T0419016

2024
Harris
New England
Manufacturers Directory

MERGENT
Exclusive Provider of
Dun & Bradstreet Library Solutions

dun&bradstreet

Published April 2024 next update April 2025

Publisher

Mergent Inc.
444 Madison Ave
New York, NY 10022

©Mergent Inc All Rights Reserved
2024 Mergent Business Press
ISSN 1080-2614
ISBN 979-8-89251-156-8

MERGENT
BUSINESS PRESS
by FTSE Russell

TABLE OF CONTENTS

SUMMARY OF CONTENTS

Number of Companies ....:.. 17,782

Number of Decision Makers 29,699

Minimum Number of Employees 7

EXPLANATORY NOTES

How to Cross-Reference in This Directory

Sequential Entry Numbers. Each establishment in the Geographic Section is numbered sequentially (G-0000). The number assigned to each establishment is referred to as its "entry number." To make cross-referencing easier, each listing in the Geographic, SIC, Alphabetic and Product Sections includes the establishment's entry number. To facilitate locating an entry in the Geographic Section, the entry numbers for the first listing on the left page and the last listing on the right page are printed at the top of the page next to the city name.

Source Suggestions Welcome

Although all known sources were used to compile this directory, it is possible that companies were inadvertently omitted. Your assistance in calling attention to such omissions would be greatly appreciated. A special form on the facing page will help you in the reporting process.

Analysis

Every effort has been made to contact all firms to verify their information. The one exception to this rule is the annual sales figure, which is considered by many companies to be confidential information. Therefore, estimated sales have been calculated by multiplying the nationwide average sales per employee for the firm's major SIC/NAICS code by the firm's number of employees. Nationwide averages for sales per employee by SIC/NAICS codes are provided by the U.S. Department of Commerce and are updated annually. All sales—sales (est)—have been estimated by this method. The exceptions are parent companies (PA), division headquarters (DH) and headquarter locations (HQ) which may include an actual corporate sales figure—sales (corporate-wide) if available.

Types of Companies

Descriptive and statistical data are included for companies in the entire state. These comprise manufacturers, machine shops, fabricators, assemblers and printers. Also identified are corporate offices in the state.

Employment Data

This directory contains companies with 7 or more employees. The employment figure shown in the Geographic Section includes male and female employees and embraces all levels of the company: administrative, clerical, sales and maintenance. This figure is for the facility listed and does not include other plants or offices. It should be recognized that these figures represent an approximate year-round average. These employment figures are broken into codes A through G and used in the Product and SIC Sections to further help you in qualifying a company. Be sure to check the footnotes on the bottom of pages for the code breakdowns.

Standard Industrial Classification (SIC)

The Standard Industrial Classification (SIC) system used in this directory was developed by the federal government for use in classifying establishments by the type of activity they are engaged in. The SIC classifications used in this directory are from the 1987 edition published by the U.S. Government's Office of Management and Budget. The SIC system separates all activities into broad industrial divisions (e.g., manufacturing, mining, retail trade). It further subdivides each division. The range of manufacturing industry classes extends from two-digit codes (major industry group) to four-digit codes (product).

For example:

Industry Breakdown	Code	Industry, Product, etc.
*Major industry group	20	Food and kindred products
Industry group	203	Canned and frozen foods
*Industry	2033	Fruits and vegetables, etc.

*Classifications used in this directory

Only two-digit and four-digit codes are used in this directory.

Arrangement

1. The **Geographic Section** contains complete in-depth corporate data. This section is sorted by cities listed in alphabetical order and companies listed alphabetically within each city. A County/City Index for referencing cities within counties precedes this section.

IMPORTANT NOTICE: It is a violation of both federal and state law to transmit an unsolicited advertisement to a facsimile machine. Any user of this product that violates such laws may be subject to civil and criminal penalties, which may exceed $500 for each transmission of an unsolicited facsimile. Mergent Inc. provides fax numbers for lawful purposes only and expressly forbids the use of these numbers in any unlawful manner.

2. The **Standard Industrial Classification (SIC) Section** lists companies under approximately 500 four-digit SIC codes. An alphabetical and a numerical index precedes this section. A company can be listed under several codes. The codes are in numerical order with companies listed alphabetically under each code.

3. The **Alphabetic Section** lists all companies with their full physical or mailing addresses and telephone number.

4. The **Product Section** lists companies under unique Harris categories. An index preceding this section lists all product categories in alphabetical order. Companies can be listed under several categories.

USER'S GUIDE TO LISTINGS

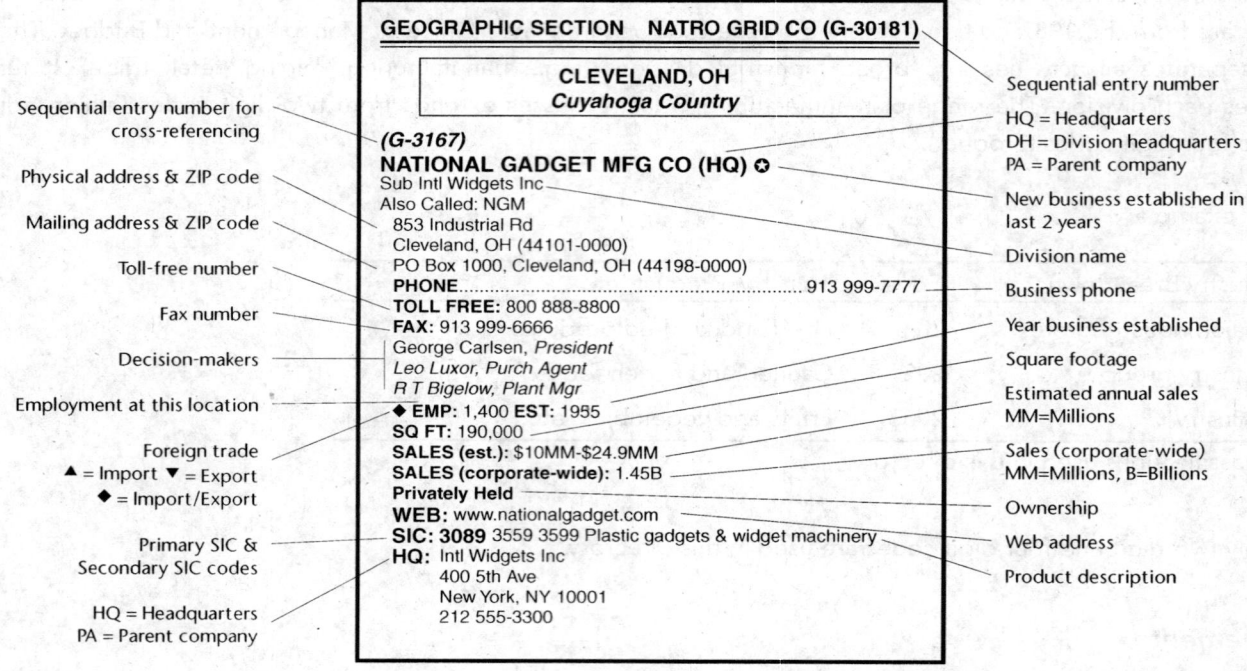

GEOGRAPHIC SECTION   NATRO GRID CO (G-30181)

Sequential entry number

CLEVELAND, OH
Cuyahoga Country

Sequential entry number for cross-referencing

Physical address & ZIP code

Mailing address & ZIP code

Toll-free number

Fax number

Decision-makers

Employment at this location

Foreign trade
▲ = Import ▼ = Export
◆ = Import/Export

Primary SIC & Secondary SIC codes

HQ = Headquarters
PA = Parent company

(G-3167)
NATIONAL GADGET MFG CO (HQ) ✪
Sub Intl Widgets Inc
Also Called: NGM
  853 Industrial Rd
  Cleveland, OH (44101-0000)
  PO Box 1000, Cleveland, OH (44198-0000)
PHONE..913 999-7777
TOLL FREE: 800 888-8800
FAX: 913 999-6666
George Carlsen, *President*
Leo Luxor, *Purch Agent*
R T Bigelow, *Plant Mgr*
◆ **EMP:** 1,400 **EST:** 1955
SQ FT: 190,000
SALES (est.): $10MM-$24.9MM
SALES (corporate-wide): 1.45B
Privately Held
WEB: www.nationalgadget.com
SIC: 3089 3559 3599 Plastic gadgets & widget machinery
HQ: Intl Widgets Inc
  400 5th Ave
  New York, NY 10001
  212 555-3300

HQ = Headquarters
DH = Division headquarters
PA = Parent company

New business established in last 2 years

Division name

Business phone

Year business established

Square footage

Estimated annual sales MM=Millions

Sales (corporate-wide) MM=Millions, B=Billions

Ownership

Web address

Product description

SIC SECTION   3089 Plastic Products, NEC

Standard Industrial Classification

Designates this location as a headquarters

3089 Plastic Products, NEC

	CITY	ST	EMP	PHONE	ENTRY#
Lees Indl Prdts Co	Albany	NY	A	518 699-3333	23054
Molded Plastics Co	Canton	OH	C	913 771-1117	27566
National Gadget Mfg (HQ)	Kansas City	KS	A	913 999-7777	39167

Employment codes
A = over 500 employees
B = 251-500, C = 101-250
D = 51-100, E = 20-50
F = 10-19, G = 1-9

Geographic Section entry number where full company information appears

Business phone

ALPHABETIC SECTION   NATIONAL GADGET MFG CO

National Gadget Mfg Co...216 999-7777
  853 Industrial Rd Cleveland, OH (44198) **(G-301801)**

National Glass Co 480 Lewis Lexington, KY (40505) **(G-20615)**..........606 477-9000

National Group Mfg 920 247-4000
  1234 W Waldo Ave Green Bay, WI (54301) **(G-36751)**

National Gypsum Wall...773 490-8888
  65 S Rio Dr Chicago, IL (6060) **(G-18901)**

Address, city & ZIP

Geographic Section entry number where full company information appears

Business phone

PRODUCT SECTION   GADGETS: Plastic

Product Category

Designates this location as a headquarters

GADGETS: PLASTIC

	CITY	ST	EMP	PHONE	ENTRY#
Nacomb Mfg Co	Decatur	IL	C	217 222-4000	29981
National Avon Inds (HQ)	Rome	GA	A	706 551-6060	30035
National Gadget Mfg (HQ)	Kansas City	KS	A	913 999-7777	39167
Nupone Plastics Inc	Dallas	TX	B	920 344-5522	30891

Employment codes
A = over 500 employees
B = 251-500, C = 101-250
D = 51-100, E = 20-50
F = 10-19, G = 1-9

Geographic Section entry number where full company information appears

Business phone

GEOGRAPHIC SECTION

Companies sorted by city in alphabetical order
In-depth company data listed

STANDARD INDUSTRIAL CLASSIFICATIONS

Alphabetical index of classification descriptions
Numerical index of classification descriptions
Companies sorted by SIC product groupings

ALPHABETIC SECTION

Company listings in alphabetical order

PRODUCT INDEX

Product categories listed in alphabetical order

PRODUCT SECTION

Companies sorted by product and manufacturing service classifications

GEOGRAPHIC

SIC

ALPHABETIC

PRDT INDEX

PRODUCT

COUNTY/CITY CROSS-REFERENCE INDEX

ENTRY #

Southwest Harbor ..... (G-5518)
Stonington ..... (G-5534)
Sunset ..... (G-5539)
Surry ..... (G-5540)
Trenton ..... (G-5553)

Kennebec

Albion ..... (G-4401)
Augusta ..... (G-4466)
Belgrade ..... (G-4539)
Benton ..... (G-4544)
Chelsea ..... (G-4687)
China ..... (G-4696)
Clinton ..... (G-4697)
Farmingdale ..... (G-4776)
Fayette ..... (G-4783)
Gardiner ..... (G-4812)
Hallowell ..... (G-4860)
Manchester ..... (G-5044)
Monmouth ..... (G-5071)
Mount Vernon ..... (G-5078)
North Monmouth ..... (G-5115)
Oakland ..... (G-5120)
Readfield ..... (G-5318)
Sidney ..... (G-5459)
South China ..... (G-5485)
Waterville ..... (G-5593)
Wayne ..... (G-5597)
Windsor ..... (G-5677)
Winslow ..... (G-5679)
Winthrop ..... (G-5690)

Knox

Appleton ..... (G-4406)
Camden ..... (G-4667)
Cushing ..... (G-4714)
Friendship ..... (G-4806)
North Haven ..... (G-5114)
Rockland ..... (G-5323)
Rockport ..... (G-5345)
Thomaston ..... (G-5541)
Vinalhaven ..... (G-5572)
Warren ..... (G-5582)
Washington ..... (G-5588)

Lincoln

Alna ..... (G-4405)
Boothbay ..... (G-4597)
Boothbay Harbor ..... (G-4599)
Bremen ..... (G-4607)
Bristol ..... (G-4630)
Damariscotta ..... (G-4715)
East Boothbay ..... (G-4736)
Edgecomb ..... (G-4747)
Jefferson ..... (G-4918)
Newcastle ..... (G-5092)
Nobleboro ..... (G-5100)
Round Pond ..... (G-5352)
South Bristol ..... (G-5483)
Waldoboro ..... (G-5573)
Walpole ..... (G-5580)
Whitefield ..... (G-5655)
Wiscasset ..... (G-5697)

Oxford

Albany Twp ..... (G-4400)
Bethel ..... (G-4552)
Brownfield ..... (G-4636)
Buckfield ..... (G-4658)
Canton ..... (G-4671)
Denmark ..... (G-4722)
Dixfield ..... (G-4727)
Fryeburg ..... (G-4807)
Greenwood ..... (G-4853)
Hartford ..... (G-4876)
Hiram ..... (G-4890)
Lovell ..... (G-5027)
Mexico ..... (G-5058)
Norway ..... (G-5116)
Oxford ..... (G-5140)
Peru ..... (G-5155)
Porter ..... (G-5165)
Rumford ..... (G-5355)
South Paris ..... (G-5488)
Sumner ..... (G-5538)
West Paris ..... (G-5612)

Penobscot

Bangor ..... (G-4487)
Brewer ..... (G-4608)
Cardville ..... (G-4673)
Chester ..... (G-4691)
Corinna ..... (G-4701)
Dexter ..... (G-4726)
Eddington ..... (G-4746)
Enfield ..... (G-4762)
Etna ..... (G-4763)
Greenbush ..... (G-4845)
Greenfield Twp ..... (G-4849)
Hampden ..... (G-4863)
Hermon ..... (G-4880)
Indian Island ..... (G-4907)
Lee ..... (G-4946)
Lincoln ..... (G-5007)
Macwahoc Plt ..... (G-5036)
Medway ..... (G-5055)
Milford ..... (G-5063)
Millinocket ..... (G-5064)
Newport ..... (G-5097)
Old Town ..... (G-5124)
Orono ..... (G-5134)
Orrington ..... (G-5139)
Patten ..... (G-5153)
Stetson ..... (G-5531)
Stillwater ..... (G-5533)
Veazie ..... (G-5570)
West Enfield ..... (G-5610)
Winn ..... (G-5678)

Piscataquis

Brownville ..... (G-4637)
Dover Foxcroft ..... (G-4729)
Greenville ..... (G-4850)
Greenville Junction ..... (G-4852)
Guilford ..... (G-4854)
Medford ..... (G-5054)
Milo ..... (G-5069)
Monson ..... (G-5074)
Sangerville ..... (G-5419)
Sebec ..... (G-5456)

Sagadahoc

Bath ..... (G-4525)
Bowdoin ..... (G-4605)
Bowdoinham ..... (G-4606)
Georgetown ..... (G-4814)
Richmond ..... (G-5320)
Topsham ..... (G-5547)
West Bath ..... (G-5609)

Somerset

Athens ..... (G-4414)
Canaan ..... (G-4669)
Cornville ..... (G-4707)
Detroit ..... (G-4725)
Fairfield ..... (G-4764)
Harmony ..... (G-4874)
Hartland ..... (G-4878)
Jackman ..... (G-4909)
Madison ..... (G-5041)
Moose River ..... (G-5076)
Norridgewock ..... (G-5103)
North Anson ..... (G-5104)
Pittsfield ..... (G-5158)
Saint Albans ..... (G-5386)
Skowhegan ..... (G-5462)
Solon ..... (G-5482)

Waldo

Belfast ..... (G-4533)
Belmont ..... (G-4542)
Burnham ..... (G-4660)
Islesboro ..... (G-4908)
Jackson ..... (G-4912)
Knox ..... (G-4943)
Liberty ..... (G-4998)
Lincolnville ..... (G-5015)
Montville ..... (G-5075)
Searsmont ..... (G-5449)
Searsport ..... (G-5451)
Unity ..... (G-5566)

Washington

Baileyville ..... (G-4482)
Beals ..... (G-4532)
Charlotte ..... (G-4686)
Cherryfield ..... (G-4688)
Columbia Falls ..... (G-4698)
Danforth ..... (G-4718)
Deblois ..... (G-4721)
East Machias ..... (G-4739)
Eastport ..... (G-4745)
Jonesboro ..... (G-4919)
Machias ..... (G-5031)
Machiasport ..... (G-5035)
Marshfield ..... (G-5046)
Milbridge ..... (G-5060)
Steuben ..... (G-5532)
Whitneyville ..... (G-5657)

York

Alfred ..... (G-4402)
Arundel ..... (G-4407)
Berwick ..... (G-4549)
Biddeford ..... (G-4553)
Buxton ..... (G-4662)
Cape Neddick ..... (G-4672)
Cornish ..... (G-4704)
Dayton ..... (G-4720)
Eliot ..... (G-4749)
Hollis Center ..... (G-4893)
Kennebunk ..... (G-4920)
Kittery ..... (G-4935)
Kittery Point ..... (G-4942)
Lebanon ..... (G-4945)
Limerick ..... (G-5000)
Limington ..... (G-5006)
Lyman ..... (G-5029)
North Berwick ..... (G-5108)
Ogunquit ..... (G-5123)
Parsonsfield ..... (G-5151)
Saco ..... (G-5363)
Sanford ..... (G-5389)
Shapleigh ..... (G-5458)
Springvale ..... (G-5520)
Waterboro ..... (G-5589)
Wells ..... (G-5598)
West Kennebunk ..... (G-5611)
York ..... (G-5711)

MASSACHUSETTS

Barnstable

Barnstable ..... (G-6199)
Bourne ..... (G-7140)
Brewster ..... (G-7215)
Buzzards Bay ..... (G-7453)
Cataumet ..... (G-7859)
Centerville ..... (G-7860)
Chatham ..... (G-7897)
Cotuit ..... (G-8146)
Dennis ..... (G-8257)
Dennis Port ..... (G-8259)
East Dennis ..... (G-8348)
East Falmouth ..... (G-8353)
East Sandwich ..... (G-8404)
Eastham ..... (G-8434)
Falmouth ..... (G-8628)
Harwich ..... (G-9066)
Harwich Port ..... (G-9070)
Hyannis ..... (G-9428)
Marstons Mills ..... (G-10247)
Mashpee ..... (G-10249)
North Falmouth ..... (G-11013)
North Truro ..... (G-11051)
Orleans ..... (G-11236)
Osterville ..... (G-11245)
Pocasset ..... (G-11486)
Provincetown ..... (G-11496)
Sagamore Beach ..... (G-11697)
Sandwich ..... (G-11747)
South Dennis ..... (G-11935)
South Orleans ..... (G-11973)
South Yarmouth ..... (G-11980)
Teaticket ..... (G-12378)
Wellfleet ..... (G-12953)
West Dennis ..... (G-12999)
West Falmouth ..... (G-13000)
West Yarmouth ..... (G-13071)
Yarmouth Port ..... (G-13846)

Berkshire

Adams ..... (G-5771)
Ashley Falls ..... (G-5970)
Berkshire ..... (G-6317)
Clarksburg ..... (G-8072)
Dalton ..... (G-8148)
East Otis ..... (G-8403)
Great Barrington ..... (G-8973)
Hancock ..... (G-9024)
Hinsdale ..... (G-9167)
Lanesborough ..... (G-9532)
Lee ..... (G-9610)
Lenox ..... (G-9624)
Lenox Dale ..... (G-9628)
North Adams ..... (G-10802)
Pittsfield ..... (G-11389)
Richmond ..... (G-11626)
Savoy ..... (G-11768)
Sheffield ..... (G-11797)
South Lee ..... (G-11972)
Southfield ..... (G-12039)
West Stockbridge ..... (G-13054)
Williamstown ..... (G-13366)

Bristol

Acushnet ..... (G-5769)
Assonet ..... (G-5972)
Attleboro ..... (G-5985)
Attleboro Falls ..... (G-6078)
Berkley ..... (G-6314)
Chartley ..... (G-7896)
Dartmouth ..... (G-8230)
Dighton ..... (G-8291)
East Freetown ..... (G-8363)
East Taunton ..... (G-8406)
Fairhaven ..... (G-8504)
Fall River ..... (G-8516)
Mansfield ..... (G-10035)
New Bedford ..... (G-10560)
North Attleboro ..... (G-10863)
North Dartmouth ..... (G-10990)
North Dighton ..... (G-11003)
North Easton ..... (G-11007)
Norton ..... (G-11122)
Raynham ..... (G-11581)
Rehoboth ..... (G-11608)
Seekonk ..... (G-11774)
Somerset ..... (G-11851)
South Dartmouth ..... (G-11916)
South Easton ..... (G-11936)
Swansea ..... (G-12302)
Taunton ..... (G-12315)
Westport ..... (G-13292)
Westport Point ..... (G-13303)

Dukes

Chilmark ..... (G-8071)
Edgartown ..... (G-8465)
Oak Bluffs ..... (G-11221)
Vineyard Haven ..... (G-12491)
West Tisbury ..... (G-13055)

Essex

Amesbury ..... (G-5827)
Andover ..... (G-5867)
Beverly ..... (G-6321)
Boxford ..... (G-7158)
Byfield ..... (G-7457)
Danvers ..... (G-8157)
Essex ..... (G-8472)
Georgetown ..... (G-8904)
Gloucester ..... (G-8916)
Groveland ..... (G-9012)
Haverhill ..... (G-9074)
Ipswich ..... (G-9477)
Lawrence ..... (G-9533)
Lynn ..... (G-9961)
Lynnfield ..... (G-9994)
Manchester ..... (G-10032)
Marblehead ..... (G-10084)
Merrimac ..... (G-10324)
Methuen ..... (G-10327)
Middleton ..... (G-10380)
Nahant ..... (G-10460)
Newbury ..... (G-10665)
Newburyport ..... (G-10666)
North Andover ..... (G-10815)
Peabody ..... (G-11292)
Rowley ..... (G-11667)
Salem ..... (G-11699)
Salisbury ..... (G-11738)
Saugus ..... (G-11754)
South Hamilton ..... (G-11969)
Swampscott ..... (G-12297)
Topsfield ..... (G-12432)
West Boxford ..... (G-12954)
West Newbury ..... (G-13006)

Franklin

ENTRY #

Ashfield (G-5954)
Colrain (G-8095)
Conway (G-8143)
Deerfield (G-8256)
Erving (G-8469)
Gill (G-8915)
Greenfield (G-8981)
Leverett (G-9718)
Millers Falls (G-10447)
Montague (G-10458)
New Salem (G-10664)
Northfield (G-11120)
Orange (G-11223)
Shelburne Falls (G-11802)
South Deerfield (G-11920)
Sunderland (G-12273)
Turners Falls (G-12444)
Whately (G-13339)

Hampden

Agawam (G-5776)
Brimfield (G-7248)
Chester (G-7996)
Chicopee (G-8004)
East Longmeadow (G-8368)
Feeding Hills (G-8636)
Granville (G-8972)
Hampden (G-9022)
Holyoke (G-9240)
Indian Orchard (G-9469)
Longmeadow (G-9848)
Ludlow (G-9937)
Monson (G-10455)
Palmer (G-11269)
Russell (G-11694)
Southwick (G-12040)
Springfield (G-12067)
Thorndike (G-12427)
Three Rivers (G-12429)
West Springfield (G-13013)
Westfield (G-13145)
Wilbraham (G-13356)

Hampshire

Amherst (G-5856)
Belchertown (G-6278)
Chesterfield (G-7997)
Cummington (G-8147)
Easthampton (G-8437)
Florence (G-8683)
Goshen (G-8966)
Granby (G-8970)
Hadley (G-9017)
Hardwick (G-9059)
Hatfield (G-9071)
Leeds (G-9620)
Montgomery (G-10459)
Northampton (G-11052)
Plainfield (G-11428)
South Hadley (G-11959)
Southampton (G-11985)
Ware (G-12824)
West Hatfield (G-13003)
Williamsburg (G-13365)

Middlesex

Acton (G-5730)
Arlington (G-5937)
Ashland (G-5956)
Auburndale (G-6130)
Ayer (G-6170)
Bedford (G-6204)
Belmont (G-6304)
Billerica (G-6395)
Boxboro (G-7144)
Boxborough (G-7146)
Burlington (G-7329)
Cambridge (G-7461)
Carlisle (G-7845)
Chelmsford (G-7901)
Chestnut Hill (G-7998)
Concord (G-8097)
Devens (G-8264)
Dracut (G-8302)
Dunstable (G-8328)
Everett (G-8481)
Framingham (G-8739)
Groton (G-9008)
Holliston (G-9197)
Hopkinton (G-9304)
Hudson (G-9350)
Lexington (G-9719)
Lincoln (G-9794)
Littleton (G-9799)
Lowell (G-9850)
Malden (G-10000)
Marlborough (G-10103)
Maynard (G-10259)
Medford (G-10278)
Melrose (G-10312)
Natick (G-10467)
Newton (G-10730)
Newton Upper Falls (G-10795)
Newtonville (G-10796)
North Billerica (G-10893)
North Chelmsford (G-10965)
North Reading (G-11037)
Pepperell (G-11380)
Reading (G-11600)
Sherborn (G-11810)
Shirley (G-11812)
Somerville (G-11858)
Stoneham (G-12173)
Stow (G-12244)
Sudbury (G-12260)
Tewksbury (G-12383)
Townsend (G-12441)
Tyngsboro (G-12456)
Waban (G-12496)
Wakefield (G-12498)
Waltham (G-12580)
Watertown (G-12854)
Wayland (G-12923)
West Groton (G-13001)
West Townsend (G-13056)
Westford (G-13224)
Weston (G-13284)
Wilmington (G-13369)
Winchester (G-13483)
Woburn (G-13494)

Nantucket

Nantucket (G-10461)

Norfolk

Avon (G-6140)
Bellingham (G-6282)
Braintree (G-7166)
Brookline (G-7317)
Canton (G-7765)
Cohasset (G-8094)
Dedham (G-8235)
East Walpole (G-8417)
East Weymouth (G-8423)
Foxboro (G-8688)
Foxborough (G-8734)
Franklin (G-8813)
Holbrook (G-9168)
Medfield (G-10269)
Medway (G-10301)
Millis (G-10448)
Milton (G-10452)
Needham (G-10502)
Needham Heights (G-10530)
Norfolk (G-10797)
North Quincy (G-11036)
Norwood (G-11151)
Plainville (G-11429)
Quincy (G-11500)
Randolph (G-11546)
Sharon (G-11791)
South Weymouth (G-11974)
Stoughton (G-12190)
Walpole (G-12545)
Wellesley (G-12933)
Wellesley Hills (G-12949)
Westwood (G-13304)
Weymouth (G-13324)
Wrentham (G-13836)

Plymouth

Abington (G-5721)
Bridgewater (G-7218)
Brockton (G-7251)
Carver (G-7852)
Duxbury (G-8329)
East Bridgewater (G-8334)
East Wareham (G-8422)
Halifax (G-9020)
Hanover (G-9026)
Hanson (G-9049)
Hingham (G-9139)
Hull (G-9427)
Kingston (G-9505)
Lakeville (G-9515)
Marion (G-10097)
Marshfield (G-10239)
Mattapoisett (G-10255)
Middleboro (G-10348)
Norwell (G-11139)
Pembroke (G-11356)
Plymouth (G-11445)
Plympton (G-11484)
Rochester (G-11631)
Rockland (G-11632)
Scituate (G-11769)
South Carver (G-11915)
Wareham (G-12828)
West Bridgewater (G-12966)
West Wareham (G-13057)
Whitman (G-13348)

Suffolk

Allston (G-5817)
Boston (G-6499)
Brighton (G-7239)
Charlestown (G-7861)
Chelsea (G-7974)
Dorchester (G-8295)
Hyde Park (G-9456)
Jamaica Plain (G-9501)
Mattapan (G-10254)
Revere (G-11616)
Roslindale (G-11666)
Roxbury (G-11688)
Roxbury Crossing (G-11693)
West Roxbury (G-13009)

Worcester

Ashburnham (G-5951)
Athol (G-5977)
Auburn (G-6097)
Baldwinville (G-6198)
Barre (G-6202)
Berlin (G-6318)
Blackstone (G-6493)
Bolton (G-6495)
Boylston (G-7162)
Brookfield (G-7315)
Charlton (G-7885)
Cherry Valley (G-7995)
Clinton (G-8075)
Dudley (G-8315)
East Douglas (G-8349)
East Templeton (G-8414)
Fiskdale (G-8638)
Fitchburg (G-8640)
Gardner (G-8878)
Gilbertville (G-8913)
Grafton (G-8968)
Harvard (G-9060)
Holden (G-9187)
Hopedale (G-9293)
Hubbardston (G-9348)
Lancaster (G-9524)
Leicester (G-9622)
Leominster (G-9629)
Lunenburg (G-9958)
Mendon (G-10320)
Milford (G-10398)
Millbury (G-10426)
Millville (G-10451)
New Braintree (G-10663)
North Brookfield (G-10964)
North Grafton (G-11018)
North Oxford (G-11031)
Northborough (G-11088)
Northbridge (G-11117)
Oxford (G-11247)
Paxton (G-11289)
Petersham (G-11388)
Princeton (G-11495)
Rochdale (G-11627)
Rutland (G-11696)
Shrewsbury (G-11825)
South Barre (G-11914)
South Grafton (G-11957)
South Lancaster (G-11970)
Southborough (G-11989)
Southbridge (G-12007)
Spencer (G-12054)
Sterling (G-12154)
Sturbridge (G-12248)
Sutton (G-12276)
Templeton (G-12380)
Upton (G-12469)
Uxbridge (G-12476)
Warren (G-12850)
Webster (G-12926)
West Boylston (G-12955)
West Brookfield (G-12991)
Westborough (G-13075)
Westminster (G-13268)
Whitinsville (G-13341)
Winchendon (G-13478)
Worcester (G-13694)

NEW HAMPSHIRE

Belknap

Alton (G-13859)
Barnstead (G-13913)
Belmont (G-13958)
Center Barnstead (G-14049)
Center Harbor (G-14056)
Gilford (G-14333)
Gilmanton (G-14339)
Gilmanton Iron Works (G-14340)
Laconia (G-14638)
Meredith (G-14968)
New Hampton (G-15195)
Northfield (G-15263)
Sanbornton (G-15577)
Tilton (G-15651)

Carroll

Albany (G-13847)
Bartlett (G-13918)
Center Conway (G-14050)
Center Ossipee (G-14057)
Center Tuftonboro (G-14059)
Chatham (G-14070)
Conway (G-14177)
Intervale (G-14561)
Jackson (G-14562)
Madison (G-14802)
Middleton (G-15008)
Moultonborough (G-15051)
North Conway (G-15246)
Ossipee (G-15282)
Sanbornville (G-15578)
Silver Lake (G-15607)
Tamworth (G-15647)
West Ossipee (G-15694)
Wolfeboro (G-15731)
Wolfeboro Falls (G-15736)

Cheshire

Alstead (G-13856)
Dublin (G-14261)
Fitzwilliam (G-14312)
Gilsum (G-14341)
Harrisville (G-14432)
Hinsdale (G-14443)
Jaffrey (G-14563)
Keene (G-14588)
Marlborough (G-14964)
Marlow (G-14966)
North Swanzey (G-15256)
North Walpole (G-15257)
Rindge (G-15459)
Spofford (G-15630)
Swanzey (G-15643)
Troy (G-15658)
Walpole (G-15659)
West Swanzey (G-15695)
Westmoreland (G-15698)
Winchester (G-15713)

Coos

Berlin (G-13978)
Colebrook (G-14103)
Dummer (G-14263)
Gorham (G-14357)
Groveton (G-14377)
Jefferson (G-14583)
Lancaster (G-14675)
Milan (G-15009)
Pittsburg (G-15328)
Stewartstown (G-15631)

ENTRY #	ENTRY #	ENTRY #	ENTRY #	ENTRY #

Whitefield .... (G-15699)

Grafton

Alexandria .... (G-13851)
Ashland .... (G-13899)
Bristol .... (G-14034)
Campton .... (G-14043)
Canaan .... (G-14045)
Enfield .... (G-14274)
Hanover .... (G-14421)
Holderness .... (G-14446)
Landaff .... (G-14682)
Lebanon .... (G-14683)
Lincoln .... (G-14707)
Lisbon .... (G-14708)
Littleton .... (G-14714)
Monroe .... (G-15047)
North Haverhill .... (G-15253)
North Woodstock .... (G-15262)
Orange .... (G-15280)
Orford .... (G-15281)
Plymouth .... (G-15354)
Rumney .... (G-15497)
Wentworth .... (G-15676)
West Lebanon .... (G-15678)
Woodsville .... (G-15737)

Hillsborough

Amherst .... (G-13860)
Antrim .... (G-13896)
Bedford .... (G-13919)
Bennington .... (G-13974)
Brookline .... (G-14038)
Deering .... (G-14187)
Goffstown .... (G-14346)
Greenfield .... (G-14364)
Greenville .... (G-14373)
Hancock .... (G-14420)
Hillsborough .... (G-14441)
Hollis .... (G-14448)
Hudson .... (G-14478)
Litchfield .... (G-14712)
Lyndeborough .... (G-14800)
Manchester .... (G-14804)
Mason .... (G-14967)
Merrimack .... (G-14971)
Milford .... (G-15010)
Mont Vernon .... (G-15048)
Nashua .... (G-15054)
New Boston .... (G-15192)
New Ipswich .... (G-15196)
Pelham .... (G-15286)
Peterborough .... (G-15311)
Weare .... (G-15668)
Wilton .... (G-15701)

Merrimack

Allenstown .... (G-13852)
Boscawen .... (G-13988)
Bow .... (G-13993)
Bradford .... (G-14017)
Chichester .... (G-14072)
Concord .... (G-14112)
Contoocook .... (G-14167)
Danbury .... (G-14184)
Dunbarton .... (G-14264)
Epsom .... (G-14278)
Franklin .... (G-14318)
Henniker .... (G-14433)
Hooksett .... (G-14462)
Hopkinton .... (G-14477)
Loudon .... (G-14793)

Manchester .... (G-14963)
New London .... (G-15202)
Newbury .... (G-15204)
North Sutton .... (G-15254)
Pembroke .... (G-15301)
Penacook .... (G-15310)
Pittsfield .... (G-15331)
Salisbury .... (G-15575)
Warner .... (G-15665)
Webster .... (G-15674)

Rockingham

Atkinson .... (G-13903)
Auburn .... (G-13906)
Brentwood .... (G-14019)
Candia .... (G-14048)
Chester .... (G-14071)
Danville .... (G-14185)
Deerfield .... (G-14186)
Derry .... (G-14189)
East Hampstead ...... (G-14269)
East Kingston .... (G-14272)
Epping .... (G-14276)
Exeter .... (G-14284)
Fremont .... (G-14326)
Greenland .... (G-14365)
Hampstead .... (G-14380)
Hampton .... (G-14396)
Hampton Falls .... (G-14418)
Kensington .... (G-14629)
Kingston .... (G-14632)
Londonderry .... (G-14726)
Newfields .... (G-15205)
Newington .... (G-15206)
Newmarket .... (G-15218)
Newton .... (G-15242)
North Hampton .... (G-15251)
Northwood .... (G-15272)
Nottingham .... (G-15276)
Plaistow .... (G-15335)
Portsmouth .... (G-15356)
Raymond .... (G-15451)
Rye .... (G-15499)
Salem .... (G-15501)
Sandown .... (G-15579)
Seabrook .... (G-15582)
South Hampton .... (G-15629)
Stratham .... (G-15633)
West Nottingham ..... (G-15693)
Windham .... (G-15719)

Strafford

Barrington .... (G-13914)
Dover .... (G-14212)
Durham .... (G-14266)
Farmington .... (G-14307)
Lee .... (G-14704)
Madbury .... (G-14801)
Milton .... (G-15045)
Rochester .... (G-15462)
Rollinsford .... (G-15495)
Somersworth .... (G-15608)
Strafford .... (G-15632)

Sullivan

Charlestown .... (G-14060)
Claremont .... (G-14074)
Cornish .... (G-14183)
Grantham .... (G-14362)
Newport .... (G-15225)
South Acworth .... (G-15628)
Sunapee .... (G-15642)

RHODE ISLAND

Bristol

Barrington .... (G-15746)
Bristol .... (G-15751)
Prudence Island ...... (G-16650)
Warren .... (G-16748)

Kent

Coventry .... (G-15806)
East Greenwich .... (G-15972)
Warwick .... (G-16774)
West Greenwich ...... (G-16881)
West Warwick .... (G-16898)

Newport

Jamestown .... (G-16068)
Little Compton .... (G-16159)
Middletown .... (G-16170)
Newport .... (G-16199)
Portsmouth .... (G-16434)
Tiverton .... (G-16734)

Providence

Central Falls .... (G-15787)
Chepachet .... (G-15803)
Cranston .... (G-15824)
Cumberland .... (G-15931)
East Providence ...... (G-15999)
Fiskeville .... (G-16053)
Glendale .... (G-16054)
Greenville .... (G-16055)
Harrisville .... (G-16064)
Johnston .... (G-16071)
Lincoln .... (G-16114)
Manville .... (G-16163)
Mapleville .... (G-16166)
North Providence .... (G-16293)
North Scituate .... (G-16314)
North Smithfield ...... (G-16318)
Oakland .... (G-16335)
Pascoag .... (G-16336)
Pawtucket .... (G-16342)
Providence .... (G-16462)
Riverside .... (G-16652)
Rumford .... (G-16661)
Slatersville .... (G-16682)
Smithfield .... (G-16684)
Woonsocket .... (G-16946)

Washington

Ashaway .... (G-15738)
Exeter .... (G-16050)
Hope Valley .... (G-16066)
Kenyon .... (G-16112)
Kingston .... (G-16113)
Narragansett .... (G-16186)
North Kingstown ..... (G-16228)
Peace Dale .... (G-16433)
Richmond .... (G-16651)
Wakefield .... (G-16740)
West Kingston .... (G-16892)
Westerly .... (G-16927)
Wyoming .... (G-16983)

VERMONT

Addison

Bristol .... (G-17112)
Ferrisburgh .... (G-17268)
Middlebury .... (G-17334)
New Haven .... (G-17394)

North Ferrisburgh .... (G-17419)
Shoreham .... (G-17567)
Starksboro .... (G-17625)
Vergennes .... (G-17655)
Weybridge .... (G-17703)
Whiting .... (G-17711)

Bennington

Arlington .... (G-16985)
Bennington .... (G-17035)
Dorset .... (G-17214)
Manchester .... (G-17323)
Manchester Center .. (G-17326)
North Bennington .... (G-17409)
Pownal .... (G-17455)
Shaftsbury .... (G-17549)
Sunderland .... (G-17635)
West Rupert .... (G-17694)

Caledonia

Barnet .... (G-16995)
East Ryegate .... (G-17219)
Groton .... (G-17278)
Hardwick .... (G-17283)
Lyndonville .... (G-17317)
Saint Johnsbury ...... (G-17537)
South Ryegate .... (G-17613)

Chittenden

Burlington .... (G-17117)
Cambridge .... (G-17168)
Charlotte .... (G-17175)
Colchester .... (G-17185)
Essex .... (G-17225)
Essex Junction .... (G-17226)
Fairfax .... (G-17254)
Hinesburg .... (G-17290)
Jericho .... (G-17308)
Milton .... (G-17353)
Richmond .... (G-17478)
Shelburne .... (G-17556)
South Burlington .... (G-17569)
St George .... (G-17624)
Underhill .... (G-17654)
Williston .... (G-17719)
Winooski .... (G-17765)

Essex

Canaan .... (G-17169)
Island Pond .... (G-17304)
Lunenburg .... (G-17316)

Franklin

Enosburg Falls .... (G-17220)
Fairfield .... (G-17266)
Highgate Center ...... (G-17288)
Montgomery Center . (G-17368)
Richford .... (G-17475)
Saint Albans .... (G-17515)
Sheldon Springs ...... (G-17566)
Swanton .... (G-17636)

Grand Isle

Alburg .... (G-16984)
South Hero .... (G-17609)

Lamoille

Belvidere Center ...... (G-17034)
Hyde Park .... (G-17299)
Jeffersonville .... (G-17306)
Johnson .... (G-17309)
Morrisville .... (G-17380)

Stowe .... (G-17629)
Waterville .... (G-17682)
Wolcott .... (G-17773)

Orange

Bradford .... (G-17061)
Chelsea .... (G-17178)
East Randolph .... (G-17218)
Fairlee .... (G-17267)
Randolph .... (G-17465)
Strafford .... (G-17634)
Topsham .... (G-17649)
Tunbridge .... (G-17651)
Wells River .... (G-17686)
West Topsham .... (G-17698)
Williamstown .... (G-17717)

Orleans

Barton .... (G-17027)
Derby .... (G-17211)
Derby Line .... (G-17213)
Irasburg .... (G-17302)
Newport .... (G-17397)
Newport Center .... (G-17408)
North Troy .... (G-17428)
Orleans .... (G-17438)
Westfield .... (G-17699)

Rutland

Benson .... (G-17058)
Brandon .... (G-17066)
Castleton .... (G-17171)
Center Rutland .... (G-17174)
Cuttingsville .... (G-17209)
Danby .... (G-17210)
Fair Haven .... (G-17250)
Florence .... (G-17270)
Forest Dale .... (G-17274)
Hydeville .... (G-17301)
Killington .... (G-17313)
North Clarendon ...... (G-17413)
Pawlet .... (G-17441)
Pittsford .... (G-17444)
Poultney .... (G-17447)
Proctor .... (G-17456)
Rutland .... (G-17488)
Tinmouth .... (G-17648)
Wallingford .... (G-17670)
West Pawlet .... (G-17691)
West Rutland .... (G-17695)

Washington

Barre .... (G-16996)
Cabot .... (G-17166)
Calais .... (G-17167)
East Barre .... (G-17215)
Graniteville .... (G-17276)
Marshfield .... (G-17333)
Middlesex .... (G-17352)
Montpelier .... (G-17370)
Northfield .... (G-17431)
Riverton .... (G-17483)
Waitsfield .... (G-17663)
Warren .... (G-17671)
Waterbury .... (G-17673)
Waterbury Center .... (G-17680)
Websterville .... (G-17683)
Worcester .... (G-17781)

Windham

Bellows Falls .... (G-17028)
Brattleboro .... (G-17072)

ENTRY #	ENTRY #	ENTRY #	ENTRY #	ENTRY #
East Dummerston .... (G-17216)	Whitingham .... (G-17713)	Brownsville .... (G-17116)	Proctorsville .... (G-17461)	Stockbridge .... (G-17628)
Grafton .... (G-17275)	Wilmington .... (G-17754)	Chester .... (G-17180)	Quechee .... (G-17462)	Taftsville .... (G-17647)
Guilford .... (G-17280)		Hartland .... (G-17286)	Rochester .... (G-17484)	White River Junction
South Londonderry . (G-17611)	**Windsor**	Ludlow .... (G-17314)	Sharon .... (G-17555)	(G-17704)
Townshend . (G-17650)		North Hartland .... (G-17420)	South Royalton .... (G-17612)	Wilder .... (G-17714)
West Dover ....(G-17689)	Ascutney .... (G-16993)	North Springfield ..... (G-17421)	South Woodstock .... (G-17615)	Windsor .... (G-17757)
Westminster .... (G-17700)	Barnard .... (G-16994)	Norwich .... (G-17437)	Springfield .... (G-17616)	Woodstock .... (G-17776)
Westminster Station . (G-17702)	Bethel .... (G-17060)	Perkinsville .... (G-17442)		
	Bridgewater .... (G-17111)			

GEOGRAPHIC SECTION

Sequential entry number for cross-referencing

Physical address & ZIP code

Mailing address & ZIP code

Toll-free number

Fax number

Decision-makers

Employment at this location

Foreign trade
▲ = Import ▼ = Export
◆ = Import/Export

Primary SIC & Secondary SIC codes

HQ = Headquarters
PA = Parent company

Designates this location as a headquarters

New business established in last 2 years

Division name

Business phone

Year business established

Square footage

Estimated annual sales MM=Millions

Ownership

Sales (corporate-wide) MM=Millions, B=Billions

Web address

Product description

CLEVELAND, OH
Cuyahoga Country

(G-3167)
NATIONAL GADGET MFG CO (HQ) ✪
Sub Intl Widgets Inc
Also Called: NGM
853 Industrial Rd
Cleveland, OH (44101-0000)
PO Box 1000, Cleveland, OH (44198-0000)
PHONE.. 913 999-7777
TOLL FREE: 800 888-8800
FAX: 913 999-6666
George Carlsen, *President*
Leo Luxor, *Purch Agent*
R T Bigelow, *Plant Mgr*
◆ **EMP:** 1,400 **EST:** 1955
SQ FT: 190,000
SALES (est.): $1MM-$4.9MM **Privately Held**
SALES (corporate-wide): 1.45B
WEB: www.nationalgadget.com
SIC: 3089 3559 3599 Plastic gadgets & widget machinery
HQ: Intl Widgets Inc
400 5th Ave
New York, NY 10001
212 555-3300

See footnotes for symbols and codes identification.
- This section is in alphabetical order by city.
- Companies are sorted alphabetically under their respective cities.
- To locate cities within a county refer to the County/City Cross Reference Index.

IMPORTANT NOTICE: It is a violation of both federal and state law to transmit an unsolicited advertisement to a facsimile machine. Any user of this product that violates such laws may be subject to civil and criminal penalties which may exceed $500 for each transmission of an unsolicited facsimile. Harris InfoSource provides fax numbers for lawful purposes only and expressly forbids the use of these numbers in any unlawful manner.

CONNECTICUT

Andover
Tolland County

(G-1)
AMERICAN DREAM UNLIMITED LLC
212 Gilead Rd (06232-1603)
PHONE.............................860 742-5055
EMP: 7 EST: 2002
SALES (est): 559.14K Privately Held
Web: www.americandreamunlimited.com
SIC: 3845 Endoscopic equipment, electromedical, nec

(G-2)
MTM CORPORATION
643 Route 6 (06232-1320)
P.O. Box 268 (06232-0268)
PHONE.............................860 742-9600
William Thurston Junior, *Pr*
EMP: 9 EST: 1979
SQ FT: 12,000
SALES (est): 941.95K Privately Held
SIC: 3728 Aircraft parts and equipment, nec

(G-3)
VERTICAL RETAIL SOLUTIONS LLC
101 Hutchinson Rd (06232-1016)
P.O. Box 87 (06232-0087)
PHONE.............................860 742-6464
Simon Cohn, *Pr*
Aron Welsh, *Ch*
Saul Bloomberg, *VP*
Sidney Zlonick, *VP*
Steven Trent, *CFO*
EMP: 608 EST: 2002
SQ FT: 400,000
SALES (est): 26.13MM Privately Held
Web: www.verticalretailsolutions.com
SIC: 2591 Blinds vertical

Ansonia
New Haven County

(G-4)
A-1 HEAT TREATING INC
22 Maple St (06401-1230)
PHONE.............................914 220-2179
John Palmiero, *Pr*
EMP: 11 EST: 2018
SALES (est): 473.09K Privately Held
Web: www.a1heattreating.com
SIC: 3398 Metal heat treating

(G-5)
AERO-MED MOLDING TECHNOLOGIES (PA)
50 Westfield Ave (06401-1121)
PHONE.............................203 735-2331
Lawrence Saffran, *Pr*
EMP: 10 EST: 1997
SQ FT: 30,000
SALES (est): 4.81MM Privately Held
Web: www.stelray.com
SIC: 3089 Injection molding of plastics

(G-6)
AMERICAN PRECISION MFG LLC
26 Beaver St Ste 1 (06401-3250)
PHONE.............................203 734-1800
EMP: 17 EST: 1997
SQ FT: 30,000
SALES (est): 904.13K Privately Held
Web: www.ap-mfg.com
SIC: 3599 Machine shop, jobbing and repair

(G-7)
ANSONIA PLASTICS LLC
Also Called: Npi Medical
401 Birmingham Blvd (06401-1035)
PHONE.............................203 736-5200
Brian Jones, *CEO*
EMP: 80 EST: 1998
SALES (est): 23.28MM
SALES (corp-wide): 568.49MM Privately Held
Web: www.westfalltechnik.com
SIC: 3086 Plastics foam products
PA: Westfall Technik, Inc.
3883 Howard Hughes Pkwy # 590
Las Vegas NV 89169
702 659-9898

(G-8)
B & J ELECTRIC MOTOR REPAIR CO INC
30 Maple St (06401-1230)
PHONE.............................203 734-1695
TOLL FREE: 800
EMP: 10
Web: www.bandjelectric.com
SIC: 5063 7694 Motors, electric; Electric motor repair

(G-9)
CASTLE BEVERAGES INC
105 Myrtle Ave (06401-2099)
PHONE.............................203 732-0883
Kenneth Dworkin, *Pr*
David Pantalone, *VP*
EMP: 9 EST: 1907
SQ FT: 96,000
SALES (est): 989.07K Privately Held
Web: www.glassbottlesoda.org
SIC: 2086 Carbonated beverages, nonalcoholic; pkged. in cans, bottles

---

(G-10)
CBS CONTRACTORS INC
Also Called: CBS Contractors
1 Riverside Dr Ste D (06401-1255)
PHONE.....................203 734-8015
Angelo Giordano, Pr
EMP: 10 **EST:** 1983
SALES (est): 992.16K **Privately Held**
Web: www.cbscontractors.net
SIC: 1711 3444　Warm air heating and air
conditioning contractor; Sheet metalwork

(G-11)
**CONNECTICUT METAL
INDUSTRIES**
1 Riverside Dr Ste G (06401-1255)
P.O. Box 234 (06468-0234)
PHONE.....................203 736-0790
Tom Mele, Prin
◆ **EMP:** 7 **EST:** 2010
SALES (est): 394.99K **Privately Held**
Web: www.ctmetal.com
SIC: 3999　Manufacturing industries, nec

(G-12)
DAWID MANUFACTURING INC
26 Beaver St (06401-3250)
PHONE.....................203 734-1800
Leigh Dawid, Pr
Karen Dawid, Treas
EMP: 8 **EST:** 1984
SQ FT: 4,000
SALES (est): 743.48K **Privately Held**
SIC: 3599 5088　Machine shop, jobbing and
repair; Marine supplies

(G-13)
**DIVERSIFIED MANUFACTURING
LLC**
1 Riverside Dr Ste H (06401-1255)
PHONE.....................203 734-0379
Kazimierz Bialczak, Pr
EMP: 10
SALES (est): 515.22K **Privately Held**
SIC: 3999　Manufacturing industries, nec

(G-14)
FARREL CORPORATION (DH)
Also Called: Farrel Pomini
1 Farrell Blvd (06401-1256)
PHONE.....................203 736-5500
Mark Meulbroek, CEO
Paul M Zepp, *
James L Burns, *
◆ **EMP:** 91 **EST:** 1848
SQ FT: 60,000
SALES (est): 47.76MM
SALES (corp-wide): 144.19K **Privately
Held**
Web: www.farrel-pomini.com
SIC: 3559 1011 3089　Rubber working
machinery, including tires; Iron ore
pelletizing; Extruded finished plastics
products, nec
HQ: Harburg-Freudenberger
Maschinenbau Gmbh
Schlachthofstr. 22
Hamburg HH 21079
40771790

(G-15)
KENSCO INC (PA)
Also Called: Tub's & Stuff Plumbing Supply
41 Clifton Ave (06401-2203)
P.O. Box 43 (06401-0043)
PHONE.....................203 734-8827
Kenneth R Shortell, Pr
Yvette Shortell, VP
EMP: 8 **EST:** 1985

SQ FT: 10,000
SALES (est): 1.02MM
SALES (corp-wide): 1.02MM **Privately
Held**
SIC: 3431 3089-5074 5999　Bathtubs:
enameled iron, cast iron, or pressed metal;
Tubs, plastics (containers); Plumbing and
hydronic heating supplies; Plumbing and
heating supplies

(G-16)
LINE SETS INC
10 Hershey Dr (06401-2312)
PHONE.....................203 732-6700
EMP: 7 **EST:** 2017
SALES (est): 228.25K **Privately Held**
Web: www.linesetsinc.com
SIC: 3999　Manufacturing industries, nec

(G-17)
**PRO COUNTERS NEW
ENGLAND LLC**
1 Chestnut St (06401-2300)
PHONE.....................203 347-8663
EMP: 7 **EST:** 2017
SALES (est): 980.88K **Privately Held**
Web: www.procountersne.com
SIC: 2541　Counter and sink tops

(G-18)
**PUMP TECHNOLOGY
INCORPORATED**
Also Called: Homa Pump Technology
390 Birmingham Blvd (06401-1032)
PHONE.....................203 736-8890
James Torony, Pr
Joanne Marino, *
◆ **EMP:** 25 **EST:** 1982
SQ FT: 38,500
SALES (est): 4.78MM **Privately Held**
Web: www.homapump.com
SIC: 5084 3561　Pumps and pumping
equipment, nec; Pumps, domestic: water or
sump

(G-19)
ROYAL WOODCRAFT INC
1 Riverside Dr (06401-1228)
PHONE.....................203 847-3461
Dominick Mudugno, Pr
EMP: 10 **EST:** 1966
SALES (est): 251.4K **Privately Held**
Web: www.royalwoodcraftinc.com
SIC: 5211 2434　Cabinets, kitchen; Vanities,
bathroom: wood

(G-20)
**STELRAY PLASTIC PRODUCTS
INC**
50 Westfield Ave (06401-1121)
PHONE.....................203 735-2331
Lawrence David Saffran, Pr
Mortimer Saffran, Ch Bd
▲ **EMP:** 48 **EST:** 1965
SQ FT: 15,000
SALES (est): 8.95MM **Privately Held**
Web: www.stelray.com
SIC: 3089 5031　Injection molding of plastics
; Molding, all materials

Ashford
Windham County

(G-21)
PITH PRODUCTS LLC
39 Nott Hwy Unit 1 (06278-1341)
PHONE.....................860 487-4859

EMP: 16 **EST:** 1991
SALES (est): 2.15MM **Privately Held**
Web: www.pithproducts.com
SIC: 2449　Rectangular boxes and crates,
wood

(G-22)
**TOOLMAX DESIGNING TOOLING
INC**
591 Ference Rd (06278-2103)
P.O. Box 103 (06084-0103)
PHONE.....................860 477-0373
Michael Tyler, Owner
Sally Ann Tyler, Ofcr
Lewis Perry, Genl Mgr
James Houge, Prd Mgr
EMP: 17 **EST:** 2005
SALES (est): 1.49MM **Privately Held**
Web: www.toolmax-inc.com
SIC: 3599 3728　Machine shop, jobbing and
repair; Blades, aircraft propeller: metal or
wood

Avon
Hartford County

(G-23)
DIRECTORY ASSISTANTS INC
34 Valley View Dr (06001-2712)
PHONE.....................860 633-0122
EMP: 12 **EST:** 1990
SALES (est): 977.26K **Privately Held**
Web: www.daiagency.com
SIC: 7311 2741　Advertising consultant;
Miscellaneous publishing

(G-24)
FLAGMAN OF AMERICA LLC
22 E Main St (06001-3801)
P.O. Box 440 (06001-0440)
PHONE.....................860 678-0275
TOLL FREE: 800
Annette Dimesky, Pt
Annette Dimesky, Mng Pt
David Dimesky, Mng Pt
James Walz, Mng Pt
EMP: 8 **EST:** 1948
SQ FT: 1,900
SALES (est): 932.2K **Privately Held**
Web: www.flagman.com
SIC: 5999 2399　Flags; Flags, fabric

(G-25)
**GENERAL DYNAMICS
ORDNANCE**
Also Called: Simunition Operations
65 Sandscreen Rd (06001-2222)
P.O. Box 576 (06001-0576)
PHONE.....................860 404-0162
EMP: 10
SALES (corp-wide): 42.27B **Publicly Held**
Web: www.gd-ots.com
SIC: 3482 8741　Small arms ammunition;
Management services
HQ: General Dynamics Ordnance And
Tactical Systems, Inc.
100 Carillon Pkwy
Saint Petersburg FL 33716
727 578-8100

(G-26)
**HARTFORD COURANT
COMPANY LLC**
Also Called: Hartford Courant
80 Darling Dr (06001-4217)
PHONE.....................860 678-1330
Bonnie Phillips, Mgr
EMP: 7

SQ FT: 500
Web: www.courant.com
SIC: 2711　Newspapers: publishing only, not
printed on site
HQ: The Hartford Courant Company Llc
285 Broad St
Hartford CT 06115
860 241-6200

(G-27)
IDEVICES LLC
50 Tower Ln (06001-4228)
PHONE.....................860 352-5252
C J Allen Senior, Pr
Christopher J Allen, Managing Member*
Warren Katz, CMO*
Kelley Mcintyre, CFO
▲ **EMP:** 100 **EST:** 2010
SALES (est): 16.26MM
SALES (corp-wide): 5.37B **Publicly Held**
Web: www.idevicesinc.com
SIC: 3625 5731　Timing devices, electronic;
Consumer electronic equipment, nec
PA: Hubbell Incorporated
40 Waterview Dr
Shelton CT 06484
475 882-4000

(G-28)
LEECO INC
5 Alexandra Ln (06001-2210)
PHONE.....................860 404-8876
Janis L Lockhart, Pr
EMP: 8 **EST:** 2003
SALES (est): 202.23K **Privately Held**
SIC: 3545　Machine tool accessories

(G-29)
LEGERE GROUP LTD
Also Called: Legere Woodworking
80 Darling Dr (06001-4217)
P.O. Box 1527 (06001-1527)
PHONE.....................860 674-0392
Joseph Legere, CEO
Ronald Legere, *
Francis Legere, *
Bill Bruneau, *
Steve Nagle, *
EMP: 54 **EST:** 1975
SQ FT: 144,000
SALES (est): 20.57MM **Privately Held**
Web: www.legeregroup.com
SIC: 2434 2431 3442 2499　Wood kitchen
cabinets; Millwork; Metal doors, sash, and
trim; Decorative wood and woodwork

(G-30)
**LUCENT SPECIALTY FIBER
TECH**
55 Darling Dr (06001-4273)
PHONE.....................320 258-3035
EMP: 8 **EST:** 2019
SALES (est): 413.31K **Privately Held**
Web: www.ofsoptics.com
SIC: 3357　Nonferrous wiredrawing and
insulating

(G-31)
MINUTEMAN PRESS
Also Called: Minuteman Press
195 W Main St Ste E (06001-3685)
PHONE.....................860 674-8700
EMP: 8 **EST:** 2011
SALES (est): 123.68K **Privately Held**
Web: www.minuteman.com
SIC: 2752　Commercial printing, lithographic

▲ = Import　▼ = Export
◆ = Import/Export

(G-32)

NATURAL NUTMEG LLC
53 Mountain View Ave (06001-3813)
PHONE...............................860 206-9500
Chris Hindman, *Prin*
EMP: 8 **EST:** 2007
SALES (est): 473.31K **Privately Held**
Web: www.naturalnutmeg.com
SIC: 2721   Magazines: publishing and
   printing

(G-33)

OFS FITEL LLC
Also Called: Ofs Specialty Photonics Div
55 Darling Dr (06001-4273)
PHONE...............................860 678-0371
Jane Cercena, *VP*
EMP: 350
Web: www.ofsoptics.com
SIC: 3357   Nonferrous wiredrawing and
   insulating
HQ: Ofs Fitel Llc
   2000 Northeast Expy
   Norcross GA 30071
   888 342-3743

(G-34)

**OLDCASTLE
INFRASTRUCTURE INC**
Also Called: Rotondo Precast
151 Old Farms Rd (06001-2253)
PHONE...............................860 673-3291
EMP: 43
SALES (corp-wide): 32.72B **Privately Held**
Web: www.oldcastleinfrastructure.com
SIC: 3272   Concrete products, nec
HQ: Oldcastle Infrastructure, Inc.
   7000 Central Pkwy Ste 800
   Atlanta GA 30328
   770 270-5000

(G-35)

ORAFOL AMERICAS INC
120 Darling Dr (06001-4217)
PHONE...............................860 676-7100
Mike Arsenault, *Dir Opers*
EMP: 143
SALES (corp-wide): 903.73MM **Privately
Held**
Web: www.orafol.com
SIC: 3081 5162 3827   Vinyl film and sheet;
   Plastics film; Lenses, optical: all types
   except ophthalmic
HQ: Orafol Americas Inc.
   1100 Oracal Pkwy
   Black Creek GA 31308
   912 851-5000

(G-36)

PMP CORPORATION
25 Security Dr (06001-4227)
P.O. Box 422 (06001-0422)
PHONE...............................860 677-9656
▲ **EMP:** 62 **EST:** 1950
SALES (est): 9.33MM **Privately Held**
Web: www.pmp-corp.com
SIC: 3559   Refinery, chemical processing,
   and similar machinery

Baltic
New London County

(G-37)

**AMGRAPH PACKAGING INC
(PA)**
90 Paper Mill Rd (06330-1436)
PHONE...............................860 822-2000
Kenneth L Fontaine, *CEO*

Robert Guertin, *VP*
Desmond P O'grady, *Treas*
Michael P Devlin, *Sec*
▲ **EMP:** 71 **EST:** 1984
SQ FT: 75,000
SALES (est): 40.47MM
SALES (corp-wide): 40.47MM **Privately
Held**
Web: www.amgraph.com
SIC: 2671 2759 2752 2673   Paper, coated or
   laminated for packaging; Commercial
   printing, nec; Commercial printing,
   lithographic; Bags: plastic, laminated, and
   coated

(G-38)

NUTMEG WIRE
14 Main St (06330-1443)
P.O. Box 719 (06330-0719)
PHONE...............................860 822-8616
Fred Stackpole, *Pr*
Sharon Stackpole, *Sec*
EMP: 10 **EST:** 1984
SQ FT: 15,400
SALES (est): 761.77K **Privately Held**
SIC: 3315   Wire products, ferrous/iron: made
   in wiredrawing plants

Beacon Falls
New Haven County

(G-39)

**ANSONIA STL FABRICATION CO
INC**
164 Pines Bridge Rd (06403-1018)
P.O. Box 175 (06403-0175)
PHONE...............................203 888-4509
Bart Hogestyn, *Pr*
William Hogestyn, *Dir*
Debra Hogestyn, *Dir*
▲ **EMP:** 20 **EST:** 1941
SQ FT: 11,000
SALES (est): 2.29MM **Privately Held**
SIC: 7692 3444 3441   Welding repair; Sheet
   metalwork; Fabricated structural metal

(G-40)

GOLDENROD CORPORATION
25 Lancaster Dr (06403-1049)
P.O. Box 95 (06403-0095)
PHONE...............................203 723-4400
Alessio Pretto, *CEO*
John Pretto, *
Stephen Pretto, *
David Sullivan, *
Judith Pretto, *
▲ **EMP:** 35 **EST:** 1986
SQ FT: 30,000
SALES (est): 11.3MM **Privately Held**
Web: www.goldenrodcorp.com
SIC: 5084 3554 3545 8711   Industrial
   machine parts; Paper industries machinery;
   Machine tool accessories; Engineering
   services

(G-41)

LIBERTY SCREEN PRINT CO LLC
Also Called: Liberty Screen Print Co
141 S Main St (06403-1469)
PHONE...............................203 632-5449
EMP: 16 **EST:** 2014
SQ FT: 10,000
SALES (est): 1.44MM **Privately Held**
Web: www.libertyprintco.com
SIC: 2752 2759   Commercial printing,
   lithographic; Screen printing

(G-42)

MAGNA STEEL SALES INC
2 Alliance Cir (06403-1054)
PHONE...............................203 888-0300
Edward Mulligan, *Pr*
Patricia Mavlouganes, *Sec*
EMP: 15 **EST:** 1984
SQ FT: 27,000
SALES (est): 2.1MM **Privately Held**
Web: www.magnasteel.com
SIC: 3441 5051   Fabricated structural metal;
   Steel

(G-43)

**MARSARS WTR RESCUE
SYSTEMS INC**
206 Skokorat Rd (06403-1413)
PHONE...............................203 924-7315
Robert E Davis, *Pr*
Michelle Davis, *VP*
EMP: 8 **EST:** 1984
SALES (est): 984.98K **Privately Held**
Web: www.marsars.com
SIC: 3561   Pumps, domestic: water or sump

(G-44)

O & G INDUSTRIES INC
105 Breault Rd (06403-1033)
PHONE...............................203 881-5192
EMP: 44
SALES (corp-wide): 496.36MM **Privately
Held**
Web: www.ogind.com
SIC: 3999   Atomizers, toiletry
PA: O & G Industries, Inc.
   112 Wall St
   Torrington CT 06790
   860 489-9261

(G-45)

O & G INDUSTRIES INC
Railroad Ave Ext (06403)
PHONE...............................203 729-4529
William Stanley, *Brnch Mgr*
EMP: 10
SALES (corp-wide): 496.36MM **Privately
Held**
Web: www.ogind.com
SIC: 3281 1542   Stone, quarrying and
   processing of own stone products;
   Commercial and office building, new
   construction
PA: O & G Industries, Inc.
   112 Wall St
   Torrington CT 06790
   860 489-9261

(G-46)

TRADEWINDS
274 Bethany Rd (06403-1402)
P.O. Box 2158 (06011-2158)
PHONE...............................203 723-6966
Kim Ashley, *Prin*
▲ **EMP:** 8 **EST:** 2006
SALES (est): 156.04K **Privately Held**
Web: www.tradewindsnews.com
SIC: 2711   Newspapers, publishing and
   printing

Berlin
Hartford County

(G-47)

ALDEN TOOL COMPANY INC
199 New Park Dr (06037-3738)
PHONE...............................860 828-3556
Daniel Muravnick, *CEO*
Charles Muravnick, *

Kathleen Muravnick, *
EMP: 30 **EST:** 1945
SQ FT: 20,000
SALES (est): 4.49MM **Privately Held**
Web: www.aldentool.com
SIC: 3545   Cutting tools for machine tools

(G-48)

ALL FIVE TOOL CO INC
Also Called: North Amercn Spring TI Co Div
169 White Oak Dr (06037-1638)
PHONE...............................860 583-1693
Joseph B Panella, *Pr*
▲ **EMP:** 15 **EST:** 1967
SQ FT: 18,000
SALES (est): 395.6K
SALES (corp-wide): 9.55MM **Privately
Held**
Web: www.siroistool.com
SIC: 3544 3545   Special dies and tools;
   Gauges (machine tool accessories)
PA: Sirois Tool Company, Inc.
   169 White Oak Dr
   Berlin CT 06037
   860 828-5327

(G-49)

**AMCO PRECISION TOOLS INC
(PA)**
Also Called: Aerospace
921 Farmington Ave (06037-2218)
P.O. Box 442 (06037-0442)
PHONE...............................860 828-5640
Aldo Zovich, *Pr*
Richard Zovich, *
Theresa Zovich, *
EMP: 31 **EST:** 1966
SQ FT: 17,000
SALES (est): 5.3MM
SALES (corp-wide): 5.3MM **Privately Held**
Web: www.amcoprecision.com
SIC: 3845 3721   Medical cleaning
   equipment, ultrasonic; Aircraft

(G-50)

**ASSA ABLOY ACC DOOR
CNTRLS GRO**
Also Called: Yale Commercial Locks & Hdwr
225 Episcopal Rd (06037-1524)
P.O. Box 4004 (06037-0512)
PHONE...............................865 986-7511
Dick Krajewski, *Mgr*
EMP: 89
SQ FT: 2,300
SALES (corp-wide): 11.51B **Privately Held**
Web: www.yalecommercial.com
SIC: 3429   Locks or lock sets
HQ: Assa Abloy Accessories And Door
   Controls Group, Inc.
   1902 Airport Rd
   Monroe NC 28110
   877 974-2255

(G-51)

**ASSA ABLOY ACCESS EGRESS
HDWR**
Also Called: Corbin Russwin Arch Hdwr
225 Episcopal Rd (06037-1524)
P.O. Box 4004 (06037-0512)
PHONE...............................860 225-7411
Martin Huddart, *Pr*
John R Carlson, *
Mike Mortillaro, *
John F Hannon, *
John C Davenport, *
◆ **EMP:** 500 **EST:** 1993
SQ FT: 1,000,000
SALES (est): 87.23MM
SALES (corp-wide): 11.51B **Privately Held**
Web: www.corbinrusswin.com

SIC: 3429 Door locks, bolts, and checks
PA: Assa Abloy Ab
    Klarabergsviadukten 90
    Stockholm 111 6
    850648500

(G-52)
BODYCOTE THERMAL PROC INC
675 Christian Ln (06037-1425)
PHONE..............................860 225-7691
Mike Sakelakos, *Brnch Mgr*
EMP: 40
SALES (corp-wide): 895.27MM **Privately Held**
Web: www.bodycote.com
SIC: 3398 Metal heat treating
HQ: Bodycote Thermal Processing, Inc.
    12750 Merit Dr Ste 1400
    Dallas TX 75251
    214 904-2420

(G-53)
BODYCOTE THERMAL PROC INC
Bodycote
675 Christian Ln (06037-1425)
PHONE..............................508 754-1724
Mike Sakelakos, *Genl Mgr*
EMP: 99
SALES (corp-wide): 895.27MM **Privately Held**
Web: www.bodycote.com
SIC: 3398 Metal heat treating
HQ: Bodycote Thermal Processing, Inc.
    12750 Merit Dr Ste 1400
    Dallas TX 75251
    214 904-2420

(G-54)
BUDNEY AEROSPACE INC
131 New Park Dr (06037-3740)
PHONE..............................860 828-0585
Kevin M Budney, *Pr*
Lisa Budney, *
Richard V Newcombe, *
EMP: 75 EST: 2007
SALES (est): 6.52MM **Privately Held**
Web: www.budneyaerospace.com
SIC: 3728 Aircraft assemblies,
    subassemblies, and parts, nec

(G-55)
BUDNEY INDUSTRIES INC
Also Called: Northeast Overhaul and Repair
40 New Park Dr (06037-3741)
P.O. Box 8316 (06037-8316)
PHONE..............................860 828-1950
EMP: 150 EST: 1984
SALES (est): 20.35MM **Privately Held**
Web: www.budney.com
SIC: 3724 Aircraft engines and engine parts

(G-56)
BUDNEY OVERHAUL & REPAIR LTD
131 New Park Dr (06037-3740)
P.O. Box 8158 (06037-8158)
PHONE..............................860 828-0585
Kevin M Budney, *Pr*
Lisa Budney, *
Richard V Newcombe, *
▲ EMP: 160 EST: 1989
SQ FT: 37,500
SALES (est): 23.43MM **Privately Held**
Web: www.budneyaerospace.com
SIC: 3599 Machine shop, jobbing and repair

(G-57)
CAMBRIDGE SPECIALTY CO INC
588 Four Rod Rd (06037-2280)
PHONE..............................860 828-3579
Peter M Campanelli, *Pr*
Lori Satkowski, *
EMP: 76 EST: 1951
SQ FT: 27,500
SALES (est): 9.84MM **Privately Held**
Web: www.cambridgespecialty.com
SIC: 3728 3724 3714 3544 Aircraft parts
    and equipment, nec; Aircraft engines and
    engine parts; Motor vehicle parts and
    accessories; Special dies, tools, jigs, and
    fixtures

(G-58)
CAPITAL STEEL LLC
190 New Park Dr (06037-3741)
P.O. Box 178 (06037-0178)
PHONE..............................860 828-9353
Oriana Fraser, *
Denise Miranda, *
EMP: 27 EST: 2021
SALES (est): 1.12MM **Privately Held**
Web: www.capitalsteelservice.com
SIC: 3441 Fabricated structural metal

(G-59)
COASTAL INDUSTRIAL DISTRS INC
Also Called: Cid Performance Tool
56 Willow Brook Dr (06037-1534)
PHONE..............................207 286-3319
John Lowery, *Pr*
EMP: 14 EST: 1986
SALES (est): 2.31MM **Privately Held**
Web: www.cidtools.com
SIC: 3541 Machine tools, metal cutting type

(G-60)
COCCOMO BROTHERS DRILLING LLC
1897 Berlin Tpke (06037-3679)
PHONE..............................860 828-1632
Thomas Coccomo, *Mng Pt*
EMP: 15 EST: 2003
SQ FT: 5,000
SALES (est): 2.21MM **Privately Held**
SIC: 1411 Limestone, dimension-quarrying

(G-61)
COMPLETE SHEET METAL LLC
500 Four Rod Rd Ste 122 (06037-2243)
PHONE..............................860 310-5447
Jeffrey Michaud, *Prin*
EMP: 8 EST: 2017
SALES (est): 577.91K **Privately Held**
Web: www.completesheetmetalct.com
SIC: 3444 Sheet metalwork

(G-62)
COMPUTER EXPRESS LLC
365 New Britain Rd Ste D (06037-1366)
PHONE..............................860 829-1310
Michael Psillas, *CEO*
▲ EMP: 14 EST: 1990
SQ FT: 8,500
SALES (est): 4.02MM **Privately Held**
Web: www.computerexpressct.com
SIC: 3577 Computer peripheral equipment,
    nec

(G-63)
CPI MANUFACTURING LLC
128 Old Brickyard Ln (06037-1465)
EMP: 18 EST: 1993
SALES (est): 2.74MM **Privately Held**
SIC: 3599 Machine shop, jobbing and repair

(G-64)
DELMAR PRODUCTS INC
Also Called: D'Andrea USA

400 Christian Ln (06037-1424)
P.O. Box 504 (06037-0504)
PHONE..............................860 828-6501
John Di Mugno Junior, *Pr*
Gale Chaplin, *Sec*
▲ EMP: 18 EST: 1966
SQ FT: 32,500
SALES (est): 8.34MM **Privately Held**
Web: www.delmarproducts.com
SIC: 5162 3089 Plastics sheets and rods;
    Laminating of plastics

(G-65)
FOCUS TECHNOLOGIES INC
600 Four Rod Rd Ste 5 (06037-3665)
PHONE..............................860 829-8998
EMP: 10 EST: 2001
SALES (est): 443.6K **Privately Held**
SIC: 3599 Machine shop, jobbing and repair

(G-66)
FORREST MACHINE INC
236 Christian Ln (06037-1420)
PHONE..............................860 563-1796
David Forrest, *Pr*
EMP: 54 EST: 1973
SQ FT: 17,250
SALES (est): 6.93MM **Privately Held**
Web: www.forrestmachine.com
SIC: 3469 3728 Machine parts, stamped or
    pressed metal; Aircraft parts and
    equipment, nec

(G-67)
FSB INC
Also Called: Fsb North America
24 New Park Dr (06037-3741)
P.O. Box 504 (06492-0504)
PHONE..............................203 404-4700
John Bergstrom, *Pr*
William S Ferguson, *VP*
▲ EMP: 11 EST: 1998
SALES (est): 2.37MM **Privately Held**
Web: www.fsbna.com
SIC: 3429 Locks or lock sets

(G-68)
GRACE MACHINE COMPANY LLC
46 Woodlawn Rd (06037-1544)
PHONE..............................860 828-8789
EMP: 10 EST: 1981
SQ FT: 5,500
SALES (est): 1.16MM **Privately Held**
Web: www.gracemachinecompany.com
SIC: 3599 Machine shop, jobbing and repair

(G-69)
HOSOKAWA MICRON INTL INC
Also Called: Hosokawa Polymer Systems Div
63 Fuller Way (06037-1540)
PHONE..............................860 828-0541
Robert Voorhees, *Pr*
EMP: 45
Web: www.polysys.com
SIC: 3089 Injection molding of plastics
HQ: Hosokawa Micron International Inc.
    10 Chatham Rd
    Summit NJ 07901
    908 273-6360

(G-70)
HW MACHINE LLC
37 Willow Brook Dr (06037-1533)
PHONE..............................860 828-7679
Walter Sewerniak, *Pr*
EMP: 8 EST: 1995
SALES (est): 753.8K **Privately Held**

SIC: 3599 Machine shop, jobbing and repair

(G-71)
INNER ARMOUR BLACK LLC
83 White Oak Dr (06037-1638)
PHONE..............................860 656-7720
Diane Lagace, *VP*
EMP: 9 EST: 2010
SALES (est): 248.65K **Privately Held**
SIC: 2023 Dietary supplements, dairy and
    non-dairy based

(G-72)
KENNEDY GUSTAFSON AND COLE INC
Also Called: Kgc
100 White Oak Dr (06037-1635)
PHONE..............................860 828-2594
Edward Charles Cole, *Pr*
Roberts T Cole, *
Pierre Joseph Roy, *
Robert Thomas Cole, *
EMP: 30 EST: 1962
SQ FT: 25,000
SALES (est): 5.46MM **Privately Held**
Web: www.kgcsheetmetal.com
SIC: 3564 Exhaust fans: industrial or
    commercial

(G-73)
KENSINGTON GL & FRMNG CO INC
124 Woodlawn Rd (06037-1536)
PHONE..............................860 828-9428
Frank Carfora Junior, *Pr*
Mary Sue Hermann, *Sec*
Frank Carfora Senior, *Treas*
EMP: 13 EST: 1976
SQ FT: 2,400
SALES (est): 1.62MM **Privately Held**
Web:
www.kensingtonglasscompany.com
SIC: 2499 5719 1793 Picture and mirror
    frames, wood; Mirrors; Glass and glazing
    work

(G-74)
LLC DOW GAGE
169 White Oak Dr 06037 (06037-1638)
PHONE..............................860 828-5327
Scott Brotherton, *Mgr*
EMP: 8 EST: 1946
SQ FT: 24,000
SALES (est): 269.76K **Privately Held**
Web: www.siroistool.com
SIC: 3545 Gauges (machine tool
    accessories)

(G-75)
LLC DOW GAGE
169 White Oak Dr (06037-1638)
PHONE..............................860 828-5327
Scott Brotherton, *Mgr*
EMP: 7 EST: 2005
SALES (est): 422.54K **Privately Held**
Web: www.siroistool.com
SIC: 3674 Strain gages, solid state

(G-76)
MIDSUN SPECIALTY PRODUCTS INC
Also Called: Tommy Tape
378 Four Rod Rd (06037-2257)
P.O. Box 864 (06489-0864)
PHONE..............................860 378-0111
Robert F Vojtila, *Ch Bd*
Mark C Hatje, *
▲ EMP: 34 EST: 1993
SQ FT: 16,600

SALES (est): 9.32MM **Privately Held**
Web:
www.midsunspecialtyproducts.com
SIC: 3069   Rubber tape
PA: Midsun Group, Inc.
135 Redstone St
Southington CT 06489

(G-77)
NATIONAL SIGN CORPORATION (PA)
Also Called: Signamerica
780 Four Rod Rd (06037-3628)
PHONE..................................860 829-9060
EMP: 17 EST: 1993
SALES (est): 4.09MM **Privately Held**
Web: www.nationalsign.net
SIC: 3993   Signs and advertising specialties

(G-78)
POINT MACHINE COMPANY
588 Four Rod Rd (06037-2280)
P.O. Box 188 (06037-0188)
PHONE..................................860 828-6901
Peter M Campanelli, *Prin*
EMP: 9 EST: 2006
SALES (est): 236.82K **Privately Held**
Web: www.cambridgespecialty.com
SIC: 3724   Aircraft engines and engine parts

(G-79)
PRECISION PUNCH + TOOLING CORP (PA)
304 Christian Ln (06037-1420)
PHONE..................................860 229-9902
Kevin Gregoire, *Pr*
Dennis Glynn, *
EMP: 66 EST: 1965
SQ FT: 44,000
SALES (est): 10.09MM
SALES (corp-wide): 10.09MM **Privately Held**
Web: www.ppunch.com
SIC: 3544   Special dies and tools

(G-80)
PRECISION PUNCH + TOOLING CORP
Eastern Industries
304 Christian Ln (06037-1420)
P.O. Box 7087 (06037-7087)
PHONE..................................860 225-4159
Kevin Gregoire, *VP*
EMP: 9
SALES (corp-wide): 8.03MM **Privately Held**
Web: www.ppunch.com
SIC: 3599   Machine shop, jobbing and repair
PA: Precision Punch + Tooling Corporation
304 Christian Ln
Berlin CT 06037
860 229-9902

(G-81)
PROMEIN STEEL LLC
76 Depot Rd (06037-1439)
P.O. Box 280 (06037-0280)
PHONE..................................860 828-1944
EMP: 11 EST: 2018
SALES (est): 2.48MM **Privately Held**
SIC: 3531   Crane carriers

(G-82)
PYC DEBORRING LLC F/K/A C &
500 Four Rod Rd Ste 114 (06037-2243)
PHONE..................................860 828-6806
Krzysztof Pyc, *Prin*
EMP: 9 EST: 2010
SALES (est): 322.13K **Privately Held**

SIC: 3559   Metal finishing equipment for plating, etc.

(G-83)
ROYAL MACHINE AND TOOL CORP
4 Willow Brook Dr (06037-1534)
P.O. Box Y (06037-0505)
PHONE..................................860 828-6555
Richard Ruscio, *Pr*
Joseph Dibattista, *
Kevin Murphy, *
EMP: 49 EST: 1952
SQ FT: 25,000
SALES (est): 8.61MM **Privately Held**
Web: www.royalworkholding.com
SIC: 3545 5084 3544   Chucks: drill, lathe, or magnetic (machine tool accessories); Industrial machinery and equipment; Special dies, tools, jigs, and fixtures

(G-84)
SANDERS ARCHTECTURAL WDWKG LLC
150 Episcopal Rd (06037-1525)
PHONE..................................860 682-5607
EMP: 7 EST: 2018
SALES (est): 258.82K **Privately Held**
SIC: 2431   Millwork

(G-85)
SIROIS TOOL COMPANY INC (PA)
169 White Oak Dr (06037-1638)
PHONE..................................860 828-5327
Alan E Ortner, *Pr*
Andre Nadeau, *
Marc Begin, *
Bruce Northrup, *
EMP: 37 EST: 1960
SQ FT: 20,000
SALES (est): 9.55MM
SALES (corp-wide): 9.55MM **Privately Held**
Web: www.siroistool.com
SIC: 3544 3545 3542 3599   Jigs and fixtures ; Gauges (machine tool accessories); Machine tools, metal forming type; Machine shop, jobbing and repair

(G-86)
SPACE ELECTRONICS LLC
81 Fuller Way (06037-1540)
PHONE..................................860 829-0001
Kurt Wiener, *Prin*
EMP: 22 EST: 1959
SQ FT: 23,000
SALES (est): 4.95MM **Privately Held**
Web: www.raptor-scientific.com
SIC: 3825 3545   Electrical power measuring equipment; Balancing machines (machine tool accessories)

(G-87)
TIGHITCO INC
Aerostructures Group
245 Old Brickyard Ln (06037-1423)
PHONE..................................860 828-0298
Tawne Castorina, *VP*
EMP: 130
SALES (corp-wide): 443.7MM **Privately Held**
Web: www.tighitco.com
SIC: 3369   Titanium castings, except die-casting
HQ: Tighitco Inc.
8450 Plmtto Commerce Pkwy
Ladson SC 29456

(G-88)
TOMZ CORPORATION
47 Episcopal Rd (06037-1522)
PHONE..................................860 829-0670
Zbig Matulaniec, *CEO*
Tom Barwinski, *
Tom Matulaniec, *
EMP: 130 EST: 1988
SQ FT: 55,000
SALES (est): 26.75MM **Privately Held**
Web: www.tomz.com
SIC: 3451   Screw machine products

(G-89)
TRIGILA CONSTRUCTION INC
30 And A Half Ripple Ct (06037)
PHONE..................................860 828-8444
Thomas Trigila, *Pr*
Tina Trigila, *VP*
EMP: 10 EST: 1987
SALES (est): 438.73K **Privately Held**
Web: www.trigilaconstruction.com
SIC: 2452 1521   Prefabricated wood buildings; General remodeling, single-family houses

(G-90)
VAS INTEGRATED LLC
600 Four Rod Rd (06037-3665)
PHONE..................................860 748-4058
Chris Parzych, *Pr*
Jim Cox, *CFO*
EMP: 7 EST: 2011
SALES (est): 189.23K **Privately Held**
Web: www.arcmedgroup.com
SIC: 3498   Manifolds, pipe: fabricated from purchased pipe

Bethany
New Haven County

(G-91)
AFCON PRODUCTS INC
35 Sargent Dr (06524-3135)
P.O. Box 490 (06410-0490)
PHONE..................................203 393-9301
John Mark Chayka, *Pr*
James Chayka, *VP*
EMP: 15 EST: 1981
SQ FT: 10,000
SALES (est): 2.37MM **Privately Held**
Web: www.afconproducts.com
SIC: 3621 3563 7629 7699   Generating apparatus and parts, electrical; Air and gas compressors; Generator repair; Industrial equipment services

(G-92)
CONNECTICUT ANALYTICAL CORP
696 Amity Rd Ste 13 (06524-3006)
PHONE..................................203 393-9666
Joseph J Bango Junior, *Prin*
Joseph J Bango Junior, *Pr*
Joseph J Bango Senior, *VP*
EMP: 17 EST: 1989
SALES (est): 702.98K **Privately Held**
Web: www.ctanalytical.com
SIC: 3812 5169 8731 8711   Search and navigation equipment; Industrial gases; Electronic research; Engineering services

(G-93)
FCMII INC
20 Sargent Dr (06524-3136)
PHONE..................................203 393-9751
John Ianiri, *Pr*
Mandy Ianiri, *Sec*

EMP: 19 EST: 1983
SQ FT: 20,000
SALES (est): 2.31MM **Privately Held**
Web: www.fcmillwork.com
SIC: 2431   Millwork

(G-94)
LATICRETE INTERNATIONAL INC (PA)
1 Laticrete Park N (06524-3444)
PHONE..................................203 393-0010
◆ EMP: 290 EST: 1956
SALES (est): 135.71MM
SALES (corp-wide): 135.71MM **Privately Held**
Web: www.laticrete.com
SIC: 2899 2891   Chemical preparations, nec ; Epoxy adhesives

(G-95)
LATICRETE SUPERCAP LLC
91 Amity Rd (06524-3423)
PHONE..................................203 393-4558
Edward Metcalf, *Pr*
EMP: 9 EST: 2017
SALES (est): 1.32MM **Privately Held**
Web: www.laticretesupercap.com
SIC: 3823   Moisture meters, industrial process type

(G-96)
NATURES HARVEST LLC
845 Carrington Rd (06524-3141)
P.O. Box 1318 (06770-1318)
PHONE..................................203 758-3725
Theron Simons, *Managing Member*
EMP: 10 EST: 2006
SALES (est): 516.15K **Privately Held**
Web: www.naturesharvestmulch.com
SIC: 2499   Mulch, wood and bark

(G-97)
PLASTIC ASSEMBLY SYSTEMS LLC
Also Called: Pas
19 Sargent Dr (06524-3135)
PHONE..................................203 393-0639
Kurt Fugal, *Managing Member*
EMP: 15 EST: 1998
SQ FT: 9,000
SALES (est): 2.16MM **Privately Held**
Web: www.heatstaking.com
SIC: 3089   Injection molding of plastics

Bethel
Fairfield County

(G-98)
24 SCITICO LLC
15 Whitney Rd (06801-1805)
PHONE..................................203 791-9055
EMP: 7 EST: 2012
SALES (est): 51.89K **Privately Held**
Web: www.dymotek.com
SIC: 3089   Injection molding of plastics

(G-99)
ALPHACOIN LLC
10 Trowbridge Dr (06801-2858)
PHONE..................................475 256-4050
EMP: 8 EST: 2017
SALES (est): 57.68K **Privately Held**
Web: www.alphametalcraft.com
SIC: 3324   Aerospace investment castings, ferrous

(G-100)
BETHEL MAIL SERVICE
Also Called: Bethel Mail Service Center
211 Greenwood Ave Ste 2 (06801-2146)
PHONE...................203 730-1399
Sivlia Duff, *Owner*
EMP: 10 **EST:** 1990
SALES (est): 955.03K **Privately Held**
SIC: 2542　Mail racks and lock boxes, postal service: except wood

(G-101)
BLACKSTONE INDUSTRIES LLC
Also Called: Foredom Electric Co
16 Stony Hill Rd (06801-1031)
PHONE...................203 792-8622
▲ **EMP:** 60 **EST:** 1984
SQ FT: 38,000
SALES (est): 11.37MM **Privately Held**
Web: www.blackstoneind.com
SIC: 3546 3425　Power-driven handtools; Saw blades, for hand or power saws

(G-102)
CHROMATICS INC
19 Francis J Clarke Cir (06801-2847)
PHONE...................203 743-6868
Stephen Newlin, *Prin*
▲ **EMP:** 68 **EST:** 1982
SQ FT: 10,000
SALES (est): 23.74MM **Publicly Held**
SIC: 2819　Industrial inorganic chemicals, nec
HQ: Colorant Chromatics Ag
　Hauptstrasse 30
　Birsfelden BL 4127

(G-103)
CONNECTICUT COINING INC
Also Called: Connecticut Coining
10 Trowbridge Dr (06801-2858)
PHONE...................203 743-3861
Gregory J Marciano, *Pr*
Elise Marciano, *
Patricia R Gershwin, *
EMP: 55 **EST:** 1963
SQ FT: 8,500
SALES (est): 5.34MM **Privately Held**
Web: www.alphametalcraft.com
SIC: 3599 3671　Machine shop, jobbing and repair; Electron tubes

(G-104)
CORONET MACHINERY CORP
8 Trowbridge Dr (06801-2858)
PHONE...................203 744-8009
EMP: 30 **EST:** 1973
SALES (est): 6.13MM **Privately Held**
Web: www.coronetmachinery.com
SIC: 3599　Machine shop, jobbing and repair

(G-105)
CVC II INC (DH)
Also Called: Customvault Convergint
4 Research Dr (06801-1040)
PHONE...................203 401-4205
◆ **EMP:** 51 **EST:** 1984
SQ FT: 3,000
SALES (est): 37.12MM
SALES (corp-wide): 3.37B **Privately Held**
Web: www.convergint.com
SIC: 3499 5044　Safes and vaults, metal; Vaults and safes
HQ: Convergint Technologies Llc
　1 Commerce Dr
　Schaumburg IL 60173
　847 620-5000

(G-106)
DCG-PMI INC
Also Called: Dcg Precision Manufacturing
9 Trowbridge Dr (06801-2858)
PHONE...................203 743-5525
Gerald Palanzo, *CEO*
Paul Sullivan, *
EMP: 49 **EST:** 1943
SQ FT: 33,000
SALES (est): 5.12MM **Privately Held**
Web: www.dcgprecision.com
SIC: 3499 3841　Machine bases, metal; Surgical and medical instruments

(G-107)
DEL-TRON PRECISION INC
5 Trowbridge Dr Ste 1 (06801-2869)
PHONE...................203 778-2727
Ralph A Mcintosh Junior, *Pr*
Edward Keane, *
Katherine Keane, *
Sally A Kelly, *Stockholder*
EMP: 50 **EST:** 1975
SQ FT: 28,000
SALES (est): 6.28MM **Privately Held**
Web: www.deltron.com
SIC: 3562 5084 3568　Roller bearings and parts; Industrial machinery and equipment; Power transmission equipment, nec

(G-108)
DRS NAVAL POWER SYSTEMS INC
11 Durant Ave (06801-1906)
PHONE...................203 366-5211
EMP: 300
SALES (corp-wide): 15.28B **Publicly Held**
Web: www.leonardodrs.com
SIC: 3812　Search and navigation equipment
HQ: Drs Naval Power Systems, Inc
　W126n7449 Flint Dr
　Menomonee Falls WI 53051
　414 875-4314

(G-109)
DUNE DENIM LLC
6 Meadow Ln (06801-1130)
PHONE...................203 241-5409
EMP: 7 **EST:** 2005
SALES (est): 162.04K **Privately Held**
SIC: 2211　Denims

(G-110)
DURACELL COMPANY
Duracell USA
Berkshire Corporate Bldg (06801)
PHONE...................203 796-4000
Ed Degrand, *VP*
EMP: 23
SALES (corp-wide): 302.09B **Publicly Held**
Web: www.duracell.com
SIC: 3691　Storage batteries
HQ: The Duracell Company
　135 S Lasalle St Ste 2250
　Chicago IL 60603
　203 796-4000

(G-111)
DURACELL INTERNATIONAL INC
14 Research Dr (06801-1067)
PHONE...................203 796-4000
▲ **EMP:** 8000
SIC: 3691　Storage batteries

(G-112)
DURACELL MANUFACTURING LLC
14 Research Dr (06801-1067)

PHONE...................203 796-4000
Mark Leckie, *Pr*
EMP: 250 **EST:** 2015
SALES (est): 138.2MM
SALES (corp-wide): 302.09B **Publicly Held**
SIC: 3691　Storage batteries
PA: Berkshire Hathaway Inc.
　3555 Farnam St Ste 1440
　Omaha NE 68131
　402 346-1400

(G-113)
DURACELL US HOLDING LLC (HQ)
14 Research Dr (06801-1067)
PHONE...................203 796-4000
Laura Becker, *Pr*
EMP: 26 **EST:** 2015
SALES (est): 10.94MM
SALES (corp-wide): 302.09B **Publicly Held**
Web: www.duracell.com
SIC: 3691　Alkaline cell storage batteries
PA: Berkshire Hathaway Inc.
　3555 Farnam St Ste 1440
　Omaha NE 68131
　402 346-1400

(G-114)
ELECTRO-LITE CORPORATION
6 Trowbridge Dr (06801-2881)
PHONE...................203 743-4059
Doctor Joshua Friedman, *CEO*
Allan Brooks, *Sr VP*
EMP: 10 **EST:** 1983
SQ FT: 6,750
SALES (est): 2.35MM **Privately Held**
Web: www.electro-lite.com
SIC: 5049 3641　Optical goods; Electric lamps

(G-115)
FOCAL METALS
11 Trowbridge Dr (06801-2858)
PHONE...................203 743-4443
Richard Varnum, *Prin*
EMP: 9 **EST:** 2016
SALES (est): 451.81K **Privately Held**
Web: www.focalmetals.com
SIC: 2434 5021 5211　Wood kitchen cabinets ; Furniture; Counter tops

(G-116)
FOCUS MEDICAL LLC
Also Called: Naturalase
23 Francis J Clarke Cir (06801-2861)
PHONE...................203 730-8885
John B Lee Junior, *CEO*
EMP: 8 **EST:** 1999
SQ FT: 4,000
SALES (est): 2.39MM **Privately Held**
Web: www.focusmedical.com
SIC: 3845　Laser systems and equipment, medical

(G-117)
GRECO INDUSTRIES INC
14 Trowbridge Dr (06801-2858)
PHONE...................203 798-7804
Hugo Greco, *Pr*
Enrico Greco, *VP*
Michael Greco, *VP*
EMP: 7 **EST:** 1985
SQ FT: 2,800
SALES (est): 620.33K **Privately Held**
Web: www.grecoindustries.com
SIC: 3499　Trophies, metal, except silver

(G-118)
GREGORY WOODWORKS LLC
6 Sympaug Park Rd (06801-2838)
PHONE...................203 794-0726
EMP: 9 **EST:** 2011
SALES (est): 908.72K **Privately Held**
Web: www.gregory-builders.com
SIC: 2521 2541　Cabinets, office: wood; Cabinets, lockers, and shelving

(G-119)
INSULATED WIRE INC
Iw Microwave Products Division
2c Park Lawn Dr (06801-1072)
PHONE...................203 791-1999
John Morelli, *Pr*
EMP: 26
SALES (corp-wide): 9.77MM **Privately Held**
Web: www.insulatedwire.com
SIC: 3357　Nonferrous wiredrawing and insulating
PA: Insulated Wire Inc.
　960 Sylvan Ave
　Bayport NY 11705
　631 472-4070

(G-120)
INTERSURFACE DYNAMICS INC
Also Called: Polypolish Products Div
21 Francis J Clarke Cir (06801-2847)
P.O. Box 181 (06801-0181)
PHONE...................203 778-9995
Jonathon J Wolk, *Pr*
Walter Wolk Junior, *VP*
▲ **EMP:** 14 **EST:** 1985
SQ FT: 20,000
SALES (est): 3.92MM
SALES (corp-wide): 113.31MM **Publicly Held**
Web: www.isurface.com
SIC: 2899　Chemical preparations, nec
PA: Amtech Systems, Inc.
　131 S Clark Dr
　Tempe AZ 85288
　480 967-5146

(G-121)
IR INDUSTRIES INC
21 Francis J Clarke Cir (06801-2847)
PHONE...................203 790-8273
Eric Rothstein, *Pr*
▲ **EMP:** 15 **EST:** 1977
SQ FT: 25,000
SALES (est): 1.64MM **Privately Held**
SIC: 3069 5113　Tape, pressure sensitive: rubber; Shipping supplies

(G-122)
J & B SERVICE COMPANY LLC
12 Trowbridge Dr (06801-2858)
P.O. Box 879 (06801-0879)
PHONE...................203 743-9357
EMP: 8 **EST:** 1971
SQ FT: 1,200
SALES (est): 778.93K **Privately Held**
Web: www.jandbservice.net
SIC: 3822 1711　Hydronic pressure or temperature controls; Warm air heating and air conditioning contractor

(G-123)
KANTHAL CORPORATION (DH)
119 Wooster St (06801-1837)
P.O. Box 281 (06801-0281)
PHONE...................203 744-1440
Parag Satpute, *CEO*
Nicklas Nilsson, *
Phil Yu, *
Edward Faustino, *

▲ **EMP:** 82 **EST:** 1982
SALES (est): 50.96MM
SALES (corp-wide): 11.77B **Privately Held**
SIC: 3316 3357 Cold finishing of steel
shapes; Nonferrous wiredrawing and
insulating
HQ: Sandvik, Inc.
1483 Dogwood Way
Mebane NC 27302
919 563-5008

(G-124)
KANTHAL CORPORATION
Also Called: Sandvik Wire and Heating Tech
119 Wooster St (06801-1837)
P.O. Box 281 (06801-0281)
PHONE......................203 744-1440
EMP: 32
SALES (corp-wide): 10.82B **Privately Held**
SIC: 3357 3316 3312 3621 Nonferrous
wiredrawing and insulating; Cold finishing
of steel shapes; Wire products, steel or iron
; Motors and generators
HQ: Kanthal Corporation
119 Wooster St
Bethel CT 06801

(G-125)
LEADING EDGE AERO LLC
15 Berkshire Blvd Ste A (06801-1052)
PHONE......................203 797-1200
EMP: 11 **EST:** 2021
SALES (est): 516.44K **Privately Held**
SIC: 3728 3724 Aircraft parts and
equipment, nec; Aircraft engines and
engine parts

(G-126)
LEADING EDGE CONCEPTS INC
15 Berkshire Blvd Ste A (06801-1052)
PHONE......................203 797-1200
Addison Unangst, *Pr*
Carolyn Mc Grath, *VP*
Rosemarie Unangst, *Sec*
EMP: 7 **EST:** 1991
SQ FT: 6,300
SALES (est): 958.36K **Privately Held**
SIC: 3728 Aircraft propellers and associated
equipment

(G-127)
LORENCO INDUSTRIES INC
25 Henry St (06801-2405)
PHONE......................203 743-6962
Jay Cugini, *Pr*
Loren Cugini, *VP*
EMP: 10 **EST:** 1977
SQ FT: 6,500
SALES (est): 1.04MM **Privately Held**
Web: www.lorenco.com
SIC: 2759 Screen printing

(G-128)
MEMRY CORPORATION (HQ)
Also Called: Saes Memry
3 Berkshire Blvd (06801-1037)
PHONE......................203 739-1100
Dean Tulumaris, *CEO*
Richard F Sowerby, *
Marcy F Macdonald, *
Nicola Dibartolomeo, *
John Schosser, *
EMP: 356 **EST:** 1981
SQ FT: 37,500
SALES (est): 94.95MM
SALES (corp-wide): 259.92MM **Privately
Held**
Web: www.memry.com
SIC: 3841 Surgical and medical instruments
PA: Saes Getters Spa
Viale Italia 3/5/7

Origgio VA 21040
02931781

(G-129)
MONO-CRETE STEP CO CT LLC
12 Trowbridge Dr (06801-2858)
P.O. Box 74 (06801-0074)
PHONE......................203 748-8419
TOLL FREE: 800
Shawn Mc Loughlin, *Prin*
EMP: 10 **EST:** 1974
SQ FT: 19,000
SALES (est): 1.4MM **Privately Held**
Web: www.monocrete.com
SIC: 3272 3446 Steps, prefabricated
concrete; Railings, prefabricated metal

(G-130)
MORRISTOWN STAR STRUCK LLC
Also Called: Star Struck
8 Francis J Clarke Cir (06801-2850)
P.O. Box 308 (06801-0308)
PHONE......................203 778-4925
Wesley Lang, *Prin*
Keith Sessler, *
Ricardo Rago, *
Richard Morris, *
Rose Mccallum, *Mgr*
▲ **EMP:** 31 **EST:** 2006
SQ FT: 20,000
SALES (est): 4.78MM **Privately Held**
Web: www.starstruckllc.com
SIC: 3873 Watches and parts, except
crystals and jewels

(G-131)
PARAMA CORPORATION
7 Trowbridge Dr (06801-2858)
PHONE......................203 790-8155
Aloyzas Petrikas, *Pr*
Aloyzas Petrikas Prestreas, *Prin*
EMP: 8 **EST:** 1978
SQ FT: 13,500
SALES (est): 212.92K **Privately Held**
SIC: 7692 Brazing

(G-132)
PRINT B2B LLC
3 Hillcrest Rd (06801-1210)
PHONE......................203 744-5435
Joseph Mccabe, *Prin*
EMP: 7 **EST:** 2016
SALES (est): 239.69K **Privately Held**
SIC: 2752 Commercial printing, lithographic

(G-133)
PROXYSOFT WORLDWIDE INC
17c Trowbridge Dr (06801-4814)
PHONE......................203 730-0084
Brett W Thornton, *Prin*
EMP: 7 **EST:** 2015
SALES (est): 252.63K **Privately Held**
Web: www.proxysoft.com
SIC: 3843 Dental equipment and supplies

(G-134)
SOUTHERN DIVERSIFIED PDTS LLC
Also Called: Mythic Paint
5 2nd Ln (06801-2852)
PHONE......................917 306-4138
James M Evans, *Managing Member*
Keir Cleinknecht, *Dir*
EMP: 10 **EST:** 1999
SALES (est): 1.8MM **Privately Held**
SIC: 2851 Paints and paint additives

(G-135)
SUMMIT STAIR INC
101 Wooster St (06801-1847)
PHONE......................203 778-2251
Al Curesky, *Pr*
EMP: 11 **EST:** 1999
SALES (est): 458.04K **Privately Held**
Web: www.summit-stair.com
SIC: 2431 Staircases and stairs, wood

(G-136)
TRINE ACCESS TECHNOLOGY INC
2 Park Lawn Dr (06801-1042)
PHONE......................203 730-1756
Fred Schildwachter Iii, *Ch Bd*
William Schildwachter, *Ch Bd*
Betsy Schildwachter, *VP*
▲ **EMP:** 19 **EST:** 1999
SQ FT: 12,000
SALES (est): 4.18MM **Privately Held**
Web: www.trineonline.com
SIC: 3699 Electrical equipment and
supplies, nec

(G-137)
TT TRADE GROUP LLC (PA)
Also Called: Powr2
185 Grassy Plain St Unit 1 (06801-4811)
PHONE......................800 354-4502
Toby Nunn, *CEO*
EMP: 17 **EST:** 2016
SALES (est): 2.84MM
SALES (corp-wide): 2.84MM **Privately
Held**
Web: www.powr2.com
SIC: 3621 1731 5063 Generators and sets,
electric; Standby or emergency power
specialization; Storage batteries, industrial

(G-138)
UNDERGROUND SYSTEMS INC (PA)
Also Called: USI
3a Trowbridge Dr (06801-2858)
PHONE......................203 792-3444
Paul A Alex, *Ch Bd*
James Shattuck, *OF Business Development*
EMP: 20 **EST:** 1975
SQ FT: 12,000
SALES (est): 15.82MM
SALES (corp-wide): 15.82MM **Privately
Held**
Web: www.usi-power.com
SIC: 5063 3823 Cable conduit; Temperature
instruments: industrial process type

(G-139)
VANDERBILT CHEMICALS LLC
Also Called: Bethel Division
31 Taylor Ave (06801-2411)
PHONE......................203 744-3900
John Eshelman, *Prin*
EMP: 188
SQ FT: 40,000
SALES (corp-wide): 266.87MM **Privately
Held**
Web: www.vanderbiltchemicals.com
SIC: 2891 2819 2869 Adhesives and
sealants; Industrial inorganic chemicals, nec
; Industrial organic chemicals, nec
HQ: Vanderbilt Chemicals, Llc
30 Winfield St
Norwalk CT 06855
203 295-2141

(G-140)
VARNUM ENTERPRISES LLC
Also Called: Danbury Sheet Metal

11 Trowbridge Dr (06801-2858)
PHONE......................203 743-4443
EMP: 18 **EST:** 1944
SQ FT: 14,000
SALES (est): 2.7MM **Privately Held**
Web: www.focalmetals.com
SIC: 3441 3699 Fabricated structural metal;
Laser welding, drilling, and cutting
equipment

(G-141)
VITTA CORPORATION
7 Trowbridge Dr Ste 2 (06801-2864)
PHONE......................203 790-8155
Aloyzas Petrikas, *Pr*
Paul Petrikas, *Sec*
▼ **EMP:** 20 **EST:** 1963
SQ FT: 20,000
SALES (est): 2.29MM **Privately Held**
Web: www.vitta.com
SIC: 3443 Weldments

Bethlehem
Litchfield County

(G-142)
AIR VALVES LLC
78 Thomson Rd (06751-2019)
PHONE......................203 266-7175
Leonard J Assard, *Prin*
EMP: 7 **EST:** 2009
SALES (est): 227.52K **Privately Held**
SIC: 3592 Valves

(G-143)
HERFF JONES LLC
39 Terrell Farm Rd (06751-1407)
PHONE......................203 266-7170
Maureen Hawthorne, *Brnch Mgr*
EMP: 8
SALES (corp-wide): 2.02B **Privately Held**
Web: www.yearbookdiscoveries.com
SIC: 2752 Commercial printing, lithographic
HQ: Herff Jones, Llc
4501 W 62nd St
Indianapolis IN 46268
317 297-3741

Bloomfield
Hartford County

(G-144)
AEROSPACE ALLOYS INC
11 Britton Dr (06002-3616)
PHONE......................860 882-0019
Christopher D Allinson, *Pr*
Robert Allinson, *
Richard M Allinson, *
EMP: 51 **EST:** 1980
SQ FT: 30,000
SALES (est): 18.08MM **Privately Held**
Web: www.aalloys.com
SIC: 5051 3449 7389 Sheets, metal;
Miscellaneous metalwork; Design services

(G-145)
AMERICAN PREFAB WOOD PDTS CO
Also Called: American Prefab
1217 Blue Hills Ave (06002-1955)
PHONE......................860 242-5468
Allen Gaudet, *Pr*
EMP: 7 **EST:** 1976
SALES (est): 548.62K **Privately Held**
SIC: 2452 Prefabricated buildings, wood

GEOGRAPHIC

(G-146)
AQUA BLASTING CORP
2 Northwood Dr (06002-1911)
PHONE.....................................860 242-8855
Victoria Stavola, *Pr*
Craig Stavola, *VP*
EMP: 12 **EST:** 1971
SQ FT: 12,000
SALES (est): 1.81MM **Privately Held**
Web: www.aquablasting.com
SIC: 3398 3471 7699   Shot peening (treating steel to reduce fatigue); Cleaning, polishing, and finishing; Engine repair and replacement, non-automotive

(G-147)
ARTEFFECTS INCORPORATED
Also Called: Artfx Signs
27 Britton Dr (06002-3616)
P.O. Box 804 (06002-0804)
PHONE.....................................860 242-0031
Lawrin Rosen, *Pr*
Mel Cornette, *
EMP: 26 **EST:** 1983
SQ FT: 14,000
SALES (est): 4.46MM **Privately Held**
Web: www.artfxsigns.com
SIC: 3993 7336   Signs, not made in custom sign painting shops; Graphic arts and related design

(G-148)
ASCEND ELEVATOR INC
Also Called: Cemcolift Elevator Systems
212 W Newberry Rd (06002-5305)
PHONE.....................................215 703-0358
Enery Wilcox, *Pr*
H Moon, *
S Choi, *
Walter J Herrmann, *
◆ **EMP:** 60 **EST:** 1999
SQ FT: 265,000
SALES (est): 4.46MM
SALES (corp-wide): 68.92B **Publicly Held**
SIC: 3534   Elevators and equipment
PA: Rtx Corporation
      1000 Wilson Blvd
      Arlington VA 22209
      781 522-3000

(G-149)
BASS PLATING COMPANY
82 Old Windsor Rd (06002-1417)
PHONE.....................................860 243-2557
Rocco Mastrobattista, *Pr*
Peter Mastrobattista, *
EMP: 33 **EST:** 1956
SQ FT: 32,000
SALES (est): 4.96MM **Privately Held**
Web: www.bassplating.com
SIC: 3471   Electroplating of metals or formed products

(G-150)
BAY STATE ELEVATOR COMPANY INC
105 W Dudley Town Rd Ste H (06002)
PHONE.....................................860 243-9030
Sal Morassi, *Superintnt*
EMP: 17
SALES (corp-wide): 13.69B **Publicly Held**
Web: www.baystateelevator.us
SIC: 1796 3534   Elevator installation and conversion; Elevators and equipment
HQ: Bay State Elevator Company, Inc.
      275 Silver St
      Agawam MA 01001
      413 786-7000

(G-151)
BECON INCORPORATED (PA)
522 Cottage Grove Rd Bldg H (06002-3111)
PHONE.....................................860 243-1428
George M Economos, *CEO*
David Archilla, *
Bess Economos, *
Maria Economos, *
▲ **EMP:** 126 **EST:** 1966
SQ FT: 65,000
SALES (est): 42.86MM
SALES (corp-wide): 42.86MM **Privately Held**
Web: www.beconinc.com
SIC: 3511   Turbines and turbine generator sets

(G-152)
BLASTECH OVERHAUL & REPR CORP
86 W Dudley Town Rd (06002-1347)
PHONE.....................................860 243-8811
Jeffrey D Wolpert, *Pr*
Karl D Wolpert, *Treas*
EMP: 22 **EST:** 1993
SQ FT: 15,000
SALES (est): 1.75MM **Privately Held**
Web: www.blastechusa.com
SIC: 3511   Turbines and turbine generator sets and parts

(G-153)
BLOOMFIELD WOOD & MELAMINE INC
1 Griffin Rd S (06002-1351)
PHONE.....................................860 243-3226
Eddie Leshem, *Pr*
Jerry Leshem, *Sec*
Steven Leshem, *VP*
EMP: 10 **EST:** 1999
SALES (est): 729.72K **Privately Held**
SIC: 2521 5072   Wood office furniture; Furniture hardware, nec

(G-154)
BRICO LLC
6c Northwood Dr (06002-1911)
PHONE.....................................860 242-7068
Blake Johnson, *Mgr*
EMP: 7 **EST:** 2005
SALES (est): 428.49K **Privately Held**
SIC: 2851   Lead-in-oil paints

(G-155)
CHILDRENS MEDICAL GROUP (PA)
6 Northwestern Dr Ste 101 (06002-3416)
PHONE.....................................860 242-8330
Doctor Lee Hoffman, *Pt*
Lee I Hoffman, *Pt*
David L Brown, *Pt*
Harry C Weinerman, *Pt*
EMP: 35 **EST:** 1957
SALES (est): 2.42MM **Privately Held**
Web: www.prohealthmd.com
SIC: 8011 2326   Pediatrician; Men's and boy's work clothing

(G-156)
COHERENT CORP
Also Called: Coherent Bloomfield
1280 Blue Hills Ave Ste A (06002-5317)
PHONE.....................................860 243-9557
Leon Newmes, *Mgr*
EMP: 144
SALES (corp-wide): 5.16B **Publicly Held**
Web: www.coherent.com

SIC: 3699 3845   Outboard motors, electric; Laser systems and equipment, medical
PA: Coherent Corp.
      375 Saxonburg Blvd
      Saxonburg PA 16056
      724 352-4455

(G-157)
COHERENT-DEOS LLC
1280 Blue Hills Ave (06002-5317)
PHONE.....................................860 243-9557
▲ **EMP:** 80 **EST:** 2001
SQ FT: 50,000
SALES (est): 4.66MM
SALES (corp-wide): 5.16B **Publicly Held**
Web: www.coherent.com
SIC: 3699   Laser systems and equipment
PA: Coherent Corp.
      375 Saxonburg Blvd
      Saxonburg PA 16056
      724 352-4455

(G-158)
DERINGER-NEY INC (PA)
353 Woodland Ave (06002-1386)
PHONE.....................................860 242-2281
Rod Lamm, *CEO*
Keith Kowalski, *
Brett Utter, *Finance**
▼ **EMP:** 175 **EST:** 1950
SQ FT: 100,000
SALES (est): 98.41MM
SALES (corp-wide): 98.41MM **Privately Held**
Web: www.deringerney.com
SIC: 3469 3316 3643 3452   Metal stampings, nec; Cold finishing of steel shapes; Contacts, electrical; Bolts, nuts, rivets, and washers

(G-159)
DERINGER-NEY INC
2 Douglas St (06002-3602)
PHONE.....................................860 242-2281
Gary Smith, *Brnch Mgr*
EMP: 160
SALES (corp-wide): 98.41MM **Privately Held**
Web: www.deringerney.com
SIC: 3643   Current-carrying wiring services
PA: Deringer-Ney Inc.
      353 Woodland Ave
      Bloomfield CT 06002
      860 242-2281

(G-160)
DUCTCO LLC
13 Britton Dr (06002-3616)
PHONE.....................................860 243-0350
EMP: 32 **EST:** 1994
SQ FT: 4,000
SALES (est): 4.78MM **Privately Held**
Web: www.ductco.com
SIC: 3444   Sheet metal specialties, not stamped

(G-161)
ENGINEERED BUILDING PDTS INC
18 Southwood Dr (06002-1952)
PHONE.....................................860 243-1110
Joel Smith, *Pr*
Joel Smith, *Pr*
Theresa J Demorais, *
EMP: 28 **EST:** 1986
SALES (est): 9.61MM **Privately Held**
Web: www.ebpfab.com
SIC: 1791 3446 3449 3444   Structural steel erection; Architectural metalwork; Miscellaneous metalwork; Sheet metalwork

(G-162)
ENJET AERO BLOOMFIELD LLC
3 Old Windsor Rd (06002-1397)
PHONE.....................................860 242-2211
Bruce Breckenridge, *Managing Member*
Christopher Ferraro, *
EMP: 130 **EST:** 1943
SQ FT: 80,000
SALES (est): 16.37MM
SALES (corp-wide): 78.96MM **Privately Held**
Web: www.birken.net
SIC: 3724 3728   Aircraft engines and engine parts; Aircraft parts and equipment, nec
PA: Enjet Aero, Llc
      9401 Indian Creek Pkwy
      Overland Park KS 66210
      913 717-7396

(G-163)
FAXON ENGINEERING COMPANY INC (PA)
17 Britton Dr (06002-3616)
P.O. Box 330337 (06133-0337)
PHONE.....................................860 236-4266
TOLL FREE: 800
John Newton Clark, *Pr*
EMP: 14 **EST:** 1946
SQ FT: 10,000
SALES (est): 6.3MM
SALES (corp-wide): 6.3MM **Privately Held**
Web: www.faxonengineering.com
SIC: 5084 3492 5085 7699   Pneumatic tools and equipment; Hose and tube fittings and assemblies, hydraulic/pneumatic; Industrial fittings; Hydraulic equipment repair

(G-164)
FEMAN STEEL LLC
107 Old Windsor Rd Ste F (06002-1400)
PHONE.....................................860 982-6393
EMP: 13 **EST:** 2007
SALES (est): 1.15MM **Privately Held**
SIC: 3446 1799 3499 3441   Stairs, fire escapes, balconies, railings, and ladders; Ornamental metal work; Fire- or burglary-resistive products; Building components, structural steel

(G-165)
FOILMARK INC
Also Called: ITW Foilmark
40 E Newberry Rd (06002-1441)
PHONE.....................................860 243-0343
EMP: 8
SALES (corp-wide): 15.93B **Publicly Held**
Web: www.itwshinemark.com
SIC: 3497 3549 3544   Metal foil and leaf; Metalworking machinery, nec; Special dies, tools, jigs, and fixtures
HQ: Foilmark, Inc.
      5 Malcolm Hoyt Dr
      Newburyport MA 01950

(G-166)
GROTE & WEIGEL INC (PA)
76 Granby St (06002-3512)
PHONE.....................................860 242-8528
Michael J Greiner, *Pr*
▲ **EMP:** 50 **EST:** 1890
SQ FT: 20,000
SALES (est): 7.42MM
SALES (corp-wide): 7.42MM **Privately Held**
Web: www.groteandweigel.com
SIC: 2013 2011   Sausages and other prepared meats; Meat packing plants

▲ = Import ▼ = Export
◆ = Import/Export

(G-167)
GUHRING INC
121 W Dudley Town Rd Ste C (06002)
PHONE................................860 216-5948
Debbie Wentworth, *Mgr*
EMP: 50
SALES (corp-wide): 1.03B Privately Held
Web: www.guhring.com
SIC: 3545 Cutting tools for machine tools
HQ: Guhring, Inc.
1445 Commerce Ave
Brookfield WI 53045
262 784-6730

(G-168)
HARTFORD AIRCRAFT PRODUCTS INC
94 Old Poquonock Rd (06002-1427)
PHONE................................860 242-8228
James P Griffin, *Pr*
Susan M Griffin, *
EMP: 24 EST: 1973
SQ FT: 13,000
SALES (est): 2.41MM Privately Held
Web: www.hartfordaircraftproducts.com
SIC: 3429 3812 Aircraft hardware; Search and navigation equipment

(G-169)
HERMELL PRODUCTS INC
9 Britton Dr (06002-3616)
P.O. Box 82 (06002-0082)
PHONE................................860 242-6550
Ronald G Pollack, *Pr*
Ronald Pollack, *
Dan Aitchison, *Development**
Lynn Polaski, *
Allie Mcconnell, *Marketing PRODUCT Development*
▲ EMP: 38 EST: 1970
SQ FT: 23,000
SALES (est): 3.99MM Privately Held
Web: www.hermell.com
SIC: 3842 Bandages and dressings

(G-170)
HISCO PUMP INCORPORATED (PA)
Also Called: Hisco
4 Mosey Dr (06002-3531)
PHONE................................860 243-2705
Joseph Montineri, *Pr*
Roy Sjolund, *VP*
▲ EMP: 18 EST: 1976
SQ FT: 54,000
SALES (est): 9.93MM
SALES (corp-wide): 9.93MM Privately Held
Web: www.hiscopump.com
SIC: 5084 3561 7699 Pumps and pumping equipment, nec; Pumps and pumping equipment; Pumps and pumping equipment repair

(G-171)
INDEPENDENT EXPLOSIVES INC
103 Old Windsor Rd (06002-1438)
PHONE................................860 243-0137
Daniel M Werner Junior, *Pr*
EMP: 8 EST: 2012
SALES (est): 108.89K Privately Held
Web: www.iexpsco.com
SIC: 2892 Explosives

(G-172)
INDUSTRIAL CNNCTONS SLTONS LLC
45 Griffin Rd S (06002-1353)

PHONE................................678 216-5817
EMP: 22
SIC: 3613 Control panels, electric
HQ: Industrial Connections & Solutions Llc
305 Gregson Dr
Cary NC 27511
203 229-3932

(G-173)
INTERNTNAL TURBINE SYSTEMS INC
131 W Dudley Town Rd (06002-5328)
PHONE................................860 761-0358
Steve Lamond, *Pr*
EMP: 15 EST: 2014
SALES (est): 755.19K Privately Held
Web: internationalturbinesystemsinc.secureserverites.net
SIC: 3511 Turbines and turbine generator sets

(G-174)
ITW HLOGRAPHIC SPECIALTY FILMS
40 E Newberry Rd (06002-1441)
PHONE................................860 243-0343
▲ EMP: 9 EST: 2007
SALES (est): 511.96K Privately Held
SIC: 3479 Metal coating and allied services

(G-175)
JACOBS VEHICLE SYSTEMS INC
Also Called: Jake Brake
22 E Dudley Town Rd (06002-1440)
PHONE................................860 243-5222
Mark Stuebe, *Pr*
Kevin Potts, *Treas*
James F O'reilly, *Sec*
Frank T Mcfaden, *Treas*
Chris Mulhall, *CFO*
◆ EMP: 420 EST: 1903
SALES (est): 95.27MM
SALES (corp-wide): 5.22B Publicly Held
Web: www.jacobsvehiclesystems.com
SIC: 3519 Engines, diesel and semi-diesel or dual-fuel
HQ: Altra Industrial Motion Corp.
300 Granite St Ste 201
Braintree MA 02184
781 917-0600

(G-176)
JAMES L HOWARD AND COMPANY INC
10 Britton Dr (06002-3617)
PHONE................................860 242-3581
Fred Rotondo Junior, *Pr*
Steven Eppler, *VP*
EMP: 30 EST: 1841
SQ FT: 18,300
SALES (est): 2.21MM Privately Held
Web: www.jameslhoward.com
SIC: 3429 3743 Keys, locks, and related hardware; Railroad equipment

(G-177)
JOHNSON GAGE COMPANY
534 Cottage Grove Rd (06002-3093)
PHONE................................860 242-5541
Lowell C Johnson, *Pr*
▼ EMP: 37 EST: 1922
SQ FT: 15,000
SALES (est): 3.98MM Privately Held
Web: www.johnsongage.com
SIC: 3545 8711 3823 Precision tools, machinists'; Machine tool design; Process control instruments

(G-178)
KAMAN ACQUISITION USA INC (HQ)
1332 Blue Hills Ave (06002-5302)
PHONE................................860 243-7100
Neal J Keating, *CEO*
EMP: 11 EST: 2019
SALES (est): 111.2MM
SALES (corp-wide): 687.96MM Publicly Held
SIC: 3728 Aircraft parts and equipment, nec
PA: Kaman Corporation
1332 Blue Hills Ave
Bloomfield CT 06002
860 243-7100

(G-179)
KAMAN AEROSPACE CORPORATION (DH)
1332 Blue Hills Ave (06002-5302)
PHONE................................860 242-4461
Ian K Walsh, *CEO*
Neal J Keating, *Ch Bd*
Gregory Steiner, *Pr*
Richard C Forsberg, *VP*
Robert D Starr, *VP*
▲ EMP: 750 EST: 1946
SQ FT: 185,000
SALES (est): 662.44MM
SALES (corp-wide): 687.96MM Publicly Held
Web: www.kaman.com
SIC: 3721 3728 Aircraft; Aircraft parts and equipment, nec
HQ: Kaman Aerospace Group, Inc.
1332 Blue Hills Ave
Bloomfield CT 06002

(G-180)
KAMAN AEROSPACE CORPORATION
Kaman Cmpsites-Connecticut Div
30 Old Windsor Rd (06002-1414)
PHONE................................860 242-4461
EMP: 29
SALES (corp-wide): 687.96MM Publicly Held
Web: www.kaman.com
SIC: 3721 3728 5085 Helicopters; Aircraft parts and equipment, nec; Bearings
HQ: Kaman Aerospace Corporation
1332 Blue Hills Ave
Bloomfield CT 06002
860 242-4461

(G-181)
KAMAN AEROSPACE CORPORATION
Air Vehicles & Mro Division
30 Old Windsor Rd (06002-1414)
P.O. Box 2 (06002)
PHONE................................860 242-4461
Salvatore Bordonaro, *Mgr*
EMP: 7
SALES (corp-wide): 687.96MM Publicly Held
Web: www.kaman.com
SIC: 3728 3721 3724 Airframe assemblies, except for guided missiles; Aircraft; Aircraft engines and engine parts
HQ: Kaman Aerospace Corporation
1332 Blue Hills Ave
Bloomfield CT 06002
860 242-4461

(G-182)
KAMAN AEROSPACE GROUP INC (HQ)
1332 Blue Hills Ave (06002-5302)

PHONE................................860 243-7100
Richard R Barnhart, *Pr*
Gregory L Steiner, *Pr*
James C Larwood Junior, *KAMAN AEROSYSTEMS*
Robert D Starr, *VP*
Richard C Forsberg, *Contracts Management Vice-President*
◆ EMP: 14 EST: 1945
SQ FT: 40,000
SALES (est): 907.3MM
SALES (corp-wide): 687.96MM Publicly Held
Web: www.kaman.com
SIC: 3721 3724 3728 3769 Aircraft; Aircraft engines and engine parts; Aircraft parts and equipment, nec; Space vehicle equipment, nec
PA: Kaman Corporation
1332 Blue Hills Ave
Bloomfield CT 06002
860 243-7100

(G-183)
KAMAN CORPORATION (PA)
Also Called: Kaman
1332 Blue Hills Ave (06002-5302)
PHONE................................860 243-7100
Ian K Walsh, *Ch Bd*
Russell J Bartlett, *Sr VP*
Shawn G Lisle, *Sr VP*
Rafael Z Cohen, *CIO*
Megan A Morgan, *Chief Human Resource Officer*
EMP: 60 EST: 1945
SQ FT: 40,000
SALES (est): 687.96MM
SALES (corp-wide): 687.96MM Publicly Held
Web: www.kaman.com
SIC: 3761 3721 3728 5085 Guided missiles and space vehicles; Helicopters; Aircraft parts and equipment, nec; Bearings

(G-184)
KAMATICS CORPORATION (DH)
Also Called: Kamatics
1330 Blue Hills Ave (06002-5303)
PHONE................................860 243-9704
Ian K Walsh, *CEO*
Robert G Paterson, *Pr*
James G Coogan, *CFO*
Jairaj Chetnani, *
Amanda Balboni, *VP Fin*
EMP: 50 EST: 1971
SQ FT: 140,000
SALES (est): 144.66MM
SALES (corp-wide): 687.96MM Publicly Held
Web: www.kaman.com
SIC: 3451 3562 3724 3728 Screw machine products; Ball and roller bearings; Aircraft engines and engine parts; Aircraft parts and equipment, nec
HQ: Kaman Aerospace Group, Inc.
1332 Blue Hills Ave
Bloomfield CT 06002

(G-185)
KAMATICS CORPORATION
1331 Blue Hills Ave (06002-1304)
PHONE................................860 243-7230
Glen Gauvin, *Genl Mgr*
EMP: 188
SALES (corp-wide): 687.96MM Publicly Held
Web: www.kaman.com
SIC: 3562 Ball and roller bearings
HQ: Kamatics Corporation
1330 Blue Hills Ave
Bloomfield CT 06002
860 243-9704

(G-186)
KOOL INK LLC
Also Called: Sir Speedy
21 Old Windsor Rd Ste B (06002-1362)
PHONE..................................860 242-0303
EMP: 13 **EST:** 1985
SQ FT: 5,000
SALES (est): 2.29MM **Privately Held**
Web: www.sirspeedy.com
SIC: 2752 2791 2789 2759   Commercial
printing, lithographic; Typesetting;
Bookbinding and related work; Commercial
printing, nec

(G-187)
LENSESONLY LLC
812 Park Ave (06002-2417)
PHONE..................................860 769-2020
Steven Abbate, *Managing Member*
EMP: 10 **EST:** 2015
SALES (est): 1.1MM **Privately Held**
Web: www.lensesonlyoptical.com
SIC: 3841 3851   Bronchoscopes, except
electromedical; Eyeglasses, lenses and
frames

(G-188)
LEPPERT/NUTMEG INC
113 W Dudley Town Rd (06002-1379)
PHONE..................................860 243-1737
Brian Scott, *Pr*
William Hartnet, *
EMP: 30 **EST:** 1964
SQ FT: 20,000
SALES (est): 4.64MM **Privately Held**
Web: www.leppert-nutmeg.com
SIC: 7629 7694 5084   Electrical equipment
repair services; Electric motor repair;
Compressors, except air conditioning

(G-189)
LESRO INDUSTRIES INC
1 Griffin Rd S (06002-1351)
PHONE..................................800 275-7545
Adam Leshem, *CEO*
Jerry Leshem, *
Alice Leshem, *
Ed Leshem, *
◆ **EMP:** 100 **EST:** 1973
SQ FT: 120,000
SALES (est): 22.76MM **Privately Held**
Web: www.lesro.com
SIC: 2521   Wood office furniture

(G-190)
LIQUIDPISTON INC
1292a Blue Hills Ave (06002-1301)
PHONE..................................860 838-2677
James Norrod, *CEO*
Alexander Shkolnik, *Pr*
Nikolay Shkolnik, *VP*
David Habiger, *Dir*
▲ **EMP:** 27 **EST:** 2004
SQ FT: 6,000
SALES (est): 5.45MM **Privately Held**
Web: www.liquidpiston.com
SIC: 3519   Internal combustion engines, nec

(G-191)
MALLACE INDUSTRIES CORP
Also Called: Iconotech
460 Woodland Ave (06002-1342)
P.O. Box 317 (06002-0317)
PHONE..................................800 521-0194
EMP: 10 **EST:** 2017
SALES (est): 492.17K **Privately Held**
Web: www.iconotech.com
SIC: 2759   Commercial printing, nec

(G-192)
MINARIK CORPORATION
Also Called: Minarik Automation & Control
1 Vision Way (06002-5321)
P.O. Box 723 (06095-0723)
PHONE..................................860 687-5000
▲ **EMP:** 250
SIC: 3625   Relays and industrial controls

(G-193)
MITTYS LLC
76 Granby St (06002-3512)
PHONE..................................516 297-9219
EMP: 25 **EST:** 2015
SALES (est): 3MM **Privately Held**
SIC: 2013   Sausages and other prepared
meats

(G-194)
MK NORTH AMERICA INC
105 Highland Park Dr (06002-1396)
PHONE..................................860 769-5500
▲ **EMP:** 40 **EST:** 1988
SALES (est): 8.76MM **Privately Held**
Web: www.mknorthamerica.com
SIC: 3535   Conveyors and conveying
equipment

(G-195)
MOTION INDUSTRIES INC
Kaman Industrial Technologies
1 Vision Way (06002-5321)
PHONE..................................860 687-5000
EMP: 1700
SALES (corp-wide): 22.1B **Publicly Held**
Web: www.motionindustries.com
SIC: 3491 5085   Industrial valves; Industrial
supplies
HQ: Motion Industries, Inc.
　1605 Alton Rd
　Birmingham AL 35210
　205 956-1122

(G-196)
NIAGARA BOTTLING LLC
380 Woodland Ave (06002-1342)
PHONE..................................909 226-7353
EMP: 7
SALES (corp-wide): 120MM **Privately
Held**
Web: www.niagarawater.com
PA: Niagara Bottling, Llc
　1440 Bridgegate Dr
　Diamond Bar CA 91765
　909 230-5000

(G-197)
OLD CAMBRIDGE PRODUCTS
CORP
244 Woodland Ave (06002-5318)
PHONE..................................860 243-1761
William Oneill, *Prin*
EMP: 10 **EST:** 2010
SALES (est): 146.58K **Privately Held**
SIC: 3643   Current-carrying wiring services

(G-198)
OTIS ELEVATOR COMPANY
Also Called: Otis Elevator Company
212 W Newberry Rd (06002-5305)
PHONE..................................860 242-3632
Tom Vaccaro, *Mgr*
EMP: 300
SQ FT: 116,000
SALES (corp-wide): 13.69B **Publicly Held**
Web: www.otis.com

SIC: 5084 1796 3534   Elevators; Elevator
installation and conversion; Elevators and
moving stairways
HQ: Otis Elevator Company
　1 Carrier Pl
　Farmington CT 06032
　860 674-3000

(G-199)
P&G METAL COMPONENTS
CORP
98 Filley St (06002-1874)
PHONE..................................860 243-2220
Andrew Ponkow, *Pr*
EMP: 19 **EST:** 2015
SQ FT: 27,500
SALES (est): 2.3MM **Privately Held**
Web: www.pgmetalcomp.com
SIC: 3469 3471 3563 4961   Stamping metal
for the trade; Plating and polishing; Air and
gas compressors including vacuum pumps;
Steam and air-conditioning supply

(G-200)
P/A INDUSTRIES INC (PA)
522 Cottage Grove Rd Bldg B (06002-3111)
PHONE..................................860 243-8306
Jerome Edward Finn, *Prin*
Edward Morris, *
◆ **EMP:** 40 **EST:** 1953
SQ FT: 30,000
SALES (est): 9.03MM
SALES (corp-wide): 9.03MM **Privately
Held**
Web: www.pa.com
SIC: 3549 3625   Coiling machinery; Relays
and industrial controls

(G-201)
PDS ENGINEERING &
CONSTRUCTION
Also Called: Pds
107 Old Windsor Rd (06002-1400)
PHONE..................................860 242-8586
TOLL FREE: 800
William Jodice, *Pr*
Ronald Jodice, *
Frank Borawski, *
William Jodice, *VP*
EMP: 46 **EST:** 1965
SQ FT: 13,000
SALES (est): 36.72MM **Privately Held**
Web: www.pdsec.com
SIC: 1541 1542 3441   Industrial buildings,
new construction, nec; Commercial and
office building, new construction; Building
components, structural steel

(G-202)
POINT LIGHTING CORPORATION
61 W Dudley Town Rd 65 (06002)
P.O. Box 686 (06070-0686)
PHONE..................................860 243-0600
Michael J Callahan, *Pr*
Robert Malley, *
Ryan Pape, *
Meghan Pugliese, *
Christine Breton, *
EMP: 32 **EST:** 1993
SQ FT: 48,000
SALES (est): 5.1MM **Privately Held**
Web: www.pointlighting.com
SIC: 3648 5063   Outdoor lighting equipment;
Lighting fixtures, commercial and industrial

(G-203)
PRATT WHTNEY MSRMENT
SYSTEMS I
66 Douglas St (06002-3619)

PHONE..................................860 286-8181
David N Stelly, *Pr*
Daniel J Tycz, *
▲ **EMP:** 24 **EST:** 2003
SQ FT: 20,000
SALES (est): 7.85MM **Privately Held**
Web: www.prattandwhitney.com
SIC: 3829   Measuring and controlling
devices, nec

(G-204)
QUALITY BEAD CRAFT INC
25 Northwood Dr (06002-1908)
P.O. Box 712 (06002-0712)
PHONE..................................860 242-2167
John J Ferguson, *Pr*
Frederick Hillier, *VP*
EMP: 9 **EST:** 1986
SQ FT: 13,500
SALES (est): 244.52K **Privately Held**
Web: www.thebeadery.com
SIC: 3999   Beads, unassembled

(G-205)
R&D DYNAMICS CORPORATION
49 W Dudley Town Rd (06002-1316)
PHONE..................................860 726-1204
Giridhari L Agrawal, *Pr*
EMP: 73 **EST:** 1990
SALES (est): 18.82MM **Privately Held**
Web: www.rddynamics.com
SIC: 8711 3511   Designing: ship, boat,
machine, and product; Turbines and turbine
generator sets

(G-206)
REILLY FOAM CORP
16 Britton Dr (06002-3617)
PHONE..................................860 243-8200
Mark S Burns, *Bmch Mgr*
EMP: 15
SALES (corp-wide): 26.42MM **Privately
Held**
Web: www.reillyfoam.com
SIC: 3069 3086   Foam rubber; Plastics foam
products
PA: Reilly Foam Corp.
　751 5th Ave
　King Of Prussia PA 19406
　610 834-1900

(G-207)
ROKR DISTRIBUTION US INC
Also Called: KMC Music
310 W Newberry Rd (06002-1393)
PHONE..................................860 509-8888
◆ **EMP:** 400
SIC: 5099 3931   Musical instruments parts
and accessories; Musical instruments

(G-208)
ROMCO CONTRACTORS INC
12 E Newberry Rd (06002-1404)
PHONE..................................860 243-8872
Keith Lacourciere, *Pr*
Steve Hansen, *VP*
EMP: 14 **EST:** 1982
SQ FT: 4,000
SALES (est): 2.52MM **Privately Held**
Web: www.romcocontractors.com
SIC: 3441   Fabricated structural metal

(G-209)
SALAMANDER DESIGNS LTD
Also Called: Salamander Designs
811 Blue Hills Ave (06002-3709)
PHONE..................................860 761-9500
▲ **EMP:** 22 **EST:** 1991
SQ FT: 85,000
SALES (est): 6.11MM **Privately Held**

Web: www.salamanderdesigns.com
SIC: 2511 2514 2521 Wood household furniture; Metal household furniture; Wood office furniture

(G-210)
SOUND CONSTRUCTION & ENGRG CO
522 Cottage Grove Rd Bldg H (06002-3111)
PHONE..............................860 242-2109
Michael G Economos, *Pr*
David Archilla, *
George Economos, *
Gary Laurito, *
EMP: 14 EST: 1978
SQ FT: 80,000
SALES (est): 765.94K
SALES (corp-wide): 42.86MM **Privately Held**
SIC: 3441 Fabricated structural metal
PA: Becon, Incorporated
522 Cottage Grove Rd
Bloomfield CT 06002
860 243-1428

(G-211)
SWIFT TEXTILE METALIZING LLC (HQ)
23 Britton Dr (06002-3616)
P.O. Box 66 (06002-0066)
PHONE..............................860 243-1122
Steven Sigmon, *CEO*
Richard Lenhardt, *
▲ EMP: 60 EST: 1997
SQ FT: 35,000
SALES (est): 24.96MM
SALES (corp-wide): 137.12MM **Privately Held**
Web: www.swift-textile.com
SIC: 2295 2297 2257 2221 Metallizing of fabrics; Nonwoven fabrics; Weft knit fabric mills; Broadwoven fabric mills, manmade
PA: Sanders Industries Holdings, Inc.
3701 E Conant St
Long Beach CA 90808
562 354-2920

(G-212)
T & A INDUSTRIES LLC
3 Maple Ave (06002-2301)
PHONE..............................860 309-9211
Timothy D Riccucci, *Admn*
EMP: 8 EST: 2015
SALES (est): 411.69K **Privately Held**
SIC: 3089 Injection molding of plastics

(G-213)
TRIUMPH GROUP INC
1395 Blue Hills Ave (06002-1309)
PHONE..............................860 726-9378
Tom Holzthum, *Brnch Mgr*
EMP: 8
Web: www.triumphgroup.com
SIC: 3728 Aircraft parts and equipment, nec
PA: Triumph Group, Inc.
555 E Lancaster Ave # 400
Radnor PA 19087

(G-214)
TURBINE CONTROLS INC (PA)
5 Old Windsor Rd (06002-1311)
PHONE..............................860 242-0448
Glen Greenberg, *Pr*
Miriam Greenberg, *
EMP: 74 EST: 1980
SQ FT: 35,000
SALES (est): 21.93MM
SALES (corp-wide): 21.93MM **Privately Held**

Web: www.tcimro.com
SIC: 3541 4581 Milling machines; Aircraft maintenance and repair services

(G-215)
UNIVERSAL FOAM PRODUCTS LLC
101 W Dudley Town Rd Unit C&D (06002)
P.O. Box 421 (06029-0421)
PHONE..............................860 216-3015
◆ EMP: 12 EST: 2014
SQ FT: 25,000
SALES (est): 1.1MM **Privately Held**
SIC: 3069 3086 Latex, foamed; Packaging and shipping materials, foamed plastics

(G-216)
WAYPOINT DISTILLERY
410 Woodland Ave (06002-1342)
PHONE..............................860 519-5390
EMP: 7 EST: 2015
SALES (est): 440.31K **Privately Held**
Web: www.drinkwaypoint.com
SIC: 2085 Distilled and blended liquors

(G-217)
WIRETEK INC
48 E Newberry Rd (06002-1404)
PHONE..............................860 242-9473
Kuldeep Singh Sandhu, *Pr*
Parminder Singh Sandhu, *VP*
EMP: 10 EST: 1997
SQ FT: 10,000
SALES (est): 1.69MM **Privately Held**
Web: www.wiretekusa.com
SIC: 3357 3315 Nonferrous wiredrawing and insulating; Wire and fabricated wire products

Bolton
Tolland County

(G-218)
ABLE COIL AND ELECTRONICS CO
25 Howard Rd (06043-7428)
P.O. Box 9127 (06043-9127)
PHONE..............................860 646-5686
Steven K Rockfeller, *Pr*
▼ EMP: 30 EST: 1969
SQ FT: 25,000
SALES (est): 8.22MM **Privately Held**
Web: www.ablecoil.com
SIC: 3677 3679 3089 3676 Filtration devices, electronic; Solenoids for electronic applications; Injection molding of plastics; Electronic resistors

(G-219)
CARLYLE JOHNSON MACHINE CO LLC (DH)
Also Called: Cjmco
291 Boston Tpke (06043-7252)
P.O. Box 9546 (06043-9546)
PHONE..............................860 643-1531
▼ EMP: 17 EST: 1903
SQ FT: 40,000
SALES (est): 12.06MM
SALES (corp-wide): 436.59MM **Privately Held**
Web: www.cjmco.com
SIC: 3568 3625 3566 5063 Clutches, except vehicular; Brakes, electromagnetic; Speed changers (power transmission equipment), except auto; Transformers and transmission equipment

HQ: Ringfeder Power Transmission Usa Corporation
291 Boston Tpke
Bolton CT 06043
201 666-3320

(G-220)
HARVARD CHEMICAL LLC (HQ)
201 Boston Trnpk (06043-7203)
P.O. Box 16458 (30321-0458)
PHONE..............................404 761-0657
EMP: 16 EST: 1986
SALES (est): 4.17MM
SALES (corp-wide): 63.21MM **Privately Held**
Web: www.simoniz.com
SIC: 2899 2841 2842 Chemical preparations, nec; Soap and other detergents; Cleaning or polishing preparations, nec
PA: Simoniz Usa Inc
201 Boston Tpke
Bolton CT 06043
860 646-0172

(G-221)
MUNSONS CANDY KITCHEN INC (PA)
Also Called: Munson's Chocolates
174 Hopriver Rd (06043-7444)
PHONE..............................860 649-4332
Robert Munson, *Pr*
Josephine Munson, *
EMP: 50 EST: 1946
SQ FT: 32,000
SALES (est): 12.07MM
SALES (corp-wide): 12.07MM **Privately Held**
Web: www.munsonschocolates.com
SIC: 5947 5441 2066 2064 Gift, novelty, and souvenir shop; Candy; Chocolate and cocoa products; Candy and other confectionery products

(G-222)
RINGFEDER PWR TRANSM USA CORP (HQ)
Also Called: Ringfeder
291 Boston Tpke (06043-7252)
PHONE..............................201 666-3320
Ross Rivard, *
Gordon Raspe, *
▲ EMP: 10 EST: 1971
SALES (est): 28.87MM
SALES (corp-wide): 436.59MM **Privately Held**
SIC: 5084 3545 Industrial machinery and equipment; Machine tool attachments and accessories
PA: Vbg Group Ab (Publ)
Kungsgatan 57
Trollhättan 461 3
521277700

(G-223)
SIMONIZ USA INC (PA)
Also Called: Washing Equipment Technologies
201 Boston Tpke (06043-7203)
PHONE..............................860 646-0172
William M Gorra, *Pr*
Christine Gorra, *
Mark Kershaw, *
Christine Brunette-gorra, *VP*
▲ EMP: 97 EST: 1952
SQ FT: 30,000
SALES (est): 63.21MM
SALES (corp-wide): 63.21MM **Privately Held**
Web: www.simoniz.com

SIC: 2842 2841 Cleaning or polishing preparations, nec; Detergents, synthetic organic or inorganic alkaline

(G-224)
W H PREUSS SONS INCORPORATED
228 Boston Tpke (06043-7204)
PHONE..............................860 643-9492
N James Preuss, *Pr*
Eleanor H Preuss, *Sec*
Sharon Preuss, *VP*
Norman J Preuss, *Treas*
EMP: 7 EST: 1911
SQ FT: 18,000
SALES (est): 826.85K **Privately Held**
Web: www.whpreuss.com
SIC: 5261 5722 7699 7629 Lawnmowers and tractors; Electric household appliances; Lawn mower repair shop; Electrical household appliance repair

Bozrah
New London County

(G-225)
AC/DC INDUSTRIAL ELECTRIC LLC
16b Stockhouse Rd (06334-1150)
PHONE..............................860 886-2232
Charles Carroll, *Managing Member*
EMP: 8 EST: 2007
SALES (est): 989.78K **Privately Held**
Web: www.acdcindustrial.com
SIC: 3621 1731 5063 Generators and sets, electric; Electric power systems contractors; Generators

(G-226)
ADELMAN SAND & GRAVEL INC
34 Bozrah St (06334-1304)
PHONE..............................860 889-3394
Linda Adelman, *Pr*
Seymour Adelman, *
Wesley Hyde, *
EMP: 18 EST: 1950
SALES (est): 825.42K **Privately Held**
Web: www.adelmaninc.com
SIC: 5032 1442 Sand, construction; Construction sand and gravel

(G-227)
COLLINS & JEWELL COMPANY INC
5 Rachel Dr (06334-1149)
PHONE..............................860 887-8813
Christopher R Jewell, *Pr*
Brian Dudek, *
EMP: 75 EST: 1946
SQ FT: 35,000
SALES (est): 23.34MM **Privately Held**
Web: www.collins-jewell.com
SIC: 3441 Fabricated structural metal

(G-228)
ELECTRO MECH SPECIALISTS LLC
6 Commerce Park Rd (06334-1122)
PHONE..............................860 887-2613
Donna Laparre, *Pr*
Mervin Laparre Ii, *C O O*
EMP: 8 EST: 2002
SQ FT: 20,000
SALES (est): 2.49MM **Privately Held**
Web: www.emechspec.com
SIC: 3699 Electrical equipment and supplies, nec

GEOGRAPHIC

(G-229)
MARTY GILMAN INCORPORATED
Also Called: Gilman Gear
1 Commerce Park Rd (06334-1122)
P.O. Box 97 (06334-0097)
PHONE..................................860 889-7334
Shirley Gilman, *Ch*
EMP: 8
SALES (corp-wide): 6.98MM **Privately Held**
Web: www.gilmangear.com
SIC: 3949 Sporting and athletic goods, nec
PA: Marty Gilman, Incorporated
30 Gilman Rd
Gilman CT 06336
860 889-7334

Branford
New Haven County

(G-230)
24/7 LLC
107 Short Beach Rd (06405-4427)
PHONE..................................203 410-5151
Paul J Intravia, *Pr*
EMP: 7 **EST:** 2017
SALES (est): 292.2K **Privately Held**
SIC: 7692 Welding repair

(G-231)
AEROMICS INC
11000 Cedar Ave Ste 270 (06405)
PHONE..................................216 772-1004
Marc Pelletier, *CEO*
Walter Boron, *Ch Bd*
John Foster, *Prin*
Peter Longo, *Prin*
Frederick Jones, *Prin*
EMP: 7 **EST:** 2006
SALES (est): 515.86K **Privately Held**
Web: www.aeromics.com
SIC: 2834 Pharmaceutical preparations

(G-232)
AIRBORNE INDUSTRIES INC
6 Sycamore Way Ste 2 (06405-6528)
PHONE..................................203 315-0200
Anthony Gentile, *Pr*
Jenny Gentile, *VP*
EMP: 10 **EST:** 1963
SQ FT: 15,000
SALES (est): 3.76MM **Privately Held**
Web: www.airborneindustries.com
SIC: 3728 2399 Aircraft body assemblies and parts; Military insignia, textile

(G-233)
ALEIAS GLUTEN FREE FOODS LLC
4 Pin Oak Dr (06405-6506)
PHONE..................................203 488-5556
Theresa Montleon, *
EMP: 36 **EST:** 2008
SQ FT: 11,000
SALES (est): 3.71MM **Privately Held**
Web: www.aleias.com
SIC: 2099 Food preparations, nec

(G-234)
ALL PANEL SYSTEMS LLC
9 Baldwin Dr Unit 1 (06405-6501)
P.O. Box 804 (06405-0804)
PHONE..................................203 208-3142
Philip P Delise, *Managing Member*
Venance Lafrancois, *
Joe Criscuolo, *
▲ **EMP:** 67 **EST:** 2009

SQ FT: 39,000
SALES (est): 7.48MM **Privately Held**
Web: www.allpanelsystems.com
SIC: 3441 Fabricated structural metal

(G-235)
AMERICAN POLYFILM INC (PA)
Also Called: API
15 Baldwin Dr (06405-6501)
PHONE..................................203 483-9797
Victor J Cassella, *Pr*
Matthew V Cassella, *VP*
Paul C Cassella, *VP*
Larysa Olenska, *Sec*
John C Ehmann, *VP*
EMP: 8 **EST:** 1998
SQ FT: 10,000
SALES (est): 5.42MM
SALES (corp-wide): 5.42MM **Privately Held**
Web: www.americanpolyfilm.com
SIC: 3081 Unsupported plastics film and sheet

(G-236)
ARECNA HOLDINGS INC
15 Commercial St (06405-2801)
PHONE..................................203 819-2322
Arjun Duraisamy Ganesan, *CEO*
Arjun Ganesan, *CEO*
Tim Hughes, *CFO*
EMP: 18 **EST:** 2012
SALES (est): 1.97MM **Privately Held**
Web: www.ancera.com
SIC: 7371 3821 Custom computer programming services; Laboratory measuring apparatus

(G-237)
ATLAS INDUSTRIAL SERVICES LLC
30 Ne Industrial Rd (06405-2845)
PHONE..................................203 315-4538
Michael C Picard, *Managing Member*
EMP: 25 **EST:** 2004
SQ FT: 20,000
SALES (est): 2.49MM **Privately Held**
SIC: 3444 1611 Guard rails, highway: sheet metal; Guardrail construction, highways

(G-238)
AUTAC INCORPORATED (PA)
25 Thompson Rd (06405-2842)
P.O. Box 306 (06471-0306)
PHONE..................................203 481-3444
Marie Burkle, *CEO*
EMP: 9 **EST:** 1947
SQ FT: 12,000
SALES (est): 2.34MM
SALES (corp-wide): 2.34MM **Privately Held**
Web: www.autacusa.com
SIC: 3357 5063 Automotive wire and cable, except ignition sets: nonferrous; Wire and cable

(G-239)
AXIOMX INC
688 E Main St (06405-2971)
PHONE..................................203 208-1034
Christopher Mcleod, *Pr*
Michael Weiner, *CSO**
EMP: 28 **EST:** 2012
SALES (est): 6.18MM
SALES (corp-wide): 435.47MM **Privately Held**
SIC: 2836 Biological products, except diagnostic
PA: Abcam Limited
Discovery Drive

Cambridge CAMBS CB2 0
122 369-6000

(G-240)
BIOMX INC
36 E Industrial Rd Ste 1 (06405-6534)
PHONE..................................203 408-3915
Jonathan Solomon, *CEO*
Russell Greig, *
Marina Wolfson, *CAO*
Assaf Oron, *Chief Business Officer*
Sailaja Puttagunta, *CMO*
EMP: 106 **EST:** 2017
SQ FT: 3,770
Web: www.biomx.com
SIC: 2836 Biological products, except diagnostic

(G-241)
BLAKESLEE PRESTRESS INC (PA)
Rt 139 At Mc Dermott Rd (06405)
P.O. Box 510 (06405-0510)
PHONE..................................203 315-7090
Mario J Bertolini, *Pr*
R W Vine, *
Vincent A Gambardella, *
Robert J Vitelli, *
Alan Vine, *
▲ **EMP:** 250 **EST:** 1976
SQ FT: 165,000
SALES (est): 25.64MM
SALES (corp-wide): 25.64MM **Privately Held**
Web: www.blakesleeprestress.com
SIC: 3272 Prestressed concrete products

(G-242)
CAS MEDICAL SYSTEMS INC
Also Called: Casmed
44 E Industrial Rd (06405-6507)
PHONE..................................203 488-6056
EMP: 26
SALES (corp-wide): 6B **Publicly Held**
Web: www.edwards.com
SIC: 3841 Blood pressure apparatus
HQ: Cas Medical Systems, Inc.
1 Edwards Way
Irvine CA 92614
203 488-6056

(G-243)
CD SOLUTIONS INC
420 E Main St Ste 16 (06405-2942)
PHONE..................................203 481-5895
David Pfrommer, *Pr*
EMP: 7 **EST:** 1994
SALES (est): 249.8K **Privately Held**
SIC: 7372 4226 Prepackaged software; Document and office records storage

(G-244)
CERRITO FURNITURE INDS INC
Also Called: Cerritos Upholstery Concepts
7 Venice St (06405-3111)
PHONE..................................203 481-2580
Ronald Cerrito, *Pr*
Robert Cerrito, *Sec*
EMP: 14 **EST:** 1976
SQ FT: 7,000
SALES (est): 597.34K **Privately Held**
Web: www.cerritofurniture.com
SIC: 2512 5712 Upholstered household furniture; Furniture stores

(G-245)
CRYSTAL JOURNEY CANDLES LLC
69 N Branford Rd (06405-2810)

PHONE..................................203 433-4735
Cosmo Coriglianao, *Owner*
▲ **EMP:** 10 **EST:** 1999
SQ FT: 5,000
SALES (est): 468.51K **Privately Held**
Web: www.crystaljourneycandles.com
SIC: 3999 5947 Candles; Gift, novelty, and souvenir shop

(G-246)
CYBERCHROME INC
19 Business Park Dr Ste B (06405-2936)
PHONE..................................203 488-9594
EMP: 34 **EST:** 1986
SALES (est): 7.78MM **Privately Held**
Web: www.cyberchrome.com
SIC: 2752 Commercial printing, lithographic

(G-247)
CYBERRESEARCH INC
29 Business Park Dr Ste D (06405-2976)
PHONE..................................203 643-5000
◆ **EMP:** 23 **EST:** 1983
SALES (est): 2.36MM **Privately Held**
Web: www.cyberresearch.com
SIC: 7373 5045 3823 3571 Computer integrated systems design; Computers, nec ; Process control instruments; Electronic computers

(G-248)
CYGNUS MEDICAL LLC
965 W Main St Ste 2 (06405-3454)
PHONE..................................800 990-7489
Walter L Maquire Junior, *Managing Member*
▲ **EMP:** 8 **EST:** 2000
SALES (est): 1.03MM **Privately Held**
Web: www.cygnusmedical.com
SIC: 3841 Surgical and medical instruments

(G-249)
DERBY TIRE COMPANY
Also Called: Whip-It Tire of Branford
34 N Main St (06405-3022)
PHONE..................................203 481-8473
David L Coventry, *Brnch Mgr*
EMP: 10
SALES (corp-wide): 1.79MM **Privately Held**
Web: www.whipittire.com
SIC: 5531 5014 7534 Automotive tires; Tires and tubes; Tire retreading and repair shops
PA: The Derby Tire Company
20 Eagle St
Waterbury CT

(G-250)
DOLTRONICS LLC
65-4 N Branford Rd (06405-2861)
PHONE..................................203 488-8766
EMP: 32 **EST:** 1981
SQ FT: 3,500
SALES (est): 925.35K **Privately Held**
Web: www.doltronics.com
SIC: 8731 3679 Electronic research; Electronic circuits

(G-251)
DORIC VAULT CONNECTICUT LLC
23 Thistle Meadow Ln (06405-4035)
PHONE..................................203 494-0172
EMP: 7 **EST:** 2007
SALES (est): 12.5K **Privately Held**
SIC: 3272 Burial vaults, concrete or precast terrazzo

(G-252)
DRM RESEARCH LABORATORIES INC
8 Juniper Point Rd (06405-5632)
PHONE...............................203 488-5555
Samuel Waknine, *Pr*
EMP: 10 EST: 1993
SALES (est): 888.7K **Privately Held**
Web: www.drmco.com
SIC: 3843 3999 8731 Dental materials; Barber and beauty shop equipment; Biotechnical research, commercial

(G-253)
ESSEX LLC
120 N Main St (06405-3011)
PHONE...............................602 374-1890
EMP: 7 EST: 2016
SALES (est): 465.35K **Privately Held**
Web: www.theessex.com
SIC: 2092 Fresh or frozen packaged fish

(G-254)
EVOLVEIMMUNE THERAPEUTICS INC
23 Business Park Dr (06405-2904)
PHONE...............................203 858-7389
Stephen Bloch, *CEO*
Rebecca Frey, *COO*
Jennifer Gabler, *CFO*
EMP: 12 EST: 2020
SALES (est): 1.17MM **Privately Held**
Web: www.evolveimmune.com
SIC: 2834 Pharmaceutical preparations

(G-255)
FABRIQUE LTD (PA)
Also Called: Fabrique
764 E Main St Ste 1 (06405-2921)
PHONE...............................203 481-2266
Su Dan, *Pr*
▲ EMP: 9 EST: 1980
SALES (est): 1.02MM **Privately Held**
Web: www.fabriqueusa.com
SIC: 3161 Cases, carrying, nec

(G-256)
FILMCO RUST PROTECTION LLC
63-5 N Branford Rd (06405-2860)
PHONE...............................203 483-5017
Michael Florio, *Prin*
EMP: 10 EST: 2016
SALES (est): 52.49K **Privately Held**
Web: www.filmcorustprotection.com
SIC: 2899 Chemical preparations, nec

(G-257)
FITZGERALD AND WOOD INC
85 Rogers St Ste 3 (06405-3674)
PHONE...............................203 488-2553
Thomas J Shanley, *Pr*
Susan Shanley, *Mgr*
EMP: 8 EST: 1924
SQ FT: 3,000
SALES (est): 732.3K **Privately Held**
Web: www.fitzwoodplumbing.com
SIC: 3432 Plumbing fixture fittings and trim

(G-258)
FREETHINK TECHNOLOGIES INC
35 Ne Industrial Rd (06405-6802)
PHONE...............................860 237-5800
K Waterman, *Pr*
Kenneth C Waterman, *CEO*
Mark Kastan, *VP*
Ken Waterman, *Pr*

Butch Waterman, *CFO*
EMP: 19 EST: 2011
SALES (est): 2.96MM **Privately Held**
Web: www.freethinktech.com
SIC: 7372 8732 Prepackaged software; Research services, except laboratory

(G-259)
FREVVO INC
500 E Main St Ste 330 (06405-2929)
PHONE...............................203 208-3117
Ashish Desphande, *CEO*
Nancy Esposito, *COO*
EMP: 18 EST: 2007
SALES (est): 1.5MM **Privately Held**
Web: www.frevvo.com
SIC: 7372 Business oriented computer software

(G-260)
FYC APPAREL GROUP LLC (PA)
Also Called: Allison Taylor
30 Thompson Rd (06405-2842)
P.O. Box 812 (06405-0812)
PHONE...............................203 481-2420
Sunny Leigh, *
Kathe Sherman, *
▲ EMP: 100 EST: 1992
SQ FT: 42,000
SALES (est): 18.8MM **Privately Held**
SIC: 2331 2335 2337 5651 Women's and misses' blouses and shirts; Women's, junior's, and misses' dresses; Women's and misses' suits and skirts; Family clothing stores

(G-261)
GILEAD SCIENCES INC
36 E Industrial Rd Ste 3 (06405-6534)
PHONE...............................203 315-1222
EMP: 7
SALES (corp-wide): 30.39B **Publicly Held**
SIC: 2836 Biological products, except diagnostic
PA: Gilead Sciences, Inc.
    333 Lakeside Dr
    Foster City CA 94404
    650 574-3000

(G-262)
GREG ROBBINS AND ASSOCIATES
15 Park Pl (06405-7726)
PHONE...............................888 699-8876
Gregory Robbins, *Prin*
EMP: 7 EST: 2011
SALES (est): 235.82K **Privately Held**
SIC: 2024 Ice cream and frozen deserts

(G-263)
HARCOSEMCO LLC
186 Cedar St (06405-6011)
P.O. Box 10 (06405-0010)
PHONE...............................203 483-3700
Raymond Laubenthal, *CEO*
Michael Milardo, *
Gregory Rufus, *
EMP: 137 EST: 1951
SQ FT: 1,200
SALES (est): 48.87MM
SALES (corp-wide): 6.58B **Publicly Held**
Web: www.harcosemco.com
SIC: 3829 Aircraft and motor vehicle measurement equipment
HQ: Transdigm, Inc.
    1301 E 9th St Ste 3000
    Cleveland OH 44114

(G-264)
HOUSTON-WEBER SYSTEMS INC
31 Business Park Dr Ste 3 (06405-2977)
PHONE...............................203 481-0115
Via Weber, *Pr*
Charles Weber, *VP*
Carol Weber, *Sec*
EMP: 8 EST: 1958
SQ FT: 13,000
SALES (est): 983.09K **Privately Held**
Web: www.ober-read.com
SIC: 3494 3599 Valves and pipe fittings, nec ; Machine shop, jobbing and repair

(G-265)
HOWMET CORPORATION
2 Commercial St (06405-2801)
PHONE...............................203 315-6150
EMP: 294
SALES (corp-wide): 5.66B **Publicly Held**
Web: www.howmet.com
SIC: 3324 Commercial investment castings, ferrous
HQ: Howmet Corporation
    1 Misco Dr
    Whitehall MI 49461
    231 894-5686

(G-266)
HOWMET CORPORATION
Howmet Trbine Cmpnents Coating
4 Commercial St (06405-2801)
PHONE...............................203 481-3451
John Schilbe, *Mgr*
EMP: 1053
SALES (corp-wide): 6.64B **Publicly Held**
Web: www.howmet.com
SIC: 3324 Commercial investment castings, ferrous
HQ: Howmet Corporation
    1 Misco Dr
    Whitehall MI 49461
    231 894-5686

(G-267)
IVY BIOMEDICAL SYSTEMS INC
11 Business Park Dr Ste 10 (06405-2959)
PHONE...............................203 481-4183
James W Biondi, *Ch*
Richard Kosmala, *
Richard A Mentelos, *
Stephen Childs, *
▲ EMP: 47 EST: 1984
SQ FT: 14,700
SALES (est): 10.13MM **Privately Held**
Web: www.ivybiomedical.com
SIC: 3845 Patient monitoring apparatus, nec

(G-268)
LQ MECHATRONICS INC
2 Sycamore Way (06405-6551)
PHONE...............................203 433-4430
Hans-elmar Kessler, *Ex VP*
▲ EMP: 9 EST: 2011
SQ FT: 27,900
SALES (est): 3.58MM
SALES (corp-wide): 56.87MM **Privately Held**
Web: www.lq-group.com
SIC: 3823 3824 3679 Process control instruments; Electromechanical counters; Harness assemblies, for electronic use: wire or cable
PA: Lq Mechatronik-Systeme Gmbh
    Carl-Benz-Str. 6
    Besigheim BW 74354
    714396830

(G-269)
LUVATA WATERBURY INC
8 Baldwin Dr (06405-6501)
PHONE...............................203 488-5956
James C Lajewski, *Brnch Mgr*
EMP: 34
Web: www.luvata.com
SIC: 3496 Miscellaneous fabricated wire products
HQ: Luvata Waterbury, Inc.
    2121 Thomaston Ave
    Waterbury CT 06704

(G-270)
MADISON COMPANY (PA)
27 Business Park Dr (06405-2954)
PHONE...............................203 488-4477
Steven Schickler, *Pr*
EMP: 44 EST: 1959
SQ FT: 20,000
SALES (est): 11.13MM
SALES (corp-wide): 11.13MM **Privately Held**
Web: www.madisonco.com
SIC: 3613 3823 Switchgear and switchboard apparatus; Liquid level instruments, industrial process type

(G-271)
MADISON POLYMERIC ENGRG INC
Also Called: M P E
965 W Main St Ste 2 (06405-3454)
PHONE...............................203 488-4554
Walter L Maguire Junior, *Pr*
Robert Hojnacki, *
EMP: 45 EST: 1976
SQ FT: 50,000
SALES (est): 8.84MM **Privately Held**
Web: www.madpoly.com
SIC: 3086 Plastics foam products

(G-272)
MOSAIC PRTG SIGNAGE MKTG SVCS
250 W Main St (06405-4032)
PHONE...............................203 483-4598
EMP: 8 EST: 2019
SALES (est): 239.22K **Privately Held**
Web: www.mosaic247.net
SIC: 2752 Offset printing

(G-273)
NEW ENGLAND BEVERAGES LLC
137 N Branford Rd (06405-2810)
PHONE...............................203 208-4517
EMP: 8 EST: 2011
SALES (est): 120.18K **Privately Held**
SIC: 2086 Carbonated beverages, nonalcoholic: pkged. in cans, bottles

(G-274)
ROBINSON TAPE & LABEL INC
32 E Industrial Rd Ste 1 (06405-6524)
PHONE...............................203 481-5581
TOLL FREE: 800
Edward A Pepe, *Pr*
Dennis Smith, *VP*
Dawn Sterns, *Stockholder*
EMP: 20 EST: 1969
SQ FT: 11,000
SALES (est): 4.64MM **Privately Held**
Web: www.robinsontapeandlabel.com
SIC: 2759 Labels and seals: printing, nsk

(G-275)
SCHMITT REALTY HOLDINGS INC
Also Called: Acitronics
746 E Main St (06405-2918)
PHONE..................................203 488-3252
Stephen Sadowski, *Brnch Mgr*
EMP: 14
SALES (corp-wide): 19.22MM **Privately Held**
Web: www.georgeschmitt.com
SIC: 2754 2796 Rotogravure printing;
Platemaking services
PA: Schmitt Realty Holdings, Inc.
251 Boston Post Rd
Guilford CT 06437
203 453-4334

(G-276)
SEMCO INSTRUMENTS INC
Also Called: Harcosemco
186 Cedar St (06405-6011)
PHONE..................................661 362-6117
Theresa V Von Szilassy, *Mgr*
EMP: 23
SALES (corp-wide): 6.58B **Publicly Held**
Web: www.harcosemco.com
SIC: 3829 Measuring and controlling
devices, nec
HQ: Semco Instruments, Inc.
186 Cedar St
Branford CT 06405
203 483-3700

(G-277)
SEMCO INSTRUMENTS INC (DH)
Also Called: Harcosemco
186 Cedar St (06405-6011)
PHONE..................................203 483-3700
Michael G Moore, *Pr*
Vincent Sandoval, *
EMP: 177 EST: 1965
SQ FT: 38,000
SALES (est): 64.21MM
SALES (corp-wide): 6.58B **Publicly Held**
Web: www.harcosemco.com
SIC: 3829 Thermometers and temperature
sensors
HQ: Transdigm, Inc.
1301 E 9th St Ste 3000
Cleveland OH 44114

(G-278)
SORBUS INC
20 Baldwin Dr (06405-6501)
PHONE..................................203 481-2810
Brian Richardson, *Pr*
EMP: 10 EST: 1981
SALES (est): 1.37MM **Privately Held**
Web: www.respondsystems.com
SIC: 8041 3845 Offices and clinics of
chiropractors; Laser systems and
equipment, medical

(G-279)
STERLING MATERIALS LLC
17 Tanglewood Dr (06405-3355)
PHONE..................................203 315-6619
Suzanne Hopkins, *Prin*
EMP: 7 EST: 2011
SALES (est): 137.41K **Privately Held**
SIC: 3273 Ready-mixed concrete

(G-280)
STONY CREEK QUARRY CORPORATION
7 Business Park Dr Ste A (06405-2926)
PHONE..................................203 483-3904
Doug Anderson, *Pr*

Bill Gaunt, *Treas*
William E Gaunt Junior, *Treas*
EMP: 9 EST: 2006
SALES (est): 1.38MM **Privately Held**
Web: www.stonycreekquarry.com
SIC: 1411 Granite, dimension-quarrying

(G-281)
TEK-MOTIVE INC
171 Turtle Bay Dr (06405-4902)
PHONE..................................203 468-2224
Thomas Moalli, *Pr*
Ronald Moalli, *
Angela R Moalli, *
Richard Moalli, *
Carol Maolli, *
EMP: 18 EST: 1981
SALES (est): 3.05MM **Privately Held**
Web: www.tek-motive.com
SIC: 5013 3714 3499 Automotive supplies
and parts; Motor vehicle brake systems and
parts; Friction material, made from
powdered metal

(G-282)
THIMBLE ISLAND BREWING COMPANY
16 Business Park Dr (06405-2924)
PHONE..................................203 208-2827
Justin Gargano, *Pr*
EMP: 25 EST: 2011
SALES (est): 2.54MM **Privately Held**
Web: www.thimbleislandbrewery.com
SIC: 5813 2082 Bars and lounges; Near
beer

(G-283)
TOTAL CONCEPT TOOL INC
2 Research Dr Ste 1 (06405-2858)
PHONE..................................203 483-1130
Albert Mirto, *Pr*
Jennifer Mirto, *VP*
EMP: 8 EST: 1989
SALES (est): 812.65K **Privately Held**
Web: www.totalconcepttool.com
SIC: 3544 3599 Special dies and tools;
Machine shop, jobbing and repair

(G-284)
VOLPE CABLE CORPORATION
201 Linden Ave (06405-5123)
PHONE..................................203 623-1818
Frank Volpe, *CEO*
▲ EMP: 115 EST: 1984
SALES (est): 10.75MM **Privately Held**
SIC: 3357 Coaxial cable, nonferrous

(G-285)
WALLINGFORD INDUSTRIES INC
31 Business Park Dr Ste 3 (06405-2977)
PHONE..................................203 481-0359
Charles Weber Junior, *Pr*
Vincea Weber, *VP*
Carol Weber, *Sec*
EMP: 10 EST: 1947
SQ FT: 15,000
SALES (est): 1.25MM **Privately Held**
SIC: 3599 Machine and other job shop work

(G-286)
WALLINGFORD PRTG BUS FORMS INC
758 E Main St (06405-2918)
PHONE..................................203 481-1911
Jennifer Bright, *Pr*
Thomas Bright, *VP*
EMP: 10 EST: 1967
SQ FT: 5,500

SALES (est): 789.38K **Privately Held**
SIC: 2761 5111 2759 Manifold business
forms; Printing and writing paper;
Commercial printing, nec

(G-287)
ZUSE INC
54 E Industrial Rd (06405-6507)
PHONE..................................203 458-3295
Ted Zuse, *Pr*
Skip Zuse, *VP*
Thatcher Zuse. *Stockholder*
EMP: 51 EST: 1989
SQ FT: 6,000
SALES (est): 6.74MM **Privately Held**
Web: www.zuse.com
SIC: 2396 2395 Screen printing on fabric
articles; Pleating and stitching

Bridgeport
Fairfield County

(G-288)
5N PLUS CORP
380 Horace St (06610-1903)
PHONE..................................608 846-1357
◆ EMP: 18 EST: 2010
SALES (est): 2.91MM **Privately Held**
Web: www.5nplus.com
SIC: 5074 2899 Heating equipment and
panels, solar; Chemical preparations, nec

(G-289)
5N PLUS WISCONSIN INC
Also Called: 5n Plus
380a Horace St (06610-1903)
PHONE..................................203 384-0331
Richard Perron, *CFO*
Paul Tancell, *VP*
◆ EMP: 16 EST: 1969
SQ FT: 40,000
SALES (est): 9.03MM
SALES (corp-wide): 264.22MM **Privately Held**
Web: www.5nplus.com
SIC: 3341 Secondary nonferrous metals
PA: 5n Plus Inc.
4385 Rue Garand
Saint-Laurent QC H4R 2
514 856-0644

(G-290)
A J R INC
Also Called: Interface Technology
67 Poland St Ste 4 (06605-3266)
PHONE..................................203 384-0400
John Vaughan, *Pr*
EMP: 10 EST: 1983
SQ FT: 7,000
SALES (est): 1.08MM **Privately Held**
Web: www.interfacetechnology.net
SIC: 3357 Coaxial cable, nonferrous

(G-291)
ABC SIGN CORPORATION
125 Front St (06606-5108)
PHONE..................................203 513-8110
Greg De Santy, *CEO*
Gus De Santy, *
Greg De Santy, *Pr*
EMP: 25 EST: 1955
SQ FT: 20,000
SALES (est): 4.66MM **Privately Held**
Web: www.abcsigncorp.com
SIC: 3993 Signs, not made in custom sign
painting shops

(G-292)
ACSON TOOL COMPANY
62 Carroll Ave (06607-2317)
PHONE..................................203 334-8050
David Deandrade, *Pr*
Antro Deandrade, *VP*
EMP: 18 EST: 1951
SALES (est): 491.89K **Privately Held**
SIC: 3544 Dies, plastics forming

(G-293)
ALUMINUM FINISHING COMPANY INC
1575 Railroad Ave (06605-2031)
P.O. Box 3379 (06605-0379)
PHONE..................................203 366-5871
Edward Sivri, *Pr*
EMP: 26 EST: 1948
SALES (est): 2.5MM **Privately Held**
Web: www.afc1948.com
SIC: 3471 Electroplating of metals or
formed products

(G-294)
AMERICAN HYDROGEN NORTHEAST
520 Savoy St (06606-4125)
PHONE..................................203 449-4614
EMP: 7 EST: 2011
SALES (est): 63.29K **Privately Held**
SIC: 3999 Manufacturing industries, nec

(G-295)
AMERICAN MOLDED PRODUCTS INC
130 Front St (06606-5109)
PHONE..................................203 333-0183
Mehmed Ramic, *Pr*
Paul Cipriono Taulo, *VP*
EMP: 10 EST: 1982
SQ FT: 4,800
SALES (est): 955.71K **Privately Held**
SIC: 3089 3544 Injection molding of plastics
; Industrial molds

(G-296)
AMODEX PRODUCTS INCORPORATED
1354 State St (06605-2003)
P.O. Box 3332 (06605-0332)
PHONE..................................203 335-1255
Sylvia Fatse, *Pr*
James Fatse, *
EMP: 30 EST: 1957
SQ FT: 1,500
SALES (est): 2.17MM **Privately Held**
Web: www.amodexusa.com
SIC: 2842 2844 2841 Stain removers;
Cosmetic preparations; Soap: granulated,
liquid, cake, flaked, or chip

(G-297)
ARCADE TECHNOLOGY LLC
Also Called: Arcade Metal Stampings
38 Union Ave (06607-2336)
PHONE..................................203 366-3871
Steve Pepe, *Managing Member*
William Rhone, *
EMP: 54 EST: 1948
SQ FT: 45,000
SALES (est): 5.85MM **Privately Held**
Web: www.arcademetalstamping.com
SIC: 3469 3644 3599 3544 Stamping metal
for the trade; Electric outlet, switch, and
fuse boxes; Electrical discharge machining
(EDM); Special dies, tools, jigs, and fixtures

▲ = Import ▼ = Export
◆ = Import/Export

(G-298)
ARCHITECTURAL STONE GROUP LLC
9 Island Brook Ave (06606-5113)
PHONE.................................203 494-5451
Tom Astram, *Prin*
EMP: 7 **EST:** 2016
SALES (est): 242.83K **Privately Held**
SIC: 3281 Cut stone and stone products

(G-299)
B & E JUICES INC
Also Called: Snapple Juices
550 Knowlton St (06608-1816)
PHONE.................................203 333-1802
Robert Clyne, *Pr*
Mitchell Clyne, *VP*
EMP: 20 **EST:** 1974
SQ FT: 40,000
SALES (est): 3.06MM **Privately Held**
Web: www.bejuice.com
SIC: 2086 Bottled and canned soft drinks

(G-300)
BARCIA LLC
50 Hurd Ave (06604-3222)
PHONE.................................203 367-1010
EMP: 13 **EST:** 2008
SALES (est): 585.22K **Privately Held**
SIC: 2258 Curtains and curtain fabrics, lace

(G-301)
BECKSON MANUFACTURING INC (PA)
165 Holland Ave (06605-2136)
P.O. Box 3336 (06605-0336)
PHONE.................................203 366-3644
Frank Sbeckerer, *Pr*
Eloise Beckerer, *
Frank S Beckerer Junior, *Sec*
◆ **EMP:** 30 **EST:** 1955
SQ FT: 15,000
SALES (est): 9.77MM
SALES (corp-wide): 9.77MM **Privately Held**
Web: www.becksonmfg.com
SIC: 3561 3429 3083 Pumps and pumping equipment; Marine hardware; Laminated plastics plate and sheet

(G-302)
BLACK ROCK TECH GROUP LLC
211 State St Ste 203 (06604-4824)
PHONE.................................203 916-7200
EMP: 12 **EST:** 2011
SQ FT: 3,000
SALES (est): 4.43MM **Privately Held**
Web: www.brtg.com
SIC: 3571 Electronic computers

(G-303)
BOSTON ENDO-SURGICAL TECH LLC
Also Called: Pep Be-St
1146 Barnum Ave (06610-2705)
PHONE.................................203 336-6479
EMP: 288 **EST:** 2012
SALES (est): 2.04MM
SALES (corp-wide): 433.51MM **Privately Held**
SIC: 3841 5047 Surgical and medical instruments; Surgical equipment and supplies
HQ: Precision Engineered Products Llc
110 Frank Mossberg Dr
Attleboro MA 02703

(G-304)
BRIDGEPORT INSULATED WIRE CO (PA)
51 Brookfield Ave (06610-3004)
P.O. Box 5217 (06610-0217)
PHONE.................................203 333-3191
Christopher Pelletier, *CEO*
Ronald A Pelletier, *Ch*
Milton L Cohn, *Sec*
EMP: 17 **EST:** 1950
SQ FT: 16,000
SALES (est): 2.55MM
SALES (corp-wide): 2.55MM **Privately Held**
Web: www.thebridgeportwireco.com
SIC: 3357 3496 3315 Nonferrous wiredrawing and insulating; Miscellaneous fabricated wire products; Steel wire and related products

(G-305)
BRIDGEPORT TL & STAMPING CORP
35 Burr Ct (06605-2204)
PHONE.................................203 336-2501
Julius Kish, *Pr*
Rolf Schmidt, *VP*
Sharon Kish, *Sec*
Darlene Kish, *Sec*
EMP: 21 **EST:** 1939
SQ FT: 14,000
SALES (est): 2.24MM **Privately Held**
Web: www.bridgeporttoolstamping.com
SIC: 3469 3544 Stamping metal for the trade ; Special dies and tools

(G-306)
BRODY PRINTING COMPANY INC
265 Central Ave (06607-2495)
PHONE.................................203 384-9313
Karen Brody Collett, *CEO*
Preseo Bonacci, *Pr*
EMP: 18 **EST:** 1971
SQ FT: 13,500
SALES (est): 2.39MM **Privately Held**
Web: www.brodyprinting.com
SIC: 2752 Offset printing

(G-307)
BUSWELL MANUFACTURING COMPANY
229 Merriam St (06604-2915)
PHONE.................................203 334-6069
Norman Buecher, *Pr*
Mildred Fitch, *VP*
EMP: 10 **EST:** 1923
SQ FT: 9,000
SALES (est): 833.04K **Privately Held**
Web: www.buswellmfg.com
SIC: 3562 3599 Ball bearings and parts; Machine shop, jobbing and repair

(G-308)
BYRNE WOODWORKING INC
170 Herbert St (06604-2903)
PHONE.................................203 953-3205
Frank Byrne, *Prin*
EMP: 8 **EST:** 2008
SALES (est): 268.86K **Privately Held**
Web: www.byrnewoodworking.com
SIC: 2431 Millwork

(G-309)
CALZONE LTD (PA)
Also Called: Calzone Case Company
225 Black Rock Ave (06605-1204)
PHONE.................................203 367-5766
Joseph Edward Calzone Iii, *Pr*

Vincent James Calzone, *
Joseph E Calzone Junior, *Sec*
Stephen Bajda, *
▲ **EMP:** 50 **EST:** 1979
SQ FT: 26,000
SALES (est): 20.3MM
SALES (corp-wide): 20.3MM **Privately Held**
Web: www.calzoneandanvil.com
SIC: 3161 Cases, carrying, nec

(G-310)
CARDINAL SHEHAN CENTER INC
1494 Main St (06604-3600)
PHONE.................................203 336-4468
Lorraine Gibbons, *Dir*
EMP: 30 **EST:** 1962
SALES (est): 2.41MM **Privately Held**
Web: www.shehancenter.org
SIC: 3999 Education aids, devices and supplies

(G-311)
CHRISTOPOULOS DESIGNS INC
195 Dewey St (06605-2114)
PHONE.................................203 576-1110
George Christopoulos, *Pr*
Nicholas Daniolos, *VP*
EMP: 10 **EST:** 1988
SQ FT: 10,000
SALES (est): 867.81K **Privately Held**
Web: www.christopoulosdesigns.com
SIC: 2511 2517 2434 End tables: wood; Television cabinets, wood; Vanities, bathroom: wood

(G-312)
CONN ANODIZING FINSHG CO INC
128 Logan St (06607-1930)
PHONE.................................203 367-1765
Victor Sinko Ii, *Pr*
EMP: 21 **EST:** 1975
SQ FT: 24,000
SALES (est): 455.54K **Privately Held**
Web: www.ctanodizing.com
SIC: 3471 Electroplating of metals or formed products

(G-313)
D&C GLOBAL ENTERPRISE LLC
290 East Ave (06610-2960)
PHONE.................................810 553-2360
David Reeves, *Managing Member*
EMP: 7 **EST:** 2021
SALES (est): 311.83K **Privately Held**
SIC: 3651 Audio electronic systems

(G-314)
DAYBRAKE DONUTS INC
941 Madison Ave (06606-5218)
PHONE.................................203 368-4962
EMP: 9 **EST:** 1992
SALES (est): 286.92K **Privately Held**
SIC: 2051 5812 Doughnuts, except frozen; Coffee shop

(G-315)
DECORATOR SERVICES INC
25 Wells St Ste 1 (06604-2800)
PHONE.................................203 384-8144
Charles Musante, *Pr*
Frances Musante, *Sec*
EMP: 7 **EST:** 1975
SQ FT: 9,500
SALES (est): 388.92K **Privately Held**
Web: www.decoratorservicesonline.com

SIC: 2391 2591 Draperies, plastic and textile: from purchased materials; Blinds vertical

(G-316)
DELTA-RAY INDUSTRIES INC
805 Housatonic Ave (06604-2807)
PHONE.................................203 367-6910
John M Ray, *Pr*
Tom Vann, *Mgr*
EMP: 10 **EST:** 1999
SALES (est): 1.85MM **Privately Held**
Web: www.delta-ray.com
SIC: 3599 Machine shop, jobbing and repair

(G-317)
DEVAR INC
706 Bostwick Ave (06605-2396)
PHONE.................................203 368-6751
A James Ruscito, *Pr*
Marianne Ruscito, *
EMP: 30 **EST:** 1954
SQ FT: 33,000
SALES (est): 2.84MM **Privately Held**
Web: www.devarinc.com
SIC: 3625 5084 3823 Electric controls and control accessories, industrial; Industrial machinery and equipment; Process control instruments

(G-318)
E&S AUTOMOTIVE OPERATIONS LLC
425 Boston Ave (06610-1701)
PHONE.................................203 332-4555
Harry Gill, *Owner*
EMP: 9 **EST:** 2008
SALES (est): 469.36K **Privately Held**
SIC: 2869 Fuels

(G-319)
EDCO INDUSTRIES INC
Also Called: Edco Industries
203 Dekalb Ave (06607-2492)
PHONE.................................203 333-8982
John Thomas Szalan, *Pr*
Anne Marie Szalan, *Finance*
▲ **EMP:** 16 **EST:** 1969
SQ FT: 13,500
SALES (est): 2.46MM **Privately Held**
Web: www.edcoindustries.com
SIC: 3089 5162 Injection molding of plastics ; Plastics materials, nec

(G-320)
ENGINEERED ELECTRIC COMPANY
Also Called: Drs Fermont
141 North Ave (06606-5120)
PHONE.................................203 366-5211
EMP: 300
SIC: 3621 Generators and sets, electric

(G-321)
FLUTED PARTITION INC
Cell Pack Div
850 Union Ave (06607-1137)
PHONE.................................203 334-3500
EMP: 71
SALES (corp-wide): 10.19MM **Privately Held**
Web: www.valleycontainer.com
SIC: 2653 Partitions, corrugated: made from purchased materials
PA: Fluted Partition, Inc.
850 Union Ave
Bridgeport CT 06607
203 368-2548

(PA)=Parent Co (HQ)=Headquarters
✪ = New Business established in last 2 years
          2024 Harris New England
          Manufacturers Directory
                                                           29

(G-322)
FLUTED PARTITION INC (PA)
850 Union Ave (06607-1137)
PHONE......................203 368-2548
Rudolph Neidermeir, *Ch*
Arthur M Vietze Junior, *Pr*
Robert Neidermeir, *
EMP: 125 **EST:** 1972
SQ FT: 120,000
SALES (est): 10.19MM
SALES (corp-wide): 10.19MM **Privately Held**
Web: www.valleycontainer.com
SIC: 2671 2653 2631 Paper; coated and laminated packaging; Partitions, corrugated: made from purchased materials ; Paperboard mills

(G-323)
GENERAL ELECTRIC COMPANY
Also Called: GE
1285 Boston Ave (06610-2612)
PHONE......................203 396-1572
Bill O'brien, *Manager*
EMP: 100
SALES (corp-wide): 76.56B **Publicly Held**
Web: www.ge.com
SIC: 3625 Relays and industrial controls
PA: General Electric Company
1 Financial Ctr Ste 3700
Boston MA 02111
617 443-3000

(G-324)
GENERAL SHEET METAL WORKS INC
120 Silliman Ave (06605-2185)
PHONE......................203 333-6111
Jeffrey D Cibulas, *Pr*
EMP: 10 **EST:** 1916
SQ FT: 6,500
SALES (est): 971.8K **Privately Held**
Web: www.generalsheet.com
SIC: 3444 1761 Ducts, sheet metal; Roofing, siding, and sheetmetal work

(G-325)
GLOBAL SCENIC SERVICES INC
46 Brookfield Ave (06610-3005)
PHONE......................203 334-2130
James Malski, *Pr*
Warren Katz, *
James Malski, *Pr*
▲ **EMP:** 46 **EST:** 2006
SQ FT: 40,000
SALES (est): 9.71MM **Privately Held**
Web: www.globalscenicservices.com
SIC: 3999 Theatrical scenery

(G-326)
GRANT MANUFACTURING AND MCH CO
90 Silliman Ave (06605-2127)
P.O. Box 3345 (06605-0345)
PHONE......................203 366-4557
Bruce W Mc Naughton, *Ch Bd*
EMP: 18 **EST:** 1904
SQ FT: 22,000
SALES (est): 1.36MM **Privately Held**
Web: www.grantriveters.com
SIC: 3542 Machine tools, metal forming type

(G-327)
HALLMARK WOODWORKERS INC
350 Fairfield Ave Ste 602 (06604-6004)
PHONE......................203 730-0535
EMP: 18 **EST:** 1995
SQ FT: 30,000

SALES (est): 990.08K **Privately Held**
SIC: 1751 2431 Cabinet building and installation; Millwork

(G-328)
HEMINGWAY CUSTOM CABINETRY LLC
3400 Fairfield Ave (06605-3225)
PHONE......................203 382-0300
George Krawiec, *Managing Member*
EMP: 35 **EST:** 2001
SQ FT: 12,500
SALES (est): 4.12MM **Privately Held**
Web: www.hemingwaycustom.com
SIC: 2434 Wood kitchen cabinets

(G-329)
HISPANIC ENTERPRISES INC
Also Called: Emtec Metal Products
200 Cogswell St (06610-1941)
PHONE......................203 588-9334
EMP: 20 **EST:** 1994
SQ FT: 12,500
SALES (est): 4.53MM **Privately Held**
SIC: 3444 Sheet metal specialties, not stamped

(G-330)
HORNBLOWER SHIPYARD LLC
731 Seaview Ave (06607-1607)
PHONE......................203 572-0378
EMP: 37 **EST:** 2021
SALES (est): 2.71MM **Privately Held**
Web: bridgeport.hornblower.com
SIC: 3731 7389 Shipbuilding and repairing; Business services, nec

(G-331)
IDENTIFICATION PRODUCTS CORP
1073 State St (06605-1504)
PHONE......................203 334-5969
Hugh F Mccann, *Mgr*
EMP: 10
SALES (corp-wide): 9.58MM **Privately Held**
Web: www.idproducts.com
SIC: 2759 3479 2671 Flexographic printing; Name plates: engraved, etched, etc.; Paper; coated and laminated packaging
PA: Identification Products Corp
1 Parrott Dr Ste 500
Shelton CT 06484
203 334-5969

(G-332)
INTEGRATED PRINT SOLUTIONS INC
Also Called: Everett Print
35 Benham Ave Ste 2 (06605-1436)
PHONE......................203 330-0200
Philip Palmieri, *Pr*
▲ **EMP:** 11 **EST:** 1998
SQ FT: 40,000
SALES (est): 2.18MM **Privately Held**
SIC: 2759 Screen printing

(G-333)
JAMES IPPOLITO & CO CONN INC
1069 Connecticut Ave Ste 16 (06607-1228)
PHONE......................203 366-3840
Gerald V Cavallo, *Pr*
EMP: 40 **EST:** 1995
SQ FT: 25,000
SALES (est): 4.9MM **Privately Held**
SIC: 3429 Aircraft hardware

(G-334)
JET CORPORATION
146 Davis Ave (06605-2557)
PHONE......................203 334-3317
Jose E Tamayo, *Pr*
Jose L Tamayo, *Sec*
EMP: 11 **EST:** 1981
SALES (est): 2.23MM **Privately Held**
Web: www.jetcorp.us
SIC: 3365 3566 Aluminum foundries; Gears, power transmission, except auto

(G-335)
JJ BOX CO INC
25 Admiral St (06605-1808)
PHONE......................203 367-1211
TOLL FREE: 800
James Garamella, *Pr*
EMP: 9 **EST:** 1984
SQ FT: 10,000
SALES (est): 950.21K **Privately Held**
Web: www.jj-box.com
SIC: 2448 Pallets, wood

(G-336)
JOHN JUNE CUSTOM CABINETRY LLC
541 Fairfield Ave (06604-3904)
PHONE......................203 334-1720
EMP: 8 **EST:** 2004
SALES (est): 620.51K **Privately Held**
Web: www.johnjunecustomcabinetry.com
SIC: 2434 Wood kitchen cabinets

(G-337)
JOZEF CUSTOM IRONWORKS INC
Also Called: Aesthetic Blacksmithing
250 Smith St (06607-2219)
PHONE......................203 384-6363
Jozef Witkowski, *Pr*
Erik Witkowski, *CEO*
▲ **EMP:** 22 **EST:** 1994
SQ FT: 40,000
SALES (est): 2.46MM **Privately Held**
Web: www.jozef.net
SIC: 3441 Fabricated structural metal

(G-338)
KAFA GROUP LLC
800 Union Ave (06607-1422)
PHONE......................475 275-0090
Steve Mckenzie, *Pr*
Nicole Mckenzie, *VP*
EMP: 8 **EST:** 2005
SQ FT: 1,200
SALES (est): 1.21MM **Privately Held**
Web: www.kafagroup.com
SIC: 1389 1542 1541 Construction, repair, and dismantling services; Commercial and office building, new construction; Industrial buildings, new construction, nec

(G-339)
KASTEN INC
Also Called: Dakota Life Sciences
304 Bishop Ave (06610-3050)
P.O. Box 3540 (89429-3540)
PHONE......................702 860-2407
Jose Delgado, *CEO*
EMP: 8 **EST:** 2017
SALES (est): 227.83K **Privately Held**
SIC: 2834 Pharmaceutical preparations

(G-340)
KITCHEN CAB RESURFACING LLC
136 Merriam St (06604-2912)

PHONE......................203 334-2857
James Svab, *Pr*
EMP: 10 **EST:** 2010
SALES (est): 615.64K **Privately Held**
Web: www.kcrct.com
SIC: 2434 Wood kitchen cabinets

(G-341)
KOLMAR AMERICAS INC (HQ)
10 Middle St Ph (06604-4229)
PHONE......................203 873-2051
Rafael Aviner, *Pr*
Paul Francis Teta, *VP*
Kevin Luddy, *CFO*
◆ **EMP:** 10 **EST:** 1997
SALES (est): 92.07MM **Privately Held**
Web: www.kolmargroup.com
SIC: 5169 2869 Chemicals and allied products, nec; Fuels
PA: Kolmar Group Ag
Baarerstrasse 18
Zug ZG 6300

(G-342)
L P MACADAMS COMPANY INC
50 Austin St (06604-5437)
P.O. Box 5540 (06610-0540)
PHONE......................203 366-3647
Lawrence P Macadams, *Pr*
Kay Macadams, *
D Paul Macadams, *
▲ **EMP:** 85 **EST:** 1925
SQ FT: 150,000
SALES (est): 6.56MM **Privately Held**
Web: www.lpmacadams.com
SIC: 2759 7331 4225 2752 Imprinting; Direct mail advertising services; General warehousing and storage; Commercial printing, lithographic

(G-343)
LACEY MANUFACTURING CO LLC
Also Called: Paragon Medical - Bridgeport
1146 Barnum Ave (06610-2794)
PHONE......................203 336-0121
▲ **EMP:** 310 **EST:** 1993
SQ FT: 100,000
SALES (est): 63.16MM
SALES (corp-wide): 433.51MM **Privately Held**
Web: www.paragonmedical.com
SIC: 3841 3089 Surgical instruments and apparatus; Injection molding of plastics
HQ: Precision Engineered Products Llc
110 Frank Mossberg Dr
Attleboro MA 02703

(G-344)
LEARNTOPROGRAMTV INCORPORATED
Also Called: Learntoprogram Media
1000 Lafayette Blvd (06604-4725)
PHONE......................860 840-7090
Mark Lassoff, *Pr*
Kevin Hernandez, *VP*
EMP: 10 **EST:** 2011
SQ FT: 1,600
SALES (est): 991.5K **Privately Held**
Web: www.dollardesignschool.com
SIC: 2741 8243 Technical manuals: publishing only, not printed on site; Operator training, computer

(G-345)
M & O CORPORATION
164 Alex St (06607-1905)
PHONE......................203 367-4292
TOLL FREE: 800
Emilio Espejo, *Pr*

Alan M Decaprio, *
Robert H Oetjen, *Stockholder**
EMP: 35 **EST:** 1976
SQ FT: 8,000
SALES (est): 4.55MM **Privately Held**
Web: www.mocorp.net
SIC: 1711 3444 Warm air heating and air conditioning contractor; Ducts, sheet metal

(G-346)
MARKAL FINISHING CO INC
400 Bostwick Ave (06605-2407)
PHONE.................................203 384-8219
Craig Sander, *Pr*
Christine Royer, *
EMP: 44 **EST:** 1961
SQ FT: 40,000
SALES (est): 4.47MM **Privately Held**
Web: www.markalfinishing.com
SIC: 2672 Paper; coated and laminated, nec

(G-347)
MILL MANUFACTURING INC
105 Willow St (06610-3220)
PHONE.................................203 367-9572
Karl E Ostberg, *Pr*
Karl E Ostberg Prestreas, *Prin*
EMP: 8 **EST:** 1979
SQ FT: 2,000
SALES (est): 720.99K **Privately Held**
SIC: 3599 Machine shop, jobbing and repair

(G-348)
MJ METAL INC
225 Howard Ave (06605-1825)
PHONE.................................203 334-3484
Jeffrey Dreyer, *Pr*
George Dreyer, *VP*
▲ **EMP:** 20 **EST:** 1983
SQ FT: 32,000
SALES (est): 2.45MM **Privately Held**
Web: www.mjmetalinc.com
SIC: 5093 4953 3341 Ferrous metal scrap and waste; Refuse systems; Secondary nonferrous metals

(G-349)
MOHAWK TOOL AND DIE MFG CO INC
25 Wells St Ste 4 (06604-2800)
PHONE.................................203 367-2181
Vincent A Bonazzo, *Pr*
Lucy R Bonazzo, *Sec*
▲ **EMP:** 13 **EST:** 1946
SQ FT: 8,000
SALES (est): 1.64MM **Privately Held**
Web: www.mohawktoolanddie.com
SIC: 3544 3089 Forms (molds), for foundry and plastics working machinery; Injection molding of plastics

(G-350)
MOORE TOOL COMPANY INC (HQ)
599 Hollister Ave (06607-1102)
PHONE.................................203 366-3224
Newman Marsilius Iii, *Pr*
Newman M Marsilius Iv, *Sec*
◆ **EMP:** 26 **EST:** 1924
SQ FT: 334,113
SALES (est): 5.18K
SALES (corp-wide): 91.35MM **Privately Held**
Web: www.mooretool.com
SIC: 3541 3544 3545 Machine tools, metal cutting: exotic (explosive, etc.); Dies and die holders for metal cutting, forming, die casting; Gauges (machine tool accessories)
PA: Pmt Group, Inc.
      800 Union Ave

Bridgeport CT 06607
203 367-8675

(G-351)
NABCO ENTRANCES INC
1556 Barnum Ave (06610-3278)
PHONE.................................262 679-0045
EMP: 14
Web: www.nabcoentrances.com
SIC: 3699 Electrical equipment and supplies, nec
HQ: Nabco Entrances, Inc.
      S82w18717 Gemini Dr
      Muskego WI 53150
      262 679-7532

(G-352)
NNTECHNOLOGY MOORE SYSTEMS LLC
800 Union Ave (06607-1422)
P.O. Box 1381 (06601-1381)
PHONE.................................203 366-3224
Ranae Wright, *Admn*
EMP: 51
SALES (corp-wide): 91.35MM **Privately Held**
Web: www.nanotechsys.com
SIC: 3827 Optical instruments and lenses
HQ: Moore Nanotechnology Systems Llc
      230 Old Homestead Hwy
      Swanzey NH 03446
      603 352-3030

(G-353)
NORTH SAILS GROUP LLC (DH)
Also Called: North Technology Group
837 Seaview Ave Ste A (06607-1607)
PHONE.................................203 874-7548
Thomas A Whidden, *CEO*
Jay Hansen, *
John Mc Clary, *
Jay Kiraly, *
◆ **EMP:** 70 **EST:** 2000
SQ FT: 3,000
SALES (est): 80.73MM **Privately Held**
Web: fr.northsails.com
SIC: 2211 2394 Sail cloth; Sails: made from purchased materials
HQ: North Technology Group, Llc
      837 Seaview Ave
      Bridgeport CT 06607
      203 877-7621

(G-354)
O & G INDUSTRIES INC
240 Bostwick Ave (06605-2434)
P.O. Box 907 (06790-0907)
PHONE.................................203 366-4586
John Leverty, *Brnch Mgr*
EMP: 262
SALES (corp-wide): 496.36MM **Privately Held**
Web: www.ogind.com
SIC: 3273 1771 1794 2951 Ready-mixed concrete; Blacktop (asphalt) work; Excavation and grading, building construction; Asphalt paving mixtures and blocks
PA: O & G Industries, Inc.
      112 Wall St
      Torrington CT 06790
      860 489-9261

(G-355)
PARK DISTRIBUTORIES INC
Also Called: Universal Relays
347 Railroad Ave (06604-5424)
P.O. Box 1020 (06601-1020)
PHONE.................................203 366-7200
EMP: 8

SALES (corp-wide): 2.42MM **Privately Held**
Web: www.parkdistributors.com
SIC: 5065 3625 Electronic parts; Relays and industrial controls
PA: Park Distributories Inc.
      347 Railroad Ave
      Bridgeport CT 06604
      203 579-2140

(G-356)
PARK DISTRIBUTORIES INC
Also Called: Electronic Finishing Company
347 Railroad Ave (06604-5424)
P.O. Box 1020 (06601-1020)
PHONE.................................203 366-7200
Allan Goodman, *Mgr*
EMP: 7
SALES (corp-wide): 2.42MM **Privately Held**
Web: www.parkdistributors.com
SIC: 3625 3679 Relays and industrial controls; Electronic circuits
PA: Park Distributories Inc.
      347 Railroad Ave
      Bridgeport CT 06604
      203 579-2140

(G-357)
PARK DISTRIBUTORIES INC (PA)
Also Called: Universal Relay Company
347 Railroad Ave (06604-5424)
P.O. Box 1020 (06601-1020)
PHONE.................................203 579-2140
Alan Goodman, *Pr*
Rick Depaulis, *Prin*
Larry Depaulis, *VP*
Joan Green, *Sec*
Ricard Depaulis, *CFO*
EMP: 9 **EST:** 1966
SQ FT: 16,000
SALES (est): 4.92MM
SALES (corp-wide): 4.92MM **Privately Held**
Web: www.parkdistributors.com
SIC: 3625 5065 Relays and industrial controls; Electronic parts

(G-358)
PEREY TURNSTILES INC
308 Bishop Ave (06610-3055)
PHONE.................................203 333-9400
M Edmund Hendrickson, *Pr*
Jeanne Hendrickson, *
EMP: 24 **EST:** 1999
SQ FT: 15,000
SALES (est): 3.44MM **Privately Held**
Web: www.turnstile.com
SIC: 3829 Turnstiles, equipped with counting mechanisms

(G-359)
PMT GROUP INC (PA)
800 Union Ave (06607-1422)
PHONE.................................203 367-8675
Newman M Marsilius Iii, *Pr*
◆ **EMP:** 110 **EST:** 1928
SQ FT: 218,000
SALES (est): 91.35MM
SALES (corp-wide): 91.35MM **Privately Held**
Web: www.pmt-group.com
SIC: 3541 3545 3544 Machine tools, metal cutting: exotic (explosive, etc.); Machine tool attachments and accessories; Special dies, tools, jigs, and fixtures

(G-360)
PRC SYNERGY CORP
Also Called: Prime Line

1100 Boston Ave Bldg 1 (06610-2654)
PHONE.................................203 331-9100
Jeffrey Lederer, *Pr*
◆ **EMP:** 500 **EST:** 1980
SQ FT: 128,000
SALES (est): 86.91MM
SALES (corp-wide): 2.19B **Privately Held**
Web: www.alphabroder.com
SIC: 3993 2759 Signs and advertising specialties; Promotional printing
HQ: Broder Bros., Co.
      6 Neshaminy Interplex Dr
      Feasterville Trevose PA 19053
      800 523-4585

(G-361)
PRECISION ENGINEERED PDTS LLC
Also Called: Boston Endo-Surgical Tech
1146 Barnum Ave (06610-2705)
PHONE.................................203 336-6479
Alan M Huffenus, *CEO*
EMP: 7
SALES (corp-wide): 433.51MM **Privately Held**
Web: www.nninc.com
SIC: 3841 5047 Surgical and medical instruments; Surgical equipment and supplies
HQ: Precision Engineered Products Llc
      110 Frank Mossberg Dr
      Attleboro MA 02703

(G-362)
PRESTIGE REMODELING LLC
66 Holland Ave (06605-2117)
PHONE.................................203 386-8426
Remy Ludwin, *Mgr*
EMP: 10 **EST:** 2011
SALES (est): 468.05K **Privately Held**
Web: www.prbyr.com
SIC: 2434 Wood kitchen cabinets

(G-363)
PRODUCTO CORPORATION (HQ)
Also Called: Producto Machine Company, The
800 Union Ave (06607-1422)
PHONE.................................203 366-3224
Newman M Marsilius Iii, *CEO*
Joanne Clark, *VP*
Jon Krchnavy, *VP*
Maynard Cotter, *VP*
Dan Kolb, *Contrlr*
EMP: 10 **EST:** 2000
SALES (est): 40.13MM
SALES (corp-wide): 91.35MM **Privately Held**
Web: www.mooretool.com
SIC: 3541 3545 3544 Machine tools, metal cutting type; Machine tool accessories; Special dies, tools, jigs, and fixtures
PA: Pmt Group, Inc.
      800 Union Ave
      Bridgeport CT 06607
      203 367-8675

(G-364)
QUALITY STAIRS INC
70 Logan St (06607-1930)
PHONE.................................203 367-8390
Lee Pereira, *Pr*
Geomar Pereira, *Sec*
Manuel Pereira, *VP*
EMP: 15 **EST:** 1985
SQ FT: 8,000
SALES (est): 4.97MM **Privately Held**
Web: www.qualitystairsinc.com
SIC: 2431 3446 Staircases and stairs, wood ; Stairs, staircases, stair treads: prefabricated metal

(G-365)
RELIABLE PLTG & POLSG CO INC
Also Called: Reliable Plating & Polishing
80 Bishop Ave (06607-1541)
PHONE..............................203 366-5261
Joseph D Bourdeau, *Ch Bd*
James Bourdeau, *
Lynn Myers, *
EMP: 35 **EST:** 1956
SQ FT: 225,000
SALES (est): 2.28MM **Privately Held**
Web: www.reliableplatingct.com
SIC: 3471   Electroplating of metals or formed products

(G-366)
ROSE SISTERS BRANDS INC
Also Called: Rose Sisters Chips
480 Barnum Ave Ste 5 (06608-2459)
PHONE..............................475 999-8115
Ann Marcus, *CEO*
Jonathan Marcus, *Pr*
Lauren Rosato, *Treas*
EMP: 11 **EST:** 2016
SALES (est): 503.97K **Privately Held**
Web: www.rosesisterschips.com
SIC: 2096   Potato chips and other potato-based snacks

(G-367)
ROTAIR AEROSPACE CORPORATION
964 Crescent Ave (06607-1066)
PHONE..............................203 576-6545
Wesley Harrington, *Pr*
Christine Kudravy, *
EMP: 46 **EST:** 1975
SQ FT: 80,000
SALES (est): 10.13MM **Privately Held**
Web: www.rotair.com
SIC: 3728   Aircraft parts and equipment, nec

(G-368)
SAVETIME CORPORATION
2710 North Ave Ste 105b (06604-2352)
PHONE..............................203 382-2991
Donna Buckenmaier, *Pr*
Erwin Theodore Buckenmaier, *Ch*
Robert Zuklie, *VP Opers*
EMP: 12 **EST:** 1983
SQ FT: 6,100
SALES (est): 665.07K **Privately Held**
Web: www.rainhandler.com
SIC: 3089 1761   Gutters (glass fiber reinforced), fiberglass or plastics; Roofing, siding, and sheetmetal work

(G-369)
SCHWERDTLE STAMP COMPANY
Also Called: Schwerdtle
41 Benham Ave (06605-1419)
P.O. Box 1461 (06601-1461)
PHONE..............................203 330-2750
TOLL FREE: 800
Katherine Saint, *Pr*
John Schwerdtle Junior, *VP*
EMP: 35 **EST:** 1879
SQ FT: 14,000
SALES (est): 4.42MM **Privately Held**
Web: www.schwerdtle.com
SIC: 3953 7336   Marking devices; Graphic arts and related design

(G-370)
SEAVIEW PLASTIC RECYCLING INC
938 Crescent Ave (06607-1024)

PHONE..............................203 367-0070
Joseph Cirillo, *Pr*
EMP: 16 **EST:** 2012
SQ FT: 58,724
SALES (est): 870.01K **Privately Held**
Web: www.seaviewplasticrecycling.com
SIC: 4953 2821 5169   Recycling, waste materials; Plastics materials and resins; Synthetic resins, rubber, and plastic materials

(G-371)
SIGN FAST
3841 Main St (06606-2813)
PHONE..............................203 549-8500
Nelson Lima, *Prin*
EMP: 7 **EST:** 2010
SALES (est): 100.21K **Privately Held**
Web: www.signfab.com
SIC: 3993   Signs and advertising specialties

(G-372)
SIKORSKY AIRCRAFT CORPORATION
1201 South Ave (06604-5246)
PHONE..............................203 384-7532
Robert Brady, *Mgr*
EMP: 54
Web: www.gyrocamsystems.com
SIC: 3721   Helicopters
HQ: Sikorsky Aircraft Corporation
6900 Main St
Stratford CT 06614

(G-373)
SOFT SERVE CT LLC
325 Cherry St (06605-2334)
PHONE..............................203 367-3000
EMP: 10 **EST:** 2009
SALES (est): 489.85K **Privately Held**
Web: new.mistersofteect.com
SIC: 2024   Ice cream and frozen deserts

(G-374)
SPEC PLATING INC
740 Seaview Ave (06607-1606)
PHONE..............................203 366-3638
EMP: 14 **EST:** 1995
SQ FT: 10,000
SALES (est): 1.62MM **Privately Held**
Web: www.specplatingct.com
SIC: 3471   Electroplating of metals or formed products

(G-375)
STERLING CUSTOM CABINETRY LLC
323 North Ave (06606-5125)
PHONE..............................203 335-5151
EMP: 19 **EST:** 2004
SALES (est): 1.31MM **Privately Held**
Web: www.sterling-custom.com
SIC: 2434   Wood kitchen cabinets

(G-376)
STONE WORKSHOP LLC
1108 Railroad Ave (06605-1835)
PHONE..............................203 362-1144
▲ **EMP:** 7 **EST:** 2003
SQ FT: 12,000
SALES (est): 846.47K **Privately Held**
Web: www.stoneworkshops.com
SIC: 3281   Granite, cut and shaped

(G-377)
STROCCHIA IRON WORKS
116 Knowlton St (06608-2105)
PHONE..............................203 296-4600
EMP: 11 **EST:** 2017

SALES (est): 1.63MM **Privately Held**
SIC: 3441   Fabricated structural metal

(G-378)
SWAGNIFICENT ENT LLC
Also Called: Ricco Vishnu Brew House
79 Sage Ave (06610-3061)
PHONE..............................203 449-0124
EMP: 7 **EST:** 2013
SALES (est): 400K **Privately Held**
SIC: 2082 5813   Malt beverages; Bars and lounges

(G-379)
THORME WALL INC
1535 Central Ave Apt 107 (06610-2847)
PHONE..............................203 583-2305
Michael Barkley Ii, *Prin*
EMP: 10 **EST:** 2021
SALES (est): 125K **Privately Held**
SIC: 2599   Food wagons, restaurant

(G-380)
TRIO COMMUNITY MEALS LLC
515 Lindley St (06606-5451)
PHONE..............................203 336-8407
Kevin Fonck, *Dir*
EMP: 18
Web: www.triocommunitymeals.com
SIC: 2099   Food preparations, nec
HQ: Trio Community Meals, Llc
100 Valley Dr Ste 200
Pearl MS 39208
844 773-0370

(G-381)
UNGER ENTERPRISES LLC (PA)
425 Asylum St (06610-2105)
PHONE..............................203 366-4884
Mark D Unger, *Pr*
◆ **EMP:** 130 **EST:** 1964
SQ FT: 70,000
SALES (est): 27.56MM
SALES (corp-wide): 27.56MM **Privately Held**
Web: www.ungerglobal.com
SIC: 3423   Hand and edge tools, nec

(G-382)
UNGER INDUSTRIAL LLC
Also Called: Unger Industrial
425 Asylum St (06610-2105)
PHONE..............................203 336-3344
EMP: 9 **EST:** 1994
SALES (est): 1.51MM **Privately Held**
Web: www.ungerconsumer.com
SIC: 3429   Hardware, nec

(G-383)
VALLEY CONTAINER INC
850 Union Ave (06607-1137)
PHONE..............................203 368-6546
Arthur Vietze Junior, *CEO*
Rudolph Neidermeir, *
Robert Neidermeir, *
Robert Vietze, *
▲ **EMP:** 45 **EST:** 1969
SQ FT: 120,000
SALES (est): 10.09MM **Privately Held**
Web: www.valleycontainer.com
SIC: 2679 7319   Corrugated paper: made from purchased material; Display advertising service

(G-384)
VINEGAR SYNDROME LLC
100 Congress St (06604-4046)
PHONE..............................475 731-1778
Joe Rubin, *Prin*

EMP: 9 **EST:** 2013
SALES (est): 1.27MM **Privately Held**
Web: www.vinegarsyndrome.com
SIC: 2099 7371   Vinegar; Computer software development and applications

(G-385)
WOOD GRINDING UNLIMITED
10 Barnum Dyke (06604-5210)
PHONE..............................203 333-9047
EMP: 7
SALES (est): 386.68K **Privately Held**
SIC: 3599   Grinding castings for the trade

(G-386)
WOODWORKERS HEAVEN INC
955 Connecticut Ave Ste 4106 (06607-1297)
PHONE..............................203 333-2778
EMP: 10 **EST:** 1996
SQ FT: 5,000
SALES (est): 828.33K **Privately Held**
Web: www.cabinetmaker.net
SIC: 2511   Wood household furniture

(G-387)
YANKEE PLAK CO INC
Also Called: Yankee Photo Service
240 Alice St (06606-5675)
PHONE..............................203 333-3168
Joseph Abruzzo Junior, *Pr*
Melanie Abruzzo, *VP*
EMP: 11 **EST:** 1977
SQ FT: 12,000
SALES (est): 882.19K **Privately Held**
Web: www.yankeeplak.com
SIC: 7384 3993   Photofinish laboratories; Signs and advertising specialties

(G-388)
YARD STICK DECORE
145 Hart St (06606-5048)
PHONE..............................203 330-0360
Joe Costa, *Managing Member*
EMP: 10 **EST:** 2010
SALES (est): 345.85K **Privately Held**
Web: yardstick-decor.tripod.com
SIC: 2391   Curtains and draperies

Bristol
Hartford County

(G-389)
A & D COMPONENTS INC
33 Stafford Ave Ste 2 (06010-4699)
PHONE..............................860 582-9541
Harold Etherington, *Pr*
Nora Etherington, *VP*
Rita Mckenzie, *Sec*
EMP: 8 **EST:** 1994
SQ FT: 25,000
SALES (est): 1.28MM **Privately Held**
Web: www.adcomponents.com
SIC: 3469   Stamping metal for the trade

(G-390)
ABEK LLC
Also Called: Thomson Linear
492 Birch St (06010-7837)
PHONE..............................860 314-3905
John B Thomson Junior, *Ch Bd*
Robert C Magee, *Vice Chairman*
Alex N Beavers, *CEO*
Jeffry Peterson, *Corporate Vice President*
Patrick Mazzeo Senior, *Corporate Vice President*
◆ **EMP:** 11 **EST:** 1976
SQ FT: 12,500

SALES (est): 4.78MM
SALES (corp-wide): 31.47B **Publicly Held**
SIC: 3562   Ball bearings and parts
PA: Danaher Corporation
  2200 Penn Ave Nw Ste 800w
  Washington DC 20037
  202 828-0850

(G-391)
**ACCUPAULO HOLDING
CORPORATION (PA)**
Also Called: Accurate Threaded Products
33 Stafford Ave Ste 5 (06010-4699)
PHONE..............................860 666-5621
Jon Omichinski, *Pr*
Harold Etherington, *
EMP: 25 EST: 1991
SALES (est): 7.18MM **Privately Held**
SIC: 3769 3599 3724   Space vehicle
  equipment, nec; Machine shop, jobbing and
  repair; Aircraft engines and engine parts

(G-392)
ACT ROBOTS INC
95 Wooster Ct (06010-6777)
PHONE..............................860 314-1557
Richard Morgan, *Pr*
Mark Zamaria, *Sec*
Katarina Zamaria, *Off Mgr*
EMP: 9 EST: 1996
SQ FT: 12,000
SALES (est): 2.09MM **Privately Held**
Web: www.actrobots.com
SIC: 8711 3569   Industrial engineers;
  Robots, assembly line: industrial and
  commercial

(G-393)
**ADVANCED PRINTING
SERVICES INC**
135 Cross St (06010-7434)
PHONE..............................860 583-1906
▲ EMP: 20
Web: www.compumail.net
SIC: 2752   Offset printing

(G-394)
ALLOY WELDING & MFG CO INC
233 Riverside Ave (06010-6319)
PHONE..............................860 582-3638
Alfred L Frechette, *Pr*
Edith Frechette, *VP*
Darren Frechette, *Genl Mgr*
EMP: 15 EST: 1937
SQ FT: 14,000
SALES (est): 2.37MM **Privately Held**
Web: www.alloyweldingmfg.com
SIC: 3441 1799   Fabricated structural metal;
  Welding on site

(G-395)
**AMERICAN BUILDING SYSTEMS
INC**
200 Terryville Ave Ste 1 (06010-1917)
PHONE..............................860 589-0215
TOLL FREE: 800
Richard E Mute, *Pr*
EMP: 7 EST: 1983
SQ FT: 2,400
SALES (est): 690K **Privately Held**
SIC: 1521 1761 2542   New construction,
  single-family houses; Roofing contractor;
  Partitions for floor attachment,
  prefabricated: except wood

(G-396)
ARNA MACHINE COMPANY
95 Wooster Ct (06010-6777)
PHONE..............................860 583-0628

Stephen B Shanahan, *Pr*
Jason G Rousseau, *Sec*
EMP: 15 EST: 1953
SQ FT: 22,000
SALES (est): 2.65MM **Privately Held**
Web: www.arnamachine.com
SIC: 3542 3599 3545   Machine tools, metal
  forming type; Custom machinery; Gauges
  (machine tool accessories)

(G-397)
**ARROW MANUFACTURING
COMPANY**
16 Jeannette St (06010-7000)
P.O. Box 9161 (06011-9161)
EMP: 24 EST: 1951
SQ FT: 40,000
SALES (est): 2.49MM **Privately Held**
Web: www.arrowmfg.com
SIC: 3469 3493 3496   Stamping metal for
  the trade; Steel springs, except wire;
  Miscellaneous fabricated wire products

(G-398)
**ARTHUR G RUSSELL COMPANY
INC**
750 Clark Ave (06010-4065)
P.O. Box 237 (06011-0237)
PHONE..............................860 583-4109
Robert J Ensminger, *CEO*
Mark Burzynski, *
William Mis, *
Edmund Mikolowski, *
Donald Talaia, *
◆ EMP: 85 EST: 1945
SQ FT: 80,000
SALES (est): 45.55MM **Privately Held**
Web: www.arthurgrussell.com
SIC: 5084 3569   Industrial machinery and
  equipment; Assembly machines, non-
  metalworking

(G-399)
**ATLANTIC PRECISION SPRING
INC**
125 Ronzo Rd (06010-8620)
PHONE..............................860 583-1864
Neil Fries, *Pr*
Terry Fries, *
Brian J Fries, *
Michael J Fries, *
EMP: 32 EST: 1958
SQ FT: 15,000
SALES (est): 4.79MM **Privately Held**
Web: www.aps-ct.com
SIC: 3493 3495 3469   Flat springs, sheet or
  strip stock; Wire springs; Metal stampings,
  nec

(G-400)
B & L FINISHING SHOP INC
400 Middle St Ste 6 (06010-8405)
P.O. Box 411 (06011-0411)
PHONE..............................860 583-1164
Hermel Lizotte, *Pr*
Rita Lizotte, *Sec*
EMP: 9 EST: 1973
SALES (est): 821.89K **Privately Held**
Web: www.bandlfinishingshopct.com
SIC: 2434   Wood kitchen cabinets

(G-401)
B & P PLATING EQUIPMENT LLC
74 Broderick Rd (06010-7736)
PHONE..............................860 589-5799
Ronald Landrette, *Managing Member*
EMP: 10 EST: 2002
SQ FT: 10,000
SALES (est): 767.65K **Privately Held**

SIC: 3471 3544   Plating of metals or formed
  products; Special dies and tools

(G-402)
B&T SCREW MACHINE CO INC
571 Broad St (06010-6662)
P.O. Box 431 (06011-0431)
PHONE..............................860 314-4410
Theresa Gokey, *Pr*
EMP: 13 EST: 1997
SQ FT: 20,000
SALES (est): 442.89K **Privately Held**
Web:
www.btscrewmachinecompany.com
SIC: 3451   Screw machine products

(G-403)
BARLOW METAL STAMPING INC
2 Barlow St (06010-4001)
P.O. Box 1397 (06011-1397)
PHONE..............................860 583-1387
Peter Gaughan, *Ch Bd*
Terry Gaughan, *Pr*
Norman Lazerow, *VP*
EMP: 20 EST: 1966
SQ FT: 15,600
SALES (est): 2.43MM **Privately Held**
Web: www.barlowmetalstamping.com
SIC: 3469   Stamping metal for the trade

(G-404)
BARNES GROUP INC
Associated Spring
18 Main St (06010-6581)
PHONE..............................860 582-9581
Paulo Coit, *Brnch Mgr*
EMP: 100
SALES (corp-wide): 1.26B **Publicly Held**
Web: www.onebarnes.com
SIC: 3469 3495   Metal stampings, nec; Wire
  springs
PA: Barnes Group Inc.
  123 Main St
  Bristol CT 06010
  860 583-7070

(G-405)
BARNES GROUP INC
Also Called: Barnes Aerospace W Chester
Div
123 Main St (06010-6376)
PHONE..............................513 759-3503
EMP: 111
SALES (corp-wide): 1.26B **Publicly Held**
Web: www.onebarnes.com
SIC: 3724   Aircraft engines and engine parts
PA: Barnes Group Inc.
  123 Main St
  Bristol CT 06010
  860 583-7070

(G-406)
BARNES GROUP INC (PA)
Also Called: Barnes
123 Main St (06010-6376)
PHONE..............................860 583-7070
Thomas J Hook, *Pr*
Thomas O Barnes, *
Julie K Streich, *Sr VP*
Jay B Knoll, *Sr VP*
Dawn N Edwards, *Senior Vice President
Human Resources*
▲ EMP: 245 EST: 1857
SALES (est): 1.26B
SALES (corp-wide): 1.26B **Publicly Held**
Web: www.onebarnes.com
SIC: 3724 3495 3469   Aircraft engines and
  engine parts; Precision springs; Stamping
  metal for the trade

(G-407)
BARON & YOUNG CO INC
400 Middle St Ste 13 (06010-8405)
PHONE..............................860 589-3235
Donald Baron, *Pr*
Dennis Dutkiewicz, *VP*
Patricia Baron, *Sec*
EMP: 9 EST: 1956
SQ FT: 10,080
SALES (est): 900K **Privately Held**
Web: www.baronandyoungco.com
SIC: 3471 3479   Buffing for the trade;
  Lacquering of metal products

(G-408)
BASS PRODUCTS LLC
435 Lake Ave (06010-7332)
P.O. Box 1359 (06011-1359)
PHONE..............................860 585-7923
EMP: 9 EST: 2001
SQ FT: 17,000
SALES (est): 1.5MM **Privately Held**
Web: www.bassproducts.com
SIC: 3613   Power circuit breakers

(G-409)
BAUER INC
175 Century Dr (06010-7482)
PHONE..............................860 583-9100
▲ EMP: 58 EST: 1968
SQ FT: 38,000
SALES (est): 23.45MM **Privately Held**
Web: www.bauerct.com
SIC: 3829   Aircraft and motor vehicle
  measurement equipment

(G-410)
BAUMER LTD (DH)
Also Called: Baumer Electric
5 Century Dr (06010-7478)
PHONE..............................860 621-2121
Milan Ralbovsky, *Pr*
Lisa Zup, *Sec*
Severino Bruno, *Treas*
▲ EMP: 10 EST: 1988
SALES (est): 26.1MM **Privately Held**
Web: www.baumer.com
SIC: 5084 3625   Measuring and testing
  equipment, electrical; Switches, electric
  power
HQ: Baumer Holding Ag
  Hummelstrasse 17
  Frauenfeld TG 8500

(G-411)
BEEKLEY CORPORATION (PA)
1 Prestige Ln (06010-7454)
PHONE..............................860 583-4700
▲ EMP: 67 EST: 1934
SALES (est): 16.12MM
SALES (corp-wide): 16.12MM **Privately
Held**
Web: www.beekley.com
SIC: 2759 2761   Business forms: printing,
  nsk; Manifold business forms

(G-412)
BEEKLEY MEDICAL
1 Prestige Ln (06010-7468)
PHONE..............................860 583-4700
Ayn Laplant, *Pr*
EMP: 23 EST: 2017
SALES (est): 3.27MM
SALES (corp-wide): 16.12MM **Privately
Held**
Web: www.beekley.com
SIC: 3841   Surgical and medical instruments
PA: Beekley Corporation
  1 Prestige Ln
  Bristol CT 06010
  860 583-4700

(G-413)

BELMONT CORPORATION

Also Called: Village Cabinets
60 Crystal Pond Pl (06010-7475)
PHONE.................................860 589-5700
TOLL FREE: 800
David T Clark, *CEO*
Bruce L Clark, *
Robert L Boutot, *
EMP: 22 EST: 1971
SQ FT: 41,000
SALES (est): 1.77MM **Privately Held**
Web: www.villagecabinets.com
SIC: 2434 2521 2517 Wood kitchen cabinets
; Wood office furniture; Wood television and
radio cabinets

(G-414)

BES-CUT INC

400 Middle St (06010-8405)
PHONE.................................860 582-8660
Jay Rasmus, *Pr*
Ed O'hannessian, *CEO*
Karen Cunningham, *VP*
EMP: 7 EST: 1992
SQ FT: 3,500
SALES (est): 959.02K **Privately Held**
SIC: 3496 Miscellaneous fabricated wire
products

(G-415)

**BETTER MOLDED PRODUCTS
INC (PA)**

95 Valley St Ste 2 (06010-4985)
P.O. Box 2141 (06011-2141)
PHONE.................................860 589-0066
Roy Izzo, *Pr*
EMP: 60 EST: 1984
SQ FT: 60,000
SALES (est): 9.41MM
SALES (corp-wide): 9.41MM **Privately
Held**
Web: www.bettermolded.com
SIC: 3089 3544 Injection molding of plastics
; Special dies, tools, jigs, and fixtures

(G-416)

BLACK PHOENIX CUSTOMS LLC

43 Elm St (06010-6334)
PHONE.................................860 681-3162
EMP: 7 EST: 2017
SALES (est): 412.78K **Privately Held**
SIC: 3484 Guns (firearms) or gun parts, 30
mm. and below

(G-417)

**BRIDGESTONE RET
OPERATIONS LLC**

Also Called: Firestone
700 Farmington Ave (06010-3914)
PHONE.................................860 584-2727
Ryan Epps, *Mgr*
EMP: 8
Web: www.bridgestoneamericas.com
SIC: 5531 7534 Automotive tires;
Rebuilding and retreading tires
HQ: Bridgestone Retail Operations, Llc
333 E Lake St Ste 300
Bloomingdale IL 60108
630 259-9000

(G-418)

**BRISTOL ADULT RESOURCE
CTR INC**

97 Peck Ln (06010-6163)
PHONE.................................860 583-8721
Ronnie Cassin, *Brnch Mgr*
EMP: 76
SALES (corp-wide): 8.9MM **Privately Held**
Web: www.bristolarc.org
SIC: 2621 Bristols
PA: Bristol Adult Resource Center, Inc.
195 Maltby St
Bristol CT 06010
860 261-5592

(G-419)

BRISTOL HOSPITALITY LLC

42 Century Dr (06010-4779)
PHONE.................................860 589-7766
EMP: 7 EST: 2016
SALES (est): 397.76K **Privately Held**
SIC: 2621 Paper mills

(G-420)

**BRISTOL INSTRUMENT GEARS
INC**

164 Central St Ste 1 (06010-6778)
P.O. Box 9248 (06011-9248)
PHONE.................................860 583-1395
James Carros, *Pr*
David Carros, *VP*
Alex Carros, *General*
James Carros Prestreas, *Prin*
EMP: 18 EST: 1951
SQ FT: 20,000
SALES (est): 445.05K **Privately Held**
SIC: 3462 Iron and steel forgings

(G-421)

BRISTOL PRESS

188 Main St (06010-6308)
PHONE.................................860 845-8686
EMP: 10 EST: 2018
SALES (est): 249.73K **Privately Held**
Web: www.bristolpress.com
SIC: 2741 Miscellaneous publishing

(G-422)

**BRISTOL RTARY SCHLRSHIP
FUND I**

123 Farmington Ave Ste 111 (06010-4200)
PHONE.................................860 314-1871
EMP: 7 EST: 2010
SALES (est): 549.28K **Privately Held**
Web: www.bristolrotaryclub.org
SIC: 2621 Bristols

(G-423)

BRISTOL TOOL & DIE COMPANY

550 Broad St Ste 13 (06010-6677)
PHONE.................................860 582-2577
Carl Guenther, *Pr*
EMP: 17 EST: 1965
SQ FT: 5,000
SALES (est): 745.29K **Privately Held**
Web: www.bristoltool.com
SIC: 3469 3599 3544 Stamping metal for
the trade; Machine and other job shop work
; Special dies and tools

(G-424)

CD MANAGEMENT LLC

Also Called: Clinical Dynamics
225 N Main St (06010-4926)
PHONE.................................203 269-0090
Joseph Rebot, *Managing Member*
EMP: 11 EST: 2009
SALES (est): 930.4K **Privately Held**
Web: www.clinicaldynamics.com
SIC: 3841 Surgical and medical instruments

(G-425)

CENTURY SPRING MFG CO INC

100 Wooster Ct (06010-6731)
P.O. Box 301 (06011-0301)
PHONE.................................860 582-3344
Walter Waseleski, *CEO*
William J Waseleski, *
Theresa Waseleski, *
EMP: 25 EST: 1975
SQ FT: 14,000
SALES (est): 4.92MM **Privately Held**
Web: www.centuryspringmfg.com
SIC: 3495 3493 3469 Mechanical springs,
precision; Steel springs, except wire; Metal
stampings, nec

(G-426)

**CHESTNUT UNITED
CORPORATION**

281 Lake Ave (06010-7322)
P.O. Box 1358 (06011-1358)
PHONE.................................860 584-0594
David Devoe, *CEO*
Richard Rubenstein, *
Lea Rubenstein, *
Arthur Difabbio, *
Jack Haber, *
EMP: 55 EST: 1958
SQ FT: 40,000
SALES (est): 11.13MM
SALES (corp-wide): 559.16MM **Privately
Held**
Web: www.plymouthspring.com
SIC: 3495 Instrument springs, precision
HQ: Lesjofors Stockholms Fjader Ab
Jamtlandsgatan 62
VAllingby 162 6
8870250

(G-427)

CLASSIC COIL COMPANY INC

205 Century Dr (06010-7486)
PHONE.................................860 583-7600
Rudolf Zeidler, *CEO*
James E Dowman, *
Richard Bisaillon, *
▲ EMP: 100 EST: 1976
SALES (est): 17.05MM **Privately Held**
Web: www.classic-coil.com
SIC: 3677 Coil windings, electronic

(G-428)

CLINICAL DYNAMICS CONN LLC

225 N Main St (06010-4984)
PHONE.................................203 269-0090
EMP: 9 EST: 2009
SALES (est): 820.06K **Privately Held**
Web: www.clinicaldynamics.com
SIC: 3841 Surgical and medical instruments

(G-429)

CMI SPECIALTY PRODUCTS INC

105 Redstone Hill Rd (06010-7799)
PHONE.................................860 585-0409
Joseph A Bozzuto, *Pr*
▲ EMP: 10 EST: 2003
SQ FT: 2,100
SALES (est): 2.27MM **Privately Held**
Web: www.cmispecialty.com
SIC: 3312 3353 Rods, iron and steel: made
in steel mills; Aluminum sheet and strip

(G-430)

**CONNECTICUT CLEAN ROOM
CORP**

32 Valley St Ste 2 (06010-4991)
P.O. Box 840 (06011-0840)
PHONE.................................860 589-0049
EMP: 26 EST: 1979
SALES (est): 3.93MM **Privately Held**
Web: www.ctcleanroom.com
SIC: 2273 2678 3081 Carpets and rugs;
Notebooks: made from purchased paper;
Unsupported plastics film and sheet

(G-431)

**CONNECTICUT TOOL & CUTTER
CO**

280 Redstone Hill Rd Ste 1 (06010-8624)
P.O. Box 368 (06062-0368)
PHONE.................................860 314-1740
Doctor Caroline Skudlarek, *Pr*
Alfonse Skudlarek Senior, *Pr*
Caroline Skudlarek, *VP*
EMP: 11 EST: 1970
SQ FT: 16,900
SALES (est): 2.36MM **Privately Held**
Web: www.ctctool.com
SIC: 3541 Machine tools, metal cutting:
exotic (explosive, etc.)

(G-432)

**CONVEYCO TECHNOLOGIES
INC (PA)**

47 Commerce Dr (06010-8608)
P.O. Box 1000 (06011-1000)
PHONE.................................860 589-8215
Raymond Cocozza, *Pr*
Doug Cartona, *Off Mgr*
Chris Benevides, *Account Executive*
Jim Benevides, *Prin*
EMP: 23 EST: 1979
SQ FT: 15,000
SALES (est): 15.1MM
SALES (corp-wide): 15.1MM **Privately
Held**
Web: www.conveyco.com
SIC: 5084 3625 Materials handling
machinery; Control equipment, electric

(G-433)

CURTIS PRODUCTS LLC

70 Halcyon Dr (06010-7464)
PHONE.................................203 754-4155
Ronald Weintraub, *Managing Member*
EMP: 18 EST: 1950
SALES (est): 2.02MM **Privately Held**
Web: www.curtisprod.com
SIC: 3451 Screw machine products

(G-434)

DACRUZ MANUFACTURING INC

100 Broderick Rd (06010-7724)
PHONE.................................860 584-5315
Victor P Dacruz, *Pr*
Chelsea E Castor, *
Betty T Dacruz, *
EMP: 43 EST: 1981
SQ FT: 33,000
SALES (est): 6.41MM **Privately Held**
Web: www.dacruzmfg.com
SIC: 3451 Screw machine products

(G-435)

**DCP SPRING ACQUISITION CO
INC**

Also Called: New England Spring
95 Valley St (06010-4980)
P.O. Box 1079 (06011-1079)
PHONE.................................860 589-3231
Jamie Valedaserra, *Pr*
William Lathrop, *Mng Pt*
Peter Desrosier, *
EMP: 35 EST: 1946
SQ FT: 33,000
SALES (est): 5.42MM **Privately Held**
Web: www.newenglandspring.com
SIC: 3495 Wire springs

(G-436)

DI-COR INDUSTRIES INC

139 Center St (06010-5074)
P.O. Box 3128 (06011-3128)
PHONE.................................860 585-5583

Harry Vassiliou, *Pr*
Tom Vassiliou, *Treas*
▼ **EMP:** 23 **EST:** 1990
SQ FT: 24,000
SALES (est): 825.11K **Privately Held**
SIC: 3441 2542 5021 Fabricated structural
metal; Racks, merchandise display or
storage: except wood; Racks

(G-437)
EMME CONTROLS LLC
32 Valley St Fl C (06010-4991)
P.O. Box 2251 (06011-2251)
PHONE..............................503 793-3792
David Cohen, *Pr*
Jon Brodeur, *CEO*
EMP: 8 **EST:** 2015
SQ FT: 12,000
SALES (est): 929.12K **Privately Held**
Web: www.getemme.com
SIC: 3822 Air flow controllers, air
conditioning and refrigeration

(G-438)
EMME E2MS LLC
32 Valley St Fl C (06010-4991)
P.O. Box 2251 (06011-2251)
PHONE..............................860 845-8810
Jonathan Brodeur, *CEO*
EMP: 10 **EST:** 2012
SQ FT: 10,000
SALES (est): 1.58MM **Privately Held**
Web: www.getemme.com
SIC: 3822 Limit controls, residential and
commercial heating types

(G-439)
EMME E2MS LLC
32 Valley St (06010-4991)
P.O. Box 2251 (06011-2251)
PHONE..............................860 845-8810
Emma Calise, *Prin*
EMP: 10 **EST:** 2012
SALES (est): 772.92K **Privately Held**
Web: www.emme-inc.com
SIC: 3822 Environmental controls

(G-440)
EMP CO INC (PA)
Also Called: Empco Prcision Swiss Screw
Mch
147 Terryville Rd (06010-4010)
P.O. Box 207 (06781-0207)
PHONE..............................860 589-3233
Henry Patnode, *Pr*
EMP: 7 **EST:** 1969
SQ FT: 1,000
SALES (est): 1.15MM
SALES (corp-wide): 1.15MM **Privately
Held**
Web: empcoinc.secureserversites.net
SIC: 3599 Machine shop, jobbing and repair

(G-441)
ENFLO CORPORATION (PA)
315 Lake Ave (06010-7397)
P.O. Box 490 (06011-0490)
PHONE..............................860 589-0014
Myron A Rudner, *Pr*
Robert E Dalton, *
Bertram Wolfson, *
▲ **EMP:** 20 **EST:** 1955
SQ FT: 25,000
SALES (est): 4.62MM
SALES (corp-wide): 4.62MM **Privately
Held**
Web: www.enflo.com
SIC: 3089 Injection molding of plastics

(G-442)
ETHERINGTON BROTHERS INC
Also Called: E B Buffing
33 Stafford Ave Ste 2 (06010-4699)
PHONE..............................860 585-5624
Nora Etherington, *Pr*
Harold Etherington, *VP*
EMP: 8 **EST:** 2005
SALES (est): 676.05K **Privately Held**
SIC: 3471 Electroplating of metals or
formed products

(G-443)
ETTER ENGINEERING
COMPANY INCORPORATED
210 Century Dr (06010-7477)
PHONE..............................860 584-8842
EMP: 20 **EST:** 1940
SALES (est): 5.29MM **Privately Held**
Web: www.etterengineering.com
SIC: 3567 5084 Industrial furnaces and
ovens; Heat exchange equipment, industrial

(G-444)
EXCEL SPRING & STAMPING
LLC
61 E Main St Ste 2 (06010-7060)
PHONE..............................860 585-1495
EMP: 9 **EST:** 2000
SQ FT: 7,500
SALES (est): 964.48K **Privately Held**
Web: www.excelspringct.com
SIC: 3469 3495 3496 3493 Perforated
metal, stamped; Precision springs; Cages,
wire; Coiled flat springs

(G-445)
FAD TOOL COMPANY LLC
95 Valley St Ste 7 (06010-4985)
P.O. Box 1117 (06011-1117)
PHONE..............................860 582-7890
David Scott, *Pr*
Rick Miner, *
EMP: 40 **EST:** 1965
SQ FT: 3,500
SALES (est): 3.48MM **Privately Held**
Web: www.fadtool.com
SIC: 3544 Special dies and tools

(G-446)
FARMINGTON MTAL
FBRICATION LLC
26 Lewis St (06010-3640)
PHONE..............................860 402-5148
John Cunningham, *Prin*
EMP: 7 **EST:** 2019
SALES (est): 499.2K **Privately Held**
SIC: 3499 Fabricated metal products, nec

(G-447)
FIRESTONE BUILDING PDTS CO
LLC
Firestone
780 James P Casey Rd Ste 4 (06010-8537)
PHONE..............................860 584-4516
William Probert, *Mgr*
EMP: 11
Web: www.holcimelevate.com
SIC: 5531 7534 5014 2952 Automotive tires
; Tire retreading and repair shops; Tires
and tubes; Asphalt felts and coatings
HQ: Holcim Solutions And Products Us, Llc
6211 N Ann Arbor Rd
Dundee MI 48131

(G-448)
FOUR STAR MANUFACTURING
CO
400 Riverside Ave (06010-8807)
PHONE..............................860 583-1614
Edward Plonski, *Pr*
Gary Plonski, *VP*
Florence Plonski, *Sec*
EMP: 39 **EST:** 1961
SQ FT: 18,000
SALES (est): 877.98K **Privately Held**
Web: www.fourstarmanufacturing.com
SIC: 3469 Stamping metal for the trade

(G-449)
FOURSLIDE SPRING STAMPING
INC
87 Cross St (06010-7434)
P.O. Box 839 (06011-0839)
PHONE..............................860 583-1688
Bryan Funk, *Pr*
Judith Schmidt, *
EMP: 25 **EST:** 1962
SQ FT: 20,000
SALES (est): 4.54MM **Privately Held**
Web: www.fourslide.com
SIC: 3493 3469 3495 Flat springs, sheet or
strip stock; Metal stampings, nec; Wire
springs

(G-450)
FUTURE MANUFACTURING INC
75 Center St (06010-4979)
P.O. Box 23 (06011-0023)
PHONE..............................860 584-0685
Denis Boroski, *Pr*
EMP: 12 **EST:** 1983
SQ FT: 10,000
SALES (est): 818.38K **Privately Held**
Web: www.futuremfg.com
SIC: 3677 Electronic coils and transformers

(G-451)
GMN USA LLC
181 Business Park Dr (06010-8628)
PHONE..............................800 686-1679
Glenn Ledoux, *Mgr*
Gary P Quirion, *Pr*
▲ **EMP:** 14 **EST:** 1998
SQ FT: 27,815
SALES (est): 4.82MM
SALES (corp-wide): 100.46MM **Privately
Held**
Web: www.gmnusa.com
SIC: 3541 Machine tools, metal cutting type
HQ: Gmn Paul Muller Industrie Gmbh &
Co. Kg
AuBere Bayreuther Str. 230
Nurnberg BY 90411
91156910

(G-452)
HARDWARE PRODUCTS
COMPANY LP
Also Called: Hardware Products Company
95 Valley St (06010-4985)
PHONE..............................617 884-9410
Ted White, *Pt*
EMP: 29 **EST:** 1866
SALES (est): 4.28MM **Privately Held**
Web: www.newenglandspring.com
SIC: 3495 Instrument springs, precision

(G-453)
HERBALIFE DISTRIBUTOR
607 King St (06010-4478)
PHONE..............................860 584-9721
Robin Plourde, *Prin*
EMP: 7 **EST:** 2017
SALES (est): 80.35K **Privately Held**
Web: www.herbalife.com
SIC: 2023 Dry, condensed and evaporated
dairy products

(G-454)
HEXCELPACK LLC
95 Wooster Ct (06010-6777)
PHONE..............................855 439-2351
David Goodrich, *Managing Member*
▼ **EMP:** 7 **EST:** 2014
SALES (est): 1.14MM **Privately Held**
Web: www.hexcelpack.com
SIC: 2621 Packaging paper

(G-455)
HRF FASTENER SYSTEMS INC
70 Horizon Dr (06010-7473)
PHONE..............................860 589-0750
Robert R Rohrs, *Pr*
Marsha Rohrs, *
EMP: 52 **EST:** 1970
SQ FT: 5,000
SALES (est): 2.42MM **Privately Held**
SIC: 3441 3546 Fabricated structural metal;
Power-driven handtools

(G-456)
IDEX HEALTH & SCIENCE LLC
Also Called: Eastern Plastics
110 Halcyon Dr (06010-7487)
PHONE..............................860 314-2880
David Kingsbury, *Dir*
EMP: 124
SALES (corp-wide): 3.18B **Publicly Held**
Web: www.idex-hs.com
SIC: 3821 3089 3494 3823 Laboratory
apparatus and furniture; Plastics processing
; Valves and pipe fittings, nec; Process
control instruments
HQ: Idex Health & Science Llc
600 Park Ct
Rohnert Park CA 94928
707 588-2000

(G-457)
INSIGHT PLUS TECHNOLOGY
LLC
747 Stafford Ave (06010-3846)
PHONE..............................860 930-4763
Thomas J Holtz, *Prin*
EMP: 9 **EST:** 2017
SALES (est): 350.43K **Privately Held**
Web: www.insightplustech.com
SIC: 3651 7382 3699 Household audio and
video equipment; Protective devices,
security; Security devices

(G-458)
JARVIS PRECISION POLISHING
190 Century Dr (06010-7491)
PHONE..............................860 589-5822
Wallace F Jarvis, *Pr*
EMP: 10 **EST:** 1992
SALES (est): 997.19K **Privately Held**
SIC: 3471 Electroplating and plating

(G-459)
JOVEK TOOL AND DIE
474 Birch St (06010-7837)
PHONE..............................860 261-5020
Joseph Longo, *Prin*
EMP: 8 **EST:** 2016
SALES (est): 637.01K **Privately Held**
Web: www.jo-vek.com
SIC: 3544 Special dies and tools

(G-460)
LAB SECURITY SYSTEMS CORP
Also Called: L A B
700 Emmett St (06010-7714)
PHONE..............................860 589-6037
Robert A Labbe, *Pr*
Gerald Roraback Junior, *VP*

GEOGRAPHIC

Richard Labbe, *
▲ EMP: 45 EST: 1957
SQ FT: 36,000
SALES (est): 6.68MM Privately Held
Web: www.labpins.com
SIC: 3429 3452 Keys, locks, and related hardware; Bolts, nuts, rivets, and washers

(G-461)
LEE SPRING COMPANY LLC
245 Lake Ave (06010-7398)
P.O. Box 1038 (06011-1038)
PHONE................................860 584-0991
Marcel Ouellette, Mgr
EMP: 17
SALES (corp-wide): 46.66MM Privately Held
Web: www.leespring.com
SIC: 3495 3493 5085 3315 Mechanical springs, precision; Steel springs, except wire; Springs; Wire and fabricated wire products
PA: Lee Spring Company Llc
　140 58th St Ste 3c
　Brooklyn NY 11220
　888 777-4647

(G-462)
LINCOLN THOMPSON
Also Called: Precision Threaded Products
220 Business Park Dr (06010-8629)
PHONE................................860 516-0472
Lincoln Thompson, Owner
EMP: 16 EST: 2010
SALES (est): 1.15MM Privately Held
Web: www.ptp-inc.com
SIC: 3399 Metal fasteners

(G-463)
LOU-JAN TOOL & DIE INC
474 Birch St (06010-7837)
P.O. Box 148 (06410-0148)
PHONE................................203 272-3536
Reita Jannetty, Pr
Louis Jannetty Junior, VP
EMP: 15 EST: 1966
SQ FT: 12,000
SALES (est): 1.3MM Privately Held
Web: www.ammo-tooling.com
SIC: 3544 3542 Special dies and tools; Machine tools, metal forming type

(G-464)
MARTIN CABINET INC
500 Broad St (06010-6638)
PHONE................................860 747-5769
Dan Chamberland, Prin
EMP: 13
SALES (corp-wide): 4.62MM Privately Held
Web: www.martincabinet.com
SIC: 2434 Vanities, bathroom: wood
PA: Martin Cabinet, Inc.
　336 S Washington St Ste 2
　Plainville CT 06062
　860 747-5769

(G-465)
MCINTIRE COMPANY (HQ)
Also Called: Western Progress
745 Clark Ave (06010-4068)
PHONE................................860 585-8559
William F Steinen, Ch
Thomas R Keenan, VP
John J Delaney Junior, Sec
▲ EMP: 15 EST: 1960
SQ FT: 12,000
SALES (est): 19.01MM
SALES (corp-wide): 22.03MM Privately Held

Web: www.mcintireco.com
SIC: 3564 3993 3842 3634 Blowers and fans ; Signs and advertising specialties; Surgical appliances and supplies; Electric housewares and fans
PA: Wm. Steinen Mfg. Co.
　29 E Halsey Rd
　Parsippany NJ 07054
　973 887-6400

(G-466)
MDF SYSTEMS INC
780 James P Casey Rd (06010-8537)
PHONE................................860 584-4750
▲ EMP: 70
SIC: 7389 2752 Advertising, promotional, and trade show services; Commercial printing, lithographic

(G-467)
MEADOW MANUFACTURING INC
106 Enterprise Dr Ste B (06010-8403)
PHONE................................860 357-3785
Brian Evans, Pr
Mark Gregoretti, Pr
Patrick D Temme, Ofcr
Joshua A Mcphail, VP
EMP: 15 EST: 2011
SALES (est): 2.89MM Privately Held
Web: www.meadowmfg.com
SIC: 3724 3429 Aircraft engines and engine parts; Aircraft hardware

(G-468)
METALLICS INC
229 Cross St (06010-7456)
PHONE................................860 589-4186
EMP: 46 EST: 1960
SALES (est): 13.36MM Privately Held
Web: www.nsiindustries.com
SIC: 3452 Screws, metal
PA: Nsi Industries, Llc
　13235 Reese Blvd W
　Huntersville NC 28078

(G-469)
MINUTEMAN PRESS OF BRISTOL
Also Called: Minuteman Press
98 Farmington Ave (06010-4218)
PHONE................................860 589-1100
EMP: 10 EST: 2011
SALES (est): 456.53K Privately Held
Web: hartford.minutemanpress.com
SIC: 2752 Commercial printing, lithographic

(G-470)
MIRABELLO HOLDINGS LLC
60 Wooster Ct (06010-6731)
PHONE................................860 582-9517
EMP: 45 EST: 1944
SALES (est): 9.53MM Privately Held
Web: www.mftech.com
SIC: 3471 Electroplating of metals or formed products

(G-471)
MONOPOL CORPORATION
394 Riverside Ave (06010-6320)
PHONE................................860 583-3852
Wesley Woisna, Pr
Lucy Woisna, Sec
EMP: 10 EST: 1984
SQ FT: 6,000
SALES (est): 764.57K Privately Held
SIC: 3841 Surgical and medical instruments

(G-472)
MORIN CORPORATION (DH)
Also Called: Morin East
685 Middle St (06010-8441)
P.O. Box 3028 (06011-3028)
PHONE................................860 584-0900
Russell Shiels, Pr
George Mcduffee, VP
Ilhan Eser, *
Richard Walker, *
▲ EMP: 60 EST: 1989
SALES (est): 40.94MM Privately Held
Web: www.kingspan.com
SIC: 3448 Prefabricated metal buildings and components
HQ: Kingspan-Medusa Inc.
　726 Summerhill Dr
　Deland FL 32724

(G-473)
MULTI-CABLE CORP
37 Horizon Dr (06010-7480)
P.O. Box 797 (06011-0797)
PHONE................................860 589-9035
Patrick Joyce, Pr
Grant Campbell, Pr
Guy Campbell, Ch
Emily S Joyce, Sec
EMP: 15 EST: 1975
SQ FT: 15,000
SALES (est): 3.74MM Privately Held
Web: www.multicable.com
SIC: 3357 Nonferrous wiredrawing and insulating

(G-474)
NELSON TOOL & MACHINE CO INC
675 Emmett St (06010-7715)
PHONE................................860 589-8004
David Florian, Prin
EMP: 7 EST: 2004
SALES (est): 116.43K Privately Held
SIC: 3728 Aircraft parts and equipment, nec

(G-475)
NEW ENGLAND MACHINE TOOLS INC
597 Middle St Ste B (06010-8400)
PHONE................................860 583-4001
Ben Thomas, Pr
Mark Knobloch, Ex VP
▲ EMP: 7 EST: 1988
SQ FT: 5,500
SALES (est): 837.09K Privately Held
Web: www.nemtusa.com
SIC: 8711 3625 3541 Consulting engineer; Control equipment, electric; Machine tools, metal cutting type

(G-476)
NOVO PRECISION LLC
150 Dolphin Rd (06010-8041)
PHONE................................860 583-0517
◆ EMP: 22 EST: 1981
SQ FT: 14,000
SALES (est): 5.51MM Privately Held
Web: www.novoprecision.com
SIC: 3496 5084 Miscellaneous fabricated wire products; Industrial machinery and equipment

(G-477)
OSCAR JOBS
Also Called: Reliable Spring Company
165 Riverside Ave (06010-6322)
P.O. Box 1952 (06011-1952)
PHONE................................860 583-7834
Oscar Jobs, Owner

EMP: 8 EST: 1981
SQ FT: 15,000
SALES (est): 891.5K Privately Held
Web: www.reliablespring.net
SIC: 3469 3493 3495 Stamping metal for the trade; Steel springs, except wire; Wire springs

(G-478)
P-Q CONTROLS INC (PA)
95 Dolphin Rd (06010-8000)
PHONE................................860 583-6994
Douglas D Schumann, Pr
Bart Matthew Guthrie, VP
▲ EMP: 38 EST: 1972
SQ FT: 20,000
SALES (est): 8.12MM
SALES (corp-wide): 8.12MM Privately Held
Web: www.pqcontrols.com
SIC: 3625 Control equipment, electric

(G-479)
PA-TED SPRING COMPANY LLC
137 Vincent P Kelly Rd (06010-7489)
PHONE................................860 582-6368
EMP: 22 EST: 1946
SALES (est): 4.11MM Privately Held
Web: www.pa-ted.com
SIC: 3469 3493 3496 5085 Metal stampings, nec; Steel springs, except wire; Miscellaneous fabricated wire products; Springs

(G-480)
PATWIL LLC
Also Called: Amstep Products
190 Century Dr Ste 102 (06010-7491)
PHONE................................860 589-9085
EMP: 8 EST: 1911
SQ FT: 6,400
SALES (est): 875.6K Privately Held
Web: www.amstep.com
SIC: 3446 Stairs, staircases, stair treads: prefabricated metal

(G-481)
PLAINVILLE MACHINE & TL CO INC
65 Ronzo Rd (06010-8621)
PHONE................................860 589-5595
Lawrence M Frey, Pr
Henry R Frey Junior, VP
EMP: 25 EST: 1965
SQ FT: 9,000
SALES (est): 2.26MM Privately Held
Web: www.plainvillemachinetool.com
SIC: 3544 Special dies and tools

(G-482)
PLYMOUTH SPRING COMPANY INC
281 Lake Ave (06010-7322)
PHONE................................860 584-0594
David Devoe, CEO
Diane Gagnon, *
EMP: 54 EST: 2021
SALES (est): 20.19MM
SALES (corp-wide): 559.16MM Privately Held
Web: www.plymouthspring.com
SIC: 3495 Wire springs
HQ: Lesjofors Ab
　Lagergrens Gata 2
　Karlstad 652 2
　54137750

(G-483)

PRECISION EXPRESS MFG LLC
80 Dolphin Rd (06010-8051)
PHONE...............................860 584-2627
EMP: 13 **EST:** 2010
SALES (est): 482.9K **Privately Held**
Web: www.precisionexpressmfg, nec
SIC: 3999 Manufacturing industries, nec

(G-484)

PRIME ENGNRED CMPNNTS - BRSTOL
231 Century Dr (06010-8401)
PHONE...............................860 584-5964
Mark D Izzo, *Pr*
EMP: 13 **EST:** 2007
SALES (est): 287.79K **Privately Held**
SIC: 3451 Screw machine products

(G-485)

QUALITY COILS INCORPORATED (PA)
748 Middle St (06010-8417)
P.O. Box 1480 (06011-1480)
PHONE...............................860 584-0927
Keith A Gibson, *Pr*
Gary A Gibson, *
Mark A Gibson, *
Joyce Achille, *
EMP: 120 **EST:** 1965
SQ FT: 30,000
SALES (est): 22.74MM
SALES (corp-wide): 22.74MM **Privately Held**
Web: www.qualitycoils.com
SIC: 3677 Coil windings, electronic

(G-486)

QUALITY WELDING LLC
61 E Main St Bldg C (06010-7060)
PHONE...............................860 585-1121
Samuel Walters, *Managing Member*
EMP: 9 **EST:** 1996
SQ FT: 1,800
SALES (est): 610.36K **Privately Held**
Web: www.qualityweldingllc.com
SIC: 7692 Welding repair

(G-487)

QUALITY WIRE EDM INC
329 Redstone Hill Rd (06010-7741)
PHONE...............................860 583-9867
Jeffrey Rimcoski, *Pr*
EMP: 9 **EST:** 1987
SQ FT: 2,000
SALES (est): 1.36MM **Privately Held**
Web: www.qualitywire-edm.com
SIC: 3599 3544 Electrical discharge machining (EDM); Special dies and tools

(G-488)

R & R CORRUGATED CONTAINER INC
360 Minor St (06010-8543)
P.O. Box 399 (06786-0399)
PHONE...............................860 584-1194
Robert J Braverman, *Pr*
EMP: 58 **EST:** 1968
SQ FT: 32,000
SALES (est): 12.21MM **Privately Held**
Web: www.randrbox.com
SIC: 2653 Boxes, corrugated: made from purchased materials

(G-489)

RADCLIFF WIRE INC
97 Ronzo Rd (06010-8619)
P.O. Box 603 (06011-0603)

PHONE...............................312 876-1754
Jean Radcliff, *CEO*
Charlie Radcliff, *
Mable Radcliff, *
Donald F Radcliff, *
▲ **EMP:** 36 **EST:** 1959
SQ FT: 25,000
SALES (est): 5.39MM **Privately Held**
Web: www.radcliffwire.com
SIC: 3357 3315 3496 Nonferrous wiredrawing and insulating; Wire, ferrous/iron; Miscellaneous fabricated wire products

(G-490)

RALPH INDUSTRIES INC
Also Called: Accurate Threaded Products Co
33 Stafford Ave Ste 5 (06010-4699)
PHONE...............................860 666-5621
Gary Fett, *Pr*
EMP: 33 **EST:** 1928
SALES (est): 800K **Privately Held**
SIC: 3599 Machine shop, jobbing and repair
PA: Atp Industries, Llc
75 Northwest Dr
Plainville CT 06062

(G-491)

REED AND STEFANOW MCH TL CO
165 Riverside Ave (06010-6322)
P.O. Box 1952 (06011-1952)
PHONE...............................860 583-7834
Joseph S Reed, *Pr*
Alice Reed, *VP*
▲ **EMP:** 44 **EST:** 1972
SQ FT: 2,000
SALES (est): 2.25MM **Privately Held**
Web: www.reedandstefanow.com
SIC: 3599 Machine shop, jobbing and repair

(G-492)

RGD TECHNOLOGIES CORP
Also Called: Nab Tool
50 Emmett St (06010-6623)
P.O. Box 9308 (06011-9308)
PHONE...............................860 589-0756
Robert G Dabkowski, *Pr*
Cynthia D Policki, *
Debra D Martin, *
▲ **EMP:** 60 **EST:** 1970
SQ FT: 200,000
SALES (est): 9.61MM **Privately Held**
Web: www.rgdtech.com
SIC: 3451 Screw machine products

(G-493)

RJ 15 INC
115 Cross St (06010-7434)
PHONE...............................860 585-0111
TOLL FREE: 800
Joseph E Palfini, *Pr*
Margaret J Palfini, *Sec*
EMP: 17 **EST:** 1976
SQ FT: 14,500
SALES (est): 4.54MM **Privately Held**
Web: www.rayjurgen.com
SIC: 3713 Truck and bus bodies

(G-494)

ROWLEY SPRING & STAMPING CORP
210 Redstone Hill Rd Ste 2 (06010-7796)
PHONE...............................860 582-8175
John Dellalana, *Pr*
Darlene B Krammer, *
William R Joyce, *
EMP: 160 **EST:** 1954
SQ FT: 150,000
SALES (est): 19.48MM **Privately Held**
Web: www.rowleyspring.com

SIC: 3495 3621 3496 3493 Mechanical springs, precision; Motors and generators; Miscellaneous fabricated wire products; Steel springs, except wire

(G-495)

ROYAL SCREW MACHINE PDTS CO
409 Lake Ave (06010-7330)
P.O. Box 1325 (06721-1325)
PHONE...............................860 845-8920
Alyssa Anderson, *Admn*
Thomas H Derwin, *
EMP: 19 **EST:** 1940
SQ FT: 20,000
SALES (est): 2.37MM **Privately Held**
Web: www.royalscrew.com
SIC: 3451 Screw machine products

(G-496)

SCOTT METAL FINISHING LLC
Also Called: Scott Metal Finishing
310 Birch St (06010-7800)
P.O. Box 9091 (06011-9091)
PHONE...............................860 589-3778
James Barnes, *Pr*
Scott Barnes, *VP*
EMP: 15 **EST:** 1978
SALES (est): 810.58K **Privately Held**
Web: www.scottmetalfinishingct.com
SIC: 3471 5051 Finishing, metals or formed products; Metals service centers and offices

(G-497)

SPRING TOLLMAN COMPANY INCORPORATED (PA)
91 Enterprise Dr (06010-7472)
PHONE...............................860 583-1326
EMP: 85 **EST:** 1945
SALES (est): 9.49MM
SALES (corp-wide): 9.49MM **Privately Held**
Web: www.tollmanspring.com
SIC: 3495 3493 3496 Wire springs; Steel springs, except wire; Miscellaneous fabricated wire products

(G-498)

SPRINGFIELD SPRING CORPORATION
24 Dell Manor Dr (06010-7436)
PHONE...............................860 584-6560
Dave Reno, *Mgr*
EMP: 13
SALES (corp-wide): 5.79MM **Privately Held**
Web: www.springfieldspring.com
SIC: 3495 Wire springs
PA: Springfield Spring Corporation
311 Shaker Rd
East Longmeadow MA 01028
413 525-6837

(G-499)

SSI MANUFACTURING TECH CORP
106 Enterprise Dr (06010-8403)
PHONE...............................860 589-8004
Gary Hutchison, *Pr*
Bob Peterson, *
Penny Hutchison, *
EMP: 36 **EST:** 1950
SQ FT: 14,000
SALES (est): 5.15MM **Privately Held**
Web: www.ssimanufacturing.com
SIC: 3599 Machine shop, jobbing and repair

(G-500)

THE PLAINVILLE ELECTRICAL PRODUCTS CO
Also Called: Pepco
435 Lake Ave (06010-7332)
P.O. Box 1359 (06011-1359)
PHONE...............................860 583-1144
EMP: 32 **EST:** 1922
SALES (est): 6.95MM **Privately Held**
Web: www.pepco-ft4.com
SIC: 3613 Control panels, electric

(G-501)

THEIS PRECISION STEEL USA INC (HQ)
Also Called: Theis Precision Steel
300 Broad St (06010-6600)
PHONE...............................860 589-5511
Robert W Garthwait Junior, *Pr*
Peter K Gersky, *
David Elliot, *
Thaddeus M Sendzimir, *
Tom Webel, *
◆ **EMP:** 210 **EST:** 1986
SQ FT: 350,000
SALES (est): 25.23MM
SALES (corp-wide): 25.23MM **Privately Held**
SIC: 3312 Blast furnaces and steel mills
PA: Tps Acquisition, Llc
151 Sharon Rd
Waterbury CT 06705
860 589-5511

(G-502)

THOMPSON AEROSPACE LLC
Also Called: Precision Threaded Products
220 Business Park Dr (06010-8629)
PHONE...............................860 516-0472
EMP: 16 **EST:** 1930
SQ FT: 16,500
SALES (est): 2.14MM **Privately Held**
Web: www.ptp-inc.com
SIC: 3728 Aircraft parts and equipment, nec

(G-503)

ULTIMATE COMPANIES INC (PA)
200 Central St (06010-6716)
PHONE...............................860 582-9111
Nancy J Brault, *Pr*
Robert P Nadeau, *VP*
EMP: 8 **EST:** 2003
SALES (est): 1.13MM
SALES (corp-wide): 1.13MM **Privately Held**
Web: www.theultimatecompanies.com
SIC: 3843 Dental equipment and supplies

(G-504)

ULTIMATE WIREFORMS INC
200 Central St (06010-6716)
PHONE...............................860 582-9111
Paul Blanchette, *Pr*
Robert Nadeau, *
Nancy Blanchette, *
EMP: 53 **EST:** 1988
SALES (est): 9.88MM **Privately Held**
Web: www.ultimatewireforms.com
SIC: 3841 8021 3843 3496 Surgical and medical instruments; Offices and clinics of dentists; Dental equipment and supplies; Miscellaneous fabricated wire products

(G-505)

WESTFALIA INC
625 Middle St (06010-8415)
P.O. Box 9529 (06011-9529)
PHONE...............................860 314-2920
Robert Crumb, *Pr*

▲ **EMP:** 26 **EST:** 1997
SQ FT: 35,000
SALES (est): 7.98MM
SALES (corp-wide): 549.14MM **Privately Held**
Web: www.westfalia-mh.com
SIC: 3714 3429　Camshafts, motor vehicle; Clamps, couplings, nozzles, and other metal hose fittings
HQ: Westfalia Metallschlauchtechnik Verwaltungs-Gmbh Konigsallee 4 Dusseldorf NW 273 328-3100

(G-506)
WHITMAN CONTROLS LLC
201 Dolphin Rd　(06010-8000)
PHONE...............................800 233-4401
Richard Sexton, *Managing Member*
EMP: 13 **EST:** 2018
SQ FT: 10,000
SALES (est): 2.54MM **Privately Held**
Web: www.whitmancontrols.com
SIC: 3823　Process control instruments

Broad Brook
Hartford County

(G-507)
ACE ENERGY LLC
152 Broad Brook Rd　(06016-9685)
P.O. Box 348　(06016-0348)
PHONE...............................860 623-3308
Catherine Ann Schantz, *Prin*
EMP: 10 **EST:** 2018
SALES (est): 3.05MM **Privately Held**
Web: www.taylorenergyct.com
SIC: 1382　Oil and gas exploration services

(G-508)
DOUBLE H ACRES LLC
47 Broad Brook Rd　(06016-9618)
P.O. Box 307　(06016-0307)
PHONE...............................860 250-3311
Herbert W Holden, *Prin*
EMP: 7 **EST:** 2010
SALES (est): 645.51K **Privately Held**
Web: www.broadbrookbeef.com
SIC: 3523　Cattle feeding, handling, and watering equipment

Brookfield
Fairfield County

(G-509)
AB ELECTRONICS LLC
61 Commerce Dr　(06804-3405)
PHONE...............................203 740-2793
EMP: 35 **EST:** 1992
SQ FT: 13,000
SALES (est): 7.42MM
SALES (corp-wide): 7.42MM **Privately Held**
Web: www.abelectronicsllc.com
SIC: 3672 3679 8711　Printed circuit boards; Electronic circuits; Electrical or electronic engineering
PA: Aragra Technologies Corporation 750 Trumbull Dr Pittsburgh PA 15205 412 505-8102

(G-510)
BOB THE BAKER LLC
Also Called: Bob The Baker
594 Federal Rd　(06804-2008)

P.O. Box 281　(06804-0281)
PHONE...............................203 775-1032
EMP: 10 **EST:** 2010
SALES (est): 959.25K **Privately Held**
SIC: 2052　Cookies

(G-511)
BOLTPRINTINGCOM
20 Old Grays Bridge Rd　(06804-2623)
PHONE...............................203 885-0571
Lana Corsano, *Owner*
▼ **EMP:** 8 **EST:** 2010
SALES (est): 311.9K **Privately Held**
Web: www.boltprinting.com
SIC: 2759　Screen printing

(G-512)
BRANSON ULTRASONICS CORP (DH)
120 Park Ridge Rd　(06804-3980)
PHONE...............................203 796-0400
Vernon Murray, *Pr*
Robert Tibbetts, *
▲ **EMP:** 275 **EST:** 1965
SALES (est): 162.36MM
SALES (corp-wide): 15.16B **Publicly Held**
Web: www.bransonultrasonics.com
SIC: 3699 3548 3541　Welding machines and equipment, ultrasonic; Welding apparatus; Machine tools, metal cutting type
HQ: Emerson Electric (U.S.) Holding Corporation 8000 West Florissant Ave Saint Louis MO 63136

(G-513)
BRIDGEWATER CHOCOLATE LLC
559 Federal Rd　(06804-2017)
PHONE...............................203 775-2286
▲ **EMP:** 8 **EST:** 1996
SQ FT: 4,800
SALES (est): 1.04MM **Privately Held**
Web: www.bridgewaterchocolate.com
SIC: 5441 2064　Candy; Candy and other confectionery products

(G-514)
BROOKFELD MDCL/SRGICAL SUP INC
Also Called: Brookfield Phrm Compounding
60 Old New Milford Rd Ste 1b (06804-2430)
PHONE...............................203 775-0862
James Cangelosi, *Pr*
Diane Cangelosi, *Sec*
EMP: 10 **EST:** 1988
SALES (est): 1.19MM **Privately Held**
Web: www.brookfieldmedical.com
SIC: 2834　Druggists' preparations (pharmaceuticals)

(G-515)
CHANNEL SOURCES LLC
Also Called: Channel Sources Company
246 Federal Rd Ste A12-1　(06804-2635)
P.O. Box 164　(06804-0164)
PHONE...............................203 775-6464
Tom Fitzsimmons, *Managing Member*
EMP: 25 **EST:** 1993
SALES (est): 660.22K **Privately Held**
Web: www.channelsources.com
SIC: 7372　Business oriented computer software

(G-516)
DAYLEEN INTIMATES INC
Also Called: Dominique Intimate Apparel
57 Commerce Dr　(06804-3405)

PHONE...............................914 969-5900
▲ **EMP:** 18 **EST:** 1995
SQ FT: 20,000
SALES (est): 2.28MM **Privately Held**
Web: www.dominiqueapparel.com
SIC: 2341 4225　Women's and children's undergarments; General warehousing and storage

(G-517)
DEFEO MANUFACTURING INC
Also Called: Xcaliber
115 Commerce Dr　(06804-3400)
PHONE...............................203 775-0254
Arturo De Feo, *Pr*
Anthony De Feo, *
◆ **EMP:** 29 **EST:** 2007
SQ FT: 14,000
SALES (est): 6.33MM **Privately Held**
Web: www.xcalibertransmission.com
SIC: 3714　Transmission housings or parts, motor vehicle

(G-518)
DSAENCORE LLC
50 Pocono Rd　(06804-3303)
PHONE...............................203 740-4200
EMP: 60
Web: www.dsaencore.com
SIC: 3679　Power supplies, all types: static

(G-519)
EASTERN PRECAST COMPANY INC
1 Commerce Dr　(06804-3405)
P.O. Box 5133　(06804-5133)
PHONE...............................203 775-0230
Richard G Ditullio Senior, *Pr*
Richard G Ditullio Junior, *Ex VP*
John J Ditullio, *Treas*
Judith H Ditullio, *Sec*
EMP: 16 **EST:** 1972
SQ FT: 3,000
SALES (est): 2.21MM **Privately Held**
Web: www.easternprecast.com
SIC: 3272　Concrete products, precast, nec

(G-520)
FOX VALLEY PAINT INC
5a Production Dr　(06804-1156)
PHONE...............................844 627-5255
Connor Mckenna, *Pr*
EMP: 69 **EST:** 2020
SALES (est): 2.76MM **Privately Held**
Web: www.foxvalleypaint.com
SIC: 2851　Paints and allied products

(G-521)
GK MECHANICAL SYSTEMS LLC
934 Federal Rd Ste 1　(06804-1143)
PHONE...............................203 775-4970
Michael Barnes, *Genl Mgr*
EMP: 8 **EST:** 2002
SQ FT: 4,500
SALES (est): 2.42MM
SALES (corp-wide): 49.07MM **Privately Held**
Web: www.gkmechanical.com
SIC: 3429　Keys, locks, and related hardware
PA: Novaria Holdings, Llc 6625 Iron Horse Blvd North Richland Hills TX 76180 817 381-3810

(G-522)
GORDON ENGINEERING CORPORATION
67 Del Mar Dr　(06804-2494)
PHONE...............................203 775-4501

Steven Weighart, *Pr*
EMP: 8 **EST:** 1971
SQ FT: 3,000
SALES (est): 470.4K **Privately Held**
Web: www.gordoneng.com
SIC: 3823 3842　Industrial process control instruments; Surgical appliances and supplies

(G-523)
GORDON PRODUCTS INCORPORATED
67 Del Mar Dr　(06804-2401)
PHONE...............................203 775-4501
Steven Weighart, *Pr*
EMP: 25 **EST:** 1979
SQ FT: 14,000
SALES (est): 2.48MM **Privately Held**
Web: www.gordonproducts.com
SIC: 3625 3674 3643　Electric controls and control accessories, industrial; Semiconductors and related devices; Current-carrying wiring services

(G-524)
GREENFIELD GLOBAL USA INC (HQ)
Also Called: Pharmco-Aaper
58 Vale Rd　(06804-3984)
PHONE...............................203 740-3471
▼ **EMP:** 14 **EST:** 1985
SALES (est): 54.42MM
SALES (corp-wide): 319.48MM **Privately Held**
Web: www.greenfield.com
SIC: 5169 2869　Industrial chemicals; Industrial organic chemicals, nec
PA: Greenfield Global Inc. 20 Toronto St Suite 1400 Toronto ON M5C 2 416 304-1700

(G-525)
IMPERIAL ELCTRNIC ASSEMBLY INC
Also Called: I E A
1000 Federal Rd　(06804-1158)
PHONE...............................203 740-8425
Tony Conte, *Pr*
Edward O'donnell, *VP*
Lisa O'donnell, *Sec*
Katie Scozzafava, *
▲ **EMP:** 93 **EST:** 1989
SQ FT: 45,000
SALES (est): 21.73MM **Privately Held**
Web: www.impea.com
SIC: 3679　Electronic circuits

(G-526)
INTERSPACE INDUSTRIES LLC
72 Grays Bridge Rd Ste 1c　(06804-2638)
PHONE...............................520 745-5009
Dave Humphryes, *Managing Member*
EMP: 20 **EST:** 2007
SALES (est): 787.19K **Privately Held**
SIC: 3651　Electronic kits for home assembly: radio, TV, phonograph

(G-527)
JENRAY PRODUCTS INC
4 Production Dr　(06804-1156)
PHONE...............................914 375-5596
Raymond D'urso, *Pr*
▲ **EMP:** 26 **EST:** 1999
SALES (est): 2.25MM **Privately Held**
Web: www.jenrayproducts.com
SIC: 3999　Sprays, artificial and preserved

(G-528)

LA PIETRA THINSTONE VENEER

Also Called: La Pietra Custom Marble & Gran
1106 Federal Rd (06804-1122)
P.O. Box 5149 (06804-5149)
PHONE..................................203 775-6162
Fabio Figueiredo, *Pr*
EMP: 11 **EST:** 2016
SALES (est): 1.5MM **Privately Held**
Web: www.thinstoneveneers.com
SIC: **3281** 5211 Marble, building: cut and
shaped; Tile, ceramic

(G-529)

MCMULLIN MANUFACTURING CORP

70 Pocono Rd (06804-3303)
P.O. Box 780 (06804-0780)
PHONE..................................203 740-3360
EMP: 31 **EST:** 1996
SQ FT: 12,800
SALES (est): 2.77MM **Privately Held**
Web: www.mcmullinmfg.com
SIC: **3469** 3444 Stamping metal for the trade
; Sheet metalwork

(G-530)

MIST HILL PROPERTY MAINT LLC

32 Mist Hill Dr (06804-1621)
PHONE..................................203 648-7434
EMP: 14 **EST:** 2018
SQ FT: 25,000
SALES (est): 2.23MM **Privately Held**
Web: www.misthillco.com
SIC: **2879** 1794 5083 0782 Insecticides and
pesticides; Excavation and grading;
building construction; Landscaping
equipment; Garden maintenance services

(G-531)

NITCH TO STITCH LLC

419 Federal Rd (06804-2090)
PHONE..................................203 948-9921
Scott Mitchell, *Mgr*
EMP: 8 **EST:** 2005
SALES (est): 127.28K **Privately Held**
SIC: **2395** Embroidery and art needlework

(G-532)

NORDEX INCORPORATED

Also Called: Nordex
426 Federal Rd (06804-2018)
PHONE..................................203 775-4877
EMP: 47 **EST:** 1960
SALES (est): 9.98MM **Privately Held**
Web: www.nordex.com
SIC: **3841** 3566 3568 3562 Surgical and
medical instruments; Speed changers,
drives, and gears; Power transmission
equipment, nec; Ball and roller bearings

(G-533)

PHOTRONICS INC (PA)

Also Called: Photronics
15 Secor Rd (06804-3937)
P.O. Box 5226 (06804-5226)
PHONE..................................203 775-9000
Frank Lee, *Pr*
Deno Macricostas, *
John P Jordan, *Ex VP*
Christopher J Progler, *Ex VP*
Richelle E Burr, *Ex VP*
EMP: 306 **EST:** 1969
SALES (est): 892.08MM
SALES (corp-wide): 892.08MM **Publicly
Held**
Web: www.photronics.com

SIC: **3674** Semiconductors and related
devices

(G-534)

PHOTRONICS TEXAS INC

15 Secor Rd (06804-3937)
PHONE..................................203 546-3039
Sean T Smith, *Prin*
EMP: 28 **EST:** 2015
SALES (est): 2.74MM
SALES (corp-wide): 892.08MM **Publicly
Held**
Web: www.photronics.com
SIC: **3674** Semiconductors and related
devices
PA: Photronics, Inc.
15 Secor Rd
Brookfield CT 06804
203 775-9000

(G-535)

PHOTRONICS TEXAS I LLC

15 Secor Rd (06804-3937)
PHONE..................................203 775-9000
EMP: 8 **EST:** 2015
SALES (est): 1.29MM
SALES (corp-wide): 892.08MM **Publicly
Held**
Web: www.photronics.com
SIC: **3674** Semiconductors and related
devices
PA: Photronics, Inc.
15 Secor Rd
Brookfield CT 06804
203 775-9000

(G-536)

RCD CHAMBERS INC

878 Federal Rd (06804-1830)
P.O. Box 280 (06804-0280)
PHONE..................................203 775-4416
Robert Ditullio Senior, *CEO*
Gina Carolan, *Pr*
Robert Ditullio Junior, *VP*
Chris Ditullio, *CFO*
▼ **EMP:** 15 **EST:** 1988
SQ FT: 12,000
SALES (est): 3.12MM **Privately Held**
Web: www.cultec.com
SIC: **3089** Washers, plastics

(G-537)

ROM TECHNOLOGIES INC

101 Silvermine Rd (06804-2047)
PHONE..................................888 374-0855
Peter Arn, *Pr*
Michael Bissonnette, *
EMP: 513 **EST:** 2020
SALES (est): 83.97MM **Privately Held**
Web: www.romtech.com
SIC: **3841** Surgical and medical instruments

(G-538)

ROTHSTEIN ASSOCIATES INC

Also Called: Rothstein Ctlog On Dsster Rcve
4 Arapaho Rd (06804-3104)
PHONE..................................203 740-7400
Philip J Rothstein, *Pr*
Carla Rothstein, *VP*
EMP: 8 **EST:** 1985
SQ FT: 1,500
SALES (est): 824.05K **Privately Held**
Web: www.rothstein.com
SIC: **8742** 2731 Management consulting
services; Books, publishing only

(G-539)

TARGET FLAVORS INC

7 Del Mar Dr (06804-2401)
PHONE..................................203 775-4727

John Maclean, *Pr*
William Maclean, *VP*
John S Maclean Junior, *VP*
Judith W Maclean, *Sec*
▲ **EMP:** 12 **EST:** 1981
SQ FT: 25,000
SALES (est): 2.48MM **Privately Held**
Web: www.targetflavors.com
SIC: **2087** Concentrates, flavoring (except
drink)

(G-540)

UNIPOWER LLC

57 Commerce Dr (06804-3405)
PHONE..................................203 740-8555
Debra Clavijo, *CEO*
EMP: 40
SALES (corp-wide): 22.76MM **Privately
Held**
Web: www.unipowerco.com
SIC: **3612** Specialty transformers
PA: Unipower, Llc
210 N University Dr # 700
Coral Springs FL 33071
954 346-2442

(G-541)

UNIVERSAL VOLTRONICS CORP

Also Called: Universal Voltronics
57 Commerce Dr (06804-3405)
PHONE..................................203 740-8555
Tom Kell, *CEO*
William T Carney, *
Rosa Feliciano, *
EMP: 55 **EST:** 1998
SQ FT: 22,000
SALES (est): 888.46K **Privately Held**
Web: www.voltronics.com
SIC: **3612** Specialty transformers

(G-542)

VALIDUS DC SYSTEMS LLC

50 Pocono Rd (06804-3303)
PHONE..................................203 448-3600
Frank Catapano, *VP*
EMP: 8 **EST:** 2003
SQ FT: 29,000
SALES (est): 497.8K **Privately Held**
Web: www.validusdc.com
SIC: **3679** Static power supply converters
for electronic applications

(G-543)

VISION DESIGNS LLC

Also Called: Vision Designs
1120 Federal Rd Ste 2 (06804-1157)
PHONE..................................203 778-9898
Scott D Johnsonmbr, *Mng Pt*
EMP: 15 **EST:** 2003
SALES (est): 2.49MM **Privately Held**
Web: www.visiondesignsct.com
SIC: **2759** 5099 Screen printing; Signs,
except electric

(G-544)

WENTWORTH LABORATORIES INC (PA)

1087 Federal Rd Ste 4 (06804-1145)
PHONE..................................203 775-0448
Stephen A A Evans, *Pr*
Stephen Evans, *
Arthur Evans, *
Robert Bollo, *
Joseph Mullaney, *
EMP: 150 **EST:** 1967
SQ FT: 25,000
SALES (est): 14.56MM
SALES (corp-wide): 14.56MM **Privately
Held**
Web: www.wentworthlabs.com

SIC: **3825** Instruments to measure electricity

Brooklyn
Windham County

(G-545)

CONTROL CONCEPTS INC (PA)

19 S Main St (06234-3400)
PHONE..................................860 928-6551
Henry D Tiffany Iii, *Pr*
Jonathan Larrabee, *Sec*
◆ **EMP:** 12 **EST:** 1992
SQ FT: 8,200
SALES (est): 5.67MM
SALES (corp-wide): 5.67MM **Privately
Held**
Web: www.controlconceptsusa.com
SIC: **3625** 3613 3566 Switches, electronic
applications; Switches, electric power
except snap, push button, etc.; Speed
changers, drives, and gears

Burlington
Hartford County

(G-546)

CASAVANT CORPORATION

5 Cricket Ln (06013-1301)
PHONE..................................860 605-5937
Brian Casavant, *Ofcr*
EMP: 7 **EST:** 2021
SALES (est): 61.91K **Privately Held**
SIC: **3732** Boatbuilding and repairing

(G-547)

CRESCENT MNFACTURING OPERATING

700 George Washington Tpke
(06013-1718)
P.O. Box 1350 (06013-0350)
PHONE..................................860 673-2591
Richard V Gates, *
James Speck, *
Joanne Gates, *
Richard Green, *
EMP: 34 **EST:** 1960
SQ FT: 18,000
SALES (est): 3.37MM **Privately Held**
Web: www.crescentmanufacturing.com
SIC: **3452** Screws, metal

(G-548)

E R HINMAN & SONS INC

Also Called: Hinman Lumber
77 Milford St (06013-1722)
PHONE..................................860 673-9170
Michael J Hinman, *Pr*
Paul Hinman, *VP*
Julia Hinman, *CEO*
EMP: 8 **EST:** 1915
SQ FT: 5,000
SALES (est): 685.02K **Privately Held**
Web: www.erhinman.com
SIC: **2421** 2426 Lumber: rough, sawed, or
planed; Hardwood dimension and flooring
mills

(G-549)

ENERGY SAVING PDTS & SLS CORP

713 George Washington Tpke
(06013-1718)
P.O. Box 2037 (06013-1037)
PHONE..................................860 675-6443
Richard Lamothe, *Pr*
Susan Lamothe, *
EMP: 50 **EST:** 1986

SQ FT: 30,000
SALES (est): 3.49MM **Privately Held**
Web: www.espcorp.com
SIC: 3579 Forms handling equipment

(G-550)
GYPSUM SYSTEMS LLC
11 Hinman Meadow Rd (06013-1739)
P.O. Box 162 (06756-0162)
PHONE...............................860 470-3916
Nicole Rodrigue, *Prin*
EMP: 9 **EST:** 2014
SALES (est): 822.13K **Privately Held**
SIC: 3599 Industrial machinery, nec

(G-551)
HARPS UNLIMITED INTL LLC
21 Highfield Dr (06013-1510)
P.O. Box 730 (94517-0730)
PHONE...............................860 675-0227
Peter Reis, *Prin*
EMP: 8 **EST:** 1999
SALES (est): 469.1K **Privately Held**
Web: www.harps-international.com
SIC: 3931 Harps and parts

Canaan
Litchfield County

(G-552)
BECTON DICKINSON AND COMPANY
Rt 7 & Grace Way (06018)
P.O. Box 749 (06018-0749)
PHONE...............................860 824-5487
Todd Zeller, *Mgr*
EMP: 51
SALES (corp-wide): 19.37B **Publicly Held**
Web: www.bd.com
SIC: 3841 3842 Hypodermic needles and syringes; Surgical appliances and supplies
PA: Becton, Dickinson And Company
1 Becton Dr
Franklin Lakes NJ 07417
201 847-6800

(G-553)
BONSAL AMERICAN INC
43 Clayton Rd (06018-2153)
P.O. Box 996 (06018-0996)
PHONE...............................860 824-7733
George Sperry, *VP*
EMP: 10
SALES (corp-wide): 32.72B **Privately Held**
SIC: 3272 Concrete products, nec
HQ: Bonsal American, Inc.
625 Griffith Rd Ste 100
Charlotte NC 28217
704 525-1621

(G-554)
CENTURY ACQUISITION
49 Clayton Rd (06018-2153)
P.O. Box 485 (06018-0485)
PHONE...............................518 758-7229
Brendan Clemente, *Owner*
EMP: 8 **EST:** 2011
SALES (est): 176.27K **Privately Held**
Web: www.21centuryconcrete.com
SIC: 3273 Ready-mixed concrete

(G-555)
HUTZLER MANUFACTURING CO INC
4 Grace Way (06018-2487)
P.O. Box 969 (06018-0969)
PHONE...............................860 824-5117
Lawrence Hutzler, *Pr*

Lillian Ehrenhuaus, *
Glenn Ehrenhuaus, *
▲ **EMP:** 25 **EST:** 1937
SQ FT: 60,000
SALES (est): 10MM **Privately Held**
Web: www.hutzlerco.com
SIC: 3089 Injection molding of plastics

(G-556)
MINTEQ INTERNATIONAL INC
Also Called: Mineral Technology
30 Daisy Hill Rd (06018-2115)
P.O. Box 667 (06018-0667)
PHONE...............................860 824-5435
Mark Lambert, *Prin*
EMP: 10
Web: www.mineralstech.com
SIC: 2851 3823 3624 Paints and allied products; Process control instruments; Carbon and graphite products
HQ: Minteq International Inc.
35 Highland Ave
Bethlehem PA 18017

(G-557)
SPECIALTY MINERALS INC
30 Daisy Hill Rd (06018-2115)
P.O. Box 667 (06018-0667)
PHONE...............................860 824-5435
EMP: 19
Web: www.mineralstech.com
SIC: 3297 2819 1422 Nonclay refractories; Industrial inorganic chemicals, nec; Crushed and broken limestone
HQ: Specialty Minerals Inc.
622 3rd Ave Fl 38
New York NY 10017

(G-558)
TALLON LUMBER INC
2 Tallon Dr (06018)
P.O. Box 1058 (06018-1058)
PHONE...............................860 824-0733
James A Tallon, *Pr*
Brion Tallon, *.
EMP: 26 **EST:** 1970
SQ FT: 1,200
SALES (est): 3.05MM **Privately Held**
Web: www.tallonlumber.com
SIC: 2421 2426 Lumber: rough, sawed, or planed; Flooring, hardwood

Canton
Hartford County

(G-559)
CONNECTICUT SOLID SURFACE LLC
Also Called: Connecticut Solid
85 Washburn Rd (06019-2218)
PHONE...............................860 410-9800
Steven Roux, *Managing Member*
Raymond Roux, *Managing Member**
Jaclyn Roux, *.
EMP: 40 **EST:** 1997
SALES (est): 4.12MM **Privately Held**
Web: www.ctsolidsurface.com
SIC: 2511 3281 2434 Wood household furniture; Cut stone and stone products; Wood kitchen cabinets

(G-560)
DELTA ELEVATOR SERVICE CORP (DH)
Also Called: Otis Elevator Company
1 Farm Springs Rd (06019)
PHONE...............................860 676-6152
Randy Wilclx, *Pr*

Chris Gouyd, *Mgr*
EMP: 20 **EST:** 1969
SALES (est): 15.78MM
SALES (corp-wide): 13.69B **Publicly Held**
Web: www.otis.com
SIC: 3625 Control equipment, electric
HQ: North American Elevator Services Company
1 Farm Springs Rd
Farmington CT 06032

(G-561)
FINISHING TOUCH WOODCRAFT
3 Noja Trl (06019-2154)
PHONE...............................860 916-2642
Robert J Donovan Junior, *Prin*
EMP: 7 **EST:** 2010
SALES (est): 127.27K **Privately Held**
Web: www.woodcraft.com
SIC: 2511 Wood household furniture

Centerbrook
Middlesex County

(G-562)
IMERCHANDISE LLC
47 Industrial Park Rd (06409-1020)
PHONE...............................860 581-8700
Doug Stoyer, *CFO*
EMP: 20 **EST:** 2015
SALES (est): 870.33K **Privately Held**
Web: www.oldglory.com
SIC: 2339 Athletic clothing: women's, misses', and juniors'

(G-563)
QUALITY CARE DRG/ CNTRBROOK LLC
33 Main St (06409-1083)
P.O. Box 540 (06441-0540)
PHONE...............................860 767-0206
Richard Allen Olson, *Managing Member*
EMP: 12 **EST:** 2013
SALES (est): 663.54K **Privately Held**
SIC: 2834 Druggists' preparations (pharmaceuticals)

(G-564)
TOWER LABORATORIES LTD (PA)
Also Called: Tower Brands
8 Industrial Park Rd (06409-1019)
P.O. Box 306 (06409-0306)
PHONE...............................860 767-2127
Norman Needleman, *Pr*
E Cook Rand, *.
◆ **EMP:** 95 **EST:** 1979
SQ FT: 38,000
SALES (est): 52.81MM
SALES (corp-wide): 52.81MM **Privately Held**
Web: www.towerlabs.com
SIC: 2834 Effervescent salts

Central Village
Windham County

(G-565)
ARNIO WELDING LLC
12 Water St (06332-3255)
P.O. Box 443 (06332-0443)
PHONE...............................860 564-7696
Brian Arnio, *Managing Member*
EMP: 10 **EST:** 1991
SQ FT: 20,994
SALES (est): 500K **Privately Held**
Web: www.arniowelding.com

SIC: 1799 3312 Welding on site; Rails, steel or iron

Cheshire
New Haven County

(G-566)
A B & F SHEET METAL
Also Called: AB&f Sheet Metal Products
327 Sandbank Rd (06410-1771)
PHONE...............................203 272-9340
Milford Armstrong, *Owner*
EMP: 7 **EST:** 1967
SQ FT: 4,500
SALES (est): 737.84K **Privately Held**
Web: www.abfsheetmetal.com
SIC: 3444 Sheet metalwork

(G-567)
A B & F SHEET METAL PDTS INC
327 Sandbank Rd Ste C3 (06410-1771)
PHONE...............................203 272-9340
Jeffrey Armstrong, *Prin*
Peter Morin, *Prin*
EMP: 7 **EST:** 1998
SALES (est): 504.44K **Privately Held**
Web: www.abfsheetmetal.com
SIC: 3444 Sheet metalwork

(G-568)
ABLE MACHINE TOOL
110 Hitchcock Ct (06410-3001)
PHONE...............................203 272-5459
EMP: 7 **EST:** 2008
SALES (est): 112.55K **Privately Held**
Web: www.ablemts.com
SIC: 3599 Machine shop, jobbing and repair

(G-569)
AI-TEK INSTRUMENTS LLC
Also Called: Ai-Tek
152 Knotter Dr (06410-1136)
P.O. Box 748 (06410-0748)
PHONE...............................203 271-6927
▼ **EMP:** 38 **EST:** 2001
SQ FT: 18,000
SALES (est): 7.55MM **Privately Held**
Web: www.aitekinstruments.com
SIC: 3823 Process control instruments

(G-570)
AIS GLOBAL HOLDINGS LLC
Also Called: Atlantic Inertial Systems
250 Knotter Dr (06410-1137)
PHONE...............................203 250-3500
Christopher Holmes, *Managing Member*
EMP: 47 **EST:** 2007
SALES (est): 6.92MM
SALES (corp-wide): 68.92B **Publicly Held**
SIC: 3812 Gyroscopes
HQ: Goodrich Corporation
2730 W Tyvola Rd
Charlotte NC 28217
704 423-7000

(G-571)
APEX MACHINE TOOL COMPANY INC
500 Knotter Dr (06410-1140)
PHONE...............................860 677-2884
Dominick A Pagano, *Pr*
Glenn L Purple, *.
EMP: 99 **EST:** 1944
SQ FT: 44,008
SALES (est): 13.83MM **Privately Held**

▲ = Import ▼ = Export
◆ = Import/Export

SIC: 3544 3545 3546 3089 Jigs and fixtures
; Precision tools, machinists'; Power-driven
handtools; Injection molded finished
plastics products, nec
HQ: Hanwha Aerospace Usa Llc
5 Mckee Pl
Cheshire CT 06410
203 806-2090

(G-572)
ATLANTIC INERTIAL SYSTEMS
INC (DH)
Also Called: Goodrich Sensors and Integrate
250 Knotter Dr (06410-1137)
PHONE..............................203 250-3500
Justin Robert Keppy, *Pr*
Richard S Caswell, *
Diana Morales, *
▲ EMP: 490 EST: 2000
SQ FT: 70,000
SALES (est): 113.31MM
SALES (corp-wide): 68.92B **Publicly Held**
Web: www.atlanticinertial.com
SIC: 3812 Gyroscopes
HQ: Goodrich Corporation
2730 W Tyvola Rd
Charlotte NC 28217
704 423-7000

(G-573)
ATLANTIC INERTIAL SYSTEMS
INC
Also Called: Cheshire Division
250 Knotter Dr (06410-1137)
PHONE..............................203 250-3500
Robert Nead, *Brnch Mgr*
EMP: 103
SALES (corp-wide): 68.92B **Publicly Held**
Web: www.atlanticinertial.com
SIC: 3812 3845 Gyroscopes;
Electromedical equipment
HQ: Atlantic Inertial Systems Inc.
250 Knotter Dr
Cheshire CT 06410
203 250-3500

(G-574)
AUTOMATED MAILING
SERVICES LLC
1687 Reinhard Rd (06410-1222)
PHONE..............................203 439-2763
EMP: 8 EST: 1985
SQ FT: 10,000
SALES (est): 863.97K **Privately Held**
Web: www.automated-mail.com
SIC: 7331 2752 Mailing service;
Promotional printing, lithographic

(G-575)
BARKER ADVG SPECIALTY CO
INC (PA)
Also Called: Barker Specialty Co
27 Realty Dr (06410-1656)
PHONE..............................203 272-2222
TOLL FREE: 800
Gerald Barker, *CEO*
Herbert Barker, *
Gloria Barker, *
Steven E Barker, *
Darlene J Bowen, *
◆ EMP: 64 EST: 1966
SQ FT: 50,000
SALES (est): 18.89MM
SALES (corp-wide): 18.89MM **Privately**
Held
Web: www.barkerspecialty.com
SIC: 7336 2741 7389 5094 Silk screen
design; Catalogs: publishing and printing;
Advertising, promotional, and trade show
services; Coins, medals, and trophies

(G-576)
BOVANO INDUSTRIES
INCORPORATED
Also Called: Bovano of Cheshire
830 S Main St Ofc A (06410-3474)
PHONE..............................203 272-3208
James A Flood, *Pr*
David Flood, *VP*
EMP: 11 EST: 1954
SQ FT: 17,000
SALES (est): 461.15K **Privately Held**
Web: www.bovano.com
SIC: 3231 5947 3229 Enameled glass; Gift
shop; Pressed and blown glass, nec

(G-577)
CARTEN CONTROLS INC
604 W Johnson Ave (06410-4500)
PHONE..............................203 699-2100
▲ EMP: 36 EST: 1990
SQ FT: 65,000
SALES (est): 1.91MM **Privately Held**
Web: www.cartenus.com
SIC: 3592 3494 Valves; Valves and pipe
fittings, nec

(G-578)
CARTEN-FUJIKIN
INCORPORATED
604 W Johnson Ave (06410-4500)
PHONE..............................203 699-2134
Seamus Sweeney, *Genl Mgr*
▲ EMP: 18 EST: 2014
SALES (est): 2.74MM **Privately Held**
Web: www.cartencontrols.com
SIC: 3674 Microcircuits, integrated
(semiconductor)

(G-579)
CHESHIRE CML LLC
21 Diana Ct (06410-1207)
PHONE..............................203 238-3482
Michael Batista, *Managing Member*
EMP: 50 EST: 2002
SALES (est): 2.45MM **Privately Held**
SIC: 2051 Bakery: wholesale or wholesale/
retail combined

(G-580)
CHESHIRE MANUFACTURING
CO INC
312 E Johnson Ave Ste 1 (06410-1297)
PHONE..............................203 272-3586
Joseph Whitright Junior, *Pr*
Dora Whitright, *Sec*
EMP: 7 EST: 1957
SQ FT: 6,500
SALES (est): 687.54K **Privately Held**
SIC: 3714 3469 7692 Motor vehicle parts
and accessories; Metal stampings, nec;
Welding repair

(G-581)
CONNTECH PRODUCTS
CORPORATION
30 Grandview Ct (06410-1261)
P.O. Box 309 (06410-0309)
PHONE..............................203 272-2261
EMP: 45 EST: 1972
SALES (est): 2.98MM **Privately Held**
Web: www.conntechproducts.com
SIC: 3449 Miscellaneous metalwork

(G-582)
CONSOLDTED INDS ACQSITION
CORP
Also Called: Consolidated Industries
677 Mixville Rd (06410-3836)

PHONE..............................203 272-5371
John David Wilbur, *Pr*
Benjamin Mark Palazzo, *
Drew Papio, *General Vice President*
▲ EMP: 100 EST: 1999
SQ FT: 87,000
SALES (est): 16.34MM **Privately Held**
Web: www.forgemetal.com
SIC: 3462 3369 Aircraft forgings, ferrous;
Aerospace castings, nonferrous: except
aluminum

(G-583)
CONSOLIDATED INDUSTRIES
INC
677 Mixville Rd (06410-3800)
PHONE..............................203 272-5371
▲ EMP: 100
SIC: 3463 Nonferrous forgings

(G-584)
CREATIVE DIMENSIONS INC
345 Mccausland Ct Ste 2 (06410-1377)
PHONE..............................203 250-6500
Joel P Roy, *Pr*
William A Violette Junior, *Prin*
▲ EMP: 37 EST: 1987
SQ FT: 48,000
SALES (est): 7.36MM **Privately Held**
Web: www.gowithcd.com
SIC: 3993 2541 Electric signs; Wood
partitions and fixtures

(G-585)
CUMMINS - ALLISON CORP
Also Called: Cummins Allison
125 Commerce Ct Ste 6 (06410-1243)
PHONE..............................203 794-9200
Tom Mack, *Mgr*
EMP: 8
SALES (corp-wide): 3.37B **Publicly Held**
Web: www.cranepi.com
SIC: 5046 5087 3519 Commercial
equipment, nec; Shredders, industrial and
commercial; Internal combustion engines,
nec
HQ: Cummins-Allison Corp.
852 Feehanville Dr
Mount Prospect IL 60056
800 786-5528

(G-586)
DALTON ENTERPRISES INC (PA)
131 Willow St (06410-2732)
PHONE..............................203 272-3221
John A Dalton, *Pr*
Barbara Alberino, *
▼ EMP: 75 EST: 1981
SALES (est): 21.61MM
SALES (corp-wide): 21.61MM **Privately**
Held
Web: www.latexite.com
SIC: 3272 Paving materials, prefabricated
concrete

(G-587)
DANJON MANUFACTURING
CORP
1075 S Main St (06410-3414)
P.O. Box 212 (06410-0212)
PHONE..............................203 272-7258
Eugene Johnson, *Pr*
Lorraine Johnson, *VP*
EMP: 35 EST: 1948
SQ FT: 4,000
SALES (est): 498.88K **Privately Held**
Web: www.danjon.com
SIC: 3545 Machine tool attachments and
accessories

(G-588)
DP FOODS L L C
152 Knotter Dr (06410-1136)
P.O. Box 748 (06410-0748)
PHONE..............................203 271-6212
Peter Sandore, *Prin*
EMP: 7 EST: 2009
SALES (est): 120.06K **Privately Held**
SIC: 2099 Food preparations, nec

(G-589)
ELECTRO-TECH INC
Also Called: E T I
408 Sandbank Rd (06410-1544)
PHONE..............................203 271-1976
Jerry F Camarota, *Pr*
Charles W Terry, *
Carol Terry, *
Roberta Camarota, *
EMP: 50 EST: 1984
SQ FT: 10,000
SALES (est): 9.82MM **Privately Held**
Web: www.eti-electrotech.com
SIC: 3451 3679 3678 Screw machine
products; Electronic circuits; Electronic
connectors

(G-590)
ENGINEERED POLYMERS INDS
INC
726 S Main St (06410-3472)
PHONE..............................203 272-2233
Len Azzaro, *Prin*
▲ EMP: 12 EST: 2015
SALES (est): 3.18MM
SALES (corp-wide): 130.85MM **Privately**
Held
Web: www.osterman-co.com
SIC: 2821 Plastics materials and resins
PA: Osterman & Company, Inc.
726 S Main St
Cheshire CT 06410
203 272-2233

(G-591)
ERICKSON METALS
CORPORATION (PA)
25 Knotter Dr (06410-1133)
P.O. Box 1941 (06011-1941)
PHONE..............................203 272-2918
Troy Erickson, *Pr*
Robert Stiles, *
Marlyn Poznanski, *
Lorna Weingart, *
Randy Adkisson, *
▲ EMP: 9 EST: 1972
SQ FT: 40,000
SALES (est): 24.05MM
SALES (corp-wide): 24.05MM **Privately**
Held
Web: www.ericksonmetals.com
SIC: 5051 3355 3444 Aluminum bars, rods,
ingots, sheets, pipes, plates, etc.;
Aluminum rolling and drawing, nec; Sheet
metalwork

(G-592)
EXCELSIOR INC
120 Braemar Dr (06410-1614)
PHONE..............................203 491-2028
EMP: 12 EST: 2001
SALES (est): 239.79K **Privately Held**
Web: www.excelsiorinc.com
SIC: 3069 Fabricated rubber products, nec

(G-593)
FIMOR NORTH AMERICA INC
(HQ)
Also Called: Fimor North America

50 Grandview Ct (06410-1261)
P.O. Box 764 (06410-0764)
PHONE.................................203 272-3219
Manuel Zuckerman, Pr
Nancy P Williams, *
Robert P Williams, *
David Corbin, *
EMP: 23 EST: 1961
SQ FT: 30,000
SALES (est): 9.61MM
SALES (corp-wide): 8.44MM Privately
Held
Web: www.fimornorthamerica.com
SIC: 3089 2821 Injection molding of plastics
; Plastics materials and resins
PA: Fimor
210 Rue Du Polygone
Le Mans 72100
243406600

(G-594)
G SCHOEPFERINC
460 Cook Hill Rd (06410-3707)
PHONE.................................203 250-7794
James Schoepfer, Pr
Dave Pagno, Sec
Mary Schoepfer, Sec
EMP: 11 EST: 1907
SQ FT: 4,000
SALES (est): 289.94K Privately Held
Web: www.schoepferseyes.com
SIC: 3229 Pressed and blown glass, nec

(G-595)
GEOSONICS INC
416 Highland Ave Ste D (06410-2527)
PHONE.................................203 271-2504
Susan Shepley, Mgr
EMP: 10
SALES (corp-wide): 9.71MM Privately
Held
Web: www.geosonicsvibratech.com
SIC: 1382 Seismograph surveys
PA: Geosonics, Inc.
359 Northgate Dr Ste 200
Warrendale PA 15086
724 934-2900

(G-596)
GRAPHICS PRESS LLC
1161 Sperry Rd (06410-3747)
P.O. Box 430 (06410-0430)
PHONE.................................203 272-9187
Edward Tufte, Managing Member
EMP: 7 EST: 1984
SALES (est): 1.08MM Privately Held
Web: www.edwardtufte.com
SIC: 2741 Miscellaneous publishing

(G-597)
HANWHA AEROSPACE USA LLC
(DH)
5 Mckee Pl (06410-1140)
PHONE.................................203 806-2090
Terry Bruni, Pr
Mike Debolt, *
EMP: 112 EST: 1946
SQ FT: 19,200
SALES (est): 104.45MM Privately Held
Web: www.hanwhaaerospaceusa.com
SIC: 3769 3541 3724 Space vehicle
equipment, nec; Machine tools, metal
cutting type; Aircraft engines and engine
parts
HQ: Hanwha Aerospace Usa Corporation
555 Theodore Fremd Ave
Rye NY 10580
860 677-2603

(G-598)
HENLAY CO
Also Called: My Pet Chicken
615 W Johnson Ave Ste 104 (06410-4532)
PHONE.................................908 795-1007
EMP: 9
SALES (corp-wide): 233.96K Privately
Held
SIC: 2679 Egg cartons, molded pulp: made
from purchased material
PA: Henlay Co
117 Rowland Rd
Brooks GA 30205
908 795-1007

(G-599)
HOB INDUSTRIES INC
25 Knotter Dr (06410-1133)
PHONE.................................203 879-3028
Francis X Macary Junior, CEO
Raymond R Macary, *
Peter Macary, *
Sarah Macary, *
EMP: 40 EST: 1975
SALES (est): 5.35MM Privately Held
Web: www.hobindustries.com
SIC: 3469 Stamping metal for the trade

(G-600)
HYLIE PRODUCTS
INCORPORATED
30 Grandview Ct (06410-1261)
P.O. Box 2015 (06770-8604)
PHONE.................................203 439-8786
Ruji Gomes, Pr
Deanne C Gauya, CEO
John C Gauya, VP
EMP: 49 EST: 1951
SQ FT: 10,000
SALES (est): 1.81MM Privately Held
SIC: 3469 Perforated metal, stamped

(G-601)
INDUSTRIAL HEATER CORP
30 Knotter Dr (06410-1122)
PHONE.................................203 250-0500
Thomas A Mcgwire Junior, Pr
Ted Mcgwire, Pr
Katherine Mcgwire, Sec
▼ EMP: 80 EST: 1921
SALES (est): 9.55MM Privately Held
Web: www.industrialheater.com
SIC: 3567 Heating units and devices,
industrial: electric

(G-602)
JOHN CANNING & CO LTD
150 Commerce Ct (06410-1253)
PHONE.................................203 272-9868
John Canning, Pr
Dorothea Hennessey, *
David Riccio, *
EMP: 25 EST: 1977
SQ FT: 7,500
SALES (est): 4.5MM Privately Held
Web: www.johncanningco.com
SIC: 1721 3299 1741 8999 Commercial
painting; Ornamental and architectural
plaster work; Masonry and other stonework;
Art restoration

(G-603)
LANE CONSTRUCTION
CORPORATION (DH)
Also Called: Lane
90 Fieldstone Ct (06410-1212)
PHONE.................................203 235-3351
Ignacio Botella, Pr
Mark Schiller, Pr

Kirk D Junco, Ex VP
Donald P Dobbs, Ex VP
Ann M Falsey, Sec
EMP: 250 EST: 1902
SQ FT: 90,000
SALES (est): 666.47MM
SALES (corp-wide): 7.95B Privately Held
Web: www.laneconstruct.com
SIC: 1622 1611 1629 3272 Highway
construction, elevated; Airport runway
construction; Subway construction; Building
materials, except block or brick: concrete
HQ: Lane Industries Incorporated
90 Fieldstone Ct
Cheshire CT 06410
203 235-3351

(G-604)
LANE INDUSTRIES
INCORPORATED (DH)
90 Fieldstone Ct (06410-1212)
PHONE.................................203 235-3351
Mark Schiller, Pr
Robert Alger, Pr
Vincent Caiola, Treas
Gianfranco Catrini, Dir
Kirk Junco, Ex VP
EMP: 7 EST: 1982
SQ FT: 18,000
SALES (est): 1.82B
SALES (corp-wide): 7.95B Privately Held
Web: www.laneconstruct.com
SIC: 1629 1622 1611 3272 Subway
construction; Highway construction,
elevated; Airport runway construction;
Building materials, except block or brick:
concrete
HQ: Salini-Impregilo Us Holdings, Inc.
90 Fieldstone Ct
Cheshire CT 06410
203 439-2900

(G-605)
MARION MANUFACTURING
COMPANY
1675 Reinhard Rd (06410-1222)
PHONE.................................203 272-5376
Douglas Johnson, Pr
Mary L Cramer, Pr
Jessica L Richard, Sec
Douglas Johnson, VP
▼ EMP: 21 EST: 2015
SQ FT: 28,000
SALES (est): 4.03MM Privately Held
Web: www.marionmfg.net
SIC: 3469 Stamping metal for the trade

(G-606)
MCGUIRE MANUFACTURING CO
INC
60 Grandview Ct (06410-1261)
P.O. Box 746 (06410-0746)
PHONE.................................203 699-1801
T Michael Mcroberts, Pr
Ken Byrant, Treasurer Finance
▲ EMP: 23 EST: 1951
SQ FT: 13,500
SALES (est): 4.6MM
SALES (corp-wide): 10.26MM Privately
Held
Web: www.mcguiremfg.com
SIC: 3432 Plumbing fixture fittings and trim
PA: Bead Industries, Inc.
11 Cascade Blvd
Milford CT 06460
203 301-0270

(G-607)
MICROTECH INC
1425 Highland Ave (06410-1233)

PHONE.................................203 272-3234
James A Mcgregor Iii, Pr
Flavio Montiero, *
EMP: 83 EST: 1955
SQ FT: 36,000
SALES (est): 14.8MM Privately Held
Web: www.microtech-inc.com
SIC: 3678 3679 3677 3663 Electronic
connectors; Waveguides and fittings;
Electronic coils and transformers; Radio
and t.v. communications equipment

(G-608)
NEW DESIGNZ REALTY LLC
Also Called: Ndz Performance
278 Sandbank Rd (06410)
PHONE.................................860 384-1809
Antonin Blazek, VP
EMP: 8 EST: 2015
SALES (est): 351.49K Privately Held
Web: www.newdesignz.com
SIC: 3484 Guns (firearms) or gun parts, 30
mm. and below

(G-609)
NUTMEG UTILITY PRODUCTS
INC (PA)
1755 Highland Ave (06410-1289)
P.O. Box 723 (06410-0723)
PHONE.................................203 250-8802
Jeannine Lavallee, CEO
Theresa Lavallee, *
▲ EMP: 34 EST: 1975
SALES (est): 4.93MM
SALES (corp-wide): 4.93MM Privately
Held
Web: www.nutmegutility.com
SIC: 3825 3669 3661 Instruments to
measure electricity; Emergency alarms;
Telephone and telegraph apparatus

(G-610)
OGS TECHNOLOGIES LLC
Also Called: Waterbury Button Company
1855 Peck Ln (06410-4411)
PHONE.................................203 271-9055
Michael L Salamone, Pr
Salvatore Geraci, *
▲ EMP: 45 EST: 1999
SQ FT: 40,000
SALES (est): 9.02MM Privately Held
Web: www.waterburybutton.com
SIC: 3993 3965 Signs and advertising
specialties; Buttons and parts

(G-611)
PRATT & WHITNEY ENG SVCS
INC
Also Called: Pratt & Whitney
500 Knotter Dr (06410-1140)
P.O. Box 786 (06410-0786)
PHONE.................................203 250-4000
Angela Megron, VP
EMP: 500
SALES (corp-wide): 68.92B Publicly Held
Web: www.prattwhitney.com
SIC: 3724 Aircraft engines and engine parts
HQ: Pratt & Whitney Engine Services, Inc.
1525 Midway Park Rd
Bridgeport WV 26330
304 842-5421

(G-612)
R & R PALLET CORP
120 Schoolhouse Rd (06410-1293)
PHONE.................................203 272-2784
Joseph Rizzo Junior, Pr
EMP: 12 EST: 1973
SQ FT: 16,000
SALES (est): 1.99MM Privately Held

▲ = Import ▼ = Export
◆ = Import/Export

Web: www.rrpalletcorp.com
SIC: 2448 Pallets, wood

(G-613)
RAND MACHINE & FABRICATION CO
1486 Highland Ave Ste 2 (06410-1200)
PHONE................................203 272-1352
Tom Saath, *Owner*
Donald J Ranaudo, *Pr*
Connie Ranaudo, *VP*
EMP: 10 **EST:** 1979
SQ FT: 4,000
SALES (est): 969.96K **Privately Held**
Web: www.randmachineco.com
SIC: 3599 Machine shop, jobbing and repair

(G-614)
RAND SHEAVES & PULLEYS LLC
1486 Highland Ave (06410-1200)
PHONE................................203 272-1352
EMP: 9 **EST:** 2010
SALES (est): 843.76K **Privately Held**
Web: www.randsheavesandpulleys.com
SIC: 3599 Machine shop, jobbing and repair

(G-615)
RM DISSOLUTION CO LLC
151 Moss Farms Rd (06410-1987)
PHONE................................203 699-9125
Cliff Perdion, *Prin*
EMP: 40 **EST:** 2010
SALES (est): 188.46K **Privately Held**
Web: www.fidmail.com
SIC: 3131 Rands

(G-616)
SALSCO INC
105 Schoolhouse Rd (06410-1241)
PHONE................................203 271-1682
EMP: 55 **EST:** 1979
SALES (est): 7.67MM **Privately Held**
Web: www.salsco.com
SIC: 7692 3524 3531 3523 Welding repair; Lawn and garden tractors and equipment; Construction machinery; Farm machinery and equipment

(G-617)
SPECTRUM VIRTUAL LLC
55 Realty Dr Ste 315 (06410-4600)
PHONE................................203 303-7540
Jonathan Reeves, *Prin*
Charles Baudinet, *Prin*
Mario Dinatale, *CIO*
EMP: 8 **EST:** 2013
SALES (est): 2.77MM **Privately Held**
Web: www.spectrumvirtual.com
SIC: 3577 7374 Data conversion equipment, media-to-media: computer; Data processing and preparation

(G-618)
TECHNOMETALPOST CONNECTICUT
766 Marion Rd (06410-3809)
PHONE................................203 228-7094
Michel Beaudoin, *Pr*
EMP: 10 **EST:** 2017
✪ **SALES (est):** 777.89K **Privately Held**
SIC: 3272 Pier footings, prefabricated concrete

(G-619)
TKH SECURITY LLC (PA)
Also Called: Park Assist
125 Commerce Ct Ste 11 (06410-1243)
PHONE................................203 220-6544
Timme Grijpink, *CEO*

▲ **EMP:** 70 **EST:** 2007
SALES (est): 10.17MM **Privately Held**
Web: www.parkassist.com
SIC: 3559 Parking facility equipment and supplies

(G-620)
TRIPLE B MEDIA LLC
195 S Main St (06410-3171)
PHONE................................917 710-2222
Anthony Bailey, *Managing Member*
EMP: 17 **EST:** 2021
SALES (est): 1.02MM **Privately Held**
Web: www.tripleb.tv
SIC: 2741 Internet publishing and broadcasting

(G-621)
WANHO MANUFACTURING LLC
154 Knotter Dr (06410-1136)
PHONE................................203 759-3744
David R Elliott, *Managing Member*
▲ **EMP:** 25 **EST:** 2004
SQ FT: 50,000
SALES (est): 23.91MM
SALES (corp-wide): 23.91MM **Privately Held**
Web: www.wanho.com
SIC: 5065 3443 Electronic parts; Cable trays, metal plate
PA: Us Capital Resources, Llc
137 Mattatuck Heights Rd
Waterbury CT 06705
203 759-3744

Chester
Middlesex County

(G-622)
AEROCISION LLC
12a Inspiration Ln (06412-1366)
PHONE................................860 526-9700
Andrew Gibson, *
Jeffrey Carpenter, *
EMP: 70 **EST:** 2004
SQ FT: 40,000
SALES (est): 20MM **Privately Held**
Web: www.aerocision.com
SIC: 3728 Aircraft parts and equipment, nec
HQ: Aerocision Parent, Llc
12a Inspiration Ln
Chester CT

(G-623)
BEN HUGHES COMMUNICATION PRODUCTS CO
Also Called: Cable Prep
207 Middlesex Ave (06412-1221)
P.O. Box 373 (06412-0373)
PHONE................................860 526-4337
EMP: 20 **EST:** 1979
SALES (est): 2.47MM **Privately Held**
Web: www.cableprep.com
SIC: 3423 Hand and edge tools, nec

(G-624)
BLACKWOLD INC
Also Called: Greenwald Industries
212 Middlesex Ave (06412-1273)
PHONE................................860 526-0800
Leonard F Leganza, *CEO*
Leonard Samela, *
Thomas W Williams, *
▲ **EMP:** 80 **EST:** 1987
SQ FT: 140,000
SALES (est): 16.56MM
SALES (corp-wide): 279.27MM **Publicly Held**

Web: www.greenwaldindustries.com
SIC: 3581 Mechanisms for coin-operated machines; Calculating and accounting equipment
PA: The Eastern Co
3 Enterprise Dr Ste 408
Shelton CT 06484
203 729-2255

(G-625)
CHAPCO INC (PA)
10 Denlar Dr (06412-1208)
P.O. Box 378 (06412-0378)
PHONE................................860 526-9535
Robert Weinstein, *Prin*
Brian Weinstein, *Prin*
Doug Berrie, *Prin*
Marianne Creeron, *Prin*
Doug Bredbury, *Prin*
▲ **EMP:** 47 **EST:** 1962
SQ FT: 22,000
SALES (est): 11.38MM
SALES (corp-wide): 11.38MM **Privately Held**
Web: www.chapcoinc.com
SIC: 3444 3599 Sheet metal specialties, not stamped; Machine shop, jobbing and repair

(G-626)
DENLAR FIRE PROTECTION LLC
20 Denlar Dr (06412-1208)
PHONE................................860 526-9846
Bryan Weinstein, *Pr*
EMP: 9 **EST:** 2011
SALES (est): 933.25K **Privately Held**
Web: www.denlarhoods.com
SIC: 3444 Hoods, range: sheet metal

(G-627)
EAST COAST PRECISION MFG
221 Middlesex Ave (06412-1221)
PHONE................................860 322-4624
EMP: 13
SALES (est): 264.96K **Privately Held**
Web: www.eastcoastmfg.com
SIC: 3999 Manufacturing industries, nec

(G-628)
EASTERN CO
Greenwald Industries, Inc Del
212 Middlesex Ave (06412-1273)
PHONE................................860 526-0800
Leonard Samela, *Pr*
EMP: 45
SALES (corp-wide): 279.27MM **Publicly Held**
Web: www.easterncompany.com
SIC: 3581 Mechanisms for coin-operated machines
PA: The Eastern Co
3 Enterprise Dr Ste 408
Shelton CT 06484
203 729-2255

(G-629)
ESICO TRITON LLC
10 Denlar Dr (06412-1208)
PHONE................................860 526-9535
EMP: 20 **EST:** 2018
SALES (est): 1.08MM **Privately Held**
Web: www.esicotriton.com
SIC: 3423 Soldering tools

(G-630)
PURIFICATION TECHNOLOGIES LLC (DH)
67 Winthrop Rd (06412-1036)
PHONE................................860 526-7801
Gerald A Richard, *Pr*
James F Lusis, *Treas*

James Lusis, *CFO*
◆ **EMP:** 13 **EST:** 2015
SQ FT: 32,000
SALES (est): 7.23MM
SALES (corp-wide): 6.97B **Publicly Held**
SIC: 2911 2899 Solvents; Chemical preparations, nec
HQ: Vwr Corporation
100 W Matsonford Rd Ste 1
Radnor PA 19087
610 386-1700

(G-631)
ROTO-FRANK OF AMERICA INC
Also Called: Roto Hardware Systems
14 Inspiration Ln (06412-1366)
PHONE................................860 526-4996
Greg Koch, *Pr*
Chrissostomos Dimou, *
Debra Brucker, *
Debra Wallis, *
Michael Stangier, *Prin*
◆ **EMP:** 120 **EST:** 1979
SQ FT: 64,000
SALES (est): 30.06MM
SALES (corp-wide): 899.96MM **Privately Held**
Web: www.rotonorthamerica.com
SIC: 2591 Window blinds
PA: Roto Frank Holding Ag
Wilhelm-Frank-Platz 1
Leinfelden-Echterdingen BW 70771
71175980

(G-632)
SAMSARA FITNESS LLC
Also Called: Trueform Runner
10 Denlar Dr (06412-1208)
PHONE................................860 895-8533
Jocelyn Coutant, *Sls Mgr*
EMP: 11 **EST:** 2015
SALES (est): 1.73MM **Privately Held**
Web: www.trueformrunner.com
SIC: 3949 Treadmills

(G-633)
WHELEN ENGINEERING COMPANY INC
Also Called: Austin Electronics
Rr 145 (06412)
PHONE................................860 526-9504
John Olson, *Brnch Mgr*
EMP: 40
SALES (corp-wide): 488.29MM **Privately Held**
Web: www.whelen.com
SIC: 3646 Commercial lighting fixtures
PA: Whelen Engineering Company, Inc.
51 Winthrop Rd
Chester CT 06412
860 526-9504

(G-634)
WHELEN ENGINEERING COMPANY INC (PA)
51 Winthrop Rd (06412-1036)
PHONE................................860 526-9504
Geoff Marsh, *Pr*
George Whelen Iv, *Ex VP*
Bob Mitchel, *CFO*
◆ **EMP:** 291 **EST:** 1952
SQ FT: 90,000
SALES (est): 488.29MM
SALES (corp-wide): 488.29MM **Privately Held**
Web: www.whelen.com
SIC: 3647 3646 3671 3651 Automotive lighting fixtures, nec; Commercial lighting fixtures; Electron tubes; Household audio and video equipment

Clinton
Middlesex County

(G-635)
AMERICAN MARKETING INTL LLC
Also Called: A.M.I. Contract Foodservice
20 Knollwood Dr (06413-1606)
PHONE..............................860 669-4100
Victor Robinson Mcgrady, *Managing Member*
◆ **EMP:** 25 **EST:** 1993
SALES (est): 6.25MM **Privately Held**
Web: www.amifood.com
SIC: 5087 7699 1542 3444 Restaurant supplies; Restaurant equipment repair; Restaurant construction; Restaurant sheet metalwork

(G-636)
ARGO TRANSDATA CORP
1 Heritage Park Rd (06413-1836)
PHONE..............................860 669-2233
▼ **EMP:** 26
Web: www.argoems.com
SIC: 3672 Printed circuit boards

(G-637)
BAUSCH ADVANCED TECH INC (PA)
115 Nod Rd (06413-1083)
PHONE..............................860 669-7380
Oliver Bausch, *Pr*
▲ **EMP:** 102 **EST:** 2003
SALES (est): 29.57MM
SALES (corp-wide): 29.57MM **Privately Held**
Web: www.bausch-group.com
SIC: 3559 3565 Sewing machines and hat and zipper making machinery; Packaging machinery

(G-638)
CLINTON INSTRUMENT COMPANY
Also Called: Clinton Instrument Company
295 E Main St (06413-2232)
PHONE..............................860 669-7548
Marianne Clinton Szreders, *Pr*
Marianne Clinton Szreders, *Pr*
Donna Langley, *VP*
EMP: 45 **EST:** 1965
SQ FT: 15,000
SALES (est): 9MM **Privately Held**
Web: www.clintoninstrument.com
SIC: 3823 3825 3829 Process control instruments; Instruments to measure electricity; Measuring and controlling devices, nec

(G-639)
COLD STONE CREAMERY
Also Called: Sweet Dreams
7 Glenwood Rd Unit F (06413-1712)
PHONE..............................860 669-7025
Christopher Anatra, *Owner*
EMP: 9 **EST:** 2001
SALES (est): 421.7K **Privately Held**
Web: www.coldstonecreamery.com
SIC: 5812 5451 2024 Ice cream stands or dairy bars; Ice cream (packaged); Ice cream and frozen deserts

(G-640)
CONOPCO INC
Unilever Home & Personal Care
1 John St (06413-1753)

PHONE..............................860 669-8601
Donald Wilbur, *Mgr*
EMP: 109
SALES (corp-wide): 62.39B **Privately Held**
Web: www.autoclor.com
SIC: 2844 Face creams or lotions
HQ: Conopco, Inc.
700 Sylvan Ave
Englewood Cliffs NJ 07632
201 894-7760

(G-641)
CUSTOM COVERS LLC
20 Riverside Dr (06413-2625)
P.O. Box 424 (06413-0424)
PHONE..............................860 669-4169
Barbara Whiting, *Owner*
EMP: 9 **EST:** 1982
SQ FT: 600
SALES (est): 495.85K **Privately Held**
Web: www.customcoverscanvas.com
SIC: 2394 Liners and covers, fabric: made from purchased materials

(G-642)
EASTERN CO
Also Called: Argo Ems
1 Heritage Park Rd (06413-1836)
PHONE..............................860 669-2233
John Hughes Iii, *Brnch Mgr*
EMP: 130
SALES (corp-wide): 279.27MM **Publicly Held**
Web: www.easterncompany.com
SIC: 3672 Printed circuit boards
PA: The Eastern Co
3 Enterprise Dr Ste 408
Shelton CT 06484
203 729-2255

(G-643)
EMI INC
4 Heritage Park Rd (06413-1836)
PHONE..............................860 669-1199
Sean Donkin, *Pr*
EMP: 8 **EST:** 1939
SALES (est): 920K **Privately Held**
Web: www.clevelandmixer.com
SIC: 3556 Mixers, commercial, food

(G-644)
HELANDER PRODUCTS INC
Also Called: Tiny-Clutch
26 Knollwood Dr (06413-1606)
P.O. Box 247 (06413-0247)
PHONE..............................860 669-7953
Gordon Helander, *Pr*
Andrew Helander, *VP*
EMP: 10 **EST:** 1964
SQ FT: 5,000
SALES (est): 1.01MM **Privately Held**
Web: www.tinyclutch.com
SIC: 3568 5084 Clutches, except vehicular; Industrial machinery and equipment

(G-645)
KENYON INTERNATIONAL INC
Also Called: Kenyon International
8 Heritage Park Rd (06413-1836)
P.O. Box 925 (06413-0925)
PHONE..............................860 664-4906
Phillip Williams, *Pr*
Mike Reischmann, *
◆ **EMP:** 33 **EST:** 1922
SQ FT: 24,000
SALES (est): 8.78MM **Privately Held**
Web: www.cookwithkenyon.com
SIC: 3631 Barbecues, grills, and braziers (outdoor cooking)

(G-646)
KINGFISHER MARINE LTD
70 Riverside Dr (06413-2625)
PHONE..............................602 409-1460
Richard Shriver, *Prin*
EMP: 8 **EST:** 2013
SALES (est): 54.34K **Privately Held**
SIC: 3069 Fabricated rubber products, nec

(G-647)
MALLACE INDUSTRIES CORP
Also Called: American Coated Products
1 Heritage Park Rd (06413-1836)
P.O. Box 918 (06413-0918)
PHONE..............................860 669-9001
Mark F Bertelsen, *CEO*
Mark F Bertelsen, *Ex VP*
Dennis R Mallace, *Pr*
Valdemar Bertelsen Iii, *VP*
Linda Bertelsen-mallace, *Sec*
▲ **EMP:** 20 **EST:** 1994
SQ FT: 20,000
SALES (est): 2.44MM **Privately Held**
SIC: 3953 Stencils, painting and marking

(G-648)
ONSITE SERVICES INC
23 Meadow Rd (06413-2265)
PHONE..............................860 669-3988
Kathleen Miller, *Pr*
David Miller, *VP*
Jonathan Miller, *VP*
EMP: 12 **EST:** 1995
SALES (est): 2.47MM **Privately Held**
Web: www.onsiteservices-signs.com
SIC: 3669 Pedestrian traffic control equipment

(G-649)
REGIONAL INDUSTRIES LLC
41 Commerce St (06413-2054)
PHONE..............................860 227-3627
EMP: 10 **EST:** 2016
SALES (est): 595.88K **Privately Held**
SIC: 3999 Manufacturing industries, nec

(G-650)
STATE WELDING & FABG INC
10 W Main St (06413-2092)
PHONE..............................203 294-4071
Charles Mascola, *Pr*
EMP: 7 **EST:** 1956
SALES (est): 800.61K **Privately Held**
Web: www.statewelding.net
SIC: 3441 7692 Building components, structural steel; Welding repair

(G-651)
TECHNIQUE PRINTERS INC
36 Old Post Rd (06413-1887)
PHONE..............................860 669-2516
Peter Hubbard, *Pr*
Thomas Snelgrove, *VP*
EMP: 7 **EST:** 2000
SQ FT: 2,300
SALES (est): 888.42K **Privately Held**
Web: www.techniqueprinters.com
SIC: 2752 7331 Offset printing; Mailing service

(G-652)
TOWER LABORATORIES LTD
7 Heritage Park Rd (06413-1836)
PHONE..............................860 669-7078
Robin Fey, *Brnch Mgr*
EMP: 20
SALES (corp-wide): 52.81MM **Privately Held**
Web: www.towerlabs.com

SIC: 2834 Pharmaceutical preparations
PA: Tower Laboratories, Ltd.
8 Industrial Park Rd
Centerbrook CT 06409
860 767-2127

Colchester
New London County

(G-653)
ACTION STEEL LLC
34 Oconnell Road Ext (06415-5011)
PHONE..............................860 537-9499
EMP: 21 **EST:** 2002
SALES (est): 2.47MM **Privately Held**
Web: www.actionsteel.net
SIC: 3441 Fabricated structural metal

(G-654)
ALPHA Q INC (PA)
87 Upton Rd (06415-2712)
P.O. Box 536 (06415-0536)
PHONE..............................860 537-4681
EMP: 75 **EST:** 1986
SALES (est): 24.64MM
SALES (corp-wide): 24.64MM **Privately Held**
Web: www.alphaqinc.com
SIC: 3812 Aircraft/aerospace flight instruments and guidance systems

(G-655)
CAREFREE BUILDING CO INC (PA)
Also Called: Conn Shed Company
48 Westchester Rd (06415-2420)
PHONE..............................860 267-7600
Norman Gustafson, *Pr*
Reynold Marvin, *Sec*
Todd Gustafson, *VP*
Brian Marvin, *VP*
EMP: 18 **EST:** 1979
SQ FT: 20,000
SALES (est): 3.15MM
SALES (corp-wide): 3.15MM **Privately Held**
Web: www.carefreebuildings.com
SIC: 2452 2511 Prefabricated buildings, wood; Lawn furniture: wood

(G-656)
EAGLE MANUFACTURING CO INC
13 Homonick Rd (06415-1911)
P.O. Box 186 (06415-0186)
PHONE..............................860 537-3759
Clifton O'donal, *Pr*
Jerry Risley, *Contrlr*
EMP: 15 **EST:** 1986
SQ FT: 10,000
SALES (est): 2.35MM **Privately Held**
SIC: 3441 Fabricated structural metal

(G-657)
ESSENTIAL TRADING SYSTEMS CORP
Also Called: Etc
188 Norwich Ave Ste 5 (06415-1256)
PHONE..............................860 295-8100
Gilbert M Smith, *CEO*
David Harding, *Pr*
Jeffrey Hasbargen, *Technology Vice President*
▲ **EMP:** 14 **EST:** 1986
SQ FT: 10,000
SALES (est): 2.45MM **Privately Held**
Web: www.essentialtel.com

▲ = Import ▼ = Export
◆ = Import/Export

SIC: 3669 Visual communication systems

(G-658)
ESSEX WOOD PRODUCTS INC
Also Called: Ewp
75 Mill St (06415-1263)
P.O. Box 513 (06415-0513)
PHONE..............................860 537-3451
Stephen Lloyd Schwartz, Pr
Michael Pasternak, *
EMP: 11 EST: 1975
SQ FT: 20,000
SALES (est): 244.74K Privately Held
SIC: 3944 2499 Craft and hobby kits and
sets; Novelties, wood fiber

(G-659)
GRANITE GROUP
WHOLESALERS LLC
Also Called: Granite Group, The
464 S Main St Ste 1 (06415-1548)
PHONE..............................860 537-7600
Robert Tellegrini, Mgr
EMP: 9
SALES (corp-wide): 187.65MM Privately
Held
Web: www.thegranitegroup.com
SIC: 5999 5074 3432 Plumbing and heating
supplies; Plumbing and hydronic heating
supplies; Plumbing fixture fittings and trim
PA: The Granite Group Wholesalers Llc
6 Storrs St
Concord NH 03301
603 545-3470

(G-660)
INNOVATIVE ENVIRONMENTAL
LLC
Also Called: Innovative Environmental
367 Lebanon Ave (06415-2111)
P.O. Box 846 (06415-0846)
PHONE..............................860 871-7582
Frank Pappalardo, Managing Member
Anthony Pappalardo, Proj Mgr
EMP: 18 EST: 1994
SQ FT: 4,000
SALES (est): 2.28MM Privately Held
Web: www.ieindustrialservices.com
SIC: 7349 4959 1389 1711 Cleaning
service, industrial or commercial;
Environmental cleanup services;
Construction, repair, and dismantling
services; Ventilation and duct work
contractor

(G-661)
INTERNATIONAL CORDAGE
EAST LTD (PA)
Also Called: Baynets Safety Systems
226 Upton Rd (06415-2712)
PHONE..............................860 537-1414
◆ EMP: 75 EST: 1995
SQ FT: 25,000
SALES (est): 23.83MM Privately Held
Web: www.incord.com
SIC: 2298 Cargo nets

(G-662)
N C T INC
Also Called: Numerical Control Technology
124 Upton Rd (06415-2712)
PHONE..............................860 666-8424
Volodymr Drobockyi, Pr
Adam Jarzebowski, Pr
Walter Jarzebowski, VP
Elizabeth Jarzebowski, VP
EMP: 11 EST: 1983
SALES (est): 861.83K Privately Held
Web: www.nctfrictionwelding.com

SIC: 7692 7629 7389 Welding repair;
Electronic equipment repair; Grinding,
precision: commercial or industrial

(G-663)
PLAY-IT PRODUCTIONS INC
167b Lebanon Ave (06415-1225)
PHONE..............................212 695-6530
Terri Tyler, VP
EMP: 10 EST: 1991
SALES (est): 760.85K Privately Held
SIC: 2752 7336 7812 7819 Commercial
printing, lithographic; Graphic arts and
related design; Audio-visual program
production; Video tape or disk reproduction

(G-664)
Q ALPHA INC
Also Called: Glastonbury Southern Gage Div
87 Upton Rd (06415-2712)
P.O. Box 531 (06415-0531)
PHONE..............................860 357-7340
Jim Klein, Mgr
EMP: 24
SQ FT: 25,000
SALES (corp-wide): 24.64MM Privately
Held
Web: www.gsgage.com
SIC: 3545 Gauges (machine tool
accessories)
PA: Alpha Q, Inc.
87 Upton Rd
Colchester CT 06415
860 537-4681

(G-665)
S & S WORLDWIDE INC
75 Mill St (06415-1263)
P.O. Box 513 (06415-0513)
PHONE..............................860 537-3451
Stephen L Schwartz, Ch
Adam L Schwartz, *
Hy J Schwartz, *
Audrey Bis, *
Allen Dyer, *
◆ EMP: 290 EST: 1906
SQ FT: 200,000
SALES (est): 192.62MM Privately Held
Web: www.ssww.com
SIC: 5199 5049 3944 Art goods; School
supplies; Games, toys, and children's
vehicles

Colebrook
Litchfield County

(G-666)
FAMP INC
Also Called: Fairchild
1 Thompson Rd Pmb 310 (06021-7057)
PHONE..............................860 379-2725
TOLL FREE: 800
Norman F Thompson, Ch Bd
Jonathan P Thompson, Pr
EMP: 22 EST: 1944
SQ FT: 16,500
SALES (est): 3.73MM Privately Held
Web: www.fairchildparts.com
SIC: 3599 Machine shop, jobbing and repair

Collinsville
Hartford County

(G-667)
KELYNIAM GLOBAL INC
97 River Rd Ste A (06019-3246)
PHONE..............................800 280-8192

Ross Bjella, CEO
EMP: 9 EST: 2005
SQ FT: 7,000
SALES (est): 1.67MM Privately Held
Web: www.kelyniam.com
SIC: 3842 Surgical appliances and supplies

(G-668)
PURITAN INDUSTRIES INC
122 Powder Mill Rd (06019-3502)
P.O. Box 186 (06022-0186)
PHONE..............................860 693-0791
Andrew P Papanek, Pr
▲ EMP: 9 EST: 1893
SQ FT: 10,000
SALES (est): 483.04K Privately Held
Web: www.puritanindustries.net
SIC: 3559 Sewing machines and
attachments, industrial, nec

Columbia
Tolland County

(G-669)
COLUMBIA MANUFACTURING
INC
165 Route 66 E (06237-1223)
P.O. Box 368 (06237-0368)
PHONE..............................860 228-2259
Kimberly Bell, Pr
Donald K Hodgins, *
John Della Ventura, *
Michael Enders, *
Samuel G Oliva, *
▲ EMP: 99 EST: 1980
SQ FT: 100,000
SALES (est): 26.23MM Privately Held
Web: www.columbiamanufacturing.net
SIC: 3724 5088 Pumps, aircraft engine;
Transportation equipment and supplies

(G-670)
HAWK INTEGRATED PLASTICS
LLC
1 Commerce Dr (06237-1231)
PHONE..............................860 337-0310
Joseph Bak, Managing Member
EMP: 12 EST: 2000
SQ FT: 12,500
SALES (est): 2.74MM Privately Held
Web: www.hawkiplas.com
SIC: 3089 Injection molding of plastics

(G-671)
WH ROSE INC
9 Route 66 E (06237-1235)
PHONE..............................860 228-8258
Lisa Rose, Pr
Christopher Rose, VP
Daniel J Marriott, VP
William Rose, Sec
EMP: 32 EST: 1943
SALES (est): 2MM Privately Held
Web: www.hpfairfield.com
SIC: 5013 7539 7692 Truck parts and
accessories; Auto front end repair;
Automotive welding

Cornwall Bridge
Litchfield County

(G-672)
STATIC SAFE PRODUCTS
COMPANY
8 Cook Rd (06754-1320)
P.O. Box 97 (06754-0097)

PHONE..............................203 937-6391
David F Greco, Pr
EMP: 10 EST: 2001
SALES (est): 1.19MM Privately Held
Web: www.staticsafeproducts.com
SIC: 2522 Office furniture, except wood

Cos Cob
Fairfield County

(G-673)
0 MOHAWK LLC
97 Valley Rd (06807-2209)
PHONE..............................203 622-7180
Grant Gyesky, Owner
EMP: 7 EST: 2014
SALES (est): 52K Privately Held
SIC: 2273 Finishers of tufted carpets and
rugs

(G-674)
CHICKEN SOUP FOR SOUL LLC
132 E Putnam Ave Ste 20 (06807-2724)
P.O. Box 700 (06807-0369)
PHONE..............................203 861-4000
William J Rouhana Junior, CEO
EMP: 50 EST: 2007
SALES (est): 9.15MM Privately Held
Web: www.chickensoup.com
SIC: 2741 Miscellaneous publishing

(G-675)
CHICKEN SOUP FOR SOUL
PRDCTONS (PA)
132 E Putnam Ave Ste 20 (06807-2744)
PHONE..............................855 398-0443
William J Rouhana Junior, CEO
EMP: 15 EST: 2014
SALES (est): 598.7MM
SALES (corp-wide): 598.7MM Publicly
Held
Web: www.cssentertainment.com
SIC: 2741 Miscellaneous publishing

(G-676)
DOONEY WOODWORKS LLC
(PA)
105 River Rd (06807-2554)
PHONE..............................203 340-9770
Peter Dewart Dooney, Managing Member
EMP: 8 EST: 2010
SALES (est): 398.12K
SALES (corp-wide): 398.12K Privately
Held
Web: www.dooneywoodworks.com
SIC: 2431 Millwork

(G-677)
DRAPERIES INTRORS
GRENWICH LLC
238 E Putnam Ave (06807-2702)
PHONE..............................203 489-3010
Donna Munzer, Mgr
EMP: 7 EST: 2020
SALES (est): 203.96K Privately Held
Web:
www.draperiesandinteriorsofgreenwich.com
SIC: 2391 Curtains and draperies

(G-678)
LIFETOKEN SOFTWARE INC
22 Daffodil Ln (06807-1409)
PHONE..............................203 515-9686
Jeff Dyment, CEO
EMP: 8 EST: 2021
SALES (est): 1MM Privately Held

SIC: **7372** 7389　Prepackaged software;
Business Activities at Non-Commercial Site

Coventry
Tolland County

(G-679)
**FOWLER D J LOG LAND
CLEARING**
150 Plains Rd (06238-3420)
PHONE..............................860 742-5842
Daniel J Fowler, *Prin*
EMP: 7 EST: 2003
SALES (est): 183.06K **Privately Held**
SIC: 2411　Logging camps and contractors

(G-680)
MIKE SADLAK
Also Called: Sadlak Innovative Design
712 Bread And Milk St Unit A6
(06238-1093)
P.O. Box 207 (06238-0207)
PHONE..............................860 742-0227
Mike Sadlak, *Owner*
EMP: 7 EST: 1989
SQ FT: 3,000
SALES (est): 302.5K **Privately Held**
Web: www.sadlak.com
SIC: 3949 8711 3484　Snow skiing
equipment and supplies, except skis;
Engineering services; Rifles or rifle parts,
30 mm. and below

(G-681)
SADLAK INDUSTRIES LLC
712 Bread And Milk St Unit A9
(06238-1093)
P.O. Box 207 (06238-0207)
PHONE..............................860 742-0227
John Barrett, *
EMP: 25 EST: 2002
SALES (est): 2.04MM **Privately Held**
Web: www.sadlak.com
SIC: 3541 3949　Machine tool replacement &
repair parts, metal cutting types; Targets,
archery and rifle shooting

(G-682)
SADLAK MANUFACTURING LLC
712 Bread And Milk St Apt 7 (06238-1093)
PHONE..............................860 742-0227
Michael Sadlak, *Managing Member*
John Barret, *
EMP: 25 EST: 2019
SALES (est): 1.16MM **Privately Held**
Web: www.sadlak.com
SIC: 3999　Manufacturing industries, nec

(G-683)
TELEFLEX INCORPORATED
Also Called: Teleflex
1295 Main St (06238-3117)
P.O. Box 219 (06238-0219)
PHONE..............................860 742-8821
Paul Jacovich, *Mgr*
EMP: 22
SALES (corp-wide): 2.79B **Publicly Held**
Web: www.teleflex.com
SIC: 3841　Surgical and medical instruments
PA: Teleflex Incorporated
550 E Swedesford Rd # 400
Wayne PA 19087
610 225-6800

Cromwell
Middlesex County

(G-684)
**ADVANCED WINDOW SYSTEMS
LLC**
14 Alcap Rdg Ste 4 (06416-1060)
PHONE..............................800 841-6544
TOLL FREE: 800
Joseph Lavoie, *Managing Member*
EMP: 15 EST: 1997
SALES (est): 2.92MM **Privately Held**
Web:
www.advancedwindowsystems.com
SIC: 3442 5031　Window and door frames;
Doors and windows

(G-685)
**ALBRAYCO TECHNOLOGIES
INC**
38 River Rd (06416-2325)
PHONE..............................860 635-3369
Allan Aylward, *Pr*
EMP: 8 EST: 2001
SQ FT: 6,500
SALES (est): 750K **Privately Held**
Web: www.moor-king.com
SIC: 3826　Laser scientific and engineering
instruments

(G-686)
APOGEE CORPORATION
Also Called: Impact Plastics
154 West St Ste C (06416-4400)
PHONE..............................860 632-3550
Steven Ryan, *Mgr*
EMP: 57
SALES (corp-wide): 9.98MM **Privately
Held**
Web: www.impactplastics.co
SIC: 3081　Unsupported plastics film and
sheet
PA: Apogee Corporation
5 Highland Dr
Putnam CT 06260
860 963-1976

(G-687)
ATLANTIC VENT & EQP CO INC
125 Sebethe Dr (06416-1033)
PHONE..............................860 635-1300
Martin F Cosker, *
Martin F Cosker, *
Keith Hellstrom, *
Jeffrey T Cosker, *
Terry L Cosker, *
EMP: 40 EST: 1965
SQ FT: 27,113
SALES (est): 4.5MM **Privately Held**
Web: www.atlanticventilating.com
SIC: 1711 3564 3444　Ventilation and duct
work contractor; Blowers and fans; Sheet
metalwork

(G-688)
BOB VESS BUILDING LLC
605 Main St (06416-1433)
PHONE..............................860 729-2536
EMP: 7 EST: 2000
SALES (est): 337.36K **Privately Held**
SIC: 3949　Sporting and athletic goods, nec

(G-689)
**CAREY MANUFACTURING CO
INC**
Also Called: Amatom Electronic Hardware
5 Pasco Hill Rd Unit B (06416-1012)
PHONE..............................860 829-1803

EMP: 10
SALES (corp-wide): 20.81MM **Privately
Held**
Web: www.careymfg.com
SIC: 5072 5999 3728　Hardware; Electronic
parts and equipment; Aircraft assemblies,
subassemblies, and parts, nec
PA: Carey Manufacturing Company, Inc.
5 Pasco Hill Rd Unit A
Cromwell CT 06416
860 829-1803

(G-690)
**CROMWELL CONCRETE
PRODUCTS INCORPORATED**
667 Main St (06416-1429)
P.O. Box 99 (06416-0099)
EMP: 34 EST: 1925
SALES (est): 3.21MM **Privately Held**
Web:
www.cromwellconcreteproducts.com
SIC: 3272 3271　Concrete products, precast,
nec; Blocks, concrete or cinder: standard

(G-691)
CRRC LLC
Also Called: Ripley
46 Nooks Hill Rd (06416-1562)
PHONE..............................860 635-2200
Kenneth Mac Cormac, *Pr*
EMP: 100
SALES (corp-wide): 24.81MM **Privately
Held**
Web: www.ripley-tools.com
SIC: 3429 3423 3634　Parachute hardware;
Hand and edge tools, nec; Blowers,
portable, electric
PA: Crrc, Llc
105 Nutmeg Rd S
South Windsor CT 06074
877 684-6464

(G-692)
**FLOYD MANUFACTURING CO
INC**
5 Pasco Hill Rd (06416-1012)
PHONE..............................860 829-1920
EMP: 38 EST: 1987
SALES (est): 2.76MM **Privately Held**
Web: www.floydmfg.com
SIC: 3545　Precision tools, machinists'

(G-693)
**GKN ARSPACE SVCS
STRCTURES LLC**
1000 Corporate Row (06416-2074)
PHONE..............................860 613-0236
David Olchowski, *CEO*
EMP: 135 EST: 2002
SQ FT: 28,500
SALES (est): 46.25MM
SALES (corp-wide): 9.07B **Privately Held**
SIC: 3724　Aircraft engines and engine parts
HQ: Gkn Limited
2nd Floor, One Central Boulevard
Solihull W MIDLANDS B90 8
121 210-9800

(G-694)
**HUBBELL POWER SYSTEMS
INC**
46 Nooks Hill Rd (06416-1562)
PHONE..............................860 635-2200
John Jutila, *Mgr*
EMP: 75
SALES (corp-wide): 5.37B **Publicly Held**
Web: www.hubbell.com

SIC: **3643** 5063 4841　Current-carrying
wiring services; Wiring devices; Cable and
other pay television services
HQ: Hubbell Power Systems, Inc.
200 Center Point Cir # 200
Columbia SC 29210
803 216-2600

(G-695)
ROSSI GROUP LLC (PA)
162 West St Ste A (06416-4405)
PHONE..............................860 632-3505
▼ **EMP: 17 EST:** 2010
SALES (est): 3.18MM **Privately Held**
Web: www.rossigroup.net
SIC: 2426　Lumber, hardwood dimension

(G-696)
RWK TOOL INC
200 Corporate Row (06416-2029)
PHONE..............................860 635-0116
William Buggie, *Pr*
Kenneth Buggie, *VP*
Donna Buggie, *Sec*
Robert V Buggie, *Dir*
EMP: 27 EST: 1978
SQ FT: 49,000
SALES (est): 444.47K **Privately Held**
Web: rwk-tool-inc.business.site
SIC: 3599　Machine shop, jobbing and repair

(G-697)
**SUPERIOR PLAS EXTRUSION
CO INC**
154 West St (06416-4400)
PHONE..............................860 234-1864
EMP: 23
Web: www.suburbanphysicaltherapy.com
SIC: 3081　Plastics film and sheet
PA: Superior Plastics Extrusion Company,
Inc.
5 Highland Dr
Putnam CT 06260

(G-698)
**UNIQUE EXTRUSIONS
INCORPORATED**
10 Countyline Dr (06416-1175)
PHONE..............................860 632-1314
Robert M Tabshey, *Pr*
Tami N Tabshey, *
Lauren Dalal, *
▲ **EMP: 25 EST:** 2004
SQ FT: 5,600
SALES (est): 4.63MM **Privately Held**
Web: www.uniqueextrusions.com
SIC: 3354　Aluminum extruded products

Danbury
Fairfield County

(G-699)
**A GUIDEPOSTS CHURCH CORP
(PA)**
Also Called: Peale Ctr For Christn Living
100 Reserve Rd Ste E200 (06810-5269)
PHONE..............................203 749-0203
John F Temple, *Pr*
Rocco Martino, *
James Asselmeyer, *
Dave Tietler, *
EMP: 125 EST: 1945
SALES (est): 22.14MM
SALES (corp-wide): 22.14MM **Privately
Held**
Web: www.guideposts.org

SIC: **8661** 2721 2731   Churches, temples, and shrines; Magazines: publishing only, not printed on site; Books, publishing only

(G-700)
A-1 STAIRS & RAILS LLC
2 Mill Plain Rd (06811-5141)
PHONE..............................203 792-7367
EMP: 8 EST: 2010
SALES (est): 79.49K **Privately Held**
SIC: 2431   Millwork

(G-701)
ABB INC
24 Commerce Dr (06810-4131)
PHONE..............................203 790-8588
Tishore Sundararajan, *Mgr*
EMP: 112
Web: new.abb.com
SIC: 3612   Transformers, except electric
HQ: Abb Inc.
    305 Gregson Dr
    Cary NC 27511

(G-702)
ABB INC
A B B Control
152 Deer Hill Ave Ste 304 (06810-7766)
PHONE..............................203 798-6210
E Santacana, *VP*
EMP: 37
Web: new.abb.com
SIC: 3625   Motor controls, electric
HQ: Abb Inc.
    305 Gregson Dr
    Cary NC 27511

(G-703)
ACCUTROL LLC
21 Commerce Dr (06810-4131)
PHONE..............................203 445-9991
Fred George, *Prin*
EMP: 28 EST: 2012
SALES (est): 2.27MM **Privately Held**
Web: www.accutrolllc.com
SIC: 3599   Air intake filters, internal combustion engine, except auto

(G-704)
ACUREN INSPECTION INC (HQ)
Also Called: Hellier
30 Main St Ste 402 (06810-3004)
PHONE..............................203 702-8740
Peter Scannell, *Pr*
Peter O Scannell, *Pr*
John P Lockwood, *VP*
Jim Gustafson, *Genl Mgr*
EMP: 532 EST: 1976
SQ FT: 30,000
SALES (est): 766.81MM
SALES (corp-wide): 1.5B **Privately Held**
Web: www.acuren.com
SIC: 1389 8071   Testing, measuring, surveying, and analysis services; Testing laboratories
PA: Rockwood Service Corporation
    43 Arch St
    Greenwich CT 06830
    203 869-6734

(G-705)
AIRGAS USA LLC
50 Mill Plain Rd (06811-5140)
PHONE..............................203 792-1834
Andrew Cichocki, *Brnch Mgr*
EMP: 227
SALES (corp-wide): 101.26MM **Privately Held**
Web: www.airgas.com

SIC: **5084** 5085 5169 2813   Welding machinery and equipment; Welding supplies ; Chemicals and allied products, nec; Industrial gases
HQ: Airgas Usa, Llc
    259 N Radnor Chester Rd
    Radnor PA 19087
    216 642-6600

(G-706)
ALLIED SINTERINGS INCORPORATED
29 Briar Ridge Rd (06810-7248)
PHONE..............................203 743-7502
Mark Foster, *Pr*
Diana Foster, *
EMP: 32 EST: 1959
SQ FT: 15,000
SALES (est): 4.3MM **Privately Held**
Web: www.alliedsinterings.com
SIC: 3399   Powder, metal

(G-707)
AMPHENOL CORPORATION
Also Called: Amphenol Rf
4 Old Newtown Rd (06810-6221)
PHONE..............................203 743-9272
Michele Vaccaro, *Dir*
EMP: 150
SALES (corp-wide): 12.62B **Publicly Held**
Web: www.amphenol.com
SIC: 3678   Electronic connectors
PA: Amphenol Corporation
    358 Hall Ave
    Wallingford CT 06492
    203 265-8900

(G-708)
APPLIED ADVERTISING INC
71 Newtown Rd Ste 5 (06810-6251)
PHONE..............................860 640-0800
Jason D Bergeron, *Pr*
EMP: 10 EST: 1999
SALES (est): 968.57K **Privately Held**
Web: www.appliedadvertisinginc.com
SIC: 3993 7319 7311   Electric signs; Transit advertising services; Advertising consultant

(G-709)
APPLIED LASER SOLUTIONS INC
28 Commerce Dr (06810-4131)
P.O. Box 1217 (06813-1217)
PHONE..............................203 739-0179
Edward Standke, *Pr*
Michele Standke, *Sec*
EMP: 8 EST: 2001
SQ FT: 22,000
SALES (est): 1MM **Privately Held**
Web: www.appliedlasersolutions.net
SIC: 3441   Fabricated structural metal

(G-710)
ARMORED AUTOGROUP PARENT INC
44 Old Ridgebury Rd Ste 300 (06810-5107)
PHONE..............................203 205-2900
Michael Klein, *CEO*
Andy Bolt, *
EMP: 164 EST: 2010
SALES (est): 1.05MM
SALES (corp-wide): 2.92B **Publicly Held**
SIC: 2842 2911 2899   Automobile polish; Fuel additives; Chemical preparations, nec
HQ: Spectrum Brands Legacy, Inc.
    3001 Deming Way
    Middleton WI 53562

(G-711)
BAGELMAN III INC
40 1/2 Padanaram Rd (06811-4840)
PHONE..............................203 792-0030
Mark L Froehlich, *Pr*
Valerie Froehlich, *VP*
EMP: 10 EST: 1989
SQ FT: 2,800
SALES (est): 481.48K **Privately Held**
Web: www.bagelmanct.com
SIC: 5812 2052   Delicatessen (eating places) ; Bakery products, dry

(G-712)
BASE-LINE II INC (PA)
Also Called: Base Line
30 Main St Ste 406 (06810-3006)
PHONE..............................203 826-7031
Howard Harper, *Pr*
Cynthia J Harper, *VP*
▲ **EMP: 20 EST:** 1948
SALES (est): 4.94MM
SALES (corp-wide): 4.94MM **Privately Held**
SIC: 3861   Graphic arts plates, sensitized

(G-713)
BEDOUKIAN RESEARCH INC (PA)
6 Commerce Dr (06810-4131)
PHONE..............................203 830-4000
Robert H Bedoukian, *Pr*
▲ **EMP: 41 EST:** 1972
SQ FT: 44,000
SALES (corp-wide): 29.6MM **Privately Held**
Web: www.bedoukian.com
SIC: 2844 2869 2879   Concentrates, perfume ; Flavors or flavoring materials, synthetic; Insecticides and pesticides

(G-714)
BEGELL HOUSE INC
50 North St (06810-5664)
PHONE..............................203 456-6161
Yelena Shafeyeva, *Pr*
EMP: 10 EST: 2005
SALES (est): 1.24MM **Privately Held**
Web: www.begellhouse.com
SIC: 2741   Miscellaneous publishing

(G-715)
BELIMO AIRCONTROLS (USA) INC (HQ)
Also Called: Belimo Air Controls USA
33 Turner Rd (06810-5101)
P.O. Box 2928 (06813-2928)
PHONE..............................800 543-9038
James Furlong, *Pr*
John Coppola, *
Richard Schneyer, *
◆ **EMP: 115 EST:** 1988
SQ FT: 44,000
SALES (est): 68.8MM **Privately Held**
Web: www.belimo.com
SIC: 3822 5075 3625   Refrigeration/air-conditioning defrost controls; Humidifiers, except portable; Relays and industrial controls
PA: Belimo Holding Ag
    Brunnenbachstrasse 1
    Hinwil ZH 8340

(G-716)
BELIMO AUTOMATION AG
33 Turner Rd (06810-5101)
PHONE..............................203 749-3319
Andreas Steiner, *Pr*

Beat Trutmann, *Sec*
▲ **EMP: 33 EST:** 2003
SALES (est): 2.04MM **Privately Held**
SIC: 3822   Refrigeration/air-conditioning defrost controls

(G-717)
BELIMO TECHNOLOGY (USA) INC
33 Turner Rd (06810-5101)
PHONE..............................203 791-9915
Alexander Van Der Weerd, *Pr*
EMP: 98 EST: 2002
SALES (est): 19.31MM **Privately Held**
Web: www.belimo.com
SIC: 3491   Industrial valves
PA: Belimo Holding Ag
    Brunnenbachstrasse 1
    Hinwil ZH 8340

(G-718)
BURLINGTON COAT FCTRY WHSE COR
Also Called: Burlington Coat Factory
1 Padanaram Rd Ste 25 (06811)
PHONE..............................203 748-8583
EMP: 49
SALES (corp-wide): 8.7B **Publicly Held**
Web: www.burlington.com
SIC: 2311   Men's and boy's suits and coats
HQ: Burlington Coat Factory Warehouse Corporation
    1830 N Route 130
    Burlington NJ 08016
    609 387-7800

(G-719)
CAM2 TECHNOLOGIES LLC
Also Called: Redwave Technology
41 Eagle Rd (06810-8802)
PHONE..............................203 628-4833
Craig Markleski, *Managing Member*
Morris Martelle, *Prin*
Jonathan Frattaroli, *Prin*
James Fitzpatrick, *Prin*
David Schiering, *Prin*
EMP: 16 EST: 2013
SALES (est): 1.46MM **Privately Held**
Web: www.redwavetech.com
SIC: 3826   Infrared analytical instruments

(G-720)
CANDLEWOOD STARS INC
Also Called: Mega Resveratrol
60 Newtown Rd Ste 32 (06810-6257)
PHONE..............................203 994-8826
EMP: 7 EST: 2010
SALES (est): 638.89K **Privately Held**
Web: www.megaresveratrol.net
SIC: 2833   Medicinals and botanicals

(G-721)
CITRA-SOLV LLC
98 Mill Plain Rd Ste 4c (06811-6101)
P.O. Box 2597 (06813-2597)
PHONE..............................203 778-0881
Steven Zeitler, *Mgr*
EMP: 7 EST: 1996
SALES (est): 814.99K **Privately Held**
Web: www.citrasolv.com
SIC: 2842   Polishes and sanitation goods

(G-722)
CONOPTICS INC
19 Eagle Rd (06810-4127)
PHONE..............................203 743-3349
Ronald Pizzo, *Pr*
Richard Kocka, *VP*
EMP: 16 EST: 1981

SQ FT: 9,000
SALES (est): 1.05MM **Privately Held**
Web: www.conoptics.com
SIC: 3827 Optical instruments and
apparatus

(G-723)
CREO MEDICAL INC
100 Reserve Rd Ste B400 (06810-5270)
PHONE..............................860 670-6054
David G Woods, *CEO*
EMP: 16 **EST:** 2018
SALES (est): 955.71K **Privately Held**
SIC: 3841 Medical instruments and
equipment, blood and bone work

(G-724)
DANBURY A LLC
Also Called: Audi Danbury
25 Sugar Hollow Rd (06810-7419)
PHONE..............................203 744-5202
EMP: 30 **EST:** 2021
SALES (est): 10.77MM **Privately Held**
Web: www.audidanbury.com
SIC: 5511 7538 3714 Automobiles, new and
used; General automotive repair shops;
Motor vehicle parts and accessories

(G-725)
DANBURY ORTHO
2 Riverview Dr (06810-6268)
PHONE..............................203 797-1500
EMP: 9 **EST:** 2017
SALES (est): 164.31K **Privately Held**
Web: www.myorthoct.com
SIC: 3842 Surgical appliances and supplies

(G-726)
DANBURY POWERSPORTS INC
41 Lake Avenue Ext (06811-5247)
PHONE..............................203 791-1310
Frank Chamberlain, *Pr*
EMP: 13 **EST:** 1998
SALES (est): 2.16MM **Privately Held**
Web: www.danburypowersports.com
SIC: 5571 3799 Motorcycles; All terrain
vehicles (ATV)

(G-727)
**DANBURY SQUARE BOX
COMPANY**
1a Broad St (06810-6204)
PHONE..............................203 744-4611
Chris Ann Allen, *Pr*
Michael Allen, *VP*
EMP: 22 **EST:** 1906
SQ FT: 37,000
SALES (est): 5.91MM **Privately Held**
Web: www.danburysquarebox.com
SIC: 2653 Boxes, corrugated: made from
purchased materials

(G-728)
DAVIS TREE & LOGGING LLC
57 North St Ste 209 (06810-5627)
PHONE..............................203 938-2153
EMP: 16 **EST:** 1989
SQ FT: 10,000
SALES (est): 858.42K **Privately Held**
Web: www.peterdavis.com
SIC: 0783 2411 0782 Planting, pruning, and
trimming services; Logging; Lawn and
garden services

(G-729)
DELCOM PRODUCTS INC
45 Backus Ave (06810-7328)
PHONE..............................914 934-5170
Doug Lovett, *Prin*

EMP: 8 **EST:** 1998
SALES (est): 692.43K **Privately Held**
Web: www.delcomproducts.com
SIC: 8711 3674 Electrical or electronic
engineering; Solid state electronic devices,
nec

(G-730)
DFS IN-HOME SERVICES
15 Great Pasture Rd (06810-8127)
PHONE..............................845 405-6464
Roman Abreu, *Prin*
EMP: 9 **EST:** 2014
SALES (est): 210.23K **Privately Held**
SIC: 3089 5033 Gutters (glass fiber
reinforced), fiberglass or plastics; Roofing
and siding materials

(G-731)
DIBA INDUSTRIES INC (HQ)
4 Precision Rd (06810-7317)
PHONE..............................203 744-0773
Timothy O'sullivan, *Pr*
Charles E Dubois, *
Sharon Gazley, *
EMP: 22 **EST:** 1986
SQ FT: 36,000
SALES (est): 56.27MM
SALES (corp-wide): 2.23B **Privately Held**
Web: www.arcmedgroup.com
SIC: 3823 3498 3083 Fluidic devices,
circuits, and systems for process control;
Fabricated pipe and fittings; Laminated
plastics plate and sheet
PA: Halma Public Limited Company
Misbourne Court Rectory Way
Amersham BUCKS HP7 0
149 472-1111

(G-732)
**DIVERSIFIED PRTG SOLUTIONS
INC**
128 E Liberty St (06810-6767)
PHONE..............................203 826-7198
EMP: 9 **EST:** 2015
SALES (est): 471.21K **Privately Held**
Web: www.diversifiedprint.com
SIC: 2752 Offset printing

(G-733)
**DMT SOLUTIONS GLOBAL
CORP (HQ)**
Also Called: Bluecrest
37 Executive Dr (06810-4147)
PHONE..............................833 874-0552
Dennis Lestrange, *CEO*
Susan Gabrielsen, *Sr VP*
Lance Arneson, *CFO*
EMP: 67 **EST:** 2018
SALES (est): 496.97MM **Privately Held**
Web: www.bluecrestinc.com
SIC: 3579 Word processing equipment
PA: Platinum Equity, Llc
360 N Crescent Dr Bldg S
Beverly Hills CA 90210

(G-734)
**DRS NAVAL POWER SYSTEMS
INC**
21 South St (06810-8147)
PHONE..............................203 798-3000
Mark Newmann, *Brnch Mgr*
EMP: 478
SALES (corp-wide): 15.28B **Publicly Held**
Web: www.leonardodrs.com
SIC: 3812 Nautical instruments
HQ: Drs Naval Power Systems, Inc
W126n7449 Flint Dr
Menomonee Falls WI 53051
414 875-4314

(G-735)
EMOSYN AMERICA INC
7 Commerce Dr (06810-4131)
PHONE..............................203 794-1100
EMP: 40
SALES (est): 24.35MM
SALES (corp-wide): 6.82B **Publicly Held**
SIC: 3674 Semiconductors and related
devices
HQ: Silicon Storage Technology, Inc.
1020 Kifer Rd
Sunnyvale CA 94086

(G-736)
ENERGIZER AUTO SALES INC
44 Old Ridgebury Rd Ste 300 (06810-5107)
PHONE..............................203 205-2900
Heather Clefisch, *Pr*
EMP: 48 **EST:** 2010
SALES (est): 4.91MM
SALES (corp-wide): 2.96B **Publicly Held**
SIC: 3714 Motor vehicle parts and
accessories
PA: Energizer Holdings, Inc.
533 Maryville Univ Dr
Saint Louis MO 63141
314 985-2000

(G-737)
ENTEGRIS INC
Also Called: Entegris
7 Commerce Dr (06810-4131)
PHONE..............................800 766-2681
EMP: 128
SALES (corp-wide): 3.28B **Publicly Held**
Web: www.entegris.com
SIC: 3089 Plastics processing
PA: Entegris, Inc.
129 Concord Rd
Billerica MA 01821
978 436-6500

(G-738)
**ENTEGRIS PROF SOLUTIONS
INC (HQ)**
Also Called: Atmi, Inc.
7 Commerce Dr (06810-4131)
PHONE..............................203 794-1100
Douglas A Neugold, *Ch Bd*
Timothy C Carlson, *
Lawrence H Dubois, *
Kathleen G Mincieli, *Senior Vice President
Human Resources*
David M Ward, *CAO*
◆ **EMP:** 105 **EST:** 1986
SQ FT: 31,000
SALES (est): 375.92MM
SALES (corp-wide): 3.52B **Publicly Held**
Web: www.entegris.com
SIC: 3674 Thin film circuits
PA: Entegris, Inc.
129 Concord Rd
Billerica MA 01821
978 436-6500

(G-739)
**ESCHENBACH OPTIK AMERICA
INC (PA)**
Also Called: Eschenbach Optik
22 Shelter Rock Ln Ste 1 (06810-8268)
PHONE..............................203 702-1600
Kenneth T Bradley, *Pr*
Charles C Keith, *VP*
▲ **EMP:** 14 **EST:** 1983
SQ FT: 10,000
SALES (est): 8.36MM
SALES (corp-wide): 8.36MM **Privately
Held**
Web: www.eschenbach.com

SIC: 3827 Optical instruments and lenses

(G-740)
**ETHAN ALLEN INTERIORS INC
(PA)**
Also Called: Ethan Allen
25 Lake Avenue Ext (06811-5286)
PHONE..............................203 743-8000
M Farooq Kathwari, *Ch Bd*
Amy Franks, *Ex VP*
Matthew J Mcnulty, *Sr VP*
EMP: 145 **EST:** 1932
SALES (est): 791.38MM **Publicly Held**
Web: www.ethanallen.com
SIC: 2512 5712 2511 Upholstered
household furniture; Furniture stores; Wood
bedroom furniture

(G-741)
ETHAN ALLEN RETAIL INC (HQ)
Also Called: Ethan Allen Home Interiors
25 Lake Avenue Ext (06811-5286)
P.O. Box 1966 (06813-1966)
PHONE..............................203 743-8000
Farooq Kathwari, *Ch Bd*
Pamela Banks, *Sec*
Ed Teplitz, *Ex VP*
Corey Whitely, *Executive Vice President
COS*
Geoffrey White, *VP Fin*
◆ **EMP:** 300 **EST:** 1932
SQ FT: 144,000
SALES (est): 455.32MM **Publicly Held**
Web: www.ethanallen.com
SIC: 5712 5719 5713 5231 Furniture stores;
Bedding (sheets, blankets, spreads, and
pillows); Carpets; Wallpaper
PA: Ethan Allen Interiors Inc.
25 Lake Avenue Ext
Danbury CT 06811

(G-742)
**EURO TECH METAL CREATIONS
INC**
2 Broad St (06810-6205)
PHONE..............................914 325-1760
Armindo Garcia, *Prin*
EMP: 7 **EST:** 2016
SALES (est): 246.33K **Privately Held**
Web: www.eurotechmetal.com
SIC: 3446 Architectural metalwork

(G-743)
EXPRESSWAY LUBE CENTERS
Also Called: Lubrication Management
225 White St (06810-6827)
PHONE..............................203 744-2511
Don Daseliva, *Mgr*
Vito Vontana, *Mgr*
EMP: 10 **EST:** 1991
SALES (est): 616.66K **Privately Held**
SIC: 3599 3714 Oil filters, internal
combustion engine, except auto; Motor
vehicle parts and accessories

(G-744)
**FAIRFIELD PROCESSING CORP
(PA)**
Also Called: Fairfield Processing
88 Rose Hill Ave (06810-5495)
P.O. Box 1157 (06813-1157)
PHONE..............................203 744-2090
Roy Young, *Ch*
Virginia Young, *
Joan Fleischman, *Information Director*
Jordan Young, *
◆ **EMP:** 150 **EST:** 1950
SQ FT: 100,000
SALES (est): 98.46MM

SALES (corp-wide): 98.46MM **Privately Held**
Web: www.fairfieldworld.com
SIC: 2824 Polyester fibers

(G-745)
FEDERAL PRISON INDUSTRIES
Also Called: Unicor
Route 37 (06811)
PHONE..................................203 743-6471
David Gold, *Superintnt*
EMP: 20
Web: www.bop.gov
SIC: 3315 9223 Cable, steel: insulated or armored; Correctional institutions
HQ: Federal Prison Industries, Inc
320 Frst St N W Fncl Mgt
Washington DC 20534

(G-746)
FLAGSHIP CONVERTERS INC
205 Shelter Rock Rd (06810-7049)
PHONE..................................203 792-0034
Frank E Gustafson, *Pr*
E Michael Davies, *
Allan Wolfe, *
James Mcavoy, *CFO*
◆ EMP: 57 EST: 1989
SQ FT: 95,000
SALES (est): 9.86MM **Privately Held**
Web: www.flagshipconverters.com
SIC: 3089 2671 7389 3081 Laminating of plastics; Paper; coated and laminated packaging; Laminating service; Unsupported plastics film and sheet

(G-747)
FOLEYS PUMP SERVICE INC
30 Miry Brook Rd (06810-7410)
PHONE..................................203 792-2236
James J Foley, *Pr*
Kevin Foley, *
EMP: 26 EST: 1982
SALES (est): 4.6MM **Privately Held**
Web: www.foleyspump.com
SIC: 3561 1799 Pumps and pumping equipment; Petroleum storage tank installation, underground

(G-748)
FUELCELL ENERGY INC (PA)
Also Called: Fuelcell Energy
3 Great Pasture Rd (06810-8153)
PHONE..................................203 825-6000
Jason B Few, *Pr*
James H England, *
Michael J Lisowski, *Ex VP*
Michael S Bishop, *Ex VP*
Anthony J Leo, *Ex VP*
EMP: 177 EST: 1969
SQ FT: 72,000
SALES (est): 123.39MM
SALES (corp-wide): 123.39MM **Publicly Held**
Web: www.fuelcellenergy.com
SIC: 3674 Semiconductors and related devices

(G-749)
G P TOOL CO INC
59 James St (06810-6196)
PHONE..................................203 744-0310
David Parille Prestreas, *Prin*
David Parille, *Pr*
Mark Parille, *VP*
EMP: 40 EST: 1947
SQ FT: 8,000
SALES (est): 890.38K **Privately Held**
Web: www.gptool.com

SIC: 3544 Special dies and tools

(G-750)
GOODRICH CORPORATION
Goodrich Arospc Flight Systems
100 Wooster Hts (06810-7509)
PHONE..................................505 345-9031
Chris Holmes, *Brnch Mgr*
EMP: 460
SALES (corp-wide): 68.92B **Publicly Held**
Web: www.collinsaerospace.com
SIC: 3679 8711 Electronic circuits; Aviation and/or aeronautical engineering
HQ: Goodrich Corporation
2730 W Tyvola Rd
Charlotte NC 28217
704 423-7000

(G-751)
GOODRICH CORPORATION
Also Called: Collins Aerospace
100 Reserve Rd Ste F2100 (06810-5281)
PHONE..................................704 423-7000
EMP: 189
SALES (corp-wide): 67.07B **Publicly Held**
Web: www.collinsaerospace.com
SIC: 3728 Aircraft parts and equipment, nec
HQ: Goodrich Corporation
2730 W Tyvola Rd
Charlotte NC 28217
704 423-7000

(G-752)
GOODRICH CORPORATION
Goodrich Optical Space Systems
100 Wooster Hts (06810-7509)
PHONE..................................203 797-5000
Tom Bergeon, *Pr*
EMP: 500
SALES (corp-wide): 68.92B **Publicly Held**
Web: www.collinsaerospace.com
SIC: 3728 Aircraft parts and equipment, nec
HQ: Goodrich Corporation
2730 W Tyvola Rd
Charlotte NC 28217
704 423-7000

(G-753)
GRANTA USA LTD
62 E Starrs Plain Rd (06810-8319)
PHONE..................................440 207-6051
Rea Hederman, *Pr*
▲ EMP: 10 EST: 1986
SALES (est): 660K **Privately Held**
SIC: 2721 Magazines: publishing only, not printed on site

(G-754)
GROLIER TELEMARKETING INC
90 Sherman Turnpike (06816)
PHONE..................................203 797-3500
Richard Robinson, *Pr*
EMP: 24 EST: 1976
SQ FT: 300,000
SALES (est): 881.08K
SALES (corp-wide): 1.7B **Publicly Held**
SIC: 2731 Books, publishing only
HQ: Scholastic Library Publishing, Inc.
90 Sherman Tpke
Danbury CT 06816
203 797-3500

(G-755)
GS THERMAL SOLUTIONS INC
144 Old Brookfield Rd Ste C (06811-4071)
PHONE..................................475 289-4625
Rick Depalma, *Pr*
EMP: 8 EST: 2016
SALES (est): 800.03K **Privately Held**
Web: www.gsthermalsolutions.com

SIC: 3645 Garden, patio, walkway and yard lighting fixtures: electric

(G-756)
HAMAR LASER INSTRUMENTS INC
5 Ye Olde Rd (06810-7322)
PHONE..................................203 730-4600
Martin Hamar, *Ch*
Roderick M Hamar, *Pr*
Anne Hamar, *VP*
EMP: 20 EST: 1967
SQ FT: 12,000
SALES (est): 9.1MM **Privately Held**
Web: www.hamarlaser.com
SIC: 5084 3699 Measuring and testing equipment, electrical; Laser systems and equipment

(G-757)
HOLOGIC INC
37 Apple Ridge Rd (06810-7301)
PHONE..................................203 790-1188
Bill Healy, *VP*
EMP: 195
SALES (corp-wide): 4.03B **Publicly Held**
Web: www.hologic.com
SIC: 3844 3841 X-ray apparatus and tubes; Surgical and medical instruments
PA: Hologic, Inc.
250 Campus Dr
Marlborough MA 01752
508 263-2900

(G-758)
IDELLE MANAGEMENT COMPANY
100 Reserve Rd Ste Cc250 (06810-5103)
EMP: 20 EST: 2003
SALES (est): 3.62MM **Privately Held**
SIC: 3999 Hair and hair-based products
HQ: Helen Of Troy Texas Corporation
1 Helen Of Troy Plz
El Paso TX 79912
915 225-8000

(G-759)
INTERLAB INCORPORATED
3 Precision Rd (06810-7391)
PHONE..................................203 794-0209
Narcissza Layton, *Ch Bd*
Howard Layton, *Prin*
Liviu Marian, *Pr*
Paul Ludanyi, *VP*
Tamas Ludanyi, *Sr VP*
EMP: 20 EST: 1958
SQ FT: 35,000
SALES (est): 2.35MM **Privately Held**
SIC: 3559 Chemical machinery and equipment

(G-760)
ITHACO SPACE SYSTEMS INC
100 Wooster Hts (06810-7509)
PHONE..................................607 272-7640
Thomas C Bergeron, *Ch*
EMP: 33 EST: 1996
SALES (est): 4.56MM
SALES (corp-wide): 68.92B **Publicly Held**
SIC: 3728 Aircraft parts and equipment, nec
HQ: Goodrich Corporation
2730 W Tyvola Rd
Charlotte NC 28217
704 423-7000

(G-761)
JEWELRY DESIGNS INC
86 Mill Plain Rd (06811-5140)
PHONE..................................203 797-0389

Robert Underhill, *Pr*
Robert Underhill, *Prin*
▲ EMP: 33 EST: 1980
SQ FT: 7,500
SALES (est): 2.2MM **Privately Held**
Web: www.jewelrydesigns.com
SIC: 5944 3911 Jewelry, precious stones and precious metals; Jewelry, precious metal

(G-762)
JOSEPH MERRITT & COMPANY INC
Also Called: Merritt, Joseph & Company
4c Christopher Columbus Ave (06810-2310)
PHONE..................................203 743-6734
Tony Texeira, *Brnch Mgr*
EMP: 7
SQ FT: 10,000
SALES (corp-wide): 23.1MM **Privately Held**
Web: www.josephmerritt.com
SIC: 2752 5049 2789 Offset printing; Engineers' equipment and supplies, nec; Bookbinding and related work
PA: Joseph Merritt & Company Incorporated
650 Franklin Ave Ste 3
Hartford CT 06114
860 296-2500

(G-763)
JOVIL UNIVERSAL LLC
10 Precision Rd (06810-2309)
PHONE..................................203 792-6700
Keith Fredlund, *Pr*
EMP: 12 EST: 2014
SQ FT: 24,000
SALES (est): 3.38MM **Privately Held**
Web: www.jovil.com
SIC: 3549 5084 Coil winding machines for springs; Industrial machinery and equipment

(G-764)
KERR CORPORATION
21 Commerce Dr (06810-4131)
PHONE..................................203 748-0030
David Giangregorio, *Mgr*
EMP: 70
Web: www.kerrdental.com
SIC: 3843 Dental laboratory equipment
HQ: Kerr Corporation
1717 W Collins Ave
Orange CA 92867
714 516-7400

(G-765)
KIMCHUK INCORPORATED
4 Finance Dr (06810-4191)
PHONE..................................203 798-0799
Jim Maquis, *Pr*
EMP: 124
SALES (corp-wide): 43.94MM **Privately Held**
Web: www.kimchuk.com
SIC: 3571 Electronic computers
PA: Kimchuk, Incorporated
1 Corporate Dr Ste 1 # 1
Danbury CT 06810
203 790-7800

(G-766)
KIMCHUK INCORPORATED (PA)
Also Called: Kimchuk
1 Corporate Dr Ste 1 (06810-4139)
PHONE..................................203 790-7800
Jim Marquis, *Pr*
William Kimbell, *Pr*
James A Marquis, *VP*

EMP: 15 EST: 1957
SQ FT: 10,000
SALES (est): 43.94MM
SALES (corp-wide): 43.94MM **Privately Held**
Web: www.kimchuk.com
SIC: 3625 7389 3312 7371   Control equipment, electric; Design, commercial and industrial; Sheet or strip, steel, cold-rolled: own hot-rolled; Custom computer programming services

(G-767)
KINGSWOOD KITCHENS CO INC
70 Beaver St (06810-5497)
PHONE...............................203 792-8700
TOLL FREE: 800
Henry Blevio, *Pr*
Richard Rausch, *Stockholder**
EMP: 75 **EST:** 1968
SQ FT: 75,000
SALES (est): 4.76MM **Privately Held**
Web: www.kingswoodkitchens.com
SIC: 2434   Vanities, bathroom: wood

(G-768)
LEICA GEOSYSTEMS INC
Also Called: LEICA GEOSYSTEMS, INC.
81 Kenosia Ave Ste 6 (06810-7361)
PHONE...............................203 744-8362
Walter Schacht, *Brnch Mgr*
EMP: 10
SALES (corp-wide): 491.93K **Privately Held**
Web: www.leica-geosystems.com
SIC: 3829   Measuring and controlling devices, nec
HQ: Leica Geosystems Inc.
    5051 Pchtree Crs Cir
    Norcross GA 30092
    770 326-9500

(G-769)
LESSER EVIL
18 Finance Dr (06810-4132)
PHONE...............................203 529-3555
Andrew Strife, *Pr*
EMP: 7 **EST:** 2015
SALES (est): 532.2K **Privately Held**
Web: www.lesserevil.com
SIC: 2099   Food preparations, nec

(G-770)
LIBERTY GARAGE INC
51 Sugar Hollow Rd Ste 1 (06810-7532)
PHONE...............................203 778-0222
Anthony Sigillito, *Pr*
EMP: 7 **EST:** 2008
SALES (est): 424.78K **Privately Held**
Web: www.libertyclosetandgarage.com
SIC: 2599   Cabinets, factory

(G-771)
LIGHT ROCK SPRING WATER CO
Also Called: Light Rock Beverage
9 Balmforth Ave (06810-5908)
PHONE...............................203 743-2251
George Antous, *Pr*
Frederick Antous, *VP*
Morris Antous, *Sec*
EMP: 15 **EST:** 1905
SQ FT: 7,500
SALES (est): 1.98MM **Privately Held**
SIC: 2086   Soft drinks: packaged in cans, bottles, etc.

(G-772)
LIMAT GRAPHICS INC
128 E Liberty St (06810-6773)
PHONE...............................203 798-9771

Edward Blasco, *Pr*
EMP: 24 **EST:** 1986
SQ FT: 6,000
SALES (est): 932.44K **Privately Held**
Web: www.limat.com
SIC: 3672   Printed circuit boards

(G-773)
LINDE ADVANCED MTL TECH INC
Also Called: Praxair
10 Riverview Dr (06810-6268)
PHONE...............................203 837-2000
EMP: 103
Web: www.linde-amt.com
SIC: 3479   Painting, coating, and hot dipping
HQ: Linde Advanced Material Technologies Inc.
    1500 Polco St
    Indianapolis IN 46222
    317 240-2500

(G-774)
LINDE GAS & EQUIPMENT INC
Also Called: Praxair
55 Old Ridgebury Rd (06810-5121)
PHONE...............................203 837-2162
Don Blanchat, *Brnch Mgr*
EMP: 7
Web: www.lindeus.com
SIC: 2813   Industrial gases
HQ: Linde Gas & Equipment Inc.
    10 Riverview Dr
    Danbury CT 06810
    844 445-4633

(G-775)
LINDE GAS & EQUIPMENT INC (DH)
Also Called: Praxair
10 Riverview Dr (06810-6268)
PHONE...............................844 445-4633
Ben Glazer, *Pr*
Anthony Pepper, *Sec*
Lisa Hurley, *Treas*
▲ **EMP:** 15 **EST:** 1969
SALES (est): 795.02MM **Privately Held**
Web: www.lindeus.com
SIC: 2813 5084 5999   Industrial gases; Welding machinery and equipment; Welding supplies
HQ: Linde Inc.
    10 Riverview Dr
    Danbury CT 06810
    203 837-2000

(G-776)
LINDE INC (HQ)
Also Called: Praxair
10 Riverview Dr (06810-6268)
PHONE...............................203 837-2000
Stephen F Angel, *Ch Bd*
Matthew J White, *Sr VP*
Karen L Keegans, *Chief Human Resources Officer*
◆ **EMP:** 400 **EST:** 1907
SALES (est): 10.59B **Privately Held**
Web: www.lindeus.com
SIC: 2813 3569 3471 3479   Industrial gases; Gas producers (machinery); Plating of metals or formed products; Coating of metals and formed products
PA: Linde Public Limited Company
    Ten
    Dublin

(G-777)
LINDE INC
Also Called: Praxair
10 Riverview Dr (06810-6268)

PHONE...............................800 772-9247
Mike Barr, *Brnch Mgr*
EMP: 30
Web: www.lindeus.com
SIC: 3842   Respiratory protection equipment, personal
HQ: Linde Inc.
    10 Riverview Dr
    Danbury CT 06810
    203 837-2000

(G-778)
LORAD CORPORATION
Also Called: Lorad Medical Systems
36 Apple Ridge Rd (06810-7301)
P.O. Box 1946 (06813-1946)
PHONE...............................203 790-5544
Raymond Calvo, *VP*
▲ **EMP:** 200 **EST:** 1984
SQ FT: 63,500
SALES (est): 38.25MM
SALES (corp-wide): 4.03B **Publicly Held**
SIC: 3844 3841   Radiographic X-ray apparatus and tubes; Biopsy instruments and equipment
PA: Hologic, Inc.
    250 Campus Dr
    Marlborough MA 01752
    508 263-2900

(G-779)
LOSTOCCO REFUSE SERVICE LLC
Also Called: Lostocco Services
79 Beaver Brook Rd (06810-6211)
P.O. Box 964 (06813-0964)
PHONE...............................203 748-9296
EMP: 20 **EST:** 1982
SQ FT: 6,000
SALES (est): 4.71MM **Privately Held**
Web: www.lostocco.com
SIC: 4953 7692 3444   Rubbish collection and disposal; Welding repair; Sheet metalwork

(G-780)
M & M PRECAST CORP
39 Padanaram Rd (06811-3701)
PHONE...............................203 743-5559
Robert Kaufman, *Pr*
Todd Kaufman, *Sec*
EMP: 33 **EST:** 1962
SQ FT: 5,000
SALES (est): 637.8K **Privately Held**
Web: www.mmprecast.com
SIC: 3272   Septic tanks, concrete

(G-781)
MANNKIND CORPORATION (PA)
Also Called: Mannkind
1 Casper St Ste 330 (06810-6903)
PHONE...............................818 661-5000
Michael E Castagna, *CEO*
James S Shannon, *
Steven B Binder, *CFO*
Stuart A Tross, *PEOPLE WORKPLACE*
David B Thomson, *Corporate Secretary*
▲ **EMP:** 58 **EST:** 1991
SQ FT: 190,000
SALES (est): 99.77MM
SALES (corp-wide): 99.77MM **Publicly Held**
Web: www.mannkindcorp.com
SIC: 2834   Pharmaceutical preparations

(G-782)
MAPLEGATE MEDIA GROUP INC
1503 Sienna Dr (06810-7156)
PHONE...............................203 826-7557
Sharon E Warner, *Pr*

EMP: 16 **EST:** 2003
SALES (est): 584.71K **Privately Held**
Web: www.maplegatemedia.com
SIC: 2721   Magazines: publishing only, not printed on site

(G-783)
MCM STAMPING CORPORATION
66 Beaver Brook Rd (06810-6298)
PHONE...............................203 792-3080
Arlene Mc Mullin, *Pr*
Kathy Timm, *Sec*
EMP: 25 **EST:** 1970
SQ FT: 10,000
SALES (est): 978.14K **Privately Held**
Web: www.mcmstamping.com
SIC: 3469   Stamping metal for the trade

(G-784)
MEGA SOUND AND LIGHT LLC
36 Mill Plain Rd Ste 312 (06811-5114)
PHONE...............................203 743-4200
▲ **EMP:** 7 **EST:** 1997
SQ FT: 3,000
SALES (est): 852.99K **Privately Held**
SIC: 5112 5111 3951 2621   Pens and/or pencils; Printing and writing paper; Pens and mechanical pencils; Stationary, envelope and tablet papers

(G-785)
MESSER LLC
10 Riverview Dr (06810-6268)
PHONE...............................908 464-8100
William Gerristead, *Mgr*
EMP: 50
SALES (corp-wide): 1.63B **Privately Held**
Web: www.messeramericas.com
SIC: 2813   Oxygen, compressed or liquefied
HQ: Messer Llc
    200 Smrst Corp Blvd # 7000
    Bridgewater NJ 08807
    800 755-9277

(G-786)
MILLER-STEPHENSON CHEMICAL COMPANY INC (PA)
55 Backus Ave (06810-7378)
PHONE...............................800 442-3424
EMP: 35 **EST:** 1955
SALES (est): 11.51MM
SALES (corp-wide): 11.51MM **Privately Held**
Web: www.miller-stephenson.com
SIC: 2819   Industrial inorganic chemicals, nec

(G-787)
MINUTEMAN PRESS
Also Called: Minuteman Press
12 Mill Plain Rd Ste 1 (06811-5135)
PHONE...............................973 748-7160
Sam Shin, *Owner*
EMP: 7 **EST:** 2011
SALES (est): 189.41K **Privately Held**
Web: www.minutemandanbury.com
SIC: 2752   Commercial printing, lithographic

(G-788)
MINUTEMAN PRESS OF DANBURY
Also Called: Minuteman Press
12 Mill Plain Rd Ste 10 (06811-5135)
PHONE...............................203 743-6755
Tom Wilson, *Pt*
EMP: 9 **EST:** 2001
SQ FT: 2,450
SALES (est): 831.64K **Privately Held**
Web: www.minutemandanbury.com

SIC: 2752   Commercial printing, lithographic

(G-789)
MUTTI USA INC
83 Wooster Hts Ste 120 (06810-7548)
PHONE.................................844 664-2630
Charles Waimon, *CEO*
EMP: 12 EST: 2017
SALES (est): 1.07MM **Privately Held**
Web: www.mutti-parma.com
SIC: 2033   Tomato products, packaged in cans, jars, etc.

(G-790)
NORDIC AMERICAN SMOKELESS INC
100 Mill Plain Rd Ste 115 (06811-5189)
PHONE.................................203 207-9977
Darren Quinn, *Pr*
EMP: 10 EST: 2008
SALES (est): 130.63K **Privately Held**
Web: www.nordicamerican.com
SIC: 2131   Chewing and smoking tobacco

(G-791)
O & G INDUSTRIES INC
9 Segar St (06810-6324)
PHONE.................................203 748-5694
Drew Oneglia, *Brnch Mgr*
EMP: 39
SALES (corp-wide): 496.36MM **Privately Held**
Web: www.ogind.com
SIC: 3273 1542   Ready-mixed concrete; Commercial and office building, new construction
PA: O & G Industries, Inc.
    112 Wall St
    Torrington CT 06790
    860 489-9261

(G-792)
ON LINE BUILDING SYSTEMS LLC
Also Called: Integ Systems
22 Shelter Rock Ln Unit 4 (06810-8268)
PHONE.................................203 798-1194
James Spinner, *Prin*
Pamela Spinner, *Sec*
EMP: 9 EST: 1982
SALES (est): 975.67K **Privately Held**
SIC: 7389 5063 7629 1731   Design, commercial and industrial; Electrical apparatus and equipment; Electrical equipment repair services; Computer power conditioning

(G-793)
OUIDAD PRODUCTS LLC
41b Eagle Rd (06810-4127)
P.O. Box 80 (06801-0080)
EMP: 8 EST: 1993
SQ FT: 4,500
SALES (est): 521.22K **Privately Held**
SIC: 3999   Hair and hair-based products

(G-794)
PARKER MEDICAL INC
Also Called: PMI
43 Old Ridgebury Rd (06810-5113)
PHONE.................................860 350-4304
▲ EMP: 80 EST: 1984
SALES (est): 9.26MM **Privately Held**
Web: www.parkermed.com
SIC: 3844   X-ray apparatus and tubes

(G-795)
PAUL DEWITT
Also Called: Economy Printing

128 E Liberty St Ste 4 (06810-6767)
PHONE.................................203 792-5610
Paul Dewitt, *Owner*
EMP: 7 EST: 1995
SALES (est): 405.11K **Privately Held**
SIC: 2752 2796 2791 2789   Offset printing; Platemaking services; Typesetting; Bookbinding and related work

(G-796)
PEROSPHERE INC
108 Mill Plain Rd Ste 3 (06811-1502)
PHONE.................................203 885-1111
Solomon S Steiner Ph.d., *CEO*
Philip N Sussman, *CFO*
EMP: 12 EST: 2011
SALES (est): 2.05MM **Privately Held**
Web: www.perosphere.com
SIC: 2834 7389   Pharmaceutical preparations; Business services, nec

(G-797)
PEROSPHERE TECHNOLOGIES INC
108 Mill Plain Rd Ste 3 (06811-1509)
PHONE.................................475 218-4600
Sasha Bakhru, *Pr*
Stefan Zappe, *Ex VP*
Steve Ward, *Ex VP*
EMP: 9 EST: 2017
SALES (est): 1.93MM **Privately Held**
Web: www.perospheretech.com
SIC: 3841   Diagnostic apparatus, medical

(G-798)
PMC ENGINEERING LLC
Also Called: P.M.c
11 Old Sugar Hollow Rd (06810-7517)
PHONE.................................203 792-8686
Robert P Knowles, *Pr*
EMP: 31 EST: 1963
SQ FT: 24,000
SALES (est): 6.6MM **Privately Held**
Web: www.pmc1.com
SIC: 3823   Pressure measurement instruments, industrial

(G-799)
PREFERRED UTILITIES MFG CORP (HQ)
Also Called: Preferred Instruments
31-35 South St (06810-8147)
PHONE.................................203 743-6741
David G Bohn, *Ch Bd*
Charles A White Iii, *Ex VP*
Gilbert Sy, *
David H Paddock, *
Dwayne Boulden, *
EMP: 60 EST: 1920
SQ FT: 44,000
SALES (est): 25.23MM **Privately Held**
Web: www.preferred-mfg.com
SIC: 3829 3433 3561 8711   Measuring and controlling devices, nec; Gas burners, industrial; Industrial pumps and parts; Designing: ship, boat, machine, and product
PA: Pumc Holding Corporation
    31-35 South St
    Danbury CT 06810

(G-800)
PRIORITY ONE INC
Also Called: Sign-A-Rama
35 Eagle Rd (06810-4127)
PHONE.................................203 244-7093
Robert Morris, *Pr*
EMP: 7 EST: 1989
SQ FT: 1,250
SALES (est): 503.74K **Privately Held**
Web: www.signarama-ct.com

SIC: 3993   Signs and advertising specialties

(G-801)
PROCESS AUTOMTN SOLUTIONS INC (HQ)
107 Mill Plain Rd Ste 301 (06811-6100)
PHONE.................................203 207-9917
Ricardo De La Cierva, *Ex VP*
EMP: 21 EST: 2001
SQ FT: 2,400
SALES (est): 14.91MM
SALES (corp-wide): 1.9B **Privately Held**
Web: www.pa-ats.com
SIC: 7373 7379 3822   Systems integration services; Computer related consulting services; Building services monitoring controls, automatic
PA: Ats Corporation
    730 Fountain St N Bldg 2
    Cambridge ON N3H 4
    604 332-2666

(G-802)
PUMC HOLDING CORPORATION (PA)
31-35 South St (06810-8147)
PHONE.................................203 743-6741
Robert G Bohn, *CEO*
David G Bohn, *Pr*
David H Paddock, *Sec*
Joshline Whyte, *Stockholder*
Cindy Robertson, *Stockholder*
EMP: 10 EST: 1929
SQ FT: 44,000
SALES (est): 25.23MM **Privately Held**
Web: www.preferred-mfg.com
SIC: 3433 8711   Gas burners, industrial; Designing: ship, boat, machine, and product

(G-803)
RANKIN TEXTILE PRINTING INC
37 Newtown Rd (06810-6219)
PHONE.................................203 743-1317
Andrew Rankin, *Pr*
Andrew Rankin, *Pr*
Susan Rankin, *Sec*
EMP: 7 EST: 1973
SQ FT: 6,400
SALES (est): 977.58K **Privately Held**
Web: www.rankintextile.com
SIC: 2759   Screen printing

(G-804)
RAZBERI TECHNOLOGIES INC
3 Corporate Dr Ste 1 (06810-4166)
PHONE.................................469 828-3380
Doug Dickerson, *CEO*
Joe Vitalone, *CSO CMO*
Thomas Galvin, *CPO*
Jerry Trojan, *
▲ EMP: 35 EST: 2011
SALES (est): 6.3MM **Privately Held**
Web: www.razberi.net
SIC: 3699 5065   Security devices; Security control equipment and systems

(G-805)
REPUBLIC FOIL INC
Also Called: Garmco
58 Longview Ave (06811-3335)
PHONE.................................203 743-2731
▲ EMP: 60
SIC: 3497 3353 3355 3354   Metal foil and leaf; Foil, aluminum; Aluminum rolling and drawing, nec; Aluminum extruded products

(G-806)
RK MANUFACTURING CORP CONN

34 Executive Dr Ste 2 (06810-4190)
PHONE.................................203 797-8700
Donna Krebs, *Pr*
John Hutter, *
EMP: 83 EST: 1981
SQ FT: 42,000
SALES (est): 9.84MM **Privately Held**
Web: www.rkmcorp.com
SIC: 3599   Machine shop, jobbing and repair

(G-807)
RSA CORP
36 Old Sherman Tpke (06810-4124)
PHONE.................................203 790-8100
Jan S Anthony, *Pr*
Stephanie Weber, *
▲ EMP: 25 EST: 1935
SQ FT: 20,000
SALES (est): 10.72MM **Privately Held**
Web: www.rsa-corporation.com
SIC: 2869   Plasticizers, organic: cyclic and acyclic

(G-808)
SANDVIKS INC (PA)
4 Mountainview Ter Ste 200 (06810-4116)
PHONE.................................866 984-0188
Marius Sandvik, *Pr*
Robert Israel, *Treas*
EMP: 9 EST: 2010
SALES (est): 2.05MM
SALES (corp-wide): 2.05MM **Privately Held**
Web: www.hookedonphonics.com
SIC: 3542   Machine tools, metal forming type

(G-809)
SCHAEFFLER AEROSPACE USA CORP (DH)
200 Park Ave (06810-7505)
P.O. Box 2449 (06813-2449)
PHONE.................................203 744-2211
Peter J Enright, *CEO*
Bruce Warmbold, *
Robert Hillstrom, *
Claus Bauer, *
Steve Crow, *
◆ EMP: 400 EST: 1942
SQ FT: 192,000
SALES (est): 91.85MM
SALES (corp-wide): 66.25B **Privately Held**
Web: www.schaeffler.us
SIC: 3562 3469 3842 3089   Ball bearings and parts; Machine parts, stamped or pressed metal; Surgical appliances and supplies; Injection molded finished plastics products, nec
HQ: Schaeffler Group Usa Inc.
    308 Springhill Farm Rd
    Fort Mill SC 29715
    803 548-8500

(G-810)
SCHAEFFLER HOLDING LLC (DH)
200 Park Ave (06810-7505)
PHONE.................................203 790-5474
Peter Enright, *Pr*
◆ EMP: 450 EST: 1920
SQ FT: 27,000
SALES (est): 297.95MM
SALES (corp-wide): 66.25B **Privately Held**
Web: www.schaeffler.us
SIC: 3562   Ball bearings and parts
HQ: Schaeffler Schweinfurt Beteiligungs Gmbh
    Georg-Schafer-Str. 30
    Schweinfurt BY 97421
    9721910

(G-811)

SCHOLASTIC INC (DH)
90 Old Sherman Tpke (06810-4124)
P.O. Box 5277 (06804-5277)
PHONE...............................212 343-6100
Barry Jones, *Pr*
Edward M Kabak, *Sec*
Edward Russo, *Treas*
▲ EMP: 89 EST: 1895
SQ FT: 300,000
SALES (est): 84.08MM
SALES (corp-wide): 1.7B Publicly Held
SIC: 5192 2741 2731 Books; Miscellaneous
   publishing; Book publishing
HQ: Scholastic Library Publishing, Inc.
   90 Sherman Tpke
   Danbury CT 06816
   203 797-3500

(G-812)

SCHOLASTIC LIBRARY PUBG INC (HQ)
90 Sherman Tpke (06816)
P.O. Box 3765 (65102-3765)
PHONE...............................203 797-3500
Dick Robinson, *Pr*
Arnaud Lagardere, *
Dominique D'hinnin, *Chairman of the Board Finance*
Lester Rackoff, *
Dante Cirilli, *Ex VP*
▲ EMP: 790 EST: 1988
SQ FT: 300,836
SALES (est): 460.79MM
SALES (corp-wide): 1.7B Publicly Held
SIC: 2731 5963 5192 2721 Books,
   publishing only; Encyclopedias, house-to-
   house; Books; Magazines: publishing only,
   not printed on site
PA: Scholastic Corporation
   557 Broadway Lbby 1
   New York NY 10012
   212 343-6100

(G-813)

SCHWING BIOSET TECHNOLOGIES
98 Mill Plain Rd Ste A (06811-6101)
PHONE...............................203 744-2100
Thomas Anderson, *Pr*
EMP: 214 EST: 2003
SALES (est): 897.23K
SALES (corp-wide): 13.01B Privately Held
Web: www.schwingbioset.com
SIC: 3592 Pistons and piston rings
HQ: Schwing America, Inc.
   5900 Centerville Rd
   Saint Paul MN 55127
   651 429-0999

(G-814)

SEALED AIR CORPORATION
10 Old Sherman Tpke (06810-4159)
PHONE...............................203 791-3597
Randy Gouveia, *VP*
EMP: 120
SALES (corp-wide): 5.64B Publicly Held
Web: www.sealedair.com
SIC: 3086 2671 Packaging and shipping
   materials, foamed plastics; Paper; coated
   and laminated packaging
PA: Sealed Air Corporation
   2415 Cascade Pointe Blvd
   Charlotte NC 28208
   980 221-3235

(G-815)

SI GROUP INC
4 Mountainview Ter Ste 200 (06810-4116)
PHONE...............................203 702-6140

Frank Bozich, *Brnch Mgr*
EMP: 150
Web: www.siigroup.com
SIC: 2822 2869 2891 2911 Ethylene-
   propylene rubbers, EPDM polymers;
   Antioxidants, rubber processing: cyclic or
   acyclic; Adhesives; Fuel additives
HQ: Si Group, Inc.
   1790 Hughes Landing Blvd # 600
   The Woodlands TX 77380
   518 347-4200

(G-816)

SI GROUP USA HLDINGS USHA CORP (DH)
Also Called: Addivant
4 Mountainview Ter Ste 200 (06810-4116)
PHONE...............................203 702-6140
Peter R Smith, *CEO*
◆ EMP: 32 EST: 2012
SALES (est): 899.06MM Privately Held
SIC: 2869 Antioxidants, rubber processing:
   cyclic or acyclic
HQ: Sk Blue Holdings, L P
   C/O Maples Corporate Services Ltd
   George Town GR CAYMAN KY1-1

(G-817)

SIGMUND SOFTWARE LLC
83 Wooster Hts Ste 210 (06810-7549)
PHONE...............................800 448-6975
EMP: 18 EST: 2002
SALES (est): 2.83MM Privately Held
Web: www.sigmundsoftware.com
SIC: 7372 Prepackaged software

(G-818)

SIMMONDS PRECISION PDTS INC
Also Called: UTC Aerospace Systems
100 Wooster Hts (06810-7509)
PHONE...............................203 797-5000
Justin Robert Keppy, *CEO*
EMP: 17
SALES (corp-wide): 68.92B Publicly Held
SIC: 3829 3694 3724 3728 Aircraft and
   motor vehicle measurement equipment;
   Ignition systems, high frequency; Aircraft
   engines and engine parts; Aircraft parts and
   equipment, nec
HQ: Simmonds Precision Products Inc
   100 Panton Rd
   Vergennes VT 05491
   802 877-4000

(G-819)

SOCIETY PLASTICS ENGINEERS INC (PA)
Also Called: S P E
83 Wooster Hts Ste 125 (06810-7550)
PHONE...............................203 740-5422
Conor Carlin, *Pr*
Susan Oderwald, *
EMP: 27 EST: 1941
SALES (est): 3.61MM
SALES (corp-wide): 3.61MM Privately Held
Web: www.4spe.org
SIC: 8621 2721 7389 2731 Engineering
   association; Trade journals: publishing only,
   not printed on site; Advertising,
   promotional, and trade show services; Book
   publishing

(G-820)

SPECTRO ANALYTICAL INSTRS INC
Also Called: SPECTRO ANALYTICAL
INSTRUMENTS, INC.

15 Roger Ave (06810-5420)
PHONE...............................203 778-8837
EMP: 13
SIC: 3826 Analytical instruments
PA: Asoma Tower, Inc.
   50 Fordham Rd
   Wilmington MA 01887

(G-821)

STANLEY ENGNERED FASTENING LLC (HQ)
Also Called: Stanley Engineered Fastening
4 Shelter Rock Ln (06810-8159)
PHONE...............................800 783-6427
Michael A Tyll, *Pr*
Charles Fenton, *VP*
Ed Delterio, *VP*
◆ EMP: 10 EST: 1902
SALES (est): 489.65MM
SALES (corp-wide): 16.95B Publicly Held
Web:
www.stanleyengineeredfastening.com
SIC: 8711 3541 Engineering services;
   Machine tools, metal cutting type
PA: Stanley Black & Decker, Inc.
   1000 Stanley Dr
   New Britain CT 06053
   860 225-5111

(G-822)

STERZINGERS WELDING LLC
28 Alan Rd (06810-8302)
PHONE...............................203 685-1575
Richard Sterzinger, *Prin*
EMP: 7 EST: 2015
SALES (est): 283.35K Privately Held
SIC: 7692 Welding repair

(G-823)

TARRY MEDICAL PRODUCTS INC
Also Called: Tarry Manufacturing
22 Shelter Rock Ln Unit 7 (06810-8268)
PHONE...............................203 791-9001
Scott Bell, *Pr*
Don Mortifoglio, *VP*
George Quatropanni, *VP*
EMP: 15 EST: 2003
SQ FT: 4,500
SALES (est): 2.73MM Privately Held
Web: www.tarrymfg.com
SIC: 3841 5047 Surgical and medical
   instruments; Medical and hospital
   equipment

(G-824)

TEKTRONIX
Also Called: Tektronix
100 Wooster Hts (06810-7509)
PHONE...............................203 730-2730
Jose Riojas, *Pr*
EMP: 17 EST: 2015
SALES (est): 243.81K Privately Held
Web: www.tek.com
SIC: 3825 Instruments to measure electricity

(G-825)

TOPEX INC
10 Precision Rd Ste 2 (06810-2309)
PHONE...............................203 748-5918
John Brenna, *Pr*
Anthony Pellegrino, *CEO*
EMP: 10 EST: 2009
SALES (est): 943.84K Privately Held
Web: www.topexmedical.com
SIC: 3844 3679 X-ray apparatus and tubes;
   Electronic loads and power supplies

(G-826)

TP CYCLE & ENGINEERING INC
Also Called: T P Engineering
4 Finance Dr (06810-4191)
PHONE...............................203 744-4960
Thomas A Pirone, *Pr*
EMP: 25 EST: 1984
SQ FT: 63,000
SALES (est): 4.93MM Privately Held
Web: www.tpengines.com
SIC: 3599 8711 Machine shop, jobbing and
   repair; Consulting engineer

(G-827)

TROPAX PRECISION MANUFACTURING
10 Precision Rd (06810-2309)
PHONE...............................203 794-0733
Bruno Tropeano, *Pr*
Mike Tropeano, *VP*
Elio Tropeano, *Sec*
EMP: 10 EST: 1980
SQ FT: 6,000
SALES (est): 1.05MM Privately Held
Web: www.jovil.net
SIC: 3599 Machine shop, jobbing and repair

(G-828)

TUDOR CONVERTED PRODUCTS INC (PA)
1305 Revere Rd (06811-2603)
PHONE...............................203 304-1875
Richard P Cuminale Junior, *Pr*
Debbie T Cuminale, *Sec*
▲ EMP: 14 EST: 1979
SALES (est): 1.12MM
SALES (corp-wide): 1.12MM Privately
Held
SIC: 2679 Paper products, converted, nec

(G-829)

U S TOOL GRINDING INC
100 Wooster Hts (06810-7509)
PHONE...............................203 797-5036
EMP: 8 EST: 2019
SALES (est): 335.05K Privately Held
SIC: 3541 Machine tools, metal cutting type

(G-830)

UNITEC
4 Larson Dr (06810-5132)
PHONE...............................203 778-0400
Albert Coccaro, *Owner*
Albert Coccaro, *Prin*
EMP: 8 EST: 1999
SALES (est): 120K Privately Held
Web: www.zendextool.com
SIC: 3714 Motor vehicle parts and
   accessories

(G-831)

VANGUARD PRODUCTS CORPORATION
87 Newtown Rd (06810-4199)
PHONE...............................203 744-7265
Robert C Benn Senior, *Ch Bd*
Robert C Benn Junior, *Pr*
Robert C Benn Senior, *Dir*
Gladys S Benn, *
▲ EMP: 75 EST: 1965
SQ FT: 51,000
SALES (est): 9.56MM Privately Held
Web: www.vanguardproducts.com
SIC: 3053 3061 Gaskets, all materials;
   Mechanical rubber goods

(G-832)

VEOLIA ES TCHNCAL SLUTIONS LLC

53 Newtown Rd (06810-6223)

PHONE.............................203 748-9116

EMP: 14

SIC: 8711 4953 2869 1799 Engineering services; Hazardous waste collection and disposal; Solvents, organic; Asbestos removal and encapsulation

HQ: Onyx Environmental Services Llc
53 State St Ste 14
Boston MA 02109
617 849-6600

(G-833)

VILLARINA PASTA & FINE FOODS (PA)

22 Shelter Rock Ln Unit 34 (06810-8267)

PHONE.............................203 917-4463

Joseph Filc, *Pr*

Joseph M Filc, *Pr*

Joseph W Filc, *VP*

EMP: 7 EST: 1990

SALES (est): 996.59K **Privately Held**

Web: www.villarinas.com

SIC: 2098 2038 Macaroni and spaghetti; Frozen specialties, nec

(G-834)

WARMUP INC

52 Federal Rd Ste 1b (06810-6162)

▲ EMP: 10 EST: 2003

SALES (est): 1.85MM **Privately Held**

Web: www.warmup.com

SIC: 3567 Heating units and devices, industrial: electric

(G-835)

WATERBURY LEATHERWORKS CO

1 Rivington Way Unit 304 (06810-5154)

PHONE.............................203 755-7789

EMP: 8 EST: 1996

SALES (est): 248.26K **Privately Held**

Web: waterburyleatherworksco.wordpress.com

SIC: 3199 Equestrian related leather articles

(G-836)

WESCONN STAIRS INC

Also Called: A-1 Stairs By Wesconn Stairs

2 Mill Plain Rd (06811-5141)

P.O. Box 2148 (06813-2148)

PHONE.............................203 792-7367

Danna Mackey, *Pr*

EMP: 7 EST: 1974

SQ FT: 3,500

SALES (est): 672.86K **Privately Held**

SIC: 2431 Staircases and stairs, wood

(G-837)

WESTCHSTER BK/RNSFORD TYPE INC

Also Called: Rainsford Type

4 Old Newtown Rd (06810-4200)

PHONE.............................203 791-0080

Dennis J Pistone, *Pr*

Nancy Rainsford-pistone, *VP*

EMP: 30 EST: 1981

SALES (est): 867.17K **Privately Held**

Web: www.westchesterpublishingservices.com

SIC: 2791 Typesetting

(G-838)

YORK INTERNATIONAL CORPORATION

86 Payne Rd (06810-4108)

PHONE.............................203 730-8100

Gary Frye, *Brnch Mgr*

EMP: 12

SIC: 3585 Refrigeration and heating equipment

HQ: York International Corporation
5005 York Dr
Norman OK 73069
800 481-9738

Danielson
Windham County

(G-839)

GREEN VALLEY PACKAGING INC

90 Wauregan Rd (06239-3712)

PHONE.............................860 779-7970

Robert A Bond, *Pr*

Craig A Bond, *VP*

▲ EMP: 8 EST: 2008

SALES (est): 1.01MM **Privately Held**

Web: www.vegware.us

SIC: 2836 Biological products, except diagnostic

(G-840)

JOLLEY PRECAST INC

463 Putnam Rd (06239-2041)

PHONE.............................860 774-9066

Clarence Jolley, *Pr*

Eleanor Jolley, *VP*

EMP: 27 EST: 1923

SQ FT: 1,080

SALES (est): 2.42MM **Privately Held**

Web: www.jolleyprecast.com

SIC: 3272 5074 Septic tanks, concrete; Pipes and fittings, plastic

(G-841)

SEISMIC MONITORING SVCS LLC

70 Black Rock Ave (06239-4102)

PHONE.............................860 753-6363

Charles A Berube Junior, *Pr*

EMP: 7 EST: 2016

SALES (est): 463.24K **Privately Held**

SIC: 1382 Seismograph surveys

(G-842)

SIRI MANUFACTURING CO INC

90 Wauregan Rd (06239-3712)

PHONE.............................860 236-5901

Roger Bond, *Pr*

Ruth Bond, *Sec*

▲ EMP: 23 EST: 1992

SQ FT: 100,000

SALES (est): 4.84MM **Privately Held**

Web: www.siriwire.com

SIC: 3496 Miscellaneous fabricated wire products

(G-843)

SIRI WIRE CO

90 Wauregan Rd (06239-3712)

PHONE.............................860 774-0607

EMP: 7 EST: 2019

SALES (est): 798.08K **Privately Held**

Web: www.siriwire.com

SIC: 3496 Miscellaneous fabricated wire products

(G-844)

SPIROL INTERNATIONAL CORP (HQ)

Also Called: Spirol

30 Rock Ave (06239-1434)

PHONE.............................860 774-8571

Jeffrey F Koehl, *Ch*

James C Shaw, *

Hans H Koehl, *HOLDING*

William R Hunt, *

Jack Ferdinandi, *

▲ EMP: 150 EST: 1945

SQ FT: 120,000

SALES (est): 229.06K

SALES (corp-wide): 65.55MM **Privately Held**

Web: www.spirol.com

SIC: 3452 3499 3469 3053 Pins; Shims, metal; Stamping metal for the trade; Gaskets, all materials

PA: Spirol International Holding Corporation
30 Rock Ave
Danielson CT 06239
860 774-8571

(G-845)

SPIROL INTL HOLDG CORP (PA)

30 Rock Ave (06239-1425)

P.O. Box 6349 (60197-6349)

PHONE.............................860 774-8571

Jeffrey F Koehl, *CEO*

Hans Koehl, *

▲ EMP: 150 EST: 1979

SQ FT: 100,000

SALES (est): 65.55MM

SALES (corp-wide): 65.55MM **Privately Held**

Web: www.globalfasternews.com

SIC: 3452 3499 3469 Pins; Shims, metal; Stamping metal for the trade

Darien
Fairfield County

(G-846)

CHAPIN PACKAGING LLC

Also Called: Chapin Printing Group

1078 Post Rd Ste 1 (06820-5424)

PHONE.............................203 202-2747

EMP: 8 EST: 2007

SALES (est): 314.95K **Privately Held**

Web: www.chapinpackaging.com

SIC: 7389 2789 Printers' services: folding, collating, etc.; Bookbinding and related work

(G-847)

HAY ISLAND HOLDING CORPORATION (PA)

20 Thorndal Cir (06820-5421)

PHONE.............................203 656-8000

◆ EMP: 160 EST: 1995

SQ FT: 7,200

SALES (est): 828.43MM **Privately Held**

SIC: 5194 2131 Tobacco and tobacco products; Chewing tobacco

(G-848)

HENKEL US OPERATIONS CORP

100 Tokeneke Rd (06820-4825)

PHONE.............................203 655-8911

Carsten Knobel, *CEO*

EMP: 700

SALES (corp-wide): 23.26B **Privately Held**

Web: www.henkel-northamerica.com

SIC: 2844 Hair preparations, including shampoos

HQ: Henkel Us Operations Corporation
1 Henkel Way
Rocky Hill CT 06067
860 571-5100

(G-849)

INFORMA TECH HOLDINGS LLC

Also Called: Cliggott Publishing

330 Post Rd Fl 2 (06820-3600)

PHONE.............................203 662-6501

Gary Marshal, *CEO*

EMP: 12

SALES (corp-wide): 2.72B **Privately Held**

Web: www.mjhlifesciences.com

SIC: 2721 2741 2731 8748 Magazines: publishing only, not printed on site; Miscellaneous publishing; Book publishing; Publishing consultant

HQ: Informa Tech Holdings Llc
1983 Marcus Ave Ste 250
New Hyde Park NY 11042
516 562-7800

(G-850)

JOY FOOD COMPANY

138 Goodwives River Rd (06820-5807)

PHONE.............................917 549-6240

Tom Arrix, *CEO*

EMP: 7 EST: 2019

SALES (est): 62.38K **Privately Held**

Web: www.getjoyfood.com

SIC: 2047 Dog food

(G-851)

LIFE STUDY FLLWSHIP FOUNDATION

90 Heights Rd (06820-4129)

PHONE.............................203 655-1436

Michael Keane, *CEO*

John J Keane Junior, *VP Fin*

EMP: 8 EST: 1939

SQ FT: 10,000

SALES (est): 1.11MM **Privately Held**

Web: www.lifestudyfellowship.com

SIC: 2731 7331 2741 Books, publishing only ; Direct mail advertising services; Miscellaneous publishing

(G-852)

MOBILE SENSE TECHNOLOGIES INC

24 Cliff Ave (06820-4914)

PHONE.............................203 914-5375

Justin Chickles, *CEO*

Ki Chon, *VP*

EMP: 10 EST: 2016

SALES (est): 219.53K **Privately Held**

Web: www.mobilesensetech.com

SIC: 3845 Cardiographs

(G-853)

PRESIDIUM USA INC

42 Beach Dr (06820-5608)

P.O. Box 2396 (06820-0396)

PHONE.............................203 803-2980

Per Sekse, *Pr*

EMP: 13 EST: 2017

SALES (est): 584.49K **Privately Held**

SIC: 2821 Polyurethane resins

(G-854)

REALHUB INC

Also Called: American Devices

30 Old Kings Hwy S Ste 155 (06820-4551)

PHONE.............................650 461-9210

Steve Chainani, *CEO*

Sanjeev Menon, *COO*

EMP: 15 EST: 1998

SQ FT: 2,000

SALES (est): 1.59MM **Privately Held**

Web: www.realhub.com

SIC: **5084** 5047 2389 2836   Safety equipment; Industrial safety devices: first aid kits and masks; Hospital gowns; Vaccines and other immunizing products

(G-855)

SMOKEY MOUNTAIN CHEW INC

365 Post Rd (06820-3606)
P.O. Box 1106 (06820-1106)
PHONE.............................203 304-9200
EMP: 18 **EST:** 1994
SALES (est): 2.6MM **Privately Held**
SIC: **2111** 5194 Cigarettes; Smokeless tobacco

(G-856)

SYZYGY GLOBAL TECHNOLOGY LLC

17 Cutrone Rd (06820)
PHONE.............................203 818-2166
EMP: 7 **EST:** 2021
SALES (est): 459.81K **Privately Held**
Web: www.syzygyglobaltechnology.com
SIC: **3541** Machine tools, metal cutting type

(G-857)

UNIWORLD BUS PUBLICATIONS INC

35 Kensett Ln (06820-2438)
PHONE.............................201 384-4900
Michael Shimkin, *Ch Bd*
Barbara Fiorito, *Sec*
EMP: 7 **EST:** 1977
SALES (est): 601.38K **Privately Held**
Web: www.uniworldonline.com
SIC: **7372** 7389 Publisher's computer software; Business Activities at Non-Commercial Site

Dayville
Windham County

(G-858)

BLACK POND BREWS

1001 Hartford Pike (06241-1749)
PHONE.............................860 207-5295
Michael Teed, *Pr*
EMP: 8 **EST:** 2015
SALES (est): 571.73K **Privately Held**
Web: www.blackpondbrews.com
SIC: **2082** Malt beverages

(G-859)

BOLLORE INC

60 Louisa Viens Dr (06241-1106)
P.O. Box 530 (06241-0530)
PHONE.............................860 774-2930
Steve Brunetti, *Pr*
Robert Vickers, *
Mark E Block, *
▲ **EMP:** 80 **EST:** 1976
SQ FT: 62,000
SALES (est): 23.29MM **Privately Held**
Web: www.bolloreinc.com
SIC: **2671** Plastic film, coated or laminated for packaging
HQ: Bollore Se
Odet
Ergue Gaberic 29500
298667200

(G-860)

BOUDREAUS WELDING CO INC

1029 N Main St (06241-2170)
P.O. Box 339 (06241-0339)
PHONE.............................860 774-2771
Ronald Jussaume, *Pr*
Ronald Jussaume, *Pr*

Monique Jussaume, *Sec*
Julie Jussaume, *VP*
Randall Jussaume, *Sec*
EMP: 12 **EST:** 1957
SQ FT: 20,600
SALES (est): 2.29MM **Privately Held**
Web: www.boudreauswelding.com
SIC: **3312** 3446 3441 3449 Structural and rail mill products; Railings, banisters, guards, etc: made from metal pipe; Building components, structural steel; Miscellaneous metalwork

(G-861)

COLTS PLASTICS COMPANY INC

969 N Main St (06241-2123)
P.O. Box 429 (06241-0429)
PHONE.............................860 774-2277
Charles W Bentley Junior, *Pr*
Patrick Garrity, *
Marc Bates, *
▲ **EMP:** 125 **EST:** 1936
SQ FT: 80,000
SALES (est): 20.87MM **Privately Held**
Web: www.coltsplastics.com
SIC: **3089** Jars, plastics

(G-862)

FERRON MOLD AND TOOL LLC

154 Louisa Viens Dr (06241-1133)
P.O. Box 144 (06241-0144)
PHONE.............................860 774-5555
Norman Ferron, *Pt*
Beverly Ferron, *Pt*
EMP: 8 **EST:** 1998
SQ FT: 6,500
SALES (est): 929.02K **Privately Held**
Web: www.ferronmold.com
SIC: **3544** Industrial molds

(G-863)

MIYOSHI AMERICA INC (HQ)

110 Louisa Viens Dr (06241-1132)
P.O. Box 859 (06241-0859)
PHONE.............................860 779-3990
Kaoru Takagi, *
Taizo Miyoshi, *
Janice Leblanc, *
▲ **EMP:** 67 **EST:** 1985
SQ FT: 82,000
SALES (est): 24.76MM **Privately Held**
Web: www.miyoshiamerica.com
SIC: **2844** 5169 Cosmetic preparations; Chemicals and allied products, nec
PA: Miyoshi Kasei,Inc.
4-3-14, Kudankita
Chiyoda-Ku TKY 102-0

(G-864)

NORTHEAST FOODS INC

Also Called: Automatic Rolls of New England
328 Lake Rd (06241-1537)
PHONE.............................860 779-1117
Fred Sexton, *Brnch Mgr*
EMP: 100
SALES (corp-wide): 301.98MM **Privately Held**
Web: www.nefoods.com
SIC: **2051** Bakery: wholesale or wholesale/retail combined
PA: Northeast Foods, Inc.
601 S Caroline St
Baltimore MD 21231
410 276-7254

(G-865)

PEPSI-COLA BTLG WORCESTER INC

Also Called: Pepsico

135 Louisa Viens Dr (06241-1105)
P.O. Box 736 (06241-0736)
PHONE.............................860 774-4007
Tim Brown, *Brnch Mgr*
EMP: 45
SALES (corp-wide): 22.65MM **Privately Held**
Web: www.pepsiworcester.com
SIC: **2086** Carbonated soft drinks, bottled and canned
PA: Pepsi-Cola Bottling Co. Of Worcester, Inc.
90 Industrial Dr
Holden MA 01520
508 829-6551

(G-866)

PLASTICS COLOR CORP INC

349 Lake Rd (06241-1551)
PHONE.............................800 922-9936
Raymond Lachapelle, *Prin*
EMP: 7 **EST:** 2016
SALES (est): 248.05K **Privately Held**
SIC: **2821** Plastics materials and resins

(G-867)

PUTNAM PLASTICS CORPORATION

40 Louisa Viens Dr (06241-1106)
PHONE.............................860 774-1559
James Binch, *
Hank Hague, *
EMP: 150 **EST:** 1984
SQ FT: 40,000
SALES (est): 48.46MM **Privately Held**
Web: www.putnamplastics.com
SIC: **3841** Surgical and medical instruments

(G-868)

ROL-VAC LIMITED PARTNERSHIP

207 Tracy Rd (06241-1123)
P.O. Box 777 (06241-0777)
PHONE.............................860 928-9929
Ron Jones, *Genl Pt*
▲ **EMP:** 12 **EST:** 1998
SQ FT: 45,000
SALES (est): 3.22MM **Privately Held**
Web: www.rolvac.com
SIC: **2671** Paper; coated and laminated packaging

(G-869)

SYMBOL MATTRESS NENG INC

312 Lake Rd (06241-1537)
P.O. Box 1050 (75151-1050)
PHONE.............................860 779-3112
EMP: 400 **EST:** 1994
SALES (corp-wide): 457.32MM **Privately Held**
Web: www.symbolmattress.com
SIC: **2515** Mattresses and foundations
HQ: Eastern Sleep Products Company
4901 Fitzhugh Ave
Richmond VA 23230
804 254-1711

(G-870)

WEB INDUSTRIES HARTFORD INC (HQ)

20 Louisa Viens Dr (06241-1106)
PHONE.............................860 779-3197
Donald Romine, *Pr*
Robert Fulton, *
James Hanrahan, *
▲ **EMP:** 32 **EST:** 1982
SQ FT: 40,000
SALES (est): 9.54MM

SALES (corp-wide): 104.33MM **Privately Held**
Web: www.webindustries.com
SIC: **3082** 5162 Unsupported plastics profile shapes; Plastics film
PA: Web Industries Inc.
293 Boston Post Rd W # 510
Marlborough MA 01752
508 898-2988

(G-871)

WINCHESTER INTERCONNECT CM CORPORATION

Also Called: C & M
349 Lake Rd (06241-1551)
PHONE.............................860 774-4812
◆ **EMP:** 250 **EST:** 2000
SALES (est): 55.57MM
SALES (corp-wide): 17.49B **Privately Held**
SIC: **3357** Communication wire
HQ: Winchester Interconnect Corporation
68 Water St
Norwalk CT 06854

Deep River
Middlesex County

(G-872)

ABSTRACT TOOL INC

500 Main St Ste 15 (06417-2000)
PHONE.............................860 526-4635
Ken Hallden, *Pr*
Glenn Guggenheim, *VP*
Janet Hallden, *Treas*
Diane Guggenheim, *Sec*
EMP: 10 **EST:** 1989
SQ FT: 6,000
SALES (est): 779.09K **Privately Held**
SIC: **3599** Machine shop, jobbing and repair

(G-873)

BELL AND HOWELL LLC

6 Winter Ave (06417-1813)
PHONE.............................860 526-9561
EMP: 27
Web: www.bellhowell.net
SIC: **3579** Paper handling machines
PA: Bell And Howell, Llc
3791 S Alston Ave
Durham NC 27713

(G-874)

CHESTER BOATWORKS

444 Main St (06417-2062)
PHONE.............................860 526-2227
Gil Bartlett, *Owner*
EMP: 8 **EST:** 2014
SALES (est): 192.35K **Privately Held**
Web: www.chesterboatworks.com
SIC: **3732** Boats, fiberglass: building and repairing

(G-875)

CONNECTICUT SIGN SERVICE LLC

500 Industrial Park Rd (06417-1698)
P.O. Box 645 (06475-0645)
PHONE.............................860 767-7446
John Morrison, *Managing Member*
EMP: 9 **EST:** 1997
SALES (est): 752.02K **Privately Held**
Web: www.ctsign.com
SIC: **3993** Signs and advertising specialties

(G-876)

CT SIGN SERVICE LLC

500 Industrial Park Rd (06417-1698)
PHONE.............................860 322-3954

John R Morrison Iii, *Pr*
EMP: 8 **EST:** 2016
SALES (est): 604.4K Privately Held
Web: www.ctsign.com
SIC: 3993 Signs and advertising specialties

(G-877)
GBR SYSTEMS CORPORATION
6 Winter Ave (06417-1813)
P.O. Box 51004 (48151-5004)
PHONE.................................860 526-9561
▲ **EMP:** 27
Web: www.gbr.com
SIC: 3579 Paper handling machines

(G-878)
INVENTEC PRFMCE CHEM USA LLC
500 Main St Ste 18 (06417-2000)
P.O. Box 989 (06417-0989)
PHONE.................................860 526-8300
Jean-noel Poirier, *CEO*
David Reitz, *CFO*
Leigh Gesick, *Dir Opers*
EMP: 20 **EST:** 2014
SQ FT: 12,000
SALES (est): 7.18MM
SALES (corp-wide): 12.11MM Privately Held
Web: www.inventecusa.com
SIC: 2899 Fluxes: brazing, soldering, galvanizing, and welding
PA: Dehon
4 Rue De La Croix Faubin
Paris
143987584

(G-879)
OLD LYME GOURMET COMPANY
Also Called: Deep River Snacks
16 Grove St (06417-1711)
P.O. Box 1127 (06417-1127)
PHONE.................................860 434-7347
Jim Golberg, *CEO*
▼ **EMP:** 28 **EST:** 2002
SQ FT: 4,000
SALES (est): 13.21MM Privately Held
Web: www.deepriversnacks.com
SIC: 5149 2096 Health foods; Potato chips and other potato-based snacks
PA: Arca Continental, S.A.B. De C.V.
Av. San Jeronimo No. 813 Poniente
Monterrey NLE 64640

(G-880)
PARASON MACHINE INC
1000 Industrial Park Rd (06417)
P.O. Box 292 (06417-0292)
PHONE.................................860 526-3565
Charles Paradis, *Pr*
Janice Paradis, *VP*
EMP: 18 **EST:** 1991
SQ FT: 10,000
SALES (est): 2.71MM Privately Held
Web: www.parasonmachine.com
SIC: 3599 Machine shop, jobbing and repair

(G-881)
SD GOODSPEED INC
12 Bridge St (06417-1704)
PHONE.................................860 526-3200
EMP: 112
SIC: 3089 Injection molding of plastics

(G-882)
SILGAN PLASTICS LLC
Also Called: Silgan
38 Bridge St (06417-1731)
P.O. Box 405 (06417)
PHONE.................................860 526-6300

Jim Leardi, *Mgr*
EMP: 170
Web: www.silganplastics.com
SIC: 3089 Plastics containers, except foam
HQ: Silgan Plastics Llc
14515 North Outer 40 Rd # 21
Chesterfield MO 63017
800 274-5426

(G-883)
SMT INTERNATIONAL LLC
Also Called: Amtech Solder
500 Main St Ste 18 (06417-2000)
P.O. Box 989 (06417-0989)
PHONE.................................860 526-8300
EMP: 10
SIC: 2899 Fluxes: brazing, soldering, galvanizing, and welding

(G-884)
SOUND VIEW PLASTICS LLC
500 Main St Ste 25a (06417-2000)
PHONE.................................860 322-4139
EMP: 11 **EST:** 2017
SALES (est): 740.96K Privately Held
Web: www.soundviewplastics.com
SIC: 3089 Injection molding of plastics

(G-885)
SWPC PLASTICS LLC (DH)
Also Called: Tri Town Precision Plastics
12 Bridge St (06417-1704)
PHONE.................................860 526-9800
Mark Smith, *CEO*
EMP: 112 **EST:** 2014
SALES (est): 33.56MM
SALES (corp-wide): 479.24MM Publicly Held
Web: www.swpc.com
SIC: 3089 Injection molding of plastics
HQ: Smith & Wesson Inc.
2100 Roosevelt Ave
Springfield MA 01104
800 331-0852

(G-886)
TRIMECH SOLUTIONS LLC
Also Called: Trimech Advanced Manufacturing
630 Industrial Park Rd (06417-1600)
PHONE.................................860 526-5869
Dan Straka, *Brnch Mgr*
EMP: 15
SALES (corp-wide): 24.06MM Privately Held
Web: www.trimech.com
SIC: 3555 Printing trades machinery
PA: Trimech Solutions, Llc
4991 Lake Brook Dr # 300
Glen Allen VA 23060
804 257-9965

(G-887)
USA BUILDERS INC
12 Belmont Ave (06417-2014)
PHONE.................................843 321-9618
Ryan Pulcini, *Pr*
EMP: 8 **EST:** 2017
SALES (est): 220K Privately Held
SIC: 1389 Construction, repair, and dismantling services

Derby
New Haven County

(G-888)
CASTLE SELTZER INC
Also Called: Arthur G Lombardi Seltzer
245 Francis St (06418-1505)

PHONE.................................203 736-6887
Brian Dworkin, *Pr*
Sharon Dworkin, *Sec*
Michelle Dworkin, *VP*
EMP: 8 **EST:** 1972
SQ FT: 8,000
SALES (est): 562.93K Privately Held
SIC: 2086 Water, natural: packaged in cans, bottles, etc.

(G-889)
GORDON RUBBER AND PKG CO INC
10 Cemetery Ave (06418-1604)
P.O. Box 298 (06418-0298)
PHONE.................................203 735-7441
John A Mazur, *Pr*
EMP: 33 **EST:** 1948
SQ FT: 20,000
SALES (est): 3.31MM Privately Held
Web: www.gordonrubber.com
SIC: 3069 5085 3544 Molded rubber products; Rubber goods, mechanical; Special dies, tools, jigs, and fixtures

(G-890)
IDA INTERNATIONAL INC
200 Roosevelt Dr (06418-1625)
P.O. Box 284 (06418-0284)
PHONE.................................203 736-9249
Norman M Harbinson, *VP*
Thomas Harbinson, *
Robert A Harbinson, *
EMP: 45 **EST:** 1995
SQ FT: 124,581
SALES (est): 10.28MM Privately Held
Web: www.ida-intl.com
SIC: 3446 Architectural metalwork

(G-891)
M & B ENTERPRISE LLC
Also Called: Wholesale Poster Frames
155 New Haven Ave (06418-2161)
PHONE.................................888 983-2670
EMP: 15 **EST:** 2004
SQ FT: 20,000
SALES (est): 2.54MM Privately Held
Web: www.frameiteasy.com
SIC: 3499 Picture frames, metal

(G-892)
SAVAGE LATINA MAGAZINE LLC
12 11th St (06418-1208)
PHONE.................................800 260-3525
Jesus Lopez, *Pr*
Aaron Charles Co, *Editor in Chief*
EMP: 8 **EST:** 2020
SALES (est): 412.54K Privately Held
Web: www.savagelatinamagazine.com
SIC: 2721 Magazines: publishing and printing

(G-893)
VALLEY PUBLISHING COMPANY INC
Also Called: Valley Times
7 Francis St (06418-1597)
PHONE.................................203 735-6696
Blaze A Garbatini, *Pr*
Romolo Garbatini, *VP*
Irene Garbatini, *Sec*
EMP: 10 **EST:** 1959
SALES (est): 975.73K Privately Held
Web: www.valleypubco.com
SIC: 2711 Newspapers, publishing and printing

(G-894)
WEIMANN BROTHERS MFG CO
247 Roosevelt Dr (06418-1626)
P.O. Box 333 (06418-0333)
PHONE.................................203 735-3311
James A Fair Senior, *Pr*
James A Fair Junior, *VP*
Marion Neville, *Sec*
Jeff Fair, *VP*
EMP: 13 **EST:** 1917
SQ FT: 12,000
SALES (est): 486.6K Privately Held
SIC: 3469 3544 Stamping metal for the trade ; Special dies and tools

(G-895)
WHALLEY GLASS COMPANY (PA)
Also Called: Curved Glass Distributors
72 Chapel St (06418-2130)
PHONE.................................203 735-9388
Mark S Vece, *Pr*
Corinne V Cacopardo, *
Blaise L Vece, *
Joyce Gaul, *
▲ **EMP:** 100 **EST:** 1970
SQ FT: 50,000
SALES (est): 15.49MM
SALES (corp-wide): 15.49MM Privately Held
Web: www.curvedglassdist.com
SIC: 3229 5023 Glass furnishings and accessories; Glassware

Durham
Middlesex County

(G-896)
CHAPMAN MANUFACTURING COMPANY
471 New Haven Rd (06422-2514)
P.O. Box 250 (06422-0250)
PHONE.................................860 349-9228
William Le Vee, *Pr*
Doris Le Vee, *VP*
Carmella Kowalski, *Prin*
EMP: 10 **EST:** 1942
SQ FT: 1,200
SALES (est): 1.36MM Privately Held
Web: www.chapmanmfg.com
SIC: 5251 3423 Tools; Screw drivers, pliers, chisels, etc. (hand tools)

(G-897)
CHEMOTEX PRTCTIVE CATINGS CORP (PA)
15 Commerce Cir (06422-1002)
PHONE.................................860 349-0144
Kevin Wise, *Pr*
EMP: 11 **EST:** 1980
SQ FT: 10,000
SALES (est): 1.19MM
SALES (corp-wide): 1.19MM Privately Held
Web: www.cpc-corp.com
SIC: 2899 Chemical preparations, nec

(G-898)
CLAREMONT SALES CORPORATION
35 Winsome Rd (06422-1315)
P.O. Box 430 (06422-0430)
PHONE.................................860 349-4499
▼ **EMP:** 30 **EST:** 1993
SQ FT: 32,000
SALES (est): 8.21MM Privately Held
Web: www.claremontcorporation.com

SIC: 3086 2221 Insulation or cushioning material, foamed plastics; Fiberglass fabrics

(G-899)
DURHAM MANUFACTURING COMPANY (PA)
201 Main St (06422-2108)
P.O. Box 230 (06422-0230)
PHONE..................................860 349-3427
Richard Patterson, *CEO*
Francis Korn, *
John Gowac, *
John Patterson, *
◆ EMP: 99 EST: 1922
SQ FT: 120,000
SALES (est): 23.79MM
SALES (corp-wide): 23.79MM **Privately Held**
Web: www.durhammfg.com
SIC: 3469 2542 2522 2514 Boxes, stamped metal; Partitions and fixtures, except wood; Office furniture, except wood; Metal household furniture

(G-900)
FLEMMING TINKER INCORPORATED
27 Parson Ln Ste G (06422-1323)
PHONE..................................860 316-2589
Flemming Tinker, *Pr*
EMP: 10 EST: 2004
SALES (est): 980.93K **Privately Held**
Web: www.apertureos.com
SIC: 3827 Optical instruments and lenses

(G-901)
HOBSON AND MOTZER INCORPORATED (PA)
30 Airline Rd (06422-1000)
PHONE..................................860 349-1756
Frank W Dworak, *Pr*
James O'brien, *VP Opers*
Donald Zak, *
EMP: 144 EST: 1912
SQ FT: 52,000
SALES (est): 23.62MM
SALES (corp-wide): 23.62MM **Privately Held**
Web: www.hobsonmotzer.com
SIC: 3469 3544 Stamping metal for the trade; Special dies and tools

(G-902)
JBSBT LLC
30 Ozick Dr Unit C (06422-1022)
P.O. Box 312 (06422-0312)
PHONE..................................860 349-0631
Jeffery B Threloff, *Managing Member*
EMP: 10 EST: 2011
SALES (est): 997.91K **Privately Held**
Web: www.versalift.com
SIC: 3599 Machine and other job shop work

(G-903)
MORGAN A M T
18 Airline Rd (06422-1000)
PHONE..................................860 349-4444
Lonnie Buff, *Prin*
EMP: 10 EST: 2015
SALES (est): 919.29K **Privately Held**
SIC: 3624 Carbon and graphite products

(G-904)
TECHNICAL MANUFACTURING CORP
Also Called: T M C
645 New Haven Rd (06422-2512)
P.O. Box 306 (06422-0306)
PHONE..................................860 349-1735

Mary Lou Bonito, *Pr*
Marylou Bonito, *
Fred Bonito, *
David Bonito, *
EMP: 30 EST: 1985
SQ FT: 70,000
SALES (est): 4.88MM **Privately Held**
Web: www.techmfgcorp.com
SIC: 3672 3679 Printed circuit boards; Harness assemblies, for electronic use: wire or cable

(G-905)
TRANSFORMER TECHNOLOGY INC
60 Commerce Cir (06422-1002)
P.O. Box 436 (06422-0436)
PHONE..................................860 349-1061
Bruce M Gueble Junior, *Pr*
Suzanne M Gueble, *Treas*
▲ EMP: 12 EST: 1973
SQ FT: 20,000
SALES (est): 2.33MM **Privately Held**
Web:
www.transformertechnologyinc.com
SIC: 3679 3612 Power supplies, all types: static; Power transformers, electric

East Berlin
Hartford County

(G-906)
ALBI PROTECTIVE COATINGS LLC
401 Berlin St (06023-1127)
PHONE..................................860 828-0571
EMP: 10 EST: 2020
SALES (est): 235.82K **Privately Held**
Web: www.albi.com
SIC: 2851 Paints and allied products

(G-907)
ASI SIGN SYSTEMS INC
100 Clark Dr (06023-1172)
PHONE..................................860 828-3331
Doden Hoff, *Mgr*
EMP: 8
Web: www.asisignage.com
SIC: 3993 Signs and advertising specialties
PA: Asi Sign Systems, Inc.
8181 Jetstar Dr Ste 100
Irving TX 75063

(G-908)
BARETTA PROVISION INC
172 Commerce St (06023-1105)
P.O. Box 344 (06023-0344)
PHONE..................................860 828-0802
William Baretta Junior, *Pr*
Carol Baretta, *Sec*
EMP: 10 EST: 1967
SQ FT: 10,000
SALES (est): 1.57MM **Privately Held**
Web: www.barettaprovision.com
SIC: 5147 2013 Meats, fresh; Sausages and related products, from purchased meat

(G-909)
DEBURRING HOUSE INC
230 Berlin St (06023-1032)
PHONE..................................860 828-0889
David Durity, *VP*
David Durity, *Pr*
Steven Cyr, *
Kevin Cyr, *
EMP: 22 EST: 1965
SQ FT: 10,000
SALES (est): 781.92K **Privately Held**

Web: www.deburringhouse.com
SIC: 3471 3484 3724 Buffing for the trade; Small arms; Aircraft engines and engine parts

(G-910)
FENN LLC
80 Clark Dr Unit 5d (06023-1157)
PHONE..................................860 259-6600
Eric Mara, *CEO*
David Somers, *
Ryan Cutter, *
▲ EMP: 30 EST: 2014
SQ FT: 22,000
SALES (est): 5.25MM
SALES (corp-wide): 2.41B **Privately Held**
Web: www.fenn-torin.com
SIC: 3542 Rebuilt machine tools, metal forming types
HQ: Quality Products, Inc.
1 Air Cargo Pkwy E
Swanton OH 43558
419 866-6301

(G-911)
FLETCHER-TERRY COMPANY LLC (PA)
91 Clark Dr (06023-1104)
PHONE..................................860 828-3400
◆ EMP: 90 EST: 2009
SALES (est): 24.19MM **Privately Held**
Web: www.fletcher-terry.com
SIC: 3423 3541 6512 3549 Hand and edge tools, nec; Machine tools, metal cutting type ; Nonresidential building operators; Metalworking machinery, nec

(G-912)
HEISE INDUSTRIES INC
196 Commerce St (06023-1105)
PHONE..................................860 828-6538
Brooks B Heise Senior, *CEO*
Brooks B Heise Junior, *Pr*
Michael Cesario, *
EMP: 60 EST: 1965
SQ FT: 25,000
SALES (est): 9.43MM **Privately Held**
Web: www.heiseindustries.com
SIC: 3544 Special dies and tools

(G-913)
LIBERTY INDUSTRIES INC
133 Commerce St (06023-1106)
P.O. Box 508 (06023-0508)
PHONE..................................860 828-6361
▲ EMP: 25 EST: 1953
SALES (est): 5.75MM **Privately Held**
Web: www.liberty-ind.com
SIC: 3564 5941 Air purification equipment; Firearms

(G-914)
PALMER MANUFACTURING CO LLC
Also Called: PALMER MANUFACTURING CO., LLC
134 Commerce St (06023-1105)
PHONE..................................860 828-0344
EMP: 11
SALES (corp-wide): 402.2MM **Privately Held**
SIC: 3724 Aircraft engines and engine parts
HQ: Palmer Manufacturing Co., Llc.
243 Medford St
Malden MA 02148
781 321-0480

(G-915)
PARADIGM PRCISION HOLDINGS LLC
Also Called: Berlin Operations
134 Commerce St (06023-1105)
PHONE..................................860 829-3663
Lester Karolek, *Brnch Mgr*
EMP: 70
SALES (corp-wide): 139.19MM **Privately Held**
Web: www.pursuitaero.com
SIC: 3545 Machine tool accessories
HQ: Paradigm Precision Holdings, Llc
404 W Guadalupe Rd
Tempe AZ 85283

(G-916)
PRECISION GRAPHICS INC
10 Clark Dr (06023-1103)
P.O. Box 248 (06023-0248)
PHONE..................................860 828-6561
Burton Johnson, *Pr*
Ross Johnson, *
Eric Johnson, *
Karen Johnson, *
EMP: 25 EST: 1965
SQ FT: 13,000
SALES (est): 2.47MM **Privately Held**
Web: www.frontpanels.com
SIC: 3613 3993 Control panels, electric; Name plates: except engraved, etched, etc.: metal

(G-917)
STANCHEM INCORPORATED
Also Called: Stanchem Polymers
401 Berlin St (06023-1127)
PHONE..................................860 828-0571
Paul Stenson, *Pr*
Kevin O'connell, *CFO*
EMP: 39 EST: 1969
SALES (est): 5.58MM
SALES (corp-wide): 5.58MM **Privately Held**
Web: www.stanchem-inc.com
SIC: 2822 Ethylene-propylene rubbers, EPDM polymers
PA: Deltech Holdings Inc.
11911 Scenic Hwy
Baton Rouge LA 70807
225 775-0150

(G-918)
STANCHEM INCORPORATED (HQ)
401 Berlin St (06023-1127)
PHONE..................................860 828-0571
◆ EMP: 37 EST: 1969
SALES (est): 21.48MM
SALES (corp-wide): 99.21MM **Privately Held**
Web: www.stanchem-inc.com
SIC: 2899 2851 2891 2821 Chemical preparations, nec; Paints and paint additives ; Adhesives and sealants; Plastics materials and resins
PA: Deltech Llc
11911 Scenic Hwy
Baton Rouge LA 70807
225 775-0150

(G-919)
T M I LIQUIDATING INC
134 Commerce St (06023-1105)
P.O. Box 278 (06023-0278)
PHONE..................................860 828-0344
Rosemarie Fischer, *CEO*
Anthony Micacci, *
Lucille Micacci, *
Tinamarie Blinn, *

Lucia Micacci Bantle, *
▲ **EMP:** 48 **EST:** 1962
SQ FT: 70,000
SALES (est): 841.63K **Privately Held**
SIC: 3599 Machine shop, jobbing and repair

(G-920)
WAD INC
Also Called: Asi Modulex
100 Clark Dr (06023-1172)
P.O. Box 504 (06023-0504)
PHONE................................860 828-3331
EMP: 19 **EST:** 1986
SQ FT: 9,000
SALES (est): 896.09K **Privately Held**
SIC: 3993 1799 Signs, not made in custom sign painting shops; Sign installation and maintenance

East Canaan
Litchfield County

(G-921)
ALLYNDALE CORPORATION
40 Allyndale Rd (06024)
P.O. Box 265 (06024-0265)
PHONE................................860 824-7959
Louis C Allyn Ii, *Pr*
Steven Allyn, *VP*
Brian Allyn, *Sec*
Leonard Allyn, *Treas*
EMP: 31 **EST:** 1961
SQ FT: 450
SALES (est): 2.21MM **Privately Held**
SIC: 1422 Agricultural limestone, ground

(G-922)
LAND OF NOD WINERY LLC
99 Lower Rd (06024-2624)
PHONE................................860 824-5225
William S Adam, *Prin*
EMP: 7 **EST:** 2000
SALES (est): 404.19K **Privately Held**
SIC: 2084 Wines

East Glastonbury
Hartford County

(G-923)
QUALITY NAME PLATE INC
Also Called: Qnp Technologies
22 Fisher Hill Rd (06025)
P.O. Box 308 (06025-0308)
PHONE................................860 633-9495
Craig O Garneau, *Pr*
Barry B Ralston, *
▲ **EMP:** 95 **EST:** 1946
SQ FT: 40,000
SALES (est): 12MM **Privately Held**
Web: www.qnp.com
SIC: 3613 3625 3083 2759 Switchgear and switchboard apparatus; Relays and industrial controls; Laminated plastics plate and sheet; Screen printing

East Granby
Hartford County

(G-924)
ACCELERON INC
21 Lordship Rd Ste 1 (06026-9589)
PHONE................................860 651-9333
Rory Montano, *Pr*
Donald Montano, *
Lance Montano, *
Donald Christensen, *

EMP: 46 **EST:** 1974
SQ FT: 60,000
SALES (est): 4.69MM **Privately Held**
Web: www.acceleroninc.com
SIC: 7692 Welding repair

(G-925)
APPLETON GRP LLC
Also Called: Egs Elctrcal Group Nlson Heat
2 Connecticut South Dr (06026-9738)
PHONE................................860 653-1603
EMP: 13
SALES (corp-wide): 15.16B **Publicly Held**
Web: appleton.emerson.com
SIC: 3823 Process control instruments
HQ: Appleton Grp Llc
9377 W Higgins Rd
Rosemont IL 60018
847 268-6000

(G-926)
BURKE PRECISION MACHINE CO INC
7 Hatchett Hill Rd (06026-9526)
P.O. Box 329 (06026-0329)
PHONE................................860 408-1394
EMP: 9 **EST:** 1995
SQ FT: 10,000
SALES (est): 832.31K **Privately Held**
Web: www.burkeprecision.com
SIC: 3599 Machine shop, jobbing and repair

(G-927)
CBS MANUFACTURING COMPANY
35 Kripes Rd (06026-9644)
PHONE................................860 653-8100
John James Lawton, *CEO*
Clifford James Lawton, *
Robert Bruce Lawton, *
Steven Eric Lawton, *
EMP: 39 **EST:** 1972
SQ FT: 16,000
SALES (est): 5.92MM **Privately Held**
Web: www.cbsmfg.com
SIC: 3724 3728 Aircraft engines and engine parts; Aircraft parts and equipment, nec

(G-928)
COHERENT INC
7 Airport Park Rd (06026-9523)
PHONE................................860 408-5066
EMP: 20 **EST:** 2018
SALES (est): 2.58MM **Privately Held**
Web: www.coherent.com
SIC: 3674 Semiconductors and related devices

(G-929)
COLOR CRAFT LTD
Also Called: Createx Colors
14 Airport Park Rd (06026-9523)
P.O. Box 120 (06026-0120)
PHONE................................800 509-6563
Vincent H Kennedy, *Pr*
Craig Kenndey, *Treas*
EMP: 13 **EST:** 1980
SQ FT: 10,000
SALES (est): 2.46MM **Privately Held**
Web: www.createxcolors.com
SIC: 3952 5199 5198 5961 Artists' materials, except pencils and leads; Artists' materials; Paints; Arts and crafts equipment and supplies, mail order

(G-930)
COMMAND CORPORATION
4 Creamery Brk (06026-8702)
P.O. Box 832 (06026-0832)

PHONE................................800 851-6012
Robert Bazyk, *Pr*
EMP: 25 **EST:** 1991
SALES (est): 3.06MM **Privately Held**
Web: www.commandco.com
SIC: 3699 1731 Security control equipment and systems; Closed circuit television installation

(G-931)
COMPUTER COMPONENTS INC
Also Called: Relays Unlimited
18 Kripes Rd (06026-9645)
P.O. Box 1378 (06026-1378)
PHONE................................860 653-9909
Gary Flor, *Pr.*
EMP: 25 **EST:** 1959
SQ FT: 6,000
SALES (est): 2.74MM
SALES (corp-wide): 35MM **Privately Held**
Web: www.relays-unlimited.com
SIC: 3625 Relays, for electronic use
PA: Comus International, Inc.
454 Allwood Rd
Clifton NJ 07012

(G-932)
COORSTEK INC
Also Called: Coorstek East Granby
10 Airport Park Rd (06026-9523)
PHONE................................860 653-8071
Janis Hunter, *Sec*
EMP: 221
SALES (corp-wide): 1.16B **Privately Held**
Web: www.coorstek.com
SIC: 3264 Porcelain electrical supplies
HQ: Coorstek, Inc.
14143 Denver West Pkwy # 400
Lakewood CO 80401
303 271-7000

(G-933)
ENVIRONMENTAL SYSTEMS PRODUCTS INC
7 Kripes Rd (06026-9720)
P.O. Box 83201 (60691-0201)
PHONE................................860 653-0081
▲ **EMP:** 108
SIC: 7549 3559 3564 Emissions testing without repairs, automotive; Ozone machines; Blowers and fans

(G-934)
GALASSO MATERIALS LLC
60 S Main St (06026-9550)
P.O. Box 1776 (06026-0676)
PHONE................................860 527-1825
EMP: 160 **EST:** 1997
SQ FT: 7,000
SALES (est): 27.31MM **Privately Held**
Web: www.galassomaterials.com
SIC: 1499 1429 1442 Asphalt mining and bituminous stone quarrying; Grits mining (crushed stone); Construction sand and gravel

(G-935)
GULFSTREAM AEROSPACE CORP
95 Old County Rd (06026-9754)
PHONE................................912 965-3000
Scott Mcdougall, *Brnch Mgr*
EMP: 16
SALES (corp-wide): 42.27B **Publicly Held**
Web: www.gulfstream.com
SIC: 3721 Aircraft
HQ: Gulfstream Aerospace Corporation
500 Gulfstream Rd
Savannah GA 31408

(G-936)
JOINING TECH AUTOMTN INC
17 Connecticut South Dr Ste B
(06026-9671)
PHONE................................860 784-1967
Dave Hudson, *Pr*
Michael Francoeur, *CEO*
EMP: 15 **EST:** 2016
SALES (est): 1.14MM **Privately Held**
Web: www.jtautomation.com
SIC: 3542 Machine tools, metal forming type

(G-937)
JOINING TECHNOLOGIES LLC
17 Connecticut South Dr Ste B
(06026-9671)
PHONE................................860 653-0111
Michael Francoeur, *Ch Bd*
David Hudson, *Pr*
Gary Francoeur, *VP*
Matthew Francoeur, *Sec*
Caitlin Scott, *Mgr*
EMP: 70 **EST:** 1992
SQ FT: 27,578
SALES (est): 23MM **Privately Held**
Web: www.joiningtech.com
SIC: 7692 5063 Welding repair; Electrical apparatus and equipment

(G-938)
JT AUTOMATION LLC
17 Connecticut South Dr (06026-9671)
PHONE................................860 784-1967
EMP: 18 **EST:** 2016
SALES (est): 1.53MM **Privately Held**
SIC: 3548 Welding apparatus

(G-939)
MAGNATECH LLC
Also Called: Magnatech Dsd Co, The
6 Kripes Rd (06026-9645)
P.O. Box 260 (06026-0260)
PHONE................................860 653-2573
▼ **EMP:** 54 **EST:** 1946
SQ FT: 24,000
SALES (est): 9.93MM **Privately Held**
Web: www.magnatechllc.com
SIC: 3548 3699 Welding apparatus; Electrical welding equipment

(G-940)
MARMON INDUS ENRGY INFRSTRCTUR ✪
20 Bradley Park Rd (06026-9789)
PHONE................................860 653-8300
Chris Venice, *Managing Member*
EMP: 50 **EST:** 2023
SALES (est): 2.79MM **Privately Held**
SIC: 3679 Electronic components, nec

(G-941)
MB AEROSPACE
99 Rainbow Rd (06026-9431)
PHONE................................860 653-0569
EMP: 38 **EST:** 2017
SALES (est): 7.51MM **Privately Held**
Web: www.barnesaero.com
SIC: 3721 Aircraft

(G-942)
MB AEROSPACE EAST GRANBY LIMITED PARTNERSHIP
39 Bradley Park Rd (06026-9789)
PHONE................................860 653-5041
EMP: 175 **EST:** 1955
SALES (est): 23.36MM **Privately Held**
Web: www.barnesaero.com

SIC: 3724 3444 3443 3728 Turbines, aircraft type; Casings, sheet metal; Fabricated plate work (boiler shop); Aircraft parts and equipment, nec

(G-943)
MB AERSPACE ACP HLDNGS III COR (PA)
39 Bradley Park Rd (06026-9789)
PHONE..................................586 772-2500
Craig Gallagher, *CEO*
Gregor Goodwin, *CFO*
EMP: 20 EST: 2013
SALES (est): 26.85MM
SALES (corp-wide): 26.85MM **Privately Held**
Web: www.barnesaero.com
SIC: 3724 Aircraft engines and engine parts

(G-944)
MP SYSTEMS INC
34 Bradley Park Rd (06026-9789)
PHONE..................................860 687-3460
EMP: 12 EST: 2007
SALES (est): 4.83MM **Privately Held**
Web: www.mp-systems.net
SIC: 3443 5078 Heat exchangers: coolers (after, inter), condensers, etc.; Beverage coolers
PA: Morris Group, Inc.
    910 Day Hill Rd
    Windsor CT 06095

(G-945)
NUFERN
Also Called: Nufern
7 Airport Park Rd (06026-9523)
PHONE..................................860 408-5000
Martin Seifert, *Pr*
Alan Levesque, *
Doctor Kanishka Tankala, *VP Opers*
Bryce Samson, *
▲ EMP: 68 EST: 2000
SQ FT: 57,000
SALES (est): 16.71MM
SALES (corp-wide): 5.16B **Publicly Held**
Web: www.coherent.com
SIC: 3229 Fiber optics strands
PA: Coherent Corp.
    375 Saxonburg Blvd
    Saxonburg PA 16056
    724 352-4455

(G-946)
OSHKOSH CORPORATION
Also Called: Oshkosh
35 Nicholson Rd (06026-9736)
P.O. Box 1126 (06026-1126)
PHONE..................................860 653-5548
Bruce Anderson, *Mgr*
EMP: 10
SALES (corp-wide): 8.28B **Publicly Held**
Web: www.oshkoshcorp.com
SIC: 3711 Motor vehicles and car bodies
PA: Oshkosh Corporation
    1917 Four Wheel Dr
    Oshkosh WI 54902
    920 502-3400

(G-947)
OVERHAUL SUPPORT SERVICES LLC (PA)
5 Connecticut South Dr (06026-9738)
PHONE..................................860 264-2101
Ken Oconnor, *Managing Member*
EMP: 76 EST: 2007
SQ FT: 10,000
SALES (est): 9.99MM **Privately Held**
Web: www.tighitco.com

SIC: 3728 Aircraft parts and equipment, nec

(G-948)
PIONEER OPTICS COMPANY INC
20 Connecticut South Dr (06026-9738)
PHONE..................................860 286-0071
Ron Hille, *Pr*
EMP: 14 EST: 1991
SALES (est): 1.34MM **Privately Held**
Web: www.pioneeroptics.com
SIC: 3845 3229 Laser systems and equipment, medical; Fiber optics strands

(G-949)
RSCC WIRE & CABLE LLC
Also Called: Rscc
27 Bradley Park Rd (06026-9789)
PHONE..................................860 653-8300
EMP: 100
SALES (corp-wide): 302.09B **Publicly Held**
Web: www.r-scc.com
SIC: 3357 Nonferrous wiredrawing and insulating
HQ: Rscc Wire & Cable Llc
    20 Bradley Park Rd
    East Granby CT 06026

(G-950)
RSCC WIRE & CABLE LLC (DH)
Also Called: Rockbestos
20 Bradley Park Rd (06026-9789)
PHONE..................................860 653-8300
▲ EMP: 263 EST: 1956
SQ FT: 140,000
SALES (est): 143.54MM
SALES (corp-wide): 302.09B **Publicly Held**
Web: www.r-scc.com
SIC: 3357 3315 Nonferrous wiredrawing and insulating; Cable, steel: insulated or armored
HQ: Marmon Holdings, Inc.
    181 W Madison St Ste 3900
    Chicago IL 60602
    312 372-9500

(G-951)
SIGNS PLUS INC (PA)
3 Turkey Hills Rd (06026-9564)
P.O. Box 560 (06026-0560)
PHONE..................................860 653-0547
Christopher Aubin, *Pr*
Barbara A Aubin, *Sec*
EMP: 7 EST: 1988
SQ FT: 3,000
SALES (est): 1.11MM
SALES (corp-wide): 1.11MM **Privately Held**
Web: www.signsplusprint.com
SIC: 3993 Signs, not made in custom sign painting shops

(G-952)
SMITHS MEDICAL
133 Hartford Ave Ste 3 (06026-9138)
PHONE..................................860 413-3230
EMP: 7 EST: 2017
SALES (est): 34.74K **Privately Held**
Web: www.smiths-medical.com
SIC: 3841 Surgical and medical instruments

(G-953)
SPECIALTY STEEL TREATING INC
Also Called: Heat Treating
12 Kripes Rd (06026-9645)
PHONE..................................860 653-0061

Dennis Kollmorgen, *Prin*
EMP: 40
SALES (corp-wide): 58.1MM **Privately Held**
Web: www.sst.net
SIC: 3398 Metal heat treating
PA: Specialty Steel Treating, Inc.
    34501 Commerce
    Fraser MI 48026
    586 293-5355

(G-954)
TILCON CONNECTICUT INC
60 S Main St (06026-9550)
P.O. Box 578 (06026-0578)
PHONE..................................860 844-7000
Don Penepent, *Mgr*
EMP: 23
SALES (corp-wide): 32.72B **Privately Held**
Web: www.tilconct.com
SIC: 5032 3273 Stone, crushed or broken; Ready-mixed concrete
HQ: Tilcon Connecticut Inc.
    642 Black Rock Ave
    New Britain CT 06052
    860 224-6010

East Haddam
Middlesex County

(G-955)
C SHERMAN JOHNSON COMPANY INC
Also Called: Johnson Marine
1 Matthews Dr (06423-1350)
P.O. Box L (06423-0296)
PHONE..................................860 873-8697
Burton Johnson, *CEO*
Curtiss Johnson Iii, *Pr*
Elsie Johnson, *Sec*
◆ EMP: 14 EST: 1957
SQ FT: 5,200
SALES (est): 2.36MM **Privately Held**
Web: www.csjohnson.com
SIC: 3429 Marine hardware

(G-956)
TEX ELM INC
136 Town St (06423-1423)
PHONE..................................860 873-9715
Luella A Lyman, *Pr*
Emmett J Lyman, *Treas*
William B Harmon, *Clerk*
EMP: 7 EST: 1974
SQ FT: 10,000
SALES (est): 119.61K **Privately Held**
SIC: 2759 Engraving, nec

East Hampton
Middlesex County

(G-957)
4 D TECHNOLOGY CORPORATION
Also Called: 4 D TECHNOLOGY CORPORATION
91 Daniel St (06424-1806)
PHONE..................................860 365-0420
James Wyant, *Brnch Mgr*
EMP: 20
SALES (corp-wide): 1.01B **Publicly Held**
Web: www.4dtechnology.com
SIC: 3827 Optical test and inspection equipment
HQ: 4d Technology Corporation
    3280 E Hmshre Loop Ste 14
    Tucson AZ 85706
    520 294-5600

(G-958)
AMERICA EXTRACT CORPORATION
31 E High St (06424-1021)
P.O. Box 319 (06424-0319)
PHONE..................................860 267-4444
Edward Jackowitz, *Pr*
EMP: 18 EST: 1987
SQ FT: 65,000
SALES (est): 276.92K **Privately Held**
Web: www.americandistilling.com
SIC: 2087 Extracts, flavoring

(G-959)
AMERICAN DISTILLING INC (PA)
31 E High St (06424-1021)
P.O. Box 319 (06424-0319)
PHONE..................................860 267-4444
Edward C Jackowitz, *Pr*
Kevin R Jackowitz, *
Bryan E Jackowitz, *
▼ EMP: 70 EST: 1866
SQ FT: 65,000
SALES (est): 15.55MM
SALES (corp-wide): 15.55MM **Privately Held**
Web: www.americandistilling.com
SIC: 2085 2833 2844 2087 Distiller's dried grains and solubles, and alcohol; Botanical products, medicinal: ground, graded, or milled; Perfumes and colognes; Flavoring extracts and syrups, nec

(G-960)
BERRY GLOBAL INC
44 Oneill Ln (06424-1111)
PHONE..................................413 529-7602
R Jones, *Mgr*
EMP: 8
Web: www.berryglobal.com
SIC: 3089 3081 Bottle caps, molded plastics ; Unsupported plastics film and sheet
HQ: Berry Global, Inc.
    101 Oakley St
    Evansville IN 47710

(G-961)
BEVIN BROS MANUFACTURING CO
Also Called: Bevin Bells
17 Watrous St (06424-1234)
P.O. Box 60 (06424-0060)
PHONE..................................860 267-4431
Stanley R Bevin, *Pr*
Alison Bevinlove, *
EMP: 40 EST: 1832
SALES (est): 5.85MM **Privately Held**
Web: www.bevinbells.com
SIC: 3699 Bells, electric

(G-962)
HUMPHREYS PHARMACAL INC
31 E High St (06424-1021)
P.O. Box 317 (06424-0317)
PHONE..................................860 267-8710
Tom Shultz, *Pr*
▼ EMP: 10 EST: 1854
SALES (est): 2.46MM
SALES (corp-wide): 2.9MM **Privately Held**
Web: www.humphreysbaby.com
SIC: 2834 Vitamin preparations
PA: Dickinson Brands Inc.
    31 E High St
    East Hampton CT 06424
    860 267-2279

(G-963)
KAHN INDUSTRIES INC
11 Hurd Park Rd (06424-3004)

P.O. Box 336 (06456-0336)
PHONE................................860 529-8643
Jeffrey S Kahn, *Pr*
David Kahn, *Sec*
Gerhard Merkle, *VP*
▼ **EMP:** 20 **EST:** 1968
SQ FT: 50,000
SALES (est): 2.16MM **Privately Held**
Web: www.kahn.com
SIC: 3829 Dynamometer instruments

(G-964)
KITCHEN LIVING LLC
21 Main St (06424-1116)
PHONE................................860 819-5847
Matthew Modglin, *Owner*
EMP: 7 **EST:** 2011
SALES (est): 408.4K **Privately Held**
Web: www.kitchenlivingdesign.com
SIC: 2434 Wood kitchen cabinets

(G-965)
ROKAP INC
Also Called: Sign Stop
127 Comstock Trl (06424-2306)
PHONE................................203 265-6895
Rosalind Kaplan, *Pr*
Russ Kaplan, *Sec*
EMP: 7 **EST:** 1985
SALES (est): 667.39K **Privately Held**
Web: www.rokap.com
SIC: 3993 7699 7532 7389 Signs, not made
in custom sign painting shops; Boat repair;
Truck painting and lettering; Engraving
service

(G-966)
T N DICKINSON COMPANY
Also Called: Dickinson's Cosmetics
31 E High St (06424-1021)
PHONE................................860 267-2279
Edward C Jackowitz, *Pr*
Kevin R Jackowitz, *VP*
Bryan E Jackowitz, *Sec*
EMP: 10 **EST:** 1888
SALES (est): 738.09K **Privately Held**
SIC: 2844 5122 Perfumes, cosmetics and
other toilet preparations; Toiletries

(G-967)
WEST SHORE LLC
70 N Main St (06424-1431)
PHONE................................860 267-1764
Gladys Yeager, *Mgr*
EMP: 7 **EST:** 2001
SALES (est): 110K **Privately Held**
SIC: 3531 Marine related equipment

(G-968)
ZATORSKI COATING CO INC
77 Wopowog Rd (06424-1674)
PHONE................................860 267-9889
Diane A Zatorski, *Pr*
Diane Achenbach-zatorski, *Pr*
Raymond Zatorski, *Sec*
EMP: 10 **EST:** 1995
SALES (est): 151.79K **Privately Held**
SIC: 3554 Coating and finishing machinery,
paper

East Hartford
Hartford County

(G-969)
ADAPTIVE OPTICS ASSOCIATES INC
Also Called: Aoa Xinetics
121 Prestige Park Cir (06108-1908)

PHONE................................860 282-4401
Rick Little, *Mgr*
EMP: 16
Web: www.aoa-supplylink.com
SIC: 3827 Optical elements and
assemblies, except ophthalmic
HQ: Adaptive Optics Associates, Inc.
115 Jackson Rd
Devens MA 01434
978 757-9600

(G-970)
ANDHER MFG LLC
24 Emely St (06108-3917)
PHONE................................860 874-8816
Andrzej Herman, *Prin*
EMP: 8 **EST:** 2012
SALES (est): 285.2K **Privately Held**
SIC: 3999 Manufacturing industries, nec

(G-971)
ARDENT INC (PA)
Also Called: Ardent Displays & Packaging
95 Leggett St (06108-1167)
PHONE................................860 528-6000
Donald Budnick, *Pr*
Matthew Pope, *VP*
▲ **EMP:** 13 **EST:** 1987
SQ FT: 55,000
SALES (est): 6.08MM **Privately Held**
Web: www.ardentdisplays.com
SIC: 2542 5046 Fixtures: display, office, or
store: except wood; Display equipment,
except refrigerated

(G-972)
ARTHUR J HURLEY COMPANY
60 Meadow St (06108-3218)
PHONE................................860 257-5505
Arthur J Hurley, *Prin*
EMP: 8 **EST:** 2016
SALES (est): 285.73K **Privately Held**
Web: www.hurleywire.com
SIC: 3699 Electrical equipment and
supplies, nec

(G-973)
ATI LADISH MACHINING INC (DH)
Also Called: ATI Forged Products
311 Prestige Park Rd (06108-1928)
PHONE................................860 688-3688
John Delaney, *Pr*
Dale G Reid, *
Jeff Cebula, *
John S Minich, *
Elliot S Davis, *
EMP: 48 **EST:** 1946
SQ FT: 40,000
SALES (est): 23.13MM **Publicly Held**
Web: www.atimaterials.com
SIC: 3724 Aircraft engines and engine parts
HQ: Ati Ladish Llc
5481 S Packard Ave
Cudahy WI 53110
414 747-2611

(G-974)
ATI LADISH MACHINING INC
Also Called: East Hartford Operations
311 Prestige Park Rd (06108-1928)
PHONE................................860 688-3688
Richard Cleary, *Brnch Mgr*
EMP: 100
Web: www.atimaterials.com
SIC: 3724 Aircraft engines and engine parts
HQ: Ati Ladish Machining, Inc.
311 Prestige Park Rd
East Hartford CT 06108
860 688-3688

(G-975)
BESSETTE HOLDINGS INC
Also Called: Connecticut Die Cutting Svc
95 Leggett St (06108-1167)
PHONE................................860 289-6000
Donald Budnick, *Managing Member*
Carmen Bessette, *
Raymond J Gruzas, *
Ken Besset, *
Gary R Bessette, *
EMP: 32 **EST:** 1959
SQ FT: 25,000
SALES (est): 1.18MM **Privately Held**
SIC: 3544 3469 3423 Dies, steel rule;
Stamping metal for the trade; Cutting dies,
except metal cutting

(G-976)
BRESCIAS PRINTING SERVICES INC
66 Connecticut Blvd (06108-3013)
PHONE................................860 528-4254
William G Brescia, *Pr*
William Brescia, *Pr*
EMP: 7 **EST:** 1945
SQ FT: 5,000
SALES (est): 818.79K **Privately Held**
Web: www.brescias.com
SIC: 2752 7334 2791 7331 Offset printing;
Photocopying and duplicating services;
Typesetting; Mailing service

(G-977)
CARDIAC PACEMAKERS INC
P.O. Box 280166 (06128-0166)
PHONE................................651 582-3201
EMP: 2300
SALES (corp-wide): 12.68B **Publicly Held**
SIC: 3845 Pacemaker, cardiac
HQ: Cardiac Pacemakers, Inc.
4100 Hamline Ave N
Saint Paul MN 55112
651 638-4000

(G-978)
CARDINAL HEALTH 414 LLC
Also Called: Cardinal Health 414
131 Hartland St Ste 8 (06108-3229)
PHONE................................860 291-9135
EMP: 9
SALES (corp-wide): 205.01B **Publicly
Held**
SIC: 2835 2834 Radioactive diagnostic
substances; Pharmaceutical preparations
HQ: Cardinal Health 414, Llc
7000 Cardinal Pl
Dublin OH 43017
614 757-5000

(G-979)
CELLU TISSUE CORPORATION
2 Forbes St (06108-3727)
PHONE................................860 289-7496
▼ **EMP:** 570
SIC: 2621 3842 2676 Tissue paper;
Bandages and dressings; Napkins, paper:
made from purchased paper

(G-980)
CENTRAL CONN COATINGS INC
52 Village St (06108-3904)
PHONE................................860 528-8281
Gene Schaeffer, *Pr*
EMP: 9 **EST:** 2007
SALES (est): 460.29K **Privately Held**
Web: www.centralctcoatings.com
SIC: 3479 Coating of metals and formed
products

(G-981)
COCA-COLA BEVS NORTHEAST INC
Also Called: E. Hartford Production
451 Main St (06118-1452)
PHONE................................860 895-5100
EMP: 27
Web: www.cokenortheast.com
SIC: 2086 Bottled and canned soft drinks
HQ: Coca-Cola Beverages Northeast, Inc.
1 Executive Park Dr # 330
Bedford NH 03110
603 627-7871

(G-982)
COCA-COLA BTLG STHSTERN NENG I
Coca-Cola
471 Main St # 471 (06118-1402)
PHONE................................860 569-0037
Jody Lemay, *Brnch Mgr*
EMP: 18
Web: www.coca-cola.com
SIC: 2086 Bottled and canned soft drinks
HQ: Coca-Cola Bottling Company Of
Southeastern New England, Inc.
150 Waterford Parkway S
Waterford CT 06385
860 443-2816

(G-983)
CS GROUP - USA INC
222 Pitkin St Ste 123 (06108-3261)
PHONE................................860 944-0041
Laurent Pieraut, *CEO*
Matthew Tkac, *Pr*
Jerome Casteret, *VP*
Arnaud Salomod, *Ch*
Madelyn S Shulman, *Sec*
EMP: 21 **EST:** 2015
SALES (est): 2.5MM **Privately Held**
Web: www.c-s-inc.us
SIC: 8711 3721 Engineering services;
Aircraft

(G-984)
CT DRIVESHAFT SERVICE LLC
77 Cherry St (06108-2053)
PHONE................................860 289-6459
Christopher Dewitt, *Prin*
EMP: 7 **EST:** 2014
SALES (est): 433.96K **Privately Held**
Web: www.ctdriveshaftservicesllc.com
SIC: 3714 Motor vehicle parts and
accessories

(G-985)
DEMUSZ MFG CO INC
303 Burnham St (06108-1183)
PHONE................................860 528-9845
Waldemar Demusz, *Pr*
Wieslaw Demusz, *
EMP: 27 **EST:** 1970
SQ FT: 12,000
SALES (est): 4.98MM **Privately Held**
Web: www.demusz.com
SIC: 3599 Machine shop, jobbing and repair

(G-986)
DRT AEROSPACE LLC
221 Burnham St (06108-1134)
PHONE................................937 298-7391
EMP: 10
Web: www.drtholdingsllc.com
SIC: 3599 Machine shop, jobbing and repair
HQ: Drt Aerospace, Llc
1950 Campbell Rd
Sidney OH 45365
937 492-6121

(G-987)

DUNN PAPER HOLDINGS INC
2 Forbes St (06108-3727)
PHONE...........................860 289-7496
Chris Fedler, *Manager*
EMP: 192
SALES (corp-wide): 109.53MM **Privately Held**
Web: www.bioriginsp.com
SIC: 2621 Towels, tissues and napkins; paper and stock
PA: Dunn Paper Holdings, Inc.
44 Milton Ave
Alpharetta GA 30009
810 984-5521

(G-988)

DUNN PAPER LLC
2 Forbes St (06108-3727)
PHONE...........................860 466-4141
EMP: 80 **EST:** 2015
SALES (est): 15.79MM
SALES (corp-wide): 109.53MM **Privately Held**
Web: www.bioriginsp.com
SIC: 2621 Paper mills
HQ: Dunn Paper, Inc.
44 Milton Ave
Alpharetta GA 30009
810 984-5521

(G-989)

DUR-A-FLEX INC (HQ)
95 Goodwin St (06108-1146)
PHONE...........................860 528-9838
TOLL FREE: 800
◆ **EMP:** 31 **EST:** 1966
SALES (est): 110.6K
SALES (corp-wide): 22.15B **Publicly Held**
Web: www.dur-a-flex.com
SIC: 2851 Epoxy coatings
PA: The Sherwin-Williams Company
101 W Prospect Ave # 1020
Cleveland OH 44115
216 566-2000

(G-990)

EBL PRODUCTS INC
22 Prestige Park Cir (06108-1917)
PHONE...........................860 290-3737
Joseph Zarrelli, *Pr*
Andrew Tremblay, *Pr*
EMP: 13 **EST:** 2005
SALES (est): 2.5MM **Privately Held**
Web: www.eblproducts.com
SIC: 3679 Piezoelectric crystals

(G-991)

ECU & US INTERNATIONAL
Also Called: US Reflector
43 Franklin St (06108-1723)
PHONE...........................860 906-3390
▲ **EMP:** 18 **EST:** 1989
SALES (est): 2.1MM **Privately Held**
Web: www.endotocorp.com
SIC: 5999 5099 3231 3647 Safety supplies and equipment; Safety equipment and supplies; Reflector glass beads, for highway signs or reflectors; Clearance lamps and reflectors, motor vehicle

(G-992)

ELJEN CORPORATION
125 Mckee St (06108-4018)
PHONE...........................860 610-0426
Joseph Glasser, *CEO*
EMP: 28
SALES (corp-wide): 2.32MM **Privately Held**
Web: www.eljen.com

SIC: 3259 Clay sewer and drainage pipe and tile
PA: Eljen Corporation
10 N Main St Ste 216
West Hartford CT
860 232-0077

(G-993)

ENVIRNMNTAL OFFICE SLTIONS INC (PA)
Also Called: E O S
130 Prestige Park Rd (06108-1922)
PHONE...........................860 291-1900
Christopher Stoddard, *Pr*
Mark Tosi, *
◆ **EMP:** 29 **EST:** 1996
SQ FT: 38,000
SALES (est): 22.22MM
SALES (corp-wide): 22.22MM **Privately Held**
Web: www.eosusa.com
SIC: 5045 5112 3955 5961 Printers, computer; Office supplies, nec; Print cartridges for laser and other computer printers; Computer equipment and electronics, mail order

(G-994)

FLUOROPOLYMER RESOURCES LLC (PA)
99 Eriver Dr Riverview Sq li (06108)
P.O. Box 875 (06371-0875)
PHONE...........................860 423-7622
EMP: 7 **EST:** 2011
SQ FT: 2,000
SALES (est): 5.17MM **Privately Held**
Web: www.frlusa.com
SIC: 3089 Injection molding of plastics

(G-995)

FSM PLASTICOID MFG INC
400 Governor St (06108-3925)
P.O. Box 1036 (49301-1036)
PHONE...........................860 623-1361
David Facchini, *Pr*
▲ **EMP:** 13 **EST:** 2013
SALES (est): 736.88K **Privately Held**
Web: www.plasticoidmfg.com
SIC: 3089 Injection molding of plastics

(G-996)

GENERAL DIGITAL CORPORATION
Also Called: Interactive Display Systems
60 Prestige Park Rd (06108-1919)
PHONE...........................860 282-2900
EMP: 85 **EST:** 1973
SALES (est): 14.4MM **Privately Held**
Web: www.generaldigital.com
SIC: 3575 3571 3577 8711 Computer terminals; Electronic computers; Computer peripheral equipment, nec; Engineering services

(G-997)

HORST ENGINEERING & MANUFACTURING CO (PA)
Also Called: Horst Engineering
141 Prestige Park Rd (06108-1923)
PHONE...........................860 289-8209
EMP: 85 **EST:** 1946
SALES (est): 20.9MM
SALES (corp-wide): 20.9MM **Privately Held**
Web: www.horstengineering.com
SIC: 3728 3452 3451 3724 Aircraft parts and equipment, nec; Bolts, nuts, rivets, and washers; Screw machine products; Aircraft engines and engine parts

(G-998)

HYAXIOM INC (HQ)
Also Called: Doosan
101 E River Dr (06108-3285)
PHONE...........................860 727-2200
Jeff Hyungrak Chung, *Pr*
Susan Yan, *
Eric Strayer, *
Minchul Kim, *
Howie Hooseok Che, *
◆ **EMP:** 36 **EST:** 2014
SQ FT: 238,711
SALES (est): 106.68MM **Privately Held**
Web: www.hyaxiom.com
SIC: 3674 7629 Fuel cells, solid state; Electronic equipment repair
PA: Doosan Corporation
275 Jangchungdan-Ro, Jung-Gu
Seoul 04563

(G-999)

HYDRO HONING LABORATORIES INC (PA)
Also Called: Peening Technologies Conn
8 Eastern Park Rd (06108-1105)
P.O. Box 280306 (06128-0306)
PHONE...........................860 289-4328
Thomas Beach, *Pr*
Richard Brooks, *
Walter Beach Junior, *VP*
Martha R Beach, *
EMP: 44 **EST:** 1966
SQ FT: 24,000
SALES (est): 6.26MM
SALES (corp-wide): 6.26MM **Privately Held**
Web: www.peentech.com
SIC: 3398 Shot peening (treating steel to reduce fatigue)

(G-1000)

IAE INTERNATIONAL AERO ENGS AG
Also Called: International Aero Engines
400 Main St (06108-0968)
PHONE...........................860 565-1773
Jon Beatty, *Pr*
Charles Ayer, *
John Green, *PROGRAMS*
Steve Burrill, *
Dave Avery, *
EMP: 150 **EST:** 1983
SQ FT: 34,900
SALES (est): 40.98MM
SALES (corp-wide): 68.92B **Publicly Held**
SIC: 3724 Aircraft engines and engine parts
PA: Rtx Corporation
1000 Wilson Blvd
Arlington VA 22209
781 522-3000

(G-1001)

IMAGE INSIGHT INC
222 Pitkin St Ste 2 # 128 (06108-3265)
PHONE...........................888 667-9244
Eric Rubenstein, *Pr*
EMP: 8 **EST:** 2011
SALES (est): 928.89K **Privately Held**
Web: www.imageinsightinc.com
SIC: 3829 Measuring and controlling devices, nec

(G-1002)

INTERNATIONAL AERO ENGINES LLC
Also Called: Iae
400 Main St (06108-0968)
PHONE...........................860 565-5515
Karen C Mccusker, *VP*

EMP: 10 **EST:** 2012
SALES (est): 10.73MM
SALES (corp-wide): 67.07B **Publicly Held**
Web: www.prattwhitney.com
SIC: 3724 Aircraft engines and engine parts
PA: Rtx Corporation
1000 Wilson Blvd
Arlington VA 22209
781 522-3000

(G-1003)

LEWIS MACHINE LLC
22 John St (06108-2118)
PHONE...........................860 289-3468
EMP: 29
SIC: 3812 3724 Search and navigation equipment; Aircraft engines and engine parts

(G-1004)

MARENA INDUSTRIES INC
Also Called: Marena Machinery Sales Div
433 School St (06108-1162)
PHONE...........................860 528-9701
Teodoro Marena, *Pr*
Fran Marena, *Sec*
EMP: 15 **EST:** 1966
SQ FT: 19,000
SALES (est): 2.22MM **Privately Held**
Web: www.marenaind.com
SIC: 3545 3541 Cutting tools for machine tools; Grinding machines, metalworking

(G-1005)

MEGOWEN LLC
Also Called: Deco Manufacturing
433 School St (06108-1135)
PHONE...........................860 528-9701
Brian Anderson, *Managing Member*
EMP: 10 **EST:** 2016
SALES (est): 561.86K **Privately Held**
SIC: 3599 Machine shop, jobbing and repair

(G-1006)

MIDWOOD QUARRY AND CNSTR INC (PA)
Also Called: Better Stones & Garden
200 Tolland St (06108-2414)
PHONE...........................860 289-1414
TOLL FREE: 800
William Smallwood, *Pr*
▲ **EMP:** 10 **EST:** 1980
SQ FT: 11,000
SALES (est): 1.44MM
SALES (corp-wide): 1.44MM **Privately Held**
SIC: 5211 5032 5261 1442 Masonry materials and supplies; Brick, stone, and related material; Retail nurseries and garden stores; Construction sand and gravel

(G-1007)

NORTHROP GRUMMAN CORPORATION
121 Prestige Park Cir (06108-1908)
PHONE...........................860 282-4461
EMP: 80
Web: www.northropgrumman.com
SIC: 3812 Search and navigation equipment
PA: Northrop Grumman Corporation
2980 Fairview Park Dr
Falls Church VA 22042

(G-1008)

OWENS CORNING SALES LLC
Also Called: Owens Corning
P.O. Box 260658 (06128)
PHONE...........................304 353-6945
EMP: 148

▲ = Import ▼ = Export
◆ = Import/Export

SIC: 3296 2952 3229 3089 Fiberglass insulation; Asphalt felts and coatings; Glass fibers, textile; Windows, plastics
HQ: Owens Corning Sales, Llc
1 Owens Corning Pkwy
Toledo OH 43659
419 248-8000

(G-1009)
PCL FIXTURES INC
Also Called: Packaging Concepts
95 Leggett St Ste 2 (06108-1167)
PHONE.................................401 334-4646
Donald Budnick, *Pr*
▲ **EMP: 23 EST:** 1973
SALES (est): 789.94K **Privately Held**
Web: www.pclfixtures.com
SIC: 2542 Cabinets: show, display, or storage: except wood

(G-1010)
PEENING TECHNOLOGIES EQP LLC
8 Eastern Park Rd (06108-1105)
PHONE.................................860 289-4328
Richard Brooks, *
EMP: 50 EST: 2012
SALES (est): 4.86MM **Privately Held**
Web: www.peentech.com
SIC: 3398 Shot peening (treating steel to reduce fatigue)

(G-1011)
PICTURE THIS HARTFORD INC
Also Called: Hartford Fine Art & Framing Co
80 Pitkin St (06108-3318)
PHONE.................................860 528-1409
William Plage, *Pr*
Lauren Plage, *VP*
EMP: 7 EST: 1981
SQ FT: 9,500
SALES (est): 684.77K **Privately Held**
Web: www.hartfordfineart.com
SIC: 5719 3999 7699 Pictures and mirrors; Framed artwork; General household repair services

(G-1012)
POPCORN MOVIE POSTER CO LLC
Also Called: Popcorn Movie Poster Co
1 Cherry St (06108-3922)
P.O. Box 1121 (06033-6121)
PHONE.................................860 610-0000
EMP: 14 EST: 2001
SQ FT: 4,500
SALES (est): 2.18MM **Privately Held**
Web: www.popcornposters.com
SIC: 2759 Poster and decal printing and engraving

(G-1013)
PRATT & WHITNEY CENCO INC
400 Main St (06108-0968)
PHONE.................................860 565-4321
EMP: 10 EST: 2013
SALES (est): 692.43K **Privately Held**
SIC: 3724 Research and development on aircraft engines and parts

(G-1014)
PRATT & WHITNEY COMPANY INC
Also Called: Middletown Engine Center
400 Main St (06108-0968)
PHONE.................................860 565-4321
Charlesa L Ceres, *Pr*
Alison Erlewein, *
Hendrikje Ganung, *

Stephanie J Weissglas, *Prin*
EMP: 12792 EST: 1986
SALES (est): 491.09MM
SALES (corp-wide): 67.07B **Publicly Held**
Web: www.rtx.com
SIC: 3724 Aircraft engines and engine parts
PA: Rtx Corporation
1000 Wilson Blvd
Arlington VA 22209
781 522-3000

(G-1015)
PRATT & WHITNEY ENG SVCS INC
Also Called: Pratt Whtney Cstmer Trning Ctr
400 Main St (06118-1888)
PHONE.................................860 565-4321
EMP: 27
SALES (corp-wide): 68.92B **Publicly Held**
Web: www.prattwhitney.com
SIC: 3724 Aircraft engines and engine parts
HQ: Pratt & Whitney Engine Services, Inc.
1525 Midway Park Rd
Bridgeport WV 26330
304 842-5421

(G-1016)
PRATT & WHITNEY ENG SVCS INC
Pratt & Whitney Power Systems
411 Silver Ln (06118-1127)
PHONE.................................860 610-7478
Robert Hobbs, *Mgr*
EMP: 43
SALES (corp-wide): 68.92B **Publicly Held**
Web: www.rtx.com
SIC: 3724 8731 Aircraft engines and engine parts; Commercial physical research
HQ: Pratt & Whitney Engine Services, Inc.
1525 Midway Park Rd
Bridgeport WV 26330
304 842-5421

(G-1017)
PRATT & WHITNEY SERVICES INC
400 Main St (06108-0968)
PHONE.................................860 565-5489
Paul Adams, *Pr*
EMP: 98 EST: 2007
SALES (est): 4.42MM
SALES (corp-wide): 67.07B **Publicly Held**
SIC: 3724 Aircraft engines and engine parts
PA: Rtx Corporation
1000 Wilson Blvd
Arlington VA 22209
781 522-3000

(G-1018)
QUEST MACHINING & MFG LLC
333 E River Dr Ste 500 (06108-4201)
PHONE.................................860 290-1145
EMP: 15 EST: 2006
SALES (est): 117.4K **Privately Held**
SIC: 3599 Machine shop, jobbing and repair

(G-1019)
RSL FIBER SYSTEMS LLC
473 Silver Ln (06118-1152)
PHONE.................................860 282-4930
EMP: 13 EST: 2001
SALES (est): 2.47MM **Privately Held**
Web: www.rslfibersystems.com
SIC: 3648 Lighting equipment, nec

(G-1020)
RTX CORPORATION
Also Called: Raytheon Technologies RES Ctr
411 Silver Ln (06118-1127)

PHONE.................................860 610-7000
Phil Podgorski, *CFO*
EMP: 1100
SALES (corp-wide): 67.07B **Publicly Held**
Web: www.rtx.com
SIC: 3724 Aircraft engines and engine parts
PA: Rtx Corporation
1000 Wilson Blvd
Arlington VA 22209
781 522-3000

(G-1021)
RTX CORPORATION
400 Main St (06108-0968)
PHONE.................................860 565-7622
Rick Silva, *Pr*
EMP: 11
SALES (corp-wide): 68.92B **Publicly Held**
Web: www.rtx.com
SIC: 3585 Refrigeration and heating equipment
PA: Rtx Corporation
1000 Wilson Blvd
Arlington VA 22209
781 522-3000

(G-1022)
STANDARD WELDING COMPANY INC
212 Prospect St (06108-1653)
PHONE.................................860 528-9628
Richard Ashlaw, *Pr*
Clifford Wayner, *Treas*
EMP: 9 EST: 1948
SQ FT: 7,000
SALES (est): 504.69K **Privately Held**
Web: www.standardweldingllc.com
SIC: 7692 7549 7513 Welding repair; Trailer maintenance; Truck rental and leasing, no drivers

(G-1023)
STP BINDERY SERVICES INC
265 Prestige Park Rd Ste 2 (06108-1939)
PHONE.................................860 528-1430
Steven Pensiero, *Pr*
EMP: 17 EST: 1986
SQ FT: 25,000
SALES (est): 440.26K **Privately Held**
SIC: 2789 Binding only: books, pamphlets, magazines, etc.

(G-1024)
STRYKER CORPORATION
155 Founders Plz (06108-8313)
PHONE.................................860 528-1111
Vince Morgera, *Brnch Mgr*
EMP: 11
SALES (corp-wide): 18.45B **Publicly Held**
Web: www.stryker.com
SIC: 3841 Surgical and medical instruments
PA: Stryker Corporation
2825 Airview Blvd
Portage MI 49002
269 385-2600

(G-1025)
SUA PRFORMANCE FABRICATION LLC
89 Charles St (06108-2022)
PHONE.................................860 904-6068
Josue Ortiz, *Prin*
EMP: 7 EST: 2013
SALES (est): 47.05K **Privately Held**
SIC: 7692 Welding repair

(G-1026)
TAYLOR COMMUNICATIONS INC
311 Prestige Park Rd (06108-1928)

PHONE.................................860 875-0731
Louis Rozie, *Brnch Mgr*
EMP: 13
SALES (corp-wide): 3.81B **Privately Held**
Web: www.taylor.com
SIC: 2761 Manifold business forms
HQ: Taylor Communications, Inc.
1725 Roe Crest Dr
North Mankato MN 56003
866 541-0937

(G-1027)
THEBEAMER LLC
87 Church St (06108-3720)
PHONE.................................860 212-5071
Peter Solomon, *CEO*
EMP: 17 EST: 2014
SQ FT: 400
SALES (est): 773.37K **Privately Held**
Web: www.thestardustmystery.com
SIC: 7372 Educational computer software

(G-1028)
TOTAL COMMUNICATIONS INC (PA)
333 Burnham St (06108-1183)
PHONE.................................860 282-9999
TOLL FREE: 800
Scott Lennon, *Pr*
EMP: 100 EST: 1980
SQ FT: 24,000
SALES (est): 53.76MM
SALES (corp-wide): 53.76MM **Privately Held**
Web: www.totalcomm.com
SIC: 3661 5065 7629 Telephone and telegraph apparatus; Telephone equipment; Telephone set repair

(G-1029)
TRENTO GROUP LLC
Also Called: Plastech Manufacturing
400 Governor St (06108-3925)
P.O. Box 997 (06088-0997)
PHONE.................................860 623-1361
Emanuele Mangiafico, *Brnch Mgr*
EMP: 9
SALES (corp-wide): 72.7K **Privately Held**
Web: www.plasticoidmfg.com
SIC: 3089 Injection molding of plastics
PA: Trento Group Llc
147 Mountain Spring Rd
Farmington CT

(G-1030)
UNAS GRINDING CORPORATION
28 Cherry St (06108-2010)
P.O. Box 280535 (06128-0535)
PHONE.................................860 289-1538
John Orzech, *Pr*
Greg Endrelunas, *
EMP: 30 EST: 1952
SQ FT: 18,500
SALES (est): 4.04MM **Privately Held**
Web: www.unasgrinding.com
SIC: 3599 Grinding castings for the trade

(G-1031)
UNCLE SAMS CONTRACTORS LLC (PA)
290 Roberts St Ste 302 (06108-3692)
PHONE.................................833 487-2776
EMP: 17 EST: 2012
SALES (est): 2.5MM
SALES (corp-wide): 2.5MM **Privately Held**
Web: www.unclesamscontractors.com
SIC: 3589 Commercial cleaning equipment

GEOGRAPHIC

(G-1032)
UNITED STEEL INC
Also Called: United Steel Erectors
164 School St (06108-1867)
PHONE..........................860 289-2323
Keith Corneau, *Pr*
Glen Corneau, *
Lynn M Caouette, *
EMP: 150 EST: 1979
SQ FT: 122,500
SALES (est): 65.86MM **Privately Held**
Web: www.unitedsteel.com
SIC: 3441 3443 3446 3444 Fabricated
structural metal; Fabricated plate work
(boiler shop); Ornamental metalwork; Sheet
metalwork

(G-1033)
WALTER A BEACH INC
8 Eastern Park Rd (06108-1105)
PHONE..........................860 282-7440
Walter A Beach, *Pr*
EMP: 7 EST: 2001
SQ FT: 20,948
SALES (est): 109.66K **Privately Held**
Web: www.peentech.com
SIC: 3398 Metal heat treating

East Haven
New Haven County

(G-1034)
ABC PRINTING INC
Also Called: A B C Printing & Mailing
875 Foxon Rd (06513-1837)
PHONE..........................203 468-1245
Salvatore L Vadala, *Pr*
Salvatore A Vadala Junior, *VP*
Julie Vadala, *Clerk*
EMP: 10 EST: 1971
SQ FT: 3,200
SALES (est): 1.63MM **Privately Held**
Web: www.abcprintingink.com
SIC: 2752 Offset printing

(G-1035)
ANGELOS ALUMINUM
55 Thompson St Apt 14g (06513-1942)
PHONE..........................203 469-3117
Angelo Tammaro, *Prin*
EMP: 7 EST: 2002
SALES (est): 178.92K **Privately Held**
SIC: 3334 Primary aluminum

(G-1036)
ASSOCIATED X-RAY CORP (PA)
Also Called: Advanced Control Systems Div
246 Dodge Ave (06512-3305)
P.O. Box 120559 (06512-0559)
PHONE..........................203 466-2446
Gary Johnson, *Pr*
EMP: 15 EST: 1988
SQ FT: 23,000
SALES (est): 2.61MM
SALES (corp-wide): 2.61MM **Privately
Held**
Web: www.axrcorp.com
SIC: 5047 3844 X-ray machines and tubes;
X-ray apparatus and tubes

(G-1037)
BARDELL PRINTING CORP
Also Called: Bardell Office Sty & Sups
42 Michael St (06513-1811)
PHONE..........................203 469-2441
Frank Gambardella, *Pr*
Adeline Gambardella, *VP*
Anthony Gambardella, *VP*

Gary Gambardella, *CFO*
EMP: 7 EST: 1978
SQ FT: 6,000
SALES (est): 868.91K **Privately Held**
Web:
www.bardellprintingandofficesupplies.com
SIC: 2752 Offset printing

(G-1038)
**CALABRO CHEESE
CORPORATION**
580 Coe Ave (06512-3850)
PHONE..........................203 469-1311
TOLL FREE: 800
EMP: 95 EST: 1951
SALES (est): 18.49MM **Privately Held**
Web: www.calabrocheese.com
SIC: 2022 Cheese; natural and processed

(G-1039)
CURRENT INC (PA)
Also Called: Current Composites
30 Tyler Street Ext (06512-3025)
P.O. Box 120183 (06512-0183)
PHONE..........................203 469-1337
▲ **EMP: 77 EST:** 1962
SALES (est): 11.74MM
SALES (corp-wide): 11.74MM **Privately
Held**
Web: www.currentcomposites.com
SIC: 3083 2821 Laminated plastics plate
and sheet; Thermosetting materials

(G-1040)
EAST SHORE WIRE ROPE
5 Old Bradley St (06512-2344)
P.O. Box 308 (06473-0308)
PHONE..........................203 469-5204
EMP: 7 EST: 2010
SALES (est): 612.94K **Privately Held**
SIC: 3462 Iron and steel forgings

(G-1041)
EDAL INDUSTRIES INC
51 Commerce St (06512-4113)
PHONE..........................203 467-2591
Andrew Esposito, *Pr*
Pat Lauria, *
▲ **EMP: 23 EST:** 1958
SQ FT: 14,000
SALES (est): 2.6MM **Privately Held**
Web: www.edal.com
SIC: 3679 3674 Rectifiers, electronic;
Semiconductors and related devices

(G-1042)
FOXON PARK BEVERAGES INC
103 Foxon Blvd (06513-1871)
PHONE..........................203 467-7874
Anthony M Naclerio, *Pr*
Raymond Naclerio, *Sec*
EMP: 8 EST: 1922
SQ FT: 6,500
SALES (est): 919.05K **Privately Held**
Web: www.foxonpark.com
SIC: 2086 Soft drinks: packaged in cans,
bottles, etc.

(G-1043)
FYC APPAREL GROUP LLC
Donno Ricco
158 Commerce St (06512-4145)
PHONE..........................203 466-6525
Maia Chiatt, *Pr*
EMP: 27
SIC: 2331 Women's and misses' blouses
and shirts
PA: Fyc Apparel Group, Llc
30 Thompson Rd
Branford CT 06405

(G-1044)
LDA CONSTRUCTION LLC
459 Main St (06512-2745)
PHONE..........................203 469-3180
Yamile Valdez, *Prin*
EMP: 12 EST: 2017
SALES (est): 1.17MM **Privately Held**
SIC: 3271 Concrete block and brick

(G-1045)
MASAS USA INC
192 Commerce St (06512-4145)
PHONE..........................305 603-8868
EMP: 49 EST: 1988
SQ FT: 15,000
SALES (est): 6.94MM **Privately Held**
SIC: 1541 2095 5499 2082 Food products
manufacturing or packing plant construction
; Coffee roasting (except by wholesale
grocers); Coffee; Malt beverages

(G-1046)
MILBAR LABS INC
20 Commerce St (06512-4145)
PHONE..........................203 467-1577
Mary Ann Emswiler, *CEO*
Edward A Zelinsky, *Sec*
Susan S Lamar, *Treas*
▲ **EMP: 15 EST:** 1988
SQ FT: 36,000
SALES (est): 4.91MM
SALES (corp-wide): 4.91MM **Privately
Held**
Web: www.dclskincare.com
SIC: 2844 Cosmetic preparations
PA: Dermatologic Cosmetic Laboratories
Ltd.
20 Commerce St
East Haven CT 06512
800 552-5060

(G-1047)
**NATIONAL SCREW
MANUFACTURING**
259 Commerce St (06512-4147)
PHONE..........................203 469-7109
Cahrles Hirsch, *Pr*
William Feingold, *VP*
Joan Hirsch, *Sec*
EMP: 15 EST: 1970
SALES (est): 198.28K **Privately Held**
SIC: 3541 Boring mills

(G-1048)
NEW HAVEN COMPANIES INC
41 Washington Ave (06512-3768)
PHONE..........................203 469-6421
EMP: 15
Web: www.newhaven-usa.com
SIC: 2299 3625 5012 3537 Pads, fiber:
henequen, sisal, istle; Control equipment,
electric; Automobiles and other motor
vehicles; Industrial trucks and tractors
PA: The New Haven Companies Inc
4820 Suthpoint Dr Ste 102
Fredericksburg VA 22407

(G-1049)
OEM DESIGN SERVICES LLC
34 Panagrosi St (06512-4143)
P.O. Box 120206 (06512-0206)
PHONE..........................203 467-5993
EMP: 9 EST: 2003
SQ FT: 4,000
SALES (est): 912.53K **Privately Held**
Web: www.oemdesignservices.com
SIC: 7699 3577 Industrial machinery and
equipment repair; Input/output equipment,
computer

(G-1050)
**SHORELINE METAL SERVICES
LLC**
250 Dodge Ave (06512-3360)
PHONE..........................203 466-7372
EMP: 8 EST: 2002
SQ FT: 10,000
SALES (est): 980.78K **Privately Held**
Web: www.shorelinemetalservices.com
SIC: 3444 Sheet metalwork

(G-1051)
SPECTRUM PRESS
Also Called: Spectrum Graphix
875 Foxon Rd (06513-1837)
PHONE..........................203 878-9090
Peter J Bonaventure, *Pt*
Kim Bonaventure, *Pt*
EMP: 15 EST: 1991
SALES (est): 1.66MM **Privately Held**
SIC: 2752 Offset printing

(G-1052)
**STEAD-FAST CUSTOM LININGS
LLC**
641 Main St (06512-2088)
PHONE..........................203 466-8000
TOLL FREE: 877
EMP: 10 EST: 1999
SALES (est): 1.01MM **Privately Held**
Web: www.steadfastlinings.com
SIC: 3563 5531 Spraying and dusting
equipment; Truck equipment and parts

(G-1053)
THERMATOOL CORP (HQ)
31 Commerce St (06512-4172)
PHONE..........................203 468-4100
Michael A Nallen, *Pr*
Laurence Krupnick, *
◆ **EMP: 65 EST:** 1952
SQ FT: 75,000
SALES (est): 28.14MM
SALES (corp-wide): 645.5MM **Privately
Held**
Web: www.thermatool.com
SIC: 3599 Machine shop, jobbing and repair
PA: Inductotherm Group, Llc
10 Indel Ave
Rancocas NJ 08073
609 267-9000

(G-1054)
**THOMSON REUTERS
CORPORATION**
250 Dodge Ave (06512-3360)
PHONE..........................203 466-5055
Estim Pop Lazarov, *Brnch Mgr*
EMP: 24
SALES (corp-wide): 10.66B **Publicly Held**
Web: www.thomsonreuters.com
SIC: 2741 Miscellaneous publishing
HQ: Thomson Reuters Corporation
333 Bay St
Toronto ON M5H 2
416 687-7500

(G-1055)
TOTAL FAB LLC
Also Called: Total Fab
140 Commerce St (06512-4145)
PHONE..........................475 238-8176
Fred Moore Junior, *Managing Member*
EMP: 10 EST: 2000
SQ FT: 3,500
SALES (est): 1.28MM **Privately Held**
Web: www.totalfabllc.com
SIC: 3441 7692 Fabricated structural metal;
Welding repair

(G-1056)
WEARSPF LLC
20 Commerce St (06512-4145)
PHONE...............................203 466-4616
Richard Dentis, *CEO*
Tim Daly, *COO*
EMP: 8 **EST:** 2021
SALES (est): 250K **Privately Held**
SIC: 2844 Cosmetic preparations

(G-1057)
XTREME DESIGNS LLC
330 Main St (06512-2920)
PHONE...............................203 773-9303
EMP: 8 **EST:** 2002
SALES (est): 656.96K **Privately Held**
Web: www.xtremedesignsnh.com
SIC: 7336 2759 Graphic arts and related design; Screen printing

East Lyme
New London County

(G-1058)
BIRK MANUFACTURING INC
14 Capitol Dr (06333-1452)
PHONE...............................800 531-2070
Norman Birk, *Pr*
Howard Birk, *
▲ **EMP:** 95 **EST:** 1989
SQ FT: 32,000
SALES (est): 11.98MM **Privately Held**
Web: www.birkmfg.com
SIC: 3567 Heating units and devices, industrial: electric

(G-1059)
HAYES SERVICES LLC
15 Colton Rd (06333-1436)
P.O. Box 365 (06333-0365)
PHONE...............................860 739-2273
Kurt J Hayes, *CEO*
EMP: 22 **EST:** 2003
SALES (est): 948.28K **Privately Held**
Web: www.hayesservicesct.com
SIC: 0781 3443 4959 Landscape services; Dumpsters, garbage; Snowplowing

(G-1060)
PAW PRINT PANTRY LLC (PA)
33 Gurley Rd (06333-1713)
PHONE...............................860 447-8442
Jennifer Mohr, *Owner*
EMP: 7 **EST:** 2013
SALES (est): 192.7K
SALES (corp-wide): 192.7K **Privately Held**
Web: www.pawprintpantry.com
SIC: 2752 Commercial printing, lithographic

(G-1061)
PHESI INC
6 Applewood Cmn (06333-1444)
PHONE...............................800 679-0068
General Li, *Pr*
Jonathan Peachey, *COO*
Paul Chew, *CMO*
Guoqiang Wu, *CIO*
EMP: 8 **EST:** 2019
SALES (est): 204.69K **Privately Held**
Web: www.phesi.com
SIC: 7372 Application computer software

(G-1062)
R-D MFG INC
6 Colton Rd (06333-1435)
PHONE...............................860 739-3986
Louis N Tashash, *Pr*
Nancy A Tashash, *Sec*
EMP: 12 **EST:** 1984
SQ FT: 13,000
SALES (est): 1.85MM **Privately Held**
Web: www.rdmfginc.com
SIC: 3444 Sheet metal specialties, not stamped

East Windsor
Hartford County

(G-1063)
A HARDIMAN MACHINE CO INC
94 Newberry Rd (06088-9544)
PHONE...............................860 623-8133
John Gould, *Pr*
Suzanne J Barstis, *VP*
EMP: 8 **EST:** 1945
SALES (est): 582.83K **Privately Held**
Web: www.hardiman.com
SIC: 3599 Machine shop, jobbing and repair

(G-1064)
AEROCOR INC
59 Newberry Rd (06088-9631)
P.O. Box 567 (06088-0567)
PHONE...............................860 281-9274
Marc Corallo, *Prin*
Daniel Corallo, *Prin*
Erica Poulin, *Prin*
EMP: 12 **EST:** 2019
SALES (est): 901.09K **Privately Held**
Web: www.aerocorinc.com
SIC: 3444 Sheet metalwork

(G-1065)
ALS BEVERAGE COMPANY INC
13 Revay Rd (06088-9688)
PHONE...............................860 627-7003
Gerald E Martin, *Pr*
Marjorie Feldman, *Pr*
EMP: 20 **EST:** 1955
SQ FT: 11,000
SALES (est): 4.9MM
SALES (corp-wide): 24.87MM **Privately Held**
Web: www.alsbeverage.com
SIC: 2086 2095 Carbonated beverages, nonalcoholic: pkged. in cans, bottles; Roasted coffee
PA: Al's Holding Inc
13 Revay Rd
East Windsor CT 06088
860 627-7003

(G-1066)
BASF CATALYSTS LLC
12 Thompson Rd (06088-9696)
PHONE...............................860 623-9901
EMP: 80
SALES (corp-wide): 90.7B **Privately Held**
Web: catalysts.basf.com
SIC: 2869 Industrial organic chemicals, nec
HQ: Basf Catalysts Llc
33 Wood Ave S
Iselin NJ 08830
732 205-5000

(G-1067)
BETHUNE NONWOVENS INC
Also Called: Suominen Nonwovens
1 Hartfield Blvd Ste 101 (06088-9500)
PHONE...............................860 386-8001
Nina Kopola, *CEO*
◆ **EMP:** 120 **EST:** 2011
SALES (est): 32.2MM
SALES (corp-wide): 512.33MM **Privately Held**
SIC: 2843 2297 Textile finishing agents; Nonwoven fabrics

HQ: Suominen Us Holding, Inc.
1 Hartfield Blvd Ste 101
East Windsor CT 06088
860 386-8001

(G-1068)
BLUE BELL MATTRESS COMPANY LLC (HQ)
Also Called: King Koil Northeast
24 Thompson Rd (06088-9698)
PHONE...............................860 292-6372
Derek Ritzel, *Pr*
Mark J Kolovson, *
Steven D Byer, *
◆ **EMP:** 36 **EST:** 1911
SQ FT: 100,000
SALES (est): 49.54MM
SALES (corp-wide): 53.78MM **Privately Held**
Web: www.bluebellmattress.com
SIC: 2515 6722 Mattresses, innerspring or box spring; Management investment, open-end
PA: Landon Capital Partners, Llc
21 Custom House St # 700
Boston MA 02110
617 412-2700

(G-1069)
BRICKENMORE EAST LLC
9 Thompson Rd (06088-9695)
P.O. Box 134 (06029-0134)
PHONE...............................860 906-6116
Michael Richey, *Ofcr*
Cynthia Richey, *Prin*
EMP: 19 **EST:** 2014
SQ FT: 25,000
SALES (est): 1.14MM **Privately Held**
Web: www.verna-mae.com
SIC: 2869 Industrial organic chemicals, nec

(G-1070)
CURTISS-WRIGHT CORPORATION
12 Thompson Rd (06088-9696)
PHONE...............................864 486-9311
Edward Mychaskiw, *Mgr*
EMP: 9
SALES (corp-wide): 2.56B **Publicly Held**
Web: www.curtisswright.com
SIC: 3491 Industrial valves
PA: Curtiss-Wright Corporation
130 Harbour Place Dr # 300
Davidson NC 28036
704 869-4600

(G-1071)
DRI-AIR INDUSTRIES INC
Also Called: Dri-Air Industries
16 Thompson Rd (06088-9696)
P.O. Box 1020 (06088-1020)
PHONE...............................860 627-5110
Jason Sears, *Pr*
Charles F Sears Junior, *Pr*
Esther Sears, *
EMP: 26 **EST:** 1985
SQ FT: 20,000
SALES (est): 6.26MM **Privately Held**
Web: www.dri-air.com
SIC: 3567 3537 Driers and redriers, industrial process; Industrial trucks and tractors

(G-1072)
EBTEC CORPORATION
68 Prospect Hill Rd (06088-9667)
PHONE...............................860 789-2462
EMP: 77 **EST:** 1969
SALES (est): 19.25MM **Privately Held**
Web: ebtec.hanwhaaerospaceusa.com

SIC: 3699 7692 Electron beam metal cutting, forming or welding machines; Welding repair
HQ: Hanwha Aerospace Usa Llc
5 Mckee Pl
Cheshire CT 06410
203 806-2090

(G-1073)
ESSEL DENTAL
44 S Main St Ste 14 (06088-1702)
PHONE...............................860 254-6955
Doctor Rakesh Kumar D.d.s., *Prin*
EMP: 8 **EST:** 2015
SALES (est): 240.68K **Privately Held**
Web: www.dentistinavonct.com
SIC: 6324 3843 8021 Dental insurance; Drills, dental; Dental clinic

(G-1074)
HANWHA AEROSPACE USA LLC
Edac Machinery
68 Prospect Hill Dr (06088-9640)
PHONE...............................860 789-2500
James Telletier, *Mgr*
EMP: 20
Web: www.hanwhaaerospaceusa.com
SIC: 3724 Aircraft engines and engine parts
HQ: Hanwha Aerospace Usa Llc
5 Mckee Pl
Cheshire CT 06410
203 806-2090

(G-1075)
HANWHA AEROSPACE USA LLC
68 Prospect Hill Rd (06088-9667)
PHONE...............................860 789-2511
EMP: 60
Web: www.hanwhaaerospaceusa.com
SIC: 3769 3541 3724 Space vehicle equipment, nec; Machine tools, metal cutting type; Aircraft engines and engine parts
HQ: Hanwha Aerospace Usa Llc
5 Mckee Pl
Cheshire CT 06410
203 806-2090

(G-1076)
HOMELAND FUNDRAISING
Also Called: Kelleher Marketing
38 Borrup Rd (06088-9605)
PHONE...............................860 386-6698
Kevin Kelleher, *Owner*
EMP: 7 **EST:** 2001
SQ FT: 2,300
SALES (est): 265.84K **Privately Held**
Web: www.homelandfundraising.com
SIC: 3949 Sporting and athletic goods, nec

(G-1077)
JMF GROUP LLC
Also Called: Al's Beverage Company
13 Revay Rd (06088-9688)
PHONE...............................860 627-7003
TOLL FREE: 888
EMP: 55 **EST:** 1996
SALES (est): 3.52MM **Privately Held**
Web: www.alsbeverage.com
SIC: 2087 5149 Beverage bases, concentrates, syrups, powders and mixes; Groceries and related products, nec

(G-1078)
KINETIC TOOL CO INC
5 Craftsman Rd Ste 7 (06088-9617)
PHONE...............................860 627-5882
Jonathan Cherpak, *Pr*
EMP: 18 **EST:** 1978
SQ FT: 4,000

SALES (est): 771.09K **Privately Held**
Web: www.kinetictoolco.com
SIC: 3545   Cutting tools for machine tools

(G-1079)
KTI INC (HQ)
3 Thompson Rd (06088-9695)
P.O. Box 658 (06088-0658)
PHONE..............................860 623-2511
Howard Orr, *Ch*
▲ **EMP:** 9 **EST:** 1966
SQ FT: 30,000
SALES (est): 2.24MM
SALES (corp-wide): 2.24MM **Privately Held**
Web: www.theperfectweld.com
SIC: 7692   Welding repair
PA: Applied Energy Corporation
    33 East St Ste 4
    Winchester MA
    781 756-1216

(G-1080)
MERCURY-EXCELUM INC
215 S Main St (06088-9701)
PHONE..............................860 292-1800
EMP: 30 **EST:** 1953
SALES (est): 6.43MM **Privately Held**
Web: www.mercuryexcelum.com
SIC: 3442 3089 5033   Screen and storm doors and windows; Windows, plastics; Siding, except wood

(G-1081)
METAL IMPROVEMENT COMPANY LLC
Curtiss-Wright Surface Tech
12 Thompson Rd (06088-9696)
PHONE..............................860 523-9901
Peter Ruggiero, *Brnch Mgr*
EMP: 70
SALES (corp-wide): 2.56B **Publicly Held**
Web: www.curtisswright.com
SIC: 3398   Shot peening (treating steel to reduce fatigue)
HQ: Metal Improvement Company, Llc
    80 E Rte 4 Ste 310
    Paramus NJ 07652
    201 843-7800

(G-1082)
MLS ACQ INC
Also Called: Max Analytical Technologies
32 North Rd (06088-9627)
P.O. Box 390 (06088-0390)
PHONE..............................860 386-6878
Anthony Smith, *Pr*
EMP: 10 **EST:** 2017
SALES (est): 1.88MM
SALES (corp-wide): 44.91B **Publicly Held**
Web: www.maxanalytical.com
SIC: 3826   Analytical instruments
PA: Thermo Fisher Scientific Inc.
    168 3rd Ave
    Waltham MA 02451
    781 622-1000

(G-1083)
R&R TOOL & DIE LLC
Also Called: R&R Tool & Die
94 Newberry Rd (06088-9544)
PHONE..............................860 627-9197
EMP: 8 **EST:** 1995
SQ FT: 2,000
SALES (est): 988.2K **Privately Held**
Web: www.rrtooldie.com
SIC: 3545 3544   Diamond cutting tools for turning, boring, burnishing, etc.; Industrial molds

(G-1084)
ROTO-DIE COMPANY INC
Also Called: Preston Engravers
7d Pasco Dr (06088-1707)
PHONE..............................860 292-7030
EMP: 33
SALES (corp-wide): 99.99MM **Privately Held**
Web: www.maxcessintl.com
SIC: 3944 2759 3544   Games, toys, and children's vehicles; Commercial printing, nec; Special dies, tools, jigs, and fixtures
PA: Roto-Die Company, Inc.
    800 Howerton Ln
    Eureka MO 63025
    636 587-3600

(G-1085)
SHOHAM MANUFACTURING INC
Also Called: P M I
32 North Rd Rear (06088-9627)
P.O. Box 450 (06088-0450)
PHONE..............................860 623-1361
Jonathan Shoham, *Pr*
Robert Shoham, *Pr*
Daniel Shoham, *VP*
▲ **EMP:** 18 **EST:** 1976
SQ FT: 16,200
SALES (est): 897.64K **Privately Held**
Web: www.spacetoys.com
SIC: 3089   Injection molding of plastics

(G-1086)
SPECIALTY PRINTING LLC
15 Thompson Rd (06088-9697)
PHONE..............................860 654-1850
EMP: 10
SALES (corp-wide): 26.86MM **Privately Held**
Web: www.specialtyprinting.net
SIC: 2752   Offset printing
PA: Specialty Printing, Llc
    123 Day Hill Rd
    Windsor CT 06095
    860 623-8870

(G-1087)
SUOMINEN US HOLDING INC (HQ)
1 Hartfield Blvd Ste 101 (06088-9500)
P.O. Box 418 (06096-0418)
PHONE..............................860 386-8001
John Bigos, *Pr*
▲ **EMP:** 20 **EST:** 2011
SALES (est): 103.62MM
SALES (corp-wide): 512.33MM **Privately Held**
Web: www.suominen.fi
SIC: 2297   Nonwoven fabrics
PA: Suominen Oyj
    Karvaamokuja 2b
    Helsinki 00380
    10214300

(G-1088)
TITANIUM METALS CORPORATION
Also Called: Timet
7 Craftsman Rd (06088-9685)
P.O. Box 2128 (89009-7003)
PHONE..............................860 627-7051
Phil Macvain, *Mgr*
EMP: 111
SQ FT: 22,000
SALES (corp-wide): 302.09B **Publicly Held**
Web: www.timet.com
SIC: 3356 5051   Nonferrous rolling and drawing, nec; Metals service centers and offices

HQ: Titanium Metals Corporation
    4832 Richmond Rd Ste 100
    Warrensville Heights OH 44128
    740 537-5600

(G-1089)
W B MASON CO INC
43 North Rd (06088-9523)
PHONE..............................888 926-2766
EMP: 68
SALES (corp-wide): 1.01B **Privately Held**
Web: www.wbmason.com
SIC: 5943 5712 2752   Office forms and supplies; Office furniture; Commercial printing, lithographic
PA: W. B. Mason Co., Inc.
    59 Centre Street
    Brockton MA 02301
    508 586-3434

(G-1090)
WINDSOR LOCKS NONWOVENS INC (DH)
Also Called: Suominen Nonwoven
1 Hartfield Blvd Ste 101 (06088-9500)
PHONE..............................860 292-5600
Nina Kopola, *CEO*
Petri Rolig, *
John Bigos, *
◆ **EMP:** 16 **EST:** 2011
SQ FT: 312,000
SALES (est): 27.92MM
SALES (corp-wide): 512.33MM **Privately Held**
Web: www.suominen.fi
SIC: 2297   Nonwoven fabrics
HQ: Suominen Us Holding, Inc.
    1 Hartfield Blvd Ste 101
    East Windsor CT 06088
    860 386-8001

Eastford
Windham County

(G-1091)
INDUSTRIAL PALLET LLC
27 Chaplin Rd (06242-9439)
P.O. Box 389 (06242-0389)
PHONE..............................860 974-0093
▲ **EMP:** 63 **EST:** 1988
SQ FT: 51,000
SALES (est): 9.88MM
SALES (corp-wide): 604.77MM **Privately Held**
SIC: 2448   Pallets, wood
PA: 48forty Solutions, Llc
    11740 Katy Fwy Ste 12
    Houston TX 77079
    678 722-3984

(G-1092)
SS FABRICATIONS INC
82 County Rd (06242-7700)
P.O. Box 37 (06242-0037)
PHONE..............................860 974-1910
David Buchholz Junior, *Pr*
EMP: 8 **EST:** 1976
SQ FT: 3,000
SALES (est): 480.04K **Privately Held**
Web: www.ssfabrications.com
SIC: 7692 3599   Welding repair; Machine shop, jobbing and repair

(G-1093)
WHITCRAFT LLC (PA)
Also Called: Pursuit Aerospace
76 County Rd (06242-7700)
P.O. Box 128 (06242-0128)

PHONE..............................860 974-0786
Colin Cooper, *CEO*
Jeff Paul, *Pr*
▲ **EMP:** 187 **EST:** 1960
SQ FT: 63,200
SALES (est): 139.19MM
SALES (corp-wide): 139.19MM **Privately Held**
Web: www.whitcraft.com
SIC: 3443 3444 3728   Weldments; Sheet metalwork; Aircraft parts and equipment, nec

(G-1094)
WHITCRAFT SCRBOROUGH/ TEMPE LLC (HQ)
76 County Rd (06242-7700)
PHONE..............................860 974-0786
Colin Cooper, *CEO*
EMP: 42 **EST:** 2019
SALES (est): 46.2MM
SALES (corp-wide): 139.19MM **Privately Held**
SIC: 3728 3443 3444   Aircraft parts and equipment, nec; Weldments; Sheet metalwork
PA: Whitcraft Llc
    76 County Rd
    Eastford CT 06242
    860 974-0786

Easton
Fairfield County

(G-1095)
FAIRFIELD MARKETING GROUP INC (PA)
830 Sport Hill Rd (06612-1241)
P.O. Box 299 (06612-0299)
PHONE..............................203 261-0884
Ed Washchilla, *Pr*
Pamela Washchilla, *Treas*
Jason Miller, *Ofcr*
Ed Washchilla Senior, *Ofcr*
EMP: 12 **EST:** 1986
SALES (est): 2.29MM
SALES (corp-wide): 2.29MM **Privately Held**
Web: www.fairfieldmarketing.com
SIC: 8742 8743 7331 2791   Marketing consulting services; Sales promotion; Direct mail advertising services; Typesetting

(G-1096)
MARITIME ACTIVITY REPORTS (PA)
60 Herrmann Ln (06612-1048)
PHONE..............................212 477-6700
John C O'malley, *VP*
EMP: 19 **EST:** 1939
SALES (est): 4.83MM
SALES (corp-wide): 4.83MM **Privately Held**
Web: www.marinelink.com
SIC: 2721   Magazines: publishing only, not printed on site

(G-1097)
POLARIS MANAGEMENT INC
30 Silver Hill Rd (06612-1114)
PHONE..............................203 261-6399
Robert G George, *Pr*
Matthew Simpson, *VP*
EMP: 7 **EST:** 2009
SALES (est): 117.61K **Privately Held**
SIC: 3621   Generating apparatus and parts, electrical

▲ = Import ▼ = Export
◆ = Import/Export

(G-1098)
WENDON COMPANY INC
16 Wimbledon Ln (06612-1238)
EMP: 18 **EST:** 1961
SALES (est): 3.34MM **Privately Held**
Web: www.wendon.net
SIC: 3599 Machine shop, jobbing and repair

Ellington
Tolland County

(G-1099)
ALL STEEL LLC
240 Crystal Lake Rd (06029-3406)
PHONE...............................860 871-6023
Eben J Holmes, *Managing Member*
EMP: 7 **EST:** 2008
SALES (est): 1.23MM **Privately Held**
SIC: 3334 Pigs, aluminum

(G-1100)
ALLYN TOOL COMPANY
164 Maple St (06029-3330)
PHONE...............................860 979-0041
EMP: 8 **EST:** 1944
SALES (est): 635.64K **Privately Held**
Web: www.allyntool.com
SIC: 3599 Machine shop, jobbing and repair

(G-1101)
ARROW DIVERSIFIED TOOLING INC
17 Pinney St (06029-3812)
P.O. Box 508 (06029-0508)
PHONE...............................860 872-9072
David Trench, *Pr*
EMP: 22 **EST:** 1970
SQ FT: 13,000
SALES (est): 1.97MM **Privately Held**
Web: www.arrowdiversified.com
SIC: 3544 3363 3542 3543 Special dies and tools; Aluminum die-castings; Machine tools, metal forming type; Industrial patterns

(G-1102)
BERGSON TIRE CO INC
40 West Rd (06029-4200)
P.O. Box 453 (06066-0453)
PHONE...............................860 872-7729
James B Wood, *Pr*
C Perry Chilberg, *
EMP: 11 **EST:** 1973
SQ FT: 46,000
SALES (est): 213.13K **Privately Held**
Web: www.bergsontire.com
SIC: 7534 5014 Tire recapping; Truck tires and tubes

(G-1103)
COUNTRY PURE FOODS INC
58 West Rd (06029-4200)
PHONE...............................330 753-2293
Kim Wilford, *Mgr*
EMP: 106
Web: www.countrypure.com
SIC: 2099 Food preparations, nec
PA: Country Pure Foods, Inc.
222 S Main St Ste 401
Akron OH 44308

(G-1104)
DYMOTEK CORPORATION
7 Main St (06029-3317)
PHONE...............................860 875-2868
Steven R Trueb, *Pr*
Thomas W Trueb, *
◆ **EMP:** 50 **EST:** 1990
SQ FT: 35,000

SALES (est): 11.87MM **Privately Held**
Web: www.dymotek.com
SIC: 3089 Injection molding of plastics

(G-1105)
ELLINGTON PRINTERY INC
Also Called: Med Print
25 West Rd Ste B (06029-4260)
P.O. Box 219 (06029-0219)
PHONE...............................860 875-3310
Carol White, *Pr*
EMP: 7 **EST:** 1984
SQ FT: 2,000
SALES (est): 525.54K **Privately Held**
Web: www.ellingtonprintery.com
SIC: 2752 Offset printing

(G-1106)
FLITSAI INC
3 Oak Hill Farms Rd (06029-4329)
PHONE...............................203 586-8201
Avishek Ganguly, *Prin*
EMP: 10
SALES (est): 378.96K **Privately Held**
SIC: 7372 7389 Business oriented computer software; Business services, nec

(G-1107)
FORTIS SOLUTIONS GROUP LLC
374 Somers Rd (06029-2628)
PHONE...............................860 872-6311
EMP: 40
Web: www.fortissolutionsgroup.com
SIC: 5131 5113 5084 2671 Labels; Boxes and containers; Processing and packaging equipment; Paper; coated and laminated packaging
PA: Fortis Solutions Group, Llc
2505 Hawkeye Ct
Virginia Beach VA 23452

(G-1108)
FOUNDATION CIGAR COMPANY LLC
Also Called: Foundation Cigar
78 Abbott Rd (06029-3602)
PHONE...............................203 738-9377
Nicholas Melillo, *Managing Member*
EMP: 7 **EST:** 2015
SALES (est): 987.39K **Privately Held**
Web: www.foundationcigarcompany.com
SIC: 2121 5194 5993 Cigars; Cigarettes; Cigar store

(G-1109)
MAYARC INDUSTRIES INC
54 Minor Hill Rd (06029-3107)
PHONE...............................860 871-1872
Mark Minor, *Prin*
Matthew Minor, *Pr*
EMP: 7 **EST:** 2005
SALES (est): 463.31K **Privately Held**
SIC: 3441 Fabricated structural metal

(G-1110)
MERCO INC
26 Village St (06029-3815)
P.O. Box 150 (06029-0150)
PHONE...............................860 871-1888
Merrill Lieberman, *Pr*
Bernard Lieberman, *VP*
EMP: 38 **EST:** 1968
SQ FT: 80,000
SALES (est): 4.76MM **Privately Held**
Web: www.merrillindustries.com
SIC: 2653 2441 3086 Boxes, corrugated: made from purchased materials; Boxes, wood; Plastics foam products

(G-1111)
MERRILL INDUSTRIES LLC
26 Village St (06029-3815)
P.O. Box 150 (06029-0150)
PHONE...............................860 871-1888
Albert Gardiner, *VP*
Richard Cobuzzi, *
EMP: 25 **EST:** 2012
SALES (est): 2.6MM **Privately Held**
Web: www.merrillind.com
SIC: 2653 Boxes, corrugated: made from purchased materials

(G-1112)
NATURAL COUNTRY FARMS INC
Also Called: Country Pure Foods
58 West Rd (06029-4200)
PHONE...............................860 872-8346
Bernie Garow, *Mgr*
EMP: 178
SQ FT: 80,000
Web: www.countrypure.com
SIC: 4222 2086 2033 Warehousing, cold storage or refrigerated; Bottled and canned soft drinks; Canned fruits and specialties
HQ: Natural Country Farms, Inc.
681 W Waterloo Rd
Akron OH 44314
330 753-2293

(G-1113)
RICE PACKAGING INC
356 Somers Rd (06029-2628)
PHONE...............................860 870-7057
Clifford Rice, *Pr*
William A Rice, *
▲ **EMP:** 100 **EST:** 1964
SQ FT: 95,000
SALES (est): 19.17MM **Privately Held**
Web: www.ricepackaging.com
SIC: 2657 2653 2652 2631 Folding paperboard boxes; Corrugated and solid fiber boxes; Setup paperboard boxes; Paperboard mills

(G-1114)
SEALS-IT INC
164 Maple St (06029-3330)
PHONE...............................860 979-0060
EMP: 9 **EST:** 2020
SALES (est): 624.02K **Privately Held**
Web: www.sealsit.com
SIC: 8711 7539 5085 3545 Engineering services; Automotive repair shops, nec; Industrial supplies; Machine tool accessories

(G-1115)
SJM PROPERTIES INC
164 Maple St (06029-3330)
PHONE...............................860 979-0060
EMP: 9 **EST:** 2005
SQ FT: 12,000
SALES (est): 726.95K **Privately Held**
SIC: 3545 Balancing machines (machine tool accessories)

(G-1116)
SOAPSTONE MEDIA INC
Also Called: Mvp Visuals
92 West Rd (06029-3722)
PHONE...............................860 749-0455
Benjamin Camerota, *Pr*
Theresa Camerota, *Prin*
EMP: 10 **EST:** 2012
SALES (est): 1.61MM **Privately Held**
Web: www.mvpvisuals.com

SIC: 5131 2399 5999 2394 Flags and banners; Banners, pennants, and flags; Banners, flags, decals, and posters; Canopies, fabric: made from purchased materials

(G-1117)
SYN-MAR PRODUCTS INC
5 Nutmeg Dr (06029-3899)
P.O. Box 333 (06029-0333)
PHONE...............................860 872-8505
Tim Hill, *Pr*
EMP: 16 **EST:** 1978
SALES (est): 2.34MM **Privately Held**
Web: www.syn-marproducts.com
SIC: 3088 3261 Tubs (bath, shower, and laundry), plastics; Sinks, vitreous china

(G-1118)
TRANS-TEK INC
10 Industrial Dr (06029-2632)
P.O. Box 338 (06029-0338)
PHONE...............................860 872-8351
Nancy Hamilton, *Pr*
James L Waters, *Sec*
EMP: 25 **EST:** 1968
SQ FT: 14,000
SALES (est): 4.23MM **Privately Held**
Web: www.transtekinc.com
SIC: 3825 3669 3829 Transducers for volts, amperes, watts, vars, frequency, etc.; Signaling apparatus, electric; Measuring and controlling devices, nec

(G-1119)
YELLOWFIN HOLDINGS INC
Yellowfin Distribution
160 West Rd (06029-3723)
P.O. Box 83 (06029-0083)
PHONE...............................866 341-0979
Joseph Teixeira, *Mgr*
EMP: 29
Web: www.yellowfindistribution.com
SIC: 3577 Bar code (magnetic ink) printers
PA: Yellowfin Holdings, Inc.
26 Main St
Ellington CT 06029

Enfield
Hartford County

(G-1120)
ADAMCZYK ENTERPRISES INC
Also Called: Enfield Collision
3 Palomba Dr (06082-3823)
P.O. Box 1143 (06083-1143)
PHONE...............................860 745-9830
Robert P Adamczyk, *Pr*
Thomas Adamczyk, *Sec*
EMP: 9 **EST:** 1991
SALES (est): 789.55K **Privately Held**
Web: www.enfieldcollision.com
SIC: 3549 Assembly machines, including robotic

(G-1121)
ATLANTIC WOODCRAFT INC
Also Called: B&C Kitchen and Bath
199 Moody Rd (06082-3209)
PHONE...............................860 749-4887
Michael St Germain, *Pr*
Genevieve St Germain, *Sec*
EMP: 15 **EST:** 2008
SALES (est): 2.4MM **Privately Held**
Web: www.bnccabinetry.com
SIC: 3423 2431 Edge tools for woodworking: augers, bits, gimlets, etc.; Millwork

---

(G-1122)
CARRIS REELS CONNECTICUT INC
Also Called: Carris Reels of CT
11 Randolph St (06082-4724)
P.O. Box 1104 (06083-1104)
PHONE..............................860 749-8308
Alberto Aguilar, *Pr*
David Fitz-gerald, *VP*
David Sunderland, *VP*
Kathy Brytowski, *Sec*
▲ **EMP:** 64 **EST:** 1868
SQ FT: 116,640
SALES (est): 10.72MM **Privately Held**
Web: www.carris.com
SIC: 2499 Spools, reels, and pulleys: wood
PA: Carris Financial Corp.
49 Main St
Proctor VT 05765

(G-1123)
CIRTEC MEDICAL CORP
99 Print Shop Rd (06082-3211)
PHONE..............................860 814-3973
Richard Nicholas, *Brnch Mgr*
EMP: 120
SALES (corp-wide): 200MM **Privately Held**
Web: www.cirtecmed.com
SIC: 3841 Surgical and medical instruments
PA: Cirtec Medical Corp.
9200 Xylon Ave N
Brooklyn Park MN 55445
763 493-8556

(G-1124)
CNC ENGINEERING INC
19 Bacon Rd (06082-2301)
PHONE..............................860 749-1780
Gary Caravella, *Pr*
Patrick Harrington, *
EMP: 32 **EST:** 1983
SQ FT: 15,000
SALES (est): 8.43MM **Privately Held**
Web: www.cnc1.com
SIC: 7699 7371 3541 Industrial machinery
and equipment repair; Computer software
development; Machine tools, metal cutting
type

(G-1125)
CONTROL MODULE INC (PA)
Also Called: CMI
89 Phoenix Ave (06082-4439)
PHONE..............................860 745-2433
▼ **EMP:** 53 **EST:** 1969
SALES (est): 9.98MM
SALES (corp-wide): 9.98MM **Privately Held**
Web: www.controlmod.com
SIC: 3577 3629 Optical scanning devices;
Battery chargers, rectifying or nonrotating

(G-1126)
CONVAL INC
96 Phoenix Ave (06082-4408)
P.O. Box 1049 (06071-4149)
PHONE..............................860 749-0761
Frank A Siver, *Ch Bd*
Donald L Curtin, *
F C Schweitzer, *
Dudley D Williams, *
Lynn A Brooks, *
▲ **EMP:** 105 **EST:** 1967
SALES (est): 20.01MM **Privately Held**
Web: www.conval.com
SIC: 3491 Industrial valves

(G-1127)
CUSTOM PRINTING & COPY INC (PA)
16 Debra St (06082-5031)
P.O. Box 280745 (06128-0745)
PHONE..............................860 290-6890
Martin Madeux, *Pr*
Bedilea Bodo, *VP*
EMP: 11 **EST:** 1988
SQ FT: 1,200
SALES (est): 1.29MM
SALES (corp-wide): 1.29MM **Privately Held**
Web: www.customprintingct.com
SIC: 2752 7334 Offset printing;
Photocopying and duplicating services

(G-1128)
EASTERN METAL TREATING INC
28 Bacon Rd (06082-2302)
PHONE..............................860 763-4311
Maureen R Lyman, *Pr*
Lawrence C Lyman, *Dir*
EMP: 10 **EST:** 1988
SQ FT: 20,000
SALES (est): 1.71MM **Privately Held**
Web: www.easternmetaltreating.com
SIC: 3398 Metal heat treating

(G-1129)
ENFIELD TRANSIT MIX INC
84 Broadbrook Rd (06082-5303)
P.O. Box 376 (06083-0376)
PHONE..............................860 763-0864
Zigmund Kertenis Junior, *Pr*
EMP: 16 **EST:** 1952
SALES (est): 2.38MM **Privately Held**
SIC: 3273 Ready-mixed concrete

(G-1130)
EPPENDORF INC (DH)
175 Freshwater Blvd (06082-4444)
PHONE..............................860 253-3400
Kirti Patel, *Pr*
▲ **EMP:** 9 **EST:** 1946
SQ FT: 320,000
SALES (est): 23.61MM
SALES (corp-wide): 2.67MM **Privately Held**
Web: www.eppendorf.com
SIC: 3821 Laboratory equipment: fume
hoods, distillation racks, etc.
HQ: Eppendorf Se
Barkhausenweg 1
Hamburg HH 22339
40538010

(G-1131)
EPPENDORF HOLDING INC (DH)
175 Freshwater Blvd (06082-4444)
PHONE..............................860 253-3417
Martin Farb, *CEO*
Christian Jaaks, *CFO*
Klaus U Theidmann, *Sec*
▲ **EMP:** 31 **EST:** 1999
SALES (est): 85.51MM
SALES (corp-wide): 2.67MM **Privately Held**
Web: corporate.eppendorf.com
SIC: 3821 Shakers and stirrers
HQ: Eppendorf Se
Barkhausenweg 1
Hamburg HH 22339
40538010

(G-1132)
EPPENDORF MANUFACTURING CORP
175 Freshwater Blvd (06082-4444)
PHONE..............................860 253-3400
Kirti Patel, *CEO*
◆ **EMP:** 170 **EST:** 2004
SALES (est): 48.36MM
SALES (corp-wide): 2.67MM **Privately Held**
Web: www.eppendorf.com
SIC: 3841 Surgical and medical instruments
HQ: Eppendorf Se
Barkhausenweg 1
Hamburg HH 22339
40538010

(G-1133)
EXTEC CORP
99 Phoenix Ave (06082-4439)
P.O. Box 1258 (06083-1258)
PHONE..............................860 741-3435
Andrea Rinaldi, *Pr*
J Ronald Rinaldi, *Pr*
▲ **EMP:** 15 **EST:** 1996
SQ FT: 10,000
SALES (est): 4.98MM **Privately Held**
Web: www.extec.com
SIC: 5162 3821 3291 2842 Plastics
materials and basic shapes; Sample
preparation apparatus; Wheels, grinding:
artificial; Polishing preparations and related
products

(G-1134)
HIGH-TECH CONVERSIONS LLC
1699 King St Ste 108 (06082-6052)
PHONE..............................860 265-2633
EMP: 27 **EST:** 2021
SALES (est): 1.17MM **Privately Held**
Web: www.high-techconversions.com
SIC: 3231 Laboratory glassware

(G-1135)
I Q TECHNOLOGY LLC
9 Moody Rd Ste 18 (06082-3120)
PHONE..............................860 749-7255
EMP: 25 **EST:** 2003
SQ FT: 10,000
SALES (est): 986.75K **Privately Held**
SIC: 3555 Printing trades machinery

(G-1136)
INTEGRAL TECHNOLOGIES INC (DH)
120 Post Rd (06082-5690)
PHONE..............................860 741-2281
Gottfried Keusters, *Pr*
Paul Lettieri, *Sec*
▲ **EMP:** 8 **EST:** 1989
SQ FT: 75,000
SALES (est): 21.64MM
SALES (corp-wide): 242.12K **Privately Held**
Web: www.ptreb.com
SIC: 3699 8731 3599 Electron beam metal
cutting, forming or welding machines;
Industrial laboratory, except testing;
Machine and other job shop work
HQ: Ptr Strahltechnik Gmbh
Am Erlenbruch 9
Langenselbold HE 63505
618420550

(G-1137)
LEGO SYSTEMS INC (DH)
Also Called: Lego Brand Retail
100 Print Shop Rd (06082-3231)
PHONE..............................860 698-9367
Preston Frank Kodak Iii, *Pr*
Nancy Sanchez, *VP*
Jared Carr, *VP*
R Scott Slifka, *Sec*
Alessandro Cardito, *Treas*
◆ **EMP:** 1350 **EST:** 1973
SQ FT: 1,000,000
SALES (est): 503.72MM **Privately Held**
Web: www.lego.com
SIC: 3944 5092 Erector sets, toy; Toys and
hobby goods and supplies
HQ: Lego A/S
Astvej 1
Billund 7190
79506070

(G-1138)
MRND LLC
75 Hazard Ave Ste 1 (06082-3866)
PHONE..............................860 749-0256
Larry Vertefeuille, *Mgr*
EMP: 7
SQ FT: 6,000
SALES (corp-wide): 8.6MM **Privately Held**
Web: www.mrnd.com
SIC: 3444 Sheet metalwork
PA: Mrnd Llc
4418 Louisburg Rd
Raleigh NC
919 862-8480

(G-1139)
MSC FILTRATION TECH INC
Also Called: M S C
198 Freshwater Blvd (06082-4455)
PHONE..............................860 745-7475
Michael Assimus, *Pr*
▼ **EMP:** 10 **EST:** 1962
SQ FT: 6,800
SALES (est): 4.84MM **Privately Held**
Web: www.mscfiltertech.com
SIC: 5085 3569 3561 5084 Filters, industrial
; Filters; Pumps and pumping equipment;
Pumps and pumping equipment, nec

(G-1140)
OLYMPIA SALES INC
Also Called: Enfield Stationers
215 Moody Rd (06082-3230)
P.O. Box 1800 (06083-1800)
PHONE..............................860 749-0751
Thomas O'hara, *Pr*
Arthur O'hara, *CEO*
◆ **EMP:** 60 **EST:** 1966
SQ FT: 90,000
SALES (est): 5.01MM **Privately Held**
Web: www.olympiasales.net
SIC: 5112 5961 7389 2771 Greeting cards;
Mail order house, nec; Fund raising
organizations; Greeting cards

(G-1141)
PHOENIX MANUFACTURING INC
250 South Rd (06082-4457)
PHONE..............................860 745-2080
Krystyna Paluch, *CEO*
Mark E Dilorenzo, *
Martha Paluch, *
EMP: 65 **EST:** 1989
SQ FT: 24,000
SALES (est): 11.67MM **Privately Held**
Web: www.phoenix-mfg-inc.com
SIC: 3599 Machine shop, jobbing and repair

(G-1142)
POLYMERIC CONVERTING LLC
5 Old Depot Hill Rd (06082-6040)
PHONE..............................860 623-1335
▲ **EMP:** 20 **EST:** 1992
SQ FT: 56,000
SALES (est): 4.66MM **Privately Held**
Web: www.polyconverting.com
SIC: 2671 3089 Plastic film, coated or
laminated for packaging; Laminating of
plastics

(G-1143)
PTI INDUSTRIES INC (HQ)
Also Called: P T I
2 Peerless Way (06082-2371)
PHONE.................................800 318-8438
Ronald Lalli, *CEO*
Harley Delude, *
Carl Muller, *
EMP: 40 **EST:** 1983
SQ FT: 19,000
SALES (est): 9.29MM
SALES (corp-wide): 672.12MM **Privately Held**
Web: www.ptiindustries.com
SIC: 3479 8734 Coating of metals and formed products; Metallurgical testing laboratory
PA: Iss 2, Llc
840 Gessner Rd Ste 950
Houston TX 77024
239 244-2244

(G-1144)
PTR - PRECISION TECHNOLOGIES INC (DH)
120 Post Rd (06082-5690)
PHONE.................................860 741-2281
▲ **EMP:** 48 **EST:** 1975
SALES (est): 21.64MM
SALES (corp-wide): 242.12K **Privately Held**
Web: www.ptreb.com
SIC: 3699 Electron beam metal cutting, forming or welding machines
HQ: Integral Technologies Inc
120 Post Rd
Enfield CT 06082

(G-1145)
QG PRINTING IL LLC
Also Called: QG PRINTING IL LLC
96 Phoenix Ave (06082-4408)
PHONE.................................860 741-0150
EMP: 90
SALES (corp-wide): 3.22B **Publicly Held**
SIC: 2752 Offset printing
HQ: Qg Printing Ii Llc
N61w23044 Harrys Way
Sussex WI 53089

(G-1146)
SCIENCE FCTION FNTSY WRTERS AM
24 Nutmeg Ave (06082-4908)
P.O. Box 215 (94580-0215)
PHONE.................................860 698-0536
EMP: 15 **EST:** 2013
SALES (est): 496.9K **Privately Held**
Web: www.sfwa.org
SIC: 2741 Miscellaneous publishing

(G-1147)
SENIOR OPERATIONS LLC
Also Called: Senior Aerospace Connecticut
4 Peerless Way (06082-2371)
PHONE.................................860 741-2546
David Squires, *Pr*
Michael Lang, *
Herbert Parsley, *
EMP: 95 **EST:** 1992
SQ FT: 55,000
SALES (est): 12.28MM **Privately Held**
Web: www.pcxaero.com
SIC: 3728 Aircraft parts and equipment, nec

(G-1148)
SENIOR OPERATIONS LLC
Also Called: Sterling Machine Division
4 Peerless Way (06082-2371)

PHONE.................................860 741-2546
EMP: 20
SALES (corp-wide): 1.02B **Privately Held**
Web: www.seniorflexonics.com
SIC: 3599 Hose, flexible metallic
HQ: Senior Operations Llc
300 E Devon Ave
Bartlett IL 60103
630 372-3500

(G-1149)
SFWA
24 Nutmeg Ave (06082-4908)
P.O. Box 215 (94580-0215)
PHONE.................................508 320-5293
EMP: 15 **EST:** 2018
SALES (est): 168.83K **Privately Held**
Web: www.sfwa.org
SIC: 2741 Miscellaneous publishing

(G-1150)
SHLOMO ENTERPRISES INC (PA)
1699 King St (06082-6051)
PHONE.................................860 265-7995
▲ **EMP:** 9 **EST:** 2020
SALES (est): 5.15MM **Privately Held**
Web: www.high-techconversions.com
SIC: 5169 2842 Sanitation preparations; Dusting cloths, chemically treated

(G-1151)
SIGN FACTORY
Also Called: Little John's Sign Factory
25 Dust House Rd (06082-4650)
PHONE.................................860 763-1085
Little John, *Owner*
EMP: 10 **EST:** 1974
SQ FT: 7,000
SALES (est): 782.82K **Privately Held**
Web: www.ljsignfactory.com
SIC: 3993 Signs and advertising specialties

(G-1152)
SIMPSON STRONG-TIE COMPANY INC
7 Pearson Way (06082-2655)
PHONE.................................860 741-8923
John Adkins, *Mgr*
EMP: 57
SALES (corp-wide): 2.12B **Publicly Held**
Web: www.strongtie.com
SIC: 3449 Miscellaneous metalwork
HQ: Simpson Strong-Tie Company Inc.
5956 W Las Positas Blvd
Pleasanton CA 94588
925 560-9000

(G-1153)
SMITHFAMILY1938 LLC
14 Hazard Ave Ste 23 (06082-3713)
PHONE.................................424 341-8876
Lenworth Smith, *CEO*
EMP: 8 **EST:** 2020
SALES (est): 288.38K **Privately Held**
SIC: 3161 5999 3589 6798 Clothing and apparel carrying cases; Sales barn; Service industry machinery, nec; Real estate investment trusts

(G-1154)
STR HOLDINGS INC (PA)
Also Called: Str
1559 King St (06082-5844)
PHONE.................................860 272-4235
Robert S Yorgensen, *Pr*
Thomas D Vitro, *CAO*
EMP: 10 **EST:** 1944
SQ FT: 69,500

SALES (est): 10.88MM **Privately Held**
SIC: 3081 Unsupported plastics film and sheet

(G-1155)
TIRE COUNTRY OF ENFIELD INC
623 Hazard Ave (06082-4232)
PHONE.................................860 763-0846
Robert Brennan, *Pr*
EMP: 7 **EST:** 1986
SQ FT: 10,000
SALES (est): 392.34K **Privately Held**
Web: www.tirecountryautorepair.com
SIC: 7538 7534 7549 5531 General automotive repair shops; Tire repair shop; Automotive maintenance services; Automotive tires

(G-1156)
U S GLASS DISTRIBUTORS INC
7 Niblick Rd (06082-4431)
PHONE.................................860 741-3658
Mark S Vece, *Pr*
Corinne Cacopardo, *VP*
Blaise Vece, *Treas*
▲ **EMP:** 20 **EST:** 1986
SQ FT: 28,000
SALES (est): 4.66MM **Privately Held**
SIC: 5039 3231 Glass construction materials ; Products of purchased glass

(G-1157)
VERICO TECHNOLOGY LLC (HQ)
230 Shaker Rd (06082-2385)
PHONE.................................860 871-1200
Yuval Dubois, *Pr*
Yuval Dubois, *Pr*
Rebecca Itkin Duffy, *
◆ **EMP:** 45 **EST:** 1987
SQ FT: 11,500
SALES (est): 93.18MM
SALES (corp-wide): 111.83MM **Privately Held**
Web: www.vericocontractcoating.com
SIC: 3577 3861 3555 Magnetic ink and optical scanning devices; Graphic arts plates, sensitized; Printing plates
PA: Mai Holdings, Inc.
10 Glenville St
Greenwich CT

(G-1158)
WEST SHORE METALS LLC
28 W Shore Dr (06082-2223)
PHONE.................................860 749-8013
Bruce Bouchard, *Prin*
EMP: 7 **EST:** 2015
SALES (est): 410.92K **Privately Held**
SIC: 3469 Metal stampings, nec

(G-1159)
WHOLE DONUT
920 Enfield St Ste A (06082-3673)
PHONE.................................860 745-3041
John Algiere, *Pr*
Joseph Algiere, *VP*
Catherine Algiere, *Sec*
Nancy Algiere, *Treas*
EMP: 18 **EST:** 1979
SQ FT: 2,000
SALES (est): 911.17K **Privately Held**
Web: www.thewholedonut.tripod.com
SIC: 5461 5812 2051 Doughnuts; Coffee shop; Doughnuts, except frozen

(G-1160)
WORLD CORD SETS INC
210 Moody Rd (06082-3206)
P.O. Box 1111 (06083-1111)
PHONE.................................860 763-2100

Edward C Smith, *Pr*
▲ **EMP:** 8 **EST:** 2002
SALES (est): 1.46MM **Privately Held**
Web: shop.worldcordsets.com
SIC: 3699 3643 Appliance cords, for household electrical equipment; Current-carrying wiring services

(G-1161)
YANKEE CASTING CO INC
243 Shaker Rd (06082-2327)
P.O. Box 813 (06083-0813)
PHONE.................................860 749-6171
Mark Vecchiarelli, *Pr*
Brian Vecchiarelli, *
Kevin Vecchiarelli, *
Timothy Vecchiarelli, *
EMP: 55 **EST:** 1961
SQ FT: 51,000
SALES (est): 5.34MM **Privately Held**
Web: www.yankeecasting.com
SIC: 3369 Castings, except die-castings, precision

Essex
Middlesex County

(G-1162)
BELL POWER SYSTEMS LLC
Also Called: John Deere Authorized Dealer
34 Plains Rd (06426-1501)
P.O. Box 980 (06426-0980)
PHONE.................................860 767-7502
▲ **EMP:** 60 **EST:** 2012
SALES (est): 9.35MM **Privately Held**
Web: www.bellpower.com
SIC: 3519 5082 Diesel, semi-diesel, or duel-fuel engines, including marine; Construction and mining machinery

(G-1163)
ESSEX CONCRETE PRODUCTS INC
141 Westbrook Rd (06426-1512)
PHONE.................................860 767-1768
Robert Vitari, *Pr*
Ruth Vitari, *Sec*
EMP: 10 **EST:** 1958
SQ FT: 5,000
SALES (est): 916.35K **Privately Held**
SIC: 3273 3272 Ready-mixed concrete; Concrete products, precast, nec

(G-1164)
FIRESTABLE INSULATION CO
36 Plains Rd (06426-1501)
PHONE.................................860 767-8773
Peter Gummo, *Prin*
EMP: 9
SALES (est): 512.24K **Privately Held**
SIC: 3999 Manufacturing industries, nec

(G-1165)
HERMETIC SOLUTIONS GROUP INC (HQ)
16 Plains Rd (06426-1501)
PHONE.................................215 645-9420
Keith Barclay, *CEO*
EMP: 15 **EST:** 2016
SALES (est): 168.44MM
SALES (corp-wide): 168.44MM **Privately Held**
Web: www.hermeticsolutions.com
SIC: 3679 Electronic circuits
PA: Qnnect, Llc
4 Embarcadero Ctr # 2660
San Francisco CA

GEOGRAPHIC

(G-1166)
HI-REL GROUP LLC
16 Plains Rd (06426-1501)
PHONE............................860 767-9031
William Hubbard, *Pr*
EMP: 7 **EST:** 2013
SALES (est): 2.48MM
SALES (corp-wide): 152.91MM **Privately Held**
Web: www.hermeticsolutions.com
SIC: 3674　Hybrid integrated circuits
HQ: Hermetic Solutions Group Inc.
　16 Plains Rd
　Essex CT 06426
　215 645-9420

(G-1167)
HI-REL PRODUCTS LLC
16 Plains Rd (06426-1501)
PHONE............................860 767-9031
William Hubbard, *Pr*
EMP: 40 **EST:** 2013
SQ FT: 16,500
SALES (est): 10.11MM
SALES (corp-wide): 152.91MM **Privately Held**
Web: www.hermeticsolutions.com
SIC: 3674　Hybrid integrated circuits
HQ: Hermetic Solutions Group Inc.
　16 Plains Rd
　Essex CT 06426
　215 645-9420

(G-1168)
JACKSON CORRUGATED CONT CORP
45 River Rd (06426-1302)
PHONE............................860 767-3373
TOLL FREE: 800
William P Herlihy, *Pr*
Paula Bingham, *
EMP: 16 **EST:** 1949
SQ FT: 60,000
SALES (est): 373.29K **Privately Held**
SIC: 2653　Boxes, corrugated: made from purchased materials

(G-1169)
PLANES ROAD ASSOCIATES LLC
38 Plains Rd (06426-1501)
PHONE............................860 469-3200
Ethan B Goller, *Mgr*
EMP: 17 **EST:** 2006
SALES (est): 260.36K **Privately Held**
Web: www.redpaperplane.com
SIC: 2759　Commercial printing, nec

(G-1170)
PROCTOR WOODWORKS LLC
53 Grandview Ter (06426-1004)
PHONE............................860 767-9881
Brian D Proctor, *Prin*
EMP: 7 **EST:** 2008
SALES (est): 227.11K **Privately Held**
SIC: 2431　Millwork

(G-1171)
SMITH HILL OF DELAWARE INC
34 Plains Rd (06426-1501)
P.O. Box 980 (06426-0980)
PHONE............................860 767-7502
Martin A Bell, *Pr*
A Arnold Bell, *
Susan E Sinagra, *
▲ **EMP:** 47 **EST:** 1967
SQ FT: 52,000
SALES (est): 1.01MM **Privately Held**
Web: www.bellpower.com

SIC: 3519　Internal combustion engines, nec

(G-1172)
STEEL MODULAR INC
124 Westbrook Rd Ste 101 (06426-1551)
PHONE............................310 227-3714
Jennifer Kelly Freis, *CEO*
Jennifer Freis, *CEO*
Al Montoya, *Dir*
Robert Easter, *Dir*
EMP: 13 **EST:** 2018
SALES (est): 874.61K **Privately Held**
Web: www.steelmodular.us
SIC: 3448　Prefabricated metal buildings

(G-1173)
WINTHROP TOOL LLC
55 Plains Rd (06426-1504)
PHONE............................860 526-9079
EMP: 7 **EST:** 1987
SQ FT: 2,500
SALES (est): 664.72K **Privately Held**
Web: www.winthroptool.com
SIC: 3599 3544　Machine shop, jobbing and repair; Special dies, tools, jigs, and fixtures

Fairfield
Fairfield County

(G-1174)
5381 PARTNERS LLC
5381 Congress St (06824-1726)
PHONE............................203 255-7985
EMP: 20
SIC: 7372　Publisher's computer software

(G-1175)
AMPLIFIED INK CO
188 Farmstead Hill Rd (06824-7119)
PHONE............................203 787-2184
Henry S Snow, *Pr*
Steven M Snow, *
Sandra Snow, *
▲ **EMP:** 101 **EST:** 1958
SQ FT: 55,000
SALES (est): 4.81MM **Privately Held**
Web: www.ctlaminating.com
SIC: 3089　Identification cards, plastics

(G-1176)
ARCAT INC
173 Sherman St (06824-5823)
PHONE............................203 929-9444
F P Jannott, *Pr*
F Rick P Jannott, *Pr*
Leslie L Jannott, *VP*
EMP: 8 **EST:** 1991
SQ FT: 1,600
SALES (est): 1.1MM **Privately Held**
Web: www.arcat.com
SIC: 2752 2741　Publication printing, lithographic; Miscellaneous publishing

(G-1177)
BELLA GRACE LLC
857 Post Rd (06824-6041)
PHONE............................929 533-2343
Julie Santaniello, *Admn*
EMP: 50 **EST:** 2019
SALES (est): 1.32MM **Privately Held**
SIC: 5999 2844　Cosmetics; Cosmetic preparations

(G-1178)
CLARKTRON PRODUCTS INC
1525 Kings Hwy Ste 7 (06824-5321)
PHONE............................203 333-6517
William F Mason Junior, *Pr*

EMP: 8 **EST:** 1950
SQ FT: 5,000
SALES (est): 982.05K **Privately Held**
Web: www.clarktron.com
SIC: 3625　Electric controls and control accessories, industrial

(G-1179)
CLEAN AIR GROUP INC (PA)
Also Called: Atmosair
418 Meadow St Ste 204 (06824-5365)
PHONE............................203 335-3700
Steve Levine, *Pr*
James Mcmanus, *CFO*
EMP: 8 **EST:** 2007
SQ FT: 1,500
SALES (est): 9.12MM **Privately Held**
Web: www.atmosair.com
SIC: 3564　Air purification equipment

(G-1180)
COMMAND CHEMICAL CORPORATION
2490 Black Rock Tpke # 359 (06825-2400)
PHONE............................203 319-1857
Robert Lesko, *Pr*
Lori Ann Lesko, *VP*
◆ **EMP:** 9 **EST:** 2002
SQ FT: 15,000
SALES (est): 2.14MM **Privately Held**
Web: www.commandchemical.com
SIC: 2899　Fire retardant chemicals

(G-1181)
DOMESTIC KITCHENS INC
515 Commerce Dr (06825-5541)
PHONE............................203 368-1651
Pasquale Staltaro, *Pr*
Frank Staltaro, *
EMP: 27 **EST:** 1973
SALES (est): 2.43MM **Privately Held**
Web: www.domestickitchens.com
SIC: 2434　Wood kitchen cabinets

(G-1182)
EARLY ADVANTAGE LLC
426 Mine Hill Rd (06824-2151)
PHONE............................203 259-6480
David Ward, *Managing Member*
▲ **EMP:** 10 **EST:** 1997
SALES (est): 966.1K **Privately Held**
Web: www.early-advantage.com
SIC: 2731　Book publishing

(G-1183)
ELINCO INTERNATIONAL JPC INC (PA)
1525 Kings Hwy (06824-5321)
PHONE............................203 334-7537
Thomas Mclaughlin, *Pr*
EMP: 8 **EST:** 2007
SQ FT: 8,000
SALES: 9.63MM
SALES (corp-wide): 9.63MM **Privately Held**
Web: www.e-jpc.com
SIC: 3621 5063　Motors and generators; Motors, electric

(G-1184)
ENEON US LLC (HQ) ✪
2150 Post Rd (06824-5669)
PHONE............................312 724-6886
Ken Franklin, *Pr*
Jason Peacock, *Marketing*
EMP: 13 **EST:** 2023
SALES (est): 3.5MM
SALES (corp-wide): 3.5MM **Privately Held**

SIC: 3825　Energy measuring equipment, electrical
PA: Us Clean Energy Llc
　2150 Post Rd
　Fairfield CT 06824
　312 724-6886

(G-1185)
FAIRFIX CT INC
Also Called: Fairfix
1134 Post Rd (06824-6006)
PHONE............................203 516-4137
Arik Yusupov, *Pr*
EMP: 10 **EST:** 2017
SALES (est): 733.16K **Privately Held**
Web: www.fairfixusa.com
SIC: 3571　Electronic computers

(G-1186)
FREEDOM GRAFIX LLC
457 Castle Ave (06825-5446)
PHONE............................815 900-6189
Timothy S Sturtevant, *CEO*
EMP: 7 **EST:** 2012
SALES (est): 79.51K **Privately Held**
Web: www.freedomgrafix.com
SIC: 3861　Photocopy machines

(G-1187)
GRAYBARK ENTERPRISES LLC
20 Governors Ln (06824-2106)
PHONE............................203 255-4503
EMP: 9 **EST:** 2009
SALES (est): 478.65K **Privately Held**
SIC: 7372　Prepackaged software

(G-1188)
HIGHLAND IMPORTS LLC
Also Called: Highland Imports
74 Linwood Ave (06824-4911)
PHONE............................203 538-6818
Oliver P Mackinnon Iii, *Pr*
Oliver P Mackinnon Junior, *Prin*
◆ **EMP:** 25 **EST:** 2011
SALES (est): 2.13MM **Privately Held**
Web: www.highlandimportsct.co
SIC: 2084　Wine cellars, bonded: engaged in blending wines

(G-1189)
IPC SYSTEMS INC
Also Called: IPC Information Systems
777 Commerce Dr Ste 100 (06825-5500)
PHONE............................860 271-4100
Peter Gyurko, *Brnch Mgr*
EMP: 49
Web: www.ipc.com
SIC: 3661　Telephone and telegraph apparatus
HQ: I.P.C. Systems, Inc.
　Harborside Fncl Plz 10 3
　Jersey City NJ 07302
　201 253-2000

(G-1190)
JAPANESE PRODUCTS CORPORATION
Also Called: Jpc Products
1525 Kings Hwy (06824-5321)
PHONE............................203 334-7537
▲ **EMP:** 12
Web: www.e-jpc.com
SIC: 5063 3621　Motors, electric; Motors and generators

(G-1191)
JOLEN CREAM BLEACH CORP
25 Walls Dr (06824-5156)
P.O. Box 458 (06824-0458)

PHONE..................203 259-8779
Evelyn Kossak, *Pr*
EMP: 7 **EST:** 1964
SQ FT: 8,000
SALES (est): 216.32K **Privately Held**
Web: www.jolenbeauty.com
SIC: 2844 Face creams or lotions

(G-1192)
JULIAN MATERIALS LLC (PA)
418 Meadow St (06824-5365)
PHONE..................203 416-5308
EMP: 10 **EST:** 2017
SALES (est): 4.59MM
SALES (corp-wide): 4.59MM **Privately Held**
Web: www.julianenterprises.com
SIC: 1411 Granite dimension stone

(G-1193)
KATONA BAKERY LLC
Also Called: Billy's Bakery
1189 Post Rd Ste 3b (06824-6046)
PHONE..................203 337-5349
EMP: 22 **EST:** 2017
SALES (est): 965.39K **Privately Held**
SIC: 2051 Bread, cake, and related products

(G-1194)
MOHICAN VALLEY CONCRETE CORP
Also Called: Mohican Valley
195 Ardmore S: (06824-6127)
PHONE..................203 254-7133
Mark Greenawalt, *CEO*
Thomas Greenawalt Ii, *VP*
Donna Sedgewick, *Treas*
Thomas Greenawalt Senior, *Stockholder*
EMP: 20 **EST:** 1956
SQ FT: 2,700
SALES (est): 2.45MM **Privately Held**
Web: www.mohicanvalley.com
SIC: 3273 Ready-mixed concrete

(G-1195)
NCI WOODWORKING LLC LLC
230 Hollydale Rd (06824-2228)
PHONE..................203 391-1614
Charles Ferreira, *Prin*
EMP: 7 **EST:** 2016
SALES (est): 189.72K **Privately Held**
SIC: 2431 Millwork

(G-1196)
PENFIELD SEARCH PARTNERS LTD
1275 Post Rd Ste 200d (06824-6057)
PHONE..................203 307-2600
Andrew Davis, *Pr*
EMP: 7 **EST:** 2012
SALES (est): 66.07K **Privately Held**
SIC: 8748 2834 Business consulting, nec;
   Pharmaceutical preparations

(G-1197)
PFM HOLDING CO
418 Meadow St Ste 201 (06824-5365)
PHONE..................203 335-3300
Steven Levine, *Pr*
EMP: 500 **EST:** 1999
SALES (est): 11.52MM **Privately Held**
SIC: 7349 7342 3585 Janitorial service,
   contract basis; Pest control services;
   Heating and air conditioning combination
   units

(G-1198)
POLSTER INDUSTRIES LLC
115 Verna Hill Rd (06824-2162)

PHONE..................203 521-8517
EMP: 8 **EST:** 2011
SALES (est): 496.11K **Privately Held**
SIC: 3999 Manufacturing industries, nec

(G-1199)
SAGEMAKER INC
883 Black Rock Tpke Ste 200
(06825-4718)
PHONE..................203 368-4888
EMP: 80 **EST:** 1995
SQ FT: 8,000
SALES (est): 3.36MM **Privately Held**
SIC: 7372 Prepackaged software

(G-1200)
SCAP MOTORS INC
Also Called: Jeep
562 Rock Ridge Rd (06824-2267)
PHONE..................203 384-0005
Geza Scap, *Pr*
Julie Scap, *
EMP: 150 **EST:** 1964
SALES (est): 46.81MM **Privately Held**
Web: www.scapauto.com
SIC: 5511 3724 Automobiles, new and used
   ; Aircraft engines and engine parts

(G-1201)
TECHNISONIC RESEARCH INC
328 Commerce Dr (06825-5560)
PHONE..................203 368-3600
Kenneth Thompson, *Pr*
Joseph Di Blasi, *VP*
EMP: 9 **EST:** 1983
SQ FT: 3,000
SALES (est): 1.04MM **Privately Held**
SIC: 3829 Ultrasonic testing equipment

(G-1202)
UNCLE WILEYS INC
1220 Post Rd (06824-6027)
PHONE..................203 256-9313
Wiley Mullins, *Pr*
Greg Hill, *Sec*
Oswald Yanez Mullins, *Prin*
EMP: 12 **EST:** 1992
SQ FT: 6,000
SALES (est): 393.53K **Privately Held**
Web: www.unclewileys.com
SIC: 2099 Seasonings and spices

(G-1203)
UNIVERSAL PRTG MILING SVCS INC
Also Called: Universal Prtg & Mailing Svcs
75 Ardmore St (06824-6127)
PHONE..................203 330-0611
Shelley Llewellyn, *Pr*
EMP: 15 **EST:** 1996
SQ FT: 6,000
SALES (est): 1.52MM **Privately Held**
Web: www.universalprinting4u.com
SIC: 2752 Offset printing

(G-1204)
UNIVERSAL THREAD GRINDING CO
30 Chambers St (06825-5594)
PHONE..................203 336-1849
William H Everett Junior, *Pr*
Carl Linley, *Treas*
EMP: 13 **EST:** 1947
SQ FT: 10,000
SALES (est): 414.28K **Privately Held**
Web: www.universal-thread.com
SIC: 3452 Screws, metal

(G-1205)
UPS AUTHORIZED RETAILER
Also Called: UPS
857 Post Rd (06824-6041)
PHONE..................203 256-9991
Ketsly Gedeon, *Prin*
EMP: 7 **EST:** 2009
SALES (est): 424.22K **Privately Held**
Web: www.theupsstore.com
SIC: 7389 2759 Mailbox rental and related
   service; Commercial printing, nec

(G-1206)
WHIFF LLC
119 Jackman Ave (06825-1725)
PHONE..................917 420-0397
Elizabeth Firgeleski, *Prin*
EMP: 10 **EST:** 2018
SALES (est): 576.5K **Privately Held**
Web: www.innrstate.com
SIC: 3999 Manufacturing industries, nec

Farmington
Hartford County

(G-1207)
B/E AEROSPACE INC
Also Called: Colins Aerospace
9 Farm Springs Rd (06032-2576)
PHONE..................410 266-2048
Kelly Ortberg, *CEO*
EMP: 75
SALES (corp-wide): 68.92B **Publicly Held**
Web: www.collinsaerospace.com
SIC: 3728 Aircraft parts and equipment, nec
HQ: B/E Aerospace, Inc.
   150 Oak Plaza Blvd # 200
   Winston Salem NC 27105
   336 747-5000

(G-1208)
BACTANA CORP
Also Called: Bactana Animal Health
400 Farmington Ave (06032-1913)
PHONE..................203 716-1230
John Kallassy, *Pr*
EMP: 8 **EST:** 2016
SALES (est): 1.72MM **Privately Held**
Web: www.bactana.com
SIC: 2836 2023 2048 Veterinary biological
   products; Dietary supplements, dairy and
   non-dairy based; Feed supplements

(G-1209)
BARNES GROUP INC
Barnes Aerospace
80 Scott Swamp Rd (06032-2847)
PHONE..................860 298-7740
EMP: 8
SALES (corp-wide): 1.26B **Publicly Held**
Web: www.onebarnes.com
SIC: 3495 3469 Wire springs; Metal
   stampings, nec
PA: Barnes Group Inc.
   123 Main St
   Bristol CT 06010
   860 583-7070

(G-1210)
BROADCASTMED LLC (PA)
195 Farmington Ave (06032-1700)
PHONE..................860 953-2900
Ross J Joel, *CEO*
Peter Gailey, *Pr*
Richard Meyer, *CFO*
EMP: 15 **EST:** 1994
SQ FT: 5,000
SALES (est): 5.1MM

SALES (corp-wide): 5.1MM **Privately Held**
Web: www.broadcastmed.com
SIC: 2741 Internet publishing and
   broadcasting

(G-1211)
CARRIER FIRE SEC AMERICAS CORP
Also Called: Edwards Detection & Alarm
30 Batterson Park Rd Ste 100
(06032-2545)
PHONE..................941 739-4200
EMP: 46
SALES (corp-wide): 20.42B **Publicly Held**
Web: corporate.carrier.com
SIC: 3669 5065 Burglar alarm apparatus,
   electric; Electronic parts and equipment, nec
HQ: Carrier Fire & Security Americas
   Corporation
   13995 Pasteur Blvd
   Palm Beach Gardens FL 33418

(G-1212)
CONNECTCUT SPRING STMPING CORP
Also Called: Connecticut Spring & Stamping
48 Spring Ln (06032-3140)
PHONE..................860 677-1341
William Stevenson, *Pr*
Peter Youmans, *Stockholder*
Steve Dicke, *
Chuck Thomas, *
David Fischler, *
▲ **EMP:** 500 **EST:** 1939
SQ FT: 150,000
SALES (est): 83.4MM **Privately Held**
Web: www.ctspring.com
SIC: 3469 3495 3493 Stamping metal for
   the trade; Wire springs; Steel springs,
   except wire

(G-1213)
CONNECTICUT CONCRETE FORM INC
168 Brickyard Rd (06032-1202)
PHONE..................860 674-1314
EMP: 14 **EST:** 1961
SQ FT: 12,000
SALES (est): 2.14MM **Privately Held**
Web: www.connecticutconcreteform.com
SIC: 3271 Blocks, concrete or cinder:
   standard

(G-1214)
DP CONCRETE LLC
Also Called: Farmington Ready Mix
164 Brickyard Rd (06032-1202)
P.O. Box 344 (06034-0344)
PHONE..................860 677-2626
EMP: 24 **EST:** 2012
SALES (est): 5.29MM **Privately Held**
Web: www.farmingtonreadymix.com
SIC: 3273 Ready-mixed concrete

(G-1215)
DRAUGHT TECHNOLOGIES LLC
592 New Britain Ave (06032)
PHONE..................860 840-7555
Steven J Salcedo, *Managing Member*
EMP: 7 **EST:** 2003
SALES (est): 593.99K **Privately Held**
SIC: 8748 3561 Business consulting, nec;
   Pumps and pumping equipment

(G-1216)
EASTERN BROACH & MACHINE LLC
24 Skyline Dr (06032-2019)
PHONE..................860 678-7490

Gregory Guay, *Owner*
EMP: 8 EST: 2018
SALES (est): 126.22K **Privately Held**
Web: www.easternbroach.com
SIC: 3599 Machine shop, jobbing and repair

(G-1217)
EBM-PAPST INC (DH)
100 Hyde Rd (06032-2835)
PHONE..............................860 674-1515
Robert Sobolewski, *CEO*
Gerhard Sturm, *
Donald Beckwith, *
William T John, *
▲ **EMP:** 300 **EST:** 1981
SALES (est): 132.11MM
SALES (corp-wide): 17.56MM **Privately
Held**
Web: www.ebmpapst.com
SIC: 5084 3564 Fans, industrial; Blowers
and fans
HQ: Ebm Industries Management Group,
Inc.
100 Hyde Rd
Farmington CT 06032

(G-1218)
EDMUNDS MANUFACTURING
COMPANY (PA)
Also Called: Edmunds Gages
45 Spring Ln (06032-3139)
P.O. Box 385 (06034-0385)
PHONE..............................860 677-2813
Robert F Edmunds Senior, *Ch Bd*
Robert F Edmunds Junior, *Ch*
Robert F Edmunds Iii, *VP*
Kenneth I Swanson, *VP*
EMP: 100 **EST:** 1971
SQ FT: 43,000
SALES (est): 12.19MM
SALES (corp-wide): 12.19MM **Privately
Held**
Web: www.edmundsgages.com
SIC: 3829 3545 Measuring and controlling
devices, nec; Machine tool accessories

(G-1219)
FARMINGTON DISPLAYS INC
Also Called: F D I
21 Hyde Rd Ste 2 (06032-2859)
PHONE..............................860 677-2497
Sabastian Ditomosso, *Pr*
Salvatore Ditomaso, *
Paul F Ditomaso Junior, *VP*
Maria Fabrizi, *
▲ **EMP:** 45 **EST:** 1973
SQ FT: 130,000
SALES (est): 8.27MM **Privately Held**
Web: www.fdi-group.com
SIC: 3993 Displays and cutouts, window
and lobby

(G-1220)
FORMATRON LTD
21 Hyde Rd Ste 3 (06032-2859)
PHONE..............................860 676-0227
Salvatore Ditommaso, *Pr*
Paul Ditommaso Junior, *Prin*
EMP: 39 **EST:** 1962
SQ FT: 25,000
SALES (est): 914.42K **Privately Held**
SIC: 2541 3999 Store and office display
cases and fixtures; Furniture, barber and
beauty shop

(G-1221)
HANWHA AEROSPACE USA LLC
1790 New Britain Ave (06032-3315)
P.O. Box 366 (06034-0366)
PHONE..............................860 677-2603

EMP: 52
Web: www.hanwhaaerospaceusa.com
SIC: 3724 Aircraft engines and engine parts
HQ: Hanwha Aerospace Usa Llc
5 Mckee Pl
Cheshire CT 06410
203 806-2090

(G-1222)
IBNR LLC
190 Farmington Ave (06032-1713)
PHONE..............................860 676-8600
Vincent J Dowling Junior, *Managing
Member*
EMP: 10 **EST:** 1999
SALES (est): 140.35K **Privately Held**
SIC: 2721 Periodicals, publishing only

(G-1223)
INTEGRITY MFG LLC
1451 New Britain Ave Ste 1 (06032-3343)
PHONE..............................860 678-1599
James Gadoury, *Managing Member*
EMP: 14 **EST:** 1998
SQ FT: 3,200
SALES (est): 1.02MM **Privately Held**
Web: www.integritymfgllc.com
SIC: 3423 Hand and edge tools, nec

(G-1224)
INTELLINET CORPORATION
10 Stanford Dr Ste 1 (06032-2451)
PHONE..............................860 677-4427
EMP: 8
SALES (corp-wide): 8.25MM **Privately
Held**
Web: www.baypointetechnology.com
SIC: 7372 Prepackaged software
PA: Intellinet Corporation
150 Center St
Chardon OH 44024
216 289-4100

(G-1225)
JOSEPH HANNOUSH FAMILY INC
Also Called: Hannoush Jewelers
500 Westfarms Mall (06032-2614)
PHONE..............................860 561-4651
Sultana Hannoush, *Pr*
Souad Hannoush, *VP*
Sharvel Hannoush, *Treas*
EMP: 10 **EST:** 2004
SALES (est): 1.3MM **Privately Held**
SIC: 5944 3911 7631 Jewelry, precious
stones and precious metals; Jewelry,
precious metal; Jewelry repair services

(G-1226)
KEENEY HOLDINGS LLC
74 Batterson Park Rd Ste 102
(06032-2565)
PHONE..............................860 666-3342
Chris Jeffers, *Managing Member*
Neal Restivo, *
EMP: 298 **EST:** 2019
SALES (est): 97.17MM
SALES (corp-wide): 304.6MM **Privately
Held**
SIC: 5074 5999 3088 Plumbing fittings and
supplies; Plumbing and heating supplies;
Plastics plumbing fixtures
PA: Oatey Co.
20600 Emerald Pkwy
Cleveland OH 44135
800 203-1155

(G-1227)
KIP INC
Also Called: Norgren
72 Spring Ln (06032-3140)

PHONE..............................860 677-0272
Nick Testanero, *Pr*
Nicholas Testanero, *
Gary Fett, *
Donald Mcmahan, *Sec*
James Etter, *
▲ **EMP:** 189 **EST:** 1962
SALES (est): 38.04MM
SALES (corp-wide): 2.47B **Privately Held**
SIC: 3491 Solenoid valves
HQ: Norgren Limited
Cross Chancellor Street
Leeds LS6 2
113 245-7587

(G-1228)
LATIN AMERICAN HOLDING INC
(HQ)
1 Carrier Pl (06032-2562)
PHONE..............................860 674-3000
Robert Galli, *Dir*
EMP: 11 **EST:** 1990
SALES (est): 10.44MM
SALES (corp-wide): 67.07B **Publicly Held**
SIC: 3585 Refrigeration and heating
equipment
PA: Rtx Corporation
1000 Wilson Blvd
Arlington VA 22209
781 522-3000

(G-1229)
LITHOGRAPHICS INC
55 Spring Ln (06032-3139)
P.O. Box 767 (06034-0767)
PHONE..............................860 678-1660
Judith A Wilson, *Pr*
Thomas R Smith, *
Glenn H Wilson, *
Jill W Kijanka, *
EMP: 21 **EST:** 1968
SQ FT: 31,800
SALES (est): 1.73MM **Privately Held**
Web: www.lithographicsinc.com
SIC: 2752 Offset printing

(G-1230)
MOTT CORPORATION (PA)
75 Spring Ln (06032-3139)
PHONE..............................860 864-5017
Boris F Levin, *CEO*
Michele A Listro, *
◆ **EMP:** 90 **EST:** 1959
SQ FT: 50,000
SALES (est): 60.39MM
SALES (corp-wide): 60.39MM **Privately
Held**
Web: www.mottcorp.com
SIC: 3569 Filters

(G-1231)
NEW ENGLAND AIRFOIL PDTS
INC
36 Spring Ln (06032-3140)
PHONE..............................860 677-1376
Michele Cassin, *Pr*
EMP: 25 **EST:** 2015
SQ FT: 100,000
SALES (est): 5.03MM
SALES (corp-wide): 64.36MM **Privately
Held**
Web:
www.newenglandairfoilproductsinc.com
SIC: 3721 3724 3795 Aircraft; Aircraft
engines and engine parts; Tanks and tank
components
HQ: Pietro Rosa T.B.M. Srl
Via Francesco Petrarca 7
Maniago PN 33085
042771503

(G-1232)
NORGREN LLC
Also Called: IMI Precision Engineering
72 Spring Ln (06032-3140)
P.O. Box 468 (06034-0468)
PHONE..............................860 677-0272
Nick Testanero, *Brnch Mgr*
EMP: 200
SALES (corp-wide): 2.47B **Privately Held**
Web: www.norgren.com
SIC: 3492 Control valves, fluid power:
hydraulic and pneumatic
HQ: Norgren Llc
5400 S Delaware St
Littleton CO 80120
303 794-5000

(G-1233)
NORTH AMERICAN ELEV SVCS
CO (DH)
Also Called: Delta Elevator Service
1 Farm Springs Rd (06032-2572)
PHONE..............................860 676-6000
Micheal Hartigan, *Pr*
Kent Brittan, *VP Fin*
Kathie Johnson, *Admn*
EMP: 20 **EST:** 1990
SALES (est): 15.78MM
SALES (corp-wide): 13.69B **Publicly Held**
SIC: 7699 3625 Elevators: inspection,
service, and repair; Control equipment,
electric
HQ: Otis Elevator Company
1 Carrier Pl
Farmington CT 06032
860 674-3000

(G-1234)
OLD DMFG INC
Also Called: Dayon Mfg., Inc.
1820 New Britain Ave (06032-3114)
P.O. Box 588 (06034-0588)
PHONE..............................860 677-8561
Kim D Sonstroem, *Pr*
Rose Marie Sonstroem, *VP*
Janice R Keller, *Sec*
▲ **EMP:** 20 **EST:** 1957
SQ FT: 17,000
SALES (est): 4.94MM
SALES (corp-wide): 46.66MM **Privately
Held**
Web: www.dayonspring.com
SIC: 3495 3493 Precision springs; Steel
springs, except wire
PA: Lee Spring Company Llc
140 58th St Ste 3c
Brooklyn NY 11220
888 777-4647

(G-1235)
OTIS ELEVATOR COMPANY (HQ)
Also Called: Otis
1 Carrier Pl (06032-2562)
P.O. Box 730400 (75373-0400)
PHONE..............................860 674-3000
Judith F Marks, *Pr*
Rahul Ghai, *Ex VP*
Todd Glance, *Ofcr*
◆ **EMP:** 132 **EST:** 1906
SALES (est): 983.44MM
SALES (corp-wide): 13.69B **Publicly Held**
Web: www.otis.com
SIC: 3534 7699 1796 7371 Elevators and
equipment; Miscellaneous building item
repair services; Elevator installation and
conversion; Computer software
development
PA: Otis Worldwide Corporation
1 Carrier Pl
Farmington CT 06032
860 674-3000

▲ = Import ▼ = Export
◆ = Import/Export

(G-1236)
OTIS ELEVATOR INTL INC
10 Farm Springs Rd (06032-2577)
PHONE................................860 676-6000
Angelo J Messina, *Pr*
Johan O Bill, *VP*
Christopher Witzky, *Treas*
EMP: 233 **EST:** 1972
SALES (est): 17.86MM
SALES (corp-wide): 13.69B **Publicly Held**
Web: www.otis.com
SIC: 3534 Elevators and moving stairways
HQ: Otis Elevator Company
1 Carrier Pl
Farmington CT 06032
860 674-3000

(G-1237)
OTIS WORLDWIDE CORPORATION (PA)
Also Called: Otis
1 Carrier Pl (06032-2562)
PHONE................................860 674-3000
Judith F Marks, *Ch Bd*
Anurag Maheshwari, *Ex VP*
Abbe Luersman, *CPO*
Peiming Zheng, *Ex VP*
Nora E Lafreniere, *Ex VP*
EMP: 562 **EST:** 1853
SALES (est): 13.69B
SALES (corp-wide): 13.69B **Publicly Held**
Web: www.otis.com
SIC: 3534 7699 Elevators and moving
stairways; Elevators: inspection, service,
and repair

(G-1238)
PANELOC CORPORATION
142 Brickyard Rd (06032-1202)
P.O. Box 547 (06034-0547)
PHONE................................860 677-6711
Courtney Crocker Iii, *Pr*
Sarah Horner, *
EMP: 32 **EST:** 1969
SQ FT: 13,000
SALES (est): 2.71MM **Privately Held**
Web: www.paneloc.com
SIC: 3429 3965 Aircraft hardware; Fasteners

(G-1239)
PAR MANUFACTURING INC
Also Called: Par Thread Grinding
1824 New Britain Ave (06032-3114)
PHONE................................860 677-1797
Ken Dimauro, *Pr*
John Vasellina Junior, *Pr*
EMP: 8 **EST:** 1951
SQ FT: 5,000
SALES (est): 675.53K **Privately Held**
Web: www.parmfg.com
SIC: 3599 Machine shop, jobbing and repair

(G-1240)
PARK AVENUE SECURITIES
197 Scott Swamp Rd (06032-3384)
PHONE................................860 677-2600
Bob Worgaftik, *Prin*
EMP: 10 **EST:** 2016
SALES (est): 504.13K **Privately Held**
Web: www.cfsllc.com
SIC: 3714 Motor vehicle parts and
accessories

(G-1241)
POLAR CORPORATION
1790 New Britain Ave (06032-3315)
PHONE................................862 225-6000
Andrew Kawalski, *CEO*
Daniel Texira, *Mgr*
EMP: 15 **EST:** 1981

SALES (est): 690.01K **Privately Held**
Web: www.polarcorporation.com
SIC: 3599 Machine shop, jobbing and repair

(G-1242)
POLYMER RESOURCES LTD (PA)
Also Called: Polymer Resources
656 New Britain Ave (06032-2146)
PHONE................................800 243-5176
Leslie M Klein, *Ch Bd*
Scott Anderson, *Pr*
▲ **EMP:** 60 **EST:** 1976
SALES (est): 44.38MM
SALES (corp-wide): 44.38MM **Privately Held**
Web: www.prlresins.com
SIC: 2821 Plastics materials and resins

(G-1243)
RAYM-CO INC
62 Spring Ln (06032-3140)
PHONE................................860 678-8292
Sarah Artibani, *Pr*
Karen Motta, *
Brandon Artibani, *
EMP: 43 **EST:** 1980
SQ FT: 35,000
SALES (est): 4.3MM **Privately Held**
Web: www.raymco.com
SIC: 3599 Machine shop, jobbing and repair

(G-1244)
RTX CORPORATION
Also Called: UTC Climate Controls & SEC
9 Farm Springs Rd Ste 3 (06032-2576)
PHONE................................954 485-6501
William Brown, *Pr*
EMP: 500
SALES (corp-wide): 67.07B **Publicly Held**
Web: www.rtx.com
SIC: 3699 3669 Security devices; Fire
detection systems, electric
PA: Rtx Corporation
1000 Wilson Blvd
Arlington VA 22209
781 522-3000

(G-1245)
RTX CORPORATION
Also Called: Carrier Commercial Rfrgn
4 Farm Springs Rd (06032-2573)
PHONE................................860 678-4500
Barbara Coccomo, *Mgr*
EMP: 250
SALES (corp-wide): 67.07B **Publicly Held**
Web: www.rtx.com
SIC: 3724 Aircraft engines and engine parts
PA: Rtx Corporation
1000 Wilson Blvd
Arlington VA 22209
781 522-3000

(G-1246)
SAAR CORPORATION
81 Spring Ln (06032-3139)
PHONE................................860 674-9440
EMP: 13 **EST:** 1995
SQ FT: 8,000
SALES (est): 2.07MM **Privately Held**
Web: www.saarcorp.com
SIC: 3841 3724 Surgical and medical
instruments; Aircraft engines and engine
parts

(G-1247)
SERVICE NETWORK INC
Also Called: Edac Machinery
21 Spring Ln (06032-3128)
PHONE................................860 679-7432

EMP: 60
SQ FT: 300,000
SALES (est): 5.77MM
SALES (corp-wide): 143.58MM **Privately Held**
SIC: 3541 Machine tools, metal cutting type
PA: Edac Technologies Llc
5 Mckee Pl
Cheshire CT 06410
203 806-2090

(G-1248)
STANLEY BLACK & DECKER INC
Also Called: Stanley Access Technologies
65 Scott Swamp Rd (Corner Of Rte 6 &
Hyde Rd) (06032-2803)
PHONE................................860 677-2861
EMP: 14
SALES (corp-wide): 16.95B **Publicly Held**
Web: www.stanleyblackanddecker.com
SIC: 5031 1751 7699 3699 Doors, nec;
Window and door installation and erection;
Door and window repair; Electrical
equipment and supplies, nec
PA: Stanley Black & Decker, Inc.
1000 Stanley Dr
New Britain CT 06053
860 225-5111

(G-1249)
SYSTEMATIC AUTOMATION INC
20 Executive Dr (06032-2838)
PHONE................................310 218-3361
Joseph J Gilberti, *Pr*
Maria Gilberti, *
EMP: 40 **EST:** 1983
SQ FT: 40,000
SALES (est): 9.21MM **Privately Held**
Web: www.systauto.com
SIC: 8711 3552 3555 2396 Designing: ship,
boat, machine, and product; Silk screens
for textile industry; Printing trades
machinery; Automotive and apparel
trimmings

(G-1250)
TAYLOR COML FOODSERVICE INC
Taylor Company
3 Farm Glen Blvd Ste 301 (06032-1981)
P.O. Box 410 (61072-0410)
PHONE................................336 245-6400
Clark Wangaard, *Pr*
EMP: 627
SQ FT: 100,000
SALES (corp-wide): 4.03B **Publicly Held**
Web: www.taylor-company.com
SIC: 3556 Ice cream manufacturing
machinery
HQ: Taylor Commercial Foodservice, Llc
750 N Blackhawk Blvd
Rockton IL 61072
815 624-8333

(G-1251)
TRANE US INC
Also Called: Trane
135 South Rd (06032-2556)
P.O. Box 977 (06034-0977)
PHONE................................860 470-3901
Kevin Mcnamara, *Brnch Mgr*
EMP: 10
Web: www.trane.com
SIC: 3585 Refrigeration and heating
equipment
HQ: Trane U.S. Inc.
800 Beaty St Ste E
Davidson NC 28036
704 655-4000

(G-1252)
TRU-PRECISION CORPORATION
1451 New Britain Ave Ste 86 (06032-3343)
PHONE................................860 269-6230
Chester Schwalenberg, *Pr*
EMP: 9 **EST:** 1985
SALES (est): 844.38K **Privately Held**
Web: www.truprecision.us
SIC: 3724 3469 Aircraft engines and engine
parts; Machine parts, stamped or pressed
metal

(G-1253)
TRUMPF INC
5 Johnson Ave (06032-2842)
PHONE................................860 255-6000
EMP: 21
SALES (corp-wide): 4.51B **Privately Held**
Web: www.trumpf.com
SIC: 3542 Sheet metalworking machines
HQ: Trumpf, Inc.
111 Hyde Rd
Farmington CT 06032
860 255-6000

(G-1254)
TRUMPF INC
1 Johnson Ave (06032-2842)
PHONE................................860 255-6000
EMP: 27
SALES (corp-wide): 4.51B **Privately Held**
Web: www.trumpf.com
SIC: 3542 3423 3546 Sheet metalworking
machines; Hand and edge tools, nec;
Power-driven handtools
HQ: Trumpf, Inc.
111 Hyde Rd
Farmington CT 06032
860 255-6000

(G-1255)
TRUMPF INC (DH)
111 Hyde Rd (06032-2851)
P.O. Box 105 (06034-0105)
PHONE................................860 255-6000
Peter Hoecklin, *Pr*
Nicola Leibinger-kammuller, *Ch Bd*
Stuart Douglas Devnew, *VP*
John Burke Doar, *Sr VP*
Bettina Steingruber, *CFO*
◆ **EMP:** 48 **EST:** 1969
SQ FT: 160,000
SALES (est): 201.82MM
SALES (corp-wide): 4.51B **Privately Held**
Web: www.trumpf.com
SIC: 3542 3423 3546 Sheet metalworking
machines; Hand and edge tools, nec;
Power-driven handtools
HQ: Trumpf International Beteiligungs-Ag
Johann-Maus-Str. 2
Ditzingen BW 71254
71563030

(G-1256)
TRUMPF PHOTONICS INC
111 Hyde Rd (06032-2834)
PHONE................................860 255-6000
Nicola Leibinger-kammuller, *CEO*
Mathias Kammuller, *CDO*
Lars Grunert, *CFO*
Christian Schmitz, *LT*
EMP: 69 **EST:** 2002
SALES (est): 5.55MM
SALES (corp-wide): 4.51B **Privately Held**
Web: www.trumpf.com
SIC: 3444 Sheet metalwork
PA: Trumpf Se + Co. Kg
Johann-Maus-Str. 2
Ditzingen BW 71254
71563030

GEOGRAPHIC

(G-1257)
TURBINE TECHNOLOGIES INC (PA)
Also Called: Burke Aerospace
126 Hyde Rd (06032-2866)
P.O. Box 1267 (06034-1267)
PHONE...............................860 678-1642
Tyler Burke, *CEO*
Brittany Isherwood, *
Justin Lamprey, *
Tyler Burke, *Bd of Dir*
Lou Auletta, *
EMP: 65 **EST:** 1991
SALES (est): 24.76MM **Privately Held**
Web: www.burkeaerospace.com
SIC: 3724 3714 Aircraft engines and engine parts; Motor vehicle parts and accessories

(G-1258)
WENDELL ENTERPRISES INC
4 Right Ln (06032-3148)
PHONE...............................860 846-0800
EMP: 238 **EST:** 1957
SALES (est): 961.29K
SALES (corp-wide): 139.19MM **Privately Held**
PA: Whitcraft Llc
76 County Rd
Eastford CT 06242
860 974-0786

Gales Ferry
New London County

(G-1259)
B&R SAND AND GRAVEL
1358 Baldwin Hill Rd (06335-1856)
PHONE...............................860 464-5099
EMP: 8 **EST:** 2016
SALES (est): 524.52K **Privately Held**
SIC: 3273 Ready-mixed concrete

(G-1260)
INTEGRATED MEDICAL SYSTEMS INC
5 Little John Ct (06335-1306)
PHONE...............................860 949-2929
EMP: 15
SIC: 3845 Electromedical equipment

(G-1261)
STONINGTON SERVICES LLC
Also Called: Brand Services
39 Kings Hwy (06335-1535)
PHONE...............................860 464-1991
Jo-ann Chiangi, *Managing Member*
John Chiangi, *
EMP: 48 **EST:** 2004
SQ FT: 4,400
SALES (est): 3.98MM **Privately Held**
Web: www.brand-svc.com
SIC: 8742 3442 Management consulting services; Fire doors, metal

(G-1262)
TOWN OF LEDYARD
Also Called: Town of Medyard, The
889 Colonel Ledyard Hwy (06339-1102)
PHONE...............................860 464-9060
Steve Maslin, *Brnch Mgr*
EMP: 10
SALES (corp-wide): 78.2MM **Privately Held**
Web: www.ledyardct.org
SIC: 3531 Road construction and maintenance machinery
PA: Town Of Ledyard
741 Colonel Ledyard Hwy

Ledyard CT 06339
860 464-3235

Gaylordsville
Litchfield County

(G-1263)
CANDLEWOOD TOOL AND MCH SP INC
24 Martha Ln (06755-1501)
PHONE...............................860 355-1892
George Christophersen, *Pr*
Joan B Christophersen, *Sec*
James Jacques, *VP*
Amy Jacques, *Treas*
EMP: 10 **EST:** 1974
SQ FT: 5,300
SALES (est): 926.49K **Privately Held**
Web: www.candlewoodtool.com
SIC: 3599 3544 Machine shop, jobbing and repair; Special dies and tools

(G-1264)
CONWAY HARDWOOD PRODUCTS LLC
Also Called: Conway Hardwood Products
37 Gaylord Rd (06755-1518)
PHONE...............................860 355-4030
Jeremiah C Conway, *Managing Member*
▲ **EMP:** 25 **EST:** 1977
SQ FT: 9,000
SALES (est): 2.49MM **Privately Held**
Web: www.conwayhardwood.com
SIC: 2426 2434 2431 5211 Flooring, hardwood; Wood kitchen cabinets; Moldings, wood: unfinished and prefinished ; Lumber products

(G-1265)
MICRO SOURCE DISCOVERY SYSTEMS
11 George Washington Plz (06755-1500)
PHONE...............................860 350-8078
John Devlin, *Pr*
Mary Ortner, *VP*
EMP: 7 **EST:** 1994
SQ FT: 2,000
SALES (est): 770.14K **Privately Held**
Web: www.msdiscovery.com
SIC: 2834 Pharmaceutical preparations

Gilman
New London County

(G-1266)
GILMAN CORPORATION
1 Polly Ln (06336)
P.O. Box 68 (06336-0068)
PHONE...............................860 887-7080
Richard Gilman, *CEO*
Elizabeth Gilman, *
▼ **EMP:** 30 **EST:** 1948
SQ FT: 32,000
SALES (est): 6.7MM **Privately Held**
Web: www.gilmancorp.com
SIC: 3086 3949 Plastics foam products; Sporting and athletic goods, nec

(G-1267)
MARTY GILMAN INCORPORATED (PA)
Also Called: Gilman Gear
30 Gilman Rd (06336-1006)
P.O. Box 97 (06336-0097)
PHONE...............................860 889-7334
Shirley Gilman, *Ch Bd*

Neil Gilman, *
Geoffrey Gilman, *
EMP: 47 **EST:** 1929
SQ FT: 20,000
SALES (est): 6.98MM
SALES (corp-wide): 6.98MM **Privately Held**
Web: www.gilmangear.com
SIC: 3949 Sporting and athletic goods, nec

(G-1268)
THE GILMAN BROTHERS COMPANY
9 Thomas Rd (06336-1008)
P.O. Box 38 (06336-0038)
PHONE...............................860 889-8444
◆ **EMP:** 69 **EST:** 1897
SALES (est): 19.02MM **Privately Held**
Web: www.gilmanbrothers.com
SIC: 3993 3086 3089 2672 Signs and advertising specialties; Plastics foam products; Plastics hardware and building products; Coated paper, except photographic, carbon, or abrasive

Glastonbury
Hartford County

(G-1269)
ACTIVE INTERNET TECH LLC (PA)
Also Called: Finalsite
655 Winding Brook Dr Ste 10 (06033-4337)
PHONE...............................800 592-2469
EMP: 109 **EST:** 2010
SALES (est): 28.44MM **Privately Held**
Web: www.finalsite.com
SIC: 7371 7372 Computer software development; Educational computer software

(G-1270)
BIOMED HEALTH INC
70 Oakwood Dr Ste 8 (06033-2459)
P.O. Box 911 (06033-0911)
PHONE...............................860 657-2258
M E Sherman, *Pr*
Generosa Mendez, *Sec*
EMP: 7 **EST:** 1992
SALES (est): 946.95K **Privately Held**
Web: www.biomed-health.com
SIC: 2833 2834 Vitamins, natural or synthetic: bulk, uncompounded; Pharmaceutical preparations

(G-1271)
BOUNCYBAND LLC
148 Eastern Blvd Ste 308 (06033)
PHONE...............................860 916-9978
EMP: 7 **EST:** 2014
SALES (est): 127.64K **Privately Held**
Web: www.bouncyband.com
SIC: 2531 School furniture

(G-1272)
BRITISH PRECISION INC
20 Sequin Dr (06033-2475)
PHONE...............................860 633-3343
Ralph Naylor, *Pr*
Mary Naylor, *
EMP: 16 **EST:** 1974
SQ FT: 11,000
SALES (est): 973.69K **Privately Held**
Web: www.britishprecision.com
SIC: 3599 Machine shop, jobbing and repair

(G-1273)
CAMERON INTERNATIONAL CORP
Also Called: Measurement Systems
256 Oakwood Dr Ste 1 (06033-2465)
PHONE...............................860 633-0277
Kim Giansianti, *Mgr*
EMP: 10
Web: www.slb.com
SIC: 3533 Oil and gas field machinery
HQ: Cameron International Corporation
1333 West Loop S Ste 1700
Houston TX 77027

(G-1274)
CLEARSPAN FABR STRCTRES INTL I
Also Called: Clearspan
703 Hebron Ave Ste 3 (06033-5001)
PHONE...............................866 643-1010
Barry Goldsher, *Pr*
Charles Clark Junior, *Sec*
EMP: 25 **EST:** 2006
SALES (est): 6.19MM **Privately Held**
Web: www.clearspan.com
SIC: 3441 Fabricated structural metal

(G-1275)
CONARD CORPORATION
101 Commerce St (06033-2312)
P.O. Box 676 (06033-0676)
PHONE...............................860 659-0591
William J Fox, *Pr*
▲ **EMP:** 23 **EST:** 1965
SQ FT: 12,000
SALES (est): 4.04MM **Privately Held**
Web: www.conardcorp.com
SIC: 3479 Etching on metals

(G-1276)
CREOLE JOS LLC
2389 Main St Ste 100 (06033-4617)
PHONE...............................203 893-2875
Joel Hamilton, *Managing Member*
EMP: 12 **EST:** 2017
SALES (est): 607.87K **Privately Held**
SIC: 2599 5812 Food wagons, restaurant; Caterers

(G-1277)
ENGINE ALLIANCE LLC
Also Called: Engine Alliance
124 Hebron Ave Ste 200 (06033)
PHONE...............................860 565-2239
Dean Athans, *Pr*
Todd Kallman, *
Willam Fehling, *
David Joyce, *
Ron Schlechtweg, *
EMP: 400 **EST:** 2003
SALES (est): 114.5MM
SALES (corp-wide): 68.92B **Publicly Held**
Web: www.enginealliance.com
SIC: 3724 Aircraft engines and engine parts
PA: Rtx Corporation
1000 Wilson Blvd
Arlington VA 22209
781 522-3000

(G-1278)
FREEDOM TECHNOLOGIES LLC
80 Timrod Trl (06033-1937)
P.O. Box 117 (06025-0117)
PHONE...............................860 633-0452
EMP: 8 **EST:** 1993
SQ FT: 5,000
SALES (est): 765.33K **Privately Held**
Web: www.freedomlaser.com

▲ = Import ▼ = Export
◆ = Import/Export

SIC: 3661 Telephone and telegraph apparatus

(G-1279)
G & G DISSOLUTION CORP
137 National Dr (06033-1211)
PHONE...............................860 633-7099
TOLL FREE: 888
▲ EMP: 35
SIC: 3089 3544 Injection molding of plastics ; Special dies, tools, jigs, and fixtures

(G-1280)
GENERAL ELECTRO COMPONENTS
Also Called: Line Electric
122 Naubuc Ave Ste A7 (06033-4226)
P.O. Box 127 (06073-0127)
PHONE...............................860 659-3573
Bill Harris, Pr
◆ EMP: 8 EST: 1980
SQ FT: 5,000
SALES (est): 886.12K Privately Held
Web: www.lineelectric.com
SIC: 3679 3625 3613 Electronic circuits; Relays, for electronic use; Switchgear and switchboard apparatus

(G-1281)
GLASTONBURY CITIZEN INC
Also Called: Glastonbury Citizen
87 Nutmeg Ln (06033-2353)
P.O. Box 373 (06033-0373)
PHONE...............................860 633-4691
Jane Hallas, Pr
James Hallas, VP
Marian Hallas, Sec
EMP: 14 EST: 1948
SQ FT: 3,200
SALES (est): 817.45K Privately Held
Web: www.glcitizen.com
SIC: 2711 Job printing and newspaper publishing combined

(G-1282)
GSS INFOTECH CT INC
41b New London Tpke Ste 7 (06033-4240)
PHONE...............................860 709-0933
EMP: 150 EST: 1995
SQ FT: 3,000
SALES (est): 21.3MM Privately Held
Web: www.gssinfotech.com
SIC: 7372 7379 8742 7371 Prepackaged software; Computer related consulting services; Management consulting services; Custom computer programming services
HQ: Gss Infotech Inc.
    2050 Brnswick Plz State H
    North Brunswick NJ 08902
    732 798-3101

(G-1283)
HABCO INDUSTRIES LLC
Also Called: Habco
172 Oak St (06033-2318)
PHONE...............................860 682-6800
Brian Montnari, CEO
Paul Rocheleau, *
Jeff Kretzmer, *
Nick Zandonella, *
EMP: 32 EST: 2013
SQ FT: 50,000
SALES (est): 6.61MM Privately Held
Web: www.habco.biz
SIC: 3824 3825 3829 Fluid meters and counting devices; Instruments to measure electricity; Measuring and controlling devices, nec

(G-1284)
HANWHA AEROSPACE USA LLC
Also Called: Edac ND
81 National Dr (06033-1211)
P.O. Box 396 (06033-0396)
PHONE...............................860 633-9474
Terry Bruni, CEO
EMP: 100 EST: 1951
SQ FT: 55,000
SALES (est): 13.93MM Privately Held
Web: www.hanwhaaerospaceusa.com
SIC: 3728 3812 3721 Aircraft assemblies, subassemblies, and parts, nec; Search and navigation equipment; Aircraft
HQ: Hanwha Aerospace Usa Llc
    5 Mckee Pl
    Cheshire CT 06410
    203 806-2090

(G-1285)
HARPOON ACQUISITION CORP
455 Winding Brook Dr (06033-4315)
PHONE...............................860 815-5736
Louis Hernandez Junior, CEO
EMP: 25 EST: 2006
SALES (est): 4.42MM
SALES (corp-wide): 17.74B Publicly Held
SIC: 7372 7373 Business oriented computer software; Systems integration services
PA: Fiserv, Inc.
    255 Fiserv Dr
    Brookfield WI 53045
    262 879-5000

(G-1286)
HIGHWAY SAFETY LLC (HQ)
Also Called: Connecticut Galvanizing
239 Commerce St (06033-2448)
P.O. Box 358 (06033-0358)
PHONE...............................860 633-9445
TOLL FREE: 800
W Patric Gregory Iii, CEO
Robert West, *
▼ EMP: 100 EST: 1978
SQ FT: 83,000
SALES (est): 80.2MM
SALES (corp-wide): 85.75MM Privately Held
Web: www.highwaysafety.net
SIC: 3444 3479 Guard rails, highway: sheet metal; Galvanizing of iron, steel, or end-formed products
PA: Race Rock Gp, L.L.C.
    1980 Post Oak Blvd # 2175
    Houston TX 77056
    832 920-1276

(G-1287)
KEM LIQUIDATING COMPANY INC
172 Oak St (06033-2318)
PHONE...............................860 430-5100
EMP: 32
SIC: 3823 3824 3825 8711 Industrial process control instruments; Fluid meters and counting devices; Instruments to measure electricity; Designing: ship, boat, machine, and product

(G-1288)
LYDALL THERMAL/ ACOUSTICAL INC
180 Glastonbury Blvd (06033-4439)
P.O. Box 151 (06045-0151)
PHONE...............................860 646-1233
Dale G Barnhart, CEO
Robert K Julian, Pr
William M Lachenmeyer, VP
James Laughlan, VP
Chad Mcdaniel, VP
EMP: 23 EST: 2006
SALES (est): 6.29MM Privately Held
Web: www.lydall.com
SIC: 2297 Nonwoven fabrics

(G-1289)
MAURER & SHEPHERD JOYNERS
122 Naubuc Ave Ste B4 (06033-4271)
PHONE...............................860 633-2383
Galen Shepherd, Pr
Donna Shepherd, VP
EMP: 10 EST: 1973
SQ FT: 3,000
SALES (est): 703.41K Privately Held
Web: www.thecoopergroupct.com
SIC: 2431 Woodwork, interior and ornamental, nec

(G-1290)
MITSUBISHI POWER AERO LLC (HQ)
628 Hebron Ave Ste 400 (06033-5018)
PHONE...............................860 368-5900
Raul Pereda, Pr
Nimesh Patel, *
Christopher Jones, *
◆ EMP: 146 EST: 1961
SQ FT: 59,954
SALES (est): 123.4MM Privately Held
Web: power.mhi.com
SIC: 3511 Turbines and turbine generator sets
PA: Mitsubishi Heavy Industries, Ltd.
    3-2-3, Marunouchi
    Chiyoda-Ku TKY 100-0

(G-1291)
NORTHEAST CIRCUIT TECH LLC
112 Sherwood Dr (06033-3724)
PHONE...............................860 633-1967
George R Willis, Prin
EMP: 7 EST: 2001
SALES (est): 193.96K Privately Held
SIC: 3672 Printed circuit boards

(G-1292)
PARTNER IN PUBLISHING LLC
1715 Main St (06033-2939)
PHONE...............................860 430-9440
EMP: 50 EST: 2011
SALES (est): 5.15MM Privately Held
Web: www.partnerinpublishing.com
SIC: 2741 Miscellaneous publishing

(G-1293)
PINTO MANUFACTURING LLC
122 Naubuc Ave (06033-4298)
PHONE...............................860 659-9543
Robert Pinto, Owner
EMP: 8 EST: 1976
SQ FT: 3,000
SALES (est): 685.7K Privately Held
Web: www.pintomanufacturing.com
SIC: 3599 Machine shop, jobbing and repair

(G-1294)
PLASTICS AND CONCEPTS CONN INC
101 Laurel Trl (06033-4055)
PHONE...............................860 657-9655
Kathleen Harris, Pr
Harold Harris, Sec
Tom Harris, VP
EMP: 9 EST: 1970
SQ FT: 3,000
SALES (est): 417.08K Privately Held
Web: plasticsandconcepts.wordpress.com

SIC: 3089 3498 Injection molding of plastics ; Tube fabricating (contract bending and shaping)

(G-1295)
PROJECTS INC
65 Sequin Dr (06033-2484)
P.O. Box 190 (06033-0190)
PHONE...............................860 633-4615
F Michael Kenyon, Pr
Adelle Kenyon, *
Joseph Kenyon, *
EMP: 102 EST: 1959
SQ FT: 36,000
SALES (est): 23.33MM Privately Held
Web: www.projectsinc.com
SIC: 3829 3599 7699 3823 Thermocouples; Machine shop, jobbing and repair; Precision instrument repair; Process control instruments

(G-1296)
R & M ASSOCIATES INC
Also Called: Close To Home
277 Hebron Ave (06033-2116)
PHONE...............................860 633-0721
Marc Gattinella, Prin
Ronald Gattinella, Pr
Marilyn Gattinella, VP
Paul Gattinella, Prin
EMP: 13 EST: 1982
SQ FT: 5,700
SALES (est): 1.36MM Privately Held
Web: www.closetohomestores.com
SIC: 5949 2591 Fabric stores piece goods; Drapery hardware and window blinds and shades

(G-1297)
REMINDER BROADCASTER
Also Called: Reminder Media
37 Cardinal Dr (06033-1753)
PHONE...............................860 875-3366
Ken Hovland, Pr
EMP: 16 EST: 2002
SALES (est): 513.06K Privately Held
Web: www.courant.com
SIC: 2711 Newspapers, publishing and printing

(G-1298)
T-SHIRTS ETC INC
74 Kreiger Ln Ste 1 (06033-2377)
P.O. Box 995 (06033-0995)
PHONE...............................860 657-3551
Paul Bowler, Pr
Debra Bowler, VP
Stacey Fagan, Mgr
EMP: 7 EST: 1989
SQ FT: 2,700
SALES (est): 462.66K Privately Held
Web: www.tseink.com
SIC: 7299 2396 Stitching, custom; Screen printing on fabric articles

(G-1299)
TOUCHE MANUFACTURING COMPANY
200 Glastonbury Blvd (06033-4418)
PHONE...............................860 254-5080
Rolando Loera, Ch Bd
Livino D Ribaya Junior, VP
Frank Ramirez Iii, VP
Charles E Shaw, VP
Robert Loera, Sec
EMP: 17 EST: 1971
SQ FT: 123,000
SALES (est): 256.75K Privately Held
SIC: 3469 Electronic enclosures, stamped or pressed metal

(G-1300)
TURBINE KINETICS INC
Also Called: Heico
60 Sequin Dr Ste 2 (06033-5042)
PHONE..................................860 633-8520
Mike Siegel, *CEO*
Bryan Peters, *Sr VP*
EMP: 11 EST: 1984
SALES (est): 12.49MM **Publicly Held**
Web: www.heico.com
SIC: 3724 Aircraft engines and engine parts
HQ: Heico Aerospace Holdings Corp.
3000 Taft St
Hollywood FL 33021
954 987-4000

(G-1301)
WALKER PRODUCTS INCORPORATED
80 Commerce St Ste C (06033-2385)
PHONE..................................860 659-3781
TOLL FREE: 800
Bernadine A Brock, *Pr*
Charles Y Brock Junior, *Sec*
▲ **EMP: 14 EST:** 1977
SQ FT: 25,000
SALES (est): 1.64MM **Privately Held**
Web: www.walkermarkerboards.com
SIC: 2675 Die-cut paper and board

Goshen
Litchfield County

(G-1302)
COUNTRY LOG HOMES INC
Also Called: Country Log Homes
27 Rockwall Ct (06756-1714)
PHONE..................................413 229-8084
Ivan Chassie, *Pr*
Doreen Chassie, *Sec*
EMP: 10 EST: 1994
SQ FT: 12,000
SALES (est): 269.52K **Privately Held**
SIC: 2452 1521 Log cabins, prefabricated, wood; Single-family housing construction

(G-1303)
L & L MECHANICAL LLC
28 Pie Hill Rd (06756-2024)
PHONE..................................860 491-4007
EMP: 11 EST: 1989
SALES (est): 1.01MM **Privately Held**
SIC: 3443 1711 Ducting, metal plate; Ventilation and duct work contractor

(G-1304)
SUNSET MEADOW FARM LLC
599 Old Middle St (06756-2205)
PHONE..................................860 201-4654
George Motel, *Asstg*
EMP: 11 EST: 2007
SALES (est): 922.7K **Privately Held**
Web: www.sunsetmeadowvineyards.com
SIC: 2084 Wines

Granby
Hartford County

(G-1305)
ARROW CONCRETE PRODUCTS INC (PA)
560 Salmon Brook St (06035-1100)
PHONE..................................860 653-5063
Kurt A Burkhart, *Pr*
Ronald Burkhart Senior, *VP*
Bertha Burkhart, *
▲ **EMP: 32 EST:** 1953
SALES (est): 12.36MM
SALES (corp-wide): 12.36MM **Privately Held**
Web: www.arrow-concrete.com
SIC: 3272 Septic tanks, concrete

(G-1306)
GRASS ROOTS CREAMERY
4 Park Pl (06035-2300)
PHONE..................................860 653-6303
Elizabeth Florian, *Prin*
EMP: 9 EST: 2015
SALES (est): 864.24K **Privately Held**
Web: www.grassrootsicecream.com
SIC: 2021 Creamery butter

(G-1307)
KRYSTAL INC LLC
Also Called: Krystal Restaurant
9a Bank St (06035-2303)
P.O. Box 14 (06035-0014)
PHONE..................................860 844-1267
Arun Lillaney, *Pr*
Ron Lira, *Genl Mgr*
EMP: 7 EST: 1986
SQ FT: 2,500
SALES (est): 502.66K **Privately Held**
Web: www.krystal.com
SIC: 5812 5731 2085 American restaurant; Video recorders, players, disc players, and accessories; Neutral spirits, except fruit

(G-1308)
REMARC LLC
46 Twilight Dr (06035-1212)
PHONE..................................860 844-8939
EMP: 7 EST: 2016
SALES (est): 97.9K **Privately Held**
Web: www.remarc.us
SIC: 3599 Machine shop, jobbing and repair

(G-1309)
VILEX LLC
18 Hartford Ave (06035-2304)
PHONE..................................860 413-9875
David Pelizzon, *Managing Member*
EMP: 20 EST: 2019
SALES (est): 995.03K **Privately Held**
SIC: 3841 Surgical and medical instruments

Greenwich
Fairfield County

(G-1310)
ACUREN INSPECTION INC
43 Arch St (06830-6512)
PHONE..................................203 869-6734
Peter Scannell, *Brnch Mgr*
EMP: 9
SALES (corp-wide): 1.5B **Privately Held**
Web: www.acuren.com
SIC: 1389 Testing, measuring, surveying, and analysis services
HQ: Acuren Inspection, Inc.
30 Main St Ste 402
Danbury CT 06810
203 702-8740

(G-1311)
AMERICAN METALS COAL INTL INC (HQ)
Also Called: A M C I
475 Steamboat Rd 2nd Fl (06830-7144)
PHONE..................................203 625-9200
Fritz Kundrun, *CEO*
Hans J Mende, *Pr*
Mike Walker, *Ex VP*

Lisa Krievel, *Sec*
Harris Antoniou, *CEO*
▲ **EMP: 13 EST:** 1987
SQ FT: 3,720
SALES (est): 42.01MM **Privately Held**
SIC: 5052 5051 1222 6512 Coal; Steel; Bituminous coal-underground mining; Commercial and industrial building operation
PA: K M Investment Corporation
475 Steamboat Rd
Greenwich CT 06830

(G-1312)
APRICOT HOME LLC
15 Sheffield Way (06831-3725)
PHONE..................................203 552-1791
Abby Pillari, *Managing Member*
▲ **EMP: 7 EST:** 2012
SALES (est): 310.67K **Privately Held**
SIC: 2273 Carpets and rugs

(G-1313)
APTUIT (SCIENTIFIC OPERATIONS) LLC
2 Greenwich Office Park (06831-5148)
PHONE..................................203 422-6600
EMP: 1725
SIC: 2834 Pharmaceutical preparations

(G-1314)
ASSET INTERNATIONAL INC
Also Called: Plan & Sponsor
125 Greenwich Ave Ste 3 (06830-5527)
PHONE..................................203 629-5014
Charles A Ruffel, *Pr*
J L Engels, *
Nicholas Platt Junior, *Ex VP*
EMP: 30 EST: 1985
SQ FT: 7,000
SALES (est): 2.49MM **Privately Held**
SIC: 2721 6282 Magazines: publishing only, not printed on site; Investment advice

(G-1315)
ATLAS AGI HOLDINGS LLC
Also Called: Agi-Shorewood U.S.
100 Northfield St (06830-4618)
PHONE..................................203 622-9138
Andrew M Bursky, *Managing Member*
Timothy J Fazio, *Managing Member**
Daniel E Cromie, *
Edward J Fletcher, *
Jacob Hudson, *
▼ **EMP: 3860 EST:** 2010
SALES (est): 115.76MM **Privately Held**
Web: www.atlasholdingsllc.com
SIC: 2671 Paper; coated and laminated packaging

(G-1316)
BEAR ISLAND PAPER COMPANY LLC
Also Called: White Birch Paper Company
80 Field Point Rd Ste 3 (06830-6416)
PHONE..................................203 661-3344
Peter Brant, *CEO*
Christopher Brant, *Pr*
Russell Lowder, *Sr VP*
Timothy Butler, *VP*
Thomas Armstrong, *Prin*
EMP: 17 EST: 2011
SALES (est): 327.86K **Privately Held**
SIC: 2621 Paper mills

(G-1317)
BERQ RNG HOLDINGS USA LLC (PA)
Also Called: Berq US Operations

591 W Putnam Ave (06830-6005)
PHONE..................................412 656-8863
Bas Van Berkel, *CEO*
EMP: 10 EST: 2021
SALES (est): 2.9MM
SALES (corp-wide): 2.9MM **Privately Held**
Web: www.berqrng.com
SIC: 1311 Crude petroleum and natural gas

(G-1318)
BH SHOE HOLDINGS INC (HQ)
124 W Putnam Ave Ste 1 (06830-5317)
PHONE..................................203 661-2424
James Issler, *Pr*
Marc Hamburg, *
J Scott Bohling, *
◆ **EMP: 50 EST:** 1992
SALES (est): 383.85MM
SALES (corp-wide): 302.09B **Publicly Held**
SIC: 3143 Men's footwear, except athletic
PA: Berkshire Hathaway Inc.
3555 Farnam St Ste 1440
Omaha NE 68131
402 346-1400

(G-1319)
BLUE SKY STUDIOS INC
Also Called: Blue Sky/Vifx
1 American Ln Ste 301 (06831-2563)
PHONE..................................203 992-6000
Robert Cohen, *Ch Bd*
Hutch Parker, *
Brian Keane, *
EMP: 200 EST: 1987
SALES (est): 39.67MM
SALES (corp-wide): 88.9B **Publicly Held**
Web: www.disney.com
SIC: 7372 7812 Prepackaged software; Motion picture and video production
HQ: Fox Entertainment Group, Llc
1211 Ave Of The Americas
New York NY 10036
212 852-7000

(G-1320)
BRANT INDUSTRIES INC (PA)
Also Called: White Birch Paper Company
80 Field Point Rd Fl 3 (06830-6416)
PHONE..................................203 661-3344
Peter M Brant, *Ch*
Christopher Brant, *Pr*
Bruno Antonios, *VP Fin*
Russell Lowder, *VP Sls*
Timothy Butler, *VP Fin*
◆ **EMP: 18 EST:** 1941
SQ FT: 4,500
SALES (est): 194.59MM
SALES (corp-wide): 194.59MM **Privately Held**
SIC: 2621 Paper mills

(G-1321)
BRANT PAPER INC
80 Field Point Rd Ste 3 (06830-6416)
PHONE..................................203 661-3344
Peter Brant, *Pr*
EMP: 16 EST: 2006
SALES (est): 891.31K **Privately Held**
SIC: 2621 Paper mills

(G-1322)
BRIDGWELL RSURCES HOLDINGS LLC (HQ)
1 Sound Shore Dr Ste 302 (06830-7251)
PHONE..................................203 622-9138
EMP: 45 EST: 2010
SALES (est): 257.62MM
SALES (corp-wide): 8.23B **Privately Held**
Web: www.atlasholdingsllc.com

SIC: **5031** 2491 5039 5153 Paneling, wood; Wood products, creosoted; Prefabricated structures; Grain and field beans
PA: Atlas Holdings, Llc
100 Northfield St
Greenwich CT 06830
203 622-9138

(G-1323)
BUFFALO GULF CAST TRMINALS LLC
100 W Putnam Ave (06830-5361)
PHONE.................................203 930-3802
EMP: 43 EST: 2012
SALES (est): 9.77MM **Publicly Held**
SIC: **1389** Oil and gas field services, nec
HQ: Buffalo Parent Gulf Coast Terminals, Llc
1201 S Sheldon Rd
Houston TX 77015
713 315-2910

(G-1324)
BUISSON JEWELERS INC
200 Railroad Ave Ste 201 (06830-6384)
PHONE.................................203 869-8895
Joel Buisson, *Pr*
Yves Buisson, *Sec*
EMP: 8 EST: 1994
SALES (est): 909.26K **Privately Held**
Web: www.buissonjewelers.com
SIC: **5944** 3961 Jewelry, precious stones and precious metals; Costume jewelry

(G-1325)
CAPRICORN INVESTORS II LP
30 E Elm St (06830-6529)
PHONE.................................203 861-6600
Herbert Winokur Junior, *Genl Pt*
Herbert Winokur Junior, *Managing General Partner*
Nathaniel A Gregory, *Genl Pt*
Dudley C Mecum, *Genl Pt*
James M Better, *Genl Pt*
EMP: 23 EST: 1988
SALES (est): 5.89MM **Privately Held**
SIC: **2676** 5461 6794 Diapers, paper (disposable): made from purchased paper; Retail bakeries; Patent owners and lessors

(G-1326)
CAPRICORN INVESTORS III LP (PA)
30 E Elm St (06830-6529)
PHONE.................................203 861-6600
Herbert Winiker, *Pt*
James Petter, *Pt*
Dudley Micum, *Pt*
▼ EMP: 10 EST: 2000
SALES (est): 17.99MM **Privately Held**
Web: www.tcby.com
SIC: **5812** 6794 3556 5046 Eating places; Patent owners and lessors; Food products machinery; Commercial equipment, nec

(G-1327)
CONNECTICUT IRON WORKS INC
59 Davenport Ave (06830-7105)
PHONE.................................203 869-0657
Albert Margenot, *Pr*
John R Margenot, *VP*
EMP: 8 EST: 1921
SQ FT: 8,800
SALES (est): 975.23K **Privately Held**
SIC: **3441** 3446 Fabricated structural metal; Ornamental metalwork

(G-1328)
DOONEY WOODWORKS LLC
55 Conyers Farm Dr (06831-2736)
PHONE.................................203 869-5457
EMP: 13
SALES (corp-wide): 398.12K **Privately Held**
Web: www.dooneywoodworks.com
SIC: **2431** Millwork
PA: Dooney Woodworks Llc
105 River Rd
Cos Cob CT 06807
203 340-9770

(G-1329)
FAIRFIELD COUNTY LOOK LLC
6 Wyckham Hill Ln (06831-3049)
PHONE.................................203 869-0077
Elaine Ubina, *Prin*
EMP: 9 EST: 2014
SALES (est): 222.21K **Privately Held**
Web: www.fairfieldcountylook.com
SIC: **2721** Magazines: publishing only, not printed on site

(G-1330)
FISHER FOOTWEAR LLC
Also Called: Marc Fisher Footwear
777 W Putnam Ave (06830-5091)
PHONE.................................203 302-2800
Marc Fisher, *CEO*
▲ EMP: 10 EST: 2004
SQ FT: 45,000
SALES (est): 2.58MM **Privately Held**
Web: www.marcfisherfootwearcorp.com
SIC: **3143** 3144 Men's footwear, except athletic; Women's footwear, except athletic

(G-1331)
FISHER SIGERSON MORRISON LLC
777 W Putnam Ave Ste 10 (06830-5014)
PHONE.................................203 302-2800
Marc Fisher, *Managing Member*
▲ EMP: 30 EST: 1990
SQ FT: 1,600
SALES (est): 9.7MM
SALES (corp-wide): 42.46MM **Privately Held**
SIC: **3144** Women's footwear, except athletic
PA: Marc Fisher Llc
777 W Putnam Ave Ste 10
Greenwich CT 06830
203 302-2800

(G-1332)
GRADUATION SOLUTIONS LLC
Also Called: Graduation Source
200 Pemberwick Rd (06831-4236)
PHONE.................................914 934-5991
▲ EMP: 30 EST: 2006
SQ FT: 3,600
SALES (est): 7.66MM **Privately Held**
Web: www.graduationsource.com
SIC: **2384** Robes and dressing gowns

(G-1333)
GREENWICH SENTINEL
28 Bruce Park Ave (06830-2728)
PHONE.................................203 883-1430
Beth Barhydt, *Owner*
EMP: 7 EST: 2017
SALES (est): 295.66K **Privately Held**
Web: www.greenwichsentinel.com
SIC: **2711** Newspapers, publishing and printing

(G-1334)
HH BROWN SHOE COMPANY INC (DH)
Also Called: Cove Shoe Company Division
124 W Putnam Ave Ste 1a (06830-5317)
PHONE.................................203 661-2424
Francis C Rooney Junior, *Ch Bd*
James Issler, *Pr*
J E Issler, *VP*
J Scott Bohling, *Ex VP*
◆ EMP: 50 EST: 1927
SQ FT: 13,000
SALES (est): 238.13MM
SALES (corp-wide): 302.09B **Publicly Held**
Web: www.hhbrown.com
SIC: **3143** 3144 Work shoes, men's; Women's footwear, except athletic
HQ: Bh Shoe Holdings, Inc.
124 W Putnam Ave Ste 1
Greenwich CT 06830

(G-1335)
ICON CAPITAL MANAGEMENT LLC
500 W Putnam Ave Ste 400 (06830-2947)
PHONE.................................203 542-7792
Kirk Mclaren, *Admn*
EMP: 7 EST: 2014
SALES (est): 522.57K **Privately Held**
SIC: **6531** 1389 Real estate agents and managers; Construction, repair, and dismantling services

(G-1336)
KAREN CALLAN DESIGNS INC
30 Field Point Dr (06830-7014)
PHONE.................................203 762-9914
Karen Callan, *Pr*
EMP: 7 EST: 1986
SQ FT: 2,200
SALES (est): 544.76K **Privately Held**
SIC: **7389** 2387 Design services; Apparel belts

(G-1337)
LAMBDA INVESTORS LLC
411 W Putnam Ave (06830-6261)
PHONE.................................203 862-7000
EMP: 10 EST: 2007
SALES (est): 582.8K **Privately Held**
SIC: **3841** 8731 Surgical and medical instruments; Medical research, commercial

(G-1338)
LITTLEJOHN PARTNERS IV LP
115 E Putnam Ave Ste 2 (06830-5643)
PHONE.................................203 552-3500
Angus C Littlejohn Junior, *Pt*
EMP: 811 EST: 1999
SQ FT: 2,500
SALES (est): 36.37MM **Privately Held**
Web: www.littlejohnllc.com
SIC: **3799** 3714 Towing bars and systems; Motor vehicle parts and accessories

(G-1339)
LONGVIEW HOLDING CORPORATION (HQ)
43 Arch St (06830-6512)
PHONE.................................203 869-6734
Peter O Scannell, *Pr*
Harald B Findlay, *Corporate Vice President*
Margaret O'brien, *Sec*
John P Lockwood, *CFO*
EMP: 7 EST: 1990
SQ FT: 3,500
SALES (est): 54.25MM
SALES (corp-wide): 1.5B **Privately Held**
SIC: **6719** 1389 Personal holding companies, except banks; Testing, measuring, surveying, and analysis services
PA: Rockwood Service Corporation
43 Arch St
Greenwich CT 06830
203 869-6734

(G-1340)
LYNCH CORP
140 Greenwich Ave Ste 3 (06830-6560)
PHONE.................................203 452-3007
Ralph Papitto, *Prin*
EMP: 10 EST: 2008
SALES (est): 314.31K **Privately Held**
Web: www.lynchcorp.com
SIC: **3559** Special industry machinery, nec

(G-1341)
MBF HOLDINGS LLC
777 W Putnam Ave (06830-5091)
PHONE.................................203 302-2812
▲ EMP: 10 EST: 2011
SQ FT: 70,000
SALES (est): 1.31MM **Privately Held**
SIC: **3143** Men's footwear, except athletic

(G-1342)
MF-TFC LLC
Also Called: Marc Fisher Footwear
777 W Putnam Ave (06830-5091)
PHONE.................................203 302-2820
EMP: 10 EST: 2015
SQ FT: 10,000
SALES (est): 1.46MM **Privately Held**
SIC: **3143** 3144 Men's footwear, except athletic; Women's footwear, except athletic

(G-1343)
POST ROAD IRON WORKS INC
345 W Putnam Ave (06830-5296)
PHONE.................................203 869-6322
EMP: 50 EST: 1927
SALES (est): 7.61MM **Privately Held**
Web: www.postroadironworks.com
SIC: **3441** 3442 Fabricated structural metal for ships; Screen and storm doors and windows

(G-1344)
PROMISIM INC
500 W Putnam Ave Ste 400 (06830-6086)
PHONE.................................203 554-2707
Aki Immonen, *Prin*
EMP: 25 EST: 2006
SALES (est): 693.68K **Privately Held**
SIC: **3841** Surgical and medical instruments
HQ: Delfin Technologies Oy
Microkatu 1
Kuopio 70210
509111199

(G-1345)
PUPPY HUGGER
Also Called: Hugger Design
15 Widgeon Way (06830-6701)
PHONE.................................203 661-4858
Elaine Doran, *Mng Pt*
Judy Mcauliff, *Mng Pt*
EMP: 8 EST: 2005
SALES (est): 304.63K **Privately Held**
Web: www.puppyhugger.com
SIC: **2399** Horse and pet accessories, textile

(G-1346)
REGENERATIVE MEDICINE LLC (PA)
Also Called: Regen Med
125 Field Point Rd Apt B5 (06830-6485)

P.O. Box 1135 (06836-1135)
PHONE..............................203 969-4877
Michael P Tierney, *CEO*
EMP: 8 **EST:** 2014
SALES (est): 926.83K
SALES (corp-wide): 926.83K **Privately Held**
SIC: 7372 7389 Prepackaged software; Business Activities at Non-Commercial Site

(G-1347)
RJTB INITIATIVES INC
200 Pemberwick Rd (06831-4236)
PHONE..............................203 531-7216
Thomas Butkiewicz, *CEO*
Ana Bangay, *CFO*
EMP: 10 **EST:** 2015
SQ FT: 400
SALES (est): 1.13MM **Privately Held**
SIC: 2844 Perfumes, cosmetics and other toilet preparations

(G-1348)
ROCKWOOD SERVICE CORPORATION (PA)
43 Arch St (06830-6512)
PHONE..............................203 869-6734
Peter Scannell, *Pr*
John Lockwood, *Treas*
Adam Bozek, *Sec*
EMP: 9 **EST:** 1986
SALES (est): 1.5B
SALES (corp-wide): 1.5B **Privately Held**
Web: www.rockwoodservice.com
SIC: 1389 Testing, measuring, surveying, and analysis services

(G-1349)
SASC LLC
Also Called: Sangari Active Science
44 Amogerone Crossway Unit 7862
(06836-8701)
PHONE..............................203 846-2274
Eric Johnson, *CEO*
Tom Pence, *Sales & Marketing*
Amy Barnes, *
David Robertshaw, *Chief Product Officer*
EMP: 27 **EST:** 2012
SALES (est): 3.13MM **Privately Held**
Web: www.activatelearning.com
SIC: 2731 Book publishing

(G-1350)
SDA LABORATORIES INC
280 Railroad Ave Ste 207 (06830-6338)
PHONE..............................203 861-0005
EMP: 10 **EST:** 1986
SQ FT: 1,200
SALES (est): 235.38K **Privately Held**
Web: www.sdalabs.com
SIC: 2834 Vitamin preparations

(G-1351)
SEWICKLEY LLC
340 North St (06830-3930)
PHONE..............................203 661-2511
Thomas Spencer Knight Junior, *Mgr*
EMP: 8 **EST:** 2013
SALES (est): 174.38K
SALES (corp-wide): 26.48B **Publicly Held**
SIC: 2033 Tomato sauce: packaged in cans, jars, etc.
PA: The Heinz Kraft Company
  1 Ppg Pl Ste 3400
  Pittsburgh PA 15222
  412 456-5700

(G-1352)
SOUNDVIEW PAPER MILLS LLC (DH)
1 Sound Shore Dr Ste 203 (06830-7251)
PHONE..............................201 796-4000
George Wurtz, *Ch*
George Wurtz, *CEO*
Karl Meyers, *Pr*
John Mclean, *VP*
Tim Crawford, *Sr VP*
EMP: 13 **EST:** 2012
SALES (est): 456.95MM
SALES (corp-wide): 467.08MM **Privately Held**
SIC: 2676 Sanitary paper products
HQ: Soundview Paper Holdings Llc
  1 Market St
  Elmwood Park NJ 07407
  201 796-4000

(G-1353)
STELLA DORO BISCUIT CO INC
8 Sound Shore Dr Ste 265 (06830-7272)
PHONE..............................718 549-3700
EMP: 160 **EST:** 1936
SALES (est): 10.2MM
SALES (corp-wide): 49.93MM **Privately Held**
SIC: 2052 2051 Cookies; Bread, cake, and related products
PA: Brynwood Partners V Limited Partnership
  8 Sound Shore Dr Ste 2
  Greenwich CT 06830
  203 622-1790

(G-1354)
STRATEGIC VALUE PARTNERS LLC (PA)
Also Called: Svp Global
100 W Putnam Ave Ste 2 (06830-5361)
PHONE..............................203 618-3500
Victor Khosla, *CEO*
Jason Clarke, *
Kevin Lydon, *
Albert Shin, *
Jumbo Tanaka, *
EMP: 81 **EST:** 2001
SQ FT: 45,000
SALES (est): 384.47MM **Privately Held**
Web: www.svpglobal.com
SIC: 6733 3444 Personal investment trust management; Sheet metalwork

(G-1355)
TAC ACQUISITION CORP
Also Called: Tensar
8 Sound Shore Dr (06830-7242)
PHONE..............................203 983-5276
Saul Rosenthal, *Pr*
EMP: 650 **EST:** 2005
SALES (est): 153.68MM
SALES (corp-wide): 8.8B **Publicly Held**
SIC: 2879 5039 Soil conditioners; Soil erosion control fabrics
PA: Commercial Metals Company
  6565 N Macarthur Blvd # 800
  Irving TX 75039
  214 689-4300

(G-1356)
TMS INTERNATIONAL LLC
165 W Putnam Ave (06830-5222)
PHONE..............................203 629-8383
EMP: 10
SIC: 3312 Blast furnaces and steel mills
HQ: Tms International, Llc
  Southside Wrks Bldg 1 3f
  Pittsburgh PA 15203
  412 678-6141

(G-1357)
TRI-STATE LED INC
255 Mill St (06830-5806)
PHONE..............................203 813-3791
Ron Young, *Pr*
Bob Ostrander, *Sec*
EMP: 14 **EST:** 2010
SALES (est): 5.11MM **Privately Held**
Web: www.ledlightingwholesale.com
SIC: 3646 Commercial lighting fixtures
PA: Revolution Lighting Technologies, Inc.
  177 Broad St Fl 12
  Stamford CT 06901

(G-1358)
TURNSTONE INC
Also Called: AlphaGraphics
500 W Putnam Ave (06830-2947)
PHONE..............................203 625-0000
Karen Brinker, *Pr*
EMP: 15 **EST:** 1990
SALES (est): 2.26MM **Privately Held**
Web: www.alphagraphics.com
SIC: 2752 Commercial printing, lithographic

(G-1359)
UST
100 W Putnam Ave (06830-5361)
PHONE..............................203 661-1100
Vincent Gierer, *Ch*
EMP: 21 **EST:** 2011
SALES (est): 986.38K **Privately Held**
SIC: 2141 Tobacco stemming and redrying

(G-1360)
WESTCHESTER INDUSTRIES INC
485 W Putnam Ave (06830-6060)
PHONE..............................203 661-0055
Joe Cotter, *Ch Bd*
EMP: 16 **EST:** 1966
SALES (est): 820.72K **Privately Held**
SIC: 2951 1611 Asphalt and asphaltic paving mixtures (not from refineries); Highway and street paving contractor

(G-1361)
WEXFORD CAPITAL LP (PA)
777 W Putnam Ave Ste 10 (06830-5014)
PHONE..............................203 862-7000
EMP: 9 **EST:** 1994
SALES (est): 35.82MM **Privately Held**
Web: www.wexford.com
SIC: 8741 6282 1221 1222 Management services; Investment advice; Bituminous coal surface mining; Bituminous coal-underground mining

(G-1362)
WIZARDS NUTS HOLDINGS LLC (PA)
100 Northfield St (06830-4618)
PHONE..............................708 483-1315
Timothy Fazio, *Managing Member*
Jacob Hudson, *Managing Member*
EMP: 60 **EST:** 2019
SALES (est): 1.09B
SALES (corp-wide): 1.09B **Privately Held**
Web: www.atlasholdingsllc.com
SIC: 6719 5411 2068 Investment holding companies, except banks; Grocery stores; Salted and roasted nuts and seeds

(G-1363)
WOOD SERVICES LLC
1 Sound Shore Dr Ste 203 (06830-7251)
PHONE..............................203 983-5752
Ed Sletcher, *Prin*
EMP: 8 **EST:** 2005

SALES (est): 112.91K **Privately Held**
SIC: 2499 Decorative wood and woodwork

Groton
New London County

(G-1364)
APPLIED PHYSICAL SCIENCES CORP (HQ)
475 Bridge St Ste 100 (06340-3780)
PHONE..............................860 448-3253
Charles N Corrado Junior, *Pr*
David Horne, *
Julie P Aslaksen, *
EMP: 75 **EST:** 2002
SQ FT: 20,000
SALES (est): 24.52MM
SALES (corp-wide): 42.27B **Publicly Held**
Web: www.aphysci.com
SIC: 8711 3669 Consulting engineer; Intercommunication systems, electric
PA: General Dynamics Corporation
  11011 Sunset Hills Rd
  Reston VA 20190
  703 876-3000

(G-1365)
B I L INC
Also Called: Legnos Boat Industries
973 North Rd (06340-3219)
PHONE..............................860 446-8058
Peter J Legnos, *Pr*
EMP: 18 **EST:** 1973
SALES (est): 9.97MM **Privately Held**
Web: www.lbifiberglass.com
SIC: 5085 5088 3732 Industrial supplies; Marine supplies; Boats, fiberglass: building and repairing

(G-1366)
DONCASTERS INC
Also Called: Doncasters Precision Castings-
835 Poquonnock Rd (06340-4537)
PHONE..............................860 446-4803
Bruce Ebright, *Opers Mgr*
EMP: 84
Web: www.doncasters.com
SIC: 3356 3369 3324 Nonferrous rolling and drawing, nec; Nonferrous foundries, nec; Steel investment foundries
PA: Doncasters Inc.
  835 Poquonnock Rd
  Groton CT 06340

(G-1367)
DONCASTERS INC (PA)
Also Called: DONCASTERS STORMS FORGE
835 Poquonnock Rd (06340-4537)
P.O. Box 1146 (06340-1146)
PHONE..............................860 449-1603
Mike Quinn, *CEO*
Ian Molyneux, *Sec*
◆ **EMP:** 60 **EST:** 1988
SQ FT: 100,000
SALES (est): 2.06K **Privately Held**
Web: www.doncasters.com
SIC: 3356 3728 7699 3511 Titanium; Aircraft parts and equipment, nec; Aircraft and heavy equipment repair services; Turbines and turbine generator sets and parts

(G-1368)
DONCASTERS US HLDINGS 2018 INC
835 Poquonnock Rd (06340-4537)
PHONE..............................860 449-1603

76   2024 Harris New England
Manufacturers Directory   ▲ = Import ▼ = Export
◆ = Import/Export

Ian Molyneux, *Pr*
Duncan Hinks, *Treas*
EMP: 10 **EST:** 2018
SALES (est): 1.51MM **Privately Held**
SIC: 3324 Aerospace investment castings, ferrous

(G-1369)
ELECTRIC BOAT CORPORATION
210 Mitchell St (06340-4075)
P.O. Box 949 (06340-0949)
PHONE...............................860 433-0503
EMP: 91
SALES (corp-wide): 42.27B **Publicly Held**
Web: www.gdeb.com
SIC: 3731 Submarines, building and repairing
HQ: Electric Boat Corporation
75 Eastern Point Rd
Groton CT 06340

(G-1370)
ELECTRIC BOAT CORPORATION (HQ)
Also Called: General Dynamics Electric Boat
75 Eastern Point Rd (06340-4905)
P.O. Box 1327 (06340-1327)
PHONE...............................860 433-3000
◆ **EMP:** 495 **EST:** 1995
SQ FT: 2,600,000
SALES (est): 473.62K
SALES (corp-wide): 42.27B **Publicly Held**
Web: www.gdeb.com
SIC: 3731 8711 Submarines, building and repairing; Engineering services
PA: General Dynamics Corporation
11011 Sunset Hills Rd
Reston VA 20190
703 876-3000

(G-1371)
ELECTRIC BOAT CORPORATION
Also Called: Electric Boat Fairwater Div
75 Eastern Point Rd (06340-4905)
PHONE...............................860 433-3000
Susan Williams, *Brnch Mgr*
EMP: 1136
SALES (corp-wide): 42.27B **Publicly Held**
Web: www.gdeb.com
SIC: 3731 8711 Submarines, building and repairing; Engineering services
HQ: Electric Boat Corporation
75 Eastern Point Rd
Groton CT 06340

(G-1372)
GENERAL DYNAMICS CORPORATION
Electric Boat Division
75 Eastern Point Rd (06340-4989)
PHONE...............................860 433-3000
John K Welch, *Pr*
EMP: 12000
SALES (corp-wide): 42.27B **Publicly Held**
Web: www.gd.com
SIC: 3731 Shipbuilding and repairing
PA: General Dynamics Corporation
11011 Sunset Hills Rd
Reston VA 20190
703 876-3000

(G-1373)
IF NOT NOW WHEN INC
Also Called: Paul's Pasta Shop
223 Thames St (06340-3955)
PHONE...............................860 445-5276
Paul Fidrych, *Pr*
Edward J Planeta, *Sr VP*
Paul T Fidrych, *Treas*
Edward J Planeta Junior, *Prin*

Dorothy P Fidrych, *Prin*
EMP: 9 **EST:** 1988
SQ FT: 2,000
SALES (est): 408.43K **Privately Held**
Web: www.paulspastashop.com
SIC: 2099 5812 Pasta, uncooked: packaged with other ingredients; Eating places

(G-1374)
INNOVATORSLINK CORPORATION
973 North Rd (06340-3272)
PHONE...............................860 446-8058
Peter Legnos, *Pr*
Peter J Legnos, *Pr*
EMP: 7 **EST:** 2019
SALES (est): 190.59K **Privately Held**
Web: www.innovatorslink.com
SIC: 3845 Ultrasonic medical equipment, except cleaning

(G-1375)
KONGSBERG DGTAL SIMULATION INC
115b Leonard Dr (06340-5336)
P.O. Box 180 (06388-0180)
PHONE...............................860 405-2300
Michael Muti, *Pr*
Herbert Taylor, *VP*
Jorunn Nyheim, *Sec*
▲ **EMP:** 18 **EST:** 1992
SALES (est): 6.5MM **Privately Held**
Web: www.navpac.com
SIC: 3824 Controls, revolution and timing instruments
HQ: Kongsberg Maritime As
Kirkegardsveien 45
Kongsberg 3616

(G-1376)
LINDE INC
Praxair
Eastern Point Rd (06340)
PHONE...............................860 623-8211
R M Mgrdichian, *Brnch Mgr*
EMP: 20
Web: www.lindeus.com
SIC: 2813 Industrial gases
HQ: Linde Inc.
10 Riverview Dr
Danbury CT 06810
203 837-2000

(G-1377)
PCC STRUCTURALS GROTON (DH)
Also Called: PCC Structurals
839 Poquonnock Rd (06340-4537)
PHONE...............................860 405-3700
Joseph B Cox, *Pr*
William C Mccormick, *Ch Bd*
▲ **EMP:** 175 **EST:** 1990
SALES (est): 261.92MM
SALES (corp-wide): 302.09B **Publicly Held**
Web: www.pccstructurals.com
SIC: 3369 Nonferrous foundries, nec
HQ: Wyman-Gordon Company
244 Worcester St
North Grafton MA 01536
508 839-8252

(G-1378)
PFIZER
Also Called: Pfizer
111 Ledgewood Rd (06340-6602)
PHONE...............................203 584-2793
EMP: 44 **EST:** 2018
SALES (est): 1.34MM **Privately Held**

Web: pfizer.dejobs.org
SIC: 2834 Pharmaceutical preparations

(G-1379)
PFIZER INC
Pfizer
257 Eastern Point Rd (06340-5050)
PHONE...............................860 441-4100
J R Schachner, *Brnch Mgr*
EMP: 111
SALES (corp-wide): 100.33B **Publicly Held**
Web: www.pfizer.com
SIC: 2834 8731 Pharmaceutical preparations; Medical research, commercial
PA: Pfizer Inc.
66 Hudson Blvd E
New York NY 10001
212 733-2323

(G-1380)
STONINGTON VINEYARDS INC
Also Called: Stonington Vineyards
328 Mitchell St (06340-4435)
PHONE...............................860 535-1222
Cornelius H Smith, *Pr*
Harriet Smith, *Sec*
EMP: 9 **EST:** 1986
SALES (est): 956.7K **Privately Held**
Web: www.stoningtonvineyards.com
SIC: 2084 Wines

(G-1381)
THAYERMAHAN INC (PA)
120b Leonard Dr (06340-5336)
PHONE...............................860 785-9994
Michael Connor, *Pr*
Ryan Koenitzer, *CFO*
Carlos Jativa, *CTRL*
Chad Sweet, *Prin*
EMP: 33 **EST:** 2016
SALES (est): 50MM
SALES (corp-wide): 50MM **Privately Held**
Web: www.thayermahan.com
SIC: 3812 8731 Search and navigation equipment; Commercial physical research

---

Guilford
New Haven County

(G-1382)
ADVANCE DEVELOPMENT & MFG CORP
325 Soundview Rd (06437-2970)
P.O. Box 396 (06437-0396)
PHONE...............................203 453-4325
Robert Fisher, *Ch*
John F Fisher, *Pr*
EMP: 10 **EST:** 1956
SQ FT: 12,000
SALES (est): 1.64MM **Privately Held**
Web: www.adammfgcorp.com
SIC: 3599 Machine shop, jobbing and repair

(G-1383)
AI THERAPEUTICS INC ✪
530 Old Whitfield St (06437-3441)
PHONE...............................203 458-7100
Elizabeth Whayland, *Sec*
David Scheer, *Ch Bd*
Elizabeth Whayland, *Sec*
EMP: 10 **EST:** 2022
SALES (est): 2.5MM **Privately Held**
Web: www.ai-therapeutics.com
SIC: 2835 In vivo diagnostics

(G-1384)
ALGONQUIN INDUSTRIES INC (HQ)
129 Soundview Rd (06437-2943)
PHONE...............................203 453-4348
Kamesh Chivukula, *Pr*
◆ **EMP:** 61 **EST:** 1968
SQ FT: 104,000
SALES (est): 24.53MM
SALES (corp-wide): 220.53MM **Privately Held**
Web: www.reawire.com
SIC: 3357 Nonferrous wiredrawing and insulating
PA: Rea Magnet Wire Company, Inc.
3400 E Coliseum Blvd # 20
Fort Wayne IN 46805
260 421-7321

(G-1385)
AUTERRA INC
333 White Birch Dr (06437-2134)
PHONE...............................518 382-9600
Eric Burnett, *Pr*
EMP: 9 **EST:** 2006
SALES (est): 2.17MM **Privately Held**
Web: www.auterrainc.com
SIC: 2819 Industrial inorganic chemicals, nec

(G-1386)
BIO-MED DEVICES INC
Also Called: Bmd
61 Soundview Rd (06437-2937)
PHONE...............................203 458-0202
Dean J Bennett Junior, *Ch Bd*
Dean J Bennett Iii, *Pr*
Doris A Bennett, *
◆ **EMP:** 67 **EST:** 1972
SQ FT: 20,000
SALES (est): 12.76MM **Privately Held**
Web: www.biomeddevices.com
SIC: 3845 3841 Electromedical equipment; Surgical and medical instruments

(G-1387)
BIOASIS BIOSCIENCES CORP
14 Water St Ste A (06437-2860)
P.O. Box 64 (06437-0064)
PHONE...............................203 533-7082
EMP: 8 **EST:** 2017
SALES (est): 421.8K **Privately Held**
Web: www.bioasis.us
SIC: 2834 Pharmaceutical preparations

(G-1388)
BROOK & WHITTLE LIMITED (PA)
20 Carter Dr (06437-2125)
PHONE...............................203 483-5602
▲ **EMP:** 413 **EST:** 1996
SALES (est): 250.23MM **Privately Held**
Web: www.brookandwhittle.com
SIC: 2754 2759 Commercial printing, gravure; Commercial printing, nec

(G-1389)
COMPETITION ENGINEERING INC
80 Carter Dr (06437-2125)
PHONE...............................203 453-5200
Richard B Moroso, *Pr*
Pamela Kiss, *Sec*
EMP: 20 **EST:** 1984
SQ FT: 70,000
SALES (est): 482.87K
SALES (corp-wide): 22.36MM **Privately Held**
Web: www.moroso.com

SIC: 3714 Motor vehicle parts and
accessories
PA: Moroso Performance Products, Inc.
80 Carter Dr
Guilford CT 06437
203 453-6571

(G-1390)
COOPERSURGICAL INC
Also Called: Lifeglobal Group, The
393 Soundview Rd (06437-2970)
PHONE.............................203 453-1700
Monica Mezezi, *Mgr*
EMP: 40
SALES (corp-wide): 3.59B **Publicly Held**
Web: www.coopersurgical.com
SIC: 2836 Biological products, except
diagnostic
HQ: Coopersurgical, Inc.
75 Corporate Dr
Trumbull CT 06611

(G-1391)
DEFIBTECH LLC (HQ)
741 Boston Post Rd Ste 201 (06437-2714)
PHONE.............................866 333-4248
Glenn W Laub, *Managing Member*
Robert Reinhardt, *
Gintaras A Vaisnys, *
EMP: 65 **EST:** 2003
SQ FT: 10,850
SALES (est): 24.47MM **Privately Held**
Web: www.defibtech.com
SIC: 3845 Defibrillator
PA: Nihon Kohden Corporation
1-31-4, Nishiochiai
Shinjuku-Ku TKY 161-0

(G-1392)
DRUG FARM USA LLC
88 Greenbrier Dr (06437-1675)
PHONE.............................617 735-5205
EMP: 7 **EST:** 2021
SALES (est): 78.66K **Privately Held**
SIC: 2834 Pharmaceutical preparations

(G-1393)
EASTWOODS ARMS LLC
37 Orcutt Dr (06437-2221)
PHONE.............................203 615-3476
Jonathan Caviola, *Prin*
EMP: 8 **EST:** 2016
SALES (est): 226.07K **Privately Held**
SIC: 2499 Wood products, nec

(G-1394)
GEORGE SCHMITT & CO INC (PA)
251 Boston Post Rd (06437-2904)
PHONE.............................203 453-4334
J Robert Gunther, *Prin*
Teresa A Gunther, *Prin*
Maurice J Resler, *Prin*
Jean Chapman, *CFO*
James Love, *VP*
◆ **EMP:** 20 **EST:** 1998
SALES (est): 7.61MM
SALES (corp-wide): 7.61MM **Privately Held**
Web: www.palmasprinting.com
SIC: 2759 2679 Screen printing; Labels,
paper: made from purchased material

(G-1395)
HYPERFINE INC (PA)
351 New Whitfield St (06437-3400)
PHONE.............................203 458-7100
Dave Scott, *CEO*
R Scott Huennekens, *Ex Ch Bd*
Alok Gupta, *CFO*

Mark Hughes, *COO*
Khan Siddiqui, *CMO CSO*
EMP: 126 **EST:** 2014
SALES (est): 6.81MM
SALES (corp-wide): 6.81MM **Publicly Held**
Web: www.hyperfine.io
SIC: 3845 Electromedical equipment

(G-1396)
HYPERFINE OPERATIONS INC
351 New Whitfield St (06437-3400)
PHONE.............................866 796-6767
Maria Sainz, *Pr*
EMP: 35 **EST:** 2014
SALES (est): 5.84MM
SALES (corp-wide): 6.81MM **Publicly Held**
Web: www.hyperfine.io
SIC: 3841 Diagnostic apparatus, medical
PA: Hyperfine, Inc.
351 New Whitfield St
Guilford CT 06437
203 458-7100

(G-1397)
IMAGE PROCESSING
251 Boston Post Rd (06437-2904)
PHONE.............................203 488-3252
Steve Cushman, *Pr*
EMP: 7 **EST:** 1983
SQ FT: 25,000
SALES (est): 241.89K **Privately Held**
Web: www.georgeschmitt.com
SIC: 7336 2791 Graphic arts and related
design; Typesetting

(G-1398)
JOSHUA LLC (PA)
Also Called: Unicast Development Co.
1930 Durham Rd (06437-1686)
PHONE.............................203 624-0080
EMP: 10 **EST:** 1958
SALES (est): 2.5MM
SALES (corp-wide): 2.5MM **Privately Held**
Web: www.mylawyerct.com
SIC: 3542 2819 3297 3624 Machine tools,
metal forming type; Catalysts, chemical;
Nonclay refractories; Carbon and graphite
products

(G-1399)
LEWMAR INC (DH)
Also Called: Lewmar Marine
2351 Boston Post Rd Ste 503
(06437-4361)
PHONE.............................203 458-6200
Peter Tierney, *Ch*
Harcourt Schutz, *Genl Mgr*
John Harsh, *Sec*
◆ **EMP:** 20 **EST:** 1967
SALES (est): 6.68MM
SALES (corp-wide): 5.21B **Publicly Held**
Web: www.lewmar.com
SIC: 3423 3429 3714 Axes and hatchets;
Hardware, nec; Motor vehicle steering
systems and parts
HQ: Lewmar Limited
Southmoor Lane
Havant HANTS PO9 1
239 247-1841

(G-1400)
MIAMI BAY BEVERAGE COMPANY LLC
Also Called: Trimino
66 High St (06437-3499)
PHONE.............................203 453-0090
Peter J Dacey, *CEO*
Casey P Hoban, *COO*

Robert J Leary. *Dir*
EMP: 10 **EST:** 2012
SALES (est): 1.2MM **Privately Held**
Web: www.drinktrimino.com
SIC: 5499 2086 Beverage stores;
Carbonated beverages, nonalcoholic:
pkged. in cans, bottles

(G-1401)
MOROSO PERFORMANCE PDTS INC (PA)
Also Called: Moroso
80 Carter Dr (06437-2116)
PHONE.............................203 453-6571
Richard B Moroso, *Pr*
Lori Moroso, *
▲ **EMP:** 170 **EST:** 1968
SQ FT: 70,000
SALES (est): 22.36MM
SALES (corp-wide): 22.36MM **Privately Held**
Web: www.moroso.com
SIC: 3714 Motor vehicle engines and parts

(G-1402)
PEXAGON TECHNOLOGY INC
Also Called: Pexagon
1 Shoreline Dr Ste 7 (06437-2978)
PHONE.............................203 458-3364
Brian R Campbell, *Pr*
Susan Campbell, *
Albert Conte, *
◆ **EMP:** 30 **EST:** 2002
SALES (est): 4.69MM **Privately Held**
Web: www.pexagontech.com
SIC: 3572 Computer storage devices

(G-1403)
RAM TECHNOLOGIES LLC
29 Soundview Rd Ste 12 (06437-2997)
PHONE.............................203 453-3916
Richard Mentelos, *Pr*
Susan Senter, *CFO*
▲ **EMP:** 10 **EST:** 1992
SQ FT: 3,000
SALES (est): 1.16MM **Privately Held**
Web: www.ramtechno.com
SIC: 3845 Electromedical apparatus

(G-1404)
REA MAGNET WIRE COMPANY INC
Algonquin Industries Division
129 Soundview Rd (06437-2972)
P.O. Box 441 (06437-0441)
PHONE.............................203 738-6100
EMP: 90
SQ FT: 104,000
SALES (corp-wide): 220.53MM **Privately Held**
Web: www.reawire.com
SIC: 3357 Nonferrous wiredrawing and
insulating
PA: Rea Magnet Wire Company, Inc.
3400 E Coliseum Blvd # 20
Fort Wayne IN 46805
260 421-7321

(G-1405)
RETCOMM INC
29 Soundview Rd (06437-2910)
PHONE.............................203 453-2389
David Moffat, *Pr*
Beth F Moffat, *Sec*
EMP: 10 **EST:** 1981
SQ FT: 5,000
SALES (est): 2.3MM **Privately Held**
Web: www.taccomm.com

SIC: 7622 3663 Radio repair shop, nec;
Radio broadcasting and communications
equipment

(G-1406)
SAYBROOK PRESS INCORPORATED
39 Chaffinch Island Rd (06437-3244)
P.O. Box 575 (06437-0575)
PHONE.............................203 458-3637
Eugene O Leary, *Pr*
Jean Oleary, *Treas*
EMP: 9 **EST:** 1970
SALES (est): 150.97K **Privately Held**
SIC: 2791 2789 2759 Typesetting;
Bookbinding and repairing: trade, edition,
library, etc.; Commercial printing, nec

(G-1407)
SCHMITT REALTY HOLDINGS INC (PA)
251 Boston Post Rd (06437-2904)
P.O. Box 448 (06437-0448)
PHONE.............................203 453-4334
William G Gunther, *CEO*
◆ **EMP:** 59 **EST:** 1874
SQ FT: 48,000
SALES (est): 19.22MM
SALES (corp-wide): 19.22MM **Privately Held**
Web: www.georgeschmitt.com
SIC: 2759 Commercial printing, nec

(G-1408)
SCHMITT REALTY HOLDINGS INC
Also Called: George Schmithet and Company
251 Boston Post Rd (06437-2904)
PHONE.............................203 453-4334
Gunther William, *Pr*
EMP: 14
SALES (corp-wide): 19.22MM **Privately Held**
Web: www.georgeschmitt.com
SIC: 2759 Labels and seals: printing, nsk
PA: Schmitt Realty Holdings, Inc.
251 Boston Post Rd
Guilford CT 06437
203 453-4334

(G-1409)
WALSTON INC
131 Nut Plains Rd (06437-2135)
PHONE.............................203 453-5929
Richard Walston, *Pr*
Marie Walston, *VP*
EMP: 9 **EST:** 1972
SQ FT: 4,500
SALES (est): 896.47K **Privately Held**
SIC: 2431 Staircases and stairs, wood

Haddam
Middlesex County

(G-1410)
TARGET CUSTOM MANUFACTURING CO
27 Swain Johnson Trl (06438-1061)
PHONE.............................860 388-5848
Neil Gallagher, *Pr*
Christine Gallagher, *VP*
Vanessa Braig, *Sec*
EMP: 9 **EST:** 1974
SALES (est): 814.88K **Privately Held**
Web: targetcustom.weebly.com
SIC: 3444 3469 Sheet metalwork; Stamping
metal for the trade

▲ = Import ▼ = Export
◆ = Import/Export

Hamden
New Haven County

(G-1411)
AMPD AIR QUALITY SERVICS LLC
51 Greenes Ridge Rd (06514-1126)
PHONE.................................203 387-1709
EMP: 7 EST: 2001
SALES (est): 469.66K Privately Held
Web: www.nationalairquality.com
SIC: 7699 2679 Cleaning services; Building, insulating, and packaging paper

(G-1412)
AMPHENOL CORPORATION
Amphenol Spctr-Strip Oprations
720 Sherman Ave (06514-1146)
P.O. Box 4340 (06514-0340)
PHONE.................................203 287-2272
Eric Juntwait, Genl Mgr
EMP: 72
SALES (corp-wide): 12.62B Publicly Held
Web: www.amphenol.com
SIC: 3678 Electronic connectors
PA: Amphenol Corporation
358 Hall Ave
Wallingford CT 06492
203 265-8900

(G-1413)
BAR-PLATE MANUFACTURING CO
1180 Sherman Ave (06514-1300)
P.O. Box 185470 (06518-0470)
PHONE.................................203 397-0033
Brian Garrity, Pr
▲ EMP: 10 EST: 1985
SQ FT: 17,000
SALES (est): 2.71MM
SALES (corp-wide): 426.63MM Privately Held
Web: www.barplate.com
SIC: 3554 Die cutting and stamping machinery, paper converting
PA: R.A.F. Industries, Inc.
50 Monument Rd Ste 303
Bala Cynwyd PA 19004
215 572-0738

(G-1414)
BRIDGESTONE RET OPERATIONS LLC
Also Called: Firestone
2300 Dixwell Ave Ste A (06514-2108)
PHONE.................................203 288-1634
Pawel Wieczerzak, Mgr
EMP: 8
Web: www.bridgestoneamericas.com
SIC: 5531 7534 Automotive tires; Rebuilding and retreading tires
HQ: Bridgestone Retail Operations, Llc
333 E Lake St Ste 300
Bloomingdale IL 60108
630 259-9000

(G-1415)
BURT PROCESS EQUIPMENT INC (PA)
100 Overlook Dr (06514-1139)
P.O. Box 185100 (06518-0100)
PHONE.................................203 287-1985
Stephen J Burt, Pr
William J Burt, CFO
Alan L Speckhart, VP
Michael E Burt, Sec
EMP: 21 EST: 1970
SQ FT: 29,000

SALES (est): 31.17MM
SALES (corp-wide): 31.17MM Privately Held
Web: www.burtprocess.com
SIC: 5085 3432 Industrial fittings; Plumbing fixture fittings and trim

(G-1416)
CARLTON INDUSTRIES CORP
33 Rossotto Dr (06514-1336)
PHONE.................................203 288-5605
◆ EMP: 49 EST: 1994
SQ FT: 27,000
SALES (est): 11.09MM Privately Held
Web: www.cicems.com
SIC: 3672 Printed circuit boards

(G-1417)
CHARLES K WHITE
Also Called: Metal Perfection
2259 State St (06517-3723)
PHONE.................................203 631-2540
EMP: 8 EST: 1994
SALES (est): 148.57K Privately Held
SIC: 2842 Metal polish

(G-1418)
COMMS AT MILL RIVER
75 Washington Ave (06518-3200)
PHONE.................................203 287-0082
Norman Osach, Prin
EMP: 7 EST: 2005
SALES (est): 239.92K Privately Held
SIC: 2711 Newspapers, publishing and printing

(G-1419)
CUSTOM & PRECISION PDTS INC
2893 State St Rear (06517-1712)
P.O. Box 5446 (06518-0446)
PHONE.................................203 281-0818
Diamante Dente, Pr
Gregory Dente, Sec
EMP: 9 EST: 1969
SQ FT: 12,000
SALES (est): 924.11K Privately Held
Web: apartments.grandview.ypeek.com
SIC: 3444 Sheet metalwork

(G-1420)
CYCLONE MICROSYSTEMS INC
25 Marne St (06514-3610)
PHONE.................................203 786-5536
Joel Zackin, Pr
EMP: 21 EST: 1986
SALES (est): 2.33MM Privately Held
Web: www.cyclone.com
SIC: 3571 3672 Personal computers (microcomputers); Printed circuit boards

(G-1421)
DEXSIL CORPORATION
1 Hamden Park Dr (06517-3150)
PHONE.................................203 288-3509
◆ EMP: 35 EST: 1977
SALES (est): 4.83MM Privately Held
Web: www.dexsil.com
SIC: 2899 3826 Chemical preparations, nec; Environmental testing equipment

(G-1422)
DUROL CO
2580 State St (06517-3009)
P.O. Box 4141 (06514-0141)
PHONE.................................203 288-3383
Cynthia Civitello, Pr
Carol D Newman, VP
EMP: 15 EST: 1962

SQ FT: 9,000
SALES (est): 1.69MM Privately Held
Web: www.durol.com
SIC: 3599 Machine shop, jobbing and repair

(G-1423)
ELECTRONIC SPC CONN INC
19 Hamden Park Dr (06517-3151)
PHONE.................................203 288-1707
William Kovacs, Pr
Duc Huu Nguyen, VP
EMP: 31 EST: 1980
SQ FT: 12,500
SALES (est): 2.06MM Privately Held
Web: www.electronicspecialties.com
SIC: 3672 Printed circuit boards

(G-1424)
ELM CITY CHEESE COMPANY INC
2240 State St (06517-3798)
PHONE.................................203 865-5768
Marjorie Weinstein-kowal, Pr
Suzanne Weinstein, Sec
EMP: 10 EST: 1896
SQ FT: 12,000
SALES (est): 1.65MM Privately Held
Web: www.elmcitycheese.com
SIC: 2022 Natural cheese

(G-1425)
ELM CITY MFG JEWELERS INC
Also Called: Elm City Management
29 Marne St (06514-3610)
PHONE.................................203 248-2195
Anthony Cuomo, Pr
Diane Orr, VP
Rosemarie Cuomo, Sec
Marianne Cuomo, Treas
EMP: 15 EST: 1957
SQ FT: 2,000
SALES (est): 1.59MM Privately Held
Web: www.elmcityapartments.com
SIC: 3911 5094 5944 Jewelry, precious metal; Jewelry; Jewelry, precious stones and precious metals

(G-1426)
GIERING METAL FINISHING INCORPORATED
2655 State St (06517-2225)
PHONE.................................203 248-5583
EMP: 37 EST: 1951
SALES (est): 4.92MM Privately Held
Web: www.gieringmetalfinishing.com
SIC: 3471 3479 Plating and polishing; Painting, coating, and hot dipping

(G-1427)
HAMDEN METAL SERVICE CO INC
2 Broadway (06518-2629)
PHONE.................................203 281-1522
Jay Hirsch, Pr
Edward Hirsch Iii, VP
Martha Hirsch, Sec
EMP: 15 EST: 1976
SALES (est): 2.27MM Privately Held
Web: www.hamdenmetal.com
SIC: 3315 3357 Wire, ferrous/iron; Building wire and cable, nonferrous

(G-1428)
HAMDEN PACKAGING INC
100 Sanford St (06514-1740)
PHONE.................................203 288-0200
Dorothy R Podgwaite, CEO
Michael J Podgwaite, *
EMP: 28 EST: 1971

SQ FT: 32,000
SALES (est): 4.72MM Privately Held
Web: www.packedge.com
SIC: 2657 2675 2679 2631 Folding paperboard boxes; Die-cut paper and board; Paper products, converted, nec; Boxboard

(G-1429)
HEALTHPER INC
24 Guenevere Ct (06518-1148)
PHONE.................................203 506-0957
David Lenihan, Prin
EMP: 21
SALES (corp-wide): 236.31K Privately Held
Web: www.healthper.com
SIC: 7372 Application computer software
PA: Healthper, Inc.
124 Brookstone Dr
Princeton NJ 08540
888 257-1804

(G-1430)
HEALTHY MOM LLC
2319 Whitney Ave Ste 1d (06518-3534)
PHONE.................................855 588-6242
EMP: 13 EST: 2019
SALES (est): 512.1K Privately Held
Web: www.maiayogurt.com
SIC: 2023 Yogurt mix

(G-1431)
HPI MANUFACTURING INC
375 Morse St (06517-3133)
P.O. Box 6157 (06517-0157)
PHONE.................................203 777-5395
Glenn M Ayer, Prin
EMP: 13 EST: 2016
SALES (est): 503.92K Privately Held
Web: www.highprecisioninc.com
SIC: 3999 Manufacturing industries, nec

(G-1432)
INSULPANE CONNECTICUT INC
Also Called: Solar Seal of Connecticut
30 Edmund St (06517-3914)
PHONE.................................800 922-3248
Paul Cody, CEO
Frederick Federico Senior, Prin
Lawrence Federico, *
Frederick Federico Junior, VP
Anthony Mancini, Treas
▲ EMP: 62 EST: 1980
SQ FT: 12,000
SALES (est): 9.52MM
SALES (corp-wide): 106.86MM Privately Held
SIC: 3211 3469 Insulating glass, sealed units; Architectural panels or parts, porcelain enameled
PA: Grey Mountain Partners, Llc
1470 Walnut St Ste 400
Boulder CO 80302
303 449-5692

(G-1433)
INTERNATIONAL PROVISIONS INC
14 Hamden Park Dr (06517-3149)
▲ EMP: 40 EST: 1992
SQ FT: 15,000
SALES (est): 2.76MM Privately Held
SIC: 2099 Food preparations, nec

(G-1434)
JEFFREY GOLD
Also Called: Laser Body Solutions
2415 Shepard Ave Apt 41 (06518-1524)
PHONE.................................203 281-5737
Jeffrey Gold, Owner

EMP: 7 **EST:** 2003
SALES (est): 933.3K **Privately Held**
Web: codeworks.cirran.net
SIC: 3845 8011　Laser systems and
　equipment, medical; Opthalmologist

(G-1435)
JFD TUBE & COIL PRODUCTS
INC
　7 Hamden Park Dr　(06517-3151)
　P.O. Box 6309　(06517-0309)
　PHONE...............................203 288-6941
　Thomas Orlowski,　*
　Daniel Orlowski,　*
　Diane Orlowski,　*
　EMP: 34 **EST:** 1983
　SQ FT: 14,200
　SALES (est): 8.25MM **Privately Held**
　Web: www.jfdcoil.com
　SIC: 3443 3498　Heat exchangers,
　　condensers, and components; Coils, pipe:
　　fabricated from purchased pipe

(G-1436)
LEED - HIMMEL INDUSTRIES
INC
　75 Leeder Hill Dr　(06517-2731)
　PHONE...............................203 288-8484
　Howard B Goldfarb,　*Pr*
　Larry Himmel,　*
　EMP: 70 **EST:** 1945
　SQ FT: 120,000
　SALES (est): 22.13MM **Privately Held**
　Web: www.leed-himmel.com
　SIC: 3446　Architectural metalwork

(G-1437)
LEGAL AFFAIRS INC
Also Called: LEGAL AFFAIRS MAGAZINE
　115 Blake Rd　(06517-3405)
　PHONE...............................203 865-2520
　Lincoln Caplan,　*Pr*
　EMP: 9 **EST:** 2000
　SALES (est): 420.22K **Privately Held**
　Web: www.legalaffairs.org
　SIC: 2721　Periodicals

(G-1438)
MARC WOODWORKS　LLC
　51 Overlook Dr　(06514-1140)
　PHONE...............................203 281-4700
　EMP: 7 **EST:** 2019
　SALES (est): 468.7K **Privately Held**
　Web: www.marcwoodworks.com
　SIC: 2431　Millwork

(G-1439)
MEDIA ONE LLC
　44 Hawley Rd　(06517-2128)
　PHONE...............................203 745-5825
　Saad Mobarak,　*CEO*
　Muhd Molla,　*Pr*
　EMP: 50 **EST:** 2015
　SALES (est): 2.35MM **Privately Held**
　SIC: 3559　Sewing machines and
　　attachments, industrial, nec

(G-1440)
MERRITT EXTRUDER CORP
　15 Marne St　(06514-3610)
　PHONE...............................203 230-8100
　Lucien D Yokana,　*Ch Bd*
　Alexander Guthrie,　*
　Thomas J Oravits,　*
　Charles Jaffin,　*
　Mark Roland,　*
　EMP: 24 **EST:** 1987
　SQ FT: 45,000
　SALES (est): 1.16MM **Privately Held**

SIC: 3559 3089 3549 3542　Fiber optics
　strand coating machinery; Extruded
　finished plastics products, nec;
　Metalworking machinery, nec; Machine
　tools, metal forming type

(G-1441)
MEYER WIRE & CABLE
COMPANY LLC
　1072 Sherman Ave　(06514-1337)
　PHONE...............................203 281-0817
　EMP: 21 **EST:** 2005
　SQ FT: 2,000
　SALES (est): 2.49MM **Privately Held**
　Web: www.meyerwirecable.com
　SIC: 3496　Miscellaneous fabricated wire
　　products

(G-1442)
MILFOAM CORPORATION
　23 Marne St　(06514-3610)
　PHONE...............................203 248-8011
　Douglas Pfenninger,　*Ch*
　Douglas Pfenninger,　*Ch Bd*
　Alfred Peterson,　*VP*
　EMP: 13 **EST:** 1962
　SQ FT: 23,000
　SALES (est): 403.16K **Privately Held**
　Web: www.milfoam.com
　SIC: 3089　Molding primary plastics

(G-1443)
MINUTE MAN PRESS
Also Called: Minuteman Press
　5 Hamden Park Dr　(06517-3150)
　PHONE...............................203 891-6251
　EMP: 9 **EST:** 2014
　SALES (est): 382.76K **Privately Held**
　Web: www.minutemanpress.com
　SIC: 2752　Commercial printing, lithographic

(G-1444)
MOON CUTTER CO　INC
　2969 State St　(06517-1712)
　PHONE...............................203 288-9249
　Eleanor Moon,　*Pr*
　Lenore Capasso,　*
　Charles Moon,　*
　EMP: 45 **EST:** 1957
　SQ FT: 54,000
　SALES (est): 4.81MM **Privately Held**
　Web: www.mooncutter.com
　SIC: 3541 3545　Machine tools, metal cutting
　　type; Machine tool accessories

(G-1445)
NDR LIUZZI INC
Also Called: Liuzzi Cheese
　86 Rossotto Dr　(06514-1335)
　PHONE...............................203 287-8477
　▲ **EMP:** 48 **EST:** 2004
　SALES (est): 6.6MM **Privately Held**
　Web: www.liuzzicheese.com
　SIC: 2022 5143　Cheese; natural and
　　processed; Cheese

(G-1446)
NEW ENGLAND CNC　INC
　46 Manila Ave　(06514-4107)
　PHONE...............................203 288-8241
　Lawrence Carrignan,　*Pr*
　Ronald Krutz,　*VP*
　EMP: 10 **EST:** 1960
　SQ FT: 6,600
　SALES (est): 986.79K **Privately Held**
　Web: www.newenglandcnc.com
　SIC: 3599 3541　Machine shop, jobbing and
　　repair; Machine tools, metal cutting type

(G-1447)
NICKS ENTERPRISES INC (PA)
Also Called: N & D Sports
　2951 State St　(06517-1712)
　PHONE...............................203 287-9990
　EMP: 14 **EST:** 1958
　SALES (est): 3MM
　SALES (corp-wide): 3MM **Privately Held**
　Web: www.nanddsports.com
　SIC: 5199 5092 5947 5136　Gifts and
　　novelties; Balloons, novelty; Gifts and
　　novelties; Sportswear, men's and boys'

(G-1448)
NQ INDUSTRIES　INC
　850 Sherman Ave　(06514-1147)
　P.O. Box 330343　(06133-0343)
　PHONE...............................860 258-3466
　William Carey,　*CEO*
　▲ **EMP:** 10 **EST:** 2006
　SQ FT: 3,000
　SALES (est): 1.41MM **Privately Held**
　Web: www.nqinc.com
　SIC: 3564　Air cleaning systems

(G-1449)
PORCELEN LIMITED
CONNECTICUT LLC (PA)
Also Called: Specrail
　333 Welton St　(06517-3934)
　P.O. Box 6308　(06517-0308)
　PHONE...............................203 248-6346
　▲ **EMP:** 64 **EST:** 1957
　SALES (est): 10MM
　SALES (corp-wide): 10MM **Privately Held**
　Web: www.specrail.com
　SIC: 3354 3471 5719 5023　Aluminum
　　extruded products; Finishing, metals or
　　formed products; Aluminumware;
　　Aluminumware

(G-1450)
PORCELEN LTD CONNECTICUT
LLC
　129 Leeder Hill Dr　(06517-2731)
　PHONE...............................203 248-6346
　Jack Pierson,　*Brnch Mgr*
　EMP: 36
　SALES (corp-wide): 14.8MM **Privately**
　Held
　Web: www.specrail.com
　SIC: 3354　Aluminum extruded products
　PA: Porcelen, Limited, Connecticut, Llc
　　333 Welton St
　　Hamden CT 06517
　　203 248-6346

(G-1451)
POROBOND PRODUCTS　LLC
　80 Sanford St　(06514-1707)
　PHONE...............................203 288-7477
　◆ **EMP:** 10 **EST:** 1996
　SQ FT: 25,000
　SALES (est): 993.81K **Privately Held**
　SIC: 3443　Heat exchangers, condensers,
　　and components

(G-1452)
RAYMON TOOL　LLC
　79 Rossotto Dr　(06514-1336)
　PHONE...............................203 248-2199
　Vincent Palumbo,　*Managing Member*
　EMP: 19 **EST:** 1997
　SQ FT: 10,000
　SALES (est): 2.2MM **Privately Held**
　Web: www.raymontool.com
　SIC: 3542　Machine tools, metal forming type

(G-1453)
RECORD PRODUCTS AMERICA
INC
Also Called: R P A
　700 Sherman Ave　(06514-1360)
　PHONE...............................203 248-6371
　Robert Roczynski,　*Pr*
　▲ **EMP:** 14 **EST:** 1977
　SQ FT: 13,000
　SALES (est): 2.24MM **Privately Held**
　Web: www.recordproducts.com
　SIC: 5084 3469　Industrial machinery and
　　equipment; Machine parts, stamped or
　　pressed metal

(G-1454)
SCREEN TEK PRINTING CO　INC
Also Called: Screen Tek
　130 Welton St　(06517-3930)
　PHONE...............................203 248-6248
　Robert Mastriano,　*Pr*
　Paul Mastriano,　*VP*
　EMP: 8 **EST:** 1972
　SQ FT: 6,000
　SALES (est): 600.39K **Privately Held**
　Web: www.screentek.net
　SIC: 2759　Screen printing

(G-1455)
SKICO MANUFACTURING CO
LLC
Also Called: Skico Manufacturing
　3 Industrial Cir　(06517-3153)
　PHONE...............................203 230-1305
　Dan Skibitcky,　*Pt*
　Tom Skibitcky,　*Pt*
　EMP: 9 **EST:** 1980
　SQ FT: 7,200
　SALES (est): 1MM **Privately Held**
　SIC: 3599 3545 3544 7699　Machine shop,
　　jobbing and repair; Precision tools,
　　machinists'; Special dies and tools; Aircraft
　　and heavy equipment repair services

(G-1456)
SPECIALTY WIRE & CORD SETS
INC
Also Called: Swc
　1 Gallagher Rd　(06517-3171)
　PHONE...............................203 498-2932
　Lynn Campo,　*Pr*
　Liborio Campo,　*VP*
　EMP: 18 **EST:** 1990
　SQ FT: 12,000
　SALES (est): 2.36MM **Privately Held**
　Web: www.specialtywire.com
　SIC: 3496　Miscellaneous fabricated wire
　　products

(G-1457)
STENT METAL CORP
Also Called: Yankee Aluminum
　9 Hamden Park Dr　(06517-3151)
　P.O. Box 6312　(06517-0312)
　PHONE...............................203 287-9007
　Glenn S Rasmussen,　*Pr*
　Glenn Rasmussen,　*
　EMP: 7 **EST:** 1988
　SQ FT: 18,000
　SALES (est): 797.77K **Privately Held**
　SIC: 3442　Store fronts, prefabricated, metal

(G-1458)
SUPERIOR PRINTING INK CO
INC
　800 Sherman Ave　(06514-1191)
　PHONE...............................203 281-1921
　Andrew Anselmo,　*Brnch Mgr*
　EMP: 26

▲ = Import ▼ = Export
◆ = Import/Export

SALES (corp-wide): 45.61MM **Privately Held**
Web: www.superiorink.com
SIC: 2893 Printing ink
PA: Superior Printing Ink Co Inc
　　10 York Ave
　　West Caldwell NJ 07006
　　201 478-5600

(G-1459)
TACHWA ENTERPRISES INC
4 Industrial Cir (06517-3152)
PHONE...............................203 691-5772
Andrew Wilkes, *VP*
James White Junior, *Pr*
EMP: 7 EST: 2003
SQ FT: 7,200
SALES (est): 991.26K **Privately Held**
Web: www.tachwa.com
SIC: 3728 Aircraft assemblies,
　　subassemblies, and parts, nec

(G-1460)
TOMTEC INC
Also Called: Tomtec
1020 Sherman Ave (06514-1337)
PHONE...............................203 281-6790
Tom Astle, *CEO*
Gade Ajeigbe, *
Joan Astle, *
▲ **EMP: 68 EST:** 1972
SQ FT: 70,000
SALES (est): 9.78MM **Privately Held**
Web: www.tomtec.com
SIC: 3845 3826 3821 Electromedical
　　apparatus; Analytical instruments;
　　Laboratory apparatus and furniture

(G-1461)
TUDOR HOUSE FURNITURE CO INC
929 Sherman Ave (06514-1150)
PHONE...............................203 288-8451
Harold Margolies, *Pr*
EMP: 11 EST: 1963
SQ FT: 20,000
SALES (est): 489.68K **Privately Held**
SIC: 2512 2511 Living room furniture:
　　upholstered on wood frames; Wood
　　household furniture

(G-1462)
W AND G MACHINE COMPANY INC
4 Hamden Park Dr (06517-3149)
P.O. Box 6187 (06517-0187)
PHONE...............................203 288-3871
Noel Mara, *Managing Member*
Jay Kroopnick, *Pr*
Robin Kroopnick, *Treas*
Sheree A Napolitan, *Sec*
EMP: 14 EST: 1952
SQ FT: 12,000
SALES (est): 4.19MM **Privately Held**
Web: www.wgmachineco.com
SIC: 3728 Aircraft parts and equipment, nec

(G-1463)
WARNER PRECISION MACHINING & F
875 Shepard Ave (06514-1356)
PHONE...............................203 281-3660
J Warner, *Prin*
EMP: 7 EST: 2008
SALES (est): 169.71K **Privately Held**
SIC: 3599 Machine shop, jobbing and repair

Hampton
Windham County

(G-1464)
BURELL BROS INC
Rr 97 (06247)
PHONE...............................860 455-9681
Frances Burell, *Pr*
Francis Burell, *Pr*
John Burell, *VP*
Carol Burell, *Sec*
EMP: 7 EST: 1970
SQ FT: 10,000
SALES (est): 957.42K **Privately Held**
SIC: 2421 Sawmills and planing mills,
　　general

(G-1465)
HAMPTON GAZETTE INC
218 W Old Route 6 (06247-1311)
P.O. Box 101 (06247-0101)
PHONE...............................860 455-0160
Susan Matejka, *Prin*
EMP: 7 EST: 2010
SALES (est): 131.72K **Privately Held**
Web: www.hamptongazette.com
SIC: 2711 Newspapers, publishing and
　　printing

Hartford
Hartford County

(G-1466)
A&P COAT APRON & LINEN SUP LLC
Also Called: Unitex Textile Rental Service
420 Ledyard St (06114-3207)
PHONE...............................914 840-3200
Raymon Neal, *Brnch Mgr*
EMP: 68
SALES (corp-wide): 96.22MM **Privately Held**
Web: www.unitex.com
SIC: 2299 7213 7218 Textile mill waste and
　　remnant processing; Uniform supply;
　　Industrial launderers
PA: A&P Coat, Apron & Linen Supply Llc
　　565 Taxter Rd Ste 620
　　Elmsford NY 10523
　　914 840-3200

(G-1467)
ADAMSAHERN SIGN SOLUTIONS INC
30 Arbor St (06106-1238)
PHONE...............................860 523-8835
Diane Ahern, *Pr*
Chris Adams, *Pr*
EMP: 14 EST: 1995
SALES (est): 1.76MM **Privately Held**
Web: www.adamsahern.com
SIC: 3993 1799 Electric signs; Sign
　　installation and maintenance

(G-1468)
AEROSPACE METALS INC
Also Called: Suisman & Blumenthal
239 W Service Rd (06120-1205)
PHONE...............................860 522-3123
Paul Haveson, *Pr*
Robert Kaseta, *CFO*
Michael Suisman, *Prin*
EMP: 965 EST: 1899
SQ FT: 225,000
SALES (est): 3.69MM **Privately Held**
Web: www.slaerospace.com
SIC: 3356 Titanium

HQ: Metal Management, Inc.
　　2425 S Wood St
　　Chicago IL 60608
　　773 890-4210

(G-1469)
ALBERT KEMPERLE INC
141 Locust St (06114-1504)
PHONE...............................860 727-0933
Ronald Kemperle, *Pr*
EMP: 17
SALES (corp-wide): 90.2MM **Privately Held**
Web: www.kemperle.com
SIC: 2851 Paints and allied products
PA: Albert Kemperle, Inc.
　　8400 New Horizons Blvd
　　Amityville NY 11701
　　631 841-1241

(G-1470)
APPELS PRTG & MAILING BUR INC
307 Homestead Ave (06112-2155)
P.O. Box 512 (06088-0512)
PHONE...............................860 522-8189
Joel Appelbaum, *Pr*
EMP: 10 EST: 1941
SQ FT: 5,000
SALES (est): 600K **Privately Held**
SIC: 2752 2791 Offset printing; Typesetting

(G-1471)
AQUILINE DRONES CORPORATION
750 Main St Ph (06103-2703)
PHONE...............................973 980-6596
Ethan James, *Admn*
Barry Alexander, *Managing Member**
EMP: 25 EST: 2019
SALES (est): 2.65MM **Privately Held**
Web: www.aquilinedrones.com
SIC: 3721 8299 7374 Nonmotorized and
　　lighter-than-air aircraft; Educational service,
　　nondegree granting: continuing educ.; Data
　　processing service

(G-1472)
AUSTIN ORGANS INCORPORATED
156 Woodland St (06105-1284)
P.O. Box 355 (06412-0355)
PHONE...............................860 522-8293
Richard G Taylor, *Ch*
Michael B Fazio, *Pr*
EMP: 19 EST: 1893
SQ FT: 35,000
SALES (est): 917.91K **Privately Held**
Web: www.austinorgans.com
SIC: 3931 Organs, all types: pipe, reed,
　　hand, electronic, etc.

(G-1473)
CAPITOL PRINTING CO INC
Also Called: Minuteman Press
52 Pratt St (06103-1601)
PHONE...............................860 522-1547
Joel Steinman, *Pr*
Steve Weber, *VP*
Amy Steinman, *Dir*
Gail Weber, *Dir*
EMP: 8 EST: 2003
SQ FT: 1,500
SALES (est): 882.32K **Privately Held**
Web: www.minutemanpress.com
SIC: 2752 Commercial printing, lithographic

(G-1474)
CMHANB LLC
1 Financial Plz Fl 16 (06103-2601)
PHONE...............................860 241-0112
James Carter, *Prin*
EMP: 9 EST: 2010
SALES (est): 221.9K **Privately Held**
SIC: 3568 Railroad car journal bearings

(G-1475)
CONNECTCUT HSPNIC YELLOW PAGES
2074 Park St Ste 2 (06106-2055)
PHONE...............................860 560-8713
Hector Torres, *Pr*
Angel Funtes, *Prin*
▲ **EMP: 10 EST:** 1997
SALES (est): 879.9K **Privately Held**
SIC: 2741 Telephone and other directory
　　publishing

(G-1476)
DLZ ARCHITECTURAL MILL WORK
510 Ledyard St (06114-3213)
PHONE...............................860 883-7562
David L Zavarella, *Pr*
EMP: 8 EST: 2014
SALES (est): 445.1K **Privately Held**
Web: www.dlzarchitecturalmillwork.com
SIC: 2431 Millwork

(G-1477)
EDI LANDSCAPE LLC
32 Belmont St (06106-2905)
PHONE...............................860 216-6871
Kimberly Colapietro, *Managing Member*
Joan M Davidson, *Pt*
Susan Mercer, *Admn*
EMP: 15 EST: 2001
SQ FT: 1,200
SALES (est): 4.32MM **Privately Held**
Web: www.edilandscape.com
SIC: 0781 0721 0783 3446 Landscape
　　services; Planting services; Planting
　　services, ornamental tree; Fences or posts,
　　ornamental iron or steel

(G-1478)
EL PASO PROD OIL GAS TEXAS LP
490 Capitol Ave (06106-1354)
PHONE...............................860 293-1990
Tom Starr, *Mgr*
EMP: 33
Web: www.kindermorgan.com
SIC: 1382 1311 Oil and gas exploration
　　services; Crude petroleum production
HQ: El Paso Production Oil & Gas Texas,
　　L.P.
　　1001 Louisiana St
　　Houston TX 77002
　　713 997-1000

(G-1479)
ENVIRONMANTAL SYSTEMS COR
18 Jansen Ct (06110-1913)
PHONE...............................860 953-5167
Donald Mccurdy, *Prin*
EMP: 36 EST: 2006
SALES (est): 1.15MM **Privately Held**
Web: www.esccontrols.com
SIC: 3569 Liquid automation machinery and
　　equipment

G
E
O
G
R
A
P
H
I
C

(G-1480)
FKA PPM INC
225 Asylum St Fl 20 (06103-1532)
PHONE........................781 871-4606
Donald R Seifel Junior, *CEO*
EMP: 46 **EST:** 1968
SQ FT: 27,000
SALES (est): 9.5MM **Privately Held**
Web: www.proppm.com
SIC: 3089 3544　Injection molding of plastics
; Special dies, tools, jigs, and fixtures

(G-1481)
FUTURAMIK INDUSTRIES INC
245 Hamilton St (06106-2939)
PHONE........................860 951-3121
▼ **EMP:** 30 **EST:** 1958
SALES (est): 2.35MM **Privately Held**
Web: www.futuramik.com
SIC: 3083　Thermosetting laminates: rods,
tubes, plates, and sheet

(G-1482)
GAMUT PUBLISHING
Also Called: Southside Media
30 Arbor St Unit 101 (06106-1241)
PHONE........................860 296-6128
Jon Harden, *Owner*
EMP: 7 **EST:** 1977
SALES (est): 235.04K **Privately Held**
SIC: 2711 2721 2731　Newspapers;
Periodicals; Book publishing

(G-1483)
GIMA LLC
Also Called: Gimasport
241 Ledyard St Ste B10 (06114-2029)
PHONE........................860 296-4441
Roberto Giansiracusa, *Prin*
George Marinelli, *Prin*
EMP: 17 **EST:** 1997
SQ FT: 20,000
SALES (est): 2.3MM **Privately Held**
Web: www.gimasport.com
SIC: 2329 5136　Men's and boys' sportswear
and athletic clothing; Gloves, men's and
boys'

(G-1484)
**GOVERNMENT SURPLUS
SALES INC**
Also Called: Government Sales
69 Francis Ave (06106-2102)
PHONE........................860 247-7787
Eric L Schweitzer, *Pr*
David H Schweitzer, *VP*
EMP: 7 **EST:** 1961
SQ FT: 15,000
SALES (est): 913.84K **Privately Held**
Web: www.aviationhelmets.com
SIC: 3469 5571　Helmets, steel; Motorcycle
parts and accessories

(G-1485)
**HARTFORD BUSINESS SUPPLY
INC**
Also Called: Printers
1718 Park St (06106-2132)
PHONE........................860 233-2138
Susan Falotico, *Pr*
Daniel J Falotico, *
EMP: 26 **EST:** 1974
SQ FT: 12,050
SALES (est): 4.43MM **Privately Held**
Web: www.budget-printers.com
SIC: 2752 5943　Offset printing; Office forms
and supplies

(G-1486)
**HARTFORD COURANT
COMPANY LLC (DH)**
285 Broad St (06115-3785)
PHONE........................860 241-6200
Rick Daniels, *CEO*
Mary Lou Stoneburner, *
David P Eldersveld, *
Thomas Brown, *
EMP: 700 **EST:** 1764
SQ FT: 293,792
SALES (est): 55.97B **Privately Held**
Web: www.courant.com
SIC: 2711　Newspapers, publishing and
printing
HQ: Tribune Publishing Company
560 W Grand Ave
Chicago IL 60654
312 222-9100

(G-1487)
HARTFORD JET CENTER LLC
20 Lindbergh Dr (06114-2132)
PHONE........................860 548-9334
EMP: 13 **EST:** 2015
SALES (est): 1.78MM **Privately Held**
Web: www.hartfordjetcenter.com
SIC: 3721　Aircraft

(G-1488)
**JOSEPH MERRITT & COMPANY
INC (PA)**
650 Franklin Ave Ste 3 (06114-3091)
PHONE........................860 296-2500
Edward W Perry, *Pr*
Patrick Freer, *
Craig Perry, *
Carla Francalangia, *Corporate Controller*
Ted J Crew, *
EMP: 40 **EST:** 1908
SQ FT: 24,000
SALES (est): 23.1MM
SALES (corp-wide): 23.1MM **Privately
Held**
Web: www.josephmerritt.com
SIC: 8748 2752 7331 7374
Communications consulting; Offset printing;
Direct mail advertising services; Computer
graphics service

(G-1489)
JWC STEEL CO LLC
540 Ledyard St (06114-3208)
PHONE........................860 296-5517
EMP: 35 **EST:** 2017
SALES (est): 2.72MM **Privately Held**
Web: www.jwcsteel.com
SIC: 1791 3441　Structural steel erection;
Fabricated structural metal

(G-1490)
LINE-X OF HARTFORD
Also Called: Line-X
192 Ledyard St (06114-2006)
PHONE........................860 216-6180
EMP: 8 **EST:** 2018
SALES (est): 229.87K **Privately Held**
Web: www.linex.com
SIC: 3479 5531　Coating of metals and
formed products; Truck equipment and parts

(G-1491)
**MARMON ENGNERED WIRE
CABLE LLC**
Also Called: Marmon Engineered Wire &
Cable
280 Trumbull St Fl 23 (06103-3599)
PHONE........................860 653-8300
Dennis Chalk, *Pr*

EMP: 12 **EST:** 2011
SALES (est): 458.24K **Privately Held**
Web: www.r-scc.com
SIC: 5063 3999　Wire and cable; Atomizers,
toiletry

(G-1492)
**MASSACHUSETTS ENVELOPE
CO INC**
General Business Envelope Co
10 Midland St (06120-1118)
P.O. Box 750 (06142-0750)
PHONE........................860 727-9100
Thomas Cummings, *Mgr*
EMP: 10
SQ FT: 34,000
SALES (corp-wide): 24.68MM **Privately
Held**
Web: www.grossmanmarketing.com
SIC: 2754 2752 5112　Commercial printing,
gravure; Commercial printing, lithographic;
Envelopes
PA: Massachusetts Envelope Company,
Inc.
10 State St Ste 100
Woburn MA 01801
617 623-8000

(G-1493)
MINIMALLY INVASIVE SURGEON
1000 Asylum Ave Lbby (06105-1701)
PHONE........................860 241-0870
Richard Newman, *Prin*
EMP: 7 **EST:** 2005
SALES (est): 665.05K **Privately Held**
SIC: 3841　Surgical and medical instruments

(G-1494)
MODERN PASTRY SHOP INC
Also Called: Modern Pastry
422 Franklin Ave (06114-2518)
PHONE........................860 296-7628
Carmelo Sardelli, *Pr*
EMP: 7 **EST:** 1958
SQ FT: 4,000
SALES (est): 253.92K **Privately Held**
Web: www.modernpastryshop.com
SIC: 5461 2052 2051　Cakes; Cookies and
crackers; Bread, cake, and related products

(G-1495)
**MOZZICATO PASTRY & BAKE
SP INC**
Also Called: Mozzict-De Psqale Bky Pstry Sp
329 Franklin Ave (06114-1851)
PHONE........................860 296-0426
Luigi Mozzicato, *Pr*
Gisella Mozzicato, *
EMP: 28 **EST:** 1908
SQ FT: 25,000
SALES (est): 2.13MM **Privately Held**
Web: www.mozzicatobakery.com
SIC: 5461 5149 2099 2052　Cakes; Bakery
products; Food preparations, nec; Cookies
and crackers

(G-1496)
**NEW ENGLAND FOAM
PRODUCTS LLC (PA)**
Also Called: New England Foam
760 Windsor St (06120-1918)
P.O. Box 583 (06095-0583)
PHONE........................860 524-0121
Christopher J Elia, *
EMP: 46 **EST:** 1987
SQ FT: 80,000
SALES (est): 9.64MM **Privately Held**
Web: www.newenglandfoam.com

SIC: 3069 3086　Foam rubber; Plastics foam
products

(G-1497)
NRG CONNECTICUT LLC
Also Called: Jewish Ledger
36 Woodland St Ste 1 (06105-2328)
PHONE........................860 231-2424
N Richard Greenfield, *Prin*
EMP: 19 **EST:** 1929
SQ FT: 2,000
SALES (est): 903.48K **Privately Held**
SIC: 2711 8661　Newspapers, publishing
and printing; Religious organizations

(G-1498)
OBERDORFER LLC
6 Central Row Fl 1 (06103-2719)
EMP: 110
SIC: 3365　Aluminum foundries

(G-1499)
PLASTONICS INC
230 Locust St (06114-2081)
PHONE........................860 249-5455
Robert B Zimmerli Junior, *Pr*
EMP: 28 **EST:** 1959
SQ FT: 32,000
SALES (est): 4.91MM **Privately Held**
Web: www.plastonics.com
SIC: 3479　Coating of metals and formed
products

(G-1500)
**PRATT & WHITNEY ENGINE LSG
LLC**
400 Main St (06118-1888)
PHONE........................860 565-4321
Shane Eddy, *Pr*
EMP: 64 **EST:** 2002
SALES (est): 1.53MM
SALES (corp-wide): 68.92B **Publicly Held**
SIC: 3724　Aircraft engines and engine parts
PA: Rtx Corporation
1000 Wilson Blvd
Arlington VA 22209
781 522-3000

(G-1501)
PYNE-DAVIDSON COMPANY
237 Weston St (06120-1209)
PHONE........................860 522-9106
Harry H Davidson, *CEO*
Daniel J Davidson, *
Jeff Milliard, *
Diane Davidson, *
EMP: 28 **EST:** 1930
SQ FT: 12,500
SALES (est): 4.47MM **Privately Held**
Web: www.pynedavidson.com
SIC: 2752　Offset printing

(G-1502)
QSR STEEL CORPORATION LLC
121 Elliott St E (06114-1515)
PHONE........................860 548-0248
EMP: 20 **EST:** 2000
SALES (est): 6.84MM **Privately Held**
Web: www.qsrsteel.com
SIC: 3441　Building components, structural
steel

(G-1503)
R L FISHER INC
Also Called: Rlf Homes
30 Bartholomew Ave (06106-2283)
PHONE........................860 951-8110
Robin Fisher, *Pr*
Philip Sarrantonio, *

EMP: 25 EST: 1985
SQ FT: 36,000
SALES (est): 2.06MM Privately Held
Web: www.rlfhome.com
SIC: 2391 2392 Curtains, window: made from purchased materials; Household furnishings, nec

(G-1504)
RELIABLE AUTO TIRE COMPANY INC
711 Maple Ave (06114-1858)
PHONE.................................860 247-7977
Jerry J Massaro Senior, Pr
Eleanor Massaro, VP
Thomas Yacavone, Sec
EMP: 7 EST: 1922
SQ FT: 5,000
SALES (est): 736.52K Privately Held
Web: www.reliableautotire.com
SIC: 5531 5014 7534 Automotive tires; Tires and tubes; Tire repair shop

(G-1505)
RELIABLE ELECTRIC MOTOR INC
285 Murphy Rd (06114-2111)
PHONE.................................860 522-2257
Brian Langille, Pr
EMP: 12 EST: 1936
SQ FT: 15,000
SALES (est): 7.81MM Privately Held
Web: www.remisi.com
SIC: 5063 7694 Motors, electric; Electric motor repair

(G-1506)
SEVERANCE FOODS INC
Also Called: Pan De Oro Brand
3478 Main St (06120-1138)
PHONE.................................860 724-7063
Richard Stevens, Pr
Leif Dana, *
EMP: 45 EST: 1984
SQ FT: 40,400
SALES (est): 9.86MM Privately Held
Web: www.severancefoods.com
SIC: 2099 Food preparations, nec

(G-1507)
SHEPARD STEEL CO INC (PA)
Also Called: Shepard Steel
110 Meadow St (06114-1598)
PHONE.................................860 525-4446
George R Beckerman, Pr
Lawrence K Schwartz, *
Keith F Wolf, *
Brian Ritchie, *
▲ EMP: 65 EST: 1959
SQ FT: 100,000
SALES (est): 510.43K
SALES (corp-wide): 510.43K Privately Held
Web: www.shepardsteel.com
SIC: 3441 3446 Building components, structural steel; Architectural metalwork

(G-1508)
SLEEP MANAGEMENT SOLUTIONS LLC (DH)
20 Church St Ste 900 (06103-1248)
PHONE.................................888 497-5337
EMP: 10 EST: 2005
SALES (est): 2.4MM
SALES (corp-wide): 139.08B Publicly Held
Web: www.carecentrix.com
SIC: 3841 8741 Diagnostic apparatus, medical; Management services

HQ: Carecentrix, Inc.
20 Church St Fl 12
Hartford CT 06103

(G-1509)
STAR TIRES PLUS WHEELS LLC
888 Wethersfield Ave (06114-3180)
PHONE.................................860 296-9799
EMP: 12 EST: 2014
SALES (est): 3MM Privately Held
Web: www.startireandwheels.com
SIC: 7534 5531 Tire repair shop; Automotive tires

(G-1510)
STOP N GO LLC
432 New Britain Ave (06106-3832)
PHONE.................................860 206-3950
Edwin R Cruz, Prin
EMP: 7 EST: 2017
SALES (est): 90.74K Privately Held
Web: www.kwiktrip.com
SIC: 2911 Petroleum refining

(G-1511)
SWING BY SWING GOLF INC
80 State House Sq Unit 158 (06123-7701)
PHONE.................................804 869-6983
Charles Cox, CEO
Charles A Cox, *
James Reid Gorman, *
EMP: 31 EST: 2012
SQ FT: 2,000
SALES (est): 2.59MM Privately Held
Web: www.swingu.com
SIC: 7372 Application computer software

(G-1512)
SYCAST INC
148 Bartholomew Ave (06106-2903)
PHONE.................................860 308-2122
Anhared Stowe, CEO
John W Stowe, Pr
EMP: 13 EST: 2010
SALES (est): 1.39MM Privately Held
Web: www.sycastinc.com
SIC: 3369 Castings, except die-castings, precision

(G-1513)
TEES & MORE LLC
306 Murphy Rd (06114-2127)
PHONE.................................860 244-2224
EMP: 9 EST: 2003
SALES (est): 840.87K Privately Held
Web: teesandmore.shop
SIC: 2262 Screen printing: manmade fiber and silk broadwoven fabrics

(G-1514)
THOMAS W RAFTERY INC
1055 Broad St (06106-2310)
PHONE.................................860 278-9870
Gary Rigoletti, CEO
Robert O'connor, Pr
EMP: 35 EST: 1963
SQ FT: 60,000
SALES (est): 4.85MM Privately Held
Web: www.twraftery.com
SIC: 2391 2392 5131 2591 Draperies, plastic and textile: from purchased materials ; Blankets, comforters and beddings; Synthetic fabrics, nec; Drapery hardware and window blinds and shades

(G-1515)
VALEN TECHNOLOGIES INC
Also Called: Valen Analytics
170 Huyshope Ave (06106-2817)

PHONE.................................720 570-3333
Dax Craig, Pr
Gale Pierce, *
Kirstin Marr, CMO*
EMP: 24 EST: 2002
SALES (est): 2.35MM Privately Held
Web: www.insurity.com
SIC: 7372 Business oriented computer software

(G-1516)
VANCE PUBLISHING CORPORATION
Also Called: Vance Publishing
100 Pearl St Fl 13 (06103-4511)
PHONE.................................847 634-2600
▲ EMP: 170
SIC: 2721 Trade journals: publishing and printing

(G-1517)
WILD CARD GOLF LLC
222 Murphy Rd (06114-2107)
PHONE.................................860 296-1661
▲ EMP: 9 EST: 2003
SALES (est): 271.22K Privately Held
Web: www.mikesgolfoutlet.com
SIC: 3949 5091 Sporting and athletic goods, nec; Golf equipment

Harwinton
Litchfield County

(G-1518)
A & H TOOL WORKS LLC
101 Rocky Rd E (06791-2911)
PHONE.................................860 302-9284
David Baril, Prin
EMP: 7 EST: 2013
SALES (est): 255.64K Privately Held
SIC: 3544 Special dies and tools

(G-1519)
EASTERN ELECTRIC CNSTR CO
75 North Rd (06791-1902)
PHONE.................................860 485-1100
Thomas Simko, Prin
EMP: 7 EST: 2010
SALES (est): 821.5K Privately Held
SIC: 3699 1731 1521 Electrical equipment and supplies, nec; Electrical work; Single-family housing construction

(G-1520)
EASTSIDE ELECTRIC INC
178 Birge Park Rd (06791-1909)
PHONE.................................860 485-0700
Gregory L Mele, Prin
EMP: 18 EST: 2013
SALES (est): 2.85MM Privately Held
Web: www.eastside-electric.com
SIC: 3699 1731 Electrical equipment and supplies, nec; Electrical work

(G-1521)
IRONHORSE INDUSTRIES LLC
357 Terryville Rd (06791-2804)
PHONE.................................203 598-8720
EMP: 7 EST: 2018
SALES (est): 492.4K Privately Held
SIC: 3999 Manufacturing industries, nec

(G-1522)
O & G INDUSTRIES INC
255 Lower Bogue Rd (06791-1626)
PHONE.................................860 485-6600
Bob Oneglia, VP
EMP: 38

SALES (corp-wide): 496.36MM Privately Held
Web: www.ogind.com
SIC: 3999 Atomizers, toiletry
PA: O & G Industries, Inc.
112 Wall St
Torrington CT 06790
860 489-9261

(G-1523)
SPRING COMPUTERIZED INDS LLC
Also Called: Csi
93 Oakwood Dr (06791-1307)
PHONE.................................860 605-9206
Elliot Cyr, Owner
Janice Syr Ofc, Mgr
EMP: 8 EST: 1993
SQ FT: 1,500
SALES (est): 630K Privately Held
SIC: 3495 3493 Wire springs; Steel springs, except wire

(G-1524)
STEVENSON GROUP CORPORATION
120 Wilson Pond Rd (06791-2815)
PHONE.................................860 689-0011
John A Stevenson, Pr
Donna B Stevenson, VP
Melissa A Stevenson, Treas
EMP: 10 EST: 2003
SALES (est): 388.98K Privately Held
SIC: 1796 2541 Elevator installation and conversion; Wood partitions and fixtures

Hebron
Tolland County

(G-1525)
BENNETTSVILLE HOLDINGS LLC
Also Called: Bennettsville Printing
33 Pendleton Dr # A (06248-1512)
P.O. Box 71 (06331-0071)
PHONE.................................860 444-9400
Victor Winogradrow, Managing Member
Carol Winogradrow, *
EMP: 10 EST: 2010
SALES (est): 770.61K Privately Held
Web: www.bennettsvilleprinting.com
SIC: 2396 Fabric printing and stamping

(G-1526)
COUNTRY CARPENTERS INC
326 Gilead St (06248-1347)
PHONE.................................860 228-2276
Roger G Barrett Junior, Pr
Lois M Barrett, VP
EMP: 8 EST: 1973
SALES (est): 1.28MM Privately Held
Web: www.countrycarpenters.com
SIC: 2491 1521 2452 2439 Poles, posts and pilings: treated wood; Single-family housing construction; Prefabricated wood buildings; Structural wood members, nec

(G-1527)
FRONT LINE APPAREL GROUP LLC
Also Called: Front Line Group, The
33 Pendleton Dr (06248-1512)
PHONE.................................860 859-3524
Ronald Levine, CEO
Victor Winogradow, VP
EMP: 10 EST: 2000
SQ FT: 75,000
SALES (est): 497.78K Privately Held

Web: www.frontlineapparel.net
SIC: 7349 0781 2311 Janitorial service,
contract basis; Landscape services; Military
uniforms, men's and youths': purchased
materials

(G-1528)
IAMAW
249 East St (06248-1311)
PHONE.................................860 228-0049
EMP: 7 EST: 2005
SALES (est): 85.7K Privately Held
Web: www.goiam.org
SIC: 3541 Vertical turning and boring
machines (metalworking)

Higganum
Middlesex County

(G-1529)
KENYON LABORATORIES LLC
Also Called: Ken-Labs
12 Scovil Rd (06441-4218)
PHONE.................................860 345-2097
EMP: 7 EST: 1951
SQ FT: 17,000
SALES (est): 915.72K Privately Held
Web: www.ken-lab.com
SIC: 3861 Photographic equipment and
supplies

Ivoryton
Middlesex County

(G-1530)
**MOELLER INSTRUMENT
COMPANY INC**
126 Main St (06442-1102)
P.O. Box 668 (06442-0668)
PHONE.................................800 243-9310
Jeff Murtz, Pr
Darcy Murtz, Sec
EMP: 11 EST: 1867
SQ FT: 5,000
SALES (est): 664.71K Privately Held
Web: www.moellerinstrument.com
SIC: 3823 Temperature measurement
instruments, industrial

(G-1531)
ORTRONICS LEGRAND
14 Windermere Way (06442-1275)
PHONE.................................860 767-3515
Mike Hines, Prin
EMP: 7 EST: 2010
SALES (est): 199.82K Privately Held
SIC: 3577 Computer peripheral equipment,
nec

(G-1532)
**RICHARD RIGGIO AND SONS
INC**
Also Called: Innovative Designs
90 Pond Meadow Rd (06442-1156)
PHONE.................................860 767-0812
Gary R Riggio, Pr
Paul Riggio, *
Julie C Ladone, *
EMP: 15 EST: 1978
SQ FT: 12,000
SALES (est): 988.8K Privately Held
Web: www.richardriggioandsons.com
SIC: 1521 2542 6552 New construction,
single-family houses; Counters or counter
display cases, except wood; Subdividers
and developers, nec

(G-1533)
THE L C DOANE COMPANY
110 Pond Meadow Rd (06442-1121)
PHONE.................................860 767-8295
William Psillos, Pr
Margaret P Eagan, *
William Psillos, VP
Nicholas Orobello, *
EMP: 99 EST: 1947
SQ FT: 140,000
SALES (est): 11.46MM Privately Held
Web: www.lcdoane.com
SIC: 3646 3647 Commercial lighting fixtures
; Boat and ship lighting fixtures

(G-1534)
**WESTBROOK
MANUFACTURING LLC**
1 Cheney St (06442-1182)
PHONE.................................860 767-2460
EMP: 12 EST: 1992
SQ FT: 1,600
SALES (est): 1.57MM Privately Held
Web: www.westbrookmfg.com
SIC: 3089 3443 3599 Plastics hardware and
building products; Metal parts; Machine
shop, jobbing and repair

Jewett City
New London County

(G-1535)
CAMARO SIGNS INC (PA)
268 Edmond Rd (06351-1310)
PHONE.................................860 886-1553
John Hansen, Pr
Erica Hansen, Sec
EMP: 7 EST: 1968
SALES (est): 956.08K
SALES (corp-wide): 956.08K Privately
Held
Web: www.camarosigns.com
SIC: 3993 Electric signs

(G-1536)
MAPLE PRINT SERVICES INC
39 Wedgewood Dr (06351-2437)
PHONE.................................860 381-5470
Mike Johnson, Pr
EMP: 7 EST: 2011
SALES (est): 207.25K Privately Held
Web: www.mapleprintservices.com
SIC: 2752 Offset printing

Kensington
Hartford County

(G-1537)
AEROCOMPOSITES INC
49 Cambridge Hts (06037-2310)
PHONE.................................860 829-6809
John Violette, Pr
Harrison Griswold, VP
Ernest Glastris, VP
EMP: 14 EST: 1998
SALES (est): 612.95K Privately Held
Web: www.rotatingcomposites.com
SIC: 3728 Aircraft propellers and associated
equipment

(G-1538)
**BERLIN STEEL CONSTRUCTION
CO (PA)**
Also Called: Berlin Steel
76 Depot Rd (06037-1439)
P.O. Box 428 (06037-0428)

PHONE.................................860 828-3531
Carl A Johnson, Pr
Robert Bailey, *
Mike Pierney, *
Michael O'sullivan, Treas
David J Baffaro, *
▲ EMP: 50 EST: 1916
SQ FT: 62,500
SALES (est): 34.88MM
SALES (corp-wide): 34.88MM Privately
Held
Web: www.berlinsteel.com
SIC: 1791 3441 Structural steel erection;
Fabricated structural metal for bridges

(G-1539)
**D&D FLTRTION CONS SPPLIERS
INC**
Also Called: D & D Filtration
612 Four Rod Rd (06037-2281)
PHONE.................................860 829-3690
Daniel Quagliaro, Pr
Debra Quagliaro, VP
EMP: 13 EST: 1988
SQ FT: 10,000
SALES (est): 4.89MM Privately Held
Web: www.danddfiltration.com
SIC: 3569 7389 8742 8748 Filters; Design,
commercial and industrial; Manufacturing
management consultant; Business
consulting, nec

(G-1540)
**ROTATING COMPOSITE TECH
LLC**
49 Cambridge Hts (06037-2310)
PHONE.................................860 829-6809
John Violette, Pr
EMP: 8 EST: 2007
SALES (est): 1.74MM Privately Held
Web: www.rotatingcomposites.com
SIC: 3728 Aircraft parts and equipment, nec

Kent
Litchfield County

(G-1541)
INDIGO COAST INC
Also Called: Trailheads
17 Meadow St (06757-1329)
PHONE.................................860 592-0088
Stephanie Raftery, Pr
Stephanie Raftery, Prin
Ed Raftery, VP
Lorienne Cote, Sec
▲ EMP: 8 EST: 2007
SALES (est): 994.03K Privately Held
Web: www.trailheads.com
SIC: 2353 7389 Hats, caps, and millinery;
Business Activities at Non-Commercial Site

(G-1542)
**KENT FALLS BREWING
COMPANY**
33 Camps Rd (06757-1901)
PHONE.................................860 398-9645
EMP: 7 EST: 2016
SALES (est): 552.57K Privately Held
Web: www.kentfallsbrewing.com
SIC: 2082 Brewers' grain

Killingworth
Middlesex County

(G-1543)
MODINE LLC

129 Chittenden Rd (06419-2428)
PHONE.................................860 452-4194
EMP: 10 EST: 2012
SALES (est): 719.1K
SALES (corp-wide): 2.3B Publicly Held
Web: www.modine.com
SIC: 3443 Fabricated plate work (boiler
shop)
PA: Modine Manufacturing Company Inc
1500 De Koven Ave
Racine WI 53403
262 636-1200

(G-1544)
NEW ENGLAND TOOLING INC
145 Chestnut Hill Rd (06419-1300)
PHONE.................................800 866-5105
Shane Springer, Pr
Jeff Springer, VP
EMP: 10 EST: 2009
SALES (est): 1.15MM Privately Held
Web: www.newenglandtooling.com
SIC: 3541 3545 2899 2843 Machine tools,
metal cutting type; Cutting tools for
machine tools; Corrosion preventive
lubricant; Soluble oils or greases

Lakeville
Litchfield County

(G-1545)
EWALD INSTRUMENTS CORP
331 Wells Hill Rd (06039-2301)
P.O. Box 398 (06756-0398)
PHONE.................................860 491-9042
Richard Vreeland, Pr
Susan Vreeland, Sec
EMP: 11 EST: 1954
SALES (est): 415.98K Privately Held
Web: www.ewaldinstruments.com
SIC: 3545 3625 7699 Cutting tools for
machine tools; Resistance welder controls;
Welding equipment repair

(G-1546)
ILLINOIS TOOL WORKS INC
ITW Impro Lakeville Operations
14 Brook St (06039-1104)
P.O. Box 1570 (06039-1570)
PHONE.................................860 435-2574
Bill Thurston, Mgr
EMP: 22
SQ FT: 20,000
SALES (corp-wide): 15.93B Publicly Held
Web: www.itw.com
SIC: 3089 Injection molding of plastics
PA: Illinois Tool Works Inc.
155 Harlem Ave
Glenview IL 60025
847 724-7500

(G-1547)
**LAKEVILLE JOURNAL
COMPANY LLC (PA)**
Also Called: WINSTED JOURNAL
33 Bissell St (06039-1212)
P.O. Box 1688 (06039-1688)
PHONE.................................860 435-9873
Will Little, Pr
EMP: 45 EST: 1897
SQ FT: 10,000
SALES (est): 1.03MM
SALES (corp-wide): 1.03MM Privately
Held
Web: www.tricornernews.com
SIC: 2711 Job printing and newspaper
publishing combined

Lebanon
New London County

(G-1548)
ANN S DAVIS
Also Called: Recognition Products
754 Exeter Rd (06249-1735)
P.O. Box 1980 (06249-1980)
PHONE...............................860 642-7228
Ann S Davis, *Owner*
EMP: 10 **EST:** 1980
SALES (est): 474.78K **Privately Held**
Web: www.rproducts.com
SIC: 3999 3479 7389 Identification tags, except paper; Name plates: engraved, etched, etc.; Engraving service

(G-1549)
MIRACLE INSTRUMENTS CO
1667 Exeter Rd (06249-1904)
PHONE...............................860 642-7745
John Ryan, *Pr*
EMP: 11 **EST:** 1967
SQ FT: 3,000
SALES (est): 1.12MM **Privately Held**
Web: www.miracleinstrument.com
SIC: 3545 3829 3699 Chucks: drill, lathe, or magnetic (machine tool accessories); Levels and tapes, surveying; Door opening and closing devices, electrical

(G-1550)
SCOTTS COMPANY LLC
20 Industrial Rd (06249-1326)
P.O. Box 143 (06249-0143)
PHONE...............................860 642-7591
Mark Kulling, *Mgr*
EMP: 50
SALES (corp-wide): 3.55B **Publicly Held**
Web: www.scotts.com
SIC: 2875 Fertilizers, mixing only
HQ: The Scotts Company Llc
14111 Scottslawn Rd
Marysville OH 43040
937 644-0011

Ledyard
New London County

(G-1551)
FORTE RTS INC
Also Called: Forte Carbon Fiber Products
14 Lorenz Industrial Pkwy (06339-1946)
PHONE...............................860 464-5221
Anthony F Delima, *Pr*
▼ **EMP:** 8 **EST:** 2006
SALES (est): 889.89K **Privately Held**
Web: www.fortecarbon.com
SIC: 3825 Spark plug testing equipment, electric

(G-1552)
JOHNSON CONTROLS INC
Also Called: Johnson Controls
39 Norwich Westerly Rd (06339-1128)
PHONE...............................860 886-9021
Tom Oneil, *Mgr*
EMP: 16
Web: www.johnsoncontrols.com
SIC: 2531 Seats, automobile
HQ: Johnson Controls, Inc.
5757 N Green Bay Ave
Milwaukee WI 53209
920 245-6409

(G-1553)
SKULL KINGDOM ENTRMT LLC
4e Flintlock Rd (06339-4812)
PHONE...............................262 804-8193
Jovaun Scully, *CEO*
Jovaun Scully, *Managing Member*
EMP: 8 **EST:** 2020
SALES (est): 339.2K **Privately Held**
SIC: 2741 7389 Music book and sheet music publishing; Music recording producer

Lisbon
New London County

(G-1554)
AMGRAPH
190 Inland Rd (06351)
PHONE...............................860 822-2000
EMP: 9 **EST:** 2016
SALES (est): 90.74K **Privately Held**
Web: www.amgraph.com
SIC: 2671 Paper; coated and laminated packaging

Litchfield
Litchfield County

(G-1555)
CUSTOM FURNITURE & DESIGN LLC
Also Called: Custom Furniture & Design
601 Bantam Rd (06759)
P.O. Box 1533 (06759-1533)
PHONE...............................860 567-3519
Mike Moskowitz, *Managing Member*
EMP: 14 **EST:** 1988
SQ FT: 6,000
SALES (est): 479.84K **Privately Held**
Web:
www.customfurnitureanddesign.com
SIC: 2434 2511 Wood kitchen cabinets; Wood household furniture

(G-1556)
EAST COAST SHEET METAL LLC
141 Woodruff St (06759-3528)
PHONE...............................860 283-1126
Lisa Patchell, *Managing Member*
David Patchell, *Managing Member*
EMP: 14 **EST:** 1992
SALES (est): 905.21K **Privately Held**
SIC: 1711 3444 Mechanical contractor; Sheet metalwork

(G-1557)
ENGINEERED COATINGS INC
272 Norfolk Rd (06759-2517)
P.O. Box 501 (06759-0501)
PHONE...............................860 567-5556
TOLL FREE: 800
Alan Landau, *Pr*
Christopher Krone, *VP*
EMP: 9 **EST:** 1961
SQ FT: 36,000
SALES (est): 992.51K **Privately Held**
Web: www.engineeredcoatingsinc.com
SIC: 2899 Concrete curing and hardening compounds

(G-1558)
KENT NUTRITION GROUP INC
99 Thomaston Rd (06759-2911)
PHONE...............................860 482-7116
Brian Lake, *Brnch Mgr*
EMP: 7

SQ FT: 1,000
SALES (corp-wide): 517.65MM **Privately Held**
Web: www.kentfeeds.com
SIC: 2048 Livestock feeds
HQ: Kent Nutrition Group, Inc.
2905 N Highway 61
Muscatine IA 52761
866 647-1212

(G-1559)
LITCHFIELD DISTILLERY
569 Bantam Rd (06759-3203)
PHONE...............................860 361-6503
EMP: 7 **EST:** 2018
SALES (est): 408.42K **Privately Held**
Web: www.litchfielddistillery.com
SIC: 2085 Distilled and blended liquors

Lyme
New London County

(G-1560)
PEELED SNACKS INC
121 Mount Archer Rd (06371-3132)
PHONE...............................773 372-3223
James Goldberg, *CEO*
Chad Denen, *CFO*
EMP: 10 **EST:** 2021
SALES (est): 232.78K **Privately Held**
Web: www.peeledsnacks.com
SIC: 2099 Food preparations, nec

Madison
New Haven County

(G-1561)
CONNECTICUT PARENT MAGAZINE
311 Bartlett Dr (06443-1787)
PHONE...............................203 483-1700
Joel Macclaren, *Prin*
EMP: 10 **EST:** 1999
SALES (est): 623.5K **Privately Held**
Web: www.ctparent.com
SIC: 2721 Magazines: publishing only, not printed on site

(G-1562)
KIRCHOFF WOHLBERG INC
897 Boston Post Rd (06443-3155)
PHONE...............................212 644-2020
Morris Kirchoff, *Pr*
Ronald Zollshan, *
EMP: 11 **EST:** 1974
SQ FT: 8,000
SALES (est): 409.84K **Privately Held**
SIC: 2731 7389 Textbooks: publishing only, not printed on site; Artists' agents and brokers

(G-1563)
MADISON MEDICAL LLC
Also Called: M E M
8 Bishop Ln Ste 4 (06443-3367)
PHONE...............................203 245-0306
▲ **EMP:** 34
SIC: 3841 8732 Surgical and medical instruments; Market analysis, business, and economic research

(G-1564)
NEW PRECISION TECHNOLOGY LLC
Also Called: USI Education & Government Sls
98 Fort Path Rd Ste B (06443-2264)

PHONE...............................800 243-4565
Nicholas Gianacoplos, *Owner*
Nicholas Gianacoplos, *Prin*
Sherri Montminy, *Prin*
EMP: 7 **EST:** 2000
SQ FT: 14,000
SALES (est): 920.73K **Privately Held**
Web: www.np-tek.com
SIC: 3083 Thermosetting laminates: rods, tubes, plates, and sheet

(G-1565)
OUTDOOR INDUSTRIES LLC
80 Devonshire Ln (06443-1681)
P.O. Box 948 (06443-0948)
PHONE...............................203 350-2275
EMP: 19
SALES (corp-wide): 440.36K **Privately Held**
Web: www.outdoorindustriesllc.com
SIC: 3999 Barber and beauty shop equipment
PA: Outdoor Industries, Llc
391 Soundview Rd
Guilford CT

(G-1566)
POWERPHONE INC
1321 Boston Post Rd (06443-3431)
PHONE...............................203 245-8911
Chris Salafia, *CEO*
Philip M Salafia Junior, *CEO*
Jerry Turk, *
EMP: 35 **EST:** 1983
SQ FT: 11,000
SALES (est): 6.07MM **Privately Held**
Web: www.powerphone.com
SIC: 8742 2741 8748 8331 Industry specialist consultants; Technical manuals: publishing only, not printed on site; Communications consulting; Job training services

(G-1567)
PRECISION X-RAY INC
Also Called: Precision X-Ray Irradiation
14 New Rd (06443-2507)
PHONE...............................203 484-2011
Viktoriya Baytser, *CEO*
William Mclaughlin, *Pr*
Paul Murtagh, *
Amy Bradley, *
EMP: 30 **EST:** 2018
SALES (est): 2.62MM **Privately Held**
Web: www.precisionxray.com
SIC: 3844 X-ray apparatus and tubes

(G-1568)
RWT CORPORATION
Also Called: Welding Works
32 New Rd (06443-2507)
PHONE...............................203 245-2731
Ross E Mccartney, *Pr*
Laurie Mccartney, *Sec*
EMP: 24 **EST:** 2018
SQ FT: 22,000
SALES (est): 5.11MM **Privately Held**
Web: www.weldingworks.com
SIC: 3441 3448 Fabricated structural metal; Prefabricated metal components

(G-1569)
SCOTT WOODFORD
817 Boston Post Rd (06443-3155)
PHONE...............................203 245-4266
Scott Woodford, *Prin*
EMP: 9 **EST:** 2006
SALES (est): 348.14K **Privately Held**
Web: www.woodforddental.com

SIC: 3843　Enamels, dentists'

(G-1570)
SHORE PUBLISHING LLC
724 Boston Post Rd (06443-3039)
P.O. Box 1010 (06443-1010)
PHONE...........................203 245-1877
James Warner, *Managing Member*
EMP: 37 EST: 1994
SQ FT: 2,500
SALES (est): 2.23MM **Privately Held**
Web: www.zip06.com
SIC: 2711　Commercial printing and
newspaper publishing combined

(G-1571)
SHUTTERCRAFT INC
15 Orchard Park Rd Ste A5 (06443-2274)
PHONE...........................203 245-2608
Colleen Murdock, *CEO*
EMP: 8
SALES (corp-wide): 986.63K **Privately
Held**
Web: www.shuttercraft.com
SIC: 2431　Millwork
PA: Shuttercraft Inc
282 Stepstone Hill Rd
Guilford CT
203 453-1973

(G-1572)
TANGO MODEM LLC
303 Race Hill Rd (06443-1628)
PHONE...........................203 421-2245
Robert Allen, *Prin*
EMP: 7 EST: 2010
SALES (est): 235.96K **Privately Held**
SIC: 3661　Modems

(G-1573)
TORINO SYSTEMS LLC
Also Called: Torino Systems
44 Pent Rd (06443-3238)
P.O. Box 4013 (06443-4000)
PHONE...........................203 871-1118
Vincent Dipaola, *Prin*
EMP: 7 EST: 2018
SALES (est): 376.1K **Privately Held**
Web: www.torino.systems
SIC: 7372　Prepackaged software

(G-1574)
ULTRA CLEAN EQUIPMENT INC
64 Wall St (06443-3150)
PHONE...........................860 669-1354
Bill Clorite, *Pr*
Christine Clorite, *Sec*
EMP: 8 EST: 1969
SALES (est): 971.73K **Privately Held**
Web: www.ultracleanequip.com
SIC: 3699　Cleaning equipment, ultrasonic,
except medical and dental

(G-1575)
UNITED PLASTICS TECH INC
6 Downing Way (06443-3447)
PHONE...........................860 224-1110
Vincent Dicioccio, *Pr*
Anthony Straska, *VP*
John Shurkus, *Sec*
Vincent Dicioccio Junior, *VP*
EMP: 15 EST: 1981
SALES (est): 828.61K **Privately Held**
SIC: 3089　Injection molding of plastics

(G-1576)
WELDING WORKS INC
32 New Rd (06443-2507)
P.O. Box 1739 (06450-8839)

PHONE...........................203 245-2731
EMP: 24
SIC: 3441 3448　Fabricated structural metal;
Prefabricated metal components

(G-1577)
**WIRE ASSOCIATION INTL INC
(PA)**
Also Called: Wai
71 Bradley Rd Unit 9 (06443-2662)
P.O. Box 578 (06437-0578)
PHONE...........................203 453-2777
Daniel Blais, *Pr*
Steven J Fetteroll, *Ex Dir*
David B Lavalley, *Treas*
EMP: 11 EST: 1930
SQ FT: 7,000
SALES (est): 31.48K
SALES (corp-wide): 31.48K **Privately Held**
Web: www.wirenet.org
SIC: 8621 2721　Professional organizations;
Magazines: publishing only, not printed on
site

(G-1578)
WIRE JOURNAL INC
71 Bradley Rd Unit 9 (06443-2662)
P.O. Box 578 (06437-0578)
PHONE...........................203 453-2777
Sanford May, *Ex Dir*
EMP: 13 EST: 1966
SQ FT: 10,000
SALES (est): 2.25MM
SALES (corp-wide): 31.48K **Privately Held**
Web: www.wirenet.org
SIC: 2721　Magazines: publishing only, not
printed on site
PA: The Wire Association International Inc
71 Bradley Rd Unit 9
Madison CT 06443
203 453-2777

Manchester
Hartford County

(G-1579)
3333 LLC
Also Called: Kaplan Tarps & Cargo Controls
42 Hilliard St (06042-3002)
PHONE...........................860 643-1384
EMP: 7 EST: 2015
SQ FT: 12,000
SALES (est): 535.24K **Privately Held**
Web: www.kaplantarps.com
SIC: 7359 2394 3792　Tent and tarpaulin
rental; Canvas covers and drop cloths;
Pickup covers, canopies or caps

(G-1580)
ABA-PGT INC (PA)
Also Called: A B A Tool & Die Div
10 Gear Dr (06042-8907)
PHONE...........................860 649-4591
Samuel D Pierson, *CEO*
Michael J Rice, *
Thomas R Peck, *
EMP: 100 EST: 1944
SQ FT: 67,000
SALES (est): 19.19MM
SALES (corp-wide): 19.19MM **Privately
Held**
Web: www.abapgt.com
SIC: 3089 3544　Injection molding of plastics
; Dies, plastics forming

(G-1581)
**ACCURATE BRAZING
CORPORATION**

4 Progress Dr (06042-2212)
PHONE...........................860 432-1840
Bob Sartori, *Mgr*
EMP: 18
SALES (corp-wide): 3.35B **Privately Held**
Web: www.aalberts-ab.us
SIC: 3398　Metal heat treating
HQ: Accurate Brazing Corporation
36 Cote Ave Ste 5
Goffstown NH 03045

(G-1582)
ACMT INC
Also Called: Aerospace Manufacturing
369 Progress Dr (06042-2296)
PHONE...........................860 645-0592
Michael Polo, *Pr*
Michael G Polo, *
Paul Polo Senior, *VP*
EMP: 90 EST: 1986
SQ FT: 48,000
SALES (est): 20.57MM **Privately Held**
Web: www.acmt.aero
SIC: 3061 3724 3728 5088　Mechanical
rubber goods; Aircraft engines and engine
parts; Aircraft parts and equipment, nec;
Helicopter parts

(G-1583)
ADVANCE MOLD & MFG INC
Also Called: Vision Technical Molding
71 Utopia Rd (06042-2192)
PHONE...........................860 432-5887
Randy Clark, *Pr*
Timothy Stewart, *
Daniel Wendler, *
EMP: 150 EST: 1959
SQ FT: 28,500
SALES (est): 49.33MM **Privately Held**
Web: www.flex.com
SIC: 3544 3089　Industrial molds; Injection
molding of plastics
HQ: Flextronics International Usa, Inc.
6201 America Center Dr
San Jose CA 95002

(G-1584)
**ALLIED PRINTING SERVICES
INC (PA)**
1 Allied Way (06042-8933)
P.O. Box 850 (06045-0850)
PHONE...........................860 643-1101
John G Sommers, *Pr*
Robert B Mc Cann, *
Bettina Sommers, *
Gerald Sommers, *
Peter Swan, *
◆ EMP: 349 EST: 1950
SALES (est): 183.31K
SALES (corp-wide): 183.31K **Privately
Held**
Web: www.alliedprinting.com
SIC: 2396 2752 2759 2789　Automotive and
apparel trimmings; Offset printing;
Commercial printing, nec; Bookbinding and
related work

(G-1585)
ALLOY SPECIALTIES LLC
110 Batson Dr (06042-1694)
PHONE...........................860 646-4587
Dawn Dimauro, *Pr*
Dennis P Dimauro, *
Sean Holly, *
EMP: 40 EST: 1981
SQ FT: 14,500
SALES (est): 6.85MM **Privately Held**
Web: www.alloysp.com

SIC: 3724 5051　Aircraft engines and engine
parts; Metals service centers and offices

(G-1586)
**BAKELITE N SUMITOMO AMER
INC (DH)**
24 Mill St (06042-2316)
PHONE...........................860 646-5500
Shintaro Ishiwata, *Ch*
Henny Van Dijk, *
Alan Houghton, *
▲ EMP: 85 EST: 2000
SALES (est): 33.76MM **Privately Held**
Web: www.sbhpp.com
SIC: 2821　Plastics materials and resins
HQ: Sumitomo Bakelite North America, Inc.
4400 Haggerty Hwy
Commerce Township MI 48390

(G-1587)
CAM GROUP LLC
130 Chapel Rd (06042-1625)
PHONE...........................860 646-2378
EMP: 10 EST: 2004
SQ FT: 2,000
SALES (est): 984.96K **Privately Held**
Web: www.camthebull.com
SIC: 3519　Jet propulsion engines

(G-1588)
CFI MILLWORK INC
Also Called: Clay Furniture
41 Chapel St (06042-7340)
PHONE...........................860 643-7580
Julie Clay, *Pr*
Richard F Clay Junior, *VP*
EMP: 10 EST: 1992
SQ FT: 15,000
SALES (est): 1.33MM **Privately Held**
Web: www.clayfurniture.com
SIC: 2521　Cabinets, office: wood

(G-1589)
CHAMPLIN-PACKRITE INC
151 Batson Dr (06042-1624)
PHONE...........................860 559-6373
Rory T Poole, *Pr*
Christine E Poole, *Sec*
Sean T Poole, *Dir*
EMP: 22 EST: 1933
SQ FT: 75,000
SALES (est): 4.16MM **Privately Held**
Web: www.champlincompany.com
SIC: 2441 2449 2653 3412　Packing cases,
wood: nailed or lock corner; Shipping cases
and drums, wood: wirebound and plywood;
Boxes, corrugated: made from purchased
materials; Metal barrels, drums, and pails

(G-1590)
**CHARLES J ANGELO MFG
GROUP LLC**
130 Chapel Rd (06042-1625)
PHONE...........................860 646-2378
EMP: 10 EST: 2003
SQ FT: 12,000
SALES (est): 1.5MM **Privately Held**
Web: www.camanufacturing.com
SIC: 3544　Special dies, tools, jigs, and
fixtures

(G-1591)
DAWN ENTERPRISES LLC
275 Progress Dr Ste B (06042-2211)
PHONE...........................860 646-8200
◆ EMP: 9 EST: 1978
SALES (est): 2.36MM **Privately Held**
Web: www.godawn.com

SIC: 3272   Cast stone, concrete

(G-1592)
DEROSA PRINTING COMPANY INC
485 Middle Tpke E (06040-3748)
P.O. Box 1567 (06045-1567)
PHONE..................................860 646-1698
Richard De Rosa, *Pr*
EMP: 12 **EST:** 1980
SQ FT: 7,000
SALES (est): 397.01K **Privately Held**
SIC: 2752 7334   Offset printing;
    Photocopying and duplicating services

(G-1593)
DONWELL COMPANY
Also Called: Donwell
130 Sheldon Rd (06042-2388)
P.O. Box 906 (06045-0906)
PHONE..................................860 649-5374
TOLL FREE: 800
Tracey B Sherman, *Pr*
Jeffrey Sherman, *
Dean A Sherman, *
EMP: 44 **EST:** 1957
SQ FT: 23,000
SALES (est): 5.39MM **Privately Held**
Web: www.donwell.com
SIC: 3479   Coating of metals and formed
    products

(G-1594)
EA PATTEN CO LLC
303 Wetherell St (06040-6349)
PHONE..................................860 649-2851
Forest E Patten, *Ch*
David W Pinette, *
Michael F Mulpeter, *
▼ **EMP:** 95 **EST:** 1945
SQ FT: 40,000
SALES (est): 29.71MM
SALES (corp-wide): 16.95B **Publicly Held**
Web: parked.sbdinc.com
SIC: 3498 3599   Tube fabricating (contract
    bending and shaping); Amusement park
    equipment
HQ: Consolidated Aerospace
    Manufacturing, Llc
    1425 S Acacia Ave
    Fullerton CA 92831
    714 989-2797

(G-1595)
ELECTROCAL INC
Also Called: ITW Graphics
375 New State Rd (06042-1818)
PHONE..................................860 646-8153
◆ **EMP:** 145
Web: www.electrocal.com
SIC: 2759 2821   Screen printing; Plastics
    materials and resins

(G-1596)
EMPIRE INDUSTRIES INC
180 Olcott St (06040-2647)
PHONE..................................860 647-1431
Mark Schauster, *Pr*
Richard Schauster, *
John Feeney, *
◆ **EMP:** 37 **EST:** 1942
SQ FT: 55,000
SALES (est): 8.66MM **Privately Held**
Web: www.empireindustries.com
SIC: 3469   Metal stampings, nec

(G-1597)
ENJET AERO MANCHESTER LLC ✪

41 Progress Dr (06042-2293)
PHONE..................................913 717-7396
Bruce Breckenridge, *CEO*
EMP: 10 **EST:** 2022
SALES (est): 1.26MM
SALES (corp-wide): 78.96MM **Privately Held**
Web: www.enjetaero.com
SIC: 3724   Aircraft engines and engine parts
PA: Enjet Aero, Llc
    9401 Indian Creek Pkwy
    Overland Park KS 66210
    913 717-7396

(G-1598)
FLUID DYNAMICS LLC
192 Sheldon Rd (06042-2319)
P.O. Box 2468 (06045-2468)
PHONE..................................860 791-6325
Paul Cooper, *Managing Member*
EMP: 10 **EST:** 1999
SQ FT: 9,000
SALES (est): 1.41MM **Privately Held**
Web: www.fluiddynamics.info
SIC: 3492 5085   Hose and tube fittings and
    assemblies, hydraulic/pneumatic; Hose,
    belting, and packing

(G-1599)
GREEN MANOR CORPORATION (PA)
Also Called: Journal Inquirer
306 Progress Dr (06042-9011)
PHONE..................................860 643-8111
Neil H Ellis, *Pr*
Elizabeth Ellis, *
Rudy Rudewicz, *
EMP: 280 **EST:** 1950
SQ FT: 36,000
SALES (est): 35.07MM
SALES (corp-wide): 35.07MM **Privately Held**
Web: www.ctinsider.com
SIC: 2711   Commercial printing and
    newspaper publishing combined

(G-1600)
HARRIS ENTERPRISE CORP
Also Called: Harris Woodworking
80 Colonial Rd (06042-2310)
P.O. Box 266 (06492-0266)
PHONE..................................860 649-4663
David Harris, *Pr*
John Harris, *
Robert Osborne, *
EMP: 22 **EST:** 1979
SQ FT: 24,380
SALES (est): 873K **Privately Held**
Web: www.harrisent.com
SIC: 5211 2499 2431   Lumber products;
    Decorative wood and woodwork; Millwork

(G-1601)
HBL AMERICA INC (HQ)
Also Called: Hbl Batteries
169 Progress Dr (06042-9019)
PHONE..................................860 257-9800
James Mcauliffe, *Pr*
Robert Herritty, *Dir*
◆ **EMP:** 7 **EST:** 2011
SALES (est): 7.33MM **Privately Held**
Web: www.hblbatteries.com
SIC: 3691   Storage batteries
PA: Hbl Power Systems Limited
    8-2-616, Plot No.4
    Hyderabad TG 50003

(G-1602)
HHC LLC
Also Called: Hydrofera

340 Progress Dr (06042-2280)
PHONE..................................860 456-0677
EMP: 20 **EST:** 1997
SQ FT: 10,000
SALES (est): 2.48MM **Privately Held**
SIC: 3086   Plastics foam products

(G-1603)
HIGHLAND MANUFACTURING INC
5 Glen Rd Ste 4 (06040-6793)
PHONE..................................860 646-5142
Christian W Queen, *Pr*
John Whitney, *
EMP: 28 **EST:** 1984
SQ FT: 16,000
SALES (est): 4.66MM **Privately Held**
Web: www.highlandmfg.com
SIC: 3545 3544   Gauges (machine tool
    accessories); Special dies and tools

(G-1604)
HYDROFERA LLC
340 Progress Dr (06042-2280)
PHONE..................................860 456-0677
Tom Drury, *CEO*
EMP: 65 **EST:** 2012
SALES (est): 9.36MM
SALES (corp-wide): 14.89B **Privately Held**
Web: www.hydrofera.com
SIC: 3086   Plastics foam products
HQ: Essity North America Inc.
    2929 Arch St Ste 2600
    Philadelphia PA 19104

(G-1605)
ILLINOIS TOOL WORKS INC
ITW Graphics
375 New State Rd (06042-1818)
PHONE..................................860 646-8153
Joe Tetrault, *Opers Mgr*
EMP: 145
SALES (corp-wide): 15.93B **Publicly Held**
Web: www.itwgraphics.com
SIC: 2672   Adhesive papers, labels, or
    tapes: from purchased material
PA: Illinois Tool Works Inc.
    155 Harlem Ave
    Glenview IL 60025
    847 724-7500

(G-1606)
ISWISS CORPORATION
161 Sanrico Dr (06042-2224)
PHONE..................................860 327-4200
Zivorad M Tomic, *Pr*
EMP: 7 **EST:** 2016
SALES (est): 414.57K **Privately Held**
Web: www.iswisstools.com
SIC: 3545   Collets (machine tool
    accessories)

(G-1607)
J & L MACHINE CO INC (PA)
62 Batson Dr (06042-1657)
PHONE..................................860 649-3539
Marian Jusko, *Pr*
Barbara Jusko, *Sec*
EMP: 48 **EST:** 1979
SQ FT: 30,000
SALES (est): 6.58MM
SALES (corp-wide): 6.58MM **Privately Held**
Web: www.jlmachineco.com
SIC: 3599   Machine shop, jobbing and repair

(G-1608)
JOURNAL PUBLISHING COMPANY INC

Also Called: Journal Inquirer
306 Progress Dr (06042-9011)
P.O. Box 510 (06045-0510)
PHONE..................................860 646-0500
Elizabeth Ellis, *Pr*
EMP: 560 **EST:** 1970
SQ FT: 36,000
SALES (est): 50.82MM
SALES (corp-wide): 50.82MM **Privately Held**
Web: www.ctinsider.com
SIC: 2711   Newspapers, publishing and
    printing
PA: Green Manor Corporation
    306 Progress Dr
    Manchester CT 06042
    860 643-8111

(G-1609)
K & G CORP
Also Called: R T G
219 Adams St (06042-1985)
P.O. Box 8267 (06040-0267)
PHONE..................................860 643-1133
Kenneth Wolf, *Pr*
Gail Wolf, *VP*
EMP: 10 **EST:** 1955
SQ FT: 6,000
SALES (est): 892.31K **Privately Held**
Web: www.rtgcoatings.com
SIC: 3479 3251   Coating of metals and
    formed products; Fireproofing tile, clay

(G-1610)
L M GILL WELDING AND MFR LLC (PA)
Also Called: Bhs-Torin
1422 Tolland Tpke (06042-1636)
PHONE..................................860 647-9931
Richard A Brink, *Pr*
Gale Brink, *Corporate Secretary*
EMP: 52 **EST:** 1978
SALES (est): 8.32MM
SALES (corp-wide): 8.32MM **Privately Held**
Web: www.lmgillwelding.com
SIC: 3542 5084 3549   Spring winding and
    forming machines; Industrial machinery and
    equipment; Metalworking machinery, nec

(G-1611)
L M GILL WELDING AND MFR LLC
Also Called: Lm Gill Welding & Mfg
1422 Tolland Tpke (06042-1636)
PHONE..................................860 647-9931
Gale Brink, *Corporate Secretary*
EMP: 68
SALES (corp-wide): 10.21MM **Privately Held**
Web: www.lmgillwelding.com
SIC: 7692 3728   Welding repair; Aircraft
    parts and equipment, nec
PA: L M Gill Welding And Manufacturer Llc
    1422 Tolland Tpke
    Manchester CT 06042
    860 647-9931

(G-1612)
LINDE ADVANCED MTL TECH INC
Also Called: Praxair
1366 Tolland Tpke (06042-8903)
PHONE..................................860 646-0700
EMP: 136
Web: www.linde-amt.com
SIC: 3479 3548   Coating of metals and
    formed products; Electric welding equipment

G
E
O
G
R
A
P
H
I
C

HQ: Linde Advanced Material Technologies
　　Inc.
　　1500 Polco St
　　Indianapolis IN 46222
　　317 240-2500

(G-1613)
LM GILL WELDING & MFG LLC
1422 Tolland Tpke (06042-1636)
PHONE...............................860 647-9931
Richard A Brink, *Owner*
EMP: 21 EST: 1997
SQ FT: 25,000
SALES (est): 2.57MM **Privately Held**
Web: www.lmgillwelding.com
SIC: 7692 3728 3731　Welding repair;
Aircraft parts and equipment, nec;
Commercial cargo ships, building and
repairing

(G-1614)
LYDALL INC (HQ)
Also Called: Alkegen
1 Colonial Rd (06042-2307)
P.O. Box 151 (06045-0151)
PHONE...............................860 646-1233
John Dandolph, *Pr*
EMP: 50 EST: 1969
SALES (est): 764.04MM **Privately Held**
Web: www.lydall.com
SIC: 3714 2899 3564　Motor vehicle parts
and accessories; Insulating compounds;
Filters, air: furnaces, air conditioning
equipment, etc.
PA: Unifrax Holding Co.
　　600 Riverwalk Pkwy
　　Tonawanda NY 14150

(G-1615)
MANCHESTER MOLDING AND MFG CO
96 Sheldon Rd (06042-2399)
PHONE...............................860 643-2141
Allan Griffin, *Pr*
Joseph Nadeau, *
Joanne Scanlon, *
EMP: 50 EST: 1967
SQ FT: 27,500
SALES (est): 4.21MM **Privately Held**
Web: www.manchestermolding.com
SIC: 3089 3544　Injection molding of plastics
; Special dies and tools

(G-1616)
MANCHESTER PACKING COMPANY INC
Also Called: Bogner's
349 Wetherell St (06040-6349)
PHONE...............................860 646-5000
Robert E Bogner, *Pr*
Kurt Bogner, *
David Bogner, *
▲ EMP: 60 EST: 1942
SQ FT: 19,000
SALES (est): 9.12MM **Privately Held**
Web: www.bognerqualitymeats.com
SIC: 2011 5147 5421 2013　Meat packing
plants; Meats, cured or smoked; Meat
markets, including freezer provisioners;
Sausages and other prepared meats

(G-1617)
METER HEALTH INC
69 Cougar Dr (06040-6379)
PHONE...............................833 638-3777
Adam Kievman, *CEO*
EMP: 7 EST: 2021
SALES (est): 500K **Privately Held**
SIC: 2834　Pharmaceutical preparations

(G-1618)
MINUTEMAN PRESS
757 Main St (06040-5102)
PHONE...............................860 646-0601
EMP: 7 EST: 2019
SALES (est): 162.93K **Privately Held**
Web: www.minutemanpress.com
SIC: 2752　Commercial printing, lithographic

(G-1619)
MOUNTAIN CREEK ENERGY INC
6 Castle Hl (06040-5657)
PHONE...............................512 990-7886
Harlan Mize, *Prin*
EMP: 7 EST: 2009
SALES (est): 129.21K **Privately Held**
Web: www.mountaincreekenergy.com
SIC: 2911　Petroleum refining

(G-1620)
NETSOURCE INC (PA)
260 Progress Dr (06042-9001)
PHONE...............................860 649-6000
Thor Swanson, *Pr*
Joline Swanson, *
EMP: 37 EST: 1993
SALES (est): 8.77MM **Privately Held**
Web: www.netsource-inc.com
SIC: 3496　Miscellaneous fabricated wire
products

(G-1621)
NEW ENGLAND TOOL CORPORATION (PA)
161 Sanrico Dr (06042-2224)
PHONE...............................860 783-5555
Zivorad M Tomic, *Pr*
Marija Tomic, *Prin*
▼ EMP: 17 EST: 1999
SQ FT: 13,000
SALES (est): 5.3MM
SALES (corp-wide): 5.3MM **Privately Held**
Web: www.netoolcorp.com
SIC: 3599　Machine shop, jobbing and repair

(G-1622)
NORWALK INDUS COMPONENTS LLC
135 Sheldon Rd (06042-2386)
P.O. Box 772 (06083-0772)
PHONE...............................860 645-5340
EMP: 9 EST: 1997
SALES (est): 1.13MM **Privately Held**
SIC: 3823　Industrial process measurement
equipment

(G-1623)
PARADIGM MANCHESTER INC (DH)
Also Called: Paradigm Precision
200 Adams St (06042-1915)
PHONE...............................772 287-7770
Michael Grunza, *Pr*
James Donahu, *
Steve Lindsey, *
William W Booth, *
Rita Lei, *
▲ EMP: 500 EST: 2004
SQ FT: 66,000
SALES (est): 114.47MM
SALES (corp-wide): 402.2MM **Privately Held**
SIC: 3728　Aircraft assemblies,
subassemblies, and parts, nec
HQ: Paradigm Precision Holdings, Llc
　　404 W Guadalupe Rd
　　Tempe AZ 85283

(G-1624)
PARADIGM MANCHESTER INC
151 Sheldon Rd (06042-2318)
PHONE...............................860 646-4048
Howard Miller, *Ch Bd*
EMP: 7
SALES (corp-wide): 402.2MM **Privately Held**
SIC: 3444　Sheet metal specialties, not
stamped
HQ: Manchester Paradigm Inc
　　200 Adams St
　　Manchester CT 06042
　　772 287-7770

(G-1625)
PARADIGM MANCHESTER INC
Also Called: Dynamic Gunver Technologies
255 Sheldon Rd Bldg 4 (06042-2322)
P.O. Box 240 (06045-0240)
PHONE...............................860 649-2888
Howard Miller, *Ch Bd*
EMP: 247
SALES (corp-wide): 402.2MM **Privately Held**
SIC: 3444 3462 3429 3398　Sheet metal
specialties, not stamped; Iron and steel
forgings; Hardware, nec; Metal heat treating
HQ: Manchester Paradigm Inc
　　200 Adams St
　　Manchester CT 06042
　　772 287-7770

(G-1626)
PARADIGM PRCISION HOLDINGS LLC
967 Parker St (06042-2208)
PHONE...............................860 649-2888
EMP: 46
SALES (corp-wide): 402.2MM **Privately Held**
Web: www.paradigmprecision.com
SIC: 3469　Machine parts, stamped or
pressed metal
HQ: Paradigm Precision Holdings, Llc
　　404 W Guadalupe Rd
　　Tempe AZ 85283

(G-1627)
PARAGON TOOL COMPANY INC
121 Adams St (06042-1919)
P.O. Box 8168 (06040-0168)
PHONE...............................860 647-9935
Valdis Klavins, *Pr*
John Zemzars, *VP*
Lorraine Amaio, *Mgr*
EMP: 8 EST: 1961
SQ FT: 7,400
SALES (est): 957.29K **Privately Held**
Web: www.paragontool.com
SIC: 3544 3728　Special dies and tools;
Aircraft parts and equipment, nec

(G-1628)
PARAMOUNT MACHINE COMPANY INC
138 Sanrico Dr (06042-9008)
PHONE...............................860 643-5549
Nicolas Djiounas, *Pr*
Andrew Djiounas, *
Nick Djiounas, *
EMP: 85 EST: 1976
SQ FT: 46,000
SALES (est): 9.36MM **Privately Held**
Web: www.paramountmachineco.com
SIC: 3599　Machine shop, jobbing and repair

(G-1629)
PAS TECHNOLOGIES INC
Also Called: Bolton Aerospace
321 Progress Dr (06042-2296)
PHONE...............................860 649-2727
EMP: 77
Web: www.standardaerocomponents.com
SIC: 3728　Ailerons, aircraft
HQ: Pas Technologies Inc.
　　1234 Atlantic Ave
　　North Kansas City MO 64116

(G-1630)
PCX AEROSYSTEMS- MANCHESTER LLC
586 Hilliard St (06042-2879)
PHONE...............................860 649-0000
Richard G Kyle, *Pr*
William R Burkhart, *
Christopher A Coughlin, *
Philip D Fracassa, *
EMP: 125 EST: 2007
SQ FT: 18,700
SALES: 26.46MM
SALES (corp-wide): 151.59MM **Privately Held**
Web: www.aerodrivesystems.com
SIC: 3724 3728　Aircraft engines and engine
parts; Aircraft body assemblies and parts
PA: Pcx Aerostructures, Llc
　　300 Fenn Rd
　　Newington CT 06111
　　860 666-2471

(G-1631)
PURDY CORPORATION
586 Hilliard St (06042-2879)
P.O. Box 1898 (06045-1898)
PHONE...............................860 649-0000
EMP: 115
SIC: 3724 3728　Aircraft engines and engine
parts; Aircraft body assemblies and parts

(G-1632)
ROYAL ICE CREAM COMPANY INC (PA)
27 Warren St (06040-6500)
PHONE...............................860 649-5358
James S Orfitelli, *Pr*
Cynthia L Orfitelli, *Sec*
▲ EMP: 10 EST: 1926
SQ FT: 12,000
SALES (est): 1.66MM
SALES (corp-wide): 1.66MM **Privately Held**
Web: www.royalicecream.com
SIC: 2024　Ice cream and ice milk

(G-1633)
RTG COATINGS
219 Adams St (06042-1985)
P.O. Box 8267 (06040-0267)
PHONE...............................860 643-1133
EMP: 7 EST: 2009
SALES (est): 211.08K **Privately Held**
Web: www.rtgcoatings.com
SIC: 3479　Coating of metals and formed
products

(G-1634)
SA MANCHESTER LLC
41 Progress Dr (06042-2293)
PHONE...............................860 533-7500
Bruce Breckenridge, *CEO*
Christopher Ferraro, *CFO*
EMP: 87 EST: 2005
SQ FT: 69,000
SALES (est): 17.65MM **Privately Held**
Web: www.enjetaero.com

▲ = Import ▼ = Export
◆ = Import/Export

SIC: **3724** 3544 3469 3769 Aircraft engines and engine parts; Special dies and tools; Metal stampings, nec; Space vehicle equipment, nec

(G-1635)
SATELLITE AEROSPACE INC
240 Chapel Rd (06042-1629)
P.O. Box 1077 (06045-1077)
PHONE...............................860 643-2771
Marianna Knec, *Pr*
Mark Knec, *Pr*
Frances Lynch, *Sec*
EMP: 22 **EST:** 1975
SQ FT: 13,000
SALES (est): 2.48MM **Privately Held**
Web: www.satelliteaerospace.com
SIC: 3469 Stamping metal for the trade

(G-1636)
SCAN-OPTICS LLC
169 Progress Dr (06042-9020)
PHONE...............................860 645-7878
Thomas Rice, *CEO*
EMP: 99 **EST:** 2005
SALES (est): 9.14MM **Privately Held**
Web: www.scanoptics.com
SIC: 3577 Optical scanning devices

(G-1637)
SPECIALTY SHOP INC
18 Sanrico Dr (06042-2225)
PHONE...............................860 647-1477
Hector Alzugaray Junior, *Pr*
Manny Rodrigues, *VP*
Hector Alzugaray Senior, *Treas*
EMP: 7 **EST:** 1967
SQ FT: 15,000
SALES (est): 981.77K **Privately Held**
Web: www.specialtyshopinc.com
SIC: 2434 2541 Wood kitchen cabinets; Counter and sink tops

(G-1638)
STANDARD WASHER & MAT INC
299 Progress Dr (06042-2211)
P.O. Box 368 (06045-0368)
PHONE...............................860 643-5125
Carl Eckblom, *Pr*
EMP: 20 **EST:** 1929
SQ FT: 15,000
SALES (est): 2.38MM **Privately Held**
Web: www.standardwasher.com
SIC: 3069 3089 3053 Washers, rubber; Washers, plastics; Gaskets, all materials

(G-1639)
STEPHENS PIPE & STEEL LLC
776 N Main St (06042-1989)
PHONE...............................877 777-8721
Eric Bronstrup, *Brnch Mgr*
EMP: 58
Web: www.spsfence.com
SIC: 5051 3315 3523 Pipe and tubing, steel; Chain link fencing; Cattle feeding, handling, and watering equipment
HQ: Stephens Pipe & Steel, Llc
2224 E Highway 619
Russell Springs KY 42642
270 866-3331

(G-1640)
VISION TECHNICAL MOLDING
20 Utopia Rd (06042-2191)
PHONE...............................860 783-5050
EMP: 8 **EST:** 2015
SALES (est): 184.75K **Privately Held**
SIC: 3089 Injection molding of plastics

(G-1641)
VISION TECHNICAL MOLDING LLC
71 Utopia Rd (06042-2192)
PHONE...............................860 647-7787
▲ **EMP:** 105
SIC: 3089 Injection molding of plastics

Marlborough
Hartford County

(G-1642)
CICI BEVIN GORDON
9 Austin Dr (06447-1375)
PHONE...............................860 365-5731
Cici Gordon, *Owner*
EMP: 8
SALES (est): 269.81K **Privately Held**
SIC: 3999 Manufacturing industries, nec

(G-1643)
HEARTWOOD CABINETRY
345 N Main St (06447-1315)
PHONE...............................860 295-0304
EMP: 8
SALES (est): 420K **Privately Held**
SIC: 2434 Wood kitchen cabinets

(G-1644)
MARLBOROUGH PLASTICS INC
350 N Main St (06447-1346)
PHONE...............................860 295-9124
Joseph J Asklar, *Pr*
Corrine Machowski, *Treas*
▲ **EMP:** 8 **EST:** 1933
SQ FT: 11,250
SALES (est): 976K **Privately Held**
Web: www.marlboroughplastics.com
SIC: 3089 Injection molded finished plastics products, nec

(G-1645)
MPS PLASTICS INCORPORATED
351 N Main St (06447-1315)
P.O. Box 59 (06447-0059)
PHONE...............................860 295-1161
▲ **EMP:** 27 **EST:** 1980
SQ FT: 18,000
SALES (est): 2.42MM **Privately Held**
Web: www.mpsplastics.com
SIC: 3089 Injection molding of plastics

(G-1646)
NOVANTA MOTION USA INC (HQ)
Also Called: I M S
370 N Main St (06447-1346)
P.O. Box 457 (06447-0457)
PHONE...............................860 295-6102
▲ **EMP:** 58 **EST:** 1986
SALES (est): 18.81MM **Publicly Held**
Web: www.novantaims.com
SIC: 3621 Motors and generators
PA: Novanta Inc.
125 Middlesex Tpke
Bedford MA 01730

Meriden
New Haven County

(G-1647)
3M COMPANY
Also Called: 3M
400 Research Pkwy (06450-7172)
PHONE...............................203 237-5541
Wei Moline, *Pr*
EMP: 15

SALES (corp-wide): 34.23B **Publicly Held**
Web: www.3m.com
SIC: 3465 Automotive stampings
PA: 3m Company
3m Center
Saint Paul MN 55144
651 733-1110

(G-1648)
3M PURIFICATION INC (HQ)
400 Research Pkwy (06450-7172)
P.O. Box 1018 (06450-1018)
PHONE...............................203 237-5541
Mike Roman, *CEO*
Mark Kachur, *
Timothy Carney, *
Frederick Flynn Junior, *VP Fin*
David Schaeffer, *
◆ **EMP:** 300 **EST:** 1912
SQ FT: 189,000
SALES (est): 469.36MM
SALES (corp-wide): 34.23B **Publicly Held**
Web: engage.3m.com
SIC: 3589 3569 Water purification equipment, household type; Filters
PA: 3m Company
3m Center
Saint Paul MN 55144
651 733-1110

(G-1649)
A G C INCORPORATED
Also Called: A G C
106 Evansville Ave (06451-5135)
PHONE...............................203 235-3361
Doris D Harms, *Prin*
R Bruce Andrews, *
Walter Layman, *
Rhoda Hurwitz, *
Shelly Anderson, *
EMP: 175 **EST:** 1951
SQ FT: 110,000
SALES (est): 23.85MM **Privately Held**
Web: www.agcincorporated.com
SIC: 3728 3444 3398 3053 Aircraft assemblies, subassemblies, and parts, nec; Sheet metalwork; Metal heat treating; Gaskets; packing and sealing devices

(G-1650)
ACCEL INTL HOLDINGS INC
Also Called: Accel International
508 N Colony St (06450-2246)
PHONE...............................203 237-2700
Anthony Oh, *Pr*
Jodi Lynn Oh, *Sec*
Kyle Scott Senk, *CMO**
▲ **EMP:** 30 **EST:** 2002
SQ FT: 150,000
SALES (est): 9.69MM **Privately Held**
SIC: 3315 Wire and fabricated wire products

(G-1651)
ACTION-DCTGRAPH TLECOMUNCATION
Also Called: Action Systems Company Div
55 Colony St (06451-3210)
PHONE...............................203 238-2326
Harris B Randall, *Pr*
EMP: 9 **EST:** 1958
SQ FT: 6,000
SALES (est): 772.26K **Privately Held**
SIC: 3661 Telephones and telephone apparatus

(G-1652)
AEROSWISS LLC
Also Called: Aeroswiss
20 Powers Dr (06451-5556)
PHONE...............................203 634-4545

EMP: 19 **EST:** 2000
SQ FT: 1,000
SALES (est): 4.26MM **Privately Held**
Web: www.aeroswissusa.com
SIC: 3599 Machine shop, jobbing and repair

(G-1653)
AGC ACQUISITION LLC
106 Evansville Ave (06451-5135)
PHONE...............................203 639-7125
Doris D Harms, *Pr*
Michael Doolan, *VP*
EMP: 112 **EST:** 2013
SALES (est): 21.73MM **Privately Held**
Web: www.agcincorporated.com
SIC: 3724 Aircraft engines and engine parts

(G-1654)
APERTURE OPTICAL SCIENCES INC (PA)
170 Pond View Dr (06450-7142)
PHONE...............................860 316-2589
Flemming Tinker, *Pr*
Lisa Tinker, *Sec*
EMP: 24 **EST:** 2010
SALES (est): 3.17MM
SALES (corp-wide): 3.17MM **Privately Held**
Web: www.apertureos.com
SIC: 3827 Optical instruments and lenses

(G-1655)
APLICARE PRODUCTS LLC (HQ)
550 Research Pkwy (06450-7172)
PHONE...............................203 630-0500
Charlie Mills, *CEO*
EMP: 55 **EST:** 2017
SQ FT: 55,416
SALES (est): 49.5MM
SALES (corp-wide): 7.75B **Privately Held**
SIC: 2834 3841 Antiseptics, medicinal; Surgical instruments and apparatus
PA: Medline Industries, Lp
3 Lakes Dr
Northfield IL 60093
847 949-5500

(G-1656)
BRAND-NU LABORATORIES LLC (PA)
Also Called: Biosolutions
377 Research Pkwy Ste 2 (06450-7155)
PHONE...............................203 235-7989
John J Gorman Iii, *Pr*
Carol A Shea, *VP*
◆ **EMP:** 20 **EST:** 1955
SQ FT: 80,000
SALES (est): 9.58MM
SALES (corp-wide): 9.58MM **Privately Held**
Web: www.brandnu.com
SIC: 2899 Chemical preparations, nec

(G-1657)
C & S ENGINEERING INC
956 Old Colony Rd (06451-7921)
PHONE...............................203 235-5727
Alfred L Cavallo, *Pr*
Michael Cavallo, *VP*
EMP: 12 **EST:** 1990
SQ FT: 20,000
SALES (est): 898.15K **Privately Held**
Web: www.c-sengineering.com
SIC: 3449 3562 3471 Miscellaneous metalwork; Ball and roller bearings; Plating and polishing

(G-1658)
CABLE MANAGEMENT LLC
290 Pratt St Ste 1108 (06450-8600)
P.O. Box 2719 (06450-1788)
PHONE..............................860 670-1890
▲ **EMP: 25 EST:** 2007
SALES (est): 3.63MM **Privately Held**
Web: www.cablemanagementusa.com
SIC: 3569 Baling machines, for scrap metal,
  paper, or similar material

(G-1659)
CENTER BROACH & MACHINE CO
525 N Colony St (06450-2287)
P.O. Box 2 (06450-0002)
PHONE..............................203 235-6329
William Phillips Iv, *VP*
EMP: 9 EST: 1962
SQ FT: 13,000
SALES (est): 673.85K **Privately Held**
Web: www.centerbroach.com
SIC: 3545 Broaches (machine tool
  accessories)

(G-1660)
CHERISE CPL LLC
57 S Broad St (06450-6544)
PHONE..............................203 238-3482
EMP: 7 EST: 2005
SALES (est): 142.28K **Privately Held**
SIC: 2052 Bakery products, dry

(G-1661)
CONNECTICUT CARPENTRY LLC
Also Called: Connecticut Carpentry
290 Pratt St Ofc (06450-8603)
PHONE..............................203 639-8585
Leo Dufour, *Owner*
EMP: 15 EST: 1985
SALES (est): 545.95K **Privately Held**
SIC: 2431 Millwork

(G-1662)
CRC CHROME CORPORATION
169 Pratt St # R (06450-4250)
PHONE..............................203 630-1008
Frank Ciarcia, *Pr*
Michael Ciarcia, *Sec*
EMP: 10 EST: 1983
SQ FT: 8,000
SALES (est): 1.01MM **Privately Held**
Web: www.crcchrome.com
SIC: 3471 Chromium plating of metals or
  formed products

(G-1663)
DOLECO USA INC
290 Pratt St (06450-8600)
PHONE..............................203 440-1940
Ralph Abato, *Pr*
EMP: 9 EST: 2013
SALES (est): 1.13MM **Privately Held**
Web: www.doleco-usa.com
SIC: 3537 Trucks, tractors, loaders, carriers,
  and similar equipment

(G-1664)
DRT AEROSPACE LLC
620 Research Pkwy (06450-7127)
PHONE..............................203 781-8020
EMP: 38
Web: www.drtholdingsllc.com
SIC: 3724 Aircraft engines and engine parts
HQ: Drt Aerospace, Llc
  1950 Campbell Rd
  Sidney OH 45365
  937 492-6121

(G-1665)
DURO HILEX POLY LLC
Also Called: Flexo Converters
850 Murdock Ave (06450-7004)
PHONE..............................203 639-7070
Stan Bikulege, *Brnch Mgr*
EMP: 70
SALES (corp-wide): 10.97B **Publicly Held**
Web: www.novolex.com
SIC: 2674 Paper bags: made from
  purchased materials
HQ: Duro Hilex Poly, Llc
  12245 S Central Ave
  Alsip IL 60803
  708 385-8674

(G-1666)
ELKS MANUFACTURING CORPORATION
290 Pratt St Ste 15 (06450-8601)
P.O. Box 2110 (06450-1210)
PHONE..............................203 235-2528
Pamela J Camire, *Pr*
EMP: 10 EST: 1983
SQ FT: 11,000
SALES (est): 381.27K **Privately Held**
SIC: 3599 Custom machinery

(G-1667)
ENVIRONMENTAL MONITOR SVC INC
87 Gypsy Ln (06450-7927)
P.O. Box 4340 (06492-7562)
PHONE..............................203 935-0102
James Cognetta, *Pr*
Ann Cognetta, *Sec*
▼ **EMP: 7 EST:** 1990
SQ FT: 6,600
SALES (est): 925.81K **Privately Held**
Web: www.emsct.com
SIC: 7699 3564 7389 Industrial equipment
  services; Air purification equipment; Air
  pollution measuring service

(G-1668)
FORM-ALL PLASTICS CORP
104 Gracey Ave (06451-2295)
PHONE..............................203 634-1137
Tim Jennings, *Pr*
EMP: 7 EST: 1963
SQ FT: 7,000
SALES (est): 784.41K **Privately Held**
Web: www.form-all.com
SIC: 3089 Injection molding of plastics

(G-1669)
IODINE HOLDINGS INC
550 Research Pkwy (06450-7172)
PHONE..............................203 630-0500
Bruce Wilson Junior, *CEO*
Philip Hamrock, *
James E Coer, *
Bruce Wilson, *
EMP: 198 EST: 1983
SQ FT: 55,416
SALES (est): 47.44MM
SALES (corp-wide): 7.39B **Publicly Held**
SIC: 3841 Surgical and medical instruments
PA: The Clorox Company
  1221 Broadway Ste 1300
  Oakland CA 94612
  510 271-7000

(G-1670)
JOHNSON CONTROLS INC
Also Called: Johnson Controls
71 Deerfield Ln (06450-7151)
PHONE..............................678 297-4040
EMP: 16

Web: www.johnsoncontrols.com
SIC: 2531 3714 3691 3822 Seats,
  automobile; Motor vehicle body
  components and frame; Lead acid batteries
  (storage batteries); Building services
  monitoring controls, automatic
HQ: Johnson Controls, Inc.
  5757 N Green Bay Ave
  Milwaukee WI 53209
  920 245-6409

(G-1671)
JONAL LABORATORIES INC
456 Center St (06450-3302)
P.O. Box 743 (06450-0743)
PHONE..............................203 634-4444
Marc Nemeth, *Pr*
Dan Clifford, *VP*
David Nemeth, *VP*
Ken Keegan, *Ex VP*
◆ **EMP: 60 EST:** 1965
SQ FT: 20,000
SALES (est): 22.91MM **Privately Held**
Web: www.jonal.com
SIC: 8711 3069 Engineering services;
  Custom compounding of rubber materials

(G-1672)
LOGAN STEEL INC (PA)
Also Called: Logan Sandblasting
119 Empire Ave (06450-1928)
PHONE..............................203 235-0811
Howard A Lohmann Junior, *Pr*
Gail Lohmann, *
Erik K Lohmann, *
EMP: 25 EST: 1975
SQ FT: 16,000
SALES (est): 20.88MM
SALES (corp-wide): 20.88MM **Privately Held**
Web: www.logansteel.com
SIC: 5051 3471 3441 Structural shapes,
  iron or steel; Sand blasting of metal parts;
  Fabricated structural metal

(G-1673)
MEGADOOR USA INC
Also Called: ABS Pumps
140 Pond View Dr (06450-7142)
PHONE..............................203 238-2700
▲ **EMP:** 175
SIC: 3561 3589 3531 Industrial pumps and
  parts; Sewage treatment equipment;
  Construction machinery

(G-1674)
MERIDEN FIRE MARSHALS OFFICE
142 E Main St (06450-5605)
PHONE..............................203 630-4010
Robert Morpurgo, *Mgr*
EMP: 10 EST: 2010
SALES (est): 161.65K **Privately Held**
Web: www.meridenct.gov
SIC: 3711 Fire department vehicles (motor
  vehicles), assembly of

(G-1675)
MERIDEN MANUFACTURING INC
230 State Street Ext (06450-3205)
P.O. Box 694 (06450-0694)
PHONE..............................203 237-7481
Sharon Fox, *CEO*
Lester Maloney, *
Sharon M Fox, *
Aedra Baston, *
James Muller, *
EMP: 86 EST: 1965
SQ FT: 27,000
SALES (est): 14.97MM **Privately Held**

Web: www.meridenmfg.com
SIC: 3469 3769 3812 Machine parts,
  stamped or pressed metal; Space vehicle
  equipment, nec; Search and navigation
  equipment

(G-1676)
MIDSTATE ARC INC
Also Called: Powers Industries & Laserpro
20 Powers Dr (06451-5556)
PHONE..............................203 238-9001
Pamela Smith, *Mgr*
EMP: 79
SALES (corp-wide): 14.74MM **Privately Held**
Web: www.midstatearc.org
SIC: 8322 3861 Social services for the
  handicapped; Photographic equipment and
  supplies
PA: Midstate Arc, Inc.
  74 S Broad St
  Meriden CT 06450
  203 237-9975

(G-1677)
MIRION TECH CANBERRA INC (DH)
Also Called: Canberra Industries
800 Research Pkwy (06450-7127)
PHONE..............................203 238-2351
Thomas Logan, *Pr*
Brian Schopfer, *
Emmanuelle Lee, *
▲ **EMP: 100 EST:** 2001
SQ FT: 170,000
SALES (est): 146.23MM
SALES (corp-wide): 717.8MM **Publicly Held**
SIC: 3829 4813 Nuclear radiation and
  testing apparatus; Voice telephone
  communications
HQ: Mirion Technologies (Us), Inc.
  3000 Executive Pkwy # 222
  San Ramon CA 94583

(G-1678)
MULTIPRINTS INC
Also Called: Barker Screen Printers
812 Old Colony Rd (06451-7929)
P.O. Box 834 (06450-0834)
PHONE..............................203 235-4409
Amy J P Barker, *Pr*
Susan Dunphy, *Sec*
EMP: 8 EST: 1984
SQ FT: 12,000
SALES (est): 433.24K **Privately Held**
Web: www.barkerspecialty.com
SIC: 2759 Screen printing

(G-1679)
NATIONAL DEFAULT SERVICING LLC
500 S Broad St Ste 1 (06450-6643)
PHONE..............................858 300-0700
EMP: 90
SALES (corp-wide): 5.03MM **Privately Held**
SIC: 1389 Roustabout service
HQ: National Default Servicing, Llc
  500 S Brd St Bldg Aste
  Meriden CT 06450
  860 368-3400

(G-1680)
NORTHEAST COMPANIES INC (PA)
Also Called: Construction
250 Pomeroy Ave (06450-8316)
PHONE..............................203 630-9675

▲ = Import ▼ = Export
◆ = Import/Export

Dominic Lapenta, *CEO*
Dominic A Lapenta, *Pr*
EMP: 16 **EST:** 2006
SALES (est): 4.45MM **Privately Held**
SIC: 1389 Construction, repair, and
dismantling services

(G-1681)
OLDANI BROTHERS LLC (PA)
735 Hanover Rd (06451-5208)
PHONE..............................203 630-6565
Peter Oldani, *Managing Member*
EMP: 7 **EST:** 2019
SALES (est): 1MM
SALES (corp-wide): 1MM **Privately Held**
Web: www.oldanibrothers.com
SIC: 3914 Trophies, silver

(G-1682)
OMERIN USA INC
Also Called: Qs Tehcnoligies Divison
95 Research Pkwy (06450-7124)
PHONE..............................475 343-3450
Xavier Omerin, *CEO*
Aurelien Paumier, *
EMP: 28 **EST:** 2014
SALES (est): 7.48MM **Privately Held**
Web: www.omerin-usa.com
SIC: 3357 Aluminum wire and cable
HQ: Omerin Sas
Omerin Div Silisol & Div Principale
Zone Industrielle
Ambert 63600
473825000

(G-1683)
ORBIT DESIGN LLC
290 Pratt St (06450-8600)
PHONE..............................203 393-0171
Ron Oren, *Managing Member*
EMP: 10 **EST:** 1984
SQ FT: 4,000
SALES (est): 1.34MM **Privately Held**
Web: www.orbitdesign.com
SIC: 3089 Injection molding of plastics

(G-1684)
PERFORMANCE CONNECTION SYSTEMS
599 W Main St (06451-2751)
P.O. Box 556 (06444-0556)
PHONE..............................203 868-5517
John Keefe, *Owner*
EMP: 8 **EST:** 2007
SALES (est): 525.6K **Privately Held**
Web: www.pcsconnectors.com
SIC: 3499 Welding tips, heat resistant: metal

(G-1685)
PRODUCTION EQUIPMENT COMPANY
401 Liberty St (06450-4500)
PHONE..............................800 758-5697
Rebecca Davis, *Pr*
Rebecca Davis, *Pr*
Roswell Davis Senior, *VP*
Stephanie Jordan, *
Roswell Davis Junior, *Treas*
EMP: 25 **EST:** 1938
SQ FT: 10,000
SALES (est): 4.73MM **Privately Held**
Web:
www.productionequipmentcompany.com
SIC: 3536 3535 Cranes, overhead traveling;
Overhead conveyor systems

(G-1686)
PYRAMID TIME SYSTEMS LLC
45 Gracey Ave (06451-2284)

PHONE..............................203 238-0550
John Augustyn, *Pr*
George Bucci, *
Bob Lennon, *
◆ **EMP:** 50 **EST:** 1969
SQ FT: 70,000
SALES (est): 9.64MM **Privately Held**
Web: www.pyramidtimesystems.com
SIC: 3579 3873 Time clocks and time
recording devices; Watches, clocks,
watchcases, and parts

(G-1687)
Q-S TECHNOLOGIES INC
602 Pomeroy Ave (06450-4872)
PHONE..............................203 237-2297
EMP: 25
Web: www.omerin-usa.com
SIC: 3315 Wire, steel: insulated or armored

(G-1688)
QUICK MACHINING SERVICES LLC
290 Pratt St Ste 4 (06450-8601)
PHONE..............................203 634-8822
EMP: 7 **EST:** 1981
SQ FT: 5,600
SALES (est): 506.56K **Privately Held**
Web: www.quickmachine.com
SIC: 3599 7699 Machine shop, jobbing and
repair; Industrial machinery and equipment
repair

(G-1689)
R & D PRECISION INC
235 Cheshire Rd (06451-5011)
PHONE..............................203 284-3396
David Harkness, *Owner*
EMP: 11 **EST:** 1987
SALES (est): 493.69K **Privately Held**
Web: www.rdprecisioninc.com
SIC: 3444 Sheet metalwork

(G-1690)
RADIO FREQUENCY SYSTEMS INC (DH)
200 Pondview Dr (06450-7195)
PHONE..............................203 630-3311
Monika Maurer, *Pr*
Wichard Von Bredow, *CFO*
Philippe Fizellier, *COO*
◆ **EMP:** 30 **EST:** 1986
SQ FT: 380,000
SALES (est): 391.26MM
SALES (corp-wide): 25.87B **Privately Held**
Web: www.rfsworld.com
SIC: 3663 3661 5045 5065 Antennas,
transmitting and communications;
Telephone and telegraph apparatus;
Computers, peripherals, and software;
Electronic parts and equipment, nec
HQ: Nokia Of America Corporation
600 Mountain Ave Ste 700
New Providence NJ 07974

(G-1691)
RAGOZZINO FOODS INC (PA)
Also Called: Ragozzino
10 Ames Ave (06451-2912)
P.O. Box 116 (06450-0116)
PHONE..............................203 238-2553
Gloria A Ragozzino, *CEO*
Nancy Ragozzino, *Pr*
John Ragozzino, *CFO*
Ellen Sattler, *VP*
Susan Darin, *VP*
EMP: 15 **EST:** 1953
SQ FT: 71,000
SALES (est): 20.95MM
SALES (corp-wide): 20.95MM **Privately Held**

Web: www.ragozzino.com
SIC: 2038 2033 Frozen specialties, nec;
Spaghetti and other pasta sauce: packaged
in cans, jars, etc

(G-1692)
RECORD-JOURNAL NEWSPAPER (PA)
Also Called: Town Times
500 S Broad St Ste 2 (06450-6643)
P.O. Box 915 (06450-0915)
PHONE..............................203 235-1661
Eliot C White, *Owner*
John Ausanka, *Sr VP*
Aliso Muschinsky, *Sec*
Leslie White, *Stockholder*
▲ **EMP:** 175 **EST:** 1867
SALES (est): 23.31MM
SALES (corp-wide): 23.31MM **Privately Held**
Web: www.ctinsider.com
SIC: 2711 2752 Commercial printing and
newspaper publishing combined; Offset
printing

(G-1693)
RGL INC
290 Pratt St Ste 51 (06450-8607)
PHONE..............................860 653-7254
Rocco G Lapenta, *Pr*
EMP: 10 **EST:** 1968
SALES (est): 471.97K **Privately Held**
SIC: 2731 2721 2741 Books, publishing only
; Periodicals, publishing only; Racing forms
and programs: publishing only, not printing

(G-1694)
RICH PLASTIC PRODUCTS INC
339 Fleming Rd (06450-7108)
PHONE..............................203 235-4241
Daniel J Rich, *Pr*
Denise Rivard, *Sec*
EMP: 7 **EST:** 1916
SALES (est): 798.17K **Privately Held**
Web: www.richplastics.net
SIC: 3822 Thermostats and other
environmental sensors

(G-1695)
S J PAPPAS INC
Also Called: Roy Tech
718 Old Colony Rd (06451-7930)
PHONE..............................203 237-7701
TOLL FREE: 800
Kalliroy Pappas, *Pr*
Stratos Pappas, *Sec*
Jack Pappas, *Treas*
Steven J Pappas, *Stockholder*
EMP: 8 **EST:** 1953
SQ FT: 27,000
SALES (est): 1.78MM **Privately Held**
Web: www.sjpappas.com
SIC: 5031 5712 1751 2521 Kitchen cabinets
; Cabinet work, custom; Cabinet building
and installation; Wood office furniture

(G-1696)
SAF INDUSTRIES LLC (HQ)
Also Called: Gar Kenyon Aerospace &
Defense
106 Evansville Ave (06451-5135)
PHONE..............................203 729-4900
Shelly Anderson, *Pr*
Jonathan Fournier, *VP*
EMP: 21 **EST:** 2003
SQ FT: 44,000
SALES (est): 3.71MM
SALES (corp-wide): 119.44MM **Privately Held**
Web: www.garkenyon.com

SIC: 3728 3812 Aircraft assemblies,
subassemblies, and parts, nec;
Acceleration indicators and systems
components, aerospace
PA: Loar Group Inc.
20 New King St
White Plains NY 10604
203 317-2683

(G-1697)
SHINER SIGNS INC
Also Called: Signage US
38 Elm St Ste 3 (06450-5704)
PHONE..............................203 634-4331
Robert Laurencelle, *Pr*
Irwin Laurencelle, *Treas*
EMP: 20 **EST:** 1904
SQ FT: 10,000
SALES (est): 1.65MM **Privately Held**
Web: www.shinersigns.com
SIC: 3993 Electric signs

(G-1698)
SILVER CITY MANUFACTURING LLC
Also Called: Silver City Manufacturing
85 Tremont St Ste 5 (06450-2273)
PHONE..............................203 238-0027
EMP: 12 **EST:** 1969
SQ FT: 3,800
SALES (est): 984.99K **Privately Held**
SIC: 3599 Machine shop, jobbing and repair

(G-1699)
SMOKELOUDZ LLC (PA)
1367 Hanover Ave Apt 801 (06451-6278)
PHONE..............................203 909-3556
EMP: 9 **EST:** 2021
SALES (est): 210.4K
SALES (corp-wide): 210.4K **Privately Held**
SIC: 3559 5199 Tobacco products
machinery; Smokers' supplies

(G-1700)
SNOW GOOSE 2019 INC
235 Cheshire Rd (06451-5011)
PHONE..............................203 237-3444
EMP: 43 **EST:** 1981
SALES (est): 4.54MM **Privately Held**
Web: www.rdprecisioninc.com
SIC: 3444 3699 Sheet metalwork; Electrical
equipment and supplies, nec

(G-1701)
SOUTHWICK & MEISTER INC
Also Called: Innovative Systems
1455 N Colony Rd (06450-1979)
P.O. Box 725 (06450-0725)
PHONE..............................203 237-0000
Robert A Meister, *Pr*
Ernest M Meister, *
Lynn M Papale, *
Barbara Meister, *
EMP: 105 **EST:** 1962
SQ FT: 45,000
SALES (est): 18.46MM **Privately Held**
Web: www.s-mcollets.com
SIC: 3545 Tools and accessories for
machine tools

(G-1702)
STONEHOUSE FINE CAKES
61 N 1st St (06451-4018)
PHONE..............................203 235-5091
Susan Stone, *Managing Member*
EMP: 10 **EST:** 1997
SALES (est): 370.15K **Privately Held**
SIC: 2051 Bakery: wholesale or wholesale/
retail combined

(G-1703)
SUZIO YORK HILL COMPANIES
975 Westfield Rd (06450-2553)
PHONE..............................888 789-4626
EMP: 10 EST: 2017
SALES (est): 582.21K Privately Held
Web: www.suzioyorkhill.com
SIC: 5032 3273 Asphalt mixture; Ready-mixed concrete

(G-1704)
TG INDUSTRIES INC
361 S Colony St Ste 1 (06451-6280)
PHONE..............................203 235-3239
Anthony Gullo, Pr
Bob Kowalski, VP
Helen Gullo, Sec
EMP: 15 EST: 1981
SQ FT: 10,000
SALES (est): 2.38MM Privately Held
Web: www.tgimachine.com
SIC: 3599 Machine shop, jobbing and repair

(G-1705)
THE L SUZIO ASPHALT CO INC
975 Westfield Rd (06450-2553)
P.O. Box 748 (06450-0748)
PHONE..............................203 237-8421
Leonardo C Suzio, Pr
Leonardo H Suzio, Sec
Scott P Suzio, VP
EMP: 28 EST: 1957
SQ FT: 10,000
SALES (est): 729.93K Privately Held
Web: www.suzioyorkhill.com
SIC: 3273 Ready-mixed concrete

(G-1706)
THE L SUZIO CONCRETE CO INC (PA)
975 Westfield Rd (06450-2553)
P.O. Box 748 (06450-0748)
PHONE..............................203 237-8421
Leonardo H Suzio, VP
Scott P Suzio, VP
Cheryl Suzio, *
Henry E Suzio, *
Henrietta R Suzio, *
EMP: 37 EST: 1898
SQ FT: 10,000
SALES (est): 10.66MM
SALES (corp-wide): 10.66MM Privately Held
Web: www.suzioyorkhill.com
SIC: 3273 Ready-mixed concrete

(G-1707)
THE LYONS TOOL & DIE COMPANY
185 Research Pkwy (06450-7124)
PHONE..............................203 238-2689
William Lyons Iii, CEO
William Lyons Iv, Pr
Neal Lyons, *
David Brown, *
Gini Selvaggi, *
EMP: 48 EST: 1951
SQ FT: 32,000
SALES (est): 8.99MM Privately Held
Web: www.lyons.com
SIC: 3469 3544 3545 Stamping metal for the trade; Special dies and tools; Gauges (machine tool accessories)

(G-1708)
THOMPSON BRANDS LLC
80 S Vine St (06451-3823)
PHONE..............................203 235-2541
◆ EMP: 85 EST: 1995

SQ FT: 114,000
SALES (est): 15.87MM Privately Held
Web: www.thompsonchocolate.com
SIC: 2064 5441 2066 5145 Candy and other confectionery products; Candy; Chocolate and cocoa products; Candy

(G-1709)
THOMPSON CANDY COMPANY
80 S Vine St (06451-3823)
PHONE..............................203 235-2541
Jeffrey H White, Pr
Allan E White, *
William Walsh, *
Amy Parrot, *
EMP: 70 EST: 1967
SQ FT: 114,000
SALES (est): 4.25MM Privately Held
Web: www.thompsonchocolate.com
SIC: 2064 5441 Candy and other confectionery products; Candy

(G-1710)
TRADEBE TREATMENT AND RECYCLING NORTHEAST LLC (DH)
Also Called: Tradebe Transportation
234 Hobart St Ste 1 (06450-4380)
P.O. Box 902 (06450-0902)
PHONE..............................203 238-8102
EMP: 55 EST: 1982
SALES (est): 101.05MM Privately Held
Web: www.tradebeusa.com
SIC: 4953 1442 4212 Recycling, waste materials; Construction sand and gravel; Hazardous waste transport
HQ: Tradebe Environmental Services, Llc
1433 E 83rd Ave Ste 200
Merrillville IN 46410

(G-1711)
UPC LLC
170 Research Pkwy (06450-7144)
PHONE..............................877 466-1137
EMP: 24 EST: 2008
SALES (est): 2.49MM Privately Held
Web: www.maagkit.com
SIC: 3089 Plastics containers, except foam

(G-1712)
YORK HILL TRAP ROCK QUARRY CO
975 Westfield Rd (06450-2553)
P.O. Box 748 (06450-0748)
PHONE..............................203 237-8421
Leonardo C Suzio, Pr
Scott P Suzio, VP
Cheryl Suzio, VP
Henry E Suzio, VP
EMP: 30 EST: 1898
SQ FT: 16,000
SALES (est): 2.08MM Privately Held
Web: www.suzioyorkhill.com
SIC: 3273 Ready-mixed concrete

Middlebury
New Haven County

(G-1713)
AMERICAN ROLLER COMPANY LLC
Also Called: Plasma Coatings
84 Turnpike Dr (06762-1819)
P.O. Box 10006 (06725-0006)
PHONE..............................203 598-3100
Gary Carlo, Manager
EMP: 21
SALES (corp-wide): 90.09MM Privately Held

Web: www.americanroller.com
SIC: 3069 3479 Rubber rolls and roll coverings; Coating of metals with plastic or resins
PA: American Roller Company, Llc
1440 13th Ave
Union Grove WI 53182
262 878-8665

(G-1714)
CHEMTURA USA CORPORATION
Also Called: Chemtura
199 Benson Rd (06762-3218)
PHONE..............................203 573-2000
◆ EMP: 2400
SIC: 2879 2869 2822 Insecticides, agricultural or household; Industrial organic chemicals, nec; Synthetic rubber

(G-1715)
KATY INDUSTRIES INC
765 Straits Tpke Bldg 2 (06762-2853)
PHONE..............................314 656-4321
Jacob Saliba, Prin
EMP: 8 EST: 2008
SALES (est): 168.93K Privately Held
SIC: 3999 Manufacturing industries, nec

(G-1716)
LEGACY WOODWORKING LLC
49 Birchwood Ter (06762-1626)
PHONE..............................203 592-8807
EMP: 7 EST: 2008
SALES (est): 82K Privately Held
SIC: 2431 Millwork

(G-1717)
MIDDLBURY BEE-INTELLIGENCER-CT
2030 Straits Tpke Ste 1 (06762-1831)
P.O. Box 10 (06762-0010)
PHONE..............................203 577-6800
EMP: 8 EST: 2010
SALES (est): 190.45K Privately Held
Web: www.bee-news.com
SIC: 2711 Job printing and newspaper publishing combined

(G-1718)
O2 CONCEPTS LLC
199 Park Road Ext Ste B (06762-1833)
PHONE..............................877 867-4008
EMP: 25
SALES (corp-wide): 21.81MM Privately Held
Web: www.o2-concepts.com
SIC: 2813 Oxygen, compressed or liquefied
PA: O2 Concepts, Llc
6303 Waterford Blvd # 150
Oklahoma City OK 73118
877 867-4008

(G-1719)
PLASMA COATINGS INC
84 Turnpike Dr (06762-1819)
PHONE..............................203 598-3100
Charles J Tasch, CEO
Michael S Felvey, Ch
EMP: 13 EST: 1969
SALES (est): 95.64K Privately Held
Web: www.americanroller.com
SIC: 3479 Painting, coating, and hot dipping

(G-1720)
ROLLER BEARING CO AMER INC
Pic Design
86 Benson Rd (06762-3215)
P.O. Box 1004 (06762-1004)

PHONE..............................203 758-8272
Jeff Post, Brnch Mgr
EMP: 16
SALES (corp-wide): 1.47B Publicly Held
Web: www.rbcbearings.com
SIC: 3568 3566 3535 3462 Power transmission equipment, nec; Speed changers, drives, and gears; Conveyors and conveying equipment; Iron and steel forgings
HQ: Roller Bearing Company Of America, Inc.
102 Willenbrock Rd
Oxford CT 06478
203 267-7001

(G-1721)
STRIDE INC
80 Turnpike Dr Ste 1 (06762-1830)
PHONE..............................203 758-8307
Roberta Nole, Pr
EMP: 14 EST: 1987
SALES (est): 810.81K Privately Held
Web: www.strideorthotics.com
SIC: 3842 Limbs, artificial

(G-1722)
TIMEX GROUP USA INC (HQ)
555 Christian Rd (06762-3206)
PHONE..............................203 346-5000
Paolo Marai, CEO
Robert Butler, *
Giorgio Galli, *
W John Dryfe, *
Louis M Galie, *
◆ EMP: 230 EST: 1854
SQ FT: 81,000
SALES (est): 460.68MM
SALES (corp-wide): 968.09K Privately Held
Web: www.timexgroup.com
SIC: 3873 Watches and parts, except crystals and jewels
PA: Tanager Group B.V.
Eduard Van Beinumstraat 28
Amsterdam NH 1077
235563660

Middlefield
Middlesex County

(G-1723)
ADVANCED SHEETMETAL ASSOC LLC
52 Industrial Park Access Rd (06455-1263)
PHONE..............................860 349-1644
EMP: 20 EST: 2014
SALES (est): 4.38MM Privately Held
Web: www.tinknockerct.com
SIC: 3444 Sheet metalwork

(G-1724)
COOPER-ATKINS CORPORATION (HQ)
33 Reeds Gap Rd (06455-1138)
PHONE..............................860 349-3473
Carol Duplessis, Corporate Secretary
Robert Nerbonne, *
◆ EMP: 115 EST: 1885
SQ FT: 40,000
SALES (est): 41.53MM
SALES (corp-wide): 15.16B Publicly Held
Web: www.cooper-atkins.com
SIC: 3829 Thermometers, including digital: clinical
PA: Emerson Electric Co.
8000 West Florissant Ave
Saint Louis MO 63136
314 553-2000

▲ = Import ▼ = Export
◆ = Import/Export

(G-1725)
LYMAN FARM INCORPORATED (PA)
Also Called: Lyman Orchards
7 Lyman Rd (06455-1254)
PHONE..............................860 349-1793
Stephen Ciskowski, Pr
John Lyman Junior, Treas
EMP: 250 EST: 1741
SQ FT: 2,000
SALES (est): 26.42MM
SALES (corp-wide): 26.42MM **Privately Held**
Web: www.lymanorchards.com
SIC: 0175 2099 5431 7992 Apple orchard; Cider, nonalcoholic; Fruit stands or markets ; Public golf courses

(G-1726)
NATIONAL WELDING LLC
48 Industrial Park Access Rd (06455-1263)
P.O. Box 452 (06457-0452)
PHONE..............................860 818-1240
Sebastiano Spada, Prin
EMP: 7 EST: 2014
SALES (est): 406.48K **Privately Held**
SIC: 7692 Welding repair

(G-1727)
POWERHOLD INC
63 Old Indian Trl (06455-1248)
P.O. Box 447 (06455-0447)
PHONE..............................860 349-1044
Richard C Spooner, Ch
R Chadwick Spooner, Pr
Marilyn D Harris, Sec
William T Spooner, VP
EMP: 24 EST: 1958
SQ FT: 14,900
SALES (est): 4.39MM **Privately Held**
Web: www.powerholdinc.com
SIC: 3545 Cutting tools for machine tools

(G-1728)
RAMAR-HALL INC
Also Called: Ramar-Hall
26 Old Indian Trl (06455-1200)
P.O. Box 218 (06455-0218)
PHONE..............................860 349-1081
David Ferraguto, Pr
Tom Varricchio, *
EMP: 28 EST: 1956
SQ FT: 9,000
SALES (est): 6.3MM **Privately Held**
Web: www.ramarhall.com
SIC: 3728 3544 3769 Aircraft parts and equipment, nec; Special dies and tools; Space vehicle equipment, nec

(G-1729)
TET MFG CO INC
Also Called: Tet Mfg Co/Machine Shop
2 Old Indian Trl (06455-1200)
PHONE..............................860 349-1004
Thomas H Cady Junior, Pr
Virginia F Cady, VP
EMP: 22 EST: 1971
SQ FT: 10,000
SALES (est): 2.44MM **Privately Held**
Web: www.tetmfg.com
SIC: 3599 Machine shop, jobbing and repair

(G-1730)
TIMES PUBLISHING LLC
Also Called: Antiqueweb.com
491 Main St (06455-1205)
P.O. Box 333 (06455-0333)
PHONE..............................860 349-8532
Robert G Ahlgren, Pr
EMP: 8 EST: 1997

SALES (est): 402.6K **Privately Held**
Web: www.monkeytv.com
SIC: 2741 Miscellaneous publishing

(G-1731)
WEPCO PLASTICS INC
27 Industrial Park Access Rd (06455-1263)
P.O. Box 182 (06455-0182)
PHONE..............................860 349-3407
Waldo Parmelee Junior, Pr
EMP: 21 EST: 1984
SQ FT: 10,350
SALES (est): 3.33MM **Privately Held**
Web: www.wepcoplastics.com
SIC: 3089 3544 Injection molding of plastics ; Special dies, tools, jigs, and fixtures

(G-1732)
ZYGO CORPORATION (HQ)
Also Called: Zygo
21 Laurel Brook Rd (06455-1291)
PHONE..............................860 347-8506
Chris Koliopoulos, Pr
▲ EMP: 8 EST: 1970
SQ FT: 153,500
SALES (est): 86.38MM
SALES (corp-wide): 6.15B **Publicly Held**
Web: www.zygo.com
SIC: 3827 Optical instruments and lenses
PA: Ametek, Inc.
       1100 Cassatt Rd
       Berwyn PA 19312
       610 647-2121

Middletown
Middlesex County

(G-1733)
AEROSPACE TECHNIQUES INC
Also Called: Aerospace Techniques
1100 Country Club Rd (06457-2306)
PHONE..............................860 347-1200
Jeffrey Lynn, CEO
Jack E Lynn, *
Robert Joseph Bosco, *
Richard B Polivy, *
Anthony Parillo Junior, CFO
EMP: 75 EST: 1965
SQ FT: 80,000
SALES (est): 10MM **Privately Held**
Web: www.aerospacetechniques.com
SIC: 3724 3599 4581 3841 Aircraft engines and engine parts; Machine shop, jobbing and repair; Aircraft maintenance and repair services; Surgical and medical instruments

(G-1734)
ALLSTATE FIRE SYSTEMS LLC
35 Phil Mack Dr (06457-1517)
PHONE..............................860 246-7711
EMP: 42 EST: 1994
SALES (est): 1MM **Privately Held**
SIC: 1711 3669 Fire sprinkler system installation; Fire alarm apparatus, electric
PA: Encore Holdings, Llc
       70 Bacon St
       Pawtucket RI 02860

(G-1735)
AMERICAN LIBRARY ASSOCIATION
Also Called: Choice Magazine
575 Main St Ste 300 (06457-2804)
PHONE..............................860 347-6933
Ervin E Rockwood, Brnch Mgr
EMP: 14
SALES (corp-wide): 61.23MM **Privately Held**

Web: www.ala.org
SIC: 2721 Magazines: publishing only, not printed on site
PA: American Library Association
       225 N Michigan Ave # 1300
       Chicago IL 60601
       800 545-2433

(G-1736)
ARMETTA LLC
Also Called: Copar Industries
90 Industrial Park Rd (06457-1521)
P.O. Box 236 (06023-0236)
PHONE..............................860 788-2369
Antonia Armetta, Pr
Kimberley Ponticelli, Acctg Mgr
EMP: 15 EST: 2010
SALES (est): 1.28MM **Privately Held**
Web: www.dumpsterrentalct.com
SIC: 1411 Granite, dimension-quarrying

(G-1737)
AUBURN MANUFACTURING COMPANY
Also Called: Auburn
29 Stack St (06457-2274)
PHONE..............................860 346-6677
Gary Mittelman, Pr
Robert L Mittelman, *
▲ EMP: 23 EST: 1878
SQ FT: 40,000
SALES (est): 4.86MM **Privately Held**
Web: www.auburn-mfg.com
SIC: 3053 5169 3069 Gasket materials; Synthetic rubber; Washers, rubber

(G-1738)
BALDWIN LAWN FURNITURE LLC
440 Middlefield St Ste 1 (06457-3551)
PHONE..............................860 347-1306
Max Baldwin, Pt
Sherry Baldwin, Managing Member
EMP: 15 EST: 1989
SQ FT: 30,000
SALES (est): 865.92K **Privately Held**
Web: www.baldwinpergolas.com
SIC: 2511 5021 Lawn furniture: wood; Outdoor and lawn furniture, nec

(G-1739)
BERGAN ARCHITECTURAL WDWKG INC
55 N Main St (06457-2228)
PHONE..............................860 346-0869
Richard Bergan, Pr
Maria Bergan, VP
EMP: 20 EST: 1976
SQ FT: 16,000
SALES (est): 2.27MM **Privately Held**
Web: www.berganwood.com
SIC: 2431 2521 2435 2434 Millwork; Wood office furniture; Hardwood veneer and plywood; Wood kitchen cabinets

(G-1740)
BIDWELL INDUSTRIAL GROUP INC
Also Called: Rapidprint
2055 S Main St (06457-6151)
PHONE..............................860 346-9283
Donald Bidwell, CEO
Donald Bidwell Junior, VP
Michael M Bidwell, *
EMP: 50 EST: 1969
SQ FT: 40,000
SALES (est): 4.73MM **Privately Held**
Web: www.bidwellinc.com

SIC: 3824 3579 3089 3861 Electromechanical counters; Duplicating machines; Organizers for closets, drawers, etc.: plastics; Photographic equipment and supplies

(G-1741)
BOURDON FORGE CO INC
99 Tuttle Rd (06457-1827)
PHONE..............................860 632-2740
Peter Bourdon, Pr
▲ EMP: 145 EST: 1969
SQ FT: 50,000
SALES (est): 23.45MM **Privately Held**
Web: www.bourdonforge.com
SIC: 3429 3462 Parachute hardware; Iron and steel forgings

(G-1742)
BULL METAL PRODUCTS INC
Also Called: Bull Display
191 Saybrook Rd (06457-4714)
P.O. Box 738 (06457-0738)
PHONE..............................860 346-9691
Steven Bull, Pr
Steven Z Bull, *
Lawrence J Malone, *
EMP: 40 EST: 1954
SQ FT: 40,000
SALES (est): 7.43MM **Privately Held**
Web: www.bulldisplay.com
SIC: 2542 3444 Cabinets: show, display, or storage: except wood; Sheet metalwork

(G-1743)
CLARKE INTERNATIONAL BUS INC
Also Called: Industrial Construction & Dev
7232 Town Pl (06457-1763)
PHONE..............................860 632-1149
Gary Clarke, Ch Bd
EMP: 50 EST: 2010
SALES (est): 2.15MM **Privately Held**
SIC: 3353 3449 1761 3446 Aluminum sheet and strip; Curtain wall, metal; Architectural sheet metal work; Architectural metalwork

(G-1744)
CONTEMPORARY PRODUCTS LLC
2055 S Main St (06457-6151)
PHONE..............................860 346-9283
EMP: 10 EST: 2003
SQ FT: 40,000
SALES (est): 210.3K **Privately Held**
Web: www.contemporaryproducts.com
SIC: 3842 3491 5047 Respiratory protection equipment, personal; Industrial valves; Medical equipment and supplies

(G-1745)
E-B MANUFACTURING COMPANY INC
825 Middle St (06457-1524)
PHONE..............................860 632-8563
Edward A Billings, Pr
Linda H Billings, *
EMP: 26 EST: 1979
SQ FT: 15,000
SALES (est): 4.04MM **Privately Held**
Web: www.ebmanufacturing.com
SIC: 3599 Machine shop, jobbing and repair

(G-1746)
FIDELUX LIGHTING LLC (PA)
Also Called: Fidelux
180 Johnson St (06457-2247)
PHONE..............................203 774-5653
Sindhu Natarajan, Pr

Jay Jayanthan, *Ofcr*
▲ **EMP:** 12 **EST:** 2012
SALES (est): 2.53MM
SALES (corp-wide): 2.53MM **Privately Held**
Web: www.fidelux.com
SIC: 3648 Lighting equipment, nec

(G-1747)
FIRST CHANCE INC
598 Washington St (06457-2513)
PHONE....................860 346-3663
Stephen Lapenta, *Pr*
EMP: 10 **EST:** 1980
SQ FT: 800
SALES (est): 1.08MM **Privately Held**
SIC: 5499 2099 Health foods; Food preparations, nec

(G-1748)
GORILLA GRAPHICS INC
52 N Main St (06457-2269)
PHONE....................860 704-8208
Geoff Konstan, *Pr*
EMP: 10 **EST:** 1996
SQ FT: 13,000
SALES (est): 979.25K **Privately Held**
Web: www.gorillagraphics.com
SIC: 2269 Linen fabrics: dyeing, finishing, and printing

(G-1749)
HABASIT ABT INC
150 Industrial Park Rd (06457-1521)
PHONE....................860 632-2211
Harry Cardillo, *CEO*
▲ **EMP:** 140 **EST:** 1990
SQ FT: 78,000
SALES (est): 21.89MM **Privately Held**
Web: www.habasitabt.com
SIC: 3496 Conveyor belts
HQ: Habasit America, Inc.
  805 Satellite Blvd Nw
  Suwanee GA 30024
  678 288-3600

(G-1750)
HABASIT AMERICA INC
150 Industrial Park Rd (06457-1521)
PHONE....................860 632-2211
Gary Peterson, *Bmch Mgr*
EMP: 171
Web: www.habasit.com
SIC: 3496 Miscellaneous fabricated wire products
HQ: Habasit America, Inc.
  805 Satellite Blvd Nw
  Suwanee GA 30024
  678 288-3600

(G-1751)
HYDRO SERVICE & SUPPLIES INC
975 Middle St Ste K (06457-7572)
PHONE....................203 265-3995
Richard Desrosiers, *Mgr*
EMP: 9
SALES (corp-wide): 11.19MM **Privately Held**
Web: www.hydroservice.com
SIC: 3589 7699 Water treatment equipment, industrial; Industrial equipment services
PA: Hydro Service & Supplies, Inc.
  513 United Dr
  Durham NC 27713
  919 544-3744

(G-1752)
HYPACK INC (HQ)
56 Bradley St (06457-1513)
PHONE....................860 635-1500
Patrick Sanders, *Pr*
EMP: 13 **EST:** 1986
SALES (est): 2.81MM **Publicly Held**
Web: www.hypack.com
SIC: 7372 Business oriented computer software
PA: Xylem Inc.
  301 Water St Se Ste 201
  Washington DC 20003

(G-1753)
IMAGE STAR LLC
35 Phil Mack Dr (06457-1517)
PHONE....................888 632-5515
EMP: 7 **EST:** 2015
SALES (est): 266.16K **Privately Held**
Web: www.imagestar.com
SIC: 3555 3552 Printing presses; Printing machinery, textile

(G-1754)
JARVIS PRODUCTS CORPORATION (HQ)
Also Called: Jarvis
33 Anderson Rd (06457-4926)
PHONE....................860 347-7271
Jonathan D Jarvis, *Pr*
Penfield Jarvis, *VP*
Robert Cornelius Danaher, *Sec*
▲ **EMP:** 10 **EST:** 1956
SQ FT: 54,800
SALES (est): 37.79MM
SALES (corp-wide): 48.88MM **Privately Held**
Web: www.jarvisproducts.com
SIC: 3556 Meat, poultry, and seafood processing machinery
PA: Penco Corporation
  229 Buckingham St
  Hartford CT
  860 278-2345

(G-1755)
KAMAN AEROSPACE CORPORATION
Precision Products Division
217 Smith St (06457-8750)
PHONE....................860 632-1000
EMP: 234
SALES (corp-wide): 687.96MM **Publicly Held**
Web: www.kaman.com
SIC: 3489 3572 3823 Ordnance and accessories, nec; Computer storage devices ; Process control instruments
HQ: Kaman Aerospace Corporation
  1332 Blue Hills Ave
  Bloomfield CT 06002
  860 242-4461

(G-1756)
KAMAN CORPORATION
217 Smith St (06457-8750)
PHONE....................860 632-1000
EMP: 28
SALES (corp-wide): 687.96MM **Publicly Held**
Web: www.kaman.com
SIC: 3812 Acceleration indicators and systems components, aerospace
PA: Kaman Corporation
  1332 Blue Hills Ave
  Bloomfield CT 06002
  860 243-7100

(G-1757)
KAMAN PRECISION PRODUCTS INC
217 Smith St (06457-8750)
PHONE....................860 632-1000
EMP: 206
SALES (corp-wide): 687.96MM **Publicly Held**
Web: www.kamansensors.com
SIC: 3812 Acceleration indicators and systems components, aerospace
HQ: Kaman Precision Products, Inc.
  6655 E Colonial Dr
  Orlando FL 32807
  407 282-1000

(G-1758)
LEGGETT & PLATT INCORPORATED
422 Timber Ridge Rd (06457-7540)
PHONE....................860 635-8811
EMP: 14
SALES (corp-wide): 5.15B **Publicly Held**
Web: www.leggett.com
SIC: 2515 Mattresses and bedsprings
PA: Leggett & Platt, Incorporated
  1 Leggett Rd
  Carthage MO 64836
  417 358-8131

(G-1759)
LEGGETT PLATT ARSPC MDDLTOWN L
Also Called: Pegasus Manufacturing
422 Timber Ridge Rd (06457-7540)
P.O. Box 501 (06023-0501)
PHONE....................860 635-8811
Chris Dipentima, *Pr*
EMP: 82
SALES (corp-wide): 5.15B **Publicly Held**
Web: www.leggettaerospace.com
SIC: 3498 Tube fabricating (contract bending and shaping)
HQ: Leggett & Platt Aerospace Middletown, Llc
  1 Leggett Rd
  Carthage MO
  417 358-8131

(G-1760)
LORD & HODGE INC
362 Industrial Park Rd Ste 4 (06457-1548)
P.O. Box 737 (06457-0737)
PHONE....................860 632-7006
Gary Lord, *Pr*
EMP: 10 **EST:** 1946
SQ FT: 9,000
SALES (est): 891.28K **Privately Held**
Web: www.lordandhodge.com
SIC: 3965 3069 3545 Fasteners, snap; Grommets, rubber; Vises, machine (machine tool accessories)

(G-1761)
LYMAN PRODUCTS CORPORATION (PA)
Also Called: Raytech Industries Div
475 Smith St (06457-1529)
PHONE....................860 632-2020
Richard Ranzinger, *Pr*
Thomas Andersen, *
Luke Fichthorn Iii, *Treas*
Edward W Wytrych, *
◆ **EMP:** 100 **EST:** 1977
SQ FT: 100,000
SALES (est): 34.43MM
SALES (corp-wide): 34.43MM **Privately Held**
Web: www.lymanproducts.com

SIC: 3559 Ammunition and explosives, loading machinery

(G-1762)
METAL IMPROVEMENT COMPANY LLC
20 Tuttle Pl Ste 6 (06457-1870)
PHONE....................860 635-9994
Paul Dimatti, *Mgr*
EMP: 25
SALES (corp-wide): 2.56B **Publicly Held**
Web: www.imrtest.com
SIC: 3398 Shot peening (treating steel to reduce fatigue)
HQ: Metal Improvement Company, Llc
  80 E Rte 4 Ste 310
  Paramus NJ 07652
  201 843-7800

(G-1763)
MHQ INC
Also Called: Natick Auto Sales
750 Newfield St (06457-1869)
PHONE....................888 242-1118
Michael Fratoni, *Prin*
EMP: 32
Web: www.buymchq.com
SIC: 5999 3711 Police supply stores; Patrol wagons (motor vehicles), assembly of
PA: Mhq, Inc.
  401 Elm St
  Marlborough MA 01752

(G-1764)
MICROSPECIALITIES INC
430 Smith St (06457-1531)
P.O. Box 1201 (06457-1201)
PHONE....................203 874-1832
Gaston Levesque, *CEO*
EMP: 10 **EST:** 1997
SQ FT: 5,200
SALES (est): 1.09MM **Privately Held**
Web: www.pro-paks.com
SIC: 3841 Surgical knife blades and handles

(G-1765)
MIDDLETOWN PRINTING CO INC
Also Called: Minuteman Press
512 Main St (06457-2810)
PHONE....................860 347-5700
Charlie Lazich, *Pr*
EMP: 12 **EST:** 2002
SALES (est): 685.47K **Privately Held**
Web: www.minuteman.com
SIC: 2752 Commercial printing, lithographic

(G-1766)
MOHAWK MANUFACTURING COMPANY
1270 Newfield St (06457-1842)
PHONE....................860 632-2345
William W Ferguson Junior, *Pr*
William P Ferguson, *VP*
Debra J Ferguson, *Sec*
EMP: 18 **EST:** 1921
SQ FT: 32,000
SALES (est): 2.34MM **Privately Held**
Web: www.mohawk-mfg.com
SIC: 3469 Stamping metal for the trade

(G-1767)
NATS USA INCORPORATED
Also Called: North American Technical Svcs
515 Centerpoint Dr Ste 108 (06457-7570)
PHONE....................860 398-0035
Syed R Maswood, *CEO*
Syed R Maswood, *Pr*
Awatef Gacem Maswood, *VP*
EMP: 11 **EST:** 2002

SQ FT: 3,000
SALES (est): 1.9MM **Privately Held**
Web: www.nats-usa.com
SIC: **8734** 3822 3826   Radiation laboratories
; Environmental controls; Elemental
analyzers

(G-1768)
NORPACO INC
Also Called: Norpaco Gourmet Foods
80 Bysiewicz Dr (06457-7564)
PHONE.................................860 632-2299
▲ EMP: 100 EST: 1959
SALES (est): 23.82MM **Privately Held**
Web: www.norpaco.com
SIC: **2035** 2013 5141   Vegetables, brined;
Smoked meats, from purchased meat;
Groceries, general line

(G-1769)
**PEGASUS MANUFACTURING
INC**
Also Called: Pegasus Manufacturing
422 Timber Ridge Rd (06457-7540)
PHONE.................................860 635-8811
▲ EMP: 50
SIC: **3498**   Tube fabricating (contract
bending and shaping)

(G-1770)
**PERKATORY PRODUCTIONS
LLC** ✪
725 Main St Unit 32 (06457-2734)
PHONE.................................860 894-6040
EMP: 7 EST: 2023
SALES (est): 288.14K **Privately Held**
SIC: **2051**   Bakery: wholesale or wholesale/
retail combined

(G-1771)
PLASTIC DESIGN INTL INC (PA)
Also Called: Pdi
111 Industrial Park Rd (06457-1520)
PHONE.................................860 632-2001
Donald A Bergeron, *Pr*
Yvonne Ledoux, *
Kimberly Guillemin, *
◆ EMP: 46 EST: 1977
SQ FT: 30,000
SALES (est): 8.3MM
SALES (corp-wide): 8.3MM **Privately Held**
Web: www.plasticdesign.com
SIC: **3089** 3544   Injection molding of plastics
; Forms (molds), for foundry and plastics
working machinery

(G-1772)
POWER-DYNE LLC
Also Called: Power-Dyne LLC/Bidwll Indstrl
2055 S Main St (06457-6151)
PHONE.................................860 346-9283
EMP: 25 EST: 1995
SQ FT: 40,000
SALES (est): 1.57MM **Privately Held**
Web: www.bidwellinc.com
SIC: **3423** 3829 7699   Wrenches, hand tools
; Gauging instruments, thickness ultrasonic;
Hydraulic equipment repair

(G-1773)
**PRATT & WHITNEY ENG SVCS
INC**
Also Called: Pratt & Whitney
1 Aircraft Rd (06457-5723)
P.O. Box 611 (06457-0611)
PHONE.................................860 344-4000
Roger Cherichoni, *Mgr*
EMP: 500
SALES (corp-wide): 68.92B **Publicly Held**

Web: www.prattwhitney.com
SIC: **3728** 3724 3714   Aircraft assemblies,
subassemblies, and parts, nec; Aircraft
engines and engine parts; Motor vehicle
parts and accessories
HQ: Pratt & Whitney Engine Services, Inc.
1525 Midway Park Rd
Bridgeport WV 26330
304 842-5421

(G-1774)
PRECISION SPEED MFG LLC
422 Timber Ridge Rd (06457-7540)
P.O. Box 501 (06023-0501)
PHONE.................................860 635-8811
EMP: 25 EST: 2004
SQ FT: 21,000
SALES (est): 906.55K **Privately Held**
SIC: **3724** 3728   Aircraft engines and engine
parts; Aircraft parts and equipment, nec

(G-1775)
QUEMERE INTERNATIONAL LLC
Also Called: Quemere
234 Middle St (06457-7517)
PHONE.................................914 934-8366
Celine Quemere, *Owner*
EMP: 8 EST: 1999
SALES (est): 583.55K **Privately Held**
Web: www.quemeredesigns.com
SIC: **3253**   Ceramic wall and floor tile

(G-1776)
RAYCO METAL FINISHING INC
134 Mill St (06457-3749)
P.O. Box 177 (06457-0177)
PHONE.................................860 347-7434
Louise Goldreich, *Ch Bd*
George Goldreich, *VP*
Mark Goldreich, *VP*
EMP: 13 EST: 1973
SQ FT: 7,500
SALES (est): 842.4K **Privately Held**
Web: www.raycometalfinishing.com
SIC: **3471**   Electroplating of metals or
formed products

(G-1777)
REAL-TIME ANALYZERS INC
362 Industrial Park Rd Ste 8 (06457-1548)
PHONE.................................860 635-9800
Doctor Stuart Farquharson, *Pr*
Stuart Farquharson, *Pr*
David Hamblen, *Sec*
EMP: 8 EST: 2001
SQ FT: 3,000
SALES (est): 1.61MM **Privately Held**
Web: www.rta.biz
SIC: **3826**   Mass spectroscopy
instrumentation

(G-1778)
RICHARD E PERSONETTE
Also Called: PIP Printing
179 Main Street Ext (06457-3814)
PHONE.................................860 344-9001
Richard E Personette, *Owner*
Richard Personette, *Owner*
EMP: 10 EST: 1984
SQ FT: 2,400
SALES (est): 695.4K **Privately Held**
Web: www.pipmid.com
SIC: **2752** 2759 2791 2789   Offset printing;
Commercial printing, nec; Typesetting;
Bookbinding and related work

(G-1779)
RTX CORPORATION
Aircraft Rd Bldg 220 (06457)
PHONE.................................860 704-7133

EMP: 214
SALES (corp-wide): 67.07B **Publicly Held**
Web: www.rtx.com
SIC: **3585**   Refrigeration and heating
equipment
PA: Rtx Corporation
1000 Wilson Blvd
Arlington VA 22209
781 522-3000

(G-1780)
SIGNS ON DEMAND USA LLC
777 Laurel Grove Rd (06457-4961)
PHONE.................................860 346-1720
Denis O'brien, *Prin*
EMP: 8 EST: 2005
SALES (est): 209.39K **Privately Held**
Web: www.signsondemandusa.com
SIC: **3993**   Signs and advertising specialties

(G-1781)
**SKYLINE EXHIBITS GRAPHICS
INC**
362 Industrial Park Rd Ste 6 (06457-1548)
PHONE.................................860 635-2400
Larry Zollo, *Pr*
EMP: 10 EST: 1995
SQ FT: 12,500
SALES (est): 924.41K **Privately Held**
Web: www.skyline-ct.com
SIC: **3993**   Signs and advertising specialties

(G-1782)
**SOMERSET PLASTICS
COMPANY INC**
454 Timber Ridge Rd (06457-7540)
P.O. Box 8446 (06037-8446)
PHONE.................................860 635-1601
Clifford F White Junior, *Pr*
Lois White, *VP*
Kim White, *Sec*
Clifford White Junior, *Pr*
EMP: 20 EST: 1980
SQ FT: 10,000
SALES (est): 2.65MM **Privately Held**
Web: www.somersetplastics.com
SIC: **3544** 3089   Forms (molds), for foundry
and plastics working machinery; Injection
molding of plastics

(G-1783)
**SPERIAN PRTCTION
INSTRMNTTION**
651 S Main St (06457-4252)
PHONE.................................860 344-1079
EMP: 80 EST: 2003
SQ FT: 75,000
SALES (est): 5.18MM
SALES (corp-wide): 35.47B **Publicly Held**
SIC: **3829** 3812 3823   Gas detectors;
Search and navigation equipment; Process
control instruments
HQ: Honeywell Analytics Inc.
405 Barclay Blvd
Lincolnshire IL 60069
847 955-4175

(G-1784)
SPREAD CHEESE CO LLC
386 Main St (06457-3360)
PHONE.................................203 982-1674
EMP: 7 EST: 2019
SALES (est): 889.65K **Privately Held**
Web: www.spreadcheeseco.com
SIC: **2022**   Spreads, cheese

(G-1785)
T & J MANUFACTURING LLP
Also Called: T&J Manufacturing

1385 Newfield St (06457-1819)
PHONE.................................860 632-8655
Mark Jablonski, *Owner*
Mark Jablonski, *Pt*
Chris Targanski, *Pt*
EMP: 25 EST: 1998
SALES (est): 2.21MM **Privately Held**
Web: www.tandjmanufacturing.com
SIC: **3599**   Machine shop, jobbing and repair

(G-1786)
TINNY CORPORATION
Also Called: Shelco Filters Division
100 Bradley St (06457-1513)
PHONE.................................860 854-6121
Robert Leconche Junior, *Pr*
Debra A Leconche, *Sec*
▲ EMP: 25 EST: 1971
SQ FT: 40,000
SALES (est): 6.3MM **Privately Held**
Web: www.shelco.com
SIC: **3569** 5074 5085   Filters, general line:
industrial; Plumbing and hydronic heating
supplies; Filters, industrial

(G-1787)
**TRIUMPH MANUFACTURING CO
INC**
422 Timber Ridge Rd (06457-7540)
P.O. Box 501 (06023-0501)
PHONE.................................860 635-8811
Vincent Dipentima, *Pr*
Todd Dipentima, *VP*
EMP: 18 EST: 1969
SQ FT: 7,100
SALES (est): 306.96K **Privately Held**
Web: www.triumph-mfg.com
SIC: **3599**   Machine shop, jobbing and repair

(G-1788)
UNITED OPHTHALMICS LLC
430 Smith St (06457-1531)
PHONE.................................203 500-3332
Gaston S Levesque, *Prin*
EMP: 10 EST: 2009
SALES (est): 377.41K **Privately Held**
Web: www.pro-paks.com
SIC: **3841**   Eye examining instruments and
apparatus

(G-1789)
VENAN ENTERTAINMENT INC
213 Court St Ste 102 (06457-3364)
PHONE.................................860 704-6330
Brandon Curiel, *Pr*
Robert Solomon, *Sec*
EMP: 7 EST: 2002
SQ FT: 2,700
SALES (est): 346.92K **Privately Held**
Web: www.venan.com
SIC: **7812** 7372   Video tape production;
Home entertainment computer software

(G-1790)
WESLEYAN UNIVERSITY
Also Called: Wes Press
110 Mount Vernon St (06457-3289)
PHONE.................................860 685-2980
Suzanna Tamminen, *Dir*
EMP: 8
SALES (corp-wide): 276.38MM **Privately
Held**
Web: www.wesleyan.edu
SIC: **2731** 8221   Book publishing; University
PA: Wesleyan University
45 Wyllys Ave
Middletown CT 06459
860 685-2000

(G-1791)
YOUNGS COMMUNICATIONS INC
Also Called: Fastsigns
182 Court St (06457-3357)
PHONE..............................860 347-8569
EMP: 10 **EST:** 1885
SQ FT: 12,000
SALES (est): 818.5K **Privately Held**
Web: www.youngsprinting.com
SIC: 2752   Offset printing

Milford
New Haven County

(G-1792)
A PLUS EXTERIOR LLC
Also Called: A Plus Exterior
215 Bridgeport Ave (06460-4116)
PHONE..............................203 516-1729
EMP: 15 **EST:** 2011
SALES (est): 1.3MM **Privately Held**
Web: www.trustinaplus.com
SIC: 1761 3444 1751 1771   Roofing, siding, and sheetmetal work; Gutters, sheet metal; Window and door installation and erection; Driveway, parking lot, and blacktop contractors

(G-1793)
ABBOTT ASSOCIATES INC
261a Pepes Farm Rd (06460-3671)
P.O. Box 5405 (06460-0706)
PHONE..............................203 878-2370
John Winfield, *Pr*
EMP: 144 **EST:** 1968
SQ FT: 10,000
SALES (est): 1.54MM **Privately Held**
Web: www.goabbott.com
SIC: 3841   Surgical and medical instruments

(G-1794)
AIR-LOCK INCORPORATED
108 Gulf St (06460-4859)
P.O. Box 592 (06460-0592)
PHONE..............................203 878-4691
Michael H Mccarthy, *Pr*
John W Bassick, *
Robert A Vincent, *
David A Sweet, *
Darlene K Ferris, *
EMP: 25 **EST:** 1951
SQ FT: 27,000
SALES (est): 4.91MM
SALES (corp-wide): 96.68MM **Privately Held**
Web: www.airlockinc.com
SIC: 3728 3429   Aircraft parts and equipment, nec; Hardware, nec
PA: David Clark Company Incorporated
360 Franklin St
Worcester MA 01604
508 756-6216

(G-1795)
ALCAT INCORPORATED
116 W Main St (06460-3310)
PHONE..............................203 878-0648
James Edwards, *Pr*
▲ **EMP:** 26 **EST:** 1963
SQ FT: 31,000
SALES (est): 1.9MM **Privately Held**
Web: www.alcatcoatings.com
SIC: 3083   Plastics finished products, laminated

(G-1796)
ALINABAL INC (HQ)
Also Called: Sterling Screw Machine Div
28 Woodmont Rd (06460-2872)
PHONE..............................203 877-3241
Samuel S Bergami Junior, *Pr*
Kevin Conlisk, *
Steven Bennett, *
▲ **EMP:** 243 **EST:** 1979
SQ FT: 110,000
SALES (est): 42.38MM
SALES (corp-wide): 56.95MM **Privately Held**
Web: www.alinabal.com
SIC: 3469 3399 3625 3728   Metal stampings, nec; Laminating steel; Electric controls and control accessories, industrial; Aircraft parts and equipment, nec
PA: Alinabal Holdings Corporation
28 Woodmont Rd
Milford CT 06460
203 877-3241

(G-1797)
ALINABAL HOLDINGS CORPORATION (PA)
28 Woodmont Rd (06460-2872)
PHONE..............................203 877-3241
Samuel Bergami, *CEO*
Samuel Bergami, *Pr*
Kevin M Conlisk, *
Bruce M Bickley, *
▲ **EMP:** 300 **EST:** 1960
SQ FT: 147,000
SALES (est): 56.95MM
SALES (corp-wide): 56.95MM **Privately Held**
Web: www.alinabal.com
SIC: 3714 3577 3399 3469   Bearings, motor vehicle; Printers, computer; Laminating steel ; Metal stampings, nec

(G-1798)
B & A COMPANY INC
160 Wampus Ln (06460-4861)
PHONE..............................203 876-7527
Richard Schwarz, *Pr*
Ronald Schwartz, *VP*
EMP: 20 **EST:** 1966
SALES (est): 2.23MM **Privately Held**
Web: www.bamachine.com
SIC: 3599   Machine shop, jobbing and repair

(G-1799)
BALDING PRECISION INC
61 Woodmont Rd (06460-2840)
PHONE..............................203 878-9135
Mike Goodman, *Pr*
EMP: 8 **EST:** 1997
SQ FT: 5,000
SALES (est): 986.13K **Privately Held**
SIC: 3599   Machine shop, jobbing and repair

(G-1800)
BARON TECHNOLOGY INC
86 Raton Rd (06461-1726)
PHONE..............................203 452-0515
David Baron, *Pr*
Ruth Baron, *
Frank Baron, *
Karlo Glad, *
EMP: 18 **EST:** 1978
SALES (est): 8.25MM **Privately Held**
Web: www.baronengraving.com
SIC: 2759 3231 2796   Engraving, nec; Products of purchased glass; Platemaking services

(G-1801)
BEAD INDUSTRIES INC (PA)
Also Called: Bead Electronics
11 Cascade Blvd (06460-2849)
PHONE..............................203 301-0270
Jill Bryant Mayer, *CEO*
Tracey Miller, *
Jill Mayer, *Prin*
Richard Cote, *Prin*
Ron Andreoli, *Prin*
◆ **EMP:** 27 **EST:** 1914
SQ FT: 75,000
SALES (est): 9.65MM
SALES (corp-wide): 9.65MM **Privately Held**
Web: www.beadelectronics.com
SIC: 3432 3679 3678 3643   Plumbing fixture fittings and trim; Electronic circuits; Electronic connectors; Current-carrying wiring services

(G-1802)
BIC CONSUMER PDTS MFG CO INC
565 Bic Dr (06461-1769)
PHONE..............................203 783-2000
Mario Guevara, *Pr*
James V Dipietro, *
Thomas M Kelleher, *
Ken Brannin, *PLANT SVCS*
Cheryl A Dubois, *
▲ **EMP:** 120 **EST:** 1999
SALES (est): 18.33MM
SALES (corp-wide): 800.85MM **Privately Held**
SIC: 3951 2899   Ball point pens and parts; Correction fluid
HQ: Bic Usa Inc.
1 Bic Way Ste 1 # 1
Shelton CT 06484
203 783-2000

(G-1803)
BRIDGESTONE RET OPERATIONS LLC
Also Called: Firestone
1063 Boston Post Rd (06460-3534)
PHONE..............................203 878-6859
Gary Carella, *Mgr*
EMP: 8
Web: www.bridgestoneamericas.com
SIC: 5531 7534   Automotive tires; Rebuilding and retreading tires
HQ: Bridgestone Retail Operations, Llc
333 E Lake St Ste 300
Bloomingdale IL 60108
630 259-9000

(G-1804)
BUCKS SPUMONI COMPANY INC
Also Called: Buck's Ice Cream
229 Pepes Farm Rd (06460-3671)
PHONE..............................203 874-2007
Charles Buck Junior, *Pr*
Lois Gosselin, *Sec*
EMP: 15 **EST:** 1954
SQ FT: 14,000
SALES (est): 1.77MM **Privately Held**
SIC: 2024   Ice cream, bulk

(G-1805)
CAAP CO INC
152 Pepes Farm Rd (06460-3670)
P.O. Box 3758 (06460-0948)
PHONE..............................203 877-0375
James F Moraveck, *Pr*
Charles Scheidler Junior, *VP*
Christine L Sledge, *VP*
Christopher J Moraveck, *VP*
Billie C Moraveck, *Sec*
▲ **EMP:** 20 **EST:** 1976
SQ FT: 10,000
SALES (est): 4.69MM **Privately Held**
Web: www.caapco.com
SIC: 2899   Waterproofing compounds

(G-1806)
CADCOM INC
110 Raton Rd (06461-1779)
PHONE..............................203 877-0640
Richard Meisenheimer, *Pr*
Daniel Meisenheimer, *VP*
Maria Sabina, *Contrlr*
EMP: 10 **EST:** 1987
SQ FT: 3,500
SALES (est): 969.43K **Privately Held**
SIC: 3451   Screw machine products

(G-1807)
CANEVARI PLASTICS INC
10 Furniture Row (06460-3607)
P.O. Box 464 (06460-0464)
PHONE..............................203 878-4319
George Canevari, *Pr*
Kevin Callahan, *VP*
Janice Canevari, *Sec*
EMP: 9 **EST:** 1980
SQ FT: 1,200
SALES (est): 1.91MM **Privately Held**
Web: www.canevariplastics.com
SIC: 3089   Molding primary plastics

(G-1808)
CARDIOPULMONARY CORP
200 Cascade Blvd Ste B (06460-8515)
PHONE..............................203 877-1999
Doctor James Biondi, *Ch Bd*
Nick Snow, *
Paul Blodgett, *
Joseph Mcguire, *Technology Vice President*
▲ **EMP:** 36 **EST:** 1988
SQ FT: 25,000
SALES (est): 2.41MM **Privately Held**
Web: www.venturi.com
SIC: 3842   Surgical appliances and supplies

(G-1809)
CARRUBBA INCORPORATED
70 Research Dr (06460-8523)
PHONE..............................203 878-0605
EMP: 59 **EST:** 1980
SALES (est): 2.98MM **Privately Held**
SIC: 2899   Chemical preparations, nec

(G-1810)
CET INC
Also Called: CET
270 Rowe Ave Ste D (06461-3085)
PHONE..............................203 882-8057
John Breger, *Pr*
EMP: 8 **EST:** 1992
SQ FT: 5,000
SALES (est): 1MM **Privately Held**
Web: www.cet-inc.net
SIC: 3625   Control equipment, electric

(G-1811)
COLONIAL COATINGS INC
66 Erna Ave (06461-3115)
PHONE..............................,203 783-9933
Russell Colon Junior, *Pr*
Russell A Colon, *
David Colon, *
Russell Colon Senior, *Stockholder*
Richard S Castorina, *
EMP: 45 **EST:** 1982
SQ FT: 17,000
SALES (est): 8.43MM **Privately Held**

Web: www.colonialcoatings.com
SIC: 3479 3471 2851 Coating of metals and formed products; Plating and polishing; Paints and allied products

(G-1812)
COMPOSITION MATERIALS CO INC
249 Pepes Farm Rd (06460-3671)
PHONE....................203 874-6500
▲ EMP: 8 EST: 1923
SALES (est): 1.76MM Privately Held
Web: www.compomat.com
SIC: 3291 5085 Abrasive products; Abrasives

(G-1813)
CONNECTCUT MCH TOLING CAST INC
93 Research Dr (06460-8525)
PHONE....................203 874-8300
George Paulis, Pr
Marolyn Paulis, Treas
George Paulis Junior, VP
EMP: 12 EST: 1980
SQ FT: 8,000
SALES (est): 420.11K Privately Held
SIC: 3599 Machine shop, jobbing and repair

(G-1814)
CONNECTICUT STONE SUPPLIES INC (PA)
Also Called: Connecticut Stone
138 Woodmont Rd (06460-2832)
PHONE....................203 882-1000
Joseph Dellacroce, Pr
Kelly Dellacroce, *
◆ EMP: 83 EST: 1952
SALES (est): 11.51MM
SALES (corp-wide): 11.51MM Privately Held
Web: www.connecticutstone.com
SIC: 3281 5032 1411 Paving blocks, cut stone; Building stone; Dimension stone

(G-1815)
D & B TOOL CO LLC
83 Erna Ave (06461-3118)
PHONE....................203 878-6026
John Butka, Owner
EMP: 8 EST: 1994
SALES (est): 684.26K Privately Held
Web: www.morningstartool.com
SIC: 3544 Special dies and tools

(G-1816)
DATA SIGNAL CORPORATION
16 Higgins Dr (06460-2853)
PHONE....................203 882-5393
Lynda Kilgore, Pr
Gerard Kilgore, Sec
EMP: 35 EST: 1980
SQ FT: 15,900
SALES (est): 815.34K Privately Held
SIC: 3679 Harness assemblies, for electronic use: wire or cable

(G-1817)
DEL ARBOUR LLC
152 Old Gate Ln (06460-3637)
PHONE....................203 882-8501
EMP: 10 EST: 1979
SQ FT: 2,500
SALES (est): 925.25K Privately Held
Web: www.delarbour.com

SIC: 2329 2339 5136 5137 Athletic clothing, except uniforms: men's, youths' and boys'; Athletic clothing: women's, misses', and juniors'; Sportswear, men's and boys'; Sportswear, women's and children's

(G-1818)
DONGHIA INC
Also Called: Donghia Furniture and Textiles
500 Bic Dr Ste 200 (06461)
PHONE....................800 366-4442
◆ EMP: 200
Web: www.kravet.com
SIC: 5198 5131 5021 2342 Wallcoverings; Piece goods and other fabrics; Furniture; Corset accessories: clasps, stays, etc.

(G-1819)
DRILL MASTERS-ELDORADO TOOL INC
336 Boston Post Rd (06460-2559)
PHONE....................203 878-1711
▲ EMP: 78 EST: 1973
SALES (est): 13.23MM Privately Held
Web: www.dmetool.com
SIC: 3545 Cutting tools for machine tools

(G-1820)
EASTERN MARBLE AND GRANITE LLC
201 Buckingham Ave (06460-4842)
PHONE....................203 882-8221
Michael Ballaro, Managing Member
▲ EMP: 10 EST: 1989
SALES (est): 1MM Privately Held
Web: www.easternmarbleandgranite.com
SIC: 3281 Marble, building: cut and shaped

(G-1821)
EASTERN METAL WORKS INC
333 Woodmont Rd (06460-2847)
PHONE....................203 878-6995
Raymond J Weiner, Pr
Christopher J Weiner, Sec
Greg Weiner, Prin
▼ EMP: 22 EST: 1983
SQ FT: 15,000
SALES (est): 7.36MM Privately Held
Web: www.easternmetalworks.com
SIC: 3449 3446 5051 Bars, concrete reinforcing: fabricated steel; Architectural metalwork; Steel

(G-1822)
EDGEWELL PER CARE BRANDS LLC
10 Leighton Rd (06460-3552)
PHONE....................203 882-2300
Joseph Lynch, Brnch Mgr
EMP: 33
SALES (corp-wide): 2.25B Publicly Held
Web: www.edgewell.com
SIC: 2844 Cosmetic preparations
HQ: Edgewell Personal Care Brands, Llc
6 Research Dr
Shelton CT 06484
203 944-5500

(G-1823)
EDGEWELL PERSONAL CARE COMPANY
10 Leighton Rd (06460-3552)
PHONE....................203 882-2308
EMP: 52
SALES (corp-wide): 2.25B Publicly Held
Web: www.edgewell.com
SIC: 3421 Razor blades and razors
PA: Edgewell Personal Care Company
6 Research Dr Ste 400

Shelton CT 06484
203 944-5500

(G-1824)
ENGINEERED INSERTS SYSTEMS INC (PA)
Also Called: Eis
26 Quirk Rd (06460-3745)
P.O. Box 610 (06795-0610)
PHONE....................203 301-3334
Teri Cook, Pr
EMP: 10 EST: 1988
SALES (est): 2.27MM
SALES (corp-wide): 2.27MM Privately Held
Web: www.eisinserts.com
SIC: 3599 Machine shop, jobbing and repair

(G-1825)
ENGINUITY PLM LLC (DH)
Also Called: IMS
440 Wheelers Farms Rd (06461-9133)
PHONE....................203 218-7225
EMP: 19 EST: 1992
SQ FT: 6,600
SALES (est): 9.21MM Privately Held
Web: www.3ds.com
SIC: 7372 7373 8734 8742 Application computer software; Systems software development services; Testing laboratories; Management consulting services
HQ: Dassault Systemes
10 Rue Marcel Dassault
Velizy Villacoublay 78140
161626162

(G-1826)
EPHEMERAL SOLUTIONS INC
Also Called: Ephemeral Tattoo
4 Oxford Rd Ste B1 (06460-3819)
PHONE....................203 312-7337
Jeffrey Liu, CEO
Brennal Pierre, *
EMP: 50 EST: 2015
SALES (est): 1.54MM Privately Held
SIC: 7299 2844 Tattoo parlor; Cosmetic preparations

(G-1827)
EXCELLO TOOL ENGRG & MFG CO
37 Warfield St (06461-2930)
PHONE....................203 878-4073
Michael Zahornacky Junior, Pr
Jeff Solomon, *
EMP: 25 EST: 1960
SALES (est): 2.45MM Privately Held
Web: www.excellotool.com
SIC: 3599 Machine shop, jobbing and repair

(G-1828)
FERRARO CUSTOM WOODWORK LLC
29 Eastern Steel Rd (06460-2837)
PHONE....................203 876-1280
Joseph Ferraro, Owner
EMP: 15 EST: 2005
SALES (est): 535.63K Privately Held
SIC: 2431 Woodwork, interior and ornamental, nec

(G-1829)
GALAXY FUEL LLC
180 New Haven Ave (06460-4829)
PHONE....................203 878-8173
Mustafa Bayram, Prin
EMP: 8 EST: 2014
SALES (est): 503.46K Privately Held
SIC: 2869 Fuels

(G-1830)
GRAPHIC IMAGE INC
561 Boston Post Rd (06460-2676)
PHONE....................203 877-8787
Leigh Danenberg, Pr
EMP: 25 EST: 1998
SQ FT: 11,000
SALES (est): 4.32MM Privately Held
Web: www.graphicimage.net
SIC: 2752 Offset printing

(G-1831)
GRILLO SERVICES LLC
1183 Oronoque Rd (06461-1714)
PHONE....................203 877-5070
John Michael Grillo, Pr
Lawrence Grillo, *
EMP: 25 EST: 1996
SALES (est): 4.6MM Privately Held
Web: www.grilloservices.com
SIC: 2875 4213 4953 5191 Potting soil, mixed; Contract haulers; Dumps, operation of; Soil, potting and planting
PA: Grillo Organic Inc.
1183 Oronoque Rd
Milford CT 06461

(G-1832)
GYBENORTH INDUSTRIES LLC
Also Called: American Dry Stripping
80 Wampus Ln Ste 13 (06460-4856)
P.O. Box 471 (06460-0471)
PHONE....................203 876-9876
Roger F Van Brussel, Prin
Roger Vanbrussel, Mgr
EMP: 12 EST: 2012
SALES (est): 1.96MM Privately Held
Web: www.americandrystripping.com
SIC: 3479 3471 Aluminum coating of metal products; Electroplating and plating

(G-1833)
HASLER INC
478 Wheelers Farms Rd (06461-9105)
PHONE....................203 301-3400
▲ EMP: 381
SIC: 5044 3565 3596 8741 Mailing machines; Packaging machinery; Industrial scales; Management services

(G-1834)
HAYWARD TURNSTILES INC
333 Quarry Rd (06460-8574)
PHONE....................203 647-9144
EMP: 8 EST: 2018
SALES (est): 172.09K Privately Held
Web: www.haywardturnstiles.com
SIC: 3829 Measuring and controlling devices, nec

(G-1835)
HE TECHNOLOGIES INC
Also Called: Hawkeye Technologies
181 Research Dr Ste 8 (06460-8549)
PHONE....................203 878-6892
Alexander Sorokin, Pr
EMP: 9 EST: 2013
SALES (est): 999.86K Privately Held
Web: www.hawkeyetechnologies.com
SIC: 3823 Absorption analyzers: infrared, x-ray, etc.: industrial

(G-1836)
I & J MACHINE TOOL COMPANY
230 Woodmont Rd Ste V (06460-2845)
PHONE....................203 877-5376
Ivan Jukic, Pt
Jure Jukic, Pt
▼ EMP: 15 EST: 1979

SQ FT: 7,200
SALES (est): 1.92MM **Privately Held**
Web: www.ijmachinetool.com
SIC: 3728 3724 Aircraft body assemblies
    and parts; Aircraft engines and engine parts

(G-1837)
**IMPERIAL GRPHIC
CMMNCTIONS INC**
Also Called: Imperial Graphics
22 Way St (06460-4200)
PHONE.............................203 650-3478
David Emery, *Pr*
Robert Emery, *VP*
EMP: 27 EST: 1929
SQ FT: 20,000
SALES (est): 766.2K **Privately Held**
Web: www.perfectdomain.com
SIC: 2752 2789 2759 Offset printing;
    Bookbinding and related work; Commercial
    printing, nec

(G-1838)
INDECO NORTH AMERICA INC
135 Research Dr (06460-2839)
PHONE.............................203 713-1030
Michael Fischer, *CEO*
Annalisa Ugalde, *
Charles Ameer, *
◆ EMP: 28 EST: 1990
SQ FT: 77,000
SALES (est): 10.56MM **Privately Held**
Web: www.indeco-breakers.com
SIC: 3531 Backhoe mounted, hydraulically
    powered attachments
PA: Indeco Ind Spa
    Viale Guglielmo Lindemann 10
    Bari BA 70132

(G-1839)
**INTERFACE DEVICES
INCORPORATED**
Also Called: IDI
230 Depot Rd (06460-3813)
PHONE.............................203 878-4648
Mark Robinson, *Pr*
Mike Hotchkiss, *VP*
Roger Dennis, *Treas*
EMP: 8 EST: 1972
SQ FT: 10,000
SALES (est): 1.45MM **Privately Held**
Web: www.interfacedevices.com
SIC: 3599 5084 Machine and other job shop
    work; Industrial machinery and equipment

(G-1840)
JGS PROPERTIES LLC
Also Called: R A Lalli
132 Shelland St (06461-1785)
PHONE.............................203 378-7508
Geza Scap, *Owner*
Geza Scap, *Pr*
Julie Scap, *VP*
EMP: 30 EST: 1953
SALES (est): 2.5MM **Privately Held**
Web: www.valleytl.com
SIC: 3444 Sheet metal specialties, not
    stamped

(G-1841)
JOEL GORKOWSKI INC
215 Pepes Farm Rd (06460-3626)
P.O. Box 3608 (06460-0945)
PHONE.............................203 877-3896
Joel B Gorkowski, *Prin*
EMP: 10 EST: 2004
SALES (est): 849.04K **Privately Held**
SIC: 2299 Crash, linen

(G-1842)
K B C ELECTRONICS INC
Also Called: Kbc Electronics
273 Pepes Farm Rd (06460-3671)
PHONE.............................203 298-9654
Kue Choi, *Owner*
EMP: 10 EST: 1986
SQ FT: 7,500
SALES (est): 2.2MM **Privately Held**
Web: www.kbcelectronics.com
SIC: 3679 3841 3842 Electronic circuits;
    Surgical and medical instruments; Surgical
    appliances and supplies

(G-1843)
LAC LANDSCAPING LLC
60 Country Ln (06461-1943)
PHONE.............................203 807-1067
EMP: 10 EST: 2005
SALES (est): 969.1K **Privately Held**
SIC: 3714 Dump truck lifting mechanism

(G-1844)
LEAP POND LLC
3 Schooner Ln Ste 15 (06460-3377)
PHONE.............................203 361-9200
Nancy Fliss, *Pr*
EMP: 8 EST: 2014
SALES (est): 276.67K **Privately Held**
Web: www.leapthepond.com
SIC: 7372 Prepackaged software

(G-1845)
LENSCRAFTERS
1201 Boston Post Rd # 20 (06460-2703)
PHONE.............................203 878-8511
EMP: 7
SALES (est): 452.06K **Privately Held**
Web: local.lenscrafters.com
SIC: 8049 5699 5047 3827 Offices of health
    practitioner; Miscellaneous apparel and
    accessory stores; Medical and hospital
    equipment; Optical instruments and lenses

(G-1846)
LITTLE TOKYO EXPRESS INC
1201 Boston Post Rd Ste 2 (06460-2700)
PHONE.............................203 878-8814
EMP: 7 EST: 2006
SALES (est): 217.33K **Privately Held**
SIC: 2741 Miscellaneous publishing

(G-1847)
MACHINE BUILDERS NENG LLC
83 Erna Ave (06461-3118)
PHONE.............................203 922-9446
EMP: 12 EST: 2002
SALES (est): 953K **Privately Held**
Web: www.machinebuildne.com
SIC: 7699 3541 Industrial equipment
    services; Milling machines

(G-1848)
MDM PRODUCTS LLC
Also Called: Rhino Shelters
105 Woodmont Rd (06460-2840)
PHONE.............................203 877-7070
◆ EMP: 11 EST: 2002
SQ FT: 65,000
SALES (est): 2.15MM **Privately Held**
Web: www.mdmshelters.com
SIC: 3448 3089 Garages, portable:
    prefabricated metal; Sponges, plastics

(G-1849)
MICROSPECIALTIES INC
264 Quarry Rd (06460-8506)
PHONE.............................203 874-1832
J Esposito, *M*

EMP: 8 EST: 1997
SALES (est): 95.34K **Privately Held**
SIC: 3841 Surgical and medical instruments

(G-1850)
MIDGET LOUVER COMPANY INC
671 Naugatuck Ave (06461-4064)
PHONE.............................203 783-1444
Michael Vignola, *Pr*
Paul Creatore, *Prin*
Delores Creatore, *Sec*
EMP: 8 EST: 1948
SQ FT: 3,300
SALES (est): 943.44K **Privately Held**
Web: www.midgetlouver.com
SIC: 3444 Sheet metalwork

(G-1851)
MIKS MIX LLC
60 Corona Dr (06460-3512)
PHONE.............................203 521-7824
Michelle Cotton, *Prin*
EMP: 8 EST: 2010
SALES (est): 286.9K **Privately Held**
Web: www.miksmixcrafts.com
SIC: 3273 Ready-mixed concrete

(G-1852)
MILFORD FABRICATING CO INC
500 Bic Dr Bldg 2 (06461-1777)
PHONE.............................203 878-2476
EMP: 80
SIC: 3444 Sheet metal specialties, not
    stamped

(G-1853)
NEW ENGLAND STONE INC
35 Higgins Dr (06460-2853)
PHONE.............................203 876-8606
John Tomlinson Junior, *Pr*
▲ EMP: 17 EST: 1990
SQ FT: 14,000
SALES (est): 2.24MM **Privately Held**
Web: www.newenglandstone.com
SIC: 1743 3281 1799 5032 Tile installation,
    ceramic; Marble, building: cut and shaped;
    Kitchen and bathroom remodeling;
    Limestone

(G-1854)
NEWHART PRODUCTS INC
80 Collingsdale Dr (06461-3054)
P.O. Box 2231 (06460-1131)
PHONE.............................203 878-3546
Thomas N D'aulizio, *Pr*
EMP: 29 EST: 1953
SQ FT: 25,000
SALES (est): 4.3MM **Privately Held**
Web: www.newhartproducts.com
SIC: 5051 3544 Stampings, metal; Special
    dies, tools, jigs, and fixtures

(G-1855)
**NORTHEAST ELECTRONICS
CORP**
Also Called: Northeast
455 Bic Dr (06461-1735)
PHONE.............................203 878-3511
Armand J Cantafio, *Ch*
Frank Gaudiano, *
John Short, *
Timothy A Cantafio, *
Philo Shelton, *
▲ EMP: 100 EST: 1961
SQ FT: 36,000
SALES (est): 18.77MM **Privately Held**
Web: www.northeast.com
SIC: 3679 Hermetic seals, for electronic
    equipment

(G-1856)
OBJECTIF LUNE INC
5 Eastern Steel Rd (06460-2873)
PHONE.............................203 878-7206
EMP: 7 EST: 2019
SALES (est): 123.92K **Privately Held**
Web: www.uplandsoftware.com
SIC: 7372 Business oriented computer
    software

(G-1857)
OEM SOURCES LLC
214 Broadway (06460-5858)
PHONE.............................203 283-5415
Thomas Bach, *Pr*
▲ EMP: 9 EST: 2001
SALES (est): 589.25K **Privately Held**
Web: www.oemsources.com
SIC: 3542 3462 3469 3451 Die casting
    machines; Iron and steel forgings; Metal
    stampings, nec; Screw machine products

(G-1858)
OLD GATE AUTOMOTIVE LLC ✪
254 Old Gate Ln (06460-8621)
PHONE.............................203 878-7688
EMP: 8 EST: 2023
SALES (est): 645.26K **Privately Held**
SIC: 3711 Automobile assembly, including
    specialty automobiles

(G-1859)
ORANGE RESEARCH INC
140 Cascade Blvd (06460-2893)
PHONE.............................203 877-5657
Paul A Hoffman, *Pr*
Leslie Hoffman, *
Mike Donovan, *
Muriel Hoffman, *
EMP: 53 EST: 1961
SQ FT: 10,000
SALES (est): 9.75MM **Privately Held**
Web: www.orangeresearch.com
SIC: 3823 Pressure measurement
    instruments, industrial

(G-1860)
OSDA INC
98 Quirk Rd (06460-3763)
P.O. Box 3048 (06460-0848)
PHONE.............................203 878-2155
David Ingraham, *Prin*
EMP: 9 EST: 2013
SALES (est): 1.03MM **Privately Held**
Web: www.osda.com
SIC: 3679 Electronic circuits

(G-1861)
OUTLAND ENGINEERING INC
167 Cherry St Pmb 280 (06460-3466)
PHONE.............................800 797-3709
▲ EMP: 12 EST: 1994
SQ FT: 54,000
SALES (est): 891.66K **Privately Held**
SIC: 3429 5075 Hardware, nec; Air
    conditioning and ventilation equipment and
    supplies

(G-1862)
PANAGRAFIX INC (PA)
75 Cascade Blvd (06460-2849)
PHONE.............................203 878-7412
Kathleen Featherston, *Pr*
Mary Kokias, *Sec*
Charles Featherston, *VP Opers*
James Featherston, *VP Sls*
EMP: 14 EST: 2014
SALES (est): 4.45MM
SALES (corp-wide): 4.45MM **Privately
Held**

Web: www.panagfx.com
SIC: 2752 Offset printing

(G-1863)
PARIDISE FOODS LLC
828 New Haven Ave (06460-3675)
P.O. Box 5178 (06460-0709)
PHONE.............................203 283-3903
Hristos Paridis, *Prin*
EMP: 7 EST: 2010
SALES (est): 182.19K Privately Held
SIC: 2099 Food preparations, nec

(G-1864)
PENNY PRESS INC
185 Plains Rd Ste 100e (06461-2480)
PHONE.............................203 866-6688
Vincent Petrecca, *Prin*
EMP: 20
SALES (corp-wide): 4.56MM Privately
Held
Web: www.pennydellpuzzles.com
SIC: 2741 Miscellaneous publishing
PA: Penny Press, Inc.
6 Prowitt St
Norwalk CT 06855
203 866-6688

(G-1865)
PENNY PUBLICATIONS LLC
185 Plains Rd Ste 201 (06461-2440)
PHONE.............................203 866-6688
Peter Kanter, *Brnch Mgr*
EMP: 25
Web: www.pennypublications.com
SIC: 2741 Miscellaneous publishing
PA: Penny Publications Llc
6 Prowitt St
Norwalk CT 06855

(G-1866)
PLASTIC MET COMPONENTS CO INC
381 Bridgeport Ave (06460-4103)
P.O. Box 312 (06460-0312)
PHONE.............................203 877-2723
John Ciesla, *Pr*
Robert E Dwyer, *Pr*
Donald Hoover, *VP*
EMP: 11 EST: 1970
SQ FT: 4,500
SALES (est): 1.84MM Privately Held
Web: www.plastic-metal-comp.com
SIC: 5072 3452 5085 5251 Hardware; Bolts,
nuts, rivets, and washers; Fasteners,
industrial: nuts, bolts, screws, etc.;
Hardware stores

(G-1867)
PRACTICAL AUTOMATION INC (HQ)
28 Woodmont Rd (06460-8502)
P.O. Box 3028 (06460-0828)
PHONE.............................203 882-5640
Samuel Bergami, *Pr*
Kevin M Conlisk, *
Bruce M Bickley, *
▲ EMP: 52 EST: 1960
SQ FT: 35,000
SALES (est): 9.97MM
SALES (corp-wide): 56.95MM Privately
Held
Web: www.practicalautomation.com
SIC: 2759 Thermography
PA: Alinabal Holdings Corporation
28 Woodmont Rd
Milford CT 06460
203 877-3241

(G-1868)
PRECISION AEROSPACE INC
220 Rock Ln (06460-3853)
PHONE.............................203 888-3022
Evan Waldman, *CEO*
Todd Waldman, *
Garrett Ferris, *General Vice President*
EMP: 41 EST: 1969
SALES (est): 8.72MM
SALES (corp-wide): 559.81MM Privately
Held
Web: www.essexindustries.com
SIC: 3599 Machine shop, jobbing and repair
HQ: Essex Industries, Inc.
7700 Gravois Rd
Saint Louis MO 63123
314 644-3000

(G-1869)
PRECISION METAL PRODUCTS INC
307 Pepes Farm Rd (06460-8605)
PHONE.............................203 877-4258
William O'brien, *Pr*
EMP: 196 EST: 1959
SQ FT: 36,000
SALES (est): 21.12MM Privately Held
Web: www.pmpinc.biz
SIC: 3599 Machine shop, jobbing and repair

(G-1870)
PRECISION SENSORS INC
340 Woodmont Rd (06460-3702)
P.O. Box 509 (06460-0509)
PHONE.............................203 877-2795
Robert D Reis, *Ch Bd*
David A Reis, *
R Tim Straub, *Marketing*
Brian Hallahan, *
▼ EMP: 39 EST: 1962
SQ FT: 10,000
SALES (est): 5.28MM
SALES (corp-wide): 39.4MM Privately
Held
Web: www.precisionsensors.com
SIC: 3829 Measuring and controlling
devices, nec
PA: United Electric Controls Company
180 Dexter Ave
Watertown MA 02472
617 926-1000

(G-1871)
PROBATTER SPORTS LLC
49 Research Dr Ste 1 (06460-2864)
PHONE.............................203 874-2500
Greg Battersby, *Managing Member*
EMP: 8 EST: 1999
SALES (est): 971.75K Privately Held
Web: www.probatter.com
SIC: 3949 5941 Baseball, softball, and
cricket sports equipment; Sporting goods
and bicycle shops

(G-1872)
PUCKS PUTTERS & FUEL LLC
10 Robert Dennis Dr (06461-2267)
PHONE.............................203 877-5457
Steven Genova, *Brnch Mgr*
EMP: 40
SALES (corp-wide): 1.41MM Privately
Held
SIC: 2869 Fuels
PA: Pucks, Putters, & Fuel, Llc
784 River Rd
Shelton CT 06484
203 494-3952

(G-1873)
QTRAN INC (PA)
155 Hill St Ste 3 (06460-3192)
PHONE.............................203 367-8777
▲ EMP: 30 EST: 1993
SQ FT: 10,000
SALES (est): 9.05MM Privately Held
Web: www.q-tran.com
SIC: 3679 3677 Electronic circuits;
Electronic coils and transformers

(G-1874)
QUADIENT INC (DH)
Also Called: Neopost
478 Wheelers Farms Rd (06461-9105)
PHONE.............................203 301-3400
Alain Fairise, *Pr*
Christopher M Obrien, *
Kirk Shankle, *
▲ EMP: 250 EST: 1933
SQ FT: 62,000
SALES (est): 397.07MM Privately Held
Web: www.quadient.com
SIC: 3579 7359 7629 Postage meters;
Business machine and electronic
equipment rental services; Business
machine repair, electric
HQ: Quadient France
7 Rue Henri Becquerel
Rueil Malmaison 92500

(G-1875)
QUADIENT FINANCE USA INC (DH)
Also Called: Neopost USA
478 Wheelers Farms Rd (06461-9105)
PHONE.............................203 301-3400
Alain Fairise, *Pr*
Carl Amacker, *VP*
Joseph Bonassar, *Sec*
EMP: 26 EST: 2006
SALES (est): 49.11MM Privately Held
Web: mail.quadient.com
SIC: 3579 Mailing machines
HQ: Quadient Holdings Usa, Inc.
478 Wheelers Farms Rd
Milford CT 06461

(G-1876)
REL-TECH ELECTRONICS INC
215 Pepes Farm Rd (06460-3626)
P.O. Box 3111 (06460-0911)
PHONE.............................203 877-8770
Ralph L Palumbo, *Pr*
Noreen C Palumbo, *
EMP: 85 EST: 1986
SQ FT: 12,000
SALES (est): 23.24MM
SALES (corp-wide): 72.17MM Publicly
Held
Web: www.rel-tech.com
SIC: 3679 5063 Harness assemblies, for
electronic use: wire or cable; Wire and cable
PA: Rf Industries, Ltd.
16868 Via Del Campo Ct
San Diego CA 92127
858 549-6340

(G-1877)
RICHARD MANUFACTURING CO INC
250 Rock Ln (06460-3853)
PHONE.............................203 874-3617
James F Steponavich, *Pr*
EMP: 35 EST: 1957
SQ FT: 13,000
SALES (est): 7.61MM Privately Held
Web: www.richardmanufacturing.com
SIC: 3728 Aircraft assemblies,
subassemblies, and parts, nec

(G-1878)
RIDGE VIEW ASSOCIATES INC
Also Called: J Burdon Division
122 Cascade Blvd (06460-2848)
PHONE.............................203 878-8560
William B Maley Junior, *Pr*
▲ EMP: 70 EST: 1959
SQ FT: 55,000
SALES (est): 9.04MM Privately Held
SIC: 3647 3546 Locomotive and railroad car
lights; Drills and drilling tools

(G-1879)
RINGS WIRE INC (PA)
257 Depot Rd (06460-3804)
P.O. Box 3013 (06460-0813)
PHONE.............................203 874-6719
Stanley Reiter, *Pr*
Howard J Reiter, *
EMP: 45 EST: 1938
SQ FT: 300,000
SALES (est): 2.89MM
SALES (corp-wide): 2.89MM Privately
Held
SIC: 3965 Fasteners, snap

(G-1880)
ROME FASTENER CORPORATION
257 Depot Rd (06460-3804)
P.O. Box 3013 (06460-0813)
PHONE.............................203 874-6719
Stanley F Reiter, *Pr*
Howard J Reiter, *
▲ EMP: 50 EST: 1945
SQ FT: 75,000
SALES (est): 4.8MM Privately Held
Web: www.romefast.com
SIC: 3999 3965 Forms: display, dress, and
show; Fasteners

(G-1881)
ROSS MFG & DESIGN LLC
124 Research Dr Ste A (06460-8571)
PHONE.............................203 878-0187
Donald Ross Mg, *Pt*
Donald Ross, *Mng Pt*
Christopher Ross, *Mng Pt*
EMP: 11 EST: 1987
SQ FT: 4,200
SALES (est): 128.94K Privately Held
SIC: 3599 Machine shop, jobbing and repair

(G-1882)
SANTEC CORPORATION
84 Old Gate Ln (06460-8622)
PHONE.............................203 878-1379
Laura Lombardo, *VP*
EMP: 12 EST: 1983
SQ FT: 14,000
SALES (est): 2.16MM Privately Held
Web: www.santec-printing-parts.com
SIC: 3555 Printing trades machinery

(G-1883)
SEI II INC
60 Commerce Park Ste 1 (06460-3513)
PHONE.............................203 877-8488
Jeffrey A Stein, *Pr*
EMP: 10 EST: 1981
SQ FT: 2,000
SALES (est): 2.43MM Privately Held
SIC: 8711 3841 Consulting engineer;
Surgical and medical instruments

(G-1884)
SHOW MOTION INC
1034 Bridgeport Ave (06460-3167)
PHONE.............................203 866-1866

William Mensching Senior, *Pr*
William Mensching, *
▲ **EMP:** 50 **EST:** 1994
SQ FT: 30,000
SALES (est): 9.99MM **Privately Held**
Web: www.showmotion.com
SIC: 3999 3531 1799 Theatrical scenery;
  Winches; Rigging, theatrical

(G-1885)
SILICON INTEGRATION INC
241 Research Dr Ste 9 (06460-8560)
PHONE...............................203 876-2844
Cary Cieciuch, *Pr*
EMP: 20 **EST:** 1997
SQ FT: 4,000
SALES (est): 2.49MM **Privately Held**
Web: www.siliconint.com
SIC: 8711 3672 Electrical or electronic
  engineering; Circuit boards, television and
  radio printed

(G-1886)
SONITEK CORPORATION
Also Called: Sonitek
84 Research Dr (06460-8523)
PHONE...............................203 878-9321
Robert James Bishop, *Pr*
Cheryl Ann Bishop, *
EMP: 30 **EST:** 1990
SQ FT: 7,500
SALES (est): 7.71MM **Privately Held**
Web: www.sonitek.com
SIC: 3548 3541 Welding apparatus;
  Ultrasonic metal cutting machine tools

(G-1887)
SPECIALTY COATING SYSTEMS INC
98 Quirk Rd (06460-3745)
PHONE...............................203 283-0087
EMP: 128
Web: www.scscoatings.com
SIC: 3674 Light emitting diodes
HQ: Specialty Coating Systems, Inc.
  7645 Woodland Dr
  Indianapolis IN 46278

(G-1888)
SPECIALTY TOOL COMPANY USA LLC
61 Erna Ave (06461-3118)
PHONE...............................203 874-2009
Richard E Fisk Mng, *Mgr*
EMP: 24 **EST:** 1968
SQ FT: 5,000
SALES (est): 860.49K **Privately Held**
Web: www.specialtytoolusa.com
SIC: 3724 Aircraft engines and engine parts

(G-1889)
SPECTRUM ASSOCIATES INC
440 New Haven Ave Ste 1 (06460-3629)
P.O. Box 470 (06460-0470)
PHONE...............................203 878-4618
Richard Meisenheimer, *Pr*
Linda Meisenheimer, *Sec*
Daniel Meisenheimer Iii, *VP*
EMP: 10 **EST:** 1969
SALES (est): 1.31MM **Privately Held**
Web: www.spectrumct.com
SIC: 3643 5084 5085 Current-carrying
  wiring services; Hydraulic systems
  equipment and supplies; Industrial supplies

(G-1890)
STEVENS MANUFACTURING CO INC
220 Rock Ln (06460-3853)

PHONE...............................203 878-2328
Stephen Fogler, *Pr*
Elizabeth Fogler, *
▲ **EMP:** 40 **EST:** 1957
SQ FT: 62,000
SALES (est): 10.33MM
SALES (corp-wide): 559.81MM **Privately Held**
Web: www.essexindustries.com
SIC: 3599 Machine shop, jobbing and repair
HQ: Essex Industries, Inc.
  7700 Gravois Rd
  Saint Louis MO 63123
  314 644-3000

(G-1891)
SUMMIT SCREW MACHINE CORP
49 Research Dr Ste 3 (06460-2864)
PHONE...............................203 693-2727
EMP: 8 **EST:** 2016
SALES (est): 173.62K **Privately Held**
Web: www.summit-os.com
SIC: 3599 Machine shop, jobbing and repair

(G-1892)
SURGIQUEST INC
488 Wheelers Farms Rd (06461-5801)
PHONE...............................203 799-2400
Kurt Azarbarzin, *
Christine Antalik, *
EMP: 83 **EST:** 2005
SALES (est): 11.69MM
SALES (corp-wide): 1.05B **Publicly Held**
Web: www.surgiquest.com
SIC: 3841 Surgical and medical instruments
PA: Conmed Corporation
  11311 Concept Blvd
  Largo FL 33773
  727 392-6464

(G-1893)
TALLINN FULFILLMENT LIMITED
Also Called: Osda
291 Pepes Farm Rd (06460-3671)
P.O. Box 3048 (06460-0848)
PHONE...............................203 878-2155
David H Ingraham, *Pr*
EMP: 25 **EST:** 1987
SQ FT: 14,000
SALES (est): 6.28MM **Privately Held**
Web: www.osda.com
SIC: 3672 Printed circuit boards

(G-1894)
THE GAS EQUIPMENT ENGINEERING CORPORATION
Also Called: Geeco
571 Plains Rd (06461-1731)
▼ **EMP:** 19
Web: www.gasequip.com
SIC: 3569 Gas producers, generators, and
  other gas related equipment

(G-1895)
THOMAS SPRING CO CONN INC
29 Seemans Ln (06460-4338)
PHONE...............................203 874-7030
Peter Tessitore, *Pr*
Gerry Tessitore, *VP*
EMP: 8 **EST:** 1961
SALES (est): 864.46K **Privately Held**
SIC: 3495 Mechanical springs, precision

(G-1896)
TINSLEY GROUP-PS&W INC (HQ)
Also Called: Olympic STEel-Ps&w
1 Eastern Steel Rd (06460-2837)

PHONE...............................919 742-5832
▲ **EMP:** 49 **EST:** 1996
SQ FT: 70,000
SALES (est): 44.31MM
SALES (corp-wide): 2.56B **Publicly Held**
SIC: 3531 7692 3441 Construction
  machinery; Welding repair; Fabricated
  structural metal
PA: Olympic Steel, Inc.
  22901 Mllcreek Blvd Ste 6
  Cleveland OH 44122
  216 292-3800

(G-1897)
VALLEY TOOL AND MFG LLC
Also Called: Milford Fabricating Co.
500 Bic Dr Bldg 2 (06461-1777)
PHONE...............................203 878-2476
EMP: 48
SALES (corp-wide): 92.77MM **Privately Held**
Web: www.valleytl.com
SIC: 3444 Sheet metalwork
HQ: Valley Tool And Manufacturing Llc
  132 Shelland St
  Milford CT 06461
  203 799-8800

(G-1898)
VALLEY TOOL AND MFG LLC (HQ)
Also Called: Milford Fabricating Co.
132 Shelland St (06461-1785)
P.O. Box 564 (06477-0564)
PHONE...............................203 799-8800
Phillip C Freidman, *CEO*
Howard Turner, *
▲ **EMP:** 49 **EST:** 2017
SQ FT: 36,000
SALES (est): 12MM
SALES (corp-wide): 92.77MM **Privately Held**
Web: www.valleytl.com
SIC: 3728 Aircraft parts and equipment, nec
PA: Harlow Aerostructures Llc
  1501 S Mclean Blvd
  Wichita KS 67213
  316 265-5268

(G-1899)
W & W MACHINE CO INC
90 Woodmont Rd (06460-2832)
▲ **EMP:** 10 **EST:** 1951
SQ FT: 7,000
SALES (est): 997.41K **Privately Held**
Web: www.wwmachine.com
SIC: 3599 Machine shop, jobbing and repair

Milldale
Hartford County

(G-1900)
CENTURY TOOL AND DESIGN INC
260 Canal St (06467)
P.O. Box 545 (06467-0545)
PHONE...............................860 621-6748
Michael Aldi, *Pr*
Raymond Koontz, *VP*
Charles Maxfield, *Sec*
EMP: 15 **EST:** 1975
SQ FT: 5,000
SALES (est): 433.27K **Privately Held**
Web: www.centtool.com
SIC: 3545 7389 Machine tool attachments
  and accessories; Design services

(G-1901)
JAY SONS SCREW MCH PDTS INC
197 Burritt St (06467)
P.O. Box 674 (06467-0674)
PHONE...............................860 621-0141
David Tellerico, *Pr*
John Spinello, *VP*
Joseph Tellerico Iii, *Sec*
EMP: 21 **EST:** 1945
SQ FT: 12,000
SALES (est): 490.46K **Privately Held**
Web: www.jaysons.com
SIC: 3451 Screw machine products

(G-1902)
MICRO INSERT INCORPORATED
183 Clark St (06467-6501)
P.O. Box 673 (06467-0673)
PHONE...............................860 621-5789
James Deangelo, *Pr*
Fred Douglas Smith, *Sec*
Kenneth Nelson, *Treas*
EMP: 9 **EST:** 1980
SQ FT: 15,000
SALES (est): 1.41MM **Privately Held**
Web: microinsertinc.blogspot.com
SIC: 3545 Tool holders

(G-1903)
TOFF INDUSTRY INC
323 Clark St (06467-6503)
P.O. Box 579 (06467-0579)
PHONE...............................860 378-0532
Harold Toffey, *Pr*
Dori Tapineau, *Off Mgr*
▲ **EMP:** 7 **EST:** 1980
SQ FT: 5,000
SALES (est): 738.14K **Privately Held**
Web: www.toffindustries.com
SIC: 2394 Awnings, fabric: made from
  purchased materials

Monroe
Fairfield County

(G-1904)
AMERICAN HEAT TREATING INC
16 Commerce Dr (06468-2601)
PHONE...............................203 268-1750
Peter J Wolcott, *Pr*
Charles Polatsek, *
John H Weiland, *
EMP: 45 **EST:** 1969
SQ FT: 32,000
SALES (est): 4.85MM **Privately Held**
Web: www.americanheattreating.com
SIC: 3398 Metal heat treating

(G-1905)
AXEL PLASTICS RES LABS INC
50 Cambridge Dr (06468-2661)
PHONE...............................718 672-8300
Franklin B K Axel, *CEO*
Jake Axel, *
Barbara Axel, *
◆ **EMP:** 32 **EST:** 1941
SQ FT: 4,500
SALES (est): 5.22MM **Privately Held**
Web: www.axelplastics.com
SIC: 2821 2992 Plastics materials and resins
  ; Lubricating oils and greases

(G-1906)
BIOMERICS LLC
Biomerics Nle
246 Main St Ste C (06468-1178)
PHONE...............................203 268-7238

Rich Rosselli, *Pr*
EMP: 60
Web: www.biomerics.com
SIC: 7389 2679 3479 3953 Engraving
   service; Labels, paper: made from
   purchased material; Name plates:
   engraved, etched, etc.; Stencils, painting
   and marking
HQ: Biomerics, Llc
   6030 W Harold Gatty Dr
   Salt Lake City UT 84116

(G-1907)
BML TOOL & MFG CORP
67 Enterprise Dr (06468-2674)
PHONE...............................203 880-9485
Philip Battaglia, *Pr*
Vincent Battaglia, *
EMP: 60 **EST:** 1968
SQ FT: 38,000
SALES (est): 5.3MM **Privately Held**
Web: 041390a.netsolhost.com
SIC: 3469 3544 Stamping metal for the trade
   ; Special dies, tools, jigs, and fixtures

(G-1908)
CARRUBBA INCORPORATED
500 Pepper St (06468-2672)
PHONE...............................203 878-0605
Duane Carrubba, *Pr*
▲ **EMP:** 55 **EST:** 1976
SALES (est): 12.15MM **Privately Held**
Web: www.carrubba.com
SIC: 2869 2844 2087 Perfumes, flavorings,
   and food additives; Perfumes, cosmetics
   and other toilet preparations; Flavoring
   extracts and syrups, nec

(G-1909)
CHURCH HILL CLASSICS LTD
Also Called: Diplomaframe.com
594 Pepper St (06468-2672)
PHONE...............................800 477-9005
▲ **EMP:** 70 **EST:** 1991
SQ FT: 25,000
SALES (est): 21.71MM **Privately Held**
Web: www.diplomaframe.com
SIC: 7699 2499 Picture framing, custom;
   Picture frame molding, finished

(G-1910)
CONNECTICUT PRECAST CORP
Also Called: CT Precast
555 Fan Hill Rd (06468-1336)
PHONE...............................203 268-8688
TOLL FREE: 800
Stephen Domizio, *Pr*
George T Domizio, *
EMP: 23 **EST:** 1952
SQ FT: 20,000
SALES (est): 5.34MM **Privately Held**
Web: www.ctprecast.com
SIC: 3272 Septic tanks, concrete

(G-1911)
CORNELL-CARR CO INC
626 Main St (06468-2808)
P.O. Box 253 (06468-0253)
PHONE...............................203 261-2529
Anton S Cornell, *Pr*
Philip H Gangnath, *
Margaret Carr, *Stockholder**
Stan Szarek, *
▲ **EMP:** 35 **EST:** 1955
SQ FT: 22,000
SALES (est): 8.88MM **Privately Held**
Web: www.cornell-carr.com
SIC: 3442 3647 3429 Metal doors; Boat and
   ship lighting fixtures; Marine hardware

(G-1912)
CUSTOM CFT KTCHENS BY RZIO BRO
8 Maple Dr (06468-1603)
PHONE...............................203 268-0271
Ralph Rizio, *Pr*
Mario E Rizio, *VP*
Angelina Rizio, *Sec*
Millie B Rizio, *Treas*
EMP: 18 **EST:** 1976
SQ FT: 18,000
SALES (est): 499.35K **Privately Held**
SIC: 2541 1799 1751 Counter and sink tops
   ; Counter top installation; Cabinet building
   and installation

(G-1913)
DR CHARLES ENVMTL CNSTR LLC
Also Called: D.R. Charles Envmtl Excav
189 Monroe Tpke (06468-2248)
PHONE...............................203 445-0412
David Charles, *Pt*
David Charles, *Managing Member*
EMP: 8 **EST:** 2001
SALES (est): 985.69K **Privately Held**
Web: www.drcharlesenviro.com
SIC: 2499 3531 8744 1794 Mulch, wood
   and bark; Plows: construction, excavating,
   and grading; Environmental remediation;
   Excavation and grading, building
   construction

(G-1914)
JURMAN METRICS INC
555 Hammertown Rd (06468-1310)
P.O. Box 223 (06468-0223)
PHONE...............................203 261-9388
David R Jurman, *Pr*
Rudolf Jurman, *VP*
Jeannette Jurman, *Sec*
EMP: 19 **EST:** 1973
SQ FT: 5,000
SALES (est): 844.36K **Privately Held**
Web: www.jurmanmetrics.com
SIC: 3829 Measuring and controlling
   devices, nec

(G-1915)
M CUBED TECHNOLOGIES INC
921 Main St (06468-2811)
PHONE...............................203 452-2333
Mark Meiberger, *Pr*
EMP: 20
SALES (corp-wide): 5.16B **Publicly Held**
Web: www.mmmt.com
SIC: 3599 Machine shop, jobbing and repair
HQ: M Cubed Technologies, Inc.
   31 Pecks Ln Ste 8
   Newtown CT 06470
   203 304-2940

(G-1916)
MC CANN BROS INC
Also Called: Mc Cann Brothers Baskets
490 Pepper St (06468-2673)
PHONE...............................203 335-8630
Fred Ryan, *Pr*
▲ **EMP:** 10 **EST:** 1975
SQ FT: 45,000
SALES (est): 1.89MM **Privately Held**
SIC: 5193 5023 2499 3269 Artificial flowers;
   Home furnishings, wicker, rattan or reed;
   Market baskets, wood; Flower pots, red
   earthenware

(G-1917)
MONROE RECYCL & AGGREGATES LLC
485 Pepper St (06468-2608)
PHONE...............................203 644-7748
EMP: 8 **EST:** 2018
SALES (est): 888.42K **Privately Held**
Web: www.monroeaggregate.com
SIC: 5032 1442 Aggregate; Construction
   sand and gravel

(G-1918)
NORTHEAST LASER ENGRAVING INC
Also Called: Nle
246 C Main St Rte 25 (06468-1178)
PHONE...............................203 268-7238
EMP: 40
Web: www.biomerics.com
SIC: 7389 2679 3479 3953 Engraving
   service; Labels, paper: made from
   purchased material; Name plates:
   engraved, etched, etc.; Stencils, painting
   and marking

(G-1919)
PRECISION ELECTRONIC ASSEMBLY
133 Bart Rd (06468-1108)
PHONE...............................203 452-1839
William Romaniello, *Pr*
EMP: 19 **EST:** 1992
SQ FT: 5,000
SALES (est): 921.3K **Privately Held**
Web: www.precisionelectronicassy.com
SIC: 3679 3575 Harness assemblies, for
   electronic use: wire or cable; Keyboards,
   computer, office machine

(G-1920)
REDCO AUDIO INC
515 Fan Hill Rd (06468-1336)
PHONE...............................203 502-7600
David Berliner, *Pr*
◆ **EMP:** 14 **EST:** 1989
SALES (est): 3.28MM **Privately Held**
Web: www.redco.com
SIC: 3496 3651 1761 Cable, uninsulated
   wire: made from purchased wire;
   Household audio equipment; Sheet metal
   work, nec

(G-1921)
SEYMOUR - SHERIDAN INCORPORATED
15 Commerce Dr (06468-2600)
PHONE...............................203 261-4009
EMP: 57 **EST:** 1965
SALES (est): 7.09MM **Privately Held**
Web: www.seymoursheridan.com
SIC: 3823 3599 Liquid level instruments,
   industrial process type; Bellows, industrial:
   metal

(G-1922)
STANCOR LP
Also Called: Stancor Pumps
515 Fan Hill Rd (06468-1336)
PHONE...............................203 268-7513
Bill Tipton, *Pt*
◆ **EMP:** 38 **EST:** 1985
SQ FT: 18,000
SALES (est): 4.95MM **Privately Held**
Web: www.flowsolutions.com
SIC: 3561 5084 Industrial pumps and parts;
   Pumps and pumping equipment, nec

(G-1923)
TEK-AIR SYSTEMS INC
600 Pepper St (06468-2671)
PHONE...............................203 791-1400
Arnold B Siemer, *Ch Bd*

Arnold B Siemer, *Ch*
Roger Bailey, *Sec*
Joseph Colletti Junior, *Pr*
▲ **EMP:** 39 **EST:** 2000
SALES (est): 2.83MM **Privately Held**
Web: www.accutrolllc.com
SIC: 3829 3823 3822 Measuring and
   controlling devices, nec; Process control
   instruments; Environmental controls

(G-1924)
TELENITY INC
755 Main St Ste 7 (06468-2830)
PHONE...............................203 445-2000
Ilhan Bagoren, *CEO*
Ilhan Bagoren, *Ch*
Esref Ozulkulu, *Sec*
EMP: 257 **EST:** 2000
SQ FT: 3,000
SALES (est): 4.97MM
SALES (corp-wide): 20.68MM **Privately Held**
Web: www.telenity.com
SIC: 7372 Application computer software
PA: I3g, Llc
   755 Main St Ste 7
   Monroe CT 06468
   203 445-2000

(G-1925)
THOUGHT OUT CO LLC
200 Main St Ste B (06468-1174)
PHONE...............................203 987-5452
Michael D Talmadge, *Prin*
EMP: 7 **EST:** 2013
SALES (est): 156.56K **Privately Held**
Web: www.thoughtout.biz
SIC: 3545 Machine tool accessories

Montville
New London County

(G-1926)
ALL-TIME MANUFACTURING CO INC
Bridge St (06353)
P.O. Box 37 (06353-0037)
PHONE...............................860 848-9258
David Brodie, *Pr*
EMP: 18 **EST:** 1946
SQ FT: 36,000
SALES (est): 2.16MM **Privately Held**
Web: www.alltimemfg.com
SIC: 3442 1751 3089 Storm doors or
   windows, metal; Window and door
   (prefabricated) installation; Window frames
   and sash, plastics

(G-1927)
RAND-WHITNEY RECYCLING LLC
370 Route 163 (06353)
PHONE...............................860 848-1900
Robert Kraft, *Pr*
◆ **EMP:** 100 **EST:** 2006
SALES (est): 23.55MM **Privately Held**
SIC: 2653 Boxes, corrugated: made from
   purchased materials
PA: Kraft Group Llc
   1 Patriot Pl
   Foxboro MA 02035

(G-1928)
RAND-WHTNEY CNTNRBARD LTD PRTN
370 Route 163 (06353-9702)
P.O. Box 336 (06353-0336)
PHONE...............................860 848-1900

EMP: 100 **EST:** 1993
SQ FT: 120,000
SALES (est): 47.93MM **Privately Held**
SIC: 2631 Container board
PA: Kraft Group Llc
  1 Patriot Pl
  Foxboro MA 02035

Moodus
Middlesex County

(G-1929)
BROWNELL & COMPANY INC
(PA)
  423 E Haddam Moodus Rd (06469-1025)
  P.O. Box 362 (06469-0362)
PHONE.....................860 873-8625
Anthony A Ferraz, *Pr*
Cynthia Stackowitz, *Sec*
Anthony A Ferraz, *Dir*
▲ **EMP:** 10 **EST:** 1844
SQ FT: 100,000
SALES (est): 817.31K
SALES (corp-wide): 817.31K **Privately
Held**
Web: www.brownellco.com
SIC: 2298 Twine, nec

Moosup
Windham County

(G-1930)
GRISWOLD LLC
Also Called: Griswold Rubber Company
  1 River St (06354-1309)
  P.O. Box 638 (06354-0638)
PHONE.....................845 986-2271
David Natorski, *CEO*
◆ **EMP:** 36 **EST:** 1949
SQ FT: 200,000
SALES (est): 9.36MM **Privately Held**
Web: www.rogerscorp.com
SIC: 3069 Sponge rubber and sponge
  rubber products
PA: Mechanical Rubber Products
  Company, Inc.
  77 Forester Ave Ste 1
  Warwick NY 10990

(G-1931)
VAPORIZER LLC
  245 Main St (06354-1249)
PHONE.....................860 564-7225
Gunther Bowerman, *Managing Member*
Joseph Ducci, *Managing Member*
Neil Cohen, *Managing Member*
◆ **EMP:** 20 **EST:** 2012
SALES (est): 9.85MM
SALES (corp-wide): 195.38MM **Privately
Held**
Web: www.vaporizericemelt.com
SIC: 2097 Manufactured ice
PA: American Rock Salt Company Llc
  5520 Geneseo Mt Morris Rd
  Mount Morris NY 14510
  585 991-6878

Morris
Litchfield County

(G-1932)
AMERICAN BACKPLANE INC
  355 Bantam Lake Rd (06763-1102)
PHONE.....................860 567-2360
Thomas L Zampini, *Pr*
Marie Zampini, *

EMP: 35 **EST:** 1982
SQ FT: 85,000
SALES (est): 5.14MM **Privately Held**
SIC: 3672 Printed circuit boards

(G-1933)
MK MILLWORK LLC
  234 Thomaston Rd (06763-1915)
PHONE.....................860 567-0173
EMP: 12 **EST:** 2017
SALES (est): 492.04K **Privately Held**
SIC: 3999 Manufacturing industries, nec

(G-1934)
SUN CORP
  27 Anderson Road Ext (06763-1910)
PHONE.....................860 567-0817
Edwin H Nearing Iii, *Pr*
EMP: 7 **EST:** 1978
SQ FT: 3,000
SALES (est): 501.53K **Privately Held**
SIC: 3451 Screw machine products

Mystic
New London County

(G-1935)
ACME WIRE PRODUCTS CO INC
  7 Broadway Avenue Ext (06355-2847)
  P.O. Box 218 (06355-0218)
PHONE.....................860 572-0511
Mary P Fitzgerald, *Pr*
Michael A Planeta, *
Edward Planeta Junior, *Sec*
▲ **EMP:** 50 **EST:** 1970
SQ FT: 73,000
SALES (est): 9.88MM **Privately Held**
Web: www.acmewire.com
SIC: 3496 7389 Miscellaneous fabricated
  wire products; Business services, nec

(G-1936)
**AQUA MASSAGE
INTERNATIONAL INC**
Also Called: A M I
  800 Flanders Rd Unit 1-3 (06355-1341)
  P.O. Box 808 (06340-0808)
PHONE.....................860 536-3735
David Cote, *Pr*
Hilaire Cote, *VP*
▲ **EMP:** 17 **EST:** 1989
SQ FT: 29,000
SALES (est): 2.31MM **Privately Held**
Web: www.aquamassage.com
SIC: 3949 Exercise equipment

(G-1937)
CARLIN MFG KITCHENS TO GO
  31 Masons Island Rd (06355-2938)
PHONE.....................413 519-2822
EMP: 7 **EST:** 2017
SALES (est): 83.18K **Privately Held**
Web: www.kitchenstogo.com
SIC: 3999 Manufacturing industries, nec

(G-1938)
J STEELE SERVICES LLC
  800 Flanders Rd Unit 5-1 (06355-1353)
PHONE.....................860 415-9720
James Lewis, *Pr*
EMP: 8 **EST:** 2009
SQ FT: 3,000
SALES (est): 976.9K **Privately Held**
Web: www.jsteeleservices.com
SIC: 3441 Fabricated structural metal

(G-1939)
MYSTIC KNOTWORK LLC
  25 Cottrell St (06355-2663)
PHONE.....................860 889-3793
EMP: 7 **EST:** 2014
SALES (est): 456.99K **Privately Held**
Web: www.mysticknotwork.com
SIC: 3961 Bracelets, except precious metal

(G-1940)
MYSTIC SEAPORT MUSEUM INC
Also Called: MYSTIC SEAPORT
  75 Greenmanville Ave (06355-1972)
  P.O. Box 6000 (06355-0990)
PHONE.....................860 572-0711
▲ **EMP:** 340 **EST:** 1930
SALES (est): 36.46MM **Privately Held**
Web: www.mysticseaport.org
SIC: 8412 5947 2731 Museum; Gift shop;
  Book publishing

(G-1941)
ORION MANUFACTURING LLC
  800 Flanders Rd Unit 4-8 (06355-1349)
PHONE.....................860 572-2921
EMP: 8 **EST:** 2009
SQ FT: 6,000
SALES (est): 845.37K **Privately Held**
SIC: 2431 Millwork

(G-1942)
SEAPORT MARINE INC
  2 Washington St (06355-2696)
PHONE.....................860 536-9651
Malcolm Robertson, *Pr*
EMP: 9 **EST:** 1914
SQ FT: 65,000
SALES (est): 865.57K **Privately Held**
Web: www.noankshipyard.com
SIC: 5551 3732 Marine supplies, nec;
  Motorized boat, building and repairing

(G-1943)
THOMAS S KLISE CO
  42 Denison Ave (06355-2728)
PHONE.....................860 536-4200
Margaret Mary Klise, *Pr*
Elizabeth Klise, *VP*
EMP: 7 **EST:** 1966
SQ FT: 10,000
SALES (est): 477.21K **Privately Held**
SIC: 3999 Education aids, devices and
  supplies

(G-1944)
VECTOR ENGINEERING INC
Also Called: Tylaska Marine Hardware
  800 Flanders Rd Unit 1-4 (06355-1341)
PHONE.....................860 572-0422
Tim Tylaska, *Pr*
▼ **EMP:** 15 **EST:** 1993
SQ FT: 70,000
SALES (est): 2.43MM **Privately Held**
Web: www.tylaska.com
SIC: 3429 8711 Hardware, nec; Engineering
  services

(G-1945)
VOICE GLANCE LLC
Also Called: Voice Glance
  12 Roosevelt Ave (06355-2809)
PHONE.....................800 260-3025
Chandrasekhar Naik, *Pr*
Thomas Longo, *VP*
EMP: 15 **EST:** 2013
SALES (est): 1.03MM **Privately Held**
Web: www.voiceglance.com
SIC: 7372 Business oriented computer
  software

Naugatuck
New Haven County

(G-1946)
**ADVANTAGE SHEET METAL
MFG LLC**
Also Called: Micro Matic
  51 Elm St (06770-4157)
PHONE.....................203 720-0929
EMP: 25 **EST:** 1997
SALES (est): 4.33MM **Privately Held**
SIC: 3444 Sheet metalwork

(G-1947)
**AHEAD COMMUNICATIONS
SYSTEMS**
  6 Rubber Ave (06770-4163)
PHONE.....................203 720-0227
Anton Kaeslin, *CEO*
EMP: 20 **EST:** 2001
SALES (est): 488.8K **Privately Held**
Web: www.aheadcommunications.com
SIC: 3661 4812 4813 Telephones and
  telephone apparatus; Radiotelephone
  communication; Telephone communication,
  except radio

(G-1948)
ANNE QUEEN WOODWORKING
  74 Great Hill Rd (06770-2224)
PHONE.....................203 720-1781
EMP: 14 **EST:** 1995
SQ FT: 5,000
SALES (est): 603.45K **Privately Held**
SIC: 2499 Decorative wood and woodwork

(G-1949)
BELLEVUE PRIVATE EQUITY INC
  39 Great Hill Rd (06770-2225)
PHONE.....................781 893-6721
James Stranberg, *Pr*
Dianne Ruggiero, *VP*
EMP: 8 **EST:** 2021
SALES (est): 168.07K **Privately Held**
SIC: 3357 Nonferrous wiredrawing and
  insulating

(G-1950)
**BUSINESS CARDS TOMORROW
INC**
Also Called: B C T
  69 Raytkwich Rd (06770-2223)
PHONE.....................203 723-5858
Jim Redwanz, *Pr*
EMP: 44
SALES (corp-wide): 455.38K **Privately
Held**
Web: www.evoprint.com
SIC: 2752 Commercial printing, lithographic
PA: Business Cards Tomorrow, Inc.
  2810 E Oklnd Prk Blvd # 308
  Fort Lauderdale FL 33306
  954 563-1224

(G-1951)
CADI CO INC (PA)
Also Called: Cadi Company
  60 Rado Dr (06770-2211)
  P.O. Box 1127 (06770-1127)
PHONE.....................203 729-1111
Rocco Capozzi, *Pr*
Dana M Capozzi, *
Peter Tatalias, *
▲ **EMP:** 33 **EST:** 1977
SQ FT: 33,000
SALES (est): 5.69MM
SALES (corp-wide): 5.69MM **Privately
Held**

▲ = Import ▼ = Export
◆ = Import/Export

Web: www.cadicompany.com
SIC: 3548 Electrode holders, for electric
welding apparatus

(G-1952)
CKS PACKAGING INC
10 Great Hill Rd (06770-2224)
P.O. Box 979 (06770-0979)
PHONE.................................203 729-0716
Bill Padgett, *Mgr*
EMP: 48
SALES (corp-wide): 483.16MM **Privately
Held**
Web: www.ckspackaging.com
SIC: 3089 Plastics containers, except foam
PA: C.K.S. Packaging, Inc.
350 Great Sw Pkwy
Atlanta GA 30336
404 691-8900

(G-1953)
CON-TEC INC
41 Raytkwich Rd (06770-2223)
PHONE.................................203 723-8942
Craig Corbett, *Pr*
EMP: 12 EST: 1984
SQ FT: 5,000
SALES (est): 2.18MM **Privately Held**
Web: www.con-tecinc.com
SIC: 3599 Flexible metal hose, tubing, and
bellows

(G-1954)
CONCENTRIC TOOL AND MFG
CO
550 Spring St (06770-1906)
PHONE.................................203 756-9145
EMP: 7 EST: 2019
SALES (est): 550.83K **Privately Held**
Web: www.concentrictoolct.com
SIC: 3999 Manufacturing industries, nec

(G-1955)
CULTURE FRESH FOODS INC
162 Spring St (06770-2921)
PHONE.................................203 632-8433
Thomas Moffitt, *CEO*
EMP: 15 EST: 2019
SALES (est): 2.74MM **Privately Held**
Web: www.culturefreshfoods.com
SIC: 2023 Dry, condensed and evaporated
dairy products

(G-1956)
EAST COAST METAL HOSE INC
41 Raytkwich Rd (06770-2223)
P.O. Box 978 (06770-0978)
PHONE.................................203 723-7459
Lloyd Corbett, *Pr*
Michelle Baranoski, *VP*
▼ EMP: 7 EST: 1979
SALES (est): 934.26K **Privately Held**
Web: www.con-tecinc.com
SIC: 3599 Hose, flexible metallic

(G-1957)
ELECTRIC CABLE
COMPOUNDS INC
108 Rado Dr (06770-2211)
PHONE.................................203 723-2590
Ida Fridland, *CEO*
Eugene Fridland, *
Anatoly Fridland, *
▼ EMP: 75 EST: 1988
SQ FT: 60,000
SALES (est): 21.88MM **Privately Held**
Web: www.electriccablecompounds.com
SIC: 2821 Plastics materials and resins

(G-1958)
FLABEG TECHNICAL GLASS US
CORP
451 Church St (06770-2834)
PHONE.................................203 729-5227
Torsten Khler, *Genl Mgr*
Vickie Waters, *
▲ EMP: 35 EST: 2008
SQ FT: 50,000
SALES (est): 4.97MM **Privately Held**
SIC: 3231 3229 3827 Products of
purchased glass; Optical glass; Mirrors,
optical

(G-1959)
FRANK SMITH
Also Called: Innovative Solutions
60 Great Hill Rd (06770-2224)
PHONE.................................203 729-6434
EMP: 48
SALES (est): 3.02MM **Privately Held**
SIC: 3823 Process control instruments

(G-1960)
GARMAC SCREW MACHINES
INC
70 Great Hill Rd (06770-2224)
P.O. Box 1338 (06770-1338)
PHONE.................................203 723-6911
Gerald Gardino, *Pr*
James Mac Burney, *VP*
Anthony Gardino, *Sec*
EMP: 16 EST: 1971
SQ FT: 5,000
SALES (est): 1.64MM **Privately Held**
SIC: 3451 Screw machine products

(G-1961)
GENERAL DATACOMM INDS INC
(PA)
6 Rubber Ave (06770-4163)
PHONE.................................203 729-0271
Howard S Modlin, *Ch Bd*
Howard S Modlin, *Ch Bd*
William G Henry, *VP Fin*
George M Gray, *VP Opers*
EMP: 11 EST: 1969
SQ FT: 360,000
SALES (est): 22.6MM
SALES (corp-wide): 22.6MM **Privately
Held**
SIC: 3661 Multiplex equipment, telephone
and telegraph

(G-1962)
H BARBER & SONS INC
15 Raytkwich Rd (06770-2223)
PHONE.................................203 729-9000
John H Barber, *Pr*
James P Barber, *VP*
◆ EMP: 20 EST: 1966
SQ FT: 5,000
SALES (est): 4.96MM **Privately Held**
Web: www.hbarber.com
SIC: 3531 Construction machinery

(G-1963)
HOWARD ENGINEERING LLC
687 Wooster St (06770-3135)
P.O. Box 6211 (06716-0211)
PHONE.................................203 729-5213
Lesley H Swirski, *CEO*
Lesley H Swirski, *CEO*
Brian N Howard, *
Holley E Duffy, *
EMP: 44 EST: 1956
SQ FT: 32,840
SALES (est): 5.23MM **Privately Held**
Web: www.howardengineering.com

SIC: 3469 3452 Stamping metal for the trade
; Rivets, metal

(G-1964)
ILLINOIS TOOL WORKS INC
Also Called: ITW Nutmeg
29 Rado Dr (06770-2220)
PHONE.................................203 720-1676
EMP: 10
SQ FT: 24,470
SALES (corp-wide): 15.93B **Publicly Held**
Web: www.itw.com
SIC: 3965 3469 3444 Fasteners, buttons,
needles, and pins; Metal stampings, nec;
Sheet metalwork
PA: Illinois Tool Works Inc.
155 Harlem Ave
Glenview IL 60025
847 724-7500

(G-1965)
INNOVATIVE FUSION INC
60 Great Hill Rd (06770-2224)
PHONE.................................203 729-3873
Daniel Budnik, *
▲ EMP: 40 EST: 1985
SQ FT: 8,000
SALES (est): 3.96MM **Privately Held**
Web: www.innovativefusion.com
SIC: 1799 3822 7692 Welding on site;
Liquid level controls, residential or
commercial heating; Welding repair

(G-1966)
INTERNATIONAL FRAMERS LLC
100 Water St 102 (06770)
PHONE.................................203 723-4564
Anthony Gallagher, *Managing Member*
EMP: 20 EST: 2015
SALES (est): 4.43MM **Privately Held**
Web: www.internationalframers.com
SIC: 2439 Timbers, structural: laminated
lumber

(G-1967)
ITW POWERTRAIN FASTENING
29 Rado Dr (06770-2220)
PHONE.................................203 720-1676
Jim Dara, *Pr*
EMP: 34 EST: 2017
SALES (est): 406.84K **Privately Held**
SIC: 3965 Fasteners

(G-1968)
K & E AUTO MACHINE L L C
Also Called: Mike's Engine Stand
628 Prospect St (06770-3120)
PHONE.................................203 723-7189
EMP: 10 EST: 2000
SALES (est): 541.87K **Privately Held**
SIC: 3599 Machine shop, jobbing and repair

(G-1969)
KAMMETAL INC (PA)
300 Great Hill Rd (06770-2000)
PHONE.................................718 722-9991
Samuel Kusack, *Pr*
Alastair Kusack, *VP*
EMP: 18 EST: 2008
SALES (est): 5.26MM **Privately Held**
Web: www.kammetal.com
SIC: 3446 Architectural metalwork

(G-1970)
LANXESS CORPORATION
400 Elm St (06770-4556)
P.O. Box 490 (06770-0490)
PHONE.................................203 714-8669
Richard Hooper, *Mgr*

EMP: 27
SALES (corp-wide): 8.4B **Privately Held**
Web: www.lanxess.com
SIC: 5169 2899 Chemicals and allied
products, nec; Chemical preparations, nec
HQ: Lanxess Corporation
111 Ridc Park West Dr
Pittsburgh PA 15275
412 809-1000

(G-1971)
MIL-CON INC
22 Great Hill Rd (06770-2224)
PHONE.................................630 595-2366
Bernard C Machura, *Ch Bd*
Micheal Machura, *
Doris Machura, *
EMP: 17 EST: 1983
SQ FT: 30,000
SALES (est): 231.58K **Privately Held**
Web: www.mil-coninc.com
SIC: 5063 5065 3613 3679 Electrical
supplies, nec; Electronic parts; Switchgear
and switchboard apparatus; Electronic
circuits

(G-1972)
MINI LLC
Also Called: Mini
66 Church St (06770-4112)
PHONE.................................203 464-5495
EMP: 8 EST: 2015
SALES (est): 592.8K **Privately Held**
SIC: 3572 Computer auxiliary storage units

(G-1973)
MJM MARGA LLC
28 Raytkwich Rd (06770-2222)
PHONE.................................203 729-0600
Mario Mazzettini, *Managing Member*
EMP: 7 EST: 2012
SALES (est): 993.16K **Privately Held**
Web: www.mjmmarga.com
SIC: 3469 Stamping metal for the trade

(G-1974)
MULTI-METAL
MANUFACTURING INC
Also Called: Precision Electronic Hardware
550 Spring St (06770-1906)
PHONE.................................203 723-8887
Ralph Minervino, *Pr*
Patrick Guarino, *
EMP: 101 EST: 1974
SQ FT: 31,000
SALES (est): 668.87K **Privately Held**
SIC: 3451 Screw machine products

(G-1975)
NAUGATUCK GLASS LLC ✪
451 Church St (06770-2834)
PHONE.................................203 729-5227
Shekhar Tewatia, *Managing Member*
Anshuman Mehrotra, *Managing Member*
EMP: 25 EST: 2022
SALES (est): 2.39MM **Privately Held**
SIC: 3231 Mirrored glass

(G-1976)
NAUGATUCK STAIR COMPANY
INC
51 Elm St (06770-4157)
P.O. Box 384 (06770-0384)
PHONE.................................203 729-7134
Henry Carrier, *Pr*
Ginette Carrier, *VP*
EMP: 11 EST: 1981
SQ FT: 7,000
SALES (est): 449.57K **Privately Held**

(PA)=Parent Co (HQ)=Headquarters
✪ = New Business established in last 2 years

Web: www.naugatuckstair.com
SIC: 2431 3446 Staircases and stairs, wood
; Stairs, staircases, stair treads:
prefabricated metal

(G-1977)
NEW CHRISTIE VENTURES LLC
31 Sheridan Dr Ste 31 (06770-2034)
PHONE............................203 720-9478
Chris Depaolo, *Mgr*
EMP: 35 EST: 1999
SQ FT: 5,000
SALES (est): 4.08MM **Privately Held**
SIC: 3089 Injection molding of plastics

(G-1978)
PALCO CONNECTOR INC
22 Great Hill Rd (06770-2224)
PHONE............................203 729-9090
▲ EMP: 47 EST: 1978
SALES (est): 7.64MM **Privately Held**
Web: www.phoenixofchicago.com
SIC: 3678 Electronic connectors

(G-1979)
PASTANCH LLC
Also Called: New Christie Ventures
31 Sheridan Dr (06770-2034)
PHONE............................203 720-9478
EMP: 30 EST: 1992
SQ FT: 52,000
SALES (est): 4.95MM **Privately Held**
Web: www.ncvpots.com
SIC: 7359 2821 3089 Equipment rental and
leasing, nec; Elastomers, nonvulcanizable
(plastics); Injection molding of plastics

(G-1980)
**PHOENIX COMPANY OF
CHICAGO INC (PA)**
22 Great Hill Rd (06770-2224)
PHONE............................630 595-2300
Michael B Machura, *Pr*
Bernard C Machura, *
Doris G Machura, *
▲ EMP: 60 EST: 1969
SQ FT: 550,000
SALES (est): 19.08MM
SALES (corp-wide): 19.08MM **Privately
Held**
Web: www.phoenixofchicago.com
SIC: 3678 5063 5065 Electronic connectors;
Electronic wire and cable; Connectors,
electronic

(G-1981)
PPI GAS DISTRIBUTION INC
33 Great Hill Rd (06770-2225)
P.O. Box 7056 (06712-0056)
EMP: 8 EST: 1995
SALES (est): 949.56K **Privately Held**
Web: www.ppigas.com
SIC: 3494 Valves and pipe fittings, nec

(G-1982)
QUALITY SHEET METAL INC
17 Clark Rd (06770-5097)
PHONE............................203 729-2244
Lawrence H Torto Junior, *Pr*
EMP: 28 EST: 1976
SQ FT: 10,000
SALES (est): 4.7MM **Privately Held**
Web: www.qualitysheetmetalinc.com
SIC: 3444 Sheet metal specialties, not
stamped

(G-1983)
RAM WELDING CO INC
Also Called: Ram Specialty Fabrication

93 Rado Dr (06770-2221)
PHONE............................203 720-0535
David J Murelli, *Pr*
Scott Murelli, *
Diane R Murelli, *
Joseph Nader, *
EMP: 50 EST: 1946
SQ FT: 40,000
SALES (est): 9.53MM **Privately Held**
Web: www.ramwelding.com
SIC: 3441 3444 7692 3353 Fabricated
structural metal; Sheet metalwork; Welding
repair; Aluminum sheet and strip

(G-1984)
**RELIABLE SILVER
CORPORATION**
302 Platts Mill Rd (06770-2036)
PHONE............................203 574-7732
Arlo Ellison, *Pr*
EMP: 11 EST: 2002
SALES (est): 5.05MM **Privately Held**
Web: www.reliablecorp.com
SIC: 3341 Secondary nonferrous metals

(G-1985)
**RONDO AMERICA
INCORPORATED**
Also Called: Rondo Packaging Systems
209 Great Hill Rd (06770-2096)
PHONE............................203 723-5831
James M Simkins, *Pr*
Morton H Simkins, *
Stephanie Simkins, *
EMP: 200 EST: 1949
SQ FT: 55,000
SALES (est): 31.15MM
SALES (corp-wide): 11.67K **Privately Held**
Web: www.rondopackaging.com
SIC: 2652 3569 Setup paperboard boxes;
Assembly machines, non-metalworking
PA: Simkins Corporation
1636 Valley Rd
Jenkintown PA 19046
215 739-4033

(G-1986)
SPERRY AUTOMATICS CO INC
1372 New Haven Rd (06770-5039)
P.O. Box 717 (06770-0717)
PHONE............................203 729-4589
Charles A Pugliese, *Pr*
David A Pugliese, *VP*
Richard Pugliese, *Treas*
EMP: 26 EST: 1963
SQ FT: 12,000
SALES (est): 798.34K **Privately Held**
Web: www.sperryautomatics.com
SIC: 3451 5085 3541 Screw machine
products; Industrial supplies; Machine tools,
metal cutting type

(G-1987)
STATELY STAIR CO INC
91 Great Hill Rd (06770-2227)
PHONE............................203 575-1966
Nick Pennacchio, *Pr*
Elizabeth Adams, *Genl Mgr*
EMP: 26 EST: 1991
SALES (est): 755.33K **Privately Held**
Web: www.statelystair.com
SIC: 2431 3446 Staircases and stairs, wood
; Stairs, staircases, stair treads:
prefabricated metal

(G-1988)
STRAN TECHNOLOGIES LLC
39 Great Hill Rd (06770-2225)
PHONE............................203 720-6500
EMP: 7 EST: 2013

SALES (est): 2.61MM
SALES (corp-wide): 12.59B **Publicly Held**
Web: www.strantech.com
SIC: 3229 Fiber optics strands
HQ: Ace And Company, Inc.
39 Great Hill Rd
Naugatuck CT 06770
203 720-6500

(G-1989)
SURFCTCOM INC
1453 New Haven Rd (06770-5040)
P.O. Box 1790 (06770-8601)
PHONE............................203 720-9209
Paul Vigario, *CEO*
EMP: 40 EST: 2003
SQ FT: 2,500
SALES (est): 6.49MM **Privately Held**
Web: www.surfct.com
SIC: 7299 3843 Information services,
consumer; Dental equipment and supplies

(G-1990)
THE YOFARM COMPANY
Also Called: Yocrunch
141a Sheridan Dr Ste A (06770-2038)
PHONE............................203 720-0000
EMP: 100
Web: www.yocrunch.com
SIC: 2026 Yogurt

(G-1991)
**UNIMETAL SURFACE FINISHING
LLC**
Also Called: Donham Crafts
15 E Waterbury Rd (06770-2138)
P.O. Box 1187 (06770-1187)
PHONE............................203 729-8244
Pat Hayden, *Pr*
EMP: 38
SALES (corp-wide): 20.44MM **Privately
Held**
Web: www.unimetal.com
SIC: 3471 Electroplating of metals or
formed products
PA: Unimetal Surface Finishing, Llc
135 S Main St
Thomaston CT 06787
860 283-0271

(G-1992)
**VITEK RESEARCH
CORPORATION**
33 Sheridan Dr (06770-2039)
P.O. Box 315 (06418-0315)
PHONE............................203 735-1813
Robert Evans, *Pr*
EMP: 13 EST: 1968
SQ FT: 10,000
SALES (est): 1.81MM **Privately Held**
Web: www.vitekres.com
SIC: 3479 8732 Coating of metals and
formed products; Business research service

(G-1993)
VIVAX MEDICAL CORPORATION
54 Great Hill Rd (06770-2253)
PHONE............................203 729-0514
Rick Swanson, *Pr*
Harold Lash, *Sec*
Mark Plaumann, *CEO*
EMP: 17 EST: 1984
SALES (est): 2.37MM **Privately Held**
Web: www.vivaxmedical.com
SIC: 7352 3841 Medical equipment rental;
Medical instruments and equipment, blood
and bone work

New Britain
Hartford County

(G-1994)
A-1 MACHINING CO LLC
Also Called: A-1 Machining Co.
235 John Downey Dr (06051-2905)
PHONE............................860 223-6420
David S Bovenizer, *CEO*
Thomas Daily, *
Van H Mai, *Sec*
◆ EMP: 52 EST: 1975
SQ FT: 36,800
SALES (est): 10.16MM
SALES (corp-wide): 41.96MM **Privately
Held**
Web: www.a1machining.com
SIC: 3724 3728 3621 Aircraft engines and
engine parts; Aircraft parts and equipment,
nec; Power generators
PA: Lionheart Holdings Llc
54 Friends Ln Ste 125
Newtown PA 18940
215 283-8400

(G-1995)
**ACME MONACO CORPORATION
(PA)**
75 Winchell Rd (06052-1097)
PHONE............................860 224-1349
Michael J Karabin, *CEO*
Thomas Sebastian, *
Lucas Karabin, *
Rebecca Karabin-ahern, *Ex VP*
▲ EMP: 125 EST: 1955
SQ FT: 37,520
SALES (est): 24.94MM
SALES (corp-wide): 24.94MM **Privately
Held**
Web: www.acmemonaco.com
SIC: 3841 3843 3469 3493 Surgical and
medical instruments; Orthodontic appliances
; Stamping metal for the trade; Steel
springs, except wire

(G-1996)
ADAM Z GOLAS (PA)
Also Called: Zag Machine & Tool Co
99 John Downey Dr (06051-2916)
P.O. Box 1120 (06050-1120)
PHONE............................860 224-7178
Adam Z Golas, *Owner*
EMP: 8 EST: 1967
SQ FT: 50,000
SALES (est): 2.17MM
SALES (corp-wide): 2.17MM **Privately
Held**
SIC: 3547 Rolling mill machinery

(G-1997)
ADKINS PRINTING COMPANY
Also Called: Adkins
40 South St Ste 2 (06051-3574)
P.O. Box 2440 (06050-2440)
PHONE............................800 228-9745
Scott Pechout, *Pr*
EMP: 13 EST: 1880
SQ FT: 18,000
SALES (est): 857.83K **Privately Held**
Web: www.adkinsinc.net
SIC: 2752 5943 5112 2789 Offset printing;
Office forms and supplies; Office supplies,
nec; Bookbinding and related work

(G-1998)
ADMILL MACHINE CO LLC
150 John Downey Dr (06051-2904)
PHONE............................860 356-0330

EMP: 134
SIC: 3728 Aircraft parts and equipment, nec

(G-1999)
AMMUNITION STOR COMPONENTS LLC
206 Newington Ave (06051-2130)
PHONE.............................860 225-3548
Barry Bergen, *Mgr*
EMP: 8 EST: 2011
SALES (est): 932.49K **Privately Held**
Web: www.ammosc.com
SIC: 3949 Sporting and athletic goods, nec

(G-2000)
ANMOR MACHINING COMPANY LLC
20 Hudson Pl (06051-4115)
PHONE.............................860 224-7774
EMP: 12
Web: www.anmorllc.com
SIC: 3599 Machine shop, jobbing and repair

(G-2001)
ARKADIA PLASTICS INC
315 John Downey Dr (06051-2907)
PHONE.............................860 612-0556
EMP: 28 EST: 2006
SALES (est): 2.13MM **Privately Held**
Web: www.arkadiaplastics.com
SIC: 2821 Plastics materials and resins

(G-2002)
ATLAS CONCRETE PRODUCTS INC
65 Burritt St (06053-4048)
PHONE.............................860 224-2244
TOLL FREE: 800
James Pryor, *Pr*
EMP: 18 EST: 1983
SQ FT: 24,000
SALES (est): 2.56MM **Privately Held**
Web: www.atlasconcrete.com
SIC: 3272 Concrete products, precast, nec

(G-2003)
ATLAS METALLIZING INC
5 East St (06051-3609)
PHONE.............................860 827-9777
Elizabeth Mierkiewicz, *Pr*
▲ EMP: 19 EST: 1994
SQ FT: 16,000
SALES (est): 2.08MM **Privately Held**
Web: www.thegriffnetwork.com
SIC: 3081 Plastics film and sheet

(G-2004)
AVNA INC (PA)
200 Ellis St (06051-3523)
P.O. Box 2470 (06050-2470)
PHONE.............................860 225-8707
EMP: 107 EST: 1968
SALES (est): 21.99MM
SALES (corp-wide): 21.99MM **Privately Held**
Web: www.avna.com
SIC: 3469 3542 Stamping metal for the trade
; Machine tools, metal forming type

(G-2005)
B & F DESIGN INCORPORATED
120 Production Ct (06051-2912)
PHONE.............................860 357-4317
EMP: 50
Web: b-and-f-design-inc.hub.biz
SIC: 8711 7389 3721 Designing: ship, boat,
machine, and product; Hand tool designers;
Aircraft

(G-2006)
B & F MACHINE CO INC (PA)
370 John Downey Dr (06051-2908)
PHONE.............................860 225-6349
Carl Francalangia, *Pr*
Carla Francalangia, *
Mario Francalangia, *
Cathy Hayden, *
▲ EMP: 158 EST: 1972
SQ FT: 37,400
SALES (est): 25.48MM
SALES (corp-wide): 25.48MM **Privately Held**
Web: www.bfmachine.com
SIC: 3599 7692 Machine shop, jobbing and
repair; Welding repair

(G-2007)
BARILE PRINTERS LLC
43 Viets St (06053-3988)
P.O. Box 2628 (06050-2628)
PHONE.............................860 224-0127
Joseph Barile, *Managing Member*
EMP: 13 EST: 1918
SQ FT: 3,000
SALES (est): 718.41K **Privately Held**
Web: www.barileprinters.com
SIC: 2752 5999 5099 Offset printing; Alarm
and safety equipment stores; Firearms and
ammunition, except sporting

(G-2008)
BLACK & DECKER (US) INC
Also Called: Stanley Black and Decker
700 Stanley Dr (06053-1679)
PHONE.............................860 225-5111
EMP: 9
SALES (corp-wide): 16.95B **Publicly Held**
Web: www.blackanddecker.com
SIC: 3546 3634 Power-driven handtools;
Electric household cooking appliances
HQ: Black & Decker (U.S.) Inc.
1000 Stanley Dr
New Britain CT 06053
860 225-5111

(G-2009)
BRIDGESTONE RET OPERATIONS LLC
Also Called: Firestone
55 Chestnut St (06051-2601)
PHONE.............................860 229-0348
Ethan Turney, *Mgr*
EMP: 10
Web: www.bridgestoneamericas.com
SIC: 5531 7534 Automotive tires;
Rebuilding and retreading tires
HQ: Bridgestone Retail Operations, Llc
333 E Lake St Ste 300
Bloomingdale IL 60108
630 259-9000

(G-2010)
CENTRAL CONN CMMUNICATIONS LLC
Also Called: New Britain Herald , The
1 Court St Fl 4 (06051-2259)
P.O. Box 1090 (06050-1090)
PHONE.............................860 225-4601
EMP: 80 EST: 2009
SALES (est): 7.93MM **Privately Held**
Web: www.centralctcommunications.com
SIC: 2711 Newspapers, publishing and
printing

(G-2011)
CENTRAL PALLET & BOX CO LLC
271 John Downey Dr (06051-2905)
PHONE.............................860 224-4416
Michael T Hannifan, *Owner*
EMP: 12 EST: 1984
SQ FT: 12,000
SALES (est): 604.22K **Privately Held**
Web: www.humanesocietybaycounty.org
SIC: 2448 Pallets, wood

(G-2012)
CONNECTICUT SHOTGUN MANUFACTURING CO
Also Called: Galazan's Gun Shop
100 Burritt St (06053-4004)
P.O. Box 1692 (06050-1692)
PHONE.............................860 225-6581
▲ EMP: 60 EST: 1976
SALES (est): 4.88MM **Privately Held**
Web: www.connecticutshotgun.co
SIC: 5941 3484 Firearms; Shotguns or
shotgun parts, 30 mm. and below

(G-2013)
CONNECTICUT VALLEY BINDERY
1 Hartford Sq Ste 1w (06052-1179)
PHONE.............................860 229-7637
Kevin Hubert, *Pr*
Tracy Hubert, *
Dan Valente, *
▼ EMP: 30 EST: 1980
SQ FT: 37,598
SALES (est): 2.21MM **Privately Held**
Web: www.connvalleybindery.com
SIC: 2789 Binding only: books, pamphlets,
magazines, etc.

(G-2014)
CONTINENTAL MACHINE TL CO INC
533 John Downey Dr (06051-2435)
PHONE.............................860 223-2896
Tadeusz Malkowski, *Pr*
Wanda Malkowski, *
EMP: 97 EST: 1983
SQ FT: 24,800
SALES (est): 8.57MM **Privately Held**
Web: www.continentalmachinetool.com
SIC: 3599 3714 3728 3484 Machine shop,
jobbing and repair; Motor vehicle parts and
accessories; Aircraft parts and equipment,
nec; Machine guns or machine gun parts,
30 mm. and below

(G-2015)
CONTORQ COMPONENTS LLC
433 John Downey Dr (06051-2918)
PHONE.............................860 225-3366
John Mccarthy Junior, *Pr*
EMP: 11 EST: 2010
SALES (est): 1.92MM **Privately Held**
Web: www.nemetalworks.com
SIC: 3452 Bolts, nuts, rivets, and washers

(G-2016)
CREED 20 LLC ✪
Also Called: Creed Monarch
1 Pucci Park (06051)
PHONE.............................860 826-4004
EMP: 8 EST: 2023
SALES (est): 589.26K **Privately Held**
SIC: 3451 Screw machine products

(G-2017)
CREED ASSETS INC
Also Called: Creed Monarch
1 Pucci Park (06051)
P.O. Box 550 (06050-0550)
PHONE.............................860 225-7884

Richard Creed, *Pr*
David Creed, *
Don Creed, *
Deborah Boynton, *
▲ EMP: 275 EST: 1952
SQ FT: 150,000
SALES (est): 49.93MM **Privately Held**
Web: www.creedmonarch.com
SIC: 3451 Screw machine products

(G-2018)
CW SOLUTIONS LLC ✪
200 Myrtle St (06053-4160)
PHONE.............................860 229-7700
William Green, *Pr*
EMP: 100 EST: 2022
SALES (est): 5MM **Privately Held**
Web: www.cwresources.org
SIC: 2099 4789 0782 7349 Food
preparations, nec; Transportation services,
nec; Lawn and garden services; Building
maintenance services, nec

(G-2019)
CYIENT DEFENSE SERVICES INC
Also Called: Tooling Division
120 Production Ct (06051-2912)
PHONE.............................860 357-4317
Ralph Noyes, *Brnch Mgr*
EMP: 50
Web: www.cyient.com
SIC: 8711 3721 7389 Designing: ship, boat,
machine, and product; Aircraft; Hand tool
designers
HQ: Cyient Defense Services, Inc.
15300 Pk Of Commerce Blvd
Jupiter FL 33478
860 729-8179

(G-2020)
DAY MACHINE SYSTEMS INC
221 South St Bldg F2 (06051-3650)
P.O. Box 2667 (06050-2667)
PHONE.............................860 229-3440
Jim Kostin, *Pr*
EMP: 13 EST: 1984
SQ FT: 14,500
SALES (est): 2.55MM **Privately Held**
Web: www.day-machine-systems.com
SIC: 3451 3559 Screw machine products;
Automotive related machinery

(G-2021)
DBF INDUSTRIES INC
Also Called: DB&f Industries
145 Edgewood Ave (06051-4109)
PHONE.............................860 827-8283
Carl Francalangia, *Pr*
Federico Bragoni, *
EMP: 13 EST: 1979
SQ FT: 7,000
SALES (est): 477.84K **Privately Held**
SIC: 7692 Brazing

(G-2022)
DEBURRING LABORATORIES INC
206 Newington Ave (06051-2130)
PHONE.............................860 829-6300
Douglas Narins, *Pr*
Nina Narins, *
EMP: 18 EST: 1961
SALES (est): 478.08K **Privately Held**
SIC: 3541 3471 Deburring machines;
Plating and polishing

(G-2023)
**DSO MANUFACTURING
COMPANY INC**
390 John Downey Dr (06051-2932)
PHONE...........................860 224-2641
Carl Bernard Deleo, *Pr*
Tina Joan Deleo, *
EMP: 25 **EST:** 1947
SQ FT: 35,000
SALES (est): 3.99MM **Privately Held**
Web: www.dsomfg.com
SIC: 3599 Machine shop, jobbing and repair

(G-2024)
E R HITCHCOCK COMPANY
Also Called: Hitchcock Printers
191 John Downey Dr (06051-2945)
PHONE...........................860 229-2024
Edward R Young, *Pr*
Dane Baclaski, *
Constance M Young, *Stockholder**
EMP: 33 **EST:** 1895
SQ FT: 22,000
SALES (est): 4.98MM **Privately Held**
Web: www.hitchcockprinting.com
SIC: 2752 2791 2789 Offset printing;
    Typesetting; Bookbinding and related work

(G-2025)
EK-RIS CABLE COMPANY INC
Also Called: Ek-Ris Cable
503 Burritt St Apt 7 (06053-3627)
PHONE...........................860 223-4327
Gary J Robinson, *Pr*
Dolores M Robinson, *
Charles Wusterbarth, *
EMP: 25 **EST:** 1987
SALES (est): 672.49K **Privately Held**
SIC: 3643 Current-carrying wiring services

(G-2026)
ENJET AERO NEW BRITAIN LLC
150 John Downey Dr (06051-2904)
PHONE...........................860 356-0330
Bruce Breckenridge, *CEO*
Christopher Ferraro, *
EMP: 134 **EST:** 2019
SQ FT: 63,000
SALES (est): 22.97MM
SALES (corp-wide): 78.96MM **Privately
Held**
Web: www.enjetaero.com
SIC: 3728 Aircraft parts and equipment, nec
PA: Enjet Aero, Llc
    9401 Indian Creek Pkwy
    Overland Park KS 66210
    913 717-7396

(G-2027)
EZ WELDING LLC
244 Garry Dr (06052-1106)
PHONE...........................860 707-3100
EMP: 14
SALES (corp-wide): 554.96K **Privately
Held**
Web: www.ezweldingct.com
SIC: 7692 Welding repair
PA: Ez Welding Llc
    47 Saint Claire Ave
    New Britain CT 06051
    860 707-3099

(G-2028)
**GUIDA-SEIBERT DAIRY
COMPANY (HQ)**
Also Called: Guida's Dairy
433 Park St (06051-2700)
PHONE...........................800 832-8929
TOLL FREE: 800

Michael Young, *Pr*
Michael J A Guida, *
James Guida, *
Pat Panko, *
Joel Clark, *
EMP: 225 **EST:** 1886
SALES (est): 99.85MM
SALES (corp-wide): 24.52B **Privately Held**
Web: www.garelickfarms.com
SIC: 2026 2033 5143 5149 Milk processing
    (pasteurizing, homogenizing, bottling); Fruit
    juices: packaged in cans, jars, etc.; Dairy
    products, except dried or canned; Juices
PA: Dairy Farmers Of America, Inc.
    1405 N 98th St
    Kansas City KS 66111
    816 801-6455

(G-2029)
HAJAN LLC
788 W Main St (06053-3856)
PHONE...........................860 223-2005
Mukhtar Ahmed, *Prin*
EMP: 10 **EST:** 2009
SALES (est): 689.11K **Privately Held**
SIC: 2869 Industrial organic chemicals, nec

(G-2030)
**HSB AIRCRAFT COMPONENTS
LLC**
80 Production Ct (06051-2917)
P.O. Box 342 (06023-0342)
PHONE...........................860 505-7349
Henry Wasik, *Managing Member*
EMP: 12 **EST:** 2006
SQ FT: 5,000
SALES (est): 407.39K **Privately Held**
SIC: 3724 Aircraft engines and engine parts

(G-2031)
ID MAIL SYSTEMS INC
515 John Downey Dr (06051-2435)
PHONE...........................860 344-3333
▲ **EMP:** 15 **EST:** 1997
SQ FT: 15,000
SALES (est): 4.05MM **Privately Held**
Web: www.idparcelandmail.com
SIC: 3579 3535 Mailing, letter handling, and
    addressing machines; Conveyors and
    conveying equipment

(G-2032)
INTEGRA-CAST INC
265 Newington Ave (06051-2129)
PHONE...........................860 225-7600
David Arcesi, *Pr*
Jennifer C Arcesi, *
EMP: 62 **EST:** 1984
SQ FT: 30,000
SALES (est): 9.8MM **Privately Held**
Web: www.integracast.com
SIC: 3365 3599 3364 3324 Aerospace
    castings, aluminum; Machine shop, jobbing
    and repair; Nonferrous die-castings except
    aluminum; Steel investment foundries

(G-2033)
**INTERNATIONAL AUTO ENTPS
INC**
Also Called: Production Dept
21 Dewey St (06051-2007)
PHONE...........................860 223-7979
EMP: 15
SALES (corp-wide): 1.96MM **Privately
Held**
Web: www.erareplicas.com
SIC: 3714 Motor vehicle parts and
    accessories

PA: International Automobile Enterprises,
    Inc.
    608 E Main St Ste 612
    New Britain CT 06051
    860 224-0253

(G-2034)
**INTERNATIONAL AUTO ENTPS
INC (PA)**
Also Called: ERA Replica Automobiles
608 E Main St Ste 612 (06051-2074)
PHONE...........................860 224-0253
Philip R Gaudette, *Pr*
Thomas Portante, *VP*
Robert Putnam. *Sec*
EMP: 13 **EST:** 1967
SQ FT: 4,000
SALES (est): 1.96MM
SALES (corp-wide): 1.96MM **Privately
Held**
Web: www.erareplicas.com
SIC: 3714 5531 Motor vehicle parts and
    accessories; Auto and home supply stores

(G-2035)
**IRWIN INDUSTRIAL TOOL
COMPANY**
700 Stanley Dr 2nd Fl (06053-1679)
PHONE...........................860 438-3460
EMP: 8 **EST:** 2017
SALES (est): 476.11K
SALES (corp-wide): 16.95B **Publicly Held**
Web: www.irwintools.com
SIC: 3423 Hand and edge tools, nec
PA: Stanley Black & Decker, Inc.
    1000 Stanley Dr
    New Britain CT 06053
    860 225-5111

(G-2036)
K AND R PRECISION GRINDING
39 John St (06051-2724)
PHONE...........................860 505-8030
Marc W Begin, *Admn*
EMP: 11 **EST:** 2017
SALES (est): 454.54K **Privately Held**
SIC: 3999 Grinding and pulverizing of
    materials, nec

(G-2037)
**LEOS KITCHEN AND STAIR
CORP**
48 John St (06051-2725)
PHONE...........................860 225-7363
Jean-paul Ayotte, *Pr*
EMP: 8 **EST:** 1950
SQ FT: 2,000
SALES (est): 660K **Privately Held**
Web: www.leoskit.com
SIC: 2434 2541 2431 Wood kitchen cabinets
    ; Table or counter tops, plastic laminated;
    Staircases and stairs, wood

(G-2038)
**LINK MECHANICAL SERVICES
INC**
Also Called: Honeywell Authorized Dealer
60 Production Ct (06051-2912)
P.O. Box 364 (06050-0364)
PHONE...........................860 826-5880
EMP: 33 **EST:** 1993
SALES (est): 7.4MM **Privately Held**
Web: www.justcalllink.com
SIC: 1711 3444 Mechanical contractor;
    Sheet metalwork

(G-2039)
MARSAM METAL FINISHING CO
206 Newington Ave (06051-2130)
P.O. Box 1975 (06050-1975)
PHONE...........................860 826-5489
EMP: 25 **EST:** 1997
SALES (est): 2.89MM **Privately Held**
Web: www.marsammetalfinishing.com
SIC: 3471 Electroplating of metals or
    formed products

(G-2040)
MARTIN ROSOLS INC
45 Grove St (06053-4198)
PHONE...........................860 223-2707
Robert C Rosol, *Ch Bd*
Robert C Rosol, *Pr*
Karen M Rosol, *
EMP: 25 **EST:** 1929
SQ FT: 85,000
SALES (est): 1.97MM **Privately Held**
Web: www.martinrosolsinc.com
SIC: 2011 5421 2013 Meat packing plants;
    Food and freezer plans, meat; Bologna,
    from purchased meat

(G-2041)
ME PRODUCTS LLC
30 Peter Ct (06051-3545)
PHONE...........................860 832-8960
Richard R Knight, *Managing Member*
John Bogart, *
▲ **EMP:** 40 **EST:** 1971
SQ FT: 4,000
SALES (est): 8.46MM **Privately Held**
Web: www.monroeengineering.com
SIC: 3648 Airport lighting fixtures: runway
    approach, taxi, or ramp

(G-2042)
**METAL IMPROVEMENT
COMPANY LLC**
E/M Coatings Solutions
1 John Downey Dr (06051-2901)
PHONE...........................860 224-9148
Eric Altomare, *Mgr*
EMP: 28
SQ FT: 10,000
SALES (corp-wide): 2.56B **Publicly Held**
Web: www.imrtest.com
SIC: 3398 Shot peening (treating steel to
    reduce fatigue)
HQ: Metal Improvement Company, Llc
    80 E Rte 4 Ste 310
    Paramus NJ 07652
    201 843-7800

(G-2043)
**METALFORM ACQUISITION LLC
(PA)**
Also Called: Metalform Company
555 John Downey Dr (06051-2435)
PHONE...........................860 224-2630
John P Mccarthy, *Prin*
Martin C Mccarthy, *Ch Bd*
EMP: 19 **EST:** 1968
SQ FT: 15,000
SALES (est): 2.3MM
SALES (corp-wide): 2.3MM **Privately Held**
Web: www.drawnshells.com
SIC: 3965 3469 3452 Fasteners, hooks and
    eyes; Stamping metal for the trade; Nuts,
    metal

(G-2044)
**METALLURGICAL PROCESSING
INCORPORATED**
Also Called: M.P.I.
68 Arthur St (06053-3902)

P.O. Box 2320 (06050-2320)
PHONE....................860 224-2648
EMP: 60 **EST:** 1957
SALES (est): 9.82MM **Privately Held**
Web: www.mpimetaltreating.com
SIC: 3398 Metal heat treating

(G-2045)
MICRO FARMINGTON SUB LLC
206 Newington Ave (06051-2130)
PHONE....................860 677-2646
Robert Mongell, *Managing Member*
Jerry Sirois, *
▼ **EMP:** 92 **EST:** 1947
SALES (est): 8.46MM **Privately Held**
Web: www.jfftool.com
SIC: 3724 Aircraft engines and engine parts

(G-2046)
NEW ENGLAND CABINET CO
580 E Main St (06051-2042)
PHONE....................860 225-8645
Joel Salwocki, *Pr*
EMP: 20 **EST:** 1985
SQ FT: 20,000
SALES (est): 868.25K **Privately Held**
Web: www.necabinetco.com
SIC: 2541 2431 Cabinets, except refrigerated: show, display, etc.: wood; Millwork

(G-2047)
ORCA INC
199 Whiting St (06051-3146)
PHONE....................860 223-4180
Gregory P Goguen, *Prin*
Gregory P Goguen, *Prin*
Kathleen Goguen, *
EMP: 30 **EST:** 1984
SQ FT: 60,000
SALES (est): 6.87MM **Privately Held**
Web: www.orca-mfg.com
SIC: 3466 Closures, stamped metal

(G-2048)
OXFORD INDUSTRIES CONN INC
Also Called: Oxford Polymers
221 South St (06051-3627)
PHONE....................860 225-3700
Nicholas L Defelice, *Pr*
David Gambardella, *
▲ **EMP:** 24 **EST:** 1980
SQ FT: 100,000
SALES (est): 6.06MM **Privately Held**
Web: www.oxfordpolymers.com
SIC: 2821 Thermoplastic materials

(G-2049)
PAINT & POWDER WORKS LLC
35 M And S Ct (06051-2320)
PHONE....................860 225-2019
Fred H Sillner, *Mgr*
EMP: 10 **EST:** 2005
SALES (est): 960.39K **Privately Held**
Web: www.ppw4services.com
SIC: 3479 Coating of metals and formed products

(G-2050)
PARKER-HANNIFIN CORPORATION
Fluid Controls Division
95 Edgewood Ave (06051-4151)
P.O. Box 1450 (06050-1450)
PHONE....................860 827-2300
Larry Ryba, *Brnch Mgr*
EMP: 250
SALES (corp-wide): 19.07B **Publicly Held**
Web: www.parker.com

SIC: 3491 3492 Solenoid valves; Fluid power valves and hose fittings
PA: Parker-Hannifin Corporation
6035 Parkland Blvd
Cleveland OH 44124
216 896-3000

(G-2051)
PETER PAUL ELECTRONICS CO INC
480 John Downey Dr (06051-2910)
P.O. Box 1180 (06050-1180)
PHONE....................860 229-4884
Paul S Mangiafico, *Pr*
Michael Mangiafico Ii, *Pr*
Mark Mangiafico, *
▲ **EMP:** 140 **EST:** 1947
SQ FT: 77,000
SALES (est): 18.54MM **Privately Held**
Web: www.peterpaul.com
SIC: 3491 Solenoid valves

(G-2052)
POLAMER PRECISION INC
105 Alton Brooks Way (06053-3359)
PHONE....................860 259-6200
Chris Galik, *CEO*
Chris Galik, *Pr*
Andrew Dulnik, *
Mario Giooo, *
EMP: 175 **EST:** 1997
SQ FT: 3,200
SALES (est): 24.2MM **Privately Held**
Web: www.polamer.us
SIC: 3728 Aircraft parts and equipment, nec

(G-2053)
POLAR CORP
33 Columbus Blvd (06051-2243)
PHONE....................860 225-6000
Val Zurawlew, *VP*
EMP: 7 **EST:** 2018
SALES (est): 279.56K **Privately Held**
Web: www.polarcorporation.com
SIC: 3724 Aircraft engines and engine parts

(G-2054)
POLAR CORPORATION
59 High St Ste 11 (06051-2279)
PHONE....................860 223-7891
Andrew Kowalski, *CEO*
Andrew Kowalski, *Pr*
Kazimiera Zamojska Kowalski, *
EMP: 45 **EST:** 1980
SQ FT: 15,000
SALES (est): 8.04MM **Privately Held**
Web: www.polarcorporation.com
SIC: 3724 3812 3728 Aircraft engines and engine parts; Search and navigation equipment; Aircraft parts and equipment, nec

(G-2055)
PRECISION GRINDING COMPANY
33 Charles St (06051-2162)
PHONE....................860 229-9652
James Weber, *Pr*
EMP: 14 **EST:** 1957
SQ FT: 4,000
SALES (est): 431.65K **Privately Held**
SIC: 3599 Machine shop, jobbing and repair

(G-2056)
RAYCO INC
48 Atlantic St (06053-3025)
PHONE....................860 357-4693
Jose Fontanez, *Pr*
EMP: 11 **EST:** 1951

SALES (est): 1.46MM **Privately Held**
SIC: 3471 Electroplating of metals or formed products

(G-2057)
RICH PRODUCTS CORPORATION
263 Myrtle St (06053-4161)
PHONE....................866 737-8884
EMP: 11
SALES (corp-wide): 4.81B **Privately Held**
Web: www.richs.com
SIC: 2053 Frozen bakery products, except bread
PA: Rich Products Corporation
1 Robert Rich Way
Buffalo NY 14213
716 878-8000

(G-2058)
SAL STEEL INC
Also Called: Sal Steel
221 South St Ste 5 (06051-3652)
PHONE....................860 826-2755
Edward Salvatore, *Pr*
EMP: 13 **EST:** 1991
SQ FT: 30,000
SALES (est): 3.2MM **Privately Held**
Web: www.salsteel.com
SIC: 3312 Blast furnaces and steel mills

(G-2059)
SALFORM INC
250 John Downey Dr (06051-2906)
PHONE....................860 559-6359
EMP: 13 **EST:** 2019
SALES (est): 533.31K **Privately Held**
Web: www.salform.com
SIC: 3599 Machine shop, jobbing and repair

(G-2060)
SEABOARD METAL FINISHING CO
Also Called: Seaboard Plating
410 John Downey Dr (06051-2910)
PHONE....................203 933-1603
Steven D Tarantino, *Pr*
Karen A Tarantino, *Sec*
EMP: 18 **EST:** 1972
SQ FT: 25,000
SALES (est): 366.67K **Privately Held**
Web: www.seaboardmetalfin.com
SIC: 3471 Electroplating of metals or formed products

(G-2061)
SOUTHPACK LLC
1 Hartford Sq Ste 14w (06052-1175)
PHONE....................860 224-2242
EMP: 25 **EST:** 1991
SQ FT: 20,000
SALES (est): 4.89MM **Privately Held**
Web: www.southpack.com
SIC: 3089 Blister or bubble formed packaging, plastics

(G-2062)
STANDARD MFG CO LLC
100 Burritt St (06053-4004)
PHONE....................860 225-3401
Louis Frutuoso, *Managing Member*
EMP: 10 **EST:** 2010
SALES (est): 2.41MM **Privately Held**
Web: www.stdgun.com
SIC: 3484 Guns (firearms) or gun parts, 30 mm. and below

(G-2063)
STANLEY BLACK & DECKER INC
480 Myrtle St (06053-4018)
PHONE....................860 225-5111
Joe Voelker, *Brnch Mgr*
EMP: 13
SALES (corp-wide): 16.95B **Publicly Held**
Web: www.stanleyblackanddecker.com
SIC: 3699 3429 Security devices; Builders' hardware
PA: Stanley Black & Decker, Inc.
1000 Stanley Dr
New Britain CT 06053
860 225-5111

(G-2064)
STANLEY BLACK & DECKER INC
100 Curtis St (06052-1326)
P.O. Box 1308 (06050-1308)
PHONE....................860 225-5111
Patrick Egan, *Brnch Mgr*
EMP: 9
SALES (corp-wide): 16.95B **Publicly Held**
Web: www.stanleyblackanddecker.com
SIC: 3429 Hardware, nec
PA: Stanley Black & Decker, Inc.
1000 Stanley Dr
New Britain CT 06053
860 225-5111

(G-2065)
STANLEY BLACK & DECKER INC (PA)
Also Called: Stanley Black & Decker
1000 Stanley Dr (06053-1675)
P.O. Box 7000 (06050-7000)
PHONE....................860 225-5111
Donald Allan Junior, *Pr*
Andrea J Ayers, *
Robert H Raff, *CCO*
Christopher J Nelson, *Ex VP*
Scot D Greulach, *CAO*
EMP: 200 **EST:** 1843
SALES (est): 16.95B
SALES (corp-wide): 16.95B **Publicly Held**
Web: www.stanleyblackanddecker.com
SIC: 3429 3546 3423 3452 Builders' hardware; Power-driven handtools; Hand and edge tools, nec; Bolts, nuts, rivets, and washers

(G-2066)
STANLEY BLACK & DECKER INC
600 Myrtle St (06053-3976)
PHONE....................860 827-5025
EMP: 10
SALES (corp-wide): 16.95B **Publicly Held**
Web: www.stanleyblackanddecker.com
SIC: 3429 5063 Builders' hardware; Alarm systems, nec
PA: Stanley Black & Decker, Inc.
1000 Stanley Dr
New Britain CT 06053
860 225-5111

(G-2067)
STANLEY BLACK & DECKER INC
Stanley Tools
480 Myrtle St (06053-4018)
P.O. Box 1308 (06050-1308)
PHONE....................860 225-5111
Thomas E Mahoney, *Brnch Mgr*
EMP: 102
SALES (corp-wide): 16.95B **Publicly Held**
Web: www.stanleyblackanddecker.com

SIC: 3429 5085 3546 3423 Builders' hardware; Industrial supplies; Power-driven handtools; Hand and edge tools, nec
PA: Stanley Black & Decker, Inc.
1000 Stanley Dr
New Britain CT 06053
860 225-5111

(G-2068)
STANLEY BLACK DCKER ASIA HLDNG (HQ)
1000 Stanley Dr (06053-1675)
PHONE..........................860 225-5111
EMP: 10 EST: 2020
SALES (est): 6.45MM
SALES (corp-wide): 16.95B **Publicly Held**
Web: www.stanleyblackanddecker.com
SIC: 3429 Builders' hardware
PA: Stanley Black & Decker, Inc.
1000 Stanley Dr
New Britain CT 06053
860 225-5111

(G-2069)
STANLEY FASTENING SYSTEMS LP
Also Called: Stanley-Bostitch
480 Myrtle St (06053-4018)
PHONE..........................860 225-5111
Bruce Behnke, *Pr*
EMP: 43
SALES (corp-wide): 16.95B **Publicly Held**
SIC: 3579 Stapling machines (hand or power)
HQ: Stanley Fastening Systems Lp
2 Briggs Dr
East Greenwich RI 02818
401 884-2500

(G-2070)
STANLEY INDUSTRIAL & AUTO LLC
Also Called: Proto Industrial Tools
480 Myrtle St (06053-4018)
PHONE..........................800 800-8005
Kate White, *Dir*
EMP: 118
SALES (corp-wide): 16.95B **Publicly Held**
Web: www.mactools.com
SIC: 3429 Hardware, nec
HQ: Stanley Industrial & Automotive, Llc
5195 Blazer Pkwy
Dublin OH 43017
614 755-7000

(G-2071)
THE COMMERCIAL FOUNDRY COMPANY
326 South St (06051-3721)
P.O. Box 97 (06050-0097)
PHONE..........................860 224-1794
EMP: 20
Web: www.commercialfoundry.com
SIC: 3369 Machinery castings, exc. die, nonferrous, exc. alum. copper

(G-2072)
TILCON CONNECTICUT INC (DH)
Also Called: Tilcon Connecticut
642 Black Rock Ave (06052-1037)
PHONE..........................860 224-6010
Carmine Abate, *Pr*
Rick Mergens, *Prin*
Dan Stover, *Prin*
▲ EMP: 100 EST: 1981
SQ FT: 2,000
SALES (est): 79.33MM
SALES (corp-wide): 32.72B **Privately Held**
Web: www.tilconct.com

SIC: 5032 1611 3273 2951 Sand, construction; Highway and street paving contractor; Ready-mixed concrete; Asphalt paving mixtures and blocks
HQ: Tilcon Inc.
301 Hartford Ave
Newington CT 06111
860 223-3651

(G-2073)
ULTRA FOOD AND FUEL
788 W Main St (06053-3856)
PHONE..........................860 223-2005
Mukhtar Ahmed, *Prin*
EMP: 7 EST: 2010
SALES (est): 161.17K **Privately Held**
SIC: 2869 Fuels

(G-2074)
VIKING KITCHEN CABINETS LLC (PA)
33 John St 39 (06051)
PHONE..........................860 223-7101
EMP: 40 EST: 1997
SQ FT: 11,000
SALES (est): 24.14MM
SALES (corp-wide): 24.14MM **Privately Held**
Web: www.vikingkitchens.com
SIC: 5031 5211 2541 2434 Kitchen cabinets ; Lumber and other building materials; Wood partitions and fixtures; Wood kitchen cabinets

(G-2075)
WINSLOW AUTOMATICS INC
23 Saint Claire Ave (06051-1630)
PHONE..........................860 225-6321
Janusz Podlasek, *CEO*
Walter Borysewicz, *
Robert Mc Nally, *
Wendi P Scata, *
J George Podlasek, *
EMP: 91 EST: 1951
SQ FT: 70,000
SALES (est): 9.41MM **Privately Held**
Web: www.winslowautomatics.com
SIC: 3841 3724 3843 3743 Surgical and medical instruments; Aircraft engines and engine parts; Dental equipment and supplies; Brakes, air and vacuum: railway

---

New Canaan
Fairfield County

(G-2076)
BOOM LLC
Also Called: Boom Creative Development
11 Forest St Ste 3 (06840-4746)
PHONE..........................212 317-2005
Art Degaetano, *Pr*
Glenn Marks, *
▲ EMP: 35 EST: 2000
SALES (est): 2.3MM **Privately Held**
Web: www.boompage.net
SIC: 3999 5122 Atomizers, toiletry; Cosmetics, perfumes, and hair products

(G-2077)
CJ FIRST CANDLE
21 Locust Ave Ste 2b (06840-4735)
PHONE..........................203 966-1300
Allison Jacobson, *CEO*
EMP: 9 EST: 2017
SALES (est): 436.67K **Privately Held**
Web: www.firstcandle.org
SIC: 3999 Candles

(G-2078)
CONTEK INTERNATIONAL CORP
Also Called: Century Products
93 Cherry St (06840-5521)
PHONE..........................203 972-7330
John Chen, *Pr*
Alice Chen, *VP*
▲ EMP: 17 EST: 1990
SQ FT: 5,000
SALES (est): 714.26K **Privately Held**
Web: www.contek.net
SIC: 3577 Computer peripheral equipment, nec

(G-2079)
COVIA FINANCE COMPANY LLC
258 Elm St (06840-5309)
PHONE..........................203 966-8880
EMP: 62 EST: 1997
SALES (est): 89.41MM
SALES (corp-wide): 1.6B **Privately Held**
SIC: 1446 Industrial sand
PA: Covia Holdings Llc
3 Summit Park Dr Ste 700
Independence OH 44131
800 255-7263

(G-2080)
COVIA SPECIALTY MINERALS INC
Also Called: Unimin Specialty Minerals Inc
258 Elm St (06840-5309)
PHONE..........................203 966-8880
▼ EMP: 50 EST: 1989
SQ FT: 30,000
SALES (est): 14.39MM
SALES (corp-wide): 1.6B **Privately Held**
SIC: 1446 Silica mining
PA: Covia Holdings Llc
3 Summit Park Dr Ste 700
Independence OH 44131
800 255-7263

(G-2081)
CRATEDIGGER INC
53 Turtle Back Rd (06840-2619)
PHONE..........................203 594-1488
Tom Kurz, *CEO*
EMP: 7 EST: 2020
SALES (est): 257.7K **Privately Held**
SIC: 7372 Application computer software

(G-2082)
MB SPORT LLC (PA)
31 Grove St (06840-5324)
PHONE..........................203 966-1985
Michael Buscher, *Managing Member*
◆ EMP: 24 EST: 1998
SQ FT: 5,500
SALES (est): 3.48MM
SALES (corp-wide): 3.48MM **Privately Held**
Web: www.mbsport.com
SIC: 2321 2337 Sport shirts, men's and boys': from purchased materials; Women's and misses' suits and coats

(G-2083)
MECHANCAL ENGNERED SYSTEMS LLC
180 Jonathan Rd (06840-2116)
PHONE..........................203 400-4658
EMP: 7 EST: 2012
SQ FT: 2,000
SALES (est): 702.61K **Privately Held**
SIC: 3564 3585 Turbo-blowers, industrial; Refrigeration and heating equipment

(G-2084)
NEW CANAAN SPORTS LLC
96 Park St (06840-5401)
PHONE..........................866 629-2453
EMP: 9 EST: 2019
SALES (est): 136.81K **Privately Held**
Web: www.newcanaanbicycles.com
SIC: 2711 Newspapers, publishing and printing

(G-2085)
PURACLENZ LLC
30 Butler Ln (06840-6817)
PHONE..........................561 213-1411
Fordyce Wendell Minnick, *Managing Member*
EMP: 8 EST: 2020
SALES (est): 1.51MM **Privately Held**
Web: www.puraclenz.com
SIC: 3634 Air purifiers, portable

(G-2086)
SLOGIC HOLDING CORP (PA)
36 Grove St (06840-5329)
PHONE..........................203 966-2800
EMP: 13 EST: 2016
SALES (est): 99.16MM
SALES (corp-wide): 99.16MM **Privately Held**
SIC: 2394 5091 Tents: made from purchased materials; Camping equipment and supplies

(G-2087)
SOUTHERN ALMNUM INTRMDTE HLDIN
130 Main St (06840-5509)
PHONE..........................870 234-8660
Allison Schultz, *CEO*
EMP: 225 EST: 2018
SALES (est): 8.77MM **Privately Held**
SIC: 2514 Metal household furniture

(G-2088)
SUPERNOVA DIAGNOSTICS INC
36 Richmond Hill Rd (06840-5301)
PHONE..........................301 792-4345
Neil J Campbell, *CEO*
Doctor Christopher M Ball, *Ex VP*
Dane Saglio, *VP*
EMP: 7 EST: 2009
SALES (est): 343.42K **Privately Held**
SIC: 3841 Diagnostic apparatus, medical

(G-2089)
TOTAL SPECIALTY CHEMICALS INC (PA)
47 Elm St (06840-5502)
PHONE..........................203 966-1525
▲ EMP: 49 EST: 1994
SALES (est): 16.64MM **Privately Held**
Web: www.totaltsc.com
SIC: 5169 2819 Chemicals and allied products, nec; Industrial inorganic chemicals, nec

(G-2090)
UNIMIN TEXAS CO LTD (HQ)
258 Elm St (06840-5309)
PHONE..........................203 966-8880
EMP: 13
SALES (est): 5.44MM
SALES (corp-wide): 117.6MM **Privately Held**
SIC: 1446 Industrial sand
PA: Scr - Sibelco Nv
Plantin En Moretuslei 1a
Antwerpen 2018
32236611

▲ = Import ▼ = Export
◆ = Import/Export

(G-2091)
UNIMIN WISCONSIN EQP CORP
258 Elm St (06840-5309) .
PHONE.....................................203 966-8880
EMP: 49 **EST:** 1990
SALES (est): 2.7MM
SALES (corp-wide): 1.6B **Privately Held**
SIC: 1446 Industrial sand
PA: Covia Holdings Llc
3 Summit Park Dr Ste 700
Independence OH 44131
800 255-7263

(G-2092)
UNISIL CORPORATION
258 Elm St (06840-5309)
PHONE.....................................203 966-8880
EMP: 31 **EST:** 1982
SALES (est): 1.83MM
SALES (corp-wide): 1.6B **Privately Held**
SIC: 1446 Industrial sand
PA: Covia Holdings Llc
3 Summit Park Dr Ste 700
Independence OH 44131
800 255-7263

(G-2093)
US CHEMICALS INC
280 Elm St (06840-5313)
PHONE.....................................203 655-8878
H T Von Oehsen, *CEO*
EMP: 9 **EST:** 2013
SALES (est): 211.3K **Privately Held**
SIC: 2911 5169 Solvents; Acids

New Fairfield
Fairfield County

(G-2094)
CUSTOM VAULT CORPORATION
6 Jeremy Dr (06812-2110)
PHONE.....................................203 746-0506
Michael Iadarola, *Prin*
EMP: 7 **EST:** 2010
SALES (est): 146.93K **Privately Held**
SIC: 3272 Concrete products, nec

(G-2095)
DANIEL F CRAPA
17 Calverton Dr (06812-3705)
PHONE.....................................203 746-5706
Daniel F Crapa, *Prin*
EMP: 7 **EST:** 2006
SALES (est): 77.6K **Privately Held**
SIC: 2431 Millwork

(G-2096)
NEW FAIRFIELD PRESS INC
3 Dunham Dr (06812-4055)
P.O. Box 8864 (06812-8864)
PHONE.....................................203 746-2700
John Paul Parille, *Pr*
Arlene Pugliatti, *VP*
EMP: 14 **EST:** 1965
SQ FT: 5,000
SALES (est): 646.13K **Privately Held**
Web: www.nfpress.com
SIC: 2759 2752 Business forms: printing,
nsk; Commercial printing, lithographic

New Hartford
Litchfield County

(G-2097)
ADVANCED PWR SYSTEMS INTL INC

18 Hemlock Dr (06057-2814)
PHONE.....................................860 921-0009
Chris Wright, *COO*
EMP: 8 **EST:** 1995
SQ FT: 3,000
SALES (est): 485.36K **Privately Held**
Web: www.fitchfuelcatalyst.com
SIC: 5084 2819 2899 2869 Engines and
transportation equipment; Catalysts,
chemical; Chemical preparations, nec;
Industrial organic chemicals, nec

(G-2098)
ALTRA INDUSTRIAL MOTION CORP
31 Industrial Park Rd (06057-2337)
PHONE.....................................860 379-1673
Donald Beall, *Brnch Mgr*
EMP: 34
SALES (corp-wide): 5.22B **Publicly Held**
Web: www.altramotion.com
SIC: 5085 3568 Power transmission
equipment and apparatus; Power
transmission equipment, nec
HQ: Altra Industrial Motion Corp.
300 Granite St Ste 201
Braintree MA 02184
781 917-0600

(G-2099)
BREWERY LEGITIMUS LLC
283 Main St (06057-2750)
PHONE.....................................860 810-8894
Christopher Sayer, *Managing Member*
EMP: 10 **EST:** 2015
SALES (est): 790.09K **Privately Held**
Web: www.brewerylegitimus.com
SIC: 2082 Beer (alcoholic beverage)

(G-2100)
EXECUTIVE GREETINGS INC (HQ)
Also Called: Baldwin Cooke
120 Industrial Park Rd (06057-2308)
P.O. Box 3669 (56002-3669)
PHONE.....................................860 379-9911
Dan Rao, *Pr*
Stephen D Roberts, *CFO*
▼ **EMP:** 450 **EST:** 1956
SQ FT: 140,000
SALES (est): 51.29MM
SALES (corp-wide): 3.81B **Privately Held**
SIC: 2741 5112 5199 2759 Miscellaneous
publishing; Greeting cards; Gifts and
novelties; Commercial printing, nec
PA: Taylor Corporation
1725 Roe Crest Dr
North Mankato MN 56003
507 625-2828

(G-2101)
HMC ENTERPRISES INC
37 Greenwoods Rd (06057-2207)
P.O. Box 366 (06057-0366)
PHONE.....................................860 379-8506
David J Hurley, *Pr*
Thomas P Hurley, *VP*
EMP: 50 **EST:** 1945
SQ FT: 22,600
SALES (est): 2.99MM **Privately Held**
Web: www.hurleyspring.com
SIC: 3493 3469 Steel springs, except wire;
Metal stampings, nec

(G-2102)
INERTIA DYNAMICS LLC
31 Industrial Park Rd (06057-2337)
PHONE.....................................860 379-1252
▲ **EMP:** 110 **EST:** 1971
SQ FT: 32,000

SALES (est): 25.95MM
SALES (corp-wide): 5.22B **Publicly Held**
Web: www.warnerelectric.com
SIC: 3625 3568 Brakes, electromagnetic;
Clutches, except vehicular
HQ: Altra Industrial Motion Corp.
300 Granite St Ste 201
Braintree MA 02184
781 917-0600

(G-2103)
INERTIA DYNAMICS INC
31 Industrial Park Rd (06057-2337)
P.O. Box 641 (61080-0641)
PHONE.....................................860 379-1252
Steve Nyquist, *Prin*
EMP: 27 **EST:** 2012
SALES (est): 4.91MM **Privately Held**
Web: www.warnerelectric.com
SIC: 3714 Motor vehicle parts and
accessories

(G-2104)
INJECTECH ENGINEERING LLC (PA)
19 Pioneer Rd (06057-4235)
PHONE.....................................860 379-9781
Kenneth Heyse, *Managing Member*
EMP: 7 **EST:** 1978
SQ FT: 7,000
SALES (est): 631.91K
SALES (corp-wide): 631.91K **Privately Held**
SIC: 3089 Injection molding of plastics

(G-2105)
L & M MANUFACTURING CO INC
37 Greenwoods Rd (06057-2207)
PHONE.....................................860 379-2751
Maurice J La Brecque, *Pr*
Joseph J Mangiome, *VP*
EMP: 22 **EST:** 1969
SQ FT: 24,000
SALES (est): 588.59K **Privately Held**
Web: www.lamyoga.com
SIC: 3452 Screws, metal

(G-2106)
NEW HARTFORD INDUSTRIAL PK INC
Also Called: Hurley Manufacturing
37 Greenwoods Rd (06057-2207)
P.O. Box 366 (06057-0366)
PHONE.....................................860 379-8506
David Hurley, *Pr*
Thomas Hurley, *
EMP: 18 **EST:** 1945
SQ FT: 30,000
SALES (est): 989.38K **Privately Held**
Web: www.hurleybusinesspark.com
SIC: 3469 Metal stampings, nec

(G-2107)
PERRY TECHNOLOGY CORPORATION
120 Industrial Park Rd (06057-2308)
P.O. Box 21 (06057-0021)
PHONE.....................................860 738-2525
Lansford Perry, *Pr*
Margaret H Perry, *
EMP: 85 **EST:** 1938
SQ FT: 55,000
SALES (est): 12.43MM **Privately Held**
Web: www.perrygear.com
SIC: 3545 3728 3568 3462 Machine tool
accessories; Gears, aircraft power
transmission; Power transmission
equipment, nec; Iron and steel forgings

(G-2108)
SCP MANAGEMENT LLC
Also Called: Syntac Coated Products
29 Industrial Park Rd (06057-2310)
PHONE.....................................860 738-2600
Curt Rutsky, *Managing Member*
Aaron Rutsky, *VP*
▲ **EMP:** 45 **EST:** 2000
SALES (est): 4.94MM **Privately Held**
Web: www.shurtape.com
SIC: 3312 Coated or plated products

New Haven
New Haven County

(G-2109)
90 RIVER STREET LLC
90 River St (06513-4382)
PHONE.....................................203 772-4700
EMP: 8 **EST:** 2006
SALES (est): 522.81K **Privately Held**
SIC: 3629 Electrical industrial apparatus,
nec

(G-2110)
A D PERKINS COMPANY
43 Elm St (06510-2032)
PHONE.....................................203 777-3456
Kirk Schroff, *Pr*
Jay Smilovich, *VP*
Nancy Schroff, *Sec*
EMP: 9 **EST:** 1876
SQ FT: 1,200
SALES (est): 663.43K **Privately Held**
Web: www.adperkins.com
SIC: 3953 3993 7389 Embossing seals and
hand stamps; Advertising novelties;
Engraving service

(G-2111)
ACCUSTANDARD INC
125 Market St (06513-3031)
PHONE.....................................203 786-5290
Michael Bolgar, *Ch*
Amy Harvey, *
Matthew Bolgar, *
Julie C Bolgar, *
EMP: 65 **EST:** 1986
SQ FT: 34,000
SALES (est): 12.34MM **Privately Held**
Web: www.accustandard.com
SIC: 8731 2869 Commercial physical
research; Industrial organic chemicals, nec

(G-2112)
ALEXION PHARMA LLC (DH)
Also Called: Alexion Rare Dsase By Astrznec
100 College St (06510-3210)
PHONE.....................................203 272-2596
Irving Adler, *Dir*
EMP: 72 **EST:** 2015
SALES (est): 177.23MM
SALES (corp-wide): 44.35B **Privately Held**
Web: www.alexion.com
SIC: 2834 8733 Pharmaceutical
preparations; Medical research
HQ: Alexion Pharmaceuticals, Inc.
121 Seaport Blvd
Boston MA 02210

(G-2113)
ALL PHASE STEEL WORKS LLC
57 Trumbull St (06510-1004)
PHONE.....................................203 375-8881
Paul J Pinto, *Prin*
EMP: 11 **EST:** 2012
SQ FT: 30,000
SALES (est): 2.27MM **Privately Held**

SIC: 3441 1791 Building components, structural steel; Building front installation, metal

(G-2114)
ALLIANCE ENERGY LLC
Also Called: Connecticut Refining Co
Merritt Parkway (06535)
P.O. Box 9545 (06535-0545)
PHONE..............................203 933-2511
Rich Hyland, *Mgr*
EMP: 137
Web: www.globalp.com
SIC: 1389 Construction, repair, and dismantling services
HQ: Alliance Energy Llc
800 South St Ste 500
Waltham MA 02453

(G-2115)
AMERICAN SIGN INC
Also Called: American Sign
614 Ferry St (06513-2924)
PHONE..............................203 624-2991
David Lafo, *Pr*
EMP: 17 **EST:** 1979
SQ FT: 10,500
SALES (est): 1.26MM **Privately Held**
Web: www.americansigninc.com
SIC: 7389 3993 3953 2394 Sign painting and lettering shop; Signs and advertising specialties; Marking devices; Canvas and related products

(G-2116)
APICELLAS BAKERY INC
365 Grand Ave (06513-3732)
PHONE..............................203 865-6204
Alphonse J Cimino, *Pr*
EMP: 20 **EST:** 1918
SQ FT: 6,000
SALES (est): 4.32MM **Privately Held**
Web: www.apicellabakery.com
SIC: 5149 5461 2051 Bakery products; Bread; Bread, cake, and related products

(G-2117)
ARGA PRSNLZED DCMENT SOLUTIONS
25 James St (06513-4218)
PHONE..............................203 401-3650
EMP: 7 **EST:** 2011
SALES (est): 169.88K **Privately Held**
SIC: 2752 Offset printing

(G-2118)
ARROW LOCK MANUFACTURING CO
110 Sargent Dr (06511-5918)
PHONE..............................203 603-5959
Michael Matteo, *Pur Agt*
EMP: 7 **EST:** 2017
SALES (est): 116.49K **Privately Held**
Web: www.arrowlock.com
SIC: 3999 Manufacturing industries, nec

(G-2119)
ARVINAS INC (PA)
Also Called: Protac
395 Winchester Ave (06511-1917)
PHONE..............................203 535-1456
John Houston, *Pr*
John Houston, *Ch Bd*
Sean Cassidy, *CFO*
Ronald Peck, *CMO*
Ian Taylor, *CSO*
EMP: 260 **EST:** 2013
SQ FT: 63,000
SALES (est): 131.4MM

SALES (corp-wide): 131.4MM **Publicly Held**
Web: www.arvinas.com
SIC: 2834 8731 Pharmaceutical preparations; Biotechnical research, commercial

(G-2120)
ASSA INC
Also Called: Assa High Security Locks
110 Sargent Dr (06511-5918)
P.O. Box 9453 (06534-0453)
PHONE..............................800 235-7482
Richard Eisen, *Pr*
Page L Heslin, *Sec*
▲ **EMP:** 12 **EST:** 1987
SQ FT: 5,000
SALES (est): 6.16MM
SALES (corp-wide): 11.51B **Privately Held**
Web: www.medeco.com
SIC: 3429 Locks or lock sets
HQ: Assa Abloy Inc.
110 Sargent Dr
New Haven CT 06511

(G-2121)
ASSA ABLOY ACC DOOR CNTRLS GRO
Also Called: Norton Door Controls
110 Sargent Dr (06511-5918)
PHONE..............................901 365-2160
EMP: 127
SALES (corp-wide): 11.51B **Privately Held**
SIC: 3429 3466 Locks or lock sets; Crowns and closures
HQ: Assa Abloy Accessories And Door Controls Group, Inc.
1902 Airport Rd
Monroe NC 28110
877 974-2255

(G-2122)
ASSA ABLOY INC (HQ)
Also Called: Assa
110 Sargent Dr (06511-5918)
PHONE..............................203 562-2151
Thanasis Molokotos, *CEO*
Lucas Boselli, *Pr*
Jeff Mereschuk, *CFO*
◆ **EMP:** 400 **EST:** 1986
SQ FT: 325,000
SALES (est): 2.03B
SALES (corp-wide): 11.51B **Privately Held**
Web: www.assaabloydss.com
SIC: 3429 3699 Keys, locks, and related hardware; Security control equipment and systems
PA: Assa Abloy Ab
Klarabergsviadukten 90
Stockholm 111 6
850648500

(G-2123)
BARNES TECHNICAL PRODUCTS LLC
15 High St (06510-2304)
PHONE..............................203 931-8852
Russell Barnes, *Managing Member*
EMP: 7 **EST:** 2001
SALES (est): 829.8K **Privately Held**
Web: www.barnestechprod.com
SIC: 3599 Machine shop, jobbing and repair

(G-2124)
BARTRON MEDICAL IMAGING LLC
91 Shelton Ave (06511-1811)
P.O. Box 16 (06418-0016)
PHONE..............................203 498-2184

EMP: 9
SQ FT: 4,500
SALES (est): 1.42MM **Privately Held**
Web: www.bartron.ws
SIC: 3841 3845 Surgical and medical instruments; Electromedical equipment

(G-2125)
BECAID LLC
Also Called: C8 Sciences
5 Science Park (06511-1967)
PHONE..............................203 915-6914
EMP: 8 **EST:** 2011
SALES (est): 465.95K **Privately Held**
SIC: 7372 Educational computer software

(G-2126)
BILCO HOLDING COMPANY
370 James St Ste 201 (06513-3090)
PHONE..............................203 507-2751
Robert S Santoro, *Prin*
EMP: 35 **EST:** 2015
SALES (est): 7.87MM
SALES (corp-wide): 861.44MM **Privately Held**
Web: www.bilco.com
SIC: 3442 Metal doors, sash, and trim
HQ: Amesbury Group, Inc.
5001 W Delbridge St
Sioux Falls SD 57107
978 388-0581

(G-2127)
BIOHAVEN PHARMACEUTICALS INC
215 Church St (06510-1803)
PHONE..............................203 404-0410
Robert Berman, *CEO*
Clifford Bechtold, *COO*
EMP: 65 **EST:** 2021
SALES (est): 22.18MM
SALES (corp-wide): 3.06MM **Privately Held**
Web: www.biohaven.com
SIC: 2834 Pharmaceutical preparations
HQ: Biohaven Pharmaceutical Holding Company Ltd.
C/O Maples Corporate Services (Bvi) Limited
Road Town

(G-2128)
BIOHAVEN PHRM HOLDG CO LTD
Also Called: Biohaven Labs
25 Science Park Ste 2d (06511-1984)
PHONE..............................203 691-6332
EMP: 14
SALES (corp-wide): 100.33B **Publicly Held**
Web: www.biohavenpharma.com
SIC: 2834 Pharmaceutical preparations
HQ: Biohaven Pharmaceutical Holding Company Ltd.
215 Church St
New Haven CT 06510
203 404-0410

(G-2129)
BIOHAVEN PHRM HOLDG CO LTD (HQ)
Also Called: Biohaven Pharmaceuticals
215 Church St (06510-1803)
PHONE..............................203 404-0410
Vlad Coric, *Ch Bd*
Matthew Buten, *CFO*
Elyse Stock, *CMO*
Charles Conway, *CSO*
Kimberly Gentile Senior, *Clinical Vice President*

EMP: 51 **EST:** 2013
SQ FT: 10,000
SALES (est): 462.51MM
SALES (corp-wide): 100.33B **Publicly Held**
Web: www.biohaven.com
SIC: 2834 Drugs acting on the central nervous system & sense organs
PA: Pfizer Inc.
66 Hudson Blvd E Fl 20
New York NY 10001
212 733-2323

(G-2130)
BIOXCEL THERAPEUTICS INC
555 Long Wharf Dr Fl 12 (06511-6104)
PHONE..............................475 238-6837
Vimal Mehta, *Pr*
Peter Mueller, *
Frank Yocca, *CSO*
Richard I Steinhart, *Sr VP*
Javier Rodriguez, *CLO*
EMP: 183 **EST:** 2017
SQ FT: 18,285
SALES (est): 375K **Privately Held**
Web: www.bioxceltherapeutics.com
SIC: 2834 Pharmaceutical preparations

(G-2131)
BOLD WOOD INTERIORS LLC
138 Haven St (06513-3522)
PHONE..............................203 907-4077
▲ **EMP:** 15 **EST:** 1991
SQ FT: 8,500
SALES (est): 2.23MM **Privately Held**
Web: www.boldwoodinteriors.com
SIC: 2521 Wood office furniture

(G-2132)
BRIDGESTONE RET OPERATIONS LLC
Also Called: Firestone
680 Chapel St (06510-3112)
PHONE..............................203 787-1208
Michael Geltman, *Mgr*
EMP: 7
Web: www.bridgestoneamericas.com
SIC: 5531 7534 Automotive tires; Rebuilding and retreading tires
HQ: Bridgestone Retail Operations, Llc
333 E Lake St Ste 300
Bloomingdale IL 60108
630 259-9000

(G-2133)
CAPITAL CITIES COMMUNICATIONS
8 Elm St (06510-2006)
PHONE..............................203 784-8800
Hank Yaggi, *Prin*
EMP: 7 **EST:** 2007
SALES (est): 111.85K **Privately Held**
Web: www.wtnh.com
SIC: 2711 Newspapers, publishing and printing

(G-2134)
CARESTREAM HLTH MLCLAR IMGING
Also Called: Carestream Molecular Imaging
4 Science Park (06511-1962)
PHONE..............................888 777-2072
Stephanie Chiang, *Prin*
Shahram Hejazi, *Prin*
Sindy Woodhams, *Prin*
EMP: 24 **EST:** 2007
SALES (est): 812.22K **Privately Held**
SIC: 3826 Analytical instruments

▲ = Import ▼ = Export
◆ = Import/Export

(G-2135)
CARLS BONED CHICKEN INC
208 Food Terminal Plz (06511-5910)
PHONE.................................203 777-9048
EMP: 47 **EST:** 1951
SALES (est): 7.3MM **Privately Held**
SIC: 5144 2015 Poultry products, nec;
  Poultry slaughtering and processing

(G-2136)
CELLDEX THERAPEUTICS INC
300 George St Ste 503 (06511-6624)
PHONE.................................203 483-3531
Larry Ellberger, *Ch*
EMP: 16
SALES (corp-wide): 2.36MM **Publicly Held**
Web: www.celldex.com
SIC: 2834 Pharmaceutical preparations
PA: Celldex Therapeutics, Inc.
  53 Frontage Rd Ste 220
  Hampton NJ 08827
  908 200-7500

(G-2137)
COGSTATE SPORT INC
195 Church St Fl 10 (06510-2009)
PHONE.................................203 773-5010
EMP: 13 **EST:** 2010
SALES (est): 286.76K **Privately Held**
Web: www.cogstate.com
SIC: 2834 8741 8734 Pharmaceutical
  preparations; Management services;
  Testing laboratories

(G-2138)
CONVEXITY SCIENTIFIC INC
85 Willow St Lbby (06511-2696)
PHONE.................................844 359-7632
Geoff Matous, *Pr*
Ralph Finger, *Managing Member*
EMP: 8 **EST:** 2014
SALES (est): 975.22K **Privately Held**
Web: www.wellinks.com
SIC: 3841 Inhalators, surgical and medical

(G-2139)
CORBIN RUSSWIN
110 Sargent Dr (06511-5918)
PHONE.................................860 225-7411
Douglas Millikan, *Prin*
EMP: 20 **EST:** 2010
SALES (est): 2.04MM **Privately Held**
SIC: 3429 Keys, locks, and related hardware

(G-2140)
CORE SITE SERVICES LLC
470 James St Ste 7 (06513-3175)
PHONE.................................475 227-9026
Allen Page, *Prin*
EMP: 7 **EST:** 2017
SALES (est): 655.05K **Privately Held**
SIC: 1794 1799 3281 Excavation work;
  Grave excavation; Curbing, paving, and
  walkway stone

(G-2141)
COVIDIEN LP
Also Called: Surgical Devices
555 Long Wharf Dr Fl 4 (06511-6102)
PHONE.................................781 839-1722
Scott Riley, *Brnch Mgr*
EMP: 149
Web: www.covidien.com
SIC: 3841 Surgical and medical instruments
HQ: Covidien Lp
  15 Hampshire St
  Mansfield MA 02048
  763 514-4000

(G-2142)
CUSTOM TEES PLUS
365 Whalley Ave (06511-3044)
PHONE.................................203 752-1071
William Gibbs, *Owner*
EMP: 7 **EST:** 1996
SALES (est): 440.55K **Privately Held**
SIC: 2759 Screen printing

(G-2143)
DOCUPRINT & IMAGING INC
Also Called: Docuprintnow
27 Whitney Ave (06510-1219)
PHONE.................................203 776-6000
Anthony Colasanto, *Pr*
EMP: 8 **EST:** 1972
SQ FT: 4,000
SALES (est): 898.55K **Privately Held**
Web: www.docuprintandimaging.com
SIC: 2752 Offset printing

(G-2144)
DOW COVER COMPANY INCORPORATED
Also Called: Dcci
373 Lexington Ave (06513-4061)
PHONE.................................203 469-5394
Mark Steinhardt, *Pr*
Barry Konet, *
▲ **EMP:** 68 **EST:** 1947
SQ FT: 38,000
SALES (est): 3.66MM **Privately Held**
Web: www.dowcover.com
SIC: 2393 Textile bags

(G-2145)
DS SEWING INC
260 Wolcott St (06513-3834)
P.O. Box 8983 (06532-0983)
PHONE.................................203 773-1344
David Steinhard, *Pr*
▲ **EMP:** 11 **EST:** 1992
SQ FT: 11,000
SALES (est): 914.81K **Privately Held**
Web: www.ds-sewing.com
SIC: 7389 2399 Sewing contractor;
  Banners, made from fabric

(G-2146)
DUROL LABORATORIES LLC
Also Called: Durol Cosmetic Laboratories
116 Welton St (06511-1524)
PHONE.................................866 611-9694
Sade Aminu, *CEO*
EMP: 10 **EST:** 2010
SQ FT: 11,000
SALES (est): 521.1K **Privately Held**
Web: www.durollabs.com
SIC: 2844 Perfumes, cosmetics and other
  toilet preparations

(G-2147)
EAST ROCK BREWING COMPANY LLC (PA)
285 Nicoll St (06511-2625)
PHONE.................................203 530-3484
Tim Wilson, *Managing Member*
EMP: 7 **EST:** 2016
SALES (est): 2.94MM
SALES (corp-wide): 2.94MM **Privately Held**
Web: www.eastrockbeer.com
SIC: 2082 Beer (alcoholic beverage)

(G-2148)
EDSAN CHEMICAL COMPANY INC
150 Whittier Rd (06515-2474)
PHONE.................................203 624-3123
Susan Fewes, *Pr*
EMP: 13 **EST:** 1948
SQ FT: 10,000
SALES (est): 209.47K **Privately Held**
SIC: 2842 5087 Polishes and sanitation
  goods; Janitors' supplies

(G-2149)
ELECTRIX LLC
45 Spring St (06519-2340)
P.O. Box 9575 (06535-0575)
PHONE.................................203 776-5577
▲ **EMP:** 54
Web: www.electrixillumination.com
SIC: 3648 Decorative area lighting fixtures

(G-2150)
ERICSSON
310 Orange St (06510-1719)
PHONE.................................203 776-0631
EMP: 48 **EST:** 2011
SALES (est): 816.7K **Privately Held**
SIC: 3663 Radio and t.v. communications
  equipment

(G-2151)
F W WEBB COMPANY
Also Called: Johnson Contrls Authorized Dlr
650 Ella T Grasso Blvd (06519-1810)
PHONE.................................203 865-6124
Michael Sewell, *Mgr*
EMP: 10
SALES (corp-wide): 1.02B **Privately Held**
Web: www.johnsoncontrols.com
SIC: 3432 5074 5251 Plumbing fixture
  fittings and trim; Plumbing fittings and
  supplies; Hardware stores
PA: F. W. Webb Company
  160 Middlesex Tpke
  Bedford MA 01730
  781 272-6600

(G-2152)
FLO-TECH LLC (PA)
545 Long Wharf Dr Ste 602 (06511-5960)
PHONE.................................860 613-3333
TOLL FREE: 800
Leo Bonetti, *CEO*
Steve Therrien, *
Arthur G Aery Junior, *CFO*
Scott Macgregor, *
Mike Assunto, *
▲ **EMP:** 76 **EST:** 1991
SALES (est): 39.35MM **Privately Held**
Web: www.flotech.net
SIC: 5045 3577 Printers, computer;
  Printers, computer

(G-2153)
GE ENGINE SVCS UNC HOLDG I INC
Also Called: GE
71 Shelton Ave (06511-1811)
Rural Route R 1 Ive D (12345-0001)
PHONE.................................518 380-0767
Randall Mcalister, *Pr*
Jonathan Goodman, *VP*
Doriann Salisbury, *Treas*
EMP: 148 **EST:** 1999
SALES (est): 29.34MM
SALES (corp-wide): 76.56B **Publicly Held**
SIC: 3511 Turbines and turbine generator
  sets
PA: General Electric Company
  1 Financial Ctr Ste 3700
  Boston MA 02111
  617 443-3000

(G-2154)
GELATO GIULIANA LLC
240 Sargent Dr Ste 9 (06511-6108)
PHONE.................................203 772-0607
EMP: 10 **EST:** 2005
SALES (est): 780.84K **Privately Held**
Web: www.gelatogiuliana.com
SIC: 2024 Dairy based frozen desserts

(G-2155)
GOODCOPY PRINTING CENTER INC
Also Called: Goodcopy Printing & Graphics
110 Hamilton St (06511-5813)
P.O. Box 8088 (06530-0088)
PHONE.................................203 624-0194
Louis Goldberg, *Pr*
Louis Goldberg, *Pr*
Edith Goldberg, *VP*
EMP: 20 **EST:** 1968
SQ FT: 10,000
SALES (est): 4.87MM **Privately Held**
Web: www.goodcopy.com
SIC: 2752 Offset printing

(G-2156)
GRACIES KITCHENS INC
211 Food Terminal Plz (06511-5911)
PHONE.................................203 773-0795
Ralph Parillo, *Pr*
EMP: 10 **EST:** 2012
SQ FT: 30,000
SALES (est): 2.4MM **Privately Held**
Web: www.gracieskitchens.com
SIC: 5148 2099 5149 Fruits, fresh;
  Vegetables, peeled for the trade; Sauces

(G-2157)
GREENLEAF BFUELS NEW HAVEN LLC
100 Waterfront St (06512-1713)
PHONE.................................203 672-9028
Mark Mccall, *Managing Member*
Augustus G Kellogg, *Mgr*
EMP: 10 **EST:** 2004
SALES (est): 1.72MM **Privately Held**
SIC: 2869 Industrial organic chemicals, nec

(G-2158)
GREY WALL SOFTWARE LLC
Also Called: Veoci.com
195 Church St Fl 14 (06510-2009)
PHONE.................................203 782-5944
Sukh Greywal, *CEO*
Brigitte Girard, *CFO*
EMP: 15 **EST:** 2011
SQ FT: 5,600
SALES (est): 2.16MM **Privately Held**
Web: www.veoci.com
SIC: 7372 Prepackaged software

(G-2159)
H KREVIT AND COMPANY INC
73 Welton St (06511-1523)
PHONE.................................203 772-3350
Thomas Ross, *Pr*
Carolyn Dechello, *
Donald Dechello, *
EMP: 44 **EST:** 1919
SQ FT: 45,000
SALES (est): 9.72MM **Privately Held**
Web: www.pvschemicals.com
SIC: 2869 2819 3589 Industrial organic
  chemicals, nec; Industrial inorganic
  chemicals, nec; Water treatment
  equipment, industrial

(G-2160)
HENRY FURTERA
45 Orchard St Fl 1 (06519-1009)
PHONE................................762 200-7318
Furtera Henry, *Prin*
EMP: 7
SALES (est): 78.66K Privately Held
SIC: 3711 Trucks, pickup, assembly of

(G-2161)
HUMMEL BROS INC
180 Sargent Dr (06511-5919)
PHONE................................203 787-4113
TOLL FREE: 800
William F Hummel, *Pr*
Kurt Hummel, *
Robert W Hummel Junior, *VP*
Mary Ellen Hummel, *
EMP: 70 EST: 1933
SQ FT: 42,000
SALES (est): 9.78MM Privately Held
Web: www.hummelbros.com
SIC: 2099 2013 Food preparations, nec;
Sausages, from purchased meat

(G-2162)
IDEAL PRINTING CO
INCORPORATED
228 Food Terminal Plz (06511-5910)
P.O. Box 8488 (06531-0488)
PHONE................................203 777-7626
Jim Cohane, *Pr*
Rocco Candela, *VP*
EMP: 7 EST: 1920
SQ FT: 7,920
SALES (est): 819.91K Privately Held
Web: www.idealprintingct.com
SIC: 2759 2752 Letterpress printing; Offset
printing

(G-2163)
INDUSTRIAL FLOW SLTONS
OPER LL
104 John W Murphy Dr (06513-3504)
PHONE................................860 399-5937
John Wilson, *Pr*
▲ EMP: 37 EST: 1983
SALES (est): 6.54MM Privately Held
Web: www.flowsolutions.com
SIC: 3561 5084 Industrial pumps and parts;
Industrial machinery and equipment

(G-2164)
JUMO HEALTH USA INC (PA)
Also Called: Jumo
470 James St (06513-3098)
PHONE................................646 895-9319
Kevin Aniskovich, *CEO*
Kate Hersov, *
Raymond N Altieri, *
Mitzie Garland, *
EMP: 49 EST: 2013
SQ FT: 1,000
SALES (est): 7.38MM
SALES (corp-wide): 7.38MM Privately
Held
Web: www.jumohealth.com
SIC: 2721 2731 Comic books: publishing
and printing; Books, publishing only

(G-2165)
KAROS PHARMACEUTICALS
INC
5 Science Park Ste 2 (06511-1989)
PHONE................................203 535-0540
A Daifotis, *Pr*
Anastasia Daifotis, *Resident Chief
Executive Officer*
Philippe Chambon, *Ch Bd*

EMP: 13 EST: 2011
SALES (est): 242.46K Privately Held
Web: www.biohaven.com
SIC: 2834 Pharmaceutical preparations

(G-2166)
KOLLTAN PHARMACEUTICALS
INC (HQ)
300 George St Ste 530 (06511-6624)
PHONE................................203 773-3000
Gerald Mcmahon, *Pr*
Jane Henderson, *Chief Financial*
Carolyn F Sidor, *Chief Medical Officer*
Ronald A Peck, *CMO*
EMP: 22 EST: 2007
SALES (est): 398.14K
SALES (corp-wide): 2.36MM Publicly
Held
SIC: 2834 Pharmaceutical preparations
PA: Celldex Therapeutics, Inc.
53 Frontage Rd Ste 220
Hampton NJ 08827
908 200-7500

(G-2167)
KUEHNE NEW HAVEN LLC
71 Welton St (06511-1523)
PHONE................................203 508-6703
EMP: 23 EST: 2019
SALES (est): 10MM
SALES (corp-wide): 86.48MM Privately
Held
SIC: 2812 2899 Chlorine, compressed or
liquefied; Sodium chloride, refined
PA: Kuehne Chemical Company, Inc.
86 N Hackensack Ave
Kearny NJ 07032
973 589-0700

(G-2168)
LATINO MULTISERVICE LLC
552 Ferry St (06513-3053)
PHONE................................203 691-9715
David Banegas, *Owner*
EMP: 7 EST: 2015
SALES (est): 544.73K Privately Held
SIC: 3663 Mobile communication equipment

(G-2169)
LAYDON INDUSTRIES LLC (PA)
299 Terminal Ln (06519-1800)
PHONE................................203 562-7283
Kristy Leydon, *
EMP: 38 EST: 2005
SALES (est): 18.48MM
SALES (corp-wide): 18.48MM Privately
Held
Web: www.laydonindustries.com
SIC: 1611 3271 1795 4213 Highway signs
and guardrails; Paving blocks, concrete;
Demolition, buildings and other structures;
Automobiles, transport and delivery

(G-2170)
LONGHINI LLC
Also Called: Longhini Sausage
41 Longhini Ln (06519-1820)
PHONE................................203 624-7110
David Kemp, *Managing Member*
Richard Longhini Junior, *Pr*
EMP: 22 EST: 2017
SQ FT: 7,500
SALES (est): 5.35MM
SALES (corp-wide): 43.03MM Privately
Held
Web: www.longhinisausage.com
SIC: 2013 Sausages and other prepared
meats
PA: Village Gourmet Holdco, Llc
32 W 39th St Ph 16

New York NY 10018
212 219-1230

(G-2171)
LUCKEY LLC
184 Chapel St (06513-4209)
P.O. Box 871 (06419-0871)
PHONE................................203 747-5270
EMP: 10 EST: 2008
SALES (est): 788.03K Privately Held
Web: www.luckeyclimbers.com
SIC: 3299 3446 2431 Architectural
sculptures: gypsum, clay, papier mache, etc.
; Architectural metalwork; Millwork

(G-2172)
LUPIS INCORPORATED
169 Washington Ave (06519-1618)
PHONE................................203 562-9491
Peter P Lupi, *Pr*
Ellen Lupi, *Sec*
EMP: 10 EST: 1935
SQ FT: 10,000
SALES (est): 502.47K Privately Held
Web: www.lupisbakery.com
SIC: 2051 5461 Bread, all types (white,
wheat, rye, etc); fresh or frozen; Retail
bakeries

(G-2173)
MCVAC ENVIRONMENTAL SVCS
INC
481 Grand Ave (06513-3800)
PHONE................................203 497-1960
Serge Demers, *Pr*
Florence Demers, *
Charles Demers, *
Joseph Barraco, *
EMP: 44 EST: 1990
SQ FT: 15,000
SALES (est): 24.54MM Privately Held
Web: www.mcvacenvironmental.com
SIC: 4959 3561 1711 Environmental
cleanup services; Pumps and pumping
equipment; Heating and air conditioning
contractors

(G-2174)
MECHA NOODLE BAR
201 Crown St (06510-2701)
PHONE................................203 691-9671
Tony Pham, *Pr*
EMP: 8 EST: 2016
SALES (est): 226.75K Privately Held
Web: www.mechanoodlebar.com
SIC: 2098 Noodles (e.g. egg, plain, and
water), dry

(G-2175)
MINIT PRINT INC
27 Whitney Ave (06510-1219)
PHONE................................203 776-6000
Antonio Colasanto, *Prin*
EMP: 9 EST: 2007
SALES (est): 488.59K Privately Held
SIC: 2752 Offset printing

(G-2176)
MLK BUSINESS FORMS INC
25 James St (06513-4218)
P.O. Box 383 (06513-0383)
PHONE................................203 624-6304
Gene Booth, *Pr*
Fred Levesh, *VP*
Craig Levesh, *Sec*
EMP: 11 EST: 1994
SQ FT: 12,500
SALES (est): 430.31K Privately Held

SIC: 2759 2761 Business forms: printing,
nsk; Manifold business forms

(G-2177)
NEW HAVEN CHEMICALS LLC
67 Welton St (06511-1521)
PHONE................................475 241-1150
Nalluru Murthy, *CEO*
EMP: 30 EST: 2016
SALES (est): 787.57K Privately Held
SIC: 7389 4231 2911 3799 Business
services, nec; Trucking terminal facilities;
Nonaromatic chemical products;
Transportation equipment, nec

(G-2178)
NEW HAVEN CHLOR-ALKALI
LLC
Also Called: H.krevit
73 Welton St (06511-1523)
PHONE................................203 772-3350
Nalluru C Murthy, *Managing Member*
EMP: 70 EST: 2015
SALES (est): 9.27MM Privately Held
SIC: 2819 Hydrofluoric acid

(G-2179)
NEW HAVEN REGISTER LLC
100 Gando Dr (06513-1014)
PHONE................................203 789-5200
TOLL FREE: 800
Kevin F Walsh, *Pr*
Thomas Rice, *
John Collins, *
▲ EMP: 590 EST: 1915
SQ FT: 250,000
SALES (est): 103.7MM
SALES (corp-wide): 4.29B Privately Held
Web: www.nhregister.com
SIC: 2711 2752 Commercial printing and
newspaper publishing combined;
Commercial printing, lithographic
PA: The Hearst Corporation
300 W 57th St Fl 42
New York NY 10019
212 649-2000

(G-2180)
NOFET LLC
227 Church St Apt 5j (06510-1825)
P.O. Box 466 (06484-0466)
PHONE................................203 848-9064
Idit Hoter-ishay, *Managing Member*
Idit Hoter Ishay, *Managing Member*
EMP: 10 EST: 2013
SALES (est): 873.92K Privately Held
Web: www.resqbattery.com
SIC: 3691 7389 Batteries, rechargeable;
Business Activities at Non-Commercial Site

(G-2181)
ONOFRIOS ULTIMATE FOODS
INC
35 Wheeler St (06512-1632)
PHONE................................203 469-4014
Richard Onofrio, *Managing Member*
EMP: 10 EST: 2004
SALES (est): 2.33MM Privately Held
Web: www.ultimatefoods.net
SIC: 2033 2035 Spaghetti and other pasta
sauce: packaged in cans, jars, etc; Soy
sauce

(G-2182)
OVERSEAS MINISTRIES STUDY
CTR
Also Called: Omsc
342 Yale Ave (06515-2233)
P.O. Box 821 (08542-0803)

PHONE..................203 624-6672
Nelson Jennings, *Dir*
Gerald H Anderson, *Dir*
Dr Charles W, *Frmn Supr*
R Mac Dougall, *Treas*
Julius Poppinga, *Sec*
▲ EMP: 15 EST: 1923
SALES (est): 3.93MM Privately Held
Web: omsc.ptsem.edu
SIC: 8299 2721 Educational service, nondegree granting: continuing educ.; Periodicals, publishing only

(G-2183)
PEPSICO
Also Called: Pepsico
150 Munson St (06511-3572)
PHONE..................203 974-8912
EMP: 23 EST: 2013
SALES (est): 448.53K Privately Held
Web: www.pepsico.com
SIC: 2086 Carbonated soft drinks, bottled and canned

(G-2184)
PFIZER INC
Also Called: Pfizer
1 Howe St (06511-5473)
PHONE..................203 401-0100
Subhashis Banerjee Md, *Mgr*
EMP: 11
SALES (corp-wide): 100.33B Publicly Held
Web: www.pfizer.com
SIC: 2834 Pharmaceutical preparations
PA: Pfizer Inc.
66 Hudson Blvd E
New York NY 10001
212 733-2323

(G-2185)
PGXHEALTHHOLDING INC (PA)
5 Science Park (06511-1966)
PHONE..................203 786-3400
Kevin Rakin, *Pr*
Gerald F Vovis, *Ex VP*
EMP: 147 EST: 1986
SQ FT: 72,000
SALES (est): 14.4MM Privately Held
SIC: 2834 Pharmaceutical preparations

(G-2186)
PHOENIX PRESS INC
15 James St (06513-4217)
P.O. Box 347 (06513-0347)
PHONE..................203 865-5555
Brian Driscoll, *Pr*
EMP: 30 EST: 1982
SQ FT: 56,000
SALES (est): 4.99MM Privately Held
Web: www.phoenixpressinc.com
SIC: 2752 2791 2789 Offset printing; Typesetting; Bookbinding and related work

(G-2187)
PRECIPIO INC (PA)
4 Science Park Ste 3 (06511-1962)
PHONE..................203 787-7888
▲ EMP: 16 EST: 1997
SQ FT: 7,630
SALES (est): 9.41MM Publicly Held
Web: www.precipiodx.com
SIC: 8734 3826 8731 Testing laboratories; Analytical instruments; Biological research

(G-2188)
PROLIANCE INTERNATIONAL INC
100 Gando Dr (06513-1049)
PHONE..................203 401-6450

Mike Paulus, *Pr*
EMP: 22 EST: 2010
SALES (est): 5.88MM Privately Held
Web: www.nhregister.com
SIC: 3433 3629 Heating equipment, except electric; Condensers, for motors or generators

(G-2189)
QUANTUM CIRCUITS INC
150 Munson St Ste 203 (06511-3572)
PHONE..................203 872-4723
Martin Mengwal, *CEO*
Evan Wischik, *Contrlr*
EMP: 22 EST: 2021
SALES (est): 2.58MM Privately Held
Web: www.quantumcircuits.com
SIC: 3572 Computer storage devices

(G-2190)
RALLYBIO CORPORATION (PA)
Also Called: Rallybio
234 Church St Ste 1020 (06510-1869)
PHONE..................203 859-3820
Stephen Uden, *Pr*
Martin W Mackay, *Ofcr*
Jeffrey M Fryer, *CFO*
Steven Ryder, *CMO*
EMP: 16 EST: 2018
SQ FT: 4,500
Web: www.rallybio.com
SIC: 2834 Pharmaceutical preparations

(G-2191)
RHEMA 320 LLC (PA)
263 Grand Ave # 101 (06513-3724)
PHONE..................475 434-8581
EMP: 7 EST: 2021
SALES (est): 75.39K
SALES (corp-wide): 75.39K Privately Held
SIC: 3589 7389 Commercial cleaning equipment; Business services, nec

(G-2192)
ROCKWOOD MANUFACTURING CO
100 Sargent Dr (06511-5918)
PHONE..................800 582-2424
EMP: 11 EST: 2018
SALES (est): 994.36K Privately Held
SIC: 3999 Manufacturing industries, nec

(G-2193)
SALSA FRESCA NEW HAVEN
51 Broadway (06511-3411)
PHONE..................301 675-6226
EMP: 8 EST: 2017
SALES (est): 110.56K Privately Held
Web: www.salsafrescagrill.com
SIC: 2099 Dips, except cheese and sour cream based

(G-2194)
SARGENT MANUFACTURING COMPANY
Also Called: Assa Abloy USA
100 Sargent Dr (06511-5943)
P.O. Box 9725 (06536-0915)
PHONE..................203 562-2151
William Grambo, *Pr*
David M Ambrosini, *
Jeffrey Mereschuk, *
◆ EMP: 900 EST: 1985
SQ FT: 344,000
SALES (est): 120.36MM
SALES (corp-wide): 11.51B Privately Held
Web: www.sargentlock.com
SIC: 3429 Locks or lock sets
HQ: Assa Abloy Inc.
110 Sargent Dr

New Haven CT 06511

(G-2195)
SCHULZ ELECTRIC COMPANY
30 Gando Dr (06513-1049)
PHONE..................203 562-5811
Robert C Davis, *Pr*
Cheryl Davis, *
◆ EMP: 126 EST: 1927
SQ FT: 50,000
SALES (est): 44.69MM
SALES (corp-wide): 4.5B Publicly Held
Web: www.schulzgroupusa.com
SIC: 3621 3613 7694 Coils, for electric motors or generators; Control panels, electric; Electric motor repair
PA: The Timken Company
4500 Mount Pleasant St Nw
North Canton OH 44720
234 262-3000

(G-2196)
SEC ELECTRICAL INC
30 Gando Dr (06513-1049)
PHONE..................203 562-5811
Robert C Davis, *Pr*
EMP: 16 EST: 1998
SQ FT: 12,000
SALES (est): 901.4K Privately Held
SIC: 5063 7694 Motors, electric; Rewinding stators

(G-2197)
SECOND WIND MEDIA LIMITED
Also Called: Business New Haven
315 Front St (06513-3200)
PHONE..................203 781-3480
Michael Bingham, *Pr*
EMP: 10 EST: 1993
SQ FT: 1,200
SALES (est): 1.86MM Privately Held
Web: www.sftimes.com
SIC: 2711 Newspapers, publishing and printing

(G-2198)
SENSOR SWITCH INC (DH)
265 Church St Fl 15 (06510-7003)
PHONE..................203 265-2842
Vernon J Nagel, *Pr*
Brian Platner, *
Beverly Platner, *
Richard K Reece, *
C Dan Smith, *
EMP: 30 EST: 1987
SQ FT: 36,000
SALES (est): 10.65MM
SALES (corp-wide): 3.95B Publicly Held
SIC: 3812 3648 Infrared object detection equipment; Lighting equipment, nec
HQ: Acuity Brands Lighting, Inc.
1 Acuity Way
Conyers GA 30012

(G-2199)
SIMKINS INDUSTRIES INC
260 East St (06511-5839)
PHONE..................203 787-7171
EMP: 16 EST: 2020
SALES (est): 486.39K Privately Held
Web: www.simkinsindustries.com
SIC: 2631 2621 Paperboard mills; Paper mills

(G-2200)
SMARTPAY SOLUTIONS LLC
470 James St Ste 7 (06513-3175)
PHONE..................860 986-7659
Robert Conerly, *CEO*
EMP: 28 EST: 2016

SALES (est): 2.72MM Privately Held
Web: www.smartpayllc.com
SIC: 7372 Prepackaged software

(G-2201)
SMM NEW ENGLAND CORPORATION
808 Washington Ave (06519-1825)
PHONE..................203 777-7445
Brian More, *Mgr*
EMP: 35
Web: www.simsmm.com
SIC: 5051 3341 Metals service centers and offices; Secondary nonferrous metals
HQ: Smm New England Corporation
234 Universal Dr
North Haven CT 06473
203 777-2591

(G-2202)
SOTO HOLDINGS INC
300 East St (06511-5801)
PHONE..................203 781-8020
John Soto, *Pr*
Adrienne Montano, *
EMP: 43 EST: 1970
SQ FT: 44,000
SALES (est): 6.2MM Privately Held
SIC: 3724 Aircraft engines and engine parts

(G-2203)
SOUTHERN NENG TELECOM CORP (HQ)
Also Called: AT&T
2 Science Park (06511-1963)
PHONE..................203 771-5200
William Blase, *Pr*
Donald Mcgregor, *VP*
Michelle Macauda, *Network Service Vice President*
EMP: 300 EST: 1878
SQ FT: 100,000
SALES (est): 548.26MM
SALES (corp-wide): 120.74B Publicly Held
SIC: 4813 4812 5065 6159 Local and long distance telephone communications; Cellular telephone services; Telephone equipment; Machinery and equipment finance leasing
PA: At&T Inc.
208 S Akard St
Dallas TX 75202
210 821-4105

(G-2204)
SURACI CORP
Also Called: Suraci Paint & Powder Coating
90 River St Ste 2 (06513-4382)
PHONE..................203 624-1345
EMP: 9 EST: 2011
SALES (est): 204.75K Privately Held
Web: www.carccoater.com
SIC: 3479 Coating of metals and formed products

(G-2205)
SYLVAN R SHEMITZ DESIGNS LLC
45 Spring St (06519-2340)
PHONE..................203 776-5577
Allison Schieffelin, *CEO*
EMP: 54
SALES (corp-wide): 23.39MM Privately Held
Web: www.thelightingquotient.com
SIC: 3648 Decorative area lighting fixtures
PA: Sylvan R. Shemitz Designs, Llc
114 Boston Post Rd

West Haven CT 06516
203 931-4455

(G-2206)
TECHNOLUTIONS INC
157 Church St Fl 22a (06510-2105)
PHONE...................................203 404-4835
Alexander Clark, *CEO*
Alexander Grant Clark, *
EMP: 80 **EST:** 2004
SALES (est): 9.69MM **Privately Held**
Web: www.technolutions.com
SIC: 7372 Application computer software

(G-2207)
TETHEREDUCATION INC
102 Audubon St Fl 2 (06510-1263)
PHONE...................................203 691-0131
Christopher Neilson, *CEO*
EMP: 20
SALES (est): 690.79K **Privately Held**
SIC: 7372 7389 Prepackaged software;
Business services, nec

(G-2208)
TFAC LLC
27 Whitney Ave (06510-1219)
PHONE...................................203 776-6000
EMP: 7 **EST:** 2009
SALES (est): 114.49K **Privately Held**
SIC: 2752 Commercial printing, lithographic

(G-2209)
THE HOFFMAN PRESS
INCORPORATED
Also Called: Hoffman Press, The
30 Printers Ln (06519-1812)
PHONE...................................203 865-0818
EMP: 10 **EST:** 1908
SALES (est): 659.29K **Privately Held**
Web: www.thehoffmanpress.com
SIC: 2759 Flexographic printing

(G-2210)
TOTO LLC
27 Whitney Ave (06510-1219)
PHONE...................................203 776-6000
Antonio Colasanto, *Managing Member*
EMP: 10 **EST:** 2010
SALES (est): 494.31K **Privately Held**
Web: www.totousa.com
SIC: 2752 Commercial printing, lithographic

(G-2211)
TRANE INC
Also Called: Trane Supply
178 Wallace St (06511-5032)
PHONE...................................860 437-6208
John Rosenboom, *Brnch Mgr*
EMP: 17
Web: www.trane.com
SIC: 3585 Refrigeration and heating
equipment
HQ: Trane Inc.
1 Centennial Ave Ste 101
Piscataway NJ 08854
732 652-7100

(G-2212)
TRELLEBORG CTD SYSTEMS
US INC
Also Called: Uretek
30 Lenox St (06513-4419)
PHONE...................................203 468-0342
Sarah Mcguire, *Brnch Mgr*
EMP: 180
SALES (corp-wide): 276.11MM **Privately
Held**
Web: www.uretek.com

SIC: 2295 Resin or plastic coated fabrics
PA: Trelleborg Coated Systems Us, Inc.
715 Railroad Ave
Rutherfordton NC 28139
828 286-9126

(G-2213)
TREVI THERAPEUTICS INC (PA)
Also Called: Trevi
195 Church St Fl 14 (06510-2064)
PHONE...................................203 304-2499
Jennifer Good, *Pr*
David Meeker, *Ch Bd*
Christopher Seiter, *CFO*
Helena Brett-smith, *CDO*
Yann Mazabraud, *CCO*
EMP: 16 **EST:** 2011
SQ FT: 5,600
Web: www.trevitherapeutics.com
SIC: 2834 Pharmaceutical preparations

(G-2214)
VEOCI INC
195 Church St Ste 1401 (06510-2063)
PHONE...................................203 782-5944
Sukhminder Grewal, *Pr*
Brigitte J Girard, *
Tamas Simon, *
EMP: 97 **EST:** 2018
SALES (est): 7.44MM **Privately Held**
Web: www.veoci.com
SIC: 7372 Publisher's computer software

(G-2215)
VESPOLI USA INC
385 Clinton Ave (06513-4812)
PHONE...................................203 773-0311
Michael Vespoli, *Pr*
Nancy P Vespoli, *
◆ **EMP:** 45 **EST:** 1980
SQ FT: 32,000
SALES (est): 4.47MM **Privately Held**
Web: www.vespoli.com
SIC: 3732 5551 Boats, fiberglass: building
and repairing; Sails and equipment

(G-2216)
YALE ALUMNI PUBLICATIONS
INC
149 York St Fl 2 (06511-8923)
P.O. Box 1905 (06509-1905)
PHONE...................................203 432-0645
J Weili Cheng, *Ch*
EMP: 9 **EST:** 1937
SALES (est): 87.33K **Privately Held**
Web: www.yalealumnimagazine.org
SIC: 2721 Magazines: publishing only, not
printed on site

(G-2217)
YALE NEW HAVEN HLTH SVCS
CORP
150 Sargent Dr Ste 1 (06511-6100)
PHONE...................................203 688-2100
EMP: 523
SALES (corp-wide): 921.33MM **Privately
Held**
Web: www.ynhh.org
SIC: 8741 8011 2752 Hospital management
; Clinic, operated by physicians;
Commercial printing, lithographic
PA: Yale New Haven Health Services
Corporation
789 Howard Ave
New Haven CT 06519
203 688-4242

(G-2218)
YALE UNIVERSITY
Also Called: Cira
135 College St Ste 200 (06510-2483)
PHONE...................................203 764-4333
Leif Mitchell, *Prin*
EMP: 48
SALES (corp-wide): 5.1B **Privately Held**
Web: www.yale.edu
SIC: 8221 2731 2721 2741 University; Book
publishing; Magazines: publishing and
printing; Catalogs: publishing and printing
PA: Yale University
105 Wall St
New Haven CT 06511
203 432-2550

(G-2219)
YALE UNIVERSITY (PA)
105 Wall St (06511-8917)
P.O. Box 208228 (06520-8228)
PHONE...................................203 432-2550
Richard C Levin, *Pr*
Dorothy Robinson, *General Vice President**
Linda Koch Lorimer, *
John E Pepper Junior, *VP Fin*
Andrew D Hamilton, *
▲ **EMP:** 50 **EST:** 1701
SALES (est): 5.1B
SALES (corp-wide): 5.1B **Privately Held**
Web: www.yale.edu
SIC: 8221 2731 2721 2741 University; Book
publishing; Magazines: publishing and
printing; Catalogs: publishing and printing

(G-2220)
YALE UNIVERSITY
Also Called: Computing and Media Center
333 Cedar St le90shm (06510-3206)
PHONE...................................203 737-1244
Susan Grajek, *Dir*
EMP: 41
SALES (corp-wide): 5.1B **Privately Held**
Web: www.yale.edu
SIC: 8221 2759 University; Commercial
printing, nec
PA: Yale University
105 Wall St
New Haven CT 06511
203 432-2550

(G-2221)
YALE UNIVERSITY
Also Called: Printing & Graphic Services
149 York St (06511-8923)
P.O. Box 208227 (06520-8227)
PHONE...................................203 432-2880
Joseph Maynard, *Brnch Mgr*
EMP: 7
SALES (corp-wide): 5.1B **Privately Held**
Web: www.yale.edu
SIC: 2711 8221 Newspapers, publishing
and printing; University
PA: Yale University
105 Wall St
New Haven CT 06511
203 432-2550

New London
New London County

(G-2222)
BAYARD INC (DH)
Also Called: Creative Communications
1 Montauk Ave Ste 3 (06320-4967)
PHONE...................................860 437-3012
Richard Johnson, *Pr*
Lise Marie C Zanghetti, *
Didier Remiot, *

Guylene Dumais, *
EMP: 40 **EST:** 2000
SALES (est): 16.13MM **Privately Held**
Web: www.bayardinc.com
SIC: 2741 Miscellaneous publishing
HQ: Bayard
18 Rue Barbes
Montrouge 92120
174316060

(G-2223)
BUON APPETITO FROM ITALY
LLC
15 Shaw St (06320-4939)
PHONE...................................860 437-3668
EMP: 8 **EST:** 2010
SALES (est): 361.42K **Privately Held**
Web: www.buonappetitoristorante.com
SIC: 1389 Construction, repair, and
dismantling services

(G-2224)
CARWILD CORPORATION (PA)
3 State Pier Rd (06320-5817)
PHONE...................................860 442-4914
Joel S Wildstein, *Ch Bd*
Thomas Mcdonald, *Dir*
Rebecca Wildstein, *
◆ **EMP:** 21 **EST:** 1977
SQ FT: 40,000
SALES (est): 8.81MM **Privately Held**
Web: www.carwild.net
SIC: 3842 3841 Surgical appliances and
supplies; Surgical and medical instruments

(G-2225)
COPY CATS INC
458 Williams St Ste 1 (06320-5860)
PHONE...................................860 442-8424
Marion Brick, *Pr*
Marion Brick, *Pr*
Alan Terris, *VP*
EMP: 17 **EST:** 1993
SQ FT: 6,000
SALES (est): 2MM **Privately Held**
Web: www.copycatsnl.com
SIC: 2759 2672 7334 3993 Commercial
printing, nec; Paper; coated and laminated,
nec; Photocopying and duplicating services
; Advertising artwork

(G-2226)
DAY PUBLISHING COMPANY
(HQ)
Also Called: Day, The
47 Eugene Oneill Dr (06320-6351)
P.O. Box 1231 (06320-1231)
PHONE...................................860 701-4200
Gary Farrugia, *Pr*
Bob Tousignant, *
Mary Jane Mcginnis, *Sec*
EMP: 352 **EST:** 1881
SQ FT: 20,000
SALES (est): 64.22MM
SALES (corp-wide): 64.22MM **Privately
Held**
Web: www.theday.com
SIC: 2711 Commercial printing and
newspaper publishing combined
PA: The Day Trust
47 Eugene Oneill Dr
New London CT 06320
860 442-2200

(G-2227)
ELECTRIC BOAT CORPORATION
Also Called: General Dynamics Electric Boat
50 Pequot Ave (06320-5410)
PHONE...................................860 433-3000
EMP: 1416

▲ = Import ▼ = Export
◆ = Import/Export

SALES (corp-wide): 39.41B **Publicly Held**
Web: www.gdeb.com
SIC: 3731 Submarines, building and repairing
HQ: Electric Boat Corporation
75 Eastern Point Rd
Groton CT 06340

(G-2228)
FIRST AID BANDAGE CO INC
Also Called: Fabco Wrap
3 State Pier Rd (06320-5817)
PHONE..............................860 443-8499
Joel S Wildstein, *Pr*
EMP: 27 EST: 1932
SQ FT: 4,000
SALES (est): 782.66K **Privately Held**
Web: www.fabcousa.net
SIC: 3842 5122 Adhesive tape and plasters, medicated or non-medicated; Drugs, proprietaries, and sundries

(G-2229)
JOSHUA FRIEDMAN & CO LLC
49 Jay St (06320-5919)
PHONE..............................860 439-1637
EMP: 10 EST: 1982
SQ FT: 11,500
SALES (est): 770.09K **Privately Held**
Web: www.joshuafriedmanandco.com
SIC: 7641 2431 Furniture repair and maintenance; Millwork

(G-2230)
MICHAELS DAIRY INC
11 Harbor Ln (06320-4324)
PHONE..............................860 443-7617
Michael Buscetto, *Pr*
Philomena Buscetto, *VP*
EMP: 34 EST: 1936
SQ FT: 1,000
SALES (est): 256.27K **Privately Held**
Web: www.mitchell.edu
SIC: 5812 2024 Ice cream stands or dairy bars; Ice cream and ice milk

(G-2231)
NEW BEDFORD THREAD COMPANY
3 State Pier Rd (06320-5817)
PHONE..............................860 333-6700
David Wildstein, *Pr*
Richard S Cody, *Sec*
Rebecca Wildstein, *Treas*
EMP: 12 EST: 2019
SALES (est): 469.3K **Privately Held**
Web: www.newbedfordthread.com
SIC: 2284 Polyester thread

(G-2232)
ORTRONICS INC (DH)
Also Called: Ortronics
125 Eugene Oneill Dr Ste 140 (06320-6417)
PHONE..............................860 445-3900
Brian Dibella, *Pr*
Jackie Thornton, *VP*
▲ EMP: 60 EST: 1966
SALES (est): 119.06MM **Privately Held**
Web: www.legrand.us
SIC: 3577 3357 Computer peripheral equipment, nec; Communication wire
HQ: Legrand Holding, Inc.
60 Woodlawn St
West Hartford CT 06110
860 233-6251

(G-2233)
SHEFFIELD PHARMACEUTICALS LLC (PA)
Also Called: Sheffield Pharmaceuticals
170 Broad St (06320-5313)
PHONE..............................860 442-4451
Jeffrey Davis, *Pr*
Anthony Sollima, *CSO**
Todd Kwait, *
James Congdon, *
Michael Clark, *PRODUCT Development**
◆ EMP: 140 EST: 1850
SQ FT: 113,618
SALES (est): 89.87MM
SALES (corp-wide): 89.87MM **Privately Held**
Web: www.sheffieldpharma.com
SIC: 2844 5122 Toothpastes or powders, dentifrices; Pharmaceuticals

(G-2234)
THAMES SHIPYARD & REPAIR CO
50 Farnsworth St (06320-4104)
P.O. Box 791 (06320-0791)
PHONE..............................860 442-5349
John P Wronowski, *Pr*
Thomas Tyreseck, *
Richard Macmurray, *
Adam C Wronowski, *
EMP: 100 EST: 1967
SQ FT: 6,000
SALES (est): 9.5MM **Privately Held**
Web: www.thames-shipyard.com
SIC: 3731 Shipbuilding and repairing

(G-2235)
TIMES COMMUNITY NEWS GROUP
47 Eugene Oneill Dr (06320-6306)
PHONE..............................860 437-1150
Howard Lee, *Prin*
EMP: 15 EST: 1999
SALES (est): 138.82K **Privately Held**
Web: www.theday.com
SIC: 2711 Newspapers, publishing and printing

New Milford
Litchfield County

(G-2236)
3 STORY SOFTWARE LLC
63 Bridge St (06776-3527)
PHONE..............................860 799-6366
Darren Reid, *Managing Member*
EMP: 8 EST: 2007
SALES (est): 2.43MM
SALES (corp-wide): 1.6B **Privately Held**
Web: www.3storysoftware.com
SIC: 7372 Prepackaged software
PA: Hays Plc
4th Floor
London NW1 3
207 383-2266

(G-2237)
ADM GROUP LLC
18 Round Table Rd (06776-2620)
PHONE..............................860 354-3208
Andrew Mcguire, *Prin*
EMP: 9 EST: 2012
SALES (est): 159.92K **Privately Held**
SIC: 2041 Flour and other grain mill products

(G-2238)
ANZ PETROLEUM INC
Also Called: Fuel Wholesale
291 Danbury Rd Unit 2a (06776-7318)
PHONE..............................860 261-4798
Riaz Uddin, *CEO*
Maruf Ahmad, *CEO*
Riaz Uddin, *Off Mgr*
EMP: 16 EST: 2014
SALES (est): 9.53MM **Privately Held**
Web: www.anzpetroleum.com
SIC: 5172 1389 Fuel oil; Construction, repair, and dismantling services

(G-2239)
BALL & ROLLER BEARING CO LLC
Also Called: Ball & Roller Bearing
46 Old State Rd Ste 4 (06776-4330)
PHONE..............................860 355-4161
David Nohe, *CEO*
EMP: 10 EST: 1985
SALES (est): 829.69K **Privately Held**
Web: www.bandrb.com
SIC: 3562 3312 5085 Ball and roller bearings; Blast furnaces and steel mills; Bearings, bushings, wheels, and gears

(G-2240)
CARLSON SHEET METAL LLC
24 Bostwick Pl (06776-3510)
PHONE..............................860 354-4660
Craig F Carlson, *Prin*
EMP: 8 EST: 2006
SALES (est): 175.21K **Privately Held**
SIC: 3444 Sheet metalwork

(G-2241)
CRYSTAL FAIRFIELD TECH LLC
8 S End Plz (06776-4200)
PHONE..............................860 354-2111
▼ EMP: 9 EST: 2004
SQ FT: 6,500
SALES (est): 1.02MM **Privately Held**
Web: www.fairfieldcrystal.com
SIC: 3827 Optical instruments and lenses

(G-2242)
EAST BRANCH ENGRG & MFG INC
57 S End Plz (06776-4244)
PHONE..............................860 355-9661
EMP: 16 EST: 1990
SQ FT: 1,500
SALES (est): 2.88MM **Privately Held**
Web: www.eastbrancheng.com
SIC: 3599 Machine shop, jobbing and repair

(G-2243)
FARRELL PRCSION MTALCRAFT CORP
192 Danbury Rd (06776-4311)
PHONE..............................860 355-2651
Michael Tkacs, *Pr*
William Farrell, *
Peter Farrell, *Prin*
Terrance Farrell, *
EMP: 41 EST: 1976
SQ FT: 17,500
SALES (est): 2.2MM **Privately Held**
Web: www.farrellprecision.com
SIC: 3444 3479 7692 Sheet metal specialties, not stamped; Painting of metal products; Welding repair

(G-2244)
GLACIER COMPUTER LLC
46 Bridge St (06776-6513)

PHONE..............................603 882-1560
Rodney Mitchell, *Brnch Mgr*
EMP: 12
SALES (corp-wide): 4.55MM **Privately Held**
Web: www.glaciercomputer.com
SIC: 3571 5734 Mainframe computers; Computer and software stores
PA: Glacier Computer, L.L.C.
46 Bridge St Ste 1
New Milford CT 06776
860 355-7552

(G-2245)
GUARDIAN ENVMTL TECH INC
208 Sawyer Hill Rd (06776-2018)
P.O. Box 2344 (06777-0344)
PHONE..............................860 350-2200
EMP: 10 EST: 1992
SQ FT: 800
SALES (est): 446.61K **Privately Held**
Web: www.guardianenvironmental.com
SIC: 3589 3564 Water filters and softeners, household type; Filters, air: furnaces, air conditioning equipment, etc.

(G-2246)
GWILLIAM COMPANY INC
46 Old State Rd (06776-4330)
PHONE..............................860 354-2884
David Nohe, *Pr*
Margaret Nohe, *Sec*
▲ EMP: 12 EST: 1929
SALES (est): 2.11MM **Privately Held**
Web: www.bandrb.com
SIC: 3562 3568 Ball bearings and parts; Power transmission equipment, nec

(G-2247)
HARRELLS LLC
458 Danbury Rd Ste D3 (06776-4380)
PHONE..............................863 680-2003
Mark Chant, *Mgr*
EMP: 18
SALES (corp-wide): 243.41MM **Privately Held**
Web: www.harrells.com
SIC: 2875 Fertilizers, mixing only
HQ: Harrell's, Llc
5105 New Tampa Hwy
Lakeland FL 33815

(G-2248)
INTACT SOLUTIONS LLC
201 Housatonic Ave (06776-5540)
PHONE..............................860 350-1900
EMP: 8 EST: 2019
SALES (est): 106.06K **Privately Held**
SIC: 3559 Pharmaceutical machinery

(G-2249)
KARAS ENGINEERING COMPANY INC
44 Old State Rd Ste 20 (06776-4339)
PHONE..............................860 355-3153
Denny Karas, *Pr*
Lisa Karas, *Sec*
EMP: 8 EST: 1973
SQ FT: 5,000
SALES (est): 715.86K **Privately Held**
Web: www.karaseng.com
SIC: 3599 Machine shop, jobbing and repair

(G-2250)
KIMBERLY-CLARK CORPORATION
Also Called: Kimberly-Clark
58 Pickett District Rd (06776-4493)
PHONE..............................860 210-1602

Wayne Sanders, *Mgr*
EMP: 54
SALES (corp-wide): 20.43B **Publicly Held**
Web: www.kimberly-clark.com
SIC: 2621 2676 Sanitary tissue paper;
　Infant and baby paper products
PA: Kimberly-Clark Corporation
　351 Phelps Dr
　Irving TX 75038
　972 281-1200

(G-2251)
LABLITE LLC
8 S Main St (06776-3508)
P.O. Box 1206 (06776-1206)
PHONE................................860 355-8817
EMP: 10 **EST:** 1995
SQ FT: 1,400
SALES (est): 975.25K **Privately Held**
Web: www.lablite.com
SIC: 7372 Application computer software

(G-2252)
LINE-X OF NEW ENGLAND LLC
Also Called: Line-X
8 Spice Ln (06776-2670)
PHONE................................860 355-6997
John Farrell, *Prin*
EMP: 8 **EST:** 2017
SALES (est): 234.7K **Privately Held**
Web: www.linex.com
SIC: 7692 5531 Welding repair; Truck
　equipment and parts

(G-2253)
MODELVISION INC
566 Danbury Rd Ste 4 (06776-4331)
PHONE................................860 355-3884
David Spiegel, *Pr*
Laura Spiegel, *Sec*
EMP: 7 **EST:** 1995
SQ FT: 7,500
SALES (est): 565.44K **Privately Held**
Web: www.modelvisioninc.com
SIC: 3999 Models, general, except toy

(G-2254)
NEELTRAN INC
71 Pickett District Rd (06776-4412)
PHONE................................860 350-5964
Antonio Capanna Junior, *Pr*
◆ **EMP:** 117 **EST:** 1973
SQ FT: 45,000
SALES (est): 36.86MM
SALES (corp-wide): 105.98MM **Publicly
Held**
Web: www.neeltran.com
SIC: 3612 3677 3679 Line voltage regulators
　; Electronic transformers; Static power
　supply converters for electronic applications
PA: American Superconductor Corporation
　114 E Main St
　Ayer MA 01432
　978 842-3000

(G-2255)
NEW MILFORD COMMISSION
Also Called: New Mlford Wtr Plltion Ctrl Au
123 West St (06776-3540)
P.O. Box 178 (06776-0178)
PHONE................................860 354-3758
Ken Bailey, *Superintnt*
EMP: 8 **EST:** 2002
SQ FT: 3,652
SALES (est): 178.24K **Privately Held**
Web: www.newmilford.org
SIC: 3589 Sewage and water treatment
　equipment

(G-2256)
NEW MILFORD FARMS INC
60 Boardman Rd (06776-5516)
PHONE................................860 210-0250
EMP: 12 **EST:** 1991
SALES (est): 3.59MM
SALES (corp-wide): 20.43B **Publicly Held**
Web: www.garick.com
SIC: 2875 Compost
HQ: Garick, Llc
　8400 Sweet Valley Dr # 408
　Cleveland OH 44125
　216 581-0100

(G-2257)
NUTEK AEROSPACE CORP
180 Sunny Valley Rd Ste 2 (06776-3361)
PHONE................................860 355-3169
Joseph Di Candido, *Pr*
Eloise Di Candido, *Sec*
EMP: 7 **EST:** 1983
SQ FT: 7,000
SALES (est): 901.28K **Privately Held**
Web: www.nutekaerospace.com
SIC: 3592 Valves, aircraft

(G-2258)
O & G INDUSTRIES INC
271 Danbury Rd (06776-4313)
PHONE................................860 354-4438
Bill Eayrs, *Brnch Mgr*
EMP: 39
SQ FT: 7,465
SALES (corp-wide): 496.36MM **Privately
Held**
Web: www.ogind.com
SIC: 2951 1542 Asphalt paving mixtures
　and blocks; Commercial and office building,
　new construction
PA: O & G Industries, Inc.
　112 Wall St
　Torrington CT 06790
　860 489-9261

(G-2259)
QUALITY MACHINE INC
87 Danbury Rd (06776-3413)
PHONE................................860 354-6794
Joseph John Mcfadden Junior, *Prin*
EMP: 7 **EST:** 2012
SALES (est): 332.05K **Privately Held**
SIC: 3599 Machine shop, jobbing and repair

(G-2260)
**SEGA READY MIX
INCORPORATED (PA)**
Also Called: Sega Ready Mix
519 Danbury Rd (06776-4392)
PHONE................................860 354-3969
Roderic Oneglia, *Pr*
EMP: 10 **EST:** 1958
SQ FT: 8,000
SALES (est): 2.19MM
SALES (corp-wide): 2.19MM **Privately
Held**
Web: www.segareadymix.com
SIC: 3273 Ready-mixed concrete

(G-2261)
TOBY PRESS LLC
Also Called: Koren Publishers
P.O. Box 8531 (06776-8531)
PHONE................................203 830-8508
Matthew Miller, *Managing Member*
EMP: 10 **EST:** 1999
SALES (est): 547.89K **Privately Held**
Web: www.korenpub.com
SIC: 2731 Book publishing

(G-2262)
TOTAL REGISTER INC
180 Sunny Valley Rd Ste 1 (06776-3361)
PHONE................................860 210-0465
Terence Gallagher, *Pr*
Daniel J Gallagher, *VP*
John Gallagher, *VP*
▲ **EMP:** 10 **EST:** 1986
SALES (est): 870K **Privately Held**
Web: www.grafixequipment.com
SIC: 3699 Laser systems and equipment

Newington
Hartford County

(G-2263)
2023 HOLDINGS LLC (PA)
Also Called: Plumb Pak Medical
1170 Main St (06111-3000)
P.O. Box 311146 (06131-1146)
PHONE................................603 239-6371
Robert S Holden, *CEO*
Jean Hanna Holden, *Ch*
Kenneth L Collett, *Treas*
James H Holden, *Ex VP*
Edwin F Atkins, *VP Sls*
▲ **EMP:** 200 **EST:** 1923
SALES (est): 48.21MM
SALES (corp-wide): 48.21MM **Privately
Held**
Web: www.elliottkieffer.com
SIC: 3432 5074 Plumbers' brass goods:
　drain cocks, faucets, spigots, etc.;
　Plumbing fittings and supplies

(G-2264)
261 PASCONE PLACE LLC
261 Pascone Pl (06111-4524)
PHONE................................860 666-7845
Nicholas Lococo, *Prin*
EMP: 8 **EST:** 2011
SALES (est): 130.32K **Privately Held**
SIC: 3585 Soda fountain and beverage
　dispensing equipment and parts

(G-2265)
**A-1 CHROME AND POLISHING
CORP**
125 Stamm Rd (06111-3619)
PHONE................................860 666-4593
Claudio Spada, *Pr*
Joseph Spada, *VP*
EMP: 12 **EST:** 1980
SQ FT: 2,400
SALES (est): 485.7K **Privately Held**
Web: www.a1chrome.com
SIC: 3471 Electroplating of metals or
　formed products

(G-2266)
ADDAMO MANUFACTURING INC
360 Stamm Rd (06111-3627)
PHONE................................860 667-2601
Sebastian Addamo, *Pr*
Paul Addamo, *VP*
Lucy Addamo, *Sec*
Sevvy Addamo, *VP*
EMP: 7 **EST:** 1960
SQ FT: 15,000
SALES (est): 642.34K **Privately Held**
Web: www.addamomfg.com
SIC: 3469 3599 Machine parts, stamped or
　pressed metal; Machine shop, jobbing and
　repair

(G-2267)
**ADVANCED ADHESIVE
SYSTEMS INC**

Also Called: A A S
681 N Mountain Rd (06111-1349)
PHONE................................860 953-4100
EMP: 28 **EST:** 1994
SALES (est): 6.02MM **Privately Held**
Web: www.advadh.com
SIC: 2891 Adhesives

(G-2268)
**ADVANCED TORQUE
PRODUCTS LLC**
56 Budney Rd (06111-5132)
P.O. Box 7241 (06037-7241)
PHONE................................860 828-1523
EMP: 8 **EST:** 2000
SQ FT: 12,146
SALES (est): 1.78MM **Privately Held**
Web: www.advancedtorque.com
SIC: 3566 7539 Torque converters, except
　auto; Torque converter repair, automotive

(G-2269)
ALKEN INDUSTRIES INC
300 Fenn Rd (06111-2277)
PHONE................................631 467-2000
Tami Senior, *Pr*
Bridgette Senior, *
EMP: 40 **EST:** 1969
SALES (est): 10.13MM
SALES (corp-wide): 151.59MM **Privately
Held**
Web: www.alkenind.com
SIC: 3728 3441 Aircraft parts and
　equipment, nec; Fabricated structural metal
PA: Pcx Aerostructures, Llc
　300 Fenn Rd
　Newington CT 06111
　860 666-2471

(G-2270)
ALLIANCE GRAPHICS INC
16 Progress Cir (06111-5545)
PHONE................................860 666-7992
Mark Bruks, *CEO*
EMP: 10 **EST:** 1980
SQ FT: 4,200
SALES (est): 977.71K **Privately Held**
Web: www.agink.com
SIC: 2752 7334 Offset printing;
　Photocopying and duplicating services

(G-2271)
ALLIED MACHINING CO INC
Also Called: Allied Engineering
50 Progress Cir Ste 3 (06111-5547)
PHONE................................860 665-1228
Katherine Nogiec, *Pr*
Katherine Jankowski, *Pr*
Chris Jankowski, *VP*
Peter Jankowski, *Sec*
EMP: 9 **EST:** 1988
SQ FT: 9,600
SALES (est): 1.81MM **Privately Held**
Web: www.alliedmachining.biz
SIC: 3599 Machine shop, jobbing and repair

(G-2272)
AMERICAN TOOL & MFG CORP
125 Rockwell Rd (06111-5535)
PHONE................................860 666-2255
Grzegorz Wolanin, *CEO*
EMP: 11 **EST:** 1992
SQ FT: 6,000
SALES (est): 1.81MM **Privately Held**
Web: www.amertool.com
SIC: 3599 Machine shop, jobbing and repair

(G-2273)
ATLAS STAMPING & MFG CORP
729 N Mountain Rd (06111-1424)
PHONE..............................860 757-3233
Kenneth Prigodich, *Pr*
EMP: 30 EST: 1969
SQ FT: 13,500
SALES (est): 5.89MM Privately Held
Web: www.atlasstamping.com
SIC: 3469 3544 Stamping metal for the trade
; Dies and die holders for metal cutting,
forming, die casting

(G-2274)
B&N AEROSPACE INC
44 Rockwell Rd (06111-5526)
PHONE..............................860 665-0134
Walter Blaszko, *Prin*
Dennis Blaszko, *
Gary Klinsman Senior, *VP*
Donna Blaszko, *
EMP: 45 EST: 1979
SQ FT: 15,000
SALES (est): 7.63MM Privately Held
Web: www.bnaerospace.com
SIC: 3728 Aircraft assemblies,
subassemblies, and parts, nec

(G-2275)
BEACON GROUP INC (PA)
549 Cedar St (06111-1814)
PHONE..............................860 594-5200
Suresh Mirchandani, *Pr*
Robert Sarkisian, *
Karishma Mirchandani, *
EMP: 27 EST: 1979
SQ FT: 100,000
SALES (est): 25.85MM
SALES (corp-wide): 25.85MM Privately
Held
Web: www.beacongp.com
SIC: 3724 3812 3053 3714 Aircraft engines
and engine parts; Search and navigation
equipment; Gaskets; packing and sealing
devices; Motor vehicle parts and
accessories

(G-2276)
BEACON INDUSTRIES INC
549 Cedar St (06111-1814)
PHONE..............................860 594-5200
Suresh Mirchandani, *CEO*
Robert S Sarkisian, *
▲ EMP: 108 EST: 1948
SQ FT: 300,000
SALES (est): 25.85MM
SALES (corp-wide): 25.85MM Privately
Held
Web: www.beacongp.com
SIC: 3728 Aircraft parts and equipment, nec
PA: The Beacon Group Inc
549 Cedar St
Newington CT 06111
860 594-5200

(G-2277)
**BRIDGESTONE RET
OPERATIONS LLC**
Also Called: Firestone
2897 Berlin Tpke (06111-4115)
PHONE..............................860 594-0594
EMP: 7
Web: www.bridgestoneamericas.com
SIC: 5531 7534 Automotive tires; Tire
retreading and repair shops
HQ: Bridgestone Retail Operations, Llc
333 E Lake St Ste 300
Bloomingdale IL 60108
630 259-9000

(G-2278)
C & A MACHINE CO INC
49 Progress Cir (06111-5532)
PHONE..............................860 667-0605
Joe Milluzzo, *Pr*
John Marut, *
EMP: 43 EST: 1980
SQ FT: 16,000
SALES (est): 5.24MM Privately Held
Web: www.ca-machine.com
SIC: 3451 3599 Screw machine products;
Machine shop, jobbing and repair

(G-2279)
**CATSKILL GRAN
COUNTERTOPS INC**
Also Called: Counters
156 Pane Rd Ste A (06111-5557)
PHONE..............................860 667-1555
Nicacio F Pinho, *Pr*
EMP: 10 EST: 2012
SALES (est): 417.85K Privately Held
Web: www.catskillgranite.com
SIC: 3131 Counters

(G-2280)
CENTRAL CONN SLS & MFG INC
37 Stanwell Rd (06111-4531)
PHONE..............................860 667-1411
Paul Campbell, *Pr*
Richard Campbell, *VP*
EMP: 7 EST: 1978
SQ FT: 6,000
SALES (est): 946.12K Privately Held
Web: centralctsales.yolasite.com
SIC: 3599 Machine shop, jobbing and repair

(G-2281)
**COMPONENT TECHNOLOGIES
INC (PA)**
Also Called: CTI
68 Holmes Rd (06111-1708)
PHONE..............................860 667-1065
Fred Viggiano, *Pr*
Fred Viggiano Junior, *Pr*
Lynn D.o.s., *VP*
Laurie D.o.s., *Treas*
Larry Hutnick, *VP*
EMP: 22 EST: 1981
SQ FT: 24,000
SALES (est): 3.68MM
SALES (corp-wide): 3.68MM Privately
Held
Web: www.motga.org
SIC: 3471 Electroplating of metals or
formed products

(G-2282)
COMPU-DATA LLC
Also Called: Intelisent
597 N Mountain Rd (06111-1418)
PHONE..............................800 666-0399
Andrew Mandell, *Pr*
Mark Mandell, *
Joyce Mandell, *
Bruce Mandell, *
Eric Springer, *
EMP: 85 EST: 1985
SQ FT: 40,000
SALES (est): 17.12MM Privately Held
Web: www.intelisent.com
SIC: 5112 3231 Business forms; Products of
purchased glass

(G-2283)
CUSTOM METAL CRAFTERS INC
Also Called: Custom Metal Crafters CMC
815 N Mountain Rd (06111-1489)
PHONE..............................860 953-4210

Jean Bourget, *Ch*
Daniel F Bourget, *Pr*
Stephen Rosner, *Pr*
Lynn M Clemente, *VP*
▲ EMP: 20 EST: 1972
SQ FT: 55,000
SALES (est): 4.47MM Privately Held
Web: www.custom-metal.com
SIC: 3364 3369 3363 Nonferrous die-
castings except aluminum; Nonferrous
foundries, nec; Aluminum die-castings

(G-2284)
CYR WOODWORKING INC
139 Summit St (06111-1715)
PHONE..............................860 232-1991
Roderique Cyr, *Pr*
EMP: 7 EST: 1966
SALES (est): 912.5K Privately Held
Web: www.cyrwoodworking.com
SIC: 2521 2434 Wood office furniture; Wood
kitchen cabinets

(G-2285)
DATA-GRAPHICS INC
240 Hartford Ave (06111-2077)
PHONE..............................860 667-0435
▲ EMP: 74 EST: 1994
SQ FT: 15,000
SALES (est): 8.35MM Privately Held
Web: www.data-mail.com
SIC: 2752 Commercial printing, lithographic

(G-2286)
**DCG-APVH ACQUISITION CO
LLC**
53 Rockwell Rd (06111-5535)
P.O. Box 188 (63351-0188)
PHONE..............................636 488-3200
Anik Patel, *Managing Member*
Jacki Brandenburg, *Acctnt*
EMP: 50 EST: 2021
SALES (est): 2.41MM Privately Held
SIC: 3554 Die cutting and stamping
machinery, paper converting

(G-2287)
**EB CARPORTS & METAL
STRUCTURES**
357 Alumni Rd (06111-1867)
PHONE..............................860 263-3797
EMP: 10 EST: 2019
SALES (est): 924.23K Privately Held
Web: www.ebcarports.com
SIC: 3448 Prefabricated metal buildings and
components

(G-2288)
ECO MILLWORK LLC
697 Cedar St (06111-1814)
PHONE..............................860 266-5744
EMP: 10 EST: 2021
SALES (est): 948.6K Privately Held
Web: eco-millwork-llc.business.site
SIC: 2431 Millwork

(G-2289)
EDCO ENGINEERING INC
100 Rockwell Rd (06111-5530)
PHONE..............................860 667-8292
EMP: 68 EST: 1977
SALES (est): 11.38MM Privately Held
Web: www.edcoengineering.com
SIC: 3544 Special dies, tools, jigs, and
fixtures

(G-2290)
EDRIVE ACTUATORS INC
385 Stamm Rd (06111-3628)

PHONE..............................860 953-0588
Richard Swanson, *Pr*
James Haury, *VP*
EMP: 8 EST: 1980
SQ FT: 3,600
SALES (est): 9.45MM
SALES (corp-wide): 3.92B Publicly Held
Web: www.edriveactuators.com
SIC: 3545 Machine tool attachments and
accessories
HQ: Joyce/Dayton Corp.
3300 S Dixie Dr Ste 101
Dayton OH 45439
937 294-6261

(G-2291)
ENJET AERO NEWINGTON INC
111 Holmes Rd (06111-1714)
PHONE..............................860 953-0686
Bruce Breckenridge, *CEO*
EMP: 55 EST: 1969
SQ FT: 8,000
SALES (est): 9.89MM
SALES (corp-wide): 78.96MM Privately
Held
Web: www.enjetaero.com
SIC: 3545 Precision tools, machinists'
HQ: Enjet Aero Acquisitions Holding Inc.
9401 Indian Creek Pkwy
Overland Park KS 66210
913 717-7396

(G-2292)
ENVELOPES & MORE INC
124 Francis Ave (06111-1216)
PHONE..............................860 286-7570
Mike Sullivan, *Pr*
John Sullivan, *Pr*
Michael Sullivan, *Pr*
Tim Sullivan, *Treas*
EMP: 17 EST: 1991
SALES (est): 781.84K Privately Held
Web: www.duplionline.com
SIC: 2759 Envelopes: printing, nsk

(G-2293)
FINE PRINT NEW ENGLAND INC
711 N Mountain Rd (06111-1424)
PHONE..............................860 953-0660
James Weber Junior, *Pr*
EMP: 8 EST: 1991
SQ FT: 7,200
SALES (est): 754.84K Privately Held
Web: www.instafax.com
SIC: 2752 Offset printing

(G-2294)
FLOW RESOURCES INC (HQ)
Also Called: Wolf Colorprint
135 Day St Ste 1 (06111-1200)
PHONE..............................860 666-1200
John W Meier, *CEO*
Glenn Basale, *
EMP: 25 EST: 1941
SQ FT: 20,000
SALES (est): 10.17MM
SALES (corp-wide): 21.88MM Privately
Held
Web: www.wolfcolorprint.com
SIC: 2752 Offset printing
PA: J.S. Mccarthy Co., Inc.
15 Darin Dr
Augusta ME 04330
207 622-6241

(G-2295)
FRASAL TOOL CO INC
14 Foster St (06111-4906)
PHONE..............................860 666-3524
Frank Giangrave, *Pr*

Pierrette Giangrave, *Sec*
▲ **EMP: 10 EST:** 1972
SALES (est): 1.88MM **Privately Held**
Web: www.frasaltool.com
SIC: 3599 3546 Machine shop, jobbing and
　repair; Power-driven handtools

(G-2296)
GKN AEROSPACE NEWINGTON LLC
76 Stanwell Rd (06111-4531)
PHONE............................860 830-5810
EMP: 10 EST: 2004
SALES (est): 204.48K **Privately Held**
SIC: 3721 Aircraft

(G-2297)
GKN AEROSPACE NEWINGTON LLC (DH)
183 Louis St (06111-4517)
PHONE............................860 667-8502
▲ **EMP: 146 EST:** 2004
SQ FT: 43,000
SALES (est): 49.51MM
SALES (corp-wide): 9.07B **Privately Held**
SIC: 3724 3728 Aircraft engines and engine
　parts; Aircraft parts and equipment, nec
　HQ: Gkn Aerospace Sweden Ab
　　Flygmotorvagen 1m
　　TrollhAttan 461 3
　　52094000

(G-2298)
HANWHA AEROSPACE USA LLC
Edac Aero
275 Richard St (06111-5046)
PHONE............................860 667-2134
Tom Mosdale, *Genl Mgr*
EMP: 92
Web: www.hanwhaaerospaceusa.com
SIC: 3728 Aircraft parts and equipment, nec
　HQ: Hanwha Aerospace Usa Llc
　　5 Mckee Pl
　　Cheshire CT 06410
　　203 806-2090

(G-2299)
HANWHA AEROSPACE USA LLC
Also Called: Mtu Aero Engine Design Inc.
275 Richard St (06111-5046)
PHONE............................860 667-2134
Ben Adams, *Pr*
Alain Derube, *　 ＊*
Thomas Seifert, *　 ＊*
▲ **EMP: 130 EST:** 1945
SALES (est): 46.07MM **Privately Held**
Web: www.hanwhaaerospaceusa.com
SIC: 3728 Aircraft parts and equipment, nec
　HQ: Hanwha Aerospace Usa Llc
　　5 Mckee Pl
　　Cheshire CT 06410
　　203 806-2090

(G-2300)
HI-TECH POLISHING INC
50 Progress Cir Ste 3 # 5 (06111-5547)
PHONE............................860 665-1399
Pasquale Griffo, *Pr*
Frances Griffo, *VP*
EMP: 18 EST: 1989
SQ FT: 1,600
SALES (est): 976.49K **Privately Held**
SIC: 3471 Tumbling (cleaning and
　polishing) of machine parts

(G-2301)
JENSEN MACHINE COMPANY
721 Russell Rd (06111-1527)
PHONE............................860 666-5438

John Andrew Jensen Junior, *Pr*
Alice Jensen, *Treas*
Audrey N Jensen, *Sec*
EMP: 9 EST: 1946
SQ FT: 15,000
SALES (est): 965.02K **Privately Held**
Web: www.jensenmachine.com
SIC: 3599 Machine shop, jobbing and repair

(G-2302)
KANIA DARIUS
75 Rockwell Rd (06111-5564)
PHONE............................860 667-4400
Darius Kania, *Prin*
EMP: 9 EST: 2011
SALES (est): 207.98K **Privately Held**
Web: www.aerospacewelding.com
SIC: 3599 Machine shop, jobbing and repair

(G-2303)
KINETIC CONCEPTS INC
Also Called: Kci
65 Louis St Ste C (06111-4598)
PHONE............................860 594-1043
Michael Mcnelly, *Genl Mgr*
EMP: 10
SALES (corp-wide): 34.23B **Publicly Held**
Web: www.acelity.com
SIC: 3841 Surgical and medical instruments
　HQ: Kinetic Concepts, Inc.
　　12930 W Interstate 10
　　San Antonio TX 78249
　　800 531-5346

(G-2304)
LYNN WELDING CO INC
75 Rockwell Rd Ste 1 (06111-5564)
PHONE............................860 667-4400
Jan Kania, *Pr*
James Inglis Senior, *Pr*
Joseph Inglis, *　 ＊*
Regina Kania, *　 ＊*
EMP: 80 EST: 1981
SQ FT: 13,900
SALES (est): 8.35MM **Privately Held**
Web: www.aerospacewelding.com
SIC: 3599 7692 Machine shop, jobbing and
　repair; Welding repair

(G-2305)
MACRISTY INDUSTRIES INC (PA)
610 N Mountain Rd (06111-1347)
PHONE............................860 225-4637
Jeff Barlow, *Pr*
Kristin Barlow, *Sec*
Jon Brad Barlow, *Sec*
▲ **EMP: 12 EST:** 1972
SQ FT: 150,000
SALES (est): 13.07MM
SALES (corp-wide): 13.07MM **Privately Held**
SIC: 3498 3432 3433 4226 Tube fabricating
　(contract bending and shaping); Plumbing
　fixture fittings and trim; Heating equipment,
　except electric; Special warehousing and
　storage, nec

(G-2306)
MEGA PRECISION LLC
56 Budney Rd Unit B (06111-5132)
PHONE............................203 887-5718
Robert Burzacki, *Prin*
EMP: 9 EST: 2015
SALES (est): 476.74K **Privately Held**
Web: www.megaprecisionllc.com
SIC: 3599 Machine shop, jobbing and repair

(G-2307)
MUIR ENVELOPE PLUS INC
Also Called: Muir Envelope Div
124 Francis Ave (06111-1216)
PHONE............................860 953-6847
Paul Klett, *Pr*
Jack Muir, *Sec*
EMP: 14 EST: 1957
SQ FT: 40,000
SALES (est): 320.68K **Privately Held**
Web: www.muirenvelope.com
SIC: 2759 2752 Commercial printing, nec;
　Commercial printing, lithographic

(G-2308)
NEW ENGLAND INDUSTRIAL SUP LLC
127 Costello Rd (06111-5109)
PHONE............................860 436-5959
Michael Clavette, *Managing Member*
Michael Kollasch, *Prin*
EMP: 10 EST: 2005
SALES (est): 1.29MM **Privately Held**
Web: www.neisupplies.com
SIC: 7363 5087 3086 7349 Office help
　supply service; Janitors' supplies;
　Packaging and shipping materials, foamed
　plastics; Janitorial service, contract basis

(G-2309)
NEW ENGLAND LIFT SYSTEMS LLC
714 N Mountain Rd (06111-1348)
PHONE............................860 372-4040
Ann M Jordan, *Pr*
EMP: 8 EST: 2016
SALES (est): 78.89K **Privately Held**
SIC: 3536 3625 Hoists, cranes, and
　monorails; Crane and hoist controls,
　including metal mill

(G-2310)
NEWINGTON MEAT CENTER
847 Main St (06111-2471)
PHONE............................860 666-3431
Vito Lattarulo, *Pt*
EMP: 7 EST: 1963
SQ FT: 1,000
SALES (est): 217.12K **Privately Held**
Web: www.newingtonmeat.com
SIC: 5421 2013 Meat markets, including
　freezer provisioners; Sausages and other
　prepared meats

(G-2311)
NOWAK PRODUCTS INC
8 Dean Dr (06111-4311)
PHONE............................860 666-9685
Gary Nowak, *Pr*
Jay Giblin, *Sec*
EMP: 9 EST: 1984
SALES (est): 1.11MM **Privately Held**
Web: www.nowakproducts.com
SIC: 3541 Machine tools, metal cutting type

(G-2312)
OMAR COFFEE COMPANY
41 Commerce Ct (06111-2246)
PHONE............................860 667-8889
TOLL FREE: 800
Diane C Bokron, *Pr*
Joann Lemnior, *　 ＊.*
Steve Costas, *　 ＊*
EMP: 50 EST: 1937
SQ FT: 30,000
SALES (est): 8.05MM **Privately Held**
Web: www.omarcoffee.com
SIC: 2095 5149 Coffee roasting (except by
　wholesale grocers); Condiments

(G-2313)
ON SITE GAS SYSTEMS INC
35 Budney Rd (06111-5133)
PHONE............................860 667-8888
◆ **EMP: 45 EST:** 1987
SALES (est): 9.62MM **Privately Held**
Web: www.onsitegas.com
SIC: 3569 Generators: steam, liquid
　oxygen, or nitrogen

(G-2314)
PAUL WELDING COMPANY INC
157 Kelsey St (06111-5419)
PHONE............................860 229-9945
Michael Paul, *Pr*
Terese Seidl, *Sec*
David Paul, *VP*
Jeffrey Paul, *VP*
EMP: 15 EST: 1947
SQ FT: 5,000
SALES (est): 462.38K **Privately Held**
Web: www.paulwelding.com
SIC: 7692 Welding repair

(G-2315)
PCX AEROSTRUCTURES LLC (PA)
300 Fenn Rd (06111-2277)
PHONE............................860 666-2471
Tom Holzthum, *CEO*
Jeff Frisby, *　 ＊*
Jeff Mcrae, *CFO*
▲ **EMP: 200 EST:** 1900
SQ FT: 145,000
SALES (est): 151.59MM
SALES (corp-wide): 151.59MM **Privately Held**
Web: www.pcxaero.com
SIC: 3728 Aircraft assemblies,
　subassemblies, and parts, nec

(G-2316)
PCX AEROSTRUCTURES LLC
Also Called: Pcx
300 Fenn Rd (06111-2277)
PHONE............................860 666-2471
EMP: 27
SALES (corp-wide): 151.59MM **Privately Held**
Web: www.pcxaero.com
SIC: 3441 Fabricated structural metal
　PA: Pcx Aerostructures, Llc
　　300 Fenn Rd
　　Newington CT 06111
　　860 666-2471

(G-2317)
PCX AEROSYSTEMS LLC
300 Fenn Rd (06111-2277)
PHONE............................860 666-2471
Jeff Frisby, *CEO*
EMP: 175 EST: 2014
SALES (est): 127.98MM
SALES (corp-wide): 710.67MM **Privately Held**
Web: www.pcxaero.com
SIC: 3365 Aerospace castings, aluminum
　PA: Equity Greenbriar Group L P
　　1 Greenwich Plz Ste 2
　　Greenwich CT 06830
　　914 925-9600

(G-2318)
PRO TOOL AND DESIGN INC
45 Maselli Rd (06111-5520)
PHONE............................860 828-4667
Michael Bosse, *Pr*
Albert Gallnot, *VP*
EMP: 10 EST: 1991
SALES (est): 928.05K **Privately Held**

Web: www.protoolanddesign.com
SIC: 3599 Machine shop, jobbing and repair

(G-2319)
PROMISE PROPANE LLC
110 Holmes Rd (06111-1713)
PHONE..............................860 685-0676
Justin Kovalcek, *Prin*
EMP: 7 EST: 2015
SALES (est): 2.31MM **Privately Held**
Web: www.promisepropane.com
SIC: 1311 Crude petroleum and natural gas

(G-2320)
PROSPECT PRODUCTS INCORPORATED
43 Kelsey St (06111-5415)
PHONE..............................860 666-0323
Richard E Carlson, *Pr*
Liza Bang, *
Jerry Johnson, *
EMP: 26 EST: 1950
SQ FT: 4,000
SALES (est): 2.44MM **Privately Held**
Web: www.prospectproductsinc.com
SIC: 3559 3826 3089 Semiconductor
  manufacturing machinery; Electrolytic
  conductivity instruments; Injection molding
  of plastics

(G-2321)
RENO MACHINE COMPANY INC
170 Pane Rd Ste 1 (06111-5537)
PHONE..............................860 666-5641
Antonio Occhialini, *Ch Bd*
Mark Occhialini, *
David Occhialini, *
▲ EMP: 65 EST: 1956
SQ FT: 68,000
SALES (est): 9.45MM **Privately Held**
Web: www.reno-machine.com
SIC: 3599 7692 3544 Machine shop,
  jobbing and repair; Welding repair; Special
  dies, tools, jigs, and fixtures

(G-2322)
RICHARDS MACHINE TOOL CO INC
187 Stamm Rd (06111-3619)
PHONE..............................860 436-2938
Lillian Bartkowicz, *Pr*
Dorothy Bartkowicz Weber, *VP*
EMP: 12 EST: 1978
SQ FT: 7,000
SALES (est): 2MM **Privately Held**
Web: www.richardscnc.com
SIC: 3599 3544 Machine shop, jobbing and
  repair; Special dies and tools

(G-2323)
SACCUZZO COMPANY INC
149 Louis St (06111-4517)
PHONE..............................860 665-1101
Vincent Saccuzzo, *Pr*
Marco Saccuzzo, *Sr VP*
▲ EMP: 7 EST: 1979
SQ FT: 16,000
SALES (est): 851.3K **Privately Held**
Web: www.icaffe.com
SIC: 2095 5046 5149 Coffee roasting
  (except by wholesale grocers); Coffee
  brewing equipment and supplies;
  Flavorings and fragrances

(G-2324)
SCHUCO USA LLLP (HQ)
Also Called: Schuco International
240 Pane Rd (06111-5527)
PHONE..............................860 666-0505

Thomas Knobloch, *CEO*
Edgar Freind, *Pt*
Dirk U Hindrichs, *Pr*
▲ EMP: 24 EST: 1997
SQ FT: 90,000
SALES (est): 35.73MM
SALES (corp-wide): 42.13MM **Privately Held**
SIC: 2431 Windows, wood
PA: Schuco International Kg
  Karolinenstr. 1-15
  Bielefeld NW 33609
  5217830

(G-2325)
SHEPARD STEEL CO INC
55 Shepard Dr (06111-1159)
PHONE..............................860 525-4446
Allen Shilosky, *Brnch Mgr*
EMP: 30
SALES (corp-wide): 510.43K **Privately Held**
Web: www.shepardsteel.com
SIC: 3316 3446 3441 Cold finishing of steel
  shapes; Architectural metalwork;
  Fabricated structural metal
PA: Shepard Steel Co. Inc.
  110 Meadow St
  Hartford CT 06114
  860 525-4446

(G-2326)
SOUSA CORP
Also Called: Heat Treating
565 Cedar St (06111-1814)
PHONE..............................860 523-9090
Amanda Eddy, *Pr*
Norman W Sousa Junior, *Pr*
Andrew Sousa, *VP*
Kathryn Desjardins, *VP*
Eric Eddy, *VP*
EMP: 20 EST: 1963
SQ FT: 37,000
SALES (est): 2.36MM **Privately Held**
Web: www.sousacorp.com
SIC: 3398 3471 8734 Metal heat treating;
  Plating and polishing; Product testing
  laboratories

(G-2327)
THE HARTFORD PRESS INC
Also Called: Service Press
105 Day St (06111-1209)
PHONE..............................860 296-3588
EMP: 20 EST: 1974
SALES (est): 2.27MM **Privately Held**
Web: www.servicepress.net
SIC: 2752 Offset printing

(G-2328)
TILCON INC (DH)
301 Hartford Ave (06111-1503)
P.O. Box 1357 (06050-1357)
PHONE..............................860 223-3651
Joseph Abate, *Pr*
Angelo Tomasso Junior, *Ch Bd*
Joseph A Abate, *
James Ryan, *
Anthony P Germano, *
EMP: 300 EST: 1979
SQ FT: 2,000
SALES (est): 458.78MM
SALES (corp-wide): 32.72B **Privately Held**
Web: www.tilconct.com
SIC: 1611 5032 3273 2951 Highway and
  street paving contractor; Sand, construction
  ; Ready-mixed concrete; Asphalt paving
  mixtures and blocks
HQ: Crh Americas, Inc.
  900 Ashwood Pkwy Ste 600
  Atlanta GA 30338
  770 804-3363

(G-2329)
TRUSS MANUFACTURING INC
97 Stanwell Rd (06111-4531)
PHONE..............................860 665-0000
Lawrence Vernon, *Pr*
Aurelien Giguere, *VP*
EMP: 13 EST: 1983
SQ FT: 8,000
SALES (est): 2.31MM **Privately Held**
Web: www.trussmfg.com
SIC: 2439 Trusses, wooden roof

(G-2330)
U S STUCCO LLC
28 Costello Pl (06111-5146)
PHONE..............................860 667-1935
EMP: 9 EST: 2009
SALES (est): 867.84K **Privately Held**
Web: www.usstucco.com
SIC: 3299 Stucco

(G-2331)
U-SEALUSA LLC
56 Fenn Rd (06111-2212)
PHONE..............................860 667-0911
EMP: 10 EST: 2011
SQ FT: 20,000
SALES (est): 232.07K **Privately Held**
SIC: 3444 Gutters, sheet metal

(G-2332)
UTC CORPORATION
25 Holly Dr (06111-2243)
PHONE..............................860 665-1770
Mark E Seli, *Dir*
EMP: 18 EST: 2015
SALES (est): 2.51MM **Privately Held**
SIC: 3812 Aircraft/aerospace flight
  instruments and guidance systems

(G-2333)
VISIONPOINT LLC
152 Rockwell Rd Ste B6 (06111-5546)
PHONE..............................860 436-9673
Kevin J Lavoie, *
EMP: 28 EST: 2003
SQ FT: 6,500
SALES (est): 8.37MM **Privately Held**
Web: www.visionpointllc.com
SIC: 7371 7373 3669 3651 Custom
  computer programming services; Systems
  integration services; Visual communication
  systems; Audio electronic systems

(G-2334)
WEST HRTFORD STIRS CBINETS INC
17 Main St (06111-1314)
P.O. Box 330118 (06133-0118)
PHONE..............................860 953-9151
TOLL FREE: 800
Andre Letourneau, *Pr*
EMP: 85 EST: 1937
SQ FT: 68,000
SALES (est): 8.37MM **Privately Held**
Web: www.stairsandcabinets.com
SIC: 2431 2434 Staircases and stairs, wood
  ; Wood kitchen cabinets

(G-2335)
ZAVARELLA WOODWORKING INC
48 Commerce Ct (06111-2246)
PHONE..............................860 666-6969
Bruno Zavarella, *Pr*
EMP: 9 EST: 2000
SALES (est): 2.28MM **Privately Held**
Web: www.zavarellawoodworking.com
SIC: 2431 Millwork

Newtown
Fairfield County

(G-2336)
CASCADES HOLDING US INC
Cascades Cntnrbard Pckg Nwtown
1 Edmund Rd (06470-1632)
PHONE..............................718 340-2136
Geoff Schiffenhaus, *Manager*
EMP: 61
SALES (corp-wide): 3.32B **Privately Held**
Web: www.cascades.com
SIC: 2653 Corrugated and solid fiber boxes
HQ: Cascades Holding Us Inc.
  4001 Packard Rd
  Niagara Falls NY 14303
  716 285-3681

(G-2337)
CHASE MEDIA GROUP
31 Pecks Ln Ste 3 (06470-5312)
PHONE..............................914 962-3871
EMP: 12 EST: 2011
SALES (est): 550.65K **Privately Held**
Web: www.chasemediagroup.com
SIC: 2711 Newspapers: publishing only, not
  printed on site

(G-2338)
HUBBELL INCORPORATED
14 Prospect Dr (06470-2338)
PHONE..............................203 426-2555
Robert Khansen, *Brnch Mgr*
EMP: 55
SALES (corp-wide): 5.37B **Publicly Held**
Web: www.hubbell.com
SIC: 3643 Connectors and terminals for
  electrical devices
PA: Hubbell Incorporated
  40 Waterview Dr
  Shelton CT 06484
  475 882-4000

(G-2339)
LMT COMMUNICATIONS INC
Also Called: L M T Magazine
84 S Main St Ste B (06470-2359)
PHONE..............................203 426-4568
Judy Fishman, *Pr*
EMP: 20 EST: 1984
SQ FT: 1,600
SALES (est): 4.01MM **Privately Held**
Web: www.lmtmag.com
SIC: 2721 7389 Magazines: publishing only,
  not printed on site; Trade show arrangement

(G-2340)
LOCTEC CORPORATION
15 Commerce Rd Ste 2 (06470-1633)
PHONE..............................203 364-1000
Victor Anderson, *Pr*
Victor Anderson, *Pr*
Steven Schoenfeld, *
EMP: 8 EST: 1990
SQ FT: 9,500
SALES (est): 261.21K **Privately Held**
SIC: 5072 3429 Security devices, locks;
  Locks or lock sets

(G-2341)
M CUBED TECHNOLOGIES INC (HQ)
Also Called: M Cubed
31 Pecks Ln Ste 8 (06470-5312)
PHONE..............................203 304-2940
Randall Price Senior, *Pr*
Jai Singh, *Ex VP*
William J Lauricella, *CFO*

▲ **EMP:** 45 **EST:** 1993
SQ FT: 110,000
SALES (est): 46.68MM
SALES (corp-wide): 5.16B **Publicly Held**
Web: www.mmmt.com
SIC: 3444 5051 3599   Sheet metalwork;
Metals service centers and offices; Machine
shop, jobbing and repair
PA: Coherent Corp.
375 Saxonburg Blvd
Saxonburg PA 16056
724 352-4455

(G-2342)
MIDWEST MOTOR SUPPLY CO
Also Called: Kimball Midwest
14 Prospect Dr (06470-2338)
PHONE.............................800 233-1294
Tracy Bosley, *Mgr*
EMP: 35
SALES (corp-wide): 129.4MM **Privately
Held**
Web: www.kimballmidwest.com
SIC: 3965   Fasteners
PA: Midwest Motor Supply Co.
4800 Roberts Rd
Columbus OH 43228
800 233-1294

(G-2343)
**NEW LEAF
PHARMACEUTICALS LLC**
77 S Main St (06470-2388)
P.O. Box 735 (06470-0735)
PHONE.............................203 270-4167
Paul Carpenter, *CEO*
EMP: 17 **EST:** 2017
SALES (est): 1.25MM **Privately Held**
Web: www.newleafpharma.com
SIC: 2834   Proprietary drug products

(G-2344)
QSONICA LLC
Also Called: Sonicators
53 Church Hill Rd (06470-1614)
PHONE.............................203 426-0101
Lauren Soloff, *Pr*
Robert Soloff, *VP*
Steven A Bowen, *CFO*
Ronald Verrilli, *Sec*
EMP: 8 **EST:** 2009
SALES (est): 2.34MM
SALES (corp-wide): 19.63MM **Privately
Held**
Web: www.sonicator.com
SIC: 3569   Liquid automation machinery and
equipment
PA: Sonics & Materials, Inc.
53 Church Hill Rd
Newtown CT 06470
203 270-4600

(G-2345)
RAND-WHITNEY GROUP LLC
Also Called: Rand-Whitney Container
Newtown
1 Edmund Rd (06470-1632)
P.O. Box 498 (06470-0498)
PHONE.............................203 426-5871
Dick Minton, *Mgr*
EMP: 36
Web: www.randwhitney.com
SIC: 2653   Boxes, corrugated: made from
purchased materials
HQ: Rand-Whitney Group Llc
1 Rand Whitney Way
Worcester MA 01607
508 791-2301

(G-2346)
SHOP SMART CENTRAL INC
Also Called: Chase Press
31 Pecks Ln (06470-5312)
PHONE.............................914 962-3871
Carla Chase, *Pr*
EMP: 7 **EST:** 2005
SALES (est): 590.52K **Privately Held**
Web: www.chasepress.com
SIC: 2741   Business service newsletters:
publishing and printing

(G-2347)
SONICS & MATERIALS INC (PA)
Also Called: Ultra Sonic Seal Co
53 Church Hill Rd (06470-1699)
PHONE.............................203 270-4600
Robert Soloff, *CEO*
Lauren H Soloff, *´*
▲ **EMP:** 60 **EST:** 1969
SQ FT: 44,000
SALES (est): 19.63MM
SALES (corp-wide): 19.63MM **Privately
Held**
Web: www.sonics.com
SIC: 3548 3569   Welding apparatus; Liquid
automation machinery and equipment

(G-2348)
**SYNCOTE CHEMICAL COMPANY
INC**
16 Greenbriar Ln (06470-2218)
PHONE.............................203 426-5526
George J Grosner, *Pr*
EMP: 9 **EST:** 1972
SALES (est): 104.58K **Privately Held**
SIC: 3291   Abrasive products

(G-2349)
TAUNTON INC
Also Called: Taunton Press
63 S Main St (06470-2355)
P.O. Box 5506 (06470-0921)
PHONE.............................203 426-8171
EMP: 844 **EST:** 1995
SQ FT: 70,000
SALES (est): 38.86MM **Privately Held**
Web: www.taunton.com
SIC: 2721 2731 7812 5963   Magazines:
publishing only, not printed on site; Books,
publishing only; Video tape production;
Direct sales, telemarketing

(G-2350)
TAUNTON PRESS INC
Also Called: THE TAUNTON PRESS, INC.
191 S Main St (06470-2733)
PHONE.............................203 426-8171
EMP: 184
SALES (corp-wide): 47.22MM **Privately
Held**
Web: www.taunton.com
SIC: 2721   Magazines: publishing only, not
printed on site
PA: The Taunton Press Inc
63 S Main St
Newtown CT 06470
203 426-8171

(G-2351)
**THE BEE PUBLISHING
COMPANY (PA)**
Also Called: Health Monitor
5 Church Hill Rd (06470-1605)
P.O. Box 5503 (06470-5503)
PHONE.............................203 426-8036
R Scudder Smith, *Pr*
Helen Smith, *´*
David Smith, *´*

Sheri Smith-baggett, *Dir*
▼ **EMP:** 49 **EST:** 1877
SQ FT: 20,000
SALES (est): 4.48MM
SALES (corp-wide): 4.48MM **Privately
Held**
Web: www.antiquesandthearts.com
SIC: 2711   Newspapers: publishing only, not
printed on site

(G-2352)
THE TAUNTON PRESS INC (PA)
63 S Main St (06470-2344)
P.O. Box 5506 (06470-0921)
PHONE.............................203 426-8171
◆ **EMP:** 185 **EST:** 1975
SALES (est): 47.22MM
SALES (corp-wide): 47.22MM **Privately
Held**
Web: www.taunton.com
SIC: 2721 2731 7812   Magazines: publishing
only, not printed on site; Books, publishing
only; Video tape production

(G-2353)
TO WIND DOWN LLC
31 Pecks Ln (06470-5312)
PHONE.............................203 426-3030
R Joseph Young, *´*
Michael Iassonga, *´*
EMP: 67 **EST:** 2003
SQ FT: 35,000
SALES (est): 9.07MM **Privately Held**
Web: www.arch-medical.com
SIC: 3599   Machine shop, jobbing and repair

(G-2354)
WIND CORPORATION
Also Called: Wind Hardware
30 Pecks Ln (06470-2361)
PHONE.............................800 946-3267
Patrick E Wind, *Pr*
Kevin Houlihan, *´*
◆ **EMP:** 28 **EST:** 1949
SQ FT: 60,000
SALES (est): 9.97MM **Privately Held**
Web: www.windhardware.com
SIC: 5072 3562   Hardware; Ball and roller
bearings

(G-2355)
ZEPHYR LOCK LLC
30 Pecks Ln (06470-2361)
PHONE.............................866 937-4971
▲ **EMP:** 12 **EST:** 2001
SQ FT: 20,000
SALES (est): 1.22MM **Privately Held**
Web: www.zephyrlock.com
SIC: 3429   Locks or lock sets

Niantic
New London County

(G-2356)
EBS ACQUISITION INC
Also Called: Energy Beam Sciences
2 Oak St (06357-2748)
PHONE.............................860 653-0411
Michael R Nesta, *Pr*
Michael Nesta, *Pr*
Michael Whittlesy, *Sec*
Paul Kenney, *Treas*
EMP: 12 **EST:** 2003
SALES (est): 923.72K **Privately Held**
SIC: 3821   Laboratory apparatus and
furniture

(G-2357)
ENERGY BEAM SCIENCES INC
Also Called: Labpulse Medical
2 Oak St (06357-2748)
PHONE.............................860 653-0411
Michael Nesta, *Pr*
Paul Kenney, *Treas*
Mike Whittlesy, *Sec*
EMP: 17 **EST:** 1989
SALES (est): 2.39MM **Privately Held**
Web: www.ebsciences.com
SIC: 3826   Analytical instruments

(G-2358)
NEPV LLC
Also Called: New England Pump and Valve
36 Industrial Park Rd Ste B (06357-1262)
PHONE.............................860 739-2200
Jeffrey Armstrong, *Pr*
Jeff Armstrong, *Managing Member*
EMP: 14 **EST:** 1986
SQ FT: 20,000
SALES (est): 2.41MM **Privately Held**
Web: www.nepv.com
SIC: 7699 7694   Valve repair, industrial;
Electric motor repair

Noank
New London County

(G-2359)
COMPONENTS FOR MFG LLC
26 High St (06340-5752)
PHONE.............................860 572-1671
Tracey Jacey, *Brnch Mgr*
EMP: 20
SALES (corp-wide): 619.94K **Privately
Held**
Web:
www.componentsformanufacturing.com
SIC: 3999   Barber and beauty shop
equipment
PA: Components For Manufacturing Llc
800 Flanders Rd Bldg 3
Mystic CT 06355
860 245-5326

Norfolk
Litchfield County

(G-2360)
KINGSLAND COMPANY
7 Colebrook Rd (06058-1332)
P.O. Box 594 (06058-0594)
PHONE.............................860 542-6981
Luke K Burke, *Pr*
Mark K Burke, *VP*
Matthew K Burke, *VP*
Liane Burke, *Sec*
EMP: 8 **EST:** 1983
SQ FT: 7,200
SALES (est): 831.02K **Privately Held**
Web: www.kingsland-shutters.com
SIC: 2431   Doors and door parts and trim,
wood

North Branford
New Haven County

(G-2361)
BROOK & WHITTLE LIMITED
260 Branford Rd (06471-1303)
PHONE.............................203 483-5602
EMP: 14
Web: www.brookandwhittle.com

▲ = Import ▼ = Export
◆ = Import/Export

SIC: 2754 2759 Commercial printing, gravure; Commercial printing, nec
PA: Brook & Whittle Limited
20 Carter Dr
Guilford CT 06437

(G-2362)
COASTLINE ENVIRONMENTAL LLC
12 Ridgetop Ln (06471-1477)
PHONE..............................203 483-6898
EMP: 9 **EST:** 2002
SALES (est): 299.97K **Privately Held**
SIC: 8999 7699 3089 Earth science services ; Septic tank cleaning service; Toilets, portable chemical: plastics

(G-2363)
CODE RED ELECTRONICS LLC
999 Foxon Rd Ste 30 (06471-1294)
▲ **EMP:** 9 **EST:** 2005
SALES (est): 983.7K **Privately Held**
Web: www.code-red-electronics.com
SIC: 3674 3676 3675 Semiconductors and related devices; Electronic resistors; Electronic capacitors

(G-2364)
CTHRU METALS INC
14 Commerce Dr (06471-1240)
PHONE..............................203 884-1017
Ronald P Delfini, *Pr*
Carmen D Ciardiello, *VP*
John Brooke Delfini, *Sec*
EMP: 15 **EST:** 2021
SALES (est): 1.22MM **Privately Held**
Web: www.cthrumetals.com
SIC: 3497 Metal foil and leaf

(G-2365)
DEPENDABLE REPAIR INC
Also Called: Dependable Hydraulics
2110 Foxon Rd (06471-1511)
PHONE..............................203 481-9706
TOLL FREE: 800
Benedict Larosa, *Owner*
EMP: 10
SALES (corp-wide): 6.54MM **Privately Held**
Web: www.dependablehydraulics.com
SIC: 7699 3599 Hydraulic equipment repair; Machine shop, jobbing and repair
PA: Dependable Repair, Inc.
18 Ranick Dr W
Amityville NY 11701
631 842-0700

(G-2366)
DWYER ALUMINUM MAST CO INC
2 Commerce Dr Ste 1 (06471-1250)
PHONE..............................203 484-0419
Robert Dwyer, *Pr*
Andrew Dwyer, *Sec*
◆ **EMP:** 10 **EST:** 1963
SQ FT: 10,500
SALES (est): 837.94K **Privately Held**
Web: www.dwyermast.com
SIC: 3365 3429 Masts, cast aluminum; Marine hardware

(G-2367)
ENGINEERING SPECIALTIES INC
Also Called: Esi
452 Twin Lakes Rd (06471-3203)
PHONE..............................203 488-2266
◆ **EMP:** 34 **EST:** 1990
SALES (est): 5.88MM **Privately Held**
Web: www.esict.com

SIC: 3495 3599 8711 Wire springs; Custom machinery; Mechanical engineering

(G-2368)
HYDROGEN HIGHWAY LLC
242 Branford Rd (06471-1340)
PHONE..............................203 871-1000
Terri S Alpert, *Mgr*
EMP: 7 **EST:** 2005
SALES (est): 243.75K **Privately Held**
Web: www.hydrogenhighway.com
SIC: 2813 Hydrogen

(G-2369)
INTERNATIONAL PIPE & STL CORP
4 Enterprise Dr (06471-1354)
PHONE..............................203 481-7102
W A Lalani, *Pr*
W A Lalani, *Pr*
Sada Lalani, *Sec*
▼ **EMP:** 10 **EST:** 1982
SQ FT: 25,000
SALES (est): 1.93MM **Privately Held**
Web: www.fence-material.com
SIC: 3446 5051 3496 3315 Architectural metalwork; Pipe and tubing, steel; Miscellaneous fabricated wire products; Steel wire and related products

(G-2370)
NATIONAL GRAPHICS INC
248 Branford Rd (06471-1328)
P.O. Box 508 (06471-0508)
PHONE..............................203 481-2351
EMP: 359 **EST:** 1980
SALES (est): 25.2MM **Privately Held**
Web: www.natgraphics.com
SIC: 2759 Commercial printing, nec

(G-2371)
PENNSYLVANIA GLOBE GASLIGHT CO
300 Shaw Rd (06471-1061)
PHONE..............................203 484-7749
EMP: 20 **EST:** 1995
SQ FT: 16,000
SALES (est): 3.66MM **Privately Held**
Web: www.pennglobe.com
SIC: 3648 5063 Outdoor lighting equipment; Lighting fixtures

(G-2372)
PRECISION X-RAY INC
15 Comm Dr Unit 1 (06471)
PHONE..............................203 484-2011
Brian P Dermott, *Pr*
Donald Santacroce, *Treas*
▲ **EMP:** 15 **EST:** 2003
SQ FT: 16,500
SALES (est): 2.22MM **Privately Held**
Web: www.precisionxray.com
SIC: 3844 X-ray apparatus and tubes

(G-2373)
PRIME TECHNOLOGY LLC
344 Twin Lakes Rd (06471-1220)
P.O. Box 185 (06471-0185)
PHONE..............................203 481-5721
Luis Lluberes, *Pr*
John Smith, *CFO*
Keith Macdowall, *VP Sls*
▲ **EMP:** 34 **EST:** 1973
SQ FT: 38,000
SALES (corp-wide): 50.21MM **Privately Held**
Web: www.primetechnology.com

SIC: 3676 3825 3823 3679 Electronic resistors; Meters: electric, pocket, portable, panelboard, etc.; Controllers, for process variables, all types; Power supplies, all types: static
PA: Cox & Company, Inc.
1664 Old Country Rd
Plainview NY 11803
212 366-0200

(G-2374)
SA CANDELORA ENTERPRISES INC
Also Called: Taconic Wire
250 Totoket Rd (06471-1035)
PHONE..............................203 484-2863
Salvatore Candelora, *Ch*
Joseph Candelora, *Sec*
Angela Watrous, *Pr*
Anthony Candelora, *VP*
◆ **EMP:** 19 **EST:** 1984
SQ FT: 30,000
SALES (est): 2.43MM **Privately Held**
Web: www.taconicwire.com
SIC: 3315 Wire, steel: insulated or armored

(G-2375)
SOURCE INC (PA)
101 Fowler Rd (06471-1556)
PHONE..............................203 488-6400
Susan Domizi, *Pr*
◆ **EMP:** 9 **EST:** 1975
SQ FT: 18,000
SALES (est): 2.15MM
SALES (corp-wide): 2.15MM **Privately Held**
Web: www.4source.com
SIC: 2048 2099 Feed supplements; Food preparations, nec

(G-2376)
T WOODWARD STAIR BUILDING LLC
10 Bailey Dr (06471-1447)
P.O. Box 939 (06419-0939)
PHONE..............................860 664-0515
Woodward Tom, *Prin*
EMP: 8 **EST:** 2002
SALES (est): 244.24K **Privately Held**
SIC: 3446 Stairs, staircases, stair treads: prefabricated metal

(G-2377)
TRANSMONDE USA INC
Also Called: Transmode USA
100 Shaw Rd (06471-1062)
PHONE..............................203 484-1528
Carol Mansfield, *Pr*
James Foley, *
Marcella Walten-sherdon, *Pr*
Marcella Sheridan, *
Mark Tracey, *
▲ **EMP:** 60 **EST:** 2000
SALES (est): 3.63MM **Privately Held**
Web: www.transmonde.com
SIC: 2752 7331 Commercial printing, lithographic; Direct mail advertising services

(G-2378)
WALTS TROPPER FACTORY LLC
44 Circle Dr (06471-1313)
PHONE..............................203 871-9254
Walter Vongher, *Pr*
EMP: 7 **EST:** 2017
SALES (est): 218.08K **Privately Held**
SIC: 3944 Electronic toys

(G-2379)
WILLCONN CONNECTIONS INC
Also Called: Dicon
33 Fowler Rd (06471-1519)
P.O. Box 190 (06471-0190)
PHONE..............................203 481-8080
Jeffrey Williams, *Pr*
Timothy Williams, *
EMP: 25 **EST:** 1990
SQ FT: 18,000
SALES (est): 1.96MM **Privately Held**
Web: www.diconnections.com
SIC: 3643 Current-carrying wiring services

(G-2380)
WITKOWSKY JOHN
73 Branford Rd (06471-1323)
PHONE..............................203 483-0152
Tiffanie Witkowsky, *Prin*
EMP: 9 **EST:** 2004
SALES (est): 392.94K **Privately Held**
SIC: 2411 Logging

North Franklin
New London County

(G-2381)
ARICO ENGINEERING INC
841 Route 32 Ste 19 (06254-1132)
PHONE..............................860 642-7040
John Arico, *Pr*
Mary Ann Arico, *VP*
EMP: 7 **EST:** 1989
SQ FT: 5,000
SALES (est): 580.89K **Privately Held**
Web: www.aricoengineering.com
SIC: 3555 7699 Printing trade parts and attachments; Industrial machinery and equipment repair

(G-2382)
M & W SHEET METAL LLC
841 Route 32 Ste 7 (06254-1132)
PHONE..............................860 642-7748
Paul Warbin, *Prin*
EMP: 8 **EST:** 2002
SALES (est): 245.03K **Privately Held**
SIC: 3444 Sheet metal specialties, not stamped

(G-2383)
MOARK LLC (HQ)
28 Under The Mountain Rd (06254-1421)
PHONE..............................951 332-3300
▲ **EMP:** 28 **EST:** 1954
SQ FT: 55,000
SALES (est): 261.82MM
SALES (corp-wide): 2.89B **Privately Held**
SIC: 5144 2048 0252 2015 Eggs; Poultry feeds; Chicken eggs; Poultry slaughtering and processing
PA: Land O'lakes, Inc.
4001 Lexington Ave N
Arden Hills MN 55126
651 375-2222

North Grosvenordale
Windham County

(G-2384)
LIBERTY GLASS AND MET INDS INC
339 Riverside Dr (06255-2160)
PHONE..............................860 923-3623
Donna Esposito, *Pr*
Edward Esposito Senior, *VP*

GEOGRAPHIC

Daniel Marschat, *
EMP: 32 **EST:** 1987
SQ FT: 52,000
SALES (est): 2.15MM **Privately Held**
Web: www.lgminc.net
SIC: 3229 3442 1793 5039 Glassware, industrial; Sash, door or window: metal; Glass and glazing work; Glass construction materials

(G-2385)
LORIC TOOL INC
95 Gaumond Rd (06255-2011)
PHONE................................860 928-0171
Ricky Smith, *Pr*
Lorraine Smith, *Sec*
EMP: 10 **EST:** 1987
SQ FT: 3,000
SALES (est): 698.75K **Privately Held**
Web: www.loricchimneyservices.com
SIC: 3599 Machine shop, jobbing and repair

(G-2386)
MERRICK SERVICES
81 Plum Rd (06255-2121)
PHONE................................508 802-3751
Hal Merreick, *Pr*
EMP: 11 **EST:** 2011
SALES (est): 375.98K **Privately Held**
SIC: 3674 5082 Fuel cells, solid state; Excavating machinery and equipment

(G-2387)
SUPERIOR BAKERY INC
Also Called: Kasanof Bread
72 Main St (06255-1712)
PHONE................................860 923-9555
Louis P Faucher, *Pr*
Michael Faucher, *
Raymond P Faucher Senior, *Sec*
EMP: 50 **EST:** 1907
SQ FT: 30,000
SALES (est): 9.86MM **Privately Held**
Web: www.superiorbakery.com
SIC: 5149 2051 Bakery products; Bread, cake, and related products

North Haven
New Haven County

(G-2388)
ADVISOR
83 State St (06473-2208)
P.O. Box 460 (06473-0460)
PHONE................................203 239-4121
Patricia Flagg, *Owner*
EMP: 9 **EST:** 1965
SALES (est): 154.93K **Privately Held**
Web: www.advisor-newspaper.com
SIC: 2711 Newspapers, publishing and printing

(G-2389)
ALCAD INC
Also Called: Alcad Standby Batteries
3 Powdered Metal Rd (06473-3209)
PHONE................................203 985-2500
Annie Sennet, *CEO*
Sara Lopofsky, *Contrlr*
▲ **EMP:** 30 **EST:** 1987
SQ FT: 28,000
SALES (est): 5.22MM
SALES (corp-wide): 7.96B **Publicly Held**
Web: www.alcadusa.com
SIC: 3691 Storage batteries
HQ: Saft America Inc
 13575 Waterworks St
 Jacksonville FL 32221
 904 861-1501

(G-2390)
ALDLAB CHEMICALS LLC
410 Sackett Point Rd (06473-3168)
P.O. Box 465 (06405-0465)
PHONE................................203 589-4934
EMP: 10 **EST:** 2009
SALES (est): 143.6K **Privately Held**
Web: www.aldlab.com
SIC: 2813 Industrial gases

(G-2391)
AMERICAN WOOD PRODUCTS
Also Called: Bar Co American
301 State St (06473-6104)
PHONE................................203 248-4433
Valerie Galleuba, *CEO*
EMP: 7 **EST:** 1995
SALES (est): 629.92K **Privately Held**
SIC: 2431 Millwork

(G-2392)
ANDERSON STAIR & RAILING
348 Sackett Point Rd (06473-3103)
PHONE................................203 288-0117
Art Anderson, *Owner*
EMP: 10 **EST:** 2001
SALES (est): 852.65K **Privately Held**
Web: www.andersonstair.com
SIC: 2431 Staircases, stairs and railings

(G-2393)
AQUALOGIC INC
30 Devine St (06473-2236)
PHONE................................203 248-8959
Nicholas Papa, *Pr*
Dorothy F Papa, *Sec*
EMP: 27 **EST:** 1966
SQ FT: 6,000
SALES (est): 1.95MM **Privately Held**
Web: www.aqualogic.com
SIC: 3589 Water treatment equipment, industrial

(G-2394)
BONITO MANUFACTURING INC
Also Called: New England Clock
445 Washington Ave (06473-1320)
PHONE................................203 234-8786
James Bonito, *Pr*
Richard Elia, *
EMP: 61 **EST:** 1992
SQ FT: 70,000
SALES (est): 6.97MM **Privately Held**
Web: www.bonitogroup.com
SIC: 2429 7641 2522 2511 Barrels and barrel parts; Reupholstery and furniture repair; Office furniture, except wood; Wood household furniture

(G-2395)
BYK USA INC
Also Called: Altana
33 Stiles Ln (06473-2274)
PHONE................................475 234-5317
EMP: 40
SALES (corp-wide): 4.22B **Privately Held**
Web: www.altana.com
SIC: 3087 Custom compound purchased resins
HQ: Byk Usa Inc.
 524 S Cherry St
 Wallingford CT 06492
 203 265-2086

(G-2396)
C COWLES & COMPANY (PA)
Also Called: Hydrolevel Div
126 Bailey Rd (06473-2612)
PHONE................................203 865-3117

Lawrence C Moon Junior, *Ch Bd*
Richard Lyons, *Pr*
Robert Gaura, *CFO*
Russell Spector, *Prin*
Jennifer Moon Lyons, *Prin*
▲ **EMP:** 75 **EST:** 1838
SQ FT: 170,000
SALES (est): 48.81MM
SALES (corp-wide): 48.81MM **Privately Held**
Web: www.ccowles.com
SIC: 3089 3465 3443 3646 Injection molding of plastics; Moldings or trim, automobile: stamped metal; Boiler shop products: boilers, smokestacks, steel tanks; Ceiling systems, luminous

(G-2397)
C S M S-I P A
127 Washington Ave Ste 3 (06473-1715)
PHONE................................203 562-7228
Lisa Guerino, *Brnch Mgr*
EMP: 9
SQ FT: 6,210
SALES (corp-wide): 1.14MM **Privately Held**
Web: www.csms-ipa.com
SIC: 8621 8099 2711 Medical field-related associations; Medical services organization ; Newspapers, publishing and printing
PA: C S M S-I P A
 1 Corporate Dr
 Shelton CT 06484
 203 225-1291

(G-2398)
COLE S CREW MACHINE PRODUCTS
69 Dodge Ave (06473-1119)
PHONE................................203 723-1418
David F Calabrese, *Pr*
Patricia Calabrese, *Sec*
EMP: 24 **EST:** 1963
SQ FT: 6,500
SALES (est): 367.98K **Privately Held**
SIC: 3451 3542 Screw machine products; Thread rolling machines

(G-2399)
CONNECTICUT CONTAINER CORP (PA)
Also Called: Unicorr Group
455 Sackett Point Rd (06473-3199)
PHONE................................203 248-2161
Harry A Perkins, *Pr*
Harry A Perkins, *Pr*
Louis Ceruzzi, *
◆ **EMP:** 132 **EST:** 1946
SQ FT: 160,000
SALES (est): 151.34MM
SALES (corp-wide): 151.34MM **Privately Held**
Web: www.unicorr.com
SIC: 2653 3993 3412 2631 Boxes, corrugated: made from purchased materials ; Signs and advertising specialties; Metal barrels, drums, and pails; Paperboard mills

(G-2400)
CONTRACTORS STEEL SUPPLY INC
111 Quinnipiac Ave (06473-3623)
PHONE................................203 782-1221
EMP: 10 **EST:** 1994
SQ FT: 7,000
SALES (est): 2.23MM **Privately Held**
Web:
www.contractorssteelcompany.com
SIC: 5051 3441 Steel; Fabricated structural metal

(G-2401)
COVIDIEN HOLDING INC
195 Mcdermott Rd (06473-3665)
PHONE................................203 492-5000
EMP: 151
Web: www.covidien.com
SIC: 3841 Surgical and medical instruments
HQ: Covidien Holding Inc.
 710 Medtronic Pkwy
 Minneapolis MN 55432

(G-2402)
COVIDIEN LP
195 Mcdermott Rd (06473-3665)
PHONE................................203 492-6332
Kenneth Niehoff, *Dir*
EMP: 430
Web: www.forcetriad.com
SIC: 3841 Surgical and medical instruments
HQ: Covidien Lp
 15 Hampshire St
 Mansfield MA 02048
 763 514-4000

(G-2403)
COVIDIEN LP
Also Called: Surgical Devices
60 Middletown Ave (06473-3908)
PHONE................................203 492-5000
Dave Bento, *Brnch Mgr*
EMP: 521
Web: www.forcetriad.com
SIC: 3841 Surgical and medical instruments
HQ: Covidien Lp
 15 Hampshire St
 Mansfield MA 02048
 763 514-4000

(G-2404)
COWLES OPERATING COMPANY
Also Called: Carlin Combustion Tech Inc
126 Bailey Rd (06473-2612)
PHONE................................203 680-9401
▲ **EMP:** 125 **EST:** 2009
SALES (est): 18.43MM
SALES (corp-wide): 48.81MM **Privately Held**
Web: www.carlincombustion.com
SIC: 3433 Gas burners, industrial
PA: C. Cowles & Company
 126 Bailey Rd
 North Haven CT 06473
 203 865-3117

(G-2405)
COWLES PRODUCTS COMPANY INC
126 Bailey Rd (06473-2612)
PHONE................................203 865-3110
Lawrence Moon, *Pr*
▲ **EMP:** 100 **EST:** 2000
SALES (est): 14.55MM
SALES (corp-wide): 48.81MM **Privately Held**
Web: www.cowlesproducts.com
SIC: 3089 Extruded finished plastics products, nec
PA: C. Cowles & Company
 126 Bailey Rd
 North Haven CT 06473
 203 865-3117

(G-2406)
COWLES STAMPING INC
126 Bailey Rd (06473-2612)
PHONE................................203 865-3117
Lawrence C Moon Junior, *Pr*
Rusell Spector, *
▲ **EMP:** 40 **EST:** 2001
SQ FT: 64,000

▲ = Import ▼ = Export
◆ = Import/Export

SALES (est): 9.89MM
SALES (corp-wide): 48.81MM **Privately Held**
Web: www.ccowles.com
SIC: 3469 Stamping metal for the trade
PA: C. Cowles & Company
126 Bailey Rd
North Haven CT 06473
203 865-3117

(G-2407)
EAST SHORE WIRE ROPE RGGING SU
78 Rebeschi Dr (06473-3934)
P.O. Box 479 (06473-0479)
PHONE...............................203 469-5204
Gary Lipkvich, *Pr*
Wayne Lipkvich, *Treas*
Richard Lipkvich, *VP*
EMP: 10 EST: 1954
SQ FT: 10,000
SALES (est): 1.11MM **Privately Held**
SIC: 5051 5072 2298 3496 Rope, wire (not insulated); Chains; Slings, rope; Miscellaneous fabricated wire products

(G-2408)
ECOCHLOR INC
285 State St Ste 8 (06473-2170)
PHONE...............................978 298-1463
Steve Candito, *CEO*
Charlie Miller, *
Peter J Bollier, *
Richard Graber, *
Charles W Miller, *
▲ EMP: 55 EST: 2013
SALES (est): 9.82MM **Privately Held**
Web: www.ecochlor.com
SIC: 3823 Water quality monitoring and control systems

(G-2409)
ELM CITY MANUFACTURING LLC
Also Called: Atlantic Millwork
370 Sackett Point Rd (06473-3106)
PHONE...............................203 248-1969
Mark Bolling, *Managing Member*
EMP: 18 EST: 1997
SQ FT: 13,000
SALES (est): 1.13MM **Privately Held**
Web: www.atlanticmillwork.net
SIC: 2499 Decorative wood and woodwork

(G-2410)
EPICUREAN FEAST MEDTRON O
195 Mcdermott Rd (06473-3665)
PHONE...............................203 492-5000
EMP: 181 EST: 2017
SALES (est): 2.74MM **Privately Held**
Web: www.medtronic.com
SIC: 3841 Surgical and medical instruments

(G-2411)
F D GRAVE & SON INC
85 State St Ste C (06473-2240)
P.O. Box 2085 (06473-8285)
PHONE...............................203 239-9394
Frederick D Grave Junior, *Pr*
EMP: 8 EST: 1884
SQ FT: 25,000
SALES (est): 982.57K **Privately Held**
Web: www.fdgrave.com
SIC: 2121 Cigars

(G-2412)
FARMINGTON ENGINEERING INC
73 Defco Park Rd (06473-1129)
PHONE...............................800 428-7584

Bob Adelson, *Prin*
▲ EMP: 7 EST: 2009
SALES (est): 705.02K **Privately Held**
Web: www.sfckoenig.com
SIC: 3499 Drain plugs, magnetic

(G-2413)
FLIGHT SUPPORT INC
101 Sackett Point Rd (06473-3211)
P.O. Box 498 (06473-0498)
PHONE...............................203 562-1415
Wayne Blake, *CEO*
Bernadette Blake, *
EMP: 50 EST: 1971
SQ FT: 17,200
SALES (est): 7.65MM **Privately Held**
Web: www.flightsupport.net
SIC: 3728 Aircraft parts and equipment, nec

(G-2414)
HYDROLEVEL COMPANY
126 Bailey Rd (06473-2612)
PHONE...............................203 776-0473
Alan C Bennett, *Ch Bd*
John Downs, *Pr*
T Richard Coss, *Treas*
James Bennett, *Sec*
▲ EMP: 10 EST: 1979
SQ FT: 5,000
SALES (est): 2.52MM
SALES (corp-wide): 48.81MM **Privately Held**
Web: www.hydrolevel.com
SIC: 3494 Valves and pipe fittings, nec
PA: C. Cowles & Company
126 Bailey Rd
North Haven CT 06473
203 865-3117

(G-2415)
INTELLGENT CLEARING NETWRK INC
110 Washington Ave (06473-1723)
PHONE...............................203 972-0861
EMP: 8 EST: 2010
SALES (est): 774.41K **Privately Held**
Web: www.icn-net.com
SIC: 7372 Application computer software

(G-2416)
INTERACTIVE MARKETING CORP
Also Called: IMC Internet
399 Sackett Point Rd (06473-3105)
PHONE...............................203 248-5324
EMP: 7 EST: 1994
SQ FT: 6,000
SALES (est): 894.25K **Privately Held**
Web: www.imchosted.com
SIC: 3571 7373 Personal computers (microcomputers); Local area network (LAN) systems integrator

(G-2417)
JENSEN INDUSTRIES INC (PA)
Also Called: Jensen Dental
50 Stillman Rd (06473-1622)
P.O. Box 514 (06473-0514)
PHONE...............................203 285-1402
David J Stine, *Pr*
Peter Kouvaris, *
Bob Lamonaca, *
Kevin Mahan, *
Peter Trefz, *
▲ EMP: 60 EST: 1976
SQ FT: 25,000
SALES (est): 14.65MM
SALES (corp-wide): 14.65MM **Privately Held**
Web: www.jensendental.com

SIC: 3843 Dental alloys for amalgams

(G-2418)
JESKEY LLC
Also Called: James Manufacturing
69 Dodge Ave (06473-1119)
PHONE...............................203 772-6675
TOLL FREE: 800
Adam Jeskey, *Managing Member*
EMP: 23 EST: 1946
SQ FT: 29,000
SALES (est): 2.64MM **Privately Held**
Web: www.jamesmfg.com
SIC: 3599 Machine shop, jobbing and repair

(G-2419)
JOHNSTONE COMPANY INC
222 Sackett Point Rd (06473-3160)
P.O. Box 472 (06473-0472)
PHONE...............................203 239-5834
David R Johnstone Junior, *Pr*
Michael Johnstone, *
Tonya Johnstone, *
▼ EMP: 26 EST: 1941
SQ FT: 20,000
SALES (est): 4.96MM **Privately Held**
Web: www.johnstonecompany.com
SIC: 3398 3559 3443 Metal heat treating; Refinery, chemical processing, and similar machinery; Fabricated plate work (boiler shop)

(G-2420)
JOSEPH COHN SON TILE TRAZO LLC
352 Sackett Point Rd (06473-3103)
PHONE...............................203 772-2420
Louis Monico, *Managing Member*
EMP: 9 EST: 2011
SALES (est): 477.15K **Privately Held**
Web: www.josephcohnandson.com
SIC: 1743 2273 Tile installation, ceramic; Floor coverings, textile fiber

(G-2421)
KOBUTA CHOPPERS LLC
439 Washington Ave (06473-1310)
PHONE...............................203 234-6047
Steve Kobuta, *Pr*
EMP: 7 EST: 2017
SALES (est): 445.38K **Privately Held**
SIC: 3751 Motorcycles and related parts

(G-2422)
MANCHESTER TL & DESIGN ADP LLC
Also Called: ADP Rivet
44 Hermitage Ln (06473-4018)
PHONE...............................860 296-6541
Peter Depaola, *Managing Member*
EMP: 7 EST: 1951
SALES (est): 823.71K **Privately Held**
Web: www.adprivet.com
SIC: 3965 3599 Fasteners; Custom machinery

(G-2423)
MARTIN PRINTING INC
100 Powdered Metal Rd (06473-3209)
PHONE...............................203 239-7991
Martin Santacroce, *Pr*
Kim Morris, *
▲ EMP: 30 EST: 1984
SQ FT: 63,000
SALES (est): 2.07MM **Privately Held**
SIC: 2752 2759 2675 Offset printing; Promotional printing; Die-cut paper and board

(G-2424)
MEDTRONIC INC
Also Called: Medtronic
60 Middletown Ave (06473-3908)
PHONE...............................203 492-5764
Holly Donahue, *Mgr*
EMP: 198
Web: www.medtronic.com
SIC: 3841 Surgical and medical instruments
HQ: Medtronic, Inc.
710 Medtronic Pkwy
Minneapolis MN 55432
763 514-4000

(G-2425)
MILLWOOD INC
33 Stiles Ln Ste 3 (06473-2274)
PHONE...............................203 248-7902
Edwin Melendez, *Brnch Mgr*
EMP: 53
Web: www.millwoodinc.com
SIC: 3565 5084 Packaging machinery; Packaging machinery and equipment
PA: Millwood, Inc.
3708 International Blvd
Vienna OH 44473

(G-2426)
NEU SPCLTY ENGINEERED MTLS LLC
15 Corporate Dr (06473-3255)
PHONE...............................203 239-9629
EMP: 12 EST: 2009
SALES (est): 5.18MM **Publicly Held**
Web: www.avient.com
SIC: 2821 3087 5162 Thermoplastic materials; Custom compound purchased resins; Resins
PA: Avient Corporation
33587 Walker Rd
Avon Lake OH 44012

(G-2427)
NEW ENGLAND CAGE & FENCE CORP
Also Called: Hartford Wire Works
230 Clintonville Ln (06473-2405)
PHONE...............................860 688-8148
EMP: 10
SALES (est): 1.86MM **Privately Held**
SIC: 3496 5039 Cages, wire; Wire fence, gates, and accessories

(G-2428)
NICOLOCK PAVING STONES NE LLC
Also Called: Nicolock Paving Stones Ne
99 Stoddard Ave (06473-2526)
PHONE...............................203 234-2800
Roberto Nicolia, *Pr*
▲ EMP: 10 EST: 2001
SALES (est): 2.4MM **Privately Held**
Web: www.nicolock.com
SIC: 3272 Concrete products, nec

(G-2429)
O F MOSSBERG & SONS INC (HQ)
7 Grasso Ave (06473-3237)
P.O. Box 497 (06473-0497)
PHONE...............................203 230-5300
A Iver Mossberg Junior, *Ch Bd*
Alan I Mossberg, *
Christopher Orlando, *General Vice President*
Joseph H Bartozzi, *
◆ EMP: 160 EST: 1919
SQ FT: 80,000
SALES (est): 97.93MM **Privately Held**

Web: www.mossberg.com
SIC: 3484 Small arms
PA: Mossberg Corporation
7 Grasso Ave
North Haven CT 06473

(G-2430)
PARKER-HANNIFIN CORPORATION
Also Called: Advanced Products Operation
33 Defco Park Rd (06473-1129)
PHONE.............................203 239-3341
Jim Randall, *Brnch Mgr*
EMP: 100
SALES (corp-wide): 19.07B **Publicly Held**
Web: www.parker.com
SIC: 3053 Gaskets, all materials
PA: Parker-Hannifin Corporation
6035 Parkland Blvd
Cleveland OH 44124
216 896-3000

(G-2431)
PLATT-LABONIA OF N HAVEN INC
Also Called: Craftline
70 Stoddard Ave (06473-2524)
P.O. Box 398 (06473-0398)
PHONE.............................203 239-5681
Guy Ferraiolo, *Pr*
Vincent Labonia Junior, *Pr*
Elizabeth Labonia, *VP*
▲ EMP: 65 EST: 1953
SQ FT: 110,000
SALES (est): 6.31MM **Privately Held**
Web: www.craftline.us
SIC: 2542 3714 Cabinets: show, display, or
storage: except wood; Motor vehicle parts
and accessories

(G-2432)
PRECISION COMBUSTION INC
410 Sackett Point Rd Ste B (06473-3168)
PHONE.............................203 287-3700
EMP: 33 EST: 1985
SALES (est): 5.15MM **Privately Held**
Web: www.precision-combustion.com
SIC: 8731 3511 Energy research; Turbines
and turbine generator sets

(G-2433)
PROFLOW INC
Also Called: Proflow Process Equipment
303 State St (06473-6104)
P.O. Box 748 (06473-0748)
PHONE.............................203 230-4700
Kurt Uihlein, *Pr*
Lawrence Bee Junior, *VP*
EMP: 47 EST: 1922
SQ FT: 18,000
SALES (est): 9.95MM **Privately Held**
Web: www.proflow-inc.com
SIC: 3823 5084 5251 3561 Industrial flow
and liquid measuring instruments; Pumps
and pumping equipment, nec; Pumps and
pumping equipment; Pumps and pumping
equipment

(G-2434)
RUSSELL PARTITION CO INC
20 Dodge Ave (06473-1124)
PHONE.............................203 239-5749
Jim Bango, *Pr*
EMP: 9 EST: 1969
SQ FT: 25,000
SALES (est): 994.41K **Privately Held**
Web: www.russellpartition.com
SIC: 2653 2631 Partitions, corrugated:
made from purchased materials;
Paperboard mills

(G-2435)
SAFT AMERICA INC
3 Powdered Metal Rd (06473-3209)
PHONE.............................203 234-8333
David Cox, *Mgr*
EMP: 35
SALES (corp-wide): 7.96B **Publicly Held**
Web: www.saft.com
SIC: 3691 Storage batteries
HQ: Saft America Inc
13575 Waterworks St
Jacksonville FL 32221
904 861-1501

(G-2436)
SFC KOENIG LLC
73 Defco Park Rd (06473-1129)
PHONE.............................203 245-1100
▲ EMP: 30 EST: 1991
SQ FT: 9,800
SALES (est): 18.76MM
SALES (corp-wide): 3.18B **Publicly Held**
Web: www.sfckoenig.com
SIC: 8742 3594 3561 Industry specialist
consultants; Motors, pneumatic; Pumps
and pumping equipment
HQ: Sfc Koenig Ag
Lagerstrasse 8
Dietikon ZH 8953

(G-2437)
SOLON MANUFACTURING
7 Grasso Ave (06473-3237)
P.O. Box 441 (06473-0441)
PHONE.............................203 230-5300
Rick Battis, *Prin*
EMP: 14 EST: 2010
SALES (est): 334.64K **Privately Held**
SIC: 3999 Manufacturing industries, nec

(G-2438)
SUPERIOR PRINTING INK CO INC
15 Bernhard Rd (06473-3906)
PHONE.............................203 777-9055
Dave Juliano, *Brnch Mgr*
EMP: 8
SALES (corp-wide): 45.61MM **Privately Held**
Web: www.superiorink.com
SIC: 2893 Printing ink
PA: Superior Printing Ink Co Inc
10 York Ave
West Caldwell NJ 07006
201 478-5600

(G-2439)
THE E J DAVIS COMPANY
10 Dodge Ave (06473-1140)
P.O. Box 326 (06473-0326)
PHONE.............................203 239-5391
Gregory J Godbout, *Pr*
Evelyn Davis Edwards, *Treas*
Barbara D Godbout, *Sec*
EMP: 30 EST: 1953
SQ FT: 62,000
SALES (est): 4.69MM **Privately Held**
Web: www.ejdavis.com
SIC: 3296 3083 2672 Fiberglass insulation;
Laminated plastics plate and sheet; Paper;
coated and laminated, nec

(G-2440)
TRI STATE MAINTENANCE SVCS LLC
356 Old Maple Ave (06473-3248)
P.O. Box 180 (06473-0180)
PHONE.............................203 691-1343
EMP: 19 EST: 2006

SALES (est): 4.35MM **Privately Held**
Web: www.tristatemain.com
SIC: 1389 1731 Construction, repair, and
dismantling services; General electrical
contractor

(G-2441)
TWELVE PERCENT LLC
Also Called: Twelve Percent Beer Project
341 State St (06473-3112)
PHONE.............................203 745-3983
EMP: 13 EST: 2007
SALES (est): 1.09MM **Privately Held**
Web: www.12percentimports.com
SIC: 2084 Wines

(G-2442)
ULBRICH STNLESS STELS SPCIAL M (PA)
153 Washington Ave (06473-1710)
P.O. Box 294 (06473-0294)
PHONE.............................203 239-4481
Frederick C Ulbrich Iii, *CEO*
Derek Ulbrich, *
Michael Petro, *
Victor D'amato, *CFO*
▲ EMP: 60 EST: 1955
SQ FT: 25,000
SALES (est): 196.78MM
SALES (corp-wide): 196.78MM **Privately Held**
Web: www.ulbrich.com
SIC: 3316 3356 5051 3341 Strip, steel, cold-
rolled, nec: from purchased hot-rolled,;
Nickel and nickel alloy: rolling, drawing, or
extruding; Strip, metal; Secondary
nonferrous metals

(G-2443)
VALLEY SAND & GRAVEL CORP
400 N Frontage Rd (06473-3620)
PHONE.............................203 562-3192
Bill Ladum, *Dir*
EMP: 14 EST: 1998
SALES (est): 522.62K **Privately Held**
Web: www.valleysandct.com
SIC: 1771 1442 Driveway, parking lot, and
blacktop contractors; Construction sand
and gravel

(G-2444)
WILDE MANUFACTURING LLC
5 Philip Pl (06473-1607)
P.O. Box 53 (06460-0053)
PHONE.............................203 693-3939
Frank Wilde, *Pr*
EMP: 7 EST: 2012
SALES (est): 708.35K **Privately Held**
SIC: 3599 Machine shop, jobbing and repair

(G-2445)
WORLD COLOR (USA) HOLDING COMPANY
291 State St (06473-2131)
PHONE.............................203 288-2468
◆ EMP: 12893
SIC: 2752 2754 Commercial printing,
lithographic; Publication printing, gravure

North Stonington
New London County

(G-2446)
AMERICAN KUHNE INC
75 Frontage Rd (06359-1769)
PHONE.............................401 326-6200
▲ EMP: 30
SIC: 3544 Extrusion dies

(G-2447)
DYNAMIC BLDG ENRGY SLTIONS LLC (PA)
183 Providence New London Tpke Ste W3
(06359-1721)
PHONE.............................860 599-1872
Julia Discuillo, *Prin*
Julia Discuillo, *Managing Member*
EMP: 10 EST: 1990
SQ FT: 5,000
SALES (est): 4.16MM **Privately Held**
Web: www.dynamicbuildingct.com
SIC: 3625 8748 Industrial controls: push
button, selector switches, pilot; Energy
conservation consultant

(G-2448)
FARIA BEEDE INSTRUMENTS INC
Also Called: Faria Marine Instruments
75 Frontage Rd Ste 106 (06359-1711)
PHONE.............................860 848-9271
Fred J Merritt, *CEO*
Kent Rice, *
▲ EMP: 165 EST: 1956
SALES (est): 23.16MM **Privately Held**
Web: www.fariabeede.com
SIC: 3824 3825 3823 3643 Tachometer,
centrifugal; Instruments to measure
electricity; Process control instruments;
Current-carrying wiring services

(G-2449)
FISHER CONTROLS INTL LLC
95 Pendleton Hill Rd (06359-1737)
PHONE.............................860 599-1140
Bill Quernemoen, *Mgr*
EMP: 13
SALES (corp-wide): 15.16B **Publicly Held**
SIC: 3491 3494 Valves, automatic control;
Valves and pipe fittings, nec
HQ: Fisher Controls International Llc
205 S Center St
Marshalltown IA 50158
641 754-3011

North Windham
Windham County

(G-2450)
BUILDERS CONCRETE EAST LLC
79 Boston Post Rd (06256-1302)
P.O. Box 133 (06226-0133)
PHONE.............................860 456-4111
Steven E Aiudi, *Managing Member*
Harold Hopkins, *
EMP: 25 EST: 1950
SQ FT: 12,000
SALES (est): 6.13MM **Privately Held**
Web: www.bceast.com
SIC: 3273 Ready-mixed concrete

(G-2451)
UNITED ABRASIVES INC (PA)
185 Boston Post Rd (06256-1302)
PHONE.............................860 456-7131
Aris Marziali, *Ch Bd*
Eric Marziali, *
◆ EMP: 280 EST: 1969
SQ FT: 300,000
SALES (est): 47.21MM
SALES (corp-wide): 47.21MM **Privately Held**
Web: www.unitedabrasives.com
SIC: 3291 3553 2296 Abrasive buffs, bricks,
cloth, paper, stones, etc.; Woodworking
machinery; Tire cord and fabrics

Northford
New Haven County

(G-2452)
FIRE-LITE ALARMS INC
Also Called: Fire-Lite
1 Fire Lite Pl (06472-1653)
PHONE........................203 484-7161
◆ EMP: 350
Web: buildings.honeywell.com
SIC: 3669 Fire detection systems, electric

(G-2453)
HONEYWELL INTERNATIONAL INC
Also Called: Honeywell
1 Fire Lite Pl (06472-1662)
PHONE........................203 484-7161
EMP: 22
SALES (corp-wide): 35.47B **Publicly Held**
Web: www.honeywell.com
SIC: 3724 Aircraft engines and engine parts
PA: Honeywell International Inc.
855 S Mint St
Charlotte NC 28202
704 627-6200

(G-2454)
HONEYWELL INTERNATIONAL INC
Also Called: Honeywell
12 Clintonville Rd (06472-1610)
PHONE........................203 484-7161
Paul Stone, *Brnch Mgr*
EMP: 450
SALES (corp-wide): 35.47B **Publicly Held**
Web: www.honeywell.com
SIC: 3724 Aircraft engines and engine parts
PA: Honeywell International Inc.
855 S Mint St
Charlotte NC 28202
704 627-6200

(G-2455)
SOLIDIFICATION PDTS INTL INC
Also Called: Solidification Products Intl
215 Village St (06472-1405)
P.O. Box 35 (06472-0035)
PHONE........................203 484-9494
William J Gannon Junior, *Pr*
EMP: 23 EST: 1991
SALES (est): 3.94MM **Privately Held**
Web: www.oilbarriers.com
SIC: 3533 Oil and gas field machinery

(G-2456)
SOLIDIFICATION PDTS INTL INC
524 Forest Rd (06472-1485)
P.O. Box 35 (06472-0035)
PHONE........................203 484-9494
William Gannon, *Pr*
Bill Gannon, *Pr*
EMP: 7 EST: 1996
SALES (est): 989.01K **Privately Held**
Web: www.oilbarriers.com
SIC: 2843 2819 3999 Oils and greases;
Industrial inorganic chemicals, nec;
Atomizers, toiletry

(G-2457)
XTRALIS INC
175 Bodwell St (06472)
PHONE........................800 229-4434
EMP: 36 EST: 1996
SALES (est): 13.84MM
SALES (corp-wide): 35.47B **Publicly Held**
Web: www.xtralis.com

SIC: 3669 Visual communication systems
PA: Honeywell International Inc.
855 S Mint St
Charlotte NC 28202
704 627-6200

Norwalk
Fairfield County

(G-2458)
ABB FINANCE (USA) INC
501 Merritt 7 (06851-7001)
PHONE........................919 856-2360
EMP: 24 EST: 2012
SALES (est): 835.73K **Privately Held**
SIC: 3613 Switchgear and switchboard
apparatus
PA: Abb Ltd
Affolternstrasse 44
ZUrich ZH 8050

(G-2459)
AIRPOT CORPORATION
35 Lois St (06851-4405)
PHONE........................800 848-7681
Mark Gaberman, *Pr*
Barbara Cohen, *
Tom Lee, *
◆ EMP: 26 EST: 1969
SQ FT: 12,000
SALES (est): 6.31MM **Privately Held**
Web: www.airpot.com
SIC: 3499 3714 3593 Machine bases, metal
; Motor vehicle parts and accessories; Fluid
power cylinders and actuators

(G-2460)
AJ CASEY LLC
Also Called: Beverly Feldman
597 Westport Ave Unit C363 (06851-4440)
PHONE........................203 226-5961
Anthony J Casey, *Managing Member*
▲ EMP: 7 EST: 2001
SQ FT: 2,100
SALES (est): 773.89K **Privately Held**
SIC: 3144 Dress shoes, women's

(G-2461)
AKADEMOS LLC
200 Connecticut Ave Ste 2b (06854-1907)
PHONE........................203 866-0190
Raj Kaji, *CEO*
Ron Kwiatkowski, *
Geoffrey Katz, *
Daniel Rubin, *Technology Vice President*
Chris Boyster, *Marketing*
EMP: 53 EST: 1999
SQ FT: 6,276
SALES (est): 16.84MM
SALES (corp-wide): 24.82MM **Privately
Held**
Web: www.akademos.com
SIC: 7372 Educational computer software
PA: Vitalsource Technologies Llc
227 Fayetteville St # 400
Raleigh NC 27601
919 755-8100

(G-2462)
APPLIED BIOSYSTEMS LLC
301 Merritt 7 Ste 23 (06851-1062)
PHONE........................781 271-0045
Tony L White, *Prin*
EMP: 17
SALES (corp-wide): 44.91B **Publicly Held**
Web: www.thermofisher.com
SIC: 3826 Analytical instruments
HQ: Applied Biosystems, Llc
5791 Van Allen Way

Carlsbad CA 92008

(G-2463)
AQUA PULSAR LLC
Also Called: Clear Water Plasma
95b Rowayton Ave Ste 1 (06853-1432)
PHONE........................772 320-9691
EMP: 7 EST: 2017
SALES (est): 228.31K **Privately Held**
Web: www.aquapulsar.com
SIC: 2836 Plasmas

(G-2464)
ARTISTIC IRON WORKS LLC
11 Reynolds St (06855-1014)
PHONE........................203 838-9200
Edward Jankowski, *Managing Member*
Renata Singh, *Managing Member*
EMP: 9 EST: 1969
SALES (est): 979.49K **Privately Held**
Web: www.artistic-iw.com
SIC: 3446 Gates, ornamental metal

(G-2465)
ASEA BROWN BOVERI INC
Also Called: A B B Power Transmission
501 Merritt 7 (06851-7000)
PHONE........................203 750-2200
Donald Aiken, *Pr*
Jeff Halsey, *Sr VP*
Han-anders Nilsson, *Sr VP*
E Barry Lyon, *VP*
Barry Wentworth, *D B Contact*
EMP: 10634 EST: 1978
SQ FT: 36,000
SALES (est): 331.27MM **Privately Held**
Web: new.abb.com
SIC: 3612 3613 5063 3511 Transformers,
except electric; Switchgear and
switchboard apparatus; Electrical apparatus
and equipment; Steam turbine generator
set units, complete
HQ: Abb Holdings Inc.
305 Gregson Dr
Cary NC 27511
919 856-2360

(G-2466)
ASPECTA NORTH AMERICA LLC
15 Oakwood Ave (06850-1365)
PHONE........................855 400-7732
EMP: 9 EST: 2014
SALES (est): 390.59K **Privately Held**
Web: www.aspectaflooring.com
SIC: 3253 Ceramic wall and floor tile

(G-2467)
AVARA PHARMACEUTICAL SVCS INC (HQ)
401 Merritt 7 (06851-1000)
PHONE........................405 217-7670
Leonard Levi, *Ch Bd*
Keith A Lyon, *
EMP: 90 EST: 2015
SALES (est): 35.38MM
SALES (corp-wide): 140.77MM **Privately
Held**
Web: www.avara.com
SIC: 2834 Pharmaceutical preparations
PA: Avara Us Holdings Llc
101 Merritt 7
Norwalk CT 06851
203 655-1333

(G-2468)
AVARA US HOLDINGS LLC (PA)
101 Merritt 7 (06851-1059)
PHONE........................203 655-1333
Timothy Tyson, *CEO*
James Scandura, *Ex VP*

Keith Lyon, *Ex VP*
William Pasek, *Chief Commercial Officer*
Donald Britt, *Chief Quality Officer*
EMP: 24 EST: 2016
SALES (est): 140.77MM
SALES (corp-wide): 140.77MM **Privately
Held**
Web: www.avara.com
SIC: 2834 6719 Druggists' preparations
(pharmaceuticals); Investment holding
companies, except banks

(G-2469)
BELVOIR MEDIA GROUP LLC
535 Connecticut Ave Ste 100 (06854)
P.O. Box 5656 (06856-5656)
PHONE........................203 857-3100
EMP: 7 EST: 1999
SALES (est): 472.25K **Privately Held**
Web: www.belvoir.com
SIC: 2731 Book publishing

(G-2470)
BELVOIR PUBLICATIONS INC (PA)
Also Called: Belvoir Media Group
800 Connecticut Ave Ste 4w02
(06854-1631)
P.O. Box 5656 (06856-5656)
PHONE........................203 857-3100
Robert Englander, *Ch*
Ron Goldberg, *
EMP: 50 EST: 1971
SQ FT: 11,000
SALES (est): 22.58MM
SALES (corp-wide): 22.58MM **Privately
Held**
Web: www.belvoir.com
SIC: 2721 Magazines: publishing only, not
printed on site

(G-2471)
BENDER MANAGEMENT INC
Also Called: Bender Showrooms
235 Westport Ave (06851-4310)
P.O. Box 857 (06852-0857)
PHONE........................203 847-3865
David Bender, *Pr*
Stephen Fecteau, *VP*
James Narduzzo, *VP*
EMP: 46 EST: 2011
SALES (est): 5.01MM **Privately Held**
Web: www.benderplumbing.com
SIC: 1799 2499 Kitchen and bathroom
remodeling; Kitchen, bathroom, and
household ware: wood

(G-2472)
BIO MED PACKAGING SYSTEMS INC
100 Pearl St (06850-1629)
PHONE........................203 846-1923
James B Brown, *Pr*
Janet Kaufman, *VP*
▼ EMP: 18 EST: 1962
SQ FT: 50,000
SALES (est): 422.02K **Privately Held**
Web: www.biomedpackaging.com
SIC: 3842 Surgical appliances and supplies

(G-2473)
BITE TECH INC
20 Glover Ave Ste 1 (06850-1234)
PHONE........................203 987-6898
Jeff Padovan, *CEO*
James Meyers, *
▼ EMP: 27 EST: 1995
SQ FT: 3,500
SALES (est): 2.93MM **Privately Held**
Web: www.bitetech.com

GEOGRAPHIC

SIC: 3069 Mouthpieces for pipes, cigarette holders, etc.: rubber

(G-2474)
BLC HOLDINGS LLC (PA)
Also Called: Benifit Port
20 Glover Ave (06850-1219)
PHONE..................................203 229-1007
Robert Milligan, *CEO*
Julie Lowitz, *Sec*
Robert J Murphy, *CFO*
EMP: 40 **EST:** 1999
SQ FT: 11,328
SALES (est): 24.72MM
SALES (corp-wide): 24.72MM **Privately Held**
SIC: 7372 6321 4813 Business oriented computer software; Accident and health insurance; Proprietary online service networks

(G-2475)
BPI REPROGRAPHICS
Also Called: American Reprographics
87 Taylor Ave (06854-2038)
PHONE..................................203 866-5600
TOLL FREE: 800
John P Schaberg, *Pr*
EMP: 10 **EST:** 1946
SQ FT: 6,000
SALES (est): 792.03K **Privately Held**
SIC: 7373 3861 7334 Computer-aided system services; Photographic equipment and supplies; Blueprinting service

(G-2476)
BRANDS TO GO INC
65 East Ave (06851-4907)
EMP: 10
SIC: 2834 Drugs acting on the central nervous system & sense organs

(G-2477)
BUCK SCIENTIFIC INC
58 Fort Point St (06855-1097)
PHONE..................................203 853-9444
Robert Anderson, *Pr*
Edward Nadeau, *
Eric Anderson, *Corporate Secretary*
EMP: 31 **EST:** 1972
SQ FT: 10,000
SALES (est): 4.41MM **Privately Held**
Web: www.bucksci.com
SIC: 3826 3823 Analytical instruments; Absorption analyzers: infrared, x-ray, etc.: industrial

(G-2478)
BUSINESS JOURNALS INC
Also Called: Travel Wear
50 Day St (06854-3100)
PHONE..................................203 853-6015
EMP: 55
Web: www.whole-dog-journal.com
SIC: 2721 2741 Trade journals: publishing only, not printed on site; Technical manuals: publishing only, not printed on site

(G-2479)
CARLUCCI WLDG FABRICATION INC
205 Wilson Ave (06854-5025)
PHONE..................................203 588-0746
Canio C Carlucci, *Pr*
EMP: 18 **EST:** 2015
SALES (est): 2.47MM **Privately Held**
Web: www.carlucciwelding.com
SIC: 7692 Welding repair

(G-2480)
CEBAL AMERICAS (PA)
Also Called: Alcan Packaging
101 Merritt 7 Ste 2 (06851-1060)
PHONE..................................203 845-6356
Christel Bories, *CEO*
EMP: 1325 **EST:** 2003
SALES (est): 58.11MM
SALES (corp-wide): 58.11MM **Privately Held**
Web: na.pechiney.com
SIC: 3082 Tubes, unsupported plastics

(G-2481)
CHRISTOPHER PEACOCK HOME LLC
9 Bettswood Rd (06851-5103)
PHONE..................................203 388-4022
EMP: 16 **EST:** 2009
SALES (est): 77.33K **Privately Held**
SIC: 2434 Wood kitchen cabinets

(G-2482)
CLARKE DISTRIBUTION CORP
64 S Main St (06854-2934)
PHONE..................................203 838-9385
Thomas Clarke, *Pr*
EMP: 7
SQ FT: 14,894
Web: www.clarkeliving.com
SIC: 3639 5722 Major kitchen appliances, except refrigerators and stoves; Electric household appliances, major
PA: Clarke Distribution Corporation
393 Fortune Blvd
Milford MA 01757

(G-2483)
CLASSIC PREP CHILDRENSWEAR INC
161 Rowayton Ave (06853-1411)
P.O. Box 142 (06853-0142)
PHONE..................................203 286-6204
Ginger Drysdale, *CEO*
EMP: 9 **EST:** 2015
SALES (est): 1.01MM **Privately Held**
Web: www.classicprep.com
SIC: 2361 5641 Girl's and children's dresses, blouses; Children's wear

(G-2484)
COBRA GREEN LLC
50 N Water St (06854-2278)
PHONE..................................203 354-5000
EMP: 600
SALES (est): 14.31MM **Privately Held**
SIC: 8748 6799 7372 8721 Business consulting, nec; Venture capital companies; Prepackaged software; Accounting, auditing, and bookkeeping

(G-2485)
CONCORD INDUSTRIES INC
Also Called: Concord Distributing
19 Willard Rd (06851-4415)
PHONE..................................203 750-6060
Karen Muller Condron, *Pr*
▲ **EMP:** 35 **EST:** 1985
SQ FT: 27,000
SALES (est): 1.67MM **Privately Held**
Web: concordind.wordpress.com
SIC: 3499 5199 3993 Novelties and giftware, including trophies; Gifts and novelties; Signs and advertising specialties

(G-2486)
CONNECTICUT TICK CONTROL LLC
Also Called: Connecticut Tick Control
15 Chapel St (06850-4113)
P.O. Box 1439 (06856-1439)
PHONE..................................203 855-7849
EMP: 17 **EST:** 1998
SALES (est): 1.98MM **Privately Held**
Web: www.nixticks.com
SIC: 7342 2879 Pest control in structures; Insecticides and pesticides

(G-2487)
CORTELYOU INC
129 Glover Ave (06850-1345)
PHONE..................................203 847-2000
EMP: 60
SIC: 2741 Miscellaneous publishing

(G-2488)
CRITERION INC
Also Called: Perfectsoftware
301 Merritt 7 (06851-1070)
PHONE..................................203 703-9000
Sunil Reddy, *CEO*
EMP: 58 **EST:** 2009
SALES (est): 9.76MM **Privately Held**
Web: www.criterionhcm.com
SIC: 7372 Business oriented computer software

(G-2489)
DATTO HOLDING CORP (DH)
Also Called: Datto
101 Merritt 7 (06851-1059)
PHONE..................................888 995-1431
Timothy Weller, *CEO*
John Abbot, *CFO*
Chris Mccloskey, *CCO*
Radhesh Menon, *CPO*
EMP: 52 **EST:** 2007
SQ FT: 134,000
SALES (est): 618.66MM
SALES (corp-wide): 655.22MM **Privately Held**
Web: www.datto.com
SIC: 7372 Prepackaged software
HQ: Knockout Parent Inc.
701 Brickell Ave Ste 400
Miami FL 33131
415 694-5700

(G-2490)
DEVINE BROTHERS INCORPORATED
38 Commerce St (06850-4109)
P.O. Box 189 (06852-0189)
PHONE..................................203 866-4421
Tom Devine, *Sec*
Michael M Devine, *
Stephen C Devine, *
Sonia M Donovan, *
Richard T Devine, *
EMP: 37 **EST:** 1918
SQ FT: 5,000
SALES (est): 7.84MM **Privately Held**
Web: www.devinebi.com
SIC: 5983 5032 5031 3273 Fuel oil dealers; Concrete mixtures; Building materials, exterior; Ready-mixed concrete

(G-2491)
DICKSON PRODUCT DEV INC
14 Perry Ave (06850-1623)
PHONE..................................203 846-2128
Maurice Bennett, *Pr*
Margaret Bennett, *VP*
EMP: 7 **EST:** 1969
SQ FT: 6,000
SALES (est): 725.41K **Privately Held**
SIC: 3599 Machine shop, jobbing and repair

(G-2492)
DOONEY & BOURKE INC (HQ)
1 Regent St (06855-1405)
P.O. Box 841 (06856-0841)
PHONE..................................203 853-7515
H Peter Dooney, *Pr*
Frederick A Bourke Junior, *Treas*
Philip R Kinsley, *
◆ **EMP:** 38 **EST:** 1975
SQ FT: 56,000
SALES (est): 42MM
SALES (corp-wide): 733.7K **Privately Held**
Web: www.dooney.com
SIC: 3171 2387 3161 3172 Handbags, women's; Apparel belts; Suitcases; Personal leather goods, nec
PA: Dooney & Bourke Italia Srl
Via I Maggio 146
Monsummano Terme PT 51015

(G-2493)
DULCE DOMUM LLC
Also Called: Cottages & Grdns Publications
40 Richards Ave Ste 4 (06854-2320)
PHONE..................................203 227-1400
EMP: 41 **EST:** 2005
SQ FT: 3,225
SALES (est): 6.5MM **Privately Held**
Web: www.cottagesgardens.com
SIC: 2721 Magazines: publishing and printing

(G-2494)
DYMO CORPORATION
383 Main Ave Ste 4 (06851-1544)
▲ **EMP:** 75
Web: www.dymo.com
SIC: 3577 3565 3555 Computer peripheral equipment, nec; Labeling machines, industrial; Printing trades machinery

(G-2495)
ECOMETICS INC
19 Concord St (06854-3706)
P.O. Box 179 (06856-0179)
PHONE..................................203 853-7856
Mark Lowenstein, *Pr*
Judith Lowenstein, *
Michael Lowenstein, *
▲ **EMP:** 30 **EST:** 1972
SQ FT: 25,000
SALES (est): 4.27MM **Privately Held**
Web: www.ecometics.com
SIC: 2844 Cosmetic preparations

(G-2496)
ELIZABETH EAKINS INC
5 Taft St (06854-4201)
PHONE..................................203 831-9347
Elizabeth Eakins, *CEO*
EMP: 41 **EST:** 1983
SALES (est): 4.07MM
SALES (corp-wide): 421.83MM **Privately Held**
SIC: 2273 5713 Rugs: twisted paper, grass, reed, coir, sisal, jute, etc.; Rugs
HQ: Holland & Sherry, Inc.
979 3rd Ave Ste 1402
New York NY 10022
877 631-0090

(G-2497)
ELOQUE LLC
201 Merritt 7 (06851-1056)
PHONE..................................203 849-5567
Ersin Uzun, *Pr*
Maulet Lee, *Prin*
EMP: 11 **EST:** 2021
SALES (est): 2.43MM
SALES (corp-wide): 7.11B **Publicly Held**

SIC: **3577** Computer peripheral equipment, nec
HQ: Xerox Corporation
201 Merritt 7 Ste 1
Norwalk CT 06851
203 849-5216

(G-2498)
EUROPEAN WOODCRAFT LLC
Also Called: European Woodcraft
9 Crockett St Ste 1 (06851)
PHONE..............................203 847-6195
EMP: 8 EST: 1993
SALES (est): 797.05K **Privately Held**
Web: www.europeanwoodcraftllc.com
SIC: **2499** 2517 2511 2434 Decorative wood and woodwork; Wood television and radio cabinets; Wood household furniture; Wood kitchen cabinets

(G-2499)
FC MEYER PACKAGING LLC (HQ)
108 Main St Ste 3 (06851-4640)
PHONE..............................203 847-8500
Kenneth Schulman, *Managing Member*
Steven Schulman, *
Steve Gilliand, *
EMP: 29 EST: 2001
SQ FT: 12,000
SALES (est): 44.36MM
SALES (corp-wide): 97.08MM **Privately Held**
Web: www.mafcote.com
SIC: **3086** Packaging and shipping materials, foamed plastics
PA: Mafcote, Inc.
108 Main St Ste 3
Norwalk CT 06851
203 847-8500

(G-2500)
FINANCIAL ACCNTING FOUNDATION (PA)
Also Called: Financial Accnting Stndards Bd
801 Main Ave (06851-1127)
P.O. Box 5116 (06856-5116)
PHONE..............................203 847-0700
Teresa S Polley, *Pr*
Jack Brennan, *Ch*
Robert Attmore, *GASB*
Leslie Seidman, *FASB*
Jeffrey W Rubin, *VP*
EMP: 165 EST: 1972
SQ FT: 60,000
SALES (est): 75.6MM
SALES (corp-wide): 75.6MM **Privately Held**
Web: www.accountingfoundation.org
SIC: **8621** 2721 Accounting association; Periodicals, publishing only

(G-2501)
FITZGERALD-NORWALK AWNG CO INC
Also Called: Norwalk Awning Company
131 Main St (06851-4628)
PHONE..............................203 847-5858
George H Genuario Junior, *Pr*
Gregory Genuario, *Sec*
Carol Genuario, *Treas*
EMP: 7 EST: 1929
SALES (est): 682.1K **Privately Held**
Web: www.fitzgeraldnorwalkawning.com
SIC: **2394** 1799 Awnings, fabric: made from purchased materials; Awning installation

(G-2502)
FOAM SYSTEMS LLC
Also Called: Spray Foam Insulation
30 Muller Ave Ste 19 (06851)
P.O. Box 1182 (06840-1182)
PHONE..............................800 853-1577
EMP: 8 EST: 2016
SALES (est): 885.15K **Privately Held**
Web: www.sprayfoamoutlets.com
SIC: **5999** 2851 Foam and foam products; Polyurethane coatings

(G-2503)
GATEWAY DIGITAL INC
Also Called: Gateway
16 Testa Pl (06854-4638)
PHONE..............................203 853-4929
EMP: 19 EST: 1993
SQ FT: 13,000
SALES (est): 2.04MM **Privately Held**
SIC: **2796** 2752 2791 2759 Color separations, for printing; Commercial printing, lithographic; Typesetting; Commercial printing, nec

(G-2504)
GENERAL ELECTRIC COMPANY
Also Called: GE
901 Main Ave Ste 103 (06851-1187)
P.O. Box 1920b (06813-1920)
PHONE..............................203 797-0840
EMP: 659
SALES (corp-wide): 76.56B **Publicly Held**
Web: www.ge.com
SIC: **3511** 3845 3533 6153 Turbines and turbine generator sets; Electromedical equipment; Oil and gas field machinery; Working capital financing
PA: General Electric Company
1 Financial Ctr Ste 3700
Boston MA 02111
617 443-3000

(G-2505)
GENERAL PACKAGING PRODUCTS INC
3 Valley View Rd Apt 9 (06851-1033)
P.O. Box 7059 (06897-7059)
PHONE..............................203 846-1340
Peter D Schonberg, *Pr*
Anthony Lorenzo, *Sec*
EMP: 9 EST: 1958
SQ FT: 1,400
SALES (est): 976.24K **Privately Held**
SIC: **3086** 2653 2671 Packaging and shipping materials, foamed plastics; Boxes, corrugated: made from purchased materials; Plastic film, coated or laminated for packaging

(G-2506)
GLOBENIX INC
9 Lois St (06851-4404)
PHONE..............................203 740-7070
Young Chun, *Pr*
EMP: 7 EST: 2013
SQ FT: 2,500
SALES (est): 706.42K **Privately Held**
Web: www.globenixvideoscope.com
SIC: **5065** 5049 3731 Communication equipment; Optical goods; Submersible marine robots, manned or unmanned

(G-2507)
GOLF GALAXY LLC
Also Called: Golfsmith
595 Connecticut Ave Ste 4 (06854-1734)
PHONE..............................203 855-0500
Steve Partin, *Prin*
EMP: 18

SALES (corp-wide): 12.37B **Publicly Held**
Web: stores.golfgalaxy.com
SIC: **3949** 5091 5941 Golf equipment; Golf equipment; Golf goods and equipment
HQ: Golf Galaxy, Llc
345 Court St
Coraopolis PA 15108

(G-2508)
GOTHAM CHEMICAL COMPANY INC
21 South St (06854-2602)
PHONE..............................203 854-6644
Richard Zane Elkin, *Pr*
Ernest Elkin, *
Richard Elkin, *
EMP: 100 EST: 1946
SQ FT: 10,000
SALES (est): 9.03MM **Privately Held**
Web: www.gothamtechnologiesinc.com
SIC: **2899** Water treating compounds

(G-2509)
GOTHAM TECHNOLOGIES INC
21 South St (06854-2602)
PHONE..............................800 468-4261
Richard Zane Elkin, *Pr*
EMP: 11 EST: 2007
SALES (est): 575.28K **Privately Held**
SIC: **3589** Sewage and water treatment equipment

(G-2510)
GREENWICH FINE WOODWORK LLC
7 Lexington Ave (06854-4310)
PHONE..............................203 987-0001
EMP: 8 EST: 2012
SALES (est): 285.51K **Privately Held**
Web: www.greenwichfinewoodwork.com
SIC: **2431** Millwork

(G-2511)
HECKMANN BUILDING PRODUCTS INC
110 Richards Ave Ste 1 (06854-1685)
PHONE..............................708 865-2403
Paul M Curtis, *CEO*
Paul G Curtis, *Pr*
▲ EMP: 24 EST: 1923
SALES (est): 460.04K **Privately Held**
Web: www.heckmannbuildingprods.com
SIC: **3429** 5039 Builders' hardware; Joists

(G-2512)
HFW INC
18 Ludlow Mnr (06855-2011)
PHONE..............................203 854-9584
Charles Walsh, *Ofcr*
EMP: 8 EST: 2014
SALES (est): 86.01K **Privately Held**
SIC: **3599** Machine shop, jobbing and repair

(G-2513)
HICKS AND OTIS PRINTS INC
9 Wilton Ave (06851-4515)
PHONE..............................203 846-2087
Harold Kaplan, *Pr*
Linwood Wade, *
Steven Crovatto, *
▲ EMP: 32 EST: 1939
SQ FT: 45,000
SALES (est): 4.09MM **Privately Held**
SIC: **3083** 3429 Plastics finished products, laminated; Hardware, nec

(G-2514)
HJ HOFFMAN COMPANY
25 Hanford Pl (06854-3017)
PHONE..............................203 853-7740
David C Hoffman, *Pr*
Michael Hoffman, *VP*
EMP: 9 EST: 1981
SQ FT: 4,000
SALES (est): 930.79K **Privately Held**
Web: www.hjhco.com
SIC: **7336** 2395 Silk screen design; Embroidery and art needlework

(G-2515)
HMTX INDUSTRIES LLC (PA)
29 Oakwood Ave (06850-1301)
PHONE..............................203 299-3100
Harlan Stone, *CEO*
John Henkel, *
EMP: 7 EST: 2020
SALES (est): 8.02MM
SALES (corp-wide): 8.02MM **Privately Held**
Web: www.hmtx.global
SIC: **2499** 2421 3253 Tiles, cork; Flooring (dressed lumber), softwood; Floor tile, ceramic

(G-2516)
IHS HEROLD INC (DH)
200 Connecticut Ave Ste 3a (06854-1907)
PHONE..............................203 857-0215
Christin Juneau, *CEO*
Donald Whelley, *
Gilbert Baliki, *
John Parry, *
Lysle Brinker, *
▼ EMP: 66 EST: 1948
SQ FT: 16,000
SALES (est): 10.57MM
SALES (corp-wide): 11.18B **Publicly Held**
Web: www.herold.com
SIC: **3826** 6282 8742 Analytical instruments; Investment research; Marketing consulting services
HQ: Ihs Global Inc.
15 Inverness Way E
Englewood CO 80112

(G-2517)
INDUSTRIAL PRESS INC
1 Chestnut St (06854-5901)
PHONE..............................888 528-7852
Michael A Backer, *Ch Bd*
Alex Luchars, *Pr*
▲ EMP: 16 EST: 1894
SQ FT: 3,400
SALES (est): 2.24MM **Privately Held**
Web: books.industrialpress.com
SIC: **2741** Miscellaneous publishing

(G-2518)
INSYS MICRO INC
40 Richards Ave Ste 3 (06854-2320)
PHONE..............................917 566-5045
Yuriy Kartoshkin, *Pr*
EMP: 7 EST: 2013
SALES (est): 492.44K **Privately Held**
SIC: **3679** 7373 Electronic components, nec; Computer integrated systems design

(G-2519)
JARDEN LLC
Also Called: Jarden Plastic Solution
301 Merritt 7 Ste 5 (06851-1051)
PHONE..............................203 845-5300
James Lillie, *Pr*
EMP: 24
SALES (corp-wide): 9.46B **Publicly Held**
Web: www.newellbrands.com

SIC: **3089** 3634 Plastics containers, except foam; Electric housewares and fans
HQ: Jarden Llc
   221 River St
   Hoboken NJ 07030

(G-2520)
JARED MANUFACTURING CO INC
25 Perry Ave (06850-1655)
P.O. Box 266 (06850)
PHONE..............................203 846-1732
Timothy C Frate, *Pr*
EMP: 36 **EST:** 1979
SQ FT: 11,000
SALES (est): 1.1MM **Privately Held**
SIC: **3444** 3599 3699 Sheet metal specialties, not stamped; Machine shop, jobbing and repair; Electrical equipment and supplies, nec

(G-2521)
K W GRIFFEN COMPANY
Also Called: Biomed Packing Systems
100 Pearl St (06850-1629)
PHONE..............................203 846-1923
James B Brown, *Pr*
Rosemary Brown, *
EMP: 40 **EST:** 1860
SQ FT: 32,000
SALES (est): 4.99MM **Privately Held**
Web: www.kwgriffen.com
SIC: **3842** Surgical appliances and supplies

(G-2522)
KARAVAS FASHIONS LTD
17 Wall St (06850-3413)
PHONE..............................203 866-4000
Stelios Paraskevas, *Pr*
Carol Paraskevas, *Sec*
EMP: 10 **EST:** 1979
SALES (est): 578.52K **Privately Held**
SIC: **3911** Jewelry, precious metal

(G-2523)
KING INDUSTRIES INC (PA)
1 Science Rd (06850-4261)
P.O. Box 588 (06852-0588)
PHONE..............................203 866-5551
◆ **EMP:** 168 **EST:** 1932
SALES (est): 48.62MM
SALES (corp-wide): 48.62MM **Privately Held**
Web: www.kingindustries.com
SIC: **2899** 2819 Rust resisting compounds; Catalysts, chemical

(G-2524)
KOLMAR AMERICAS
383 Main Ave (06851-1543)
PHONE..............................203 840-5337
EMP: 9 **EST:** 2019
SALES (est): 1.67MM **Privately Held**
Web: www.kolmargroup.com
SIC: **1389** Oil and gas field services, nec

(G-2525)
LAJOIE AUTO WRECKING CO INC
Also Called: La Joies Auto Scrap & Recycl
40 Meadow St (06854-4501)
PHONE..............................203 870-0641
Donald L La Joie, *Pr*
James Murphy, *
EMP: 25 **EST:** 1933
SQ FT: 3,750
SALES (est): 2.43MM **Privately Held**
Web: www.lajoies.com

SIC: **5093** 3341 Automotive wrecking for scrap; Secondary nonferrous metals

(G-2526)
LEEJAY INDUSTRIES LLC
151 Woodward Ave (06854-4721)
P.O. Box 1406 (06856-1406)
PHONE..............................203 847-3660
EMP: 25 **EST:** 1985
SALES (est): 1.46MM **Privately Held**
SIC: **2752** 2789 Commercial printing, lithographic; Bookbinding and related work

(G-2527)
LEEK BUILDING PRODUCTS INC
205 Wilson Ave Ste 3 (06854-5025)
PHONE..............................203 853-3883
William A Leek Junior, *Pr*
Martha K Leek, *Sec*
▲ **EMP:** 20 **EST:** 1986
SQ FT: 10,000
SALES (est): 2.45MM **Privately Held**
Web: www.leekbuildingproducts.com
SIC: **3446** 3444 3296 5211 Architectural metalwork; Sheet metalwork; Mineral wool; Door and window products

(G-2528)
LINKS POINT INC
1 Selleck St Ste 330 (06855-1118)
PHONE..............................203 853-4600
Strite H Potter, *Pr*
Scott T Potter, *Chief Technical Officer*
Michael Ippolito, *Prin*
EMP: 20 **EST:** 1999
SALES (est): 2.1MM **Privately Held**
Web: www.linkspoint.com
SIC: **3663** Mobile communication equipment

(G-2529)
LOREX PLASTICS CO INC
221 Wilson Ave (06854-5026)
PHONE..............................203 286-0020
Ed Abdelnour, *Owner*
EMP: 12 **EST:** 2014
SALES (est): 1.06MM **Privately Held**
Web: www.lorexplastics.com
SIC: **3089** Injection molding of plastics

(G-2530)
MAFCOTE INC (PA)
Also Called: Miami Wabash Paper
108 Main St Ste 3 (06851-4640)
PHONE..............................203 847-8500
EMP: 28 **EST:** 1975
SALES (est): 97.08MM
SALES (corp-wide): 97.08MM **Privately Held**
Web: www.mafcote.com
SIC: **2631** 2657 2679 2671 Paperboard mills; Folding paperboard boxes; Doilies, paper: made from purchased material; Wrapping paper, waterproof or coated

(G-2531)
MAFCOTE INDUSTRIES
108 Main St Ste 3 (06851-4640)
PHONE..............................601 776-9006
EMP: 14 **EST:** 2010
SALES (est): 410.99K **Privately Held**
Web: www.mafcote.com
SIC: **3999** Manufacturing industries, nec

(G-2532)
MAFCOTE INTERNATIONAL INC (HQ)
108 Main St Ste 3 (06851-4640)
PHONE..............................203 644-1200
Steven A Schulnan, *Pr*

Steven A Schulnan, *Pr*
Miles Hisiger, *Treas*
EMP: 24 **EST:** 1998
SALES (est): 3.57MM
SALES (corp-wide): 97.08MM **Privately Held**
Web: www.mafcote.com
SIC: **2621** Paper mills
PA: Mafcote, Inc.
   108 Main St Ste 3
   Norwalk CT 06851
   203 847-8500

(G-2533)
MANUP LLC
345 Wilson Ave (06854-4666)
PHONE..............................203 588-9861
EMP: 8 **EST:** 2009
SQ FT: 14,500
SALES (est): 2.8MM **Privately Held**
Web: www.lax.com
SIC: **5941** 7382 2353 3161 Specialty sport supplies, nec; Security systems services; Hats, caps, and millinery; Luggage

(G-2534)
MAYAN CORPORATION
79 Day St (06854-3733)
PHONE..............................203 854-4711
Luis M Huerta, *Pr*
Ronald E Pair, *Sec*
EMP: 15 **EST:** 1993
SQ FT: 6,800
SALES (est): 1.09MM **Privately Held**
Web: www.mayanet.net
SIC: **3172** Personal leather goods, nec

(G-2535)
MEDIANEWS GROUP INC
Also Called: Connecticut Post
301 Merritt 7 Ste 1 (06851-1051)
PHONE..............................203 333-0161
Robert Laska, *Brnch Mgr*
EMP: 10
SALES (corp-wide): 1.96B **Privately Held**
Web: www.medianewsgroup.com
SIC: **2711** Newspapers, publishing and printing
HQ: Medianews Group, Inc.
   5990 Washington St
   Denver CO 80216

(G-2536)
METSA BOARD AMERICAS CORP
301 Merritt 7 Ste 2 (06851-1051)
PHONE..............................203 229-0037
◆ **EMP:** 69 **EST:** 1978
SQ FT: 12,000
SALES (est): 51.37MM
SALES (corp-wide): 7.25B **Privately Held**
SIC: **2631** Paperboard mills
HQ: Metsa Board Oyj
   Revontulenpuisto 2
   Espoo 02100
   104611

(G-2537)
MIAMI WABASH PAPER LLC (HQ)
108 Main St Ste 3 (06851-4640)
PHONE..............................203 847-8500
EMP: 31 **EST:** 2000
SQ FT: 12,000
SALES (est): 16.82MM
SALES (corp-wide): 97.08MM **Privately Held**
Web: www.mafcote.com
SIC: **2621** Paper mills
PA: Mafcote, Inc.
   108 Main St Ste 3

Norwalk CT 06851
203 847-8500

(G-2538)
MINUTEMAN LAND SERVICES INC
377 Highland Ave (06854-3439)
PHONE..............................203 854-4949
Jordan Grant, *Prin*
EMP: 7 **EST:** 2016
SALES (est): 226.68K **Privately Held**
Web: www.minutemenlandservices.com
SIC: **2752** Offset printing

(G-2539)
MOAB OIL INC
20 Marshall St Ste 200 (06854-2281)
PHONE..............................203 857-6622
Kenneth T Utting, *Pr*
Donald L Linsley, *VP*
Michael A Fabacher, *VP*
EMP: 15 **EST:** 2003
SALES (est): 2.47MM
SALES (corp-wide): 5.02B **Publicly Held**
Web: www.moaboil.com
SIC: **1382** Oil and gas exploration services
HQ: Tp Icap Group Services Limited
   2 Floor
   London EC2M
   207200700

(G-2540)
MY SLIDE LINES LLC
173 Main St (06851-3606)
PHONE..............................203 324-1642
EMP: 10 **EST:** 2014
SALES (est): 1.97MM **Privately Held**
SIC: **1389** Construction, repair, and dismantling services

(G-2541)
MYLLYKOSKI NORTH AMERICA
Also Called: Joint Venture Madison Intl
101 Merritt Ste 7 (06851)
▲ **EMP:** 30 **EST:** 1988
SALES (est): 2.02MM **Privately Held**
SIC: **3291** Paper, abrasive: garnet, emery, aluminum oxide coated

(G-2542)
NC BRANDS LP
40 Richards Ave Ste 2 (06854-2320)
PHONE..............................203 295-2300
Robert Kulperger, *CEO*
Mark Munford, *Pr*
Debra Gordon, *CFO*
EMP: 85 **EST:** 2012
SQ FT: 3,500
SALES (est): 19.64MM
SALES (corp-wide): 2.39B **Privately Held**
Web: www.naturalchemistry.com
SIC: **2842** Polishes and sanitation goods
HQ: Bio-Lab, Inc.
   1725 N Brown Rd
   Lawrenceville GA 30043
   678 502-4000

(G-2543)
NCI HOLDINGS INC (PA)
40 Richards Ave Ste 2 (06854-2320)
PHONE..............................203 295-2300
Robert J Kulperger, *CEO*
Debbie Gordon, *
▲ **EMP:** 52 **EST:** 1989
SALES (est): 18.27MM **Privately Held**
SIC: **2842** Polishes and sanitation goods

▲ = Import ▼ = Export
◆ = Import/Export

(G-2544)
NEW CANAAN NEWS
301 Merritt 7 Ste 1 (06851-1051)
PHONE...............................203 842-2582
EMP: 7 **EST:** 2017
SALES (est): 150.82K **Privately Held**
Web: www.ncadvertiser.com
SIC: 2711 Newspapers, publishing and
printing

(G-2545)
NEWS 12 CONNECTICUT LLC
28 Cross St (06851-4632)
PHONE...............................203 849-1321
EMP: 24 **EST:** 2008
SALES (est): 676.07K **Privately Held**
Web: connecticut.news12.com
SIC: 2711 Newspapers, publishing and
printing

(G-2546)
NORFIELD DATA PRODUCTS INC
Also Called: Cofmic Computers
181 Main St Ste 2 (06851-3624)
PHONE...............................203 849-0292
Hasmukh Parikh, *Pr*
Hasmukh Parikh, *Pr*
Richard C Miller, *VP*
Jayshree Parikh, *Sec*
EMP: 10 **EST:** 1984
SQ FT: 2,500
SALES (est): 982.8K **Privately Held**
Web: www.norfielddp.com
SIC: 7379 7373 7372 3672 Computer
related maintenance services; Systems
software development services;
Prepackaged software; Printed circuit
boards

(G-2547)
OASIS COFFEE CORP
327 Main Ave (06851-6156)
PHONE...............................203 847-0554
Ralph Sandolo, *Pr*
Veronica Rondini, *VP*
Joseph Sandolo, *VP*
EMP: 9 **EST:** 1988
SQ FT: 6,000
SALES (est): 734.05K **Privately Held**
Web: www.oasiscoffeect.com
SIC: 2095 2098 5461 Roasted coffee;
Macaroni and spaghetti; Bread

(G-2548)
OMEGA ENGINEERING INC
Also Called: Newport Electronics
800 Connecticut Ave Ste 5n1 (06854)
PHONE...............................714 540-4914
Bill Keating, *Genl Mgr*
EMP: 70
SALES (corp-wide): 653.43MM **Privately
Held**
Web: www.omega.com
SIC: 3559 3829 3822 3825 Electronic
component making machinery;
Temperature sensors, except industrial
process and aircraft; Temperature controls,
automatic; Measuring instruments and
meters, electric
HQ: Omega Engineering, Inc.
800 Connecticut Ave 5n01
Norwalk CT 06854
203 359-1660

(G-2549)
OMEGA ENGINEERING INC (DH)
Also Called: Omegadyne
800 Connecticut Ave Ste 5n01
(06854-1631)
P.O. Box 4047 (06907-0047)

PHONE...............................203 359-1660
James R Dale, *Pr*
◆ **EMP:** 233 **EST:** 1962
SALES (est): 128.05MM
SALES (corp-wide): 653.43MM **Privately
Held**
Web: www.omega.com
SIC: 3823 3575 3577 3433 Temperature
measurement instruments, industrial;
Computer terminals; Printers, computer;
Heating equipment, except electric
HQ: Dwyer Instruments, Llc
102 Indiana Highway 212
Michigan City IN 46360
219 879-8868

(G-2550)
**PACO ASSENSIO
WOODWORKING LLC**
15 Meadow St (06854-4504)
PHONE...............................203 536-2608
Francisco Paco Fernandez, *Prin*
EMP: 7 **EST:** 2014
SALES (est): 452.07K **Privately Held**
SIC: 2431 Millwork

(G-2551)
**PALMERS ELC MTRS & PUMPS
INC**
40 Osborne Ave (06855-1021)
PHONE...............................203 348-7378
Michael Peterson, *Pr*
Carlton Brown, *VP*
Lorraine Vigneault, *Treas*
Clive Hyde, *VP*
EMP: 7 **EST:** 1971
SQ FT: 6,600
SALES (est): 896.21K **Privately Held**
Web: www.palmerselectric.com
SIC: 7694 5063 5999 Electric motor repair;
Motors, electric; Motors, electric

(G-2552)
PDC INTERNATIONAL CORP
8 Sheehan Ave (06854-4659)
P.O. Box 492 (06856-0492)
PHONE...............................203 853-1516
Neal A Konstantin, *CEO*
Neal Konstantin, *
Gary Tantimonico, *
EMP: 55 **EST:** 1968
SQ FT: 19,000
SALES (est): 13.7MM **Privately Held**
Web: www.pdc-corp.com
SIC: 3565 Packing and wrapping machinery

(G-2553)
**PENNY MARKETING LTD
PARTNR (PA)**
6 Prowitt St (06855-1204)
PHONE...............................203 866-6688
EMP: 21 **EST:** 1993
SALES (est): 2.77MM **Privately Held**
Web: www.pennydellpuzzles.com
SIC: 2721 Magazines: publishing only, not
printed on site

(G-2554)
PENNY PRESS INC (PA)
6 Prowitt St (06855-1220)
PHONE...............................203 866-6688
William E Kanter, *Ch Bd*
Peter A Kanter, *
Selma Kanter, *
EMP: 130 **EST:** 1940
SQ FT: 20,000
SALES (est): 4.56MM
SALES (corp-wide): 4.56MM **Privately
Held**

Web: www.pennydellpuzzles.com
SIC: 2721 Magazines: publishing only, not
printed on site

(G-2555)
PENNY PUBLICATIONS LLC (PA)
6 Prowitt St (06855-1204)
PHONE...............................203 866-6688
EMP: 100 **EST:** 1998
SALES (est): 17.34MM **Privately Held**
Web: www.pennypublications.com
SIC: 2741 Miscellaneous publishing

(G-2556)
**PEPPERIDGE FARM
INCORPORATED (HQ)**
Also Called: Pepperidge Farm
595 Westport Ave (06851-4413)
PHONE...............................203 846-7000
Christopher D Foley, *Pr*
Tom Smith, *
Richard J Landers, *
Ashok Madhavan, *
Kathleen Gibson, *
◆ **EMP:** 700 **EST:** 1937
SQ FT: 71,000
SALES (est): 833.49MM
SALES (corp-wide): 9.36B **Publicly Held**
Web: www.pepperidgefarm.com
SIC: 2099 Food preparations, nec
PA: Campbell Soup Company
1 Campbell Pl
Camden NJ 08103
856 342-4800

(G-2557)
**PHOENIX ASSETS HOLDINGS
LTD**
68 Water St (06854-3071)
PHONE...............................800 323-9562
Michael Manchura, *Prin*
EMP: 45 **EST:** 2002
SALES (est): 251K
SALES (corp-wide): 17.49B **Privately Held**
SIC: 3643 Current-carrying wiring services
HQ: Winchester Holding, Inc.
68 Water St
Norwalk CT

(G-2558)
PIC20 GROUP LLC
Also Called: Ranger Ready Repellents
155 Woodward Ave Ste 3 (06854-4731)
PHONE...............................203 957-3555
Chris L Fuentes, *Pr*
Ted Kespen, *COO*
EMP: 18 **EST:** 2016
SQ FT: 5,000
SALES (est): 1.37MM **Privately Held**
Web: www.rangerready.com
SIC: 2879 5191 5999 Insecticides and
pesticides; Insecticides; Insecticide

(G-2559)
PORTFOLIO ARTS GROUP LTD
Also Called: New York Graphic Society
129 Glover Ave (06850-1345)
PHONE...............................203 847-2000
Richard Fleischmann, *Pr*
EMP: 15 **EST:** 2007
SALES (est): 481.37K **Privately Held**
SIC: 2741 Miscellaneous publishing

(G-2560)
PROFESSIONAL GRAPHICS INC
25 Perry Ave (06850-1655)
PHONE...............................203 846-4291
Thomas Bumbolow, *Pr*
Anthony Federici, *VP*

EMP: 19 **EST:** 1979
SQ FT: 9,000
SALES (est): 877.21K **Privately Held**
Web: www.professionalgraph.com
SIC: 2752 2791 Offset printing; Typesetting

(G-2561)
R F H COMPANY INC
79 Rockland Rd Ste 3 (06854-4628)
PHONE...............................203 853-2863
Pamela Falcone, *Pr*
Blake Billmeyer, *VP*
EMP: 10 **EST:** 1979
SQ FT: 5,000
SALES (est): 492.91K **Privately Held**
Web: www.shoprfhcompany.com
SIC: 2395 2396 Embroidery products,
except Schiffli machine; Automotive and
apparel trimmings

(G-2562)
RED 7 MEDIA LLC (HQ)
10 Norden Pl Ste 202 (06855-1445)
PHONE...............................203 853-2474
EMP: 38 **EST:** 2002
SQ FT: 5,000
SALES (est): 9.65MM
SALES (corp-wide): 45.62MM **Privately
Held**
Web: www.accessintel.com
SIC: 2721 Magazines: publishing and
printing
PA: Access Intelligence Llc
9211 Corporate Blvd Fl 4
Rockville MD 20850
301 354-2000

(G-2563)
REEDS INC
201 Merritt 7 (06851-1056)
PHONE...............................800 997-3337
Norman E Snyder Junior, *CEO*
John J Bello, *Ch Bd*
Neal Cohane, *CSO*
Christopher Burleson, *CCO*
Joann Tinnelly, *Interim Chief Financial
Officer*
◆ **EMP:** 31 **EST:** 1987
SQ FT: 8,620
SALES (est): 53.04MM **Privately Held**
Web: www.reedsinc.com
SIC: 2086 2064 2024 Soft drinks: packaged
in cans, bottles, etc.; Candy and other
confectionery products; Ice cream and ice
milk

(G-2564)
**RELOCATION INFORMATION
SVC INC**
Also Called: National Relocation & RE Mag
69 East Ave Ste 4 (06851-4904)
PHONE...............................203 855-1234
John Featherston, *Pr*
Darryl Mcpherson, *Ex VP*
EMP: 10 **EST:** 1980
SALES (est): 381.85K **Privately Held**
Web: www.realestateservicespro.com
SIC: 2721 2741 8742 Magazines: publishing
only, not printed on site; Directories, nec:
publishing only, not printed on site: Industry
specialist consultants

(G-2565)
RELX INC
Reed Exhibitions
383 Main Ave Fl 3 (06851-6404)
PHONE...............................203 840-4800
Jacqueline Boswick, *Mgr*
EMP: 4000
SQ FT: 238,000

SALES (corp-wide): 10.3B **Privately Held**
Web: www.lexisnexis.com
SIC: 2721 Periodicals
HQ: Relx Inc.
230 Park Ave Ste 700
New York NY 10169
212 309-8100

(G-2566)
REMA DRI-VAC CORP
45 Ruby St (06850-1614)
P.O. Box 86 (06852-0086)
PHONE..................................203 847-2464
F W Petri, *Pr*
James J Reed Junior, *VP*
James Flynn, *Treas*
Barry Gunterson, *VP*
▲ **EMP: 15 EST:** 1947
SQ FT: 9,300
SALES (est): 2.27MM **Privately Held**
Web: www.remadrivac.com
SIC: 3582 5084 Drycleaning equipment and
machinery, commercial, nec; Water pumps
(industrial)

(G-2567)
ROYAL CONSUMER PRODUCTS LLC (HQ)
Also Called: Geographics Australia
108 Main St Ste 3 (06851-4640)
P.O. Box 25118 Network Pl (60673-0001)
PHONE..................................203 847-8500
▲ **EMP: 40 EST:** 2000
SQ FT: 1,000
SALES (est): 23.8MM
SALES (corp-wide): 97.08MM **Privately Held**
Web: www.geographics.com
SIC: 2679 2621 Tags and labels, paper;
Stationary, envelope and tablet papers
PA: Mafcote, Inc.
108 Main St Ste 3
Norwalk CT 06851
203 847-8500

(G-2568)
RT VANDERBILT HOLDING CO INC (PA)
30 Winfield St (06855-1329)
PHONE..................................203 295-2141
Hugh Vanderbilt Junior, *CEO*
Hugh B Vanderbilt Junior, *Ch Bd*
Randall L Johnson, *Pr*
Joseph Denaro, *Ex VP*
Paul R Vanderbilt, *Ex VP*
◆ **EMP: 12 EST:** 1916
SALES (est): 266.87MM
SALES (corp-wide): 266.87MM **Privately Held**
Web: www.rtvanderbilt.com
SIC: 2869 2819 1499 1459 Laboratory
chemicals, organic; Industrial inorganic
chemicals, nec; Talc mining; Clays
(common) quarrying

(G-2569)
SAM & TY LLC (PA)
Also Called: Tailor Vintage
12 S Main St Ste 403 (06854-2980)
PHONE..................................212 840-1871
Richard Rosenthal, *Managing Member*
◆ **EMP: 8 EST:** 2008
SALES (est): 748.54K **Privately Held**
SIC: 2396 Linings, apparel: made from
purchased materials

(G-2570)
SERVERS STORAGE NETWORKING LLC
26 Pearl St Ste 101 (06850-1647)
PHONE..................................203 433-0808
EMP: 8 EST: 2014
SALES (est): 2.31MM **Privately Held**
Web: www.ssnus.com
SIC: 3674 5065 Solid state electronic
devices, nec; Electronic parts

(G-2571)
SHIBUMICOM INC
50 Washington St Ste 302e (06854-2792)
PHONE..................................855 744-2864
Robert Nahmias, *CEO*
EMP: 10 EST: 2011
SQ FT: 6,000
SALES (est): 1.06MM **Privately Held**
Web: www.shibumi.com
SIC: 7372 7374 Business oriented computer
software; Data processing and preparation

(G-2572)
SHOW MANAGEMENT ASSOCIATES LLC
10 Wall St Apt 201 (06850-3434)
PHONE..................................203 939-9901
EMP: 7 EST: 2003
SALES (est): 458.22K **Privately Held**
Web: www.smashows.com
SIC: 7389 2721 Trade show arrangement;
Magazines: publishing and printing

(G-2573)
SIGMA TANKERS INC
20 Glover Ave Ste 5 (06850-1234)
EMP: 20 EST: 2007
SALES (est): 3.57MM **Privately Held**
SIC: 1389 Oil field services, nec
HQ: Heidmar Inc.
20 Glover Ave Ste 14
Norwalk CT 06850

(G-2574)
STATHAM WOODWORK
38 Hemlock Pl (06854-4331)
PHONE..................................203 831-0629
Gary Statham, *Pr*
Emily Statham, *VP*
EMP: 7 EST: 1980
SQ FT: 7,000
SALES (est): 768.74K **Privately Held**
Web: www.stathamwoodwork.com
SIC: 2434 Wood kitchen cabinets

(G-2575)
TECHNICAL REPRODUCTIONS INC
326 Main Ave (06851-6108)
PHONE..................................203 849-9100
William R Boczer, *CEO*
Karyn Boczer, *Pr*
Holly Boczer, *VP*
Amy Boczer, *VP*
Patricia Boczer, *Stockholder*
EMP: 14 EST: 1971
SQ FT: 7,500
SALES (est): 1.5MM **Privately Held**
Web: www.trepro.net
SIC: 5999 5049 5199 2752 Architectural
supplies; Engineers' equipment and
supplies, nec; Architects' supplies (non-
durable); Offset printing

(G-2576)
TEGU
319 Rowayton Ave (06853-1023)
PHONE..................................877 834-8869
William Haughey, *CEO*
Christopher Haughey, *
▲ **EMP: 69 EST:** 2009

SALES (est): 4.63MM **Privately Held**
Web: www.tegu.com
SIC: 3944 Games, toys, and children's
vehicles

(G-2577)
TELEDYNE BOLT INC
4 Duke Pl (06854-4632)
PHONE..................................203 853-0700
▼ **EMP: 201**
SIC: 3829 3678 3694 Measuring and
controlling devices, nec; Electronic
connectors; Engine electrical equipment

(G-2578)
TEREX CORPORATION (PA)
Also Called: TEREX
45 Glover Ave Fl 4 (06850-1238)
PHONE..................................203 222-7170
John L Garrison Junior, *Ch Bd*
Julie Beck, *Sr VP*
Amy George, *Senior Vice President Human Resources*
Scott Posner, *Sr VP*
Stephen A Johnston, *CAO*
◆ **EMP: 15 EST:** 1983
SALES (est): 5.15B
SALES (corp-wide): 5.15B **Publicly Held**
Web: www.terex.com
SIC: 3537 3531 3569 3536 Industrial trucks
and tractors; Cranes, nec; Bridge or gate
machinery, hydraulic; Hoists, cranes, and
monorails

(G-2579)
TEREX USA LLC (HQ)
Also Called: Terex Awp North America
45 Glover Ave Ste 4 (06850-1238)
P.O. Box 42269 (46242-0269)
PHONE..................................203 222-7170
Julie Ann Beck, *
◆ **EMP: 335 EST:** 1923
SALES (est): 223.47MM
SALES (corp-wide): 4.42B **Publicly Held**
Web: www.terex.com
SIC: 3531 Construction machinery
PA: Terex Corporation
45 Glover Ave Ste 2
Norwalk CT 06850
203 222-7170

(G-2580)
TERO DESIGN HOLDINGS LLC
Also Called: Teroforma
66 Fort Point St Ste 2 (06855-1217)
PHONE..................................203 899-9950
◆ **EMP: 8 EST:** 2006
SALES (est): 847.83K **Privately Held**
Web: www.teroforma.com
SIC: 3229 3914 3263 5023 Tableware,
glass or glass ceramic; Flatware, plated (all
metals); Semivitreous table and kitchenware
; Kitchenware

(G-2581)
TEXAS DIE CASTING LLC
8 Knobhill Rd (06851-3303)
PHONE..................................903 845-2224
John Oxton, *VP*
Pat Burke, *
EMP: 120 EST: 2013
SALES (est): 7.83MM **Privately Held**
SIC: 3363 Aluminum die-castings

(G-2582)
TITANIUM ELECTRIC LLC
15 Arbor Dr (06854-3407)
PHONE..................................203 810-4050
Riccardo Arruzza, *Admn*
EMP: 7 EST: 2011

SALES (est): 507.38K **Privately Held**
SIC: 3356 Titanium

(G-2583)
TL PARTNERS LLC
227 Wilson Ave (06854-5026)
PHONE..................................203 956-6181
Peter Tucci, *Managing Member*
EMP: 8 EST: 2010
SQ FT: 10,300
SALES (est): 927.84K **Privately Held**
Web: www.tlbats.com
SIC: 3949 5941 Baseball equipment and
supplies, general; Baseball equipment

(G-2584)
TM WARD CO CONNECTICUT LLC
5 Wilbur St (06854-4112)
PHONE..................................203 866-9203
EMP: 7 EST: 2006
SALES (est): 673.69K **Privately Held**
Web: www.tmwardcoffee.com
SIC: 2095 Coffee roasting (except by
wholesale grocers)

(G-2585)
TOOL LOGISTICS II
46 Chestnut St (06854-3623)
PHONE..................................203 855-9754
Cawthon Smith, *Owner*
EMP: 10 EST: 2000
SALES (est): 758.38K **Privately Held**
SIC: 3599 3315 Machine shop, jobbing and
repair; Welded steel wire fabric

(G-2586)
TOWER OPTICAL COMPANY INC
275 East Ave Fl 2 (06855-1924)
P.O. Box 251 (06856-0251)
PHONE..................................203 866-4535
Bonnie Rising, *Pr*
Gregory Rising, *Sec*
EMP: 7 EST: 1933
SQ FT: 4,000
SALES (est): 710.18K **Privately Held**
Web: www.toweropticalco.com
SIC: 3827 5049 Binoculars; Scientific and
engineering equipment and supplies

(G-2587)
TRIRX PHARMACEUTICAL SVCS LLC (PA)
101 Merritt 7 (06851-1059)
PHONE..................................256 489-8867
Tim Tyson, *CEO*
EMP: 29 EST: 2019
SALES (est): 97.57MM
SALES (corp-wide): 97.57MM **Privately Held**
Web: www.trirx.com
SIC: 2834 Pharmaceutical preparations

(G-2588)
TWENTY-FIVE COMMERCE INC
Also Called: Cico
25 Commerce St (06850-4163)
P.O. Box 146 (06852-0146)
PHONE..................................203 866-0540
Robert Slapin, *Pr*
EMP: 8 EST: 1924
SALES (est): 739.6K **Privately Held**
SIC: 2097 Ice cubes

(G-2589)
VANDERBILT CHEMICALS LLC (HQ)
30 Winfield St (06855-1329)

▲ = Import ▼ = Export
◆ = Import/Export

P.O. Box 5150 (06856-5150)
PHONE..............................203 295-2141
Jon Eshelman, *
◆ **EMP: 49 EST:** 2012
SALES (est): 175.62MM
SALES (corp-wide): 266.87MM **Privately Held**
Web: www.vanderbiltchemicals.com
SIC: 2819 2869 5169 Industrial inorganic chemicals, nec; Industrial organic chemicals, nec; Chemicals and allied products, nec
PA: R.T. Vanderbilt Holding Company, Inc.
30 Winfield St
Norwalk CT 06855
203 295-2141

(G-2590)
VANDERBILT MINERALS LLC (HQ)
33 Winfield St (06855-1307)
P.O. Box 5150 (06856-5150)
PHONE..............................203 295-2140
James Ian Begley, *Pr*
Jeffrey Brohel, *Sec*
Peter Ciullo, *Asst Tr*
▼ **EMP: 20 EST:** 2012
SALES (est): 44.88MM
SALES (corp-wide): 266.87MM **Privately Held**
Web: www.vanderbiltminerals.com
SIC: 1459 Bentonite mining
PA: R.T. Vanderbilt Holding Company, Inc.
30 Winfield St
Norwalk CT 06855
203 295-2141

(G-2591)
VENTUS TECHNOLOGIES LLC
333 Wilson Ave (06854-4616)
PHONE..............................203 642-2800
Keith Charette, *Managing Member*
EMP: 10 **EST:** 2016
SALES (est): 1.76MM **Privately Held**
Web: www.ventusgns.com
SIC: 8731 3577 Computer (hardware) development; Computer peripheral equipment, nec

(G-2592)
VERSIMEDIA
63 Glover Ave (06850-1203)
PHONE..............................203 604-8094
John Babina Iii, *Pr*
EMP: 7 **EST:** 2008
SALES (est): 178.86K **Privately Held**
SIC: 2741 Miscellaneous publishing

(G-2593)
W B MASON CO INC
151 Woodward Ave (06854-4721)
PHONE..............................888 926-2766
EMP: 45
SALES (corp-wide): 1.01B **Privately Held**
Web: www.wbmason.com
SIC: 5943 5712 2752 Office forms and supplies; Office furniture; Commercial printing, lithographic
PA: W. B. Mason Co., Inc.
59 Centre Street
Brockton MA 02301
508 586-3434

(G-2594)
WDSS CORPORATION
7 Old Well Ct (06855-2014)
PHONE..............................203 854-5930
Wayne Nasution, *Pr*
EMP: 10 **EST:** 2009
SALES (est): 550.32K **Privately Held**

SIC: 3599 Industrial machinery, nec

(G-2595)
WINCHESTER INTERCONNECT CORP (DH)
Also Called: Winchester Interconnect
68 Water St (06854-3071)
PHONE..............................203 741-5400
Kevin S Perhamus, *Pr*
John Sickler, *
EMP: 45 **EST:** 2006
SALES (est): 513.49MM
SALES (corp-wide): 17.49B **Privately Held**
Web: www.winconn.com
SIC: 3678 Electronic connectors
HQ: Aptiv Corporation
5725 Innovation Dr
Troy MI 48098

(G-2596)
WINCHSTER INTERCONNECT RF CORP (DH)
Also Called: Winchester Interconnect
68 Water St (06854-3071)
P.O. Box 842464 (02284-2464)
PHONE..............................978 532-0775
Timothy S O'neil, *Pr*
Anthony Martiniello, *
▼ **EMP:** 65 **EST:** 1951
SQ FT: 40,000
SALES (est): 20MM
SALES (corp-wide): 17.49B **Privately Held**
Web: www.winconn.com
SIC: 3643 3678 Connectors and terminals for electrical devices; Electronic connectors
HQ: Winchester Interconnect Corporation
68 Water St
Norwalk CT 06854

(G-2597)
WINDHOVER INFORMATION INC (DH)
Also Called: Windhver Rvw-Emerging Med Vent
383 Main Ave (06851-1543)
PHONE..............................203 838-4401
Roger Longman, *Pr*
David Cassak, *
Peter Stelling, *CFO*
▼ **EMP:** 30 **EST:** 1983
SQ FT: 5,000
SALES (est): 22.01MM
SALES (corp-wide): 10.3B **Privately Held**
SIC: 2721 2731 7375 Magazines: publishing only, not printed on site; Books, publishing only; Data base information retrieval
HQ: Elsevier Inc.
230 Park Ave Fl 7
New York NY 10169
212 309-8100

(G-2598)
XEROX CORPORATION (HQ)
Also Called: Xerox
201 Merritt 7 (06851-1047)
P.O. Box 4505 (06856-4505)
PHONE..............................203 849-5216
Steven J Bandrowczak, *CEO*
A Scott Letier, *
John G Bruno, *Pr*
Xavier Heiss, *Ex VP*
Naresh K Shanker, *Sr VP*
EMP: 475 **EST:** 1906
SALES (est): 7.11B
SALES (corp-wide): 7.11B **Publicly Held**
Web: www.xerox.com
SIC: 3577 3861 3579 7629 Computer peripheral equipment, nec; Photocopy machines; Paper handling machines; Business machine repair, electric

PA: Xerox Holdings Corporation
201 Merritt 7 Ste 1
Norwalk CT 06851
203 849-5216

(G-2599)
XEROX HOLDINGS INC
201 Merritt 7 (06851-1047)
PHONE..............................203 968-3000
Giovanni Visentin, *V Ch Bd*
▲ **EMP:** 5400 **EST:** 1985
SALES (est): 414.9MM
SALES (corp-wide): 7.11B **Publicly Held**
SIC: 3577 3861 3579 7629 Computer peripheral equipment, nec; Photocopy machines; Paper handling machines; Business machine repair, electric
HQ: Xerox Corporation
201 Merritt 7 Ste 1
Norwalk CT 06851
203 849-5216

(G-2600)
XEROX HOLDINGS CORPORATION (PA)
Also Called: Xerox
201 Merritt 7 (06851-1047)
P.O. Box 4505 (06856-4505)
PHONE..............................203 849-5216
Steven Bandrowczak, *CEO*
Scott Letier, *Ch Bd*
John Bruno, *Pr*
Louie Chief Transformation Pas tor, *Administrative Officer*
Mirlanda Gecaj, *CAO*
EMP: 353 **EST:** 1906
SALES (est): 7.11B
SALES (corp-wide): 7.11B **Publicly Held**
Web: www.xerox.com
SIC: 3577 3861 3579 7629 Computer peripheral equipment, nec; Photocopy machines; Paper handling machines; Business machine repair, electric

---

Norwich
New London County

(G-2601)
AP DISPOSITION LLC
387 N Main St (06360-3917)
PHONE..............................860 889-1344
◆ **EMP:** 13 **EST:** 2004
SALES (est): 690.52K **Privately Held**
SIC: 2653 Boxes, corrugated: made from purchased materials

(G-2602)
AVIAN VACCINE SERVICES LLC (PA)
Also Called: Avs Bio
1 Wisconsin Ave (06360-1515)
PHONE..............................860 889-1389
Debra Tosto, *Managing Member*
EMP: 61 **EST:** 1963
SALES (est): 8.87MM
SALES (corp-wide): 8.87MM **Privately Held**
Web: www.avsbio.com
SIC: 2836 0252 Biological products, except diagnostic; Chicken eggs

(G-2603)
CAG IMAGING LLC
387 N Main St (06360-3917)
PHONE..............................860 887-0836
Frank Fazenbaker, *VP*
Stuart Swan, *Prin*
EMP: 8 **EST:** 2004

SALES (est): 297.83K **Privately Held**
SIC: 2752 3861 7335 Photo-offset printing; Enlargers, photographic; Color separation, photographic and movie film

(G-2604)
CONTINUUM
34 Thomas Ave (06360-5315)
PHONE..............................860 383-2562
EMP: 7 **EST:** 2016
SALES (est): 71.46K **Privately Held**
Web: www.continuumct.org
SIC: 7372 Prepackaged software

(G-2605)
FRANKLIN IMPRESSIONS INC
327 Laurel Hill Ave (06360-6928)
P.O. Box 175 (06360-0175)
PHONE..............................860 887-1661
Merrill Keeley, *CEO*
Kenneth Keeley, *Pr*
EMP: 14 **EST:** 1917
SQ FT: 8,200
SALES (est): 1.2MM **Privately Held**
SIC: 2752 7336 Offset printing; Graphic arts and related design

(G-2606)
GATEHOUSE MEDIA LLC
Norwich Bulletin, The
10 Railroad Ave (06360-5829)
PHONE..............................860 886-0106
Ellen Lind, *Bmch Mgr*
EMP: 59
SALES (corp-wide): 2.95B **Publicly Held**
Web: www.norwichbulletin.com
SIC: 2711 Newspapers, publishing and printing
HQ: Gatehouse Media, Llc
175 Sullys Trl Ste 203
Pittsford NY 14534
585 598-0030

(G-2607)
INCJET
31 Clinton Ave Ste 2 (06360-2165)
PHONE..............................860 823-1427
EMP: 19 **EST:** 2019
SALES (est): 924.09K **Privately Held**
Web: www.guntherintl.com
SIC: 3429 Hardware, nec

(G-2608)
J & M PLUMBING & CNSTR LLC
16 West St (06360-6120)
PHONE..............................860 319-3082
EMP: 8 **EST:** 2015
SALES (est): 2MM **Privately Held**
Web: www.jmplumbingconstruction.com
SIC: 1389 1799 1711 Construction, repair, and dismantling services; Construction site cleanup; Plumbing contractors

(G-2609)
NALAS ENGINEERING SERVICES
1 Winnenden Rd (06360-1513)
PHONE..............................860 861-3691
Jerry Salan, *CEO*
David Am Ende, *Pr*
Kerri Salan, *
Shilpa Amato, *
EMP: 52 **EST:** 2008
SALES (est): 8.44MM **Privately Held**
Web: www.nalasengineering.com
SIC: 2869 Industrial organic chemicals, nec

(PA)=Parent Co (HQ)=Headquarters
✿ = New Business established in last 2 years

2024 Harris New England
Manufacturers Directory

131

GEOGRAPHIC

(G-2610)
NORDSON EFD LLC
10 Connecticut Ave (06360-1502)
PHONE.....................860 889-3383
◆ **EMP:** 75
SALES (corp-wide): 2.63B **Publicly Held**
Web: www.nordson.com
SIC: 3563   Air and gas compressors
HQ: Nordson Efd Llc
   40 Catamore Blvd
   East Providence RI 02914
   401 431-7000

(G-2611)
NORWICH PRINTING COMPANY INC
Also Called: Minuteman Press
595 W Main St Ste 2 (06360-5300)
P.O. Box 165 (06357-0165)
PHONE.....................860 887-7468
Steve Weber, Pr
Gail Weber, VP
EMP: 10 **EST:** 1992
SQ FT: 4,300
SALES (est): 1.05MM **Privately Held**
Web: www.minuteman.com
SIC: 2789 2752   Bookbinding and related work; Commercial printing, lithographic

(G-2612)
NORWIX INC
Also Called: Norwix Marking Systems
31 Clinton Ave Ste 2 (06360-2165)
PHONE.....................860 823-3090
Marc Perkins, Pr
EMP: 239 **EST:** 2001
SALES (est): 9.55MM
SALES (corp-wide): 17.65MM **Privately Held**
Web: www.norwix.com
SIC: 3229   Stationers' glassware: inkwells, clip cups, etc.
PA: Inc.Jet Holding, Inc.
   1 Winnenden Rd
   Norwich CT 06360
   860 823-1427

(G-2613)
NUTRON MANUFACTURING INC
5 Wisconsin Ave (06360-1515)
P.O. Box 314 (06385-0314)
PHONE.....................860 887-4550
Jack Edward Feinberg, Pr
Mark L Favalora, *
Joseph L Feinberg, *
Phyllis P Feinberg, *
Gail B Feinberg, *
▲ **EMP:** 24 **EST:** 1960
SQ FT: 95,000
SALES (est): 2.76MM **Privately Held**
Web: www.nutron-mfg.com
SIC: 3646   Commercial lighting fixtures

(G-2614)
ONE & CO INC
Also Called: Eon Designs
154 N Main St (06360-5121)
PHONE.....................860 892-5180
Gordon Kyle, Pr
Mark Stasko, VP
EMP: 7 **EST:** 1992
SQ FT: 16,000
SALES (est): 469.76K **Privately Held**
Web: www.eondesigns.com
SIC: 2522 2541   Office furniture, except wood; Wood partitions and fixtures

(G-2615)
SAINT VINCENT DE PAUL PLACE
120 Cliff St (06360-5155)
PHONE.....................860 889-7374
Jillian Corbin, Dir
EMP: 8 **EST:** 1978
SALES (est): 1.39MM **Privately Held**
Web: www.svdpp.org
SIC: 8322 2759   Social service center; Commercial printing, nec

(G-2616)
SHEFFIELD PHARMACEUTICALS LLC
9 Wisconsin Ave (06360-1562)
PHONE.....................860 442-4451
Jeffrey Davis, Pr
EMP: 10
SALES (corp-wide): 89.87MM **Privately Held**
Web: www.sheffieldpharma.com
SIC: 2834   Pharmaceutical preparations
PA: Sheffield Pharmaceuticals, Llc
   170 Broad St
   New London CT 06320
   860 442-4451

(G-2617)
SKURGE OF SEA LLC
11 Barnsider Ln (06360-1403)
PHONE.....................860 887-7679
Michael Vitagliano, Prin
EMP: 8 **EST:** 2011
SALES (est): 236.69K **Privately Held**
Web: www.skurgeofthesea.com
SIC: 2323   Men's and boy's neckwear

(G-2618)
VERMONT PALLET AND SKID SP INC
104 Baltic Rd (06360-9409)
P.O. Box 646 (06330-0646)
PHONE.....................860 822-6949
James Adams, Pr
Inez Urso, Sec
Dave Renfahw, VP
EMP: 9 **EST:** 1981
SQ FT: 3,200
SALES (est): 947.02K **Privately Held**
Web: www.vermontpalletandskid.com
SIC: 2448 2441 2449   Pallets, wood; Boxes, wood; Wood containers, nec

(G-2619)
W B MASON CO INC
2 Consumers Ave (06360-7521)
PHONE.....................888 926-2766
EMP: 101
SALES (corp-wide): 1.01B **Privately Held**
Web: www.wbmason.com
SIC: 5943 5712 2752   Office forms and supplies; Office furniture; Commercial printing, lithographic
PA: W. B. Mason Co., Inc.
   59 Centre Street
   Brockton MA 02301
   508 586-3434

Oakdale
New London County

(G-2620)
BOVE BROTHERS LLC
18 Sachatello Industrial Dr (06370-1860)
PHONE.....................860 443-9200
EMP: 25 **EST:** 2021
SALES (est): 2.5MM **Privately Held**

SIC: 3532   Washers, aggregate and sand

(G-2621)
E B ASPHALT & LANDSCAPING LLC
1650 Old Colchester Rd Unit 1 (06370-1065)
PHONE.....................860 639-1921
Rickie Emmons Junior, Managing Member
EMP: 10 **EST:** 2016
SALES (est): 1.27MM **Privately Held**
Web: www.eb-asphalt.com
SIC: 2951 0781   Asphalt paving mixtures and blocks; Landscape services

(G-2622)
INCORD LTD
430 Chapel Hill Rd (06370-1425)
PHONE.....................860 537-1414
EMP: 10 **EST:** 2017
SALES (est): 637.86K **Privately Held**
Web: www.incord.com
SIC: 3999   Manufacturing industries, nec

(G-2623)
PEMAC CONSTRUCTION
15 Lakewood Dr Unit 17 (06370-1858)
PHONE.....................860 437-0007
Edilberto Peralta, Pr
EMP: 10 **EST:** 2012
SALES (est): 686.77K **Privately Held**
Web: www.pemacny.com
SIC: 1751 2541 5712 2542   Carpentry work; Store and office display cases and fixtures; Cabinet work, custom; Showcases (not refrigerated): except wood

Oakville
Litchfield County

(G-2624)
NORWALK WILBERT VAULT CO LLC
Also Called: Norwalk Vault Company
760 Frost Bridge Rd (06779-1493)
PHONE.....................203 366-5678
EMP: 35 **EST:** 1932
SQ FT: 65,000
SALES (est): 4.92MM **Privately Held**
Web: www.norwalkwilbert.com
SIC: 3272   Burial vaults, concrete or precast terrazzo

(G-2625)
QUALITY AUTOMATICS INC (PA)
15 Mclennan Dr (06779-1428)
P.O. Box 11190 (06703-0190)
PHONE.....................860 945-4795
Stephen White, Pr
Robert Cermola, VP
EMP: 19 **EST:** 1980
SQ FT: 25,000
SALES (est): 2.51MM
SALES (corp-wide): 2.51MM **Privately Held**
Web: www.curtisprod.com
SIC: 3451   Screw machine products

(G-2626)
RAMDY CORPORATION
40 Mclennan Dr (06779-1429)
P.O. Box 834 (06795-0834)
PHONE.....................860 274-3716
John Mendicino, Pr
Allen Thornberg, Pr
Jill A Shaw, Sec
Paul Thornberg, VP
Richard J Klipp, Pr

EMP: 20 **EST:** 1988
SQ FT: 10,000
SALES (est): 4.68MM **Privately Held**
Web: www.ramdycorp.com
SIC: 3541   Machine tools, metal cutting type

(G-2627)
T & J SCREW MACHINE PDTS LLC
27 Main St (06779-1703)
PHONE.....................860 417-3801
EMP: 11 **EST:** 2006
SALES (est): 1.09MM **Privately Held**
SIC: 3451   Screw machine products

(G-2628)
UNIVERSAL BODY AND EQP CO LLC
17 Di Nunzio Rd (06779-1407)
PHONE.....................860 274-7541
TOLL FREE: 800
Todd Richards, Managing Member
EMP: 16 **EST:** 1975
SQ FT: 6,000
SALES (est): 2.28MM **Privately Held**
Web: www.universal-body.com
SIC: 3713 3711   Truck bodies (motor vehicles); Snow plows (motor vehicles), assembly of

(G-2629)
WHQ WOODWORKS LLC
28 Main St Ste 3 (06779-1704)
PHONE.....................203 756-3011
Wesley Quigley Senior, Pr
Wesley Quigley Iii, VP
Jean H Quigley, Sec
EMP: 7 **EST:** 1989
SQ FT: 3,000
SALES (est): 488.75K **Privately Held**
Web: www.whqwoodworks.com
SIC: 2431   Millwork

Old Greenwich
Fairfield County

(G-2630)
BOND PAINTING COMPANY INC
27 Meadowbank Rd (06870-2311)
PHONE.....................212 944-0070
Stuart Feld, Pr
EMP: 21 **EST:** 1990
SALES (est): 2.25MM **Privately Held**
Web: www.bondpaintingcompany.com
SIC: 1721 2211   Commercial painting; Upholstery, tapestry and wall coverings: cotton

(G-2631)
COSS SYSTEMS INC (NOT INC)
26 Arcadia Rd (06870-1721)
PHONE.....................732 447-7724
Antonia Spitzer, Prin
EMP: 7 **EST:** 2006
SALES (est): 570.32K **Privately Held**
Web: www.cosserp.com
SIC: 7372   Prepackaged software

(G-2632)
DIGIRAD HEALTH LLC
53 Forest Ave (06870-1526)
PHONE.....................800 947-6134
Martin Shirley, Managing Member
EMP: 331 **EST:** 2018
SALES (est): 1.4MM
SALES (corp-wide): 56.66MM **Privately Held**

SIC: 3845 Electromedical equipment
PA: Ttg Imaging Solutions, Llc
    2403 Sidney St Ste 220
    Pittsburgh PA 15203
    412 481-0600

(G-2633)
GRILL DADDY BRUSH COMPANY
29 Arcadia Rd (06870-1701)
PHONE..................................888 840-7552
Michael A Wales, *Pr*
▲ EMP: 30 EST: 2006
SQ FT: 2,000
SALES (est): 2.39MM **Privately Held**
Web: www.buygrilldaddy.com
SIC: 2842 Cleaning or polishing
    preparations, nec

(G-2634)
NAVTECH SYSTEMS INC
322 Sound Beach Ave (06870-1931)
PHONE..................................203 661-7800
Sushil Advaney, *Pr*
EMP: 8 EST: 1999
SALES (est): 415.61K **Privately Held**
SIC: 7372 Prepackaged software

(G-2635)
STAR EQUITY HOLDINGS INC
(PA)
Also Called: Star Equity Holdings
53 Forest Ave Ste 101 (06870-1537)
PHONE..................................203 489-9500
Richard K Coleman Junior, *CEO*
Jeffrey E Eberwein, *
David J Noble, *CFO*
EMP: 66 EST: 1985
SQ FT: 1,344
SALES (est): 112.15MM
SALES (corp-wide): 112.15MM **Publicly
Held**
Web: www.starequity.com
SIC: 3845 3829 Electromedical equipment;
    Medical diagnostic systems, nuclear

Old Lyme
New London County

(G-2636)
CALLAWAY CARS INC
3 High St (06371-1529)
PHONE..................................860 434-9002
E Reeves Callaway, *Pr*
E Reeves Callaway Iii, *Pr*
Michael Zoner, *Sec*
EMP: 18 EST: 1976
SQ FT: 10,000
SALES (est): 8.84MM **Privately Held**
Web: www.callawaycars.com
SIC: 3714 Motor vehicle engines and parts
PA: The Callaway Companies Inc
    3 High St
    Old Lyme CT 06371

(G-2637)
CALLAWAY COMPANIES INC
(PA)
3 High St (06371-1529)
PHONE..................................860 434-9002
E Reeves Callaway Iii, *Pr*
▲ EMP: 15 EST: 1978
SQ FT: 16,300
SALES (est): 13.24MM **Privately Held**
Web: www.callawaycars.com
SIC: 3714 8732 Motor vehicle engines and
    parts; Research services, except laboratory

(G-2638)
CUMMINS ENVIRO TECH INC
Also Called: Cummins
29 Mile Creek Rd (06371-1710)
PHONE..................................860 388-6377
Hansen Cummins, *Pr*
EMP: 7 EST: 2004
SALES (est): 199.66K **Privately Held**
Web: www.cumminsenvirotech.com
SIC: 8711 3519 Consulting engineer;
    Internal combustion engines, nec

(G-2639)
**CUSTOM DESIGN
WOODWORKS LLC**
10 Maywood Dr (06371-1523)
P.O. Box 376 (06371-0376)
PHONE..................................860 434-0515
Christopher Defiore, *Prin*
EMP: 8 EST: 2011
SALES (est): 397.88K **Privately Held**
SIC: 2431 Millwork

(G-2640)
**DESIGN LABEL
MANUFACTURING INC**
12 Nottingham Dr (06371-1820)
PHONE..................................860 739-6266
TOLL FREE: 800
EMP: 38
Web: www.dlmillc.com
SIC: 2672 2759 Adhesive papers, labels, or
    tapes: from purchased material; Labels and
    seals: printing, nsk

(G-2641)
FIBERQA LLC
10 Vista Dr Unit 101 (06371-5110)
PHONE..................................860 254-7275
Douglas Wilson, *Pt*
EMP: 20 EST: 2012
SALES (est): 2.66MM **Privately Held**
Web: www.fiberqa.com
SIC: 3357 Fiber optic cable (insulated)

(G-2642)
GENERATORS ON DEMAND LLC
61-1 Buttonball Rd (06371-1761)
PHONE..................................860 662-4090
EMP: 14 EST: 2011
SALES (est): 2.19MM **Privately Held**
Web: www.generatorsondemand.com
SIC: 3621 Motors and generators

(G-2643)
**NANCY LARSON PUBLISHERS
INC**
27 Talcott Farm Rd (06371-1474)
P.O. Box 688 (06371-0688)
PHONE..................................860 434-0800
Nancy A Larson, *Pr*
EMP: 22 EST: 2007
SALES (est): 1.56MM **Privately Held**
Web: www.nancylarsonpublishers.com
SIC: 2741 Miscellaneous publishing

(G-2644)
**PATRICIA SPRATT FOR HOME
LLC**
Also Called: Patricia Spratt For The Home
60 Lyme St (06371-2332)
PHONE..................................860 434-9291
EMP: 10 EST: 1993
SQ FT: 1,000
SALES (est): 856.99K **Privately Held**
Web: www.patriciasprattforthehome.com
SIC: 2392 5131 Tablecloths and table
    settings; Linen piece goods, woven

Old Saybrook
Middlesex County

(G-2645)
BFF HOLDINGS INC (HQ)
Also Called: B L R
141 Mill Rock Rd E (06475-4217)
PHONE..................................860 510-0100
Robert L Brady, *Pr*
J Michael Brady, *
Brian E Gurnham, *
EMP: 175 EST: 1977
SQ FT: 75,000
SALES (est): 24.84MM **Privately Held**
SIC: 2721 2731 7812 3652 Periodicals;
    Book publishing; Motion picture and video
    production; Prerecorded records and tapes
PA: Simplify Compliance, Llc
    5511 Virginia Way Ste 150
    Brentwood TN 37027

(G-2646)
BRANNKEY INC
137 Mill Rock Rd E (06475-4217)
PHONE..................................860 510-0501
Anthony Carambot, *Brnch Mgr*
EMP: 41
SALES (corp-wide): 8.76MM **Privately
Held**
SIC: 3911 Jewelry, precious metal
PA: Brannkey Inc.
    1385 Broadway Fl 14
    New York NY 10018
    212 371-1515

(G-2647)
**EZFLOW LIMITED
PARTNERSHIP (DH)**
4 Business Park Rd (06475-4238)
P.O. Box 768 (06475-0768)
PHONE..................................860 577-7064
Roy E Moore, *CEO*
Bryan Coppes, *VP*
EMP: 50 EST: 2009
SALES (est): 10.97MM
SALES (corp-wide): 3.07B **Publicly Held**
Web: www.infiltratorwater.com
SIC: 3531 Construction machinery
HQ: Infiltrator Water Technologies, Llc
    4 Business Park Rd
    Old Saybrook CT 06475
    860 577-7000

(G-2648)
FORTUNE PLASTICS INC
1 Williams Ln (06475-4233)
P.O. Box 637 (06475-0637)
PHONE..................................800 243-0306
◆ EMP: 398
Web: www.fortuneplastics.com
SIC: 2673 3081 Plastic bags: made from
    purchased materials; Unsupported plastics
    film and sheet

(G-2649)
**GREGS OUTBOARD SERVICE
LLC**
304 Boston Post Rd (06475-1561)
PHONE..................................860 339-5139
Gregory Andrew Fiorelli, *Prin*
EMP: 8 EST: 2015
SALES (est): 449.78K **Privately Held**
SIC: 3732 Non-motorized boat, building and
    repairing

(G-2650)
**HANFORD CABINET & WDWKG
CO INC**
Also Called: Hanford Cabinet & Woodworking
102 Ingham Hill Rd (06475-4115)
PHONE..................................860 388-5055
Steve Hanford, *Pr*
EMP: 7 EST: 1969
SQ FT: 6,000
SALES (est): 862K **Privately Held**
Web: www.hanfordcabinet.com
SIC: 2434 1521 Wood kitchen cabinets;
    Single-family housing construction

(G-2651)
**INFILTRATOR WATER
TECHNOLOGIES LLC (HQ)**
Also Called: Champion Polymers Recycling
4 Business Park Rd (06475-4238)
P.O. Box 768 (06475-0768)
PHONE..................................860 577-7000
◆ EMP: 55 EST: 1986
SALES (est): 93.79MM
SALES (corp-wide): 3.07B **Publicly Held**
Web: www.infiltratorwater.com
SIC: 3089 Septic tanks, plastics
PA: Advanced Drainage Systems, Inc.
    4640 Trueman Blvd
    Hilliard OH 43026
    614 658-0050

(G-2652)
IPC SYSTEMS INC
Also Called: IPC Information Systems
8 Custom Dr (06475-4009)
PHONE..................................860 952-9575
Antoine Verzilli, *Brnch Mgr*
EMP: 15
Web: www.ipc.com
SIC: 3661 Telephone and telegraph
    apparatus
HQ: I.P.C. Systems, Inc.
    Harborside Fncl Plz 10 3
    Jersey City NJ 07302
    201 253-2000

(G-2653)
ITERUM THERAPEUTICS INC
20 Research Pkwy (06475-4214)
PHONE..................................860 391-8349
Jeff Schaffnit, *CCO*
EMP: 9 EST: 2016
SALES (est): 656.87K **Privately Held**
Web: www.iterumtx.com
SIC: 2834 Pharmaceutical preparations

(G-2654)
LIFTLINE CAPITAL LLC
Also Called: Stencil Ease
7 Center Rd W (06475-4053)
P.O. Box 1127 (06475-5127)
PHONE..................................860 395-0150
▼ EMP: 19 EST: 1990
SQ FT: 30,000
SALES (est): 4.8MM **Privately Held**
Web: www.stencilease.com
SIC: 2675 3991 3953 Stencils and lettering
    materials: die-cut; Paintbrushes; Stencils,
    painting and marking

(G-2655)
METALPRO INC
50 School House Rd (06475-4029)
PHONE..................................860 388-1811
Thomas Wright, *Pr*
Elizabeth Wright, *VP*
EMP: 23 EST: 1994
SQ FT: 45,000
SALES (est): 571.77K **Privately Held**

SIC: 3599　Machine shop, jobbing and repair

(G-2656)
NORTHSIDE MINIS LLC
27 Bellaire Dr (06475-2703)
PHONE..............................860 388-6871
Robert Preece, *Prin*
EMP: 7 EST: 2011
SALES (est): 158.77K **Privately Held**
SIC: 3537　Trucks, tractors, loaders, carriers, and similar equipment

(G-2657)
OASIS TRUCK TIRE SERVICE LLC (PA)
104 Old Sea Ln (06475-1954)
PHONE..............................860 296-8749
EMP: 7 EST: 1992
SALES (est): 999.04K **Privately Held**
Web: www.oasistrucktires.com
SIC: 7534　Tire repair shop

(G-2658)
PASTA VITA INC
225 Elm St (06475-4135)
P.O. Box 523 (06475-0523)
PHONE..............................860 395-1452
Richard Cersosimo, *Pr*
EMP: 7 EST: 1992
SQ FT: 3,000
SALES (est): 834.01K **Privately Held**
Web: www.pastavita.com
SIC: 2099 5149　Pasta, uncooked: packaged with other ingredients; Pasta and rice

(G-2659)
PATHWAY LIGHTING PRODUCTS INC
35 Research Pkwy (06475-4211)
P.O. Box 591 (06475-0591)
PHONE..............................860 388-6881
Frederick W Stark Iii, *Pr*
Jill Elizabeth Coan, *
▲ EMP: 85 EST: 1989
SALES (est): 20.83MM **Privately Held**
Web: www.pathwaylighting.com
SIC: 3648 5063 3646　Lighting equipment, nec; Electrical apparatus and equipment; Commercial lighting fixtures

(G-2660)
PAUL H GESSWEIN & COMPANY INC
40 River St (06475-1513)
PHONE..............................860 388-0652
John Hoadley, *Mgr*
EMP: 8
SALES (corp-wide): 593.19K **Privately Held**
Web: www.gesswein.com
SIC: 3281　Stone, quarrying and processing of own stone products
PA: Paul H. Gesswein & Company, Inc.
201 Hancock Ave
Bridgeport CT 06605
203 366-5400

(G-2661)
PRIVATEER LLC
5 Center Rd W (06475-4053)
PHONE..............................860 526-1838
Richard Wilczewski, *Pr*
EMP: 18 EST: 2005 *
SQ FT: 10,000
SALES (est): 4.92MM
SALES (corp-wide): 51.43MM **Privately Held**
Web: www.privateerusa.com

SIC: 2759　Labels and seals: printing, nsk
PA: Premium Label & Packaging Solutions, Llc
411 Theodore Fremd Ave
Rye NY 10580
914 967-1390

(G-2662)
SOUND MANUFACTURING INC
1 Williams Ln (06475-4233)
PHONE..............................860 388-4466
Kelli Vallieries, *CEO*
Brian E Cote, *
John A Vallieres, *
▲ EMP: 81 EST: 1984
SALES (est): 20.15MM **Privately Held**
Web: www.soundmfg.com
SIC: 3444　Sheet metalwork

(G-2663)
STI INCORPORATED
6 Business Park Rd (06475-4238)
PHONE..............................860 577-7000
James Nichols, *Pr*
Robert Mchugh, *Sec*
Brian Coppes, *Treas*
EMP: 40 EST: 1984
SALES (est): 1.85MM
SALES (corp-wide): 3.07B **Publicly Held**
SIC: 3089　Septic tanks, plastics
PA: Advanced Drainage Systems, Inc.
4640 Trueman Blvd
Hilliard OH 43026
614 658-0050

(G-2664)
TANTOR MEDIA INCORPORATED
6 Business Park Rd (06475-4238)
PHONE..............................860 395-1155
Kevin Colebank, *CEO*
Laura Colebank, *
▼ EMP: 123 EST: 2004
SALES (est): 22.87MM **Privately Held**
Web: www.tantor.com
SIC: 2731　Books, publishing only
PA: Recorded Books Inc.
8400 Corporate Dr Ste 100
Hyattsville MD 20785

Orange
New Haven County

(G-2665)
ADVANCED DECISIONS INC
350 Woodland Ln (06477-3038)
PHONE..............................203 402-0603
Michael R Landino, *Pr*
Gary Felberbaum, *VP*
EMP: 7 EST: 1971
SALES (est): 160.8K **Privately Held**
Web: www.advanceddecisions.com
SIC: 7372 7379　Application computer software; Computer hardware requirements analysis

(G-2666)
ALVAREZ INDUSTRIES LLC
312 Boston Post Rd (06477-3505)
P.O. Box 964 (06477-0964)
PHONE..............................203 799-2356
Lenny Alvarez, *Brnch Mgr*
EMP: 72
SALES (corp-wide): 8.46MM **Privately Held**
SIC: 3499　Metal household articles
PA: Alvarez Industries Llc
26 Brownell St Fl 3

New Haven CT 06511
203 401-1152

(G-2667)
AMERICAN SEAL AND ENGRG CO INC
295 Indian River Rd (06477-3609)
PHONE..............................203 789-8819
Thomas Kinisky, *Pr*
Joseph Kedues, *
EMP: 40 EST: 1971
SQ FT: 30,000
SALES (est): 10.47MM
SALES (corp-wide): 397.78MM **Privately Held**
Web: www.omniseal-solutions.com
SIC: 3053　Gaskets and sealing devices
HQ: Saint-Gobain Corporation
20 Moores Rd
Malvern PA 19355

(G-2668)
F & W RENTALS INC
164 Boston Post Rd (06477-3234)
PHONE..............................203 795-0591
Harold R Funk, *Pr*
Harold R Funk Prestreas, *Prin*
EMP: 14 EST: 1939
SQ FT: 15,000
SALES (est): 455.11K **Privately Held**
SIC: 7692 5084　Welding repair; Industrial machine parts

(G-2669)
FOX STEEL PRODUCTS LLC
312 Boston Post Rd (06477-3505)
P.O. Box 592 (06477-0592)
PHONE..............................203 799-2356
Peter Cosentino, *Managing Member*
EMP: 10 EST: 1940
SQ FT: 6,500
SALES (est): 1.9MM **Privately Held**
SIC: 5051 3441　Bars, metal; Fabricated structural metal

(G-2670)
ITC GROUP LLC
378 Boston Post Rd Ste 101 (06477-3523)
PHONE..............................203 260-5101
Frank Betancourt, *Mgr*
EMP: 8 EST: 2020
SALES (est): 366.95K **Privately Held**
SIC: 2834　Pharmaceutical preparations

(G-2671)
KCO NUMET INC
235 Edison Rd (06477-3603)
PHONE..............................203 375-4995
Mark Roscio, *CEO*
Andrew Gale, *
Antonio Neto, *
Dennis Nolan, *
Scott Kokosa, *
EMP: 32 EST: 2011
SQ FT: 40,000
SALES (est): 4.84MM **Privately Held**
Web: www.thebromfordgroup.com
SIC: 3519 6719　Jet propulsion engines; Investment holding companies, except banks

(G-2672)
KI INC
342 Cedarwood Dr (06477-1665)
PHONE..............................203 641-5492
Rondi D'agostino, *Pr*
▲ EMP: 67 EST: 1980
SALES (est): 906.05K **Privately Held**

SIC: 3651　Amplifiers: radio, public address, or musical instrument

(G-2673)
KRELL INDUSTRIES LLC
45 Connair Rd (06477-3681)
PHONE..............................203 298-4000
Rondi D'agostino, *Managing Member*
EMP: 16 EST: 2009
SQ FT: 10,000
SALES (est): 1.8MM **Privately Held**
Web: www.krellhifi.com
SIC: 3651　Amplifiers: radio, public address, or musical instrument

(G-2674)
LCD LIGHTING INC
Also Called: Voltarc
37 Robinson Blvd (06477-3623)
P.O. Box 948 (06477-0948)
PHONE..............................203 799-7877
Christian L Sauska, *CEO*
▲ EMP: 110 EST: 1990
SQ FT: 75,000
SALES (est): 19.22MM **Privately Held**
Web: www.light-sources.com
SIC: 3641 3646　Electric lamps and parts for generalized applications; Commercial lighting fixtures

(G-2675)
MARENNA AMUSEMENTS LLC
88 Marsh Hill Rd (06477-3625)
P.O. Box 788 (06477-0788)
PHONE..............................203 623-4386
EMP: 10 EST: 1997
SALES (est): 1.14MM **Privately Held**
Web: www.marennaamusements.com
SIC: 3599　Carnival machines and equipment, amusement park, nec

(G-2676)
MAURER METALCRAFT INC
22 Prindle Hill Rd (06477-3615)
PHONE..............................203 799-8800
EMP: 9 EST: 2019
SALES (est): 255.41K **Privately Held**
Web: www.valleytl.com
SIC: 3469　Stamping metal for the trade

(G-2677)
MCWEENEY MARKETING GROUP INC
53 Robinson Blvd (06477-3623)
P.O. Box 989 (06477-0989)
PHONE..............................203 891-8100
George E Mcweeney Junior, *Pr*
EMP: 9 EST: 1990
SQ FT: 3,000
SALES (est): 1.19MM **Privately Held**
SIC: 2759 5199　Commercial printing, nec; Advertising specialties

(G-2678)
NATURES FIRST INC (PA)
58 Robinson Blvd Ste C (06477-3647)
PHONE..............................203 795-8400
Harjit Singh, *Pr*
▼ EMP: 18 EST: 1997
SQ FT: 12,000
SALES (est): 3.83MM
SALES (corp-wide): 3.83MM **Privately Held**
Web: www.naturesfirst.com
SIC: 2023　Dietary supplements, dairy and non-dairy based

(G-2679)
NUMET MACHINING TECHNIQUES LLC
235 Edison Rd (06477-3603)
PHONE..............................203 375-4995
Tim Ulles, *
Joseph Satori, *
Anthony Guarascio, *
▲ EMP: 32 EST: 1983
SQ FT: 40,000
SALES (est): 9.62MM Privately Held
Web: www.thebromfordgroup.com
SIC: 3724 Aircraft engines and engine parts
HQ: Aerocision Parent, Llc
    12a Inspiration Ln
    Chester CT

(G-2680)
PEZ CANDY INC (HQ)
Also Called: Pez
35 Prindle Hill Rd (06477-3616)
PHONE..............................203 795-0531
Christian Jegen, CEO
Brian Fry, *
Christof Ebersberg, *
▲ EMP: 52 EST: 1953
SALES (est): 25.35MM Privately Held
Web: us.pez.com
SIC: 2064 Candy and other confectionery
    products
PA: Pez Inter Holding Ag
    C/O Globaltax Gmbh
    ZUrich ZH

(G-2681)
PEZ MANUFACTURING CORP
35 Prindle Hill Rd (06477-3616)
PHONE..............................203 795-0531
Christian Jegen, CEO
Peter Graf, *
Brian Fry, *
▲ EMP: 100 EST: 1973
SQ FT: 50,000
SALES (est): 10.12MM Privately Held
Web: us.pez.com
SIC: 2064 Candy and other confectionery
    products
HQ: Pez Candy, Inc.
    35 Prindle Hill Rd
    Orange CT 06477
    203 795-0531

(G-2682)
RESAVUE INC
Also Called: Resavue Exhibits
48 Grannis Rd (06477-1908)
PHONE..............................203 878-0944
TOLL FREE: 800
John B Kelman, CEO
Christine Kelman, Sec
◆ EMP: 10 EST: 1984
SALES (est): 936.31K Privately Held
Web: www.resavue.com
SIC: 3577 7319 Graphic displays, except
    graphic terminals; Display advertising
    service

(G-2683)
VALLEY TOOL & MANUFACTURING INC
22 Prindle Hill Rd (06477-3615)
P.O. Box 564 (06477-0564)
PHONE..............................203 799-8800
▲ EMP: 72
SIC: 3469 Metal stampings, nec

Oxford
New Haven County

(G-2684)
ADVANCED SONICS LLC
Also Called: Advanced Sonic Proc Systems
324 Christian St (06478-1023)
PHONE..............................203 266-4440
David Hunicke, Managing Member
EMP: 7 EST: 1992
SQ FT: 17,500
SALES (est): 934.48K Privately Held
Web: www.advancedsonics.com
SIC: 3629 7379 Electronic generation
    equipment; Data processing consultant

(G-2685)
ANVIL CT LLP
324 Christian St (06478-1023)
PHONE..............................860 619-0589
EMP: 11 EST: 2018
SALES (est): 946.77K Privately Held
Web: www.anvilct.com
SIC: 2431 Millwork

(G-2686)
ARP WELDING LLC
6 Fox Hollow Rd (06478-3161)
PHONE..............................203 344-7528
Adam Patrick, Managing Member
EMP: 18 EST: 2015
SALES (est): 1.49MM Privately Held
SIC: 7692 Welding repair

(G-2687)
BALFOR INDUSTRIES INC
327 Riggs St (06478-1129)
PHONE..............................203 828-6473
Richard Ballot, Pr
EMP: 15 EST: 1955
SQ FT: 17,500
SALES (est): 1.51MM Privately Held
Web: www.balfor.com
SIC: 3089 Molding primary plastics

(G-2688)
CAST GLOBAL MANUFACTURING CORP
Also Called: Met-Craft
66 Prokop Rd (06478-1107)
PHONE..............................203 828-6147
Chung Hsuen Hu, Pr
EMP: 10 EST: 2009
SALES (est): 341.51K Privately Held
SIC: 3452 Bolts, nuts, rivets, and washers

(G-2689)
CATACHEM INC
353 Christian St Ste 2 (06478-1053)
PHONE..............................203 262-0330
Luis P Leon, Pr
Luis P Leon, Pr
David Templeton, COO
▲ EMP: 7 EST: 1984
SQ FT: 3,500
SALES (est): 980.64K Privately Held
Web: www.catachem.com
SIC: 3841 Diagnostic apparatus, medical

(G-2690)
COLORGRAPHIX LLC
91 Willenbrock Rd Ste B5 (06478-1036)
P.O. Box 545 (06488-0545)
PHONE..............................203 264-5212
Jeff Jones, Managing Member
EMP: 8 EST: 1987
SQ FT: 4,500
SALES (est): 1.05MM Privately Held

Web: www.colorgraphix.com
SIC: 2759 Screen printing

(G-2691)
CONSULTING ENGRG DEV SVCS INC
Also Called: C E D
3 Fox Hollow Rd (06478-3162)
PHONE..............................203 828-6528
Steven G Meyer, Pr
EMP: 55 EST: 1982
SQ FT: 20,000
SALES (est): 8.69MM Privately Held
Web: www.cedmachining.com
SIC: 3599 3469 Machine shop, jobbing and
    repair; Machine parts, stamped or pressed
    metal

(G-2692)
CV INDUSTRIES CORPORATION
2 Fox Hollow Rd (06478-3161)
PHONE..............................203 828-6566
Dean Contaxis, Ex Dir
Dean Contaxis, Pr
Tom Villano, *
Theresa Contaxis, *
EMP: 34 EST: 1961
SQ FT: 30,000
SALES (est): 4.98MM Privately Held
Web: www.gen-el-mec.com
SIC: 3999 Barber and beauty shop
    equipment

(G-2693)
DIGITALDRUKER INC
Also Called: AlphaGraphics
11 Old Farm Rd (06478-1704)
PHONE..............................203 888-6001
Robert J Talbot, Pr
EMP: 11 EST: 2014
SALES (est): 216.93K Privately Held
Web: www.alphagraphics.com
SIC: 2752 Commercial printing, lithographic

(G-2694)
GEN-EL-MEC ASSOCIATES LLC ✪
2 Fox Hollow Rd (06478-3161)
PHONE..............................203 828-6566
Dean Contaxis, Managing Member
EMP: 32 EST: 2023
SALES (est): 1.34MM Privately Held
Web: www.gen-el-mec.com
SIC: 3599 Machine shop, jobbing and repair

(G-2695)
GRAND EMBROIDERY INC
Also Called: Grand Imprints
225 Christian St (06478-1252)
PHONE..............................203 888-7484
EMP: 12 EST: 1993
SQ FT: 6,300
SALES (est): 470.45K Privately Held
Web: www.grandembroidery.com
SIC: 2395 2269 Embroidery and art
    needlework; Finishing plants, nec

(G-2696)
HART TOOL & ENGINEERING
339 Christian St (06478-1084)
PHONE..............................203 264-9776
Gilbert Hart, Owner
EMP: 7 EST: 1975
SQ FT: 2,500
SALES (est): 736.65K Privately Held
Web: www.harttools.com
SIC: 3423 Hand and edge tools, nec

(G-2697)
HAYNES AGGRGTES - DEEP RVER LL
220 Main St Ste 2f (06478-1065)
PHONE..............................203 888-8100
Thomas Haynes, Prin
EMP: 7 EST: 2008
SALES (est): 581.75K Privately Held
SIC: 1481 Nonmetallic mineral services

(G-2698)
HUSKY FUEL LLC
62 Larkey Rd (06478-3149)
PHONE..............................203 783-0783
Robert James Hofmiller, Prin
EMP: 9 EST: 2016
SALES (est): 2.03MM Privately Held
Web: www.huskyfuel.com
SIC: 2869 Fuels

(G-2699)
INDUSTRIAL TECTO
1 Tribiology Ctr (06478-1035)
PHONE..............................310 537-3750
EMP: 11 EST: 2013
SALES (est): 1.25MM Privately Held
SIC: 3568 Bearings, bushings, and blocks

(G-2700)
INTERNATIONAL CONTACT TECH INC
Also Called: I C T
6 Pheasant Run Dr Unit 4 (06478-1066)
PHONE..............................203 264-5757
Joseph Baker, Pr
Paul J Geary, VP
▲ EMP: 9 EST: 1993
SALES (est): 879.52K Privately Held
Web: www.ict-probe.com
SIC: 3825 Test equipment for electronic and
    electric measurement

(G-2701)
JESCO IRON CRAFTS INC
Also Called: Jescraft
116 Willenbrock Rd (06478-1031)
PHONE..............................201 488-4545
Michael Brown, Pr
EMP: 15 EST: 1946
SALES (est): 2.48MM Privately Held
Web: www.jescraft.com
SIC: 3423 3444 Hand and edge tools, nec;
    Sheet metalwork

(G-2702)
KENNETH LYNCH & SONS INC
114 Willenbrock Rd (06478-1031)
PHONE..............................203 762-8363
Timothy A Lynch, Pr
◆ EMP: 9 EST: 1946
SQ FT: 30,000
SALES (est): 1.46MM Privately Held
Web: www.klynchandsons.com
SIC: 3446 3281 Architectural metalwork;
    Stone, quarrying and processing of own
    stone products

(G-2703)
MACTON OXFORD LLC
116 Willenbrock Rd (06478-1031)
PHONE..............................203 267-1500
David Perkins, Prin
EMP: 25 EST: 2006
SALES (est): 923.05K Privately Held
SIC: 3599 Machine shop, jobbing and repair

(G-2704)
MODERN METAL FINISHING LLC
✪
110 Willenbrock Rd (06478-1031)
PHONE..............................203 267-1510
Jonathan Wilcox, *Managing Member*
EMP: 49 **EST:** 2023
SALES (est): 1.54MM **Privately Held**
SIC: 3559 Electroplating machinery and
equipment

(G-2705)
MORSE WATCHMANS INC
2 Morse Rd (06478-1040)
PHONE..............................203 264-4949
Manuel Pires, *Pr*
Fernando Pires, *
▲ **EMP:** 50 **EST:** 1882
SQ FT: 20,000
SALES (est): 10.17MM **Privately Held**
Web: www.morsewatchmans.com
SIC: 3699 3577 Security control equipment
and systems; Computer peripheral
equipment, nec

(G-2706)
NAC INDUSTRIES INC
112 Hurley Rd (06478-1027)
PHONE..............................845 214-0659
EMP: 10 **EST:** 2007
SALES (est): 463.5K **Privately Held**
SIC: 3999 Candles

(G-2707)
OXFORD SCIENCE INC
1 Old Moose Hill Rd (06478-6137)
PHONE..............................203 881-3115
Edward L Carver Junior, *Pr*
EMP: 19 **EST:** 1990
SALES (est): 812.4K **Privately Held**
Web: www.oxfordscienceinc.com
SIC: 3841 Surgical and medical instruments

(G-2708)
PRO SCIENTIFIC INC
99 Willenbrock Rd (06478-1032)
P.O. Box 448 (06468-0448)
PHONE..............................203 267-4600
Richard Yacko, *Pr*
Patricia Yacko, *VP*
EMP: 10 **EST:** 1992
SALES (est): 2MM **Privately Held**
Web: www.proscientific.com
SIC: 3556 Homogenizing machinery: dairy,
fruit, vegetable

(G-2709)
PTA CORPORATION (PA)
Also Called: Pta Plastics
148 Christian St (06478-1221)
PHONE..............................203 888-0585
▲ **EMP:** 80 **EST:** 1954
SALES (est): 30.31MM **Privately Held**
Web: www.ptaplastics.com
SIC: 3089 7389 8711 Injection molding of
plastics; Design, commercial and industrial;
Engineering services

(G-2710)
RBC BEARINGS
INCORPORATED (PA)
Also Called: Rbc
1 Tribology Ctr (06478-1035)
PHONE..............................203 267-7001
Michael J Hartnett, *Pr*
Daniel A Bergeron, *VP*
Robert M Sullivan, *VP*
John J Feeney, *VP*
Patrick S Bannon, *General Vice President*

EMP: 151 **EST:** 1919
SQ FT: 70,000
SALES (est): 1.47B
SALES (corp-wide): 1.47B **Publicly Held**
Web: www.rbcbearings.com
SIC: 3562 5085 3728 Ball and roller
bearings; Bearings; Aircraft parts and
equipment, nec

(G-2711)
SARGENT CONTROLS AND
AEROSPACE
1 Tribology Ctr (06478-1035)
PHONE..............................520 744-1000
EMP: 9 **EST:** 2018
SALES (est): 265.24K **Privately Held**
Web: www.sargentaerospace.com
SIC: 3728 Aircraft parts and equipment, nec

(G-2712)
STIHL INCORPORATED
Also Called: Northeast Stihl
2 Patriot Way (06478-1274)
PHONE..............................203 929-8488
Nick Jiannas, *Brnch Mgr*
EMP: 23
SALES (corp-wide): 3.65B **Privately Held**
Web: www.stihl.com
SIC: 3546 5083 Power-driven handtools;
Farm and garden machinery
HQ: Stihl Incorporated
536 Viking Dr
Virginia Beach VA 23452
757 486-9100

(G-2713)
TURBINE COMPONENTS INC
Also Called: T C I
102 Willenbrock Rd (06478-1033)
PHONE..............................858 678-8568
Raffee Esmailians, *Pr*
Tom Hughes, *
EMP: 48 **EST:** 2006
SALES (est): 12.75MM
SALES (corp-wide): 1.47B **Publicly Held**
Web: www.turbinecomponents.com
SIC: 3724 Turbines, aircraft type
PA: Rbc Bearings Incorporated
1 Tribology Ctr
Oxford CT 06478
203 267-7001

(G-2714)
WALZ & KRENZER INC
Also Called: Pilgrim Nuts
91 Willenbrock Rd Ste B4 (06478-1036)
PHONE..............................203 267-5712
Benjamin Rising, *Pr*
EMP: 9
SALES (est): 2.6MM **Privately Held**
Web: www.wkdoors.com
SIC: 3443 Water tanks, metal plate
PA: Walz & Krenzer, Inc.
91 Willenbrock Rd Ste B4
Oxford CT 06478
203 267-5712

(G-2715)
ZACKIN PUBLICATIONS INC
Also Called: Alternative Energy Retailer
100 Willenbrock Rd (06478-1044)
P.O. Box 2180 (06722-2180)
PHONE..............................203 262-4670
David Zackin, *Pr*
Linda Zackin, *
Paul M Zackin, *
Jennifer Zackin, *
EMP: 24 **EST:** 1967
SQ FT: 2,000
SALES (est): 2.46MM **Privately Held**

Web: www.zackinpublications.com
SIC: 2721 Trade journals: publishing only,
not printed on site

Pawcatuck
New London County

(G-2716)
COOPER GROUP LLC
25 White Rock Bridge Rd (06379-1312)
PHONE..............................860 599-2481
Kenneth Cooper, *Pr*
EMP: 18 **EST:** 2019
SALES (est): 2.82MM **Privately Held**
Web: www.thecoopergroupct.com
SIC: 3442 Window and door frames

(G-2717)
DAVIS-STANDARD LLC (HQ)
Also Called: Harrel
1 Extrusion Dr (06379-2327)
PHONE..............................860 300-3928
Giovanni Spitale, *CEO*
Michael Roe, *
◆ **EMP:** 398 **EST:** 1995
SALES (est): 141.68MM **Privately Held**
SIC: 3089 Extruded finished plastics
products, nec
PA: Davis-Standard Holdings, Inc.
1 Extrusion Dr
Pawcatuck CT 06379

(G-2718)
DAVIS-STANDARD HOLDINGS
INC (PA)
Also Called: Egan, Strling Nrm Kllion Ltol
1 Extrusion Dr (06379-2327)
PHONE..............................860 599-1010
Charles Buckley, *Pr*
Hassan Helmy, *
Ernest Plasse, *
Mark Panozzo, *
James Murphy, *
◆ **EMP:** 400 **EST:** 1994
SQ FT: 170,000
SALES (est): 265.5MM **Privately Held**
SIC: 3559 Plastics working machinery

(G-2719)
DESCHENES & COOPER
ARCHITECTUR
25 White Rock Bridge Rd (06379-1312)
P.O. Box 9222 (06340-9222)
PHONE..............................860 599-2481
Brian Cooper, *Pr*
EMP: 8 **EST:** 1973
SQ FT: 10,000
SALES (est): 706.57K **Privately Held**
Web: www.thecoopergroupct.com
SIC: 2431 1521 Doors, wood; General
remodeling, single-family houses

(G-2720)
GENERAL DYNAMICS INFO
TECH INC
100 Mechanic St (06379-2163)
PHONE..............................860 441-2400
Joseph M Marino, *Brnch Mgr*
EMP: 99
SQ FT: 10,000
SALES (corp-wide): 42.27B **Publicly Held**
Web: www.gdit.com
SIC: 7379 8711 7373 3444 Computer
related maintenance services; Engineering
services; Computer integrated systems
design; Sheet metalwork

HQ: General Dynamics Information
Technology, Inc.
3150 Fairview Park Dr
Falls Church VA 22042
703 995-8700

(G-2721)
GUIDERA MARKETING
SERVICES
Also Called: Fabricgraphics
21 Pawcatuck Ave (06379-2421)
P.O. Box 108 (06378-0108)
PHONE..............................860 599-8880
Timothy Guidera, *Pr*
Pamela Guidera, *VP*
EMP: 12 **EST:** 1979
SQ FT: 2,500
SALES (est): 377.23K **Privately Held**
Web: www.fabrigraphics.com
SIC: 2395 Embroidery and art needlework

(G-2722)
HI TECH PROFILES INC
185 S Broad St Ste 301 (06379-1997)
PHONE..............................401 377-2040
Sherry Quinlan, *Prin*
EMP: 7 **EST:** 2016
SALES (est): 215.82K **Privately Held**
Web: www.hitechprofiles.com
SIC: 3089 Injection molding of plastics

(G-2723)
LEHVOSS NORTH AMERICA LLC
185 S Broad St Ste 2b (06379-1997)
PHONE..............................860 495-2046
▲ **EMP:** 12 **EST:** 2013
SALES (est): 4.34MM
SALES (corp-wide): 212.03MM **Privately
Held**
Web: www.lehvoss.us
SIC: 3089 Thermoformed finished plastics
products, nec
PA: Lehmann & Voss & Co. Kg
Alsterufer 19
Hamburg HH 20354
40441970

(G-2724)
OLIVE CAPIZZANO OILS &
VINEGAR
5 Coggswell St Ste 1 (06379-1672)
PHONE..............................860 495-2187
Stephen Capizzano, *Prin*
EMP: 7 **EST:** 2014
SALES (est): 415K **Privately Held**
Web: www.capizzanoco.com
SIC: 2079 Olive oil

(G-2725)
RITE-SOLUTIONS INC (PA)
185 S Broad St (06379-1997)
P.O. Box 1060 (06379-0060)
PHONE..............................401 847-3399
Joe Marino, *CEO*
Joe Marino, *Ch Bd*
Dennis Mclaughlin, *CEO*
Michael Coffey, *Ex VP*
Michael Taylor, *Sr VP*
EMP: 15 **EST:** 1999
SQ FT: 3,300
SALES (est): 42.96MM
SALES (corp-wide): 42.96MM **Privately
Held**
Web: www.rite-solutions.com
SIC: 7372 7373 8711 Prepackaged software
; Computer integrated systems design;
Engineering services

(G-2726)
**THAVENET MACHINE
COMPANY INC**
12 Chase St Ste 14 (06379-2127)
PHONE..............................860 599-4495
Louis Thavenet Junior, *Pr*
Evelyn Thavenet, *Sec*
Eric Thavenet, *VP*
EMP: 8 EST: 1922
SQ FT: 4,000
SALES (est): 854.89K **Privately Held**
Web: www.thavenetmachine.com
SIC: 3599 5084 Machine shop, jobbing and
repair; Welding machinery and equipment

(G-2727)
**VACCA ARCHITECTURAL
WDWKG LLC**
9 Coggswell St (06379-1626)
PHONE..............................860 599-3677
EMP: 8 EST: 2001
SQ FT: 6,958
SALES (est): 662K **Privately Held**
SIC: 2499 Decorative wood and woodwork

(G-2728)
WESCON CORP OF CONN
Elmata Ave (06379)
P.O. Box 296 (02891-0296)
PHONE..............................860 599-2500
Paul Lynch, *Pr*
Steven Lynch, *Sec*
EMP: 8 EST: 1947
SQ FT: 1,200
SALES (est): 1.24MM
SALES (corp-wide): 48.18MM **Privately
Held**
SIC: 2951 Asphalt and asphaltic paving
mixtures (not from refineries)
PA: J.H. Lynch & Sons, Inc.
50 Lynch Pl
Cumberland RI 02864
401 333-4300

Pine Meadow
Litchfield County

(G-2729)
TRD SPECIALTIES INC
Also Called: T R D Specialities
8 Wickett St (06061-2039)
P.O. Box 80 (06061-0080)
PHONE..............................860 738-4505
Thomas Reading, *Pr*
Albert De Gaeta, *Treas*
▲ **EMP: 8 EST:** 1993
SQ FT: 7,500
SALES (est): 956.99K **Privately Held**
Web: www.trdspecialties.com
SIC: 3399 Steel balls

Plainfield
Windham County

(G-2730)
AMTEC CORPORATION
30 Center Pkwy (06374-2051)
PHONE..............................860 230-0006
David E Fallon, *Pr*
Donna M Hunt, *
EMP: 30 EST: 1988
SQ FT: 15,000
SALES (est): 3.71MM **Privately Held**
Web: www.amtecgrips.com
SIC: 3496 Woven wire products, nec

(G-2731)
APCM MANUFACTURING LLC
Also Called: Adhesives Prepregs
1366 Norwich Rd (06374-1931)
P.O. Box 264 (06374-0264)
PHONE..............................860 564-7817
EMP: 8 EST: 1992
SQ FT: 7,000
SALES (est): 1.03MM **Privately Held**
Web: www.prepregs.com
SIC: 2891 Adhesives

(G-2732)
ARS PRODUCTS INC
43 Lathrop Road Ext (06374-1965)
P.O. Box 288 (06374-0288)
PHONE..............................860 564-0208
EMP: 43 EST: 2003
SALES (est): 7.05MM **Privately Held**
Web: www.arsproducts.com
SIC: 3825 Analog-digital converters,
electronic instrumentation type

(G-2733)
ASAP MCH SP FABRICATION INC
89 Mill Brook Rd (06374-1967)
PHONE..............................860 564-4114
EMP: 7 EST: 2007
SALES (est): 652.19K **Privately Held**
Web: www.brooklynfarmandpets.com
SIC: 3599 Machine shop, jobbing and repair

(G-2734)
B S T SYSTEMS INC
78 Plainfield Pike (06374-1700)
PHONE..............................860 564-4078
Kenneth P Avery, *Pr*
Thomas T Terjesen, *
Michael A Solis, *
Edward J Mulvey, *
▲ **EMP: 55 EST:** 1983
SQ FT: 27,000
SALES (est): 9.6MM **Privately Held**
Web: www.bstsys.com
SIC: 3692 3691 3629 Primary batteries, dry
and wet; Storage batteries; Electronic
generation equipment

(G-2735)
BAY STATE MACHINE INC
21 Center Pkwy (06374-2054)
PHONE..............................860 230-0054
Robert Stafford, *Pr*
Pamela Stafford, *Sec*
EMP: 8 EST: 1970
SQ FT: 2,000
SALES (est): 854.39K **Privately Held**
SIC: 3599 Machine shop, jobbing and repair

(G-2736)
**LINEMASTER SWITCH
CORPORATION**
16 Center Pkwy (06374-2051)
PHONE..............................860 564-7713
▲ **EMP: 8 EST:** 2009
SALES (est): 380.16K **Privately Held**
Web: www.linemaster.com
SIC: 3679 Electronic switches

(G-2737)
**PRO-MANUFACTURED
PRODUCTS INC**
29 Center Pkwy (06374-2054)
P.O. Box 359 (06795-0359)
PHONE..............................860 564-2197
Ward E Walker, *Pr*
Kristin D Walker, *Sec*
EMP: 8 EST: 1992
SQ FT: 5,250

SALES (est): 1.36MM
SALES (corp-wide): 49.87MM **Privately
Held**
SIC: 3451 Screw machine products
PA: Kksp Precision Machining, Llc
1688 Glen Ellyn Rd
Glendale Heights IL 60139
630 260-1735

(G-2738)
RADECO INC
17 West Pkwy (06374-2048)
P.O. Box 1304 (02644-0715)
PHONE..............................860 823-1220
Paul Lovendale, *Pr*
Ann Lovendale, *Sec*
Keith Lovendale, *VP Opers*
Brad Lovendale, *VP Sls*
▼ **EMP: 7 EST:** 1971
SQ FT: 6,000
SALES (est): 994.01K **Privately Held**
Web: www.radecoinc.com
SIC: 3674 Radiation sensors

(G-2739)
**SCOPE TECHNOLOGY
INCORPORATED**
8 Center Pkwy (06374-2051)
PHONE..............................860 963-1141
EMP: 10 EST: 1982
SQ FT: 4,000
SALES (est): 943.05K **Privately Held**
Web: www.scopetech.com
SIC: 3827 Magnifying instruments, nec,
optical

(G-2740)
STM IMP AND EXP CORP
Also Called: Mk Wood Cabinets
55 Lathrop Road Ext (06374-1965)
PHONE..............................973 450-5110
EMP: 9 EST: 2019
SALES (est): 483.81K **Privately Held**
Web: www.mkwoodcabinets.com
SIC: 2434 2521 Wood kitchen cabinets;
Cabinets, office: wood

(G-2741)
WESTMINSTER TOOL INC
5 East Pkwy (06374-2046)
PHONE..............................860 564-6966
Raymond S Coombs Junior, *Pr*
Paul L Szydlo, *
Sherry L Appleton, *
▲ **EMP: 40 EST:** 1997
SQ FT: 4,500
SALES (est): 10.5MM **Privately Held**
Web: www.westminstertool.com
SIC: 3544 Industrial molds

Plainville
Hartford County

(G-2742)
A AIUDI & SONS LLC (PA)
190 Camp St (06062-1612)
P.O. Box 279 (06062-0279)
PHONE..............................860 747-5534
EMP: 9 EST: 1945
SQ FT: 3,000
SALES (est): 1.93MM
SALES (corp-wide): 1.93MM **Privately
Held**
Web: www.aiudiconcrete.com
SIC: 1771 3273 Concrete work; Ready-
mixed concrete

(G-2743)
A D GRINDING
54 Lewis St (06062-2049)
PHONE..............................860 747-6630
Anthony Loumbard, *Pr*
Dan Haag, *Sec*
EMP: 14 EST: 2005
SALES (est): 446.29K **Privately Held**
SIC: 3599 Grinding castings for the trade

(G-2744)
**ABB ENTERPRISE SOFTWARE
INC**
Also Called: GE
41 Woodford Ave (06062-2372)
PHONE..............................860 747-7111
Lloyd G Trotter, *Brnch Mgr*
EMP: 900
Web: new.abb.com
SIC: 3613 7361 3643 Switches, electric
power except snap, push button, etc.;
Employment agencies; Current-carrying
wiring services
HQ: Abb Inc.
305 Gregson Dr
Cary NC 27511

(G-2745)
ACCURATE BURRING CO LLC
161 Woodford Ave Ste 19 (06062-2368)
PHONE..............................860 747-8640
Robert Beaudoin, *Owner*
EMP: 12 EST: 1983
SQ FT: 20,000
SALES (est): 1.19MM **Privately Held**
Web: www.accurateburring.com
SIC: 3471 Finishing, metals or formed
products

(G-2746)
**ALPHA PLATING AND
FINISHING CO**
169 W Main St (06062-1925)
P.O. Box 89 (06062-0089)
PHONE..............................860 747-5002
Rafael Bawabe, *Pr*
EMP: 24 EST: 1976
SQ FT: 15,000
SALES (est): 422.75K **Privately Held**
SIC: 3471 Electroplating of metals or
formed products

(G-2747)
APP POLONIA LLC
Also Called: App Polonia Trading
95 Metacomet Rd (06062-1424)
PHONE..............................860 747-3397
EMP: 7 EST: 2004
SALES (est): 115.99K **Privately Held**
SIC: 2911 5147 Diesel fuels; Meats and
meat products

(G-2748)
ATP INDUSTRIES LLC (PA)
75 Northwest Dr (06062-1101)
PHONE..............................860 479-5007
EMP: 16 EST: 2009
SQ FT: 20,000
SALES (est): 5.54MM **Privately Held**
Web: www.atp-ind.com
SIC: 3541 3492 8711 3451 Vertical turning
and boring machines (metalworking); Fluid
power valves and hose fittings; Mechanical
engineering; Screw machine products

(G-2749)
**BRIARWOOD PRINTING
COMPANY INC**

301 Farmington Ave (06062-1398)
PHONE........................860 747-6805
David M Drew, *Pr*
Brian Kupchik, *VP*
EMP: 11 EST: 1960
SQ FT: 10,000
SALES (est): 506.91K **Privately Held**
Web: www.briarwoodprinting.com
SIC: 2752 Offset printing

(G-2750)
CARLING TECHNOLOGIES INC
(HQ)
Also Called: LITTELFUSE
60 Johnson Ave (06062-1181)
PHONE........................860 793-9281
Richard W Sorenson, *Pr*
Paul Soucy, *
Edward Rosenthal, *
Richard Sorenson Junior, *Ex VP*
Jennifer Buddenhagen, *
▲ **EMP: 175 EST:** 1920
SQ FT: 135,000
SALES (est): 2.08MM
SALES (corp-wide): 2.51B **Publicly Held**
Web: www.carlingtech.com
SIC: 3643 3613 3612 Electric switches;
  Power circuit breakers; Transformers,
  except electric
PA: Littelfuse, Inc.
  8755 W Higgins Rd Ste 500
  Chicago IL 60631
  773 628-1000

(G-2751)
CONNECTICUT TOOL & MFG CO
LLC
Also Called: Whitcraft Central Connecticut
35 Corp Ave (06062)
PHONE........................860 846-0800
Doug Folsom, *Prin*
▲ **EMP: 70 EST:** 2004
SQ FT: 29,000
SALES (est): 20.36MM
SALES (corp-wide): 139.19MM **Privately Held**
SIC: 3728 Aircraft assemblies,
  subassemblies, and parts, nec
PA: Whitcraft Llc
  76 County Rd
  Eastford CT 06242
  860 974-0786

(G-2752)
CT HONE INC
9 Grace Ave (06062-2849)
P.O. Box 263 (06062-0263)
PHONE........................860 747-3884
Douglas Simard, *VP*
Gregory Simard, *VP*
Bert Simard, *Pr*
EMP: 7 EST: 1971
SQ FT: 2,500
SALES (est): 698.3K **Privately Held**
Web: www.cthone.com
SIC: 3599 Machine shop, jobbing and repair

(G-2753)
DELL ACQUISITION LLC
Also Called: Dell Manufacturing
35 Corporate Ave (06062-1194)
PHONE........................860 677-8545
Joe Maisto, *Prin*
EMP: 14 EST: 2011
SALES (est): 474.08K **Privately Held**
SIC: 3599 Machine shop, jobbing and repair

(G-2754)
DISPLAYCRAFT INC
335 S Washington St (06062-2729)
PHONE........................860 747-9110
Richard Seigars, *Pr*
Rui Carvalho, *Ex VP*
▲ **EMP: 20 EST:** 1958
SQ FT: 80,000
SALES (est): 2.57MM **Privately Held**
Web: www.displaycraft.com
SIC: 3993 2542 Displays and cutouts,
  window and lobby; Partitions and fixtures,
  except wood

(G-2755)
EASTERN BROACH INC
10 Sparks St (06062-2052)
PHONE........................860 828-4800
Robert Tarver, *Pr*
Ivor Tarver, *Pr*
Robert Tarver, *VP*
Malcolm Tarver, *Sec*
Charles H Tarver, *Stockholder*
EMP: 14 EST: 1972
SQ FT: 6,000
SALES (est): 455.16K **Privately Held**
Web: www.easternbroach.com
SIC: 3545 7699 Broaches (machine tool
  accessories); Tool repair services

(G-2756)
ECLAS REALTY CORPORATION
Also Called: Hygrade
329 Cooke St (06062-1448)
PHONE........................860 747-5773
John A Salce, *CEO*
Stephen L Saltzman, *Sec*
Richard J Cleary, *
EMP: 28 EST: 1962
SQ FT: 40,000
SALES (est): 2.29MM **Privately Held**
Web: www.hygrade.com
SIC: 3599 Machine shop, jobbing and repair

(G-2757)
EDISON COATINGS INC
3 Northwest Dr (06062-1336)
PHONE........................860 747-2220
Michael Edison, *Pr*
Leya Edison, *VP*
◆ **EMP: 13 EST:** 1981
SQ FT: 20,000
SALES (est): 2.51MM **Privately Held**
Web: www.edisoncoatings.com
SIC: 2891 Adhesives

(G-2758)
ELLIS MANUFACTURING LLC
161 Woodford Ave (06062-2370)
PHONE........................865 518-0531
Robert Knowlton, *Prin*
EMP: 7 EST: 2010
SALES (est): 384.69K **Privately Held**
Web: www.ellismanufacturingllc.com
SIC: 3999 Manufacturing industries, nec

(G-2759)
FABTRON INCORPORATED
80 Farmington Valley Dr (06062-1193)
PHONE........................860 410-1801
Garret J Maino, *Pr*
Joseph H Maino, *VP*
Jeffrey P Maino, *Treas*
EMP: 9 EST: 1962
SQ FT: 31,000
SALES (est): 976.54K **Privately Held**
Web: www.fabtronusa.com
SIC: 1761 7692 Sheet metal work, nec;
  Welding repair

(G-2760)
FORESTVILLE MACHINE
COMPANY
355 S Washington St (06062-2742)
PHONE........................860 747-6000
John Ingulli, *CEO*
EMP: 14 EST: 1945
SALES (est): 267.6K **Privately Held**
Web: www.forestvillemachine.com
SIC: 3451 Screw machine products

(G-2761)
GEMS SENSORS INC (HQ)
Also Called: Gems Sensors & Controls
1 Cowles Rd (06062-1107)
PHONE........................860 747-3000
Jeffrey Townsend, *Pr*
▲ **EMP: 325 EST:** 1959
SALES (est): 135.22MM
SALES (corp-wide): 5.83B **Publicly Held**
Web: www.gemssensors.com
SIC: 3824 5084 3812 3625 Fluid meters
  and counting devices; Industrial machinery
  and equipment; Search and navigation
  equipment; Relays and industrial controls
PA: Fortive Corporation
  6920 Seaway Blvd
  Everett WA 98203
  425 446-5000

(G-2762)
GERDAU AMERISTEEL US INC
75 Neal Ct (06062-1622)
PHONE........................860 351-9029
EMP: 8
Web: www.gerdau.com
SIC: 3312 Iron and steel products, hot-rolled
HQ: Gerdau Ameristeel Us Inc.
  4221 W Boy Scout Blvd # 600
  Tampa FL 33607
  813 286-8383

(G-2763)
HARTFORD FIRE EQUIPMENT
394 East St (06062-3238)
P.O. Box 457 (06062-0457)
PHONE........................860 747-2757
TOLL FREE: 800
Jeff Wells, *Pr*
EMP: 10 EST: 1975
SALES (est): 82.67K **Privately Held**
SIC: 7349 1231 5063 Cleaning service,
  industrial or commercial; Anthracite mining;
  Electrical apparatus and equipment

(G-2764)
HYGRADE PRECISION TECH
LLC
329 Cooke St (06062-1448)
P.O. Box 568 (06062-0568)
PHONE........................860 747-5773
EMP: 30 EST: 2019
SALES (est): 6.26MM **Privately Held**
Web: www.hygrade.com
SIC: 3599 Machine shop, jobbing and repair

(G-2765)
J & P MANUFACTURING LLC
125 Robert Jackson Way Unit F
(06062-2663)
PHONE........................860 919-8287
Pawel Surowaniec, *Managing Member*
EMP: 13 EST: 2006
SALES (est): 1.02MM **Privately Held**
SIC: 3549 Assembly machines, including
  robotic

(G-2766)
KING NETWORK SERVICES INC
336 S Washington St Ste R (06062-2752)
PHONE........................860 479-8029
EMP: 10 EST: 2013
SALES (est): 2.12MM **Privately Held**
Web: www.knsinc.net
SIC: 3357 Communication wire

(G-2767)
LAROSA MANUFACTURING LLC
15 Hultenius St (06062-2878)
PHONE........................860 819-7066
EMP: 8 EST: 2015
SALES (est): 193.44K **Privately Held**
SIC: 3544 Special dies, tools, jigs, and
  fixtures

(G-2768)
LASSY TOOLS INC
96 Bohemia St (06062-2122)
P.O. Box G (06062-0956)
PHONE........................860 747-2748
William Lassy, *Pr*
Marc Lassy, *VP*
Gail Sjogren, *Sec*
EMP: 7 EST: 1938
SQ FT: 10,000
SALES (est): 645.65K **Privately Held**
Web: www.lassytools.com
SIC: 3429 3544 Clamps, metal; Special dies
  and tools

(G-2769)
LDM MANUFACTURING INC
20 Hultenius St Ste S (06062-2883)
PHONE........................860 410-9804
Julie Desimone, *VP*
Benjamin Desimone, *Dir*
Katey Desimone, *Dir*
EMP: 8 EST: 2015
SALES (est): 504.4K **Privately Held**
Web: www.ldmmanufacturing.com
SIC: 3999 Manufacturing industries, nec

(G-2770)
LPG METAL CRAFTS LLC
54 Carol Dr (06062-3206)
PHONE........................860 982-3573
Leonard Gale, *Managing Member*
EMP: 7 EST: 2006
SALES (est): 505.22K **Privately Held**
SIC: 3446 Architectural metalwork

(G-2771)
MARETRON LLP
60 Johnson Ave (06062-1181)
PHONE........................602 861-1707
Mark Biegel, *VP*
▲ **EMP: 10 EST:** 2003
SALES (est): 414.03K **Privately Held**
Web: www.maretron.com
SIC: 3531 Marine related equipment

(G-2772)
MARTIN CABINET INC (PA)
336 S Washington St Ste 2 (06062-2752)
PHONE........................860 747-5769
Jean Martin, *Pr*
Brian Martin, *Sec*
EMP: 47 EST: 1971
SQ FT: 5,000
SALES (est): 4.62MM
SALES (corp-wide): 4.62MM **Privately Held**
Web: www.martincabinet.com
SIC: 2434 5211 Wood kitchen cabinets;
  Cabinets, kitchen

▲ = Import ▼ = Export
◆ = Import/Export

(G-2773)
MCKINNON DESIGN LLC ✪
Also Called: Modern Woodcrafts
72 Woodford Dr (06062-1164)
PHONE.....................860 677-7371
EMP: 7 EST: 2023
SALES (est): 299.06K **Privately Held**
SIC: 2541 2431 Wood partitions and fixtures
; Millwork

(G-2774)
NICKSON INDUSTRIES INC
336 Woodford Ave (06062-2487)
PHONE.....................860 747-1671
Ilan Ginga, *Pr*
▲ EMP: 48 EST: 1968
SQ FT: 100,000
SALES (est): 10.06MM
SALES (corp-wide): 30.48MM **Privately
Held**
Web: www.nickson.com
SIC: 3714 Motor vehicle parts and
accessories
PA: Metapoint Partners, A Limited
Partnership
108 Beach St
Manchester MA 01944
978 531-1398

(G-2775)
OLSON BROTHERS COMPANY
272 Camp St (06062-1612)
P.O. Box 188 (06062-0188)
PHONE.....................860 747-6844
Robert R Carroll, *CEO*
Christopher Carroll, *Pr*
EMP: 19 EST: 1924
SQ FT: 7,000
SALES (est): 907.24K **Privately Held**
Web: www.obcinc.net
SIC: 3451 Screw machine products

(G-2776)
**PLAINVILLE PLATING
COMPANY INC**
21 Forestville Ave (06062-2159)
P.O. Box 219 (06062-0219)
PHONE.....................860 747-1624
Gerald Glassman, *Ch Bd*
Charles L Pratt, *Pr*
Jay R Fienman, *Treas*
George Urbanowicz, *Dir*
Roy Manzie, *Dir*
EMP: 60 EST: 1920
SQ FT: 23,000
SALES (est): 4.82MM **Privately Held**
Web: www.plainvilleplating.com
SIC: 3471 Electroplating of metals or
formed products

(G-2777)
PLAINVILLE SPECIAL TOOL LLC
63 N Washington St (06062-1972)
PHONE.....................860 747-2736
EMP: 13 EST: 2014
SALES (est): 2.45MM **Privately Held**
Web: www.pstct.com
SIC: 3312 Tool and die steel and alloys

(G-2778)
PRALINES OF PLAINVILLE
107 New Britain Ave (06062-2073)
PHONE.....................860 410-1151
Jim Scarfo, *Owner*
EMP: 7 EST: 2010
SALES (est): 146.08K **Privately Held**
SIC: 2024 Ice cream, bulk

(G-2779)
RD VENTURES INC
1 Northwest Dr (06062-1340)
PHONE.....................860 747-2709
Richard Williams, *Pr*
David Williams, *VP*
Arthur Williams, *VP*
▼ EMP: 18 EST: 1938
SQ FT: 15,000
SALES (est): 2.47MM **Privately Held**
Web: www.drtempleman.com
SIC: 3495 Mechanical springs, precision

(G-2780)
SHUSTER-METTLER CORP
Also Called: Shuster Machines
10 Sparks St (06062-2052)
P.O. Box 883 (06504-0883)
PHONE.....................203 562-3178
Dennis Polio, *Pr*
Joyce Polio, *
EMP: 30 EST: 1947
SQ FT: 20,000
SALES (est): 3.8MM **Privately Held**
Web: www.shustermettler.com
SIC: 5084 3541 3315 3549 Machine tools
and accessories; Machine tools, metal
cutting type; Steel wire and related products
; Cutting and slitting machinery

(G-2781)
STYLAIR LLC
161 Woodford Ave (06062-2370)
P.O. Box 7014 (06062-7014)
PHONE.....................860 747-4588
EMP: 15 EST: 1992
SQ FT: 8,000
SALES (est): 4.98MM **Privately Held**
Web: www.stylair.com
SIC: 3564 3563 Blowers and fans; Air and
gas compressors

(G-2782)
TACO FASTENERS INC
71 Northwest Dr (06062-1101)
P.O. Box 338 (06062-0338)
PHONE.....................860 747-5597
Arnold Finn, *Pr*
Marguerite Finn, *Sec*
EMP: 10 EST: 1970
SQ FT: 10,000
SALES (est): 967.19K **Privately Held**
Web: www.tacofasteners.com
SIC: 3469 3544 Stamping metal for the trade
; Special dies and tools

(G-2783)
TETCO INC
4 Northwest Dr (06062-1311)
PHONE.....................860 747-1280
Sandra T Simmons, *Pr*
Sandra Thibault, *Pr*
George Simmons, *VP*
EMP: 36 EST: 1979
SQ FT: 14,000
SALES (est): 792.59K **Privately Held**
Web: www.tetcoinc.com
SIC: 3541 Grinding machines, metalworking

(G-2784)
**TOP FLIGHT MACHINE TOOL
LLC**
Also Called: Aircraft
90 Robert Jackson Way (06062-2650)
PHONE.....................860 747-4726
EMP: 9 EST: 2005
SALES (est): 851.14K **Privately Held**
SIC: 3599 Machine shop, jobbing and repair

(G-2785)
TRANSIT SYSTEMS INC
161 Woodford Ave Ste 34 (06062-2369)
PHONE.....................860 747-3669
Jeffrey Yost, *Pr*
Walter J Lappen, *VP*
EMP: 7 EST: 1986
SQ FT: 8,000
SALES (est): 846.98K **Privately Held**
Web: www.transitsys.com
SIC: 3743 Interurban cars and car
equipment

(G-2786)
TRUMPF INC
3 Johnson Ave (06062-1115)
PHONE.....................860 255-6000
EMP: 7
SALES (corp-wide): 4.51B **Privately Held**
Web: www.trumpf.com
SIC: 3542 3546 3423 Sheet metalworking
machines; Power-driven handtools; Hand
and edge tools, nec
HQ: Trumpf, Inc.
111 Hyde Rd
Farmington CT 06032
860 255-6000

(G-2787)
VIGUE HOLDING COMPANY INC
355 S Washington St (06062-2742)
PHONE.....................860 747-6000
Jeffrey Paul Hamel, *Pr*
Peter Lionell Vigue, *
▲ EMP: 45 EST: 1945
SQ FT: 28,000
SALES (est): 8.21MM **Privately Held**
Web: www.forestvillemachine.com
SIC: 3451 Screw machine products

(G-2788)
**WASHINGTON CONCRETE PDTS
INC**
328 S Washington St (06062-2752)
P.O. Box 176 (06062-0176)
PHONE.....................860 747-5242
Richard M Sewell, *Pr*
Nancy Sewell, *Sec*
EMP: 15 EST: 1960
SQ FT: 15,000
SALES (est): 2.5MM **Privately Held**
Web: www.washingtonconcrete.com
SIC: 5032 5999 3446 3272 Concrete and
cinder building products; Concrete
products, pre-cast; Architectural metalwork;
Concrete products, nec

Plantsville
Hartford County

(G-2789)
ATHENS INDUSTRIES INC
220 West St (06479-1145)
P.O. Box 487 (06489-0487)
PHONE.....................860 621-8957
Richard Emmings Senior, *Pr*
EMP: 9 EST: 1980
SQ FT: 5,000
SALES (est): 1.82MM **Privately Held**
Web: www.athensind.com
SIC: 3728 Aircraft assemblies,
subassemblies, and parts, nec

(G-2790)
DEBURR CO
201 Atwater St (06479-1653)
P.O. Box 24 (06479-0024)
PHONE.....................860 621-6634

Ben Divalentino, *Pr*
Gino Brino, *
EMP: 13 EST: 1976
SQ FT: 6,500
SALES (est): 383.97K **Privately Held**
SIC: 3471 Finishing, metals or formed
products

(G-2791)
**FORRATI MANUFACTURING &
TL LLC**
411 Summer St (06479-1122)
PHONE.....................860 426-1105
Mark Forauer, *Managing Member*
EMP: 7 EST: 2004
SALES (est): 484.05K **Privately Held**
SIC: 3599 Machine shop, jobbing and repair

(G-2792)
G M T MANUFACTURING CO INC
Also Called: Gmt Mfg
220 West St (06479-1145)
P.O. Box 324 (06479-0324)
PHONE.....................860 628-6757
Guy Touma, *Pr*
EMP: 8 EST: 1947
SQ FT: 11,000
SALES (est): 594.62K **Privately Held**
SIC: 3451 Screw machine products

(G-2793)
J J RYAN CORPORATION
Also Called: Rex Forge Div
355 Atwater St (06479-1653)
P.O. Box 39 (06479-0039)
PHONE.....................860 628-0393
Ronald Fontanella, *Pr*
Joseph P Polzella, *
EMP: 170 EST: 1975
SQ FT: 150,000
SALES (est): 22.55MM **Privately Held**
Web: www.rexforge.com
SIC: 3312 3423 3451 3462 Forgings, iron
and steel; Mechanics' hand tools; Screw
machine products; Iron and steel forgings

(G-2794)
**PRECISION FIRE FABRICATION
LLC**
8 West St (06479-1141)
PHONE.....................203 706-0749
EMP: 10 EST: 2017
SALES (est): 401.41K **Privately Held**
SIC: 3999 Manufacturing industries, nec

(G-2795)
SIGN PRO INC
60 Westfield Dr (06479-1753)
PHONE.....................860 229-1812
Peter Rappoccio, *Pr*
Suzanne Rappoccio, *Sec*
Keith Dubois, *Genl Mgr*
EMP: 15 EST: 1990
SQ FT: 16,000
SALES (est): 4.74MM **Privately Held**
Web: www.signpro-usa.com
SIC: 3993 Signs, not made in custom sign
painting shops

(G-2796)
**SOUTHINGTON TOOL & MFG
CORP**
Also Called: Stmc
300 Atwater St (06479-1643)
P.O. Box 595 (06489-0595)
PHONE.....................860 276-0021
Lynette Nadeau, *Pr*
Edward Kalat, *
EMP: 37 EST: 1970

SQ FT: 25,000
SALES (est): 5.59MM **Privately Held**
Web: www.stmc.com
SIC: 3841 3469 3495　Surgical stapling
　devices; Stamping metal for the trade; Wire
　springs

(G-2797)
SUPREME-LAKE MFG INC
455 Atwater St (06479-1642)
P.O. Box 19 (06479-0019)
PHONE......................860 621-8911
Gary N Dobrindt, *Pr*
David A Cano, *
Kevin Dobrindt, *
Richard L Fazzone, *
Robert C Fazzone, *
▲ **EMP:** 85 **EST:** 1965
SQ FT: 42,739
SALES (est): 8.49MM **Privately Held**
Web: www.supremelake.com
SIC: 3451　Screw machine products

(G-2798)
TIGER ENTERPRISES INC
379 Summer St (06479-1149)
PHONE......................860 621-9155
Rex Florian, *Pr*
Lance Florian, *
EMP: 28 **EST:** 1978
SQ FT: 30,000
SALES (est): 4.81MM **Privately Held**
Web: www.tigerstamping.com
SIC: 3469 3496 3429 3423　Stamping metal
　for the trade; Miscellaneous fabricated wire
　products; Hardware, nec; Hand and edge
　tools, nec

(G-2799)
TORREY S CRANE COMPANY
492 Summer St (06479-1123)
P.O. Box 374 (06479-0374)
PHONE......................860 628-4778
David Baker, *Pr*
Barbara Baker, *VP*
▲ **EMP:** 20 **EST:** 1933
SQ FT: 10,000
SALES (est): 4.2MM **Privately Held**
Web: www.torreycrane.com
SIC: 3356　Solder: wire, bar, acid core, and
　rosin core

Pleasant Valley
Litchfield County

(G-2800)
CENTURY WOODWORKING INC
40 River Rd (06063-3315)
P.O. Box 1097 (06083-1097)
PHONE......................860 379-7538
TOLL FREE: 800
Paul Richardson, *Pr*
Bradford W Hamel, *VP*
Ellyn Hamel, *Sec*
EMP: 19 **EST:** 1983
SQ FT: 12,000
SALES (est): 515.12K **Privately Held**
Web: www.centurywoodworking.com
SIC: 2431　Millwork

(G-2801)
GOULET ENTERPRISES INC
Also Called: Goulet Printery
115 New Hartford Rd (06063-3350)
PHONE......................860 379-0793
Paul Goulet, *Pr*
Barbara Goulet, *Sec*
Dennis M Goulet, *VP*
Cyril Goulet, *Sec*

Richard Goulet, *Asst Tr*
EMP: 16 **EST:** 1965
SQ FT: 10,000
SALES (est): 2.38MM **Privately Held**
Web: www.gouletprinting.com
SIC: 2752　Offset printing

(G-2802)
LIGHTSTAT INC
22 W West Hill Rd (06063-3221)
PHONE......................860 738-4111
EMP: 33 **EST:** 1983
SALES (est): 6.19MM **Privately Held**
Web: www.lightstat.com
SIC: 3822　Temperature controls, automatic

(G-2803)
**PLEASANT VALLEY FENCE CO
INC**
Also Called: Bazzano, J Cedar Products
Route 181 (06063)
P.O. Box 153 (06063-0153)
PHONE......................860 379-0088
Katherine Bazzano, *Pr*
Richard Bazzano, *VP*
Pat Bazzano, *Treas*
Pasquale Bazzano, *Sec*
EMP: 9 **EST:** 1949
SQ FT: 1,115
SALES (est): 481.19K **Privately Held**
Web: www.pleasantvalleyfence.net
SIC: 2499 3999　Fencing, wood; Pet supplies

(G-2804)
STERLING ENGINEERING CORP
236 New Hartford Rd (06063-3345)
P.O. Box 559 (06098-0559)
PHONE......................860 379-3366
John N Lavieri, *Pr*
Patricia L Minton, *
▲ **EMP:** 105 **EST:** 1946
SQ FT: 75,000
SALES (est): 15.6MM **Publicly Held**
Web: www.airindustriesgroup.com
SIC: 3599 3769　Machine shop, jobbing and
　repair; Space vehicle equipment, nec
PA: Air Industries Group
　1460 5th Ave
　Bay Shore NY 11706

(G-2805)
TRU-HITCH INC
16 W West Hill Rd (06063-3221)
PHONE......................860 379-7772
Martin Marola, *Pr*
Anthony Cuozzo, *Sec*
EMP: 12 **EST:** 1991
SQ FT: 13,000
SALES (est): 2.13MM **Privately Held**
Web: www.truhitch.com
SIC: 3714　Fifth wheel, motor vehicle

Plymouth
Litchfield County

(G-2806)
**CT CRANE AND HOIST SERVICE
LLC**
19 Burr Rd (06782-2220)
PHONE......................860 283-4320
George Frost, *Pr*
EMP: 7 **EST:** 1992
SALES (est): 784.85K **Privately Held**
Web: www.ctcrane.com
SIC: 5084 3531　Cranes, industrial;
　Backhoes, tractors, cranes, plows, and
　similar equipment

Pomfret
Windham County

(G-2807)
**FIBEROPTICS TECHNOLOGY
INC (PA)**
1 Quasset Rd (06258)
P.O. Box 286 (06258-0286)
PHONE......................860 928-0443
Steve Giamundo, *Pr*
Joan Loos, *
▲ **EMP:** 110 **EST:** 1977
SQ FT: 62,000
SALES (est): 37.12MM
SALES (corp-wide): 37.12MM **Privately
Held**
Web: www.fiberopticstech.com
SIC: 5065 3827　Electronic parts and
　equipment, nec; Optical instruments and
　apparatus

(G-2808)
**FIBEROPTICS TECHNOLOGY
INC**
1 Fiber Rd (06258-8003)
PHONE......................860 928-0443
August Loos, *Brnch Mgr*
EMP: 16
SALES (corp-wide): 37.12MM **Privately
Held**
Web: www.fiberopticstech.com
SIC: 3229　Glass fibers, textile
PA: Fiberoptics Technology, Inc.
　1 Quasset Rd
　Pomfret CT 06258
　860 928-0443

(G-2809)
LOOS & CO INC (PA)
Also Called: Wire Rope Div
16b Mashamoquet Rd (06258)
P.O. Box 98 (06258-0098)
PHONE......................860 928-7981
William Loos, *CEO*
Richard Griswold, *
Laura Taylor, *
◆ **EMP:** 300 **EST:** 1989
SQ FT: 175,000
SALES (est): 85.46MM
SALES (corp-wide): 85.46MM **Privately
Held**
Web: www.loosco.com
SIC: 3315 2298 5051 3357　Wire, ferrous/iron
　; Cordage and twine; Cable, wire;
　Nonferrous wiredrawing and insulating

(G-2810)
LOOS & CO INC
Jewel Wire Company
Rte 101 (06258)
P.O. Box 282 (06258-0282)
PHONE......................860 928-6681
Samuel Dixon, *Genl Mgr*
EMP: 57
SALES (corp-wide): 85.46MM **Privately
Held**
Web: www.loosco.com
SIC: 3315 3991　Wire, ferrous/iron; Brooms
　and brushes
PA: Loos & Co., Inc.
　16b Mashamoquet Rd
　Pomfret CT 06258
　860 928-7981

(G-2811)
SHARPE HILL VINEYARD INC
108 Wade Rd (06258)
P.O. Box 1 (06258-0001)

PHONE......................860 974-3549
Steven Vollweiler, *Pr*
Catherine Vollweiler, *
Jill R Vollweiler, *
EMP: 16 **EST:** 1993
SQ FT: 11,000
SALES (est): 534.88K **Privately Held**
Web: www.sharpehill.com
SIC: 2084 5812　Wines; Eating places

Pomfret Center
Windham County

(G-2812)
HULL FOREST PRODUCTS INC
101 Hampton Rd (06259-1712)
PHONE......................860 974-0127
William Boston Hull, *CEO*
Samuel I Hull, *
Jeffrey M Durst, *
◆ **EMP:** 42 **EST:** 1965
SQ FT: 61,000
SALES (est): 16.07MM **Privately Held**
Web: www.hullforest.com
SIC: 5031 2421 2426　Lumber: rough,
　dressed, and finished; Sawmills and
　planing mills, general; Hardwood dimension
　and flooring mills

(G-2813)
NESTLE USA INC
151 Mashamoquet Rd (06259-1727)
PHONE......................860 928-0082
Peter Argentine, *Brnch Mgr*
EMP: 81
Web: www.nestleusa.com
SIC: 2023　Evaporated milk
HQ: Nestle Usa, Inc.
　1812 N Moore St
　Arlington VA 22209
　703 682-4600

(G-2814)
WATERCURE FARM LLC
94 Hampton Rd (06259-1717)
PHONE......................860 208-4083
EMP: 7 **EST:** 2018
SALES (est): 490.66K **Privately Held**
Web: www.watercurefarm.com
SIC: 3556　Distillery machinery

Poquonock
Hartford County

(G-2815)
**PREVENTATIVE MAINTENANCE
CORP**
55 Tunxis St (06064)
PHONE......................860 683-1180
Richard Rzasa, *Pr*
Pamela Rzasa, *VP*
▲ **EMP:** 10 **EST:** 1987
SQ FT: 3,000
SALES (est): 781.3K **Privately Held**
SIC: 3471　Cleaning and descaling metal
　products

Portland
Middlesex County

(G-2816)
**AIREX RUBBER PRODUCTS
CORPORATION**
100 Indian Hill Ave (06480-1159)
P.O. Box 273 (06480-0273)

PHONE............860 342-0850
▼ EMP: 30 EST: 1943
SALES (est): 4.56MM Privately Held
Web: www.airexrubber.com
SIC: 3069 3544 3061 Molded rubber products; Special dies, tools, jigs, and fixtures; Mechanical rubber goods

(G-2817)
B & B EQUIPMENT LLC
80 Main St Ste D (06480-4825)
PHONE............860 342-5773
EMP: 8 EST: 2001
SQ FT: 45,000
SALES (est): 924.14K Privately Held
Web: www.bandbequip.com
SIC: 3565 Packaging machinery

(G-2818)
CONNECTICUT DEPARTMENT TRNSP
Also Called: Portland Connecticut Mch Sp
263 Freestone Ave (06480-1641)
PHONE............860 342-5996
Peter Mrowka, Mgr
EMP: 7
SALES (corp-wide): 40.68B Privately Held
Web: www.ct.gov
SIC: 3599 9621 Machine shop, jobbing and repair; Regulation, administration of transportation
HQ: Connecticut Department Of Transportation
2800 Berlin Tpke
Newington CT 06111

(G-2819)
ELITE GROUP MANUFACTURING LLC
173 E Cotton Hill Rd (06480-1036)
PHONE............860 788-6413
Catherine Ksiazek, Prin
EMP: 9 EST: 2012
SALES (est): 374.46K Privately Held
SIC: 3999 Manufacturing industries, nec

(G-2820)
JARVIS AIRFOIL INC
528 Glastonbury Tpke (06480-1099)
PHONE............860 342-5000
Wal Jarvis, Pr
▲ EMP: 88 EST: 1954
SQ FT: 50,000
SALES (est): 10.65MM
SALES (corp-wide): 18.45MM Privately Held
Web: www.jarvisairfoil.com
SIC: 3728 Aircraft assemblies, subassemblies, and parts, nec
PA: Jarvis Group, Inc.
229 Buckingham St
Hartford CT
860 278-2353

(G-2821)
PRECISION PLASTIC PRODUCTS INC
151 Freestone Ave (06480-1641)
PHONE............860 342-2233
Edward Organek Senior, Pr
Edward Organek Junior, VP
Rosemarie Organek, Sec
▲ EMP: 14 EST: 1981
SQ FT: 17,000
SALES (est): 2.43MM Privately Held
Web: www.pppinc.org
SIC: 3089 Injection molding of plastics

(G-2822)
REALEJO DONUTS INC
Also Called: Dunkin' Donuts
860 Portland Cobalt Rd (06480-1731)
PHONE............860 342-5120
Joseph Realejo, Owner
Frank Realejo, Pr
EMP: 11 EST: 1998
SALES (est): 179.37K Privately Held
Web: www.dunkindonuts.com
SIC: 5461 2051 Doughnuts; Doughnuts, except frozen

(G-2823)
REDIFOILS LLC
193 Pickering St (06480-1961)
PHONE............860 342-1500
◆ EMP: 10 EST: 2008
SQ FT: 10,000
SALES (est): 949.15K Privately Held
Web: www.redifoilsllc.com
SIC: 3312 Sheet or strip, steel, cold-rolled: own hot-rolled

(G-2824)
ROLLTECH PRECISION METALS
193 Pickering St (06480-1961)
PHONE............412 246-8846
EMP: 7 EST: 2017
SALES (est): 320.78K Privately Held
Web: www.rolltech.us
SIC: 3312 Blast furnaces and steel mills

(G-2825)
STANDARD KNAPP INC
Also Called: Standard-Knapp, Inc.
63 Pickering St (06480-1957)
PHONE............860 342-1100
James Michael Weaver, Pr
Robert Roiger, CEO
Mark Jehinges, COO
▲ EMP: 55 EST: 1893
SQ FT: 50,000
SALES (est): 19.27MM
SALES (corp-wide): 355.83K Privately Held
Web: www.standard-knapp.com
SIC: 3565 Packaging machinery
PA: Eol Packaging Experts Gmbh
Industriestr. 11-13
Kirchlengern NW 32278
522387910

(G-2826)
SUMMIT PLASTICS LLC
91 Main St (06480-1825)
PHONE............860 740-4482
EMP: 7 EST: 2016
SALES (est): 75.21K Privately Held
Web: www.summitplastic.com
SIC: 2821 Plastics materials and resins

(G-2827)
TILCON CONNECTICUT INC
Also Called: Tilcon Connecticut Portland
Black Rock Av (06480)
P.O. Box 311228 (06131-1228)
PHONE............860 342-1096
Joel Edman, Mgr
EMP: 8
SALES (corp-wide): 32.72B Privately Held
Web: www.tilconct.com
SIC: 3273 Ready-mixed concrete
HQ: Tilcon Connecticut Inc.
642 Black Rock Ave
New Britain CT 06052
860 224-6010

Preston
New London County

(G-2828)
PIELA ELECTRIC INC
16 Halls Mill Rd (06365-8503)
PHONE............860 889-8476
Joseph W Piela, Pr
Joanne Piela, Treas
Judith Piela Yasi, Sec
EMP: 15 EST: 1932
SQ FT: 50,000
SALES (est): 3.21MM Privately Held
Web: www.pielaelectric.com
SIC: 5063 7694 Motors, electric; Rewinding stators

Prospect
New Haven County

(G-2829)
BEN-ART MANUFACTURING CO INC
109 Waterbury Rd (06712-1295)
P.O. Box 7013 (06712-0013)
PHONE............203 758-4435
Benny A Paventy, Pr
Albert M Paventy, VP
Robert Paventy, Sec
EMP: 7 EST: 1952
SQ FT: 9,900
SALES (est): 800K Privately Held
SIC: 3469 Stamping metal for the trade

(G-2830)
BIG DIPPER ICE CREAM FCTRY INC
Also Called: Big Dipper
91 Waterbury Rd (06712-1223)
P.O. Box 7305 (06712-0305)
PHONE............203 758-3200
Barbara Rowe, Pr
Harry W Rowe Iii, VP
EMP: 18 EST: 1986
SQ FT: 2,880
SALES (est): 468.67K Privately Held
Web: www.bigdipper.com
SIC: 5812 2024 Ice cream stands or dairy bars; Ice cream and frozen deserts

(G-2831)
COMMSCOPE TECHNOLOGIES LLC
33 Union City Rd Ste 2 (06712-1550)
PHONE............203 699-4100
Peter Sandore, Brnch Mgr
EMP: 10
SIC: 3663 Radio and t.v. communications equipment
HQ: Commscope Technologies Llc
4 Westbrook Corp Ctr
Westchester IL 60154
800 366-3891

(G-2832)
CURTISS WOODWORKING INC
Also Called: Curtiss Woodworking
123 Union City Road, Route 68 (06712-1030)
PHONE............203 527-9305
Dale R Curtiss, Pr
Lisa Curtiss, VP
Isabelle Curtiss, Sec
EMP: 52 EST: 1990
SQ FT: 10,000
SALES (est): 1.89MM Privately Held
Web: www.curtisswoodworking.com
SIC: 2599 2431 Cabinets, factory; Millwork

(G-2833)
DEPENDABLE ENERGY INCORPORATED
Also Called: Dependable Fuel
9 Gramar Ave (06712-1017)
P.O. Box 7187 (06712-0187)
PHONE............203 758-5831
Glen Noble, Pr
EMP: 7 EST: 1989
SALES (est): 1.33MM Privately Held
Web: www.dependableenergy.net
SIC: 2869 1711 Fuels; Heating and air conditioning contractors

(G-2834)
ESI ELECTRONIC PRODUCTS CORP
109 Waterbury Rd (06712-1223)
P.O. Box 7326 (06712-0326)
PHONE............203 758-4401
Reza Khani, CEO
Donald Janezic, Treas
EMP: 29 EST: 1982
SQ FT: 20,000
SALES (est): 2.72MM Privately Held
Web: www.esielectronic.com
SIC: 3679 8711 Electronic circuits; Engineering services

(G-2835)
HIGHLAND WOODWORKING LLC
21 Gramar Ave (06712-1017)
PHONE............203 758-6625
Arthur Tyrrell, Prin
EMP: 11 EST: 2008
SALES (est): 448.84K Privately Held
SIC: 2431 Millwork

(G-2836)
MAX-TEK LLC
Also Called: Max-Tek Ue Superabrasive Mch
59 Cherry Cir (06712-6409)
PHONE............860 372-4900
Edward Elie, Pr
▲ EMP: 10 EST: 2004
SALES (est): 1.02MM Privately Held
SIC: 3599 Machine shop, jobbing and repair

(G-2837)
OXFORD GENERAL INDUSTRIES INC
3 Gramar Ave (06712-1017)
P.O. Box 7033 (06712-0033)
PHONE............203 758-4467
Donna Carnaroli, VP
Gordon Eckman, MFTG
Brian Barrett, VP
EMP: 11 EST: 1950
SQ FT: 25,000
SALES (est): 2.17MM Privately Held
Web: www.ogict.com
SIC: 3499 3544 3542 Machine bases, metal ; Special dies, tools, jigs, and fixtures; Machine tools, metal forming type

(G-2838)
P I LIQUIDATING INC (PA)
32 Gramar Ave (06712-1016)
P.O. Box 7075 (06712-0075)
PHONE............203 758-6651
David L Lewis, Pr
Eugene R Lewis, *
▲ EMP: 35 EST: 1978
SALES (est): 6.17MM
SALES (corp-wide): 6.17MM Privately Held

Web: www.polarcentral.com
SIC: 2821 Polystyrene resins

(G-2839)
PACKARD INC
Also Called: Packard Specialties
6 Industrial Rd (06712-1018)
P.O. Box 7238 (06712-0238)
PHONE..............................203 758-6219
John F Jones, *Pr*
Carol Jones, *VP*
EMP: 20 EST: 1980
SQ FT: 15,000
SALES (est): 2.11MM **Privately Held**
Web:
www.automationmachinebuilders.com
SIC: 3565 3569 Packaging machinery;
　Assembly machines, non-metalworking

(G-2840)
PROSPECT MACHINE PRODUCTS INC
139 Union City Rd (06712-1031)
P.O. Box 7016 (06712-0016)
PHONE..............................203 758-4448
Richard Laurenzi, *CEO*
EMP: 15 EST: 1949
SQ FT: 20,000
SALES (est): 4.51MM **Privately Held**
Web: www.pmpdeepdraw.com
SIC: 3469 8711 Stamping metal for the trade
　; Machine tool design

(G-2841)
PROSPECT PRINTING LLC
16 Waterbury Rd (06712-1255)
P.O. Box 7242 (06712-0242)
PHONE..............................203 758-6007
EMP: 10 EST: 1982
SQ FT: 5,500
SALES (est): 1.02MM **Privately Held**
Web: www.prospectprinting.net
SIC: 2752 Offset printing

(G-2842)
SGA COMPONENTS GROUP LLC
13 Gramar Ave (06712-1017)
PHONE..............................203 758-3702
EMP: 8 EST: 1983
SQ FT: 5,000
SALES (est): 600K **Privately Held**
Web: www.sgalt.com
SIC: 3451 Screw machine products

(G-2843)
SHELDON PRECISION LLC
10 Industrial Rd (06712-1018)
PHONE..............................203 758-4441
John Hoskins Junior, *CEO*
EMP: 50 EST: 2014
SQ FT: 17,500
SALES (est): 12MM **Privately Held**
Web: www.sheldonprecision.com
SIC: 3451 Screw machine products

(G-2844)
TSS & A INC
Also Called: Triple Stitch Sportswear
100 Union City Rd (06712-1027)
P.O. Box 7036 (06712-0036)
PHONE..............................203 758-6303
EMP: 13 EST: 1992
SQ FT: 3,000
SALES (est): 2.97MM **Privately Held**
Web: www.triplestitch.com
SIC: 2395 7336 Embroidery products,
　except Schiffli machine; Silk screen design

Putnam
Windham County

(G-2845)
AEROTECH FASTENERS INC
1 Ridge Rd (06260-3034)
PHONE..............................860 928-6300
Frank Dirienzo, *Pr*
Erik Sandberg-diment, *Pr*
Frank Di Rienzo, *VP*
EMP: 13 EST: 1991
SQ FT: 18,000
SALES (est): 2.03MM **Privately Held**
Web: www.aerotechfasteners.us
SIC: 3452 Screws, metal

(G-2846)
BARNES CONCRETE CO INC
873 Providence Pike (06260-2606)
PHONE..............................860 928-7242
David Barnes, *Pr*
Bruce Barnes, *VP*
EMP: 35 EST: 1968
SQ FT: 2,500
SALES (est): 3.96MM **Privately Held**
Web: www.barnesconcreteco.com
SIC: 3273 Ready-mixed concrete

(G-2847)
CAROLINA PRECISION TECHNOLOGIE
51 Ridge Rd (06260-3034)
PHONE..............................860 315-9017
EMP: 12 EST: 2020
SALES (est): 948.18K **Privately Held**
Web: www.carolinaprecision.com
SIC: 3599 Machine shop, jobbing and repair

(G-2848)
CENTRAL CONSTRUCTION INDS LLC
Also Called: CCI
30 Harris St (06260-1907)
P.O. Box 229 (06260-0229)
PHONE..............................860 963-8902
Bruce Richards, *Managing Member*
EMP: 20 EST: 1996
SALES (est): 9.53MM **Privately Held**
Web: www.ccict.com
SIC: 1542 1521 3441 Commercial and
　office building, new construction; Single-
　family housing construction; Fabricated
　structural metal

(G-2849)
CHASE GRAPHICS INC
124 School St (06260-1613)
PHONE..............................860 315-9006
James St Jean, *Pr*
Debra St Jean, *VP*
EMP: 16 EST: 1966
SQ FT: 4,500
SALES (est): 2.33MM **Privately Held**
Web: www.chasegraphics.net
SIC: 2752 Offset printing

(G-2850)
CONNECTICUT TOOL CO INC
6 Highland Dr (06260-3007)
P.O. Box 90 (06260-0090)
PHONE..............................860 928-0565
Philip Durand, *Ch*
Claire Durand, *Sec*
EMP: 20 EST: 1981
SQ FT: 13,500
SALES (est): 2.05MM **Privately Held**
Web: www.conntool.com

SIC: 3089 3544 Injection molding of plastics
　; Special dies, tools, jigs, and fixtures

(G-2851)
CONNTROL INTERNATIONAL INC
135 Park Rd (06260-3032)
P.O. Box 645 (06260-0645)
PHONE..............................860 928-0567
Ronald Braaten, *Pr*
Willie O Pritchard, *Sec*
EMP: 12 EST: 1985
SQ FT: 13,000
SALES (est): 2.21MM **Privately Held**
Web: www.conntrol.com
SIC: 3625 Relays and industrial controls

(G-2852)
D & M GROUP LLC
Also Called: Putnam Science Academy
18 Maple St (06260-1816)
PHONE..............................860 928-5010
Tieqiang Ding, *Pr*
Ying Ma, *Pr*
EMP: 11 EST: 2015
SALES (est): 781.64K **Privately Held**
SIC: 3621 Synchros

(G-2853)
DIMENSION-POLYANT INC
78 Highland Dr (06260-3037)
PHONE..............................860 928-8314
John E Gluek Junior, *Pr*
Karin Ruckwardt, *
Don E Swanson, *
▲ **EMP: 40 EST:** 1979
SQ FT: 50,000
SALES (est): 6.91MM **Privately Held**
Web: www.dimension-polyant.com
SIC: 2211 2221 2394 Sail cloth;
　Broadwoven fabric mills, manmade;
　Canvas and related products

(G-2854)
ENSINGER PRCSION CMPONENTS INC (DH)
Also Called: Plastock
11 Danco Rd (06260-3001)
PHONE..............................860 928-7911
Matt Mckenney, *Genl Mgr*
▲ **EMP: 65 EST:** 1996
SQ FT: 66,000
SALES (est): 16.88MM
SALES (corp-wide): 632.07MM **Privately Held**
Web: www.ensinger-pc.com
SIC: 3089 Injection molding of plastics
HQ: Ensinger Industries, Inc.
　365 Meadowlands Blvd
　Washington PA 15301
　724 746-6050

(G-2855)
FOSTER CORPORATION (HQ)
Also Called: Foster Delivery Science
45 Ridge Rd (06260-3034)
PHONE..............................860 928-4102
Larry Acquarulo, *CEO*
Hank Hague, *
▲ **EMP: 30 EST:** 1989
SQ FT: 43,000
SALES (est): 25.82MM **Privately Held**
Web: www.fostercomp.com
SIC: 3087 Custom compound purchased
　resins
PA: Polymedex Discovery Group, Inc.
　45 Ridge Rd
　Putnam CT 06260

(G-2856)
FOSTER CORPORATION
38 Ridge Rd (06260-3035)
PHONE..............................860 377-7117
EMP: 34
SIC: 3087 Custom compound purchased
　resins
HQ: Foster Corporation
　45 Ridge Rd
　Putnam CT 06260

(G-2857)
FOSTER DELIVERY SCIENCE INC (HQ)
Also Called: Sever Pharma Solutions
36 Ridge Rd (06260-3035)
PHONE..............................860 541-5280
Kenneth Stokholm, *CEO*
Kenneth Stokholm, *Pr*
EMP: 10 EST: 2015
SALES (est): 5.62MM
SALES (corp-wide): 1.1MM **Privately Held**
Web: www.fosterdeliveryscience.com
SIC: 2834 Pharmaceutical preparations
PA: If Metall Klubben Sever Pharma
　Solutions
　Agneslundsvagen 27
　MalmO 212 1

(G-2858)
FOSTER DELIVERY SCIENCE INC
45 Ridge Rd (06260-3034)
PHONE..............................860 630-4515
Lawrence Acquarulo, *CEO*
EMP: 20
SALES (corp-wide): 1.1MM **Privately Held**
Web: www.fostercomp.com
SIC: 2834 Tablets, pharmaceutical
HQ: Foster Delivery Science, Inc.
　36 Ridge Rd
　Putnam CT 06260
　860 541-5280

(G-2859)
HARDING COMPANY INC (HQ)
58 Highland Dr (06260-3007)
PHONE..............................603 778-7070
Reitzel O Swaim, *Pr*
EMP: 7 EST: 1959
SALES (est): 5.51MM
SALES (corp-wide): 50.56MM **Privately Held**
SIC: 3496 Miscellaneous fabricated wire
　products
PA: Alp Industries, Inc.
　512 N Market St Ste 100
　Lancaster PA 17603
　610 384-1300

(G-2860)
HARDING COMPANY INC
Also Called: Cableworks
58 Highland Dr (06260-3007)
PHONE..............................860 928-0475
Shawn L Ober, *Pr*
EMP: 12
SALES (corp-wide): 50.56MM **Privately Held**
SIC: 3496 5131 Miscellaneous fabricated
　wire products; Nylon piece goods, woven
HQ: Harding Company, Inc.
　58 Highland Dr
　Putnam CT 06260

(G-2861)
INTERNATIONAL PAPER COMPANY
International Paper

175 Park Rd (06260-3040)
PHONE..............................860 928-7901
Don Davis, *Mgr*
EMP: 109
SALES (corp-wide): 21.16B **Publicly Held**
Web: www.internationalpaper.com
SIC: 2621 Paper mills
PA: International Paper Company
6400 Poplar Ave
Memphis TN 38197
901 419-7000

(G-2862)

JAMES WRIGHT PRECISION PDTS

20 Mechanics St (06260-1315)
P.O. Box 924 (06260-0924)
PHONE..............................860 928-7756
Robert A Main Junior, *Pr*
William Main, *
Susan Main, *
EMP: 43 **EST:** 1975
SQ FT: 7,500
SALES (est): 324.75K
SALES (corp-wide): 31.25MM **Privately Held**
Web: www.jwpp.com
SIC: 3451 Screw machine products
PA: Main, Robert A & Sons Holding
Company Inc
20-21 Wagaraw Rd
Fair Lawn NJ 07410
201 447-3700

(G-2863)

LEISURE ZONE STORES INC

Also Called: Leisure Zone
164 Providence Pike (06260-2529)
P.O. Box 489 (11040-0489)
PHONE..............................860 963-1181
Bob Quier, *Pr*
Denise Wellspeak, *Sec*
EMP: 10 **EST:** 1997
SQ FT: 3,400
SALES (est): 1.03MM **Privately Held**
Web: www.onsitedesigns.com
SIC: 3088 Hot tubs, plastics or fiberglass

(G-2864)

MAGNETIC TECHNOLOGIES LTD

31 Highland Dr (06260-3010)
P.O. Box 257 (01540-0257)
PHONE..............................508 987-3303
John E Deluca, *Pr*
Jonathan Ely, *Dir*
Karen J Deluca, *Sec*
▲ **EMP:** 15 **EST:** 1984
SQ FT: 13,000
SALES (est): 4.09MM **Privately Held**
Web: www.magnetictech.com
SIC: 3568 3625 Clutches, except vehicular;
Relays and industrial controls

(G-2865)

NATIONAL CHROMIUM COMPANY INC

Also Called: National Chromium Co Inc Conn
10 Senexet Rd (06260-1039)
PHONE..............................860 928-7965
John Miller, *Pr*
Whitby K Ellsworth, *Sec*
EMP: 22 **EST:** 1941
SQ FT: 9,000
SALES (est): 1.08MM **Privately Held**
Web: www.nationalchromium.com
SIC: 3471 Electroplating of metals or
formed products

(G-2866)

NEW ENGLAND PLASMA DEV CORP

14 Highland Dr (06260-3007)
P.O. Box 369 (06260-0369)
PHONE..............................860 928-6561
Peter J Olshewski, *Pr*
Maureen Olshewski, *VP*
EMP: 10 **EST:** 1988
SQ FT: 3,800
SALES (est): 1.87MM **Privately Held**
Web: www.neplasma.com
SIC: 3541 Machine tools, metal cutting type

(G-2867)

NUTMEG CONTAINER CORPORATION (HQ)

Also Called: Unicorr Packaging
100 Canal St (06260-1912)
PHONE..............................860 963-6727
Harry A Perkins, *CEO*
Charles Pious, *
James Pious, *
EMP: 100 **EST:** 1986
SQ FT: 25,000
SALES: 51.61MM
SALES (corp-wide): 151.34MM **Privately Held**
Web: www.unicorr.com
SIC: 2653 Boxes, corrugated: made from
purchased materials
PA: Connecticut Container Corp.
455 Sackett Point Rd
North Haven CT 06473
203 248-2161

(G-2868)

OPTICONX INC

45 Danco Rd (06260-3001)
PHONE..............................888 748-6855
EMP: 25 **EST:** 1996
SQ FT: 16,000
SALES (est): 4.79MM **Privately Held**
Web: www.opticonx.com
SIC: 3661 Fiber optics communications
equipment

(G-2869)

PALLFLEX PRODUCTS COMPANY

125 Kennedy Dr (06260-1945)
PHONE..............................860 928-7761
Ronald Hoffman, *Ch*
Lawrence J Kingsley, *
Lisa Mcdermott, *CFO*
▲ **EMP:** 50 **EST:** 1990
SALES (est): 11.41MM
SALES (corp-wide): 31.47B **Publicly Held**
SIC: 3569 Filters, general line: industrial
HQ: Pall Corporation
25 Harbor Park Dr
Port Washington NY 11050
516 484-5400

(G-2870)

POLYMEDEX DISCOVERY GROUP INC (PA)

45 Ridge Rd (06260-3034)
PHONE..............................860 928-4102
Lawrence A Acquarulo Junior, *Pr*
James V Dandeneau, *VP*
Hank Hague, *COO*
EMP: 131 **EST:** 2009
SALES (est): 41.62MM **Privately Held**
Web: www.fostercomp.com
SIC: 3082 3083 6719 Tubes, unsupported
plastics; Laminated plastics plate and sheet
; Investment holding companies, except
banks

(G-2871)

R W E INC

91 Highland Dr (06260-3010)
P.O. Box 431 (06260-0431)
PHONE..............................860 974-1101
Eric Whittenburg, *Pr*
Robin Whittenburg, *
EMP: 34 **EST:** 1985
SQ FT: 15,000
SALES (est): 6.33MM **Privately Held**
Web: www.erwinc.com
SIC: 3444 Sheet metal specialties, not
stamped

(G-2872)

RAWSON DEVELOPMENT INC

205 Munyan Rd (06260-2508)
PHONE..............................860 928-4536
Allan Rawson, *Pr*
Richard A Rawson, *VP*
Kathleen Rawson, *Treas*
Harold Hopkins, *VP*
EMP: 16 **EST:** 1946
SQ FT: 1,500
SALES (est): 1.49MM **Privately Held**
SIC: 1442 5032 5211 Construction sand
and gravel; Sand, construction; Sand and
gravel

(G-2873)

RENCHEL TOOL LLC

51 Ridge Rd (06260-3034)
PHONE..............................,,860 315-9017
Ronald Williams, *Pr*
Brenda Williams, *Sec*
Robert Mccurry, *VP*
Shane Szall, *VP*
EMP: 12 **EST:** 1982
SQ FT: 3,000
SALES (est): 2.11MM **Privately Held**
Web: www.carolinaprecision.com
SIC: 3599 Machine shop, jobbing and repair

(G-2874)

SHOPPER-TURNPIKE CORPORATION

Also Called: Shoppers Guide
70 Main St (06260-1918)
P.O. Box 529 (06260-0529)
PHONE..............................860 928-3040
Dennis E Neumann, *Pr*
Wilbur D Neumann, *Pr*
EMP: 10 **EST:** 1956
SQ FT: 2,000
SALES (est): 272.1K **Privately Held**
Web: www.shopperturnpike.com
SIC: 2741 Guides: publishing only, not
printed on site

(G-2875)

SONOCO PRTECTIVE SOLUTIONS INC

29 Park Rd (06260-3044)
PHONE..............................860 928-7795
Ken Blandina, *Manager*
EMP: 51
SQ FT: 80,000
SALES (corp-wide): 7.25B **Publicly Held**
Web: www.sonoco.com
SIC: 3086 2821 2671 Packaging and
shipping materials, foamed plastics;
Plastics materials and resins; Paper;
coated and laminated packaging
HQ: Sonoco Protective Solutions, Inc.
3930 N Ventura Dr
Arlington Heights IL 60004
847 398-0110

(G-2876)

SPECTRAL LLC

Also Called: Spectral Products
111 Highland Dr (06260-3010)
PHONE..............................860 928-7726
▲ **EMP:** 10 **EST:** 2003
SALES (est): 1.77MM **Privately Held**
Web: www.spectralproducts.com
SIC: 3826 Analytical instruments

(G-2877)

SUPERIOR PLAS EXTRUSION CO INC (PA)

Also Called: Town of Putnam
5 Highland Dr (06260-3010)
PHONE..............................860 963-1976
David P Kingeter, *Pr*
Steven M Ryan, *
Denis A Chaves, *
▲ **EMP:** 21 **EST:** 1997
SQ FT: 50,000
SALES (est): 7.6MM **Privately Held**
Web: www.impactplastics.co
SIC: 3089 Injection molding of plastics

(G-2878)

US BUTTON CORPORATION

328 Kennedy Dr (06260-1629)
PHONE..............................860 928-2707
Larry Jacobs, *Pr*
◆ **EMP:** 140 **EST:** 1990
SQ FT: 100,000
SALES (est): 9.46MM **Privately Held**
Web: www.usbutton.com
SIC: 3965 Buttons and parts

(G-2879)

WINDHAM CONTAINER CORPORATION

30 Park Rd (06260-3030)
P.O. Box 944 (06260-0944)
PHONE..............................860 928-7934
Gordie Mauer, *Pr*
Jeanine Mauer, *Treas*
EMP: 19 **EST:** 1958
SQ FT: 45,000
SALES (est): 1.03MM **Privately Held**
Web: www.windhamcontainer.com
SIC: 2653 2671 Boxes, corrugated: made
from purchased materials; Paper; coated
and laminated packaging

Redding
Fairfield County

(G-2880)

AMERICAN ACTUATOR CORPORATION

292 Newtown Tpke (06896-2418)
P.O. Box 41 (10804-0041)
PHONE..............................203 324-6334
Joseph Fowler, *Pr*
Evelyn Fowler, *Sec*
EMP: 9 **EST:** 1951
SQ FT: 1,800
SALES (est): 203.48K **Privately Held**
Web: www.americanactuator.com
SIC: 3542 Machine tools, metal forming type

(G-2881)

ARMORED SHIELD TECHNOLOGIES

Also Called: Cable Manufacturing Business
3655 W Mcfadden Ave (06896)
PHONE..............................714 848-5796
Christopher Badinelli, *Pr*
▲ **EMP:** 19 **EST:** 1998

SQ FT: 10,000
SALES (est): 502.3K **Privately Held**
SIC: 3496 Cable, uninsulated wire: made from purchased wire

(G-2882)
GOLD LINE CONNECTOR INC (PA)
Also Called: Gold Line
40 Great Pasture Rd (06896-2303)
PHONE...............................203 938-2588
Martin Miller, *Pr*
Marjorie Miller, *
EMP: 25 **EST:** 1961
SALES (est): 2.28MM
SALES (corp-wide): 2.28MM **Privately Held**
Web: www.gold-line.com
SIC: 3825 3663 3643 3829 Radio apparatus analyzers, nec; Citizens' band (CB) radio; Cord connectors, electric; Measuring and controlling devices, nec

(G-2883)
SCHARF AND BREIT INC
9 High Ridge Rd (06896-2020)
PHONE...............................516 282-0287
Christopher Aives, *Pr*
EMP: 7 **EST:** 1939
SALES (est): 235.21K **Privately Held**
SIC: 2329 Sweaters and sweater jackets, men's and boys'

Ridgefield
Fairfield County

(G-2884)
360ALUMNI LLC
85 Ethan Allen Hwy (06877-6226)
PHONE...............................203 253-5860
Christina Balotescu, *CEO*
EMP: 15 **EST:** 2014
SQ FT: 1,200
SALES (est): 1.15MM **Privately Held**
Web: www.360alumni.com
SIC: 7372 Prepackaged software

(G-2885)
AMY KAHN RUSSELL LLC (PA)
225 S Salem Rd (06877-4832)
PHONE...............................203 438-2133
Amy Kahn Russell, *Owner*
EMP: 10 **EST:** 1985
SALES (est): 1.05MM
SALES (corp-wide): 1.05MM **Privately Held**
Web: www.amykahnrussell.com
SIC: 3911 Jewelry, precious metal

(G-2886)
BOEHRINGER INGELHEIM CORP (DH)
900 Ridgebury Rd (06877-1058)
P.O. Box 368 (06877-0368)
PHONE...............................203 798-9988
Paul Fonteyne, *Prin*
Stefan Rinn, *
◆ **EMP:** 1500 **EST:** 1984
SQ FT: 266,000
SALES (est): 2.12B
SALES (corp-wide): 23.34B **Privately Held**
Web: www.boehringer-ingelheim.com
SIC: 2834 6221 Medicines, capsuled or ampuled; Commodity traders, contracts
HQ: Boehringer Ingelheim Usa Corporation
900 Ridgebury Rd
Ridgefield CT 06877

(G-2887)
BOEHRINGER INGELHEIM DATA DIME
900 Ridgebury Rd (06877-1058)
P.O. Box 1088 (06877-9088)
PHONE...............................800 203-2916
EMP: 14 **EST:** 2011
SALES (est): 1.84MM **Privately Held**
SIC: 2834 Pharmaceutical preparations

(G-2888)
BOEHRINGER INGELHEIM USA CORP (DH)
Also Called: Boehringer Ingelheim
900 Ridgebury Rd (06877-1058)
P.O. Box 368 (06877-0368)
PHONE...............................203 798-9988
Andreas Barner, *Ch Bd*
Paul Fonteyne, *CEO*
Marla S Persky, *Sr VP*
Stefan Rinn, *Sr VP*
▲ **EMP:** 26 **EST:** 2006
SALES (est): 2.13B
SALES (corp-wide): 23.34B **Privately Held**
Web: www.boehringer-ingelheim.com
SIC: 2834 Medicines, capsuled or ampuled
HQ: Boehringer Ingelheim
Auslandsbeteiligungs Gmbh
Binger Str. 173
Ingelheim Am Rhein RP 55218
6132770

(G-2889)
BOEHRNGER INGELHEIM ROXANE INC
900 Ridgebury Rd (06877-1058)
P.O. Box 1088 (06877-9088)
PHONE...............................800 243-0127
Glenn Marina, *Pr*
EMP: 30 **EST:** 2009
SIC: 2834 Pharmaceutical preparations

(G-2890)
BOEHRNGER INGLHEIM PHRMCTCALS
39 Briar Ridge Rd (06877-1005)
PHONE...............................203 798-9988
EMP: 174
SALES (corp-wide): 23.34B **Privately Held**
Web: www.bi-animalhealth.com
SIC: 2834 Drugs acting on the cardiovascular system, except diagnostic
HQ: Boehringer Ingelheim Pharmaceuticals, Inc.
900 Ridgebury Rd
Ridgefield CT 06877

(G-2891)
BOEHRNGER INGLHEIM PHRMCTCALS (DH)
Also Called: Boehringer Ingelheim
900 Ridgebury Rd (06877-1058)
P.O. Box 368 (06877-0368)
PHONE...............................203 798-9988
Paul Fonteyne, *CEO*
Andreas Barner, *Pr*
Stefan Rinn Senior, *VP*
▲ **EMP:** 1300 **EST:** 1971
SQ FT: 1,326,000
SALES (est): 1.07B
SALES (corp-wide): 23.34B **Privately Held**
Web: www.bi-animalhealth.com
SIC: 2834 Drugs acting on the cardiovascular system, except diagnostic
HQ: Boehringer Ingelheim Corporation
900 Ridgebury Rd
Ridgefield CT 06877
203 798-9988

(G-2892)
BRANDSTROM INSTRUMENTS INC
85 Ethan Allen Hwy (06877-6226)
PHONE...............................203 544-9341
Arvid A Brandstrom, *CEO*
Thomas Allard, *
▼ **EMP:** 25 **EST:** 1972
SQ FT: 5,000
SALES (est): 2.56MM **Privately Held**
Web: www.brandstrominstruments.com
SIC: 3728 3812 Aircraft parts and equipment, nec; Infrared object detection equipment

(G-2893)
CONTINUITY ENGINE INC
426 Main St # 2 (06877-4508)
PHONE...............................866 631-5556
Andy Greenawalt, *CEO*
EMP: 11 **EST:** 2012
SALES (est): 266.51K **Privately Held**
Web: www.continuityengine.com
SIC: 3599 7372 Machine and other job shop work; Business oriented computer software

(G-2894)
CUSTOM TS N MORE LLC
135 Ethan Allen Hwy (06877-6207)
PHONE...............................203 438-1592
Arthur F Crabtree, *Owner*
EMP: 8 **EST:** 2009
SALES (est): 397.84K **Privately Held**
Web: www.tsandmore.com
SIC: 2759 Screen printing

(G-2895)
CV CUSTOM VOLT
162 Danbury Rd (06877)
PHONE...............................203 431-7646
Thomas P Brennan, *Pr*
EMP: 8 **EST:** 2007
SALES (est): 97.89K **Privately Held**
SIC: 3272 Burial vaults, concrete or precast terrazzo

(G-2896)
DONELAN FMLY WINE CELLARS LLC
34 Circle Dr E (06877-1920)
PHONE...............................707 591-0782
EMP: 7 **EST:** 2010
SALES (est): 269.41K **Privately Held**
SIC: 2084 Wines

(G-2897)
EXPLAIN EVERYTHING SALES INC
54 Danbury Rd Unit 425 (06877-4019)
P.O. Box 1019 (06877-9019)
PHONE...............................646 825-8552
Reshan Richards, *CEO*
EMP: 7 **EST:** 2015
SALES (est): 56.54K **Privately Held**
Web: www.explaineverything.com
SIC: 7372 Business oriented computer software

(G-2898)
HERSAM ACORN CMNTY PUBG LLC (HQ)
16 Bailey Ave (06877-4512)
PHONE...............................203 438-6544
EMP: 9 **EST:** 2007
SALES (est): 4.81MM
SALES (corp-wide): 9.7MM **Privately Held**
Web: www.acorn-online.com

SIC: 2711 Newspapers, publishing and printing
PA: Hersam Acorn Newspapers, Llc
16 Bailey Ave
Ridgefield CT 06877
203 438-6000

(G-2899)
HERSAM ACORN NEWSPAPERS LLC (PA)
16 Bailey Ave (06877-4512)
P.O. Box 605 (06840-0605)
PHONE...............................203 438-6000
Martin Hersam, *Pt*
Thomas Nash, *Pt*
EMP: 10 **EST:** 1997
SALES (est): 9.7MM
SALES (corp-wide): 9.7MM **Privately Held**
SIC: 2711 Commercial printing and newspaper publishing combined

(G-2900)
KCR TIRE & AUTO INC
861 Ethan Allen Hwy (06877-2801)
PHONE...............................203 438-4042
Richard Desrochers, *Admn*
EMP: 11 **EST:** 2014
SALES (est): 758.68K **Privately Held**
Web: www.acetireauto.com
SIC: 3011 Automobile tires, pneumatic

(G-2901)
LITIGATION ANALYTICS INC (PA)
127 Main St (06877-4932)
P.O. Box 1105 (06877-9105)
PHONE...............................203 431-0300
John Scarbrough, *Pr*
John Morsen, *Sec*
EMP: 8 **EST:** 1990
SQ FT: 3,000
SALES (est): 1.8MM **Privately Held**
Web: www.litigationanalytics.com
SIC: 8732 7372 Business analysis; Prepackaged software

(G-2902)
MARCO INTERNATIONAL INC
Also Called: Marco Manufacturing
100 Danbury Rd Ste 101 (06877-4122)
PHONE...............................203 894-8000
Claude L Buller, *Pr*
Sally Hubiak, *CFO*
▼ **EMP:** 75 **EST:** 1991
SQ FT: 5,300
SALES (est): 25MM **Privately Held**
SIC: 5045 5065 3577 3674 Computers, peripherals, and software; Electronic parts and equipment, nec; Computer peripheral equipment, nec; Semiconductors and related devices

(G-2903)
NORTHERN TIER ENERGY LLC (DH)
38c Grove St Ste 5 (06877-4669)
PHONE...............................203 244-6550
EMP: 14 **EST:** 2010
SALES (est): 761.07MM **Publicly Held**
SIC: 1311 Crude petroleum production
HQ: Northern Tier Energy Lp
1250 W Washington St # 300
Tempe AZ 85288
602 302-5450

(G-2904)
PLANET BIOPHARMACEUTICALS INC
96 Danbury Rd (06877-4069)
PHONE...............................800 255-3749

EMP: 8 **EST:** 2008
SALES (est): 153.52K **Privately Held**
SIC: 3564   Blowers and fans

(G-2905)
PLANET TECHNOLOGIES INC
96 Danbury Rd (06877-4069)
PHONE..............................800 255-3749
Edward J Steube, *Pr*
Scott L Glenn, *
Francesca Dinota, *CAO**
Bret Megargel, *
EMP: 60 **EST:** 1991
SQ FT: 13,317
SALES (est): 3.88MM **Privately Held**
SIC: 3564   Air cleaning systems

(G-2906)
R4 TECHNOLOGIES INC (PA)
Also Called: Conversion Marketing
38c Grove St Ste 201 (06877-4667)
PHONE..............................203 461-7100
Paul Breitenbach, *Pr*
Matthew Breitenbach, *
Lisa Lersner, *
▲ **EMP:** 39 **EST:** 2001
SQ FT: 2,500
SALES (est): 5.13MM
SALES (corp-wide): 5.13MM **Privately Held**
Web: www.r4.ai
SIC: 8742 7372 8748 7371   Marketing consulting services; Prepackaged software; Business consulting, nec; Custom computer programming services

(G-2907)
SEWN IN AMERICA INC (PA)
Also Called: Sia
54 Danbury Rd Ste 240 (06877-4019)
PHONE..............................203 438-9149
John Mc Loughlin, *Pr*
▲ **EMP:** 80 **EST:** 2005
SALES (est): 4.85MM **Privately Held**
Web: www.sewninamerica.com
SIC: 2326   Men's and boy's work clothing

(G-2908)
ULLMAN DEVICES CORPORATION
664 Danbury Rd (06877-2720)
P.O. Box 398 (06877-0398)
PHONE..............................203 438-6577
Edward Coleman, *Pr*
Steve Gorden, *
Benjamin Ungar, *
Janet Lemma, *
Bernard Jaffe, *
▲ **EMP:** 70 **EST:** 1935
SQ FT: 15,000
SALES (est): 8.49MM **Privately Held**
Web: www.saundersmidwest.com
SIC: 3423   Mechanics' hand tools

(G-2909)
WALPOLE OUTDOORS LLC
Also Called: Walpole Fence Company
346 Ethan Allen Hwy (06877-4703)
PHONE..............................508 668-2800
Robert Booth, *Brnch Mgr*
EMP: 20
SQ FT: 1,000
SALES (corp-wide): 50.41MM **Privately Held**
Web: www.walpoleoutdoors.com
SIC: 2499 5211 5712 2452   Fencing, wood; Fencing; Outdoor and garden furniture; Prefabricated wood buildings
PA: Walpole Outdoors Llc
   255 Patriot Pl

Foxboro MA 02035
508 668-2800

Riverside
Fairfield County

(G-2910)
PORCELANOSA NEW YORK INC
1063 E Putnam Ave (06878-1305)
PHONE..............................203 698-7618
Reana Coursey, *Brnch Mgr*
EMP: 11
Web: www.porcelanosa-usa.com
SIC: 5032 3253   Ceramic wall and floor tile, nec; Ceramic wall and floor tile
HQ: Porcelanosa New York, Inc.
   600 State Rt 17
   Ramsey NJ 07446
   408 467-9400

(G-2911)
WEIGH & TEST SYSTEMS INC
Also Called: Wagner Instruments
17 Wilmot Ln Ste 2 (06878-1633)
P.O. Box 1217 (06836-1217)
PHONE..............................203 698-9681
William B Wagner, *Pr*
Pierrette Wagner, *VP*
▲ **EMP:** 10 **EST:** 1969
SQ FT: 2,000
SALES (est): 965.97K **Privately Held**
SIC: 3829   Measuring and controlling devices, nec

Riverton
Litchfield County

(G-2912)
DURALITE INCORPORATED
15 School St (06065-1013)
PHONE..............................860 379-3113
Mark Jessen, *Pr*
Elliott E Jessen, *Ch Bd*
Carolyn M Jessen, *Sec*
Jeanette Smith, *Treas*
Dale L Smith, *VP*
▲ **EMP:** 10 **EST:** 1946
SQ FT: 5,500
SALES (est): 2MM **Privately Held**
Web: www.duralite.com
SIC: 3567   Heating units and devices, industrial: electric

Rockfall
Middlesex County

(G-2913)
CONNECTICUT FOREST PK ASSN INC
Also Called: CFPA
16 Meriden Rd (06481-2945)
PHONE..............................860 346-2372
E Hammerling, *Ex Dir*
Eric Hammerling, *Ex Dir*
EMP: 10 **EST:** 1895
SALES (est): 1.68MM **Privately Held**
Web: www.ctwoodlands.org
SIC: 8999 2721   Natural resource preservation service; Periodicals

(G-2914)
LOYAL FENCE COMPANY LLC
1 Lorraine Ter (06481-2067)
PHONE..............................203 530-7046
EMP: 7 **EST:** 2013

SALES (est): 460.84K **Privately Held**
SIC: 3446   Fences, gates, posts, and flagpoles

(G-2915)
ROGERS MANUFACTURING COMPANY
Also Called: Mery Manufacturing
72 Main St (06481-2001)
P.O. Box 155 (06481-0155)
PHONE..............................860 346-8648
Vincent J Bitel Junior, *Pr*
Vincent J Bitel Senior Stkhdr, *Prin*
Elaine B Cunningham, *
▲ **EMP:** 100 **EST:** 1891
SQ FT: 65,000
SALES (est): 20.95MM **Privately Held**
Web: www.therogersmanufacturingcompany.com
SIC: 3089   Injection molded finished plastics products, nec

(G-2916)
WADSWORTH FALLS MFG CO
72 Main St (06481-2001)
P.O. Box 155 (06481-0155)
PHONE..............................860 346-3644
Vincent J Bitel, *Pr*
EMP: 10 **EST:** 1978
SALES (est): 1.59MM **Privately Held**
Web: www.therogersmanufacturingcompany.com
SIC: 5085 3423   Tools, nec; Hand and edge tools, nec

Rocky Hill
Hartford County

(G-2917)
CCO LLC
Also Called: Sams Food Stores
2138 Silas Deane Hwy Ste 101 (06067-2317)
PHONE..............................860 757-3434
Nasim Khalid, *Managing Member*
EMP: 17 **EST:** 2010
SALES (est): 2.12MM **Privately Held**
Web: www.samsfoodstores.com
SIC: 5411 3496   Convenience stores, independent; Grocery carts, made from purchased wire

(G-2918)
CLEARY MILLWORK COMPANY INC
2049 Silas Deane Hwy Ste 1 (06067-2368)
PHONE..............................800 486-7600
James Lyke, *VP*
EMP: 9 **EST:** 1922
SQ FT: 120,000
SALES (est): 946.72K **Privately Held**
Web: www.clearymillwork.com
SIC: 2431   Millwork

(G-2919)
CONNECTICUT RADIO INC
1208 Cromwell Ave Ste C (06067-3436)
P.O. Box 487 (06067-0487)
PHONE..............................860 563-4867
TOLL FREE: 800
Don Bighinatti, *Pr*
Bill Charamut, *VP*
EMP: 8 **EST:** 1989
SQ FT: 1,000
SALES (est): 1.52MM **Privately Held**
Web: www.connradio.com

SIC: 5065 3663   Communication equipment; Radio broadcasting and communications equipment

(G-2920)
CUMMINS INC
Also Called: Metropower
914 Cromwell Ave (06067-3004)
PHONE..............................860 529-7474
Rusty Graham, *Brnch Mgr*
EMP: 14
SALES (corp-wide): 34.06B **Publicly Held**
Web: www.cummins.com
SIC: 5084 3519   Engines, gasoline; Internal combustion engines, nec
PA: Cummins Inc.
   500 Jackson St
   Columbus IN 47201
   812 377-5000

(G-2921)
D&R MARINE UPHOLSTERY & CANVAS
369 Old Main St (06067-1507)
PHONE..............................860 989-9646
Raymond Accardo, *Owner*
EMP: 8 **EST:** 2013
SALES (est): 262.21K **Privately Held**
SIC: 2211   Canvas

(G-2922)
FRONTIER VISION TECH INC
Also Called: Evogence
2049 Silas Deane Hwy Ste 1c (06067-2332)
PHONE..............................860 953-0240
EMP: 43 **EST:** 1996
SALES (est): 5.02MM **Privately Held**
Web: www.evogence.com
SIC: 3571 3577 7378 5045   Computers, digital, analog or hybrid; Graphic displays, except graphic terminals; Computer maintenance and repair; Computers, peripherals, and software

(G-2923)
GULF MANUFACTURING INC
645 Cromwell Ave (06067-1807)
P.O. Box 430 (06067-0430)
PHONE..............................860 529-8601
James Murphy, *Pr*
Julie Murphy, *Sec*
James Murphy, *VP*
EMP: 32 **EST:** 1968
SQ FT: 8,000
SALES (est): 2.42MM **Privately Held**
Web: www.gulfmfg.com
SIC: 3441 3599   Fabricated structural metal; Machine shop, jobbing and repair

(G-2924)
HARTFORD TECHNOLOGIES INC
1022 Elm St (06067-1809)
PHONE..............................860 571-3602
Laura T Grondin, *Pr*
Lincoln Thomson, *
▲ **EMP:** 27 **EST:** 2004
SALES (est): 4.87MM
SALES (corp-wide): 67.02MM **Privately Held**
Web: www.hartfordtechnologies.com
SIC: 3562 3399   Ball and roller bearings; Steel balls
PA: Virginia Industries, Inc.
   1022 Elm St
   Rocky Hill CT 06067
   860 571-3600

(G-2925)
HENKEL LOCTITE CORPORATION (DH)
Also Called: Henkel Loctite
1 Henkel Way (06067-3581)
PHONE..............................860 571-5100
Carsten Knobel, *Ch Bd*
◆ **EMP: 71 EST:** 1987
SQ FT: 500,000
SALES (est): 32.62MM
SALES (corp-wide): 23.26B **Privately Held**
Web: www.henkel-adhesives.com
SIC: 8711 3677 2891 8731   Engineering
services; Inductors, electronic; Adhesives;
Commercial physical research
HQ: Henkel Us Operations Corporation
1 Henkel Way
Rocky Hill CT 06067
860 571-5100

(G-2926)
HENKEL OF AMERICA INC (HQ)
1 Henkel Way (06067-3581)
PHONE..............................860 615-3395
Carsten Knobel, *CEO*
Carsten Knobel, *Ch Bd*
Steven Essick, *
Robert Mcnamee, *Sec*
Burak Yildirim, *
◆ **EMP: 421 EST:** 1979
SQ FT: 60,000
SALES (est): 1.97B
SALES (corp-wide): 23.26B **Privately Held**
Web: www.henkel-northamerica.com
SIC: 2843 2821 2833 2899   Surface active
agents; Plastics materials and resins;
Medicinals and botanicals; Chemical
preparations, nec
PA: Henkel Ag & Co. Kgaa
Henkelstr. 67
Dusseldorf NW 40589
2117970

(G-2927)
HENKEL US OPERATIONS CORP (DH)
1 Henkel Way (06067-3581)
PHONE..............................860 571-5100
Seven Essick, *Pr*
Kathrin Menges, *
Jochen Krautter, *
Raphaela Dohm, *
Michael Acampora, *
◆ **EMP: 400 EST:** 1970
SQ FT: 60,000
SALES (est): 1.38B
SALES (corp-wide): 23.26B **Privately Held**
Web: www.henkel.com
SIC: 2843 2821 2833 2899   Surface active
agents; Plastics materials and resins;
Medicinals and botanicals; Chemical
preparations, nec
HQ: Henkel Of America, Inc.
1 Henkel Way
Rocky Hill CT 06067
860 615-3395

(G-2928)
HEXPLORA LLC
10 Waterchase Dr (06067-2100)
PHONE..............................860 760-7601
Srinivas Pendyala, *CEO*
Sai Alahari, *Prin*
Ravi Obbu, *
EMP: 60 EST: 2013
SQ FT: 2,700
SALES (est): 4.1MM **Privately Held**
Web: www.hexplora.com
SIC: 7372 7374   Application computer
software; Data processing service

(G-2929)
IDEMIA IDENTITY & SEC USA LLC
101 Hammer Mill Rd (06067-3771)
PHONE..............................860 529-2559
Jim Lyons, *Brnch Mgr*
EMP: 14
SALES (corp-wide): 2.44B **Privately Held**
Web: www.idemia.com
SIC: 3089   Identification cards, plastics
HQ: Idemia Identity & Security Usa Llc
11951 Freedom Dr Ste 1800
Reston VA 20190

(G-2930)
JOHNSON CONTROLS INC
Also Called: Johnson Controls
27 Inwood Rd (06067-3412)
PHONE..............................860 571-3300
Dave Clark, *VP*
EMP: 19
Web: www.johnsoncontrols.com
SIC: 2531   Seats, automobile
HQ: Johnson Controls, Inc.
5757 N Green Bay Ave
Milwaukee WI 53209
920 245-6409

(G-2931)
MTU AERO ENGINES N AMER INC
795 Brook St # 5 (06067-3403)
PHONE..............................860 258-9700
Alarm Eerube, *Pr*
EMP: 158
SALES (corp-wide): 5.54B **Privately Held**
Web: www.mtuusa.com
SIC: 3812   Airspeed instrumentation
(aeronautical instruments)
HQ: Mtu Aero Engines North America Inc.
400 Capital Blvd Ste 300
Rocky Hill CT 06067

(G-2932)
PDQ INC (PA)
24 Evans Rd (06067-3734)
PHONE..............................860 529-9051
Ronald Gronback Junior, *Pr*
Ronald G Gronback Junior, *Pr*
Ronald Gronback Senior, *Genl Mgr*
Jeffrey W Gronback, *
EMP: 24 EST: 1989
SQ FT: 6,000
SALES (est): 4.59MM **Privately Held**
Web: www.pdqcorp.com
SIC: 3724   Aircraft engines and engine parts

(G-2933)
RARE REMINDER INCORPORATED
222 Dividend Rd (06067-3740)
P.O. Box 289 (06067-0289)
PHONE..............................860 563-9386
Kevin Rarey, *Pr*
James Klatt, *
EMP: 27 EST: 1953
SQ FT: 14,300
SALES (est): 973.29K **Privately Held**
Web: www.rarereminder.com
SIC: 2741 2752   Shopping news: publishing
and printing; Offset printing

(G-2934)
ROYALTY CONSULTING LLC
Also Called: Royalty Consulting
750 Old Main St (06067-1567)
PHONE..............................800 474-5157
Francisco Santos, *CEO*
EMP: 15 EST: 2021

SALES (est): 710.63K **Privately Held**
SIC: 8748 1389 6531 0783   Business
consulting, nec; Construction, repair, and
dismantling services; Real estate leasing
and rentals; Tree trimming services for
public utility lines

(G-2935)
STORMTECH LLC
70 Inwood Rd Ste 3 (06067-3441)
PHONE..............................860 529-8188
Ron Vitarelli, *Managing Member*
▲ **EMP: 30 EST:** 2003
SALES (est): 2.16MM **Privately Held**
Web: www.adspipe.com
SIC: 3589   Sewage and water treatment
equipment

(G-2936)
TECH II BUSINESS SERVICES INC
400 Capital Blvd (06067-3599)
PHONE..............................518 587-1565
Daniel Bardin, *CEO*
Eric Guby, *
EMP: 28 EST: 1983
SALES (est): 7.45MM **Privately Held**
Web: www.tech-ii.com
SIC: 7629 3575 5065   Telephone set repair;
Computer terminals, monitors and
components; Telephone and telegraphic
equipment
PA: Adnet Technologies, Llc
400 Capital Blvd Ste 101
Rocky Hill CT 06067

(G-2937)
TORNIK INC
16 Old Forge Rd # B (06067-3729)
PHONE..............................860 282-6081
▲ **EMP: 110 EST:** 1990
SQ FT: 21,000
SALES (est): 21.29MM **Privately Held**
Web: www.tornik.com
SIC: 3679 8711   Harness assemblies, for
electronic use: wire or cable; Electrical or
electronic engineering

(G-2938)
TORNIK LLC
16 Old Forge Rd Ste B (06067-3729)
PHONE..............................860 282-6081
Edward S Stephens, *Managing Member*
EMP: 11 EST: 2012
SALES (est): 1.01MM **Privately Held**
Web: www.tornik.com
SIC: 3679   Harness assemblies, for
electronic use: wire or cable

(G-2939)
TRANE TECHNOLOGIES COMPANY LLC
Also Called: Ingersoll-Rand
716 Brook St Ste 130 (06067-3433)
PHONE..............................860 616-6600
Mike Carey, *Mgr*
EMP: 16
Web: www.trane.com
SIC: 3561   Pumps and pumping equipment
HQ: Trane Technologies Company Llc
800 Beaty St Ste E
Davidson NC 28036
704 655-4000

(G-2940)
UNITED SEATING & MOBILITY LLC
Also Called: Numotion
65 Inwood Rd (06067-3440)

PHONE..............................806 761-0700
EMP: 66
SALES (corp-wide): 491.33MM **Privately
Held**
Web: www.numotion.com
SIC: 3842   Wheelchairs
PA: United Seating & Mobility Llc
155 Franklin Rd Ste 300
Brentwood TN 37027
860 656-0702

(G-2941)
WETHERSFIELD PRINTING CO INC
1795 Silas Deane Hwy (06067-1305)
PHONE..............................860 721-8236
Joseph Amaio, *Pr*
Barbara Amaio, *Sec*
EMP: 15 EST: 1987
SQ FT: 7,500
SALES (est): 318.73K **Privately Held**
SIC: 2752   Offset printing

(G-2942)
WIREMOLD COMPANY
Also Called: THE WIREMOLD COMPANY
777 Brook St (06067-3403)
PHONE..............................860 233-6251
Greg Stepeck, *Mgr*
EMP: 70
Web: www.wiremoldproducts.com
SIC: 3644   Insulators and insulation
materials, electrical
HQ: Wiremold Company
60 Woodlawn St
West Hartford CT 06110
860 233-6251

Rogers
Windham County

(G-2943)
ROGERS CORPORATION
Advanced Circuit Materials Div
1 Technology Dr (06263)
PHONE..............................860 774-9605
EMP: 158
SALES (corp-wide): 971.17MM **Publicly
Held**
Web: www.rogerscorp.com
SIC: 3679   Electronic circuits
PA: Rogers Corporation
2225 W Chandler Blvd
Chandler AZ 85224
480 917-6000

Roxbury
Litchfield County

(G-2944)
FUTURE CLASSICS USA LLC (PA)
1030 Washington Woodbury Rd
(06783-1200)
P.O. Box 1254 (06793-0254)
PHONE..............................860 838-4688
EMP: 13 EST: 2017
SALES (est): 1.42MM
SALES (corp-wide): 1.42MM **Privately
Held**
Web: www.dado-usa.com
SIC: 2511 3272   Wood household furniture;
Bathtubs, concrete

Salem
New London County

(G-2945)
RIGHT OF WAY SOLUTIONS LLC
595 Norwich Rd (06420-3729)
PHONE...............................860 917-0608
EMP: 7 **EST:** 2018
SALES (est): 991.06K **Privately Held**
SIC: 4911 1731 1389 Transmission, electric power; Electric power systems contractors; Testing, measuring, surveying, and analysis services

(G-2946)
SALEM PRIME CUTS INCORPORATED
12 New London Rd Ste 5 (06420-4019)
PHONE...............................860 859-0741
John Fusaro, *Pr*
Thomas Rozanski, *Sec*
EMP: 14 **EST:** 1961
SALES (est): 1.61MM **Privately Held**
SIC: 2011 Meat packing plants

(G-2947)
SALEM VLY FARMS ICE CREAM INC
20 Darling Rd (06420-3906)
PHONE...............................860 859-2980
David Bingham, *Pr*
Tiffany B.Cunningham, *VP*
Anne W Bingham, *Sec*
EMP: 11 **EST:** 1988
SALES (est): 208.67K **Privately Held**
Web:
www.salemvalleyfarmsicecream.com
SIC: 2024 Ice cream, bulk

Sandy Hook
Fairfield County

(G-2948)
CONN ENGINEERING ASSOC CORP
27 Philo Curtis Rd (06482-1245)
P.O. Box 656 (06482-0656)
PHONE...............................203 426-4733
Gregory Jossick, *Pr*
Jeffrey Jossick, *VP*
Greg Jossick, *Sec*
Sandra Jossick, *Sec*
▲ **EMP:** 14 **EST:** 1967
SQ FT: 6,000
SALES (est): 2.23MM **Privately Held**
Web: www.ceacpowders.com
SIC: 3399 Powder, metal

(G-2949)
CURTIS CORPORATION A DEL CORP
44 Berkshire Rd (06482-1499)
PHONE...............................203 426-5861
Donald Droppo, *Pr*
William Peck, *Sec*
EMP: 155 **EST:** 1836
SQ FT: 112,000
SALES (est): 6.59K **Privately Held**
Web: www.curtispackaging.com
SIC: 2657 Folding paperboard boxes

(G-2950)
CURTIS PACKAGING CORPORATION
44 Berkshire Rd (06482-1428)

PHONE...............................203 426-5861
Donald R Droppo Junior, *Ch Bd*
William F Peck, *
Donald Droppo Junior, *Pr*
Robert T Johnson, *
▲ **EMP:** 130 **EST:** 1845
SQ FT: 150,000
SALES (est): 22.16MM **Privately Held**
Web: www.curtispackaging.com
SIC: 2657 Folding paperboard boxes

(G-2951)
FORECAST INTERNATIONAL INC
75 Glen Rd Ste 302 (06482-1173)
PHONE...............................203 426-0800
Edward M Nebinger, *CEO*
Douglas A Nebinger, *
EMP: 48 **EST:** 1973
SALES (est): 7.88MM **Privately Held**
Web: www.forecastinternational.com
SIC: 2731 8742 Book publishing; Management consulting services

(G-2952)
MAPLE CRAFT FOODS LLC
6 Cider Mill Rd (06482-1587)
PHONE...............................203 913-7066
EMP: 9 **EST:** 2016
SALES (est): 521K **Privately Held**
Web: www.maplecraftfoods.com
SIC: 2099 Food preparations, nec

Scotland
Windham County

(G-2953)
HARDWOOD LUMBER MANUFACTURING
Also Called: Scotland Hardwoods
111 Ziegler Rd (06247-2002)
P.O. Box 328 (06264-0328)
PHONE...............................860 423-2447
EMP: 290
SALES (corp-wide): 46.88MM **Privately Held**
Web: www.ahwood.com
SIC: 5031 2421 Lumber: rough, dressed, and finished; Sawmills and planing mills, general
PA: Hardwood Lumber Manufacturing, Inc
567 N Charlotte Ave
Waynesboro VA 22980
540 946-9150

(G-2954)
SCOTLAND HARDWOODS LLC
Also Called: Scotland Hardwoods
117 Ziegler Rd (06247-2002)
P.O. Box 328 (06264-0328)
PHONE...............................860 423-1233
Peter J Rossi, *Managing Member*
▼ **EMP:** 34 **EST:** 2002
SQ FT: 45,000
SALES: 5.18MM
SALES (corp-wide): 5.18MM **Privately Held**
Web: www.scotlandhardwoods.com
SIC: 2421 Lumber: rough, sawed, or planed
PA: New England Timber Resources Inc
162 West St Ste A
Cromwell CT 06416
860 632-3505

Seymour
New Haven County

(G-2955)
AIR-VAC ENGINEERING CO INC (PA)
30 Progress Ave Ste 2 (06483-3935)
P.O. Box 216 (06483-0216)
PHONE...............................203 888-9900
Clifford S Lasto, *Pr*
Jeffrey S Duhaime, *VP*
Gary R Duhaime, *Sec*
Howard C Lasto, *Treas*
EMP: 22 **EST:** 1959
SQ FT: 25,000
SALES (est): 7.68MM
SALES (corp-wide): 7.68MM **Privately Held**
Web: www.air-vac-eng.com
SIC: 3548 Soldering equipment, except hand soldering irons

(G-2956)
CANOGA PERKINS CORPORATION
100 Bank St (06483-2806)
PHONE...............................203 888-7914
Steve Hannay, *Brnch Mgr*
EMP: 9
SALES (corp-wide): 645.5MM **Privately Held**
Web: www.canoga.com
SIC: 3661 Modems
HQ: Canoga Perkins Corporation
20600 Prairie St
Chatsworth CA 91311
818 718-6300

(G-2957)
CASPARI INC (PA)
99 Cogwheel Ln (06483-3900)
PHONE...............................203 888-1100
Douglas H Stevens, *Ch Bd*
Lisa Fingeret, *VP*
Caralyn Stevens, *VP*
◆ **EMP:** 16 **EST:** 1945
SQ FT: 35,000
SALES (est): 23.17MM
SALES (corp-wide): 23.17MM **Privately Held**
Web: www.casparionline.com
SIC: 2771 Greeting cards

(G-2958)
CIRCUIT BREAKER SALES NE LLC
Also Called: Circuit Breaker Sales Ne Inc.
79 Main St (06483-3122)
PHONE...............................203 888-7500
John Degenova, *Pr*
Brian Constantino, *
Thomas Cheaney, *
EMP: 92 **EST:** 2014
SALES (est): 30MM **Privately Held**
Web: www.circuitbreakersalesne.com
SIC: 5063 3699 Electrical supplies, nec; Electrical equipment and supplies, nec
PA: Group Cbs, Llc
1315 Columbine Dr
Gainesville TX 76240

(G-2959)
CONNECTICUT BASEMENT SYSTEMS INC
Also Called: Total Basement Finishing
60 Silvermine Rd (06483-3931)
PHONE...............................203 881-5090
▲ **EMP:** 117 **EST:** 1987

SALES (est): 12.53MM **Privately Held**
Web:
www.connecticutbasementsystems.com
SIC: 1799 1741 1771 3561 Decontamination services; Foundation and retaining wall construction; Flooring contractor; Pumps, domestic: water or sump

(G-2960)
DEKARZ CORPORATION
Also Called: Dekarz Engineering
31 Silvermine Rd (06483-3906)
PHONE...............................203 888-3102
FAX: 203 888-4940
EMP: 11
SQ FT: 6,000
SALES (est): 790K **Privately Held**
SIC: 3089 Injection molding of plastics

(G-2961)
GREENWICH WORKSHOP INC (PA)
Also Called: Gws Marketing Associates
151 Main St (06483-3137)
P.O. Box 231 (06483-0231)
PHONE...............................203 881-3336
Vincent Grabowski, *Pr*
Michael Meskill, *
▲ **EMP:** 20 **EST:** 1972
SQ FT: 28,000
SALES (est): 9.65MM
SALES (corp-wide): 9.65MM **Privately Held**
Web: www.greenwichworkshop.com
SIC: 5199 5999 8412 2731 Art goods; Art dealers; Art gallery; Book publishing

(G-2962)
JV PRECISION MACHINE CO
71 Cogwheel Ln (06483-3919)
PHONE...............................203 888-0748
Josef Visinski Junior, *Pr*
Andrew Visinski, *
EMP: 30 **EST:** 1974
SQ FT: 42,000
SALES (est): 4.65MM **Privately Held**
Web: www.jvprecision.net
SIC: 3599 Machine shop, jobbing and repair

(G-2963)
LA PIETRA THINSTONE OF CT LLC
15 Franklin St (06483-2809)
PHONE...............................203 948-3756
Marcio Figueiredo, *Pr*
EMP: 12 **EST:** 2020
SALES (est): 1.09MM **Privately Held**
SIC: 2499 Furniture inlays (veneers)

(G-2964)
MATTHEW WARREN INC
Also Called: Raf Electronic Hardware
95 Silvermine Rd Ste 1 (06483-3915)
PHONE...............................203 888-2133
EMP: 8
SALES (corp-wide): 1.05B **Privately Held**
Web: www.mwcomponents.com
SIC: 3451 3452 Screw machine products; Bolts, nuts, rivets, and washers
HQ: Matthew Warren, Inc.
3426 Toringdon Way # 100
Charlotte NC 28277
704 837-0331

(G-2965)
MICROBOARD PROCESSING INC
Also Called: M P I
36 Cogwheel Ln (06483-3922)
PHONE...............................203 881-4300

Craig Hoekenga, *Ch Bd*
Nicole Russo, *
Ted Labowski, *Quality Vice President*
Sandra Hoekenga, *
▲ **EMP: 105 EST: 1983**
SQ FT: 60,000
SALES (est): 47.61MM Privately Held
Web: www.microboard.com
SIC: 3672 7629 Circuit boards, television
and radio printed; Circuit board repair

(G-2966)
PLASTIC MOLDING
TECHNOLOGY
92 Cogwheel Ln (06483-3937)
PHONE..................203 881-1811
Charles Sholtis, *Prin*
EMP: 9 EST: 2010
SALES (est): 240.31K Privately Held
SIC: 3089 Injection molding of plastics

(G-2967)
PORTA DOOR CO
65 Cogwheel Ln (06483-3919)
PHONE..................203 888-6191
Peter Romanos, *Pr*
Chris Malizia, *
EMP: 22 EST: 1973
SQ FT: 20,000
SALES (est): 2.92MM Privately Held
Web: www.portadoor.com
SIC: 2434 5712 2431 Wood kitchen cabinets
; Furniture stores; Millwork

(G-2968)
RETINA SYSTEMS INC
146 Day St (06483-3403)
PHONE..................203 881-1311
Floyd Moir, *Pr*
Janice Moir, *
▲ **EMP: 25 EST: 1987**
SQ FT: 14,000
SALES (est): 2.32MM Privately Held
Web: www.retinasystems.com
SIC: 3827 Lenses, optical: all types except
ophthalmic

(G-2969)
SLICKBAR PRODUCTS CORP
18 Beach St (06484-3702)
PHONE..................203 888-7700
Dave Bakalar, *Prd Mgr*
EMP: 8 EST: 1988
SALES (est): 290.7K Privately Held
Web: www.slickbar.com
SIC: 3533 Oil and gas field machinery

(G-2970)
THE A H EMERY COMPANY (PA)
Also Called: Emery Winslow Scale Co
73 Cogwheel Ln (06483-3930)
PHONE..................203 881-9333
◆ **EMP: 30 EST: 1868**
SALES (est): 9.95MM
SALES (corp-wide): 9.95MM Privately
Held
SIC: 3596 Industrial scales

(G-2971)
THULE INC (DH)
42 Silvermine Rd (06483-3928)
PHONE..................203 881-9600
Fred Clark, *Pr*
Bruce Bossidy, *
Fred Wyckoff, *
◆ **EMP: 157 EST: 1992**
SALES (est): 109.65MM Privately Held
Web: www.thule.com

SIC: 3714 5021 Tops, motor vehicle; Racks
HQ: Thule Holding, Inc.
42 Silvermine Rd
Seymour CT 06483

(G-2972)
THULE HOLDING INC (DH)
42 Silvermine Rd (06483-3928)
PHONE..................203 881-9600
Fred Clark, *Pr*
Moreen Parente, *VP*
EMP: 27 EST: 2004
SALES (est): 336.49MM Privately Held
SIC: 3792 3714 Travel trailers and campers;
Tops, motor vehicle
HQ: Thule Holding Ab
Fosievagen 13
MalmO
406359000

(G-2973)
TRI-STAR INDUSTRIES INC
95 Silvermine Rd # 1 (06483-3915)
PHONE..................860 828-7570
Andrew Nowakowski, *VP*
EMP: 35 EST: 1991
SALES (est): 4.65MM
SALES (corp-wide): 1.05B Privately Held
Web: www.mwcomponents.com
SIC: 3451 Screw machine products
HQ: Mw Industries, Inc.
2400 Farrell Rd
Houston TX 28277
800 875-3510

(G-2974)
UNITED AVIONICS INC
Also Called: Ua
181 Mountain Rd (06483-2339)
PHONE..................203 723-1404
Richard F Nicolari, *Pr*
Louis Nicoletti, *
William Nicoletti, *
Thomas D Bunk, *
Joseph Cardella Senior, *VP*
EMP: 48 EST: 1981
SALES (est): 9.81MM Privately Held
Web: www.unitedavionicsinc.com
SIC: 3728 Aircraft parts and equipment, nec

(G-2975)
VERNIER METAL FABRICATING
INC
Also Called: V M F
26 Progress Ave (06483-3921)
PHONE..................203 881-3133
Edward Zerjav, *Pr*
John J Zerjav, *
Barbara Zerjav, *
Robert Zerjav, *
EMP: 70 EST: 1964
SQ FT: 54,000
SALES (est): 8.84MM Privately Held
Web: www.verniermetal.com
SIC: 3441 3444 Fabricated structural metal;
Sheet metalwork

(G-2976)
XAMAX INDUSTRIES INC
Also Called: Xamax
63 Silvermine Rd (06483-3915)
PHONE..................203 888-7200
Martin J Weinberg, *Pr*
Margaret Pederson, *
◆ **EMP: 50 EST: 1974**
SQ FT: 36,000
SALES (est): 9.47MM Privately Held
Web: www.xamax.com
SIC: 2621 2297 Insulation siding, paper;
Nonwoven fabrics

Shelton
Fairfield County

(G-2977)
A & I CONCENTRATE LLC
2 Corporate Dr Ste 136 (06484-6274)
PHONE..................203 447-1938
Don Vultaggio, *Managing Member*
EMP: 21 EST: 2007
SALES (est): 835.13K Privately Held
SIC: 3556 5181 Food products machinery;
Beer and ale

(G-2978)
ACME UNITED CORPORATION
(PA)
1 Waterview Dr Ste 200 (06484-4368)
PHONE..................203 254-6060
Walter C Johnsen, *Ch Bd*
Brian S Olschan, *
Paul G Driscoll, *VP*
◆ **EMP: 96 EST: 1867**
SQ FT: 15,400
SALES (est): 193.96MM
SALES (corp-wide): 193.96MM Publicly
Held
Web: www.acmeunited.com
SIC: 3421 2499 3842 3579 Scissors, hand;
Rulers and rules, wood; First aid, snake
bite, and burn kits; Pencil sharpeners

(G-2979)
AL-LYNN SALES LLC
Also Called: Al-Lynn Sales
25 Brook St Ste 102 (06484-2332)
PHONE..................203 922-7840
TOLL FREE: 800
EMP: 9 EST: 1992
SQ FT: 2,000
SALES (est): 926.32K Privately Held
Web: www.al-lynn.com
SIC: 5699 2395 Uniforms; Embroidery
products, except Schiffli machine

(G-2980)
ALPHA-CORE INC
6 Waterview Dr (06484-4300)
PHONE..................203 954-0050
Peder Ulrik Poulsen, *Pr*
Sandu Pescaru, *
◆ **EMP: 45 EST: 1981**
SQ FT: 25,000
SALES (est): 799.53K Privately Held
Web: www.bridgeportmagnetics.com
SIC: 3679 5731 3612 3549 Cores, magnetic
; Radio, television, and electronic stores;
Transformers, except electric; Metalworking
machinery, nec

(G-2981)
ANCO ENGINEERING INC
Also Called: Anco
217 Long Hill Cross Rd (06484-6145)
PHONE..................203 925-9235
Lucian S Leszczynski, *Pr*
Lucian Leszczynski Junior, *VP*
Ann Leszczynski, *
Daniel Leszczynski, *
EMP: 85 EST: 1981
SQ FT: 100,000
SALES (est): 22.04MM Privately Held
Web: www.ancoeng.com
SIC: 3441 3444 Fabricated structural metal;
Sheet metal specialties, not stamped

(G-2982)
ARCADIA CHEM PRESERVATIVE
LLC

100 Beard Sawmill Rd Ste 348 (06484)
PHONE..................203 717-4750
Sujanan Tuthanppurayil, *CEO*
Richard Rofe, *Managing Member*
EMP: 13 EST: 2015
SQ FT: 3,000
SALES (est): 2.55MM Privately Held
Web: www.arcadiacap.com
SIC: 2869 5169 Industrial organic
chemicals, nec; Alkalines and chlorine

(G-2983)
BETA SHIM CO
11 Progress Dr (06484-6218)
PHONE..................203 926-1150
John P Mccue, *Pr*
Mark Lovallo, *
Zach Pratt, *
Scott Mccue, *VP*
EMP: 47 EST: 1974
SQ FT: 21,000
SALES (est): 9.53MM Privately Held
Web: www.betashim.com
SIC: 3499 3469 Shims, metal; Metal
stampings, nec

(G-2984)
BIC CONSUMER PDTS MFG CO
INC (DH)
1 Bic Way Ste 1 (06484-6223)
PHONE..................203 783-2000
Bruno Bich, *Ch Bd*
▲ **EMP: 61 EST: 1999**
SALES (est): 24.34MM
SALES (corp-wide): 800.85MM Privately
Held
Web: us.bic.com
SIC: 3951 Ball point pens and parts
HQ: Bic Usa Inc.
1 Bic Way Ste 1 # 1
Shelton CT 06484
203 783-2000

(G-2985)
BIC CORPORATION (HQ)
Also Called: Bic Graphic USA
1 Bic Way Ste 1 (06484-6223)
PHONE..................203 783-2000
Bruno Bich, *Ch Bd*
Mario Guevara, *
Thomas M Kelleher, *
Paul Russo, *Senior Vice President Human*
Resources
Francois Bich, *
◆ **EMP: 900 EST: 1958**
SQ FT: 800,000
SALES (est): 1.43B
SALES (corp-wide): 800.85MM Privately
Held
Web: corporate.bic.com
SIC: 3951 2899 3999 3421 Ball point pens
and parts; Correction fluid; Cigarette
lighters, except precious metal; Razor
blades and razors
PA: Societe Bic
12 22
Clichy 92110
145195200

(G-2986)
BIC USA INC (DH)
1 Bic Way Ste 1 (06484-6223)
PHONE..................203 783-2000
Kazufumi Ikeda, *Ch Bd*
Don Cummins, *
David T Kimball, *
Barry Johnson, *
Steven A Burkhart, *
▲ **EMP: 200 EST: 1999**
SQ FT: 15,000

▲ = Import ▼ = Export
◆ = Import/Export

SALES (est): 119.87MM
SALES (corp-wide): 800.85MM **Privately Held**
Web: uslogolighter.bic.com
SIC: 3951 2899 3999 3421   Ball point pens and parts; Correction fluid; Cigarette lighters, except precious metal; Razor blades and razors
HQ: Bic Corporation
1 Bic Way Ste 1 # 1
Shelton CT 06484
203 783-2000

(G-2987)
BRENNAN REALTY LLC (PA)
Also Called: Aggregate Products
70 Platt Rd (06484-5339)
P.O. Box 788 (06484-0788)
PHONE..................................203 929-6314
EMP: 112 EST: 1958
SQ FT: 25,000
SALES (est): 24.68MM
SALES (corp-wide): 24.68MM **Privately Held**
Web: www.jjbrennan.com
SIC: 1623 1542 1442 8741   Water, sewer, and utility lines; Commercial and office building, new construction; Sand mining; Management services

(G-2988)
BRIDGEPORT MAGNETICS GROUP INC
Also Called: Bridgeport Magnetics Group
6 Waterview Dr (06484-4300)
PHONE..................................203 954-0050
Ulrik Poulsen, *Pr*
Sandu Pescaru, *
Charlotte Poulsen, *
▲ EMP: 27 EST: 2008
SALES (est): 4.38MM **Privately Held**
Web: www.bridgepmagnetics.com
SIC: 3357 3679 3612   Magnet wire, nonferrous; Cores, magnetic; Power transformers, electric

(G-2989)
CCL INDUSTRIES CORPORATION
15 Controls Dr (06484-6111)
PHONE..................................203 926-1253
EMP: 4974
SALES (corp-wide): 4.75B **Privately Held**
Web: www.cclind.com
SIC: 2759   Flexographic printing
HQ: Ccl Industries Corporation
161 Worcester Rd Ste 403
Framingham MA 01701

(G-2990)
CCL LABEL INC
15 Controls Dr (06484-6111)
PHONE..................................203 926-1253
EMP: 16
SALES (corp-wide): 4.75B **Privately Held**
Web: www.cclind.com
SIC: 2759 3411 2671   Flexographic printing; Aluminum cans; Paper; coated and laminated packaging
HQ: Ccl Label, Inc.
161 Worcester Rd Ste 403
Framingham MA 01701
508 872-4511

(G-2991)
CENTRIX INC
Also Called: Centrix
770 River Rd (06484-5430)
PHONE..................................203 929-5582
William B Dragan, *Pr*

William B Dragan, *Prin*
John J Discko Junior, *VP*
Paul Fattibene, *
▲ EMP: 103 EST: 1970
SQ FT: 50,000
SALES (est): 20.33MM **Privately Held**
Web: www.centrixdental.com
SIC: 3843   Dental equipment

(G-2992)
CHROMALLOY COMPONENT SVCS INC
415 Howe Ave (06484-3166)
PHONE..................................203 924-1666
Dan Martin, *Brnch Mgr*
EMP: 60
SALES (corp-wide): 1.2B **Privately Held**
Web: www.chromalloy.com
SIC: 3471   Electroplating of metals or formed products
HQ: Chromalloy Component Services, Inc.
303 Industrial Park Rd
San Antonio TX 78226
210 331-2300

(G-2993)
COMET TECHNOLOGIES USA INC (DH)
Also Called: Yxlon International
100 Trap Falls Road Ext (06484-4646)
PHONE..................................203 447-3200
Robert Jardim, *Pr*
◆ EMP: 30 EST: 1997
SQ FT: 16,421
SALES (est): 94.17MM **Privately Held**
Web: pct.comet.tech
SIC: 3674   Semiconductors and related devices
HQ: Comet Ag
Herrengasse 10
Flamatt FR 3175

(G-2994)
CYA TECHNOLOGIES INC
3 Enterprise Dr Ste 408 (06484-4696)
PHONE..................................203 513-3111
Wayne Crandall, *Pr*
EMP: 18 EST: 2000
SALES (est): 896.38K **Privately Held**
SIC: 7372   Application computer software

(G-2995)
DAC SYSTEMS INC
Also Called: Telliris
2 Corporate Dr Ste 949 (06484-6274)
PHONE..................................203 924-7000
Mark Nickson, *Pr*
Mark G Nickson, *Pr*
EMP: 10 EST: 1988
SALES (est): 947.16K **Privately Held**
Web: www.dacsystems.it
SIC: 3661   Telephones and telephone apparatus

(G-2996)
DAN BEARD INC
Also Called: Island Sand & Gravel Pit
64 Hawthorne Ave (06484-4437)
P.O. Box 71 (06484-0071)
PHONE..................................203 924-4346
Jeff Rhodes, *Mgr*
EMP: 20
SALES (corp-wide): 2.31MM **Privately Held**
SIC: 3281 5032 1442   Cut stone and stone products; Brick, stone, and related material; Construction sand and gravel
PA: Dan Beard, Inc.
Mary St
Shelton CT 06484
203 924-1575

(G-2997)
DARK FIELD TECHNOLOGIES INC
5 Research Dr (06484-6232)
PHONE..................................203 298-0731
Timothy A Potts, *Pr*
Jamila E Potts, *VP*
EMP: 15 EST: 1997
SQ FT: 10,000
SALES (est): 2.45MM **Privately Held**
Web: www.darkfield.com
SIC: 8711 3577   Electrical or electronic engineering; Optical scanning devices

(G-2998)
DDK INDUSTRIES LLC
70 Center St (06484-3242)
PHONE..................................203 641-4218
Kevin Zdanowicz, *Prin*
EMP: 7 EST: 2014
SALES (est): 286.86K **Privately Held**
SIC: 3999   Manufacturing industries, nec

(G-2999)
DERBY CELLULAR PRODUCTS INC
680 Bridgeport Ave Ste 3 (06484-4705)
PHONE..................................203 735-4661
EMP: 50 EST: 1947
SQ FT: 161,000
SALES (est): 1MM **Privately Held**
SIC: 3053   Gaskets and sealing devices

(G-3000)
DIGATRON POWER ELECTRONICS INC
240 Long Hill Cross Rd (06484-6161)
PHONE..................................203 446-8000
Rolf Beckers, *
◆ EMP: 35 EST: 1962
SQ FT: 16,000
SALES (est): 15.89MM
SALES (corp-wide): 711.66K **Privately Held**
Web: www.digatron.com
SIC: 3629 3625 3825   Battery chargers, rectifying or nonrotating; Motor controls, electric; Battery testers, electrical
HQ: Digatron Power Electronics Gmbh
Tempelhofer Str. 12-14
Aachen NW 52068
241168090

(G-3001)
EASTERN CO (PA)
3 Enterprise Dr Ste 408 (06484-4696)
P.O. Box 460 (06770-0460)
PHONE..................................203 729-2255
August M Vlak, *Pr*
James A Mitarotonda, *
James P Woidke, *COO*
Peter O'hara, *CFO*
EMP: 40 EST: 1858
SQ FT: 8,000
SALES (est): 279.27MM
SALES (corp-wide): 279.27MM **Publicly Held**
Web: www.easterncompany.com
SIC: 3452 3316 2439 3429   Bolts, nuts, rivets, and washers; Cold finishing of steel shapes; Structural wood members, nec; Locks or lock sets

(G-3002)
EDGEWELL PER CARE BRANDS LLC (HQ)
Also Called: Energizer
6 Research Dr (06484-6228)
PHONE..................................203 944-5500

Ward Klein, *Ch Bd*
David Hatfield, *
Daniel J Sescleifer, *
◆ EMP: 370 EST: 1986
SALES (est): 3.24B
SALES (corp-wide): 2.25B **Publicly Held**
Web: www.edgewell.com
SIC: 3421 2844 2676   Razor blades and razors; Lotions, shaving; Tampons, sanitary: made from purchased paper
PA: Edgewell Personal Care Company
6 Research Dr Ste 400
Shelton CT 06484
203 944-5500

(G-3003)
EDGEWELL PERSONAL CARE COMPANY (PA)
Also Called: EDGEWELL
6 Research Dr Ste 400 (06484-6228)
PHONE..................................203 944-5500
Rod R Little, *Pr*
John C Hunter Iii, *Non-Executive Chairman of the Board*
Daniel J Sullivan, *CAO*
John N Hill, *Chief Human Resources Officer*
Latanya Langley, *CLO*
▼ EMP: 25 EST: 1772
SALES (est): 2.25B
SALES (corp-wide): 2.25B **Publicly Held**
Web: www.edgewell.com
SIC: 2844 3421 2676 3069   Perfumes, cosmetics and other toilet preparations; Razor blades and razors; Tampons, sanitary: made from purchased paper; Nipples, rubber

(G-3004)
ENERGIZER HOLDINGS
6 Research Dr Ste 400 (06484-6228)
PHONE..................................314 985-2000
Ward Klein, *CEO*
David Hatfield, *Pr*
EMP: 33 EST: 2014
SALES (est): 1.09MM **Privately Held**
Web: www.energizerholdings.com
SIC: 3421   Cutlery

(G-3005)
ENGINEERED FIBERS TECH LLC
88 Long Hill Cross Rd Ste 4 (06484-4783)
PHONE..................................203 922-1810
Robert E Evans, *Managing Member*
Andy Honkamp Actt, *Mgr*
▲ EMP: 12 EST: 1998
SQ FT: 18,000
SALES (est): 2.32MM
SALES (corp-wide): 9.64MM **Privately Held**
Web: www.eftfibers.com
SIC: 8711 5169 2299   Engineering services; Manmade fibers; Flock (recovered textile fibers)
PA: Cellusuede Products, Inc.
1515 Elmwood Rd
Rockford IL 61103
815 964-8619

(G-3006)
FIVE STAR PRODUCTS INC
2 Enterprise Dr Ste 303 (06484-4656)
PHONE..................................203 336-7900
David S Babcock, *Ch*
Wilfred A Martinez, *
David Babcock, *
Brian R Feidt, *
Terry Stysly, *
▲ EMP: 30 EST: 1980
SALES (est): 13.07MM **Privately Held**
Web: www.fivestarproducts.com

GEOGRAPHIC

SIC: **3273** 2891 2899 2851　Ready-mixed concrete; Adhesives and sealants; Chemical preparations, nec; Paints and allied products

(G-3007)
FLEXIINTERNATIONAL SFTWR INC (PA)
Also Called: Flexiinternational
2 Trap Falls Rd (06484-7623)
PHONE..............................203 925-3040
Stefan R Bothe, *Ch Bd*
Dmitry G Trudov, *
Maureen M Okerstrom, *
EMP: 34 EST: 1990
SQ FT: 25,000
SALES (est): 9.38MM **Privately Held**
Web: www.flexi.com
SIC: 7372　Application computer software

(G-3008)
GELDER AEROSPACE LLC
Also Called: United Aero Group
50 Waterview Dr Ste 120 (06484-4377)
PHONE..............................203 283-9524
Joshua Gelder, *Pr*
James Gelder, *Pr*
Joshua Gelder, *COO*
EMP: 8 EST: 2007
SALES (est): 2.4MM
SALES (corp-wide): 4.39MM **Privately Held**
Web: www.unitedaerogroup.com
SIC: 3728　Aircraft parts and equipment, nec
PA: Brightwater Uag, Llc
　　7199 Conway Rd
　　Orlando FL 32812
　　203 283-9524

(G-3009)
GRAYWOLF SENSING SOLUTIONS LLC (PA)
6 Research Dr Ste 110 (06484-6228)
PHONE..............................203 402-0477
Richard T Stonier, *Pr*
EMP: 8 EST: 1997
SALES (est): 2.32MM
SALES (corp-wide): 2.32MM **Privately Held**
Web: www.graywolfsensing.com
SIC: 3829　Measuring and controlling devices, nec

(G-3010)
GREAT LAKES CHEMICAL CORP (DH)
2 Armstrong Rd Ste 101 (06484-4735)
PHONE..............................203 573-2000
Craig Rogerson, *CEO*
Anne Noonan, *
◆ **EMP: 50 EST:** 1932
SALES (est): 262.8MM
SALES (corp-wide): 8.4B **Privately Held**
SIC: 2842 2899　Sanitation preparations, disinfectants and deodorants; Fire retardant chemicals
HQ: Lanxess Corporation
　　111 Ridc Park West Dr
　　Pittsburgh PA 15275
　　412 809-1000

(G-3011)
H J BAKER & BROTHER INC
2 Corporate Dr Ste 545 (06484-6279)
PHONE..............................501 664-4870
Mark Hohnbaum, *Pr*
EMP: 10 EST: 2018
SALES (est): 680.16K **Privately Held**
Web: www.hjbaker.com

SIC: **2048**　Prepared feeds, nec

(G-3012)
HAMWORTHY PEABODY COMBUSTN INC (DH)
Also Called: John Zink Company
6 Armstrong Rd Ste 2 (06484-4722)
PHONE..............................203 922-1199
Lawrence Berry, *Pr*
Anthony R Baker, *VP*
▲ **EMP: 23 EST:** 1920
SALES (est): 11.98MM
SALES (corp-wide): 36.93B **Privately Held**
SIC: 3433 3567 3561　Gas burners, industrial ; Industrial furnaces and ovens; Pumps and pumping equipment
HQ: John Zink Company, Llc
　　11920 E Apache St
　　Tulsa OK 74116
　　918 234-1800

(G-3013)
HIPOTRONICS INC (HQ)
Also Called: Hipotronics
40 Waterview Dr (06484-4300)
P.O. Box 414 (10509-0414)
PHONE..............................845 279-3644
Richard Davies, *Pr*
Timothy H Powers, *
Jeff Brown, *
◆ **EMP: 115 EST:** 1962
SALES (est): 48.39MM
SALES (corp-wide): 5.37B **Publicly Held**
Web: www.hubbell.com
SIC: 3825 3679 3829 3677　Test equipment for electronic and electrical circuits; Power supplies, all types: static; Measuring and controlling devices, nec; Electronic coils and transformers
PA: Hubbell Incorporated
　　40 Waterview Dr
　　Shelton CT 06484
　　475 882-4000

(G-3014)
HJ BAKER & BRO LLC (PA)
2 Corporate Dr Ste 545 (06484-6279)
PHONE..............................203 682-9200
Christopher Smith, *CEO*
David Smith, *
Jack L Williams, *
Stuart Adendorff, *
Mary Deegan, *
◆ **EMP: 40 EST:** 1850
SQ FT: 12,500
SALES (est): 110.47MM
SALES (corp-wide): 110.47MM **Privately Held**
Web: www.hjbaker.com
SIC: 5191 5052 2048　Feed; Sulfur; Feed supplements

(G-3015)
HJ BAKER INTERNATIONAL INC
2 Corporate Dr Ste 545 (06484-6279)
PHONE..............................203 682-9200
Christopher V B Smith, *Pr*
Timothy Puglielli, *VP*
EMP: 12 EST: 2013
SALES (est): 380.07K **Privately Held**
Web: www.hjbaker.com
SIC: 2048　Poultry feeds

(G-3016)
HOT TOPS LLC
240 Long Hill Cross Rd Ste 4 (06484-6161)
PHONE..............................203 926-2067
EMP: 10 EST: 1979
SQ FT: 9,000
SALES (est): 890.37K **Privately Held**

Web: www.hottops.com
SIC: 7336 3993 2396 2395　Silk screen design; Signs and advertising specialties; Automotive and apparel trimmings; Pleating and stitching

(G-3017)
HUBBELL INCORPORATED (PA)
Also Called: Hubbell
40 Waterview Dr (06484-4300)
PHONE..............................475 882-4000
Gerben W Bakker, *Ch Bd*
William R Sperry, *Ex VP*
Stephen M Mais, *Sr VP*
Katherine A Lane, *VP*
Jonathan M Del Nero, *CAO*
EMP: 639 EST: 1888
SALES (est): 5.37B
SALES (corp-wide): 5.37B **Publicly Held**
Web: www.hubbell.com
SIC: 3678 3699　Electronic connectors; Electrical equipment and supplies, nec

(G-3018)
HUBBELL INCORPORATED DELAWARE (HQ)
Also Called: Hubbell Raco Division
40 Waterview Dr (06484-4300)
PHONE..............................475 882-4000
David G Nord, *Pr*
▲ **EMP: 484 EST:** 1933
SQ FT: 350,000
SALES (est): 330.9MM
SALES (corp-wide): 5.37B **Publicly Held**
Web: www.hubbell.com
SIC: 3644 3699 3613　Outlet boxes (electric wiring devices); Electrical equipment and supplies, nec; Switchgear and switchboard apparatus
PA: Hubbell Incorporated
　　40 Waterview Dr
　　Shelton CT 06484
　　475 882-4000

(G-3019)
IDENTIFICATION PRODUCTS CORP (PA)
Also Called: ID Products.com
1 Parrott Dr Ste 500 (06484-4896)
P.O. Box 3276 (06605-0276)
PHONE..............................203 334-5969
EMP: 35 EST: 1973
SALES (est): 9.58MM
SALES (corp-wide): 9.58MM **Privately Held**
Web: www.idproducts.com
SIC: 2759 3479 3993 2671　Commercial printing, nec; Name plates: engraved, etched, etc.; Signs and advertising specialties; Paper; coated and laminated packaging

(G-3020)
INFORM INC
Also Called: Visible Record Systems
25 Brook St Ste 200 (06484-2332)
P.O. Box 785 (06484-0785)
PHONE..............................203 924-9929
Bill Carlson, *Pr*
David Carlson, *Sec*
EMP: 8 EST: 1992
SQ FT: 10,000
SALES (est): 946.63K **Privately Held**
Web: www.informprinting.com
SIC: 2752　Offset and photolithographic printing

(G-3021)
INLINE PLASTICS CORP
470 Bridgeport Ave (06484-4713)
PHONE..............................800 826-5567
EMP: 22
SALES (corp-wide): 146.76MM **Privately Held**
Web: www.inlineplastics.com
SIC: 3089　Injection molding of plastics
PA: Inline Plastics Corp.
　　42 Canal St
　　Shelton CT 06484
　　203 924-5933

(G-3022)
INLINE PLASTICS CORP (PA)
Also Called: Surelock Division
42 Canal St (06484-3265)
PHONE..............................203 924-5933
Thomas Orkisz, *Pr*
Edward A Colombo, *
◆ **EMP: 190 EST:** 1968
SQ FT: 312,000
SALES (est): 146.76MM
SALES (corp-wide): 146.76MM **Privately Held**
Web: www.inlineplastics.com
SIC: 3089　Injection molding of plastics

(G-3023)
INTENSITY THERAPEUTICS INC
1 Enterprise Dr Ste 430 (06484-4779)
PHONE..............................203 221-7381
Lewis H Bender, *Ch Bd*
Ian B Walters, *CMO*
James M Ahlers, *CFO*
John Wesolowski, *CAO*
Joseph Talamo, *CFO*
EMP: 16 EST: 2012
SQ FT: 4,100
Web: www.intensitytherapeutics.com
SIC: 2836　Biological products, except diagnostic

(G-3024)
ITT WATER & WASTEWATER USA INC (HQ)
1 Greenwich Pl Ste 2 (06484-7603)
PHONE..............................262 548-8181
Ron Port, *Pr*
Jonny Sandstedt, *
Frank Oliveira, *
◆ **EMP: 70 EST:** 1957
SQ FT: 35,000
SALES (est): 47.24MM
SALES (corp-wide): 3.28B **Publicly Held**
SIC: 3561　Pumps and pumping equipment
PA: Itt Inc.
　　100 Washington Blvd Fl 6
　　Stamford CT 06902
　　914 641-2000

(G-3025)
JOHN ZINK COMPANY LLC
Also Called: John Zink -Todd Combustn Group
2 Armstrong Rd Bldg 3 (06484-4735)
PHONE..............................203 925-0380
EMP: 24 EST: 1993
SQ FT: 45,000
SALES (est): 240.16K **Privately Held**
Web: www.johnzinkhamworthy.com
SIC: 3433 8711 5074　Oil burners, domestic or industrial; Engineering services; Oil burners

(G-3026)
KENO GRAPHIC SERVICES INC
1 Parrott Dr Ste 100 (06484-4853)
PHONE..............................203 925-7722

▲ = Import ▼ = Export
◆ = Import/Export

Daniel Kennedy, *Pr*
Thomas Kennedy, *
William Kennedy Junior, *Treas*
EMP: 27 **EST:** 1990
SALES (est): 2.85MM **Privately Held**
Web: www.kenographics.com
SIC: 2752   Offset printing

(G-3027)
LANXESS SOLUTIONS US INC
Also Called: Chemtura USA
2 Armstrong Rd Ste 101 (06484-4735)
PHONE..................................203 573-2000
EMP: 2500
Web: www.lanxess.com
SIC: 2869 2843 2821 2911   Industrial
organic chemicals, nec; Surface active
agents; Plastics materials and resins;
Residues

(G-3028)
LIFTWING LLC
12 Commerce Dr (06484-6202)
PHONE..................................203 913-2308
EMP: 10 **EST:** 2017
SALES (est): 904.61K **Privately Held**
Web: www.liftwing.com
SIC: 3728   Aircraft parts and equipment, nec

(G-3029)
LOANWORKS SERVICING LLC
3 Corporate Dr Ste 208 (06484-6278)
PHONE..................................203 402-7304
Joe Caravetta, *Dir*
EMP: 15 **EST:** 2009
SALES (est): 496.03K **Privately Held**
SIC: 1389   Roustabout service

(G-3030)
MERCANTILE DEVELOPMENT INC
10 Waterview Dr (06484-4300)
P.O. Box 825 (06484-0825)
PHONE..................................203 922-8880
F Alan Fankhanel, *Pr*
Lucia Furman, *
◆ **EMP:** 38 **EST:** 1947
SQ FT: 138,960
SALES (est): 10.6MM **Privately Held**
Web: www.mdiwipers.com
SIC: 2679   Paper products, converted, nec

(G-3031)
MICA CORPORATION
9 Mountain View Dr (06484-6404)
PHONE..................................203 922-8888
◆ **EMP:** 25 **EST:** 1971
SALES (est): 4.11MM **Privately Held**
Web: www.mica-corp.com
SIC: 2891   Adhesives

(G-3032)
MICROPHASE CORPORATION
100 Trap Falls Road Ext Ste 400
(06484-4646)
PHONE..................................203 866-8000
Amos Kohn, *CEO*
Necdet F Ergul, *
James Ashman, *
Jeffrey R F Peterson, *
EMP: 26 **EST:** 1955
SQ FT: 23,898
SALES (est): 8.82MM
SALES (corp-wide): 134.33MM **Publicly Held**
Web: www.microphase.com

SIC: 3663 3677 3674 3661   Microwave
communication equipment; Electronic coils
and transformers; Semiconductors and
related devices; Telephone and telegraph
apparatus
HQ: Coolisys Technologies, Inc.
1635 S Main St
Milpitas CA 95035
877 634-0982

(G-3033)
NAIAD DYNAMICS US INC (HQ)
Also Called: Naiad Marine Systems
50 Parrott Dr (06484-4733)
PHONE..................................203 929-6355
John D Venables, *Pr*
▲ **EMP:** 50 **EST:** 2008
SQ FT: 26,500
SALES (est): 15.27MM **Privately Held**
Web: www.naiadmfg.com
SIC: 3531 3625 3569 3599   Marine related
equipment; Marine and navy auxiliary
controls; Assembly machines, non-
metalworking; Machine and other job shop
work
PA: Naiad Maritime Group, Inc.
50 Parrott Dr
Shelton CT 06484

(G-3034)
NAIAD MARITIME GROUP INC (PA)
Also Called: Naiad Dynamics
50 Parrott Dr (06484-4733)
PHONE..................................203 944-1932
EMP: 50 **EST:** 2008
SALES (est): 29.26MM **Privately Held**
Web: www.naiad.com
SIC: 6719 3731 3531   Personal holding
companies, except banks; Shipbuilding and
repairing; Marine related equipment

(G-3035)
NATIONAL PUBLISHER SVCS LLC
Also Called: NPS Media Group
2 Enterprise Dr Ste 420 (06484-4656)
PHONE..................................917 902-9590
Mark Harris, *CEO*
Bob Mcilwain, *CFO*
EMP: 12 **EST:** 2017
SALES (est): 554.32K **Privately Held**
Web: www.npsmediagroup.com
SIC: 2741   Miscellaneous publishing

(G-3036)
NATIONAL SHTING SPT FNDTION IN
6 Corporate Dr Ste 650 (06484-6271)
PHONE..................................203 426-1320
Joseph Bartozzi, *CEO*
Nancy Coburn, *
Steve Sanetti, *
EMP: 52 **EST:** 1961
SQ FT: 20,000
SALES (est): 51.69MM **Privately Held**
Web: www.nssf.org
SIC: 2721 8611 2741   Magazines: publishing
only, not printed on site; Trade associations
; Miscellaneous publishing

(G-3037)
NEVAMAR COMPANY LLC (HQ)
Also Called: Nevamar Distributors
2 Corporate Dr Ste 946 (06484-6274)
PHONE..................................203 925-1556
Jeffrey Muller, *Managing Member*
Jim Tees, *
◆ **EMP:** 300 **EST:** 2002

SALES (est): 104.16MM **Privately Held**
Web: www.panolam.com
SIC: 3089 5162   Panels, building: plastics,
nec; Plastics materials and basic shapes
PA: Panolam Industries International, Inc.
2 Corporate Dr Ste 946
Shelton CT 06484

(G-3038)
NEW ENGLAND STAIR COMPANY INC
1 White St (06484-3117)
P.O. Box 763 (06484-0763)
PHONE..................................203 924-0606
TOLL FREE: 800
William J Sylvia, *Pr*
Matthew Sylvia, *Sec*
EMP: 21 **EST:** 1976
SQ FT: 25,000
SALES (est): 2.52MM **Privately Held**
Web: www.newenglandstair.com
SIC: 2431   Staircases and stairs, wood

(G-3039)
NEWCO CONDENSER INC
40 Waterview Dr (06484-4300)
PHONE..................................475 882-4000
EMP: 18 **EST:** 2007
SALES (est): 554.11K
SALES (corp-wide): 4.95B **Publicly Held**
SIC: 3264 3699 3675 3674   Insulators,
electrical: porcelain; Electrical equipment
and supplies, nec; Electronic capacitors;
Semiconductors and related devices
PA: Hubbell Incorporated
40 Waterview Dr
Shelton CT 06484
475 882-4000

(G-3040)
NNI LIQUIDATION CORP
7 Progress Dr (06484-6218)
PHONE..................................203 929-2221
EMP: 10 **EST:** 2019
SALES (est): 193.88K **Privately Held**
Web: www.ensightsolutions.us
SIC: 3549   Metalworking machinery, nec

(G-3041)
NOVAMONT NORTH AMERICA INC
1000 Bridgeport Ave Ste 304 (06484-4660)
PHONE..................................203 744-8801
Gaetano Lo Monaco, *Prin*
Alessandro Ferlito, *Pr*
EMP: 16 **EST:** 2010
SALES (est): 1.81MM
SALES (corp-wide): 137.63B **Privately Held**
Web: northamerica.novamont.com
SIC: 3821   Chemical laboratory apparatus,
nec
HQ: Novamont Spa
Via Giacomo Fauser 8
Novara NO 28100
032 169-9600

(G-3042)
O E M CONTROLS INC (PA)
10 Controls Dr (06484-6100)
P.O. Box 894 (06484-0894)
PHONE..................................203 929-8431
S Brian Simons, *Pr*
Keith T Simons, *
Sam Simons, *
Samuel R N Simons, *
EMP: 196 **EST:** 1966
SQ FT: 56,000
SALES (est): 32.72MM
SALES (corp-wide): 32.72MM **Privately Held**

Web: www.oemcontrols.com
SIC: 3625 3229 3577   Electric controls and
control accessories, industrial; Fiber optics
strands; Computer peripheral equipment,
nec

(G-3043)
OERLIKON AM MEDICAL INC
Also Called: (Parent Is Oerlikon Usa Holding
Inc, Trafford, Pa.)
10 Constitution Blvd S (06484-4302)
PHONE..................................203 712-1030
Ottavio Disanto, *CEO*
Thomas Barret, *
Nancy Theodorides, *Treas*
Mark Zembrzuski, *Sec*
EMP: 75 **EST:** 1984
SQ FT: 30,000
SALES (est): 14.39MM
SALES (corp-wide): 2.87B **Privately Held**
SIC: 3841   Surgical instruments and
apparatus
PA: Oc Oerlikon Corporation Ag, Pfaffikon
Churerstrasse 120
PfAffikon SZ 8808
583609696

(G-3044)
PANOLAM INDUSTRIES INC (HQ)
Also Called: Panolam Surface System
2 Corporate Dr Ste 946 (06484-6274)
PHONE..................................203 925-1556
Robert Muller, *Pr*
Alan S Kabus, *
Lawrence Grossman, *
Jeffery Muller, *
Vincent Miceli, *
▲ **EMP:** 40 **EST:** 1996
SALES (est): 101MM **Privately Held**
Web: www.panolam.com
SIC: 3089 3083   Panels, building: plastics,
nec; Laminated plastics plate and sheet
PA: Panolam Industries International, Inc.
2 Corporate Dr Ste 946
Shelton CT 06484

(G-3045)
PANOLAM INDUSTRIES INTL INC (PA)
Also Called: Panolam Surface Systems
2 Corporate Dr Ste 946 (06484-6274)
PHONE..................................203 925-1556
◆ **EMP:** 40 **EST:** 1997
SALES (est): 419.38MM **Privately Held**
Web: www.panolam.com
SIC: 2493 3089   Particleboard products;
Panels, building: plastics, nec

(G-3046)
PERKINELMER US LLC (PA) ✪
710 Bridgeport Ave (06484-4794)
PHONE..................................203 925-4600
Jessica Higgins, *Managing Member*
EMP: 33 **EST:** 2023
SALES (est): 50.26MM
SALES (corp-wide): 50.26MM **Privately Held**
SIC: 3826   Analytical instruments

(G-3047)
PIONEER PLASTICS CORPORATION (HQ)
Also Called: Pionite Decorative Surfaces
2 Corporate Dr Ste 946 (06484-6274)
PHONE..................................203 925-1556
Alan S Kabus, *Pr*
Robert Muller, *
Jeffrey Muller, *

Vincent Miceli, *
Larry Grossman, *
◆ **EMP: 50 EST:** 1946
SQ FT: 560,000
SALES (est): 204.06MM **Privately Held**
Web: www.panolam.com
SIC: 3083 3087 Laminated plastics plate
and sheet; Custom compound purchased
resins
PA: Panolam Industries International, Inc.
2 Corporate Dr Ste 946
Shelton CT 06484

(G-3048)
PITNEY BOWES INC
Pitney Bowes
27 Waterview Dr (06484-4361)
PHONE..........................203 356-5000
EMP: 8
SALES (corp-wide): 3.54B **Publicly Held**
Web: www.pitneybowes.com
SIC: 3579 Postage meters
PA: Pitney Bowes Inc.
3001 Summer St
Stamford CT 06905
203 356-5000

(G-3049)
PITNEY BOWES INC
Also Called: Pitney Bowes
27 Waterview Dr (06484-4361)
PHONE..........................203 922-4000
Brian Baxendale, *Brnch Mgr*
EMP: 35
SALES (corp-wide): 3.54B **Publicly Held**
Web: www.pitneybowes.com
SIC: 3579 Postage meters
PA: Pitney Bowes Inc.
3001 Summer St
Stamford CT 06905
203 356-5000

(G-3050)
PLAYTEX PRODUCTS LLC (HQ)
6 Research Dr Ste 400 (06484-6228)
P.O. Box 889 (06484-0889)
PHONE..........................203 944-5500
Neil P Defeo, *Managing Member*
▼ **EMP: 100 EST:** 1932
SQ FT: 59,100
SALES (est): 413.9MM
SALES (corp-wide): 2.25B **Publicly Held**
SIC: 2676 3069 2844 3842 Tampons,
sanitary: made from purchased paper;
Nipples, rubber; Suntan lotions and oils;
Gloves, safety
PA: Edgewell Personal Care Company
6 Research Dr Ste 400
Shelton CT 06484
203 944-5500

(G-3051)
**PR-MX HOLDINGS COMPANY
LLC (HQ)**
Also Called: Precision Resource Mexico
25 Forest Pkwy (06484-6122)
PHONE..........................203 925-0012
EMP: 78 EST: 2005
SQ FT: 70,000
SALES (est): 7.14MM
SALES (corp-wide): 125.54MM **Privately
Held**
SIC: 3469 Stamping metal for the trade
PA: Precision Resource, Inc.
25 Forest Pkwy
Shelton CT 06484
203 925-0012

(G-3052)
**PRECISE CIRCUIT COMPANY
INC**
155 Myrtle St (06484-4062)
PHONE..........................203 924-2512
Thomas Misencik, *Pr*
Roseann Misencik, *Sec*
EMP: 32 EST: 1984
SQ FT: 15,000
SALES (est): 2.48MM **Privately Held**
Web: www.precisecircuit.com
SIC: 3672 Circuit boards, television and
radio printed

(G-3053)
PRECISION RESOURCE INC (PA)
25 Forest Pkwy (06484-6122)
PHONE..........................203 925-0012
Peter Wolcott, *CEO*
Charles Polatsek, *
John Weiland, *
▲ **EMP: 176 EST:** 1953
SQ FT: 100,000
SALES (est): 125.54MM
SALES (corp-wide): 125.54MM **Privately
Held**
Web: www.precisionresource.com
SIC: 3469 Stamping metal for the trade

(G-3054)
**PREFERRED TOOL & DIE INC
(PA)**
Also Called: Preferred Precision
30 Forest Pkwy (06484-6122)
PHONE..........................203 925-8525
Michael Fortin, *Pr*
Wayne Fortin, *
Virginia Fortin, *
EMP: 42 EST: 1965
SQ FT: 26,000
SALES (est): 9.53MM
SALES (corp-wide): 9.53MM **Privately
Held**
Web: www.preferredtool.com
SIC: 3469 3544 Stamping metal for the trade
; Special dies and tools

(G-3055)
PREFERRED TOOL & DIE INC
Preferred Precision
19 Forest Pkwy (06484-6135)
PHONE..........................203 925-8525
Mark Testani, *Brnch Mgr*
EMP: 40
SALES (corp-wide): 9.53MM **Privately
Held**
Web: www.preferredtool.com
SIC: 3545 Precision tools, machinists'
PA: Preferred Tool & Die, Inc.
30 Forest Pkwy
Shelton CT 06484
203 925-8525

(G-3056)
**PRESTIGE INDUSTRIAL FINSHG
CO**
511 River Rd (06484-4521)
P.O. Box 287 (06484-0287)
PHONE..........................203 924-7720
Michele Proto, *Pr*
James Osso, *VP*
EMP: 29 EST: 1981
SQ FT: 5,000
SALES (est): 948.33K **Privately Held**
Web:
www.prestigeindustrialfinishing.com
SIC: 3479 Coating of metals and formed
products

(G-3057)
QDS LLC
120 Long Hill Cross Rd (06484-6180)
PHONE..........................203 338-9668
Paul Christian, *Prin*
EMP: 7 EST: 2015
SALES (est): 252.12K **Privately Held**
Web: www.qds-mfg.com
SIC: 3999 Manufacturing industries, nec

(G-3058)
QUALEDI INC
Also Called: QUALEDI INC
1 Trap Falls Rd Ste 206 (06484-4672)
P.O. Box 623 (06615-0623)
PHONE..........................203 538-5320
Stephen A Morocco, *Brnch Mgr*
EMP: 8
SALES (corp-wide): 990.72K **Privately
Held**
Web: www.qualedi.com
SIC: 7372 Prepackaged software
PA: Qualedi, Inc.
121 W Main St Ste 4
Milford CT

(G-3059)
RCD LLC
230 Long Hill Cross Rd (06484-6160)
PHONE..........................203 712-1900
Harry Holiday Iii, *Brnch Mgr*
EMP: 31
Web: www.dtengineering.com
SIC: 3312 Tool and die steel and alloys
PA: Rcd Llc
1107 Springfield Rd
Lebanon MO 65536

(G-3060)
REVVITY INC
Perkinelmer Life and Analytic
710 Bridgeport Ave (06484-4750)
P.O. Box 520 (06410-0520)
PHONE..........................203 925-4600
EMP: 8
SALES (corp-wide): 3.31B **Publicly Held**
Web: www.perkinelmer.com
SIC: 3826 Analytical instruments
PA: Revvity, Inc.
940 Winter St
Waltham MA 02451
781 663-6900

(G-3061)
**REVVITY HEALTH SCIENCES
INC**
710 Bridgeport Ave (06484-4750)
PHONE..........................203 925-4600
EMP: 135
SALES (corp-wide): 3.31B **Publicly Held**
Web: www.perkinelmer.com
SIC: 3826 Analytical instruments
HQ: Revvity Health Sciences, Inc.
940 Winter St
Waltham MA 02451
781 663-6900

(G-3062)
**SIKORSKY AIRCRAFT
CORPORATION**
1 Far Mill Xing (06484-6121)
PHONE..........................203 386-7861
Filmson Alexander, *Brnch Mgr*
EMP: 13
Web: www.gyrocamsystems.com
SIC: 3721 Helicopters
HQ: Sikorsky Aircraft Corporation
6900 Main St
Stratford CT 06614

(G-3063)
**SIKORSKY AIRCRAFT
CORPORATION**
33 Platt Rd (06615-9129)
P.O. Box 9729 (06615-9129)
PHONE..........................203 386-4000
Deborah Torrice, *Plng Mgr*
EMP: 24
Web: www.lockheedmartin.com
SIC: 3721 Helicopters
HQ: Sikorsky Aircraft Corporation
6900 Main St
Stratford CT 06614

(G-3064)
SPINE WAVE INC
3 Enterprise Dr Ste 210 (06484-4696)
PHONE..........................203 944-9494
Mark Loguidice, *Pr*
EMP: 100 EST: 2001
SALES (est): 21.64MM **Privately Held**
Web: www.spinewave.com
SIC: 3841 Surgical and medical instruments

(G-3065)
SPM MANAGEMENT INC
Also Called: Success Printing and Mailing
3 Enterprise Dr (06484-7620)
PHONE..........................203 847-1112
Robert Hurwitz, *Pr*
William Roos, *VP*
EMP: 12 EST: 1989
SALES (est): 2.37MM **Privately Held**
Web: www.successprint.com
SIC: 2752 2796 7336 Offset printing;
Platemaking services; Commercial art and
graphic design

(G-3066)
SUMNER COMMUNICATIONS INC
6 Research Dr Ste 420 (06484-6228)
PHONE..........................203 748-2050
Eugene Scott Sumner, *Pr*
Sherwood S Sumner, *VP*
EMP: 20 EST: 1988
SQ FT: 5,000
SALES (est): 2.22MM **Privately Held**
Web: www.sumnercom.com
SIC: 2721 Magazines: publishing only, not
printed on site

(G-3067)
TALALAY GLOBAL INC (DH)
Also Called: Latex Foam Products
510 River Rd (06484-4517)
PHONE..........................203 924-0700
Marc Navarre, *CEO*
Steve Turner, *
◆ **EMP: 15 EST:** 2020
SALES (est): 53.56MM
SALES (corp-wide): 250.72K **Privately
Held**
Web: www.talalayglobal.com
SIC: 2392 3069 Household furnishings, nec;
Foam rubber
HQ: Artilat
Breugelhoevestraat 135
Nijlen 2560
34101300

(G-3068)
THE VIKING TOOL COMPANY
435 Access Rd (06484-5302)
P.O. Box 808 (06484-0808)
PHONE..........................203 929-1457
Ole C Severson Junior, *Pr*
Ole C Severson Iii, *Treas*
James J Severson, *Sec*
EMP: 20 EST: 1946
SQ FT: 10,000

SALES (est): 424.22K **Privately Held**
Web: www.vikingtool.com
SIC: 3541 5084 3545 Machine tools, metal cutting type; Industrial machinery and equipment; Machine tool accessories

(G-3069)
TIGER-SUL PRODUCTS LLC
4 Armstrong Rd Ste 220 (06484-4721)
P.O. Box 5 (36504-0005)
PHONE.........................203 635-0190
Don Cherry, *Pr*
▼ **EMP:** 50 **EST:** 1975
SALES (est): 12.64MM
SALES (corp-wide): 23.24MM **Privately Held**
Web: www.tigersul.com
SIC: 2819 Sulfur, recovered or refined, incl. from sour natural gas
PA: Platte River Equity Iii, L.P.
200 Fillmore St Ste 200 # 200
Denver CO 80206
303 292-7300

(G-3070)
TORTRAN INC
Also Called: Bridgeport Magnetics
6 Waterview Dr (06484-4300)
PHONE.........................203 538-5062
FAX: 203 384-8120
▲ **EMP:** 10
SQ FT: 18,000
SALES (est): 1.8MM **Privately Held**
Web: www.tortran.com
SIC: 3612 3677 Transformers, except electric; Electronic coils and transformers

(G-3071)
TRANSWITCH CORPORATION
3 Enterprise Dr (06484-4696)
PHONE.........................203 929-8810
EMP: 112
Web: www.transwitch.com
SIC: 3674 Semiconductors and related devices

(G-3072)
TREIF USA INC
50 Waterview Dr Ste 130 (06484-4377)
PHONE.........................203 929-9930
Guenter Becker, *Pr*
▲ **EMP:** 15 **EST:** 1992
SQ FT: 12,000
SALES (est): 4.95MM
SALES (corp-wide): 1.77B **Privately Held**
Web: www.treifusa.com
SIC: 3556 5046 Food products machinery; Commercial equipment, nec
HQ: Marel Treif Gmbh
Toni-Reifenhauser-Str. 1
Oberlahr RP 57641
268 594-4389

(G-3073)
UNILEVER ASCC AG
3 Corporate Dr (06484-6222)
PHONE.........................203 381-2482
EMP: 300
SALES (corp-wide): 62.39B **Privately Held**
Web: www.unilever.ch
SIC: 2841 2099 Soap and other detergents; Syrups
HQ: Unilever Ascc Ag
Spitalstrasse 5
Schaffhausen SH

(G-3074)
URBAN EXPOSITION LLC (DH)
Also Called: Clarion Ux
6 Research Dr (06484-6228)

PHONE.........................203 242-8717
▲ **EMP:** 25 **EST:** 1995
SALES (est): 10.48MM
SALES (corp-wide): 541.63MM **Privately Held**
Web: us.clarionevents.com
SIC: 7389 8741 2721 7299 Convention and show services; Management services; Magazines: publishing and printing; Party planning service
HQ: Clarion Events Limited
Bedford House
London SW6 3
207 370-8200

(G-3075)
VIDENDUM PROD SOLUTIONS INC (HQ)
Also Called: Vitec Production Solutions Inc
14 Progress Dr (06484-6216)
P.O. Box 827 (06484-0827)
PHONE.........................203 929-1100
Dan Fitzpatrick, *Pr*
Michael Accardi, *
Matthew Danilowicz, *
Micheal L Martell, *
Curt Dann, *
▲ **EMP:** 41 **EST:** 1970
SALES (est): 48.98MM
SALES (corp-wide): 543.23MM **Privately Held**
Web: www.antonbauer.com
SIC: 3861 3692 Cameras and related equipment; Primary batteries, dry and wet
PA: Videndum Plc
Bridge House
Richmond TW9 1
208 332-4600

(G-3076)
VISHAY AMERICAS INC (HQ)
Also Called: Vishay
1 Greenwich Pl (06484-7603)
PHONE.........................203 452-5648
Gerald Paul, *CEO*
Marc Zandman, *CDO*
EMP: 500 **EST:** 1999
SALES (est): 294.2MM
SALES (corp-wide): 3.5B **Publicly Held**
Web: www.vishay.com
SIC: 3676 3674 Electronic resistors; Semiconductors and related devices
PA: Vishay Intertechnology, Inc.
63 Lancaster Ave
Malvern PA 19355
610 644-1300

(G-3077)
WEST-CONN TOOL AND DIE INC
128 Long Hill Cross Rd (06484-6169)
PHONE.........................203 538-5081
Laura Marasco, *CEO*
David Marasco, *
EMP: 40 **EST:** 1983
SQ FT: 15,900
SALES (est): 4.96MM **Privately Held**
Web: www.westconntool.com
SIC: 3544 3841 3999 Special dies and tools; Surgical instruments and apparatus; Barber and beauty shop equipment

(G-3078)
WICKS BUSINESS INFORMATION LLC (PA)
Also Called: Treasury & Risk Management
4 Research Dr Ste 402 (06484-6242)
PHONE.........................203 334-2002
EMP: 10 **EST:** 1999

SIC: 2721 2711 Magazines: publishing only, not printed on site; Newspapers: publishing only, not printed on site

(G-3079)
WIFFLE BALL INCORPORATED
275 Bridgeport Ave (06484-3827)
P.O. Box 193 (06484-0193)
PHONE.........................203 924-4643
David J Mullany, *Pr*
Stephen A Mullany, *VP*
EMP: 15 **EST:** 1953
SQ FT: 20,000
SALES (est): 2.52MM **Privately Held**
Web: www.wiffle.com
SIC: 3949 Sporting and athletic goods, nec

(G-3080)
XYLEM WATER SOLUTIONS USA INC
1000 Bridgeport Ave Ste 402 (06484-4660)
PHONE.........................203 450-3715
EMP: 47
Web: www.xylem.com
SIC: 3561 Pumps and pumping equipment
HQ: Xylem Water Solutions U.S.A., Inc.
4828 Parkway Plaza Blvd # 200
Charlotte NC 28217

(G-3081)
YXLON
100 Trap Falls Road Ext (06484-4646)
PHONE.........................234 284-7862
Chris Warren, *Prin*
EMP: 8 **EST:** 2014
SALES (est): 240.72K **Privately Held**
Web: yxlon.comet.tech
SIC: 3844 X-ray apparatus and tubes

Sherman
Fairfield County

(G-3082)
PHOCUSWRIGHT INC (HQ)
1 Route 37 E Ste 200 (06784-1406)
P.O. Box 760 (06784-0760)
PHONE.........................860 350-4084
EMP: 18 **EST:** 1994
SALES (est): 11.4MM
SALES (corp-wide): 110.19MM **Privately Held**
Web: www.phocuswright.com
SIC: 8742 2759 Marketing consulting services; Publication printing
PA: Northstar Travel Media, Llc
100 Lighting Way Ste 200
Secaucus NJ 07094
201 902-2000

Simsbury
Hartford County

(G-3083)
BMI CAD SERVICES INC
8a Herman Dr (06070-1404)
P.O. Box 522 (06070-0522)
PHONE.........................860 658-0808
Bradford T Martin, *Pr*
Karen A Martin, *VP*
EMP: 10 **EST:** 1993
SALES (est): 1.63MM **Privately Held**
Web: www.bmicad.com
SIC: 3599 Machine shop, jobbing and repair

(G-3084)
BONDI BAND LLC
24 Metacom Dr (06070-1850)
PHONE.........................207 576-4191
EMP: 15 **EST:** 2006
SALES (est): 436.58K **Privately Held**
Web: www.bondiband.com
SIC: 7929 Entertainment service; Men's miscellaneous accessories; Apparel accessories

(G-3085)
DYNO NOBEL INC
660 Hopmeadow St (06070-2420)
P.O. Box 2006 (06070-7603)
PHONE.........................860 843-2000
Jock Muir, *Brnch Mgr*
EMP: 150
Web: www.dynonobel.com
SIC: 2892 Detonators and detonating caps
HQ: Dyno Nobel Inc.
6440 S Millrock Dr # 150
Salt Lake City UT 84121
801 364-4800

(G-3086)
EASCO HAND TOOLS INC
Also Called: Danaher Tool Group
125 Powder Forest Dr (06070)
PHONE.........................860 843-7351
◆ **EMP:** 1400
SIC: 3423 Wrenches, hand tools

(G-3087)
ENSIGN BICKFORD INDUSTRIES
100 Grist Mill Ln (06070-2484)
P.O. Box 7 (06070-0007)
PHONE.........................203 843-2126
EMP: 20 **EST:** 2009
SALES (est): 1.55MM **Privately Held**
Web: www.ebad.com
SIC: 3999 Manufacturing industries, nec

(G-3088)
ENSIGN-BCKFORD RNWBLE ENRGIES
125 Powder Forest Dr (06070)
PHONE.........................860 843-2000
Caleb E White, *Pr*
Dorothy Hammett, *Sec*
Scott M Deakin, *VP*
EMP: 9 **EST:** 2009
SALES (est): 2.02MM
SALES (corp-wide): 696.33MM **Privately Held**
Web: www.ensign-bickfordind.com
SIC: 2421 Wood chips, produced at mill
PA: Ensign-Bickford Industries, Inc.
999 17th St Ste 900
Denver CO 80202
860 843-2000

(G-3089)
ENSIGN-BICKFORD AROSPC DEF CO (HQ)
Also Called: EBA&d
640 Hopmeadow St (06070-2420)
P.O. Box 429 (06070-0429)
PHONE.........................860 843-2289
Brendan Walsh, *Pr*
Brendan M Walsh, *
Denise M Grant, *
Dorothy T Hammett, *
▲ **EMP:** 51 **EST:** 2000
SQ FT: 150,000
SALES (est): 115.27MM
SALES (corp-wide): 696.33MM **Privately Held**
Web: www.ebad.com

GEOGRAPHIC

SIC: 3812 Search and navigation equipment
PA: Ensign-Bickford Industries, Inc.
999 17th St Ste 900
Denver CO 80202
860 843-2000

(G-3090)
ENSIGN-BICKFORD COMPANY (HQ)
125 Powder Forest Dr (06070)
P.O. Box 711 (06070-0711)
PHONE..........................860 843-2001
Scott M Deakin, *Pr*
Charles Difatta, *
Dorothy Hammett, *
◆ **EMP: 16 EST:** 1971
SQ FT: 11,000
SALES (est): 26.01MM
SALES (corp-wide): 696.33MM **Privately Held**
Web: www.ensign-bickfordind.com
SIC: 3812 Search and navigation equipment
PA: Ensign-Bickford Industries, Inc.
999 17th St Ste 900
Denver CO 80202
860 843-2000

(G-3091)
INTEGRITY GRAPHICS INC
42 Carver Cir (06070-2020)
PHONE..........................800 343-1248
Joseph E La Valla, *Pr*
Michael Hart, *
EMP: 105 EST: 1988
SALES (est): 10.94MM **Privately Held**
Web: telling-secrets.blogspot.com
SIC: 2752 Offset printing

(G-3092)
J FOSTER ICE CREAM
894 Hopmeadow St (06070-1825)
PHONE..........................860 651-1499
John Darcangelo, *Brnch Mgr*
EMP: 73
Web: www.jfostericecream.com
SIC: 2024 5812 Ice cream and frozen deserts; Ice cream stands or dairy bars
PA: J Foster Ice Cream
4 Bailey Rd
Avon CT 06001

(G-3093)
MICROSEMI CORPORATION
Also Called: Microsemi
90 Wolcott Rd (06070-1462)
P.O. Box 549 (06070-0549)
PHONE..........................860 651-0211
EMP: 79
SALES (corp-wide): 8.44B **Publicly Held**
Web: www.microsemi.com
SIC: 3679 Waveguides and fittings
HQ: Microsemi Corporation
11861 Western Ave
Garden Grove CA 92841
949 380-6100

(G-3094)
MICROTOOLS INC
714 Hopmeadow St Ste 14 (06070-2234)
P.O. Box 624 (06070-0624)
PHONE..........................860 651-6170
Bob Japenga, *Pr*
Joseph Lehman, *Sec*
Nancy Lehman, *Stockholder*
Barbara Japenga, *Stockholder*
EMP: 8 EST: 1989
SQ FT: 900
SALES (est): 975.42K **Privately Held**
Web: www.microtoolsinc.com

SIC: 7371 3825 Computer software development; Test equipment for electronic and electrical circuits

(G-3095)
PHARMAVITE CORP
10 Station St (06070-2258)
PHONE..........................860 651-1885
Thomas Leloup, *Prin*
EMP: 39 EST: 1997
SALES (est): 226.66K **Privately Held**
SIC: 2834 Vitamin preparations

(G-3096)
SHELBRACK WOODWORKING
15 Nod Brook Dr (06070-3015)
PHONE..........................860 431-5028
Wayne S Shelbrack, *Prin*
EMP: 7 **EST:** 2010
SALES (est): 218.88K **Privately Held**
SIC: 2431 Millwork

(G-3097)
SIMSBURY PRECISION PDTS INC
11 Herman Dr Ste C (06070-1463)
PHONE..........................860 658-6909
Bruce Staubley, *Pr*
EMP: 8 EST: 1966
SQ FT: 4,800
SALES (est): 859.07K **Privately Held**
Web: www.simsburyprecision.com
SIC: 3599 Machine shop, jobbing and repair

Somers
Tolland County

(G-3098)
CT FIBEROPTICS INC
64 Field Rd Ste 5a (06071-2043)
PHONE..........................860 763-4341
John Plocharczyk, *Pr*
EMP: 10 EST: 1987
SQ FT: 4,500
SALES (est): 819.58K **Privately Held**
Web: www.ctfiberoptics.com
SIC: 3827 Optical instruments and lenses

(G-3099)
PARKER SEPTIC LLC
Also Called: Parker Saw Mill
77 South Rd (06071-2109)
PHONE..........................860 749-8220
Perlin A Parker Junior, *Pt*
Susan Parker, *Pt*
EMP: 7 **EST:** 1980
SALES (est): 196.8K **Privately Held**
SIC: 7699 2421 Septic tank cleaning service ; Sawmills and planing mills, general

(G-3100)
STAR STEEL STRUCTURES INC
392 Four Bridges Rd (06071-1107)
P.O. Box 535 (06071-0535)
PHONE..........................860 763-5681
Karl Milikowski, *Ch*
Kurt Knoefel, *Pr*
Mark Milikowski, *Sec*
Neal Farnham, *VP*
EMP: 9 EST: 1984
SQ FT: 9,000
SALES (est): 908.08K **Privately Held**
SIC: 3448 Greenhouses, prefabricated metal

Somersville
Tolland County

(G-3101)
CARBON PRODUCTS INC
40 Scitico Rd (06072)
P.O. Box N (06072-0914)
PHONE..........................860 749-0614
Peter Ouellet, *Pr*
◆ **EMP: 9 EST:** 1960
SQ FT: 18,000
SALES (est): 797.76K **Privately Held**
SIC: 3624 Carbon and graphite products

South Windham
Windham County

(G-3102)
HARWEST HOLDINGS ONE INC
1102 Windham Rd (06266-1131)
P.O. Box 96 (06266-0096)
PHONE..........................860 423-8334
Robert Mongell, *Pr*
Anthony Williams, *Ch*
Joseph Loffredo, *VP*
EMP: 23 EST: 1994
SALES (est): 649.53K **Privately Held**
Web: www.microprecisiongroup.com
SIC: 3599 Machine shop, jobbing and repair

(G-3103)
MICRO PRECISION LLC
1102 Windham Rd (06266-1131)
P.O. Box 96 (06266-0096)
PHONE..........................860 423-4575
EMP: 29 EST: 2011
SALES (est): 5.39MM **Privately Held**
Web: www.microprecisiongroup.com
SIC: 3599 Machine shop, jobbing and repair

(G-3104)
WENTWORTH MANUFACTURING LLC
Also Called: Wentworth
1102 Windham Rd (06266-1131)
P.O. Box 96 (06266-0096)
PHONE..........................860 423-4575
EMP: 92 EST: 1981
SQ FT: 7,000
SALES (est): 6.94MM **Privately Held**
Web: www.microprecisiongroup.com
SIC: 3599 Machine shop, jobbing and repair

(G-3105)
WINDHAM AUTOMATED MACHINES INC
Also Called: W A M
1102 Windham Rd (06266-1131)
PHONE..........................860 208-5297
Christopher H Ramm, *Pr*
EMP: 20 EST: 1985
SALES (est): 279.08K **Privately Held**
SIC: 3559 Automotive related machinery

South Windsor
Hartford County

(G-3106)
ACCUTURN MANUFACTURING CO LLC
100 Commerce Way (06074-1151)
PHONE..........................860 289-6355
EMP: 16 EST: 1997
SQ FT: 2,000

SALES (est): 1.8MM **Privately Held**
Web: www.accuturnmfg.com
SIC: 3599 Machine shop, jobbing and repair

(G-3107)
AERO TUBE TECHNOLOGIES LLC
425 Sullivan Ave (06074-1947)
PHONE..........................860 289-2520
EMP: 25
Web: www.aerotubetech.com
SIC: 3728 Aircraft parts and equipment, nec

(G-3108)
AERO-MED LLC
571 Nutmeg Rd N (06074-2461)
PHONE..........................860 659-2270
Daniel Del Mastro, *Brnch Mgr*
EMP: 10
SALES (corp-wide): 205.01B **Publicly Held**
Web: www.aero-med.com
SIC: 3843 Dental equipment and supplies
HQ: Aero-Med, Llc
65 Old Roberts St
East Hartford CT 06108
860 659-0602

(G-3109)
AGREDA & SON INC
425 Sullivan Ave Ste 5 (06074-1947)
PHONE..........................860 289-2520
Pedro J Agreda, *Pr*
Juan C Agreda, *
EMP: 65 EST: 1992
SALES (est): 8.6MM **Privately Held**
SIC: 3599 Machine shop, jobbing and repair

(G-3110)
AGREDA INDUSTRIES LLC
Also Called: Empire Manufacturing
425 Sullivan Ave Ste 6 (06074-1947)
PHONE..........................860 436-5551
EMP: 25 EST: 1977
SALES (est): 2.41MM **Privately Held**
SIC: 3724 3728 Engine mount parts, aircraft ; Aircraft parts and equipment, nec

(G-3111)
ALLIED METAL FINISHING LLC
379 Chapel Rd (06074-4104)
P.O. Box 1181 (06074-7181)
PHONE..........................860 290-8865
Joseph A Toce, *Managing Member*
EMP: 8 EST: 1997
SALES (est): 908.65K **Privately Held**
Web: www.toceperformance.com
SIC: 3471 Electroplating of metals or formed products

(G-3112)
AMERICAN DESIGN & MFG INC
Also Called: AM
145 Commerce Way (06074-1152)
PHONE..........................860 282-2719
Daniel Lessard, *VP*
Adam Vyskocil, *
Daniel W Jordan, *
EMP: 35 EST: 1991
SQ FT: 33,000
SALES (est): 5.4MM **Privately Held**
Web: www.americandes-mfg.com
SIC: 3829 3724 Testers for checking hydraulic controls on aircraft; Aircraft engines and engine parts

(G-3113)
AMK WELDING INC
Also Called: Amk Technical Services

283 Sullivan Ave (06074-1914)
P.O. Box 663 (06074-0663)
PHONE.................................860 289-5634
Daniel R Godin, *Pr*
EMP: 30 **EST:** 2009
SALES (est): 5.04MM
SALES (corp-wide): 344.81MM **Privately Held**
Web: www.meyertool.com
SIC: 7692 3398 7699 Welding repair; Metal heat treating; Aviation propeller and blade repair
PA: Meyer Tool, Inc.
3055 Colerain Ave
Cincinnati OH 45225
513 681-7362

(G-3114)
AMOUN PITA & DISTRIBUTION LLC
Also Called: Amoun Bakery & Distribution
361 Pleasant Valley Rd (06074-3427)
PHONE.................................866 239-9990
Mohsen Youssef, *Pr*
EMP: 16 **EST:** 2010
SQ FT: 9,000
SALES (est): 388.1K **Privately Held**
Web: www.amounfoods.com
SIC: 2051 5461 Bread, cake, and related products; Bread

(G-3115)
ANDRE FURNITURE INDUSTRIES LLC
55 Sandra Dr (06074-1039)
PHONE.................................860 528-8826
EMP: 8 **EST:** 1978
SQ FT: 12,000
SALES (est): 514.35K **Privately Held**
SIC: 2511 Wood household furniture

(G-3116)
ATI LADISH MACHINING INC
Also Called: Aerex Manufacturing
34 S Satellite Rd (06074-3445)
PHONE.................................860 688-3688
Richard Cleary, *Brnch Mgr*
EMP: 95
Web: www.atimaterials.com
SIC: 3724 Aircraft engines and engine parts
HQ: Ati Ladish Machining, Inc.
311 Prestige Park Rd
East Hartford CT 06108
860 688-3688

(G-3117)
ATLANTIC FABRICATING CO INC
71 Edwin Rd (06074-2476)
P.O. Box 433 (06074-0433)
PHONE.................................860 291-9882
William S Johnson, *Pr*
Susan Johnson, *Sec*
EMP: 10 **EST:** 1986
SQ FT: 7,500
SALES (est): 1.39MM **Privately Held**
Web: www.atlanticfabricating.com
SIC: 3441 Fabricated structural metal

(G-3118)
ATLAS METAL WORKS LLC
Also Called: Atlas Metal Works
48 Commerce Way (06074-1151)
PHONE.................................860 282-1030
Gary Allard, *Managing Member*
EMP: 12 **EST:** 1995
SALES (est): 2.42MM **Privately Held**
Web: www.atlasmetalworksllc.com

SIC: 3441 Fabricated structural metal

(G-3119)
ATLAS PRECISION MFG LLC
Also Called: Atlas Precision Manufacturing
508 Burnham St (06074-4102)
PHONE.................................860 290-9114
EMP: 25 **EST:** 1997
SQ FT: 20,000
SALES (est): 2.42MM **Privately Held**
Web: www.atlasprecmfg.com
SIC: 3599 Machine shop, jobbing and repair

(G-3120)
BLOOMY CONTROLS INC (PA)
Also Called: Bloomy Energy Systems
68 Nutmeg Rd S (06074-3469)
PHONE.................................860 298-9925
Peter Blume, *Pr*
Robert Cornwell, *
EMP: 36 **EST:** 1992
SQ FT: 6,000
SALES (est): 24.5MM **Privately Held**
Web: www.bloomy.com
SIC: 5084 3825 3679 Industrial machinery and equipment; Instruments to measure electricity; Electronic switches

(G-3121)
BODYCOTE THERMAL PROC INC
45 Connecticut Ave (06074-3475)
PHONE.................................860 282-1371
EMP: 48
SALES (corp-wide): 895.27MM **Privately Held**
Web: www.bodycote.com
SIC: 3398 Brazing (hardening) of metal
HQ: Bodycote Thermal Processing, Inc.
12750 Merit Dr Ste 1400
Dallas TX 75251
214 904-2420

(G-3122)
BROADRDGE CSTMER CMMNCTONS E L (PA)
125 Ellington Rd (06074-4112)
PHONE.................................860 290-7000
EMP: 20 **EST:** 1979
SQ FT: 30,000
SALES (est): 9.08MM
SALES (corp-wide): 9.08MM **Privately Held**
Web: www.broadridge.com
SIC: 2759 Laser printing

(G-3123)
C & T PRINT FINISHING INC
67 Commerce Way (06074-1152)
PHONE.................................860 282-0616
Jeffrey Cole, *Pr*
Mary Ann Cole, *Sec*
EMP: 10 **EST:** 1979
SQ FT: 9,500
SALES (est): 1.81MM **Privately Held**
Web: www.ctpf.com
SIC: 2675 Paper die-cutting

(G-3124)
C MATHER COMPANY INC
Also Called: Mathertops
339 Chapel Rd (06074-4104)
PHONE.................................860 528-5667
Thomas Mather, *Pr*
James Fromerth, *VP*
Richard Mather, *Sec*
EMP: 9 **EST:** 1959
SQ FT: 10,000
SALES (est): 999.41K **Privately Held**
Web: www.mathertops.com

SIC: 2542 2821 2541 Counters or counter display cases, except wood; Plastics materials and resins; Wood partitions and fixtures

(G-3125)
CAMETOID TECHNOLOGIES INC
45 S Satellite Rd Unit D (06074-5407)
P.O. Box 1409 (06074-7409)
PHONE.................................860 646-4667
John W Adams, *Pr*
Robert Sanderson, *
EMP: 35 **EST:** 1988
SQ FT: 18,000
SALES (est): 4.92MM **Privately Held**
Web: www.cametoidtechnologies.com
SIC: 3479 Coating of metals and formed products

(G-3126)
CAPEWELL AERIAL SYSTEMS LLC (PA)
105 Nutmeg Rd S (06074-5400)
PHONE.................................860 610-0700
Richard Wheeler, *Managing Member*
▲ **EMP:** 100 **EST:** 2014
SALES (est): 43.78MM
SALES (corp-wide): 43.78MM **Privately Held**
Web: www.capewell.com
SIC: 3531 Aerial work platforms: hydraulic/ elec. truck/carrier mounted

(G-3127)
CENTRAL CONN COOPERATIVE FARME
1050 Sullivan Ave Ste A3 (06074-2000)
P.O. Box 8500 (06074)
PHONE.................................860 649-4523
Daniel Logue, *Pr*
Walter Bradway, *
Harold Liebman, *
Donald Domina, *
John Collins, *
EMP: 40 **EST:** 1938
SQ FT: 35,000
SALES (est): 6.96MM **Privately Held**
SIC: 5191 5153 2041 Feed; Grains; Flour and other grain mill products

(G-3128)
CLEAR EDGE POWER INTERNATIONAL SERVICE LLC
195 Governors Hwy (06074-2419)
PHONE.................................860 727-2200
EMP: 148
SIC: 8731 3674 Commercial physical research; Fuel cells, solid state

(G-3129)
COBURN TECHNOLOGIES INC (DH)
83 Gerber Rd W (06074-3230)
PHONE.................................860 648-6600
▲ **EMP:** 40 **EST:** 2010
SALES (est): 38.74MM **Privately Held**
Web: www.coburntechnologies.com
SIC: 3851 3827 Ophthalmic goods; Optical instruments and lenses
HQ: Sdc Technologies, Inc.
45 Parker Ste 100
Irvine CA 92618
714 939-8300

(G-3130)
COBURN TECHNOLOGIES INTL INC (DH)
55 Gerber Rd E (06074-3244)

PHONE.................................860 648-6600
EMP: 18 **EST:** 1976
SQ FT: 65,000
SALES (est): 9.61MM **Privately Held**
Web: www.coburntechnologies.com
SIC: 5049 3827 7699 Optical goods; Optical instruments and lenses; Optical instrument repair
HQ: Coburn Technologies, Inc.
83 Gerber Rd W
South Windsor CT 06074

(G-3131)
COCA-COLA BEVS NORTHEAST INC
Also Called: Coca-Cola
359 Ellington Rd (06074-4116)
PHONE.................................800 241-2653
EMP: 23
Web: www.cokenortheast.com
SIC: 2086 Bottled and canned soft drinks
HQ: Coca-Cola Beverages Northeast, Inc.
1 Executive Park Dr # 330
Bedford NH 03110
603 627-7871

(G-3132)
CONNECTICUT PLASMA TECH LLC
273 Chapel Rd (06074-4104)
P.O. Box 58 (06074-0058)
PHONE.................................860 289-5500
James J Jasmin, *Managing Member*
Robert Lempicki, *Managing Member*
EMP: 16 **EST:** 2004
SALES (est): 951.65K **Privately Held**
Web:
www.connecticutplasmatechnologies.com
SIC: 3479 Coating of metals and formed products

(G-3133)
COSTA PACKAGING LLC
70 Bidwell Rd (06074-2412)
PHONE.................................860 282-2535
▲ **EMP:** 14 **EST:** 1997
SQ FT: 21,000
SALES (est): 2.45MM **Privately Held**
Web: www.eagletissue.com
SIC: 2679 Wrappers, paper (unprinted): made from purchased material

(G-3134)
CP FOODS LLC
Also Called: Carla's Pasta
50 Talbot Ln (06074-5401)
PHONE.................................860 436-4042
Brian Durst, *CEO*
EMP: 139 **EST:** 2021
SALES (est): 25.56MM
SALES (corp-wide): 49.35MM **Privately Held**
Web: www.carlaspasta.com
SIC: 2038 Spaghetti and meatballs, frozen
PA: Tribe 9 Foods Llc
2901 Progress Rd
Madison WI 53716
608 257-7216

(G-3135)
CRAMER COMPANY
105 Nutmeg Rd S (06074-5400)
PHONE.................................860 291-8402
Kenneth Mac Cormac, *Pr*
EMP: 10 **EST:** 2005
SALES (est): 118.43K **Privately Held**
SIC: 3621 Motors and generators

(G-3136)
CRRC LLC (PA)
Also Called: Capewell
105 Nutmeg Rd S (06074-5400)
PHONE..................877 684-6464
◆ EMP: 100 EST: 1881
SALES (est): 24.81MM
SALES (corp-wide): 24.81MM **Privately Held**
Web: www.capewell.com
SIC: 3423 3621 3625 3429 Hand and edge tools, nec; Motors, electric; Timing devices, electronic; Parachute hardware

(G-3137)
CT COMPOSITES & MARINE SVC LLC
620 Sullivan Ave (06074-1919)
PHONE..................860 282-0100
EMP: 8 EST: 2009
SALES (est): 554.15K **Privately Held**
Web: www.ctcomposites.com
SIC: 3083 Laminated plastics plate and sheet

(G-3138)
DYCO INDUSTRIES INC
229 S Satellite Rd (06074-3474)
PHONE..................860 289-4957
David Dyke, *Pr*
Barbara Dyke, *
Kaylin S Dyke, *
EMP: 30 EST: 1977
SQ FT: 24,000
SALES (est): 4.39MM **Privately Held**
Web: www.dycoind.com
SIC: 3446 7692 3444 Architectural metalwork; Welding repair; Sheet metalwork

(G-3139)
EAST WINDSOR METAL FABG INC
91 Glendale Rd (06074-2415)
P.O. Box 357 (06028-0357)
PHONE..................860 528-7107
Peter Hughes, *Pr*
Mary Ellen Brennan, *VP*
James Hughes, *VP*
Josephine Hughes, *Sec*
EMP: 11 EST: 1970
SQ FT: 20,000
SALES (est): 2MM **Privately Held**
SIC: 3444 7692 3446 3441 Metal housings, enclosures, casings, and other containers; Welding repair; Architectural metalwork; Fabricated structural metal

(G-3140)
ELECTRO-METHODS INC
525 Nutmeg Rd N (06074-2461)
P.O. Box 54 (06074-0054)
PHONE..................860 289-8661
Randall Fries, *Brnch Mgr*
EMP: 21
SALES (corp-wide): 26.74MM **Privately Held**
Web: www.electro-methods.com
SIC: 3724 Aircraft engines and engine parts
PA: Electro-Methods, Inc.
330 Governors Hwy
South Windsor CT 06074
860 289-8661

(G-3141)
ELECTRO-METHODS INC (PA)
330 Governors Hwy (06074-2422)
P.O. Box 54 (06074-0054)
PHONE..................860 289-8661
Randall Fries, *Pr*

Paul D Keller, *
Dani Stephens, *
William W Soucy, *
Lisa G Ford, *
EMP: 179 EST: 1965
SQ FT: 101,000
SALES (est): 26.74MM
SALES (corp-wide): 26.74MM **Privately Held**
Web: www.electro-methods.com
SIC: 3724 7629 3728 3829 Aircraft engines and engine parts; Aircraft electrical equipment repair; Panel assembly (hydromatic propeller test stands), aircraft; Testing equipment: abrasion, shearing strength, etc.

(G-3142)
ELECTROSTATIC COATING TECHNOLOGIES CORP
Also Called: Ect
1265 John Fitch Blvd Ste 12 (06074-2456)
PHONE..................860 610-9097
EMP: 14
Web: www.ectoilers.com
SIC: 3479 Coating of metals and formed products

(G-3143)
ENCORE OPTICS
140 Commerce Way (06074-1151)
PHONE..................860 282-0082
Paul Zito, *Owner*
▲ EMP: 9 EST: 2003
SALES (est): 479.94K **Privately Held**
Web: www.encoreoptics.com
SIC: 3851 Eyeglasses, lenses and frames

(G-3144)
ENGINEERING SERVICES & PDTS CO (PA)
Also Called: Clearspan
1395 John Fitch Blvd (06074-1029)
PHONE..................860 528-1119
Barry Goldsher, *Pr*
Matthew K Niaura, *
Charles R Clark Junior, *Sec*
◆ EMP: 85 EST: 1981
SQ FT: 51,281
SALES (est): 103.33MM
SALES (corp-wide): 103.33MM **Privately Held**
Web: www.esapco.com
SIC: 3081 3523 5083 Polyethylene film; Dairy equipment (farm), nec; Poultry equipment

(G-3145)
ESTEEM MANUFACTURING CORP
175 S Satellite Rd (06074-3474)
PHONE..................860 282-9964
David Kostyk, *Pr*
Suzanne Kostyk, *
Shawn Dietz, *
EMP: 44 EST: 1981
SQ FT: 10,000
SALES (est): 5.64MM **Privately Held**
Web: www.esteemmfg.com
SIC: 3599 Machine shop, jobbing and repair

(G-3146)
EVOQUA WATER TECHNOLOGIES LLC
88 Nutmeg Rd S (06074-3469)
PHONE..................860 528-6512
Robert Rohan, *Mgr*
EMP: 52
Web: www.evoqua.com

SIC: 3589 Water treatment equipment, industrial
HQ: Evoqua Water Technologies Llc
210 6th Ave Ste 3300
Pittsburgh PA 15222
724 772-0044

(G-3147)
EXPERMENTAL PROTOTYPE PDTS INC
248 Chapel Rd (06074-4103)
P.O. Box 1021 (06074-7021)
PHONE..................860 289-4948
Robert H Ainsworth Junior, *Pr*
William Ainsworth Senior, *VP*
Robert Ainsworth Senior, *Sec*
EMP: 10 EST: 1976
SQ FT: 2,500
SALES (est): 891.45K **Privately Held**
Web: www.ex-proproducts.com
SIC: 3599 Machine shop, jobbing and repair

(G-3148)
F W MANUFACTURING & ENGRG CO
1505 John Fitch Blvd (06074-1035)
PHONE..................860 291-8580
Regina Aszklar, *Pr*
Frank Aszklar, *VP*
EMP: 11 EST: 1993
SALES (est): 340.5K **Privately Held**
SIC: 3599 Machine shop, jobbing and repair

(G-3149)
GENERAL SEATING SOLUTIONS LLC
45 S Satellite Rd Ste 5 (06074-5407)
PHONE..................860 242-3307
EMP: 10 EST: 2001
SALES (est): 852.21K **Privately Held**
Web: www.generalseatingsolutions.com
SIC: 2599 7641 Restaurant furniture, wood or metal; Reupholstery

(G-3150)
GERBER COBURN OPTICAL INC (DH)
55 Gerber Rd E (06074-3244)
PHONE..................800 843-1479
Alex Incera, *Pr*
Wayne Labrecque, *
Nick Coppola, *Prin*
◆ EMP: 120 EST: 1990
SQ FT: 60,000
SALES (est): 22.39MM **Privately Held**
Web: www.coburntechnologies.com
SIC: 3851 3827 Ophthalmic goods; Optical instruments and lenses
HQ: Coburn Technologies, Inc.
83 Gerber Rd W
South Windsor CT 06074

(G-3151)
GLOBAL TRBINE CMPNENT TECH LLC
125 S Satellite Rd (06074-3474)
P.O. Box 923 (06074-0923)
PHONE..................860 528-4722
EMP: 25 EST: 1991
SQ FT: 20,000
SALES (est): 2.41MM **Privately Held**
SIC: 3728 3724 Aircraft parts and equipment, nec; Aircraft engines and engine parts

(G-3152)
GROWSPAN LLC
Also Called: Growspan Greenhouse Structures

1395 John Fitch Blvd (06074-1029)
PHONE..................877 835-9996
Daniel Ebrahimi, *Mgr*
EMP: 14 EST: 2015
SALES (est): 256.93K **Privately Held**
Web: www.growspan.com
SIC: 3272 Concrete structural support and building material

(G-3153)
H & B TOOL & ENG CO INC
481 Sullivan Ave (06074-1942)
P.O. Box 717 (06074-0717)
PHONE..................860 528-9341
Janice Proll, *Pr*
Michael Giannelli, *
EMP: 50 EST: 1960
SQ FT: 33,000
SALES (est): 5.86MM **Privately Held**
Web: www.h-btool.com
SIC: 3599 3823 3728 3545 Machine shop, jobbing and repair; Process control instruments; Aircraft parts and equipment, nec; Machine tool accessories

(G-3154)
HERMAN SCHMIDT PRECISION WORKH
26 Sea Pave Rd (06074-4155)
PHONE..................860 289-3347
Thomas Duff Iii, *Pr*
EMP: 8 EST: 2017
SALES (est): 790.98K **Privately Held**
Web: www.hschmidt.com
SIC: 3544 Special dies, tools, jigs, and fixtures

(G-3155)
HERMANN SCHMIDT COMPANY INC
Also Called: Hermann Schmidt
26 Sea Pave Rd (06074-4155)
PHONE..................860 289-3347
Peter Schmidt, *Pr*
EMP: 10 EST: 1962
SALES (est): 906.01K **Privately Held**
Web: www.hschmidt.com
SIC: 3545 Precision measuring tools

(G-3156)
HEXCEL CORPORATION
250 Nutmeg Rd S (06074-3498)
PHONE..................925 520-3232
Jason Eddy, *Pr*
Nick Stanage, *
EMP: 99 EST: 2017
SALES (est): 21.82MM
SALES (corp-wide): 1.58B **Publicly Held**
Web: www.hexcel.com
SIC: 3324 Aerospace investment castings, ferrous
PA: Hexcel Corporation
281 Tresser Blvd 16
Stamford CT 06901
203 969-0666

(G-3157)
HOYA CORPORATION
Also Called: Hoya Optcal Labs Amrc-Hartford
580 Nutmeg Rd N (06074-2458)
PHONE..................860 289-5379
Joe Bassler, *Brnch Mgr*
EMP: 30
Web: www.hoyavision.com
SIC: 3851 5049 Ophthalmic goods; Optical goods
HQ: Hoya Corporation
651 E Corporate Dr
Lewisville TX 75057
972 221-4141

2024 Harris New England
Manufacturers Directory
▲ = Import ▼ = Export
◆ = Import/Export

(G-3158)
JAD LLC
Also Called: Industronics Service
489 Sullivan Ave (06074-1942)
P.O. Box 649 (06074-0649)
PHONE..................................860 289-1551
James L Wyse, *Pr*
Dean P Hills, *Managing Member**
EMP: 25 **EST:** 1958
SQ FT: 14,000
SALES (est): 5.59MM **Privately Held**
Web: www.industronics.com
SIC: 3823 3567 5084 3433   Temperature
   instruments: industrial process type;
   Industrial furnaces and ovens; Controlling
   instruments and accessories; Heating
   equipment, except electric

(G-3159)
JHS RESTORATION INC
170 Strong Rd (06074-1013)
PHONE..................................860 757-3870
EMP: 10 **EST:** 2010
SALES (est): 1.27MM **Privately Held**
Web: www.jhsrestoration.com
SIC: 3444 1761   Roof deck, sheet metal;
   Roofing, siding, and sheetmetal work

(G-3160)
**KEYSTONE PAPER & BOX CO
LLC (HQ)**
Also Called: Keystone Paper & Box Co Inc
31 Edwin Rd (06074-2413)
P.O. Box 355 (06028-0355)
PHONE..................................860 291-0027
James Rutt, *Pr*
EMP: 19 **EST:** 1944
SQ FT: 61,000
SALES (est): 11.05MM
SALES (corp-wide): 110.2MM **Privately
Held**
Web: www.keystonepaperbox.com
SIC: 2657 2631   Folding paperboard boxes;
   Container, packaging, and boxboard
PA: Mill Rock Packaging Partners Llc
   667 Madison Ave
   New York NY 10065
   212 763-7740

(G-3161)
**LIGHTHOUSE INTERNATIONAL
LLC**
125 S Satellite Rd (06074-3474)
PHONE..................................860 528-4722
EMP: 17 **EST:** 2005
SALES (est): 580.07K **Privately Held**
SIC: 3724   Aircraft engines and engine parts

(G-3162)
MASSCONN DISTRIBUTE CPL
12 Commerce Way (06074-1151)
PHONE..................................860 882-0717
Brian Hastings, *Dir*
EMP: 85 **EST:** 2007
SALES (est): 3.89MM **Privately Held**
SIC: 2051   Doughnuts, except frozen

(G-3163)
MEYER GAGE CO INC
230 Burnham St (06074-4193)
PHONE..................................860 528-6526
John Meyer, *CEO*
John Meyer, *Pr*
James Meyer, *VP*
▲ **EMP:** 18 **EST:** 1960
SQ FT: 28,000
SALES (est): 1.94MM **Privately Held**
Web: www.meyergage.com

SIC: 3545   Machine tool accessories

(G-3164)
MH RHODES CRAMER LLC
105 Nutmeg Rd S (06074-5400)
PHONE..................................860 291-8402
▲ **EMP:** 9 **EST:** 2014
SALES (est): 247.01K **Privately Held**
Web: www.mhrhodes.com
SIC: 3613 5012   Time switches, electrical
   switchgear apparatus; Motorized cycles

(G-3165)
MICHAEL ZOPPA
Also Called: Zoppa Studio
23 Sea Pave Rd (06074-4156)
PHONE..................................860 289-5881
Michael Zoppa, *Owner*
EMP: 9 **EST:** 1980
SQ FT: 3,800
SALES (est): 751.56K **Privately Held**
Web: www.zoppastudio.com
SIC: 7336 3993 2396   Silk screen design;
   Signs and advertising specialties;
   Automotive and apparel trimmings

(G-3166)
**NUCOR HRRIS RBAR
NORTHEAST LLC**
30 Talbot Ln (06074-5401)
PHONE..................................860 282-1860
EMP: 65
SALES (corp-wide): 41.51B **Publicly Held**
Web: www.harrisrebar.com
SIC: 3449 5085   Bars, concrete reinforcing:
   fabricated steel; Industrial supplies
HQ: Nucor Harris Rebar Northeast Llc
   55 Sumner St Ste 1
   Milford MA 01757
   800 370-0132

(G-3167)
NUWAY TOBACCO COMPANY
200 Sullivan Ave Ste 2 (06074-1953)
P.O. Box 415 (06028-0415)
PHONE..................................860 289-6414
Raymond A Voorhies, *CEO*
Anne S King, *
Charles B Shepard, *
James T Farrell, *
Jean E Shepard Iii, *Asst Tr*
◆ **EMP:** 85 **EST:** 1951
SQ FT: 65,000
SALES (est): 15.62MM **Privately Held**
SIC: 2131 5159   Chewing and smoking
   tobacco; Tobacco, leaf

(G-3168)
O & W HEAT TREAT INC
Also Called: Ohlheiser, H R Jr Pe
1 Bidwell Rd (06074-2411)
PHONE..................................860 528-9239
Harold R Ohlheiser Junior, *Pr*
Patrick Ohlheiser, *VP*
Vicky Sanborn, *Mgr*
EMP: 23 **EST:** 1963
SQ FT: 10,500
SALES (est): 2.94MM **Privately Held**
Web: www.owheattreat.com
SIC: 8742 3398   Management consulting
   services; Brazing (hardening) of metal

(G-3169)
**OXFORD PERFORMANCE MTLS
INC**
30 S Satellite Rd (06074-3445)
PHONE..................................860 698-9300
◆ **EMP:** 35 **EST:** 2011
SQ FT: 16,000

SALES (est): 5.15MM **Privately Held**
Web: www.oxfordpm.com
SIC: 2821   Plastics materials and resins

(G-3170)
**OXPEKK PERFORMANCE MTLS
INC**
30 S Satellite Rd (06074-3445)
PHONE..................................860 698-9300
Scott Defelice, *Pr*
EMP: 21 **EST:** 2000
SALES (est): 512.07K **Privately Held**
Web: www.oxfordpm.com
SIC: 2821   Thermoplastic materials

(G-3171)
PH PRODUCTION CT LLC
Also Called: Powder Hollow Brewery
46 Schwier Rd (06074-1902)
PHONE..................................860 205-0942
Michael Mcmanus, *Prin*
EMP: 8 **EST:** 2017
SALES (est): 469.68K **Privately Held**
SIC: 2082   Malt beverages

(G-3172)
PLAS-TEC COATINGS INC
68 Mascolo Rd (06074-3312)
PHONE..................................860 289-6029
Richard Cyr, *Pr*
Brian Cyr, *VP*
Sandra Cyr, *VP*
EMP: 10 **EST:** 1977
SQ FT: 10,000
SALES (est): 945.63K **Privately Held**
Web: www.plas-teccoatings.com
SIC: 3479   Coating of metals and formed
   products

(G-3173)
**PLASMA TECHNOLOGY
INCORPORATED**
70 Rye St (06074-1218)
PHONE..................................860 282-0659
Richard Petersen, *Brnch Mgr*
EMP: 29
SQ FT: 12,000
SALES (corp-wide): 12.34MM **Privately
Held**
Web: www.ptise.com
SIC: 2836 3471   Plasmas; Plating and
   polishing
PA: Plasma Technology Incorporated
   1754 Crenshaw Blvd
   Torrance CA 90501
   310 320-3373

(G-3174)
PRESSURE BLAST MFG CO INC
205 Nutmeg Rd S Ste E (06074-5406)
PHONE..................................800 722-5278
Lowell W Mc Mullen Iii, *Ch Bd*
Ted Clifford, *Treas*
Stephen Zavarella, *Sec*
EMP: 15 **EST:** 1958
SQ FT: 25,000
SALES (est): 665.36K **Privately Held**
Web: www.pressureblast.com
SIC: 3629 3469 3291   Blasting machines,
   electrical; Machine parts, stamped or
   pressed metal; Abrasive products

(G-3175)
PRINTED COMMUNICATIONS
400 Chapel Rd Ste L1 (06074-4159)
PHONE..................................860 436-9619
Wayne Egienbaum, *Mgr*
Wayne Egienbaum, *Pr*
EMP: 7 **EST:** 2002

SALES (est): 275.6K **Privately Held**
SIC: 2711   Commercial printing and
   newspaper publishing combined

(G-3176)
**PROGRESSIVE SHEETMETAL
LLC**
36 Mascolo Rd (06074-3312)
PHONE..................................860 436-9884
Keith Beaulieu, *Managing Member*
Andrea Beaulieu, *
EMP: 36 **EST:** 1996
SQ FT: 13,600
SALES (est): 4.41MM **Privately Held**
SIC: 3444   Sheet metalwork

(G-3177)
REDLAND BRICK INC
Also Called: K F Brick Plant
1440 John Fitch Blvd (06074-1036)
PHONE..................................860 528-1311
Simon Whalley, *Dir*
EMP: 33
SALES (corp-wide): 140.04MM **Privately
Held**
SIC: 3255 3251   Brick, clay refractory; Brick
   and structural clay tile
HQ: Redland Brick Inc.
   15718 Clear Spring Rd
   Williamsport MD 21795
   301 223-7700

(G-3178)
SATELLITE TOOL & MCH CO INC
571 Nutmeg Rd N (06074-2461)
PHONE..................................860 290-8558
J Mark Lukasik, *CEO*
Jan Lukasik, *
Jack Lukasik, *
Monica Marselli, *
EMP: 50 **EST:** 1975
SQ FT: 10,000
SALES (est): 8.41MM **Privately Held**
Web: www.satellitetoolmachine.net
SIC: 3599   Machine shop, jobbing and repair

(G-3179)
SIFTEX EQUIPMENT COMPANY
Also Called: American Pulley Cover
52 Connecticut Ave Ste D (06074-3484)
PHONE..................................860 289-8779
Steven Weil, *Pr*
◆ **EMP:** 25 **EST:** 1983
SQ FT: 12,000
SALES (est): 5.47MM **Privately Held**
Web: www.siftex.com
SIC: 3089   Ducting, plastics

(G-3180)
**SKILLCRAFT MACHINE TOOL
CO**
255 Nutmeg Rd S (06074-5403)
PHONE..................................860 953-1246
Thomas Litke, *Pr*
Salvatore Di Fabio, *Sec*
Lisa Litke, *Sec*
EMP: 15 **EST:** 1946
SALES (est): 2.45MM **Privately Held**
Web: www.skillcraftmachine.com
SIC: 3423 3544   Wrenches, hand tools;
   Special dies and tools

(G-3181)
SMR METAL TECHNOLOGY LLC
524 Sullivan Ave Ste 15 (06074-1946)
PHONE..................................860 291-8259
Sharon M Riley, *Owner*
EMP: 7 **EST:** 1999
SALES (est): 928.2K **Privately Held**

Web: www.smrmanufacturing.com
SIC: 3443 Metal parts

(G-3182)
SOUTH WINDSOR GOLF COURSE LLC
Also Called: Topstone Golf Course
516 Griffin Rd (06074-1324)
PHONE...................................860 648-4653
John J Kelly Senior, *Managing Member*
EMP: 60 **EST:** 1996
SALES (est): 2.3MM **Privately Held**
Web: www.topstonegc.com
SIC: 7997 3631 Golf club, membership;
　Barbecues, grills, and braziers (outdoor
　cooking)

(G-3183)
STACHE CO LLC
71 Edwin Rd Ste 2 (06074-2476)
PHONE...................................860 719-1727
Aidan Mannarino, *Prin*
EMP: 8 **EST:** 2018
SALES (est): 310.25K **Privately Held**
Web: www.stacheco.com
SIC: 3949 Sporting and athletic goods, nec

(G-3184)
STEELTECH BUILDING PDTS INC
636 Nutmeg Rd N (06074-2433)
PHONE...................................860 290-8930
TOLL FREE: 800
J Robert Denton, *Ch*
Steve Rich, *
Steve Iacino, *
EMP: 51 **EST:** 1965
SQ FT: 38,000
SALES (est): 9.68MM **Privately Held**
Web: www.steeltechbp.com
SIC: 3441 1791 5072 5031 Fabricated
　structural metal; Structural steel erection;
　Hardware; Doors, nec

(G-3185)
TELEFUNKEN USA LLC
Also Called: Telefunken Elektro Acoustic
300 Pleasant Valley Rd Ste E (06074-5408)
PHONE...................................860 882-5919
▲ **EMP:** 15 **EST:** 2005
SQ FT: 10,000
SALES (est): 2.47MM **Privately Held**
Web: www.telefunken-elektroakustik.com
SIC: 3651 Microphones

(G-3186)
TRUE POSITION MFG LLC
40 Sandra Dr Ste 3 (06074-1043)
PHONE...................................860 291-2987
EMP: 8 **EST:** 1999
SQ FT: 2,000
SALES (est): 895.84K **Privately Held**
SIC: 3549 Metalworking machinery, nec

(G-3187)
TWIN MFG CO DBA TWIN MRO
273 Chapel Rd (06074-4165)
PHONE...................................860 289-6041
Craig Wurmnest, *Pr*
▼ **EMP:** 75 **EST:** 1986
SQ FT: 36,000
SALES (est): 10MM **Privately Held**
Web: www.twinmro.com
SIC: 3599 Machine and other job shop work

(G-3188)
US AVIONICS INC / SUPERABR
Also Called: US Avionics
1265 John Fitch Blvd Ste 3 (06074-2456)
P.O. Box 599 (06074-0599)

PHONE...................................860 528-1114
Sari Alt, *Prin*
EMP: 8 **EST:** 2006
SALES (est): 423.57K **Privately Held**
Web: www.salt-superabrasives.com
SIC: 3541 Grinding machines, metalworking

(G-3189)
WAYBEST FOODS INC
1510 John Fitch Blvd (06074-1019)
EMP: 9 **EST:** 1971
SALES (est): 859.32K **Privately Held**
SIC: 2015 Poultry sausage, luncheon
　meats, and other poultry products

(G-3190)
WEBILENT TECHNOLOGY INC
225 Oakland Rd Ste 106 (06074-2896)
PHONE...................................860 254-6169
Anil Mallavarapu, *CEO*
EMP: 48 **EST:** 2001
SALES (est): 1.07MM **Privately Held**
Web: www.webilent.com
SIC: 7372 Prepackaged software

(G-3191)
WHITCRAFT SOUTH WINDSOR LLC
Also Called: Whitcraft South Windsor
425 Sullivan Ave (06074-1947)
PHONE...................................860 436-5551
Doug Folsom, *CEO*
Joe Maisto, *CFO*
EMP: 381 **EST:** 2019
SALES (est): 8.61MM
SALES (corp-wide): 139.19MM **Privately Held**
Web: www.pursuitaero.com
SIC: 3728 Aircraft parts and equipment, nec
PA: Whitcraft Llc
　76 County Rd
　Eastford CT 06242
　860 974-0786

Southbury
New Haven County

(G-3192)
COMSAT INC
Also Called: Comsat Inc.
2120 River Rd (06488-1147)
PHONE...................................203 264-4091
Guy White, *Brnch Mgr*
EMP: 14
SALES (corp-wide): 34.53MM **Privately Held**
Web: www.satcomdirect.com
SIC: 3663 Radio and t.v. communications
　equipment
HQ: Comsat, Inc.
　1050 Satcom Ln
　Melbourne FL 32940
　321 525-4504

(G-3193)
EDGE2WEB INC
800 Main St S (06488-4212)
PHONE...................................203 770-2588
Frederick Holahan, *CEO*
Christopher Keller, *VP*
EMP: 7 **EST:** 2016
SALES (est): 154.38K **Privately Held**
Web: www.edge2web.com
SIC: 7372 Prepackaged software

(G-3194)
GYRE9 LLC
1200 Main St S (06488-4173)

PHONE...................................203 702-4010
Edward Gilchrest, *Pr*
Edward Gilchrist, *
EMP: 34 **EST:** 2012
SALES (est): 4.46MM **Privately Held**
Web: www.gyre9.com
SIC: 7389 3569 Design services; Assembly
　machines, non-metalworking

(G-3195)
HI STONE & SON INC
313 Main St N (06488-1805)
PHONE...................................203 264-8656
Harry H Stone Ii, *Pr*
Harry H Stone Ii, *Pr*
Harry H Stone Iii, *VP*
Jeremy L Stone, *
EMP: 26 **EST:** 1955
SALES (est): 30.23MM **Privately Held**
Web: www.histoneson.com
SIC: 4212 4953 3443 1794 Dump truck
　haulage; Sludge disposal sites; Dumpsters,
　garbage; Excavation work

(G-3196)
HOPP COMPANIES INC (PA)
519 Heritage Rd Ste 2e (06488-1699)
PHONE...................................800 889-8425
EMP: 7 **EST:** 1993
SQ FT: 5,000
SALES (est): 2.51MM **Privately Held**
Web: www.hoppcompanies.com
SIC: 3578 3086 Point-of-sale devices;
　Plastics foam products

(G-3197)
O & G INDUSTRIES INC
236 Roxbury Rd (06488-1234)
PHONE...................................203 263-2195
TOLL FREE: 800
John Jenkins, *Brnch Mgr*
EMP: 44
SALES (corp-wide): 496.36MM **Privately Held**
Web: www.ogind.com
SIC: 5032 2951 1542 Sand, construction;
　Asphalt paving mixtures and blocks;
　Commercial and office building, new
　construction
PA: O & G Industries, Inc.
　112 Wall St
　Torrington CT 06790
　860 489-9261

(G-3198)
SOUTHBURY PRINTING CENTRE INC
385 Main St S (06488-4292)
PHONE...................................203 264-0102
Fredrick Plescia Junior, *Pr*
EMP: 9 **EST:** 1986
SQ FT: 1,500
SALES (est): 940.23K **Privately Held**
Web: www.spcink.com
SIC: 2752 Offset printing

(G-3199)
THE ROMATIC MANUFACTURING COMPANY
1200 Main St S (06488-2159)
P.O. Box 28 (06488-0028)
PHONE...................................203 264-8203
EMP: 210
SIC: 3469 2396 3471 Stamping metal for
　the trade; Automotive and apparel trimmings
　; Plating and polishing

Southington
Hartford County

(G-3200)
ABBOTT DIAGNOSTICS
178 Old Cider Mill Rd (06489-1874)
PHONE...................................860 463-0767
EMP: 7 **EST:** 2018
SALES (est): 254.35K **Privately Held**
Web: www.corelaboratory.abbott
SIC: 2834 Pharmaceutical preparations

(G-3201)
ACUCUT INC
200 Town Line Rd (06489-1145)
PHONE...................................860 793-7012
Scott Barmore, *CEO*
Judith Barmore, *
Larry Mc Nellis, *
Michael Barmore, *
Ray Lemay, *
EMP: 48 **EST:** 1978
SQ FT: 30,000
SALES (est): 6.9MM **Privately Held**
Web: www.acucut.com
SIC: 3599 Machine shop, jobbing and repair

(G-3202)
AFFORDABLE CONVEYOR SVCS LLC
72 Industrial Dr (06489-1125)
P.O. Box 2252 (06011-2252)
PHONE...................................860 582-1800
EMP: 10 **EST:** 2003
SALES (est): 2.02MM **Privately Held**
Web: www.affordableconveyor.com
SIC: 3535 Conveyors and conveying
　equipment

(G-3203)
AMERICAN STANDARD COMPANY
Also Called: Florian Tools
85 Ladyslipper Ln (06489-1082)
PHONE...................................860 628-9643
Nathaniel Florian, *CEO*
Sean E Florian, *
Judith B Florian, *
Beth C Florian, *
◆ **EMP:** 25 **EST:** 1937
SALES (est): 2.56MM **Privately Held**
Web:
www.americanstandardcompany.com
SIC: 3469 3312 5261 Spinning metal for the
　trade; Tool and die steel; Garden supplies
　and tools, nec

(G-3204)
BRACONE METAL SPINNING INC
39 Depaolo Dr (06489-1021)
PHONE...................................860 628-5927
Christina Bracone, *Pr*
EMP: 20 **EST:** 1984
SQ FT: 15,000
SALES (est): 3.31MM **Privately Held**
Web: www.bmsaerospace.com
SIC: 3599 3469 Machine and other job shop
　work; Spinning metal for the trade

(G-3205)
BRIDGESTONE RET OPERATIONS LLC
Also Called: Firestone
288 Queen St (06489-1901)
PHONE...................................860 628-9621
David Carrier, *Mgr*

EMP: 8
Web: www.bridgestoneamericas.com
SIC: 5531 7534 7539 Automotive tires; Rebuilding and retreading tires; Brake services
HQ: Bridgestone Retail Operations, Llc
333 E Lake St Ste 300
Bloomingdale IL 60108
630 259-9000

(G-3206)
C V TOOL COMPANY INC (PA)
44 Robert Porter Rd (06489-1159)
PHONE................................978 353-7901
Carmine Votino, *Pr*
Assunta Votino, *
EMP: 32 **EST:** 1980
SQ FT: 35,000
SALES (est): 9.64MM
SALES (corp-wide): 9.64MM **Privately Held**
Web: www.cvtool.com
SIC: 3599 3728 7692 3544 Machine shop, jobbing and repair; Aircraft parts and equipment, nec; Welding repair; Special dies, tools, jigs, and fixtures

(G-3207)
COMPANION INDUSTRIES INC
891 W Queen St (06489-1094)
PHONE................................860 628-0504
Ken Paul, *Pr*
Steve Tosta, *
Vincent Roy, *
EMP: 70 **EST:** 1973
SQ FT: 34,000
SALES (est): 8.19MM **Privately Held**
Web: www.companionind.com
SIC: 3469 Stamping metal for the trade

(G-3208)
ETHICON INC
Also Called: Ethicon Endo - Surgery
201 W Queen St (06489-1138)
PHONE................................860 621-9111
John Callen, *Mgr*
EMP: 300
SALES (corp-wide): 94.94B **Publicly Held**
SIC: 3842 Ligatures, medical
HQ: Ethicon Inc.
1000 Route 202
Raritan NJ 08869
800 384-4266

(G-3209)
F F SCREW PRODUCTS INC
Also Called: Ff Screw Products
888 W Queen St (06489-1033)
PHONE................................860 621-4567
Frank Fragola, *Pr*
Mary Fragola, *
▲ **EMP:** 25 **EST:** 1973
SQ FT: 15,000
SALES (est): 4.71MM **Privately Held**
Web:
www.fragolaperformancesystems.com
SIC: 3089 3451 Fittings for pipe, plastics; Screw machine products

(G-3210)
F-K BEARINGS INC
865 W Queen St (06489-1032)
PHONE................................860 621-4567
Frank Fragola, *CEO*
Alfonso Fragola, *VP*
▲ **EMP:** 15 **EST:** 1983
SQ FT: 15,000
SALES (est): 3.88MM **Privately Held**
Web: www.fkrodends.com

SIC: 5085 3568 Bearings; Power transmission equipment, nec

(G-3211)
GEMCO MANUFACTURING CO INC
555 W Queen St (06489-1178)
PHONE................................860 628-5529
Mark Divenere, *Pr*
EMP: 21 **EST:** 1943
SQ FT: 40,000
SALES (est): 4.69MM **Privately Held**
Web: www.gemcomfg.com
SIC: 3469 3495 3496 Stamping metal for the trade; Wire springs; Woven wire products, nec

(G-3212)
GENERAL MACHINE COMPANY INC
1223 Mount Vernon Rd (06489-2116)
PHONE................................860 426-9295
Mary Grzegorzk, *Pr*
Walentyn Grzegorzk, *VP*
EMP: 10 **EST:** 1981
SQ FT: 2,500
SALES (est): 961.26K **Privately Held**
SIC: 3599 Machine shop, jobbing and repair

(G-3213)
GLOBE TOOL & MET STAMPG CO INC
95 Robert Porter Rd (06489-1161)
PHONE................................860 621-6807
Reginald J Cote, *CEO*
Michelle Cote Knuth, *
Paul Cote, *
Phyllis B Cote, *
EMP: 24 **EST:** 1945
SQ FT: 31,000
SALES (est): 773.86K **Privately Held**
Web: www.globe-tool.com
SIC: 3469 3544 Stamping metal for the trade ; Die sets for metal stamping (presses)

(G-3214)
GORDON CORPORATION
170 Spring St Unit 3 (06489-1532)
PHONE................................860 628-4775
Anthony Prepiatti, *Pr*
EMP: 79 **EST:** 1979
SQ FT: 50,000
SALES (est): 8.93MM **Privately Held**
Web: www.gordoncelladoor.com
SIC: 3317 3442 Steel pipe and tubes; Metal doors

(G-3215)
HANDYSCAPE LLC
43 Sandy Pine Dr (06489-6016)
PHONE................................860 318-1067
Alan Seibert, *Prin*
EMP: 7 **EST:** 2012
SALES (est): 224.04K **Privately Held**
SIC: 2851 Removers and cleaners

(G-3216)
HOLM CORRUGATED CONTAINER INC
Metals Dr (06489)
P.O. Box 477 (06489-0477)
PHONE................................860 628-5559
Douglas Holm, *Pr*
Francine Holm, *
EMP: 26 **EST:** 1973
SQ FT: 25,000
SALES (est): 4.07MM **Privately Held**
SIC: 2653 Boxes, corrugated: made from purchased materials

(G-3217)
JETCT INC
125 W Queen St (06489-1126)
PHONE................................860 621-5381
Ronald Sanzone, *CEO*
Todd Sanzone, *Pr*
Christy Sanzone, *Sec*
EMP: 24 **EST:** 1971
SQ FT: 3,400
SALES (est): 3MM **Privately Held**
Web: www.jettool.com
SIC: 3545 Machine tool accessories

(G-3218)
JJIOC INC
125 W Queen St (06489-1126)
PHONE................................860 628-4655
Todd Sanzone, *Pr*
Kathleen Sanzone, *VP*
Christy Sanzone, *Sec*
EMP: 41 **EST:** 1968
SQ FT: 2,000
SALES (est): 4.42MM **Privately Held**
Web: www.jjind.com
SIC: 3545 Machine tool accessories

(G-3219)
LIGHT METALS COLORING CO INC
Also Called: L M C
270 Spring St (06489-1589)
PHONE................................860 621-0145
Richard William Fleet, *Pr*
Mark Thomas, *
EMP: 100 **EST:** 1945
SQ FT: 27,000
SALES (est): 13.9MM **Privately Held**
Web: www.lightmetalscoloring.com
SIC: 3471 Electroplating of metals or formed products

(G-3220)
MASTERCRAFT TOOL AND MCH CO
100 Newell St (06489-1123)
PHONE................................860 628-5551
Stephen Lassy, *Pr*
Michael Lassy, *VP*
Brian J Lassy, *VP*
EMP: 19 **EST:** 1968
SALES (est): 2.45MM **Privately Held**
Web: www.mastercrafttool-mach.com
SIC: 3469 3443 3544 Stamping metal for the trade; Air coolers, metal plate; Special dies and tools

(G-3221)
MATTHEW WARREN INC
Also Called: Economy Spring
75 Aircraft Rd Ste 1 (06489-1443)
PHONE................................860 621-7358
Leonide Charette, *Brnch Mgr*
EMP: 89
SALES (corp-wide): 1.05B **Privately Held**
Web: www.mwcomponents.com
SIC: 3495 3493 Precision springs; Steel springs, except wire
HQ: Matthew Warren, Inc.
3426 Toringdon Way # 100
Charlotte NC 28277
704 837-0331

(G-3222)
METTLER PACKAGING LLC
100 Queen St Ste 5 (06489-2052)
PHONE................................860 628-6193
EMP: 8 **EST:** 2019
SALES (est): 154.64K **Privately Held**
Web: www.papier-mettler.com

SIC: 2674 Bags: uncoated paper and multiwall

(G-3223)
NECST INC
Also Called: Springs Manufacturer Supply Co
525 W Queen St (06489-1178)
P.O. Box 1998 (06013-0998)
PHONE................................860 628-2515
William Lyons Iii, *Pr*
Ralph Parlado, *VP*
Marianne Caiaze, *Off Mgr*
EMP: 18 **EST:** 1969
SQ FT: 10,000
SALES (est): 756.83K **Privately Held**
Web: www.springmsc.com
SIC: 3599 Machine shop, jobbing and repair

(G-3224)
NEWCOMB SPRING CORP
235 Spring St (06489-1542)
PHONE................................860 621-0111
EMP: 56
SALES (corp-wide): 60.18MM **Privately Held**
Web: www.newcombspring.com
SIC: 3495 3493 Wire springs; Steel springs, except wire
PA: Newcomb Spring Corp.
3155 North Point Pkwy G220
Alpharetta GA 30005
770 981-2803

(G-3225)
NEWCOMB SPRINGS CONNECTICUT
Also Called: Newcomb Springs
235 Spring St (06489-1542)
PHONE................................860 621-0111
Robert Jacobson, *Pr*
Donald Jacobson, *Ch*
EMP: 50 **EST:** 1969
SQ FT: 80,000
SALES (est): 4.68MM **Privately Held**
Web: www.newcombspring.com
SIC: 3495 Wire springs

(G-3226)
NORTHEASTERN SHAPED WIRE INC
411 N Main St (06489-2519)
PHONE................................860 621-8991
EMP: 38 **EST:** 1976
SALES (est): 4.91MM **Privately Held**
Web: www.neswire.com
SIC: 3496 Miscellaneous fabricated wire products

(G-3227)
OWEN TOOL AND MFG CO INC
149 Aircraft Rd (06489-1404)
P.O. Box 8 (06062-0008)
PHONE................................860 628-6540
Thomas Owen, *Pr*
EMP: 8 **EST:** 1941
SQ FT: 10,000
SALES (est): 757.9K **Privately Held**
Web: www.owen-tool.com
SIC: 3469 Stamping metal for the trade

(G-3228)
PEPSI COLA BOTTLING CO BRISTOL
Also Called: Pepsico
110 Corporate Dr (06489-1086)
PHONE................................860 628-8200
Charles T Tenney Junior, *Pr*
Thomas Strahle, *
EMP: 25 **EST:** 1935

SQ FT: 50,000
SALES (est): 1.69MM Privately Held
Web: www.pepsicolaofbristol.com
SIC: 2086   Carbonated soft drinks, bottled
and canned

(G-3229)
PROTEK SKI RACING INC
85 Ladyslipper Ln (06489-1082)
PHONE.................................860 628-9643
Sean Florian, *Pr*
Beth Florian, *Prin*
EMP: 7 EST: 2011
SALES (est): 74.38K Privately Held
Web: www.protekskiracing.com
SIC: 3949 5085   Ice skates, parts and
accessories; Gears

(G-3230)
**QUANTUM BPOWER
SOUTHINGTON LLC**
Also Called: Quantum Biopower
49 Depaolo Dr (06489-1021)
PHONE.................................860 201-0621
EMP: 13 EST: 2016
SALES (est): 1.82MM Privately Held
Web: www.quantumbiopower.com
SIC: 3572   Computer storage devices

(G-3231)
REM CHEMICALS INC (PA)
Also Called: R E M
325 W Queen St (06489-1177)
PHONE.................................860 621-6755
Mark D Michaud, *Pr*
Louise B Michaud, *Sec*
▲ EMP: 17 EST: 1965
SQ FT: 14,500
SALES (est): 8.8MM
SALES (corp-wide): 8.8MM Privately Held
Web: www.remchem.com
SIC: 2899   Chemical preparations, nec

(G-3232)
SMITHS MEDICAL ASD INC
Also Called: Medex Southington
201 W Queen St (06489-1194)
PHONE.................................860 621-9111
John Hemsted, *Brnch Mgr*
EMP: 44
SALES (corp-wide): 2.28B Publicly Held
SIC: 3841   IV transfusion apparatus
HQ: Smiths Medical Asd, Inc.
6000 Nathan Ln N
Plymouth MN 55442
763 383-3000

(G-3233)
SOUTHINGTON METAL FABG CO
95 Corporate Dr (06489-1085)
P.O. Box 456 (06489-0456)
PHONE.................................860 621-0149
John Brunalli, *Pr*
James Needham, *Sec*
EMP: 10 EST: 1967
SQ FT: 17,500
SALES (est): 1.11MM Privately Held
Web: www.southington.org
SIC: 3446   Stairs, fire escapes, balconies,
railings, and ladders

(G-3234)
ST LIQUIDATION CORPORATION
445 W Queen St Ste 100 (06489-1171)
PHONE.................................860 628-9090
Anthony Amato, *Pr*
Pat Clavet, *Sec*
▲ EMP: 18 EST: 1986
SALES (est): 7.56MM Privately Held
Web: www.stamptechinc.com

SIC: 5051 3542   Metals service centers and
offices; Machine tools, metal forming type

(G-3235)
**STANLEY BLACK & DECKER
INC**
400 Executive Blvd (06489-6027)
PHONE.................................860 460-9122
EMP: 11
SALES (est): 2.49MM Privately Held
Web: www.stanleyblackanddecker.com
SIC: 3546   Power-driven handtools

(G-3236)
THOMAS PRODUCTS LTD
987 West St (06489-1023)
PHONE.................................860 621-9101
Thomas Duksa, *Pr*
EMP: 13 EST: 1980
SQ FT: 20,000
SALES (est): 4.23MM Privately Held
Web: www.thomasprod.com
SIC: 3625 3643   Flow actuated electrical
switches; Current-carrying wiring services

(G-3237)
THORNTON AND COMPANY INC
132 Main St Ste 2a # 3 (06489-2561)
PHONE.................................860 628-6771
◆ EMP: 10 EST: 1994
SQ FT: 3,000
SALES (est): 3.12MM Privately Held
SIC: 2821 5162   Polyethylene resins;
Plastics products, nec

(G-3238)
**TRI-MAR MANUFACTURING
COMPANY**
191 Captain Lewis Dr (06489-1144)
PHONE.................................860 628-4791
Keith Martinelli, *Pr*
Kevin Martinelli, *VP*
Martin Martinelli, *Sec*
David Martinelli, *Asst Tr*
EMP: 29 EST: 1980
SQ FT: 6,000
SALES (est): 1.16MM Privately Held
SIC: 3599   Machine shop, jobbing and repair

(G-3239)
**VANGUARD PLASTICS
CORPORATION**
100 Robert Porter Rd (06489-1160)
PHONE.................................860 628-4736
Lawrence J Budnick Junior, *CEO*
Christopher Budnick, *Pr*
Marsha A Budnick, *VP*
Kimberly Lagace, *VP*
Daren Fippinger, *VP*
▲ EMP: 45 EST: 1972
SQ FT: 22,500
SALES (est): 8.96MM Privately Held
Web: www.vanguardplastics.com
SIC: 3089   Injection molding of plastics

(G-3240)
WELD-ALL INC
987 West St (06489-1023)
PHONE.................................860 621-3156
Thomas R Duksa, *Pr*
Clara Duksa, *Sec*
EMP: 9 EST: 1973
SQ FT: 10,000
SALES (est): 223.63K Privately Held
Web: www.thomasprod.com
SIC: 3599 7692   Machine shop, jobbing and
repair; Welding repair

(G-3241)
YARDE METALS INC (HQ)
45 Newell St (06489-1424)
PHONE.................................860 406-6061
TOLL FREE: 800
Matthew Smith, *Pr*
William A Smith Ii, *VP*
Karla R Lewis, *VP*
Virginia Fitzgerald, *CFO*
◆ EMP: 425 EST: 1976
SQ FT: 500,000
SALES (est): 240.19MM
SALES (corp-wide): 17.02B Publicly Held
Web: www.yarde.com
SIC: 3499 5051   Safe deposit boxes or
chests, metal; Aluminum bars, rods, ingots,
sheets, pipes, plates, etc.
PA: Reliance Steel & Aluminum Co.
16100 N 71st St Ste 400
Scottsdale AZ 85254
480 564-5700

Southport
Fairfield County

(G-3242)
BEQOM NORTH AMERICA INC ✪
132 Old Post Rd (06890-1302)
PHONE.................................888 995-3028
Brad Perry, *Ofcr*
EMP: 26 EST: 2023
SALES (est): 1.04MM Privately Held
SIC: 7372   Prepackaged software

(G-3243)
**BERNHARD THMAS BLDG
SYSTEMS LL**
Also Called: B T Building Systems
281 Pequot Ave (06890-1360)
PHONE.................................203 925-0414
Harold C Thomas, *Prin*
Van H Bernhard, *
Bryan Maloney, *
EMP: 14 EST: 1998
SQ FT: 110,000
SALES (est): 448.52K Privately Held
SIC: 2439 5211 2435   Trusses, wooden roof;
Home centers; Hardwood veneer and
plywood

(G-3244)
C O JELLIFF CORPORATION (PA)
Also Called: Jelliff
354 Pequot Ave Ste 300 (06890-1485)
PHONE.................................203 259-1615
TOLL FREE: 800
Geoffrey Wheeler, *Pr*
Wilmot F Wheeler Junior, *Ch Bd*
Halsted W Wheeler, *
Rand Glucroft, *
▲ EMP: 28 EST: 1880
SQ FT: 40,000
SALES (est): 9.42MM
SALES (corp-wide): 9.42MM Privately
Held
Web: www.jelliff.com
SIC: 3496   Woven wire products, nec

(G-3245)
CENTER FOR DISCOVERY
1320 Mill Hill Rd (06890-3017)
PHONE.................................203 955-1381
Alyse Peekman, *Prin*
EMP: 20 EST: 2012
SALES (est): 242.9K Privately Held
Web: www.centerfordiscovery.com

SIC: 3822   Liquid level controls, residential
or commercial heating

(G-3246)
**STURM RUGER & COMPANY
INC**
1 Lazy Pl (06890)
PHONE.................................203 256-3895
Steve Sanetti, *Brnch Mgr*
EMP: 368
SALES (corp-wide): 595.84MM Publicly
Held
Web: www.ruger.com
SIC: 3484   Guns (firearms) or gun parts, 30
mm. and below
PA: Sturm, Ruger & Company, Inc.
1 Lacey Pl
Southport CT 06890
203 259-7843

(G-3247)
**STURM RUGER & COMPANY
INC (PA)**
Also Called: Ruger
1 Lacey Pl (06890-1207)
PHONE.................................203 259-7843
Christopher J Killoy, *Pr*
Ronald C Whitaker, *Non-Executive
Chairman of the Board**
John A Cosentino Junior, *V Ch Bd*
Thomas A Dineen, *Sr VP*
Kevin B Reid Senior, *Corporate Secretary*
▲ EMP: 271 EST: 1949
SQ FT: 25,000
SALES (est): 595.84MM
SALES (corp-wide): 595.84MM Publicly
Held
Web: www.ruger.com
SIC: 3484 3324   Small arms; Commercial
investment castings, ferrous

(G-3248)
SUPERIOR PLATING COMPANY
2 Lacey Pl (06890-1241)
PHONE.................................203 255-1501
John L Raymond, *Pr*
EMP: 75 EST: 1945
SQ FT: 20,000
SALES (est): 9.87MM
SALES (corp-wide): 18.45MM Privately
Held
Web: www.superiorplating.biz
SIC: 3471   Electroplating of metals or
formed products
PA: Superior Technology Corp.
Lacey Pl
Southport CT 06890
203 255-1501

(G-3249)
**SUPERIOR TECHNOLOGY CORP
(PA)**
Lacey Place (06890)
PHONE.................................203 255-1501
John L Raymond, *Pr*
EMP: 119 EST: 1974
SQ FT: 30,000
SALES (est): 18.73MM
SALES (corp-wide): 18.73MM Privately
Held
SIC: 3471   Electroplating of metals or
formed products

(G-3250)
THINK ENERGY LLC
Also Called: Think Energy
107 John St (06890-1466)
PHONE.................................917 202-3574
EMP: 60 EST: 2011

SALES (est): 16.77MM
SALES (corp-wide): 16.77MM **Privately Held**
SIC: 3825 Digital panel meters, electricity measuring
PA: Energywell Parent Llc
107 John St
Southport CT 06890
917 202-3574

Stafford
Tolland County

(G-3251)
TTM TECHNOLOGIES INC
4 Old Monson Rd (06075)
P.O. Box 145 (06075-0145)
PHONE..................................860 684-5881
Phil Titterton, *Genl Mgr*
EMP: 400
SALES (corp-wide): 2.5B **Publicly Held**
Web: www.ttm.com
SIC: 3672 Printed circuit boards
PA: Ttm Technologies, Inc.
200 Sandpointe Ave # 400
Santa Ana CA 92707
714 327-3000

Stafford Springs
Tolland County

(G-3252)
3M PURIFICATION INC
Also Called: 3M
32 River Rd (06076-1500)
PHONE..................................860 684-8628
Michael Bristol, *Mgr*
EMP: 251
SALES (corp-wide): 34.23B **Publicly Held**
Web: engage.3m.com
SIC: 3677 Filtration devices, electronic
HQ: 3m Purification Inc.
400 Research Pkwy
Meriden CT 06450
203 237-5541

(G-3253)
AMERICAN SLEEVE BEARING LLC
Also Called: American Sleeve Bearing
1 Spring St (06076-1504)
PHONE..................................860 684-8060
▲ EMP: 35 EST: 1982
SQ FT: 60,000
SALES (est): 4.74MM **Privately Held**
Web: www.asbbearings.com
SIC: 3568 3366 Bearings, plain; Copper foundries

(G-3254)
DIVISION 5 LLC
Also Called: SBE-CT
99 Cooper Ln (06076-1312)
PHONE..................................860 752-4127
Alex Pumiglia, *Operations*
Shane West, *Estimator*
EMP: 17 EST: 2013
SQ FT: 6,000
SALES (est): 3.5MM **Privately Held**
Web: www.division5ct.com
SIC: 3441 Fabricated structural metal

(G-3255)
EI-REC LLC
Also Called: Rec Components
17 Middle River Dr (06076-1034)
PHONE..................................860 851-9014

▲ EMP: 15 EST: 1997
SQ FT: 15,000
SALES (est): 2.41MM **Privately Held**
Web: www.reelseats.com
SIC: 3949 Fishing equipment

(G-3256)
HOBBS MEDICAL INC
8 Spring St (06076-1505)
PHONE..................................860 684-5875
Joanna Warner, *Pr*
EMP: 22 EST: 1982
SQ FT: 10,000
SALES (est): 4.27MM **Privately Held**
Web: www.hobbsmedical.com
SIC: 3841 3845 Surgical and medical instruments; Electromedical equipment

(G-3257)
MSJ INVESTMENTS INC
Also Called: Rmi
72 W Stafford Rd Ste 3 (06076-1000)
PHONE..................................860 684-9956
EMP: 10 EST: 1993
SQ FT: 4,000
SALES (est): 1.11MM **Privately Held**
SIC: 3724 3812 Aircraft engines and engine parts; Aircraft/aerospace flight instruments and guidance systems

(G-3258)
NEW ENGLAND MEAT PACKING LLC
30 Furnace Hollow Rd (06076-4306)
PHONE..................................860 684-3505
Memet Beqiri, *Prin*
EMP: 14 EST: 2007
SALES (est): 2.14MM **Privately Held**
Web: www.newenglandmeatpacking.com
SIC: 2011 Meat packing plants

(G-3259)
SKYLINE QUARRY LLC
110 Conklin Rd (06076-4204)
PHONE..................................860 875-3580
Wayne C Williams, *Pt*
Carolyn Williams, *Pt*
EMP: 10 EST: 1981
SQ FT: 1,500
SALES (est): 892.17K **Privately Held**
Web: www.skylinequarry.com
SIC: 3281 1442 1423 5032 Stone, quarrying and processing of own stone products; Construction sand and gravel; Crushed and broken granite; Building stone

(G-3260)
TE CONNECTIVITY CORPORATION
Tyco Elec Stafford Sprng Div
15 Tyco Dr (06076)
PHONE..................................860 684-8000
Robert Peirce, *Genl Mgr*
EMP: 25
Web: www.te.com
SIC: 3549 3672 Assembly machines, including robotic; Printed circuit boards
HQ: Te Connectivity Corporation
1050 Westlakes Dr
Berwyn PA 19312
610 893-9800

(G-3261)
TTM PRINTED CIRCUIT GROUP INC
15 Industrial Park Dr (06076-3612)
PHONE..................................860 684-8000
Bob Pierce, *Genl Mgr*
EMP: 149

SALES (corp-wide): 2.5B **Publicly Held**
Web: www.ttm.com
SIC: 3672 Printed circuit boards
HQ: Ttm Printed Circuit Group, Inc.
2630 S Harbor Blvd
Santa Ana CA 92704

(G-3262)
TTM TECHNOLOGIES INC
20 Industrial Park Dr (06076-3613)
PHONE..................................860 684-8000
Keith Wood, *Brnch Mgr*
EMP: 100
SALES (corp-wide): 2.5B **Publicly Held**
Web: www.ttm.com
SIC: 3672 Printed circuit boards
PA: Ttm Technologies, Inc.
200 Sandpointe Ave # 400
Santa Ana CA 92707
714 327-3000

(G-3263)
URG GRAPHICS INC (PA)
12 Fox Hill Dr (06076-3742)
PHONE..................................860 928-0835
Arthur Etchells, *CEO*
Rennie Cercone, *
J Paul Etchells, *
Helen R Etchells, *
EMP: 24 EST: 1963
SQ FT: 19,000
SALES (est): 2.19MM
SALES (corp-wide): 2.19MM **Privately Held**
Web: www.urggraphicsinc.com
SIC: 2796 Engraving platemaking services

(G-3264)
WILLINGTON NAMEPLATE INC
Also Called: Willington Companies
11 Middle River Dr (06076-1034)
PHONE..................................860 684-4281
EMP: 63 EST: 1965
SALES (est): 8.93MM **Privately Held**
Web: www.wnpinc.com
SIC: 3479 Name plates: engraved, etched, etc.

Stamford
Fairfield County

(G-3265)
116 LENOX EO LLC
707 Summer St Fl 5 (06901-1057)
PHONE..................................973 854-1999
Ron Kutas, *Prin*
EMP: 7 EST: 2016
SALES (est): 376.39K **Privately Held**
SIC: 3585 Refrigeration and heating equipment

(G-3266)
20/20 SOFTWARE INC
2001 W Main St Ste 270 (06902-4540)
PHONE..................................203 316-5500
Donald Resnick, *Pr*
Sheron Resnick, *VP*
EMP: 8 EST: 1982
SQ FT: 1,200
SALES (est): 825.02K **Privately Held**
Web: www.twensoft.com
SIC: 3695 7389 4813 Computer software tape and disks: blank, rigid, and floppy; Design services; Internet host services

(G-3267)
A TO A STUDIO SOLUTIONS LTD
47 Euclid Ave (06902-6230)

PHONE..................................203 388-9050
EMP: 10 EST: 2008
SALES (est): 860.85K **Privately Held**
Web: www.a2a.com
SIC: 7374 2759 2791 7336 Computer graphics service; Laser printing; Typographic composition, for the printing trade; Graphic arts and related design

(G-3268)
ABB ENTERPRISE SOFTWARE INC
Also Called: ABB ENTERPRISE SOFTWARE INC.
900 Long Ridge Rd (06902-1139)
PHONE..................................203 329-8771
John W Cutler Junior, *Brnch Mgr*
EMP: 10
Web: new.abb.com
SIC: 3612 Transformers, except electric
HQ: Abb Inc.
305 Gregson Dr
Cary NC 27511

(G-3269)
ABYRX INC
700 Fairfield Ave Ste 1 (06902-7541)
PHONE..................................855 475-9175
John Pacifico, *CEO*
John Pacifico, *Pr*
EMP: 11 EST: 2013
SALES (est): 1.56MM **Privately Held**
Web: www.abyrx.com
SIC: 3841 Surgical instruments and apparatus

(G-3270)
ACCURATE TOOL & DIE INC
16 Leon Pl (06902-5508)
PHONE..................................203 967-1200
Jeffrey Salvatore, *Pr*
▲ EMP: 22 EST: 1956
SQ FT: 14,500
SALES (est): 2.48MM **Privately Held**
Web: www.accuratetoolanddie.com
SIC: 3599 3544 Machine shop, jobbing and repair; Special dies and tools

(G-3271)
ACI INDUSTRIES CONVERTING LTD
1266 E Main St Ste 700r (06902-3507)
PHONE..................................740 368-4166
EMP: 18
SALES (corp-wide): 10MM **Privately Held**
Web: www.aci-industries.com
SIC: 2676 Towels, napkins, and tissue paper products
HQ: Aci Industries Converting, Ltd.
970 Pittsburgh Dr
Delaware OH 43015

(G-3272)
ACME SIGN CO (PA)
12 Research Dr (06906-1419)
P.O. Box 2345 (06906-0345)
PHONE..................................203 324-2263
TOLL FREE: 800
Stephen Trell, *Pr*
Jeff Trell, *VP*
EMP: 16 EST: 1977
SQ FT: 7,000
SALES (est): 2.32MM
SALES (corp-wide): 2.32MM **Privately Held**
Web: www.acmesignco.com
SIC: 3993 3953 5099 5719 Signs and advertising specialties; Textile marking stamps, hand: rubber or metal; Signs, except electric; Lighting fixtures

GEOGRAPHIC

(G-3273)
ACTION LETTER INC (PA)
11 Elm Ct (06902-5117)
PHONE....................203 323-2466
Ellen Connery, *Pr*
EMP: 45 **EST:** 1961
SALES (est): 4.85MM
SALES (corp-wide): 4.85MM **Privately Held**
Web: www.actionletter.com
SIC: 7331 7334 2791 2752 Mailing list compilers; Photocopying and duplicating services; Typesetting; Commercial printing, lithographic

(G-3274)
AG SEMICONDUCTOR SERVICES LLC
1111 Summer St Fl 4 (06905-5508)
P.O. Box 4484 (06907-0484)
PHONE....................203 322-5300
▼ **EMP:** 30 **EST:** 2005
SQ FT: 10,000
SALES (est): 3.65MM **Privately Held**
Web: www.agsemiconductor.com
SIC: 3674 Semiconductors and related devices

(G-3275)
AGI-SHOREWOOD GROUP US LLC
Also Called: Agi-Shorewood
300 Atlantic St Ste 206 (06901-3514)
PHONE....................203 324-4839
Donald K Eldert, *CFO*
Timothy J Facio, *
Jacob D Hudson, *
Philip E Schuch, *
◆ **EMP:** 1005 **EST:** 1966
SALES (est): 123.82MM
SALES (corp-wide): 8.23B **Privately Held**
SIC: 2671 2652 2657 Paper; coated and laminated packaging; Setup paperboard boxes; Folding paperboard boxes
PA: Atlas Holdings, Llc
100 Northfield St
Greenwich CT 06830
203 622-9138

(G-3276)
AIRCASTLE ADVISOR LLC
Also Called: Aircastle
201 Tresser Blvd Ste 400 (06901-3435)
PHONE....................203 504-1020
Ron Wainshal, *Managing Member*
J Robert Peart, *CIO*
Michael Kriedberg, *CCO*
EMP: 78 **EST:** 2004
SALES (est): 23.58MM **Privately Held**
Web: www.aircastle.com
SIC: 7359 3721 Aircraft rental; Aircraft
PA: Aircastle Limited
201 Tresser Blvd Ste 400
Stamford CT 06901

(G-3277)
ALLIED CONTROLS INC
25 Forest St Apt 14a (06901-1860)
PHONE....................860 628-8443
EMP: 11
SQ FT: 25,000
SALES (est): 596.68K **Privately Held**
Web: www.alliedcontrols.com
SIC: 3643 3613 3625 Current-carrying wiring services; Switchgear and switchboard apparatus; Relays, for electronic use

(G-3278)
ALPHAGRAPHICS
Also Called: AlphaGraphics
16 Dyke Ln (06902-7313)
PHONE....................203 847-8884
EMP: 8 **EST:** 2019
SALES (est): 365.07K **Privately Held**
Web: www.alphagraphics.com
SIC: 2752 Commercial printing, lithographic

(G-3279)
ALTUS IL LLC
2200 Atlantic St Fl 6 (06902-6834)
PHONE....................203 698-0090
EMP: 8 **EST:** 2021
SALES (est): 538.58K **Privately Held**
SIC: 3612 Power and distribution transformers

(G-3280)
AMERPET LLC
Also Called: Manufacturing
48 Union St Ste 2d (06906-1342)
PHONE....................475 619-9512
John Peterson, *Pr*
EMP: 9 **EST:** 2020
SALES (est): 530.64K **Privately Held**
Web: www.amerpet.net
SIC: 3999 Pet supplies

(G-3281)
AMPHENOL CORPORATION
Also Called: Amphenol Nexus Technologies
316 Courtland Ave Ste 100 (06906-2269)
PHONE....................203 327-7300
Gregory Diblasi, *Genl Mgr*
EMP: 70
SALES (corp-wide): 12.62B **Publicly Held**
Web: www.nexus.com
SIC: 3643 Electric switches
PA: Amphenol Corporation
358 Hall Ave
Wallingford CT 06492
203 265-8900

(G-3282)
ANOTHERCREATIONBYMICHELE
1351 Riverbank Rd (06903-2026)
PHONE....................203 322-4277
Michele Pulver, *Managing Member*
EMP: 7 **EST:** 1988
SALES (est): 224.63K **Privately Held**
Web: www.anothercreation.com
SIC: 2771 Greeting cards

(G-3283)
API WIZARD LLC
1127 High Ridge Rd Ste 238 (06905-1203)
PHONE....................800 691-8714
Rcihard Volpitta, *Managing Member*
EMP: 25 **EST:** 2011
SALES (est): 1.25MM **Privately Held**
Web: www.api-wizard.com
SIC: 7372 7389 Utility computer software; Business Activities at Non-Commercial Site

(G-3284)
APIJECT SYSTEMS CORP (PA)
2 High Ridge Park Fl 1 (06905-1349)
PHONE....................203 461-7121
Jay Walker, *CEO*
James A Garrett, *CCO*
Craig Cohon, *CSO*
EMP: 58 **EST:** 2018
SALES (est): 8.85MM
SALES (corp-wide): 8.85MM **Privately Held**
Web: www.apiject.com

SIC: 3841 Surgical and medical instruments

(G-3285)
ARCADIA ARCHITECTURAL PDTS INC
110 Viaduct Rd (06907-2707)
PHONE....................203 316-8000
◆ **EMP:** 25 **EST:** 1996
SALES (est): 2.44MM **Privately Held**
Web: www.arcadiaproducts.com
SIC: 3442 Metal doors, sash, and trim

(G-3286)
ARCCOS GOLF LLC (PA)
700 Canal St Ste 19 (06902-5921)
PHONE....................844 692-7226
Ammad Faisal, *COO*
Sal Syed, *
EMP: 24 **EST:** 2012
SQ FT: 4,500
SALES (est): 5.08MM
SALES (corp-wide): 5.08MM **Privately Held**
Web: www.arccosgolf.com
SIC: 3679 Electronic circuits

(G-3287)
ATACCAMA CORP US
263 Tresser Blvd Fl 9 (06901-3236)
PHONE....................203 564-1488
Michal Klaus, *CEO*
EMP: 21 **EST:** 2010
SALES (est): 3.34MM **Privately Held**
Web: www.ataccama.com
SIC: 7372 Prepackaged software

(G-3288)
ATCONSULTING LLC
Also Called: E-Z Audit
151 Cascade Rd (06903-4225)
P.O. Box 8176 (06905-8176)
PHONE....................203 987-5355
EMP: 7 **EST:** 2002
SALES (est): 347.49K **Privately Held**
Web: www.ezaudit.net
SIC: 7372 Prepackaged software

(G-3289)
ATLANTIC STREET CAPITL MGT LLC (PA)
281 Tresser Blvd Fl 6 (06901-3246)
PHONE....................203 428-3158
Timothy Lewis, *
Andy Wilkins, *
Brian Cooper, *
Iris Rosken, *
EMP: 50 **EST:** 2006
SALES (est): 545.74MM **Privately Held**
Web: www.atlanticstreetcapital.com
SIC: 6799 2099 Venture capital companies; Food preparations, nec

(G-3290)
BAL INTERNATIONAL INC
281 Tresser Blvd Fl 12 (06901-3238)
PHONE....................203 359-6775
EMP: 29 **EST:** 1992
SALES (est): 995.75K **Privately Held**
Web: www.balnet.com
SIC: 3339 Precious metals

(G-3291)
BEIERSDORF INC (DH)
301 Tresser Blvd Ste 1500 (06901-3280)
PHONE....................203 563-5800
Joerg Disseld, *CFO*
Amy Nenner, *VP*
Kathy Shea, *VP*
◆ **EMP:** 9 **EST:** 1928

SALES (est): 221.15MM
SALES (corp-wide): 12.51B **Privately Held**
Web: www.beiersdorfusa.com
SIC: 2844 Face creams or lotions
HQ: Beiersdorf North America Inc.
301 Tresser Blvd Ste 1500
Stamford CT 06901
203 563-5800

(G-3292)
BEIERSDORF NORTH AMERICA INC (DH)
301 Tresser Blvd Ste 1500 (06901-3280)
PHONE....................203 563-5800
James A Kenton, *CEO*
Bill Graham, *Pr*
Magnus Jonsson, *VP*
Tina Jackse, *VP*
Raymond Engelbrecht, *CFO*
◆ **EMP:** 10 **EST:** 1998
SALES (est): 464.18MM
SALES (corp-wide): 12.51B **Privately Held**
Web: www.beiersdorfusa.com
SIC: 2844 5122 3842 2841 Face creams or lotions; Antiseptics; Bandages and dressings; Soap: granulated, liquid, cake, flaked, or chip
HQ: Beiersdorf Ag
Beiersdorfstr. 1-9
Hamburg HH 22529
4049090

(G-3293)
BELDOTTI BAKERIES LLC
Also Called: Cerbone Bakery
605 Newfield Ave (06905-3302)
PHONE....................203 348-9029
James Beldotti Junior, *Pt*
Michael Beldotti, *Pt*
EMP: 15 **EST:** 1979
SQ FT: 3,000
SALES (est): 965.29K **Privately Held**
Web: www.goodbreadbakery.com
SIC: 2051 2052 Bakery: wholesale or wholesale/retail combined; Cookies and crackers

(G-3294)
BETTER LISTS INCORPORATED
64 Sunnyside Ave (06902-7641)
PHONE....................203 324-4171
EMP: 25
Web: www.betterlists.com
SIC: 7331 7374 4215 2759 Direct mail advertising services; Data processing and preparation; Courier services, except by air; Commercial printing, nec

(G-3295)
BLUETRITON BRANDS INC
Also Called: Blue Triton Brands
900 Long Ridge Rd (06902-1139)
PHONE....................203 531-4100
Andrew Walpole, *Acctg Mgr*
EMP: 11
SALES (corp-wide): 1.3B **Privately Held**
Web: www.nestle-watersna.com
SIC: 5963 2086 Bottled water delivery; Water, natural: packaged in cans, bottles, etc.
HQ: Bluetriton Brands, Inc.
900 Long Ridge Rd Bldg 2
Stamford CT 06902

(G-3296)
BLUETRITON BRANDS INC (HQ)
Also Called: Perrier Water
900 Long Ridge Rd Bldg 2 (06902-1140)
PHONE....................888 747-7437
Jorge Mesquita, *CEO*

Charlie Broll, *
David Colville, *
Heidi Paul, *
Bill Pearson, *
◆ **EMP:** 320 **EST:** 1986
SQ FT: 81,225
SALES (est): 991.99MM
SALES (corp-wide): 1.3B **Privately Held**
Web: www.bluetriton.com
SIC: 2086 5963 Water, natural: packaged in
   cans, bottles, etc.; Bottled water delivery
PA: Bluetriton Brands Holdings, Inc.
   900 Long Ridge Rd Bldg 2
   Stamford CT 06902
   203 531-4100

(G-3297)
BROOKSIDE FLVORS
INGRDENTS LLC (HQ)
201 Tresser Blvd Ste 320 (06901-3435)
PHONE..................203 595-4520
Rudy Dieperink, *CEO*
Donald L Hawks Iii, *Ch Bd*
William Gambrell, *
Gaetan Sourceau, *
Richard Nikola, *
EMP: 8 **EST:** 2015
SALES (est): 19.23MM
SALES (corp-wide): 19.23MM **Privately
Held**
SIC: 2087 Flavoring extracts and syrups,
   nec
PA: Bep Flavor Holdings Llc
   201 Tresser Blvd Ste 320
   Stamford CT 06901
   203 595-4520

(G-3298)
BUITONI FOOD COMPANY (PA)
1 High Ridge Park Ste 201 (06905-1323)
PHONE..................475 210-0128
Graham Corneck, *Pr*
Peter Wilson, *Ch Bd*
Kyle Moran, *CFO*
EMP: 20 **EST:** 2020
SALES (est): 96.1MM
SALES (corp-wide): 96.1MM **Privately
Held**
Web: www.buitoni.com
SIC: 2098 Macaroni and spaghetti

(G-3299)
C SPEAKER CORP
46 Southfield Ave Ste 300 (06902-7256)
▲ **EMP:** 246
SIC: 3651 Speaker systems

(G-3300)
CADMUS
200 Stamford Pl Fl 2 (06902-6753)
PHONE..................203 595-3000
Scott J Goodwin, *CFO*
EMP: 17 **EST:** 2014
SALES (est): 215.5K **Privately Held**
Web: www.cadmusgroup.com
SIC: 2752 Commercial printing, lithographic

(G-3301)
CANIDAE LLC
Also Called: Canidae Pet Foods
1 Dock St Ste 502 (06902-5838)
P.O. Box 3610 (93403-3610)
PHONE..................475 208-1789
Bret Furio, *CEO*
John Gordon, *
Scott Whipple, *
EMP: 100 **EST:** 1963
SALES (est): 44.62MM **Privately Held**
Web: www.canidae.com

SIC: 2047 Dog and cat food

(G-3302)
CARA THERAPEUTICS INC
Also Called: Cara
400 Atlantic St Ste 500 (06901-3512)
PHONE..................203 406-3700
Christopher Posner, *CEO*
Frederique Menzaghi, *Research &
Development*
Ryan Maynard, *CFO*
Joana Goncalves, *CMO*
Scott M Terrillion, *CCO*
EMP: 80 **EST:** 2004
SQ FT: 36,000
SALES (est): 41.87MM **Privately Held**
Web: www.caratherapeutics.com
SIC: 2834 8731 Pharmaceutical
   preparations; Commercial physical research

(G-3303)
CASE CONCEPTS INTL LLC
112 Prospect St Unit A (06901-1207)
PHONE..................203 883-8602
▲ **EMP:** 16 **EST:** 1995
SQ FT: 7,500
SALES (est): 1.01MM **Privately Held**
Web: www.caseconcepts.com
SIC: 3161 Attache' cases

(G-3304)
CCI CORPUS CHRISTI LLC
2200 Atlantic St Ste 800 (06902-6834)
PHONE..................203 564-8100
Michale Dowling, *Pr*
EMP: 15 **EST:** 2014
SALES (est): 2.4MM **Privately Held**
SIC: 2911 Petroleum refining
PA: Castleton Commodities International
   Llc
   2200 Atlantic St Ste 800
   Stamford CT 06902

(G-3305)
CCI CYRUS RIVER TERMINAL
LLC
2200 Atlantic St Ste 800 (06902-6834)
PHONE..................203 761-8000
William C Reed Ii, *Pr*
EMP: 9 **EST:** 2008
SALES (est): 2.9MM **Privately Held**
Web: www.ccci.com
SIC: 3999 Dock equipment and supplies,
   industrial
HQ: Cci Us Asset Holdings Llc
   2200 Atlantic St Ste 800
   Stamford CT 06902
   203 564-8100

(G-3306)
CCI ROBINSONS BEND LLC
2200 Atlantic St Ste 800 (06902-6834)
PHONE..................203 564-8571
Craig Jarchow, *Pr*
EMP: 22 **EST:** 2013
SALES (est): 1.68MM **Privately Held**
SIC: 1311 Crude petroleum and natural gas
PA: Castleton Commodities International
   Llc
   2200 Atlantic St Ste 800
   Stamford CT 06902

(G-3307)
CENVEO CORPORATION
200 Stamford Pl Fl 2 (06902)
PHONE..................303 790-8023
EMP: 6380
Web: www.cenveo.com

SIC: 2677 2752 2759 Envelopes;
   Commercial printing, lithographic; Labels
   and seals: printing, nsk

(G-3308)
CENVEO ENTERPRISES INC
(PA)
200 Stamford Pl 2nd Fl (06902-6753)
PHONE..................203 595-3000
Robert G Burton Junior, *CEO*
Mike Burton, *Pr*
Mark Hiltwein, *CFO*
Ayman Zameli, *CSO*
EMP: 52 **EST:** 2018
SALES (est): 1.04B
SALES (corp-wide): 1.04B **Privately Held**
Web: www.cenveo.com
SIC: 2677 2679 Envelopes; Tags and
   labels, paper

(G-3309)
CENVEO WORLDWIDE LIMITED
(DH)
Also Called: Discount Labels Montgomery Co
200 Stamford Pl (06902-6753)
PHONE..................203 595-3000
Robert Burton Junior, *CEO*
Michael G Burton, *
Mark Hiltwein, *
EMP: 27 **EST:** 2018
SALES (est): 671.31MM
SALES (corp-wide): 1.04B **Privately Held**
Web: www.cenveo.com
SIC: 2677 2679 Envelopes; Tags and
   labels, paper
HQ: Cwl Enterprises, Inc.
   200 First Stamford Pl # 2
   Stamford CT 06902
   303 790-8023

(G-3310)
CHIEF EXECUTIVE GROUP LLC
(PA)
Also Called: Chief Executive Group
9 W Broad St Ste 430 (06902-3764)
PHONE..................785 832-0303
Wayne Cooper, *Managing Member*
Dan Bigman, *Chief Content Officer*
EMP: 40 **EST:** 2009
SQ FT: 4,200
SALES (est): 8.98MM
SALES (corp-wide): 8.98MM **Privately
Held**
Web: www.chiefexecutive.net
SIC: 2721 2741 7319 8611 Magazines:
   publishing only, not printed on site;
   Business service newsletters: publishing
   and printing; Media buying service;
   Business associations

(G-3311)
CHIEF EXECUTIVE GROUP LP
(PA)
Also Called: Chief Executive Magazine
9 W Broad.St Ste 430 (06902-3764)
PHONE..................203 930-2700
Edward Kopko, *CEO*
EMP: 9 **EST:** 1972
SQ FT: 6,600
SALES (est): 2.44MM
SALES (corp-wide): 2.44MM **Privately
Held**
SIC: 2721 8742 Magazines: publishing only,
   not printed on site; Management consulting
   services

(G-3312)
CINE MAGNETICS INC (HQ)
Also Called: CMI Media Management

9 W Broad St Ste 730 (06902-3780)
P.O. Box 862 (10504-0862)
PHONE..................914 273-7600
Joseph J Barber Junior, *Ch*
Robert Pastore, *Pr*
Stephen Kushel, *Sec*
▲ **EMP:** 54 **EST:** 1961
SQ FT: 62,282
SALES (est): 17.08MM **Privately Held**
Web: www.premieredigital.com
SIC: 7819 7221 3861 7384 Video tape or
   disk reproduction; Photographer, still or
   video; Photographic processing chemicals;
   Photofinish laboratories
PA: Premiere Digital Services, Inc.
   5900 Wilshire Blvd # 1700
   Los Angeles CA 90036

(G-3313)
CITY CARTING INC
Also Called: City Carting
8 Viaduct Rd (06907-2707)
P.O. Box 17250 (06907-7250)
PHONE..................888 413-3344
EMP: 92 **EST:** 1975
SALES (est): 46.07MM **Privately Held**
Web: www.citycarting.net
SIC: 4953 2611 Refuse collection and
   disposal services; Pulp manufactured from
   waste or recycled paper

(G-3314)
CJS MILLWORK INC
425 Fairfield Ave Ste 12 (06902-7588)
PHONE..................203 708-0080
Chris Sculti, *Pr*
EMP: 10 **EST:** 1996
SALES (est): 998.92K **Privately Held**
Web: www.cjsmillwork.com
SIC: 2431 Millwork

(G-3315)
CLASSIC GRAPHICS CORP
Also Called: Copy Art
652 Glenbrook Rd Ste 3-308 (06906-1427)
PHONE..................203 323-6635
George F Nix Junior, *Pr*
George F Nix Senior, *VP*
EMP: 8 **EST:** 1975
SQ FT: 5,000
SALES (est): 848.22K **Privately Held**
Web: www.classicgraphicscorp.com
SIC: 3993 Signs and advertising specialties

(G-3316)
COFCO AMERICAS
RESOURCES CORP (HQ)
Also Called: Cofco-Gri Cof Cot Grins Sug Di
107 Elm St Fl 11 (06902-3834)
PHONE..................203 658-2820
EMP: 10 **EST:** 2011
SQ FT: 48,060
SALES (est): 301.86MM **Privately Held**
SIC: 6221 5153 5149 2099 Commodity
   dealers, contracts; Grain and field beans;
   Cocoa; Sugar
PA: Cofco Corporation
   No.8, Nan Street, Chaoyangmen,
   Chaoyang District
   Beijing BJ 10002

(G-3317)
COLONIAL WOODWORKING INC
841 Cove Rd (06902-9422)
PHONE..................203 866-5844
Frank Carlucci, *Pr*
Nancy Carlucci, *VP*
Veronica Mahan, *Sec*
Peter Carlucci, *VP*
EMP: 27 **EST:** 1975

SALES (est): 3.47MM **Privately Held**
SIC: 2431　Staircases and stairs, wood

(G-3318)
COMICANA INC
61 Studio Rd (06903-4724)
PHONE..................................203 968-0748
Mort Walker, *Pr*
Greg Walker, *VP*
Brian Walker, *Sec*
EMP: 9 **EST:** 1979
SALES (est): 507.74K **Privately Held**
SIC: 2721 2731　Comic books: publishing only, not printed on site; Books, publishing and printing

(G-3319)
COMPUTER PRGRM & SYSTEMS INC (PA)
Also Called: Actuaries Division
1011 High Ridge Rd Ste 208 (06905-1604)
PHONE..................................203 324-9203
Samuel Urda, *Pr*
Allan Aferrone, *VP*
Peter O'karma, *VP*
EMP: 7 **EST:** 1967
SQ FT: 3,000
SALES (est): 981.67K
SALES (corp-wide): 981.67K **Privately Held**
Web: www.cpsincorp.com
SIC: 7372 8742 8999　Prepackaged software ; Management consulting services; Actuarial consultant

(G-3320)
CONAIR LLC (HQ)
Also Called: Personal Care Appliances Div
1 Cummings Point Rd (06902-7901)
PHONE..................................203 351-9000
Kristie Juster, *Pr*
Ronald Diamond, *Vice Chairman*
James Dubin, *Ofcr*
John Dourdis, *
Michael Baldino, *CORP FINANCIAL REPORTING*
◆ **EMP:** 366 **EST:** 1959
SALES (est): 2B **Privately Held**
Web: validate.perfdrive.com
SIC: 3631 3999 3634 3639　Household cooking equipment; Barber and beauty shop equipment; Electric housewares and fans; Major kitchen appliances, except refrigerators and stoves
PA: American Securities Llc
　590 Madison Ave Fl 38
　New York NY 10022

(G-3321)
CONAIR LLC
Also Called: Euro -Coiffeur
1 Cummings Point Rd (06902-7901)
PHONE..................................203 348-6684
EMP: 10
Web: validate.perfdrive.com
SIC: 3634　Electric housewares and fans
HQ: Conair Llc
　1 Cummings Point Rd
　Stamford CT 06902
　203 351-9000

(G-3322)
CONTINENTAL FRAGRANCES LTD
Also Called: Continental Consumer Products
333 Ludlow St Ste 2 (06902-6987)
PHONE..................................800 542-5903
M Benjamin Jones, *Prin*
EMP: 37 **EST:** 1983
SQ FT: 56,000

SALES (est): 1.66MM
SALES (corp-wide): 20.29MM **Privately Held**
SIC: 2844　Hair coloring preparations
HQ: Hrb Winddown, Inc.
　333 Ludlow St Ste 2
　Stamford CT 06902

(G-3323)
CPI OPERATIONS LLC
Also Called: Nustar
750 Wshngton Blvd Ste 600 (06901)
Rural Route 781609 (78278)
PHONE..................................210 249-9988
EMP: 210
SIC: 2911　Petroleum refining

(G-3324)
CRAFTSMEN PRINTING GROUP INC
104 Lincoln Ave (06902-3121)
PHONE..................................203 327-2817
James Zygmont, *Pr*
Marcia Gogliettino, *Treas*
EMP: 7 **EST:** 1986
SQ FT: 1,600
SALES (est): 506.76K **Privately Held**
SIC: 2752　Offset printing

(G-3325)
CRANE AEROSPACE INC (DH)
100 Stamford Pl (06902-6740)
PHONE..................................203 363-7300
EMP: 106 **EST:** 2002
SALES (est): 45.37MM
SALES (corp-wide): 2.04B **Publicly Held**
Web: www.craneco.com
SIC: 3492 3728　Control valves, fluid power: hydraulic and pneumatic; Aircraft parts and equipment, nec
HQ: Crane International Holdings, Inc.
　100 Stamford Pl
　Stamford CT 06902

(G-3326)
CRANE COMPANY (PA)
100 Stamford Pl Ste 300 (06902-6747)
PHONE..................................203 363-7300
Max H Mitchell, *Pr*
James L L Tullis, *Ch Bd*
Richard A Maue, *CAO*
Tami Polmanteer, *Chief Human Resources Officer*
Alejandro Alcala, *Ex VP*
EMP: 98 **EST:** 1855
SALES (est): 2.04B
SALES (corp-wide): 2.04B **Publicly Held**
Web: www.craneco.com
SIC: 3812 3826 7373　Aircraft/aerospace flight instruments and guidance systems; Laser scientific and engineering instruments ; Systems engineering, computer related

(G-3327)
CRANE CONTROLS INC (DH)
100 Stamford Pl (06902-6740)
PHONE..................................203 363-7300
EMP: 247 **EST:** 2003
SALES (est): 86.69MM
SALES (corp-wide): 2.04B **Publicly Held**
Web: www.craneco.com
SIC: 3492　Control valves, fluid power: hydraulic and pneumatic
HQ: Crane International Holdings, Inc.
　100 Stamford Pl
　Stamford CT 06902

(G-3328)
CRANE INTL HOLDINGS INC (HQ)
Also Called: Crane
100 Stamford Pl (06902-6740)
PHONE..................................203 363-7300
EMP: 170 **EST:** 1997
SALES (est): 499.1MM
SALES (corp-wide): 2.04B **Publicly Held**
SIC: 3492　Control valves, fluid power: hydraulic and pneumatic
PA: Crane Company
　100 First Stamford Pl # 40
　Stamford CT 06902
　203 363-7300

(G-3329)
CRANE MERGER CO LLC
100 Stamford Pl (06902-6740)
PHONE..................................203 363-7300
EMP: 15 **EST:** 2010
SALES (est): 1.2MM
SALES (corp-wide): 3.37B **Publicly Held**
SIC: 3492　Control valves, fluid power: hydraulic and pneumatic
PA: Crane Nxt, Co.
　950 Winter St Fl 4
　Waltham MA 02451
　610 430-2510

(G-3330)
CRANE OVERSEAS LLC (HQ)
100 Stamford Pl (06902-6740)
PHONE..................................203 363-7300
EMP: 34 **EST:** 2010
SALES (est): 8.95MM
SALES (corp-wide): 3.37B **Publicly Held**
SIC: 3492　Control valves, fluid power: hydraulic and pneumatic
PA: Crane Nxt, Co.
　950 Winter St Fl 4
　Waltham MA 02451
　610 430-2510

(G-3331)
CUBICO PALMETTO HOLDINGS LLC
208 Harbor Dr (06902-7467)
PHONE..................................646 513-4981
EMP: 24
SALES (est): 1.31MM **Privately Held**
SIC: 3621　Windmills, electric generating

(G-3332)
CWL ENTERPRISES INC (HQ)
200 Stamford Pl 2nd Fl (06902-6753)
PHONE..................................303 790-8023
Robert G Burton Junior, *CEO*
Mike Burton, *Pr*
Mark Hiltwein, *CFO*
EMP: 13 **EST:** 2018
SALES (est): 1.04B
SALES (corp-wide): 1.04B **Privately Held**
SIC: 2677 2679　Envelopes; Tags and labels, paper
PA: Cenveo Enterprises, Inc.
　200 First Stamford Pl # 2
　Stamford CT 06902
　203 595-3000

(G-3333)
CYTEC INDUSTRIES INC
1937 W Main St Ste 1 (06902-4578)
P.O. Box 60 (06904-0060)
PHONE..................................203 321-2200
Bill Moore, *Mgr*
EMP: 92
SALES (corp-wide): 146.05MM **Privately Held**

Web: www.solvay.com
SIC: 2899 8731　Chemical preparations, nec ; Commercial physical research
HQ: Cytec Industries Inc.
　504 Carnegie Ctr
　Princeton NJ 08540

(G-3334)
DATAQUEST KOREA INC
56 Top Gallant Rd (06902-7747)
PHONE..................................239 561-4862
Christopher J Lafond, *Prin*
EMP: 22 **EST:** 2001
SALES (est): 261.04K **Privately Held**
Web: www.gartner.com
SIC: 3695　Computer software tape and disks: blank, rigid, and floppy

(G-3335)
DEANE INC
1267 E Main St (06902-3538)
PHONE..................................203 327-7008
Peter M Dean, *Mgr*
Carrie Ann Deane, *Prin*
EMP: 22 **EST:** 1980
SQ FT: 2,500
SALES (est): 1.37MM **Privately Held**
Web: www.deaneinc.com
SIC: 5712 2431　Cabinet work, custom; Millwork

(G-3336)
DEER CREEK FABRICS INC
11b Riverbend Dr S (06907-2524)
PHONE..................................203 964-0922
Steven Lucier, *Pr*
Mary Ann Lucier, *VP*
Jill Cooper, *VP*
EMP: 7 **EST:** 1980
SALES (est): 856.44K **Privately Held**
Web: www.deercreekfabrics.com
SIC: 2221　Broadwoven fabric mills, manmade

(G-3337)
DIAGEO INVESTMENT CORPORATION
200 Elm St Ste 200 (06902-3826)
PHONE..................................203 229-2100
Jeff Millstein, *Ex VP*
◆ **EMP:** 25 **EST:** 2007
SALES (est): 485.4K
SALES (corp-wide): 21.15B **Privately Held**
SIC: 2082　Malt beverages
PA: Diageo Plc
　16 Great Marlborough Street
　London W1F 7
　845 751-5101

(G-3338)
DIRECT ENERGY INC (HQ)
263 Tresser Blvd Fl 8 (06901-3236)
PHONE..................................800 260-0300
Badar Khan, *Pr*
Scott Boose, *COO*
▲ **EMP:** 23 **EST:** 2004
SALES (est): 175.15MM **Publicly Held**
Web: www.directenergy.com
SIC: 4911 1311　Electric services; Natural gas production
PA: Nrg Energy, Inc.
　910 Louisiana St Ste B200
　Houston TX 77002

(G-3339)
DT HOLDINGS INCORPORATED
72 Camp Ave (06907-1852)
PHONE..................................203 602-6969
Marc Kuppersmith, *CEO*
EMP: 16 **EST:** 1999

SQ FT: 4,700
SALES (est): 1.8MM **Privately Held**
SIC: 3911 5944 8741 3961 Jewelry, precious metal; Jewelry stores; Management services; Costume jewelry

(G-3340)
EAGLE SHIP MANAGEMENT LLC (HQ)
300 Stamford Pl (06902-6765)
PHONE.....................203 276-8100
Gary Vogel, *CEO*
EMP: 127 EST: 2009
SALES (est): 7.68MM
SALES (corp-wide): 719.85MM **Publicly Held**
Web: www.eagleships.com
SIC: 4424 5172 1321 1221 Coastwise transportation, freight; Crude oil; Natural gasoline production; Bituminous coal surface mining
PA: Eagle Bulk Shipping Inc.
300 Frst Stamford Pl Fl 5 Flr 5
Stamford CT 06902
203 276-8100

(G-3341)
EBREVIA INC
6 Landmark Sq Ste B (06901-2516)
PHONE.....................203 870-3000
EMP: 17 EST: 2019
SALES (est): 531.73K **Privately Held**
Web: www.dfinsolutions.com
SIC: 7372 Prepackaged software

(G-3342)
ECOLOGIC ENERGY SOLUTIONS LLC
48 Union St Ste 14 (06906-1342)
PHONE.....................203 889-0505
EMP: 53 EST: 2007
SALES (est): 3.43MM
SALES (corp-wide): 2.67B **Publicly Held**
Web: www.ecologices.com
SIC: 3296 1742 Fiberglass insulation; Insulation, buildings
PA: Installed Building Products, Inc.
495 S High St Ste 50
Columbus OH 43215
614 221-3399

(G-3343)
EOWS MIDLAND INC
1 Landmark Sq Fl 11 (06901-2603)
PHONE.....................203 358-5705
Charles Drimal, *Pr*
EMP: 13 EST: 2001
SALES (est): 753.7K **Privately Held**
SIC: 1381 Drilling oil and gas wells

(G-3344)
EQUINOR PIPELINES LLC
600 Washington Blvd 8th Fl (06901)
PHONE.....................203 978-6900
Charles O'brien, *Dir*
EMP: 150 EST: 2008
SALES (est): 16.52MM **Privately Held**
SIC: 1382 Oil and gas exploration services
HQ: Equinor Us Holdings Inc.
600 Wshington Blvd Fl 8 Flr 8
Stamford CT 06901
203 978-6900

(G-3345)
EQUINOR US HOLDINGS INC (DH)
600 Washington Blvd 8th Fl (06901)
PHONE.....................203 978-6900
Bent Rune Solheim, *Pr*

Todd Walls, *DOWNSTREAM*
Kathleen Parchinski, *TAX*
Josh Kaplan, *Sec*
▲ EMP: 119 EST: 1987
SQ FT: 56,000
SALES (est): 10.6B **Privately Held**
Web: www.equinor.com
SIC: 5172 1382 Crude oil; Oil and gas exploration services
HQ: Equinor Energy As
Forusbeen 50
Stavanger 4035

(G-3346)
EVERCEL INC
1055 Washington Blvd Fl 8 (06901-2251)
PHONE.....................781 741-8800
Garry A Prime, *Pr*
James D Gerson, *
Anthony P Kiernan, *CFO*
Daniel J Mccarthy, *COO*
EMP: 116 EST: 1999
SALES (est): 13.15MM **Privately Held**
SIC: 3691 Alkaline cell storage batteries

(G-3347)
EVERGREEN PRINTING
61 Seaview Ave (06902-6021)
PHONE.....................203 323-4717
EMP: 7 EST: 2013
SALES (est): 118.59K **Privately Held**
SIC: 2752 Offset printing

(G-3348)
FRC FOUNDERS CORPORATION (PA)
Also Called: F R C
290 Harbor Dr (06902-8700)
PHONE.....................203 661-6601
EMP: 30 EST: 1987
SALES (est): 84MM
SALES (corp-wide): 84MM **Privately Held**
Web: www.firstreserve.com
SIC: 8741 1311 1389 8731 Financial management for business; Crude petroleum and natural gas; Oil field services, nec; Energy research

(G-3349)
FREDERICK PURDUE COMPANY INC (PA)
Also Called: Purdue Pharma
201 Tresser Blvd (06901-3435)
PHONE.....................203 588-8000
John H Stewart, *Pr*
Edward B Mahony, *
Stuart D Baker, *
Jim Dolan, *
David Long, *
▲ EMP: 310 EST: 2004
SQ FT: 90,000
SALES (est): 90.5MM
SALES (corp-wide): 90.5MM **Privately Held**
Web: www.purduepharma.com
SIC: 2834 5122 Pharmaceutical preparations; Pharmaceuticals

(G-3350)
FREEPOINT ECO-SYSTEMS LLC
58 Commerce Rd (06902-4506)
PHONE.....................203 542-6000
EMP: 12 EST: 2020
SALES (est): 4.9MM
SALES (corp-wide): 524.75MM **Privately Held**
Web: www.freepoint.com
SIC: 2611 Pulp mills, mechanical and recycling processing
HQ: Freepoint Commodities Llc
58 Commerce Rd

Stamford CT 06902

(G-3351)
FREMCO LLC
25 Washington Ct Apt 7-6 (06902-2334)
P.O. Box 791 (06877-0791)
PHONE.....................203 857-0522
Lloyd Fremed, *CEO*
EMP: 10 EST: 2005
SQ FT: 1,600
SALES (est): 617.36K **Privately Held**
SIC: 3577 7379 Printers, computer; Online services technology consultants

(G-3352)
FUJIFILM ELCTRNIC MTLS USA INC
Also Called: Fujifilm NDT Systems
419 West Ave (06902-6343)
PHONE.....................203 363-3360
EMP: 28
Web: www.fujifilm-ffem.com
SIC: 5043 3861 Photographic equipment and supplies; Photographic equipment and supplies
HQ: Fujifilm Electronic Materials U.S.A., Inc.
80 Circuit Dr
North Kingstown RI 02852
401 522-9499

(G-3353)
FURCI COMMUNICATIONS INC
Also Called: Printech
652 Glenbrook Rd Ste 4-101 (06906-1438)
PHONE.....................203 961-1800
▲ EMP: 50
SIC: 2752 Offset printing

(G-3354)
GENERAL ELECTRIC COMPANY
Also Called: GE
1600 Summer St Ste 2 (06905-5125)
PHONE.....................866 419-4096
Denis J Nayden, *Mgr*
EMP: 10
SALES (corp-wide): 76.56B **Publicly Held**
Web: www.gecapital.com
SIC: 3511 3845 3533 3724 Turbines and turbine generator sets; Electromedical equipment; Oil and gas field machinery; Airfoils, aircraft engine
PA: General Electric Company
1 Financial Ctr Ste 3700
Boston MA 02111
617 443-3000

(G-3355)
GENEVE CORPORATION (HQ)
96 Cummings Point Rd (06902-7975)
PHONE.....................203 358-8000
F Peter Zoch Iii, *Pr*
Edward Netter, *Ch Bd*
Ronald G Strackbein, *Ex VP*
Robert T Keiser, *Sr VP*
Steven P Lapin, *Sr VP*
EMP: 20 EST: 1971
SQ FT: 12,000
SALES (est): 279.97MM
SALES (corp-wide): 775.69MM **Privately Held**
SIC: 5961 3483 6282 Educational supplies and equipment, mail order; Ammunition components; Investment counselors
PA: Geneve Holdings, Inc.
96 Cummings Point Rd
Stamford CT 06902
203 358-8000

(G-3356)
GOLDEN SUN INC
Also Called: Newhall Labs
5 High Ridge Park Ste 200 (06905-1326)
PHONE.....................800 575-7960
Dario Margve, *Ch*
Jon Achenbaum, *CEO*
Chris Conley, *CFO*
Ian Mactaggart, *VP*
▲ EMP: 20 EST: 1975
SQ FT: 20,000
SALES (est): 3.47MM **Privately Held**
Web: www.newhalllabs.com
SIC: 2844 Hair preparations, including shampoos
HQ: Golden Sun Holdings, Inc.
5 High Ridge Park Ste 100
Stamford CT 06905
203 595-5228

(G-3357)
GOLDEN SUN HOLDINGS INC (HQ)
5 High Ridge Park Ste 100 (06905-1329)
PHONE.....................203 595-5228
Hendrik Hartong Iii, *Mng Pt*
Ian Mactaggart, *Mng Pt*
Dario Margve, *Mng Pt*
Hendrik Hartong Junior, *Mng Pt*
Nicholas Dicarlo, *CFO*
EMP: 15 EST: 2011
SALES (est): 9.37MM **Privately Held**
SIC: 2844 Perfumes, cosmetics and other toilet preparations
PA: Brynwood Partners Vii L.P.
8 Sound Shore Dr Ste 265
Greenwich CT 06830

(G-3358)
GOODWAY TECHNOLOGIES CORPORATION (PA)
Also Called: Goodway
420 West Ave (06902-6329)
PHONE.....................203 359-4708
◆ EMP: 68 EST: 1966
SALES (est): 15.63MM
SALES (corp-wide): 15.63MM **Privately Held**
Web: www.goodway.com
SIC: 3589 High pressure cleaning equipment

(G-3359)
GREENWICH TIME
44 Columbus Pl Apt 9 (06907-1614)
PHONE.....................203 253-2922
Katelyn L Imbornoni, *Prin*
EMP: 8 EST: 2011
SALES (est): 117.04K **Privately Held**
Web: www.greenwichtime.com
SIC: 2711 Newspapers, publishing and printing

(G-3360)
H G STEINMETZ MCH WORKS INC
Also Called: Steinmetz Machine Works
184 Jonathan Dr (06903-1508)
PHONE.....................203 794-1880
William Michelotti, *Pr*
EMP: 25 EST: 1946
SALES (est): 874.48K **Privately Held**
Web: www.steinmetzmachine.com
SIC: 3599 3499 7699 7692 Machine shop, jobbing and repair; Strapping, metal; Industrial machinery and equipment repair; Welding repair

(G-3361)

HALO TECHNOLOGY HOLDINGS INC
1266 E Main St Ste 700r (06902-3507)
PHONE.................................203 422-2950
Rodney A Bienvenu Junior, *Ch Bd*
Ernest C Mysogland, *CLO*
Mark Finkel, *CFO*
Brian J Sisko, *COO*
Takeshi Taniguchi, *Interim CAO*
EMP: 234 EST: 2000
SQ FT: 4,466
SALES (est): 11.22MM **Privately Held**
SIC: 7372 Prepackaged software

(G-3362)

HARMAN BCKER AUTO SYSTEMS MFG
400 Atlantic St Ste 15 (06901-3533)
PHONE.................................203 328-3501
EMP: 9 EST: 2016
SALES (est): 416.54K **Privately Held**
SIC: 3651 Household audio and video
    equipment
HQ: Harman International Industries
    Incorporated
    400 Atlantic St Ste 15
    Stamford CT 06901
    203 328-3500

(G-3363)

HARMAN CONSUMER INC
Also Called: Jbl
400 Atlantic St Ste 1500 (06901-3512)
PHONE.................................203 328-3500
Dinesh Paliwal, *CEO*
EMP: 38 EST: 1979
SALES (est): 1.72MM **Privately Held**
Web: www.harman.com
SIC: 3651 Audio electronic systems

(G-3364)

HARMAN INTERNATIONAL INDS INC
Also Called: Harman Consumer Group
Division
400 Atlantic St Ste 15 (06901-3533)
PHONE.................................203 328-3500
EMP: 33
Web: www.harman.com
SIC: 3651 Household audio equipment
HQ: Harman International Industries
    Incorporated
    400 Atlantic St Ste 15
    Stamford CT 06901
    203 328-3500

(G-3365)

HARMAN INTERNATIONAL INDS INC (HQ)
Also Called: Harman
400 Atlantic St Ste 15 (06901-3533)
PHONE.................................203 328-3500
Michael Mauser, *Pr*
Young Sohn, *
Mark Hartje, *
James Ahn, *
▲ EMP: 15206 EST: 1980
SALES (est): 1.7B **Privately Held**
Web: www.harman.com
SIC: 3651 Household audio equipment
PA: Samsung Electronics Co., Ltd.
    129 Samsung-Ro, Yeongtong-Gu
    Suwon 16677

(G-3366)

HARMAN KG HOLDING LLC (DH)

(G-3361) (continued)
400 Atlantic St Ste 1500 (06901-3512)
PHONE.................................203 328-3500
Dinesh C Paliwal, *Ch Bd*
EMP: 64 EST: 2009
SALES (est): 1.24MM **Privately Held**
Web: www.harman.com
SIC: 3651 Household audio equipment
HQ: Harman International Industries
    Incorporated
    400 Atlantic St Ste 15
    Stamford CT 06901
    203 328-3500

(G-3367)

HARVEST HILL HOLDINGS LLC (PA)
1 High Ridge Park Fl 2 (06905-1330)
PHONE.................................203 914-1620
Tim Voelkerding, *Pr*
EMP: 19 EST: 2014
SALES (est): 491.93MM
SALES (corp-wide): 491.93MM **Privately Held**
SIC: 2086 5499 Fruit drinks (less than 100% juice): packaged in cans, etc.; Soft drinks

(G-3368)

HAT ATTACK INC (PA)
Also Called: Hat Attack I Bujibaja
52b Poplar St (06907-2705)
PHONE.................................718 994-1000
William Gedney, *Pr*
Barbara J Gedney, *VP*
◆ EMP: 20 EST: 1981
SALES (est): 2.06MM
SALES (corp-wide): 2.06MM **Privately Held**
Web: www.hatattack.com
SIC: 3111 2353 Bag leather; Hats, caps, and millinery

(G-3369)

HCRX INVESTMENTS HOLDCO LP
300 Atlantic St Ste 600 (06901-3514)
PHONE.................................203 487-8300
EMP: 7 EST: 2021
SALES (est): 446.85K **Privately Held**
SIC: 2834 Pharmaceutical preparations

(G-3370)

HCRX MASTER GP LLC
300 Atlantic St Ste 600 (06901-3514)
PHONE.................................203 487-8300
EMP: 18 EST: 2021
SALES (est): 220.29K
SALES (corp-wide): 2.67MM **Privately Held**
SIC: 2834 Pharmaceutical preparations
PA: Healthcare Royalty, Inc.
    300 Atlantic St Ste 600
    Stamford CT 06901
    203 487-8300

(G-3371)

HEALTHCARE ROYALTY INC (PA)
Also Called: Healthcare Royalty
300 Atlantic St Ste 600 (06901-3514)
PHONE.................................203 487-8300
Clarke B Futch, *Ch Bd*
Christopher A White, *Pr*
Thomas K Conner, *CAO*
Carlos M Almodovar, *Chief Business Officer*
EMP: 7 EST: 2006
SALES (est): 2.67MM
SALES (corp-wide): 2.67MM **Privately Held**
Web: www.hcrx.com

SIC: 2834 Pharmaceutical preparations

(G-3372)

HEARTH KITCHEN PRODUCTS INC
Also Called: Hearth Kitchen Co
226 Selleck St # B (06902-6420)
PHONE.................................203 325-8800
Sally Russell, *Pr*
Lewis White, *COO*
EMP: 7 EST: 2000
SQ FT: 3,600
SALES (est): 760K **Privately Held**
SIC: 3567 5719 Ceramic kilns and furnaces; Kitchenware

(G-3373)

HENKEL CONSUMER GOODS INC (DH)
Also Called: Henkel
200 Elm St (06902-3800)
PHONE.................................475 210-0230
Norbert Koll, *Pr*
Paul R Berry, *
Raphaela Lessmann, *
Brad A Gazaway, *
Christopher J Littlefield, *
◆ EMP: 600 EST: 2004
SALES (est): 1.13B
SALES (corp-wide): 23.26B **Privately Held**
Web: www.henkel-northamerica.com
SIC: 2841 Soap and other detergents
HQ: Henkel Us Operations Corporation
    1 Henkel Way
    Rocky Hill CT 06067
    860 571-5100

(G-3374)

HEXCEL CORPORATION (PA)
Also Called: HEXCEL
281 Tresser Blvd # 16 (06901-3284)
PHONE.................................203 969-0666
Nick L Stanage, *Ch Bd*
Patrick J Winterlich, *Ex VP*
Robert G Hennemuth, *Chief of Staff*
Gail E Lehman, *Ex VP*
Gina Fitzsimons, *Chief Human Resources Officer*
EMP: 26 EST: 1946
SALES (est): 1.79B
SALES (corp-wide): 1.79B **Publicly Held**
Web: www.hexcel.com
SIC: 3728 3089 3624 2891 Aircraft parts
    and equipment, nec; Fiberglass doors;
    Fibers, carbon and graphite; Adhesives

(G-3375)

HEXCEL POTTSVILLE CORPORATION
Two Stamford Plaza 16th Floor 281 Tresser
Boulevard (06901-3263)
PHONE.................................203 969-0666
Wayne C Pensky, *Pr*
EMP: 28 EST: 1998
SALES (est): 1.71MM
SALES (corp-wide): 1.58B **Publicly Held**
Web: www.hexcel.com
SIC: 3728 Aircraft parts and equipment, nec
PA: Hexcel Corporation
    281 Tresser Blvd 16
    Stamford CT 06901
    203 969-0666

(G-3376)

HIGH RIDGE COPY INC
Also Called: High Ridge Printing & Copy Ctr
351 Woodbine Rd (06903-1904)
PHONE.................................203 329-1889
Jon De Crescenzo, *Pr*

Christine De Crescenzo, *Sec*
EMP: 10 EST: 1987
SALES (est): 933.91K **Privately Held**
Web: www.highridgeprinting.com
SIC: 2752 Offset printing

(G-3377)

HISPANIC COMMUNICATIONS LLC
400 Main St (06901-3004)
PHONE.................................203 674-6793
Norma Rodriguez, *Pr*
EMP: 7 EST: 2006
SALES (est): 102.01K **Privately Held**
Web: www.lavozhispanact.com
SIC: 2711 Newspapers, publishing and printing

(G-3378)

HOFFMAN ENGINEERING LLC (DH)
8 Riverbend Dr (06907)
P.O. Box 4430 (06907-0430)
PHONE.................................203 425-8900
Andrew Sadlon, *
EMP: 63 EST: 1987
SQ FT: 30,000
SALES (est): 17.74MM
SALES (corp-wide): 4.01MM **Privately Held**
Web: www.hoffmanengineering.com
SIC: 8734 3647 3826 3825 Testing
    laboratories; Aircraft lighting fixtures;
    Photometers; Instruments to measure
    electricity
HQ: Aeronautical & Gi Holdings Limited
    Fleets Point House
    Poole BH15
    120 268-5661

(G-3379)

HRB WINDDOWN INC (HQ)
333 Ludlow St Ste 2 (06902-6991)
PHONE.................................203 674-8080
EMP: 65 EST: 2008
SALES (est): 20MM
SALES (corp-wide): 20.29MM **Privately Held**
Web: www.hrbbrands.com
SIC: 2844 Perfumes, cosmetics and other
    toilet preparations
PA: Hrb Buyer, Inc.
    333 Ludlow St 2nd
    Stamford CT

(G-3380)

IMBRIUM THERAPEUTICS LP (DH)
201 Tresser Blvd (06901-3435)
PHONE.................................888 827-0622
P Medeiros, *Pt*
M Kesselman, *
P Strassburger, *
J Renger, *
J Lowne, *
EMP: 34 EST: 2018
SALES (est): 23.73MM
SALES (corp-wide): 790.3MM **Privately Held**
Web: www.purduepharma.com
SIC: 8731 2834 Commercial physical
    research; Pharmaceutical preparations
HQ: Purdue Pharma L.P.
    201 Tresser Blvd Fl 1
    Stamford CT 06901

(G-3381)

IMMUCOR TRNSPLANT DGNSTICS INC (DH)

▲ = Import ▼ = Export
◆ = Import/Export

550 West Ave (06902-6352)
PHONE...............................203 328-9500
Carl Hull, *Pr*
Bullion Keith, *
EMP: 63 **EST:** 2003
SALES (est): 23.04MM
SALES (corp-wide): 4.03B **Publicly Held**
SIC: 8071 3944 Testing laboratories;
  Science kits: microscopes, chemistry sets,
  etc.
HQ: Gen-Probe Incorporated
  250 Campus Dr
  Marlborough MA 01752
  508 263-8937

(G-3382)
IMPRESSION POINT INC
500 West Ave (06902-6360)
PHONE...............................203 353-8800
Robert Labanca, *CEO*
Robert Labanca, *Prin*
Mary Labanca, *Treas*
EMP: 8 **EST:** 2003
SQ FT: 5,000
SALES (est): 803.05K **Privately Held**
Web: www.impressionpt.com
SIC: 2752 Offset printing

(G-3383)
INFORMA BUSINESS MEDIA INC
National Ctr For Database Mktg
11 Riverbend Dr S (06906)
P.O. Box 4949 (06907-0949)
PHONE...............................203 358-9900
EMP: 110
SALES (corp-wide): 2.72B **Privately Held**
Web: www.informa.com
SIC: 2721 Periodicals
HQ: Informa Business Media, Inc.
  605 3rd Ave Fl 22
  New York NY 10158
  212 204-4200

(G-3384)
**INTERNATIONAL MKTG
STRATEGIES**
Also Called: Marine Money
62 Southfield Ave Ste 214 (06902-7229)
PHONE...............................203 406-0106
James Lawrence, *Ch*
James Lawrence, *Pr*
Jill Lawrence, *VP*
EMP: 11 **EST:** 1987
SQ FT: 4,000
SALES (est): 2.31MM **Privately Held**
Web: www.marinemoney.com
SIC: 2721 Trade journals: publishing only,
  not printed on site

(G-3385)
INTERNATIONAL ROBOTICS INC
Also Called: Robotics
761 Stillwater Rd (06902-1726)
PHONE...............................914 630-1060
EMP: 10 **EST:** 2011
SALES (est): 636.98K **Privately Held**
Web: www.internationalrobotics.com
SIC: 3535 Robotic conveyors

(G-3386)
ISUPPORTWS INC
Also Called: JI Services
1 Barry Pl (06902-7534)
PHONE...............................203 569-7600
Joseph Liscek, *Pr*
EMP: 12 **EST:** 2005
SQ FT: 5,000
SALES (est): 825.71K **Privately Held**
Web: www.isupport.ws

SIC: 7379 7371 3699 6211 Computer
related consulting services; Computer
software development and applications;
Security devices; Distributors, security

(G-3387)
ITT GOULDS PUMPS INC (HQ)
100 Washington Blvd Fl 6 (06902)
PHONE...............................315 568-2811
George Abdo Hanna, *Ch Bd*
EMP: 50 **EST:** 2004
SALES (est): 1.31B
SALES (corp-wide): 2.99B **Publicly Held**
Web: www.gouldspumps.com
SIC: 3561 5084 Pumps and pumping
  equipment; Industrial machinery and
  equipment
PA: Itt Inc.
  100 Washington Blvd Fl 6
  Stamford CT 06902
  914 641-2000

(G-3388)
ITT INC (PA)
Also Called: ITT
100 Washington Blvd Fl 6 (06902-9302)
PHONE...............................914 641-2000
Luca Savi, *Pr*
Timothy H Powers, *
Emmanuel Caprais, *Sr VP*
Maurine C Lembesis, *Chief Human
Resources Officer*
Lori B Marino, *Sr VP*
EMP: 221 **EST:** 1920
SALES (est): 2.99B
SALES (corp-wide): 2.99B **Publicly Held**
Web: www.itt.com
SIC: 3594 3625 3823 3812 Fluid power
  pumps and motors; Control equipment,
  electric; Fluidic devices, circuits, and
  systems for process control; Radar systems
  and equipment

(G-3389)
**ITT INDUSTRIES HOLDINGS INC
(DH)**
100 Washington Blvd Fl 6 (06902)
PHONE...............................914 641-2000
Mary Beth Gustafsson, *Pr*
Steve Giuliano, *Sr VP*
Lori Marino, *Sec*
Thomas Scalera, *Sr VP*
Michael Savinelli, *Tax Vice President*
EMP: 8 **EST:** 2004
SALES (est): 49.6MM
SALES (corp-wide): 2.99B **Publicly Held**
SIC: 2611 4731 Pulp mills; Freight
  consolidation
HQ: International Standard Electric
  Corporation
  1105 N Market St Ste 1217
  Wilmington DE 19801
  302 427-3769

(G-3390)
JBS AVES LTDA
680 E Main St Ste A Pmb 650
(06901-2113)
PHONE...............................203 357-5920
EMP: 15 **EST:** 1953
SALES (est): 2.37MM **Publicly Held**
SIC: 5147 2011 Meats and meat products;
  Beef products, from beef slaughtered on site
PA: Jbs S/A
  Av. Marginal Direita Do Tiete 500
  Sao Paulo SP 05118

(G-3391)
JERA INDUSTRIES LLC
27 Wind Mill Cir (06903-3103)

PHONE...............................203 428-6588
David Shulman, *Prin*
EMP: 9 **EST:** 2012
SALES (est): 98K **Privately Held**
SIC: 3999 Manufacturing industries, nec

(G-3392)
JKL SPECIALTY FOODS INC
456 Glenbrook Rd Ste 2 (06906-1800)
P.O. Box 4607 (06907-0607)
PHONE...............................203 541-3990
▼ **EMP:** 10 **EST:** 1983
SALES (est): 954.71K **Privately Held**
Web: www.asianmenusauces.com
SIC: 2099 Food preparations, nec

(G-3393)
**JORNIK MANUFACTURING
CORP**
652 Glenbrook Rd Ste 8-201 (06906-1424)
PHONE...............................203 969-0500
Jacqueline Herz, *Pr*
Peter Herz, *Sec*
▲ **EMP:** 19 **EST:** 1992
SQ FT: 7,500
SALES (est): 2.46MM **Privately Held**
Web: www.jornik.com
SIC: 3993 2396 Signs and advertising
  specialties; Automotive and apparel
  trimmings

(G-3394)
K A F MANUFACTURING CO INC
14 Fahey St (06907-2216)
PHONE...............................203 324-3012
John Feighery, *Pr*
Sharon Feighery, *Sec*
Brian Feighery, *Prin*
EMP: 22 **EST:** 1971
SQ FT: 11,500
SALES (est): 2.43MM **Privately Held**
Web: www.kaf.com
SIC: 3826 3562 Analytical instruments; Ball
  and roller bearings

(G-3395)
KNOA PHARMA LLC (PA)
201 Tresser Blvd (06901-3442)
PHONE...............................203 588-8000
Craig Landau, *Pr*
Mark Kesselman, *VP*
Jon Lowne, *VP*
EMP: 27 **EST:** 2021
SALES (est): 790.3MM
SALES (corp-wide): 790.3MM **Privately
Held**
Web: www.purduepharma.com
SIC: 2834 5122 Pharmaceutical
  preparations; Pharmaceuticals

(G-3396)
LANDMARK PRINT INC
Also Called: Landmark Document Services
375 Fairfield Ave Bldg 3 (06902-7220)
PHONE...............................800 499-3808
TOLL FREE: 800
Michael Dimitriou, *Pr*
Carmine Iannacchino, *
Robert J Nizolek, *
EMP: 65 **EST:** 1986
SQ FT: 30,000
SALES (est): 16.97MM **Privately Held**
Web: www.landmarkprint.com
SIC: 2752 2732 Offset printing; Book printing

(G-3397)
**LEISURE LEARNING
PRODUCTS INC**
Also Called: Leisure Group

652 Glenbrook Rd Bldg 8 (06906-1410)
P.O. Box 2697 (06906-0697)
PHONE...............................203 325-2800
Richard Bendett, *Pr*
Christine Binsteiner, *VP*
▲ **EMP:** 18 **EST:** 1976
SQ FT: 15,000
SALES (est): 265.23K **Privately Held**
Web: www.mightymind.com
SIC: 3999 5092 Education aids, devices
  and supplies; Toys and games

(G-3398)
LESCO
52b Poplar St (06907-2718)
PHONE...............................203 353-0061
Rick Linsaoey, *Sec*
EMP: 7 **EST:** 2015
SALES (est): 75.67K **Privately Held**
Web: www.lesco.com
SIC: 3999 Manufacturing industries, nec

(G-3399)
LESSONBEE INC
700 Canal St Ste 42a (06902-5921)
PHONE...............................646 582-2040
Reva Mcpollom, *CEO*
EMP: 9 **EST:** 2018
SALES (est): 430.85K **Privately Held**
Web: www.lessonbee.com
SIC: 7372 Educational computer software

(G-3400)
**LETTERING INC OF NEW YORK
(PA)**
255 Mill Rd (06903-1625)
PHONE...............................203 329-7759
Karin Krumpelbeck, *Pr*
John Krumpelbeck, *VP*
EMP: 22 **EST:** 1939
SALES (est): 2.07MM
SALES (corp-wide): 2.07MM **Privately
Held**
Web: www.izett.com
SIC: 7336 2791 Commercial art and graphic
  design; Typesetting

(G-3401)
LINDEN VFT LLC
800 Long Ridge Rd (06902-1227)
PHONE...............................203 357-4740
Daniel Walsh, *Managing Member*
EMP: 10 **EST:** 2007
SQ FT: 50,000
SALES (est): 988.85K **Privately Held**
SIC: 3612 Distribution transformers, electric

(G-3402)
LOCALLIVE NETWORKS INC
Also Called: Locallive Networks
175 Atlantic St Ste 15 (06901-3530)
PHONE...............................877 355-6225
Nelson Santos, *CEO*
EMP: 19 **EST:** 2017
SALES (est): 1.33MM **Privately Held**
Web: www.locallive.tv
SIC: 7372 Application computer software

(G-3403)
LOCK IT DOWN INC
54 Research Dr (06906-1428)
PHONE...............................203 313-6454
Michael G Bushnell, *Pr*
EMP: 9 **EST:** 2016
SALES (est): 354.47K **Privately Held**
SIC: 2082 Malt beverages

(G-3404)
LOVESAC COMPANY (PA)
2 Landmark Sq Ste 300 (06901-2410)
PHONE...........................888 636-1223
Shawn Nelson, *CEO*
Andrew R Heyer, *Ch Bd*
Mary Fox, *Pr*
Keith Siegner, *Ex VP*
EMP: 84 **EST:** 1995
SQ FT: 22,480
SALES (est): 651.18MM
SALES (corp-wide): 651.18MM **Publicly Held**
Web: www.lovesac.com
SIC: 5712 2519   Furniture stores; Bean bag Chairs

(G-3405)
LOXO ONCOLOGY INC (HQ)
281 Tresser Blvd Fl 9 (06901-3238)
PHONE...........................203 653-3880
Joshua H Bilenker Md, *Pr*
Jacob S Van Naarden, *
Nisha Nanda, *Chief Development Officer*
EMP: 47 **EST:** 2013
SQ FT: 36,400
SALES (est): 49.33MM
SALES (corp-wide): 28.54B **Publicly Held**
Web: www.loxooncology.com
SIC: 2834   Pharmaceutical preparations
PA: Eli Lilly And Company
       Lilly Corporate Ctr
       Indianapolis IN 46285
       317 276-2000

(G-3406)
MADD GEAR LLC
8 Hedge Brook Ln (06903-2029)
PHONE...........................410 800-4423
Brian Anderson, *CEO*
Todd Suskin, *SALES*
▲ **EMP:** 12 **EST:** 2010
SQ FT: 5,000
SALES (est): 2.77MM **Privately Held**
SIC: 3751   Motor scooters and parts
HQ: Madd Gear Pty. Ltd.
       Unit 5 4 Kirkham Road
       Dandenong South VIC 3175

(G-3407)
MAGIK EYE INC
1055 Washington Blvd Fl 5 (06901-2219)
PHONE...........................917 676-7436
Takeo Miyazawa, *CEO*
Julien Beguin, *Vice President of Product & Engineering*
EMP: 9 **EST:** 2014
SALES (est): 369.65K **Privately Held**
Web: www.magik-eye.com
SIC: 3669   Visual communication systems

(G-3408)
MARINERO EXPRESS 809 EAST
809 E Main St (06902-3807)
PHONE...........................203 487-0636
Jose L Marinero, *Prin*
EMP: 12 **EST:** 2009
SALES (est): 636.26K **Privately Held**
SIC: 3578   Automatic teller machines (ATM)

(G-3409)
MAYBORN USA INC
Also Called: Mayborn Group
1010 Washington Blvd Fl 9 (06901-2202)
P.O. Box 5003 (06881-5003)
PHONE...........................781 269-7490
Steve Parkin, *CEO*
Brenda O'grady Liistro, *Pr*
George Idicula, *Sec*
▲ **EMP:** 13 **EST:** 1946
SQ FT: 3,000
SALES (est): 10.81MM
SALES (corp-wide): 265.67MM **Privately Held**
Web: www.mayborngroup.com
SIC: 3069 3085 3634 3821   Baby pacifiers, rubber; Plastics bottles; Bottle warmers, electric: household; Sterilizers
HQ: Mayborn Group Limited
       Ayborn House, Balliol Business Park
       Newcastle-Upon-Tyne NE12
       191 250-1864

(G-3410)
MEDITERRANEAN SNACK FD CO LLC
1111 Summer St (06905-5508)
PHONE...........................973 402-2644
◆ **EMP:** 11 **EST:** 2012
SQ FT: 2,500
SALES (est): 2.22MM
SALES (corp-wide): 17.26MM **Privately Held**
SIC: 2096   Potato chips and similar snacks
PA: American Halal Company, Inc
       1111 Summer St Fl 5
       Stamford CT 06905
       203 961-1954

(G-3411)
MILDRED COPPOLA (PA)
Also Called: Coppola Marble
64 Research Dr (06906-1419)
PHONE...........................203 967-9300
Mildred Coppola, *Owner*
EMP: 16 **EST:** 1992
SQ FT: 5,000
SALES (est): 2.44MM
SALES (corp-wide): 2.44MM **Privately Held**
SIC: 5032 5713 3281 2541   Tile, clay or other ceramic, excluding refractory; Floor tile; Marble, building: cut and shaped; Wood partitions and fixtures

(G-3412)
MILTON & GOOSE LLC
65 High Ridge Rd Ste 369 (06905-3800)
PHONE...........................203 539-1073
Shari Raymond, *Managing Member*
EMP: 7 **EST:** 2017
SALES (est): 478.74K **Privately Held**
Web: www.miltonandgoose.com
SIC: 2434 3944   Wood kitchen cabinets; Blocks, toy

(G-3413)
MOWMEDIA LLC
85 Camp Ave Apt 10l (06907-1839)
PHONE...........................203 240-6416
EMP: 8 **EST:** 2019
SALES (est): 491.76K **Privately Held**
Web: www.mowmedia.com
SIC: 2741   Internet publishing and broadcasting

(G-3414)
MUNK PACK INC
76 Progress Dr Ste 263 (06902-3698)
PHONE...........................203 769-5005
Michelle Leutzinger, *CEO*
Tobias Glienke, *Pr*
EMP: 10 **EST:** 2013
SALES (est): 2.02MM **Privately Held**
Web: store.munkpack.com
SIC: 2043   Oatmeal: prepared as cereal breakfast food

(G-3415)
NEAR OAK LLC
Also Called: Amber Synthetics
1011 High Ridge Rd (06905-1610)
PHONE...........................203 329-6500
Thomas J Castrovinci, *Pr*
Diane M Castrovinci, *Sec*
◆ **EMP:** 7 **EST:** 1992
SALES (est): 1.93MM **Privately Held**
SIC: 5169 2899   Chemicals, industrial and heavy; Chemical preparations, nec

(G-3416)
NEW HORIZON MACHINE CO INC
36 Ludlow St (06902-6914)
PHONE...........................203 316-9355
Antoinette Balbi, *Pr*
Carmello Balbi, *VP*
EMP: 8 **EST:** 1978
SQ FT: 5,500
SALES (est): 863.9K **Privately Held**
Web: www.newhorizonmachine.com
SIC: 3599   Machine shop, jobbing and repair

(G-3417)
NEWSPAPER SPACE BUYERS LLC
1 Station Pl Ste 5 (06902-6893)
PHONE...........................203 967-6452
Paul C Wilkinson, *Prin*
EMP: 8 **EST:** 2009
SALES (est): 255.52K **Privately Held**
Web: www.newspaperspacebuyers.com
SIC: 2711   Newspapers

(G-3418)
NEXVUE INFORMATION SYSTEMS INC
65 Broad St (06901-2374)
P.O. Box 110462 (06911-0462)
PHONE...........................203 327-0800
Dan Schwartz, *Pr*
Gary Frey, *VP*
EMP: 20 **EST:** 1984
SALES (est): 2.62MM **Privately Held**
Web: www.nexvue.com
SIC: 7372   Business oriented computer software

(G-3419)
NORTHEASTERN METALS CORP
130 Lenox Ave Ste 23 (06906-2337)
PHONE...........................203 348-8088
Charles Schemera, *Pr*
Fred Lorenzen, *Sec*
EMP: 7 **EST:** 1975
SQ FT: 2,500
SALES (est): 719.93K **Privately Held**
Web: www.northeasternmetals.net
SIC: 3339 5094 5084   Precious metals; Precious metals; Cleaning equipment, high pressure, sand or steam

(G-3420)
NUTMEG ARCHITECTURAL WDWRK INC
48 Union St Ste 14 (06906-1342)
PHONE...........................203 325-4434
Tito Cerretani, *Pr*
Glenn Silkman, *VP*
EMP: 14 **EST:** 1998
SQ FT: 22,300
SALES (est): 482.05K **Privately Held**
SIC: 2522   Cabinets, office: except wood

(G-3421)
O & G INDUSTRIES INC
686 Canal St (06902-5904)

PHONE...........................203 977-1618
Ray Oneglia, *Brnch Mgr*
EMP: 58
SALES (corp-wide): 496.36MM **Privately Held**
Web: www.ogind.com
SIC: 3273   Ready-mixed concrete
PA: O & G Industries, Inc.
       112 Wall St
       Torrington CT 06790
       860 489-9261

(G-3422)
O & G INDUSTRIES INC
40 Meadow St (06902-5919)
PHONE...........................203 323-1111
Jack Harding, *Brnch Mgr*
EMP: 77
SQ FT: 10,000
SALES (corp-wide): 496.36MM **Privately Held**
Web: mason.ogind.com
SIC: 5211 3273 1542 3281   Brick; Ready-mixed concrete; Commercial and office building, new construction; Cut stone and stone products
PA: O & G Industries, Inc.
       112 Wall St
       Torrington CT 06790
       860 489-9261

(G-3423)
ODOROX IAQ INC
1266 E Main St Ste 700r (06902-3507)
PHONE...........................203 541-5577
EMP: 9 **EST:** 2010
SALES (est): 114.48K **Privately Held**
Web: www.odoroxiaq.com
SIC: 3442   Molding, trim, and stripping

(G-3424)
OMEGA ENGINEERING INC
1 Omega Dr (06907-2336)
P.O. Box 2699 (06906-0699)
PHONE...........................203 359-7922
EMP: 133
SALES (corp-wide): 653.43MM **Privately Held**
Web: www.omega.com
SIC: 3823   Process control instruments
HQ: Omega Engineering, Inc.
       800 Connecticut Ave 5n01
       Norwalk CT 06854
       203 359-1660

(G-3425)
P C I GROUP
652 Glenbrook Rd Ste 3-301 (06906-1443)
PHONE...........................203 327-0410
Mary Ferrara, *Pr*
EMP: 10 **EST:** 1985
SQ FT: 4,500
SALES (est): 799.43K **Privately Held**
Web: www.pcigroup.net
SIC: 2752 7336   Offset printing; Graphic arts and related design

(G-3426)
PARFUMS DE COEUR LTD (PA)
Also Called: PDC Brands
750 E Main St Ste 1000 (06902-3872)
PHONE...........................203 655-8807
Peter Columbia, *CEO*
Mark A Laracy, *
James Stammer, *
Edward Kaminski, *
James E Rogers, *
◆ **EMP:** 30 **EST:** 1981
SQ FT: 13,000
SALES (est): 41.1MM

▲ = Import ▼ = Export
◆ = Import/Export

SALES (corp-wide): 41.1MM **Privately Held**
Web: www.pdcwellness.com
SIC: 2844 Perfumes, natural or synthetic

(G-3427)
PAULS MARBLE DEPOT LLC
Also Called: Extile.com
40 Warshaw Pl Ste 1 (06902-6354)
PHONE...............................203 978-0669
Parag Adalja, *Managing Member*
▲ EMP: 15 EST: 2003
SQ FT: 28,000
SALES (est): 941.35K **Privately Held**
Web: www.marble-depot.com
SIC: 3272 5032 Tile, precast terrazzo or
concrete; Marble building stone

(G-3428)
**PEERLESS SYSTEMS
CORPORATION (DH)**
Also Called: Peerless
1055 Washington Blvd Fl 8 (06901-2251)
PHONE...............................203 350-0040
Anthony Bonid, *CEO*
Lodovico De Visconti, *Pr*
EMP: 9 EST: 1982
SQ FT: 1,200
SALES (est): 64.36MM
SALES (corp-wide): 67.93MM **Privately Held**
Web: www.peerless.com
SIC: 7372 7371 Prepackaged software;
Custom computer programming services
HQ: Mobius Acquisition, Llc
1000 Mcknight Park Dr # 10
Pittsburgh PA 15237
412 281-7000

(G-3429)
**PEGASUS CAPITAL ADVISORS
LP (PA)**
750 E Main St Ste 600 (06902-3872)
PHONE...............................203 869-4400
Craig Cogut, *Mng Pt*
Daniel Stencel, *CFO*
Greg Gish, *VP*
EMP: 10 EST: 1995
SALES (est): 19.59MM **Privately Held**
Web: www.pcalp.com
SIC: 3646 3648 Commercial lighting fixtures
; Street lighting fixtures

(G-3430)
PF LABORATORIES INC (DH)
201 Tresser Blvd Ste 324 (06901-3435)
PHONE...............................973 256-3100
John Stewart, *Pr*
Edward Mahony, *
David Long, *
Russ Gasdia, *
Bert Weinstein, *
EMP: 150 EST: 1976
SQ FT: 300,000
SALES (est): 41.02MM
SALES (corp-wide): 790.3MM **Privately Held**
SIC: 2834 Pharmaceutical preparations
HQ: Purdue Pharma L.P.
201 Tresser Blvd Fl 1
Stamford CT 06901

(G-3431)
**PHARMACEUTICAL RES ASSOC
INC**
201 Tresser Blvd (06901-3435)
PHONE...............................203 588-8000
Stuart Baker, *Asst VP*
Howard Udell, *VP*

EMP: 675 EST: 1945
SQ FT: 90,000
SALES (est): 298.76MM
SALES (corp-wide): 790.3MM **Privately Held**
Web: www.purduepharma.com
SIC: 2834 5122 Pharmaceutical
preparations; Pharmaceuticals
HQ: Purdue Pharma L.P.
201 Tresser Blvd Fl 1
Stamford CT 06901

(G-3432)
PHILIP MORRIS INTL INC (PA)
Also Called: Philip Morris
677 Washington Blvd Ste 1100 (06901)
PHONE...............................203 905-2410
Jacek Olczak, *CEO*
Andre Calantzopoulos, *Ex Ch Bd*
Emmanuel Babeau, *CFO*
Stefano Volpetti, *CCO*
Yann Guerin, *Sr VP*
EMP: 1061 EST: 1987
SALES (est): 31.76B
SALES (corp-wide): 31.76B **Publicly Held**
Web: www.pmi.com
SIC: 2111 Cigarettes

(G-3433)
PITNEY BOWES INC (PA)
Also Called: Pitney Bowes
3001 Summer St (06905-4317)
P.O. Box 371896 (15250-7896)
PHONE...............................203 356-5000
Jason C Dies, *Interim Chief Executive
Officer*
Mary J Steele Guilfoile, *Non-Executive
Chairman of the Board**
Ana Maria Chadwick, *Ex VP*
Daniel J Goldstein, *CLO*
James Fairweather, *CIO*
◆ EMP: 3500 EST: 1920
SALES (est): 3.54B
SALES (corp-wide): 3.54B **Publicly Held**
Web: www.pitneybowes.com
SIC: 3579 7359 3661 8744 Mailing
machines; Business machine and
electronic equipment rental services;
Facsimile equipment; Facilities support
services

(G-3434)
PITNEY BOWES RE FING CORP
Also Called: Pitney Bowes
300 Stamford Pl Ste 200 (06902-6735)
PHONE...............................203 356-5000
EMP: 102 EST: 1986
SALES (est): 10.35MM **Privately Held**
Web: www.pitneybowes.com
SIC: 3579 Postage meters

(G-3435)
PRA HOLDINGS INC
1 Stamford Forum (06901-3516)
PHONE...............................203 853-0123
Stuart Baker, *Pr*
Howard Udell, *
EMP: 675 EST: 1987
SQ FT: 90,000
SALES (est): 144.6MM **Privately Held**
SIC: 2834 5122 8742 Pharmaceutical
preparations; Pharmaceuticals; Industry
specialist consultants
HQ: Pra Health Sciences, Inc.
4131 Parklake Ave Ste 600
Raleigh NC 27612
919 786-8200

(G-3436)
PRINT PROMOWEAR LLC
169 Canfield Dr (06902-1336)
PHONE...............................203 504-2858
Donald Richner, *Prin*
EMP: 7 EST: 2011
SALES (est): 299.45K **Privately Held**
Web: www.printpromowear.com
SIC: 2759 Screen printing

(G-3437)
PRINTER TECHS LLC
44 Commerce Rd (06902-4561)
PHONE...............................203 322-1160
Nicholas J Santagata Junior, *Mgr*
EMP: 7 EST: 2005
SALES (est): 133.87K **Privately Held**
Web: www.printertechs.com
SIC: 2752 Commercial printing, lithographic

(G-3438)
PROTEGRITY USA INC (PA)
333 Ludlow St Ste 8 (06902-6991)
PHONE...............................203 326-7200
Paul Mountford, *CEO*
Eileen Garry, *CMO*
Jay Wolf, *Contrlr*
Christian Carnell, *CFO*
Dante Malagrino, *CPO*
EMP: 22 EST: 2004
SALES (est): 16.94MM
SALES (corp-wide): 16.94MM **Privately Held**
Web: www.protegrity.com
SIC: 7372 Prepackaged software

(G-3439)
PURDUE PHARMA LP (HQ)
201 Tresser Blvd (06901-3432)
PHONE...............................203 588-8000
▲ EMP: 107 EST: 1991
SQ FT: 500,000
SALES (est): 790.3MM
SALES (corp-wide): 790.3MM **Privately Held**
Web: www.purduepharma.com
SIC: 2834 5122 Pharmaceutical
preparations; Pharmaceuticals
PA: Knoa Pharma Llc
201 Tresser Blvd
Stamford CT 06901
203 588-8000

(G-3440)
**PURDUE PHARMA
MANUFACTURING LP**
201 Tresser Blvd (06901-3432)
PHONE...............................252 265-1924
David Lundie Senior, *VP*
David Lundie, *Sr VP*
Phillip Strassburger, *VP*
Stuart D Baker, *VP*
Edward Mahony, *VP*
▲ EMP: 17 EST: 2013
SALES (est): 4.75MM
SALES (corp-wide): 790.3MM **Privately Held**
Web: www.purduepharma.com
SIC: 2834 Chlorination tablets and kits
(water purification)
HQ: Purdue Pharma L.P.
201 Tresser Blvd Fl 1
Stamford CT 06901

(G-3441)
**PURDUE PHARMA
TECHNOLOGIES INC**
Also Called: Purdue Pharma
1 Stamford Forum (06901-3516)

PHONE...............................203 588-8000
John Stewart, *Pr*
Edward Mahony, *
EMP: 1000 EST: 1970
SALES (est): 37.95MM **Privately Held**
Web: www.purduepharma.com
SIC: 2834 Pharmaceutical preparations

(G-3442)
PURDUE PRODUCTS LP
Also Called: Avrio Health L.P.
201 Tresser Blvd Fl 1 (06901-3435)
PHONE...............................888 827-0624
John Stewart, *Mng Pt*
Edward Mahony, *
EMP: 1500 EST: 2002
SALES (est): 173.99MM
SALES (corp-wide): 790.3MM **Privately Held**
Web: www.purduepharma.com
SIC: 2834 Pharmaceutical preparations
HQ: Purdue Pharma L.P.
201 Tresser Blvd Fl 1
Stamford CT 06901

(G-3443)
RAIN COMMODITIES (USA) INC
10 Signal Rd (06902-7909)
PHONE...............................203 406-0535
EMP: 13 EST: 2005
SALES (est): 567.98K **Privately Held**
SIC: 3312 Coke, produced in chemical
recovery coke ovens

(G-3444)
RAPID USA INC
2 High Ridge Park Fl 1 (06905-1349)
PHONE...............................203 461-7121
Jay Walker, *Pr*
Karen Romaine, *Treas*
EMP: 10 EST: 2020
SALES (est): 578.81K **Privately Held**
SIC: 3841 Surgical and medical instruments

(G-3445)
REDCO CORPORATION (HQ)
Also Called: Crane
100 Stamford Pl (06902-6740)
PHONE...............................203 363-7300
Max H Mitchell, *Pr*
Richard A Maue, *
Anthony M D'iorio, *Sr VP*
Christina Cristiano, *CAO**
Edward S Switter, *
▲ EMP: 56 EST: 1855
SALES (est): 1.4B
SALES (corp-wide): 3.37B **Privately Held**
Web: www.craneco.com
SIC: 3492 3494 3594 3589 Control valves,
fluid power: hydraulic and pneumatic; Pipe
fittings; Pumps, hydraulic power transfer;
Water treatment equipment, industrial
PA: Spruce Lake Liability Management
Holdco Llc
1345 Ave Of The Americas
New York NY

(G-3446)
**RESINALL CORP NORTH
CAROLINA (DH)**
Also Called: Resinall Corp.
3065 High Ridge Rd (06903-1301)
P.O. Box 1639 (39215-1639)
PHONE...............................203 329-7100
Elaine Godina, *Pr*
Lee T Godina, *Sec*
▼ EMP: 10 EST: 1968
SQ FT: 4,000
SALES (est): 84.13MM
SALES (corp-wide): 1.43B **Privately Held**

Web: www.ergon.com
SIC: 2821 Thermosetting materials
HQ: Ergon Chemicals, Llc
　　2829 Lakeland Dr Ste 2000
　　Flowood MS 39232
　　601 933-3000

(G-3447)
REVOLUTION LIGHTING TECH INC (PA)
177 Broad St Fl 12 (06901-5002)
PHONE..............................877 578-2536
Robert V Lapenta, *Ch Bd*
Joan Nano, *
EMP: 50 EST: 1991
SQ FT: 16,626
SALES (est): 82.31MM **Privately Held**
Web: www.energysourcegroup.com
SIC: 3674 3641 3993　Light emitting diodes;
　Electric light bulbs, complete; Signs and
　advertising specialties

(G-3448)
RHODES PHARMACEUTICALS LP
201 Tresser Blvd (06901-3435)
PHONE..............................888 827-0616
EMP: 12
SALES (corp-wide): 790.3MM **Privately
Held**
Web: www.purduepharma.com
SIC: 2834 Pharmaceutical preparations
HQ: Rhodes Pharmaceuticals L.P.
　　4701 Intl Blvd Pmb 307 307 Pmb
　　Wilson NC 27893

(G-3449)
RISEANDSHINE CORPORATION (PA)
Also Called: Rise Brewing Co
425 Fairfield Ave 1a11 (06902-7538)
PHONE..............................917 599-7541
Grant Gyesky, *CEO*
EMP: 18 **EST:** 2015
SALES (est): 2.55MM
SALES (corp-wide): 2.55MM **Privately
Held**
Web: www.risebrewingco.com
SIC: 2095 Instant coffee

(G-3450)
ROBERT L LOVALLO
Also Called: Roblo Woodworks
127 Myrtle Ave (06902-3906)
PHONE..............................203 324-6655
Robert L Lovallo, *Owner*
EMP: 7 **EST:** 1956
SQ FT: 2,500
SALES (est): 453.35K **Privately Held**
SIC: 2434 2541 2431　Wood kitchen cabinets
　; Wood partitions and fixtures; Staircases
　and stairs, wood
PA: Jm Family Enterprises, Inc.
　　100 Jim Moran Blvd
　　Deerfield Beach FL 33442
　　954 429-2000

(G-3451)
ROLLEASE ACMEDA INC (HQ)
750 E Main St Fl 7 (06902-3872)
PHONE..............................203 964-1573
Brent Burns, *Pr*
◆ **EMP:** 80 **EST:** 1980
SQ FT: 54,000
SALES (est): 46.69MM
SALES (corp-wide): 1.49B **Privately Held**
Web: www.rolleaseacmeda.com
SIC: 3568 2591　Clutches, except vehicular;
　Drapery hardware and window blinds and
　shades
PA: Jm Family Enterprises, Inc.
　　100 Jim Moran Blvd
　　Deerfield Beach FL 33442
　　954 429-2000

(G-3452)
ROSCO LABORATORIES INC (HQ)
Also Called: Rosco
52 Harbor View Ave (06902-5947)
PHONE..............................203 708-8900
Mark Engel, *Pr*
Stanford Miller, *
Stan Schwartz, *
Rosemary Schlotter, *
Rich Luce, *
▲ **EMP:** 26 **EST:** 1910
SQ FT: 40,000
SALES (est): 27.41MM **Privately Held**
Web: www.roscodigital.com
SIC: 3861　Motion picture apparatus and
　equipment
PA: Sixmil Holdings, Inc.
　　52 Harbor View Ave
　　Stamford CT 06902

(G-3453)
ROTAD INC
52 Harbor View Ave (06902-5914)
PHONE..............................203 708-8900
▲ **EMP:** 14
SQ FT: 15,000
SALES (est): 1.83MM
SALES (corp-wide): 10.43MM **Privately
Held**
SIC: 3549　Assembly machines, including
　robotic
HQ: Rosco Laboratories, Inc.
　　52 Harbor View Ave
　　Stamford CT 06902
　　203 708-8900

(G-3454)
SEESMART INC
Also Called: Revolution Lighting
263 Tresser Blvd (06901-3236)
PHONE..............................203 504-1111
James Depalma, *Pr*
Ken Ames, *
Jonathan Miller, *
Patrick Doehner, *
▲ **EMP:** 27 **EST:** 2009
SALES (est): 10.03MM **Privately Held**
SIC: 3645 3646　Residential lighting fixtures;
　Commercial lighting fixtures
PA: Revolution Lighting Technologies, Inc.
　　177 Broad St Fl 12
　　Stamford CT 06901

(G-3455)
SENIOR NETWORK INC
777 Summer St Ste 103 (06901-1018)
PHONE..............................203 969-2700
Frederick Adler, *Pr*
Larry Brown, *
EMP: 10 **EST:** 1990
SALES (est): 729.21K **Privately Held**
SIC: 2741　Miscellaneous publishing

(G-3456)
SIGG SWITZERLAND (USA) INC
1177 High Ridge Rd (06905-1221)
PHONE..............................203 321-1232
Daniel Mcnamara, *VP*
▲ **EMP:** 18 **EST:** 2006
SALES (est): 587.5K **Privately Held**
Web: www.sigg.com
SIC: 2086　Bottled and canned soft drinks

(G-3457)
SILGAN CLOSURES INTL HOLDG CO
4 Landmark Sq (06901-2502)
PHONE..............................203 975-7110

EMP: 10
SALES (est): 4.66MM **Publicly Held**
Web: www.silganholdings.com
SIC: 3411　Metal cans
PA: Silgan Holdings Inc.
　　4 Landmark Sq Ste 400
　　Stamford CT 06901

(G-3458)
SILGAN CONTAINERS CORPORATION
Also Called: Silgan
4 Landmark Sq (06901-2502)
PHONE..............................203 975-7110
EMP: 3774
Web: www.silgancontainers.com
SIC: 3411　Metal cans
HQ: Silgan Containers Corporation
　　21600 Oxnard St Ste 1600
　　Woodland Hills CA 91367
　　818 710-3700

(G-3459)
SILGAN HOLDINGS INC (PA)
4 Landmark Sq Ste 400 (06901-2502)
PHONE..............................203 975-7110
Adam J Greenlee, *Pr*
Anthony J Allott, *Ex Ch Bd*
Robert B Lewis, *Ex VP*
Frank W Hogan Iii, *Sr VP*
Kimberly I Ulmer, *VP Fin*
EMP: 143 **EST:** 1987
SALES (est): 6.41B **Publicly Held**
Web: www.silganholdings.com
SIC: 3411 3085 3089　Food and beverage
　containers; Plastics bottles; Plastics
　containers, except foam

(G-3460)
SILGAN WHITE CAP CORPORATION
4 Landmark Sq Ste 400 (06901-2502)
PHONE..............................630 515-8383
Anthony J Allott, *CEO*
Robert B Lewis, *VP*
▲ **EMP:** 127 **EST:** 2003
SALES (est): 18.58MM **Publicly Held**
Web: www.silgan.com
SIC: 3411　Metal cans
PA: Silgan Holdings Inc.
　　4 Landmark Sq Ste 400
　　Stamford CT 06901

(G-3461)
SIX ONE CMMODITIES US TRDG LLC
1 Dock St Ste 412 (06902-5839)
PHONE..............................203 409-2079
EMP: 34 **EST:** 2021
SALES (est): 3.68MM **Privately Held**
SIC: 1321　Natural gas liquids

(G-3462)
SIXMIL HOLDINGS INC (PA)
52 Harbor View Ave (06902-5914)
PHONE..............................203 708-8900
Stanford Miller, *Pr*
Stan Schwartz, *
Mark Engel, *
Rosemary Schlotter, *
▲ **EMP:** 60 **EST:** 1958
SQ FT: 20,000
SALES (est): 27.41MM **Privately Held**
Web: us.rosco.com
SIC: 3861　Motion picture apparatus and
　equipment

(G-3463)
SOLAIS LIGHTING INC
650 West Ave (06902-6325)
PHONE..............................203 683-6222
James Leahy, *Pr*
Glenn Bordfeld, *VP*
EMP: 10 **EST:** 2009
SALES (est): 2.42MM
SALES (corp-wide): 29.28B **Publicly Held**
Web: www.solais.com
SIC: 3648　Lighting equipment, nec
HQ: Powersecure, Inc.
　　4068 Stirrup Creek Dr
　　Durham NC 27703
　　919 556-3056

(G-3464)
SOLVAY
1937 W Main St (06902-4578)
PHONE..............................203 321-2292
Gerald Brzoska Junior, *Prin*
EMP: 24 **EST:** 2018
SALES (est): 4.41MM **Privately Held**
SIC: 2819　Industrial inorganic chemicals,
　nec

(G-3465)
SOLVE ADVISORS INC (PA)
600 Summer St Ste 503 (06901-1419)
PHONE..............................646 699-5041
Yevgeniy Grinberg, *Pr*
Gerard Nealon, *Pr*
EMP: 13 **EST:** 2011
SALES (est): 10.59MM
SALES (corp-wide): 10.59MM **Privately
Held**
Web: www.solvefixedincome.com
SIC: 7372　Business oriented computer
　software

(G-3466)
SOUTHERN CONN NEWSPAPERS INC
Also Called: Stamford Advocate, The
1055 Washington Blvd L (06901-2216)
PHONE..............................203 964-2200
Durham Monsma, *Pr*
Joseph Pisani, *
Robert A Amos Junior, *VP*
Robert T Hughes, *
Craig L Allen, *
EMP: 437 **EST:** 1829
SQ FT: 150,000
SALES (est): 45.17MM
SALES (corp-wide): 930.82MM **Privately
Held**
SIC: 2711　Newspapers, publishing and
　printing
PA: Los Angeles Times Communications,
　Llc
　　2300 E Imperial Hwy
　　El Segundo CA 90245
　　213 237-5000

(G-3467)
SPARTECH LLC
Also Called: Polycast
69 Southfield Ave (06902-7614)
PHONE..............................203 327-6010
Julie A Mcalindon, *Mgr*
EMP: 106
SALES (corp-wide): 344.31MM **Privately
Held**
Web: www.spartech.com
SIC: 3089 3081 2821　Plastics processing;
　Unsupported plastics film and sheet;
　Plastics materials and resins
PA: Spartech Llc
　　11650 Lkeside Crossing Ct
　　Saint Louis MO 63146
　　314 569-7400

▲ = Import ▼ = Export
◆ = Import/Export

(G-3468)

SPARTECH POLYCAST INC
70 Carlisle Pl (06902-7630)
PHONE..............................203 327-6010
◆ **EMP:** 110
SIC: 3089 Molding primary plastics

(G-3469)

STAMFORD CAPITAL GROUP INC (PA)
1266 E Main St (06902-3546)
PHONE..............................800 977-7837
EMP: 18 **EST:** 1994
SALES (est): 53.51MM **Privately Held**
SIC: 2741 6211 Guides: publishing only, not printed on site; Investment bankers

(G-3470)

STAMFORD IRON & STL WORKS INC
347 Courtland Ave (06906-2201)
P.O. Box 2190 (06906-0190)
PHONE..............................203 324-6751
Joseph Fuss Senior, *Pr*
Thomas Pettit Junior, *VP*
EMP: 27 **EST:** 1957
SQ FT: 4,500
SALES (est): 962.7K **Privately Held**
Web: www.stamfordiron.com
SIC: 3441 Fabricated structural metal

(G-3471)

STAMFORD MDIA CTR PRDCTONS LLC
307 Atlantic St (06901-3506)
PHONE..............................203 905-4000
EMP: 9 **EST:** 1998
SALES (est): 252.62K **Privately Held**
Web: www.stamfordtvtickets.com
SIC: 7922 3663 Television program, including commercial producers; Studio equipment, radio and television broadcasting

(G-3472)

STAMFORD RISK ANALYTICS LLC
263 Tresser Blvd 9th Fl (06901-3236)
PHONE..............................203 559-0883
Ali Samad-khan, *Managing Member*
EMP: 11 **EST:** 2004
SALES (est): 1.09MM **Privately Held**
Web: www.stamfordrisk.com
SIC: 7372 Business oriented computer software

(G-3473)

STAR GROUP LP (PA)
9 W Broad St Ste 310 (06902-3758)
PHONE..............................203 328-7310
EMP: 90 **EST:** 1995
SALES (est): 1.95B **Publicly Held**
Web: www.stargrouplp.com
SIC: 2911 Petroleum refining

(G-3474)

STERLING GAS DRLG FUND 1982 LP
1 Landmark Sq (06901-2603)
PHONE..............................203 358-5700
Charles E Drimal Junior, *CEO*
EMP: 7 **EST:** 2009
SALES (est): 202.76K **Privately Held**
SIC: 1381 Drilling oil and gas wells

(G-3475)

SWEET LEAF TEA COMPANY (DH)
900 Long Ridge Rd Bldg 2 (06902-1140)
PHONE..............................203 863-0263
Dan Costello, *CEO*
Clayton Christopher, *Pr*
David Smith, *VP*
Brian Goldberg, *CFO*
▲ **EMP:** 11 **EST:** 2002
SQ FT: 2,000
SALES (est): 15.95MM
SALES (corp-wide): 1.3B **Privately Held**
Web: www.purityorganic.com
SIC: 2086 Iced tea and fruit drinks, bottled and canned
HQ: Bluetriton Brands, Inc.
900 Long Ridge Rd Bldg 2
Stamford CT 06902

(G-3476)

SYMBOL TECHNOLOGIES LLC
6 Landmark Sq 4th Fl (06901-2704)
PHONE..............................203 359-5677
EMP: 27
SALES (corp-wide): 5.78B **Publicly Held**
SIC: 3577 3663 Computer peripheral equipment, nec; Radio and t.v. communications equipment
HQ: Symbol Technologies, Llc
3 Overlook Pt
Lincolnshire IL 60069
877 208-7756

(G-3477)

SYSDYNE TECHNOLOGIES LLC
9 Riverbend Dr S (06907-2528)
PHONE..............................203 327-3649
▲ **EMP:** 10 **EST:** 2002
SQ FT: 3,500
SALES (est): 2.25MM **Privately Held**
Web: www.sysdynetechnologies.com
SIC: 3679 Commutators, electronic

(G-3478)

TECH-REPRO INC
Also Called: Rapid Press
555 Summer St Ste 1 (06901-1413)
PHONE..............................203 348-8884
William Fishman, *Pr*
Hillary Huaman, *VP*
EMP: 10 **EST:** 1979
SALES (est): 822.8K **Privately Held**
SIC: 7334 2752 2791 2789 Photocopying and duplicating services; Offset printing; Typesetting; Bookbinding and related work

(G-3479)

TEK WIRE AND CABLE CORP
77 Havemeyer Ln Unit 422 (06902-2177)
PHONE..............................914 663-2100
EMP: 26 **EST:** 1991
SALES (est): 2.59MM **Privately Held**
SIC: 3357 Nonferrous wiredrawing and insulating

(G-3480)

THE SUN PRODUCTS CORPORATION
200 Elm St Ste 600 (06902-3862)
PHONE..............................203 254-6700
◆ **EMP:** 48
SIC: 2841 Detergents, synthetic organic or inorganic alkaline

(G-3481)

THIS OLD HOUSE VENTURES LLC

2 Harbor Dr (06902-7445)
PHONE..............................475 209-8665
EMP: 50 **EST:** 2008
SALES (est): 9.18MM **Privately Held**
Web: www.thisoldhouse.com
SIC: 2721 7299 Magazines: publishing only, not printed on site; Home improvement and renovation contractor agency

(G-3482)

THOMSON REUTERS RISK MGT INC
1 Station Pl (06902-6800)
PHONE..............................203 539-8000
Jamie A Kagan, *Pr*
Sean Cannizzaro, *Sec*
EMP: 12 **EST:** 2012
SALES (est): 93.48K **Privately Held**
Web: www.thomsonreuters.com
SIC: 2711 Newspapers, publishing and printing

(G-3483)

THOMSON REUTERS US LLC (DH)
1 Station Pl Ste 6 (06902-6893)
PHONE..............................203 539-8000
EMP: 72 **EST:** 1996
SALES (est): 469.13MM
SALES (corp-wide): 10.66B **Publicly Held**
Web: www.thomsonreuters.com
SIC: 2711 Newspapers, publishing and printing
HQ: Thomson Reuters Corporation
333 Bay St
Toronto ON M5H 2
416 687-7500

(G-3484)

TORQMASTER INC
Also Called: Torqmaster International
200 Harvard Ave (06902-6348)
PHONE..............................203 326-5945
Garrett Bebell, *Pr*
Doctor Martin Waine, *VP*
◆ **EMP:** 45 **EST:** 1997
SQ FT: 20,000
SALES (est): 5.07MM **Privately Held**
Web: www.torqmaster.com
SIC: 3499 Friction material, made from powdered metal

(G-3485)

TRANSOM SYMPHONY OPCO LLC (PA)
Also Called: Beauty Quest Group
120 Long Ridge Rd (06902-1839)
PHONE..............................203 503-7938
John Costanza, *CEO*
James Oh, *VP*
EMP: 83 **EST:** 2019
SALES (est): 54.19MM
SALES (corp-wide): 54.19MM **Privately Held**
Web: www.beautyquestgroup.com
SIC: 2844 Toilet preparations

(G-3486)

TRONOX INCORPORATED (DH)
263 Tresser Blvd Ste 1100 (06901-3227)
PHONE..............................203 705-3800
Timothy C Carlson, *
◆ **EMP:** 200 **EST:** 1964
SALES (est): 455.57MM
SALES (corp-wide): 3.45B **Privately Held**
Web: www.tronox.com
SIC: 2421 2819 Railroad ties, sawed; Sodium compounds or salts, inorg., ex. refined sod. chloride

HQ: Tronox Us Holdings Inc.
3301 Nw 150th St
Oklahoma City OK 73134
405 775-5000

(G-3487)

TRONOX LLC (PA)
Also Called: Tronox
263 Tresser Blvd Ste 1100 (06901-3227)
PHONE..............................203 705-3800
John D Romano, *CEO*
Jean-franois Turgeon, *CEO*
Russ Austin, *Sr VP*
Jeff Engle, *Sr VP*
Jeffrey Neuman, *Sr VP*
EMP: 19 **EST:** 1997
SALES (est): 10.89MM
SALES (corp-wide): 10.89MM **Privately Held**
Web: www.tronox.com
SIC: 1442 1241 Sand mining; Coal mining services

(G-3488)

US GAMES SYSTEMS INC
Also Called: Cove Press
179 Ludlow St (06902-6900)
PHONE..............................800 544-2637
Stuart R Kaplan, *Ch Bd*
Marilyn Kaplan, *
Ricardo Cruz, *
◆ **EMP:** 41 **EST:** 1968
SQ FT: 22,000
SALES (est): 4.81MM **Privately Held**
Web: www.usgamesinc.com
SIC: 2741 5092 3944 2752 Miscellaneous publishing; Playing cards; Games, toys, and children's vehicles; Commercial printing, lithographic

(G-3489)

UST LLC
6 High Ridge Park Bldg A (06905-1327)
P.O. Box 85107 (23285-5107)
PHONE..............................203 817-3000
Rich A Kohlberger, *Ex VP*
Richard A Kohlberger, *
Raymond P Silcock, *
Gary B Glass, *
◆ **EMP:** 4610 **EST:** 1986
SALES (est): 255.22MM
SALES (corp-wide): 25.1B **Publicly Held**
Web: www.ustinc.com
SIC: 2131 2084 2621 3999 Chewing and smoking tobacco; Wines, brandy, and brandy spirits; Cigarette paper; Pipe cleaners
PA: Altria Group, Inc.
6601 W Broad St
Richmond VA 23230
804 274-2200

(G-3490)

VALLEYLAB
74 Putter Dr (06907-1241)
PHONE..............................203 461-9075
Mike Coppola, *Mgr*
EMP: 27 **EST:** 2011
SALES (est): 571.96K **Privately Held**
SIC: 3841 Surgical and medical instruments

(G-3491)

VERBIO NORTH AMERICA LLC (PA)
9 W Broad St Ste 400 (06902-3764)
PHONE..............................866 306-4777
Greg Northrup, *CEO*
Rand Dueweke, *VP*
Alicia Webber, *CFO*
EMP: 20 **EST:** 2018

SALES (est): 67.3MM
SALES (corp-wide): 67.3MM **Privately Held**
Web: www.verbio-north-america.com
SIC: 1389 Cementing oil and gas well casings

(G-3492)
VERBIO NORTH AMERICAN HOLDINGS
9 W Broad St Ste 400 (06902-3764)
PHONE..................866 306-4777
Greg Northrup, *Pr*
Alicia Webber, *Treas*
Oliver Luedtke, *Dir*
Stefan Schreiber, *Dir*
Theodor Niesmann, *Dir*
EMP: 40 EST: 2021
SALES (est): 1.06MM **Privately Held**
SIC: 2823 Cellulosic manmade fibers

(G-3493)
WEEKLY READER CORP
200 Stamford Pl Ste 200 (06902-6753)
PHONE..................203 705-3500
EMP: 10 EST: 2019
SALES (est): 480.38K **Privately Held**
Web: www.scholastic.com
SIC: 2731 Books, publishing only

(G-3494)
WESTROCK COMMERCIAL LLC
1635 Coining Dr (06902)
PHONE..................203 595-3130
EMP: 8 EST: 2013
SALES (est): 248.54K **Privately Held**
SIC: 2752 Offset printing

(G-3495)
WILSON PARTITIONS INC
Also Called: Arcadia
120 Viaduct Rd (06907-2707)
PHONE..................203 316-8033
Jim Schladen, *Owner*
▼ **EMP: 19 EST:** 2001
SALES (est): 905.25K **Privately Held**
Web: www.wilsonpart.com
SIC: 3334 Primary aluminum

(G-3496)
WOOLWORKS INTERNATIONAL LTD
379 Old Long Ridge Rd (06903-1133)
PHONE..................203 661-7076
EMP: 8 EST: 1992
SALES (est): 237.12K **Privately Held**
SIC: 2721 Periodicals

(G-3497)
WORLD WRESTLING ENTRMT LLC (DH)
1241 E Main St (06902-3520)
PHONE..................203 352-8600
Nick Khan, *Pr*
Frank A Riddick Iii, *Pr*
Paul Levesque, *CCO*
Karen Mullane, *CAO*
▲ **EMP: 120 EST:** 1980
SALES (est): 1.29B
SALES (corp-wide): 5.27B **Publicly Held**
Web: www.wwe.com
SIC: 7812 7929 2721 Television film production; Entertainment group; Magazines: publishing only, not printed on site
HQ: Tko Group Holdings, Inc.
200 5th Ave Fl 7
New York NY 10010
646 558-8333

(G-3498)
ZIMMER & ROHDE LTD (DH)
30 Buxton Farm Rd Ste 110 (06905-1206)
PHONE..................203 327-1400
Andreas Zimmer, *Pr*
Dorothy Kostek, *Dir*
▲ **EMP: 12 EST:** 1947
SQ FT: 800
SALES (est): 4.94MM
SALES (corp-wide): 349.55K **Privately Held**
Web: www.zimmer-rohde.com
SIC: 2211 Apparel and outerwear fabrics, cotton
HQ: Zimmer + Rohde Gmbh
Zimmersmuhlenweg 14-18
Oberursel (Taunus) HE 61440
617163202

Sterling
Windham County

(G-3499)
AUSTIN POWDER COMPANY
332 Ekonk Hill Rd (06377)
PHONE..................860 564-5466
EMP: 26
SALES (corp-wide): 749.73MM **Privately Held**
Web: www.austinpowder.com
SIC: 2892 Explosives
HQ: Austin Powder Company
25800 Science Park Dr # 300
Cleveland OH 44122
216 464-2400

(G-3500)
DETOTEC NORTH AMERICA INC
401 Snake Meadow Hill Rd (06377-1713)
P.O. Box 276 (06377-0276)
PHONE..................860 564-1012
Tim Obrien, *Pr*
Martha Obrien, *Sec*
▲ **EMP: 9 EST:** 1996
SQ FT: 100
SALES (est): 2.59MM **Privately Held**
Web: www.detotec.com
SIC: 2298 Cordage and twine

(G-3501)
JORDAN SAW MILL LLC
Also Called: Jordan Sawmill
201 Saw Mill Hill Rd (06377-1405)
PHONE..................860 774-0247
Kevin Jordan, *Managing Member*
EMP: 10 EST: 1976
SQ FT: 20,000
SALES (est): 972.32K **Privately Held**
Web: www.suntelhouseplans.com
SIC: 2421 Sawmills and planing mills, general

(G-3502)
MAXAM INITIATION SYSTEMS LLC
74 Dixon Rd (06377-1503)
PHONE..................860 556-4064
◆ **EMP: 28 EST:** 2001
SALES (est): 1.57MM
SALES (corp-wide): 27.56MM **Privately Held**
SIC: 2892 Explosives
PA: Maxam North America, Inc.
133 River Park Rd Ste 106
Mooresville NC 28117
214 736-8100

(G-3503)
NU-STONE MFG & DISTRG LLC
160 Sterling Rd (06377-2006)
PHONE..................860 564-6555
Charlie Corson, *Owner*
EMP: 7
SALES (est): 644.83K **Privately Held**
SIC: 1429 Igneus rock, crushed and broken-quarrying

(G-3504)
STERLING PRCSION MACHINING INC
Also Called: Sterling Precision Machining
112 Industrial Park Rd (06377-1802)
P.O. Box 236 (06377-0236)
PHONE..................860 564-4043
Carmine Demarco, *Pr*
Dave Demarco, *Sec*
Rick Demarco, *Treas*
EMP: 13 EST: 1987
SQ FT: 12,000
SALES (est): 1.81MM **Privately Held**
Web: www.sterlingct.us
SIC: 3599 Machine shop, jobbing and repair

(G-3505)
WESTMINSTER TOOL INC
51 Industrial Park Rd (06377-1804)
PHONE..................860 317-1039
EMP: 8 EST: 2014
SALES (est): 124.13K **Privately Held**
Web: www.westminstertool.com
SIC: 3599 Machine shop, jobbing and repair

Stevenson
Fairfield County

(G-3506)
ANODIC INCORPORATED
1480 Monroe Tpke (06491)
P.O. Box 52 (06491-0052)
PHONE..................203 268-9966
Ronald Buttner, *Pr*
EMP: 18 EST: 1951
SQ FT: 16,000
SALES (est): 925.39K **Privately Held**
Web: www.anodic.com
SIC: 3471 Finishing, metals or formed products

Stonington
New London County

(G-3507)
BEERD BREWING CO LLC (PA)
22 Bayview Ave (06378-1143)
PHONE..................860 857-1014
Aaren Simoncini, *Managing Member*
EMP: 22 EST: 2012
SALES (est): 4MM
SALES (corp-wide): 4MM **Privately Held**
Web: www.beerdbrewing.com
SIC: 5813 2082 Bars and lounges; Beer (alcoholic beverage)

(G-3508)
DODSON BOATYARD LLC
194 Water St (06378-1209)
P.O. Box 272 (06378-0272)
PHONE..................860 535-1507
EMP: 28 EST: 1851
SQ FT: 20,000
SALES (est): 7.68MM **Privately Held**
Web: www.dodsonboatyard.com

SIC: 5551 4493 7699 3732 Marine supplies, nec; Marinas; Nautical repair services; Boatbuilding and repairing

(G-3509)
GREENHAVEN CABINETRY MLLWK LLC
338 Elm St (06378-2926)
PHONE..................860 535-1106
Robert D Wood, *Prin*
EMP: 8 EST: 2006
SALES (est): 310.08K **Privately Held**
SIC: 2434 Wood kitchen cabinets

Storrs
Tolland County

(G-3510)
CHAMPION ENTERPRISES INC
19 Greenfield Ln (06268-1250)
PHONE..................860 429-3537
Nayna Chheda, *Prin*
EMP: 8 EST: 2011
SALES (est): 227.28K **Privately Held**
SIC: 2451 Mobile homes

(G-3511)
CHARLES RIVER LABORATORIES INC
67 Baxter Rd (06268-1109)
PHONE..................860 429-7261
Seador Girshick, *Mgr*
EMP: 10
SALES (corp-wide): 3.98B **Publicly Held**
Web: www.criver.com
SIC: 8731 2835 Commercial physical research; Diagnostic substances
HQ: Charles River Laboratories, Inc.
251 Ballardvale St
Wilmington MA 01887
781 222-6000

Storrs Mansfield
Tolland County

(G-3512)
DESIATO SAND & GRAVEL CORP
999 Stafford Rd (06268-1803)
PHONE..................860 429-6479
Phillip Desiato, *Pr*
Sam Schrager, *Sec*
EMP: 23 EST: 1955
SQ FT: 8,600
SALES (est): 2.31MM **Privately Held**
Web: www.desiatosandandgravel.com
SIC: 1794 5211 5032 1442 Excavation work; Sand and gravel; Brick, stone, and related material; Construction sand and gravel

(G-3513)
WILLARD J STEARNS & SONS INC
Also Called: Mountain Dairy
50 Stearns Rd (06268-2701)
P.O. Box 96 (06268-0096)
PHONE..................860 423-9289
Willard C Stearns, *CEO*
David Stearns, *
James W Stearns, *
Arthur B Stearns, *
EMP: 35 EST: 1871
SALES (est): 2.87MM **Privately Held**
Web: www.mountaindairy.com
SIC: 2026 0241 Fluid milk; Dairy farms

Stratford
Fairfield County

(G-3514)
300 WOOD AVENUE LLC
45 Plane Tree Rd (06614-1826)
PHONE....................763 479-6605
Linden Higgins, *Prin*
EMP: 7 EST: 2010
SALES (est): 97.3K Privately Held
Web: www.axiominternet.com
SIC: 3599 Industrial machinery, nec

(G-3515)
ADVANCED GRAPHICS INCORPORATED
55 Old South Ave (06615-7368)
P.O. Box 656 (06615-0656)
PHONE....................203 378-0471
John Alesevich Junior, *Pr*
John Alesevich, *Pr*
Bonnie Alesevich, *
EMP: 24 EST: 1976
SQ FT: 11,000
SALES (est): 2.66MM Privately Held
Web: www.advanced-graphics.com
SIC: 3479 2759 2396 Painting of metal
products; Screen printing; Automotive and
apparel trimmings

(G-3516)
AGISSAR CORPORATION
526 Benton St (06615-7351)
PHONE....................203 375-8662
Ryan Foley, *Pr*
Suzanne Rassiga, *
Stephanie Foley, *
EMP: 44 EST: 1977
SQ FT: 15,500
SALES (est): 4.45MM Privately Held
Web: www.agissar.com
SIC: 3579 7629 5044 Mailing machines;
Business machine repair, electric; Office
equipment

(G-3517)
ASHCROFT INC (DH)
250 E Main St (06614-5145)
PHONE....................203 378-8281
Steven Culmone, *CEO*
John Vouno, *CFO*
◆ EMP: 450 EST: 2005
SQ FT: 325,000
SALES (est): 195.77MM Privately Held
Web: www.ashcroft.com
SIC: 3823 3679 3663 3625 Pressure
gauges, dial and digital; Transducers,
electrical; Transmitter-receivers, radio;
Switches, electric power
HQ: Ashcroft-Nagano Keiki Holdings, Inc.
250 E Main St
Stratford CT 06614

(G-3518)
BARGAIN NEWS FREE CLSSFIED ADV
720 Barnum Avenue Cutoff Ofc
(06614-5037)
PHONE....................203 377-3000
EMP: 12 EST: 1971
SALES (est): 179.44K Privately Held
Web: www.bargainnews.com
SIC: 2711 2721 Newspapers, publishing
and printing; Periodicals

(G-3519)
BENEFIT COATINGS INC
550 Long Beach Blvd (06615-7179)
PHONE....................203 572-0660
Adam Berry, *CEO*
Craig Berry, *COO*
EMP: 15 EST: 2018
SALES (est): 2.31MM Privately Held
SIC: 2834 Pharmaceutical preparations

(G-3520)
BLASE MANUFACTURING COMPANY (PA)
Also Called: Blase Tool & Manufacturing Co
60 Watson Blvd (06615-7165)
PHONE....................203 375-5646
John Blase, *Pr*
EMP: 42 EST: 1947
SQ FT: 60,000
SALES (est): 5.53MM
SALES (corp-wide): 5.53MM Privately
Held
Web: www.blasemanufacturing.com
SIC: 3469 Stamping metal for the trade

(G-3521)
BREMSER TECHNOLOGIES INC
305 Sniffens Ln (06615-7558)
PHONE....................203 378-8486
Helma Chartier, *Pr*
Eric Chartier, *VP*
Eric Helma, *VP*
EMP: 10 EST: 1949
SQ FT: 5,000
SALES (est): 908.51K Privately Held
Web: www.bremsertech.com
SIC: 3544 5084 Special dies and tools;
Industrial machinery and equipment

(G-3522)
BRIDGEPORT FITTINGS LLC
Also Called: Bridgeport
705 Lordship Blvd (06615-7313)
P.O. Box 619 (06601-0619)
PHONE....................203 377-5944
Paul Suzio, *Pr*
▲ EMP: 200 EST: 1925
SQ FT: 135,000
SALES (est): 48.89MM Privately Held
Web: www.nsiindustries.com
SIC: 3644 Electric conduits and fittings
PA: Nsi Industries, Llc
13235 Reese Blvd W
Huntersville NC 28078

(G-3523)
BRIDGEPORT INSULATED WIRE CO
Also Called: The Bridgeport Insulated Wire
Company
514 Surf Ave (06615-6725)
PHONE....................203 375-9579
Wayne Gombar, *Mgr*
EMP: 8
SQ FT: 2,200
SALES (corp-wide): 2.55MM Privately
Held
Web: www.thebridgeportwireco.com
SIC: 3357 3496 Nonferrous wiredrawing
and insulating; Miscellaneous fabricated
wire products
PA: The Bridgeport Insulated Wire
Company
51 Brookfield Ave
Bridgeport CT 06610
203 333-3191

(G-3524)
BUCKLEY ASSOCIATES INC
350 Long Beach Blvd (06615-7167)
PHONE....................203 380-2405
Mike Gajnon, *Brnch Mgr*
EMP: 9
SALES (corp-wide): 92.59MM Privately
Held
Web: www.buckleyonline.com
SIC: 5075 3444 Warm air heating
equipment and supplies; Ducts, sheet metal
PA: Buckley Associates, Inc.
385 King St
Hanover MA 02339
781 878-5000

(G-3525)
CARBTROL CORPORATION
200 Benton St (06615-7330)
PHONE....................203 337-4340
Chris Rotondo, *Pr*
Austin Shepherd, *
Heather Mroz, *
Brian Murray, *
EMP: 30 EST: 1983
SALES (est): 4.77MM Privately Held
Web: www.carbtrol.com
SIC: 2819 Charcoal (carbon), activated

(G-3526)
CHRIS CROSS LLC
Also Called: Prestige Remodeling
294 Benton St (06615-7330)
P.O. Box 321135 (06825-6135)
PHONE....................203 386-8426
John Cross, *Mgr*
EMP: 10 EST: 2005
SALES (est): 604.63K Privately Held
SIC: 2434 Wood kitchen cabinets

(G-3527)
CLARITY OUTPUT SOLUTIONS LLC
Also Called: Premier Prtg Mailing Solutions
860 Honeyspot Rd (06615-7159)
PHONE....................800 414-1624
EMP: 55 EST: 1988
SQ FT: 33,000
SALES (est): 15.26MM Privately Held
Web: www.clarityosl.com
SIC: 2752 Offset printing

(G-3528)
COATING DESIGN GROUP INC
430 Sniffens Ln (06615-7559)
PHONE....................203 878-3663
William L Roy, *Pr*
Kathryn G Cunningham, *Sec*
EMP: 20 EST: 1988
SQ FT: 11,500
SALES (est): 2.45MM Privately Held
Web: www.coatingdesigngroup.com
SIC: 3827 3089 Optical instruments and
lenses; Coloring and finishing of plastics
products

(G-3529)
COBER INC
30 Moffitt St (06615-6718)
PHONE....................203 855-8755
EMP: 21 EST: 1966
SALES (est): 2.27MM Privately Held
Web: www.cober.com
SIC: 3567 Dielectric heating equipment

(G-3530)
CONNECTICUT MACHINE & WELDING
Also Called: Rollins Transmission Service

425 Harding Ave (06615-7248)
P.O. Box 249 (06615-0249)
PHONE....................203 502-2605
Wayne J Rollins, *Pr*
Glenn A Rollins, *Sec*
Hattie-jane Rollins, *VP*
Gary Rollins, *Treas*
EMP: 9 EST: 1989
SQ FT: 7,000
SALES (est): 217.68K Privately Held
SIC: 7692 Welding repair

(G-3531)
CONSUMER PRODUCT DISTRS LLC
1075 Honeyspot Rd (06615-7113)
PHONE....................203 378-2193
EMP: 8
SALES (corp-wide): 639.12MM Privately
Held
Web: www.thencd.com
SIC: 5194 5099 2111 Tobacco and tobacco
products; Brass goods; Cigarettes
HQ: Consumer Product Distributors, Llc
705 Meadow St
Chicopee MA 01013
413 592-4141

(G-3532)
CUESCRIPT INC
555 Lordship Blvd Unit G (06615-7156)
PHONE....................203 763-4030
Michael Accardi, *Pr*
EMP: 7 EST: 2014
SALES (est): 786.2K Privately Held
Web: www.cuescript.tv
SIC: 3663 Radio and t.v. communications
equipment

(G-3533)
DICTAPHONE CORPORATION (DH)
3191 Broadbridge Ave (06614-2566)
PHONE....................203 381-7000
Daniel P Hart, *Sr VP*
Robert Schwager, *
Joseph Delaney, *
Thomas C Hodge, *
Ed Rucinski, *
▲ EMP: 200 EST: 1881
SQ FT: 100,000
SALES (est): 167.35MM
SALES (corp-wide): 211.91B Publicly
Held
Web: www.dictaphone.com
SIC: 3579 3825 3695 3577 Dictating
machines; Instruments to measure
electricity; Magnetic and optical recording
media; Computer peripheral equipment, nec
HQ: Nuance Communications, Inc.
1 Wayside Rd
Burlington MA 01803

(G-3534)
ELECTRIC ENTERPRISE INC
1410 Stratford Ave (06615-6417)
PHONE....................203 378-7311
Raymond J Sierakowski, *Pr*
Mary Jo Sierakowski, *Sec*
EMP: 11 EST: 1955
SQ FT: 3,200
SALES (est): 577.79K Privately Held
Web:
www.industrialmachinerepairus.com
SIC: 7694 5063 Electric motor repair;
Motors, electric

(G-3535)
FAIRFIELD WOODWORKS LLC
Also Called: Fairfield Wood Works

365 Sniffens Ln (06615-7558)
PHONE..................................203 380-9842
EMP: 18 **EST:** 1992
SQ FT: 10,500
SALES (est): 1.84MM **Privately Held**
SIC: 2431   Millwork

(G-3536)
FG SIGNS LLC
1895 Stratford Ave (06615-6426)
PHONE..................................203 612-4447
Geovanna Granda, *Managing Member*
EMP: 8 **EST:** 2014
SALES (est): 221.37K **Privately Held**
SIC: 3993   Signs and advertising specialties

(G-3537)
FOOD ATMTN - SVC TCHNIQUES LLC (PA)
Also Called: Fast
905 Honeyspot Rd (06615-7140)
PHONE..................................203 377-4414
Christian Koether, *CEO*
George F Koether, *
Joan G Koether, *
Mike Keefe, *
John Balkonis, *
◆ **EMP:** 30 **EST:** 1969
SQ FT: 100,000
SALES (est): 49.87MM
SALES (corp-wide): 49.87MM **Privately Held**
Web: www.kitchenbrains.com
SIC: 3823 3822   Time cycle and program
  controllers, industrial process type;
  Temperature controls, automatic

(G-3538)
FORCE3 PRO GEAR LLC
Also Called: Force3 Pro Gear
240 Hathaway Dr (06615-7361)
PHONE..................................315 367-2331
Jason Klein, *Pt*
Michael Klein, *Ltd Pt*
James Evans, *Ltd Pt*
Cole Flowers, *Ltd Pt*
EMP: 16 **EST:** 2017
SALES (est): 1.21MM **Privately Held**
Web: www.force3progear.com
SIC: 3949   Baseball, softball, and cricket
  sports equipment

(G-3539)
FRANK ROTH CO INC
1795 Stratford Ave (06615-6442)
PHONE..................................203 377-2155
Walker Woodworth, *Pr*
Cornelia Toffolo, *
Marissa Woodworth, *
▲ **EMP:** 60 **EST:** 1934
SQ FT: 14,000
SALES (est): 8.42MM **Privately Held**
Web: www.frankroth.com
SIC: 3599 3325 3841 3751   Machine shop,
  jobbing and repair; Alloy steel castings,
  except investment; Surgical and medical
  instruments; Motorcycles, bicycles and parts

(G-3540)
GARY TOOL COMPANY
26 Grant St (06615-6188)
PHONE..................................203 377-3077
Raymond Anderson Junior, *Pr*
Cristine Ansder, *VP*
EMP: 7 **EST:** 1947
SQ FT: 10,000
SALES (est): 534.19K **Privately Held**
SIC: 3541 3544   Machine tools, metal
  cutting: exotic (explosive, etc.); Jigs and
  fixtures

(G-3541)
GEORGE H OLSON STEEL COMPANY
Also Called: Olson, G H Steel
245 Access Rd (06615-7414)
PHONE..................................203 375-5656
George H Olson, *Pr*
Mary Ann Gentile, *Sec*
EMP: 15 **EST:** 1944
SQ FT: 2,800
SALES (est): 943.28K **Privately Held**
SIC: 1791 3441   Structural steel erection;
  Fabricated structural metal

(G-3542)
GLYNE MANUFACTURING CO INC
380 E Main St (06614-5145)
PHONE..................................203 375-4495
Bruce Mcgalliard, *Pr*
Thomas Frei, *VP*
EMP: 16 **EST:** 1966
SQ FT: 9,600
SALES (est): 2.4MM **Privately Held**
Web: www.glyne.com
SIC: 3728   Aircraft parts and equipment, nec

(G-3543)
GRAFTED COATINGS INC
Also Called: We Make Paint
400 Surf Ave (06615-6723)
PHONE..................................203 377-9979
James A Bolton, *Pr*
Alice Irene Bolton, *Sec*
Joanne M Young, *Treas*
EMP: 8 **EST:** 1992
SQ FT: 12,000
SALES (est): 432.99K **Privately Held**
Web: www.graftedcoatings.com
SIC: 2891 5198   Sealants; Paints

(G-3544)
HAMPFORD RESEARCH INC (PA)
54 Veterans Blvd (06615-5111)
PHONE..................................203 375-1137
Kate Hampford Donahue, *CEO*
Lloyd Lirio, *
Anne B Hampford, *
▲ **EMP:** 32 **EST:** 1982
SQ FT: 100,000
SALES (est): 8.29MM
SALES (corp-wide): 8.29MM **Privately Held**
Web: www.hampfordresearch.com
SIC: 2869 8731   Industrial organic
  chemicals, nec; Commercial physical
  research

(G-3545)
HAUSER EQP & WLDG SVCS INC
Also Called: Hauser Equipment & Welding
45 Embree St (06615-6710)
PHONE..................................203 377-7072
Robert J Hauser, *Pr*
Tom Sullivan, *Treas*
Gretchen Hauser, *Stockholder*
EMP: 12 **EST:** 1994
SQ FT: 1,200
SALES (est): 2.25MM **Privately Held**
SIC: 5084 7699 7692   Materials handling
  machinery; Industrial machinery and
  equipment repair; Welding repair

(G-3546)
HERFF JONES LLC
71 Vought Pl (06614-2949)
PHONE..................................203 368-9344
Herff Jones, *Brnch Mgr*

EMP: 10
SALES (corp-wide): 2.02B **Privately Held**
Web: www.yearbookdiscoveries.com
SIC: 2752   Commercial printing, lithographic
HQ: Herff Jones, Llc
  4501 W 62nd St
  Indianapolis IN 46268
  317 297-3741

(G-3547)
HI-TECH PACKAGING INC
1 Bruce Ave (06615-6102)
PHONE..................................203 378-2700
Michael Rappa, *Pr*
Alfred Thibault, *
EMP: 28 **EST:** 1986
SQ FT: 40,000
SALES (est): 6.78MM **Privately Held**
Web: www.hitechpackaging.com
SIC: 2448 2653 3086   Pallets, wood; Boxes,
  corrugated: made from purchased materials
  ; Carpet and rug cushions, foamed plastics

(G-3548)
HUDSON PAPER COMPANY (PA)
Also Called: Hupaco
1341 W Broad St (06615-5761)
PHONE..................................203 378-8759
Richard Wilk, *Pr*
Richard Wilk, *Pr*
Bonnie S Wilk, *
Brian Wilk, *
▲ **EMP:** 35 **EST:** 1908
SQ FT: 80,000
SALES (est): 17.13MM
SALES (corp-wide): 17.13MM **Privately Held**
Web: www.hudsonpaper.com
SIC: 5113 5199 5947 2674   Bags, paper and
  disposable plastic; Packaging materials;
  Party favors; Bags: uncoated paper and
  multiwall

(G-3549)
IMPERIAL METAL FINISHING INC
920 Honeyspot Rd (06615-7112)
PHONE..................................203 377-1229
Vincent Bevacqua, *Pr*
Frank Bevacqua, *VP*
John Bevacqua Junior, *VP*
EMP: 9 **EST:** 1969
SQ FT: 13,000
SALES (est): 967.68K **Privately Held**
Web: www.imperialmetalfinishing.com
SIC: 3479   Painting of metal products

(G-3550)
J PALMERO SALES COMPANY INC
Also Called: Palmero Health Care
120 Goodwin Pl (06615-6713)
PHONE..................................203 377-6424
▲ **EMP:** 18
SIC: 3843   Dental equipment and supplies

(G-3551)
J R MERRITT CONTROLS INC (PA)
55 Sperry Ave (06615-7317)
PHONE..................................203 381-0100
▲ **EMP:** 27 **EST:** 1986
SALES (est): 9.9MM
SALES (corp-wide): 9.9MM **Privately Held**
Web: www.jrmerritt.com
SIC: 3572 3625   Computer storage devices;
  Relays and industrial controls

(G-3552)
KINGSLEY PRINTING ASSOC LLC
4883 Main St (06614-3646)
PHONE..................................203 345-6046
David Kingsley Adnett, *Brnch Mgr*
EMP: 16
SALES (corp-wide): 89.14K **Privately Held**
SIC: 2752   Commercial printing, lithographic
PA: Kingsley Printing Associates Llc
  165 Hemlock Hills Rd S
  Fairfield CT

(G-3553)
KUB TECHNOLOGIES INC
Also Called: Kubtec
111 Research Dr (06615-7126)
PHONE..................................203 364-8544
Vikram Butani, *Pr*
Preeti Butani, *
▼ **EMP:** 28 **EST:** 2004
SQ FT: 10,000
SALES (est): 5.17MM **Privately Held**
Web: www.kubtec.com
SIC: 3844   X-ray apparatus and tubes

(G-3554)
M & D COATINGS LLC
300 Long Beach Blvd (06615-7153)
PHONE..................................203 380-9466
Jeffrey Dumas, *Mgr*
▲ **EMP:** 9 **EST:** 2005
SALES (est): 960.34K **Privately Held**
Web: www.rdcoatingsusa.com
SIC: 2851   Paints, waterproof

(G-3555)
MCMELLON BROS INCORPORATED
915 Honeyspot Rd (06615-7192)
PHONE..................................203 375-5685
Thomas Miller, *Pr*
Hans Hanshaffner, *
Reberta Miller, *
Thomas Kaskie, *
EMP: 27 **EST:** 1951
SQ FT: 20,000
SALES (est): 6.5MM **Privately Held**
Web: www.mcmellonbros.com
SIC: 3728 3452   Aircraft parts and
  equipment, nec; Bolts, nuts, rivets, and
  washers

(G-3556)
MERCURY CABLING SYSTEMS LLC
Also Called: Mercury Group The
300 Avon St (06615-6734)
PHONE..................................203 378-9008
EMP: 40 **EST:** 1999
SQ FT: 20,000
SALES (est): 9.67MM **Privately Held**
Web: www.mercury-group.com
SIC: 1731 8748 4813 3661   Electrical work;
  Communications consulting; Data
  telephone communications; Fiber optics
  communications equipment

(G-3557)
MERRILL ANDERSON COMPANY INC
1166 Barnum Ave (06614-5427)
PHONE..................................203 377-4996
Thomas Gerrity, *Pr*
Samuel H Heitzman, *Ch Bd*
James B Gust, *Sec*
Samuel Simpson, *Treas*
EMP: 20 **EST:** 1934
SQ FT: 7,500

▲ = Import ▼ = Export
◆ = Import/Export

SALES (est): 1.1MM **Privately Held**
Web: www.merrillanderson.com
SIC: **2741** 8742   Business service
newsletters: publishing and printing;
Marketing consulting services

(G-3558)
NORTHASTERN COMMUNICATIONS INC
255 Hathaway Dr Ste 3 (06615-7370)
PHONE..................................203 381-9008
Julie Reibold, *Brnch Mgr*
EMP: 10
SALES (corp-wide): 9.05MM **Privately Held**
Web: www.norcomct.com
SIC: **5999** 3663   Telephone and
communication equipment; Radio
broadcasting and communications
equipment
PA: Northeastern Communications, Inc.
7 Great Hill Rd
Naugatuck CT 06770
203 575-9008

(G-3559)
NORWALK COMPRESEER COMPANY
1650 Stratford Ave (06615-6419)
PHONE..................................203 386-1234
Arthur Mccauley, *Ch Bd*
▼ EMP: 45 EST: 1864
SQ FT: 33,000
SALES (est): 5.67MM **Privately Held**
SIC: **3563**   Air and gas compressors

(G-3560)
NORWALK POWDERED METALS INC
Also Called: Npm
30 Moffitt St (06615-6718)
PHONE..................................203 338-8000
Thomas A Blumenthal, *Pr*
Richard Webb, *
Henry Adams, *
Ann Blumenthal, *
EMP: 70 EST: 1957
SQ FT: 34,000
SALES (est): 8.76MM **Privately Held**
Web: www.norwalkpm.com
SIC: **3399**   Powder, metal

(G-3561)
NUOVO PASTA PRODUCTIONS LTD
1330 Honeyspot Road Ext (06615-7115)
PHONE..................................203 380-4090
Carl L Zuanelli, *Pr*
Tom Quinn, *
◆ EMP: 150 EST: 1989
SQ FT: 40,000
SALES (est): 36MM **Privately Held**
Web: www.nuovopasta.com
SIC: **2099**   Pasta, rice, and potato, packaged
combination products

(G-3562)
PALMERO HEALTHCARE LLC
120 Goodwin Pl (06615-6790)
PHONE..................................203 377-6424
Karen Neiner, *Pr*
Bernie Dutton, *COO*
EMP: 13 EST: 2016
SALES (est): 2.17MM **Privately Held**
Web: www.palmerohealth.com
SIC: **3843**   Dental equipment and supplies

(G-3563)
PAR PHRMCEUTICAL COMPANIES INC
Also Called: Par Pharmaceutical Companies,
Inc.
555 Lordship Blvd (06615-7156)
PHONE..................................203 290-6261
EMP: 58
SIC: **2834**   Pharmaceutical preparations
HQ: Endo Generics Holdings, Inc.
300 Tice Blvd Ste 230
Woodcliff Lake NJ 07677
845 573-5500

(G-3564)
PARK CITY PACKAGING INC (PA)
Also Called: Pack Center , The
480 Sniffens Ln (06615-7559)
PHONE..................................203 378-7384
C Richard Polzello, *CEO*
EMP: 35 EST: 1954
SQ FT: 25,000
SALES (est): 8.58MM
SALES (corp-wide): 8.58MM **Privately
Held**
Web: www.thepackcenter.com
SIC: **4783** 5199 2679   Packing goods for
shipping; Packaging materials; Corrugated
paper: made from purchased material

(G-3565)
PENMAR INDUSTRIES INC
Also Called: Spec Label Systems
35 Ontario St (06615-7135)
PHONE..................................203 853-4868
TOLL FREE: 800
Elizabeth Soegaard, *Pr*
Javier A Soegaard, *Sec*
Jose A Soegaard Iii, *Treas*
Eddy W Rodriguez, *Pr*
Jeffrey Dais, *Prin*
EMP: 14 EST: 1967
SQ FT: 11,500
SALES (est): 5MM **Privately Held**
Web: www.penmar-industries.com
SIC: **5199** 5113 2671   Packaging materials;
Shipping supplies; Paper; coated and
laminated packaging

(G-3566)
PEPSI-COLA METRO BTLG CO INC
Also Called: Pepsico
355 Benton St (06615-7329)
PHONE..................................203 375-2484
Todd Bixby, *Mgr*
EMP: 23
SALES (corp-wide): 86.39B **Publicly Held**
Web: www.pepsico.com
SIC: **2086**   Carbonated soft drinks, bottled
and canned
HQ: Pepsi-Cola Metropolitan Bottling
Company, Inc.
700 Anderson Hill Rd
Purchase NY 10577
914 767-6000

(G-3567)
PHILLIPS FUEL SYSTEMS INC
25 Sherman St (06615-6240)
PHONE..................................203 908-3323
Rodolfo Garcia, *Prin*
EMP: 13 EST: 2021
SALES (est): 2.64MM **Privately Held**
Web: www.phillipsfuelsystems.com
SIC: **3714**   Filters: oil, fuel, and air, motor
vehicle

(G-3568)
PROFESSIONAL MKTG SVCS INC
Also Called: Pmsi
300 Long Beach Blvd Ste 6 (06615-7153)
PHONE..................................203 610-6222
Marty Bear, *Pr*
EMP: 10 EST: 1983
SQ FT: 3,500
SALES (est): 2.24MM **Privately Held**
Web: www.callpmsi.com
SIC: **5199** 2678   Advertising specialties;
Stationery products

(G-3569)
PROTECTION INDUSTRIES CORP (PA)
2897 Main St (06614-4938)
P.O. Box 1832 (10156-1832)
PHONE..................................203 375-9393
William J Hill, *Ch Bd*
William J Hill, *Ch*
Donna Z Hill, *Pr*
EMP: 25 EST: 1979
SALES (est): 2.54MM
SALES (corp-wide): 2.54MM **Privately
Held**
SIC: **5063** 3669   Control and signal wire and
cable, including coaxial; Fire detection
systems, electric

(G-3570)
SCHWEIZER AIRCRAFT CORP
Also Called: Smcc
6900 Main St (06614-1378)
P.O. Box 9729 (06615-9129)
PHONE..................................203 386-4356
◆ EMP: 500
SIC: **3721** 3728   Airplanes, fixed or rotary
wing; Aircraft body and wing assemblies
and parts

(G-3571)
SIKORSKY AIRCRAFT CORPORATION (HQ)
Also Called: Sikorsky
6900 Main St (06614-1385)
P.O. Box 9729 (06615-9129)
PHONE..................................203 386-4000
Daniel Schultz, *Pr*
John Palumbo, *
Judith E Bankowski, *
Mark F Miller, *
Mary Gallagher, *
◆ EMP: 509 EST: 1994
SALES (est): 2.16B **Publicly Held**
Web: www.lockheedmartin.com
SIC: **3721** 4581 5599   Helicopters; Aircraft
maintenance and repair services; Aircraft
dealers
PA: Lockheed Martin Corporation
6801 Rockledge Dr
Bethesda MD 20817

(G-3572)
SIKORSKY AIRCRAFT CORPORATION
1825 Main St (06615-6528)
P.O. Box 9729 (06615-9129)
PHONE..................................203 386-4000
Steven Finger, *Pr*
EMP: 22
Web: www.lockheedmartin.com
SIC: **3724**   Aircraft engines and engine parts
HQ: Sikorsky Aircraft Corporation
6900 Main St
Stratford CT 06614

(G-3573)
SIKORSKY AIRCRAFT CORPORATION
3191 Broadbridge Ave (06614-2566)
PHONE..................................203 380-3142
Jorge Herrera, *Brnch Mgr*
EMP: 20
Web: www.gyrocamsystems.com
SIC: **3812**   Search and navigation equipment
HQ: Sikorsky Aircraft Corporation
6900 Main St
Stratford CT 06614

(G-3574)
SIKORSKY EXPORT CORPORATION
6900 Main St (06614-1378)
PHONE..................................203 386-4000
Mick Maurer, *Pr*
◆ EMP: 95 EST: 1975
SALES (est): 3.91MM **Publicly Held**
SIC: **3721**   Helicopters
HQ: Sikorsky Aircraft Corporation
6900 Main St
Stratford CT 06614

(G-3575)
SONIC CORP
1 Research Dr (06615-7184)
PHONE..................................203 375-0063
Robert Brakeman Iii, *Pr*
Claire C Skidd, *Sec*
EMP: 12 EST: 1957
SQ FT: 10,000
SALES (est): 4.73MM **Privately Held**
Web: www.sonicmixing.com
SIC: **3561** 3552 3554 3556   Pumps and
pumping equipment; Textile machinery;
Paper industries machinery; Homogenizing
machinery: dairy, fruit, vegetable

(G-3576)
STRATFORD STEEL LLC
185 Masarik Ave (06615-7252)
PHONE..................................203 612-7350
Michael Matkovic, *Managing Member*
EMP: 40 EST: 2014
SQ FT: 13,000
SALES (est): 7.32MM **Privately Held**
Web: www.stratfordsteel.com
SIC: **3441**   Fabricated structural metal

(G-3577)
STRATFORD STL FABRICATION LLC
214 Benton St (06615-7330)
PHONE..................................203 612-7350
Michael Matkovic, *Prin*
EMP: 11 EST: 2019
SALES (est): 857.95K **Privately Held**
Web: www.stratfordsteel.com
SIC: **3441**   Fabricated structural metal

(G-3578)
STRATON INDUSTRIES INC
180 Surf Ave (06615-7137)
PHONE..................................203 375-4488
Edward Cremin, *CEO*
David Cremin, *
Kathleen Mccann, *VP*
EMP: 74 EST: 1961
SQ FT: 12,000
SALES (est): 22.1MM **Privately Held**
Web: www.straton.com
SIC: **3544** 3599 3721 3728   Special dies and
tools; Machine and other job shop work;
Research and development on aircraft by
the manufacturer; Alighting (landing gear)
assemblies, aircraft

(G-3579)

SUPER SEAL COMPANY LLC
45 Seymour St (06615-6170)
P.O. Box 394 (06615-0394)
PHONE..................................203 378-5015
William Newbauer Junior, *Pr*
Einer Dineson, *Sec*
▲ **EMP:** 10 **EST:** 1985
SQ FT: 12,000
SALES (est): 981.19K **Privately Held**
Web: www.supersealcorp.com
SIC: 3089 Molding primary plastics

(G-3580)

THE ELECTRIC HEATER COMPANY
Also Called: Hubbell-Electric Heater Co
45 Seymour St (06615-6170)
P.O. Box 288 (06615-0288)
PHONE..................................800 647-3165
EMP: 88 **EST:** 1937
SALES (est): 25.2MM
SALES (corp-wide): 51.44MM **Privately Held**
Web: www.rentawaterheater.com
SIC: 3639 3822 Hot water heaters, household; Water heater controls
PA: The Nudyne Group Llc
45 Seymour St
Stratford CT 06615
203 378-2659

(G-3581)

TYGER TOOL INC
45 Sperry Ave (06615-7317)
PHONE..................................203 375-4344
Mark Bracchi, *Pr*
Paul Ferencz, *VP*
Darrell Ingram, *Sec*
Jackie Mata, *Off Mgr*
EMP: 10 **EST:** 1990
SQ FT: 4,800
SALES (est): 917.24K **Privately Held**
Web: www.tygertool.com
SIC: 3469 3549 Machine parts, stamped or pressed metal; Metalworking machinery, nec

(G-3582)

VIDEO MESSENGERCOM CORP
Also Called: Video Messenger Co
862 Judson Pl (06615-5933)
PHONE..................................203 358-8842
Joe Romano, *Pr*
Charles Corsello, *VP*
EMP: 8 **EST:** 1988
SQ FT: 5,000
SALES (est): 222.2K **Privately Held**
Web: www.videomessenger.com
SIC: 7941 6719 3663 Sports promotion; Investment holding companies, except banks; Encryption devices

(G-3583)

WESTPORT PRECISION LLC
Also Called: Westport Precision
280 Hathaway Dr (06615-7344)
PHONE..................................203 378-2175
Robert Zawadski, *
EMP: 53 **EST:** 1979
SQ FT: 25,000
SALES (est): 9.18MM **Privately Held**
Web: www.westportprecision.com
SIC: 3599 Machine shop, jobbing and repair

(G-3584)

WILLCO SALES & SERVICE INC (PA)
18 King St (06615-5827)

P.O. Box 320003 (06825-0003)
PHONE..................................203 366-3895
Laura Walker, *Pr*
Donald Tague, *Pr*
Daniel A Gorman, *VP*
Barbara Tague, *Sec*
EMP: 12 **EST:** 1956
SQ FT: 3,500
SALES (est): 5.49MM
SALES (corp-wide): 5.49MM **Privately Held**
Web: www.willcosales.com
SIC: 5031 5084 2522 Doors, nec; Waste compactors; Panel systems and partitions, office: except wood

(G-3585)

WJ KETTLEWORKS LLC
55 Sperry Ave (06615-7317)
PHONE..................................203 377-5000
EMP: 7 **EST:** 2011
SALES (est): 445.22K **Privately Held**
SIC: 3272 Concrete structural support and building material

(G-3586)

XG INDUSTRIES LLC
53 Hancock St (06615-6204)
PHONE..................................475 282-4643
EMP: 11 **EST:** 2016
SALES (est): 1.75MM **Privately Held**
Web: www.xgindustries.com
SIC: 2891 Adhesives and sealants

Suffield
Hartford County

(G-3587)

ARCOR LASER SERVICES LLC
4 Kenny Roberts Memorial Dr (06078-2529)
PHONE..................................860 370-9780
EMP: 80
Web: www.arcorlaser.com
SIC: 3699 Laser welding, drilling, and cutting equipment

(G-3588)

ARCOR SYSTEMS LLC
4 Kenny Roberts Memorial Dr (06078-2529)
PHONE..................................860 370-9780
EMP: 9 **EST:** 2014
SALES (est): 495.54K **Privately Held**
SIC: 3599 Machine shop, jobbing and repair

(G-3589)

CADENCE CT INC
4 Kenny Roberts Memorial Dr (06078-2529)
PHONE..................................860 370-9780
EMP: 75 **EST:** 2019
SQ FT: 30,000
SALES (est): 11.38MM
SALES (corp-wide): 105.16MM **Privately Held**
Web: www.cadencedevice.com
SIC: 3699 Laser welding, drilling, and cutting equipment
PA: Cadence, Inc.
9 Technology Dr
Staunton VA 24401
540 248-2200

(G-3590)

ENVIRO-FUELS LLC
700 Hale St (06078-2508)
PHONE..................................860 242-2325

Joseph Rouleau, *Bd of Dir*
EMP: 8 **EST:** 2019
SALES (est): 253.42K **Privately Held**
SIC: 2911 Petroleum refining

(G-3591)

HP HOOD LLC
Ice Cream Division
1250 East St S (06078-2498)
PHONE..................................860 623-4435
Rick Kovarik, *Opers Mgr*
EMP: 225
SQ FT: 147,000
SALES (corp-wide): 2.21B **Privately Held**
Web: www.hood.com
SIC: 2024 Ice cream and frozen deserts
PA: Hp Hood Llc
6 Kimball Ln Ste 400
Lynnfield MA 01940
617 887-3000

(G-3592)

KONGSBERG ACTTION SYSTEMS II L (PA)
Also Called: Kongsberg Automotive
1 Firestone Dr (06078-2611)
PHONE..................................860 668-1285
Hennings Jensen, *CEO*
Jonathan Day, *Pr*
Rachel Baxter, *Sec*
James Fuda, *Treas*
▲ **EMP:** 58 **EST:** 1981
SALES (est): 30.29MM **Privately Held**
SIC: 3714 Motor vehicle parts and accessories

(G-3593)

METAL FINISH EQP & SUP CO INC
Also Called: Metfin Shot Blast Systems
19 Kenny Roberts Memorial Dr (06078-2500)
PHONE..................................860 668-1050
Richard Rush, *CEO*
Richard Rush, *Pr*
Robert Rush, *
▲ **EMP:** 27 **EST:** 1983
SQ FT: 10,000
SALES (est): 9.16MM **Privately Held**
Web: www.metfin.com
SIC: 5084 2892 Materials handling machinery; Explosives

(G-3594)

MOBILE MINI INC
911 S St Mach 1 Industrial Park (06078)
PHONE..................................860 668-1888
Brian Lowder, *Mgr*
EMP: 7
SALES (corp-wide): 2.14B **Publicly Held**
Web: www.mobilemini.com
SIC: 3448 3441 3412 7359 Buildings, portable: prefabricated metal; Fabricated structural metal; Drums, shipping: metal; Shipping container leasing
HQ: Mobile Mini, Inc.
4646 E Van Buren St # 400
Phoenix AZ 85008
480 894-6311

(G-3595)

STONE IMAGE CUSTOM CON LLC
1186 Old Coach Xing (06078-1538)
PHONE..................................860 668-2434
Robert Heim, *Prin*
EMP: 8 **EST:** 2006
SALES (est): 187.88K **Privately Held**

SIC: 3272 Cast stone, concrete

(G-3596)

UNITED GEAR AND MACHINE CO INC
1087 East St S (06078-2405)
PHONE..................................860 623-6618
Kurt Malec, *VP*
William J Malec, *Pr*
Genevieve Malec, *Sec*
EMP: 17 **EST:** 1955
SALES (est): 1.87MM **Privately Held**
Web: www.unitedgearct.com
SIC: 3599 3462 3724 3764 Machine shop, jobbing and repair; Gears, forged steel; Aircraft engines and engine parts; Space propulsion units and parts

---

Taftville
New London County

(G-3597)

GP INDUSTRIES
500 Norwich Ave Ste 7 (06380-1335)
PHONE..................................860 859-9938
Vesselin Zaprianov, *Pr*
EMP: 16 **EST:** 2002
SALES (est): 547.08K **Privately Held**
Web: www.airportlinktaximnusa.com
SIC: 3089 Battery cases, plastics or plastics combination

Tariffville
Hartford County

(G-3598)

APPLIED POROUS TECH INC
2 Tunxis Rd Ste 103 (06081-9687)
P.O. Box 569 (06081-0569)
PHONE..................................860 408-9793
Edward Swiniarski, *Pr*
Heidi Eisenhaure, *VP*
▲ **EMP:** 15 **EST:** 2000
SQ FT: 7,500
SALES (est): 1.8MM **Privately Held**
Web: www.appliedporous.com
SIC: 3569 Filters, general line: industrial

Terryville
Litchfield County

(G-3599)

ADVANCED MICRO CONTROLS INC
Also Called: Amci
20 Gear Dr (06786-7314)
PHONE..................................860 585-1254
William Erb, *Pr*
Peter Serev, *
◆ **EMP:** 38 **EST:** 1985
SQ FT: 16,000
SALES (est): 7.27MM **Privately Held**
Web: www.amci.com
SIC: 3625 Controls for adjustable speed drives

(G-3600)

ALLREAD PRODUCTS CO LLC
22 S Main St (06786-6212)
PHONE..................................860 589-3566
EMP: 18 **EST:** 1974
SQ FT: 8,000
SALES (est): 1.03MM **Privately Held**
SIC: 3399 2821 Powder, metal; Plastics materials and resins

(G-3601)
ELM PRESS INCORPORATED
16 Tremco Dr (06786-7312)
PHONE..................................860 583-3600
Victor Losure, *Pr*
Victor L Losure, *
Joel A Zinn, *
EMP: 40 **EST:** 1961
SQ FT: 13,200
SALES (est): 6.51MM **Privately Held**
Web: www.elmpress.com
SIC: 2752 2791 2789 2759 Offset printing;
Typesetting; Bookbinding and related work;
Commercial printing, nec

(G-3602)
ES METAL FABRICATIONS INC
11 Allread Dr (06786-7300)
PHONE..................................860 585-6067
Eric Schleich, *Pr*
Russell Schleich, *VP*
▲ **EMP:** 22 **EST:** 1984
SQ FT: 6,000
SALES (est): 805.27K **Privately Held**
Web: www.esmetal.com
SIC: 3441 Fabricated structural metal

(G-3603)
FURNACE SOURCE LLC
99 Agney Ave (06786-6224)
PHONE..................................860 582-4201
EMP: 18 **EST:** 2002
SALES (est): 2.36MM **Privately Held**
Web: www.thefurnacesource.com
SIC: 3567 3841 Industrial furnaces and
ovens; Medical instruments and equipment,
blood and bone work

(G-3604)
GENOVESE MANUFACTURING CO
8 Bombard Ct (06786-4403)
P.O. Box 2112 (06011-2112)
PHONE..................................860 582-9944
Vincent Genovese, *Pr*
Mike Genovese, *VP*
Vincent Genovese Junior, *Stockholder*
EMP: 10 **EST:** 1985
SQ FT: 15,000
SALES (est): 934.49K **Privately Held**
SIC: 3599 Machine shop, jobbing and repair

(G-3605)
LAURETANO SIGN GROUP INC
1 Tremco Dr (06786-7311)
PHONE..................................860 582-0233
Michael Lauretano, *Pr*
Joanne West, *
Patrick Byrne, *
EMP: 50 **EST:** 1991
SQ FT: 28,000
SALES (est): 8.42MM **Privately Held**
Web: www.lauretano.com
SIC: 3993 Electric signs

(G-3606)
NAPCO PLASTICS LLC
75 Napco Dr (06786-7305)
PHONE..................................860 261-4819
EMP: 10 **EST:** 2019
SALES (est): 536.26K **Privately Held**
Web: www.napcoplastics.com
SIC: 3089 Injection molding of plastics

(G-3607)
NORTH-EAST FASTENERS CORP
8 Tremco Dr (06786-7312)
P.O. Box 322 (06786-0322)
PHONE..................................860 589-3242
Eric Webster, *Pr*
Diane Webster, *VP*
▲ **EMP:** 22 **EST:** 1963
SQ FT: 9,000
SALES (est): 2.45MM **Privately Held**
Web: www.nef1.com
SIC: 3452 3316 Screws, metal; Cold
finishing of steel shapes

(G-3608)
R & I MANUFACTURING CO
118 Napco Dr (06786-7309)
PHONE..................................860 589-6364
Bruce Czatlicki, *Owner*
EMP: 10 **EST:** 1968
SQ FT: 2,400
SALES (est): 998.26K **Privately Held**
Web: www.rimfg.com
SIC: 3599 Machine shop, jobbing and repair

(G-3609)
SPARGO MACHINE PRODUCTS INC
6 Gear Dr (06786-7314)
PHONE..................................860 583-3925
Randy Spargo, *Pr*
Carole Spargo, *Sec*
EMP: 18 **EST:** 1986
SALES (est): 975.58K **Privately Held**
Web: www.spargomachineproducts.com
SIC: 3599 Machine shop, jobbing and repair

(G-3610)
SUNNYCOR INCORPORATED
60 Napco Dr (06786-7307)
PHONE..................................860 582-9667
John W Cole, *Pr*
Danielle K Cole, *Sec*
EMP: 14 **EST:** 1993
SQ FT: 7,000
SALES (est): 2.37MM **Privately Held**
Web: www.sunnycor.com
SIC: 3599 Machine shop, jobbing and repair

(G-3611)
TECHNOLOGY PLASTICS LLC
75 Napco Dr (06786-7305)
PHONE..................................860 583-1590
Tom Fernandes, *CEO*
▲ **EMP:** 15 **EST:** 2002
SQ FT: 46,000
SALES (est): 1.74MM **Privately Held**
SIC: 3089 Injection molding of plastics

(G-3612)
TRIEM INDUSTRIES LLC
105 Napco Dr (06786-7310)
PHONE..................................203 888-1212
▲ **EMP:** 28 **EST:** 1996
SQ FT: 23,000
SALES (est): 4.92MM **Privately Held**
Web: www.triemindustries.com
SIC: 3451 Screw machine products

(G-3613)
UNIPRISE INTERNATIONAL INC
Also Called: Uniprise Sales
50 Napco Dr (06786-7307)
P.O. Box 369 (06786-0369)
PHONE..................................860 589-7262
Philip Porter, *Pr*
Douglas Porter, *
EMP: 24 **EST:** 1976
SQ FT: 10,000
SALES (est): 2.9MM **Privately Held**
Web: www.unipriseinc.com
SIC: 3599 3423 Tubing, flexible metallic;
Soldering tools

(G-3614)
VICTORY FUEL LLC
248 Main St (06786-5901)
PHONE..................................860 585-0532
Samuel J Gizzie Junior, *Owner*
EMP: 7 **EST:** 2011
SALES (est): 244.78K **Privately Held**
SIC: 2869 Fuels

Thomaston
Litchfield County

(G-3615)
BROOKFIELD INDUSTRIES INC
99 W Hillside Ave (06787-1433)
PHONE..................................860 283-6211
Karl P Kinzer, *Pr*
Chris S Kinzer, *
EMP: 25 **EST:** 1974
SQ FT: 10,000
SALES (est): 5.92MM **Privately Held**
Web: www.bfimfg.com
SIC: 3699 3429 Electrical equipment and
supplies, nec; Hardware, nec

(G-3616)
CHAPMAN LUMBER INC
Also Called: Ace Hardware
224 Watertown Rd (06787-1920)
PHONE..................................860 283-6213
David Chapman, *Pr*
Stuart Chapman, *
EMP: 30 **EST:** 1952
SQ FT: 50,000
SALES (est): 5.33MM **Privately Held**
Web: www.chapmanlumberinc.com
SIC: 5211 2431 5231 Millwork and lumber;
Millwork; Paint, glass, and wallpaper stores

(G-3617)
CORESLAB STRUCTURES CONN INC
1023 Waterbury Rd (06787-2028)
P.O. Box 279 (06787-0279)
PHONE..................................860 283-8281
Mario Franciosa, *Pr*
Leon Grant, *
Frank Franciosa, *
EMP: 80 **EST:** 1997
SQ FT: 45,000
SALES (est): 21.77MM
SALES (corp-wide): 27.34MM **Privately Held**
Web: www.coreslab.com
SIC: 8712 1771 3272 Architectural services;
Concrete work; Precast terrazzo or
concrete products
HQ: Coreslab Structures (Ont) Inc
205 Coreslab Dr
Dundas ON L9H 0
905 689-3993

(G-3618)
EDWARD SEGAL INC
360 Reynolds Bridge Rd (06787-1914)
P.O. Box 429 (06787-0429)
PHONE..................................860 283-5821
David Segal, *Pr*
Richard Segal, *Stockholder*
Leslie Segal, *Sec*
▲ **EMP:** 20 **EST:** 1942
SQ FT: 20,000
SALES (est): 4.47MM **Privately Held**
Web: www.edwardsegalinc.com
SIC: 3559 Buttonhole and eyelet machines
and attachments, industrial

(G-3619)
ELEMENT 119 LLC
Also Called: Element 119
296 Reynolds Bridge Rd (06787-1996)
P.O. Box 100 (06787-0100)
PHONE..................................860 358-0119
Andrew Zeppa, *Pr*
EMP: 10 **EST:** 2010
SQ FT: 4,000
SALES (est): 2.13MM **Privately Held**
Web: www.element119.com
SIC: 2851 Undercoatings, paint

(G-3620)
GK AUTOMATICS INCORPORATED
Also Called: Thomaston Swiss
437 S Main St (06787-1816)
P.O. Box 247 (06787-0247)
PHONE..................................860 283-5878
George Kowaleski, *Pr*
EMP: 14 **EST:** 1947
SQ FT: 20,000
SALES (est): 475.88K **Privately Held**
Web: www.tbwprecision.com
SIC: 3451 Screw machine products

(G-3621)
HDB INC
Also Called: Homer D Bronson Company, The
135 S Main St Ste 1 (06787-1754)
PHONE..................................860 379-9901
John Zoldy, *Pr*
Bob Pulford, *VP*
EMP: 15 **EST:** 1839
SQ FT: 77,000
SALES (est): 910.89K **Privately Held**
SIC: 3429 3444 Hardware, nec; Sheet metal
specialties, not stamped

(G-3622)
J&J PRECISION INC
116 Waterbury Rd (06787-1829)
PHONE..................................860 283-8243
John Stephen Maxwell, *Pr*
EMP: 70 **EST:** 1971
SQ FT: 3,000
SALES (est): 7.71MM **Privately Held**
Web: www.jjprecision.com
SIC: 3965 2834 3469 Eyelets, metal:
clothing, fabrics, boots, or shoes;
Pharmaceutical preparations; Stamping
metal for the trade

(G-3623)
LASER TOOL CO INC
98 N Main St (06787-1654)
P.O. Box 278 (06787-0278)
PHONE..................................860 283-8284
Faye Duquette, *Pr*
EMP: 14 **EST:** 1948
SQ FT: 4,840
SALES (est): 805.36K **Privately Held**
Web: www.lasertoolco.com
SIC: 3541 Machine tools, metal cutting type

(G-3624)
METALLON INC
1415 Waterbury Rd (06787-2030)
PHONE..................................860 283-8265
Paul P Ayoub, *Prin*
Alexander Ayoub, *Prin*
Kimberly Ayoub, *Prin*
EMP: 50 **EST:** 1964
SQ FT: 30,000
SALES (est): 9.5MM **Privately Held**
Web: www.metallon.com

SIC: **3469** 3728   Stamping metal for the trade
; Aircraft assemblies, subassemblies, and
parts, nec

(G-3625)
NATIONAL SPRING & STAMPING INC
135 S Main St Ste 8 (06787-1754)
P.O. Box 369 (06787-0369)
PHONE...............................860 283-0203
Walter Janczyk, *Pr*
Raymond Kowalec, *VP*
William Yeske Iii, *Sec*
EMP: 15 **EST:** 1984
SQ FT: 8,000
SALES (est): 495.85K **Privately Held**
SIC: 3495 3469   Wire springs; Stamping
metal for the trade

(G-3626)
QUALITY ROLLING DEBURRING INC
135 S Main St Ste 3 (06787-1754)
P.O. Box 128 (06787-0128)
PHONE...............................860 283-0271
George Lacapra, *Ch Bd*
George Lacapra Junior, *Pr*
Ronald Stango, *
EMP: 44 **EST:** 1949
SQ FT: 110,000
SALES (est): 2.38MM **Privately Held**
Web: www.unimetal.com
SIC: 3471   Electroplating of metals or
formed products

(G-3627)
REYNOLDS CARBIDE DIE CO INC
27 Reynolds Bridge Rd (06787-1910)
P.O. Box 326 (06787-0326)
PHONE...............................860 283-8246
James Zaccaria, *Pr*
Michael Masi Junior, *VP*
EMP: 26 **EST:** 1971
SQ FT: 12,000
SALES (est): 1.15MM **Privately Held**
Web: www.reynoldscarbide.com
SIC: 3552 3544   Textile machinery; Special
dies and tools

(G-3628)
SELECTIVES LLC
166 Litchfield St (06787-1427)
P.O. Box 336 (06787-0336)
PHONE...............................860 585-1956
Ernie Coss, *Owner*
EMP: 7 **EST:** 2011
SALES (est): 220.39K **Privately Held**
SIC: 3089   Plastics products, nec

(G-3629)
SILGAN DSPNSING SYSTEMS CVIT A
Also Called: Albea Metal Americas
60 Electric Ave (06787-1617)
PHONE...............................860 274-6791
Henry F Seebach Junior, *Pr*
John Spino, *
▲ **EMP:** 375 **EST:** 2011
SALES (est): 128.7MM
SALES (corp-wide): 355.83K **Privately
Held**
SIC: 3086   Packaging and shipping
materials, foamed plastics
HQ: Albea Services
Zac Des Barbanniers Le Signac
Gennevilliers 92230
181932000

(G-3630)
SILGAN DSPNSING SYSTEMS THMSTO
Also Called: Albea
60 Electric Ave (06787-1617)
PHONE...............................860 283-2000
Francois Luscan, *CEO*
▲ **EMP:** 370 **EST:** 1991
SQ FT: 150,000
SALES (est): 92.94MM
SALES (corp-wide): 355.83K **Privately
Held**
Web: www.silgandispensing.com
SIC: 2844   Cosmetic preparations
HQ: Albea Americas, Inc.
191 State Route 31 N
Washington NJ 07882

(G-3631)
STEVENS COMPANY INCORPORATED
1085 Waterbury Rd # 1 (06787-2028)
P.O. Box 428 (06787-0428)
PHONE...............................860 283-8201
Doug Stevens, *Pr*
Jannette Stevens, *
Michele Caulfield, *
▲ **EMP:** 65 **EST:** 1950
SQ FT: 40,000
SALES (est): 8.51MM **Privately Held**
Web: www.stevenscompanyinc.com
SIC: 3469 3965   Stamping metal for the trade
; Eyelets, metal: clothing, fabrics, boots, or
shoes

(G-3632)
STEWART EFI LLC
332 Reynolds Bridge Rd (06787-1914)
PHONE...............................860 283-2523
Daniel Stokes, *Mgr*
EMP: 10
SALES (corp-wide): 98.16MM **Privately
Held**
Web: www.stewartefi.com
SIC: 3469   Stamping metal for the trade
PA: Stewart Efi, Llc
45 Old Waterbury Rd
Thomaston CT 06787
860 283-8213

(G-3633)
STEWART EFI LLC (PA)
45 Old Waterbury Rd (06787-1903)
PHONE...............................860 283-8213
Mike Morrissey, *Managing Member*
Dan Stokes, *Managing Member**
Bernie Rosselli, *
Phillip Rejeski, *
John Labis, *
EMP: 105 **EST:** 2003
SQ FT: 98,000
SALES (est): 98.16MM
SALES (corp-wide): 98.16MM **Privately
Held**
Web: www.stewartefi.com
SIC: 3469   Stamping metal for the trade

(G-3634)
STEWART EFI CONNECTICUT LLC
45 Old Waterbury Rd (06787-1903)
PHONE...............................860 283-8213
Daniel Stokes, *Managing Member*
EMP: 110 **EST:** 2003
SQ FT: 98,000
SALES (est): 17.59MM
SALES (corp-wide): 98.16MM **Privately
Held**
Web: www.stewartefi.com

SIC: **3469**   Stamping metal for the trade
PA: Stewart Efi, Llc
45 Old Waterbury Rd
Thomaston CT 06787
860 283-8213

(G-3635)
SUMMIT CORPORATION OF AMERICA
Also Called: Summit Finishing Division
1430 Waterbury Rd (06787-2098)
PHONE...............................860 283-4391
Harry M Scoble, *Pr*
Larry Buhl, *
Daniel Stokes, *
Linda L Scapellati, *
▲ **EMP:** 83 **EST:** 1948
SQ FT: 140,000
SALES (est): 10MM **Privately Held**
Web: www.summitplating.com
SIC: 3471 3479   Electroplating of metals or
formed products; Etching on metals

(G-3636)
THE PETIT TOOL CO
1387 Waterbury Rd (06787-2030)
P.O. Box 206 (06787-0206)
PHONE...............................860 283-9626
EMP: 30 **EST:** 1963
SALES (est): 4.31MM **Privately Held**
Web: www.petittool.com
SIC: 1761 5033 3444 3354   Roofing, siding,
and sheetmetal work; Roofing, siding, and
insulation; Sheet metalwork; Aluminum
extruded products

(G-3637)
THOMASTN-MDTOWN SCREW MCH PDTS
550 N Main St (06787-1315)
P.O. Box 249 (06787-0249)
PHONE...............................860 283-9796
Robert P Lyman, *Pr*
Celeste Parsons, *VP*
EMP: 15 **EST:** 1963
SQ FT: 7,500
SALES (est): 373.01K **Privately Held**
Web: www.screwmachineproducts.net
SIC: 3451   Screw machine products

(G-3638)
THOMASTON INDUSTRIES INC
41 Electric Ave (06787-1651)
P.O. Box 308 (06787-0308)
PHONE...............................860 283-4358
Dennis Diemand, *Pr*
EMP: 10 **EST:** 1801
SALES (est): 902.97K **Privately Held**
Web: www.thomastonindustries.com
SIC: 3451 3999   Screw machine products;
Barber and beauty shop equipment

(G-3639)
TREADWELL CORPORATION
341 Railroad St (06787-1667)
P.O. Box 458 (06787-0458)
PHONE...............................860 283-7600
Robert Johnson, *CEO*
John A Johnson, *CEO*
Robert Johnson, *COO*
Steven Malaspina, *Ex VP*
Michael Patruski, *VP*
EMP: 22 **EST:** 1900
SQ FT: 30,000
SALES (est): 4.82MM **Privately Held**
Web: www.treadwellcorp.com
SIC: 3564   Air purification equipment

(G-3640)
UNIMETAL SURFACE FINISHING LLC (PA)
135 S Main St (06787-1754)
P.O. Box 902 (06787-0902)
PHONE...............................860 283-0271
George Lacapra Junior, *Managing Member*
EMP: 42 **EST:** 2011
SALES (est): 20.44MM
SALES (corp-wide): 20.44MM **Privately
Held**
Web: www.unimetal.com
SIC: 2843   Finishing agents

(G-3641)
WARD LEONARD CT LLC (DH)
401 Watertown Rd (06787-1990)
PHONE...............................860 283-5801
George Whittier, *CEO*
Chris Spafford, *Prin*
Pat Bussie, *Pr*
Jared Barefield, *VP*
◆ **EMP:** 56 **EST:** 1955
SQ FT: 135,000
SALES (est): 55.54MM
SALES (corp-wide): 653.43MM **Privately
Held**
Web: www.fairbanksmorsedefense.com
SIC: 3621 3625   Motors, electric; Motor
controls, electric
HQ: Ward Leonard Operating Llc
401 Watertown Rd
Thomaston CT 06787
860 283-5801

(G-3642)
WARD LEONARD CT LLC
401 Watertown Rd (06787-1990)
PHONE...............................860 283-2294
George Whittier, *CEO*
EMP: 24
SQ FT: 150,000
SALES (corp-wide): 653.43MM **Privately
Held**
Web: www.fairbanksmorsedefense.com
SIC: 3621   Generators and sets, electric
HQ: Ward Leonard Ct Llc
401 Watertown Rd
Thomaston CT 06787
860 283-5801

(G-3643)
WARD LEONARD OPERATING LLC (DH)
401 Watertown Rd (06787-1990)
PHONE...............................860 283-5801
George Whittier, *CEO*
EMP: 25 **EST:** 1994
SALES (est): 55.54MM
SALES (corp-wide): 653.43MM **Privately
Held**
Web: www.fairbanksmorsedefense.com
SIC: 1731 3621 7694   Electrical work;
Motors and generators; Armature rewinding
shops
HQ: Fairbanks Morse, Llc
701 White Ave
Beloit WI 53511
800 356-6955

(G-3644)
WARD LONARD HOUMA HOLDINGS LLC
401 Watertown Rd (06787-1990)
PHONE...............................860 283-5801
Mike Clute, *Pr*
EMP: 52 **EST:** 2015
SALES (est): 1.56MM
SALES (corp-wide): 4.99MM **Privately
Held**

Web: www.fairbanksmorsedefense.com
SIC: **1731** 3621 7694   Electrical work;
Motors and generators; Armature rewinding
shops
HQ: WI Intermediate Holdings, Llc
401 Watertown Rd
Thomaston CT 06787
860 283-5801

(G-3645)
WHYCO FINISHING TECH LLC
670 Waterbury Rd (06787-2099)
PHONE..............................860 283-5826
EMP: 47 **EST:** 2009
SQ FT: 100,000
SALES (est): 10.28MM **Privately Held**
Web: www.whyco.com
SIC: **3471**   Electroplating of metals or
formed products

(G-3646)
WOODCRAFTERS LLP
118 Williams St (06787-1544)
PHONE..............................860 355-1022
Craig Zenobia, *Owner*
EMP: 7 **EST:** 2004
SALES (est): 74K **Privately Held**
SIC: **3553**   Cabinet makers' machinery

(G-3647)
ZERO CHECK LLC
Also Called: Zero Check
297 Reynolds Bridge Rd (06787-1974)
P.O. Box 903 (06787-0903)
PHONE..............................860 283-5629
EMP: 8 **EST:** 1983
SQ FT: 8,600
SALES (est): 969.46K **Privately Held**
Web: www.zerocheck.com
SIC: **3545**   Gauges (machine tool
accessories)

Thompson
Windham County

(G-3648)
CENTURY TOOL CO INC
753 Thompson Rd (06277-1939)
P.O. Box 314 (06277-0314)
PHONE..............................860 923-9523
Joseph Simonelli, *Pr*
EMP: 18 **EST:** 1973
SQ FT: 8,000
SALES (est): 2.63MM **Privately Held**
Web: www.centurytoolusa.com
SIC: **3544**   Special dies and tools

(G-3649)
DELTA TOOL CO INC
Rr 193 (06277)
PHONE..............................860 923-2012
Joseph Simonelli, *Pr*
Kathie Swanson, *Treas*
EMP: 8 **EST:** 1983
SQ FT: 4,000
SALES (est): 749.63K **Privately Held**
SIC: **3544**   Special dies and tools

(G-3650)
IVANHOE TOOL & DIE
COMPANY INC
590 Thompson Rd (06277-2237)
P.O. Box 218 (06277-0218)
PHONE..............................860 923-9541
EMP: 30 **EST:** 1952
SALES (est): 4.95MM **Privately Held**
Web: www.ivanhoetool.com
SIC: **3544**   Industrial molds

(G-3651)
MOLDVISION LLC
316 County Home Rd (06277-2845)
PHONE..............................860 315-1025
John Carpenter, *Pr*
EMP: 8 **EST:** 2016
SALES (est): 283.19K **Privately Held**
Web: www.envbrinc.com
SIC: **3544**   Industrial molds

(G-3652)
NUMA TOOL COMPANY (PA)
646 Thompson Rd (06277-2252)
P.O. Box 348 (06277-0348)
PHONE..............................860 923-9551
Ralph H Leonard, *Pr*
Mark Stickney, *
▼ **EMP:** 75 **EST:** 1967
SQ FT: 52,000
SALES (est): 23.62MM
SALES (corp-wide): 23.62MM **Privately
Held**
Web: www.numahammers.com
SIC: **3532** 3531 3533 5082   Drills and drilling
equipment, mining (except oil and gas);
Hammer mills (rock and ore crushing
machines), portable; Oil and gas field
machinery; General construction machinery
and equipment

(G-3653)
TOTAL DRILLING SUPPLY LLC
144 New Rd (06277-1913)
PHONE..............................860 923-1091
Robert Neundorf, *Pr*
Debra Neundorf, *CFO*
EMP: 10 **EST:** 2012
SALES (est): 985.96K **Privately Held**
Web: www.totaldrillingsupply.com
SIC: **1381**   Drilling oil and gas wells

Tolland
Tolland County

(G-3654)
ACCU-RITE TOOL & MFG CO
23 Industrial Park Rd W Ste A
(06084-2861)
PHONE..............................860 688-4844
Steve Gessay, *Pr*
Christophe Gessay, *VP*
EMP: 11 **EST:** 1956
SQ FT: 6,500
SALES (est): 2.1MM **Privately Held**
Web: www.accuritetool.com
SIC: **3545**   Machine tool attachments and
accessories

(G-3655)
B & D MACHINE INC
30 Industrial Park Rd E (06084-2874)
P.O. Box 791 (06084-0791)
PHONE..............................860 871-9226
Robert Stutz, *Pr*
Donald Gagnon, *VP*
Kenneth Gibbons, *Treas*
EMP: 24 **EST:** 1960
SQ FT: 9,000
SALES (est): 907.29K **Privately Held**
Web: www.banddmachine.com
SIC: **3544**   Special dies and tools

(G-3656)
DATA TECHNOLOGY INC
24 Industrial Park Rd W (06084-2806)
PHONE..............................860 871-8082
David Buckley, *Training Chief Executive
Officer*

David Buckley, *Pr*
Steve Gore, *
EMP: 1710 **EST:** 1960
SQ FT: 29,000
SALES (est): 2.47MM
SALES (corp-wide): 258.77MM **Privately
Held**
SIC: **3577** 3829 3827   Computer peripheral
equipment, nec; Surveying instruments and
accessories; Optical instruments and lenses
PA: Gerber Scientific Llc
24 Indl Pk Rd W
Tolland CT 06084
860 871-8082

(G-3657)
DDM METAL FINISHING
COMPANY
25 Industrial Park Rd W (06084-2806)
P.O. Box 687 (06084-0687)
PHONE..............................860 872-4683
Daniel R Castonguay, *Pr*
EMP: 8 **EST:** 1974
SQ FT: 2,500
SALES (est): 865.58K **Privately Held**
SIC: **3471**   Buffing for the trade

(G-3658)
E & S GAGE INC
38 Gerber Dr (06084-2851)
PHONE..............................860 872-5917
Kevin Hilinski, *Prin*
Kyle Percy, *Prin*
Elizabeth Furey, *Prin*
EMP: 15 **EST:** 2006
SALES (est): 920.49K **Privately Held**
Web: www.esgage.com
SIC: **3423**   Hand and edge tools, nec

(G-3659)
E AND S GAGE INC
Also Called: E & S Gauge Company
38 Gerber Dr (06084-2851)
PHONE..............................860 872-5917
Kevin S Hilinski, *Pr*
EMP: 12 **EST:** 1953
SQ FT: 2,500
SALES (est): 1.49MM **Privately Held**
Web: www.esgage.com
SIC: **3545** 3544   Gauges (machine tool
accessories); Special dies, tools, jigs, and
fixtures

(G-3660)
ENVIRONICS INC
69 Industrial Park Rd E (06084-2873)
PHONE..............................860 872-1111
Rachel Stansel, *Pr*
Catherine S Dunn, *CEO*
Terrence P Dunn, *COO*
Rachel M Stansel, *VP*
EMP: 18 **EST:** 1986
SQ FT: 15,000
SALES (est): 4.4MM **Privately Held**
Web: www.environics.com
SIC: **3823** 3821   Gas flow computers,
industrial process type; Calibration tapes,
for physical testing machines

(G-3661)
GERBER SCIENTIFIC LLC (PA)
24 Industrial Park Rd W (06084)
PHONE..............................860 871-8082
Michael Elia, *Pr*
John Capasso, *
Karen Watson, *Corporate Vice President*
James Martin, *
◆ **EMP:** 200 **EST:** 1948
SQ FT: 250,000
SALES (est): 258.77MM

SALES (corp-wide): 258.77MM **Privately
Held**
Web: www.lectra.com
SIC: **3993** 7336 3851 7372   Signs and
advertising specialties; Commercial art and
graphic design; Lenses, ophthalmic;
Prepackaged software

(G-3662)
GERBER TECHNOLOGY LLC
(HQ)
Also Called: Gerber Scientific
24 Industrial Park Rd W (06084-2806)
PHONE..............................800 321-2448
Mohit Uberoi, *CEO*
James Martin, *VP*
Patricia L Burmahl, *Sr VP*
Theresa J Kenny, *Treas*
David Kralic, *CFO*
◆ **EMP:** 344 **EST:** 1968
SQ FT: 260,000
SALES (est): 207.72MM
SALES (corp-wide): 218.21MM **Privately
Held**
Web: www.lectra.com
SIC: **3559** 7371   Foundry machinery and
equipment; Custom computer programming
services
PA: Lectra
Nu 16 A 18
Paris 75116
153644200

(G-3663)
IREX MACHINING INC
4 Midland Dr (06084-2505)
PHONE..............................860 870-1885
Ireneusz Kotlewski, *Prin*
EMP: 7 **EST:** 2015
SALES (est): 34.7K **Privately Held**
Web: irex-machine-inc.hub.biz
SIC: **3599**   Machine shop, jobbing and repair

(G-3664)
SOLDREAM SPCIAL PROCESS -
WLDG
203 Hartford Tpke (06084-2821)
PHONE..............................860 858-5247
EMP: 8 **EST:** 2018
SALES (est): 241.23K **Privately Held**
Web: www.soldream.com
SIC: **3599**   Machine shop, jobbing and repair

Torrington
Litchfield County

(G-3665)
2600 ALBANY AVENUE LLC
1688 E Main St (06790-3519)
PHONE..............................336 632-0005
Maria Domack, *Prin*
EMP: 8 **EST:** 2009
SALES (est): 341.81K **Privately Held**
SIC: **3561**   Pumps and pumping equipment

(G-3666)
A V I INTERNATIONAL INC
3240 Winsted Rd (06790-2233)
PHONE..............................860 482-8345
Clifford W Burrell, *Pr*
Deborah A Burrell, *Sec*
Adon Burrell, *Treas*
◆ **EMP:** 8 **EST:** 1993
SQ FT: 4,600
SALES (est): 2.12MM **Privately Held**
Web: www.avipumps.com

SIC: **7699** 3561　Pumps and pumping
equipment repair; Pumps and pumping
equipment

(G-3667)
ALLIANCE CARPET CUSHION CO (HQ)
180 Church St (06790-5225)
P.O. Box 1174 (06790-1174)
PHONE..................................860 489-4273
Jack Lens, *Supervisor*
▲ **EMP:** 60 **EST:** 1998
SALES (est): 9.83MM **Publicly Held**
SIC: **1771** 2273　Flooring contractor; Carpets
and rugs
PA: Mohawk Industries, Inc.
160 S Industrial Blvd
Calhoun GA 30701

(G-3668)
ALTEK COMPANY
89 Commercial Blvd Ste 1 (06790-7215)
P.O. Box 1128 (06790-1128)
PHONE..................................860 482-7626
Stephen Altschuler, *Pr*
Joan Altschuler, *
EMP: 180 **EST:** 1972
SALES (est): 23.74MM **Privately Held**
Web: www.altekelectronics.com
SIC: **3625**　Relays and industrial controls

(G-3669)
ALTEK ELECTRONICS INC
89 Commercial Blvd (06790-7215)
P.O. Box 1128 (06790-1128)
PHONE..................................860 482-7626
Stephen Altschuler, *Ch Bd*
David Altschuler, *
Sabrina Beck, *
▲ **EMP:** 170 **EST:** 1972
SQ FT: 65,000
SALES (est): 46.36MM **Privately Held**
Web: www.altekelectronics.com
SIC: **3825** 3599 3625 3672　Measuring
instruments and meters, electric; Machine
and other job shop work; Control
equipment, electric; Printed circuit boards

(G-3670)
ANDRITZ SHW INC
90 Commercial Blvd (06790-3097)
P.O. Box 238 (06790-0238)
PHONE..................................860 496-8888
George Shank, *CEO*
George L Shank, *
Ulrich Severing, *
▲ **EMP:** 30 **EST:** 2005
SQ FT: 50,000
SALES (est): 10.32MM
SALES (corp-wide): 355.83K **Privately Held**
SIC: **3554**　Paper industries machinery
HQ: Shw Casting Technologies Gmbh
Stiewingstr. 101
Aalen BW 73433

(G-3671)
BERKSHIRE PHOTONICS LLC
89 Commercial Blvd Ste 4 (06790-7215)
P.O. Box 595 (06794-0595)
PHONE..................................860 868-0412
Jeffrey Miller, *Pr*
EMP: 8 **EST:** 2004
SQ FT: 2,200
SALES (est): 1.69MM **Privately Held**
Web: www.berkshirephotonics.com
SIC: **3559**　Optical lens machinery

(G-3672)
BICRON ELECTRONICS LLC (HQ)
427 Goshen Rd (06790-2601)
PHONE..................................860 482-2524
Sarah Harris, *Pr*
▲ **EMP:** 79 **EST:** 1964
SQ FT: 30,000
SALES (est): 11.7MM
SALES (corp-wide): 36.11MM **Privately Held**
Web: www.bicronusa.com
SIC: **3612** 3679 3677　Power transformers,
electric; Solenoids for electronic applications
; Electronic coils and transformers
PA: Incrore, Llc
311 Sinclair Rd
Bristol PA 19007
267 557-3901

(G-3673)
BRISTOL PRESS
Also Called: Thomaston Express, The Div
188 Main St (06790-5201)
P.O. Box 2158 (06011-2158)
PHONE..................................860 584-0501
Robert Jelenic, *Pr*
EMP: 87 **EST:** 1871
SQ FT: 24,000
SALES (est): 849.99K
SALES (corp-wide): 293.08MM **Privately Held**
Web: www.bristolpress.com
SIC: **2711**　Commercial printing and
newspaper publishing combined
PA: Journal Register Company
5 Hanover Sq Fl 25
New York NY 10004
212 257-7212

(G-3674)
COLONIAL BRONZE COMPANY
511 Winsted Rd (06790-2932)
P.O. Box 207 (06790-0207)
PHONE..................................860 489-9233
Jamie V Gregg, *CEO*
▲ **EMP:** 55 **EST:** 1927
SQ FT: 50,000
SALES (est): 9.58MM **Privately Held**
Web: www.colonialbronze.com
SIC: **3429** 3432　Builders' hardware;
Plumbing fixture fittings and trim

(G-3675)
COMMERCIAL SEWING INC
65 Grant St (06790-6899)
P.O. Box 1173 (06790-1173)
PHONE..................................860 482-5509
Samuel G Mazzarelli, *CEO*
Greg Perosino, *
Stephen Mazzarelli, *
David Mazzarelli, *
▲ **EMP:** 140 **EST:** 1967
SQ FT: 30,000
SALES (est): 24.86MM **Privately Held**
Web: www.commercialsewing.com
SIC: **3161** 2394　Luggage; Liners and
covers, fabric: made from purchased
materials

(G-3676)
CONAIR LLC
Also Called: Waring Products Division
314 Ella Grasso Ave (06790-2345)
P.O. Box 3201 (06790-8181)
PHONE..................................800 492-7464
Richard Dombroski, *Mgr*
EMP: 66
Web: validate.perfdrive.com

SIC: **3634** 5064 8741 7629　Electric
housewares and fans; Electrical
appliances, television and radio;
Management services; Electrical repair
shops
HQ: Conair Llc
1 Cummings Point Rd
Stamford CT 06902
203 351-9000

(G-3677)
DYMAX OLIGOMERS & COATINGS
318 Industrial Ln (06790-7709)
PHONE..................................860 626-7006
Greg Bachmann, *Ch*
Roberta E Hagstrom, *Pr*
▲ **EMP:** 10 **EST:** 1987
SQ FT: 15,000
SALES (est): 6.14MM
SALES (corp-wide): 125.44MM **Privately Held**
Web: www.bomar-chem.com
SIC: **2869**　Industrial organic chemicals, nec
HQ: Dymax Materials, Inc.
51 Greenwoods Rd
Torrington CT 06790

(G-3678)
FCT ELECTRONICS LP
Also Called: Fct
187 Commercial Blvd (06790-3098)
PHONE..................................860 482-2800
Toni Kling, *Mng Pt*
Daniel J Schreck, *
Siegfried Ratzel, *
Anton Kling, *
▲ **EMP:** 55 **EST:** 1999
SQ FT: 26,500
SALES (est): 10.99MM **Privately Held**
SIC: **5065** 3678　Connectors, electronic;
Electronic connectors

(G-3679)
FCT ELECTRONICS MANAGEMENT INC
187 Commercial Blvd (06790-3098)
PHONE..................................860 482-2800
Daniel Schreck, *Pr*
Siegfried Ratzel, *Treas*
EMP: 15 **EST:** 1999
SALES (est): 107.49K **Privately Held**
SIC: **3678**　Electronic connectors

(G-3680)
FEDERAL BUSINESS PRODUCTS INC
368 Ella Grasso Ave (06790-2345)
PHONE..................................860 482-6231
Bob Beltrandi, *Bmch Mgr*
EMP: 20
SQ FT: 32,500
SALES (corp-wide): 20MM **Privately Held**
Web: www.feddirect.com
SIC: **7389** 2761　Personal service agents,
brokers, and bureaus; Manifold business
forms
PA: Federal Business Products Inc
150 Clove Rd Ste 5
Little Falls NJ 07424
973 667-9800

(G-3681)
FRANKLIN PRODUCTS INC (PA)
153 Water St (06790-5339)
P.O. Box 117 (06790-0117)
PHONE..................................860 482-0266
◆ **EMP:** 49 **EST:** 1988
SALES (est): 22.14MM

SALES (corp-wide): 22.14MM **Privately Held**
Web: www.franklinproductsinc.com
SIC: **2531**　Seats, aircraft

(G-3682)
FUELCELL ENERGY INC
Also Called: Fuel Cell Manufacturing
539 Technology Park Dr (06790-2594)
PHONE..................................860 496-1111
Christopher R Bentley, *Pr*
EMP: 35
SALES (corp-wide): 123.39MM **Publicly Held**
Web: www.fuelcellenergy.com
SIC: **3674** 3621 3699　Fuel cells, solid state;
Motors and generators; Electrical
equipment and supplies, nec
PA: Fuelcell Energy, Inc.
3 Great Pasture Rd
Danbury CT 06810
203 825-6000

(G-3683)
GREGOR TECHNOLOGIES LLC
529 Technology Park Dr (06790-2594)
PHONE..................................860 482-2569
David H Hannah, *Managing Member*
Janice Gregorich, *
John Gregorich, *
Karla R Lewis, *
EMP: 49 **EST:** 1989
SQ FT: 40,000
SALES (est): 11.78MM
SALES (corp-wide): 17.02B **Publicly Held**
Web: www.gregortech.com
SIC: **3599**　Machine shop, jobbing and repair
HQ: Metals Usa Holdings Corp.
4901 Nw 17th Way Ste 405
Fort Lauderdale FL 33309

(G-3684)
IFFLAND LUMBER COMPANY INC
747 S Main St (06790-6926)
P.O. Box 477 (06790-0477)
PHONE..................................860 489-9218
TOLL FREE: 800
Earl Iffland, *Pr*
Thomas Iffland, *
EMP: 35 **EST:** 1972
SQ FT: 100,000
SALES (est): 4.63MM **Privately Held**
Web: www.ifflandlumber.com
SIC: **5211** 3273　Planing mill products and
lumber; Ready-mixed concrete

(G-3685)
JAMES A BEAN CORPORATION
89 Commercial Blvd Ste 3 (06790-7215)
PHONE..................................860 489-1404
James A Bean, *Pr*
Jim Bean, *Pr*
Alan Bean, *Sec*
EMP: 17 **EST:** 1989
SQ FT: 26,000
SALES (est): 3.2MM **Privately Held**
Web: www.questplastics.com
SIC: **3089** 3559　Injection molding of plastics
; Glass making machinery: blowing,
molding, forming, etc.

(G-3686)
JEFF MFG INC
679 Riverside Ave (06790-4535)
PHONE..................................860 482-1387
Jeff Roesing, *Pr*
Jeff Currier, *VP*
EMP: 10 **EST:** 1994
SQ FT: 2,000

SALES (est): 750.31K **Privately Held**
Web: www.jeffmfg.com
SIC: 7692 3599   Welding repair; Machine and other job shop work

(G-3687)

K-TECH INTERNATIONAL INC

56 Ella Grasso Ave (06790-2341)
PHONE..................860 489-9399
Samuel J Massameno, *Pr*
Samuel Massameno, *
Kay E Massameno, *
EMP: 25 **EST:** 1981
SQ FT: 10,800
SALES (est): 4.11MM **Privately Held**
Web: www.ktechonline.com
SIC: 3534 3661 3499   Elevators and equipment; Telephone and telegraph apparatus; Barricades, metal

(G-3688)

KENT SCIENTIFIC CORPORATION

1116 Litchfield St (06790-6029)
PHONE..................860 626-1172
Andrew H Ide, *Pr*
Deborah Ide, *VP*
Cindy Lundgern, *Mgr*
▲ **EMP:** 15 **EST:** 1989
SQ FT: 4,500
SALES (est): 4.26MM **Privately Held**
Web: www.kentscientific.com
SIC: 5999 5961 3821   Medical apparatus and supplies; Electronic shopping; Laboratory apparatus and furniture

(G-3689)

O & G INDUSTRIES INC (PA)

112 Wall St (06790-5464)
PHONE..................860 489-9261
◆ **EMP:** 70 **EST:** 1923
SALES (est): 496.36MM
SALES (corp-wide): 496.36MM **Privately Held**
Web: www.ogind.com
SIC: 1542 1541 1611 1623   Commercial and office building, new construction; Industrial buildings, new construction, nec; General contractor, highway and street construction; Sewer line construction

(G-3690)

ODDO PRINT SHOP INC

Also Called: Oddo Print Shop & Copy Center
142 E Main St (06790-5429)
PHONE..................860 489-6585
Patricia Meneguzzo, *Pr*
Lisa Meneguzzo, *Sec*
EMP: 8 **EST:** 1946
SALES (est): 962.47K **Privately Held**
SIC: 2752 7334 2791 7331   Offset printing; Photocopying and duplicating services; Typesetting; Mailing service

(G-3691)

PANACOL-USA INC

142 Industrial Ln (06790-2325)
PHONE..................860 738-7449
EMP: 15 **EST:** 1994
SQ FT: 34,000
SALES (est): 2.31MM **Privately Held**
Web: www.panacol-usa.com
SIC: 2891   Adhesives and sealants

(G-3692)

RBC AIRCRAFT PRODUCTS INC

2788 Winsted Rd (06790-2427)
PHONE..................860 626-7800
Fred Pasler, *Brnch Mgr*
EMP: 93

SALES (corp-wide): 1.47B **Publicly Held**
Web: www.rbcbearings.com
SIC: 5085 3562   Bearings; Ball and roller bearings
HQ: Rbc Aircraft Products, Inc.
1 Tribiology Ctr
Oxford CT 06478
203 267-7001

(G-3693)

REGISTER CITIZEN PUBLISHING

Also Called: Torrington Register Citizen
59 Field St (06790-4942)
P.O. Box 58 (06790-0058)
PHONE..................860 489-3121
FAX: 860 489-6790
EMP: 120
SQ FT: 50,000
SALES (est): 5.87MM
SALES (corp-wide): 6.5B **Privately Held**
SIC: 2711   Commercial printing and newspaper publishing combined
PA: The Hearst Corporation
300 W 57th St Fl 42
New York NY 10019
212 649-2000

(G-3694)

REIDVILLE HYDRAULICS & MFG INC

175 Industrial Ln (06790-2326)
PHONE..................860 496-1133
Larry J Becker, *Prin*
Larry J Becker, *Pr*
Jeanette Becker, *
▲ **EMP:** 25 **EST:** 1955
SQ FT: 23,000
SALES (est): 4.84MM **Privately Held**
Web: www.reidvillehydraulics.com
SIC: 3594 3599   Motors: hydraulic, fluid power, or air; Machine shop, jobbing and repair

(G-3695)

SEITZ LLC

212 Industrial Ln (06790-2325)
PHONE..................860 489-0476
Brian Anderson, *Pr*
▲ **EMP:** 155 **EST:** 1949
SQ FT: 80,000
SALES (est): 43.61MM
SALES (corp-wide): 61.99MM **Privately Held**
Web: www.moldeddevices.com
SIC: 5084   Industrial machine parts; Injection molded finished plastics products, nec
PA: Molded Devices, Inc.
740 W Knox Rd
Tempe AZ 85284
480 785-9100

(G-3696)

SILGAN DISPENSING

669 Prospect St (06790-4917)
PHONE..................860 283-2025
EMP: 11 **EST:** 2020
SALES (est): 2.36MM **Privately Held**
Web: www.silgandispensing.com
SIC: 3089   Plastics containers, except foam

(G-3697)

STRATIS VISUALS LLC (PA)

129 Industrial Ln (06790-2326)
PHONE..................860 482-1208
EMP: 44 **EST:** 1975
SALES (est): 9.85MM
SALES (corp-wide): 9.85MM **Privately Held**
Web: www.mccoyprinting.com

SIC: 2752 2759   Commercial printing, lithographic; Screen printing

(G-3698)

TECHNICAL INDUSTRIES INC (PA)

336 Pinewoods Rd (06790-2350)
PHONE..................860 489-2160
EMP: 336 **EST:** 1994
SQ FT: 25,000
SALES (est): 23.11MM **Privately Held**
Web: www.technicalindustriesinc.com
SIC: 3089   Injection molding of plastics

(G-3699)

THERAP TECHNE LLC ✪

333 Kennedy Dr Ste R101 (06790-3060)
PHONE..................203 596-7553
James Kelly, *Managing Member*
EMP: 8 **EST:** 2023
SALES (est): 348.5K **Privately Held**
SIC: 3577   Data conversion equipment, media-to-media: computer

(G-3700)

TOCE BROTHERS INCORPORATED (PA)

145 E Main St (06790-5432)
PHONE..................860 496-2080
TOLL FREE: 800
Russell Barrett, *Pr*
Debra A Lopardo, *
Dominic Toce, *
▲ **EMP:** 30 **EST:** 1924
SQ FT: 13,800
SALES (est): 5.1MM
SALES (corp-wide): 5.1MM **Privately Held**
Web: www.barnwelltire.com
SIC: 5531 5014 3011   Automotive tires; Tires and tubes; Tires and inner tubes

(G-3701)

TORRINGTON DISTRIBUTORS INC (PA)

Also Called: Tdi
43 Norfolk St (06790-4825)
PHONE..................860 482-4464
James A Mazzarelli, *Pr*
James A Mazzarelli, *Pr*
Teresa L Asklar, *
James Allen Mazzarelli, *Pr*
▲ **EMP:** 24 **EST:** 1974
SQ FT: 17,000
SALES (est): 4.78MM
SALES (corp-wide): 4.78MM **Privately Held**
Web: www.torringtondistributors.com
SIC: 2531   Seats, aircraft

(G-3702)

TRANE TECHNOLOGIES COMPANY LLC

Also Called: Ingersoll-Rand
70 North St (06790-4907)
PHONE..................860 626-2085
Pauline Johnson, *Mgr*
EMP: 9
Web: www.tranetechnologies.com
SIC: 3561   Pumps and pumping equipment
HQ: Trane Technologies Company Llc
800 Beaty St Ste E
Davidson NC 28036
704 655-4000

(G-3703)

TSMC INC

100 Lawton St (06790-6715)
PHONE..................860 283-8265
Allen M Sperry Senior, *Ch Bd*

Paul Ayoub, *Pr*
▲ **EMP:** 634 **EST:** 1848
SQ FT: 345,000
SALES (est): 5.3MM **Privately Held**
SIC: 3315 5051   Nails, steel: wire or cut; Cable, wire

(G-3704)

UNISOFT MEDICAL CORPORATION

65 New Litchfield St (06790-6414)
PHONE..................860 482-6848
Stacey Dubell Mileti, *CEO*
Robert Mileti, *Pr*
EMP: 10 **EST:** 2016
SALES (est): 597.7K **Privately Held**
Web: www.unisoftmedical.com
SIC: 3842   Surgical appliances and supplies

(G-3705)

UPRISING LLC

207 Doman Dr (06790-3489)
PHONE..................860 960-3781
Peterson Joseph, *Managing Member*
EMP: 15 **EST:** 2021
SALES (est): 525.36K **Privately Held**
SIC: 3471   Cleaning, polishing, and finishing

(G-3706)

VR INDUSTRIES LLC

27 Elton St (06790-6702)
P.O. Box 1147 (06790-1147)
PHONE..................860 618-2772
Mark Bastiaanse, *Owner*
EMP: 7 **EST:** 2016
SALES (est): 61.03K **Privately Held**
Web: www.vrindustries.com
SIC: 3999   Manufacturing industries, nec

(G-3707)

WHITE DOG WOODWORKING LLC

59 Field St Ste 140 (06790-4955)
PHONE..................860 482-3776
EMP: 13 **EST:** 2006
SALES (est): 434.06K **Privately Held**
SIC: 2431   Millwork

(G-3708)

WITTMANN USA INC (DH)

1 Technology Park Dr (06790-2594)
PHONE..................860 496-9603
Michael Wittmann, *CEO*
David C Preusse, *
Jacqueline Powers, *
▲ **EMP:** 80 **EST:** 1989
SQ FT: 40,000
SALES (est): 88.87MM
SALES (corp-wide): 2.67MM **Privately Held**
Web: www.wittmann-group.com
SIC: 3559 5084   Robots, molding and forming plastics; Industrial machinery and equipment
HQ: Wittmann Technology Gmbh
Lichtblaustraße 10
Wien 1220
1250390

Trumbull
Fairfield County

(G-3709)

AEGEA MEDICAL INC

50 Corporate Dr (06611-1349)
PHONE..................650 701-1125
Maria Sainz, *CEO*
EMP: 21 **EST:** 2007

SALES (est): 4.42MM
SALES (corp-wide): 3.59B **Publicly Held**
Web: www.maratreatment.com
SIC: 3841 Surgical and medical instruments
HQ: Coopersurgical, Inc.
75 Corporate Dr
Trumbull CT 06611

(G-3710)
AMERICAN GRIPPERS INC
Also Called: A G I Automation
171 Spring Hill Rd (06611-1327)
PHONE.....................203 459-8345
Peter Farkas, *Pr*
John Barnes, *VP*
EMP: 17 **EST:** 1997
SALES (est): 466.61K **Privately Held**
Web: www.agi-automatiom.com
SIC: 3545 Machine tool accessories

(G-3711)
ANSEL LABEL AND PACKAGING CORP
204 Spring Hill Rd Ste 3 (06611-1356)
PHONE.....................203 452-0311
Jeff San Fan Andre, *Pr*
William San Fan Andre, *Ch Bd*
Clifford Albers, *VP Sls*
Harold Smyth, *Sec*
EMP: 22 **EST:** 1992
SQ FT: 13,364
SALES (est): 2.31MM **Privately Held**
Web: www.ansellabel.com
SIC: 2759 2671 Labels and seals: printing, nsk; Paper; coated and laminated packaging

(G-3712)
APTARGROUP INC
Aptar Stratford
60 Commerce Dr # 1 (06611-5403)
PHONE.....................203 377-8100
EMP: 350
Web: www.aptar.com
SIC: 3089 3499 Closures, plastics; Aerosol valves, metal
PA: Aptargroup, Inc.
265 Exchange Dr Ste 100
Crystal Lake IL 60014

(G-3713)
AVERY ABRASIVES INC
2225 Reservoir Ave Ste 1 (06611-4795)
PHONE.....................203 372-3513
Craig F Avery, *Pr*
Robert J Berta, *
Philip Archard, *
▲ **EMP:** 35 **EST:** 1960
SQ FT: 42,000
SALES (est): 4.45MM **Privately Held**
Web: www.averyabrasives.com
SIC: 3291 Wheels, abrasive

(G-3714)
BLAIRDEN PRECISION INSTRUMENTS INC
Also Called: Cooper Surgical
95 Corporate Dr (06611-1350)
PHONE.....................203 799-2000
▲ **EMP:** 9
SIC: 3841 Surgical instruments and apparatus

(G-3715)
COOPERSURGICAL INC
Also Called: Wallach Surgical
120 Corporate Dr (06611-1387)
PHONE.....................203 601-5200
EMP: 7

(G-3716)
COOPERSURGICAL INC (DH)
75 Corporate Dr (06611-1350)
PHONE.....................203 601-5200
Holly Sheffield, *Pr*
Robert D Auerbach, *
Kerry Blair, *
Cheryl H Bogardus, *
Alan T Tucker, *
◆ **EMP:** 180 **EST:** 1990
SQ FT: 92,000
SALES (est): 184.17MM
SALES (corp-wide): 3.59B **Publicly Held**
Web: www.coopersurgical.com
SIC: 5047 3842 3841 3845 Medical equipment and supplies; Gynecological supplies and appliances; Surgical and medical instruments; Electromedical equipment
HQ: Cooper Medical, Inc.
6140 Stnrdge Mall Rd Ste
Pleasanton CA 94588
925 460-3600

(G-3717)
DELCON INDUSTRIES
31 Frenchtown Rd (06611-4729)
PHONE.....................203 371-5711
EMP: 7 **EST:** 2010
SALES (est): 167.35K **Privately Held**
Web: www.delconindustrial.com
SIC: 3999 Manufacturing industries, nec

(G-3718)
E-LITE TECHNOLOGIES INC
2285 Reservoir Ave (06611-4752)
PHONE.....................203 371-2070
Gustaf T Appelberg, *Ch*
Mark Appelberg, *Pr*
EMP: 26 **EST:** 1993
SQ FT: 10,600
SALES (est): 921.45K **Privately Held**
SIC: 3645 Residential lighting fixtures

(G-3719)
ENFIELD TECHNOLOGIES LLC
35 Nutmeg Dr Ste 130 (06611-5451)
PHONE.....................203 375-3100
▼ **EMP:** 10 **EST:** 2002
SQ FT: 6,000
SALES (est): 2.36MM **Privately Held**
Web: www.enfieldtech.com
SIC: 3492 3494 Fluid power valves and hose fittings; Valves and pipe fittings, nec

(G-3720)
FIRE PREVENTION SERVICES
20 Indian Rd (06611-2724)
PHONE.....................203 866-6357
Andrew Delcarmine, *Owner*
EMP: 10 **EST:** 2010
SALES (est): 994.21K **Privately Held**
SIC: 3999 Fire extinguishers, portable

(G-3721)
HELICOPTER SUPPORT INC (DH)
Also Called: Sikorsky Commercial
124 Quarry Rd (06611-4816)
P.O. Box 111068 (06611-0868)
PHONE.....................203 416-4000
David Adler, *Pr*

Christopher Bogan, *VP*
John Chimini, *VP*
Peter Graber-lipperman, *Sec*
Ari David, *Sec*
◆ **EMP:** 265 **EST:** 1978
SQ FT: 183,000
SALES (est): 84.22MM **Publicly Held**
SIC: 5088 4581 3728 Helicopter parts; Aircraft maintenance and repair services; Aircraft parts and equipment, nec
HQ: Sikorsky Aircraft Corporation
6900 Main St
Stratford CT 06614

(G-3722)
HERSAM ACORN CMNTY PUBG LLC
Also Called: Trumbull Printing
205 Spring Hill Rd (06611-1327)
PHONE.....................203 261-2548
Gus Semon, *Mgr*
EMP: 11
SALES (corp-wide): 9.7MM **Privately Held**
Web: www.acorn-online.com
SIC: 2711 Newspapers, publishing and printing
HQ: Hersam Acorn Community Publishing, Llc
16 Bailey Ave
Ridgefield CT 06877

(G-3723)
LEX PRODUCTS LLC (PA)
Also Called: Lex
35 Nutmeg Dr Ste 205 (06611-5495)
PHONE.....................203 363-3738
Robert R Luther, *Managing Member*
Elizabeth A Luther, *
◆ **EMP:** 150 **EST:** 1989
SQ FT: 18,000
SALES (est): 93.22MM **Privately Held**
Web: www.lexproducts.com
SIC: 3829 3315 3643 3613 Measuring and controlling devices, nec; Cable, steel: insulated or armored; Current-carrying wiring services; Switchboards and parts, power

(G-3724)
M T D CORPORATION
171 Spring Hill Rd (06611-1327)
PHONE.....................203 261-3721
Dorothy Bertini, *Pr*
Milo Bertini, *VP*
EMP: 25 **EST:** 1965
SQ FT: 9,000
SALES (est): 494.41K **Privately Held**
SIC: 3599 Machine shop, jobbing and repair

(G-3725)
MINUTEMAN PRESS
14 Kitcher Ct (06611-1015)
PHONE.....................203 261-8318
EMP: 7 **EST:** 2018
SALES (est): 83.91K **Privately Held**
Web: www.minutemanpress.com
SIC: 2752 2741 Commercial printing, lithographic; Miscellaneous publishing

(G-3726)
OCE-USA HOLDING INC
100 Oakview Dr (06611-4724)
PHONE.....................773 714-8500
◆ **EMP:** 11000
Web: www.cpp.canon
SIC: 3861 5044 Photographic film, plate, and paper holders; Copying equipment

---

(G-3727)
ORIGIO MIDATLANTIC DEVICES INC
75 Corporate Dr (06611-1350)
PHONE.....................856 762-2000
Paul Rennell, *CEO*
Terrance J Fortino, *
◆ **EMP:** 70 **EST:** 1989
SQ FT: 11,000
SALES (est): 4.26MM
SALES (corp-wide): 3.59B **Publicly Held**
SIC: 3821 5047 Laboratory equipment: fume hoods, distillation racks, etc.; Medical laboratory equipment
HQ: Origio Inc.
2400 Hunters Way
Charlottesville VA 22911

(G-3728)
PREFERRED PRINTING CO INC
140 Corporate Dr (06611-1387)
EMP: 23 **EST:** 1983
SALES (est): 2.86MM **Privately Held**
Web: www.preferredprinting.com
SIC: 2752 Offset printing

(G-3729)
PREUSSER RESEARCH GROUP INC (PA)
115 Technology Dr Unit B307 (06611-6339)
PHONE.....................203 459-8700
EMP: 10 **EST:** 1990
SALES (est): 2.43MM **Privately Held**
Web: www.preussergroup.com
SIC: 8748 3669 Traffic consultant; Pedestrian traffic control equipment

(G-3730)
RAMPAGE LLC
38 Palisade Ave (06611-3040)
PHONE.....................203 521-1645
EMP: 8 **EST:** 1994
SALES (est): 400.09K **Privately Held**
Web: www.skateparkramps.com
SIC: 3949 Skateboards

(G-3731)
SCAN TOOL & MOLD INC
2 Trefoil Dr (06611-1330)
PHONE.....................203 459-4950
John F Gotch Junior, *Pr*
▲ **EMP:** 26 **EST:** 1972
SQ FT: 32,500
SALES (est): 4.54MM **Privately Held**
Web: www.scantoolinc.com
SIC: 3089 3544 Injection molding of plastics ; Industrial molds

(G-3732)
SECUREMARK DECAL CORP
20 Nutmeg Dr (06611-5414)
PHONE.....................203 333-5503
Norman Hoffderg, *Pr*
EMP: 16 **EST:** 2005
SALES (est): 1.35MM **Privately Held**
Web: www.surys.com
SIC: 2672 Labels (unprinted), gummed: made from purchased materials

(G-3733)
SIKORSKY AIRCRAFT CORPORATION
124 Quarry Rd (06611-4816)
PHONE.....................203 386-7794
EMP: 7
Web: www.gyrocamsystems.com
SIC: 3812 Search and navigation equipment
HQ: Sikorsky Aircraft Corporation
6900 Main St

▲ = Import ▼ = Export
◆ = Import/Export

Stratford CT 06614

(G-3734)
SURYS INC
20 Nutmeg Dr (06611-5414)
PHONE...............................203 333-5503
Frederic Trojani, *Pr*
Fabio Tremolada, *
▲ **EMP:** 202 **EST:** 2009
SALES (est): 54.28MM
SALES (corp-wide): 44.72MM **Privately Held**
Web: www.surys.com
SIC: 2679 2759 Tags and labels, paper; Labels and seals: printing, nsk
PA: Surys
Parc D Activite G Eiffel
Bussy Saint Georges 77600
164763100

(G-3735)
TRUMBULL PRINTING INC
205 Spring Hill Rd (06611-1327)
PHONE...............................203 261-2548
Steve Huhta, *Pr*
EMP: 150 **EST:** 1951
SQ FT: 80,000
SALES (est): 8.78MM **Privately Held**
Web: www.trumbullprinting.com
SIC: 2752 Offset printing

(G-3736)
UNILEVER HOME AND PER CARE NA
Also Called: Unilever Hpc NA
75 Merritt Blvd (06611-5435)
PHONE...............................203 502-0086
Frederick Baumer, *Prin*
◆ **EMP:** 25 **EST:** 2005
SALES (est): 1.87MM **Privately Held**
SIC: 2841 2844 Soap and other detergents; Shampoos, rinses, conditioners: hair

(G-3737)
UNILEVER HPC USA
45 Commerce Dr (06611-5403)
PHONE...............................203 381-3311
Richard Mcnabb, *Dir*
EMP: 83 **EST:** 2010
SALES (est): 478.41K **Privately Held**
SIC: 2844 Deodorants, personal

(G-3738)
UNILEVER TRUMBULL RES SVCS INC
Also Called: Unilever Hpc USA
40 Merritt Blvd (06611-5413)
PHONE...............................203 502-0086
Peter Gallagher, *Pr*
Christine Koch, *VP*
Wolfgang Bergmann, *VP*
EMP: 80 **EST:** 2002
SALES (est): 4.73MM
SALES (corp-wide): 62.39B **Privately Held**
SIC: 2844 Toilet preparations
PA: Unilever Plc
Unilever House
London EC4Y
207 572-1202

(G-3739)
UNITED STTES SIGN FBRCTION COR
Also Called: US Sign
1 Trefoil Dr Ste 2 (06611-6352)
PHONE...............................203 601-1000
George Holley, *Ch Bd*
Ron Eppert, *VP Opers*
Alan Posner, *CFO*

EMP: 18 **EST:** 1991
SQ FT: 40,000
SALES (est): 772.13K **Privately Held**
Web: www.ussign.com
SIC: 3953 3993 3444 3356 Marking devices ; Signs and advertising specialties; Sheet metalwork; Nonferrous rolling and drawing, nec

(G-3740)
WALLACH SURGICAL DEVICES INC (PA)
75 Corporate Dr (06611-1350)
PHONE...............................203 799-2000
Nicholas J Pichotta, *CEO*
Paul L Remmell, *
Carol R Kaufman, *
Dan Wallach, *
▲ **EMP:** 44 **EST:** 1980
SQ FT: 40,000
SALES (est): 4.59MM
SALES (corp-wide): 4.59MM **Privately Held**
Web: www.coopersurgical.com
SIC: 3841 Surgical and medical instruments

Uncasville
New London County

(G-3741)
MOHEGAN DIGITAL SERVICES LLC
1 Mohegan Sun Blvd (06382-1355)
PHONE...............................888 226-7711
Richard Roberts, *Pr*
EMP: 7 **EST:** 2021
SALES (est): 531.99K
SALES (corp-wide): 1.59B **Privately Held**
SIC: 3571 Computers, digital, analog or hybrid
PA: Mohegan Tribal Gaming Authority
1 Mohegan Sun Blvd
Uncasville CT 06382
860 862-8000

(G-3742)
NORTHEAST WOOD PRODUCTS LLC
Also Called: Thermaglo
13 Crow Hill Rd (06382-1118)
PHONE...............................860 862-6350
Guy J Mozzicato, *Pr*
Michael D Reid, *Sr VP*
Kenneth N Wycherley, *Sr VP*
EMP: 13 **EST:** 2013
SQ FT: 20,000
SALES (est): 784.29K **Privately Held**
SIC: 3999 Burnt wood articles

(G-3743)
PEPSI-COLA METRO BTLG CO INC
Also Called: Pepsi-Cola
260 Gallivan Ln (06382-1121)
PHONE...............................860 848-1231
Paul Andreotta, *Mgr*
EMP: 22
SALES (corp-wide): 86.39B **Publicly Held**
Web: www.pepsico.com
SIC: 2086 Carbonated soft drinks, bottled and canned
HQ: Pepsi-Cola Metropolitan Bottling Company, Inc.
700 Anderson Hill Rd
Purchase NY 10577
914 767-6000

(G-3744)
TECH-AIR INCORPORATED
152 Route 163 (06382-2118)
P.O. Box 363 (06382-0363)
PHONE...............................860 848-1287
Richard Hubbert, *Pr*
Michael F Hubbert, *
Donald L Hubbert, *
Jeanette B Hubbert, *
EMP: 27 **EST:** 1978
SQ FT: 13,000
SALES (est): 1.18MM **Privately Held**
SIC: 3444 1761 Sheet metalwork; Sheet metal work, nec

(G-3745)
TOWN OF MONTVILLE
Also Called: Montville Sewer Plant
83 Pink Row (06382-2427)
PHONE...............................860 848-3830
Mike Didato, *Mgr*
EMP: 95
SALES (corp-wide): 76.97MM **Privately Held**
Web: www.townofmontville.org
SIC: 3589 Water treatment equipment, industrial
PA: Town Of Montville
310 Nrwich New Lndon Tpke
Uncasville CT 06382
860 848-3030

Unionville
Hartford County

(G-3746)
AIR TOOL SALES & SVC CO INC (PA)
1 Burnham Ave (06085-1225)
P.O. Box 218 (06085-0218)
PHONE...............................860 673-2714
Niles O Lindstedt, *Pr*
EMP: 9 **EST:** 1976
SQ FT: 15,000
SALES (est): 1.39MM
SALES (corp-wide): 1.39MM **Privately Held**
Web: www.vintagemodifieds.com
SIC: 3546 5084 5072 7699 Power-driven handtools; Pneumatic tools and equipment; Power tools and accessories; Power tool repair

(G-3747)
AUTOMATECH INC
21 Westview Ter (06085-1459)
PHONE...............................860 673-5940
John Murry, *Mgr*
EMP: 10
Web: www.automatech.com
SIC: 7372 Prepackaged software
PA: Automatech, Inc.
138 Industrial Park Rd
Plymouth MA 02360

(G-3748)
DATA MANAGEMENT INCORPORATED
Also Called: Threshold Visitor MGT Systems
537 New Britain Ave (06085-1482)
P.O. Box 789 (06034-0789)
PHONE...............................860 677-8586
Daniel A Hincks, *CEO*
Brian Gallagher, *Pr*
EMP: 45 **EST:** 1961
SQ FT: 6,000
SALES (est): 11MM
SALES (corp-wide): 4.75B **Privately Held**

Web: www.datamanage.com
SIC: 2752 2782 Offset printing; Account books
PA: Ccl Industries Inc.
111 Gordon Baker Rd Suite 801
Toronto ON M2H 3
416 756-8500

(G-3749)
MADIGAN MILLWORKS INC
Also Called: Madigan Millwork
150 New Britain Ave (06085-1221)
PHONE...............................860 673-7601
James Madigan, *Pr*
Regina Madigan, *Sec*
EMP: 9 **EST:** 1980
SQ FT: 20,000
SALES (est): 1.6MM **Privately Held**
SIC: 2431 2511 Woodwork, interior and ornamental, nec; Wood household furniture

(G-3750)
NOVA MACHINING LLC
16 E Shore Blvd (06085-1510)
PHONE...............................860 675-8131
EMP: 8
SALES (est): 180K **Privately Held**
Web: www.novamachining.com
SIC: 3599 Machine shop, jobbing and repair

Vernon
Tolland County

(G-3751)
BNL INDUSTRIES INC
30 Industrial Park Rd (06066-5523)
PHONE...............................860 870-6222
Leonard Bosh Junior, *Pr*
Patricia C Paro, *V PES**
Leonard Bosh, *
EMP: 40 **EST:** 1987
SQ FT: 27,000
SALES (est): 9.88MM **Privately Held**
Web: www.bnl.com
SIC: 3491 Industrial valves

(G-3752)
BRAVO LLC
Also Called: Manchester Packing
1084 Hartford Tpke (06066-4413)
PHONE...............................860 896-1899
David Bogner, *Mgr*
EMP: 10
SALES (corp-wide): 30.02MM **Privately Held**
Web: www.bravorawdiet.com
SIC: 2047 Dog food
HQ: Bravo, Llc
2425 W Dorothy Ln
Moraine OH 45439
866 922-9222

(G-3753)
CONNECTICUT MILLWORK INC
80 Spring St (06066-3452)
PHONE...............................860 875-2860
EMP: 9 **EST:** 1994
SQ FT: 6,000
SALES (est): 712.68K **Privately Held**
SIC: 2431 Millwork

(G-3754)
MIKRO INDUSTRIAL FINISHING CO
170 W Main St (06066-3560)
PHONE...............................860 875-6357
Steven Wakefield, *Pr*
Carla Wakefield, *VP*

EMP: 9 **EST:** 1983
SQ FT: 10,500
SALES (est): 2.31MM **Privately Held**
Web: www.mikro1.com
SIC: 5084 3559 Machine tools and
metalworking machinery; Metal finishing
equipment for plating, etc.

(G-3755)
NEISS CORP
29 Naek Rd (06066-3990)
PHONE..........................860 872-8528
John Cratty, *Pr*
Bonnie Cratty, *Sec*
EMP: 10 **EST:** 1971
SQ FT: 8,000
SALES (est): 1.01MM **Privately Held**
SIC: 2521 Panel systems and partitions
(free-standing), office: wood

(G-3756)
ROCKVILLE TECHNOLOGY LLC
✿
129 Reservoir Rd (06066-5705)
PHONE..........................860 871-6883
Steven Tanzi, *Managing Member*
EMP: 30 **EST:** 2023
SALES (est): 1.21MM **Privately Held**
SIC: 3724 Aircraft engines and engine parts

(G-3757)
TEAM LOGIC IT
428 Hartford Tpke Ste 107 (06066-4841)
PHONE..........................320 760-9084
EMP: 7 **EST:** 2019
SALES (est): 171.82K **Privately Held**
Web: www.teamlogicit.com
SIC: 3577 Computer peripheral equipment,
nec

(G-3758)
TOWN OF VERNON
Also Called: Water Treatment Plant
100 Windsorville Rd (06066-2315)
PHONE..........................860 870-3545
Robert Grasis, *Genl Mgr*
EMP: 81
SALES (corp-wide): 130.44MM **Privately Held**
Web: www.vernon-ct.gov
SIC: 3589 Water treatment equipment,
industrial
PA: Town Of Vernon
14 Park Pl
Vernon CT 06066
860 870-3690

Vernon Rockville
Tolland County

(G-3759)
AMERBELLE TEXTILES LLC
104 E Main St (06066-3336)
EMP: 75
SIC: 2261 Finishing plants, cotton

(G-3760)
BNL MANUFACTURING LLC
30 Industrial Park Rd (06066-5523)
PHONE..........................860 870-6222
EMP: 7 **EST:** 2013
SALES (est): 62.54K **Privately Held**
Web: www.bnl.com
SIC: 3999 Manufacturing industries, nec

(G-3761)
RMI INC
Also Called: Stafford Reminder
130 Old Town Rd (06066-2322)
P.O. Box 27 (06066-0027)
PHONE..........................860 875-3366
EMP: 200
SIC: 2711 2752 Newspapers, publishing
and printing; Offset printing

(G-3762)
SOLDREAM INC
129 Reservoir Rd (06066-5705)
PHONE..........................860 871-6883
▼ **EMP:** 49 **EST:** 1993
SQ FT: 20,000
SALES (est): 9.59MM **Privately Held**
Web: www.soldream.com
SIC: 3829 Measuring and controlling
devices, nec

(G-3763)
TEK INDUSTRIES INC
166 Tunnel Rd (06066-5505)
PHONE..........................860 870-0001
Mark Matheny, *Pr*
Deborah Gordon, *
EMP: 32 **EST:** 1990
SALES (est): 4.63MM **Privately Held**
Web: www.tekind.com
SIC: 3672 7373 8711 Printed circuit boards;
Turnkey vendors, computer systems;
Designing: ship, boat, machine, and product

Versailles
New London County

(G-3764)
FUSION PAPERBOARD
CONNECTICUT LLC
Also Called: Fusion Paperboard
130 Inland Rd (06383-8306)
PHONE..........................888 283-3617
EMP: 150
SIC: 2652 2631 Setup paperboard boxes;
Boxboard

(G-3765)
FUSION PAPERBOARD US INC
130 Inland Rd (06383-8306)
PHONE..........................859 586-1100
▲ **EMP:** 250
SIC: 2657 2759 2752 2631 Folding
paperboard boxes; Commercial printing, nec
; Commercial printing, lithographic;
Paperboard mills

Wallingford
New Haven County

(G-3766)
3M COMPANY
Also Called: 3M
100 Barnes Rd (06492-1897)
PHONE..........................203 949-1630
Dominic Magisano, *Mgr*
EMP: 11
SALES (corp-wide): 34.23B **Publicly Held**
Web: www.3m.com
SIC: 3841 5045 Surgical instruments and
apparatus; Computer software
PA: 3m Company
3m Center
Saint Paul MN 55144
651 733-1110

(G-3767)
ADVANCED TURBINE SERVICES
LLC
Also Called: Ats
856 N Main Street Ext (06492-2419)
PHONE..........................203 269-7977
EMP: 7 **EST:** 1995
SQ FT: 5,000
SALES (est): 795.55K **Privately Held**
Web: www.aux-pwr.com
SIC: 3511 Turbines and turbine generator
sets

(G-3768)
AERO-PRECISION MFG LLC
71 S Turnpike Rd (06492-3421)
PHONE..........................203 675-7625
Frank Jukic, *Prin*
EMP: 8 **EST:** 2007
SALES (est): 889.7K **Privately Held**
SIC: 3999 Manufacturing industries, nec

(G-3769)
ALLNEX USA INC
Also Called: Evonic Cyro
528 S Cherry St (06492-4458)
PHONE..........................203 269-4481
Linda Harroch, *CEO*
EMP: 62
Web: www.allnex.com
SIC: 2821 Plastics materials and resins
HQ: Allnex Usa Inc.
9005 Westside Pkwy
Alpharetta GA
770 280-8300

(G-3770)
AMETEK INC
Also Called: Ametek Specialty Metal Pdts
21 Toelles Rd (06492-4456)
P.O. Box 5807 (06492-7607)
PHONE..........................203 265-6731
Bob Deshenes, *Brnch Mgr*
EMP: 105
SALES (corp-wide): 6.15B **Publicly Held**
Web: www.ametek.com
SIC: 3452 3823 3399 3331 Bolts, metal;
Process control instruments; Iron, powdered
; Primary copper
PA: Ametek, Inc.
1100 Cassatt Rd
Berwyn PA 19312
610 647-2121

(G-3771)
AMPHENOL CORPORATION (PA)
Also Called: AMPHENOL
358 Hall Ave (06492-3574)
P.O. Box 5030 (06492-7530)
PHONE..........................203 265-8900
R Adam Norwitt, *Pr*
Martin H Loeffler, *
Craig A Lampo, *Sr VP*
Lance E D'amico, *Sr VP*
David Silverman, *Senior Vice President
Human Resources*
▼ **EMP:** 85 **EST:** 1932
SALES (est): 12.62B
SALES (corp-wide): 12.62B **Publicly Held**
Web: www.amphenol.com
SIC: 3678 3643 3661 Electronic connectors;
Connectors and terminals for electrical
devices; Fiber optics communications
equipment

(G-3772)
AMPHENOL INTERNATIONAL
LTD (HQ)
358 Hall Ave (06492-3574)

PHONE..........................203 265-8900
EMP: 27 **EST:** 1980
SALES (est): 22.76MM
SALES (corp-wide): 12.62B **Publicly Held**
Web: www.amphenolmao.com
SIC: 3678 Electronic connectors
PA: Amphenol Corporation
358 Hall Ave
Wallingford CT 06492
203 265-8900

(G-3773)
APCT-WALLINGFORD INC
Also Called: Tech Circuits
340 Quinnipiac St Unit 25 (06492-4050)
P.O. Box 309 (06492-0309)
PHONE..........................203 269-3311
Steve Robinson, *Pr*
Greg Elder, *
EMP: 45 **EST:** 1979
SQ FT: 46,000
SALES (est): 10.41MM
SALES (corp-wide): 87.73MM **Privately
Held**
Web: www.apct.com
SIC: 3672 Circuit boards, television and
radio printed
HQ: Apct, Inc.
3495 De La Cruz Blvd
Santa Clara CA 95054
408 727-6442

(G-3774)
AQUACOMFORT SOLUTIONS
LLC
8 Fairfield Blvd Ste 115 (06492-1890)
PHONE..........................203 265-0100
Carol Yeager, *CFO*
EMP: 8 **EST:** 2017
SALES (est): 169.72K **Privately Held**
Web: www.aquacomfort.com
SIC: 3433 Heaters, swimming pool: oil or
gas

(G-3775)
ARNCO SIGN COMPANY
1133 S Broad St (06492-1713)
PHONE..........................203 238-1224
Paul Cohen, *Pr*
Marc Cohen, *
EMP: 26 **EST:** 1952
SQ FT: 15,000
SALES (est): 848.53K **Privately Held**
Web: www.arncosign.com
SIC: 7389 3993 Crane and aerial lift service;
Electric signs

(G-3776)
ARRIS TECHNOLOGY INC
15 Sterling Dr (06492-1967)
PHONE..........................678 473-8493
EMP: 22 **EST:** 2017
SALES (est): 1.25MM **Privately Held**
SIC: 3663 Radio and t.v. communications
equipment

(G-3777)
ATLANTIC EQP INSTALLERS INC
55 N Plains Industrial Rd (06492-5812)
P.O. Box 547 (06492-0547)
PHONE..........................203 284-0402
Robert J Huelsman, *Pr*
Donald J Huelsman, *VP*
Robert K Huelsman, *Stockholder*
William E Bohne, *CFO*
EMP: 22 **EST:** 1981
SQ FT: 12,000
SALES (est): 4.57MM **Privately Held**
Web: www.atlequip.com

▲ = Import ▼ = Export
◆ = Import/Export

SIC: 3441 1796 Fabricated structural metal; Installing building equipment

(G-3778)
ATLAS FILTRI NORTH AMERICA LLC
1068 N Farms Rd Ste 3 (06492-5939)
PHONE.................................203 284-0080
Gary Fappino, *Managing Member*
Daniele Costantini, *VP*
EMP: 12 EST: 2016
SQ FT: 24,000
SALES (est): 1.38MM Privately Held
Web: us.atlasfiltri.com
SIC: 3589 Water treatment equipment, industrial

(G-3779)
AUTOMATED LOGIC CORPORATION
23 Village Ln (06492-2426)
PHONE.................................203 284-0100
EMP: 20
SALES (corp-wide): 22.1B Publicly Held
Web: www.automatedlogic.com
SIC: 3822 Temperature controls, automatic
HQ: Automated Logic Corporation
1150 Roberts Blvd Nw
Kennesaw GA 30144
770 429-3000

(G-3780)
BEI HOLDINGS INC
Also Called: Business Electronics
6 Capital Dr (06492-2318)
PHONE.................................203 741-9300
Michael Salamone, *Prin*
EMP: 15 EST: 1976
SALES (est): 1.37MM Privately Held
Web: www.beiinc.com
SIC: 7382 3572 5999 Protective devices, security; Tape recorders for computers; Alarm and safety equipment stores

(G-3781)
BLP TECHNOLOGIES INC
Also Called: Sensorworx
2a Research Pkwy (06492-1965)
PHONE.................................203 678-4224
Benjamin Hahn, *Pr*
EMP: 27 EST: 2017
SALES (est): 7.51MM Privately Held
Web: www.sensorworx.com
SIC: 3648 Lighting equipment, nec

(G-3782)
BOARDMAN SILVERSMITHS INC
22 N Plains Industrial Rd Ste 6c (06492-2341)
PHONE.................................203 265-9978
Burton Boardman, *Pr*
EMP: 11 EST: 1990
SALES (est): 591.59K Privately Held
Web: www.boardmansilversmiths.com
SIC: 3914 Silverware

(G-3783)
BRIT SYSTEMS LLC
135 N Plains Industrial Rd (06492-2332)
PHONE.................................214 630-0636
EMP: 10 EST: 1993
SQ FT: 11,000
SALES (est): 4.94MM Privately Held
Web: www.brit.com
SIC: 5047 7372 Hospital equipment and furniture; Prepackaged software

(G-3784)
BROAD PEAK MANUFACTURING LLC
Also Called: Broad Peak
10 Beaumont Rd Ste 1 (06492-2455)
PHONE.................................203 678-4664
EMP: 20 EST: 2015
SALES (est): 1.88MM Privately Held
SIC: 3471 Cleaning, polishing, and finishing

(G-3785)
CABINETS TO GO LLC
10 Technology Dr (06492-1955)
PHONE.................................800 222-4638
Thomas D Sullivan, *Pt*
EMP: 24 EST: 2016
SALES (est): 963.56K Privately Held
Web: www.cabinetstogo.com
SIC: 2434 Wood kitchen cabinets

(G-3786)
CIDRA CHEMICAL MANAGEMENT INC (HQ)
50 Barnes Park Rd N Ste 103 (06492-5920)
PHONE.................................203 265-0035
F Kevin Didden, *Pr*
Michael Grillo, *
Gary Hokunson, *
John Viega, *
EMP: 70 EST: 2008
SALES (est): 23.35MM Privately Held
Web: www.cidra.com
SIC: 3823 Flow instruments, industrial process type
PA: Cidra Holdings Llc
50 Barnes Park Rd N # 103
Wallingford CT 06492

(G-3787)
CIDRA CORPORATE SERVICES INC (HQ)
50 Barnes Park Rd N (06492-5920)
PHONE.................................203 265-0035
F Kevin Didden, *Pr*
Michael Grillo, *
John Viega, *
Gary Hokunson, *
Paul Rothman, *Pr*
EMP: 50 EST: 1999
SALES (est): 28.07MM Privately Held
Web: www.cidra.com
SIC: 3823 Industrial flow and liquid measuring instruments
PA: Cidra Holdings Llc
50 Barnes Park Rd N # 103
Wallingford CT 06492

(G-3788)
CIDRA CORPORATION
50 Barnes Park Rd N Ste 103 (06492-5920)
PHONE.................................203 265-0035
F Kevin Didden, *CEO*
Patrick Curry, *
Michael Grillo, *CAO*
John Viega, *
Gary Hokunson, *
▼ EMP: 95 EST: 1996
SALES (est): 22.07MM Privately Held
Web: www.cidra.com
SIC: 3823 Industrial flow and liquid measuring instruments

(G-3789)
CIDRA MINERALS PROCESSING INC
50 Barnes Park Rd N (06492-5920)
PHONE.................................203 265-0035

F Kevin Didden, *Pr*
Michael Grillo, *VP*
Gary Hokunson, *CFO*
EMP: 20 EST: 2008
SALES (est): 3.48MM Privately Held
Web: www.cidra.com
SIC: 3823 Flow instruments, industrial process type
HQ: Cidra Corporate Services Inc.
50 Barnes Park Rd N
Wallingford CT 06492

(G-3790)
COASTAL EXTERIORS LLC
Also Called: Coastal Exteriors
10 Winding Brook Ln (06492-3355)
PHONE.................................203 626-5396
Brian Gazlay, *Managing Member*
EMP: 11 EST: 2006
SALES (est): 776.25K Privately Held
Web: www.coastalexteriorsllc.com
SIC: 1521 1761 1522 3444 Single-family housing construction; Roofing contractor; Remodeling, multi-family dwellings; Metal roofing and roof drainage equipment

(G-3791)
COMPONENT ENGINEERS INC
Also Called: C E I
108 N Plains Industrial Rd (06492-2334)
PHONE.................................203 269-0557
Ronald Hansen Junior, *CEO*
Rick Griffin, *
Clayton Oliver, *
◆ EMP: 95 EST: 1981
SQ FT: 52,000
SALES (est): 18.01MM Privately Held
Web: www.ceiprecision.com
SIC: 3469 Stamping metal for the trade

(G-3792)
CONNECTICUT HYPODERMICS INC
519 Main St (06492-1723)
PHONE.................................203 265-4881
Steven Tutolo, *Pr*
Mark Tutolo, *
Chris Tutolo, *
Leonard Tutolo, *
◆ EMP: 90 EST: 1979
SQ FT: 30,000
SALES (est): 10.07MM Privately Held
Web: www.connhypo.com
SIC: 3841 Hypodermic needles and syringes

(G-3793)
CONNECTICUT PLASTICS INC
1264 Old Colony Rd (06492-1711)
PHONE.................................203 265-3299
EMP: 34
SIC: 3089 Plastics processing

(G-3794)
CONTROLLED FLUIDICS LLC
1262 Old Colony Rd (06492-1711)
PHONE.................................603 673-4323
Christopher Connor, *Brnch Mgr*
EMP: 17
SALES (corp-wide): 3.84MM Privately Held
Web: www.controlledfluidics.com
SIC: 3599 Machine shop, jobbing and repair
PA: Controlled Fluidics Llc
18 Hollow Oak Ln
Milford NH 03055
603 673-4323

(G-3795)
CORRU-SEALS INC
24 Capital Dr (06492-2318)
PHONE.................................203 265-9331
Michael Fabiani, *Pr*
EMP: 12 EST: 1977
SQ FT: 8,000
SALES (est): 874.74K Privately Held
Web: www.nicholsons.com
SIC: 3053 Gaskets, all materials

(G-3796)
CST INCORPORATED
65 N Plains Industrial Rd Ste 3 (06492-5832)
PHONE.................................203 949-9900
TOLL FREE: 800
Basil Minickene, *Managing Member*
Basil G Minickene, *CEO*
John Minickene, *CIO*
Sylvia Minickene, *Stockholder*
Gennaro Minickene, *Stockholder*
EMP: 14 EST: 1989
SQ FT: 3,400
SALES (est): 2.17MM Privately Held
Web: www.managedbycst.com
SIC: 7379 7372 4813 7375 Online services technology consultants; Business oriented computer software; Internet connectivity services; Remote data base information retrieval

(G-3797)
CT ACQUISITIONS LLC
Also Called: Danver
1 Grand St (06492-3509)
PHONE.................................888 441-0537
Mitchell Slater, *Managing Member*
EMP: 50 EST: 1998
SQ FT: 52,000
SALES (est): 9.12MM Privately Held
Web: www.danver.com
SIC: 2514 Kitchen cabinets: metal

(G-3798)
CUSTOM CHROME PLATING
400 S Orchard St (06492-4500)
PHONE.................................203 265-5667
Jerry Sofocli, *Mgr*
EMP: 8 EST: 1994
SALES (est): 139.55K Privately Held
Web: www.crcchrome.com
SIC: 3471 Electroplating of metals or formed products

(G-3799)
DANAHER TOOL GROUP
61 Barnes Industrial Park N (06492-1845)
PHONE.................................203 284-7000
Lawrence Culp Junior, *CEO*
EMP: 12 EST: 2005
SALES (est): 603.97K Privately Held
Web: www.holo-krome.com
SIC: 3823 Water quality monitoring and control systems

(G-3800)
DEXMET CORPORATION
22 Barnes Industrial Rd S (06492-2462)
PHONE.................................203 294-4440
▲ EMP: 65 EST: 2006
SALES (est): 12.5MM
SALES (corp-wide): 17.65B Publicly Held
Web: www.dexmet.com
SIC: 3497 Metal foil and leaf
PA: Ppg Industries, Inc.
1 Ppg Pl
Pittsburgh PA 15272
412 434-3131

(G-3801)

DIRECTIONAL TECHNOLOGIES INC

89 N Main St (06492-3709)
PHONE..............................203 294-9200
Katherine M Sequino, *Prin*
EMP: 7 **EST:** 2016
SALES (est): 318.81K **Privately Held**
Web: www.directionaltech.com
SIC: 1381 Directional drilling oil and gas
    wells

(G-3802)

E & A ENTERPRISES INC

Also Called: Northeast Thermography
10 Capital Dr # A (06492-2318)
PHONE..............................203 250-8050
EMP: 7 **EST:** 1986
SQ FT: 10,000
SALES (est): 220.46K **Privately Held**
Web: www.hodginsengraving.com
SIC: 2752 Offset printing

(G-3803)

E-J ELECTRIC T & D LLC

53 N Plains Industrial Rd (06492-5808)
PHONE..............................203 626-9625
EMP: 80 **EST:** 2009
SALES (est): 7.77MM **Privately Held**
Web: www.ej1899.com
SIC: 3699 1731 Electrical equipment and
    supplies, nec; Electrical work

(G-3804)

EVEREST ISLES LLC

616 N Elm St (06492-3270)
PHONE..............................203 561-5128
Jeffrey Hladky, *Pr*
EMP: 7 **EST:** 2012
SALES (est): 450K **Privately Held**
Web: www.everestisles.com
SIC: 2329 Bathing suits and swimwear:
    men's and boys'

(G-3805)

EXPERT EMBROIDERY LLC

121 N Plains Industrial Rd Ste G
(06492-5883)
PHONE..............................203 269-9675
Chris Fjuer, *Pr*
EMP: 8 **EST:** 1997
SALES (est): 282.84K **Privately Held**
SIC: 2395 Embroidery products, except
    Schiffli machine

(G-3806)

EYLWARD TIMBER CO

13 Quince St (06492-2964)
PHONE..............................203 265-4276
Mike Eylward, *Owner*
EMP: 9 **EST:** 1998
SALES (est): 496.93K **Privately Held**
SIC: 2421 5099 Sawmills and planing mills,
    general; Firewood

(G-3807)

FOUGERA PHARMACEUTICALS INC

Byk-Chemie USA
524 S Cherry St (06492-4453)
P.O. Box 5670 (06492-7651)
PHONE..............................203 265-2086
Wolfgang Zinnert, *Mgr*
EMP: 104
Web: www.altana.com
SIC: 2851 Paints and allied products
HQ: Fougera Pharmaceuticals Inc.
    60 Baylis Rd
    Melville NY 11747
    631 454-7677

(G-3808)

FREVVO LLC

82 Anderson Rd (06492-5503)
PHONE..............................203 208-3117
Ashish Deshpande, *Prin*
EMP: 7 **EST:** 2007
SALES (est): 125.38K **Privately Held**
Web: www.frevvo.com
SIC: 7372 Prepackaged software

(G-3809)

GKN ARSPACE SVCS STRCTURES LLC

14 Research Pkwy (06492-1931)
PHONE..............................203 303-1408
Lindsay Phillips, *VP*
EMP: 265 **EST:** 2003
SALES (est): 10.12MM **Privately Held**
SIC: 3724 Aircraft engines and engine parts

(G-3810)

GLASS INDUSTRIES AMERICA LLC

340 Quinnipiac St Unit 9 (06492-4050)
PHONE..............................203 269-6700
EMP: 7 **EST:** 2002
SALES (est): 253.79K **Privately Held**
SIC: 3231 5023 Decorated glassware:
    chipped, engraved, etched, etc.;
    Kitchenware

(G-3811)

HARBY POWER SOLUTIONS LLC

105 S Elm St (06492-4705)
PHONE..............................203 265-0012
Byron Brewer Junior, *Prin*
EMP: 9 **EST:** 2010
SALES (est): 272.62K **Privately Held**
Web: www.northeastmarketing.com
SIC: 3629 Electrical industrial apparatus,
    nec

(G-3812)

HERBASWAY LABORATORIES LLC

Also Called: Herbasway
101 N Plains Industrial Rd Ste 3
(06492-2360)
PHONE..............................203 269-6991
▲ **EMP:** 10 **EST:** 1996
SALES (est): 2.06MM **Privately Held**
Web: www.herbasway.com
SIC: 2099 8731 2087 5149 Tea blending;
    Commercial physical research; Flavoring
    extracts and syrups, nec; Organic and diet
    food

(G-3813)

HITACHI ALOKA MEDICAL LTD

10 Fairfield Blvd (06492-5903)
PHONE..............................203 269-5088
EMP: 19 **EST:** 1991
SALES (est): 355.83K **Privately Held**
Web: www.hitachi-aloka.com
SIC: 3841 5047 3829 Surgical and medical
    instruments; Hospital equipment and
    furniture; Measuring and controlling
    devices, nec

(G-3814)

HITACHI ALOKA MEDICAL AMER INC

Also Called: Hitachi Aloka Medical
10 Fairfield Blvd (06492-5903)
PHONE..............................800 872-5652
David R Famiglietti, *Pr*
Ray Koba, *VP*

EMP: 99 **EST:** 2014
SALES (est): 10.53MM **Privately Held**
Web: www.hitachi-aloka.com
SIC: 3841 5047 3829 Surgical and medical
    instruments; Hospital equipment and
    furniture; Measuring and controlling
    devices, nec
PA: Hitachi, Ltd.
    1-6-6, Marunouchi
    Chiyoda-Ku TKY 100-0

(G-3815)

HOLO-KROME USA

61 Barnes Industrial Park N (06492-1845)
PHONE..............................800 879-6205
Orlando Castaneda, *Mgr*
EMP: 30 **EST:** 2018
SALES (est): 2.7MM **Privately Held**
Web: www.holo-krome.com
SIC: 3452 Bolts, nuts, rivets, and washers

(G-3816)

I2S LLC

1070 N Farms Rd Ste 3 (06492-5931)
PHONE..............................203 265-5684
◆ **EMP:** 150
Web: www.tenova.com
SIC: 3444 5051 Sheet metalwork; Ferrous
    metals

(G-3817)

IDEX HEALTH & SCIENCE LLC

50 Barnes Park Rd N (06492-5920)
PHONE..............................203 774-4422
EMP: 24
SALES (corp-wide): 3.18B **Publicly Held**
Web: www.idex-hs.com
SIC: 3561 Industrial pumps and parts
HQ: Idex Health & Science Llc
    600 Park Ct
    Rohnert Park CA 94928
    707 588-2000

(G-3818)

INTERACTER INC

10 Beaumont St A (06492-2455)
PHONE..............................203 949-0199
EMP: 13 **EST:** 1990
SALES (est): 780.07K **Privately Held**
Web: www.interacter.com
SIC: 3629 Battery chargers, rectifying or
    nonrotating

(G-3819)

ITS NEW ENGLAND INC

8 Capital Dr (06492-2318)
PHONE..............................203 265-8100
Brian Russell, *Pr*
EMP: 11 **EST:** 2010
SALES (est): 405.62K **Privately Held**
SIC: 3579 Office machines, nec

(G-3820)

J & L TOOL COMPANY INC

368 N Cherry Street Ext (06492-2309)
PHONE..............................203 265-6237
Leonard Rossicone Senior, *Pr*
Leonard Rossicone Senior, *Pr*
Nancy Rossicone, *VP*
Leonard Rossicone Junior, *VP*
Sheri Lynn Rossicone, *VP*
EMP: 26 **EST:** 1976
SQ FT: 12,000
SALES (est): 713.75K **Privately Held**
Web: www.jlmolding.com
SIC: 3544 Industrial molds

(G-3821)

J&L PLASTIC MOLDING LLC

368 N Cherry Street Ext (06492-2309)
PHONE..............................203 265-6237
▲ **EMP:** 7 **EST:** 1999
SQ FT: 12,000
SALES (est): 1.34MM **Privately Held**
Web: www.jlmolding.com
SIC: 3089 Molding primary plastics

(G-3822)

JAWOR LUMBER INC

1068 N Farms Rd Ste 1 (06492-5939)
P.O. Box 9 (06492-0009)
PHONE..............................203 269-4431
Walter Jawor, *Pr*
Walter J Jawor, *Pr*
Barbara M Jawor, *Sec*
Walter E Jawor, *VP*
EMP: 10 **EST:** 1922
SQ FT: 12,000
SALES (est): 951.78K **Privately Held**
Web: www.jaworlumber.com
SIC: 2431 Millwork

(G-3823)

JET PROCESS CORPORATION

126 S Turnpike Rd (06492-4369)
PHONE..............................203 985-6000
Richard Hart, *Ch Bd*
EMP: 8 **EST:** 1984
SALES (est): 889.27K **Privately Held**
Web: www.jetprocess.com
SIC: 3559 3479 8731 2851 Semiconductor
    manufacturing machinery; Painting,
    coating, and hot dipping; Commercial
    physical research; Paints and allied
    products

(G-3824)

KINAMOR INCORPORATED

Also Called: Kinamor Plastics
63 N Plains Industrial Rd (06492-5841)
PHONE..............................203 269-0380
John Romanik Senior, *CEO*
Mary Romanik, *
John Romanik Junior, *VP*
▲ **EMP:** 29 **EST:** 1974
SQ FT: 15,000
SALES (est): 2.39MM **Privately Held**
Web: www.kinamorinc.com
SIC: 3089 3441 2396 Injection molding of
    plastics; Fabricated structural metal;
    Automotive and apparel trimmings

(G-3825)

KOVACS MACHINE AND TOOL CO

50 N Plains Industrial Rd (06492-2372)
PHONE..............................203 269-4949
Allen Cuccaro, *Pr*
Peter Albrycht, *
Michael Frank, *
EMP: 19 **EST:** 1967
SQ FT: 8,000
SALES (est): 998.96K **Privately Held**
Web: www.kovacsmachine.com
SIC: 3599 3544 Machine shop, jobbing and
    repair; Special dies, tools, jigs, and fixtures

(G-3826)

LAWRENCE HOLDINGS INC

34b Barnes Industrial Rd S (06492-2438)
P.O. Box 336 (48066-0336)
PHONE..............................203 949-1600
Lawrence Buhl Iii, *CEO*
K C Jones, *CFO*
EMP: 13 **EST:** 2006
SALES (est): 372.32K **Privately Held**
Web: www.lawrenceholdings.com

SIC: 3469 3089 3544 Stamping metal for the trade; Automotive parts, plastic; Special dies, tools, jigs, and fixtures

(G-3827)
LEE MANUFACTURING INC
46 Barnes Industrial Rd S (06492-2438)
P.O. Box 758 (06492-0758)
PHONE..............................203 284-0466
George M Eames Iv, *Pr*
George M Eames Iii, *Dir*
EMP: 60 EST: 1998
SQ FT: 40,000
SALES (est): 5.56MM **Privately Held**
Web: www.leemanufacturing.com
SIC: 3444 Metal housings, enclosures, casings, and other containers

(G-3828)
LINGOL CORPORATION
415 S Cherry St (06492-4428)
P.O. Box 791 (06492-0791)
PHONE..............................203 265-3608
Peter W Lindenfelser, *VP*
Ruth B Lindenfelser, *Sec*
EMP: 10 EST: 1974
SALES (est): 1MM **Privately Held**
Web: www.lingolcorp.com
SIC: 3089 Injection molding of plastics

(G-3829)
MAGNETEC CORPORATION
Also Called: Ithaca Peripherals Div
7 Laser Ln (06492-1928)
PHONE..............................203 949-9933
Bart C Shuldman, *Pr*
Richard Cote, *Ex VP*
John Cygielnik, *Sr VP*
Lucy H Staley, *Sr VP*
Michael Kumpf, *Sr VP*
EMP: 70 EST: 1973
SQ FT: 44,000
SALES (est): 836.1K **Publicly Held**
SIC: 3577 Printers, computer
PA: Transact Technologies Incorporated
1 Hamden Ctr
Hamden CT 06518

(G-3830)
MATTHEWS PRINTING CO
10 Marshall St (06492-4097)
P.O. Box 456 (06492-0456)
PHONE..............................203 265-0363
Dean De Negris, *Pr*
Gail De Negris, *Sec*
EMP: 10 EST: 1960
SQ FT: 4,000
SALES (est): 836.09K **Privately Held**
SIC: 2752 2759 Offset printing; Letterpress printing

(G-3831)
MEASUREMENT SYSTEMS INC
Also Called: Ultra Elec Measurement Systems
50 Barnes Park Rd N Ste 101
(06492-5920)
PHONE..............................203 949-3500
Peter Crawford, *Pr*
Ken L Tasch, *
EMP: 42 EST: 1960
SQ FT: 19,500
SALES (est): 12MM
SALES (corp-wide): 2.67MM **Privately Held**
Web: www.ultra.group
SIC: 3625 3577 Electric controls and control accessories, industrial; Computer peripheral equipment, nec
HQ: Ultra Electronics Holdings Limited

Unit C1 Knaves Beech Business Centre
High Wycombe BUCKS HP10
208 813-4321

(G-3832)
MIDSTATE ELECTRONICS CO
71 S Turnpike Rd Ste 2 (06492-3421)
PHONE..............................203 265-9900
Josh Reed, *Pr*
▲ EMP: 18 EST: 1977
SQ FT: 7,774
SALES (est): 4.5MM **Privately Held**
Web: www.midstateelectronics.com
SIC: 5065 3672 Electronic parts; Printed circuit boards

(G-3833)
MIKCO MANUFACTURING INC
14 Village Ln (06492-2427)
P.O. Box 764 (06492-0764)
PHONE..............................203 269-2250
Michael J Boissy, *Pr*
Michael S Boissy, *VP*
Betty J Boissy, *Stockholder*
EMP: 14 EST: 1977
SQ FT: 9,000
SALES (est): 2.1MM **Privately Held**
SIC: 3599 Machine shop, jobbing and repair

(G-3834)
NEW DESIGNZ INC
Also Called: Manufacturing
1068 N Farms Rd Ste 2 (06492-5939)
PHONE..............................203 439-7784
EMP: 14 EST: 2004
SALES (est): 4.11MM **Privately Held**
Web: www.newdesignz.com
SIC: 3599 Machine shop, jobbing and repair

(G-3835)
NN INC
6 Northrop Industrial Park Rd W
(06492-1962)
PHONE..............................203 793-7132
EMP: 11
SALES (corp-wide): 498.74MM **Publicly Held**
Web: www.nninc.com
SIC: 3562 Ball bearings and parts
PA: Nn, Inc.
6210 Ardrey Kell Rd # 600
Charlotte NC 28277
980 264-4300

(G-3836)
NUCOR STEEL CONNECTICUT INC
Also Called: Nucor Bar Mill Group
35 Toelles Rd (06492-4419)
P.O. Box 928 (06492-0928)
PHONE..............................203 265-0615
Aymond S Napolitan, *Pr*
Tomas A Miller, *
◆ EMP: 157 EST: 1983
SQ FT: 227,120
SALES (est): 52.24MM
SALES (corp-wide): 41.51B **Publicly Held**
Web: www.nucor.com
SIC: 3312 3449 3496 Rods, iron and steel: made in steel mills; Bars, concrete reinforcing: fabricated steel; Mesh, made from purchased wire
PA: Nucor Corporation
1915 Rexford Rd Ste 400
Charlotte NC 28211
704 366-7000

(G-3837)
PAUWAY CORP
63 N Cherry St Ste 2 (06492-2363)
PHONE..............................203 265-3939
Wayne Rydzy, *Pr*
Paulette Rydzy, *Sec*
EMP: 15 EST: 1978
SALES (est): 2.14MM **Privately Held**
Web: www.pauwaycorp.com
SIC: 3479 Coating of metals and formed products

(G-3838)
PRALINES INC
Also Called: Pralines Central
30 N Plains Industrial Rd Ste 12
(06492-2357)
PHONE..............................203 284-8847
Donna Torre, *Pr*
Dana Torre, *Pr*
EMP: 11 EST: 1984
SQ FT: 1,900
SALES (est): 965.79K **Privately Held**
Web: www.pralinesownmade.com
SIC: 2024 Ice cream, bulk

(G-3839)
PRECISION DEVICES INC (PA)
55 N Plains Industrial Rd (06492-5812)
PHONE..............................203 265-9308
William P Bacha Junior, *Pr*
Mark Hoover, *VP*
Christine Bacha, *Sec*
EMP: 17 EST: 1981
SQ FT: 8,000
SALES (est): 4.86MM
SALES (corp-wide): 4.86MM **Privately Held**
Web: www.precisiondevices.com
SIC: 7694 5063 Electric motor repair; Electrical apparatus and equipment

(G-3840)
PRECISION ENGINEERED PDTS LLC
Also Called: Pep Connecticut Plastics
6 Northrop Industrial Park Rd W
(06492-1962)
PHONE..............................203 265-3299
Claire Webb Cust, *Svc Mgr*
EMP: 40
SALES (corp-wide): 433.51MM **Privately Held**
Web: www.nninc.com
SIC: 3089 Injection molding of plastics
HQ: Precision Engineered Products Llc
110 Frank Mossberg Dr
Attleboro MA 02703

(G-3841)
PROTON ENERGY SYSTEMS INC
Also Called: Nel Hydrogen US
10 Technology Dr (06492-1955)
PHONE..............................203 678-2000
▲ EMP: 132 EST: 1996
SQ FT: 98,703
SALES (est): 50.68MM
SALES (corp-wide): 4.87B **Privately Held**
Web: www.protononsite.com
SIC: 3569 Gas producers, generators, and other gas related equipment
HQ: Nel Asa
Karenslyst Alle 49
Oslo 0279

(G-3842)
PROTRONIX INC
Also Called: Protronix

28 Parker St (06492-2320)
PHONE..............................203 269-5858
Don Rosadini Junior, *Pr*
Janis Rosadini, *Sec*
EMP: 10 EST: 1986
SQ FT: 3,500
SALES (est): 1.6MM **Privately Held**
Web: www.protronix.us
SIC: 3679 Electronic circuits

(G-3843)
QUALITY ENGINEERING SVCS INC
122 N Plains Industrial Rd (06492-2386)
PHONE..............................203 269-5054
Richard Addy, *Pr*
Harold Addy, *
Gregory Whitehouse, *
EMP: 30 EST: 1971
SQ FT: 10,000
SALES (est): 4.48MM **Privately Held**
Web: www.qes1.com
SIC: 8711 3449 3544 Mechanical engineering; Miscellaneous metalwork; Special dies, tools, jigs, and fixtures

(G-3844)
R & D PRECISION INC
63 N Cherry St Ste 1 (06492-2363)
PHONE..............................203 284-3396
William D Harkness, *Pr*
Robin Harkness, *Sec*
EMP: 19 EST: 1987
SQ FT: 14,000
SALES (est): 2.22MM **Privately Held**
Web: www.rdprecisioninc.com
SIC: 3444 Sheet metal specialties, not stamped

(G-3845)
RACING TIMES
428 Main St (06492-2275)
PHONE..............................203 298-2899
Alan Joseph Piquette, *Pt*
EMP: 8 EST: 2009
SQ FT: 2,300
SALES (est): 133.46K **Privately Held**
SIC: 2721 Magazines: publishing and printing

(G-3846)
ROEHM AMERICA LLC
528 S Cherry St (06492-4458)
PHONE..............................203 269-4481
EMP: 50
SALES (corp-wide): 2.67MM **Privately Held**
Web: www.roehm.com
SIC: 2821 Plastics materials and resins
HQ: Roehm America Llc
8 Campus Dr Ste 1
Parsippany NJ 07054
800 225-0172

(G-3847)
RUSSELL ORGANICS LLC
329 Main St Ste 208 (06492-2273)
PHONE..............................203 285-6633
◆ EMP: 7 EST: 2009
SALES (est): 505.99K **Privately Held**
Web: www.russellorganics.com
SIC: 2844 Cosmetic preparations

(G-3848)
SIMSON CORPORATION
50 N Plains Industrial Rd (06492-2333)
PHONE..............................203 265-9882
Allen Cuccaro, *Pr*
Michael Frank, *Sec*
EMP: 13 EST: 1976

SALES (est): 538.7K **Privately Held**
Web: www.simsonproducts.com
SIC: 3599 Machine shop, jobbing and repair

(G-3849)
SJD TECH INC
Also Called: Orafol
320 Barnes Rd (06492-1804)
PHONE..................................203 269-9500
Randall Mertz, *CEO*
◆ **EMP:** 75 **EST:** 1948
SQ FT: 70,000
SALES (est): 29.47MM
SALES (corp-wide): 903.73MM **Privately Held**
Web: www.orafol.com
SIC: 2821 Plastics materials and resins
HQ: Orafol Americas Inc.
1100 Oracal Pkwy
Black Creek GA 31308
912 851-5000

(G-3850)
SORRENTO FINE WOODWORK LLC
340 Quinnipiac St Bldg 43l (06492-4050)
PHONE..................................203 741-9263
Mark Burlison, *Prin*
Mike Zurlis, *Prin*
EMP: 10 **EST:** 2019
SALES (est): 441.01K **Privately Held**
Web: www.sorrentofinewoodwork.com
SIC: 2431 Millwork

(G-3851)
SOUTHERN CONN PALLET CO INC
346 Quinnipiac St (06492-4053)
P.O. Box 4566 (06492-7566)
PHONE..................................203 265-1313
James Waldeck, *Pr*
EMP: 7 **EST:** 1980
SQ FT: 10,000
SALES (est): 910.35K **Privately Held**
Web:
www.southernconnecticutpallet.com
SIC: 2448 Pallets, wood

(G-3852)
SPECIALTY CABLE CORP
2 Tower Dr (06492-1877)
P.O. Box 50 (06492-0050)
PHONE..................................203 265-7126
Kim Bowen, *CEO*
Carl Shanahan, *
Carl Shanahan Junior, *Sec*
EMP: 70 **EST:** 1986
SQ FT: 65,000
SALES (est): 21.63MM **Privately Held**
Web: www.specialtycable.com
SIC: 3357 3315 5063 Nonferrous
wiredrawing and insulating; Cable, steel:
insulated or armored; Wire and cable

(G-3853)
SPECIALTY COMPONENTS INC
14 Village Ln Ste 1 (06492-2459)
PHONE..................................203 284-9112
Marc Hadarik, *Pr*
Amy Hadarik, *Sec*
EMP: 9 **EST:** 1975
SQ FT: 17,000
SALES (est): 1MM **Privately Held**
Web: www.specialtycomponents.com
SIC: 3599 Machine shop, jobbing and repair

(G-3854)
STABAN ENGINEERING CORP
65 N Plains Industrial Rd (06492-5832)

P.O. Box 8 (06492-0008)
PHONE..................................203 294-1997
Dennis Bandecchi, *Pr*
Todd Widener, *VP*
EMP: 14 **EST:** 1992
SQ FT: 16,500
SALES (est): 2.39MM **Privately Held**
Web: www.staban.com
SIC: 3565 Packing and wrapping machinery

(G-3855)
STRAIN MEASUREMENT DEVICES INC
55 Barnes Park Rd N (06492-1883)
PHONE..................................203 294-5800
Frederick E Jackson, *Pr*
Daniel Shapiro, *
Barrie Hopewell, *
EMP: 25 **EST:** 1979
SQ FT: 14,000
SALES (est): 6.47MM **Privately Held**
Web: www.smdsensors.com
SIC: 3674 Semiconductors and related devices

(G-3856)
SULZER PUMP SOLUTIONS US INC (PA)
108 Leigus Rd (06492-6062)
PHONE..................................203 238-2700
John Everhart, *Pr*
Stefan Baumgaertner, *
▲ **EMP:** 25 **EST:** 2011
SALES (est): 8.81MM
SALES (corp-wide): 8.81MM **Privately Held**
SIC: 3561 5251 5084 Industrial pumps and parts; Pumps and pumping equipment; Pumps and pumping equipment, nec

(G-3857)
TECHNICAL METAL FINISHING INC
Also Called: T M F
29 Capital Dr (06492-5818)
PHONE..................................203 284-7825
Levi Citarella, *Pr*
Phillip Milidaneri, *
Alfred Matarese, *
EMP: 23 **EST:** 2008
SALES (est): 2.35MM **Privately Held**
Web: www.sintoamerica.com
SIC: 3471 Electroplating of metals or formed products

(G-3858)
TELECT MFG LLC
358 Hall Ave (06492-3574)
PHONE..................................877 858-3855
EMP: 11 **EST:** 2019
SALES (est): 2.21MM
SALES (corp-wide): 12.62B **Publicly Held**
SIC: 3678 Electronic connectors
PA: Amphenol Corporation
358 Hall Ave
Wallingford CT 06492
203 265-8900

(G-3859)
TENOVA INC
1070 N Farms Rd Ste 3b (06492-5931)
PHONE..................................203 265-5684
Frank Byus, *Prin*
EMP: 20
Web: www.tenova.com
SIC: 8711 5084 3325 Industrial engineers; Industrial machinery and equipment; Rolling mill rolls, cast steel
HQ: Tenova Inc.
100 Corporate Center Dr # 100

Coraopolis PA 15108
412 262-2240

(G-3860)
THATS GREAT NEWS LLC
900 Northrop Rd Ste F (06492-1900)
P.O. Box 5021 (06492-7521)
PHONE..................................203 649-4900
EMP: 24 **EST:** 2003
SALES (est): 4.74MM **Privately Held**
Web: www.thatsgreatnews.com
SIC: 2711 Newspapers, publishing and printing

(G-3861)
THERMOSPAS HOT TUB PRODUCTS
47 N Plains Industrial Rd (06492-5831)
PHONE..................................203 303-0005
Andrew Tournas, *Pr*
EMP: 35 **EST:** 2012
SALES (est): 10.33MM
SALES (corp-wide): 423.13K **Privately Held**
Web: online.thermospas.com
SIC: 3999 Hot tubs
HQ: Sundance Spas, Inc.
17872 Gillette Ave # 300
Irvine CA 92614
909 606-7733

(G-3862)
THOMAS KEEGAN & SONS INC
Also Called: Keegan Construction
38 Evanwood Dr (06492-2057)
PHONE..................................203 239-9248
Terrence Keegan, *Pr*
Mary L Keegan, *Sec*
Terrence J Keegan, *Pr*
EMP: 19 **EST:** 1966
SALES (est): 2.26MM **Privately Held**
Web: www.keeganmaterials.com
SIC: 7359 4212 1794 1442 Equipment rental and leasing, nec; Local trucking, without storage; Excavation work; Construction sand and gravel

(G-3863)
THYSSENKRUPP MATERIALS NA INC
Copper and Brass Sales Div
5 Sterling Dr (06492-1843)
PHONE..................................610 586-1800
Frank Kavani, *Brnch Mgr*
EMP: 43
SALES (corp-wide): 40.78B **Privately Held**
Web:
www.thyssenkrupp-materials-na.com
SIC: 3341 5051 Secondary nonferrous metals; Iron and steel (ferrous) products
HQ: Thyssenkrupp Materials Na, Inc.
22355 W 11 Mile Rd
Southfield MI 48033
248 233-5600

(G-3864)
TICO TITANIUM INC (PA)
Also Called: Lhi Metals
34b Barnes Industrial Rd S (06492-2438)
P.O. Box 336 (48066-0336)
PHONE..................................248 446-0400
Lawrence Buhl Iii, *CEO*
Gary C Johnson, *
Jeffrey A White, *
Lawrence Coassin, *
James D Morell, *
▲ **EMP:** 31 **EST:** 1957
SQ FT: 60,500
SALES (est): 8.85MM
SALES (corp-wide): 8.85MM **Privately Held**

SIC: 5051 3452 3441 3356 Nonferrous metal sheets, bars, rods, etc., nec; Bolts, nuts, rivets, and washers; Fabricated structural metal; Nonferrous rolling and drawing, nec

(G-3865)
TIMES FIBER COMMUNICATIONS INC (HQ)
358 Hall Ave (06492-3574)
P.O. Box 384 (06492-7006)
PHONE..................................800 677-2288
Adam Norwitt, *Pr*
Craig Lampo, *
◆ **EMP:** 54 **EST:** 1948
SQ FT: 15,000
SALES (est): 203.7MM
SALES (corp-wide): 12.62B **Publicly Held**
Web: www.amphenolbroadband.com
SIC: 3357 Coaxial cable, nonferrous
PA: Amphenol Corporation
358 Hall Ave
Wallingford CT 06492
203 265-8900

(G-3866)
TIMES MICROWAVE SYSTEMS INC (HQ)
Also Called: Times Microwave Systems
358 Hall Ave (06492-3574)
P.O. Box 5039 (06492-7539)
PHONE..................................203 949-8400
Bill Callahan, *Genl Mgr*
Dominique Thompson, *
David Kiesling, *
▲ **EMP:** 300 **EST:** 1948
SQ FT: 154,000
SALES (est): 91.81MM
SALES (corp-wide): 12.62B **Publicly Held**
Web: www.timesmicrowave.com
SIC: 3679 3357 3678 Microwave components; Appliance fixture wire, nonferrous; Electronic connectors
PA: Amphenol Corporation
358 Hall Ave
Wallingford CT 06492
203 265-8900

(G-3867)
TIMES WIRE AND CABLE COMPANY (HQ)
Also Called: Amphenol
358 Hall Ave (06492-3574)
PHONE..................................203 949-8400
EMP: 62 **EST:** 2008
SALES (est): 3.32MM
SALES (corp-wide): 12.62B **Publicly Held**
Web: www.amphenol.com
SIC: 3643 5063 Current-carrying wiring services; Electronic wire and cable
PA: Amphenol Corporation
358 Hall Ave
Wallingford CT 06492
203 265-8900

(G-3868)
TIMNA MANUFACTURING INC
208 N Plains Industrial Rd (06492-2358)
PHONE..................................203 265-4656
Sharon A Nagy, *Pr*
Frank A Nagy, *VP*
EMP: 9 **EST:** 1979
SALES (est): 883.52K **Privately Held**
SIC: 3599 Machine shop, jobbing and repair

(G-3869)
TMC LIQUIDATING CORP
Also Called: Marlin Company, The
10 Research Pkwy Ste 100 (06492-1963)

PHONE...................800 344-5901
▲ **EMP:** 85
Web: www.appspace.com
SIC: 7372 Prepackaged software

(G-3870)
TRUE PUBLISHING COMPANY
Also Called: Cheshire Herald
125 Grandview Ave (06492-5157)
P.O. Box 247 (06410-0247)
PHONE...................203 272-5316
Joseph Jakubisyn, *Owner*
Joseph Jakubisyn, *Pr*
Maureen Jakubisyn, *Sec*
EMP: 15 **EST:** 1953
SALES (est): 869.88K **Privately Held**
Web: www.cheshireherald.com
SIC: 2711 Newspapers: publishing only, not printed on site

(G-3871)
ULBRICH STAINLESS STEELS
Also Called: Ulbrich Steel
1 Dudley Ave (06492-4457)
P.O. Box 610 (06492-0610)
PHONE...................203 269-2507
Rob Giapponi, *Mgr*
EMP: 180
SALES (corp-wide): 196.78MM **Privately Held**
Web: www.ulbrich.com
SIC: 3316 3547 3356 3339 Cold finishing of steel shapes; Rolling mill machinery; Nonferrous rolling and drawing, nec; Primary nonferrous metals, nec
PA: Ulbrich Stainless Steels & Special Metals, Inc.
153 Washington Ave
North Haven CT 06473
203 239-4481

(G-3872)
UNHOLTZ-DICKIE CORPORATION
6 Brookside Dr (06492-1893)
PHONE...................203 265-3929
Michael K Reen, *Pr*
Gerald K Reen, *
◆ **EMP:** 48 **EST:** 1958
SQ FT: 40,000
SALES (est): 9.65MM **Privately Held**
Web: www.udco.com
SIC: 3829 Vibration meters, analyzers, and calibrators

(G-3873)
VALUE PRINT INCORPORATED
34 Mellor Dr (06492-4953)
PHONE...................203 265-1371
John L Kastukevich, *Pr*
Mary R Kastukevich, *Sec*
EMP: 7 **EST:** 1976
SQ FT: 5,000
SALES (est): 174.1K **Privately Held**
SIC: 2752 Offset printing

(G-3874)
VERTIV CORPORATION
Also Called: Vertiv
8 Fairfield Blvd Ste 4 (06492-1890)
PHONE...................203 294-6020
EMP: 10
SALES (corp-wide): 5.69B **Publicly Held**
Web: www.vertiv.com
SIC: 3823 Process control instruments
HQ: Vertiv Corporation
505 N Cleveland Ave
Westerville OH 43082
614 888-0246

(G-3875)
WEATHERFORD INTERNATIONAL LLC
8 Enterprise Rd (06492-1835)
PHONE...................203 294-0190
Kevin Didden, *Brnch Mgr*
EMP: 25
Web: www.weatherford.com
SIC: 1389 Oil field services, nec
HQ: Weatherford International, Llc
2000 Saint James Pl
Houston TX 77056
713 693-4000

(G-3876)
Z-MEDICA LLC
4 Fairfield Blvd Ste 1 (06492-1857)
PHONE...................203 294-0000
Eric Compton, *CEO*
David Dean, *CFO*
▲ **EMP:** 68 **EST:** 2012
SQ FT: 20,000
SALES (est): 24.57MM
SALES (corp-wide): 2.79B **Publicly Held**
Web: www.quikclot.com
SIC: 5047 2211 Medical equipment and supplies; Bandages, gauzes and surgical fabrics, cotton
PA: Teleflex Incorporated
550 E Swedesford Rd # 400
Wayne PA 19087
610 225-6800

Washington Depot
Litchfield County

(G-3877)
NICHOLS WOODWORKING LLC
P.O. Box 618 (06794-0618)
PHONE...................860 350-4223
EMP: 35
SALES (corp-wide): 185.76K **Privately Held**
Web: www.nicholswoodworking.com
SIC: 2431 Millwork
PA: Nichol's Woodworking Llc
136 Walker Brook Rd S
Washington Depot CT 06794
860 350-4223

Waterbury
New Haven County

(G-3878)
77 MATTATUCK HEIGHTS LLC
77 Mattatuck Heights Rd (06705-3832)
PHONE...................203 597-9338
▲ **EMP:** 8 **EST:** 1998
SALES (est): 429.55K **Privately Held**
SIC: 2431 Woodwork, interior and ornamental, nec

(G-3879)
ALENT INC
245 Freight St (06702-1818)
PHONE...................203 575-5980
Allan Macdonald, *Prin*
EMP: 84 **EST:** 1986
SALES (est): 22.78MM
SALES (corp-wide): 2.55B **Publicly Held**
Web: www.macdermid.com
SIC: 3699 Electrical equipment and supplies, nec
HQ: Macdermid, Incorporated
245 Freight St
Waterbury CT 06702
203 575-5700

(G-3880)
ALENT USA HOLDING INC
245 Freight St (06702-1818)
PHONE...................203 575-5727
Steven Corbett, *Pr*
Robert Landry, *
William Gorgone, *
Allan Macdonald, *
Joseph M Creighton, *
EMP: 25 **EST:** 2012
SALES (est): 1.75MM
SALES (corp-wide): 2.55B **Publicly Held**
SIC: 3699 3356 3341 3313 Electrical equipment and supplies, nec; Solder: wire, bar, acid core, and rosin core; Lead smelting and refining (secondary); Alloys, additive, except copper: not made in blast furnaces
PA: Element Solutions Inc
500 E Broward Blvd # 1860
Fort Lauderdale FL 33394
561 207-9600

(G-3881)
ALPHA ASSEMBLY SOLUTIONS INC
Also Called: Alpha Advanced Materials
245 Freight St (06702-1818)
PHONE...................203 575-5696
EMP: 27
SALES (corp-wide): 2.55B **Publicly Held**
Web: www.macdermidalpha.com
SIC: 3356 Solder: wire, bar, acid core, and rosin core
HQ: Alpha Assembly Solutions Inc.
4100 6th Ave
Altoona PA 16602
814 946-1611

(G-3882)
AMERICAN ELECTRO PRODUCTS INC
Also Called: American Electro Products
1358 Thomaston Ave (06704-1791)
P.O. Box 4129 (06704-0129)
PHONE...................203 756-7051
Dennis Burke, *Pr*
John Krin, *
EMP: 135 **EST:** 1950
SALES (est): 21.63MM
SALES (corp-wide): 48.04MM **Privately Held**
Web: www.americanelectro.com
SIC: 3471 Electroplating of metals or formed products
PA: National Integrated Industries, Inc.
322 Main St
Farmington CT 06032
860 677-7995

(G-3883)
AMERICAN PLASTIC PRODUCTS INC
2114 Thomaston Ave (06704-1013)
P.O. Box 4429 (06704-0429)
PHONE...................203 596-2410
Dennis M Burke, *Pr*
EMP: 135 **EST:** 1950
SQ FT: 5,000
SALES (est): 26.42MM
SALES (corp-wide): 48.04MM **Privately Held**
Web: www.americanplasticproductsinc.com
SIC: 3089 Injection molding of plastics
PA: National Integrated Industries, Inc.
322 Main St
Farmington CT 06032
860 677-7995

(G-3884)
AMERICAN-REPUBLICAN INC (PA)
Also Called: Republican-American
389 Meadow St (06702-1808)
P.O. Box 2090 (06722-2090)
PHONE...................203 574-3636
William B Pape, *Pr*
EMP: 185 **EST:** 1923
SQ FT: 110
SALES (est): 39.14MM
SALES (corp-wide): 39.14MM **Privately Held**
Web: www.rep-am.com
SIC: 2711 2752 Newspapers, publishing and printing; Commercial printing, lithographic

(G-3885)
ANGEL FUEL LLC
56 Knoll St (06705-1813)
PHONE...................203 597-8759
Angel L Morales, *Mgr*
EMP: 8 **EST:** 2005
SALES (est): 401.7K **Privately Held**
SIC: 3443 Fuel tanks (oil, gas, etc.), metal plate

(G-3886)
ARCHITECTURAL SUPPLEMENTS LLC
567 S Leonard St Bldg 1b (06708-4300)
PHONE...................203 591-5505
Phil Feinman, *Ch Bd*
Steven C Decker, *Pt*
▲ **EMP:** 18 **EST:** 1997
SQ FT: 50,000
SALES (est): 4.38MM **Privately Held**
Web: www.architecturalsupplements.com
SIC: 3089 3412 Plastics containers, except foam; Metal barrels, drums, and pails

(G-3887)
ASEPSIS INC
199 Benson Rd (06749-0001)
PHONE...................203 573-2000
Billie S Flaherty, *Prin*
EMP: 14 **EST:** 1960
SALES (est): 201.89K **Privately Held**
SIC: 2834 Pharmaceutical preparations

(G-3888)
ATI FLAT RLLED PDTS HLDNGS LLC
Also Called: ATI Flat Rolled Products
271 Railroad Hill St (06708-4306)
PHONE...................203 756-7414
Jose Reyes, *Mgr*
EMP: 10
Web: www.atimaterials.com
SIC: 3312 5051 Stainless steel; Steel
HQ: Ati Flat Rolled Products Holdings, Llc
1000 Six Ppg Pl
Pittsburgh PA 15222
412 394-3047

(G-3889)
BAR WORK MANUFACTURING CO INC
1198 Highland Ave (06708-4911)
PHONE...................203 753-4103
William Steinen Junior, *Pr*
John J Scopelliti, *VP*
John B Dangler, *Sec*
EMP: 44 **EST:** 1951
SQ FT: 24,000
SALES (est): 2.41MM
SALES (corp-wide): 22.03MM **Privately Held**

Web: www.tbwprecision.com
SIC: 3451 Screw machine products
PA: Wm. Steinen Mfg. Co.
    29 E Halsey Rd
    Parsippany NJ 07054
    973 887-6400

(G-3890)
BERKLEY ASSOCIATES INC
2712 S Main St (06706-2647)
P.O. Box 2542 (06723-2542)
PHONE..............................203 757-9221
William E Finkenzeller, *VP*
Robert A Finkenzeller, *
Harriet Finkenzeller, *
Frank T Healey, *
EMP: 65 EST: 1963
SQ FT: 30,000
SALES (est): 6.78MM **Privately Held**
Web: www.eyeletcrafters.com
SIC: 3469 3471 Stamping metal for the trade
; Finishing, metals or formed products

(G-3891)
BPREX HALTHCARE
BROOKVILLE INC
574 E Main St (06702-1706)
P.O. Box 808 (06720-0808)
PHONE..............................203 754-4141
Kevin Edwards, *Mgr*
EMP: 262
SQ FT: 100,000
SIC: 3089 Caps, plastics
HQ: Bprex Healthcare Brookville Inc.
    1899 N Wilkinson Way
    Perrysburg OH 43551

(G-3892)
BRASS CITY TILE DESIGNS LLC
29 S Commons Rd Ste 3 (06704-1060)
PHONE..............................203 597-8764
Martin Niatopsky, *Owner*
EMP: 7 EST: 2015
SALES (est): 249.97K **Privately Held**
Web: www.brasscitiledesigns.com
SIC: 2499 3253 5032 Tiles, cork; Ceramic
wall and floor tile; Ceramic wall and floor
tile, nec

(G-3893)
BRIDGESTONE RET
OPERATIONS LLC
Also Called: Firestone
809 Wolcott St (06705-1313)
PHONE..............................203 754-6119
Raymond Jones, *Mgr*
EMP: 10
Web: www.bridgestoneamericas.com
SIC: 5531 7534 Automotive tires;
Rebuilding and retreading tires
HQ: Bridgestone Retail Operations, Llc
    333 E Lake St Ste 300
    Bloomingdale IL 60108
    630 259-9000

(G-3894)
BYRNE GROUP INC
Also Called: Minuteman Tress
156 Grand St (06702-1909)
PHONE..............................203 573-0100
Matt Byrne, *Pr*
Tiffany Byrne, *VP*
EMP: 17 EST: 2016
SALES (est): 969.27K **Privately Held**
Web: www.minutemanpress.com
SIC: 2752 Commercial printing, lithographic

(G-3895)
C F D ENGINEERING COMPANY
Naugatuck Manufacturing Div
105 Avenue Of Industry (06705-3902)
P.O. Box 3175 (06705-0175)
PHONE..............................203 754-2807
Chuck Adminson, *Mgr*
EMP: 16
SALES (corp-wide): 1.88MM **Privately
Held**
Web: www.naugatuckmfg.com
SIC: 3823 Industrial flow and liquid
measuring instruments
PA: The C F D Engineering Company
    194 Cook Rd
    Prospect CT 06712
    203 758-4148

(G-3896)
CARLSON FUEL OF MERIDEN
INC
532 S Leonard St (06708-4317)
P.O. Box 40 (06492-0040)
PHONE..............................203 574-9396
Christopher T Carr, *Prin*
EMP: 11 EST: 2008
SALES (est): 500.35K **Privately Held**
SIC: 2869 Fuels

(G-3897)
CARPIN MANUFACTURING INC
Also Called: Carpin
411 Austin Rd (06705-3763)
P.O. Box 471 (06720-0471)
PHONE..............................203 574-2556
Ralph Carpinella, *Ch Bd*
David Ferraro, *Pr*
Rachel S Albanese, *Treas*
▲ EMP: 90 EST: 1984
SQ FT: 60,000
SALES (est): 19.3MM **Privately Held**
Web: www.carpin.com
SIC: 3469 3089 3441 Metal stampings, nec;
Injection molding of plastics; Fabricated
structural metal

(G-3898)
CLY-DEL MANUFACTURING
COMPANY
151 Sharon Rd (06705-4041)
P.O. Box 1367 (06721-1367)
PHONE..............................203 574-2100
Robert W Garthwait, *Ch*
Robert W Garthwait Junior, *Pr*
Charles W Henry, *Sec*
▲ EMP: 215 EST: 1939
SQ FT: 185,000
SALES (est): 25.21MM **Privately Held**
Web: www.cly-del.com
SIC: 3469 Stamping metal for the trade

(G-3899)
COLONIAL CORRUGATED PDTS
INC
118 Railroad Hill St (06708-4320)
P.O. Box 2753 (06723-2753)
PHONE..............................203 597-1707
Jack Bair, *Pr*
Angela Derkins, *
EMP: 33 EST: 1980
SALES (est): 732.37K **Privately Held**
SIC: 2653 Boxes, corrugated: made from
purchased materials

(G-3900)
COMPUGRAPHICS USA INC (HQ)
Also Called: Compugraphics
245 Freight St (06702-1818)
PHONE..............................510 249-2600

Lawrence Amon, *Pr*
EMP: 56 EST: 1983
SALES (est): 11.25MM
SALES (corp-wide): 2.55B **Publicly Held**
Web: www.compsus.com
SIC: 3674 Integrated circuits,
semiconductor networks, etc.
PA: Element Solutions Inc
    500 E Broward Blvd # 1860
    Fort Lauderdale FL 33394
    561 207-9600

(G-3901)
CONCENTRIC TOOL & MFG CO
INC
133 S Leonard St (06708-4246)
PHONE..............................203 756-9145
Klaus D Babiarz, *Pr*
EMP: 13 EST: 1972
SQ FT: 7,000
SALES (est): 2.45MM **Privately Held**
Web: www.concentrictoolct.com
SIC: 3599 Machine shop, jobbing and repair

(G-3902)
CUSTOMIZED FOODS MFG LLC
8 S Commons Rd (06704-1035)
PHONE..............................203 759-1645
Al Poe, *Pr*
EMP: 8 EST: 2006
SALES (est): 526.49K **Privately Held**
SIC: 3999 Manufacturing industries, nec

(G-3903)
D & M PACKING LLC
407 Brookside Rd Ste 1 (06708-1453)
P.O. Box 4038 (06704-0038)
PHONE..............................203 591-8986
David Miller, *Pr*
Aziz Debbagh, *
▲ EMP: 28 EST: 2013
SALES (est): 2.88MM **Privately Held**
Web: www.dandmpacking.com
SIC: 5149 2032 Organic and diet food;
Ethnic foods, canned, jarred, etc.

(G-3904)
DASCO WELDED PRODUCTS
INC
2038 Thomaston Ave (06704-1036)
PHONE..............................203 754-9353
Daren Edward Thornberg, *Pr*
EMP: 11 EST: 1993
SQ FT: 3,000
SALES (est): 2.86MM **Privately Held**
Web: www.dascowelding.com
SIC: 7692 Welding repair

(G-3905)
DENOMINATOR COMPANY INC
20 S Commons Rd (06704-1035)
P.O. Box 5004 (06798-5004)
PHONE..............................203 263-3210
Thomas C Clark, *Pr*
EMP: 15 EST: 1961
SALES (est): 1.52MM **Privately Held**
SIC: 3824 Mechanical counters

(G-3906)
DEVIVO INDUSTRIES INC
211 Brookside Rd (06708-1428)
PHONE..............................203 270-1552
Anthony Rosati, *Pr*
EMP: 21 EST: 1966
SQ FT: 39,000
SALES (est): 4.16MM
SALES (corp-wide): 10.87MM **Privately
Held**

SIC: 3589 3559 Garbage disposers and
compactors, commercial; Recycling
machinery
PA: Hi-Rise Recycling Companies, Inc.
    148 E Liberty St Ste 210
    Wooster OH

(G-3907)
DIASYS CORP
21 W Main St (06702-2013)
PHONE..............................302 636-5400
EMP: 16 EST: 2009
SALES (est): 320.37K **Privately Held**
Web: www.diasys-diagnostics.com
SIC: 3826 Analytical instruments

(G-3908)
DURCO MANUFACTURING CO
INC
493 S Leonard St (06708-4315)
PHONE..............................203 575-0446
Sebastian Corona, *Pr*
F Donald Ek, *CEO*
EMP: 8 EST: 1987
SQ FT: 5,000
SALES (est): 913.15K **Privately Held**
Web: www.durcomfg.com
SIC: 3451 Screw machine products

(G-3909)
E & J PARTS CLEANING INC
1669 Thomaston Ave (06704-1026)
P.O. Box 4250 (06704-0250)
PHONE..............................203 757-1716
Everett Hardick, *Pr*
EMP: 11 EST: 1993
SALES (est): 1.45MM **Privately Held**
Web: www.ejpartscleaning.com
SIC: 3471 7349 Cleaning and descaling
metal products; Cleaning service, industrial
or commercial

(G-3910)
EEMAX INC
400 Captain Neville Dr (06705-3811)
PHONE..............................203 267-7890
Kevin M Ruppelt, *Pr*
◆ EMP: 80 EST: 1988
SQ FT: 16,000
SALES (est): 20.44MM **Privately Held**
Web: www.eemax.com
SIC: 3639 Hot water heaters, household
HQ: Rheem Manufacturing Company Inc
    1100 Abernathy Rd # 1700
    Atlanta GA 30328
    770 351-3000

(G-3911)
EYELET DESIGN INC
2223 Thomaston Ave (06704-1000)
P.O. Box 808 (06720-0808)
PHONE..............................203 754-4141
Robert L Hughes, *Pr*
Claudia M Hughes, *
EMP: 100 EST: 1993
SALES (est): 8.21MM **Privately Held**
Web: www.eyeletdesign.com
SIC: 3469 3466 Stamping metal for the trade
; Crowns and closures

(G-3912)
FASCIAS CHOCOLATES INC
44 Chase River Rd (06704-1408)
PHONE..............................203 753-0515
Carmen Romeo, *Pr*
Lynne Fascia Moanes, *VP*
Louise Fascia Romeo, *Sec*
EMP: 14 EST: 1964
SQ FT: 18,000
SALES (est): 890.58K **Privately Held**

▲ = Import ▼ = Export
◆ = Import/Export

Web: www.faschoc.com
SIC: **5441** 2064 Confectionery produced for direct sale on the premises; Candy and other confectionery products

(G-3913)
FORUM PLASTICS LLC
105 Progress Ln (06705-3878)
PHONE.................................203 754-0777
Joseph Pasqualucci, *Prin*
EMP: 50 **EST:** 2011
SALES (est): 27.14MM **Privately Held**
Web: www.forummolding.com
SIC: **2821** Thermoplastic materials

(G-3914)
GEM MANUFACTURING LLC
Also Called: Gem
78 Brookside Rd (06708-1402)
P.O. Box 4550 (06704-0550)
PHONE.................................203 574-1466
Robert C Caulfield, *Pr*
Mark G Caulfield, *
Nicholas Longtin, *
◆ **EMP:** 100 **EST:** 1950
SQ FT: 84,000
SALES (est): 10.74MM **Privately Held**
Web: www.gemmfg.com
SIC: **3469** Stamping metal for the trade

(G-3915)
GROTTO ALWAYS INC
Also Called: Tasteful Gift Baskets By Mrs G
634 Watertown Ave (06708-2207)
PHONE.................................203 754-0295
TOLL FREE: 800
Joseph Graziosa, *Pr*
Bernadette Graziosa, *VP*
EMP: 10 **EST:** 1938
SQ FT: 3,000
SALES (est): 465.17K **Privately Held**
SIC: **5812** 5499 2098 2097 Italian restaurant ; Food gift baskets; Macaroni and spaghetti; Manufactured ice

(G-3916)
H&T WATERBURY INC
Also Called: Bouffard Metal Goods
984 Waterville St (06710-1015)
P.O. Box 4700 (06704-0700)
PHONE.................................203 574-2240
Christian Diemer, *Prin*
Ronald T Turmel, *
Daniel D Moffa, *
▲ **EMP:** 159 **EST:** 1976
SQ FT: 128,000
SALES (est): 44.56MM **Privately Held**
Web: www.ht-group.com
SIC: **3469** Stamping metal for the trade
PA: Sdruzeni Firem Heitkamp&Thumann Group
Havlickova 540/28
Hustopece

(G-3917)
HALCO INC
Also Called: Waterbury Plating
114 Porter St (06708-3819)
P.O. Box 2545 (06723-2545)
PHONE.................................203 575-9450
Glen Harper, *Pr*
Bob Lanz, *
EMP: 75 **EST:** 1941
SQ FT: 55,000
SALES (est): 9.26MM **Privately Held**
Web: www.nemetalworks.com
SIC: **3471** 3479 Electroplating of metals or formed products; Painting of metal products

(G-3918)
HAYDON KERK MTION SLUTIONS INC (HQ)
1500 Meriden Rd (06705-3982)
P.O. Box 3329 (06705-0329)
PHONE.................................203 756-7441
John P Norris, *Pr*
Kathryn E Sena, *
William J Burke, *
Robert S Feit, *
▲ **EMP:** 97 **EST:** 1963
SQ FT: 42,000
SALES (est): 39.19MM
SALES (corp-wide): 6.15B **Publicly Held**
Web: www.haydonkerkpittman.com
SIC: **3823** Process control instruments
PA: Ametek, Inc.
1100 Cassatt Rd
Berwyn PA 19312
610 647-2121

(G-3919)
HUBBARD-HALL INC (PA)
Also Called: Hubbard-Hall
563 S Leonard St (06708-4316)
P.O. Box 790 (06720-0790)
PHONE.................................203 756-5521
Molly Kellogg, *Pr*
Charles T Kellogg, *
Jeff Davis, *
Gerard Mastropietro, *
Robert Farrell, *
◆ **EMP:** 70 **EST:** 1971
SQ FT: 90,000
SALES (corp-wide): 105.87MM **Privately Held**
Web: www.hubbardhall.com
SIC: **5169** 3471 2899 2842 Chemicals, industrial and heavy; Finishing, metals or formed products; Chemical preparations, nec; Polishes and sanitation goods

(G-3920)
ILLINOIS TOOL WORKS INC
ITW Drawform Waterbury
1240 Wolcott St (06705-1320)
PHONE.................................203 574-2119
Rob Webber, *Brnch Mgr*
EMP: 140
SALES (corp-wide): 15.93B **Publicly Held**
Web: www.itw.com
SIC: **3482** 3469 3448 Small arms ammunition; Metal stampings, nec; Prefabricated metal buildings and components
PA: Illinois Tool Works Inc.
155 Harlem Ave
Glenview IL 60025
847 724-7500

(G-3921)
INDUSTRIAL DRIVES CONTRLS INC (PA)
165 Homer St (06704-1729)
PHONE.................................203 753-5103
Jack Traver Junior, *Pr*
Elaine Traver, *Sec*
Jack Traver Senior, *Treas*
EMP: 11 **EST:** 1980
SQ FT: 5,000
SALES (est): 9.75MM
SALES (corp-wide): 9.75MM **Privately Held**
SIC: **5063** 7694 Motors, electric; Electric motor repair

(G-3922)
INFINITY STONE INC
1261 Meriden Rd Ste 1 (06705-3637)
PHONE.................................203 575-9484
Michael Amendola, *Pr*
EMP: 10 **EST:** 2014
SALES (est): 899.63K **Privately Held**
Web: www.infinitysba.com
SIC: **1411** 3944 Marble, dimension-quarrying ; Marbles (toys)

(G-3923)
ITW HIGHLAND MANUFACTURING INC
Also Called: ITW Highland
1240 Wolcott St (06705-1320)
PHONE.................................203 574-3200
Gills Boehm, *Prin*
EMP: 62 **EST:** 2011
SALES (est): 13.73MM
SALES (corp-wide): 15.93B **Publicly Held**
Web: www.itwdrawform.com
SIC: **3469** Stamping metal for the trade
PA: Illinois Tool Works Inc.
155 Harlem Ave
Glenview IL 60025
847 724-7500

(G-3924)
J & L MFG WATERTOWN INC
2714 E Main St (06705-2839)
PHONE.................................203 591-9124
James Binkoski, *Pr*
Donald R Martelli, *
EMP: 25 **EST:** 1983
SQ FT: 13,000
SALES (est): 2.8MM **Privately Held**
SIC: **3599** 3541 7692 3544 Machine shop, jobbing and repair; Milling machines; Welding repair; Special dies, tools, jigs, and fixtures

(G-3925)
JL LUCAS MACHINERY CO INC
429 Brookside Rd (06708-1418)
P.O. Box 4220 (06704-0220)
PHONE.................................203 597-1300
John Pelletier, *Pr*
Judy Pelletier, *Sec*
▲ **EMP:** 18 **EST:** 1987
SQ FT: 20,000
SALES (est): 2.67MM **Privately Held**
Web: www.jllucas.com
SIC: **3541** 5084 Machine tools, metal cutting type; Machine tools and accessories

(G-3926)
JOMA INCORPORATED
185 Interstate Ln (06705-2640)
PHONE.................................203 759-0848
Francis X Macary, *Pr*
▲ **EMP:** 25 **EST:** 1953
SALES (est): 3.7MM **Privately Held**
Web: www.jomaincorporated.com
SIC: **3469** Stamping metal for the trade

(G-3927)
K4 MACHINING LLC
217 Interstate Ln (06705-2642)
PHONE.................................203 437-8764
Anna Leszczynski, *CEO*
Lou Leszczynski, *Managing Member*
EMP: 10 **EST:** 2018
SALES (est): 1.59MM **Privately Held**
Web: www.k4machining.com
SIC: **3599** Machine shop, jobbing and repair

(G-3928)
KING INDUSTRIES
800 Chase Pkwy (06708-3031)
PHONE.................................203 527-7380
EMP: 11 **EST:** 2019
SALES (est): 444.75K **Privately Held**
Web: www.kingindustries.com
SIC: **2591** Drapery hardware and window blinds and shades

(G-3929)
KRAFT HEINZ FOODS COMPANY
Also Called: Kraft Foods
67 Freight St (06702-1802)
PHONE.................................203 597-9109
Tom Konetsky, *Mgr*
EMP: 7
SALES (corp-wide): 26.48B **Publicly Held**
Web: www.kraftfoodsgroup.com
SIC: **2033** Canned fruits and specialties
HQ: Kraft Heinz Foods Company
1 Ppg Pl Ste 3400
Pittsburgh PA 15222
412 456-5700

(G-3930)
L C M TOOL CO
68 Diane Ter (06705-3523)
P.O. Box 3245 (06705-0245)
PHONE.................................203 757-1575
Dante Carrafa, *Pr*
Sebastian Longo, *Treas*
Michele Longo, *VP*
Mario Longo, *Sec*
EMP: 9 **EST:** 1966
SALES (est): 749.23K **Privately Held**
Web: www.lcmtool.com
SIC: **3541** Screw and thread machines

(G-3931)
LUVATA WATERBURY INC (HQ)
2121 Thomaston Ave (06704-1037)
PHONE.................................203 753-5215
Pekka Kleemola, *Pr*
James C Lajewski, *Prin*
Kati Mannisto, *Sr VP*
Annamari Ahlmark, *CCO*
Olli Naukkarinen, *Sr VP*
◆ **EMP:** 77 **EST:** 2001
SQ FT: 210,000
SALES (est): 27.14MM **Privately Held**
Web: www.luvata.com
SIC: **3357** 3643 3674 3699 Magnet wire, nonferrous; Electric connectors; Semiconductors and related devices; Electrical welding equipment
PA: Mitsubishi Materials Corporation
3-2-3, Marunouchi
Chiyoda-Ku TKY 100-0

(G-3932)
LYONS SLITTING INC
46 Mattatuck Heights Rd (06705-3831)
PHONE.................................203 755-4564
EMP: 10 **EST:** 1994
SQ FT: 12,000
SALES (est): 760.67K **Privately Held**
Web: www.lyonsslitting.com
SIC: **7389** 3444 Metal slitting and shearing; Sheet metalwork

(G-3933)
MACDERMID INCORPORATED (HQ)
Also Called: Macdermid Prfmce Solutions
245 Freight St (06702-1818)
P.O. Box 671 (06720-0671)
PHONE.................................203 575-5700
Scot Benson, *Pr*
Denis Brauer, *

John Capps, *
◆ **EMP: 200 EST:** 1922
SQ FT: 51,700
SALES (est): 421.85MM
SALES (corp-wide): 2.55B **Publicly Held**
Web: www.macdermid.com
SIC: 2842 2992 2752 3577 Cleaning or polishing preparations, nec; Lubricating oils ; Offset and photolithographic printing; Printers and plotters
PA: Element Solutions Inc
    500 E Broward Blvd # 1860
    Fort Lauderdale FL 33394
    561 207-9600

(G-3934)
MACDERMID ACUMEN INC
245 Freight St (06702-1818)
PHONE..................203 575-5700
EMP: 41 EST: 1997
SALES (est): 2.47MM
SALES (corp-wide): 2.55B **Publicly Held**
Web: www.macdermid.com
SIC: 2899 Chemical preparations, nec
PA: Element Solutions Inc
    500 E Broward Blvd # 1860
    Fort Lauderdale FL 33394
    561 207-9600

(G-3935)
MACDERMID AG SOLUTIONS INC (HQ)
Also Called: Agriphar Crop Solutions
245 Freight St (06702-1818)
PHONE..................203 575-5727
Frank Monteiro, *Pr*
John Cordani, *Sec*
Michael Kennedy, *Treas*
EMP: 14 EST: 2019
SQ FT: 50,000
SALES (est): 9.56MM **Privately Held**
Web: www.macdermid.com
SIC: 2899 Chemical preparations, nec
PA: Upl Limited
    Upl House, 610 B/2, Bandra Village,
    Mumbai MH 40005

(G-3936)
MACDERMID ANION INC
245 Freight St (06702-1818)
PHONE..................203 575-5700
EMP: 105 EST: 2002
SALES (est): 13.34MM
SALES (corp-wide): 2.55B **Publicly Held**
Web: www.macdermid.com
SIC: 2899 Chemical preparations, nec
PA: Element Solutions Inc
    500 E Broward Blvd # 1860
    Fort Lauderdale FL 33394
    561 207-9600

(G-3937)
MACDERMID AUTOTYPE INC
245 Freight St (06702-1818)
PHONE..................847 818-8262
Frank J Monteiro, *Pr*
EMP: 48 EST: 1970
SALES (est): 3.6MM
SALES (corp-wide): 2.55B **Publicly Held**
Web: www.macdermid.com
SIC: 2899 Chemical preparations, nec
PA: Element Solutions Inc
    500 E Broward Blvd # 1860
    Fort Lauderdale FL 33394
    561 207-9600

(G-3938)
MACDERMID BRAZIL INC
245 Freight St (06702-1818)
PHONE..................203 575-5700

EMP: 104 EST: 2002
SALES (est): 20.62MM
SALES (corp-wide): 2.55B **Publicly Held**
Web: www.macdermid.com
SIC: 2869 Hydraulic fluids, synthetic base
PA: Element Solutions Inc
    500 E Broward Blvd # 1860
    Fort Lauderdale FL 33394
    561 207-9600

(G-3939)
MACDERMID HOLDINGS LLC
245 Freight St (06702-1818)
PHONE..................203 575-5700
EMP: 39 EST: 2006
SALES (est): 446.61K **Privately Held**
Web: www.macdermid.com
SIC: 2899 Chemical preparations, nec

(G-3940)
MACDERMID OVERSEAS ASIA LTD (HQ)
245 Freight St (06702-1818)
PHONE..................203 575-5799
EMP: 23 EST: 1983
SALES (est): 13.9MM
SALES (corp-wide): 2.55B **Publicly Held**
Web: www.macdermid.com
SIC: 2899 Chemical preparations, nec
PA: Element Solutions Inc
    500 E Broward Blvd # 1860
    Fort Lauderdale FL 33394
    561 207-9600

(G-3941)
MACDERMID PRTG SLTONS ACMEN IN
245 Freight St (06702-1818)
PHONE..................203 575-5700
EMP: 109 EST: 2003
SALES (est): 25.33MM
SALES (corp-wide): 2.55B **Publicly Held**
Web: www.macdermid.com
SIC: 2899 Chemical preparations, nec
PA: Element Solutions Inc
    500 E Broward Blvd # 1860
    Fort Lauderdale FL 33394
    561 207-9600

(G-3942)
MARJAN INC
44 Railroad Hill St (06708-4320)
P.O. Box 2420 (06722-2420)
PHONE..................203 573-1742
George Strobel Senior, *Pr*
William C Strobel, *VP*
Richard Strobel, *Sec*
George Strobel Junior, *Treas*
▲ **EMP: 31 EST:** 1972
SQ FT: 17,000
SALES (est): 2.12MM **Privately Held**
Web: www.marjaninc.com
SIC: 3479 Hot dip coating of metals or formed products

(G-3943)
MARVEL SCREW MACHINE PDTS INC
58 Lafayette St (06708-3802)
PHONE..................203 756-7058
David Perriello, *Pr*
Joyce Folo, *VP*
Margaret Perriello Ii, *Sec*
EMP: 22 EST: 1954
SQ FT: 15,000
SALES (est): 454.43K **Privately Held**
Web: www.wsmpco.com.
SIC: 3451 Screw machine products

(G-3944)
MICROBEST INC
Also Called: Microbest
670 Captain Neville Dr Ste 1 (06705-3855)
PHONE..................203 597-0355
Shaun Gaus, *CEO*
Steven Griffin, *
Elaine M Studwell, *
Jim Tata, *
Edward Mcnerney, *Pr*
EMP: 250 EST: 1960
SQ FT: 43,000
SALES (est): 34.4MM **Privately Held**
Web: www.microbest.com
SIC: 3541 3451 3452 3599 Machine tools, metal cutting type; Screw machine products ; Bolts, nuts, rivets, and washers; Amusement park equipment

(G-3945)
MIRROR POLISHING & PLTG CO INC
346 Huntingdon Ave (06708-1430)
PHONE..................203 574-5400
Gary Nalband, *Pr*
◆ **EMP: 40 EST:** 1953
SQ FT: 85,000
SALES (est): 8.88MM **Privately Held**
Web: www.mpp.net
SIC: 3471 5719 Chromium plating of metals or formed products; Mirrors

(G-3946)
MITCHELL-BATE COMPANY
365 Thomaston Ave (06702-1024)
P.O. Box 1707 (06721-1707)
PHONE..................203 233-0862
Donald C Lang Junior, *Pr*
Scott Lang, *
EMP: 27 EST: 1955
SQ FT: 15,000
SALES (est): 786.7K **Privately Held**
SIC: 2542 3479 3443 Racks, merchandise display or storage: except wood; Coating of metals with plastic or resins; Fabricated plate work (boiler shop)

(G-3947)
MY CITIZENS NEWS
389 Meadow St (06702-1808)
PHONE..................203 729-2228
Paul Roth, *Publisher*
EMP: 12 EST: 2008
SALES (est): 324.17K **Privately Held**
Web: www.mycitizensnews.com
SIC: 2711 Newspapers: publishing only, not printed on site

(G-3948)
NELSON HEAT TREATING CO INC
2046 N Main St (06704-2365)
PHONE..................203 754-0670
James La France, *Pr*
James Lafrance, *Pr*
EMP: 11 EST: 1993
SQ FT: 6,000
SALES (est): 1.57MM **Privately Held**
Web: www.nelsonheattreating.com
SIC: 3398 Metal heat treating

(G-3949)
NEOPERL INC
171 Mattatuck Heights Rd (06705-3832)
PHONE..................203 756-8891
Michael Moraniec, *Sr VP*
Marie Helene Pernin, *VP*
Oliver Myer, *Treas*
▲ **EMP: 60 EST:** 1927

SQ FT: 60,000
SALES (est): 12.28MM **Privately Held**
Web: www.neoperl.com
SIC: 3432 5074 3088 Plumbers' brass goods: drain cocks, faucets, spigots, etc.; Plumbers' brass goods and fittings; Plastics plumbing fixtures
PA: Neoperl Group Ag
    Pfeffingerstrasse 21
    Reinach BL 4153

(G-3950)
NEW ENGLAND DIE CO INC
48 Ford Ave (06708-1408)
PHONE..................203 574-5140
Joseph Almeida, *Pr*
Joseph Almeida Junior, *Pr*
Shelly Almeida, *Sec*
EMP: 14 EST: 1941
SQ FT: 10,000
SALES (est): 719.31K **Privately Held**
Web: www.newenglanddie.com
SIC: 3541 Electrical discharge erosion machines

(G-3951)
NEWMARK MEDICAL COMPONENTS INC
2670 S Main St (06706-2616)
P.O. Box 1030 (06721-1030)
PHONE..................203 753-1158
David W Mieczkowski, *Pr*
James Behuniak, *Ch Bd*
Thomas Tassis, *Sec*
EMP: 14 EST: 2010
SQ FT: 15,000
SALES (est): 1.98MM
SALES (corp-wide): 27,58MM **Privately Held**
Web: www.newmarkmc.com
SIC: 3841 Medical instruments and equipment, blood and bone work
PA: The Platt Brothers & Company
    2670 S Main St
    Waterbury CT 06706
    203 753-4194

(G-3952)
NOUJAIM TOOL CO INC
412 Chase River Rd (06704-1401)
PHONE..................203 753-4441
Joseph Noujaim, *Pr*
Daad Noujaim, *Treas*
Naim Noujaim, *VP*
Selim G Noujaim, *Ex VP*
EMP: 23 EST: 1985
SQ FT: 5,500
SALES (est): 3.78MM **Privately Held**
Web: www.noujaimtools.com
SIC: 3599 3544 Machine shop, jobbing and repair; Special dies, tools, jigs, and fixtures

(G-3953)
NVI WELD TECHNOLOGY LLC
15 Maplerow Ave (06705-1731)
PHONE..................203 707-0587
EMP: 7 EST: 2021
SALES (est): 253.86K **Privately Held**
SIC: 1799 3499 3599 3317 Special trade contractors, nec; Fabricated metal products, nec; Flexible metal hose, tubing, and bellows; Welded pipe and tubes

(G-3954)
OAKVILLE QUALITY PRODUCTS LLC
Also Called: Bobkin Automatics
1495 Thomaston Ave Ste 2 (06704-1744)
PHONE..................203 757-5525
Mark Newton, *Pr*

▲ = Import ▼ = Export
◆ = Import/Export

EMP: 13 EST: 2012
SALES (est): 2.06MM **Privately Held**
Web: www.oakvillequality.com
SIC: 3599 Machine shop, jobbing and repair

(G-3955)
OIL PURIFICATION SYSTEMS INC
2176 Thomaston Ave (06704-1013)
PHONE.................................203 346-1800
Greg Slawson, *CEO*
William F Esposito, *Pr*
Mark Smith, *CFO*
◆ EMP: 15 EST: 2002
SQ FT: 1,200
SALES (est): 2.33MM **Privately Held**
Web: www.pittsburghpower.com
SIC: 3533 Oil field machinery and equipment

(G-3956)
OLIVE OIL FACTORY LLC
Also Called: Olive Oil Factory
197 Huntingdon Ave (06708-1413)
PHONE.................................203 437-8286
Laura Miller, *CFO*
▲ EMP: 23 EST: 1995
SQ FT: 2,000
SALES (est): 854.53K **Privately Held**
Web: www.shopdelavignes.com
SIC: 7389 5812 2079 Packaging and labeling services; Eating places; Olive oil

(G-3957)
OPTICARE HEALTH SYSTEMS INC (DH)
Also Called: Opticare
87 Grandview Ave (06708-2523)
PHONE.................................203 574-2020
Nancy Noll, *Pr*
Brian M Wood, *
Mary Graveline, *
EMP: 150 EST: 1999
SALES (est): 25.7MM **Privately Held**
Web: waterbury.refocuseyedoctors.com
SIC: 8042 5995 3841 Offices and clinics of optometrists; Optical goods stores; Eye examining instruments and apparatus
HQ: Refac Optical Group
1 Harmon Dr
Blackwood NJ 08012
856 228-1000

(G-3958)
PALLADIN PRECISION PDTS INC
57 Bristol St (06708-4901)
PHONE.................................203 574-0246
Anthony Palladino, *Pr*
Lynne R Palladino, *
Dean Palladino, *
EMP: 25 EST: 1963
SQ FT: 20,000
SALES (est): 4.95MM **Privately Held**
Web: www.palladin.com
SIC: 3451 Screw machine products

(G-3959)
PHARMACAL RESEARCH LABS INC
562 Captain Neville Dr Ste 1 (06705-3875)
P.O. Box 369 (06770-0369)
PHONE.................................203 755-4908
Kenneth Shapiro, *Pr*
Bill Fleischer, *
Jerry Shapiro, *
◆ EMP: 34 EST: 1976
SQ FT: 14,500
SALES (est): 7.51MM **Privately Held**
Web: www.pharmacal.com

SIC: 2841 Soap and other detergents

(G-3960)
PHILIPS ULTRASOUND INC
Igc Advanced Superconductors
1875 Thomaston Ave Ste 5 (06704-1034)
PHONE.................................203 753-5215
EMP: 109
SALES (corp-wide): 18.51B **Privately Held**
Web: usa.philips.com
SIC: 3845 Electromedical equipment
HQ: Philips Ultrasound Llc
22100 Bothell Everett Hwy
Bothell WA 98021
800 982-2011

(G-3961)
PLASMA COATINGS INC
758 E Main St (06702-1712)
P.O. Box 10006 (06725-0006)
PHONE.................................203 598-3100
Gary Carlo, *Pr*
EMP: 8 EST: 2013
SALES (est): 170.11K **Privately Held**
Web: www.americanroller.com
SIC: 3479 Coating of metals and formed products

(G-3962)
PLATT & LABONIA COMPANY LLC
182 E Aurora St (06708-2024)
PHONE.................................800 505-9099
Guy A Ferraiolo, *Pr*
EMP: 45 EST: 2015
SALES (est): 2.62MM **Privately Held**
Web: www.plattlabonia.com
SIC: 3441 Fabricated structural metal

(G-3963)
PLATT BROTHERS & COMPANY (PA)
2670 S Main St (06706-2616)
PHONE.................................203 753-4194
Milton Grile, *Ch Bd*
James P Behuniak, *
David W Mieczkowski, *
John Greaney, *
Mark J Wrenn, *
EMP: 71 EST: 1830
SQ FT: 120,000
SALES (est): 27.58MM
SALES (corp-wide): 27.58MM **Privately Held**
Web: www.plattbros.com
SIC: 3356 3357 3965 3272 Zinc and zinc alloy: rolling, drawing, or extruding; Nonferrous wiredrawing and insulating; Eyelets, metal: clothing, fabrics, boots, or shoes; Terrazzo products, precast, nec

(G-3964)
PREMIERE PACKG PARTNERS LLC
197 Huntingdon Ave (06708-1413)
PHONE.................................203 694-0003
EMP: 25 EST: 2018
SALES (est): 2.38MM **Privately Held**
Web: www.ppp-foods.com
SIC: 2099 Food preparations, nec

(G-3965)
RAND-WHITNEY CONTAINER LLC
118 Railroad Hill St (06708-4320)
PHONE.................................203 597-1707
EMP: 28
Web: www.randwhitney.com

SIC: 2653 Boxes, corrugated: made from purchased materials
HQ: Rand-Whitney Container Llc
1 Rand Whitney Way
Worcester MA 01607
508 890-7000

(G-3966)
RINTEC CORPORATION
165 Haddad Rd (06708-1897)
PHONE.................................860 274-3697
Antonio F Rinaldi, *Pr*
Veronica S Rinaldi, *VP*
EMP: 10 EST: 1986
SALES (est): 974.4K **Privately Held**
Web: www.rintec.net
SIC: 3544 Special dies and tools

(G-3967)
SANDUR TOOL CO
853 Hamilton Ave (06706-1998)
PHONE.................................203 753-0004
Anthony Durso Junior, *Pr*
EMP: 7 EST: 1955
SQ FT: 5,000
SALES (est): 833.02K **Privately Held**
Web: www.sandurtool.com
SIC: 3544 Special dies and tools

(G-3968)
SEGA READY MIX INCORPORATED
Also Called: Sega Ready Mix
310 Chase River Rd (06704-1401)
PHONE.................................203 465-1052
Mark Whitlock, *Mgr*
EMP: 8
SALES (corp-wide): 2.19MM **Privately Held**
Web: www.segareadymix.com
SIC: 3273 Ready-mixed concrete
PA: Sega Ready Mix, Incorporated
519 Danbury Rd
New Milford CT 06776
860 354-3969

(G-3969)
SEIDEL LLC
2223 Thomaston Ave (06704-1000)
PHONE.................................203 757-7349
Michael Ritzenhoff, *Pr*
▲ EMP: 70 EST: 1986
SQ FT: 75,000
SALES (est): 9.93MM **Privately Held**
Web: www.seidelgroup.com
SIC: 3471 Electroplating of metals or formed products

(G-3970)
SOMMA TOOL COMPANY
109 Scott Rd (06705-3202)
P.O. Box 2559 (06723-2559)
PHONE.................................203 753-2114
Eric A Somma, *Pr*
Thomas R Minuto, *
Jerry Somma, *
Gerard H Somma, *
EMP: 25 EST: 1939
SQ FT: 27,000
SALES (est): 4.98MM **Privately Held**
Web: www.sommatool.com
SIC: 3545 Cutting tools for machine tools

(G-3971)
SYFERLOCK TECHNOLOGY CORP
31 Stowe Rd (06704-1154)
PHONE.................................203 292-5441
Robert D Russo, *Pr*

EMP: 7 EST: 2008
SALES (est): 907.71K **Privately Held**
Web: www.syferlock.com
SIC: 3577 5045 Computer peripheral equipment, nec; Computer software

(G-3972)
T & A SCREW PRODUCTS INC
64 Avenue Of Industry (06705-3901)
PHONE.................................203 756-2770
EMP: 19 EST: 1981
SALES (est): 719.44K **Privately Held**
Web: t-a-screw-products-inc-ct.hub.biz
SIC: 3451 Screw machine products

(G-3973)
TOO SWEETS LLC ✪
1348 N Main St (06704-3132)
PHONE.................................203 578-6493
Shomari Beamon, *Managing Member*
EMP: 7 EST: 2023
SALES (est): 642.81K **Privately Held**
SIC: 2499 2099 Food handling and processing products, wood; Food preparations, nec

(G-3974)
TRAVER ELECTRIC MOTOR CO INC
151 Homer St (06704-1729)
PHONE.................................203 753-5103
Jack E Traver, *Pr*
Elaine Traver, *
EMP: 25 EST: 1940
SQ FT: 14,000
SALES (est): 4.76MM **Privately Held**
Web: www.traveridc.com
SIC: 7694 5063 Electric motor repair; Electrical supplies, nec

(G-3975)
TREMCO SWISS INC
43 Mattatuck Heights Rd (06705-3832)
P.O. Box 3128 (06705-0128)
PHONE.................................203 573-8584
Neil Tremaglio Junior, *Pr*
Alba Tremaglio, *
EMP: 27 EST: 1950
SQ FT: 11,500
SALES (est): 4.87MM **Privately Held**
Web: www.waterburyswiss.com
SIC: 3451 Screw machine products

(G-3976)
TRI TEC ELECTRONICS INC
33 5th St (06708-4207)
PHONE.................................203 573-8491
T Canu, *Pr*
EMP: 8 EST: 1995
SALES (est): 307.75K **Privately Held**
Web: www.tritecelectronics.com
SIC: 3679 Electronic components, nec

(G-3977)
TRITEX CORPORATION
Also Called: Haydon Motion Europe
1500 Meriden Rd (06705-3982)
P.O. Box 3329 (06705-0329)
PHONE.................................203 756-7441
John Norris, *Pr*
▲ EMP: 250 EST: 1985
SQ FT: 42,000
SALES (est): 18.7MM **Privately Held**
Web: www.tritexcorporation.com
SIC: 3679 3621 Switches, stepping; Motors, electric

(G-3978)
UNIPHARM INC
Also Called: Ameripharma
75 Progress Ln (06705-3866)
PHONE..................203 528-3230
Victor Sapritsky, *Pr*
EMP: 24
Web: www.unipharmus.com
SIC: 2023 2834 3559 Dietary supplements, dairy and non-dairy based; Pharmaceutical preparations; Pharmaceutical machinery
PA: Unipharm, Inc.
      350 5th Ave Ste 6701
      New York NY 10118

(G-3979)
VILLE SWISS AUTOMATICS INC
205 Cherry St (06702-1610)
P.O. Box 4068 (06704-0068)
PHONE..................203 756-2825
John Petro, *Pr*
Miriam Hernandez, *Sec*
EMP: 14 **EST:** 1985
SQ FT: 7,800
SALES (est): 1.59MM **Privately Held**
Web: www.villeswiss.com
SIC: 3451 Screw machine products

(G-3980)
WATERBURY COMPANIES INC
64 Avenue Of Industry (06705-3901)
P.O. Box 629 (06488-0629)
◆ **EMP:** 180
Web: www.waterburybuttons.com
SIC: 2879 3499 5191 Pesticides, agricultural or household; Nozzles, spray: aerosol, paint, or insecticide; Pesticides

(G-3981)
WATERBURY ROLLING MILLS INC
215 Piedmont St (06706-2152)
P.O. Box 550 (06720-0550)
PHONE..................203 597-5000
Pat Kelly, *Genl Mgr*
EMP: 87 **EST:** 1906
SQ FT: 100,000
SALES (est): 4.37MM
SALES (corp-wide): 9.38B **Publicly Held**
SIC: 3351 3312 3356 Bronze rolling and drawing; Blast furnaces and steel mills; Nickel and nickel alloy: rolling, drawing, or extruding
PA: Olin Corporation
      190 Carondelet Plz # 1530
      Saint Louis MO 63105
      314 480-1400

(G-3982)
WATERBURY SCREW MCH PDTS CO
311 Thomaston Ave Ste 319 (06702-1024)
P.O. Box 2576 (06723-2576)
PHONE..................203 756-8084
Matthew Corcoran, *Pr*
EMP: 20 **EST:** 1938
SQ FT: 13,500
SALES (est): 980.76K **Privately Held**
Web: www.wsmpco.com
SIC: 3451 Screw machine products

(G-3983)
WCES INC
Also Called: Inc, Wtrbury Cntract Eylets St
225 S Leonard St (06708-4247)
P.O. Box 33 (06720-0033)
PHONE..................203 573-1325
Lisa Meyer, *Pr*
EMP: 14 **EST:** 1978

SQ FT: 18,000
SALES (est): 2.39MM **Privately Held**
Web: www.waterburycontract.com
SIC: 3469 Stamping metal for the trade

(G-3984)
WHITE WELDING COMPANY
44 N Elm St (06702-1512)
P.O. Box 1710 (06721-1710)
PHONE..................203 753-1197
Robert Tomaiolo, *VP*
Robert Tomaiolo, *VP*
Mark Krause, *VP*
Leo Tomaiolo, *Sec*
EMP: 8 **EST:** 1986
SQ FT: 10,000
SALES (est): 920.61K **Privately Held**
Web: www.whitewelding.com
SIC: 3444 7692 Metal housings, enclosures, casings, and other containers; Welding repair

(G-3985)
WOODFREE CRATING SYSTEMS INC
150 Mattatuck Heights Rd (06705-3893)
PHONE..................203 759-1799
David Goodrich, *Pr*
Michael Jackson, *Sec*
EMP: 12 **EST:** 2003
SQ FT: 17,900
SALES (est): 1.24MM **Privately Held**
Web: www.pactww.com
SIC: 2449 Rectangular boxes and crates, wood

Waterford
New London County

(G-3986)
COASTAL STEEL CORPORATION
10 Mallard Ln (06385-1110)
PHONE..................860 443-4073
Glenn Ahnert, *Pr*
Susan Ahnert, *Sec*
EMP: 10 **EST:** 1964
SQ FT: 22,000
SALES (est): 347.61K **Privately Held**
SIC: 3441 Fabricated structural metal

(G-3987)
COCA-COLA BOTTLING COMPANY OF SOUTHEASTERN NEW ENGLAND INC (DH)
Also Called: Coca-Cola
150 Waterford Parkway S (06385-1219)
P.O. Box 1310 (06320-1310)
PHONE..................860 443-2816
▲ **EMP:** 12 **EST:** 1938
SALES (est): 8.54MM **Privately Held**
Web: www.cocacolaofsene.com
SIC: 2086 5962 Soft drinks: packaged in cans, bottles, etc.; Merchandising machine operators
HQ: Coca-Cola Beverages Northeast, Inc.
      1 Executive Park Dr # 330
      Bedford NH 03110
      603 627-7871

(G-3988)
CRITICAL SCRN PRINTG & EMB
82 Boston Post Rd (06385-2425)
PHONE..................860 443-4327
James Monahan, *Pr*
EMP: 7 **EST:** 2014
SALES (est): 351.6K **Privately Held**
SIC: 2759 Screen printing

(G-3989)
DEFENDER INDUSTRIES INC
Also Called: Defender Warehouse Outlet Str
42 Great Neck Rd (06385-3334)
PHONE..................860 701-3400
Stephan Lance, *Pr*
◆ **EMP:** 120 **EST:** 1938
SQ FT: 109,000
SALES (est): 47.12MM **Privately Held**
Web: www.defender.com
SIC: 5551 5961 5088 2394 Marine supplies, nec; Mail order house, nec; Marine supplies ; Canvas and related products
HQ: Boutique Linus Inc
      255 Boul Decarie
      Saint-Laurent QC H4N 2
      514 600-1747

(G-3990)
JAYPRO SPORTS LLC
Also Called: US Athletic Equipment
976 Hartford Tpke Ste B (06385-4044)
PHONE..................860 447-3001
▲ **EMP:** 50 **EST:** 1953
SALES (est): 4.46MM **Privately Held**
Web: www.jayprosports.com
SIC: 3949 5091 Sporting and athletic goods, nec; Sporting and recreation goods

(G-3991)
KOBYLUCK READY-MIX INC
24 Industrial Dr (06385-4026)
PHONE..................860 444-9604
Matthew T Kobyluck, *Pr*
Daniel W Kobyluck, *VP*
Maureen A Kobyluck, *VP*
Joshua E Kobyluck, *VP*
Mark N Kobyluck, *VP*
EMP: 10 **EST:** 1995
SALES (est): 1.76MM **Privately Held**
Web: www.kobyluckinc.com
SIC: 3271 Blocks, concrete or cinder: standard

(G-3992)
KOBYLUCK SAND AND GRAVEL INC
24 Industrial Dr (06385-4026)
PHONE..................860 444-9600
Daniel W Kobyluck, *Pr*
Maureen Kobyluck, *Sec*
EMP: 17 **EST:** 1979
SALES (est): 932.91K **Privately Held**
Web: www.kobyluckinc.com
SIC: 1442 Common sand mining

(G-3993)
SECONN AUTOMATION SOLUTIONS
147 Cross Rd (06385-1216)
P.O. Box 294 (06385-0294)
PHONE..................860 442-4325
Robert Mareli, *CEO*
EMP: 23 **EST:** 1956
SQ FT: 2,600
SALES (est): 490.75K **Privately Held**
Web: www.seconn.com
SIC: 3444 Sheet metalwork

(G-3994)
SECONN FABRICATION LLC
180 Cross Rd (06385-1215)
PHONE..................860 443-0000
EMP: 65 **EST:** 2003
SQ FT: 60,000
SALES (est): 14.72MM **Privately Held**
Web: www.seconn.com
SIC: 3444 Sheet metal specialties, not stamped

(G-3995)
SINGER COMPANY INC
Also Called: Salem Stone Design
18a Industrial Dr (06385-4026)
PHONE..................860 439-1234
John Kim, *Pr*
Arthur Singer, *Pr*
William Singer, *VP*
Stacey Singer, *Sec*
EMP: 10 **EST:** 2001
SQ FT: 5,000
SALES (est): 989.22K **Privately Held**
Web: www.salemstonedesign.com
SIC: 1799 3281 3269 Counter top installation; Granite, cut and shaped; Cookware: stoneware, coarse earthenware, and pottery

(G-3996)
SMOOTHIE KING
Also Called: Smoothie King
106 Boston Post Rd Ste A (06385-2426)
PHONE..................860 574-9382
EMP: 13 **EST:** 2017
SALES (est): 91.32K **Privately Held**
Web: www.smoothieking.com
SIC: 5812 2024 Ice cream, soft drink and soda fountain stands; Ice cream and frozen deserts

(G-3997)
SONALYSTS INC (PA)
215 Parkway N (06385)
P.O. Box 280 (06385-0280)
PHONE..................860 442-4355
Lawrence F Clark, *Ch Bd*
Andrew N Toriello, *
Milton L Stretton, *
David R Samuelson, *
Miroslaw Fal, *
▲ **EMP:** 275 **EST:** 1973
SQ FT: 38,000
SALES (est): 56.43MM
SALES (corp-wide): 56.43MM **Privately Held**
Web: www.sonalysts.com
SIC: 8711 7373 8748 8732 Consulting engineer; Systems engineering, computer related; Systems engineering consultant, ex. computer or professional; Business research service

(G-3998)
UNIFIED SPORTS INCORPORATED (PA)
Also Called: Jaypro Sports
976 Hartford Tpke Ste B (06385-4044)
P.O. Box 400 (06385-0400)
PHONE..................860 447-3001
▲ **EMP:** 49 **EST:** 1986
SALES (est): 8.79MM **Privately Held**
Web: www.jayprosports.com
SIC: 3949 Basketball equipment and supplies, general

(G-3999)
WHALING CITY GRAPHICS LLC
Also Called: Fastsigns
217 Boston Post Rd # 1 (06385-2201)
P.O. Box 622 (06385-0622)
PHONE..................860 437-7446
Anthony Sabilia, *Mng Pt*
EMP: 12 **EST:** 2011
SALES (est): 256.32K **Privately Held**
Web: www.fastsigns.com
SIC: 3993 Signs and advertising specialties

(G-4000)
YOST MANUFACTURING & SUP INC
1018 Hartford Tpke (06385-4032)
P.O. Box 263 (06385-0263)
PHONE................................800 872-9678
George P Yost, *Pr*
Albert G Yost Junior, *VP*
EMP: 10 **EST:** 1985
SQ FT: 5,000
SALES (est): 932.79K **Privately Held**
Web: www.yostmfg.com
SIC: 3444 Gutters, sheet metal

Watertown
Litchfield County

(G-4001)
ADVANCED SPECIALIST LLC
162 Commercial St (06795-3309)
PHONE................................860 945-9125
Gardner W Gage, *Prin*
▲ **EMP:** 8 **EST:** 2009
SALES (est): 796.26K **Privately Held**
SIC: 3999 Manufacturing industries, nec

(G-4002)
ARROW SHED LLC
150 Callender Rd (06795-1628)
PHONE................................800 560-8383
EMP: 10 **EST:** 2010
SALES (est): 250.93K **Privately Held**
SIC: 2394 Tents: made from purchased materials

(G-4003)
BRAXTON MANUFACTURING CO INC
858 Echo Lake Rd (06795-1636)
P.O. Box 429 (06795-0429)
PHONE................................860 274-6781
Thomas Ordway, *Pr*
Joseph E Triano, *
Robert G Dionne, *
EMP: 170 **EST:** 1964
SQ FT: 60,000
SALES (est): 24.48MM **Privately Held**
Web: www.braxtonmfg.com
SIC: 3965 3769 3577 Eyelets, metal: clothing, fabrics, boots, or shoes; Space vehicle equipment, nec; Computer peripheral equipment, nec

(G-4004)
BRISTOL INC (HQ)
Also Called: Emerson Rmote Automtn Solution
1100 Buckingham St (06795-6622)
P.O. Box 36911 (63136-9011)
PHONE................................860 945-2200
Craig T Llewlyn, *Pr*
Craig Llewlyn, *
Warren Howard, *
Teresa A Burnett, *
▲ **EMP:** 300 **EST:** 1980
SQ FT: 190,000
SALES (est): 91.58MM
SALES (corp-wide): 15.16B **Publicly Held**
SIC: 3823 Industrial process control instruments
PA: Emerson Electric Co.
8000 West Florissant Ave
Saint Louis MO 63136
314 553-2000

(G-4005)
CLICK BOND INC
18 Park Rd (06795-1618)
PHONE................................860 274-5435
Charles G Hutter Iii, *CEO*
EMP: 50
SALES (corp-wide): 92.29MM **Privately Held**
Web: www.clickbond.com
SIC: 3452 Bolts, metal
HQ: Click Bond, Inc.
2151 Lockheed Way
Carson City NV 89706
775 885-8000

(G-4006)
CRYSTAL ROCK HOLDINGS INC
1050 Buckingham St (06795-6602)
PHONE................................860 945-0661
▲ **EMP:** 294
Web: www.crystalrock.com
SIC: 2086 3589 Mineral water, carbonated: packaged in cans, bottles, etc.; Coffee brewing equipment

(G-4007)
CRYSTAL ROCK SPRING WATER CO
Also Called: Crystal Rock Water & Coffee Co
1050 Buckingham St (06795-6602)
PHONE................................860 945-0661
Peter Baker, *Pr*
Jack Baker, *
John B Baker, *
Bruce Macdonald, *
▲ **EMP:** 315 **EST:** 1914
SQ FT: 67,000
SALES (est): 65.48MM **Privately Held**
Web: www.crystalrock.com
SIC: 5149 5499 2086 2899 Mineral or spring water bottling; Water: distilled mineral or spring; Bottled and canned soft drinks; Chemical preparations, nec

(G-4008)
DEMSEY MANUFACTURING CO INC
78 New Wood Rd (06795-3339)
PHONE................................860 274-6209
Richard A Demsey, *Pr*
Scott Demsey, *
EMP: 35 **EST:** 1954
SQ FT: 35,000
SALES (est): 5.07MM **Privately Held**
Web: www.demseymfg.com
SIC: 3469 Stamping metal for the trade

(G-4009)
DS SERVICES OF AMERICA INC
Also Called: Primo Water North America
1050 Buckingham St (06795-6602)
PHONE................................860 945-0661
Jerry Fowden, *Brnch Mgr*
EMP: 294
SALES (corp-wide): 2.22B **Publicly Held**
Web: www.water.com
SIC: 2086 3589 Mineral water, carbonated: packaged in cans, bottles, etc.; Coffee brewing equipment
HQ: Ds Services Of America, Inc.
1150 Assembly Dr Ste 800
Tampa FL 33607
770 933-1400

(G-4010)
E COOK ASSOCIATES INC
15 Mountain View Rd (06795-1648)
P.O. Box 116 (06787-0116)
PHONE................................860 283-9849

Edward Cook, *Pr*
Irma Diaz, *VP*
EMP: 12 **EST:** 1991
SQ FT: 13,000
SALES (est): 2.49MM **Privately Held**
Web: www.eciscreenprint.com
SIC: 2759 Screen printing

(G-4011)
EASTERN AWNING SYSTEMS INC
843 Echo Lake Rd (06795-1637)
PHONE................................860 274-9218
▲ **EMP:** 10 **EST:** 1961
SALES (est): 1.77MM **Privately Held**
Web: www.easternawning.com
SIC: 2394 Awnings, fabric: made from purchased materials

(G-4012)
EYELET TOOLMAKERS INC
40 Callender Rd (06795-6619)
P.O. Box 402 (06795-0402)
PHONE................................860 274-5423
Albinas Rickevicius, *Pr*
Linda Rickevicius, *
Anna Rickevicius, *
EMP: 32 **EST:** 1972
SQ FT: 30,000
SALES (est): 919.87K **Privately Held**
SIC: 3469 Stamping metal for the trade

(G-4013)
G L C INC
Also Called: Anco Tool & Manufacturing
1094 Echo Lake Rd (06795-1635)
P.O. Box 698 (06795-0698)
PHONE................................860 945-6166
Charles G Lacombe, *Pr*
Charles J Lacombe, *VP*
Donald Melason, *VP*
EMP: 12 **EST:** 1956
SALES (est): 1.75MM **Privately Held**
Web: www.ancotool.com
SIC: 3544 3599 3469 Special dies and tools ; Electrical discharge machining (EDM); Metal stampings, nec

(G-4014)
GENERAL WLDG & FABRICATION INC
977 Echo Lake Rd (06795-1639)
PHONE................................860 274-9668
Holly A Herbert, *Pr*
Jay N Herbert, *
EMP: 30 **EST:** 1995
SQ FT: 12,400
SALES (est): 9.28MM **Privately Held**
Web: www.gwfab.com
SIC: 1791 3499 3441 2431 Building front installation, metal; Fire- or burglary-resistive products; Fabricated structural metal for ships; Staircases, stairs and railings

(G-4015)
HAWK RIDGE WINERY LLC
28 Plungis Rd (06795-1321)
P.O. Box 410 (06795-0410)
PHONE................................860 274-7440
John M Mchugh, *Prin*
EMP: 8 **EST:** 2017
SALES (est): 265.77K **Privately Held**
Web: www.hawkridgewinery.net
SIC: 2084 Wines

(G-4016)
KKSP PRECISION MACHINING LLC
1012 Buckingham St (06795-6602)

PHONE................................860 274-6773
Mark Izzo, *Brnch Mgr*
EMP: 55
SALES (corp-wide): 49.87MM **Privately Held**
Web: www.kksp.com
SIC: 3599 Machine shop, jobbing and repair
PA: Kksp Precision Machining, Llc
1688 Glen Ellyn Rd
Glendale Heights IL 60139
630 260-1735

(G-4017)
KOSTER KEUNEN INC
1021 Echo Lake Rd (06795-1639)
PHONE................................860 945-3333
John Koster, *Ch Bd*
EMP: 58 **EST:** 1980
SALES (est): 6.29MM **Privately Held**
Web: www.kosterkeunen.com
SIC: 2911 Mineral waxes, natural

(G-4018)
KOSTER KEUNEN LLC (PA)
1021 Echo Lake Rd (06795-1639)
PHONE................................860 945-3333
◆ **EMP:** 37 **EST:** 2004
SALES (est): 9.89MM **Privately Held**
Web: www.kosterkeunen.com
SIC: 2999 2834 2671 2842 Waxes, petroleum: not produced in petroleum refineries; Pharmaceutical preparations; Bread wrappers, waxed or laminated: purchased material; Floor waxes

(G-4019)
KOSTER KEUNEN MFG INC
Also Called: Koster Keunen
1021 Echo Lake Rd (06795-1639)
P.O. Box 69 (06795-0069)
PHONE................................860 945-3333
John F Koster, *Pr*
◆ **EMP:** 60 **EST:** 1980
SQ FT: 100,000
SALES (est): 9.63MM **Privately Held**
Web: www.kosterkeunen.com
SIC: 2911 Mineral waxes, natural

(G-4020)
NIEM HOLDINGS INC
569 Lake Winnemaug Rd (06795-3051)
PHONE................................203 267-1510
Bruno S Perin, *Pr*
David Murelli, *
EMP: 49 **EST:** 1985
SALES (est): 5.01MM **Privately Held**
Web: www.mmfinc.com
SIC: 3479 Coating of metals and formed products

(G-4021)
PACKAGING AND CRATING TECH LLC
1100 Buckingham St Ste 4 (06795-6622)
PHONE................................203 759-1799
EMP: 10 **EST:** 2012
SALES (est): 1.44MM **Privately Held**
Web: www.pactww.com
SIC: 2671 3089 Paper; coated and laminated packaging; Blister or bubble formed packaging, plastics

(G-4022)
PACT INC
1100 Buckingham St Ste 4 (06795-6622)
PHONE................................203 759-1799
EMP: 10 **EST:** 2009
SALES (est): 2.4MM **Privately Held**
Web: www.pactww.com

(PA)=Parent Co (HQ)=Headquarters
✪ = New Business established in last 2 years

SIC: 2631　Packaging board

(G-4023)
PEACHWAVE OF WATERTOWN
1156 Main St (06795-2938)
PHONE...............................203 942-4949
Kelly Dun, *Mng Pt*
EMP: 7 EST: 2012
SALES (est): 228.61K Privately Held
Web: www.peachwaveyogurt.com
SIC: 2026　Yogurt

(G-4024)
PETRON AUTOMATION INC
65 Mountain View Rd (06795-1648)
P.O. Box 399 (06795-0399)
PHONE...............................860 274-9091
Michael Petro Senior, *Pr*
Patricia Petro, *
EMP: 24 EST: 1980
SQ FT: 7,500
SALES (est): 2.44MM Privately Held
Web: www.petronautomation.com
SIC: 3451　Screw machine products

(G-4025)
PRIME ENGNEERED COMPONENTS INC
Also Called: Prime Engineered Components
1012 Buckingham St (06795-6602)
P.O. Box 359 (06795-0359)
PHONE...............................860 274-6773
TOLL FREE: 800
Dennis Izzo, *Pr*
Mark Izzo, *
Prima Izzo, *
EMP: 61 EST: 1967
SQ FT: 32,000
SALES (est): 5.22MM Privately Held
Web: www.primeeci.com
SIC: 3451　Screw machine products

(G-4026)
PROFESSIONAL TRADES NETWRK LLC
1100 Buckingham St (06795-6621)
P.O. Box 327 (06795-0327)
PHONE...............................860 567-0173
EMP: 9 EST: 2009
SALES (est): 637.31K Privately Held
SIC: 2521 5031　Wood office furniture; Kitchen cabinets

(G-4027)
PROTOPAC INC
Also Called: Protopac Printing Services
120 Echo Lake Rd (06795-2664)
PHONE...............................860 274-6796
Hugh J Langin, *Pr*
Susan Langin, *Sec*
Stephen Langin, *Treas*
Hugh F Langin, *Contrlr*
EMP: 9 EST: 1979
SQ FT: 3,000
SALES (est): 889.89K Privately Held
Web: www.pro4print.com
SIC: 3496 2752　Wire winding; Offset printing

(G-4028)
SHELTERLOGIC CORP (HQ)
150 Callender Rd (06795-1628)
PHONE...............................860 945-6442
James Raymond, *CEO*
Robert J Silinski, *Pr*
Paul Hatty, *CFO*
◆ EMP: 25 EST: 2011
SALES (est): 98.3MM
SALES (corp-wide): 99.16MM Privately Held

Web: www.shelterlogic.com
SIC: 2394 5091　Tents: made from purchased materials; Camping equipment and supplies
PA: Slogic Holding Corp.
36 Grove St
New Canaan CT 06840
203 966-2800

(G-4029)
SIEMON COMPANY (PA)
Also Called: Siemon Global Project Services
101 Siemon Company Dr (06795-2651)
PHONE...............................860 945-4200
Henry Siemon, *Pr*
John Siemon, *VP Engg*
Ck Siemon, *Pr*
Kevin Gokey, *CFO*
◆ EMP: 537 EST: 1903
SQ FT: 200,000
SALES (est): 108.61MM
SALES (corp-wide): 108.61MM Privately Held
Web: www.siemon.com
SIC: 3643 3089 3679 3469　Electric connectors; Thermoformed finished plastics products, nec; Harness assemblies, for electronic use: wire or cable; Metal stampings, nec

(G-4030)
SOLLA EYELET PRODUCTS INC
Also Called: Solla Eyelet Products
50 Seemar Rd (06795-1638)
PHONE...............................860 274-5729
Louis Luigi Solla, *CEO*
Salvatore L Solla, *VP*
EMP: 40 EST: 1978
SQ FT: 9,000
SALES (est): 1.75MM Privately Held
Web: www.thomas-holding.com
SIC: 3469　Stamping metal for the trade

(G-4031)
TEAM TECHNOLOGIES INC
162 Commercial St (06795-3309)
PHONE...............................860 945-9125
Steven Henrikso, *Owner*
EMP: 8 EST: 2018
SALES (est): 148.61K Privately Held
Web: www.teamtech.com
SIC: 3841　Surgical and medical instruments

(G-4032)
THE CARBY CORPORATION
Also Called: Carby
1121 Echo Lake Rd (06795-1693)
P.O. Box 427 (06795-0427)
PHONE...............................860 274-6741
EMP: 75 EST: 1980
SALES (est): 8.17MM Privately Held
Web: www.carbycorp.com
SIC: 3449　Miscellaneous metalwork

(G-4033)
TRIPLE PLAY SPORTS
16 Straits Tpke (06795-3119)
PHONE...............................860 417-2877
Tom Daddona, *Pt*
EMP: 10 EST: 2009
SALES (est): 511.39K Privately Held
Web: www.tripleplaybargrille.com
SIC: 2599　Bar, restaurant and cafeteria furniture

(G-4034)
TRUELOVE & MACLEAN INC
57 Callender Rd (06795-1627)
P.O. Box 268 (06795-0268)
PHONE...............................860 274-9600

Richard L Bouffard, *Pr*
Grant Demerchant, *
Mario Lambiase, *
Wayne Bouffard, *
Charles Henry, *
▲ EMP: 137 EST: 1998
SQ FT: 105,000
SALES (est): 24.8MM Privately Held
Web: www.trueloveandmaclean.com
SIC: 3469　Stamping metal for the trade
PA: Sfs Group Ag
Rosenbergsaustrasse 8
Heerbrugg SG 9435

(G-4035)
UTITEC INC (HQ)
169 Callender Rd Ste 3 (06795-6620)
P.O. Box 370 (06795-0370)
PHONE...............................860 945-0605
Carl Contadini, *Pr*
EMP: 58 EST: 1979
SALES (est): 10.9MM
SALES (corp-wide): 116.24MM Privately Held
Web: www.utitec.com
SIC: 3841 3341 3469　Surgical and medical instruments; Platinum group metals, smelting and refining (secondary); Pressure cookers, stamped or drawn metal
PA: Cadence, Inc.
9 Technology Dr
Staunton VA 24401
540 248-2200

(G-4036)
UTITEC HOLDINGS INC
169 Callender Rd Ste 3 (06795-6620)
P.O. Box 370 (06795-0370)
PHONE...............................860 945-0601
Ronald Lipeika, *COO*
Mike Mcgregor, *Contrlr*
Bob Oppici, *
EMP: 75 EST: 2012
SALES (est): 3.16MM Privately Held
Web: www.utitec.com
SIC: 3841 3469　Surgical and medical instruments; Pressure cookers, stamped or drawn metal

(G-4037)
WATERTOWN JIG BORE SERVICE INC
29 New Wood Rd (06795-3314)
PHONE...............................860 274-5898
Michael Schlosky, *Pr*
Nicole Carroll, *Sec*
EMP: 24 EST: 1963
SQ FT: 7,000
SALES (est): 508.97K Privately Held
SIC: 3544 3541　Special dies and tools; Milling machines

(G-4038)
WATERTOWN PLASTICS INC
830 Echo Lake Rd (06795-1636)
P.O. Box 309 (06795-0309)
PHONE...............................860 274-7535
Jonathan Andrew, *Pr*
Edward Nickles, *
Diane Andrew, *
EMP: 36 EST: 1984
SQ FT: 15,000
SALES (est): 8.4MM Privately Held
Web: www.watertownplastics.com
SIC: 3089 3544　Injection molding of plastics; Industrial molds

Wauregan
Windham County

(G-4039)
BROOKWOOD LAMINATING INC
Also Called: Brookwood Roll Goods Group
275 Putnam Rd (06387-8716)
PHONE...............................860 774-5001
Amber M Brookman, *Pr*
Joseph Trumpetto, *
Robert Vander Meulen, *
▲ EMP: 65 EST: 1995
SQ FT: 50,000
SALES (est): 23.43MM Privately Held
Web: www.brookwoodcompanies.com
SIC: 2295 2269　Laminating of fabrics; Finishing plants, nec
HQ: Brookwood Companies Incorporated
485 Madison Ave Ste 500
New York NY 10022
212 551-0100

(G-4040)
FORTERRA PIPE & PRECAST LLC
174 All Hallows Rd (06387)
PHONE...............................860 564-9000
George Stevens, *Genl Mgr*
EMP: 9
Web: www.rinkerpipe.com
SIC: 3272　Concrete products, precast, nec
HQ: Forterra Pipe & Precast, Llc
511 E John Carpenter Fwy
Irving TX 75062
469 458-7973

(G-4041)
QUIKRETE COMPANIES INC
Also Called: Quikrete Connecticut ME
541 Green Hollow Rd (06387)
P.O. Box 381 (06387-0381)
PHONE...............................860 564-3308
FAX: 860 564-1874
EMP: 10
SQ FT: 3,520
SIC: 3272 5032 3273　Concrete products, nec; Cement; Ready-mixed concrete
HQ: The Quikrete Companies Llc
5 Concourse Pkwy Ste 1900
Atlanta GA 30328
404 634-9100

Weatogue
Hartford County

(G-4042)
RC CONNECTORS LLC
146 Hopmeadow St (06089-7908)
PHONE...............................860 413-2196
John D Ritson, *Prin*
EMP: 8 EST: 2012
SALES (est): 289.06K Privately Held
SIC: 3678　Electronic connectors

(G-4043)
VEEDER-ROOT COMPANY (HQ)
Also Called: Veeder-Root
125 Powder Forest Dr Fl 1 (06089-7943)
P.O. Box 2003 (06070-7684)
PHONE...............................860 651-2700
Brian Burnett, *Pr*
◆ EMP: 80 EST: 1890
SQ FT: 25,000
SALES (est): 176.79MM
SALES (corp-wide): 3.1B Publicly Held
Web: www.veeder.com

SIC: **3823** 3824   Process control instruments
; Mechanical measuring meters
PA: Vontier Corporation
5438 Wade Park Blvd # 601
Raleigh NC 27607
984 275-6000

West Cornwall
Litchfield County

(G-4044)
IAN INGERSOLL CABINETMAKER
422 Sharon Goshen Tpke (06796-1122)
PHONE...............................860 672-6334
Ian Ingersoll, *Owner*
EMP: 10 EST: 1975
SQ FT: 2,000
SALES (est): 464.02K **Privately Held**
Web: www.ianingersoll.com
SIC: **5712** 2511   Cabinet work, custom;
Chairs, household, except upholstered:
wood

West Hartford
Hartford County

(G-4045)
A PIECE OF PZZLE BHVRAL INTRVN
1100 New Britain Ave Ste 105
(06110-2427)
PHONE...............................860 250-8054
Amy Lavoie, *Prin*
EMP: 13 EST: 2017
SALES (est): 691.82K **Privately Held**
SIC: **3944**   Puzzles

(G-4046)
ABBOTT BALL COMPANY
19 Railroad Pl (06110-2384)
P.O. Box 330100 (06133-0100)
PHONE...............................860 236-5901
Craig W Bond, *Pr*
▲ EMP: 75 EST: 1918
SALES (est): 20.87MM **Privately Held**
Web: www.abbottball.com
SIC: **3399**   Steel balls

(G-4047)
ADAMS AHERN SIGN SOLUTIONS
120 Vanderbilt Ave (06110-1513)
PHONE...............................860 523-8835
EMP: 7 EST: 2019
SALES (est): 263.04K **Privately Held**
Web: www.adamsahern.com
SIC: **3993**   Signs and advertising specialties

(G-4048)
AUTOMATION INC
707 Oakwood Ave (06110-1508)
P.O. Box 330346 (06133-0346)
PHONE...............................860 236-5991
Ronald D Hall, *Pr*
Robert C Dodge, *VP*
Alice L Hall, *Sec*
EMP: 30 EST: 1963
SQ FT: 5,000
SALES (est): 4.47MM **Privately Held**
Web: www.automationincct.com
SIC: **3569** 5085   Lubrication equipment,
industrial; Industrial supplies

(G-4049)
CABINET HARWARD SPECIALTI
50 Chelton Ave (06110-1205)
PHONE...............................860 231-1192
Art Roth, *Owner*
EMP: 7 EST: 1998
SALES (est): 467.6K **Privately Held**
SIC: **2434**   Wood kitchen cabinets

(G-4050)
CAPITOL GLASS COMPANY INC
75 Grassmere Ave (06110-1296)
P.O. Box 330311 (06133-0311)
PHONE...............................860 236-1936
Gregory Gagnon, *Managing Member*
Claude A Gagnon, *Pr*
Pamela C Gagnon, *Sec*
Greg Gagnon, *VP*
Eric Gagnon, *VP*
EMP: 15 EST: 1970
SQ FT: 7,000
SALES (est): 1.1MM **Privately Held**
Web: www.capitolglass.com
SIC: **5231** 7536 1793 3442   Glass;
Automotive glass replacement shops;
Glass and glazing work; Store fronts,
prefabricated, metal

(G-4051)
CAPTIVATING KITCHENS
555 New Park Ave (06110-1348)
PHONE...............................860 236-6500
Tony Rogers, *Sales & Marketing*
EMP: 7 EST: 2015
SALES (est): 112.26K **Privately Held**
Web: www.ctshowerandbath.com
SIC: **2434**   Wood kitchen cabinets

(G-4052)
CCR PRODUCTS LLC
175 South St (06110-1928)
P.O. Box 330186 (06133-0186)
PHONE...............................860 953-0499
▲ EMP: 20 EST: 2003
SALES (est): 2.46MM **Privately Held**
Web: www.ccrproducts.com
SIC: **3312** 3399   Iron and steel products, hot-
rolled; Tacks, nonferrous metal or wire

(G-4053)
COLT DEFENSE LLC (HQ)
Also Called: Colt Defense Holding
547 New Park Ave (06110-1336)
PHONE...............................860 232-4489
Dennis Veilleux, *Managing Member*
James R Battaglini, */**
Richard Harris In, *CFO*
EMP: 380 EST: 2002
SQ FT: 250,000
SALES (est): 94.15MM **Privately Held**
Web: www.colt.com
SIC: **3484**   Machine guns or machine gun
parts, 30 mm. and below
PA: Colt Defense Holding Llc
547 New Park Ave
W Hartford CT 06110

(G-4054)
CONNECTCUT BOILER REPR MFG INC
Also Called: Cbr
694 Oakwood Ave (06110-1507)
PHONE...............................860 953-9117
Peter J Royer, *Pr*
Irene L Royer, *Treas*
Sharon E Royer, *Sec*
EMP: 20 EST: 1950
SQ FT: 12,000
SALES (est): 2.19MM **Privately Held**
Web: www.ct-boiler.com

SIC: **7699** 1711 3443   Boiler repair shop;
Boiler and furnace contractors;
Smokestacks, boiler plate

(G-4055)
CRICKET PRESS INC
236 Park Rd (06119-2018)
PHONE...............................860 521-9279
Michelle Confessore, *Pr*
Greg Confessore, *VP*
Carol Teasdale, *Treas*
EMP: 10 EST: 1971
SQ FT: 2,000
SALES (est): 947.02K **Privately Held**
Web: www.cricketpress.biz
SIC: **2752**   Offset printing

(G-4056)
DELTA-SOURCE LLC
138 Beacon Hill Dr (06117-1006)
PHONE...............................860 461-1600
Daniel Barash, *Prin*
EMP: 10 EST: 2010
SALES (est): 408.98K **Privately Held**
SIC: **3999**   Manufacturing industries, nec

(G-4057)
EAGLE INVESTMENT SYSTEMS LLC
65 Lasalle Rd Ste 305 (06107-2325)
PHONE...............................860 561-4602
EMP: 16
SALES (corp-wide): 19.99B **Publicly Held**
Web: www.eagleinvsys.com
SIC: **7299** 6282 8721 7372   Debt counseling
or adjustment service, individuals;
Investment advisory service; Accounting
services, except auditing; Business
oriented computer software
HQ: Eagle Investment Systems Llc
45 William St
Wellesley MA 02481

(G-4058)
EL MAR INC
Also Called: Uncle Bill's Tweezers
38 Cody St # 2 (06110-1904)
P.O. Box 925 (06001-0925)
PHONE...............................860 729-7232
Glen Baron, *Pr*
EMP: 9 EST: 1983
SQ FT: 5,000
SALES (est): 695.88K **Privately Held**
Web: www.slivergripper.com
SIC: **3599**   Machine and other job shop work

(G-4059)
ELM-CAP INDUSTRIES INC
111 South St (06110-1928)
P.O. Box 330099 (06133-0099)
PHONE...............................860 953-1060
R Thomas Abbate, *Pr*
EMP: 45 EST: 1914
SALES (est): 4.04MM **Privately Held**
Web: www.elmcap.net
SIC: **3272**   Burial vaults, concrete or precast
terrazzo

(G-4060)
ENVIRONMENTAL SYSTEMS CORP
Also Called: Honeywell Authorized Dealer
18 Jansen Ct (06110-1958)
PHONE...............................860 953-8800
EMP: 150 EST: 1963
SALES (est): 16.66MM
SALES (corp-wide): 121.26MM **Privately Held**
Web: www.esccontrols.com

SIC: **7373** 7376 7379 7382   Turnkey
vendors, computer systems; Computer
facilities management; Computer related
maintenance services; Security systems
services
PA: Fidelity Engineering, Llc
25 Loveton Cir
Sparks MD 21152
410 771-9400

(G-4061)
FRESH INK LLC
216 Park Rd Ste 3 (06119-2046)
PHONE...............................860 656-7013
EMP: 9 EST: 2010
SALES (est): 149.15K **Privately Held**
Web: www.freshinkllc.com
SIC: **2759**   Screen printing

(G-4062)
GREENMAKER INDUSTRIES CONN LLC
Also Called: Greenmaker Industries
697 Oakwood Ave (06110-1506)
PHONE...............................860 761-2830
Sarah Beatty, *Managing Member*
EMP: 10 EST: 2011
SALES (est): 1.68MM **Privately Held**
Web: www.greenmakerindustries.com
SIC: **2851**   Paints and allied products

(G-4063)
HAR-CONN CHROME COMPANY (PA)
603 New Park Ave (06110-1380)
P.O. Box 330189 (06133-0189)
PHONE...............................860 236-6801
Kent N Backus, *CEO*
Tim Backus, ***
Daniel Backus, ***
Donald Vye, ***
Fred Gariepy, ***
EMP: 70 EST: 1948
SQ FT: 40,000
SALES (est): 11.24MM
SALES (corp-wide): 11.24MM **Privately Held**
Web: www.har-conn.com
SIC: **3471**   Plating of metals or formed
products

(G-4064)
HARTFORD COMPRESSORS INC
179 South St (06110-1928)
P.O. Box 330389 (06133-0389)
▲ EMP: 43 EST: 1995
SQ FT: 124,000
SALES (est): 16.25MM
SALES (corp-wide): 846.3MM **Privately Held**
SIC: **3585**   Compressors for refrigeration
and air conditioning equipment
HQ: Dunham-Bush International (Cayman)
Limited
C/O: Close Brothers (Cayman) Ltd
George Town GR CAYMAN

(G-4065)
JOBIN MACHINE INC
836 Farmington Ave (06119-1574)
PHONE...............................860 953-1631
George Kiss, *Pr*
Erica Kiss Ames, ***
EMP: 28 EST: 1967
SALES (est): 3.95MM **Privately Held**
Web: www.jobinmachine.com
SIC: **3728** 3714   Aircraft parts and
equipment, nec; Motor vehicle parts and
accessories

(G-4066)

LEBON PRESS INCORPORATED

Also Called: Lebon Press
30 Osage Rd (06117-1334)
PHONE..............................860 278-6355
EMP: 25
Web: lebon.openfos.com
SIC: 2752   Offset printing

(G-4067)

LEGRAND HOLDING INC (DH)

60 Woodlawn St (06110-2326)
PHONE..............................860 233-6251
John P Selldorff, *CEO*
Giles Schnep, *
Antoine Burel, *
Robert Julian, *
Franck Lemery, *
▲ **EMP:** 30 **EST:** 1984
SALES (est): 2.43B **Privately Held**
Web: www.legrand.us
SIC: 3643 6719   Current-carrying wiring
   services; Investment holding companies,
   except banks
HQ: Legrand France
   128 Av Du Mal De Lattre De Tassigny
   Limoges 87000
   555068787

(G-4068)

LEWTAN INDUSTRIES CORPORATION

Also Called: Abbott Manufacturing
57 Loomis Dr Apt A1 (06107-2035)
P.O. Box 4694 (06831-0412)
PHONE..............................860 278-9800
Marvin Lewtan, *Ch Bd*
Douglas Lewtan, *
▲ **EMP:** 22 **EST:** 1947
SQ FT: 35,000
SALES (est): 368.83K **Privately Held**
SIC: 3993   Signs and advertising specialties

(G-4069)

LIFE PUBLICATIONS

Also Called: White Publishing
106 South St Ste 5 (06110-1965)
PHONE..............................860 953-0444
Christopher White, *Owner*
EMP: 10 **EST:** 1997
SALES (est): 461.87K **Privately Held**
Web: www.lifepublications.com
SIC: 2711   Newspapers, publishing and
   printing

(G-4070)

MANUFACTURERS COML FIN LLC

Also Called: Electro-Flex Heat
1022 Boulevard (06119-1801)
P.O. Box 88 (06002-0088)
PHONE..............................860 242-6287
EMP: 31 **EST:** 2010
SALES (est): 3.27MM **Privately Held**
Web: www.electroflexheat.com
SIC: 3567   Heating units and devices,
   industrial: electric

(G-4071)

MBSW INC

41 Plainfield Rd (06117-1936)
PHONE..............................860 243-0303
Theodore L Zachs, *Pr*
Ross Zachs, *
Jed Zachs, *
▲ **EMP:** 21 **EST:** 1939
SQ FT: 45,000
SALES (est): 367.44K **Privately Held**

SIC: 3089 3953 2782   Injection molded
   finished plastics products, nec; Stencils,
   painting and marking; Scrapbooks, albums,
   and diaries

(G-4072)

METALLIZING SVC HOLDINGS LLC (PA)

11 Cody St (06110-1949)
PHONE..............................860 953-1144
David S Gollob, *Pr*
David S Gollob, *Pr*
Rona B Gollob, *
EMP: 84 **EST:** 1940
SQ FT: 14,000
SALES (est): 9.71MM
SALES (corp-wide): 9.71MM **Privately Held**
Web: www.mscplasma.com
SIC: 3479   Coating of metals and formed
   products

(G-4073)

METALLURGICAL PROCESSING

11 Ritoli Rdg (06117-1860)
PHONE..............................860 916-5015
EMP: 7 **EST:** 2018
SALES (est): 446.85K **Privately Held**
Web: www.mpimetaltreating.com
SIC: 3398   Metal heat treating

(G-4074)

NEW COLT HOLDING CORP

545 New Park Ave (06110-1336)
P.O. Box 1868 (06144-1868)
PHONE..............................860 236-6311
EMP: 18 **EST:** 1994
SALES (est): 88.73K **Privately Held**
SIC: 3484   Small arms
HQ: Colt Defense Llc
   547 New Park Ave
   West Hartford CT 06110
   860 232-4489

(G-4075)

NUMMY LLC

1160 New Britain Ave (06110-2413)
PHONE..............................608 801-9850
Ronak Patel, *Prin*
EMP: 7 **EST:** 2017
SALES (est): 283.66K **Privately Held**
Web: www.nummy.com
SIC: 2045   Prepared flour mixes and doughs

(G-4076)

ORTRONICS INC

Also Called: Legrand
60 Woodlawn St (06110-2326)
PHONE..............................877 295-3472
EMP: 12
Web: www.legrand.us
SIC: 3577 3357   Computer peripheral
   equipment, nec; Communication wire
HQ: Ortronics, Inc.
   125 Eugene Oneill Dr # 140
   New London CT 06320
   860 445-3900

(G-4077)

PALADIN COMMERCIAL PRTRS LLC

Also Called: Paladin Commercial Printers
109 Talcott Rd (06110-1228)
PHONE..............................860 953-4900
EMP: 12 **EST:** 1989
SALES (est): 532.55K **Privately Held**
Web: www.paladinp.com
SIC: 2752   Offset printing

(G-4078)

PETRUNTI DESIGN & WDWKG LLC

23c Andover Dr (06110-1524)
PHONE..............................860 953-5332
EMP: 8 **EST:** 2006
SALES (est): 476.59K **Privately Held**
Web: www.petruntidesign.com
SIC: 2431   Millwork

(G-4079)

READY TOOL COMPANY

1 Carney Rd (06110-1937)
PHONE..............................860 524-7811
Joseph Wagner, *Pr*
EMP: 20 **EST:** 1908
SQ FT: 40,000
SALES (est): 2.64MM
SALES (corp-wide): 24.77MM **Privately Held**
Web: www.readytool.net
SIC: 3541   Machine tools, metal cutting type
PA: The United Tool & Die Company
   1 Carney Rd
   West Hartford CT 06110
   860 246-6531

(G-4080)

RECREATIONAL EQUIPMENT INC

1417 New Britain Ave (06110-1659)
PHONE..............................860 313-0128
EMP: 12 **EST:** 2018
SALES (est): 313.98K **Privately Held**
SIC: 3949   Sporting and athletic goods, nec

(G-4081)

SORENSON LIGHTED CONTROLS INC (PA)

Also Called: Solico
100 Shield St (06110-1920)
PHONE..............................860 527-3092
Robert C Sorenson, *Pr*
Fred Kundahl, *
John D Gallery, *
Julia Sorenson, *
Robert C Sorenson Junior, *VP*
▲ **EMP:** 85 **EST:** 1960
SQ FT: 25,000
SALES (est): 9.23MM
SALES (corp-wide): 9.23MM **Privately Held**
Web: www.solico.com
SIC: 3648   Lighting equipment, nec

(G-4082)

SPENCER NORB

17 Oakwood Ave Ste 2 (06119-2182)
PHONE..............................860 231-8079
Norb Spencer, *Prin*
EMP: 10 **EST:** 2007
SALES (est): 218.53K **Privately Held**
Web: www.signs-on-site.com
SIC: 3993   Signs and advertising specialties

(G-4083)

SPV INDUSTRIES LLC

9 Tolles St (06110-1504)
PHONE..............................860 953-5928
EMP: 7 **EST:** 2009
SALES (est): 245.89K **Privately Held**
Web: spv-industries-llc.hub.biz
SIC: 3999   Manufacturing industries, nec

(G-4084)

SWANSON TOOL MANUFACTURING INC

71 Custer St (06110-1908)

P.O. Box 330318 (06133-0318)
PHONE..............................860 953-1641
Kenneth Swanson Junior, *CEO*
Kenneth W Swanson Senior, *CEO*
Annlouise Swanson, *
EMP: 25 **EST:** 1967
SQ FT: 19,000
SALES (est): 2.31MM **Privately Held**
Web: www.swansonsage.com
SIC: 3545 5084 5251   Threading tools
   (machine tool accessories); Threading tools
   ; Tools

(G-4085)

TRIATIC INC

22 Grassmere Ave (06110-1251)
PHONE..............................860 236-2298
EMP: 11 **EST:** 1992
SQ FT: 10,000
SALES (est): 1.3MM **Privately Held**
Web: www.triaticinc.com
SIC: 3291   Artificial abrasives

(G-4086)

TRIUMPH ENG CTRL SYSTEMS LLC

110 Talcott Rd (06110-1232)
PHONE..............................860 597-7173
EMP: 490
SIC: 3728   Aircraft parts and equipment, nec
HQ: Triumph Engine Control Systems, Llc
   1 Charter Oak Blvd
   West Hartford CT 06110
   860 236-0651

(G-4087)

TRIUMPH ENG CTRL SYSTEMS LLC (HQ)

Also Called: Goodrich
1 Charter Oak Blvd (06110-1328)
PHONE..............................860 236-0651
Alec Searle, *VP*
EMP: 69 **EST:** 2013
SALES (est): 144.58MM **Publicly Held**
SIC: 3728 3724 3812   Aircraft body and wing
   assemblies and parts; Aircraft engines and
   engine parts; Aircraft control instruments
PA: Triumph Group, Inc.
   555 E Lancaster Ave # 400
   Radnor PA 19087

(G-4088)

UNITED TOOL & DIE COMPANY (PA)

1 Carney Rd (06110-1982)
PHONE..............................860 246-6531
David Hussey, *Pr*
Julie Susan Wagner, *
Joseph Wagner, *
Charles Zien, *
David Hussey, *Sec*
EMP: 110 **EST:** 1923
SQ FT: 150,000
SALES (est): 24.77MM
SALES (corp-wide): 24.77MM **Privately Held**
Web: www.utdco.com
SIC: 3724 3541 3769   Aircraft engines and
   engine parts; Machine tools, metal cutting
   type; Space vehicle equipment, nec

(G-4089)

WEST HARTFORD LOCK CO LLC

11 Sherman St (06110-1914)
PHONE..............................860 236-0671
EMP: 13 **EST:** 1947
SQ FT: 3,000
SALES (est): 2.25MM **Privately Held**

▲ = Import ▼ = Export
◆ = Import/Export

Web: www.westhartfordlock.com
SIC: **5999** 5031 7699 3873 Architectural
supplies; Lumber, plywood, and millwork;
Locksmith shop; Watches, clocks,
watchcases, and parts

(G-4090)
WIPL-D (USA) LLC
103 High Ridge Rd (06117-1815)
PHONE.................................860 570-0678
Zoran Maricevic, *Prin*
EMP: 16 **EST:** 2013
SALES (est): 121.87K **Privately Held**
Web: www.wipl-d.com
SIC: **7372** Prepackaged software

(G-4091)
WIREMOLD COMPANY (DH)
60 Woodlawn St (06110-2383)
PHONE.................................860 233-6251
John P Selldorff, *CEO*
Brian Dibella, *
Virdi Sneh, *
Steve Schneider, *
◆ **EMP:** 750 **EST:** 1919
SQ FT: 226,000
SALES (est): 356.08MM **Privately Held**
Web: www.legrand.us
SIC: **3643** 3496 3315 3644 Current-carrying
wiring services; Miscellaneous fabricated
wire products; Steel wire and related
products; Raceways
HQ: Legrand Holding, Inc.
60 Woodlawn St
West Hartford CT 06110
860 233-6251

(G-4092)
WIREMOLD COMPANY
Also Called: The Wiremold Company
21 Railroad Pl (06110-2344)
PHONE.................................860 263-3115
John P Selldorff, *CEO*
EMP: 50
Web: www.wiremoldproducts.com
SIC: **3644** Noncurrent-carrying wiring
devices
HQ: Wiremold Company
60 Woodlawn St
West Hartford CT 06110
860 233-6251

(G-4093)
WROUGHT IRON WORKS LLC
600 Oakwood Ave (06110-1520)
PHONE.................................860 523-4457
EMP: 25 **EST:** 2000
SALES (est): 2.36MM **Privately Held**
Web: www.wroughtironworksct.com
SIC: **3446** Architectural metalwork

West Haven
New Haven County

(G-4094)
AMERIFIX LLC
278 Washington Ave (06516-5327)
PHONE.................................203 931-7290
EMP: 9 **EST:** 2004
SQ FT: 22,000
SALES (est): 1.02MM **Privately Held**
SIC: **2491** Millwork, treated wood

(G-4095)
**BRIDGESTONE RET
OPERATIONS LLC**
Also Called: Firestone
525 Saw Mill Rd (06516-4045)

PHONE.................................203 933-7750
EMP: 7
Web: www.bridgestoneamericas.com
SIC: **5531** 7538 7537 7534 Automotive tires
; General automotive repair shops;
Automotiv e transmission repair shops; Tire
retreading and repair shops
HQ: Bridgestone Retail Operations, Llc
333 E Lake St Ste 300
Bloomingdale IL 60108
630 259-9000

(G-4096)
CANNELLI PRINTING CO INC
39 Wood St (06516-3843)
PHONE.................................203 932-1719
Victor Cannelli, *Pr*
Rose Cannelli, *VP*
EMP: 9 **EST:** 1911
SALES (est): 1.54MM **Privately Held**
Web: www.cannelli.com
SIC: **2752** 2759 Offset printing; Card
printing and engraving, except greeting

(G-4097)
**COLONIAL WOOD PRODUCTS
INC**
250 Callegari Dr (06516-6234)
PHONE.................................203 932-9003
Kevin Donovan, *Pr*
William Donovan Junior, *VP*
EMP: 9 **EST:** 1938
SQ FT: 10,000
SALES (est): 436.84K **Privately Held**
SIC: **2431** 2441 Millwork; Boxes, wood

(G-4098)
CONCO WOOD WORKING INC
755 1st Ave (06516-2712)
P.O. Box 17176 (06907-7176)
PHONE.................................203 934-9665
EMP: 9 **EST:** 1994
SQ FT: 27,000
SALES (est): 1.03MM **Privately Held**
Web: www.concowoodworking.com
SIC: **2521** 2522 Wood office furniture; Office
furniture, except wood

(G-4099)
COSMOS FOOD PRODUCTS INC
200 Callegari Dr (06516-6234)
PHONE.................................800 942-6766
Cosmo N Laudano, *Pr*
Lisa L Laudano, *
Lauren N Laudano, *
Mark C Laudano, *
▲ **EMP:** 40 **EST:** 1973
SQ FT: 25,000
SALES (est): 8.84MM **Privately Held**
SIC: **2033** Canned fruits and specialties

(G-4100)
COVER-IT INC
17 Wood St (06516-3843)
P.O. Box 06037 (06516)
PHONE.................................203 931-4747
Susan Smith, *Pr*
Marguerite Starr, *
EMP: 105 **EST:** 1990
SALES (est): 11.46MM **Privately Held**
SIC: **3448** Prefabricated metal buildings

(G-4101)
DANDREA CORPORATION (PA)
Also Called: Dunkin' Donuts
985 Boston Post Rd (06516-1727)
PHONE.................................203 932-6000
EMP: 7 **EST:** 1979
SALES (est): 3.65MM **Privately Held**
Web: www.dandreagroupct.com

SIC: **5461** 2051 Doughnuts; Doughnuts,
except frozen

(G-4102)
**DEITSCH PLASTIC COMPANY
INC**
14 Farwell St (06516-1717)
P.O. Box 26005 (06516-8005)
PHONE.................................203 934-6601
Mordecoi Deitsch, *Pr*
Joseph Deitsch, *
Joshua Sandman, *
◆ **EMP:** 68 **EST:** 1954
SQ FT: 200,000
SALES (est): 6.84MM **Privately Held**
Web: www.deitschplastic.com
SIC: **2221** 2295 Broadwoven fabric mills,
manmade; Plastic coated yarns or fabrics

(G-4103)
DEVICE42 INC
600 Saw Mill Rd (06516-4007)
PHONE.................................203 409-7242
Raj Jalen, *CEO*
Stephen Timms, *CRO*
EMP: 14 **EST:** 2010
SALES (est): 2.67MM **Privately Held**
Web: www.device42.com
SIC: **7372** Prepackaged software

(G-4104)
DIETZGEN CORPORATION
351 Morgan Ln (06516-4135)
PHONE.................................813 849-4334
EMP: 10 **EST:** 2017
SALES (est): 831.52K **Privately Held**
Web: www.dietzgen.com
SIC: **2679** Paper products, converted, nec

(G-4105)
**E O MANUFACTURING
COMPANY INC**
474 Frontage Rd (06516-4154)
PHONE.................................203 932-5981
Peter Lemere Junior, *Pr*
EMP: 40 **EST:** 1945
SQ FT: 8,748
SALES (est): 501.16K **Privately Held**
SIC: **3599** Machine shop, jobbing and repair

(G-4106)
ERA WIRE INC
19 Locust St (06516-2022)
PHONE.................................203 933-0480
Richard T Rae, *Pr*
Katherine Rae, *VP*
EMP: 11 **EST:** 1988
SQ FT: 5,000
SALES (est): 2.69MM **Privately Held**
Web: www.erawire.com
SIC: **3496** Miscellaneous fabricated wire
products

(G-4107)
GHP MEDIA INC (PA)
Also Called: Ghp
475 Heffernan Dr (06516-4161)
PHONE.................................203 479-7500
John Robinson, *CEO*
Fred Hoxsie, *Mng Pt*
EMP: 65 **EST:** 1991
SQ FT: 11,000
SALES (est): 31.41MM **Privately Held**
Web: www.ghpmedia.com
SIC: **2752** 2796 Offset printing; Color
separations, for printing

(G-4108)
**JUPITER COMMUNICATIONS
LLC**
755 1st Ave (06516-2712)
PHONE.................................475 238-7082
Ethan Odin, *Managing Member*
EMP: 12 **EST:** 1975
SQ FT: 16,000
SALES (est): 885.13K **Privately Held**
SIC: **2752** 2791 Offset printing; Typesetting,
computer controlled

(G-4109)
**KEMPER MANUFACTURING
CORP**
5 Clinton Pl (06516-2808)
PHONE.................................203 934-1600
Cathy Harter, *Pr*
▲ **EMP:** 20 **EST:** 1977
SQ FT: 10,000
SALES (est): 1.06MM **Privately Held**
Web: www.straplady.com
SIC: **2399** Belting and belt products

(G-4110)
**KRAMER PRINTING COMPANY
INC**
270 Front Ave (06516-2836)
P.O. Box 27155 (06516-0970)
PHONE.................................203 933-5416
Richard Kramer, *Pr*
Marcy Kramer-ide, *Sec*
EMP: 18 **EST:** 1945
SQ FT: 7,800
SALES (est): 454.96K **Privately Held**
Web: kramer.typepad.com
SIC: **2752** 2759 Offset printing; Promotional
printing

(G-4111)
KX TECHNOLOGIES LLC (DH)
55 Railroad Ave (06516-4143)
PHONE.................................203 799-9000
John J Goody, *Managing Member*
Bruce R Belcher, *
▲ **EMP:** 46 **EST:** 2004
SQ FT: 67,000
SALES (est): 24.3MM
SALES (corp-wide): 302.09B **Publicly
Held**
Web: www.kxtech.com
SIC: **3589** Water purification equipment,
household type
HQ: Marmon Water Llc
1769a Jamestown Rd
Williamsburg VA 23185

(G-4112)
MACDERMID ENTHONE INC (HQ)
Also Called: Macdermid Enthone Indus Sltons
350 Frontage Rd (06516-4130)
PHONE.................................203 934-8611
Scott Benson, *Pr*
Ted Ericson, *
◆ **EMP:** 158 **EST:** 1946
SALES (est): 167.27MM
SALES (corp-wide): 2.55B **Publicly Held**
Web: industrial.macdermidenthone.com
SIC: **2899** Chemical preparations, nec
PA: Element Solutions Inc
500 E Broward Blvd # 1860
Fort Lauderdale FL 33394
561 207-9600

(G-4113)
**MANUFACTURERS
ASSOCIATES INC**
45 Railroad Ave (06516-4143)
P.O. Box 4419 (06514-0419)

PHONE...................203 931-4344
Lonnie Parillo, Pr
EMP: 25 **EST:** 1996
SQ FT: 25,000
SALES (est): 893.96K **Privately Held**
Web: www.manufacturersassociates.com
SIC: 3451 Screw machine products

(G-4114)
MAREL CORPORATION
5 Saw Mill Rd (06516-4111)
PHONE...................203 934-8187
John Rice, Pr
Tim Mcneil, VP
Elizabeth Rice, Sec
EMP: 9 **EST:** 1998
SALES (est): 459.49K **Privately Held**
Web: www.marel.com
SIC: 3841 5047 Surgical and medical
instruments; Hospital equipment and
furniture

(G-4115)
MCNEIL HEALTHCARE INC
5 Saw Mill Rd (06516-4111)
P.O. Box 351 (07936-0351)
PHONE...................203 934-8187
Tim Mcneil, Pr
EMP: 599 **EST:** 2000
SALES (est): 695.13K
SALES (corp-wide): 1.41B **Publicly Held**
Web: www.mcneilhealthcare.com
SIC: 3842 Surgical appliances and supplies
PA: Kenvue Inc.
199 Grandview Rd
Skillman NJ 08558
908 874-1200

(G-4116)
NEW ENGLAND NONWOVENS
LLC
283 Dogburn Rd (06516-2101)
PHONE...................203 891-0851
John Guchmanowicz, Managing Member
EMP: 19 **EST:** 2008
SALES (est): 996.88K **Privately Held**
Web: www.newenglandnonwovens.com
SIC: 2297 Nonwoven fabrics

(G-4117)
O BERK COMPANY NENG LLC
300 Callegari Dr (06516-6255)
PHONE...................203 932-8000
▲ **EMP:** 10 **EST:** 1933
SALES (est): 4.71MM
SALES (corp-wide): 52.84MM **Privately
Held**
Web: www.oberk.com
SIC: 5085 2759 3999 5047 Bottler supplies;
Screen printing; Gold stamping, except
books; Hospital equipment and supplies,
nec
PA: The O Berk Company L L C
3 Milltown Ct
Union NJ 07083
800 631-7392

(G-4118)
PANAGRAFIX INC
Also Called: USA Notepads
50 Fresh Meadow Rd (06516-1445)
PHONE...................203 691-5529
EMP: 26
SALES (corp-wide): 4.45MM **Privately
Held**
Web: www.usa-notepads.com
SIC: 2678 Tablets and pads, book and
writing: from purchased materials
PA: Panagrafix, Inc.
75 Cascade Blvd

Milford CT 06460
203 878-7412

(G-4119)
POLYMER FILMS INC
301 Heffernan Dr (06516-4163)
PHONE...................203 932-3000
John Watson, Pr
Robert Watson, *
Mary Watson, *
James Watson, *
EMP: 25 **EST:** 1963
SQ FT: 88,000
SALES (est): 248.28K **Privately Held**
Web: www.glanbianutritionals.com
SIC: 3081 2671 Plastics film and sheet;
Paper; coated and laminated packaging

(G-4120)
QUEEN GRAPHICS
PRINTWORKS INC
Also Called: Queen Graphics
738 Washington Ave (06516-3754)
PHONE...................203 464-7337
Kursad Ece, Pr
EMP: 10 **EST:** 2012
SALES (est): 639.91K **Privately Held**
Web: www.queengraphics.com
SIC: 7384 2759 Film developing and printing
; Advertising literature: printing, nsk

(G-4121)
ROBERT-KENNETH ANDRADE
LLC
975 Campbell Ave (06516-2707)
PHONE...................203 937-8697
Robert B Andrade, Mgr
EMP: 8 **EST:** 2001
SALES (est): 125.03K **Privately Held**
SIC: 3713 Automobile wrecker truck bodies

(G-4122)
SABATINO NORTH AMERICA
LLC (PA)
Also Called: Speedy Food Group USA
135 Front Ave (06516-2811)
P.O. Box 505 (06516-0505)
PHONE...................718 328-4120
Federico Balestra, CEO
▲ **EMP:** 80 **EST:** 2006
SQ FT: 42,000
SALES (est): 20MM **Privately Held**
Web: www.sabatinotruffles.com
SIC: 2033 Mushrooms: packaged in cans,
jars, etc.

(G-4123)
SAVIN ROCK PRINTING
145 Boston Post Rd (06516-2059)
PHONE...................203 500-1577
EMP: 7 **EST:** 2017
SALES (est): 438.56K **Privately Held**
SIC: 2752 Commercial printing, lithographic

(G-4124)
SCHRAFEL PPRBD
CONVERTING CORP
82 W Clark St Ste 1 (06516-3559)
P.O. Box 419 (06516-0419)
PHONE...................203 931-1700
Richard B Schrafel, Pr
Robert A Schrafel, Sec
EMP: 21 **EST:** 1996
SQ FT: 101,000
SALES (est): 1.76MM **Privately Held**
Web: www.schrafelpaper.com
SIC: 2679 2631 Paperboard products,
converted, nec; Paperboard mills

(G-4125)
SEONGYUN CORPORATION
21 Elm St (06516-3808)
PHONE...................203 668-6803
Seongyun Choi, CEO
Jae Choi, Prin
EMP: 15 **EST:** 2007
SALES (est): 682.18K **Privately Held**
Web: www.e-nosk.com
SIC: 3842 Surgical appliances and supplies

(G-4126)
SKIN & CO NORTH AMERICA
LLC
135 Front Ave (06516-2811)
PHONE...................888 444-9971
EMP: 9 **EST:** 2017
SALES (est): 247.01K **Privately Held**
Web: www.sabatinotruffles.com
SIC: 2844 2836 7389 Face creams or lotions
; Serums; Cosmetic kits, assembling and
packaging

(G-4127)
SYLVAN R SHEMITZ DESIGNS
LLC (PA)
Also Called: Lighting Quotient, The
114 Boston Post Rd (06516-2043)
PHONE...................203 931-4455
Allison Schieffelin, CEO
Andreas Novotny, *
▲ **EMP:** 98 **EST:** 2014
SALES (est): 24.82MM
SALES (corp-wide): 24.82MM **Privately
Held**
Web: www.thelightingquotient.com
SIC: 3646 Commercial lighting fixtures

(G-4128)
THE BILCO COMPANY (DH)
Also Called: Permentry
37 Water St (06516-3837)
P.O. Box 1203 (06505-1203)
PHONE...................203 934-6363
◆ **EMP:** 140 **EST:** 1926
SALES (est): 49.56MM
SALES (corp-wide): 861.44MM **Privately
Held**
Web: www.bilco.com
SIC: 3442 3446 3444 6794 Metal doors;
Stairs, staircases, stair treads:
prefabricated metal; Metal roofing and roof
drainage equipment; Franchises, selling or
licensing
HQ: Truth Hardware Corporation
3600 Minnesota Dr Ste 800
Edina MN 55435

(G-4129)
THERACOUR PHARMA INC
135 Wood St Ste 8 (06516-3700)
PHONE...................203 937-6137
Anil Diwan, Pr
EMP: 7 **EST:** 2005
SALES (est): 88.36K **Privately Held**
SIC: 2834 Pharmaceutical preparations

(G-4130)
THERMAXX LLC (HQ)
14 Farwell St (06516-1717)
PHONE...................203 672-1021
Mike Bannon, CEO
Brian Bannon, Pr
Philip Johns, VP
EMP: 7 **EST:** 2008
SALES (est): 6.88MM
SALES (corp-wide): 144.65MM **Privately
Held**
Web: www.thermaxxjackets.com

SIC: 3443 Jackets, industrial: metal plate
PA: Spi Llc
2101 Rexford Rd Ste 300e
Charlotte NC 28211
704 336-9555

(G-4131)
UNIVERSAL PRINTING SVCS INC
Also Called: Universal Graphic
375 Morgan Ln Ste 203 (06516-4158)
PHONE...................203 934-4275
Thomas Morgillo, Pr
Eileen Morgillo, VP
Michael F Morgillo, Sec
EMP: 21 **EST:** 1982
SQ FT: 3,500
SALES (est): 3.67MM **Privately Held**
Web: www.univgraph.com
SIC: 2791 2789 2759 2752 Typesetting,
computer controlled; Bookbinding and
related work; Commercial printing, nec;
Commercial printing, lithographic

(G-4132)
WATSON LLC (DH)
Also Called: Watson
301 Heffernan Dr (06516-4163)
PHONE...................203 932-3000
James Watson, Pr
Gavin Watson, COO
◆ **EMP:** 37 **EST:** 2015
SQ FT: 220,000
SALES (est): 83.63MM **Privately Held**
Web: www.glanbianutritionals.com
SIC: 2045 2833 2087 2051 Prepared flour
mixes and doughs; Vitamins, natural or
synthetic: bulk, uncompounded; Flavoring
extracts and syrups, nec; Bread, cake, and
related products
HQ: Glanbia Nutritionals (Na), Inc.
1900 S Spresser St
Taylorville IL 62568
760 438-0089

(G-4133)
WOODLAND POWER
PRODUCTS INC
Also Called: Cyclone Rake
72 Acton St (06516-1704)
PHONE...................888 531-7253
James Whitney Ph.d., Pr
Ethan Hershman, *
▲ **EMP:** 33 **EST:** 1997
SQ FT: 15,000
SALES (est): 9.56MM **Privately Held**
Web: www.cyclonerake.com
SIC: 3524 Lawn and garden equipment

(G-4134)
YOLANDA DUBOSE RECORDS
AND
105 W Prospect St (06516-3540)
P.O. Box 5034 (06460-1434)
PHONE...................203 823-6699
Yolanda Dubose, Managing Member
EMP: 10 **EST:** 2009
SALES (est): 720.52K **Privately Held**
SIC: 2782 7929 7389 Record albums;
Entertainment service; Business services,
nec

Westbrook
Middlesex County

(G-4135)
AGW CLSSIC HARDWOOD
FLOORS LLC
1871 Boston Post Rd (06498-2183)

PHONE...............................203 640-3106
EMP: 8 **EST:** 2003
SALES (est): 426.21K **Privately Held**
Web: www.covenantkitchens.com
SIC: 1751 1752 2499 5713 Carpentry work;
Wood floor installation and refinishing;
Decorative wood and woodwork; Floor
covering stores

(G-4136)
AIUDI CONCRETE INC
129 Norris Ave (06498-1567)
PHONE...............................860 399-9289
Elmo Aiudi, *Pr*
EMP: 8 **EST:** 1982
SQ FT: 1,939
SALES (est): 843.53K **Privately Held**
SIC: 3273 Ready-mixed concrete

(G-4137)
**CLINTON NURSERY PRODUCTS
INC (PA)**
517 Pond Meadow Rd (06498-1493)
P.O. Box 679 (06498-0679)
PHONE...............................860 399-3000
David Richards, *Pr*
Warren Richards Junior, *Ch*
Peter Richards, *
Jim Galvin, *
EMP: 250 **EST:** 1948
SQ FT: 50,000
SALES (est): 22.73MM
SALES (corp-wide): 22.73MM **Privately
Held**
SIC: 5191 2879 5193 2875 Fertilizer and
fertilizer materials; Agricultural chemicals,
nec; Nursery stock; Potting soil, mixed

(G-4138)
GARDEN IRON LLC
47 Westbrook Indust Park Rd (06498-1524)
PHONE...............................860 767-9917
EMP: 7 **EST:** 1982
SALES (est): 848.06K **Privately Held**
Web: www.gardeniron.com
SIC: 1799 3446 Ornamental metal work;
Ornamental metalwork

(G-4139)
LEE COMPANY
22 Pequot Park Rd (06498-1466)
PHONE...............................860 399-6281
Ed Jones, *Brnch Mgr*
EMP: 20
SALES (corp-wide): 175.86MM **Privately
Held**
Web: www.theleeco.com
SIC: 3823 Process control instruments
PA: The Lee Company
2 Pettipaug Rd
Westbrook CT 06498
860 399-6281

(G-4140)
LEE COMPANY (PA)
2 Pettipaug Rd (06498-1500)
P.O. Box 424 (06498-0424)
PHONE...............................860 399-6281
William W Lee, *Pr*
Leighton Lee Iii, *Ch*
James Stamos, *
Robert M Lee, *
Thomas Lee, *
▲ **EMP:** 775 **EST:** 1949
SQ FT: 365,000
SALES (est): 175.86MM
SALES (corp-wide): 175.86MM **Privately
Held**
Web: www.theleeco.com

SIC: 3823 3841 3812 3728 Fluidic devices,
circuits, and systems for process control;
Surgical and medical instruments; Search
and navigation equipment; Aircraft parts
and equipment, nec

(G-4141)
LEE COMPANY HC
2 Pettipaug Rd (06498-1500)
PHONE...............................860 399-6281
Leighton Lee Iii, *Dir*
EMP: 11 **EST:** 2018
SALES (est): 194.55K **Privately Held**
Web: www.theleeco.com
SIC: 3823 Process control instruments

(G-4142)
SCRAPBOOK CLUBHOUSE
20 Westbrook Pl (06498-3902)
PHONE...............................860 399-4443
Sharon Cooke, *Owner*
EMP: 10 **EST:** 2005
SALES (est): 659.5K **Privately Held**
Web: www.papercraftclubhouse.com
SIC: 2782 Scrapbooks

(G-4143)
SSHC INC
Also Called: Solid State Heating
1244 Old Clinton Rd (06498-1871)
P.O. Box 769 (06475-0769)
PHONE...............................860 399-5434
Susan Watson, *VP*
Richard Watson, *Pr*
William C Bieluch Junior, *Sec*
EMP: 15 **EST:** 1989
SALES (est): 2.47MM **Privately Held**
Web: www.sshcinc.com
SIC: 3567 1711 Heating units and devices,
industrial: electric; Plumbing, heating, air-
conditioning

(G-4144)
TOPSIDE CANVAS & UPHL INC
768 Boston Post Rd (06498-1846)
PHONE...............................860 399-4845
Robert Ramsdell, *Pr*
Maureen Ramsdell, *Pr*
EMP: 7 **EST:** 1984
SQ FT: 2,400
SALES (est): 458.87K **Privately Held**
Web: www.topsidecanvasct.com
SIC: 2394 Canvas and related products

(G-4145)
TRIAD CONCEPTS INC
51 Brookwood Dr (06498-1576)
PHONE...............................860 399-4045
Arno E Utegg Senior, *Pr*
EMP: 7 **EST:** 2004
SALES (est): 160.32K **Privately Held**
SIC: 3569 Filters and strainers, pipeline

(G-4146)
**WESTBROOK CON BLOCK CO
INC**
Cold Spring Brook Industrial Park (06498)
PHONE...............................860 399-6201
Rose Maksin, *Mgr*
EMP: 25
SALES (corp-wide): 4.7MM **Privately Held**
Web: www.westbrookblock.com
SIC: 3271 Blocks, concrete or cinder:
standard
PA: Westbrook Concrete Block Company,
Inc.
439 Spencer Plains Rd
Westbrook CT
860 399-6201

Weston
Fairfield County

(G-4147)
CAPSTAN INC
263 Georgetown Rd (06883-1226)
PHONE...............................508 384-3100
W Macleod Snaith, *Pr*
EMP: 10 **EST:** 1995
SALES (est): 125.43K **Privately Held**
Web: www.capstan.be
SIC: 3441 Fabricated structural metal

(G-4148)
CELL NIQUE
12 Old Stage Coach Rd (06883-1908)
P.O. Box 1131 (06883-0131)
PHONE...............................888 417-9343
EMP: 7 **EST:** 2018
SALES (est): 438.7K **Privately Held**
Web: www.hudsonriverfoods.com
SIC: 2086 Bottled and canned soft drinks

(G-4149)
**CREATIVE MEDIA
APPLICATIONS**
22 Old Orchard Dr (06883-1309)
PHONE...............................203 226-0544
Barbara Stewart, *Pr*
Daniel Oelsen, *VP*
Lary Rosenblatt, *VP*
EMP: 7 **EST:** 1990
SQ FT: 1,500
SALES (est): 117.26K **Privately Held**
Web: www.cmacontent.com
SIC: 2731 Book publishing

(G-4150)
JACOBY
11 Blueberry Hill Rd (06883-2402)
PHONE...............................203 227-2220
Douglas Jacoby, *Pr*
EMP: 11 **EST:** 2017
SALES (est): 97.91K **Privately Held**
SIC: 2741 Miscellaneous publishing

(G-4151)
PMC TECHNOLOGIES LLC
31 Glenwood Rd (06883-2310)
PHONE...............................203 222-0000
EMP: 7 **EST:** 2011
SALES (est): 375.26K **Privately Held**
Web: www.pmctechnologies.net
SIC: 3651 Household audio and video
equipment

(G-4152)
**ROBERT MILLER ASSOCIATES
LLC**
127 Lords Hwy (06883-1751)
PHONE...............................718 392-1640
EMP: 15 **EST:** 1996
SALES (est): 756.08K **Privately Held**
SIC: 2389 Men's miscellaneous accessories

(G-4153)
SHIPPINGINSIGHT
21 Davis Hill Rd (06883-1902)
PHONE...............................203 260-0480
Carleen Lyden Walker, *Prin*
EMP: 8 **EST:** 2018
SALES (est): 387.89K **Privately Held**
Web: www.shippinginsight.com
SIC: 7372 Prepackaged software

(G-4154)
**VAN DEUSEN & LEVITT ASSOC
INC**
14 Wood Hill Rd (06883-1603)
P.O. Box 1257 (06883-0257)
PHONE...............................203 445-6244
Glenn C Van Deusen, *Pr*
EMP: 7 **EST:** 2009
SALES (est): 186.74K **Privately Held**
Web: www.vdla-inc.com
SIC: 3953 Irons, marking or branding

(G-4155)
VERTICAL VENTURES INTL LLC
40 Hackberry Hill Rd (06883-1825)
PHONE...............................203 227-1364
J Hough, *Prin*
EMP: 8 **EST:** 2004
SALES (est): 161K **Privately Held**
SIC: 2591 Drapery hardware and window
blinds and shades

Westport
Fairfield County

(G-4156)
**AMERICAN NATURAL SODA
ASH CORP (PA)**
Also Called: Ansac
15 Riverside Ave Ste 2 (06880-4245)
PHONE...............................203 226-9056
John M Andrews, *Pr*
Samuel R Blood, *VP*
Daniel Martinez, *VP*
Danny Sin, *VP*
◆ **EMP:** 20 **EST:** 1981
SQ FT: 9,000
SALES (est): 10.97MM
SALES (corp-wide): 10.97MM **Privately
Held**
Web: www.ansac.com
SIC: 1474 Soda ash (natural) mining

(G-4157)
**BAKER GRAPHICS
CORPORATION**
Also Called: Baker Grphics Reproduction Ctr
1753 Post Rd E (06880-5606)
PHONE...............................203 226-6928
Richard Baker, *Pr*
Marita Baker, *VP*
EMP: 11 **EST:** 1976
SQ FT: 6,500
SALES (est): 480.1K **Privately Held**
Web: www.bakergraphics.net
SIC: 7334 2752 Photocopying and
duplicating services; Offset printing

(G-4158)
**BIOSIG TECHNOLOGIES INC
(PA)**
Also Called: Biosig Technologies
55 Greens Farms Rd Ste 1 (06880-6149)
PHONE...............................203 409-5444
Kenneth L Londoner, *Ex Ch Bd*
Kenneth L Londoner, *Ex Ch Bd*
Steve Chaussy, *CFO*
John Sieckhaus, *COO*
EMP: 39 **EST:** 2009
SQ FT: 6,590
SALES (est): 286K
SALES (corp-wide): 286K **Publicly Held**
Web: www.biosig.com
SIC: 3841 Surgical and medical instruments

GEOGRAPHIC

(G-4159)
BOOKTRIBLIFECOM LLC
155 Post Rd E (06880-3412)
PHONE..............................203 226-0199
Meryl Moss, *Pr*
EMP: 10 EST: 2013
SALES (est): 214.3K **Privately Held**
SIC: 2741 Miscellaneous publishing

(G-4160)
CHESSCO INDUSTRIES INC (PA)
1330 Post Rd E Ste 2 (06880-5539)
PHONE..............................203 255-2804
Jeffrey Radler, *Pr*
Louis Radler, *
Albert J Kleban, *
Michael J Daly, *
▲ EMP: 41 EST: 1968
SQ FT: 2,000
SALES (est): 8.2MM
SALES (corp-wide): 8.2MM **Privately Held**
SIC: 3291 2911 2992 2899 Abrasive
products; Oils, lubricating; Cutting oils,
blending: made from purchased materials;
Chemical preparations, nec

(G-4161)
CLOUD PEAK ENERGY INC (PA)
606 Post Rd E # 624 (06880-4540)
P.O. Box 3001 (82717-3001)
PHONE..............................307 687-6000
Todd Myers, *Pr*
Heath Hill, *
Bryan Pechersky, *Corporate Secretary*
EMP: 86 EST: 1993
SQ FT: 32,000
SALES (est): 1.04B **Privately Held**
SIC: 1221 Bituminous coal and lignite-
surface mining

(G-4162)
**COMPASS GROUP
MANAGEMENT LLC (PA)**
301 Riverside Ave (06880-4806)
PHONE..............................203 221-1703
EMP: 16 EST: 1998
SALES (est): 22.56MM
SALES (corp-wide): 22.56MM **Privately Held**
Web: www.compassdiversified.com
SIC: 6282 3547 Investment advisory service
; Rolling mill machinery

(G-4163)
CSC SUGAR LLC (PA)
Also Called: CSC El Paso
33 Riverside Ave Ste 101 (06880-4226)
PHONE..............................203 846-5610
Paul J Farmer, *Pr*
Francis X Claps, *CFO*
◆ EMP: 20 EST: 2004
SALES (est): 134.53MM
SALES (corp-wide): 134.53MM **Privately Held**
Web: www.cscsugar.com
SIC: 5159 2063 2062 Sugar, raw; Liquid
sugar, from sugar beets; Refined cane
sugar, from purchased raw sugar or syrup

(G-4164)
DCA BUSINESS MEDIA LLC
256 Post Rd E Ste 206 (06880-3617)
PHONE..............................203 227-1699
Patrick Toole, *Prin*
EMP: 14 EST: 2007
SALES (est): 385.34K **Privately Held**
Web: www.shootonline.com

(G-4165)
DOMINO MEDIA GROUP INC
Also Called: Domino.com
16 Taylor Pl (06880-4313)
PHONE..............................877 223-7844
Cliff Sirlin, *CEO*
Aaron Wallace, *
Andy Appelbaum, *
EMP: 17 EST: 2012
SQ FT: 1,500
SALES (est): 168.31K **Privately Held**
Web: www.domino.com
SIC: 2721 5712 Magazines: publishing only,
not printed on site; Furniture stores

(G-4166)
EARNIX INC
191 Post Rd W (06880-4625)
PHONE..............................203 557-8077
Meryl Golden, *Brnch Mgr*
EMP: 10
Web: www.earnix.com
SIC: 7372 Business oriented computer
software
PA: Earnix Ltd
2 Jabotinsky
Ramat Gan

(G-4167)
ECONOMY ENERGY LLC
11 Ferry Ln W (06880-5808)
PHONE..............................203 227-5181
James Donaher, *Prin*
EMP: 7 EST: 2016
SALES (est): 600.17K **Privately Held**
SIC: 1382 Oil and gas exploration services

(G-4168)
FIRST EQUITY GROUP INC (PA)
15 Riverside Ave Ste 2 (06880-4245)
PHONE..............................203 291-7700
EMP: 15 EST: 1994
SQ FT: 3,000
SALES (est): 17.97MM **Privately Held**
Web: www.firstequity.com
SIC: 3724 7389 Aircraft engines and engine
parts; Brokers, business: buying and selling
business enterprises

(G-4169)
**GENIE LEASE MANAGEMENT
LLC**
200 Nyala Farms Rd (06880-6265)
PHONE..............................203 222-7170
Timothy A Ford, *Prin*
EMP: 7 EST: 2008
SALES (est): 250.71K **Privately Held**
SIC: 3536 Hoists, cranes, and monorails

(G-4170)
GOOD EARTH MILLWORK LLC
292 Post Rd E (06880-3628)
PHONE..............................203 226-7958
Michael Greenberg, *Mgr*
EMP: 8 EST: 2005
SALES (est): 153.31K **Privately Held**
SIC: 2431 Millwork

(G-4171)
H J BAKER & BRO INC
228 Saugatuck Ave Ste A (06880-6444)
PHONE..............................203 682-9200
Christopher Smith, *CEO*
EMP: 274 EST: 1996
SALES (est): 17.72MM **Privately Held**

Web: www.hjbaker.com
SIC: 2048 5052 5191 Poultry feeds; Sulfur;
Feed

(G-4172)
HEAVY INC
Also Called: Heavy.com
55 Post Rd W Fl 2 (06880-4235)
P.O. Box 1018 (10018-0013)
PHONE..............................646 806-2113
Michael Donn, *Admn*
Simon Assaad, *CEO*
▲ EMP: 10 EST: 1999
SQ FT: 12,000
SALES (est): 2.74MM **Privately Held**
Web: www.heavy.com
SIC: 2741 Internet publishing and
broadcasting

(G-4173)
**HILLS POINT INDUSTRIES LLC
(PA)**
Also Called: Gorilla Grip
20 Ketchum St (06880-5939)
PHONE..............................800 807-8579
Marissa Saporta, *Managing Member*
▼ EMP: 14 EST: 2014
SALES (est): 5.14MM
SALES (corp-wide): 5.14MM **Privately
Held**
Web: www.gorillacommerce.co
SIC: 2392 Household furnishings, nec

(G-4174)
IN STORE EXPERIENCE INC
Also Called: In Store Experience
37 Franklin St (06880-5938)
PHONE..............................203 221-4777
Christopher S Anderson, *CEO*
Deborah Anderson, *Research*
Adam Silverstein, *Design Vice President*
Frank Cirillo, *VP*
George Martocchio, *Retail Vice President*
▲ EMP: 26 EST: 2006
SALES (est): 8.89MM **Privately Held**
Web: www.instoreexperience.com
SIC: 2542 Fixtures, store: except wood

(G-4175)
INDUSTRIAL SALES CORP (PA)
Also Called: Industrial Sales Supply
727 Post Rd E (06880-5219)
PHONE..............................203 227-5988
James Hornung, *Pr*
Robert Hornung, *VP*
▲ EMP: 11 EST: 1979
SALES (est): 4.86MM
SALES (corp-wide): 4.86MM **Privately
Held**
Web: www.iscamerica.com
SIC: 2431 Windows and window parts and
trim, wood

(G-4176)
INFIRST HEALTHCARE INC
Also Called: Infirst Healthcare
8 Church Ln (06880-3508)
P.O. Box 715 (06897-0715)
PHONE..............................203 222-1300
James Barickman, *CEO*
EMP: 14 EST: 2010
SQ FT: 5,000
SALES (est): 2.58MM **Privately Held**
Web: www.infirst-usa.com
SIC: 2834 Antacids

(G-4177)
KERRY R WOOD
2 Hideaway Ln (06880-6115)
PHONE..............................203 221-7780

Kerry Wood, *Owner*
EMP: 7 EST: 2007
SALES (est): 305.09K **Privately Held**
Web:
www.sandersdiscountplumbing.com
SIC: 2035 2099 Dressings, salad: raw and
cooked (except dry mixes); Salads, fresh or
refrigerated

(G-4178)
KIDS DISCOVER LLC
606 Post Rd E Ste 3 (06880-4540)
PHONE..............................212 677-4457
Theodore Levine, *Managing Member*
EMP: 11 EST: 2014
SALES (est): 285.54K **Privately Held**
Web: www.kidsdiscover.com
SIC: 2721 Magazines: publishing only, not
printed on site

(G-4179)
KTCR HOLDING
4 Pheasant Ln (06880-1709)
PHONE..............................203 227-4115
Joshua Rizack, *Owner*
EMP: 8 EST: 2009
SALES (est): 327.19K **Privately Held**
SIC: 3621 Motors and generators

(G-4180)
**LH GAULT & SON
INCORPORATED**
Also Called: Gault
11 Ferry Ln W (06880-5808)
P.O. Box 2030 (06880-0030)
PHONE..............................203 227-5181
William L Gault, *Ch*
Samuel M Gault, *
▲ EMP: 65 EST: 1932
SQ FT: 40,000
SALES (est): 37.63MM **Privately Held**
Web: www.gaultenergy.com
SIC: 1411 5032 3441 5211 Granite
dimension stone; Building stone; Fabricated
structural metal; Sand and gravel

(G-4181)
LUMENDI LLC
253 Post Rd W (06880-4737)
PHONE..............................203 528-0316
Michael Parrilla, *COO*
EMP: 7 EST: 2015
SQ FT: 4,000
SALES (est): 1.33MM **Privately Held**
Web: www.lumendi.com
SIC: 3841 Surgical and medical instruments

(G-4182)
**MANTROSE-HAEUSER CO INC
(HQ)**
100 Nyala Farms Rd (06880-6266)
PHONE..............................203 454-1800
Michael Matthews, *Pr*
Stephen A Santos, *
Sue C O'rourke, *Treas*
Ron Rice, *
▲ EMP: 29 EST: 1992
SALES (est): 62.03MM
SALES (corp-wide): 7.26B **Publicly Held**
Web: www.mantrose.com
SIC: 2064 2066 2851 0723 Candy and other
confectionery products; Chocolate and
cocoa products; Paints and allied products;
Crop preparation services for market
PA: Rpm International Inc.
2628 Pearl Rd
Medina OH 44256
330 273-5090

▲ = Import ▼ = Export
◆ = Import/Export

(G-4183)
MATTHEW PORIO
367 Main St (06880-2417)
PHONE.....................203 227-3695
Matthew Porio, *Prin*
EMP: 10 **EST:** 2005
SALES (est): 391.43K **Privately Held**
SIC: 3544 Special dies, tools, jigs, and fixtures

(G-4184)
MD SOLARSCIENCES CORPORATION
88 Post Rd W Ste 3 (06880-4238)
PHONE.....................203 857-0095
Renee Plato, *CEO*
Scott Friedman, *VP*
Paul Ainsworth, *Pr*
▲ **EMP:** 12 **EST:** 2007
SQ FT: 2,500
SALES (est): 3.01MM **Privately Held**
Web: www.mdsolarsciences.com
SIC: 2834 Pharmaceutical preparations

(G-4185)
MINUTEMAN NEWSPAPER (PA)
1175 Post Rd E Ste 3e (06880-5400)
PHONE.....................203 226-8877
Paula Walsh, *Mgr*
EMP: 24 **EST:** 1993
SALES (est): 1.16MM **Privately Held**
SIC: 2711 Newspapers, publishing and printing

(G-4186)
MOBILE GLOBAL ESPORTS INC
500 Post Rd E Fl 2 (06880-4431)
PHONE.....................475 666-8401
Sunny Bhandarkar, *CEO*
Marco Welch, *Ch Bd*
Kiki Benson, *CFO*
EMP: 12 **EST:** 2021
SIC: 7372 Home entertainment computer software

(G-4187)
MOFFLY PUBLICATIONS INC
Also Called: Greenwich Magazine
205 Main St Ste 1 (06880-3206)
PHONE.....................203 222-0600
Jonathan Moffly, *CEO*
John W Moffly Iv, *Ch*
Donna C Moffly, *
Elena Moffly, *
EMP: 47 **EST:** 1947
SQ FT: 4,500
SALES (est): 4.69MM **Privately Held**
Web: www.mofflylifestylemedia.com
SIC: 2721 Magazines: publishing only, not printed on site

(G-4188)
NATIONAL PUBLISHING CO INC
Also Called: Npc Inserts
64 Post Rd W (06880-4208)
P.O. Box 5186 (06881-5186)
PHONE.....................203 221-2300
Paul Cohen, *Pr*
EMP: 30 **EST:** 1979
SQ FT: 5,000
SALES (est): 2.39MM **Privately Held**
SIC: 2741 7319 Miscellaneous publishing; Media buying service

(G-4189)
NATURESEAL INC
1175 Post Rd E Ste 3b (06880-5424)
PHONE.....................203 454-1800
William J Barrie, *Pr*

Sue O'rourke, *VP*
Edward W'Moore, *
EMP: 12 **EST:** 2008
SALES (est): 2.3MM
SALES (corp-wide): 7.26B **Publicly Held**
Web: www.natureseal.com
SIC: 0723 2037 Crop preparation services for market; Frozen fruits and vegetables
HQ: Mantrose-Haeuser Co., Inc.
100 Nyala Farms Rd
Westport CT 06880

(G-4190)
NEWMANS OWN INC (PA)
Also Called: Newman's Own Organics
1 Morningside Dr N Ste 1 (06880-3847)
PHONE.....................203 222-0136
David Best, *CEO*
William Lee, *
Joan Williams, *
Michael Havard, *Acting Vice President*
Jamie Gerard, *
▼ **EMP:** 16 **EST:** 1982
SQ FT: 4,200
SALES (est): 23.46MM
SALES (corp-wide): 23.46MM **Privately Held**
Web: www.newmansown.com
SIC: 2035 2086 Dressings, salad: raw and cooked (except dry mixes); Lemonade: packaged in cans, bottles, etc.

(G-4191)
ONLINE RIVER LLC
606 Post Rd E Ste 723 (06880-4540)
PHONE.....................203 801-5900
EMP: 12 **EST:** 2003
SALES (est): 874.73K **Privately Held**
Web: www.onlineriver.com
SIC: 5099 3829 5045 3577 Novelties, durable; Turnstiles, equipped with counting mechanisms; Computer software; Computer peripheral equipment, nec

(G-4192)
PACKEDGE INC ✪
54 Maple Ave S (06880-5629)
PHONE.....................203 288-0200
Adam Aron, *Pr*
EMP: 13 **EST:** 2022
SALES (est): 857.04K **Privately Held**
SIC: 2671 Paper, coated or laminated for packaging

(G-4193)
PROVISIONAIRE & CO LLC
Also Called: Field Trip
151 Post Rd E (06880-3410)
P.O. Box 710 (06881-0710)
PHONE.....................646 681-8600
Thomas Donigan, *Managing Member*
EMP: 20 **EST:** 2010
SALES (est): 969.65K **Privately Held**
Web: www.fieldtripsnacks.com
SIC: 5812 2013 Snack bar; Snack sticks, including jerky: from purchased meat

(G-4194)
RECYCLE 4 VETS LLC
Also Called: R4v
518 Riverside Ave Ste 1 (06880-5741)
PHONE.....................203 222-7300
EMP: 7 **EST:** 2012
SALES (est): 485.01K **Privately Held**
Web: www.recycle4vets.com
SIC: 5112 3861 3577 Stationery and office supplies; Photographic processing chemicals; Readers, sorters, or inscribers, magnetic ink

(G-4195)
ROBERT WARREN LLC (PA)
Also Called: Lance International
1 Sprucewood Ln (06880-4022)
PHONE.....................203 247-3347
EMP: 50 **EST:** 1974
SQ FT: 18,000
SALES (est): 9.8MM
SALES (corp-wide): 9.8MM **Privately Held**
Web: www.lanceintl.com
SIC: 3679 Harness assemblies, for electronic use: wire or cable

(G-4196)
SIGMAVOIP LLC
980 Post Rd E (06880-5300)
P.O. Box 309 (06455-0309)
PHONE.....................203 541-5450
Charles Ambrosecchia, *Pt*
EMP: 7 **EST:** 2012
SALES (est): 493.7K **Privately Held**
Web: www.sigmavoip.com
SIC: 4813 3661 Voice telephone communications; Telephones and telephone apparatus

(G-4197)
STOWED LLC (PA)
Also Called: Stowed Home
12 Elm St (06880-3305)
PHONE.....................203 346-5687
Elissia Sigalow, *Managing Member*
EMP: 7 **EST:** 2019
SALES (est): 78.03K
SALES (corp-wide): 78.03K **Privately Held**
SIC: 2511 Bed frames, except water bed frames: wood

(G-4198)
TEREX ADVANCE MIXER INC
500 Post Rd E (06880-4431)
PHONE.....................203 222-7170
EMP: 48 **EST:** 1995
SALES (est): 3.81MM
SALES (corp-wide): 5.15B **Publicly Held**
SIC: 3531 Construction machinery
PA: Terex Corporation
45 Glover Ave Ste 2
Norwalk CT 06850
203 222-7170

(G-4199)
TEXTSPEAK CORPORATION
Also Called: Textspeak Design
55 Post Rd W Fl 2 (06880-4235)
PHONE.....................203 803-1069
Nancy Stogel, *Pr*
Scott Stogel, *VP*
EMP: 11 **EST:** 2000
SALES (est): 2.06MM **Privately Held**
Web: www.textspeak.com
SIC: 4899 3845 Communication signal enhancement network services; Audiological equipment, electromedical

(G-4200)
WASHINGTON TEREX INC
200 Nyala Farms Rd Ste 2 (06880-6261)
PHONE.....................203 222-7170
John Garrison, *CEO*
EMP: 14 **EST:** 2019
SALES (est): 4.73MM
SALES (corp-wide): 5.15B **Publicly Held**
SIC: 3531 Construction machinery
PA: Terex Corporation
45 Glover Ave Ste 2
Norwalk CT 06850
203 222-7170

(G-4201)
WESTPORT SUMMIT 7 LLC
1365 Post Rd E (06880-5506)
PHONE.....................917 370-2244
Camilla Gazal, *CEO*
EMP: 7 **EST:** 2015
SALES (est): 342.72K **Privately Held**
SIC: 2711 Newspapers, publishing and printing

Wethersfield
Hartford County

(G-4202)
ARROW WIN SHADE MFG OF MRDEN I
47 Oxford St (06109-1724)
PHONE.....................860 563-4035
Oscar Laraia, *Pr*
EMP: 9 **EST:** 1961
SALES (est): 143.75K **Privately Held**
SIC: 2591 5719 Venetian blinds; Venetian blinds

(G-4203)
CKH INDUSTRIES INC
365 Silas Deane Hwy Ste 1 (06109-2121)
PHONE.....................860 563-2999
Kenneth Cline, *Brnch Mgr*
EMP: 51
SALES (corp-wide): 4.31MM **Privately Held**
Web: www.ckhindustries.com
SIC: 3442 Window and door frames
PA: Ckh Industries Inc
520 Temple Hill Rd
New Windsor NY 12553
845 561-9000

(G-4204)
EASTWOOD PRINTING INC
501 Middletown Ave (06109-3809)
P.O. Box 290271 (06129-0271)
PHONE.....................860 529-6673
Lewis Eastwood, *Pr*
Ellen Eastwood, *Sec*
EMP: 10 **EST:** 1986
SQ FT: 2,500
SALES (est): 983.01K **Privately Held**
Web: www.ewoodoutput.com
SIC: 2759 Commercial printing, nec

(G-4205)
HEDGES & HEDGES LTD
Also Called: Copies Now
1155 Silas Deane Hwy Ste 4 (06109-4331)
PHONE.....................860 257-3170
Robert Hedges, *Pr*
EMP: 8 **EST:** 1988
SQ FT: 1,800
SALES (est): 541.73K **Privately Held**
Web: www.hedgesandhedgesltd.com
SIC: 7334 2791 Photocopying and duplicating services; Typesetting

(G-4206)
J & T PRINTING LLC
81 Wolcott Hill Rd (06109-1268)
PHONE.....................860 529-4628
Jeffrey W Foley, *Prin*
EMP: 11 **EST:** 2015
SALES (est): 518.62K **Privately Held**
SIC: 2752 Commercial printing, lithographic

(G-4207)
JOHN OLDHAM STUDIOS INC
888 Wells Rd (06109-2417)
PHONE.....................860 529-3331

G
E
O
G
R
A
P
H
I
C

John W Oldham Junior, *Pr*
Patrica Oldham, *
Mark Oldham, *
▲ **EMP: 24 EST:** 1931
SQ FT: 86,000
SALES (est): 2.66MM **Privately Held**
Web: www.oldhamstudios.com
SIC: 3993 7389 Displays and cutouts, window and lobby; Design services

(G-4208)
KAHN INSTRUMENTS INCORPORATED
885 Wells Rd (06109-2416)
P.O. Box 336 (06456-0336)
PHONE...............................860 529-8643
Jeffrey Kahn, *Pr*
EMP: 7 EST: 1982
SQ FT: 50,000
SALES (est): 1.81MM **Privately Held**
SIC: 5084 3823 Instruments and control equipment; Moisture meters, industrial process type

(G-4209)
KELL-STROM TOOL CO INC (PA)
214 Church St (06109-2397)
PHONE...............................860 529-6851
Francis P Kelly, *Pr*
Robert Kelly, *
Peter J Kelly, *
Thomas J Kelly, *
EMP: 16 EST: 1942
SALES (est): 8.43MM **Privately Held**
Web: www.kell-strom.com
SIC: 3429 3599 3423 Aircraft hardware; Machine shop, jobbing and repair; Hand and edge tools, nec

(G-4210)
KELL-STROM TOOL INTL INC
214 Church St (06109-2316)
PHONE...............................860 529-6851
Francis P Kelly, *Pr*
Thomas J Kelly, *Treas*
Robert M Kelly, *VP*
Peter J Kelly, *Sec*
EMP: 16 EST: 1942
SQ FT: 30,000
SALES (est): 2.4MM **Privately Held**
Web: www.kell-strom.com
SIC: 3429 3599 5072 5085 Aircraft hardware; Machine shop, jobbing and repair; Hand tools; Industrial supplies
PA: The Kell-Strom Tool Co Incorporated
    214 Church St
    Wethersfield CT 06109

(G-4211)
MINUTEMAN PRESS
Also Called: Minuteman Press
81 Wolcott Hill Rd (06109-1268)
PHONE...............................860 529-4628
Taunya Foley, *Owner*
Taunya Foley, *Prin*
EMP: 16 EST: 2008
SALES (est): 429.83K **Privately Held**
Web: www.minutemanpress.com
SIC: 2752 Commercial printing, lithographic

(G-4212)
MOZZICATO FMLY INVESTMENTS LLC
Also Called: Sam Maulucci & Sons
631 Ridge Rd (06109-2617)
PHONE...............................860 296-0426
Rino Mozzicato, *Managing Member*
EMP: 10 EST: 2000
SQ FT: 1,200
SALES (est): 856.06K **Privately Held**

SIC: 2022 5143 Cheese; natural and processed; Cheese

(G-4213)
REAC READY LLC
51 Clovercrest Rd (06109-3519)
PHONE...............................860 550-5049
Eddie Brady White, *Managing Member*
EMP: 7 EST: 2009
SALES (est): 1.85MM **Privately Held**
Web: www.reacreadyllc.com
SIC: 1389 8742 Construction, repair, and dismantling services; Training and development consultant

(G-4214)
REFLEX LTG GROUP OF CT LLC
1290 Silas Deane Hwy Ste 1a (06109-4337)
PHONE...............................860 666-1548
EMP: 9 EST: 2010
SALES (est): 203.87K **Privately Held**
Web: www.reflexlighting.com
SIC: 3648 Lighting equipment, nec

(G-4215)
WINGSITE DISPLAYS INC
1060 Silas Deane Hwy (06109-4231)
PHONE...............................860 257-3300
▲ **EMP: 20 EST:** 1992
SALES (est): 2.31MM **Privately Held**
Web: www.wingsitedisplays.com
SIC: 3993 7389 Signs and advertising specialties; Advertising, promotional, and trade show services

Willimantic
Windham County

(G-4216)
ARCH PARENT INC
82 Storrs Rd (06226-4001)
PHONE...............................860 336-4856
EMP: 12898
SALES (corp-wide): 116.71MM **Privately Held**
SIC: 2752 Commercial printing, lithographic
PA: Arch Parent Inc.
    9 W 57th St Fl 31
    New York NY 10019
    212 796-8500

(G-4217)
CHRONICLE PRINTING COMPANY
Also Called: Chronicle, The
1 Chronicle Rd (06226-1932)
P.O. Box 229 (06226-0229)
PHONE...............................860 423-8466
Lucy B Crosbie, *Pr*
EMP: 22 EST: 1877
SQ FT: 22,000
SALES (est): 841.89K **Privately Held**
Web: www.thechronicle.com
SIC: 2711 Commercial printing and newspaper publishing combined

(G-4218)
GULEMO INC
Also Called: Willimatic Instant Print
2 Birch St (06226-2103)
P.O. Box 467 (06226-0467)
PHONE...............................860 456-1151
Gunnel Stenberg, *Pr*
Lena Fontaine, *Sec*
EMP: 8 EST: 1994
SALES (est): 849.88K **Privately Held**
Web: www.gulemo.com

SIC: 2752 Offset printing

(G-4219)
HORIZONS UNLIMITED INC
Also Called: Quality Sign Crafters
90 S Park St Ste 1 (06226-3336)
P.O. Box 35 (06226-0035)
PHONE...............................860 423-1931
Richard Napolitano, *Pr*
Lisa Napolitano, *Sec*
EMP: 12 EST: 1995
SQ FT: 15,000
SALES (est): 983.75K **Privately Held**
SIC: 3993 Signs and advertising specialties

(G-4220)
PRYSMIAN CBLES SYSTEMS USA LLC
Also Called: Willimantic, CT Plant
1600 Main St (06226-1128)
PHONE...............................860 456-8000
Jim Barney, *Pr*
EMP: 148
Web: na.prysmian.com
SIC: 3496 3357 Miscellaneous fabricated wire products; Communication wire
HQ: Prysmian Cables And Systems Usa, Llc
    4 Tesseneer Dr
    Highland Heights KY 41076
    859 572-8000

(G-4221)
WILLIMANTIC WASTE PAPER CO INC (HQ)
121 Chronicle Rd (06226)
P.O. Box 239 (06226-0239)
PHONE...............................860 423-4527
Thomas E Devivo, *Pr*
▲ **EMP: 110 EST:** 1946
SQ FT: 70,000
SALES (est): 97.91MM **Publicly Held**
Web: www.williwaste.com
SIC: 5093 3341 2611 Waste paper; Secondary nonferrous metals; Pulp mills
PA: Casella Waste Systems, Inc.
    25 Greens Hill Ln
    Rutland VT 05701

(G-4222)
WINDHAM MATERIALS LLC (PA)
79 Boston Post Rd (06226-1808)
P.O. Box 346 (06226-0346)
PHONE...............................860 456-4111
Steve Aiudi, *Pr*
Dave Doremus, *Asst VP*
EMP: 20 EST: 1956
SQ FT: 12,000
SALES (est): 12.06MM
SALES (corp-wide): 12.06MM **Privately Held**
Web: www.windhammaterials.com
SIC: 5032 5211 1542 3273 Sand, construction; Sand and gravel; Institutional building construction; Ready-mixed concrete

(G-4223)
WINDHAM MATERIALS LLC
360 Plains Rd (06226-3722)
PHONE...............................860 456-3277
Steve Aiudi, *Brnch Mgr*
EMP: 80
SALES (corp-wide): 12.06MM **Privately Held**
Web: www.windhammaterials.com
SIC: 3273 Ready-mixed concrete
PA: Windham Materials, Llc
    79 Boston Post Rd
    Willimantic CT 06226
    860 456-4111

Willington
Tolland County

(G-4224)
CABLE TECHNOLOGY INC
73 River Rd (06279-1830)
PHONE...............................860 429-7889
Michael Cariglia, *Pr*
Carl Beyor, *
EMP: 25 EST: 1982
SQ FT: 35,000
SALES (est): 4.99MM **Privately Held**
Web: www.cabletechnologyinc.com
SIC: 3677 3357 Electronic coils and transformers; Nonferrous wiredrawing and insulating

(G-4225)
INNOVATIV HOISTING LLC
16 Tolland Tpke (06279-1313)
PHONE...............................860 969-4477
EMP: 12 EST: 2018
SALES (est): 1.48MM **Privately Held**
Web: www.innovativ-hoisting.com
SIC: 3537 Industrial trucks and tractors

(G-4226)
PJ SPECIALTIES
7 Luchon Rd (06279-1616)
P.O. Box 41 (06279-0041)
PHONE...............................860 429-7626
William Hodge, *Owner*
EMP: 10 EST: 1997
SALES (est): 423.61K **Privately Held**
Web: pjprinting.espwebsite.com
SIC: 7336 2395 Silk screen design; Embroidery and art needlework

(G-4227)
WHITNEY PRATT
64 Cemetery Rd (06279-2300)
PHONE...............................860 565-6431
Peter Kelly, *Prin*
EMP: 7 EST: 2018
SALES (est): 193.41K **Privately Held**
SIC: 3724 Aircraft engines and engine parts

Wilton
Fairfield County

(G-4228)
21ST CENTURY FOX AMERICA INC
Also Called: News America
20 Westport Rd (06897-4549)
PHONE...............................203 563-6600
Carey Chase, *Ch*
EMP: 8
SALES (corp-wide): 88.9B **Publicly Held**
Web: www.foxnews.com
SIC: 2711 Newspapers: publishing only, not printed on site
HQ: News America Incorporated
    1211 Ave Of The Americas
    New York NY 10036
    212 852-7000

(G-4229)
AIR AGE INC
88 Danbury Rd Ste 2b (06897-4423)
PHONE...............................203 431-9000
Louis Defrancesco Junior, *Pr*
Louis De Francesco Junior, *Pr*
Yvonne De Francesco, *
Carol Shepherd, *
EMP: 27 EST: 1929

SQ FT: 9,675
SALES (est): 3.93MM Privately Held
Web: www.airage.com
SIC: 2721 2731 Magazines: publishing only, not printed on site; Books, publishing and printing

(G-4230)
ARISTA INDUSTRIES INC (PA)
187 Danbury Rd Ste 3a (06897-4079)
PHONE..............................203 761-1009
Alan Weitzer, *Pr*
Charles Hillyer, *
◆ EMP: 25 EST: 1930
SQ FT: 4,500
SALES (est): 9.62MM
SALES (corp-wide): 9.62MM Privately Held
Web: www.aristaindustries.com
SIC: 2021 2079 Butter oil; Vegetable refined oils (except corn oil)

(G-4231)
ASML US LLC
Asml
77 Danbury Rd (06897-4407)
PHONE..............................203 761-4000
Noreen Harned, *VP*
EMP: 800
SALES (corp-wide): 21.99B Privately Held
Web: www.asml.com
SIC: 3559 Semiconductor manufacturing machinery
HQ: Asml Us, Llc
2625 W Geronimo Pl
Chandler AZ 85224
480 696-2888

(G-4232)
BIOWAVE INNOVATIONS LLC
274 Ridgefield Rd (06897-2335)
PHONE..............................203 982-8157
EMP: 191 EST: 2010
SALES (est): 8.09MM Privately Held
SIC: 3844 X-ray apparatus and tubes

(G-4233)
BLUE BUFFALO COMPANY LTD (DH)
11 River Rd Ste 200 (06897-6011)
PHONE..............................203 762-9751
Bill Bishop, *Ch*
Kurt Schmidt, *
Jennifer Stites, *
Mike Nathenson, *
EMP: 98 EST: 2003
SALES (est): 481.75MM
SALES (corp-wide): 20.09B Publicly Held
Web: www.bluebuffalo.com
SIC: 2047 5149 Dog and cat food; Pet foods
HQ: Blue Buffalo Pet Products, Inc.
11 River Rd Ste 103
Wilton CT 06897
203 762-9751

(G-4234)
BLUE BUFFALO PET PRODUCTS INC (HQ)
11 River Rd Ste 103 (06897-6011)
P.O. Box 770 (06897-0770)
PHONE..............................203 762-9751
William Bishop Junior, *Pr*
Mike Nathenson, *Treas*
Larry Miller, *Sec*
EMP: 39 EST: 2002
SQ FT: 41,000
SALES (est): 1B
SALES (corp-wide): 20.09B Publicly Held
Web: www.bluebuffalo.com

(G-4235)
CAPITOL ELECTRONICS INC
18 Keelers Ridge Rd (06897-1607)
PHONE..............................203 744-3300
Richard Warren, *Pr*
EMP: 10 EST: 1997
SALES (est): 1MM Privately Held
Web: www.capitolelectronics.com
SIC: 3613 Switchgear and switchgear accessories, nec

(G-4236)
CHILDRENS HEALTH MARKET INC
27 Cannon Rd Ste 1b (06897-2627)
P.O. Box 7294 (06897-7294)
PHONE..............................203 762-2938
Nancy M Grace, *Pr*
James C Grace, *Sec*
Timothy C Grace, *Prin*
EMP: 7 EST: 1987
SQ FT: 1,400
SALES (est): 910.26K Privately Held
Web: www.thegreatbodyshop.net
SIC: 2741 8748 Miscellaneous publishing; Business consulting, nec

(G-4237)
CORTINA LEARNING INTL INC (PA)
Also Called: Cortina Famous Schools
33 Catalpa Rd (06897-2002)
PHONE..............................800 245-2145
Robert E Livesey, *Pr*
Magdalen B Livesey, *Sec*
Robert Ellis, *VP*
EMP: 12 EST: 1882
SALES (est): 2.35MM
SALES (corp-wide): 2.35MM Privately Held
Web: www.cortinalearning.com
SIC: 2731 8249 Books, publishing only; Correspondence school

(G-4238)
CYCLING SPORTS GROUP INC (HQ)
Also Called: Cannondale Sports Group
1 Cannondale Way (06897-4319)
PHONE..............................203 845-8300
Peter Woods, *Pr*
Sean Jacobs, *CFO*
Nico Zimmerman, *Sec*
◆ EMP: 70 EST: 2003
SQ FT: 32,500
SALES (est): 134.08MM
SALES (corp-wide): 419.36K Privately Held
Web: privacy.ponbike.com
SIC: 3751 2329 Bicycles and related parts; Men's and boys' sportswear and athletic clothing
PA: Pon Holdings
10 Greenbrier Pl
Regina SK S4S 7
306 586-6738

(G-4239)
FEDERICI BRANDS LLC (PA)
195 Danbury Rd 3rd Fl (06897-4075)
PHONE..............................203 762-7667
James Federici, *Prin*

SIC: 2048 Canned pet food (except dog and cat)
PA: General Mills, Inc.
1 General Mills Blvd
Minneapolis MN 55426
763 764-7600

▲ EMP: 12 EST: 2009
SALES (est): 22.89MM
SALES (corp-wide): 22.89MM Privately Held
Web: www.federicibrands.com
SIC: 3273 Ready-mixed concrete

(G-4240)
GRACENOTE MEDIA SERVICES LLC
40 Danbury Rd (06897-4441)
PHONE..............................518 223-1993
Karthik Rao, *Pr*
Amilcar Perez, *CFO*
Kay Johansson, *COO*
EMP: 18 EST: 1933
SALES (est): 1.3MM Privately Held
SIC: 2721 Periodicals

(G-4241)
L & L CAPITAL PARTNERS LLC
57 Danbury Rd Ste 3 (06897-4439)
PHONE..............................203 834-6222
Bulkeley Griswold, *Pt*
EMP: 17 EST: 1984
SQ FT: 2,500
SALES (est): 2.28MM Privately Held
Web: www.llcapitalpartners.com
SIC: 6726 2511 Investment offices, nec; Wood household furniture

(G-4242)
LOUIS DREYFUS HOLDG CO US LLC (HQ)
40 Danbury Rd (06897-4441)
PHONE..............................203 761-2000
Carol Aronoff, *
◆ EMP: 350 EST: 1976
SQ FT: 70,000
SALES (est): 161.08MM
SALES (corp-wide): 2.24MM Privately Held
SIC: 6221 5153 6512 6531 Commodity traders, contracts; Grains; Commercial and industrial building operation; Real estate managers
PA: Impala Sas
4 Rue Euler
Paris 75008
145623786

(G-4243)
LTI PORTFOLIO MANAGEMENT CORP
221 Danbury Rd (06897-4090)
PHONE..............................203 563-1100
EMP: 17 EST: 1988
SALES (est): 3.34MM
SALES (corp-wide): 6.27MM Privately Held
SIC: 3577 Computer peripheral equipment, nec
PA: Leasing Technologies International, Inc.
24 Danbury Rd Ste 7
Wilton CT 06897
203 563-1100

(G-4244)
OLIN CORPORATION
Also Called: Olin Chlor Alkali Products
88 Danbury Rd Ste 1a (06897-4423)
PHONE..............................203 750-3100
Joseph D Rupp, *CEO*
EMP: 25 EST: 2008
SALES (est): 10.89MM Privately Held
Web: www.olin.com
SIC: 2869 Industrial organic chemicals, nec

(G-4245)
RAVAGO AMERICAS LLC
Muehlstein
10 Westport Rd (06897-4543)
PHONE..............................203 855-6000
EMP: 100
Web: www.amcopolymers.com
SIC: 2821 Plastics materials and resins
HQ: Ravago Americas Llc
1900 Smmit Twr Blvd Ste 9
Orlando FL 32810
407 773-7777

(G-4246)
RC INDUSTRIES INC
4 Erdmann Ln (06897-4611)
PHONE..............................203 423-9419
Randy Pape, *Prin*
EMP: 11 EST: 2010
SALES (est): 50K Privately Held
SIC: 3999 Manufacturing industries, nec

(G-4247)
SHILLER AND COMPANY INC
Also Called: Shillermath
258 Thunder Lake Rd (06897-1339)
PHONE..............................203 210-5208
Larry Shiller, *Pr*
EMP: 15 EST: 2007
SALES (est): 405.63K Privately Held
SIC: 2741 Miscellaneous publishing

(G-4248)
STARTECH ENVIRONMENTAL CORP (PA)
88 Danbury Rd Ste 2b (06897-4423)
PHONE..............................203 762-2499
Joseph F Longo, *Ch Bd*
Peter J Scanlon, *VP*
EMP: 16 EST: 1991
SQ FT: 5,612
SALES (est): 2.33MM Privately Held
SIC: 3559 Recycling machinery

Windsor
Hartford County

(G-4249)
A&S INNERSPRINGS USA LLC
4 Market Cir (06095-1422)
PHONE..............................860 298-0401
Deborah Covey, *Managing Member*
EMP: 13 EST: 2016
SALES (est): 4.28MM
SALES (corp-wide): 229.54MM Privately Held
Web: www.asinnersprings.com
SIC: 2515 Mattresses and bedsprings
PA: Agro Holding Gmbh
Senfdamm 21
Bad Essen NI 49152
547294200

(G-4250)
AAR GOVERNMENT SERVICES INC
Also Called: AAR Defense Systems Logistics
754 Rainbow Rd Ste C (06095-1004)
PHONE..............................860 298-0144
Cheryl Keith, *Brnch Mgr*
EMP: 10
SALES (corp-wide): 1.99B Publicly Held
Web: www.aarcorp.com
SIC: 3728 Aircraft parts and equipment, nec
HQ: Aar Government Services, Inc.
1100 N Wood Dale Rd
Wood Dale IL 60191
630 227-2000

(G-4251)
ABB INC
Also Called: Corporate
5 Waterside Xing Ste 204a (06095-1594)
PHONE...................................860 285-0183
Steve Alger, *Brnch Mgr*
EMP: 112
Web: new.abb.com
SIC: 3612 Transformers, except electric
HQ: Abb Inc.
   305 Gregson Dr
   Cary NC 27511

(G-4252)
ACCU-TIME SYSTEMS INC (DH)
Also Called: A T S
20 International Dr (06095-1044)
PHONE...................................860 870-5000
James Mchale, *CEO*
David Hopkins, *
Thomas Benton, *
Lawrence Feuer, *
Lisa Gladysz, *
▲ **EMP:** 36 **EST:** 1991
SALES (est): 18.8MM **Privately Held**
Web: www.accu-time.com
SIC: 3579 3873 Time clocks and time
   recording devices; Watches, clocks,
   watchcases, and parts
HQ: Amano Usa Holdings, Inc.
   29j Commerce Way
   Totowa NJ 07512

(G-4253)
ACCUTRON INC (PA)
149 Addison Rd (06095-2102)
PHONE...................................860 683-8300
Vijay R Faldu, *Pr*
Bharat R Faldu, *
Bhagwati R Faldu, *
Kamlesh R Faldu, *
▼ **EMP:** 95 **EST:** 1989
SQ FT: 55,000
SALES (est): 31.96MM **Privately Held**
Web: www.accutroninc.com
SIC: 3672 3613 3441 Printed circuit boards;
   Control panels, electric; Fabricated
   structural metal

(G-4254)
**ACUTEK ADHESIVE
SPECIALTIES**
Also Called: Acutek
111 Great Pond Dr (06095-1527)
PHONE...................................310 419-0190
Jerry Muchin, *Pr*
Karen Kline, *
EMP: 16 **EST:** 1967
SALES (est): 458.97K **Privately Held**
SIC: 3069 Medical sundries, rubber

(G-4255)
AERO GEAR INCORPORATED
1050 Day Hill Rd (06095-4728)
PHONE...................................860 688-0888
Douglas B Rose, *Pr*
Craig W Scott, *
◆ **EMP:** 140 **EST:** 1981
SQ FT: 78,000
SALES (est): 31.4MM **Privately Held**
Web: www.aerogear.com
SIC: 3728 Gears, aircraft power
   transmission

(G-4256)
AKO INC
Also Called: Torque Specialties
50 Baker Hollow Rd (06095-2133)
P.O. Box 1283 (06083-1283)
PHONE...................................860 298-9765

Rachel Leclerc, *Pr*
Sylvia Leclerc, *Sec*
James Wininger, *Dir Opers*
EMP: 20 **EST:** 1923
SQ FT: 17,800
SALES (est): 4.29MM **Privately Held**
Web: www.akotorque.com
SIC: 3829 8734 Measuring and controlling
   devices, nec; Product testing laboratories

(G-4257)
ALSTOM POWER CO
175 Addison Rd (06095-2178)
PHONE...................................860 688-1911
EMP: 24 **EST:** 2015
SALES (est): 2.02MM
SALES (corp-wide): 76.56B **Publicly Held**
SIC: 3569 8711 Liquid automation
   machinery and equipment; Professional
   engineer
PA: General Electric Company
   1 Financial Ctr Ste 3700
   Boston MA 02111
   617 443-3000

(G-4258)
ALTIUM PACKAGING
ALTIUM PACKAGING
4 Market Cir (06095-1422)
PHONE...................................860 683-8560
Roy Provost, *Mgr*
EMP: 18
SALES (corp-wide): 15.9B **Publicly Held**
Web: www.altiumpkg.com
SIC: 3089 3085 Blow molded finished
   plastics products, nec; Plastics bottles
HQ: Altium Packaging Llc
   2500 Windy Ridge Pkwy Se # 1400
   Atlanta GA 30339
   678 742-4600

(G-4259)
ALVEST (USA) INC (DH)
812 Bloomfield Ave (06095-2340)
PHONE...................................860 602-3400
Mark Garlasco, *CEO*
EMP: 26 **EST:** 1991
SALES (est): 279.12MM
SALES (corp-wide): 675.45K **Privately
Held**
SIC: 3585 3535 Air conditioning equipment,
   complete; Unit handling conveying systems
HQ: Lbo France Gestion
   148 Rue De L Universite
   Paris 75007

(G-4260)
APCOMPOWER INC (PA)
200 Great Pond Dr (06095-4806)
P.O. Box 500 (06095-0711)
PHONE...................................860 688-1911
Eric A Heruser, *Pr*
Jeff Skipton, *
Thomas Kehoe, *
James M Carroll, *
Theordore P Sharp, *
EMP: 47 **EST:** 1990
SQ FT: 58,000
SALES (est): 24.02MM **Privately Held**
Web: www.apcompower.com
SIC: 8711 3443 1629 Engineering services;
   Fabricated plate work (boiler shop); Power
   plant construction

(G-4261)
**APPLIED RUBBER & PLASTICS
INC**
100 Skitchewaug St (06095-4605)
PHONE...................................860 987-9018
Brendan Ward Farrell, *Pr*

Patricia C Farrell, *Sec*
▲ **EMP:** 15 **EST:** 1988
SQ FT: 20,000
SALES (est): 4.32MM **Privately Held**
Web: www.appliedrubber.com
SIC: 3061 5085 Mechanical rubber goods;
   Rubber goods, mechanical

(G-4262)
BARNES GROUP INC
Also Called: Barnes Aerospace
169 Kennedy Rd (06095-2043)
PHONE...................................860 298-7740
EMP: 1434
SQ FT: 160,000
SALES (corp-wide): 1.26B **Publicly Held**
Web: www.onebarnes.com
SIC: 3728 Aircraft parts and equipment, nec
PA: Barnes Group Inc.
   123 Main St
   Bristol CT 06010
   860 583-7070

(G-4263)
C & C LOGGING
416 Pigeon Hill Rd (06095-2157)
PHONE...................................860 683-0071
Grace Cranouski, *Prin*
EMP: 9 **EST:** 2001
SALES (est): 858.42K **Privately Held**
SIC: 2411 Logging camps and contractors

(G-4264)
CARBIDE SOLUTIONS LLC
800 Marshall Phelps Rd (06095-2143)
PHONE...................................860 515-8665
Alan M Stanek, *Prin*
EMP: 8 **EST:** 2015
SALES (est): 931.91K **Privately Held**
SIC: 2819 Carbides

(G-4265)
CERTUSS AMERICA LP
800 Marshall Phelps Rd (06095-2143)
PHONE...................................440 454-6172
Shawn Hartigan, *Mgr*
EMP: 7 **EST:** 2014
SALES (est): 210.4K **Privately Held**
Web: www.certuss-america.com
SIC: 3443 Boiler and boiler shop work

(G-4266)
**CHROMALLOY COMPONENT
SVCS INC**
Chromalloy Connecticuit
601 Marshall Phelps Rd (06095-5716)
PHONE...................................860 688-7798
Robert Jones, *Mgr*
EMP: 34
SQ FT: 50,000
SALES (corp-wide): 1.2B **Privately Held**
Web: www.chromalloy.com
SIC: 3724 3812 2851 Aircraft engines and
   engine parts; Search and navigation
   equipment; Paints and allied products
HQ: Chromalloy Component Services, Inc.
   303 Industrial Park Rd
   San Antonio TX 78226
   210 331-2300

(G-4267)
**CHROMALLOY GAS TURBINE
LLC**
Also Called: Chromalloy Connecticut
601 Marshall Phelps Rd (06095-5716)
P.O. Box 748 (06492-0748)
PHONE...................................860 688-7798
Clive Bailey, *Prin*
EMP: 77

SALES (corp-wide): 1.2B **Privately Held**
Web: www.chromalloy.com
SIC: 3724 Aircraft engines and engine parts
HQ: Chromalloy Gas Turbine Llc
   4100 Rca Blvd
   Palm Beach Gardens FL 33410
   561 935-3571

(G-4268)
COOPER CROUSE-HINDS LLC
Airport Lighting Division
1200 Kennedy Rd (06095-1384)
PHONE...................................860 683-4300
Jason Smith, *Business Unit Manager*
EMP: 92
SQ FT: 66,000
Web: www.coopercrouse-hinds.com
SIC: 3069 3648 Hard rubber and molded
   rubber products; Airport lighting fixtures:
   runway approach, taxi, or ramp
HQ: Cooper Crouse-Hinds, Llc
   1201 Wolf St
   Syracuse NY 13208
   315 477-7000

(G-4269)
**DARLY CUSTOM TECHNOLOGY
INC**
276 Addison Rd (06095-2334)
P.O. Box 527 (06095-0527)
PHONE...................................860 298-7966
Yimou Yang, *Pr*
Stanley J Misunas, *Product Vice President*
Yao Kuang Yang, *Treas*
Hei-ju Yang, *Stockholder*
Li-chiung Chi Yang, *Stockholder*
▲ **EMP:** 13 **EST:** 1981
SQ FT: 15,000
SALES (est): 800.82K **Privately Held**
Web: www.darlytech.com
SIC: 3599 Custom machinery

(G-4270)
DEMARTINO FIXTURE CO INC
Also Called: Chefs Equipment Emporium
360 Bloomfield Ave Ste 301 (06095-2700)
PHONE...................................203 628-4899
TOLL FREE: 800
Dominick Demartino, *Pr*
Pasquale Salvatore, *VP*
Michele Salvatore, *Sec*
EMP: 12 **EST:** 1967
SQ FT: 150,000
SALES (est): 4.39MM **Privately Held**
Web:
demartino-fixtures.squarespace.com
SIC: 3585 Refrigeration equipment,
   complete

(G-4271)
**EATON ELECTRIC HOLDINGS
LLC**
Crouse-Hinds Airport Lighting
1200 Kennedy Rd (06095-1384)
PHONE...................................860 683-4300
Jack Bac, *Brnch Mgr*
EMP: 16
Web: www.eaton.com
SIC: 3648 Airport lighting fixtures: runway
   approach, taxi, or ramp
HQ: Eaton Electric Holdings Llc
   1000 Eaton Blvd
   Cleveland OH 44122

(G-4272)
EMHART GLASS INC (DH)
123 Great Pond Dr (06095-1569)
P.O. Box 220 (06095-0220)
PHONE...................................860 298-7340
Joseph Laundry, *Pr*

▲ = Import ▼ = Export
◆ = Import/Export

◆ **EMP:** 65 **EST:** 1940
SALES (est): 121.51MM **Privately Held**
Web: www.emhartglass.com
SIC: 3559 Glass making machinery:
blowing, molding, forming, etc.
HQ: Emhart Glass Sa
Hinterbergstrasse 22
Steinhausen ZG 6312

(G-4273)
EMHART GLASS
MANUFACTURING INC (DH)
123 Great Pond Dr (06095-1569)
P.O. Box 220 (06095-0220)
PHONE....................860 298-7340
Martin Jetter, *Pr*
Christer Hermannsson, *VP*
William Grninger, *VP*
Jeffrey D Hartung, *VP*
Edward P Munz, *VP*
▲ **EMP:** 20 **EST:** 1994
SALES (est): 101.1MM **Privately Held**
Web: www.emhartglass.com
SIC: 3221 Glass containers
HQ: Emhart Glass Inc.
123 Great Pond Dr
Windsor CT 06095
860 298-7340

(G-4274)
EXPRESS LUBE & TIRE LLC
35 Philip Henry Cir (06095-3979)
PHONE....................860 690-3066
David Mccarthy, *Managing Member*
EMP: 7
SALES (est): 242.16K **Privately Held**
SIC: 3714 Motor vehicle parts and
accessories

(G-4275)
FABBRICA LLC (PA)
1 Market Cir (06095-1423)
PHONE....................860 253-4136
EMP: 130 **EST:** 2015
SALES (est): 16.84MM
SALES (corp-wide): 16.84MM **Privately
Held**
Web: www.fabbricausa.com
SIC: 3448 Prefabricated metal buildings

(G-4276)
FISCHER TECHNOLOGY INC
(DH)
750 Marshall Phelps Rd (06095-2199)
PHONE....................860 683-0781
EMP: 30 **EST:** 1979
SALES (est): 14.02MM
SALES (corp-wide): 16.9MM **Privately
Held**
Web: www.fischer-technology.com
SIC: 3829 Measuring and controlling
devices, nec
HQ: Helmut Fischer Gmbh
Industriestr. 21
Sindelfingen BW
703 130-3527

(G-4277)
GARF TRUCKING INC
462 Palisado Ave (06095-2023)
PHONE....................860 558-8487
Nancy Garthwaite, *Pr*
Robert Garthwaite, *VP*
EMP: 7 **EST:** 1986
SALES (est): 1.11MM **Privately Held**
Web: www.garftrucking.com
SIC: 1442 Construction sand and gravel

(G-4278)
GE GRID SOLUTIONS LLC
175 Addison Rd (06095-2178)
PHONE....................425 250-2695
EMP: 9 **EST:** 2017
SALES (est): 189.22K **Privately Held**
Web: www.gegridsolutions.com
SIC: 3613 Power circuit breakers

(G-4279)
GE STEAM POWER INC (HQ)
Also Called: Alstom Power Co
200 Great Pond Dr (06095-4806)
PHONE....................866 257-8664
Conor Begley, *Pr*
Jeffrey Allen, *
Jorge Cavazos, *
Francois Berthiaume, *
Bruce Moffat, *
◆ **EMP:** 1200 **EST:** 1999
SQ FT: 286,000
SALES (est): 1.15B
SALES (corp-wide): 76.56B **Publicly Held**
Web: gefreight.ardmorelogistics.com
SIC: 3621 3823 8711 4931 Motors and
generators; Process control instruments;
Engineering services; Cogeneration of
electric power
PA: General Electric Company
1 Financial Ctr Ste 3700
Boston MA 02111
617 443-3000

(G-4280)
HFO CHICAGO LLC
910 Day Hill Rd (06095-5727)
PHONE....................860 285-0709
Bradley R Morris, *Mgr*
EMP: 9 **EST:** 2009
SALES (est): 408.84K **Privately Held**
Web: www.morrisgroupinc.com
SIC: 3599 Machine shop, jobbing and repair

(G-4281)
HOWDEN ROOTS LLC
Also Called: Howden Amricas Cmpsr -
Windsor
600 Day Hill Rd (06095-1703)
PHONE....................860 688-8361
Anthony Mancini, *Mgr*
EMP: 85
SALES (corp-wide): 5.92B **Publicly Held**
Web: www.chartindustries.com
SIC: 3589 3564 3498 5084 Vacuum
cleaners and sweepers, electric: industrial;
Turbo-blowers, industrial; Tube fabricating
(contract bending and shaping);
Compressors, except air conditioning
HQ: Howden Roots Llc
900 W Mount St
Connersville IN 47331
765 827-9200

(G-4282)
HURLEY MTAL FBRICATION
MFG LLC
725 Marshall Phelps Rd (06095-2105)
PHONE....................860 688-8844
EMP: 15 **EST:** 1995
SQ FT: 40,000
SALES (est): 1.19MM **Privately Held**
Web: www.hurleymetalfab.com
SIC: 7692 Welding repair

(G-4283)
INDUSTRIAL MAGNETICS INC
Also Called: Walker Magnetics
600 Day Hill Rd (06095-1703)
PHONE....................508 853-3232
EMP: 90

SALES (corp-wide): 50.34MM **Privately
Held**
Web: www.magnetics.com
SIC: 3545 3559 3845 3535 Machine tool
attachments and accessories; Separation
equipment, magnetic; Electromedical
equipment; Conveyors and conveying
equipment
PA: Industrial Magnetics, Inc.
1385 S M 75
Boyne City MI 49712
231 582-3100

(G-4284)
INTERSTATE ELEC SVCS CORP
800 Marshall Phelps Rd # 2 (06095-2143)
PHONE....................860 243-5644
John Sloane, *Brnch Mgr*
EMP: 49
SALES (corp-wide): 122.73MM **Privately
Held**
Web: www.iesc1.com
SIC: 1731 3531 Electronic controls
installation; Cranes, nec
PA: Interstate Electrical Services
Corporation
70 Treble Cove Rd
North Billerica MA 01862
978 667-5200

(G-4285)
LAMAR ADVERTISING
COMPANY
Also Called: Lamar Advertising
32 Midland St (06095-4334)
PHONE....................860 246-6546
Steve Hebert, *Mgr*
EMP: 9
Web: www.lamar.com
SIC: 7312 3993 Billboard advertising; Signs
and advertising specialties
PA: Lamar Advertising Company
5321 Corporate Blvd
Baton Rouge LA 70808

(G-4286)
LEIPOLD INC
545 Marshall Phelps Rd (06095-1702)
PHONE....................860 298-9791
Pascal Schiefer, *Managing Member*
Pascal Schiefer, *Pr*
Thomas Fees, *
Christoph Lange, *
▲ **EMP:** 30 **EST:** 1997
SALES (est): 14.36MM
SALES (corp-wide): 67.98MM **Privately
Held**
Web: www.leipold.com
SIC: 3451 Screw machine products
PA: Carl Leipold Gmbh
Schiltacher Str. 5
Wolfach BW 77709
783483950

(G-4287)
LIMRA INTERNATIONAL INC (PA)
300 Day Hill Rd (06095-4761)
P.O. Box 208 (06141-0208)
PHONE....................860 688-3358
EMP: 25 **EST:** 1917
SALES (est): 52.82MM
SALES (corp-wide): 52.82MM **Privately
Held**
Web: www.limra.com
SIC: 8611 2721 Trade associations;
Periodicals

(G-4288)
MANUFACTURING PDT
SYSTEMS INC

910 Day Hill Rd (06095-5727)
PHONE....................877 689-1860
Bradley Morris, *CEO*
EMP: 10 **EST:** 1972
SALES (est): 1.05MM **Privately Held**
SIC: 3433 Boilers, low-pressure heating:
steam or hot water

(G-4289)
MATERION LRGE AREA
CATINGS LLC (DH)
300 Lamberton Rd (06095-2131)
PHONE....................216 486-4200
▲ **EMP:** 53 **EST:** 1996
SQ FT: 30,000
SALES (est): 17.91MM **Publicly Held**
SIC: 3479 Coating of metals and formed
products
HQ: Materion Advanced Materials
Technologies And Services Inc.
2978 Main St
Buffalo NY 14214
800 327-1355

(G-4290)
MEDIA LINKS INC
431 Hayden Station Rd Ste C (06095-1393)
PHONE....................860 206-9163
Takatsugu Ono, *CEO*
John Dale Iii, *VP*
EMP: 14 **EST:** 2005
SQ FT: 10,000
SALES (est): 4.88MM **Privately Held**
Web: www.medialinks.com
SIC: 3663 Television broadcasting and
communications equipment
PA: Media Links Co., Ltd.
580-16, Horikawacho, Saiwai-Ku
Kawasaki KNG 212-0

(G-4291)
METAL IMPROVEMENT
COMPANY LLC
145 Addison Rd (06095-2102)
PHONE....................860 688-6201
Kelly Hoffman, *Mgr*
EMP: 28
SALES (corp-wide): 2.56B **Publicly Held**
Web: www.curtisswright.com
SIC: 3398 Shot peening (treating steel to
reduce fatigue)
HQ: Metal Improvement Company, Llc
80 E Rte 4 Ste 310
Paramus NJ 07652
201 843-7800

(G-4292)
O S WALKER COMPANY INC
(HQ)
600 Day Hill Rd (06095-1703)
PHONE....................508 853-3232
Richard Longo, *Pr*
Debra Krikorian, *Sec*
Ken Wanko, *Dir*
◆ **EMP:** 27 **EST:** 1896
SALES (est): 9.8MM
SALES (corp-wide): 55.92MM **Privately
Held**
Web: www.drownemachinery.com
SIC: 3545 Chucks: drill, lathe, or magnetic
(machine tool accessories)
PA: Industrial Magnetics, Inc.
1385 S M 75
Boyne City MI 49712
231 582-3100

(G-4293)
OSF FLAVORS INC (PA)
40 Baker Hollow Rd (06095-2133)

P.O. Box 591 (06095-0591)
PHONE.................................860 298-8350
Olivier De Botton, *CEO*
Eduardo De Botao, *Pr*
▲ **EMP:** 15 **EST:** 1983
SQ FT: 18,000
SALES (est): 7.11MM
SALES (corp-wide): 7.11MM **Privately Held**
Web: www.osfflavors.com
SIC: 2087 Flavoring extracts and syrups, nec

(G-4294)
PEPSI-COLA METRO BTLG CO INC
Also Called: Pepsico
55 International Dr (06095-1062)
PHONE.................................860 688-6281
David Cronin, *Mgr*
EMP: 51
SALES (corp-wide): 86.39B **Publicly Held**
Web: www.pepsico.com
SIC: 2086 Carbonated soft drinks, bottled and canned
HQ: Pepsi-Cola Metropolitan Bottling Company, Inc.
700 Anderson Hill Rd
Purchase NY 10577
914 767-6000

(G-4295)
PRECISION FINISHING SVCS INC
60 Ezra Silva Ln (06095-2122)
P.O. Box 189 (06060-0189)
PHONE.................................860 882-1073
EMP: 20 **EST:** 1995
SQ FT: 33,000
SALES (est): 2.02MM **Privately Held**
Web: www.surfaceprepne.com
SIC: 3471 Plating of metals or formed products

(G-4296)
PRIMATICS FINANCIAL LLC (HQ)
80 Lamberton Rd Fl 1 (06095-2142)
PHONE.................................703 342-0040
Kevin J Hesselbirg, *CEO*
Jeff Sant, *
Abbs Valliani, *Managing Member**
Michael Therrien, *
Umar Syyid, *
EMP: 37 **EST:** 2006
SALES (est): 22.35MM
SALES (corp-wide): 5.28B **Publicly Held**
Web: www.primaticsfinancial.com
SIC: 7372 Prepackaged software
PA: Ss&C Technologies Holdings, Inc.
80 Lamberton Rd Fl 1
Windsor CT 06095
860 298-4500

(G-4297)
PROLIANCE INTERNATIONAL INC
436 Hayden Station Rd (06095-1388)
PHONE.................................860 688-7644
Romero Rasho, *Prin*
EMP: 7 **EST:** 2016
SALES (est): 127.79K **Privately Held**
SIC: 3714 Motor vehicle parts and accessories

(G-4298)
SCAPA HOLDINGS INC (DH)
111 Great Pond Dr (06095-1527)
PHONE.................................860 688-8000
Steve Lennon, *Chief*
EMP: 96 **EST:** 1999
SALES (est): 107.46MM **Publicly Held**

Web: www.scapa.com
SIC: 2672 Paper; coated and laminated, nec
HQ: Scapa Group Limited
Manchester Road
Manchester OL7 0
161 301-7400

(G-4299)
SECURITIES SOFTWARE & CONSULTI
80 Lamberton Rd (06095-2136)
PHONE.................................860 298-4500
William C Stone, *Prin*
EMP: 28 **EST:** 2002
SALES (est): 999K **Privately Held**
Web: www.ssctech.com
SIC: 7372 Prepackaged software

(G-4300)
SPECIALTY PRINTING LLC (PA)
Also Called: S P
123 Day Hill Rd (06095-1709)
PHONE.................................860 623-8870
William T Bailey, *Managing Member*
Francis Poirier, *
Edward Poirier, *
EMP: 92 **EST:** 1977
SQ FT: 40,000
SALES (est): 26.86MM
SALES (corp-wide): 26.86MM **Privately Held**
Web: www.specialtyprinting.net
SIC: 2679 2759 2672 Labels, paper: made from purchased material; Labels and seals: printing, nsk; Paper; coated and laminated, nec

(G-4301)
SPENCER TURBINE COMPANY (DH)
600 Day Hill Rd (06095-4706)
PHONE.................................860 688-8361
TOLL FREE: 800
Antonio Mancini, *Pr*
▲ **EMP:** 35 **EST:** 1892
SQ FT: 200,000
SALES (est): 52.68MM **Privately Held**
Web: www.chartindustries.com
SIC: 3589 3564 3498 5084 Vacuum cleaners and sweepers, electric: industrial; Turbo-blowers, industrial; Tube fabricating (contract bending and shaping); Compressors, except air conditioning
HQ: Howden Group Limited
Old Govan Road
Renfrew PA4 8
141 885-7500

(G-4302)
SS&C TECHNOLOGIES INC (HQ)
80 Lamberton Rd (06095-2142)
PHONE.................................800 234-0556
William Stone, *Ch Bd*
Normand Boulanger, *Pr*
Patrick Pedonti, *Sr VP*
Stephen Whitman, *Sr VP*
Campbell Dyer, *Prin*
EMP: 200 **EST:** 1996
SQ FT: 73,000
SALES (est): 617.71MM
SALES (corp-wide): 5.28B **Publicly Held**
Web: www.ssctech.com
SIC: 7372 7371 8741 Prepackaged software ; Custom computer programming services; Management services
PA: Ss&C Technologies Holdings, Inc.
80 Lamberton Rd Fl 1
Windsor CT 06095
860 298-4500

(G-4303)
SS&C TECHNOLOGIES HOLDINGS INC (PA)
Also Called: SS&C HOLDINGS
80 Lamberton Rd (06095-2142)
PHONE.................................860 298-4500
William C Stone, *Ch Bd*
Normand A Boulanger, *Vice Chairman*
Rahul Kanwar, *Pr*
Patrick J Pedonti, *Sr VP*
Jason White, *Sr VP*
EMP: 515 **EST:** 1986
SQ FT: 93,500
SALES (est): 5.28B
SALES (corp-wide): 5.28B **Publicly Held**
Web: www.ssctech.com
SIC: 7372 Prepackaged software

(G-4304)
STAUFFER SHEET METAL LLC
Also Called: Stauffer Sheet Metal
56 Depot St (06006-0001)
PHONE.................................860 623-0518
EMP: 9 **EST:** 1984
SQ FT: 10,400
SALES (est): 878.93K **Privately Held**
Web: www.stauffersheetmetal.com
SIC: 3444 Sheet metalwork

(G-4305)
SUBINAS USA LLC
4 Market Cir (06095-1422)
PHONE.................................860 298-0401
Daniel Herran, *Managing Member*
▲ **EMP:** 10 **EST:** 2012
SALES (est): 870.09K **Privately Held**
Web: www.subinas.es
SIC: 2515 Mattresses, innerspring or box spring

(G-4306)
T & T AUTOMATION INC
88 Pierson Ln (06095-2049)
PHONE.................................860 683-8788
Ben Terkildsen, *Pr*
EMP: 17 **EST:** 1992
SQ FT: 8,000
SALES (est): 729.62K **Privately Held**
SIC: 3625 Control equipment, electric

(G-4307)
TAYLOR & FENN COMPANY
22 Deerfield Rd (06095-4237)
PHONE.................................860 219-9393
Brian Butler, *CEO*
Brian Butler, *Ch*
Edgar B Butler Junior, *V Ch Bd*
◆ **EMP:** 49 **EST:** 1901
SQ FT: 130,000
SALES (est): 9.13MM **Privately Held**
Web: www.taylorfenn.com
SIC: 3321 Gray iron castings, nec

(G-4308)
TELLING INDUSTRIES LLC
1050 Kennedy Rd (06095-1303)
PHONE.................................860 731-7975
Satry Perleini, *Genl Mgr*
EMP: 36
SALES (corp-wide): 31.59MM **Privately Held**
Web: www.tellingindustries.com
SIC: 3316 Cold finishing of steel shapes
PA: Telling Industries, Llc
4420 Sherwin Rd Ste 4
Willoughby OH 44094
440 974-3370

(G-4309)
TLD AMERICA CORPORATION (DH)
Also Called: Tld Group
812 Bloomfield Ave (06095-2340)
PHONE.................................860 602-3400
Mark L Garlasco, *Pr*
David Wells, *
Debbie Dorman, *
Antoine Maguin, *
◆ **EMP:** 18 **EST:** 1966
SQ FT: 20,000
SALES (est): 189.77MM
SALES (corp-wide): 675.45K **Privately Held**
SIC: 5088 3728 7629 Aircraft and parts, nec ; Aircraft parts and equipment, nec; Aircraft electrical equipment repair
HQ: Alvest (Usa) Inc.
812 Bloomfield Ave
Windsor CT 06095

(G-4310)
TRIUMPH ACTTION SYSTEMS - CONN (HQ)
Also Called: Triumph Actuation Systems
175 Addison Rd Ste 4 (06095-2178)
PHONE.................................860 687-5412
Daniel Crowley, *CEO*
Richard C III, *
Jeffry D Frisby, *
Tom Holtzum, *
M David Kornblatt, *
▲ **EMP:** 85 **EST:** 1998
SALES (est): 53.21MM **Publicly Held**
SIC: 3728 Aircraft parts and equipment, nec
PA: Triumph Group, Inc.
555 E Lancaster Ave # 400
Radnor PA 19087

(G-4311)
ULTRA FLOW DISPENSE LLC
820 Prospect Hill Rd (06095-1559)
P.O. Box 565 (06002-0565)
PHONE.................................866 827-2534
EMP: 14 **EST:** 2013
SALES (est): 2.01MM **Privately Held**
Web: www.ultraflow.com
SIC: 3585 Beer dispensing equipment

(G-4312)
VERTAFORE INC
5 Waterside Xing Fl 2 (06095-1577)
PHONE.................................860 602-6000
Johanna Carpino, *Brnch Mgr*
EMP: 46
SALES (corp-wide): 5.37B **Publicly Held**
Web: www.vertafore.com
SIC: 7371 8711 7373 7372 Computer software development; Engineering services ; Computer integrated systems design; Prepackaged software
HQ: Vertafore, Inc.
999 18th St Ste 400
Denver CO 80202
800 444-4813

(G-4313)
VULCAN INDUSTRIES INC
651 Day Hill Rd (06095-1798)
PHONE.................................860 683-2005
EMP: 150 **EST:** 1970
SQ FT: 33,000
SALES (est): 1.28MM
SALES (corp-wide): 10.1MM **Privately Held**
SIC: 3714 3444 3443 Motor vehicle parts and accessories; Sheet metalwork; Fabricated plate work (boiler shop)
PA: Thermodynetics, Inc.
651 Day Hill Rd

▲ = Import ▼ = Export
◆ = Import/Export

Windsor CT 06095
860 683-2005

(G-4314)
WALKER MAGNETICS GROUP INC
600 Day Hill Rd (06095-1703)
PHONE...............................508 853-3232
◆ **EMP:** 90
Web: www.walkermagnet.com
SIC: 3545 3559 3845 3535 Machine tool attachments and accessories; Separation equipment, magnetic; Electromedical equipment; Conveyors and conveying equipment

(G-4315)
WPCS INTERNATIONAL-HARTFORD INC (HQ)
427 Hayden Station Rd Ste B (06095-1335)
TOLL FREE: 800
EMP: 46 **EST:** 1995
SALES (est): 914.74K
SALES (corp-wide): 2.99MM **Publicly Held**
Web: www.wpcs-solutions.com
SIC: 3663 4812 Radio broadcasting and communications equipment; Cellular telephone services
PA: Ayro, Inc.
900 E Old Settlers Blvd
Round Rock TX 78664
512 994-4917

(G-4316)
YOSI KOSHER CATERING LLC
598 Hayden Station Rd (06095-1309)
PHONE...............................860 688-6677
EMP: 12 **EST:** 2003
SALES (est): 805.53K **Privately Held**
Web: www.yosikitchen.com
SIC: 5812 2099 Caterers; Box lunches, for sale off premises

Windsor Locks
Hartford County

(G-4317)
ACCURATE WELDING SERVICES LLC
7 Industrial Rd (06096-1101)
PHONE...............................860 623-9500
EMP: 10 **EST:** 1997
SALES (est): 614.7K **Privately Held**
Web: www.electronbeamct.com
SIC: 7692 Welding repair

(G-4318)
AHLSTROM NONWOVENS LLC (DH)
Also Called: Ahlstrom-Munksjo Nonwovens LLC
2 Elm St (06096-2335)
PHONE...............................860 654-8300
◆ **EMP:** 264 **EST:** 2000
SALES (est): 211.48MM
SALES (corp-wide): 2.67MM **Privately Held**
Web: www.ahlstrom.com
SIC: 2591 3291 Drapery hardware and window blinds and shades; Abrasive products
HQ: Ahlstrom Usa Inc.
2 Elm St
Windsor Locks CT 06096

(G-4319)
AHLSTROM USA INC (DH)
Also Called: Ahlstrom-Munksjo USA Inc.
2 Elm St (06096-2335)
P.O. Box 270 (06096-0270)
PHONE...............................860 654-8300
William Casey, Pr
David T Pluta, VP
Leonard H Mirahver, VP
Christopher Coates, VP
Gustav Adlercreutz, Sec
◆ **EMP:** 11 **EST:** 1989
SALES (est): 465.05MM
SALES (corp-wide): 2.67MM **Privately Held**
Web: www.ahlstrom.com
SIC: 2621 Specialty or chemically treated papers
HQ: Ahlstrom Oyj
Alvar Aallon Katu 3c
Helsinki 00100
108880

(G-4320)
AHLSTROM-MUNKSJO NONWOVENS LLC
Also Called: AHLSTROM-MUNKSJO NONWOVENS LLC
11 Canal Bank Rd (06096-2300)
PHONE...............................860 654-8300
Gary Blevins, Pr
EMP: 18
SALES (corp-wide): 2.67MM **Privately Held**
Web: www.ahlstrom.com
SIC: 2621 Paper mills
HQ: Ahlstrom Nonwovens Llc
2 Elm St
Windsor Locks CT 06096
860 654-8300

(G-4321)
AHLSTROM-MUNKSJO PAPER INC
2 Elm St (06096-2335)
PHONE...............................860 654-8300
Jan Alston, Dir
Andrew J Rice, Pr
Kim Henriksson, Ex VP
Caspar Callerstrm, Dir
◆ **EMP:** 10 **EST:** 2002
SQ FT: 1,200
SALES (est): 8.29MM
SALES (corp-wide): 145.85K **Privately Held**
SIC: 2621 Paper mills
HQ: Munksjo Germany Holding Gmbh
Nordlicher Stadtgraben 4
Aalen BW 73430
736 150-6111

(G-4322)
AIR TRANSPORT INTL INC
100 Cargo Rd (06096)
PHONE...............................937 287-8455
EMP: 7 **EST:** 2012
SALES (est): 73.45K **Privately Held**
SIC: 3724 Aircraft engines and engine parts

(G-4323)
AIW-ALTON INC
545 Spring St Unit E (06096-1106)
P.O. Box 130 (06095-0130)
EMP: 8 **EST:** 1930
SQ FT: 23,000
SALES (est): 983.88K **Privately Held**
Web: www.aiwalton.com
SIC: 3599 Machine shop, jobbing and repair

(G-4324)
EMBRAER EXECUTIVE JET SVCS LLC
Also Called: Embraer Executive Jets
41 Perimeter Rd (06096-1069)
PHONE...............................860 804-4600
Eric Pettersen, Mgr
EMP: 8
SIC: 3721 Aircraft
HQ: Embraer Executive Jet Services, Llc
2008 General Aviation Dr
Melbourne FL 32935
321 751-5050

(G-4325)
GENUINE PARTS COMPANY
Also Called: NAPA Auto Parts
508 Spring St Ste 2 (06096-1148)
PHONE...............................860 623-4479
Don Wright, Genl Mgr
EMP: 8
SALES (corp-wide): 22.1B **Publicly Held**
Web: www.genpt.com
SIC: 5531 5013 3714 Automotive parts; Automotive supplies and parts; Motor vehicle parts and accessories
PA: Genuine Parts Company
2999 Wildwood Pkwy
Atlanta GA 30339
678 934-5000

(G-4326)
GIRARDIN MOULDING INC
564 Halfway House Rd (06096-1500)
P.O. Box 577 (06096-0577)
PHONE...............................860 623-4486
Gaston Girardin, Pr
Daniel Girardin, VP
Gail Girardin, Sec
EMP: 13 **EST:** 1952
SQ FT: 55,000
SALES (est): 488.19K **Privately Held**
Web: www.girardinmoulding.com
SIC: 3442 Metal doors, sash, and trim

(G-4327)
GREIF INC
Also Called: Greif Global Industrial Packg
491 North St (06096-1140)
PHONE...............................740 549-6000
David Russolski, Mgr
EMP: 53
SALES (corp-wide): 5.22B **Publicly Held**
Web: www.greif.com
SIC: 2655 Fiber cans, drums, and similar products
PA: Greif, Inc.
425 Winter Rd
Delaware OH 43015
740 549-6000

(G-4328)
HAMILTON SNDSTRAND SPACE SYSTE
1 Hamilton Rd (06096-1000)
PHONE...............................860 654-6000
Edward Francis, Pr
Daneil Lee, *
Jeffery Chanin, *
Marlin Knight, *
Paul Carew, *
▲ **EMP:** 24 **EST:** 1994
SQ FT: 230,000
SALES (est): 994.06K **Privately Held**
SIC: 3841 3826 Diagnostic apparatus, medical; Thermal analysis instruments, laboratory type

(G-4329)
HAMILTON STANDARD SPACE
1 Hamilton Rd (06096-1010)
PHONE...............................860 654-6000
Harry Garfinkel, Pr
Chester Paul Beach Junior, Sec
EMP: 24 **EST:** 1994
SALES (est): 821.65K **Privately Held**
SIC: 3822 3728 3842 3569 Environmental controls; Oxygen systems, aircraft; Space suits; Gas producers, generators, and other gas related equipment

(G-4330)
HAMILTON SUNDSTRAND CORP (HQ)
Also Called: Collins Aerospace
1 Hamilton Rd (06096-1000)
PHONE...............................619 714-9442
Stephen Timm, CEO
◆ **EMP:** 800 **EST:** 1999
SALES (est): 1.89B
SALES (corp-wide): 67.07B **Publicly Held**
Web: www.collinsaerospace.com
SIC: 3621 3625 3728 3594 Frequency converters (electric generators); Actuators, industrial; Gears, aircraft power transmission; Fluid power pumps and motors
PA: Rtx Corporation
1000 Wilson Blvd
Arlington VA 22209
781 522-3000

(G-4331)
LEARJET INC
Also Called: Bombardier
85-173 Bradley Intl Airport (06096-1071)
PHONE...............................860 627-9491
Jim Scavotta, Mgr
EMP: 150
SQ FT: 65,000
SALES (corp-wide): 6.91B **Privately Held**
Web: www.bombardier.com
SIC: 3721 Aircraft
HQ: Learjet Inc.
1 Learjet Way
Wichita KS 67209
316 946-2000

(G-4332)
QUICK TURN MACHINE COMPANY INC
1000 Old County Cir Ste 105 (06096-1570)
PHONE...............................860 623-2569
Maria Rafalowski, Pr
Stanley Rafalowski, VP
EMP: 19 **EST:** 1986
SQ FT: 21,000
SALES (est): 829.85K **Privately Held**
Web: www.quickturnmfg.com
SIC: 3599 Machine shop, jobbing and repair

(G-4333)
RTX CORPORATION
UTC Aerospace Systems
1 Hamilton Rd (06096-1000)
PHONE...............................860 654-7519
Chuck Catania, Prin
EMP: 91
SALES (corp-wide): 68.92B **Publicly Held**
Web: www.rtx.com
SIC: 3724 Aircraft engines and engine parts
PA: Rtx Corporation
1000 Wilson Blvd
Arlington VA 22209
781 522-3000

(G-4334)
**SPECTRUM MACHINE &
DESIGN LLC**
800 Old County Cir (06096-1575)
P.O. Box 4144 (06096-4144)
PHONE...............................860 386-6490
Gary Poesnecker, *Mgr*
EMP: 32 EST: 1999
SQ FT: 4,000
SALES (est): 5.05MM **Privately Held**
Web: www.wemachine.com
SIC: 3599 Machine shop, jobbing and repair

(G-4335)
STANDARD BELLOWS CO (PA)
375 Ella Grasso Tpke (06096-1003)
P.O. Box 66 (06096-0066)
PHONE...............................860 623-2307
Stanley E Tkacz Junior, *Pr*
Thomas J Tkacz, *Sec*
EMP: 20 EST: 1961
SQ FT: 18,400
SALES (est): 3.35MM
SALES (corp-wide): 3.35MM **Privately
Held**
Web: www.std-bellows.com
SIC: 3599 Bellows, industrial: metal

(G-4336)
**UNITED TECHNOLOGIES
OPTICAL SYSTEMS INC**
1 Hamilton Rd (06096-1000)
PHONE...............................860 654-6000
▲ **EMP:** 246
SIC: 3827 Optical instruments and
apparatus

(G-4337)
**WOOD GROUP PRATT &
WHITNEY**
147 Addison Rd (06096)
PHONE...............................860 687-1686
Bob Hutchinson, *Dir*
EMP: 9
SALES (corp-wide): 31.05MM **Privately
Held**
Web: www.wgpw.com
SIC: 3511 Turbines and turbine generator
sets
PA: Wood Group Pratt & Whitney Industrial
Turbine Services, Llc
1460 Blue Hills Ave
Bloomfield CT 06002
860 286-4600

Winsted
Litchfield County

(G-4338)
**AMERICAN COLLARS
COUPLINGS INC**
88 Hubbard St (06098-1050)
PHONE...............................860 379-7043
Shirley A Clarke, *Pr*
Michael A Clarke, *VP*
Linda Stommel, *VP*
▲ **EMP:** 16 EST: 1983
SQ FT: 8,000
SALES (est): 461.23K **Privately Held**
SIC: 3568 Collars, shaft (power
transmission equipment)

(G-4339)
BKMFG CORP
Also Called: Broil King
200 International Way (06098-2252)
PHONE...............................860 738-2200

Michael Shanahan, *Pr*
Michael Bosson, *
▲ **EMP:** 35 EST: 1964
SQ FT: 30,000
SALES (est): 4.53MM
SALES (corp-wide): 10.88MM **Privately
Held**
Web: www.broilking.com
SIC: 3634 Broilers, electric
PA: Cadco, Ltd.
200 International Way
Winsted CT 06098
860 738-2500

(G-4340)
**DUFRANE NUCLEAR
SHIELDING INC**
150 Price Rd (06098-2265)
PHONE...............................860 379-2318
Joshua Brooks, *Pr*
Dan Brooks, *VP*
EMP: 15 EST: 1987
SQ FT: 2,000
SALES (est): 2.49MM **Privately Held**
Web: www.dufrane.com
SIC: 7389 3444 3312 8711   Design services;
Metal housings, enclosures, casings, and
other containers; Stainless steel;
Mechanical engineering

(G-4341)
DUFRANE TECHNOLOGIES LLC
150 Price Rd (06098-2265)
PHONE...............................860 379-2318
Joshua Brooks, *Managing Member*
EMP: 15 EST: 2018
SALES (est): 1.02MM **Privately Held**
Web: www.dufranetechnologies.com
SIC: 3625 Brakes, electromagnetic

(G-4342)
E & E TOOL & MFG CO INC
100 International Way (06098-2251)
PHONE...............................860 738-8577
Edward Clark, *Pr*
William Clark, *VP*
EMP: 12 EST: 1972
SQ FT: 7,500
SALES (est): 1.1MM **Privately Held**
SIC: 3469 3544 Metal stampings, nec;
Special dies and tools

(G-4343)
**EAST COAST LIGHTNING EQP
INC**
Also Called: East Coast Roof Specialties
24 Lanson Dr (06098-2072)
PHONE...............................860 379-9072
Mark P Morgan, *Pr*
Jennifer Morgan, *Sec*
EMP: 24 EST: 1985
SQ FT: 20,000
SALES (est): 5.44MM **Privately Held**
Web: www.ecle.biz
SIC: 3643 5072 Lightning protection
equipment; Miscellaneous fasteners

(G-4344)
**ELECTRIC MOTION COMPANY
INC (DH)**
110 Groppo Dr (06098)
P.O. Box 626 (06098-0626)
PHONE...............................860 379-8515
▲ **EMP:** 124 EST: 1979
SALES (est): 50.21MM
SALES (corp-wide): 4.95B **Publicly Held**
Web: www.hubbell.com
SIC: 3643 Ground clamps (electric wiring
devices)

HQ: Hubbell Power Systems, Inc.
200 Center Point Cir # 200
Columbia SC 29210
803 216-2600

(G-4345)
FAIRCHILD INDUSTRIES INC
Also Called: Fairchild Auto-Mated Parts
10 White St (06098-2132)
PHONE...............................860 379-2725
Leland Lecciardi, *Dir*
EMP: 12 EST: 2021
SALES (est): 822.83K **Privately Held**
Web: www.fairchildparts.com
SIC: 3599 Machine shop, jobbing and repair

(G-4346)
H-O PRODUCTS CORPORATION
12 Munro St (06098-1423)
PHONE...............................860 379-9875
Chris Olson, *Pr*
Robert Carfiro, *
Walter Emmett D.o.s., *Prin*
EMP: 26 EST: 1971
SQ FT: 50,000
SALES (est): 5.02MM **Privately Held**
Web: www.h-oproducts.com
SIC: 3069 3086 3053 2672 Weather strip,
sponge rubber; Insulation or cushioning
material, foamed plastics; Gaskets and
sealing devices; Adhesive papers, labels,
or tapes: from purchased material

(G-4347)
HOWMET AEROSPACE INC
Also Called: HOWMET AEROSPACE INC
145 Price Rd (06098-2240)
PHONE...............................860 379-3314
Klaus Kleinfield, *Brnch Mgr*
EMP: 21
SALES (corp-wide): 6.64B **Publicly Held**
Web: www.howmet.com
SIC: 3334 Primary aluminum
PA: Howmet Aerospace Inc.
201 Isabella St Ste 200
Pittsburgh PA 15212
412 553-1950

(G-4348)
M & J SHEET METAL LLC
41 Meadow St (06098-1438)
PHONE...............................860 379-2907
EMP: 8 EST: 2003
SALES (est): 94.54K **Privately Held**
SIC: 3444 Sheet metalwork

(G-4349)
METAMORPHIC MATERIALS INC
122 Colebrook River Rd (06098-2205)
PHONE...............................860 738-8638
Jay K Martin, *Pr*
▲ **EMP:** 9 EST: 2012
SALES (est): 2.31MM **Privately Held**
Web: www.metamorphicmaterials.com
SIC: 2819 2891 3479 Inorganic acids
except nitric and phosphoric; Adhesives
and sealants; Etching and engraving

(G-4350)
**NANNI MANUFACTURING CO
INC**
200 Price Rd (06098-2236)
P.O. Box 556 (06098-0556)
▲ **EMP:** 27
SIC: 3728 Aircraft parts and equipment, nec

(G-4351)
NARRAGANSETT SCREW CO
119 Rowley St (06098-2068)

PHONE...............................860 379-4059
Charlie Rhoades, *Pr*
EMP: 13 EST: 1960
SQ FT: 27,000
SALES (est): 1.82MM **Privately Held**
Web: www.narragansettscrew.com
SIC: 3452 3364 3354 Screws, metal;
Nonferrous die-castings except aluminum;
Aluminum extruded products

(G-4352)
NORTHWEST CONN MFG CO INC
95 Beech Hill Rd (06098)
PHONE...............................860 379-1553
Louis Fasano Junior, *Pr*
Jane Fasano, *Sec*
EMP: 8 EST: 1974
SQ FT: 5,200
SALES (est): 764.9K **Privately Held**
SIC: 3599 Machine shop, jobbing and repair

(G-4353)
**PRECISION METALS AND
PLASTICS**
Also Called: Precision Metals and Plas Mfg
118 Colebrook River Rd Ste 7
(06098-2241)
P.O. Box 7264 (06037-7264)
PHONE...............................860 238-4320
William Bonk, *Prin*
EMP: 9 EST: 2008
SALES (est): 654.11K **Privately Held**
Web: www.metalsplastics.com
SIC: 3728 Aircraft assemblies,
subassemblies, and parts, nec

(G-4354)
**SCHAEFFLER AEROSPACE USA
CORP**
Also Called: Winsted Precision Ball
159 Colebrook River Rd (06098-2203)
PHONE...............................860 379-7558
Roman Czarniecki, *Genl Mgr*
EMP: 71
SALES (corp-wide): 66.25B **Privately Held**
Web: www.schaeffler.us
SIC: 3562 3399 3229 Ball bearings and
parts; Steel balls; Pressed and blown glass,
nec
HQ: Schaeffler Aerospace Usa Corporation
200 Park Ave
Danbury CT 06810
203 744-2211

(G-4355)
SKF SPECIALTY BALLS
149 Colebrook River Rd (06098-2203)
PHONE...............................860 379-8511
EMP: 10 EST: 2018
SALES (est): 583.27K **Privately Held**
SIC: 3562 Ball and roller bearings

(G-4356)
SKF USA INC
149 Colebrook River Rd (06098-2203)
PHONE...............................860 379-8511
Frank Baker, *Brnch Mgr*
EMP: 41
SALES (corp-wide): 9.24B **Privately Held**
Web: www.skf.com
SIC: 3562 3053 Ball and roller bearings;
Gaskets and sealing devices
HQ: Skf Usa Inc.
890 Forty Foot Rd
Lansdale PA 19446
267 436-6000

(G-4357)
STERLING SINTERED TECHNOLOGIES INC
249 Rockwell St (06098-1946)
PHONE..................................860 379-2753
EMP: 52 **EST:** 1985
SALES (est): 7MM **Privately Held**
Web: www.sterlingsintered.com
SIC: 3399   Powder, metal

(G-4358)
WESTWOOD PRODUCTS INC
167 Torrington Rd (06098-2087)
P.O. Box 933 (06098-0933)
PHONE..................................860 379-9401
Brian Tarbox, *Pr*
Sara Westervelt, *Off Mgr*
EMP: 10 **EST:** 1988
SQ FT: 8,000
SALES (est): 809.1K **Privately Held**
Web: www.westwoodproductsinc.com
SIC: 2441 2448 2449   Boxes, wood; Pallets, wood; Wood containers, nec

(G-4359)
WINCHESTER INDUSTRIES INC
106 John G Groppo Dr (06098-2249)
PHONE..................................860 379-5336
Peter Toomey, *Pr*
EMP: 7 **EST:** 1987
SALES (est): 863.21K **Privately Held**
Web: www.railroadgage.com
SIC: 3743   Railroad equipment

Wolcott
New Haven County

(G-4360)
ACUTE CARE GASES OF CT LLC
23 Nutmeg Valley Rd (06716-2621)
PHONE..................................855 399-1224
Ben Cohen, *Prin*
EMP: 13 **EST:** 2016
SALES (est): 1.13MM **Privately Held**
Web: www.acgases.com
SIC: 3845   Respiratory analysis equipment, electromedical

(G-4361)
ALDEN CORPORATION
Also Called: Drill-Out
1 Hillside Dr (06716-2403)
P.O. Box 6262 (06716-0262)
PHONE..................................203 879-8830
Yvon J Desaulniers, *Pr*
▲ **EMP:** 60 **EST:** 1990
SQ FT: 40,000
SALES (est): 8.53MM **Privately Held**
Web: www.drillout.com
SIC: 3545 3546   Cutting tools for machine tools; Drill attachments, portable

(G-4362)
COILS PLUS INC
30 Town Line Rd (06716-2624)
PHONE..................................203 879-0755
Michael Mennillo, *Pr*
Daniel J Mennillo Junior, *VP*
EMP: 28 **EST:** 1984
SQ FT: 13,000
SALES (est): 3.28MM **Privately Held**
Web: www.coilsplus.com
SIC: 3621 3677   Coils, for electric motors or generators; Electronic coils and transformers

(G-4363)
DEVON PRECISION INDUSTRIES INC
Also Called: Devon Precision Industries.
251 Munson Rd (06716-2728)
P.O. Box 6555 (06716-0555)
PHONE..................................203 879-1437
Yvon J Desaulniers, *CEO*
Lorraine Desaulniers, *
Donald J Desaulniers, *
David J Desaulniers, *
EMP: 65 **EST:** 1967
SQ FT: 55,000
SALES (est): 6.37MM **Privately Held**
Web: www.devonprecision.com
SIC: 3451   Screw machine products

(G-4364)
EDSON MANUFACTURING INC
10 Venus Dr (06716-2627)
P.O. Box 6211 (06716-0211)
PHONE..................................203 879-1411
Lee Gaw, *Pr*
John Famiglietti, *Sec*
▲ **EMP:** 10 **EST:** 1997
SQ FT: 6,200
SALES (est): 2.96MM **Privately Held**
Web: www.edsonmfg.com
SIC: 3452   Rivets, metal

(G-4365)
EYELET TECH LLC
10 Venus Dr (06716-2627)
PHONE..................................203 879-5306
Scott Allen, *Managing Member*
EMP: 20 **EST:** 2000
SALES (est): 797.04K **Privately Held**
SIC: 3542 3965 3469   Brakes, metal forming ; Eyelets, metal: clothing, fabrics, boots, or shoes; Metal stampings, nec

(G-4366)
JAN MANUFACTURING CO
Also Called: Connecticut Cue Parts
14 Town Line Rd Ste 8 (06716-2635)
PHONE..................................203 879-0580
John Ciavarella Junior, *Pr*
EMP: 7 **EST:** 1978
SQ FT: 3,500
SALES (est): 562.78K **Privately Held**
Web: www.janmfg.com
SIC: 3599 7694   Machine shop, jobbing and repair; Coil winding service

(G-4367)
MAILLY MFG CO INC
54 Wakelee Rd (06716-2620)
P.O. Box 6143 (06716-0143)
PHONE..................................203 879-1445
John Mailly, *Pr*
Richard Mailly, *VP*
Janet Corden, *Sec*
EMP: 7 **EST:** 1945
SQ FT: 8,000
SALES (est): 625.82K **Privately Held**
Web: www.maillymfg.com
SIC: 3451   Screw machine products

(G-4368)
MILITE BAKERY
Also Called: Arturo Milite and Spinella Bky
26 Evers Dr (06716-2506)
PHONE..................................203 753-9451
Ralph Spinella, *Owner*
EMP: 8 **EST:** 1932
SALES (est): 504.74K **Privately Held**
SIC: 2051 5461   Bread, all types (white, wheat, rye, etc); fresh or frozen; Retail bakeries

(G-4369)
MUSANO INC
Also Called: Neslo Manufacturing
373 Woodtick Rd (06716-2824)
P.O. Box 6205 (06716-0205)
PHONE..................................203 879-4651
TOLL FREE: 800
Fred Musano Junior, *Pr*
Anthony Musano, *VP*
Patricia Musano, *Sec*
EMP: 24 **EST:** 1967
SQ FT: 10,000
SALES (est): 4.19MM **Privately Held**
Web: www.neslo.com
SIC: 1542 2542 3446   Commercial and office buildings, renovation and repair; Partitions for floor attachment, prefabricated: except wood; Architectural metalwork

(G-4370)
NATIONAL DIE COMPANY
64 Wolcott Rd (06716-2612)
P.O. Box 6281 (06716-0281)
PHONE..................................203 879-1408
John J Ernst, *CEO*
Paul Cote, *Pr*
EMP: 9 **EST:** 1945
SQ FT: 15,000
SALES (est): 1.66MM **Privately Held**
Web: www.nationaldieco.com
SIC: 3469   Stamping metal for the trade

(G-4371)
NUCAP US INC (DH)
238 Wolcott Rd (06716-2617)
PHONE..................................203 879-1423
David Weichenberg, *CEO*
▲ **EMP:** 30 **EST:** 1994
SQ FT: 56,000
SALES (est): 24.63MM
SALES (corp-wide): 95.03MM **Privately Held**
SIC: 3965 3452 3469 3714   Eyelets, metal: clothing, fabrics, boots, or shoes; Rivets, metal; Metal stampings, nec; Motor vehicle parts and accessories
HQ: Nucap Industries Inc
   3370 Pharmacy Ave
   Scarborough ON M1W 3
   416 494-1444

(G-4372)
P-A-R PRECISION INC
15 Town Line Rd (06716-2625)
P.O. Box 6127 (06716-0127)
PHONE..................................860 491-4181
Robert L Clement, *Pr*
Patrick Galvin, *
Alex Zambetti, *
EMP: 10 **EST:** 1973
SQ FT: 8,000
SALES (est): 459.6K **Privately Held**
Web: www.p-a-r.com
SIC: 3451 3541   Screw machine products; Machine tools, metal cutting type

(G-4373)
PRECISION METHODS INCORPORATED
Also Called: PMI
40 North St (06716-1332)
P.O. Box 6445 (06716-0445)
PHONE..................................203 879-1429
C Thomas Accuosti, *Pr*
Thomas D Accuosti, *VP*
EMP: 19 **EST:** 1971
SQ FT: 10,000
SALES (est): 2.41MM **Privately Held**
Web: www.precisionmethods.com

SIC: 3451   Screw machine products

(G-4374)
RICHARDS METAL PRODUCTS INC
14 Swiss Ln (06716-2622)
P.O. Box 6290 (06716-0290)
PHONE..................................203 879-2555
Christopher Cobb, *Pr*
EMP: 12 **EST:** 1965
SQ FT: 10,000
SALES (est): 2.44MM **Privately Held**
Web: www.richardsmetalproducts.com
SIC: 3469   Stamping metal for the trade

(G-4375)
SECONDARIES INC
15 Venus Dr (06716-2607)
PHONE..................................203 879-4633
Robert A Ferry, *Pr*
John A Karas, *VP*
EMP: 7 **EST:** 1962
SQ FT: 6,400
SALES (est): 798.32K **Privately Held**
Web: www.secondariesinc.com
SIC: 3599 3462   Machine shop, jobbing and repair; Flange, valve, and pipe fitting forgings, ferrous

(G-4376)
SELECTCOM MANUFACTURING CO INC
29 Nutmeg Valley Rd (06716-2621)
PHONE..................................203 879-9900
Brian Lanese, *Pr*
Arthur Lanese Junior, *VP*
Sheila Lanese, *Sec*
EMP: 7 **EST:** 1970
SQ FT: 7,500
SALES (est): 691.41K **Privately Held**
Web: www.selectcommfg.com
SIC: 3451   Screw machine products

(G-4377)
SEQUEL SPECIAL PRODUCTS LLC
Also Called: Nissha Medical Technologies
1 Hillside Dr (06716-2403)
PHONE..................................203 759-1020
EMP: 81 **EST:** 1994
SQ FT: 20,000
SALES (est): 9.56MM **Privately Held**
Web: dm.nisshamedical.com
SIC: 3841   Surgical and medical instruments

Woodbridge
New Haven County

(G-4378)
CLASSIC LABEL INC
10 Research Dr (06525-2347)
PHONE..................................203 389-3535
Louis Fantarella, *Pr*
Laura Fantarella, *Sec*
▲ **EMP:** 9 **EST:** 1988
SQ FT: 10,000
SALES (est): 1.68MM **Privately Held**
Web: www.classiclabel.net
SIC: 2752   Offset printing

(G-4379)
KOL LLC
12 Cassway Rd (06525-1215)
PHONE..................................203 393-2924
Christopher Neumann, *Managing Member*
Michael Toscani, *Dir*
EMP: 10 **EST:** 2004

SQ FT: 3,000
SALES (est): 156.8K **Privately Held**
Web: www.kolonline.com
SIC: 7372 Business oriented computer
  software

(G-4380)
LIFE CHEMICALS USA INC
26 Selden St Ste B (06525-2219)
PHONE..................................203 693-4563
Irina Chabanny, *Prin*
EMP: 7 **EST:** 2018
SALES (est): 174.03K **Privately Held**
SIC: 2834 Pharmaceutical preparations

(G-4381)
MANUFACTURERS SERVICE CO INC
Also Called: Air Handling Systems
5 Lunar Dr (06525-2320)
PHONE..................................203 389-9595
David Edward Scott, *Pr*
Patricia Scott, *Treas*
Jamison Scott, *VP*
▼ **EMP:** 8 **EST:** 1965
SQ FT: 12,800
SALES (est): 1.19MM **Privately Held**
Web: www.airhand.com
SIC: 3444 Ducts, sheet metal

(G-4382)
PLASTIC FORMING COMPANY INC (PA)
20 S Bradley Rd (06525-2330)
PHONE..................................203 397-1338
John Womer, *Pr*
Peter T Schurman, *
Gary Amatrudo, *
Mike Warth, *
▲ **EMP:** 25 **EST:** 1966
SQ FT: 60,000
SALES (est): 9.86MM
SALES (corp-wide): 9.86MM **Privately Held**
Web: www.pfccases.com
SIC: 3089 3086 Blow molded finished
  plastics products, nec; Plastics foam
  products

(G-4383)
TRANSATLANTIC BUBBLES LLC
935 Greenway Rd (06525-2412)
PHONE..................................203 464-0051
Michael Carleton, *Prin*
EMP: 7 **EST:** 2010
SALES (est): 200.03K **Privately Held**
Web: www.transatlanticbubbles.com
SIC: 2087 Beverage bases

Woodbury
Litchfield County

(G-4384)
A X M S INC
27 Woodside Cir (06798-1528)
PHONE..................................203 263-5046
Emilia Corey, *Pr*
▲ **EMP:** 7 **EST:** 2004
SALES (est): 382.73K **Privately Held**
Web: www.axms.com
SIC: 3199 Leather garments

(G-4385)
COGZ SYSTEMS LLC
58 Steeple View Ln (06798-3300)
PHONE..................................203 263-7882
Jay Ambrose, *Owner*
EMP: 10 **EST:** 1989

SALES (est): 773.66K **Privately Held**
Web: www.cogz.com
SIC: 3695 5961 Computer software tape
  and disks: blank, rigid, and floppy;
  Computer software, mail order

(G-4386)
COMPUWEIGH CORPORATION (PA)
50 Middle Quarter Rd (06798-3901)
PHONE..................................203 262-9400
Robin B Sax, *CEO*
Harold Ecke, *Pr*
EMP: 17 **EST:** 1984
SQ FT: 15,000
SALES (est): 6.52MM
SALES (corp-wide): 6.52MM **Privately Held**
Web: www.compuweigh.com
SIC: 7371 Computer software
  development; Industrial scales

(G-4387)
DUDA AND GOODWIN INCORPORATED
Also Called: Dg Precision Manufacturing
90 Washington Rd (06798-2804)
P.O. Box 349 (06798-0349)
PHONE..................................203 263-4353
David S Duda, *Pr*
Brian P Duda, *VP*
Peggy Nelson, *Mgr*
EMP: 10 **EST:** 1945
SQ FT: 8,000
SALES (est): 2.23MM **Privately Held**
Web: www.dgprecision.com
SIC: 3451 Screw machine products

(G-4388)
PROJECT GRAPHICS INC
Also Called: Project Graphics
41 Stone Pit Rd (06798-2717)
P.O. Box 370 (06798-0370)
PHONE..................................802 488-8789
Andrew Riecker, *Pr*
Andrew Riecker, *Pr*
Gregory Mckim, *VP*
▲ **EMP:** 23 **EST:** 1993
SQ FT: 19,000
SALES (est): 2.41MM **Privately Held**
Web: www.projectgraphics.com
SIC: 7336 2752 3993 2396 Graphic arts and
  related design; Commercial printing,
  lithographic; Signs and advertising
  specialties; Automotive and apparel
  trimmings

(G-4389)
WOODBURY PEWTERERS INC
860 Main St S (06798-3706)
P.O. Box 482 (06798-0482)
PHONE..................................203 263-2668
Paul Titcomb, *Pr*
Paul Titcomb, *Pr*
Linda Charbonneau, *
EMP: 32 **EST:** 1952
SQ FT: 10,000
SALES (est): 2.03MM **Privately Held**
Web: www.woodburypewter.com
SIC: 3914 Pewter ware

Woodstock
Windham County

(G-4390)
AARDVARK POLYMERS
Also Called: Gapolymer
73 Underwood Rd Ste 13 (06281-3518)

PHONE..................................609 483-1013
Mike Gehrig, *Owner*
EMP: 9 **EST:** 1983
SQ FT: 14,000
SALES (est): 567.76K **Privately Held**
SIC: 2822 Ethylene-propylene rubbers,
  EPDM polymers

(G-4391)
BROOKE TAYLOR FARM LLC (PA)
Also Called: Taylor Brooke Winery
848 Route 171 (06281-2930)
PHONE..................................860 974-1263
Linda Auger, *Managing Member*
EMP: 8 **EST:** 2002
SALES (est): 1.95MM
SALES (corp-wide): 1.95MM **Privately Held**
Web: www.taylorbrookewinery.com
SIC: 2084 Wines

(G-4392)
BRUNARHANS INC
263 Woodstock Rd (06281-1815)
P.O. Box 208 (06244-0208)
PHONE..................................860 928-0887
TOLL FREE: 800
Dennis Tucker, *Pr*
EMP: 9 **EST:** 1967
SQ FT: 18,000
SALES (est): 922.63K **Privately Held**
Web: www.brunarhans.com
SIC: 2434 Wood kitchen cabinets

(G-4393)
CRABTREE & EVELYN LTD (DH)
102 Peake Brook Rd (06281-3429)
PHONE..................................800 272-2873
Kevin J Coen, *Pr*
Colleen Creevy Cording, *Sec*
Karen Barlow, *Asst Tr*
Koh Han Seow, *Treas*
◆ **EMP:** 250 **EST:** 1975
SQ FT: 80,000
SALES (est): 299.37MM **Privately Held**
Web: www.crabtree-evelyn.com
SIC: 5122 5149 2844 Toilet soap; Pickles,
  preserves, jellies, and jams; Perfumes,
  cosmetics and other toilet preparations
HQ: Crabtree Evelyn Investment (Hk)
  Limited
  12/F The Octagon
  Tsuen Wan NT

(G-4394)
FOCUS FABRICATION LLC
76 Pole Bridge Rd (06281-1223)
PHONE..................................860 604-8018
Dennis Defocy, *Prin*
EMP: 8 **EST:** 2018
SALES (est): 230.38K **Privately Held**
Web: www.focusfabrication.com
SIC: 3441 Fabricated structural metal

(G-4395)
LINEMASTER SWITCH CORPORATION
29 Plaine Hill Rd (06281-2913)
P.O. Box 238 (06281-0238)
PHONE..................................860 630-4920
Joseph J Carlone, *CEO*
Joseph J Carlone Junior, *Pr*
Marilyn J Mancini, *
▲ **EMP:** 160 **EST:** 1952
SQ FT: 55,000
SALES (est): 47.75MM **Privately Held**
Web: www.linemaster.com
SIC: 3625 Switches, electric power

(G-4396)
ROGERS CORPORATION
Elastomeric Mtl Solution Div
245 Woodstock Rd (06281-1815)
P.O. Box 188 (06281-0188)
PHONE..................................860 928-3622
Peter Kaczmarek, *Sr VP*
EMP: 103
SALES (corp-wide): 971.17MM **Publicly Held**
Web: www.rogerscorp.com
SIC: 2821 Plastics materials and resins
PA: Rogers Corporation
  2225 W Chandler Blvd
  Chandler AZ 85224
  480 917-6000

Yalesville
New Haven County

(G-4397)
G & G BEVERAGE DISTRIBUTORS
Also Called: G & G Recycling Center
207 Church St (06492-6202)
P.O. Box 4488 (06492-7565)
PHONE..................................203 949-6220
Mark Gingras, *Pr*
Chris Gingras, *
▲ **EMP:** 31 **EST:** 1976
SQ FT: 54,000
SALES (est): 20.46MM **Privately Held**
Web: www.ggbeverage.com
SIC: 5181 5149 4953 2086 Beer and other
  fermented malt liquors; Soft drinks;
  Recycling, waste materials; Bottled and
  canned soft drinks

(G-4398)
JOVAL MACHINE CO INC
Also Called: Pac Products
515 Main St (06492-1736)
PHONE..................................203 284-0082
Gerald A Chase, *Pr*
Joyce Chase, *
Jeffrey Chase, *
EMP: 25 **EST:** 1964
SQ FT: 25,000
SALES (est): 2.73MM **Privately Held**
Web: www.jovalmachine.com
SIC: 3599 Machine shop, jobbing and repair

(G-4399)
UNITED CONCRETE PRODUCTS INC
173 Church St (06492-2267)
PHONE..................................203 269-3119
EMP: 175 **EST:** 1953
SALES (est): 25.26MM **Privately Held**
Web: www.unitedconcrete.com
SIC: 3272 Concrete products, precast, nec

MAINE

Albany Twp
Oxford County

(G-4400)
CITIZEN PRINTERS INCORPORATED
Also Called: Bethel Citizen
19 Crooked River Cswy (04217-6300)
P.O. Box 109 (04217-0109)
PHONE..................................207 824-2444
Edward Snook, *Pr*
Michael Daniels, *Mgr*

EMP: 7 EST: 1927
SQ FT: 4,900
SALES (est): 510.27K **Privately Held**
Web: www.sunjournal.com
SIC: 2711 Newspapers, publishing and printing

Albion
Kennebec County

(G-4401)
UNIQUE SPIRAL STAIRS INC
Also Called: Xander Performance
117 Benton Rd (04910-6164)
PHONE.............................207 437-2415
▼ **EMP: 8 EST:** 1996
SQ FT: 6,000
SALES (est): 859.24K **Privately Held**
Web: www.uniquespiralstairs.com
SIC: 2431 Staircases and stairs, wood

Alfred
York County

(G-4402)
ALFREDS UPHLSTRING CSTM FBRCTI
Also Called: Alfred's Upholstrey and Co.
181 Waterboro Rd (04002-3236)
P.O. Box 1065 (04002-1065)
PHONE.............................207 536-5565
EMP: 12 EST: 2010
SQ FT: 8,000
SALES (est): 911.23K **Privately Held**
Web: www.alfredsupholstery.com
SIC: 2512 2431 2211 Upholstered household furniture; Interior and ornamental woodwork and trim; Upholstery fabrics, cotton

(G-4403)
NEW ENGLAND STL FBRICATORS INC
342 Jordan Springs Rd (04002-3532)
PHONE.............................207 324-1846
Jason M Payeur, *Prin*
EMP: 10 EST: 2019
SALES (est): 985.68K **Privately Held**
Web:
www.newenglandsteelfabricators.com
SIC: 3441 Fabricated structural metal

Allagash
Aroostook County

(G-4404)
SYL-VER LOGGING INC
206 Allagash Rd (04774-4014)
PHONE.............................207 398-3158
Sylvia Pelletier, *Owner*
EMP: 7 EST: 2004
SALES (est): 205.1K **Privately Held**
SIC: 2411 Logging camps and contractors

Alna
Lincoln County

(G-4405)
PORT-LITE LLC
957 Alna Rd (04535-3809)
PHONE.............................678 575-9065
Christopher Audy, *Asst Sec*
Claudine Audy, *Ex Sec*
EMP: 9 EST: 2017

SALES (est): 316.52K **Privately Held**
Web: www.port-lite.com
SIC: 3792 Campers, for mounting on trucks

Appleton
Knox County

(G-4406)
TRANZTAPE LLC
317 Town Hill Rd (04862-6630)
PHONE.............................207 785-2467
EMP: 8 EST: 2017
SALES (est): 1.87MM **Privately Held**
SIC: 2396 7389 Bindings, bias: made from purchased materials; Business services, nec

Arundel
York County

(G-4407)
ALIGN PRECISION - ARUNDEL LLC
20 Technology Dr (04046-7979)
PHONE.............................207 985-8555
Mark Cherry, *CEO*
Marcel Bertrand, *
Timothy Smith, *
EMP: 110 EST: 2019
SALES (est): 24.84MM
SALES (corp-wide): 1.83B **Privately Held**
SIC: 3599 Machine and other job shop work
HQ: Align Precision Corp.
730 W 22nd St
Tempe AZ 85282
480 968-1778

(G-4408)
ARUNDEL HOLDINGS INC
20 Technology Dr (04046-7979)
PHONE.............................207 985-8555
Marcel Bertrand, *Prin*
Marcel Bertrand, *Pr*
Ray Bertrand, *
EMP: 90 EST: 1984
SQ FT: 30,000
SALES (est): 8.38MM **Privately Held**
Web: www.arundelmachine.com
SIC: 3599 3451 3812 3795 Machine shop, jobbing and repair; Screw machine products ; Missile guidance systems and equipment; Amphibian tanks, military

(G-4409)
C B P CORP (PA)
Also Called: Port Canvas Company
39 Limerick Rd Unit 2 (04046-8158)
PHONE.............................207 985-9767
Margot L Thompson, *Pr*
Ned Thompson, *Pr*
EMP: 10 EST: 1989
SQ FT: 3,200
SALES (est): 1.17MM
SALES (corp-wide): 1.17MM **Privately Held**
SIC: 2211 3161 2394 2393 Canvas; Luggage; Canvas and related products; Textile bags

(G-4410)
LANK MACHINING CO LLC
113 Mountain Rd (04046-8330)
PHONE.............................207 286-9549
EMP: 7 EST: 1987
SQ FT: 6,000
SALES (est): 661.34K **Privately Held**
Web: www.lankmachining.com

SIC: 3599 Machine shop, jobbing and repair

Ashland
Aroostook County

(G-4411)
MOOSEWOOD MILLWORKS LLC
42 American Realty Rd. (04732)
PHONE.............................207 435-4950
John Mcnulty, *Managing Member*
EMP: 8 EST: 2012
SALES (est): 259.84K
SALES (corp-wide): 7.79MM **Privately Held**
SIC: 2426 Flooring, hardwood
HQ: Seven Islands Land Company
112 Broadway
Bangor ME 04401
207 947-0541

(G-4412)
NORTHEAST PELLETS LLC
53 Realty Rd (04732-3101)
P.O. Box 19 (04732-0019)
PHONE.............................207 435-6230
EMP: 13 EST: 2005
SQ FT: 10,000
SALES (est): 1.28MM **Privately Held**
Web: www.northeastpellets.net
SIC: 3532 Pellet mills (mining machinery)

(G-4413)
PERLEYS LOGGING INC
150 Rafford Rd (04732)
P.O. Box 791 (04732-0791)
PHONE.............................207 227-0513
Gayle Burby, *Prin*
EMP: 9 EST: 2010
SALES (est): 297.82K **Privately Held**
SIC: 2411 Logging camps and contractors

Athens
Somerset County

(G-4414)
LINKLETTER & SONS INC
115 Harmony Rd (04912-4629)
P.O. Box 135 (04912-0135)
PHONE.............................207 654-2301
Richard Linkletter, *Pr*
Robert Linkletter, *
Sandra Linkletter, *
Bruce Linkletter, *
EMP: 21 EST: 1961
SALES (est): 824.02K **Privately Held**
SIC: 2421 Wood chips, produced at mill

(G-4415)
MAINE WOODS PELLET COMPANY LLC
164 Harmony Rd (04912-4631)
PHONE.............................207 654-2237
George Rybarczyk, *Managing Member*
Robert Linkletter, *Managing Member**
▲ **EMP: 47 EST:** 2006
SALES (est): 6.79MM **Privately Held**
Web: www.mwpellet.com
SIC: 2499 Laundry products, wood

Auburn
Androscoggin County

(G-4416)
AC ELECTRIC CORP (PA)
Also Called: AC

120 Merrow Rd (04210-8896)
P.O. Box 1508 (04211-1508)
PHONE.............................207 784-7341
Dan Parsons, *Pr*
Marcia Clark, *
▲ **EMP: 27 EST:** 1994
SQ FT: 17,000
SALES (est): 9.11MM
SALES (corp-wide): 9.11MM **Privately Held**
Web: www.acelec.com
SIC: 7694 5063 7629 Rebuilding motors, except automotive; Motors, electric; Circuit board repair

(G-4417)
AFFORDABLE EXHIBIT DISPLAYS
142 Turner St (04210-5956)
PHONE.............................207 782-6175
EMP: 10 EST: 2012
SALES (est): 746.24K **Privately Held**
Web: www.affordabledisplays.com
SIC: 3993 Signs and advertising specialties

(G-4418)
AMERICAN CONCRETE INDS INC (PA)
982 Minot Ave (04210-3719)
PHONE.............................207 947-8334
TOLL FREE: 800
Shawn Macdonald, *Pr*
Kimberly Macdonald, *Treas*
EMP: 20 EST: 1951
SQ FT: 82,000
Web: www.americanconcrete.com
SIC: 3272 Concrete products, precast, nec

(G-4419)
ANGOSTURA INTERNATIONAL LTD
176 First Flight Dr (04210-9055)
PHONE.............................207 786-3200
Steve Angostura, *Pr*
▲ **EMP: 11 EST:** 2005
SALES (est): 529.78K **Privately Held**
Web: www.angostura.com
SIC: 2013 Sausages and related products, from purchased meat

(G-4420)
ANGSTROM FIBER AUBURN LLC ✪
125 Allied Rd (04210-7985)
PHONE.............................734 756-1164
Nagesh K Palakurthi, *Managing Member*
EMP: 80 EST: 2022
SALES (est): 18.58MM
SALES (corp-wide): 39.93MM **Privately Held**
SIC: 3714 Motor vehicle body components and frame
PA: Angstrom 2021 Holdings, Llc
2000 Town Ctr Ste 1100
Southfield MI 48075
313 295-0100

(G-4421)
AUBURN ASPHALT LLC
3189 Hotel Rd (04210)
PHONE.............................207 894-5040
EMP: 11 EST: 2015
SALES (est): 48.02K **Privately Held**
Web: www.asmg.com
SIC: 3999 Manufacturing industries, nec

GEOGRAPHIC

(G-4422)
AUBURN SPRING WATER COMPANY (PA)
24 Brickyard Cir (04210-4853)
P.O. Box 1450 (04211-1450)
PHONE............................207 782-1521
TOLL FREE: 800
Peter Bornstein, *Pr*
Richard Bornstein, *Treas*
Derek Laliberta, *Genl Mgr*
EMP: 8 **EST:** 1986
SQ FT: 10,000
SALES (est): 1.85MM
SALES (corp-wide): 1.85MM **Privately Held**
Web: www.crystalspringwaterco.com
SIC: 2086 5499 Pasteurized and mineral waters, bottled and canned; Soft drinks

(G-4423)
CASCADES AUBURN FIBER INC
586 Lewiston Junction Rd (04210-8847)
PHONE............................207 753-5300
Paul Deraich, *Prin*
EMP: 40 **EST:** 1998
SALES (est): 11.15MM
SALES (corp-wide): 3.32B **Privately Held**
SIC: 2621 8711 Paper mills; Engineering services
PA: Cascades Inc
　　404 Boul Marie-Victorin
　　Kingsey Falls QC J0A 1
　　819 363-5100

(G-4424)
CONFORM AUTOMOTIVE LLC
Also Called: Conform Automotive
125 Allied Rd (04210-7985)
P.O. Box 1300 (04211-1300)
PHONE..............................207 784-1118
Steven Philips, *Prin*
EMP: 384
Web: www.conformgroup.com
SIC: 2823 2824 3089 Cellulosic manmade fibers; Polyester fibers; Fiber, vulcanized
PA: Conform Automotive, Llc
　　32500 Telg Rd Ste 207
　　Bingham Farms MI 48025

(G-4425)
CRESCENT INDUSTRIES COMPANY
191 Washington St S (04210-4821)
PHONE............................207 777-3500
Rex Bradbury, *Pr*
EMP: 8 **EST:** 1976
SQ FT: 3,500
SALES (est): 979.1K **Privately Held**
Web: www.crescentindustries.com
SIC: 3714 Motor vehicle electrical equipment

(G-4426)
DESIGN FAB INC
928 Minot Ave (04210-3719)
PHONE............................207 786-2446
Leo Roche, *Pr*
EMP: 14 **EST:** 2012
SALES (est): 207.56K **Privately Held**
Web: www.newfabinc.com
SIC: 3441 Fabricated structural metal

(G-4427)
DUNKIN DONUTS (PA)
360 Center St (04210-6115)
PHONE............................207 783-0408
EMP: 23 **EST:** 1984
SQ FT: 2,200
SALES (est): 3.14MM **Privately Held**
Web: www.dunkindonuts.com

SIC: 5461 2051 Doughnuts; Doughnuts, except frozen

(G-4428)
ENEFCO INTERNATIONAL INC (PA)
Also Called: Globaldie
1130 Minot Ave (04210-3739)
P.O. Box 1120 (04211-1120)
PHONE............................207 514-7218
Peter Klein, *Pr*
Marc Fontaine, *
Timothy Smith, *
▲ **EMP:** 40 **EST:** 2003
SQ FT: 78,000
SALES (est): 17.89MM
SALES (corp-wide): 17.89MM **Privately Held**
Web: www.enefco.com
SIC: 3131 7389 5999 5719 Footwear cut stock; Textile and apparel services; Toiletries, cosmetics, and perfumes; Bath accessories

(G-4429)
ENERCON
234 First Flight Dr (04210-9056)
P.O. Box 665 (04039-0665)
PHONE............................207 657-7001
Roger Wincox, *Brnch Mgr*
EMP: 24
SALES (corp-wide): 102.95MM **Privately Held**
Web: www.enercontechnologies.com
SIC: 3672 5063 Printed circuit boards; Electrical apparatus and equipment
HQ: Enercon
　　25 Northbrook Dr
　　Gray ME 04039
　　207 657-7000

(G-4430)
EVERGREEN CUSTOM PRINTING INC
63 Broad St (04210-6814)
P.O. Box 755 (04212-0755)
PHONE............................207 782-2327
Donald Cote, *Pr*
Laurie Hickot Production, *Asstg*
EMP: 8 **EST:** 1984
SQ FT: 3,000
SALES (est): 700.1K **Privately Held**
Web: www.evergreencustomprinting.com
SIC: 2752 2759 Offset printing; Invitation and stationery printing and engraving

(G-4431)
FALCON PERFORMANCE FTWR LLC
27 Wrights Lndg (04210-8308)
PHONE............................207 784-9186
▲ **EMP:** 9 **EST:** 2007
SALES (est): 340.15K **Privately Held**
SIC: 3143 Men's footwear, except athletic

(G-4432)
FLUE GAS SOLUTIONS INC
3161 Hotel Rd (04210-8398)
PHONE............................207 893-1510
Bruce Harlow, *Pr*
EMP: 8 **EST:** 2007
SQ FT: 160,000
SALES (est): 861.03K **Privately Held**
Web: www.opennetme.com
SIC: 3494 Expansion joints, pipe

(G-4433)
FORMED FIBER TECHNOLOGIES INC

Also Called: Conform Automotive
125 Allied Rd (04210-7985)
P.O. Box 1300 (04211-1300)
PHONE............................207 784-1118
▲ **EMP:** 900
SIC: 2824 3089 2823 Polyester fibers; Fiber, vulcanized; Cellulosic manmade fibers

(G-4434)
FUTUREGUARD BUILDING PDTS INC (PA)
Also Called: Nuimage Awnings
101 Merrow Rd (04210-8319)
P.O. Box 2030 (04211-2030)
PHONE............................800 858-5818
◆ **EMP:** 48 **EST:** 1996
SQ FT: 163,000
SALES (est): 24.18MM **Privately Held**
Web: www.futureguard.net
SIC: 3444 3479 Awnings and canopies; Etching and engraving

(G-4435)
GAGNE & SON CON BLOCKS INC
270 Riverside Dr (04210-9629)
PHONE............................207 495-3313
TOLL FREE: 800
George Allen, *Mgr*
EMP: 7
SALES (corp-wide): 9.83MM **Privately Held**
Web: www.gagneandson.com
SIC: 3271 5211 5039 3444 Blocks, concrete or cinder: standard; Masonry materials and supplies; Septic tanks; Concrete forms, sheet metal
PA: Gagne & Son Concrete Blocks, Inc.
　　28 Old Rte 27 Rd
　　Belgrade ME 04917
　　207 495-3313

(G-4436)
GENERAL ELECTRIC COMPANY
Also Called: GE
135 Rodman Rd (04210-3831)
PHONE............................207 786-5100
Fletch Rickman, *Mgr*
EMP: 155
SALES (corp-wide): 76.56B **Publicly Held**
Web: www.ge.com
SIC: 3613 3643 Power circuit breakers; Current-carrying wiring services
PA: General Electric Company
　　1 Financial Ctr Ste 3700
　　Boston MA 02111
　　617 443-3000

(G-4437)
GLOBE FOOTWEAR LLC (HQ)
27 Wrights Lndg (04210-8308)
PHONE............................207 784-9186
Tom Vetras, *Pr*
◆ **EMP:** 51 **EST:** 2006
SALES (est): 15.28MM
SALES (corp-wide): 1.53B **Publicly Held**
SIC: 3842 Suits, firefighting (asbestos)
PA: Msa Safety Incorporated
　　1000 Cranberry Woods Dr
　　Cranberry Township PA 16066
　　724 776-8600

(G-4438)
INTERNATIONAL PAPER COMPANY
Also Called: International Paper
175 Allied Rd (04210-7985)
P.O. Box 238 (04212-0238)

PHONE............................207 784-4051
Bob Ritter, *Mgr*
EMP: 130
SALES (corp-wide): 21.16B **Publicly Held**
Web: www.internationalpaper.com
SIC: 2621 Paper mills
PA: International Paper Company
　　6400 Poplar Ave
　　Memphis TN 38197
　　901 419-7000

(G-4439)
LAPOINT INDUSTRIES INC (PA)
65 First Flight Dr (04210-9049)
P.O. Box 1970 (04211-1970)
PHONE............................207 777-3100
Alan Lapoint, *Pr*
EMP: 80 **EST:** 1998
SQ FT: 820,000
SALES (est): 25.25MM
SALES (corp-wide): 25.25MM **Privately Held**
Web: www.strainrite.com
SIC: 3569 2393 2655 5085 Filters, general line: industrial; Bags and containers, except sleeping bags: textile; Containers, liquid tight fiber: from purchased material; Filters, industrial

(G-4440)
LEPAGE BAKERIES INC
Also Called: Country Kitchen
11 Adamian Dr (04210-8304)
P.O. Box 1900 (04211-1900)
PHONE............................207 783-9161
EMP: 525
SIC: 2051 5461 Bread, cake, and related products; Retail bakeries

(G-4441)
LEPAGE BAKERIES PARK ST LLC
Also Called: Green Mountain Baking Co
11 Adamian Dr (04210-8304)
PHONE............................207 783-9161
EMP: 19
SALES (corp-wide): 4.81B **Publicly Held**
SIC: 2051 5461 Bakery: wholesale or wholesale/retail combined; Retail bakeries
HQ: Lepage Bakeries Park Street Llc
　　415 Lisbon St 4
　　Lewiston ME 04240
　　207 783-9161

(G-4442)
MAINE METAL RECYCLING INC
Also Called: Krushco
522 Washington St N (04210-3856)
P.O. Box 1478 (04211-1478)
PHONE............................207 786-3531
TOLL FREE: 800
David A Murphy, *Pr*
EMP: 18 **EST:** 1952
SQ FT: 30,000
SALES (est): 2.22MM
SALES (corp-wide): 2.88B **Publicly Held**
SIC: 5093 3341 Junk and scrap; Secondary nonferrous metals
PA: Schnitzer Steel Industries, Inc.
　　299 Sw Clay St Ste 400
　　Portland OR 97201
　　503 224-9900

(G-4443)
MAINE SCALE LLC
Also Called: Mainecal
4 Washington St N Ste 1 (04210-4859)
PHONE............................207 777-9500
EMP: 10 **EST:** 2013
SALES (est): 597.14K **Privately Held**

Web: www.mainescale.me
SIC: **3545** Scales, measuring (machinists'
precision tools)

(G-4444)
METAL SPECIALTIES INC
300 Rodman Rd (04210-3898)
PHONE............................207 786-4268
Mark Hodsdon, *Pr*
Irving Isaacson, *Clerk*
EMP: 20 **EST:** 1968
SQ FT: 13,000
SALES (est): 432.52K **Privately Held**
Web: www.colmet.com
SIC: **3599** Machine shop, jobbing and repair

(G-4445)
MIZKAN AMERICAS INC
176 First Flight Dr (04210-9055)
PHONE............................207 786-3200
Michael J Quinlan, *Pr*
EMP: 49 **EST:** 2010
SALES (est): 3.49MM **Privately Held**
Web: www.mizkan.com
SIC: **2099** Food preparations, nec

(G-4446)
MOUNTAIN MACHINE WORKS
Also Called: Mountain Fluid Power
2589 Hotel Rd (04210-8822)
PHONE............................207 783-6680
TOLL FREE: 800
Bruce R Tisdale, *Pr*
Charles Gillis, *
Rebecca Cote, *
Scott Pelchat, *
EMP: 24 **EST:** 1982
SQ FT: 5,500
SALES (est): 4.71MM **Privately Held**
Web: www.mountainmachineworks.com
SIC: **3599** Machine shop, jobbing and repair

(G-4447)
MS AMBROGIO NORTH AMERICA LLC
135 Rodman Rd (04210-3831)
PHONE............................832 834-3641
EMP: 29 **EST:** 2021
SALES (est): 23MM **Privately Held**
Web:
msambrogionorthamericallc.easyapply.co
SIC: **3714** Motor vehicle engines and parts
HQ: M.S. Ambrogio Spa
Via Tre Fontane 20
Cisano Bergamasco BG 24034

(G-4448)
NORTH E WLDG & FABRICATION INC
Also Called: Newfab
928 Minot Ave (04210-3719)
PHONE............................207 786-2446
Leo Roche, *Pr*
Leon V White, *
EMP: 25 **EST:** 1977
SQ FT: 29,400
SALES (est): 4.18MM **Privately Held**
Web: www.newfabinc.com
SIC: **7692** 3441 3531 3444 Welding repair;
Fabricated structural metal; Construction
machinery; Sheet metalwork

(G-4449)
PACKGEN INC
Also Called: Packgen
160 Cascades Dr (04210-7830)
P.O. Box 1970 (04211-1970)
PHONE............................207 784-4195
John H Lapoint Iii, *Pr*

◆ **EMP:** 30 **EST:** 1978
SQ FT: 86,000
SALES (est): 7.51MM **Privately Held**
Web: www.packgen.com
SIC: **7389** 3089 Packaging and labeling
services; Boxes, plastics

(G-4450)
PAINE PRODUCTS INC
Also Called: Paine Incense Co
17 Sunset Ave (04210-4127)
P.O. Box 1056 (04211-1056)
PHONE............................207 782-0931
Ann Loomis, *Pr*
John Vigue, *VP*
David Vigue, *Treas*
▲ **EMP:** 19 **EST:** 1931
SQ FT: 10,000
SALES (est): 884.56K **Privately Held**
Web: www.burnonlythegoodstuff.com
SIC: **2899** Incense

(G-4451)
PANOLAM SURFACE SYSTEMS
1 Pionite Rd (04210-3800)
PHONE............................203 925-1556
EMP: 18 **EST:** 2018
SALES (est): 800.95K **Privately Held**
Web: www.panolam.com
SIC: **3089** Plastics products, nec

(G-4452)
PEPSI-COLA METRO BTLG CO INC
Also Called: Pepsi-Cola
191 Merrow Rd (04210-8319)
P.O. Box 1090 (04211-1090)
PHONE............................207 784-5791
Brian Garrison, *Brnch Mgr*
EMP: 46
SALES (corp-wide): 86.39B **Publicly Held**
Web: www.pepsico.com
SIC: **2086** Soft drinks: packaged in cans,
bottles, etc.
HQ: Pepsi-Cola Metropolitan Bottling
Company, Inc.
700 Anderson Hill Rd
Purchase NY 10577
914 767-6000

(G-4453)
PERFORMANCE PRODUCTS PAINTING
63 Omni Cir (04210-8310)
P.O. Box 2030 (04211-2030)
PHONE............................207 783-4222
David Sullivan, *Pr*
Paul Lavoie, *Sec*
EMP: 20 **EST:** 1987
SQ FT: 20,000
SALES (est): 2.51MM **Privately Held**
SIC: **3479** Painting of metal products
PA: Futureguard Building Products, Inc.
101 Merrow Rd
Auburn ME 04210

(G-4454)
PIONEER PLASTICS CORPORATION
Also Called: Pioneer Plastics
1 Pionite Rd (04210-3840)
PHONE............................207 784-9111
Pete Roseno, *Mgr*
EMP: 200
Web: www.pioneerplastics.com
SIC: **3083** 3087 Laminated plastics plate
and sheet; Custom compound purchased
resins
HQ: Pioneer Plastics Corporation
2 Corporate Dr Ste 946

Shelton CT 06484
203 925-1556

(G-4455)
PRE-HUNG DOORS INC
353 Riverside Dr (C4210-9704)
PHONE............................207 783-3881
James F Murphy, *Pr*
James Jim F Murphy, *Pr*
Norman Rattey Clrk, *Prin*
Whitney Drake, *Stockholder*
EMP: 15 **EST:** 1987
SQ FT: 35,000
SALES (est): 2.32MM **Privately Held**
SIC: **5211** 5031 2431 Doors, storm: wood or
metal; Doors, nec; Millwork

(G-4456)
PROCTER & GAMBLE COMPANY
Also Called: Procter & Gamble
2879 Hotel Rd (04210-8823)
PHONE............................207 753-4000
Mike Caron, *Brnch Mgr*
EMP: 150
SALES (corp-wide): 82.01B **Publicly Held**
Web: us.pg.com
SIC: **2844** Deodorants, personal
PA: The Procter & Gamble Company
1 Procter And Gamble Plz
Cincinnati OH 45202
513 983-1100

(G-4457)
R A CUMMINGS INC
Also Called: Auburn Concrete
82 Goldthwaite Rd (04210-3812)
P.O. Box 1747 (04211-1747)
PHONE............................207 777-7100
Rodney Cummings, *Pr*
Joel Cummings, *VP*
Lori Cummings, *VP*
EMP: 20 **EST:** 1972
SQ FT: 3,000
SALES (est): 3.37MM **Privately Held**
Web: www.auburnconcrete.com
SIC: **3273** Ready-mixed concrete

(G-4458)
REGGIES SALES & SERVICE
1334 Minot Ave (04210-3724)
PHONE............................207 783-0558
Reginald Emery Junior, *Pr*
Cathy Emery, *VP*
EMP: 7 **EST:** 1989
SALES (est): 593.7K **Privately Held**
Web: www.reggiessales.com
SIC: **7699** 5999 5261 3546 Engine repair
and replacement, non-automotive; Engine
and motor equipment and supplies; Retail
nurseries and garden stores; Saws and
sawing equipment

(G-4459)
RJF - MORIN BRICK LLC
Also Called: La Chance Brick
130 Morin Brick Rd (04210)
PHONE............................207 784-9375
Norman Davis, *Pr*
▲ **EMP:** 89 **EST:** 1934
SQ FT: 44,000
SALES (est): 8.52MM **Privately Held**
Web: www.morinbrick.com
SIC: **3271** 5032 3251 5211 Brick, concrete;
Masons' materials; Brick and structural clay
tile; Masonry materials and supplies

(G-4460)
SEASMOKE EXTRACTS INC
230 Merrow Rd (04210-8896)
PHONE............................207 819-4114

Scott Howard Opts, *Mgr*
EMP: 12 **EST:** 2018
SALES (est): 553.18K **Privately Held**
SIC: **2833** Medicinal chemicals

(G-4461)
TRI STATE STEEL INC
24 Chasse St (04210-3842)
P.O. Box 1207 (04211-1207)
PHONE............................207 784-9371
TOLL FREE: 800
Frank V Hiltz Iii, *Pr*
EMP: 9 **EST:** 1974
SQ FT: 12,500
SALES (est): 753.08K **Privately Held**
Web: www.tssteelmaine.com
SIC: **3441** Fabricated structural metal

(G-4462)
TWIN CITY TIMES
64 Jennifer Dr (04210-9057)
PHONE............................207 795-5017
Peter A Steele, *Owner*
EMP: 7 **EST:** 2005
SALES (est): 513.69K **Privately Held**
Web: www.twincitytimes.com
SIC: **2711** Newspapers: publishing only, not
printed on site

(G-4463)
UNITED FBRCNTS STRAINRITE CORP (HQ)
Also Called: Strainrite
65 First Flight Dr (04210-9049)
P.O. Box 1970 (04211-1970)
PHONE............................207 376-1600
Alan Lapoint, *Pr*
Alan Roberts, *Mgr*
David M Thompson, *Mgr*
Janet Allen, *Mgr*
John Reid, *Mgr*
▲ **EMP:** 75 **EST:** 1978
SQ FT: 82,000
SALES (est): 24.62MM
SALES (corp-wide): 25.25MM **Privately Held**
Web: www.strainrite.com
SIC: **3569** 5078 Filters, general line:
industrial; Drinking water coolers,
mechanical
PA: Lapoint Industries, Inc.
65 First Flight Dr
Auburn ME 04210
207 777-3100

(G-4464)
WORLD HARBORS LLC
176 First Flight Dr (04210-9055)
P.O. Box 1405 (04039-1405)
PHONE............................207 786-3200
EMP: 109 **EST:** 2021
SALES (est): 1.24MM
SALES (corp-wide): 3.46MM **Privately Held**
Web: www.worldharbors.com
SIC: **2035** Dressings, salad: raw and
cooked (except dry mixes)
PA: Kitchen Partners Llc
176 First Flight Dr
Auburn ME 04210
207 786-3200

(G-4465)
ZAMPELL REFRACTORIES INC
192 First Flight Dr (04210-9055)
PHONE............................207 786-2400
Sean Case, *Mgr*
EMP: 18
SALES (corp-wide): 45.44MM **Privately Held**

Web: www.zampell.com
SIC: 3255 1742 Tile and brick refractories, except plastic; Insulation, buildings
PA: Zampell Refractories, Inc.
9 Stanley Tucker Dr
Newburyport MA 01950
978 465-0055

Augusta
Kennebec County

(G-4466)
ADVANCED INDUS SOLUTIONS INC (PA)
Also Called: Custom Cordage, LLC
36 Anthony Ave (04330-7891)
PHONE.........................207 623-9599
EMP: 11 **EST:** 2009
SALES (est): 2.26MM **Privately Held**
Web: www.aisinc.me
SIC: 7389 3423 Design services; Cutting dies, except metal cutting

(G-4467)
ARTCO OFFSET INC
15 Darin Dr (04330-7815)
PHONE.........................781 830-7900
Daniel L Bauman, *Pr*
EMP: 41 **EST:** 1973
SALES (est): 740K **Privately Held**
Web: www.jsmccarthy.com
SIC: 2752 Offset printing

(G-4468)
CHANGE HLTHCARE PHRM SLTONS IN
Also Called: Ghs Data Management
45 Commerce Dr Ste 5 (04330-7889)
P.O. Box 1090 (04332-1090)
PHONE.........................207 622-7153
James Clair, *CEO*
Victoria Mulkern, *
John Grotton, *Executive Pharm Vice President*
William G Waldron Junior, *Ch Bd*
Dan Hardin, *
EMP: 82 **EST:** 2013
SQ FT: 28,000
SALES (est): 10.56MM
SALES (corp-wide): 324.16B **Publicly Held**
SIC: 8742 7372 Hospital and health services consultant; Prepackaged software
HQ: Change Healthcare Solutions, Llc
424 Church St Ste 1400
Nashville TN 37219

(G-4469)
CIVES CORPORATION
Also Called: Cives Steel
103 Lipman Rd (04330-8322)
P.O. Box 1077 (04332-1077)
PHONE.........................207 622-6141
Lawrence J Morgan, *Pr*
EMP: 140
SALES (corp-wide): 562.61MM **Privately Held**
Web: www.vikingcives.com
SIC: 3441 3446 Fabricated structural metal; Architectural metalwork
PA: Cives Corporation
3700 Mansell Rd Ste 500
Alpharetta GA 30022
770 993-4424

(G-4470)
CPK MANUFACTURING LLC
Also Called: Kenway Composites

681 Riverside Dr (04330-8300)
PHONE.........................207 622-6229
Ian Kopp, *Brnch Mgr*
EMP: 35
SALES (corp-wide): 881.42MM **Privately Held**
Web: www.creativecompositesgroup.com
SIC: 3089 Hardware, plastics
HQ: Cpk Manufacturing, Llc
214 Industrial Ln
Alum Bank PA 15521
814 839-4186

(G-4471)
ELECTRNIC MOBILITY CONTRLS LLC
Also Called: EMC
26 Gabriel Dr (04330-7853)
PHONE.........................207 512-8009
Scott Bolduc, *Owner*
EMP: 14 **EST:** 1992
SQ FT: 12,000
SALES (est): 2.29MM **Privately Held**
Web: www.electronicmobilitycontrols.com
SIC: 3714 3845 3625 Motor vehicle parts and accessories; Electromedical equipment ; Relays and industrial controls

(G-4472)
HARVEY INDUSTRIES INC
Also Called: Harvey Building Products
80 Anthony Ave (04330-7882)
PHONE.........................207 629-3737
EMP: 10
SALES (corp-wide): 1.2B **Privately Held**
Web: www.harveybp.com
SIC: 5031 5033 3442 2431 Windows; Roofing, asphalt and sheet metal; Storm doors or windows, metal; Windows, wood
PA: Harvey Industries, Llc
1400 Main St Fl 3
Waltham MA 02451
800 598-5400

(G-4473)
JS MCCARTHY CO INC (PA)
Also Called: J.S. McCarthy Printers
15 Darin Dr (04330-7815)
PHONE.........................207 622-6241
TOLL FREE: 888
Jonathan Tardiff, *Pr*
Conrad Ayott, *
Bill White, *
EMP: 100 **EST:** 1960
SQ FT: 90,000
SALES (est): 21.88MM
SALES (corp-wide): 21.88MM **Privately Held**
Web: www.jsmccarthy.com
SIC: 2791 2752 2789 2759 Typesetting, computer controlled; Offset printing; Beveling of cards; Business forms: printing, nsk

(G-4474)
KENNEBEC TECHNOLOGIES
150 Church Hill Rd (04330-8261)
P.O. Box 470 (04212-0470)
PHONE.........................207 626-0188
Charles Johnson, *Pr*
Steve Lee, *VP Fin*
Bart Haley, *VP Sls*
Richard L Trafton, *Clerk*
▲ **EMP:** 65 **EST:** 1972
SQ FT: 25,000
SALES (est): 9.36MM **Privately Held**
Web: www.kennebec.com
SIC: 3544 3599 Special dies and tools; Custom machinery

(G-4475)
LETTER SYSTEMS INC (PA)
Also Called: J S McCarthy Printing
15 Darin Dr (04330-7815)
PHONE.........................207 622-7126
Richard Tardiff, *Pr*
Conrad Ayotte, *
EMP: 160 **EST:** 1973
SQ FT: 90,000
SALES (est): 23.43MM
SALES (corp-wide): 23.43MM **Privately Held**
Web: www.jsmccarthy.com
SIC: 2752 Offset printing

(G-4476)
MAINE INDUSTRIAL REPAIR SERVICE INC
Also Called: Mirs
60 Darin Dr (04330-7817)
P.O. Box 6929 (44706-0929)
PHONE.........................207 623-7500
EMP: 25
Web: www.schulzgroupusa.com
SIC: 7699 7694 Industrial equipment services; Electric motor repair

(G-4477)
MAINE TIRE & APPLIANCE CO
Also Called: Goodyear
300 State St (04330-7035)
PHONE.........................207 623-1171
Dale Cushman, *Mgr*
EMP: 8
SALES (corp-wide): 4.59MM **Privately Held**
Web: www.sullivantire.com
SIC: 5531 7534 Automotive tires; Tire repair shop
PA: Maine Tire & Appliance Co
251 Us Route 1 Ste 9
Falmouth ME 04105
207 781-3136

(G-4478)
MCLEOD OPTICAL COMPANY INC
179 Mount Vernon Ave (04330-4233)
PHONE.........................207 623-3841
Donald J Mcleod, *Pr*
EMP: 7
SQ FT: 1,300
SALES (corp-wide): 2.97MM **Privately Held**
Web: www.mcleodoptical.com
SIC: 3851 5048 Eyeglasses, lenses and frames; Optometric equipment and supplies
PA: Mcleod Optical Company, Inc.
50 Jefferson Park Rd
Warwick RI 02888
401 467-3000

(G-4479)
PURBECK ISLE INC (PA)
36 Anthony Ave Ste 104 (04330-7891)
PHONE.........................207 623-5119
David Hinson, *Pr*
Eric Dick, *
▼ **EMP:** 32 **EST:** 1997
SQ FT: 20,000
SALES (est): 2.45MM **Privately Held**
SIC: 2037 Frozen fruits and vegetables

(G-4480)
SEATTLE TIMES COMPANY
Also Called: Blethen Maine Newspapers
274 Western Ave (04330-4976)
PHONE.........................207 623-3811
John Christie, *Mgr*

EMP: 138
SALES (corp-wide): 224.06MM **Privately Held**
Web: www.seattletimes.com
SIC: 2711 Newspapers, publishing and printing
PA: Seattle Times Company
1000 Denny Way Ste 501
Seattle WA 98109
206 464-2111

(G-4481)
W B MASON CO INC
188 Water St (04330-4614)
PHONE.........................888 926-2766
EMP: 34
SALES (corp-wide): 1.01B **Privately Held**
Web: www.wbmason.com
SIC: 5943 5712 2752 Office forms and supplies; Office furniture; Commercial printing, lithographic
PA: W. B. Mason Co., Inc.
59 Centre Street
Brockton MA 02301
508 586-3434

Baileyville
Washington County

(G-4482)
DOMTAR PAPER COMPANY LLC
144 Main St (04694-3529)
PHONE.........................207 427-6400
Mona W Moorman, *Brnch Mgr*
EMP: 108
Web: www.domtar.com
SIC: 2621 Printing paper
HQ: Domtar Paper Company, Llc
234 Kingsley Park Dr
Fort Mill SC 29715

(G-4483)
FULGHUM FIBRES INC
224 Main St (04694-3552)
P.O. Box 727 (04694-0727)
PHONE.........................207 427-6560
Mark Seaby, *Mgr*
EMP: 7
SALES (corp-wide): 152.14MM **Privately Held**
Web: www.thepricecompanies.com
SIC: 2421 Sawmills and planing mills, general
HQ: Fulghum Fibres, Inc.
333 S Grand Ave Ste 4100
Los Angeles CA 90071

(G-4484)
GEORGIA-PACIFIC LLC
Also Called: Georgia-Pacific
144 Main St (04694-3545)
P.O. Box 759 (04694-0759)
PHONE.........................207 427-4077
Jim Runyan, *Mgr*
EMP: 8
SALES (corp-wide): 36.93B **Privately Held**
Web: www.gp.com
SIC: 2431 2621 2631 2421 Millwork; Paper mills; Container board; Lumber: rough, sawed, or planed
HQ: Georgia-Pacific Llc
133 Peachtree St Nw
Atlanta GA 30303
404 652-4000

(G-4485)
TRANS UTILITY INC
Also Called: Trans-Utility Services
197 Houlton Rd (04694-3621)

P.O. Box 543 (04619-0543)
PHONE..............................207 454-1162
Tony Leavitt, *Pr*
EMP: 8 **EST:** 2016
SQ FT: 8,000
SALES (est): 2.2MM **Privately Held**
Web: www.trans-utility.com
SIC: 3612 Transformers, except electric

(G-4486)
WOODLAND PULP LLC (PA)
144 Main St (04694-3529)
PHONE..............................207 427-3311
Scott Beal, *
◆ **EMP:** 299 **EST:** 2001
SALES (est): 102.21MM
SALES (corp-wide): 102.21MM **Privately Held**
Web: www.woodlandpulp.com
SIC: 2611 Pulp mills

Bangor
Penobscot County

(G-4487)
AC ELECTRIC CORP
Also Called: AC Electric
40 Target Cir (04401-5798)
PHONE..............................207 945-9487
Dan Parsons, *Pr*
EMP: 18
SALES (corp-wide): 9.11MM **Privately Held**
Web: www.acelec.com
SIC: 7694 5085 Electric motor repair; Industrial supplies
PA: A.C. Electric Corp.
120 Merrow Rd
Auburn ME 04210
207 784-7341

(G-4488)
AMERICAN CONCRETE INDS INC
Also Called: Shawnee Steps
1717 Stillwater Ave (04401-2671)
PHONE..............................207 947-8334
TOLL FREE: 800
Shawn Mcdonald, *Brnch Mgr*
EMP: 55
Web: www.americanconcrete.com
SIC: 3272 5211 Concrete products, precast, nec; Masonry materials and supplies
PA: American Concrete Industries, Inc.
982 Minot Ave
Auburn ME 04210
207 947-8334

(G-4489)
BAFS INC (PA)
Also Called: Birch Stream Farms
61 Florida Ave Ste 101 (04401-3005)
PHONE..............................207 942-5226
Allon R Fish Junior, *Pr*
EMP: 18 **EST:** 1999
SQ FT: 36,000
SALES (est): 7.54MM
SALES (corp-wide): 7.54MM **Privately Held**
Web: www.bafsinc.com
SIC: 2038 Frozen specialties, nec

(G-4490)
BANGOR LTR SP & COLOR COPY CTR
99 Washington St (04401-6518)
PHONE..............................207 945-9311
Irvine W Marsters Junior, *Pr*
EMP: 9 **EST:** 1950

SALES (est): 1.31MM **Privately Held**
Web: www.bangorlettershop.com
SIC: 7331 2759 Direct mail advertising services; Commercial printing, nec

(G-4491)
BANGOR MILLWORK & SUPPLY INC (PA)
Also Called: Bangor Wholesale Laminates
355 Target Cir (04401-5721)
PHONE..............................207 947-6019
Layton Day, *Pr*
Roland Day, *VP*
EMP: 15 **EST:** 1977
SQ FT: 10,000
SALES (est): 3.08MM
SALES (corp-wide): 3.08MM **Privately Held**
Web: www.bangorwholesalelaminates.com
SIC: 5211 2431 Counter tops; Millwork

(G-4492)
BANGOR NEON
1567 Hammond St (04401-5793)
PHONE..............................207 947-2766
TOLL FREE: 800
Gayle Treworgy Hansen, *Pr*
Grace C Treworgy, *Dir*
Joel Hansen, *VP*
EMP: 10 **EST:** 1948
SQ FT: 5,000
SALES (est): 1MM **Privately Held**
Web: www.bangorneon.com
SIC: 3993 7389 Electric signs; Lettering and sign painting services

(G-4493)
BANGOR PUBLISHING COMPANY (PA)
Also Called: Bangor Daily News
1 Merchants Plz (04401-8302)
P.O. Box 1329 (04402-1329)
PHONE..............................207 990-8000
Todd Benoit, *Pr*
Arthur E Mc Kenzie, *
Susan Coffman, *
Tim Reynolds, *
▲ **EMP:** 200 **EST:** 1889
SQ FT: 60,000
SALES (est): 39.35MM
SALES (corp-wide): 39.35MM **Privately Held**
Web: www.bangornews.com
SIC: 2711 Commercial printing and newspaper publishing combined

(G-4494)
BANGOR STEEL SERVICE INC
123 Dowd Rd (04401-6733)
P.O. Box 1900 (04402-1900)
PHONE..............................207 947-2773
TOLL FREE: 800
Paula G Nickerson, *Pr*
EMP: 20 **EST:** 1978
SQ FT: 14,000
SALES (est): 8.84MM **Privately Held**
Web: www.bangorsteel.com
SIC: 5051 3441 5719 Steel; Fabricated structural metal; Metalware

(G-4495)
CENTRAL STREET CORPORATION
Also Called: Northeast Reprographics
80 Central St (04401-5110)
P.O. Box 2008 (04402-2008)
PHONE..............................207 947-8049
TOLL FREE: 800
Vernon Haynes, *Pr*

Ken Rogers Junior, *Treas*
Paul Weeks, *Clerk*
EMP: 10 **EST:** 1969
SQ FT: 3,500
SALES (est): 963.57K **Privately Held**
Web: www.printbangor.com
SIC: 2741 2752 7334 Miscellaneous publishing; Photolithographic printing; Blueprinting service

(G-4496)
CREATIVE DIGITAL IMAGING
Also Called: Creative Companies, The
24 Dowd Rd (04401-6700)
P.O. Box 1296 (04402-1296)
PHONE..............................207 973-0500
Micheal Bazinet, *CEO*
EMP: 36 **EST:** 1997
SALES (est): 4.92MM **Privately Held**
Web: www.creativedi.com
SIC: 2759 Commercial printing, nec

(G-4497)
CROSBYS WELDING LLC
99 Farm Rd (04401-6831)
PHONE..............................207 974-7815
Jesse Crosby, *Prin*
EMP: 7 **EST:** 2014
SALES (est): 254.88K **Privately Held**
SIC: 7692 Welding repair

(G-4498)
EDGE MEDIA GROUP
1 Cumberland Pl Ste 204 (04401-5090)
P.O. Box 2639 (04402-2639)
PHONE..............................207 942-2901
Michael Fern, *Pr*
Deandra Briggs, *VP*
Kimberly Whitmore, *VP*
EMP: 10 **EST:** 2006
SALES (est): 502.32K **Privately Held**
Web: www.themaineedge.com
SIC: 7374 2711 Computer graphics service; Newspapers: publishing only, not printed on site

(G-4499)
ELDUR CORPORATION
Also Called: Eldur AG
448 Griffin Rd (04401-3031)
PHONE..............................207 942-6592
▲ **EMP:** 21 **EST:** 1996
SQ FT: 33,000
SALES (est): 4.81MM **Privately Held**
Web: www.dietzegroup.com
SIC: 3357 Communication wire
PA: Eldur Ag, Maienfeld
Industriestrasse 4
Maienfeld GR 7304

(G-4500)
EZTOUSECOM DIRECTORIES
592 Hammond St (04401-4545)
PHONE..............................207 974-3171
Nicole Lozier, *Prin*
Nicole Lozier, *Mgr*
EMP: 7 **EST:** 2012
SALES (est): 247.08K **Privately Held**
SIC: 2741 Telephone and other directory publishing

(G-4501)
FLEXWARE CONTROL TECH LLC
40 Johnson St (04401-3391)
PHONE..............................207 262-9682
James Labrecque, *Pr*
James Labrecque, *Managing Member*
EMP: 8 **EST:** 2018
SALES (est): 557.57K **Privately Held**

SIC: 5078 3585 Commercial refrigeration equipment; Refrigeration and heating equipment

(G-4502)
FRANKS BAKE SHOP INC
Also Called: Frank's Bake Shop & Catering
199 State St (04401-5410)
P.O. Box 1108 (04402-1108)
PHONE..............................207 947-4594
Richard Soucy, *Pr*
Theresa Soucy, *Treas*
EMP: 9 **EST:** 1945
SQ FT: 2,200
SALES (est): 936.73K **Privately Held**
Web: www.franksbakery.com
SIC: 5461 5812 2024 5451 Bread; Caterers; Ice cream, bulk; Ice cream (packaged)

(G-4503)
FURBUSH ROBERTS PRTG CO INC
435 Odlin Rd (04401-6705)
PHONE..............................207 945-9409
Thomas C Roberts, *Pr*
Caitline Sullivan, *VP*
EMP: 9 **EST:** 1939
SQ FT: 12,700
SALES (est): 911.01K **Privately Held**
Web: www.maineprinters.com
SIC: 2752 Offset printing

(G-4504)
GAFTEK INC
160 Perry Rd (04401-6722)
PHONE..............................207 217-6515
Burnham William Gaff Junior, *Brnch Mgr*
EMP: 22
SALES (corp-wide): 13.83MM **Privately Held**
Web: www.gaftek.com
SIC: 2911 Diesel fuels
PA: Gaftek, Inc.
2083 Dover Rd
Epsom NH 03234
207 217-6515

(G-4505)
GENERAL ELECTRIC COMPANY
Also Called: GE
534 Griffin Rd (04401-3086)
PHONE..............................207 941-2500
Brackett Denniston, *Brnch Mgr*
EMP: 1074
SALES (corp-wide): 76.56B **Publicly Held**
Web: www.ge.com
SIC: 3511 3563 Turbines and turbine generator sets; Air and gas compressors
PA: General Electric Company
1 Financial Ctr Ste 3700
Boston MA 02111
617 443-3000

(G-4506)
JAMES W SEWALL COMPANY
77 Exchange St Ste 401 (04401-6618)
PHONE..............................207 817-5410
George N Campbell Junior, *Pr*
EMP: 7
SALES (corp-wide): 8.46MM **Privately Held**
Web: www.sewall.com
SIC: 8711 0851 7335 1382 Engineering services; Forestry services; Commercial photography; Oil and gas exploration services
PA: James W. Sewall Company
136 Center St
Old Town ME 04468
207 827-4456

(G-4507)
JIFFY PRINT INC
494 Broadway (04401-3468)
PHONE..............................207 947-4490
Mark D Grandchamp, *Pr*
EMP: 9 EST: 2003
SQ FT: 6,000
SALES (est): 960.13K **Privately Held**
Web: www.jiffyprint.com
SIC: 2752 Offset printing

(G-4508)
LANE CONSTRUCTION CORPORATION
Also Called: Hermon Plant Site
953 Odlin Rd (04401-6715)
P.O. Box 103 (04402-0103)
PHONE..............................207 945-0850
Ken Anderson, *Mgr*
EMP: 280
SALES (corp-wide): 7.95B **Privately Held**
Web: www.laneconstruct.com
SIC: 1611 2951 1442 Highway and street
paving contractor; Asphalt paving mixtures
and blocks; Construction sand and gravel
HQ: The Lane Construction Corporation
90 Fieldstone Ct
Cheshire CT 06410
203 235-3351

(G-4509)
LEES CONCRETE INC
974 Odlin Rd (04401-6716)
PHONE..............................207 974-4936
Margaret Lee, *Prin*
EMP: 8 EST: 2016
SALES (est): 251.75K **Privately Held**
SIC: 3273 Ready-mixed concrete

(G-4510)
ME TITLE
543 Hammond St (04401-4511)
PHONE..............................207 942-1988
EMP: 7 EST: 2019
SALES (est): 883.68K **Privately Held**
Web: www.metitle.net
SIC: 3625 Motor controls and accessories

(G-4511)
NAUTEL MAINE INC
Also Called: Nautel
201 Target Cir (04401-5799)
PHONE..............................207 947-8200
Peter Conlon, *Ch Bd*
Darlene Fowlow, *
Doreen Commeau, *
▼ EMP: 175 EST: 1975
SQ FT: 24,000
SALES (est): 25.47MM
SALES (corp-wide): 1.39MM **Privately Held**
Web: www.nautel.com
SIC: 3663 Transmitting apparatus, radio or
television
HQ: Nautel Limited
10089 Peggys Cove Rd Hwy 333
Hacketts Cove NS B3Z 3
902 823-3900

(G-4512)
NYLE INTERNATIONAL CORP (PA)
195 Thatcher St Ste 2 (04401-6874)
PHONE..............................207 989-4335
Samuel Nyer, *Ch Bd*
Donald C Lewis, *Pr*
EMP: 242 EST: 1963
SQ FT: 800
SALES (est): 23.54MM

SALES (corp-wide): 23.54MM **Privately Held**
Web: www.nyle.com
SIC: 5047 3585 Medical equipment and
supplies; Humidifiers and dehumidifiers

(G-4513)
NYLE SYSTEMS LLC
Also Called: Nyle Systems
690 Maine Ave (04401-3021)
PHONE..............................207 989-4335
Antonius Mathissen, *Managing Member*
◆ EMP: 43 EST: 2008
SALES (est): 7.69MM **Privately Held**
Web: www.nyle.com
SIC: 3585 Heat pumps, electric

(G-4514)
PINELAND FARMS DAIRY COMPANY
1 Milk St (04401-5768)
PHONE..............................207 922-4036
Mark Whitney, *Pr*
EMP: 15 EST: 2017
SALES (est): 1.94MM **Privately Held**
Web: www.pinelandfarmsdairy.com
SIC: 2023 2022 Condensed, concentrated,
and evaporated milk products; Cheese;
natural and processed

(G-4515)
PRINT BANGOR
Also Called: Northeast Reprographics
80 Central St (04401-5110)
PHONE..............................207 947-8049
Benjamin Metzger, *Pr*
Elena Metzger, *VP*
EMP: 9 EST: 2014
SQ FT: 4,000
SALES (est): 957.65K **Privately Held**
Web: www.printbangor.com
SIC: 7389 2759 7334 Design services;
Commercial printing, nec; Photocopying
and duplicating services

(G-4516)
TISSUE PLUS LLC
Also Called: Paper Source
39 Hildreth St N (04401-5732)
PHONE..............................978 524-0550
Marc Cooper, *Managing Member*
EMP: 14 EST: 2019
SALES (est): 2.41MM **Privately Held**
Web: www.tissueplus.com
SIC: 2621 2675 Specialty papers; Die-cut
paper and board

(G-4517)
TYLER TECHNOLOGIES INC
Advanced Data Systems
700 Mount Hope Ave Ste 101 (04401)
PHONE..............................207 947-4494
Duane Graves, *Brnch Mgr*
EMP: 10
SALES (corp-wide): 1.85B **Publicly Held**
Web: www.tylertech.com
SIC: 7372 7371 1731 7378 Prepackaged
software; Computer software development;
Computer installation; Computer and data
processing equipment repair/maintenance
PA: Tyler Technologies, Inc.
5101 Tennyson Pkwy
Plano TX 75024
972 713-3700

(G-4518)
UMAMI NOODLE
1 Main St (04401-6303)
PHONE..............................207 947-9991
Thinda Cristana, *Owner*

EMP: 10 EST: 2014
SALES (est): 504.04K **Privately Held**
SIC: 2098 Noodles (e.g. egg, plain, and
water), dry

(G-4519)
VLD INC
Also Called: Equipment Depot
163 Hildreth St N (04401-5953)
PHONE..............................207 947-6148
TOLL FREE: 800
Verle Drinkwater, *Pr*
George Eaton Iii, *Clerk*
EMP: 9 EST: 1994
SQ FT: 1,800
SALES (est): 977.69K **Privately Held**
SIC: 5012 5013 3713 Truck bodies; Truck
parts and accessories; Truck bodies and
parts

(G-4520)
W B MASON CO INC
78 Rice St (04401-5730)
PHONE..............................888 926-2766
EMP: 34
SALES (corp-wide): 1.01B **Privately Held**
Web: www.wbmason.com
SIC: 5943 5712 2752 Office forms and
supplies; Office furniture; Commercial
printing, lithographic
PA: W. B. Mason Co., Inc.
59 Centre Street
Brockton MA 02301
508 586-3434

(G-4521)
WATERWORKS
Also Called: Bed Works, The
25 Dowd Rd (04401-6733)
PHONE..............................207 941-8306
EMP: 14
SALES (corp-wide): 2.78MM **Privately Held**
Web: www.thebedworksofmaine.com
SIC: 2511 Wood household furniture
PA: The Waterworks
270 State St
Brewer ME 04412
207 989-3233

Bar Harbor
Hancock County

(G-4522)
CELLARS
854 State Highway 3 (04609-7238)
PHONE..............................207 288-3907
Bruce Stevens, *Prin*
EMP: 7 EST: 2011
SALES (est): 123.03K **Privately Held**
Web: www.barharborcellars.com
SIC: 2084 Wines

(G-4523)
MOUNT DESERT ISLAND ICE CREAM
325 Main St (04609-1640)
PHONE..............................207 460-5515
EMP: 7 EST: 2015
SALES (est): 265.25K **Privately Held**
Web: www.fearlessflavor.com
SIC: 2024 Ice cream and frozen deserts

Bass Harbor
Hancock County

(G-4524)
MY EASE INC (PA)
53 Granville Rd (04653-3233)
P.O. Box 395 (04653-0395)
PHONE..............................207 667-6235
Doug Metchick, *CEO*
Dewitt C Morris, *Pr*
Cuyler Morris, *Pr*
Justine M Morris, *Treas*
▼ EMP: 51 EST: 1972
SALES (est): 5.65MM
SALES (corp-wide): 5.65MM **Privately Held**
Web: www.morrisyachts.com
SIC: 3732 Sailboats, building and repairing

Bath
Sagadahoc County

(G-4525)
BATH IRON WORKS CORPORATION (HQ)
700 Washington St (04530-2556)
PHONE..............................207 443-3311
Jay L Johnson, *Ch*
Jeffrey S Geiger, *
Phebe N Novakovic, *
Thomas A Brown, *
▲ EMP: 772 EST: 1886
SALES (est): 477.87MM
SALES (corp-wide): 42.27B **Publicly Held**
Web: www.gdbiw.com
SIC: 3731 8711 Combat vessels, building
and repairing; Consulting engineer
PA: General Dynamics Corporation
11011 Sunset Hills Rd
Reston VA 20190
703 876-3000

(G-4526)
DIRECT DISPLAY PUBLISHING CO
765 High St Ste 5 (04530-2459)
P.O. Box 3 (04086-0003)
PHONE..............................207 443-4800
Spencer Richie, *Pr*
Bebera Mosher, *Mgr*
EMP: 8 EST: 1995
SALES (est): 653.69K **Privately Held**
Web: www.direct-display.com
SIC: 2741 Directories, nec: publishing and
printing

(G-4527)
KENNEBEC CABINETRY INC
Also Called: Kennebec Company, The
37 Wing Farm Pkwy (04530-1515)
PHONE..............................207 442-0813
James Stewart, *Prin*
EMP: 10 EST: 2014
SQ FT: 15,651
SALES (est): 488.5K **Privately Held**
Web: www.kennebeccompany.com
SIC: 2434 Wood kitchen cabinets

(G-4528)
KENNEBEC COMPANY
Also Called: Kennebec Cabinet Company
1 Front St Ste 3 (04530-2562)
PHONE..............................207 443-2131
J D Leonard, *Owner*
EMP: 17 EST: 1973
SQ FT: 16,000
SALES (est): 2.24MM **Privately Held**

▲ = Import ▼ = Export
◆ = Import/Export

GEOGRAPHIC

Web: www.kennebeccompany.com
SIC: 2434 Wood kitchen cabinets

(G-4529)
LOCKHEED MARTIN CORPORATION
Also Called: Lockheed/Ms2-Baltimore
700 Washington St (04530-2574)
PHONE..............................207 442-3125
EMP: 8 EST: 2019
SALES (est): 239.04K Privately Held
Web: www.lockheedmartinjobs.com
SIC: 3812 Search and navigation equipment

(G-4530)
NORTHROP GRMMN SPCE & MSSN SYS
Also Called: Precommissioning Unit TAC 1
P.O. Box 286 (04530-0286)
PHONE..............................207 442-5097
EMP: 140
SIC: 3812 Defense systems and equipment
HQ: Northrop Grumman Space & Mission
Systems Corp.
6379 San Ignacio Ave
San Jose CA 95119
703 280-2900

(G-4531)
VIRGINIA PROJECT INC
Also Called: MAINE'S FIRST SHIP
229 Washington St (04530-1638)
P.O. Box 358 (04562-0358)
PHONE..............................207 443-4242
Orman Hines, Prin
Jeremy Blaiklock, Prin
Lori Benson, Prin
Allison Hepler, Prin
Dan Burchstead, Prin
EMP: 15 EST: 1997
SALES (est): 160.47K Privately Held
SIC: 3731 Shipbuilding and repairing

Beals
Washington County

(G-4532)
CARVER SHELLFISH INC
Also Called: A.C.
125 Black Duck Cove Rd (04611)
P.O. Box 187 (04611-0187)
PHONE..............................207 497-2261
Albert Carver, Pr
Patrick Robinson, *
Karla Alley, *
EMP: 22 EST: 1945
SQ FT: 20,000
SALES (est): 7.5MM Privately Held
Web: www.acincshellfish.com
SIC: 5146 2092 2091 Seafoods; Seafoods,
fresh: prepared; Seafood products:
packaged in cans, jars, etc.

Belfast
Waldo County

(G-4533)
FRENCH WEBB & CO INC
21 Front St (04915-6836)
PHONE..............................207 338-6706
EMP: 11 EST: 1996
SALES (est): 387.05K Privately Held
Web: www.frenchwebb.com
SIC: 3732 Boatbuilding and repairing

(G-4534)
G + O LOGIC LLC
137 High St (04915-6358)
P.O. Box 567 (04915-0567)
PHONE..............................413 588-8079
Matthew Omalia, Prin
▲ EMP: 20 EST: 2008
SALES (est): 2.36MM Privately Held
Web: www.gologic.us
SIC: 2452 Prefabricated buildings, wood

(G-4535)
MATHEWS BROTHERS COMPANY (PA)
Also Called: Mathews Brothers
22 Perkins Rd (04915-6034)
P.O. Box 345 (04915-0345)
PHONE..............................207 338-3360
John Hawthorne, CEO
Scott Hawthorne, *
Brent West, *
Alex Hawthorne, *
▲ EMP: 130 EST: 1854
SQ FT: 100,000
SALES (est): 36.48MM
SALES (corp-wide): 36.48MM Privately
Held
Web: www.mathewsbrothers.com
SIC: 2431 3089 Window frames, wood;
Windows, plastics

(G-4536)
MOWI DUCKTRAP LLC
61 Little River Dr (04915-6035)
PHONE..............................207 338-6280
Jose Fidalgo, Managing Member
EMP: 61
SIC: 2091 Fish, smoked
HQ: Mowi Ducktrap, Llc
57 Little River Dr
Belfast ME 04915
207 338-6280

(G-4537)
MOWI DUCKTRAP LLC
Also Called: Ducktrap River of Maine, LLC
57 Little River Dr (04915-6035)
PHONE..............................207 338-6280
Jose Fidalgo, Managing Member
◆ EMP: 130 EST: 1978
SQ FT: 70,000
SALES (est): 36.14MM Privately Held
Web: www.ducktrap.com
SIC: 2091 2092 Fish, smoked; Fresh or
frozen packaged fish
HQ: Mowi Usa Holding, Llc
57 Little River Dr
Belfast ME

(G-4538)
STATE SAND & GRAVEL CO INC
185 Belmont Ave (04915-7558)
P.O. Box 420 (04915-0420)
PHONE..............................207 338-4070
Gari Oxton, Pr
Richard Oxton Junior, VP
David Oxton, *
Susan Oxton, *
Debora Riley, *
EMP: 10 EST: 1920
SQ FT: 1,500
SALES (est): 964.32K Privately Held
Web: www.expiredwixdomain.com
SIC: 5211 3273 1442 Sand and gravel;
Ready-mixed concrete; Construction sand
and gravel

Belgrade
Kennebec County

(G-4539)
GAGNE & SON CONCRETE BLOCKS INC (PA)
28 Old Rte 27 Rd (04917-3708)
PHONE..............................207 495-3313
EMP: 50 EST: 1970
SALES (est): 9.83MM
SALES (corp-wide): 9.83MM Privately
Held
Web: www.gagneandson.com
SIC: 3271 5211 Blocks, concrete or cinder:
standard; Concrete and cinder block

(G-4540)
HAMMOND LUMBER COMPANY (PA)
Also Called: Benjamin Moore Authorized Ret
2 Hammond Dr (04917-4152)
P.O. Box 500 (04917-0500)
PHONE..............................207 495-3303
TOLL FREE: 800
Michael J Hammond, Pr
Donald C Hammond, *
Robert Thing, *
EMP: 150 EST: 1947
SQ FT: 50,000
SALES (est): 81.74MM
SALES (corp-wide): 81.74MM Privately
Held
Web: www.hammondlumber.com
SIC: 5251 2421 5031 5231 Hardware stores
; Sawmills and planing mills, general;
Lumber: rough, dressed, and finished;
Paint, glass, and wallpaper stores

(G-4541)
KEVIN S HAWES
652 Manchester Rd (04917-3828)
PHONE..............................207 495-3412
Kevin S Hawes, Prin
EMP: 7 EST: 2004
SALES (est): 204.69K Privately Held
SIC: 2411 Logging

Belmont
Waldo County

(G-4542)
BELMONT BOATWORKS LLC
163 Augusta Rd (04952-3005)
PHONE..............................207 342-2885
Daniel Miller, Owner
EMP: 10 EST: 2011
SQ FT: 144
SALES (est): 838.22K Privately Held
Web: www.belmontboatworks.com
SIC: 3732 Boatbuilding and repairing

(G-4543)
CREATIVE APPAREL ASSOC LLC
Also Called: Creative Apparel
318 Augusta Rd (04952-3015)
P.O. Box 301 (04668-0301)
PHONE..............................207 342-2814
▲ EMP: 300 EST: 1989
SQ FT: 15,000
SALES (est): 524.26K
SALES (corp-wide): 576.69K Privately
Held
Web: www.creativeaa.com

SIC: 2339 2329 Athletic clothing: women's,
misses', and juniors'; Athletic clothing,
except uniforms: men's, youths' and boys'
PA: Passamaquoddy Tribe At Indian
Township
8 Kennabasis Rd
Princeton ME 04668
207 796-5004

Benton
Kennebec County

(G-4544)
B & B PRECISE PRODUCTS INC
25 Neck Rd (04901-3546)
PHONE..............................207 453-8118
Welman Rood, Pr
EMP: 45 EST: 1990
SQ FT: 16,000
SALES (est): 9.97MM Privately Held
Web: www.bbprecise.com
SIC: 7389 3599 Grinding, precision:
commercial or industrial; Machine shop,
jobbing and repair

(G-4545)
GOSSAMER PRESS
6 Albion Rd (04901-3640)
PHONE..............................207 827-9881
EMP: 8 EST: 1996
SALES (est): 550.86K Privately Held
Web: www.gossamerpress.com
SIC: 2759 7334 Screen printing;
Photocopying and duplicating services

(G-4546)
MAINELY GATES & HANDRAILS
263 Neck Rd (04901-3541)
PHONE..............................207 314-1083
James Gates, Prin
EMP: 8 EST: 2013
SALES (est): 376.83K Privately Held
SIC: 3446 Architectural metalwork

Bernard
Hancock County

(G-4547)
BYER MANUFACTURING COMPANY
Also Called: Byer of Maine
41 Gunlow Pond Rd (04612-3673)
P.O. Box 100 (04473-0100)
PHONE..............................207 866-2171
James P Shields, Pr
◆ EMP: 26 EST: 1880
SALES (est): 618.55K Privately Held
Web: www.byerofmaine.com
SIC: 3161 2511 2394 2393 Luggage; Camp
furniture: wood; Canvas and related
products; Textile bags

(G-4548)
JAMES H RICH BOATYARD
Rte 102 Main St (04612)
P.O. Box 297 (04612-0297)
PHONE..............................207 244-3208
Nancy Thurlow, Owner
EMP: 8 EST: 1957
SALES (est): 845.15K Privately Held
SIC: 3732 4493 Boatbuilding and repairing;
Boat yards, storage and incidental repair

Berwick
York County

(G-4549)
COLLINS SHEET METAL INC
510 Portland St (03901-2873)
P.O. Box 1248 (03901-1248)
PHONE..............................207 384-4428
Gary Collins Senior, *Pr*
Pat Collins, *VP*
EMP: 10 **EST:** 1985
SQ FT: 5,000
SALES (est): 1.3MM **Privately Held**
Web: www.collinssheetmetal.com
SIC: 3444 Sheet metal specialties, not
   stamped

(G-4550)
LITTLE HARBOR WINDOW CO INC
Also Called: Little Harbor Window Company
11 Little Harbor Rd (03901-2456)
P.O. Box 1188 (03901-1188)
PHONE..............................207 698-1332
James Eaton, *Pr*
John Royal, *CFO*
EMP: 27 **EST:** 1982
SQ FT: 6,000
SALES (est): 938K **Privately Held**
Web: www.littleharborwindow.com
SIC: 2431 Doors, wood

(G-4551)
MBW TRACTOR SALES LLC
540 Route 4 (03901-2800)
PHONE..............................207 384-2001
EMP: 10 **EST:** 2005
SALES (est): 951.87K **Privately Held**
Web: www.mickbodyworks.com
SIC: 3471 7532 Plating and polishing;
   Collision shops, automotive

Bethel
Oxford County

(G-4552)
COLEMAN CONCRETE
Also Called: Alvin J Coleman
Nwbethel Rd (04217)
PHONE..............................207 824-6300
Buzz Coleman, *Owner*
EMP: 9 **EST:** 2001
SALES (est): 588.87K **Privately Held**
Web: www.colemanconcrete.com
SIC: 3273 Ready-mixed concrete

Biddeford
York County

(G-4553)
32 NORTH CORPORATION
Also Called: Stabil
16 Pomerleau St (04005-9457)
PHONE..............................207 284-5010
John Milburn, *Pr*
Anne Gould, *CFO*
▲ **EMP:** 8 **EST:** 1990
SQ FT: 10,000
SALES (est): 2.56MM
SALES (corp-wide): 300MM **Privately Held**
Web: www.32north.com
SIC: 3021 Protective footwear, rubber or
   plastic
HQ: Implus, Llc
   2001 Tw Alexander Dr

Durham NC 27709
919 544-7900

(G-4554)
AMERICAN RHNMETALL SYSTEMS LLC
15 Morin St Ste B (04005-4403)
PHONE..............................207 571-5850
EMP: 40 **EST:** 2007
SQ FT: 35,000
SALES (est): 10.45MM
SALES (corp-wide): 10.45MM **Privately Held**
Web: www.rheinmetall.com
SIC: 3812 Defense systems and equipment
PA: American Rheinmetall Defense, Inc.
   11180 Sunrise Valley Dr # 2
   Reston VA 20191
   571 867-0047

(G-4555)
B PEACHEE INC
Also Called: Angelrox
40 Main St Ste 13-109 (04005-5178)
PHONE..............................207 602-6262
Roxi Suger, *Pr*
EMP: 9 **EST:** 2013
SALES (est): 155.59K **Privately Held**
Web: www.angelrox.com
SIC: 5621 2331 Boutiques; Women's and
   misses' blouses and shirts

(G-4556)
BARRETTE OUTDOOR LIVING INC
8 Morin St (04005-4413)
PHONE..............................800 866-8101
Steve Hanscom, *Mgr*
EMP: 35
SALES (corp-wide): 32.72B **Privately Held**
Web: www.barretteoutdoorliving.com
SIC: 3499 Fire- or burglary-resistive
   products
HQ: Barrette Outdoor Living, Inc.
   7830 Freeway Cir
   Middleburg Heights OH 44130
   440 891-0790

(G-4557)
BEACON PRESS INC
Also Called: Northern Light
457 Alfred St (04005-9447)
P.O. Box 627 (04005-0627)
PHONE..............................207 282-1535
George Sample, *Pr*
EMP: 44 **EST:** 1884
SALES (est): 2.4MM **Privately Held**
Web: www.pressherald.com
SIC: 2711 Commercial printing and
   newspaper publishing combined

(G-4558)
CRI-SIL LLC
Also Called: Cri-Sil Silicone Technologies
359 Hill St (04005-3949)
PHONE..............................207 283-6422
▲ **EMP:** 32 **EST:** 1994
SQ FT: 35,000
SALES (est): 8.64MM **Privately Held**
Web: www.crisil-silicones.com
SIC: 2822 Synthetic rubber

(G-4559)
DEEPWATER BUOYANCY INC
Also Called: Deepwater
394 Hill St (04005-4341)
P.O. Box 2190 (04005-8190)
PHONE..............................207 468-2565
David Capotosto, *Pr*

EMP: 10 **EST:** 2013
SQ FT: 35,000
SALES (est): 2.46MM **Privately Held**
Web: www.deepwaterbuoyancy.com
SIC: 3086 5085 3533 Plastics foam products
   ; Industrial supplies; Oil and gas field
   machinery

(G-4560)
DRAGON PRODUCTS COMPANY LLC (DH)
2 Main St Ste 18-221 (04005-3098)
PHONE..............................207 594-5555
Terrence L Veysey, *Pr*
David S Grinnell, *VP*
John Slagle, *Prs Dir*
◆ **EMP:** 25 **EST:** 1988
SALES (est): 49.06MM **Privately Held**
Web: www.dragonproducts.com
SIC: 3273 3241 3281 3274 Ready-mixed
   concrete; Portland cement; Cut stone and
   stone products; Lime
HQ: Giant Cement Holding, Inc.
   396 W Greens Rd Ste 300
   Houston TX 77067

(G-4561)
DSM METAL FABRICATION INC
Also Called: Metal Fabrications
129 Precourt St (04005-4343)
P.O. Box 404 (04005-0404)
PHONE..............................207 282-6740
Bob Standard, *Pr*
William Cain, *
Paula Hayward, *
Tom Hopkins, *
EMP: 45 **EST:** 1977
SQ FT: 30,000
SALES (est): 9.81MM **Privately Held**
Web: www.dsmmetalfabrication.com
SIC: 3444 1711 Sheet metal specialties, not
   stamped; Warm air heating and air
   conditioning contractor

(G-4562)
EAMI INC
Also Called: E A M
19 Pomerleau St (04005-9457)
P.O. Box 519 (04005-0519)
PHONE..............................207 283-3001
Stephen G Swinburne, *CEO*
Jim Robinson, *CFO*
EMP: 16 **EST:** 1988
SQ FT: 15,000
SALES (est): 22.35MM
SALES (corp-wide): 22.35MM **Privately Held**
Web: www.eaminc.com
SIC: 3699 3565 Electrical equipment and
   supplies, nec; Packaging machinery
PA: Prescott Metal
   565 Elm St
   Biddeford ME 04005
   207 283-0115

(G-4563)
ELM STREET VAULT INC
38 Landry St (04005-4310)
PHONE..............................207 284-4855
Donald Daigle, *Pr*
Christiane Daigle, *Sec*
David Daigle, *Mgr*
EMP: 8 **EST:** 1971
SQ FT: 5,000
SALES (est): 712.94K **Privately Held**
SIC: 3272 5039 Burial vaults, concrete or
   precast terrazzo; Septic tanks

(G-4564)
FIBER MATERIALS INC (DH)
5 Morin St (04005-4414)
PHONE..............................207 282-5911
Mark Miklos, *Pr*
Mark Niklos, *
EMP: 153 **EST:** 2011
SQ FT: 40,000
SALES (est): 98.06MM **Publicly Held**
Web: www.spiritaero.com
SIC: 3769 2299 7389 5131 Guided missile
   and space vehicle parts and aux. equip.,
   R&D; Insulating felts; Inspection and testing
   services; Broadwoven fabrics
HQ: Spirit Aerosystems, Inc.
   3801 S Oliver St
   Wichita KS 67210
   316 526-9000

(G-4565)
FLOTATION TECHNOLOGIES LLC
20 Morin St (04005-4413)
PHONE..............................207 282-7749
◆ **EMP:** 56
Web: www.deepwaterbuoyancy.com
SIC: 3089 Casting of plastics

(G-4566)
FOOTWEAR SPECIALTIES INC
16 Pomerleau St (04005-9457)
PHONE..............................207 284-5003
EMP: 9 **EST:** 1995
SQ FT: 10,000
SALES (est): 207.1K **Privately Held**
Web: www.surewerxfootwear.com
SIC: 3143 3144 Work shoes, men's;
   Women's footwear, except athletic

(G-4567)
G PRO INDUSTRIAL SERVICES
5 Drapeau St (04005-4411)
P.O. Box 1362 (04005-1362)
PHONE..............................207 766-1671
EMP: 8 **EST:** 2013
SALES (est): 428.4K **Privately Held**
Web: www.greatlakescustomworks.com
SIC: 3089 Injection molding of plastics

(G-4568)
GENERAL MARINE INC
56 Landry St (04005-4321)
PHONE..............................207 284-7517
Stacey Raymond, *Pr*
▲ **EMP:** 7 **EST:** 1982
SQ FT: 6,000
SALES (est): 640K **Privately Held**
Web: www.generalmarine.com
SIC: 3732 Motorboats, inboard or outboard:
   building and repairing

(G-4569)
HIGHTECH EXTRACTS LLC
5 Drapeau St (04005-4411)
PHONE..............................207 590-3251
Paul Gelardi, *Prin*
EMP: 10 **EST:** 2017
SALES (est): 2.79MM **Privately Held**
Web: www.hightechextracts.com
SIC: 2836 Extracts

(G-4570)
HYPERLITE MOUNTAIN GEAR INC
Also Called: Hmg
40 Main St Ste 13-120 (04005-5178)
PHONE..............................800 464-9208
EMP: 75 **EST:** 2010
SQ FT: 20,000

SALES (est): 8.79MM Privately Held
Web: www.hyperlitemountaingear.com
SIC: 5941 3949 5091 Specialty sport supplies, nec; Sporting and athletic goods, nec; Sporting and recreation goods

(G-4571)
INTEGRITY COMPOSITES LLC
8 Morin St (04005-4413)
PHONE.....................207 571-0743
Matt Bevin, *Managing Member*
EMP: 15 EST: 2012
SQ FT: 100,000
SALES (est): 1.35MM Privately Held
Web: www.barretteoutdoorliving.com
SIC: 2491 1521 Wood preserving; Patio and deck construction and repair

(G-4572)
INTERMAT
389 Hill St (04005-4335)
PHONE.....................207 283-1156
David Loper, *Pr*
Maynard Forbes, *
EMP: 24 EST: 1996
SQ FT: 33,000
SALES (est): 4.97MM Publicly Held
Web: www.intermatwrestle.com
SIC: 8711 3769 Engineering services; Guided missile and space vehicle parts and aux. equip., R&D
HQ: Fiber Materials Inc.
5 Morin St
Biddeford ME 04005
207 282-5911

(G-4573)
JUNORA LTD
16 Pomerleau St (04005-9457)
PHONE.....................207 284-4900
Dean Plaisted, *CEO*
EMP: 16 EST: 2017
SALES (est): 2.66MM Privately Held
Web: www.junoraltd.com
SIC: 3339 Precious metals

(G-4574)
KYOCERA AVX CMPNNTS BDDFORD CO
Also Called: A V X
401 Hill St (04005-4335)
PHONE.....................207 282-5111
John Sarvis, *Ch*
▲ EMP: 135 EST: 1987
SQ FT: 75,000
SALES (est): 25.76MM Privately Held
Web: www.kyocera-avx.com
SIC: 3675 3629 Electronic capacitors; Capacitors and condensers
HQ: Kyocera Avx Components Corporation
1 Avx Blvd
Fountain Inn SC 29644
864 967-2150

(G-4575)
LINDE ADVANCED MTL TECH INC
Also Called: Praxair
24 Landry St (04005-4310)
PHONE.....................207 282-3787
Roger Dumas, *Ltd Pt*
EMP: 100
Web: www.linde-amt.com
SIC: 3479 7692 Coating, rust preventive; Welding repair
HQ: Linde Advanced Material Technologies Inc.
1500 Polco St
Indianapolis IN 46222
317 240-2500

(G-4576)
MAINELY MEDIA
457 Alfred St (04005-9447)
PHONE.....................207 282-4337
EMP: 27 EST: 2019
SALES (est): 222.34K Privately Held
Web: www.pressherald.com
SIC: 2711 Newspapers, publishing and printing

(G-4577)
MAINELY NEWSPAPERS INC
Also Called: Biddeford Saco Courier
180 Main St (04005-2410)
P.O. Box 1894 (04005-1894)
PHONE.....................207 282-4337
TOLL FREE: 800
David Flood, *Pr*
Carolyn Flood, *Sec*
EMP: 23 EST: 1989
SQ FT: 11,000
SALES (est): 477.46K Privately Held
SIC: 2711 Newspapers, publishing and printing

(G-4578)
MCALLISTER MACHINE INC
7 Pomerleau St # 102 (04005-9457)
PHONE.....................207 282-8655
James A Mcallister, *Pr*
Donna Mcallister, *Treas*
EMP: 20 EST: 1983
SALES (est): 1.8MM Privately Held
Web: www.mcallistermachine.com
SIC: 3599 Machine shop, jobbing and repair

(G-4579)
ME INDUSTRIES
Also Called: Donovan Marine-Atlantic
19 Pomerleau St (04005-9457)
PHONE.....................207 286-2030
Thomas Norton, *Mgr*
▲ EMP: 8 EST: 2006
SALES (est): 545.68K Privately Held
Web: www.oemshafting.com
SIC: 3462 Iron and steel forgings

(G-4580)
OCEAN APPROVED INC
Also Called: Atlantic Sea Farms
20 Pomerleau St (04005-9457)
P.O. Box 8129 (04104-8129)
PHONE.....................207 701-1576
Briana Warner, *CEO*
EMP: 9 EST: 2006
SALES (est): 1.2MM Privately Held
Web: www.oceanapproved.com
SIC: 0919 2038 Seaweed, gathering of; Breakfasts, frozen and packaged

(G-4581)
OCEANS BALANCE
10 W Point Ln Bldg 10 (04005-3770)
P.O. Box 2150 (04116-2150)
PHONE.....................207 370-4874
Mitchell Lench, *Pr*
Tollef Olson, *Prin*
EMP: 9 EST: 2016
SALES (est): 605.37K Privately Held
Web: www.oceansbalance.com
SIC: 2034 Dried and dehydrated vegetables

(G-4582)
PORTLAND MATTRESS MAKERS (PA)
Also Called: Maine Bedding & Furniture Co.
25 Edwards Ave (04005-3709)
PHONE.....................207 282-9583
George Samaras, *Pr*

EMP: 10 EST: 1938
SALES (est): 1MM
SALES (corp-wide): 1MM Privately Held
Web: www.portlandmattressmakers.com
SIC: 2515 5712 Mattresses, containing felt, foam rubber, urethane, etc.; Furniture stores

(G-4583)
PRECISION SCREW MCH PDTS INC
Also Called: P S M P
30 Gooch St (04005-2015)
P.O. Box 1944 (04005-1944)
PHONE.....................207 283-0121
Joseph Moreshead, *Pr*
Andrea C Moreshead, *
EMP: 30 EST: 1961
SQ FT: 28,000
SALES (est): 4.72MM Privately Held
Web: www.psmp.com
SIC: 3599 Machine shop, jobbing and repair

(G-4584)
PRESCOTT METAL (PA)
565 Elm St (04005-4324)
P.O. Box 519 (04005-0519)
PHONE.....................207 283-0115
John Grondin, *Pr*
EMP: 26 EST: 1964
SQ FT: 30,000
SALES (est): 22.35MM
SALES (corp-wide): 22.35MM Privately Held
Web: www.prescottmetal.com
SIC: 3441 3444 Fabricated structural metal; Sheet metalwork

(G-4585)
RICHARDSON-ALLEN INC
38 Pearl St (04005-2040)
P.O. Box 236 (04072-0236)
PHONE.....................207 284-8402
EMP: 9 EST: 1989
SQ FT: 9,000
SALES (est): 464.19K Privately Held
Web: www.richardsonallen.com
SIC: 2511 Lawn furniture: wood

(G-4586)
ROPELESS SYSTEMS INC
6 Apostolic Way (04005-9419)
PHONE.....................207 468-8545
David A Capotosto, *Prin*
Harold Vincent, *Prin*
George Raftopoulos, *Prin*
EMP: 7 EST: 2021
SALES (est): 225.58K Privately Held
Web: www.ropeless.us
SIC: 3812 Search and navigation equipment

(G-4587)
SACRED PROFANE LLC
50 Washington St (04005-2523)
PHONE.....................508 259-3052
Brienne Allen, *Managing Member*
EMP: 8 EST: 2021
SALES (est): 723.78K Privately Held
Web: www.mwhossconstruction.com
SIC: 2082 Beer (alcoholic beverage)

(G-4588)
SOLERAS ADVANCED COATINGS LTD (PA)
589 Elm St (04005-4417)
P.O. Box 1867 (04005-1867)
PHONE.....................207 282-5699
Jeff Edel, *Pr*
Anders Svensson, *CFO*
Ivan Van De Putte, *Business Director*

Bob Lin, *Chief Manager*
▲ EMP: 48 EST: 1977
SQ FT: 25,000
SALES (est): 13.62MM
SALES (corp-wide): 13.62MM Privately Held
Web: www.soleras.com
SIC: 3599 Custom machinery

(G-4589)
SPURWINK CORDAGE INC
27 Landry St (04005-4309)
P.O. Box 856 (04005-0856)
PHONE.....................207 284-5894
Robert Rice, *Pr*
Michael Stetson, *VP*
Robert Cyr, *Sec*
▲ EMP: 7 EST: 1932
SALES (est): 471.24K Privately Held
SIC: 2298 Cord, braided

(G-4590)
STERLING ROPE COMPANY INC
26 Morin St (04005-4413)
PHONE.....................800 788-7673
Tripp Wyckoff, *Pr*
◆ EMP: 8 EST: 1996
SALES (est): 5.54MM
SALES (corp-wide): 109.31MM Privately Held
Web: www.sterlingrope.com
SIC: 2298 Rope, except asbestos and wire
HQ: Sherrill, Inc.
496 Gallimore Dairy Rd D
Greensboro NC 27409
336 378-0444

(G-4591)
THERMOFORMED PLASTICS NENG LLC
362 Hill St (04005-4341)
PHONE.....................207 286-1775
Paul Tyson, *Managing Member*
EMP: 12 EST: 2002
SALES (est): 2.33MM Privately Held
Web: www.tpne.com
SIC: 3089 Injection molding of plastics

(G-4592)
TRIANGLE DESIGN GROUP LLC
649 Elm St (04005-4421)
PHONE.....................207 776-3177
EMP: 10 EST: 2019
SALES (est): 2.41MM Privately Held
Web: www.triangledesigngroup.com
SIC: 3613 Control panels, electric

(G-4593)
VALMET INC
516 Alfred St (04005-9432)
PHONE.....................207 282-1521
Thomas Claus, *Prin*
EMP: 182
SALES (corp-wide): 5.27B Privately Held
Web: www.valmet.com
SIC: 3554 Paper industries machinery
HQ: Valmet, Inc.
3720 Davinci Ct Ste 300
Norcross GA 30092
770 263-7863

(G-4594)
VOLK PACKAGING CORPORATION
11 Morin St Biddeford Industrial Park (04005-4498)
P.O. Box 1011 (04005-1011)
PHONE.....................207 282-6151
Douglas A Volk, *CEO*

Gerk Volk, *
Doug Hellstrom, *
Derek Volk, *
EMP: 74 **EST:** 1967
SQ FT: 140,000
SALES (est): 19.72MM **Privately Held**
Web: www.volkboxes.com
SIC: 2653 2657 2652 Boxes, corrugated:
    made from purchased materials; Folding
    paperboard boxes; Setup paperboard boxes

Blue Hill
Hancock County

(G-4595)
BOREALIS PRESS INC
35 Tenney Hl (04614-5948)
P.O. Box 1988 (04416-1988)
PHONE.............................800 669-6845
Mark Baldwin, *Pr*
EMP: 9 **EST:** 1983
SALES (est): 817.98K **Privately Held**
Web: www.borealispress.net
SIC: 2771 Greeting cards

(G-4596)
SISTERS SALSA INC
689 Hinckley Ridge Rd (04614-5701)
PHONE.............................207 374-2170
James Buddington, *Pr*
EMP: 8 **EST:** 2009
SALES (est): 725.74K **Privately Held**
Web: www.sisterssalsa.com
SIC: 2099 Food preparations, nec

Boothbay
Lincoln County

(G-4597)
ELKINS & CO INC
103 Industrial Park Rd (04537-4670)
PHONE.............................207 633-0109
Michael R Elkins, *Pr*
Jennifer B Elkins, *Treas*
EMP: 10 **EST:** 1992
SQ FT: 7,700
SALES (est): 836.52K **Privately Held**
Web: www.mainecabinetmaker.com
SIC: 2426 Furniture stock and parts,
    hardwood

(G-4598)
KNICKERBOCKER GROUP INC
Also Called: Boothbay Home Builders
8 Builders Sq (04537-5161)
PHONE.............................207 541-9333
Stephen Malcom, *CEO*
Danielle Betts, *
EMP: 75 **EST:** 1978
SALES (est): 4.89MM **Privately Held**
Web: www.knickerbockergroup.com
SIC: 7389 2451 Interior design services;
    Mobile homes

Boothbay Harbor
Lincoln County

(G-4599)
A SILVER LINING INC
Also Called: Maine Bracelet Company, The
17 Townsend Ave (04538-1840)
P.O. Box 477 (04538-0477)
PHONE.............................207 633-4103
Anthony Heyl, *Pr*
EMP: 7 **EST:** 1977
SALES (est): 621.89K **Privately Held**

Web: www.asilverlining.com
SIC: 5944 3911 5094 Jewelry, precious
    stones and precious metals; Jewelry,
    precious metal; Jewelry

(G-4600)
ALLEY ROAD LLC
120 Commercial St (04538-1823)
P.O. Box 462 (04538-0462)
PHONE.............................207 633-3171
EMP: 18 **EST:** 2008
SALES (est): 492.54K **Privately Held**
SIC: 3732 Boatbuilding and repairing

(G-4601)
BBH APPAREL
45 Commercial St (04538-1826)
PHONE.............................207 633-0601
EMP: 10 **EST:** 1996
SQ FT: 1,300
SALES (est): 739.36K **Privately Held**
Web: www.bbhapparel.com
SIC: 2395 7336 7389 Embroidery products,
    except Schiffli machine; Silk screen design;
    Embroidery advertising

(G-4602)
MAINE-OK ENTERPRISES INC
Also Called: Wiscasset Newspaper
97 Townsend Ave (04538-1843)
P.O. Box 357 (04538-0357)
PHONE.............................207 633-4620
A R Tandy, *Pr*
EMP: 17
SALES (est): 728.65K **Privately Held**
Web: www.boothbayregister.com
SIC: 2711 Newspapers, publishing and
    printing

(G-4603)
MCDONALD STAIN GLASS LTD
7 Wall Point Rd (04538-2308)
PHONE.............................207 633-4815
Richard Macdonald, *Pr*
EMP: 7 **EST:** 1970
SALES (est): 490.29K **Privately Held**
Web: www.macdonaldglass.com
SIC: 3229 3231 Novelty glassware;
    Products of purchased glass

(G-4604)
**SHIPYARD IN BOOTHBAY HBR
LLC**
Also Called: Boothbay Harbor Shipyard
120 Commercial St (04538-1823)
PHONE.............................207 633-3171
Andy Tyska, *Prin*
EMP: 20 **EST:** 2017
SALES (est): 470.48K
SALES (corp-wide): 6.75MM **Privately
Held**
Web: www.boothbayharbormarina.com
SIC: 4493 3732 Marinas; Sailboats, building
    and repairing
PA: Lenmarine, Inc.
    99 Poppasquash Rd Ste 1
    Bristol RI 02809
    401 253-2200

Bowdoin
Sagadahoc County

(G-4605)
FHC INC (PA)
1201 Main St (04287-7302)
PHONE.............................207 666-8190
Frederick Haer, *Ch*
Stephanie Dundas, *Finance**

EMP: 85 **EST:** 1986
SQ FT: 35,000
SALES (est): 21.47MM
SALES (corp-wide): 21.47MM **Privately
Held**
Web: www.fh-co.com
SIC: 3845 3826 Electromedical equipment;
    Analytical instruments

Bowdoinham
Sagadahoc County

(G-4606)
RICHMOND CONTRACT MFG
85 White Rd (04008-5422)
P.O. Box 247 (04357-0247)
PHONE.............................207 737-4385
Wayne Bodge, *Pr*
Linda Douglass, *VP*
Jim Margetts, *VP*
Jim Margette, *Prin*
EMP: 11 **EST:** 1999
SQ FT: 27,500
SALES (est): 379.74K **Privately Held**
SIC: 3625 Control circuit devices, magnet
    and solid state

Bremen
Lincoln County

(G-4607)
COMMUNITY SHELLFISH CO LLC
656 Waldoboro Rd (04551-3221)
P.O. Box 106 (04551-0106)
PHONE.............................207 529-2700
John Marsh, *Prin*
Gary Worthley, *Prin*
EMP: 25 **EST:** 2007
SALES (est): 1.62MM **Privately Held**
Web: www.communityshellfish.com
SIC: 2091 Broth, fish and seafood:
    packaged in cans, jars, etc.

Brewer
Penobscot County

(G-4608)
ALAN S BOLSTER
Also Called: Aerus
413 Wilson St (04412-1521)
PHONE.............................207 989-5143
Alan S Bolster, *Owner*
Alan S Bolster, *Prin*
EMP: 10 **EST:** 2007
SALES (est): 644.13K **Privately Held**
Web: www.beyondbyaerus.com
SIC: 1799 3589 5999 Decontamination
    services; Water filters and softeners,
    household type; Air purification equipment

(G-4609)
AMERICAN NAMEPLATE
103 Center St (04412-2603)
P.O. Box 291 (04412-0291)
PHONE.............................207 848-7187
EMP: 8
SALES (corp-wide): 244.72K **Privately
Held**
Web: www.amernameplate.com
SIC: 3993 Signs and advertising specialties
PA: American Nameplate
    21 White Pine Rd Ste 1
    Hermon ME 04401
    207 848-7187

(G-4610)
BIOTRONIK INC
3 Clover Ln (04412-1301)
PHONE.............................207 944-5515
EMP: 7 **EST:** 2018
SALES (est): 72.52K **Privately Held**
Web: www.biotronik.com
SIC: 3841 Surgical and medical instruments

(G-4611)
**DOWN EAST SHTMTL & CERTIF
WLDG**
19 Sparks Ave (04412-1446)
P.O. Box 332 (04412-0332)
PHONE.............................207 989-3443
James Hillman, *Pr*
EMP: 9 **EST:** 1990
SALES (est): 950.79K **Privately Held**
Web: www.downeastsheetmetal.com
SIC: 3444 7692 Sheet metal specialties, not
    stamped; Welding repair

(G-4612)
FAULKNER CORPORATION
Also Called: R.D. Faulkner
146 Parkway S (04412-1655)
PHONE.............................207 989-3792
Reginald Faulkner, *Pr*
▲ **EMP:** 9 **EST:** 1961
SQ FT: 28,000
SALES (est): 711.61K **Privately Held**
Web: www.rdfaulkner.com
SIC: 5084 3949 Chainsaws; Sporting and
    athletic goods, nec

(G-4613)
GETCHELL BROS INC (PA)
1 Union St (04412-2040)
P.O. Box 8 (04412-0008)
PHONE.............................800 949-4423
Douglas Farnham, *Pr*
EMP: 20 **EST:** 1888
SQ FT: 20,000
SALES (est): 9.16MM
SALES (corp-wide): 9.16MM **Privately
Held**
Web: www.arcticglacier.com
SIC: 5143 2097 Ice cream and ices; Block
    ice

(G-4614)
**HIGHLAND BELTS & FINE LEA
GDS**
96 Parkway S (04412-1685)
PHONE.............................207 989-2597
Adam Sutton, *Owner*
EMP: 15 **EST:** 2015
SALES (est): 1.31MM **Privately Held**
SIC: 5136 2387 2389 Apparel belts, men's
    and boys'; Apparel belts; Men's
    miscellaneous accessories

(G-4615)
L H THOMPSON INC
Also Called: Thompson Printing
54 Wilson St (04412-2024)
PHONE.............................207 989-3280
Paul Kenneth Smith, *Pr*
Thomas E Needham, *Clerk*
EMP: 16 **EST:** 1902
SALES (est): 328.33K **Privately Held**
SIC: 2752 Offset printing

(G-4616)
**LANE CONVEYORS & DRIVES
INC**
Also Called: Lane Supply Company
15 Industrial Plaza Dr (04412-2241)

▲ = Import ▼ = Export
◆ = Import/Export

P.O. Box 218 (04412-0218)
PHONE..............................207 989-4560
EMP: 52
SIC: 5085 3441 3599   Industrial supplies;
Fabricated structural metal; Machine shop,
jobbing and repair

(G-4617)
M & S ENTERPRISES INC
Also Called: Evergreen Home & Hearth
603 Wilson St (04412-1418)
PHONE..............................207 989-0077
Matthew J Scott, *Prin*
EMP: 9 **EST:** 2016
SALES (est): 1.52MM **Privately Held**
Web: www.mainestoves.com
SIC: 5074 2449 3631   Stoves, wood burning;
Tubs, wood: coopered; Barbecues, grills,
and braziers (outdoor cooking)

(G-4618)
M DRUG LLC
Also Called: Miller Drug Whiting Hill Phrm
33 Whiting Hill Rd Ste 4 (04412-1022)
PHONE..............................207 973-9444
EMP: 8 **EST:** 2010
SALES (est): 426.01K **Privately Held**
SIC: 2834   Pharmaceutical preparations

(G-4619)
SOMIC AMERICA INC
6 Baker Blvd (04412-2253)
PHONE..............................207 989-1759
EMP: 100
Web: www.somicamerica.com
SIC: 3714   Motor vehicle parts and
accessories
HQ: Somic America, Inc.
343 E Lee Trinkle Dr
Wytheville VA 24382

(G-4620)
T J RYAN LLC
Also Called: Kickit Sports
90 Acme Rd (04412-1523)
PHONE..............................207 989-7183
Louis Janicki, *Pt*
Caryle Janicki, *Pt*
EMP: 10 **EST:** 1994
SQ FT: 35,000
SALES (est): 625.34K **Privately Held**
SIC: 5941 2759 7941 8661   Soccer supplies;
Screen printing; Ice hockey club; Religious
organizations

(G-4621)
TIS BREWER LLC
Also Called: Troy Industrial Solutions
15 Industrial Plaza Dr (04412-2241)
PHONE..............................207 989-4560
Jason Smith, *Pr*
EMP: 50 **EST:** 2015
SALES (est): 8.19MM **Privately Held**
SIC: 5085 3441 3599   Industrial supplies;
Fabricated structural metal; Machine shop,
jobbing and repair

(G-4622)
TURBINE SPECIALISTS LLC
55 Baker Blvd (04412-2200)
PHONE..............................207 947-9327
▲ **EMP:** 17 **EST:** 2000
SQ FT: 5,000
SALES (est): 385.59K **Privately Held**
SIC: 3471   Finishing, metals or formed
products

(G-4623)
**W S EMERSON COMPANY INC
(PA)**
15 Acme Rd (04412-1500)
P.O. Box 10 (04412-0010)
PHONE..............................207 989-3410
John A Vickery, *Pr*
Russel M Vicery, *
John A Vickery Junior, *VP*
EMP: 41 **EST:** 1921
SQ FT: 35,000
SALES (est): 9.92MM
SALES (corp-wide): 9.92MM **Privately
Held**
Web: www.wsemerson.com
SIC: 2759   Screen printing

(G-4624)
WESTMOR INDUSTRIES LLC
42 Coffin Ave (04412-2271)
PHONE..............................207 989-0100
Kenneth Peters, *Pr*
EMP: 50
SALES (corp-wide): 344.76MM **Privately
Held**
Web: www.westmor-ind.com
SIC: 3443   Tanks for tank trucks, metal plate
HQ: Westmor Industries, Llc
7 Industrial Blvd
Morris MN 56267
320 589-2100

Bridgewater
Aroostook County

(G-4625)
**E G W BRADBURY
ENTERPRISES INC**
Also Called: Bradbury Barrel Co
100 Main St (04735-3011)
P.O. Box 129 (04735-0129)
PHONE..............................207 429-8141
Adelle F Bradbury, *Pr*
D Wayne Bradbury, *VP*
William Yerxa, *Sec*
EMP: 16 **EST:** 1974
SQ FT: 12,000
SALES (est): 701.9K **Privately Held**
SIC: 2541 2542 2449   Store fixtures, wood;
Partitions and fixtures, except wood; Wood
containers, nec

Bridgton
Cumberland County

(G-4626)
**BRIDGTON NEWS
CORPORATION**
Also Called: Bridgton News The
118 Main St (04009-1127)
P.O. Box 244 (04009-0244)
PHONE..............................207 647-2851
Stephen Shorey, *Pr*
Eric Gulberndsen, *Adm/Asst*
EMP: 12 **EST:** 1870
SQ FT: 3,000
SALES (est): 335.63K **Privately Held**
Web: www.bridgton.com
SIC: 2711   Newspapers, publishing and
printing

(G-4627)
**CUSTOM CANVAS &
UPHOLSTERY LLC**
721 Portland Rd (04009-4221)
P.O. Box 877 (04009-0877)

PHONE..............................207 241-8518
EMP: 15 **EST:** 2011
SALES (est): 668.34K **Privately Held**
Web: www.customcanvasupholstery.com
SIC: 2512 2394 5999 5714   Upholstered
household furniture; Canvas and related
products; Canvas products; Upholstery
materials

(G-4628)
EVERETT MCCABE
Also Called: McCabe Logging and Tree Svc
21 Smith Ave (04009-1326)
P.O. Box 131 (04267-0131)
PHONE..............................207 890-9174
Everett Mccabe, *Prin*
EMP: 7 **EST:** 2016
SALES (est): 255.48K **Privately Held**
Web:
www.mccabeloggingandtreeservice.com
SIC: 2411   Logging

(G-4629)
**HOWELL LABORATORIES INC
(PA)**
Also Called: Conservation Systems
188 Harrison Rd (04009-4748)
P.O. Box 389 (04009-0389)
PHONE..............................207 647-3327
David Allen, *Pr*
Paul A Wescott, *
Carl H Bishop, *
Martyn Gregory, *
◆ **EMP:** 48 **EST:** 1964
SQ FT: 33,000
SALES (est): 26.48MM
SALES (corp-wide): 26.48MM **Privately
Held**
Web: www.howelllabs.com
SIC: 5551 3663   Marine supplies and
equipment; Antennas, transmitting and
communications

Bristol
Lincoln County

(G-4630)
HANLEY CONSTRUCTION INC
1829 Bristol Rd (04539-3511)
PHONE..............................207 677-2207
Mark Hanley, *Pr*
EMP: 10 **EST:** 1953
SQ FT: 1,120
SALES (est): 1.6MM **Privately Held**
Web: www.hanleyconstructioninc.com
SIC: 1794 1442   Excavation and grading,
building construction; Gravel mining

(G-4631)
MASTERS MACHINE COMPANY
500 Lower Round Pond Rd (04539-3219)
P.O. Box 16 (04564-0016)
PHONE..............................207 529-5191
Debra Stacy, *CFO*
▲ **EMP:** 114 **EST:** 1957
SQ FT: 120,000
SALES (est): 24.16MM **Privately Held**
Web: www.mastersmachine.com
SIC: 3599   Machine shop, jobbing and repair

Brooklin
Hancock County

(G-4632)
BROOKLIN BOAT YARD INC (PA)
Also Called: Stephens, Waring and White
44 Center Harbor Rd Ste 44 (04616-3511)

P.O. Box 143 (04616-0143)
PHONE..............................207 359-2236
J Steven White, *Pr*
Frank C Hull, *
EMP: 49 **EST:** 1960
SQ FT: 15,000
SALES (est): 6.64MM
SALES (corp-wide): 6.64MM **Privately
Held**
Web: www.brooklinboatyard.com
SIC: 3732 4493   Yachts, building and
repairing; Boat yards, storage and
incidental repair

(G-4633)
CROSSFOX INC
Flye Point Rd (04616)
P.O. Box 217 (04616-0217)
PHONE..............................207 664-2900
O D Hopkins, *CEO*
EMP: 12 **EST:** 1995
SALES (est): 405.09K **Privately Held**
Web: www.atlanticboat.com
SIC: 3732   Boats, fiberglass: building and
repairing

(G-4634)
OFF CENTER HARBOR LLC
7 Bay Rd (04616)
PHONE..............................401 487-2090
Steven Stone, *CEO*
EMP: 8 **EST:** 2011
SALES (est): 740.8K **Privately Held**
Web: www.offcenterharbor.com
SIC: 3069   Fabricated rubber products, nec

(G-4635)
**WOODENBOAT PUBLICATIONS
INC**
Also Called: Professional Boat Builder
41 Wooden Boat Ln (04616-3371)
P.O. Box 78 (04616-0078)
PHONE..............................207 359-4651
TOLL FREE: 800
James Miller, *Pr*
Jonathan A Wilson, *
▲ **EMP:** 45 **EST:** 1974
SQ FT: 12,000
SALES (est): 7.16MM **Privately Held**
Web: www.woodenboat.com
SIC: 2721   Magazines: publishing only, not
printed on site

Brownfield
Oxford County

(G-4636)
LAWRENCE PARSON
Also Called: Parson's Kitchen
510 Hampshire Rd (04010-4031)
PHONE..............................207 935-3737
Lawrence Parson, *Owner*
EMP: 9 **EST:** 1982
SQ FT: 3,000
SALES (est): 1.16MM **Privately Held**
Web: www.parsonskitchens.com
SIC: 2434   Wood kitchen cabinets

Brownville
Piscataquis County

(G-4637)
EARL W GERRISH & SONS
2 Charlottes Rd (04414-3002)
P.O. Box 630 (04414-0630)
PHONE..............................207 965-2171
Earl W Gerrish Junior, *Pr*

GEOGRAPHIC

Earl W Gerrish Junior, *Pr*
Daniel Gerrish Senior, *VP*
Ronald Gerrish, *VP*
Peter Gerrish, *VP*
EMP: 15 EST: 1949
SALES (est): 1.02MM **Privately Held**
SIC: 1442 4212 0711 1711　Construction sand and gravel; Lumber and timber trucking; Plowing services; Septic system construction

(G-4638)
S & K UNLIMITED　LLC
Also Called: Trilliam Solutions
33 Front St　(04414-3702)
PHONE..............................207 965-6137
EMP: 14 EST: 2008
SQ FT: 5,000
SALES (est): 1.16MM **Privately Held**
SIC: 2992 8742 7374 8711　Lubricating oils and greases; Marketing consulting services ; Computer graphics service; Engineering services

Brunswick
Cumberland County

(G-4639)
ALLIANCE PRINTERS　LLC
Also Called: Alliance Press, The
3 Business Pkwy Ste 1　(04011-7549)
P.O. Box 10　(04011-1302)
PHONE..............................207 504-8200
Chris P Mile, *CEO*
▲ **EMP: 9 EST:** 2012
SALES (est): 387.08K **Privately Held**
SIC: 2752　Offset printing

(G-4640)
ARTFORMS (PA)
128 Maine St　(04011-2011)
PHONE..............................800 828-8518
Joanne Malia, *Dir*
◆ **EMP: 7 EST:** 2012
SALES (est): 4.91MM
SALES (corp-wide): 4.91MM **Privately Held**
Web: www.artformsinc.com
SIC: 2759　Screen printing

(G-4641)
BATH IRON WORKS CORPORATION
Mallet Park　(04011)
PHONE..............................207 442-1266
Chris Marco, *Brnch Mgr*
EMP: 24
SALES (corp-wide): 42.27B **Publicly Held**
Web: www.gdbiw.com
SIC: 3731　Shipbuilding and repairing
HQ: Bath Iron Works Corporation
　　700 Washington St Stop 1
　　Bath ME 04530
　　207 443-3311

(G-4642)
BLUSHIFT AEROSPACE INC
2 Pegasus St Ste 2　(04011-5018)
PHONE..............................207 619-1703
Sascha Deri, *CEO*
EMP: 13 EST: 2014
SALES (est): 2.24MM **Privately Held**
Web: www.blushiftaerospace.com
SIC: 3764 3761　Rocket motors, guided missiles; Rockets, space and military, complete

(G-4643)
BRUNSWICK PUBLISHING LLC
3 Business Pkwy　(04011-7549)
P.O. Box 10　(04011-1302)
PHONE..............................207 729-3311
EMP: 19 EST: 2007
SALES (est): 786.33K **Privately Held**
SIC: 2711　Newspapers, publishing and printing

(G-4644)
CLAMAR FLOATS INC
74 Orion St　(04011-5031)
PHONE..............................603 828-5373
EMP: 7 EST: 2018
SALES (est): 761.56K **Privately Held**
Web: www.clamarfloats.com
SIC: 3728　Aircraft parts and equipment, nec

(G-4645)
ERIC T VANNAH
Also Called: Vannah Logging
8 Oakwood Ter　(04011-1629)
PHONE..............................207 631-2475
Eric Vannah, *Prin*
EMP: 7 EST: 2016
SALES (est): 353.32K **Privately Held**
SIC: 2411　Logging

(G-4646)
IDENTITY GROUP HOLDINGS CORP
Also Called: Allen Screen Printing
43 Bibber Pkwy　(04011-7357)
PHONE..............................207 510-6800
Josh Wolfgram, *Brnch Mgr*
EMP: 40
SALES (corp-wide): 127.27MM **Privately Held**
Web: www.identitygroup.com
SIC: 2759　Screen printing
PA: Identity Group Holdings Corp.
　　1480 Gould Dr
　　Cookeville TN 38506
　　931 432-4000

(G-4647)
L L BEAN　INC
Also Called: LL Bean Mfg Bus
8 Industrial Pkwy　(04011-7314)
PHONE..............................207 725-0300
Mike Laflamme, *Dir*
EMP: 16
SALES (corp-wide): 593.78MM **Privately Held**
Web: www.llbean.com
SIC: 3143 3144 3161 2384　Men's footwear, except athletic; Women's footwear, except athletic; Luggage; Robes and dressing gowns
PA: L. L. Bean, Inc.
　　15 Casco St
　　Freeport ME 04033
　　207 552-2000

(G-4648)
MAINE NATURAL GAS CORPORATION
9 Industrial Pkwy　(04011-7550)
PHONE..............................207 729-0420
Dennis V Arriola, *CEO*
EMP: 16 EST: 1998
SALES (est): 81.96K **Privately Held**
Web: www.mainenaturalgas.com
SIC: 1311　Natural gas production

(G-4649)
MAINE WOOLENS　LLC
15 Paul St　(04011-2807)

P.O. Box 221　(04011-0221)
PHONE..............................207 725-7900
EMP: 30 EST: 2008
SALES (est): 2.36MM **Privately Held**
SIC: 2211　Blankets and blanketings, cotton

(G-4650)
MEDICAL RESOURCES　INC
Also Called: Inside Premier Health
11 Medical Center Dr Ste 1　(04011-3061)
PHONE..............................207 721-1110
Cristy Joubert, *Ex Dir*
EMP: 28
SALES (corp-wide): 49.65MM **Privately Held**
Web: www.medicalresources.com
SIC: 3841　Diagnostic apparatus, medical
PA: Medical Resources, Inc.
　　1455 Broad St Ste 4
　　Bloomfield NJ 07003
　　973 707-1100

(G-4651)
NATURAL SELECTION　INC
Also Called: Wild Oats Bakery
166 Admiral Fitch Ave　(04011-2793)
PHONE..............................207 725-6287
David Shepherd, *Pr*
Rebecca Shepherd, *
Marshall Shepherd, *
EMP: 26 EST: 1981
SQ FT: 2,250
SALES (est): 2.4MM **Privately Held**
Web: www.wildoatsbakery.com
SIC: 5461 5812 2051 5411　Retail bakeries; Restaurant, family: independent; Cakes, bakery: except frozen; Delicatessen stores

(G-4652)
NORTHERN TURF PRFESSIONALS INC
251 Old Portland Rd　(04011-7273)
P.O. Box 285　(04011-0285)
PHONE..............................207 522-8598
EMP: 11 EST: 2010
SALES (est): 515.47K **Privately Held**
SIC: 2879 0782　Insecticides and pesticides; Fertilizing services, lawn

(G-4653)
OCV FABRICS US　INC
43 Bibber Pkwy　(04011-7357)
PHONE..............................207 729-7792
Phil Harmon, *Pr*
◆ **EMP: 93 EST:** 1984
SQ FT: 50,000
SALES (est): 25.94MM **Publicly Held**
SIC: 2221　Broadwoven fabric mills, manmade
PA: Owens Corning
　　1 Owens Corning Pkwy
　　Toledo OH 43659

(G-4654)
RAVEN TECHNOLOGY LLC
14 Industrial Pkwy　(04011-7358)
PHONE..............................207 729-7904
Christopher Tupper, *Dir*
EMP: 10 EST: 1999
SQ FT: 3,600
SALES (est): 983.85K **Privately Held**
Web: www.raventechpower.com
SIC: 3621　Generators and sets, electric

(G-4655)
STARC SYSTEMS　INC
112 Orion St Ste 100　(04011-5004)
PHONE..............................844 596-1784
Timothy Hebert, *CEO*
Bruce Bickford, *

Chris Mackenzie, *
EMP: 82 EST: 2014
SALES (est): 13.52MM **Privately Held**
Web: www.starcsystems.com
SIC: 2542　Fixtures, office: except wood

(G-4656)
SYLLAWORKS LLC
Also Called: Syllametrics
1 Laurel Rd　(04011-3419)
PHONE..............................617 564-3727
EMP: 11 EST: 2016
SALES (est): 322.48K **Privately Held**
SIC: 7372　Educational computer software

(G-4657)
WESTCON MFG INC
Also Called: Theam
22 Bibber Pkwy　(04011-7357)
PHONE..............................207 725-5537
John Garrec, *Pr*
Lolly Garrec, *
▲ **EMP: 25 EST:** 1981
SALES (est): 3.01MM **Privately Held**
Web: www.theamconveyors.com
SIC: 3555　Printing trades machinery

Buckfield
Oxford County

(G-4658)
R E LOWELL LUMBER　CO INC
132 N Hill Rd　(04220-4312)
P.O. Box 336　(04220-0336)
PHONE..............................207 336-2901
Edith Lowell, *VP*
Dana Lowell, *
Rebecca Lowell, *
Edith Pepin, *
EMP: 27 EST: 1948
SQ FT: 3,000
SALES (est): 4.84MM **Privately Held**
Web: www.lowelllumber.com
SIC: 5251 5211 5031 2421　Hardware stores ; Millwork and lumber; Millwork; Sawmills and planing mills, general

(G-4659)
TURNING ACQUISITIONS LLC
Also Called: Wells Wood Turning & Finishing
46 John Ellingwood Rd　(04220-4360)
P.O. Box 220　(04220-0220)
PHONE..............................207 336-2400
Simon Varney, *
EMP: 16 EST: 2005
SALES (est): 1.68MM **Privately Held**
Web: www.wellswoodturning.com
SIC: 2426 2499　Turnings, furniture: wood; Carved and turned wood

Burnham
Waldo County

(G-4660)
MEDALIST CORP
Also Called: Medalist Corp
10 N Main St　(04922-3300)
PHONE..............................615 620-8280
James Stutts Junior, *Admn*
EMP: 32
SIC: 3339　Primary nonferrous metals, nec
PA: Macneill Pride Group Corp.
　　2236 Rutherford Rd # 107
　　Carlsbad CA 92008

▲ = Import ▼ = Export
◆ = Import/Export

(G-4661)
PRIDE MANUFACTURING CO LLC (PA)
Also Called: Pride Sports
10 N Main St (04922-3300)
PHONE...............................207 487-3322
Richard Dupont, *
▲ EMP: 120 EST: 1930
SQ FT: 87,000
SALES (est): 49.85MM
SALES (corp-wide): 49.85MM Privately Held
SIC: 2411 3949   Handle bolts, wood: hewn; Bags, golf

Buxton
York County

(G-4662)
DONUT HOLE INC
Also Called: Donut Hole
4 Pierce Dr (04093-6018)
PHONE...............................207 929-5060
Ronald J Arborio, Pr
George F Burns, Clerk
EMP: 10 EST: 1981
SALES (est): 563.03K Privately Held
Web: www.donuthole.com
SIC: 5461 2051   Doughnuts; Bread, cake, and related products

(G-4663)
MAINE BUNK BEDS LLC
355 Joy Valley Rd (04093-6235)
PHONE...............................207 929-4499
Jim Steffensen, Managing Member
EMP: 12 EST: 2012
SALES (est): 449.75K Privately Held
Web: www.mainebunkbeds.com
SIC: 2511 5712   Wood household furniture; Beds and accessories

(G-4664)
SACO BAY MILLWORK CO
20 Tory Hill Dr (04093-6155)
P.O. Box 86 (04004-0086)
PHONE...............................207 929-8400
Dave Durrell, VP
Dave Burrell, VP
Tim Flynn, Pr
EMP: 8 EST: 2006
SALES (est): 224.47K Privately Held
SIC: 2431   Millwork

(G-4665)
TEM INC
Also Called: T E M
8 Pierce Dr (04093-6018)
PHONE...............................207 929-8700
Eric Nelson, Pr
▲ EMP: 29 EST: 1976
SQ FT: 26,000
SALES (est): 33.62K Privately Held
Web: www.temmachining.com
SIC: 3724 3462 3463   Aircraft engines and engine parts; Turbine engine forgings, ferrous; Nonferrous forgings

(G-4666)
VITAMINSEA LLC
369 Beech Plain Rd (04093-6320)
PHONE...............................207 671-0955
EMP: 8 EST: 2012
SALES (est): 940K Privately Held
Web: www.vitaminseaseaweed.com
SIC: 3519   Marine engines

Camden
Knox County

(G-4667)
LYMAN MORSE BOATBUILDING INC
59 Sea St (04843-1731)
PHONE...............................207 236-4378
Lyman Cabot, Prin
EMP: 12
SALES (corp-wide): 24.89MM Privately Held
Web: www.lymanmorse.com
SIC: 3732   Yachts, building and repairing
PA: Lyman Morse Boatbuilding, Inc.
84 Knox St
Thomaston ME 04861
207 354-6904

(G-4668)
SIERRA PEAKS CORPORATION
5 Colcord Ave (04843-2005)
P.O. Box 1096 (04843-1096)
PHONE...............................207 236-3301
EMP: 48 EST: 2007
SALES (est): 1.41MM Privately Held
Web: www.sierra-peaks.com
SIC: 3669   Intercommunication systems, electric
PA: Sierra Peaks Corporation
4801 Lincoln Rd Ne
Albuquerque NM 87109

Canaan
Somerset County

(G-4669)
GOOD CRUST LLC
70 Pinnacle Rd (04924-3019)
PHONE...............................207 522-4872
Heather R Kerner, Managing Member
EMP: 9 EST: 2020
SALES (est): 452.88K Privately Held
Web: www.thegoodcrust.com
SIC: 2045   Pizza doughs, prepared: from purchased flour

(G-4670)
OLSON S LOGGING LLC
15 Strickland Rd (04924-3032)
PHONE...............................207 474-8835
Daim Meyer, Prin
EMP: 7 EST: 2014
SALES (est): 325.08K Privately Held
SIC: 2411   Logging

Canton
Oxford County

(G-4671)
KW PRODUCTS LLC
4 Golden Pond Rd (04221-3158)
PHONE...............................207 357-3798
Kevin White, Prin
EMP: 7 EST: 2016
SALES (est): 132.88K Privately Held
Web: www.kwproducts.org
SIC: 3599   Machine shop, jobbing and repair

Cape Neddick
York County

(G-4672)
RAWZ NATURAL PET FOOD (PA)
40 Adams Rd (03902-7173)
PHONE...............................207 363-0684
Jim Scott, CEO
EMP: 12 EST: 2014
SALES (est): 1.06MM
SALES (corp-wide): 1.06MM Privately Held
Web: www.rawznaturalpetfood.com
SIC: 2048   Frozen pet food (except dog and cat)

Cardville
Penobscot County

(G-4673)
STEPHEN F MADDEN
183 Greenfield Rd (04418-3501)
P.O. Box 59 (04418-0059)
PHONE...............................207 827-5737
EMP: 7 EST: 1972
SALES (est): 410.19K Privately Held
SIC: 2411   Logging camps and contractors

Caribou
Aroostook County

(G-4674)
COUNTY QWIK PRINT INC
56 Sweden St (04736-2110)
P.O. Box 621 (04736-0621)
PHONE...............................207 492-0360
Dave Levesque, Pr
Anissa Levesque, Ex VP
EMP: 10 EST: 1990
SQ FT: 5,000
SALES (est): 2.27MM Privately Held
Web: www.countyqwikprint.com
SIC: 2752   Offset printing

(G-4675)
GARY RAYMOND
Also Called: Gary's Sales and Service
1121 Presque Isle Rd (04736-4202)
PHONE...............................207 498-2549
Gary Raymond, Owner
Mary Raymond, Owner
EMP: 7 EST: 1982
SALES (est): 969.36K Privately Held
Web: www.garysautocaribou.com
SIC: 5571 5251 5561 5261   Motorcycle dealers; Tools; Recreational vehicle parts and accessories; Lawnmowers and tractors

(G-4676)
MAINE POTATO GROWERS INC
Also Called: Maine Bag Co
56 Sincock St (04736-2344)
PHONE...............................207 764-3131
Lester Hersey, Mgr
EMP: 14
SALES (corp-wide): 28.4MM Privately Held
Web: www.mpgco-op.com
SIC: 2674 5199   Bags: uncoated paper and multiwall; Packaging materials
PA: Maine Potato Growers, Inc.
261 Main St
Presque Isle ME 04769
207 764-3131

(G-4677)
NORTHEAST PUBLISHING COMPANY
Also Called: Aroostook Republic and News
159 Bennett Dr (04736-2049)
P.O. Box 510 (04769-0510)
PHONE...............................207 496-3251
Andrew Bearden, Prin
EMP: 9
SALES (corp-wide): 39.35MM Privately Held
SIC: 7311 2711   Advertising agencies; Commercial printing and newspaper publishing combined
HQ: Northeast Publishing Company Inc
260 Missile St
Presque Isle ME 04769
207 764-4471

(G-4678)
ONIX CORPORATION
71 Main St (04736-4159)
P.O. Box 270 (04736-0270)
PHONE...............................866 290-5362
Charles Verhoff, Pr
Charles Verhoff, CEO
Chris Osborne, *
Janet Marr, *
EMP: 12 EST: 1992
SQ FT: 100,000
SALES (est): 329.31K Privately Held
Web: www.theonixcorp.com
SIC: 3567 3433 3443   Industrial furnaces and ovens; Heating equipment, except electric; Boilers: industrial, power, or marine

(G-4679)
PORVAIR FILTRATION GROUP INC
15 Armco Ave (04736-1601)
PHONE...............................207 493-3027
EMP: 10
SALES (corp-wide): 197.94MM Privately Held
Web: www.porvairfiltration.com
SIC: 3677   Filtration devices, electronic
HQ: Porvair Filtration Group, Inc.
301 Business Ln
Ashland VA 23005
804 550-1600

Carrabassett Valley
Franklin County

(G-4680)
SUGARLOAF AMBULANCE AND RESCUE
1003 Carriage Rd (04947-5328)
PHONE...............................207 235-2222
Steven Achilles, Dir
EMP: 13 EST: 1972
SALES (est): 166.26K Privately Held
Web: www.sugarloaf.com
SIC: 4119 3711   Ambulance service; Ambulances (motor vehicles), assembly of

Casco
Cumberland County

(G-4681)
JZ INC
46 Red Mill Rd (04015-3544)
P.O. Box 1000 (04077-1000)
PHONE...............................207 655-7520
Kermit A Schott, Pr

Kermit A Schott, *Pr*
EMP: 7 **EST:** 1979
SQ FT: 4,000
SALES (est): 765.38K **Privately Held**
Web: www.redmilllumber.com
SIC: 2421 Sawmills and planing mills, general

(G-4682)
NORTHEAST MILL WORK INC
22 Industrial Way (04015-3551)
P.O. Box 423 (04077-0423)
PHONE................................207 655-1202
EMP: 7 **EST:** 2017
SALES (est): 225.03K **Privately Held**
SIC: 2431 Millwork

(G-4683)
RIDLONS METAL SHOP
627 Roosevelt Trl (04015-3509)
PHONE................................207 655-7997
Mike Ridlon, *Owner*
EMP: 7 **EST:** 2000
SALES (est): 259.31K **Privately Held**
SIC: 3444 Sheet metalwork

(G-4684)
WILBERT SWANS VAULT CO
13 Scott Dr (04015-3525)
PHONE................................207 854-5324
Stephen Swan, *Pr*
Frank Frye, *Sec*
Susan Swan, *VP*
EMP: 20 **EST:** 1947
SALES (est): 999.16K **Privately Held**
SIC: 3272 5211 Burial vaults, concrete or precast terrazzo; Concrete and cinder block

(G-4685)
YANKEE MACHINE INC
1300 Poland Springs Rd Rte 11 (04015-3226)
P.O. Box 10 (04015-0010)
PHONE................................207 627-4277
Phillip N Hanson, *Pr*
Richard Thompson, *Clerk*
EMP: 22 **EST:** 1972
SQ FT: 8,600
SALES (est): 458.37K **Privately Held**
SIC: 3599 Machine shop, jobbing and repair

Charlotte
Washington County

(G-4686)
SKF
35 Sandy Beach Ln (04666-6311)
PHONE................................207 454-8078
EMP: 19 **EST:** 2018
SALES (est): 234.54K **Privately Held**
Web: www.skf.com
SIC: 3569 General industrial machinery, nec

Chelsea
Kennebec County

(G-4687)
NEW ENGLAND RENT TO OWN LLC
65 River Rd (04330-1013)
PHONE................................207 399-6181
EMP: 7 **EST:** 2019
SALES (est): 443.68K **Privately Held**
Web: www.newenglandrenttoown.com
SIC: 2452 Prefabricated wood buildings

Cherryfield
Washington County

(G-4688)
CHERRYFIELD FOODS INC (DH)
320 Ridge Rd (04622-4030)
P.O. Box 128 (04622-0128)
PHONE................................207 546-7573
John Bragg, *Pr*
Ragnar Kamp, *
Peter Durand, *
Milton Wood, *
Matthew Bragg, *
◆ **EMP:** 73 **EST:** 1991
SQ FT: 35,000
SALES (est): 59.34MM
SALES (corp-wide): 3.35MM **Privately Held**
Web: www.oxfordfrozenfoods.com
SIC: 2033 Fruits: packaged in cans, jars, etc.
HQ: Oxford Frozen Foods Limited
4881 Main St
Oxford NS B0M 1
902 447-2100

(G-4689)
JASPER WYMAN & SON
Rte 193 (04622)
P.O. Box 100 (04658-0100)
PHONE................................207 546-3381
Homer Woodward, *Brnch Mgr*
EMP: 11
SALES (corp-wide): 27.24MM **Privately Held**
Web: www.wymans.com
SIC: 2033 Canned fruits and specialties
PA: Jasper Wyman & Son
7 Wyman Rd
Milbridge ME 04658
207 546-3800

(G-4690)
JASPER WYMAN & SON
178 Main St (04622-4212)
PHONE................................207 546-3381
EMP: 25
SALES (corp-wide): 27.24MM **Privately Held**
Web: www.wymans.com
SIC: 2033 Canned fruits and specialties
PA: Jasper Wyman & Son
7 Wyman Rd
Milbridge ME 04658
207 546-3800

Chester
Penobscot County

(G-4691)
DAVIS BROTHERS INC
Also Called: Dbi
86 Access Rd (04457-5503)
PHONE................................207 794-1001
Heath Joe Davis, *Pr*
Tyler Davis, *VP*
EMP: 15 **EST:** 2000
SQ FT: 5,000
SALES (est): 2.47MM **Privately Held**
Web: www.davisbrothersinc.com
SIC: 7692 Welding repair

(G-4692)
DELAITE TRUCKING INC
Also Called: Delaite Trucking
45 Gray Rd (04457-5561)
P.O. Box 410 (04457-0410)
PHONE................................207 794-6844

Richard Delaitte, *Pr*
Judith Delaite, *Pt*
Richard Delaitte, *Pt*
Dave Delaite, *Pt*
EMP: 11 **EST:** 2001
SALES (est): 527.87K **Privately Held**
Web: www.delaitetrucking.com
SIC: 2411 Logging camps and contractors

(G-4693)
GARDNER CHPMLLS MLLINOCKET LLC
820 S Chesterrd (04457-5521)
P.O. Box 189 (04457-0189)
PHONE................................207 794-2223
Tom Gardner, *Prin*
EMP: 16 **EST:** 2005
SALES (est): 351.71K **Privately Held**
SIC: 3999 Manufacturing industries, nec

(G-4694)
WALPOLE OUTDOORS LLC
235 N Chester Rd (04457-5725)
PHONE................................207 794-2248
EMP: 20
SALES (corp-wide): 50.41MM **Privately Held**
Web: www.walpoleoutdoors.com
SIC: 2499 5211 5712 2452 Fencing, wood; Fencing; Outdoor and garden furniture; Prefabricated wood buildings
PA: Walpole Outdoors Llc
255 Patriot Pl
Foxboro MA 02035
508 668-2800

Chesterville
Franklin County

(G-4695)
WOOD-MIZER HOLDINGS INC
Also Called: Pine Tree Lumber
541 Borough Rd (04938-3301)
PHONE................................207 645-2072
Ross Clair, *Owner*
EMP: 18
SALES (corp-wide): 133.23MM **Privately Held**
Web: www.woodmizer.com
SIC: 2421 Custom sawmill
PA: Wood-Mizer Holdings, Inc.
8180 W 10th St
Indianapolis IN 46214
317 271-1542

China
Kennebec County

(G-4696)
M A HASKELL & SONS LLC
174 Mann Rd (04358-4435)
PHONE................................207 993-2265
William R Peebles, *Prin*
EMP: 9 **EST:** 2010
SALES (est): 1.88MM **Privately Held**
Web: www.haskelltrucking.com
SIC: 2869 Fuels

Clinton
Kennebec County

(G-4697)
A W CHAFFEE
163 Hinckley Rd (04927-3601)
P.O. Box 69 (04963-0069)

PHONE................................207 426-8588
Lowell Hall, *Mgr*
EMP: 35
SALES (corp-wide): 2.64MM **Privately Held**
SIC: 2421 Wood chips, produced at mill
PA: A W Chaffee
164 Belgrade Rd
Oakland ME 04963
207 465-3234

Columbia Falls
Washington County

(G-4698)
COUNTY CONCRETE & CNSTR CO
125 Pit Rd (04623-5116)
PHONE................................207 483-4409
Morrill Worcester, *Pr*
EMP: 21 **EST:** 1974
SQ FT: 3,360
SALES (est): 978.04K **Privately Held**
Web: www.usecounty.com
SIC: 3273 3531 1611 3275 Ready-mixed concrete; Asphalt plant, including gravel-mix type; Surfacing and paving; Wallboard, gypsum

(G-4699)
EPPING VOLUNTEER FIRE DISTRICT
Also Called: Epping Vfd
392 Us Rte-1 (04623)
P.O. Box 204 (04623-0204)
PHONE................................207 483-2036
Mark Howe, *Pr*
EMP: 7 **EST:** 2014
SALES (est): 89.74K **Privately Held**
SIC: 3711 Fire department vehicles (motor vehicles), assembly of

Connor Twp
Aroostook County

(G-4700)
ARCH PARENT INC
25 Emond Rd (04736-6634)
PHONE................................207 492-5414
Kermit Staples, *Brnch Mgr*
EMP: 12898
SALES (corp-wide): 499.13MM **Privately Held**
SIC: 2752 Commercial printing, lithographic
PA: Arch Parent Inc.
9 W 57th St Fl 31
New York NY 10019
212 796-8500

Corinna
Penobscot County

(G-4701)
MCKENNEY MACHINE & TOOL CO
Also Called: Mc Kenney Machine & Tool Co
400 Exeter Rd (04928-3514)
PHONE................................207 278-7091
Galen Mc Kenney, *Owner*
EMP: 15 **EST:** 1980
SQ FT: 5,000
SALES (est): 554.21K **Privately Held**
Web: www.mckenneymachine.com
SIC: 3599 Machine shop, jobbing and repair

(G-4702)
MELVIN L YODER
16 Bolstridge Rd (04928-3209)
PHONE..............................207 278-3539
Melvin L Yoder, *Prin*
EMP: 11 **EST:** 2001
SALES (est): 815.19K **Privately Held**
SIC: 2421 Sawmills and planing mills, general

(G-4703)
PERFECT FIT
39 Stetson Rd (04928-3617)
P.O. Box 439 (04928-0439)
PHONE..............................207 278-3333
◆ **EMP:** 18 **EST:** 1991
SQ FT: 13,000
SALES (est): 2.1MM **Privately Held**
Web: www.perfectfitusa.com
SIC: 3172 3199 Personal leather goods, nec ; Leather garments

Cornish
York County

(G-4704)
CONTOUR360 CORP
5 Industrial Way (04020-3246)
PHONE..............................207 625-4000
John Moller, *Pr*
Thomas Gleason, *
EMP: 40 **EST:** 1979
SQ FT: 15,000
SALES (est): 4.62MM **Privately Held**
Web: www.archcuttingtools.com
SIC: 7389 5049 3545 Grinding, precision: commercial or industrial; Precision tools; Machine tool accessories

(G-4705)
HIGHLAND FARMS LOGGING LLC
104 Towles Hill Rd (04020-3137)
PHONE..............................207 239-2977
David Pike, *Prin*
Daniel Palmer, *Prin*
Lorie Pike, *Prin*
Libby Bleakney, *Prin*
EMP: 11 **EST:** 2014
SALES (est): 744.22K **Privately Held**
Web: www.highlandfarmlogging.com
SIC: 2411 Logging

(G-4706)
NURSERY SUPPLIES INC
18 High Rd (04020-3205)
PHONE..............................207 625-9373
R Rodriguez, *Sls Mgr*
EMP: 7 **EST:** 2017
SALES (est): 132K **Privately Held**
Web: www.nurserysupplies.com
SIC: 3089 Plastics products, nec

Cornville
Somerset County

(G-4707)
TOMATERO PUBLICATIONS INC
300 Beckwith Rd (04976-6355)
PHONE..............................207 474-6300
EMP: 7 **EST:** 2016
SALES (est): 250.29K **Privately Held**
SIC: 2759 Publication printing

Cumberland Center
Cumberland County

(G-4708)
DELKIN INC
286 Harris Rd (04021-3723)
PHONE..............................207 370-0703
John Lindsey, *Prin*
EMP: 7 **EST:** 2014
SALES (est): 58.12K **Privately Held**
Web: www.delkin.com
SIC: 3674 Semiconductors and related devices

(G-4709)
MAINE TURNPIKE AUTHORITY
108 Blackstrap Rd (04021-3030)
PHONE..............................207 829-4531
Greg Hinds, *Dir*
EMP: 81
SALES (corp-wide): 170.56MM **Privately Held**
Web: www.maineturnpike.com
SIC: 2499 7349 Signboards, wood; Building maintenance services, nec
PA: Maine Turnpike Authority
2360 Congress St
Portland ME 04102
207 842-4030

(G-4710)
REXX COMPANY INC
Also Called: Rexx Home Systems, Inc.
18 Frye Dr (04021-3528)
PHONE..............................207 200-9000
Jason Record, *Pr*
EMP: 10 **EST:** 2003
SALES (est): 897.71K **Privately Held**
SIC: 3822 Environmental controls

(G-4711)
WINTER PEOPLE INC
Also Called: Winter People
389 Main St (04021-3911)
PHONE..............................207 865-6636
Dale Bouton, *CEO*
Carol A Bouton, *Pr*
Patricia M Bouton, *Treas*
Jack Mercier, *CFO*
Cley Bouton, *VP*
EMP: 22 **EST:** 1987
SALES (est): 1.92MM **Privately Held**
Web: claybouton.geiger.com
SIC: 5699 7375 7336 3993 Uniforms and work clothing; Information retrieval services ; Commercial art and graphic design; Signs and advertising specialties

Cumberland Foreside
Cumberland County

(G-4712)
LGC CLINICAL DIAGNOSTICS INC
Also Called: Maine Standards Company, LLC
221 Us Route 1 (04110-1345)
PHONE..............................207 892-1300
Thomas Happe, *Managing Member*
Dean Miller, *
EMP: 54 **EST:** 2000
SQ FT: 28,000
SALES (est): 11.25MM
SALES (corp-wide): 17.31MM **Privately Held**
Web: www.mainestandards.com
SIC: 8731 2835 Medical research, commercial; In vitro diagnostics

PA: Lgc Science Group Limited
Queens Road
Teddington MIDDX TW11
208 943-7000

(G-4713)
PRECISION MILLWORK INC
12 Sky View Dr (04110-1340)
P.O. Box 2729 (04116-2729)
PHONE..............................207 761-3997
EMP: 8 **EST:** 2010
SALES (est): 435.2K **Privately Held**
Web: www.cookandboardman.com
SIC: 2431 Millwork

Cushing
Knox County

(G-4714)
PJ SCHWALBENBERG & ASSOC INC
26 Spear Mill Rd (04563-3144)
PHONE..............................207 354-0700
Peter Schwalbenberg, *Pr*
EMP: 9 **EST:** 2002
SQ FT: 3,200
SALES (est): 981.58K **Privately Held**
Web: www.turbinesandgears.com
SIC: 3511 Steam turbine generator set units, complete

Damariscotta
Lincoln County

(G-4715)
HODGDON SHIPBUILDING LLC
6 Angell Ln (04543-4507)
PHONE..............................207 563-7033
EMP: 74
SALES (corp-wide): 23.48MM **Privately Held**
Web: www.hodgdonyachts.com
SIC: 3732 Boatbuilding and repairing
HQ: Hodgdon Shipbuilding, Llc
100 Ebenecook Rd
Southport ME 04576

(G-4716)
N C HUNT INC
237 Route One (04543-4529)
PHONE..............................207 563-8503
David Smith, *Brnch Mgr*
EMP: 32
SALES (corp-wide): 21.65MM **Privately Held**
Web: www.nchuntlumber.com
SIC: 2421 5211 Sawmills and planing mills, general; Lumber and other building materials
PA: N. C. Hunt, Inc.
200 S Clary Rd
Jefferson ME 04348
207 549-0922

(G-4717)
ROUND TOP ICE CREAM INC
526 Main St (04543-4680)
PHONE..............................207 563-5307
Gary Woodcock, *Pr*
Brenda Woodcock, *VP*
Rob Gregory, *Sec*
EMP: 13 **EST:** 1924
SQ FT: 4,000
SALES (est): 503.89K **Privately Held**
SIC: 2024 5812 Ice cream and frozen deserts; Ice cream stands or dairy bars

Danforth
Washington County

(G-4718)
DAVIS FORESTRY PRODUCTS INC
P.O. Box 96 (04424-0096)
PHONE..............................207 448-2625
Carl Davis, *Pr*
EMP: 10 **EST:** 1995
SALES (est): 989.3K **Privately Held**
SIC: 2411 Logging

(G-4719)
PFC LOGGING INC
46 Snow Farm Rd (04424-3129)
PHONE..............................207 448-7998
EMP: 8 **EST:** 2009
SALES (est): 235.39K **Privately Held**
SIC: 2411 Logging

Dayton
York County

(G-4720)
DAYTON SAND & GRAVEL INC
928 Goodwins Mills Rd (04005-7352)
PHONE..............................207 499-2306
Russell Keene, *Pr*
EMP: 75 **EST:** 1966
SQ FT: 1,200
SALES (est): 8.95MM **Privately Held**
Web: www.daytonsandandgravel.com
SIC: 3273 2951 1442 Ready-mixed concrete ; Asphalt paving mixtures and blocks; Construction sand and gravel

Deblois
Washington County

(G-4721)
JASPER WYMAN & SON
Also Called: C & D
601 Rte 193 (04622-3507)
PHONE..............................207 638-2201
Darren Hammen, *Mgr*
EMP: 15
SALES (corp-wide): 27.24MM **Privately Held**
Web: www.wymans.com
SIC: 2033 0171 Fruits: packaged in cans, jars, etc.; Berry crops
PA: Jasper Wyman & Son
7 Wyman Rd
Milbridge ME 04658
207 546-3800

Denmark
Oxford County

(G-4722)
JOHN KHIEL III LOG CHPPING INC
65 Bull Ring Rd (04022-5300)
P.O. Box 85 (04022-0085)
PHONE..............................207 452-2157
John Khiel Iii, *Pr*
Travis Khiel, *
EMP: 40 **EST:** 1994
SALES (est): 4.46MM **Privately Held**
Web: www.khiellogging.com
SIC: 2411 1794 Logging camps and contractors; Excavation work

(G-4723)
K W AGGREGATES
65 Bull Ring Rd (04022-5300)
PHONE..............................207 452-8888
EMP: 8 EST: 2016
SALES (est): 784.69K Privately Held
Web: www.kandwaggregates.com
SIC: 1442 Construction sand and gravel

(G-4724)
MINUTEMAN PRESS
33 E Main St (04022-5500)
PHONE..............................207 517-5355
EMP: 8 EST: 1975
SALES (est): 76.51K Privately Held
Web: www.minutemanpress.com
SIC: 2752 Commercial printing, lithographic

Detroit
Somerset County

(G-4725)
SOMATEX INC
70 North Rd (04929-3227)
P.O. Box 487 (04967-0487)
PHONE..............................207 487-6141
Laurie Ferland, CEO
Jason Kamara, *
▼ EMP: 26 EST: 1989
SQ FT: 12,000
SALES (est): 7.98MM Privately Held
Web: www.somatexinc.com
SIC: 3531 3536 5084 7389 Cranes, nec;
Hoists; Cranes, industrial; Crane and aerial
lift service

Dexter
Penobscot County

(G-4726)
CMD ENTERPRISES LLC
Also Called: Cmd
363 Garland Rd (04930-2650)
P.O. Box 453 (04930-0453)
PHONE..............................207 745-9985
Cheryl Breton, Managing Member
EMP: 8 EST: 2005
SALES (est): 290.58K Privately Held
SIC: 3312 Structural shapes and pilings,
steel

Dixfield
Oxford County

(G-4727)
RIVERBEND FIBERGLASS INC
16 Carter Rd (04224-4411)
PHONE..............................207 562-7103
EMP: 8 EST: 1985
SQ FT: 18,000
SALES (est): 759.35K Privately Held
Web: www.riverbendfiberglass.com
SIC: 3089 Air mattresses, plastics

(G-4728)
ROLAND H TYLER LOGGING INC
Canton Point Rd (04224)
P.O. Box 818 (04224-0818)
PHONE..............................207 562-7282
Roland H Tyler, Pr
George A Hess, Clerk
EMP: 9 EST: 1960
SALES (est): 1MM Privately Held

SIC: 2411 4212 Logging camps and
contractors; Lumber (log) trucking, local

Dover Foxcroft
Piscataquis County

(G-4729)
MOOSE RIVER LUMBER COMPANY INC
432 Milo Rd (04426-3339)
P.O. Box 454 (04945-0454)
PHONE..............................207 668-4426
Charles Lumbert, Pr
Jeff Defjardins, *
EMP: 75 EST: 1976
SQ FT: 11,000
SALES (est): 34.66MM Privately Held
Web: www.mooseriverlumber.com
SIC: 2421 Lumber: rough, sawed, or planed

(G-4730)
NORTHEAST PUBLISHING COMPANY
Also Called: Piscataquis Observer
12 E Main St Ste A (04426-1414)
P.O. Box 30 (04426-0030)
PHONE..............................207 564-8355
Roger Tremblay, Dir
EMP: 9
SALES (corp-wide): 39.35MM Privately Held
Web: www.thecounty.me
SIC: 2752 7334 7313 4822 Offset printing;
Photocopying and duplicating services;
Newspaper advertising representative;
Facsimile transmission services
HQ: Northeast Publishing Company Inc
260 Missile St
Presque Isle ME 04769
207 764-4471

(G-4731)
PLEASANT RIVER LUMBER COMPANY (PA)
432 Milo Rd (04426-3339)
P.O. Box 68 (04426-0068)
PHONE..............................207 564-8520
Luke Brochu, Pr
Jason Brochu, *
Christopher Brochu, *
EMP: 35 EST: 1991
SQ FT: 100,000
SALES (est): 27.61MM
SALES (corp-wide): 27.61MM Privately Held
Web: www.pleasantriverlumber.com
SIC: 2421 Sawmills and planing mills,
general

Durham
Androscoggin County

(G-4732)
COPP EXCAVATING INC
190 Pinkham Brook Rd (04222-5429)
P.O. Box 285 (04250-0285)
PHONE..............................207 926-4988
Micheal S Copp, Pr
EMP: 20 EST: 1987
SALES (est): 948.99K Privately Held
SIC: 1389 4959 Excavating slush pits and
cellars; Snowplowing

(G-4733)
MAINE CUSTOM WOODLANDS LLC

1326 Hallowell Rd (04222-5376)
PHONE..............................207 353-9020
Thomas Cushman, Prin
EMP: 13 EST: 1998
SALES (est): 2.19MM Privately Held
Web: www.mainecustomwoodlands.com
SIC: 2411 Logging

Eagle Lake
Aroostook County

(G-4734)
CHOPPER ONE INC
215 Old Main St (04739-3304)
P.O. Box 396 (04739-0396)
PHONE..............................207 444-5476
Reynold Blair, Pr
Mary Blair, Treas
Jeff Blair, VP
EMP: 7 EST: 1991
SALES (est): 697.17K Privately Held
SIC: 2411 Logging

East Baldwin
Cumberland County

(G-4735)
ROBBINS LUMBER E BALDWIN LLC
Also Called: Limington Lumber
411 Pequawket Trl (04024-4143)
P.O. Box 47 (04024-0047)
PHONE..............................207 625-3286
Winthrop Smith, Pr
James Henderson, *
EMP: 41 EST: 2021
SQ FT: 700
SALES (est): 5.87MM
SALES (corp-wide): 28.95MM Privately Held
SIC: 2421 Sawmills and planing mills,
general
PA: Robbins Lumber, Inc.
53 Ghent Rd
Searsmont ME 04973
207 342-5221

East Boothbay
Lincoln County

(G-4736)
HODGDON YACHTS INC (PA)
14 School St (04544-6029)
PHONE..............................207 737-2802
▲ EMP: 76 EST: 1816
SALES (est): 23.48MM
SALES (corp-wide): 23.48MM Privately Held
Web: www.hodgdonyachts.com
SIC: 3732 Fishing boats: lobster, crab,
oyster, etc.: small

(G-4737)
WASHBURN & DOUGHTY ASSOC INC
7 Enterprise St (04544-6045)
P.O. Box 296 (04544-0296)
PHONE..............................207 633-6517
Bruce H Doughty, CEO
Bruce D Washburn, *
▲ EMP: 55 EST: 1977
SQ FT: 50,000
SALES (est): 9.67MM Privately Held
Web: www.washburndoughty.com

SIC: 3731 3732 Sailing vessels,
commercial: building and repairing;
Boatbuilding and repairing

(G-4738)
WILLIAMS PARTNERS LTD
Also Called: Sullivan Associates
29 Lincoln St (04544-6035)
P.O. Box 514 (04544-0514)
PHONE..............................207 633-3111
Pete Williams, Pr
EMP: 7 EST: 1975
SQ FT: 1,200
SALES (est): 883.19K Privately Held
SIC: 3589 Water treatment equipment,
industrial

East Machias
Washington County

(G-4739)
ASHLEY & HARMON LOGGING INC
230 Chases Mill Rd (04630-3804)
PHONE..............................207 259-2043
George Harmon, Pr
Kathy Harmon, Treas
Thomas Ashley, VP
EMP: 10 EST: 1987
SALES (est): 1.02MM Privately Held
SIC: 2411 Logging camps and contractors

(G-4740)
LYLE GUPTILL
Also Called: Guptill's Logging Supply
343 Scotts Hill Rd (04630-4131)
P.O. Box 226 (04630-0226)
PHONE..............................207 255-4130
Lyle Guptill, Owner
EMP: 12 EST: 1974
SQ FT: 18,600
SALES (est): 2.3MM Privately Held
Web: www.guptills.com
SIC: 5083 5091 2411 5561 Farm and
garden machinery; Sporting and recreation
goods; Logging camps and contractors;
Recreational vehicle dealers

East Wilton
Franklin County

(G-4741)
JARDEN LLC
Also Called: Unimark Plastics
5 Mill Street (04234)
PHONE..............................207 645-2574
John Beach, Mgr
EMP: 17
SALES (corp-wide): 9.46B Publicly Held
Web: www.newellbrands.com
SIC: 2033 3089 3356 3479 Preserves,
including imitation: in cans, jars, etc.;
Plastics containers, except foam; Zinc and
zinc alloy bars, plates, sheets, etc.;
Painting, coating, and hot dipping
HQ: Jarden Llc
221 River St
Hoboken NJ 07030

Easton
Aroostook County

(G-4742)
HUBER ENGINEERED WOODS LLC

333 Station Rd (04740-4005)
P.O. Box 69 (04740-0069)
PHONE.....................207 488-6700
John Goding, *Mgr*
EMP: 78
SALES (corp-wide): 1.24B **Privately Held**
Web: www.huberwood.com
SIC: 2493 3613 Reconstituted wood
products; Panel and distribution boards and
other related apparatus
HQ: Huber Engineered Woods Llc
10925 David Taylor Dr # 3
Charlotte NC 28262
800 933-9220

(G-4743)
MCCAIN FOODS USA INC
319 Richardson Rd (04740-4056)
P.O. Box 159 (04740-0159)
PHONE.....................207 488-2561
Conrad Caron, *Bmch Mgr*
EMP: 129
SALES (corp-wide): 19.5B **Privately Held**
Web: www.mccainusafoodservice.com
SIC: 2037 2038 2033 Frozen fruits and
vegetables; Frozen specialties, nec;
Canned fruits and specialties
HQ: Mccain Foods Usa, Inc.
10973 State Highway 54 E
Wisconsin Rapids WI 54494
630 955-0400

(G-4744)
MCCAIN FOODS USA INC
Station Rd (04740)
PHONE.....................207 488-2561
EMP: 16
SALES (corp-wide): 19.5B **Privately Held**
Web: www.mccainusafoodservice.com
SIC: 2037 Potato products, quick frozen and
cold pack
HQ: Mccain Foods Usa, Inc.
10973 State Highway 54 E
Wisconsin Rapids WI 54494
630 955-0400

Eastport
Washington County

(G-4745)
J W RAYE & CO INC
Also Called: Raye's Mustard
83 Washington St (04631-1226)
P.O. Box 2 (04631-0002)
PHONE.....................207 853-4451
Nancy Raye, *Pr*
Karen Raye, *Pr*
Caroline Raye, *Clerk*
Donald Raye, *Treas*
EMP: 16 **EST:** 1903
SQ FT: 5,000
SALES (est): 2.13MM **Privately Held**
Web: www.rayesmustard.com
SIC: 2035 Mustard, prepared (wet)

Eddington
Penobscot County

(G-4746)
**PEAVEY MANUFACTURING
COMPANY**
526 Main Rd (04428-3211)
P.O. Box 129 (04428-0129)
PHONE.....................207 843-7861
Raymond F Delano, *Pr*
Rodney Buswell, *General Vice President*
Rena Delano, *

▲ **EMP:** 45 **EST:** 1857
SALES (est): 4.91MM **Privately Held**
Web: www.peaveymfg.com
SIC: 2499 3545 3423 Tool handles, wood;
Machine tool accessories; Hand and edge
tools, nec

Edgecomb
Lincoln County

(G-4747)
EBW WINDUP
957 Boothbay Rd (04556-3320)
PHONE.....................207 882-5038
Michael Mayne, *Pr*
EMP: 7 **EST:** 1991
SALES (est): 537.84K **Privately Held**
Web: www.edgecombboatworks.net
SIC: 3732 Boatbuilding and repairing

(G-4748)
**SHEEPSCOT RIVER POTTERY
(PA)**
34 Route One (04556-3003)
PHONE.....................207 882-9410
John Okie, *Pr*
Karen Okie, *VP*
Bill Logan, *Clerk*
EMP: 14 **EST:** 1974
SQ FT: 5,000
SALES (est): 1.71MM **Privately Held**
Web: www.sheepscotriverpottery.com
SIC: 5719 5945 3269 5023 Pottery; Arts
and crafts supplies; Pottery cooking and
kitchen articles; Pottery

Eliot
York County

(G-4749)
BEV-TECH INC
56 Julie Ln (03903-1427)
P.O. Box 479 (03903-0479)
PHONE.....................207 439-8061
TOLL FREE: 800
Martin T Mcnerney, *Pr*
Veronica A Mcnerney, *VP*
▲ **EMP:** 12 **EST:** 1985
SQ FT: 11,500
SALES (est): 3.73MM **Privately Held**
Web: portal.odeko.com
SIC: 5084 5078 2087 Food industry
machinery; Ice making machines; Beverage
bases, concentrates, syrups, powders and
mixes

(G-4750)
MODERNIST PANTRY LLC
25 Harold L Dow Hwy (03903-2081)
PHONE.....................207 200-3817
Jieming Wang, *Managing Member*
▲ **EMP:** 9 **EST:** 2011
SALES (est): 1.06MM **Privately Held**
Web: www.modernistpantry.com
SIC: 2099 5499 Almond pastes; Dried fruit

(G-4751)
VENTECH INDUSTRIES INC
384 Harold L Dow Hwy Unit 1 (03903)
PHONE.....................207 439-0069
Michael A Varney, *Pr*
EMP: 8 **EST:** 2002
SQ FT: 6,000
SALES (est): 582.13K **Privately Held**
Web: www.ventechindustries.com

SIC: 3251 3253 3585 Structural brick and
blocks; Ceramic wall and floor tile; Parts for
heating, cooling, and refrigerating
equipment

(G-4752)
**YORK WOODS TREE SERVICE
LLC**
Also Called: York Woods Tree and Products
300 Harold L Dow Hwy (03903-1438)
PHONE.....................207 703-0150
EMP: 16 **EST:** 1996
SALES (est): 2.03MM **Privately Held**
Web: www.yorkwoodstree.com
SIC: 0783 1629 2499 Removal services,
bush and tree; Land clearing contractor;
Mulch or sawdust products, wood

Ellsworth
Hancock County

(G-4753)
**ALLENS BLUEBERRY FREEZER
INC (HQ)**
244 Main St (04605-1698)
P.O. Box 536 (04605-0536)
PHONE.....................207 667-5561
Roy Allen, *Pr*
▼ **EMP:** 25 **EST:** 1956
SQ FT: 18,000
SALES (est): 4.44MM
SALES (corp-wide): 27.24MM **Privately
Held**
Web: www.allensblueberries.com
SIC: 2037 Fruits, quick frozen and cold pack
(frozen)
PA: Jasper Wyman & Son
7 Wyman Rd
Milbridge ME 04658
207 546-3800

(G-4754)
BALD HILL REACH INC
1 Printing House Sq (04605-2044)
P.O. Box 509 (04605-0509)
PHONE.....................207 667-2576
Alan Baker, *Pr*
EMP: 60 **EST:** 1851
SALES (est): 4.88MM **Privately Held**
Web: www.ellsworthamerican.com
SIC: 2711 7375 Newspapers, publishing
and printing; Information retrieval services

(G-4755)
**BANGOR PUBLISHING
COMPANY**
Also Called: Bangor Daily News Hancock Bur
98 Main St Ste B (04605-1930)
PHONE.....................207 667-9393
Kathy Cook, *Mgr*
EMP: 7
SALES (corp-wide): 39.35MM **Privately
Held**
Web: www.bangornews.com
SIC: 2711 Newspapers, publishing and
printing
PA: Bangor Publishing Company
1 Merchants Plz
Bangor ME 04401
207 990-8000

(G-4756)
DESERT HARVEST INC
192 Main St (04605-1976)
P.O. Box 86 (04605-0086)
PHONE.....................919 245-1853
Heather Florio, *CEO*
▲ **EMP:** 10 **EST:** 1993

SQ FT: 11,800
SALES (est): 5MM **Privately Held**
Web: www.desertharvest.com
SIC: 5961 5122 2834 Pharmaceuticals, mail
order; Medicinals and botanicals; Extracts
of botanicals: powdered, pilular, solid, or
fluid

(G-4757)
**DOWNEAST GRAPHICS & PRTG
INC**
477 Washington Junction Rd (04605)
P.O. Box 1103 (04605-1103)
PHONE.....................207 667-5582
Charles E Ferden, *Pr*
James Patterson Esq, *Sec*
EMP: 12 **EST:** 1968
SQ FT: 16,500
SALES (est): 953.72K **Privately Held**
Web: www.downeastgraphics.com
SIC: 2752 2759 Offset printing; Commercial
printing, nec

(G-4758)
E SKIP GRINDLE & SONS
485 North St (04605-3454)
PHONE.....................207 460-0334
E Grindle, *Owner*
EMP: 11 **EST:** 2014
SALES (est): 495.69K **Privately Held**
SIC: 3949 5932 4959 Snow skiing
equipment and supplies, except skis;
Building materials, secondhand;
Snowplowing

(G-4759)
MOUNT DESERT ISLANDER
1 Printing House Sq (04605-2044)
P.O. Box 900 (04609-0900)
PHONE.....................207 288-0556
Earl Brechlin, *CEO*
EMP: 7 **EST:** 2002
SALES (est): 589.79K **Privately Held**
Web: www.mdislander.com
SIC: 2711 Newspapers, publishing and
printing

(G-4760)
**SUPERIOR WLDG FABRICATION
INC**
Also Called: Superior Docks
420 Christian Ridge Rd (04605-3218)
PHONE.....................207 664-2121
Richard Newman, *Pr*
▲ **EMP:** 19 **EST:** 1986
SQ FT: 3,600
SALES (est): 847.97K **Privately Held**
Web: www.gangways.biz
SIC: 3479 Aluminum coating of metal
products

(G-4761)
WOODLAND STUDIOS INC
406 State St (04605-3331)
PHONE.....................207 667-3286
Chris Feldkamp, *Pr*
Thomas Feldkamp, *VP*
Cathy Feldkamp, *Sec*
EMP: 10 **EST:** 1983
SQ FT: 5,000
SALES (est): 606.51K **Privately Held**
Web: www.woodlandstudios.com
SIC: 2395 5136 2759 Emblems,
embroidered; Men's and boys' outerwear;
Screen printing

Enfield
Penobscot County

(G-4762)
PLEASANT RIVER LUMBER COMPANY
542 Hammett Rd (04493-4301)
PHONE..........................207 403-1507
EMP: 7
SALES (corp-wide): 27.61MM Privately Held
Web: www.pleasantriverlumber.com
SIC: 2421 Sawmills and planing mills, general
PA: Pleasant River Lumber Company
　432 Milo Rd
　Dover Foxcroft ME 04426
　207 564-8520

Etna
Penobscot County

(G-4763)
FAMILY YARNS INC
15 Family Cir (04434-3448)
PHONE..........................207 269-3852
Joe Marchelletta, Pr
Gary Marchelletta, VP
Michael Marchelletta, Sec
Antonio Marchelletta, Stockholder
EMP: 8 EST: 1998
SQ FT: 26,000
SALES (est): 594.53K Privately Held
SIC: 2281 Yarn spinning mills

Fairfield
Somerset County

(G-4764)
MAINELY HANDRAILS LLC
52 West St (04937-1345)
PHONE..........................207 314-1083
EMP: 11 EST: 2020
SALES (est): 1.22MM Privately Held
Web: www.mainelyhandrailsllc.com
SIC: 3446 Architectural metalwork

(G-4765)
SHERIDAN CORPORATION (HQ)
33 Sheridan Rd (04937-3315)
P.O. Box 359 (04937-0359)
PHONE..........................207 453-9311
Brad Nelson, Pr
Mithcell Sammons, *
Dan Wildes, *
EMP: 28 EST: 1947
SQ FT: 38,500
SALES (est): 31.51MM
SALES (corp-wide): 47.46MM Privately Held
Web: www.sheridancorp.com
SIC: 1541 1542 3448 Industrial buildings, new construction, nec; Commercial and office building, new construction; Prefabricated metal buildings and components
PA: Sheri - Key
　33 Sheridan Rd
　Fairfield ME 04937
　207 453-9313

(G-4766)
SOYAZ
7 Truss Ln (04937-1180)
P.O. Box 377 (04937-0377)
PHONE..........................207 453-4911
Michael Boulet, Pr
EMP: 33 EST: 1991
SQ FT: 19,000
SALES (est): 1.7MM Privately Held
Web: www.mainelytrusses.com
SIC: 2439 Trusses, wooden roof

Falmouth
Cumberland County

(G-4767)
ANODYNE HEALTH PARTNERS INC (HQ)
400 Us Route 1 Ste 1 (04105-1319)
PHONE..........................207 347-7400
Michael Funk, CEO
Gil Kochman, *
Brad Clark, *
M Sean Molley, *
EMP: 50 EST: 2003
SQ FT: 7,351
SALES (est): 9.31MM
SALES (corp-wide): 1.33B Privately Held
Web: www.athenahealth.com
SIC: 8721 7372 Billing and bookkeeping service; Prepackaged software
PA: Athenahealth, Inc.
　80 Guest St
　Boston MA 02135
　617 402-1000

(G-4768)
F O BAILEY CO INC
35 Depot Rd (04105-1715)
PHONE..........................207 781-8001
Joy Piscopo, Pr
Carmine Piscopo, Treas
EMP: 9 EST: 1912
SQ FT: 7,500
SALES (est): 620.08K Privately Held
Web: www.fobaileyrealestate.com
SIC: 7389 5932 7641 2842 Auctioneers, fee basis; Antiques; Antique furniture repair and restoration; Furniture polish or wax

(G-4769)
MAINE TIRE & APPLIANCE CO (PA)
Also Called: Goodyear
251 Us Route 1 Ste 9 (04105-1322)
PHONE..........................207 781-3136
Frederick J Haley Junior, Pr
▼ EMP: 10 EST: 1970
SQ FT: 10,000
SALES (est): 4.59MM
SALES (corp-wide): 4.59MM Privately Held
Web: www.goodyear.com
SIC: 5531 7534 5014 Automotive tires; Tire retreading and repair shops; Tires and tubes

(G-4770)
NEW PORTLAND PUBLISHING INC
Also Called: Portland Phoenix
251 Us Route 1 Ste 204 (04105-1322)
PHONE..........................207 536-5210
Marian Mccue, VP
Karen Wood, Publisher
EMP: 7 EST: 2019
SALES (est): 60K Privately Held
SIC: 3999 Manufacturing industries, nec

(G-4771)
SIEMENS INDUSTRY INC
9 Sunset Rd (04105-2433)
PHONE..........................207 878-3367
EMP: 92
SALES (corp-wide): 84.48B Privately Held
Web: www.siemens.com
SIC: 3613 Switchgear and switchgear accessories, nec
HQ: Siemens Industry, Inc.
　100 Technology Dr
　Alpharetta GA 30005
　847 215-1000

(G-4772)
SOUTHWORTH INTL GROUP INC (PA)
11 Gray Rd (04105-2027)
P.O. Box 1380 (04104-1380)
PHONE..........................207 878-0700
James Cabot, Pr
John Morton, CFO
Scott Beaudin, Dir Fin
◆ EMP: 65 EST: 1986
SQ FT: 15,000
SALES (est): 57.73MM
SALES (corp-wide): 57.73MM Privately Held
Web: www.southworthproducts.com
SIC: 3537 3625 3554 2822 Tables, lift: hydraulic; Relays and industrial controls; Paper industries machinery; Synthetic rubber

(G-4773)
SOUTHWORTH PRODUCTS CORP (HQ)
Also Called: Southworth
11 Gray Rd (04105-2027)
P.O. Box 1380 (04104-1380)
PHONE..........................207 878-0700
James Cabot, Pr
John Morton, *
Scott Beaudin, *
▲ EMP: 40 EST: 1986
SQ FT: 15,000
SALES (est): 40MM
SALES (corp-wide): 57.73MM Privately Held
Web: www.southworthproducts.com
SIC: 3537 5084 Straddle carriers, mobile; Lift trucks and parts
PA: Southworth International Group, Inc.
　11 Gray Rd
　Falmouth ME 04105
　207 878-0700

(G-4774)
TOZIER GROUP INC
Also Called: Tozier Group, The
185 Mountain Rd (04105-2573)
PHONE..........................207 838-7939
Ronald R Tozier, Pr
Leonard Nelson, Clerk
EMP: 12 EST: 1981
SALES (est): 578.89K Privately Held
SIC: 2541 1521 Cabinets, except refrigerated: show, display, etc.: wood; Single-family home remodeling, additions, and repairs

(G-4775)
WB ENGINEERING INC (HQ)
Also Called: Presto Lifts
11 Gray Rd (04105-2027)
PHONE..........................207 878-0700
James Cabot, Pr
John Morton, *
Scott Beaudin, *
EMP: 50 EST: 2002
SALES (est): 17.34MM
SALES (corp-wide): 57.73MM Privately Held
SIC: 3537 Lift trucks, industrial: fork, platform, straddle, etc.
PA: Southworth International Group, Inc.
　11 Gray Rd
　Falmouth ME 04105
　207 878-0700

Farmingdale
Kennebec County

(G-4776)
CORE CUTTER LLC
362 Maine Ave (04344-2915)
PHONE..........................207 588-7519
EMP: 11 EST: 2016
SALES (est): 710.02K Privately Held
Web: www.corecutterusa.com
SIC: 3545 Cutting tools for machine tools

Farmington
Franklin County

(G-4777)
BRUCE A MANZER INC
189 Main St (04938-5842)
PHONE..........................207 696-5881
Bruce A Manzer, Pr
Crystal Manzer, *
EMP: 43 EST: 1999
SALES (est): 4.29MM Privately Held
Web: www.pavingmaine.com
SIC: 1611 2951 Surfacing and paving; Paving mixtures

(G-4778)
FARMINGTON CHIPPING ENTP INC
Also Called: Farmington Chipping Ent
Town Farm Rd (04938)
P.O. Box 488 (04945-0488)
PHONE..........................207 778-4888
EMP: 9 EST: 1994
SALES (est): 1.03MM Privately Held
SIC: 2411 Wood chips, produced in the field

(G-4779)
FARMINGTON COCA COLA BTLG DSTR
Also Called: Coca-Cola
282 Farmington Falls Rd (04938-6434)
PHONE..........................207 778-4733
Allen Trask, Pr
Jim Sweet, VP
Sherry Walker, Treas
EMP: 10 EST: 1922
SQ FT: 6,000
SALES (est): 473.29K Privately Held
Web: www.coca-cola.com
SIC: 2086 Bottled and canned soft drinks

(G-4780)
FRANKLIN GROUP
Also Called: Franklin Journal, The
187 Wilton Rd (04938-6120)
P.O. Box 750 (04938-0750)
PHONE..........................207 778-2075
Barbara Zelasko, Prin
EMP: 22 EST: 2008
SALES (est): 168.53K Privately Held
Web: www.sunjournal.com
SIC: 2711 Commercial printing and newspaper publishing combined

(G-4781)
HALEY CONSTRUCTION INC
Also Called: HALEY CONSTRUCTION, INC.

▲ = Import ▼ = Export
◆ = Import/Export

116 Pierpole Rd (04938-5517)
PHONE..............................207 778-9990
Jan Carter, *Brnch Mgr*
EMP: 7
SALES (corp-wide): 5.32MM **Privately Held**
Web: www.haleyconstructioninc.com
SIC: 3273 Ready-mixed concrete
PA: Haley's Inc.
165 Main Rd
Sangerville ME 04479
207 876-4412

(G-4782)
NEMI PUBLISHING INC
Also Called: Franklin's Printing
553 Wilton Rd (04938-6126)
P.O. Box 568 (04938-0568)
PHONE..............................207 778-4801
Gregory Nemi, *Pr*
Richard Nemi, *
Patrick Joyce, *
EMP: 49 **EST:** 1948
SQ FT: 28,000
SALES (est): 10.57MM **Privately Held**
Web: www.franklinprinting.com
SIC: 2752 Offset printing

Fayette
Kennebec County

(G-4783)
**MAINE MARKET
REFRIGERATION LLC (PA)**
98 Morris Springer Rd (04349-3709)
PHONE..............................207 685-3504
Mike Reeve, *Managing Member*
EMP: 38 **EST:** 1999
SQ FT: 3,200
SALES (est): 4.76MM
SALES (corp-wide): 4.76MM **Privately Held**
Web: www.mainemarketrefrigeration.com
SIC: 3585 Air conditioning equipment, complete

Fort Fairfield
Aroostook County

(G-4784)
INGREDION INCORPORATED
145 Presque Isle St (04742-1074)
PHONE..............................207 472-1250
Richard Pfeffer, *Pr*
EMP: 22
SALES (corp-wide): 7.95B **Publicly Held**
Web: www.ingredion.com
SIC: 2046 Potato starch
PA: Ingredion Incorporated
5 Westbrook Corporate Ctr
Westchester IL 60154
708 551-2600

(G-4785)
LUCERNE FARMS
40 Easton Line Rd (04742)
P.O. Box 510 (04742-0510)
PHONE..............................207 488-2520
George James, *Pr*
Allen White, *Prin*
EMP: 20 **EST:** 1989
SQ FT: 500
SALES (est): 2.34MM **Privately Held**
Web: www.lucernefarms.com
SIC: 2499 0191 Mulch or sawdust products, wood; General farms, primarily crop

Fort Kent
Aroostook County

(G-4786)
D R LOGGING INC
11 Pinette Ln (04743-2056)
P.O. Box 268 (04743-0268)
PHONE..............................207 316-6434
EMP: 7 **EST:** 2015
SALES (est): 238.98K **Privately Held**
SIC: 2411 Logging

(G-4787)
FIDDLEHEAD FOCUS
90 E Main St # 1 (04743-1436)
PHONE..............................207 316-2243
Andrew Birden, *Prin*
EMP: 8 **EST:** 2012
SALES (est): 193.94K **Privately Held**
Web: www.fiddleheadfocus.com
SIC: 2711 Newspapers, publishing and printing

(G-4788)
FIRST MILE BREWING CO LLC
28 Market St Ste 103 (04743-1417)
PHONE..............................207 231-4579
Travis Guy, *Prin*
David Saucier, *Prin*
Rodney Lahren, *Prin*
Travis Jandreau, *Prin*
Mathew Deprey, *Prin*
EMP: 8 **EST:** 2017
SALES (est): 465.72K **Privately Held**
Web: www.firstmilebrewing.com
SIC: 2082 Malt beverages

(G-4789)
G V LOGGING INC
399 Aroostook Rd (04743-2101)
P.O. Box 125 (04743-0125)
PHONE..............................207 231-1003
EMP: 7 **EST:** 2016
SALES (est): 295.26K **Privately Held**
SIC: 2411 Logging

(G-4790)
MORIN BROTHERS
41 Charette Hill Rd (04743-1438)
P.O. Box 68 (04744-0068)
PHONE..............................207 834-5361
Robbie Morin, *Pt*
EMP: 8 **EST:** 2001
SALES (est): 769.35K **Privately Held**
SIC: 2951 Asphalt paving mixtures and blocks

(G-4791)
NADEAU LOGGING INC
48 Summer Ave (04743-1619)
P.O. Box 106 (04743-0106)
PHONE..............................207 834-6338
Paul J Nadeau Junior, *Pr*
EMP: 10 **EST:** 1980
SALES (est): 803.69K **Privately Held**
Web: www.fortkentchamber.com
SIC: 2411 Logging camps and contractors

(G-4792)
PELLETIER & PELLETIER
14 E Main St (04743-1305)
PHONE..............................207 834-2296
James Pelletier, *Pr*
Keith Pelletier, *
Steven Pelletier, *
Rina Pelletier, *
EMP: 19 **EST:** 1955
SALES (est): 898.49K **Privately Held**

Web: www.pelletierford.com
SIC: 2411 Logging camps and contractors

(G-4793)
ROBERT MCBREAIRTY JR SONS
260 St John Rd (04743-2210)
PHONE..............................207 834-3257
Robert Mcbreairty, *Prin*
EMP: 7 **EST:** 2020
SALES (est): 461.57K **Privately Held**
SIC: 2411 Logging camps and contractors

(G-4794)
STEVEN PELLETIER
Also Called: Vallet Motors
82 W Main St (04743-1233)
PHONE..............................207 834-3191
Steven Pelletier, *Owner*
EMP: 19 **EST:** 2015
SQ FT: 15,000
SALES (est): 3.19MM **Privately Held**
Web: www.valleymotorsgm.com
SIC: 5511 7538 7534 Automobiles, new and used; General automotive repair shops; Tire repair shop

(G-4795)
UP NORTH CORP
185 Pleasant St (04743-1502)
PHONE..............................207 834-6178
Leroy R Martin, *Pr*
Mary L Martin, *Treas*
EMP: 10 **EST:** 1979
SQ FT: 2,925
SALES (est): 459.12K **Privately Held**
SIC: 2411 0722 Pulpwood contractors engaged in cutting; Crop harvesting

Franklin
Hancock County

(G-4796)
SEA & REEF AQUACULTURE LLC
Also Called: Sea & Reef Aquaculture
33 Salmon Farm Rd (04634-3144)
PHONE..............................207 422-2422
Soren Hansen, *CEO*
EMP: 12 **EST:** 2003
SALES (est): 984.83K **Privately Held**
Web: www.seaandreef.com
SIC: 2092 0273 Fish, fresh: prepared; Tropical fish farm

Freeport
Cumberland County

(G-4797)
BETTY REEZ WHOOPIEZ
67 Carter Rd (04032-6889)
PHONE..............................207 865-1735
Betty Ree Zolla, *Prin*
EMP: 8 **EST:** 2010
SALES (est): 290.33K **Privately Held**
Web: www.bettyreez.com
SIC: 2051 Cakes, bakery: except frozen

(G-4798)
BIGELOW MOUNTAIN PARTNERS LLC
Also Called: Winterstick Snowboards
208 Us Route 1 (04032-7014)
PHONE..............................207 865-9208
Christopher P Lorenz, *Managing Member*
EMP: 10 **EST:** 2000
SALES (est): 398.2K **Privately Held**

SIC: 3949 Winter sports equipment

(G-4799)
BROWN GOLDSMITHS & CO INC
11 Mechanic St (04032-1526)
PHONE..............................207 865-4126
TOLL FREE: 800
Stephen Brown, *Pr*
Judith Brown, *VP*
EMP: 10 **EST:** 1968
SQ FT: 1,000
SALES (est): 970.29K **Privately Held**
Web: www.browngoldsmiths.com
SIC: 5944 7631 3911 Jewelry, precious stones and precious metals; Jewelry repair services; Jewelry, precious metal

(G-4800)
CHILTON PAINT CO INC ME
Also Called: Chilton Furniture and Paint
184 Lower Main St (04032-1008)
PHONE..............................207 865-4443
Todd Davis, *Mgr*
EMP: 8
SALES (corp-wide): 2.51MM **Privately Held**
Web: www.chiltons.com
SIC: 2851 5198 5712 Paints and allied products; Paints, varnishes, and supplies; Unfinished furniture
PA: Chilton Paint Co Inc Me
410 Payne Rd
Scarborough ME 04074
207 883-3366

(G-4801)
MAINE BEER COMPANY LLC
525 Us Route 1 (04032-7009)
PHONE..............................207 221-5711
Peter Walker, *Prin*
EMP: 38 **EST:** 2009
SALES (est): 5.4MM **Privately Held**
Web: www.mainebeercompany.com
SIC: 2082 Beer (alcoholic beverage)

(G-4802)
MOMS ORGANIC MUNCHIES INC
174 Lower Main St Ste 21 (04032-1001)
PHONE..............................207 869-4078
Betty Crush, *Owner*
EMP: 7 **EST:** 2009
SALES (est): 494.32K **Privately Held**
Web: www.momsorganicmunchies.com
SIC: 2052 Cookies

(G-4803)
SEA BAGS INC
Also Called: SEA BAGS, INC.
6 Bow St (04032-1515)
PHONE..............................207 939-3679
Sokunthy Yean, *Brnch Mgr*
EMP: 11
SALES (corp-wide): 6.35MM **Privately Held**
Web: www.seabags.com
SIC: 3161 5948 Luggage; Luggage, except footlockers and trunks
PA: Sea Bags, Llc
25 Custom House Wharf
Portland ME 04101
207 780-0744

(G-4804)
WAYSIDE PUBLISHING
2 Stonewood Dr (04032-7024)
PHONE..............................888 302-2519
Greg Greuel, *Pr*
EMP: 11 **EST:** 1987
SALES (est): 2.57MM **Privately Held**

Web: www.waysidepublishing.com
SIC: 2731　Books, publishing only

(G-4805)
WILBURS ME CHOCLAT CONFECTIONS
174 Lower Main St (04032-1001)
PHONE..................207 865-4071
EMP: 11 EST: 2010
SALES (est): 979.33K Privately Held
Web: www.wilburs.com
SIC: 5441 2064 5145　Candy; Chocolate candy, except solid chocolate; Confectionery

Friendship
Knox County

(G-4806)
FTC INC (PA)
570 Cushing Rd (04547-4146)
PHONE..................207 354-2545
Chris Anderson, Pr
J Pike Bartlett Junior, Pr
▲ EMP: 35 EST: 1977
SQ FT: 16,000
SALES (est): 4.15MM
SALES (corp-wide): 4.15MM Privately Held
Web: www.friendshiptrap.com
SIC: 3496 5051　Traps, animal and fish; Wire, nec

Fryeburg
Oxford County

(G-4807)
BEAR PAW LUMBER CORP (PA)
103 Main St (04037-1154)
P.O. Box 522 (04037-0522)
PHONE..................207 935-3052
Dennis Keaten, Pr
Gregory Kellough, VP
Lisa Lovejoy, Treas
EMP: 10 EST: 1977
SQ FT: 3,600
SALES (est): 1.49MM
SALES (corp-wide): 1.49MM Privately Held
SIC: 2426 5031 2435　Lumber, hardwood dimension; Lumber, plywood, and millwork; Hardwood veneer and plywood

(G-4808)
DEARBORN BORTEC LLC
Also Called: Dearborn Bortec
12 Budrich Dr (04037-1287)
P.O. Box 310 (04037-0310)
PHONE..................207 935-2502
Kenneth Albert, Managing Member
Deborah Kelly, Pr
Joseph Keaney, Treas
EMP: 14 EST: 2010
SALES (est): 2.4MM Privately Held
Web: www.dearbornbortec.com
SIC: 3599　Machine shop, jobbing and repair

(G-4809)
HUNTING DEARBORN INC
6 Dearborn Dr (04037-1609)
PHONE..................207 935-2171
Bill Findeisen, Pr
David Pasquale, *
Robert F Newton, *
▲ EMP: 150 EST: 1944
SQ FT: 212,000
SALES (est): 39.74MM

SALES (corp-wide): 725.8MM Privately Held
Web: www.huntingplc.com
SIC: 3599 1382 3812　Machine shop, jobbing and repair; Oil and gas exploration services; Acceleration indicators and systems components, aerospace
PA: Hunting Plc
　5th Floor
　London SW1Y
　207 321-0123

(G-4810)
SACO RIVER BREWING LLC
10 Jockey Cap Ln (04037-1428)
PHONE..................207 256-3028
EMP: 17 EST: 2016
SALES (est): 447.12K Privately Held
Web: www.sacoriverbrewing.com
SIC: 5813 2082　Bars and lounges; Beer (alcoholic beverage)

(G-4811)
WESTERN MAINE TIMBERLANDS INC
278 Mcneil Rd (04037-4709)
PHONE..................207 925-1138
Marc Graney, Pr
Jennifer Graney, Sec
EMP: 10 EST: 2001
SALES (est): 1.47MM Privately Held
Web: www.westernmainetimberlands.com
SIC: 2411　Logging camps and contractors

Gardiner
Kennebec County

(G-4812)
BLIND PIG TAVERN
266 Water St (04345-2110)
PHONE..................207 592-0776
EMP: 7 EST: 2020
SALES (est): 185.21K Privately Held
Web: www.blindpigtavern.com
SIC: 2591　Window blinds

(G-4813)
ZOULAMIS FINE WOODWORKING
521 Water St (04345-2040)
PHONE..................207 449-1680
Greg Zoulamis, Prin
EMP: 8 EST: 2015
SALES (est): 603.1K Privately Held
Web: www.zoulamisfinewoodworking.com
SIC: 2431　Millwork

Georgetown
Sagadahoc County

(G-4814)
GEORGETOWN POTTERY
755 Five Islands Rd (04548-3304)
P.O. Box 151 (04548-0151)
PHONE..................207 371-2801
Jeffrey Peters, Owner
▲ EMP: 9 EST: 1971
SQ FT: 4,500
SALES (est): 433.93K Privately Held
Web: www.georgetownpottery.com
SIC: 3269 5719　Pottery cooking and kitchen articles; Pottery

(G-4815)
WOODEX BEARING COMPANY INC
216 Bay Point Rd (04548-3509)
PHONE..................207 371-2210
Glenn R Irish, Pr
Stephen Williams, *
EMP: 28 EST: 1905
SQ FT: 28,390
SALES (est): 4.5MM Privately Held
Web: www.woodexbearing.com
SIC: 3053 3568 2499　Gaskets and sealing devices; Power transmission equipment, nec; Bearings, wood

Gorham
Cumberland County

(G-4816)
ATLANTIC PRECISION SERVICES
397 Ossipee Trl (04038-2133)
P.O. Box 132 (04038-0132)
PHONE..................207 329-1043
Jacob Nicely, Prin
EMP: 8 EST: 2018
SALES (est): 481.88K Privately Held
Web: www.atlanticprecisionservices.com
SIC: 3578　Automatic teller machines (ATM)

(G-4817)
D AND GM ACHINE PRODUCTS
20 Hutcherson Dr (04038-2643)
PHONE..................207 854-1500
EMP: 8 EST: 2020
SALES (est): 212.53K Privately Held
Web: www.dgmachine.com
SIC: 3599　Machine shop, jobbing and repair

(G-4818)
EMERSON APPARATUS COMPANY
59 Sanford Dr Unit 12 (04038-2667)
PHONE..................207 856-0055
Kimberly Miller, Pr
Jack Miller, VP
EMP: 15 EST: 2006
SQ FT: 7,500
SALES (est): 2.02MM Privately Held
Web: www.emersonapparatus.com
SIC: 3821　Laboratory apparatus and furniture

(G-4819)
ERIN FLETT
2 Main St (04038-1302)
PHONE..................207 887-9253
Erin Flett, Prin
EMP: 7 EST: 2014
SALES (est): 353.13K Privately Held
Web: www.erinflett.com
SIC: 7389 2399　Design services; Fabricated textile products, nec

(G-4820)
GOODWILL INDUSTRIES NTHRN NENG (PA)
Also Called: Goodwill Northern New England
34 Hutcherson Dr (04038-2743)
PHONE..................207 774-6323
Anne Roosevelt, CEO
◆ EMP: 100 EST: 1933
SQ FT: 53,097
SALES (est): 85.18MM
SALES (corp-wide): 85.18MM Privately Held
Web: www.goodwillnne.org

SIC: 8331 2392　Vocational rehabilitation agency; Household furnishings, nec

(G-4821)
GORHAM TIMES INC
77 South St (04038-1715)
P.O. Box 401 (04038-0401)
PHONE..................207 839-8390
EMP: 49 EST: 2010
SALES (est): 1.99MM Privately Held
Web: www.gorhamtimes.com
SIC: 2711　Newspapers, publishing and printing

(G-4822)
HILL-LOMA INC
Also Called: Hill Acme Company
20 Hutcherson Dr (04038-2643)
P.O. Box 189 (04038-0189)
PHONE..................207 854-9791
Cathy Goldman, Prin
David Goldman, *
EMP: 47 EST: 1986
SALES (est): 2.65MM Privately Held
SIC: 3549　Metalworking machinery, nec

(G-4823)
JOTUL NORTH AMERICA INC
55 Hutcherson Dr (04038-2644)
PHONE..................207 797-5912
Bret Watson, Pr
Jim Merkel, *
▲ EMP: 85 EST: 1980
SQ FT: 117,000
SALES (est): 21.02MM
SALES (corp-wide): 355.83K Privately Held
Web: www.jotul.com
SIC: 3433　Heating equipment, except electric
HQ: Jotul As
　Langoyveien
　Krakeroy 1678

(G-4824)
KNOWLTON MACHINE COMPANY
Also Called: Knowlton Machine Engineering
5 Sanford Dr (04038-2647)
P.O. Box 190 (04038-0190)
PHONE..................207 854-8471
Normand R Trudel, Pr
David Miller, *
EMP: 31 EST: 1864
SQ FT: 25,000
SALES (est): 1.05MM Privately Held
Web: www.capedetailing.com
SIC: 3599 7699 8711 3444　Machine shop, jobbing and repair; Valve repair, industrial; Engineering services; Sheet metalwork

(G-4825)
MAINE VALVE REBUILDERS
5 Sanford Dr (04038-2647)
PHONE..................207 856-6735
Normand Trudel, Pr
EMP: 7 EST: 2011
SALES (est): 144.99K Privately Held
Web: www.kmaine.com
SIC: 3592　Valves

(G-4826)
MC FAULKNER & SONS INC
5 Shaws Mill Rd (04038-2137)
PHONE..................207 929-4545
Mark C Faulkner, Pr
Susan Williams, VP
EMP: 11 EST: 1995
SALES (est): 1.07MM Privately Held
Web: www.srsattachments.com

SIC: 3444 Sheet metalwork

(G-4827)
MONTALVO CORPORATION
50 Hutcherson Dr (04038-2645)
PHONE................................207 856-2501
Margaret B Montalvo, *CEO*
Edwin J Montalvo Junior, *Pr*
Margaret M Denham, *
▲ **EMP**: 32 **EST**: 1947
SQ FT: 25,000
SALES (est): 6.62MM **Privately Held**
Web: www.montalvo.com
SIC: 3599 3568 3625 3823 Machine and
other job shop work; Power transmission
equipment, nec; Relays and industrial
controls; Process control instruments

(G-4828)
ODAT MACHINE INC
20 Sanford Dr (04038-2646)
PHONE................................207 854-2455
Richard C Pratt, *Pr*
Roxana E Pratt, *
EMP: 40 **EST**: 1992
SQ FT: 10,000
SALES (est): 4.99MM **Privately Held**
Web: www.odatmachine.com
SIC: 3599 Machine shop, jobbing and repair

(G-4829)
PHINNEY LUMBER CO
519 Fort Hill Rd (04038-2270)
PHONE................................207 839-3336
Michael J Phinney, *Pr*
EMP: 31 **EST**: 1928
SQ FT: 5,000
SALES (est): 2.16MM **Privately Held**
Web: www.phinneylumber.com
SIC: 2421 5211 Sawmills and planing mills,
general; Lumber products

(G-4830)
**PHOCAM MANUFACTURING
LLC**
Also Called: Marca Machine Engineering
5 Sanford Dr (04038-2647)
PHONE................................207 854-8471
Frederick Veitch, *CEO*
John Shaw, *Genl Mgr*
EMP: 10 **EST**: 2010
SALES (est): 721.83K **Privately Held**
Web: www.marcacoating.com
SIC: 3999 Barber and beauty shop
equipment

(G-4831)
POOL ENVIRONMENTS INC
Also Called: Efficient Air Systems
10 Elm St (04038-1506)
PHONE................................207 839-8225
William Chase, *Pr*
EMP: 13 **EST**: 2003
SALES (est): 485.57K **Privately Held**
Web: www.poolenvironments.com
SIC: 3585 Humidifiers and dehumidifiers

(G-4832)
**PRC ACQUISITION COMPANY
INC**
Hydraulic Hose & Assemblies
639 Main St (04038-2623)
PHONE................................207 854-3702
Kevin Easler, *Genl Mgr*
EMP: 11
SALES (corp-wide): 4.71B **Privately Held**
Web: www.prcindustrial.com

SIC: 5084 5085 3492 Hydraulic systems
equipment and supplies; Industrial supplies;
Hose and tube fittings and assemblies,
hydraulic/pneumatic
HQ: Prc Acquisition Company, Inc.
15 Saunders Way
Westbrook ME 04092
207 774-3993

(G-4833)
PRIME ELECTRIC MOTORS
72 Sanford Dr (04038-2646)
PHONE................................207 591-7800
Daniel Furrow, *Pr*
EMP: 10 **EST**: 2005
SALES (est): 1.06MM **Privately Held**
Web: www.primeelectricmotor.com
SIC: 7694 Electric motor repair

(G-4834)
**SEBAGO BREWING COMPANY
(PA)**
616 Main St (04038-2620)
P.O. Box 1054 (04070-1054)
PHONE................................207 856-2537
Brad Monarch, *Pr*
Tim Haines, *
Kai Adams, *
EMP: 50 **EST**: 1998
SQ FT: 7,700
SALES (est): 13.14MM
SALES (corp-wide): 13.14MM **Privately
Held**
Web: www.sebagobrewing.com
SIC: 2082 Malt beverages

(G-4835)
**SHAW BROTHERS
CONSTRUCTION INC (PA)**
Also Called: Commercial Paving
341 Mosher Rd (04038-2626)
P.O. Box 69 (04038-0069)
PHONE................................207 839-2552
TOLL FREE: 800
Jonathan Shaw, *Pr*
Jonathan E Shaw, *
Daniel H Shaw, *
Thomas Biegel, *
▲ **EMP**: 175 **EST**: 1977
SQ FT: 75,000
SALES (est): 42.17MM
SALES (corp-wide): 42.17MM **Privately
Held**
Web: www.shawbrothers.com
SIC: 1611 1794 1623 2951 General
contractor, highway and street construction;
Excavation work; Water, sewer, and utility
lines; Paving blocks

(G-4836)
TOWN OF GORHAM (PA)
75 South St Ste 1 (04038-1737)
PHONE................................207 222-1610
David O Cole, *Town Manager*
EMP: 50 **EST**: 1764
SQ FT: 3,000
SALES (est): 79.82MM
SALES (corp-wide): 79.82MM **Privately
Held**
Web: www.gorham-me.org
SIC: 2741 Miscellaneous publishing

(G-4837)
TRANSFORMIT (PA)
33 Sanford Dr (04038-2647)
PHONE................................207 856-9911
Cynthia Thompson, *Pr*
EMP: 45 **EST**: 1988
SQ FT: 11,200
SALES (est): 4.59MM **Privately Held**

Web: www.transformit.com
SIC: 7389 3993 Design, commercial and
industrial; Signs and advertising specialties

Gouldsboro
Hancock County

(G-4838)
C A CONSTRUCTION INC
Also Called: Tucker Mountain Log Homes
41 Tucker Mountain Rd (04607)
P.O. Box 76 (04607-0076)
PHONE................................207 422-3493
Cliff Albee, *Pr*
John Albee, *VP*
Judy Albee, *Sec*
Richard Macdaniels, *Mgr*
EMP: 8 **EST**: 1984
SQ FT: 2,400
SALES (est): 433.71K **Privately Held**
Web: www.tuckermtnloghomes.com
SIC: 1521 2452 New construction, single-
family houses; Log cabins, prefabricated,
wood

(G-4839)
**ELSCOTT MANUFACTURING
LLC (PA)**
Also Called: Downeast Manufacturing
38 Route 1 (04607-3015)
PHONE................................207 422-6747
Leah Hurlburt, *Managing Member*
Will Taylor, *
EMP: 30 **EST**: 1976
SQ FT: 6,000
SALES (est): 7.03MM
SALES (corp-wide): 7.03MM **Privately
Held**
Web: www.elscott.com
SIC: 3672 3625 Printed circuit boards;
Resistors and resistor units

(G-4840)
OFFSHORE FUEL
130 Route 1 (04607-3017)
PHONE................................207 963-7068
EMP: 8 **EST**: 2007
SALES (est): 612.78K **Privately Held**
SIC: 2869 Fuels

Gray
Cumberland County

(G-4841)
ENERCON (HQ)
Also Called: Enercon Technologies
25 Northbrook Dr (04039-9451)
P.O. Box 665 (04039-0665)
PHONE................................207 657-7000
Ronald Marcotte, *Pr*
Walter Hebold, *VP*
▲ **EMP**: 80 **EST**: 1980
SQ FT: 32,000
SALES (est): 59.44MM
SALES (corp-wide): 102.95MM **Privately
Held**
Web: www.enercontechnologies.com
SIC: 3672 5063 3699 3545 Printed circuit
boards; Electrical apparatus and equipment
; Electrical equipment and supplies, nec;
Machine tool accessories
PA: Healthcare Ew Partners L P
75 Rockefeller Plz # 1700
New York NY 10019
646 429-1251

(G-4842)
LIBERTY MACHINE INC
189 Yarmouth Rd (04039-9513)
PHONE................................207 376-6224
EMP: 9 **EST**: 2019
SALES (est): 204.63K **Privately Held**
Web: www.libertymachineinc.com
SIC: 3599 Machine shop, jobbing and repair

(G-4843)
PEMBERTONS FOOD INC
Also Called: Pemberton's Gourmet
32 Lewiston Rd Bldg 1b (04039-7583)
P.O. Box 1405 (04039-1405)
PHONE................................207 657-6446
David Fillinger, *Pr*
▼ **EMP**: 8 **EST**: 1985
SQ FT: 3,500
SALES (est): 750K **Privately Held**
Web:
www.pembertonsgourmetfoods.com
SIC: 2033 Jams, jellies, and preserves,
packaged in cans, jars, etc.

(G-4844)
VUETEK SCIENTIFIC LLC
Also Called: Spirometrics
22 Shaker Rd (04039-6702)
P.O. Box 680 (04039-0680)
PHONE................................207 657-6565
Ronald P Marcotte, *Managing Member*
EMP: 9 **EST**: 1987
SALES (est): 303.98K **Privately Held**
Web: www.vuetekscientific.com
SIC: 3845 Electromedical equipment

Greenbush
Penobscot County

(G-4845)
SF MADDEN INC
183 Greenfield Rd (04418-3501)
PHONE................................207 852-2525
Stephen Madden, *Prin*
EMP: 9 **EST**: 1990
SALES (est): 821.51K **Privately Held**
SIC: 2411 Logging

Greene
Androscoggin County

(G-4846)
KJPL RESTAURANTS INC
Also Called: Hurricane's Cafe and Deli
682 Route 202 (04236-4228)
P.O. Box 28 (04236-0028)
PHONE................................207 577-1728
Kirsten Wilbur, *Prin*
EMP: 18 **EST**: 2007
SALES (est): 305.75K **Privately Held**
SIC: 5812 2099 Delicatessen (eating places)
; Ready-to-eat meals, salads, and
sandwiches

(G-4847)
MAINE POLY AQUISITION CORP
Also Called: Mpac
933 Route 202 (04236-3489)
PHONE................................207 946-7000
Kimball H Dunton, *Pr*
EMP: 9 **EST**: 2002
SQ FT: 64,000
SALES (est): 189.02K **Privately Held**
SIC: 2759 Flexographic printing

(PA)=Parent Co (HQ)=Headquarters
✪ = New Business established in last 2 years

2024 Harris New England
Manufacturers Directory

233

GEOGRAPHIC

(G-4848)
TECHNICAL SALES & SVC OF NENG
Also Called: Tne
170 N Daggett Hill Rd (04236-4123)
PHONE..............................207 946-5506
William George, *Pr*
EMP: 10 **EST:** 1987
SQ FT: 12,000
SALES (est): 991.93K **Privately Held**
Web: www.tneinc.com
SIC: 3599 Machine shop, jobbing and repair

Greenfield Twp
Penobscot County

(G-4849)
ALEXANDERS WELDING & MCH INC
Also Called: Alexanders Mech Solutions
1462 Greenfield Rd (04418-7022)
PHONE..............................207 827-3300
Denise Alexander, *Admn*
James E Alexander Junior, *Pr*
EMP: 10 **EST:** 1994
SALES (est): 1.38MM **Privately Held**
Web:
www.alexandersmechanicalsolutions.com
SIC: 3599 3999 Machine shop, jobbing and repair; Barber and beauty shop equipment

Greenville
Piscataquis County

(G-4850)
LANDER GROUP LLC
36a Chipmunk Ln W (04441-3191)
PHONE..............................207 974-3104
Leslie Edgell, *Dir Opers*
EMP: 13 **EST:** 2005
SALES (est): 4.52MM **Privately Held**
Web: www.thelandergroup.com
SIC: 1542 3812 1629 1541 Commercial and office buildings, prefabricated erection; Search and navigation equipment; Dams, waterways, docks, and other marine construction; Industrial buildings and warehouses

(G-4851)
MOOSEHEAD COUNTRY LOG HOMES
Greenville Industral Park (04441)
P.O. Box 1285 (04441-1285)
PHONE..............................207 695-3730
Randall E Comber, *Pr*
Lucille Comber, *VP*
EMP: 8 **EST:** 1986
SALES (est): 320.17K **Privately Held**
Web: www.mclh.net
SIC: 2452 Log cabins, prefabricated, wood

Greenville Junction
Piscataquis County

(G-4852)
MOOSEHEAD WOOD COMPONENTS INC
Also Called: Moosehead Cedar Log Homes
441 Pritham Ave (04442-3085)
P.O. Box 1285 (04441-1285)
PHONE..............................207 695-3730
Randy Comber, *Pr*
Lucy Comber, *VP*
EMP: 17 **EST:** 1996

SALES (est): 762.53K **Privately Held**
SIC: 2452 Log cabins, prefabricated, wood

Greenwood
Oxford County

(G-4853)
SAUNDERS AT LOCKE MILLS LLC
256 Main St (04255-3014)
PHONE..............................207 875-2853
EMP: 9 **EST:** 2010
SALES (est): 96.56K **Privately Held**
SIC: 2493 Reconstituted wood products

Guilford
Piscataquis County

(G-4854)
HARDWOOD PRODUCTS COMPANY LLC ✪
30 School St (04443-6388)
P.O. Box 88 (04443-0088)
PHONE..............................207 876-3312
Rachael Davis, *Managing Member*
EMP: 20 **EST:** 2022
SALES (est): 3.71MM **Privately Held**
Web: www.hardwoodproductsco.com
SIC: 2499 Woodenware, kitchen and household

(G-4855)
PRIDE MANUFACTURING CO LLC
Also Called: Pride Manufacturing Machine Sp
169 Water St (04443-6333)
PHONE..............................207 876-2719
Brad Coburn, *Brnch Mgr*
EMP: 10
SALES (corp-wide): 49.85MM **Privately Held**
SIC: 2411 2426 Handle bolts, wood: hewn; Turnings, furniture: wood
PA: Pride Manufacturing Company Llc
10 N Main St
Burnham ME 04922
207 487-3322

(G-4856)
PURITAN MEDICAL PDTS CO I LP
Also Called: Puritan Medical Products
31 School St (04443-6388)
P.O. Box 149 (04443-0149)
PHONE..............................207 876-3311
Timothy Templet, *Pt*
Scott Wellman, *
◆ **EMP:** 382 **EST:** 1919
SQ FT: 482,000
SALES (est): 98.91MM **Privately Held**
Web: www.puritanmedproducts.com
SIC: 3842 2499 Surgical appliances and supplies; Handles, poles, dowels and stakes: wood

(G-4857)
PURITAN MEDICAL PDTS CO LLC (PA)
31 School St (04443-6388)
P.O. Box 149 (04443-0149)
PHONE..............................207 876-3311
Terry Young, *Managing Member*
EMP: 470 **EST:** 2002
SALES (est): 55.93MM
SALES (corp-wide): 55.93MM **Privately Held**

Web: www.puritanmedproducts.com
SIC: 3842 Surgical appliances and supplies

(G-4858)
R A THOMAS LOGGING INC
58 Butter St (04443-6039)
PHONE..............................207 876-2722
Richard Thomas, *Pr*
Roberta Thomas, *Treas*
Phyllis Dyer, *Sec*
EMP: 7 **EST:** 1963
SALES (est): 678.63K **Privately Held**
SIC: 2411 1611 Wooden logs; Highway and street construction

(G-4859)
THOMAS LOGGING & FORESTRY INC
58 Butter St (04443-6039)
PHONE..............................207 876-2722
Thomas Douglass, *Pr*
James L Morin, *Pr*
EMP: 7 **EST:** 2014
SALES (est): 552.31K **Privately Held**
SIC: 2411 Logging camps and contractors

Hallowell
Kennebec County

(G-4860)
MELTON SALES AND SERVICE INC
Also Called: Butler & Macmaster Engines
323 Water St (04347-1341)
PHONE..............................207 623-8895
John F Melton, *Pr*
EMP: 8 **EST:** 2012
SQ FT: 50,000
SALES (est): 223.95K **Privately Held**
SIC: 3519 3599 7538 5084 Internal combustion engines, nec; Air intake filters, internal combustion engine, except auto; Engine repair, except diesel: automotive; Engines and parts, diesel

(G-4861)
QUALITY COPY INC
Also Called: Quality Copy and Digital Print
4 North St (04347-1417)
PHONE..............................207 622-7447
David C Wheelock Iii, *Pr*
Catherine Wheelock, *VP*
EMP: 7 **EST:** 1985
SQ FT: 2,000
SALES (est): 617.73K **Privately Held**
Web: www.qualitycopymaine.com
SIC: 2752 Offset printing

(G-4862)
QUARRY TAP ROOM LLC
122 Water St (04347-1313)
PHONE..............................207 213-6173
Chris Vallee, *Managing Member*
EMP: 9 **EST:** 2015
SALES (est): 238.9K **Privately Held**
Web: www.quarrytaproom.com
SIC: 2599 Bar, restaurant and cafeteria furniture

Hampden
Penobscot County

(G-4863)
EXTREME DIM WILDLIFE CALLS LLC
208 Kennebec Rd (04444-1318)

P.O. Box 220 (04444-0220)
PHONE..............................207 862-2825
▲ **EMP:** 8 **EST:** 1999
SQ FT: 6,000
SALES (est): 189.91K **Privately Held**
Web: www.harmonscents.com
SIC: 3949 Hunting equipment

(G-4864)
HUGHES BROTHERS INC
719 Main Rd N (04444-1901)
PHONE..............................207 659-3417
Peter Hughes, *Pr*
EMP: 45 **EST:** 1931
SQ FT: 16,800
SALES (est): 9.28MM **Privately Held**
Web: www.hughesbrosinc.com
SIC: 1442 1794 Construction sand and gravel; Excavation work

(G-4865) ·
PEPSI-COLA METRO BTLG CO INC
Pepsi-Cola
19 Penobscot Meadow Dr (04444-1933)
PHONE..............................207 973-2217
Bob Bates, *Mgr*
EMP: 28
SALES (corp-wide): 86.39B **Publicly Held**
Web: www.pepsico.com
SIC: 2086 Carbonated soft drinks, bottled and canned
HQ: Pepsi-Cola Metropolitan Bottling Company, Inc.
700 Anderson Hill Rd
Purchase NY 10577
914 767-6000

(G-4866)
PUFFIN BOATS LLC
Also Called: Puffin Boat Company
100 Marina Rd (04444-1825)
PHONE..............................207 907-4385
Katherine Higgins, *Managing Member*
EMP: 8 **EST:** 2013
SALES (est): 891.45K **Privately Held**
Web: www.puffinboatcompany.com
SIC: 5088 3732 Boats, non-recreational; Dinghies, building and repairing

(G-4867)
REVISION HEAT LLC
188 Emerson Mill Rd (04444-1018)
PHONE..............................207 221-5677
Lee Landry, *Prin*
▲ **EMP:** 7 **EST:** 2012
SALES (est): 670.85K **Privately Held**
Web: www.revisionheat.com
SIC: 1311 Natural gas production

Hancock
Hancock County

(G-4868)
COASTAL BLUEBERRY SERVICE INC (PA)
Also Called: Merrill Blueberry Farms
Rural Rte 4 Thorsen Rd (04640)
P.O. Box 149 (04605-0149)
PHONE..............................207 667-9750
Delmont Merrill, *Pr*
Richard Merrill, *VP*
Roger W Dow, *Clerk*
EMP: 10 **EST:** 1965
SQ FT: 1,200
SALES (est): 1.38MM
SALES (corp-wide): 1.38MM **Privately Held**

SIC: 2037 Frozen fruits and vegetables

(G-4869)
HAROLD MACQUINN INCORPORATED (PA)
127 Macquinn Rd (04640-3026)
P.O. Box 789 (04605-0789)
PHONE...............................207 667-4654
Ronald P Quinn Mac, *Pr*
Paul Mac Quinn, *
EMP: 30 **EST:** 1936
SQ FT: 1,500
SALES (est): 10.32MM
SALES (corp-wide): 10.32MM **Privately Held**
Web: www.haroldmacquinn.com
SIC: 1611 1623 1542 1521 Highway and street paving contractor; Sewer line construction; Nonresidential construction, nec; Single-family housing construction

(G-4870)
JASPER WYMAN & SON
37 Wymans Rd (04640-3208)
PHONE...............................207 546-3381
Shannon Fickett, *Mgr*
EMP: 8
SALES (corp-wide): 27.24MM **Privately Held**
Web: www.wymans.com
SIC: 2037 Fruits, quick frozen and cold pack (frozen)
PA: Jasper Wyman & Son
7 Wyman Rd
Milbridge ME 04658
207 546-3800

(G-4871)
MAINE COAST SEA VEGETABLES INC
430 Washington Jctn Rd (04640-3116)
PHONE...............................207 412-0094
Shepard Erhart, *Pr*
Mary Ellen Lasell, *Treas*
Seraphina Erhart, *Sec*
EMP: 20 **EST:** 1972
SQ FT: 9,000
SALES (est): 4.5MM **Privately Held**
Web: www.seaveg.com
SIC: 5149 2034 Natural and organic foods; Dried and dehydrated vegetables

(G-4872)
MERRILL BLUEBERRY FARMS INC
63 Thorsen Rd (04640-3141)
P.O. Box 149 (04605-0149)
PHONE...............................207 667-2541
Todd Merrill, *Pr*
Richard O Merrill, *VP*
EMP: 17 **EST:** 1946
SQ FT: 50,000
SALES (est): 461.26K **Privately Held**
Web: www.merrillwildblueberries.com
SIC: 2037 4222 Frozen fruits and vegetables ; Refrigerated warehousing and storage

(G-4873)
PRL HANCOCK LLC
Also Called: Pleasant River Pine
71 Salems Rd/Washington Jctn Rd (04640)
PHONE...............................207 564-8520
EMP: 8 **EST:** 2011
SALES (est): 199.45K **Privately Held**
SIC: 2421 Sawmills and planing mills, general

Harmony
Somerset County

(G-4874)
TRACY J MORRISON
Also Called: Morrison's Forest Products
26 Wellington Rd (04942-7600)
PHONE...............................207 683-2371
Tracy J Morrison, *Pr*
EMP: 8 **EST:** 1988
SALES (est): 795K **Privately Held**
SIC: 2411 4212 Logging camps and contractors; Lumber (log) trucking, local

Harrison
Cumberland County

(G-4875)
ELMS PUZZLES INC
Hobbs Hill Ln (04040)
P.O. Box 537 (04040-0537)
PHONE...............................207 583-6262
Elizabeth Stuart, *Pr*
Frederick E Stuart Junior, *VP*
Patricia Peard, *Clerk*
EMP: 10 **EST:** 1987
SALES (est): 505.27K **Privately Held**
Web: www.waterfordpuzzles.com
SIC: 3944 Puzzles

Hartford
Oxford County

(G-4876)
MAINE MOLD & MACHINE INC
208 Town Farm Rd (04220-5160)
PHONE...............................207 388-2732
David Bullecks, *Pr*
Colleen Bullecks, *Off Mgr*
EMP: 7 **EST:** 1985
SALES (est): 727.39K **Privately Held**
Web: www.mainemold.com
SIC: 3544 3089 Forms (molds), for foundry and plastics working machinery; Injection molding of plastics

(G-4877)
TERRENCE L HAYFORD
Also Called: Hayford Logging
74 Moses Young Rd (04220-5012)
PHONE...............................207 357-0142
Terry Hayford, *Prin*
EMP: 8 **EST:** 2015
SALES (est): 259.56K **Privately Held**
SIC: 2411 Logging

Hartland
Somerset County

(G-4878)
TASMAN INDUSTRIES INC
Also Called: Prime Tanning Compan
9 Main St (04943-3759)
PHONE...............................207 938-4491
EMP: 8
SALES (corp-wide): 43.78MM **Privately Held**
Web: www.tasmanusa.com
SIC: 3111 5199 Tanneries, leather; Leather and cut stock
PA: Tasman Industries, Inc.
930 Geiger St
Louisville KY 40206
502 785-7477

(G-4879)
TASMAN LEATHER GROUP LLC
Also Called: Acadia Leather
9 Main St (04943-3759)
P.O. Box 400 (04943-0400)
PHONE...............................207 553-3700
▲ **EMP:** 164 **EST:** 2010
SALES (est): 2.64MM
SALES (corp-wide): 43.78MM **Privately Held**
Web: www.tasmanusa.com
SIC: 3111 Leather tanning and finishing
PA: Tasman Industries, Inc.
930 Geiger St
Louisville KY 40206
502 785-7477

Hermon
Penobscot County

(G-4880)
ARMSTRONG FAMILY INDS INC
Also Called: Snowman's Printing & Stamps
1 Printers Dr (04401-1333)
PHONE...............................207 848-7300
Edward J Armstrong, *Pr*
Richard G Armstrong, *
Mark Armstrong, *
Mary Armstrong, *Stockholder**
▲ **EMP:** 30 **EST:** 1932
SQ FT: 17,000
SALES (est): 2.42MM **Privately Held**
Web: www.snowprint.com
SIC: 2752 3953 2759 Offset printing; Marking devices; Letterpress printing

(G-4881)
EUROVIA ATLANTIC COAST LLC
1067 Odlin Rd (04401-7201)
PHONE...............................703 230-0850
EMP: 28
SALES (corp-wide): 16.98MM **Privately Held**
Web: www.virginiapaving.com
SIC: 2951 Asphalt and asphaltic paving mixtures (not from refineries)
HQ: Eurovia Atlantic Coast Llc
14500 Avion Pkwy Ste 310
Chantilly VA 20151
703 230-0850

(G-4882)
GARY M POMEROY LOGGING INC
1909 Hammond St (04401-1116)
PHONE...............................207 848-3171
Gary M Pomeroy, *Pr*
Gayle M Pomeroy, *VP*
EMP: 16 **EST:** 1977
SALES (est): 2.24MM **Privately Held**
Web: www.garypomeroy.com
SIC: 2411 Logging

(G-4883)
HERMON SAND & GRAVEL LLC
23 Timberview Dr (04401-0460)
PHONE...............................207 848-5977
EMP: 10 **EST:** 2003
SALES (est): 962.03K **Privately Held**
SIC: 1442 Construction sand and gravel

(G-4884)
HOWARD TOOL COMPANY
78 Freedom Pkwy (04401-1105)
PHONE...............................207 942-1203
Marty H Arsenault, *Owner*
EMP: 20 **EST:** 1985
SALES (est): 2.25MM **Privately Held**
Web: www.howardtool.com
SIC: 3599 Machine shop, jobbing and repair

(G-4885)
MAINE COMMERCIAL TIRE INC (PA)
55 Freedom Pkwy (04401-1100)
P.O. Box 941 (04402-0941)
PHONE...............................207 848-5540
James Lynch, *Pr*
James Mccurdy, *VP*
EMP: 30 **EST:** 1990
SQ FT: 24,000
SALES (est): 12.69MM **Privately Held**
Web: www.mctire.com
SIC: 7534 5014 Tire retreading and repair shops; Truck tires and tubes

(G-4886)
NAHEKS INC
Also Called: Invironments
15 Elaine Dr (04401-1129)
PHONE...............................207 848-7770
Robert Skehan, *Prin*
EMP: 15 **EST:** 2005
SALES (est): 483.42K **Privately Held**
SIC: 2434 Wood kitchen cabinets

(G-4887)
NTENSION CORP
18 White Pine Rd (04401-0258)
PHONE...............................207 848-7700
Scott Biehn, *Pr*
Melissa Biehn, *
EMP: 45 **EST:** 2006
SQ FT: 40,000
SALES (est): 5.67MM **Privately Held**
Web: www.ntension.com
SIC: 2389 Disposable garments and accessories

(G-4888)
OVERHEAD DOOR CO BANGOR INC
Also Called: Overhead Doors
56 Liberty Dr (04401-1130)
PHONE...............................207 848-7200
TOLL FREE: 800
David Ripley, *Pr*
Bernhoff A Dahl, *Pr*
L Mark Talon, *VP*
▲ **EMP:** 19 **EST:** 1980
SALES (est): 960.67K **Privately Held**
Web: www.overheaddoorofbangor.com
SIC: 1751 3442 Garage door, installation or erection; Garage doors, overhead: metal

(G-4889)
SNOWMAN GROUP
Also Called: Presort Express
1 Printers Dr (04401-1333)
PHONE...............................207 848-7300
Ed Armstrong, *Ch Bd*
Richard Armstrong, *
Mark Armstrong, *
EMP: 38 **EST:** 1996
SQ FT: 18,000
SALES (est): 2.53MM **Privately Held**
Web: www.snowprint.com
SIC: 2752 Offset printing

Hiram
Oxford County

(G-4890)
GRANDY ORGANICS LLC (PA)
Also Called: Grandyoats
34 Schoolhouse Rd (04041-3262)

PHONE...................207 935-7415
Nathaniel Peirce, *Pr*
Aaron Anker, *Managing Member*
EMP: 29 EST: 1996
SALES (est): 3.76MM
SALES (corp-wide): 3.76MM Privately Held
Web: www.grandyorganics.com
SIC: 2043 5145   Granola and muesli, except bars and clusters; Snack foods

Hodgdon
Aroostook County

(G-4891)
ELVES & ANGELS INC
506 White Settlement Rd (04730-4432)
PHONE...................207 456-7575
David Smalley, *Pr*
EMP: 7 EST: 1989
SALES (est): 738.99K Privately Held
Web: www.elvesandangels.com
SIC: 5945 3944 5092   Children's toys and games, except dolls; Games, toys, and children's vehicles; Toys and hobby goods and supplies

(G-4892)
WA LOGGING LLC
634 White Settlement Rd (04730-4434)
PHONE...................207 694-2921
Weldon L Willette, *Owner*
EMP: 7 EST: 2013
SALES (est): 530.26K Privately Held
SIC: 2411   Logging

Hollis Center
York County

(G-4893)
EAGLE INDUSTRIES INC
118 Hollis Rd (04042-4010)
P.O. Box 179 (04042-0179)
PHONE...................207 929-3700
Jon Sjulander, *Pr*
▼ **EMP: 25 EST: 1973**
SQ FT: 27,000
SALES (est): 5.79MM Privately Held
Web: www.eagleinds.com
SIC: 3444   Sheet metalwork

(G-4894)
MID-CAPE RESTORATION INC
335 Cape Rd (04042-3703)
PHONE...................207 929-4759
Lloyd Bradbury, *Pr*
Cathy Bradbury, *Treas*
EMP: 9 EST: 1999
SALES (est): 485.34K Privately Held
Web: www.midcaperestoration.com
SIC: 3559   Metal finishing equipment for plating, etc.

Houlton
Aroostook County

(G-4895)
A E STALEY MANUFACTURING CO
48 Morningstar Rd (04730-3039)
PHONE...................207 532-9523
Sue Carr, *Mgr*
EMP: 8 EST: 2017
SALES (est): 39.59K Privately Held
Web: www.tateandlyle.com

SIC: 2046   Wet corn milling

(G-4896)
BAUDE INC
76 Smyrna St (04730-1843)
P.O. Box 280 (04730-0280)
PHONE...................207 532-6571
Gemma Bartley, *Pr*
EMP: 10 EST: 2006
SQ FT: 1,500
SALES (est): 818.84K Privately Held
SIC: 7534 5531 7513   Tire retreading and repair shops; Automotive tires; Truck rental and leasing, no drivers

(G-4897)
BISON PUMPS
98 Bangor St (04730-1603)
P.O. Box 977 (04730-0977)
PHONE...................207 532-2600
Kim Folsom, *Prin*
EMP: 11 EST: 2011
SALES (est): 580.16K Privately Held
Web: www.bisonpumps.com
SIC: 3561   Pumps and pumping equipment

(G-4898)
BROWN CONSTRUCTION INC
68 Bangor St (04730-1641)
PHONE...................207 532-0910
James Brown, *Pr*
EMP: 11 EST: 2017
SALES (est): 2MM Privately Held
SIC: 1794 1751 1611 3537   Excavation and grading, building construction; Carpentry work; Gravel or dirt road construction; Trucks, tractors, loaders, carriers, and similar equipment

(G-4899)
DARRELL C MCGUIRE & SONS INC
1157 Hodgdon Corner Rd (04730)
PHONE...................207 532-0511
Douglas Mcguire, *Pr*
Brent Mcguire, *Sec*
Jonathan Mcguire, *VP*
EMP: 11 EST: 1960
SALES (est): 511.2K Privately Held
SIC: 2411   Logging camps and contractors

(G-4900)
HOULTON FARMS DAIRY INC (PA)
Also Called: Houlton Farms Dairy
25 Commonwealth Ave (04730-2347)
P.O. Box 429 (04730-0429)
PHONE...................207 532-3170
Alice M Lincoln, *Pr*
Leonard Lincoln, *VP*
Eric Lincoln, *Asst Tr*
James Lincoln, *Sec*
EMP: 15 EST: 1981
SQ FT: 8,400
SALES (est): 4.72MM
SALES (corp-wide): 4.72MM Privately Held
Web: www.houltonfarmsdairy.com
SIC: 2026   Cream, sweet

(G-4901)
MCQUADE TIDD INDUSTRIES
Also Called: Steelstone Industries
154 Steelstone St (04730)
P.O. Box 746 (04730-0746)
PHONE...................207 532-2675
Blake Mcquade, *Pr*
EMP: 11 EST: 2009
SALES (est): 306.55K Privately Held

SIC: 2046   Wet corn milling

(G-4902)
MCQUADE TIDD INDUSTRIES
Houlton Tire Co
76 Smyrna St (04730-1843)
PHONE...................207 532-6571
Michael Hawkes, *Mgr*
EMP: 10
SALES (corp-wide): 4.97MM Privately Held
SIC: 7534 5531   Tire retreading and repair shops; Automotive tires
PA: Mcquade Tidd Industries
154 Steelstone St
Houlton ME 04730
207 532-2675

(G-4903)
NORTHEAST PUBLISHING COMPANY
Also Called: Houlton Pioneer Times
23 Court St (04730-1745)
P.O. Box 456 (04730-0456)
PHONE...................207 532-2281
Mark Putman, *Mgr*
EMP: 9
SALES (corp-wide): 39.35MM Privately Held
Web: www.thecounty.me
SIC: 2711   Newspapers, publishing and printing
HQ: Northeast Publishing Company Inc
260 Missile St
Presque Isle ME 04769
207 764-4471

(G-4904)
PRIMARY PDTS INGRDNTS AMRCAS L
48 Morningstar Rd (04730-3039)
PHONE...................207 532-9523
Thomas Strong, *Mgr*
EMP: 35
SALES (corp-wide): 1.16B Privately Held
Web: www.tateandlyle.com
SIC: 2046   Wet corn milling
HQ: Primary Products Ingredients Americas Llc
2200 E Eldorado St
Decatur IL 62521
217 423-4411

(G-4905)
TINY HOMES OF MAINE LLC
66 Industrial Dr # 4 (04730-3319)
P.O. Box 1604 (04730-5604)
PHONE...................207 619-4108
Corinne Watson, *Managing Member*
EMP: 9 EST: 2016
SALES (est): 500K Privately Held
Web: www.tinyhomesofmaine.com
SIC: 2451   Mobile homes

(G-4906)
WLHC INC (PA)
Also Called: Ward Cedar Log Homes
37 Bangor St (04730-1739)
P.O. Box 72 (04730-0072)
PHONE...................207 532-6531
Jay Mclaughlin, *Pr*
Dana Delano, *VP*
EMP: 7 EST: 1923
SQ FT: 3,200
SALES (est): 1.98MM
SALES (corp-wide): 1.98MM Privately Held
Web: www.wardcedarloghomes.com

SIC: 1442   Construction sand and gravel

SIC: 2452 1521   Log cabins, prefabricated, wood; New construction, single-family houses

Indian Island
Penobscot County

(G-4907)
FEDERAL PROGRAM INTEGRATORS LLC
12 Wabanaki Way (04468-1254)
EMP: 12 EST: 2009
SALES (est): 2.28MM Privately Held
Web: www.fedintegrators.com
SIC: 2499   Fencing, docks, and other outdoor wood structural products
PA: Penobscot Indian Nation Enterprises
31 Wabanaki Way
Indian Island ME 04468

Islesboro
Waldo County

(G-4908)
DARK HARBOR BOATYARD CORP
700 Acre Is (04848)
P.O. Box 25 (04849-0025)
PHONE...................207 734-2246
Ethan Emery, *Pr*
EMP: 10 EST: 1970
SQ FT: 5,000
SALES (est): 953.78K Privately Held
Web: www.darkharborboatyard.com
SIC: 3732 4493 5541 5551   Boatbuilding and repairing; Boat yards, storage and incidental repair; Marine service station; Marine supplies, nec

Jackman
Somerset County

(G-4909)
E J CARRIER INC
Rte 201 (04945)
P.O. Box 489 (04945-0489)
PHONE...................207 668-4457
Jacquelin Carrier, *Pr*
EMP: 49 EST: 1972
SQ FT: 10,000
SALES (est): 3.72MM Privately Held
SIC: 2411   Logging camps and contractors

(G-4910)
EDMOND ROY & SONS INC
101 Main Street (04945-5301)
P.O. Box 192 (04945-0192)
PHONE...................877 425-8491
Germain Roy, *Pr*
Yzan Roy, *Off Mgr*
EMP: 8 EST: 1971
SALES (est): 187.12K Privately Held
SIC: 0851 0831 2411   Forestry services; Forest products; Logging camps and contractors

(G-4911)
JACKMAN LUMBER INC (PA)
Also Called: Jackman Cash Fuel
548 Main St (04945-5222)
P.O. Box 425 (04945-0425)
PHONE...................207 668-4407
Reginald Griffin, *Pr*
Linda Griffin, *
Russell Griffin, *

EMP: 27 EST: 1980
SQ FT: 500
SALES (est): 2.26MM
SALES (corp-wide): 2.26MM **Privately Held**
SIC: 2411 2421   Logging camps and contractors; Sawmills and planing mills, general

---

Jackson
Waldo County

(G-4912)
FC WORK & SONS INCORPORATED
Also Called: F C Work and Sons
774 Moosehead Trl (04921-3319)
PHONE..............................207 722-3206
John Work, *Pr*
Jennifer Work, *Sec*
EMP: 10 **EST:** 1970
SQ FT: 9,000
SALES (est): 1.28MM **Privately Held**
SIC: 1794 3272 5082   Excavation and grading, building construction; Culvert pipe, concrete; Road construction and maintenance machinery

---

Jay
Franklin County

(G-4913)
HOWIES WLDG & FABRICATION INC
1148 Main St (04239-4220)
PHONE..............................207 645-2581
Mary Howes, *Pr*
EMP: 9 **EST:** 1983
SQ FT: 9,200
SALES (est): 626.84K **Privately Held**
SIC: 7692 3441   Welding repair; Fabricated structural metal

(G-4914)
PIXELLE ANDROSCOGGIN LLC (HQ)
300 Riley Rd (04239-4840)
PHONE..............................207 897-3431
EMP: 80 **EST:** 2010
SALES (est): 19.43MM
SALES (corp-wide): 760.06MM **Privately Held**
SIC: 2621   Paper mills
PA: Pixelle Specialty Solutions Llc
228 S Main St
Spring Grove PA 17362
717 225-4711

(G-4915)
PIXELLE SPCIALTY SOLUTIONS LLC
300 Riley Rd (04239-4840)
PHONE..............................207 897-3431
EMP: 348
SALES (corp-wide): 760.06MM **Privately Held**
Web: www.pixelle.com
SIC: 2621   Specialty or chemically treated papers
PA: Pixelle Specialty Solutions Llc
228 S Main St
Spring Grove PA 17362
717 225-4711

(G-4916)
SPECIALTY MINERALS INC
Riley Rd Gate 15 (04239)
P.O. Box 329 (04239-0329)
PHONE..............................207 897-4492
Robert Door, *Mgr*
EMP: 7
Web: www.mineralstech.com
SIC: 2819   Calcium compounds and salts, inorganic, nec
HQ: Specialty Minerals Inc.
622 3rd Ave Fl 38
New York NY 10017

(G-4917)
VERSO PAPER HOLDING LLC
Also Called: Verso Paper Holding Llc
300 Riley Rd (04239-4840)
P.O. Box 20 (04239-0020)
PHONE..............................207 897-3431
Marc Connor, *Brnch Mgr*
EMP: 800
SALES (corp-wide): 4.06B **Privately Held**
Web: www.versoco.com
SIC: 2671 2672 2621   Paper, coated or laminated for packaging; Paper; coated and laminated, nec; Paper mills
HQ: Billerud U.S. Production Holding Llc
8540 Gander Creek Dr
Miamisburg OH 45342
877 855-7243

Jefferson
Lincoln County

(G-4918)
N C HUNT INC (PA)
Also Called: NC Hunt Lumber Company
200 S Clary Rd (04348-4128)
P.O. Box 3 (04348-0003)
PHONE..............................207 549-0922
Robert E Hunt, *Pr*
EMP: 43 **EST:** 1987
SQ FT: 1,000
SALES (est): 21.65MM
SALES (corp-wide): 21.65MM **Privately Held**
Web: www.nchuntlumber.com
SIC: 5251 2421   Hardware stores; Sawmills and planing mills, general

---

Jonesboro
Washington County

(G-4919)
JASPER WYMAN & SON
10 Bluebird Dr (04648)
PHONE..............................207 546-3381
Shannon Fickett, *Brnch Mgr*
EMP: 8
SALES (corp-wide): 27.24MM **Privately Held**
Web: www.wymans.com
SIC: 2037   Fruits, quick frozen and cold pack (frozen)
PA: Jasper Wyman & Son
7 Wyman Rd
Milbridge ME 04658
207 546-3800

Kennebunk
York County

(G-4920)
ANCHOR CORPORATION
Also Called: Anchor Fence

2 Bragdon Ln 1 (04043-7230)
P.O. Box 1117 (04043-1117)
PHONE..............................207 985-6018
TOLL FREE: 800
Mat Chase, *Pr*
EMP: 10 **EST:** 1981
SQ FT: 2,000
SALES (est): 1.6MM **Privately Held**
Web: www.anchorfencemaine.com
SIC: 1799 5211 5039 3496   Fence construction; Fencing; Wire fence, gates, and accessories; Miscellaneous fabricated wire products

(G-4921)
ASHLEIGH INC (PA)
Also Called: Kennebunkport Brewing Company
8 Western Ave Ste 6 (04043-7756)
PHONE..............................207 967-4311
Fred Frosley, *Pr*
EMP: 28 **EST:** 1987
SQ FT: 2,000
SALES (est): 10.14MM **Privately Held**
Web: www.federaljacks.com
SIC: 2082 5813 5812   Ale (alcoholic beverage); Drinking places; Eating places

(G-4922)
BEER SAVER USA
16 Sylvan Cir (04043-6917)
PHONE..............................207 299-2826
Larry Gumb, *CEO*
EMP: 10 **EST:** 2009
SALES (est): 821.36K **Privately Held**
Web: www.beersaverusa.com
SIC: 3585   Soda fountain and beverage dispensing equipment and parts

(G-4923)
CANVASWORKS INC
8 Bragdon Ln (04043-7230)
PHONE..............................207 985-2419
Stephen R Eberle, *Pr*
EMP: 7 **EST:** 1983
SQ FT: 3,500
SALES (est): 847.93K **Privately Held**
Web: www.canvasworksinc.com
SIC: 2394   Awnings, fabric: made from purchased materials

(G-4924)
CORNING INCORPORATED
Also Called: Corning
2 Alfred Rd (04043-6266)
PHONE..............................207 985-3111
Ken Walker, *Prin*
EMP: 60
SQ FT: 90,000
SALES (corp-wide): 12.59B **Publicly Held**
Web: www.corning.com
SIC: 3229   Pressed and blown glass, nec
PA: Corning Incorporated
1 Riverfront Plz
Corning NY 14831
607 974-9000

(G-4925)
G & G PRODUCTS LLC
Also Called: G & G Machining
70 Twine Mill Rd Ste 1 (04043-6359)
PHONE..............................207 985-9100
Gary Gagnon, *Managing Member*
✪ **EMP:** 27 **EST:** 1999
SQ FT: 23,000
SALES (est): 2.5MM **Privately Held**
Web: www.ggproductsllc.com
SIC: 3089 2821   Injection molding of plastics ; Molding compounds, plastics

(G-4926)
MALINGS WELDING SVC INC
115 York St (04043-7104)
PHONE..............................207 985-9769
Greg Maling, *Owner*
EMP: 7 **EST:** 1995
SALES (est): 132.2K **Privately Held**
SIC: 3441   Fabricated structural metal

(G-4927)
NORTHEAST COATING TECH INC
Also Called: Nct
105 York St (04043-7104)
P.O. Box 539 (04043-0539)
PHONE..............................207 985-3232
▲ **EMP:** 50 **EST:** 1994
SQ FT: 30,000
SALES (est): 14.27MM
SALES (corp-wide): 8.86MM **Privately Held**
Web: www.northeastcoating.com
SIC: 3479   Coating of metals and formed products
PA: Hef M&S Services
69 Avenue Benoit Fourneyron
Andrezieux Boutheon 42160
477555222

(G-4928)
RAMBLERS WAY FARM INC (PA)
2 Storer St Ste 207 (04043-6882)
PHONE..............................207 467-8118
Tom Chappell, *CEO*
EMP: 9 **EST:** 2008
SALES (est): 754.06K **Privately Held**
Web: www.ramblersway.com
SIC: 2231   Apparel and outerwear broadwoven fabrics

(G-4929)
RICH ASSOCIATES INCORPORATED
Also Called: Hunter Editions
759 Alewive Rd (04043-6008)
PHONE..............................207 985-5999
EMP: 7 **EST:** 1994
SQ FT: 3,200
SALES (est): 430K **Privately Held**
Web: www.huntereditions.com
SIC: 7999 2741   Art gallery, commercial; Art copy and poster publishing

(G-4930)
TOMS OF MAINE INC (HQ)
Also Called: Tom's Natural Soap
2 Storer St Ste 302 (04043-6883)
PHONE..............................207 985-2944
Tom Obrien, *CEO*
Astrid Hermann, *
▲ **EMP:** 95 **EST:** 1970
SQ FT: 20,000
SALES (est): 48.63MM
SALES (corp-wide): 17.97B **Publicly Held**
Web: www.tomsofmaine.com
SIC: 2844   Cosmetic preparations
PA: Colgate-Palmolive Company
300 Park Ave Fl 8
New York NY 10022
212 310-2000

(G-4931)
YORK COUNTY COAST STAR INC
39 Main St (04043-7081)
P.O. Box 979 (04043-0979)
PHONE..............................207 985-5901
EMP: 8 **EST:** 1996
SALES (est): 92.08K **Privately Held**

Web: www.seacoastonline.com
SIC: 2711 Newspapers, publishing and printing

Kingfield
Franklin County

(G-4932)
ADVANCED RSRCES CNSTR ENTPS IN
Also Called: ARC Enterprises
27 Commercial Rd (04947)
P.O. Box 120 (04947-0120)
PHONE..........................207 265-2646
Walter P Kilbreth, Pr
EMP: 25 EST: 1980
SQ FT: 18,000
SALES (est): 5.19MM Privately Held
Web: www.arcenterprisesinc.com
SIC: 3441 Fabricated structural metal

(G-4933)
FRONTIER FORGE INC
Also Called: Kingfield Wood Products
37 Depot St (04947-4208)
PHONE..........................207 265-2151
Phillip Kennedy, Pr
EMP: 17 EST: 1984
SQ FT: 35,000
SALES (est): 952.7K Privately Held
Web: www.kingfieldwoodproducts.com
SIC: 2499 Spools, wood

(G-4934)
NEW ENGLAND WIRE PRODUCTS INC
49 Depot St (04947-4208)
PHONE..........................207 265-2176
Charles Peters, Brnch Mgr
EMP: 37
SALES (corp-wide): 38.98MM Privately Held
Web: www.displayracks.com
SIC: 3496 Miscellaneous fabricated wire products
PA: New England Wire Products, Inc.
9 Mohawk Dr
Leominster MA 01453
800 254-9473

Kittery
York County

(G-4935)
GOOD TO-GO LLC
Also Called: Good To-Go
484 Us Route 1 (03904-5507)
PHONE..........................207 451-9060
Jennifer Scism, Pr
David Koorits, VP
EMP: 10 EST: 2013
SQ FT: 3,000
SALES (est): 1.07MM Privately Held
Web: www.goodto-go.com
SIC: 2032 Ethnic foods, canned, jarred, etc.

(G-4936)
LAUNCHPAD ELECTRIC SOLUTIONS
Also Called: Ev Launchpad
24 Hillcrest Ave (03904-1444)
PHONE..........................603 828-2919
James Penfold, CEO
EMP: 10 EST: 2017
SALES (est): 1MM Privately Held

SIC: 3694 Battery charging generators, automobile and aircraft

(G-4937)
MESSER LLC
9 Ranger Dr (03904-1055)
PHONE..........................207 475-3102
Daryl Souzer, Brnch Mgr
EMP: 38
SALES (corp-wide): 1.63B Privately Held
Web: www.messeramericas.com
SIC: 2813 Nitrogen
HQ: Messer Llc
200 Smrst Corp Blvd # 7000
Bridgewater NJ 08807
800 755-9277

(G-4938)
PARKER-HANNIFIN CORPORATION
Pneumatic North America
9 Cutts Rd (03904-5567)
PHONE..........................207 439-9511
Bill Treacy, Mgr
EMP: 82
SALES (corp-wide): 19.07B Publicly Held
Web: www.parker.com
SIC: 3822 1711 3612 3564 Building services monitoring controls, automatic; Mechanical contractor; Transformers, except electric; Blowers and fans
PA: Parker-Hannifin Corporation
6035 Parkland Blvd
Cleveland OH 44124
216 896-3000

(G-4939)
PATTEN TOOL AND ENGRG INC
Also Called: Pte Precision Machining
22 Route 236 (03904-5525)
P.O. Box 478 (03904-0478)
PHONE..........................207 439-1555
Kevin R Stine, Pr
Herbert A Marsh, VP
H Allen Marsh, VP
EMP: 14 EST: 1972
SALES (est): 2.48MM Privately Held
Web: www.pte-precision-machining.com
SIC: 8711 3599 Designing: ship, boat, machine, and product; Machine shop, jobbing and repair

(G-4940)
VILLEROY & BOCH USA INC
Also Called: House of Villeroy & Boch
360 Us Route 1 (03904-6502)
PHONE..........................207 439-6440
Mary Hui, Mgr
EMP: 10
SALES (corp-wide): 1.03B Privately Held
Web: www.villeroy-boch.com
SIC: 3089 Tableware, plastics
HQ: Villeroy & Boch Usa, Inc.
3a S Middlesex Ave
Monroe Township NJ 08831
800 536-2284

(G-4941)
YORK HARBOR BREWING COMPANY
8 Blueberry Ln (03904-5453)
PHONE..........................207 703-8060
David Albert Dauteuil, Pr
EMP: 9 EST: 2015
SALES (est): 320K Privately Held
SIC: 2082 Malt beverages

Kittery Point
York County

(G-4942)
SYNERGY PRINTING
89 Goodwin Rd (03905-5224)
P.O. Box 25 (03905-0025)
PHONE..........................207 703-2782
EMP: 7 EST: 2017
SALES (est): 121.14K Privately Held
Web: hemmons.geiger.com
SIC: 2759 Commercial printing, nec

Knox
Waldo County

(G-4943)
CENTER POINT INC
Also Called: Center Point Publishing
600 Brooks Rd (04986-4210)
P.O. Box 1 (04986-0001)
PHONE..........................207 568-3717
◆ EMP: 22 EST: 1988
SALES (est): 2.16MM Privately Held
Web: www.centerpointlargeprint.com
SIC: 2741 2732 Miscellaneous publishing; Books, printing only

Lamoine
Hancock County

(G-4944)
SW BOATWORKS
358 Douglas Hwy (04605-4248)
PHONE..........................207 667-7427
Stewart Workman, Pr
EMP: 14 EST: 2005
SALES (est): 1.03MM Privately Held
Web: www.swboatworks.com
SIC: 3732 Boats, fiberglass: building and repairing

Lebanon
York County

(G-4945)
NEW ENGLAND POWDER COATING
172 Creamery Hill Rd (04027-3436)
PHONE..........................207 432-6679
William Larose, Prin
EMP: 10 EST: 2014
SALES (est): 117.62K Privately Held
Web: www.bellspowdercoating.com
SIC: 3479 Painting, coating, and hot dipping

Lee
Penobscot County

(G-4946)
T RAYMOND FOREST PRODUCTS INC
Also Called: T Raymond Forest Products
260 Arab Rd (04455-4519)
PHONE..........................207 738-2313
Terry R Raymond, Pr
Paula Raymonds, VP
EMP: 10 EST: 1977
SALES (est): 468.15K Privately Held
Web: www.denverneph.net
SIC: 2411 Logging camps and contractors

(G-4947)
YATES LUMBER INC
137 Winn Rd (04455-4202)
P.O. Box 137 (04455-0137)
PHONE..........................207 738-2331
EMP: 10 EST: 1996
SALES (est): 714K Privately Held
SIC: 2421 Wood chips, produced at mill

Leeds
Androscoggin County

(G-4948)
GERRITY COMPANY INCORPORATED
Also Called: Dayken Pallet
152 Bog Rd (04263-3736)
P.O. Box 121 (04259-0121)
PHONE..........................207 933-2804
TOLL FREE: 877
Peter F Gerrity, Pr
Peter J Young, *
J F Gerrity Iii, Treas
EMP: 40 EST: 1950
SQ FT: 40,000
SALES (est): 9.05MM
SALES (corp-wide): 20.36MM Privately Held
Web: www.gerrityindustries.com
SIC: 2448 2421 Pallets, wood; Sawmills and planing mills, general
PA: Gerrity Enterprises, Incorporated
63b Bedford St
Lakeville MA 02347
617 916-0776

Lewiston
Androscoggin County

(G-4949)
ACTION SCREEN PRINTING
41 Chestnut St Ste 5 (04240-7779)
PHONE..........................207 795-7786
EMP: 7 EST: 1996
SALES (est): 490.98K Privately Held
Web: www.actionscreenprinting.net
SIC: 2759 Screen printing

(G-4950)
ALLEN MANUFACTURING INC
41 Canal St (04240-7764)
PHONE..........................207 333-3385
David Allen, Pr
▲ EMP: 14 EST: 2011
SALES (est): 232.44K Privately Held
Web: www.allenmfgusa.com
SIC: 2399 Fabricated textile products, nec

(G-4951)
AVIENT COLORANTS USA LLC
17 Foss Rd (04240-1303)
PHONE..........................207 784-0733
Russ Neal, Genl Mgr
EMP: 259
Web: www.avient.com
SIC: 2865 5169 Dyes and pigments; Synthetic resins, rubber, and plastic materials
HQ: Avient Colorants Usa Llc
85 Industrial Dr
Holden MA 01520
508 829-6321

(G-4952)
B&T PALLET RECYCLING INC
13 Fireslate Pl (04240-2310)

P.O. Box 1120 (04243-1120)
PHONE..............................207 784-9048
EMP: 7 **EST:** 1991
SQ FT: 45,000
SALES (est): 622.03K **Privately Held**
SIC: 2448 Pallets, wood

(G-4953)
BELL MANUFACTURING CO
Also Called: Bell Label Co.
777 Main St (04240-5803)
P.O. Box 196 (04243-0196)
PHONE..............................207 784-2961
Tom Seder, *Pr*
◆ **EMP:** 9 **EST:** 1947
SQ FT: 30,000
SALES (est): 635.38K **Privately Held**
Web: www.belllabel.com
SIC: 2241 2759 Labels, woven; Tags:
printing, nsk
PA: Sml Usa Inc.
1 Harmon Plz Fl 6
Secaucus NJ 07094

(G-4954)
**CHANDLER SECURITY
SYSTEMS INC**
1260 Lisbon St (04240-3962)
PHONE..............................207 576-3418
Richard Rodrigue, *Owner*
EMP: 9 **EST:** 2012
SALES (est): 332.38K **Privately Held**
Web: www.chandlersecuritysystems.com
SIC: 3699 Security control equipment and
systems

(G-4955)
**DESIGN ARCHITECTURAL
HEATING**
141 Howe St (04240-6422)
P.O. Box 7110 (04243-7110)
PHONE..............................207 784-0309
Paul Roy, *Pr*
▲ **EMP:** 10 **EST:** 1993
SQ FT: 8,000
SALES (est): 851.19K **Privately Held**
Web:
www.designarchitecturalheating.com
SIC: 3699 Heat emission operating
apparatus

(G-4956)
DINGLEY PRESS INC
40 Westminster St (04240-3532)
PHONE..............................207 782-1529
Christopher A Pierce, *Pr*
EMP: 219
SALES (corp-wide): 46.82MM **Privately
Held**
Web: www.dingley.com
SIC: 2752 Offset printing
PA: The Dingley Press Inc
119 Lisbon St
Lisbon ME 04250
207 353-1500

(G-4957)
DVE MANUFACTURING INC
550 Lisbon St (04240-6580)
P.O. Box 2005 (04241-2005)
PHONE..............................207 783-9895
Donald Loiselle, *Pr*
EMP: 8 **EST:** 1982
SQ FT: 49,000
SALES (est): 476.77K **Privately Held**
Web: www.dvemfg.com
SIC: 2353 7336 2396 Caps: cloth, straw,
and felt; Silk screen design; Automotive
and apparel trimmings

(G-4958)
ELEMENT ALL STARS
746 Main St (04240-5807)
PHONE..............................207 576-6931
Andrea Kenebous, *Prin*
EMP: 8 **EST:** 2018
SALES (est): 938.99K **Privately Held**
Web: www.elementallstarsme.com
SIC: 2819 Elements

(G-4959)
ELMET TECHNOLOGIES INC
1560 Lisbon St (04240-3519)
PHONE..............................207 784-3591
◆ **EMP:** 232
SIC: 3451 3356 Screw machine products;
Tungsten, basic shapes

(G-4960)
**ELMET TECHNOLOGIES LLC
(PA)**
Also Called: Elmet Technologies
1560 Lisbon St (04240-3519)
PHONE..............................207 333-6100
Andrew D R Nichols, *CEO*
Marc Lamare, *S&M/VP*
Derek Fox, *CFO*
◆ **EMP:** 207 **EST:** 2015
SQ FT: 220,000
SALES (est): 77.73MM
SALES (corp-wide): 77.73MM **Privately
Held**
Web: www.elmettechnologies.com
SIC: 3356 3499 3769 3599 Nonferrous
rolling and drawing, nec; Friction material,
made from powdered metal; Space vehicle
equipment, nec; Machine and other job
shop work

(G-4961)
**ENTERPRISE CASTING
CORPORATION**
40 South Ave (04240-5756)
PHONE..............................207 782-5511
Jason Schmertman, *Pr*
EMP: 42 **EST:** 2020
SALES (est): 3.29MM **Privately Held**
Web: www.enterprisefoundry.com
SIC: 2899 2891 5084 3398 Core oil or
binders; Epoxy adhesives; Smelting
machinery and equipment; Metal heat
treating

(G-4962)
GEIGER BROS (PA)
Also Called: Crestline
70 Mount Hope Ave (04240-1021)
P.O. Box 1609 (04241-1609)
PHONE..............................207 755-2000
Jo-an G Lantz, *CEO*
Eugene G Geiger, *
Peter E Geiger, *Marketing GRP*
Ronald G Giard, *PROD GRP*
Tuan Huynh, *CIO*
▲ **EMP:** 325 **EST:** 1878
SQ FT: 144,000
SALES (est): 146.45MM
SALES (corp-wide): 146.45MM **Privately
Held**
Web: www.crestline.com
SIC: 5199 3993 2752 2782 Advertising
specialties; Advertising novelties;
Calendars, lithographed; Blankbooks and
looseleaf binders

(G-4963)
HAHNEL BROS CO (PA)
Also Called: Hbc
46 Strawberry Ave (04240-5942)

P.O. Box 1160 (04243-1160)
PHONE..............................207 784-6477
Alan R Hahnel, *Pr*
William H Hunter, *Ex VP*
EMP: 107 **EST:** 1916
SQ FT: 35,000
SALES (est): 19.19MM
SALES (corp-wide): 19.19MM **Privately
Held**
Web: www.hbcme.com
SIC: 1761 3444 Roofing contractor; Sheet
metalwork

(G-4964)
HUHTAMAKI INC
11 Fireslate Pl (04240-2310)
PHONE..............................207 795-6000
EMP: 25
SALES (corp-wide): 4.65B **Privately Held**
Web: www.huhtamaki.com
SIC: 2671 Paper; coated and laminated
packaging
HQ: Huhtamaki, Inc.
9201 Packaging Dr
De Soto KS 66018
913 583-3025

(G-4965)
INFAB REFRACTORIES INC
150 Summer St (04240-7532)
PHONE..............................207 783-2075
David Collins, *CEO*
Richard Marston, *Treas*
Jean Bergeron, *VP*
EMP: 8 **EST:** 2004
SQ FT: 12,600
SALES (est): 848.14K **Privately Held**
Web: www.infabrefractories.com
SIC: 3297 Nonclay refractories

(G-4966)
INSULSAFE TEXTILES INC
55 Holland St (04240-7515)
P.O. Box 149 (04236-0149)
PHONE..............................207 782-7011
Charles Gillis, *Pr*
Bruce Bubier, *VP*
Joyce Graham, *VP Sls*
▲ **EMP:** 20 **EST:** 1992
SQ FT: 45,000
SALES (est): 4.34MM **Privately Held**
Web: www.insulsafe.com
SIC: 2297 2211 Bonded-fiber fabrics, except
felt; Broadwoven fabric mills, cotton

(G-4967)
ITALIAN BAKERY PRODUCTS CO
Also Called: Italian Bakery Products
225 Bartlett St (04240-6502)
PHONE..............................207 782-8312
Frank Chiaravelotti, *Owner*
EMP: 10 **EST:** 1959
SQ FT: 2,400
SALES (est): 489.73K **Privately Held**
Web: www.theitalianbakeryme.com
SIC: 2051 5461 Bakery: wholesale or
wholesale/retail combined; Bread

(G-4968)
**JOHNS MANVILLE
CORPORATION**
51 Lexington St (04240-3529)
PHONE..............................207 784-0123
Tim Olehowski, *Mgr*
EMP: 50
SALES (corp-wide): 302.09B **Publicly
Held**
Web: www.jm.com
SIC: 3296 Mineral wool
HQ: Johns Manville Corporation
717 17th St Ste 800

Denver CO 80202
303 978-2000

(G-4969)
**KULLSON ENGINEERED TECH
INC**
Also Called: Purestat Engineered Tech
10 Gould Rd (04240-1402)
PHONE..............................207 576-9808
Richard Kullson, *Pr*
Keith Donaldson, *
▼ **EMP:** 29 **EST:** 2011
SALES (est): 3.6MM **Privately Held**
Web: www.transcendia.com
SIC: 2671 6719 Paper; coated and
laminated packaging; Investment holding
companies, except banks

(G-4970)
LASERWORDS MAINE
1775 Lisbon St (04240-3523)
PHONE..............................207 782-9595
Vellayan Subbiah, *Pr*
Daniel Boilard, *VP*
EMP: 18 **EST:** 1973
SQ FT: 5,000
SALES (est): 981.12K **Privately Held**
SIC: 2791 Typesetting, computer controlled

(G-4971)
**LEPAGE BAKERIES PARK ST
LLC (HQ)**
415 Lisbon St # 4 (04240-7617)
P.O. Box 1900 (04211-1900)
PHONE..............................207 783-9161
EMP: 40 **EST:** 2012
SQ FT: 20,000
SALES (est): 186.72MM
SALES (corp-wide): 4.81B **Publicly Held**
SIC: 2051 5461 Bread, cake, and related
products; Retail bakeries
PA: Flowers Foods, Inc.
1919 Flowers Cir
Thomasville GA 31757
229 226-9110

(G-4972)
**LEPAGE BAKERIES PARK ST
LLC**
Also Called: Country Kitchen
354 Lisbon St (04240-7306)
P.O. Box 1900 (04211-1900)
PHONE..............................207 783-9161
Thomas Mato, *Mgr*
EMP: 100
SALES (corp-wide): 4.81B **Publicly Held**
Web: www.flowersfoods.com
SIC: 2051 Bread, all types (white, wheat,
rye, etc); fresh or frozen
HQ: Lepage Bakeries Park Street Llc
415 Lisbon St 4
Lewiston ME 04240
207 783-9161

(G-4973)
LEWISTON DAILY SUN (PA)
Also Called: Sun Journal
104 Park St (04240-7202)
P.O. Box 4400 (04243-4400)
PHONE..............................207 784-3555
TOLL FREE: 800
James R Costello, *Pr*
James Thornton, *
Edward M Snook, *
Janice Costello, *Stockholder*
Stephen Costello, *
EMP: 245 **EST:** 1898
SQ FT: 16,000
SALES (est): 12.96MM

SALES (corp-wide): 12.96MM **Privately Held**
Web: www.sunjournal.com
SIC: 2711 Commercial printing and newspaper publishing combined

(G-4974)
LEWISTON-AUBURN TENT & AWNG CO
Also Called: L & A Tent Awning
240 River Rd (04240-1019)
PHONE..................................207 784-7353
Barry Richardson, *Pr*
Malcolm W Philbrook, *Clerk*
EMP: 8 EST: 1946
SQ FT: 5,000
SALES (est): 852.34K **Privately Held**
SIC: 2394 Awnings, fabric: made from purchased materials

(G-4975)
MICRONETIXX TECHNOLOGIES LLC
70 Commercial St Ste 1 (04240-3958)
P.O. Box 2114 (04241-2114)
PHONE..................................207 786-2000
George M Harris, *Managing Member*
▼ **EMP: 9 EST:** 2009
SQ FT: 8,500
SALES (est): 1.07MM **Privately Held**
Web: www.micronetixx.com
SIC: 3589 3825 Microwave ovens (cooking equipment), commercial; Oscillators, audio and radio frequency (instrument types)

(G-4976)
MODULA INC (DH)
Also Called: Diamond Systems
90 Alfred A Plourde Pkwy (04240-1027)
PHONE..................................207 440-5100
◆ **EMP: 63 EST:** 1995
SQ FT: 105,000
SALES (est): 61.75MM **Privately Held**
Web: www.modula.us
SIC: 8711 3535 Engineering services; Conveyors and conveying equipment
HQ: Modula Spa
Via San Lorenzo 41
Casalgrande RE 42013
052 277-4111

(G-4977)
MOTOR POWER INC
1505 Lisbon St (04240-3594)
PHONE..................................207 782-0616
TOLL FREE: 800
Ronald Guay, *Pr*
EMP: 8 EST: 1968
SQ FT: 2,500
SALES (est): 1MM **Privately Held**
Web: www.motorpwr.com
SIC: 5999 7694 Motors, electric; Electric motor repair

(G-4978)
MR BOSTON BRANDS LLC (HQ)
Also Called: Boston Brands of Maine
21 Saratoga St (04240-3527)
P.O. Box 2359 (04241-2359)
PHONE..................................207 783-1433
William Goldring, *Ch*
▲ **EMP: 10 EST:** 2015
SALES (est): 9.95MM
SALES (corp-wide): 1.28B **Privately Held**
SIC: 2085 2084 Grain alcohol for beverage purposes; Brandy
PA: Sazerac Company, Inc.
101 Magazine St Fl 5
New Orleans LA 70130
866 729-3722

(G-4979)
NEAL SPECIALTY COMPOUNDING LLC
Also Called: Compounding Solutions
258 Goddard Rd (04240-1000)
PHONE..................................207 777-1122
TOLL FREE: 877
Scott Neal, *Managing Member*
▲ **EMP: 70 EST:** 1999
SQ FT: 60,000
SALES (est): 34.61MM **Privately Held**
Web: www.compoundingsolutions.net
SIC: 2821 Plastics materials and resins

(G-4980)
NEOKRAFT SIGNS INC
647 Pleasant St (04240-3914)
P.O. Box 336 (04243-0336)
PHONE..................................207 782-9654
TOLL FREE: 800
Peter Murphy, *Pr*
Paul Lessard, *
Phil Bolduc, *
EMP: 36 EST: 1947
SALES (est): 4.47MM **Privately Held**
Web: www.neokraft.com
SIC: 3993 Neon signs

(G-4981)
OBRIEN CONSOLIDATED INDS
680 Lisbon St Ste 1 (04240-6509)
P.O. Box 139 (04243-0139)
PHONE..................................207 783-8543
Susan D Lagueux, *Pr*
Annette Dallaire, *Treas*
EMP: 27 EST: 1964
SQ FT: 22,000
SALES (est): 996.81K **Privately Held**
Web: www.obrienconsolidated.com
SIC: 3541 3544 3599 Machine tools, metal cutting type; Special dies, tools, jigs, and fixtures; Machine and other job shop work

(G-4982)
PAMCO MACHINE COMPANY INC
41 Chestnut St Ste 1a (04240-7779)
P.O. Box 1565 (04241-1565)
PHONE..................................207 783-1763
Maurice R Cote Prestreas, *Prin*
Brenda F Cote, *VP*
Peter M Garcia, *Clerk*
Maurice R Cote, *
▲ **EMP: 18 EST:** 1960
SALES (est): 2.23MM **Privately Held**
SIC: 5084 3559 Shoe manufacturing and repairing machinery; Shoe making and repairing machinery

(G-4983)
PANTHEON GUITARS LLC
Also Called: Bourgeois Guitars
41 Canal St (04240-7764)
PHONE..................................207 755-0003
EMP: 10 EST: 2000
SQ FT: 7,000
SALES (est): 967.79K **Privately Held**
Web: www.pantheonguitars.com
SIC: 3931 5099 Guitars and parts, electric and nonelectric; Musical instruments

(G-4984)
PENMOR LITHOGRAPHERS INC
Also Called: Western Maine Graphics
8 Lexington St (04240-3500)
P.O. Box 2003 (04241-2003)
PHONE..................................207 784-1341
TOLL FREE: 800
Joseph Fillion, *CEO*
Paul Fillion, *
Karen Nicole, *
Glen Fillion, *
Wayne Fillion, *Information Technology Vice President*
EMP: 50 EST: 1969
SQ FT: 42,000
SALES (est): 8.58MM **Privately Held**
Web: www.penmor.com
SIC: 2752 2789 Lithographing on metal; Bookbinding and related work

(G-4985)
PRR ENTERPRISE INC
40 South Ave (04240-5756)
P.O. Box 1564 (04241-1564)
PHONE..................................207 783-2991
EMP: 35
SIC: 3321 Gray and ductile iron foundries

(G-4986)
PUBLIC SCALES
32 Lexington St (04240-3510)
PHONE..................................207 784-9466
Robert Blanchette, *Pr*
EMP: 10 EST: 1991
SALES (est): 536.86K **Privately Held**
Web:
www.blanchettemovingandstorage.com
SIC: 3596 5046 Scales and balances, except laboratory; Scales, except laboratory

(G-4987)
PURE-STAT TECHNOLOGIES INC
Also Called: Purestat
11 Fireslate Pl (04240-2310)
PHONE..................................207 795-6000
EMP: 34
SIC: 2671 Paper; coated and laminated packaging

(G-4988)
QSA OPTICAL CO INC
Also Called: Hoya Vision Care
1567 Lisbon St Ste 5 (04240-3545)
PHONE..................................207 783-8523
Buster Walloff, *Mgr*
EMP: 40
SALES (corp-wide): 5.18MM **Privately Held**
SIC: 5049 3851 3842 Optical goods; Ophthalmic goods; Surgical appliances and supplies
PA: Qsa Optical Co, Inc
580 Nutmeg Rd N
South Windsor CT
860 289-5367

(G-4989)
RANCOURT & CO SHOECRAFTERS INC
Also Called: Rancourt & Co.
9 Bridge St (04240-7505)
P.O. Box 9739 (04104-5039)
PHONE..................................855 999-3544
Michael Rancourt, *Pr*
Kyle Rancourt, *VP*
▲ **EMP: 19 EST:** 2009
SQ FT: 25,000
SALES (est): 2.07MM **Privately Held**
Web: www.rancourtandcompany.com
SIC: 3143 Dress shoes, men's

(G-4990)
RODCO ENTERPRISES
Also Called: Rogue Wear
9 Westminster St (04240-3531)
P.O. Box 1750 (04241-1750)
PHONE..................................207 786-2931
Lionel G Rodrigue, *Pr*
Mark L Rodrigue, *
Diane D Rodrigue, *
Susan M Mulligan, *
EMP: 15 EST: 1969
SQ FT: 32,000
SALES (est): 4.65MM **Privately Held**
Web: www.roguewear.com
SIC: 5136 2393 2329 2395 Sportswear, men's and boys'; Textile bags; Jackets (suede, leatherette, etc.), sport: men's and boys'; Emblems, embroidered

(G-4991)
SAMS ITALIAN FOODS INC (PA)
Also Called: Sam's Italian Sandwich Shop
268 Main St (04240-7024)
PHONE..................................207 782-9145
Gerald C Clements, *Pr*
Phillip Libby, *Treas*
EMP: 15 EST: 1939
SQ FT: 2,000
SALES (est): 9.98MM
SALES (corp-wide): 9.98MM **Privately Held**
Web: www.samsitalian.com
SIC: 5812 2032 Italian restaurant; Italian foods, nec: packaged in cans, jars, etc.

(G-4992)
SENIOR OPERATIONS LLC
Also Called: Senior Flxnics Pthway Mtroflex
29 Lexington St (04240-3511)
PHONE..................................207 784-2338
EMP: 31
SALES (corp-wide): 1.02B **Privately Held**
Web: www.seniorflexonics.com
SIC: 3441 3822 8711 Expansion joints (structural shapes), iron or steel; Damper operators: pneumatic, thermostatic, electric; Industrial engineers
HQ: Senior Operations Llc
300 E Devon Ave
Bartlett IL 60103
630 372-3500

(G-4993)
SML INC
777 Main St (04240-5803)
P.O. Box 1020 (04250-1020)
PHONE..................................207 784-2961
▲ **EMP: 56 EST:** 2011
SALES (est): 2.36MM **Privately Held**
SIC: 2241 Narrow fabric mills

(G-4994)
TRANSCENDIA INC
21 Old Farm Rd (04240-2302)
PHONE..................................207 786-4790
EMP: 58
SALES (corp-wide): 290.26MM **Privately Held**
Web: www.transcendia.com
SIC: 2671 Paper; coated and laminated packaging
PA: Transcendia, Inc.
9201 Belmont Ave Ste 100a
Franklin Park IL 60131
847 678-1800

(G-4995)
WAHLCOMETROFLEX INC
Also Called: Senior Flexonics Pthwy
29 Lexington St (04240-3533)
PHONE..................................207 784-2338
John Powell, *Pr*
John W Bader, *
Roger Poulin, *
◆ **EMP: 300 EST:** 2000
SQ FT: 73,000
SALES (est): 49.85MM

SALES (corp-wide): 1.02B **Privately Held**
Web: www.sfpathway.com
SIC: 3441 3822 8711 Expansion joints (structural shapes), iron or steel; Damper operators: pneumatic, thermostatic, electric; Industrial engineers
HQ: Senior Operations Llc
   300 E Devon Ave
   Bartlett IL 60103
   630 372-3500

(G-4996)
WHEELCHAIR
192 Russell St (04240-5435)
PHONE................................207 782-8400
EMP: 11 EST: 2011
SALES (est): 91.83K **Privately Held**
Web: www.unitedambulance.com
SIC: 3842 Wheelchairs

(G-4997)
WHITE ROCK DISTILLERIES INC
Also Called: Lawrence & Co
21 Saratoga St (04240-3527)
P.O. Box 2586 (04241-2586)
PHONE................................207 783-1433
◆ EMP: 205
Web: www.whiterockdistilleries.com
SIC: 2085 Distilled and blended liquors

Liberty
Waldo County

(G-4998)
DEWEYS LUMBER LLC
140 Kager Mountain Rd (04949-3205)
P.O. Box 281 (04949-0281)
PHONE................................207 589-4126
Duane Jewett, *Prin*
EMP: 8 EST: 2008
SALES (est): 858.3K **Privately Held**
Web: www.deweyslumber.com
SIC: 2421 5211 Lumber: rough, sawed, or planed; Planing mill products and lumber

(G-4999)
LIBERTY GRAPHICS INC
Also Called: Liberty Graphics
Main St (04949)
P.O. Box 5 (04949-0005)
PHONE................................207 589-4596
Tom Opper, *Pr*
EMP: 19 EST: 1978
SQ FT: 12,000
SALES (est): 1.79MM **Privately Held**
Web: www.lgtees.com
SIC: 2759 2396 Screen printing; Automotive and apparel trimmings

Limerick
York County

(G-5000)
BOSAL FOAM AND FIBER (PA)
Also Called: Bosal Foam Products
171 Washington St (04048-3545)
P.O. Box 489 (04048-0489)
PHONE................................207 793-2245
TOLL FREE: 800
Robert J Harrisburg, *Pr*
▼ EMP: 25 EST: 2001
SQ FT: 163,000
SALES (est): 4.44MM
SALES (corp-wide): 4.44MM **Privately Held**
Web: www.bosalfoam.com

SIC: 3069 5131 6512 5199 Foam rubber; Upholstery fabrics, woven; Commercial and industrial building operation; Foams and rubber

(G-5001)
F R CARROLL INC
25 Doles Ridge Rd (04048-3400)
P.O. Box 9 (04048-0009)
PHONE................................207 793-8615
Francis R Carroll, *Pr*
Barbara A Carroll, *
EMP: 33 EST: 1952
SQ FT: 2,500
SALES (est): 4.18MM **Privately Held**
Web: www.frcarroll.com
SIC: 3273 1442 1771 2951 Ready-mixed concrete; Construction sand and gravel; Concrete work; Asphalt paving mixtures and blocks

(G-5002)
L M C LIGHT IRON INC
151 E Range Rd (04048-4220)
P.O. Box 521 (04048-0521)
PHONE................................207 793-9957
Steve Hamilton, *Pr*
EMP: 10 EST: 1996
SQ FT: 6,000
SALES (est): 1.09MM **Privately Held**
SIC: 3441 2431 Fabricated structural metal; Staircases, stairs and railings

(G-5003)
LIMERICK MACHINE COMPANY INC
Also Called: Limerick Machine Co
81 Central Ave (04048-3204)
P.O. Box 534 (04048-0534)
PHONE................................207 793-2288
Thomas C West, *Prin*
EMP: 28 EST: 2000
SQ FT: 13,000
SALES (est): 8.25MM **Privately Held**
Web: www.limerickmachine.com
SIC: 3599 Machine shop, jobbing and repair

Limestone
Aroostook County

(G-5004)
GRAPHIC UTILITIES INCORPORATED
191 Development Dr (04750-6114)
PHONE................................207 370-9178
Jacob Leby, *Pr*
Nancy Leby, *VP*
▲ EMP: 15 EST: 1985
SALES (est): 686.38K **Privately Held**
Web: www.graphicutilities.com
SIC: 2893 Printing ink

(G-5005)
STAINLESS FDSRVICE EQP MFG INC
Also Called: SFE Mfg
14 Connecticut Rd (04750-6160)
PHONE................................207 227-7747
Doug Morrell, *Pr*
William Busse, *Clerk*
EMP: 17 EST: 1991
SALES (est): 991.71K **Privately Held**
Web: www.sfemanufacturing.com
SIC: 2542 Office and store showcases and display fixtures

Limington
York County

(G-5006)
TRICO MILLWORKS INC
300 Hardscrabble Rd (04049-3011)
P.O. Box 69 (04049-0069)
PHONE................................207 637-2711
Dave Baker, *Pr*
Gordon Leach, *
EMP: 24 EST: 2000
SQ FT: 15,000
SALES (est): 2.18MM **Privately Held**
Web: www.tricomillwork.com
SIC: 2434 Wood kitchen cabinets

Lincoln
Penobscot County

(G-5007)
FASTCO FABRICATION INC
Also Called: Fastco
675 W Broadway (04457-4104)
PHONE................................207 794-3030
Allen Smith, *Pr*
Scott Smith, *
EMP: 25 EST: 1988
SALES (est): 4.64MM **Privately Held**
Web: www.fastco-corp.com
SIC: 1711 3444 Mechanical contractor; Sheet metalwork

(G-5008)
FOREST CHESTER PRODUCTS INC
Rte 116 (04457)
P.O. Box 189 (04457-0189)
PHONE................................207 794-2303
EMP: 26 EST: 1991
SQ FT: 12,000
SALES (est): 2.49MM **Privately Held**
SIC: 2411 2421 Wood chips, produced in the field; Sawmills and planing mills, general

(G-5009)
JOHNSTON DANDY COMPANY (PA)
Also Called: E.F. Cook Company
148 Main St (04457-1523)
P.O. Box 670 (04457-0670)
PHONE................................207 794-6571
Robert A Johnston, *Pr*
Daniel J Johnston, *
Kyle Johnston, *
◆ EMP: 25 EST: 1955
SQ FT: 30,000
SALES (est): 5.77MM
SALES (corp-wide): 5.77MM **Privately Held**
Web: www.johnstondandy.com
SIC: 3554 Paper mill machinery: plating, slitting, waxing, etc.

(G-5010)
LINCOLN NEWS
Also Called: Gateway Press
78 W Broadway (04457-1312)
P.O. Box 35 (04457-0035)
PHONE................................207 794-6532
Kevin Tenggren, *Owner*
EMP: 9 EST: 1961
SQ FT: 1,000
SALES (est): 246.92K **Privately Held**
Web: www.lincnews.com
SIC: 2711 Job printing and newspaper publishing combined

(G-5011)
LINCOLN PAPER AND TISSUE LLC
50 Katadin Ave (04457-1307)
P.O. Box 490 (04457-0490)
PHONE................................207 794-0600
◆ EMP: 400
Web: www.lpt.com
SIC: 2621 Tissue paper

(G-5012)
RAMSAYS WELDING & MACHINE INC
289 Enfield Rd (04457-4136)
P.O. Box 298 (04457-0298)
PHONE................................207 794-8839
Jeffrey L Fogg, *Pr*
Cynthia A Fogg, *VP*
EMP: 19 EST: 1966
SQ FT: 12,000
SALES (est): 480.56K **Privately Held**
Web: www.ramsayweldingandmachine.com
SIC: 3599 3441 7692 Machine shop, jobbing and repair; Fabricated structural metal; Welding repair

(G-5013)
S W COLLINS
Also Called: Do It Best
431 Main St (04457-4701)
P.O. Box 280 (04457-0280)
PHONE................................207 794-6113
Robert Haskell, *Pr*
Jay C Mcfalls, *VP*
Frederick Haskell, *Treas*
EMP: 21 EST: 1924
SQ FT: 5,000
SALES (est): 3.64MM **Privately Held**
Web: www.swcollins.com
SIC: 5251 5031 2421 2426 Hardware stores ; Lumber: rough, dressed, and finished; Lumber: rough, sawed, or planed; Hardwood dimension and flooring mills

(G-5014)
THOMPSON TRUCKING INC
Also Called: Thompson Forest Services
725 Enfield Rd (04457-4143)
P.O. Box 206 (04457-0206)
PHONE................................207 794-6101
Mary Keegan, *Pr*
George Keegan, *
EMP: 15 EST: 1965
SQ FT: 2,500
SALES (est): 860.28K **Privately Held**
SIC: 2411 4212 Logging camps and contractors; Lumber (log) trucking, local

Lincolnville
Waldo County

(G-5015)
MAINE CAT
380 Hope Rd (04849-5918)
PHONE................................207 529-6500
Dick Vermeulen, *Pr*
EMP: 11 EST: 1991
SALES (est): 410.6K **Privately Held**
Web: www.mecat.com
SIC: 3732 Yachts, building and repairing

GEOGRAPHIC

Lisbon
Androscoggin County

(G-5016)
SHERIDAN ME INC
119 Lisbon St (04250-6041)
PHONE................................207 353-1500
Eric Lane, *Pr*
EMP: 7 **EST:** 2004
SALES (est): 843.88K **Privately Held**
Web: www.dingley.com
SIC: 2752 Offset printing

(G-5017)
SPRINGWORKS FARM MAINE INC
347 Lisbon St (04250-6821)
P.O. Box 233 (04250-0233)
PHONE................................207 407-4207
Dave Kenkel, *Prin*
Stephanie Kenkel, *Prin*
EMP: 15 **EST:** 2015
SALES (est): 7.93MM **Privately Held**
Web: www.springworksfarm.com
SIC: 0191 2099 General farms, primarily crop; Salads, fresh or refrigerated

(G-5018)
THE DINGLEY PRESS INC (PA)
119 Lisbon St (04250-6005)
PHONE................................207 353-1500
EMP: 181 **EST:** 1955
SALES (est): 46.82MM
SALES (corp-wide): 46.82MM **Privately Held**
Web: www.dingley.com
SIC: 2752 2789 2732 Offset printing; Bookbinding and related work; Book printing

Lisbon Falls
Androscoggin County

(G-5019)
BLUE OX MALTHOUSE LLC
41 Capital Ave (04252-1102)
PHONE................................207 649-0018
Steve Culver, *CFO*
EMP: 12 **EST:** 2013
SALES (est): 861.52K **Privately Held**
Web: www.blueoxmalthouse.com
SIC: 2083 Barley malt

(G-5020)
FIRST CHOICE PRINTING INC
60 Capital Ave (04252-1102)
PHONE................................207 353-8006
Steven A Samson, *Pr*
EMP: 7 **EST:** 1989
SQ FT: 2,500
SALES (est): 730.48K **Privately Held**
Web: www.firstchoiceprinting.net
SIC: 2752 7334 Offset printing; Photocopying and duplicating services

(G-5021)
HARPSWELL HOUSE INC
52 Capital Ave (04252-1102)
P.O. Box 305 (04086-0305)
PHONE................................207 353-2385
Karen Brown, *Pr*
EMP: 7 **EST:** 1959
SQ FT: 9,000
SALES (est): 991.64K **Privately Held**
Web: www.harpswellhouse.com
SIC: 5199 3281 Advertising specialties; Slate products

(G-5022)
MAINE TOOL & MACHINE LLC
27 Canal St (04252-1823)
P.O. Box 129 (04252-0129)
PHONE................................207 576-4319
EMP: 9 **EST:** 2003
SQ FT: 17,000
SALES (est): 800K **Privately Held**
Web: www.mainetoolmachine.com
SIC: 3599 Machine shop, jobbing and repair

(G-5023)
MILLER INDUSTRIES INC
Also Called: Edwards Home Furnishings
Canal St Rr 196 (04252)
PHONE................................207 353-4371
FAX: 207 353-5900
EMP: 290 **EST:** 1929
SQ FT: 315,000
SALES (est): 20.28MM **Privately Held**
Web: www.mjblankets.com
SIC: 2211 2282 Broadwoven fabric mills, cotton; Wool yarn: twisting, winding, or spooling

Livermore
Androscoggin County

(G-5024)
JOHNNY H CASTONGUAY
140 Shackley Hill Rd (04253-3703)
PHONE................................207 897-5945
Johnny Castonguay, *Prin*
EMP: 8 **EST:** 2001
SALES (est): 407.29K **Privately Held**
SIC: 2411 Logging camps and contractors

Livermore Falls
Androscoggin County

(G-5025)
PINE TREE ORTHOPEDIC LAB INC
175 Park St (04254-4125)
PHONE................................207 897-5558
Bruce L Macdonald, *Pr*
▲ **EMP:** 15 **EST:** 2006
SQ FT: 10,000
SALES (est): 2.38MM **Privately Held**
Web: www.pinetreeorthopedic.com
SIC: 3842 5661 Orthopedic appliances; Footwear, athletic

(G-5026)
TM AND TM INC
Also Called: Tm & Tm
49 Gilbert St (04254-4238)
PHONE................................207 897-3442
Anthony Maxwell, *Pr*
Teri Maxwell, *VP*
EMP: 10 **EST:** 1946
SALES (est): 590.39K **Privately Held**
SIC: 2051 Rolls, bread type: fresh or frozen

Lovell
Oxford County

(G-5027)
LOVELL LUMBER COMPANY
3 Mill Rd (04051)
P.O. Box 106 (04051-0106)
PHONE................................207 925-6455
Mark Woodbrey, *Pr*
Helen A Woodbrey, *Ch Bd*
EMP: 22 **EST:** 1935

SQ FT: 1,200
SALES (est): 2.18MM **Privately Held**
Web: www.lovelllumber.com
SIC: 2426 2421 Lumber, hardwood dimension: Sawmills and planing mills, general

Ludlow
Aroostook County

(G-5028)
MAINE CEDAR SPECIALTY PRODUCTS
1938 Ludlow Rd (04730-7841)
PHONE................................207 532-4034
Gary Brewer, *Pr*
Andy Brewer, *VP*
EMP: 7 **EST:** 1996
SQ FT: 10,000
SALES (est): 693.11K **Privately Held**
Web: www.mainecedar.com
SIC: 2421 Sawmills and planing mills, general

Lyman
York County

(G-5029)
J AND L SAND
221 S Waterboro Rd (04002-7300)
PHONE................................207 499-2545
Jeffery Mcdonald, *Owner*
Lesley Leighton, *Owner*
EMP: 7 **EST:** 2002
SALES (est): 177.77K **Privately Held**
SIC: 1442 Construction sand and gravel

(G-5030)
MAINE HOMESTEAD INC
Also Called: Maine Homestead
1773 Alfred Rd (04002-7792)
PHONE................................207 344-9274
Krista Gagne, *Pr*
EMP: 11 **EST:** 2012
SALES (est): 995.16K **Privately Held**
Web: www.mainehomesteadmarket.com
SIC: 2033 Fruits and fruit products, in cans, jars, etc.

Machias
Washington County

(G-5031)
LOOKS GOURMET FOOD CO INC (HQ)
Also Called: Bar Harbor Foods
17 Stackpole Dr (04654-7009)
PHONE................................207 259-3341
Michael Cote, *Pr*
EMP: 19 **EST:** 2005
SQ FT: 10,000
SALES: 5.14MM
SALES (corp-wide): 99.75MM **Privately Held**
Web: www.barharborfoods.com
SIC: 2091 5146 Canned and cured fish and seafoods; Fish and seafoods
PA: Sea Watch International, Ltd.
8978 Glebe Park Dr
Easton MD 21601
410 822-7501

(G-5032)
MAINE WILD BLUEBERRY COMPANY

50 Elm St (04654-1415)
PHONE................................207 255-8364
Regner Kemps, *Opers Mgr*
EMP: 55
SALES (corp-wide): 3.35MM **Privately Held**
Web: www.machiasblueberry.com
SIC: 2037 2034 2033 Frozen fruits and vegetables; Dried and dehydrated fruits, vegetables and soup mixes; Canned fruits and specialties
HQ: Maine Wild Blueberry Company Inc
78 Elm St
Machias ME 04654
207 255-8364

(G-5033)
MAINE WILD BLUEBERRY COMPANY (DH)
78 Elm St (04654-1415)
P.O. Box 100 (04468-0100)
PHONE................................207 255-8364
John Bragg, *Pr*
Geoff Baldwin, *
Ragner Kamp, *
EMP: 100 **EST:** 1983
SQ FT: 120,000
SALES (est): 29.73MM
SALES (corp-wide): 3.35MM **Privately Held**
Web: www.wildblueberries.com
SIC: 2037 2033 Fruits, quick frozen and cold pack (frozen); Fruits: packaged in cans, jars, etc.
HQ: Oxford Frozen Foods Limited
4881 Main St
Oxford NS B0M 1
902 447-2100

(G-5034)
SHANNON DRILLING
684 Route 1 (04654)
P.O. Box 870 (04654-0870)
PHONE................................207 255-6149
Christopher Getchell, *Owner*
EMP: 7 **EST:** 2012
SALES (est): 444.44K **Privately Held**
SIC: 3533 Water well drilling equipment

Machiasport
Washington County

(G-5035)
MAINE COAST NORDIC
133 Smalls Point Rd (04655-3231)
PHONE................................207 255-6714
Glen Cooke, *Pr*
EMP: 10 **EST:** 1987
SALES (est): 791.79K **Privately Held**
SIC: 2092 Fresh or frozen packaged fish

Macwahoc Plt
Penobscot County

(G-5036)
HANINGTON BROS INC
488 Us Hwy 2 (04451-4019)
PHONE................................207 765-2681
Stephen Hanington, *Pr*
EMP: 17 **EST:** 1958
SQ FT: 10,000
SALES (est): 901.87K **Privately Held**
Web: www.haningtonbrothers.com
SIC: 2411 Logging camps and contractors

▲ = Import ▼ = Export
◆ = Import/Export

Madawaska
Aroostook County

(G-5037)
EVERGREEN MANUFACTURING GROUP LLC
791 Main St (04756-3101)
PHONE..............................207 728-4900
▲ **EMP:** 31
SIC: 2844 4731 7389   Perfumes, cosmetics and other toilet preparations; Truck transportation brokers; Cosmetic kits, assembling and packaging

(G-5038)
MADTOWN LOGGING LLC
185 Lavoie Ave (04756-1315)
PHONE..............................207 728-6260
Susan Violette, *Prin*
EMP: 7 **EST:** 2013
SALES (est): 246.09K **Privately Held**
SIC: 2411   Logging camps and contractors

(G-5039)
TWIN RIVERS PAPER COMPANY CORP
82 Bridge Ave (04756-1229)
PHONE..............................207 523-2350
EMP: 667 **EST:** 2010
SALES (est): 68.54MM **Privately Held**
Web: www.twinriverspaper.com
SIC: 2621   Paper mills

(G-5040)
TWIN RIVERS PAPER COMPANY LLC (PA)
82 Bridge Ave (04756-1229)
PHONE..............................207 728-3321
◆ **EMP:** 40 **EST:** 2010
SALES (est): 215.33MM **Privately Held**
Web: www.twinriverspaper.com
SIC: 2621   Paper mills

Madison
Somerset County

(G-5041)
BURGER-ROY INC
Also Called: Agway
66 Main St (04950-1223)
PHONE..............................207 696-3978
Brent Burger, *Pr*
EMP: 31 **EST:** 2000
SQ FT: 600
SALES (est): 387.1K **Privately Held**
Web: www.truevaluecompany.com
SIC: 2511 5261   Wood lawn and garden furniture; Retail nurseries and garden stores

(G-5042)
MADISON UPM
Also Called: Madison Paper Industries
1 Main St (04950-1220)
P.O. Box 129 (04950-0129)
PHONE..............................207 696-3307
▲ **EMP:** 225
Web: www.m-realusa.com
SIC: 2621   Paper mills

(G-5043)
T R DILLON LOGGING INC (PA)
138 Main St (04950-1523)
PHONE..............................207 696-8137
Thomas R Dillon, *Pr*
Joyce G Dillon, *VP*

EMP: 10 **EST:** 1981
SALES (est): 1.19MM **Privately Held**
SIC: 2411   Logging camps and contractors

Manchester
Kennebec County

(G-5044)
D R DESIGNS INC
980 Western Ave (04351-3406)
PHONE..............................207 622-3303
Rachel Bernier, *CEO*
EMP: 8 **EST:** 2003
SALES (est): 586.25K **Privately Held**
Web: www.drdesignsonline.com
SIC: 2395 2759 5999   Embroidery products, except Schiffli machine; Promotional printing; Alcoholic beverage making equipment and supplies

Mapleton
Aroostook County

(G-5045)
FLAGSTONE INC
235 Griffin Ridge Rd (04757-4405)
PHONE..............................207 227-5883
Victor Winslow, *Owner*
EMP: 7 **EST:** 2014
SALES (est): 99.27K **Privately Held**
SIC: 3281   Flagstones

Marshfield
Washington County

(G-5046)
HANSCOM CONSTRUCTION INC
Also Called: Valley Truck Parts and Service
384 Ridge Rd (04654-5124)
PHONE..............................207 255-8067
Donald Hanscom, *Pr*
Herb A Hanscom Junior, *VP*
Debra Hanscom, *Sec*
EMP: 19 **EST:** 1947
SQ FT: 5,100
SALES (est): 863.3K **Privately Held**
Web: www.hanscomconstruction.com
SIC: 1794 5211 5531 7538   Excavation and grading, building construction; Lumber products; Truck equipment and parts; General truck repair

Masardis
Aroostook County

(G-5047)
DAAQUAM LUMBER MAINE INC (HQ)
1203 Aroostook Scenic Hwy (04732)
P.O. Box 749 (04732-0749)
PHONE..............................207 435-6401
Patrick Labonte, *Dir*
▲ **EMP:** 132 **EST:** 1979
SQ FT: 50,000
SALES (est): 33.99MM
SALES (corp-wide): 118.32MM **Privately Held**
Web: www.groupelebel.com
SIC: 2421   Lumber: rough, sawed, or planed
PA: Groupe Lebel Inc.
54 Rue Amyot
Riviere-Du-Loup QC G5R 3
877 567-5910

Mechanic Falls
Androscoggin County

(G-5048)
AUBURN MANUFACTURING INC
5125 Walker Rd (04256)
P.O. Box 220 (04256-0220)
PHONE..............................207 345-8271
Kathie Leonard, *Pr*
EMP: 65
SALES (corp-wide): 12.99MM **Privately Held**
Web: www.auburnmfg.com
SIC: 2262   Fire resistance finishing: manmade and silk broadwoven
PA: Auburn Manufacturing Incorporated
34 Walker Rd
Mechanic Falls ME 04256
207 345-8271

(G-5049)
AUBURN MANUFACTURING INC (PA)
34 Walker Rd (04256-5340)
P.O. Box 220 (04256-0220)
PHONE..............................207 345-8271
Kathie M Leonard, *Pr*
▲ **EMP:** 30 **EST:** 1979
SQ FT: 60,000
SALES (est): 12.99MM
SALES (corp-wide): 12.99MM **Privately Held**
Web: www.auburnmfg.com
SIC: 2262 2298 2295 2241   Fire resistance finishing: manmade and silk broadwoven; Cordage and twine; Coated fabrics, not rubberized; Narrow fabric mills

(G-5050)
DOWNEAST MACHINE & ENGRG INC (PA)
Also Called: Deme
26 Maple St (04256-6113)
PHONE..............................207 345-8111
Keith Beaule, *Pr*
Steve Hussey, *VP*
Michael Hamlyn, *Treas*
EMP: 17 **EST:** 1972
SQ FT: 25,000
SALES (est): 4.76MM
SALES (corp-wide): 4.76MM **Privately Held**
Web: www.downeastmachine.com
SIC: 3553 5084   Sawmill machines; Paper, sawmill, and woodworking machinery

(G-5051)
ILLINOIS TOOL WORKS INC
Electro Static Technology
31 Winterbrook Rd (04256-5724)
PHONE..............................207 998-5140
William Oh, *Genl Mgr*
EMP: 45
SALES (corp-wide): 15.93B **Publicly Held**
Web: www.itw.com
SIC: 3629 3829 3625   Static elimination equipment, industrial; Measuring and controlling devices, nec; Relays and industrial controls
PA: Illinois Tool Works Inc.
155 Harlem Ave
Glenview IL 60025
847 724-7500

(G-5052)
MAINE WOOD TREATERS INC
58 Walker Rd (04256-5340)
PHONE..............................207 345-8411

Harold Bumby, *Pr*
John Bumby, *
EMP: 30 **EST:** 1983
SQ FT: 33,710
SALES (est): 13.21MM **Privately Held**
Web: www.mainewoodtreaters.com
SIC: 2491   Poles, posts and pilings: treated wood

(G-5053)
PARENT LUMBER COMPANY INC
355 Pigeon Hill Rd (04256-5737)
PHONE..............................207 998-2322
Richard Parent, *Pr*
EMP: 7 **EST:** 1940
SQ FT: 2,400
SALES (est): 936.23K **Privately Held**
SIC: 5211 5031 2421   Planing mill products and lumber; Lumber: rough, dressed, and finished; Sawmills and planing mills, general

Medford
Piscataquis County

(G-5054)
DEWITT MCH & FABRICATION INC
1152 Medford Center Rd (04463-6208)
PHONE..............................207 732-3530
EMP: 7 **EST:** 1996
SQ FT: 80,000
SALES (est): 791.7K **Privately Held**
SIC: 3599   Machine shop, jobbing and repair

Medway
Penobscot County

(G-5055)
ELLEN MCLAUGHLIN
Rte 157 (04460)
P.O. Box 637 (04460-0637)
PHONE..............................207 746-3398
EMP: 7 **EST:** 1978
SALES (est): 389.81K **Privately Held**
SIC: 2411   Logging camps and contractors

(G-5056)
H ARTHUR YORK LOGGING INC (PA)
157 Main Rd (04460-3130)
P.O. Box 89 (04460-0089)
PHONE..............................207 746-5883
Howard Arthur York, *Pr*
Wakine Tameous, *Treas*
EMP: 11 **EST:** 1977
SALES (est): 1.31MM
SALES (corp-wide): 1.31MM **Privately Held**
SIC: 2411   Logging camps and contractors

(G-5057)
H ARTHUR YORK LOGGING INC
163 Turnpike Rd (04460-3240)
PHONE..............................207 746-5912
Arthur York, *Prin*
EMP: 14
SALES (corp-wide): 1.31MM **Privately Held**
SIC: 2411   Logging camps and contractors
PA: H Arthur York Logging Inc
157 Main Rd
Medway ME 04460
207 746-5883

Mexico
Oxford County

(G-5058)
NICOLS BROTHERS LOGGING INC
197 Poplar Hill Rd (04257-3108)
P.O. Box 12 (04257-0012)
PHONE..............................207 364-8685
James Nicols, *Pr*
James Nicols Junior, *Pr*
Billy Joe Nicols, *VP*
EMP: 14 **EST:** 1981
SALES (est): 676.42K **Privately Held**
Web: www.nicolsbrothersinc.com
SIC: 2411 Logging camps and contractors

(G-5059)
WAUGHS MOUNTAINVIEW ELEC
246 Roxbury Rd (04257-1116)
P.O. Box 97 (04276-0097)
PHONE..............................207 545-2421
Bruce Waugh, *Pr*
EMP: 10 **EST:** 2004
SQ FT: 6,000
SALES (est): 1.62MM **Privately Held**
Web: www.waughselectric.com
SIC: 3699 Electrical equipment and supplies, nec

Milbridge
Washington County

(G-5060)
CHERRY POINT PRODUCTS INC
54 Wyman Rd (04658-3608)
PHONE..............................207 546-0930
EMP: 10 **EST:** 1994
SALES (est): 359.8K **Privately Held**
SIC: 2091 2099 Canned and cured fish and seafoods; Food preparations, nec

(G-5061)
KELCO INDUSTRIES
Also Called: Sunrise County Evergreens
58 Main St (04658-3511)
P.O. Box 160 (04658-0160)
PHONE..............................207 546-7562
Dugald Kell Senior, *Pr*
Dugald Kell Junior, *VP*
Liliane Kell, *
◆ **EMP:** 25 **EST:** 1955
SQ FT: 10,000
SALES (est): 2.39MM **Privately Held**
Web: www.kelcomaine.com
SIC: 5961 3315 5199 5251 Mail order house, nec; Wire products, ferrous/iron: made in wiredrawing plants; Christmas novelties; Tools, hand

(G-5062)
L RAY PACKING COMPANY
314 Wyman Rd (04658-3612)
PHONE..............................207 546-2355
Ivan H Ray, *Pr*
Arletta R Tucker, *Treas*
EMP: 7 **EST:** 1929
SALES (est): 875.6K **Privately Held**
SIC: 2091 Sardines: packaged in cans, jars, etc.

Milford
Penobscot County

(G-5063)
WEYMOUTHS GARAGE INC
8 Weymouth Way (04461-3255)
PHONE..............................207 827-2069
Francis Weymouth, *Pr*
Chuck Yanush, *VP*
Patty Weymouth, *Sec*
EMP: 7 **EST:** 1971
SQ FT: 2,000
SALES (est): 944.69K **Privately Held**
SIC: 7538 7692 General automotive repair shops; Automotive welding

Millinocket
Penobscot County

(G-5064)
BEAR SWAMP POWER COMPANY LLC
1024 Central St (04462-2111)
PHONE..............................207 723-4341
Jerome Montpetit, *Dir*
EMP: 10 **EST:** 2006
SALES (est): 151.32K **Privately Held**
SIC: 3621 Power generators

(G-5065)
JM HUBER CORPORATION
Rte 157 (04462)
PHONE..............................207 723-9291
EMP: 42
SALES (corp-wide): 1.24B **Privately Held**
Web: www.huber.com
SIC: 1455 Kaolin mining
PA: J.M. Huber Corporation
3100 Cumberland Blvd Se # 600
Atlanta GA 30339
678 247-7300

(G-5066)
MAINE HERITAGE TIMBER LLC
Also Called: Timberchic
102 Penobscot Ave (04462-1322)
P.O. Box 778 (04462-0778)
PHONE..............................207 723-9200
EMP: 20 **EST:** 2010
SQ FT: 10,000
SALES (est): 2.46MM **Privately Held**
Web: www.timberchic.com
SIC: 2499 Decorative wood and woodwork

(G-5067)
MILLINCKET FABRICATION MCH INC (PA)
432 Katahdin Ave (04462-1624)
PHONE..............................207 723-9733
Fred Lewis, *Pr*
EMP: 20 **EST:** 1909
SQ FT: 40,000
SALES (corp-wide): 4.18MM
SALES (corp-wide): 4.18MM **Privately Held**
Web: www.millinocketfab.com
SIC: 3312 3599 3321 3443 Stainless steel; Machine and other job shop work; Gray iron castings, nec; Tanks, standard or custom fabricated: metal plate

(G-5068)
PELLETIER MANUFACTURING INC
400 Golden Rd (04462)
P.O. Box 859 (04462-0859)
PHONE..............................207 723-6500
Jeffrey Pelletier, *Managing Member*
EMP: 11 **EST:** 2010
SQ FT: 25,000
SALES (est): 821.18K **Privately Held**
Web: www.pelletiermanufacturing.com
SIC: 3715 Truck trailers

Milo
Piscataquis County

(G-5069)
EASTERN ME SHOOTING SUPS INC
Also Called: Eastern Maine Industries
71 Main St (04463-1128)
PHONE..............................207 943-8808
Brent A Bailey, *Prin*
EMP: 10 **EST:** 2005
SALES (est): 425.96K **Privately Held**
Web: www.emshootingsupplies.com
SIC: 3949 Sporting and athletic goods, nec

(G-5070)
JSI STORE FIXTURES INC (HQ)
140 Park St (04463-1740)
P.O. Box 38 (04463-0038)
PHONE..............................207 943-5203
Terry Awalt, *CEO*
Mark Awalt, *
▲ **EMP:** 124 **EST:** 2006
SQ FT: 75,000
SALES (est): 79.39MM
SALES (corp-wide): 496.98MM **Publicly Held**
Web: www.jsistorefixtures.com
SIC: 2541 2499 5046 2542 Display fixtures, wood; Bakers' equipment, wood; Store fixtures; Partitions and fixtures, except wood
PA: Lsi Industries Inc.
10000 Alliance Rd
Blue Ash OH 45242
513 793-3200

Monmouth
Kennebec County

(G-5071)
MAINE HERITAGE WEAVERS
904 Main St (04259-7017)
P.O. Box 149 (04259-0149)
PHONE..............................207 933-2605
Linda Cloutier, *Pr*
EMP: 26 **EST:** 2002
SALES (est): 930.69K **Privately Held**
Web: www.maineheritageweavers.com
SIC: 2211 Bed sheeting, cotton

(G-5072)
SPORTS FIELDS INC
242 Warren Rd (04259-7507)
P.O. Box 118 (04259-0118)
PHONE..............................207 933-3547
James Vickerson, *Pr*
James J Vickerson Junior, *Pr*
Eugene Duplessis, *VP*
EMP: 10 **EST:** 1980
SALES (est): 995.96K **Privately Held**
Web: www.sportsfieldsinc.net
SIC: 0782 3949 5191 Turf installation services, except artificial; Track and field athletic equipment; Fertilizer and fertilizer materials

(G-5073)
STEVENS ELECTRIC PUMP SERVICE
18 Berry Rd (04259-7001)
P.O. Box 238 (04259-0238)
PHONE..............................207 933-2143
Timothy Stevens, *Pr*
Cindy Stevens, *Sec*
Sandra Stevens, *Treas*
EMP: 9 **EST:** 2001
SALES (est): 553.4K **Privately Held**
Web: www.stevenselectricandpump.com
SIC: 3561 Pumps and pumping equipment

Monson
Piscataquis County

(G-5074)
SHELDON SLATE PRODUCTS CO INC
38 Farm Quarry Rd (04464-7035)
P.O. Box 245 (04464-0245)
PHONE..............................207 997-3615
John Tatko, *Prin*
EMP: 12 **EST:** 1994
SALES (est): 483.27K **Privately Held**
Web: www.sheldonslate.com
SIC: 3281 Cut stone and stone products

Montville
Waldo County

(G-5075)
PIECEWORKS INC
418 Acadia Hwy (04941-4714)
P.O. Box 133 (04949-0133)
PHONE..............................207 589-3451
Cathy Roberts, *Pr*
EMP: 7 **EST:** 1996
SQ FT: 3,000
SALES (est): 1.11MM **Privately Held**
SIC: 5085 3999 Industrial supplies; Atomizers, toiletry

Moose River
Somerset County

(G-5076)
BOUNDARY CO
Also Called: Moose River Lumber Company
25 Talpey Rd (04945-4016)
PHONE..............................207 668-4193
Nicholas Fontaine, *Pr*
EMP: 60 **EST:** 1976
SALES (est): 4.54MM **Privately Held**
Web: www.pleasantriverlumber.com
SIC: 2421 Sawmills and planing mills, general

Mount Desert
Hancock County

(G-5077)
JOHN M WILLIAMS COMPANY
Also Called: John Williams Boat
17 Shipwright Ln (04660-6243)
P.O. Box 80 (04660-0080)
PHONE..............................207 244-7854
John Williams, *Pr*
EMP: 18 **EST:** 1972
SQ FT: 630
SALES (est): 996.56K **Privately Held**
Web: www.jwboatco.com
SIC: 4493 3732 5088 5551 Boat yards, storage and incidental repair; Boats, fiberglass: building and repairing; Boats, non-recreational; Boat dealers

Mount Vernon
Kennebec County

(G-5078)
WJB ASSOCIATES INC
290 Belgrade Rd (04352-3246)
P.O. Box 297 (04352-0297)
PHONE..............................207 293-2457
William Brinton, *Pr*
EMP: 8 **EST:** 1981
SALES (est): 2.12MM **Privately Held**
Web: www.woodsend.com
SIC: 8731 8734 3826   Agricultural research;
Soil analysis; Colorimeters (optical
instruments)

Naples
Cumberland County

(G-5079)
BRAYS BREWING COMPANY
Also Called: Bray's Brew Pub & Eatery
678 Roosevelt Trl (04055-5335)
P.O. Box 548 (04055-0548)
PHONE..............................207 693-6806
EMP: 25 **EST:** 1995
SQ FT: 5,000
SALES (est): 468.76K **Privately Held**
Web: www.braysbrewingcompany.com
SIC: 5812 5813 2082   Chicken restaurant;
Bars and lounges; Beer (alcoholic
beverage)

(G-5080)
**GREAT NORTHERN DOCKS INC
(PA)**
1114 Roosevelt Trl (04055-3137)
P.O. Box 1615 (04055-1615)
PHONE..............................207 693-3770
Sam Merriam, *Pr*
Fremont Merriam, *Stockholder*
EMP: 9 **EST:** 1986
SQ FT: 9,500
SALES (est): 1.9MM
SALES (corp-wide): 1.9MM **Privately Held**
Web: www.greatnortherndocks.com
SIC: 3448   Docks, prefabricated metal

(G-5081)
P & K SAND AND GRAVEL INC
234 Casco Rd (04055-5209)
PHONE..............................207 693-6765
Cory J Mitchell, *Pr*
EMP: 44 **EST:** 1970
SQ FT: 5,800
SALES (est): 5.67MM **Privately Held**
Web: www.pksandgravel.com
SIC: 4959 1794 3273 1442   Snowplowing;
Excavation work; Ready-mixed concrete;
Construction sand and gravel

New Canada
Aroostook County

(G-5082)
VOISINE BROS INC (PA)
768 Strip Rd (04743-3038)
P.O. Box 160 (04744-0160)
PHONE..............................207 231-0220
Ben Voisine, *Pr*
EMP: 7 **EST:** 1999
SALES (est): 1.62MM
SALES (corp-wide): 1.62MM **Privately
Held**

SIC: 0851 2411   Forest management
services; Logging

New Gloucester
Cumberland County

(G-5083)
BACHMANN INDUSTRIES INC
Also Called: Clyde Bergemann Bachmann
60 Pineland Dr Ste 230 (04260-5145)
P.O. Box 2150 (04211-2150)
PHONE..............................207 440-2888
EMP: 42 **EST:** 1991
SQ FT: 26,983
SALES (est): 10.87MM **Privately Held**
Web: www.bachmannusa.com
SIC: 8711 3441   Consulting engineer;
Expansion joints (structural shapes), iron or
steel
HQ: Clyde Bergemann Gmbh Maschinen-
Und Apparatebau
Schillwiese 20
Wesel NW 46485
2818150

(G-5084)
**DAVIS ZAC FINE
WOODWORKING**
321 Gloucester Hill Rd (04260-3858)
PHONE..............................207 926-4710
EMP: 7 **EST:** 1995
SALES (est): 699.59K **Privately Held**
Web: www.davisfinewoodworking.com
SIC: 1522 2499   Residential construction,
nec; Decorative wood and woodwork

(G-5085)
J F HUTCHINSON CO
Also Called: Jim's Metal Fabrication
616b Lewiston Rd (04260-4003)
P.O. Box 175 (04260-0175)
PHONE..............................207 926-3676
EMP: 10 **EST:** 1991
SALES (est): 923.32K **Privately Held**
SIC: 3441   Fabricated structural metal

(G-5086)
**MASCHINO & SONS LUMBER
CO INC**
79 Morse Rd (04260-4414)
PHONE..............................207 926-4288
George Maschino Junior, *Pr*
Duane Maschino, *VP*
EMP: 18 **EST:** 1930
SQ FT: 4,800
SALES (est): 1.49MM **Privately Held**
Web: www.maschinolbr.com
SIC: 5211 2421   Millwork and lumber;
Lumber: rough, sawed, or planed

(G-5087)
MCCANN FABRICATION
1027 Lewiston Rd (04260-3412)
P.O. Box 169 (04260-0169)
PHONE..............................207 926-4118
Dick Mccann, *Pr*
EMP: 30 **EST:** 1983
SQ FT: 22,000
SALES (est): 7.5MM **Privately Held**
Web: www.mccannfabrication.com
SIC: 3441   Fabricated structural metal

(G-5088)
**QUARTER POINT
WOODWORKING LLC (PA)**
483 Intervale Rd (04260-3647)
PHONE..............................207 926-1032

Bob Small, *Prin*
EMP: 8 **EST:** 2013
SALES (est): 152.09K
SALES (corp-wide): 152.09K **Privately
Held**
Web: www.oceanpro.com.my
SIC: 2431   Millwork

(G-5089)
SUN DIAGNOSTICS LLC
60 Pineland Dr Ste 305 (04260)
PHONE..............................207 926-1125
Kwok Yeung, *CEO*
John Contois, *Pr*
EMP: 8 **EST:** 2012
SALES (est): 892.22K **Privately Held**
Web: www.sundiagnostics.us
SIC: 2835   In vitro diagnostics

New Sharon
Franklin County

(G-5090)
IMELDAS FABRICS & DESIGNS
5 Starks Rd (04955-3314)
PHONE..............................207 778-0665
Janet Kennedy, *Prin*
EMP: 7 **EST:** 2007
SALES (est): 146.08K **Privately Held**
Web: www.imeldasfabric.com
SIC: 2321 2331 2369 5137   Men's and boy's
furnishings; Women's and misses' blouses
and shirts; Girl's and children's outerwear,
nec; Women's and children's clothing

New Vineyard
Franklin County

(G-5091)
MAINE WOOD TURNING INC
Also Called: Sawmill
Lake Street Rte 234 (04956)
PHONE..............................207 652-2320
EMP: 8
SALES (corp-wide): 9.42MM **Privately
Held**
Web: www.mainewoodconcepts.com
SIC: 2499   Novelties, wood fiber
PA: Maine Wood Turning, Inc.
1687 New Vineyard Rd
New Vineyard ME
207 652-2441

Newcastle
Lincoln County

(G-5092)
**BOTTLE KING REDEMPTION
CENTER**
116 Mills Rd (04553-3408)
PHONE..............................207 563-1520
EMP: 9 **EST:** 2016
SALES (est): 307.69K **Privately Held**
Web: www.lcnme.com
SIC: 2711   Newspapers, publishing and
printing

(G-5093)
**LINCOLN COUNTY PUBLISHING
CO**
Also Called: Lincoln County News
116 Mills Rd (04553-3408)
P.O. Box 36 (04543-0036)
PHONE..............................207 563-3171
TOLL FREE: 800

Christopher Roberts, *Pr*
Francis Roberts, *
EMP: 45 **EST:** 1875
SALES (est): 1.63MM **Privately Held**
Web: www.lcnme.com
SIC: 2752 2711   Commercial printing,
lithographic; Newspapers, publishing and
printing

(G-5094)
LU-DZ LLC
Also Called: Split Rock Distilling
16 Osprey Point Rd (04553-3962)
PHONE..............................207 563-2669
EMP: 8 **EST:** 2016
SALES (est): 522.88K **Privately Held**
Web: www.splitrockdistilling.com
SIC: 2085   Distilled and blended liquors

(G-5095)
MAINE INDUSTRIAL P & R CORP
21 Teague St (04553)
P.O. Box 381 (04553-0381)
PHONE..............................207 563-5532
Henry G Lee, *Pr*
Katherine C Lee, *Treas*
EMP: 7 **EST:** 1980
SALES (est): 972.08K **Privately Held**
Web: www.miprcorp.com
SIC: 3069   Hard rubber products, nec

(G-5096)
**SHEEPSCOT MACHINE WORKS
LLC**
Also Called: Exact Dispensing Systems
1130 Route 1 (04553-3956)
PHONE..............................207 563-2299
EMP: 7 **EST:** 2010
SALES (est): 3.15MM
SALES (corp-wide): 286.84MM **Privately
Held**
Web: www.exactdispensing.com
SIC: 2891   Adhesives
PA: Tasi Holdings, Inc.
40 Locke Dr Ste B
Marlborough MA 01752
513 202-5182

Newport
Penobscot County

(G-5097)
NIF INC
445 Elm St (04953-3311)
P.O. Box D (04953-0423)
PHONE..............................207 368-4344
Daniel Gerry, *Pr*
EMP: 37 **EST:** 1997
SQ FT: 31,000
SALES (est): 6.19MM **Privately Held**
Web: www.nif-inc.com
SIC: 3441   Building components, structural
steel

(G-5098)
ROLLING THUNDER PRESS INC
Also Called: Rolling Thunder Express
134 Main St A (04953-3105)
P.O. Box 480 (04953-0480)
PHONE..............................207 368-2028
Sylvia Angel, *Pr*
EMP: 9 **EST:** 1978
SALES (est): 493.8K **Privately Held**
Web: www.rollingthunderexpress.com
SIC: 2711   Newspapers, publishing and
printing

(G-5099)
VIC FIRTH MANUFACTURING INC
Also Called: Vic Firth Gourmet
34 Progress Park S (04953-4153)
PHONE..................................207 368-4358
Vic Firth, *CEO*
Tracy K Firth, *
Merle E Wood, *
▲ EMP: 39 EST: 1994
SALES (est): 4.27MM Privately Held
Web: vicfirth.zildjian.com
SIC: 2426 Turnings, furniture: wood

Nobleboro
Lincoln County

(G-5100)
COASTAL WOODWORKING INC
Also Called: Coastal Woodworks & Display
16 Sand Hill Dr (04555-9051)
P.O. Box 137 (04555-0137)
PHONE..................................207 563-1072
Charles Agnew, *Pr*
EMP: 20 EST: 1990
SQ FT: 13,000
SALES (est): 1.77MM Privately Held
Web: www.coastalwoodworks.com
SIC: 2499 2431 Decorative wood and
woodwork; Millwork

(G-5101)
SPEAR FARMS INC
14 Eugley Hill Rd (04555-9547)
PHONE..................................207 832-4488
EMP: 20 EST: 1966
SALES (est): 2.71MM Privately Held
Web: www.spearsfarmstand.com
SIC: 5148 2011 0254 Vegetables; Beef
products, from beef slaughtered on site;
Chicken hatchery

(G-5102)
TEAM AUGMENTED REALITY INC
Also Called: Teamar
440 E Neck Rd (04555-8423)
P.O. Box F (04011-0587)
PHONE..................................207 350-0460
Charles Benton, *Prin*
EMP: 7 EST: 2014
SALES (est): 141.66K Privately Held
SIC: 7372 7371 Application computer
software; Computer software development
and applications

Norridgewock
Somerset County

(G-5103)
NEW BALANCE ATHLETICS INC
20 Depot St (04957-3952)
PHONE..................................207 634-3033
Jeff Williams, *Mgr*
EMP: 28
SALES (corp-wide): 17.22MM Privately
Held
Web: www.newbalance.com
SIC: 3149 3144 3143 3021 Athletic shoes,
except rubber or plastic; Women's
footwear, except athletic; Men's footwear,
except athletic; Rubber and plastics
footwear
HQ: New Balance Athletics, Inc.
100 Guest St
Boston MA 02135
617 783-4000

North Anson
Somerset County

(G-5104)
COUSINEAU WOOD PRODUCTS ME LLC
Also Called: Manufacturing
3 Valley Rd (04958-7208)
P.O. Box 58 (04958-0058)
PHONE..................................207 635-4445
Brody Cousineau, *
Randy Hau, *
EMP: 35 EST: 2001
SALES (est): 4.83MM Privately Held
Web: www.cousineaus.com
SIC: 2421 2499 Lumber: rough, sawed, or
planed; Laundry products, wood

(G-5105)
FROST CEDAR PRODUCTS INC
Fahi Pond Rd (04958)
PHONE..................................207 566-5912
R Frank Frost, *Pr*
Debra S Frost, *Sec*
EMP: 8 EST: 1960
SALES (est): 942.82K Privately Held
SIC: 2499 Fencing, wood

(G-5106)
KANGAS INC
51 New Portland Rd (04958-7401)
P.O. Box 616 (04958-0616)
PHONE..................................207 635-3745
Pete Kangas, *Pr*
EMP: 8 EST: 1989
SQ FT: 1,200
SALES (est): 818.5K Privately Held
SIC: 2499 Handles, poles, dowels and
stakes: wood

(G-5107)
MATTINGLY PRODUCTS COMPANY
25 Folon Rd (04958)
P.O. Box 105 (04958-0105)
PHONE..................................207 635-2719
Philip Mattingly, *Pr*
EMP: 31 EST: 1984
SALES (est): 1.78MM Privately Held
Web: www.mattinglyproducts.com
SIC: 3273 3272 2951 Ready-mixed concrete
; Concrete products, nec; Asphalt paving
mixtures and blocks

North Berwick
York County

(G-5108)
HUSSEY CORPORATION (PA)
Also Called: Hussey Seating Co
38 Dyer St Ext (03906-6763)
PHONE..................................207 676-2271
Tim Hussey, *Pr*
Garri Marill, *
Todd M Pierce, *
Jack F Rogers, *
◆ EMP: 300 EST: 1835
SQ FT: 12,000
SALES (est): 167.09MM
SALES (corp-wide): 167.09MM Privately
Held
Web: www.husseyseating.com
SIC: 2531 Stadium seating

(G-5109)
HUSSEY SEATING COMPANY
38 Dyer St Ext (03906-6763)
PHONE..................................207 676-2271
Brian Deveaux, *CEO*
Timothy B Hussey, *
Todd Pierce, *
Jack Rogers, *
Charles W Nadeau, *
◆ EMP: 302 EST: 1980
SQ FT: 200,000
SALES (est): 104.67MM
SALES (corp-wide): 167.09MM Privately
Held
Web: www.husseyseating.com
SIC: 2531 Stadium seating
PA: Hussey Corporation
38 Dyer St Ext
North Berwick ME 03906
207 676-2271

(G-5110)
J B J MACHINE COMPANY
12 Elm St (03906-6725)
P.O. Box 640 (03906-0640)
PHONE..................................207 676-3380
John Doiron, *Pr*
EMP: 7 EST: 1986
SALES (est): 600.47K Privately Held
SIC: 3599 Machine shop, jobbing and repair

(G-5111)
PARSHLEY STEEL FABRICATORS INC
12 Elm St (03906-6725)
P.O. Box 385 (03906-0385)
PHONE..................................207 957-4040
Gregory Parshley, *Prin*
EMP: 9 EST: 2019
SALES (est): 312.94K Privately Held
SIC: 3312 Blast furnaces and steel mills

(G-5112)
PRATT & WHITNEY ENG SVCS INC
Also Called: United Technologies
113 Wells St (03906-6751)
PHONE..................................207 676-4100
Peter Borgel, *Genl Mgr*
EMP: 450
SALES (corp-wide): 68.92B Publicly Held
Web: www.prattwhitney.com
SIC: 3724 Engine mount parts, aircraft
HQ: Pratt & Whitney Engine Services, Inc.
1525 Midway Park Rd
Bridgeport WV 26330
304 842-5421

(G-5113)
SOUTHERN MAINE ATV CLUB
43 Mckinnon Ln (03906-5737)
PHONE..................................207 676-1152
Michael Lanouette, *Treas*
EMP: 8 EST: 2010
SALES (est): 161.33K Privately Held
Web: www.southernmaineatv.com
SIC: 7997 3799 Membership sports and
recreation clubs; All terrain vehicles (ATV)

North Haven
Knox County

(G-5114)
J O BROWN & SON INC
Also Called: Brown Shop
1 Main St (04853-3316)
P.O. Box 525 (04853-0525)
PHONE..................................207 867-4621
Foy Brown, *Pr*
Karen Cooper, *Sec*
Kim Alexander, *Bookkpr*
EMP: 7 EST: 1888
SQ FT: 3,600
SALES (est): 845.63K Privately Held
Web: www.brownsboatyard.com
SIC: 3732 5551 4493 7538 Boatbuilding
and repairing; Marine supplies, nec; Boat
yards, storage and incidental repair;
General automotive repair shops

North Monmouth
Kennebec County

(G-5115)
TEX-TECH INDUSTRIES INC
105 N Main St (04265-6222)
PHONE..................................336 992-7495
Kelton Moore, *Managing Member*
EMP: 40
Web: www.textechindustries.com
SIC: 2655 Fiber cans, drums, and similar
products
PA: Tex-Tech Industries, Inc.
1350 Bridgeport Dr Ste 1
Kernersville NC 27284

Norway
Oxford County

(G-5116)
JAMES NEWSPAPERS INC (PA)
Also Called: The Rumford Falls Times
1 Pikes Hl (04268-4350)
PHONE..................................207 743-7011
Howard A James, *Pr*
EMP: 28 EST: 1976
SQ FT: 7,000
SALES (est): 2.48MM
SALES (corp-wide): 2.48MM Privately
Held
Web: www.sunjournal.com
SIC: 2711 Newspapers, publishing and
printing

(G-5117)
MW TRUCKING AND LOGGING INC
74 Frost Hill Rd (04268-5239)
P.O. Box 221 (04268-0221)
PHONE..................................207 890-3592
Milo Washer, *Prin*
EMP: 7 EST: 2015
SALES (est): 211.17K Privately Held
SIC: 2411 Logging

(G-5118)
SET CONNECTORS INC
36 Holman Ln (04268-4515)
PHONE..................................207 527-2876
EMP: 8 EST: 2013
SALES (est): 826.18K Privately Held
Web: www.setconnectors.com
SIC: 3678 Electronic connectors

Oakfield
Aroostook County

(G-5119)
KATAHDIN FOREST PRODUCTS CO (PA)
Also Called: Katahdin Cedar Log Homes
205 Smyrna Rd (04763)
P.O. Box 145 (04763-0145)

PHONE...................800 845-4533
David Gordon, *Pr*
Barry Ivey, *
EMP: 93 **EST:** 1973
SALES (est): 13.93MM
SALES (corp-wide): 13.93MM **Privately Held**
Web: www.katahdincedarloghomes.com
SIC: 2452 2499 Log cabins, prefabricated, wood; Fencing, wood

Oakland
Kennebec County

(G-5120)
MACHINING INNOVATIONS INC
279 Summer St (04963-4518)
PHONE...................207 465-2500
Curtis Fisher, *Pr*
EMP: 9 **EST:** 2006
SALES (est): 837.88K **Privately Held**
Web: www.machininginnovations.com
SIC: 3599 3511 3524 Machine shop, jobbing and repair; Turbines and turbine generator sets and parts; Lawn and garden tractors and equipment

(G-5121)
TIRE CHAINS REQUIREDCOM
1010 Kennedy Memorial Dr (04963-4830)
PHONE...................207 465-7276
EMP: 7 **EST:** 2004
SALES (est): 62.55K **Privately Held**
Web: www.tirechainsrequired.com
SIC: 3496 Tire chains

(G-5122)
WRABACON INC
150 Old Waterville Rd (04963-5358)
P.O. Box 7 (04963-0007)
PHONE...................207 465-2068
Robert Bartlett, *Pr*
Bob Bartlett Junior, *VP*
EMP: 16 **EST:** 1985
SQ FT: 16,000
SALES (est): 2.77MM **Privately Held**
Web: www.wrabacon.com
SIC: 3565 3569 Packaging machinery; Robots, assembly line: industrial and commercial

Ogunquit
York County

(G-5123)
HARBOR CANDY SHOP INC
Also Called: H & M Crumpets
248 Main St (03907-3203)
P.O. Box 2064 (03907-2064)
PHONE...................207 646-8078
E Sotiropoulos-foss, *Pr*
Eugenie Sotiropoulos-foss, *Pr*
EMP: 10 **EST:** 1956
SALES (est): 911.04K **Privately Held**
Web: www.harborcandy.com
SIC: 2064 5441 5947 2066 Candy and other confectionery products; Confectionery produced for direct sale on the premises; Gift shop; Chocolate and cocoa products

Old Town
Penobscot County

(G-5124)
BOBGUIDE PUBLISHING
478 Beechwood Ave (04468-3403)

PHONE...................207 827-3782
Bob Duchesne, *Prin*
EMP: 7 **EST:** 2009
SALES (est): 116.25K **Privately Held**
Web: www.districtwinery.com
SIC: 2741 Miscellaneous publishing

(G-5125)
JAMES W SEWALL COMPANY (PA)
136 Center St (04468-1577)
P.O. Box 433 (04468-0433)
PHONE...................207 827-4456
EMP: 21 **EST:** 1880
SALES (est): 8.46MM
SALES (corp-wide): 8.46MM **Privately Held**
Web: www.sewall.com
SIC: 8711 0851 7335 1382 Engineering services; Timber valuation services; Commercial photography; Geophysical exploration, oil and gas field

(G-5126)
JOHNSON OTDOORS WATERCRAFT INC (HQ)
Also Called: Old Town Canoe
125 Gilman Falls Ave Bldg B (04468-1325)
PHONE...................207 827-5513
Helen P Johnson-leipold, *CEO*
Del Mcalpine, *VP*
Paul Lehmann, *
Caroll Russell, *
Anthony Manzo, *
◆ **EMP:** 43 **EST:** 1898
SQ FT: 186,000
SALES (est): 24.96MM
SALES (corp-wide): 663.84MM **Publicly Held**
Web: oldtownwatercraft.johnsonoutdoors.com
SIC: 3732 Canoes, building and repairing
PA: Johnson Outdoors Inc.
555 Main St
Racine WI 53403
262 631-6600

(G-5127)
JOHNSON OUTDOORS INC
125 Gilman Falls Ave (04468-1325)
PHONE...................603 518-1634
EMP: 13
SALES (corp-wide): 663.84MM **Publicly Held**
Web: www.johnsonoutdoors.com
SIC: 3949 Fishing equipment
PA: Johnson Outdoors Inc.
555 Main St
Racine WI 53403
262 631-6600

(G-5128)
KELLY LUMBER SALES INC
101 Brunswick St (04468-1409)
P.O. Box 288 (04732-0288)
PHONE...................207 435-4950
Mike Kelly, *Pr*
Timothy Kelly, *VP*
Terry Kelly, *Opers Mgr*
▲ **EMP:** 8 **EST:** 1989
SQ FT: 120,000
SALES (est): 352.58K **Privately Held**
SIC: 2426 5031 Flooring, hardwood; Lumber, plywood, and millwork

(G-5129)
ND OTM LLC
24 Portland St (04468-2024)
P.O. Box 546 (04468-0546)
PHONE...................207 401-2879

Ken Liu, *CEO*
EMP: 120 **EST:** 2018
SALES (est): 23.82MM **Privately Held**
Web: us.ndpaper.com
SIC: 2611 Pulp mills
HQ: Nd Paper Inc.
2001 Spring Rd Ste 500
Oak Brook IL 60523
513 200-0908

(G-5130)
ND PAPER INC
24 Portland St (04468-2024)
PHONE...................207 401-2920
EMP: 242
Web: us.ndpaper.com
SIC: 2621 Paper mills
HQ: Nd Paper Inc.
2001 Spring Rd Ste 500
Oak Brook IL 60523
513 200-0908

(G-5131)
OWEN J FOLSOM INC
Also Called: Round Rock Concrete
299 Gilman Falls Ave (04468-1310)
P.O. Box 206 (04489-0206)
PHONE...................207 827-7625
Owen J Folsom, *Pr*
Rosemary Folsom, *Treas*
EMP: 20 **EST:** 1914
SQ FT: 4,800
SALES (est): 3.28MM **Privately Held**
Web: www.ojf-inc.com
SIC: 3273 Ready-mixed concrete

Orland
Hancock County

(G-5132)
FRESHWATER STONE & BRICKWORK
4 Upper Falls Rd (04472-4116)
P.O. Box 15 (04472-0015)
PHONE...................207 469-6331
Jeffrey Gammelin, *Pr*
Candace Gammelin, *
▲ **EMP:** 40 **EST:** 1988
SQ FT: 4,000
SALES (est): 9.65MM **Privately Held**
Web: www.freshwaterstone.com
SIC: 1741 3281 Masonry and other stonework; Cut stone and stone products

(G-5133)
G M ALLEN & SON INC
Also Called: G M Allen
267 Front Ridge Rd (04472-4341)
P.O. Box 454 (04614-0454)
PHONE...................207 469-7060
Ruth Allen-gray, *Sec*
Kermit Allen, *Treas*
Annie Allen, *Mgr*
Wayne Allen, *Pr*
EMP: 7 **EST:** 1912
SALES (est): 626.38K **Privately Held**
Web: www.gmallenwildblueberries.com
SIC: 2037 Fruits, quick frozen and cold pack (frozen)

Orono
Penobscot County

(G-5134)
COURSESTORM INC
148 Main St (04473-3873)
PHONE...................207 866-0328

Brian Rahill, *CEO*
EMP: 15 **EST:** 2015
SALES (est): 1.63MM **Privately Held**
Web: www.coursestorm.com
SIC: 7372 7389 Educational computer software; Business Activities at Non-Commercial Site

(G-5135)
ORONO HOUSE OF PIZZA
154 Park St (04473-4600)
PHONE...................207 866-5505
Thomas Shanos, *Owner*
EMP: 10 **EST:** 2013
SALES (est): 218.07K **Privately Held**
Web: www.oronohouseofpizza.com
SIC: 2038 5812 Pizza, frozen; Fast food restaurants and stands

(G-5136)
S P HOLT CORPORATION
Also Called: Shaw & Tenney
20 Water St (04473-4069)
P.O. Box 213 (04473-0213)
PHONE...................207 866-4867
Steven Holt, *Pr*
Nancy Forster-holt, *VP*
EMP: 9 **EST:** 1858
SQ FT: 8,000
SALES (est): 813.13K **Privately Held**
Web: www.shawandtenney.com
SIC: 2499 Oars and paddles, wood

(G-5137)
SENSOR RESEARCH AND DEV CORP
Also Called: Srd
5 Godfrey Dr (04473-3607)
PHONE...................207 866-0100
EMP: 7 **EST:** 1993
SQ FT: 4,633
SALES (est): 1.32MM **Privately Held**
Web: www.srdcorp.com
SIC: 8733 3829 Noncommercial research organizations; Gas detectors

(G-5138)
UNIVERSITY OF MAINE SYSTEM
Also Called: Wood Science/Technology
5755 Nutting Hall (04469-5755)
PHONE...................207 581-2843
Doug Gardener, *Mgr*
EMP: 10
SALES (corp-wide): 331.99MM **Privately Held**
Web: www.maine.edu
SIC: 2491 8221 Wood preserving; University
PA: University Of Maine Systems Inc
5703 Alumni Hall Ste 101
Orono ME 04469
207 973-3300

Orrington
Penobscot County

(G-5139)
T AND P LUMBER INC (PA)
Also Called: Crescent Lumber & Building Sup
60 Fowler Rd (04474-3549)
P.O. Box 1401 (04402-1401)
PHONE...................207 825-3317
EMP: 22 **EST:** 1961
SALES (est): 9.72MM
SALES (corp-wide): 9.72MM **Privately Held**
SIC: 5031 5211 2439 Lumber: rough, dressed, and finished; Millwork and lumber; Trusses, wooden roof

Oxford
Oxford County

(G-5140)
ARCAST INC
264 Main St (04270-3134)
PHONE..............................207 539-9638
▼ EMP: 9 EST: 2010
SALES (est): 984.82K **Privately Held**
Web: www.arcastinc.com
SIC: 3559 Foundry machinery and
equipment

(G-5141)
ARCAST INC
5 Park Rd (04270-3580)
PHONE..............................207 539-9638
Rayland O'neil, *CEO*
EMP: 14 EST: 2010
SALES (est): 1.01MM **Privately Held**
Web: www.arcastinc.com
SIC: 3567 Industrial furnaces and ovens

(G-5142)
C J CRANAM INC
Also Called: Valley View Orchard Pies
15 Madison Ave (04270-3579)
P.O. Box 467 (04270-0467)
PHONE..............................207 739-1016
Cynthia Johnston, *Pr*
Lisa Dunham, *VP*
EMP: 25 EST: 2018
SALES (est): 2.48MM **Privately Held**
Web: www.valleyvieworchardpies.com
SIC: 2051 2053 Cakes, pies, and pastries;
Cakes, bakery: frozen

(G-5143)
EXCEL HOMES OF MAINE LLC
Also Called: Keiser Homes
56 Mechanic Falls Rd (04270-3117)
P.O. Box 9000 (04270-9000)
PHONE..............................207 539-8883
EMP: 200
SIC: 2452 Modular homes, prefabricated,
wood

(G-5144)
**GROVER GNDRILLING
HOLDINGS LLC (PA)**
59 Industrial Dr (04270-3536)
PHONE..............................207 743-7051
Christian Hester, *Managing Member*
EMP: 39 EST: 2012
SALES (est): 24.9MM
SALES (corp-wide): 24.9MM **Privately
Held**
Web: www.groverprecision.com
SIC: 3317 Steel pipe and tubes

(G-5145)
GROVER GUNDRILLING LLC
59 Industrial Dr (04270-3536)
PHONE..............................207 743-7051
Garth Grover, *Pr*
Rupert Grover, *
Suzanne Grover, *
Jessicca Grover, *Stockholder*
Karen Vasil Busch, *
▲ EMP: 40 EST: 1983
SQ FT: 24,000
SALES (est): 5.22MM **Privately Held**
Web: www.groverprecision.com
SIC: 3599 Machine shop, jobbing and repair

(G-5146)
JACKSON CALDWELL
Also Called: Breezy Hill
266 Hebron Rd (04270-2516)
PHONE..............................207 539-2325
Caldwell Jackson, *Owner*
EMP: 7 EST: 1988
SQ FT: 5,500
SALES (est): 337.2K **Privately Held**
SIC: 2511 2512 5021 Wood household
furniture; Upholstered household furniture;
Furniture

(G-5147)
M G A CAST STONE INC
7 Oxford Homes Ln (04270-3590)
P.O. Box 207 (04270-0207)
PHONE..............................207 926-5993
Greg Hamann, *CEO*
Tom Hamann, *
David Swasey, *
EMP: 26 EST: 2006
SALES (est): 4.92MM **Privately Held**
Web: www.mgacaststone.com
SIC: 3272 Silo staves, cast stone or
concrete

(G-5148)
OXFORD TIMBER INC
60 E Oxford Rd (04270-2925)
P.O. Box 1097 (04270-1097)
PHONE..............................207 539-9656
Michael Record, *Pr*
Merle Record, *VP*
Jean L Record, *Sec*
▲ EMP: 14 EST: 1980
SQ FT: 800
SALES (est): 2.12MM **Privately Held**
Web: www.oxfordtimber.com
SIC: 2421 5031 2491 Lumber: rough,
sawed, or planed; Lumber, plywood, and
millwork; Structural lumber and timber,
treated wood

(G-5149)
SCHIAVI HOMES LLC
Also Called: Schiavi Homes
754 Main St (04270-3561)
PHONE..............................207 539-9600
EMP: 29 EST: 1996
SALES (est): 1.19MM **Privately Held**
Web: www.schiavicustombuilders.com
SIC: 2452 1521 Modular homes,
prefabricated, wood; Single-family housing
construction

(G-5150)
SEAWAY BOATS INC
59 Industrial Dr (04270-3536)
PHONE..............................207 539-8116
Harry Farmer, *Pr*
Jaqueline A Farmer, *CFO*
EMP: 19 EST: 1999
SQ FT: 3,000
SALES (est): 1.63MM **Privately Held**
SIC: 3732 Boatbuilding and repairing

Parsonsfield
York County

(G-5151)
M B EASTMAN LOGGING INC
146 North Rd (04047-6009)
PHONE..............................207 625-8020
Jennifer E Thomas, *Prin*
EMP: 8 EST: 2005
SALES (est): 212.76K **Privately Held**

SIC: 2411 4212 Logging camps and
contractors; Lumber and timber trucking

(G-5152)
M H HUMPHREY & SONS INC
92 Mudgett Rd (04047-6149)
P.O. Box 101 (04047-0101)
PHONE..............................207 625-4965
EMP: 10 EST: 1996
SALES (est): 866.81K **Privately Held**
SIC: 2411 Logging

Patten
Penobscot County

(G-5153)
HAYMART LLC
19 Mill St (04765-3159)
P.O. Box 445 (04765-0445)
PHONE..............................207 528-2058
Paul Vambutas, *Managing Member*
Kristen Wittine, *Off Mgr*
EMP: 8 EST: 2013
SALES (est): 224.44K **Privately Held**
Web: www.haymart.com
SIC: 0191 2411 3532 General farms,
primarily crop; Fuel wood harvesting; Pellet
mills (mining machinery)

(G-5154)
**SAVAGE & SAVAGE LOGGING
INC**
20 Valley St (04765-3156)
PHONE..............................207 528-2974
Scott Savage, *Pr*
Kim Savage, *Sec*
Michael Savage, *VP*
EMP: 9 EST: 1990
SALES (est): 1.09MM **Privately Held**
SIC: 2411 Logging camps and contractors

Peru
Oxford County

(G-5155)
ANDREW IRISH LOGGING
1264 Auburn Rd (04290-3409)
P.O. Box 184 (04290-0184)
PHONE..............................207 562-8839
Andrew Irish, *Owner*
EMP: 10 EST: 1981
SALES (est): 846.01K **Privately Held**
SIC: 2411 Logging camps and contractors

(G-5156)
DIMENSION LUMBER
85 Jug Hill Rd (04290)
PHONE..............................207 897-9973
Ceylon Putnam, *Owner*
EMP: 8 EST: 1998
SALES (est): 639.66K **Privately Held**
SIC: 2421 Sawmills and planing mills,
general

Phillips
Franklin County

(G-5157)
REGAN S PINGREE
989 Park St (04966)
PHONE..............................207 639-5706
Regan S Pingree, *Owner*
EMP: 10 EST: 1985
SALES (est): 603.45K **Privately Held**

SIC: 2411 Logging

Pittsfield
Somerset County

(G-5158)
**CIANBRO FBRCATION COATING
CORP**
335 Hunnewell Ave (04967-3511)
P.O. Box 1000 (04967-1000)
PHONE..............................207 487-3311
Peter A Vigue, *Pr*
Peter G Vigue, *
Kyle K Holmstrom, *CFO*
Jack A Klimp, *General Vice President*
Michael W Bennett, *Res Vice President*
EMP: 147 EST: 2002
SALES (est): 16.6MM
SALES (corp-wide): 1.16B **Privately Held**
Web: www.cianbro.com
SIC: 3441 3479 Fabricated structural metal;
Coating of metals and formed products
PA: The Cianbro Companies
1 Hunnewell Ave
Pittsfield ME 04967
207 487-3311

(G-5159)
CM ALMY & SON INC
133 Ruth St (04967-4113)
P.O. Box 148 (04967-0148)
PHONE..............................207 487-3232
Michael Fendler, *VP*
EMP: 105
SALES (corp-wide): 24.01MM **Privately
Held**
Web: www.almy.com
SIC: 2389 Clergymen's vestments
PA: C.M. Almy & Son, Inc.
28 Kaysal Ct Ste 1
Armonk NY 10504
914 864-9120

(G-5160)
INNOVATIVE SPECIALTIES LLC
Also Called: Nitro Trailers
140 Business Ct (04967-4933)
PHONE..............................207 948-1500
Chad Dow, *Managing Member*
EMP: 18 EST: 2013
SQ FT: 5,000
SALES (est): 3MM **Privately Held**
Web: www.nitrotrailers.com
SIC: 5599 3715 5012 Utility trailers; Truck
trailers; Trailers for trucks, new and used

Poland
Androscoggin County

(G-5161)
MAINE CONTAINER LLC
115 Poland Spring Dr (04274-5327)
PHONE..............................603 888-1315
EMP: 20 EST: 2005
SALES (est): 880.05K **Privately Held**
SIC: 3089 Plastics containers, except foam
PA: Carr Management, Inc.
1 Tara Blvd Ste 303
Nashua NH 03062

(G-5162)
SAFE-APPROACH INC
206 Mechanic Falls Rd (04274-6555)
PHONE..............................207 345-9900
Roger Dargie, *Pr*
▲ EMP: 18 EST: 1992
SQ FT: 12,760

SALES (est): 2.3MM **Privately Held**
Web: www.safeapproach.com
SIC: 3199   Leather belting and strapping

Poland Spring
Androscoggin County

(G-5163)
BLUETRITON BRANDS INC
Also Called: Poland Spring Bottling
109 Poland Spring Dr (04274-5327)
PHONE.................................207 998-4315
Lori Schmitz, *Prin*
EMP: 125
SQ FT: 6,000
SALES (corp-wide): 1.3B **Privately Held**
Web: www.bluetriton.com
SIC: 2086   Mineral water, carbonated:
packaged in cans, bottles, etc.
HQ: Bluetriton Brands, Inc.
900 Long Ridge Rd Bldg 2
Stamford CT 06902

Portage
Aroostook County

(G-5164)
MAINE WOODS COMPANY LLC
Also Called: Maine Wood Flooring
92 Fish Lake Rd (04768-8814)
PHONE.................................207 435-4393
Scott Ferland, *Genl Mgr*
EMP: 19 EST: 2017
SALES (est): 7.54MM **Privately Held**
Web: www.mainewoodscompany.com
SIC: 2421   Sawmills and planing mills,
general

Porter
Oxford County

(G-5165)
CHIPPING & LOGGING
37 Cross Rd (04068-3340)
P.O. Box 24 (04068-0024)
PHONE.................................207 625-4056
Laurence Taylor Junior, *Pr*
Dennis Scott, *VP*
Gary Taylor, *VP*
EMP: 8 EST: 1982
SALES (est): 530.1K **Privately Held**
SIC: 2411   Logging camps and contractors

(G-5166)
L E TAYLOR AND SONS INC
37 Cross Rd (04068-3340)
P.O. Box 24 (04068-0024)
PHONE.................................207 625-4056
Lawrence Taylor Junior, *Pr*
Brenda Taylor, *Treas*
Malcolm W Philbrook Junior, *Clerk*
EMP: 8 EST: 1960
SALES (est): 826.75K **Privately Held**
Web: www.letaylorandsonsinc.com
SIC: 2411   Logging camps and contractors

(G-5167)
**NORTHEAST STRUCTURES
BARNS LLC**
202 Colcord Pond Rd (04068-3431)
PHONE.................................207 512-0503
EMP: 8 EST: 2016
SALES (est): 815.83K **Privately Held**

SIC: 3523 7011 2452   Barn, silo, poultry,
dairy, and livestock machinery; Tourist
camps, cabins, cottages, and courts; Farm
buildings, prefabricated or portable: wood

(G-5168)
R C MCLUCAS TRUCKING INC
Route 25 (04068)
P.O. Box 67 (04068-0067)
PHONE.................................207 625-8915
Richard Mclucas, *Pr*
Gayla Mclucas, *Sec*
EMP: 50 EST: 1989
SALES (est): 2.68MM **Privately Held**
Web: www.rcmclucastrucking.com
SIC: 4212 2411   Lumber and timber trucking;
Logging

(G-5169)
ROBERT W LIBBY
Also Called: Robert W Libby and Sons
483 Old Meetinghouse Rd (04068-3206)
PHONE.................................207 625-8285
Robert W Libby, *Owner*
EMP: 9 EST: 1980
SALES (est): 1.05MM **Privately Held**
SIC: 2411 2421 1629   Logging camps and
contractors; Chipper mill; Land clearing
contractor

(G-5170)
ROBERT W LIBBY & SONS INC
483 Old Meetinghouse Rd (04068-3206)
PHONE.................................207 284-3668
Robert W Libby, *Prin*
EMP: 8 EST: 2002
SALES (est): 554.36K **Privately Held**
SIC: 2411   Logging camps and contractors

(G-5171)
**VULCAN ELECTRIC COMPANY
(PA)**
Also Called: Vulcan
28 Endfield St (04068-3502)
PHONE.................................207 625-3231
Michael Quick, *Ch Bd*
Fred Conroy, *
Paul Wieszeck, *
EMP: 95 EST: 1927
SQ FT: 40,000
SALES (est): 19.07MM
SALES (corp-wide): 19.07MM **Privately
Held**
Web: www.vulcanelectric.com
SIC: 3567   Heating units and devices,
industrial: electric

(G-5172)
VULCAN FLEX CIRCUIT CORP
28 Endfield St (04068-3502)
PHONE.................................603 883-1500
Michael Quick, *CEO*
Stanley Haupt, *
William Benger, *
Normand Sirois, *
EMP: 70 EST: 2006
SQ FT: 45,000
SALES (est): 9.89MM
SALES (corp-wide): 19.07MM **Privately
Held**
Web: www.vulcanelectric.com
SIC: 3674   Thin film circuits
PA: Vulcan Electric Company
28 Endfield St
Porter ME 04068
207 625-3231

(G-5173)
WILLIAM A DAY JR & SONS INC
28 Wild Turkey Ln (04068-3663)
PHONE.................................207 625-8181
EMP: 18 EST: 1973
SALES (est): 2.12MM **Privately Held**
Web: www.daylogging.com
SIC: 2411   Logging

Portland
Cumberland County

(G-5174)
ABACUS LABS INC
320 Cumberland Ave (04101-4928)
PHONE.................................917 426-6642
Omar Qari, *Pr*
Ted Power, *Chief Product Officer**
Josh Halickman, *
EMP: 30 EST: 2013
SALES (est): 4.47MM
SALES (corp-wide): 14.34MM **Privately
Held**
Web: www.abacus.com
SIC: 7372   Business oriented computer
software
PA: Certify, Inc.
320 Cumberland Ave
Portland ME 04101
207 773-6100

(G-5175)
ADVANCEPIERRE FOODS INC
54 Saint John St (04102-3018)
PHONE.................................207 541-2800
EMP: 679
SALES (corp-wide): 52.88B **Publicly Held**
Web: www.tysonfoodservice.com
SIC: 2015   Chicken slaughtering and
processing
HQ: Advancepierre Foods, Inc.
9990 Prnceton Glendale Rd
West Chester OH 45246
513 874-8741

(G-5176)
ALLAGASH INTERNATIONAL INC
Also Called: Allagash International
70 Ingersol Dr (04103-1093)
PHONE.................................207 781-8831
◆ EMP: 8
Web: www.noreastcontrols.com
SIC: 3491   Industrial valves

(G-5177)
ALTIUM PACKAGING LLC
Also Called: Maine Plastics
364 Forest Ave (04101-2035)
PHONE.................................207 772-7468
EMP: 43
SALES (corp-wide): 15.9B **Publicly Held**
Web: www.altiumpkg.com
SIC: 3089   Plastics containers, except foam
HQ: Altium Packaging Llc
2500 Windy Ridge Pkwy Se # 1400
Atlanta GA 30339
678 742-4600

(G-5178)
ATLANTIC SPORTSWEAR INC
Also Called: Atlantic Cotton Company
36 Waldron Way (04103-5944)
PHONE.................................207 797-5028
John Fay, *Pr*
EMP: 23 EST: 1984
SQ FT: 7,500
SALES (est): 4.67MM **Privately Held**
Web: www.atlanticsportswear.com

SIC: 2759 2396   Screen printing; Automotive
and apparel trimmings

(G-5179)
**ATLANTIC STANDARD
MOLDING INC**
380 Warren Ave Apt 2 (04103-1192)
PHONE.................................207 797-0727
James P Blanchard, *Pr*
EMP: 10 EST: 1989
SQ FT: 10,750
SALES (est): 468.86K **Privately Held**
SIC: 3944   Board games, puzzles, and
models, except electronic

(G-5180)
B&G FOODS INC
Also Called: Burnham & Morrill
1 Beanpot Cir (04103-5304)
PHONE.................................207 772-8341
John Manoush, *Prin*
EMP: 160
SALES (corp-wide): 2.16B **Publicly Held**
Web: www.bgfoods.com
SIC: 2033 2087 2051   Canned fruits and
specialties; Flavoring extracts and syrups,
nec; Bread, cake, and related products
PA: B&G Foods, Inc.
4 Gatehall Dr Ste 110
Parsippany NJ 07054
973 401-6500

(G-5181)
**BANGOR MILLWORK & SUPPLY
INC**
460 Riverside St (04103-1069)
PHONE.................................207 878-8548
Mark Cameron, *Mgr*
EMP: 9
SALES (corp-wide): 3.08MM **Privately
Held**
Web:
www.bangorwholesalelaminates.com
SIC: 2541   Table or counter tops, plastic
laminated
PA: Bangor Millwork & Supply, Inc.
355 Target Cir
Bangor ME 04401
207 947-6019

(G-5182)
BARBER FOODS LLC
70 Saint John St (04102-3018)
P.O. Box 4821 (04112-4821)
PHONE.................................207 772-1934
EMP: 603
SALES (corp-wide): 52.88B **Publicly Held**
Web: www.barberfoods.com
SIC: 2015 2038   Poultry, processed, nsk;
Frozen specialties, nec
HQ: Barber Foods, Llc
56 Milliken St
Portland ME 04103
207 482-5500

(G-5183)
BARBER FOODS LLC (DH)
56 Milliken St (04103-1530)
P.O. Box 4821 (04112-4821)
PHONE.................................207 482-5500
David Barber, *Pr*
Vicki Mann, *
Bruce Codgeshell, *
EMP: 50 EST: 1955
SQ FT: 16,000
SALES (est): 51.16MM
SALES (corp-wide): 52.88B **Publicly Held**
Web: www.barberfoods.com
SIC: 2015   Poultry, processed: frozen
HQ: Advancepierre Foods, Inc.
9990 Prnceton Glendale Rd

West Chester OH 45246
513 874-8741

(G-5184)
BARRETT MADE (PA)
65 Hanover St (04101-1932)
PHONE..............................207 650-6500
Rob Barrett, *CEO*
EMP: 25 EST: 2015
SALES (est): 1K
SALES (corp-wide): 1K **Privately Held**
Web: www.barrettmade.com
SIC: 8712 8742 2421 7389　Architectural services; Construction project management consultant; Flooring (dressed lumber), softwood; Interior design services

(G-5185)
BEACON SALES ACQUISITION INC
Also Called: Applicator Sales & Service
400 Warren Ave (04103-1109)
PHONE..............................207 797-7950
EMP: 10
SALES (corp-wide): 8.43B **Publicly Held**
Web: www.becn.com
SIC: 5033 3089　Siding, except wood; Doors, folding: plastics or plastics coated fabric
HQ: Beacon Sales Acquisition, Inc.
505 Huntmar Park Dr # 300
Herndon VA 20170
714 633-6330

(G-5186)
BELLEFLOWER BREWING CO LLC ✪
66 Cove St (04101-2514)
PHONE..............................617 365-9536
EMP: 12 EST: 2022
SALES (est): 878.35K **Privately Held**
Web: www.portlandoldport.com
SIC: 2082　Beer (alcoholic beverage)

(G-5187)
BIOPROCESSING INC
1045 Riverside St (04103-1065)
PHONE..............................207 457-0025
Gary Goodrich, *Pr*
Katherine Daigle, *VP*
EMP: 12 EST: 1991
SQ FT: 10,000
SALES (est): 910.92K **Privately Held**
Web: www.bioprocessinginc.com
SIC: 2835　Diagnostic substances

(G-5188)
BLETHEN MAINE NEWSPAPERS INC
390 Congress St (04101-3514)
P.O. Box 1460 (04104-5009)
PHONE..............................207 791-6650
Charles Cochrane, *CEO*
EMP: 14 EST: 2013
SALES (est): 247.47K **Privately Held**
Web: www.blethenmainenewspapers.com
SIC: 2711　Newspapers, publishing and printing

(G-5189)
BLUE LOBSTER WINE COMPANY
219 Anderson St Ste 2 (04101-1401)
PHONE..............................207 671-1154
EMP: 10 EST: 2017
SALES (est): 218.69K **Privately Held**
Web: www.bluelobsterwines.com
SIC: 2084　Wines

(G-5190)
BLUE SKY INC
Also Called: GA Gear
987 Riverside St (04103-1070)
P.O. Box 724 (04021-0724)
PHONE..............................207 772-0073
▼ EMP: 8 EST: 1999
SALES (est): 805.31K **Privately Held**
Web: www.gagear.com
SIC: 2759　Screen printing

(G-5191)
BRADY ENTERPRISES INC
80 Exchange St Ste 30 (04101-5035)
P.O. Box 7486 (04112-7486)
PHONE..............................207 653-9990
James Brady, *Prin*
EMP: 7 EST: 2014
SALES (est): 76.95K **Privately Held**
Web: www.bradyenterprises.com
SIC: 3599　Machine shop, jobbing and repair

(G-5192)
BRISTOL SEAFOOD LLC (HQ)
5 Portland Fish Pier (04101-4620)
P.O. Box 486 (04112-0486)
PHONE..............................207 761-4251
Bristol Seafood, *Ch*
Darrell Pardy, *
Jennifer Cyr, *
EMP: 11 EST: 2013
SQ FT: 30,000
SALES (est): 43.96MM **Privately Held**
Web: www.bristolseafood.com
SIC: 2092 5146　Fresh or frozen packaged fish; Fish, fresh
PA: Bristol Seafood Holdings Inc.
5 Portland Fish Pier
Portland ME 04101

(G-5193)
BRISTOL SEAFOOD HOLDINGS INC (PA)
5 Portland Fish Pier (04101-4620)
P.O. Box 486 (04112-0486)
PHONE..............................207 761-4251
Ray Swenton, *Ch Bd*
Darrell Pardy, *
Jeniffer Cyr, *
▲ EMP: 60 EST: 1990
SQ FT: 30,000
SALES (est): 51.45MM **Privately Held**
Web: www.bristolseafood.com
SIC: 5146 2092　Fish, fresh; Fresh or frozen packaged fish

(G-5194)
BROWNE TRADING CO
260 Commercial St (04101-4671)
PHONE..............................207 766-2402
Rod Mitchell, *CEO*
▲ EMP: 43 EST: 1991
SQ FT: 15,000
SALES (est): 21.25MM **Privately Held**
Web: www.brownetrading.com
SIC: 5146 2091　Seafoods; Fish, canned and cured

(G-5195)
CARLISLE CONSTRUCTION MTLS LLC
Also Called: Hunter Panels
15 Franklin St (04101-4169)
PHONE..............................888 746-1114
EMP: 250
SALES (corp-wide): 6.59B **Publicly Held**
Web: www.hunterpanels.com
SIC: 3086　Insulation or cushioning material, foamed plastics
HQ: Carlisle Construction Materials, Llc
1285 Ritner Hwy
Carlisle PA 17013

(G-5196)
CASCO BAY SBSTNCE ABUSE RSRCES
Also Called: Health Pro
205 Ocean Ave (04103-5712)
PHONE..............................207 773-7993
James Weaver, *Owner*
EMP: 12 EST: 1977
SALES (est): 238.6K **Privately Held**
SIC: 2721　Magazines: publishing only, not printed on site

(G-5197)
CERTIFY INC (PA)
320 Cumberland Ave (04101-4928)
PHONE..............................207 773-6100
Robert Neveu, *Pr*
EMP: 27 EST: 2014
SALES (est): 14.64MM
SALES (corp-wide): 14.64MM **Privately Held**
Web: www.certify.com
SIC: 7372　Business oriented computer software

(G-5198)
CHECKSFORLESSCOM
200 Riverside Industrial Pkwy (04103-1414)
PHONE..............................800 245-5775
Chris Lefevre, *Pr*
EMP: 10 EST: 2012
SALES (est): 622.7K **Privately Held**
Web: www.checksforless.com
SIC: 2752　Offset printing

(G-5199)
CLARIOS LLC
Also Called: Johnson Controls
477 Congress St 6th Fl (04101-3427)
PHONE..............................603 222-2400
EMP: 38
SALES (corp-wide): 1.54B **Privately Held**
Web: www.clarios.com
SIC: 2531　Seats, automobile
HQ: Clarios, Llc
5757 N Green Bay Ave
Milwaukee WI 53209

(G-5200)
COFFEE BY DESIGN INC (PA)
1 Diamond St (04101-2515)
PHONE..............................207 879-2233
EMP: 9 EST: 1995
SQ FT: 2,000
SALES (est): 5.52MM **Privately Held**
Web: www.coffeebydesign.com
SIC: 5812 2099 2095　Coffee shop; Tea blending; Roasted coffee

(G-5201)
COMNAV ENGINEERING INC
Also Called: Geesaman Software, Inc.
430 Riverside St (04103-1035)
PHONE..............................207 221-8524
EMP: 37 EST: 1996
SALES (est): 4.63MM **Privately Held**
Web: www.comnav-eng.com
SIC: 3569 5065 8711　Filters; Electronic parts and equipment, nec; Engineering services

(G-5202)
COVETRUS NORTH AMERICA LLC (PA)
Also Called: Covetrus

12 Mountfort St (04101-4307)
PHONE..............................888 280-2221
Benjamin Wolin, *Managing Member*
EMP: 150 EST: 1940
SALES (est): 4.58B
SALES (corp-wide): 4.58B **Privately Held**
Web: www.covetrus.com
SIC: 2834 2835 8734 0742　Veterinary pharmaceutical preparations; Veterinary diagnostic substances; Veterinary testing; Veterinary services, specialties

(G-5203)
CURRY PRINTING & COPY CENTER
10 City Ctr (04101-4006)
PHONE..............................207 772-5897
TOLL FREE: 800
John Mina, *Pr*
Evelyn Mina, *Treas*
EMP: 13 EST: 1976
SQ FT: 7,000
SALES (est): 2.01MM **Privately Held**
Web: www.curryprinting.biz
SIC: 2752 7334　Offset printing; Photocopying and duplicating services

(G-5204)
DALE RAND PRINTING INC
508 Riverside St Ste A (04103-1277)
PHONE..............................207 773-8198
Dale Rand, *Pr*
EMP: 8 EST: 1980
SALES (est): 788.04K **Privately Held**
Web: www.dalerandprinting.com
SIC: 2752　Offset printing

(G-5205)
DAUNIS
Also Called: Daunis Fine Jewelry
616 Congress St Ste 2 (04101-3374)
P.O. Box 5066 (04101-0766)
PHONE..............................207 773-6011
Patricia Daunis Dunning, *Pr*
William Dunning, *VP*
John F Loyd Junior, *Clerk*
EMP: 10 EST: 1974
SQ FT: 2,300
SALES (est): 497.85K **Privately Held**
Web: www.daunis.com
SIC: 3911 5944　Jewelry, precious metal; Jewelry stores

(G-5206)
DAVIC INC
Also Called: Bayside Print Services
417 Congress St (04101-3505)
PHONE..............................207 774-0093
David White, *Pr*
EMP: 9 EST: 1986
SQ FT: 1,616
SALES (est): 482.17K **Privately Held**
Web: www.baysideme.com
SIC: 2752 2791 2789　Offset printing; Typesetting; Bookbinding and related work

(G-5207)
DEFINITIVE BREWING COMPANY LLC
35 Industrial Way (04103-1071)
PHONE..............................207 446-4746
EMP: 13 EST: 2017
SALES (est): 401.84K **Privately Held**
Web: www.definitivebrewing.com
SIC: 2082　Beer (alcoholic beverage)

(G-5208)
DESK TOP GRAPHICS INC
Also Called: Spire Express

▲ = Import ▼ = Export
◆ = Import/Export

477 Congress St (04101-3427)
PHONE...............................207 828-0041
EMP: 12
SALES (corp-wide): 45.5MM Privately
Held
Web: www.spireexpress.com
SIC: 2796 Platemaking services
HQ: Desk Top Graphics Inc
1 1st Ave
Peabody MA 01960
617 832-1927

(G-5209)
DIVERSIFIED
COMMUNICATIONS (HQ)
Also Called: Diversified Bus Communications
121 Free St (04101-3919)
P.O. Box 7437 (04112-7437)
PHONE...............................207 842-5500
Theodore Wirth, Pr
Horace A Hildreth Junior, Ch
Whit Mitchell, *
EMP: 27 EST: 1970
SQ FT: 43,000
SALES (est): 53.95MM
SALES (corp-wide): 53.95MM Privately
Held
Web: www.divcom.com
SIC: 4833 2721 7389 6712 Television
broadcasting stations; Magazines:
publishing only, not printed on site; Trade
show arrangement; Bank holding
companies
PA: Diversified Holding Co.
121 Free St
Portland ME 04101
207 842-5400

(G-5210)
DOUGLAS BROTHERS
GEORGIA INC
423 Riverside Industrial Pkwy (04103-1433)
P.O. Box 8008 (04104-8008)
PHONE...............................800 341-0926
Arthur Dubois, Pr
EMP: 12 EST: 2010
SALES (est): 108.28K Privately Held
Web: www.dbpipinggroup.com
SIC: 3441 Fabricated structural metal

(G-5211)
DR PEPPER BOTTLING CO
PORTLAND
Also Called: Dr Pepper
250 Canco Rd (04103-4221)
PHONE...............................207 773-4258
Marcus Day, Prin
EMP: 10 EST: 2010
SALES (est): 149.41K Privately Held
Web: www.drpepper.com
SIC: 2086 Soft drinks: packaged in cans,
bottles, etc.

(G-5212)
DRAGON PRODUCTS
COMPANY LLC
960 Ocean Ave (04103-4703)
PHONE...............................207 879-2328
EMP: 35
Web: www.dragonproducts.com
SIC: 3273 Ready-mixed concrete
HQ: Dragon Products Company, Llc
2 Main St Ste 18-221
Biddeford ME 04005

(G-5213)
E I PRINTING CO
200 Riverside Industrial Pkwy (04103-1414)
PHONE...............................207 797-4838

Christopher Lefevere, Mgr
EMP: 16 EST: 1997
SALES (est): 756.13K Privately Held
Web: www.eiprinting.com
SIC: 2752 Offset printing

(G-5214)
EIMSKIP USA INC
468 Commercial St (04101-4637)
PHONE...............................207 221-5268
EMP: 14 EST: 2015
SALES (est): 942.82K Privately Held
Web: www.eimskip.com
SIC: 3799 4783 Trailers and trailer
equipment; Crating goods for shipping

(G-5215)
ENVIROLOGIX INC (PA)
500 Riverside Industrial Pkwy (04103-1486)
PHONE...............................207 797-0300
EMP: 40 EST: 1996
SQ FT: 26,000
SALES (est): 47.31MM Privately Held
Web: www.envirologix.com
SIC: 3826 Environmental testing equipment

(G-5216)
FIZZ LLC
Also Called: Vena's Fizz House
28 Colonial Rd (04102-2010)
PHONE...............................207 887-9618
EMP: 22
SALES (corp-wide): 347.87K Privately
Held
Web: www.venasfizzhouse.com
SIC: 2087 Cocktail mixes, nonalcoholic
PA: Fizz Llc
90 Bridge St Ste 355
Westbrook ME 04092
207 887-9618

(G-5217)
FOUNDATION BREWING
COMPANY
1 Industrial Way (04103-1072)
PHONE...............................207 370-8187
Joel Mahaffey, Pr
EMP: 16 EST: 2012
SALES (est): 1.05MM Privately Held
Web: www.foundationbrew.com
SIC: 2082 Brewers' grain

(G-5218)
GELATO FIASCO INC
22 Vesper St Apt 1 (04101-2082)
PHONE...............................207 607-4002
Bruno Tropeano, Pr
Joshua Davis, CFO
◆ EMP: 8 EST: 2007
SALES (est): 1.38MM Privately Held
Web: www.gelatofiasco.com
SIC: 5812 2024 Ice cream stands or dairy
bars; Ice cream and frozen deserts

(G-5219)
GOWEN INC
Also Called: Gowen Marine
400 Commercial St Ste 101 (04101-4660)
P.O. Box 3542 (04104-3542)
PHONE...............................207 773-1761
TOLL FREE: 800
Joseph Schmader, Pr
Joseph Schmader, Ch Bd
John Mcveigh, Clerk
EMP: 17 EST: 1969
SQ FT: 4,000
SALES (est): 2.46MM Privately Held
Web: www.gowenmarine.com

SIC: 3732 5063 5551 4493 Boatbuilding
and repairing; Generators; Boat dealers;
Boat yards, storage and incidental repair

(G-5220)
GRS GROUP INC
Also Called: Beau Tech
98 Elm St (04101-2432)
PHONE...............................207 775-6139
Peter B Garsoe, Pr
▲ EMP: 10 EST: 1975
SQ FT: 2,300
SALES (est): 1MM Privately Held
Web: menda.descoindustries.com
SIC: 7359 3423 Equipment rental and
leasing, nec; Hand and edge tools, nec

(G-5221)
HIGHBYTE INC
52 Alder St (04101-1983)
PHONE...............................844 328-2677
Tony Paine, CEO
Torey Penrod-cambra, Marketing
Betsy Peteres, Ch Bd
Corson Ellis, Bd of Dir
John Harrington Sales, Prin
EMP: 18 EST: 2018
SALES (est): 1.51MM Privately Held
Web: www.highbyte.com
SIC: 7372 Prepackaged software

(G-5222)
HIL TECHNOLOGY INC (DH)
Also Called: Hydro International Stormwater
94 Hutchins Dr (04102-1930)
PHONE...............................207 756-6200
Stephen Hides, CEO
Anthony Hollox, *
◆ EMP: 14 EST: 1986
SQ FT: 9,920
SALES (est): 18MM
SALES (corp-wide): 3.74MM Privately
Held
Web: www.hydro-int.com
SIC: 3589 Water purification equipment,
household type
HQ: Hydro International Limited
Shearwater House
Clevedon BS21
127 587-8371

(G-5223)
HOLY DONUT INC (PA)
194 Park Ave (04102-2910)
PHONE...............................207 761-7775
Jeff Buckwalter, CEO
Leigh Kellis, Pr
EMP: 26 EST: 2011
SALES (est): 4.42MM
SALES (corp-wide): 4.42MM Privately
Held
Web: www.theholydonut.com
SIC: 5461 2051 Doughnuts; Doughnuts,
except frozen

(G-5224)
HUNTER DATHAN HAIR
ARTISTRY
4 Milk St (04101-4236)
PHONE...............................207 774-8887
Dathan Hunter, Owner
EMP: 8 EST: 2002
SALES (est): 171.61K Privately Held
Web: www.dathanhunter.com
SIC: 7231 2844 3952 Unisex hair salons;
Hair coloring preparations; Wax, artists'

(G-5225)
HUNTER PANELS LLC
Also Called: Hunter Panels
15 Franklin St (04101-7119)
P.O. Box 1319 (17013-6319)
PHONE...............................888 746-1114
EMP: 250
Web: www.hunterpanels.com
SIC: 3086 Insulation or cushioning material,
foamed plastics

(G-5226)
IMMUCELL CORPORATION
33 Caddie Ln (04103-1296)
PHONE...............................207 878-2770
EMP: 24
SALES (corp-wide): 18.57MM Publicly
Held
Web: www.immucell.com
SIC: 2835 Veterinary diagnostic substances
PA: Immucell Corporation
56 Evergreen Dr
Portland ME 04103
207 878-2770

(G-5227)
IMMUCELL CORPORATION (PA)
56 Evergreen Dr (04103-5907)
PHONE...............................207 878-2770
Michael F Brigham, Pr
Michael F Brigham, Pr
David S Tomsche, Ch Bd
Bobbi Jo Brockmann, S&M/VP
Elizabeth L Williams, Manufacturing
Operations Vice President
▲ EMP: 29 EST: 1982
SQ FT: 35,000
SALES (est): 18.57MM
SALES (corp-wide): 18.57MM Publicly
Held
Web: www.immucell.com
SIC: 2835 Veterinary diagnostic substances

(G-5228)
ISF TRADING INC
390 Commercial St (04101-4610)
P.O. Box 772 (04104-0772)
PHONE...............................207 879-1575
Atsshi Tamaki, Pr
◆ EMP: 170 EST: 1989
SALES (est): 24.21MM Privately Held
Web: www.seaurchinmaine.com
SIC: 5146 2092 Seafoods; Fresh or frozen
packaged fish

(G-5229)
JOURNAL PUBLISHING
COMPANY
Also Called: Administrative Professionals
121 Free St Ste A (04101-3919)
PHONE...............................800 873-1272
EMP: 127
SALES (corp-wide): 58.72MM Privately
Held
Web: www.apcevent.com
SIC: 2741 Miscellaneous publishing
HQ: Journal Publishing Company
7777 Jefferson St Ne
Albuquerque NM 87109
505 823-3800

(G-5230)
K & R HOLDINGS INC
Also Called: Paradigm Solutions
400 Warren Ave (04103-1109)
P.O. Box 10109 (04104-0109)
PHONE...............................207 797-7950
TOLL FREE: 800
Scott Koocher, Pr
Richard Robinov, *

Jerry Robinov, *
EMP: 135 **EST:** 1958
SQ FT: 35,000
SALES (est): 24.92MM
SALES (corp-wide): 8.43B **Publicly Held**
Web: www.ceoapplicatorssales.com
SIC: 5033 3089 Siding, except wood;
Doors, folding: plastics or plastics coated
fabric
PA: Beacon Roofing Supply, Inc.
505 Huntmar Park Dr # 300
Herndon VA 20170
571 323-3939

(G-5231)
KERRY INC
Also Called: X Cafe
40 Quarry Rd Ste 200 (04103-3460)
PHONE..............................207 775-7060
EMP: 30
Web: www.kerry.com
SIC: 2095 Coffee extracts
HQ: Kerry Inc.
3400 Millington Rd
Beloit WI 53511
608 363-1200

(G-5232)
KINOTEK INC
22 Monument Sq Ste 201 (04101-5160)
PHONE..............................207 805-1919
Justin Hafner, *CEO*
David Holomakoff, *COO*
William Breeding, *Prin*
Jonathan Gagnon, *Prin*
EMP: 12 **EST:** 2018
SALES (est): 792.43K **Privately Held**
Web: www.kinotek.com
SIC: 7372 Prepackaged software

(G-5233)
LEAVITT & PARRIS INC
256 Read St (04103-3446)
PHONE..............................207 797-0100
John Hutchins, *Pr*
Lucretia Hutchins, *VP*
EMP: 15 **EST:** 1919
SQ FT: 27,000
SALES (est): 2.11MM **Privately Held**
Web: www.leavittandparris.com
SIC: 2394 7359 7699 Awnings, fabric: made
from purchased materials; Tent and
tarpaulin rental; Awning repair shop

(G-5234)
LTS INC
37 Danforth St (04101-4501)
PHONE..............................207 774-1104
Linda Tobey, *Pr*
K C Hughes, *VP*
EMP: 25 **EST:** 1991
SQ FT: 7,500
SALES (est): 1.96MM **Privately Held**
Web: www.ltsmaine.com
SIC: 2759 Screen printing

(G-5235)
LUX BOX COMPANY INC
517 Forest Ave Ste 1 (04101-1536)
PHONE..............................301 832-0622
Anne Marie Blatchford, *Pr*
Chloe Blatchford, *VP*
Olivia Jette, *Sec*
EMP: 9 **EST:** 2016
SALES (est): 919.82K **Privately Held**
Web: www.luxboxco.com
SIC: 5199 3999 Gifts and novelties;
Novelties, bric-a-brac, and hobby kits

(G-5236)
MAINE ARTFL LIMB ORTHOTICS CO
Also Called: Maine Artfl Limb & Orthotics
959 Brighton Ave Rear (04102-1041)
PHONE..............................207 773-4963
Marc N Karn, *Pr*
Wade Bonneson, *COO*
EMP: 10 **EST:** 1970
SQ FT: 6,500
SALES (est): 485.93K **Privately Held**
SIC: 3842 5999 Limbs, artificial; Artificial
limbs

(G-5237)
MAINE BAY CANVAS INC
53 Industrial Way (04103-1071)
PHONE..............................207 878-8888
TOLL FREE: 800
Ronald B Lehr, *Pr*
Ronald B Lehr, *Pr*
Charles Shumway, *Clerk*
Daniel Gauvin, *Genl Mgr*
EMP: 10 **EST:** 1979
SQ FT: 7,000
SALES (est): 412.95K **Privately Held**
Web: www.mainebaycanvas.com
SIC: 7359 2394 Tent and tarpaulin rental;
Canvas and related products

(G-5238)
MAINE BIO-FUEL INC
Also Called: Maine Standard Biofuels
51 Ingersol Dr (04103-1093)
PHONE..............................207 878-3001
James Kaltsas, *Owner*
Chris Geele, *VP*
Richard Bradsky, *Sec*
EMP: 11 **EST:** 2006
SQ FT: 2,000
SALES (est): 3.34MM **Privately Held**
Web: www.mainestandardbiofuels.com
SIC: 2869 2911 Fuels; Diesel fuels

(G-5239)
MAINE BIOTECHNOLOGY SVCS INC
Also Called: Bbi Solutions
1037r Forest Ave (04103-3395)
PHONE..............................207 797-5454
Joseph Chandler, *Pr*
Michael High, *
▼ **EMP:** 13 **EST:** 1990
SQ FT: 12,000
SALES (est): 5.68MM **Privately Held**
Web: www.bbisolutions.com
SIC: 2835 2834 In vitro diagnostics;
Pharmaceutical preparations

(G-5240)
MAINE CRAFT DISTILLING LLC
123 Washington Ave Ste 1 (04101-2471)
PHONE..............................207 798-2528
Luke Davidson, *Owner*
Thomas John Dupree, *Pt*
EMP: 8 **EST:** 2012
SQ FT: 2,800
SALES (est): 1.01MM **Privately Held**
Web: www.mainecraftdistilling.com
SIC: 2084 Wines

(G-5241)
MAINE ORTHTIC PRSTHTIC RHAB SV
Also Called: Maine Orthotic Lab
300 Park Ave (04102-2914)
PHONE..............................207 773-8818
Kenneth Perkins, *Pr*
Allison Perkins, *CEO*

Kyle Perkins, *COO*
EMP: 14 **EST:** 1983
SQ FT: 4,000
SALES (est): 970.88K **Privately Held**
Web:
www.maineorthoticsandprosthetics.com
SIC: 8049 5047 8731 3842 Physical
therapist; Medical and hospital equipment;
Commercial physical research; Surgical
appliances and supplies

(G-5242)
MAINE PARTS & MACHINE INC
68 Waldron Way (04103-5944)
PHONE..............................207 797-0024
William W Kelton, *Pr*
Deborah P Kelton, *Treas*
▲ **EMP:** 23 **EST:** 1985
SQ FT: 15,000
SALES (est): 1.96MM **Privately Held**
Web: www.maineparts.com
SIC: 3599 Machine shop, jobbing and repair

(G-5243)
MAINE VISUAL
13 Emerson St Apt 204 (04101-3286)
PHONE..............................207 553-0798
Follyvi Alognon, *Prin*
EMP: 7 **EST:** 2017
SALES (est): 68.22K **Privately Held**
Web: www.theumva.org
SIC: 2711 Newspapers, publishing and
printing

(G-5244)
MEDRHYTHMS INC
183 Middle St Ste 300 (04101-4064)
PHONE..............................207 447-2177
Owen Mccarthy, *Pr*
EMP: 45 **EST:** 2015
SALES (est): 1.92MM **Privately Held**
Web: www.medrhythms.com
SIC: 3845 Audiological equipment,
electromedical

(G-5245)
MILNE SPIRIT WORKS LLC
Also Called: Hardshore Distilling
53 Washington Ave (04101-2617)
PHONE..............................207 536-0592
EMP: 7
SALES (est): 73.45K **Privately Held**
SIC: 2085 Distilled and blended liquors

(G-5246)
MPX
Also Called: Mpx
2301 Congress St (04102-1907)
PHONE..............................207 774-6116
Ryan Jackson, *CEO*
Robert Wiilis, *Pr*
Thomas Donhauser, *VP*
Joan Tishkevich, *VP*
EMP: 67 **EST:** 1990
SALES (est): 10.54MM **Privately Held**
Web: www.mpxlinq.com
SIC: 2752 Offset printing

(G-5247)
MTM OLDCO INC (PA)
Also Called: Maine Sunday Telegram
1 City Ctr Fl 5 (04101-4070)
PHONE..............................207 791-6650
Charles Cochrane, *CEO*
EMP: 465 **EST:** 1998
SALES (est): 90.53MM
SALES (corp-wide): 90.53MM **Privately
Held**
Web: www.pressherald.com

SIC: 2711 Commercial printing and
newspaper publishing combined

(G-5248)
NANOSCALE COMPONENTS INC
P.O. Box 418 (06033-0418)
PHONE..............................207 671-7028
Ronald Wohl, *Prin*
EMP: 10 **EST:** 2011
SALES (est): 153.93K **Privately Held**
SIC: 3674 Semiconductors and related
devices

(G-5249)
NAVIGATOR PUBLISHING LLC
Also Called: Ocean Navigator
30 Danforth St Ste 307 (04101-4574)
P.O. Box 4733 (04112-4733)
PHONE..............................207 822-4350
EMP: 22 **EST:** 1984
SQ FT: 5,000
SALES (est): 4.74MM **Privately Held**
Web: www.navigatorpublishing.com
SIC: 2721 5551 Magazines: publishing only,
not printed on site; Boat dealers

(G-5250)
NEARPEER INC
63 Federal St (04101-4222)
PHONE..............................207 615-0414
Dustin Manocha, *CEO*
EMP: 8 **EST:** 2017
SALES (est): 460.84K **Privately Held**
Web: www.nearpeer.com
SIC: 7372 Application computer software

(G-5251)
NICHOLS PORTLAND LLC (PA)
2400 Congress St (04102-1949)
PHONE..............................207 774-6121
Thomas K Houck, *Pr*
EMP: 346 **EST:** 2016
SQ FT: 200,000
SALES (est): 50.39MM
SALES (corp-wide): 50.39MM **Privately
Held**
Web: www.nicholsportland.com
SIC: 3714 8711 Motor vehicle parts and
accessories; Engineering services

(G-5252)
NORTH ATLANTIC INC
2 Portland Fish Pier Ste 308 (04101-4633)
P.O. Box 682 (04104-0682)
PHONE..............................207 774-6025
Gerald Knecht, *Pr*
◆ **EMP:** 8 **EST:** 1982
SQ FT: 1,500
SALES (est): 2.25MM **Privately Held**
Web: www.northatlanticseafoodllc.com
SIC: 2092 5146 Seafoods, fresh: prepared;
Fish and seafoods

(G-5253)
OAKHURST DAIRY (HQ)
Also Called: Smiley's Dairy
364 Forest Ave (04101-2092)
PHONE..............................207 772-7468
TOLL FREE: 800
EMP: 195 **EST:** 1921
SALES (est): 37.08MM
SALES (corp-wide): 24.52B **Privately Held**
Web: www.oakhurstdairy.com
SIC: 2026 5143 Milk processing
(pasteurizing, homogenizing, bottling);
Dairy products, except dried or canned
PA: Dairy Farmers Of America, Inc.
1405 N 98th St
Kansas City KS 66111
816 801-6455

▲ = Import ▼ = Export
◆ = Import/Export

(G-5254)
ORANGE BIKE BREWING CO
31 Diamond St Ste D (04101-7505)
PHONE..............................207 391-4343
Thomas Ruff, Pr
EMP: 7
SALES (est): 308.61K Privately Held
SIC: 2082 Malt beverages

(G-5255)
PARADIGM OPERATING COMPANY LLC
Also Called: Cwindows
56 Milliken St (04103-1530)
P.O. Box 10109 (04104-0109)
PHONE..............................877 994-6369
EMP: 153 EST: 2003
SALES (est): 31.76MM Privately Held
Web: www.paradigmwindows.com
SIC: 5031 3089 Windows; Window frames and sash, plastics

(G-5256)
PIPING SPECIALTIES INC
Also Called: PSI Controls
36 Rainmaker Dr (04103-1291)
PHONE..............................207 878-3955
Mike Alt, Mgr
EMP: 10
SALES (corp-wide): 9.61MM Privately Held
Web: www.psi-team.com
SIC: 2891 Sealing compounds for pipe threads or joints
PA: Piping Specialties, Inc.
250 North St Ste B10
Danvers MA 01923
978 774-1300

(G-5257)
PORTLAND COMPANY
100 W Commercial St (04102-4019)
PHONE..............................207 774-1067
Phineas Sprague Junior, Pr
Clint Marshall, CFO
EMP: 49 EST: 2017
SALES (est): 2.4MM Privately Held
Web: www.theportlandnewchurch.com
SIC: 3732 Boatbuilding and repairing

(G-5258)
PORTLAND DRY GOODS INC
237 Commercial St (04101-4621)
PHONE..............................207 699-5575
David Hodgkins, Prin
EMP: 8 EST: 2010
SALES (est): 940.12K Privately Held
Web: www.portlanddrygoods.com
SIC: 5941 2389 Sporting goods and bicycle shops; Apparel for handicapped

(G-5259)
PORTLAND MONTHLY INC
Also Called: Portland Magazine
722 Congress St (04102-3306)
PHONE..............................207 775-4339
Collin Sargent, Pr
Nancy Sargent, VP
EMP: 8 EST: 1986
SQ FT: 3,400
SALES (est): 982.35K Privately Held
Web: www.portlandmonthly.com
SIC: 2721 Magazines: publishing only, not printed on site

(G-5260)
PORTLAND PRINTING GROUP
116 Riverside Industrial Pkwy (04103-1431)
PHONE..............................207 347-5700

Jon Webel, Prin
EMP: 7 EST: 2018
SALES (est): 92.07K Privately Held
Web: www.minutemanteam.com
SIC: 2752 Offset printing

(G-5261)
PORTLAND STONE WORKS INC
Also Called: Portland Stoneworks
50 Allen Ave (04103-3742)
PHONE..............................207 878-6832
Paul G White, Pr
Richard Gadboif, Clerk
EMP: 8 EST: 1998
SALES (est): 421.66K Privately Held
Web: www.pdxstoneworks.com
SIC: 2541 Counter and sink tops

(G-5262)
PRINT-MAIL OF MAINE INC
Also Called: Sign Solutions
75 Bishop St (04103-2614)
PHONE..............................207 878-8000
Ronald Nevers, Pr
Pauline Nevers, Treas
EMP: 16 EST: 1989
SALES (est): 795.5K Privately Held
Web: www.printmailofmaine.com
SIC: 7331 2752 3993 Mailing service; Commercial printing, lithographic; Signs and advertising specialties

(G-5263)
PROTEIN HOLDINGS INC (PA)
10 Moulton St Ste 5 (04101-5039)
PHONE..............................207 771-0965
Whit Gallagher, CEO
Stephan Lanfer, Ch Bd
Frank Ruch, Pr
Andrew Pease, Ex VP
Scott W Andrews, CFO
▲ EMP: 11 EST: 1997
SALES (est): 653.99K
SALES (corp-wide): 653.99K Privately Held
Web: www.proteinresearch.net
SIC: 2026 2024 Milk processing (pasteurizing, homogenizing, bottling); Ice cream, packaged: molded, on sticks, etc.

(G-5264)
PYRAMID CHECKS & PRINTING
208 Riverside Industrial Pkwy (04103-1414)
PHONE..............................207 878-9832
Carl J Lefevre, Pr
Christopher J Lefevre, *
EMP: 80 EST: 1992
SQ FT: 20,000
SALES (est): 9.01MM Privately Held
Web: www.pyramidchecks-printing.com
SIC: 2752 Offset printing

(G-5265)
RISING TIDE BREWING CO LLC
103 Fox St (04101-2539)
PHONE..............................207 370-2337
Nathan Sanborn, Prin
EMP: 19 EST: 2010
SALES (est): 4.99MM Privately Held
Web: www.risingtidebrewing.com
SIC: 5813 2082 Bars and lounges; Beer (alcoholic beverage)

(G-5266)
ROBERT MITCHELL CO INC (DH)
Also Called: Douglas Bros Div
423 Riverside Industrial Pkwy (04103-1485)
PHONE..............................207 797-6771
William Mackeil, Genl Mgr
EMP: 18 EST: 1972

SQ FT: 24,000
SALES (est): 10MM
SALES (corp-wide): 625.37MM Privately Held
SIC: 3441 Fabricated structural metal
HQ: Robert Mitchell Inc
350 Boul Decarie
Saint-Laurent QC H4L 3
514 747-2471

(G-5267)
ROCKSTEP SOLUTIONS INC (PA)
48 Free St Ste 200 (04101-3872)
PHONE..............................844 800-7625
Charles Donnelly, Pt
EMP: 14 EST: 2014
SALES (est): 1.24MM
SALES (corp-wide): 1.24MM Privately Held
Web: www.rockstepsolutions.com
SIC: 7372 7389 Application computer software; Business services, nec

(G-5268)
SEA BAGS LLC (PA)
25 Custom House Wharf (04101-4708)
PHONE..............................207 780-0744
Elizabeth Shissler, Pr
▼ EMP: 18 EST: 2006
SALES (est): 6.35MM
SALES (corp-wide): 6.35MM Privately Held
Web: www.seabags.com
SIC: 2299 5632 Batting, wadding, padding and fillings; Handbags

(G-5269)
SECURECASH ADVANTAGE
200 Riverside Industrial Pkwy (04103-1414)
PHONE..............................207 797-4838
EMP: 7 EST: 2011
SALES (est): 162.1K Privately Held
SIC: 3578 Accounting machines and cash registers

(G-5270)
SHIP-PAC CORP
Also Called: Maine Shipping & Packaging Sup
460 Riverside St (04103-1069)
PHONE..............................207 797-7444
TOLL FREE: 800
Jeffrey Bryant, Pr
EMP: 9 EST: 1979
SQ FT: 5,500
SALES (est): 2.2MM Privately Held
Web: www.maineshipping.com
SIC: 5199 2653 Packaging materials; Boxes, corrugated: made from purchased materials

(G-5271)
SIGN CONCEPTS LLC
Also Called: Axewraps
342 Warren Ave (04103-1183)
PHONE..............................207 699-2920
Steve Emma, VP
EMP: 10 EST: 2010
SALES (est): 423.55K Privately Held
Web: www.signconceptsmaine.com
SIC: 3993 Signs and advertising specialties

(G-5272)
SIGN DESIGN INC
306 Warren Ave Ste 3 (04103-1191)
P.O. Box 207 (04112-0207)
PHONE..............................207 856-2600
Roger Flannery, Pr
EMP: 10 EST: 1990
SALES (est): 432.63K Privately Held

Web: www.signsinmaine.com
SIC: 3993 Electric signs

(G-5273)
SLAB LLC
Also Called: Slab Sicilian Street Food
25 Preble St (04101-4910)
PHONE..............................207 245-3088
Todd Ketchum, Prin
EMP: 20 EST: 2013
SALES (est): 536.09K Privately Held
Web: www.slabportland.com
SIC: 5812 2038 Pizza restaurants; Pizza, frozen

(G-5274)
SOCK SHACK
564 Congress St (04101-3311)
PHONE..............................207 805-1348
Lori Dorr, Prin
EMP: 7 EST: 2016
SALES (est): 118.22K Privately Held
Web: www.thesockshack.com
SIC: 2252 Socks

(G-5275)
SONIC BLUE AEROSPACE INC
80 Exchange St Ste 36 (04101-5035)
PHONE..............................207 776-2471
Richard H Lugg, Pr
James Belanger, Corporate Secretary
EMP: 8 EST: 2004
SALES (est): 883.63K Privately Held
SIC: 3721 Aircraft

(G-5276)
STROUDWATER DISTILLERY
Thompsons Pt (04102)
PHONE..............................207 272-7327
EMP: 11 EST: 2016
SALES (est): 476.6K Privately Held
Web: www.stroudwaterspirits.com
SIC: 2085 Distilled and blended liquors

(G-5277)
SUNRISE GUIDE LLC
Also Called: Local Guides Publishing
503 Woodford St (04103-2439)
P.O. Box 163 (04098-0163)
PHONE..............................207 221-3450
Heather Chandler, Pr
EMP: 9 EST: 2008
SALES (est): 246.81K Privately Held
Web: www.thesunriseguide.com
SIC: 2711 Newspapers, publishing and printing

(G-5278)
SWEETGRASS FARM WINERY & DIST
324 Fore St (04101-4111)
PHONE..............................207 761-8446
EMP: 7 EST: 2014
SALES (est): 110.28K Privately Held
Web: www.sweetgrasswinery.com
SIC: 2084 Wines

(G-5279)
T R SIGN DESIGN INC
306 Warren Ave Ste 3 (04103-1191)
PHONE..............................207 856-2600
Roger Flannery, Pr
Tim Flannery, Pr
EMP: 8 EST: 1990
SQ FT: 30,000
SALES (est): 220.22K Privately Held
SIC: 3993 Signs and advertising specialties

GEOGRAPHIC

(G-5280)
TAPROOT
49 Fox St (04101-2500)
PHONE..........................802 472-1617
Veronica Medwid, *Prin*
EMP: 9 **EST:** 2015
SALES (est): 481.31K **Privately Held**
Web: www.taprootmag.com
SIC: 2721 Magazines: publishing only, not printed on site

(G-5281)
THORS SKYR LLC
68 Commercial St (04101-5089)
P.O. Box 364 (13685-0364)
PHONE..........................315 955-9418
EMP: 10 **EST:** 2021
SALES (est): 555.85K **Privately Held**
Web: www.thorsskyr.com
SIC: 2026 Yogurt

(G-5282)
TIGPRO INC
21 Tee Dr (04103-1299)
PHONE..........................207 878-1190
Ken Welton, *Pr*
EMP: 8 **EST:** 2003
SQ FT: 4,000
SALES (est): 994.46K **Privately Held**
Web: www.tigpro.com
SIC: 1711 3441 Process piping contractor; Fabricated structural metal

(G-5283)
TILLAMOOK COUNTY CREAMERY ASSN
190 Riverside St Unit 6a (04103-1073)
PHONE..........................503 815-1300
EMP: 8
SALES (corp-wide): 182.67MM **Privately Held**
Web: www.tillamook.com
SIC: 2022 Cheese; natural and processed
PA: Tillamook County Creamery Association
4185 Highway 101 N
Tillamook OR 97141
503 842-4481

(G-5284)
TIMKEN MOTOR & CRANE SVCS LLC
Also Called: Stultz Electric
190 Riverside St Unit 4a (04103-1073)
PHONE..........................207 699-2501
EMP: 15
SALES (corp-wide): 4.5B **Publicly Held**
Web: www.hnelectric.com
SIC: 7694 7699 Electric motor repair; Professional instrument repair services
HQ: Timken Motor & Crane Services, Llc
11575 Teller St
Broomfield CO 80020
303 623-8658

(G-5285)
TONYS DONUT SHOP
9 Bolton St (04102-2501)
PHONE..........................207 772-2727
Richard Fournier, *Pr*
EMP: 7 **EST:** 1964
SQ FT: 675
SALES (est): 251.69K **Privately Held**
Web: www.tonysdonutshop.com
SIC: 5461 2051 Doughnuts; Doughnuts, except frozen

(G-5286)
TRUELINE PUBLISHING LLC
561 Congress St (04101-3308)
PHONE..........................207 510-4099
EMP: 40 **EST:** 2010
SALES (est): 3.88MM **Privately Held**
Web: www.wearetrueline.com
SIC: 2721 Trade journals: publishing and printing

(G-5287)
TYLER TECHNOLOGIES INC
2275 Congress St (04102-1907)
PHONE..........................207 879-7243
EMP: 24
SALES (corp-wide): 1.85B **Publicly Held**
Web: www.tylertech.com
SIC: 7372 Prepackaged software
PA: Tyler Technologies, Inc.
5101 Tennyson Pkwy
Plano TX 75024
972 713-3700

(G-5288)
W B MASON CO INC
106 Pine Tree Industrial Pkwy (04102-1400)
PHONE..........................888 926-2766
EMP: 34
SALES (corp-wide): 1.01B **Privately Held**
Web: www.wbmason.com
SIC: 5943 5712 2752 Office forms and supplies; Office furniture; Commercial printing, lithographic
PA: W. B. Mason Co., Inc.
59 Centre Street
Brockton MA 02301
508 586-3434

(G-5289)
WILD OCEAN AQUACULTURE LLC
Also Called: Bangs Island Mussels
72 Commercial St # 15 (04101-4749)
PHONE..........................207 458-6288
EMP: 11 **EST:** 2010
SALES (est): 766.06K **Privately Held**
Web: www.bangsislandmussels.com
SIC: 2091 Seafood products: packaged in cans, jars, etc.

(G-5290)
WISE BUSINESS FORMS INC
Also Called: E P X Group
2301 Congress St (04102-1907)
PHONE..........................207 774-6560
Harold Pechie, *Brnch Mgr*
EMP: 150
SALES (corp-wide): 106.09MM **Privately Held**
Web: www.wbf.com
SIC: 5112 2761 Stationery and office supplies; Manifold business forms
PA: Wise Business Forms Incorporated
555 Mcfarland 400 Dr
Alpharetta GA 30004
770 442-1060

(G-5291)
WOODLAB LLC
299 Presumpscot St (04103-5224)
PHONE..........................207 536-7542
EMP: 8 **EST:** 2016
SALES (est): 529.03K **Privately Held**
Web: www.woodlab.me
SIC: 2499 Wood products, nec

(G-5292)
YORK-CMBRLAND ASSN FOR HNDCPPE (PA)
Also Called: Saco Bay Provisioners
619 Brighton Ave (04102-2373)
PHONE..........................207 879-1140
Heidi Howard, *Ex Dir*
Edward Mcgeachey, *Pr*
EMP: 24 **EST:** 1967
SQ FT: 15,000
SALES (est): 36.47MM
SALES (corp-wide): 36.47MM **Privately Held**
SIC: 5021 2426 8322 3421 Furniture; Hardwood dimension and flooring mills; Individual and family services; Cutlery

(G-5293)
ZOOTILITY CO
2301 Congress St Ste 3 (04102-1907)
PHONE..........................207 536-0639
Nathan Barr, *Pr*
EMP: 13 **EST:** 2011
SQ FT: 1,000
SALES (est): 2.46MM **Privately Held**
Web: www.zootility.com
SIC: 3421 Knife blades and blanks

Pownal
Cumberland County

(G-5294)
VINTAGE MAINE KITCHEN LLC
83 Fickett Rd (04069-6155)
PHONE..........................207 317-2536
EMP: 7 **EST:** 2018
SALES (est): 498.88K **Privately Held**
Web: www.vintagemainekitchen.com
SIC: 2096 Potato chips and similar snacks

Presque Isle
Aroostook County

(G-5295)
ALLENS ENVIRONMENTAL SVCS INC
Also Called: Allen's Drain Cleaning Service
75 Davis St (04769-2255)
P.O. Box 109 (04769-0109)
PHONE..........................207 764-9336
EMP: 9 **EST:** 2006
SALES (est): 334.19K **Privately Held**
SIC: 2842 Drain pipe solvents or cleaners

(G-5296)
AROOSTACAST INC
217 Parsons Rd (04769-5116)
PHONE..........................207 764-0077
Timothy Wilcox, *Pr*
Tim Wilcox, *Pr*
Mary Wilcox, *Sec*
EMP: 10 **EST:** 1965
SQ FT: 12,000
SALES (est): 990.62K **Privately Held**
Web: www.aroostacast.com
SIC: 3272 Concrete products, precast, nec

(G-5297)
AROOSTOOK TRUSSES INC
Also Called: Aroostook Shredding
655 Missile St (04769-2083)
P.O. Box 548 (04769-0548)
PHONE..........................207 768-5817
Gary Nelson, *Pr*
Harris Nickerson, *VP*
EMP: 20 **EST:** 1997

SQ FT: 12,000
SALES (est): 4.02MM **Privately Held**
Web: www.aroostooktrusses.com
SIC: 2439 Trusses, wooden roof

(G-5298)
COCA-COLA BEVS NORTHEAST INC
Also Called: Coca-Cola
991 Skyway St (04769-2081)
PHONE..........................207 764-4481
Wesley Elmer, *Mgr*
EMP: 24
Web: www.coca-cola.com
SIC: 2086 Bottled and canned soft drinks
HQ: Coca-Cola Beverages Northeast, Inc.
1 Executive Park Dr # 330
Bedford NH 03110
603 627-7871

(G-5299)
COLUMBIA FOREST PRODUCTS INC
Also Called: Veneer Division
395 Missile St (04769-2084)
P.O. Box 848 (04769-0848)
PHONE..........................207 760-3800
Mark Kelly, *Brnch Mgr*
EMP: 141
SALES (corp-wide): 494.11K **Privately Held**
Web: cfp.venveodev.com
SIC: 2435 2426 Hardwood veneer and plywood; Hardwood dimension and flooring mills
PA: Columbia Forest Products, Inc.
7900 Mccloud Rd Ste 200
Greensboro NC 27409
336 605-0429

(G-5300)
HAROLD HAINES INC
Also Called: Haines Manufacturing Co
243 Main St (04769-2858)
PHONE..........................207 762-1411
Fredrick Haines, *Pr*
Harold F Haines Junior, *VP*
Jacqueline Haines, *Treas*
EMP: 19 **EST:** 1930
SQ FT: 25,000
SALES (est): 1.66MM **Privately Held**
SIC: 3523 Grading, cleaning, sorting machines, fruit, grain, vegetable

(G-5301)
LANE CONSTRUCTION CORPORATION
458 Reach Rd (04769-5004)
P.O. Box 627 (04769-0627)
PHONE..........................207 764-4137
Kim Ring, *Mgr*
EMP: 21
SALES (corp-wide): 7.95B **Privately Held**
Web: www.laneconstruct.com
SIC: 1611 3273 2951 Highway and street paving contractor; Ready-mixed concrete; Asphalt paving mixtures and blocks
HQ: The Lane Construction Corporation
90 Fieldstone Ct
Cheshire CT 06410
203 235-3351

(G-5302)
LOCKWOOD MFG INC
135 Parsons St (04769-2130)
PHONE..........................207 764-4196
Chuck Crary, *Pr*
EMP: 8 **EST:** 2003
SALES (est): 248.36K **Privately Held**

Web: www.lockwoodmfg.com
SIC: 3999   Manufacturing industries, nec

(G-5303)
M & M MACHINE INC
1215 Airport Dr (04769-2051)
PHONE................................207 764-4199
Marc C Brown, *Pr*
Mark E Jones, *VP*
EMP: 7 EST: 1994
SQ FT: 6,000
SALES (est): 627.15K **Privately Held**
SIC: 3599   Machine shop, jobbing and repair

(G-5304)
MAINE & MARITIMES
CORPORATION (PA)
209 State St (04769-2663)
PHONE................................207 760-2499
Brent M Boyles, *Pr*
Michael I Williams, *Sr VP*
Randi J Arthurs, *VP Acctg*
Patrick C Cannon, *General Vice President*
Tim D Brown, *Operations*
EMP: 16 EST: 2003
SALES (est): 49.73MM
SALES (corp-wide): 49.73MM **Privately Held**
SIC: 4911 7372 7539   Distribution, electric power; Prepackaged software; Electrical services

(G-5305)
NORTHEAST PACKAGING CO
(PA)
Also Called: Nepco
875 Skyway St (04769-2063)
P.O. Box 328 (04769-0328)
PHONE................................207 764-6271
Robert Umphrey, *Pr*
▲ EMP: 45 EST: 1972
SQ FT: 60,000
SALES (est): 10.49MM
SALES (corp-wide): 10.49MM **Privately Held**
Web: www.nepcobags.com
SIC: 2673 2674   Plastic bags: made from purchased materials; Paper bags: made from purchased materials

(G-5306)
NORTHEAST PUBLISHING
COMPANY
Also Called: Starherald Newspaper Pubg
40 North St Ste 2 (04769-2269)
P.O. Box 510 (04769-0510)
PHONE................................207 768-5431
Jim Berry, *Mgr*
EMP: 9
SALES (corp-wide): 39.35MM **Privately Held**
Web: www.thecounty.me
SIC: 2711   Newspapers, publishing and printing
HQ: Northeast Publishing Company Inc
260 Missile St
Presque Isle ME 04769
207 764-4471

(G-5307)
NORTHEAST PUBLISHING
COMPANY (HQ)
Also Called: Aroostook Republican
260 Missile St (04769-2069)
P.O. Box 510 (04769-0510)
PHONE................................207 764-4471
Richard J Warren, *Pr*
EMP: 60 EST: 1965
SQ FT: 48,000

SALES (est): 10.54MM
SALES (corp-wide): 39.35MM **Privately Held**
Web: www.thecounty.me
SIC: 2711   Newspapers, publishing and printing
PA: Bangor Publishing Company
1 Merchants Plz
Bangor ME 04401
207 990-8000

(G-5308)
NORTHEAST PUBLISHING
COMPANY
Also Called: Print Works
260 Missile St (04769-2069)
P.O. Box 510 (04769-0510)
PHONE................................207 764-4471
Pam Lynch, *Mgr*
EMP: 9
SALES (corp-wide): 39.35MM **Privately Held**
Web: www.thecounty.me
SIC: 2759   Commercial printing, nec
HQ: Northeast Publishing Company Inc
260 Missile St
Presque Isle ME 04769
207 764-4471

(G-5309)
PEPSI COLA BOTTLING
AROOSTOOK
Also Called: Pepsico
52 Industrial St (04769-2598)
PHONE................................207 760-3000
J Gregory Freeman, *Pr*
Anne M Freeman, *
Katherine Freeman, *
EMP: 18 EST: 1946
SQ FT: 35,000
SALES (est): 417.76K **Privately Held**
Web: www.pepsico.com
SIC: 2086   Carbonated soft drinks, bottled and canned

(G-5310)
SUNNY SIDE LAND HOLDINGS
LLC
Also Called: AR Walton Construction
9 Parsons St (04769-2331)
PHONE................................207 768-1020
Adam Walton, *Managing Member*
EMP: 10 EST: 2009
SALES (est): 1.12MM **Privately Held**
Web: www.arwaltonconstruction.com
SIC: 1442 1799 8742 5211   Construction sand and gravel; Parking lot maintenance; Maintenance management consultant; Modular homes

(G-5311)
VALT ENTERPRIZES INC
1030 Airport Dr Unit 1 (04769-2048)
PHONE................................207 560-5188
EMP: 13 EST: 2014
SALES (est): 1.51MM **Privately Held**
Web: www.valt-ent.com
SIC: 3761 7389   Space vehicles, complete; Business Activities at Non-Commercial Site

Rangeley
Franklin County

(G-5312)
M & H LOGGING LLC
Also Called: M & H Construction
3039 Main St (04970-4205)
P.O. Box 565 (04970-0565)

PHONE................................207 864-5617
David Haley, *Pt*
EMP: 50 EST: 1980
SQ FT: 4,000
SALES (est): 7.65MM **Privately Held**
Web: www.rangeleyexcavation.com
SIC: 1611 2411 1542   Highway and street construction; Logging; Nonresidential construction, nec

(G-5313)
PATHIAKIS NICKOLAS
94 Stratton Rd (04970-4136)
PHONE................................207 864-3474
Nick Pathiakis, *Prin*
EMP: 7 EST: 2016
SALES (est): 206.91K **Privately Held**
SIC: 3489   Ordnance and accessories, nec

Raymond
Cumberland County

(G-5314)
PEARPOINT INC
28 Tower Rd (04071-6440)
PHONE................................760 343-7350
EMP: 7 EST: 2013
SALES (est): 99.9K **Privately Held**
Web: www.radiodetection.com
SIC: 3663   Radio and t.v. communications equipment

(G-5315)
SABRA CORPORATION
Also Called: Sabre Yachts
12 Hawthorne St (04071-6704)
P.O. Box 134 (04077-0134)
PHONE................................207 655-3831
EMP: 145 EST: 1970
SALES (est): 19.94MM **Privately Held**
Web: www.sabreyachts.com
SIC: 3732   Sailboats, building and repairing

(G-5316)
SPX CORPORATION
Radiodetection
28 Tower Rd (04071-6440)
PHONE................................207 655-8525
Zenya Brackett, *Brnch Mgr*
EMP: 40
SALES (corp-wide): 1.46B **Publicly Held**
Web: www.spx.com
SIC: 3661   Telephone and telegraph apparatus
HQ: Canvas Sx, Llc
6325 Ardrey Kell Rd Ste 4
Charlotte NC 28277
980 474-3700

(G-5317)
SPX CORPORATION
Also Called: Radiodetection
22 Tower Rd (04071-6440)
P.O. Box 949 (04071-0949)
PHONE................................207 655-8100
Garrett Van Atta, *Mgr*
EMP: 126
SQ FT: 7,500
SALES (corp-wide): 1.46B **Publicly Held**
Web: www.spx.com
SIC: 3663   Antennas, transmitting and communications
HQ: Canvas Sx, Llc
6325 Ardrey Kell Rd Ste 4
Charlotte NC 28277
980 474-3700

Readfield
Kennebec County

(G-5318)
SAUNDERS MFG CO INC (PA)
Also Called: Saunders Manufacturing & Mktg
65 Nickerson Hill Rd (04355-3924)
PHONE................................207 685-9860
John Rosmarin, *Pr*
David Lipman, *
Donn Harriman, *
▲ EMP: 43 EST: 1946
SQ FT: 40,000
SALES (est): 13.54MM
SALES (corp-wide): 13.54MM **Privately Held**
Web: www.saundersmidwest.com
SIC: 3499   Novelties and specialties, metal

Reed Plt
Aroostook County

(G-5319)
WILLARD S HANINGTON & SON
INC
1619 Military Rd (04497-6024)
P.O. Box 70 (04497-0070)
PHONE................................207 456-7511
Willard Hanington Junior, *Pr*
Willard S Hanington, *
EMP: 12 EST: 1981
SQ FT: 336
SALES (est): 643.13K **Privately Held**
SIC: 2411   Logging camps and contractors

Richmond
Sagadahoc County

(G-5320)
CALLAWAY GOLF BALL
OPRTONS INC
County Rd (04357)
PHONE................................207 737-4324
Thomas Whitiker, *Brnch Mgr*
EMP: 127
SALES (corp-wide): 4B **Publicly Held**
SIC: 3149   Athletic shoes, except rubber or plastic
HQ: Callaway Golf Ball Operations, Inc.
425 Meadow St
Chicopee MA 01013
413 536-1200

(G-5321)
KEITH A GILPATRICK
Also Called: J R Felix Co
373 Lincoln St (04357-3534)
PHONE................................207 737-4286
EMP: 7 EST: 1999
SALES (est): 57.81K **Privately Held**
Web: www.gilpatricksons.com
SIC: 2421   Sawmills and planing mills, general

(G-5322)
KENNEBEC RIVER
BIOSCIENCES INC
Also Called: Kennebec River Biosciences
41 Main St (04357-1108)
PHONE................................207 737-2637
EMP: 13 EST: 1996
SQ FT: 629
SALES (est): 2.35MM **Privately Held**
Web: www.kennebecbio.com

SIC: **8071** 8734 8748 2836 Testing laboratories; Testing laboratories; Testing services; Biological products, except diagnostic

Rockland
Knox County

(G-5323)
BIXBY & CO LLC
Also Called: Bixby Chocolate
1 Sea Street Pl (04841-3412)
PHONE.................................207 691-1778
Donna Mcaleer, *Managing Member*
EMP: 8 EST: 2013
SQ FT: 3,000
SALES (est): 1.4MM **Privately Held**
Web: www.bixbychocolate.com
SIC: **2066** 2064 Chocolate and cocoa products; Candy and other confectionery products

(G-5324)
CEDARWORKS OF MAINE INC
Also Called: Cedarworks Playsets
12 Merrill Dr (04841-2144)
PHONE.................................207 596-0771
Donald Protheroe, *Brnch Mgr*
EMP: 25
SALES (corp-wide): 9.4MM **Privately Held**
Web: www.cedarworks.com
SIC: **3949** Playground equipment
PA: Cedarworks Of Maine Inc
　799 Commercial St
　Rockport ME 04856
　207 596-1010

(G-5325)
DOUGLAS DYNAMICS LLC
Also Called: Fisher Engineering Division
50 Gordon Dr (04841-2139)
P.O. Box 529 (04841-0529)
PHONE.................................207 701-4200
Raymond S Littlefield, *Prin*
EMP: 19
Web: www.douglasdynamics.com
SIC: **3711** 3531 3524 Snow plows (motor vehicles), assembly of; Construction machinery; Lawn and garden equipment
HQ: Douglas Dynamics, L.L.C.
　11270 W Park Pl Ste 300
　Milwaukee WI 53224
　414 354-2310

(G-5326)
ELECTROTECH INC
344 Park St (04841-5303)
P.O. Box 1038 (04841-1038)
PHONE.................................207 596-0556
Thomas Levasseur, *Pr*
Beryl Levasseur, *Treas*
Shawn Levasseur, *VP*
EMP: 16 EST: 1983
SQ FT: 15,000
SALES (est): 2.48MM **Privately Held**
Web: www.electrotechassembly.com
SIC: **3699** Electrical equipment and supplies, nec

(G-5327)
FERRAIOLO CONSTRUCTION INC
262 Pleasant St (04841-5304)
PHONE.................................207 594-9840
TOLL FREE: 800
Vincent Ferraiolo, *Pr*
Frank Ferraiolo,　*
John Ferraiolo,　*

Filomena Ferraiolo, *Stockholder*
▲ **EMP: 50 EST:** 1968
SQ FT: 5,000
SALES (est): 9.73MM **Privately Held**
Web: www.ferraioloinc.com
SIC: **1794** 3273 Excavation work; Ready-mixed concrete

(G-5328)
FISHER ENGINEERING
Also Called: Fisher
50 Gordon Dr (04841-2168)
PHONE.................................207 701-4200
Jim Janik, *Pr*
▼ **EMP: 250 EST:** 1984
SALES (est): 51.45MM **Publicly Held**
Web: www.fisherplows.com
SIC: **3585** Snowmaking machinery
HQ: Douglas Dynamics, L.L.C.
　11270 W Park Pl Ste 300
　Milwaukee WI 53224
　414 354-2310

(G-5329)
FMC CORPORATION
Also Called: F M C Marine Colloid Division
341 Park St (04841-5302)
P.O. Box 308 (04841-0308)
PHONE.................................207 594-3200
Kiran O'dwyer, *Brnch Mgr*
EMP: 72
SALES (corp-wide): 5.8B **Publicly Held**
Web: www.fmc.com
SIC: **2869** 3295 2899 2087 Industrial organic chemicals, nec; Minerals, ground or treated; Chemical preparations, nec; Flavoring extracts and syrups, nec
PA: Fmc Corporation
　2929 Walnut St
　Philadelphia PA 19104
　215 299-6000

(G-5330)
FREE PRESS INC
8 N Main St Ste 101 (04841-3154)
P.O. Box 1076 (04843-1076)
PHONE.................................207 594-4408
Reade Brower, *Pr*
EMP: 13 EST: 1985
SQ FT: 6,000
SALES (est): 472.6K **Privately Held**
Web: www.freepressonline.com
SIC: **2711** Newspapers, publishing and printing

(G-5331)
GOODKIND PEN COMPANY INC
500 Main St (04841-3343)
PHONE.................................207 594-6207
Ian Lebauer, *Pr*
EMP: 25 EST: 1992
SQ FT: 21,000
SALES (est): 940.28K **Privately Held**
SIC: **3951** 3952 Pens and mechanical pencils; Lead pencils and art goods

(G-5332)
GS INC
12 Moran Dr Ste A1 (04841-2164)
PHONE.................................207 593-7730
Renee Philbrook, *Treas*
EMP: 7 EST: 2009
SALES (est): 432.67K **Privately Held**
SIC: **3433** 4832 Solar heaters and collectors ; Educational

(G-5333)
IMAGINEERING INC
Also Called: Weatherend Estate Furniture
6 Gordon Dr (04841-2137)

PHONE.................................207 596-6483
Gil Harper, *Pr*
EMP: 12 EST: 1983
SALES (est): 760.1K **Privately Held**
Web: www.weatherend.com
SIC: **2511** Wood household furniture

(G-5334)
ISLAND INSTITUTE
Also Called: Maine Island Trail Assctn-Cncl
386 Main St (04841-3345)
P.O. Box 648 (04841-0648)
PHONE.................................207 594-9209
Anthony Chatwin, *Pr*
Phillip Conkling,　*
Horace Hildreth,　*
John Higgins,　*
Donna Damon,　*
EMP: 40 EST: 1983
SQ FT: 14,000
SALES (est): 7.83MM **Privately Held**
Web: www.islandinstitute.org
SIC: **8641** 2731 Environmental protection organization; Book publishing

(G-5335)
JOHANSONS BOATWORKS
11 Farwell Dr (04841-6313)
PHONE.................................207 596-7060
Peter Johanson, *Pt*
Mary Johanson, *Pt*
EMP: 10 EST: 1977
SALES (est): 971.17K **Privately Held**
Web: www.jboatworks.com
SIC: **3732** Boatbuilding and repairing

(G-5336)
KENNISTON MACHINE & ENGRG
Also Called: Kennison Machine Company
30 Moran Dr (04841-2147)
PHONE.................................207 594-7810
Toby Kenniston, *Pr*
Toby W Kenniston, *Owner*
EMP: 8 EST: 1988
SALES (est): 716.22K **Privately Held**
Web: www.kennistonmachine.com
SIC: **3599** Machine shop, jobbing and repair

(G-5337)
LONZA BIO SCIENCE ROCKLAND INC
191 Thomaston St (04841-2130)
PHONE.................................207 594-3400
EMP: 25 EST: 2007
SALES (est): 728.31K **Privately Held**
Web: www.lonza.com
SIC: **2834** Pharmaceutical preparations
PA: Lonza Group Ag
　Munchensteinerstrasse 38
　Basel BS 4052

(G-5338)
LONZA ROCKLAND INC
191 Thomaston St (04841-2130)
PHONE.................................207 594-3400
Stephan Borgas, *CEO*
EMP: 65 EST: 1998
SQ FT: 40,000
SALES (est): 22.03MM **Privately Held**
Web: www.lonza.com
SIC: **2834** Pharmaceutical preparations
HQ: Lonza Usa Inc.
　412 Mount Kemble Ave 200s
　Morristown NJ 07960
　201 316-9200

(G-5339)
MARKETING WORLDWIDE CORP (PA)

423 Main St Ste 3 (04841-3383)
PHONE.................................631 444-8090
Charles Pinkerton, *CEO*
Michael Winzkowski, *Ch Bd*
EMP: 9 EST: 1996
SQ FT: 3,000
SALES (est): 2.01MM
SALES (corp-wide): 2.01MM **Publicly Held**
SIC: **3714** 7532 Motor vehicle parts and accessories; Paint shop, automotive

(G-5340)
NORTH END COMPOSITES LLC
Also Called: Back Cove Yachts
23 Merrill Dr (04841-2142)
P.O. Box 548 (04841-0548)
PHONE.................................207 594-8427
Christopher Evans, *Pr*
Jason Constantine,　*
Nancy Basselet,　*
EMP: 163 EST: 1976
SQ FT: 15,000
SALES (est): 22.29MM **Privately Held**
Web: www.backcoveyachts.com
SIC: **3732** Boats, fiberglass: building and repairing

(G-5341)
ROCKLAND MARINE CORPORATION
79 Mechanic St (04841-3513)
P.O. Box 309 (04841-0309)
PHONE.................................207 594-7860
Perry Holmes, *Pr*
EMP: 50 EST: 1991
SALES (est): 7.69MM **Privately Held**
Web: www.rocklandmarinecorp.com
SIC: **3731** Shipbuilding and repairing

(G-5342)
STEEL-PRO INC
Also Called: Steel Pro Services
771 Main St (04841-3427)
P.O. Box 449 (04841-0449)
PHONE.................................207 596-0061
Chris Beebe, *Ch Bd*
Chris Beebe,　*
Jeanne Rimm,　*
Steve Ladd,　*
Craig Wells,　*
EMP: 45 EST: 1978
SQ FT: 21,000
SALES (est): 11.21MM **Privately Held**
Web: www.steelprousa.com
SIC: **3443** 3441 Industrial vessels, tanks, and containers; Fabricated structural metal

(G-5343)
TREMS INC
Also Called: Brio Promotions
19 Merrill Dr (04841-2142)
P.O. Box 667 (04841-0667)
PHONE.................................207 596-6989
Jeffrey Thibodeau, *Pr*
Marli Thibodeau, *VP*
Jeffrey Thibodeau Persident, *Prin*
EMP: 9 EST: 2015
SALES (est): 607K **Privately Held**
Web: www.briocustom.com
SIC: **2759** Promotional printing

(G-5344)
US OCEANS LLC
Also Called: Alaskan Captain ME Lobster CLB
230 Park St (04841-2126)
P.O. Box 193 (04856-0193)
PHONE.................................207 596-3603
EMP: 10 EST: 2018
SALES (est): 995.82K **Privately Held**

Web: www.alaskancaptain.com
SIC: 2092 Fresh or frozen packaged fish

Rockport
Knox County

(G-5345)
CEDARWORKS OF MAINE INC (PA)
Also Called: Cedarworks Playsets
799 Commercial St (04856-4204)
P.O. Box 990 (04856-0990)
PHONE...........................207 596-1010
Duncan Brown, *Ch*
Barrett Brown, *
Susan Brown, *Stockholder*
EMP: 25 **EST:** 1982
SQ FT: 2,500
SALES (est): 9.4MM
SALES (corp-wide): 9.4MM **Privately Held**
Web: www.cedarworks.com
SIC: 2511 Children's wood furniture

(G-5346)
D E ENTERPRISE INC
Also Called: Fly Rod & Reel
680 Commercial St (04856-4201)
P.O. Box 679 (04843-0679)
PHONE...........................207 594-9544
Robert Fernald, *Pr*
H Allen Fernald, *Ch Bd*
James E Butler, *VP Opers*
Melissa Koester, *Sec*
▲ **EMP:** 50 **EST:** 1954
SQ FT: 25,000
SALES (est): 3.33MM **Privately Held**
Web: www.downeast.com
SIC: 2721 2731 7389 Magazines: publishing only, not printed on site; Book music: publishing only, not printed on site; Advertising, promotional, and trade show services

(G-5347)
DANICA DESIGN
Also Called: Danica Candle Works
569 West St (04856-5308)
P.O. Box 206 (04865-0206)
PHONE...........................207 236-3060
Erik Laustsen, *Pr*
Cindy Laustsen, *VP*
EMP: 20 **EST:** 1986
SQ FT: 4,000
SALES (est): 1.54MM **Privately Held**
Web: www.danicacandleworks.com
SIC: 3999 Candles

(G-5348)
DOWN EAST ENTERPRISE INC
Also Called: American College & Schl Press
680 Commercial St (04856-4201)
P.O. Box 679 (04843-0679)
PHONE...........................207 594-9544
Robert Fernald, *Pr*
Jim Butler, *
▲ **EMP:** 48 **EST:** 1977
SALES (est): 4.51MM **Privately Held**
Web: www.downeast.com
SIC: 2721 Magazines: publishing only, not printed on site

(G-5349)
GLOVER COMPANY INC
Also Called: Rockport Steel
17 Rockville St (04856-4409)
P.O. Box 1200 (04856-1200)
PHONE...........................207 236-8644
William Glover, *Pr*

Diana Glover, *VP*
▼ **EMP:** 12 **EST:** 1980
SALES (est): 1.08MM **Privately Held**
Web: www.rockportsteel.com
SIC: 3441 Fabricated structural metal

(G-5350)
HEIWA TOFU INC
Also Called: Heiwa Soy Beanery
201 West St (04856-5710)
PHONE...........................207 236-8638
Jeff Wolovitz, *Managing Member*
Jeff Molovitz, *Managing Member*
EMP: 8 **EST:** 2008
SALES (est): 511.11K **Privately Held**
Web: www.heiwatofu.com
SIC: 2099 Tofu, except frozen desserts

(G-5351)
REDDEN PUBLISHING CO LLC
160 Mistic Ave (04856-5730)
PHONE...........................207 236-0767
Dan Redden, *Owner*
EMP: 8 **EST:** 2003
SALES (est): 457.67K **Privately Held**
Web: www.yeegoconnect.com
SIC: 2741 Miscellaneous publishing

Round Pond
Lincoln County

(G-5352)
DANA ROBES BOAT BUILDERS
75 Southern Point Rd (04564-3703)
PHONE...........................207 529-2433
Dana Robes, *Pt*
Martha Robes, *Pt*
EMP: 7 **EST:** 2000
SALES (est): 487.98K **Privately Held**
SIC: 3732 Boatbuilding and repairing

(G-5353)
NORTH COUNTRY WIND BELLS INC
544 State Route 32 (04564-3728)
PHONE...........................207 677-2224
James L Davidson, *Pr*
May B Davidson, *VP*
Timothy Southwick, *Stockholder*
Constance Southwick, *Stockholder*
EMP: 12 **EST:** 1950
SALES (est): 1.88MM **Privately Held**
Web: www.northcountrywindbells.com
SIC: 3599 Machine shop, jobbing and repair

(G-5354)
PADEBCO CUSTOM BOATS
Anchor Inn Rd (04564)
P.O. Box 197 (04564-0197)
PHONE...........................207 529-5106
S Bruce Cunningham, *Pr*
Paul Cunningham, *Treas*
Debra Cunningham, *Sec*
EMP: 7 **EST:** 1961
SQ FT: 4,000
SALES (est): 590.15K **Privately Held**
Web: www.padebco.com
SIC: 3732 4213 Boatbuilding and repairing; Heavy hauling, nec

Rumford
Oxford County

(G-5355)
CLINTON G BRADBURY INC
Also Called: Bradbury Enterprises

1180 Route 2 Ste 5 (04276-3644)
PHONE...........................207 562-8014
EMP: 9 **EST:** 1973
SALES (est): 961.08K **Privately Held**
SIC: 2411 Logging

(G-5356)
HOPE ASSOCIATION (PA)
85 Lincoln Ave (04276-1844)
PHONE...........................207 364-4561
Joseph Sirois, *Dir*
EMP: 35 **EST:** 1961
SALES (est): 5.02MM
SALES (corp-wide): 5.02MM **Privately Held**
Web: www.hopeassociation.org
SIC: 3999 8322 Education aids, devices and supplies; Self-help organization, nec

(G-5357)
JAMES NEWSPAPERS INC
Also Called: Rumford Falls Times
69 Congress St (04276-2015)
PHONE...........................207 364-7893
Bruce Farrin, *Mgr*
EMP: 7
SALES (corp-wide): 2.48MM **Privately Held**
Web: www.sunjournal.com
SIC: 2759 Publication printing
PA: James Newspapers, Inc
1 Pikes HI
Norway ME 04268
207 743-7011

(G-5358)
MEAD PAPERS GROUP
35 Hartford St (04276-1000)
PHONE...........................207 369-2390
Tim Barclay, *Prin*
EMP: 7 **EST:** 2008
SALES (est): 105.47K **Privately Held**
SIC: 2741 Miscellaneous publishing

(G-5359)
ND PAPER INC
Also Called: Nine Dragons Paper - Rumford
35 Hartford St (04276-2045)
PHONE...........................207 364-4521
Randy Chicoine, *Mgr*
EMP: 278
Web: us.ndpaper.com
SIC: 2611 Pulp manufactured from waste or recycled paper
HQ: Nd Paper Inc.
2001 Spring Rd Ste 500
Oak Brook IL 60523
513 200-0908

(G-5360)
ND PAPER LLC
35 Hartford St (04276-2045)
PHONE...........................207 364-4521
Ken Liu, *CEO*
EMP: 650
Web: www.ndpaper.com
SIC: 2621 Paper mills
HQ: Nd Paper Llc
2001 Spring Rd Ste 500
Oak Brook IL 60523
937 528-3870

(G-5361)
NICOLS BROTHERS INC
29 Industrial Park Rd (04276-3436)
P.O. Box 12 (04257-0012)
PHONE...........................207 364-7032
James Nicols, *Prin*
James Nicols, *Pr*
Carlene Nicols, *Off Mgr*

EMP: 9 **EST:** 2005
SALES (est): 255.51K **Privately Held**
Web: www.nicolsbrothersinc.com
SIC: 2411 Logging camps and contractors

Sabattus
Androscoggin County

(G-5362)
SABATTUS MACHINE WORKS INC
62 Greene St (04280-4039)
PHONE...........................207 375-6222
EMP: 9 **EST:** 2020
SALES (est): 253.64K **Privately Held**
Web: www.sabattusmachine.com
SIC: 3599 Machine shop, jobbing and repair

Saco
York County

(G-5363)
BIODESIGN INTERNATIONAL
60 Industrial Park Rd (04072-1840)
PHONE...........................207 283-6500
Gerard Blain, *Treas*
EMP: 33 **EST:** 1987
SQ FT: 10,000
SALES (est): 662.6K
SALES (corp-wide): 333.02MM **Privately Held**
SIC: 2833 8731 2834 Antibiotics; Commercial physical research; Pharmaceutical preparations
PA: Meridian Bioscience, Inc.
3471 River Hills Dr
Cincinnati OH 45244
513 271-3700

(G-5364)
C P TECHNOLOGIES INC (PA)
Also Called: C P Tek
64 Industrial Park Rd (04072-1840)
PHONE...........................207 286-1167
Robert Levasseur, *Pr*
Lee Adams, *Mgr*
EMP: 13 **EST:** 1987
SQ FT: 8,000
SALES (est): 4.4MM **Privately Held**
Web: www.cptek.com
SIC: 7699 5085 8711 3554 Knife, saw and tool sharpening and repair; Industrial tools; Designing: ship, boat, machine, and product ; Paper industries machinery

(G-5365)
DER-TEX CORPORATION
Also Called: Frelonic
1 Lehner Rd (04072-1837)
PHONE...........................207 284-5931
Michael E Lunder, *Pr*
Cheryl Lunder, *
◆ **EMP:** 45 **EST:** 1943
SQ FT: 100,000
SALES (est): 8.18MM **Privately Held**
Web: www.dertexcorp.com
SIC: 3086 Padding, foamed plastics

(G-5366)
FRANKLIN GRID SOLUTIONS LLC (HQ)
Also Called: Intelligent Controls, Inc.
34 Spring Hill Rd (04072-8607)
P.O. Box 638 (04072-0638)
PHONE...........................207 571-1123
Scott Trumbull, *Pr*
Scott Trumbull, *CEO*

GEOGRAPHIC

Greg Sengstack, *
▲ **EMP:** 35 **EST:** 1978
SQ FT: 13,000
SALES (est): 11.68MM
SALES (corp-wide): 2.04B **Publicly Held**
SIC: 3829 Measuring and controlling
  devices, nec
PA: Franklin Electric Co., Inc.
  9255 Coverdale Rd
  Fort Wayne IN 46809
  260 824-2900

(G-5367)
GARLAND MANUFACTURING CO
55 Industrial Park Rd (04072-1804)
P.O. Box 538 (04072-0538)
PHONE..............................207 283-3693
▲ **EMP:** 39 **EST:** 1866
SALES (est): 4.54MM **Privately Held**
Web: www.garlandmfg.com
SIC: 3423 Hammers (hand tools)

(G-5368)
GENERAL DYNAMICS OTS CAL INC
Also Called: GENERAL DYNAMICS OTS
(CALIFORNIA), INC.
291 North St (04072-1809)
PHONE..............................207 283-3611
Gary Laperriere, *Manager*
EMP: 174
SALES (corp-wide): 42.27B **Publicly Held**
Web: www.gd-ots.com
SIC: 3728 3812 Military aircraft equipment
  and armament; Search and navigation
  equipment
HQ: General Dynamics-Ots, Inc.
  100 Carillon Pkwy Ste 100 # 100
  Saint Petersburg FL 33716
  727 578-8100

(G-5369)
H4 HOLDINGS LLC
Also Called: Signarama Saco
24 Industrial Park Rd Unit 2 (04072-1817)
PHONE..............................207 494-8085
Mindy Hittle, *Prin*
EMP: 7 **EST:** 2015
SALES (est): 376.96K **Privately Held**
Web: www.signarama.com
SIC: 3993 Signs and advertising specialties

(G-5370)
JOHNS MANVILLE CORPORATION
Also Called: N R G Barriers
15 Lund Rd (04072-1806)
P.O. Box 5108 (80217-5108)
PHONE..............................207 283-8000
Michael Edwards, *Mgr*
EMP: 17
SALES (corp-wide): 302.09B **Publicly Held**
Web: www.jm.com
SIC: 3086 Insulation or cushioning material,
  foamed plastics
HQ: Johns Manville Corporation
  717 17th St Ste 800
  Denver CO 80202
  303 978-2000

(G-5371)
LUNDER MANUFACTURING INC
Also Called: Lunder Manufacturing Company
44 Spring Hill Rd (04072-9651)
PHONE..............................207 284-5961
Todd Gillis, *Pr*
▲ **EMP:** 35 **EST:** 1958
SQ FT: 55,000
SALES (est): 2.26MM **Privately Held**

Web: www.lundermanufacturing.com
SIC: 3131 Bows, shoe

(G-5372)
MAINE SEAFOOD VENTURES LLC
1016 Portland Rd (04072-4000)
PHONE..............................207 303-0165
John Ready, *Managing Member*
EMP: 9 **EST:** 2011
SALES (est): 1.01MM **Privately Held**
Web: www.readyseafood.com
SIC: 2092 Seafoods, fresh: prepared

(G-5373)
MERIDIAN LIFE SCIENCE INC (HQ)
Also Called: O.E.M. Concepts, Inc.
60 Industrial Park Rd (04072-1840)
PHONE..............................207 283-6500
Susan Gibney, *Pr*
Sheila Lathrop, *VP*
EMP: 7 **EST:** 1983
SQ FT: 4,200
SALES (est): 23.75MM
SALES (corp-wide): 333.02MM **Privately Held**
Web: www.meridianbioscience.com
SIC: 5122 2835 Biologicals and allied
  products; Microbiology and virology
  diagnostic products
PA: Meridian Bioscience, Inc.
  3471 River Hills Dr
  Cincinnati OH 45244
  513 271-3700

(G-5374)
MINUTEMAN PRESS OF SACO
Also Called: Minuteman Press
110 Main St Ste 1207 (04072-3516)
PHONE..............................207 282-6480
EMP: 7 **EST:** 2019
SALES (est): 83.91K **Privately Held**
Web: www.minutemanpress.com
SIC: 2752 Commercial printing, lithographic

(G-5375)
NIKEL PRECISION GROUP LLC
Also Called: Precision Mfg Solutions
19 Mill Brook Rd (04072-9806)
P.O. Box 974 (04005-0974)
PHONE..............................207 282-6080
John Strautnieks, *Pr*
▲ **EMP:** 70 **EST:** 2003
SQ FT: 30,000
SALES (est): 13.16MM **Privately Held**
Web: www.npg-mfg.com
SIC: 3599 7389 Custom machinery;
  Grinding, precision: commercial or industrial

(G-5376)
POND COVE MILLWORK INC
22 Mill Brook Rd (04072-9806)
PHONE..............................207 773-6819
Peter Flaherty, *Pr*
Tracy Chadbourne, *
EMP: 40 **EST:** 1963
SQ FT: 31,000
SALES (est): 5.21MM **Privately Held**
Web:
www.mainearchitecturalwoodwork.com
SIC: 2431 Millwork

(G-5377)
POWR PT GENERATOR PWR SYSTEMS
11 Mill Brook Rd (04072-8833)
PHONE..............................207 864-2787
EMP: 11 **EST:** 2019

SALES (est): 5.12MM **Privately Held**
Web: www.powrpoint.com
SIC: 3621 Power generators

(G-5378)
QUINCE & COMPANY INC
Also Called: Quince & Co.
102 Main St (04072-3500)
PHONE..............................207 210-6630
Michelle Kohanzo, *CEO*
▲ **EMP:** 26 **EST:** 2010
SALES (est): 3.15MM
SALES (corp-wide): 21.98MM **Privately Held**
Web: www.quinceandco.com
SIC: 5199 2281 Yarns, nec; Wool yarn, spun
PA: Orchard Yarn And Thread Company
  Inc.
  125 Chubb Ave Fl 3
  Lyndhurst NJ 07071
  800 804-3999

(G-5379)
SHED HAPPENS INC (PA)
Also Called: H2ohh
730 Portland Rd (04072-9662)
PHONE..............................207 494-7546
Michael Doherty, *Pr*
Dennis Doherty, *VP*
Tracy Doherty, *Treas*
EMP: 15 **EST:** 1981
SALES (est): 2.13MM **Privately Held**
Web: www.shedhappens.com
SIC: 2511 Wood household furniture

(G-5380)
TRANSPARENT AUDIO INC
47 Industrial Park Rd (04072-1804)
PHONE..............................207 284-1100
Karen J Sumner, *Pr*
Charlton S Smith, *
Charles M Sumner, *
▲ **EMP:** 40 **EST:** 1981
SALES (est): 4.63MM **Privately Held**
Web: www.transparentcable.com
SIC: 3651 3357 Audio electronic systems;
  Nonferrous wiredrawing and insulating

(G-5381)
WENTWORTH TECHNOLOGY INC
331 North St (04072-1815)
PHONE..............................207 571-9744
Dick Hale, *CEO*
Jennifer Barconi, *VP*
Lisa Keslar, *VP*
EMP: 7 **EST:** 2010
SALES (est): 627.99K **Privately Held**
Web: www.speedthrupro.com
SIC: 3669 Intercommunication systems,
  electric

(G-5382)
XURON CORP
62 Industrial Park Rd (04072-1865)
PHONE..............................207 283-1401
Dennis Shores, *Pr*
Robert Dube, *General Vice President*
▲ **EMP:** 40 **EST:** 1971
SQ FT: 8,600
SALES (est): 2.96MM **Privately Held**
Web: www.xuron.com
SIC: 3423 3545 Hand and edge tools, nec;
  Machine tool accessories

(G-5383)
YALE CORDAGE INC
77 Industrial Park Rd (04072-1804)
PHONE..............................207 282-3396
Thomas L Yale, *Pr*

Richard Hildebrand, *
Edward M Schumacher, *
▲ **EMP:** 55 **EST:** 1952
SQ FT: 40,000
SALES (est): 19.2MM **Privately Held**
Web: www.yalecordage.com
SIC: 2298 Twine, nec

(G-5384)
ZAJAC LLC
92 Industrial Park Rd (04072-1861)
PHONE..............................207 286-9100
Matt Reichl, *Genl Mgr*
EMP: 35 **EST:** 2003
SQ FT: 14,000
SALES (est): 10.17MM **Privately Held**
Web: www.zajacllc.com
SIC: 3565 8743 8711 Packaging machinery;
  Sales promotion; Industrial engineers

Saint Agatha
Aroostook County

(G-5385)
AROOSTOOK WOODSMITHS
149 Main St (04772-6142)
P.O. Box 188 (04772-0188)
PHONE..............................207 728-7100
EMP: 7 **EST:** 2010
SALES (est): 230.12K **Privately Held**
Web: www.rfchamberland.com
SIC: 2499 Decorative wood and woodwork

Saint Albans
Somerset County

(G-5386)
SEBASTICOOK LUMBER LLC
446 Hartland Rd (04971-7432)
P.O. Box 51 (04971-0051)
PHONE..............................207 660-1360
EMP: 7 **EST:** 2016
SALES (est): 485.48K **Privately Held**
SIC: 2421 Sawmills and planing mills,
  general

Saint Francis
Aroostook County

(G-5387)
BP LOGGING
562 Main St (04774-3114)
PHONE..............................207 398-4457
Buddy Pelletier, *Prin*
EMP: 7 **EST:** 2010
SALES (est): 165.6K **Privately Held**
SIC: 2411 Logging camps and contractors

(G-5388)
ROBERT MCBREAIRTY JR SONS INC
1013 Main St (04774-3201)
PHONE..............................207 834-3257
Robert Mc Breairty Junior, *Pr*
Beverly Mc Breairty, *Treas*
EMP: 15 **EST:** 1972
SQ FT: 500
SALES (est): 1.93MM **Privately Held**
SIC: 1794 2411 Excavation work; Logging
  camps and contractors

▲ = Import ▼ = Export
◆ = Import/Export

Sanford
York County

(G-5389)
ADVANCED BUILDING PRODUCTS INC
95 Cyro Dr (04073-2551)
P.O. Box 98 (04083-0098)
PHONE..............................207 490-2306
Richard Lolley, *Pr*
Kenneth Roy, *Ex VP*
▲ EMP: 16 EST: 1989
SQ FT: 30,000
SALES (est): 5.07MM Privately Held
Web:
www.advancedbuildingproducts.com
SIC: 3351 3083 Copper rolling and drawing;
Plastics finished products, laminated

(G-5390)
BAKER COMPANY INC (PA)
Also Called: Baker Company, The
175 Gate House Rd (04073-2482)
PHONE..............................207 324-8773
Dennis Eagleson, *Ch Bd*
David C Eagleson, *
Sidney St Felix Thaxter Ii, *Clerk*
◆ EMP: 144 EST: 1949
SQ FT: 140,000
SALES (est): 38.27MM
SALES (corp-wide): 38.27MM Privately
Held
Web: www.bakerco.com
SIC: 3821 3644 5047 Laboratory apparatus
and furniture; Noncurrent-carrying wiring
devices; Medical equipment and supplies

(G-5391)
CENTRAL TIRE CO INC (PA)
1307 Main St (04073-3633)
P.O. Box 152 (04073-0152)
PHONE..............................207 324-4250
Rene Therrien, *Pr*
Douglas Therrien, *
Jeff Therrien, *
▲ EMP: 23 EST: 1939
SQ FT: 20,000
SALES (est): 10.81MM
SALES (corp-wide): 10.81MM Privately
Held
Web: www.mainehost.com
SIC: 5014 7534 5531 7538 Automobile tires
and tubes; Rebuilding and retreading tires;
Automotive tires; General automotive repair
shops

(G-5392)
COLGATE - PALMOLIVE COMPANY
27 Community Dr (04073-5809)
PHONE..............................207 467-2224
EMP: 8 EST: 2014
SALES (est): 433.79K Privately Held
Web: www.tomsofmaine.com
SIC: 2844 Perfumes, cosmetics and other
toilet preparations

(G-5393)
CYRO INDUSTRY
1796 Main St (04073-2458)
PHONE..............................207 324-6000
Ralph Stevens, *Prin*
EMP: 10 EST: 2015
SALES (est): 829.4K Privately Held
Web: www.cyplus.com
SIC: 2821 Plastics materials and resins

(G-5394)
EKTO MANUFACTURING CORP
83 Eagle Dr (04073-5814)
P.O. Box 449 (04073-0449)
PHONE..............................207 324-4427
Karl F Epper, *Pr*
Jacqueline Epper, *
Karen Littlefield, *
▼ EMP: 22 EST: 1968
SQ FT: 50,000
SALES (est): 2.43MM Privately Held
Web: www.ekto.com
SIC: 3448 3444 Buildings, portable:
prefabricated metal; Sheet metalwork

(G-5395)
EXPANDED RUBBER PRODUCTS INC (PA)
41 Industrial Ave (04073-5820)
P.O. Box 1070 (04073-1070)
PHONE..............................207 324-8226
Barbara G Ney, *Pr*
J Clayton Ney Junior, *VP*
Robert Ney, *
Yvonne M Ney, *
EMP: 42 EST: 1968
SQ FT: 42,000
SALES (est): 6.12MM
SALES (corp-wide): 6.12MM Privately
Held
Web:
www.expandedrubberproducts.com
SIC: 3069 Sponge rubber and sponge
rubber products

(G-5396)
FLEMISH MASTER WEAVERS INC
96 Gate House Rd (04073-2484)
PHONE..............................207 324-6600
Johan Moulin, *Pr*
Ellen Ross, *
Michael Litner, *
▲ EMP: 150 EST: 1988
SQ FT: 150,000
SALES (est): 25.32MM
SALES (corp-wide): 5.26K Privately Held
Web: www.rainbowrugs.com
SIC: 2273 Rugs, hand and machine made
PA: Natco Products Corporation
155 Brookside Ave
West Warwick RI 02893
401 828-0300

(G-5397)
GETCHELL BROS INC
1913 Main St (04073-4407)
PHONE..............................207 490-0809
TOLL FREE: 800
Bob Morse, *CEO*
EMP: 15
SALES (corp-wide): 9.16MM Privately
Held
Web: www.arcticglacier.com
SIC: 2097 5143 5142 5999 Manufactured ice
; Dairy products, except dried or canned;
Packaged frozen goods; Ice
PA: Getchell Bros. Inc.
1 Union St
Brewer ME 04412
800 949-4423

(G-5398)
MAINE MANUFACTURING LLC
Also Called: Gvs North America
63 Community Dr (04073-5809)
PHONE..............................207 324-1754
Bill Emhiser, *Pr*
Craig Cunningham, *
▲ EMP: 97 EST: 2006

SALES (est): 23.58MM Privately Held
Web: www.gvs.com
SIC: 3089 Injection molded finished plastics
products, nec
HQ: Gvs Spa
Via Roma 50
Zola Predosa BO 40069
051 616-6527

(G-5399)
MAINE STOVE & CHIMNEY LLC
Also Called: Flue Master
1438 Main St (04073-2426)
P.O. Box 498 (04020-0498)
PHONE..............................207 324-4440
EMP: 8 EST: 2007
SALES (est): 915.33K Privately Held
Web: www.mainestoveandchimney.com
SIC: 1741 3433 Chimney construction and
maintenance; Stoves, wood and coal
burning

(G-5400)
MARJA CORPORATION
Also Called: Electronic Assembly Service
14 Dale St (04073-3108)
P.O. Box 431 (04073-0431)
PHONE..............................207 324-2994
Anna Grondin, *Pr*
Robert Frechette Junior, *VP*
Anna Grondin, *Sec*
EMP: 16 EST: 1986
SQ FT: 6,000
SALES (est): 2.24MM Privately Held
Web: www.marja.com
SIC: 3672 Printed circuit boards

(G-5401)
NEW ENGLAND BUILDING MATERIALS LLC
Also Called: True Value
563 New Dam Rd (04073-5703)
PHONE..............................207 324-3350
TOLL FREE: 800
EMP: 253
SIC: 5211 2421 Millwork and lumber;
Lumber: rough, sawed, or planed

(G-5402)
NEW ENGLAND TRCK TIRE CTRS INC (PA)
38 Rainbow Ln (04073-2492)
PHONE..............................207 324-2262
John Stevens, *Pr*
Jd Stevens, *Treas*
Robert Tellefsen, *Sec*
Brian Davis, *CFO*
EMP: 22 EST: 1994
SQ FT: 26,000
SALES (est): 32.45MM Privately Held
Web: www.netrucktire.com
SIC: 5014 3011 7534 Automobile tires and
tubes; Retreading materials, tire; Tire
retreading and repair shops

(G-5403)
NORTH COUNTRY TRACTOR INC
Also Called: John Deere Authorized Dealer
8 Shaws Ridge Rd (04073-6210)
PHONE..............................207 324-5646
Tom Swan, *Brnch Mgr*
EMP: 10
Web: www.deere.com
SIC: 3537 5082 Industrial trucks and tractors
; Construction and mining machinery
PA: North Country Tractor, Inc.
149 Sheep Davis Rd
Pembroke NH 03275

(G-5404)
OIZERO9 INC
Also Called: Province Automation
31 Smada Dr (04073-5824)
P.O. Box 690 (04073-0690)
PHONE..............................207 324-3582
Dan Richer, *Pr*
EMP: 22 EST: 2004
SQ FT: 16,000
SALES (est): 1.99MM Privately Held
Web: www.provinceautomation.com
SIC: 3569 3599 5084 8711 Assembly
machines, non-metalworking; Machine
shop, jobbing and repair; Processing and
packaging equipment; Mechanical
engineering

(G-5405)
PEPIN PRECAST INC
59 Shaw Rd (04073-6201)
PHONE..............................207 324-6125
David Pepin, *Prin*
Matthew Pepin, *Prin*
Luke Pepin, *Prin*
EMP: 12 EST: 2016
SALES (est): 696.07K Privately Held
SIC: 3272 Concrete products, nec

(G-5406)
PRINTEMSCOM
2066 Main St (04073-4444)
PHONE..............................207 490-5118
EMP: 8 EST: 2017
SALES (est): 131.12K Privately Held
Web: www.printems.com
SIC: 2752 Offset printing

(G-5407)
R PEPIN & SONS INC
59 Shaw Rd (04073-6201)
P.O. Box 729 (04073-0729)
PHONE..............................207 324-6125
David Pepin, *Pr*
Rudy Pepin, *
EMP: 25 EST: 1952
SQ FT: 4,000
SALES (est): 4.26MM Privately Held
Web: www.rpepin.com
SIC: 3273 5032 Ready-mixed concrete;
Gravel

(G-5408)
R&V INDUSTRIES INC
Also Called: Shape Global Technologies
90 Community Dr (04073-5810)
PHONE..............................207 324-5200
Vincent Boragine, *Pr*
Richard Courcy, *
EMP: 31 EST: 2001
SQ FT: 44,000
SALES (est): 1.05MM Privately Held
SIC: 3089 Injection molding of plastics

(G-5409)
RENAISSANCE GREETING CARDS INC
Also Called: Renaissance Greeting Cards
10 Renaissance Way (04073-3636)
PHONE..............................207 324-4153
Dan Stevers, *Pr*
◆ EMP: 25 EST: 1977
SQ FT: 35,000
SALES (est): 821.16K Privately Held
Web: www.securerms.com
SIC: 2771 5947 Greeting cards; Greeting
cards

(G-5410)
RH ROSENFIELD CO
Also Called: Edison Press
2066 Main St (04073-4444)
PHONE.................................207 324-1798
Robert H Rosenfield, *Pr*
Ronald Bourque, *
Susan Rosenfield, *
EMP: 30 **EST:** 1978
SQ FT: 4,000
SALES (est): 4.98MM **Privately Held**
Web: www.edisonpress.com
SIC: 2752 2711 Offset printing; Commercial
    printing and newspaper publishing
    combined

(G-5411)
RICHARD GENEST INC
Also Called: Genest Precast
238 Country Club Rd (04073-5225)
PHONE.................................207 324-7215
Richard Genest, *Pr*
Rita Genest, *VP*
EMP: 13 **EST:** 1984
SQ FT: 13,000
SALES (est): 2.36MM **Privately Held**
Web: www.genestprecast.com
SIC: 3272 Septic tanks, concrete

(G-5412)
ROEHM AMERICA LLC
Also Called: Sanford Manufacturing Facility
1796 Main St (04073-2458)
PHONE.................................207 324-6000
Richard Healy, *Mgr*
EMP: 48
SALES (corp-wide): 2.67MM **Privately Held**
Web: www.roehm.com
SIC: 2821 Plastics materials and resins
HQ: Roehm America Llc
    8 Campus Dr Ste 1
    Parsippany NJ 07054
    800 225-0172

(G-5413)
RUBB INC
Also Called: Rubb Building Systems
1 Rubb Ln (04073-2231)
P.O. Box 711 (04073-0711)
PHONE.................................207 324-2877
David Nickerson, *Pr*
Jacqueline Berard, *
▲ **EMP:** 55 **EST:** 1983
SALES (est): 17.39MM **Privately Held**
Web: www.rubbindustries.com
SIC: 3448 Prefabricated metal buildings

(G-5414)
SALTY CULTIVATION LLC
72 Emery St Ste 14 (04073-3160)
PHONE.................................207 752-7549
Justin Graves, *Managing Member*
EMP: 10 **EST:** 2018
SALES (est): 357.85K **Privately Held**
SIC: 7372 Prepackaged software

(G-5415)
SHAINS
Also Called: Shain's of Maine Ice Cream
1491 Main St (04073-2460)
P.O. Box 610 (04073-0610)
PHONE.................................207 324-1449
Rodney A Shain Senior, *Pr*
Jeffrey Shain, *
Rodney A Shain Junior, *Clerk*
EMP: 53 **EST:** 1968
SQ FT: 7,000
SALES (est): 1.09MM **Privately Held**

SIC: 5812 5451 5143 2024 Restaurant,
    family: independent; Ice cream (packaged);
    Ice cream and ices; Ice cream and frozen
    deserts

(G-5416)
U S FELT COMPANY INC
61 Industrial Ave (04073-5820)
PHONE.................................207 324-0063
Vincent Boragine, *Pr*
EMP: 42 **EST:** 2007
SALES (est): 4.38MM **Privately Held**
Web: www.usfelt.com
SIC: 2231 5199 Felts, woven: wool, mohair,
    or similar fibers; Felt

(G-5417)
W S BESSETT INC
1923 Main St (04073-4407)
PHONE.................................207 324-9232
Harold E Waitt, *Pr*
Gerry Waitt, *Treas*
Michael Waitt, *VP*
EMP: 20 **EST:** 1925
SQ FT: 9,600
SALES (est): 945.64K **Privately Held**
Web: www.wsbessett.com
SIC: 3639 3599 5722 Sewing machines and
    attachments, domestic; Machine shop,
    jobbing and repair; Sewing machines

(G-5418)
YORK MANUFACTURING INC
43 Community Dr (04073-5809)
PHONE.................................207 324-1300
Geoffrey G Magnuson, *CEO*
Craig Wetmore, *Pr*
EMP: 12 **EST:** 1935
SQ FT: 21,000
SALES (est): 227.23K **Privately Held**
Web: www.yorkflashings.com
SIC: 3351 3083 Copper rolling and drawing;
    Plastics finished products, laminated

Sangerville
Piscataquis County

(G-5419)
ERNEST R PALMER LUMBER CO INC
30 N Dexter Rd (04479-3309)
P.O. Box 128 (04479-0128)
PHONE.................................207 876-2725
John Armstrong, *Pr*
David E Armstrong, *VP*
EMP: 8 **EST:** 1930
SALES (est): 735.88K **Privately Held**
SIC: 2426 5211 Furniture squares,
    hardwood; Planing mill products and lumber

(G-5420)
NUMBERALL STAMP & TOOL CO
1 High St (04479-3124)
P.O. Box 187 (04479-0187)
PHONE.................................207 876-3541
Herman Bayerdorffer, *Pr*
Cynthia Bayerdorffer, *Treas*
EMP: 19 **EST:** 1930
SQ FT: 18,000
SALES (est): 2.25MM **Privately Held**
Web: www.numberall.com
SIC: 3469 Stamping metal for the trade

Scarborough
Cumberland County

(G-5421)
ALERE INC
10 Southgate Rd (04074-8303)
PHONE.................................207 730-5714
EMP: 51 **EST:** 2016
SALES (est): 909.45K **Privately Held**
Web: www.globalpointofcare.abbott
SIC: 2835 Diagnostic substances

(G-5422)
ALLEN SCREEN PRINTING
Also Called: Allen Science With Impact
25 Washington Ave (04074-9782)
PHONE.................................207 510-6800
EMP: 40
SIC: 2759 Screen printing

(G-5423)
AMERICAN HEALTHCARE
6 Lincoln Ave (04074-7706)
PHONE.................................888 567-7733
Jeff Lord, *Pr*
EMP: 12 **EST:** 1998
SALES (est): 631.85K **Privately Held**
SIC: 3826 Automatic chemical analyzers

(G-5424)
BARRINGER INDUSTRIES LLC
Also Called: Rainbow Intl Greater Portland
2 Washington Ave (04074-8310)
PHONE.................................207 730-7125
Benjamin Barringer, *Pr*
EMP: 12 **EST:** 2011
SALES (est): 1.04MM **Privately Held**
Web: www.rainbowgreaterportland.com
SIC: 3999 Manufacturing industries, nec

(G-5425)
BLACK COVE CABINETRY
137 Pleasant Hill Rd (04074-9309)
PHONE.................................207 883-8901
Bill Livendosky, *Owner*
Bill Levandowski, *Owner*
EMP: 8 **EST:** 2001
SALES (est): 386.54K **Privately Held**
SIC: 2434 Wood kitchen cabinets

(G-5426)
BLUE BARN LLC
Also Called: Bluet
15 Washington Ave Unit 9 (04074-8280)
P.O. Box 95 (94559-0095)
PHONE.................................207 536-8002
Michael Terrien, *Prin*
Eric Martin, *Prin*
EMP: 9 **EST:** 2016
SALES (est): 413.23K **Privately Held**
Web: www.bluet.me
SIC: 2084 Wine cellars, bonded: engaged in
    blending wines

(G-5427)
CASELLA RECYCLING LLC (HQ)
13 Gibson Rd (04074-8333)
P.O. Box 1364 (05495-1364)
PHONE.................................207 883-4600
John Casella, *Managing Member*
▲ **EMP:** 23 **EST:** 1919
SQ FT: 60,000
SALES (est): 22.18MM **Publicly Held**
SIC: 5093 2611 Waste paper; Pulp mills
PA: Casella Waste Systems, Inc.
    25 Greens Hill Ln
    Rutland VT 05701

(G-5428)
CHEP
7 Washington Ave (04074-9782)
PHONE.................................207 883-0244
EMP: 7 **EST:** 2017
SALES (est): 83.07K **Privately Held**
SIC: 2448 Pallets, wood

(G-5429)
CROWN EQUIPMENT CORPORATION
Also Called: Crown Lift Trucks
165 Innovation Way (04074-6502)
PHONE.................................207 773-4049
TOLL FREE: 888
EMP: 46
SALES (corp-wide): 7.12B **Privately Held**
Web: www.crown.com
SIC: 3537 Lift trucks, industrial: fork,
    platform, straddle, etc.
PA: Crown Equipment Corporation
    44 S Washington St
    New Bremen OH 45869
    419 629-2311

(G-5430)
DAVIS-JONCAS ENTERPRISES INC
Also Called: Welch Stencil Company
7 Lincoln Ave (04074-9783)
PHONE.................................207 883-6200
TOLL FREE: 800
EMP: 27
SIC: 3993 7312 3953 Signs and advertising
    specialties; Outdoor advertising services;
    Postmark stamps, hand: rubber or metal

(G-5431)
DERMALOGIX PARTNERS INC
672 Us Route 1 (04074-9745)
PHONE.................................207 883-4103
James Kerr, *Pr*
George Kerr, *Pr*
EMP: 14 **EST:** 1996
SALES (est): 874.25K **Privately Held**
Web: www.dermazinc.com
SIC: 2834 Pharmaceutical preparations

(G-5432)
GAUSS CORPORATION
Also Called: Electrodyne Systems
1 Gibson Rd (04074-8333)
P.O. Box 877 (74067-0877)
PHONE.................................207 883-4121
Robert D Sampson, *Pr*
Robert D Sampson, *Pr*
Robert C Robinson, *Clerk*
EMP: 15 **EST:** 1979
SALES (est): 1.78MM **Privately Held**
Web: www.electrodyneinc.com
SIC: 3694 Alternators, automotive

(G-5433)
GLIDDEN SIGNS INC
Also Called: Burr Signs
40a Manson Libby Rd (04074-7985)
PHONE.................................207 396-6111
Jess Glidden, *Pr*
EMP: 12 **EST:** 2016
SALES (est): 916.6K **Privately Held**
SIC: 3993 Electric signs

(G-5434)
ITLLBE LLC
Also Called: It'll Be Pizza
5 Lincoln Ave (04074-9783)
PHONE.................................207 730-7301
EMP: 8 **EST:** 2003
SALES (est): 2.45MM **Privately Held**

Web: www.itllbe.com
SIC: 2041 Pizza dough, prepared

(G-5435)
JAMES A MCBRADY INC
29 Parkway Dr (04074-7155)
P.O. Box 8239 (04104-8239)
PHONE..............................207 883-4176
James Mcbrady Junior, *Pr*
Helen Mcbrady, *VP*
EMP: 20 EST: 1954
SQ FT: 50,000
SALES (est): 4.46MM **Privately Held**
Web: www.mcbradysteel.com
SIC: 3441 1791 Fabricated structural metal;
  Structural steel erection

(G-5436)
KINETICS GROUP INC
3 Glasgow Rd (04074-8781)
PHONE..............................207 541-4712
Ken Brousseau, *Mgr*
EMP: 10 EST: 2005
SALES (est): 871.08K **Privately Held**
Web: www.kinetics.net
SIC: 3444 Sheet metalwork

(G-5437)
LEN LIBBYS INC
Also Called: Len Libby Candy Shops
419 Us Route 1 (04074-9705)
P.O. Box 657 (04070-0657)
PHONE..............................207 883-4897
Maureen Hemond, *Pr*
EMP: 13 EST: 1926
SQ FT: 5,000
SALES (est): 346.93K **Privately Held**
Web: www.lenlibby.com
SIC: 2064 5441 Candy and other
  confectionery products; Confectionery

(G-5438)
MAINE RADIO
68 Mussey Rd (04074-8921)
P.O. Box 7264 (04070-7264)
PHONE..............................207 883-2929
TOLL FREE: 800
EMP: 10 EST: 1995
SQ FT: 4,000
SALES (est): 2.06MM **Privately Held**
Web: www.maineradios.com
SIC: 3663 4812 Radio broadcasting and
  communications equipment;
  Radiotelephone communication

(G-5439)
N E TECH-AIR INC
Also Called: N.E. Tech Air
16 Manson Libby Rd (04074-9820)
PHONE..............................207 347-7577
Robert Lilly, *Pr*
Norman Locke, *
EMP: 168 EST: 1986
SQ FT: 12,960
SALES (est): 25.53MM **Privately Held**
Web: www.netechair.com
SIC: 1761 3585 3567 3564 Sheet metal
  work; Refrigeration and heating
  equipment; Industrial furnaces and ovens;
  Blowers and fans

(G-5440)
**NONESUCH RIVER BREWING
LLC**
201 Gorham Rd (04074-8970)
PHONE..............................207 219-8948
EMP: 26 EST: 2019
SALES (est): 1.8MM **Privately Held**
Web: www.nonesuchriverbrewing.com

SIC: 5813 2082 Bar (drinking places); Beer
  (alcoholic beverage)

(G-5441)
**NORTH AMERICAN SUPAFLU
SYSTEMS**
15 Holly St Ste 201b (04074-8867)
PHONE..............................207 883-1155
TOLL FREE: 800
Frederick E Howes, *Pr*
EMP: 10 EST: 1995
SQ FT: 4,000
SALES (est): 671.23K **Privately Held**
Web: www.supaflu.com
SIC: 3259 5039 1741 Clay chimney products
  ; Flue linings; Chimney construction and
  maintenance

(G-5442)
NOVEL BEVERAGE CO
137 Pleasant Hill Rd (04074-9309)
PHONE..............................207 798-9610
Matthew Hawes, *CEO*
Richard Rohl, *COO*
EMP: 7 EST: 2020
SALES (est): 455.78K **Privately Held**
Web: www.novelbeverage.com
SIC: 2833 Medicinals and botanicals

(G-5443)
STERN SEAFOOD INC
96 King St (04074-9292)
PHONE..............................207 303-8466
Susan Clough, *Prin*
Vincent Clough, *Prin*
William Bayley, *Prin*
EMP: 8 EST: 2019
SALES (est): 538.83K **Privately Held**
Web: www.sternseafood.com
SIC: 2092 Fresh or frozen packaged fish

(G-5444)
**TA PROPERTY MAINTENANCE
LLC**
81 Sawyer Rd (04074-9143)
PHONE..............................207 289-7158
Caden Ta, *Prin*
EMP: 11 EST: 2019
SALES (est): 588.32K **Privately Held**
SIC: 2952 7389 Asphalt felts and coatings;
  Business services, nec

(G-5445)
THOMAS HALL
Also Called: Local207
175 Black Point Rd (04074-9351)
P.O. Box 6877 (04070-6877)
PHONE..............................207 956-0020
Thomas Hall, *Pr*
EMP: 16 EST: 2000
SALES (est): 1.22MM **Privately Held**
Web: www.hallme.com
SIC: 3949 8742 Surfboards; Marketing
  consulting services

(G-5446)
TRI-STATE PACKING SUPPLY
158 Pleasant Hill Rd (04074-8764)
P.O. Box 416 (04070-0416)
PHONE..............................207 883-5218
James Finley, *Pr*
William Finley, *VP*
Verna Finley, *Treas*
Richard Davis, *Clerk*
EMP: 11 EST: 1973
SQ FT: 15,000
SALES (est): 2.02MM **Privately Held**
Web: www.tristatepacking.com

SIC: 5085 3599 Seals, industrial; Machine
  shop, jobbing and repair

(G-5447)
WESTROCK
16 Washington Ave (04074-8311)
PHONE..............................770 448-2193
Robert Swift, *Prin*
EMP: 11 EST: 2019
SALES (est): 892.84K **Privately Held**
Web: www.westrock.com
SIC: 2653 Boxes, corrugated: made from
  purchased materials

(G-5448)
**YOKOGAWA FLUID IMGING
TECH INC**
200 Enterprise Dr (04074-7636)
PHONE..............................207 289-3200
Kent Peterson, *CEO*
Christian K Sieracki, *Pr*
Ali Naqui, *COO*
EMP: 28 EST: 1999
SALES (est): 11.4MM **Privately Held**
Web: www.fluidimaging.com
SIC: 3826 Analytical instruments
PA: Yokogawa Electric Corporation
  2-9-32, Nakacho
  Musashino TKY 180-0

Searsmont
Waldo County

(G-5449)
ECOCOR LLC
22 Main St N (04973-3409)
PHONE..............................207 342-2085
Christian Corson, *Managing Member*
EMP: 20 EST: 2013
SALES (est): 2.4MM **Privately Held**
Web: www.ecocor.us
SIC: 1522 2452 Residential construction,
  nec; Prefabricated wood buildings

(G-5450)
ROBBINS LUMBER INC (PA)
Also Called: Lumber Manufacturer
53 Ghent Rd (04973-3123)
PHONE..............................207 342-5221
James A Robbins, *Pr*
Alden J Robbins, *
EMP: 125 EST: 1881
SQ FT: 2,400
SALES (est): 28.95MM
SALES (corp-wide): 28.95MM **Privately
Held**
Web: www.rlco.com
SIC: 2421 2611 Lumber: rough, sawed, or
  planed; Pulp mills

Searsport
Waldo County

(G-5451)
BLUEJACKET INC
Also Called: Laughing Whale
160 E Main St (04974-3311)
PHONE..............................207 548-9970
EMP: 10 EST: 1991
SQ FT: 5,500
SALES (est): 720.04K **Privately Held**
Web: www.bluejacketinc.com
SIC: 3944 5945 5092 Boat and ship models,
  toy and hobby; Models, toy and hobby;
  Model kits

(G-5452)
DALEGIP AMERICA INC
34 Kidder Point Rd (04974-3111)
PHONE..............................207 323-1880
Hector Rivadeneyra Diaz, *Pr*
▲ **EMP: 20 EST:** 2012
SALES (est): 2.39MM **Privately Held**
Web: www.gacchemical.com
SIC: 2819 Industrial inorganic chemicals,
  nec

(G-5453)
**GAC CHEMICAL CORPORATION
(PA)**
34 Kidder Point Rd (04974-3111)
PHONE..............................207 548-2525
James A Poure, *CEO*
Barbara Haase, *
David Colter, *
◆ **EMP: 55 EST:** 1994
SALES (est): 24.01MM **Privately Held**
Web: www.gacchemical.com
SIC: 2819 2873 5169 5084 Aluminum sulfate
  ; Ammonium nitrate, ammonium sulfate;
  Chemicals and allied products, nec;
  Chemical process equipment

(G-5454)
**GENERAL ALUM NEW
ENGLAND CORP**
Also Called: Gac Chemical
34 Kidder Point Rd (04974-3111)
PHONE..............................207 548-2525
David Colter, *CEO*
James A Poure, *
David M Colter, *
Barbara S Haase, *
▼ **EMP: 60 EST:** 1978
SQ FT: 3,000
SALES (est): 10.06MM **Privately Held**
Web: www.gacchemical.com
SIC: 2819 Aluminum sulfate
PA: Gac Chemical Corporation
  34 Kidder Point Rd
  Searsport ME 04974

(G-5455)
IMERYS
70 Trundy Rd (04974-6300)
PHONE..............................207 548-0900
EMP: 8 EST: 2016
SALES (est): 111.35K **Privately Held**
Web: www.imerys.com
SIC: 3295 Minerals, ground or treated

Sebec
Piscataquis County

(G-5456)
BEN SAVAGE LOGGING INC
30 North Rd (04481-3009)
PHONE..............................207 735-6699
Ben Savage, *Prin*
EMP: 7 EST: 2013
SALES (est): 223.44K **Privately Held**
SIC: 2411 Logging camps and contractors

(G-5457)
SDR LOGGING INC
Also Called: Ames Construction
629 Sebec Village Rd (04481-3104)
PHONE..............................207 564-8534
EMP: 30 EST: 1986
SALES (est): 2.5MM **Privately Held**
SIC: 2411 Logging camps and contractors

GEOGRAPHIC

Shapleigh
York County

(G-5458)
NORMAN WHITE INC
Also Called: White's Logging & Chipping
28 Grant Rd (04076-4137)
PHONE.............................207 636-1636
David White, *Pr*
Sandy White, *Treas*
EMP: 7 **EST:** 1985
SALES (est): 996.43K **Privately Held**
SIC: 2411　Logging camps and contractors

Sidney
Kennebec County

(G-5459)
J & M LOGGING INC
35 Harold Dr (04330-2012)
PHONE.............................207 622-6353
James Hasco, *Pr*
EMP: 7 **EST:** 1983
SALES (est): 296.45K **Privately Held**
SIC: 2411　Logging camps and contractors

(G-5460)
R N HASKINS PRINTING INC
1795 Pond Rd (04330-1932)
P.O. Box 97 (04963-0097)
PHONE.............................207 465-2155
Richard Haskins, *Pr*
Barbara Haskins, *VP*
EMP: 10 **EST:** 1987
SQ FT: 10,000
SALES (est): 790.16K **Privately Held**
Web: www.rnhaskins.com
SIC: 2752　Offset printing

(G-5461)
**TREES LTD A PARTNR
CONSISTING**
2506 Middle Rd (04330-2840)
PHONE.............................207 547-3168
Donny Cole, *Pr*
EMP: 7 **EST:** 2001
SALES (est): 839.54K **Privately Held**
SIC: 2411　Logging camps and contractors

Skowhegan
Somerset County

(G-5462)
AMBROSE G MCCARTHY JR
Also Called: CAM Logging
228 North Ave (04976-2144)
PHONE.............................207 474-8837
Ambrose G Mccarthy Junior, *Owner*
Ambrose G Mccarthy, *Owner*
EMP: 8 **EST:** 1971
SQ FT: 5,400
SALES (est): 374.84K **Privately Held**
Web: www.centralmainewreath.com
SIC: 2411 7389 5499 5199　Logging; Bottle
　exchange; Soft drinks; Christmas novelties

(G-5463)
BROMAR
Also Called: Skowhegan Press
17 Parlin St (04976-2142)
PHONE.............................207 474-3784
Jeremy Martinez, *Pr*
Joseph Breault, *VP*
EMP: 7 **EST:** 1925
SQ FT: 4,800

SALES (est): 993.31K **Privately Held**
Web: www.bromarprinting.com
SIC: 2752　Offset printing

(G-5464)
CARRIER CHIPPING INC
100 Carrier Ln (04976)
PHONE.............................207 858-4277
Suzanne Carrier, *Pr*
EMP: 9 **EST:** 1989
SALES (est): 379.05K **Privately Held**
SIC: 2421　Chipper mill

(G-5465)
CENTRAL MAINE DAIRY EQP INC
Also Called: Farmhand Express
793 Skowhegan Rd (04976)
P.O. Box 73 (04944-0073)
PHONE.............................207 453-6727
EMP: 9 **EST:** 2016
SALES (est): 371.29K **Privately Held**
SIC: 3523　Dairy equipment (farm), nec

(G-5466)
DIRIGO STITCHING INC
40 Dane Ave (04976-2048)
P.O. Box 447 (04976-0447)
PHONE.............................207 474-8421
TOLL FREE: 800
Peter Schultz, *Pr*
Caesar J Schiraldi, *
Herbert E Paradis, *
EMP: 25 **EST:** 1979
SQ FT: 53,000
SALES (est): 446.51K **Privately Held**
Web: www.mainestitching.com
SIC: 2391 2392　Curtains and draperies;
　Household furnishings, nec

(G-5467)
GENPLEX INC
7 Industrial Park Rd Ste 1 (04976-4016)
PHONE.............................207 474-3500
EMP: 7 **EST:** 1993
SQ FT: 10,000
SALES (est): 1.04MM **Privately Held**
Web: www.genplex.com
SIC: 3089　Extruded finished plastics
　products, nec

(G-5468)
HOWARD P FAIRFIELD LLC (DH)
Also Called: Skowhegan Machine
9 Green St (04976-1159)
P.O. Box 188 (04976-0188)
PHONE.............................207 474-9836
Ron Woodbrey, *Ex VP*
Howard E Sevey, *Managing Member*
EMP: 45 **EST:** 1951
SQ FT: 74,000
SALES (est): 9MM
SALES (corp-wide): 1.51B **Publicly Held**
Web: www.hpfairfield.com
SIC: 3531 3991　Blades for graders,
　scrapers, dozers, and snow plows; Street
　sweeping brooms, hand or machine
HQ: Alamo Group (Usa) Inc.
　1627 E Walnut St
　Seguin TX 78155
　830 379-1480

(G-5469)
IMERYS USA INC
1329 Waterville Rd (04976-4908)
PHONE.............................207 238-9267
Mike Blevins, *Brnch Mgr*
EMP: 24
SALES (corp-wide): 3.28MM **Privately
Held**
Web: www.imerys.com

SIC: 2819　Industrial inorganic chemicals,
　nec
HQ: Imerys Usa, Inc.
　100 Mansell Ct E Ste 300
　Roswell GA 30076
　770 645-3300

(G-5470)
J & M MACHINING INC
Also Called: Precision Programming
313 North Ave (04976-4021)
PHONE.............................207 474-7300
Mark Hunter, *Pr*
Danny Slaney, *VP*
EMP: 13 **EST:** 2000
SQ FT: 10,000
SALES (est): 2.36MM **Privately Held**
Web: www.jmmach.com
SIC: 3599 7389　Machine shop, jobbing and
　repair; Finishing services

(G-5471)
MAINE GRAINS INC
42 Court St (04976-1808)
PHONE.............................207 474-8001
Amber Lambke, *Pr*
Michael Scholz, *VP*
EMP: 20 **EST:** 2008
SALES (est): 1.5MM **Privately Held**
Web: www.mainegrains.com
SIC: 2041 0723　Flour mills, cereal (except
　rice); Flour milling, custom services

(G-5472)
MAINE STITCHING SPC LLC
Also Called: Maine Innkeepers Association
40 Dane Ave (04976-2048)
P.O. Box 256 (04947-0256)
PHONE.............................207 812-5207
William Swain, *Managing Member*
EMP: 13 **EST:** 2014
SQ FT: 45,000
SALES (est): 880.53K **Privately Held**
Web: www.mainestitching.com
SIC: 3552 5714　Finishing machinery, textile;
　Drapery and upholstery stores

(G-5473)
MASTERCRAFT INC
371 W Front St (04976-5102)
PHONE.............................207 431-2056
Brandon Craft, *Prin*
EMP: 10 **EST:** 2015
SALES (est): 325K **Privately Held**
SIC: 3732　Boatbuilding and repairing

(G-5474)
NEW BALANCE ATHLETICS INC
Also Called: Showhegan New Balance
10 Walnut St (04976-1513)
PHONE.............................207 474-2042
Sheldon Kilkenny, *Mgr*
EMP: 15
SALES (corp-wide): 17.22MM **Privately
Held**
Web: www.newbalance.com
SIC: 3149 3021　Athletic shoes, except
　rubber or plastic; Rubber and plastics
　footwear
HQ: New Balance Athletics, Inc.
　100 Guest St
　Boston MA 02135
　617 783-4000

(G-5475)
NORTHEAST DORAN INC
North Ave Industrial Park (04976)
P.O. Box 1042 (04976-1042)
PHONE.............................207 474-2000
Donald Williams, *Pr*

EMP: 8 **EST:** 1990
SQ FT: 3,000
SALES (est): 958.9K **Privately Held**
Web: www.northeastdoran.com
SIC: 3599　Machine shop, jobbing and repair

(G-5476)
**NORTHEAST MERCHANDISING
CORP**
Also Called: Northeast Coffee Company
60 Southgate Pkwy (04976-4975)
P.O. Box 446 (04976-0446)
PHONE.............................207 474-3321
TOLL FREE: 800
Daniel R Davis, *Pr*
John A Davis Senior, *Ch Bd*
Donald Davis, *
David Davis, *
EMP: 35 **EST:** 1973
SQ FT: 15,000
SALES (est): 4.63MM **Privately Held**
SIC: 5149 2086　Coffee, green or roasted;
　Water, natural: packaged in cans, bottles,
　etc.

(G-5477)
SAPPI NORTH AMERICA INC
Also Called: Sappi
98 North Ave (04976-1942)
PHONE.............................207 858-4201
Bruce Hanson, *VP*
EMP: 68
Web: www.sappi.com
SIC: 2621　Paper mills
HQ: Sappi North America, Inc.
　255 State St Fl 4
　Boston MA 02109
　617 423-7300

(G-5478)
SAPPI NORTH AMERICA INC
Also Called: Sappi Fine Paper North America
1329 Waterville Rd (04976-4999)
PHONE.............................207 238-3000
EMP: 725
Web: www.sappi.com
SIC: 2679 2674 2672 2621　Paper products,
　converted, nec; Bags: uncoated paper and
　multiwall; Coated paper, except
　photographic, carbon, or abrasive; Paper
　mills
HQ: Sappi North America, Inc.
　255 State St Fl 4
　Boston MA 02109
　617 423-7300

(G-5479)
TKI INC
Also Called: Tire King
309 North Ave (04976-4021)
PHONE.............................207 474-5322
EMP: 8 **EST:** 2005
SALES (est): 247.97K **Privately Held**
SIC: 7534 5531　Tire repair shop;
　Automotive tires

Smyrna Mills
Aroostook County

(G-5480)
HERBERT L HARDY & SON INC
1454 Dyerbrook (04780)
P.O. Box 164 (04780-0164)
PHONE.............................207 757-8550
Herbert L Hardy, *Pr*
Kerry Hardy, *VP*
Florence Hardy, *Treas*
EMP: 7 **EST:** 1957

SALES (est): 744.92K **Privately Held**
SIC: 2411 Logging

(G-5481)
K B LOGGING INC
Also Called: KB Logging
3276 Us Route 2 (04780-5013)
P.O. Box 189 (04780-0189)
PHONE..............................207 757-8818
Kevin Brannen, *Pr*
Kristy Brannen, *Sec*
EMP: 10 **EST:** 1978
SALES (est): 776.64K **Privately Held**
SIC: 2411 2426 2421 Logging camps and contractors; Hardwood dimension and flooring mills; Sawmills and planing mills, general

Solon
Somerset County

(G-5482)
SOLON CTR FOR RES & PUBLISHIG
Also Called: Polar Bear & Company
8 Brook St (04979-3000)
P.O. Box 311 (04979-0311)
PHONE..............................207 319-4727
Ramona Duhoux, *CEO*
Paul V Cornell Du Houx, *CEO*
Delores Cornell Du Houx, *Pr*
EMP: 12 **EST:** 1997
SALES (est): 607.93K **Privately Held**
Web: www.polarbearandco.com
SIC: 2731 Book publishing

South Bristol
Lincoln County

(G-5483)
JK CUSTOM WOODWORKING LLC
51 Sloop Nellie Rd (04568-4251)
PHONE..............................207 644-1127
Jonathan Kelsey, *Owner*
EMP: 7 **EST:** 2004
SALES (est): 213.54K **Privately Held**
Web: www.jkcustomwoodworking.com
SIC: 2431 Millwork

South Casco
Cumberland County

(G-5484)
SABRE YACHTS INC
Hawthorne Rd (04077)
PHONE..............................207 655-3831
▼ **EMP:** 150
Web: www.sabreyachts.com
SIC: 3732 Sailboats, building and repairing

South China
Kennebec County

(G-5485)
COMPREHENSIVE LAND TECH INC
Also Called: J.A. Tyler Forest Products
665 Rte 3 (04358-5652)
P.O. Box 146 (04358-0146)
PHONE..............................207 445-3151
Jason Tyler, *Pr*
EMP: 38 **EST:** 2005

SALES (est): 5.98MM **Privately Held**
Web: www.cltenv.com
SIC: 1629 2499 Land clearing contractor; Logs of sawdust and wood particles, pressed

South Harpswell
Cumberland County

(G-5486)
COLE GUNSMITHING INC
21 Bog Hollow Rd (04079-3091)
P.O. Box 197 (04079-0197)
PHONE..............................207 833-5027
Richard Cole, *Pr*
EMP: 7 **EST:** 1986
SQ FT: 3,702
SALES (est): 682.07K **Privately Held**
Web: www.colegun.com
SIC: 7699 3599 Gunsmith shop; Machine and other job shop work

(G-5487)
F V TIGGER
45a Ellen Way (04079-4141)
PHONE..............................207 721-0875
Jeffrey Hurd, *Owner*
EMP: 9 **EST:** 2004
SALES (est): 120K **Privately Held**
SIC: 3732 Fishing boats: lobster, crab, oyster, etc.: small

South Paris
Oxford County

(G-5488)
KBS BUILDERS INC
300 Park St (04281-6417)
P.O. Box 220 (04281-0220)
PHONE..............................207 739-2400
Thatcher Butcher, *Pr*
David Noble, *
EMP: 135 **EST:** 2014
SALES (est): 12.29MM **Privately Held**
Web: www.kbsbuildersinc.com
SIC: 2452 7389 Modular homes, prefabricated, wood; Business services, nec

(G-5489)
MAINE MACHINE PRODUCTS COMPANY (PA)
Also Called: Precinmac Precision Machining
79 Prospect Ave (04281-1108)
P.O. Box 260 (04281-0260)
PHONE..............................207 743-6344
David Macmahon, *Pr*
▲ **EMP:** 106 **EST:** 1956
SQ FT: 75,000
SALES (est): 155.26MM
SALES (corp-wide): 155.26MM **Privately Held**
Web: www.precinmac.com
SIC: 3599 Machine shop, jobbing and repair

(G-5490)
MODULAR FUN I INC
300 Park St (04281-6417)
P.O. Box 220 (04281-0220)
PHONE..............................207 739-2400
Thatcher Butcher, *Pr*
EMP: 195 **EST:** 2002
SALES (est): 47.75MM
SALES (corp-wide): 112.15MM **Publicly Held**
Web: www.kbsbuildersinc.com
SIC: 2452 Prefabricated wood buildings
PA: Star Equity Holdings, Inc.
53 Forest Ave Ste 101

Old Greenwich CT 06870
203 489-9500

South Portland
Cumberland County

(G-5491)
ALLEN UNIFORMS INC
Also Called: Allen Uniform Sales
385 Main St Rear 3 (04106-5517)
PHONE..............................207 775-7364
TOLL FREE: 800
Thomas Allen, *Pr*
EMP: 7 **EST:** 1960
SQ FT: 2,000
SALES (est): 756.92K **Privately Held**
Web: www.allenuniform.com
SIC: 5699 2759 Uniforms; Commercial printing, nec

(G-5492)
BRICKELL BRANDS LLC
Also Called: Brickell Men's Products
167 Rumery St (04106-6254)
PHONE..............................877 598-0060
Joshua Meyer, *CEO*
Joshua Meyer, *Managing Member*
Matthew Bolduc, *
EMP: 60 **EST:** 2014
SALES (est): 8.48MM **Privately Held**
Web: www.brickellmensproducts.com
SIC: 2844 5999 5122 Perfumes, cosmetics and other toilet preparations; Toiletries, cosmetics, and perfumes; Cosmetics, perfumes, and hair products

(G-5493)
CAPE WHPIE MNES GRMET WHPIE PI
185 Cottage Rd (04106-3719)
PHONE..............................207 799-9207
Marcia E Wiggins, *Managing Member*
EMP: 11 **EST:** 2013
SALES (est): 386.58K **Privately Held**
Web: www.capewhoopies.com
SIC: 5461 2051 Retail bakeries; Bread, cake, and related products

(G-5494)
CASCO BAY STEEL STRUCTURES INC
1 Wallace Ave (04106-6176)
PHONE..............................207 780-6722
Brian Tate, *Pr*
Wendy Tate, *VP*
EMP: 10 **EST:** 1997
SALES (est): 3.69MM **Privately Held**
Web: www.cascobaysteel.com
SIC: 3441 Fabricated structural metal for bridges

(G-5495)
COCA-COLA BEVS NORTHEAST INC
Also Called: Coca-Cola
316 Western Ave (04106-1701)
PHONE..............................207 773-5505
Alton Hartt, *Brnch Mgr*
EMP: 20
Web: www.coca-cola.com
SIC: 2086 Bottled and canned soft drinks
HQ: Coca-Cola Beverages Northeast, Inc.
1 Executive Park Dr # 330
Bedford NH 03110
603 627-7871

(G-5496)
CYBERNORTH LLC
15 Cottage Rd Unit 2433 (04116-4015)
PHONE..............................207 331-3310
Jeremy Lombardo, *Pr*
EMP: 9 **EST:** 2015
SALES (est): 10.1MM **Privately Held**
Web: www.cybernorth.com
SIC: 8748 7371 7379 3572 Systems engineering consultant, ex. computer or professional; Computer software systems analysis and design, custom; Computer hardware requirements analysis; Computer storage devices

(G-5497)
DAVID SAUNDERS INC
Also Called: Saunders Electronics
192 Gannett Dr (04106-6938)
PHONE..............................207 228-1888
David Saunders, *Pr*
Jean Saunders, *
EMP: 25 **EST:** 1979
SQ FT: 9,000
SALES (est): 5.85MM **Privately Held**
Web: www.saunderselectronics.com
SIC: 3845 3672 3823 8731 Electromedical equipment; Printed circuit boards; Process control instruments; Electronic research

(G-5498)
DJ PRINTING INC
800 Main St Ste 1 (04106-6050)
PHONE..............................207 773-0439
David Ducharme, *Pr*
Joan M Ducharme, *Treas*
EMP: 8 **EST:** 1987
SQ FT: 2,000
SALES (est): 730.97K **Privately Held**
Web: www.partnersprintingme.com
SIC: 2752 Offset printing

(G-5499)
FAIRCHILD ENERGY LLC
82 Running Hill Rd (04106-3383)
PHONE..............................207 775-8100
Mark S Thompson, *CEO*
EMP: 23 **EST:** 2005
SALES (est): 5.1MM
SALES (corp-wide): 8.25B **Publicly Held**
SIC: 3674 Semiconductors and related devices
HQ: Fairchild Semiconductor International, Inc.
1272 Borregas Ave
Sunnyvale CA 94089
408 822-2000

(G-5500)
FAIRCHILD SEMICONDUCTOR CORP
333 Western Ave (04106-0022)
PHONE..............................801 562-7000
EMP: 145
SQ FT: 279,692
SALES (corp-wide): 3.91B **Publicly Held**
SIC: 3674 Semiconductors and related devices
HQ: Fairchild Semiconductor Corporation
82 Running Hill Rd
South Portland ME 04106
207 775-8100

(G-5501)
FAIRCHILD SEMICONDUCTOR CORP
Also Called: On Semiconductor
333 Western Ave (04106-0022)
PHONE..............................207 775-8100

Izak Bencuya, *Brnch Mgr*
EMP: 250
SALES (corp-wide): 8.25B **Publicly Held**
Web: www.onsemi.com
SIC: 3674 Semiconductors and related devices
HQ: Fairchild Semiconductor Corporation
　82 Running Hill Rd
　South Portland ME 04106
　207 775-8100

(G-5502)
FAIRCHILD SEMICONDUCTOR CORP (DH)
82 Running Hill Rd (04106-3293)
PHONE...................207 775-8100
Mark Thompson, *Ch*
Kevin B London, *
Vijay Ullal, *
Mark S Frey, *
Justin Chiang, *
▲ **EMP:** 400 **EST:** 1997
SQ FT: 129,000
SALES (est): 423.72MM
SALES (corp-wide): 8.25B **Publicly Held**
Web: www.onsemi.com
SIC: 3674 Metal oxide silicon (MOS) devices
HQ: Fairchild Semiconductor International, Inc.
　1272 Borregas Ave
　Sunnyvale CA 94089
　408 822-2000

(G-5503)
FORECASTER PUBLISHING INC
Also Called: Forecaster
295 Gannett Dr (04106-6910)
P.O. Box 66797 (04105-6797)
PHONE...................207 781-3661
David Costello, *Pr*
Marian Mccue, *Prin*
EMP: 33 **EST:** 1984
SALES (est): 733.43K **Privately Held**
Web: www.pressherald.com
SIC: 2711 Commercial printing and newspaper publishing combined

(G-5504)
GRIPWET INC
55 Devereaux Cir (04106-1812)
P.O. Box 2292 (04116-2292)
PHONE...................207 239-0486
EMP: 7 **EST:** 2010
SALES (est): 237.17K **Privately Held**
SIC: 2891 Sealing compounds, synthetic rubber or plastic

(G-5505)
HCB HOLDINGS INC (PA)
190 Rumery St (04106-6230)
PHONE...................207 767-2136
TOLL FREE: 800
Robert E Hews, *Pr*
Charles Hews, *
EMP: 37 **EST:** 1927
SQ FT: 30,000
SALES (est): 21.82MM
SALES (corp-wide): 21.82MM **Privately Held**
SIC: 5012 7538 3713 Truck bodies; General truck repair; Truck and bus bodies

(G-5506)
INLAND FRESH SFOOD CORP AMER I
Inland Seafood
116 Dartmouth St Ste 2 (04106-6210)
P.O. Box 172 (04658-0172)
PHONE...................207 546-7591
John Maloney, *Mgr*

EMP: 11
SALES (corp-wide): 206.94MM **Privately Held**
Web: www.inlandfoods.com
SIC: 5146 2092 Seafoods; Fresh or frozen packaged fish
PA: Inland Fresh Seafood Corporation Of America, Inc.
　1651 Montreal Cir
　Tucker GA 30084
　404 350-5850

(G-5507)
MAINE BEVERAGE ASSOCIATION
Also Called: Coca-Cola
316 Western Ave (04106-1720)
PHONE...................207 773-5505
Oakley Jones, *State Manager*
Oakley Jones, *State Manager*
EMP: 13 **EST:** 1989
SALES (est): 446.96K **Privately Held**
Web: us.coca-cola.com
SIC: 2086 Bottled and canned soft drinks

(G-5508)
MATHEMTICS PROBLEM SOLVING LLC
Also Called: J. Weston Walch, Publisher
35 Foden Rd (04106-1723)
PHONE...................207 772-2846
Albert Noyes, *Managing Member*
Peter S Walch, *Ch Bd*
Carolyn Slayman, *V Ch Bd*
Charles Thomas, *Product Vice President*
EMP: 58 **EST:** 1927
SALES (est): 11.33MM **Privately Held**
Web: www.bwwalch.com
SIC: 2731 2732 2759 7372 Books, publishing and printing; Book printing; Commercial printing, nec; Educational computer software

(G-5509)
NORTHEAST PATIENTS GROUP
Also Called: Wellness Connection of Maine
29 Western Ave (04106-2419)
PHONE...................855 848-6740
EMP: 38
SALES (corp-wide): 6MM **Privately Held**
Web: www.mainewellness.org
SIC: 3999
PA: Northeast Patients Group
　506 Main St Ste 28
　Westbrook ME 04092
　855 848-6740

(G-5510)
P S HOLDING COMPANY INC
110 Dartmouth St (04106-6210)
P.O. Box 11015 (04104-7015)
PHONE...................207 799-9290
EMP: 120
SIC: 2091 Crabmeat, preserved and cured

(G-5511)
P-CUBE INC
125 John Roberts Rd Ste 11 (04106-3295)
P.O. Box 487 (04071-0487)
PHONE...................207 318-3349
EMP: 10 **EST:** 2012
SALES (est): 777.36K **Privately Held**
SIC: 3663 Radio and t.v. communications equipment

(G-5512)
PORTLAND PLASTIC PIPE
444 Lincoln Street Ext (04106-5632)
P.O. Box 3907 (04104-3907)

PHONE...................207 774-0364
Frederick J Olsen, *Pr*
Roger Chaisson, *VP*
EMP: 9 **EST:** 1975
SQ FT: 15,000
SALES (est): 1.01MM **Privately Held**
Web: www.portlandplasticpipe.com
SIC: 3089 Injection molding of plastics

(G-5513)
SAPPI NORTH AMERICA INC
Also Called: Sappi Fine Paper North America
179 John Roberts Rd (04106-6990)
PHONE...................207 854-7000
Jeff Wright, *Brnch Mgr*
EMP: 64
Web: www.sappi.com
SIC: 2679 2674 2672 2621 Paper products, converted, nec; Bags: uncoated paper and multiwall; Coated paper, except photographic, carbon, or abrasive; Paper mills
HQ: Sappi North America, Inc.
　255 State St Fl 4
　Boston MA 02109
　617 423-7300

(G-5514)
SELLERS PUBLISHING INC
Also Called: Ronnie Sellers Productions
161 John Roberts Rd Ste 1 (04106-3280)
PHONE...................207 772-6833
Ronnie Sellers, *Pr*
▲ **EMP:** 79 **EST:** 1993
SQ FT: 3,000
SALES (est): 13.04MM **Privately Held**
Web: www.rsvp.com
SIC: 2741 5942 Miscellaneous publishing; Book stores

(G-5515)
SUPERMEDIA LLC
600 Southborough Dr Ste 101 (04106)
PHONE...................207 828-6100
EMP: 10
SALES (corp-wide): 1.2B **Publicly Held**
SIC: 2741 Directories, telephone: publishing only, not printed on site
HQ: Supermedia Llc
　2200 W Airfield Dr
　Dfw Airport TX 75261
　972 453-7000

(G-5516)
TEVELLE PHARMACEUTICALS LLC
200 John Roberts Rd (04106-3366)
PHONE...................207 808-9771
EMP: 7 **EST:** 2021
SALES (est): 61.36K **Privately Held**
SIC: 2834 Pharmaceutical preparations

(G-5517)
WATERFRONT GRAPHICS & PRTG LLC
104 Ocean St (04106-2832)
P.O. Box 2105 (04116-2105)
PHONE...................207 799-3519
James Brown, *Managing Member*
EMP: 8 **EST:** 1976
SQ FT: 3,500
SALES (est): 540.01K **Privately Held**
Web: www.waterfrontgraphics.com
SIC: 2752 2759 Offset printing; Commercial printing, nec

Southwest Harbor
Hancock County

(G-5518)
ELLIS BOAT CO INC
265 Seawall Rd (04679-4043)
PHONE...................207 244-9221
Donald R Ellis, *Pr*
EMP: 15 **EST:** 1948
SQ FT: 6,472
SALES (est): 603.82K **Privately Held**
Web: www.ellisboat.com
SIC: 3732 4493 Boatbuilding and repairing; Boat yards, storage and incidental repair

(G-5519)
TALARIA COMPANY LLC
Also Called: Hinckley Yacht Services
130 Shore Rd (04679-4056)
PHONE...................207 244-5572
▲ **EMP:** 43 **EST:** 1999
SQ FT: 43,560
SALES (est): 2.47MM **Privately Held**
Web: www.hinckleyyachts.com
SIC: 3732 Yachts, building and repairing

Springvale
York County

(G-5520)
JAGGER BROTHERS
Also Called: Jagger Spun Division
5 Water St (04083-1329)
P.O. Box 188 (04083-0188)
PHONE...................207 324-5622
David M Jagger, *Pr*
Margaret Bullens, *
▲ **EMP:** 45 **EST:** 1898
SQ FT: 60,000
SALES (est): 3.5MM **Privately Held**
Web: www.jaggeryarn.com
SIC: 2281 Yarn spinning mills

(G-5521)
MOUSAM VALLEY MILLWORK
282 River St (04083-1219)
PHONE...................207 324-2951
Lisa Gerard, *Pr*
EMP: 20 **EST:** 2013
SALES (est): 1.32MM **Privately Held**
Web: www.mousamvalleymillwork.com
SIC: 2431 Millwork

(G-5522)
NEW ENGLAND WOODWORKS
10 Coleco Ln (04083-1203)
PHONE...................207 324-6343
Lewis Libby, *Owner*
EMP: 8 **EST:** 2004
SALES (est): 303.59K **Privately Held**
Web: www.newenglandwoodworksinc.com
SIC: 2431 Millwork

(G-5523)
WORSTED SPINNING NENG LLC
5 Water St (04083-1329)
PHONE...................207 324-5622
Greg Fall, *Managing Member*
EMP: 9 **EST:** 2019
SALES (est): 480.33K **Privately Held**
Web: www.jaggeryarn.com
SIC: 2281 Yarn spinning mills

▲ = Import ▼ = Export
◆ = Import/Export

St John Plt
Aroostook County

(G-5524)
ALLAGASH TIMBERLANDS LP
1798 St John Road St J (04743-4022)
PHONE................................207 834-6348
Winfred A Stevens, *Pt*
EMP: 9 **EST:** 1999
SALES (est): 233.5K **Privately Held**
SIC: 3523 Harvesters, fruit, vegetable, tobacco, etc.

(G-5525)
IRVING WOODLANDS LLC (HQ)
1798 St John Road St J (04743-4022)
P.O. Box 240 (04743-0240)
PHONE................................207 834-5767
James K Irving, *Managing Member*
▲ **EMP:** 40 **EST:** 1971
SQ FT: 15,000
SALES (est): 26.04MM
SALES (corp-wide): 2.89B **Privately Held**
Web: www.fortkentchamber.com
SIC: 2421 Sawmills and planing mills, general
PA: J. D. Irving Limited
300 Union St
Saint John NB E2L 4
506 632-7777

Standish
Cumberland County

(G-5526)
CELLBLOCK FCS LLC
234 Northeast Rd Ste 5 (04084-6945)
PHONE................................800 440-4119
EMP: 30 **EST:** 2017
SALES (est): 2.41MM **Privately Held**
Web: www.cellblockfcs.com
SIC: 3999 Barber and beauty shop equipment

(G-5527)
JAMES EATON
20 Shannons Way (04084-5270)
PHONE................................207 522-3944
Lisa Bosse, *Prin*
EMP: 11 **EST:** 2012
SALES (est): 1.29MM **Privately Held**
SIC: 3625 Relays and industrial controls

(G-5528)
NEW ENGLAND CASTINGS LLC
234 Northeast Rd Ste 2 (04084-6945)
PHONE................................207 642-3029
EMP: 23 **EST:** 1986
SQ FT: 6,000
SALES (est): 4.25MM **Privately Held**
Web: www.newenglandcastings.com
SIC: 3324 Commercial investment castings, ferrous

(G-5529)
TOWER PUBLISHING (PA)
Also Called: Rogue Industries
650 Cape Rd (04084-6265)
PHONE................................207 642-5400
Michael Lyons, *Pr*
EMP: 12 **EST:** 1920
SALES (est): 2.34MM
SALES (corp-wide): 2.34MM **Privately Held**
Web: www.towerpub.com

SIC: 7375 2741 8732 Data base information retrieval; Directories, nec: publishing only, not printed on site; Market analysis, business, and economic research

(G-5530)
WIRELESS CONSTRUCTION INC
40 Blake Rd (04084-6415)
PHONE................................207 642-5751
Michael Sullivan, *Pr*
Stanley Brown, *
Douglas Wright, *
EMP: 40 **EST:** 2005
SALES (est): 7.44MM **Privately Held**
Web: www.wcitowers.com
SIC: 1389 1629 Construction, repair, and dismantling services; Caisson drilling

Stetson
Penobscot County

(G-5531)
SIGN SERVICES INC
512 Wolfboro Rd (04488-3124)
PHONE................................207 296-2400
Samuel Hands, *Pr*
Ellen Hands, *Treas*
EMP: 14 **EST:** 1990
SQ FT: 3,200
SALES (est): 772.27K **Privately Held**
Web: www.signservicesofmaine.com
SIC: 3993 1799 Electric signs; Sign installation and maintenance

Steuben
Washington County

(G-5532)
H & H MARINE INC
932 Us Route 1 Ste 1 (04680-2942)
PHONE................................207 546-7477
Eric Moores, *Pr*
Anne Ray, *Sec*
Bruce Grindle, *VP*
EMP: 10 **EST:** 1984
SQ FT: 20,000
SALES (est): 434.6K **Privately Held**
Web: www.hhmarineinc.com
SIC: 3732 Fishing boats: lobster, crab, oyster, etc.: small

Stillwater
Penobscot County

(G-5533)
CENTRAL EQUIPMENT COMPANY
Also Called: White Sign Division
45 Dempsey-Greaves Ln (04489-5109)
P.O. Box 261 (04489-0261)
PHONE................................207 827-6193
Ralph Leonard, *Pr*
Kent Leonard, *Ex VP*
Anita Leonard, *Treas*
EMP: 18 **EST:** 1959
SQ FT: 24,000
SALES (est): 4.53MM **Privately Held**
Web: www.white-sign.com
SIC: 7353 3993 Heavy construction equipment rental; Signs, not made in custom sign painting shops

Stonington
Hancock County

(G-5534)
PENOBSCOT BAY PRESS (PA)
Also Called: Island Ad-Vantages
138 Main St (04681)
P.O. Box 36 (04681-0036)
PHONE................................207 367-2200
R Nathaniel Barrows, *Pr*
Katie Frasier, *Treas*
EMP: 19 **EST:** 1935
SALES (est): 1.62MM
SALES (corp-wide): 1.62MM **Privately Held**
Web: www.islandadvantages.com
SIC: 2711 2759 2731 Newspapers: publishing only, not printed on site; Commercial printing, nec; Books, publishing only

Stratton
Franklin County

(G-5535)
STRATTON LUMBER INC (HQ)
66 Fontaine Rd (04982)
P.O. Box 160 (04982-0160)
PHONE................................207 246-4500
EMP: 38 **EST:** 1979
SALES (est): 21.42MM
SALES (corp-wide): 7.79MM **Privately Held**
Web: www.timber-resource.com
SIC: 2421 Sawmills and planing mills, general
PA: Fontaine Inc
850 Rue Fontaine
Woburn QC G0Y 1
819 544-4801

Strong
Franklin County

(G-5536)
LIGNETICS OF MAINE
30 Norton Hill Rd (04983-3325)
PHONE................................207 684-3457
EMP: 13 **EST:** 2015
SALES (est): 949.71K **Privately Held**
Web: www.lignetics.com
SIC: 2499 Wood products, nec

(G-5537)
TRACY L GORDON
68 Norton Hill Rd (04983-3325)
P.O. Box 483 (04983-0483)
PHONE................................207 684-4462
Tracy L Gordon, *Prin*
EMP: 8 **EST:** 2005
SALES (est): 251.62K **Privately Held**
SIC: 2411 Logging

Sumner
Oxford County

(G-5538)
EUGENE CORSON
38 Cottage Rd (04292-3801)
P.O. Box 38 (04292-0038)
PHONE................................207 446-6489
Eugene Corson, *Owner*
EMP: 7 **EST:** 2012
SALES (est): 179.77K **Privately Held**

SIC: 2411 Logging

Sunset
Hancock County

(G-5539)
ISLAND APPROACHES
Also Called: Maine Camp Outfitters
300 Sunset Rd (04683-3800)
P.O. Box 67 (04683-0067)
PHONE................................207 348-2459
Andrew Fuller, *CEO*
EMP: 12 **EST:** 1990
SALES (est): 770.55K **Privately Held**
Web: www.maine-camp.com
SIC: 2759 5961 Screen printing; Fishing, hunting and camping equipment and supplies: by mail

Surry
Hancock County

(G-5540)
WESMAC CUSTOM BOATS INC
Also Called: Wesmac Customs Bulds
Route 172 (04684)
PHONE................................207 667-4822
EMP: 13
Web: www.wesmac.com
SIC: 3732 Boatbuilding and repairing
PA: Wesmac Custom Boats, Inc.
158 Blue Hill Rd
Surry ME 04684

Thomaston
Knox County

(G-5541)
BEST FELTS LIQUIDATION CORP
17 Dexter St (04861-3159)
P.O. Box 266 (04861-0266)
PHONE................................207 596-0566
John G Rosseel, *Pr*
Sherly Hocking, *Sec*
EMP: 10 **EST:** 1983
SQ FT: 2,500
SALES (est): 778.82K **Privately Held**
Web: www.edwardhbest.com
SIC: 2299 Felts and felt products

(G-5542)
BROOKS INC (PA)
Also Called: Brooks Trap Mill
211 Beechwood St (04861-3013)
PHONE................................207 354-8763
Mark Brooks, *Pr*
Stephen Brooks, *
Julie Brooks, *
◆ **EMP:** 30 **EST:** 1930
SQ FT: 37,000
SALES (est): 7.28MM
SALES (corp-wide): 7.28MM **Privately Held**
Web: www.brookstrapmill.com
SIC: 3499 0919 Fire- or burglary-resistive products; Whale fishing and whale products

(G-5543)
DICAPERL MINERALS
94 Buttermilk Ln (04861-3204)
PHONE................................207 594-8225
Frank G Bertrand, *Prin*
EMP: 9 **EST:** 2010
SALES (est): 475.43K **Privately Held**
Web: www.dicalite.com

SIC: 3295 Minerals, ground or treated

(G-5544)
DRAGON PRODUCTS COMPANY LLC
107 New County Rd (04861-3113)
PHONE..............................207 594-5555
Terry Veysey, *Brnch Mgr*
EMP: 41
Web: www.dragonproducts.com
SIC: 3273 3241 1442 1422 Ready-mixed concrete; Cement, hydraulic; Construction sand and gravel; Crushed and broken limestone
HQ: Dragon Products Company, Llc
   2 Main St Ste 18-221
   Biddeford ME 04005

(G-5545)
LYMAN MORSE BOATBUILDING INC
19 Elltee Cir (04861-3218)
PHONE..............................207 354-6904
Derw Lyman, *Brnch Mgr*
EMP: 12
SALES (corp-wide): 24.89MM **Privately Held**
Web: www.lymanmorse.com
SIC: 3732 Boatbuilding and repairing
PA: Lyman Morse Boatbuilding, Inc.
   84 Knox St
   Thomaston ME 04861
   207 354-6904

(G-5546)
LYMAN MORSE BOATBUILDING INC (PA)
84 Knox St (04861-3714)
PHONE..............................207 354-6904
Drew Lyman, *Pr*
Heidi Lyman, *
EMP: 124 EST: 1959
SQ FT: 90,000
SALES (est): 24.89MM
SALES (corp-wide): 24.89MM **Privately Held**
Web: www.lymanmorse.com
SIC: 3732 Yachts, building and repairing

Topsham
Sagadahoc County

(G-5547)
COASTAL METAL FAB
Also Called: Downeaster, The
120 Old Lisbon Rd (04086-6262)
PHONE..............................207 729-5101
Norman Lauze, *Pr*
Jack Harlow, *
EMP: 27 EST: 1979
SQ FT: 30,000
SALES (est): 5.44MM **Privately Held**
Web: www.downeastermfg.com
SIC: 5531 3714 Auto and truck equipment and parts; Motor vehicle parts and accessories

(G-5548)
LAG INC (PA)
Also Called: Lee Tire
27 Monument Pl (04086-1238)
P.O. Box 386 (04086-0386)
PHONE..............................207 729-1676
Wayne Gagne, *Pr*
Leonce Gagne, *VP*
EMP: 8 EST: 1984
SQ FT: 7,700
SALES (est): 15.04MM

SALES (corp-wide): 15.04MM **Privately Held**
Web: www.alltuneandlube.com
SIC: 5014 5531 7534 Automobile tires and tubes; Automotive tires; Rebuilding and retreading tires

(G-5549)
LEES TIRE
27 Monument Pl (04086-1238)
P.O. Box 386 (04086-0386)
PHONE..............................207 729-1676
Leonce A Gagne, *Pr*
Mary H Gagne, *Treas*
Linda Beal, *Treas*
Leonce A Gagne, *Owner*
EMP: 40 EST: 1932
SALES (est): 4.49MM
SALES (corp-wide): 15.04MM **Privately Held**
Web: www.leestiremaine.com
SIC: 5531 7538 7534 Automotive tires; General automotive repair shops; Tire repair shop
PA: Lag, Inc
   27 Monument Pl
   Topsham ME 04086
   207 729-1676

(G-5550)
MEGQUIER & JONES INC
72 Ivanhoe Dr (04086-6113)
PHONE..............................207 799-8555
EMP: 35
Web: www.perfectdomain.com
SIC: 3449 3441 Miscellaneous metalwork; Fabricated structural metal

(G-5551)
MORNINGSTAR MARBLE & GRAN INC
Also Called: Morningstar Stone & Tile
47 Park Dr (04086-1737)
PHONE..............................207 725-7309
John N Whatley, *Pr*
Nick Whatley, *Pr*
Laura Whatley, *VP*
▲ EMP: 19 EST: 1983
SALES (est): 2.49MM **Privately Held**
Web: www.morningstarmarble.com
SIC: 3281 1743 5032 Altars, cut stone; Marble installation, interior; Aggregate

(G-5552)
SANDELIN FOUNDATION INC
82 Old Augusta Rd (04086-1141)
P.O. Box 224 (04086-0224)
PHONE..............................207 725-7004
TOLL FREE: 800
Harold D Sandelin, *Pr*
Barbara J Sandelin, *VP*
EMP: 10 EST: 1973
SQ FT: 7,000
SALES (est): 1.05MM **Privately Held**
Web: www.sandelinprecast.com
SIC: 3272 1771 Septic tanks, concrete; Foundation and footing contractor

Trenton
Hancock County

(G-5553)
DOWNEAST FISHING GEAR
12 Bar Harbor Rd (04605-5800)
P.O. Box 1283 (04605-1283)
PHONE..............................207 667-3131
Alicin Holmquist, *Mgr*
▲ EMP: 20 EST: 1993

SQ FT: 5,000
SALES (est): 2.28MM **Privately Held**
SIC: 3496 5941 5091 Traps, animal and fish ; Fishing equipment; Fishing equipment and supplies

(G-5554)
GALLERY LEATHER DIRECT INC
8 Industrial Way (04605-6029)
PHONE..............................207 667-9474
Jeff Plourde, *Pr*
EMP: 35 EST: 2019
SALES (est): 1.23MM **Privately Held**
SIC: 3111 2782 Bookbinders' leather; Scrapbooks

(G-5555)
GALLERY LEATHER MFG INC
27 Industrial Way (04605-6028)
PHONE..............................207 667-9474
Jeff Plourde, *Pr*
EMP: 35 EST: 2019
SALES (est): 1.62MM **Privately Held**
SIC: 3111 5112 Bookbinders' leather; Stationery

(G-5556)
JOHN SEAVEY ACADIA FUEL
711 Bar Harbor Rd (04605-5926)
PHONE..............................207 664-6050
EMP: 7 EST: 2010
SALES (est): 244.32K **Privately Held**
SIC: 2869 Fuels

(G-5557)
MY EASE INC
27 Ramp Rd (04605-6031)
PHONE..............................207 667-8237
EMP: 12
SALES (corp-wide): 5.65MM **Privately Held**
Web: www.morrisyachts.com
SIC: 3732 Boatbuilding and repairing
PA: My Ease, Inc.
   53 Granville Rd
   Bass Harbor ME 04653
   207 667-6235

(G-5558)
TALARIA COMPANY LLC
Also Called: Hinckley Company, The
40 Industrial Way (04605-6029)
PHONE..............................207 667-1891
Paul Fredrick, *Mgr*
EMP: 91
SALES (corp-wide): 92.75MM **Privately Held**
Web: www.hinckleyyachts.com
SIC: 3732 Boatbuilding and repairing
PA: The Talaria Company Llc
   1 Little Harbor Lndg
   Portsmouth RI 02871
   401 683-7100

(G-5559)
TEMPSHIELD LLC
Also Called: Tempshield
23 Industrial Way (04605-6028)
P.O. Box 199 (04660-0199)
PHONE..............................207 667-9696
EMP: 14 EST: 2017
SALES (est): 2.14MM **Privately Held**
Web: www.tempshield.com
SIC: 2326 Work apparel, except uniforms

Turner
Androscoggin County

(G-5560)
BEAR POND DUMPSTER LLC
250 Bear Pond Rd (04282-3510)
PHONE..............................207 224-0337
Stephen Jones, *Prin*
EMP: 8 EST: 2017
SALES (est): 249.1K **Privately Held**
SIC: 3443 Dumpsters, garbage

(G-5561)
CLARK METAL FABRICATION INC
1463 Auburn Rd (04282-3617)
P.O. Box 399 (04282-0399)
PHONE..............................207 330-6322
William W Clark Junior, *Pr*
EMP: 8 EST: 1999
SALES (est): 1.04MM **Privately Held**
Web: www.clarkmetalfab.net
SIC: 3441 3446 Fabricated structural metal; Railings, banisters, guards, etc: made from metal pipe

(G-5562)
GLOBAL METAL FABRICATION LLC
302b Auburn Rd (04282-4124)
PHONE..............................207 753-0001
EMP: 9 EST: 2005
SALES (est): 152.56K **Privately Held**
SIC: 3441 Fabricated structural metal

(G-5563)
TRI STAR SHEET METAL COMPANY
1817 Auburn Rd (04282-3408)
P.O. Box 400 (04282-0400)
PHONE..............................207 225-2043
EMP: 10 EST: 1996
SQ FT: 25,000
SALES (est): 935.18K **Privately Held**
SIC: 3444 Sheet metalwork

(G-5564)
TURNER PUBLISHING INC
Also Called: Country Courier
5 Fern St (04282-4028)
P.O. Box 214 (04282-0214)
PHONE..............................207 225-2076
Steve Cornelio, *Pr*
Jodi Cornelio, *CFO*
EMP: 19 EST: 2002
SALES (est): 854.38K **Privately Held**
Web: www.turnerpublishing.net
SIC: 2711 7331 Newspapers: publishing only, not printed on site; Direct mail advertising services

(G-5565)
TWO RIVERS PET PRODUCTS INC
Also Called: Pussums Cat Company
469 N Parish Rd (04282-3217)
PHONE..............................207 225-3965
Susan Shaw, *CEO*
Eben Shaw, *CFO*
EMP: 21 EST: 2017
SQ FT: 1,500
SALES (est): 202.45K **Privately Held**
SIC: 3999 2392 5999 Pet supplies; Pillowcases: made from purchased materials; Pets and pet supplies

▲ = Import ▼ = Export
◆ = Import/Export

Unity
Waldo County

(G-5566)
MAINE ALPACA EXPERIENCE LLC
141 Crosby Brook Rd (04988-4020)
PHONE.................................207 356-4146
Robin L Fowler Pratt, *Owner*
EMP: 8 **EST:** 2017
SALES (est): 252.9K Privately Held
Web: www.mainealpacaexperience.com
SIC: 2231 Alpacas, mohair: woven

(G-5567)
R & N INC
557 Albion Rd (04988-3210)
P.O. Box 180 (04988-0180)
PHONE.................................207 948-2613
Ralph Nason, *Pr*
Nancy Nason, *Treas*
EMP: 8 **EST:** 1982
SQ FT: 9,000
SALES (est): 764.2K Privately Held
SIC: 2099 5149 Cole slaw, in bulk; Salad dressing

(G-5568)
WIN-PRESSOR LLC
336 Stagecoach Rd (04988-4117)
PHONE.................................207 948-4800
Ervin Hochstetler, *Prin*
EMP: 7 **EST:** 2011
SALES (est): 210.35K Privately Held
SIC: 3442 Window and door frames

Van Buren
Aroostook County

(G-5569)
KEVLAUR INDUSTRIES INC
336 Champlain St (04785-1399)
P.O. Box 954 (92067-0954)
PHONE.................................207 868-2761
Alban Cyr, *Pr*
Alban Cyr Junior, *Pr*
Beverly Hamilton, *
Richard Engels, *
Ron Schroeder, *Stockholder*
EMP: 45 **EST:** 1991
SQ FT: 30,000
SALES (est): 1.58MM Privately Held
SIC: 2499 2421 Mulch, wood and bark; Sawmills and planing mills, general

Veazie
Penobscot County

(G-5570)
COLLABRIC
Also Called: Fabric Craftsman
1017 School St (04401-6983)
P.O. Box 818 (04402-0818)
PHONE.................................207 945-5095
Mark Sampson, *Pr*
EMP: 11 **EST:** 1997
SALES (est): 983.56K Privately Held
Web: www.collabric.net
SIC: 2394 Awnings, fabric: made from purchased materials

(G-5571)
FRAZIER SIGNAL TECH LLC (PA)
✪
1506 State St (04401-7001)

PHONE.................................207 991-0543
EMP: 8 **EST:** 2022
SALES (est): 536.56K
SALES (corp-wide): 536.56K Privately Held
SIC: 3669 Traffic signals, electric

Vinalhaven
Knox County

(G-5572)
CASSIOPAE US INC
183 Roberts Cemetery Rd (04863-3614)
PHONE.................................435 647-9940
EMP: 7 **EST:** 2006
SALES (est): 224.1K
SALES (corp-wide): 1.96B Privately Held
SIC: 7372 Prepackaged software
HQ: Sopra Banking Software
Petite Avenue
Annecy 74940
450333030

Waldoboro
Lincoln County

(G-5573)
ADVANCED INDUS SOLUTIONS INC
Also Called: Custom Cordage LLC
151 One Pie Rd (04572-5927)
P.O. Box 1387 (04572-1387)
PHONE.................................207 832-0569
Maurice Maheux, *CEO*
EMP: 23
Web: www.aisinc.me
SIC: 2298 5085 Twine, cord and cordage; Rope, cord, and thread
PA: Advanced Industrial Solutions, Inc.
36 Anthony Ave
Augusta ME 04330

(G-5574)
ATLANTIC LABORATORIES INC
Also Called: North American Kelp
41 Cross St (04572-5634)
PHONE.................................207 832-5376
Robert Morse Junior, *Pr*
EMP: 8 **EST:** 1971
SQ FT: 12,000
SALES (est): 1.74MM Privately Held
Web: www.noamkelp.com
SIC: 2048 Prepared feeds, nec

(G-5575)
DAVID BIRD LLC
Also Called: Thomas Taylor Braid
151 One Pie Rd (04572-5927)
P.O. Box 1387 (04572-1387)
PHONE.................................207 832-0569
▲ **EMP:** 16 **EST:** 1998
SQ FT: 13,550
SALES (est): 500.39K Privately Held
Web: www.customcordage.com
SIC: 2298 Cordage and twine

(G-5576)
FLAME GRILLING PRODUCTS INC
2500 Winslows Mills Rd (04572-3045)
P.O. Box 452 (04619-0452)
PHONE.................................800 724-5510
Theobald Kenneth C Junior, *Pr*
Pamela L Theobald, *VP*
Kenneth Theobald, *Prin*
EMP: 18 **EST:** 2014
SALES (est): 477.85K Privately Held

Web: www.flamegrillingproducts.com
SIC: 5812 2091 Barbecue restaurant; Seafood products: packaged in cans, jars, etc.

(G-5577)
KWS INC
110 One Pie Rd (04572-5925)
P.O. Box 1313 (04572-1313)
PHONE.................................207 832-5095
Kimberley Sweetser, *Pr*
Seth Sweetser, *Dir*
EMP: 7 **EST:** 1997
SQ FT: 8,000
SALES (est): 498.7K Privately Held
Web: www.kws.com
SIC: 2299 Rugbacking, jute or other fiber

(G-5578)
MAINE ANTIQUE DIGEST INC
911 Main St (04572-6042)
P.O. Box 1429 (04572-1429)
PHONE.................................207 832-7534
Samuel Pennington, *Pr*
Sally Pennington, *VP*
Robert Cumler, *Clerk*
EMP: 13 **EST:** 1973
SQ FT: 6,500
SALES (est): 634.3K Privately Held
Web: www.maineantiquedigest.com
SIC: 2721 5932 2711 Magazines: publishing only, not printed on site; Used merchandise stores; Newspapers

(G-5579)
TSS-MAINE LLC
Also Called: Daedalon
299 Atlantic Hwy (04572-6411)
PHONE.................................207 832-6344
▲ **EMP:** 35
SIC: 3999 Education aids, devices and supplies

Walpole
Lincoln County

(G-5580)
AMBASSADOR WOODWORKS INC
44 Sproul Rd (04573-3116)
PHONE.................................916 858-1092
EMP: 7 **EST:** 1992
SALES (est): 628.66K Privately Held
Web: www.ambassadorwoodworks.com
SIC: 1751 2511 Cabinet building and installation; Wood household furniture

(G-5581)
FLOWERS BOAT WORKS INC
21 Ridge Rd (04573-3319)
PHONE.................................207 563-7404
David Flower, *Pr*
Candy Flower, *Treas*
EMP: 7 **EST:** 1981
SQ FT: 7,000
SALES (est): 605.81K Privately Held
SIC: 3732 Boatbuilding and repairing

Warren
Knox County

(G-5582)
KNOX MACHINE COMPANY
936 Eastern Rd (04864-4573)
P.O. Box 68 (04864-0068)
PHONE.................................207 273-2296

Richard B Maxcy, *Pr*
Charles D Maxcy, *
EMP: 60 **EST:** 1977
SQ FT: 28,500
SALES (est): 9.7MM Privately Held
Web: www.knoxmachine.com
SIC: 3599 Machine shop, jobbing and repair

(G-5583)
LELAND BOGGS II
Also Called: Boggs Mobile Homes
715 Camden Rd (04864-4211)
P.O. Box 177 (04864-0177)
PHONE.................................207 273-2610
Leland Boggs Ii, *Pt*
Valerie Boggs, *Pt*
EMP: 8 **EST:** 1958
SQ FT: 2,400
SALES (est): 987.35K Privately Held
Web: www.boggshomes.com
SIC: 2452 6531 Modular homes, prefabricated, wood; Real estate agents and managers

(G-5584)
LIE-NIELSEN TOOLWORKS INC
264 Stirling Rd (04864-4384)
P.O. Box 9 (04864-0009)
PHONE.................................800 327-2520
Thomas Lie-nielsen, *Pr*
Joe Butler, *
▲ **EMP:** 90 **EST:** 1980
SQ FT: 15,000
SALES (est): 9.02MM Privately Held
Web: www.lie-nielsen.com
SIC: 3425 3423 3999 Saws, hand: metalworking or woodworking; Hand and edge tools, nec; Education aids, devices and supplies

(G-5585)
ON THE ROAD INC
2243 Camden Rd (04864-4113)
P.O. Box 271 (04864-0271)
PHONE.................................207 273-3780
TOLL FREE: 888
Matt Mcconnell, *Pr*
Peter C Armstrong, *Pr*
Lauren S Armstrong, *Treas*
Stephen A Little, *Clerk*
EMP: 20 **EST:** 1985
SQ FT: 7,800
SALES (est): 1.81MM Privately Held
Web: www.on-the-road.net
SIC: 3715 5599 4213 Truck trailers; Utility trailers; Heavy hauling, nec

(G-5586)
PERSEUS PARTNERS LLC
Also Called: On The Road
2243 Camden Rd (04864-4113)
PHONE.................................207 273-3780
Matthew Mcconnell, *Mgr*
EMP: 10
SALES (est): 768.85K Privately Held
SIC: 3792 Travel trailers and campers

Washburn
Aroostook County

(G-5587)
PENOBSCOT MCCRUM LLC
2326 Parsons Rd (04786-3340)
P.O. Box 220 (04786-0220)
PHONE.................................207 338-4360
Jay Mccrum, *CEO*
EMP: 175 **EST:** 2003
SQ FT: 56,000
SALES (est): 26.62MM Privately Held

GEOGRAPHIC

Web: www.penobscotmccrum.com
SIC: 2037 Potato products, quick frozen and cold pack

Washington
Knox County

(G-5588)
SEACOLORS
45 Hopkins Rd (04574-3237)
P.O. Box 303 (04574-0303)
PHONE.....................................207 845-2587
Anne B Kennedy, *Owner*
EMP: 8 **EST:** 2009
SALES (est): 294.46K **Privately Held**
Web: www.getwool.com
SIC: 2269 Finishing plants, nec

Waterboro
York County

(G-5589)
ARCHITECTURAL SKYLIGHT CO INC
Also Called: E-Skylight.com
661 Main St (04087-3002)
PHONE.....................................207 247-6747
Adrian Ayotte, *Pr*
Francis O'neill, *VP*
EMP: 27 **EST:** 1989
SQ FT: 43,000
SALES (est): 869.46K **Privately Held**
SIC: 3444 Skylights, sheet metal

(G-5590)
CUSTOM MILLING & MACHINING INC
1087 Main St (04087-3103)
PHONE.....................................207 776-8137
Erik J Triance, *CEO*
EMP: 7
SALES (est): 509.88K **Privately Held**
Web: www.cmmi.me
SIC: 3599 Machine shop, jobbing and repair

(G-5591)
HOWE & HOWE TECHNOLOGIES INC
661 Main St (04087-3002)
PHONE.....................................207 247-2777
Geoffrey S Howe, *CEO*
Michael Howe, *Pr*
EMP: 17 **EST:** 2006
SQ FT: 48,000
SALES (est): 4.99MM
SALES (corp-wide): 12.87B **Publicly Held**
Web: www.howeandhowe.com
SIC: 8732 3795 Research services, except laboratory; Tanks and tank components
PA: Textron Inc.
    40 Westminster St
    Providence RI 02903
    401 421-2800

(G-5592)
TK MACHINING INC
Also Called: T K Machining
4 Dyer Ln (04087-3052)
P.O. Box 556 (04087-0556)
PHONE.....................................207 247-3114
Robert J Dewitt, *Pr*
EMP: 11 **EST:** 1987
SALES (est): 1.24MM **Privately Held**
Web: www.tkmachining.net
SIC: 3599 Machine shop, jobbing and repair

Waterville
Kennebec County

(G-5593)
CENTRAL MAINE MORNING SENTINEL
Also Called: Morning Sentinel
31 Front St (04901-6626)
PHONE.....................................207 873-3341
James Shaffer, *S*
John Christie, *Pr*
EMP: 23 **EST:** 1904
SALES (est): 471.83K **Privately Held**
Web: www.centralmaine.com
SIC: 2711 Newspapers, publishing and printing

(G-5594)
CHINETCO
242 College Ave (04901-6226)
PHONE.....................................207 873-3351
Mark Staton, *CEO*
EMP: 9 **EST:** 2017
SALES (est): 293.88K **Privately Held**
SIC: 2621 Paper mills

(G-5595)
MAINE COMMERCIAL TIRE INC
30 Industrial St (04901-5774)
PHONE.....................................207 622-3200
Brent Hart, *Brnch Mgr*
EMP: 10
Web: www.mctire.com
SIC: 5014 7534 Automobile tires and tubes; Tire retreading and repair shops
PA: Maine Commercial Tire, Inc.
    55 Freedom Pkwy
    Hermon ME 04401

(G-5596)
SHYFT GROUP INC
Also Called: Duramag
977 W River Rd Unit 3 (04901-4486)
PHONE.....................................207 692-7178
EMP: 200
SALES (corp-wide): 1.03B **Publicly Held**
Web: www.duramagbodies.com
SIC: 3713 Truck bodies (motor vehicles)
PA: The Shyft Group Inc
    41280 Bridge St
    Novi MI 48375
    517 543-6400

Wayne
Kennebec County

(G-5597)
LOCKHEED MARTIN
9 Craig Brook Trl (04284-3523)
PHONE.....................................603 966-6031
EMP: 41 **EST:** 2018
SALES (est): 326.3K **Privately Held**
SIC: 3721 Aircraft

Wells
York County

(G-5598)
CARON ENGINEERING INC
116 Willie Hill Rd (04090-6848)
P.O. Box 1529 (04090-1529)
PHONE.....................................207 646-6071
Robert Caron, *CEO*
Robert Caron, *Pr*
Carolyn Caron-stratos, *Treas*

Joe Lenkowski, *
EMP: 37 **EST:** 1987
SQ FT: 3,000
SALES (est): 5.01MM **Privately Held**
Web: www.caroneng.com
SIC: 7373 3625 Systems integration services; Relays and industrial controls

(G-5599)
CYNTHIA CARROLL PALLIAN
Also Called: Pallian & Company
2049 Post Rd (04090-4717)
P.O. Box 1704 (04090-1704)
PHONE.....................................207 646-1600
Cynthia C Pallian, *Owner*
EMP: 7 **EST:** 1988
SALES (est): 486.13K **Privately Held**
SIC: 3499 Novelties and giftware, including trophies

(G-5600)
MAGCO INC
85 Spencer Dr Unit A (04090-9317)
P.O. Box 559 (04090-0559)
PHONE.....................................207 324-8060
◆ **EMP:** 100
SIC: 3441 Fabricated structural metal

(G-5601)
MAINE PET SUPPLY
179 Sanford Rd (04090-5542)
PHONE.....................................207 360-0005
EMP: 7 **EST:** 2019
SALES (est): 93.17K **Privately Held**
Web: www.mainepetsupply.com
SIC: 3999 Pet supplies

(G-5602)
MARY BREEN & COMPANY INC
616 Post Rd (04090-4022)
PHONE.....................................207 646-4227
Mary Breen, *Pr*
EMP: 9 **EST:** 2017
SALES (est): 619.24K **Privately Held**
SIC: 2051 Bakery: wholesale or wholesale/retail combined

(G-5603)
MORSE HARDWARE & LUMBER LLC
Also Called: Benjamin Moore Authorized Ret
1259 Post Rd (04090-4514)
PHONE.....................................207 646-5700
Martin E Morse, *Prin*
EMP: 10 **EST:** 2006
SALES (est): 240.76K **Privately Held**
Web: www.benjaminmoore.com
SIC: 3429 5211 5231 Hardware, nec; Lumber products; Paint, glass, and wallpaper stores

(G-5604)
PIKE INDUSTRIES INC
81 Boyd Rd (04090-7128)
PHONE.....................................207 676-9973
EMP: 10
SALES (corp-wide): 32.72B **Privately Held**
Web: www.pikeindustries.com
SIC: 1611 5032 2951 Highway and street paving contractor; Sand, construction; Asphalt paving mixtures and blocks
HQ: Pike Industries, Inc.
    3 Eastgate Park Dr
    Belmont NH 03220
    603 527-5100

(G-5605)
SHORELINE PUBLICATIONS
Also Called: Weekly Sentinel, The

952 Post Rd Unit 10 (04090-4142)
PHONE.....................................207 646-8448
Carol Brennan, *Pr*
EMP: 12 **EST:** 2005
SQ FT: 1,000
SALES (est): 551.3K **Privately Held**
Web: www.theweeklysentinel.com
SIC: 2759 2711 Publication printing; Newspapers, publishing and printing

(G-5606)
STONEWALL KITCHEN LLC
Also Called: Village Candle
90 Spencer Dr (04090-5548)
PHONE.....................................207 251-4800
Jay Dowling, *Brnch Mgr*
EMP: 80
Web: www.stonewallkitchen.com
SIC: 3999 Barber and beauty shop equipment
PA: Stonewall Kitchen, Llc
    2 Stonewall Ln
    York ME 03909

(G-5607)
VELUX AMERICA LLC
Also Called: Wasco Products
85 Spencer Dr Unit A (04090-9317)
PHONE.....................................207 216-4500
Jeff Frank, *Mgr*
EMP: 95
SQ FT: 56,000
Web: www.veluxusa.com
SIC: 3441 Fabricated structural metal
HQ: Velux America Llc
    450 Old Brickyard Rd
    Greenwood SC 29649
    864 941-4700

(G-5608)
VILLAGE CANDLE INC
Also Called: Camden Designs
90 Spencer Dr (04090-5548)
PHONE.....................................207 251-4800
◆ **EMP:** 110
Web: www.stonewallkitchen.com
SIC: 3999 Barber and beauty shop equipment

West Bath
Sagadahoc County

(G-5609)
TRINKEN BREWING CO LLC
144 State Rd (04530-6315)
PHONE.....................................207 389-6360
EMP: 8 **EST:** 2019
SALES (est): 265.12K **Privately Held**
Web: www.trinkenbrewingco.com
SIC: 2082 Malt beverages

West Enfield
Penobscot County

(G-5610)
NORTHWOODS PUBLICATIONS LLC
Also Called: Northwoods Sporting Journal
57 Old County Rd N (04493-4525)
P.O. Box 195 (04493-0195)
PHONE.....................................207 732-4880
Victor Morin, *Managing Member*
EMP: 16 **EST:** 1993
SALES (est): 1.18MM **Privately Held**
Web: www.sportingjournal.com
SIC: 2711 Newspapers, publishing and printing

West Kennebunk
York County

(G-5611)
WILLIAM ARTHUR INC
Also Called: Ten Bamboo Studio
7 Alewive Park Rd (04094)
PHONE..............................413 684-2600
Stephen P Defalco, *CEO*
Beth Madore, *
Hank Beresin, *
Lisa Blinn, *
Dorothy Leavitt, *
▲ **EMP:** 63 **EST:** 1949
SQ FT: 30,000
SALES (est): 4.48MM
SALES (corp-wide): 2.72B **Privately Held**
Web: www.crane.com
SIC: 2771 2678 Greeting cards; Stationery
products
PA: Hallmark Cards, Incorporated
2501 Mcgee St
Kansas City MO 64108
816 274-5111

West Paris
Oxford County

(G-5612)
MAINE BALSAM FIR PRODCTS
Also Called: Maine Balsam Fir Products
16 Morse Hill Rd (04289-5317)
P.O. Box 9 (04289-0009)
PHONE..............................207 674-5090
TOLL FREE: 800
Wendy Newmeyer, *Pr*
Wendy Newmeyer, *Owner*
Jack Newmeyer, *Treas*
EMP: 10 **EST:** 1983
SQ FT: 5,000
SALES (est): 465.06K **Privately Held**
Web: www.mainebalsam.com
SIC: 2299 2392 Pillow fillings: curled hair,
cotton waste, moss, hemp tow; Household
furnishings, nec

Westbrook
Cumberland County

(G-5613)
320 INK LLC
2 Karen Dr (04092-1919)
PHONE..............................207 835-0038
EMP: 8 **EST:** 2019
SALES (est): 504.07K **Privately Held**
Web: www.320ink.com
SIC: 2759 Screen printing

(G-5614)
ARTEL INC
25 Bradley Dr (04092-2013)
PHONE..............................207 854-0860
Richard Curtis, *Ch Bd*
Kirby Pilcher, *
EMP: 38 **EST:** 1982
SALES (est): 8.43MM **Privately Held**
Web: www.aicompanies.com
SIC: 3845 3679 3826 Electromedical
equipment; Electronic circuits; Analytical
instruments

(G-5615)
ASML US LLC
590 County Rd (04092-1914)
PHONE..............................207 541-5000
David Price, *Mgr*
EMP: 8
SALES (corp-wide): 21.99B **Privately Held**
Web: www.asml.com
SIC: 5065 3674 Semiconductor devices;
Semiconductors and related devices
HQ: Asml Us, Llc
2625 W Geronimo Pl
Chandler AZ 85224
480 696-2888

(G-5616)
BAGALA WINDOW WORKS
677 Main St (04092-4125)
PHONE..............................207 887-9231
Marc Bagala, *Pr*
EMP: 7 **EST:** 2015
SALES (est): 922.6K **Privately Held**
Web: www.bagalawindowworks.com
SIC: 5031 2499 1751 Windows; Decorative
wood and woodwork; Carpentry work

(G-5617)
BAILEY SIGN INC
9 Thomas Dr (04092-3826)
PHONE..............................207 774-2843
Bruce W Bailey, *Pr*
Ralph Hutchenson, *
EMP: 25 **EST:** 1975
SALES (est): 2.66MM **Privately Held**
Web: www.baileysign.com
SIC: 2399 1799 3993 Banners, pennants,
and flags; Sign installation and maintenance
; Electric signs

(G-5618)
BRACKETT MACHINE INC
355 Saco St (04092-2003)
P.O. Box 7 (04098-0007)
PHONE..............................207 854-9789
Herbert Howard, *Pr*
Betty Howard, *Treas*
EMP: 20 **EST:** 1982
SALES (est): 2.12MM **Privately Held**
Web: www.aod-tuyere.com
SIC: 3599 Machine shop, jobbing and repair

(G-5619)
BURR SIGNS
2 Karen Dr Stop 4 (04092-1919)
PHONE..............................207 396-6111
Mason Legendre, *Prin*
EMP: 9 **EST:** 2012
SALES (est): 451.04K **Privately Held**
Web: www.burrsigns.com
SIC: 3993 Electric signs

(G-5620)
**CASCO BAY BUTTER
COMPANY INC**
Also Called: Casco Bay Creamery
25 Thomas Dr (04092-3853)
PHONE..............................207 712-9148
Alicia Menard, *CEO*
EMP: 9 **EST:** 2012
SALES (est): 3.63MM **Privately Held**
Web: www.cascobaycreamery.com
SIC: 2021 5143 Creamery butter; Butter

(G-5621)
CLEARH2O INC
85 Bradley Dr (04092-2013)
PHONE..............................207 221-0039
Kathie Dioli, *Prin*
Linda Pollock, *Prin*
EMP: 25 **EST:** 2005
SALES (est): 12.12MM **Privately Held**
Web: www.clearh2o.com
SIC: 2834 Pharmaceutical preparations

(G-5622)
**CONTROLLED ENVMT EQP
CORP**
55 Bradley Dr (04092-2080)
PHONE..............................207 854-9126
Joseph Davin, *Pr*
Eric Springer, *Sec*
EMP: 14 **EST:** 1988
SQ FT: 11,000
SALES (est): 3.04MM **Publicly Held**
Web: www.ceecusa.com
SIC: 2842 7218 Polishes and sanitation
goods; Clean room apparel supply
HQ: Scapa North America Inc
111 Great Pond Dr
Windsor CT 06095
860 688-8000

(G-5623)
CYBERCOPY INC
Also Called: B Copy
55 Bradley Dr Ste A (04092-2080)
PHONE..............................207 775-2679
Brad Burns, *Pr*
Thomas Black, *Pr*
Jamie Mclean, *Genl Mgr*
EMP: 9 **EST:** 1999
SALES (est): 634.17K **Privately Held**
Web: www.cybercopyme.com
SIC: 2752 Photo-offset printing

(G-5624)
D & G MACHINE PRODUCTS INC
Also Called: D & G
50 Eisenhower Dr (04092-2009)
PHONE..............................207 854-1500
Duane Gushee, *Pr*
Charles Tarling Iii, *Pr*
Charles Tarling, *VP*
Steven Sullivan, *
◆ **EMP:** 100 **EST:** 1967
SQ FT: 90,000
SALES (est): 24.07MM **Privately Held**
Web: www.dgmachine.com
SIC: 3599 Machine shop, jobbing and repair

(G-5625)
**DIRECTIONS TO MAINE
DOVETAIL**
36 Rochester St (04092-4236)
PHONE..............................207 829-2759
Ann Pollak, *Owner*
EMP: 7 **EST:** 2011
SALES (est): 246.26K **Privately Held**
Web: www.mainedovetail.com
SIC: 2434 Wood kitchen cabinets

(G-5626)
FULL COURT PRESS
855 Main St Ste 2 (04092-3069)
PHONE..............................207 464-0002
Gerald Sands, *Pr*
Edward Symbol, *VP*
EMP: 12 **EST:** 1998
SQ FT: 9,000
SALES (est): 879.92K **Privately Held**
Web: www.fullcourtpress.biz
SIC: 2752 Offset printing

(G-5627)
HARCROS CHEMICALS INC
50 Larrabee Rd (04092-4752)
PHONE..............................207 856-6756
TOLL FREE: 800
Frank Lemanski, *Brnch Mgr*
EMP: 7
SQ FT: 1,000
SALES (corp-wide): 498.13MM **Privately
Held**
Web: www.harcros.com
SIC: 5169 2869 Industrial chemicals;
Industrial organic chemicals, nec
PA: Harcros Chemicals Inc.
5200 Speaker Rd
Kansas City KS 66106
913 321-3131

(G-5628)
HAWKIN DYNAMICS LLC
90 Bridge St Ste 230 (04092-2990)
PHONE..............................207 405-9142
EMP: 18 **EST:** 2017
SALES (est): 1.04MM **Privately Held**
Web: www.hawkindynamics.com
SIC: 5734 7371 3845 Software, business
and non-game; Computer software
development and applications; Patient
monitoring apparatus, nec

(G-5629)
**HILLSIDE LUMBER COMPANY
INC**
781 County Rd (04092-1910)
PHONE..............................207 839-2575
Marsha Knight, *Pr*
EMP: 25 **EST:** 1976
SQ FT: 10,000
SALES (est): 2.74MM **Privately Held**
Web: www.hillsidelumber.com
SIC: 5211 5031 2421 Planing mill products
and lumber; Lumber: rough, dressed, and
finished; Sawmills and planing mills, general

(G-5630)
IDEXX DISTRIBUTION INC
Also Called: Idexx Reference Laboratories
1 Idexx Dr (04092-2040)
PHONE..............................207 556-0300
Jonathan Ayers, *Pr*
EMP: 80 **EST:** 2002
SALES (est): 26.8MM
SALES (corp-wide): 3.37B **Publicly Held**
Web: www.idexx.com
SIC: 3841 3826 3829 2835 Surgical and
medical instruments; Analytical instruments
; Measuring and controlling devices, nec;
Diagnostic substances
PA: Idexx Laboratories, Inc.
1 Idexx Dr
Westbrook ME 04092
207 556-0300

(G-5631)
IDEXX LABORATORIES INC (PA)
Also Called: Idexx
1 Idexx Dr (04092-2041)
PHONE..............................207 556-0300
Jonathan J Mazelsky, *Pr*
Lawrence D Kingsley, *Non-Executive
Chairman of the Board*
Brian P Mckeon, *Ex VP*
James F Polewaczyk, *CCO*
Tina Hunt, *Ex VP*
▲ **EMP:** 710 **EST:** 1983
SALES (est): 3.37B
SALES (corp-wide): 3.37B **Publicly Held**
Web: www.idexx.com
SIC: 0741 2834 2835 0219 Veterinary
services for livestock; Veterinary
pharmaceutical preparations; Veterinary
diagnostic substances; General livestock,
nec

(G-5632)
IDEXX OPERATIONS INC (HQ)
1 Idexx Dr (04092-2040)
PHONE..............................207 556-4388
Bruce Gardner, *CEO*
◆ **EMP:** 27 **EST:** 1997

SALES (est): 47.57MM
SALES (corp-wide): 3.37B **Publicly Held**
Web: www.idexx.dk
SIC: **3826** Analytical instruments
PA: Idexx Laboratories, Inc.
1 Idexx Dr
Westbrook ME 04092
207 556-0300

(G-5633)
KARDEX REMSTAR LLC (HQ)
41 Eisenhower Dr (04092-2032)
PHONE....................207 854-1861
Jens Fankhnel, *
▲ **EMP:** 46 **EST:** 1982
SQ FT: 55,000
SALES (est): 63.8MM **Privately Held**
Web: www.kardex.com
SIC: **5084 3496 2542** Materials handling
machinery; Miscellaneous fabricated wire
products; Partitions and fixtures, except
wood
PA: Kardex Holding Ag
Thurgauerstrasse 40
ZUrich ZH 8050

(G-5634)
KSD ATL TRNSPT SYSTEMS INC
Also Called: Trucking , Distribution
84g Warren Ave (04092-4433)
PHONE....................207 591-4150
TOLL FREE: 800
Michael Dore, *Pr*
Michael Dore, *VP*
Micheal Dore, *
EMP: 75 **EST:** 1992
SALES (est): 6.79MM **Privately Held**
Web: www.atlantictransportsystems.com
SIC: **3537** Trucks, tractors, loaders, carriers,
and similar equipment

(G-5635)
LANCO ASSEMBLY SYSTEMS INC (PA)
Also Called: Lanco Integrated
12 Thomas Dr (04092-3824)
PHONE....................207 773-2060
Edward Karabec, *Pr*
▲ **EMP:** 75 **EST:** 1983
SQ FT: 50,000
SALES (est): 32.78MM
SALES (corp-wide): 32.78MM **Privately Held**
Web: www.lancointegrated.com
SIC: **3559** Robots, molding and forming
plastics

(G-5636)
LLC PARK HILL
40 Fieldstone Dr (04092-3210)
PHONE....................207 239-7741
EMP: 7 **EST:** 2018
SALES (est): 117.85K **Privately Held**
SIC: **3999** Manufacturing industries, nec

(G-5637)
MATHEWS BAKERY INC
Also Called: Botto's Bakery
5 Karen Dr (04092-1925)
PHONE....................207 773-9647
Robert Mathews, *Pr*
Margaret Mathews, *Sec*
Everett Mathews, *VP*
Stevens Mathews, *Treas*
EMP: 13 **EST:** 1945
SALES (est): 599.66K **Privately Held**
Web: www.bottosbakery.com
SIC: **2051** Bread, all types (white, wheat,
rye, etc); fresh or frozen

(G-5638)
MESSER TRUCK EQUIPMENT (PA)
Also Called: Messer Petroleum Equipment
170 Warren Ave (04092-4439)
PHONE....................207 854-9751
TOLL FREE: 800
Jeffrey Messer, *Pr*
EMP: 21 **EST:** 1899
SQ FT: 34,000
SALES (est): 7.93MM
SALES (corp-wide): 7.93MM **Privately Held**
Web: www.messertruckequipment.com
SIC: **3711 3713** Snow plows (motor
vehicles), assembly of; Truck bodies and
parts

(G-5639)
MOORE-CLARK USA INC
Also Called: Bio-Oregon
15 Saunders Way Ste 500 (04092-4835)
PHONE....................207 591-7077
Ron Gowan, *CEO*
EMP: 8
Web: www.bio-oregon.com
SIC: **3999** Pet supplies
HQ: Moore-Clark U.S.A., Inc.
1140 Industrial Way
Longview WA 98632
360 425-6715

(G-5640)
NATIVE MAINE OPERATIONS INC
10 Bradley Dr (04092-2011)
PHONE....................207 856-1100
Ross Foca, *CEO*
EMP: 35 **EST:** 2017
SALES (est): 2.51MM **Privately Held**
Web: www.nativeme.com
SIC: **2023 5147 5149 5148** Dry, condensed
and evaporated dairy products; Meats and
meat products; Specialty food items; Fresh
fruits and vegetables

(G-5641)
PIKA ENERGY INC
35 Bradley Dr Stop 1 (04092-2026)
PHONE....................207 887-9105
EMP: 10 **EST:** 2010
SALES (est): 4.07MM **Publicly Held**
Web: www.generac.com
SIC: **3511** Turbines and turbine generator
sets
PA: Generac Holdings Inc.
S45w29290 Hwy 59
Waukesha WI 53189

(G-5642)
PLANET VENTURES INC (PA)
Also Called: Planet Dog-Cancelled
85 Bradley Dr (04092-2013)
PHONE....................207 761-1515
Colleen Mccrasken, *CEO*
Sean Callahan, *Dir Opers*
Alex Fisher, *COO*
▲ **EMP:** 15 **EST:** 1997
SQ FT: 3,000
SALES (est): 33
SALES (corp-wide): 33 **Privately Held**
SIC: **3999** Pet supplies

(G-5643)
PRESUMPSCOT WATER POWER CO
89 Cumberland St (04092-3592)
PHONE....................207 856-4000
Sarah Manchester, *Prin*

EMP: 64 **EST:** 1878
SALES (est): 916.2K **Privately Held**
SIC: **2621** Paper mills
HQ: Sappi North America, Inc.
255 State St Fl 4
Boston MA 02109
617 423-7300

(G-5644)
R G EATON WOODWORKS INC
Also Called: Stonecoast MARble& Granite
12 Rochester St (04092-4236)
P.O. Box 437 (04098-0437)
PHONE....................207 883-3398
Robert G Eaton, *Pr*
EMP: 9 **EST:** 1984
SQ FT: 6,500
SALES (est): 773.63K **Privately Held**
SIC: **1751 2434 2431** Cabinet building and
installation; Wood kitchen cabinets; Millwork

(G-5645)
SAPPI FINE PAPER TECH CTR
300 Warren Ave (04092-4439)
PHONE....................207 239-6071
EMP: 23 **EST:** 2017
SALES (est): 15.34MM **Privately Held**
Web: www.sappi.com
SIC: **2621** Paper mills

(G-5646)
SAPPI NORTH AMERICA INC
Also Called: Sappi North America
89 Cumberland St (04092-3592)
P.O. Box 5000 (04098-5000)
PHONE....................207 856-4000
EMP: 350
Web: www.sappi.com
SIC: **2621** Paper mills
HQ: Sappi North America, Inc.
255 State St Fl 4
Boston MA 02109
617 423-7300

(G-5647)
SAPPI NORTH AMERICA INC
Also Called: Sappi Fine Ppr Westbrook Mill
89 Cumberland St (04092-3592)
PHONE....................207 856-4911
EMP: 240
Web: www.sappi.com
SIC: **2679 2674 2672 2621** Paper products,
converted, nec; Bags: uncoated paper and
multiwall; Coated paper, except
photographic, carbon, or abrasive; Paper
mills
HQ: Sappi North America, Inc.
255 State St Fl 4
Boston MA 02109
617 423-7300

(G-5648)
SIGCO LLC
600 County Rd (04092-1932)
PHONE....................207 775-2676
EMP: 40
SALES (corp-wide): 1.5B **Privately Held**
Web: www.sigcoinc.com
SIC: **3231 3446** Insulating glass: made from
purchased glass; Architectural metalwork
HQ: Sigco, Llc
48 Spiller Dr
Westbrook ME 04092
207 775-2676

(G-5649)
SIGCO LLC (HQ)
Also Called: Sigco
48 Spiller Dr (04092-2099)
PHONE....................207 775-2676

Dave Mcelhenny, *CEO*
▲ **EMP:** 240 **EST:** 1985
SQ FT: 55,000
SALES (est): 35.15MM
SALES (corp-wide): 1.5B **Privately Held**
Web: www.sigcoinc.com
SIC: **3231 3446** Insulating glass: made from
purchased glass; Architectural metalwork
PA: Oldcastle Buildingenvelope, Inc.
5005 Lyndon B Johnson Fwy
Dallas TX 75244
214 273-3400

(G-5650)
SILVEX INCORPORATED
45 Thomas Dr (04092-3833)
PHONE....................207 761-0392
Richard Atkinson, *CEO*
Philip Ridley, *
Dan Atkinson, *
Beverly Atkinson, *
EMP: 78 **EST:** 1957
SQ FT: 40,000
SALES (est): 9.48MM **Privately Held**
Web: www.silvexinc.com
SIC: **3471** Electroplating of metals or
formed products

(G-5651)
TITAN MACHINE PRODUCTS INC
600 County Rd (04092-1932)
PHONE....................207 775-0011
EMP: 55
SIC: **3599** Machine shop, jobbing and repair

(G-5652)
TRANE US INC
Also Called: Trane
860 Spring St # 1 (04092-3820)
PHONE....................844 807-2282
Jack Borgschulte, *Brnch Mgr*
EMP: 16
Web: www.trane.com
SIC: **3585** Refrigeration and heating
equipment
HQ: Trane U.S. Inc.
800 Beaty St Ste E
Davidson NC 28036
704 655-4000

(G-5653)
WORKGROUP TECH PARTNERS INC (PA)
Also Called: Wgtech
207 Larrabee Rd (04092-4812)
P.O. Box 110 (04098-0110)
PHONE....................207 856-5312
EMP: 42 **EST:** 1994
SQ FT: 30,000
SALES (est): 9.65MM **Privately Held**
Web: www.wgtech.com
SIC: **7373 7372** Value-added resellers,
computer systems; Application computer
software

(G-5654)
XTREME SCREEN & SPORTSWEAR LLC
937 Main St (04092-2825)
PHONE....................207 857-9200
Geoff Sawyer, *Prin*
Michelle Lebeau, *Prin*
EMP: 10 **EST:** 2011
SALES (est): 770.17K **Privately Held**
Web: www.xtremescreenprint.com
SIC: **2759** Screen printing

▲ = Import ▼ = Export
◆ = Import/Export

Whitefield
Lincoln County

(G-5655)
LITTLE ENTERPRISES LLC
Also Called: Little Enterprises North
208 Rockland Rd (04353-3157)
PHONE..............................207 549-7232
Scott Little, *Pr*
EMP: 19
SALES (corp-wide): 149.03MM **Privately Held**
Web: www.mmgmfg.com
SIC: 3599 Machine shop, jobbing and repair
HQ: Little Enterprises, Llc
31 Locust Rd
Ipswich MA 01938

(G-5656)
PROKNEE CORP
Also Called: Proknee
137 Devine Rd (04353-3207)
PHONE..............................207 549-5018
Lee Richards, *Pr*
Michael Levy, *
Julie Clark, *
Jayson Abbott, *
EMP: 27 **EST:** 1985
SQ FT: 2,400
SALES (est): 2.39MM **Privately Held**
Web: www.proknee.com
SIC: 5713 1752 3069 Floor covering stores;
Floor laying and floor work, nec; Kneeling
pads, rubber

Whitneyville
Washington County

(G-5657)
WHITNEY ORIGINALS
600 Us Route 1 (04654)
P.O. Box 157 (04654-0157)
PHONE..............................207 255-5857
David Whitney, *Pr*
David Whitney, *Pr*
Dale Whitney, *
Daniel Mckay, *Clerk*
▲ **EMP:** 80 **EST:** 1991
SQ FT: 21,000
SALES (est): 4.92MM **Privately Held**
Web: www.whitneywreath.com
SIC: 3999 Wreaths, artificial

Wilton
Franklin County

(G-5658)
MINUTEMAN METAL LLC
469 Depot St (04294-6608)
P.O. Box 207 (04270-0207)
PHONE..............................207 217-8908
Evan Coleman, *Prin*
Dan Fletcher, *Prin*
EMP: 8 **EST:** 2018
SALES (est): 476.53K **Privately Held**
SIC: 3499 Fabricated metal products, nec

(G-5659)
SALT AND PEPPER ME LLC
Also Called: Salt & Pepper and Sugar Too
843 Us Route 2 E (04294-6649)
PHONE..............................207 645-7035
EMP: 12 **EST:** 2018
SALES (est): 835.86K **Privately Held**
Web: www.saltandpepperme.com

SIC: 2899 Chemical preparations, nec

Windham
Cumberland County

(G-5660)
ERIN MURPHY
824 Roosevelt Trl (04062-5370)
PHONE..............................928 525-2056
Erin Murphy, *Prin*
EMP: 7 **EST:** 2005
SALES (est): 471.14K **Privately Held**
Web: www.emliterary.com
SIC: 2759 Advertising literature: printing, nsk

(G-5661)
F W WEBB COMPANY
Also Called: Johnson Contrls Authorized Dlr
3 Danielle Dr (04062-6933)
PHONE..............................207 892-5302
EMP: 10
SALES (corp-wide): 1.02B **Privately Held**
Web: www.johnsoncontrols.com
SIC: 5251 5074 3432 Pumps and pumping
equipment; Plumbing fittings and supplies;
Plumbing fixture fittings and trim
PA: F. W. Webb Company
160 Middlesex Tpke
Bedford MA 01730
781 272-6600

(G-5662)
IBCONTROLS
Also Called: Intelligent Building Controls
3 Pope Rd (04062-2309)
PHONE..............................207 893-0080
James Evers, *Pr*
EMP: 35 **EST:** 2000
SQ FT: 8,000
SALES (est): 3.85MM **Privately Held**
Web: www.ibcontrols.com
SIC: 3829 7373 Measuring and controlling
devices, nec; Local area network (LAN)
systems integrator

(G-5663)
K & D MILLWORKS INC
Also Called: K & D Distributing
7 Danielle Dr (04062-6933)
PHONE..............................207 892-5188
Dennis Dyer, *Pr*
Kelly C Dyer, *VP*
EMP: 22 **EST:** 1989
SALES (est): 1.67MM **Privately Held**
Web: www.kdcountertops.com
SIC: 2541 5031 Counter and sink tops;
Kitchen cabinets

(G-5664)
LH LIQUIDATION LLC
765 Roosevelt Trl (04062-5341)
P.O. Box 1206 (04062-1206)
PHONE..............................207 893-8233
Dennis C Leiner, *Pr*
Mark Waite, *
EMP: 30 **EST:** 2010
SQ FT: 3,000
SALES (est): 6.06MM **Privately Held**
Web: www.lighthouseoptics.com
SIC: 3827 3845 Optical instruments and
apparatus; Endoscopic equipment,
electromedical, nec

(G-5665)
MILLS & CO INC
778 Roosevelt Trl Ste 1 (04062-5376)
PHONE..............................207 893-1115
Diana N Mills, *Pr*

Robert Mills, *VP*
EMP: 7 **EST:** 2002
SQ FT: 6,000
SALES (est): 630K **Privately Held**
Web: www.millsandcomaine.com
SIC: 3634 Housewares, excluding cooking
appliances and utensils

(G-5666)
MWAVE INDUSTRIES LLC
Also Called: Alaris USA
33r Main St Ste 1 (04062-4474)
PHONE..............................207 892-0011
Peter Farnum, *Prin*
Ralph Prigge, *VP*
▲ **EMP:** 20 **EST:** 2004
SALES (est): 2.46MM **Privately Held**
Web: www.mwavellc.com
SIC: 3663 Radio and t.v. communications
equipment

(G-5667)
**QUARTER POINT
WOODWORKING LLC**
7b Commons Ave (04062-5293)
PHONE..............................207 892-7022
EMP: 10
SALES (corp-wide): 152.09K **Privately
Held**
Web: www.oceanpro.com.my
SIC: 2431 Millwork
PA: Quarter Point Woodworking Llc
483 Intervale Rd
New Gloucester ME 04260
207 926-1032

(G-5668)
RBW INC
Also Called: Design Fab
113 Nash Rd (04062-4500)
PHONE..............................207 786-2446
Dennis E Worster, *Pr*
EMP: 11 **EST:** 1984
SALES (est): 473.56K **Privately Held**
SIC: 3441 Expansion joints (structural
shapes), iron or steel

(G-5669)
**SOUTHERN MAINE INDUSTRIES
CORP**
68 Outlet Cove Rd (04062-5536)
PHONE..............................207 856-7391
Cheryl A Bolduc V, *Pr*
EMP: 15 **EST:** 1987
SQ FT: 22,000
SALES (est): 828.88K **Privately Held**
Web: www.southernmaineindustries.com
SIC: 3471 Electroplating of metals or
formed products

(G-5670)
STANDARD MERGER SUB LLC
Also Called: Strategic Bio Solutions
52 Anderson Rd (04062-4010)
PHONE..............................207 856-6151
Jeff Thompson, *Mgr*
EMP: 51
SALES (corp-wide): 415.01MM **Publicly
Held**
SIC: 2836 3841 Serums; Surgical and
medical instruments
HQ: Standard Merger Sub, Llc
155 Mineola Blvd
Mineola NY 11501
302 248-1100

(G-5671)
TENA GROUP LLC
Also Called: Finetone

2 Plaza Dr (04062-5927)
PHONE..............................207 893-2920
Edouard A Gauthier, *Prin*
EMP: 8 **EST:** 2011
SALES (est): 495.09K **Privately Held**
SIC: 3842 Hearing aids

(G-5672)
TIME4PRINTING INC
588 Roosevelt Trl (04062-4904)
PHONE..............................207 838-1496
Kelly Mank, *Owner*
EMP: 10 **EST:** 2015
SALES (est): 448.32K **Privately Held**
Web: www.time4printing.com
SIC: 2752 Offset printing

(G-5673)
**TUBE HOLLOWS
INTERNATIONAL**
Also Called: Confluent Maine
39 Enterprise Dr Ste 2 (04062-5697)
PHONE..............................844 721-8823
EMP: 45 **EST:** 2011
SQ FT: 50,000
SALES (est): 11.03MM **Privately Held**
Web: www.confluentmedical.com
SIC: 3599 Machine shop, jobbing and repair
PA: Confluent Medical Technologies, Inc.
6263 N Scottsdale Rd # 2
Scottsdale AZ 85250

(G-5674)
WARDWELL PIPING INC
Also Called: Ata Piping
194 Roosevelt Trl (04062-3396)
PHONE..............................207 892-0034
Nathan Wardwell, *Pr*
Andrea Wardwell, *Off Mgr*
EMP: 14 **EST:** 1990
SQ FT: 6,000
SALES (est): 917.66K **Privately Held**
SIC: 3498 1711 Fabricated pipe and fittings;
Process piping contractor

(G-5675)
WINDHAM MILLWORK INC
Also Called: UNI-Sim
4 Architectural Dr (04062-5483)
P.O. Box 1358 (04062-1358)
PHONE..............................207 892-3238
Bruce Pulkkinen Senior, *Pr*
Bruce Pulkkinen Senior, *CEO*
Bruce Pulkkinen Junior, *Pr*
Michael Mcnally, *CFO*
Scott Gordan, *Prin*
EMP: 68 **EST:** 1958
SQ FT: 42,000
SALES (est): 8.67MM **Privately Held**
Web: www.windhammillwork.com
SIC: 2431 Millwork

(G-5676)
WINDHAM WEAPONRY INC
Also Called: Windham Weaponry
999 Roosevelt Trl Ste 22 (04062-5651)
P.O. Box 1900 (04062-1900)
PHONE..............................207 893-2223
EMP: 8 **EST:** 2011
SQ FT: 16,000
SALES (est): 1.94MM **Privately Held**
Web: www.windhamweaponry.com
SIC: 3484 Guns (firearms) or gun parts, 30
mm. and below

Windsor
Kennebec County

(G-5677)
AIR CONTROL INDUSTRIES INC
76 Augusta Rockland Rd (04363-3625)
PHONE....................207 445-2518
Mark A Scribner, Pr
▲ EMP: 9 EST: 2008
SALES (est): 1.7MM **Privately Held**
Web: www.aircontrolindustries.com
SIC: 3564 Aircurtains (blower)

Winn
Penobscot County

(G-5678)
HERBERT C HAYNES INC (PA)
Also Called: H C Haynes
40 Route 168 (04495-5217)
P.O. Box 96 (04495-0096)
PHONE....................207 736-3412
Herbert C Haynes, Pr
Ginger Haynes Maxwell, *
Virginia Haynes, *
EMP: 36 EST: 1930
SQ FT: 1,200
SALES (est): 4.68MM
SALES (corp-wide): 4.68MM **Privately Held**
Web: www.registrar-transfers.com
SIC: 2411 Pulpwood contractors engaged in cutting

Winslow
Kennebec County

(G-5679)
ALBION MANUFACTURING
133 Halifax St (04901-7655)
P.O. Box 39 (04910-0039)
PHONE....................207 873-5633
Mike Cothran, Pr
EMP: 7 EST: 1999
SALES (est): 964.3K **Privately Held**
Web: www.albionmfgco.com
SIC: 3599 Machine shop, jobbing and repair

(G-5680)
ALCOM LLC (PA)
Also Called: Machine Trailers
6 Millennium Dr (04901-0777)
PHONE....................207 861-9800
Tratper Clark, Pr
▼ EMP: 20 EST: 2005
SALES (est): 52.26MM **Privately Held**
Web: www.alcomusa.com
SIC: 3715 Trailer bodies

(G-5681)
BABAC INC
166 China Rd (04901-0615)
PHONE....................207 872-0889
John Wallingford, Pr
Donald B Kingsbury, VP
▲ EMP: 10 EST: 1987
SQ FT: 3,000
SALES (est): 682.7K **Privately Held**
Web: www.babac.com
SIC: 3842 Traction apparatus

(G-5682)
F W WEBB COMPANY
Also Called: Johnson Contrls Authorized Dlr
37 Heywood Rd (04901-2639)
PHONE....................207 873-7741
Jeff Peters, Genl Mgr
EMP: 37
SALES (corp-wide): 1.02B **Privately Held**
Web: www.fwwebb.com
SIC: 5074 3823 3625 Plumbing fittings and supplies; Process control instruments; Relays and industrial controls
PA: F. W. Webb Company
160 Middlesex Tpke
Bedford MA 01730
781 272-6600

(G-5683)
LOHMANN ANIMAL HEALTH INTL INC
Also Called: Biologics Production
375 China Rd (04901-0632)
PHONE....................207 873-3989
David Zacek, CEO
Frank Sterner, *
Dianna Rafue, *
Crystal Olsen, *
▲ EMP: 112 EST: 1932
SQ FT: 30,000
SALES (est): 27.09MM
SALES (corp-wide): 4.41B **Publicly Held**
SIC: 2836 Biological products, except diagnostic
HQ: Lohmann Animal Health Gmbh
Heinz-Lohmann-Str. 4
Cuxhaven NI 27472
472 174-7000

(G-5684)
MCSWAIN MANUFACTURING INC
83 Verti Dr (04901-0727)
PHONE....................513 619-1222
EMP: 8 EST: 2019
SALES (est): 499.65K **Privately Held**
SIC: 3999 Manufacturing industries, nec

(G-5685)
MID STATE MACHINE PRODUCTS (PA)
83 Verti Dr (04901-0727)
PHONE....................207 873-6136
Duane Pekar, Pr
▲ EMP: 160 EST: 1967
SQ FT: 85,000
SALES (est): 52.18MM
SALES (corp-wide): 52.18MM **Privately Held**
Web: www.midstateusa.com
SIC: 3599 3545 Machine shop, jobbing and repair; Machine tool attachments and accessories

(G-5686)
NORTHEAST LABORATORY SVCS INC (PA)
227 China Rd (04901-0629)
P.O. Box 788 (04903-0788)
PHONE....................207 873-7711
TOLL FREE: 800
Rodney E Mears, Pr
Kenneth Eskelund, Stockholder*
Richard Eskelund, Stockholder*
Donald Eskelund, Stockholder*
Melissa Higgins, *
EMP: 67 EST: 1972
SQ FT: 26,000
SALES (est): 16.86MM
SALES (corp-wide): 16.86MM **Privately Held**
Web: www.nelabservices.com
SIC: 2836 8734 Culture media; Testing laboratories

(G-5687)
ORION ROPEWORKS INC (HQ)
Also Called: Orion Cordage
953 Benton Ave (04901-2618)
PHONE....................207 877-2224
▲ EMP: 10 EST: 2005
SALES (est): 17.39MM
SALES (corp-wide): 23.75MM **Privately Held**
Web: www.orioncordage.com
SIC: 2298 Ropes and fiber cables
PA: Canada Cordage Inc
70 Dundas St
Deseronto ON K0K 1
877 224-2673

(G-5688)
ORION ROPEWORKS LLC
953 Benton Ave (04901-2618)
PHONE....................207 877-2224
◆ EMP: 55 EST: 2002
SQ FT: 144,000
SALES (est): 17.39MM
SALES (corp-wide): 23.75MM **Privately Held**
Web: www.orioncordage.com
SIC: 3552 Rope and cordage machines
HQ: Orion Ropeworks, Inc.
953 Benton Ave
Winslow ME 04901

(G-5689)
WATERVILLE WINDOW CO INC
22 Verti Dr (04901-0728)
P.O. Box 724 (04903-0724)
PHONE....................207 873-0159
EMP: 25
Web: www.watervillewindow.com
SIC: 3081 Vinyl film and sheet

Winthrop
Kennebec County

(G-5690)
ALTERNATIVE MANUFACTURING INC
Also Called: A M I
30 Summer St Ste B (04364-1253)
PHONE....................207 377-9377
Kim Vandermeulen, Ch Bd
Greg Boyd, *
Steve Martin, *
Scot Story, *
EMP: 85 EST: 1989
SQ FT: 70,000
SALES (est): 23.59MM **Privately Held**
Web: www.amiems.com
SIC: 3672 Circuit boards, television and radio printed

(G-5691)
COPY CENTER (PA)
Also Called: Copy Center Plus The
1921 Us Route 202 (04364-3351)
P.O. Box 17 (04364-0017)
PHONE....................207 623-1452
Peter Mccarthy, Pr
Kevin Mccarthy, VP
Michael Mccarthy, VP
EMP: 10 EST: 1976
SQ FT: 20,000
SALES (est): 2.22MM
SALES (corp-wide): 2.22MM **Privately Held**
Web: www.thecopycenterplus.com
SIC: 7334 2752 Blueprinting service; Color lithography

(G-5692)
FABCO INC
30 Summer St Ste G (04364-1253)
P.O. Box 485 (04364-0485)
PHONE....................207 377-6909
◆ EMP: 25
Web: www.fabcomaine.com
SIC: 3541 Machine tool replacement & repair parts, metal cutting types

(G-5693)
MICRONICS ENGNRED FLTRTION GRO
40 Winada Dr (04364-3882)
PHONE....................207 377-2626
EMP: 10
SALES (corp-wide): 187MM **Privately Held**
Web: www.micronicsinc.com
SIC: 3569 Filters, general line: industrial
PA: Micronics Engineered Filtration Group, Inc.
1201 Riverfront Pkwy A
Chattanooga TN 37402
423 320-1787

(G-5694)
MICRONICS ENGNRED FLTRTION GRO
12 Winada Dr (04364-3882)
PHONE....................207 377-2626
EMP: 70
SALES (corp-wide): 187MM **Privately Held**
Web: www.micronicsinc.com
SIC: 3569 Filters, general line: industrial
PA: Micronics Engineered Filtration Group, Inc.
1201 Riverfront Pkwy A
Chattanooga TN 37402
423 320-1787

(G-5695)
NATIONAL FILTER MEDIA CORP
12 Winada Dr (04364-3882)
PHONE....................207 327-2626
EMP: 140
Web: www.micronicsinc.com
SIC: 3569 Filters, general line: industrial
HQ: The National Filter Media Corporation
1201 Riverfront Pkwy
Chattanooga TN 37402
801 363-6736

(G-5696)
VALMET INC
Also Called: Metso Fabric
30 Summer St Ste G (04364-1253)
P.O. Box 485 (04364-0485)
PHONE....................207 377-6909
Greg Stewart, Brnch Mgr
EMP: 95
SALES (corp-wide): 5.27B **Privately Held**
Web: www.valmet.com
SIC: 3541 Machine tool replacement & repair parts, metal cutting types
HQ: Valmet, Inc.
3720 Davinci Ct Ste 300
Norcross GA 30092
770 263-7863

Wiscasset
Lincoln County

(G-5697)
COASTAL BUSINESS CENTER INC

Also Called: Copy Shop, The
62 Old Ferry Rd (04578-4809)
P.O. Box 246 (04578-0246)
PHONE..............................207 882-7197
Christine Hallowell, *Pr*
EMP: 7 EST: 1974
SALES (est): 535.88K **Privately Held**
Web: www.copyshopme.com
SIC: 7334 2752 Photocopying and
 duplicating services; Offset printing

(G-5698)
MACHINERY SERVICE CO INC
166 W Alna Rd (04578-4092)
PHONE..............................207 882-6788
Kenneth R Boudin Junior, *Pr*
EMP: 9 EST: 1985
SQ FT: 11,900
SALES (est): 794.63K **Privately Held**
SIC: 3553 7699 3599 Sawmill machines;
 Industrial machinery and equipment repair;
 Machine shop, jobbing and repair

(G-5699)
PEREGRINE TURBINE TECH LLC
29 S Point Dr (04578-3260)
PHONE..............................207 687-8333
David Stapp, *CEO*
EMP: 10 EST: 2012
SALES (est): 1.27MM **Privately Held**
Web: www.peregrineturbine.com
SIC: 3511 Gas turbine generator set units,
 complete

(G-5700)
RYNEL INC
11 Twin Rivers Dr (04578-4943)
PHONE..............................207 882-0200
◆ **EMP:** 100
SIC: 3086 2821 Packaging and shipping
 materials, foamed plastics; Polyurethane
 resins

Wytopitlock
Aroostook County

(G-5701)
HANINGTON TIMBERLANDS
95 Main St (04497)
P.O. Box 90 (04497-0090)
PHONE..............................207 456-7003
Scott Hanington, *Pr*
Lorie Hanington, *VP*
EMP: 11 EST: 1994
SALES (est): 473.86K **Privately Held**
SIC: 2411 Logging camps and contractors

Yarmouth
Cumberland County

(G-5702)
CASCON INC
Also Called: Cascon Pump
65 Forest Falls Dr (04096-6906)
PHONE..............................207 846-6202
Edward Gervais, *Pr*
Edward Gervais Iii, *VP*
Bruce A Coggeshall, *Clerk*
Joyce Gervais, *Dir*
EMP: 16 EST: 1988
SQ FT: 2,400
SALES (est): 6.5MM **Privately Held**
Web: www.casconpump.com
SIC: 5084 3561 Pumps and pumping
 equipment, nec; Industrial pumps and parts

(G-5703)
DOWNEAST CONCEPTS INC
Also Called: Cape Shore
86 Downeast Dr (04096-7533)
PHONE..............................207 846-3726
John E Palmer Junior, *Ch Bd*
Frederick Palmer, *
Patricia Palmer, *Stockholder**
Peter Chapman, *Stockholder**
◆ **EMP: 21 EST:** 1946
SQ FT: 43,000
SALES (est): 9.52MM **Privately Held**
Web: www.cape-shore.com
SIC: 5199 5122 5092 2678 Gifts and
 novelties; Toilet soap; Educational toys;
 Stationery products

(G-5704)
GARMIN INTERNATIONAL INC
2 Delorme Dr (04096-6968)
PHONE..............................800 561-5105
EMP: 304
Web: www.garmin.com
SIC: 2741 2731 7371 Maps: publishing only,
 not printed on site; Book publishing;
 Computer software systems analysis and
 design, custom
HQ: Garmin International, Inc.
 1200 E 151st St
 Olathe KS 66062

(G-5705)
GREENE MARINE INC
343 Gilman Road (04096-5739)
PHONE..............................207 846-3184
Walter Greene, *Pr*
Joan Greene, *Clerk*
EMP: 9 EST: 1980
SQ FT: 2,400
SALES (est): 558.14K **Privately Held**
Web: www.greene-marine.com
SIC: 3732 Boatbuilding and repairing

(G-5706)
QUALITY CONTAINERS OF NENG
247 Portland St Ste 2 (04096-8130)
PHONE..............................207 846-5420
Gregory H Leonard, *Pr*
Kevin Burns, *VP*
EMP: 8 EST: 1920
SQ FT: 7,000
SALES (est): 943.29K **Privately Held**
Web:
www.qualitycontainersofnewengland.com
SIC: 3085 5085 Plastics bottles;
 Commercial containers

(G-5707)
SHEARWATER ALLERGY LLC
10 Forest Falls Dr Stop 9 (04096-4900)
P.O. Box 1298 (04096-2298)
PHONE..............................207 846-7676
EMP: 7 EST: 2019
SALES (est): 235.46K **Privately Held**
Web: www.shearwaterallergy.com
SIC: 8011 2834 Allergist; Pharmaceutical
 preparations

(G-5708)
TYLER TECHNOLOGIES INC
Also Called: Munis
1 Tyler Dr (04096-6828)
PHONE..............................207 781-2260
EMP: 236
SALES (corp-wide): 1.85B **Publicly Held**
Web: www.tylertech.com
SIC: 7372 Prepackaged software
PA: Tyler Technologies, Inc.
 5101 Tennyson Pkwy

Plano TX 75024
972 713-3700

(G-5709)
UNITED PUBLICATIONS INC
Also Called: Golf Course News
106 Lafayette St (04096-6125)
P.O. Box 995 (04096-1995)
PHONE..............................207 846-0600
Brook Taliaferro, *CEO*
EMP: 30 EST: 1981
SQ FT: 10,000
SALES (est): 4.86MM **Privately Held**
Web: www.unitedpublications.com
SIC: 2721 Magazines: publishing only, not
 printed on site

(G-5710)
YANKEE MARINA INC
Also Called: Yankee Marina and Billliards
142 Lafayette St (04096-6123)
P.O. Box 548 (04096-0548)
PHONE..............................207 846-9120
Deborah Delp, *Pr*
Suzanne Stevens, *Treas*
EMP: 23 EST: 1968
SQ FT: 30,000
SALES (est): 1.69MM **Privately Held**
Web: www.yankeemarina.com
SIC: 3731 4493 Shipbuilding and repairing;
 Boat yards, storage and incidental repair

York
York County

(G-5711)
COASTAL TRAFFIC
26 Brickyard Ct Ste 1 (03909-1657)
PHONE..............................207 351-8673
Terri Miller, *Pr*
EMP: 10 EST: 2012
SALES (est): 499.27K **Privately Held**
Web: www.coastaltrafficinc.com
SIC: 3669 Traffic signals, electric

(G-5712)
HAWK MOTORS INC
1100 Us Route 1 (03909-5822)
PHONE..............................207 363-4716
John Hawk, *Owner*
EMP: 7 EST: 2006
SALES (est): 137.9K **Privately Held**
Web: www.hawkmotors.com
SIC: 3369 Nonferrous foundries, nec

(G-5713)
HOMEGROWN FOR GOOD LLC
275 Cider Hill Rd (03909-5462)
PHONE..............................857 540-6361
Timothy Gibb, *CEO*
Timothy Gibb, *COO*
EMP: 10 EST: 2014
SALES (est): 998.05K **Privately Held**
Web: www.tidalnewyork.com
SIC: 3021 Rubber and plastics footwear

(G-5714)
MUMS CHEESECAKE
463 Us Route 1 (03909-1638)
PHONE..............................207 351-8543
Kimberly Bukowiec, *Prin*
EMP: 7 EST: 2017
SALES (est): 80.36K **Privately Held**
SIC: 2591 Window blinds

(G-5715)
OFFSHORE MARINE OUTFITTERS

15 Hannaford Dr (03909-1667)
PHONE..............................207 363-8862
Matt Nagy, *Prin*
EMP: 7 EST: 2010
SALES (est): 100.9K **Privately Held**
SIC: 2048 Fish food

(G-5716)
SANDS BUSINESS EQP & SUPS LLC
11 Payneton Hill Rd (03909-5401)
P.O. Box 266 (03908-0266)
PHONE..............................207 351-3334
Karen Tabora, *Managing Member*
EMP: 10 EST: 2002
SQ FT: 3,000
SALES (est): 9MM **Privately Held**
Web:
www.sands-business-equipment.com
SIC: 5044 3425 3429 3545 Photocopy
 machines; Saw blades and handsaws;
 Hardware, nec; Machine tool accessories

(G-5717)
STONEWALL KITCHEN LLC (PA)
Also Called: Vermont Village
2 Stonewall Ln (03909-1665)
PHONE..............................207 351-2713
◆ **EMP: 120 EST:** 1991
SQ FT: 12,000
SALES (est): 119.77MM **Privately Held**
Web: www.stonewallkitchen.com
SIC: 2033 2035 2032 5149 Jams, jellies,
 and preserves, packaged in cans, jars, etc.;
 Pickled fruits and vegetables; Canned
 specialties; Spices and seasonings

(G-5718)
WIGGLY BRIDGE DISTILLERIES LLC
441 Us Route 1 (03909-1638)
PHONE..............................207 363-9322
EMP: 20
SALES (corp-wide): 509.39K **Privately Held**
Web: www.wigglybridgedistillery.com
SIC: 2085 Distilled and blended liquors
PA: Wiggly Bridge Distilleries, Llc
 19 Railroad Ave
 York ME 03909
 207 363-9322

(G-5719)
WPF LIQUIDATING CO INC (PA)
Also Called: When Pigs Fly
40 Brickyard Ct (03909-1601)
PHONE..............................207 363-0612
▲ **EMP: 56 EST:** 1993
SQ FT: 25,000
SALES (est): 5.02MM **Privately Held**
Web: www.sendbread.com
SIC: 5812 2051 Eating places; Breads, rolls,
 and buns

(G-5720)
YOC
21 Railroad Ave (03909-6535)
PHONE..............................207 363-9322
Oliver Borrmann, *Prin*
EMP: 8 EST: 2005
SALES (est): 122.26K **Privately Held**
Web: www.yorkbirding.org.uk
SIC: 2869 Fuels

GEOGRAPHIC

MASSACHUSETTS

Abington
Plymouth County

(G-5721)
ADVANCED AIR SYSTEMS INC
43 Highland Rd Ste J (02351-3014)
PHONE..............................781 878-5733
Edward J Cardinal, *Pr*
EMP: 10 **EST:** 2003
SALES (est): 670K **Privately Held**
SIC: 3444　Furnace casings, sheet metal

(G-5722)
CAPE COD LUMBER CO INC
225 Groveland St (02351-2123)
P.O. Box 2013 (02351-0513)
PHONE..............................781 878-0715
Harvey L Hurvitz, *Pr*
Melvin Westerman, *
Richard Saladyga, *
Victor Fernandes, *
EMP: 156 **EST:** 1950
SQ FT: 130,000
SALES (est): 29.27MM **Privately Held**
Web: www.capecodlumber.com
SIC: 5211 2431 2541　Lumber products;
Doors and door parts and trim, wood; Wood
partitions and fixtures

(G-5723)
DILLON LABORATORIES INC
Also Called: Dillon Dental Laboratories
4 Thicket St (02351-1027)
PHONE..............................781 871-2333
William H Dillon Iii, *Pr*
EMP: 8 **EST:** 1963
SQ FT: 14,000
SALES (est): 119.02K **Privately Held**
SIC: 3843 8072　Dental equipment and
supplies; Dental laboratories

(G-5724)
DIXON BROS MILLWORK INC
200 Wales St (02351-5804)
PHONE..............................781 261-9962
Andrew Dixon, *Pr*
EMP: 8 **EST:** 1975
SQ FT: 7,000
SALES (est): 796.24K **Privately Held**
SIC: 2431 2434　Doors, wood; Wood kitchen
cabinets

(G-5725)
LE BEL INC
Also Called: Walsh Mechanical Conractors
380 North Ave (02351-1817)
PHONE..............................781 878-7279
Paul M Lebel, *Pr*
EMP: 97 **EST:** 1918
SQ FT: 28,000
SALES (est): 24.39MM **Privately Held**
SIC: 1711 3444　Mechanical contractor;
Sheet metalwork

(G-5726)
NEW ENGLAND ART
PUBLISHERS INC
Also Called: Birchcraft Studios
10 Railroad St (02351-1705)
PHONE..............................781 878-5151
◆ **EMP:** 250
Web: www.dfsonline.com
SIC: 2771 2759　Greeting cards;
Thermography

(G-5727)
PRECAST SPECIALTIES CORP
999 Adams St (02351-1058)
P.O. Box 86 (02351-0086)
PHONE..............................781 878-7220
Robert Bouchard, *Pr*
Guy Bouchard, *
EMP: 30 **EST:** 1983
SALES (est): 5.04MM **Privately Held**
Web: www.precastspecialtiescorp.com
SIC: 3272　Concrete products, precast, nec

(G-5728)
SCHUERCH CORPORATION
Also Called: Schuremed
452 Randolph St (02351-1170)
PHONE..............................781 982-7000
EMP: 26 **EST:** 1994
SQ FT: 20,000
SALES (est): 5.14MM **Privately Held**
Web: www.schuremed.com
SIC: 3841　Surgical and medical instruments

(G-5729)
XYZ SHEET METAL INC
281 Washington St (02351-2415)
P.O. Box 391 (02370-0391)
PHONE..............................781 878-1419
Gary Macwilliams, *Pr*
EMP: 15 **EST:** 2003
SQ FT: 7,700
SALES (est): 2.36MM **Privately Held**
Web: www.xyzsheetmetal.com
SIC: 3444　Metal ventilating equipment

Acton
Middlesex County

(G-5730)
ABISEE INC
30 Sudbury Rd Ste 1b (01720-5954)
P.O. Box 140 (01776-0140)
PHONE..............................978 637-2900
Leon Reznik, *Pr*
Helen Reznik, *
▲ **EMP:** 22 **EST:** 2006
SQ FT: 5,000
SALES (est): 586.06K **Privately Held**
Web: www.freedomscientific.com
SIC: 3699　Household electrical equipment

(G-5731)
ACTON RESEARCH
CORPORATION
15 Discovery Way (01720-4482)
PHONE..............................941 556-2601
Donald Templenan, *Pr*
EMP: 25 **EST:** 1998
SQ FT: 32,500
SALES (est): 11.56MM
SALES (corp-wide): 5.37B **Publicly Held**
Web: www.actonoptics.com
SIC: 3827 3826 3648 3231　Optical
instruments and lenses; Analytical
instruments; Lighting equipment, nec;
Products of purchased glass
PA: Roper Technologies, Inc.
6901 Prof Pkwy E Ste 200
Sarasota FL 34240
941 556-2601

(G-5732)
ACTON WOODWORKS INC
2 School St (01720-3605)
PHONE..............................978 263-0222
TOLL FREE: 800
Glenn Berger, *Pr*
EMP: 7 **EST:** 1983

SQ FT: 4,400
SALES (est): 678.48K **Privately Held**
Web: www.actonwoodworks.com
SIC: 2511 5712 1542 1521　Wood
household furniture; Furniture stores;
Commercial and office building, new
construction; New construction, single-
family houses

(G-5733)
ALL METAL FABRICATORS INC
82 Hayward Rd (01720-3006)
P.O. Box 954 (01720-0954)
PHONE..............................978 263-3904
Donald E Robertson, *Pr*
Bradford P Robertson, *VP*
EMP: 12 **EST:** 1976
SQ FT: 12,000
SALES (est): 1.91MM **Privately Held**
Web: www.allmetalfab.net
SIC: 3443 3444　Fabricated plate work
(boiler shop); Sheet metalwork

(G-5734)
ALLEN MEDICAL SYSTEMS INC
(DH)
100 Discovery Way Ste 100 (01720-4483)
PHONE..............................978 263-7727
Robert J Tennison, *Pr*
Jason Krieser, *VP*
Mark Cole, *Ex Dir*
Pete Richardson, *Ex Dir*
Michael Nordling, *Ex Dir*
▲ **EMP:** 10 **EST:** 1994
SALES (est): 11.55MM
SALES (corp-wide): 14.81B **Publicly Held**
SIC: 3841　Surgical and medical instruments
HQ: Hill-Rom, Inc.
1069 State Route 46 E
Batesville IN 47006
812 934-7777

(G-5735)
ALPHA INSTRUMENTS INC
468 Great Rd Ste 3 (01720-4187)
PHONE..............................978 264-2966
Da Ke Li, *Pr*
EMP: 8 **EST:** 2005
SALES (est): 196.06K **Privately Held**
Web: www.alphainstruments.com
SIC: 3585　Heating equipment, complete

(G-5736)
AMATECH CORPORATION (DH)
Also Called: Amatech International
100 Discovery Way (01720-4483)
PHONE..............................978 263-5401
John J Greisch, *Pr*
Jason Krieser, *
EMP: 25 **EST:** 2000
SQ FT: 40,000
SALES (est): 11.55MM
SALES (corp-wide): 14.81B **Publicly Held**
Web: www.hillrom.com
SIC: 3842　Surgical appliances and supplies
HQ: Allen Medical Systems, Inc.
100 Discovery Way Ste 100 # 100
Acton MA 01720
978 263-7727

(G-5737)
AMATECH CORPORATION
531 Main St (01720-3940)
PHONE..............................978 263-5401
EMP: 55
SALES (corp-wide): 14.81B **Publicly Held**
Web: www.hillrom.com
SIC: 3842 5047　Surgical appliances and
supplies; Medical and hospital equipment
HQ: Amatech Corporation
100 Discovery Way

Acton MA 01720
978 263-5401

(G-5738)
ASSOCIATED ENVMTL
SYSTEMS INC (PA)
Also Called: Associated Envmtl Systems
8 Post Office Sq (01720-3966)
PHONE..............................978 772-0022
EMP: 130 **EST:** 1974
SQ FT: 200,000
SALES (est): 26.72MM **Privately Held**
Web:
www.associatedenvironmentalsystems.com
SIC: 3829　Measuring and controlling
devices, nec

(G-5739)
BANZAN INTL GROUP CORP
Also Called: Banzan International Group
15 Craig Rd (01720-5404)
PHONE..............................978 263-3186
Honghai Bi, *Pr*
Li Wang, *Sec*
EMP: 18 **EST:** 2014
SALES (est): 5.01MM **Privately Held**
Web: www.banzan.us
SIC: 2821　Acrylic resins
PA: Shanghai Banzan Macromolecule
Material Co., Ltd.
14th Floor, Building 11, Hi-Tech Park,
Caohejing Development Zon
Shanghai SH 20160

(G-5740)
BIG FOOT MOVING & STORAGE
INC
5 Craig Rd (01720-5404)
PHONE..............................781 488-3090
Mike Bavuso, *Pr*
EMP: 30 **EST:** 2003
SQ FT: 15,000
SALES (est): 2.79MM **Privately Held**
Web: www.bigfootmoving.com
SIC: 2653 4783 4212 4225　Corrugated and
solid fiber boxes; Packing and crating;
Furniture moving, local: without storage;
General warehousing and storage

(G-5741)
BRANSON ULTRASONICS CORP
58 Skyline Dr (01720-4090)
PHONE..............................978 262-9040
Steve Galligan, *Mgr*
EMP: 8
SALES (corp-wide): 15.16B **Publicly Held**
Web: www.bransonic.com
SIC: 3699　Electrical equipment and
supplies, nec
HQ: Branson Ultrasonics Corporation
120 Park Ridge Rd
Brookfield CT 06804
203 796-0400

(G-5742)
CAMI RESEARCH INC
42 Nagog Park Ste 115 (01720-3445)
P.O. Box 2346 (01720-6346)
PHONE..............................978 266-2655
Christopher Strangio, *Pr*
▲ **EMP:** 11 **EST:** 1984
SQ FT: 7,500
SALES (est): 1.75MM **Privately Held**
Web: www.camiresearch.com
SIC: 7371 3825　Computer software
development; Test equipment for electronic
and electric measurement

(G-5743)
CHECK POINT SOFTWARE TECH INC
179 Great Rd Ste 111a (01720-5740)
PHONE..................978 635-0300
Helen Edwards, *Brnch Mgr*
EMP: 61
Web: www.checkpoint.com
SIC: 7372 Prepackaged software
HQ: Check Point Software Technologies, Inc.
959 Skyway Rd Ste 300
San Carlos CA 94070

(G-5744)
EARTHLINK
4 Saint James Cir (01720-3622)
PHONE..................508 735-1508
EMP: 7 **EST:** 2018
SALES (est): 80.85K **Privately Held**
SIC: 2741 Miscellaneous publishing

(G-5745)
ENOS ENGINEERING LLC
914 Main St (01720-5808)
PHONE..................978 654-6522
EMP: 7 **EST:** 2016
SALES (est): 725.03K **Privately Held**
Web: www.enosengineering.com
SIC: 3599 3827 Custom machinery; Optical test and inspection equipment

(G-5746)
EO VISTA LLC
42 Nagog Park Ste 200 (01720-3445)
PHONE..................978 635-8080
EMP: 40 **EST:** 2013
SALES (est): 8.53MM **Privately Held**
Web: www.eovista.com
SIC: 3827 Optical instruments and apparatus
HQ: General Atomics
3550 General Atomics Ct
San Diego CA 92121
858 455-2810

(G-5747)
EQUIPE COMMUNICATIONS CORP
100 Nagog Park # 2 (01720-3428)
PHONE..................978 635-1999
Dennis Rainville, *Pr*
David M Robert, *
Steve Noyes, *
EMP: 108 **EST:** 1999
SQ FT: 29,000
SALES (est): 8.97MM **Privately Held**
Web: www.equipecom.com
SIC: 3577 3661 3643 Computer peripheral equipment, nec; Telephone and telegraph apparatus; Current-carrying wiring services

(G-5748)
GEORGE HOWELL COFFEE CO LLC
Also Called: Terroir Coffee
312 School St (01720-5414)
PHONE..................978 635-9033
George H Howell, *Managing Member*
Laurie A Howell, *Managing Member*
EMP: 15 **EST:** 2003
SQ FT: 5,500
SALES (est): 2.38MM **Privately Held**
Web: www.georgehowellcoffee.com
SIC: 2095 5149 Roasted coffee; Coffee, green or roasted

(G-5749)
GRIDEDGE NETWORKS INC
40 Nagog Park Ste 105 (01720-3425)
PHONE..................978 569-2000
Nachum Sadan, *CEO*
Ken Pryde, *CFO*
Victor Brown, *VP*
EMP: 10 **EST:** 2001
SALES (est): 930.99K **Privately Held**
Web: www.gridedgenetworks.com
SIC: 4813 3674 Proprietary online service networks; Integrated circuits, semiconductor networks, etc.

(G-5750)
HAARTZ CORPORATION
Also Called: Haartz
20 Craig Rd (01720-5405)
PHONE..................978 264-2607
EMP: 35
SALES (corp-wide): 120.93MM **Privately Held**
Web: www.haartz.com
SIC: 2295 Resin or plastic coated fabrics
PA: The Haartz Corporation
87 Hayward Rd
Acton MA 01720
978 264-2600

(G-5751)
HAARTZ CORPORATION (PA)
Also Called: Haartz Auto Fabric
87 Hayward Rd (01720-3000)
PHONE..................978 264-2600
John Fox, *Pr*
Eric R Haartz, *
Charles Quimby, *
◆ **EMP:** 314 **EST:** 1922
SQ FT: 265,000
SALES (est): 120.93MM
SALES (corp-wide): 120.93MM **Privately Held**
Web: www.haartz.com
SIC: 2295 3069 Resin or plastic coated fabrics; Rubberized fabrics

(G-5752)
HIGGINS LOCATION LLC
898 Main St (01720-5865)
PHONE..................978 266-1200
John R Higgins, *Managing Member*
EMP: 34 **EST:** 1981
SQ FT: 20,000
SALES (est): 772.16K **Privately Held**
Web: www.sathorncorporation.com
SIC: 3599 3993 Machine shop, jobbing and repair; Signs and advertising specialties

(G-5753)
HIRSCH RETAIL STORE INC
Also Called: Great Wine, The
52 Eaton Dr (01719)
PHONE..................978 621-4634
Robert Hirsch, *Pr*
EMP: 7 **EST:** 2009
SALES (est): 428.09K **Privately Held**
SIC: 2084 Wines, brandy, and brandy spirits

(G-5754)
HONEYWELL DATA INSTRUMENTS INC
100 Discovery Way (01720-4483)
PHONE..................978 264-9550
▼ **EMP:** 46 **EST:** 1966
SQ FT: 80,000
SALES (est): 1.71MM **Privately Held**
Web: www.honeywell.com

SIC: 3825 3823 3842 Instruments to measure electricity; Industrial process control instruments; Personal safety equipment

(G-5755)
INSULET CORPORATION (PA)
100 Nagog Park (01720-3428)
PHONE..................978 600-7000
James R Hollingshead, *Pr*
Timothy J Scannell, *
Eric Benjamin, *Ex VP*
John Kapples, *Sr VP*
Dan Manea, *Chief Human Resource Officer*
▲ **EMP:** 500 **EST:** 2000
SQ FT: 350,000
SALES (est): 1.31B
SALES (corp-wide): 1.31B **Publicly Held**
Web: www.insulet.com
SIC: 3841 Surgical and medical instruments

(G-5756)
INTECH INC
Also Called: Acra-Cut
979 Main St (01720-5898)
PHONE..................978 263-2210
John W Baker, *Pr*
EMP: 30 **EST:** 1966
SQ FT: 22,000
SALES (est): 2.53MM **Privately Held**
Web: www.intechweb.com
SIC: 3599 3541 3841 Machine shop, jobbing and repair; Saws and sawing machines; Surgical and medical instruments

(G-5757)
LIQUID METRONICS INCORPORATED
Also Called: L M I
8 Post Office Sq Ste 1 (01720-3966)
PHONE..................978 263-9800
Jean-claude Pharmont, *Pr*
Thomas Rogan, *
Michael Monts, *
▲ **EMP:** 45 **EST:** 1984
SQ FT: 72,000
SALES (est): 9.14MM
SALES (corp-wide): 5.92B **Publicly Held**
SIC: 3586 3823 Measuring and dispensing pumps; Process control instruments
HQ: Milton Roy Llc
201 Ivyland Rd
Ivyland PA 18974
215 441-0800

(G-5758)
MARZAE LLC
55 Knox Trl Ste 407 (01720-5948)
PHONE..................630 915-0352
EMP: 10
SALES (corp-wide): 83.62K **Privately Held**
SIC: 2084 Wines, brandy, and brandy spirits
PA: Marzae, Llc
8 Gould Rd
Bedford MA 01730
619 915-0352

(G-5759)
NEW ENGLAND COUNTRY PIES LLC
18 Knowlton Dr (01720-2918)
PHONE..................781 596-0176
Kent Issenberg, *Managing Member*
EMP: 10 **EST:** 2012
SALES (est): 921.44K **Privately Held**
SIC: 2053 Pies, bakery; frozen

(G-5760)
NOVOTECH INC
916 Main St (01720-5808)
PHONE..................978 929-9458
Funsho Ojebuoboh, *Pr*
Michael Hulen, *VP*
Stephen G Mcneill, *CFO*
EMP: 18 **EST:** 1996
SQ FT: 7,000
SALES (est): 4.1MM **Privately Held**
Web: www.novotech.net
SIC: 3827 Optical instruments and lenses

(G-5761)
POLY-CEL INC
6 Eastern Rd (01720-5801)
P.O. Box 41 (01775-0041)
PHONE..................508 229-8310
Denise Kelly, *Pr*
Mike Kelly, *VP*
EMP: 12 **EST:** 1992
SALES (est): 2.27MM **Privately Held**
Web: www.polycelinc.com
SIC: 3089 Plastics processing

(G-5762)
REX LUMBER COMPANY (PA)
840 Main St (01720-5804)
P.O. Box 2860 (01720-6860)
PHONE..................800 343-0567
Benjamin Forester, *Pr*
A Ledyard Smith Junior, *VP*
William Clark, *VP*
Craig Forester, *Sec*
◆ **EMP:** 100 **EST:** 1946
SQ FT: 10,584
SALES (est): 47.14MM
SALES (corp-wide): 47.14MM **Privately Held**
Web: www.rexlumber.com
SIC: 2421 2431 Custom sawmill; Millwork

(G-5763)
SANOVA BIOSCIENCE INC
42 Nagog Park (01720-3445)
PHONE..................978 429-8079
Xingfu Feng, *Pr*
Lihua Xie, *VP*
Xianfeng Zhou, *Sec*
Bing Liu, *Treas*
Veronica Zhu, *Dir*
EMP: 10 **EST:** 2014
SALES (est): 138.54K **Privately Held**
Web: www.sanovabio.com
SIC: 2834 Dermatologicals

(G-5764)
SB DEVELOPMENT CORP
Also Called: Minuteman Pre-Hung Door Co
17 Craig Rd (01720-5404)
PHONE..................978 263-2744
John Brislouf, *Pr*
EMP: 9 **EST:** 1984
SQ FT: 11,000
SALES (est): 895.85K **Privately Held**
SIC: 2431 Doors, wood

(G-5765)
SEAVUS USA INC
179 High St (01720-4217)
PHONE..................888 573-2887
Robert H Lord, *Pr*
EMP: 11 **EST:** 2004
SALES (est): 569.02K **Privately Held**
SIC: 7372 Prepackaged software

(G-5766)
TREBIA NETWORKS INC
33 Nagog Park (01720-3421)

PHONE...............................978 264-3700
Ruediger Stroh, *Pr*
Martin Riegel, *
Willie Anderson, *
Al Litchfield, *
EMP: 50 **EST:** 2000
SQ FT: 7,000
SALES (est): 4.19MM **Privately Held**
Web: www.trebia.com
SIC: 3674　Semiconductor circuit networks

(G-5767)
TRIPLE SEAT SOFTWARE LLC
6 Ashwood Rd (01720-4402)
PHONE...............................978 635-0615
EMP: 14 **EST:** 2009
SALES (est): 246.69K **Privately Held**
Web: www.tripleseat.com
SIC: 7372　Business oriented computer
software

(G-5768)
**WINTRISS CONTROLS GROUP
LLC**
100 Discovery Way Ste 110 (01720-4483)
PHONE...............................978 268-2700
▲ **EMP:** 31 **EST:** 2009
SQ FT: 15,000
SALES (est): 5.2MM **Privately Held**
Web: www.wintriss.com
SIC: 3823　Computer interface equipment,
for industrial process control

Acushnet
Bristol County

(G-5769)
ACUSHNET COMPANY
Titleist
4 Slocum St (02743-2714)
PHONE...............................508 979-2000
Eric Bartsch, *Brnch Mgr*
EMP: 10
Web: www.titleist.com
SIC: 3949　Shafts, golf club
HQ: Acushnet Company
333 Bridge St
Fairhaven MA 02719
508 979-2000

(G-5770)
CENTURY FOOD SERVICE INC
107 S Main St (02743-2838)
PHONE...............................508 995-3221
Michael A Goulart, *Pr*
Jeffrey M Goulart, *Treas*
EMP: 10 **EST:** 1991
SALES (est): 646.01K **Privately Held**
Web: www.centuryfoodservice.com
SIC: 3581　Automatic vending machines

Adams
Berkshire County

(G-5771)
**B&B MICRO MANUFACTURING
INC**
201 Howland Ave (01220-1102)
PHONE...............................413 281-9431
Mitchell Bresett, *Pr*
Mitchell Bresett, *Pr*
Jason Koperniak, *
Christopher St Cyr, *
EMP: 30 **EST:** 2017
SALES (est): 2.78MM **Privately Held**
Web: www.bbtinyhouses.com

SIC: 2541 5012　Cabinets, except
refrigerated: show, display, etc.: wood;
Recreational vehicles, motor homes, and
trailers

(G-5772)
GEORGE APKIN & SONS INC
17 Depot St Ste 1 (01220-1857)
P.O. Box 509 (01247-0509)
PHONE...............................413 664-4936
William Apkin, *Pr*
Joseph Apkin, *Sec*
EMP: 17 **EST:** 1954
SQ FT: 10,000
SALES (est): 2.37MM **Privately Held**
Web: www.apkin.com
SIC: 3341 5093　Secondary nonferrous
metals; Ferrous metal scrap and waste

(G-5773)
HOLLAND COMPANY INC
Also Called: PCA Systems
153 Howland Ave (01220-1199)
PHONE...............................413 743-1292
Thomas J Holland, *Pr*
Daniel J Holland, *
◆ **EMP:** 30 **EST:** 1967
SQ FT: 75,000
SALES (est): 9.23MM **Privately Held**
Web: www.hollandcompany.com
SIC: 2899 2819　Chemical preparations, nec
; Industrial inorganic chemicals, nec

(G-5774)
MRA LABORATORIES INC
15 Printworks Dr (01220-1220)
PHONE...............................413 743-3927
▲ **EMP:** 17
SIC: 8731 2865　Commercial physical
research; Dyes and pigments

(G-5775)
SPECIALTY MINERALS INC
260 Columbia St (01220-1399)
PHONE...............................413 743-0591
Steve Thompson, *Brnch Mgr*
EMP: 200
Web: www.mineralstech.com
SIC: 5032 3274 1422　Lime building products
; Lime; Crushed and broken limestone
HQ: Specialty Minerals Inc.
622 3rd Ave Fl 38
New York NY 10017

Agawam
Hampden County

(G-5776)
325 SILVER STREET INC
Also Called: O-A
325 Silver St (01001-2919)
P.O. Box 250 (01001-0250)
PHONE...............................413 789-1800
Tim Mccarthy, *Genl Mgr*
Philip A Vecchiarelli, *
EMP: 30 **EST:** 1986
SQ FT: 37,000
SALES (est): 4.91MM **Privately Held**
Web: www.perfectdomain.com
SIC: 3599 3728 3724 3769　Machine shop,
jobbing and repair; Aircraft parts and
equipment, nec; Aircraft engines and
engine parts; Space vehicle equipment, nec

(G-5777)
ACE PRECISION INC
1123 Suffield St (01001-3816)
P.O. Box 309 (01001-0309)

PHONE...............................413 789-7536
Geraldine A Elias, *Sec*
Antoine S Elias, *Treas*
EMP: 18 **EST:** 1997
SQ FT: 12,000
SALES (est): 4.86MM **Privately Held**
Web: www.acepreisioninc.com
SIC: 3599　Machine shop, jobbing and repair

(G-5778)
ANCHOR ELECTRIC LLC
687 Silver St (01001-2993)
PHONE...............................413 786-6788
TOLL FREE: 800
EMP: 7 **EST:** 1948
SQ FT: 7,500
SALES (est): 1.86MM **Privately Held**
Web: www.anchorelectricmotors.com
SIC: 5063 7694　Motors, electric; Electric
motor repair

(G-5779)
**BAY STATE ELEVATOR
COMPANY INC (HQ)**
275 Silver St (01001-2982)
P.O. Box 910 (01001-0910)
PHONE...............................413 786-7000
Harold F Potts Junior, *Pr*
James H Horth Junior, *VP*
James H Horth Iii, *VP*
Roger T Duval, *VP*
Francis M Potts, *Treas*
EMP: 20 **EST:** 1909
SQ FT: 14,000
SALES (est): 13.52MM
SALES (corp-wide): 13.69B **Publicly Held**
Web: www.baystateelevator.us
SIC: 3534 7699 1796 3842　Elevators and
equipment; Elevators: inspection, service,
and repair; Elevator installation and
conversion; Surgical appliances and
supplies
PA: Otis Worldwide Corporation
1 Carrier Pl
Farmington CT 06032
860 674-3000

(G-5780)
BELT TECHNOLOGIES INC (PA)
11 Bowles Rd (01001-3812)
PHONE...............................413 786-9922
Alan Wosky, *Pr*
Denis Gagnon Junior, *CEO*
Brian Stefano, *Treas*
Cindy Gadbois, *Acctg*
◆ **EMP:** 38 **EST:** 2000
SQ FT: 22,000
SALES (est): 9.47MM **Privately Held**
Web: www.belttechnologies.com
SIC: 3568 3535　Belting, chain; Conveyors
and conveying equipment

(G-5781)
**BEN FRANKLIN DESIGN MFG
CO INC**
Also Called: Ben Franklin Manufacturing
938 Suffield St (01001-2930)
P.O. Box 502 (01001-0502)
PHONE...............................413 786-4220
Edward Leyden, *Pr*
EMP: 15 **EST:** 1978
SQ FT: 12,000
SALES (est): 2.48MM **Privately Held**
SIC: 3625 3545　Numerical controls;
Precision tools, machinists'

(G-5782)
BRIDGEPORT NAT BINDERY INC
662 Silver St (01001-2987)
P.O. Box 289 (01001-0289)

PHONE...............................413 789-1981
TOLL FREE: 800
James M Larsen, *Pr*
Bruce F Jacobsen, *
▲ **EMP:** 100 **EST:** 1947
SQ FT: 54,000
SALES (est): 24.99MM **Privately Held**
Web: www.bnbindery.com
SIC: 2789　Binding only: books, pamphlets,
magazines, etc.

(G-5783)
CAMBREX
104 Gold St (01001-3807)
PHONE...............................413 786-1680
EMP: 27 **EST:** 2020
SALES (est): 6.95MM **Privately Held**
Web: www.cambrex.com
SIC: 2834　Pharmaceutical preparations

(G-5784)
**CARANDO GOURMET FOODS
CORP (PA)**
Also Called: Carando Gourmet Frozen Foods
175 Main St (01001-1870)
PHONE...............................413 737-0183
Michael Carando, *Owner*
Dino Carando, *
Raymond Gianantoni, *
EMP: 30 **EST:** 1979
SQ FT: 15,000
SALES (est): 11.56MM
SALES (corp-wide): 11.56MM **Privately
Held**
Web: www.cgfamilyfoods.com
SIC: 2013　Roast beef, from purchased meat

(G-5785)
**CATALYST ACOUSTICS GROUP
INC**
50 Almgren Dr S (01001-2971)
PHONE...............................413 789-1770
Joseph Lupone, *CEO*
Robert Armstrong, *CFO*
EMP: 129 **EST:** 2019
SALES (est): 110.5MM **Privately Held**
Web: www.catalystacoustics.com
SIC: 3229　Glass fiber products
PA: The Stephens Group Llc
100 Rver Bluff Dr Ste 500
Little Rock AR 72202

(G-5786)
**CATALYST ACUSTICS
HOLDINGS INC (HQ)**
50 Almgren Dr S (01001-2971)
PHONE...............................413 789-1770
Joe Lupone, *CEO*
Robert M Armstrong, *CFO*
EMP: 68 **EST:** 1978
SALES (est): 47.42MM **Privately Held**
Web: www.soundseal.com
SIC: 3229　Glass fiber products
PA: The Stephens Group Llc
100 Rver Bluff Dr Ste 500
Little Rock AR 72202

(G-5787)
**COMMERCIAL SCALE BALANCE
INC**
36 Russo Cir (01001-1542)
P.O. Box 268 (01001-0268)
PHONE...............................413 789-9990
TOLL FREE: 877
Jim Irwin, *Pr*
EMP: 10 **EST:** 1999
SQ FT: 6,000
SALES (est): 911.47K **Privately Held**
Web: www.csbco.com

SIC: 7699 3596 Scale repair service; Scales and balances, except laboratory

(G-5788)
CONRAD FAFARD INC
Also Called: Fafard
770 Silver St (01001-2907)
P.O. Box 790 (01001-0790)
PHONE.............................413 786-4343
◆ EMP: 1000
Web: www.fafard.com
SIC: 5191 2875 Farm supplies; Fertilizers, mixing only

(G-5789)
DFF CORP
59 Gen Creighton W Abrams Dr (01001-2956)
P.O. Box 285 (01001-0285)
PHONE.............................413 786-8880
William Marganti, Pr
▲ EMP: 198 EST: 1969
SQ FT: 303,000
SALES (est): 51.28MM
SALES (corp-wide): 839.87MM Privately Held
Web: www.cadrex.com
SIC: 3824 3545 Mechanical and electromechanical counters and devices; Precision tools, machinists'
HQ: Cgi Automated Manufacturing, Llc
275 Innovation Dr
Romeoville IL 60446
815 221-5307

(G-5790)
FAFARD INC
770 Silver St (01001-2907)
P.O. Box 790 (01001-0790)
PHONE.............................413 786-4343
▲ EMP: 70
SIC: 2875 Fertilizers, mixing only

(G-5791)
GOVERNORS AMERICA CORPORATION
Also Called: Gac
720 Silver St (01001-2907)
PHONE.............................413 233-1888
▲ EMP: 124 EST: 1986
SALES (est): 16.17MM Privately Held
Web: www.governors-america.com
SIC: 3519 Parts and accessories, internal combustion engines

(G-5792)
HAMPDEN FENCE SUPPLY INC
80 Industrial Ln (01001-3634)
P.O. Box 452 (01001-0452)
PHONE.............................413 786-4390
James Crawford, CEO
Rudika Ward-horner, Pr
EMP: 10 EST: 1946
SQ FT: 22,400
SALES (est): 2MM Privately Held
Web: www.hampdenfence.com
SIC: 3499 3315 Metal household articles; Fence gates, posts, and fittings: steel

(G-5793)
ILS BUSINESS SERVICES INC
570 Silver St (01001-2924)
PHONE.............................413 789-4555
Irene Scalise, Pr
Robert Scalise, VP
EMP: 8 EST: 1981
SQ FT: 10,000
SALES (est): 686.56K Privately Held
Web: www.ilsmail.com

SIC: 2752 7331 5112 Offset printing; Mailing service; Office supplies, nec

(G-5794)
INTERSTATE DESIGN COMPANY INC
84 Gold St (01001-2978)
PHONE.............................413 786-7730
Keith Stone, Pr
EMP: 20 EST: 1973
SQ FT: 10,000
SALES (est): 370.59K Privately Held
Web: www.interstatecorps.com
SIC: 3544 8711 Special dies and tools; Designing: ship, boat, machine, and product

(G-5795)
INTERSTATE MFG CO INC
84 Gold St (01001-2978)
PHONE.............................413 789-8674
Keith J Stone, Pr
EMP: 9 EST: 1998
SQ FT: 6,000
SALES (est): 1.24MM Privately Held
Web: www.interstatecorps.com
SIC: 3544 Special dies and tools

(G-5796)
ISLAND POND INDUSTRIES INC
270 Main St (01001-1853)
PHONE.............................413 732-6625
Richard Gavoni, Pr
EMP: 8 EST: 2017
SQ FT: 12,000
SALES (est): 468.89K Privately Held
SIC: 2431 3442 Doors, wood; Metal doors

(G-5797)
J-K TOOL CO INC
41 Russo Cir (01001-1542)
PHONE.............................413 789-0613
Joseph Kowal, Pr
Christopher J Kowal, Sec
EMP: 20 EST: 1982
SQ FT: 5,000
SALES (est): 2.86MM Privately Held
Web: www.j-ktool.com
SIC: 3544 Special dies and tools

(G-5798)
JET INDUSTRIES INC
307 Silver St (01001-2919)
P.O. Box 345 (01001-0345)
PHONE.............................413 786-2010
Michael Turrini, Pr
John Turrini, *
EMP: 50 EST: 1963
SQ FT: 22,000
SALES (est): 4.84MM Privately Held
Web: www.jetind.com
SIC: 3724 3511 3728 Aircraft engines and engine parts; Turbines and turbine generator sets and parts; Aircraft parts and equipment, nec

(G-5799)
LITRON LLC
207 Bowles Rd (01001-2964)
EMP: 66 EST: 1997
SQ FT: 23,000
SALES (est): 11.59MM
SALES (corp-wide): 168.44MM Privately Held
Web: www.hermeticsolutions.com
SIC: 3699 Laser welding, drilling, and cutting equipment
HQ: Hermetic Solutions Group Inc.
16 Plains Rd
Essex CT 06426
215 645-9420

(G-5800)
LUDLOW TOOL INC
46 Moylan Ln (01001-4606)
PHONE.............................413 786-6415
Jason Lucas, Owner
EMP: 12 EST: 1981
SQ FT: 12,800
SALES (est): 2.31MM Privately Held
Web: www.ludlowtool.com
SIC: 3312 Tool and die steel

(G-5801)
MILLENNIUM PRESS INC
570 Silver St (01001-2924)
PHONE.............................413 821-0028
TOLL FREE: 800
James E Sullivan, Pr
Kelly Sullivan, VP
EMP: 21 EST: 1989
SQ FT: 11,500
SALES (est): 2.23MM Privately Held
Web: www.millprinting.com
SIC: 2752 Offset printing

(G-5802)
OMG INC
Also Called: Omg
95 Bowles Rd (01001-2925)
PHONE.............................413 786-0516
EMP: 7
SQ FT: 24,228
SALES (corp-wide): 1.7B Publicly Held
Web: www.omginc.com
SIC: 3531 Construction machinery
HQ: Omg, Inc.
153 Bowles Rd
Agawam MA 01001
413 789-0252

(G-5803)
OMG INC (DH)
Also Called: Omg Manufacturing, Inc.
153 Bowles Rd (01001-2908)
PHONE.............................413 789-0252
Hubert T Mcgovern, Pr
Edward C Woodbridge, *
Ted Yerdon, *
Glen M Kassan, *
James F Mccabe Junior, Sr VP
◆ EMP: 280 EST: 1994
SQ FT: 58,000
SALES (est): 200.36MM
SALES (corp-wide): 1.7B Publicly Held
Web: www.omginc.com
SIC: 3452 3444 2952 3531 Bolts, nuts, rivets, and washers; Sheet metalwork; Asphalt felts and coatings; Construction machinery
HQ: Handy & Harman
C/O Steel Partners
New York NY 10022
212 520-2300

(G-5804)
OPTIMUM PARTS COMPANY
104 Ramah Cir S (01001-1559)
PHONE.............................413 273-1865
David N Moore, Prin
Martin P Tanguay, Prin
Samantha Tanguay, Prin
Pollee E Moore, Prin
EMP: 7 EST: 2015
SALES (est): 671.01K Privately Held
SIC: 3599 Machine shop, jobbing and repair

(G-5805)
PARTS TOOL AND DIE INC
344 Shoemaker Ln (01001-3618)
PHONE.............................413 821-9718
EMP: 25 EST: 1994

SQ FT: 12,000
SALES (est): 2.57MM Privately Held
Web: www.ptdinc.net
SIC: 3728 3324 3365 3369 Aircraft parts and equipment, nec; Aerospace investment castings, ferrous; Aerospace castings, aluminum; Aerospace castings, nonferrous: except aluminum

(G-5806)
SANTO C DE SPIRT MARBLE & GRAN
2 S Bridge Dr (01001-2015)
PHONE.............................413 786-7073
Philip S Schoville, Pr
Laura De Spirt, Sec
Alicia Horning, VP
EMP: 7 EST: 1978
SQ FT: 12,000
SALES (est): 1.05MM Privately Held
Web: www.santocdespirt.com
SIC: 3281 5999 Marble, building: cut and shaped; Monuments and tombstones

(G-5807)
SOUTHWORTH COMPANY
Also Called: Turner Falls Paper
265 Main St (01001-1822)
PHONE.............................413 789-1200
◆ EMP: 190
Web: www.southworth.com
SIC: 2621 5961 Bond paper; Catalog and mail-order houses

(G-5808)
SUDDEKOR LLC (DH)
240 Bowles Rd (01001-2963)
PHONE.............................413 821-9000
◆ EMP: 37 EST: 1999
SQ FT: 65,000
SALES (est): 11.17MM
SALES (corp-wide): 246.55MM Privately Held
Web: www.surteco.com
SIC: 2672 Paper; coated and laminated, nec
HQ: Omnova North America, Inc.
1175 Harrelson Blvd
Myrtle Beach SC 29577
843 848-3000

(G-5809)
SUN GRO HOLDINGS INC
770 Silver St (01001-2907)
PHONE.............................413 786-4343
Ken Blsbury, Pr
EMP: 49 EST: 2002
SALES (est): 8.45MM Privately Held
Web: www.sungro.com
SIC: 2875 5191 Potting soil, mixed; Garden supplies
HQ: Sun Gro Horticulture Canada Ltd
1900 Minnesota Crt Suite 200
Mississauga ON L5N 3
780 797-3019

(G-5810)
SUN GRO HORTICULTURE DIST INC (HQ)
Also Called: Sunshine
770 Silver St (01001-2907)
PHONE.............................413 786-4343
John Hill, Pr
Andrew Soward, Vice Treasurer*
Hris Bednar, *
◆ EMP: 45 EST: 2002
SALES (est): 446.34MM Privately Held
Web: www.sungro.com
SIC: 2875 Fertilizers, mixing only
PA: Hines Horticulture, Inc.
12621 Jeffery Rd

Irvine CA 92620

(G-5811)
SUN GRO HORTICULTURE DIST INC
Also Called: Sun Gro Horticulture Proc
770 Silver St (01001-2907)
PHONE.............................800 732-8667
Daniel Byarley, *Genl Mgr*
EMP: 36
Web: www.sungro.com
SIC: 1499 2875　Peat mining and processing
; Fertilizers, mixing only
HQ: Sun Gro Horticulture Distribution Inc.
770 Silver St
Agawam MA 01001

(G-5812)
SUN GRO HORTICULTURE DIST INC
Also Called: Inc, Sun Gro Horticulture
770 Silver St (01001-2907)
PHONE.............................864 224-7989
EMP: 58
Web: www.sungro.com
SIC: 1499 2875　Peat grinding; Fertilizers,
mixing only
HQ: Sun Gro Horticulture Distribution Inc.
770 Silver St
Agawam MA 01001

(G-5813)
TOPPER & GRIGGS GROUP LLC
36 Russo Cir (01001-1542)
PHONE.............................860 747-5737
EMP: 39
SIC: 1791 3441　Structural steel erection;
Fabricated structural metal

(G-5814)
VAUPELL INDUSTRIAL PLAS INC
Golston Product Solutions
101 Almgren Dr (01001-3828)
PHONE.............................413 233-3801
Danny Keller, *Pr*
EMP: 53
SALES (corp-wide): 23.65MM **Privately Held**
Web: www.vaupell.com
SIC: 3089　Injection molding of plastics
PA: Vaupell Industrial Plastics, Inc.
1144 Nw 53rd St
Seattle WA 98107
206 784-9050

(G-5815)
VERTICAL & MINI BLIND FACTORY
1443 Main St (01001-2509)
PHONE.............................413 789-2343
Jeff Passo, *Prin*
EMP: 9 EST: 1989
SALES (est): 107.08K **Privately Held**
SIC: 2591　Mini blinds

(G-5816)
WYZ MACHINE CO INC
95 Industrial Ln (01001-3635)
P.O. Box 404 (01001-0404)
PHONE.............................413 786-6816
Stephen J Wyzga, *Pr*
EMP: 10 EST: 1978
SQ FT: 2,400
SALES (est): 803.68K **Privately Held**
SIC: 3599　Machine shop, jobbing and repair

Allston
Suffolk County

(G-5817)
3D DIAGNOSTIX INC
Also Called: 3ddx
24 Denby Rd (02134-1606)
PHONE.............................617 820-5279
Khaled Elsaid, *Pr*
Khaled Galal Elsaid, *Pr*
EMP: 19 EST: 2005
SALES (est): 1.65MM **Privately Held**
Web: www.3ddx.com
SIC: 3843　Dental equipment and supplies

(G-5818)
73-75 MAGAZINE STREET LLC
1125 Commonwealth Ave (02134-3201)
PHONE.............................617 787-1913
Russell L Peterson, *Prin*
EMP: 7 EST: 2010
SALES (est): 167.08K **Privately Held**
SIC: 2721　Periodicals

(G-5819)
BIODEVEK INC
127 Western Ave (02134-1008)
PHONE.............................617 768-8246
EMP: 7 EST: 2018
SALES (est): 388.55K **Privately Held**
Web: www.biodevek.com
SIC: 3841　Surgical and medical instruments

(G-5820)
BOSTON KOREAN
161 Harvard Ave Ste 13 (02134-2724)
PHONE.............................617 254-4654
Myong Sool Chang, *Owner*
EMP: 7 EST: 2007
SALES (est): 474.55K **Privately Held**
Web: www.bostonkorea.com
SIC: 2711　Newspapers, publishing and
printing

(G-5821)
GENZYME CORPORATION
114 Western Ave (02134-1015)
PHONE.............................617 252-7500
EMP: 36
Web: www.sanofi.com
SIC: 2834　Pharmaceutical preparations
HQ: Genzyme Corporation
450 Water St
Cambridge MA 02141
617 252-7500

(G-5822)
KS MANUFACTURING INC
9 Sawyer Ter (02134-1803)
PHONE.............................508 427-5727
Tao Dang, *Pr*
Victor Medeiros, *
▲ **EMP:** 7 EST: 2003
SQ FT: 3,500
SALES (est): 218.98K **Privately Held**
Web: www.ksmfginc.com
SIC: 3841　Diagnostic apparatus, medical

(G-5823)
MAUNA KEA TECHNOLOGIES INC
24 Denby Rd Ste 140 (02134-1606)
PHONE.............................617 216-4263
Chris Tihansky, *Pr*
EMP: 9 EST: 2008
SALES: 4.47MM
SALES (corp-wide): 5.54MM **Privately Held**

SIC: 3841　Diagnostic apparatus, medical
PA: Mauna Kea Technologies
9 Rue D Enghien
Paris 75010
148241168

(G-5824)
MIXX FROZEN YOGURT INC (PA)
66 Brighton Ave (02134-2101)
PHONE.............................617 782-6499
Jimmy Nguyen, *Pr*
EMP: 15 EST: 2010
SQ FT: 1,200
SALES (est): 1.12MM **Privately Held**
Web: www.mixxboston.com
SIC: 2024　Ice cream and frozen deserts

(G-5825)
SALK COMPANY INC
119 Braintree St Ste 151 (02134-1628)
PHONE.............................617 782-4030
Gilbert Salk, *Ch Bd*
Lawrence H Salk, *
Michael Goshko, *
EMP: 10 EST: 1935
SQ FT: 24,000
SALES (est): 392.93K **Privately Held**
Web: www.larrysalk.com
SIC: 3842 2326　Clothing, fire resistant and
protective; Men's and boy's work clothing

(G-5826)
SCHOLASTIC CORPORATION
1200 Soldiers Field Rd # 1 (02134-1021)
PHONE.............................617 924-3846
Richard Robinson, *Brnch Mgr*
EMP: 9
SALES (corp-wide): 1.7B **Publicly Held**
Web: www.scholastic.com
SIC: 2731　Books, publishing only
PA: Scholastic Corporation
557 Broadway Lbby 1
New York NY 10012
212 343-6100

Amesbury
Essex County

(G-5827)
AMESBURY COMMUNITY TELEVI
5 Highland St (01913-2215)
PHONE.............................978 388-5900
EMP: 7 EST: 2019
SALES (est): 235.74K **Privately Held**
Web: www.amesburyctv.org
SIC: 2741　Miscellaneous publishing

(G-5828)
APPLIED GRAPHICS INC
61 S Hunt Rd (01913-4417)
PHONE.............................978 241-5300
Barbara Burnim, *Pr*
Paul Burnim, *
▲ **EMP:** 47 EST: 1975
SQ FT: 33,200
SALES (est): 5.56MM **Privately Held**
Web: www.appliedgraphics.com
SIC: 3479 2759　Coating of metals and
formed products; Screen printing

(G-5829)
AQUA LABORATORIES INC
8 Industrial Way (01913-3223)
P.O. Box 645 (01913-0015)
PHONE.............................978 388-3989
Thomas R Cass, *Pr*
Marjorie Cass, *VP*
EMP: 21 EST: 1968

SQ FT: 11,500
SALES (est): 4.89MM **Privately Held**
Web: www.aqualaboratories.com
SIC: 2899 8748　Water treating compounds;
Energy conservation consultant

(G-5830)
ARC TECHNOLOGIES LLC (HQ)
37 S Hunt Rd (01913-4423)
PHONE.............................978 388-2993
EMP: 60 EST: 1988
SALES (est): 90.58MM
SALES (corp-wide): 1.79B **Publicly Held**
Web: www.hexcel.com
SIC: 3825　Radar testing instruments, electric
PA: Hexcel Corporation
281 Tresser Blvd 16
Stamford CT 06901
203 969-0666

(G-5831)
BARTLEY MACHINE & MFG CO INC
35 Water St (01913-2914)
P.O. Box 677 (01913-0677)
▲ **EMP:** 50
Web: www.schoolbussigns.net
SIC: 3599　Machine shop, jobbing and repair

(G-5832)
CELGENE CORPORATION
100 Macy St Unit F174 (01913-4315)
PHONE.............................857 225-2309
EMP: 12
SALES (corp-wide): 45.01B **Publicly Held**
Web: www.bms.com
SIC: 2834　Pharmaceutical preparations
HQ: Celgene Corporation
86 Morris Ave
Summit NJ 07901
908 673-9000

(G-5833)
DALTON MANUFACTURING CO INC
6 Clark St (01913-2521)
P.O. Box 3 (01913-0001)
PHONE.............................978 388-2227
Howard G Dalton, *Pr*
EMP: 18 EST: 1939
SQ FT: 3,600
SALES (est): 474.53K **Privately Held**
Web: www.daltonco.com
SIC: 3599　Machine shop, jobbing and repair

(G-5834)
DALTON MANUFACTURING GROUP INC
6 Clark St (01913-2521)
P.O. Box 3 (01913-0001)
PHONE.............................978 388-2227
Seth Rogers, *Pr*
EMP: 15 EST: 2019
SALES (est): 1.06MM **Privately Held**
Web: www.daltonco.com
SIC: 3999 3599　Manufacturing industries,
nec; Machine shop, jobbing and repair

(G-5835)
GALAXY STONE INC
23 Noel St (01913-3630)
PHONE.............................617 461-2790
Francisco M Landaverde, *Prin*
EMP: 8 EST: 2014
SALES (est): 153.47K **Privately Held**
SIC: 3281　Cut stone and stone products

(G-5836)
HAWKES & HUBERDEAU WDWKG INC
23 Noel St Ste 5 (01913-3628)
PHONE......................978 388-7747
Nathan Hawkes, *Pr*
EMP: 7 **EST:** 2006
SALES (est): 669.18K **Privately Held**
Web: www.hhmillwork.com
SIC: 2431 Millwork

(G-5837)
INERT CORPORATION
1 Industrial Way (01913-3223)
PHONE......................978 462-4415
Timothy Michael, *Pr*
Deborah Johnson, *Sec*
Jermie Mosnier, *Treas*
Amaud Guirouvet, *Dir*
▲ **EMP:** 22 **EST:** 1982
SQ FT: 20,400
SALES (est): 6.18MM **Privately Held**
Web: www.inertcorp.com
SIC: 3821 7699 5047 5999 Laboratory apparatus and furniture; Medical equipment repair, non-electric; Medical equipment and supplies; Medical apparatus and supplies

(G-5838)
IPSUMM INC (PA)
10 Industrial Way Ste 1 (01913-3222)
PHONE......................603 570-4050
John Kodzis, *Pr*
EMP: 28 **EST:** 2011
SQ FT: 21,000
SALES (est): 3.82MM
SALES (corp-wide): 3.82MM **Privately Held**
Web: www.ipsumm.com
SIC: 8711 3569 Machine tool design; Assembly machines, non-metalworking

(G-5839)
J G MACLELLAN CON CO INC
Also Called: Maclellan Concrete Co
91 Haverhill Rd (01913-3916)
PHONE......................978 458-1223
John Mac Lellan Iii, *Pr*
EMP: 10
SALES (corp-wide): 10.15MM **Privately Held**
Web: www.jgmaclellanconcrete.com
SIC: 5032 1771 3273 Concrete building products; Concrete work; Ready-mixed concrete
PA: J. G. Maclellan Concrete Co., Inc.
180 Phoenix Ave
Lowell MA 01852
978 458-1223

(G-5840)
KRAMER SCIENTIFIC LLC
91 High St Ste 1 (01913-1440)
PHONE......................978 388-7159
Lois Porter, *Pr*
Alan Porter, *VP*
EMP: 8 **EST:** 1947
SQ FT: 18,000
SALES (est): 424.63K **Privately Held**
Web: www.kramerscientific.com
SIC: 3826 Analytical instruments
PA: Merrimac Tool Company, Inc.
91 High St Ste 1
Amesbury MA 01913

(G-5841)
LEGACY MACHINE & MFG LLC
43 Clinton St (01913-1234)
PHONE......................978 388-0956
Louis Bartley, *Prin*

EMP: 8 **EST:** 2016
SALES (est): 929.03K **Privately Held**
Web: www.foldingschoolbussign.com
SIC: 3599 Machine shop, jobbing and repair

(G-5842)
LIFECLOUD INC ✿
6 Lancewood Dr (01913-2197)
PHONE......................978 621-9572
John Lunny, *Pr*
Charles D Johnson, *Sec*
Damon R Pender, *Treas*
EMP: 9 **EST:** 2022
SALES (est): 330.14K **Privately Held**
SIC: 7372 7389 Application computer software; Business Activities at Non-Commercial Site

(G-5843)
MERRIMAC TOOL COMPANY INC (PA)
91 High St Ste 1 (01913-1440)
PHONE......................978 388-7159
Alan Porter, *Pr*
▲ **EMP:** 9 **EST:** 1988
SQ FT: 8,000
SALES (est): 1.2MM **Privately Held**
Web: www.merrimactool.com
SIC: 3599 Machine shop, jobbing and repair

(G-5844)
MUNTERS CORPORATION
Also Called: Munters Zeol
79 Monroe St (01913-3204)
PHONE......................978 388-2666
Derrick Drohan, *Mgr*
EMP: 10
SALES (corp-wide): 990.05MM **Privately Held**
Web: www.munters.us
SIC: 3585 Refrigeration and heating equipment
HQ: Munters Corporation
79 Monroe St
Amesbury MA 01913

(G-5845)
MUNTERS CORPORATION (DH)
Also Called: Air Treatment Division
79 Monroe St (01913-3204)
PHONE......................978 241-1100
▲ **EMP:** 150 **EST:** 1980
SQ FT: 125,000
SALES (est): 200.17MM
SALES (corp-wide): 990.05MM **Privately Held**
Web: www.munters.us
SIC: 3585 3822 3569 3564 Humidifiers and dehumidifiers; Air flow controllers, air conditioning and refrigeration; Filters, general line: industrial; Blowers and fans
HQ: Munters Ab
Borgarfjordsgatan 16
Kista 164 4
86266300

(G-5846)
MUNTERS CORPORATION
Munters Corp Cargo Care Div
79 Monroe St (01913-3204)
P.O. Box 640 (01913-0640)
PHONE......................978 241-1100
Michael Mcdonald, *Pr*
EMP: 22
SALES (corp-wide): 990.05MM **Privately Held**
Web: www.munters.us
SIC: 3585 Dehumidifiers electric, except portable
HQ: Munters Corporation
79 Monroe St

Amesbury MA 01913

(G-5847)
MUNTERS USA INC
Also Called: Munters Cargocaire
79 Monroe St (01913-3204)
PHONE......................978 241-1100
Lennart Lindquist, *Pr*
Ulf Nordling, *Sec*
▲ **EMP:** 700 **EST:** 1982
SALES (est): 68.28MM
SALES (corp-wide): 990.05MM **Privately Held**
Web: www.munters.com
SIC: 3585 Refrigeration equipment, complete
HQ: Munters Ab
Borgarfjordsgatan 16
Kista 164 4
86266300

(G-5848)
NEWCASTLE SYSTEMS INC
34 S Hunt Rd (01913-4416)
PHONE......................781 935-3450
John O'kelly, *Pr*
EMP: 20 **EST:** 2005
SALES (est): 7.59MM **Privately Held**
Web: www.newcastlesys.com
SIC: 3577 Punch card equipment: readers, tabulators, sorters, etc.

(G-5849)
PP SYSTEMS INTERNATIONAL INC
Also Called: Pp Systems
110 Haverhill Rd Ste 301 (01913-2122)
PHONE......................978 834-0505
Michael L Doyle, *Pr*
Keith J Parkinson, *Dir*
EMP: 7 **EST:** 1993
SQ FT: 3,000
SALES (est): 5.4MM **Privately Held**
Web: www.ppsystems.com
SIC: 3826 Analytical instruments

(G-5850)
REK INC
73 Merrimac St (01913-4000)
PHONE......................978 388-1826
Joy Kimball, *Pr*
EMP: 7 **EST:** 1956
SQ FT: 10,000
SALES (est): 544.8K **Privately Held**
Web: www.rekimballinc.com
SIC: 2033 2035 Preserves, including imitation: in cans, jars, etc.; Relishes, fruit and vegetable

(G-5851)
SHEA CONCRETE PRODUCTS INC (PA)
87 Haverhill Rd (01913-3916)
PHONE......................978 658-2645
Ed Shea, *Pr*
Judi Shea, *
Brenda S Stratis, *
EMP: 50 **EST:** 1975
SALES (est): 19.86MM
SALES (corp-wide): 19.86MM **Privately Held**
Web: www.sheaconcrete.com
SIC: 3272 Housing components, prefabricated concrete

(G-5852)
SHEA CONCRETE PRODUCTS INC
Also Called: E F Shea Neng Con Pdts I

87 Haverhill Rd (01913-3916)
P.O. Box 807 (01913-0018)
PHONE......................978 388-1509
Gregory Stratis, *Brnch Mgr*
EMP: 40
SALES (corp-wide): 19.86MM **Privately Held**
Web: www.sheaconcrete.com
SIC: 3272 5211 Housing components, prefabricated concrete; Masonry materials and supplies
PA: Shea Concrete Products, Inc.
87 Haverhill Rd
Amesbury MA 01913
978 658-2645

(G-5853)
SPECIALTY MANUFACTURING INC
Also Called: SMI Podwer Coating
40 Water St (01913-2915)
PHONE......................978 388-1601
James Bartley, *Pr*
EMP: 18 **EST:** 1979
SALES (est): 927.04K **Privately Held**
SIC: 3599 2759 2396 Machine shop, jobbing and repair; Commercial printing, nec ; Automotive and apparel trimmings

(G-5854)
VT INDUSTRIES INC
12 Merrill Ave (01913-2220)
P.O. Box 540 (01913-0012)
PHONE......................978 388-3792
Charles Little, *Pr*
Eric Danis, *VP*
▲ **EMP:** 20 **EST:** 1965
SQ FT: 26,000
SALES (est): 2.28MM **Privately Held**
Web: www.valiantind.com
SIC: 2431 2541 Millwork; Store and office display cases and fixtures

(G-5855)
WIRE TECHNIQUES LTD
11 Chestnut St (01913-3024)
PHONE......................978 372-1300
David E Ahearn, *Managing Member*
David E Ahearn, *Pt*
EMP: 22 **EST:** 1986
SQ FT: 14,000
SALES (est): 2.26MM **Privately Held**
Web: www.wiretechniques.com
SIC: 3699 Electrical equipment and supplies, nec

Amherst
Hampshire County

(G-5856)
AMHERST BREWING CO INC
36 N Pleasant St (01002-1703)
PHONE......................413 253-4400
John Korpita, *Pr*
Mark Parent, *
Jake Bishop, *
EMP: 45 **EST:** 1997
SQ FT: 6,000
SALES (est): 3.07MM **Privately Held**
Web: www.amherstbrewing.com
SIC: 2082 5812 5813 Beer (alcoholic beverage); Eating places; Drinking places

(G-5857)
AMHERST COLLEGE PUBLIC AFFAIRS
306 Converse Hall (01002)
PHONE......................413 542-2321

Stacey Schmeidel, *Dir*
EMP: 10 **EST:** 1821
SALES (est): 248.41K **Privately Held**
Web: www.amherst.edu
SIC: **2711** Job printing and newspaper
publishing combined

(G-5858)
AMHERST MACHINE CO
16 Cowls Rd (01002-1014)
P.O. Box 9507 (01059-9507)
PHONE.............................413 549-4551
James Bernotas, *Owner*
EMP: 16 **EST:** 1980
SQ FT: 3,200
SALES (est): 418.33K **Privately Held**
Web: www.amherstmachine.com
SIC: **3541** 3544 Machine tools, metal.cutting
type; Special dies, tools, jigs, and fixtures

(G-5859)
ATKINS FRUIT BOWL INC
Also Called: Atkins Farm Country Market
1150 West St (01002-3394)
PHONE.............................413 253-9528
Pauline Lannon, *Pr*
Harold Gould, *
David Thornton, *Stockholder*
EMP: 150 **EST:** 1969
SQ FT: 15,000
SALES (est): 13.61MM **Privately Held**
Web: www.atkinsfarms.com
SIC: **5431** 5411 2051 Fruit stands or markets
; Delicatessen stores; Bakery: wholesale or
wholesale/retail combined

(G-5860)
BAGEL WORKS INC
Also Called: Works Bakery Cafe, The
48 N Pleasant St (01002-1738)
PHONE.............................413 835-0561
Hannah Speither, *Asst Mgr*
EMP: 13
Web: www.workscafe.com
SIC: **5461** 2051 Bagels; Bagels, fresh or
frozen
PA: Bagel Works, Inc.
120 Main St
Keene NH 03431

(G-5861)
KIND GRIND INCORPORATED
Also Called: Share Coffee
178 N Pleasant St (01002-1978)
PHONE.............................413 367-2478
Robert A Lowry, *Prin*
EMP: 17 **EST:** 2010
SALES (est): 1.82MM **Privately Held**
SIC: **3599** Grinding castings for the trade

(G-5862)
MASSACHUSETTS REVIEW INC
Also Called: MASSACHUSETTS REVIEW,
THE
211 Hicks Way (01003-9371)
PHONE.............................413 545-2689
Jim Hicks, *Pr*
Neal Abraham, *Prin*
Frank Couvares, *Prin*
Mary Russo, *Prin*
Kevin Quashie, *Prin*
EMP: 8 **EST:** 1959
SALES (est): 199.68K **Privately Held**
Web: www.massreview.org
SIC: **2721** Magazines: publishing and
printing

(G-5863)
PROSENSING INC
107 Sunderland Rd (01002-1098)

PHONE.............................413 549-4402
James B Mead, *Pr*
Andrew Pazmany, *VP*
Ivan Popstefanija, *Treas*
▼ **EMP:** 15 **EST:** 1982
SQ FT: 5,500
SALES (est): 2.5MM **Privately Held**
Web: www.prosensing.com
SIC: **3812** Radar systems and equipment

(G-5864)
SCIDOSE LLC
196 N Pleasant St Ste 16 (01002-1721)
PHONE.............................866 956-4333
Negesh Palepu, *Managing Member*
EMP: 12 **EST:** 2006
SALES (est): 1.25MM **Privately Held**
SIC: **2834** 7389 Pharmaceutical
preparations; Business services, nec

(G-5865)
**TRANSITIONS ABROAD PUBG
INC**
18 Hulst Rd (01002-3523)
P.O. Box 1369 (01004-1369)
PHONE.............................413 992-6486
Clayton Hubbs, *Pr*
EMP: 9 **EST:** 1977
SALES (est): 500K **Privately Held**
Web: www.transitionsabroad.com
SIC: **2721** 2731 Magazines: publishing only,
not printed on site; Book clubs: publishing
only, not printed on site

(G-5866)
UM FOOD SCIENCES
228 Chenowith (01002)
PHONE.............................413 545-2276
EMP: 30 **EST:** 1863
SALES (est): 1.31MM **Privately Held**
SIC: **5411** 2869 8299 Grocery stores;
Industrial organic chemicals, nec; Schools
and educational services, nec

Andover
Essex County

(G-5867)
**ADVANCED DEVICE
TECHNOLOGY**
6 Yardley Rd (01810-5846)
PHONE.............................603 894-1402
Peter J Kannam, *Pr*
Jim Wilen, *Dir*
EMP: 8 **EST:** 1982
SALES (est): 650.01K **Privately Held**
SIC: **3812** Infrared object detection
equipment

(G-5868)
AGILENT TECHNOLOGIES INC
40 Shattuck Rd Ste 201 (01810-2455)
PHONE.............................978 794-3664
Carl Witonsky, *Brnch Mgr*
EMP: 24
SALES (corp-wide): 6.83B **Publicly Held**
Web: www.agilent.com
SIC: **3825** Instruments to measure electricity
PA: Agilent Technologies, Inc.
5301 Stevens Creek Blvd
Santa Clara CA 95051
800 227-9770

(G-5869)
AGRI-MARK INC (PA)
Also Called: Cabot Creamery
40 Shattuck Rd Ste 301 (01810-2456)
PHONE.............................978 552-5500

James Jacquier, *CEO*
Margaret H Bertolino, *
Doctor Richard Stammer, *VP Mktg*
William Banker, *
Mike Barnes, *
◆ **EMP:** 64 **EST:** 1980
SQ FT: 28,000
SALES (est): 305.86MM
SALES (corp-wide): 305.86MM **Privately
Held**
Web: www.agrimark.net
SIC: **2026** 2022 Milk processing
(pasteurizing, homogenizing, bottling);
Cheese; natural and processed

(G-5870)
ANDOVER PRINTING INC
Also Called: Minuteman Press
79 N Main St (01810-3510)
PHONE.............................978 475-4945
Philip N Heffernan, *Pr*
EMP: 10 **EST:** 2016
SALES (est): 807.67K **Privately Held**
Web: www.mmpand.com
SIC: **2752** Offset printing

(G-5871)
AURORA WIND PROJECT LLC
100 Brickstone Sq Ste 300 (01810)
PHONE.............................978 409-9712
EMP: 25 **EST:** 2016
SALES (est): 8.02MM
SALES (corp-wide): 120.53MM **Privately
Held**
SIC: **3621** Power generators
HQ: Tradewind Energy, Inc.
16105 W 113th St Ste 105
Lenexa KS 66219
913 888-9463

(G-5872)
BLUBOX SECURITY INC
1 Tech Dr Ste 110 (01810-2452)
PHONE.............................508 414-3517
Patrick J Barry, *Pr*
Patrick Decavaignac, *COO*
EMP: 40 **EST:** 2013
SALES (est): 3.39MM **Privately Held**
Web: www.blub0x.com
SIC: **7372** Business oriented computer
software

(G-5873)
BODYCOTE IMT INC (DH)
Also Called: Bodycote Andover
155 River St (01810-5923)
PHONE.............................978 470-0876
Dominique Yates, *Pr*
Edmond J Tenerini, *VP Opers*
David Landless, *VP*
Yale Curtis, *VP*
Stephanie Edgar, *Sec*
▲ **EMP:** 57 **EST:** 1968
SQ FT: 63,000
SALES (est): 42.61MM
SALES (corp-wide): 895.27MM **Privately
Held**
Web: www.bodycote.com
SIC: **3398** 3269 Metal heat treating;
Laboratory and industrial pottery
HQ: Bodycote Usa, Inc.
12750 Merit Dr Ste 1400
Dallas TX 75251
214 904-2420

(G-5874)
BROADCOM CORPORATION
200 Brickstone Sq Ste 401 (01810-1429)
PHONE.............................978 719-1300
Doug Grearson, *Pr*

EMP: 105
SALES (corp-wide): 35.82B **Publicly Held**
Web: www.broadcom.com
SIC: **3674** Integrated circuits,
semiconductor networks, etc.
HQ: Broadcom Corporation
1320 Ridder Park Dr
San Jose CA 95131

(G-5875)
**BYRNA TECHNOLOGIES INC
(PA)**
100 Burtt Rd Ste 115 (01810-5915)
PHONE.............................978 868-5011
EMP: 126 **EST:** 2005
SALES (est): 48.04MM **Publicly Held**
Web: le.byrna.com
SIC: **3699** Security control equipment and
systems

(G-5876)
CALIFORNIA PAINT
150 Dascomb Rd (01810-5873)
PHONE.............................978 965-2122
Joseph Deangelis, *VP*
EMP: 10 **EST:** 2018
SALES (est): 498.21K **Privately Held**
Web: www.californiapaints.com
SIC: **2851** Paints and allied products

(G-5877)
CASA SYSTEMS INC (PA)
Also Called: Casa Systems
100 River Rd (01810-1030)
PHONE.............................978 688-6706
Michael Glickman, *CEO*
Edward Durkin, *CFO*
Philip E Paro Junior, *CAO*
Sanjay Kaul, *CRO*
▲ **EMP:** 292 **EST:** 2003
SQ FT: 122,000
SALES (est): 286.54MM **Publicly Held**
Web: www.casa-systems.com
SIC: **3663** Radio and t.v. communications
equipment

(G-5878)
**CGI INFORMATION SYSTEMS &
MANAGEMENT CONSULTANTS
INC**
Also Called: Cgi
600 Federal St (01810-1064)
PHONE.............................978 946-3000
EMP: 1254
SIC: **7374** 3577 7373 Data processing
service; Data conversion equipment, media-
to-media: computer; Computer integrated
systems design

(G-5879)
COMPART NORTH AMERICA INC
6 Wild Rose Dr (01810-4613)
P.O. Box 185 (03782-0185)
PHONE.............................877 237-2725
Brian Gasteier, *CEO*
John Lynch, *Technology Vice President*
Christof Mayer, *
EMP: 25 **EST:** 2008
SALES (est): 5.07MM
SALES (corp-wide): 2.67MM **Privately
Held**
SIC: **5045** 7372 8243 Computer software;
Prepackaged software; Software training,
computer
HQ: Compart Gmbh
Otto-Lilienthal-Str. 38
Boblingen BW 71034
703162050

(G-5880)
DRAEGER MEDICAL SYSTEMS INC
6 Tech Dr (01810-2434)
PHONE.....................800 437-2437
Stefan Drager, *Ch Bd*
Ruben Derderian, *
▲ **EMP:** 380 **EST:** 2006
SQ FT: 80,000
SALES (est): 27.33MM
SALES (corp-wide): 3.16B **Privately Held**
SIC: 3841 Anesthesia apparatus
HQ: Draeger, Inc.
3135 Quarry Rd
Telford PA 18969
800 437-2437

(G-5881)
EPC SPACE LLC
200 Bulfinch Dr (01810-1140)
PHONE.....................978 208-1334
EMP: 16 **EST:** 2020
SALES (est): 2.62MM **Privately Held**
Web: www.epc.space
SIC: 3575 Computer terminals

(G-5882)
FIBERLOCK TECHNOLOGIES INC
150 Dascomb Rd (01810-5873)
PHONE.....................978 623-9987
Joseph E Connor, *Pr*
EMP: 10 **EST:** 1985
SQ FT: 3,000
SALES (est): 5.83MM
SALES (corp-wide): 923.49MM **Privately Held**
Web: www.fiberlock.com
SIC: 3826 2819 Environmental testing equipment; Industrial inorganic chemicals, nec
HQ: Icp Construction, Inc.
150 Dascomb Rd
Andover MA 01810
978 623-9980

(G-5883)
FISHMAN TRANSDUCERS INC
3 Riverside Dr Ste 1 (01810-1141)
PHONE.....................978 988-9199
Lawrence Fishman, *Pr*
Maurice Fishman, *
▲ **EMP:** 64 **EST:** 1980
SALES (est): 10.72MM **Privately Held**
Web: www.fishman.com
SIC: 3825 3931 3651 Transducers for volts, amperes, watts, vars, frequency, etc.; Musical instruments; Amplifiers: radio, public address, or musical instrument

(G-5884)
GANADO STORAGE LLC
100 Brickstone Sq Ste 300 (01810-1456)
PHONE.....................617 605-4322
Mark Mcgrail, *CEO*
EMP: 100 **EST:** 2020
SALES (est): 6.97MM **Privately Held**
SIC: 3433 Solar heaters and collectors

(G-5885)
HARRIS ENVMTL SYSTEMS INC
11 Connector Rd (01810-5926)
PHONE.....................978 470-8600
Alexander Murray, *Pr*
Yury Zlobinsky, *
EMP: 90 **EST:** 1940
SQ FT: 42,000
SALES (est): 20.55MM **Privately Held**
Web: www.harrisenv.com

(G-5886)
HH BROWN SHOE COMPANY INC
100 Brickstone Sq Ste 100 (01810-1456)
PHONE.....................978 933-4700
EMP: 45
SALES (corp-wide): 302.09B **Publicly Held**
Web: www.hhbrown.com
SIC: 3143 3144 Men's footwear, except athletic; Women's footwear, except athletic
HQ: H.H. Brown Shoe Company, Inc.
124 W Putnam Ave Ste 1a
Greenwich CT 06830
203 661-2424

(G-5887)
ICP CONSTRUCTION INC (HQ)
Also Called: Arizona Polymer Flooring
150 Dascomb Rd (01810-5873)
PHONE.....................978 623-9980
Douglas Mattscheck, *Pr*
Sven Doerge, *
Peter Longo, *
◆ **EMP:** 115 **EST:** 1926
SQ FT: 168,000
SALES (est): 141.54MM
SALES (corp-wide): 923.49MM **Privately Held**
Web: www.icpgroup.com
SIC: 2851 Paints and paint additives
PA: Innovative Chemical Products Group, Llc
150 Dascomb Rd
Andover MA 01810
978 623-9980

(G-5888)
INFINEON TECH AMERICAS CORP
Also Called: Infineon Technologies
35 New England Business Center Dr Ste 110 (01810)
PHONE.....................978 851-1298
EMP: 9
SALES (corp-wide): 17.72B **Privately Held**
Web: www.infineon.com
SIC: 3674 Semiconductors and related devices
HQ: Infineon Technologies Americas Corp.
101 N Pacific Coast Hwy
El Segundo CA 90245
310 726-8200

(G-5889)
INNOVATIVE CHEM PDTS GROUP LLC (PA)
Also Called: ICP Group
150 Dascomb Rd (01810-5873)
PHONE.....................978 623-9980
Doug Mattscheck, *Pr*
EMP: 29 **EST:** 2015
SALES (est): 923.49MM
SALES (corp-wide): 923.49MM **Privately Held**
Web: www.icpgroup.com
SIC: 8742 2891 Marketing consulting services; Adhesives

(G-5890)
JULIE INDUSTRIES INC (PA)
Also Called: Staticsmart Flooring
2 Dundee Park Dr Ste 302a (01810-3725)
P.O. Box 153 (01864-0153)
PHONE.....................978 276-0820
Jerry M Giuliano, *Pr*

▼ **EMP:** 8 **EST:** 1973
SALES (est): 2.28MM
SALES (corp-wide): 2.28MM **Privately Held**
Web: www.staticsmart.com
SIC: 2273 Carpets and rugs

(G-5891)
LOCKHEED MARTIN CORPORATION
160 Dascomb Rd Ste 1 (01810-0044)
PHONE.....................407 356-2374
Call Site, *CEO*
David Leckie, *VP*
EMP: 22 **EST:** 1995
SALES (est): 1.69MM **Privately Held**
SIC: 3721 Aircraft

(G-5892)
MASTER CONTAINERS INC
200 Brickstone Sq Ste G05 (01810-1439)
PHONE.....................800 881-6847
▼ **EMP:** 75
SIC: 3086 Cups and plates, foamed plastics

(G-5893)
MATERIALS DEVELOPMENT CORP
10 Lowell Junction Rd (01810-5906)
PHONE.....................781 391-0400
Christopher E Cataldo, *Prin*
Paul Doherty, *
Chris Cataldo, *
EMP: 58 **EST:** 1966
SQ FT: 25,000
SALES (est): 1MM
SALES (corp-wide): 5.02MM **Privately Held**
Web: www.materialsdevelopment.com
SIC: 3398 3724 Metal heat treating; Aircraft engines and engine parts
PA: Consolidated Investors Corporation
10 Lowell Junction Rd
Andover MA 01810
781 391-0400

(G-5894)
MELANIE CASEY LLC
18 Red Spring Rd Ste 102 (01810-3449)
PHONE.....................781 640-8910
Melanie Casey, *Managing Member*
EMP: 24 **EST:** 2016
SALES (est): 2.58MM **Privately Held**
Web: www.melaniecasey.com
SIC: 3911 Jewelry, precious metal

(G-5895)
MEMED US INC
200 Brickstone Sq Ste 106 (01810-1459)
PHONE.....................617 335-0349
Ethan Suttles, *Dir*
Troy Boutelle, *Genl Mgr*
Jim Kathrein, *VP*
EMP: 25 **EST:** 2018
SALES (est): 2.39MM **Privately Held**
Web: www.me-med.com
SIC: 2835 3826 Diagnostic substances; Analytical instruments

(G-5896)
MERCURY SYSTEMS INC (PA)
50 Minuteman Rd (01810-1008)
PHONE.....................978 256-1300
William L Ballhaus, *Pr*
William K O'brien, *Ch Bd*
Christopher C Cambria, *Ex VP*
David E Farnsworth, *
Christine F Harbison, *CGO*
▼ **EMP:** 366 **EST:** 1981

SQ FT: 145,262
SALES (est): 973.88MM
SALES (corp-wide): 973.88MM **Publicly Held**
Web: www.mrcy.com
SIC: 3672 7372 Printed circuit boards; Prepackaged software

(G-5897)
MERRILL CORP
35 New England Business Center Dr Ste 150 (01810)
PHONE.....................978 725-3700
Rose Quast, *Prin*
Patricia Elias, *VP*
EMP: 10 **EST:** 2016
SALES (est): 699.71K **Privately Held**
Web: www.merrillinc.com
SIC: 2759 Publication printing

(G-5898)
MKS INSTRUMENTS INC
6 Shattuck Rd (01810-2449)
PHONE.....................978 645-5500
Kathleen F Burke, *Mgr*
EMP: 20
SALES (corp-wide): 3.55B **Publicly Held**
Web: www.mks.com
SIC: 3823 3491 3494 Pressure measurement instruments, industrial; Industrial valves; Valves and pipe fittings, nec
PA: Mks Instruments, Inc.
2 Tech Dr Ste 201
Andover MA 01810
978 645-5500

(G-5899)
MKS INSTRUMENTS INC (PA)
Also Called: M K S
2 Tech Dr Ste 201 (01810-2489)
PHONE.....................978 645-5500
John T C Lee, *Pr*
Gerald G Colella, *
Seth H Bagshaw, *Ex VP*
James A Schreiner, *Sr VP*
Kathleen F Burke, *Sr VP*
◆ **EMP:** 350 **EST:** 1961
SQ FT: 158,000
SALES (est): 3.55B
SALES (corp-wide): 3.55B **Publicly Held**
Web: www.mks.com
SIC: 3823 3491 3494 Pressure measurement instruments, industrial; Industrial valves; Valves and pipe fittings, nec

(G-5900)
NEW ENGLAND ORTHDONTIC LAB INC
3 Riverside Dr Ste 1 (01810-1141)
P.O. Box 4064 (01888-4064)
PHONE.....................800 922-6365
William Saurman, *Pr*
Ann Saurman, *
EMP: 26 **EST:** 1977
SALES (est): 900K **Privately Held**
Web: www.neolab.com
SIC: 3843 8072 Orthodontic appliances; Orthodontic appliance production

(G-5901)
NORTHAST DCMENT CNSRVTION CTR
100 Brickstone Sq Ste 401 (01810-1428)
PHONE.....................978 470-1010
William Veillette, *Ex Dir*
Rob Maier, *
Michael Comeau, *
Daria D'arienzo, *Sec*

EMP: 40 **EST:** 1973
SQ FT: 20,000
SALES (est): 5.36MM **Privately Held**
Web: www.nedcc.org
SIC: 2789 7334 2631   Binding and repair of
books, magazines, and pamphlets;
Photocopying and duplicating services;
Paperboard mills

(G-5902)
NSIGHT INC
Also Called: Cohesion
300 Brickstone Sq Ste 201 (01810-1497)
PHONE.................................781 273-6300
John Owens, *Finance & Operations*
John Larson, *Sales & Marketing**
Tess Kastning, *
EMP: 35 **EST:** 1982
SQ FT: 5,400
SALES (est): 4.76MM **Privately Held**
Web: www.nsightworks.com
SIC: 2731 7338 7363 8748   Pamphlets:
publishing and printing; Editing service;
Temporary help service; Publishing
consultant

(G-5903)
OMNIFY SOFTWARE INC
1 Tech Dr (01810-2453)
PHONE.................................508 527-1956
EMP: 8 **EST:** 2018
SALES (est): 301.9K **Privately Held**
SIC: 7372   Prepackaged software

(G-5904)
ONCORUS INC (PA)
Also Called: ONCORUS
4 Corporate Dr (01810-2441)
PHONE.................................857 334-9077
Theodore Ashburn, *Pr*
Mitchell Finer, *Ex Ch Bd*
Steve Harbin, *COO*
John Mccabe, *Corporate Secretary*
Christophe Queva, *CSO*
EMP: 30 **EST:** 2015
SQ FT: 17,800
Web: www.oncorus.com
SIC: 2834   Pharmaceutical preparations

(G-5905)
PCA LLC
5 Harper Cir (01810-2331)
PHONE.................................978 494-0550
Kevin Hall, *Prin*
EMP: 11 **EST:** 2015
SALES (est): 147.13K **Privately Held**
Web: www.pca-llc.com
SIC: 3679   Harness assemblies, for
electronic use: wire or cable

(G-5906)
PFIZER INC
Also Called: Pfizer
1 Burtt Rd (01810-5901)
PHONE.................................978 247-1000
EMP: 146
SALES (corp-wide): 100.33B **Publicly
Held**
Web: www.pfizer.com
SIC: 2834   Pharmaceutical preparations
PA: Pfizer Inc.
66 Hudson Blvd E
New York NY 10001
212 733-2323

(G-5907)
PHYSICAL SCIENCES INC (PA)
20 New England Business Center Dr
(01810)
PHONE.................................978 689-0003

David Green, *CEO*
Doctor Michael L Finson, *Ch Bd*
George Caledonia, *
Robert F Weiss, *
Deborah A Boucher, *
EMP: 100 **EST:** 1973
SQ FT: 65,000
SALES (est): 55.58MM
SALES (corp-wide): 55.58MM **Privately
Held**
Web: www.psicorp.com
SIC: 8731 8742 8711 3826   Commercial
physical research; Public utilities consultant
; Engineering services; Analytical optical
instruments

(G-5908)
PROCTER & GAMBLE MFG CO
Also Called: Procter & Gamble
30 Burtt Rd (01810-5909)
PHONE.................................978 749-5547
EMP: 51
SALES (corp-wide): 82.01B **Publicly Held**
Web: us.pg.com
SIC: 2844   Toilet preparations
HQ: The Procter & Gamble Manufacturing
Company
1 Procter And Gamble Plz
Cincinnati OH 45202
513 983-1100

(G-5909)
RAYTHEON COMPANY
Also Called: Raytheon
350 Lowell St (01810-4495)
PHONE.................................978 470-5000
EMP: 132
SALES (corp-wide): 68.92B **Publicly Held**
Web: www.rtx.com
SIC: 3812   Electronic detection systems
(aeronautical)
HQ: Raytheon Company
870 Winter St
Waltham MA 02451
781 522-3000

(G-5910)
RAYTHEON ITALY LIAISON
COMPANY
Also Called: Raytheon
358 Lowell St (01810-4490)
PHONE.................................978 684-5300
James W Carter, *Prin*
Donna Mccullough, *Prin*
EMP: 99 **EST:** 2005
SALES (est): 41.26K
SALES (corp-wide): 68.92B **Publicly Held**
SIC: 3812   Search and navigation equipment
HQ: Raytheon Company
870 Winter St
Waltham MA 02451
781 522-3000

(G-5911)
RESPIRONICS NOVAMETRIX
LLC
Also Called: Philips Medical Systems
3000 Minuteman Rd (01810-1032)
PHONE.................................724 882-4120
Zita Yurko, *Admn*
Zita Yurko, *Dir*
Agnes Szoboszlai, *Dir*
▲ **EMP:** 2000 **EST:** 2002
SQ FT: 53,000
SALES (est): 179.1MM
SALES (corp-wide): 18.51B **Privately Held**
SIC: 3845 3841   Electromedical equipment;
Surgical and medical instruments
HQ: Philips Rs North America Llc
6501 Living Pl

Pittsburgh PA 15206
800 263-3342

(G-5912)
ROCK-TRED 2 LLC
Also Called: Ora Holdings
150 Dascomb Rd (01810-5873)
PHONE.................................888 762-5873
Chris O'brien, *CEO*
Mark Moran, *
EMP: 35 **EST:** 1939
SALES (est): 2.35MM **Privately Held**
Web: www.rocktred.com
SIC: 2842 2851   Polishes and sanitation
goods; Polyurethane coatings

(G-5913)
ROCKSTAR NEW ENGLAND INC
3 Dundee Park Dr Ste 102 (01810-3723)
PHONE.................................978 409-6272
Ann Davis, *Prin*
EMP: 40 **EST:** 1999
SALES (est): 1.85MM **Publicly Held**
Web: www.rockstargames.com
SIC: 7372 7371   Prepackaged software;
Custom computer programming services
HQ: Rockstar Games, Inc.
622 Broadway Fl 4
New York NY 10012
212 334-6633

(G-5914)
SAREPTA THERAPEUTICS INC
100 Federal St (01810-1036)
PHONE.................................978 662-4800
John Mills, *Mgr*
EMP: 194
SALES (corp-wide): 933.01MM **Publicly
Held**
Web: www.sarepta.com
SIC: 2834 8731   Medicines, capsuled or
ampuled; Biological research
PA: Sarepta Therapeutics, Inc.
215 1st St Ste 415
Cambridge MA 02142
617 274-4000

(G-5915)
SCHNEIDER AUTOMATION INC
Also Called: Engineering
800 Federal St (01810-1067)
PHONE.................................978 975-9600
EMP: 199
SALES (corp-wide): 82.05K **Privately Held**
Web: www.telemecanique.com
SIC: 3699   Electrical equipment and
supplies, nec
HQ: Schneider Automation Inc.
800 Federal St
Andover MA 01810
978 794-0800

(G-5916)
SEAVUS GROUP
45 W Parish Dr (01810-3338)
PHONE.................................978 623-7221
Igor Lestar, *Prin*
EMP: 24 **EST:** 2016
SALES (est): 310.17K **Privately Held**
Web: www.qinshift.com
SIC: 7372   Prepackaged software

(G-5917)
SEVENTY NINE N MAIN ST PRTG
Also Called: Minuteman Press
79 N Main St (01810-3510)
PHONE.................................978 475-4945
TOLL FREE: 800
Tom Heffernan, *Pr*
EMP: 9 **EST:** 1986

SALES (est): 1.37MM **Privately Held**
Web: www.mmpand.com
SIC: 2752   Commercial printing, lithographic

(G-5918)
SHAWSHEEN RUBBER CO INC
Also Called: Arrowhead Athletics
220 Andover St (01810-5695)
P.O. Box 4296 (01810-0814)
PHONE.................................978 470-1760
Denis J Kelley, *Pr*
Walter P Nugent, *
▲ **EMP:** 52 **EST:** 1939
SQ FT: 60,000
SALES (est): 9.68MM **Privately Held**
Web: www.bsct.us
SIC: 2672   Paper; coated and laminated, nec

(G-5919)
SIEMENS HLTHCARE
DGNOSTICS INC
6 Tech Dr (01810-2434)
PHONE.................................212 258-4000
David Pacitti, *CEO*
EMP: 19 **EST:** 2018
SALES (est): 179.11K **Privately Held**
SIC: 8099 3569   Health and allied services,
nec; Heaters, swimming pool: electric

(G-5920)
SIGE SEMICONDUCTOR INC
(HQ)
300 Federal St (01810-1038)
PHONE.................................978 327-6850
Sohail Khan, *Pr*
EMP: 23 **EST:** 2002
SALES (est): 7.77MM
SALES (corp-wide): 4.77B **Publicly Held**
Web: www.skyworksinc.com
SIC: 3674   Semiconductors and related
devices
PA: Skyworks Solutions, Inc.
5260 California Ave # 100
Irvine CA 92617
949 231-3000

(G-5921)
SKYWORKS SOLUTIONS INC
300 Federal St # 100 (01810-1038)
PHONE.................................978 327-6850
William Vaillancourt, *Brnch Mgr*
EMP: 13
SALES (corp-wide): 4.77B **Publicly Held**
Web: www.skyworksinc.com
SIC: 3674   Semiconductors and related
devices
PA: Skyworks Solutions, Inc.
5260 California Ave # 100
Irvine CA 92617
949 231-3000

(G-5922)
SLOAN VALVE COMPANY
19 Connector Rd Ste 4 (01810-5933)
PHONE.................................617 796-9001
Amy Parsons, *Mgr*
EMP: 219
SALES (corp-wide): 192.74MM **Privately
Held**
Web: www.sloan.com
SIC: 3494   Valves and pipe fittings, nec
PA: Sloan Valve Company
10500 Seymour Ave
Franklin Park IL 60131
847 671-4300

(G-5923)
SMITH & NEPHEW INC
150 Minuteman Rd (01810-1031)

▲ = Import ▼ = Export
◆ = Import/Export

PHONE.................978 749-1000
EMP: 50
SALES (corp-wide): 5.21B **Privately Held**
Web: www.ceosmith-nephew.com
SIC: 3841 Surgical instruments and apparatus
HQ: Smith & Nephew, Inc.
    1450 E Brooks Rd
    Memphis TN 38116
    901 396-2121

(G-5924)
SMITH & NEPHEW ENDOSCOPY INC
150 Minuteman Rd (01810-1031)
PHONE.................978 749-1000
Charles Federico, *Pr*
Olivier Bohuon, *
Sir John Buchanan, *
Julie Brown, *
▲ **EMP:** 237 **EST:** 1964
SALES (est): 47.3MM
SALES (corp-wide): 5.21B **Privately Held**
SIC: 3841 3845 Surgical instruments and apparatus; Electromedical equipment
HQ: Smith & Nephew, Inc.
    1450 E Brooks Rd
    Memphis TN 38116
    901 396-2121

(G-5925)
SPIRIT FOODSERVICE LLC
Also Called: Wna
200 Brickstone Sq Ste G05 (01810-1439)
P.O. Box 5040 (60045-5040)
PHONE.................978 964-1551
▲ **EMP:** 225
Web: www.one800parties.com
SIC: 3089 Novelties, plastics

(G-5926)
STICKAMAYKA PACKAGING INC
7 Connector Rd (01810-5922)
P.O. Box 4247 (01810-0814)
PHONE.................978 474-1930
Stephen R Dunlevy, *Pr*
EMP: 48 **EST:** 1972
SQ FT: 35,000
SALES (est): 10.53MM **Privately Held**
SIC: 2759 3479 3993 2752 Labels and seals: printing, nsk; Name plates: engraved, etched, etc.; Signs and advertising specialties; Commercial printing, lithographic
PA: Resource Label Group, Llc
    2550 Meridian Blvd # 370
    Franklin TN 37067

(G-5927)
STRAUMANN USA LLC
60 Minuteman Rd (01810-1008)
PHONE.................978 747-2500
Jim Frontero, *
Thomas Dressendrfer, *
Andreas L Meier, *
Beat Spalinger, *
EMP: 200 **EST:** 1989
SQ FT: 20,000
SALES (est): 95.9MM **Privately Held**
Web: www.straumann.com
SIC: 5047 3843 Medical equipment and supplies; Dental equipment and supplies
PA: Straumann Holding Ag
    Peter Merian-Weg 12
    Basel BS 4002

(G-5928)
SUNDANCE WIND PROJECT LLC
100 Brickstone Sq (01810-1438)

PHONE.................978 409-9712
EMP: 54 **EST:** 2015
SALES (est): 1.26MM
SALES (corp-wide): 120.53MM **Privately Held**
SIC: 3829 Measuring and controlling devices, nec
HQ: Enel Kansas, Llc
    100 Brickstone Sq
    Andover MA 01810
    978 409-9712

(G-5929)
SYNTONIC MICROWAVE LLC
50 Minuteman Rd (01810-1008)
P.O. Box 12228 (97212-0228)
PHONE.................408 866-5900
Jay Goodfriend, *Pr*
EMP: 7 **EST:** 2003
SALES (est): 4.94MM
SALES (corp-wide): 973.88MM **Publicly Held**
Web: www.mrcy.com
SIC: 3663 Microwave communication equipment
PA: Mercury Systems, Inc.
    50 Minuteman Rd
    Andover MA 01810
    978 256-1300

(G-5930)
TRANSCAT INC
Also Called: Transcat Calibration Services
149 River St Ste 3 (01810-5935)
PHONE.................888 975-5061
Jeremy Kraft, *Brnch Mgr*
EMP: 15
SALES (corp-wide): 230.57MM **Publicly Held**
Web: www.transcat.com
SIC: 3825 Instruments to measure electricity
PA: Transcat, Inc.
    35 Vantage Point Dr
    Rochester NY 14624
    800 828-1470

(G-5931)
TRANSMEDICS INC (PA)
Also Called: Transmedics
200 Minuteman Rd Ste 302 (01810-1046)
PHONE.................978 552-0443
Waleed Hassanein, *Pr*
Dominic Micale, *CFO*
Travis Rhodes, *Dir*
Jeffrey E Young, *Dir*
EMP: 131 **EST:** 1998
SQ FT: 32,000
SALES (est): 64.1MM
SALES (corp-wide): 64.1MM **Privately Held**
Web: www.transmedics.com
SIC: 3845 Electromedical equipment

(G-5932)
VARIAN SEMICDTR EQP ASSOC INC
Also Called: Applied Mtls Vrian Smicdtr Eqp
41 Juniper Rd (01810-2817)
PHONE.................978 282-2807
Nan Zeng, *Brnch Mgr*
EMP: 9
SALES (corp-wide): 26.52B **Publicly Held**
SIC: 3674 Semiconductors and related devices
HQ: Varian Semiconductor Equipment Associates, Inc.
    35 Dory Rd
    Gloucester MA 01930
    978 282-2000

(G-5933)
VICOR CORPORATION (PA)
Also Called: VICOR
25 Frontage Rd (01810-5499)
PHONE.................978 470-2900
Patrizio Vinciarelli, *Ch Bd*
Patrizio Vinciarelli, *Ch Bd*
James F Schmidt, *Corporate Vice President**
Alvaro Doyle, *Corporate Vice President*
Quentin A Fendelet, *Corporate Vice President*
EMP: 712 **EST:** 1981
SQ FT: 90,000
SALES (est): 399.08MM
SALES (corp-wide): 399.08MM **Publicly Held**
Web: www.vicorpower.com
SIC: 3679 3613 Electronic loads and power supplies; Switches, electric power except snap, push button, etc.

(G-5934)
WATER ANALYTICS INC
100 School St (01810-3924)
PHONE.................978 749-9949
Mark Spencer, *Pr*
▼ **EMP:** 10 **EST:** 2010
SQ FT: 8,200
SALES (est): 1.97MM **Privately Held**
Web: www.wateranalytics.net
SIC: 3823 Water quality monitoring and control systems

(G-5935)
WINGED PEGASUS CONSULTING INC
8 Bobby Jones Dr (01810-2880)
PHONE.................978 667-0600
◆ **EMP:** 20
SIC: 2893 Printing ink

(G-5936)
WYETH PHARMACEUTICALS LLC
Also Called: Wyeth Biopharma Division
1 Burtt Rd (01810-5901)
PHONE.................978 475-9214
Michelle Barrows, *Mgr*
EMP: 20
SALES (corp-wide): 100.33B **Publicly Held**
SIC: 2834 Pharmaceutical preparations
HQ: Wyeth Pharmaceuticals Llc
    500 Arcola Rd
    Collegeville PA 19426
    484 865-5000

Arlington
Middlesex County

(G-5937)
A TO Z FOODS INC
797 Massachusetts Ave (02476-4732)
PHONE.................781 413-0221
Wagih Morcos, *Prin*
EMP: 7 **EST:** 2008
SALES (est): 244.59K **Privately Held**
SIC: 2099 Food preparations, nec

(G-5938)
ACTUALITY SYSTEMS INC
1337 Massachusetts Ave (02476-4101)
PHONE.................617 325-9230
Michael Goldstein, *Pr*
Gregg Favalora, *VP*
Robert Ryan, *VP*
▲ **EMP:** 9 **EST:** 1997

SQ FT: 10,000
SALES (est): 925.19K **Privately Held**
SIC: 3575 7372 Computer terminals; Prepackaged software

(G-5939)
BRIGHAMS INC (HQ)
Also Called: Brigham's
30 Mill St (02476-4757)
PHONE.................800 242-2423
Robert Wexler, *CEO*
Roger Theriault, *Pr*
Claudia Kost, *VP Mfg*
EMP: 10 **EST:** 1914
SQ FT: 80,000
SALES (est): 9.3MM
SALES (corp-wide): 130.16MM **Privately Held**
Web: www.brighamsquare.com
SIC: 5143 5812 6794 2087 Ice cream and ices; Ice cream stands or dairy bars; Franchises, selling or licensing; Flavoring extracts and syrups, nec
PA: Wood Partners, L.L.C.
    3715 Northside Pkwy Nw
    Atlanta GA 30327
    404 965-9965

(G-5940)
FORCED EXPOSURE INC
60 Lowell St (02476-4160)
PHONE.................781 321-0320
James F Johnson, *Pr*
▲ **EMP:** 20 **EST:** 1982
SQ FT: 40,000
SALES (est): 2.43MM **Privately Held**
Web: www.forcedexposure.com
SIC: 2721 5099 5961 Magazines: publishing only, not printed on site; Compact discs; Record and/or tape (music or video) club, mail order

(G-5941)
FORGE BAKING COMPANY INC
12 Elder Ter (02474-2701)
PHONE.................617 764-5365
Jennifer A Park, *Prin*
EMP: 7 **EST:** 2014
SALES (est): 279.66K **Privately Held**
Web: www.forgebakingco.com
SIC: 2051 Bread, cake, and related products

(G-5942)
KALA PHARMACEUTICALS INC (PA)
Also Called: KALA
1167 Massachusetts Ave (02476-4346)
PHONE.................781 996-5252
Mark Iwicki, *Ch Bd*
Mary Reumuth, *CFO*
Todd Bazemore, *COO*
Kim Brazzell, *CMO*
Hongming Chen, *CSO*
EMP: 186 **EST:** 2009
SQ FT: 66,052
SALES (est): 3.89MM **Publicly Held**
Web: www.kalarx.com
SIC: 2834 Pharmaceutical preparations

(G-5943)
KINTENT INC
16 Spy Pond Pkwy (02474-8223)
PHONE.................512 294-4201
EMP: 16 **EST:** 2020
SALES (est): 315.44K **Privately Held**
Web: www.trustcloud.ai
SIC: 7372 Prepackaged software

GEOGRAPHIC

(G-5944)
PELLION TECHNOLOGIES INC
1337 Massachusetts Ave (02476-4101)
EMP: 20 **EST:** 2009
SALES (est): 2.23MM **Privately Held**
Web: www.pelliontech.com
SIC: 3694 8731　Battery charging
generators, automobile and aircraft;
Commercial research laboratory

(G-5945)
REAL RELATIONAL SOLUTIONS LLC
754 Massachusetts Ave (02476-4712)
PHONE..................................781 646-7326
EMP: 7 **EST:** 2008
SALES (est): 229.1K **Privately Held**
Web: www.realrelational.com
SIC: 7372　Prepackaged software

(G-5946)
SAFERECIPES LLC (PA)
37 Varnum St (02474-8712)
PHONE..................................617 448-6085
EMP: 7 **EST:** 2018
SALES (est): 129.42K
SALES (corp-wide): 129.42K **Privately Held**
SIC: 2741　Internet publishing and broadcasting

(G-5947)
SKELMIR LLC
81 Park Ave (02476-5962)
PHONE..................................617 625-1551
Mimir Reynnison, *Managing Member*
EMP: 15 **EST:** 1990
SALES (est): 1.26MM **Privately Held**
Web: www.skelmir.com
SIC: 7372　Business oriented computer software

(G-5948)
SYBERWORKS INC
1 Epping St (02474-2013)
PHONE..................................781 891-1999
David Boggs, *Pr*
EMP: 20 **EST:** 1995
SQ FT: 3,000
SALES (est): 2.05MM **Privately Held**
Web: www.syberworks.com
SIC: 7373 7372 8748 8299　Computer integrated systems design; Prepackaged software; Business consulting, nec; Airline training

(G-5949)
TETRAGENETICS INC
91 Mystic St Ste 1 (02474-1157)
PHONE..................................617 500-7471
Richard Douglas Kahn, *Pr*
Carl Hansen, *CEO*
Veronique Lecault, *COO*
Tryn Stimart, *Corporate Secretary*
Andrew Booth, *CFO*
EMP: 13 **EST:** 2008
SQ FT: 5,400
SALES (est): 4.83MM
SALES (corp-wide): 485.42MM **Privately Held**
Web: www.abcellera.com
SIC: 2836　Vaccines
PA: Abcellera Biologics Inc
2215 Yukon St
Vancouver BC V5Y 0
604 559-9005

(G-5950)
WELLS DEVELOPMENT L L C
32 Devereaux St (02476-8128)
PHONE..................................781 727-5560
Frederick Wells, *Sls Dir*
Frederick Wells, *Managing Member*
EMP: 8 **EST:** 1998
SALES (est): 650.6K **Privately Held**
SIC: 6552 1611 2434　Land subdividers and developers, commercial; General contractor, highway and street construction; Wood kitchen cabinets

Ashburnham
Worcester County

(G-5951)
ABCROSBY & COMPANY INC
20 S Maple Ave (01430-1639)
PHONE..................................978 827-6064
Andrew B Crosby, *Pr*
EMP: 8 **EST:** 2004
SQ FT: 22,000
SALES (est): 991.33K **Privately Held**
Web: www.abcrosby.com
SIC: 2511　Wood household furniture

(G-5952)
FLO CHEMICAL CORP
Also Called: Flow Chemicals
20 Puffer St (01430-1267)
P.O. Box 51 (01430-0051)
PHONE..................................978 827-5101
Rachel Freedman, *Pr*
EMP: 11 **EST:** 1976
SALES (est): 2.56MM **Privately Held**
Web: www.zeinproducts.com
SIC: 1541 2834 2851 2064　Food products manufacturing or packing plant construction; Pharmaceutical preparations; Shellac (protective coating); Candy and other confectionery products

(G-5953)
SALEM VILLAGE CRAFTSMEN INC (PA)
Also Called: Shaker Workshops
14 S Pleasant St (01430-1649)
P.O. Box 548 (01430-0548)
PHONE..................................833 827-7267
TOLL FREE: 800
Richard C Dabrowski, *Pr*
EMP: 10 **EST:** 1970
SQ FT: 44,000
SALES (est): 2.18MM
SALES (corp-wide): 2.18MM **Privately Held**
Web: www.shakerworkshops.com
SIC: 2511　Wood household furniture

Ashfield
Franklin County

(G-5954)
ERATECH INC
Also Called: World Satellite Media
225 Smith Rd (01330-9503)
P.O. Box 292 (01330-0292)
PHONE..................................413 628-3219
John Angleman, *Pr*
EMP: 10 **EST:** 2001
SALES (est): 442.61K **Privately Held**
SIC: 3993　Signs, not made in custom sign painting shops

(G-5955)
ROBERTS BROTHERS LUMBER CO INC
1450 Spruce Corner Rd (01330-9747)
PHONE..................................413 628-3333
Leonard Roberts, *Pr*
Joan Roberts, *Clerk*
EMP: 14 **EST:** 1946
SQ FT: 20,000
SALES (est): 831.24K **Privately Held**
Web: www.robertslumber.com
SIC: 2421 2426 2411　Lumber: rough, sawed, or planed; Hardwood dimension and flooring mills; Logging

Ashland
Middlesex County

(G-5956)
DIVINE STONEWORKS LLC
60 Pleasant St (01721-3127)
PHONE..................................774 221-6006
Michelle Campos Coelho, *Managing Member*
EMP: 17 **EST:** 2016
SALES (est): 1.45MM **Privately Held**
Web: www.divinestoneworks.com
SIC: 3281　Granite, cut and shaped

(G-5957)
DYNEX/RIVETT INC
54 Nickerson Rd (01721-1912)
PHONE..................................508 881-5110
Chuck Meserve, *Mgr*
EMP: 9
SQ FT: 15,000
SALES (corp-wide): 9.09MM **Privately Held**
Web: www.dynexhydraulics.com
SIC: 3714　Hydraulic fluid power pumps, for auto steering mechanism
PA: Dynex/Rivett Inc.
770 Capitol Dr
Pewaukee WI 53072
262 691-0300

(G-5958)
FORTERRA PIPE & PRECAST LLC
Fenwal Div
400 Main St (01721-2150)
PHONE..................................508 881-2000
William F Johnston, *Brnch Mgr*
EMP: 104
SQ FT: 500,000
Web: www.rinkerpipe.com
SIC: 3272　Concrete products, nec
HQ: Forterra Pipe & Precast, Llc
511 E John Carpenter Fwy
Irving TX 75062
469 458-7973

(G-5959)
FREEDOM DIGITAL PRINTING LLC
200 Butterfield Dr Ste A2 (01721-2060)
PHONE..................................508 881-6940
EMP: 10 **EST:** 2001
SALES (est): 849.02K **Privately Held**
Web: www.freedomdigitalprinting.com
SIC: 2752　Offset printing

(G-5960)
KIDDE-FENWAL INC (HQ)
Also Called: Kidde Fire System
400 Main St (01721-2150)
PHONE..................................508 881-2000

Arumugam Balakrishnan, *Pr*
John Vernon, *
Alex Troise, *
Martin Fernandez, *
◆ **EMP:** 600 **EST:** 1917
SQ FT: 220,000
SALES (est): 163.09MM
SALES (corp-wide): 20.42B **Publicly Held**
Web: www.kidde-fenwal.com
SIC: 3669 3823 3825 3822　Fire detection systems, electric; Temperature instruments: industrial process type; Instruments to measure electricity; Environmental controls
PA: Carrier Global Corporation
13995 Pasteur Blvd
Palm Beach Gardens FL 33418
561 365-2000

(G-5961)
LENTROS ENGINEERING INC
280 Eliot St (01721-2392)
PHONE..................................508 881-1160
Peter G Lentros, *Pr*
Kimberley A Lentros, *
▲ **EMP:** 43 **EST:** 1958
SQ FT: 28,000
SALES (est): 9.07MM **Privately Held**
Web: lentros-engineering.business.site
SIC: 3599　Machine shop, jobbing and repair

(G-5962)
MONTEFERRO PRESS
49 Half Crown Cir (01721-3922)
PHONE..................................508 944-8587
Michael Isenberg, *Prin*
EMP: 7 **EST:** 2018
SALES (est): 80.3K **Privately Held**
Web: www.monteferropress.com
SIC: 2741　Miscellaneous publishing

(G-5963)
NANOAL LLC (HQ)
260 Eliot St # 4a (01721-2445)
PHONE..................................774 777-3369
Nhon Q Vo, *CEO*
David C Dunand, *CSO*
David N Seidman, *CSO*
EMP: 8 **EST:** 2013
SALES (est): 2.18MM
SALES (corp-wide): 10.88MM **Privately Held**
Web: www.nanoal.com
SIC: 3365　Aluminum and aluminum-based alloy castings
PA: Unity Aluminum Inc,
9300 Shelbyville Rd # 401
Louisville KY 40222
606 420-4645

(G-5964)
NOKONA USA BASEBALL
60 Pleasant St (01721-3127)
PHONE..................................508 309-3527
EMP: 7 **EST:** 2015
SALES (est): 154.31K **Privately Held**
Web: www.nokonabaseballclub.com
SIC: 3949 7941　Baseball equipment and supplies, general; Baseball club, professional and semi-professional

(G-5965)
NYACOL NANO TECHNOLOGIES INC
211 Megunko Rd (01721-1426)
P.O. Box 349 (01721-0349)
PHONE..................................508 881-2220
Robert Nehring, *Pr*
Audrey Colson, *
◆ **EMP:** 29 **EST:** 1969
SQ FT: 35,000

SALES (est): 9.76MM **Privately Held**
Web: www.nyacol.com
SIC: 2819 Silica compounds

(G-5966)
RELIABLE FNCE C/WSTERN DIV INC
231 Pond St (01721-2017)
PHONE..................................508 877-1200
TOLL FREE: 800
Raymond G Pelletier, *Pr*
EMP: 10 EST: 1980
SQ FT: 15,000
SALES (est): 1.18MM **Privately Held**
Web: www.reliablefences.com
SIC: 5211 3496 2499 Fencing; Fencing, made from purchased wire; Fencing, wood

(G-5967)
STAT PRODUCTS INC
200 Butterfield Dr Ste D (01721-2060)
PHONE..................................508 881-8022
David Franco, *Pr*
John Franco, *VP*
EMP: 23 EST: 1962
SQ FT: 10,000
SALES (est): 2.24MM **Privately Held**
Web: www.statproducts.com
SIC: 2761 2754 Continuous forms, office and business; Labels: gravure printing

(G-5968)
TEKNI-PLEX INC
150 Homer Ave (01721-1770)
PHONE..................................508 881-2440
EMP: 44
SALES (corp-wide): 996.3MM **Privately Held**
Web: www.tekni-plex.com
SIC: 3081 2759 2672 Packing materials, plastics sheet; Commercial printing, nec; Paper; coated and laminated, nec
PA: Tekni-Plex, Inc.
460 E Swedesford Rd # 300
Wayne PA 19087
484 690-1520

(G-5969)
VARIAN MEDICAL SYSTEMS INC
200 Butterfield Dr Ste B (01721-2060)
PHONE..................................650 493-4000
Rocco Amico, *Brnch Mgr*
EMP: 7
SALES (corp-wide): 84.48B **Privately Held**
Web: www.varian.com
SIC: 3841 Surgical and medical instruments
HQ: Varian Medical Systems, Inc.
3100 Hansen Way
Palo Alto CA 94304
650 493-4000

Ashley Falls
Berkshire County

(G-5970)
GINGRAS LUMBER INC
77 Clayton Rd (01222-9713)
P.O. Box 232 (01222-0232)
PHONE..................................413 229-2182
David Rood, *Pr*
Robert Beham, *VP*
EMP: 9 EST: 1963
SALES (est): 666.86K **Privately Held**
SIC: 2421 Custom sawmill

(G-5971)
JACQUIER WELDING LLC
79 Clayton Rd (01222-9713)

PHONE..................................413 248-1204
John Jacquier, *Mgr*
EMP: 7 EST: 2017
SALES (est): 488.73K **Privately Held**
Web: www.jacquierwelding.com
SIC: 7692 Welding repair

Assonet
Bristol County

(G-5972)
BRIGHTMAN CORPORATION
Also Called: Brightman Lumber Co
181 S Main St (02702-1648)
PHONE..................................508 644-2620
John Brightman Junior, *Pr*
John Brightman Iii, *VP*
Edward Brightman, *VP*
Nancy Brightman, *Treas*
EMP: 14 EST: 1965
SQ FT: 2,000
SALES (est): 992.48K **Privately Held**
Web: www.brightmanlumber.com
SIC: 2411 5211 Wooden logs; Lumber and other building materials

(G-5973)
FAR INDUSTRIES INC
11 Ridge Hill Rd (02702-1667)
P.O. Box 574 (02702-0899)
PHONE..................................508 644-3122
Joseph A Ferrazza, *Pr*
Albano P Robens, *VP*
▲ EMP: 16 EST: 1986
SQ FT: 12,000
SALES (est): 739.13K **Privately Held**
SIC: 3442 3469 3444 Casements, aluminum ; Metal stampings, nec; Sheet metalwork

(G-5974)
ISP FREETOWN FINE CHEM INC
238 S Main St (02702-1657)
PHONE..................................508 672-0634
John E Panichella, *Pr*
Steven E Post, *
J Kevin Willis, *
Scott A Gregg, *
Lynn P Freeman, *
▲ EMP: 75 EST: 1997
SALES (est): 21.56MM
SALES (corp-wide): 2.19B **Publicly Held**
SIC: 2869 2821 2911 2843 Amines, acids, salts, esters; Plastics materials and resins; Solvents; Surface active agents
PA: Ashland Inc.
8145 Blazer Dr
Wilmington DE 19808
302 995-3000

(G-5975)
KLA SYSTEMS INC
31 Mill St (02702-1123)
P.O. Box 940 (02702-0896)
PHONE..................................508 644-5555
Mark E Neville, *Pr*
Fred Siino, *VP*
Sandra Matrone Mack, *Sec*
◆ EMP: 8 EST: 2001
SQ FT: 3,000
SALES (est): 1.74MM **Privately Held**
Web: www.klasystems.com
SIC: 3589 Water treatment equipment, industrial

(G-5976)
PIPING SYSTEMS INC
32 Mill St (02702-1104)
P.O. Box 409 (02702-0409)
PHONE..................................508 644-2221

Pauline Lally, *Owner*
Michael Moreira, *
Pierrette Lemieux Vi, *Pr*
EMP: 50 EST: 1971
SQ FT: 12,000
SALES (est): 13.24MM **Privately Held**
Web: www.pipingsystemsins.com
SIC: 1711 3498 Heating systems repair and maintenance; Fabricated pipe and fittings

Athol
Worcester County

(G-5977)
CUTTING EDGE CARBIDE TECH INC
438 Wallingford Ave (01331-1516)
PHONE..................................888 210-9670
William C S Weir, *Pr*
David P Bodanza, *Treas*
EMP: 8 EST: 2015
SALES (est): 288.69K **Privately Held**
Web: www.cecarbide.com
SIC: 2819 3545 Carbides; Diamond cutting tools for turning, boring, burnishing, etc.

(G-5978)
E W SYKES GENERAL CONTRACTORS
Also Called: E W Sykes
5567 S Athol Rd (01331-9305)
P.O. Box 178 (01331-0178)
PHONE..................................978 249-7655
E William Sykes, *Pr*
Clinton Sykes, *VP*
Cathi Sykes, *Treas*
Klint Sykes, *VP*
EMP: 27 EST: 1954
SALES (est): 2.57MM **Privately Held**
SIC: 3281 1794 Stone, quarrying and processing of own stone products; Excavation and grading, building construction

(G-5979)
FILTRONA EXTRUSION OF MASSACHUSETTS LLC
764 S Athol Rd (01331-9812)
P.O. Box 659 (01331-0659)
PHONE..................................978 249-5343
▲ EMP: 196
SIC: 3089 Extruded finished plastics products, nec

(G-5980)
LS STARRETT COMPANY
Also Called: Repair Dept
121 Crescent St (01331-1915)
PHONE..................................978 249-3551
Diane Mcdonald, *Mgr*
EMP: 7
SALES (corp-wide): 256.18MM **Publicly Held**
Web: www.starrett.com
SIC: 3545 Machine tool accessories
PA: The L S Starrett Company
121 Crescent St
Athol MA 01331
978 249-3551

(G-5981)
LS STARRETT COMPANY (PA)
Also Called: Starrett
121 Crescent St (01331-1915)
PHONE..................................978 249-3551
Douglas A Starrett, *Ch Bd*
John C Tripp, *CFO*
Christian Arnsten, *VP*

David T Allen, *VP*
▲ EMP: 1000 EST: 1880
SQ FT: 535,000
SALES (est): 256.18MM
SALES (corp-wide): 256.18MM **Publicly Held**
Web: www.starrett.com
SIC: 3545 3423 3999 3425 Precision measuring tools; Rules or rulers, metal; Tape measures; Saw blades, for hand or power saws

(G-5982)
PEXCO LLC
764 S Athol Rd (01331-9812)
PHONE..................................978 249-5343
EMP: 126
SALES (corp-wide): 295.68MM **Privately Held**
Web: www.pexco.com
SIC: 3089 Injection molding of plastics
PA: Pexco Llc
6470 E Johns Xing Ste 430
Johns Creek GA 30097
678 990-1523

(G-5983)
PRODUCTION TOOL & GRINDING
273 Main St (01331-2237)
P.O. Box 440 (01364-0440)
PHONE..................................978 544-8206
Rolland F Rochon, *VP*
Michael Miller, *Pr*
▲ EMP: 21 EST: 1986
SQ FT: 8,000
SALES (est): 745.05K **Privately Held**
Web: ma-athol.pacifica.org.au
SIC: 3541 Machine tools, metal cutting type

(G-5984)
WHIPPS INC
Also Called: Whipps
370 S Athol Rd (01331-2728)
P.O. Box 1058 (01331-5058)
PHONE..................................978 249-7924
EMP: 52 EST: 1977
SALES (est): 10.85MM **Privately Held**
Web: www.whipps.com
SIC: 3589 Sewage treatment equipment

Attleboro
Bristol County

(G-5985)
295 TREMONT INC
711 Park St (02703-3211)
PHONE..................................508 222-2884
David Bliss, *Pr*
Thomas K Bliss Junior, *Treas*
EMP: 70 EST: 1920
SQ FT: 25,000
SALES (est): 19.01MM
SALES (corp-wide): 46.45MM **Privately Held**
Web: www.blissdairy.com
SIC: 5143 5451 5812 2026 Ice cream and ices; Dairy products stores; Eating places; Fluid milk
PA: New England Ice Cream Corporation
222 Mansfield Ave
Norton MA 02766
508 824-0500

(G-5986)
3-D WELDING INC
5 Howard Ireland Dr (02703-4600)
PHONE..................................508 222-2500

Kevin Donahue, *Pr*
Greg Donahue, *VP*
EMP: 16 **EST:** 1983
SALES (est): 2.28MM **Privately Held**
Web: www.3dweldinginc.com
SIC: 3441 Fabricated structural metal

(G-5987)
A YOUNG CASTING
35 County St (02703-2126)
P.O. Box 540 (02703-0009)
PHONE..............................508 222-8188
Nancy Young, *Owner*
EMP: 13 **EST:** 1983
SALES (est): 241.58K **Privately Held**
SIC: 3324 Commercial investment castings,
  ferrous

(G-5988)
A&G VINEYARD INC
1 North Ave (02703-1307)
PHONE..............................508 226-4483
EMP: 7 **EST:** 2006
SALES (est): 367.7K **Privately Held**
SIC: 2084 Wines, brandy, and brandy spirits

(G-5989)
AB GROUP INC
40 John Williams St (02703-3707)
PHONE..............................508 222-1404
Jason Arenburg, *Pr*
▲ **EMP:** 7 **EST:** 1974
SALES (est): 238.11K **Privately Held**
SIC: 3961 3911 Earrings, except precious
  metal; Jewelry, precious metal

(G-5990)
ABBOTT-ACTION INC (PA)
Also Called: Action Container
3 Venus Way (02703-8149)
P.O. Box 2306 (02861-0306)
PHONE..............................401 722-2100
John S Abbott, *Pr*
Glen Gardiner, *
Gail G Conca, *
John S Abbott, *CEO*
EMP: 40 **EST:** 1976
SQ FT: 50,000
SALES (est): 21.46MM
SALES (corp-wide): 21.46MM **Privately
Held**
Web: www.abbottaction.com
SIC: 2653 Boxes, corrugated: made from
  purchased materials

(G-5991)
ADT/DIVERSITY INC
50 Perry Ave (02703-2418)
PHONE..............................508 222-9601
Enzo Lucciola, *Pr*
EMP: 8 **EST:** 1987
SQ FT: 5,000
SALES (est): 872.19K **Privately Held**
SIC: 3544 Special dies and tools

(G-5992)
ALVITI CREATIONS INC
Also Called: Alviti Creations
67 Mechanic St Unit 4 (02703-2036)
PHONE..............................508 222-4030
Ralph Alviti, *Pr*
EMP: 8 **EST:** 1959
SALES (est): 686.22K **Privately Held**
Web: www.alviti.com
SIC: 3914 Ecclesiastical ware, plated (all
  metals)

(G-5993)
APCO MOSSBERG CO
104 County St (02703-2159)
PHONE..............................508 222-0340
Betty Lou Mckearney, *Pr*
James Mckearney, *VP*
EMP: 8 **EST:** 1893
SQ FT: 15,000
SALES (est): 2.25MM **Privately Held**
Web: www.apcomossberg.com
SIC: 5072 3423 Hardware; Screw drivers,
  pliers, chisels, etc. (hand tools)

(G-5994)
**APPLIED PRECISION
TECHNOLOGY**
Also Called: Liberty Plastics Company
81 West St (02703-1618)
PHONE..............................508 226-8700
Peter Desimone, *Pr*
Donald Jeppe, *VP Mfg*
EMP: 16 **EST:** 1990
SQ FT: 70,000
SALES (est): 482.02K **Privately Held**
Web: www.apt-liberty.com
SIC: 3599 Machine shop, jobbing and repair

(G-5995)
**ATTLEBORO SAND & GRAVEL
CORP**
125 Tiffany St (02703-6349)
P.O. Box 2189 (02762-0296)
PHONE..............................508 222-2870
Gerard C Lorusso, *Pr*
EMP: 11 **EST:** 1973
SALES (est): 353.48K **Privately Held**
SIC: 1442 Construction sand and gravel

(G-5996)
AUTOMATED FINISHING CO INC
90 County St (02703-2120)
PHONE..............................508 222-6262
Roy Lambert, *Pr*
Justin Lambert, *
EMP: 21 **EST:** 1991
SQ FT: 30,000
SALES (est): 1.57MM **Privately Held**
Web: www.automatedfinishingco.com
SIC: 3479 3471 Etching and engraving;
  Depolishing metal

(G-5997)
BOSTON FABRICATIONS
39 Franklin R Mckay Rd (02703-4625)
P.O. Box 8 (02062-0008)
PHONE..............................781 762-9185
Allen Brauneis, *Pr*
EMP: 10 **EST:** 1984
SQ FT: 5,500
SALES (est): 988.01K **Privately Held**
Web: www.bostonfab.com
SIC: 2541 Table or counter tops, plastic
  laminated

(G-5998)
**BRAININ-ADVANCE INDUSTRIES
LLC (HQ)**
Also Called: Pep Brainin
48 Frank Mossberg Dr (02703-4696)
PHONE..............................508 226-1200
▲ **EMP:** 195 **EST:** 1985
SALES (est): 52.1MM
SALES (corp-wide): 498.74MM **Publicly
Held**
Web: www.nninc.com
SIC: 3469 3643 Stamping metal for the trade
  ; Contacts, electrical
PA: Nn, Inc.
  6210 Ardrey Kell Rd # 600

Charlotte NC 28277
980 264-4300

(G-5999)
**BRUCE DIAMOND
CORPORATION**
Also Called: D&S Engineered Products
1231 County St (02703-6101)
PHONE..............................508 222-3755
Stephen V Puleston, *Pr*
James Jerome Coogan, *
Robert B Puleston, *
EMP: 40 **EST:** 1955
SQ FT: 68,000
SALES (est): 6.8MM **Privately Held**
Web: www.brucediamond.com
SIC: 3599 Machine shop, jobbing and repair

(G-6000)
CASTECHNOLOGIES INC
40 Townsend Rd (02703-4628)
P.O. Box 478 (02703-0008)
PHONE..............................508 222-2915
James W Tenglin, *Pr*
Malcolm C Tenglin, *Treas*
Roger F Tenglin, *Clerk*
David Goncalves, *Pr*
EMP: 19 **EST:** 1988
SQ FT: 5,600
SALES (est): 2.24MM **Privately Held**
Web: www.castechnologies.com
SIC: 3369 Zinc and zinc-base alloy
  castings, except die-castings

(G-6001)
CHARLES THOMAE & SON INC
15 Maynard St (02703-3005)
PHONE..............................508 222-0785
Charles F Thomae, *Pr*
Diane Thomae, *Treas*
EMP: 14 **EST:** 1920
SQ FT: 5,000
SALES (est): 487.02K **Privately Held**
Web: www.chasthomae.com
SIC: 3911 5944 3965 3961 Jewelry,
  precious metal; Jewelry stores; Fasteners,
  buttons, needles, and pins; Costume jewelry

(G-6002)
CHECON LLC
527 Pleasant St Bldg 11 (02703-2463)
PHONE..............................508 838-2060
EMP: 13
SALES (corp-wide): 1.13MM **Privately
Held**
Web: www.checon.com
SIC: 3643 Current-carrying wiring services
PA: Checon, Llc
  30 Larsen Way
  North Attleboro MA 02763
  508 809-5112

(G-6003)
**CHEMICAL SYSTEMS SERVICES
INC**
12 Field Rd (02703-2466)
PHONE..............................508 431-9995
Mounir Mazzawi, *Pr*
EMP: 18 **EST:** 2002
SALES (est): 2.25MM **Privately Held**
Web: www.chemicalsystems.net
SIC: 8711 3559 Engineering services;
  Chemical machinery and equipment

(G-6004)
CITIWORKS CORP
Also Called: Citiworks RI
20 Rutledge Dr (02703-7835)
P.O. Box 3025 (02703-0906)

PHONE..............................508 761-7400
John A Chatfield, *Pr*
EMP: 18 **EST:** 1885
SQ FT: 14,000
SALES (est): 4.21MM **Privately Held**
Web: www.citiworks.com
SIC: 3496 8742 5063 1731 Mesh, made
  from purchased wire; Materials mgmt.
  (purchasing, handling, inventory) consultant
  ; Fire alarm systems; Access control
  systems specialization

(G-6005)
CMT MATERIALS INC
Also Called: Engineered Syntactic Systems
107 Frank Mossberg Dr (02703-4615)
PHONE..............................508 226-3901
Anthony Colageo, *Pr*
Noel Tessier, *Sec*
Philip Rhodes, *Dir*
▲ **EMP:** 19 **EST:** 1998
SQ FT: 20,000
SALES (est): 5.35MM **Privately Held**
Web: cmt.globecomposite.com
SIC: 3089 Injection molding of plastics

(G-6006)
COLONIAL LITHOGRAPH INC
129 Bank St Ste 5 (02703-1763)
P.O. Box 449 (02703-0008)
PHONE..............................508 222-1832
Charles Guillette, *Pr*
David H Redding, *VP Prd*
Catherine La Salandra, *VP Fin*
EMP: 10 **EST:** 1932
SQ FT: 7,200
SALES (est): 768.35K **Privately Held**
Web: www.colonial-litho.com
SIC: 2752 Lithographing on metal

(G-6007)
COMTRAN CABLE LLC
330 Turner St (02703-7714)
PHONE..............................800 842-7809
Dimitri Maistrellis, *Pr*
Robert W Webb, *
David A Allegrezza, *
▲ **EMP:** 130 **EST:** 1985
SQ FT: 150,000
SALES (est): 46.66MM
SALES (corp-wide): 302.09B **Publicly
Held**
Web: www.comtrancorp.com
SIC: 3356 Lead and lead alloy: rolling,
  drawing, or extruding
HQ: Marmon Holdings, Inc.
  181 W Madison St Ste 3900
  Chicago IL 60602
  312 372-9500

(G-6008)
CRAFT INC
Also Called: Crafts Technology
1929 County St (02703-8107)
P.O. Box 3049 (02703-0912)
PHONE..............................508 761-7917
Eric J Roy, *Pr*
Raymond G Roy, *Stockholder*
◆ **EMP:** 36 **EST:** 1950
SQ FT: 67,000
SALES (est): 4.44MM **Privately Held**
Web: www.craft-inc.com
SIC: 3429 3469 Hardware, nec; Metal
  stampings, nec

(G-6009)
DILON COMPANY INC
65 Newcomb St (02703-1403)
P.O. Box 2838 (02763-0898)
PHONE..............................508 223-3400

George Dichristofaro, *Pr*
EMP: 8 **EST:** 1987
SQ FT: 2,500
SALES (est): 921.3K **Privately Held**
SIC: 3911 Jewelry, precious metal

(G-6010)
E A DION INC
33 Franklin R Mckay Rd (02703-4625)
P.O. Box 2098 (02703-0035)
PHONE.................................800 445-1007
Edward A Dion Junior, *Pr*
Dennis W Dion, *
Melissa Carvalho, *
▲ **EMP:** 105 **EST:** 1968
SQ FT: 30,000
SALES (est): 14.76MM **Privately Held**
Web: www.eadion.com
SIC: 3911 3993 Jewelry, precious metal;
Signs and advertising specialties

(G-6011)
EF LEACH & COMPANY
Also Called: General Findings
8 N Main St Ste 500 (02703-2282)
P.O. Box 358 (02703-0006)
PHONE.................................508 643-3309
Edwin F Leach Ii, *Pr*
Joe Sisto, *
Richard St Pierre, *
▲ **EMP:** 132 **EST:** 1899
SQ FT: 100,000
SALES (est): 23.17MM
SALES (corp-wide): 302.09B **Publicly
Held**
SIC: 3356 3911 3915 3951 Gold and gold
alloy bars, sheets, strip, etc.; Earrings,
precious metal; Jewelers' findings and
materials; Ball point pens and parts
HQ: Leachgarner, Inc.
49 Pearl St
Attleboro MA 02703

(G-6012)
EMS ENGNRED MTLS
SOLUTIONS LLC (DH)
Also Called: Engineered Materials Solutions
39 Perry Ave (02703-2417)
PHONE.................................508 342-2100
Paul Duffy, *COO*
◆ **EMP:** 200 **EST:** 2007
SALES (est): 102MM
SALES (corp-wide): 335.52MM **Privately
Held**
Web: www.emsclad.com
SIC: 3351 Copper and copper alloy sheet,
strip, plate, and products
HQ: Wickeder Westfalenstahl Gmbh
Hauptstr. 6
Wickede (Ruhr) NW 58739
23779170

(G-6013)
ENGINRED SYNTACTIC
SYSTEMS LLC
107 Frank Mossberg Dr (02703-4615)
PHONE.................................508 226-3907
Thomas J Murray, *Managing Member*
▲ **EMP:** 8 **EST:** 2009
SALES (est): 956.21K **Privately Held**
Web: www.esyntactic.com
SIC: 2821 Plastics materials and resins

(G-6014)
FETERIA TOOL & FINDINGS
1285 County St (02703-6103)
PHONE.................................508 222-7788
John Feteria, *Owner*
EMP: 9 **EST:** 1995
SQ FT: 50,000

SALES (est): 1.06MM **Privately Held**
Web: www.feteiratool.com
SIC: 3423 7389 Jewelers' hand tools;
Packaging and labeling services

(G-6015)
FINDINGS INCORPORATED
1231 County St (02703-6101)
P.O. Box 605 (02703-0011)
PHONE.................................508 222-7449
EMP: 93
SALES (corp-wide): 302.09B **Publicly
Held**
SIC: 5944 5094 3911 Jewelry stores;
Jewelry and precious stones; Jewelry,
precious metal
HQ: Findings Incorporated
1701 S Flagler Dr Apt 502
West Palm Beach FL 33401
800 343-0806

(G-6016)
FINE EDGE TOOL COMPANY INC
13 Maynard St (02703-3005)
PHONE.................................508 222-7511
Messias C Vasconcelos, *Pr*
EMP: 8 **EST:** 1989
SQ FT: 6,000
SALES (est): 684.88K **Privately Held**
Web: www.fineedgetool.com
SIC: 3423 3469 Jewelers' hand tools; Metal
stampings, nec

(G-6017)
FIREBALL HEAT TREATING CO
INC
34 John Williams St (02703-3707)
PHONE.................................508 222-2617
Thomas Thomson, *Pr*
EMP: 8 **EST:** 1970
SQ FT: 5,000
SALES (est): 891.55K **Privately Held**
Web: www.fireballheattreating.com
SIC: 3398 Metal heat treating

(G-6018)
FORTIFIBER LLC
55 Starkey Ave (02703-1813)
P.O. Box 959 (02703-0959)
PHONE.................................508 222-3500
Steve Fisk, *Brnch Mgr*
EMP: 27
SQ FT: 20,000
SALES (corp-wide): 6.59B **Publicly Held**
Web: www.fortifiber.com
SIC: 2671 2672 2621 Paper, coated or
laminated for packaging; Paper; coated and
laminated, nec; Building and roofing paper,
felts and insulation siding
HQ: Fortifiber, Llc
300 Industrial Dr
Fernley NV 89408
800 773-4777

(G-6019)
G AUSTIN YOUNG INC
Also Called: Attleboro's Jewelry Makers
35 County St (02703-2126)
P.O. Box 540 (02703-0009)
PHONE.................................508 222-4700
Nancy Young, *Pr*
EMP: 9 **EST:** 1993
SALES (est): 964.66K **Privately Held**
SIC: 5944 3911 Jewelry, precious stones
and precious metals; Jewelry, precious
metal

(G-6020)
GENERAL METAL FINISHING
LLC
Also Called: Pep General Metal Finishing
42 Frank Mossberg Dr (02703-4697)
PHONE.................................508 222-9683
EMP: 98 **EST:** 1974
SQ FT: 30,000
SALES (est): 14.76MM
SALES (corp-wide): 498.74MM **Publicly
Held**
Web: www.nninc.com
SIC: 3471 Electroplating of metals or
formed products
PA: Nn, Inc.
6210 Ardrey Kell Rd # 600
Charlotte NC 28277
980 264-4300

(G-6021)
GLINES & RHODES INC
189 East St (02703-4299)
P.O. Box 2285 (02703-0039)
PHONE.................................508 226-2000
EMP: 28 **EST:** 1915
SALES (est): 12.12MM **Privately Held**
Web: www.glinesandrhodes.com
SIC: 3339 Precious metals

(G-6022)
GUYOT BROTHERS COMPANY
INC
20 John Williams St (02703-3707)
P.O. Box 2378 (02703-0040)
PHONE.................................508 222-2000
Stephen Guyot, *Pr*
Andrea Twombly, *VP*
Marsha Leary, *Sec*
Marshall A Guyot, *Treas*
EMP: 21 **EST:** 1904
SQ FT: 26,000
SALES (est): 378.86K **Privately Held**
SIC: 3915 Jewelers' materials and lapidary
work

(G-6023)
HI-TECH INC
50 Perry Ave (02703-2418)
PHONE.................................401 454-4086
John B Lavin, *Pr*
Judy Lavin, *VP*
EMP: 12 **EST:** 1981
SQ FT: 10,000
SALES (est): 2.42MM **Privately Held**
Web: www.hi-techstampings.com
SIC: 3469 3714 Stamping metal for the trade
; Motor vehicle parts and accessories

(G-6024)
HY TEMP INC
34 John Williams St (02703-3707)
PHONE.................................508 222-6626
Bruce Sargeant, *Pr*
Bruce Sargeant, *Pr*
Jane Sargeant, *VP*
EMP: 12 **EST:** 1977
SQ FT: 2,500
SALES (est): 331.78K **Privately Held**
Web: www.hytemp.net
SIC: 3398 Metal heat treating

(G-6025)
INTERPLEX ETCH LOGIC LLC
54 Venus Way (02703-8126)
PHONE.................................508 399-6810
EMP: 35 **EST:** 1999
SALES (est): 4.93MM **Privately Held**
Web: www.interplex.com

SIC: 3469 Stamping metal for the trade

(G-6026)
INVERNESS CORPORATION (DH)
49 Pearl St (02703-3940)
PHONE.................................774 203-1130
William Mead, *Pr*
◆ **EMP:** 8 **EST:** 1974
SQ FT: 30,000
SALES (est): 4.25MM
SALES (corp-wide): 302.09B **Publicly
Held**
Web: www.invernesscorp.com
SIC: 3999 Barber and beauty shop
equipment
HQ: Richline Group, Inc.
1385 Broadway Fl 14
New York NY 10018

(G-6027)
JAB INDUSTRIES INC
185 Washington St (02703-5550)
PHONE.................................401 447-9668
Carla M Bouthillette, *Prin*
EMP: 10 **EST:** 2012
SALES (est): 438.15K **Privately Held**
SIC: 3999 Manufacturing industries, nec

(G-6028)
JNJ GLOBAL ENTERPRISES LLC
47 Semple Village Rd (02703-1082)
PHONE.................................508 455-4945
EMP: 9 **EST:** 2018
SALES (est): 358.46K **Privately Held**
SIC: 2834 Pharmaceutical preparations

(G-6029)
KNOBBY KRAFTERS INC
129 Bank St Ste 5 (02703-1763)
P.O. Box 1899 (02703-0032)
PHONE.................................508 222-7272
Nicholas W Nerney, *Pr*
Dexter P Nerney, *
▲ **EMP:** 12 **EST:** 1924
SALES (est): 461.55K **Privately Held**
Web: www.knobbykrafters.com
SIC: 3089 Injection molding of plastics

(G-6030)
LANDES ENTERPRISES LLC
Also Called: Landes Family Automobile Sales
859 Washington St (02703-7550)
PHONE.................................508 761-7800
Brent Landes, *Managing Member*
EMP: 8 **EST:** 2011
SALES (est): 2.19MM **Privately Held**
Web: www.familyautoma.com
SIC: 5521 7694 Automobiles, used cars only
; Motor repair services

(G-6031)
LARSON TOOL & STAMPING
COMPANY
90 Olive St (02703-3802)
PHONE.................................508 222-0897
Charles Cederberg, *Pr*
Daniel G Larson, *
William E Larson, *
▲ **EMP:** 70 **EST:** 1920
SQ FT: 90,000
SALES (est): 213.28K **Privately Held**
Web: www.larsontool.com
SIC: 3469 3443 Stamping metal for the trade
; Cylinders, pressure: metal plate

(G-6032)
M S COMPANY
61 School St (02703-3931)
P.O. Box 298 (02703-0005)

GEOGRAPHIC

PHONE..................508 222-1700
Kurt R Schweinshaut, *Pr*
Mark Schweinshaut, *
Carl M Schweinshaut, *
▲ **EMP:** 75 **EST:** 1913
SQ FT: 45,000
SALES (est): 8.56MM **Privately Held**
Web: www.mscompany.net
SIC: 3911 3915   Jewelry, precious metal;
   Jewelers' findings and materials

(G-6033)
MANTROSE-HAEUSER CO INC
113 Olive St (02703-3801)
PHONE...................203 454-1800
Donald Young, *Prin*
EMP: 49
SALES (corp-wide): 7.26B **Publicly Held**
Web: www.mantrose.com
SIC: 2851   Paints and allied products
HQ: Mantrose-Haeuser Co., Inc.
   100 Nyala Farms Rd
   Westport CT 06880

(G-6034)
MARATHON CO
Also Called: Marathon
90 Oneil Blvd (02703-4218)
P.O. Box 419 (02703-0007)
PHONE...................508 222-5544
Roger Forman, *Pr*
Guy Forman, *
Audrey Robbins, *
▲ **EMP:** 125 **EST:** 1897
SQ FT: 50,000
SALES (est): 8.85MM **Privately Held**
Web: www.marathon-co.com
SIC: 3911   Jewelry, precious metal

(G-6035)
MATRIX METAL PRODUCTS INC
53 County St (02703-2127)
P.O. Box 2173 (02703-0037)
PHONE...................508 226-2374
Robert H Hanson Junior, *Pr*
Robert H Hanson, *Sec*
EMP: 17 **EST:** 1984
SQ FT: 4,000
SALES (est): 2.43MM **Privately Held**
Web: www.matrixmetals.com
SIC: 3469   Stamping metal for the trade

(G-6036)
MCVAN INC
35 Frank Mossberg Dr (02703-4623)
PHONE...................508 431-2400
Frederick Adler, *Pr*
Craig Adler, *
▲ **EMP:** 18 **EST:** 1946
SQ FT: 12,000
SALES (est): 4.19MM **Privately Held**
Web: www.mcvaninc.com
SIC: 3911 5049   Rosaries or other small
   religious articles, precious metal; Religious
   supplies

(G-6037)
MINI-SYSTEMS INC
Also Called: Thin Film Division
45 Frank Mossberg Dr (02703-4623)
PHONE...................508 695-0203
Robert Lamar, *VP*
EMP: 41
Web: www.mini-systemsinc.com
SIC: 3676   Electronic resistors
PA: Mini-Systems, Inc.
   20 David Rd
   North Attleboro MA 02760
   508 695-1420

(G-6038)
MORSE SAND & GRAVEL CORP
125 Tiffany St (02703-6349)
PHONE...................508 809-4644
TOLL FREE: 800
Leo Barry, *Pr*
EMP: 19 **EST:** 1926
SQ FT: 1,000
SALES (est): 456.13K **Privately Held**
SIC: 3273 5211   Ready-mixed concrete;
   Sand and gravel

(G-6039)
MR IDEA INC
Also Called: Storm Duds Raingear
100 Frank Mossberg Dr (02703-4632)
PHONE...................508 222-0155
Gary Libman, *Pr*
Timothy N Baurley, *
▲ **EMP:** 30 **EST:** 1989
SQ FT: 20,000
SALES (est): 4.42MM **Privately Held**
Web: www.stormduds.com
SIC: 3911 2385 5023   Trimmings for canes,
   umbrellas, etc.: precious metal; Raincoats,
   except vulcanized rubber: purchased
   materials; Linens and towels

(G-6040)
NATIONAL VAN SALES INC
80 Pine St (02703-3907)
PHONE...................508 222-2272
Samuel Perlman, *Pr*
EMP: 14 **EST:** 1992
SALES (est): 404.97K **Privately Held**
Web: www.nationalvans.com
SIC: 7532 5013 3716   Van conversion;
   Motor vehicle supplies and new parts;
   Motor homes

(G-6041)
NEW AGE TECHNOLOGIES INC
Also Called: New Age Ems
527 Pleasant St (02703-2463)
PHONE...................508 226-6090
EMP: 33 **EST:** 1988
SALES (est): 2.14MM **Privately Held**
SIC: 3672   Printed circuit boards

(G-6042)
NEW ENGLAND MKTG & PRTG INC
41 Deerfield Rd Unit 11 (02703-7871)
PHONE...................917 582-1029
EMP: 27
SALES (corp-wide): 229.64K **Privately Held**
SIC: 2752   Commercial printing, lithographic
PA: New England Marketing And Printing,
   Inc.
   792 West St
   Mansfield MA

(G-6043)
NORKING COMPANY INC
53 County St (02703-2127)
P.O. Box 446 (02703-0008)
PHONE...................508 222-3100
Robert H Hanson, *Pr*
Chris Hanson, *Sls Mgr*
EMP: 22 **EST:** 1985
SQ FT: 8,000
SALES (est): 2.34MM **Privately Held**
Web: www.norkingco.com
SIC: 3469 3398   Stamping metal for the trade
   ; Metal heat treating

(G-6044)
NORTH ATTLEBORO JEWELRY CO INC
112 Bank St (02703-1738)
PHONE...................508 222-4660
William Romero Junior, *Pr*
▲ **EMP:** 9 **EST:** 1969
SQ FT: 10,000
SALES (est): 897.46K **Privately Held**
Web: www.najc.net
SIC: 3911 3961   Jewelry, precious metal;
   Costume jewelry

(G-6045)
OMV
679 Washington St (02703-8406)
PHONE...................508 243-6236
Don Coelho, *Prin*
EMP: 7 **EST:** 2011
SALES (est): 101.86K **Privately Held**
Web: www.omv.at
SIC: 3714   Motor vehicle parts and
   accessories

(G-6046)
PEP INDUSTRIES LLC
110 Frank Mossberg Dr (02703-4632)
PHONE...................508 226-5600
Alan Huffenus, *CEO*
John Manci Prin=, *Prin*
EMP: 17 **EST:** 2010
SALES (est): 555.3K **Privately Held**
SIC: 3089 3351 3469 3471   Plastics
   containers, except foam; Copper rolling and
   drawing; Stamping metal for the trade;
   Plating and polishing

(G-6047)
PERFECT EMPANADA LLC (PA)
8 Blackstone Rd (02703-2612)
PHONE...................508 241-5150
Pablo Mastandrea, *Mgr*
EMP: 7 **EST:** 2021
SALES (est): 119.35K
SALES (corp-wide): 119.35K **Privately Held**
SIC: 2038 2099   Ethnic foods, nec, frozen;
   Ready-to-eat meals, salads, and
   sandwiches

(G-6048)
PLASMA BIOLIFE SERVICES L P
287 Washington St Ste 5 (02703-5524)
PHONE...................508 761-2902
Michaela Perry, *Bmch Mgr*
EMP: 50 **EST:** 1994
SALES (est): 17.68MM **Privately Held**
SIC: 2834   Pharmaceutical preparations
HQ: Biolife Plasma Services L.P.
   1200 Lakeside Dr
   Bannockburn IL 60015
   224 940-2000

(G-6049)
PLASTIC CRAFT NOVELTY CO INC
Also Called: P Craft Jewelry
12 Dunham St Apt A (02703-2946)
PHONE...................508 222-1486
Peter Manickas Iii, *CEO*
EMP: 17 **EST:** 1931
SQ FT: 35,000
SALES (est): 251.87K **Privately Held**
SIC: 3961 5944   Costume jewelry; Jewelry
   stores

(G-6050)
POWER EQUIPMENT CO INC (PA)

Also Called: Superior Power Systems
7 Franklin R Mckay Rd (02703-4692)
PHONE...................508 226-3410
Paul Toher, *Pr*
EMP: 27 **EST:** 1961
SQ FT: 15,000
SALES (est): 3.34MM
SALES (corp-wide): 3.34MM **Privately Held**
Web: www.4genset.com
SIC: 3621   Power generators

(G-6051)
PRECISION ENGINEERED PDTS LLC (DH)
Also Called: P E P
110 Frank Mossberg Dr (02703-4632)
EMP: 9 **EST:** 2002
SQ FT: 12,000
SALES (est): 256.23MM
SALES (corp-wide): 433.51MM **Privately Held**
Web: www.nninc.com
SIC: 3643 3469 3841 3471   Contacts,
   electrical; Stamping metal for the trade;
   Surgical and medical instruments; Plating
   and polishing
HQ: Precision Engineered Products
   Holdings, Inc.
   42 Frank Mossberg Dr
   Attleboro MA 02703
   508 226-5600

(G-6052)
R L BARRY INC
60 Walton St (02703-1408)
PHONE...................508 226-3350
Richard L Barry, *Pr*
James Soares, *VP Opers*
EMP: 10 **EST:** 1980
SALES (est): 691.96K **Privately Held**
SIC: 3599 3471   Machine shop, jobbing and
   repair; Plating and polishing

(G-6053)
REEVES COMPANY INC
51 Newcomb St (02703-1420)
P.O. Box 509 (02703-0009)
PHONE...................508 222-2877
Rachel Benavides, *Pr*
Thomas Reeves, *Pr*
M Cronin, *Clerk*
EMP: 14 **EST:** 1947
SQ FT: 17,000
SALES (est): 678.05K **Privately Held**
Web: www.reevesnamepins.com
SIC: 3993 3965 3452 3089   Name plates:
   except engraved, etched, etc.: metal;
   Fasteners, buttons, needles, and pins;
   Bolts, nuts, rivets, and washers;
   Identification cards, plastics

(G-6054)
RHODE ISLAND MKTG & PRTG INC
Also Called: AlphaGraphics
41 Deerfield Rd Unit 11 (02703-7871)
PHONE...................917 582-1029
Brian Decamp, *Pr*
EMP: 7 **EST:** 2015
SALES (est): 446.66K **Privately Held**
Web: www.alphagraphics.com
SIC: 2752   Commercial printing, lithographic

(G-6055)
RICHLINE GROUP INC
49 Pearl St (02703-3940)
PHONE...................774 203-1199
EMP: 17
SALES (corp-wide): 302.09B **Publicly Held**

Web: www.richlinegroup.com
SIC: 3911 Jewelry, precious metal
HQ: Richline Group, Inc.
1385 Broadway Fl 14
New York NY 10018

(G-6056)
RIKA DENSHI AMERICA INC
112 Frank Mossberg Dr (02703-4632)
PHONE................................508 226-2080
Yasuko Toda, *Pr*
EMP: 20 EST: 1991
SQ FT: 18,000
SALES (est): 3.18MM **Privately Held**
Web: www.testprobe.com
SIC: 3825 Test equipment for electronic and
electric measurement

(G-6057)
RLB INDUSTRIES INC
115 Berwick Rd (02703-2011)
PHONE................................508 226-3350
Richard L Barry, *Pr*
EMP: 75 EST: 1977
SQ FT: 30,000
SALES (est): 14.75MM **Privately Held**
Web: www.barryind.com
SIC: 3625 3672 Resistors and resistor units;
Printed circuit boards

(G-6058)
ROBBINS COMPANY
Also Called: Engage2excel
400 Oneil Blvd (02703-5147)
P.O. Box 1843 (28687-1843)
PHONE................................508 222-2900
G Brett Tharpe, *Pr*
Joel Kepley, *Sr VP*
▲ EMP: 185 EST: 1892
SQ FT: 100,000
SALES (est): 22.13MM **Privately Held**
Web: www.engage2excel.com
SIC: 3911 Pins (jewelry), precious metal
PA: Engage2excel, Inc.
115 Corporate Center Dr E
Mooresville NC 28117

(G-6059)
RONALD PRATT COMPANY INC
50 Perry Ave (02703-2418)
PHONE................................508 222-9601
Michael Reil, *Pr*
EMP: 25 EST: 2013
SALES (est): 2.49MM **Privately Held**
SIC: 3915 Jewelers' materials and lapidary
work

(G-6060)
**RUSTOLEUM ATTLEBORO
PLANT**
113 Olive St (02703-3801)
PHONE................................508 222-3710
Mike Jurist, *Prin*
◆ EMP: 9 EST: 2010
SALES (est): 799.66K **Privately Held**
SIC: 2851 Paints and allied products

(G-6061)
SCHRADER ELECTRONICS INC
Also Called: Trico
529 Pleasant St (02703-2421)
PHONE................................615 384-0089
▲ EMP: 300
SIC: 3462 Automotive and internal
combustion engine forgings

(G-6062)
**SENSATA TECHNOLOGIES INC
(HQ)**

529 Pleasant St (02703-2421)
PHONE................................508 236-3800
Jeffrey J Cote, *CEO*
Paul Vasington, *
Steven Beringhause, *
Allisha Elliott, *
◆ EMP: 800 EST: 2006
SQ FT: 22,000
SALES (est): 1.17B
SALES (corp-wide): 4.03B **Privately Held**
Web: www.sensata.com
SIC: 3679 Electronic circuits
PA: Sensata Technologies Holding Plc
Interface House
Swindon WILTS SN4 8
179 325-0031

(G-6063)
**SENSATA TECHNOLOGIES IND
INC (DH)**
529 Pleasant St (02703-2421)
PHONE................................508 236-3800
EMP: 45 EST: 2008
SALES (est): 213.99MM
SALES (corp-wide): 4.03B **Privately Held**
Web: www.sensata.com
SIC: 3676 3625 Thermistors, except
temperature sensors; Flow actuated
electrical switches
HQ: Sensata Technologies, Inc.
529 Pleasant St
Attleboro MA 02703

(G-6064)
**SENSATA TECHNOLOGIES
MASS INC (DH)**
529 Pleasant St (02703-2421)
P.O. Box 2964 (02703-0964)
PHONE................................508 236-3800
Thomas Wroe, *Ch Bd*
▲ EMP: 49 EST: 2007
SALES (est): 28.73MM
SALES (corp-wide): 4.03B **Privately Held**
Web: www.sensata.com
SIC: 3679 Electronic circuits
HQ: Sensata Technologies, Inc.
529 Pleasant St
Attleboro MA 02703

(G-6065)
**STERGIS ALUMINUM
PRODUCTS CORP**
Also Called: Stergis/Alliance
79 Walton St (02703-1418)
PHONE................................508 455-0661
Augustus J Stergis, *Pr*
Kathleen Courtney, *
John N Altomare, *
Michael Murphy, *
EMP: 48 EST: 1962
SQ FT: 48,000
SALES (est): 9.42MM **Privately Held**
Web: www.stergis.com
SIC: 3442 3089 Metal doors, sash, and trim;
Windows, plastics

(G-6066)
STERNGOLD DENTAL LLC
Also Called: A P M Sterngold
23 Frank Mossberg Dr (02703-4653)
PHONE................................508 226-5660
Gordon Craig, *CEO*
Christopher Franklin, *
David Skalrski, *Managing Member*
Ryan Mansfield, *
Dulcina Jorge, *
▲ EMP: 25 EST: 2002
SQ FT: 30,000
SALES (est): 4.41MM **Privately Held**
Web: www.sterngold.com

SIC: 3843 Dental equipment and supplies

(G-6067)
SUPERIOR DIE & STAMPING INC
Also Called: Superior Die
96 County St (02703-2120)
PHONE................................774 203-3674
Fred Capriccio, *Owner*
Stephen Quaglia, *Pr*
EMP: 9 EST: 1978
SQ FT: 3,000
SALES (est): 765.33K **Privately Held**
SIC: 3544 Special dies and tools

(G-6068)
SWEET METAL FINISHING INC
Also Called: SMP DBA A BAND FOR
BROTHERS
28 John Williams St (02703-3707)
P.O. Box 400 (02703-0007)
PHONE................................508 226-4359
Scott Sweet, *Pr*
EMP: 13 EST: 1980
SQ FT: 7,500
SALES (est): 425.26K **Privately Held**
Web: sweet-metal-finishing-inc.hub.biz
SIC: 3961 3911 3471 Costume jewelry, ex.
precious metal and semiprecious stones;
Jewelry, precious metal; Plating and
polishing

(G-6069)
**TECHNCAL HRDFCING
MCHINING INC**
Also Called: T H M
35 Extension St (02703-4642)
PHONE................................508 223-2900
Paul Egasti, *Pr*
John Mcentee, *Dir*
EMP: 15 EST: 1985
SQ FT: 18,000
SALES (est): 2.58MM **Privately Held**
Web: www.thmonline.com
SIC: 3599 3469 Machine shop, jobbing and
repair; Machine parts, stamped or pressed
metal

(G-6070)
**TEXAS INSTRUMENTS
INCORPORATED**
Also Called: Texas Instruments
529 Pleasant St (02703-2421)
P.O. Box 2964 (02703-0964)
PHONE................................508 236-3800
Tom Connors, *Mgr*
EMP: 44
SALES (corp-wide): 17.52B **Publicly Held**
Web: www.ti.com
SIC: 3679 3678 3674 3643 Electronic
circuits; Electronic connectors;
Semiconductors and related devices;
Current-carrying wiring services
PA: Texas Instruments Incorporated
12500 Ti Blvd
Dallas TX 75243
214 479-3773

(G-6071)
**UNITED COMMUNICATIONS
CORP**
Sun Chronicle, The
34 S Main St (02703-2920)
P.O. Box 600 (02703-0600)
PHONE................................508 222-7000
Oreste D'arconte, *Brnch Mgr*
EMP: 119
SALES (corp-wide): 20.73MM **Privately
Held**
Web: www.kenoshanews.com

SIC: 2711 Newspapers, publishing and
printing
PA: United Communications Corporation
5800 7th Ave
Kenosha WI 53140
262 657-1000

(G-6072)
V-TRON ELECTRONICS CORP
10 Venus Way (02703-8126)
PHONE................................508 761-9100
Doug Gobin, *Pr*
Rebekah Puleo, *
▼ EMP: 100 EST: 1970
SQ FT: 43,000
SALES (est): 23.94MM **Privately Held**
Web: www.v-tron.com
SIC: 3357 3679 Nonferrous wiredrawing
and insulating; Harness assemblies, for
electronic use: wire or cable

(G-6073)
W D C HOLDINGS INC
Also Called: Whiting & Davis Safety
200 John J Dietsch Blvd (02703)
P.O. Box 1270 (02763-0270)
PHONE................................508 699-4412
Curtis R Smith, *Pr*
John H Boyles, *
EMP: 21 EST: 1876
SQ FT: 50,000
SALES (est): 920.91K **Privately Held**
SIC: 3842 3496 3171 2326 Gloves, safety;
Miscellaneous fabricated wire products;
Women's handbags and purses; Men's and
boy's work clothing

(G-6074)
W E RICHARDS CO INC
Also Called: A B Group
40 John Williams St (02703-3707)
P.O. Box 546 (02703-0010)
PHONE................................508 226-1036
Robert Arenburg, *Pr*
Robert Arenburg, *Owner*
Jason Arenburg, *Pr*
EMP: 8 EST: 1900
SQ FT: 6,400
SALES (est): 472.05K **Privately Held**
Web: www.kellywaters.com
SIC: 3911 Jewelry, precious metal

(G-6075)
**WABASH TECHNOLOGIES INC
(DH)**
529 Pleasant St (02703-2421)
PHONE................................260 355-4100
Stephen Dow, *Pr*
Casey Kroll, *
Tom Martin, *
Lawrence Denbo, *
James Butler, *
▲ EMP: 90 EST: 1999
SQ FT: 100,000
SALES (est): 102.64MM
SALES (corp-wide): 4.03B **Privately Held**
Web: www.sensata.com
SIC: 3625 3676 Flow actuated electrical
switches; Thermistors, except temperature
sensors
HQ: Sensata Technologies Indiana, Inc.
529 Pleasant St
Attleboro MA 02703

(G-6076)
WILLIAM J HIRTEN CO LLC
Also Called: William J. Hirten Co.
96 Frank Mossberg Dr (02703-4632)
PHONE................................401 334-5370
James Dean, *Managing Member*

▲ **EMP:** 17 **EST:** 2007
SQ FT: 50,000
SALES (est): 2.92MM **Privately Held**
Web: www.wjhirten.com
SIC: 5049 3911 Religious supplies;
  Rosaries or other small religious articles,
  precious metal

(G-6077)
WILLOW TREE POULTRY FARM INC
997 S Main St (02703-6292)
PHONE.................................508 222-2479
Chester Cekala, *CEO*
Walter Cekala, *
Eileen Cekala, *
EMP: 80 **EST:** 1954
SALES (est): 12.41MM **Privately Held**
Web: www.willowtreefarm.com
SIC: 5499 5142 2015 Eggs and poultry;
  Poultry, frozen: packaged; Poultry
  slaughtering and processing

Attleboro Falls
Bristol County

(G-6078)
ADVANCED ELECTRONIC DESIGN INC
Also Called: Patrol
344 John L Dietsch Blvd (02763-1072)
PHONE.................................508 699-0249
David Swithers, *Pr*
EMP: 25 **EST:** 1997
SQ FT: 1,600
SALES (est): 5.06MM **Privately Held**
Web: www.patrolpc.com
SIC: 3571 8748 Computers, digital, analog
  or hybrid; Systems analysis and
  engineering consulting services

(G-6079)
BELLS POWDER COATING INC
500,John L Dietsch Blvd (02763-1080)
PHONE.................................508 643-2222
Nancy Bellham, *Pr*
Paul Bellham, *VP*
EMP: 18 **EST:** 1998
SQ FT: 56,000
SALES (est): 4.57MM **Privately Held**
Web: www.bellspowdercoating.com
SIC: 1799 7424 Coating, caulking, and
  weather, water, and fireproofing; Aluminum
  coating of metal products

(G-6080)
BUDGETCARD INC
171 Commonwealth Ave (02763-1178)
PHONE.................................508 695-8762
Christopher Roche, *Pr*
Paul J Roche, *Sec*
Christopher J Roche, *Treas*
▲ **EMP:** 14 **EST:** 1997
SQ FT: 8,000
SALES (est): 4.84MM **Privately Held**
Web: www.budgetcard.com
SIC: 3089 Identification cards, plastics

(G-6081)
CAPE HOUSE REALTY INC
Also Called: Sousa & Demayo
266 John L Dietsch Blvd (02763-1077)
PHONE.................................508 695-6800
EMP: 48 **EST:** 1961
SQ FT: 26,800
SALES (est): 9MM **Privately Held**
Web: www.sousademayo.com

SIC: 3441 Fabricated structural metal

(G-6082)
CONCERT MEDICAL LLC
452 John L Dietsch Blvd (02763-1079)
PHONE.................................781 261-7400
Howard W Donnelly, *Managing Member*
Normand P Collard, *Prin*
Patrick J Kinney Junior, *Prin*
▲ **EMP:** 30 **EST:** 2005
SALES (est): 7.81MM **Privately Held**
Web: www.concertmedical.com
SIC: 3841 Surgical and medical instruments

(G-6083)
DELTRAN INC
65 John L Dietsch Blvd Ste A (02763-1087)
PHONE.................................508 699-7506
Francis P Defino, *Pr*
EMP: 15 **EST:** 2007
SALES (est): 1.25MM **Privately Held**
Web: www.deltran.com
SIC: 3469 Stamping metal for the trade

(G-6084)
DISTRON CORPORATION
87 John L Dietsch Sq (02763-1027)
PHONE.................................508 695-8786
Robert Donovan, *Pr*
EMP: 110 **EST:** 1970
SQ FT: 30,000
SALES (est): 27.2MM **Privately Held**
Web: www.distron.com
SIC: 8711 3674 3672 Industrial engineers;
  Microprocessors; Printed circuit boards

(G-6085)
GARLAN CHAIN CO INC
417 John L Dietsch Blvd (02763-1000)
PHONE.................................508 399-7288
Richard Gariepy, *Pr*
David Gariepy, *VP*
▲ **EMP:** 7 **EST:** 1967
SQ FT: 7,500
SALES (est): 677.88K **Privately Held**
Web: www.garlanchain.com
SIC: 3961 3496 Necklaces, except precious
  metal; Woven wire products, nec

(G-6086)
GREENWOOD EMRGNCY VEHICLES LLC (HQ)
530 John L Dietsch Blvd (02763-1080)
PHONE.................................508 695-7138
Mark Macdonald, *Pr*
EMP: 75 **EST:** 2016
SALES (est): 12.49MM
SALES (corp-wide): 23.92MM **Privately Held**
Web: www.greenwoodev.com
SIC: 3537 5087 5012 3711 Industrial trucks
  and tractors; Firefighting equipment; Fire
  trucks; Motor vehicles and car bodies
PA: Emergency Vehicles Holdings, Llc
  30 Monument Sq Ste 302
  Concord MA 01742
  617 956-1336

(G-6087)
HUNTER INDUSTRIES INC
266 John L Dietsch Blvd (02763-1077)
PHONE.................................508 695-6800
EMP: 10 **EST:** 2016
SALES (est): 633.7K **Privately Held**
SIC: 3441 Fabricated structural metal

(G-6088)
J T INMAN CO INC
31 Larsen Way (02763-1068)

PHONE.................................508 226-0080
John L Reynolds, *Pr*
Kathryn Thorpe, *
John L Reynolds Prestreas, *Prin*
EMP: 25 **EST:** 1971
SQ FT: 10,000
SALES (est): 1.42MM **Privately Held**
Web: www.jtinman.com
SIC: 3911 3339 3914 Jewelry, precious
  metal; Primary nonferrous metals, nec;
  Silverware

(G-6089)
MARTRAN CORP
65 John L Dietsch Blvd Ste A (02763-1032)
PHONE.................................508 699-7506
Mark Cobb, *Pr*
EMP: 18 **EST:** 1961
SQ FT: 22,000
SALES (est): 1.6MM **Privately Held**
SIC: 3545 3469 Precision tools, machinists';
  Metal stampings, nec

(G-6090)
MC EMBOSSING INC
200 John L Dietsch Blvd (02763-1077)
PHONE.................................781 821-3088
Susan Nalband, *Prin*
EMP: 7 **EST:** 2010
SALES (est): 127.73K **Privately Held**
SIC: 2759 Letterpress printing

(G-6091)
METFAB ENGINEERING INC
332 John L Dietsch Blvd (02763-1078)
PHONE.................................508 695-1007
Edward Urquhart, *Pr*
Nancy J Berndt, *
EMP: 50 **EST:** 1971
SQ FT: 48,000
SALES (est): 7.42MM **Privately Held**
Web: www.metfabeng.com
SIC: 3441 Fabricated structural metal

(G-6092)
NATIONAL SIGN CORP
21 Larsen Way (02763-1068)
PHONE.................................508 809-4638
Chris Joyal, *Genl Mgr*
EMP: 25 **EST:** 2008
SALES (est): 866.11K **Privately Held**
Web: www.nationalsign.com
SIC: 3993 Signs and advertising specialties

(G-6093)
OUELLETTE INDUSTRIES INC
100 John L Dietsch Blvd Ste B
(02763-1063)
P.O. Box 2780 (02763-0897)
PHONE.................................508 695-0964
Ronald Boccanfuso, *Pr*
EMP: 7 **EST:** 1984
SALES (est): 482.71K **Privately Held**
Web: www.ouelletteindustries.com
SIC: 2399 3471 Emblems, badges, and
  insignia; Finishing, metals or formed
  products

(G-6094)
PANELTEK INC
10 Larsen Way (02763-1055)
PHONE.................................920 906-9457
Dale Gamberini, *Pr*
EMP: 18 **EST:** 2000
SALES (est): 4.89MM **Privately Held**
Web: www.paneltekllc.com
SIC: 3643 Lightning protection equipment

(G-6095)
PANELTEK LLC
10 Larsen Way (02763-1055)
PHONE.................................920 906-9457
EMP: 19 **EST:** 2017
SALES (est): 3.01MM **Privately Held**
Web: www.paneltekllc.com
SIC: 3643 7373 Lightning protection
  equipment; Systems software development
  services

(G-6096)
VH BLACKINTON & CO INC
221 John L Dietsch Blvd (02763-1031)
P.O. Box 1300 (02763-0300)
PHONE.................................508 699-4436
Peter A Roque, *Pr*
Carl R Croce, *
Mario A Roque, *
Ronald Oreilly, *
Louise J Farrands, *
EMP: 200 **EST:** 1852
SQ FT: 52,000
SALES (est): 22.09MM **Privately Held**
Web: www.blackinton.com
SIC: 2399 3499 Emblems, badges, and
  insignia: from purchased materials;
  Trophies, metal, except silver

Auburn
Worcester County

(G-6097)
ACCELERATED MEDIA TECH INC
19 Technology Dr (01501-3210)
PHONE.................................508 459-0300
EMP: 50 **EST:** 2010
SALES (est): 8.73MM **Privately Held**
Web: www.acceleratedmt.com
SIC: 3663 Satellites, communications

(G-6098)
AEARO TECHNOLOGIES LLC
Also Called: Aearo Technologies
48 Sword St Ste 101 (01501-2162)
PHONE.................................317 692-6645
Barbar Brodeur, *Brnch Mgr*
EMP: 271
SALES (corp-wide): 34.23B **Publicly Held**
Web: www.aearotechnologies.com
SIC: 3842 3851 Surgical appliances and
  supplies; Ophthalmic goods
HQ: Aearo Technologies Llc
  7911 Zionsville Rd
  Indianapolis IN 46268

(G-6099)
AIMTEK INC (PA)
Also Called: Aimco
201 Washington St (01501-3224)
PHONE.................................508 832-5035
Amar Kapur, *Pr*
Ani Kapur, *VP*
EMP: 21 **EST:** 1973
SQ FT: 20,000
SALES (est): 19.04MM
SALES (corp-wide): 19.04MM **Privately Held**
Web: www.aimtek.com
SIC: 3351 Rolled or drawn shapes, nec,
  copper and copper alloy

(G-6100)
ALLIED MACHINED PRODUCTS CORP
4 Westec Dr (01501-3041)
P.O. Box 70569 (01607-0569)
PHONE.................................508 756-4290

▲ = Import ▼ = Export
◆ = Import/Export

Ann Marie Weber, *Pr*
Joseph L Wetton, *
Ann M Weber, *Treas*
▲ **EMP:** 85 **EST:** 1945
SQ FT: 49,500
SALES (est): 10.93MM **Privately Held**
Web: www.alliedmp.com
SIC: 3599 Machine shop, jobbing and repair

(G-6101)
AMERICAN INDUSTRIAL & MED PDTS (PA)
Also Called: Aim Products
201 Washington St (01501-3224)
PHONE.................................508 832-5785
Amar Kapur, *Pr*
Ani Kapur, *VP*
EMP: 18 **EST:** 1973
SQ FT: 10,000
SALES (est): 5.14MM
SALES (corp-wide): 5.14MM **Privately Held**
Web: www.aimtek.com
SIC: 5084 2813 5047 Safety equipment; Industrial gases; Medical equipment and supplies

(G-6102)
AMERICAN PRTG & ENVELOPE INC
211 Southbridge St (01501-2548)
P.O. Box 347 (01501-0347)
PHONE.................................508 832-6100
Anthony Penny, *Pr*
David Penny, *
Francis T Penny, *
Joseph H Penny, *
EMP: 25 **EST:** 1988
SQ FT: 15,400
SALES (est): 2.32MM **Privately Held**
Web: www.american211.com
SIC: 2752 2791 2789 2677 Offset printing; Typesetting; Bookbinding and related work; Envelopes

(G-6103)
ARCADE INDUSTRIES INC
Also Called: Arcade Snacks & Dried Fruits
205 Southbridge St (01501-2548)
P.O. Box 375 (01501-0375)
PHONE.................................508 832-6300
Richard J Haufe, *Pr*
Barret H Ethier, *VP*
Ann F Ethier, *Sec*
EMP: 18 **EST:** 1986
SQ FT: 1,880
SALES (est): 4.84MM **Privately Held**
Web: www.arcadesnacks.com
SIC: 2068 2034 Salted and roasted nuts and seeds; Dried and dehydrated fruits

(G-6104)
ARCHITCTRAL FIREPLACES OF NENG
4 Washington St (01501-3012)
PHONE.................................508 757-0622
Lori O'brien, *Prin*
EMP: 11 **EST:** 2004
SALES (est): 913.2K **Privately Held**
Web: www.arc-fire.com
SIC: 8712 3429 5023 5719 Architectural services; Fireplace equipment, hardware: andirons, grates, screens; Kitchenware; Fireplaces and wood burning stoves

(G-6105)
ARONSON TIRE COMPANY INC
510 Washington St (01501-2704)
P.O. Box 291 (01501-0291)

PHONE.................................508 832-3244
Robert J Aronson, *Pr*
EMP: 50 **EST:** 1919
SQ FT: 38,000
SALES (est): 928.84K **Privately Held**
SIC: 7534 5531 5014 Tire retreading and repair shops; Automotive tires; Automobile tires and tubes

(G-6106)
ATLAS DISTRIBUTING INC
44 Southbridge St (01501-2582)
P.O. Box 420 (01501-0420)
PHONE.................................508 791-6221
Ronald J Salois Junior, *Pr*
John Sadowsky, *
John Lepore, *
◆ **EMP:** 160 **EST:** 1933
SQ FT: 130,000
SALES (est): 49.3MM **Privately Held**
Web: www.atlasdistributing.com
SIC: 2082 Beer (alcoholic beverage)

(G-6107)
BAY STATE SURFACE TECHNOLOGIES
201 Washington St (01501-3224)
PHONE.................................508 832-5035
Amar Kapur, *Pr*
Ani Kapur, *VP*
EMP: 10 **EST:** 2000
SALES (est): 2.01MM
SALES (corp-wide): 19.04MM **Privately Held**
Web: www.baystatesurfacetech.com
SIC: 3479 Coating of metals and formed products
PA: Aimtek, Inc.
201 Washington St
Auburn MA 01501
508 832-5035

(G-6108)
BRADEN MANUFACTURING LLC
Also Called: Consolidated Fabricators
17 Saint Mark St (01501-3237)
PHONE.................................508 797-8000
Brian Nason, *Genl Mgr*
EMP: 70
SALES (corp-wide): 10.62MM **Privately Held**
SIC: 3443 3444 Tanks, standard or custom fabricated: metal plate; Sheet metalwork
HQ: Braden Manufacturing, L.L.C.
5199 N Mingo Rd
Tulsa OK 74117
800 272-3360

(G-6109)
BRADY-BUILT INC
Also Called: Brady-Built Sunrooms
160 Southbridge St (01501-2583)
PHONE.................................508 798-2600
Nathaniel Cosper, *Pr*
EMP: 8 **EST:** 2017
SALES (est): 493.25K **Privately Held**
Web: www.sunroomsbybrady.com
SIC: 3448 Sunrooms, prefabricated metal

(G-6110)
BRIDGESTONE RET OPERATIONS LLC
Also Called: Firestone
450 Southbridge St (01501-2442)
PHONE.................................508 832-9671
Roger Lebel, *Mgr*
EMP: 8
Web: www.bridgestoneamericas.com
SIC: 5531 7534 Automotive tires; Rebuilding and retreading tires

HQ: Bridgestone Retail Operations, Llc
333 E Lake St Ste 300
Bloomingdale IL 60108
630 259-9000

(G-6111)
D & S MANUFACTURING COMPANY INCORPORATED
14 Sword St Ste 4 (01501-2170)
PHONE.................................508 799-7812
▲ **EMP:** 15
SALES (est): 940.12K **Privately Held**
SIC: 3423 Knives, agricultural or industrial

(G-6112)
ENDOWMENTSOLUTIONS LLC
Also Called: Endowmentsolutions
8 Booth Rd (01501-3324)
PHONE.................................617 308-7231
Michael Jarvis, *Prin*
EMP: 7 **EST:** 2016
SALES (est): 419.97K **Privately Held**
Web: www.endowmentsolutions.com
SIC: 7372 Prepackaged software

(G-6113)
FLOORING PRO INDUSTRIES LLC
Also Called: Flooring Pro Fastening
27 Elm St (01501-2715)
PHONE.................................704 736-1004
EMP: 8 **EST:** 2015
SALES (est): 143.07K **Privately Held**
SIC: 3315 Staples, steel: wire or cut

(G-6114)
ICARUS CORPORATION
93 Bancroft St (01501-2467)
P.O. Box 145 (01501-0145)
PHONE.................................508 832-3481
William D Rogers Junior, *CEO*
William P Rogan, *Pr*
EMP: 19 **EST:** 1949
SQ FT: 14,000
SALES (est): 8.89MM
SALES (corp-wide): 135.91MM **Privately Held**
Web: www.brisconelectric.com
SIC: 3496 3965 Staples, made from purchased wire; Fasteners
PA: Ecm Industries, Llc
16250 W Woods Edge Rd
New Berlin WI 53151
262 317-8700

(G-6115)
KADANT INC
Webb Systems
35 Sword St (01501-2146)
P.O. Box 269 (01501-0269)
PHONE.................................508 791-8171
EMP: 150
Web: www.kadant.com
SIC: 3554 Paper industries machinery
PA: Kadant Inc.
1 Technology Park Dr # 210
Westford MA 01886

(G-6116)
KADANT INC
AES
35 Sword St (01501-2146)
P.O. Box 7010 (12801-7010)
PHONE.................................508 791-8171
Jeffery Bachand, *Mgr*
EMP: 130
Web: www.kadant.com

SIC: 3554 5084 Paper industries machinery; Industrial machinery and equipment
PA: Kadant Inc.
1 Technology Park Dr # 210
Westford MA 01886

(G-6117)
KARL STORZ ENDSCPY- AMERICA INC
28 Millbury St (01501-3204)
PHONE.................................508 248-9011
EMP: 125
SALES (corp-wide): 2.14B **Privately Held**
Web: www.karlstorz.com
SIC: 3841 Surgical and medical instruments
HQ: Karl Storz Endoscopy-America, Inc.
2151 E Grand Ave
El Segundo CA 90245
424 218-8100

(G-6118)
KILLEEN MACHINE AND TL CO INC
43 Sword St (01501-2146)
PHONE.................................508 754-1714
Gene A Degre, *Prin*
Aline Doucet, *
EMP: 59 **EST:** 1924
SALES (est): 9.76MM **Privately Held**
Web: www.killeenmanufacturing.com
SIC: 3469 Stamping metal for the trade

(G-6119)
MARVIC INC
Also Called: Brady-Built Sunrooms
160 Southbridge St (01501-2583)
PHONE.................................508 798-2600
TOLL FREE: 877
EMP: 35 **EST:** 1995
SQ FT: 28,564
SALES (est): 4.98MM **Privately Held**
Web: www.sunroomsbybrady.com
SIC: 2452 Panels and sections, prefabricated, wood

(G-6120)
MILES PRESS INC
14 Sword St Ste 5 (01501-2171)
PHONE.................................508 752-6430
Peter Martinson, *Pr*
Nancy Martinson, *Treas*
EMP: 10 **EST:** 1967
SQ FT: 7,500
SALES (est): 953.84K **Privately Held**
Web: www.milespress.us
SIC: 2752 2789 Offset printing; Bookbinding and related work

(G-6121)
MISTRAS GROUP INC
Also Called: Mistras Services
2 Millbury St (01501-3204)
PHONE.................................508 832-5500
Dave Orlossky, *Mgr*
EMP: 56
Web: www.mistrasgroup.com
SIC: 3829 Measuring and controlling devices, nec
PA: Mistras Group, Inc.
195 Clarksville Rd
Princeton Junction NJ 08550

(G-6122)
OTIS ELEVATOR COMPANY
34 Sword St (01501-2144)
PHONE.................................401 232-7282
Matthew Salvo, *Brnch Mgr*
EMP: 15
SALES (corp-wide): 13.69B **Publicly Held**

Web: www.otis.com
SIC: 5084 3534　Elevators; Elevators and equipment
HQ: Otis Elevator Company
　　1 Carrier Pl
　　Farmington CT 06032
　　860 674-3000

(G-6123)
PCC SPECIALTY PRODUCTS INC
28 Sword St　(01501-2128)
PHONE.....................503 417-4800
Mike Donningen, *Pr*
Shawn Hagel, *
▲ **EMP:** 160 **EST:** 1995
SQ FT: 16,200
SALES (est): 24.14MM
SALES (corp-wide): 302.09B **Publicly Held**
SIC: 3542　Thread rolling machines
HQ: Precision Castparts Corp.
　　5885 Meadows Rd Ste 620
　　Lake Oswego OR 97035
　　503 946-4800

(G-6124)
PROPHET CORP
191 West St　(01501-1016)
PHONE.....................774 253-0909
Eric J Peterson, *Prin*
EMP: 11 **EST:** 2005
SALES (est): 116.93K **Privately Held**
Web: www.prophetize.com
SIC: 7372　Business oriented computer software

(G-6125)
SHEPPARD ENVELOPE COMPANY INC
133 Southbridge St　(01501-2503)
P.O. Box 358　(01501-0358)
PHONE.....................508 791-5588
J Lincoln Spaulding, *Ch Bd*
L Brook Spaulding, *Pr*
Robin F Spaulding, *Sec*
Frederick Crocker, *Dir*
EMP: 20 **EST:** 1921
SALES (est): 3.48MM **Privately Held**
Web: www.sheppardenvelope.com
SIC: 2677　Envelopes

(G-6126)
SRC PUBLISHING INC
23 Midstate Dr Ste 114　(01501-1857)
PHONE.....................508 749-3212
Dennis Hofmaier, *Pr*
EMP: 9 **EST:** 2006
SALES (est): 232.28K **Privately Held**
SIC: 2741　Miscellaneous publishing

(G-6127)
WEBER REALTY TRUST
Also Called: Allied Metel Products
4 Westec Dr　(01501-3041)
P.O. Box 70569　(01607-0569)
PHONE.....................508 756-4290
Peter Weber, *Pr*
Ruth B Weber, *
EMP: 17 **EST:** 1946
SALES (est): 850.49K **Privately Held**
Web: www.alliedmp.com
SIC: 6512 6531 3451　Commercial and industrial building operation; Real estate brokers and agents; Screw machine products

(G-6128)
WORCESTER ENVELOPE COMPANY
22 Millbury St　(01501-3200)
P.O. Box 406　(01501-0406)
PHONE.....................508 832-5394
TOLL FREE: 800
E Dexter Pond Junior, *Ch Bd*
E Dexter Pond Junior, *Ch*
Eldon D Pond Iii, *Pr*
Richard P Waterhouse, *
Derek P Waterhouse, *
EMP: 155 **EST:** 1893
SQ FT: 180,000
SALES (est): 35.78MM **Privately Held**
Web: www.worcesterenvelope.com
SIC: 2677　Envelopes

(G-6129)
WS ANDERSON ASSOCIATES INC
303 Washington St # 313　(01501-3245)
PHONE.....................508 832-5550
Ricard J Shea, *Pr*
EMP: 34 **EST:** 1982
SQ FT: 44,000
SALES (est): 4.94MM **Privately Held**
Web: www.wsanderson.net
SIC: 3599　Machine shop, jobbing and repair

Auburndale
Middlesex County

(G-6130)
CLEMENTIA PHRMCUTICALS USA INC
275 Grove St Ste 2400　(02466-2273)
PHONE.....................857 226-5588
EMP: 10 **EST:** 2018
SALES (est): 235.84K **Privately Held**
SIC: 2834　Pharmaceutical preparations

(G-6131)
CORINDUS INC (HQ)
275 Grove St Ste 1110　(02466-2275)
PHONE.....................508 653-3335
Mark Toland, *CEO*
Tal Wenderoe, *
David Long, *
▲ **EMP:** 25 **EST:** 2005
SQ FT: 9,000
SALES (est): 20.92MM
SALES (corp-wide): 32.93MM **Privately Held**
Web: www.siemens-healthineers.com
SIC: 3826 3569　Laser scientific and engineering instruments; Robots, assembly line: industrial and commercial
PA: Corindus Vascular Robotics, Inc.
　　275 Grove St Ste 1100
　　Auburndale MA 02466
　　508 653-3335

(G-6132)
CORINDUS VASCULAR ROBOTICS INC (PA)
275 Grove St Ste 1100　(02466-2276)
PHONE.....................508 653-3335
Mark J Toland, *Pr*
Jeffrey C Lightcap, *Non-Executive Chairman of the Board*
Douglas Teany, *COO*
David W Long, *Sr VP*
EMP: 34 **EST:** 2011
SALES (est): 32.93MM
SALES (corp-wide): 32.93MM **Privately Held**
Web: www.siemens-healthineers.com

SIC: 3841　Surgical and medical instruments

(G-6133)
FIG CITY NEWS INC ✪
389 Central St　(02466-2232)
PHONE.....................617 610-1093
Amy Sangiolo, *Pr*
EMP: 7 **EST:** 2022
SALES (est): 299.79K **Privately Held**
SIC: 2711　Newspapers

(G-6134)
GINER ELX SUB LLC
89 Rumford Ave　(02466-1311)
PHONE.....................781 392-0300
Andrew Belt, *CEO*
EMP: 15 **EST:** 2020
SALES (est): 9.58MM
SALES (corp-wide): 701.44MM **Publicly Held**
SIC: 3699 1731　Electrical equipment and supplies, nec; General electrical contractor
PA: Plug Power Inc.
　　968 Albany Shaker Rd
　　Latham NY 12110
　　518 782-7700

(G-6135)
GINER LIFE SCIENCES INC
Also Called: Ginerlabs
89 Rumford Ave　(02466-1311)
PHONE.....................781 529-0576
Andrew Belt, *Pr*
Theresa Scavone, *Sec*
EMP: 10 **EST:** 2017
SALES (est): 2.14MM **Privately Held**
Web: www.ginerinc.com
SIC: 2869　Laboratory chemicals, organic

(G-6136)
HC STARCK TUNGSTEN LLC
275 Grove St Ste 2400　(02466-2273)
PHONE.....................617 630-4843
EMP: 20 **EST:** 2009
SALES (est): 11.76MM **Privately Held**
Web: www.hcstarck.com
SIC: 3339　Primary nonferrous metals, nec
HQ: H.C . Starck Tungsten Gmbh
　　Im Schleeke 78-91
　　Goslar NI 38642
　　53217510

(G-6137)
MEITU
275 Grove St Ste 2400　(02466-2273)
PHONE.....................781 898-7655
Paul Stephen Nolan, *Prin*
EMP: 8 **EST:** 2015
SALES (est): 203.82K **Privately Held**
Web: www.meitucorporation.com
SIC: 2599　Furniture and fixtures, nec

(G-6138)
OCTO TELEMATICS NORTH AMER LLC
134 Rumford Ave Ste 302　(02466-1378)
PHONE.....................617 916-1080
Michael Gabardi, *Finance*
EMP: 8 **EST:** 2010
SQ FT: 2,500
SALES (est): 4.46MM
SALES (corp-wide): 121.86MM **Privately Held**
Web: www.octotelematics.com
SIC: 7379 7372　Computer related maintenance services; Business oriented computer software
HQ: Octo Telematics Spa
　　Via Vincenzo Lamaro 51
　　Roma RM 00173

(G-6139)
TELEVEH INC
132 Charles St Ste 201　(02466-1743)
PHONE.....................857 400-1938
Xinye Li, *CEO*
EMP: 10 **EST:** 2015
SALES (est): 295.29K **Privately Held**
Web: www.televeh.com
SIC: 7372　Prepackaged software

Avon
Norfolk County

(G-6140)
ACCUROUNDS INC
15 Doherty Ave　(02322-1186)
PHONE.....................508 587-3500
Michael Tamasi, *CEO*
EMP: 70 **EST:** 2010
SALES (est): 9.75MM **Privately Held**
Web: www.accurounds.com
SIC: 3599　Machine shop, jobbing and repair

(G-6141)
ALLIANCE SHEET METAL INC
21 Ledin Dr　(02322-1128)
PHONE.....................508 587-0314
Robert J Johnson, *Prin*
EMP: 8 **EST:** 2013
SALES (est): 888.68K **Privately Held**
Web: www.alliancesheetmetal.com
SIC: 3499　Fabricated metal products, nec

(G-6142)
ARCHITCTRAL GLZING SYSTEMS INC
40 Murphy Dr　(02322-1147)
PHONE.....................508 588-4845
Joseph Belanger, *Pr*
Brian Long, *VP*
Patricia Belanger, *Treas*
EMP: 22 **EST:** 1992
SALES (est): 2.38MM **Privately Held**
Web: www.archglazing.com
SIC: 3442　Window and door frames

(G-6143)
AVON CSTM EMB & SCREENPRINTING
Also Called: Avon Custom EMB & Screen Prtg
4 Brentwood Ave　(02322-1602)
PHONE.....................781 341-4663
Carol Merlo, *Pr*
EMP: 8 **EST:** 1987
SALES (est): 247.65K **Privately Held**
SIC: 2395 2759　Embroidery and art needlework; Screen printing

(G-6144)
BE PETERSON INC
40 Murphy Dr Ste 2　(02322-1147)
PHONE.....................508 436-7900
Terry Moore, *Pr*
Steven Dasaro, *
EMP: 80 **EST:** 1935
SQ FT: 88,000
SALES (est): 17.51MM **Privately Held**
Web: www.bepeterson.com
SIC: 3443　Fabricated plate work (boiler shop)

(G-6145)
BOSTON CENTERLESS INC
Also Called: Accurounds
15 Doherty Ave　(02322-1124)
PHONE.....................508 587-3500
Michael Tamasi, *Brnch Mgr*

EMP: 50
SQ FT: 26,300
SALES (corp-wide): 27.01MM **Privately Held**
Web: www.bostoncenterless.com
SIC: 3599 3451 Machine shop, jobbing and repair; Screw machine products
PA: Boston Centerless, Inc.
11 Presidential Way
Woburn MA 01801
781 994-5000

(G-6146)
CA J&L ENTERPRISES INC
Also Called: Marshall Paper Tube Co
225 Bodwell St (02322-1148)
P.O. Box 304 (02368-0304)
PHONE.................................781 963-6666
Jeffrey S Lepes, *Pr*
Elayne M Lepes, *
▲ **EMP:** 30 EST: 1948
SALES (est): 4.99MM **Privately Held**
SIC: 2655 Tubes, fiber or paper: made from purchased material

(G-6147)
CHAPMAN MANUFACTURING COMPANY INC (PA)
Also Called: Kochlowy
481 W Main St (02322-1695)
P.O. Box 359 (02322-0359)
PHONE.................................508 588-3200
▲ **EMP:** 43 EST: 1942
SALES (est): 9.38MM
SALES (corp-wide): 9.38MM **Privately Held**
Web: www.chapmanco.com
SIC: 3645 5021 Lamp and light shades; Household furniture

(G-6148)
DESIGN COMMUNICATIONS LTD (PA)
85 Bodwell St Ste 1 (02322-1112)
PHONE.................................617 542-9620
Craig H Kutner, *CEO*
Mark Andreasson, *
▼ **EMP:** 65 EST: 1984
SQ FT: 72,792
SALES (est): 62.12MM
SALES (corp-wide): 62.12MM **Privately Held**
Web:
www.designcommunicationsltd.com
SIC: 3993 Electric signs

(G-6149)
DRESSER MSNLAN CTRL VLVES AVON (DH)
Also Called: Dresser Measurement Control
85 Bodwell St (02322-1112)
PHONE.................................508 586-4600
Andrew Norman, *Pr*
▲ **EMP:** 74 EST: 2005
SALES (est): 54.02MM
SALES (corp-wide): 25.51B **Publicly Held**
SIC: 3569 Bridge or gate machinery, hydraulic
HQ: Dresser, Llc
4425 Westway Park Blvd
Houston TX 77041
262 549-2626

(G-6150)
EASTERN SLING & SUPPLY
230 Bodwell St (02322-1119)
PHONE.................................617 464-4422
George Jones, *Owner*
EMP: 13 EST: 1970
SALES (est): 559.57K **Privately Held**

Web: www.easternsling.com
SIC: 3496 Miscellaneous fabricated wire products

(G-6151)
INTEGRTED WEB FNSHG SYSTEMS IN
Also Called: I-Web
175 Bodwell St (02322-1114)
PHONE.................................508 580-5809
EMP: 26 EST: 1979
SALES (est): 5.43MM **Privately Held**
Web: www.iwebus.com
SIC: 3555 Printing trades machinery

(G-6152)
JELD-WEN INC
9 Teddy Dr (02322-1151)
PHONE.................................541 882-3451
EMP: 12
Web: www.jeld-wen.com
SIC: 3442 Shutters, door or window: metal
HQ: Jeld-Wen, Inc.
2645 Silver Crescent Dr
Charlotte NC 28273
800 535-3936

(G-6153)
JET GRAPHICS LLC
175 Bodwell St Ste 1 (02322-1122)
PHONE.................................508 580-5809
Robert Williams, *Pr*
EMP: 9 EST: 1996
SQ FT: 2,000
SALES (est): 380.8K **Privately Held**
SIC: 3555 Printing trades machinery

(G-6154)
NATIONAL STORE FRONTS CO INC
10 Tracy Dr (02322-1198)
PHONE.................................508 584-8880
EMP: 10 EST: 1995
SALES (est): 147.66K **Privately Held**
SIC: 3442 Metal doors, sash, and trim

(G-6155)
NEW ENGLAND WELDING INC
145 Bodwell St (02322-1179)
PHONE.................................508 580-2024
Ken Mcintire, *Pr*
EMP: 17 EST: 2001
SALES (est): 1.25MM **Privately Held**
Web: www.newelding.com
SIC: 7692 Welding repair

(G-6156)
OLIVENATION LLC (PA)
Also Called: Online Ret Bkg Cking Ingrdents
13 Robbie Rd Unit A4 (02322-1122)
PHONE.................................781 351-1499
Amit Mitra, *Managing Member*
Chiara Frenquellucci, *Managing Member*
◆ **EMP:** 10 EST: 2007
SQ FT: 2,000
SALES (est): 2.2MM
SALES (corp-wide): 2.2MM **Privately Held**
Web: www.olivenation.com
SIC: 5499 5149 2051 Spices and herbs; Spices and seasonings; Bakery: wholesale or wholesale/retail combined

(G-6157)
PORTAL INC
10 Tracy Dr (02322-1265)
PHONE.................................800 966-3030
Erik Naisuler, *Prin*
▲ **EMP:** 50 EST: 1972
SQ FT: 50,000

SALES (est): 4.86MM **Privately Held**
Web: www.portalincorporated.com
SIC: 3442 Metal doors

(G-6158)
R & B SPLICER SYSTEMS INC
145 Bodwell St (02322-1179)
PHONE.................................508 580-3500
Ernest D Rowe, *Pr*
EMP: 8 EST: 2005
SALES (est): 889.49K **Privately Held**
Web: www.rbsplicersystems.com
SIC: 3861 Editing equipment, motion picture: viewers, splicers, etc.

(G-6159)
RANFAC CORP
30 Doherty Ave Ste A (02322-1125)
P.O. Box 635 (02322-0635)
PHONE.................................508 588-4400
Robert M Adler, *Pr*
David C Fixler, *Sec*
EMP: 75 EST: 1888
SQ FT: 40,000
SALES (est): 16.09MM **Privately Held**
Web: www.ranfac.com
SIC: 3841 8011 3842 Surgical and medical instruments; Offices and clinics of medical doctors; Surgical appliances and supplies

(G-6160)
ROADSAFE TRAFFIC SYSTEMS INC
55 Bodwell St (02322-1112)
PHONE.................................508 580-6700
Mark Dimartino, *Brnch Mgr*
EMP: 100
Web: www.roadsafetraffic.com
SIC: 7389 1721 3993 Flagging service (traffic control); Pavement marking contractor; Signs and advertising specialties
PA: Roadsafe Traffic Systems, Inc.
8750 W Bryn Mawr Ave
Chicago IL 60631

(G-6161)
SCRATCH ART COMPANY INC (PA)
11 Robbie Rd Ste A (02322-1100)
P.O. Box 590 (06881-0590)
PHONE.................................508 583-8085
Nathan Polsky, *Pr*
Janet Polsky, *Treas*
Harvey Schwartz, *VP*
▲ **EMP:** 15 EST: 1964
SQ FT: 25,000
SALES (est): 1.33MM
SALES (corp-wide): 1.33MM **Privately Held**
Web: www.scratchart.com
SIC: 3952 Lead pencils and art goods

(G-6162)
STAR KITCHEN CABINETS INC
75 Stockwell Dr Ste H (02322-1170)
PHONE.................................508 510-3123
Xiaoqing Wu, *Prin*
▲ **EMP:** 7 EST: 2015
SALES (est): 262.03K **Privately Held**
Web: www.starkitchencabinets.com
SIC: 2434 Wood kitchen cabinets

(G-6163)
SYMMONS INDUSTRIES INC
275 Bodwell St (02322-1139)
PHONE.................................508 857-2352
EMP: 64
SALES (corp-wide): 55.34MM **Privately Held**

Web: www.symmons.com
SIC: 5074 3432 Plumbing fittings and supplies; Plumbing fixture fittings and trim
PA: Symmons Industries, Inc.
31 Brooks Dr
Braintree MA 02184
800 796-6667

(G-6164)
TAYLOR COMMUNICATIONS INC
81 Uraco Way (02322-1140)
PHONE.................................508 584-0102
Chuck Rozie, *Mgr*
EMP: 19
SALES (corp-wide): 3.81B **Privately Held**
Web: www.taylor.com
SIC: 2761 2759 2752 Manifold business forms; Commercial printing, nec; Commercial printing, lithographic
HQ: Taylor Communications, Inc.
1725 Roe Crest Dr
North Mankato MN 56003
866 541-0937

(G-6165)
TYCO FIRE PRODUCTS LP
Also Called: Tyco Fire Protection Products
27 Doherty Ave (02322-1124)
PHONE.................................508 583-8447
Derek Gimler, *Mgr*
EMP: 8
Web: www.tyco-fire.com
SIC: 3569 Sprinkler systems, fire: automatic
HQ: Tyco Fire Products Lp
1467 Elmwood Ave
Cranston RI 02910
215 362-0700

(G-6166)
UNITED CURTAIN CO INC (PA)
91 Wales Ave Ste 1 (02322-1004)
P.O. Box 2583 (02090-7583)
PHONE.................................508 588-4100
Joseph N Resha Junior, *Pr*
Thomas M Resha, *VP*
▲ **EMP:** 20 EST: 1939
SQ FT: 15,000
SALES (est): 2.08MM
SALES (corp-wide): 2.08MM **Privately Held**
SIC: 2391 Curtains and draperies

(G-6167)
WEISS SHEET METAL INC
105 Bodwell St (02322-1112)
PHONE.................................508 583-8300
Wayne Delano, *Pr*
Brian Delano, *VP*
EMP: 20 EST: 1965
SQ FT: 26,000
SALES (est): 3.3MM **Privately Held**
Web: www.weiss-sheetmetal.com
SIC: 3444 Sheet metalwork

(G-6168)
WESTERBEKE CORPORATION
41 Ledin Dr Avon Industrial Park (02322)
PHONE.................................508 823-7677
EMP: 30
SALES (corp-wide): 10.35MM **Privately Held**
Web: www.westerbeke.com
SIC: 3519 Gasoline engines
PA: Westerbeke Corporation
150 John Hancock Rd
Taunton MA 02780
508 977-4273

(G-6169)
WROBEL ENGINEERING CO INC
154 Bodwell St (02322-1160)
PHONE...................................508 586-8338
Elizabeth Wrobel, *Pr*
Edward Wrobel, *
EMP: 100 **EST:** 1976
SQ FT: 60,000
SALES (est): 20.96MM **Privately Held**
Web: www.wrobeleng.com
SIC: 3444 Sheet metalwork

Ayer
Middlesex County

(G-6170)
AJINOMOTO CAMBROOKE INC (DH)
Also Called: Cambrooke Foods
4 Copeland Dr (01432-1751)
PHONE...................................508 782-2300
Howard Lossing, *CEO*
Chuck Sizer, *
▲ **EMP:** 45 **EST:** 2000
SQ FT: 65,000
SALES (est): 27.63MM **Privately Held**
Web: www.cambrooke.com
SIC: 2023 Dietary supplements, dairy and non-dairy based
HQ: Ajinomoto Health & Nutrition North America, Inc.
250 E Devon Ave
Itasca IL 60143
630 931-6800

(G-6171)
AMERICAN SUPERCONDUCTOR CORP (PA)
Also Called: Amsc
114 E Main St (01432-1832)
PHONE...................................978 842-3000
Daniel P Mcgahn, *Ch Bd*
John W Kosiba Junior, *Sr VP*
▲ **EMP:** 88 **EST:** 1987
SQ FT: 88,000
SALES (est): 105.98MM
SALES (corp-wide): 105.98MM **Publicly Held**
Web: www.amsc.com
SIC: 3621 3674 Motors and generators; Semiconductors and related devices

(G-6172)
ANDREW ROLDEN PC
39 Main St (01432-1378)
PHONE...................................978 391-4655
Andrew Olden, *Prin*
EMP: 7 **EST:** 2010
SALES (est): 559.75K **Privately Held**
Web: www.oldencpa.com
SIC: 3089 Identification cards, plastics

(G-6173)
ANDREWS HOLDINGS INC
2 New England Way (01432-1514)
PHONE...................................978 772-4444
J Raymond Andrews, *Pr*
Richard Osterberg, *Clerk*
EMP: 44 **EST:** 1951
SQ FT: 20,000
SALES (est): 2.17MM **Privately Held**
SIC: 3241 Portland cement

(G-6174)
AVS INCORPORATED
Also Called: Advanced Vacuum Systems
60 Fitchburg Rd (01432-1049)
PHONE...................................978 772-0710
Steven Levesque, *Pr*
Charles Creeden, *
Irene Buck, *
◆ **EMP:** 100 **EST:** 1967
SQ FT: 34,000
SALES (est): 17.99MM **Privately Held**
Web: www.avsinc.com
SIC: 3567 Vacuum furnaces and ovens

(G-6175)
BMAC INC
Also Called: Bryant Manufacturing Assoc
31 Willow Rd (01432-5510)
PHONE...................................978 772-3310
EMP: 22
SIC: 3826 2542 1799 8734 Environmental testing equipment; Partitions for floor attachment, prefabricated: except wood; Demountable partition installation; Testing laboratories

(G-6176)
CAPACITEC INC (PA)
87 Fitchburg Rd (01432-1003)
P.O. Box 819 (01432-0819)
PHONE...................................978 772-6033
Robert L Foster, *Pr*
Joan M Foster, *Treas*
Donna M Mulrooney, *Off Mgr*
EMP: 13 **EST:** 1986
SQ FT: 12,000
SALES (est): 2.45MM
SALES (corp-wide): 2.45MM **Privately Held**
Web: www.capacitec.com
SIC: 3829 Measuring and controlling devices, nec

(G-6177)
CATANIA-SPAGNA CORPORATION
Also Called: Catania Oils
90 Nemco Way (01432-1541)
P.O. Box 847315 (02284-7315)
PHONE...................................978 772-7900
Anthony Basile, *CEO*
Joseph Basile, *
Stephen Basile, *
Robert Basile, *
William Reilly, *
◆ **EMP:** 45 **EST:** 1933
SALES (est): 94.73MM **Privately Held**
Web: www.cataniaoils.com
SIC: 2079 Vegetable refined oils (except corn oil)

(G-6178)
CERIC FABRICATION CO INC
Also Called: Ceric Fab Systems
70 Nemco Way (01432-1537)
PHONE...................................978 772-9034
Seth Wesson, *Pr*
Seth K Wesson Junior, *VP*
Carol Wesson, *
Judith W Candage, *
Eric J Wesson, *
EMP: 50 **EST:** 1962
SQ FT: 25,000
SALES (est): 753.78K **Privately Held**
Web: www.cericfab.com
SIC: 3444 Sheet metal specialties, not stamped

(G-6179)
CPI ESSCO INC
90 Nemco Way (01432-1541)
PHONE...................................978 568-5100
Thomas J Casale, *Pr*
◆ **EMP:** 230 **EST:** 1961
SQ FT: 30,000
SALES (est): 47.1MM **Privately Held**
SIC: 3711 3663 Motor vehicles and car bodies; Radio and t.v. communications equipment
HQ: Communications & Power Industries Llc
811 Hansen Way
Palo Alto CA 94304

(G-6180)
CREATIVE MATERIALS INC
Also Called: CMI
12 Willow Rd (01432-5513)
PHONE...................................978 391-4700
Silvio Morano, *Pr*
Janet K Morano, *
Stuart H Ganslaw, *
EMP: 30 **EST:** 1987
SQ FT: 26,000
SALES (est): 5.4MM **Privately Held**
Web: www.creativematerials.com
SIC: 8731 2891 2899 Chemical laboratory, except testing; Adhesives; Chemical preparations, nec

(G-6181)
ECKEL INDUSTRIES INC (PA)
Also Called: Eckoustic Division
100 Groton Shirley Rd (01432-1047)
PHONE...................................978 772-0840
Alex Eckel, *Pr*
Jeff Morris, *VP*
Joseph Tunnera, *Treas*
Richard Bland, *Sec*
John Flood, *VP*
▲ **EMP:** 12 **EST:** 1952
SQ FT: 38,000
SALES (est): 9.65MM
SALES (corp-wide): 9.65MM **Privately Held**
Web: www.eckelacoustics.com
SIC: 3296 3446 3444 Acoustical board and tile, mineral wool; Partitions and supports/ studs, including acoustical systems; Forming machine work, sheet metal

(G-6182)
EPIC ENTERPRISES INC
11 Copeland Dr (01432-1767)
PHONE...................................978 772-2340
T Tenney, *Pr*
Robert H Rauh Junior, *Pr*
Donald Sorrie, *
William Leader Junior, *Dir*
David R Coffman, *
EMP: 85 **EST:** 1967
SQ FT: 500,000
SALES (est): 26.8MM
SALES (corp-wide): 86.39B **Publicly Held**
Web: www.epicenterprisesinc.com
SIC: 2086 Carbonated beverages, nonalcoholic: pkged. in cans, bottles
PA: Pepsico, Inc.
700 Anderson Hill Rd
Purchase NY 10577
914 253-2000

(G-6183)
J&S BUSINESS PRODUCTS INC
17 Main St Ste 5 (01432-1383)
PHONE...................................877 425-4049
Jose Banchs Iii, *Pr*
EMP: 8 **EST:** 2008
SALES (est): 486.43K **Privately Held**
Web: www.jsbusinessproducts.com
SIC: 2752 Offset printing

(G-6184)
K & W TIRE COMPANY INC
6 Willow Rd (01432-5513)
PHONE...................................978 772-5700
Chris Klotz, *Brnch Mgr*
EMP: 13
SALES (corp-wide): 48.44MM **Privately Held**
Web: www.kwtirestore.com
SIC: 5531 5014 7534 Automotive tires; Automobile tires and tubes; Rebuilding and retreading tires
PA: K & W Tire Company, Inc.
735 N Prince St
Lancaster PA 17603
717 397-3596

(G-6185)
LOWELL SUN PUBLISHING COMPANY
69 Fitchburg Rd (01432-1003)
PHONE...................................978 433-6685
William Singleton, *Brnch Mgr*
EMP: 108
SALES (corp-wide): 1.96B **Privately Held**
Web: www.lowellsun.com
SIC: 2711 7313 Newspapers, publishing and printing; Newspaper advertising representative
HQ: Lowell Sun Publishing Company
491 Dutton St Ste 2
Lowell MA 01854
978 459-1300

(G-6186)
MICRON PLASTICS INC
30 Faulkner St (01432-1612)
PHONE...................................978 772-6900
Harold E Braselman, *Pr*
EMP: 7 **EST:** 1985
SQ FT: 27,000
SALES (est): 415.17K **Privately Held**
Web: www.micron-plastics.com
SIC: 3081 Unsupported plastics film and sheet

(G-6187)
NASOYA FOODS USA LLC
1 New England Way (01432-1514)
PHONE...................................978 772-6880
Ross Gatta, *Pr*
Thomas Perry, *
EMP: 160 **EST:** 2016
SQ FT: 140,000
SALES (est): 49.69MM **Privately Held**
Web: www.nasoya.com
SIC: 2099 Tofu, except frozen desserts
HQ: Pulmuone Foods Usa, Inc.
2315 Moore Ave
Fullerton CA 92833

(G-6188)
NEWEDGE SIGNAL SOLUTIONS LLC (PA)
323 W Main St Ste 1 (01432-1240)
PHONE...................................978 425-5400
EMP: 7 **EST:** 2011
SALES (est): 1.44MM **Privately Held**
Web: www.newedges2.com
SIC: 3663 Radio and t.v. communications equipment

(G-6189)
NORTHEAST HOT-FILL CO-OP INC
25 Copeland Dr (01432-1790)
PHONE...................................978 772-9287
Michael Matney, *Prin*
Marc Ladd, *Prin*
EMP: 45 **EST:** 1994
SQ FT: 321,000
SALES (est): 9.85MM **Privately Held**

Web: www.cpf-nehf.com
SIC: 2086 Tea, iced: packaged in cans,
bottles, etc.

(G-6190)
ORION INDUSTRIES INCORPORATED
1 Orion Park Dr (01432-1582)
PHONE.............................978 772-0020
Francis J Widmayer, *Pr*
Michael J Widmayer, *
Stuart Husmer, *
Kathryn Waller, *
Frank Widmayer, *Prin*
EMP: 33 EST: 1973
SQ FT: 17,000
SALES (est): 5.97MM Privately Held
Web: www.orionindustries.com
SIC: 3679 Electronic circuits

(G-6191)
PLASTIC ASSEMBLY CORPORATION
Also Called: Blinky Products
1 Sculley Rd Unit A (01432-1238)
P.O. Box 632 (01432-0632)
PHONE.............................978 772-4725
Regis M Magnus, *Pr*
▲ EMP: 18 EST: 1978
SQ FT: 2,500
SALES (est): 573.16K Privately Held
Web: www.blinkyproducts.com
SIC: 3089 Blow molded finished plastics
products, nec

(G-6192)
RESIN DISTRIBUTION INC
1 Sculley Rd Unit A (01432-1238)
PHONE.............................978 772-1616
Regis M Magnus, *Dir*
David Hazel, *Pr*
Janet M Gelinas, *CFO*
Norman P Gariepy, *Treas*
Michael Smith, *Treas*
EMP: 12 EST: 2003
SQ FT: 2,000
SALES (est): 3.07MM Privately Held
Web: www.resindistributioninc.com
SIC: 2821 Plastics materials and resins

(G-6193)
SEALED AIR CORPORATION
100 Westford Rd (01432-1534)
PHONE.............................508 521-5694
EMP: 34
SALES (corp-wide): 5.64B Publicly Held
Web: www.sealedair.com
SIC: 3086 Packaging and shipping
materials, foamed plastics
PA: Sealed Air Corporation
2415 Cascade Pointe Blvd
Charlotte NC 28208
980 221-3235

(G-6194)
SHANKLIN CORPORATION (HQ)
Also Called: Shrink Equipment
100 Westford Rd (01432-1552)
PHONE.............................978 487-2204
Lawrence J Pillote, *Pr*
Jonathan B Baker, *
Sarah W Shanklin, *
Kenneth Chrisman, *
Sean E Dempsey, *
◆ EMP: 160 EST: 2000
SQ FT: 170,000
SALES (est): 48.63MM
SALES (corp-wide): 5.64B Publicly Held
Web: www.shrink-pkg.com

SIC: 3565 Packaging machinery
PA: Sealed Air Corporation
2415 Cascade Pointe Blvd
Charlotte NC 28208
980 221-3235

(G-6195)
SHANKLIN RESEARCH CORPORATION
Also Called: Shanklin
100 Westford Rd (01432-1534)
PHONE.............................978 772-2090
Norman D Shanklin, *Pr*
EMP: 7 EST: 1961
SQ FT: 2,000
SALES (est): 904.59K Privately Held
SIC: 3549 Metalworking machinery, nec

(G-6196)
SILPRO LLC (PA)
2 New England Way (01432-1548)
PHONE.............................978 772-4444
◆ EMP: 24 EST: 2009
SALES (est): 4.88MM Privately Held
Web: www.silpro.com
SIC: 3423 Masons' hand tools

(G-6197)
SUPERCONDUCTIVITY INC (HQ)
Also Called: Integrated Electronics
114 E Main St (01432-1832)
PHONE.............................608 831-5773
Greg Yurek, *Pr*
▲ EMP: 89 EST: 1988
SALES (est): 26.03MM
SALES (corp-wide): 105.98MM Publicly
Held
Web: www.amsc.com
SIC: 3629 Electronic generation equipment
PA: American Superconductor Corporation
114 E Main St
Ayer MA 01432
978 842-3000

Baldwinville
Worcester County

(G-6198)
SEAMAN PAPER COMPANY MASS INC
51 Main St (01436-1158)
PHONE.............................978 939-5356
Frank Hogan, *Brnch Mgr*
EMP: 100
SALES (corp-wide): 131.46MM Privately
Held
Web: www.seamanpaper.com
SIC: 2621 Paper mills
PA: Seaman Paper Company Of
Massachusetts, Inc.
35 Wilkins Rd
Gardner MA 01440
978 632-1513

Barnstable
Barnstable County

(G-6199)
CAPE LIGHT COMPACT
3195 Main St (02630-1105)
P.O. Box 427 (02630-0427)
PHONE.............................508 375-6703
Maggie Downey, *Admn*
EMP: 17 EST: 2010
SQ FT: 10,000
SALES (est): 486.14K Privately Held
Web: www.capelightcompact.org

SIC: 1711 3679 Solar energy contractor;
Static power supply converters for
electronic applications

(G-6200)
GARBAGE GONE INC
Also Called: Waste Management
75 Old Phinneys Ln (02630-1308)
P.O. Box 237 (02601-0237)
PHONE.............................508 737-4995
Joel P Coelho Senior, *Pr*
Joel P Coelho Senior, *Pr*
Joel P Coelho Junior, *Sec*
EMP: 7 EST: 2012
SALES (est): 502.5K Privately Held
Web: www.garbagegonecapecod.com
SIC: 4953 3443 4212 Refuse systems;
Dumpsters, garbage; Dump truck haulage

(G-6201)
ROBERTS LDSCP DESIGN & CNSTR
120 Cobblestone Rd (02630-1621)
PHONE.............................508 364-4878
Dilmar Ribeiro, *Prin*
EMP: 16 EST: 2015
SALES (est): 1.04MM Privately Held
Web: www.roberts-landscape.com
SIC: 0781 3271 Landscape services;
Blocks, concrete: landscape or retaining
wall

Barre
Worcester County

(G-6202)
CHAS G ALLEN REALTY LLC
25 Williamsville Rd (01005-9502)
PHONE.............................978 355-2911
David E Krupp, *Pr*
David E Krupp, *Dir*
Gary A Boudreau, *
Charles R Sargent, *
▲ EMP: 55 EST: 1874
SQ FT: 90,000
SALES (est): 8.77MM Privately Held
Web: www.chasgallen.com
SIC: 3599 7699 3291 1796 Machine shop,
jobbing and repair; Pumps and pumping
equipment repair; Abrasive products;
Installing building equipment

(G-6203)
R J MCDONALD INC
71 Worcester Rd (01005-9108)
PHONE.............................978 355-6649
Richard J Mc Donald, *Pr*
Elizabeth Mc Donald, *Clerk*
EMP: 11 EST: 1953
SQ FT: 5,000
SALES (est): 376.56K Privately Held
Web: www.rjmenergy.com
SIC: 5983 1429 1794 1623 Fuel oil dealers;
Boulder, crushed and broken-quarrying;
Excavation work; Water main construction

Bedford
Middlesex County

(G-6204)
A B E ENTERPRISES LLC
Also Called: Carolina Binding & Textile
4 Preston Ct Ste 200 (01730-2356)
P.O. Box 249 (01730-0249)
PHONE.............................781 271-0000
EMP: 70

SIC: 2261 2396 2221 2211 Finishing plants,
cotton; Bindings, bias: made from
purchased materials; Broadwoven fabric
mills, manmade; Broadwoven fabric mills,
cotton

(G-6205)
ACME PACKET INC
100 Crosby Dr (01730-1438)
PHONE.............................781 328-4400
EMP: 880
SIC: 7372 Application computer software

(G-6206)
AERIS HEALTH INC
8 Crosby Dr (01730-1402)
PHONE.............................917 685-6504
Pierre Bi, *CEO*
Scott Trowbridge, *VP*
Elad Nehorai, *Dir*
Constantin Overlack, *COO*
EMP: 10 EST: 2020
SALES (est): 867.12K Privately Held
SIC: 3634 Air purifiers, portable

(G-6207)
ANIKA THERAPEUTICS INC (PA)
Also Called: Anika
32 Wiggins Ave (01730-2315)
PHONE.............................781 457-9000
Cheryl R Blanchard, *Pr*
Jeffery S Thompson, *
Michael L Levitz, *Ex VP*
David Colleran, *Ex VP*
Thomas Finnerty, *Ex VP*
▲ EMP: 133 EST: 1983
SQ FT: 134,000
SALES (est): 156.24MM Publicly Held
Web: www.anika.com
SIC: 3841 Surgical and medical instruments

(G-6208)
APAMA INC
14 Oak Park Dr (01730-1414)
PHONE.............................781 280-4000
EMP: 14 EST: 1999
SALES (est): 2.23MM
SALES (corp-wide): 602.01MM Publicly
Held
SIC: 7372 7371 Prepackaged software;
Custom computer programming services
PA: Progress Software Corporation
15 Wayside Rd Ste 4
Burlington MA 01803
781 280-4000

(G-6209)
APPLIED BIOSYSTEMS LLC
Also Called: Applied Bosystems Part Lf Tech
2 Preston Ct (01730-2334)
PHONE.............................781 271-0045
Tony White, *Brnch Mgr*
EMP: 19
SALES (corp-wide): 44.91B Publicly Held
Web: www.thermofisher.com
SIC: 3826 Analytical instruments
HQ: Applied Biosystems, Llc
5791 Van Allen Way
Carlsbad CA 92008

(G-6210)
ARA DELL EMC MA RSA BEDFO
174 Middlesex Tpke (01730-1408)
PHONE.............................508 431-4084
EMP: 10 EST: 2019
SALES (est): 265.89K Privately Held
Web: www.rsa.com
SIC: 3572 Computer storage devices

(G-6211)
ASPEN TECHNOLOGY INC (HQ)
Also Called: Massachusetts Aspen Tech Inc
20 Crosby Dr (01730-1402)
PHONE................................781 221-6400
Antonio Pietri, *Pr*
Jill D Smith, *Ch Bd*
Christopher Stagno, *Interim Chief Financial Officer*
Manish Chawla, *CRO*
Mark Mouritsen, *CLO*
EMP: 51 **EST:** 1981
SALES (est): 1.04B
SALES (corp-wide): 15.16B **Publicly Held**
Web: www.aspentech.com
SIC: 7371 7372 Custom computer programming services; Prepackaged software
PA: Emerson Electric Co.
    8000 West Florissant Ave
    Saint Louis MO 63136
    314 553-2000

(G-6212)
ASPENTECH CORPORATION (DH)
Also Called: Aspenone
20 Crosby Dr (01730-1402)
PHONE................................781 221-6400
Antonio J Pietri, *Pr*
John W Hague, *Ofcr*
Chantelle Breithaupt, *
Frederic G Hammond, *
EMP: 219 **EST:** 1981
SQ FT: 143,000
SALES (est): 709.38MM
SALES (corp-wide): 15.16B **Publicly Held**
Web: www.aspentech.com
SIC: 7371 7372 Custom computer programming services; Prepackaged software
HQ: Aspen Technology, Inc.
    20 Crosby Dr
    Bedford MA 01730
    781 221-6400

(G-6213)
AWARE INC (PA)
Also Called: Aware
40 Middlesex Tpke (01730-1404)
PHONE................................781 276-4000
Robert A Eckel, *Pr*
Brent P Johnstone, *
David B Barcelo, *CFO*
Robert M Mungovan, *CCO*
▲ **EMP:** 43 **EST:** 1986
SQ FT: 72,000
SALES (est): 16.01MM
SALES (corp-wide): 16.01MM **Publicly Held**
Web: www.aware.com
SIC: 7372 3674 Business oriented computer software; Semiconductors and related devices

(G-6214)
BERKSHIRE GREY INC (PA)
140 South Rd (01730-2344)
PHONE................................833 848-9900
Thomas Wagner, *CEO*
Steven Johnson, *Pr*
Mark Fidler, *CFO*
EMP: 27 **EST:** 2013
SQ FT: 70,000
SALES (est): 65.85MM
SALES (corp-wide): 65.85MM **Privately Held**
Web: www.berkshiregrey.com

SIC: 3569 8742 Robots, assembly line: industrial and commercial; Automation and robotics consultant

(G-6215)
BIOKIT U S A INC
180 Hartwell Rd (01730-2443)
PHONE................................781 861-4064
Jose Maria Rubiralta, *Pr*
EMP: 8 **EST:** 1985
SALES (est): 3.42MM **Privately Held**
Web: www.biokitusa.com
SIC: 5047 8741 2835 Medical laboratory equipment; Management services; Diagnostic substances
HQ: Biokit Sa
    Lugar Masia Can Malet, S/N
    LliCa D'amunt B 08186

(G-6216)
BRAND & OPPENHEIMER CO INC
Also Called: Cutting Edge Texstyles
4 Preston Ct Ste 200 (01730-2356)
PHONE................................781 271-0000
EMP: 20
Web: www.osinnovate.com
SIC: 2261 2396 2221 2211 Finishing plants, cotton; Bindings, bias: made from purchased materials; Broadwoven fabric mills, manmade; Broadwoven fabric mills, cotton
PA: Brand & Oppenheimer Co., Inc.
    208 Clock Tower Sq
    Portsmouth RI 02871

(G-6217)
CASENET LLC (HQ)
34 Crosby Dr Ste 100 (01730-1428)
PHONE................................781 357-2700
Sanjay Govil, *CEO*
Tim Rosner, *
EMP: 30 **EST:** 2005
SALES (est): 23.04MM
SALES (corp-wide): 23.04MM **Privately Held**
Web: www.zyter.com
SIC: 7372 Business oriented computer software
PA: Zyter, Inc.
    2600 Twr Oaks Blvd Ste 70
    Rockville MD 20852
    301 355-7760

(G-6218)
CUBICPV INC (PA)
6-8 Preston Ct (01730-2334)
PHONE................................781 861-1611
Frank Van Mierlo, *Pr*
▲ **EMP:** 17 **EST:** 2007
SALES (est): 5.91MM **Privately Held**
Web: www.cubicpv.com
SIC: 3674 Solar cells

(G-6219)
CURA SOFTWARE SOLUTIONS CO
34 Crosby Dr (01730-1449)
PHONE................................781 325-7158
EMP: 10 **EST:** 2005
SQ FT: 4,200
SALES (est): 2.84MM **Privately Held**
Web: www.curasoftware.com
SIC: 7372 Business oriented computer software
PA: Cura Risk Management Software (Pty) Ltd
    No 195 Jan Smuts Av, 1st Floor Kaya Hse Bldg Gauteng
    Johannesburg GP

(G-6220)
CYTONOME/ST LLC
9 Oak Park Dr (01730-1413)
PHONE................................617 330-5030
John C Sharpe, *CEO*
EMP: 15 **EST:** 2009
SQ FT: 18,000
SALES (est): 4.8MM **Privately Held**
Web: www.cytonome.com
SIC: 3841 Surgical and medical instruments

(G-6221)
DALE ENGINEERING & SON INC
3 Alfred Cir (01730-2318)
PHONE................................781 541-6055
Christopher Hawkes, *Pr*
Hollis Dale Hawkes, *VP*
Dorothy Hawkes, *Sec*
EMP: 14 **EST:** 1986
SQ FT: 10,000
SALES (est): 2.02MM **Privately Held**
Web: www.daleengineering.com
SIC: 3599 8711 Machine shop, jobbing and repair; Engineering services

(G-6222)
DATAWATCH CORPORATION (HQ)
4 Crosby Dr (01730-1402)
PHONE................................978 441-2200
Michael A Morrison, *Pr*
Ken Tacelli, *
James Eliason, *
Jon Pilkington, *Chief Product Officer*
EMP: 78 **EST:** 1985
SQ FT: 20,360
SALES (est): 41.68MM
SALES (corp-wide): 572.22MM **Publicly Held**
SIC: 7372 Business oriented computer software
PA: Altair Engineering Inc.
    1820 E Big Beaver Rd
    Troy MI 48083
    248 614-2400

(G-6223)
EM4 INC (DH)
Also Called: Gooch & Housego Baltimore
7 Oak Park Dr (01730-1413)
PHONE................................781 275-7501
Mark Webster, *CEO*
Christopher Jewell, *
EMP: 30 **EST:** 2000
SQ FT: 29,300
SALES (est): 16.47MM
SALES (corp-wide): 187.38MM **Privately Held**
Web: www.gandh.com
SIC: 3661 Fiber optics communications equipment
HQ: G&H Capital Holdings (Florida), Inc.
    4632 36th St
    Orlando FL

(G-6224)
EMD MILLIPORE CORPORATION
80 Ashby Rd (01730-2200)
PHONE................................781 533-6000
Martin Madaus, *Pr*
EMP: 200
SALES (corp-wide): 23.09B **Privately Held**
Web: www.millipore.com
SIC: 3826 Analytical instruments
HQ: Emd Millipore Corporation
    400 Summit Dr
    Burlington MA 01803
    800 645-5476

(G-6225)
EMD MILLIPORE CORPORATION
75 Wiggins Ave (01730-2337)
PHONE................................781 533-6000
Mike Titus, *Brnch Mgr*
EMP: 234
SALES (corp-wide): 23.09B **Privately Held**
Web: www.millipore.com
SIC: 3826 Analytical instruments
HQ: Emd Millipore Corporation
    400 Summit Dr
    Burlington MA 01803
    800 645-5476

(G-6226)
EXCEL TECHNOLOGY INC (HQ)
125 Middlesex Tpke (01730-1409)
PHONE................................781 266-5700
Antoine Dominic, *CEO*
Deborah A Mulryan, *VP*
Peter Chang, *VP*
Alice H Varisano, *CFO*
EMP: 75 **EST:** 1985
SQ FT: 65,000
SALES (est): 229.26MM **Publicly Held**
SIC: 3699 3827 Laser systems and equipment; Optical instruments and apparatus
PA: Novanta Inc.
    125 Middlesex Tpke
    Bedford MA 01730

(G-6227)
FOLIA MATERIALS INC
Also Called: Folia Water
3 Loomis St (01730-2216)
PHONE................................315 559-2135
Theresa Dankovich, *CEO*
Cantwell Carson, *COO*
John Rossmiller, *CFO*
EMP: 8 **EST:** 2016
SALES (est): 804.48K **Privately Held**
Web: www.folia-ppe.com
SIC: 8731 2679 Biological research; Filter paper: made from purchased material

(G-6228)
FUJIFILM RCRDING MEDIA USA INC (DH)
Also Called: Fujifilm Microdisks U.S.a
45 Crosby Dr (01730-1401)
PHONE................................781 271-4400
Norio Shibata, *Pr*
Hironobu Taketomi, *
Shigeru Sano, *
Suguru Enomoto, *
Ryutaro Hosoda, *
◆ **EMP:** 75 **EST:** 1990
SQ FT: 135,000
SALES (est): 48.03MM **Privately Held**
Web: global.fujifilm.com
SIC: 3577 Key-tape equipment, except drives
HQ: Fujifilm Holdings America Corporation
    200 Summit Lake Dr Fl 2
    Valhalla NY 10595

(G-6229)
HOMOLOGY MEDICINES INC
1 Patriots Park (01730-2326)
PHONE................................781 301-7277
Arthur O Tzianabos, *CEO*
Albert Seymour, *Pr*
W Bradford Smith, *CFO*
Julie Jordan, *Chief Medical Officer*
Tim Kelly, *COO*
EMP: 124 **EST:** 2015
SQ FT: 67,000
SALES (est): 3.21MM **Privately Held**
Web: www.homologymedicines.com

SIC: 8731 2834   Biological research;
   Pharmaceutical preparations

(G-6230)
HUBER + SHNER PLATIS PHOTONICS
213 Burlington Rd Ste 123 (01730-1468)
PHONE.............................781 275-5080
Gerald Wesel, *Pr*
Jeffery Farmer, *VP*
Martin Stephenson, *CFO*
Arron Bent, *VP Mktg*
EMP: 10 EST: 1998
SALES (est): 4.72MM **Privately Held**
Web: www.polatis.com
SIC: 3674   Semiconductors and related
   devices
HQ: Huber+Suhner Polatis, Inc.
   213 Burlington Rd Ste 123
   Bedford MA 01730
   781 275-5080

(G-6231)
HUBER+SUHNER POLATIS INC (DH)
213 Burlington Rd Ste 123 (01730-1468)
PHONE.............................781 275-5080
Gerald Wesel, *Pr*
Martin Stephenson, *CFO*
EMP: 36 EST: 2005
SQ FT: 25,000
SALES (est): 32.24MM **Privately Held**
Web: www.polatis.com
SIC: 3613   Switchboards and parts, power
HQ: Huber + Suhner (North America)
   Corporation
   8530 Steele Creek Pl
   Charlotte NC 28273

(G-6232)
INFRAREDX INC
28 Crosby Dr Ste 100 (01730-1450)
PHONE.............................781 221-0053
Nozomu Fujita, *CEO*
Paul Mcdermott, *Contrlr*
EMP: 80 EST: 1998
SALES (est): 23.53MM **Privately Held**
Web: www.infraredx.com
SIC: 3845   Electromedical equipment
PA: Nipro Corporation
   3-26, Senriokashinmachi
   Settsu OSK 566-0

(G-6233)
INSTRUMENTATION LABORATORY CO (DH)
Also Called: Werfen
180 Hartwell Rd (01730-2443)
PHONE.............................781 861-0710
Ramon E Benet, *Pr*
Jose Luis Martin, *VP*
James A Clayton Junior, *Sec*
Javier Gomez, *CFO*
▲ EMP: 700 EST: 1959
SALES (est): 436.34MM **Privately Held**
Web: www.werfen.com
SIC: 3841 2819 8731 2835   Diagnostic
   apparatus, medical; Chemicals, reagent
   grade: refined from technical grade;
   Commercial physical research; Diagnostic
   substances
HQ: Instrumentation Laboratory Spa
   Viale Monza 338
   Milano MI 20128
   0225221

(G-6234)
INTEGRAL BIOSYSTEMS LLC
23 Crosby Dr Ste 100a (01730-1423)

PHONE.............................781 275-8059
Shikha Barman, *Managing Member*
EMP: 10 EST: 2006
SQ FT: 9,800
SALES (est): 1.62MM **Privately Held**
Web: www.integralbiosystems.com
SIC: 8731 2834   Biotechnical research,
   commercial; Pharmaceutical preparations

(G-6235)
IROBOT CORPORATION (PA)
Also Called: Irobot
8 Crosby Dr (01730-1402)
PHONE.............................781 430-3000
Colin M Angle, *Ch Bd*
Julie Zeiler, *Ex VP*
Glen Weinstein, *CLO*
Jean Jacques Blanc, *CCO*
Keith Hartsfield, *CPO*
▲ EMP: 472 EST: 1990
SQ FT: 270,000
SALES (est): 1.18B **Publicly Held**
Web: www.irobot.com
SIC: 3635 3569   Household vacuum cleaners
   ; Robots, assembly line: industrial and
   commercial

(G-6236)
KADANT FIBERGEN INC (HQ)
8 Alfred Cir (01730-2340)
PHONE.............................781 275-3600
▼ EMP: 10 EST: 1996
SALES (est): 13.19MM **Publicly Held**
SIC: 3823   Process control instruments
PA: Kadant Inc.
   1 Technology Park Dr # 210
   Westford MA 01886

(G-6237)
LOCKHEED MARTIN CORPORATION
Also Called: Lockheed Martin
P.O. Box 855 (01730-0855)
PHONE.............................781 863-5235
EMP: 1261
Web: www.gyrocamsystems.com
SIC: 3812   Search and navigation equipment
PA: Lockheed Martin Corporation
   6801 Rockledge Dr
   Bethesda MD 20817

(G-6238)
MARZAE LLC (PA)
8 Gould Rd (01730-1214)
PHONE.............................619 915-0352
Eliot Maxwell Martin, *Managing Member*
EMP: 8 EST: 2021
SALES (est): 83.62K
SALES (corp-wide): 83.62K **Privately Held**
SIC: 2084   Wines, brandy, and brandy spirits

(G-6239)
MAYFLOWER COMMUNICATIONS INC
11 Oak Park Dr Ste 200 (01730-1413)
PHONE.............................781 359-9500
Naresh Babu N Jarmale, *VP*
Vasant Somaiya, *
Kaplesh Kumar, *
Bruce C Warwick, *
Triveni N Upadhyay, *
EMP: 37 EST: 1985
SQ FT: 15,000
SALES (est): 9.21MM **Privately Held**
Web: www.mayflowercom.com
SIC: 3661   Telephone and telegraph
   apparatus

(G-6240)
MEDICA CORPORATION (PA)
Also Called: Medica
5 Oak Park Dr Ste 1 (01730-1430)
PHONE.............................781 275-4892
▲ EMP: 104 EST: 1983
SALES (est): 24.89MM
SALES (corp-wide): 24.89MM **Privately
Held**
Web: www.medicacorp.com
SIC: 3826   Blood testing apparatus

(G-6241)
MEGAPULSE INCORPORATED
23 Crosby Dr (01730-1423)
PHONE.............................781 538-5299
Paul Johannessen, *Ch*
Eric Johannessen, *Pr*
Robert Rines, *Sec*
EMP: 39 EST: 1970
SQ FT: 40,000
SALES (est): 3.3MM **Privately Held**
Web: www.megapulse.com
SIC: 3812 3663   Navigational systems and
   instruments; Radio and t.v. communications
   equipment

(G-6242)
MERCK GROUP
80 Ashby Rd (01730-2200)
PHONE.............................781 858-3284
EMP: 21 EST: 2018
SALES (est): 1.07MM **Privately Held**
Web: www.merck.com
SIC: 2834   Pharmaceutical preparations

(G-6243)
MLS SHEET METAL LLC
39 Crosby Dr (01730-1401)
PHONE.............................781 275-2265
Kevin Leonard Senior, *Managing Member*
EMP: 16 EST: 2006
SQ FT: 5,500
SALES (est): 2.05MM **Privately Held**
Web: www.mlssheetmetal.com
SIC: 3444   Sheet metalwork

(G-6244)
N2 BIOMEDICAL LLC
One Patriots Pk (01730-2326)
PHONE.............................781 275-6001
Keith Edwards, *Pr*
EMP: 27 EST: 2013
SALES (est): 7.49MM
SALES (corp-wide): 47.68MM **Privately
Held**
Web: www.precisioncoating.com
SIC: 3479   Etching and engraving
PA: Katahdin Industries, Inc.
   51 Parmenter Rd
   Hudson MA 01749
   781 329-1420

(G-6245)
NOVANTA CORPORATION (HQ)
Also Called: Lumonics Corp Indus Pdts Div
125 Middlesex Tpke (01730-1409)
PHONE.............................781 266-5700
Matthijs Glastra, *CEO*
Robert Buckley, *CFO*
Timothy Spinella, *Treas*
▲ EMP: 104 EST: 1967
SQ FT: 147,000
SALES (est): 388.09MM **Publicly Held**
Web: www.novanta.com
SIC: 3699   Laser systems and equipment
PA: Novanta Inc.
   125 Middlesex Tpke
   Bedford MA 01730

(G-6246)
NOVANTA INC (PA)
Also Called: Novanta
125 Middlesex Tpke (01730-1409)
PHONE.............................781 266-5700
Matthijs Glastra, *Ch Bd*
Robert J Buckley, *CFO*
Brian S Young, *Chief Human Resources
Officer*
Michele D Welsh, *Corporate Secretary*
EMP: 114 EST: 1968
SQ FT: 147,000
SALES (est): 860.9MM **Publicly Held**
Web: www.novanta.com
SIC: 3699 3845   Laser systems and
   equipment; Laser systems and equipment,
   medical

(G-6247)
NOVANTA INC
Also Called: Celera Motion
125 Middlesex Tpke (01730-1409)
PHONE.............................781 266-5200
Matthijs Glasta, *CEO*
EMP: 50
Web: www.celeramotion.com
SIC: 3829   Measuring and controlling
   devices, nec
PA: Novanta Inc.
   125 Middlesex Tpke
   Bedford MA 01730

(G-6248)
NOVANTA INC
125 Middlesex Tpke (01730-1409)
PHONE.............................781 266-5700
EMP: 188
Web: www.novanta.com
SIC: 3829   Measuring and controlling
   devices, nec
PA: Novanta Inc.
   125 Middlesex Tpke
   Bedford MA 01730

(G-6249)
NYOBOLT INC
Also Called: Nyobolt
4 Crosby Dr (01730-1402)
PHONE.............................978 884-2220
Sai Shivareddy, *CEO*
Prashant Patel, *Prin*
Brian Barnett, *Treas*
Andy Matthes, *Prin*
EMP: 8 EST: 2020
SALES (est): 1.11MM **Privately Held**
Web: www.nyobolt.com
SIC: 3691   Storage batteries

(G-6250)
OCULAR THERAPEUTIX INC (PA)
Also Called: Ocular Therapeutix
24 Crosby Dr (01730-1402)
PHONE.............................781 357-4000
Antony C Mattessich, *Pr*
Charles Warden, *
Donald Notman, *CFO*
Michael Goldstein, *CMO*
EMP: 40 EST: 2006
SALES (est): 51.49MM
SALES (corp-wide): 51.49MM **Publicly
Held**
Web: www.ocutx.com
SIC: 2834   Druggists' preparations
   (pharmaceuticals)

(G-6251)
ORACLE AMERICA INC
100 Crosby Dr (01730-1438)
PHONE.............................781 328-4770

EMP: 25
SALES (corp-wide): 49.95B **Publicly Held**
Web: www.oracle.com
SIC: 3571 Minicomputers
HQ: Oracle America, Inc.
500 Oracle Pkwy
Redwood City CA 94065
650 506-7000

(G-6252)
PERMA INCORPORATED
Also Called: Industrial Floor Finishes, Div
605 Springs Rd (01730-1195)
PHONE.....................978 667-5161
Peter H Stevens, *Pr*
Dorothy Stevens, *Stockholder*
EMP: 16 **EST:** 1950
SQ FT: 12,400
SALES (est): 2.2MM **Privately Held**
Web: www.perma.com
SIC: 2842 2851 Cleaning or polishing
preparations, nec; Lacquers, varnishes,
enamels, and other coatings

(G-6253)
PORT OIL CORP
60 Carlisle Rd (01730-1568)
PHONE.....................617 926-3500
Daniel Goodrich, *Prin*
EMP: 7 **EST:** 1965
SALES (est): 273.87K **Privately Held**
SIC: 1389 Oil field services, nec

(G-6254)
PULMATRIX INC (PA)
36 Crosby Dr Ste 100 (01730-1447)
PHONE.....................781 357-2333
Ted Raad, *CEO*
Mark Iwicki, *Ch Bd*
William E Duke Junior, *CFO*
James Roach, *CMO*
EMP: 16 **EST:** 2013
SQ FT: 21,810
SALES (est): 6.07MM
SALES (corp-wide): 6.07MM **Publicly Held**
Web: www.pulmatrix.com
SIC: 2834 Druggists' preparations
(pharmaceuticals)

(G-6255)
RAAGA GO LLC
213 Burlington Rd (01730-1468)
PHONE.....................505 983-5555
Pramod Rawal, *Organizer*
EMP: 8 **EST:** 2018
SALES (est): 114.3K **Privately Held**
Web: www.raagatogo.com
SIC: 2045 Prepared flour mixes and doughs

(G-6256)
**RAYTHEON LGSTICS SPPORT
TRNING (DH)**
180 Hartwell Rd (01730-2443)
PHONE.....................310 647-9438
William H Swanson, *Pr*
EMP: 11 **EST:** 1980
SALES (est): 145.05K
SALES (corp-wide): 68.92B **Publicly Held**
SIC: 3761 Guided missiles and space
vehicles, research and development
HQ: Raytheon Company
870 Winter St
Waltham MA 02451
781 522-3000

(G-6257)
REDSTONE AGGREGATOR LP
174 Middlesex Tpke (01730-1408)
PHONE.....................781 515-5000

Rohit Ghai, *CEO*
EMP: 23
SALES (est): 442.47K
SALES (corp-wide): 1.44B **Privately Held**
SIC: 7372 Prepackaged software
PA: Rsa Security Llc
176 Middlesex Tpke
Bedford MA 01730
800 995-5095

(G-6258)
REDSTONE BUYER LLC
174 Middlesex Tpke (01730-1408)
PHONE.....................781 515-5000
Rohit Ghai, *Managing Member*
EMP: 28 **EST:** 2020
SALES (est): 1.08MM
SALES (corp-wide): 1.44B **Privately Held**
SIC: 7372 Prepackaged software
PA: Rsa Security Llc
176 Middlesex Tpke
Bedford MA 01730
800 995-5095

(G-6259)
REDSTONE GP HOLDCO 1 LLC
174 Middlesex Tpke (01730-1408)
PHONE.....................781 515-5000
Rohit Ghai, *CEO*
EMP: 24
SALES (est): 481.91K
SALES (corp-wide): 1.44B **Privately Held**
SIC: 7372 Prepackaged software
PA: Rsa Security Llc
176 Middlesex Tpke
Bedford MA 01730
800 995-5095

(G-6260)
REDSTONE GP HOLDCO 2 LLC
174 Middlesex Tpke (01730-1408)
PHONE.....................781 515-5000
Rohit Ghai, *CEO*
EMP: 24
SALES (est): 481.91K
SALES (corp-wide): 1.44B **Privately Held**
SIC: 7372 Prepackaged software
PA: Rsa Security Llc
176 Middlesex Tpke
Bedford MA 01730
800 995-5095

(G-6261)
REDSTONE HOLDCO 1 LP
174 Middlesex Tpke (01730-1408)
PHONE.....................781 515-5000
Rohit Ghai, *CEO*
EMP: 23
SALES (est): 436.16K
SALES (corp-wide): 1.44B **Privately Held**
SIC: 7372 Prepackaged software
PA: Rsa Security Llc
176 Middlesex Tpke
Bedford MA 01730
800 995-5095

(G-6262)
REDSTONE HOLDCO 2 LP
174 Middlesex Tpke (01730-1408)
PHONE.....................781 515-5000
Rohit Ghai, *CEO*
EMP: 23 **EST:** 2020
SALES (est): 436.16K
SALES (corp-wide): 1.44B **Privately Held**
SIC: 7372 Prepackaged software
PA: Rsa Security Llc
176 Middlesex Tpke
Bedford MA 01730
800 995-5095

(G-6263)
**REDSTONE INTRMDATE
ARCHER HLDC**
174 Middlesex Tpke (01730-1408)
PHONE.....................781 515-5000
Rohit Ghai, *CEO*
EMP: 11
SALES (est): 587.71K
SALES (corp-wide): 1.44B **Privately Held**
SIC: 7372 Prepackaged software
PA: Rsa Security Llc
176 Middlesex Tpke
Bedford MA 01730
800 995-5095

(G-6264)
**REDSTONE INTRMDATE FRI
HLDCO L**
174 Middlesex Tpke (01730-1408)
PHONE.....................781 515-5000
Rohit Ghai, *CEO*
EMP: 11
SALES (est): 463.85K
SALES (corp-wide): 1.44B **Privately Held**
SIC: 7372 Prepackaged software
PA: Rsa Security Llc
176 Middlesex Tpke
Bedford MA 01730
800 995-5095

(G-6265)
**REDSTONE INTRMDATE SCRID
HLDCO**
174 Middlesex Tpke (01730-1408)
PHONE.....................781 515-5000
Rohit Ghai, *CEO*
EMP: 10
SALES (est): 587.71K
SALES (corp-wide): 1.44B **Privately Held**
SIC: 7372 Prepackaged software
PA: Rsa Security Llc
176 Middlesex Tpke
Bedford MA 01730
800 995-5095

(G-6266)
REDSTONE PARENT LP
174 Middlesex Tpke (01730-1408)
PHONE.....................781 515-5000
Rohit Ghai, *CEO*
EMP: 23
SALES (est): 436.16K
SALES (corp-wide): 1.44B **Privately Held**
SIC: 7372 Prepackaged software
PA: Rsa Security Llc
176 Middlesex Tpke
Bedford MA 01730
800 995-5095

(G-6267)
RHEALTH CORPORATION
1 Oak Park Dr Ste 2 (01730-1421)
PHONE.....................617 913-7630
Eugene Chan, *CEO*
EMP: 22 **EST:** 2014
SALES (est): 1.37MM **Privately Held**
Web: www.rhealth.com
SIC: 3841 Surgical and medical instruments

(G-6268)
RSA SECURITY LLC (PA)
176 Middlesex Tpke (01730-1408)
P.O. Box 530234 (30353-0234)
PHONE.....................800 995-5095
Rohit Ghai, *CEO*
Stuart Weigensber, *
▲ **EMP:** 750 **EST:** 1986
SQ FT: 328,000
SALES (est): 1.44B

SALES (corp-wide): 1.44B **Privately Held**
Web: www.rsa.com
SIC: 3577 7372 7373 Computer peripheral
equipment, nec; Prepackaged software;
Computer integrated systems design

(G-6269)
SOFT ROBOTICS INC
32 Crosby Dr Ste 101 (01730-1448)
PHONE.....................617 391-0612
Carl Vause, *CEO*
Peter Biro, *
Mark Chiappetta, *
Patti Modzelewski, *
EMP: 56 **EST:** 2012
SALES (est): 5.68MM **Privately Held**
Web: www.softroboticsinc.com
SIC: 8731 3549 3569 Commercial physical
research; Assembly machines, including
robotic; Robots, assembly line: industrial
and commercial

(G-6270)
**SPERRY PRODUCT INNOVATION
INC**
12 Deangelo Dr (01730-2204)
PHONE.....................781 271-1400
Laurence Sperry, *Pr*
Dana Calumby Ctrl, *Prin*
▲ **EMP:** 11 **EST:** 1989
SQ FT: 6,500
SALES (est): 1.88MM **Privately Held**
Web: www.sperryinc.com
SIC: 3565 Packaging machinery

(G-6271)
SPIRE SOLAR INC (HQ)
1 Patriots Park (01730-2326)
P.O. Box 9 (01730-0009)
PHONE.....................781 275-6000
Roger Little, *CEO*
EMP: 9 **EST:** 2003
SALES (est): 3.25MM
SALES (corp-wide): 32.62MM **Privately
Held**
Web: www.eternalsun.com
SIC: 3433 5074 8731 Solar heaters and
collectors; Heating equipment and panels,
solar; Energy research
PA: Spire Corporation
25 Linnell Cir
Billerica MA 01821
978 584-3958

(G-6272)
SUDBURY SYSTEMS INC
Also Called: Rtas Systems
200 Great Rd Ste 211 (01730-2799)
P.O. Box 428 (01730-0428)
PHONE.....................800 876-8888
Gerald T Delaney, *CEO*
EMP: 29 **EST:** 1972
SQ FT: 7,920
SALES (est): 869.57K **Privately Held**
Web: www.rtas.com
SIC: 3579 3572 Dictating machines;
Computer storage devices

(G-6273)
**THERMACELL REPELLENTS
INC**
32 Crosby Dr Ste 101 (01730-1448)
PHONE.....................781 541-6900
Christian Gradlmuller, *CEO*
Juliana Haddad Litterior, *Pr*
Mark Dahms, *CFO*
Rebecca Illsley, *COO*
Grant Mansfield, *CIO*
▲ **EMP:** 66 **EST:** 1981
SALES (est): 29.47MM **Privately Held**

Web: www.thermacell.com
SIC: 2879 Pesticides, agricultural or household

(G-6274)
TOXIKON CORPORATION
15 Wiggins Ave (01730-2314)
PHONE...............................978 942-5554
EMP: 69 EST: 1982
SALES (est): 2.65MM Privately Held
Web: medtech.labcorp.com
SIC: 3841 Surgical and medical instruments

(G-6275)
TROPICAL PARADISE INC
Also Called: Cool Tropics
213 Burlington Rd Ste 109 (01730-1468)
PHONE...............................781 357-1210
Fadi Massabni, *Pr*
Christy Venskus Ctrl, *Prin*
Steve Dancey, *COO*
▲ EMP: 19 EST: 1993
SQ FT: 3,084
SALES (est): 22MM Privately Held
Web: www.cool-tropics.com
SIC: 2086 Iced tea and fruit drinks, bottled and canned

(G-6276)
WERFEN USA LLC
180 Hartwell Rd (01730-2443)
PHONE...............................781 861-0710
EMP: 250 EST: 2012
SALES (est): 67.17MM Privately Held
SIC: 2835 In vitro diagnostics
PA: Werfen S.A.
    Plaza Europa, 21 - 23
    L'hospitalet De Llobregat B 08908

(G-6277)
WORDSTOCK INC
1 Sherman Ln (01730-1109)
PHONE...............................781 646-7700
Glen Legere, *Treas*
Norman Gosselin Junior, *Pr*
Michael Legere, *
EMP: 10 EST: 1984
SALES (est): 365.96K Privately Held
Web: www.wordstock.com
SIC: 5045 7372 Computer software; Prepackaged software

Belchertown
Hampshire County

(G-6278)
BASSETTE PRINTERS LLC
326 Barton Ave (01007-9277)
PHONE...............................413 781-7140
▲ EMP: 37 EST: 1898
SQ FT: 48,000
SALES (est): 1.74MM Privately Held
Web: www.bassettecompany.com
SIC: 2752 Offset printing

(G-6279)
CRAUFURD MANUFACTURING LLC
Also Called: Crauford Mfg
401 Mill Valley Rd (01007-9212)
PHONE...............................413 323-4628
Bill Lavelle, *Managing Member*
EMP: 16 EST: 2007
SQ FT: 25,000
SALES (est): 2.03MM Privately Held
SIC: 3537 Truck trailers, used in plants, docks, terminals, etc.

(G-6280)
HUMAN RESOURCE DEV PRESS (PA)
Also Called: Hrd Press
468 Amherst Rd (01007-9351)
P.O. Box 2600 (01004-2600)
PHONE...............................413 253-3488
Robert R Carkhuff, *Pr*
Gregory Carkhuff, *CFO*
Robert W Carkhuff, *Publisher*
EMP: 20 EST: 1972
SQ FT: 6,000
SALES (est): 2.15MM
SALES (corp-wide): 2.15MM Privately Held
Web: www.hrdpress.com
SIC: 2731 7812 7371 Books, publishing only ; Video tape production; Computer software development

(G-6281)
NORTHEAST TREATERS INC (HQ)
201 Springfield Rd (01007-9039)
P.O. Box 802 (01007-0802)
PHONE...............................413 323-7811
David A Reed, *Pr*
Douglas C Elder, *
Charles Geiger, *
Henry G Page Junior, *Dir*
David Sutherland, *
EMP: 25 EST: 1985
SQ FT: 6,100
SALES (est): 11.6MM
SALES (corp-wide): 183.72MM Privately Held
Web: www.culpeperwood.com
SIC: 2491 Wood preserving
PA: Jefferson Homebuilders, Inc.
    501 N Main St
    Culpeper VA 22701
    540 825-5898

Bellingham
Norfolk County

(G-6282)
AERIAL WIRELESS SERVICES LLC
125 Depot St (02019-1460)
PHONE...............................508 657-1213
Cory Gaffney, *CEO*
John Kilcoyne, *
EMP: 85 EST: 2013
SALES (est): 8.11MM Privately Held
Web: www.qualtekservices.com
SIC: 1731 1611 3663 Electrical work; General contractor, highway and street construction; Antennas, transmitting and communications

(G-6283)
ALGONQUIN INDUSTRIES INC (PA)
139 Farm St (02019-1266)
P.O. Box 176 (02019-0176)
PHONE...............................508 966-4600
Kazmier J Kasper, *Pr*
Eddie Frietas, *
Doreen L Porter, *
EMP: 49 EST: 1974
SQ FT: 45,000
SALES (est): 12MM
SALES (corp-wide): 12MM Privately Held
Web: www.algonquinindustries.com
SIC: 3444 Sheet metalwork

(G-6284)
ALLEN WOODWORKING LLC
200 Center St (02019-1804)
PHONE...............................617 306-6479
Daniel Allen Ritts, *Prin*
EMP: 8 EST: 2014
SALES (est): 316.48K Privately Held
SIC: 2431 Millwork

(G-6285)
ANTRON ENGRG & MCH CO INC
170 Mechanic St (02019-3106)
PHONE...............................508 966-2803
Anthony F Denietolis, *Pr*
John Kauker Iv, *Treas*
Lillian T Kauker, *
Allen Massie, *
EMP: 85 EST: 1985
SQ FT: 30,000
SALES (est): 18.58MM Privately Held
Web: www.antroneng.com
SIC: 3599 Machine shop, jobbing and repair

(G-6286)
B & L MANUFACTURING INC
8 William Way (02019-1527)
PHONE...............................508 966-3066
Lawrence Lowther, *Pr*
EMP: 9 EST: 1983
SQ FT: 6,000
SALES (est): 314.37K Privately Held
SIC: 3911 Jewelry, precious metal

(G-6287)
BOSTON PIEZO-OPTICS INC
38b Maple St (02019-3011)
P.O. Box 80 (02053-0080)
PHONE...............................508 966-4988
EMP: 12 EST: 1994
SQ FT: 10,000
SALES (est): 1.8MM Privately Held
Web: www.bostonpiezooptics.com
SIC: 3826 3827 5049 Spectroscopic and other optical properties measuring equip.; Optical instruments and lenses; Optical goods

(G-6288)
CHOCORUA VALLEY LUMBER COMPANY
1210 Pulaski Blvd (02019-2127)
PHONE...............................508 883-6878
Lloyd E Rhodes, *Pr*
Daniel Rhodes, *VP*
Barbara Rhodes, *Sec*
Steve Goldman, *Clerk*
EMP: 12 EST: 1948
SQ FT: 9,600
SALES (est): 451.08K Privately Held
Web: www.bellinghamlumber.com
SIC: 2421 Sawmills and planing mills, general

(G-6289)
DAUPHINAIS CONCRETE
79 Hartford Ave (02019-1026)
PHONE...............................508 657-0941
EMP: 7 EST: 2016
SALES (est): 225.94K Privately Held
Web: www.dauphinaisconcrete.com
SIC: 5211 5032 3273 Cement; Concrete and cinder building products; Ready-mixed concrete

(G-6290)
GRAYCER SCREW PRODUCTS CO INC
113 Depot St (02019-1460)
P.O. Box 677 (02019-0677)

PHONE...............................508 966-1810
James J Cerutti, *Pr*
◆ EMP: 31 EST: 1955
SQ FT: 15,000
SALES (est): 4.68MM Privately Held
Web: www.graycer.com
SIC: 3599 Machine shop, jobbing and repair

(G-6291)
HI-TECH METALS INC
Also Called: Hitech Metals
139 Farm St (02019-1266)
P.O. Box 176 (02019-0176)
PHONE...............................508 966-0332
Kazmier J Kasper, *Pr*
Kazmier Kasper, *
Joseph Kasper, *
EMP: 60 EST: 1985
SQ FT: 45,000
SALES (est): 7.15MM Privately Held
Web: www.algonquinindustries.com
SIC: 3444 Sheet metalwork

(G-6292)
HILLIARD PRECISION PRODUCTS LLC
Also Called: Ace Torwel
125 Depot St (02019-1460)
PHONE...............................508 541-9100
EMP: 25
SIC: 3914 Stainless steel ware

(G-6293)
MANNING WAY CPITL PARTNERS LLC
Also Called: Consolidated Coating Company
5 Williams Way (02019-1527)
P.O. Box 747 (02019-0747)
PHONE...............................508 966-4800
Jeffrey Rudman, *Pr*
EMP: 25 EST: 1979
SQ FT: 31,000
SALES (est): 4MM Privately Held
Web: www.consolidatedcoating.com
SIC: 3479 Coating of metals and formed products

(G-6294)
MASSACHUSETTS BEV ALIANCE LLC
190 Mechanic St (02019-3161)
PHONE...............................617 701-6238
EMP: 16 EST: 2011
SALES (est): 2.85MM Privately Held
Web: www.hgd.beer
SIC: 2082 Beer (alcoholic beverage)

(G-6295)
MEDICAL CMPNENT SPCIALISTS INC (PA)
42 William Way (02019-1527)
PHONE...............................508 966-0992
Jim Moore, *Pr*
Linda Rubin, *Off Mgr*
EMP: 20 EST: 2006
SQ FT: 3,874
SALES (est): 2.66MM Privately Held
Web: www.medicalcomponentspecialists.com
SIC: 3479 Coating of metals and formed products

(G-6296)
MESSER LLC
Also Called: Boc Gases
92a Depot St (02019-1439)
PHONE...............................508 966-3148
Joe Marchetti, *Mgr*
EMP: 10

SALES (corp-wide): 1.63B **Privately Held**
Web: www.messeramericas.com
SIC: 2813 Industrial gases
HQ: Messer Llc
    200 Smrst Corp Blvd # 7000
    Bridgewater NJ 08807
    800 755-9277

(G-6297)
NEFAB PACKAGING NORTH EAST LLC
23 Williams Way (02019-1527)
PHONE..............................800 258-4692
Mike Pectorelli, *Mgr*
EMP: 27 **EST:** 2015
SALES (est): 412.92K
SALES (corp-wide): 903.19MM **Privately Held**
SIC: 2448 2449 2441 Pallets, wood; Rectangular boxes and crates, wood; Nailed wood boxes and shook
HQ: Nefab Packaging, Inc.
    204 Airline Dr Ste 100
    Coppell TX 75019
    469 444-5268

(G-6298)
NEWPRO OPERATING LLC
Also Called: Newpro Mfg
26 Williams Way (02019-1527)
PHONE..............................781 933-4100
EMP: 14
SALES (corp-wide): 25.79MM **Privately Held**
Web: www.newpro.com
SIC: 2431 Windows and window parts and trim, wood
PA: Newpro Operating, Llc
    26 Cedar St
    Woburn MA 01801
    781 933-4100

(G-6299)
OLIMPIA INDUSTRIES INC
175 North St (02019-1756)
PHONE..............................508 966-3392
James Mcgrath, *Owner*
EMP: 10 **EST:** 2009
SALES (est): 391.67K **Privately Held**
SIC: 3999 Manufacturing industries, nec

(G-6300)
SCANDIA KITCHENS INC
38 Maple St (02019-3011)
P.O. Box 456 (02019-0456)
PHONE..............................508 966-0300
David Dorrer, *Pr*
Linda Dorrer, *Sec*
EMP: 20 **EST:** 1968
SQ FT: 22,000
SALES (est): 641.47K **Privately Held**
Web: www.scandiakitchens.com
SIC: 2434 Wood kitchen cabinets

(G-6301)
VAN - WAL MACHINE INC
97 Depot St (02019-1437)
P.O. Box 800 (02019-0800)
PHONE..............................508 966-0733
John Van Der Wal, *Pr*
Karin Van Der Wal, *Clerk*
Eric Van Der Wal, *Prin*
Johann Van Der Wal, *Prin*
Leo Van Der Wal, *Prin*
EMP: 18 **EST:** 1972
SQ FT: 10,000
SALES (est): 2.23MM **Privately Held**
Web: www.vanwalmachine.com
SIC: 3599 Machine shop, jobbing and repair

(G-6302)
VARNEY BROS SAND & GRAVEL INC
Also Called: Varney Bros Concrete
79 Hartford Ave (02019-1026)
P.O. Box 94 (02019-0094)
PHONE..............................508 966-1313
Linda Varney, *Pr*
EMP: 15 **EST:** 1938
SQ FT: 1,800
SALES (est): 913.42K **Privately Held**
SIC: 3273 1442 Ready-mixed concrete; Sand mining

(G-6303)
WRENTHAM TOOL GROUP LLC
155 Farm St (02019-1105)
PHONE..............................508 966-2332
EMP: 40 **EST:** 1948
SQ FT: 18,000
SALES (est): 9.71MM **Privately Held**
Web: www.wrenthamtool.com
SIC: 3423 Hand and edge tools, nec

Belmont
Middlesex County

(G-6304)
BELMONT PRINTING COMPANY
46 Brighton St (02478-4172)
PHONE..............................617 484-0833
Stanley D Garfield, *Owner*
EMP: 8 **EST:** 1965
SQ FT: 8,000
SALES (est): 489.36K **Privately Held**
Web: www.belmontprinting.com
SIC: 2752 2796 2759 2791 Offset printing; Platemaking services; Letterpress printing; Typesetting

(G-6305)
CUSTOM LEARNING DESIGNS INC
375 Concord Ave Ste 101 (02478-3045)
PHONE..............................617 489-1702
Donna M Kilcoyne, *Pr*
EMP: 75 **EST:** 1979
SQ FT: 23,025
SALES (est): 7.15MM **Privately Held**
Web: www.cldinc.com
SIC: 3999 Education aids, devices and supplies

(G-6306)
HORIZON INTERNATIONAL INC
385 Concord Ave Ste 104 (02478-3037)
PHONE..............................617 489-6666
Ram Ghanta, *Prin*
EMP: 13 **EST:** 2013
SALES (est): 980.72K **Privately Held**
Web: www.horizon-international.com
SIC: 7372 Prepackaged software

(G-6307)
LONGRUN LLC
Also Called: Extra Origin Foods
464 Common St U 207 (02478-2704)
PHONE..............................617 758-8674
EMP: 13 **EST:** 2007
SQ FT: 1,000
SALES (est): 1.61MM **Privately Held**
SIC: 2099 Food preparations, nec

(G-6308)
MYSTIC VALLEY WHEEL WORKS INC (PA)
Also Called: Belmont Wheel Works

480 Trapelo Rd (02478-1422)
PHONE..............................617 489-3577
Clinton Paige, *Pr*
Peter Mooney, *VP*
EMP: 32 **EST:** 1977
SQ FT: 9,000
SALES (est): 4.53MM
SALES (corp-wide): 4.53MM **Privately Held**
Web: www.wheelworks.com
SIC: 5941 7699 3751 Bicycle and bicycle parts; Bicycle repair shop; Bicycles and related parts

(G-6309)
PURECOAT INTERNATIONAL LLC
30 Brighton St (02478-4172)
PHONE..............................561 844-0100
Thomas Mahoney, *Brnch Mgr*
EMP: 44
SALES (corp-wide): 6.32MM **Privately Held**
Web: www.purecoat.com
SIC: 3313 3559 Electrometallurgical products; Metal finishing equipment for plating, etc.
PA: Purecoat International, Llc
    3301 Elec Way Ste B
    West Palm Beach FL 33407
    561 844-0100

(G-6310)
PURECOAT NORTH LLC
39 Hittinger St (02478-4039)
P.O. Box 107 (02478-0902)
PHONE..............................617 489-2750
Marshall Menachem, *
▼ **EMP:** 55 **EST:** 2002
SQ FT: 40,000
SALES (est): 5.22MM **Privately Held**
Web: www.purecoatnorth.com
SIC: 3471 Electroplating of metals or formed products

(G-6311)
RADIANT SAGE VENTURES LLC
464 Common St Pmb 133 (02478-2704)
PHONE..............................855 723-7243
Venkatesan Thangaraj, *CEO*
Chander Jain, *COO*
EMP: 22 **EST:** 2009
SALES (est): 1.52MM **Privately Held**
Web: www.radiantsage.com
SIC: 7372 Prepackaged software

(G-6312)
SMART SOFTWARE INC
4 Hill Rd Ste 2 (02478-4351)
PHONE..............................617 489-2743
Greg Hartunian, *Pr*
Nelson Hartunian, *Ch Bd*
Thomas R Willemain, *Senior Vice President Development*
Kate Afonso, *VP*
EMP: 22 **EST:** 1981
SQ FT: 4,200
SALES (est): 3.06MM **Privately Held**
Web: www.smartcorp.com
SIC: 7372 Business oriented computer software

(G-6313)
TAKEDA
33 Brighton St (02478-4169)
PHONE..............................617 594-7199
EMP: 9 **EST:** 2019
SALES (est): 178.23K **Privately Held**
Web: jobs.takeda.com

SIC: 2834 Pharmaceutical preparations

Berkley
Bristol County

(G-6314)
COMMON CROSSING INC
11 N Main St (02779-1312)
PHONE..............................508 822-8225
Elizabeth Jackson, *Prin*
EMP: 7 **EST:** 2010
SALES (est): 222.39K **Privately Held**
SIC: 2082 Beer (alcoholic beverage)

(G-6315)
CORRUGATED STITCHER SERVICE
88 Jerome St (02779-1007)
PHONE..............................508 823-2844
Charles Laplante, *Prin*
EMP: 7 **EST:** 2008
SALES (est): 110.46K **Privately Held**
SIC: 2653 Boxes, corrugated: made from purchased materials

(G-6316)
J & R PRE-CAST INC
16 County St (02779-1206)
PHONE..............................508 822-3311
Robert Katon, *Pr*
Robert Katon Junior, *VP*
Judith Katon, *Treas*
EMP: 12 **EST:** 1954
SQ FT: 4,000
SALES (est): 1.88MM **Privately Held**
Web: www.jrprecast.com
SIC: 3272 Concrete products, precast, nec

Berkshire
Berkshire County

(G-6317)
SHIRE CITY HERBALS INC
87 Old State Rd (01224-9539)
PHONE..............................413 344-4740
Amy Huebner, *Admn*
EMP: 19 **EST:** 2011
SALES (est): 2.32MM **Privately Held**
SIC: 2099 Food preparations, nec

Berlin
Worcester County

(G-6318)
A1 PALLETS INC
163 River Rd W (01503-1648)
P.O. Box 1263 (05757-1263)
PHONE..............................978 838-2720
EMP: 7
SALES (est): 864.52K **Privately Held**
SIC: 2448 Pallets, wood and wood with metal

(G-6319)
MASSACHUSETTS BROKEN STONE CO (PA)
Also Called: Holden Trap Rock Company
332 Sawyerhill Rd (01503-1206)
P.O. Box 276 (01503-0276)
PHONE..............................978 838-9999
Andrew Forest, *Pr*
Richard Harrison, *Treas*
EMP: 7 **EST:** 1908
SQ FT: 5,000
SALES (est): 4.38MM

SALES (corp-wide): 4.38MM **Privately Held**
Web: www.massbroken.com
SIC: **2951 1429** Concrete, bituminous; Igneus rock, crushed and broken-quarrying

(G-6320)
ORGANOMATION ASSOCIATES INC
266 River Rd W (01503-1699)
PHONE..................................978 838-7300
Andrew R Mcniven, *Pr*
Heather A King, *Dir*
David Oliva, *Mktg Mgr*
EMP: 15 EST: 1959
SQ FT: 5,500
SALES (est): 2MM **Privately Held**
Web: www.organomation.com
SIC: **5049 3826** Laboratory equipment, except medical or dental; Chromatographic equipment, laboratory type

---

Beverly
Essex County

(G-6321)
3EO HEALTH INC
48 Dunham Rd Ste 4350 (01915-1844)
PHONE..................................508 308-4805
Jeremy Schubert, *CEO*
John Wu, *
EMP: 28 EST: 2020
SALES (est): 2.28MM **Privately Held**
SIC: **3841** Surgical and medical instruments

(G-6322)
7AC TECHNOLOGIES INC
100 Cummings Ctr Ste 265g (01915-6143)
PHONE..................................781 574-1348
Jed Swan, *CEO*
Shawn Montgomery, *COO*
EMP: 15 EST: 2009
SALES (est): 3.24MM
SALES (corp-wide): 15.16B **Publicly Held**
Web: www.7actech.com
SIC: **3822 3585 3564** Air flow controllers, air conditioning and refrigeration; Heating and air conditioning combination units; Filters, air: furnaces, air conditioning equipment, etc.
PA: Emerson Electric Co.
8000 West Florissant Ave
Saint Louis MO 63136
314 553-2000

(G-6323)
AERO MANUFACTURING CORP
100 Sam Fonzo Dr Ste 1 (01915-1059)
PHONE..................................978 720-1000
Salvatore Fonzo, *CEO*
David Fonzo, *
EMP: 80 EST: 1962
SQ FT: 30,000
SALES (est): 18.23MM **Privately Held**
Web: www.aeromanufacturing.com
SIC: **3444 3469 7692** Forming machine work, sheet metal; Stamping metal for the trade; Brazing

(G-6324)
AMERICAN & SCHOEN MACHINERY CO
100 Cummings Ctr Ste 140a (01915-6135)
PHONE..................................978 524-0168
Edmund Skoniecki Junior, *Pr*
Jerry Hughes, *
Debra Turner, *
Georg Nikel, *

Juergen Schneider, *
▲ EMP: 25 EST: 1971
SQ FT: 28,000
SALES (est): 5.87MM **Privately Held**
Web: www.asm-schoen.com
SIC: **3559** Shoe making and repairing machinery
HQ: Schoen + Sandt Machinery Gmbh
Lemberger Str. 82
Pirmasens RP 66955

(G-6325)
ARCHERDX INC
123 Brimbal Ave (01915-1869)
PHONE..................................978 232-3570
Jason Myers, *CEO*
EMP: 10 EST: 2014
SQ FT: 5,000
SALES (est): 404.42K **Privately Held**
Web: www.archerdx.com
SIC: **2282** Knitting yarn: twisting, winding, or spooling

(G-6326)
ARMSTRONG MACHINE CO INC
117 Elliott St Ste 3 (01915-3252)
PHONE..................................978 232-9466
Raymond Armstrong, *Pr*
EMP: 14 EST: 1985
SQ FT: 14,000
SALES (est): 729.47K **Privately Held**
SIC: **3569 3555** Filters; Printing trades machinery

(G-6327)
AUBURN FILTERSENSE LLC
Also Called: Filtersense
800 Cummings Ctr Ste 355w (01915-6174)
PHONE..................................978 777-2460
EMP: 47 EST: 2017
SALES (est): 10.16MM **Privately Held**
Web: www.filtersense.com
SIC: **3829** Thermometers and temperature sensors
HQ: Nederman Holding Usa, Inc.
4404a Chesapeake Dr
Charlotte NC 28216
704 859-2723

(G-6328)
AUBURN INTERNATIONAL INC
800 Cummings Ctr Ste 355w (01915-6174)
PHONE..................................978 777-2460
Ronald L Dechene, *Pr*
▼ EMP: 14 EST: 1973
SQ FT: 23,000
SALES (est): 473.42K **Privately Held**
SIC: **3823** Industrial flow and liquid measuring instruments

(G-6329)
AUBURN SYSTEMS LLC
800 Cummings Ctr Ste 355w (01915-6174)
P.O. Box 2008 (01923-5008)
PHONE..................................978 777-2460
Ronald L Dechene, *Pr*
EMP: 7 EST: 1999
SQ FT: 10,000
SALES (est): 1.25MM **Privately Held**
Web: www.auburnfiltersense.com
SIC: **3823 5084** Industrial flow and liquid measuring instruments; Industrial machinery and equipment

(G-6330)
AXCELIS TECHNOLOGIES INC (PA)
Also Called: Axcelis
108 Cherry Hill Dr (01915-1066)
PHONE..................................978 787-4000

Russell J Low, *Pr*
Mary G Puma, *
Kevin J Brewer, *Ex VP*
Lynnette C Fallon, *Corporate Secretary*
Douglas A Lawson, *Corporate Marketing Vice President*
▲ EMP: 582 EST: 1978
SQ FT: 417,000
SALES (est): 920MM
SALES (corp-wide): 920MM **Publicly Held**
Web: www.axcelis.com
SIC: **3559 3829** Semiconductor manufacturing machinery; Ion chambers

(G-6331)
AXYA MEDICAL INC
100 Cummings Ctr Ste 444c (01915-6132)
PHONE..................................978 232-9997
EMP: 17 EST: 1996
SQ FT: 17,000
SALES (est): 329.25K **Privately Held**
SIC: **3841 3845 3842** Surgical and medical instruments; Electromedical equipment; Surgical appliances and supplies

(G-6332)
BEVERLY CITIZEN
48 Dunham Rd (01915-1844)
PHONE..................................978 927-2777
EMP: 8 EST: 1996
SALES (est): 128.27K **Privately Held**
SIC: **2711** Newspapers, publishing and printing

(G-6333)
BIOHELIX CORPORATION
500 Cummings Ctr Ste 5550 (01915-6517)
PHONE..................................978 927-5056
Huimin Kong Ph.d., *Pr*
EMP: 13 EST: 2004
SQ FT: 15,000
SALES (corp-wide): 4.38MM
SALES (corp-wide): 3.27B **Publicly Held**
Web: www.quidelortho.com
SIC: **2836** Biological products, except diagnostic
HQ: Quidel Corporation
9975 Summers Ridge Rd
San Diego CA 92121
858 552-1100

(G-6334)
BLUEFIN BIOMEDICINE INC
32 Tozer Rd (01915-5510)
PHONE..................................925 524-3417
John Zicaro, *Mgr*
EMP: 25 EST: 2016
SALES (est): 4.92MM **Privately Held**
Web: www.bluefinbiomed.com
SIC: **2834** Pharmaceutical preparations

(G-6335)
BOSTON BRISKET COMPANY INC
323 Dodge St (01915-1262)
PHONE..................................617 442-8814
Jack Epstein, *Pr*
EMP: 10 EST: 1984
SALES (est): 1.07MM **Privately Held**
Web: www.bostonbrisket.com
SIC: **2011** Meat packing plants

(G-6336)
BUSINESS AND PROF EXCH INC
Also Called: Melros-Wakefield Answering Svc
100 Cummings Ctr Ste 344c (01915-6136)
PHONE..................................978 556-4100
EMP: 40 EST: 1976
SQ FT: 3,000
SALES (est): 6.71MM **Privately Held**

Web: www.bpeinc.com
SIC: **7389 3829 3826 3825** Telephone answering service; Measuring and controlling devices, nec; Analytical instruments; Instruments to measure electricity

(G-6337)
CELLANYX DIAGNOSTICS LLC
100 Cummings Ctr Ste 451d (01915-6115)
PHONE..................................571 212-9991
Jonathan Varsanik, *VP*
Michael Manak, *VP*
Delaney Berger, *VP*
Mani Foroohar, *Sec*
EMP: 9 EST: 2013
SQ FT: 500
SALES (est): 756.45K **Privately Held**
Web: www.cellanyx.com
SIC: **2835 5047** In vitro diagnostics; Diagnostic equipment, medical

(G-6338)
CENTERLINE MACHINE COMPANY INC
60 Park St (01915-4217)
PHONE..................................978 524-8842
EMP: 16 EST: 2006
SQ FT: 6,000
SALES (est): 764.87K **Privately Held**
SIC: **3873 7539** Watches, clocks, watchcases, and parts; Machine shop, automotive

(G-6339)
CLC BIO LLC
100 Cummings Ctr Ste 407j (01915-6101)
PHONE..................................617 945-0178
EMP: 17 EST: 2006
SALES (est): 1.83MM **Privately Held**
Web: digitalinsights.qiagen.com
SIC: **7372 7371** Business oriented computer software; Custom computer programming services

(G-6340)
COMMUNICATIONS & PWR INDS LLC
CPI Beverly Microwave Division
150 Sohier Rd (01915-5536)
PHONE..................................978 922-6000
Don Coleman, *Genl Mgr*
EMP: 300
Web: www.cpii.com
SIC: **3663** Radio and t.v. communications equipment
HQ: Communications & Power Industries Llc
811 Hansen Way
Palo Alto CA 94304

(G-6341)
CONQUEST BUSINESS MEDIA INC
152 Conant St Ste 3 (01915-1659)
PHONE..................................978 299-1200
Glen White, *CEO*
Stuart Bidgood, *
John Blatnik, *
EMP: 38 EST: 2001
SQ FT: 1,800
SALES (est): 2.1MM **Privately Held**
SIC: **2721** Magazines: publishing and printing

(G-6342)
CONTRACT ENGINEERING INC
128 Park St Ste B5 (01915-3274)
PHONE..................................978 921-0501

James Robichau, *Pr*
John Galvi, *VP*
EMP: 10 **EST:** 1989
SALES (est): 463.29K **Privately Held**
SIC: 3599 Machine shop, jobbing and repair

(G-6343)
CORNELL ORTHOTICS PROSTHETICS (PA)
100 Cummings Ctr Ste 207h (01915-6104)
PHONE........................978 922-2866
Keith Cornell, *Pr*
EMP: 8 **EST:** 1985
SALES (est): 2.35MM
SALES (corp-wide): 2.35MM **Privately Held**
Web: www.cornelloandp.com
SIC: 3842 Braces, orthopedic

(G-6344)
DANVERS INDUSTRIAL PACKG CORP
39 Tozer Rd (01915-5513)
PHONE........................978 777-0020
Leo Chester Thibeault Junior, *CEO*
Jeffrey Denoncour, *
EMP: 49 **EST:** 1966
SQ FT: 85,300
SALES (est): 10.07MM **Privately Held**
Web: www.danpack.com
SIC: 3086 2631 5199 Packaging and shipping materials, foamed plastics; Container, packaging, and boxboard; Packaging materials

(G-6345)
DELTA ELECTRONICS MFG CORP
416 Cabot St (01915-3152)
P.O. Box 53 (01915-0053)
PHONE........................978 927-1060
Diane J Delaney, *Pr*
Diane J Delaney, *Treas*
Edward J Skurski, *General Vice President*
Justin Delaney, *
William H Sweeney, *
▲ **EMP:** 115 **EST:** 1955
SQ FT: 65,000
SALES (est): 21.93MM **Privately Held**
Web: www.deltarf.com
SIC: 3678 3679 Electronic connectors; Microwave components

(G-6346)
ENON COPY INC (PA)
Also Called: Minuteman Press
409 Cabot St Ste 4 (01915-3177)
P.O. Box 89 (01915-0002)
PHONE........................978 927-8757
Joseph Bubriski, *Pr*
Judith H Bubriski, *VP*
EMP: 8 **EST:** 1982
SQ FT: 5,000
SALES (est): 1.17MM
SALES (corp-wide): 1.17MM **Privately Held**
Web: www.minutemanpress.com
SIC: 2752 Commercial printing, lithographic

(G-6347)
FEMTONICS USA INC
100 Cummings Ctr Ste 265f (01915-6144)
PHONE........................361 210-3349
Gergely Katona, *CEO*
Joseph Mercurio, *Sec*
EMP: 45
SALES (est): 1.28MM **Privately Held**
SIC: 3841 Corneal microscopes

(G-6348)
FLOW CONTROL LLC
Also Called: Flojet
100 Cummings Ctr (01915-6115)
PHONE........................978 281-0440
John Sullivan, *VP*
◆ **EMP:** 50 **EST:** 2011
SALES (est): 24.56MM **Publicly Held**
SIC: 3561 Pumps and pumping equipment
PA: Xylem Inc.
301 Water St Se Ste 201
Washington DC 20003

(G-6349)
FREUDENBERG MEDICAL LLC
Also Called: Freudenberg Nok
40 Sam Fonzo Dr (01915-1034)
PHONE........................978 281-2023
Edward Callahan, *VP*
EMP: 174
SALES (corp-wide): 12.23B **Privately Held**
Web: www.freudenbergmedical.com
SIC: 3842 Prosthetic appliances
HQ: Freudenberg Medical, Llc
1110 Mark Ave
Carpinteria CA 93013
805 684-3304

(G-6350)
GATEHOUSE MEDIA MASS I INC (HQ)
Also Called: Community Newspaper
48 Dunham Rd (01915-1844)
PHONE........................585 598-0030
Garrett J Cummings Attorney, *Prin*
Kirk Davis, *
EMP: 1200 **EST:** 2001
SALES (est): 217.83MM
SALES (corp-wide): 2.95B **Publicly Held**
Web: www.ghmne.com
SIC: 2711 Commercial printing and newspaper publishing combined
PA: Gannett Co., Inc.
7950 Jones Branch Dr Fl 8
Mc Lean VA 22102
703 854-6000

(G-6351)
GLYCOZYM USA INC
Also Called: Glycozym
100 Cummings Ctr Ste 430j (01915-6122)
PHONE........................425 985-2556
EMP: 7 **EST:** 2009
SALES (est): 471.28K **Privately Held**
SIC: 2835 Diagnostic substances

(G-6352)
HAMILTON THORNE INC (PA)
100 Cummings Ctr Ste 465e (01915-6143)
PHONE........................978 921-2050
David Wolf, *CEO*
Meg Spencer, *Ch Bd*
Diarmaid H Douglas Hamilton, *Treas*
Michael W Bruns, *CFO*
Keith F Edwards, *Sr VP*
▼ **EMP:** 30 **EST:** 1997
SQ FT: 6,000
SALES (est): 7.66MM
SALES (corp-wide): 7.66MM **Privately Held**
Web: www.hamiltonthorne.com
SIC: 3829 3841 Measuring and controlling devices, nec; Diagnostic apparatus, medical

(G-6353)
HARMONIC DRIVE LLC (HQ)
42 Dunham Rd (01915-1844)
PHONE........................978 532-1800
▲ **EMP:** 74 **EST:** 1963
SQ FT: 34,300

SALES (est): 57.07MM **Privately Held**
Web: www.harmonicdrive.net
SIC: 3566 Speed changers, drives, and gears
PA: Harmonic Drive Systems Inc.
6-25-3, Minamioi
Shinagawa-Ku TKY 140-0

(G-6354)
HEALTHQUARTERS INC
900 Cummings Ctr (01915-6198)
PHONE........................978 922-4490
Gabrielle C Ross, *Ex Dir*
EMP: 14
SALES (corp-wide): 4.34MM **Privately Held**
Web: www.healthq.org
SIC: 3131 Quarters
PA: Healthquarters, Inc.
100 Cummings Ctr Ste 220b
Beverly MA 01915
978 927-9824

(G-6355)
HEART VALVE SOCIETY
500 Cummings Ctr Ste 4400 (01915-6518)
PHONE........................212 561-9879
Jeffrey S Borer, *Prin*
EMP: 14 **EST:** 2004
SALES (est): 143.15K **Privately Held**
Web:
www.heartvalvesocietyofamerica.org
SIC: 3592 Valves

(G-6356)
IMPOLIT ENVMTL CTRL CORP
Also Called: Filtersense
800 Cummings Ctr Ste 355 (01915-6174)
PHONE........................978 927-4304
EMP: 26 **EST:** 1994
SQ FT: 10,000
SALES (est): 1.38MM **Privately Held**
Web: www.filtersense.com
SIC: 3823 3564 Process control instruments ; Blowers and fans

(G-6357)
IXYS INTGRTED CIRCUITS DIV LLC (DH)
78 Cherry Hill Dr (01915-1065)
PHONE........................978 524-6700
Nathan Zommer, *Pr*
Arnold Agbayani, *
◆ **EMP:** 99 **EST:** 1937
SQ FT: 83,000
SALES (est): 28.25MM
SALES (corp-wide): 2.51B **Publicly Held**
Web: www.ixys.net
SIC: 3674 Semiconductors and related devices
HQ: Ixys, Llc
1590 Buckeye Dr
Milpitas CA 95035
408 457-9000

(G-6358)
JULES A GOURDEAU INC
94 Corning St (01915-3837)
P.O. Box 3 (01915-0001)
PHONE........................978 922-0102
David Kampersal, *Pr*
EMP: 8 **EST:** 1945
SQ FT: 7,500
SALES (est): 956.88K **Privately Held**
SIC: 2541 Cabinets, except refrigerated: show, display, etc.: wood

(G-6359)
KOOVERA INTERNATIONAL
186 Cabot St (01915-5846)
PHONE........................978 867-0867
EMP: 30 **EST:** 2018
SALES (est): 1.05MM **Privately Held**
SIC: 3613 Distribution boards, electric

(G-6360)
KROHNE INC (DH)
Also Called: Krohne America
55 Cherry Hill Dr (01915-1068)
PHONE........................978 535-6060
▲ **EMP:** 45 **EST:** 1981
SALES (est): 60MM
SALES (corp-wide): 719.1MM **Privately Held**
Web: us.krohne.com
SIC: 3823 Flow instruments, industrial process type
HQ: Krohne Ag
Uferstrasse 90
Basel BS 4057

(G-6361)
LAUNCHWORKS LLC
Also Called: Launchworks Manufacturing Lab
123 Brimbal Ave (01915-1869)
PHONE........................978 338-3045
Maurice Barakat, *Managing Member*
EMP: 35 **EST:** 2016
SALES (est): 8.8MM
SALES (corp-wide): 50.25MM **Privately Held**
Web: www.launchworkscdmo.com
SIC: 2836 Veterinary biological products
PA: Integreon Global, Inc.
551 Raritan Center Pkwy
Edison NJ 08837
848 229-2466

(G-6362)
LIBERTY PUBLISHING INC
100 Cummings Ctr (01915-6115)
PHONE........................978 777-8200
M Jeffrey Rosen, *Pr*
EMP: 18 **EST:** 1981
SQ FT: 6,500
SALES (est): 2.48MM **Privately Held**
Web: www.libertyink.com
SIC: 2741 2721 7319 Business service newsletters: publishing and printing; Periodicals; Distribution of advertising material or sample services

(G-6363)
MACHINE TECHNOLOGY INC
148 Sohier Rd (01915-5536)
PHONE........................978 927-1900
Danial Shatford, *Pr*
Patricia M Shatford, *Pr*
Keith Shatford, *VP*
EMP: 31 **EST:** 1977
SQ FT: 6,500
SALES (est): 460.81K **Privately Held**
Web: www.machinete.com
SIC: 3599 Machine shop, jobbing and repair

(G-6364)
MICROLINE SURGICAL INC (HQ)
Also Called: MSI
50 Dunham Rd Ste 1500 (01915-1882)
PHONE........................978 922-9810
Jean Luc Boulnois, *Ch Bd*
Sharad H Joshi, *Pr*
Jose Falcao, *CFO*
▼ **EMP:** 159 **EST:** 1987
SQ FT: 75,000
SALES (est): 50.49MM **Privately Held**
Web: www.microlinesurgical.com

SIC: 3841 Surgical and medical instruments
PA: Hoya Corporation
6-10-1, Nishishinjuku
Shinjuku-Ku TKY 160-0

(G-6365)
MICROSEMI CORPORATION
163 Cabot St (01915-5906)
PHONE...............................978 232-0040
Stephen Ouellette, *Prin*
EMP: 8
SALES (corp-wide): 8.44B **Publicly Held**
Web: www.microsemi.com
SIC: 3674 Semiconductors and related
devices
HQ: Microsemi Corporation
11861 Western Ave
Garden Grove CA 92841
949 380-6100

(G-6366)
**MICROSEMI FREQUENCY TIME
CORP**
Also Called: Microsemi
34 Tozer Rd (01915-5510)
PHONE...............................978 232-0040
Paul Bya, *Brnch Mgr*
EMP: 40
SALES (corp-wide): 8.44B **Publicly Held**
Web: www.microsemi.com
SIC: 3825 7371 Instruments to measure
electricity; Custom computer programming
services
HQ: Microsemi Frequency And Time
Corporation
3870 N 1st St
San Jose CA 95134
480 792-7200

(G-6367)
**MRP TRADING INNOVATIONS
LLC**
85 Sam Fonzo Dr (01915-1072)
PHONE...............................978 762-3900
▲ EMP: 10 EST: 2013
SQ FT: 1,200
SALES (est): 823.24K **Privately Held**
Web: www.trymilkstraws.com
SIC: 2087 Concentrates, drink

(G-6368)
**NOVA ANALYTICS
CORPORATION**
100 Cummings Ctr Ste 535n (01915-6231)
PHONE...............................781 897-1208
Jim Barbookles, *Brnch Mgr*
EMP: 31
Web: www.novavg.com
SIC: 3541 Electrochemical milling machines
HQ: Nova Analytics Corporation
11390 Amalgam Way
Gold River CA 95670
866 664-6682

(G-6369)
OAK BARREL IMPORTS LLC
421r Essex St (01915-1334)
PHONE...............................617 286-2524
▲ EMP: 8 EST: 2009
SALES (est): 456.35K **Privately Held**
Web: www.oakbarrelimports.com
SIC: 2084 Wines

(G-6370)
OBJECT FIRST (US) INC
100 Cummings Ctr Ste 207p (01915-6113)
PHONE...............................844 569-0653
David Bennett, *CEO*
EMP: 22

SALES (est): 1.29MM **Privately Held**
SIC: 7372 Business oriented computer
software

(G-6371)
PARLEE COMPOSITES INC ✪
Also Called: Parlee Cycles Inc
69 Federal St (01915-5708)
PHONE...............................978 998-4880
Robert John Harrison, *CEO*
Noelle Leblanc, *VP*
EMP: 13 EST: 2023
SALES (est): 529.33K **Privately Held**
SIC: 3751 Bicycles and related parts

(G-6372)
**PROTEUS MANUFACTURING
COMPANY INC**
100 Cummings Ctr Ste 327g (01915-6123)
PHONE...............................781 939-0919
EMP: 34
SIC: 3599 Machine shop, jobbing and repair

(G-6373)
QIAGEN BEVERLY LLC
100 Cummings Ctr Ste 407j (01915-6101)
PHONE...............................978 927-7027
George Von Oertezn, *Genl Mgr*
Michael Nolan, *
Jack Percoskie, *
▼ EMP: 65 EST: 2005
SALES (est): 21MM **Privately Held**
Web: www.enzymatics.com
SIC: 2836 Biological products, except
diagnostic
PA: Qiagen N.V.
Hulsterweg 82
Venlo LI 5912

(G-6374)
QUARTO PUBG GROUP USA INC
100 Cummings Ctr Ste 265g (01915-6143)
PHONE...............................978 282-9590
Ken Fund, *Pr*
EMP: 22
SALES (corp-wide): 92.94MM **Privately
Held**
Web: www.quarto.com
SIC: 2731 Books, publishing only
HQ: Quarto Publishing Group Usa Inc.
401 2nd Ave N Ste 310
Minneapolis MN 55401
612 344-8100

(G-6375)
QUARTO PUBG GROUP USA INC
Also Called: BECker&mayer
100 Cummings Ctr Ste 253c (01915-6133)
PHONE...............................425 827-7120
Marcus Leaver, *COO*
EMP: 27
SALES (corp-wide): 92.94MM **Privately
Held**
Web: www.quarto.com
SIC: 2732 7336 5192 Books, printing and
binding; Commercial art and graphic design
; Books, periodicals, and newspapers
HQ: Quarto Publishing Group Usa Inc.
401 2nd Ave N Ste 310
Minneapolis MN 55401
612 344-8100

(G-6376)
QUAYSIDE PUBLISHING GROUP
Also Called: Rockport Publishing
100 Cummings Ctr Ste 406l (01915-6101)
PHONE...............................978 282-9590
Peter Read, *Ch*
Ken Fund, *Prin*
Mary D Aarons, *Dir*

Kevin Hamric, *VP*
▲ EMP: 9 EST: 2010
SALES (est): 220.18K
SALES (corp-wide): 92.94MM **Privately
Held**
SIC: 2731 2741 Books, publishing only;
Miscellaneous publishing
PA: Quarto Group Inc
276 5th Ave Rm 205
New York NY 10001
212 779-0700

(G-6377)
QUIDEL CORPORATION
500 Cummings Ctr Ste 55500
(01915-6142)
PHONE...............................866 800-5458
EMP: 13
SALES (corp-wide): 3.27B **Publicly Held**
Web: www.quidelortho.com
SIC: 2835 Diagnostic substances
HQ: Quidel Corporation
9975 Summers Ridge Rd
San Diego CA 92121
858 552-1100

(G-6378)
**RED DERBY INCORPORATED
EMBRDRY**
140 Elliott St Bldg E (01915-3247)
PHONE...............................978 927-4838
Gary Beck, *Pr*
EMP: 8 EST: 2010
SALES (est): 203.36K **Privately Held**
Web:
red-derby-incorporated-embrdry.hub.biz
SIC: 2395 Embroidery products, except
Schiffli machine

(G-6379)
ROBERTS MACHINE SHOP INC
117 Elliott St Ste 7 (01915-3252)
P.O. Box 84 (01915-0002)
PHONE...............................978 927-6111
Paul Sidilou, *Pr*
Peter Sidilou, *VP*
EMP: 7 EST: 1974
SQ FT: 3,800
SALES (est): 747.5K **Privately Held**
SIC: 3599 Machine shop, jobbing and repair

(G-6380)
SAGE SCIENCE INC
500 Cummings Ctr Ste 2400 (01915-6538)
PHONE...............................617 922-1832
Gary P Magnant, *Pr*
John D Curtin, *Ch*
Todd Barbera, *Treas*
EMP: 12 EST: 2005
SALES (est): 4.56MM **Privately Held**
Web: www.sagescience.com
SIC: 5049 3826 Scientific instruments;
Analytical instruments

(G-6381)
SALEM NEWS ARCHIVES
112 Sohier Rd (01915-5534)
PHONE...............................978 922-8303
EMP: 9 EST: 2018
SALES (est): 265.09K **Privately Held**
Web: www.salemnews.com
SIC: 2711 Newspapers, publishing and
printing

(G-6382)
**SEABORN NETWORKS
HOLDINGS LLC (PA)**
Also Called: Seaborn Networks
600 Cummings Ctr Fl 2 (01915-6194)

PHONE...............................978 471-3171
Steve Orlando, *CEO*
Sean Mcneill, *CFO*
◆ EMP: 18 EST: 2013
SALES (est): 9.31MM
SALES (corp-wide): 9.31MM **Privately
Held**
Web: www.seabornnetworks.com
SIC: 3661 Fiber optics communications
equipment

(G-6383)
SENSITECH INC (DH)
800 Cummings Ctr Ste 258x (01915-6197)
PHONE...............................978 927-7033
Alice Debiasio, *Pr*
Ronnie Morrison, *
Mike Nickerson, *
Lincoln Cheng, *
Diana Morales, *
◆ EMP: 70 EST: 1990
SQ FT: 30,000
SALES (est): 134.22MM
SALES (corp-wide): 22.1B **Publicly Held**
Web: www.sensitech.com
SIC: 3826 3823 3822 Environmental testing
equipment; Process control instruments;
Environmental controls
HQ: Carrier Corporation
13995 Pasteur Blvd
Palm Beach Gardens FL 33418
800 379-6484

(G-6384)
SIONYX LLC (PA)
100 Cummings Ctr Ste 303b (01915-6107)
PHONE...............................978 922-0684
Stephen Saylor, *CEO*
James E Carry Iii, *Sec*
EMP: 13 EST: 2005
SQ FT: 11,000
SALES (est): 7.73MM
SALES (corp-wide): 7.73MM **Privately
Held**
Web: www.sionyx.com
SIC: 3674 Semiconductors and related
devices

(G-6385)
**STANDLEY BROS MACHINE CO
INC**
96 Park St (01915-4312)
P.O. Box 85 (01915-0002)
PHONE...............................978 927-0278
John G Standley Junior, *Pr*
Carl W Standley, *VP*
David C Standley, *Stockholder*
EMP: 31 EST: 1956
SQ FT: 15,500
SALES (est): 2.66MM **Privately Held**
Web: www.standleybros.com
SIC: 3599 Machine shop, jobbing and repair

(G-6386)
TAUTEN INC
100 Cummings Ctr Ste 215f (01915-6123)
PHONE...............................978 961-3272
EMP: 9 EST: 2013
SALES (est): 247.69K **Privately Held**
Web: www.tauten.com
SIC: 2298 Fishing lines, nets, seines: made
in cordage or twine mills

(G-6387)
**THERMO FISHER SCIENTIFIC
INC**
Alko Diagnostic
100 Cummings Ctr Ste 166 (01915-6135)
PHONE...............................978 232-6000
Jim Barbookles, *Mgr*

EMP: 200
SALES (corp-wide): 44.91B **Publicly Held**
Web: www.thermofisher.com
SIC: 3821 3841 2899 Laboratory apparatus
  and furniture; Surgical and medical
  instruments; Chemical preparations, nec
PA: Thermo Fisher Scientific Inc.
  168 3rd Ave
  Waltham MA 02451
  781 622-1000

(G-6388)
THRIVE BIOSCIENCE INC
100 Cummings Ctr (01915-6107)
PHONE.............................978 720-8048
Gary Magnant, *CEO*
Brian Foley, *VP*
Tom Farb, *CFO*
EMP: 8 EST: 2014
SALES (est): 1.43MM **Privately Held**
Web: www.thrivebio.com
SIC: 3826 Analytical instruments

(G-6389)
TK&K SERVICES LLC
Also Called: Environmental Division
719 Hale St Ste 3 (01915-2199)
PHONE.............................770 844-8710
EMP: 80
Web: www.tkandkservices.com
SIC: 2869 8711 Fuels; Consulting engineer
PA: Tk&K Services, L.L.C.
  11675 Century Dr Unit A
  Alpharetta GA

(G-6390)
TMD TECHNOLOGIES LLC
150 Sohier Rd (01915-5536)
PHONE.............................978 922-6000
Michael Farley, *Pr*
David Holt, *
EMP: 222 EST: 2011
SALES (est): 13.86MM **Privately Held**
Web: www.cpii.com
SIC: 3812 3679 Search and navigation
  equipment; Electronic loads and power
  supplies
HQ: Communications & Power Industries
  Llc
  811 Hansen Way
  Palo Alto CA 94304

(G-6391)
US POLYMERS INC
100 Cummings Ctr Ste 326g (01915-6123)
PHONE.............................978 921-8000
Randy Haight, *Pr*
EMP: 7 EST: 1980
SALES (est): 904.92K **Privately Held**
Web: www.uspolymers.com
SIC: 2821 Plastics materials and resins

(G-6392)
**VASO ACTIVE
PHRMACEUTICALS INC**
100 Cummings Ctr Ste 243c (01915-6278)
PHONE.............................978 750-1991
Joseph Frattaroli, *Pr*
Doctor Stephen Carter, *VP*
Robert E Anderson, *Ch Bd*
EMP: 9 EST: 2003
SQ FT: 6,800
SALES (est): 902.45K **Privately Held**
Web: www.vasoactive.us
SIC: 2834 8731 Pharmaceutical
  preparations; Medical research, commercial

(G-6393)
VIBRATION & SHOCK TECH LLC
13 Arbella Dr (01915-1401)
PHONE.............................781 281-0721
▼ **EMP:** 7 EST: 2011
SALES (est): 476.38K **Privately Held**
Web: www.emersonapparatus.com
SIC: 3599 Machine shop, jobbing and repair

(G-6394)
WAFER LLC
32 Dunham Rd (01915-1844)
P.O. Box 86 (03755-0086)
PHONE.............................978 304-3821
Eric Doesburg, *Genl Mgr*
EMP: 10 EST: 2016
SQ FT: 70,000
SALES (est): 1.5MM **Privately Held**
Web: www.wafer.tech
SIC: 3629 Electronic generation equipment

Billerica
Middlesex County

(G-6395)
ABSOLUTE SHEET METAL
559 Boston Rd (01821-3713)
PHONE.............................978 667-0236
Mary Barry, *Owner*
EMP: 7 EST: 1999
SALES (est): 230.37K **Privately Held**
Web: www.absolutesheetmetal.com
SIC: 3444 Sheet metalwork

(G-6396)
**ACME BOOKBINDING
COMPANY INC**
Also Called: Acme Bookbinding
27 Woodcliff Dr (01821-5005)
PHONE.............................617 242-1100
Angelo Parisi, *Pr*
Paul Parisi, *
John Parisi, *
Antoinette Parisi, *
EMP: 100 EST: 1959
SALES (est): 12.23MM **Privately Held**
Web: www.hfgroup.com
SIC: 2789 Binding only: books, pamphlets,
  magazines, etc.
PA: Hf Group, Llc
  400 Arora Cmmons Cir Unit
  Aurora OH 44202

(G-6397)
AETRUIM INCORPORATED
4 Federal St (01821-3569)
PHONE.............................651 773-4200
Joe Levesque, *Pr*
Dean Hedstrom, *
Tim Foley, *
EMP: 29 EST: 1978
SQ FT: 61,500
SALES (est): 4.9MM
SALES (corp-wide): 112.15MM **Publicly Held**
Web: www.bostonsemiequipment.com
SIC: 3825 3674 7389 Test equipment for
  electronic and electrical circuits; Solid state
  electronic devices, nec; Inspection and
  testing services
HQ: Atrm Holdings, Inc.
  5215 Gershwin Ave N
  Oakdale MN 55128
  651 704-1800

(G-6398)
AIRGAS USA LLC
1 Plank St (01821-5726)

PHONE.............................978 439-1344
Josh Santerre, *Mgr*
EMP: 20
SALES (corp-wide): 101.26MM **Privately
Held**
Web: www.airgas.com
SIC: 2813 5169 5085 Industrial gases;
  Industrial gases; Industrial supplies
HQ: Airgas Usa, Llc
  259 N Radnor Chester Rd
  Radnor PA 19087
  216 642-6600

(G-6399)
**AMERICAN FLWFORM
MACHINING LLC (HQ)**
12 Suburban Park Dr (01821-3903)
PHONE.............................978 667-0202
Kelly P Pasterick, *Mgr*
Scott A Minder, *
Lauren S Mcandrews, *Mgr*
Amanda Skov, *
Mary Beth Moore, *
▲ **EMP:** 37 EST: 1973
SQ FT: 43,500
SALES (est): 10.56MM
SALES (corp-wide): 10.56MM **Privately
Held**
Web: www.flowform.com
SIC: 3542 Machine tools, metal forming type
PA: Consolidated Boring, Inc.
  12 Suburban Park Dr
  Billerica MA

(G-6400)
ANOKIWAVE INC
296 Concord Rd Ste 300 (01821-3487)
PHONE.............................781 820-1049
Gary St Onge, *Brnch Mgr*
EMP: 68
SALES (corp-wide): 11.36MM **Privately
Held**
Web: www.anokiwave.com
SIC: 3674 Semiconductors and related
  devices
PA: Anokiwave, Inc.
  5355 Mira Sorrento Pl # 300
  San Diego CA 92121
  858 792-9910

(G-6401)
AOTCO HOLDINGS LLC (PA)
11 Suburban Park Dr (01821-3997)
PHONE.............................978 667-8298
Matthew Smith, *Managing Member*
EMP: 10 EST: 2020
SALES (est): 9.15MM
SALES (corp-wide): 9.15MM **Privately
Held**
Web: www.aotco.com
SIC: 3471 Electroplating of metals or
  formed products

(G-6402)
AOTCO METAL FINISHING LLC
11 Suburban Park Dr (01821-3997)
PHONE.............................978 667-8298
Matthew Smith, *Pr*
Charlie Bourque, *
EMP: 55 EST: 2018
SALES (est): 9.15MM
SALES (corp-wide): 9.15MM **Privately
Held**
Web: www.aotco.com
SIC: 3471 Electroplating of metals or
  formed products
PA: Aotco Holdings, Llc
  11 Suburban Park Dr
  Billerica MA 01821
  978 667-8298

(G-6403)
**APPLIED NNSTRCTRED
SLTIONS LLC**
157 Concord Rd (01821-4600)
PHONE.............................978 670-6959
EMP: 20 EST: 2010
SALES (est): 350K
SALES (corp-wide): 3.93B **Publicly Held**
SIC: 3624 3081 3084 Carbon and graphite
  products; Plastics film and sheet; Plastics
  pipe
PA: Cabot Corporation
  2 Seaport Ln Ste 1300
  Boston MA 02210
  617 345-0100

(G-6404)
APPLIED SCIENCE GROUP INC
Also Called: Applied Science Laboratories
900 Middlesex Tpke Bldg 5 (01821-3929)
PHONE.............................781 275-4000
Valerie Sinclair, *Pr*
Robert Sinclair, *
Mark Crowley, *
EMP: 25 EST: 1984
SQ FT: 12,000
SALES (est): 4.87MM **Privately Held**
Web: www.a-s-l.com
SIC: 3827 8748 Optical instruments and
  lenses; Systems analysis and engineering
  consulting services

(G-6405)
**APRIL TWENTY ONE
CORPORATION**
Also Called: Swing Center Factory Outlet
749 Boston Rd (01821-5933)
PHONE.............................978 667-8472
EMP: 7 EST: 1994
SQ FT: 12,000
SALES (est): 647.27K **Privately Held**
Web: www.theswingcenter.com
SIC: 2499 5941 Fencing, docks, and other
  outdoor wood structural products; Sporting
  goods and bicycle shops

(G-6406)
ASMPT NEXX INC
Also Called: Nexx
900 Middlesex Tpke Bldg 6 (01821-3929)
PHONE.............................978 436-4600
Thomas Walsh, *Pr*
▲ **EMP:** 38 EST: 2001
SQ FT: 15,000
SALES (est): 10.53MM **Privately Held**
Web: www.asmpt.com
SIC: 3674 Semiconductor circuit networks
PA: Asmpt Limited
  19/F Gateway Ts
  Tsing Yi Island NT

(G-6407)
AVAYA LLC
Also Called: Avaya
600 Technology Park Dr Ste 1
(01821-4126)
PHONE.............................908 953-6000
Christie Blake, *Prin*
EMP: 11
Web: www.avaya.com
SIC: 3661 Telephone and telegraph
  apparatus
HQ: Avaya Llc
  350 Mount Kemble Ave # 1
  Morristown NJ 07960
  908 953-6000

▲ = Import ▼ = Export
◆ = Import/Export

(G-6408)
AXSUN TECHNOLOGIES INC
1 Fortune Dr (01821-3923)
PHONE..................................978 262-0049
▲ EMP: 90
Web: www.excelitas.com
SIC: 3827 Optical instruments and lenses

(G-6409)
BELMONT INSTRUMENT LLC (PA)
Also Called: Belmont Medical Technologies
780 Boston Rd Ste 3 (01821-5939)
PHONE..................................978 663-0212
Brian Ellacott, *CEO*
Jeffrey Forward, *
EMP: 29 EST: 1999
SQ FT: 15,200
SALES (est): 10.24MM
SALES (corp-wide): 10.24MM **Privately Held**
Web: www.belmontmedtech.com
SIC: 3845 3841 Electromedical apparatus;
  Surgical and medical instruments

(G-6410)
BIOVIEW (USA) INC
44 Manning Rd Ste 104 (01821-3931)
PHONE..................................978 670-4741
Emmanuel Gill, *Ch Bd*
Opher Shapira, *Pr*
Allen Schwevel, *VP*
Yuval Harrari, *VP*
EMP: 9 EST: 2002
SALES (est): 1.31MM **Privately Held**
Web: www.bioview.com
SIC: 3845 Ultrasonic scanning devices,
  medical

(G-6411)
BOSTON MATERIALS INC
8 Federal St # A (01821-3570)
PHONE..................................617 306-2396
Anvesh Gurijala, *CEO*
Michael Segal, *COO*
EMP: 15 EST: 2018
SALES (est): 260.75K **Privately Held**
Web: www.bomaterials.com
SIC: 2295 Coated fabrics, not rubberized

(G-6412)
BRUKER BIOSPIN CORPORATION (HQ)
15 Fortune Dr (01821-3958)
PHONE..................................978 667-9580
▲ EMP: 115 EST: 1968
SALES (est): 88.95MM
SALES (corp-wide): 2.53B **Publicly Held**
Web: www.bruker.com
SIC: 3826 Analytical instruments
PA: Bruker Corporation
  40 Manning Rd
  Billerica MA 01821
  978 663-3660

(G-6413)
BRUKER BIOSPIN MRI INC
15 Fortune Dr (01821-3958)
PHONE..................................978 667-9580
Joerg Laukien, *Pr*
Frank H Laukien, *Genl Mgr*
Barbara Burgess, *Treas*
▲ EMP: 10 EST: 1997
SQ FT: 1,000
SALES (est): 5.55MM
SALES (corp-wide): 2.53B **Publicly Held**
Web: www.bruker.com
SIC: 3826 Analytical instruments
PA: Bruker Corporation
  40 Manning Rd

Billerica MA 01821
978 663-3660

(G-6414)
BRUKER CORPORATION (PA)
Also Called: Bruker
40 Manning Rd (01821-3915)
PHONE..................................978 663-3660
Frank H Laukien, *Ch Bd*
Gerald N Herman, *Ex VP*
Mark R Munch, *Ex VP*
▲ EMP: 878 EST: 1991
SALES (est): 2.53B
SALES (corp-wide): 2.53B **Publicly Held**
Web: www.bruker.com
SIC: 3826 3844 Analytical instruments; X-
  ray apparatus and tubes

(G-6415)
BRUKER CORPORATION
40 Manning Rd (01821-3915)
PHONE..................................978 663-3660
EMP: 245
SALES (est): 2.53B **Publicly Held**
Web: www.bruker.com
SIC: 3826 Spectrometers
PA: Bruker Corporation
  40 Manning Rd
  Billerica MA 01821
  978 663-3660

(G-6416)
BRUKER DETECTION CORPORATION
40 Manning Rd (01821-3915)
PHONE..................................978 663-3660
William Knight, *Pr*
James Oneill, *Contrlr*
EMP: 13 EST: 2005
SALES (est): 4.26MM
SALES (corp-wide): 2.53B **Publicly Held**
Web: www.bruker.com
SIC: 3826 Analytical instruments
PA: Bruker Corporation
  40 Manning Rd
  Billerica MA 01821
  978 663-3660

(G-6417)
BRUKER ENRGY SUPERCON TECH INC (HQ)
15 Fortune Dr (01821-3958)
PHONE..................................978 901-7550
EMP: 100 EST: 2008
SALES (est): 18.65MM
SALES (corp-wide): 2.53B **Publicly Held**
Web: www.bruker.com
SIC: 3826 Analytical instruments
PA: Bruker Corporation
  40 Manning Rd
  Billerica MA 01821
  978 663-3660

(G-6418)
BRUKER SCIENTIFIC LLC
40 Manning Rd (01821-3915)
P.O. Box 83228 (01813-3228)
PHONE..................................978 667-9580
▲ EMP: 663
Web: www.bruker.com
SIC: 3826 5049 Spectrometers; Analytical
  instruments

(G-6419)
BRUKER SCIENTIFIC LLC (HQ)
40 Manning Rd (01821-3915)
PHONE..................................978 439-9899
▲ EMP: 6000 EST: 1995
SQ FT: 20,000

SALES (est): 447.15MM
SALES (corp-wide): 2.53B **Publicly Held**
Web: www.bruker.com
SIC: 5049 3826 Scientific instruments;
  Analytical instruments
PA: Bruker Corporation
  40 Manning Rd
  Billerica MA 01821
  978 663-3660

(G-6420)
C-R MACHINE CO INC (PA)
13 Alexander Rd Ste 10 (01821-5000)
PHONE..................................978 663-3989
Gary Rigoli, *Pr*
Julie Rigoli, *
EMP: 58 EST: 1974
SQ FT: 10,000
SALES (est): 9.61MM
SALES (corp-wide): 9.61MM **Privately
Held**
Web: www.crmach.com
SIC: 3599 Machine shop, jobbing and repair

(G-6421)
CABOT CORPORATION
Also Called: Cabot
157 Concord Rd (01821-4698)
P.O. Box 7001 (01821-7001)
PHONE..................................978 671-4000
Steve Reznek, *Mgr*
EMP: 25
SALES (corp-wide): 3.93B **Publicly Held**
Web: www.cabotcorp.com
SIC: 2895 2899 Carbon black; Chemical
  preparations, nec
PA: Cabot Corporation
  2 Seaport Ln Ste 1300
  Boston MA 02210
  617 345-0100

(G-6422)
CHEMGENES CORPORATION
Also Called: Chemgenes
900 Middlesex Tpke Bldg 2 (01821-3929)
PHONE..................................978 694-4500
Suresh C Srivastava, *Pr*
Sunita Srivastava, *
Amar Raj, *
▲ EMP: 50 EST: 1981
SQ FT: 30,000
SALES (est): 18.68MM **Privately Held**
Web: www.chemgenes.com
SIC: 8731 2865 Biotechnical research,
  commercial; Cyclic crudes and
  intermediates
PA: Esbi Transmissions Private Limited
  8, 6th Floor, Suit No 4
  Kolkata WB

(G-6423)
CLEARMOTION INC (PA)
Also Called: Clearmotion
805 Middlesex Tpke (01821-3914)
PHONE..................................617 313-0822
Christian Steinmann, *CEO*
Shakeel Avadhany, *Chief Business Officer*
Zackary Anderson, *COO*
Carl-peter Forster, *Dir*
EMP: 7 EST: 2008
SALES (est): 5.51MM **Privately Held**
Web: www.clearmotion.com
SIC: 3714 Motor vehicle parts and
  accessories

(G-6424)
CMC MATERIALS INC (HQ)
129 Concord Rd (01821-4612)
PHONE..................................978 436-6500
David H Li, *Pr*

William P Noglows, *Non-Executive
Chairman of the Board*
Jeanette A Press, *CAO*
H Carol Bernstein, *VP*
◆ EMP: 61 EST: 1999
SALES (est): 1.2B
SALES (corp-wide): 3.52B **Publicly Held**
Web: www.entegris.com
SIC: 3674 Semiconductors and related
  devices
PA: Entegris, Inc.
  129 Concord Rd
  Billerica MA 01821
  978 436-6500

(G-6425)
CMO PARTNERS INC
8 Cook St 10 (01821-6064)
PHONE..................................617 875-5449
Anand Panchu, *CEO*
Rajiv Panchu, *Dir*
EMP: 10 EST: 2021
SALES (est): 1.05MM **Privately Held**
SIC: 2819 Industrial inorganic chemicals,
  nec

(G-6426)
COLDSNAP CORP
6 Enterprise Rd (01821-5735)
PHONE..................................617 733-9935
EMP: 37 EST: 2018
SALES (est): 5.05MM **Privately Held**
Web: www.coldsnap.com
SIC: 3632 Household refrigerators and
  freezers

(G-6427)
CONFORMIS INC (HQ)
Also Called: Conformis
600 Technology Park Dr Ste 3
(01821-4154)
PHONE..................................781 345-9001
Mark A Augusti, *Pr*
Kenneth P Fallon Iii, *Ch Bd*
Robert S Howe, *CFO*
J Brent Alldredge, *CLO*
Michael Fillion, *COO*
EMP: 60 EST: 2004
SQ FT: 45,000
SALES (est): 62.05MM
SALES (corp-wide): 76.72MM **Privately
Held**
Web: www.conformis.com
SIC: 3841 Medical instruments and
  equipment, blood and bone work
PA: Restor3d, Inc.
  4001 Nc Hwy 54 Ste 3160
  Durham NC 27709
  678 469-0395

(G-6428)
CONSOLIDATED MACHINE CORPORATION
Also Called: Consolidated Sterilizer Systems
3 Enterprise Rd 3c (01821-5735)
P.O. Box 297 (02134-0003)
PHONE..................................617 732-6072
EMP: 50 EST: 1948
SALES (est): 9.29MM **Privately Held**
Web: www.consteril.com
SIC: 3821 3443 3559 Sterilizers; Stills,
  pressure: metal plate; Surgical appliances
  and supplies; Food products machinery

(G-6429)
CONTRACT GLASS SERVICE INC
44 Dunham Rd (01821-5727)
P.O. Box 16613 (03106-6613)
PHONE..................................978 262-1323
William Crawford, *Pr*

Mary Best, *Owner*
EMP: 22 **EST:** 1985
SQ FT: 16,000
SALES (est): 938.28K **Privately Held**
Web: www.contractglass.com
SIC: 3211 1793 Insulating glass, sealed units; Glass and glazing work

(G-6430)
CROSSTEK MEMBRANE TECH LLC
900 Technology Park Dr Ste 101 (01821-4167)
PHONE...............................978 761-9601
Bruce Bishop, *CEO*
EMP: 11 **EST:** 2016
SALES (est): 1.98MM **Privately Held**
Web: www.crosstek.com
SIC: 3589 Sewage and water treatment equipment

(G-6431)
DODGE COMPANY INC (PA)
9 Progress Rd (01821-5731)
PHONE...............................800 443-6343
Debrah Dodge, *Pr*
John Dodge, *VP*
Patrick J Hurley, *VP*
Kristie Dodge, *VP*
George B Dodge Junior, *Treas*
◆ **EMP:** 10 **EST:** 1893
SALES (est): 8.4MM
SALES (corp-wide): 8.4MM **Privately Held**
Web: www.dodgeco.com
SIC: 2869 5087 Embalming fluids; Funeral director's equipment and supplies

(G-6432)
DRUCK LLC (HQ)
Also Called: GE Measurement & Control
1100 Technology Park Dr Ste 300 (01821-4111)
PHONE...............................978 437-1000
Brian Palmer, *Pr*
Jessica Wenzell, *VP*
Kris Mcbride, *CFO*
◆ **EMP:** 101 **EST:** 1978
SALES (est): 24.81MM
SALES (corp-wide): 25.51B **Publicly Held**
Web: www.druckinc.com
SIC: 3829 3823 3824 3674 Pressure transducers; Process control instruments; Controls, revolution and timing instruments; Radiation sensors
PA: Baker Hughes Company
    575 N Dairy Ashford Rd # 100
    Houston TX 77079
    713 439-8600

(G-6433)
DURRIDGE COMPANY INC (PA)
Also Called: Sensory Acquisition Co
900 Technology Park Dr (01821-4167)
PHONE...............................978 667-9556
Wendell Clough, *Pr*
Wendell Clough, *Pr*
Ronda Wang, *VP*
EMP: 10 **EST:** 1997
SQ FT: 2,000
SALES (est): 3.52MM
SALES (corp-wide): 3.52MM **Privately Held**
Web: www.durridge.com
SIC: 3825 Analog-digital converters, electronic instrumentation type

(G-6434)
DUSA PHARMACEUTICALS INC (DH)
29 Dunham Rd (01821-5729)

PHONE...............................978 657-7500
Robert F Doman, *Pr*
Richard Christopher, *
William F O'dell, *Executive Sales & Marketing Vice President*
Michael J Todisco, *
EMP: 52 **EST:** 1991
SALES (est): 23.74MM **Privately Held**
Web: www.levulan.com
SIC: 2834 Pharmaceutical preparations
HQ: Sun Pharmaceutical Industries, Inc.
    2 Independence Way
    Princeton NJ 08540
    609 495-2800

(G-6435)
DYNISCO INSTRUMENTS LLC
Dj Instruments
37 Manning Rd Ste 2 (01821-3950)
PHONE...............................978 215-3401
Steve Debries, *Brnch Mgr*
EMP: 33
SALES (corp-wide): 223.55MM **Privately Held**
Web: www.dynisco.com
SIC: 3829 Measuring and controlling devices, nec
HQ: Dynisco Instruments Llc
    38 Forge Pkwy
    Franklin MA 02038
    508 541-9400

(G-6436)
DYNISCO PARENT INC
37 Manning Rd Ste 2 (01821-3950)
PHONE...............................978 667-5301
Michael Testa, *Mgr*
EMP: 371
SALES (corp-wide): 5.37B **Publicly Held**
Web: www.dynisco.com
SIC: 3823 3829 Industrial process control instruments; Pressure transducers
HQ: Dynisco Parent, Inc.
    38 Forge Pkwy
    Franklin MA 02038

(G-6437)
E INK CORPORATION
1000 Technology Park Dr (01821-4165)
PHONE...............................617 499-6000
Felix Ho, *Pr*
Kenneth H Titlebaum, *
Russell J Wilcox, *General Vice President*
Paul G Apen, *CSO*
Lynne C Garone, *
▲ **EMP:** 55 **EST:** 1997
SQ FT: 45,000
SALES (est): 79.93MM **Privately Held**
Web: www.eink.com
SIC: 2653 Display items, corrugated: made from purchased materials
PA: E Ink Holdings Inc.
    3, Li Shin Rd. 1, Science-Based. Industrial Park
    Hsinchu City 30078

(G-6438)
EMD MILLIPORE CORPORATION
290 Concord Rd # 2 (01821-3405)
PHONE...............................978 715-4321
EMP: 317
SALES (corp-wide): 23.09B **Privately Held**
Web: www.millipore.com
SIC: 3826 Liquid testing apparatus
HQ: Emd Millipore Corporation
    400 Summit Dr
    Burlington MA 01803
    800 645-5476

(G-6439)
EMD SERONO INC
290 Concord Rd (01821-3405)
PHONE...............................781 982-9000
EMP: 16
SALES (corp-wide): 23.09B **Privately Held**
Web: us.fertility.com
SIC: 2834 Pharmaceutical preparations
HQ: Emd Serono, Inc.
    1 Technology Pl
    Rockland MA 02370
    781 982-9000

(G-6440)
EMD SERONO BIOTECH CENTER INC
45a Middlesex Tpke (01821-3936)
PHONE...............................978 294-1100
Stephen Arkinstall, *Pr*
EMP: 21
SALES (corp-wide): 23.09B **Privately Held**
SIC: 2834 Pharmaceutical preparations
HQ: Emd Serono Biotech Center, Inc.
    1 Technology Pl
    Rockland MA 02370
    800 283-8088

(G-6441)
EMD SERONO RES & DEV INST INC
Also Called: EMD Srdi
45 Middlesex Tpke (01821-3936)
PHONE...............................978 294-1100
Paris Panayiotopoulos, *Pr*
Stephen D Gillies, *
EMP: 75 **EST:** 1992
SQ FT: 58,000
SALES (est): 22.54MM
SALES (corp-wide): 23.09B **Privately Held**
SIC: 2834 Pharmaceutical preparations
PA: Merck Kg Auf Aktien
    Frankfurter Str. 250
    Darmstadt HE 64293
    6151720

(G-6442)
ENTEGRIS INC
Also Called: Mykrolis
129 Concord Rd Bldg 2 (01821-4615)
PHONE...............................978 436-6500
EMP: 41
SQ FT: 175,000
SALES (corp-wide): 3.52B **Publicly Held**
Web: www.entegris.com
SIC: 3823 Process control instruments
PA: Entegris, Inc.
    129 Concord Rd
    Billerica MA 01821
    978 436-6500

(G-6443)
ENTEGRIS INC (PA)
Also Called: ENTEGRIS
129 Concord Rd (01821-4612)
PHONE...............................978 436-6500
Bertrand Loy, *Pr*
Gregory B Graves, *Sr VP*
Joe Colella, *Sr VP*
Michael D Sauer, *CAO*
Jim O'neill, *Sr VP*
◆ **EMP:** 1050 **EST:** 1966
SQ FT: 175,000
SALES (est): 3.52B
SALES (corp-wide): 3.52B **Publicly Held**
Web: www.entegris.com
SIC: 3089 3081 3674 Plastics processing; Plastics film and sheet; Semiconductors and related devices

(G-6444)
EPOXY TECHNOLOGY INC (PA)
Also Called: Epo-Tek
14 Fortune Dr (01821-3972)
PHONE...............................978 667-3805
Daniel Pelton, *CEO*
Andrew R Horne, *Pr*
Roy Seroussi, *VP*
John Knudsen, *Treas*
EMP: 29 **EST:** 1966
SQ FT: 40,000
SALES (est): 14.68MM
SALES (corp-wide): 14.68MM **Privately Held**
Web: www.epotek.com
SIC: 2891 2834 2869 Epoxy adhesives; Pharmaceutical preparations; Industrial organic chemicals, nec

(G-6445)
EVOTEXT INC
357 Boston Rd (01821-1802)
PHONE...............................781 272-1830
Johanna Wetmore, *CEO*
Christopher Robert, *COO*
Michael F Johnson, *Pr*
EMP: 15 **EST:** 2012
SALES (est): 3.88MM **Privately Held**
Web: www.evotext.com
SIC: 5045 4813 7372 8748 Computer software; Proprietary online service networks; Business oriented computer software; Educational consultant

(G-6446)
EXCELITAS TECHNOLOGIES CORP
1 Fortune Dr (01821-3923)
PHONE...............................978 262-0049
Jonathan Hartmann, *Brnch Mgr*
EMP: 90
SALES (corp-wide): 1.48B **Privately Held**
Web: www.excelitas.com
SIC: 3827 Optical instruments and lenses
HQ: Excelitas Technologies Corp.
    200 West St Ste 4
    Waltham MA 02451

(G-6447)
FISHER SCIENTIFIC INTL LLC
900 Middlesex Tpke Bldg 8-1 (01821-3929)
PHONE...............................978 670-7460
Hunsoo Kim, *Brnch Mgr*
EMP: 12
SALES (corp-wide): 44.91B **Publicly Held**
Web: www.thermofisher.com
SIC: 3826 Analytical instruments
HQ: Fisher Scientific International Llc
    81 Wyman St
    Waltham MA 02451

(G-6448)
FLUID MANAGEMENT SYSTEMS INC
Also Called: F M S
900 Technology Park Dr Ste 101 (01821-4167)
PHONE...............................617 393-2396
Hamid Shirkhan, *Pr*
EMP: 25 **EST:** 1986
SALES (est): 4.72MM **Privately Held**
Web: www.fms-inc.com
SIC: 3826 Analytical instruments

(G-6449)
HF GROUP LLC
Also Called: Acme Bookbinding Company
27 Woodcliff Dr (01821-5005)
PHONE...............................617 242-1100

EMP: 157
Web: www.hfgroup.com
SIC: 2789 Bookbinding and related work
PA: Hf Group, Llc
400 Arora Cmmons Cir Unit
Aurora OH 44202

(G-6450)
HOCKEY12COM
12 Beaumont Ave (01821-5913)
PHONE.................................781 910-2877
Stephen Sheridan, *Prin*
EMP: 7 **EST:** 2010
SALES (est): 236.61K **Privately Held**
Web: www.studio12sports.com
SIC: 2836 Culture media

(G-6451)
IMABIOTECH CORP
44 Manning Rd (01821-3935)
PHONE.................................978 362-1825
Jonathan Stauber, *CEO*
EMP: 13 **EST:** 2015
SALES (est): 373.23K **Privately Held**
Web: www.aliribio.com
SIC: 2834 Pharmaceutical preparations

(G-6452)
INNOVIVE LLC
129 Concord Rd (01821-4612)
PHONE.................................617 500-1691
William Zebuhr, *Prin*
EMP: 7
Web: www.innovive.com
SIC: 3496 Cages, wire
PA: Innovive, Llc
10019 Waples Ct
San Diego CA 92121

(G-6453)
INSULET MA SECURITIES CORP
600 Technology Park Dr Ste 200
(01821-4150)
PHONE.................................978 600-7000
Patrick J Sullivan, *Pr*
Michael L Levitz, *CFO*
David Colleran, *Sec*
EMP: 20 **EST:** 2009
SALES (est): 680.97K
SALES (corp-wide): 1.31B **Publicly Held**
Web: www.insulet.com
SIC: 3841 Surgical and medical instruments
PA: Insulet Corporation
100 Nagog Park
Acton MA 01720
978 600-7000

(G-6454)
INTEGRIS INC
296 Concord Rd Ste 180 (01821-3487)
PHONE.................................978 294-2633
David W Bradbury, *Prin*
EMP: 9 **EST:** 2009
SALES (est): 268.21K **Privately Held**
Web: www.entegris.com
SIC: 3674 Semiconductors and related
devices

(G-6455)
INTERSENSE INCORPORATED
700 Technology Park Dr Ste 102
(01821-4153)
PHONE.................................781 541-6330
EMP: 50 **EST:** 1996
SQ FT: 13,000
SALES (est): 4.9MM
SALES (corp-wide): 95.04MM **Privately
Held**
Web: www.intersense.com

SIC: 3643 Current-carrying wiring services
PA: Gentex Corporation
324 Main St
Simpson PA 18407
570 282-3550

(G-6456)
IONSENSE INC
40 Manning Rd (01821-3915)
PHONE.................................781 231-1739
Brian Musselman, *Pr*
Curtis Lintvedt, *VP*
EMP: 14 **EST:** 2004
SALES (est): 2.27MM **Privately Held**
Web: www.ionsense.com
SIC: 3826 Analytical instruments

(G-6457)
JEIO TECH INC
19 Alexander Rd Ste 7 (01821-5094)
PHONE.................................781 376-0700
Gisung Kim, *CEO*
Sangyong Kim, *CEO*
Hyunjoo Shin, *VP*
◆ **EMP:** 9 **EST:** 2008
SALES (est): 2.58MM **Privately Held**
Web: www.jeiotech.com
SIC: 5049 5084 3821 Laboratory
equipment, except medical or dental;
Industrial machinery and equipment;
Laboratory equipment: fume hoods,
distillation racks, etc.
PA: Jeiotech Co.,Ltd
153 Techno 2-Ro, Yuseong-Gu
Daejeon 34025

(G-6458)
**LAB MEDICAL
MANUFACTURING INC**
28 Cook St (01821-6060)
PHONE.................................978 663-2475
Leon W Bester, *Pr*
EMP: 80 **EST:** 1986
SQ FT: 29,200
SALES (est): 9.11MM **Privately Held**
Web: www.labmedical.com
SIC: 3841 Surgical instruments and
apparatus

(G-6459)
LUTRONIC USA
19 Fortune Dr (01821-3923)
PHONE.................................888 588-7644
EMP: 18 **EST:** 2015
SALES (est): 2.67MM **Privately Held**
Web: us.aesthetic.lutronic.com
SIC: 2834 Pharmaceutical preparations

(G-6460)
**METTLER-TOLEDO THORNTON
INC (DH)**
900 Middlesex Tpke Bldg 8-1 (01821-3943)
PHONE.................................978 262-0210
James L Bryant, *Pr*
Richard Brouillette, *
Charles O Staples, *
Michelle Proia, *
Mary Finnegan, *
EMP: 74 **EST:** 1964
SQ FT: 41,500
SALES (est): 24.73MM
SALES (corp-wide): 3.79B **Publicly Held**
SIC: 3823 5084 3812 3613 Controllers, for
process variables, all types; Industrial
machinery and equipment; Search and
navigation equipment; Switchgear and
switchboard apparatus
HQ: Mettler-Toledo, Llc
1900 Polaris Pkwy Fl 6
Columbus OH 43240
614 438-4511

(G-6461)
**METTLR-TLEDO PRCESS
ANLYTICS I**
900 Middlesex Tpke Bldg 8-1 (01821-3929)
PHONE.................................781 301-8800
James L Bryant, *Pr*
Rich Brouillette, *
Mary Finnegan, *
Michelle Proia, *
Evelyn Smith, *
EMP: 100 **EST:** 1966
SQ FT: 41,500
SALES (est): 28.37MM
SALES (corp-wide): 3.79B **Publicly Held**
Web: www.mt.com
SIC: 3699 3845 3822 Electrical equipment
and supplies, nec; Electromedical
equipment; Environmental controls
HQ: Mettler-Toledo, Llc
1900 Polaris Pkwy Fl 6
Columbus OH 43240
614 438-4511

(G-6462)
**NEW ENGLAND WHEELS INC
(PA)**
Also Called: New England Wheels
33 Manning Rd (01821-3925)
PHONE.................................978 663-9724
Paul Larose, *Pr*
EMP: 39 **EST:** 1981
SQ FT: 62,500
SALES (est): 6.05MM
SALES (corp-wide): 6.05MM **Privately
Held**
Web: www.frontrunnerbus.com
SIC: 3713 Van bodies

(G-6463)
**NOVA BIOMEDICAL
CORPORATION**
39 Manning Rd (01821-3925)
PHONE.................................781 894-0800
EMP: 54
SALES (corp-wide): 307.6MM **Privately
Held**
Web: www.novabiomedical.com
SIC: 2833 Medicinals and botanicals
PA: Nova Biomedical Corporation
200 Prospect St
Waltham MA 02453
781 894-0800

(G-6464)
**NOVA BIOMEDICAL
CORPORATION**
4 Enterprise Rd (01821-5735)
PHONE.................................781 647-3700
Tom Larkin, *Brnch Mgr*
EMP: 100
SALES (corp-wide): 307.6MM **Privately
Held**
Web: www.novabiomedical.com
SIC: 2833 Medicinal chemicals
PA: Nova Biomedical Corporation
200 Prospect St
Waltham MA 02453
781 894-0800

(G-6465)
NUVERA FUEL CELLS LLC (HQ)
Also Called: Nuvera
129 Concord Rd Bldg 1 (01821-4615)
PHONE.................................617 245-7500
Jon Taylor, *
▲ **EMP:** 148 **EST:** 1997
SALES (est): 74.38MM **Publicly Held**
Web: www.nuvera.com

SIC: 1382 Oil and gas exploration services
PA: Hyster-Yale Materials Handling, Inc.
5875 Landerbrook Dr # 300
Cleveland OH 44124

(G-6466)
ORBOTECH INC (DH)
Also Called: Orbotech
44 Manning Rd (01821-3990)
PHONE.................................978 667-6037
Raanan Cohen, *Pr*
Milton Bordwin, *
Amichai Steinberg, *
Ken Maylor, *
Margaret Duncan, *
▲ **EMP:** 100 **EST:** 1984
SALES (est): 185.19MM
SALES (corp-wide): 10.5B **Publicly Held**
Web: www.kla.com
SIC: 5065 3823 3674 Electronic parts and
equipment, nec; Process control
instruments; Solid state electronic devices,
nec
HQ: Orbotech Ltd.
7 Hasanhedrin Blvd.
Yavne 81215

(G-6467)
ORPRO VISION LLC
44 Manning Rd Ste 1 (01821-3931)
PHONE.................................617 676-1101
EMP: 7 **EST:** 2009
SALES (est): 448.7K **Privately Held**
SIC: 3827 Optical instruments and lenses

(G-6468)
PANAMETRICS LLC (DH)
1100 Technology Park Dr Ste 100
(01821-4111)
P.O. Box 370049 (02241-0001)
PHONE.................................978 437-1000
Kristopher Mcbride, *Managing Member*
Barbara Cameron, *
Jessica Wenzell, *
◆ **EMP:** 600 **EST:** 1968
SQ FT: 300,000
SALES (est): 225.16MM
SALES (corp-wide): 25.51B **Publicly Held**
Web: www.panametrics.com
SIC: 3823 5084 3699 3674 Moisture
meters, industrial process type; Industrial
machinery and equipment; Electrical
equipment and supplies, nec;
Semiconductors and related devices
HQ: Baker Hughes Holdings Llc
17021 Aldine Westfield Rd
Houston TX 77073
713 439-8600

(G-6469)
**PAREXEL INTERNATIONAL
CORP**
Also Called: Paraxel International
1 Federal St (01821-3582)
PHONE.................................978 313-3900
EMP: 91
SALES (corp-wide): 2.44B **Privately Held**
Web: www.parexel.com
SIC: 2834 Pharmaceutical preparations
HQ: Parexel International (Ma) Corporation
275 Grove St Ste 3101
Auburndale MA 02466
617 454-9300

(G-6470)
**PHILIPS ADVANCED
METROLOGY SYS**
47 Manning Rd (01821-3978)
PHONE.................................508 647-8400
David A Dripchak, *Pr*

Doctor Christopher J L Moore, *Pr*
Mark Heber, *Dir*
Joseph Innamorati, *Sr VP*
EMP: 17 **EST:** 1995
SALES (est): 192.7K **Privately Held**
SIC: 3674　Wafers (semiconductor devices)

(G-6471)
PHOTONIC SYSTEMS INC
900 Middlesex Tpke Ste 5-2 (01821-3929)
PHONE..........................978 670-4990
Charles Cox Iii, *CEO*
Carol Cox, *VP*
Edward Ackerman, *VP*
Douglas Dillon, *VP*
EMP: 10 **EST:** 1999
SQ FT: 5,697
SALES (est): 1.76MM **Privately Held**
Web: www.photonicsinc.com
SIC: 2298　Cable, fiber

(G-6472)
PION INC
10 Cook St Ste 6 (01821-6000)
PHONE..........................978 528-2020
EMP: 12 **EST:** 1996
SALES (est): 4.19MM **Privately Held**
Web: www.pion-inc.com
SIC: 5049 3826 8731　Laboratory
equipment, except medical or dental;
Analytical instruments; Commercial
research laboratory

(G-6473)
PRODUCTION BASICS INC
31 Dunham Rd Ste 3 (01821-5701)
PHONE..........................617 926-8100
▲ **EMP:** 20 **EST:** 1994
SQ FT: 40,000
SALES (est): 5.52MM **Privately Held**
Web: www.pbasics.com
SIC: 2522 3499 2531　Office furniture,
except wood; Furniture parts, metal; Public
building and related furniture

(G-6474)
PSJL CORPORATION
780 Boston Rd Ste 4 (01821-5939)
PHONE..........................978 313-2500
Peter Schofield, *Pr*
Jeffrey Lang, *＊*
▲ **EMP:** 250 **EST:** 1994
SQ FT: 31,000
SALES (est): 22.22MM **Privately Held**
SIC: 3577 3599 5065　Computer peripheral
equipment, nec; Custom machinery;
Electronic parts

(G-6475)
RAPISCAN SYSTEMS INC
829 Middlesex Tpke (01821-3907)
PHONE..........................978 933-4375
EMP: 16
SALES (est): 7.69MM **Privately Held**
Web: www.rapiscan-ase.com
SIC: 3577　Computer peripheral equipment,
nec

(G-6476)
RESONANCE RESEARCH INC
Also Called: R R I
31 Dunham Rd Ste 1 (01821-5701)
PHONE..........................978 671-0811
Piotr M Starewicz, *Pr*
David F Hillenbrand, *VP*
Stana Mihajlovic, *Sec*
Robert L Mackeen, *VP*
Jane Punchard, *Sec*
EMP: 20 **EST:** 1993
SQ FT: 10,000

SALES (est): 4.62MM **Privately Held**
Web: www.rricorp.com
SIC: 3826　Analytical instruments

(G-6477)
REVVITY INC
Also Called: Packard Biochip
40 Linnell Cir (01821-3901)
PHONE..........................978 439-5511
Mike Catalano, *Mgr*
EMP: 50
SALES (corp-wide): 3.31B **Publicly Held**
Web: www.perkinelmer.com
SIC: 3826　Analytical instruments
PA: Revvity, Inc.
940 Winter St
Waltham MA 02451
781 663-6900

(G-6478)
RUBIL ASSOCIATES INC
Also Called: Spectro-Film
34 Dunham Rd (01821-5727)
PHONE..........................978 670-7192
Ruth Constant, *Pr*
William White, *VP*
EMP: 13 **EST:** 1969
SQ FT: 6,100
SALES (est): 803.74K **Privately Held**
Web: www.spectrofilm.com
SIC: 3827　Optical instruments and lenses

(G-6479)
SEMILAB USA LLC
47 Manning Rd (01821-3925)
PHONE..........................508 647-8400
EMP: 40
Web: www.semilab.com
SIC: 3823　Analyzers, industrial process type

(G-6480)
SHAW WELDING COMPANY INC
7 Innis Dr (01821-2604)
P.O. Box 435 (01821-0435)
PHONE..........................978 667-0197
Richard Shaw, *CEO*
EMP: 24 **EST:** 1980
SQ FT: 3,500
SALES (est): 2.28MM **Privately Held**
Web: www.shawwelding.com
SIC: 7692　Welding repair

(G-6481)
SHEAUMANN LASER INC
5 Federal St Ste 1 (01821-3571)
PHONE..........................508 970-0600
Jim Hsieh, *CEO*
Frank C Hsieh, *＊*
Gary Sousa, *＊*
Tim Shea, *Vice-President New Business Development＊*
Edward N Gadsby Junior, *Sec*
EMP: 40 **EST:** 2005
SALES (est): 4.55MM **Privately Held**
Web: www.sheaumann.com
SIC: 3674　Semiconductor diodes and
rectifiers

(G-6482)
SIMFER PRECISION MACHINE CO
42 Manning Rd (01821-3915)
PHONE..........................978 667-1138
Enzo Ferrara, *Pt*
Pompeo Simeone, *Pt*
EMP: 7 **EST:** 1988
SQ FT: 7,500
SALES (est): 731.78K **Privately Held**
Web: www.simferprecision.com

SIC: 3599　Machine shop, jobbing and repair

(G-6483)
SOLCHROMA TECHNOLOGIES INC
12 Dunham Rd Ste 1 (01821-5745)
PHONE..........................401 829-0024
Roger Diebold, *CEO*
Matthew Aprea, *VP*
Guy Danner, *Dir*
EMP: 9 **EST:** 2015
SALES (est): 975.07K **Privately Held**
Web: www.solchroma.com
SIC: 3999　Advertising display products

(G-6484)
SPIRE CORPORATION (PA)
25 Linnell Cir (01821-3928)
P.O. Box 9 (01730-0009)
PHONE..........................978 584-3958
Rodger W Lafavre, *Pr*
Robert S Lieberman, *CAO*
▲ **EMP:** 80 **EST:** 1969
SQ FT: 144,230
SALES (est): 32.62MM
SALES (corp-wide): 32.62MM **Privately Held**
Web: www.eternalsunspire.com
SIC: 3674　Solar cells

(G-6485)
TANYX MEASUREMENTS INC
Also Called: East Tronix
505 Middlesex Tpke Unit 9 (01821-3578)
PHONE..........................978 671-0183
EMP: 8 **EST:** 1995
SALES (est): 462.6K **Privately Held**
Web: www.tanyx.com
SIC: 3694 7389　Ignition apparatus and
distributors; Design services

(G-6486)
TARK INC
35 Dunham Rd Ste 7 (01821-5711)
PHONE..........................978 663-8074
Al Robins, *Mgr*
EMP: 12
SALES (corp-wide): 9.05MM **Privately Held**
Web: www.tarkinc.com
SIC: 3561　Pumps and pumping equipment
PA: Tark, Inc.
9273 Byers Rd
Miamisburg OH 45342
937 434-6766

(G-6487)
TEL MNFACTURING ENGRG AMER INC
900 Middlesex Tpke Ste 6-1 (01821-3929)
PHONE..........................978 436-2300
EMP: 50
Web: www.tel.com
SIC: 3674 3081 5012 3699　Semiconductors
and related devices; Plastics film and sheet
; Automobiles and other motor vehicles;
Electrical equipment and supplies, nec
HQ: Tel Manufacturing And Engineering Of
America, Inc.
3455 Lyman Blvd
Chaska MN 55318
952 448-5440

(G-6488)
TOWN OF BILLERICA
Also Called: Water Billing Dept
365 Boston Rd Ste 207 (01821-1882)
P.O. Box 986535 (02298-6535)
PHONE..........................978 671-0954

David Genereux, *Mgr*
EMP: 10
SALES (corp-wide): 210.44MM **Privately Held**
Web: town.billerica.ma.us
SIC: 9511 7372　Water control and quality
agency, government; Prepackaged software
PA: Town Of Billerica
365 Boston Rd Ste 207
Billerica MA 01821
978 671-0928

(G-6489)
WEAVR HEALTH CORP
44 Manning Rd (01821-3931)
PHONE..........................617 430-6920
Linh Hoang, *CEO*
Linh Hoang, *Pr*
Janine Buonomo, *Sec*
Christine Griggs, *Treas*
Louis Nunes, *Dir*
EMP: 20 **EST:** 2007
SALES (est): 2.17MM **Privately Held**
SIC: 3841　Diagnostic apparatus, medical

(G-6490)
WHIFFLETREE CNTRY STR GIFT SP
Also Called: Whiffle Tree Candle
101 Andover Rd (01821-1932)
PHONE..........................978 663-6346
Stephen Blinn, *Pr*
Susan Blinn, *VP*
EMP: 8 **EST:** 1969
SQ FT: 6,800
SALES (est): 874.47K **Privately Held**
Web: www.whiffletreecandles.com
SIC: 3999 5947　Candles; Gift shop

(G-6491)
WILEVCO INC
10 Fortune Dr (01821-3996)
PHONE..........................978 667-0400
Leverett P Flint, *Pr*
Putnam P Flint, *Ch*
John A Whitmore, *VP*
David Marrotta, *VP*
Charles Gulino Esq, *VP*
▲ **EMP:** 27 **EST:** 1961
SQ FT: 16,400
SALES (est): 5.71MM **Privately Held**
Web: www.wilevco.com
SIC: 3556 7359 2045　Mixers, commercial,
food; Equipment rental and leasing, nec;
Bread and bread type roll mixes: from
purchased flour

(G-6492)
ZINK IMAGING INC
37 Manning Rd (01821-3950)
PHONE..........................781 761-5400
Mary Jeffries, *Ch*
Ira Parker, *＊*
Wendy Caswell, *＊*
Paul Baker, *＊*
EMP: 134 **EST:** 2005
SALES (est): 14.35MM **Privately Held**
Web: www.zink.com
SIC: 8713 3299　Ariel digital imaging;
Images, small: gypsum, clay, or papier
mache

Blackstone
Worcester County

(G-6493)
CHARLES RIVER DOOR WORKS
3 Austin St (01504-1704)

▲ = Import ▼ = Export
◆ = Import/Export

PHONE................................617 828-3946
EMP: 7 **EST:** 2016
SALES (est): 92.36K **Privately Held**
SIC: 2431   Millwork

(G-6494)
H LAROSEE AND SONS INC
35 Reilly Ave (01504-1616)
PHONE................................978 562-9417
Stephen G Larosee, *Pr*
Stephen G Larosee Prestreas, *Prin*
EMP: 16 **EST:** 1903
SALES (est): 435.23K **Privately Held**
Web: www.hlaroseeandsons.com
SIC: 3471   Plating of metals or formed
products

Bolton
Worcester County

(G-6495)
BROOMFIELD LABORATORIES INC (PA)
164 Still River Rd (01740-1073)
P.O. Box 157 (01740-0157)
PHONE................................978 779-6600
Thomas L Broomfield, *Pr*
Andrew Broomfield, *VP*
Donna M Broomfield, *Sec*
EMP: 10 **EST:** 1958
SQ FT: 60,000
SALES (est): 8.94MM
SALES (corp-wide): 8.94MM **Privately
Held**
Web: www.broomfieldusa.com
SIC: 3549   Coiling machinery

(G-6496)
ECPI INC
83 Wilder Rd (01740-1241)
PHONE................................774 823-6368
Martha Norris, *Dir*
EMP: 10 **EST:** 2017
SALES (est): 263.94K **Privately Held**
SIC: 1771 2899 3531   Concrete repair;
Concrete curing and hardening compounds
; Surfacers, concrete grinding

(G-6497)
HEADWALL PHOTONICS INC
580 Main St (01740-1368)
PHONE................................978 353-4100
David Bannon, *CEO*
James Gennari, *CFO*
EMP: 60 **EST:** 1976
SQ FT: 6,250
SALES (est): 7.32MM **Privately Held**
Web: www.headwallphotonics.com
SIC: 3827   Optical instruments and lenses

(G-6498)
NASHOBA VALLEY SPIRITS LIMITED
Also Called: Nashoba Valley Winery
100 Wattaquadock Hill Rd (01740-1238)
PHONE................................978 779-5521
Richard A Pelletier, *Pr*
Cindy Pelletier, *
EMP: 50 **EST:** 1995
SQ FT: 10,000
SALES (est): 7.29MM **Privately Held**
Web: www.nashobawinery.com
SIC: 2084 5431   Wines; Fruit and vegetable
markets

Boston
Suffolk County

(G-6499)
21ST CENTURY SOFTWARE TECH INC
Also Called: 21st Century Software
6 Liberty Sq (02109-5800)
PHONE................................610 341-9017
Rebecca Levesque, *Pr*
Danielle Dickie, *CFO*
EMP: 95 **EST:** 1998
SALES (est): 10.42MM **Privately Held**
Web: www.21cs.com
SIC: 7371 7372 7379   Computer software
development; Publisher's computer software
; Computer related maintenance services

(G-6500)
3DFORTIFY INC
75 Hood Park Dr Fl 1 (02129-1002)
PHONE................................857 274-0483
Joshua Martin, *Pr*
Karlo Delos Reyes, *Sec*
EMP: 18 **EST:** 2018
SALES (est): 3.01MM **Privately Held**
Web: www.3dfortify.com
SIC: 3089   Injection molding of plastics

(G-6501)
47 BRAND LLC
19 Jersey St (02215-4147)
PHONE................................617 437-1384
Arthur D'angelo, *Managing Member*
EMP: 74
SALES (corp-wide): 62.92MM **Privately
Held**
Web: www.47brand.com
SIC: 5099 5947 2395   Souvenirs; Souvenirs;
Pleating and stitching
PA: '47 Brand, Llc
15 S West Park
Westwood MA 02090
781 702-2921

(G-6502)
ABB ENTERPRISE SOFTWARE INC
Also Called: ABB ENTERPRISE SOFTWARE
.INC.
2 Oliver St (02109-4901)
PHONE................................617 574-1130
Arun Nayar, *Brnch Mgr*
EMP: 37
Web: new.abb.com
SIC: 3674   Microcircuits, integrated
(semiconductor)
HQ: Abb Inc.
305 Gregson Dr
Cary NC 27511

(G-6503)
ABCORP NA INC
225 Rivermoor St (02132-4905)
PHONE................................617 325-9600
William Brown, *Ch*
Elena Skaritanov, *
▲ **EMP:** 300 **EST:** 1935
SQ FT: 120,000
SALES (est): 104.82MM
SALES (corp-wide): 263.55MM **Privately
Held**
Web: www.abcorp.com
SIC: 2821   Thermoplastic materials
PA: American Banknote Corporation
1055 Washington Blvd Fl 6
Stamford CT 06901
617 325-9600

(G-6504)
ABFERO PHARMACEUTICALS INC (PA)
867 Boylston St Fl 5 (02116-2774)
PHONE................................781 266-7297
Thomas Neenan, *Prin*
EMP: 8 **EST:** 2016
SALES (est): 1.03MM
SALES (corp-wide): 1.03MM **Privately
Held**
Web: www.abferopharmaceuticals.com
SIC: 2834   Pharmaceutical preparations

(G-6505)
ABP CORPORATION (PA)
Also Called: Au Bon Pain
19 Fid Kennedy Ave (02210-2427)
PHONE................................617 423-0629
▲ **EMP:** 200 **EST:** 2005
SALES (est): 241.74MM **Privately Held**
Web: www.aubonpain.com
SIC: 5461 5812 2051   Retail bakeries;
Eating places; Bread, cake, and related
products

(G-6506)
ABRY PARTNERS V L P
111 Huntington Ave Fl 30 (02199-7685)
PHONE................................617 859-2959
Royce Yudkoff, *Pt*
Peggy Koenig, *Pt*
EMP: 840 **EST:** 2004
SALES (est): 72.86MM **Privately Held**
Web: www.abry.com
SIC: 6799 2731 2721   Venture capital
companies; Books, publishing only;
Magazines: publishing only, not printed on
site
PA: Abry Partners, Llc
888 Boylston St Ste 1600
Boston MA 02199

(G-6507)
ACCELERON HOLDING LTD
33 Avenue Louis Pasteur (02115-5727)
PHONE................................617 649-9200
EMP: 9 **EST:** 2020
SALES (est): 74.42K **Privately Held**
SIC: 2836   Biological products, except
diagnostic

(G-6508)
ACCELERON PHARMA INC (HQ)
Also Called: Acceleron
33 Avenue Louis Pasteur (02115-5727)
PHONE................................617 649-9200
Habib J Dable, *Pr*
Sujay R Kango, *CCO**
Kevin F Mclaughlin, *Sr VP*
Adam M Veness, *
EMP: 67 **EST:** 2020
SALES (est): 92.52MM
SALES (corp-wide): 59.28B **Publicly Held**
Web: www.merck.com
SIC: 2834 2836   Pharmaceutical
preparations; Biological products, except
diagnostic
PA: Merck & Co., Inc.
126 E Lincoln Ave
Rahway NJ 07065
908 740-4000

(G-6509)
ACCELEVENTS INC
10 Post Office Sq Ste 800 (02109-4603)
P.O. Box 583 (02653-0583)
PHONE................................857 254-8035
Jonathan Kazarian, *CEO*
EMP: 51 **EST:** 2015
SALES (est): 9.88MM **Privately Held**
Web: www.accelevents.com
SIC: 7372   Application computer software

(G-6510)
ACCESS ADVANCE LLC
100 Cambridge St Ste 21400 (02114)
PHONE................................617 367-4802
EMP: 10 **EST:** 2014
SALES (est): 898.81K **Privately Held**
Web: www.accessadvance.com
SIC: 3651   Audio electronic systems

(G-6511)
ACQUIA INC (PA)
53 State St Ste 1101 (02109-2300)
PHONE................................888 922-7842
Michael Sullivan, *CEO*
Eric Sikola, *Sr VP*
Chris Andersen, *CFO*
Stephen Reny, *COO*
EMP: 813 **EST:** 2007
SALES (est): 75.25K
SALES (corp-wide): 75.25K **Privately Held**
Web: www.acquia.com
SIC: 7372   Business oriented computer
software

(G-6512)
ACS DIVISION BIOCHEMICAL TECH
42 Chauncy St Ste 10a (02111-2308)
PHONE................................617 216-6144
David Roush, *Ch*
David Roush, *Ch Bd*
EMP: 15
SALES (est): 704.27K **Privately Held**
SIC: 2836   Biological products, except
diagnostic

(G-6513)
ACTIV SURGICAL INC
Also Called: Ai
30 Thomson Pl (02210-1281)
PHONE................................202 688-5648
Todd Usen, *CEO*
Peter Kim, *Pr*
Manisha Shah-bugaj, *COO*
EMP: 58 **EST:** 2015
SALES (est): 5.69MM **Privately Held**
Web: www.activsurgical.com
SIC: 3841   Surgical and medical instruments

(G-6514)
ADCOTRON EMS INC
12 Channel St Marine Industrial Park
(02210)
PHONE................................617 598-3000
▲ **EMP:** 230
Web: www.ewmfg.com
SIC: 3679 3672   Electronic circuits; Printed
circuit boards

(G-6515)
ADDISON-WESLEY
501 Boylston St Ste 900 (02116-3769)
PHONE................................617 848-6300
Greg Tobin, *Prin*
EMP: 7 **EST:** 2017
SALES (est): 33.35K **Privately Held**
SIC: 2731   Book publishing

(G-6516)
ADICET BIO INC (PA)
500 Boylston St Ste 1300 (02116-3791)
PHONE................................857 315-5528
Chen Schor, *Pr*
Lloyd Klickstein, *CSO CIO*
Stewart Abbot, *CSO*
Francesco Galimi, *CMO*

Carrie Krehlik, *Chief Human Resources Officer*
EMP: 9 **EST:** 2016
SQ FT: 9,501
SALES (est): 24.99MM
SALES (corp-wide): 24.99MM **Publicly Held**
Web: www.adicetbio.com
SIC: 2834 8731 Pharmaceutical preparations; Biotechnical research, commercial

(G-6517)
ADVANCED ENTP SYSTEMS CORP
Also Called: Utility Cloud
179 Lincoln St (02111-2425)
PHONE....................508 431-7607
Mark Moreau, *CEO*
EMP: 20 **EST:** 2011
SALES (est): 1.03MM **Privately Held**
Web: www.utilitycloud.us
SIC: 7372 Prepackaged software

(G-6518)
ADVANTAGE DATA INC (HQ)
1 Federal St Fl 25 (02110-2048)
P.O. Box 961210 (02196-1210)
PHONE....................212 227-8870
Rene Robert, *Pr*
Gina L Robert, *COO*
Richard Farrell, *Dir*
Daniel Smythe, *Dir*
EMP: 18 **EST:** 1997
SALES (est): 6.07MM
SALES (corp-wide): 10.59MM **Privately Held**
Web: www.solvefixedincome.com
SIC: 7372 Prepackaged software
PA: Solve Advisors Inc.
600 Summer St Ste 503
Stamford CT 06901
646 699-5041

(G-6519)
ADVENT TECHNOLOGIES INC (PA)
500 Rutherford Ave Ste 101 (02129-1682)
PHONE....................617 655-6000
Vasilis Gregoriou, *CEO*
Emory De Castro, *COO*
EMP: 17 **EST:** 2012
SALES (est): 2.33MM
SALES (corp-wide): 2.33MM **Privately Held**
Web: www.advent.energy
SIC: 8731 3679 Energy research; Loads, electronic

(G-6520)
AEROVATE THERAPEUTICS INC (PA)
200 Berkeley St Ste 18 (02116-5035)
PHONE....................858 443-2400
Timothy P Noyes, *CEO*
Mark Iwicki, *Ch Bd*
Benjamin T Dake, *Pr*
George A Eldridge, *CFO*
Hunter Gillies, *CMO*
EMP: 8 **EST:** 2018
Web: www.aerovatetx.com
SIC: 2834 Pharmaceutical preparations

(G-6521)
AGILONE INC (HQ)
53 State St 10th Fl (02109-2820)
PHONE....................877 769-3047
Omer Artun, *CEO*
Ted Farrell, *

EMP: 48 **EST:** 2005
SQ FT: 6,000
SALES (est): 11.9MM
SALES (corp-wide): 75.25K **Privately Held**
Web: www.acquia.com
SIC: 3826 Analytical instruments
PA: Acquia Inc.
53 State St Ste 1101
Boston MA 02109
888 922-7842

(G-6522)
AILERON THERAPEUTICS INC (PA)
Also Called: Aileron Therapeutics
285 Summer St Ste 101 (02210-1518)
PHONE....................617 995-0900
Manuel C Alves Aivado, *Pr*
Jeffrey A Bailey, *Ch Bd*
Vojislav Vukovic, *CMO*
D Allen Annis, *Senior Vice President Research*
Susan L Drexler, *Interim Chief Financial Officer*
EMP: 8 **EST:** 2001
SQ FT: 3,365
Web: www.aileronrx.com
SIC: 2834 8731 Pharmaceutical preparations; Biotechnical research, commercial

(G-6523)
AIR CANADA
200 Terminal B Ste 5 (02128-2003)
PHONE....................617 567-7157
EMP: 8 **EST:** 2018
SALES (est): 274.75K **Privately Held**
Web: www.aircanada.com
SIC: 3944 Airplane models, toy and hobby

(G-6524)
AIRWORKS SOLUTIONS INC
226 Causeway St Ste 1 (02114-2155)
PHONE....................857 990-1060
David Morczinek, *CEO*
Adam Kersnowski, *COO*
EMP: 23 **EST:** 2017
SQ FT: 900
SALES (est): 2.63MM **Privately Held**
Web: www.airworks.io
SIC: 7372 7389 8713 Application computer software; Mapmaking or drafting, including aerial; Ariel digital imaging

(G-6525)
AISLEBUYER LLLC
321 Summer St Fl 8 (02210-1725)
PHONE....................617 606-7062
Andrew Paradise, *Managing Member*
EMP: 16 **EST:** 2009
SALES (est): 447.25K
SALES (corp-wide): 14.37B **Publicly Held**
SIC: 7372 Business oriented computer software
PA: Intuit Inc.
2700 Coast Ave
Mountain View CA 94043
650 944-6000

(G-6526)
AIVEN INC
1 Lincoln St (02111-2901)
PHONE....................860 908-6924
Oskari Saarenmaa, *Pr*
EMP: 22 **EST:** 2018
SALES (est): 1MM
SALES (corp-wide): 68.91MM **Privately Held**
Web: www.aiven.io

SIC: 7372 Prepackaged software
PA: Aiven Oy
Antinkatu 1
Helsinki 00100
401964488

(G-6527)
AKILI INC (PA)
125 Broad St Fl 5 (02110-3042)
PHONE....................617 313-8853
Matthew Franklin, *CEO*
Matthew Franklin, *Pr*
W Edward Martucci, *Ch Bd*
Santosh Shanbhag, *CFO*
Jacqueline Studer, *CLO*
EMP: 28 **EST:** 2011
SQ FT: 7,800
SALES (est): 323K
SALES (corp-wide): 323K **Publicly Held**
SIC: 3841 Surgical and medical instruments

(G-6528)
AKOUOS INC (PA)
Also Called: Akouos
645 Summer St Ste 200 (02210-2135)
PHONE....................857 410-1818
Emmanuel Simons, *Pr*
Jennifer Wellman, *COO*
Sachiyo Minegishi, *CFO*
Michael Mckenna, *CMO*
Rabia Gurses Ozden, *CDO*
EMP: 41 **EST:** 2016
SQ FT: 37,500
Web: www.akouos.com
SIC: 2834 Pharmaceutical preparations

(G-6529)
ALAIMO FUEL CORP
165 Norfolk St (02124-3334)
PHONE....................617 436-3600
EMP: 8 **EST:** 2009
SALES (est): 122.52K **Privately Held**
SIC: 2869 Fuels

(G-6530)
ALBERTO VASALLO JR
Also Called: Caribe Communications
175 Wlliam F Mcclllan Hwy (02128-1185)
PHONE....................617 522-5060
EMP: 9 **EST:** 1972
SALES (est): 598.65K **Privately Held**
Web: www.elmundoboston.com
SIC: 2711 Newspapers: publishing only, not printed on site

(G-6531)
ALBIREO PHARMA INC (DH)
53 State St Fl 19 (02109-2820)
PHONE....................857 254-5555
Christelle Huguet, *Pr*
Jennifer Benenson, *Sr VP*
EMP: 20 **EST:** 2003
SALES (est): 40.58MM **Privately Held**
Web: www.albireopharma.com
SIC: 2834 Pharmaceutical preparations
HQ: Ipsen Biopharmaceuticals, Inc.
1 Main St Ste 700
Cambridge MA 02142
973 903-4442

(G-6532)
ALEXION PHARMACEUTICALS INC (HQ)
Also Called: Alexion
121 Seaport Blvd (02210-2050)
PHONE....................475 230-2596
Ludwig N Hantson, *CEO*
David R Brennan, *Ch Bd*
Aradhana Sarin, *Ex VP*
Ellen Chiniara, *CLO*

Brian M Goff, *COMMERCIAL GLOBAL*
EMP: 593 **EST:** 2021
SQ FT: 150,000
SALES (est): 6.07B
SALES (corp-wide): 44.35B **Privately Held**
Web: www.alexion.com
SIC: 2834 Pharmaceutical preparations
PA: Astrazeneca Plc
1 Francis Crick Avenue
Cambridge CAMBS CB2 0
203 749-5000

(G-6533)
ALGORITHMIA INC
Also Called: Algorithmia
225 Franklin St (02110-2804)
PHONE....................415 741-1491
Diego Oppenheimer, *CEO*
John Combs, *VP Opers*
EMP: 9 **EST:** 2012
SALES (est): 2.38MM
SALES (corp-wide): 183.94K **Privately Held**
Web: www.datarobot.com
SIC: 7372 Utility computer software
PA: Datarobot, Inc.
225 Franklin St Ste 1300
Boston MA 02110
617 765-4500

(G-6534)
ALIGNABLE INC
205 Portland St Ste 500 (02114-1708)
PHONE....................978 376-5852
Eric Groves, *Pr*
Venkat Krishnamurthy, *COO*
EMP: 10 **EST:** 2012
SALES (est): 1.52MM **Privately Held**
Web: www.alignable.com
SIC: 7372 Business oriented computer software

(G-6535)
ALLBIRDS INC
205 Newbury St (02116-2579)
PHONE....................617 430-4500
EMP: 19
SALES (corp-wide): 297.77MM **Publicly Held**
Web: www.allbirds.com
SIC: 3143 Men's footwear, except athletic
PA: Allbirds, Inc.
730 Montgomery St
San Francisco CA 94111
628 225-4848

(G-6536)
ALLBIRDS INC
800 Boylston St (02199-1900)
PHONE....................857 990-1373
EMP: 19
SALES (corp-wide): 297.77MM **Publicly Held**
Web: www.allbirds.com
SIC: 3143 Men's footwear, except athletic
PA: Allbirds, Inc.
730 Montgomery St
San Francisco CA 94111
628 225-4848

(G-6537)
ALLISON ADVERTISING INC
Also Called: Allison Associates
123 South St Ste 7 (02111-2846)
PHONE....................617 368-6800
George S Golabek, *Pr*
EMP: 16 **EST:** 1967
SQ FT: 3,000
SALES (est): 965.9K **Privately Held**

SIC: **7311** 2791 7336   Advertising consultant
; Typesetting; Graphic arts and related
design

(G-6538)
ALTAIR PARAMOUNT LLC
225 Franklin St Ste 2330 (02110-2804)
PHONE..............................617 889-7300
EMP: 7 **EST:** 2021
SALES (est): 259.73K **Privately Held**
SIC: 2911   Diesel fuels

(G-6539)
ALTIUM ACQISITION HOLDINGS INC
Also Called: CCC Acquisition Holdings, Inc.
200 Clarendon St (02116-5021)
PHONE..............................617 516-2000
Seth Meisel, *CEO*
Jeffrey Greene, *
Richard Sehring, *
Stephen Zide, *
Robert Quandt, *
EMP: 4690 **EST:** 2012
SALES (corp-wide): 1.8MM **Privately Held**
SIC: 6719 2821   Investment holding
companies, except banks; Polyvinyl
chloride resins, PVC
HQ: Bain Capital Private Equity, Lp
200 Clarendon St
Boston MA 02116

(G-6540)
AMERICAN CRANE AND HOIST CORP
Also Called: Bellamy-Robie
1234 Washington St (02118-2109)
PHONE..............................617 482-8383
Arthur Leon, *Pr*
Robert C Carmichael, *
James Leon, *
▲ **EMP:** 112 **EST:** 1912
SQ FT: 80,000
SALES (est): 15.37MM **Privately Held**
Web: www.ac-h.com
SIC: 3536 3531   Cranes, overhead traveling;
Construction machinery

(G-6541)
AMERICAN MTEOROLOGICAL SOC INC (PA)
Also Called: AMS
45 Beacon St (02108-3693)
PHONE..............................617 227-2425
Keith Feitter, *Ex Dir*
Doctor Kenneth C Spengler, *Ex Dir*
Charles Paxton, *
David Cook, *
David Rahn, *
EMP: 52 **EST:** 1919
SQ FT: 14,000
SALES (est): 17.07MM
SALES (corp-wide): 17.07MM **Privately Held**
Web: www.ametsoc.org
SIC: 2721 8621   Trade journals: publishing
only, not printed on site; Scientific
membership association

(G-6542)
AMERICAN SOC LAW MDCINE ETHICS
765 Commonwealth Ave Ste 1634
(02215-1401)
PHONE..............................617 262-4990
T Hutchinson, *Ex Dir*
Ted Hutchinson, *Ex Dir*
EMP: 7 **EST:** 1972
SQ FT: 3,000

SALES (est): 445.18K **Privately Held**
Web: www.aslme.org
SIC: 8621 2721   Medical field-related
associations; Comic books: publishing only,
not printed on site

(G-6543)
AMERICAN WELL CORPORATION (PA)
Also Called: Amwell
75 State St Fl 26 (02109-1827)
PHONE..............................617 204-3500
Ido Schoenberg, *Ch Bd*
Roy Schoenberg, *
Keith W Anderson, *CFO*
Kurt Knight, *COO*
EMP: 332 **EST:** 2006
SALES (est): 277.19MM **Publicly Held**
Web: business.amwell.com
SIC: 7372 5045   Application computer
software; Computer software

(G-6544)
AMERICAS TEST KITCHEN LIMITED PARTNERSHIP
Also Called: America's Test Kitchen
21 Drydock Ave Ste 210 (02210-2554)
PHONE..............................617 232-1000
▲ **EMP:** 140 **EST:** 1989
SALES (est): 26.59MM **Privately Held**
Web: www.americastestkitchen.com
SIC: 2731 7922 7389   Book publishing;
Television program, including commercial
producers; Inspection and testing services

(G-6545)
AMEX INC
256 Marginal St Ste 3 (02128-2800)
PHONE..............................617 569-5630
John Flanagan, *Pr*
Paul Flanagan, *
EMP: 30 **EST:** 1980
SQ FT: 2,500
SALES (est): 9.11MM **Privately Held**
Web: www.amexinc.net
SIC: 3479   Coating of metals and formed
products

(G-6546)
AMPLITUDE VASCULAR SYSTEMS INC
451 D St Ste 802 (02210-1931)
PHONE..............................754 755-1530
Mark Toland, *CEO*
Hitinder Gurm Md, *Pr*
Sean Gilligan, *COO*
Robert Chisena, *Engr*
EMP: 10 **EST:** 2019
SALES (est): 606.82K **Privately Held**
Web: www.avspulse.com
SIC: 3841   Surgical and medical instruments

(G-6547)
AMRYT PHARMACEUTICALS INC (DH)
160 Federal St Fl 21 (02110-1700)
PHONE..............................877 764-3131
Joe Wiley, *CEO*
Gregory Perry, *CFO*
John Orloff, *Ex VP*
Remi Menes, *CMO*
EMP: 11 **EST:** 2005
SQ FT: 62,271
SALES (est): 10.47MM
SALES (corp-wide): 2.86B **Privately Held**
Web: www.amrytpharma.com
SIC: 2834   Pharmaceutical preparations
HQ: Amryt Pharma Limited
Dept 920a 196 High Road

London N22 8
160 454-9952

(G-6548)
ANDREW T JOHNSON COMPANY INC (PA)
Also Called: Wales Copy Center
15 Tremont Pl (02108-4096)
PHONE..............................617 742-1610
Robert Leslie, *Pr*
Warren K Leslie, *Pr*
Helene Gerstein, *Treas*
EMP: 19 **EST:** 1938
SQ FT: 15,000
SALES (est): 3.52MM
SALES (corp-wide): 3.52MM **Privately Held**
Web: www.andrewtjohnson.com
SIC: 2791 2789 2752 7334   Typesetting;
Bookbinding and related work; Commercial
printing, lithographic; Blueprinting service

(G-6549)
ANTEC (USA) LLC
Also Called: Antec Scientific USA
1 Boston Pl Fl 26 (02108-4407)
PHONE..............................888 572-0012
EMP: 9 **EST:** 2008
SALES (est): 881.92K **Privately Held**
Web: www.myantec.com
SIC: 3826   Analytical instruments

(G-6550)
APIFIA INC
Also Called: Mavrck
200 State St. Marketplace Center N Bld,
3rd Fl (02109)
PHONE..............................585 506-2787
Lyle Stevens, *Pr*
Sean Naegeli, *
EMP: 35 **EST:** 2014
SALES (est): 4.88MM **Privately Held**
Web: www.mavrck.co
SIC: 3993 7372   Signs and advertising
specialties; Prepackaged software

(G-6551)
APIPHANI INC
Also Called: Apiphani
53 State St Fl 5 (02109-2820)
P.O. Box 51190 (02205-1190)
PHONE..............................800 215-0811
Justin Folkers, *CEO*
EMP: 50 **EST:** 2018
SALES (est): 2.63MM **Privately Held**
Web: www.apiphani.io
SIC: 7371 7379 7372 8742   Custom
computer programming services; Computer
related consulting services; Application
computer software; Management
information systems consultant

(G-6552)
APRYSE CORP
530 Harrison Ave Ste 2 (02118-2816)
PHONE..............................617 982-2646
Cassidy Smirnow, *CEO*
Bruno Lowagie, *Pr*
Ingeborg Willaert, *CFO*
EMP: 23 **EST:** 2009
SALES (est): 2.21MM **Privately Held**
Web: www.itextpdf.com
SIC: 7372   Prepackaged software

(G-6553)
APTIV SERVICES US LLC
100 Northern Ave (02210-1980)
PHONE..............................781 864-9230
Kerry Hart, *Mgr*
EMP: 59

SALES (corp-wide): 17.49B **Privately Held**
Web: www.aptiv.com
SIC: 3714   Motor vehicle engines and parts
HQ: Aptiv Services Us, Llc
5725 Innovation Dr
Troy MI 48098

(G-6554)
ARATANA THERAPEUTICS INC
200 Clarendon St 54th Fl (02116-5021)
PHONE..............................617 425-9226
EMP: 7
SALES (corp-wide): 4.41B **Publicly Held**
Web: investor.elanco.com
SIC: 2834   Pharmaceutical preparations
HQ: Aratana Therapeutics, Inc.
2500 Innovation Way N
Greenfield IN 46140
913 353-1000

(G-6555)
ARCHAEOLOGICAL INSTITUTE AMER
44 Beacon St (02108-3614)
PHONE..............................617 353-9361
Brian Rose, *Pr*
EMP: 15 **EST:** 1906
SQ FT: 6,000
SALES (est): 8.12MM **Privately Held**
Web: www.archaeological.org
SIC: 8621 2721   Scientific membership
association; Trade journals: publishing and
printing

(G-6556)
ARCHER ROOSE INC
Also Called: Archer Roose Wine
6 Liberty Sq (02109-5800)
PHONE..............................646 283-4152
Marian Leitner, *CEO*
◆ **EMP:** 14 **EST:** 2014
SALES (est): 2.5MM **Privately Held**
Web: www.archerroose.com
SIC: 2084   Wines

(G-6557)
ARCLIGHT ENRGY PRTNERS FUND VI (PA)
200 Clarendon St 55th Fl (02116-5021)
PHONE..............................617 531-6300
EMP: 20 **EST:** 2015
SALES (est): 32.51MM
SALES (corp-wide): 32.51MM **Privately Held**
Web: www.arclight.com
SIC: 6722 5172 1389   Money market mutual
funds; Gases, liquefied petroleum (propane)
; Processing service, gas

(G-6558)
ARMY & ROCHE LLC
1 Beacon St Fl 23 (02108-3106)
PHONE..............................617 936-0114
Lucia Strout, *Prin*
EMP: 9 **EST:** 2019
SALES (est): 504.06K **Privately Held**
Web: armyandroche.squarespace.com
SIC: 2834   Pharmaceutical preparations

(G-6559)
ARTEMIS CAPITAL PARTNERS LLC (PA)
160 Federal St 23rd (02110-1700)
PHONE..............................857 327-5606
Peter A Hunter, *Managing Member*
EMP: 9 **EST:** 2006
SALES (est): 22.73MM
SALES (corp-wide): 22.73MM **Privately Held**

Web: www.artemislp.com
SIC: 3829 Measuring and controlling
   devices, nec

(G-6560)
**ASIAN AMERICAN CIVIC ASSN
INC (PA)**
Also Called: SAMPANN NEWSPAPER
87 Tyler St Ste 5f (02111-1833)
PHONE................................617 426-9492
Mary Chin, *Pr*
EMP: 27 EST: 1968
SQ FT: 10,000
SALES (est): 4.74MM
SALES (corp-wide): 4.74MM **Privately
Held**
Web: www.aaca-boston.org
SIC: 8641 2711 8331 Civic associations;
   Newspapers; Community service
   employment training program

(G-6561)
ASIMOV INC
201 Brookline Ave (02215-4157)
PHONE................................339 532-9982
EMP: 25 EST: 2017
SALES (est): 3.85MM **Privately Held**
Web: www.asimov.com
SIC: 2835 Microbiology and virology
   diagnostic products

(G-6562)
**ASTRIA THERAPEUTICS INC
(PA)**
75 State St Ste 1400 (02109-1943)
PHONE................................617 349-1971
Jill C Milne, *Pr*
Kenneth Bate, *Ch Bd*
Noah Clauser, *CFO*
Benjamin Harshbarger, *CLO*
Andrea Matthews, *Chief Business Officer*
EMP: 39 EST: 2008
SQ FT: 11,000
Web: www.astriatx.com
SIC: 2834 Pharmaceutical preparations

(G-6563)
ATC PONDEROSA B-I LLC
116 Huntington Ave (02116-5749)
PHONE................................617 375-7500
EMP: 11 EST: 2018
SALES (est): 2.12MM **Publicly Held**
SIC: 3663 Radio broadcasting and
   communications equipment
PA: American Tower Corporation
   116 Huntington Ave # 1100
   Boston MA 02116

(G-6564)
ATC PONDEROSA B-II LLC
116 Huntington Ave (02116-5749)
PHONE................................617 375-7500
James Tacilet, *CEO*
EMP: 13 EST: 2018
SALES (est): 2.04MM **Publicly Held**
Web: www.americantower.com
SIC: 3663 Radio broadcasting and
   communications equipment
PA: American Tower Corporation
   116 Huntington Ave # 1100
   Boston MA 02116

(G-6565)
ATC PONDEROSA H-I LLC
116 Huntington Ave (02116-5749)
PHONE................................617 375-7500
James Tacilet, *CEO*
EMP: 19 EST: 2018
SALES (est): 1.73MM **Publicly Held**

Web: www.americantower.com
SIC: 3663 Radio broadcasting and
   communications equipment
PA: American Tower Corporation
   116 Huntington Ave # 1100
   Boston MA 02116

(G-6566)
ATC PONDEROSA H-II LLC
116 Huntington Ave (02116-5749)
PHONE................................617 375-7500
James Tacilet, *CEO*
EMP: 13 EST: 2018
SALES (est): 2.18MM **Publicly Held**
SIC: 3663 Radio broadcasting and
   communications equipment
PA: American Tower Corporation
   116 Huntington Ave # 1100
   Boston MA 02116

(G-6567)
ATC PONDEROSA K LLC
116 Huntington Ave (02116-5749)
PHONE................................617 375-7500
James Tacilet, *CEO*
EMP: 9 EST: 2018
SALES (est): 4.47MM **Publicly Held**
Web: www.americantower.com
SIC: 3663 Radio broadcasting and
   communications equipment
PA: American Tower Corporation
   116 Huntington Ave # 1100
   Boston MA 02116

(G-6568)
ATC PONDEROSA K OHIO LLC
116 Huntington Ave (02116-5749)
PHONE................................617 375-7500
James Tacilet, *CEO*
EMP: 14 EST: 2018
SALES (est): 1.73MM **Publicly Held**
SIC: 3663 Radio broadcasting and
   communications equipment
PA: American Tower Corporation
   116 Huntington Ave # 1100
   Boston MA 02116

(G-6569)
ATC SEQUOIA LLC
116 Huntington Ave (02116-5749)
PHONE................................617 375-7500
EMP: 18 EST: 2015
SALES (est): 2.1MM **Publicly Held**
SIC: 4813 3663 Internet connectivity
   services; Radio broadcasting and
   communications equipment
PA: American Tower Corporation
   116 Huntington Ave # 1100
   Boston MA 02116

(G-6570)
ATC TOWER SERVICES LLC
116 Huntington Ave Ste 1100 (02116-5786)
PHONE................................617 375-7500
Edmund Disanto, *Prin*
James D Taiclet Junior, *Ch Bd*
EMP: 25 EST: 2015
SALES (est): 5.4MM **Publicly Held**
SIC: 4813 3663 Telephone communication,
   except radio; Radio and t.v.
   communications equipment
PA: American Tower Corporation
   116 Huntington Ave # 1100
   Boston MA 02116

(G-6571)
**ATEA PHARMACEUTICALS INC
(PA)**
Also Called: ATEA PHARMACEUTICALS
225 Franklin St Ste 2100 (02110-2856)

PHONE................................857 284-8891
Jean-pierre Sommadossi, *Ch Bd*
Jean-pierre Sommadossi, *Ch Bd*
Janet Hammond, *CDO*
Maria Arantxa Horga, *CMO*
John Vavricka, *CCO*
EMP: 39 EST: 2014
SQ FT: 5,634
Web: www.ateapharma.com
SIC: 2834 8731 Pharmaceutical
   preparations; Biotechnical research,
   commercial

(G-6572)
ATHENAHEALTH INC (PA)
80 Guest St (02135-2071)
PHONE................................617 402-1000
Robert E Segert, *CEO*
Jessica Collins, *Sec*
Marc A Levine, *Ex VP*
Bill Conway, *CSO*
John Hofmann, *COO*
EMP: 494 EST: 1997
SQ FT: 551,984
SALES (est): 1.33B
SALES (corp-wide): 1.33B **Privately Held**
Web: www.athenahealth.com
SIC: 7372 Business oriented computer
   software

(G-6573)
ATIIM INC
399 Boylston St Fl 6 (02116-3325)
PHONE................................800 735-4071
Kyle Silberbauer, *CEO*
EMP: 10 EST: 2015
SALES (est): 2.48MM
SALES (corp-wide): 17.61B **Publicly Held**
Web: www.atiim.com
SIC: 7372 Prepackaged software
HQ: Workfront, Inc.
   3301 N Thanksgivng Way # 50
   Lehi UT 84043
   801 373-3266

(G-6574)
ATLANTIC ACM
Also Called: Atlantic-Acm
31 State St Ste 2 (02109-2722)
PHONE................................617 720-3700
Judy Reed Smith, *CEO*
Normand Fedor Smith Iv, *Pr*
EMP: 11 EST: 1996
SQ FT: 2,000
SALES (est): 2.41MM **Privately Held**
Web: www.atlantic-acm.com
SIC: 8742 2741 Marketing consulting
   services; Miscellaneous publishing

(G-6575)
ATLASSIAN PTY LTD
239 Causeway St Ste 300 (02114-2130)
PHONE................................401 864-1481
Rachel Reilly, *Prin*
EMP: 9
Web: www.atlassian.com
SIC: 7372 Business oriented computer
   software
HQ: Atlassian Pty Ltd
   L 6 341 George St
   Sydney NSW 2000

(G-6576)
ATTIVIO INC
100 Summer St Ste 3100 (02110-2154)
P.O. Box 731 (01742-0731)
PHONE................................857 226-5040
Stephen Baker, *CEO*
Peter Lee, *
Alan Cooke, *

Will Johnson, *
EMP: 100 EST: 2007
SQ FT: 5,600
SALES (est): 17MM **Privately Held**
Web: www.attivio.com
SIC: 7372 Application computer software

(G-6577)
AURA BIOSCIENCES INC (PA)
Also Called: AURA
80 Guest St Fl 5 (02135-2071)
PHONE................................617 500-8864
Elisabet De Los Pinos, *CEO*
David Johnson, *Non-Executive Chairman of
the Board*
Julie Feder, *CFO*
Mark De Rosch, *COO*
Christopher Primiano, *Chief Business
Officer*
EMP: 18 EST: 2009
SQ FT: 29,836
Web: www.aurabiosciences.com
SIC: 8731 2836 Biotechnical research,
   commercial; Biological products, except
   diagnostic

(G-6578)
AUTODESK INC
23 Drydock Ave Ste 610e (02210-2543)
PHONE................................857 233-4149
David Lemont, *Mgr*
EMP: 24
SALES (corp-wide): 4.39B **Publicly Held**
Web: www.autodesk.com
SIC: 7372 Prepackaged software
PA: Autodesk, Inc.
   1 Market St Ste 400
   San Francisco CA 94105
   415 507-5000

(G-6579)
AUTONODYNE LLC (PA)
320 Congress St Fl 1 (02210-1250)
PHONE................................321 751-8402
Harry Ericson, *CFO*
EMP: 24 EST: 2014
SQ FT: 30,000
SALES (est): 2.11MM
SALES (corp-wide): 2.11MM **Privately
Held**
Web: www.autonodyne.ai
SIC: 3812 Aircraft/aerospace flight
   instruments and guidance systems

(G-6580)
**AVEO PHARMACEUTICALS INC
(HQ)**
Also Called: Aveo Oncology
1 Marina Park Dr Fl 12 (02210-1832)
PHONE................................857 400-0101
Michael P Bailey, *Pr*
Erick J Lucera, *CFO*
Michael J Ferraresso, *CCO*
Jebediah Ledell, *COO*
EMP: 19 EST: 2001
SQ FT: 10,158
SALES (est): 42.3MM **Privately Held**
Web: www.aveooncology.com
SIC: 2834 Pharmaceutical preparations
PA: Lg Chem, Ltd.
   128 Yeoui-Daero, Yeongdeungpo-Gu
   Seoul 07336

(G-6581)
BA-INSIGHT INC
401 Congress St Ste 1850 (02210-2800)
PHONE................................339 368-7234
Massood Zarrabian, *CEO*
EMP: 75 EST: 2010
SALES (est): 10.54MM **Publicly Held**

Web: www.bainsight.com
SIC: 3812 Search and navigation equipment
PA: Upland Software, Inc.
401 Congress Ave Ste 1850
Austin TX 78701

(G-6582)
BAKERY TO GO INC
Also Called: East Meets West
314 Shawmut Ave (02118-2190)
PHONE...............................617 482-1015
Scott Popkowski, *Pr*
EMP: 8 EST: 1986
SQ FT: 1,000
SALES (est): 562.77K **Privately Held**
SIC: 2051 5812 Bakery: wholesale or wholesale/retail combined; Caterers

(G-6583)
BARMAKIAN BROTHERS LTD PARTNR
333 Washington St Ste 720 (02108-5191)
PHONE...............................617 227-3724
Ara Barmakian, *Pt*
Diran Barmakian, *Pt*
Vahan Barmakian, *Pt*
Adam Barmakian, *Pt*
EMP: 50 EST: 1910
SQ FT: 15,000
SALES (est): 2.59MM **Privately Held**
Web: www.barmakian.com
SIC: 3911 5944 Jewelry, precious metal; Jewelry, precious stones and precious metals

(G-6584)
BAY COLONY ASSOCIATES (PA)
818 William T Morrissey Blvd (02122-3404)
PHONE...............................617 287-9100
Philip A Strazzula Junior, *Pr*
EMP: 8 EST: 1971
SQ FT: 1,200
SALES (est): 19.57MM
SALES (corp-wide): 19.57MM **Privately Held**
Web: www.wyndhamhotels.com
SIC: 7011 2064 7933 5812 Hotels and motels; Candy and other confectionery products; Bowling centers; Eating places

(G-6585)
BCPE SEMINOLE HOLDINGS LP (PA)
200 Clarendon St (02116-5021)
PHONE...............................617 516-2000
Christopher R Gordon, *Pr*
Andrew Kaplan, *Sec*
EMP: 12 EST: 2017
SALES (est): 357.64MM
SALES (corp-wide): 357.64MM **Privately Held**
SIC: 8062 3851 6799 General medical and surgical hospitals; Ophthalmic goods; Venture capital companies

(G-6586)
BEACON BIOSIGNALS INC
80 Revere St Apt 10 (02114-4419)
PHONE...............................401 225-5782
Jacob Donoghue, *CEO*
Sydney Cash, *
Jarrett Revels, *
Christine Vietz, *Research & Development* *
EMP: 62 EST: 2019
SALES (est): 6.3MM **Privately Held**
Web: www.beacon.bio
SIC: 7372 Prepackaged software

(G-6587)
BEDROCK BRANDS LLC
Also Called: St. Josephs
20 Custom House St # 920 (02110-3513)
PHONE...............................914 231-9550
Robert Bailey, *Ex Dir*
EMP: 7 EST: 2012
SQ FT: 5,000
SALES (est): 100.55K **Privately Held**
SIC: 5122 2834 Drugs and drug proprietaries; Proprietary drug products

(G-6588)
BEGUM BRANDS CORPORATION
Also Called: Leo's Bakery
60 Old Colony Ave (02127-2406)
PHONE...............................617 269-8400
Zaki Enayetullah, *Pr*
Zaki Enayetullah, *CEO*
Shabbir Ahmed, *
EMP: 35 EST: 1958
SQ FT: 25,000
SALES (est): 2.73MM **Privately Held**
Web: www.leosbakery.com
SIC: 2051 Bread, cake, and related products

(G-6589)
BERRY TWIST
200 Faneuil Hall Market Pl (02109-1634)
PHONE...............................857 362-7455
Sergio Gonsalves, *Owner*
EMP: 7 EST: 2008
SALES (est): 504.58K **Privately Held**
SIC: 2024 Ice cream, packaged: molded, on sticks, etc.

(G-6590)
BEST MARINE AND OUTDOORS INC
100 Cambridge St (02114-2509)
PHONE...............................617 644-7711
Mark M Gilmore, *Dir*
Kevin P Shea, *Dir*
EMP: 9 EST: 2016
SALES (est): 405.89K **Privately Held**
Web: www.bestmarineandoutdoors.com
SIC: 3732 Kayaks, building and repairing

(G-6591)
BFI PRINT COMMUNICATIONS INC (PA)
Also Called: Fastforms
255 State St Fl 7 (02109-2618)
P.O. Box 455 (02382-0455)
PHONE...............................781 447-1199
Donna Anderson, *Pr*
Arthur Graham Junior, *Pr*
EMP: 30 EST: 1981
SALES (est): 4.5MM
SALES (corp-wide): 4.5MM **Privately Held**
Web: www.bfiprint.com
SIC: 2761 Manifold business forms

(G-6592)
BI-SAM
53 State St Ste 1203 (02109-2307)
PHONE...............................617 933-4400
EMP: 10 EST: 2015
SALES (est): 183.42K **Privately Held**
SIC: 7372 Prepackaged software

(G-6593)
BICON LLC (PA)
Also Called: Bicon Dental Implants
501 Arborway (02130-3663)
PHONE...............................617 524-4443
▲ EMP: 70 EST: 1994
SQ FT: 2,000
SALES (est): 9.87MM **Privately Held**

Web: www.bicon.com
SIC: 3843 Dental equipment

(G-6594)
BIGTIME SOFTWARE INC
98 N Washington St Ste 410 (02114-1918)
PHONE...............................781 859-5308
Charles Moylan, *Pr*
EMP: 20
SALES (corp-wide): 11.82MM **Privately Held**
SIC: 7372 Prepackaged software
PA: Bigtime Software, Inc.
311 S Wacker Dr Ste 2300
Chicago IL 60606
312 346-4646

(G-6595)
BIOBRIGHT LLC (HQ)
Also Called: Biobright
85 Merrimac St Ste 200 (02114-4715)
PHONE...............................617 444-9007
Charles Fracchia, *CEO*
EMP: 8 EST: 2013
SALES (est): 4.07MM
SALES (corp-wide): 201.3MM **Privately Held**
Web: www.biobright.com
SIC: 7372 7371 Prepackaged software; Computer software development and applications
PA: Insightful Science Holdings, Llc
225 Franklin St
Boston MA 02110
858 454-5577

(G-6596)
BLANCHE P FIELD LLC
22 Elkins St Ste 2 (02127-1620)
PHONE...............................617 423-0715
◆ EMP: 10 EST: 1905
SALES (est): 2.06MM **Privately Held**
Web: www.blanchefield.com
SIC: 3999 5023 7629 3645 Shades, lamp and candle; Lamps: floor, boudoir, desk; Lamp repair and mounting; Residential lighting fixtures

(G-6597)
BLAUER MANUFACTURING CO INC (PA)
Also Called: Blauer
20 Aberdeen St (02215-3800)
PHONE...............................800 225-6715
Charles Blauer, *Pr*
Michael Blauer, *
Stephen Blauer, *
Richard W Wennett, *
Michael A Simons, *
◆ EMP: 30 EST: 1936
SQ FT: 22,000
SALES (est): 48.76MM
SALES (corp-wide): 48.76MM **Privately Held**
Web: www.blauer.com
SIC: 5099 3842 2337 Safety equipment and supplies; Clothing, fire resistant and protective; Uniforms, except athletic: women's, misses', and juniors'

(G-6598)
BLUE ATLANTIC FABRICATORS LLC
256 Marginal St Ste 2 (02128-2800)
PHONE...............................617 874-8503
EMP: 10 EST: 2018
SALES (est): 2.48MM **Privately Held**
Web: www.blueatlanticfab.com
SIC: 3441 Fabricated structural metal

(G-6599)
BLUECONIC INC
179 Lincoln St Ste 501 (02111-2426)
PHONE...............................888 440-2583
Bart Heilbron, *CEO*
Harmen Haarman, *CFO*
EMP: 22 EST: 2014
SQ FT: 4,900
SALES (est): 2MM
SALES (corp-wide): 30.46MM **Privately Held**
Web: www.blueconic.com
SIC: 7372 Business oriented computer software
PA: Blueconic Holding, Inc.
179 Lincoln St Ste 501
Boston MA 02111
888 440-2583

(G-6600)
BOMBARDIER SERVICES CORP
Also Called: Bombardier Mass Transit
2 Frontage Rd (02118-2803)
PHONE...............................617 464-0323
Phil Pronchuk, *Brnch Mgr*
EMP: 119
SALES (corp-wide): 6.91B **Privately Held**
Web: www.bombardier.com
SIC: 3721 Aircraft
HQ: Bombardier Services Corp
2400 Aviation Way
Bridgeport WV 26330

(G-6601)
BOSTON ACADEMIC PUBLISHING
175 Portland St Fl 2 (02114-1713)
PHONE...............................617 851-8655
EMP: 7 EST: 2018
SALES (est): 423.96K **Privately Held**
Web: www.bacademic.com
SIC: 2741 Miscellaneous publishing

(G-6602)
BOSTON BEER COMPANY INC
30 Germania St Ste 1 (02130-2312)
PHONE...............................617 368-5080
David Grinneli, *Mgr*
EMP: 10
Web: www.bostonbeer.com
SIC: 2082 Beer (alcoholic beverage)
PA: The Boston Beer Company Inc
1 Design Center Pl # 850
Boston MA 02210

(G-6603)
BOSTON BEER COMPANY INC (PA)
Also Called: Boston Beer
1 Design Center Pl Ste 850 (02210-2300)
PHONE...............................617 368-5000
David A Burwick, *Pr*
C James Koch, *
Frank H Smalla, *CFO*
John C Geist, *CSO*
Lesya Lysyj, *CMO*
◆ EMP: 1172 EST: 1984
SQ FT: 54,200
SALES (est): 2.09B **Publicly Held**
Web: www.bostonbeer.com
SIC: 2082 Beer (alcoholic beverage)

(G-6604)
BOSTON BEER CORPORATION (DH)
1 Design Center Pl Ste 850 (02210-2300)
PHONE...............................617 368-5000
William F Urich, *Treas*
Kathleen H Wade, *

GEOGRAPHIC

EMP: 150 **EST:** 2000
SALES (est): 430.01MM **Publicly Held**
Web: www.brewbound.com
SIC: 2082 Beer (alcoholic beverage)
HQ: Boston Brewing Co Inc
    1 Design Center Pl # 850
    Boston MA 02210

(G-6605)
BOSTON BUSINESS JOURNAL INC
70 Franklin St Ste 800 (02110-1313)
PHONE...............................617 330-1000
Mike Olivieri, *Pr*
Ray Schaw, *Ch Bd*
EMP: 393 **EST:** 1980
SQ FT: 9,500
SALES (est): 2.52MM
SALES (corp-wide): 2.88B **Privately Held**
Web: www.bostonbusinessjournal.com
SIC: 2711 Newspapers, publishing and
    printing
HQ: American City Business Journals, Inc.
    120 W Morehead St Ste 400
    Charlotte NC 28202
    704 973-1000

(G-6606)
BOSTON BUSINESS PRINTING INC
115 Broad St (02110-3061)
PHONE...............................617 482-7955
Theresaa Joseph, *Pr*
Sheryl Read, *Pr*
William Joseph, *VP*
▲ **EMP:** 10 **EST:** 1971
SQ FT: 6,000
SALES (est): 884.03K **Privately Held**
Web: www.bostonbusinessprinting.com
SIC: 7334 2752 7331 5999 Photocopying
    and duplicating services; Offset printing;
    Mailing service; Banners, flags, decals, and
    posters

(G-6607)
BOSTON CHIPYARD THE INC
Also Called: Boston Chipyard
257 Faneuil Hall Market Pl (02109-1634)
PHONE...............................617 742-9537
Dana Joly, *Genl Mgr*
EMP: 24
SALES (corp-wide): 1.05MM **Privately Held**
Web: www.chipyard.com
SIC: 2052 5461 5149 Cookies; Cookies;
    Crackers, cookies, and bakery products
PA: Boston Chipyard, The Inc
    100 W Chapman Ave
    Orange CA 92866
    714 547-0262

(G-6608)
BOSTON GLOBE LLC
53 State St Lbby 2& (02109-2820)
PHONE...............................617 929-2684
Michael Sheehan, *CEO*
James Levy, *
EMP: 2200 **EST:** 2013
SALES (est): 176.49MM
SALES (corp-wide): 453.36MM **Privately Held**
Web: www.bostonglobe.com
SIC: 2711 Commercial printing and
    newspaper publishing combined
PA: Ne Media Group Inc.
    1 Exchange Pl Ste 201
    Boston MA 02109
    617 929-2000

(G-6609)
BOSTON GLOBE MDIA PARTNERS LLC
Also Called: Boston Globe, The
1 Exchange Pl Ste 201 (02109-2132)
P.O. Box 55819 (02205-5819)
PHONE...............................617 929-2000
Linda Pizzuti Henry, *CEO*
Peggy Byrd, *CMO*
EMP: 423 **EST:** 2013
SALES (est): 11MM **Privately Held**
Web: www.bostonglobe.com
SIC: 2711 Job printing and newspaper
    publishing combined

(G-6610)
BOSTON LEGION LLC
6 Liberty Sq (02109-5800)
PHONE...............................508 718-8912
EMP: 17 **EST:** 2017
SALES (est): 429.13K **Privately Held**
SIC: 2711 Newspapers, publishing and
    printing

(G-6611)
BOSTON NEIGHBORHOOD NEWS INC
Also Called: Boston Hatian Reporter
150 Mount Vernon St Ste 120 (02125)
PHONE...............................617 436-1222
William Forry, *Pr*
Ed Forry, *VP*
EMP: 8 **EST:** 1973
SQ FT: 2,000
SALES (est): 852.13K **Privately Held**
Web: www.bostonirish.com
SIC: 2711 Commercial printing and
    newspaper publishing combined

(G-6612)
BOSTON PAPER BOARD CORP
40 Roland St (02129-1222)
P.O. Box 290086 (02129-0202)
PHONE...............................617 666-1154
Mark Feinberg, *Pr*
▲ **EMP:** 18 **EST:** 1908
SQ FT: 75,000
SALES (est): 460.6K **Privately Held**
SIC: 2621 Specialty or chemically treated
    papers

(G-6613)
BOSTON PRINT SPECIALISTS LLC
Also Called: AlphaGraphics
12 Channel St Ste 804 (02210-2517)
PHONE...............................617 742-9585
EMP: 9 **EST:** 2002
SQ FT: 5,000
SALES (est): 2.34MM **Privately Held**
Web: www.alphagraphicsboston.com
SIC: 2752 Commercial printing, lithographic

(G-6614)
BOSTON SALADS AND PROVS INC
26 Chesterton St (02119-2906)
PHONE...............................617 541-9054
Claudia Stohrer, *Mgr*
EMP: 18
Web: www.bostonsalads.com
SIC: 2099 Salads, fresh or refrigerated
PA: Boston Salads And Provisions, Inc.
    225 Southampton St
    Boston MA 02118

(G-6615)
BOSTON SALADS AND PROVS INC (PA)
Also Called: Boston Salads
225 Southampton St (02118-2715)
PHONE...............................617 307-6340
John A Zofchak, *CEO*
Tom Watson, *
Lynn A Zofchak, *
EMP: 32 **EST:** 1991
SALES (est): 10.62MM **Privately Held**
Web: www.bostonsalads.com
SIC: 2099 Salads, fresh or refrigerated

(G-6616)
BOSTON SAND & GRAVEL COMPANY (PA)
100 N Washington St 2nd Fl (02114-1712)
P.O. Box 9187 (02114-9187)
PHONE...............................617 227-9000
Dean M Boylan Senior, *Ch Bd*
Dean M Boylan, *Sec*
David B Mcneil, *Sr VP*
Jeanne-marie Boylan, *VP*
EMP: 35 **EST:** 1914
SQ FT: 6,000
SALES (est): 100.01K
SALES (corp-wide): 100.01K **Privately Held**
Web: www.bostonsand.com
SIC: 3273 1442 Ready-mixed concrete;
    Construction sand mining

(G-6617)
BOSTON SHIP REPAIR LLC
32a Drydock Ave (02210-2308)
PHONE...............................617 330-5045
◆ **EMP:** 130 **EST:** 1995
SQ FT: 17,000
SALES (est): 26.62MM **Privately Held**
Web: www.nashiprepair.com
SIC: 3731 Shipbuilding and repairing
PA: Northeast Ship Repair, Inc.
    32a Drydock Ave
    Boston MA 02210

(G-6618)
BOSTON SIGN COMPANY INC
Also Called: Architectural Elements
40 Plympton St Ste 1 (02118-2554)
PHONE...............................617 338-2114
EMP: 7 **EST:** 1989
SQ FT: 4,000
SALES (est): 988.01K **Privately Held**
Web: www.bostonsign.com
SIC: 8712 3993 Architectural services;
    Signs and advertising specialties

(G-6619)
BOSTON SMOKED FISH COMPANY LLC
20 Fish Pier St W (02210)
PHONE...............................617 819-5476
Matthew Baumann, *CEO*
EMP: 15 **EST:** 2013
SQ FT: 9,000
SALES (est): 1.83MM **Privately Held**
Web: www.bostonsmokedfish.com
SIC: 2091 Fish, smoked

(G-6620)
BOSTONCOM LLC
320 Congress St Fl 2 (02210-1250)
PHONE...............................617 929-8593
EMP: 7 **EST:** 2019
SALES (est): 333.3K **Privately Held**
Web: www.boston.com
SIC: 2711 Newspapers, publishing and
    printing

(G-6621)
BOSTONIA WELDING SUPPLY INC
61 Dorchester Ave (02127-1023)
PHONE...............................617 268-1025
Bradley C Bankman, *Pr*
EMP: 7 **EST:** 2001
SALES (est): 86.77K **Privately Held**
SIC: 7692 Welding repair

(G-6622)
BRIDGESTONE RET OPERATIONS LLC
Also Called: Firestone
1528a Vfw Pkwy (02132-5500)
PHONE...............................617 327-1100
Joseph Marder, *Mgr*
EMP: 8
Web: www.bridgestoneamericas.com
SIC: 5531 7534 Automotive tires;
    Rebuilding and retreading tires
HQ: Bridgestone Retail Operations, Llc
    333 E Lake St Ste 300
    Bloomingdale IL 60108
    630 259-9000

(G-6623)
BRIGHTCOVE INC (PA)
Also Called: Brightcove
281 Summer St (02210-1509)
PHONE...............................888 882-1880
Marc Debevoise, *CEO*
Robert Noreck, *Ex VP*
David Plotkin, *CLO*
EMP: 393 **EST:** 2004
SALES (est): 211.01MM
SALES (corp-wide): 211.01MM **Publicly Held**
Web: www.brightcove.com
SIC: 4813 7372 Online service providers;
    Prepackaged software

(G-6624)
BRILL USA INC
Also Called: Brill Academic Publishers
10 Liberty Sq (02109-5801)
PHONE...............................617 263-2323
Steve Dane, *VP*
EMP: 10 **EST:** 1986
SALES (est): 4.16MM
SALES (corp-wide): 355.83K **Privately Held**
SIC: 2731 Books, publishing only
HQ: Koninklijke Brill N.V.
    Plantijnstraat 2
    Leiden ZH
    715353500

(G-6625)
BROWN INNOVATIONS INC (PA)
369 Congress St Fl 4 (02210-1837)
PHONE...............................773 477-7500
▲ **EMP:** 9 **EST:** 1991
SQ FT: 3,000
SALES (est): 1.59MM **Privately Held**
Web: www.browninnovations.com
SIC: 8711 3651 Acoustical engineering;
    Household audio and video equipment

(G-6626)
BROWNMED INC (PA)
Also Called: Brown Med
101 Federal St Fl 29 (02110-1873)
PHONE...............................857 317-3354
Ivan E Brown, *CEO*
Kylia Garver, *Pr*
Brandon Rodriguez, *Prod Management Vice-President*
Matt Garver, *VP Mktg*

▲ **EMP:** 50 **EST:** 1965
SQ FT: 30,000
SALES (est): 8.21MM
SALES (corp-wide): 8.21MM **Privately Held**
Web: www.brownmed.com
SIC: 3842 5047 Orthopedic appliances; Medical and hospital equipment

(G-6627)
BUILDIUM LLC
3 Center Plz Ste 400 (02108-2010)
PHONE....................888 414-1988
Christopher Litster, *CEO*
EMP: 9 **EST:** 2004
SALES (est): 5.39MM **Privately Held**
Web: www.buildium.com
SIC: 7372 Business oriented computer software
HQ: Realpage, Inc.
     2201 Lakeside Blvd
     Richardson TX 75082
     972 820-3000

(G-6628)
BULLHORN INC (PA)
100 Summer St Ste 1700 (02110-2106)
PHONE....................617 478-9100
Arthur Papas, *CEO*
Matt Fischer, *COO*
Tom Sheehan, *CFO*
Alan Cline, *Dir*
Arthur Papas, *BRIAN SHETH*
EMP: 59 **EST:** 1999
SQ FT: 20,000
SALES (est): 84.43MM
SALES (corp-wide): 84.43MM **Privately Held**
Web: www.bullhorn.com
SIC: 7372 Prepackaged software

(G-6629)
BV INVESTMENT PARTNERS LP (PA)
125 High St Ste 1711 (02110-2548)
PHONE....................617 224-0057
Marco J Ferrari, *Prin*
Matthew J Kinsey, *Prin*
EMP: 25 **EST:** 1983
SALES (est): 24.25MM **Privately Held**
Web: www.bvlp.com
SIC: 6799 2721 Venture capital companies; Television schedules: publishing only, not printed on site

(G-6630)
BYNDER LLC
321 Summer St Fl 1 (02210-1725)
PHONE....................857 310-5434
EMP: 190 **EST:** 2014
SALES (est): 13.15MM **Privately Held**
Web: www.bynder.com
SIC: 7371 5045 7372 Computer software systems analysis and design, custom; Computer software; Application computer software
HQ: Bynder Holding B.V.
     Max Euweplein 46
     Amsterdam NH

(G-6631)
CABOT CORPORATION (PA)
Also Called: CABOT
2 Seaport Ln Ste 1300 (02210-2019)
PHONE....................617 345-0100
Sean D Keohane, *Pr*
Sue H Rataj, *Non-Executive Chairman of the Board*
Erica Mclaughlin, *Sr VP*
Karen A Kalita, *Sr VP*

Hobart C Kalkstein, *Sr VP*
◆ **EMP:** 140 **EST:** 1882
SALES (est): 3.93B
SALES (corp-wide): 3.93B **Publicly Held**
Web: www.cabotcorp.com
SIC: 2895 3081 3084 2819 Carbon black; Polyethylene film; Plastics pipe; Silica, amorphous

(G-6632)
CABOT HOLDINGS LLC
2 Seaport Ln Ste 1300 (02210-2058)
PHONE....................617 345-0100
EMP: 8 **EST:** 2014
SALES (est): 1.17MM
SALES (corp-wide): 3.93B **Publicly Held**
SIC: 2819 Industrial inorganic chemicals, nec
PA: Cabot Corporation
     2 Seaport Ln Ste 1300
     Boston MA 02210
     617 345-0100

(G-6633)
CABOT II-TN1W09 LLC
Also Called: Cabot
1 Beacon St Ste 1700 (02108-3106)
PHONE....................617 723-7400
EMP: 10 **EST:** 2017
SIC: 2819 Industrial inorganic chemicals, nec

(G-6634)
CABOT SPECIALTY CHEMICALS INC (HQ)
2 Seaport Ln Ste 1300 (02210-2058)
PHONE....................617 345-0100
▲ **EMP:** 14 **EST:** 1969
SALES (est): 55.2MM
SALES (corp-wide): 3.93B **Publicly Held**
SIC: 2819 Industrial inorganic chemicals, nec
PA: Cabot Corporation
     2 Seaport Ln Ste 1300
     Boston MA 02210
     617 345-0100

(G-6635)
CAMBRIDGE PACKING CO INC
4143 Food Mart Rd (02118-2806)
PHONE....................617 464-6000
Christopher Pappas, *CEO*
Bruce Rodman, *Pr*
Alan Roberts, *VP*
EMP: 62 **EST:** 1923
SQ FT: 55,000
SALES (est): 25.23MM **Publicly Held**
Web: www.chefswarehouse.com
SIC: 5147 5142 5146 5141 Meats, fresh; Meat, frozen: packaged; Fish, fresh; Groceries, general line
PA: The Chefs' Warehouse Inc
     100 E Ridge Rd
     Ridgefield CT 06877

(G-6636)
CAMBRIDGE SEMANTICS INC (PA)
1 Beacon St Ste 3400 (02108-3107)
PHONE....................617 245-0517
Brian D Owen, *CEO*
Chuck Pieper, *
Alok Prasad, *
John O'sullivan, *VP*
EMP: 65 **EST:** 2007
SALES (est): 10.8MM **Privately Held**
Web: www.cambridgesemantics.com
SIC: 7372 Application computer software

(G-6637)
CANVAS GFX INC
192 South St Ste 250 (02111-2736)
P.O. Box 94112 (98124-6412)
PHONE....................833 721-0829
Patricia Hume, *CEO*
Peter Schroer, *
Phil Landman, *
John Yee, *
EMP: 30 **EST:** 1985
SQ FT: 100
SALES (est): 6.18MM **Privately Held**
Web: www.canvasgfx.com
SIC: 7372 7371 7373 5045 Publisher's computer software; Computer software development; Computer systems analysis and design; Computer software

(G-6638)
CARIBE CMMNCTONS PBLCTIONS INC
Also Called: El Mundo Newspapers
175 William F Mcclellan Hwy Ste 1 (02128-1185)
PHONE....................617 522-5060
Alberto Vasallo Iii, *Pr*
Alberto Vasallo Junior, *Pr*
EMP: 23 **EST:** 1977
SALES (est): 4.03MM **Privately Held**
Web: www.elmundoboston.com
SIC: 2711 Newspapers, publishing and printing

(G-6639)
CARL SWANSON HARP RENTALS INC (PA)
137 Webster St (02128-2810)
PHONE....................617 569-6642
Carl Swanson, *Pr*
Patrick Dougal, *VP*
EMP: 7 **EST:** 1989
SALES (est): 250.1K **Privately Held**
Web: www.swansonharp.com
SIC: 3931 7699 Harps and parts; Musical instrument repair services

(G-6640)
CARRIER EQ LLC
Also Called: Airfox
186 Lincoln St Fl 3 (02111-2403)
PHONE....................617 841-7207
Victor Santos, *CSO*
Douglas De Carvalho Lopes, *
EMP: 99 **EST:** 2016
SQ FT: 6,651
SIC: 7372 Prepackaged software

(G-6641)
CATALOG TECHNOLOGIES INC
529 Main St Ste 127 (02129-1118)
PHONE....................617 768-7222
Hyunjun Park, *CEO*
EMP: 10 **EST:** 2016
SALES (est): 1.93MM **Privately Held**
Web: www.catalogdna.com
SIC: 3663 Digital encoders

(G-6642)
CATAPULT SPORTS INC (HQ)
Also Called: Xos Digital
10 Post Office Square Fl 9 (02109-4642)
PHONE....................978 447-5220
Matthew Bairos, *CEO*
Steve Quinn, *
Steve Bayne, *CAO*
EMP: 33 **EST:** 2005
SQ FT: 10,000
SALES (est): 31.42MM **Privately Held**
Web: www.catapult.com

SIC: 2741 7371 Internet publishing and broadcasting; Computer software development and applications
PA: Catapult Group International Ltd
     75 High St
     Prahran VIC 3181

(G-6643)
CATAPULT SPORTS LLC
10 Post Office Sq Ste 900s (02109-4642)
PHONE....................312 762-5332
Brian Kopp, *Managing Member*
EMP: 30 **EST:** 2011
SALES (est): 7.16MM **Privately Held**
Web: www.catapult.com
SIC: 3599 Catapults
HQ: Catapult Sports Pty. Ltd.
     75-83 High St
     Prahran VIC 3181

(G-6644)
CELYAD INC
2 Seaport Ln (02210-2001)
PHONE....................857 990-6900
Patrick Jeanmart, *Pr*
Richard Mountfield, *VP*
Graham Morrell, *VP*
EMP: 8 **EST:** 2011
SALES (est): 1.1MM **Privately Held**
Web: www.celyad.com
SIC: 2834 Pharmaceutical preparations

(G-6645)
CENGAGE LEARNING INC
Delmar Learning
200 Pier 4 Blvd Ste 200 (02210-2457)
PHONE....................518 348-2300
EMP: 10
Web: www.cengage.com
SIC: 8249 8331 2731 8221 Business training services; Job training and related services; Textbooks: publishing and printing; Professional schools
HQ: Cengage Learning, Inc.
     5191 Natorp Blvd
     Mason OH 45040

(G-6646)
CENTREXION THERAPEUTICS CORP
200 State St Ste 6 (02109-2696)
PHONE....................617 837-6911
Jeffrey B Kindler, *CEO*
Sol J Barer, *Ch Bd*
Isaac Blech, *V Ch Bd*
James N Campbell, *CSO*
B Nicholas Harvey, *Ex VP*
EMP: 14 **EST:** 2013
SQ FT: 11,486
SALES (est): 2.45MM **Privately Held**
Web: www.centrexion.com
SIC: 2834 Pharmaceutical preparations

(G-6647)
CERULLI ASSOCIATES INC (PA)
699 Boylston St Ste 1100 (02116-4804)
PHONE....................617 437-0084
Kurt Cerulli, *Pr*
EMP: 41 **EST:** 1992
SQ FT: 12,000
SALES (est): 13.91MM **Privately Held**
Web: www.cerulli.com
SIC: 8742 2721 Business management consultant; Statistical reports (periodicals): publishing only

(G-6648)
CHANNEL FISH CO INC
370 E Eagle St (02128-2571)
PHONE....................617 569-3200

Louis A Silvestro, *Pr*
Rosario Silvestro, *
▲ **EMP:** 65 **EST:** 1962
SQ FT: 2,500
SALES (est): 14.12MM **Privately Held**
Web: www.channelfishco.com
SIC: 2048 2092 2047   Prepared feeds, nec;
Fresh or frozen packaged fish; Dog and cat
food

(G-6649)
CHENG & TSUI CO INC
25 West St (02111-1239)
PHONE......................617 988-2400
Jill Tsui Cheng, *Pr*
Hung Cheng, *Treas*
▲ **EMP:** 17 **EST:** 1969
SALES (est): 3.08MM **Privately Held**
Web: www.cheng-tsui.com
SIC: 2731 5192   Books, publishing only;
Books

(G-6650)
CHEW LLC
1255 Boylston St Ste 3 (02215-3468)
PHONE......................617 945-1868
EMP: 40 **EST:** 2014
SALES (est): 4.96MM **Privately Held**
Web: www.chewinnovation.com
SIC: 2099   Food preparations, nec

(G-6651)
CHIESI VENTURES INC
10 Post Office Sq Ste 1305 (02109-4603)
PHONE......................919 998-3330
Giacomo Chiesi, *Managing Member*
EMP: 7 **EST:** 2014
SALES (est): 2.23MM
SALES (corp-wide): 2.86B **Privately Held**
Web: www.chiesiventures.com
SIC: 2834   Pharmaceutical preparations
HQ: Chiesi Farmaceutici Spa
Via Palermo 26/A
Parma PR 43122
05212791

(G-6652)
**CHINAMERICA FD
MANUFACTURE INC**
133 Newmarket Sq (02118-2603)
PHONE......................617 426-1818
Roman W Chan, *Pr*
Wan Sum Ng, *Treas*
Shi Hoi Chan, *Sec*
Shi Keung Chan, *Dir*
Xiao Dan Chen, *Dir*
EMP: 10 **EST:** 1993
SALES (est): 753.18K **Privately Held**
SIC: 2038 2099   Ethnic foods, nec, frozen;
Food preparations, nec

(G-6653)
**CHINESE SPAGHETTI FACTORY
INC**
83 Newmarket Sq (02118-2619)
PHONE......................617 445-7714
Lai Fou Sou, *Pr*
Irene Sou, *Treas*
▲ **EMP:** 10 **EST:** 1983
SQ FT: 2,000
SALES (est): 830.49K **Privately Held**
Web: www.chinese-spaghetti.com
SIC: 2098   Noodles (e.g. egg, plain, and
water), dry

(G-6654)
**CHMC OTLRYNGLGIC
FUNDATION INC (PA)**
Also Called: BOSTON'S CHILDREN
HOSPTIAL

300 Longwood Ave Rm 273 (02115-5724)
PHONE......................617 355-8290
Pedro Deonido Doctor, *Chief*
EMP: 15 **EST:** 1982
SQ FT: 8,000
SALES (est): 34.97MM **Privately Held**
Web: www.childrenshospital.org
SIC: 3841   Surgical and medical instruments

(G-6655)
**CHRISTIAN SCIENCE PUBG
SOC (PA)**
Also Called: Christian Science Monitor
210 Massachusetts Ave (02115-3012)
PHONE......................617 450-2000
John L Selover, *Mgr*
Nathan A Talbot, *Trst*
Margaret Campbell, *Trst*
Karen Craft, *Trst*
EMP: 280 **EST:** 1888
SALES (est): 33.16MM
SALES (corp-wide): 33.16MM **Privately
Held**
Web: www.christianscience.com
SIC: 2711 2721 4833 4832   Newspapers:
publishing only, not printed on site;
Magazines: publishing only, not printed on
site; Television broadcasting stations; Radio
broadcasting stations

(G-6656)
**CISCO BRWERS DSTLRS
VNTNERS SP**
85 Northern Ave (02210-1801)
PHONE......................508 325-5929
Jason Harman, *Mgr*
EMP: 38
SALES (corp-wide): 62.38K **Privately Held**
SIC: 2085   Distilled and blended liquors
PA: Cisco Brewers, Distillers, Vintners,
Seaport, Inc.
5 Bartlett Farm Rd
Nantucket MA 02554
508 325-5929

(G-6657)
CITY OF BOSTON
Graphic Arts Printing
174 North St (02109-1405)
PHONE......................617 635-3700
Paul Dennehy, *Mgr*
EMP: 120
SALES (corp-wide): 4.17MM **Privately
Held**
Web: www.boston.gov
SIC: 9199 2752   General government
administration; Forms, business:
lithographed
PA: City Of Boston
1 City Hall Sq Ste 242
Boston MA 02201
617 635-4545

(G-6658)
CITY WINERY BOSTON LLC
80 Beverly St (02114-2134)
PHONE......................617 933-8047
EMP: 24 **EST:** 2017
SALES (est): 762.62K **Privately Held**
Web: www.citywinery.com
SIC: 5813 2084   Wine bar; Wines, brandy,
and brandy spirits

(G-6659)
CLADE THERAPEUTICS INC
201 Brookline Ave Ste 1002 (02215-4153)
PHONE......................617 546-7460
Chad A Cowen, *Pr*
Leandro A Vetcher, *VP*
EMP: 36 **EST:** 2020

SALES (est): 9.94MM **Privately Held**
Web: www.cladetx.com
SIC: 2834   Pharmaceutical preparations

(G-6660)
CODISCOPE LLC
20 Park Plz Ste 1400 (02116-4311)
PHONE......................617 804-5428
EMP: 18 **EST:** 2015
SALES (est): 522.9K **Privately Held**
Web: www.synopsys.com
SIC: 7372   Application computer software

(G-6661)
**COHEN SLVSTRI ROGOFF
HAMMER PC**
3 Post Office Sq Ste 900 (02109-3932)
PHONE......................617 426-6011
Anthony Silvestri, *Pr*
Doctor Gary Rogoff, *Prin*
Doctor Norman Hammer, *Prin*
Doctor Steven Cohen, *Prin*
EMP: 20 **EST:** 1979
SALES (est): 389.1K **Privately Held**
SIC: 8021 3842   Dentists' office; Prosthetic
appliances

(G-6662)
COLE HERSEE COMPANY (HQ)
20 Old Colony Ave (02127-2405)
PHONE......................617 268-2100
▲ **EMP:** 58 **EST:** 1924
SALES (est): 42.79MM
SALES (corp-wide): 2.51B **Publicly Held**
Web: www.littelfuse.com
SIC: 3643 3613   Current-carrying wiring
services; Switchgear and switchboard
apparatus
PA: Littelfuse, Inc.
8755 W Higgins Rd Ste 500
Chicago IL 60631
773 628-1000

(G-6663)
**COLOR-TEX INTERNATIONAL
INC**
Also Called: New England Bias Binding
28 Damrell St (02127-2775)
PHONE......................617 269-8020
EMP: 120 **EST:** 1918
SQ FT: 30,000
SALES (est): 6.5MM **Privately Held**
SIC: 2261 2396   Finishing plants, cotton;
Bindings, bias: made from purchased
materials

(G-6664)
**COMPUTER SOFTWARE
ASSOCIATES**
Also Called: Global I.P. Net
31 Saint James Ave Ste 1100 (02116-4101)
PHONE......................808 891-0099
Anthony De Andrade, *Pr*
Anthony Deandrade, *Pr*
EMP: 13 **EST:** 1984
SALES (est): 700K **Privately Held**
SIC: 7372   Prepackaged software

(G-6665)
**CONNELL LIMITED
PARTNERSHIP (PA)**
Also Called: Danly IEM
1 International Pl 31th Fl (02110-2602)
PHONE......................617 737-2700
Margot C Connell, *Pt*
Frank A Doyle, *Pt*
Kurt Keady, *Pt*
Catherine R Gallagher, *Pt*
◆ **EMP:** 15 **EST:** 1987

SQ FT: 11,000
SALES (est): 376.52MM
SALES (corp-wide): 376.52MM **Privately
Held**
Web: www.connell-lp.com
SIC: 3443 3444 3341 3544   Heat
exchangers, condensers, anc components;
Sheet metalwork; Aluminum smelting and
refining (secondary); Die sets for metal
stamping (presses)

(G-6666)
**CONSTLLTION
PHRMACEUTICALS INC (DH)**
470 Atlantic Ave Ste 1401 (02210-2264)
PHONE......................844 667-1992
Jigar Raythatha, *Pr*
Mark A Goldsmith, *
Emma Reeve, *Sr VP*
Adrian Senderowicz, *CMO*
Karen Valentine, *CLO*
EMP: 22 **EST:** 2008
SALES (corp-wide): 289.01MM **Privately
Held**
Web: www.morphosys.com
SIC: 2834   Pharmaceutical preparations
HQ: Morphosys Us Inc.
470 Atlantic Ave Ste 1401
Boston MA 02210
862 294-2150

(G-6667)
CONVERGENT NETWORKS INC
500 Boylston St Fl 4 (02116-3740)
PHONE......................978 262-0231
Surya Panditi, *Pr*
Bing Yang, *
John Collins, *Treas*
Robert Chow, *Secretary General*
EMP: 19 **EST:** 1998
SQ FT: 72,000
SALES (est): 479.12K **Privately Held**
Web: www.convergentnet.com
SIC: 3669   Intercommunication systems,
electric

(G-6668)
**COPLEY FURNITURE COMPANY
INC**
Also Called: Copley Apholstery Company
120 Landseer St (02132-3437)
PHONE......................617 566-1000
Richard Hinkley, *Pr*
Bonnie Prendergast, *VP*
EMP: 7 **EST:** 1959
SQ FT: 10,000
SALES (est): 216.86K **Privately Held**
SIC: 7641 2512   Furniture repair and
maintenance; Upholstered household
furniture

(G-6669)
**COPY COP THE DIGITAL
PRINTING COMPANY LLC**
Also Called: Copycop
12 Channel St (02210-2323)
PHONE......................617 267-8899
EMP: 38
SIC: 7334 2752 2789   Photocopying and
duplicating services; Offset printing;
Bookbinding and related work

(G-6670)
CORE SDI INC (PA)
Also Called: Core Security Technologies
41 Farnsworth St Fl 6 (02210-1320)
PHONE......................617 695-1109
Mark Hatton, *CEO*
John O'brien, *CFO*

EMP: 9 EST: 1996
SALES (est): 1.15MM
SALES (corp-wide): 1.15MM Privately Held
SIC: 7372 Prepackaged software

(G-6671)
COREDGE NETWORKS INC
Also Called: Slt Logic
50 Commonwealth Ave # 504 (02116-3025)
PHONE.................................617 267-5205
William Chu, *Pr*
EMP: 19 EST: 2004
SALES (est): 553.06K Privately Held
SIC: 3669 Intercommunication systems, electric

(G-6672)
CORIUM LLC ✪
Also Called: Corium
11 Farnsworth St Fl 4 (02210-1210)
PHONE.................................855 253-2407
Mark Sirgo, *CEO*
Perry Sternberg, *
Robert S Breuil, *
Joseph J Sarret, *Chief Business Officer**
Parminder Singh, *
EMP: 185 EST: 2022
SALES (est): 44.59MM
SALES (corp-wide): 75.8MM Privately Held
Web: www.corium.com
SIC: 2834 8731 2836 Pharmaceutical preparations; Biological research; Biological products, except diagnostic
PA: Gurnet Point Capital Llc
55 Cambridge Pkwy Ste 401
Cambridge MA 02142
617 588-4902

(G-6673)
COVALENT NETWORKS INC
24 Hanson St (02118-3602)
PHONE.................................781 296-7952
Andrew Knez, *CEO*
Matthew Delaney, *Prin*
EMP: 11 EST: 2019
SALES (est): 1.03MM Privately Held
Web: www.covalentnetworks.com
SIC: 3652 5734 Prerecorded records and tapes; Software, business and non-game

(G-6674)
CRANE CURRENCY US LLC
1 Beacon St (02108-3107)
PHONE.................................617 648-3710
Stephen Defalco, *CEO*
EMP: 18 EST: 2012
SALES (est): 2MM
SALES (corp-wide): 3.37B Publicly Held
SIC: 2759 Bank notes: engraved
PA: Crane Nxt, Co.
950 Winter St Fl 4
Waltham MA 02451
610 430-2510

(G-6675)
CREATION TECHNOLOGIES INC (PA)
1 Beacon St Fl 23 (02108-3106)
PHONE.................................877 734-7456
Stephen P Defalco, *Ch*
Patrick Freytag, *CFO*
Todd Baggett, *COO*
David Longshore Csmo, *Prin*
Liam Weston, *Chief Human Resource Officer*
EMP: 24 EST: 2019
SALES (est): 273.39MM
SALES (corp-wide): 273.39MM Privately Held

Web: www.creationtech.com
SIC: 3672 Printed circuit boards

(G-6676)
CREATION TECHNOLOGIES INTL INC (PA)
1 Beacon St (02108-3107)
PHONE.................................877 734-7456
Stephen P Defalco, *Ch*
EMP: 29 EST: 2003
SALES (est): 647.89MM
SALES (corp-wide): 647.89MM Privately Held
Web: www.creationtech.com
SIC: 3672 3679 Printed circuit boards; Electronic circuits

(G-6677)
CRIO INC
177 Huntington Ave Ste 1703 Pmb 32876 (02115-3134)
PHONE.................................617 302-9845
Raymond Nomizu, *CEO*
Daniel Oberlin, *
EMP: 30 EST: 2016
SALES (est): 4.73MM Privately Held
Web: www.clinicalresearch.io
SIC: 7372 Business oriented computer software

(G-6678)
CURRENT LIGHTING SOLUTIONS LLC
745 Atlantic Ave (02111-2735)
PHONE.................................713 521-6500
EMP: 10 EST: 2019
SALES (est): 440.44K Privately Held
Web: www.led.com
SIC: 3648 5063 Lighting equipment, nec; Lighting fixtures

(G-6679)
CURRENT LTG EMPLOYEECO LLC
745 Atlantic Ave (02111-2735)
PHONE.................................216 266-2906
Maryrose Sylvester, *Pr*
John Irvine, *
Janine Dascenzo, *Corporate Secretary**
Sok Cheng Soh, *
EMP: 1100 EST: 2018
SALES (est): 275.84MM
SALES (corp-wide): 1.6B Privately Held
SIC: 3648 Lighting equipment, nec; Lighting fixtures
PA: Current Lighting Employeeco, Inc.
25825 Science Park Dr # 400
Beachwood OH 44122
216 462-4700

(G-6680)
CYBERBIT INC
71 Commercial St Ste 26 (02109-1320)
PHONE.................................415 960-5750
Caleb Barlow, *CEO*
Oscar Williams, *Prin*
EMP: 27 EST: 2016
SALES (est): 563.16K Privately Held
SIC: 7372 Business oriented computer software

(G-6681)
CYBEREASON GOVERNMENT INC
200 Berkeley St (02116-5022)
PHONE.................................978 618-6992
Samuel Curry, *Pr*
Nathan Russ, *VP*
Timothy Kochis Dof, *Prin*

EMP: 15 EST: 2021
SALES (est): 528.69K Privately Held
Web: www.cybereason.com
SIC: 7372 Prepackaged software

(G-6682)
CYDUCT DIAGNOSTICS INC
Also Called: Solos Endoscopy
65 Sprague St (02136-2061)
PHONE.................................617 360-9700
Dom Gatto, *CEO*
Amanda B Segersten, *Co-Treasurer*
Fred Schiemann, *Co-Treasurer*
EMP: 8 EST: 1991
SQ FT: 7,000
SALES (est): 2.43MM
SALES (corp-wide): 2.43MM Privately Held
Web: www.solosendoscopy.com
SIC: 3845 5049 7699 Endoscopic equipment, electromedical, nec; Optical goods; Optical instrument repair
PA: American Medical Group Llc
1698 Post Rd E
Westport CT 06880
203 292-8444

(G-6683)
DASHBOARD ADVANTAGE LLC
207 Webster St (02128-2818)
PHONE.................................949 232-7409
EMP: 7 EST: 2016
SALES (est): 79.7K Privately Held
Web: www.zenput.com
SIC: 7372 Prepackaged software

(G-6684)
DATAROBOT INC (PA)
225 Franklin St Fl 13 (02110-2850)
PHONE.................................617 765-4500
Daniel Wright, *CEO*
Debanjan Saha, *Pr*
Elise Leung Cole, *CPO*
Michael Schmidt, *
Nick King, *CMO*
EMP: 100 EST: 2012
SALES (est): 183.94K
SALES (corp-wide): 183.94K Privately Held
Web: www.datarobot.com
SIC: 7371 7372 7379 8243 Software programming applications; Prepackaged software; Computer related maintenance services; Software training, computer

(G-6685)
DEBT EXCHANGE INC
Also Called: Debtx
225 Franklin St Fl 26 (02110-2853)
PHONE.................................617 531-3400
William Looney, *CEO*
J Kingsley Greenland Ii, *CEO*
William F Looney, *
Thomas R Goodwin, *
Troy Quimby, *
EMP: 51 EST: 2000
SALES (est): 24.86MM Privately Held
Web: www.debtx.com
SIC: 6211 6282 7375 8742 Security brokers and dealers; Investment advisory service; On-line data base information retrieval; General management consultant

(G-6686)
DECIBEL THERAPEUTICS INC (HQ)
1325 Boylston St Ste 500 (02215-3900)
PHONE.................................617 370-8701
Laurence Reid, *Pr*
John Lee, *Interim Vice President*

Elisabeth Leiderman, *CFO*
Anna Trask, *PEOPLE COMMUNITY CULTURE*
Ronald Vigliotta, *VP*
EMP: 25 EST: 2013
SQ FT: 49,000
SALES (corp-wide): 12.17B Publicly Held
Web: www.decibeltx.com
SIC: 2834 Pharmaceutical preparations
PA: Regeneron Pharmaceuticals Inc
777 Old Saw Mill River Rd # 10
Tarrytown NY 10591
914 847-7000

(G-6687)
DEEPCURE INC
100 City Hall Plz (02108-2105)
PHONE.................................617 417-2345
Kfir Schreiber, *CEO*
Joseph Jacobson, *CSO*
Gerald Chan, *Dir*
Stephen Bruso, *Dir*
EMP: 8 EST: 2018
SALES (est): 2.58MM Privately Held
Web: www.deepcure.ai
SIC: 2834 Druggists' preparations (pharmaceuticals)

(G-6688)
DEFENSECOM INC
17 Claremont Park (02118-3001)
PHONE.................................203 912-8679
Scott Lush, *Prin*
EMP: 9 EST: 2010
SALES (est): 113.12K Privately Held
SIC: 3812 Defense systems and equipment

(G-6689)
DELVE LABS INC
31 Saint James Ave (02116-4101)
PHONE.................................617 820-9798
Gabriel Tremblay, *CEO*
EMP: 11 EST: 2017
SALES (est): 613.94K Privately Held
SIC: 7372 Prepackaged software

(G-6690)
DENTOVATIONS INC
1 Beacon St (02108-3107)
PHONE.................................617 737-1199
Damon Brown, *Pr*
Adam Diasti, *Pr*
Damon Brown, *VP*
Terek Diasti, *VP*
Tim Diasti, *VP*
▲ **EMP: 10 EST: 2001**
SQ FT: 1,000
SALES (est): 1.26MM Privately Held
Web: www.dentovations.com
SIC: 3843 Dental equipment and supplies

(G-6691)
DENTOVATIONS INC
Also Called: Dentovations Company
1 Beacon St Fl 15 (02108-3107)
PHONE.................................617 737-1199
◆ **EMP: 8 EST: 2001**
SALES (est): 879.62K Privately Held
Web: www.dentovations.com
SIC: 5047 2844 Dental equipment and supplies; Toothpastes or powders, dentifrices

(G-6692)
DIACRITECH INC
Also Called: Diacritech
1 S Market St Ste 4 (02109-6201)
PHONE.................................617 236-7500
Madhusudhanan Rajamani, *Pr*
EMP: 16 EST: 2004

SALES (est): 671.18K **Privately Held**
Web: www.diacritech.com
SIC: 2721 2731 2741 7371 Trade journals: publishing only, not printed on site; Books, publishing only; Miscellaneous publishing; Custom computer programming services

(G-6693)
DIAMOND WINDOWS DOORS MFG INC
Also Called: Diamond Windows
99 E Cottage St (02125-2622)
PHONE.............................617 282-1688
Yu Liang Tseng, *Pr*
▲ **EMP:** 30 **EST:** 1992
SQ FT: 20,000
SALES (est): 8.48MM **Privately Held**
Web: www.diamondwindows.com
SIC: 3089 3231 3442 Windows, plastics; Products of purchased glass; Storm doors or windows, metal

(G-6694)
DIG PUBLISHING LLC
242 E Berkeley St Ste 2 (02118-2797)
PHONE.............................617 426-8942
EMP: 16 **EST:** 1996
SALES (est): 1.4MM **Privately Held**
Web: www.digmedia.com
SIC: 2711 Newspapers, publishing and printing

(G-6695)
DIGBOSTON
242 E Berkeley St (02118-2480)
PHONE.............................617 426-8942
EMP: 17 **EST:** 2019
SALES (est): 348.85K **Privately Held**
Web: www.digboston.com
SIC: 2711 Newspapers, publishing and printing

(G-6696)
DIGITAL LUMENS INCORPORATED
374 Congress St Ste 601 (02210-1807)
▲ **EMP:** 111 **EST:** 2008
SQ FT: 16,000
SALES (est): 23.39MM **Privately Held**
Web: www.digitallumens.com
SIC: 3674 Semiconductors and related devices

(G-6697)
DIGITAL STREAM ENERGY INC
160 Federal St Fl 18 (02110-1700)
PHONE.............................310 488-2743
Amir Chaluts, *Dir*
EMP: 9 **EST:** 2019
SALES (est): 1.51MM **Privately Held**
Web: www.digitalstreamenergy.com
SIC: 1389 Oil and gas field services, nec

(G-6698)
DORCHESTER BEER HOLDINGS LLC
1250 Massachusetts Ave (02125-1608)
PHONE.............................617 869-7092
Travis Lee, *Prin*
EMP: 11 **EST:** 2015
SALES (est): 513.88K **Privately Held**
Web: www.dorchesterbrewing.com
SIC: 2082 Near beer

(G-6699)
DOUBLEYARD INC (PA)
201 Washington St Ste 3630 (02108)
PHONE.............................857 314-1400

Tatsuya Yasunaga, *Pr*
EMP: 15 **EST:** 2020
SALES (est): 1.03MM
SALES (corp-wide): 1.03MM **Privately Held**
SIC: 7372 Business oriented computer software

(G-6700)
DOWNEAST CIDER HOUSE LLC (PA)
256 Marginal St Ste 2 (02128-2871)
PHONE.............................857 301-8881
EMP: 9 **EST:** 2011
SALES (est): 14.29MM
SALES (corp-wide): 14.29MM **Privately Held**
Web: www.downeastcider.com
SIC: 2082 2085 Beer (alcoholic beverage); Applejack (alcoholic beverage)

(G-6701)
DPB CERAMICS LLC
800 Boylston St Ste 200 (02199-8176)
PHONE.............................617 259-1084
Sergio Guzman, *Prin*
EMP: 8 **EST:** 2012
SALES (est): 257.64K **Privately Held**
Web: www.dentalpartnersofboston.com
SIC: 3269 Pottery products, nec

(G-6702)
DRAKA CABLETEQ USA INC
Also Called: Draka
PHONE.............................888 520-1200
◆ **EMP:** 384 **EST:** 1992
SALES (est): 103.45MM **Privately Held**
Web: www.drakausa.com
SIC: 3357 Building wire and cable, nonferrous
HQ: Draka Holding B.V.
Schieweg 9
Delft ZH
888084444

(G-6703)
DRIZLY LLC (HQ)
334 Boylston St Ste 301 (02116-3496)
PHONE.............................774 234-1033
Dara Khosrowshahi, *CEO*
EMP: 32 **EST:** 2012
SALES (est): 24.37MM
SALES (corp-wide): 31.88B **Publicly Held**
Web: www.drizly.com
SIC: 7372 7389 Application computer software; Business Activities at Non-Commercial Site
PA: Uber Technologies, Inc.
1515 3rd St
San Francisco CA 94158
415 612-8582

(G-6704)
DUCK CREEK TECHNOLOGIES INC (HQ)
Also Called: Duck Creek
22 Boston Wharf Rd Fl 10 (02210-3032)
PHONE.............................949 214-1000
Michael Jackowski, *CEO*
Jason Wright, *Ch Bd*
Teresa M Kim, *CFO*
Matthew Foster, *COO*
Eugene Van Biert Junior, *CRO*
EMP: 16 **EST:** 2016
SQ FT: 30,000
SALES (est): 302.92MM
SALES (corp-wide): 1.65B **Privately Held**
Web: www.duckcreek.com
SIC: 7372 Prepackaged software
PA: Vista Equity Partners Management, Llc
401 Congress Ave Ste 3100

Austin TX 78701
512 730-2400

(G-6705)
DUCK CREEK TECHNOLOGIES LLC (DH)
22 Boston Wharf Rd Fl 10 (02210-3032)
PHONE.............................833 798-7789
Michael A Jackowski, *CEO*
EMP: 23 **EST:** 2015
SQ FT: 30,000
SALES (est): 31.34MM
SALES (corp-wide): 1.65B **Privately Held**
Web: www.duckcreek.com
SIC: 7372 Prepackaged software
HQ: Duck Creek Technologies, Inc.
22 Boston Wharf Rd Fl 10
Boston MA 02210
949 214-1000

(G-6706)
EAST WEST BOSTON LLC
12 Channel St Ste 301 (02210-2323)
PHONE.............................617 598-3000
Agnes Young, *Brnch Mgr*
EMP: 90
SALES (corp-wide): 490.36MM **Privately Held**
SIC: 3679 3672 Electronic circuits; Printed circuit boards
HQ: East West Boston, Llc
4170 Ashford Dnwody Rd Ne
Brookhaven GA 30319
404 252-9441

(G-6707)
ECLYPSES INC
33 Broad St Ste 1100 (02109-4230)
PHONE.............................719 323-6680
John Nachef, *CEO*
Steve Russo, *
EMP: 30 **EST:** 2017
SALES (est): 2.13MM **Privately Held**
Web: www.eclypses.com
SIC: 8731 8711 7372 7373 Electronic research; Electrical or electronic engineering; Application computer software ; Systems software development services

(G-6708)
EIDP INC
Also Called: Dupont
123 E Dedham St (02118-2856)
PHONE.............................617 482-9595
EMP: 15
SALES (corp-wide): 17.23B **Publicly Held**
Web: www.dupont.com
SIC: 2819 Industrial inorganic chemicals, nec
HQ: Eidp, Inc.
9330 Zionsville Rd
Indianapolis IN 46268
833 267-8382

(G-6709)
EKITON CORPORATION
Also Called: Eastern Sling & Supply
17 Power House St R (02127-1600)
PHONE.............................617 464-4422
George T Jones, *Pr*
Nancy J Jones, *Sec*
G Thomas Jones, *Treas*
George T Jones, *Dir*
EMP: 7 **EST:** 1973
SQ FT: 11,000
SALES (est): 944.17K **Privately Held**
SIC: 3496 Miscellaneous fabricated wire products

(G-6710)
ELECTRA VEHICLES INC (PA)
Also Called: Electra
110 K St Ste 330 (02127-1619)
PHONE.............................617 313-7842
Fabrizio Martini, *CEO*
EMP: 14 **EST:** 2015
SALES (est): 1.18MM
SALES (corp-wide): 1.18MM **Privately Held**
Web: www.electravehicles.com
SIC: 7372 Prepackaged software

(G-6711)
ELECTROSONICS MEDICAL INC
2 Oliver St Ste 616 (02109-49C1)
PHONE.............................216 357-3310
Trevor O Jones, *CEO*
Bob Purcell, *Pr*
EMP: 7 **EST:** 1998
SQ FT: 5,000
SALES (est): 757.66K **Privately Held**
SIC: 3845 Electromedical equipment

(G-6712)
ELLOIT WRIGHT WORKROOM INC
535 Albany St Ste 18 (02118-2557)
PHONE.............................617 542-3605
Elliot Wright, *Pr*
EMP: 12 **EST:** 1995
SALES (est): 1.07MM **Privately Held**
Web: www.historicdistrict.com
SIC: 2258 Curtains and curtain fabrics, lace

(G-6713)
EMC1 CONTINENTAL AVE LLC
529 Columbus Ave Apt 18 (02118-3455)
PHONE.............................617 875-2687
EMP: 7 **EST:** 2019
SALES (est): 547.87K **Privately Held**
SIC: 3572 Computer storage devices

(G-6714)
ENBW NORTH AMERICA INC
311 Summer St Ste 200 (02210-1747)
PHONE.............................857 753-4623
William H White Junior, *Dir*
EMP: 10 **EST:** 2019
SALES (est): 2.74MM
SALES (corp-wide): 58.16B **Privately Held**
Web: www.enbw.com
SIC: 3621 Windmills, electric generating
PA: Enbw Energie Baden-Wurttemberg Ag
Durlacher Allee 93
Karlsruhe BW 76131
7216300

(G-6715)
ENTERPRISE GVRNNCE SYSTEMS COR (PA)
399 Boylston St (02116-3305)
PHONE.............................888 655-4125
Jacob Braun, *Pr*
EMP: 8 **EST:** 2021
SALES (est): 71.56K
SALES (corp-wide): 71.56K **Privately Held**
SIC: 7372 Prepackaged software

(G-6716)
ENTERPRISE GVRNNCE SYSTEMS COR
33 Arch St Ste 1600 (02110-1461)
PHONE.............................888 655-4125
Jacob Braun, *Pr*
EMP: 22
SALES (corp-wide): 71.56K **Privately Held**

SIC: 7372 Prepackaged software
PA: Enterprise Governance Systems
Corporation
399 Boylston St
Boston MA 02116
888 655-4125

(G-6717)
ENTRADA THERAPEUTICS INC (PA)
6 Tide St Ste 1 (02210-2658)
PHONE...............................857 520-9158
Dipal Doshi, *CEO*
Kush M Parmar, *Ch Bd*
Nathan J Dowden, *Pr*
Kory Wentworth, *CFO*
Nerissa C Kreher, *CMO*
EMP: 78 **EST:** 2016
Web: www.entradatx.com
SIC: 2834 Pharmaceutical preparations

(G-6718)
ERECRUIT HOLDINGS LLC
Also Called: Erecruit
100 Summer St Ste 1700 (02110-2105)
PHONE...............................617 535-3720
David Perotti, *CEO*
Greg Stott, *
EMP: 60 **EST:** 2009
SALES (est): 17.04MM
SALES (corp-wide): 84.43MM **Privately Held**
Web: www.erecruit.com
SIC: 7372 Prepackaged software
PA: Bullhorn, Inc.
100 Summer St
Boston MA 02110
617 478-9100

(G-6719)
ESKILL CORPORATION
177 Huntington Ave Ste 1703 (02115-3134)
P.O. Box 55177 (02205-5177)
PHONE...............................978 649-8010
Eric Friedman, *CEO*
EMP: 15 **EST:** 2004
SALES (est): 2.57MM **Privately Held**
Web: www.eskill.com
SIC: 7372 Business oriented computer software

(G-6720)
EURO INTERNATIONAL LTD
Also Called: Aroma Therapy International
150 Staniford St Apt 632 (02114-2597)
PHONE...............................617 670-2265
William Georgaqui, *Owner*
EMP: 10 **EST:** 1978
SQ FT: 2,000
SALES (est): 391.47K **Privately Held**
SIC: 8732 2038 Market analysis or research; Frozen specialties, nec

(G-6721)
EUROPEAN CUBICLES LLC
Also Called: Thrislington Cubicles
38 3rd Ave Ste 100w (02129-4503)
PHONE...............................617 681-6700
EMP: 9 **EST:** 2014
SALES (est): 693.15K **Privately Held**
Web: www.europeancubicles.com
SIC: 2844 Perfumes, cosmetics and other toilet preparations

(G-6722)
EXARI GROUP INC
745 Boylston St (02116-2636)
PHONE...............................617 938-3777
William M Hewitt, *CEO*
Terence Lee, *Pr*

Joe Bradley, *CFO*
EMP: 37 **EST:** 2000
SALES (est): 4.83MM
SALES (corp-wide): 536.16MM **Privately Held**
Web: www.coupa.com
SIC: 7372 Application computer software
HQ: Coupa Software Incorporated
1855 S Grant St
San Mateo CA 94402

(G-6723)
EXARI SYSTEMS INC
745 Boylston St Ste 201 (02116-2614)
PHONE...............................617 938-3777
William Hewitt, *CEO*
Mike Maziarz, *CMO**
EMP: 68 **EST:** 2000
SQ FT: 10,000
SALES (est): 15.46MM
SALES (corp-wide): 536.16MM **Privately Held**
Web: www.coupa.com
SIC: 7372 Business oriented computer software
HQ: Coupa Software Incorporated
1855 S Grant St
San Mateo CA 94402

(G-6724)
EXINDA INC
8 Faneuil Hall Market Pl 3rd Fl (02109-6114)
PHONE...............................617 973-6477
Michael Sharma, *Pr*
Efrem Ainsley, *Sec*
EMP: 8 **EST:** 2007
SALES (est): 137.22K **Privately Held**
Web: www.gfi.com
SIC: 3825 Network analyzers

(G-6725)
EXONY INC
60 State St Ste 700 (02109-1894)
PHONE...............................617 854-7486
Ian Ashby, *Pr*
EMP: 21 **EST:** 2006
SALES (est): 2.04MM
SALES (corp-wide): 98.01MM **Publicly Held**
SIC: 7372 Application computer software
HQ: Exony Limited
St Catherines House
Newbury BERKS RG14

(G-6726)
EZE CASTLE SOFTWARE INC (DH)
50 Milk St Fl 7 (02109-5000)
PHONE...............................617 316-1100
Pete Sinisgalli, *CEO*
Thomas P Gavin, *
Jeffrey Shoreman, *Pr*
Heather A Sisler, *
Peter Cameron Hyzer, *
EMP: 125 **EST:** 1999
SALES (est): 29.67MM
SALES (corp-wide): 2.96B **Publicly Held**
Web: www.ezesoft.com
SIC: 7372 Prepackaged software
HQ: Tpg Capital Management, L.P.
301 Commerce St Ste 3300
Fort Worth TX 76102

(G-6727)
EZE CASTLE SOFTWARE LLC (DH)
Also Called: Eze C.S.
50 Milk St Fl 7 (02109-5000)
PHONE...............................617 316-1100

Joseph M Velli, *Managing Member*
EMP: 9 **EST:** 2006
SALES (est): 29.65MM
SALES (corp-wide): 5.28B **Publicly Held**
Web: www.ezesoft.com
SIC: 7372 Prepackaged software
HQ: Eze Software Group Llc
50 Milk St Fl 7
Boston MA 02109
617 316-1000

(G-6728)
FA FINALE INC
24 Prime Park Way Ste 305 (02116)
PHONE...............................617 226-7888
TOLL FREE: 800
▲ **EMP:** 41 **EST:** 1995
SALES (est): 6.44MM
SALES (corp-wide): 302.09B **Publicly Held**
SIC: 3931 5099 Musical instruments; Musical instruments
HQ: Jazwares, Llc
1067 Shotgun Rd
Sunrise FL 33326

(G-6729)
FAIRMARKIT INC (PA)
1 Beacon St Fl 15 (02108-3107)
P.O. Box 393 (02148-0004)
PHONE...............................774 364-4446
Kevin Frechette, *CEO*
Tarek Alaruri, *
Victor Kushch, *
EMP: 95 **EST:** 2017
SALES (est): 10.2MM
SALES (corp-wide): 10.2MM **Privately Held**
Web: www.fairmarkit.com
SIC: 7372 Business oriented computer software

(G-6730)
FAMILY EDUCATION NETWORK INC
50 Congress St Ste 1025 (02109-4022)
PHONE...............................617 671-3435
James Tenner, *Pr*
◆ **EMP:** 40 **EST:** 1990
SQ FT: 40,000
SALES (est): 975.59K
SALES (corp-wide): 15.56MM **Privately Held**
Web: www.fen.com
SIC: 4813 2721 Internet host services; Periodicals, publishing only
PA: Sandbox Networks Inc.
745 Atlantic Ave Fl 8
Boston MA 02111
800 498-3264

(G-6731)
FARGO TA LLC
Also Called: Tivoli Audio
745 Atlantic Ave Fl 8 (02111-2735)
PHONE...............................617 345-0066
Lisa Kaufman, *CEO*
Stacey Kerek, *
Bob Brown, *
Jeffrey Stone, *
Wayne Garrett, *
▲ **EMP:** 23 **EST:** 2000
SQ FT: 3,600
SALES (est): 880.3K **Privately Held**
SIC: 3651 5731 Audio electronic systems; Radio, television, and electronic stores

(G-6732)
FAVERCO INC
Also Called: Flying Colors

16 Aberdeen St (02215-3800)
PHONE...............................617 247-1440
Mark Favermann, *Pr*
Barbara Lewis, *Treas*
EMP: 8 **EST:** 1977
SQ FT: 5,000
SALES (est): 478.45K **Privately Held**
Web: www.favermanndesign.com
SIC: 2399 8712 Banners, made from fabric; Architectural services

(G-6733)
FBNE LLC
Also Called: Falk Built New England
112 Beach St Unit A (02111-2543)
PHONE...............................617 571-6443
Michael P Macdonald, *Mgr*
EMP: 12 **EST:** 2020
SALES (est): 568.92K **Privately Held**
SIC: 3272 1793 Housing components, prefabricated concrete; Glass and glazing work

(G-6734)
FENWAY CMMUNICATIONS GROUP INC
Also Called: Minuteman Press
870 Commonwealth Ave Ste F (02215-1233)
PHONE...............................617 226-1900
EMP: 28 **EST:** 1999
SQ FT: 4,050
SALES (est): 5.51MM **Privately Held**
Web: www.fenway-group.com
SIC: 2752 Commercial printing, lithographic

(G-6735)
FIL-TECH INC
6 Pinckney St (02114-4800)
PHONE...............................617 227-1133
G Paul Becker, *Pr*
Paula L Becker, *VP*
Diana Becker, *Treas*
▲ **EMP:** 9 **EST:** 1969
SALES (est): 1.1MM **Privately Held**
Web: www.filtech.com
SIC: 3671 3625 Vacuum tubes; Vacuum relays

(G-6736)
FIRST CH OF CHRST SCNTIST IN B (PA)
Also Called: First Ch of Chrst Scientist
210 Massachusetts Ave (02115-3012)
PHONE...............................617 450-2000
Mark Swinney, *Pr*
Mary Trammell, *
J Edward Odegaard, *
Nathan Talbot, *
▲ **EMP:** 40 **EST:** 1879
SALES (est): 43.2MM
SALES (corp-wide): 43.2MM **Privately Held**
Web: www.christianscience.com
SIC: 8661 2741 Christian Science Church; Miscellaneous publishing

(G-6737)
FIS SYSTEMS INTERNATIONAL LLC
Also Called: Sungard
75-101 Federal Street (02110-1913)
PHONE...............................617 728-7722
EMP: 9
SALES (corp-wide): 14.53B **Publicly Held**
SIC: 7372 Business oriented computer software
HQ: Fis Systems International Llc
200 Campus Dr

Collegeville PA 19426
484 582-2000

(G-6738)
FITBIT INC
Also Called: FITBIT, INC.
1 Marina Park Dr Ste 701 (02210-1873)
PHONE..............................857 277-0594
EMP: 73
SALES (corp-wide): 282.84B **Publicly Held**
Web: www.fitbit.com
SIC: 3829 Measuring and controlling devices, nec
HQ: Fitbit Llc
199 Fremont St Fl 14
San Francisco CA 94105

(G-6739)
FITNOW INC
Also Called: Lose It
101 Tremont St Fl 9 (02108-5003)
PHONE..............................617 699-5585
EMP: 46 EST: 2008
SQ FT: 1,000
SALES (est): 1.46MM **Privately Held**
Web: www.loseit.com
SIC: 3949 Dumbbells and other weightlifting equipment

(G-6740)
FLATWORLD
175 Portland St Fl 2 (02114-1713)
PHONE..............................781 974-9927
EMP: 49 EST: 2020
SALES (est): 998.26K **Privately Held**
Web: catalog.flatworldknowledge.com
SIC: 2731 Textbooks: publishing and printing

(G-6741)
FLUX CYBER INC ✪
275 Newbury St Ste 3 (02116-2486)
PHONE..............................617 440-4655
Edward Julian, *CEO*
EMP: 8 EST: 2022
SALES (est): 322.63K **Privately Held**
SIC: 7372 Prepackaged software

(G-6742)
FOCUSED IMPRESSIONS TECH LLC
800 Boylston St Fl 16 (02199-1902)
PHONE..............................857 453-6771
Craig Stockmal, *CEO*
Charles Robinson, *
EMP: 27 EST: 2014
SALES (est): 5MM **Privately Held**
Web: www.focuspointsap.com
SIC: 7372 7389 Application computer software; Business services, nec

(G-6743)
FOODBERRY INC
Also Called: Foodberry
75 Sprague St (02136-2021)
PHONE..............................617 491-6600
Kevin B Murphy, *Pr*
Jonathan Huot, *
David Edwards, *
Terry Maguire, *
Joseph Speroni, *
EMP: 35 EST: 2012
SQ FT: 27,680
SALES (est): 2.97MM **Privately Held**
Web: www.foodberry.co
SIC: 2024 Ice cream and frozen deserts

(G-6744)
FORMATION INC
Also Called: Formation Systems
200 Pier 4 Blvd Ste 1000 (02210-2655)
PHONE..............................650 257-2277
Christian Hansen, *CEO*
Christian Selchau-hansen, *CEO*
Ammon Haggerty, *
EMP: 87 EST: 2017
SALES (est): 3.72MM **Privately Held**
Web: www.formation.ai
SIC: 7372 Business oriented computer software

(G-6745)
FORT POINT CABINET MAKERS LLC
21 Drydock Ave Ste 340e (02210-2704)
PHONE..............................617 338-9487
Richard Oedel, *Prin*
Matt Huffman, *Prin*
Lance Patterson, *Prin*
John Payne, *Prin*
EMP: 8 EST: 2018
SALES (est): 343.89K **Privately Held**
Web: www.fortpointcabinetmakers.com
SIC: 2434 Wood kitchen cabinets

(G-6746)
FOUNDATION DEVICES INC
6 Liberty Sq Ste 6018 (02109-5800)
PHONE..............................617 283-8306
Zachary Herbert, *CEO*
EMP: 17 EST: 2020
SALES (est): 2.03MM **Privately Held**
Web: www.foundationdevices.com
SIC: 3571 Computers, digital, analog or hybrid

(G-6747)
FREE SOFTWARE FOUNDATION INC
51 Franklin St Ste 500 (02110-1335)
PHONE..............................617 542-5942
Zo Kooyman, *Ex Dir*
EMP: 11 EST: 1985
SQ FT: 1,510
SALES (est): 1.35MM **Privately Held**
Web: www.fsf.org
SIC: 5045 5734 7372 2721 Computer software; Software, business and non-game ; Prepackaged software; Periodicals

(G-6748)
FREIGHT FARMS INC
Also Called: Freight Farms
20 Old Colony Ave Ste 201 (02127-2405)
PHONE..............................877 687-4326
Rick Vanzura, *CEO*
Jon Friedma, *
Heather Onstott, *
Jon Friedman, *
EMP: 40 EST: 2012
SQ FT: 2,000
SALES (est): 5.64MM **Privately Held**
Web: www.freightfarms.com
SIC: 3448 0182 Buildings, portable: prefabricated metal; Mushrooms, grown under cover

(G-6749)
FULL CIRCLE TECHNOLOGIES INC
11 Beacon St Ste 340 (02108-3024)
PHONE..............................617 722-0100
Rajan Nanda, *Pr*
Lars Matsson, *CEO*
EMP: 20 EST: 1993
SQ FT: 2,800

SALES (est): 856.28K **Privately Held**
Web: www.fullcircletech.com
SIC: 7371 5045 2761 7372 Computer software systems analysis and design, custom; Computer software; Computer forms, manifold or continuous; Application computer software

(G-6750)
FUSION PHARMACEUTICALS US INC
451 D St Ste 930 (02210-1950)
PHONE..............................617 420-5698
John Valliant, *Pr*
EMP: 18 EST: 2020
SALES (est): 2.74MM **Privately Held**
SIC: 2834 Pharmaceutical preparations
PA: Fusion Pharmaceuticals Inc
270 Longwood Rd S
Hamilton ON L8P 0
289 799-0891

(G-6751)
GAIN LIFE INC
55 Court St Ste 200 (02108-2104)
PHONE..............................888 412-6041
Sean Eldridge, *Pr*
Majid R Boroujerdi, *Treas*
EMP: 13 EST: 2013
SALES (est): 383.36K **Privately Held**
Web: www.gainlife.com
SIC: 7372 Prepackaged software

(G-6752)
GE ENERGY PARTS INTL LLC
41 Farnsworth St (02210-1236)
PHONE..............................617 443-3000
EMP: 34 EST: 2006
SALES (est): 2.43MM
SALES (corp-wide): 76.56B **Publicly Held**
SIC: 3511 Steam turbines
PA: General Electric Company
1 Financial Ctr Ste 3700
Boston MA 02111
617 443-3000

(G-6753)
GE MEDCAL SYSTEMS INFO TECH IN
Also Called: GE
116 Huntington Ave Ste 903 (02116-5749)
PHONE..............................617 424-6800
Jim Corrigin, *Brnch Mgr*
EMP: 350
SALES (corp-wide): 19.55B **Publicly Held**
SIC: 3845 Patient monitoring apparatus, nec
HQ: Ge Medical Systems Information Technologies, Inc.
3114 N Grandview Blvd
Waukesha WI 53188
262 544-3011

(G-6754)
GENERAL ELECTRIC COMPANY (PA)
Also Called: GE
1 Financial Ctr Ste 3700 (02111-2641)
PHONE..............................617 443-3000
H Lawrence Culp Junior, *Ch Bd*
Rahul Ghai, *Sr VP*
L Kevin Cox, *Chief Human Resources Officer*
Michael J Holston, *Sr VP*
Thomas S Timko, *CAO*
EMP: 11000 EST: 1892
SALES (est): 76.56B
SALES (corp-wide): 76.56B **Publicly Held**
Web: www.ge.com

SIC: 3511 3845 3533 3631 Turbines and turbine generator sets; Electromedical equipment; Oil and gas field machinery; Household cooking equipment

(G-6755)
GENTEX CORPORATION
Also Called: Ops-Core
12 Channel St Ste 901 (02210)
PHONE..............................617 670-3547
Heather Acker, *Mgr*
EMP: 13
SALES (corp-wide): 101.3MM **Privately Held**
Web: www.gentexcorp.com
SIC: 8731 2295 3842 Commercial physical research; Coated fabrics, not rubberized; Helmets, space
PA: Gentex Corporation
324 Main St
Simpson PA 18407
570 282-3550

(G-6756)
GEORGES BANK LLC
310 Northern Ave (02210-2316)
PHONE..............................617 423-3474
Mike Geraty, *Managing Member*
EMP: 11 EST: 2012
SALES (est): 188.48K **Privately Held**
Web: www.summershackrestaurant.com
SIC: 2092 Seafoods, fresh: prepared

(G-6757)
GETRESKILLED
800 Boylston St Ste 1600 (02199-8034)
PHONE..............................617 901-9268
EMP: 7 EST: 2018
SALES (est): 721.91K **Privately Held**
Web: www.getreskilled.com
SIC: 2834 Pharmaceutical preparations

(G-6758)
GILLETTE COMPANY (HQ)
Also Called: Gillette
1 Gillette Park (02127-1096)
PHONE..............................617 463-3000
Gary Coombe, *CEO*
Mark M Leckie, *
Terry Overbey, *
Joseph Schena, *
William J Mostyn, *
◆ EMP: 550 EST: 1901
SQ FT: 278,000
SALES (est): 960.3MM
SALES (corp-wide): 82.01B **Publicly Held**
Web: www.gillette.com
SIC: 3421 3634 2844 3951 Razor blades and razors; Electric housewares and fans; Toilet preparations; Pens and mechanical pencils
PA: The Procter & Gamble Company
1 Procter And Gamble Plz
Cincinnati OH 45202
513 983-1100

(G-6759)
GILLETTE DE MEXICO INC
800 Boylston St (02199-1900)
PHONE..............................617 421-7000
Edward Degaraan, *Pr*
EMP: 29 EST: 1982
SALES (est): 7.56MM
SALES (corp-wide): 82.01B **Publicly Held**
SIC: 3421 Cutlery
HQ: The Gillette Company
1 Gillette Park
Boston MA 02127
617 463-3000

▲ = Import ▼ = Export
◆ = Import/Export

(G-6760)
GINGER ACQUISITION INC ✪
22 Boston Wharf Rd Fl 7 (02210-3032)
PHONE...............................617 551-4000
Scott Briggs, *Pr*
EMP: 300 EST: 2022
SIC: 6719 2834 8731 Investment holding
companies, except banks; Pharmaceutical
preparations; Medical research, commercial

(G-6761)
GINKGO BIOWORKS INC (HQ)
27 Drydock Ave (02210-2377)
PHONE...............................877 422-5362
Jason Kelly, *CEO*
Reshma Shetty, *
Thomas Knight, *
Austin Che, *
Bartholomew Canton, *
EMP: 300 EST: 2008
SALES (est): 198.4MM
SALES (corp-wide): 477.71MM **Publicly
Held**
Web: www.ginkgobioworks.com
SIC: 2836 Biological products, except
diagnostic
PA: Ginkgo Bioworks Holdings, Inc.
27 Drydock Ave Ste 8
Boston MA 02210
877 422-5362

(G-6762)
**GINKGO BIOWORKS
HOLDINGS INC (PA)**
27 Drydock Ave Ste 8 (02210-2383)
PHONE...............................877 422-5362
Jason Kelly, *CEO*
Marijn Dekkers, *Ch Bd*
Reshma Shetty, *Pr*
Mark Dmytruk, *CFO*
EMP: 70 EST: 2008
SQ FT: 325,000
SALES (est): 477.71MM
SALES (corp-wide): 477.71MM **Publicly
Held**
Web: www.ginkgobioworks.com
SIC: 2836 Biological products, except
diagnostic

(G-6763)
**GLENNS GARDENING &
WOODWORKING**
491 Arborway Apt 20 (02130-3658)
PHONE...............................617 548-7977
Glenn Inghram, *Prin*
EMP: 8 EST: 2012
SALES (est): 210.49K **Privately Held**
Web: glennsgardening.vpweb.com
SIC: 2431 Millwork

(G-6764)
**GLOBAL TOWER HOLDINGS
LLC**
116 Huntington Ave (02116-5749)
PHONE...............................617 375-7500
James Tacilet, *CEO*
EMP: 12 EST: 2018
SALES (est): 2.14MM **Publicly Held**
SIC: 3663 Radio broadcasting and
communications equipment
PA: American Tower Corporation
116 Huntington Ave # 1100
Boston MA 02116

(G-6765)
**GMO THRESHOLD LOGGING
LLC**
40 Rowes Wharf Ste 600 (02110-3327)
PHONE...............................617 330-7500

EMP: 8 EST: 2006
SALES (est): 176.63K **Privately Held**
SIC: 2411 Logging camps and contractors

(G-6766)
**GMO THRSHOLD TMBER
HLDINGS LLC**
40 Rowes Wharf Ste 600 (02110-3327)
PHONE...............................617 330-7500
Eran Baruch, *Prin*
EMP: 9 EST: 2007
SALES (est): 400.76K **Privately Held**
SIC: 2411 Logging camps and contractors

(G-6767)
**GORDON BROTHERS INTL LLC
(HQ)**
800 Boylston St Spc 27 (02199-7016)
PHONE...............................888 424-1903
Mitchell H Cohen, *
Malcolm Macaulay, *
Robert L Paglia, *
Robert C Sager, *
EMP: 62 EST: 1998
SALES (est): 46.98MM
SALES (corp-wide): 336.39MM **Privately
Held**
SIC: 5311 3582 6531 Department stores;
Commercial laundry equipment; Real
estate agents and managers
PA: Gordon Brothers Group, Llc
101 Huntington Ave # 1100
Boston MA 02199
888 424-1903

(G-6768)
GOTO GROUP INC (PA)
Also Called: Goto
333 Summer St (02210-1702)
▲ **EMP: 3361 EST:** 2003
SQ FT: 220,000
SALES (est): 989.79MM
SALES (corp-wide): 989.79MM **Privately
Held**
Web: www.goto.com
SIC: 7372 7379 Prepackaged software;
Computer related consulting services

(G-6769)
**GRANDSTREAM NETWORKS
INC (PA)**
126 Brookline Ave Ste 3 (02215-3920)
PHONE...............................617 566-9300
David Xiabin Li, *Pr*
Xiang Wei, *Dir*
Xiaomei Li, *Treas*
▲ **EMP: 42 EST:** 2002
SALES (est): 40.85MM
SALES (corp-wide): 40.85MM **Privately
Held**
Web: www.grandstream.com
SIC: 4813 3661 Internet connectivity
services; Headsets, telephone

(G-6770)
GRANDTEN DISTILLING LLC
Also Called: Grandten Distilling
383 Dorchester Ave Ste 130 (02127-2422)
PHONE...............................617 269-0497
Matthew Nuernberger, *Prin*
EMP: 7 EST: 2012
SALES (est): 426.49K **Privately Held**
Web: www.grandten.com
SIC: 3556 Distillery machinery

(G-6771)
**GREAT NORTHERN INDUSTRIES
INC (PA)**
266 Beacon St Ste 2 (02116-1287)

PHONE...............................617 262-4314
M Leonard Lewis, *Pr*
M Leonard Lewis, *Pr*
Richard Secor, *
EMP: 174 EST: 1961
SQ FT: 1,000
SALES (est): 9.18MM
SALES (corp-wide): 9.18MM **Privately
Held**
SIC: 3965 3089 2678 Eyelets, metal:
clothing, fabrics, boots, or shoes; Injection
molding of plastics; Stationery: made from
purchased materials

(G-6772)
**GREENWOOD PUBLISHING
GROUP LLC (DH)**
125 High St (02110-2704)
PHONE...............................617 351-5000
Lesa Scott, *Pr*
Eric Shuman, *Ex VP*
William Bayers, *Ex VP*
Michael Dolan, *Sr VP*
Joseph Flaherty, *Sr VP*
EMP: 7 EST: 1985
SALES (est): 7.44MM
SALES (corp-wide): 1.05B **Privately Held**
Web: www.hmco.com
SIC: 2731 Books, publishing only
HQ: Hmh Publishers Llc
125 High St
Boston MA 02110
617 351-5000

(G-6773)
GRIP SECURITY INC ✪
50 Milk St Fl 16 (02109-5002)
PHONE...............................757 439-5650
Lior Yaari, *CEO*
Danny Yelin, *VP Fin*
EMP: 20 EST: 2022
SALES (est): 1.4MM **Privately Held**
SIC: 7372 Application computer software

(G-6774)
**GROOMING VENTURES - FL LLC
(HQ)**
1 Gillette Park (02127-1028)
PHONE...............................305 593-0667
▲ **EMP: 100 EST:** 1996
SALES (est): 51.77MM
SALES (corp-wide): 82.01B **Publicly Held**
Web: www.artofshaving.com
SIC: 5999 2844 3421 5122 Hair care
products; Perfumes, cosmetics and other
toilet preparations; Razor blades and razors
; Razor blades
PA: The Procter & Gamble Company
1 Procter And Gamble Plz
Cincinnati OH 45202
513 983-1100

(G-6775)
GROUPGLOBALNET CORP
768 Morton St (02126-1847)
P.O. Box 300446 (02130-0004)
PHONE...............................857 212-4012
Claretta Taylor Webb, *Pr*
EMP: 7 EST: 1998
SALES (est): 394.82K **Privately Held**
SIC: 2741 Miscellaneous publishing

(G-6776)
GROWTH I M33 L P
888 Boylston St Ste 500 (02199-8198)
PHONE...............................617 877-0046
EMP: 24 EST: 2017
SALES (est): 2.63MM **Privately Held**
Web: www.m33growth.com

SIC: 3519 Engines, diesel and semi-diesel
or dual-fuel

(G-6777)
GT SPIRITS INC
Also Called: Ghost Tequila
862 E 2nd St (02127-2427)
PHONE...............................617 276-5209
Chris Moran, *CEO*
David Moran, *CFO*
EMP: 20 EST: 2015
SALES (est): 2.67MM **Privately Held**
Web: www.ghosttequila.com
SIC: 5921 2085 Liquor stores; Distilled and
blended liquors

(G-6778)
**GTY TECHNOLOGY HOLDINGS
INC (PA)**
Also Called: Gty Technology
800 Boylston St Fl 16 (02199-1900)
PHONE...............................702 945-2898
Tj Parass, *Pr*
Justin Kerr, *CAO*
Jon Bourne, *Sec*
John Curran, *Treas*
Travis Pearson, *Dir*
EMP: 11 EST: 2018
SALES (est): 84.64MM
SALES (corp-wide): 84.64MM **Privately
Held**
Web: www.eunasolutions.com
SIC: 7374 7372 Data processing and
preparation; Prepackaged software

(G-6779)
GUARDICORE INC
100 Summer St Ste 1600 (02110-2104)
PHONE...............................781 789-8904
Pavel Gurvich, *Pr*
Yaron Bartov, *Treas*
EMP: 10 EST: 2020
SALES (est): 3.02MM
SALES (corp-wide): 3.62B **Publicly Held**
SIC: 7372 Application computer software
PA: Akamai Technologies, Inc.
145 Broadway
Cambridge MA 02142
617 444-3000

(G-6780)
**HAEMONETICS CORPORATION
(PA)**
Also Called: Haemonetics
125 Summer St Ste 1800 (02110-1613)
PHONE...............................781 848-7100
Christopher A Simon, *Pr*
Ellen M Zane, *
James C D'arecca, *Ex VP*
Anila Lingamneni, *Ex VP*
Michelle L Basil, *Ex VP*
▲ **EMP: 509 EST:** 1971
SALES (est): 1.17B
SALES (corp-wide): 1.17B **Publicly Held**
Web: www.haemonetics.com
SIC: 3841 3845 Medical instruments and
equipment, blood and bone work;
Electromedical equipment

(G-6781)
**HARPOON DISTRIBUTING CO
INC**
Also Called: Clown Shoes Beer
306 Northern Ave Ste 2 (02210-2367)
PHONE...............................617 574-9551
Dan Kanery, *CEO*
Charles Storey, *Pr*
Warren G Dibble, *CFO*
Ed Balenta, *Genl Mgr*

▲ **EMP:** 17 **EST:** 2002
SQ FT: 5,500
SALES (est): 6.48MM
SALES (corp-wide): 49.92MM **Privately Held**
Web: www.harpoonbrewery.com
SIC: 5181 2082　Beer and other fermented malt liquors; Beer (alcoholic beverage)
PA: Mass. Bay Brewing Company, Inc.
　306 Northern Ave
　Boston MA 02210
　617 574-9551

(G-6782)
HARRY MILLER CO LLC
Also Called: We Palmer Co
850 Albany St　(02119-2545)
P.O. Box 191490　(02119-0029)
PHONE.................................617 427-2300
Fred Barkstale, *Contrlr*
EMP: 11
SALES (corp-wide): 9.57MM **Privately Held**
Web: www.harrymiller.com
SIC: 2394　Awnings, fabric: made from purchased materials
PA: Harry Miller Co., Llc
　19 Hampden St
　Boston MA 02119
　617 427-2300

(G-6783)
HARRY MILLER CO LLC (PA)
Also Called: American Canvas Co
19 Hampden St　(02119-2911)
P.O. Box 191480　(02119-0028)
PHONE.................................617 427-2300
Harry Miller, *Pr*
Harry Miller, *Pr*
Suzanne Nadeski, *CFO*
▲ **EMP:** 40 **EST:** 1910
SQ FT: 40,000
SALES (est): 9.57MM
SALES (corp-wide): 9.57MM **Privately Held**
Web: www.harrymiller.com
SIC: 2394　Awnings, fabric: made from purchased materials

(G-6784)
HARVARD BUS SCHL STDNT ASSN IN
70 N Harvard St　(02163)
PHONE.................................617 495-6812
Karima Meguid, *Brnch Mgr*
EMP: 100
SALES (corp-wide): 6.1B **Privately Held**
Web: alumni.hbs.edu
SIC: 2731　Books, publishing and printing
HQ: Harvard Business School Student Association, Inc.
　Soldiers Fld
　Boston MA 02163

(G-6785)
HAYSTACK ID
100 Franklin St　(02110-1537)
PHONE.................................617 422-0075
EMP: 15 **EST:** 2012
SALES (est): 569.74K **Privately Held**
Web: www.haystackid.com
SIC: 7372　Prepackaged software

(G-6786)
HERCULES PRESS
91 Spring St　(02132-4315)
PHONE.................................617 323-1950
Michael Macrides, *Owner*
EMP: 7 **EST:** 1973
SQ FT: 2,700

SALES (est): 476.86K **Privately Held**
Web: www.herculespress.com
SIC: 2759 7334　Screen printing; Photocopying and duplicating services

(G-6787)
HILLEVAX INC
Also Called: Hillevax
321 Harrison Ave Ste 500　(02118-4679)
PHONE.................................617 213-5054
Robert Hershberg, *Ch Bd*
Sean Mcloughlin, *COO*
Shane Maltbie, *CFO*
Astrid Borkowski, *CMO*
EMP: 62 **EST:** 2020
Web: www.hillevax.com
SIC: 2836　Biological products, except diagnostic

(G-6788)
HM PUBLISHING CORP
222 Berkeley St　(02116-3748)
PHONE.................................617 251-5000
Stephen Richards, *Co-Vice President*
Stephen Richards, *Ex VP*
Gerald Hughes, *Senior Vice President Human Resources*
Paul Weaver, *Sr VP*
▲ **EMP:** 3546 **EST:** 2003
SQ FT: 246,000
SALES (est): 2.81MM
SALES (corp-wide): 460.36MM **Privately Held**
Web: www.hmco.com
SIC: 2731　Textbooks: publishing only, not printed on site
PA: Houghton Mifflin Holdings Inc
　125 High St Ste 900
　Boston MA 02110
　617 351-5000

(G-6789)
HMH PUBLISHERS LLC (DH)
Also Called: Houghton Mfflin Hrcurt Pbls In
125 High St　(02110-2704)
PHONE.................................617 351-5000
Eric Shuman, *Ex VP*
William Bayers, *Ex VP*
Michael Dolan, *Sr VP*
Joseph Flaherty, *Sr VP*
David Mills, *Asst Tr*
EMP: 19 **EST:** 2012
SALES (est): 58.63MM
SALES (corp-wide): 1.05B **Privately Held**
Web: www.hmhco.com
SIC: 2731　Books, publishing only
HQ: Houghton Mifflin Harcourt Publishers Inc.
　125 High St Ste 900
　Boston MA 02110

(G-6790)
HO YUEN BAKERY INC
54 Beach St Ste 1　(02111-2086)
PHONE.................................617 426-8320
Julie T L Lee, *Owner*
EMP: 9 **EST:** 1973
SQ FT: 1,500
SALES (est): 501.08K **Privately Held**
Web: www.etuckerdesign.com
SIC: 2051　Bakery: wholesale or wholesale/retail combined

(G-6791)
HORN BOOK INC
Also Called: Horn Book Magazine
300 Fenway Ste P311　(02115-5820)
PHONE.................................617 278-0225
Thomas Todd, *Pr*
Jane Manthorne, *VP*

EMP: 16 **EST:** 1924
SALES (est): 474.44K
SALES (corp-wide): 958.25K **Privately Held**
Web: www.hbook.com
SIC: 2721　Magazines: publishing only, not printed on site
PA: Media Source Inc.
　7858 Industrial Pkwy
　Plain City OH 43064
　646 380-0747

(G-6792)
HOUGHTON MFFLIN HRCURT FNDTION
125 High St Ste 900　(02110-2777)
PHONE.................................617 351-5000
Gordon Crovitz, *Pr*
Eric Shuman, *Ex VP*
Joseph Flaherty, *Sr VP*
William Bayers, *Sec*
EMP: 15 **EST:** 2008
SALES (est): 306.21K **Privately Held**
Web: www.hmhco.com
SIC: 2731　Book publishing

(G-6793)
HOUGHTON MFFLIN HRCURT PBLS IN (DH)
125 High St Ste 900　(02110-2777)
PHONE.................................617 351-5000
EMP: 659
SALES (est): 1.51B
SALES (corp-wide): 1.05B **Privately Held**
Web: www.houghtonmifflinbooks.com
SIC: 2731　Textbooks: publishing and printing
HQ: Houghton Mifflin Harcourt Company
　125 High St Ste 900
　Boston MA 02110
　617 351-5000

(G-6794)
HOUGHTON MIFFLIN LLC
222 Berkeley St Lbby 1　(02116-3748)
PHONE.................................617 351-5000
EMP: 59 **EST:** 2007
SALES (est): 3.54MM **Privately Held**
Web: www.hmhco.com
SIC: 2731　Book publishing

(G-6795)
HOUGHTON MIFFLIN CO INTL INC
222 Berkeley St　(02116-3748)
PHONE.................................617 351-5000
Eric Shuman, *Ex VP*
William Bayers, *Ex VP*
Michael Dolan, *Sr VP*
Joseph Flaherty, *Sr VP*
David Mills, *Asst Tr*
EMP: 38 **EST:** 1992
SALES (est): 6.1MM
SALES (corp-wide): 1.05B **Privately Held**
SIC: 2731　Book publishing
HQ: Houghton Mifflin Harcourt Publishing Company
　125 High St Ste 900
　Boston MA 02110
　617 351-5000

(G-6796)
HOUGHTON MIFFLIN HARCOURT CO (HQ)
Also Called: Hmh
125 High St Ste 900　(02110-2777)
PHONE.................................617 351-5000
John J Lynch Junior, *Pr*
Joseph P Abbott Junior, *Ex VP*
William F Bayers, *Ex VP*

Michael E Evans, *CRO*
Alejandro Reyes, *CPO*
▲ **EMP:** 92 **EST:** 2009
SALES (est): 1.05B
SALES (corp-wide): 1.05B **Privately Held**
Web: ir.hmhco.com
SIC: 2731 3999　Book publishing; Education aids, devices and supplies
PA: Harbor Holding Corp.
　9 W 57th St Fl 32
　New York NY 10019
　212 415-6700

(G-6797)
HOUGHTON MIFFLIN HARCOURT PUBG (DH)
Also Called: Houghton Mifflin Publ shing
125 High St Ste 900　(02110-2777)
PHONE.................................617 351-5000
John J Lynch Junior, *Pr*
William Bayers, *
Joseph Abbott, *
Mary Cullinane, *CCO**
John K Dragoon, *CMO**
◆ **EMP:** 717 **EST:** 1908
SQ FT: 246,000
SALES (est): 443.16MM
SALES (corp-wide): 1.05B **Privately Held**
Web: www.hmhco.com
SIC: 2731　Textbooks: publishing only, not printed on site
HQ: Houghton Mifflin Harcourt Company
　125 High St Ste 900
　Boston MA 02110
　617 351-5000

(G-6798)
HOUGHTON MIFFLIN HOLDING COMPANY INC
Also Called: Houghton Mifflin Harcourt
222 Berkeley St　(02116-3748)
PHONE.................................617 351-5000
EMP: 3550
SIC: 2731　Book publishing

(G-6799)
HUMAN CARE SYSTEMS INC (HQ)
1 Faneuil Hall Sq　(02109-1604)
PHONE.................................617 720-7838
Matthew P Hall, *Pr*
Thomas S Doyle, *Prin*
Nancy Santilli, *VP*
Courtney Saye, *COO*
EMP: 10 **EST:** 2007
SALES (est): 11.01MM
SALES (corp-wide): 34.9MM **Privately Held**
Web: www.caremetx.com
SIC: 7372　Prepackaged software
PA: Caremetx, Llc
　6931 Arlington Rd Ste 400
　Bethesda MD 20814
　877 690-0220

(G-6800)
HUMANSCALE CORPORATION
179 South St Fl 1　(02111-2729)
PHONE.................................617 338-0077
Jenniffer Harris, *Brnch Mgr*
EMP: 55
SALES (corp-wide): 344.09MM **Privately Held**
Web: www.humanscale.com
SIC: 3577　Computer peripheral equipment, nec
PA: Humanscale Corporation
　1114 Avenue Of The Americ
　New York NY 10036
　212 725-4749

(G-6801)
HYCU INC (DH)
27 Wormwood St Ste 600 (02210-1621)
PHONE...................................617 681-9100
Simon Taylor, *Pr*
Terry Curtis Junior, *Treas*
Susan Fletcher, *
Nathan Owen, *
Justin Schumacher, *
EMP: 197 **EST:** 2007
SALES (est): 173.3MM **Privately Held**
Web: www.hycu.com
SIC: 7372 Business oriented computer software
HQ: Comtrade Group B.V.
Prins Bernhardplein 200
Amsterdam NH 1097
205706810

(G-6802)
IDG
Also Called: International Data Group
1 Exeter Plz 15th Fl (02116-2856)
PHONE...................................508 875-5000
Ted Bloom, *Pr*
Jim Ghirardi, *VP*
EMP: 48 **EST:** 2000
SALES (est): 3.32MM
SALES (corp-wide): 8.52B **Publicly Held**
Web: www.idg.com
SIC: 2721 Periodicals
HQ: International Data Group, Inc.
140 Kendrick St Bldg B
Needham MA 02494
508 875-5000

(G-6803)
IDG NEWS SERVICE
699 Boylston St Ste 15 (02116-2848)
PHONE...................................617 423-9030
Elizabeth Heichler, *Prin*
EMP: 40 **EST:** 2005
SALES (est): 6.26MM
SALES (corp-wide): 8.52B **Publicly Held**
Web: www.idg.com
SIC: 2741 Newsletter publishing
HQ: International Data Group, Inc.
140 Kendrick St Bldg B
Needham MA 02494
508 875-5000

(G-6804)
IDP HOLDINGS INC (PA)
1 Beacon St (02108-3107)
◆ **EMP:** 9 **EST:** 2006
SQ FT: 5,100
SALES (est): 23K **Privately Held**
Web: www.ideapaint.com
SIC: 2851 Paint driers

(G-6805)
IFM THERAPEUTICS LLC
855 Boylston St Ste 1103 (02116-2622)
PHONE...................................857 327-9903
Gary Glick, *CEO*
Michael Cooke, *
EMP: 27 **EST:** 2017
SALES (est): 7.06MM
SALES (corp-wide): 45.01B **Publicly Held**
Web: www.ifmthera.com
SIC: 2834 Pharmaceutical preparations
PA: Bristol-Myers Squibb Company
430 E 29th St Fl 14
New York NY 10016
212 546-4000

(G-6806)
IKENA ONCOLOGY INC (PA)
Also Called: IKENA ONCOLOGY
645 Summer St Ste 1 (02210-2135)

PHONE...................................857 273-8343
Mark Manfredi, *Pr*
Ronald C Renaud Junior, *Ch Bd*
Jotin Marango, *CFO*
Jeffrey Ecsedy, *CDO*
Sergio Santillana, *CMO*
EMP: 31 **EST:** 2016
SQ FT: 20,752
SALES (est): 15.62MM
SALES (corp-wide): 15.62MM **Publicly Held**
Web: www.ikenaoncology.com
SIC: 2836 Biological products, except diagnostic

(G-6807)
ILAB SOLUTIONS LLC
217 W Springfield St # 2 (02118-3446)
PHONE...................................617 297-2805
Tad Andrew Fallows, *Prin*
EMP: 13 **EST:** 2008
SALES (est): 604.87K **Privately Held**
SIC: 3825 Instruments to measure electricity

(G-6808)
IMBRIA PHARMACEUTICALS INC
265 Franklin St Ste 1702 (02110-3144)
PHONE...................................617 941-3000
David-alexandre Gros, *CEO*
EMP: 9 **EST:** 2018
SALES (est): 992.96K **Privately Held**
Web: www.imbria.com
SIC: 8731 2834 Biotechnical research, commercial; Pharmaceutical preparations

(G-6809)
INGENICO INC
101 Federal St Ste 700 (02110-1852)
PHONE...................................888 589-5885
Jacques Guerin, *Brnch Mgr*
EMP: 40
Web: www.ingenico.com
SIC: 7372 Application computer software
HQ: Ingenico Inc.
3025 Windward Plz Ste 600
Alpharetta GA 30005
678 456-1200

(G-6810)
INNONEO HEALTH TECH INC (PA)
1 Boston Pl Ste 2600 (02108-4420)
PHONE...................................617 336-3202
Vaman Rao, *Ch*
Mary E Joseph Corporate, *Operations*
Dinesh Venkataraman Corporate, *Finance*
EMP: 70 **EST:** 2016
SALES (est): 8.21MM
SALES (corp-wide): 8.21MM **Privately Held**
Web: www.innoneo.com
SIC: 7372 8011 8099 8742 Prepackaged software; Offices and clinics of medical doctors; Health screening service; Hospital and health services consultant

(G-6811)
INNOVASEA SYSTEMS INC (PA)
266 Summer St Fl 2 (02210-1127)
PHONE...................................207 322-3219
Langley Gace, *Pr*
David Kelly, *COO*
Frank Fay, *CFO*
Traci Sheldon, *Prin*
EMP: 23 **EST:** 2014
SQ FT: 2,000
SALES (est): 11.6MM
SALES (corp-wide): 11.6MM **Privately Held**

SIC: 5084 8748 3523 Fish processing machinery, equipment and supplies; Business consulting, nec; Farm machinery and equipment

(G-6812)
INNOVATIVE CHEM PDTS GROUP LLC
Also Called: Ideapaint
1 Beacon St (02108-3107)
PHONE...................................800 393-5250
Doug Mattscheck, *CEO*
EMP: 18
SALES (corp-wide): 923.49MM **Privately Held**
Web: www.icpgroup.com
SIC: 2851 Paints and allied products
PA: Innovative Chemical Products Group, Llc
150 Dascomb Rd
Andover MA 01810
978 623-9980

(G-6813)
INSPIREMD INC (PA)
321 Columbus Ave (02116-5168)
P.O. Box 51 (01752-0051)
PHONE...................................857 305-2410
EMP: 33 **EST:** 2008
SQ FT: 1,580
SALES (est): 1.89MM
SALES (corp-wide): 1.89MM **Privately Held**
SIC: 3841 Surgical and medical instruments

(G-6814)
INSTITUTE FOR APPLIED NTWRK SE
Also Called: Ians
2 Center Plz Ste 500a (02108-1921)
PHONE...................................617 399-8100
EMP: 50 **EST:** 2001
SQ FT: 4,176
SALES (est): 20MM **Privately Held**
Web: www.iansresearch.com
SIC: 7389 2721 Trade show arrangement; Trade journals: publishing and printing

(G-6815)
INTEGRA LIFESCIENCES
7 Elkins St (02127-8777)
PHONE...................................617 268-1616
Carroll Lachance, *Prin*
EMP: 11 **EST:** 2018
SALES (est): 1.34MM **Privately Held**
Web: integralife.dejobs.org
SIC: 3841 Surgical and medical instruments

(G-6816)
IONE PRESS INC
138 Ipswich St (02215-3534)
PHONE...................................617 236-1935
Robert A Schuneman, *Pr*
EMP: 9 **EST:** 1964
SQ FT: 5,000
SALES (est): 614.05K **Privately Held**
SIC: 2741 Music, sheet: publishing only, not printed on site
PA: Ecs Publishing Corporation
138 Ipswich St
Boston MA

(G-6817)
IQBAL SHAHEEN
Also Called: Deep Blue Sea Trading
315 Freeport St Apt 3 (02122-3580)
PHONE...................................857 415-7585
Iqbal Shaheen, *Owner*
EMP: 7 **EST:** 2021

SALES (est): 312.6K **Privately Held**
SIC: 2091 Tuna fish, preserved and cured

(G-6818)
IRONWOOD PHARMACEUTICALS INC (PA)
Also Called: Ironwood
100 Summer St Ste 2300 (02110-2156)
PHONE...................................617 621-7722
Thomas Mccourt, *CEO*
Thomas A Mccourt, *CEO*
Julie H Mchugh, *Ch Bd*
Gina Consylman, *Sr VP*
Jason Rickard, *Sr VP*
EMP: 174 **EST:** 1998
SQ FT: 39,000
SALES (est): 410.6MM
SALES (corp-wide): 410.6MM **Publicly Held**
Web: www.ironwoodpharma.com
SIC: 2834 8731 Pharmaceutical preparations; Commercial physical research

(G-6819)
ITRICA CORP
125 High St 2nd Fl (02110-2704)
PHONE...................................617 340-7777
Richard Palumbo, *Pr*
EMP: 8 **EST:** 2008
SQ FT: 1,800
SALES (est): 1.1MM **Privately Held**
Web: www.itrica.com
SIC: 7372 Application computer software

(G-6820)
IVORY ONYX
320 D St Unit 403 (02127-1281)
PHONE...................................617 454-4980
Daniel Mugure, *Prin*
EMP: 11 **EST:** 2016
SALES (est): 858.11K **Privately Held**
SIC: 7379 7372 7371 5045 Online services technology consultants; Business oriented computer software; Computer software systems analysis and design, custom; Computer software

(G-6821)
JBT AEROTECH CORP
121 Frankfort St (02128-3215)
PHONE...................................857 574-3170
EMP: 23 **EST:** 2019
SALES (est): 2.3MM **Privately Held**
Web: www.jbtc.com
SIC: 3556 Food products machinery

(G-6822)
JENZABAR INC (PA)
101 Huntington Ave Ste 2200 (02199-7629)
PHONE...................................617 492-9099
Robert Maginn Junior, *Ch Bd*
Ling Chai, *
Mimi Flanagan, *
EMP: 100 **EST:** 1998
SALES (est): 375.6K
SALES (corp-wide): 375.6K **Privately Held**
Web: www.jenzabar.com
SIC: 7372 Educational computer software

(G-6823)
JEWISH ADVOCATE PUBG CORP
Also Called: Jewish Times
15 School St (02108-4315)
PHONE...................................617 523-6232
Grand Rabbi Korff, *Pr*
EMP: 18 **EST:** 1902
SQ FT: 7,000
SALES (est): 368.8K **Privately Held**
Web: www.thejewishadvocate.com

SIC: **2711** 6512 Commercial printing and newspaper publishing combined; Commercial and industrial building operation

(G-6824)
JEWISH ADVOCATE RELIGIOUS
15 School St (02108-4315)
PHONE..........................617 227-8200
Rabbi Grand R Korff, *Pr*
Grand Rabbi Y A Korff, *Pr*
EMP: 8 **EST:** 2015
SALES (est): 322.15K **Privately Held**
Web: www.thejewishadvocate.com
SIC: **2711** Newspapers, publishing and printing

(G-6825)
JIBO INC
230 Congress St Ste 900 (02110-2467)
P.O. Box 729 (01740-0729)
PHONE..........................617 542-5426
EMP: 100 **EST:** 2010
SQ FT: 16,000
SALES (est): 9.6MM **Privately Held**
Web: www.jibo.com
SIC: **3429** Hardware, nec

(G-6826)
JOHN BROWN US LLC
1 South Sta Fl 3 (02110-2253)
PHONE..........................617 449-4354
EMP: 10 **EST:** 2015
SALES (est): 3.33MM **Privately Held**
Web: www.johnbrownmedia.com
SIC: **2759** Publication printing
HQ: Dentsu International Limited
10 Triton Street Regents Place
London NW1 3
207 070-7700

(G-6827)
JOHN P POW COMPANY INC
49 D St (02127-2401)
PHONE..........................617 269-6040
John F Pow, *Pr*
Thomas Finneran Junior, *Clerk*
EMP: 32 **EST:** 1935
SQ FT: 13,390
SALES (est): 2.14MM **Privately Held**
Web: www.jppow.com
SIC: **2752** Offset printing

(G-6828)
JOHNSON CONTROLS INC
Also Called: Johnson Controls
1 Copley Pl Fl 4 (02116-6599)
PHONE..........................617 424-6601
EMP: 16
Web: www.johnsoncontrols.com
SIC: **2531** Seats, automobile
HQ: Johnson Controls, Inc.
5757 N Green Bay Ave
Milwaukee WI 53209
920 245-6409

(G-6829)
JOHNSON CONTROLS INC
Also Called: Johnson Controls
33 Avenue Louis Pasteur (02115-5727)
PHONE..........................617 992-2073
EMP: 17
Web: www.johnsoncontrols.com
SIC: **2531** Seats, automobile
HQ: Johnson Controls, Inc.
5757 N Green Bay Ave
Milwaukee WI 53209
920 245-6409

(G-6830)
JOHNSONS FOOD PRODUCTS CORP
1 Mount Vernon St (02108-1405)
PHONE..........................617 265-3400
Chris P Anton, *Pr*
Helen Anton, *Treas*
John Anton, *Sls Mgr*
Peter Anton, *VP*
Dieter Anton, *VP*
EMP: 12 **EST:** 1940
SQ FT: 15,000
SALES (est): 464.97K **Privately Held**
SIC: **2026** Cream, whipped

(G-6831)
JORDAN BROS SEAFOOD CO INC
Also Called: Jordan Brothers Seafood
314 Northern Ave (02210-2316)
P.O. Box 101 (02072-0101)
PHONE..........................508 583-9797
Thomas J Jordan Iii, *CEO*
Robert Jordan, *Treas*
EMP: 10 **EST:** 1988
SALES (est): 579.39K **Privately Held**
Web: www.jordanbrothersseafood.com
SIC: **2092** 5146 Fresh or frozen packaged fish; Fish and seafoods

(G-6832)
JOYN BIO LLC
27 Drydock Ave Ste 8 (02210-2383)
PHONE..........................978 549-3723
Mike Mille, *CEO*
Laurelin Wyntre, *Opers Mgr*
EMP: 20 **EST:** 2017
SALES (est): 4.68MM **Privately Held**
Web: www.ginkgobioworks.com
SIC: **2836** Biological products, except diagnostic

(G-6833)
JRNI INC
320 Congress St (02210-1250)
PHONE..........................857 305-6477
Jaime Ellertson, *Interim Chief Executive Officer*
Glenn Shoosmith, *Pr*
Andy Watt, *CFO*
Gary Phillips, *Interim CAO*
Yuan Cheng, *Interim Chief Technology Officer*
EMP: 44 **EST:** 2015
SALES (est): 4.28MM **Privately Held**
Web: www.jrni.com
SIC: **7372** Business oriented computer software

(G-6834)
JUGOS
145 Dartmouth St Ste 3 (02116-5162)
PHONE..........................617 418-9879
EMP: 7 **EST:** 2014
SALES (est): 145.06K **Privately Held**
Web: www.visitjugos.com
SIC: **2033** Fruit juices: fresh

(G-6835)
JULESAN INC
Also Called: Gnomon Color
325 Huntington Ave (02115-4401)
PHONE..........................617 437-6860
Julie M Knapp, *Pr*
Julie Knapp, *Pr*
EMP: 22 **EST:** 1987
SQ FT: 525
SALES (est): 1.74MM **Privately Held**
Web: www.gnomoncopy.biz

SIC: **2759** 5812 Laser printing; Pizza restaurants

(G-6836)
JUMPTAP INC
155 Seaport Blvd 8th Fl (02210-2619)
PHONE..........................617 301-4550
EMP: 30
SIC: **7372** Business oriented computer software

(G-6837)
JUNIPER PHARMACEUTICALS INC (DH)
Also Called: Juniper Pharmaceuticals
33 Arch St Ste 3110 (02110-1424)
PHONE..........................617 639-1500
Nikin Patel, *Pr*
Robert Harris, *Chief Technical Officer*
EMP: 88 **EST:** 1986
SQ FT: 7,050
SALES (est): 25.97MM **Publicly Held**
Web: www.catalent.com
SIC: **2834** Pharmaceutical preparations
HQ: Catalent Pharma Solutions, Inc.
14 Schoolhouse Rd
Somerset NJ 08873

(G-6838)
JURIBA LIMITED
30 Newbury St (02116-3239)
PHONE..........................617 356-8681
Barry Angell, *Mgr*
EMP: 30 **EST:** 2014
SALES (est): 2.05MM **Privately Held**
Web: www.juriba.com
SIC: **7372** Prepackaged software

(G-6839)
KAMROWSKI METAL REFINISHING
80 K Street Pl (02127-1613)
PHONE..........................508 877-0367
EMP: 7 **EST:** 1980
SALES (est): 441.58K **Privately Held**
Web: www.drbfacilityservices.com
SIC: **3549** Metalworking machinery, nec

(G-6840)
KARUNA THERAPEUTICS INC (PA)
99 High St Fl 26 (02110-2377)
PHONE..........................857 449-2244
Steven Paul, *Ch Bd*
Andrew Miller, *COO*
Stephen Brannan, *CMO*
Jason Brown, *CFO*
Charmaine Lykins, *CCO*
EMP: 38 **EST:** 2009
SQ FT: 11,225
SALES (est): 10.64MM **Publicly Held**
Web: www.karunatx.com
SIC: **2834** Pharmaceutical preparations

(G-6841)
KIMBLE APPLICATIONS INC
99 Chauncy St Ste 500 (02111-1760)
PHONE..........................617 651-5600
Michael Speranza, *CEO*
Steve Sharp, *
Geoff Pople, *Chief Customer Officer**
David Scott, *
Sarah Edwards, *PRODUCT**
EMP: 50 **EST:** 2012
SALES (est): 9.55MM
SALES (corp-wide): 112.03MM **Privately Held**
SIC: **7372** Prepackaged software
HQ: Kimble Applications Limited
100 Union Street

London SE1 0
203 006-9222

(G-6842)
KINETIC SYSTEMS INC
20 Arboretum Rd (02131-1102)
PHONE..........................617 522-8700
Alan D Gertel, *CEO*
Peter M Maris, *
Judith Solomon, *
◆ **EMP:** 45 **EST:** 1968
SQ FT: 24,000
SALES (est): 8.8MM **Privately Held**
Web: www.kineticsystems.com
SIC: **3829** 3827 3821 3571 Vibration meters, analyzers, and calibrators; Optical instruments and lenses; Laboratory apparatus and furniture; Electronic computers

(G-6843)
KITEWHEEL LLC
24 School St Fl 6 (02108-5113)
PHONE..........................617 447-2138
Lawrence Smith, *CEO*
Mark Smith, *
EMP: 25 **EST:** 2013
SALES (est): 4.94MM **Publicly Held**
Web: www.csgi.com
SIC: **7372** Business oriented computer software
PA: Csg Systems International, Inc.
169 Inverness Dr W # 300
Englewood CO 80112

(G-6844)
KLIKS INC
867 Boylston St (02116-2774)
PHONE..........................617 230-0544
Calvin Koo, *CEO*
EMP: 15 **EST:** 2020
SALES (est): 512.58K **Privately Held**
SIC: **7372** Business oriented computer software

(G-6845)
KNOWLEDGE AI INC (PA)
58 Winter St (02108-4714)
PHONE..........................415 321-9059
Joonhee Won, *CEO*
EMP: 98 **EST:** 2019
SALES (est): 4.74MM
SALES (corp-wide): 4.74MM **Privately Held**
Web: www.kaitsolutions.com
SIC: **7372** Educational computer software

(G-6846)
KOPLOW GAMES INC
369 Congress St Fl 5 (02210-1871)
P.O. Box 965 (02045-0965)
PHONE..........................617 482-4011
James H Koplow, *Pr*
▲ **EMP:** 12 **EST:** 1974
SQ FT: 7,000
SALES (est): 1.1MM **Privately Held**
Web: koplow.ecadv.com
SIC: **3944** Dice and dice cups

(G-6847)
KRUEGER INTERNATIONAL INC
109 Broad St (02110-3008)
PHONE..........................617 542-4043
Paul Whalen, *Prin*
EMP: 7
SALES (corp-wide): 682.99MM **Privately Held**
Web: www.ki.com
SIC: **2522** Office furniture, except wood
PA: Krueger International, Inc.
1330 Bellevue St

▲ = Import ▼ = Export
◆ = Import/Export

Green Bay WI 54302
920 468-8100

(G-6848)
KS BAXTER LOGISTICS CO INC
6 Liberty Sq (02109-5800)
PHONE...............................607 203-5921
Shonette Tomlinson, *Pr*
EMP: 10
SALES (est): 413.57K **Privately Held**
SIC: 3537   Trucks, tractors, loaders, carriers, and similar equipment

(G-6849)
KYRUUS INC
100 Franklin St Ste 803 (02110-1537)
PHONE...............................617 419-2060
Graham Gardener, *CEO*
Paul Merrild, *Pr*
Edmond Furlong, *CFO*
Julie Yoo, *CPO*
EMP: 135 **EST:** 2010
SALES (est): 23.22MM **Privately Held**
Web: www.kyruushealth.com
SIC: 7375 7372   Information retrieval services; Business oriented computer software

(G-6850)
LA BURDICK BOSTON LLC
Also Called: L.a Burdick Chocolate Shop
220 Clarendon St (02116-3709)
PHONE...............................617 303-0113
Yoon Chang, *Prin*
EMP: 8 **EST:** 2011
SALES (est): 171.18K **Privately Held**
SIC: 2066   Chocolate

(G-6851)
LAKESIDE SOFTWARE LLC (PA)
2 Oliver St Ste 700 (02109-4909)
PHONE...............................248 686-1700
Michael Schumacher, *CEO*
EMP: 30 **EST:** 1997
SALES (est): 26.42MM
SALES (corp-wide): 26.42MM **Privately Held**
Web: www.lakesidesoftware.com
SIC: 7372   Business oriented computer software

(G-6852)
LAMINAM USA INC
156 State St Fl 5 (02109-2585)
PHONE...............................905 669-6679
EMP: 17 **EST:** 2017
SALES (est): 805.35K
SALES (corp-wide): 2.67MM **Privately Held**
SIC: 3253   Ceramic wall and floor tile
HQ: Laminam Spa
Via Ghiarola Nuova 258
Fiorano Modenese MO 41042
05361844200

(G-6853)
LAWYERS WEEKLY LLC (PA)
40 Court St Fl 5 (02108-2202)
PHONE...............................617 451-7300
EMP: 80 **EST:** 1996
SALES (est): 9.58MM
SALES (corp-wide): 9.58MM **Privately Held**
Web: www.masslawyersweekly.com
SIC: 2711   Newspapers, publishing and printing

(G-6854)
LEADING MARKET TECH INC
58 Winter St Ste 5 (02108-4770)
PHONE...............................617 494-4747
Jay Kemp Smith, *CEO*
EMP: 32 **EST:** 1987
SQ FT: 5,000
SALES (est): 2.55MM **Privately Held**
Web: www.lmtech.com
SIC: 7372   Business oriented computer software

(G-6855)
LEARNING POOL INC (PA)
77 Sleeper St (02210-1359)
PHONE...............................857 284-1420
Ben Betts, *CEO*
EMP: 11 **EST:** 2017
SALES (est): 10.45MM
SALES (corp-wide): 10.45MM **Privately Held**
Web: www.learningpool.com
SIC: 7372   Educational computer software

(G-6856)
LEON EG COMPANY INC
Also Called: Leon Electric
1234 Washington St (02118-2192)
P.O. Box 181248 (02118-0013)
PHONE...............................617 482-8383
Arthur J Leon, *Pr*
EMP: 24 **EST:** 1935
SQ FT: 50,000
SALES (est): 435.44K **Privately Held**
Web: www.leonelectric.com
SIC: 1711 1731 3536   Mechanical contractor ; General electrical contractor; Hoists, cranes, and monorails

(G-6857)
LIBERTY MTALS MIN HOLDINGS LLC
175 Berkeley St (02116-5066)
PHONE...............................617 654-4374
A Alexander Fontanes, *Mgr*
EMP: 10 **EST:** 2012
SALES (est): 860.93K **Privately Held**
Web: www.libertymutualgroup.com
SIC: 1081   Metal mining services

(G-6858)
LIFE FORCE BEVERAGES LLC
Also Called: Jubali
196 Quincy St (02121-1996)
PHONE...............................551 265-9482
Liam Madden, *Pr*
EMP: 9 **EST:** 2014
SALES (est): 610.26K **Privately Held**
Web: www.blenderreviews.us
SIC: 2082   Malt beverage products

(G-6859)
LIGHTMATTER INC
100 Summer St Ste 1850 (02110-2100)
PHONE...............................857 244-0460
Nicholas C Harris, *CEO*
Nicholas C Harris, *Pr*
Thomas Graham, *
EMP: 85 **EST:** 2018
SALES (est): 10.58MM **Privately Held**
Web: www.lightmatter.co
SIC: 3674   Semiconductors and related devices

(G-6860)
LISTEN INC
580 Harrison Ave Ste 3w (02118-2637)
PHONE...............................617 556-4104
Stephen F Temme, *Pr*

EMP: 25 **EST:** 1995
SALES (est): 5.54MM **Privately Held**
Web: www.listeninc.com
SIC: 3826   Analytical instruments

(G-6861)
LOGAN STAMP WORKS INC
104 Meridian St 106 (02128-1972)
P.O. Box 521 (02128-0006)
PHONE...............................617 569-2121
Robert Vitale, *Pr*
Gary Vitale, *VP*
Tillie Vitale, *Treas*
Janice Vitale, *Clerk*
Robert Vitale, *Pr*
EMP: 7 **EST:** 1968
SQ FT: 2,800
SALES (est): 508.54K **Privately Held**
Web: www.wbmason.com
SIC: 3953   Embossing seals and hand stamps

(G-6862)
LOGICMANAGER INC
5 Drydock Ave Ste 2080 (02210-2303)
PHONE...............................617 530-1200
Steven Minsky, *CEO*
EMP: 50 **EST:** 2005
SALES (est): 5.11MM **Privately Held**
Web: www.logicmanager.com
SIC: 8741 7372 7374   Business management ; Business oriented computer software; Data processing and preparation

(G-6863)
LOUIS W MIAN INCORPORATED (PA)
547 Rutherford Ave (02129-1680)
PHONE...............................617 241-7900
Bill Mian, *Pr*
Louis W Mian Junior, *Pr*
▲ **EMP:** 19 **EST:** 1954
SQ FT: 4,423
SALES (est): 2.12MM
SALES (corp-wide): 2.12MM **Privately Held**
Web: www.louismian.com
SIC: 3281 5032 5211 1743   Marble, building: cut and shaped; Marble building stone; Tile, ceramic; Marble installation, interior

(G-6864)
LOVEPOP INC (PA)
Also Called: Lovepop
68 Harrison Ave Ste 501 (02111-1929)
PHONE...............................888 687-9589
John Wise, *Pr*
Wombi Rose, *VP*
EMP: 8 **EST:** 2014
SALES (est): 4.71MM
SALES (corp-wide): 4.71MM **Privately Held**
Web: www.lovepop.com
SIC: 5112 2771 3842   Greeting cards; Greeting cards; Personal safety equipment

(G-6865)
LUMENPULSE LIGHTING CORP
14 Beacon St Ste 301 (02108-3749)
PHONE...............................617 307-5700
Francois-xavier Souvay, *Pr*
EMP: 44 **EST:** 2010
SALES (est): 8.99MM
SALES (corp-wide): 70.73MM **Privately Held**
Web: www.lumenpulse.com
SIC: 3646   Commercial lighting fixtures
PA: Lmpg Inc
1220 Boul Marie-Victorin
Longueuil QC J4G 2
514 937-3003

(G-6866)
LUZY TECHNOLOGIES LLC
778 Boylston St Apt 6b (02199-7844)
PHONE...............................514 577-2295
EMP: 30 **EST:** 2018
SALES (est): 1.07MM **Privately Held**
SIC: 7372   Application computer software

(G-6867)
MACMILLAN PUBLISHING GROUP LLC
Bedford Books St Martins Press
75 Arlington St 8th Fl (02116-3936)
PHONE...............................646 307-5617
Joan Fineberg, *Genl Mgr*
EMP: 93
SQ FT: 3,000
SALES (corp-wide): 1.81B **Privately Held**
Web: us.macmillan.com
SIC: 2731   Books, publishing only
HQ: Macmillan Publishing Group, Llc
120 Broadway Fl 22
New York NY 10271
212 674-5151

(G-6868)
MAGELLAN DISTRIBUTION CORP
12 Channel St Ste 803 (02210-2517)
PHONE...............................617 399-7900
James Russell, *CEO*
Tara T Healey, *Pr*
EMP: 10 **EST:** 2001
SQ FT: 11,750
SALES (est): 4.47MM **Privately Held**
Web: www.magellandc.com
SIC: 5065 3674 3675 3676   Electronic parts and equipment, nec; Semiconductors and related devices; Electronic capacitors; Electronic resistors

(G-6869)
MARTINS NEWS SHOP
143 Hemenway St Apt 4 (02115-3741)
PHONE...............................617 267-1334
Paula Depina, *Prin*
EMP: 8 **EST:** 2008
SALES (est): 64.6K **Privately Held**
Web: www.newsshops.net
SIC: 2711   Newspapers, publishing and printing

(G-6870)
MASS BAY BREWING COMPANY INC (PA)
Also Called: Harpoon Brewery
306 Northern Ave (02210-2330)
PHONE...............................617 574-9551
Charlie Storey, *Pr*
Daniel Kenary, *
Warren Dibble, *
▲ **EMP:** 125 **EST:** 1986
SQ FT: 45,000
SALES (est): 49.92MM
SALES (corp-wide): 49.92MM **Privately Held**
Web: www.harpoonbrewery.com
SIC: 2082 5921   Beer (alcoholic beverage); Beer (packaged)

(G-6871)
MASSACHSTTS CNTNING LGAL EDCAT
Also Called: MCLE
10 Winter Pl (02108-4733)
PHONE...............................617 482-2205
John M Reilly, *Ex Dir*
John M Reilly, *Prin*
Janice Bassil, *

Richard S Milstein, *
Stephen Lindsay, *
EMP: 39 **EST:** 1969
SQ FT: 33,000
SALES (est): 5.81MM **Privately Held**
Web: www.mcle.org
SIC: 8299 8111 2731　Educational services;
　Legal services; Book publishing

(G-6872)
MASSACHSTTS SOC FOR PRVNTION C (PA)
Also Called: ANIMAL MAGAZINE
350 S Huntington Ave　(02130-4803)
PHONE..............................617 522-7282
Gus W Thornton D.v.m., *Pr*
Robert S Cummings, *
EMP: 246 **EST:** 1868
SQ FT: 15,000
SALES (est): 95.96MM
SALES (corp-wide): 95.96MM **Privately Held**
Web: www.mspca.org
SIC: 8699 0742 2721　Animal humane
　society; Animal hospital services, pets and
　other animal specialties; Magazines:
　publishing only, not printed on site

(G-6873)
MASSACHUSETTS CLEAN ENERGY CTR
Also Called: Masscec
63 Franklin St 3rd Fl　(02110-1301)
P.O. Box 120459　(02112-0459)
PHONE..............................617 315-9355
EMP: 50 **EST:** 2010
SALES (est): 9.88MM **Privately Held**
Web: www.masscec.com
SIC: 3822　Environmental controls

(G-6874)
MASSACHUSETTS MEDICAL SOCIETY
Also Called: New England Journal Medicine
10 Shattuck St　(02115-6030)
PHONE..............................617 734-9800
Jeff Drazen, *Mgr*
EMP: 49
SALES (corp-wide): 77.29K **Privately Held**
Web: www.massmed.org
SIC: 2721 8621　Magazines: publishing only,
　not printed on site; Health association
PA: Massachusetts Medical Society Inc
　860 Winter St
　Waltham MA 02451
　781 893-4610

(G-6875)
MASSACHUSETTS PORT AUTHORITY
Also Called: Boston Logan Intl Arprt
200 Terminal B　(02128-2003)
PHONE..............................617 561-9300
EMP: 148
SALES (corp-wide): 824.51MM **Privately Held**
Web: www.massport.com
SIC: 2711　Newspapers, publishing and
　printing
PA: Massachusetts Port Authority
　1 Harborside Dr Ste 200
　Boston MA 02128
　617 561-1600

(G-6876)
MASSACHUSETTS REPRO LTD
Also Called: Sir Speedy
1 Milk St Lbby Lbby　(02109-5403)
P.O. Box 961406　(02196-1406)

PHONE..............................617 227-2237
Linda A Borash, *Pr*
Mark A Borash, *Treas*
EMP: 11 **EST:** 1972
SQ FT: 5,000
SALES (est): 1.9MM **Privately Held**
Web: www.sirspeedy.com
SIC: 2752 2791 2789　Commercial printing,
　lithographic; Typesetting; Bookbinding and
　related work

(G-6877)
MASSBIOLOGICS
Also Called: Massbiologics
460 Walk Hill St　(02126-3120)
PHONE..............................617 474-3000
Michael F Collins, *Chancellor*
John Finch, *
EMP: 200 **EST:** 2001
SALES (est): 45.58MM
SALES (corp-wide): 2.87B **Privately Held**
Web: www.umassmed.edu
SIC: 2836 8071　Vaccines; Medical
　laboratories
PA: University Of Massachusetts
　Incorporated
　1 Beacon St
　Boston MA 02108
　617 287-7000

(G-6878)
MASTV / EL PLANETA LLC
399 Boylston St Fl 6　(02116-3305)
PHONE..............................617 379-0210
Javier Marin, *CEO*
EMP: 15 **EST:** 2012
SALES (est): 1.07MM **Privately Held**
Web: www.elplaneta.com
SIC: 2711　Newspapers, publishing and
　printing

(G-6879)
MATERIAL IMPACT INC
Also Called: Spoiler Alert
131 Dartmouth St Fl 3　(02116-5385)
PHONE..............................617 917-4123
Richard Ashenfelter, *CEO*
Emily Malina, *CPO*
Marty Sirkin, *
EMP: 40 **EST:** 2014
SALES (est): 5.92MM **Privately Held**
Web: www.materialimpact.com
SIC: 7374 7372 8742　Data processing
　service; Application computer software;
　Management consulting services

(G-6880)
MATRIVAX RESEARCH & DEV CORP
650 Albany St Ste 117　(02118-2518)
PHONE..............................617 385-7640
Yichen Lu, *Pr*
EMP: 8 **EST:** 2007
SQ FT: 1,200
SALES (est): 1.64MM **Privately Held**
Web: www.matrivax.com
SIC: 2834　Pharmaceutical preparations

(G-6881)
MBM BUILDING SYSTEMS LTD
160 Federal St　(02110-1700)
PHONE..............................617 478-3466
EMP: 10 **EST:** 2017
SALES (est): 200K **Privately Held**
Web: www.arckit.com
SIC: 3999 7389　Boat models, except toy;
　Business services, nec

(G-6882)
MENDIX INC
22 Boston Wharf Rd Fl 8　(02210-3032)
PHONE..............................857 263-8200
EMP: 120 **EST:** 2007
SALES (est): 22.88MM
SALES (corp-wide): 84.48B **Privately Held**
Web: new.siemens.com
SIC: 7372　Prepackaged software
PA: Siemens Ag
　Werner-Von-Siemens-Str. 1
　Munchen BY 80333
　893 803-5491

(G-6883)
MERCK RESEARCH LABORATORIES
33 Avenue Louis Pasteur　(02115-5727)
PHONE..............................617 992-2000
Christophe Winkelmann, *Owner*
EMP: 16 **EST:** 2016
SALES (est): 4.99MM **Privately Held**
Web: www.merck.com
SIC: 2834　Pharmaceutical preparations

(G-6884)
MERCK SHARP & DOHME CORP
33 Avenue Louis Pasteur　(02115-5727)
P.O. Box 982121　(79998-2121)
PHONE..............................617 992-2000
Jared Chellevold, *Mgr*
EMP: 25 **EST:** 2016
SALES (est): 9.26MM
SALES (corp-wide): 59.28B **Publicly Held**
Web: www.msd.ch
SIC: 2834　Pharmaceutical preparations
PA: Merck & Co., Inc.
　126 E Lincoln Ave
　Rahway NJ 07065
　908 740-4000

(G-6885)
MERIDA MERIDIAN INC
1 Design Center Pl Ste 714　(02210-2313)
PHONE..............................617 464-5400
◆ **EMP:** 50
Web: www.meridameridian.com
SIC: 5023 5198 2273 2591　Carpets;
　Wallcoverings; Carpets and rugs; Drapery
　hardware and window blinds and shades

(G-6886)
MICROSOL
2 Oliver St Ste 10c　(02109-4904)
PHONE..............................857 263-7249
EMP: 7 **EST:** 2015
SALES (est): 87.38K **Privately Held**
Web: www.microsolresources.com
SIC: 7372　Prepackaged software

(G-6887)
MIDDLESEX TRUCK & AUTO BODY
Also Called: Middlesex Truck & Coach
65 Gerard St　(02119-2938)
PHONE..............................617 442-3000
Brian A Maloney, *Pr*
Brian A Maloney, *Pr*
Sandra Maloney, *
EMP: 42 **EST:** 1965
SQ FT: 40,000
SALES (est): 4.61MM **Privately Held**
Web: www.middlesextruckcoach.com
SIC: 3713 7532 5531　Truck bodies (motor
　vehicles); Exterior repair services; Truck
　equipment and parts

(G-6888)
MILK STREET PRESS INC
Also Called: Allegra Print & Imaging
8 Faneuil Hall Market Pl 3rd Fl
　(02109-6114)
PHONE..............................617 742-7900
Jeffrey Hostage, *Dir*
Jonathan Hostage, *VP*
Roseanne Dimino, *Acctnt*
EMP: 16 **EST:** 1985
SALES (est): 998.46K **Privately Held**
Web: www.allegramarketingprint.com
SIC: 2752 8744 7334　Offset printing;
　Facilities support services; Photocopying
　and duplicating services

(G-6889)
MIXFIT INC
51 Melcher St　(02210-1508)
PHONE..............................617 902-8082
Reza Zanjani, *CEO*
Reza Zanjani, *Pr*
Ashfin Islam, *VP*
EMP: 7 **EST:** 2015
SALES (est): 943.13K **Privately Held**
Web: www.gomixfit.com
SIC: 7372　Application computer software

(G-6890)
MM REIF LTD
850 Albany St　(02119-2545)
P.O. Box 191490　(02119-0029)
PHONE..............................617 442-9500
Sydney Miller, *Ch Bd*
Harry Miller, *
▲ **EMP:** 100 **EST:** 1999
SALES (est): 6.44MM **Privately Held**
Web: www.mmreif.com
SIC: 2394 2393 2241　Awnings, fabric: made
　from purchased materials; Textile bags;
　Narrow fabric mills

(G-6891)
MOBILE MESSAGING SOLUTIONS
Also Called: MMS
745 Atlantic Ave Fl 2　(02111-2735)
PHONE..............................857 202-3132
EMP: 13 **EST:** 2016
SALES (est): 114.4K **Privately Held**
Web: www.mms.us
SIC: 7372　Application computer software

(G-6892)
MOBILE SOFTWARE INC
110 K St　(02127-1619)
PHONE..............................617 719-8660
Russell P Karlberg, *Pr*
Karen Brown, *VP Opers*
EMP: 8 **EST:** 1993
SQ FT: 1,800
SALES (est): 338.02K **Privately Held**
Web: www.mobilesoftware.com
SIC: 7379 7372　Computer related
　consulting services; Prepackaged software

(G-6893)
MOCA SYSTEMS INC (PA)
Also Called: Moca
50 Congress St Ste 630　(02109-4042)
PHONE..............................617 581-6622
Sandy Hamby, *CEO*
John Strauss, *Ch Bd*
James Phayre, *CFO*
EMP: 20 **EST:** 1999
SALES (est): 15.34MM
SALES (corp-wide): 15.34MM **Privately Held**
Web: www.moca-pm.com

SIC: **8712** 7372 Architectural services; Application computer software

(G-6894)
MOLECULAR HEALTH INC
1 Beacon St Fl 15 (02108-3107)
PHONE..................................832 482-3898
EMP: 90 **EST:** 2008
SALES (est): 10.22MM **Privately Held**
Web: www.molecularhealth.com
SIC: 3822 Sequencing controls for electric heat

(G-6895)
MONTE ROSA THERAPEUTICS INC (PA)
321 Harrison Ave Ste 900 (02118-4680)
PHONE..................................617 949-2643
Markus Warmuth, *Pr*
Alexander Mayweg, *Non-Executive Chairman of the Board*
Ajim Tamboli, *CFO*
Owen B Wallace, *CSO*
EMP: 75 **EST:** 2019
SQ FT: 16,748
Web: www.monterosatx.com
SIC: 2836 Biological products, except diagnostic

(G-6896)
MORPHISEC INC
Also Called: Morphi
11 Beacon St Ste 735 (02108-3052)
PHONE..................................617 826-1212
Yoav Tzruya, *Dir*
EMP: 20 **EST:** 2016
SALES (est): 4.74MM **Privately Held**
Web: www.morphisec.com
SIC: 7372 Prepackaged software
PA: Morphisec Information Security 2014 Ltd
   77 Haenergia
   Beer Sheva 84709

(G-6897)
MOTIVE POWER
34 Farnsworth St (02210-1288)
PHONE..................................857 350-3765
Paul Rosie, *Prin*
EMP: 10 **EST:** 2011
SALES (est): 198.98K **Privately Held**
SIC: 3743 Locomotives and parts

(G-6898)
MUSETTE BRIDAL INC
123 Newbury St (02116-2936)
PHONE..................................617 424-1070
Salwa Khoory, *Pr*
Salwa Khoory, *Prin*
EMP: 20 **EST:** 2012
SALES (est): 1.54MM **Privately Held**
Web: www.musettebridal.com
SIC: 2335 Bridal and formal gowns

(G-6899)
MUTUAL BEEF CO INC
Also Called: Victoria Brand
126 Newmarket Sq (02118-2603)
PHONE..................................617 442-3238
Augustus D Martucci, *Pr*
Anthony E Martucci, *Dir*
EMP: 15 **EST:** 1988
SQ FT: 7,200
SALES (est): 2.22MM **Privately Held**
SIC: 2011 Meat packing plants

(G-6900)
MYOMO INC (PA)
Also Called: Myomo

137 Portland St Fl 4 (02114-1702)
PHONE..................................617 996-9058
Paul R Gudonis, *Ch Bd*
David A Henry, *CFO*
Micah J Mitchell, *CCO*
Harry Kovelman, *Chief Medical Officer*
EMP: 59 **EST:** 2004
SQ FT: 9,094
SALES (est): 15.56MM
SALES (corp-wide): 15.56MM **Publicly Held**
Web: www.myomo.com
SIC: 3842 Orthopedic appliances

(G-6901)
N3K INFORMATIK INC
Also Called: N3k
470 Atlantic Ave Fl 4 (02210-2241)
PHONE..................................617 289-9282
Alan Swan, *COO*
Rainer Maurer, *Prin*
EMP: 10 **EST:** 2000
SALES (est): 378.73K **Privately Held**
Web: www.n3k.com
SIC: 2631 3577 Chip board; Computer peripheral equipment, nec

(G-6902)
NARA LOGICS INC
186 South St Ste 402 (02111-2701)
PHONE..................................617 945-2049
Jana Eggers, *CEO*
EMP: 12 **EST:** 2011
SALES (est): 2.55MM **Privately Held**
Web: www.naralogics.com
SIC: 7371 7372 Computer software development; Application computer software

(G-6903)
NATIONAL BRAILLE PRESS INC
88 Saint Stephen St (02115-4302)
PHONE..................................617 425-2400
Brian A Macdonald, *Pr*
Paul Parravano, *
Neal Rosen, *
Kimberley Ballard, *
Jennifer Stewart, *
EMP: 65 **EST:** 1927
SQ FT: 14,000
SALES (est): 5.18MM **Privately Held**
Web: www.nbp.org
SIC: 2721 2731 Magazines: publishing and printing; Books, publishing only

(G-6904)
NATIONAL REPROGRAPHICS INC
Also Called: Bluedge
21 Drydock Ave Ste 310e (02210-2397)
PHONE..................................857 383-3700
EMP: 11
SALES (corp-wide): 47.18MM **Privately Held**
Web: www.bluedge.com
SIC: 2791 7379 5199 5999 Hand composition typesetting; Computer related maintenance services; Art goods and supplies; Banners, flags, decals, and posters
PA: National Reprographics Inc.
   575 8th Ave Fl 8
   New York NY 10018
   212 366-7250

(G-6905)
NATIVE INSTRUMENTS USA INC (PA)
2 Avenue De Lafayette (02111-1750)
P.O. Box 121232 (02112-1232)
PHONE..................................617 577-7799

Mark S Ethier, *Pr*
Jeremy G Todd, *
John Bigay, *
Gerry Caron, *Chief Product Officer*
Tony Callini, *
EMP: 83 **EST:** 2008
SALES (est): 27.47MM **Privately Held**
Web: www.izotope.com
SIC: 7372 Home entertainment computer software

(G-6906)
NE MEDIA GROUP INC (PA)
Also Called: Boston Globe
1 Exchange Pl Ste 201 (02109-2132)
PHONE..................................617 929-2000
Michael J Sheehan, *CEO*
Kenneth A Richieri, *Asset President*
Christopher Mayer, *
R Anthony Benten, *
Christopher Hall, *
EMP: 100 **EST:** 1989
SQ FT: 669,000
SALES (est): 453.36MM
SALES (corp-wide): 453.36MM **Privately Held**
SIC: 2711 Newspapers, publishing and printing

(G-6907)
NEON LABS LLC
210 South St Unit 113 (02111-2718)
PHONE..................................847 867-4370
EMP: 9
SALES (corp-wide): 102.24K **Privately Held**
SIC: 2813 Neon
PA: Neon Labs Llc
   2406 S 5th St Unit A
   Austin TX 78704
   847 867-4370

(G-6908)
NEOVII BIOTECH NA INC
6 Liberty Sq (02109-5800)
PHONE..................................781 966-3830
Nadia Solomon, *Asstg*
Nadia Solomon Assit, *Prin*
Martin Devine, *Dir Fin*
EMP: 44 **EST:** 2004
SALES (est): 14.09MM **Privately Held**
Web: www.neovii.com
SIC: 2834 5812 Pharmaceutical preparations; Eating places
HQ: Neovii Biotech Gmbh
   Am Haag 6+
   Grafelfing BY 82166
   898988880

(G-6909)
NEPTUNE GARMENT COMPANY
242 E Berkeley St Ste 3 (02118-2797)
PHONE..................................617 482-3980
John Kindregan, *Pr*
EMP: 100 **EST:** 1922
SQ FT: 20,000
SALES (est): 4.89MM **Privately Held**
Web:
neptune-garment-company.sbcontract.com
SIC: 2311 2385 Men's and boys' uniforms; Raincoats, except vulcanized rubber: purchased materials

(G-6910)
NETSUITE
268 Summer St Ste 400 (02210-1108)
PHONE..................................877 638-7848
EMP: 24 **EST:** 2013
SALES (est): 635.82K **Privately Held**
Web: www.netsuite.com

SIC: 7372 Prepackaged software

(G-6911)
NEUROBO THERAPEUTICS INC
177 Huntington Ave Ste 1700 (02115-3134)
PHONE..................................617 313-7331
Jeong Gu Kang, *Interim Chief Financial Officer*
Jeong Gu Kang, *Interim Chief Financial Officer*
Yeon Kim, *Ch Bd*
Mark Versavel, *CMO*
Nicola Shannon, *Clinical Vice President*
EMP: 13 **EST:** 2017
SALES (est): 2.86MM **Publicly Held**
Web: www.neurobopharma.com
SIC: 2834 Pharmaceutical preparations
PA: Neurobo Pharmaceuticals, Inc.
   545 Concord Ave Ste 210
   Cambridge MA 02138
   617 864-2880

(G-6912)
NEUROMOTION INC
Also Called: Neuromotion Labs
186 Lincoln St (02111-2403)
PHONE..................................415 676-9326
Craig Lund, *CEO*
Jason Kahn, *CSO*
Trevor Stricker, *Technology Vice President*
EMP: 12 **EST:** 2014
SALES (est): 2.71MM **Privately Held**
Web: www.mightier.com
SIC: 3944 7371 Electronic games and toys; Computer software development and applications

(G-6913)
NEW BALANCE ATHLETICS INC (HQ)
100 Guest St (02135-2088)
PHONE..................................617 783-4000
Joseph Preston, *Pr*
James S Davis, *
Paul R Gauron, *
Kevin Doyle, *
John K Withee, *
◆ **EMP:** 400 **EST:** 1953
SQ FT: 115,000
SALES (est): 72.35MM
SALES (corp-wide): 17.22MM **Privately Held**
Web: www.newbalance.com
SIC: 2321 2329 2339 Men's and boys' sports and polo shirts; Jackets (suede, leatherette, etc.), sport: men's and boys'; Sportswear, women's
PA: New Balance, Inc.
   100 Guest St
   Brighton MA 02135
   617 783-4000

(G-6914)
NEW BEVERAGE PUBLICATIONS INC
Also Called: Massachusetts Beverage Bus
55 Clarendon St Ste 1 (02116-6067)
PHONE..................................617 598-1900
EMP: 7 **EST:** 1992
SALES (est): 793.6K **Privately Held**
Web: www.beveragebusiness.com
SIC: 2721 Periodicals

(G-6915)
NEW ENGLAND CMPUNDING PHRM INC
Also Called: New England Compounding Center
100 High St Ste 2400 (02110-1767)

PHONE.................................800 994-6322
Barry J Cadden, *Dir*
Carla Donigliaro, *Dir*
EMP: 33 **EST:** 1998
SQ FT: 3,000
SALES (est): 745.59K **Privately Held**
SIC: 2834 Pharmaceutical preparations

(G-6916)
NEW ENGLAND SPT VENTURES LLC
4 Jersey St (02215-4148)
PHONE.................................617 267-9440
John W Henry, *Owner*
EMP: 11 **EST:** 2001
SALES (est): 421.71K **Privately Held**
Web: www.mlb.com
SIC: 3949 Darts and table sports equipment and supplies

(G-6917)
NEW ENGLAND TORTILLA INC
Also Called: Tortilleria MI Nina
74a Clarendon St, (02116-6004)
PHONE.................................617 889-6462
Jamie Mammano, *CEO*
EMP: 25 **EST:** 2011
SALES (est): 9.45MM **Privately Held**
SIC: 5153 2096 Corn; Corn chips and other corn-based snacks

(G-6918)
NEW GENERATION RESEARCH INC
Also Called: Turnaround Letter, The
88 Broad St Fl 2 (02110-3403)
PHONE.................................617 573-9550
James Hammond, *CEO*
J Linzee Brown, *Pr*
EMP: 10 **EST:** 1986
SQ FT: 1,000
SALES (est): 1.47MM **Privately Held**
Web: www.newgenerationresearch.com
SIC: 2721 6211 Periodicals, publishing only; Security brokers and dealers

(G-6919)
NEW VECTRIX LLC
197 Portland St Ste 4 (02114-1716)
PHONE.................................858 674-6099
EMP: 26
SIC: 3751 Motor scooters and parts

(G-6920)
NEW VIEW SURGICAL INC
555 Massachusetts Ave Unit 5 (02118)
PHONE.................................774 284-2283
Bryce Klontz, *Prin*
EMP: 10 **EST:** 2017
SALES (est): 427.68K **Privately Held**
Web: www.newviewsurg.com
SIC: 3841 Surgical and medical instruments

(G-6921)
NEXTHINK INC
501 Boylston St Ste 4102 (02116-3796)
PHONE.................................617 861-8257
Pedro Bados, *CEO*
Sacha Herrmann, *
EMP: 25 **EST:** 2012
SALES (est): 11.69MM **Privately Held**
SIC: 7372 Publisher's computer software
PA: Nexthink Sa
Chemin Du Viaduc 1
Prilly VD 1008

(G-6922)
NIMBUS LAKSHMI INC
Also Called: Nimbus

22 Boston Wharf Rd (02210-3032)
PHONE.................................857 999-2009
Jeb Keiper, *Pr*
Jeb Keiper, *CEO*
Annie Chen, *Pr*
Holly Whittemore, *CFO*
Peter Tummino, *CSO*
EMP: 54 **EST:** 2010
SALES (est): 42.07MM **Privately Held**
Web: www.nimbustx.com
SIC: 2834 Druggists' preparations (pharmaceuticals)
PA: Takeda Pharmaceutical Company Limited
2-1-1, Nihombashihoncho
Chuo-Ku TKY 103-0

(G-6923)
NKT PHOTONICS INC (DH)
23 Drydock Ave Ste 23-410e (02210-2336)
PHONE.................................503 444-8404
Basil Garabet, *CEO*
Karen Scammell, *VP*
EMP: 10 **EST:** 2007
SALES (est): 8.62MM
SALES (corp-wide): 2.16B **Privately Held**
Web: www.nktphotonics.com
SIC: 3699 Electrical equipment and supplies, nec
HQ: Nkt Photonics A/S
Blokken 84
Birkerod 3460
43483900

(G-6924)
NORTEKUSA INC
21 Drydock Ave Ste 740e (02210-4508)
PHONE.................................617 206-5755
Atle Lohrmann, *Pr*
Jannicke Koch Hagan, *Treas*
Dan Goddard, *Sec*
EMP: 8 **EST:** 2014
SALES (est): 996.26K **Privately Held**
Web: www.nortekgroup.com
SIC: 3829 Geophysical or meteorological electronic equipment

(G-6925)
NORTH COAST SEA-FOODS CORP (PA)
5 Drydock Ave (02210-2303)
PHONE.................................617 345-4400
Norman A Stavis, *Pr*
James M Stavis, *
◆ **EMP:** 149 **EST:** 1957
SQ FT: 100,000
SALES (est): 49.83MM **Privately Held**
Web: www.northcoastseafoods.com
SIC: 2092 5146 Seafoods, fresh: prepared; Seafoods

(G-6926)
NOVABIOTICS INC
Also Called: Novabiotics
1 Boston Pl (02108-4407)
PHONE.................................866 259-4527
Deborah O'neil, *CEO*
Margaret Scott, *Corporate Secretary*
Sean King Attorney, *Prin*
EMP: 99 **EST:** 2014
SQ FT: 1,000
SALES (est): 6.8MM **Privately Held**
Web: www.novabiotics.co.uk
SIC: 2834 Pharmaceutical preparations

(G-6927)
NTT DATA INTL SVCS INC (DH)
100 City Sq (02129-3721)
PHONE.................................800 745-3263
John W Mccain, *CEO*

Tim Conway, *
Amir Durrani, *
John M Dick, *
Robert W Gray, *
EMP: 370 **EST:** 1993
SQ FT: 4,400
SALES (est): 184.94MM **Privately Held**
SIC: 7371 7372 Computer software systems analysis and design, custom; Prepackaged software
HQ: Ntt Data Group Corporation
3-3-3, Toyosu
Koto-Ku TKY 135-0

(G-6928)
OLDE BOSTONIAN
66 Von Hillern St (02125-1182)
PHONE.................................617 282-9300
TOLL FREE: 800
David Greenwood, *Owner*
EMP: 9 **EST:** 1980
SQ FT: 5,000
SALES (est): 663.31K **Privately Held**
Web: www.oldebostonian.com
SIC: 2431 Millwork

(G-6929)
OMNIVIEW SPORTS INC
Also Called: Omniview
6 Liberty Sq (02109-5800)
PHONE.................................781 583-3534
Nikhil Patel, *CEO*
EMP: 7 **EST:** 2020
SALES (est): 654.18K **Privately Held**
Web: www.ovszone.com
SIC: 5699 4832 3695 5734 Sports apparel; Sports; Computer software tape and disks: blank, rigid, and floppy; Software, computer games

(G-6930)
ON THE EDGE NUTRITION LLC
283 Old Colony Ave (02127-3520)
PHONE.................................617 752-4056
Santa Nunez, *Mgr*
EMP: 7 **EST:** 2021
SALES (est): 231.04K **Privately Held**
SIC: 2023 Dietary supplements, dairy and non-dairy based

(G-6931)
ON-SIGHT INSIGHT
38 Chauncy St (02111-2301)
PHONE.................................617 502-5985
David Whiston, *Prin*
EMP: 9 **EST:** 2012
SALES (est): 216.14K **Privately Held**
SIC: 3822 1799 Building services monitoring controls, automatic; Building site preparation

(G-6932)
ONAPSIS INC (PA)
Also Called: Onapsis
101 Federal St Ste 1800 (02110-1813)
PHONE.................................617 603-9932
Mariano Nunez, *CEO*
Bob Darabant, *VP*
Victor Hugo Montero, *COO*
Gordon Pothier, *CFO*
EMP: 15 **EST:** 2012
SALES: 5.77MM
SALES (corp-wide): 5.77MM **Privately Held**
Web: www.onapsis.com
SIC: 7372 Business oriented computer software

(G-6933)
ONCOPEPTIDES INC
111 Huntington Ave (02199-7626)
PHONE.................................866 596-6626
Mohamed Ladha, *Pr*
EMP: 124 **EST:** 2018
SALES (est): 21.99MM **Privately Held**
Web: www.oncopeptides.com
SIC: 2834 Pharmaceutical preparations
PA: Oncopeptides Ab
Luntmakargatan 46
Stockholm 111 3

(G-6934)
ONE HIPPO
71 Summer St (02110-1022)
PHONE.................................857 233-4886
EMP: 7 **EST:** 2016
SALES (est): 239.81K **Privately Held**
SIC: 7372 Prepackaged software

(G-6935)
ONSHAPE INC
121 Seaport Blvd (02210-2050)
PHONE.................................844 667-4273
Jon Hirschtick, *CEO*
EMP: 14 **EST:** 2013
SALES (est): 5.34MM
SALES (corp-wide): 2.1B **Publicly Held**
Web: www.onshape.com
SIC: 7372 Prepackaged software
PA: Ptc Inc.
121 Seaport Blvd
Boston MA 02210
781 370-5000

(G-6936)
ONYX ENVIRONMENTAL SVCS LLC (DH)
53 State St Ste 14 (02109-3205)
PHONE.................................617 849-6600
Robert Cappadona, *Managing Member*
◆ **EMP:** 20 **EST:** 1999
SQ FT: 13,000
SALES (est): 490.16MM **Privately Held**
SIC: 8711 4953 2869 1799 Engineering services; Hazardous waste collection and disposal; Solvents, organic; Asbestos removal and encapsulation
HQ: Veolia Environmental Services North America Llc
53 State St Ste 14
Boston MA 02109
617 849-6600

(G-6937)
OPENAIR INC
211 Congress St 8th Fl (02110-2410)
PHONE.................................617 351-0232
Morris J Panner, *CEO*
Tom Brennan, *
EMP: 36 **EST:** 1999
SQ FT: 10,000
SALES (est): 1.48MM **Privately Held**
Web: www.openair.com
SIC: 7372 Business oriented computer software

(G-6938)
OPENBRIDGE INC
119 Braintree St Ste 413 (02134-1697)
P.O. Box 990811 (02199-0811)
PHONE.................................857 234-1008
Thomas Spicer, *CEO*
EMP: 7 **EST:** 2013
SQ FT: 1,500
SALES (est): 491.06K **Privately Held**
Web: www.openbridge.com

SIC: 7372 Application computer software

(G-6939)
OPPORTUNITYSPACE INC
Also Called: Tomeli
295 Devonshire St Fl 4 (02110-1266)
PHONE..............................857 366-1666
Andrew Kieve, *CEO*
Alexander Kapur, *CEO*
EMP: 20 **EST:** 2013
SQ FT: 20,000
SALES (est): 665.18K **Privately Held**
Web: www.opportunityspace.org
SIC: 7379 7372 Online services technology consultants; Application computer software

(G-6940)
OPS-CORE INC
12 Channel St Ste 901b (02210-2323)
PHONE..............................617 670-3547
L P Frieder Iii, *Pr*
Heather M Acker, *Sec*
David Garvey, *Dir*
▲ **EMP:** 18 **EST:** 2005
SALES (est): 757.8K **Privately Held**
Web: www.gentexcorp.com
SIC: 3842 Respiratory protection equipment, personal

(G-6941)
OPSEC SECURITY INC
330 Congress St Fl 3 (02210-1216)
PHONE..............................617 226-3000
Jeffery Unger, *Brnch Mgr*
EMP: 7
Web: www.opsecsecurity.com
SIC: 2671 3953 Paper; coated and laminated packaging; Embossing seals and hand stamps
HQ: Opsec Security, Inc.
1857 Colonial Village Ln
Lancaster PA 17601

(G-6942)
OPTIRTC INC
98 N Washington St (02114-1913)
PHONE..............................844 678-4782
David Rubinstein, *CEO*
Jon Dickinson, *Sec*
David Rubinstein, *Pr*
EMP: 15 **EST:** 2014
SALES (est): 2.47MM **Privately Held**
Web: www.optirtc.com
SIC: 7372 Application computer software

(G-6943)
ORACLE SYSTEMS CORPORATION
Also Called: Oracle
222 Berkeley St Ste 1200 (02116-3733)
PHONE..............................617 247-7900
Jason M Lipman, *Prin*
EMP: 16
SALES (corp-wide): 49.95B **Publicly Held**
SIC: 7372 Prepackaged software
HQ: Oracle Systems Corporation
500 Oracle Pkwy
Redwood City CA 94065

(G-6944)
OREILLY MEDIA INC
Also Called: O'Reilly Media
2 Avenue De Lafayette Fl 6 (02111-1750)
PHONE..............................617 354-5800
EMP: 250
SALES (corp-wide): 191.55MM **Privately Held**
Web: www.oreilly.com

SIC: 2731 2741 Books, publishing only; Miscellaneous publishing
PA: O'reilly Media, Inc.
1005 Gravenstein Hwy N
Sebastopol CA 95472
707 827-7000

(G-6945)
OUTCOMES4ME INC
33 Arch St Fl 17 (02110-1424)
PHONE..............................617 812-1010
Maya Said, *Pr*
EMP: 30 **EST:** 2017
SALES (est): 7.41MM **Privately Held**
Web: www.outcomes4me.com
SIC: 8099 7372 Health and allied services, nec; Application computer software

(G-6946)
OUTSYSTEMS INC (PA)
55 Thomson Pl Fl 2 (02210-1244)
PHONE..............................617 837-6840
Paulo Rosado, *Pr*
Rui Pereira, *VP*
Carlos Alves, *Sec*
Timothy Maccarrick, *Treas*
Mike Lambert, *CRO*
EMP: 66 **EST:** 2004
SALES (est): 10.9MM
SALES (corp-wide): 10.9MM **Privately Held**
Web: www.outsystems.com
SIC: 7372 Application computer software

(G-6947)
OVERLAND PHRMACEUTICALS US INC
200 Clarendon St 25th Fl (02116-5021)
PHONE..............................508 827-8686
EMP: 11 **EST:** 2020
SALES (est): 2.46MM **Privately Held**
Web: www.overlandpharma.com
SIC: 2834 Pharmaceutical preparations

(G-6948)
OXEIA BIOPHARMACEUTICALS INC
361 Newbury St Ste 500 (02115-2738)
PHONE..............................619 213-7697
Kartik K Shah, *CEO*
EMP: 7 **EST:** 2014
SALES (est): 543.11K **Privately Held**
Web: www.oxeiabiopharma.com
SIC: 2834 Pharmaceutical preparations

(G-6949)
OZCAN JEWELERS INC
387 Washington St Ste 516 (02108)
PHONE..............................617 338-6844
Varujan Ozcan, *Pr*
EMP: 10 **EST:** 1982
SQ FT: 850
SALES (est): 401.52K **Privately Held**
Web: www.ozcaninc.com
SIC: 7631 3911 5094 Jewelry repair services; Jewel settings and mountings, precious metal; Jewelry and precious stones

(G-6950)
OZONE TECHNOLOGIES INC
75 Arlington St Lbby (02116-3955)
PHONE..............................617 955-4188
Max Wolff, *CEO*
EMP: 8 **EST:** 2021
SALES (est): 323.14K **Privately Held**
SIC: 7372 7389 Application computer software; Business services, nec

(G-6951)
PANALGO LLC
265 Franklin St Ste 1101 (02110-3113)
PHONE..............................781 290-0808
EMP: 12 **EST:** 1996
SALES (est): 2.68MM **Privately Held**
Web: www.panalgo.com
SIC: 7372 Application computer software

(G-6952)
PARAMETRIC TECHNOLOGY CORP
121 Seaport Blvd (02210-2050)
PHONE..............................781 370-5000
EMP: 62 **EST:** 2012
SALES (est): 25.4MM
SALES (corp-wide): 1.93B **Publicly Held**
Web: www.ptc.com
SIC: 7372 Prepackaged software
PA: Ptc Inc.
121 Seaport Blvd
Boston MA 02210
781 370-5000

(G-6953)
PARAMOUNT SOUTH BOSTON
667 E Broadway (02127-1503)
PHONE..............................617 269-9999
Joe Green, *Owner*
EMP: 11 **EST:** 2015
SALES (est): 311.62K **Privately Held**
Web: www.paramountboston.com
SIC: 2038 5812 Breakfasts, frozen and packaged; Eating places

(G-6954)
PARATEK PHARMACEUTICALS INC (DH)
75 Park Plz Ste 3 (02116-3934)
PHONE..............................617 807-6600
Evan Loh, *CEO*
Michael F Bigham, *Ch Bd*
Douglas W Pagan, *CFO*
William M Haskel, *CCO*
Adam Woodrow, *CCO*
EMP: 8 **EST:** 1996
SQ FT: 4,000
SALES (est): 160.27MM
SALES (corp-wide): 29.08B **Privately Held**
Web: www.paratekpharma.com
SIC: 2834 Pharmaceutical preparations
HQ: Novo Holdings A/S
Tuborg Havnevej 19
Hellerup 2900
35276500

(G-6955)
PARTNERS CAPITAL INV GROUP LLP
600 Atlantic Ave Ste 3001 (02210-2234)
PHONE..............................617 292-2570
Stan Miranda, *CEO*
EMP: 12 **EST:** 2016
SALES (est): 2.19MM
SALES (corp-wide): 5.47MM **Privately Held**
Web: www.partners-cap.com
SIC: 6282 7372 Investment advisory service; Application computer software
PA: Partners Capital Investment Group Llc
600 Atlantic Ave Fl 30th
Boston MA 02210
617 292-2570

(G-6956)
PATHAI INC (PA)
1325 Boylston St Ste 1000 (02215-3973)
PHONE..............................617 543-5250
Andrew Beck, *Pr*

Eric Walk, *CMO*
EMP: 25 **EST:** 2016
SALES (est): 4.22MM
SALES (corp-wide): 4.22MM **Privately Held**
Web: www.pathai.com
SIC: 7372 7379 Application computer software; Computer related consulting services

(G-6957)
PEARSON CUSTOM PUBLISHING
501 Boylston St (02116-3769)
PHONE..............................781 248-2721
EMP: 23 **EST:** 2010
SALES (est): 342.86K **Privately Held**
SIC: 2741 Miscellaneous publishing

(G-6958)
PEARSON EDUCATION INC
Also Called: Pearson Eductl Measurement
501 Boylston St (02116-3769)
PHONE..............................617 848-6000
Donald Kilburn, *Brnch Mgr*
EMP: 20
SALES (corp-wide): 4.62B **Privately Held**
Web: www.pearson.com
SIC: 2741 2731 Miscellaneous publishing; Book publishing
HQ: Pearson Education, Inc.
221 River St Ste 2
Hoboken NJ 07030
201 236-7000

(G-6959)
PEARSON EDUCATION HOLDINGS INC
Prentice Hall
501 Boylston St Ste 900 (02116-3769)
PHONE..............................617 671-2000
Will Ethridge, *Pr*
EMP: 3988
SALES (corp-wide): 4.62B **Privately Held**
Web: www.pearson.com
SIC: 2731 Book publishing
HQ: Pearson Education Holdings Inc.
330 Hudson St Fl 9
New York NY 10013
201 236-6716

(G-6960)
PEARSON LEARNING SOLUTIONS
31 Saint James Ave # 725 (02116-4101)
PHONE..............................617 671-3253
EMP: 7 **EST:** 2017
SALES (est): 293.36K **Privately Held**
SIC: 2741 Miscellaneous publishing

(G-6961)
PEERGRADE INC (PA)
361 Newbury St Ste 412 (02115-2738)
PHONE..............................857 302-4023
David Kofoed Wind, *CEO*
Victor Wang, *VP*
EMP: 7 **EST:** 2017
SALES (est): 730.71K
SALES (corp-wide): 730.71K **Privately Held**
Web: www.peergrade.io
SIC: 7372 Educational computer software

(G-6962)
PEPGEN INC
321 Harrison Ave Ste 800 (02118-4680)
PHONE..............................781 797-0979
James Mcarthur, *Pr*
Noel P Donnelly, *CFO*
Jaya Goyal, *Research Vice President*

Niels Svenstrup, *Sr VP*
Michelle L Mellion, *Sr VP*
EMP: 31 **EST:** 2018
SQ FT: 800
Web: www.pepgen.com
SIC: 8731 2834 Biotechnical research, commercial; Pharmaceutical preparations

(G-6963)
PEPSICO
Also Called: Pepsico
108 Jersey St (02215-4836)
PHONE.............................857 233-2421
EMP: 7 **EST:** 2018
SALES (est): 138.63K **Privately Held**
Web: www.pepsico.com
SIC: 2086 Carbonated soft drinks, bottled and canned

(G-6964)
PET POCKETBOOK INC
398 Columbus Ave Pmb 341 (02116-6008)
PHONE.............................857 246-9884
Diana Akelman, *CEO*
EMP: 7 **EST:** 2014
SALES (est): 501.58K **Privately Held**
SIC: 7372 Prepackaged software

(G-6965)
PHILLIPS CANDY HOUSE INC
Also Called: Phillips Chocolates
818 William T Morrissey Blvd (02122-3404)
PHONE.............................617 282-2090
Phillip A Strazzula, *Pr*
Joseph Sammartino, *Clerk*
EMP: 23 **EST:** 1952
SQ FT: 5,000
SALES (est): 2.85MM
SALES (corp-wide): 19.57MM **Privately Held**
Web: www.phillipschocolate.com
SIC: 2064 5813 5812 2066 Candy and other confectionery products; Drinking places; Eating places; Chocolate and cocoa products
PA: Bay Colony Associates
818 Wlliam T Mrrssey Blvd
Boston MA 02122
617 287-9100

(G-6966)
PISON TECHNOLOGY INC
179 Lincoln St (02111-2425)
PHONE.............................540 394-0998
Dexter Ang, *CEO*
EMP: 8 **EST:** 2016
SALES (est): 1.16MM **Privately Held**
Web: www.pisontechnology.com
SIC: 3577 Input/output equipment, computer

(G-6967)
POINTILLIST INC
321 Summer St Fl 8 (02210-1725)
PHONE.............................617 752-2214
Ronald Ruccico, *CEO*
EMP: 35 **EST:** 2019
SALES (est): 5.3MM
SALES (corp-wide): 220.02MM **Privately Held**
Web: www.genesys.com
SIC: 7372 Business oriented computer software
HQ: Genesys Cloud Services, Inc.
1302 El Cmino Real Ste 30
Menlo Park CA 94025

(G-6968)
POLKA DOG DESIGNS LLC (PA)
Also Called: Polka Dog Bakery
256 Shawmut Ave Ste 1 (02118-3582)

PHONE.............................617 338-5155
▲ **EMP:** 8 **EST:** 2002
SALES (est): 9.69MM
SALES (corp-wide): 9.69MM **Privately Held**
Web: www.polkadog.com
SIC: 2047 Dog and cat food

(G-6969)
POLKA DOG DESIGNS LLC
Also Called: Polka Dog Bakery
212 Northern Ave (02210-2089)
PHONE.............................617 307-6733
EMP: 14
SALES (corp-wide): 9.69MM **Privately Held**
Web: www.polkadog.com
SIC: 2047 Dog and cat food
PA: Polka Dog Designs, Llc
256 Shawmut Ave Ste 1
Boston MA 02118
617 338-5155

(G-6970)
POTOMAC ELECTRIC CORP
1 Westinghouse Plz Ste 17 (02136-2075)
PHONE.............................617 364-0400
▲ **EMP:** 20 **EST:** 1992
SQ FT: 18,000
SALES (est): 8.31MM **Privately Held**
Web: www.potomacelectric.com
SIC: 7694 Electric motor repair

(G-6971)
POWER ADVOCATE INC (HQ)
Also Called: Poweradvocate
179 Lincoln St (02111-2410)
PHONE.............................857 453-5700
Daniel Sullivan, *Pr*
Charles Korn, *CFO*
Timothy J Dorsey, *Sec*
Charles H M Korn, *Treas*
EMP: 73 **EST:** 2000
SALES (est): 22.3MM **Publicly Held**
Web: www.woodmac.com
SIC: 8732 2911 Commercial nonphysical research; Petroleum refining
PA: Verisk Analytics, Inc.
545 Washington Blvd
Jersey City NJ 07310

(G-6972)
POWERHYDRANT LLC (PA)
11 Elkins St Ste 310 (02127-1628)
PHONE.............................617 686-9632
Kevin Leary, *Prin*
EMP: 8 **EST:** 2009
SALES (est): 242.02K **Privately Held**
Web: www.powerhydrant.com
SIC: 3825 Instruments to measure electricity

(G-6973)
POWEROPTIONS INC
Also Called: MASSHEFA
129 South St Fl 5 (02111-2837)
PHONE.............................617 737-8480
Cynthia Arcate, *Pr*
EMP: 7 **EST:** 1997
SALES (est): 3.79MM **Privately Held**
Web: www.poweroptions.org
SIC: 1311 Natural gas production

(G-6974)
PRAXIS PRECISION MEDICINES INC (PA)
Also Called: Praxis
99 High St Ste 30 (02110-2345)
PHONE.............................617 300-8460
Marcio Souza, *Pr*
Dean Mitchell, *Non-Executive Chairman of the Board*

Timothy E Kelly, *CFO*
Bernard Ravina, *CMO*
Nicole Sweeny, *CCO*
EMP: 29 **EST:** 2016
Web: www.praxismedicines.com
SIC: 2834 8731 Pharmaceutical preparations; Commercial physical research

(G-6975)
PRESERVICA INC
50 Milk St Fl 16 (02109-5002)
PHONE.............................617 294-6676
Michael Thuman, *Prin*
Jonathan Tilbury, *Prin*
Paul Allman, *CFO*
EMP: 39 **EST:** 2014
SALES (est): 8.8MM
SALES (corp-wide): 13.87MM **Privately Held**
Web: www.preservica.com
SIC: 7372 Application computer software
PA: Preservica Ltd
32 The Quadrant
Abingdon OXON OX14
123 542-8900

(G-6976)
PRESIDENT FLLOWS HRVARD CLLEGE
Also Called: Harvard Business School
1 Soldiers Field Rd Ste 20 (02134-1805)
PHONE.............................617 495-5581
EMP: 102
SALES (corp-wide): 6.1B **Privately Held**
Web: www.harvarduniversity.com
SIC: 8221 8732 2721 University; Commercial nonphysical research; Periodicals
PA: President And Fellows Of Harvard College
1350 Massachusetts Ave
Cambridge MA 02138
617 496-4873

(G-6977)
PRESS GANEY ASSOCIATES INC
53 State St Fl 2 (02109-3105)
PHONE.............................781 295-5000
EMP: 7 **EST:** 2019
SALES (est): 194.68K **Privately Held**
Web: www.pressganey.com
SIC: 2741 Miscellaneous publishing

(G-6978)
PRESSED FOR TIME PRINTING INC
Also Called: Proprint
133 South St (02111-2802)
PHONE.............................617 267-4113
Joseph H Arthur, *Pr*
EMP: 10 **EST:** 1994
SALES (est): 432.41K **Privately Held**
Web: www.proprintboston.com
SIC: 2752 Offset printing

(G-6979)
PRETTY INSTANT LLC
300 Summer St Apt 14b (02210-1115)
PHONE.............................888 551-6765
Christopher Thomas, *Prin*
EMP: 10 **EST:** 2014
SALES (est): 511.5K **Privately Held**
Web: www.snappr.com
SIC: 2752 Commercial printing, lithographic

(G-6980)
PRFRRED LANCASTER PARTNERS LLC
200 Berkeley St (02116-5022)

PHONE.............................717 299-0782
Joseph Handerhan, *Managing Member*
James Frantz, *Managing Member*
▲ **EMP:** 17 **EST:** 2002
SQ FT: 260,000
SALES (est): 1.01MM **Privately Held**
SIC: 3711 Chassis, motor vehicle

(G-6981)
PRISCILLA OF BOSTON INC
801 Boylston St Fl 3 (02116-2682)
PHONE.............................857 366-4109
Nicole Rotonda, *Mgr*
EMP: 10
Web: www.priscillaofboston.com
SIC: 2335 2396 Wedding gowns and dresses; Automotive and apparel trimmings
HQ: Priscilla Of Boston, Inc.
1001 Washington St
Conshohocken PA 19428
610 943-5000

(G-6982)
PROGDERM INC
33 Arch St (02110-1424)
PHONE.............................617 419-1800
J Michael Delmage, *CEO*
EMP: 14 **EST:** 2008
SALES (est): 119.19K **Privately Held**
Web: www.novarepharma.com
SIC: 2834 3842 5122 Drugs acting on the respiratory system; Cosmetic restorations; Drugs and drug proprietaries

(G-6983)
PTC INC (PA)
121 Seaport Blvd (02210-2050)
PHONE.............................781 370-5000
James Heppelmann, *Ch Bd*
Michael Ditullio, *Pr*
Kristian Talvitie, *Ex VP*
Catherine Kniker, *STRAT SUSTAIN*
Aaron Von Staats, *Ex VP*
EMP: 1300 **EST:** 1985
SQ FT: 250,000
SALES (est): 2.1B
SALES (corp-wide): 2.1B **Publicly Held**
Web: www.ptc.com
SIC: 7373 7371 7372 Computer-aided system services; Computer software development and applications; Application computer software

(G-6984)
PURETECH HEALTH LLC (HQ)
Also Called: Bio Pharmaceutical
6 Tide St Ste 400 (02210-2658)
PHONE.............................617 482-2333
Stephen Muniz, *COO*
Joep Muijrers, *CFO*
▲ **EMP:** 62 **EST:** 2000
SQ FT: 4,712
SALES (est): 54.53MM
SALES (corp-wide): 15.62MM **Privately Held**
Web: www.puretechhealth.com
SIC: 2836 Biological products, except diagnostic
PA: Puretech Health Plc
C/O Tmf Group,
London EC2R

(G-6985)
PURETECH HEALTH PLC
6 Tide St Ste 400 (02210-2658)
PHONE.............................617 482-2333
Daphne Zohar, *CEO*
EMP: 61
SALES (corp-wide): 15.62MM **Privately Held**

Web: www.puretechhealth.com
SIC: 2834 Pharmaceutical preparations
PA: Puretech Health Plc
C/O Tmf Group,
London EC2R

(G-6986)
PURITAN ICE CREAM BOSTON INC
3895 Washington St (02131-1297)
PHONE..............................617 524-3580
Charles Rando Junior, *Pr*
Stephen Rando, *Treas*
Katherine Coats, *Clerk*
EMP: 9 EST: 1919
SQ FT: 25,000
SALES (est): 945.49K **Privately Held**
SIC: 2024 Ice cream and frozen deserts

(G-6987)
PYXIS ONCOLOGY INC (PA)
Also Called: Pyxis Oncology
321 Harrison Ave (02118-4677)
PHONE..............................617 221-9059
Lara Sullivan, *CEO*
David Steinberg, *Ch Bd*
Pamela Connealy, *CFO*
Ritu Shah, *COO*
Jay Feingold, *CMO*
EMP: 21 EST: 2018
Web: www.pyxisoncology.com
SIC: 2834 2836 Pharmaceutical
preparations; Biological products, except
diagnostic

(G-6988)
QUALCOMM TECHNOLOGIES INC
77 Summer St Fl 8-9 (02110-1006)
PHONE..............................617 447-9846
EMP: 32
SALES (corp-wide): 35.82B **Publicly Held**
Web: www.qualcomm.com
SIC: 3674 Integrated circuits,
semiconductor networks, etc.
HQ: Qualcomm Technologies, Inc.
5775 Morehouse Dr
San Diego CA 92121
858 587-1121

(G-6989)
QUANTUM DISCOVERIES INC
53 State St Ste 500 (02109-3111)
PHONE..............................857 272-9998
Ilan Naor, *Pr*
EMP: 7 EST: 2017
SALES (est): 538.99K **Privately Held**
Web: www.quantum-discoveries.com
SIC: 1382 1021 Oil and gas exploration
services; Copper ores

(G-6990)
QUANTUM SIMULATION TECH INC
Also Called: Qsimulate
20 Guest St Ste 101 (02135-2048)
PHONE..............................847 626-5535
Toru Shiozaki, *CEO*
Garnet Chan, *Prin*
Guanhua Chen, *Prin*
EMP: 16 EST: 2019
SALES (est): 885.36K **Privately Held**
Web: www.qsimulate.com
SIC: 7372 Prepackaged software

(G-6991)
QUICKBASE INC (PA)
290 Congress St Fl 4 (02210-1005)
P.O. Box 962077 (02196-2077)

PHONE..............................855 725-2293
Rick Willett, *Ch Bd*
Allison Mnookin, *
Ed Jennings, *
Matthew Hoogerland, *
Doug Wendell, *
EMP: 400 EST: 2016
SALES (est): 95.79MM
SALES (corp-wide): 95.79MM **Privately Held**
Web: www.quickbase.com
SIC: 7372 Prepackaged software

(G-6992)
R R DONNELLEY & SONS COMPANY
Donnelley Financial
20 Custom House St Ste 650 (02110-3513)
PHONE..............................617 345-4300
Robert Smithson, *Prin*
EMP: 60
SALES (corp-wide): 15B **Privately Held**
Web: www.rrd.com
SIC: 2759 Financial note and certificate
printing and engraving
HQ: R. R. Donnelley & Sons Company
35 W Wacker Dr
Chicago IL 60601
800 782-4892

(G-6993)
RADERS ENGRAVING INC
Also Called: Rader's Engraving
333 Washington St Ste 539 (02108-5188)
PHONE..............................617 227-2921
EMP: 8 EST: 1967
SQ FT: 3,000
SALES (est): 872.04K **Privately Held**
Web: www.engraving.cc
SIC: 7389 3993 Engraving service; Signs
and advertising specialties

(G-6994)
RADIUS HEALTH INC (PA)
Also Called: Radius
22 Boston Wharf Rd Fl 7 (02210-3032)
PHONE..............................617 551-4000
G Kelly Martin, *Pr*
Owen Hughes, *
Chhaya Shah, *Chief Business Officer*
Mike Conley, *VP*
EMP: 275 EST: 2003
SQ FT: 2,500
SALES (est): 229.97MM
SALES (corp-wide): 229.97MM **Privately Held**
Web: www.radiuspharm.com
SIC: 2834 8731 Pharmaceutical
preparations; Medical research, commercial

(G-6995)
RAINBOW VISIONS INC
161 Harvard Ave Ste 13b (02134-2724)
P.O. Box 800 (02134-0017)
PHONE..............................617 787-4084
EMP: 7
SALES (est): 387.57K **Privately Held**
SIC: 5699 3089 T-shirts, custom printed;
Novelties, plastics

(G-6996)
RAPID7 INC (PA)
120 Causeway St Ste 400 (02114-1314)
PHONE..............................617 247-1717
Corey E Thomas, *Ch Bd*
Andrew Burton, *Pr*
Tim Adams, *CFO*
Christina Luconi, *CPO*
EMP: 257 EST: 2000
SQ FT: 214,000

SALES (est): 685.08MM
SALES (corp-wide): 685.08MM **Publicly Held**
Web: www.rapid7.com
SIC: 7372 Business oriented computer
software

(G-6997)
RAPID7 LLC (HQ)
120 Causeway St Ste 400 (02114-1314)
PHONE..............................617 247-1717
Corey E Thomas, *Pr*
Alan Matthews, *
Jay Leader, *CIO*
EMP: 9 EST: 2000
SALES (est): 512.84MM
SALES (corp-wide): 685.08MM **Publicly Held**
Web: www.rapid7.com
SIC: 7372 Business oriented computer
software
PA: Rapid7, Inc.
120 Causeway St Ste 400
Boston MA 02114
617 247-1717

(G-6998)
RAPPORT THERAPEUTICS INC ✪
1325 Boylston St Ste 401 (02215-3900)
PHONE..............................512 636-1706
Abraham Ceesay, *CEO*
Troy Ignelzi, *CFO*
EMP: 20 EST: 2022
SALES (est): 1.09MM **Privately Held**
SIC: 2834 Pharmaceutical preparations

(G-6999)
REBISCAN INC
Also Called: Rebion
100 Cambridge St # 14 (02114-2509)
PHONE..............................857 600-0982
Justin Shaka, *CEO*
David G Hunter, *Ch Bd*
EMP: 11 EST: 2009
SALES (est): 1.09MM **Privately Held**
Web: www.rebion.net
SIC: 3841 Surgical and medical instruments

(G-7000)
RED FRAMES INC
Also Called: Apperian
285 Summer St Fl 2 (02210-1518)
PHONE..............................617 477-8740
Mark Lorion, *Pr*
Brian Day, *CFO*
EMP: 22 EST: 2009
SALES (est): 4.59MM
SALES (corp-wide): 19.36MM **Privately Held**
SIC: 7372 Application computer software
PA: Arxan Technologies, Inc.
285 Summer St F 2
Boston MA 02210
415 247-0900

(G-7001)
REDI2 TECHNOLOGIES INC (HQ)
205 Portland St Ste 202 (02114-1708)
PHONE..............................617 910-3282
Seth B Johnson, *CEO*
EMP: 37 EST: 2002
SALES (est): 8.98MM
SALES (corp-wide): 1.24B **Publicly Held**
Web: www.redi2.com
SIC: 7372 Business oriented computer
software
PA: Envestnet, Inc.
1000 Chesterbrook Blvd # 250
Berwyn PA 19312
312 827-2800

(G-7002)
REEBOK INTERNATIONAL LTD LLC (HQ)
Also Called: Reebok International Ltd.
25 Drydock Ave Ste 110e (02210-2344)
PHONE..............................781 401-5000
Mark King, *Pr*
Ulrich Becker, *CEO*
Terry R Pillow, *RALPH LAUREN FOOTWEAR*
David A Pace, *Sr VP*
Suzanne Biszantz, *GREG NORMAN*
◆ EMP: 400 EST: 1895
SQ FT: 13,272
SALES (est): 1.28B **Privately Held**
Web: www.reebok.com
SIC: 3149 3143 3144 2329 Athletic shoes,
except rubber or plastic; Dress shoes,
men's; Dress shoes, women's; Athletic
clothing, except uniforms: men's, youths'
and boys'
PA: Authentic Brands Group Llc
1411 Broadway Fl 4
New York NY 10018

(G-7003)
REIFY HEALTH INC (PA)
33 Arch St Fl 17 (02110-1424)
PHONE..............................617 861-8261
Ralph Passarella, *CEO*
Michael Lin, *Pr*
EMP: 114 EST: 2012
SALES (est): 49.26MM
SALES (corp-wide): 49.26MM **Privately Held**
Web: www.reifyhealth.com
SIC: 7372 Prepackaged software

(G-7004)
REISTONE BIOPHARMA INC
1 Lincoln St Fl 24 (02111-2901)
PHONE..............................978 429-5824
EMP: 13 EST: 2018
SALES (est): 466.08K **Privately Held**
Web: www.reistonebio.com
SIC: 2834 Pharmaceutical preparations

(G-7005)
REPUBLIC MIDSTREAM MKTG LLC
200 Clarendon St (02116-5021)
PHONE..............................617 531-6300
Robert M Trevisani, *Prin*
EMP: 10 EST: 2014
SALES (est): 528.11K **Privately Held**
Web: www.arclight.com
SIC: 1382 Oil and gas exploration services

(G-7006)
RESCOR INC (PA)
254 Faneuil Hall Mkt Pl (02109-1634)
PHONE..............................617 723-3635
Ron Young, *Pr*
EMP: 10 EST: 1985
SQ FT: 2,000
SALES (est): 1.18MM
SALES (corp-wide): 1.18MM **Privately Held**
SIC: 5812 2024 Ice cream stands or dairy
bars; Ice cream, packaged: molded, on
sticks, etc.

(G-7007)
RESEARCH APPLCTONS FNCL TRCKIN
Also Called: Bioraft
3 Center Plz Ste 501 (02108-2021)
PHONE..............................800 939-7238
Nathan Watson, *Pr*

Ben Benone, *VP*
Pramilla Sundaresh, *
Jon Zibell, *
Jeff Mohan, *
EMP: 29 **EST:** 2006
SALES (est): 4.21MM **Privately Held**
Web: www.bioraft.com
SIC: 7371 7372   Computer software development; Prepackaged software

(G-7008)
RETHINK ROBOTICS INC
27-43 Wormwood St (02210-1619)
PHONE...............................617 500-2487
EMP: 12
Web: www.rethinkrobotics.com
SIC: 3559   Robots, molding and forming plastics

(G-7009)
REVVITY INC
549 Albany St (02118-2512)
PHONE...............................617 596-9909
EMP: 25
SALES (corp-wide): 3.31B **Publicly Held**
Web: www.perkinelmer.com
SIC: 3826   Analytical instruments
PA: Revvity, Inc.
940 Winter St
Waltham MA 02451
781 663-6900

(G-7010)
ROBBINS BEEF CO INC
35 Food Mart Rd 37 (02118-2801)
PHONE...............................617 269-1826
Jeff Corin, *Pr*
EMP: 18 **EST:** 1943
SQ FT: 6,000
SALES (est): 2.26MM **Privately Held**
Web: www.robbinsbeef.com
SIC: 2011   Meat packing plants

(G-7011)
ROGERSON ORTHOPEDIC APPLS INC
483 Southampton St (02127-2798)
PHONE...............................617 268-1135
Peter Rogerson, *Pr*
John Rogerson, *VP*
Paula Doherty, *Sec*
EMP: 10 **EST:** 1940
SQ FT: 1,600
SALES (est): 940.97K **Privately Held**
Web: www.rogersonoandp.com
SIC: 3842   Orthopedic appliances

(G-7012)
ROGUE AMOEBA SOFTWARE INC
536 Commercial St (02109-1017)
PHONE...............................609 213-4380
EMP: 8 **EST:** 2017
SALES (est): 125.16K **Privately Held**
Web: www.rogueamoeba.com
SIC: 7372   Prepackaged software

(G-7013)
ROPES WEALTH ADVISORS LLC
800 Boylston St (02199-1900)
PHONE...............................617 951-7217
Robert N Shapiro, *CEO*
EMP: 20 **EST:** 2014
SALES (est): 1.85MM **Privately Held**
Web: www.ropeswealthadvisors.com
SIC: 2298   Ropes and fiber cables

(G-7014)
ROSEMATHREE INC
10 Dorrance St (02129-1027)
EMP: 35 **EST:** 1976
SQ FT: 16,000
SALES (est): 4.43MM **Privately Held**
Web: www.mamarosies.com
SIC: 2038   Frozen specialties, nec

(G-7015)
ROYAL BUSINESS GROUP INC
8 Newbury St Frnt (02116-3203)
PHONE...............................617 542-4100
Real O Roy, *Ch Bd*
EMP: 225 **EST:** 1948
SQ FT: 700
SALES (est): 17.38MM **Privately Held**
SIC: 2451 2452   Mobile homes; Modular homes, prefabricated, wood

(G-7016)
ROYAL FOOD IMPORT CORPORATION
100 Franklin St Ste 702 (02110-1538)
P.O. Box 117 (03049-0117)
PHONE...............................617 482-3826
EMP: 17 **EST:** 2001
SALES (est): 1.77MM **Privately Held**
Web: www.royalfoodimport.com
SIC: 2032   Canned specialties

(G-7017)
ROYAL LABEL CO INC
50 Park St Ste 3 (02122-3287)
PHONE...............................617 825-6050
Paul Clifford, *Pr*
Eileen Ezepik, *Treas*
EMP: 18 **EST:** 1958
SQ FT: 20,000
SALES (est): 2.15MM **Privately Held**
Web: www.royallabel.com
SIC: 2752   Offset printing

(G-7018)
RUSSELL JAMES ENGINEERING WORKS INC
9 Dewar St (02125-1542)
PHONE...............................617 265-2240
EMP: 32
SIC: 3443 3569   Cryogenic tanks, for liquids and gases; Gas producers, generators, and other gas related equipment

(G-7019)
S M LORUSSO & SONS INC
Also Called: West Roxbury Crushed Stone Div
10 Grove St (02132-4510)
PHONE...............................617 323-6380
Edward Sonia, *Genl Mgr*
EMP: 14
SALES (corp-wide): 22.19MM **Privately Held**
SIC: 1442   Gravel mining
PA: S. M. Lorusso & Sons, Inc.
331 West St
Walpole MA 02081
508 668-2600

(G-7020)
SAGE LEARNING INC
Also Called: Sophya
125 Western Ave (02163-1002)
PHONE...............................778 951-9312
EMP: 11 **EST:** 2018
SALES (est): 961K **Privately Held**
SIC: 7372   Prepackaged software

(G-7021)
SALEM PREFERRED PARTNERS LLC (PA)
200 Berkeley St Ste 1 (02116-5022)
PHONE...............................540 389-3922
EMP: 150 **EST:** 2002
SQ FT: 140,000
SALES (est): 21.3MM
SALES (corp-wide): 21.3MM **Privately Held**
SIC: 3519   Diesel, semi-diesel, or duel-fuel engines, including marine

(G-7022)
SALESFORCECOM INC
Also Called: SALESFORCE.COM, INC.
500 Boylston St Fl 19 (02116-3740)
PHONE...............................857 415-3510
EMP: 12
SALES (corp-wide): 31.35B **Publicly Held**
Web: www.salesforce.com
SIC: 7372   Business oriented computer software
PA: Salesforce, Inc.
415 Mission St Fl 3
San Francisco CA 94105
415 901-7000

(G-7023)
SAPPHIROS AI BIO LLC
27 Drydock Ave (02210-2377)
PHONE...............................617 297-7993
Namal Nawana, *Ch Bd*
EMP: 17 **EST:** 2021
SALES (est): 1.1MM **Privately Held**
SIC: 3841   Diagnostic apparatus, medical

(G-7024)
SAPPI NA FINANCE LLC
255 State St (02109-2617)
PHONE...............................617 423-5439
EMP: 9 **EST:** 2011
SALES (est): 1.08MM **Privately Held**
Web: www.sappi.com
SIC: 2679   Paper products, converted, nec

(G-7025)
SARA CAMPBELL LTD (PA)
67 Kemble St Ste 4 (02119-2841)
PHONE...............................617 423-3134
Sara Campbell, *Pr*
Kenneth Maloney, *Treas*
Amy Mac F Burbott, *Sec*
▲ **EMP:** 8 **EST:** 1985
SQ FT: 10,000
SALES (est): 4.83MM
SALES (corp-wide): 4.83MM **Privately Held**
Web: www.saracampbell.com
SIC: 2337 7389   Women's and misses' suits and coats; Apparel designers, commercial

(G-7026)
SCHNEIDER ELECTRIC USA INC (DH)
Also Called: Schneider Electric
1 Boston Pl Ste 2700 (02108-4411)
PHONE...............................978 975-9600
Annette Clayton, *Pr*
Robert Murray, *
Mary Kibble, *
James Danley, *
Lionel Finidori, *
◆ **EMP:** 600 **EST:** 1989
SALES (est): 1B
SALES (corp-wide): 82.05K **Publicly Held**
Web: www.se.com

SIC: 3643 3612 3823 3625   Bus bars (electrical conductors); Power transformers, electric; Controllers, for process variables, all types; Relays and industrial controls
HQ: Schneider Electric Holdings, Inc.
1111 Pasquinelli Dr
Westmont IL 60559

(G-7027)
SCIENTIFIC INSTRUMENT FACILITY
590 Commonwealth Ave Rm 255 (02215-2521)
PHONE...............................617 353-5056
Mike Mckanna, *Dir*
EMP: 10 **EST:** 1987
SQ FT: 12,000
SALES (est): 592.15K **Privately Held**
Web: sif.bu.edu
SIC: 3826   Analytical instruments

(G-7028)
SDW HOLDINGS CORPORATION
255 State St Fl 7 (02109-2618)
PHONE...............................617 423-5400
◆ **EMP:** 2500
SIC: 2621   Paper mills

(G-7029)
SEACHANGE INTERNATIONAL INC (PA)
Also Called: Seachange
177 Huntington Ave Ste 1703 Pmb 73480 (02115-3134)
PHONE...............................978 897-0100
Peter D Aquino, *Pr*
Kathleen Mosher, *Sr VP*
▲ **EMP:** 59 **EST:** 1993
SQ FT: 17,077
SALES (est): 32.49MM **Publicly Held**
Web: www.seachange.com
SIC: 3663 7822 7371   Television broadcasting and communications equipment; Television and video tape distribution; Computer software development

(G-7030)
SECURE CODE WARRIOR INC
265 Franklin St Ste 1702 (02110-3144)
PHONE...............................617 901-3005
Pieter Danhieux, *Pr*
Pieter Danhieux, *CEO*
John Fitzgerald, *
Eddie Sheehy, *
EMP: 34 **EST:** 2017
SALES (est): 5.29MM **Privately Held**
Web: www.securecodewarrior.com
SIC: 8243 7372   Software training, computer ; Educational computer software

(G-7031)
SECURE POINT TECHNOLOGIES INC
Also Called: Imx
207 Union Wharf (02109-1205)
PHONE...............................978 752-1700
William J Mcgann, *CEO*
Robert P Liscouski, *
Todd A Silvestri, *
Roger P Deschenes, *
EMP: 75 **EST:** 1984
SQ FT: 58,000
SALES (est): 37.66MM
SALES (corp-wide): 17.06B **Publicly Held**
SIC: 3812 3829   Detection apparatus: electronic/magnetic field, light/heat; Measuring and controlling devices, nec
HQ: L3 Technologies, Inc.
600 3rd Ave Fl 34

New York NY 10016
321 727-9100

(G-7032)
SELVITA INC
100 Cambridge St Ste 14010 (02114-2509)
PHONE.............................857 998-4075
Peter N Barnes-brown, *Prin*
EMP: 19 **EST:** 2015
SALES (est): 5.31MM **Privately Held**
Web: www.selvita.com
SIC: 2834 Pharmaceutical preparations
PA: Selvita S A
Ul. Podole 79
Krakow 30-39

(G-7033)
SEMRUSH HOLDINGS INC (PA)
800 Boylston St Ste 2475 (02199-8051)
PHONE.............................800 815-9959
Oleg Shchegolev, *Pr*
Dmitry Melnikov, *COO*
Vitalii Obishchenko, *CPO*
Delbert Humenik, *CRO*
Eugene Levin, *STRAT*
EMP: 278 **EST:** 2019
SQ FT: 7,234
SALES (est): 254.32MM
SALES (corp-wide): 254.32MM **Publicly Held**
Web: www.semrush.com
SIC: 7372 Prepackaged software

(G-7034)
SERVIER US INC (PA)
200 Pier 4 Blvd 7th Fl (02210-2453)
PHONE.............................610 506-8203
EMP: 10 **EST:** 2018
SALES (est): 2.78MM
SALES (corp-wide): 2.78MM **Privately Held**
Web: www.servier.us
SIC: 2834 Pharmaceutical preparations

(G-7035)
SHAMBHALA PUBLICATIONS
300 Massachusetts Ave (02115-4544)
PHONE.............................617 424-0030
EMP: 8 **EST:** 2019
SALES (est): 891.42K **Privately Held**
Web: www.shambhala.com
SIC: 2741 Miscellaneous publishing

(G-7036)
SIGNIFY NORTH AMERICA CORP
10 Milk St (02108-4600)
PHONE.............................617 423-9999
EMP: 134
Web: www.signify.com
SIC: 3646 Commercial lighting fixtures
HQ: Signify North America Corporation
400 Crossing Blvd Ste 600
Bridgewater NJ 08807
732 563-3000

(G-7037)
SIGNS BY J INC
100 Tenean St (02122-3620)
PHONE.............................617 825-9855
Edmund P A Jagiello, *Pr*
Mike Cohen, *VP*
EMP: 7 **EST:** 1966
SQ FT: 9,000
SALES (est): 755.92K **Privately Held**
Web: www.signsbyj.com
SIC: 3993 2394 Signs and advertising specialties; Canvas awnings and canopies

(G-7038)
SILEX MICROSYSTEMS INC
9 Hamilton Pl Ste 300 (02108-4715)
PHONE.............................617 834-7197
Gary Johnson, *Pr*
Edvard Kalvesten, *Dir*
Susanne Palo, *Sec*
Roland Nilsson, *Treas*
EMP: 16 **EST:** 2005
SALES (est): 2.04MM **Privately Held**
Web: www.silexmicrosystems.com
SIC: 3674 Semiconductors and related devices

(G-7039)
SIMON PEARCE US INC
Also Called: SIMON PEARCE U.S., INC.
115 Newbury St Ste 1 (02116-2970)
PHONE.............................617 450-8388
EMP: 8
SALES (corp-wide): 49.22MM **Privately Held**
Web: www.simonpearce.com
SIC: 3229 Pressed and blown glass, nec
PA: Simon Pearce (U.S.), Inc.
109 Park Rd
Windsor VT 05089
802 674-6280

(G-7040)
SLESAR BROS BREWING CO INC
Also Called: Salem Beer Works
90 Canal St (02114-2022)
PHONE.............................978 745-2337
EMP: 18
SIC: 2082 5812 Beer (alcoholic beverage); Eating places
PA: Slesar Bros. Brewing Company, Inc.
110 Canal St
Boston MA

(G-7041)
SMARTER TRAVEL MEDIA LLC
Also Called: Smarter Living
226 Causeway St Ste 3 (02114-2283)
PHONE.............................617 886-5555
Daniel Saul, *Managing Member*
EMP: 130 **EST:** 1998
SALES (est): 22.67MM
SALES (corp-wide): 1.49B **Publicly Held**
Web: www.smartertravel.com
SIC: 2721 4724 Magazines: publishing only, not printed on site; Travel agencies
HQ: Tripadvisor, Inc.
400 1st Ave
Needham MA 02494
781 800-5000

(G-7042)
SNYK INC (HQ)
100 Summer St Fl 7 (02110-2106)
PHONE.............................786 506-2615
Guy Podjarny, *Pr*
EMP: 73 **EST:** 2016
SALES (est): 11.06MM
SALES (corp-wide): 147.01MM **Privately Held**
Web: www.snyk.io
SIC: 2741 Internet publishing and broadcasting
PA: Snyk Limited
7th Floor Suite 4
London SW1H
752 063-2695

(G-7043)
SOFT10 INC
83 Chestnut St (02108-1121)
PHONE.............................857 263-7375
EMP: 8 **EST:** 2014
SALES (est): 188.87K **Privately Held**
Web: www.soft10ware.com
SIC: 7372 Prepackaged software

(G-7044)
SOLUTEK CORPORATION
94 Shirley St (02119-3029)
PHONE.............................617 445-5335
Marlowe Sigal, *Pr*
◆ **EMP:** 30 **EST:** 1946
SQ FT: 29,200
SALES (est): 2.47MM **Privately Held**
Web: www.solutekcorporation.com
SIC: 3861 Photographic processing chemicals

(G-7045)
SOMERVILLE LIVE POULTRY CO INC
Also Called: Mayflower Poultry
139 Newmarket Sq (02118-2603)
PHONE.............................617 547-9191
James Gould, *Pr*
EMP: 9 **EST:** 1932
SALES (est): 982.43K **Privately Held**
Web: www.mayflowerpoultry.com
SIC: 5499 5144 2015 Eggs and poultry; Poultry: live, dressed or frozen (unpackaged); Poultry, slaughtered and dressed

(G-7046)
SONIVIE INC
50 Milk St Fl 16 (02109-5002)
PHONE.............................857 415-4814
Init Yariv, *Pr*
EMP: 21 **EST:** 2016
SALES (est): 2.48MM **Privately Held**
Web: www.sonivie.com
SIC: 3841 Surgical and medical instruments
PA: Sonivie Ltd
2 Holzman Haim
Rehovot 76704

(G-7047)
SOS GROUP INC
529 Main St Ste 102 (02129-1101)
PHONE.............................978 496-7947
Julian Chu, *COO*
EMP: 7 **EST:** 2018
SALES (est): 258.02K **Privately Held**
Web: www.worldofsos.com
SIC: 3581 Automatic vending machines

(G-7048)
SOUTH BOSTON TODAY
396 W 4th St (02127-2622)
PHONE.............................617 268-4032
EMP: 7 **EST:** 2013
SALES (est): 102.44K **Privately Held**
Web: www.southbostontoday.com
SIC: 2711 Newspapers, publishing and printing

(G-7049)
SPECTRAGRAPHIC NEW ENGLAND INC
451 D St Ste 200 (02210-1964)
PHONE.............................617 737-3575
Nolan Meredith, *Pr*
Geoffrey R Gough, *
EMP: 25 **EST:** 1975
SQ FT: 6,000
SALES (est): 2.55MM
SALES (corp-wide): 13.55MM **Privately Held**
SIC: 2796 Color separations, for printing
PA: The Spectra Group Ltd
4 Brayton Ct

Commack NY 11725
631 499-3100

(G-7050)
SPECTRSITE BRADCAST TOWERS INC
116 Huntington Ave 11th Fl (02116-5749)
P.O. Box 60828 (28260-0828)
PHONE.............................888 498-3667
William Hess, *Sec*
EMP: 10 **EST:** 2000
SALES (est): 183.83K **Privately Held**
SIC: 3661 Telephone and telegraph apparatus

(G-7051)
SPECTRUM PHARMACEUTICALS INC (PA)
Also Called: Spectrum
2 Atlantic Ave Fl 6 (02110-3976)
PHONE.............................617 586-3900
Joseph W Turgeon, *Pr*
William L Ashton, *
Thomas J Riga, *CCO*
Kurt A Gustafson, *Ex VP*
Francois J Lebel, *CMO*
EMP: 38 **EST:** 1987
SQ FT: 8,000
SALES (est): 10.11MM **Privately Held**
Web: www.sppirx.com
SIC: 2834 Pharmaceutical preparations

(G-7052)
SPIKE AEROSPACE INC
292 Newbury St (02115-2863)
PHONE.............................617 338-1400
Vik Kachoria, *CEO*
EMP: 14 **EST:** 2013
SQ FT: 5,000
SALES (est): 463.11K **Privately Held**
Web: www.spikeaerospace.com
SIC: 3721 3812 Research and development on aircraft by the manufacturer; Aircraft/ aerospace flight instruments and guidance systems

(G-7053)
SPINELLI RAVIOLI MFG CO INC
Also Called: Spinelli Bky Ravioli Pastry Sp
282 Bennington St (02128-1447)
PHONE.............................617 567-1992
Rita Roberto, *Pr*
Louis Roberto, *
EMP: 25 **EST:** 1938
SQ FT: 7,000
SALES (est): 2.24MM **Privately Held**
Web: www.spinellis.com
SIC: 2098 2033 5812 2051 Macaroni and spaghetti; Tomato sauce: packaged in cans, jars, etc.; Caterers; Bread, cake, and related products

(G-7054)
SPINNAKERVIDEO INC
Also Called: A1 Beyond Video Services
529 Main St Ste 109 (02129-1112)
PHONE.............................617 591-2200
Terry Cullen, *Pr*
EMP: 15 **EST:** 1996
SALES (est): 2.45MM **Privately Held**
Web: www.crestron.com
SIC: 3861 Editing equipment, motion picture: viewers, splicers, etc.

(G-7055)
SPRINGLEAF THERAPEUTICS INC
8 Saint Marys St Ste 601 (02215-2421)
EMP: 12 **EST:** 2007

SALES (est): 1.99MM **Privately Held**
Web: www.springleaftx.com
SIC: **2834** Pharmaceutical preparations

(G-7056)
SPROUT USA LLC
117 Huntington Ave (02199-7602)
PHONE.................................617 650-1958
Rose Sherry, *Opers Mgr*
Michael Barbarita, *CFO*
EMP: 7 EST: 2016
SALES (est): 193.93K **Privately Held**
Web: www.sproutworld.com
SIC: **3952** Pencils and pencil parts, artists'

(G-7057)
SQUAREWORKS CONSULTING LLC
101 Arch St Fl 8 (02110-7500)
PHONE.................................800 779-6285
Bernardo Enciso, *Prin*
EMP: 34 EST: 2016
SALES (est): 1.11MM **Privately Held**
Web: www.squareworks.com
SIC: **7372** 7371 7379 Prepackaged software
; Computer software development and
applications; Computer related consulting
services

(G-7058)
STANDARD PUBLISHING CORP (PA)
10 High St Ste 1107 (02110-1752)
PHONE.................................617 457-0600
John Cross, *CEO*
John C Cross, *CEO*
Gorham L Cross, *Treas*
Theodore L Cross, *Stockholder*
EMP: 7 EST: 1865
SQ FT: 5,000
SALES (est): 50K
SALES (corp-wide): 50K **Privately Held**
Web: www.spcpub.com
SIC: **2741** Miscellaneous publishing

(G-7059)
STANLEY BLACK & DECKER
23 Drydock Ave Ste 720w (02210-3500)
PHONE.................................781 460-4511
John-paul Perron, *Prin*
EMP: 7 EST: 2018
SALES (est): 231.63K **Privately Held**
Web: www.stanleyblackanddecker.com
SIC: **3546** Power-driven handtools

(G-7060)
STATISYS INC
Also Called: Statisy
33 Arch St (02110-1424)
PHONE.................................617 804-1284
David Casion, *Pr*
Dana Stanley, *VP*
EMP: 8 EST: 2014
SALES (est): 168.17K **Privately Held**
SIC: **7372** Prepackaged software

(G-7061)
STERLINGWEAR OF BOSTON INC (PA)
175 William F Mcclellan Hwy (02128-1185)
P.O. Box 156 (02128-0009)
PHONE.................................617 567-2100
Frank G Fredella, *Pr*
Gina Fredella Tenaglia, *
▲ EMP: 199 EST: 1982
SALES (est): 17.34MM
SALES (corp-wide): 17.34MM **Privately Held**
Web: www.sterlingwear.com

SIC: **2337** 2385 2311 Women's and misses'
suits and coats; Waterproof outerwear;
Men's and boy's suits and coats

(G-7062)
STILISTI
116 Newbury St Fl 2 (02116-2948)
PHONE.................................617 262-2234
Marrisa Morleno, *Owner*
EMP: 8 EST: 2014
SALES (est): 445.61K **Privately Held**
Web: www.stilistiboston.com
SIC: **3999** 7231 Hair driers, designed for
beauty parlors; Beauty shops

(G-7063)
STREETWISE MEDIA INC
1 Marina Park Dr (02210-1832)
PHONE.................................857 265-3269
Chase Garbarino, *Pr*
EMP: 190 EST: 2006
SALES (est): 2.19MM
SALES (corp-wide): 2.88B **Privately Held**
Web: www.americaninno.com
SIC: **2711** Newspapers: publishing only, not
printed on site
HQ: American City Business Journals, Inc.
120 W Morehead St Ste 400
Charlotte NC 28202
704 973-1000

(G-7064)
SUNDAY RIVER BREWING CO INC
Also Called: Moose's Tale Food & Ale
320 D St Unit 426 (02127-1283)
PHONE.................................207 824-4253
Grant L Wilson, *Pr*
EMP: 9 EST: 1992
SQ FT: 10,000
SALES (est): 179.32K **Privately Held**
SIC: **2082** 5812 5921 5813 Malt beverages;
Eating places; Liquor stores; Drinking
places

(G-7065)
SUNDENSITY INC (PA)
100 William T Morrissey Blvd Ste 166
(02125)
PHONE.................................617 642-1767
Nishikant Sonwalkar, *Pr*
EMP: 10 EST: 2016
SALES (est): 2.8MM
SALES (corp-wide): 2.8MM **Privately Held**
Web: www.sundensity.net
SIC: **4911** 3231
; Products of purchased glass

(G-7066)
SWISSBAKERS INC
168 Western Ave (02134-1037)
PHONE.................................781 354-6989
Helene Stohr, *Pr*
EMP: 16 EST: 2008
SALES (est): 1.24MM **Privately Held**
Web: www.swissbakers.com
SIC: **2052** Bakery products, dry

(G-7067)
TAGUP INC
361 Newbury St Ste 300 (02115-2738)
PHONE.................................513 262-0159
William Vega Brown, *Prin*
EMP: 27 EST: 2016
SALES (est): 833.08K **Privately Held**
Web: www.tagup.io
SIC: **7372** Prepackaged software

(G-7068)
TALL GUY WOODWORKING INC
1349 Commonwealth Ave (02134-3301)
PHONE.................................617 901-2166
Blair R Toland, *Prin*
EMP: 7 EST: 2008
SALES (est): 176.81K **Privately Held**
Web: www.tallguywoodworking.com
SIC: **2431** Millwork

(G-7069)
TANGO THERAPEUTICS INC (PA)
Also Called: TANGO THERAPEUTICS
201 W Brookline St Ste 901 (02215-4159)
PHONE.................................857 302-4900
Barbara Weber, *Pr*
Alexis Borisy, *Non-Executive Chairman of
the Board*
Daniella Beckman, *CFO*
Alan Huang, *CSO*
EMP: 12 EST: 2021
SQ FT: 22,383
SALES (est): 24.86MM
SALES (corp-wide): 24.86MM **Publicly
Held**
Web: www.tangotx.com
SIC: **2834** 8731 Pharmaceutical
preparations; Biotechnical research,
commercial

(G-7070)
TATTE HOLDINGS LLC
Also Called: Tatte Bakery and Cafe
320 Congress St Fl 5 (02210-1250)
PHONE.................................617 577-1111
EMP: 120
Web: www.tattebakery.com
SIC: **5812** 5149 2052 Cafe; Bakery products
; Cookies
HQ: Tatte Holdings, Llc
318 3rd St
Cambridge MA 02142
617 354-4200

(G-7071)
TAUSIGHT INC
10-24 School St (02108-5140)
PHONE.................................339 364-1246
Eric Goode, *Managing Member*
EMP: 24 EST: 2018
SALES (est): 1.16MM **Privately Held**
Web: www.tausight.com
SIC: **7372** Prepackaged software

(G-7072)
TEI BIOSCIENCES INC (DH)
7 Elkins St (02127-8777)
PHONE.................................617 268-1616
Peter Arduini, *CEO*
Glen Coleman, *CFO*
Nancy Toledo, *Administrative Supervisor*
EMP: 58 EST: 1991
SQ FT: 36,000
SALES (est): 21.71MM **Publicly Held**
SIC: **3841** Surgical instruments and
apparatus
HQ: Integra Lifesciences Corporation
1100 Campus Rd
Princeton NJ 08540
609 275-0500

(G-7073)
TELETYPESETTING COMPANY INC
Also Called: Books On Disk
10 Post Office Sq Ste 800s (02109-4603)
PHONE.................................617 542-6220
Edward Friedman, *Pr*

Marlene Winer, *VP*
EMP: 10 EST: 1981
SALES (est): 1.1MM **Privately Held**
SIC: **7372** 2791 Publisher's computer
software; Typesetting

(G-7074)
TERADYNE INC
P.O. Box 3644 (02241-3644)
PHONE.................................978 370-2700
EMP: 7
SALES (corp-wide): 3.16B **Publicly Held**
Web: www.teradyne.com
SIC: **3825** 3643 3674 Semiconductor test
equipment; Connectors and terminals for
electrical devices; Semiconductors and
related devices
PA: Teradyne, Inc.
600 Riverpark Dr
North Reading MA 01864
978 370-2700

(G-7075)
TEXTILE BUFF & WHEEL CO INC
511 Medford St (02129-1495)
P.O. Box 290060 (02129-0201)
PHONE.................................617 241-8100
Andrew Wise, *Pr*
Karen Wise, *
EMP: 13 EST: 1946
SQ FT: 59,000
SALES (est): 856.08K **Privately Held**
Web: www.textilewastesupply.com
SIC: **3291** Buffing or polishing wheels,
abrasive or nonabrasive

(G-7076)
TEXTILE WASTE SUPPLY LLC
511 Medford St (02129-1495)
P.O. Box 290060 (02129-0201)
PHONE.................................617 241-8100
Jerold Wise, *Pt*
EMP: 25 EST: 1920
SQ FT: 50,000
SALES (est): 1.62MM **Privately Held**
SIC: **2211** Bathmats, cotton

(G-7077)
THL-NORTEK INVESTORS LLC (PA)
100 Federal St Ste 3700 (02110-1847)
PHONE.................................617 227-1050
Joseph L Bower, *Managing Member*
Stanley A Feldberg, *
Vernon R Alden, *
Thomas Lee, *
▲ EMP: 70 EST: 2004
SALES (est): 334.75MM **Privately Held**
SIC: **3585** 3444 3634 2431 Refrigeration
and heating equipment; Sheet metalwork;
Electric housewares and fans; Millwork

(G-7078)
THOMAS H LEE EQUITY FUND V LP
100 Federal St Ste 3500 (02110-1802)
PHONE.................................617 227-1050
EMP: 23
SALES (est): 501.36K **Privately Held**
SIC: **3585** Refrigeration and heating
equipment

(G-7079)
TOAST INC (PA)
Also Called: Toast
401 Park Dr Ste 801 (02215-3372)
PHONE.................................617 297-1005
Christopher P Comparato, *Ch Bd*
Stephen Fredette, *

Aman Narang, *
Elena Gomez, *CFO*
EMP: 1755 **EST:** 2011
SALES (est): 2.73B
SALES (corp-wide): 2.73B **Publicly Held**
Web: pos.toasttab.com
SIC: 7374 7372 Data processing and preparation; Application computer software

(G-7080)
TOMORROW COMPANIES INC
Also Called: Tomorrow.io
9 Channel Ctr St Fl 7 (02210-3428)
P.O. Box 52150 (02205-2150)
PHONE......................800 735-7075
Shimon Elkabetz, *CEO*
Rei Goffer, *Pr*
EMP: 16 **EST:** 2015
SALES (est): 4.86MM **Privately Held**
Web: www.tomorrow.io
SIC: 8999 7372 7371 Weather forecasting; Prepackaged software; Computer software development and applications

(G-7081)
TOOLSGROUP INC
75 Federal St Ste 920 (02110-1938)
PHONE......................617 263-0080
Joseph Shamir, *CEO*
Eugenio Cornacchia, *
Caroline Proctor, *CMO*
Roberto Miani, *
EMP: 26 **EST:** 2005
SQ FT: 8,000
SALES (est): 5.55MM **Privately Held**
Web: www.toolsgroup.com
SIC: 7372 Business oriented computer software

(G-7082)
TOUCH AHEAD SOFTWARE LLC
10 Post Office Sq Ste 800s (02109-4603)
PHONE......................866 960-9301
Nancy Keddy, *CEO*
EMP: 12 **EST:** 2008
SALES (est): 747.75K **Privately Held**
Web: www.touchahead.com
SIC: 7372 Prepackaged software

(G-7083)
TRACKSMITH CORPORATION (PA)
285 Newbury St (02115-2809)
PHONE......................781 235-0037
Matt Taylor, *CEO*
EMP: 7 **EST:** 2013
SALES (est): 2.58MM
SALES (corp-wide): 2.58MM **Privately Held**
Web: studiorotate-tracksmith-com-split-test.layer0-limelight.link
SIC: 2329 2339 Men's and boys' sportswear and athletic clothing; Women's and misses' athletic clothing and sportswear

(G-7084)
TRANSPARENCY-ONE INC
100 Cambridge St Ste 1310 (02114-2548)
PHONE......................617 645-2176
Chris Morrison, *CEO*
EMP: 25 **EST:** 2016
SALES (est): 1.16MM **Privately Held**
Web: www.transparency-one.com
SIC: 7372 Prepackaged software

(G-7085)
TREMONT STREET LQ GROUP INC (PA)

Also Called: Wine Emporium, The
607 Tremont St (02118-1719)
PHONE......................617 262-0379
Jewel Saeed, *Pr*
EMP: 15 **EST:** 1973
SALES (est): 2.4MM
SALES (corp-wide): 2.4MM **Privately Held**
Web: www.bostonwineemporium.com
SIC: 5921 2084 Hard liquor; Wines, brandy, and brandy spirits

(G-7086)
TRIPLESHOT LLC
21 School St (02108-4319)
PHONE......................646 812-7548
EMP: 8 **EST:** 2011
SALES (est): 114.61K **Privately Held**
Web: www.tripleshot.com
SIC: 7372 Prepackaged software

(G-7087)
TUCKERMAN STEEL FABRICATORS INC
256 Marginal St Ste 2 (02128-2800)
PHONE......................617 569-8373
EMP: 75 **EST:** 1983
SALES (est): 6.14MM **Privately Held**
Web: www.tuckermansteel.com
SIC: 3441 Fabricated structural metal

(G-7088)
TUFIN SOFTWARE NORTH AMER INC
Also Called: Tufin Software Technologies
10 Summer St (02110-1291)
PHONE......................877 270-7711
Ruvi Kitov, *Pr*
Steve Moscarelli, *VP*
EMP: 18 **EST:** 2008
SALES (est): 5.05MM **Privately Held**
Web: www.tufin.com
SIC: 7372 Prepackaged software
PA: Tufin Software Technologies Ltd
5 Hashalom Rd.
Tel Aviv-Jaffa 67892

(G-7089)
TURTLE SWAMP BREWING LLC
3377 Washington St (02130-2617)
PHONE......................617 314-2952
John Lincecum, *Managing Member*
EMP: 15 **EST:** 2015
SQ FT: 6,800
SALES (est): 940.97K **Privately Held**
Web: www.turtleswampbrewing.com
SIC: 2082 5813 Beer (alcoholic beverage); Beer garden (drinking places)

(G-7090)
UNION MINIERE
Semiconductor Processing Co
12 Channel St Ste 702 (02210-2331)
PHONE......................617 960-5900
EMP: 23
SALES (corp-wide): 6.78B **Privately Held**
Web: www.umicore.com
SIC: 3674 Semiconductors and related devices
PA: Umicore
Rue Du Marais 31
Bruxelles 1000
22277111

(G-7091)
UNISITE LLC
116 Huntington Ave Ste 1750 (02116-5749)
PHONE......................781 926-7135
EMP: 34 **EST:** 1994
SALES (est): 2.06MM **Publicly Held**

SIC: 3663 Radio and t.v. communications equipment
PA: American Tower Corporation
116 Huntington Ave # 1100
Boston MA 02116

(G-7092)
UNITARIAN UNIVERSALIST ASSN (PA)
Also Called: BEACON PRESS
24 Farnsworth St (02210-1264)
PHONE......................617 742-2100
Peter Morales, *Pr*
Reverend William G Sinkford, *Pr*
Kathleen Montgomery, *
Kaitthy Brennan, *
Larry Ladd, *
▲ **EMP:** 150 **EST:** 1961
SQ FT: 37,000
SALES (est): 15.67MM
SALES (corp-wide): 15.67MM **Privately Held**
Web: www.uua.org
SIC: 8661 2731 Miscellaneous denomination church; Books, publishing only

(G-7093)
UNITED FOODS INCORPORATED (PA)
Also Called: Sun Hing Noodle Co
170 Lincoln St (02111-2404)
PHONE......................617 482-9879
Ngar Wong, *Pr*
Robert Ung, *Clerk*
EMP: 7 **EST:** 1978
SALES (est): 1.53MM
SALES (corp-wide): 1.53MM **Privately Held**
Web: www.unitedfoodscorporation.com
SIC: 2099 Food preparations, nec

(G-7094)
UNIVERSAL HARDWOOD FLOORING
85 Arlington St (02135-2152)
PHONE......................617 783-2307
Nee Tran, *Mgr*
EMP: 8 **EST:** 2004
SALES (est): 528.4K **Privately Held**
SIC: 2426 Flooring, hardwood

(G-7095)
UNIVERSITY WAFER INC
11 Elkins St Ste 330 (02127-1628)
PHONE......................800 713-9375
Chris Baker, *CEO*
EMP: 20 **EST:** 2004
SALES (est): 2.47MM **Privately Held**
Web: www.universitywafer.com
SIC: 3674 Semiconductors and related devices

(G-7096)
VALO HEALTH INC (PA)
399 Boylston St Ste 505 (02116-3325)
PHONE......................617 237-6080
Graeme Bell, *Interim Chief Executive Officer*
David Berry, *Pr*
Christian Schade, *Ex Ch Bd*
EMP: 29 **EST:** 2019
SALES (est): 15.54MM
SALES (corp-wide): 15.54MM **Privately Held**
Web: www.valohealth.com
SIC: 8733 2834 2833 Noncommercial research organizations; Pharmaceutical preparations; Medicinal chemicals

(G-7097)
VEOLIA N AMER RGNRTION SVCS LL (DH)
53 State St Ste 14 (02109-2820)
PHONE......................312 552-2800
Gregg Macqueen, *Pr*
EMP: 93 **EST:** 2016
SALES (est): 127.68MM **Privately Held**
Web: www.veolianorthamerica.com
SIC: 2819 Sulfuric acid, oleum
HQ: Veolia North America, Llc
53 State St Ste 14
Boston MA 02109

(G-7098)
VERITY LLC (PA)
Also Called: Mackeyrms
867 Boylston St Ste 500 (02116-2774)
PHONE......................617 482-2634
Adi Filipovic, *Managing Member*
Christopher Mackey, *
EMP: 85 **EST:** 2011
SALES (est): 8.54MM
SALES (corp-wide): 8.54MM **Privately Held**
Web: www.verityplatform.com
SIC: 7372 Business oriented computer software

(G-7099)
VERMILION SOFTWARE
50 Congress St Ste 500 (02109-4005)
PHONE......................617 279-0799
Ben Mccormack, *Pr*
EMP: 7 **EST:** 2014
SALES (est): 221.72K **Privately Held**
SIC: 7372 Business oriented computer software

(G-7100)
VERTEX PHARMACEUTICALS DEL LLC
50 Northern Ave (02210-1862)
PHONE......................617 341-6100
EMP: 10
SALES (est): 1.31MM **Publicly Held**
Web: www.vrtx.com
SIC: 2834 Pharmaceutical preparations
PA: Vertex Pharmaceuticals Incorporated
50 Northern Ave
Boston MA 02210

(G-7101)
VERTEX PHARMACEUTICALS INC (PA)
Also Called: Vertex
50 Northern Ave (02210-1862)
PHONE......................617 341-6100
Reshma Kewalramani, *Pr*
Jeffrey M Leiden, *
Stuart A Arbuckle, *Ex VP*
Charles F Wagner Junior, *Ex VP*
David Altshuler, *CSO*
◆ **EMP:** 1367 **EST:** 1989
SQ FT: 1,100,000
SALES (est): 8.93B **Publicly Held**
Web: www.vrtx.com
SIC: 2834 8731 Pharmaceutical preparations; Biotechnical research, commercial

(G-7102)
VERTEX PHARMACEUTICALS PR LLC
50 Northern Ave (02210-1862)
PHONE......................617 341-6100
EMP: 26 **EST:** 2015
SALES (est): 1.74MM **Publicly Held**
Web: www.vrtx.com

SIC: **2834**　Pharmaceutical preparations
PA: Vertex Pharmaceuticals Incorporated
　50 Northern Ave
　Boston MA 02210

(G-7103)
VERTEX PHRMACEUTICALS DIST INC
50 Northern Ave (02210-1862)
PHONE..............................617 341-6100
EMP: **36 EST:** 2012
SALES (est): 5.35MM **Publicly Held**
Web: www.vrtx.com
SIC: **2834**　Pharmaceutical preparations
PA: Vertex Pharmaceuticals Incorporated
　50 Northern Ave
　Boston MA 02210

(G-7104)
VILLAGE FORGE INC
51 Industrial Dr (02136-2355)
P.O. Box 55 (02137-0055)
PHONE..............................617 361-2591
Christine M Killeen, *Pr*
EMP: **17 EST:** 1952
SQ FT: 32,000
SALES (est): 2.64MM **Privately Held**
Web: www.villageforge.net
SIC: **3441** 3446　Fabricated structural metal;
　Architectural metalwork

(G-7105)
VISIBLE MEASURES CORP (PA)
745 Atlantic Ave Fl 9 (02111-2735)
PHONE..............................617 482-0222
Brian Shin, *Pr*
Ronald Tache, *
Rishi Dean, *
Matt Cutler, *
Jeff Wakely, *
EMP: **45 EST:** 2005
SQ FT: 5,000
SALES (est): 10.22MM
SALES (corp-wide): 10.22MM **Privately Held**
SIC: **7372**　Application computer software

(G-7106)
VISIBLE SYSTEMS CORPORATION (PA)
24 School St Fl 2 (02108-5140)
PHONE..............................617 902-0767
Michael Cesino, *CEO*
George Cagliuso, *Pr*
Ellen Shoner, *CFO*
EMP: **20 EST:** 1981
SQ FT: 6,000
SALES (est): 2.61MM
SALES (corp-wide): 2.61MM **Privately Held**
SIC: **7372** 5045 8748　Prepackaged software
　; Computer software; Systems analysis or
　design

(G-7107)
VITAL BIOSCIENCES INC
268 Summer St (02210-1108)
PHONE..............................415 910-2994
Srinivas Nadella, *Prin*
Behnoud Kazenzadeh, *Prin*
Iman Khodadad, *Prin*
EMP: **7 EST:** 2019
SALES (est): 178.49K **Privately Held**
SIC: **2835**　Diagnostic substances

(G-7108)
VIVA BEVERAGES INC
1 Marina Park Dr Ste 1410 (02210-1874)
PHONE..............................617 712-3488

Stephen Thurston, *CEO*
Stephen M Thurston, *CEO*
Christopher Pronchik, *CFO*
EMP: **13 EST:** 2020
SALES (est): 1.12MM **Privately Held**
SIC: **2085** 5182　Distilled and blended liquors
　; Cocktails, alcoholic: premixed

(G-7109)
VIVANTIO INC
200 Portland St Ste 500 (02114-1715)
PHONE..............................617 982-0390
Greg Rich, *CEO*
EMP: **35 EST:** 2012
SALES (est): 4.6MM
SALES (corp-wide): 1.27MM **Privately Held**
Web: www.vivantio.com
SIC: **7372**　Prepackaged software
HQ: Vivantio Limited
　Redwood House
　Bristol BS32

(G-7110)
VMS SOFTWARE INC
6 Liberty Sq Pmb 294 (02109-5800)
PHONE..............................425 766-1692
David Sweeney, *CEO*
Duane P Harris, *CEO*
Eddie Orcutt, *VP*
Susan Skonetski, *VP*
Clair Grant, *Dir*
EMP: **65 EST:** 2014
SALES (est): 8.95MM **Privately Held**
Web: www.vmssoftware.com
SIC: **7372** 7371　Operating systems
　computer software; Software programming
　applications

(G-7111)
VOATZ INC
Also Called: Voatz
50 Milk St Fl 16 (02109-5002)
PHONE..............................617 395-8091
Nimit S Sawhney, *CEO*
Simer Sawhney, *Dir*
Matt Mosman, *Dir*
Kahlil Byrd, *Dir*
EMP: **7 EST:** 2016
SALES (est): 2.49MM **Privately Held**
Web: www.voatz.com
SIC: **7372**　Application computer software

(G-7112)
WALTER DE GRUYTER INC
Also Called: Birkhauser
121 High St Fl 3 (02110-2475)
PHONE..............................857 284-7073
Carsten Tuhr, *CEO*
EMP: **8 EST:** 2011
SALES (est): 3.34MM
SALES (corp-wide): 89.66MM **Privately Held**
Web: www.degruyter.com
SIC: **2741**　Miscellaneous publishing
PA: Walter De Gruyter Gmbh
　Genthiner Str. 13
　Berlin BE 10785
　30260050

(G-7113)
WARRIOR SPORTS INC (DH)
Also Called: Warrior Sports
100 Guest St (02135-2028)
PHONE..............................800 968-7845
James S Davis, *Pr*
Paul R Gauron, *
Joseph Preston, *
Cindy Abbott, *
Kevin Doyle, *

◆ EMP: **102 EST:** 1992
SQ FT: 120,000
SALES (est): 50.81MM
SALES (corp-wide): 17.22MM **Privately Held**
Web: www.warrior.com
SIC: **3949** 3149　Hockey equipment and
　supplies, general; Athletic shoes, except
　rubber or plastic
HQ: New Balance Athletics, Inc.
　100 Guest St
　Boston MA 02135
　617 783-4000

(G-7114)
WASHINGTON ABC IMAGING INC
Also Called: ABC Imaging
274 Summer St (02210-1106)
PHONE..............................857 753-4241
Medi Falsafi, *Prin*
EMP: **18 EST:** 2014
SALES (est): 2.54MM
SALES (corp-wide): 129.31MM **Privately Held**
Web: www.abcimaging.com
SIC: **2759**　Advertising literature: printing, nsk
PA: Abc Imaging Of Washington, Inc
　5290 Shawnee Rd Ste 300
　Alexandria VA 22312
　202 429-8870

(G-7115)
WEALTH2KCOM INC
75 Arlington St Ste 5000 (02116-3987)
PHONE..............................781 989-5200
David Macchia, *Pr*
Brian Donahue, *Dir*
Michael J Filosa, *VP*
Paul H Lefevre, *Genl Mgr*
EMP: **10 EST:** 2000
SQ FT: 4,000
SALES (est): 1.18MM **Privately Held**
SIC: **7372**　Application computer software

(G-7116)
WELLESLEY INFORMATION SVCS LLC
50 Congress St Ste 300 (02109-4069)
PHONE..............................781 407-9013
EMP: **49**
SALES (corp-wide): 91.63MM **Privately Held**
Web: www.sapinsider.org
SIC: **2731**　Books, publishing only
HQ: Wellesley Information Services, Llc
　Dedham MA 02026
　781 353-8941

(G-7117)
WESPIRE INC
50 Milk St Fl 16 (02109-5002)
PHONE..............................617 531-8970
Susan Hunt Stevens, *CEO*
EMP: **30 EST:** 2011
SALES (est): 4.65MM **Privately Held**
Web: www.wespire.com
SIC: **7372**　Application computer software

(G-7118)
WESTON PRESIDIO MGT CO INC (PA)
Also Called: Weston Presidio Capital
200 Clarendon St Ste 5000 (02116-5050)
PHONE..............................617 988-2500
Michael F Cronin, *Pr*
Kevin M Hayes, *
Therese Mrozek, *
EMP: **40 EST:** 1991
SQ FT: 10,000
SALES (est): 464.15MM **Privately Held**

Web: www.presidio.com
SIC: **6799** 3944 2519 3085　Venture capital
　companies; Games, toys, anc children's
　vehicles; Fiberglass and plastic furniture;
　Plastics bottles

(G-7119)
WESTREX INTERNATIONAL INC
25 Denby Rd (02134-1605)
PHONE..............................617 254-1200
Domenic P Emello, *Pr*
▲ EMP: **12 EST:** 1967
SQ FT: 17,160
SALES (est): 373.2K **Privately Held**
Web: www.ceowestrex.com
SIC: **2752** 5045 7379　Offset printing;
　Printers, computer; Computer related
　consulting services

(G-7120)
WESTROCK - SOUTHERN CONT LLC
84 State St (02109-2202)
PHONE..............................978 772-5050
Steve Grossman, *Mgr*
EMP: **34**
SALES (corp-wide): 20.31B **Publicly Held**
Web: www.westrock.com
SIC: **2679** 2653　Corrugated paper: made
　from purchased material; Corrugated and
　solid fiber boxes
HQ: Westrock - Southern Container, Llc
　1000 Abernathy Rd
　Atlanta GA 30328
　770 448-2193

(G-7121)
WHERE INC
1 International Pl Ste 315 (02110-2602)
PHONE..............................617 502-3100
Walter A Doyle Junior, *CEO*
Jerry King, *COO*
Naill Hawkins, *VP Fin*
Mok Oh, *Chief Innovation Officer*
Craig Forman, *
EMP: **16 EST:** 2003
SQ FT: 1,000
SALES (est): 752.46K **Privately Held**
SIC: **3812**　Radar systems and equipment

(G-7122)
WHOOP INC (PA)
1 Kenmore Sq Ste 601 (02215-2767)
PHONE..............................617 670-1074
William Ahmed, *Pr*
Tricia Gugler, *
EMP: **497 EST:** 2011
SALES (est): 289.28MM
SALES (corp-wide): 289.28MM **Privately Held**
Web: www.whoop.com
SIC: **3829** 3559　Accelerometers; Watch rate
　recorders

(G-7123)
WIIISDOM USA INC
53 State St Ste 500 (02109-3111)
PHONE..............................617 319-3563
Sebastien Goiffon, *CEO*
Bruno Masek, *VP*
EMP: **11 EST:** 2014
SQ FT: 1,000
SALES (est): 5.53MM
SALES (corp-wide): 1.18MM **Privately Held**
Web: www.wiiisdom.com
SIC: **7372**　Prepackaged software
HQ: Wiiisdom France
　63 Place Saint Hubert
　Lille 59800
　320314615

(G-7124)
WILLIAM & CO FOODS INC
135 Newmarket Sq (02118-2603)
PHONE..............................617 442-2112
William P Kinnealey, *Pr*
Carol Faye, *
EMP: 25 **EST:** 1998
SQ FT: 20,000
SALES (est): 2.76MM **Privately Held**
Web: www.wcofoods.com
SIC: 2011 Meat packing plants

(G-7125)
WILLIAMS LEA BOSTON
260 Franklin St Ste 730 (02110-3112)
PHONE..............................617 371-2300
EMP: 20 **EST:** 2008
SALES (est): 669.49K **Privately Held**
SIC: 3577 Printers and plotters

(G-7126)
WILMINGTON COMPLIANCE WEEK
129 Portland St Ste 600 (02114-2012)
PHONE..............................617 570-8600
EMP: 8 **EST:** 2018
SALES (est): 204.14K **Privately Held**
Web: www.complianceweek.com
SIC: 2721 Periodicals

(G-7127)
WILMINGTON COMPLIANCE WEEK INC
Also Called: Compliance Week
77 N Washington St Ste 201 (02114-1908)
PHONE..............................888 519-9200
Donna Rice, *VP*
Anthony Foye, *CFO*
EMP: 46 **EST:** 2013
SALES (est): 1.31MM **Privately Held**
Web: www.complianceweek.com
SIC: 2721 Magazines: publishing only, not printed on site

(G-7128)
WINDESCO INC
265 Franklin St Ste 1702 (02110-3144)
PHONE..............................617 480-9379
EMP: 7 **EST:** 2018
SALES (est): 374.44K **Privately Held**
Web: www.windesco.com
SIC: 7372 Prepackaged software

(G-7129)
WITH WELD
11 Elkins St Ste 210 (02127-1628)
PHONE..............................800 288-6016
EMP: 12 **EST:** 2016
SALES (est): 406.52K **Privately Held**
Web: www.weldpower.com
SIC: 7692 Welding repair

(G-7130)
WORDSTREAM INC
101 Huntington Ave Fl 7 (02199-7603)
PHONE..............................617 963-0555
Howard Kogan, *CEO*
EMP: 10 **EST:** 2008
SALES (est): 4.83MM
SALES (corp-wide): 2.95B **Publicly Held**
Web: www.wordstream.com
SIC: 7372 Prepackaged software
HQ: Gannett Media Corp.
7950 Jones Branch Dr Fl 8
Mc Lean VA 22102
703 854-6000

(G-7131)
WORLD ASSET MANAGEMENT LLC
225 Franklin St Ste 2320 (02110-2880)
PHONE..............................617 889-7300
EMP: 13 **EST:** 2009
SQ FT: 8,000
SALES (est): 2.46MM **Privately Held**
SIC: 2869 Industrial organic chemicals, nec

(G-7132)
WORLD ENERGY LLC
225 Franklin St Ste 2330 (02110-2804)
PHONE..............................617 889-7300
EMP: 500 **EST:** 2017
SALES (est): 26.04MM **Privately Held**
Web: www.worldenergy.net
SIC: 1321 Natural gasoline production

(G-7133)
WORLD ENERGY BIOX BIOFUELS LLC (PA)
Also Called: World Energy
225 Franklin St Ste 2330 (02110-2804)
PHONE..............................617 889-7300
EMP: 16 **EST:** 2016
SALES (est): 80.16MM
SALES (corp-wide): 80.16MM **Privately Held**
Web: www.worldenergy.net
SIC: 2869 Industrial organic chemicals, nec

(G-7134)
WORLD ENERGY ROME LLC
Also Called: World Enegry
225 Franklin St Ste 2320 (02110-2880)
PHONE..............................706 291-4829
Gene Gebolys, *Managing Member*
EMP: 9 **EST:** 2003
SALES (est): 2.24MM **Privately Held**
Web: www.usbiofuelsinc.com
SIC: 2869 Fuels

(G-7135)
X4 PHARMACEUTICALS INC (PA)
Also Called: X4
61 North Beacon St Fl 4 (02134-1912)
PHONE..............................857 529-8300
Paula Ragan, *Corporate President*
Michael S Wyzga, *Ch Bd*
Mary Dibiase, *COO*
Adam S Mostafa, *CFO*
EMP: 52 **EST:** 2010
Web: www.x4pharma.com
SIC: 2836 Biological products, except diagnostic

(G-7136)
XENOTHERAPEUTICS LLC
21 Drydock Ave Ste 610e (02210-4501)
PHONE..............................617 750-1907
Paul Holzer, *CEO*
Jonathan Adkins, *COO*
EMP: 8 **EST:** 2015
SALES (est): 143.05K **Privately Held**
Web: www.xenotx.org
SIC: 3841 Surgical and medical instruments

(G-7137)
YIELDX INC
1 Marina Park Dr (02210-1985)
PHONE..............................646 328-9803
Adam Green, *Pr*
EMP: 26 **EST:** 2019
SALES (est): 10.44MM **Privately Held**
Web: www.yieldx.app

SIC: 7372 Application computer software
HQ: Fnz Germany Holdco Limited
10th Floor
London EC2M
303 333-3330

(G-7138)
YORK ATHLETICS MFG INC
535 Albany St Ste 200 (02118-2557)
PHONE..............................617 777-3125
Travis C York, *Sec*
▲ **EMP:** 10 **EST:** 2015
SALES (est): 427.82K **Privately Held**
Web: www.yorkathleticsmfg.com
SIC: 3999 Manufacturing industries, nec

(G-7139)
ZF CHASSIS COMPONENTS LLC
P.O. Box 6459 (02114-0017)
PHONE..............................859 334-3834
EMP: 19
SALES (corp-wide): 144.19K **Privately Held**
SIC: 3714 Motor vehicle parts and accessories
HQ: Zf Chassis Components, Llc
3300 John Conley Dr
Lapeer MI 48446
810 245-2000

Bourne
Barnstable County

(G-7140)
METAL TECH INDUSTRIES INC
4 Katie Marie Dr (02532-8342)
PHONE..............................508 566-8132
Marc P Larochelle, *Prin*
EMP: 7 **EST:** 2016
SALES (est): 436.06K **Privately Held**
SIC: 3499 Fabricated metal products, nec

(G-7141)
ONSET COMPUTER CORPORATION
Also Called: Hobo
470 Macarthur Blvd (02532-3838)
P.O. Box 3450 (02559-3450)
PHONE..............................508 759-9500
James Towey, *Pr*
Lon O Hocker, *
Ellen G Hocker, *
Michael Tobin, *
◆ **EMP:** 183 **EST:** 1980
SQ FT: 40,000
SALES (est): 48.83MM **Privately Held**
Web: www.onsetcomp.com
SIC: 3823 Process control instruments

(G-7142)
SOUTHEASTERN MILLWORK CO INC
150 State Rd (02532)
PHONE..............................508 888-6038
Charles S Cooper, *Pr*
Thomas P Dudgeon, *Treas*
EMP: 18 **EST:** 1979
SQ FT: 17,000
SALES (est): 717.97K **Privately Held**
Web: www.southeasternmillwork.com
SIC: 2431 5211 Millwork; Lumber and other building materials

(G-7143)
WOODS HOLE GROUP INC (DH)
Also Called: Woods Hole Group
107 Waterhouse Rd (02532-3890)
PHONE..............................301 925-4411

Robert Hamilton Junior, *Pr*
Robert Hamilton, *Junior President*
Carine Foulquier, *
EMP: 31 **EST:** 1986
SQ FT: 15,000
SALES (est): 22MM
SALES (corp-wide): 2.23MM **Privately Held**
Web: www.woodsholegroup.com
SIC: 8711 1382 Consulting engineer; Oil and gas exploration services
HQ: Collecte Localisation Satellites
Parc Technologique Du Canal
Ramonville St Agne 31520
561395000

Boxboro
Middlesex County

(G-7144)
IDSS HOLDINGS INC
85 Swanson Rd Ste 110 (01719-1442)
PHONE..............................978 237-0236
Jeffrey Hamel, *Pr*
EMP: 51 **EST:** 2012
SALES (est): 6.57MM **Privately Held**
Web: www.idsscorp.net
SIC: 7382 3812 Security systems services; Defense systems and equipment
PA: Tek84 Inc.
13495 Gregg St
Poway CA 92064

(G-7145)
SETRA SYSTEMS INC
159 Swanson Rd Ste 1 (01719-1304)
PHONE..............................978 263-1400
David C Carr, *Pr*
Robert S Lutz, *VP*
Frank T Mcfaden, *Treas*
James F O'reilly, *Sec*
◆ **EMP:** 10 **EST:** 1967
SQ FT: 102,000
SALES (est): 9.64MM
SALES (corp-wide): 5.83B **Publicly Held**
Web: www.setra.com
SIC: 3829 3821 3824 3823 Pressure transducers; Balances, laboratory; Mechanical and electromechanical counters and devices; Process control instruments
PA: Fortive Corporation
6920 Seaway Blvd
Everett WA 98203
425 446-5000

Boxborough
Middlesex County

(G-7146)
ADVANCED MICRO DEVICES INC
90 Central St (01719-1252)
PHONE..............................978 795-2500
Gordon Glover, *Brnch Mgr*
EMP: 65
SALES (corp-wide): 22.68B **Publicly Held**
Web: www.amd.com
SIC: 3674 Microcircuits, integrated (semiconductor)
PA: Advanced Micro Devices, Inc.
2485 Augustine Dr
Santa Clara CA 95054
408 749-4000

(G-7147)
ASSABET MACHINE CORP
1145 Massachusetts Ave (01719-1408)
P.O. Box 467 (01749-0467)
PHONE............................978 263-2900
Neal M Dougherty, *Pr*
Deborah J Lutz, *Sec*
EMP: 20 **EST:** 1976
SQ FT: 19,800
SALES (est): 3.85MM **Privately Held**
Web: www.assabetmachine.com
SIC: 3599 Machine shop, jobbing and repair

(G-7148)
ASTRO WELDING & FABG INC
Also Called: Astro Welding
200 Codman Hill Rd (01719-1741)
P.O. Box 372 (01775-0372)
PHONE............................978 429-8666
Richard E Marshall, *Pr*
Martin E Wright Junior, *Treas*
EMP: 10 **EST:** 1981
SQ FT: 15,000
SALES (est): 2.78MM **Privately Held**
Web: www.astrocrane.com
SIC: 5082 7692 3441 Cranes, construction; Welding repair; Fabricated structural metal

(G-7149)
CISCO SYSTEMS INC
Cisco Systems
500 Beaver Brook Rd R (01719-2225)
PHONE............................978 936-0000
George Wright, *Mgr*
EMP: 10
SALES (corp-wide): 57B **Publicly Held**
Web: www.cisco.com
SIC: 3577 8748 5045 4899 Data conversion equipment, media-to-media: computer; Business consulting, nec; Computer software; Data communication services
PA: Cisco Systems, Inc.
170 W Tasman Dr
San Jose CA 95134
408 526-4000

(G-7150)
CROWN CSTLE FIBR HOLDINGS CORP (HQ)
Also Called: LTS Group Holdings LLC
80 Central St Ste 240 (01719-1245)
PHONE............................978 264-6001
Robert Shanahan, *CEO*
Eric Sandman, *CFO*
EMP: 11 **EST:** 2014
SALES (est): 515.91MM
SALES (corp-wide): 6.99B **Publicly Held**
SIC: 3661 Fiber optics communications equipment
PA: Crown Castle Inc.
8020 Katy Fwy
Houston TX 77024
713 570-3000

(G-7151)
DOLAN-JENNER INDUSTRIES INC
159 Swanson Rd (01719-1316)
PHONE............................978 263-1400
Mike Balas, *Pr*
Steven M Rales, *Ch Bd*
Mitchell P Rales, *Ch*
Charles G Clarkson, *Genl Mgr*
▲ **EMP:** 39 **EST:** 1962
SQ FT: 60,000
SALES (est): 4.2MM
SALES (corp-wide): 31.47B **Publicly Held**
Web: www.dolan-jenner.com

SIC: 3823 3625 3648 3674 Process control instruments; Relays and industrial controls; Lighting equipment, nec; Light sensitive devices
PA: Danaher Corporation
2200 Penn Ave Nw Ste 800w
Washington DC 20037
202 828-0850

(G-7152)
INVETECH INC
Also Called: Dover Motion
159 Swanson Rd (01719-1316)
PHONE............................508 475-3400
Mark Wilson Gnr, *Mgr*
EMP: 22
SALES (corp-wide): 5.83B **Publicly Held**
Web: www.invetechgroup.com
SIC: 3823 3625 Process control instruments ; Positioning controls, electric
HQ: Invetech, Inc.
9980 Huennekens St # 140
San Diego CA 92121
858 768-3232

(G-7153)
PERFORMANCE MOTION DEVICES INC
80 Central St Ste 200 (01719-1245)
PHONE............................978 266-1210
Chuck Lewin, *Pr*
EMP: 20 **EST:** 1994
SALES (est): 5.38MM **Privately Held**
Web: www.pmdcorp.com
SIC: 3625 3823 3674 Control equipment, electric; Process control instruments; Semiconductors and related devices

(G-7154)
PHOTO DIAGNOSTIC SYSTEMS INC
85 Swanson Rd Ste 110 (01719-1442)
PHONE............................978 266-0420
EMP: 22 **EST:** 2009
SALES (est): 4.91MM **Privately Held**
Web: www.photodiagnostic.com
SIC: 3841 Medical instruments and equipment, blood and bone work

(G-7155)
SYNQOR INC (PA)
155 Swanson Rd (01719-1316)
PHONE............................978 849-0600
Martin F Schlecht, *Ch Bd*
Rene Hemond, *
Buzz Hofmann, *
EMP: 225 **EST:** 1997
SQ FT: 25,000
SALES (est): 93.8MM
SALES (corp-wide): 93.8MM **Privately Held**
Web: www.synqor.com
SIC: 3679 Power supplies, all types: static

(G-7156)
SYNQOR HOLDINGS LLC
155 Swanson Rd (01719-1316)
PHONE............................978 849-0600
Martin Schlecht, *Pr*
Suzanne Carroll, *
EMP: 16 **EST:** 1997
SQ FT: 100,000
SALES (est): 238.79K **Privately Held**
SIC: 3679 Power supplies, all types: static

(G-7157)
VIBALOGICS US INC
1414 Massachusetts Ave (01719-2226)
PHONE............................252 903-2213

Tom Hochuli, *CEO*
EMP: 10 **EST:** 2020
SALES (est): 6.34MM
SALES (corp-wide): 112.13MM **Privately Held**
Web: www.reciphram.com
SIC: 2834 Pharmaceutical preparations
HQ: Reciphram Ab
Vasagatan 10
Stockholm 111 2

Boxford
Essex County

(G-7158)
CELLARIA BIOSCIENCES LLC
26 Bennett Rd (01921-2243)
PHONE............................617 981-4208
EMP: 9 **EST:** 2013
SALES (est): 913.09K **Privately Held**
SIC: 2836 Biological products, except diagnostic

(G-7159)
CREATIVE MKTG CONCEPTS CORP
167 Killam Hill Rd (01921-1718)
PHONE............................800 272-8267
Carol Abramo, *Pr*
◆ **EMP:** 8 **EST:** 1980
SQ FT: 10,000
SALES (est): 793.28K **Privately Held**
SIC: 5064 3648 Suntanning equipment and supplies; Sun tanning equipment, incl. tanning beds

(G-7160)
ESSEX COUNTY BREWING CO LLC
154 Ipswich Rd (01921-2030)
PHONE............................978 587-2254
Paul E Donhauser, *CEO*
EMP: 8 **EST:** 2018
SALES (est): 425.43K **Privately Held**
Web: www.essexcountybrewing.com
SIC: 2082 Beer (alcoholic beverage)

(G-7161)
NOBLE TREE LLC
37 Glen Forest Dr (01921-1913)
PHONE............................978 590-5101
Gregory Gagne, *Prin*
EMP: 7 **EST:** 2016
SALES (est): 249.35K **Privately Held**
Web: www.nobletree.us
SIC: 2411 Logging

Boylston
Worcester County

(G-7162)
HONEMATIC MACHINE CORPORATION
222 Shrewsbury St (01505-1404)
P.O. Box 1100 (01505-1800)
PHONE............................508 869-2131
Joseph J Cusimano, *CEO*
Joseph J Cusimano Junior, *Pr*
Patricia A Cusimano, *Dir*
Gregory Cusimano, *VP*
▲ **EMP:** 25 **EST:** 1956
SQ FT: 28,000
SALES (est): 5.17MM
SALES (corp-wide): 151.59MM **Privately Held**
Web: www.honematic.com

SIC: 3599 Machine shop, jobbing and repair
PA: Pcx Aerostructures, Llc
300 Fenn Rd
Newington CT 06111
860 666-2471

(G-7163)
PCX AEROSTRUCTURES LLC
Also Called: Pcx Aerosystems
222 Shrewsbury St (01505-1404)
PHONE............................508 869-2131
EMP: 55
SALES (corp-wide): 151.59MM **Privately Held**
Web: www.pcxaero.com
SIC: 3728 Aircraft assemblies, subassemblies, and parts, nec
PA: Pcx Aerostructures, Llc
300 Fenn Rd
Newington CT 06111
860 666-2471

(G-7164)
PHILLIPS PRECISION INC
240 Shrewsbury St (01505-1403)
P.O. Box 1094 (01505-1694)
PHONE............................508 369-3344
Steven Phillips, *CEO*
Cathrine Phillips, *CFO*
EMP: 10 **EST:** 1997
SQ FT: 9,000
SALES (est): 1.92MM **Privately Held**
Web: www.phillips-precision.com
SIC: 3599 Machine shop, jobbing and repair

(G-7165)
PHILLIPS PRECISION INC
141 Shrewsbury St (01505-1710)
PHONE............................508 869-0373
EMP: 9 **EST:** 2018
SALES (est): 437.76K **Privately Held**
Web: www.phillips-precision.com
SIC: 3599 Machine shop, jobbing and repair

Braintree
Norfolk County

(G-7166)
A GRAZIANO INC
71 Adams St (02184-1903)
PHONE............................781 843-7300
James A Graziano, *Pr*
Richard Graziano, *
Paul E Mackenzie Clrk, *Prin*
Dennis Graziano, *Stockholder**
EMP: 40 **EST:** 1935
SALES (est): 3.88MM **Privately Held**
Web: www.grazianoconcrete.com
SIC: 3273 5032 Ready-mixed concrete; Sand, construction

(G-7167)
ALTRA INDUSTRIAL MOTION CORP (HQ)
Also Called: Altra
300 Granite St Ste 201 (02184-3950)
PHONE............................781 917-0600
Carl R Christenson, *CEO*
Glenn E Deegan, *Legal*
Todd B Patriacca, *Ex VP*
Craig Schuele, *Business Development*
EMP: 108 **EST:** 2004
SQ FT: 119,492
SALES (est): 1.95B
SALES (corp-wide): 5.22B **Publicly Held**
Web: www.altramotion.com

SIC: **3568** 5085 3542 3625   Power transmission equipment, nec; Power transmission equipment and apparatus; Brakes, metal forming; Brakes, electromagnetic
PA: Regal Rexnord Corporation
111 W Michigan St
Milwaukee WI 53203
608 364-8800

(G-7168)
ALTRA POWER TRANSMISSION INC
300 Granite St Ste 201 (02184-3950)
PHONE...............................781 917-0600
▲ **EMP:** 476
SIC: **3568** 5085   Power transmission equipment, nec; Power transmission equipment and apparatus

(G-7169)
BAUER GEAR MOTOR LLC
300 Granite St Ste 201 (02184-3950)
PHONE...............................732 469-8770
Carl Christenson, *CEO*
▲ **EMP:** 10 **EST:** 2011
SALES (est): 6.97MM
SALES (corp-wide): 5.22B **Publicly Held**
Web: www.altramotion.com
SIC: **3568**   Power transmission equipment, nec
HQ: Altra Industrial Motion Corp.
300 Granite St Ste 201
Braintree MA 02184
781 917-0600

(G-7170)
BOSTONIAN CLG RESTORATION INC
26 Quincy Ave (02184-4404)
PHONE...............................781 356-3303
Carol Barry, *Pr*
Robert Barry, *Treas*
EMP: 10 **EST:** 1974
SQ FT: 8,000
SALES (est): 2.13MM **Privately Held**
Web: www.bostonianrestoration.com
SIC: **1521** 8744 1389 1771   Repairing fire damage, single-family houses; Environmental remediation; Construction, repair, and dismantling services; Flooring contractor

(G-7171)
BRAINTREE PRINTING INC
230 Wood Rd (02184-2408)
PHONE...............................781 848-5300
Jose Tafur, *CEO*
Jerry Hogan, *
James Corliss, *
EMP: 26 **EST:** 1989
SQ FT: 10,000
SALES (est): 4.72MM **Privately Held**
Web: www.braintreeprintingblog.com
SIC: **2752**   Offset printing

(G-7172)
BRIDGESTONE RET OPERATIONS LLC
Also Called: Firestone
535 Granite St (02184-3936)
PHONE...............................781 843-2870
Michael Crowley, *Mgr*
EMP: 8
Web: www.bridgestoneamericas.com
SIC: **5531** 7534   Automotive tires; Rebuilding and retreading tires
HQ: Bridgestone Retail Operations, Llc
333 E Lake St Ste 300

Bloomingdale IL 60108
630 259-9000

(G-7173)
CITRA LABS LLC
55 Messina Dr Ste 4 (02184-6784)
PHONE...............................781 848-9386
EMP: 39 **EST:** 2010
SALES (est): 5.61MM **Privately Held**
Web: www.zimmerbiomet.com
SIC: **2834**   Solutions, pharmaceutical

(G-7174)
CONSOLDTED PRECISION PDTS CORP
205 Wood Rd (02184-2407)
PHONE...............................781 848-3333
EMP: 46
SALES (corp-wide): 2.07B **Privately Held**
Web: www.cppcorp.com
SIC: **3324** 3365   Steel investment foundries; Aluminum foundries
PA: Consolidated Precision Products Corp.
1621 Euclid Ave Ste 1850
Cleveland OH 44115
216 453-4800

(G-7175)
CREATICS LLC
60 Columbian St (02184-7342)
PHONE...............................781 843-2202
Tom Kelly, *Prin*
Mark Cleveland, *Prin*
EMP: 10 **EST:** 2012
SALES (est): 700.5K **Privately Held**
SIC: **2835**   In vitro diagnostics

(G-7176)
CUMMINS NORTHEAST LLC (HQ)
Also Called: Cummins
30 Braintree Hill Park Ste 101 (02184-8747)
PHONE...............................781 801-1700
EMP: 50 **EST:** 2010
SQ FT: 36,800
SALES (est): 48.43MM
SALES (corp-wide): 34.06B **Publicly Held**
Web: www.cumminseasternmarine.com
SIC: **5084** 5063 3519   Engines and parts, diesel; Generators; Internal combustion engines, nec
PA: Cummins Inc.
500 Jackson St
Columbus IN 47201
812 377-5000

(G-7177)
CUSTOMINK LLC
30 Forbes Rd Ste H (02184-2647)
PHONE...............................781 205-4035
Logan Perryman, *Brnch Mgr*
EMP: 19
Web: www.customink.com
SIC: **2759**   Screen printing
PA: Customink, Llc
2910 District Ave
Fairfax VA 22031

(G-7178)
CYTOSOL LABORATORIES INC
55 Messina Dr (02184-6775)
PHONE...............................781 848-9386
William J Fileti, *CEO*
EMP: 40 **EST:** 1983
SQ FT: 13,500
SALES (est): 8.94MM
SALES (corp-wide): 6.94B **Publicly Held**
Web: www.eyesolutions.com

SIC: **2834**   Solutions, pharmaceutical
HQ: Biomet, Inc.
345 E Main St
Warsaw IN 46580
574 267-6639

(G-7179)
ELCOM INTERNATIONAL INC (PA)
Also Called: Elcom
50 Braintree Hill Park Ste 309 (02184-8724)
PHONE...............................781 501-4000
William Lock, *CEO*
David Elliott, *VP Fin*
EMP: 18 **EST:** 1992
SALES (est): 6.49MM **Privately Held**
Web: www.elcom.com
SIC: **8748** 7372   Systems analysis and engineering consulting services; Prepackaged software

(G-7180)
ENCYTE SYSTEMS INC
55 Messina Dr (02184-6783)
PHONE...............................781 848-6772
Ronald Lewis, *Pr*
EMP: 8 **EST:** 1971
SALES (est): 410.51K **Privately Held**
SIC: **5122** 2834   Pharmaceuticals; Pharmaceutical preparations

(G-7181)
ENGAGESMART INC (PA)
Also Called: Engagesmart
30 Braintree Hill Park Ste 101 (02184-8747)
PHONE...............................781 848-3733
Robert P Bennett, *CEO*
Paul G Stamas, *Ch Bd*
Cassandra Hudson, *CFO*
Scott Semel, *Sr VP*
EMP: 21 **EST:** 2018
SQ FT: 20,443
SALES (est): 303.92MM
SALES (corp-wide): 303.92MM **Privately Held**
Web: www.engagesmart.com
SIC: **7372**   Prepackaged software

(G-7182)
ETEX CORPORATION
Also Called: Etex
55 Messina Dr Ste 1 (02184-6784)
PHONE...............................617 577-7270
David A Nolan Junior, *Pr*
Jeffrey A Wellkamp, *
Richard Kim, *
EMP: 50 **EST:** 1989
SQ FT: 8,100
SALES (est): 15MM
SALES (corp-wide): 6.94B **Publicly Held**
Web: www.zimmerbiomet.com
SIC: **3841**   Medical instruments and equipment, blood and bone work
PA: Zimmer Biomet Holdings, Inc.
345 E Main St
Warsaw IN 46580
574 267-6131

(G-7183)
FIRST ELECTRONICS CORPORATION
400 Wood Rd (02184-2412)
PHONE...............................617 704-4248
Alex Durso, *Mgr*
EMP: 83
SALES (corp-wide): 2.8B **Privately Held**
Web: www.feccables.com

SIC: **3679**   Harness assemblies, for electronic use: wire or cable
HQ: The First Electronics Corporation
71 Von Hillern St Ste 1
Dorchester MA 02125
617 288-2430

(G-7184)
GEORGE H DEAN CO
140 Wood Rd Ste 105 (02184-2512)
PHONE...............................781 544-3782
Kenneth A Michaud, *CEO*
Bruce E Michaud, *
Ralph J Rivkind, *
G Earle Michaud, *
James B Burokas, *
▲ **EMP:** 85 **EST:** 1889
SQ FT: 75,000
SALES (est): 8.48MM **Privately Held**
Web: www.whatnetworkph.com
SIC: **2752** 2761 2396   Offset printing; Manifold business forms; Automotive and apparel trimmings

(G-7185)
GUESS INC
Also Called: GUESS?, INC.
250 Granite St Ste B (02184-2834)
PHONE...............................781 843-3147
EMP: 25
SALES (corp-wide): 2.69B **Publicly Held**
Web: stores.guessfactory.com
SIC: **2325**   Men's and boys' jeans and dungarees
PA: Guess , Inc.
1444 S Alameda St
Los Angeles CA 90021
213 765-3100

(G-7186)
HAEMONETICS ASIA INCORPORATED (HQ)
400 Wood Rd (02184-2486)
PHONE...............................781 848-7100
EMP: 13 **EST:** 1996
SALES (est): 2.41MM
SALES (corp-wide): 1.17B **Publicly Held**
Web: www.haemonetics.com
SIC: **3841** 3845   Medical instruments and equipment, blood and bone work; Electromedical equipment
PA: Haemonetics Corporation
125 Summer St Ste 1800
Boston MA 02110
781 848-7100

(G-7187)
HEALTHSTAR INC
62 Johnson Ln (02184-6702)
PHONE...............................781 428-3696
William J Grabowski, *Pr*
Leslie R Eliopoulos, *
EMP: 25 **EST:** 1983
SQ FT: 7,000
SALES (est): 4.31MM **Privately Held**
Web: www.healthstaronline.com
SIC: **3559**   Pharmaceutical machinery

(G-7188)
IGT GLOBAL SOLUTIONS CORP
Also Called: Gtech
60 Columbian St (02184-7342)
PHONE...............................781 849-5642
Patrick Mchugh, *Brnch Mgr*
EMP: 9
SALES (corp-wide): 4.22B **Privately Held**
Web: www.igt.com
SIC: **3575**   Computer terminals
HQ: Igt Global Solutions Corporation
10 Memorial Blvd

Providence RI 02903
401 392-7077

(G-7189)
JAMES CABLE LLC
Also Called: James Communications
15 Braintree Hill Park (02184-8722)
P.O. Box 536 (08833-0536)
PHONE.............................781 356-8701
Daniel Shoemaker, *Managing Member*
EMP: 50 **EST:** 2003
SALES (est): 7.08MM **Privately Held**
SIC: 3315　Wire and fabricated wire products

(G-7190)
JEDWARDS INTERNATIONAL INC
65 Bay State Dr (02184-5228)
PHONE.............................617 340-9461
Christos Iorio, *Pr*
EMP: 8
Web: www.bulknaturaloils.com
SIC: 2066　Cocoa butter
PA: Jedwards International, Inc.
　141 Campanelli Dr
　Braintree MA 02184

(G-7191)
JEDWARDS INTERNATIONAL INC (PA)
141 Campanelli Dr (02184-5206)
PHONE.............................617 340-9461
◆ **EMP:** 24 **EST:** 1994
SQ FT: 15,000
SALES (est): 15.09MM **Privately Held**
Web: www.bulknaturaloils.com
SIC: 2066 5149　Cocoa butter; Specialty
　food items

(G-7192)
JOHN HARVARDS BREWHOUSE LLC
Also Called: John Harvard's Brew House
36 Grove Cir (02184-7624)
PHONE.............................508 875-2337
EMP: 260
SIC: 2082 5812　Beer (alcoholic beverage);
　Steak restaurant
PA: John Harvard's Brewhouse, Llc
　1 Federal St
　Boston MA

(G-7193)
LOGAN INSTRUMENTS INC
101a French Ave (02184-6503)
P.O. Box 490951 (02149-0016)
PHONE.............................617 394-0601
Charles Gambale, *Pr*
EMP: 17 **EST:** 1969
SALES (est): 340.2K **Privately Held**
Web:
www.logansurgicalinstruments.com
SIC: 3841 8733　Surgical and medical
　instruments; Medical research

(G-7194)
MEANS PRE-CAST CO INC
151 Adams St (02184-1917)
PHONE.............................781 843-1909
Brian Ricciardi, *Pr*
Mark Ricciardi, *Clerk*
EMP: 7 **EST:** 1972
SQ FT: 3,000
SALES (est): 856.34K **Privately Held**
Web: www.meansprecast.com
SIC: 3272　Concrete products, precast, nec

(G-7195)
MERLINONE INC (PA)
Also Called: Merlinone
50 Braintree Hill Park Ste 308
(02184-8734)
PHONE.............................617 328-6645
David Tenenbaum, *Pr*
Jan Tenenbaum, *VP*
Shevawn Hardesty, *CFO*
EMP: 11 **EST:** 1986
SALES (est): 2.91MM **Privately Held**
Web: www.merlinone.com
SIC: 7372　Application computer software

(G-7196)
NIDEC AMERICA CORPORATION (HQ)
50 Braintree Hill Park Ste 110 (02184-8735)
PHONE.............................781 848-0970
◆ **EMP:** 20 **EST:** 1983
SALES (est): 21.87MM **Privately Held**
Web: www.nidec.com
SIC: 5084 5722 3621　Machine tools and
　metalworking machinery; Household
　appliance stores; Motors and generators
PA: Nidec Corporation
　338, Kuzetonoshirocho, Minami-Ku
　Kyoto KYO 601-8

(G-7197)
NORTHAST CAB CNTRTOP DSTRS INC
140 Campanelli Dr Ste 1 (02184-5240)
PHONE.............................617 296-2100
Stewart M Rosen, *Pr*
EMP: 10 **EST:** 2003
SALES (est): 474.97K **Privately Held**
Web:
www.northeastcabinetandcountertop.com
SIC: 2434　Wood kitchen cabinets

(G-7198)
PLANON CORPORATION
45 Braintree Hill Park Ste 400
(02184-8723)
PHONE.............................781 356-0999
Jim Nauen, *Prin*
EMP: 19 **EST:** 2006
SALES (est): 6.01MM
SALES (corp-wide): 121.67MM **Privately
Held**
Web: www.planonsoftware.com
SIC: 7372　Business oriented computer
　software
HQ: Planon Group B.V.
　Wijchenseweg 8
　Nijmegen GE 6537
　246413135

(G-7199)
RICHELIEU FOODS INC (DH)
222 Forbes Rd Ste 401 (02184-2717)
PHONE.............................781 786-6800
William Fox, *Pr*
◆ **EMP:** 20 **EST:** 1997
SQ FT: 7,500
SALES (est): 196.21MM
SALES (corp-wide): 2.04MM **Privately
Held**
Web: www.richelieufoods.com
SIC: 2099　Food preparations, nec
HQ: Freiberger Usa Inc.
　6 Upper Pond Rd Ste 3a
　Parsippany NJ 07054

(G-7200)
RIVER ST METAL FINISHING INC
35 Johnson Ln (02184-6701)
PHONE.............................781 843-9351

Brian Reeves, *Pr*
Pamela Reeves, *Treas*
EMP: 11 **EST:** 1991
SQ FT: 7,500
SALES (est): 1.52MM **Privately Held**
Web: www.riverstreetmetalfinishing.com
SIC: 3471　Electroplating of metals or
　formed products

(G-7201)
ROCKLAND INDUSTRIES INC
405 Washington St Ste 3 (02184-4786)
PHONE.............................781 849-7918
Steven Striar, *Prin*
EMP: 7 **EST:** 2008
SALES (est): 172.14K **Privately Held**
SIC: 3999　Manufacturing industries, nec

(G-7202)
SIR SPEEDY
529 Washington St (02184-5627)
PHONE.............................781 848-0990
Jerry Hogan, *Pr*
EMP: 9 **EST:** 2018
SALES (est): 245.19K **Privately Held**
Web: www.sirspeedy.com
SIC: 2752　Commercial printing, lithographic

(G-7203)
SPEEDY SIGN-A-RAMA USA
Also Called: Sign-A-Rama
130 Wood Rd (02184-2502)
PHONE.............................781 849-1181
Mike Sepinuck, *Owner*
EMP: 7 **EST:** 1990
SALES (est): 446.42K **Privately Held**
Web: www.signarama.com
SIC: 3993 1799　Signs and advertising
　specialties; Sign installation and
　maintenance

(G-7204)
SUPERIOR BINDERY INC
Also Called: Superior Packaging & Finishing
1 Federal Dr (02184-5238)
PHONE.............................781 303-0022
Donald Charlebois, *Pr*
▲ **EMP:** 101 **EST:** 1990
SQ FT: 16,000
SALES (est): 17.35MM **Privately Held**
Web:
www.superiorpackagingandfinishing.com
SIC: 2789　Binding only: books, pamphlets,
　magazines, etc.

(G-7205)
SUPERMEDIA LLC
186 Forbes Rd (02184-2612)
PHONE.............................781 849-7670
Jeff Rodenbush, *Brnch Mgr*
EMP: 10
SALES (corp-wide): 1.2B **Publicly Held**
SIC: 2741　Directories, telephone: publishing
　only, not printed on site
HQ: Supermedia Llc
　2200 W Airfield Dr
　Dfw Airport TX 75261
　972 453-7000

(G-7206)
SURVEY SOFTWARE SERVICES
220 Forbes Rd Ste 400 (02184-2739)
PHONE.............................781 849-8118
Oleg Matsko, *CEO*
EMP: 9 **EST:** 2013
SALES (est): 136.44K **Privately Held**
Web: www.keysurvey.com
SIC: 7372　Prepackaged software

(G-7207)
SYMMONS INDUSTRIES INC (PA)
31 Brooks Dr (02184-3804)
PHONE.............................800 796-6667
Timothy O'keefe, *CEO*
John Graves, *
William O'keeffe, *Sec*
Paula O'keeffe, *Dir*
R Ian Keeffe, *
▲ **EMP:** 245 **EST:** 1939
SQ FT: 88,000
SALES (est): 55.34MM
SALES (corp-wide): 55.34MM **Privately
Held**
Web: www.symmons.com
SIC: 3494 3432　Plumbing and heating
　valves; Faucets and spigots, metal and
　plastic

(G-7208)
TAYLOR COMMUNICATIONS INC
400 Washington St (02184-4729)
PHONE.............................781 843-0250
Chris Copley, *Brnch Mgr*
EMP: 13
SALES (corp-wide): 3.81B **Privately Held**
Web: www.taylor.com
SIC: 2761　Manifold business forms
HQ: Taylor Communications, Inc.
　1725 Roe Crest Dr
　North Mankato MN 56003
　866 541-0937

(G-7209)
TB WOODS CORPORATION
300 Granite St Ste 201 (02184-3950)
PHONE.............................781 917-0600
Carl Christenson, *CEO*
Christian Storch, *CFO*
Glenn Deegan, *Sec*
Todd B Patriacca, *Contrlr*
EMP: 43 **EST:** 1995
SALES (est): 6.06MM
SALES (corp-wide): 5.22B **Publicly Held**
Web: www.altramotion.com
SIC: 3568　Power transmission equipment,
　nec
HQ: Altra Industrial Motion Corp.
　300 Granite St Ste 201
　Braintree MA 02184
　781 917-0600

(G-7210)
TWIN CY UPHOLSTERING MAT INC
476 Quincy Ave (02184-1346)
PHONE.............................781 843-1780
George J Dubois Junior, *CEO*
James Dubois, *Treas*
EMP: 10 **EST:** 1946
SQ FT: 9,600
SALES (est): 825.84K **Privately Held**
Web: www.twincityupholstering.com
SIC: 2512 5712 2515　Living room furniture:
　upholstered on wood frames; Furniture
　stores; Mattresses, innerspring or box
　spring

(G-7211)
ULTRA ELEC OCEAN SYSTEMS INC (DH)
115 Bay State Dr (02184-5203)
PHONE.............................781 848-3400
William Terry, *Pr*
Thomas P Bourgault, *
Carlos Santiago, *
Leland Kollmorgen, *
Richard Speer, *

▲ = Import ▼ = Export
◆ = Import/Export

▲ **EMP:** 82 **EST:** 2003
SQ FT: 50,000
SALES (est): 59.38MM
SALES (corp-wide): 2.67MM **Privately
Held**
Web: www.umaritime.com
SIC: 3812   Search and navigation equipment
HQ: Ultra Electronics Defense Inc.
4101 Smith School Rd
Austin TX 78744
512 327-6795

(G-7212)
WARNER ELECTRIC
300 Granite St Ste 201 (02184-3950)
PHONE...................................781 917-0600
EMP: 52 **EST:** 1999
SALES (est): 10.37MM
SALES (corp-wide): 5.22B **Publicly Held**
Web: www.altramotion.com
SIC: 3568 5085 3542 3625   Power
transmission equipment, nec; Power
transmission equipment and apparatus;
Brakes, metal forming; Brakes,
electromagnetic
HQ: Altra Industrial Motion Corp.
300 Granite St Ste 201
Braintree MA 02184
781 917-0600

(G-7213)
WHYTE ELECTRIC LLC
95 Shaw St (02184-4311)
PHONE...................................781 348-6239
Daniel E Whyte, *Prin*
EMP: 9 **EST:** 2015
SALES (est): 987.67K **Privately Held**
SIC: 3699 1731   Electrical equipment and
supplies, nec; Electrical work

(G-7214)
WOLLASTON ALLOYS INC
Also Called: Cpp-Boston
205 Wood Rd (02184-2498)
PHONE...................................781 848-3333
William Francis Earley, *Pr*
David Andrew Adams, *
David Andrew Moreland, *
Ali Ghavami, *
Ron Hamilton, *
▲ **EMP:** 180 **EST:** 1947
SALES (est): 46.6MM
SALES (corp-wide): 820.44MM **Privately
Held**
Web: www.cppcorp.com
SIC: 3325 3369   Alloy steel castings, except
investment; Nonferrous foundries, nec
HQ: Cfhc Holdings, Inc.
1621 Euclid Ave Ste 1850
Cleveland OH

Brewster
Barnstable County

(G-7215)
MUSSEL BOUND LLC
80 Joe Long Rd (02631-2074)
P.O. Box 749 (02631-0749)
PHONE...................................774 212-5488
Terry M Jones, *Pr*
Carla S Jones, *Sec*
EMP: 8 **EST:** 2010
SQ FT: 2,000
SALES (est): 836.75K **Privately Held**
Web: www.musselbound.com
SIC: 2891   Adhesives and sealants

(G-7216)
PARACLETE PRESS INC (HQ)
36 Southern Eagle Cartway (02631-1558)
P.O. Box 1568 (02653-1568)
PHONE...................................508 255-4685
Robert J Edmonson, *Pr*
Pamela Jordan, *
Sarah Andre, *
Danielle W Bushnell, *
Betty C Pugsley, *
▲ **EMP:** 40 **EST:** 1983
SQ FT: 15,000
SALES (est): 10.02MM
SALES (corp-wide): 10.02MM **Privately
Held**
Web: www.paracletepress.com
SIC: 2741   Miscellaneous publishing
PA: The Community Of Jesus Inc
5 Bay View Dr
Orleans MA 02653
508 255-1094

(G-7217)
THE POHLY COMPANY
Also Called: Custom Publishing
42 Konohassett Cartway (02631-2555)
P.O. Box 1320 (02631-7320)
PHONE...................................617 451-1700
EMP: 10
Web: www.pohlyco.com
SIC: 2721   Magazines: publishing only, not
printed on site

Bridgewater
Plymouth County

(G-7218)
**A LUONGO & SONS
INCORPORATED**
160 Fireworks Cir (02324-3036)
P.O. Box 1051 (02703-0018)
PHONE...................................508 226-0788
Frank Luongo, *Pr*
Tony Luongo, *VP*
Peter Luongo, *Treas*
EMP: 8 **EST:** 1977
SQ FT: 15,000
SALES (est): 985K **Privately Held**
Web: www.aluongo.com
SIC: 3544 3469   Special dies and tools;
Metal stampings, nec

(G-7219)
ALLEN MORGAN
Also Called: Tsi/Protherm
32 Scotland Blvd (02324-4302)
PHONE...................................714 538-7492
Allen Morgan, *Owner*
EMP: 7 **EST:** 1991
SALES (est): 864.35K **Privately Held**
Web: www.allenmorgan.com
SIC: 3567   Heating units and devices,
industrial: electric

(G-7220)
**ASHMONT WELDING COMPANY
INC**
10 Cranmore Dr (02324-2157)
P.O. Box 5 (02324-0005)
PHONE...................................508 279-1977
Jim Welch, *Pr*
EMP: 12 **EST:** 2003
SALES (est): 908.29K **Privately Held**
Web: www.ashmontironworks.com
SIC: 7692 5084   Welding repair; Welding
machinery and equipment

(G-7221)
B R S INC
Also Called: Bridgewater Raynham Sand
Stone
1453 Plymouth St (02324-2098)
P.O. Box 187 (02324-0187)
PHONE...................................508 697-5448
EMP: 20 **EST:** 1994
SALES (est): 2.97MM **Privately Held**
Web: www.brsandstone.com
SIC: 3281 5032 1442   Cut stone and stone
products; Stone, crushed or broken;
Construction sand and gravel

(G-7222)
BAY STEEL CO INC
81 Bridge St (02324-1903)
PHONE...................................508 697-7083
EMP: 10
SALES (corp-wide): 1.25MM **Privately
Held**
SIC: 3441   Fabricated structural metal
PA: Bay Steel Co. Inc.
87 Lake St
Halifax MA 02338
781 294-8308

(G-7223)
**BAYSTATE LGHTNING
PRTCTION INC**
55 Three Rivers Dr (02324-1961)
PHONE...................................508 697-7727
James R Smith, *Pr*
EMP: 8 **EST:** 2005
SALES (est): 790.44K **Privately Held**
Web:
www.baystatelightningprotection.com
SIC: 3643   Lightning protection equipment

(G-7224)
BOSTON AREA DOOR COMPANY
Also Called: Boston Area Door Company
75 1st St Unit 3 (02324-1059)
PHONE...................................508 857-4722
Kevin Pearce, *Managing Member*
EMP: 8 **EST:** 2013
SALES (est): 1.61MM
SALES (corp-wide): 1.61MM **Privately
Held**
Web: www.badcodoors.com
SIC: 5211 5039 2431   Garage doors, sale
and installation; Construction materials, nec
; Doors and door parts and trim, wood
PA: Pearce Services Llc, Dba Boston
465 Turnpike St 650
Canton MA 02021
781 562-0892

(G-7225)
**BRIDGEWATER PRTG COPY
CTR LLC**
100 Broad St (02324-1797)
PHONE...................................508 697-5227
EMP: 9 **EST:** 2005
SALES (est): 325.68K **Privately Held**
Web: www.bridgewaterprint.com
SIC: 2752   Offset printing

(G-7226)
CIM INDUSTRIES INC
26 Summer St (02325-1218)
PHONE...................................800 543-3458
Peter R Chase, *Prin*
EMP: 20 **EST:** 2010
SALES (est): 3.05MM **Publicly Held**
Web: www.chasecorp.com
SIC: 3999   Manufacturing industries, nec
HQ: Chase Corporation
375 University Ave

Westwood MA 02090
781 332-0700

(G-7227)
CODMAN & SHURTLEFF INC
Also Called: CODMAN & SHURTLEFF INC
50 Scotland Park Dr (02324)
PHONE...................................508 880-8100
EMP: 72
SALES (corp-wide): 94.94B **Publicly Held**
SIC: 3841   Surgical and medical instruments
HQ: Cerenovus, Inc.
6303 Wtrford Dst Dr Ste 3
Miami FL 33126

(G-7228)
CONTROL 7 INC
Also Called: C7
55 Scotland Blvd (02324-2302)
PHONE...................................508 697-3197
Mark W Jacoby, *Pr*
John Nelson, *Stockholder*
EMP: 20 **EST:** 1983
SQ FT: 12,500
SALES (est): 8.71MM **Privately Held**
Web: www.control7.com
SIC: 3613   Control panels, electric

(G-7229)
FIBERTEC INC
35 Scotland Blvd (02324-2302)
PHONE...................................508 697-5100
Joseph Aten, *Pr*
◆ **EMP:** 55 **EST:** 1986
SQ FT: 52,500
SALES (est): 8.41MM **Privately Held**
Web: www.fibertecinc.com
SIC: 3089 3231   Plastics hardware and
building products; Products of purchased
glass

(G-7230)
HENRY PERKINS COMPANY
180 Broad St (02324-1751)
P.O. Box 215 (02324-0215)
PHONE...................................508 697-6978
Tom Perkins, *Pr*
David Perkins Junior, *VP*
Peter Perkins, *Treas*
▼ **EMP:** 11 **EST:** 1848
SQ FT: 3,000
SALES (est): 2.23MM **Privately Held**
Web: www.henryperkinsco.com
SIC: 3321   Gray iron castings, nec

(G-7231)
INSULATION TECHNOLOGY INC
35 1st St (02324-1054)
P.O. Box 578 (02324-0578)
PHONE...................................508 697-6926
Nancy Barone, *Pr*
▲ **EMP:** 7 **EST:** 1977
SQ FT: 20,000
SALES (est): 927.87K **Privately Held**
Web: www.insultech-eps.com
SIC: 3086   Insulation or cushioning material,
foamed plastics

(G-7232)
INTENT AI LLC
739 Main St (02324-1348)
PHONE...................................415 871-0605
Levon Harutyunyan, *CEO*
EMP: 8 **EST:** 2021
SALES (est): 330.21K **Privately Held**
SIC: 7372   Prepackaged software

(G-7233)
JEDWARDS INTERNATIONAL INC
1025 Elm St Ste 2 (02324-1078)
PHONE...............................617 340-9461
Christos Iorio, *Pr*
EMP: 8
Web: www.bulknaturaloils.com
SIC: 2066 Cocoa butter
PA: Jedwards International, Inc.
141 Campanelli Dr
Braintree MA 02184

(G-7234)
JOHNSON JOHNSON HEALTHCAR
50 Scotland Blvd (02324-2303)
PHONE...............................508 828-6194
EMP: 35 EST: 2018
SALES (est): 1.34MM **Privately Held**
SIC: 3841 Surgical and medical instruments

(G-7235)
JP PLASTICS INC
45 1st St (02324-1054)
P.O. Box 579 (02324-0579)
PHONE...............................508 697-4202
John P Cheever, *Pr*
Nicole Cheever, *VP*
EMP: 8 EST: 1957
SQ FT: 17,000
SALES (est): 968.56K **Privately Held**
Web: www.jpplasticsusa.com
SIC: 3081 Packing materials, plastics sheet

(G-7236)
PAUL MCNAMARA
Also Called: P M Tile and Grout Care
110 Dundee Dr (02324-2208)
PHONE...............................508 245-5654
Paul S Mcnamara, *Owner*
EMP: 10 EST: 1997
SALES (est): 508.95K **Privately Held**
SIC: 3471 Cleaning, polishing, and finishing

(G-7237)
ROYSTON LABORATORIES
26 Summer St (02325-1218)
PHONE...............................412 828-1500
Kenneth Duman, *CFO*
EMP: 8 EST: 2015
SALES (est): 185.64K **Privately Held**
Web: www.chasecorp.com
SIC: 2821 Plastics materials and resins

(G-7238)
STILES & HART BRICK COMPANY
127 Cook St (02324-3307)
P.O. Box 367 (02324-0367)
PHONE...............................508 697-6928
Jean Andrews, *Pr*
Francis Mansfield, *
James Kenn, *
◆ EMP: 44 EST: 1894
SQ FT: 2,500
SALES (est): 5.93MM **Privately Held**
Web: www.stilesandhart.com
SIC: 3271 3229 2426 3251 Concrete block and brick; Pressed and blown glass, nec; Hardwood dimension and flooring mills; Brick clay: common face, glazed, vitrified, or hollow

Brighton
Suffolk County

(G-7239)
COMPASS THERAPEUTICS INC (PA)
80 Guest St (02135-2071)
PHONE...............................617 500-8099
Vered Bisker-leib, *CEO*
EMP: 7 EST: 2018
Web: www.compasstherapeutics.com
SIC: 2836 Biological products, except diagnostic

(G-7240)
FUEL AMERICA
152 Chestnut Hill Ave (02135-4639)
PHONE...............................617 782-0999
EMP: 8 EST: 2011
SALES (est): 1.02MM **Privately Held**
Web: www.fuelamericacoffee.com
SIC: 2869 Fuels

(G-7241)
HARVARD BUS SCHL PUBG CORP (HQ)
Also Called: HARVARD UNIVERSITY
20 Guest St Ste 700 (02135-2063)
PHONE...............................617 783-7400
David Wan, *Pr*
Raymond Carvey, *
Paul Bills, *
▲ EMP: 150 EST: 1994
SALES (est): 307.66MM
SALES (corp-wide): 6.1B **Privately Held**
Web: www.harvardbusiness.org
SIC: 2721 2731 2741 Magazines: publishing only, not printed on site; Books, publishing only; Newsletter publishing
PA: President And Fellows Of Harvard College
1350 Massachusetts Ave
Cambridge MA 02138
617 496-4873

(G-7242)
HDM SYSTEMS CORPORATION
84 Lincoln St (02135-1409)
PHONE...............................617 562-4054
Aileen Liu, *Pr*
Chi Fu Yeh, *Sec*
▲ EMP: 12 EST: 2002
SQ FT: 12,000
SALES (est): 2.46MM **Privately Held**
Web: www.hdm-sys.com
SIC: 3679 Electronic circuits

(G-7243)
PECO PALLET
34 Lake St Apt 2 (02135-3819)
PHONE...............................845 642-2780
EMP: 7 EST: 2018
SALES (est): 218.9K **Privately Held**
Web: www.pecopallet.com
SIC: 2448 Pallets, wood

(G-7244)
REGOR THERAPEUTICS INC
50 Soldiers Field Pl (02135-1104)
PHONE...............................617 407-4737
EMP: 10 EST: 2018
SALES (est): 464.61K **Privately Held**
Web: www.qlregor.com
SIC: 2834 Pharmaceutical preparations

(G-7245)
ROCHE DGNOSTICS HEMATOLOGY INC
80 Guest St # 6 (02135-2071)
PHONE...............................508 329-2450
EMP: 80 EST: 2008
SALES (est): 11.68MM **Privately Held**
SIC: 2834 Pharmaceutical preparations
HQ: F. Hoffmann-La Roche Ag
Grenzacherstrasse 124
Basel BS 4058

(G-7246)
VINEYARD BRANDS
40 Adair Rd (02135-1728)
PHONE...............................617 901-3597
EMP: 9 EST: 2018
SALES (est): 66K **Privately Held**
SIC: 2084 Wines

(G-7247)
XL HYBRIDS INC (HQ)
Also Called: Xl Fleet
145 Newton St (02135-1508)
PHONE...............................617 718-0329
Dimitri Kazarinoff, *CEO*
Thomas J Hynes, *Chief Strategy Officer*
Clayton W Siegert, *
James Breyer, *
Kristin Brief, *
EMP: 21 EST: 2009
SALES (est): 7.86MM
SALES (corp-wide): 23.19MM **Publicly Held**
Web: www.xlfleet.com
SIC: 3714 Motor vehicle parts and accessories
PA: Spruce Power Holding Corporation
47000 Liberty Dr
Wixom MI 48393
617 718-0329

Brimfield
Hampden County

(G-7248)
ACCELLENT LLC
68 Mill Ln (01010-9749)
PHONE...............................413 245-7144
Richard Campbell, *CEO*
EMP: 10
SALES (corp-wide): 1.38B **Publicly Held**
SIC: 3841 Surgical and medical instruments
HQ: Accellent Llc
10000 Fordham Rd
Clarence NY 75024
978 570-6900

(G-7249)
BRIMFIELD PRECISION LLC
68 Mill Ln (01010-9749)
PHONE...............................413 245-7144
Donald J Spence, *Ch*
EMP: 151 EST: 1965
SQ FT: 32,500
SALES (est): 1.77MM
SALES (corp-wide): 1.38B **Publicly Held**
SIC: 3841 3842 Surgical and medical instruments; Implants, surgical
HQ: Medsource Technologies, Llc
100 Fordham Rd Ste 1
Wilmington MA 01887
978 570-6900

(G-7250)
MK FUEL INC
341 Sturbridge Rd (01010-9640)
PHONE...............................413 245-7507

Anwar Afrede, *Pr*
EMP: 10 EST: 2010
SALES (est): 479.81K **Privately Held**
SIC: 2869 Fuels

Brockton
Plymouth County

(G-7251)
A W MCMULLEN CO INC
Also Called: Prospect Hill Company
12 Field St (02301-2416)
PHONE...............................508 583-2072
TOLL FREE: 800
Timothy Mc Mullen, *Pr*
Susan Mc Mullen, *VP*
EMP: 10 EST: 1951
SALES (est): 1.49MM **Privately Held**
Web: www.prospecthillco.com
SIC: 5049 2759 Religious supplies; Business forms: printing, nsk

(G-7252)
ACUSHNET COMPANY
Also Called: Titalist and Footjoy Worldwide
144 Field St (02302-1608)
PHONE...............................508 979-2309
EMP: 11
Web: www.titleist.com
SIC: 3949 Balls: baseball, football, basketball, etc.
HQ: Acushnet Company
333 Bridge St
Fairhaven MA 02719
508 979-2000

(G-7253)
AERIAL SKYVERTISING INC
55 Boyle Rd (02302-1118)
PHONE...............................508 536-4076
Ronald Mahan, *Pr*
EMP: 7 EST: 1970
SALES (est): 638.28K **Privately Held**
Web: www.skyvertising.com
SIC: 7319 3993 Shopping news, advertising and distributing service; Signs and advertising specialties

(G-7254)
AGM INDUSTRIES INC
16 Jonathan Dr (02301-5549)
PHONE...............................508 587-3900
Tom Karjama, *CEO*
Kenneth Reale, *
Ernst Hatz, *
Norma Searle, *
EMP: 30 EST: 1961
SQ FT: 30,000
SALES (est): 4.21MM **Privately Held**
Web: www.agmind.com
SIC: 3548 Welding apparatus

(G-7255)
AMPHENOL ALDEN PRODUCTS CO (HQ)
Also Called: Amphenol Alden
117 N Main St (02301-3908)
PHONE...............................508 427-7000
R Adam Norwitt, *Pr*
Elizabeth Alden, *Ch Bd*
Martin H Loeffler, *Prin*
Edward C Wetmore, *Sec*
David J Jositas, *Treas*
▲ EMP: 126 EST: 1929
SQ FT: 60,000
SALES (est): 44.21MM
SALES (corp-wide): 12.62B **Publicly Held**
Web: www.amphenolalden.com

SIC: **3678** Electronic connectors
PA: Amphenol Corporation
358 Hall Ave
Wallingford CT 06492
203 265-8900

(G-7256)
AMS PRECISION MACHINING INC
959 W Chestnut St Ste 1 (02301-5559)
PHONE...............................508 588-2283
Antonio Sousa, *Pr*
Diane Sousa, *Treas*
Jose Romao, *Stockholder*
EMP: 7 EST: 1982
SQ FT: 5,500
SALES (est): 874.58K **Privately Held**
SIC: **3599** Machine shop, jobbing and repair

(G-7257)
ANTENNA ASSOCIATES INC
21 Burke Dr (02301-5504)
PHONE...............................508 583-3241
Ronald A Sandquist, *Pr*
Dana Sandquist, *
Clement M Frazier, *
EMP: 25 EST: 1979
SQ FT: 20,000
SALES (est): 4.66MM **Privately Held**
Web: www.antennaassociates.com
SIC: **3452** 3568 Bolts, nuts, rivets, and washers; Power transmission equipment, nec

(G-7258)
ATRENNE CMPT SOLUTIONS LLC
11 Burke Dr (02301-5504)
PHONE...............................508 588-6110
EMP: 54
SALES (corp-wide): 422MM **Privately Held**
Web: www.atrenne.com
SIC: **3354** Aluminum extruded products
HQ: Atrenne Computing Solutions, Llc
10 Mupac Dr
Brockton MA 02301
508 588-6110

(G-7259)
ATRENNE CMPT SOLUTIONS LLC (DH)
10 Mupac Dr (02301-5548)
PHONE...............................508 588-6110
Chris Boutilier, *Pr*
EMP: 273 EST: 2008
SALES (est): 64MM
SALES (corp-wide): 422MM **Privately Held**
Web: www.atrenne.com
SIC: **3354** 3469 3429 Aluminum extruded products; Metal stampings, nec; Hardware, nec
HQ: Atrenne Integrated Solutions, Inc.
9210 Science Center Dr
New Hope MN 55428
763 533-3533

(G-7260)
BARBOUR CORPORATION (PA)
Also Called: Barbour Plastics
1001 N Montello St (02301-1640)
P.O. Box 2158 (02305-2158)
PHONE...............................508 583-8200
Richard K Hynes, *Pr*
Bruce Pearson, *
Rick Bowen, *
◆ **EMP: 97 EST:** 1892
SQ FT: 130,000

SALES (est): 24.32MM
SALES (corp-wide): 24.32MM **Privately Held**
Web: www.barbourcorp.com
SIC: **3131** Welting, cut stock and finding

(G-7261)
BILTRITE CORPORATION (PA)
1350 Belmont St (02301-4430)
PHONE...............................781 647-1700
Stanley J Bernstein, *CEO*
Stephen A Fine, *COO*
Richard Bakos, *CFO*
▲ **EMP: 10 EST:** 1908
SQ FT: 8,000
SALES (est): 8.76MM
SALES (corp-wide): 8.76MM **Privately Held**
Web: www.biltrite.com
SIC: **3061** Mechanical rubber goods

(G-7262)
BRIDGESTONE RET OPERATIONS LLC
Also Called: Firestone
126 Warren Ave (02301-3833)
PHONE...............................508 588-8866
Javier Millan, *Mgr*
EMP: 8
Web: www.bridgestoneamericas.com
SIC: **5531** 7534 Automotive tires; Rebuilding and retreading tires
HQ: Bridgestone Retail Operations, Llc
333 E Lake St Ste 300
Bloomingdale IL 60108
630 259-9000

(G-7263)
BROCKTON BEER COMPANY LLC
121 Main St (02301-4047)
PHONE...............................508 521-9711
Edmund Cabellon, *Managing Member*
EMP: 7 EST: 2018
SALES (est): 1.47MM **Privately Held**
Web: www.brocktonbeer.com
SIC: **5921** 2082 Beer (packaged); Malt beverages

(G-7264)
BROCKTON PLASTICS
230 Elliot St (02302-2314)
PHONE...............................508 587-2290
EMP: 7 EST: 2019
SALES (est): 244.73K **Privately Held**
Web: www.rextrude.com
SIC: **3089** Plastics products, nec

(G-7265)
BSP GROUP INC
135 Oak Hill Way (02301-8119)
PHONE...............................508 587-1101
Edward J Twohig, *Pr*
John E Twohig, *
EMP: 60 EST: 1992
SQ FT: 16,000
SALES (est): 6.1MM **Privately Held**
SIC: **3089** Injection molding of plastics

(G-7266)
CDI LLC A VALLEY FORGE CO
637 N Montello St (02454-2454)
PHONE...............................508 587-7000
Diana Dobin Kauppinen, *Managing Member*
EMP: 120 EST: 2017
SALES (est): 17.24MM
SALES (corp-wide): 50.16MM **Privately Held**
Web: www.valleyforge.com

SIC: **2591** Drapery hardware and window blinds and shades
PA: Valley Forge Fabrics, Inc.
1650 W Mcnab Rd
Fort Lauderdale FL 33309
954 971-1776

(G-7267)
CDP MANUFACTURING LLC
15 Jonathan Dr Ste 6 (02301-5566)
PHONE...............................508 588-6400
Mark P Cutting, *Managing Member*
Paul S Wagner, *Managing Member*
EMP: 10 EST: 2004
SQ FT: 200,000
SALES (est): 785.77K **Privately Held**
SIC: **3449** Miscellaneous metalwork

(G-7268)
CHATHAM PLASTIC VENTURES INC
Also Called: Chatco
1200 W Chestnut St (02301-5574)
PHONE...............................518 392-5761
Daniel Crellin, *Pr*
EMP: 14 EST: 2004
SALES (est): 498.33K **Privately Held**
SIC: **3089** Injection molding of plastics

(G-7269)
CONCORD FOODS LLC (PA)
Also Called: Red-E-Made
10 Minuteman Way (02301-7508)
PHONE...............................508 580-1700
Robert Geoffrey Neville, *Ch*
Peter E Neville, *Pr*
Joel H Fishman, *Sec*
◆ **EMP: 218 EST:** 1968
SQ FT: 255,000
SALES (est): 90.52MM
SALES (corp-wide): 90.52MM **Privately Held**
Web: www.concordfoods.com
SIC: **2099** 2045 Dessert mixes and fillings; Prepared flour mixes and doughs

(G-7270)
CONTRACT DECOR INTL INC
637 N Montello St (02301-2454)
PHONE...............................508 587-7000
Laurence Handler, *Pr*
Michael Handler, *
◆ **EMP: 100 EST:** 1993
SQ FT: 23,000
SALES (est): 17.91MM
SALES (corp-wide): 50.16MM **Privately Held**
Web: www.valleyforge.com
SIC: **2211** Draperies and drapery fabrics, cotton
PA: Valley Forge Fabrics, Inc.
1650 W Mcnab Rd
Fort Lauderdale FL 33309
954 971-1776

(G-7271)
CREATIVE EXTRUSION & TECH INC
230 Elliot St (02302-2314)
PHONE...............................508 587-2290
John D Hopkins Junior, *Pr*
David Flynn, *
Melissa Hopkins, *
▲ **EMP: 25 EST:** 1952
SQ FT: 57,000
SALES (est): 8.25MM **Privately Held**
Web: www.creativeet.com
SIC: **3089** Injection molding of plastics

(G-7272)
CUSTOM BLENDS INC
Also Called: Cindy's Kitchen
40 Industrial Blvd (02301-7154)
PHONE...............................508 583-2995
EMP: 15 EST: 1990
SALES (est): 2.75MM **Privately Held**
Web: www.cindyskitchen.com
SIC: **2099** Food preparations, nec

(G-7273)
DRA-COR INDUSTRIES INC
65 N Main St (02301-3906)
PHONE...............................508 580-3770
Ralph Brancaccio, *Pr*
Ralph Brancaccio, *Pr*
Vincent Brancaccio, *
EMP: 25 EST: 1998
SQ FT: 30,000
SALES (est): 2.31MM **Privately Held**
Web: www.dra-cor.com
SIC: **2391** Curtains and draperies

(G-7274)
EAST COAST INDUCTION INC
506 N Warren Ave (02301-2684)
P.O. Box 2039 (02305-2039)
PHONE...............................508 587-2800
Sheldon Nitenson, *Pr*
Alan Prodouz, *General Vice President*
EMP: 11 EST: 1963
SQ FT: 75,000
SALES (est): 1.2MM **Privately Held**
Web: www.eastcoastinduction.com
SIC: **3567** Induction heating equipment

(G-7275)
EJ USA INC
1125 Pearl St (02301-5406)
PHONE...............................508 586-3130
T L Gasse, *Mgr*
EMP: 16
Web: www.ejco.com
SIC: **3321** Manhole covers, metal
HQ: Ej Usa, Inc.
301 Spring St
East Jordan MI 49727
800 874-4100

(G-7276)
ELIE BAKING CORPORATION
Also Called: Near East Bakery
204 N Montello St (02301-3918)
PHONE...............................508 584-4890
Elie T Ata, *Pr*
Ibrahim T Ata, *Sec*
Abe Ata, *VP*
EMP: 17 EST: 1992
SALES (est): 2.32MM **Privately Held**
Web: www.eliebaking.com
SIC: **2051** Bread, cake, and related products

(G-7277)
EVANS MACHINE CO INC
Also Called: Evans Machine
32 N Manchester St (02302-2354)
PHONE...............................508 584-8085
Daniel Evans Junior, *Pr*
Daniel Evans Senior, *Stockholder*
▲ **EMP: 35 EST:** 1970
SQ FT: 10,000
SALES (est): 7.37MM **Privately Held**
Web: www.emievans.com
SIC: **3599** Machine shop, jobbing and repair

(G-7278)
FASPRINT INC (PA)
Also Called: Allegra Print & Imaging
195 Liberty St Ste 1 (02301-5555)

PHONE..............................508 588-9961
Tony Ward, *Pr*
EMP: 11 **EST:** 1971
SQ FT: 2,000
SALES (est): 2.19MM
SALES (corp-wide): 2.19MM **Privately Held**
Web: www.allegramarketingprint.com
SIC: 2752 7334 2791 Offset printing; Photocopying and duplicating services; Typesetting

(G-7279)
G T R FINISHING CORPORATION
1 Jonathan Dr (02301-5549)
PHONE..............................508 588-3240
Raymond J Timmons, *CEO*
Richard G Barnard, *Ex VP*
Corinne King, *Pr*
James Craig, *VP*
Bill Klaila, *Sec*
EMP: 36 **EST:** 1979
SQ FT: 10,000
SALES (est): 801.34K **Privately Held**
Web: www.gtrmfg.com
SIC: 3479 Coating of metals and formed products

(G-7280)
GEO KNIGHT & CO INC
52 Perkins St (02302-3540)
PHONE..............................508 588-0186
Chesterton S Knight, *Pr*
Aaron Knight, *
▲ **EMP:** 32 **EST:** 1885
SQ FT: 46,000
SALES (est): 5.31MM **Privately Held**
Web: www.heatpress.com
SIC: 3443 Heat exchangers, plate type

(G-7281)
GILL METAL FAB INC
Also Called: Moduline
170 Oak Hill Way (02301-7124)
P.O. Box 339 (02379-0339)
PHONE..............................508 580-4445
Paul Gill, *Pr*
EMP: 30 **EST:** 1987
SQ FT: 18,000
SALES (est): 4.98MM **Privately Held**
Web: www.gillmetal.com
SIC: 7692 3443 3599 2521 Welding repair; Fabricated plate work (boiler shop); Machine and other job shop work; Cabinets, office: wood

(G-7282)
GTR MANUFACTURING LLC
1 Jonathan Dr (02301-5549)
PHONE..............................508 588-3240
James E Craig, *Pr*
Corinne King, *
William R Klaila, *
Daniel E Almeida, *
EMP: 63 **EST:** 1973
SQ FT: 52,000
SALES (est): 20.13MM **Privately Held**
Web: www.gtrmfg.com
SIC: 3444 Sheet metal specialties, not stamped

(G-7283)
HESS OIL
296 N Pearl St (02301-1712)
PHONE..............................508 587-8325
John Hess, *Pr*
EMP: 7 **EST:** 2005
SALES (est): 264.72K **Privately Held**
SIC: 1382 Oil and gas exploration services

(G-7284)
INKSTONE INC
Also Called: Inkstone Printing
129 Liberty St (02301-5518)
PHONE..............................508 587-5200
Robert P Donahoe, *Pr*
EMP: 14 **EST:** 1986
SQ FT: 18,000
SALES (est): 487.59K **Privately Held**
Web: www.inkstone.com
SIC: 2752 Offset printing

(G-7285)
IRVINGS HOME CENTER INC
Also Called: Ace Hardware
10 N Main St (02301-3907)
PHONE..............................508 583-4421
Richard J Sena, *Pr*
David Sena, *VP*
EMP: 9 **EST:** 1961
SQ FT: 10,000
SALES (est): 473.39K **Privately Held**
Web: www.irvingshomecenter.com
SIC: 5713 5714 5251 2434 Floor covering stores; Draperies; Hardware stores; Wood kitchen cabinets

(G-7286)
ITE LLC
Also Called: Industrial Trucks & Equipment
140 Manley St (02301-5509)
PHONE..............................508 313-5600
EMP: 7 **EST:** 2003
SQ FT: 16,000
SALES (est): 211.01K **Privately Held**
Web: www.prodigypd.com
SIC: 3537 Lift trucks, industrial: fork, platform, straddle, etc.

(G-7287)
JONES & VINING INCORPORATED (PA)
1115 W Chestnut St Ste 2 (02301-7501)
PHONE..............................508 232-7470
Mark A Krentzman, *Ch Bd*
Patricia Moretti, *CFO*
James R Salzano, *Prin*
Thomas Shields, *Prin*
Frederic J Marx, *Prin*
◆ **EMP:** 21 **EST:** 1930
SALES (est): 24.6MM
SALES (corp-wide): 24.6MM **Privately Held**
Web: www.jonesandvining.com
SIC: 2499 3131 Lasts, boot and shoe; Boot and shoe accessories

(G-7288)
KROHN-HITE CORPORATION
15 Jonathan Dr Ste 4 (02301-5566)
PHONE..............................508 580-1660
Richard M Haddad, *Pr*
EMP: 18 **EST:** 1949
SQ FT: 10,000
SALES (est): 2.4MM **Privately Held**
Web: www.krohn-hite.com
SIC: 3829 3825 3826 Measuring and controlling devices, nec; Measuring instruments and meters, electric; Analytical instruments

(G-7289)
LD PLASTICS INC
1130 Pearl St (02301-5409)
PHONE..............................508 584-7651
Charles Harlfinger, *Pr*
Kenneth B Smith, *
EMP: 30 **EST:** 1975
SQ FT: 28,800
SALES (est): 5.08MM **Privately Held**

Web: www.ldplastics.net
SIC: 3089 Plastics hardware and building products

(G-7290)
LEO F MACIVER CO INC
75 Ames St (02302-2025)
P.O. Box 2086 (02305-2086)
PHONE..............................508 583-2501
Donald L Maciver, *Pr*
Donald Maciver, *
Brian Mac Iver, *VP*
EMP: 7 **EST:** 1951
SQ FT: 22,000
SALES (est): 489.55K **Privately Held**
Web: www.lfmaciver.com
SIC: 5961 3131 Mail order house, nec; Inner parts for shoes

(G-7291)
LIBERTY PRINTING CO INC
99 Lawrence St (02302-3550)
P.O. Box 726 (02303-0726)
PHONE..............................508 586-6810
Diane Barbour, *Pr*
Joseph Barbour, *VP*
Chris Barbour, *VP*
Matt Barbour, *Genl Mgr*
EMP: 8 **EST:** 1901
SQ FT: 5,000
SALES (est): 915.7K **Privately Held**
Web: www.libertyprintinginc.com
SIC: 2752 2759 Offset printing; Letterpress printing

(G-7292)
LYNE LABORATORIES INC
Also Called: Pharmaceutical Resources
10 Burke Dr (02301-5505)
PHONE..............................508 583-8700
Stephen Tarallo, *Pr*
Robert Tarallo, *
Philip J Tarallo, *
Robert J Walker, *
Philip Tarallo, *
▲ **EMP:** 68 **EST:** 1964
SQ FT: 67,000
SALES (est): 23.23MM **Privately Held**
Web: www.lyne.com
SIC: 2834 8731 Pharmaceutical preparations; Commercial physical research

(G-7293)
M & S ELECTRICAL CONTRS LLC
116 Intervale St (02302-1760)
PHONE..............................781 389-4465
Laura Brown, *Prin*
EMP: 7 **EST:** 2014
SALES (est): 981.35K **Privately Held**
Web: www.ms-electric.com
SIC: 3699 1731 Electrical equipment and supplies, nec; Electrical work

(G-7294)
MAIR-MAC MACHINE COMPANY INC
86 N Montello St (02301-3916)
PHONE..............................508 895-9001
Mary A Macdonald, *Pr*
Edward Mac Donald, *Treas*
Ed Macdonald, *VP*
EMP: 15 **EST:** 1984
SQ FT: 9,000
SALES (est): 2.4MM **Privately Held**
Web: www.mairmac.com
SIC: 3443 3089 3599 Metal parts; Plastics processing; Machine shop, jobbing and repair

(G-7295)
MERIDIAN CUSTOM WDWKG INC
443 Summer St # 1 (02302-4118)
PHONE..............................508 587-4400
Allen W Cayer, *Pr*
James P Bentley, *Prin*
EMP: 7 **EST:** 2005
SALES (est): 239.11K **Privately Held**
Web: meridian-custom-woodworking-inc.business.site
SIC: 2431 Millwork

(G-7296)
MONTELLO HEEL MFG INC
Also Called: Colt Heel Div Montello Heel
13 Emerson Ave Ste 4 (02301-2455)
P.O. Box 2116 (02305-2116)
PHONE..............................508 586-0603
J Richard Pearson, *Pr*
▲ **EMP:** 50 **EST:** 1959
SQ FT: 10,000
SALES (est): 5.12MM **Privately Held**
Web: www.montelloheel.com
SIC: 3131 3172 Heels, shoe and boot: leather or wood; Personal leather goods, nec

(G-7297)
MONTILIO BAKING CO INC
Also Called: Montilio's Baking Company
134 Spark St (02302-1621)
PHONE..............................508 894-8855
George Montilio, *Pr*
Bryan Mclaughin, *Pr*
EMP: 78 **EST:** 1999
SALES (est): 9.05MM **Privately Held**
Web: www.montilios.com
SIC: 2051 Cakes, pies, and pastries

(G-7298)
MOONLIGHT LTD
244 Liberty St Ste 11 (02301-5561)
PHONE..............................508 584-0094
Anthony Galante, *Owner*
EMP: 9 **EST:** 2007
SALES (est): 439.35K **Privately Held**
Web: www.moonlightlimited.com
SIC: 2759 Screen printing

(G-7299)
MUTUAL OIL LEASING CO INC
863 Crescent St (02302-3401)
PHONE..............................508 583-5777
Edward A Rachins, *Pr*
EMP: 14 **EST:** 1942
SALES (est): 1.11MM **Privately Held**
SIC: 1389 Oil field services, nec

(G-7300)
PASTA BENE INC
1050 Pearl St Ste 1 (02301-5401)
PHONE..............................508 583-1515
Benjamin Alvanese, *Pr*
Joyce Alvanese, *Prin*
EMP: 10 **EST:** 1981
SALES (est): 741.62K **Privately Held**
SIC: 2099 5149 Pasta, uncooked: packaged with other ingredients; Pasta and rice

(G-7301)
PRINT SYNERGY SOLUTIONS LLC
Also Called: Printsynergy Solutions
129 Liberty St (02301-5518)
PHONE..............................508 587-5200
Robert P Donahoe, *Managing Member*
Paul A Cicone, *Managing Member*
Heather Hanson, *Managing Member*

EMP: 18 **EST:** 2011
SALES (est): 4.12MM **Privately Held**
Web: www.printsynergysolutions.com
SIC: 2752   Offset printing

(G-7302)
RESTMORE INC
Also Called: Ther-A-Pedic Sleep Products
135 Spark St (02302-1620)
PHONE..............................508 559-9944
▼ **EMP:** 55
Web: www.reynoldsphotovideo.com
SIC: 2515 5021   Mattresses, innerspring or
   box spring; Beds and bedding

(G-7303)
SCHOLZ FRANK X RAY CORP
244 Liberty St Ste 3a (02301-5561)
EMP: 18 **EST:** 1936
SALES (est): 1.86MM **Privately Held**
SIC: 3844   X-ray apparatus and tubes

(G-7304)
SHARON VACUUM CO INC
69 Falmouth Ave (02301-3403)
PHONE..............................508 588-2323
Lawrence A Resnick, *Pr*
Patricia Mcmahon, *Treas*
EMP: 10 **EST:** 1967
SQ FT: 6,000
SALES (est): 923.83K **Privately Held**
Web: www.sharonvacuum.com
SIC: 3443   High vacuum coaters, metal plate

(G-7305)
**SIE COMPUTING SOLUTIONS
INC**
10 Mupac Dr (02301-5548)
PHONE..............................508 588-6110
Chris Boutilier, *Pr*
Mark Sullivan, *
Udo Filzmaier, *
Markus Gfall, *
James Tierney, *
▲ **EMP:** 75 **EST:** 1972
SQ FT: 55,000
SALES (est): 19.59MM
SALES (corp-wide): 355.83K **Privately
Held**
Web: www.atrenne.com
SIC: 3571 3679   Electronic computers;
   Electronic circuits
HQ: Ft Ag
   HohenemserstraBe 21
   Lustenau 6890
   557789900

(G-7306)
SIGN DESIGN INC
Also Called: Alumasign
170 Liberty St (02301-5522)
PHONE..............................508 580-0094
Whitney Ferrigno, *Pr*
Ron Ferrigno, *
EMP: 70 **EST:** 1988
SQ FT: 30,000
SALES (est): 10.23MM **Privately Held**
Web: www.signdesign.com
SIC: 3993   Signs, not made in custom sign
   painting shops

(G-7307)
SOUTH SHORE PACKING INC
Also Called: South Shore Meat
12 Taylor Ave (02302-3622)
PHONE..............................508 941-0458
EMP: 30
SIC: 3556   Meat processing machinery

(G-7308)
SPENCE & CO LTD
76 Campanelli Industrial Dr (02301-1851)
PHONE..............................508 427-5577
Charles Alan Spence, *Pr*
◆ **EMP:** 45 **EST:** 1991
SQ FT: 20,000
SALES (est): 11.41MM
SALES (corp-wide): 58.54MM **Privately
Held**
Web: www.spenceltd.com
SIC: 2091 2092   Fish, smoked; Fresh or
   frozen packaged fish
PA: Acme Smoked Fish Corp.
   30 Gem St Ste 56
   Brooklyn NY 11222
   718 383-8585

(G-7309)
**SPILLDAM ENVIRONMENTAL
INC**
Also Called: Spilldam
89 N Montello St (02301-3938)
P.O. Box 960 (02303-0960)
PHONE..............................508 583-7850
Timothy Prevost, *Pr*
Patti S Prevost, *Sec*
▼ **EMP:** 12 **EST:** 1991
SQ FT: 40,000
SALES (est): 2.29MM **Privately Held**
Web: www.spilldam.com
SIC: 3589 4959   Water treatment equipment,
   industrial; Oil spill cleanup

(G-7310)
SUPERIOR BAKING CO INC
176 N Warren Ave (02301-3431)
PHONE..............................508 586-6601
Michael Debenedictis, *Pr*
Joseph Ferrini Junior, *Sec*
Robert De Benedictis, *
EMP: 50 **EST:** 1916
SQ FT: 15,000
SALES (est): 4.68MM **Privately Held**
Web: www.superiorbakingco.com
SIC: 2051 5461   Breads, rolls, and buns;
   Bread

(G-7311)
**THERAPEDIC OF NEW
ENGLAND LLC**
135 Spark St (02302-1620)
PHONE..............................508 559-9944
EMP: 13 **EST:** 2012
SALES (est): 959.81K **Privately Held**
Web: www.restmore.store
SIC: 2392 2515   Blankets, comforters and
   beddings; Mattresses and bedsprings

(G-7312)
**TIRE & AUTO SERVICE
CENTERS**
Also Called: Westgate Tire & Auto Center
98 Westgate Dr Ste 2 (02301-1824)
PHONE..............................508 559-6802
Susan Clark, *Owner*
EMP: 7 **EST:** 1986
SQ FT: 7,500
SALES (est): 657.19K **Privately Held**
Web: www.westgatetire.com
SIC: 7539 7534   Automotive repair shops,
   nec; Tire repair shop

(G-7313)
**TRIPLE P PACKG & PPR PDTS
INC**
20 Burke Dr (02301-5505)
PHONE..............................508 588-0444
Richard M Shaughnessy, *Pr*

Gregory M O'connell, *VP*
EMP: 53 **EST:** 1963
SQ FT: 66,000
SALES (est): 8.11MM **Privately Held**
Web: www.tripleppackaging.com
SIC: 2653   Boxes, corrugated: made from
   purchased materials

(G-7314)
YSNC FUEL INC
64 N Montello St (02301-3915)
PHONE..............................508 436-2716
Yaniv Sostiel, *Prin*
EMP: 11 **EST:** 2009
SALES (est): 1.13MM **Privately Held**
SIC: 2869   Fuels

Brookfield
Worcester County

(G-7315)
ROBERTS WELDING INC
32 W Main St (01506-1513)
P.O. Box 281 (01506-0281)
PHONE..............................508 867-7640
Robert Pawlowski, *Pr*
Rosemarie Pawlowski, *VP*
EMP: 26 **EST:** 1975
SQ FT: 2,000
SALES (est): 957.17K **Privately Held**
SIC: 3444   Sheet metalwork

(G-7316)
**SPENCER METAL FINISHING
INC (HQ)**
55 Mill St (01506-1516)
PHONE..............................508 885-6477
EMP: 20 **EST:** 1967
SALES (est): 2.38MM **Privately Held**
SIC: 3479 3471   Coating of metals and
   formed products; Plating and polishing

Brookline
Norfolk County

(G-7317)
BRUMBERG PUBLICATIONS INC
124 Harvard St Ste 9 (02446-6439)
PHONE..............................617 734-1979
Bruce Brumberg, *Pr*
EMP: 10 **EST:** 1986
SQ FT: 800
SALES (est): 216.2K **Privately Held**
Web: www.brumbergpublications.com
SIC: 2741   Miscellaneous publishing

(G-7318)
**HERB CHAMBERS BROOKLINE
INC**
308 Boylston St (02445-7603)
PHONE..............................617 278-3920
Herbert G Chambers, *Pr*
EMP: 99 **EST:** 2014
SALES (est): 2.35MM
SALES (corp-wide): 313.81MM **Privately
Held**
Web: www.herbchambers.com
SIC: 3443   Chambers and caissons
PA: Herb Chambers I-93, Inc.
   259 Mcgrath Hwy
   Somerville MA 02143
   617 666-4100

(G-7319)
JUST PUBLICATIONS INC
Also Called: Just Rentals

8 Alton Pl Ste 2 (02446-6448)
PHONE..............................617 739-5878
Matthew Newman, *Pr*
EMP: 8 **EST:** 1987
SQ FT: 1,500
SALES (est): 928.4K **Privately Held**
Web: www.prudentialboston.com
SIC: 2721 6531   Magazines: publishing only,
   not printed on site; Real estate agents and
   managers

(G-7320)
MICHEAL JOHN
Also Called: My Kidz App
1842 Beacon St (02445-1930)
PHONE..............................857 239-0277
John Micheal, *Owner*
EMP: 30 **EST:** 2020
SALES (est): 1.41MM **Privately Held**
SIC: 3612   Distribution transformers, electric

(G-7321)
MYSTOCKPLANCOM INC
Also Called: Mystockoptions.com
124 Harvard St Ste 9 (02446-6439)
PHONE..............................617 734-1979
Bruce Brumberg, *Pr*
Karen Axelrod, *Project Assistant*
EMP: 10 **EST:** 2000
SALES (est): 996.43K **Privately Held**
Web: www.mystockoptions.com
SIC: 2741   Miscellaneous publishing

(G-7322)
ODWALLA INC
102 Longwood Ave (02446-6696)
PHONE..............................336 877-1634
John Sunderman, *Brnch Mgr*
EMP: 34
SALES (corp-wide): 43B **Publicly Held**
Web: www.odwalla.com
SIC: 2033   Fruit juices: packaged in cans,
   jars, etc.
HQ: Odwalla, Inc.
   1 Coca Cola Plz Nw
   Atlanta GA 30313
   479 721-6260

(G-7323)
OYO SPORTSTOYS INC
1309 Beacon St Ste 300 (02446-5252)
PHONE..............................978 264-2000
Thomas K Skripps, *Pr*
▲ **EMP:** 75 **EST:** 2013
SALES (est): 10.23MM **Privately Held**
SIC: 3942 3944   Dolls and stuffed toys;
   Games, toys, and children's vehicles

(G-7324)
PADAKSHEP
1530 Beacon St Apt 201 (02446-2624)
PHONE..............................801 652-5589
Arka Santra, *Ch Bd*
EMP: 7 **EST:** 2009
SALES (est): 102.65K **Privately Held**
Web: www.padakshep.org
SIC: 8699 7372   Charitable organization;
   Application computer software

(G-7325)
PLATINUM INVESTMENTS LTD
Also Called: Real Estate Investment and MGT
1357 Beacon St (02446-4909)
PHONE..............................617 731-2447
Tariq Sobhi, *Pr*
EMP: 13 **EST:** 2019
SALES (est): 979.67K **Privately Held**

SIC: **6799** 6531 6722 1389　Investors, nec; Real estate brokers and agents; Management investment, open-end; Construction, repair, and dismantling services

(G-7326)
RADIO ACT CORPORATION
101 Winthrop Rd　(02445-4589)
PHONE...............................617 731-6542
Arkady Pittel, *CEO*
EMP: **7 EST:** 2003
SALES (est): 399.8K **Privately Held**
SIC: **3674**　Radiation sensors

(G-7327)
YOWAY LLC
1376 Beacon St　(02446-2807)
PHONE...............................617 505-5158
EMP: 32
SALES (corp-wide): 449.9K **Privately Held**
Web: www.yowayworcester.com
SIC: **2026**　Yogurt
PA: Yoway Llc
　395 Park Ave Ste 2
　Worcester MA 01610
　508 459-0611

(G-7328)
ZENNA NOODLE BAR
1374 Beacon St　(02446-2807)
PHONE...............................781 883-8624
Tien Trong, *Prin*
EMP: **8 EST:** 2006
SALES (est): 564.21K **Privately Held**
SIC: **2098**　Noodles (e.g. egg, plain, and water), dry

Burlington
Middlesex County

(G-7329)
10BEAUTY INC ✪
10 Ray Ave　(01803-4721)
PHONE...............................215 356-8680
Alexander Shashou, *CEO*
EMP: **20 EST:** 2022
SALES (est): 1.13MM **Privately Held**
SIC: **3999**　Barber and beauty shop equipment

(G-7330)
ABBOTT
168 Middlesex Tpke　(01803-4403)
PHONE...............................978 387-5652
Elvin Rivera, *Prin*
EMP: **9 EST:** 2019
SALES (est): 826.95K **Privately Held**
Web: www.abbott.com
SIC: **2834**　Pharmaceutical preparations

(G-7331)
ACRONIS INC
1 Van De Graaff Dr Ste 301　(01803-5171)
PHONE...............................781 782-9100
Michael Inbar, *Brnch Mgr*
EMP: 26
Web: www.acronis.com
SIC: **7372**　Prepackaged software
HQ: Acronis, Inc.
　1 Van De Graaff Dr # 301
　Burlington MA 01803
　781 782-9000

(G-7332)
ADVANSTAR COMMUNICATIONS INC
70 Blanchard Rd Ste 301　(01803-5100)

PHONE...............................339 298-4200
Kathy Coffey, *Brnch Mgr*
EMP: 15
SALES (corp-wide): 2.72B **Privately Held**
Web: epay.advanstar.com
SIC: **2721**　Magazines: publishing only, not printed on site
HQ: Advanstar Communications Inc.
　2501 Colorado Ave Ste 280
　Santa Monica CA 90404
　310 857-7500

(G-7333)
AEROVIRONMENT INC
141 S Bedford St Ste 250　(01803-5291)
PHONE...............................805 520-8350
Tom Vaneck, *Brnch Mgr*
EMP: 20
SALES (corp-wide): 540.54MM **Publicly Held**
Web: www.avinc.com
SIC: **3721**　Aircraft
PA: Aerovironment, Inc.
　241 18th St S Ste 415
　Arlington VA 22202
　805 520-8350

(G-7334)
AQUILA TECHNOLOGY CORP
Also Called: Aquila Technology
20 Burlington Mall Rd Ste 230　(01803-4129)
PHONE...............................781 993-9004
Thomas Willson, *Pr*
EMP: **35 EST:** 1987
SQ FT: 1,200
SALES (est): 6.24MM **Privately Held**
Web: www.aquila.technology
SIC: **7371** 3679 7375 4899　Computer software development; Commutators, electronic; Information retrieval services; Data communication services
HQ: Psi Holding Group, Inc.
　4 Technology Dr
　Westborough MA 01581
　508 621-5100

(G-7335)
ARQULE INC (HQ)
Also Called: Arqule
1 Wall St Ste 603　(01803-4769)
PHONE...............................781 994-0300
Rita Karachun, *Pr*
Caroline Litchfield, *
Jon Filderman, *
▲ EMP: **36 EST:** 1993
SALES (est): 58.78MM
SALES (corp-wide): 59.28B **Publicly Held**
Web: www.arqule.com
SIC: **2834** 8731　Pharmaceutical preparations; Biotechnical research, commercial
PA: Merck & Co., Inc.
　126 E Lincoln Ave
　Rahway NJ 07065
　908 740-4000

(G-7336)
ATTUNITY INC (DH)
70 Blanchard Rd　(01803-5100)
PHONE...............................781 730-4070
Shimon Alon, *CEO*
Mark Logan, *
Dror Harel-elkayam, *CFO*
EMP: **25 EST:** 1985
SQ FT: 7,000
SALES (est): 42.73MM
SALES (corp-wide): 728.39MM **Privately Held**
Web: www.qlik.com

SIC: **7372**　Prepackaged software
HQ: Qlik Technologies Inc.
　211 S Gulph Rd Ste 500
　King Of Prussia PA 19406

(G-7337)
AVEDRO INC (HQ)
30 North Ave Ste 1　(01803-3327)
PHONE...............................781 768-3400
Reza Zadno, *Pr*
Robert J Palmisano, *
Thomas E Griffin, *CFO*
David First, *Chief Human Resources Officer*
Rajesh K Rajpal, *CMO*
▼ EMP: **122 EST:** 2002
SALES (est): 27.67MM
SALES (corp-wide): 282.86MM **Publicly Held**
Web: www.glaukos.com
SIC: **2834** 5048 3841　Pharmaceutical preparations; Ophthalmic goods; Ophthalmic instruments and apparatus
PA: Glaukos Corporation
　1 Glaukos Way
　Aliso Viejo CA 92656
　949 367-9600

(G-7338)
AVID TECHNOLOGY INC (PA)
75 Blue Sky Dr　(01803-2770)
PHONE...............................978 640-3000
Jeff Rosica, *Pr*
Kenneth L Gayron, *Corporate Treasurer*
Tom Cordiner, *CRO*
Kevin W Riley, *Sr VP*
Mariesa Victoria, *CAO*
▲ EMP: **950 EST:** 1987
SALES (est): 417.41MM
SALES (corp-wide): 417.41MM **Privately Held**
Web: www.avid.com
SIC: **3861** 7372　Editing equipment, motion picture: viewers, splicers, etc.; Prepackaged software

(G-7339)
AZENTA INC (PA)
200 Summit Dr Ste 600　(01803-5268)
PHONE...............................978 262-2400
Stephen S Schwartz, *Pr*
Herman Cueto, *Ex VP*
Olga Pirogova, *Chief Human Resource Officer*
Jason W Joseph, *Sr VP*
Violetta Hughes, *CAO PAO*
▲ EMP: **512 EST:** 1978
SQ FT: 298,000
SALES (est): 665.07MM **Publicly Held**
Web: www.azenta.com
SIC: **3559** 3563 3823 7699　Semiconductor manufacturing machinery; Vacuum pumps, except laboratory; Thermal conductivity instruments, industrial process type; Industrial equipment services

(G-7340)
BENU NETWORKS INC
154 Middlesex Tpke Ste 2　(01803-4469)
PHONE...............................978 223-4700
Ajay Manuja, *CEO*
EMP: **56 EST:** 2010
SALES (est): 10.14MM **Publicly Held**
Web: www.benunetworks.com
SIC: **4813** 3663　Internet connectivity services; Mobile communication equipment
PA: Ciena Corporation
　7035 Ridge Rd
　Hanover MD 21076

(G-7341)
BFLY OPERATIONS INC
1600 District Ave　(01803-5232)
PHONE...............................781 557-4800
EMP: 7
SALES (est): 73.45K **Privately Held**
SIC: **3841**　Diagnostic apparatus, medical

(G-7342)
CAMBRIDGE INTERVENTIONAL LLC
78 Cambridge St　(01803-4137)
PHONE...............................978 793-2674
Briana Morey, *null Elec*
EMP: **12 EST:** 2017
SALES (est): 998.87K **Privately Held**
Web: www.cambridgeinterventional.com
SIC: **3841**　Surgical and medical instruments

(G-7343)
CERENCE INC (PA)
Also Called: Cerence
1 Burlington Woods Dr Ste 301a　(01803-4503)
PHONE...............................857 362-7300
Stefan Ortmanns, *Pr*
Arun Sarin, *Ch Bd*
Thomas Beaudoin, *CFO*
Christophe Couvreur, *Sr VP*
EMP: **54 EST:** 2019
SALES (est): 294.48MM
SALES (corp-wide): 294.48MM **Publicly Held**
Web: www.cerence.com
SIC: **7372**　Application computer software

(G-7344)
CERENCE OPERATING COMPANY (HQ)
1 Burlington Woods Dr Ste 301a　(01803-4535)
PHONE...............................857 362-7300
Stefan Ortmanns, *CEO*
Thomas Beaudoin, *
EMP: **21 EST:** 2019
SALES (est): 23.74MM
SALES (corp-wide): 294.48MM **Publicly Held**
Web: www.cerence.com
SIC: **7372**　Prepackaged software
PA: Cerence Inc.
　1 Burlington Woods Dr # 301
　Burlington MA 01803
　857 362-7300

(G-7345)
CERTEON INC
5 Wall St Fl 5　(01803-4771)
PHONE...............................781 425-5099
Massood Zarrabian, *Ch Bd*
Jeffrey Black, *Treas*
EMP: **10 EST:** 2003
SQ FT: 10,000
SALES (est): 1.01MM **Privately Held**
Web: www.certeon.com
SIC: **7372**　Business oriented computer software

(G-7346)
CHEF SOFTWARE INC (HQ)
Also Called: Opscode
15 Wayside Rd Ste 400　(01803-4620)
PHONE...............................206 508-4799
EMP: **107 EST:** 2008
SALES (est): 24.36MM
SALES (corp-wide): 694.44MM **Publicly Held**
Web: www.chef.io

SIC: 7372 Business oriented computer software
PA: Progress Software Corporation
15 Wayside Rd Ste 4
Burlington MA 01803
781 280-4000

(G-7347)
CHERRYBROOK KITCHEN LLC
Also Called: Charles Rosenberg
20 Mall Rd Ste 410 (01803-4129)
P.O. Box 8301 (01614-8301)
PHONE..............................781 272-0400
Chip Rosenberg, *Managing Member*
EMP: 7 **EST:** 2003
SQ FT: 3,000
SALES (est): 804.57K **Privately Held**
Web: www.cherrybrookkitchen.com
SIC: 2099 Dessert mixes and fillings

(G-7348)
CIRCOR LLC
Also Called: Circor International
30 Corporate Dr Ste 200 (01803-4252)
PHONE..............................781 270-1200
Scott Buckhout, *Managing Member*
Alan Glass, *Managing Member*
Frederic Burditt, *Managing Member*
Richard Broughton, *Managing Member*
EMP: 49 **EST:** 1999
SALES (est): 11.02MM **Publicly Held**
Web: www.circor.com
SIC: 3492 5085 Control valves, fluid power: hydraulic and pneumatic; Valves and fittings
HQ: Circor International, Inc.
30 Corporate Dr Ste 200
Burlington MA 01803
781 270-1200

(G-7349)
CIRCOR ENERGY LLC
30 Corporate Dr Ste 200 (01803-4252)
PHONE..............................781 270-1200
EMP: 18
SALES (est): 4.05MM **Publicly Held**
Web: www.circor.com
SIC: 3491 Industrial valves
HQ: Circor International, Inc.
30 Corporate Dr Ste 200
Burlington MA 01803
781 270-1200

(G-7350)
CIRCOR GERMAN HOLDINGS LLC (DH)
30 Corporate Dr Ste 200 (01803-4252)
PHONE..............................781 270-1200
Erik Wiik, *Pr*
EMP: 93 **EST:** 2001
SALES (est): 141.51MM **Publicly Held**
Web: www.circor.com
SIC: 3491 Industrial valves
HQ: Circor International, Inc.
30 Corporate Dr Ste 200
Burlington MA 01803
781 270-1200

(G-7351)
CIRCOR INTERNATIONAL INC (HQ)
Also Called: Circor
30 Corporate Dr Ste 200 (01803-4252)
P.O. Box 146699 (02114-0019)
PHONE..............................781 270-1200
Tony Najjar, *Pr*
Helmuth Ludwig, *
Arjun Sharma, *CFO*
Jessica Wenzell, *CPO*
Amit Goel, *CAO*
EMP: 38 **EST:** 1999

SALES (est): 786.92MM **Publicly Held**
Web: www.circor.com
SIC: 3491 Industrial valves
PA: Kkr & Co. Inc.
30 Hudson Yards
New York NY 10001

(G-7352)
CLINICAL INSTRUMENTS INTL
63 2nd Ave (01803-4413)
PHONE..............................781 221-2266
Jerome Priest, *Pr*
Rudra Tamm, *Treas*
EMP: 11 **EST:** 1989
SQ FT: 3,000
SALES (est): 221.84K **Privately Held**
SIC: 3841 Catheters

(G-7353)
COLOR KINETICS
1 Van De Graaff Dr (01803-5176)
PHONE..............................617 423-9999
EMP: 77 **EST:** 2019
SALES (est): 979.79K **Privately Held**
Web: www.colorkinetics.com
SIC: 3648 3645 Lighting equipment, nec; Residential lighting fixtures

(G-7354)
COMPREHENSIVE IDENTIFICATION PRODUCTS INC
209 Middlesex Tpke (01803-3325)
P.O. Box 571 (53201-0571)
PHONE..............................781 229-8780
TOLL FREE: 800
▲ **EMP:** 110
SIC: 5043 3861 3089 3496 Photographic equipment and supplies; Cameras and related equipment; Identification cards, plastics; Miscellaneous fabricated wire products

(G-7355)
COMPUTER IMPRNTBLE LBEL SYSTEM
Also Called: Manufacturing
1500 District Ave (01803-5069)
PHONE..............................877 512-8763
Graham Tunks, *Mgr*
Matt Parker, *Acctg Mgr*
EMP: 10 **EST:** 1997
SALES (est): 1.29MM **Privately Held**
Web: www.cils-international.com
SIC: 2759 Labels and seals: printing, nsk

(G-7356)
CSR TECHNOLOGY INC
1 Wall St (01803-4769)
PHONE..............................781 791-6000
EMP: 24
SALES (corp-wide): 6.77MM **Privately Held**
SIC: 3679 Electronic loads and power supplies
HQ: Csr Technology Inc.
1060 Rincon Cir
San Jose CA 95131

(G-7357)
CURIA GLOBAL INC
20 Blanchard Rd (01803-6809)
PHONE..............................781 205-1691
EMP: 7
SALES (corp-wide): 927.92MM **Privately Held**
Web: www.curiaglobal.com
SIC: 2836 8731 Biological products, except diagnostic; Biotechnical research, commercial

HQ: Curia Global, Inc.
26 Corporate Cir
Albany NY 12203

(G-7358)
CURIA MASSACHUSETTS INC (DH)
Also Called: Amri Global
99 S Bedford St (01803-5179)
PHONE..............................781 270-7900
Thomas E D'ambra, *CEO*
William Marth, *
Bruce J Sargent Ph.d., *Sr VP*
Michael M Nolan, *
Brian D Russell, *
EMP: 29 **EST:** 1999
SALES (est): 24.2MM
SALES (corp-wide): 927.92MM **Privately Held**
Web: www.curiaglobal.com
SIC: 2834 Pharmaceutical preparations
HQ: Curia Global, Inc.
26 Corporate Cir
Albany NY 12203

(G-7359)
CUSTOMERGAUGE USA LLC
3 Burlington Woods Dr Ste 302 (01803-4532)
PHONE..............................844 211-3932
EMP: 7 **EST:** 2013
SALES (est): 1.39MM **Privately Held**
Web: www.customergauge.com
SIC: 7372 Business oriented computer software
HQ: Directness B.V.
Lauriergracht 91
Amsterdam NH
629436360

(G-7360)
DEMANDWARE LLC (HQ)
5 Wall St Fl 2 (01803-4774)
PHONE..............................888 553-9216
Thomas D Ebling, *Pr*
Jeffrey Barnett, *
Timothy M Adams, *
Wayne R Whitcomb, *
Nick Camelio, *Chief Talent Officer*
EMP: 54 **EST:** 2004
SQ FT: 116,650
SALES (est): 175.24MM
SALES (corp-wide): 31.35B **Publicly Held**
Web: www.salesforce.com
SIC: 7371 7372 Computer software systems analysis and design, custom; Prepackaged software
PA: Salesforce, Inc.
415 Mission St Fl 3
San Francisco CA 94105
415 901-7000

(G-7361)
DESKTOP METAL INC (PA)
63 3rd Ave (01803-4430)
PHONE..............................978 224-1244
Ric Fulop, *Ch Bd*
Jason Cole, *CFO*
Thomas Nogueira, *COO*
EMP: 220 **EST:** 2015
SQ FT: 110,000
SALES (est): 209.02MM
SALES (corp-wide): 209.02MM **Publicly Held**
Web: www.desktopmetal.com
SIC: 3313 Alloys, additive, except copper: not made in blast furnaces

(G-7362)
DESKTOP METAL OPERATING INC (HQ)
63 3rd Ave (01803-4430)
PHONE..............................978 224-1244
Ric Fulop, *CEO*
Jonah Myerberg, *
Rick Chin, *
EMP: 141 **EST:** 2015
SQ FT: 10,000
SALES (est): 41.2MM
SALES (corp-wide): 209.02MM **Publicly Held**
Web: www.desktopmetal.com
SIC: 3541 Machine tools, metal cutting type
PA: Desktop Metal, Inc.
63 3rd Ave
Burlington MA 01803
978 224-1244

(G-7363)
DIGITAL IMMUNITY LLC
Also Called: Digital Immunity
60 Mall Rd Ste 309 (01803-4549)
PHONE..............................508 630-0321
John Murgo, *CEO*
EMP: 8
SALES (est): 888.19K **Privately Held**
Web: www.digitalimmunity.com
SIC: 7372 Business oriented computer software

(G-7364)
DIMENSIONAL INSIGHT INC (PA)
60 Mall Rd Ste 210 (01803-4548)
PHONE..............................781 229-9111
Frederick A Powers, *Pr*
Stan Zanarotti, *
EMP: 40 **EST:** 1989
SQ FT: 7,500
SALES (est): 16.44MM **Privately Held**
Web: www.dimins.com
SIC: 7372 Prepackaged software

(G-7365)
DOUBLE-TAKE SOFTWARE INC (DH)
Also Called: Double-Take
1700 District Ave Ste 300 (01803-5231)
PHONE..............................949 253-6500
EMP: 157 **EST:** 1991
SALES (est): 88.5MM
SALES (corp-wide): 832.31MM **Privately Held**
Web: www.carbonite.com
SIC: 7372 7373 5045 7371 Prepackaged software; Computer-aided system services; Computer software; Custom computer programming services
HQ: Carbonite, Inc.
8470 Allison Pointe Blvd # 300
Indianapolis IN 46250
617 587-1100

(G-7366)
DYNAMICOPS INC
1 Wall St Ste 201 (01803-4773)
PHONE..............................781 221-2136
Pei Ma, *Pr*
EMP: 23 **EST:** 2012
SALES (est): 693.85K **Privately Held**
Web: www.vmware.com
SIC: 7372 Business oriented computer software

(G-7367)
ECONIQ
101 Cambridge St Ste 385 (01803-3767)
PHONE..............................781 588-2223

EMP: 7 **EST:** 2018
SALES (est): 235.35K **Privately Held**
Web: www.themeetingshub.com
SIC: 7372 Prepackaged software

(G-7368)
EMD SERONO INC
Also Called: EMD Pharmaceuticals
400 Summit Dr Fl 4 (01803-5258)
PHONE..............................978 715-1804
EMP: 16
SALES (corp-wide): 23.09B **Privately Held**
Web: us.fertility.com
SIC: 2834 Pharmaceutical preparations
HQ: Emd Serono, Inc.
1 Technology Pl
Rockland MA 02370
781 982-9000

(G-7369)
ENDURANCE INTL GROUP-WEST INC
10 Corporate Dr Ste 300 (01803-4200)
PHONE..............................781 852-3200
EMP: 225 **EST:** 2004
SALES (est): 3.86MM **Privately Held**
SIC: 7372 Prepackaged software
HQ: Newfold Digital Holdings Group, Inc.
10 Corporate Dr Ste 300
Burlington MA 01803
781 852-3200

(G-7370)
ENDURE DGTAL INTRMDATE HLDNGS
10 Corp Dr Ste 300 (01803)
PHONE..............................781 852-3200
Behdad Eghbali, *Pr*
EMP: 3762 **EST:** 2020
SALES (est): 49.88MM **Privately Held**
SIC: 7372 Prepackaged software

(G-7371)
EXA CORPORATION (DH)
55 Network Dr (01803-2765)
PHONE..............................781 564-0200
Stephen A Remondi, *Pr*
John J Shields Iii, *Non-Executive Chairman of the Board*
Richard F Gilbody, *CFO*
Hudong Chen, *CSO*
Joel F Dube, *CAO*
EMP: 24 **EST:** 1991
SQ FT: 44,000
SALES (est): 104.57MM **Privately Held**
SIC: 7372 7373 Prepackaged software;
Computer-aided engineering (CAE)
systems service
HQ: Dassault Systemes Simulia Corp.
1301 Atwood Ave Ste 101w
Johnston RI 02919
401 531-5000

(G-7372)
EXATEL VISUAL SYSTEMS INC
111 S Bedford St Ste 201 (01803-5145)
PHONE..............................781 221-7400
Eli Warsawski, *Pr*
EMP: 8 **EST:** 1999
SALES (est): 203.76K **Privately Held**
SIC: 3699 Electrical equipment and
supplies, nec

(G-7373)
FINASTRA USA CORPORATION
55 Network Dr (01803-2765)
PHONE..............................781 203-9200
EMP: 83
SALES (corp-wide): 1.65B **Privately Held**

SIC: 7372 Prepackaged software
HQ: Finastra Usa Corporation
555 Sw Morrison St # 300
Portland OR 97204
407 804-6600

(G-7374)
FLEXION THRPTICS SCRITIES CORP
10 Mall Rd Ste 301 (01803-4131)
PHONE..............................781 305-7777
Michael D Clayman, *Prin*
EMP: 154 **EST:** 2015
SALES (est): 3.01MM **Publicly Held**
Web: www.pacira.com
SIC: 2834 Pharmaceutical preparations
HQ: Pacira Therapeutics, Inc.
5 Sylvan Way
Parsippany NJ 07054

(G-7375)
GALAXIE LABS INC
18 A St (01803-3418)
PHONE..............................781 272-3750
Peter Tocci, *Pr*
Kristine Tocci, *VP*
EMP: 7 **EST:** 1962
SQ FT: 13,000
SALES (est): 990.98K **Privately Held**
Web: www.galaxielabs.com
SIC: 3599 Machine shop, jobbing and repair

(G-7376)
HEALTHEDGE SOFTWARE INC (HQ)
Also Called: Healthedge
30 Corporate Dr Ste 150 (01803-4257)
PHONE..............................781 285-1300
Rob Gillette, *Pr*
Matt Mclaughlin, *CFO*
Matt Kuntz, *
Dan Welch, *
Ray Desrochers, *
EMP: 77 **EST:** 2004
SALES (est): 1.09B
SALES (corp-wide): 8.52B **Publicly Held**
Web: www.healthedge.com
SIC: 7372 Application computer software
PA: Blackstone Inc.
345 Park Ave
New York NY 10154
212 583-5000

(G-7377)
I ROBOT CORP - CLOSED
63 South Ave (01803-4946)
PHONE..............................781 345-0200
EMP: 11 **EST:** 2018
SALES (est): 2.37MM **Privately Held**
SIC: 3589 Service industry machinery, nec

(G-7378)
I-OPTICS CORP
Also Called: I-Optics
1 Wall St Fl 6 (01803-4769)
PHONE..............................508 366-1600
Jeroen Cammeraat, *CEO*
Erik Valks, *Ex VP*
Stephen Morris, *VP*
Joris Vogels, *VP*
Thomas Van Elzakker, *COO*
EMP: 8 **EST:** 2012
SALES (est): 374.6K **Privately Held**
SIC: 3827 Optical instruments and lenses

(G-7379)
INFOGIX INC (HQ)
Also Called: Infogix
1700 District Ave Ste 300 (01803-5231)

PHONE..............................630 505-1800
Early Stephens, *CEO*
Sumit Nijhawan, *
John Mcdonell, *CFO*
Paul Skordilis, *Marketing Business Development*
Angsuman Dutta, *OF CUSTOMER Development*
EMP: 155 **EST:** 1982
SALES (est): 50.36MM
SALES (corp-wide): 446.91MM **Privately Held**
Web: www.precisely.com
SIC: 7372 8742 Business oriented computer software; Management consulting services
PA: Precisely Software Incorporated
1700 District Ave Ste 300
Burlington MA 01803
978 436-8900

(G-7380)
INTEGRA LFSCNCES HOLDINGS CORP
207d Cambridge St (01803-2538)
PHONE..............................800 466-6814
EMP: 8
Web: www.acell.com
SIC: 3841 Surgical and medical instruments
PA: Integra Lifesciences Holdings Corporation
1100 Campus Rd
Princeton NJ 08540

(G-7381)
ISUBSCRIBED INC
15 Network Dr 3rd Fl (01803-2766)
PHONE..............................617 750-4975
Hari Ravichandran, *Ex Dir*
Trevor Oelschig, *Dir*
Blake Cunneen, *Dir*
Albert Sokol, *Dir*
Ryan Toohil, *COO*
EMP: 20 **EST:** 2017
SALES (est): 1.04MM **Privately Held**
Web: www.aura.com
SIC: 7372 Prepackaged software

(G-7382)
JONES & BARTLETT LEARNING LLC (PA)
25 Mall Rd (01803-4134)
P.O. Box 417289 (02241-7289)
PHONE..............................978 443-5000
Gregory Sabasky, *CEO*
▲ **EMP:** 150 **EST:** 2007
SALES (est): 49.98MM
SALES (corp-wide): 49.98MM **Privately Held**
Web: www.jblearning.com
SIC: 2741 Miscellaneous publishing

(G-7383)
KASALIS INC
11 North Ave (01803-3305)
PHONE..............................781 273-6200
Justin Roe, *Pr*
Aaron Israelski, *
Mark Kozak, *
Richard By, *
EMP: 27 **EST:** 2011
SALES (est): 8.71MM
SALES (corp-wide): 34.7B **Publicly Held**
Web: www.kasalis.com
SIC: 3861 Photographic equipment and supplies
PA: Jabil Inc.
10800 Roosevelt Blvd N
Saint Petersburg FL 33716
727 577-9749

(G-7384)
KEURIG DR PEPPER INC (PA)
Also Called: Keurig Dr Pepper
53 South Ave (01803-4903)
PHONE..............................781 418-7000
Robert J Gamgort, *Ex Ch Bd*
Robert J Gamgort, *Ex Ch Bd*
Sudhanshu Priyadarshi, *INTL*
Anthony Shoemaker, *CLO*
Justin Whitmore, *CSO*
◆ **EMP:** 100 **EST:** 1981
SALES (est): 14.06B **Publicly Held**
Web: www.keurigdrpepper.com
SIC: 2086 2087 Bottled and canned soft drinks; Beverage bases, concentrates, syrups, powders and mixes

(G-7385)
KEURIG GREEN MOUNTAIN INC
Also Called: Green Mountain Coffee Roasters
53 South Ave (01803-4903)
PHONE..............................781 246-3466
EMP: 57
Web: www.keurig.com
SIC: 2086 Carbonated beverages, nonalcoholic: pkged. in cans, bottles
HQ: Keurig Green Mountain, Inc.
1 Rotarian Pl
Waterbury VT 05676
877 879-2326

(G-7386)
KEYSTONE DENTAL INC (PA)
154 Middlesex Tpke Ste 2 (01803-4469)
PHONE..............................781 328-3300
Rolf Nilsson, *Pr*
Michael Nealon, *
Michael Gibbs, *
Sean Carney, *
EMP: 71 **EST:** 2006
SALES (est): 39.4MM **Privately Held**
Web: www.keystonedental.com
SIC: 3843 Enamels, dentists'

(G-7387)
KOGNITO SOLUTIONS LLC
Also Called: Kognito
25 Mall Rd Ste 600 (01803-4134)
PHONE..............................212 675-2651
EMP: 20 **EST:** 2003
SALES (est): 2.14MM **Privately Held**
Web: www.kognito.com
SIC: 7371 7372 8742 Computer software systems analysis and design, custom; Application computer software; Management consulting services

(G-7388)
KOHLER SGNTURE STR BY SUP NENG
19 3rd Ave (01803-4427)
PHONE..............................781 365-0168
EMP: 9 **EST:** 2017
SALES (est): 707K **Privately Held**
Web: www.kohler.com
SIC: 3431 Metal sanitary ware

(G-7389)
LEMAITRE VASCULAR INC (PA)
Also Called: LEMAITRE
63 2nd Ave (01803-4413)
PHONE..............................781 221-2266
George W Lemaitre, *Ch Bd*
David B Roberts, *
Joseph P Pellegrino Junior, *CFO*
Trent G Kamke, *VP Opers*
Laurie A Churchill, *Sr VP*
EMP: 43 **EST:** 1983
SQ FT: 27,098
SALES (est): 161.65MM

SALES (corp-wide): 161.65MM **Publicly Held**
Web: www.lemaitre.com
SIC: 3841 5047   Surgical and medical instruments; Instruments, surgical and medical

(G-7390)
LOADSPRING SOLUTIONS INC (PA)
1500 District Ave Pmb 1060 (01803)
PHONE..............................978 685-9715
Russ Blattner, *Ch Bd*
Eric Leighton, *Pr*
Al Marshall, *Ex VP*
Cameron Vixie, *VP*
Michael Foresteire, *Sec*
EMP: 17 **EST:** 1999
SQ FT: 7,219
SALES (est): 27.37MM
SALES (corp-wide): 27.37MM **Privately Held**
Web: www.loadspring.com
SIC: 7372   Prepackaged software

(G-7391)
MAGNITUDE SOFTWARE INC
2400 District Ave Ste 320 (01803-5210)
PHONE..............................781 202-3200
EMP: 21
SALES (corp-wide): 51.78MM **Privately Held**
Web: www.insightsoftware.com
SIC: 7372   Prepackaged software
HQ: Magnitude Software, Inc.
    8904 Westminster Glen Ave
    Austin TX 78730
    866 466-3849

(G-7392)
MEMENTO INC
55 Network Dr (01803-2765)
PHONE..............................781 221-3030
John E Omalley, *CEO*
James Glover, *VP*
Maria Loughlin, *VP*
Paul Whitelam, *VP*
Mike Braatz, *VP*
▼ **EMP:** 40 **EST:** 2002
SQ FT: 18,000
SALES (est): 1.78MM **Privately Held**
Web: www.fisglobal.com
SIC: 7372   Business oriented computer software

(G-7393)
META SOFTWARE CORPORATION (PA)
15 New England Executive Park (01803-5202)
PHONE..............................781 238-0293
Robert Shapiro, *Ch*
Robert Seltzer, *Pr*
EMP: 10 **EST:** 1985
SQ FT: 10,656
SALES (est): 2.07MM
SALES (corp-wide): 2.07MM **Privately Held**
Web: www.metasoftware.com
SIC: 7372 7371   Prepackaged software; Computer software development

(G-7394)
MINUTEMAN PRESS
Also Called: Minuteman Press
169 Bedford St Ste 4 (01803-2700)
PHONE..............................781 273-1155
EMP: 7 **EST:** 2018
SALES (est): 92.3K **Privately Held**
Web: www.minuteman.com

SIC: 2752   Commercial printing, lithographic

(G-7395)
N-ABLE TECHNOLOGIES INC ✪
30 Corporate Dr Ste 400 (01803-4252)
PHONE..............................855 679-0817
EMP: 1580 **EST:** 2022
SALES (est): 55.88MM **Privately Held**
Web: www.n-able.com
SIC: 7372   Prepackaged software

(G-7396)
NEDAP INC
Also Called: Nedap Retail North America
25 Corporate Dr Ste 101 (01803-4238)
PHONE..............................844 876-3327
Kay Derksen, *Pr*
Martin Bomers, *Pr*
EMP: 14 **EST:** 2013
SALES (est): 5.18MM
SALES (corp-wide): 234.29MM **Privately Held**
Web: www.nedap.com
SIC: 3648 1731 5083   Lighting equipment, nec; Access control systems specialization; Livestock equipment
PA: Nedap N.V.
    Parallelweg 2
    Groenlo GE 7141
    544471111

(G-7397)
NETBRAIN TECHNOLOGIES INC (PA)
15 Network Dr Ste 2 (01803-2766)
PHONE..............................781 221-7199
Lingping Gao, *CEO*
Jeffery Basile, *CFO*
Steven Bachert, *CRO*
EMP: 160 **EST:** 2004
SQ FT: 13,864
SALES (est): 53.77MM **Privately Held**
Web: www.netbraintech.com
SIC: 7372   Application computer software

(G-7398)
NETZSCH INSTRUMENTS N AMER LLC (DH)
Also Called: Netzsch
129 Middlesex Tpke (01803-4404)
PHONE..............................781 272-5353
Marc-antoine Thermitus, *Managing Member*
Doctor Juergen Blumm, *Managing Member*
EMP: 22 **EST:** 2001
SQ FT: 15,000
SALES (est): 13.97MM
SALES (corp-wide): 770.45MM **Privately Held**
Web: www.netzsch.com
SIC: 3823 8734   Thermal conductivity instruments, industrial process type; Testing laboratories
HQ: Netzsch - Geratebau Gesellschaft Mit Beschrankter Haftung
    Wittelsbacherstr. 42
    Selb BY
    92878810

(G-7399)
NEWFOLD DGTAL HLDNGS GROUP INC (HQ)
Also Called: Endurance
10 Corporate Dr Ste 300 (01803-4200)
PHONE..............................781 852-3200
Sharon Rowlands, *CEO*
EMP: 125 **EST:** 1997
SQ FT: 115,000
SALES (est): 1.18B **Privately Held**
Web: www.newfold.com

SIC: 7372   Prepackaged software
PA: Clearlake Capital Group, L.P.
    233 Wilshire Blvd Ste 800
    Santa Monica CA 90401

(G-7400)
NGAC LLC
Also Called: Nextgen Adhesive
25 B St (01803-3401)
P.O. Box 535 (02420-0005)
PHONE..............................781 258-0008
EMP: 20 **EST:** 2007
SALES (est): 2.28MM **Privately Held**
Web: www.nextgenadhesives.com
SIC: 2891   Adhesives and sealants

(G-7401)
NUANCE COMMUNICATIONS INC (HQ)
Also Called: Nuance
1 Wayside Rd (01803-4609)
PHONE..............................781 565-5000
Mark D Benjamin, *CEO*
Daniel Tempesta, *
Joseph Petro, *
Wendy Cassity, *CLO**
Robert Dahdah, *CRO**
▲ **EMP:** 700 **EST:** 1995
SALES (est): 1.75B
SALES (corp-wide): 211.91B **Publicly Held**
Web: www.nuance.com
SIC: 7372   Prepackaged software
PA: Microsoft Corporation
    1 Microsoft Way
    Redmond WA 98052
    425 882-8080

(G-7402)
NUANCE HLTHCARE DGNSTICS SLTON
1 Wayside Rd (01803-4609)
PHONE..............................404 575-4222
Willie Tillery, *CEO*
Chad Terry, *CFO*
Arman Sharafshahi, *Sec*
Scott Sobera, *Ex VP*
EMP: 23 **EST:** 2000
SALES (est): 2.16MM
SALES (corp-wide): 211.91B **Publicly Held**
SIC: 7372   Prepackaged software
HQ: Nuance Communications, Inc.
    1 Wayside Rd
    Burlington MA 01803

(G-7403)
OFFICEWORKS INC (PA)
149 Middlesex Tpke (01803-4400)
PHONE..............................781 270-9000
Mark Loughlin, *Pr*
David Quinn, *VP*
Felicia Miano-poles, *VP*
EMP: 17 **EST:** 1995
SALES (est): 21.45MM
SALES (corp-wide): 21.45MM **Privately Held**
Web: www.officeworksinc.com
SIC: 5712 2522 2521   Office furniture; Office furniture, except wood; Wood office furniture

(G-7404)
ORACLE AMERICA INC
4 Van De Graaff Dr Ste 1 (01803-5158)
PHONE..............................650 506-7000
EMP: 51
SALES (corp-wide): 49.95B **Publicly Held**
Web: www.oracle.com
SIC: 7372   Prepackaged software
HQ: Oracle America, Inc.
    500 Oracle Pkwy

Redwood City CA 94065
650 506-7000

(G-7405)
ORACLE AMERICA INC
95 Network Dr (01803-2770)
PHONE..............................281 710-2881
EMP: 9
SALES (corp-wide): 49.95B **Publicly Held**
Web: www.oracle.com
SIC: 3571   Minicomputers
HQ: Oracle America, Inc.
    500 Oracle Pkwy
    Redwood City CA 94065
    650 506-7000

(G-7406)
ORACLE CORPORATION
Also Called: Oracle
10 Van De Graaff Dr Ste 1 (01803-6816)
PHONE..............................678 815-6637
EMP: 51
SALES (corp-wide): 49.95B **Publicly Held**
Web: www.oracle.com
SIC: 3571   Minicomputers
PA: Oracle Corporation
    2300 Oracle Way
    Austin TX 78741
    737 867-1000

(G-7407)
ORACLE CORPORATION
Also Called: Oracle
6 Van De Graaff Dr (01803-6811)
PHONE..............................650 506-7000
EMP: 7
SALES (corp-wide): 49.95B **Publicly Held**
Web: www.oracle.com
SIC: 7372   Prepackaged software
PA: Oracle Corporation
    2300 Oracle Way
    Austin TX 78741
    737 867-1000

(G-7408)
PALOMAR MEDICAL PRODUCTS LLC
15 Network Dr (01803-2766)
PHONE..............................781 993-2300
Joseph Caruso, *Pr*
Paul Weiner, *
Patricia Davis, *
EMP: 44 **EST:** 1997
SQ FT: 25,000
SALES (est): 983.59K
SALES (corp-wide): 287.73MM **Privately Held**
SIC: 3842 3845   Surgical appliances and supplies; Laser systems and equipment, medical
HQ: Palomar Medical Technologies, Llc
    15 Network Dr
    Burlington MA 01803
    781 993-2330

(G-7409)
PALOMAR MEDICAL TECH LLC (DH)
15 Network Dr (01803-2766)
PHONE..............................781 993-2330
Michael Davin, *CEO*
Joseph Caruso, *Pr*
Timothy Baker, *Ex VP*
▲ **EMP:** 204 **EST:** 2013
SALES (est): 41.42MM
SALES (corp-wide): 287.73MM **Privately Held**
SIC: 3841 3845   Surgical lasers; Laser systems and equipment, medical
HQ: Cynosure, Llc
    5 Carlisle Rd

Westford MA 01886

(G-7410)
PERCUSSION SOFTWARE INC
Also Called: Percussion
100 Summit Dr Ste 100 (01803-5197)
P.O. Box 767 (01803-5767)
PHONE..............................781 438-9900
EMP: 10 **EST:** 1994
SALES (est): 2.45MM **Privately Held**
Web: www.percussion.com
SIC: 7372 Prepackaged software

(G-7411)
PHILIPS COLORKINETICS
3 Burlington Woods Dr (01803-4532)
PHONE..............................323 251-4758
EMP: 8 **EST:** 2019
SALES (est): 776.1K **Privately Held**
Web: www.colorkinetics.com
SIC: 3646 Commercial lighting fixtures

(G-7412)
POLY6 TECHNOLOGIES INC
Also Called: Poly6
164 Middlesex Tpke Ste 1 (01803-4420)
PHONE..............................339 234-9300
James V Stewart, *CEO*
EMP: 15 **EST:** 2015
SALES (est): 2.66MM
SALES (corp-wide): 2.07B **Privately Held**
Web: www.poly6.com
SIC: 3089 Automotive parts, plastic
PA: Consolidated Precision Products Corp.
　1621 Euclid Ave Ste 1850
　Cleveland OH 44115
　216 453-4800

(G-7413)
PROGRESS SOFTWARE CORPORATION (PA)
Also Called: Progress
15 Wayside Rd Ste 4 (01803-4521)
P.O. Box 845828 (02284-5828)
PHONE..............................781 280-4000
Yogesh K Gupta, *Pr*
John R Egan, *Non-Executive Chairman of the Board*
Anthony Folger, *Ex VP*
Yufan Stephanie Wang, *CLO*
Domenic Lococo, *CAO*
EMP: 241 **EST:** 1981
SQ FT: 33,000
SALES (est): 694.44MM
SALES (corp-wide): 694.44MM **Publicly Held**
Web: www.progress.com
SIC: 7372 7371 Prepackaged software;
　Custom computer programming services

(G-7414)
PROTAGENE US INC
Also Called: Accelerating Biologics
4 Burlington Woods Dr (01803-4511)
PHONE..............................857 829-3200
Kirtland Poss, *CEO*
John Ziolkowski, *
EMP: 25 **EST:** 2013
SALES (est): 5.26MM **Privately Held**
Web: www.protagene.com
SIC: 2836 Biological products, except
　diagnostic

(G-7415)
PUBLISHING SOLUTIONS GROUP
15 Wall St (01803-4781)
PHONE..............................781 552-5568
Lori Becker, *Pr*

EMP: 18 **EST:** 2017
SALES (est): 850.93K **Privately Held**
Web:
www.publishingsolutionsgroup.com
SIC: 2741 Miscellaneous publishing

(G-7416)
QSA GLOBAL INC (HQ)
40 North Ave Ste 2 (01803-3391)
PHONE..............................781 272-2000
Larry Swift, *Pr*
Ted Panagiotopoulos, *
Andrew Stark, *
Maria Green, *
◆ **EMP:** 70 **EST:** 1994
SQ FT: 40,000
SALES (est): 22.66MM
SALES (corp-wide): 15.93B **Publicly Held**
Web: www.qsa-global.com
SIC: 3844 2835 2819 Radiographic X-ray
　apparatus and tubes; Radioactive
　diagnostic substances; Industrial inorganic
　chemicals, nec
PA: Illinois Tool Works Inc.
　155 Harlem Ave
　Glenview IL 60025
　847 724-7500

(G-7417)
QUADRAMED QUANTIM CORPORATION
1 Wayside Rd (01803-4609)
PHONE..............................781 565-5000
EMP: 18 **EST:** 2011
SALES (est): 3.2MM
SALES (corp-wide): 211.91B **Publicly Held**
SIC: 7372 Prepackaged software
HQ: Nuance Communications, Inc.
　1 Wayside Rd
　Burlington MA 01803

(G-7418)
QUALCOMM TECHNOLOGIES INC
1 Wall St (01803-4769)
PHONE..............................781 791-6000
EMP: 19
SALES (corp-wide): 35.82B **Publicly Held**
Web: www.qualcomm.com
SIC: 3674 7372 6794 Integrated circuits,
　semiconductor networks, etc.; Business
　oriented computer software; Patent buying,
　licensing, leasing
HQ: Qualcomm Technologies, Inc.
　5775 Morehouse Dr
　San Diego CA 92121
　858 587-1121

(G-7419)
RACHAD FUEL INC
161 Bedford St (01803-2737)
PHONE..............................781 273-0292
Nizar Abdallah, *Pr*
EMP: 15 **EST:** 2011
SALES (est): 2.07MM **Privately Held**
SIC: 2869 Fuels

(G-7420)
SAFC BIOSCIENCES INC
400 Summit Dr (01803-5258)
PHONE..............................978 715-1700
EMP: 10 **EST:** 2004
SALES (est): 231.37K **Privately Held**
SIC: 2836 Biological products, except
　diagnostic

(G-7421)
SANTHERA PHARMACEUTICALS USA
25 Corporate Dr (01803-4240)
PHONE..............................781 552-5145
EMP: 7 **EST:** 2017
SALES (est): 1.02MM **Privately Held**
Web: www.santhera.com
SIC: 2834 Pharmaceutical preparations

(G-7422)
SAREPTA THERAPEUTICS
55 Network Dr (01803-2765)
PHONE..............................781 221-7805
EMP: 14 **EST:** 2019
SALES (est): 4.41MM **Privately Held**
Web: www.sarepta.com
SIC: 2834 Pharmaceutical preparations

(G-7423)
SCAN SOFT INC
1 Wayside Rd (01803-4609)
PHONE..............................781 565-5000
John Freker, *Prin*
EMP: 53 **EST:** 2016
SALES (est): 1.01MM **Privately Held**
Web: www.nuance.com
SIC: 7372 Prepackaged software

(G-7424)
SCIENCEOPEN INC
155 Middlesex Tpke Ste 4 (01803-4412)
PHONE..............................781 222-5200
EMP: 7 **EST:** 2017
SALES (est): 84.69K **Privately Held**
Web: www.scienceopen.com
SIC: 2731 Book publishing

(G-7425)
SCPHARMACEUTICALS INC
Also Called: SCPHARMACEUTICALS
25 Mall Rd Ste 203 (01803-4150)
PHONE..............................617 517-0730
John H Tucker, *Pr*
Jack A Khattar, *Ch Bd*
Rachael Nokes, *CFO*
EMP: 23 **EST:** 2013
SQ FT: 13,066
Web: www.scpharmaceuticals.com
SIC: 2834 Pharmaceutical preparations

(G-7426)
SEKISUI DIAGNOSTICS LLC (DH)
1 Wall St Ste 301 (01803-4775)
PHONE..............................781 652-7800
▲ **EMP:** 82 **EST:** 2008
SALES (est): 138.75MM **Privately Held**
Web: www.sekisuidiagnostics.com
SIC: 3841 Diagnostic apparatus, medical
HQ: Sekisui America Corporation
　300 Lighting Way Ste 320
　Secaucus NJ 07094
　201 423-7960

(G-7427)
SIGMA-ALDRICH CORPORATION
400 Summit Dr (01803-5258)
PHONE..............................978 715-1804
Chris Platts, *Brnch Mgr*
EMP: 68
SALES (corp-wide): 23.09B **Privately Held**
Web: www.sigmaaldrich.com
SIC: 2899 Chemical preparations, nec
HQ: Sigma-Aldrich Corporation
　3050 Spruce St
　Saint Louis MO 63103
　314 771-5765

(G-7428)
SIGNIFY NORTH AMERICA CORP
Also Called: Lightolier
300 Burlington Woods Dr Fl 4 (01803)
PHONE..............................508 679-8131
Mary Donelan, *Brnch Mgr*
EMP: 286
Web: www.signify.com
SIC: 3646 Commercial lighting fixtures
HQ: Signify North America Corporation
　400 Crossing Blvd Ste 600
　Bridgewater NJ 08807
　732 563-3000

(G-7429)
SIMILARWEB INC
800 District Ave Ste 120 (01803-5003)
PHONE..............................800 540-1086
Donna Dror, *Brnch Mgr*
EMP: 12
Web: www.similarweb.com
SIC: 7372 Prepackaged software
HQ: Similarweb, Inc.
　16 E 34th St Fl 15
　New York NY 10016
　347 685-5422

(G-7430)
SOAPSTONE NETWORKS INC
15 New England Executive Park
(01803-5202)
PHONE..............................617 719-3897
William J Leighton Ph.d., *Pr*
Richard T Liebhaber, *Ch Bd*
William J Stuart, *VP Fin*
Esmeralda S Swartz, *Business
Development*
T S Ramesh, *CAO*
EMP: 100 **EST:** 1996
SQ FT: 57,000
SALES (est): 2.37MM **Privately Held**
SIC: 7373 7372 Systems software
　development services; Prepackaged
　software

(G-7431)
SOFTINWAY INC
20 Mall Rd Ste 450 (01803-4123)
PHONE..............................781 328-4310
Leonid Moroz, *Pr*
Olga Moroz, *Sec*
Valentine Moroz, *CEO*
EMP: 17 **EST:** 1999
SALES (est): 2.53MM **Privately Held**
Web: www.softinway.com
SIC: 8711 7372 Consulting engineer;
　Application computer software

(G-7432)
SPEECHWORKS INTERNATIONAL
Also Called: Applied Language Technologies
1 Wayside Rd (01803-4609)
PHONE..............................781 565-5000
EMP: 25 **EST:** 1994
SQ FT: 53,600
SALES (est): 2.31MM
SALES (corp-wide): 211.91B **Publicly
Held**
SIC: 7371 7373 7372 Computer software
　development; Computer integrated systems
　design; Prepackaged software
HQ: Nuance Communications, Inc.
　1 Wayside Rd
　Burlington MA 01803

(G-7433)
SQ INNOVATION INC
20 Mall Rd Ste 220 (01803-4127)
PHONE..............................617 500-0121

Pieter Muntendam, *Pr*
EMP: 7 **EST:** 2019
SQ FT: 3,500
SALES (est): 1.13MM **Privately Held**
SIC: 2834 Pharmaceutical preparations

(G-7434)
SS&C TECHNOLOGIES INC
3 Burlington Woods Dr (01803-4532)
PHONE...................781 654-6498
EMP: 10
SALES (corp-wide): 5.28B **Publicly Held**
Web: www.ssctech.com
SIC: 7372 Prepackaged software
HQ: Ss&C Technologies, Inc.
80 Lamberton Rd Fl 1
Windsor CT 06095
800 234-0556

(G-7435)
STMICROELECTRONICS INC
200 Summit Dr (01803-5289)
PHONE...................781 861-2650
John North, *Mgr*
EMP: 9
SALES (corp-wide): 16.13B **Privately Held**
SIC: 5065 7371 3674 Semiconductor
devices; Custom computer programming
services; Semiconductors and related
devices
HQ: Stmicroelectronics, Inc.
750 Canyon Dr Ste 300
Coppell TX 75019
972 466-6000

(G-7436)
SURMET CORP (PA)
31 B St (01803-3406)
PHONE...................781 345-5721
EMP: 32 **EST:** 1982
SALES (est): 8.31MM
SALES (corp-wide): 8.31MM **Privately
Held**
Web: www.surmet.com
SIC: 3443 8711 2891 High vacuum coaters,
metal plate; Engineering services;
Adhesives and sealants

(G-7437)
TAPCOENPRO TRACKER LLC
30 Corporate Dr Ste 200 (01803-4252)
P.O. Box 146699 (02114-0019)
PHONE...................781 270-1200
EMP: 7 **EST:** 2017
SALES (est): 1.57MM **Publicly Held**
SIC: 3492 Fluid power valves and hose
fittings
HQ: Circor International, Inc.
30 Corporate Dr Ste 200
Burlington MA 01803
781 270-1200

(G-7438)
TERATECH CORPORATION
Also Called: Terason Ultrasound
77 Terrace Hall Ave (01803)
PHONE...................781 270-4143
Alice Chiang, *Pr*
Nicholas Collins, *
▲ **EMP:** 50 **EST:** 1993
SQ FT: 20,000
SALES (est): 9.73MM **Privately Held**
Web: www.terason.com
SIC: 3841 Surgical and medical instruments

(G-7439)
THORATEC LLC
168 Middlesex Tpke (01803-4403)
PHONE...................781 272-0139
EMP: 118

SALES (corp-wide): 43.65B **Publicly Held**
SIC: 3845 Electromedical equipment
HQ: Thoratec Llc
6035 Stoneridge Dr
Pleasanton CA 94588
925 847-8600

(G-7440)
THORATEC LLC
23 4th Ave Ste 2 (01803-3326)
PHONE...................781 272-0139
Ted Naughton, *Brnch Mgr*
EMP: 172
SALES (corp-wide): 43.65B **Publicly Held**
SIC: 3845 3826 Electromedical equipment;
Analytical instruments
HQ: Thoratec Llc
6035 Stoneridge Dr
Pleasanton CA 94588
925 847-8600

(G-7441)
UNIT4 BUSINESS SOFTWARE INC (PA)
3 Burlington Woods Dr Ste 201
(01803-4532)
PHONE...................877 704-5974
Lars Noreng, *Pr*
EMP: 10 **EST:** 2000
SALES (est): 13.55MM
SALES (corp-wide): 13.55MM **Privately
Held**
Web: www.unit4.com
SIC: 7372 Business oriented computer
software

(G-7442)
VARSTREET INC
67 S Bedford St Ste 400w (01803-5177)
PHONE...................781 262-0610
Shiv Agarwal, *Ex Dir*
Gopalan Shankar, *Pr*
EMP: 18 **EST:** 2011
SALES (est): 986.28K **Privately Held**
Web: www.varstreetinc.com
SIC: 7372 Application computer software

(G-7443)
VERADIGM INC
1 Burlington Woods Dr Ste 3 (01803-4535)
PHONE...................800 720-7351
Paul Reilly, *Prin*
EMP: 17
SALES (corp-wide): 1.5B **Publicly Held**
Web: www.allscripts.com
SIC: 7372 Prepackaged software
PA: Veradigm Inc.
222 Merchandise Mart Plz
Chicago IL 60654
800 334-8534

(G-7444)
VERSUM MATERIALS US LLC
400 Summit Dr (01803-5258)
PHONE...................978 715-1614
EMP: 50
SALES (corp-wide): 23.09B **Privately Held**
SIC: 2842 Ammonia, household
HQ: Versum Materials Us, Llc
8555 S River Pkwy
Tempe AZ 85284
602 282-1000

(G-7445)
VIKEN DETECTION CORPORATION
Also Called: Heuresis
21 North Ave (01803-3305)
PHONE...................617 467-5526

Jim Ryan, *CEO*
Jeffrey Warming, *
Peter Rothschild, *
EMP: 45 **EST:** 2012
SALES (est): 7.66MM **Privately Held**
Web: www.vikendetection.com
SIC: 3826 Mass spectroscopy
instrumentation

(G-7446)
VMTURBO INC
1 Burlington Woods Dr Ste 101
(01803-4535)
PHONE...................914 584-5263
EMP: 38 **EST:** 2017
SALES (est): 211.28K **Privately Held**
Web: www.ibm.com
SIC: 7372 Prepackaged software

(G-7447)
VOLICON INC
99 S Bedford St Ste 209 (01803-5153)
PHONE...................781 221-7400
Eli Warsawski, *Pr*
Ishai Gandelsman, *
EMP: 50 **EST:** 2003
SALES (est): 4.34MM
SALES (corp-wide): 338.6MM **Publicly
Held**
SIC: 3651 Household audio and video
equipment
HQ: Edgecast Inc.
13031 W Jefferson Blvd
Los Angeles CA 90094

(G-7448)
WELLNESS PET LLC (PA)
77 S Bedford St Ste 201 (01803-5115)
PHONE...................877 869-2971
William Mcdonald, *Managing Member*
▲ **EMP:** 90 **EST:** 1926
SALES (est): 101.78MM
SALES (corp-wide): 101.78MM **Privately
Held**
Web: www.wellnesspet.com
SIC: 2047 Dog and cat food

(G-7449)
WINSHUTTLE LLC (HQ)
1700 District Ave Ste 300 (01803-5231)
PHONE...................425 368-2708
John Pierson, *CEO*
Lewis Carpenter, *
Jeff Bergstrom, *
Matthew Moore, *
Vikram Chalana, *Chief Customer Officer*
EMP: 92 **EST:** 2003
SALES (est): 21.24MM
SALES (corp-wide): 446.91MM **Privately
Held**
Web: www.precisely.com
SIC: 7372 Business oriented computer
software
PA: Precisely Software Incorporated
1700 District Ave Ste 300
Burlington MA 01803
978 436-8900

(G-7450)
ZAPPIX INC
25 Mall Rd (01803-4199)
PHONE...................781 214-8124
Gal Steinberg, *VP*
Yossi Abraham, *Pr*
EMP: 21 **EST:** 2012
SQ FT: 3,000
SALES (est): 743.05K **Privately Held**
Web: www.zappix.com
SIC: 7372 Application computer software

(G-7451)
ZOLL MEDICAL CORPORATION
32 2nd Ave (01803-4416)
PHONE...................781 229-0020
Donald Fiaschetti, *Brnch Mgr*
EMP: 108
Web: www.zoll.com
SIC: 3845 Electromedical equipment
HQ: Zoll Medical Corporation
269 Mill Rd
Chelmsford MA 01824
978 421-9655

(G-7452)
ZORAN CORPORATION
Also Called: Imaging Division
1 Wall St Ste 10 (01803-4769)
PHONE...................408 523-6500
EMP: 21
SALES (corp-wide): 33.57B **Publicly Held**
SIC: 7372 Prepackaged software
HQ: Zoran Corporation
1060 Rincon Cir
San Jose CA 95131
972 673-1600

Buzzards Bay
Barnstable County

(G-7453)
BREAKTHROUGH COATINGS INC
Also Called: Breakthrough Coatings
169 Clay Pond Rd Ste 1 (02532-8303)
PHONE...................866 608-7625
Jason Larosa, *Pr*
EMP: 10 **EST:** 2017
SALES (est): 1.62MM **Privately Held**
Web: www.coloredepoxies.com
SIC: 2865 2851 Isocyanates; Epoxy coatings

(G-7454)
CONFERENCE MEDAL & TROPHY CO
530 Macarthur Blvd (02532-3839)
P.O. Box 3137 (02559-3137)
PHONE...................508 563-3600
Kevin Healy, *Pr*
Lillian Healy, *Treas*
Michael Healy, *VP*
EMP: 17 **EST:** 1951
SQ FT: 8,000
SALES (est): 476.53K **Privately Held**
SIC: 3499 3914 Trophies, metal, except
silver; Trophies, nsk

(G-7455)
MV3 LLC
Also Called: Freeaire Refrigeration
11 Mizzen Ln (02532-3313)
PHONE...................617 658-4420
EMP: 7 **EST:** 2014
SALES (est): 335.41K **Privately Held**
Web: www.freeaire.com
SIC: 3822 5078 Refrigeration controls
(pressure); Refrigeration equipment and
supplies

(G-7456)
REMOTE SENSING SOLUTIONS INC
1 Technology Park Dr Ste A (02532-8338)
PHONE...................508 362-9400
Michel Fernandes, *CEO*
James R Carswell, *Pr*
James Canniff, *CFO*
EMP: 13 **EST:** 2002

SALES (est): 1.38MM **Privately Held**
Web: www.tomorrow.io
SIC: 3674 8731 3812 Radiation sensors;
Environmental research; Radar systems
and equipment

Byfield
Essex County

(G-7457)
DIEMAT INC
19 Central St Ste 9 (01922-1233)
PHONE..............................978 499-0900
Raymond Deitz, *Pr*
EMP: 10 **EST:** 1988
SQ FT: 1,876
SALES (est): 3.1MM **Privately Held**
Web: www.namics.co.jp
SIC: 2891 Adhesives
HQ: Namics Corporation
3993, Nigorikawa, Kita-Ku
Niigata NIG 950-3

(G-7458)
**METROMATIC
MANUFACTURING COMPANY
INC**
Also Called: Waterair Supply Co
78 Elm St (01922-2812)
PHONE..............................781 396-5300
EMP: 16
SIC: 5074 3585 3433 5075 Oil burners;
Furnaces, warm air: electric; Gas burners,
domestic; Condensing units, air conditioning

(G-7459)
STARENSIER INC (PA)
Also Called: Cosmo
12 Kent Way Ste 201 (01922-1244)
P.O. Box 737 (01922-0737)
PHONE..............................978 462-7311
Richard Van Dernoot, *Ch Bd*
Joshua Van Dernoot, *Pr*
▲ **EMP:** 7 **EST:** 1985
SQ FT: 4,630
SALES (est): 1.73MM
SALES (corp-wide): 1.73MM **Privately
Held**
Web: www.cosmofabric.net
SIC: 2261 2262 2295 Chemical coating or
treating of cotton broadwoven fabrics;
Chemical coating or treating of manmade
broadwoven fabrics; Laminating of fabrics

(G-7460)
**THREE DIMENSIONAL
GRAPHICS CORP**
3 Austin Ln (01922-1600)
PHONE..............................978 774-8595
▲ **EMP:** 37
Web: www.threedimensionalink.com
SIC: 2893 Printing ink

Cambridge
Middlesex County

(G-7461)
24M TECHNOLOGIES INC (PA)
130 Brookline St Ste 200 (02139-4505)
PHONE..............................617 553-1012
▲ **EMP:** 48 **EST:** 2010
SQ FT: 10,000
SALES (est): 23.2MM **Privately Held**
Web: www.24-m.com
SIC: 3691 Storage batteries

(G-7462)
2SEVENTY BIO INC (PA)
Also Called: BLUEBIRD BIO
60 Binney St (02142-1512)
PHONE..............................339 499-9300
Nick Leschly, *Pr*
Daniel S Lynch, *Ch Bd*
William D Baird Iii, *COO*
Philip Gregory D Phil, *CSO*
EMP: 60 **EST:** 2021
SQ FT: 253,108
SALES (est): 91.5MM
SALES (corp-wide): 91.5MM **Publicly
Held**
Web: www.2seventybio.com
SIC: 2834 Pharmaceutical preparations

(G-7463)
3DM INC
Also Called: 3d-Matrix
245 1st St (02142-1200)
P.O. Box 425025 (02142-0001)
PHONE..............................617 875-6204
Keiji Nagano, *Pr*
Alex Rich Md, *Ch*
EMP: 8 **EST:** 2001
SALES (est): 1.53MM **Privately Held**
Web: www.3dmatrix.com
SIC: 2836 Biological products, except
diagnostic

(G-7464)
3RD MILLENNIUM INC
125 Cambridgepark Dr Ste 301
(02140-2392)
PHONE..............................781 890-4440
Ousama Shamma, *CEO*
Ousama Shamma, *Pr*
Roland Carel, *Ex VP*
EMP: 10 **EST:** 1994
SQ FT: 3,000
SALES (est): 987.17K **Privately Held**
Web: www.3rdmill.com
SIC: 7372 Publisher's computer software

(G-7465)
ACCELERON PHARMA INC
149 Sidney St (02139-4237)
PHONE..............................617 576-2220
John L Knopf, *Brnch Mgr*
EMP: 245
SALES (corp-wide): 59.28B **Publicly Held**
Web: www.merck.com
SIC: 2834 Pharmaceutical preparations
HQ: Acceleron Pharma Inc.
33 Avenue Louis Pasteur
Boston MA 02115
617 649-9200

(G-7466)
**ACENTECH INCORPORATED
(PA)**
33 Moulton St (02138-1118)
PHONE..............................617 499-8000
Jeffrey A Zapfe, *Pr*
Christopher Savereid, *
Richard Fine, *
Jeffry A Zapfe, *
Robert S Berens, *
EMP: 42 **EST:** 1948
SQ FT: 17,000
SALES (est): 10.71MM **Privately Held**
Web: www.acentech.com
SIC: 8742 3824 3825 Management
consulting services; Fluid meters and
counting devices; Test equipment for
electronic and electric measurement

(G-7467)
ACTNANO INC (PA)
Also Called: Actnano
85 Bolton St Ste 105 (02140-3367)
PHONE..............................857 333-8631
S Taymur Ahmad, *Pr*
James Sheridan Junior, *COO*
Bruce Acton, *APPS Technology*
Robert Dobkin, *Prin*
EMP: 13 **EST:** 2012
SALES (est): 3.62MM
SALES (corp-wide): 3.62MM **Privately
Held**
Web: www.actnano.com
SIC: 3479 Coating of metals and formed
products

(G-7468)
AERODESIGNS INC
161 1st St Ste 3 (02142-1211)
PHONE..............................617 491-6600
▲ **EMP:** 22
Web: www.aerodesigns.com
SIC: 2834 Vitamin, nutrient, and hematinic
preparations for human use

(G-7469)
AFFINIVAX INC
301 Binney St Ste 302 (02142-1071)
PHONE..............................617 465-0865
Steven Brugger, *Pr*
Kamran Tavangar, *COO*
Stuart Chaffee, *Chief Business Officer*
Elizabeth Radcliffe, *CFO*
Kara Bickham, *Chief Medical Officer*
EMP: 167 **EST:** 2014
SALES (est): 50.1MM
SALES (corp-wide): 35.31B **Privately Held**
Web: www.affinivax.com
SIC: 2836 Vaccines
PA: Gsk Plc
G S K House
Brentford MIDDX TW8 9
208 047-5000

(G-7470)
**AGIOS PHARMACEUTICALS
INC (PA)**
Also Called: Agios
88 Sidney St (02139-4137)
PHONE..............................617 649-8600
Brian Goff, *CEO*
Jacqualyn A Fouse, *
Cecilia Jones, *CFO*
James Burns, *CLO*
Sarah Gheuens, *CMO*
EMP: 345 **EST:** 2008
SQ FT: 146,000
SALES (est): 5.61MM
SALES (corp-wide): 5.61MM **Publicly
Held**
Web: www.agios.com
SIC: 2834 8731 Pharmaceutical
preparations; Biotechnical research,
commercial

(G-7471)
AKAMAI TECHNOLOGIES INC
1 Hampshire St Ste 6 (02139-1579)
PHONE..............................203 969-5161
Jorge Garcia, *Brnch Mgr*
EMP: 9
SALES (corp-wide): 3.62B **Publicly Held**
Web: www.akamai.com
SIC: 7372 Prepackaged software
PA: Akamai Technologies, Inc.
145 Broadway
Cambridge MA 02142
617 444-3000

(G-7472)
AKAMAI TECHNOLOGIES INC
Acerno
8 Cambridge Ctr (02142-1413)
PHONE..............................415 994-2299
EMP: 31
SALES (corp-wide): 3.62B **Publicly Held**
Web: www.akamai.com
SIC: 7372 Prepackaged software
PA: Akamai Technologies, Inc.
145 Broadway
Cambridge MA 02142
617 444-3000

(G-7473)
**AKAMAI TECHNOLOGIES INC
(PA)**
145 Broadway (02142-1058)
PHONE..............................617 444-3000
F Thomson Leighton, *CEO*
Daniel Hesse, *
Edward Mcgowan, *Ex VP*
Aaron Ahola, *Corporate Secretary*
Robert Blumofe, *Ex VP*
▲ **EMP:** 500 **EST:** 1998
SQ FT: 659,000
SALES (est): 3.62B
SALES (corp-wide): 3.62B **Publicly Held**
Web: www.akamai.com
SIC: 7372 7374 Prepackaged software;
Data processing and preparation

(G-7474)
**AKEBIA THERAPEUTICS INC
(PA)**
245 1st St Ste 1400 (02142-1292)
PHONE..............................617 871-2098
John P Butler, *Pr*
Michel Dahan, *Sr VP*
David A Spellman, *Sr VP*
Steven K Burke, *Research & Development*
Dell Faulkingham, *CCO*
EMP: 111 **EST:** 2007
SQ FT: 65,167
SALES (est): 292.6MM **Publicly Held**
Web: www.akebia.com
SIC: 2834 Pharmaceutical preparations

(G-7475)
ALKERMES INC
30 Rindge Ave Apt 2 (02140-1921)
PHONE..............................617 441-3092
Anne Giovanoni, *Brnch Mgr*
EMP: 117
Web: www.alkermes.com
SIC: 2834 Pharmaceutical preparations
HQ: Alkermes, Inc.
900 Winter St
Waltham MA 02451
781 609-6000

(G-7476)
ALLBIRDS INC
29 Brattle St (02138-3709)
PHONE..............................617 315-4210
EMP: 19
SALES (corp-wide): 297.77MM **Publicly
Held**
Web: www.allbirds.com
SIC: 3143 Men's footwear, except athletic
PA: Allbirds, Inc.
730 Montgomery St
San Francisco CA 94111
628 225-4848

(G-7477)
ALLM USA INC
125 Cambridgepark Dr (02140-2329)
PHONE..............................857 209-5065

▲ = Import ▼ = Export
◆ = Import/Export

Harry Reddy, *CEO*
EMP: 10 **EST:** 2015
SALES (est): 1.02MM **Privately Held**
Web: www.allm.us
SIC: 3829 Medical diagnostic systems, nuclear

(G-7478)
ALNYLAM PHARMACEUTICALS INC (PA)
Also Called: Alnylam
675 W Kendall St (02142-1168)
PHONE.............................617 551-8200
Yvonne L Greenstreet, *CEO*
Amy W Schulman, *
Akshay K Vaishnaw, *Pr*
Jeffrey V Poulton, *Ex VP*
Indrani L Franchini, *CLO*
EMP: 251 **EST:** 2002
SQ FT: 295,000
SALES (est): 1.04B
SALES (corp-wide): 1.04B **Publicly Held**
Web: www.alnylam.com
SIC: 2834 8731 Pharmaceutical preparations; Biotechnical research, commercial

(G-7479)
ALNYLAM PHARMACEUTICALS INC
Also Called: Alnylam Alewife Mfg Fcilty
665 Concord Ave (02138-1047)
PHONE.............................617 551-8200
Mark Johnson, *Mgr*
EMP: 15
SALES (corp-wide): 1.04B **Publicly Held**
Web: www.alnylam.com
SIC: 2834 Pharmaceutical preparations
PA: Alnylam Pharmaceuticals, Inc.
675 W Kendall St
Cambridge MA 02142
617 551-8200

(G-7480)
ALNYLAM PHARMACEUTICALS INC
300 3rd St (02142-1103)
PHONE.............................617 551-8200
John M Maraganore, *CEO*
EMP: 50
SALES (corp-wide): 1.04B **Publicly Held**
Web: www.alnylam.com
SIC: 2834 Pharmaceutical preparations
PA: Alnylam Pharmaceuticals, Inc.
675 W Kendall St
Cambridge MA 02142
617 551-8200

(G-7481)
ALNYLAM US INC (HQ)
675 W Kendall St (02142-1168)
PHONE.............................617 551-8200
John A Maraganore, *Pr*
EMP: 49 **EST:** 2002
SALES (est): 137.54MM
SALES (corp-wide): 1.04B **Publicly Held**
Web: www.alnylam.com
SIC: 2834 Pharmaceutical preparations
PA: Alnylam Pharmaceuticals, Inc.
675 W Kendall St
Cambridge MA 02142
617 551-8200

(G-7482)
ALOPEXX PHARMACEUTICALS LLC
Also Called: Alopexx
50 Buckingham St (02138-2228)
PHONE.............................617 945-2510

EMP: 10 **EST:** 2006
SALES (est): 846.35K **Privately Held**
Web: www.alopexx.com
SIC: 2834 Pharmaceutical preparations

(G-7483)
AMGEN INC
Also Called: Amgen
360 Binney St (02142-1011)
PHONE.............................617 444-5000
David Armistead, *Brnch Mgr*
EMP: 40
SALES (corp-wide): 26.32B **Publicly Held**
Web: www.amgen.com
SIC: 2834 Pharmaceutical preparations
PA: Amgen Inc.
1 Amgen Center Dr
Thousand Oaks CA 91320
805 447-1000

(G-7484)
AMIDE TECHNOLOGIES INC
750 Main St Ste 328 (02139-3544)
PHONE.............................508 245-6839
Brad Pentelute, *Prin*
Jeremy Wertheimer, *Prin*
EMP: 12 **EST:** 2017
SALES (est): 1.11MM **Privately Held**
Web: www.amidetech.com
SIC: 3841 Surgical and medical instruments

(G-7485)
AMPLITUDE LASER INC
Also Called: Continuum
185 Alewife Brook Pkwy (02138-1100)
PHONE.............................857 285-5952
EMP: 13
SALES (corp-wide): 22.19MM **Privately Held**
Web: www.amplitude-laser.com
SIC: 3827 Optical instruments and apparatus
PA: Amplitude Laser, Inc.
532 Gibraltar Dr
Milpitas CA 95035
408 727-3240

(G-7486)
AMYLYX PHARMACEUTICALS INC (PA)
Also Called: Amylyx
43 Thorndike St Ste 12 (02141-1764)
PHONE.............................617 682-0917
George Mclean Milne Junior, *Ch Bd*
James Frates, *CFO*
Margaret Olinger, *CCO*
EMP: 168 **EST:** 2014
SQ FT: 8,850
SALES (est): 22.23MM
SALES (corp-wide): 22.23MM **Publicly Held**
Web: www.amylyx.com
SIC: 2834 5122 8731 Pharmaceutical preparations; Pharmaceuticals; Biotechnical research, commercial

(G-7487)
ANTOLRX INC
1 Kendall Sq Bldg 1400 (02139-1562)
PHONE.............................617 902-0601
Mark Carthy, *Pr*
EMP: 9 **EST:** 2016
SALES (est): 181.45K **Privately Held**
Web: www.antolrx.com
SIC: 2834 Pharmaceutical preparations

(G-7488)
AQUINNAH PHARMACEUTICALS INC

700 Main St (02139-3543)
PHONE.............................617 416-0530
Glenn Larsen, *Dir*
EMP: 11 **EST:** 2015
SALES (est): 4.87MM **Privately Held**
Web: www.aquinnahpharma.com
SIC: 2834 Pharmaceutical preparations

(G-7489)
ARBOR BIOTECHNOLOGIES INC
Also Called: Biotech
20 Acorn Park Dr Ste 500 (02140-2133)
PHONE.............................857 301-6366
Devyn Smith, *CEO*
David Cheng, *
David Scott, *
Michaela Smith, *
Winston Yan, *
EMP: 48 **EST:** 2016
SALES (est): 5.85MM **Privately Held**
Web: www.arbor.bio
SIC: 2834 Pharmaceutical preparations

(G-7490)
ARIAD PHARMACEUTICALS INC
40 Landsdowne St (02139-4234)
EMP: 459 **EST:** 1991
SQ FT: 100,000
SALES (est): 164.31MM **Privately Held**
Web: www.takedaoncology.com
SIC: 2836 8731 Biological products, except diagnostic; Medical research, commercial
PA: Takeda Pharmaceutical Company Limited
2-1-1, Nihombashihoncho
Chuo-Ku TKY 103-0

(G-7491)
ASCEND ROBOTICS LLC
245 1st St Ste 18 (02142-1292)
PHONE.............................978 451-0170
David Askey, *Managing Member*
EMP: 18 **EST:** 2015
SALES (est): 2.06MM **Privately Held**
Web: www.ascendrobotics.com
SIC: 3535 Robotic conveyors

(G-7492)
ATERNITY INC
125 Cambridgepark Dr Ste 402 (02140-2392)
PHONE.............................508 475-0414
Trevor Matz, *CEO*
EMP: 140 **EST:** 2004
SQ FT: 9,800
SALES (est): 18.96MM **Privately Held**
Web: www.riverbed.com
SIC: 7372 Application computer software

(G-7493)
ATERNITY LLC (DH)
125 Cambridgepark Dr (02140-2392)
PHONE.............................617 250-5309
Bill Hewitt, *Pr*
Sean Lannan, *CFO*
EMP: 20 **EST:** 2020
SALES (est): 75MM
SALES (corp-wide): 912.58MM **Privately Held**
Web: www.riverbed.com
SIC: 7372 Business oriented computer software
HQ: Riverbed Technology Llc
680 Folsom St Ste 600
San Francisco CA 94107
415 247-8800

(G-7494)
ATHINIA TECHNOLOGIES LLC
245 1st St Ste 18 (02142-1292)
PHONE.............................781 491-4189
James Kugler, *Managing Member*
EMP: 10 **EST:** 2021
SALES (est): 78.66K **Privately Held**
SIC: 3674 Semiconductors and related devices

(G-7495)
AVROBIO INC (PA)
1 Kendall Sq Ste B2001 (02139-1597)
PHONE.............................617 914-8420
Erik Ostrowski, *Interim Chief Executive Officer*
Erik Ostrowski, *Interim Chief Executive Officer*
Bruce Booth, *Ch Bd*
Katina Dorton, *CFO*
Nerissa Kreher, *CMO*
EMP: 25 **EST:** 2015
SQ FT: 11,218
Web: www.avrobio.com
SIC: 2834 Pharmaceutical preparations

(G-7496)
AXCELLA HEALTH INC (PA)
Also Called: Axcella
840 Memorial Dr Ste 3 (02139-3771)
PHONE.............................857 320-2200
William R Hinshaw Junior, *Pr*
Paul Fehlner, *CLO*
Margaret James Koziel, *CMO*
EMP: 7 **EST:** 2008
SQ FT: 19,200
Web: www.axcellatx.com
SIC: 8731 2836 Commercial physical research; Biological products, except diagnostic

(G-7497)
BARRETT TECHNOLOGY INC
139 Main St (02142-1530)
PHONE.............................617 252-9000
William T Townsend, *Prin*
EMP: 10 **EST:** 2011
SALES (est): 237.94K **Privately Held**
Web: medical.barrett.com
SIC: 3535 Robotic conveyors

(G-7498)
BAXALTA US INC
650 E Kendall St (02142)
PHONE.............................312 656-8021
EMP: 384
SIC: 2834 Pharmaceutical preparations
HQ: Baxalta Us Inc.
1200 Lakeside Dr
Bannockburn IL 60015
224 948-2000

(G-7499)
BB WALPOLE LIQUIDATION NH INC
52d Brattle St (02138-3731)
PHONE.............................617 491-4340
Larry Burdick, *Owner*
EMP: 8
Web: www.47mainwalpole.com
SIC: 2066 5441 Chocolate; Candy
PA: Bb Walpole Liquidation Nh, Inc.
47 Main St Unit 1
Walpole NH 03608

(G-7500)
BEAM THERAPEUTICS INC (PA)
Also Called: Beam Therapeutics
238 Main St (02142-1099)

PHONE..............................857 327-8775
John Evans, *CEO*
Giuseppe Ciaramella, *CSO*
Terry-ann Burrell, *CFO*
Amy Simon, *Chief Medical Officer*
EMP: 68 EST: 2017
SQ FT: 38,203
SALES (est): 60.92MM
SALES (corp-wide): 60.92MM **Publicly Held**
Web: www.beamtx.com
SIC: 2836 Biological products, except diagnostic

(G-7501)
BEARER INC
185 Alewife Brook Pkwy (02138-1100)
PHONE..............................657 297-5335
Guillaume Montard, *CEO*
EMP: 12
SALES (est): 552.11K **Privately Held**
SIC: 7372 Application computer software

(G-7502)
BEIGENE US MFG CO INC
55 Cambrdge Pkwy Ste 700w (02142)
PHONE..............................781 801-1800
Titus Ball, *VP Acctg*
EMP: 70 EST: 2021
SALES (est): 1.88MM **Privately Held**
SIC: 2834 Pharmaceutical preparations

(G-7503)
BEIGENE USA INC (HQ)
55 Cambridge Pkwy Ste 700w (02142)
PHONE..............................781 801-1887
Scott Samuels, *Pr*
Aijun Wang, *CFO*
Jane Huang, *Chief Medical Officer*
Yong Ben, *Chief Medical Officer*
EMP: 21 EST: 2017
SALES (est): 389.03MM **Privately Held**
Web: www.beigene.com
SIC: 2834 5122 8731 Pharmaceutical preparations; Pharmaceuticals; Commercial research laboratory
PA: Beigene Ltd.
    C/O Mourant Governance Services (Cayman) Limited
    Camana Bay GR CAYMAN KY1-1

(G-7504)
BELLE ARTFL INTELLIGENCE CORP
245 1st St Ste 18 (02142-1200)
PHONE..............................650 291-9410
Ly Tran, *CEO*
EMP: 10 EST: 2020
SALES (est): 690.08K **Privately Held**
SIC: 7371 7372 7373 7379 Software programming applications; Prepackaged software; Systems engineering, computer related; Computer related consulting services

(G-7505)
BIAL - BIOTECH INVESTMENTS INC
19 Blackstone St Fl 2 (02139-3709)
PHONE..............................508 332-9103
EMP: 14
SALES (est): 2.49MM **Privately Held**
SIC: 2834 Pharmaceutical preparations

(G-7506)
BICARA THERAPEUTICS INC
245 Main St (02142-1064)
PHONE..............................860 882-7478
Claire Mazumdar, *CEO*

Ryan Cohlhepp, *Pr*
Ivan Hyep, *CFO*
EMP: 9 EST: 2018
SALES (est): 3.48MM **Privately Held**
Web: www.bicara.com
SIC: 2834 Pharmaceutical preparations

(G-7507)
BIND BIOSCIENCES INC
325 Vassar St (02139-4980)
PHONE..............................617 679-9600
Scott Minick, *CEO*
EMP: 17 EST: 2019
SALES (est): 874.55K **Privately Held**
Web: www.bindtherapeutics.com
SIC: 2834 Pharmaceutical preparations

(G-7508)
BIOBOHEMIA INC
1 Broadway Ste 14 (02142-1187)
PHONE..............................617 958-7900
EMP: 7 EST: 2019
SALES (est): 74.42K **Privately Held**
Web: www.biobohemia.com
SIC: 2836 Vaccines

(G-7509)
BIOCON BIOLOGICS INC
245 Main St Fl 2 (02142-1064)
PHONE..............................857 706-2596
Arun Suresh Chandavarkar, *Pr*
Paul Vazhayil Thomas, *Sec*
Chinappa Mb, *Dir*
EMP: 99 EST: 2019
SALES (est): 23.31MM **Privately Held**
Web: www.biocon.com
SIC: 2834 Pharmaceutical preparations
HQ: Biocon Biologics Limited
    Biocon House, Ground Floor, Tower-3, Semicon Park
    Bengaluru KA 56010

(G-7510)
BIODATA INC
625 Massachusetts Ave Ste 1 (02139-3357)
PHONE..............................512 593-5521
Louis Culot, *CEO*
Gal Finkelstein, *VP*
EMP: 12 EST: 1987
SALES (est): 806.28K **Privately Held**
Web: www.labguru.com
SIC: 2721 Periodicals

(G-7511)
BIOGEN INC (PA)
Also Called: Biogen
225 Binney St (02142-1031)
P.O. Box 425025 (02142-0001)
PHONE..............................617 679-2000
Christopher A Viehbacher, *Pr*
Christopher A Viehbacher, *Pr*
Stelios Papadopoulos, *
Michael R Mcdonnell, *Ex VP*
Susan H Alexander, *CLO*
◆ **EMP:** 348 **EST:** 1978
SQ FT: 1,072,000
SALES (est): 9.84MM
SALES (corp-wide): 9.84MM **Publicly Held**
Web: www.biogen.com
SIC: 2836 2834 8731 Biological products, except diagnostic; Pharmaceutical preparations; Biological research

(G-7512)
BIOGEN INC
6 Cambridge Ctr (02142-1401)
PHONE..............................617 914-8888
EMP: 84

SALES (corp-wide): 10.17B **Publicly Held**
Web: www.biogen.com
SIC: 2834 Pharmaceutical preparations
PA: Biogen Inc.
    225 Binney St
    Cambridge MA 02142
    617 679-2000

(G-7513)
BIOGEN MA INC
225 Binney St (02142-1031)
PHONE..............................781 464-2000
Paul J Clancy, *Mgr*
EMP: 100
SALES (corp-wide): 9.84MM **Publicly Held**
Web: www.biogen.com
SIC: 2836 6794 Biological products, except diagnostic; Patent buying, licensing, leasing
HQ: Biogen Ma Inc.
    225 Binney St
    Cambridge MA 02142
    617 679-2000

(G-7514)
BIOGEN MA INC (HQ)
225 Binney St (02142-1031)
PHONE..............................617 679-2000
George A Scangos Ph.d., *CEO*
Susan H Alexander, *
John G Cox, *
Kenneth Dipietro, *
Steven H Holtzman, *
▲ **EMP:** 180 **EST:** 1978
SQ FT: 150,000
SALES (est): 462.57MM
SALES (corp-wide): 9.84MM **Publicly Held**
Web: www.biogen.com
SIC: 2836 8731 Biological products, except diagnostic; Commercial research laboratory
PA: Biogen Inc.
    225 Binney St
    Cambridge MA 02142
    617 679-2000

(G-7515)
BIONTECH US INC (HQ)
40 Erie St Ste 110 (02139-4254)
PHONE..............................617 337-4701
Richard Gaynor, *Research & Development*
Jolie M Siegel, *VP*
EMP: 25 EST: 2013
SQ FT: 26,806
SALES (corp-wide): 17.98B **Privately Held**
SIC: 2836 8731 Biological products, except diagnostic; Biotechnical research, commercial
PA: Biontech Se
    An Der Goldgrube 12
    Mainz RP 55131
    613190840

(G-7516)
BIONX MEDICAL TECHNOLOGIES INC
Also Called: Biom
27 Moulton St (02138-1118)
EMP: 51 EST: 2006
SQ FT: 1,900
SALES (est): 12.47MM
SALES (corp-wide): 1.35B **Privately Held**
Web: www.ottobock.com
SIC: 3842 Surgical appliances and supplies
HQ: Ottobock Se & Co. Kgaa
    Max-Nader-Str. 15
    Duderstadt NI 37115
    55278480

(G-7517)
BLACK DIAMOND THERAPEUTICS INC (PA)
Also Called: Black Diamond Therapeutics
1 Main St Ste 1040 (02142-1599)
PHONE..............................617 252-0848
Mark Velleca, *CEO*
Thomas Leggett, *CFO*
Brent Hatzis-schoch, *COO*
Christopher D Roberts, *CSO*
Sergey Yurasov, *CMO*
EMP: 11 EST: 2014
SQ FT: 2,357
Web: www.blackdiamondtherapeutics.com
SIC: 2834 2836 Pharmaceutical preparations; Biological products, except diagnostic

(G-7518)
BLUEPRINT MEDICINES CORP (PA)
45 Sidney St (02139-4133)
PHONE..............................617 374-7580
Jeffrey W Albers, *Pr*
Daniel S Lynch, *Pr*
Kathryn Haviland, *COO*
Michael Landsittel, *CFO*
Becker Hewes, *CMO*
EMP: 529 EST: 2008
SQ FT: 99,833
SALES (est): 204.04MM
SALES (corp-wide): 204.04MM **Publicly Held**
Web: www.blueprintmedicines.com
SIC: 2834 Pharmaceutical preparations

(G-7519)
BOOMERANGS
563 Massachusetts Ave (02139-4030)
PHONE..............................617 758-6128
EMP: 7 EST: 2018
SALES (est): 74.19K **Privately Held**
Web: www.shopboomerangs.org
SIC: 3949 Boomerangs

(G-7520)
BOSTON FOOD COOPERATIVE (PA)
Also Called: Harvest Co-Operative Sprmkt
580 Massachusetts Ave (02139-3307)
PHONE..............................617 661-1580
Sliza Strode, *Pr*
Mike Wiercek, *
EMP: 135 EST: 1972
SQ FT: 24,000
SALES (est): 9.62MM
SALES (corp-wide): 9.62MM **Privately Held**
Web: www.slowfoodboston.org
SIC: 5411 2051 2052 Cooperative food stores; Bread, cake, and related products; Cookies and crackers

(G-7521)
BOSTON ONCOLOGY LLC
245 1st St Ste 1800 (02142-1292)
PHONE..............................857 209-5052
Abdullah Baaj, *Managing Member*
EMP: 11 EST: 2012
SALES (est): 513.25K **Privately Held**
Web: www.bostononcology.com
SIC: 2834 Pharmaceutical preparations

(G-7522)
BOTIFY CORPORATION
185 Alewife Brook Pkwy Ste 210 (02138-1100)
PHONE..............................617 576-2005
Adrien Menard, *Pr*

EMP: 8 EST: 2015
SALES (est): 2.53MM
SALES (corp-wide): 2.11MM **Privately Held**
Web: www.botify.com
SIC: 7372 Business oriented computer software
PA: Botify
12 Rue D Amsterdam
Paris 75009
183629078

(G-7523)
BRAMMER BIO HOLDING CO LLC (HQ)
250 Binney St (02142-1026)
PHONE.............................386 418-8199
Mark R Bamforth, *Pr*
Christopher K Murphy, *COO*
Steven J Favaloro, *CFO*
Steve Falcone, *Chief Quality Officer*
EMP: 33 EST: 2016
SQ FT: 300,000
SALES (est): 90.67MM
SALES (corp-wide): 44.91B **Publicly Held**
Web: www.patheon.com
SIC: 8731 2834 Medical research, commercial; Medicines, capsuled or ampuled
PA: Thermo Fisher Scientific Inc.
168 3rd Ave
Waltham MA 02451
781 622-1000

(G-7524)
BRAMMER BIO MA LLC (HQ)
250 Binney St (02142-1026)
PHONE.............................877 765-7676
Chris Murphy, *General Vice President**
EMP: 485 EST: 2017
SALES (est): 103.24MM
SALES (corp-wide): 44.91B **Publicly Held**
Web: www.patheon.com
SIC: 3826 8731 Analytical instruments; Biotechnical research, commercial
PA: Thermo Fisher Scientific Inc.
168 3rd Ave
Waltham MA 02451
781 622-1000

(G-7525)
BRIGHT HORIZONS AT BIOGEN IDEC
105 Broadway (02142-1023)
PHONE.............................617 621-3383
Burt Adelman, *Pr*
EMP: 16 EST: 2017
SALES (est): 3.71MM **Privately Held**
Web: www.biogen.com
SIC: 2834 Pharmaceutical preparations

(G-7526)
CADENT THERAPEUTICS INC
Also Called: Nemosyne Therapeutics
250 Massachusetts Ave (02139-4229)
PHONE.............................617 949-5529
EMP: 10 EST: 2010
SALES (est): 1.3MM **Privately Held**
Web: www.novartis.com
SIC: 2834 Pharmaceutical preparations

(G-7527)
CAMBRIDGE BRANDS MFG INC
810 Main St (02139-3588)
PHONE.............................617 491-2500
Ellen R Gordon, *Pr*
EMP: 200
SALES (corp-wide): 686.97MM **Publicly Held**

SIC: 2064 2066 Candy and other confectionery products; Chocolate and cocoa products
HQ: Cambridge Brands Manufacturing, Inc.
7401 S Cicero Ave
Chicago IL 60629

(G-7528)
CAMBRIDGE BREWING CO INC
1 Kendall Sq Ste B1102 (02139-1592)
PHONE.............................617 494-1994
Phillip C Bannatyne, *Pr*
EMP: 45 EST: 1989
SQ FT: 4,000
SALES (est): 4.74MM **Privately Held**
Web:
www.cambridgebrewingcompany.com
SIC: 2082 5812 Ale (alcoholic beverage); Eating places

(G-7529)
CAMBRIDGE CHEMICAL CO CORP
Also Called: Cambridge Chemical Company
58 Dudley St (02140-2404)
PHONE.............................617 876-4484
Michael Martorano, *Pr*
Peter A Marto, *VP*
Jacalyn Marto, *Sec*
EMP: 14 EST: 1928
SQ FT: 1,000
SALES (est): 246.59K **Privately Held**
SIC: 7342 2879 Exterminating and fumigating; Exterminating products, for household or industrial use

(G-7530)
CAMBRIDGE GL FCTRY CONDO LLC
169 Monsignor Obrien Hwy (02141-1289)
PHONE.............................617 576-6701
Jeff Goldfarb, *VP*
EMP: 13 EST: 1985
SALES (est): 312.33K **Privately Held**
SIC: 3231 Products of purchased glass

(G-7531)
CAMBRIDGEEDITORS
293 Sidney St (02139-4825)
PHONE.............................617 876-2855
Harte Weiner, *Prin*
EMP: 9 EST: 2016
SALES (est): 153.77K **Privately Held**
Web: www.cambridgeeditors.com
SIC: 2741 Miscellaneous publishing

(G-7532)
CARISMA THERAPEUTICS INC
245 1st St Ste 1800 (02142-1292)
PHONE.............................617 444-8550
EMP: 17 EST: 2008
SALES (est): 40MM **Privately Held**
Web: www.sesenbio.com
SIC: 2834 Pharmaceutical preparations

(G-7533)
CEDILLA THERAPEUTICS INC
245 1st St Ste 300 (02142-1292)
PHONE.............................617 581-9333
Alexandra Glucksmann, *Pr*
Colleen Desimone, *Interim Dean*
Neil Exter, *INTERIM CHIEF BUSINESS OFFICER*
EMP: 25 EST: 2018
SALES (est): 4.62MM **Privately Held**
Web: www.cedillatx.com
SIC: 2834 Pharmaceutical preparations

(G-7534)
CELL PRESS INC
50 Hampshire St (02139-1895)
PHONE.............................617 397-2800
Lynne Herndon, *CEO*
▲ **EMP: 102 EST:** 1974
SALES (est): 7.07MM
SALES (corp-wide): 10.3B **Privately Held**
SIC: 2721 Magazines: publishing only, not printed on site
HQ: Elsevier Inc.
230 Park Ave Fl 7
New York NY 10169
212 309-8100

(G-7535)
CELLAY LLC
100 Inman St Ste 207 (02139-1295)
PHONE.............................617 995-1307
EMP: 10 EST: 2009
SALES (est): 926.19K **Privately Held**
Web: www.cellayinc.com
SIC: 2835 Diagnostic substances

(G-7536)
CEREVEL THRPUTICS HOLDINGS INC (PA)
222 Jacobs St Unit 200 (02141-2297)
PHONE.............................844 304-2048
N Anthony Coles, *Ch Bd*
Abraham Ceesay, *Pr*
Susan Altschuller, *CFO*
Kenneth Dipietro, *Chief Human Resources Officer*
Scott Akamine, *CLO*
EMP: 11 EST: 2018
SQ FT: 61,000
Web: www.cerevel.com
SIC: 2834 Pharmaceutical preparations

(G-7537)
CHANG SHING TOFU INC
37 Rogers St (02142-1511)
PHONE.............................617 868-8878
Albert Dao, *Pr*
Kathy Huynh, *Treas*
◆ **EMP: 7 EST:** 1987
SQ FT: 16,679
SALES (est): 674.98K **Privately Held**
SIC: 2099 Tofu, except frozen desserts

(G-7538)
CHANNELWAVE SOFTWARE INC (DH)
1 Kendall Sq Bldg 200 (02139-1562)
PHONE.............................617 621-1700
Robert Hagen, *CEO*
Chris Heidelberger, ***
EMP: 37 EST: 1994
SQ FT: 25,000
SALES (est): 51.38K **Privately Held**
Web: www.channelwave.com
SIC: 7371 7372 Computer software development and applications; Business oriented computer software
HQ: Digital River, Inc.
10380 Bren Rd W
Minnetonka MN 55343

(G-7539)
CHECKMATE PHARMACEUTICALS INC
Also Called: Checkmate
245 Main St Fl 2 (02142-1064)
PHONE.............................617 682-3625
Robert Landry, ***
EMP: 31 EST: 2015
SQ FT: 1,163
SALES (corp-wide): 12.17B **Publicly Held**

Web: www.regeneron.com
SIC: 2836 8731 Biological products, except diagnostic; Medical research, commercial
PA: Regeneron Pharmaceuticals Inc
777 Old Saw Mill River Rd # 10
Tarrytown NY 10591
914 847-7000

(G-7540)
CICOR AMERICAS INC
185 Alewife Brook Pkwy Ste 410 (02138-1100)
PHONE.............................617 576-2005
EMP: 11 EST: 2017
SALES (est): 323.6K **Privately Held**
Web: www.cicor.com
SIC: 3674 Semiconductors and related devices

(G-7541)
CIRCLE LABS BIO INC ✪
400 Technology Sq Ste 602 (02139-3583)
PHONE.............................516 660-6045
Josef Feldman, *CEO*
EMP: 8 EST: 2023
SALES (est): 729.77K **Privately Held**
SIC: 2836 7371 Plasmas; Computer software development

(G-7542)
CODIAK BIOSCIENCES INC (PA)
35 Cambridgepark Dr Ste 500 (02140-2325)
PHONE.............................617 949-4100
Paul Huygens, *CRO*
Douglas E Williams, ***
Steven Gillis, ***
Linda C Bain, *CFO*
EMP: 48 EST: 2015
SQ FT: 68,258
SALES (est): 22.93MM
SALES (corp-wide): 22.93MM **Publicly Held**
Web: www.codiakbio.com
SIC: 2836 Biological products, except diagnostic

(G-7543)
COLUCID PHARMACEUTICALS INC
222 3rd St Ste 1320 (02142-1188)
P.O. Box 14401 (27709-4401)
PHONE.............................857 285-6495
EMP: 7 EST: 2006
SQ FT: 2,455
SALES (est): 4.72MM
SALES (corp-wide): 28.54B **Publicly Held**
Web: www.lilly.com
SIC: 2834 Druggists' preparations (pharmaceuticals)
PA: Eli Lilly And Company
Lilly Corporate Ctr
Indianapolis IN 46285
317 276-2000

(G-7544)
CREAMER ASSOCIATES INC
Also Called: Pageworks
501 Cambridge St Ste 101 (02141-1104)
PHONE.............................617 374-6000
Ronald Creamer Junior, *Pr*
EMP: 9 EST: 1985
SQ FT: 13,500
SALES (est): 429.18K **Privately Held**
SIC: 7336 2752 7374 Commercial art and graphic design; Offset printing; Data processing and preparation

(G-7545)
CUE BIOPHARMA INC (PA)
21 Erie St Ste 1 (02139-4223)
PHONE..................................617 949-2680
Daniel R Passeri, *Pr*
Barry Simon, *Ch Bd*
Ken Pienta, *CMO*
Anish Suri, *CSO*
Colin G Sandercock, *Sr VP*
EMP: 24 **EST:** 2014
SQ FT: 19,800
SALES (est): 1.25MM
SALES (corp-wide): 1.25MM **Publicly Held**
Web: www.cuebiopharma.com
SIC: 2834 Pharmaceutical preparations

(G-7546)
CULLINAN ONCOLOGY INC (PA)
1 Main St Ste 1350 (02142-1531)
PHONE..................................617 410-4650
Nadim Ahmed, *Pr*
Anthony Rosenberg, *Non-Executive Chairman of the Board*
Jeffrey Trigilio, *CFO*
Jeffrey Jones, *CMO*
Jacquelyn Sumer, *CLO CCO*
EMP: 19 **EST:** 2016
SQ FT: 7,531
Web: www.mpmcapital.com
SIC: 2836 Biological products, except diagnostic

(G-7547)
CYCLERION THERAPEUTICS INC (PA)
Also Called: Cyclerion
245 1st St Ste 18 (02142-1292)
PHONE..................................857 327-8778
Regina Graul, *Pr*
Marsha Fanucci, *Ch Bd*
Cheryl Gault, *COO*
Andreas Busch, *CSO*
EMP: 22 **EST:** 2018
SQ FT: 114,000
SALES (est): 1.63MM
SALES (corp-wide): 1.63MM **Publicly Held**
Web: www.cyclerion.com
SIC: 2834 Pharmaceutical preparations

(G-7548)
DAEDALUS SOFTWARE INC
215 First St Ste 7 (02142-1213)
P.O. Box 425857 (02142-0016)
PHONE..................................617 851-5157
Azita Sharif, *CEO*
EMP: 13 **EST:** 2000
SQ FT: 4,000
SALES (est): 693.8K **Privately Held**
Web: www.daedalussoftware.com
SIC: 7372 Business oriented computer software

(G-7549)
DAKTARI DIAGNOSTICS INC
85 Bolton St Ste 229 (02140-3370)
PHONE..................................617 336-3299
Donald B Hawthorne, *Pr*
EMP: 13 **EST:** 2008
SALES (est): 2.05MM **Privately Held**
Web: www.daktaridx.com
SIC: 2835 Diagnostic substances

(G-7550)
DIGI-BLOCK INC
122 Brattle St (02138-3423)
P.O. Box 380247 (02238-0247)
PHONE..................................617 926-9300
Gaby Kohoberg, *CEO*
Bill Rosenthal, *CEO*
▲ **EMP:** 22 **EST:** 1999
SALES (est): 1.55MM **Privately Held**
Web: www.digiblock.com
SIC: 5092 5945 3944 Educational toys; Hobby, toy, and game shops; Games, toys, and children's vehicles

(G-7551)
DISSERTATION EDITOR LLC
1 Mifflin Pl Ste 400 (02138-4946)
PHONE..................................857 600-2241
Doctor Allen Roda, *Prin*
EMP: 10 **EST:** 2016
SALES (est): 1.18MM
SALES (corp-wide): 1.18MM **Privately Held**
Web: www.dissertation-editor.com
SIC: 2741 Miscellaneous publishing
PA: Phd Advantage Llc
1 Miffin Pl Ste 400
Cambridge MA 02138
857 600-2241

(G-7552)
DLRC INCORPORATED ✪
1 Broadway (02142-1100)
PHONE..................................617 999-3340
Gregory Dombal, *Pr*
EMP: 7 **EST:** 2023
SALES (est): 78.66K **Privately Held**
SIC: 2834 5047 Pharmaceutical preparations; Medical and hospital equipment

(G-7553)
DROPGENIE INC
750 Main St (02139-3544)
PHONE..................................617 901-7422
EMP: 7 **EST:** 2019
SALES (est): 384.61K **Privately Held**
Web: www.drop-genie.com
SIC: 7372 Application computer software

(G-7554)
EDIGENE INC
700 Main St (02139-3543)
PHONE..................................617 682-5731
Tetsuya Yamagata, *Prin*
EMP: 13 **EST:** 2016
SALES (est): 864.5K **Privately Held**
Web: www.modalistx.com
SIC: 2514 Medicine cabinets and vanities: metal

(G-7555)
EDITAS MEDICINE INC (PA)
Also Called: Editas
11 Hurley St (02141-2110)
PHONE..................................617 401-9000
Gilmore O'neill, *Pr*
James C Mullen, *Ex Ch Bd*
Bruce Eaton, *Chief Business Officer*
Erick J Lucera, *Ex VP*
Baisong Mei, *CMO*
EMP: 226 **EST:** 2013
SQ FT: 59,783
SALES (est): 19.71MM
SALES (corp-wide): 19.71MM **Publicly Held**
Web: www.editasmedicine.com
SIC: 2836 Biological products, except diagnostic

(G-7556)
EISAI INC
35 Cambridgepark Dr Ste 200 (02140-2325)
PHONE..................................978 837-4616
Frank Aiesi, *Brnch Mgr*
EMP: 11
Web: www.eisai.com
SIC: 2834 Pharmaceutical preparations
HQ: Eisai Inc.
200 Metro Blvd
Nutley NJ 07110
201 692-1100

(G-7557)
ELAN PHARMA
300 Technology Sq Ste 3 (02139-3520)
PHONE..................................415 885-6780
EMP: 10 **EST:** 2014
SALES (est): 498.37K **Privately Held**
SIC: 2834 Pharmaceutical preparations
PA: Perrigo Company Public Limited Company
Treasury Building
Dublin 2

(G-7558)
ELAN PHARMACEUTICALS INC
Also Called: Elan
300 Technology Sq Ste 1 (02139-3520)
▲ **EMP:** 727
SIC: 2834 Drugs acting on the central nervous system & sense organs

(G-7559)
ELEVATEBIO LLC (PA)
Also Called: Elevatebio Base Camp
139 Main St Ste 500 (02142-1529)
PHONE..................................413 297-7151
Moranajovan Embiricos, *Prin*
Chris Alfieri, *Prin*
EMP: 25 **EST:** 2018
SALES (est): 10.7MM
SALES (corp-wide): 10.7MM **Privately Held**
Web: www.elevate.bio
SIC: 8731 2834 2836 Biotechnical research, commercial; Pharmaceutical preparations; Biological products, except diagnostic

(G-7560)
ELSEVIER INC
50 Hampshire St 5th Fl (02139-1893)
PHONE..................................781 663-5200
EMP: 57
SALES (corp-wide): 10.3B **Privately Held**
Web: www.elsevier.com
SIC: 2741 Miscellaneous publishing
HQ: Elsevier Inc.
230 Park Ave Fl 7
New York NY 10169
212 309-8100

(G-7561)
EMOTIONRX INC
Also Called: Emotionrx
245 Main St Fl 2 (02142-1064)
PHONE..................................617 500-5976
Phil Kongtcheu, *Managing Member*
EMP: 12 **EST:** 2018
SALES (est): 890.95K **Privately Held**
Web: emotionrx.pfktech.com
SIC: 3842 2392 Surgical appliances and supplies; Household furnishings, nec

(G-7562)
EOS IMAGING INC
185 Alewife Brook Pkwy Ste 210 (02138-1100)
PHONE..................................678 564-5400
Gisela Bryant, *Opers Mgr*
EMP: 12
Web: www.eos-imaging.com
SIC: 3841 Surgical and medical instruments
PA: Eos Imaging
10 Rue Mercoeur
Paris 75011

(G-7563)
EPIZYME INC
Also Called: Epizyme
400 Technology Sq Ste 4 (02139-3584)
PHONE..................................617 229-5872
Grant Bogle, *Pr*
David M Mott, *
Jerald Korn, *COO*
Jeffery L Kutok, *CSO*
Shefali Agarwal, *MEDICAL*
EMP: 203 **EST:** 2007
SQ FT: 43,066
SALES (est): 37.43MM **Privately Held**
Web: www.ipsen.com
SIC: 2834 8731 Pharmaceutical preparations; Biotechnical research, commercial
PA: Ipsen
65 Quai Georges Gorse
Boulogne Billancourt 92100

(G-7564)
EQRX INC (HQ)
Also Called: Eqrx
50 Hampshire St Ste 700 (02139-1893)
PHONE..................................617 315-2255
Melanie Nallicheri, *Pr*
Alexis Borisy, *Ex Ch Bd*
Jami Rubin, *CFO*
EMP: 26 **EST:** 2019
SQ FT: 33,539
SALES (corp-wide): 35.38MM **Publicly Held**
Web: www.eqrx.com
SIC: 2834 Pharmaceutical preparations
PA: Revolution Medicines, Inc.
700 Saginaw Dr
Redwood City CA 94063
650 481-6801

(G-7565)
ERYTECH PHARMA INC
Also Called: Erytech
1 Main St Ste 300 (02142-1599)
P.O. Box 507 (01462-0507)
PHONE..................................360 320-3325
Gil Beyen, *CEO*
Eric Soyer, *CFO*
EMP: 17 **EST:** 2014
SALES (est): 9.51MM
SALES (corp-wide): 1.01MM **Privately Held**
Web: www.erytech.com
SIC: 2834 Druggists' preparations (pharmaceuticals)
PA: Phaxiam Therapeutics
Erytech Pharma
Lyon 69008
478744438

(G-7566)
ETA DEVICES INC
245 1st St (02142-1200)
PHONE..................................617 577-8300
EMP: 17 **EST:** 2010
SQ FT: 2,000
SALES (est): 3.33MM
SALES (corp-wide): 25.87B **Privately Held**
Web: www.etawireless.com
SIC: 3674 Monolithic integrated circuits (solid state)
PA: Nokia Oyj
Karakaari 7
Espoo 02610
104488000

(G-7567)

EUTHYMICS BIOSCIENCE INC

43 Thorndike St Ste 21 (02141-1762)
PHONE.................................617 758-0300
Anthony A Mckinney, *Pr*
Pierre Tran, *Chief Medical Officer*
Thomas A Shea, *CFO*
EMP: 10 **EST:** 1995
SQ FT: 133,686
SALES (est): 436.53K **Privately Held**
Web: www.shoppinginfarmacia.it
SIC: 2834 Drugs acting on the central
nervous system & sense organs

(G-7568)

EXO THERAPEUTICS INC

150 Cambridgepark Dr (02140-2370)
PHONE.................................860 908-6508
EMP: 13 **EST:** 2018
SALES (est): 2.45MM **Privately Held**
Web: www.exo-therapeutics.com
SIC: 2834 Pharmaceutical preparations

(G-7569)

FERGENE INC

245 Main St 11th Fl (02142-1064)
PHONE.................................973 796-1600
David Meek, *CEO*
Ambaw Bellete, *COO*
EMP: 16 **EST:** 2019
SALES (est): 1.53MM **Privately Held**
SIC: 2834 Pharmaceutical preparations

(G-7570)

FLASHPRINT GRAPHICS INC

Also Called: Flash Print
99 Mount Auburn St Ste 3 (02138-4945)
PHONE.................................617 492-7767
EMP: 8 **EST:** 1991
SALES (est): 449.51K **Privately Held**
Web: www.flashprint.com
SIC: 7334 2759 Photocopying and
duplicating services; Commercial printing,
nec

(G-7571)

FOG PHARMACEUTICALS INC

30 Acorn Park Dr (02140)
PHONE.................................617 945-9510
Gregory Verdine, *Pr*
Weiqing Zhou, *
Milenko Cicmil V Pres Translat ional
Biology, *Prin*
Michael Hale, *Chemistry Vice President**
EMP: 70 **EST:** 2017
SALES (est): 13.05MM **Privately Held**
Web: www.fogpharma.com
SIC: 2834 Pharmaceutical preparations

(G-7572)

FOGHORN THERAPEUTICS INC (PA)

Also Called: FOGHORN THERAPEUTICS
500 Technology Sq Ste 700 (02139-3521)
PHONE.................................617 586-3100
Adrian Gottschalk, *Pr*
Stephen J Dipalma, *Interim Chief Financial
Officer*
Samuel Agresta, *CMO*
EMP: 45 **EST:** 2015
SQ FT: 81,441
SALES (est): 19.23MM
SALES (corp-wide): 19.23MM **Publicly
Held**
Web: www.foghorntx.com
SIC: 2834 Pharmaceutical preparations

(G-7573)

FOLDRX PHARMACEUTICALS INC (HQ)

100 Acorn Park Dr # 5 (02140-2303)
PHONE.................................617 252-5500
Richard Labaudiniere Ph.d., *CEO*
Richard Labaudiniere Ph.d., *Pr*
William E Aliski, *Chief Commercial Officer**
Christoph M Adams Ph.d., *Chief Business
Officer*
EMP: 15 **EST:** 2004
SQ FT: 20,000
SALES (est): 725.56K
SALES (corp-wide): 100.33B **Publicly
Held**
SIC: 2834 Pharmaceutical preparations
PA: Pfizer Inc.
66 Hudson Blvd E
New York NY 10001
212 733-2323

(G-7574)

FOUNDTION FOR DMCRACY IN UKRIN

79 Jfk St (02138-5801)
PHONE.................................617 496-8816
George Grabowizz, *Dir*
Prof William Hogan, *Dir*
EMP: 9 **EST:** 1990
SALES (est): 178.79K **Privately Held**
SIC: 8748 2721 Business consulting, nec;
Trade journals: publishing only, not printed
on site

(G-7575)

FULCRUM THERAPEUTICS INC (PA)

26 Landsdowne St Ste 525 (02139-4216)
PHONE.................................617 651-8851
Robert J Gould, *Interim Chief Executive
Officer*
Mark Levin, *Ofcr*
Judith A Dunn, *Research & Development*
Alan A Musso, *CFO*
EMP: 38 **EST:** 2015
SQ FT: 28,731
SALES (est): 6.34MM
SALES (corp-wide): 6.34MM **Publicly
Held**
Web: www.fulcrumtx.com
SIC: 2834 Pharmaceutical preparations

(G-7576)

FULCRUM THRPTICS SCRITIES CORP

26 Landsdowne St Ste 525 (02139-4249)
PHONE.................................617 651-8851
Robert J Gould, *Pr*
EMP: 35 **EST:** 2019
SALES (est): 2.26MM
SALES (corp-wide): 6.34MM **Publicly
Held**
Web: www.fulcrumtx.com
SIC: 2833 Medicinal chemicals
PA: Fulcrum Therapeutics, Inc.
26 Landsdowne St
Cambridge MA 02139
617 651-8851

(G-7577)

FURNISHED QUARTERS LLC

303 3rd St (02142-1156)
PHONE.................................212 367-9400
EMP: 49
SALES (corp-wide): 23.69MM **Privately
Held**
Web: www.furnishedquarters.com
SIC: 3131 Quarters
PA: Furnished Quarters, Llc
104 W 27th St
New York NY 10001
212 367-9400

(G-7578)

GCP APPLIED TECHNOLOGIES INC

62 Whittemore Ave (02140-1623)
PHONE.................................617 876-1400
EMP: 23
SALES (corp-wide): 397.78MM **Privately
Held**
Web: www.gcpat.com
SIC: 2819 Industrial inorganic chemicals,
nec
HQ: Gcp Applied Technologies Inc.
2325 Lakeview Pkwy # 450
Alpharetta GA 30009
617 876-1400

(G-7579)

GE DIGITAL LLC (HQ)

58 Charles St (02141-2128)
PHONE.................................925 242-6200
H Lawrence Culp Junior, *Ch Bd*
EMP: 22 **EST:** 2015
SALES (est): 70.63MM
SALES (corp-wide): 76.56B **Publicly Held**
Web: www.ge.com
SIC: 7372 Business oriented computer
software
PA: General Electric Company
1 Financial Ctr Ste 3700
Boston MA 02111
617 443-3000

(G-7580)

GE VERNOVA INTERNATIONAL LLC (HQ)

Also Called: General Electric Intl Inc
58 Charles St (02141-2128)
PHONE.................................617 443-3000
Scott Strazik, *CEO*
Jessica Uhl, *Pr*
Steven Baert, *CPO*
Kristin Carvell, *CCO*
Kenneth Sparks, *CFO*
◆ **EMP:** 222 **EST:** 1961
SALES (est): 806.71MM
SALES (corp-wide): 76.56B **Publicly Held**
SIC: 8711 3511 3533 Engineering services;
Turbines and turbine generator sets; Oil
and gas field machinery
PA: General Electric Company
1 Financial Ctr Ste 3700
Boston MA 02111
617 443-3000

(G-7581)

GENERATION BIO CO (PA)

301 Binney St Ste 3 (02142-1071)
PHONE.................................617 655-7500
Geoff Mcdonough, *Pr*
Jason Rhodes, *Ch Bd*
Matthew Norkunas, *CFO*
Matthew Stanton, *CSO*
Douglas Kerr, *CMO*
EMP: 99 **EST:** 2016
SQ FT: 71,562
Web: www.generationbio.com
SIC: 2834 Pharmaceutical preparations

(G-7582)

GENOCEA BIOSCIENCES INC (PA)

Also Called: Genocea
100 Acorn Park Dr Fl 5 (02140-2303)
PHONE.................................617 876-8191
William Clark, *Pr*
Kenneth Bate, *

New York NY 10001
212 367-9400
Diantha Duvall, *CFO*
Jessica Baker Flechtner, *CSO*
Girish Aakalu, *Chief Business Officer*
EMP: 38 **EST:** 2006
SQ FT: 34,200
SALES (est): 1.64MM **Publicly Held**
Web: www.genocea.com
SIC: 2836 2834 Biological products, except
diagnostic; Pharmaceutical preparations

(G-7583)

GENZYME CORPORATION

Also Called: Genzyme Biosurgery
55 Cambridge Pkwy Ste 19 (02142-1234)
PHONE.................................508 271-2919
Robert Pelletier, *Mgr*
EMP: 148
Web: www.sanofi.us
SIC: 2834 Pharmaceutical preparations
HQ: Genzyme Corporation
450 Water St
Cambridge MA 02141
617 252-7500

(G-7584)

GENZYME CORPORATION

Genzyme Tissue Repair Division
500 Kendall St (02142)
PHONE.................................617 494-8484
David Meaker, *VP*
EMP: 300
Web: www.sanofi.us
SIC: 2834 Pharmaceutical preparations
HQ: Genzyme Corporation
450 Water St
Cambridge MA 02141
617 252-7500

(G-7585)

GENZYME CORPORATION (DH)

Also Called: Genzyme Therapeutics Division
450 Water St (02141-2288)
PHONE.................................617 252-7500
Christopher A Viehbacher, *CEO*
▲ **EMP:** 600 **EST:** 1991
SALES (est): 1.51B **Privately Held**
Web: www.sanofi.com
SIC: 2835 2834 8071 3842 Enzyme and
isoenzyme diagnostic agents;
Pharmaceutical preparations; Biological
laboratory; Surgical appliances and supplies
HQ: Sanofi Us Services Inc.
55 Corporate Dr
Bridgewater NJ 08807
800 981-2491

(G-7586)

GENZYME CORPORATION

1 Kendall Sq Ste 113 (02139-1562)
PHONE.................................617 252-7500
Frank Ollington, *Pr*
EMP: 61
Web: www.sanofi.us
SIC: 2834 Pharmaceutical preparations
HQ: Genzyme Corporation
450 Water St
Cambridge MA 02141
617 252-7500

(G-7587)

GENZYME CORPORATION

Also Called: Genzyme Biosurgery
64 Sidney St Ste 400 (02139-4170)
PHONE.................................617 252-7999
Tim Surgenor, *Mgr*
EMP: 72
Web: www.sanofi.com
SIC: 2834 Pharmaceutical preparations
HQ: Genzyme Corporation
450 Water St

Cambridge MA 02141
617 252-7500

(G-7588)
GENZYME CORPORATION
Also Called: Sanofi Genzyme
350 Water St (02141-2287)
PHONE..................................617 252-7500
Scott Schaefer, *Brnch Mgr*
EMP: 84
Web: www.sanofi.us
SIC: 2834 Pharmaceutical preparations
HQ: Genzyme Corporation
450 Water St
Cambridge MA 02141
617 252-7500

(G-7589)
GENZYME CORPORATION
1 Kendall Sq (02139-1562)
PHONE..................................508 872-8400
Peter Cook, *Brnch Mgr*
EMP: 106
Web: www.sanofi.us
SIC: 2834 Pharmaceutical preparations
HQ: Genzyme Corporation
450 Water St
Cambridge MA 02141
617 252-7500

(G-7590)
GENZYME SECURITIES CORPORATION
50 Binney St (02142-1512)
PHONE..................................617 252-7500
Joanne M Vasily Cioffi, *Sec*
EMP: 13 **EST:** 2014
SQ FT: 267,278
SALES (est): 170.38K **Privately Held**
SIC: 2834 Pharmaceutical preparations

(G-7591)
GINKGO BIOWORKS INC
45 Moulton St (02138-1118)
PHONE..................................617 633-7972
EMP: 12 **EST:** 2008
SALES (est): 465.06K **Privately Held**
Web: www.ginkgobioworks.com
SIC: 2836 Biological products, except diagnostic

(G-7592)
GLOUCESTER PHARMACEUTICALS INC
1 Broadway Fl 14 (02142-1187)
PHONE..................................617 583-1300
Alan Colowick, *CEO*
Jean C Nichols, *Pr*
William Mcculloch, *CMO*
Peter Biewald, *CFO*
EMP: 14 **EST:** 2004
SQ FT: 400
SALES (est): 10.94MM
SALES (corp-wide): 45.01B **Publicly Held**
SIC: 2834 Pharmaceutical preparations
HQ: Celgene Corporation
86 Morris Ave
Summit NJ 07901
908 673-9000

(G-7593)
GRACE LEE DESIGNS SHILLING
309 Huron Ave (02138-6892)
PHONE..................................617 661-7090
Lee Mei Hua Chang, *Pr*
EMP: 8 **EST:** 1991
SQ FT: 6,500
SALES (est): 242.64K **Privately Held**

SIC: 5712 2512 2511 Custom made furniture, except cabinets; Upholstered household furniture; Wood household furniture

(G-7594)
GSK
200 Cambridgepark Dr (02140-2307)
PHONE..................................781 795-4165
EMP: 11 **EST:** 2018
SALES (est): 1.25MM **Privately Held**
Web: us.gsk.com
SIC: 2834 Pharmaceutical preparations

(G-7595)
GURNET HOLDING COMPANY
55 Cambridge Pkwy Ste 401 (02142-1263)
PHONE..................................617 588-4900
EMP: 212 **EST:** 2018
Web: www.gurnetpointcapital.com
SIC: 6719 2834 8731 Investment holding companies, except banks; Pharmaceutical preparations; Biological research

(G-7596)
GVD CORPORATION (PA)
45 Spinelli Pl (02138-1046)
PHONE..................................617 661-0060
Hilton Pryce Lewis, *Pr*
Karen Gleason, *Sec*
EMP: 11 **EST:** 2001
SALES (est): 4.01MM
SALES (corp-wide): 4.01MM **Privately Held**
Web: www.gvdcorp.com
SIC: 3479 Painting, coating, and hot dipping

(G-7597)
GXT GREEN INC
20 Bryant St (02138-2018)
PHONE..................................978 735-4367
Manas Chatterjee, *CEO*
EMP: 10 **EST:** 2016
SALES (est): 437.46K **Privately Held**
Web: www.gxtgreen.com
SIC: 2821 Plasticizer/additive based plastic materials

(G-7598)
HARBOUR BIOMED US INC
1 Broadway Ste 14 (02142-1187)
PHONE..................................617 682-3679
Jingsong Wang, *CEO*
EMP: 15 **EST:** 2017
SALES (est): 2.17MM **Privately Held**
Web: www.harbourbiomed.com
SIC: 2834 Pharmaceutical preparations

(G-7599)
HARTWELL ASSCOIATES
24 Thorndike St (02141-1882)
PHONE..................................617 686-7571
Stephen Hartwell, *Prin*
EMP: 7 **EST:** 2010
SALES (est): 172.8K **Privately Held**
SIC: 3081 Plastics film and sheet

(G-7600)
HARVARD DEBATE INCORPORATED
490 Adams Mail Ctr (02138-7533)
PHONE..................................617 876-5003
EMP: 9 **EST:** 2010
SALES (est): 1.29MM **Privately Held**
Web: www.hdcsw.org
SIC: 8299 2759 7999 Educational services; Publication printing; Instruction schools, camps, and services

(G-7601)
HARVARD INDEPENDENT INC
371 Harvard St Apt 2d (02138-4119)
PHONE..................................617 495-3682
Will Reckler, *Pr*
▲ **EMP:** 30 **EST:** 1969
SALES (est): 1.82MM **Privately Held**
Web: www.harvardindependent.com
SIC: 2711 2741 Newspapers; Miscellaneous publishing

(G-7602)
HARVARD LAMPOON INC
44 Bow St (02138-5108)
PHONE..................................617 495-7801
Elmer Green, *Pr*
EMP: 35 **EST:** 1876
SQ FT: 15,000
SALES (est): 167.87K **Privately Held**
Web: www.harvardlampoon.com
SIC: 2721 Magazines: publishing only, not printed on site

(G-7603)
HARVARD MAGAZINE INC
7 Ware St (02138-4037)
PHONE..................................617 495-5746
Irina Kuksin, *Pr*
John Rosenberg, *Editor*
EMP: 22 **EST:** 1898
SQ FT: 9,000
SALES (est): 3.61MM **Privately Held**
Web: www.harvardmagazine.com
SIC: 2721 Magazines: publishing only, not printed on site

(G-7604)
HARVARD SCIENTIFIC CORPORATION
799 Concord Ave (02138-1048)
P.O. Box 391651 (02139-0030)
PHONE..................................617 876-5033
Jacob Dahan, *Pr*
EMP: 10 **EST:** 1993
SQ FT: 1,000
SALES (est): 437.41K **Privately Held**
Web: www.harvardscientific.com
SIC: 3679 Waveguides and fittings

(G-7605)
HUBENGAGE INC
1035 Cambridge St Ste 1 (02141-1154)
P.O. Box 4228 (78630-4228)
PHONE..................................877 704-6662
Tushneem Dharmagadda, *Pr*
Erick Michael Crowell, *
Tushneem Dharmagadda, *CEO*
EMP: 40 **EST:** 2018
SALES (est): 2.58MM **Privately Held**
Web: www.hubengage.com
SIC: 7372 Business oriented computer software

(G-7606)
HUBSPOT INC (PA)
25 1st St Ste 200 (02141-1802)
PHONE..................................888 482-7768
Yamini Rangan, *CEO*
Brian Halligan, *
Dharmesh Shah, *
Kate Bueker, *CFO*
EMP: 550 **EST:** 2005
SQ FT: 443,000
SALES (est): 2.17B
SALES (corp-wide): 2.17B **Publicly Held**
Web: www.hubspot.com
SIC: 7372 Prepackaged software

(G-7607)
HYPERION CATALYSIS INTL INC (PA)
38 Smith Pl (02138-1008)
PHONE..................................617 354-9678
Samuel Wohlstadter, *Pr*
Nadine H Wohlstadter, *
Bob Hoch, *
▲ **EMP:** 52 **EST:** 1984
SQ FT: 50,000
SALES (est): 9.02MM
SALES (corp-wide): 9.02MM **Privately Held**
Web: www.hyperioncatalysis.com
SIC: 3624 Carbon specialties for electrical use

(G-7608)
I2O THERAPEUTICS INC
700 Main St (02139-3543)
PHONE..................................303 596-0402
EMP: 11 **EST:** 2019
SALES (est): 3.3MM **Privately Held**
Web: www.i2obio.com
SIC: 2834 Pharmaceutical preparations

(G-7609)
IDENIX PHARMACEUTICALS INC (HQ)
320 Bent St (02141-2005)
PHONE..................................617 995-9800
Ronald C Renaud Junior, *Pr*
Jacques Dumas, *CSO*
Douglas Mayers, *Vice-President Clinical Development*
EMP: 24 **EST:** 2002
SQ FT: 46,418
SALES (est): 27.51MM
SALES (corp-wide): 59.28B **Publicly Held**
SIC: 2834 Drugs affecting parasitic and infective diseases
PA: Merck & Co., Inc.
126 E Lincoln Ave
Rahway NJ 07065
908 740-4000

(G-7610)
IGGYS BREAD LTD (PA)
Also Called: Iggy's Bread of The World
130 Fawcett St (02138-1112)
PHONE..................................617 491-7600
Klaus Nygaard, *Pr*
Igor Ivanovic, *
▲ **EMP:** 75 **EST:** 1994
SQ FT: 30,000
SALES (est): 9.75MM **Privately Held**
Web: www.iggysbread.com
SIC: 2051 5461 Breads, rolls, and buns; Bread

(G-7611)
IMACTIS INC
185 Alewife Brook Pkwy Ste 210 (02138-1100)
PHONE..................................617 576-2005
Georges Tabary, *Managing Member*
EMP: 7 **EST:** 2019
SALES (est): 217.16K **Privately Held**
Web: www.gehealthcare.com
SIC: 3845 Audiological equipment, electromedical

(G-7612)
IMMUNEERING CORPORATION
Also Called: Immuneering
245 Main St Fl 2 (02142-1064)
PHONE..................................617 500-8080
Benjamin J Zeskind, *Pr*
Robert J Carpenter, *Non-Executive Chairman of the Board*

Biren Amin, *CFO*
Scott Barrett, *CMO*
Brett Hall, *CSO*
EMP: 34 **EST:** 2008
SQ FT: 586
SALES (est): 316.95K **Privately Held**
Web: www.immuneering.com
SIC: 2834 8731 Pharmaceutical
  preparations; Biotechnical research,
  commercial

(G-7613)
INFINITE FOREST INC (PA)
Also Called: Betterhalf.ai
172 Charles St Ste B (02141-2118)
  PHONE..............................617 299-1382
Pawan Gupta, *CEO*
EMP: 11 **EST:** 2016
SALES (est): 563.1K
  SALES (corp-wide): 563.1K **Privately Held**
SIC: 7372 Application computer software

(G-7614)
INFINITY PHARMACEUTICALS INC (PA)
Also Called: Infinity Pharmaceuticals
1100 Mass Ave Ste 4 (02138-5241)
Seth Tasker, *CEO*
EMP: 10 **EST:** 1995
SQ FT: 10,097
SALES (est): 2.59MM **Publicly Held**
Web: www.infi.com
SIC: 2834 8731 Pharmaceutical
  preparations; Commercial physical research

(G-7615)
INSTITUTE FOR FGN PLICY ANALIS (PA)
675 Massachusetts Ave Ste 10 (02139)
P.O. Box 390960 (02139-0021)
  PHONE..............................617 492-2116
Robert L Pfaltzgraph, *Pr*
Doctor Jacquelyn K Davis, *Ex VP*
Doctor Charles M Perry, *VP*
EMP: 20 **EST:** 1976
SALES (est): 1.88MM
  SALES (corp-wide): 1.88MM **Privately Held**
Web: www.ifpa.org
SIC: 8733 2731 7389 Educational research
  agency; Books, publishing only; Lecture
  bureau

(G-7616)
INTELLIA THERAPEUTICS INC (PA)
40 Erie St Ste 130 (02139-4254)
  PHONE..............................857 285-6200
John M Leonard, *Pr*
Frank Verwiel, *Ch Bd*
Glenn G Goddard, *Ex VP*
Eliana Clark, *Ex VP*
David Lebwohl, *CMO*
EMP: 148 **EST:** 2014
SQ FT: 65,000
SALES (est): 52.12MM
  SALES (corp-wide): 52.12MM **Publicly Held**
Web: www.intelliatx.com
SIC: 2835 8731 Diagnostic substances;
  Biotechnical research, commercial

(G-7617)
IPSEN BIOPHARMACEUTICALS INC (HQ)
1 Main St Ste 700 (02142-1531)
  PHONE..............................973 903-4442
Richard Paulson, *Ex VP*
Cynthia Schwalm, *

Jennifer Benenson, *
Elaine Yi, *
Habib Rameani, *
EMP: 215 **EST:** 2001
SQ FT: 32,600
SALES (est): 90.75MM **Privately Held**
Web: www.ipsen.com
SIC: 2833 2834 Endocrine products;
  Pharmaceutical preparations
PA: Ipsen
  65 Quai Georges Gorse
  Boulogne Billancourt 92100

(G-7618)
IPSEN BIOSCIENCE INC
1 Kendall Sq Ste B7401 (02139-1599)
  PHONE..............................617 679-8500
John Kehoe, *VP*
EMP: 41
Web: www.ipsen.com
SIC: 2834 Proprietary drug products
HQ: Ipsen Bioscience, Inc.
  1 Main St Ste 7
  Cambridge MA 02142
  617 679-8500

(G-7619)
JOHN KARL DIETRICH & ASSOC
Also Called: Classic Copy & Printing
26 Central Sq (02139-3311)
  PHONE..............................617 868-4140
EMP: 7 **EST:** 1984
SQ FT: 1,600
SALES (est): 228.34K **Privately Held**
SIC: 2791 2759 7334 Typographic
  composition, for the printing trade;
  Commercial printing, nec; Photocopying
  and duplicating services

(G-7620)
JOUNCE THERAPEUTICS INC (PA)
Also Called: Jounce Therapeutics
780 Memorial Dr (02139-4613)
  PHONE..............................857 259-3840
Richard Murray, *Pr*
Perry A Karsen, *
Kim C Drapkin, *CFO*
Elizabeth G Trehu, *CMO*
Deborah Law, *CSO*
EMP: 51 **EST:** 2012
SQ FT: 51,000
SALES (est): 82MM
  SALES (corp-wide): 82MM **Privately Held**
Web: www.concentrabiosciences.com
SIC: 2836 8731 Biological products, except
  diagnostic; Commercial physical research

(G-7621)
KALVISTA PHARMACEUTICALS INC (PA)
Also Called: Kalvista
55 Cambridge Pkwy Ste 900 (02142)
  PHONE..............................857 999-0075
T Andrew Crockett, *CEO*
Brian Jg Pereira, *Ch Bd*
Benjamin L Palleiko, *Chief Business Officer*
Edward P Feener, *CSO*
Paul K Audhya, *CMO*
EMP: 21 **EST:** 2004
SQ FT: 2,700
Web: www.kalvista.com
SIC: 2834 8071 Pharmaceutical
  preparations; Biological laboratory

(G-7622)
KERYX BIOPHARMACEUTICALS INC (HQ)

245 1st St (02142-1200)
  PHONE..............................617 871-2098
Nicole R Hadas, *Pr*
Jodie P Morrison, *Interim Chief Executive
  Officer*
Scott A Holmes, *
Christine Carberry, *
John F Neylan, *CMO*
EMP: 11 **EST:** 1998
SQ FT: 27,300
SALES (est): 56.14MM **Publicly Held**
Web: www.akebia.com
SIC: 2834 Pharmaceutical preparations
PA: Akebia Therapeutics, Inc.
  245 1st St Ste 1400
  Cambridge MA 02142

(G-7623)
KIQ BIO LLC
200 Cambridgepark Dr Ste 3100 (02140)
  PHONE..............................617 945-5576
Charles Wilson, *Pr*
EMP: 56 **EST:** 2020
SALES (est): 7.49MM **Publicly Held**
SIC: 2834 Pharmaceutical preparations
PA: Cogent Biosciences, Inc.
  275 Wyman St Fl 3
  Waltham MA 02451
  617 945-5576

(G-7624)
KORRO BIO INC (PA)
1 Kendall Sq Bldg 600-700 (02139-1562)
  PHONE..............................617 468-1999
Ram Aiyar, *Pr*
Vineet Agarwal, *CFO*
Todd Chappell, *COO*
Steve Colletti, *CSO*
Shelby J Walker, *Corporate Secretary*
EMP: 81 **EST:** 2014
SQ FT: 22,500
Web: www.frequencytx.com
SIC: 2834 Pharmaceutical preparations

(G-7625)
KSPLICE INC
1 Main St Ste 7f (02142-1599)
  PHONE..............................765 577-5423
Jeff Arnold, *Pr*
EMP: 9 **EST:** 2009
SALES (est): 1.04MM
  SALES (corp-wide): 49.95B **Publicly Held**
Web: ksplice.oracle.com
SIC: 7372 Prepackaged software
PA: Oracle Corporation
  2300 Oracle Way
  Austin TX 78741
  737 867-1000

(G-7626)
LABCENTRAL INC (PA)
Also Called: K2b Therapeutics
700 Main St N (02139-3543)
  PHONE..............................617 863-3650
Johannes Fruehauf, *CEO*
Peter Parker, *
Celina Chang, *
EMP: 27 **EST:** 2012
SALES (est): 21.8MM
  SALES (corp-wide): 21.8MM **Privately Held**
Web: www.labcentral.org
SIC: 6732 3821 Trusts: educational,
  religious, etc.; Laboratory apparatus,
  except heating and measuring

(G-7627)
LAMBIENT TECHNOLOGIES LLC
649 Massachusetts Ave Ste 4 (02139)
  PHONE..............................857 242-3963

Huan Lee, *Managing Member*
Stephen W Pomeroy, *Managing Member*
EMP: 8 **EST:** 2010
SALES (est): 589.03K **Privately Held**
Web: www.lambient.com
SIC: 3559 Screening equipment, electric

(G-7628)
LAMPLIGHTER BREWING CO LLC
110 N First St (02141-2293)
  PHONE..............................617 945-2743
John Hunsicker, *Brnch Mgr*
EMP: 22
SALES (corp-wide): 7.49MM **Privately
  Held**
Web: www.lamplighterbrewing.com
SIC: 2082 Malt beverages
PA: Lamplighter Brewing Co., Llc
  284 Broadway
  Cambridge MA 02139
  207 650-3325

(G-7629)
LAMPLIGHTER BREWING CO LLC (PA)
Also Called: Lamplighter Brewing Co.
284 Broadway (02139-1808)
  PHONE..............................207 650-3325
EMP: 24 **EST:** 2014
SQ FT: 10,003
SALES (est): 7.49MM
  SALES (corp-wide): 7.49MM **Privately
  Held**
Web: www.lamplighterbrewing.com
SIC: 2082 Beer (alcoholic beverage)

(G-7630)
LEAP THERAPEUTICS INC (PA)
Also Called: Leap Therapeutics
47 Thorndike St Ste B1-1 (02141-1799)
  PHONE..............................617 714-0360
Douglas E Onsi, *Pr*
Christopher K Mirabelli, *Ch Bd*
Augustine Lawlor, *COO*
Cynthia Sirard, *CMO*
Mark O'mahony, *MFG*
EMP: 11 **EST:** 2011
SQ FT: 7,667
Web: www.leaptx.com
SIC: 2834 Pharmaceutical preparations

(G-7631)
LETS GO INC
67 Mount Auburn St (02138-4961)
  PHONE..............................617 495-9659
Anne Chisholm, *Genl Mgr*
EMP: 1000 **EST:** 1960
SQ FT: 5,000
SALES (est): 2.58MM
  SALES (corp-wide): 2.58MM **Privately
  Held**
Web: www.letsgo.com
SIC: 2741 Miscellaneous publishing
PA: Harvard Student Agencies Inc
  67 Mount Auburn St
  Cambridge MA 02138
  617 495-3030

(G-7632)
LIBRING TECHNOLOGIES INC
1 Broadway Fl 14 (02142-1187)
  PHONE..............................617 553-1015
EMP: 13 **EST:** 2008
SALES (est): 1.89MM
  SALES (corp-wide): 177.38K **Privately
  Held**
Web: www.ballestiero.com
SIC: 7372 Prepackaged software
HQ: App Annie Inc.
  44 Montgomery St Ste 3

San Francisco CA 94104
844 277-2664

(G-7633)
LIQUIGLIDE INC
75 Sidney St 5th Fl (02139-4134)
PHONE...............................617 901-0700
Jonathan David Smith, *Pr*
EMP: 32 **EST:** 2012
SQ FT: 4,000
SALES (est): 5.72MM **Privately Held**
Web: www.liquiglide.com
SIC: 2869 3721   Industrial organic
   chemicals, nec; Aircraft

(G-7634)
LONZA BIOLOGICS INC
50 Hampshire St Ste 401 (02139-1893)
PHONE...............................608 630-3758
EMP: 71
SALES (corp-wide): 14.86MM **Privately
Held**
Web: www.lonza.com
SIC: 2834   Pharmaceutical preparations
PA: Lonza Biologics Inc.
   1978 W Winton Ave
   Hayward CA 94545
   510 731-3500

(G-7635)
**LUCKWEL PHARMACEUTICALS
INC**
125 Cambridgepark Dr Ste 301 (02140)
PHONE...............................617 430-5222
Kingrich Lee, *CEO*
Mark Carrao, *CFO*
EMP: 8 **EST:** 2013
SALES (est): 74.42K **Privately Held**
Web: www.luckwel.com
SIC: 2834   Pharmaceutical preparations

(G-7636)
M & C PRESS INC
Also Called: Kendall Press
1 Main St Ste 105 (02142-1531)
PHONE...............................617 354-2584
Mark D Lemley, *Pr*
Cheryl A Lemley, *Sr VP*
EMP: 12 **EST:** 1984
SQ FT: 3,500
SALES (est): 2.38MM **Privately Held**
SIC: 2752   Offset printing

(G-7637)
**MASSACHUSETTS INSTITUTE
TECH**
Also Called: Mit Press, The
1 Rogers St (02142-1209)
PHONE...............................617 253-5646
Ellen Faran, *Dir*
EMP: 104
SALES (corp-wide): 4.27B **Privately Held**
Web: web.mit.edu
SIC: 2721 8221   Periodicals; University
PA: Massachusetts Institute Of Technology
   77 Massachusetts Ave
   Cambridge MA 02139
   617 253-1000

(G-7638)
**MASSACHUSETTS INSTITUTE
TECH**
Also Called: Sloan MGT Review
77 Max Ave Ste E60 (02139-4307)
PHONE...............................617 253-7183
Stephen Alter, *Prin*
EMP: 9
SALES (corp-wide): 4.27B **Privately Held**
Web: web.mit.edu

SIC: 2711 8221   Newspapers, publishing
   and printing; University
PA: Massachusetts Institute Of Technology
   77 Massachusetts Ave
   Cambridge MA 02139
   617 253-1000

(G-7639)
MAZU NETWORKS LLC
125 Cambridgepark Dr Ste 14
(02140-2365)
PHONE...............................617 354-9292
EMP: 45 **EST:** 2000
SALES (est): 9.01MM
SALES (corp-wide): 912.58MM **Privately
Held**
Web: www.riverbed.com
SIC: 3577   Computer peripheral equipment,
   nec
HQ: Riverbed Technology Llc
   680 Folsom St Ste 600
   San Francisco CA 94107
   415 247-8800

(G-7640)
**MERRIMACK
PHARMACEUTICALS INC (PA)**
Also Called: Merrimack
1 Broadway Fl 14 (02142-1187)
PHONE...............................617 441-1000
Gary Crocker, *Ch Bd*
Gary L Crocker, *Ch Bd*
Jean M Franchi, *CFO*
Sergio L Santillana, *CMO*
EMP: 42 **EST:** 1993
SQ FT: 112,300
Web: www.merrimack.com
SIC: 2834   Druggists' preparations
   (pharmaceuticals)

(G-7641)
**MERSANA THERAPEUTICS INC
(PA)**
Also Called: Mersana Therapeutics
840 Memorial Dr (02139-3860)
PHONE...............................617 498-0020
Martin Huber, *Pr*
David Mott, *
Alejandra Carvajal, *CLO*
Timothy B Lowinger, *SCIENCE*
Tushar Misra Chief Manufacturi ng, *Ofcr*
EMP: 57 **EST:** 2001
SQ FT: 45,000
SALES (est): 26.58MM **Publicly Held**
Web: www.mersana.com
SIC: 2834 8731   Pharmaceutical
   preparations; Biotechnical research,
   commercial

(G-7642)
**METALMARK INNOVATIONS
PBC**
767 Concord Ave Ste 2-1 (02138-1044)
PHONE...............................617 714-4026
Sissi Liu, *CEO*
Joanna Aizenberg, *Pr*
Tanya Shirman, *Dir*
Elijah Shirman, *Dir*
EMP: 7 **EST:** 2017
SALES (est): 942.11K **Privately Held**
Web: www.metalmark.xyz
SIC: 3564 7371   Air purification equipment;
   Computer software development and
   applications

(G-7643)
MICROSOFT CORPORATION
Also Called: Microsoft
255 Main St Ste 401 (02142-1036)

PHONE...............................781 398-4600
Sven Ingard, *Mgr*
EMP: 20
SALES (corp-wide): 211.91B **Publicly
Held**
Web: www.microsoft.pl
SIC: 7372   Application computer software
PA: Microsoft Corporation
   1 Microsoft Way
   Redmond WA 98052
   425 882-8080

(G-7644)
MICROSOFT CORPORATION
Also Called: Microsoft
1 Memorial Dr Ste 1 (02142-1346)
PHONE...............................857 453-6000
Henry Cohn, *Brnch Mgr*
EMP: 21
SALES (corp-wide): 211.91B **Publicly
Held**
Web: www.microsoftnewengland.com
SIC: 7372   Application computer software
PA: Microsoft Corporation
   1 Microsoft Way
   Redmond WA 98052
   425 882-8080

(G-7645)
**MILLENNIUM
PHARMACEUTICALS INC**
640 Memorial Dr Ste 3w (02139-4853)
PHONE...............................617 679-7000
Ray Roane, *Mgr*
EMP: 119
Web: www.takedaoncology.com
SIC: 2834   Pharmaceutical preparations
HQ: Millennium Pharmaceuticals, Inc.
   40 Landsdowne St
   Cambridge MA 02139

(G-7646)
**MILLENNIUM
PHARMACEUTICALS INC (HQ)**
Also Called: Takeda Oncology
40 Landsdowne St (02139-4234)
PHONE...............................617 679-7000
Deborah Dunsire, *Pr*
Christophe Bianchi, *Executive Commercial
Vice President*
Marsha H Fanucci, *Sr VP*
Stephen M Gansler, *Senior Vice President
Human Resources*
Laurie B Keating, *Sec*
▲ **EMP:** 166 **EST:** 1993
SQ FT: 585,441
SALES (est): 405.56MM **Privately Held**
Web: www.takedaoncology.com
SIC: 2834   Pharmaceutical preparations
PA: Takeda Pharmaceutical Company
   Limited
   2-1-1, Nihombashihoncho
   Chuo-Ku TKY 103-0

(G-7647)
**MILLENNIUM
PHARMACEUTICALS INC**
35 Landsdowne St (02139-4232)
PHONE...............................617 679-7000
George Mulligan, *Brnch Mgr*
EMP: 127
Web: www.takedaoncology.com
SIC: 2834 8731   Pharmaceutical
   preparations; Commercial physical research
HQ: Millennium Pharmaceuticals, Inc.
   40 Landsdowne St
   Cambridge MA 02139

(G-7648)
**MILLENNIUM
PHARMACEUTICALS INC**
300 Massachusetts Ave (02139-4130)
PHONE...............................617 679-7000
EMP: 82
Web: www.takedaoncology.com
SIC: 2834   Pharmaceutical preparations
HQ: Millennium Pharmaceuticals, Inc.
   40 Landsdowne St
   Cambridge MA 02139

(G-7649)
**MILLENNIUM
PHARMACEUTICALS INC**
45 Sidney St (02139-4133)
PHONE...............................617 679-7000
Mark J Levin, *Ch Bd*
EMP: 87
Web: www.takedaoncology.com
SIC: 2834   Pharmaceutical preparations
HQ: Millennium Pharmaceuticals, Inc.
   40 Landsdowne St
   Cambridge MA 02139

(G-7650)
**MILLENNIUM
PHARMACEUTICALS INC**
1 Kendall Sq Bldg 200 (02139-1562)
PHONE...............................617 679-7000
Mark J Levin, *Ch Bd*
EMP: 97
Web: www.takedaoncology.com
SIC: 2834   Pharmaceutical preparations
HQ: Millennium Pharmaceuticals, Inc.
   40 Landsdowne St
   Cambridge MA 02139

(G-7651)
**MILLENNIUM
PHARMACEUTICALS INC**
125 Binney St (02142-1123)
PHONE...............................617 679-7000
EMP: 100
Web: www.takedaoncology.com
SIC: 2834   Pharmaceutical preparations
HQ: Millennium Pharmaceuticals, Inc.
   40 Landsdowne St
   Cambridge MA 02139

(G-7652)
**MITSUBSHI TNABE PHRMA
AMER INC**
21 Erie St (02139-4260)
PHONE...............................210 897-3473
EMP: 12 **EST:** 2017
SALES (est): 534.81K **Privately Held**
Web:
mtpa.preview2.ascenderstudios.com
SIC: 2834   Pharmaceutical preparations

(G-7653)
MODERNA INC (PA)
Also Called: Moderna
200 Technology Sq (02139-3578)
PHONE...............................617 714-6500
Stephane Bancel, *CEO*
Noubar B Afeyan, *Non-Executive Chairman
of the Board**
Stephen Hoge, *Pr*
James Mock, *CFO*
Jerh Collins, *CQO*
EMP: 296 **EST:** 2009
SALES (est): 19.26B
SALES (corp-wide): 19.26B **Publicly Held**
Web: www.modernatx.com

SIC: 2836 2834 Biological products, except diagnostic; Pharmaceutical preparations

(G-7654)
MOMENTA PHARMACEUTICALS INC (HQ)
301 Binney St (02142-1071)
PHONE...............................617 491-9700
Craig A Wheeler, *Pr*
James R Sulat, *Ch Bd*
Michelle Robertson, *CAO*
Santiago Arroyo, *Senior Vice President Development*
Young Kwon, *Chief Financial*
EMP: 94 EST: 2002
SQ FT: 78,500
SALES (est): 23.87MM
SALES (corp-wide): 94.94B **Publicly Held**
Web: www.momentapharma.com
SIC: 2834 Pharmaceutical preparations
PA: Johnson & Johnson
1 Johnson And Johnson Plz
New Brunswick NJ 08933
732 524-0400

(G-7655)
MONTAGUE CORPORATION
Also Called: Montague USA
1035 Cambridge St Ste 29 (02141-1154)
P.O. Box 381118 (02238-1118)
PHONE...............................617 491-7200
Harry Montague, *CEO*
David Montague, *Pr*
◆ EMP: 10 EST: 1988
SQ FT: 12,000
SALES (est): 987.2K **Privately Held**
Web: www.montaguebikes.com
SIC: 5091 3751 Bicycles; Motorcycles, bicycles and parts

(G-7656)
MONTAI HEALTH INC
26 Landsdowne St (02139-4216)
PHONE...............................617 293-0578
EMP: 26 EST: 2019
SALES (est): 2.96MM **Privately Held**
Web: www.montai.com
SIC: 2834 Pharmaceutical preparations

(G-7657)
MTOZ BIOLABS INC
210 Broadway 201 (02139-1959)
PHONE...............................617 401-8103
Alex Cheung, *CEO*
EMP: 50 EST: 2018
SALES (est): 1.74MM **Privately Held**
Web: www.mtoz-biolabs.com
SIC: 3826 Protein analyzers, laboratory type

(G-7658)
MYJOVE CORPORATION
Also Called: Jove
625 Massachusetts Ave Fl 2 (02139)
PHONE...............................617 945-9051
Moshe Pritsker, *CEO*
EMP: 55 EST: 2008
SALES (est): 10.95MM **Privately Held**
Web: www.jove.com
SIC: 2741 Miscellaneous publishing

(G-7659)
NANOBIOSYM INC
245 1st St Ste 18 (02142-1292)
PHONE...............................781 391-7979
EMP: 20
SALES (corp-wide): 9.62MM **Privately Held**
Web: www.nanobiosym.com

Web: www.netgworld.com
SIC: 3577 Computer peripheral equipment, nec
PA: Nanobiosym, Inc.
200 Boston Ave Ste 4700
Medford MA 02155
781 391-7979

(G-7660)
NAVITOR PHARMACEUTICALS INC
1030 Massachusetts Ave (02138-5388)
PHONE...............................857 285-4300
Thomas E Hughes, *CEO*
James Randall Owen, *CMO*
EMP: 13 EST: 2016
SALES (est): 4.33MM **Privately Held**
Web: www.navitorpharma.com
SIC: 2834 Pharmaceutical preparations

(G-7661)
NEENAS LIGHTING
57 Jfk St (02138-4954)
PHONE...............................617 864-5757
EMP: 7 EST: 2005
SALES (est): 15.4K **Privately Held**
SIC: 3641 3999 5023 Electric lamps; Lamp shade frames; Lamps: floor, boudoir, desk

(G-7662)
NETTWERK MUSIC GROUP LLC
15 Richdale Ave (02140-2600)
PHONE...............................617 497-8200
Dalton Sim, *Brnch Mgr*
EMP: 23
SALES (corp-wide): 19.68MM **Privately Held**
Web: www.nettwerk.com
SIC: 2782 Blankbooks and looseleaf binders
HQ: Nettwerk Music Group Llc
1545 Wilcox Ave Ste 103
Los Angeles CA 90028
323 301-4200

(G-7663)
NEURO PHAGE PHRMACEUTICALS INC
222 3rd St (02142-1102)
PHONE...............................617 941-7004
Jonathan Solomon, *CEO*
Franz Hefti, *Pr*
John F Dee, *Ch Bd*
EMP: 10 EST: 2011
SALES (est): 815.7K **Privately Held**
Web: www.neurophage.com
SIC: 2834 Pharmaceutical preparations

(G-7664)
NEUROBO PHARMACEUTICALS INC (PA)
Also Called: Neurobo
545 Concord Ave Ste 210 (02138-1132)
PHONE...............................617 864-2880
Hyung Heon, *Pr*
Yeon Kim, *Ch Bd*
Jeong Gu Kang, *Interim Chief Financial Officer*
Mark Versavel, *CMO*
Nicola Shannon, *Clinical Vice President*
EMP: 10 EST: 2008
Web: www.neurobopharma.com
SIC: 2834 Pharmaceutical preparations

(G-7665)
NEW ENGLAND TECHNOLOGY GROUP
1 Davenport St Ste 1 (02140-1415)
PHONE...............................617 864-5551
Steven K Gregory, *Pr*
EMP: 10 EST: 1981
SALES (est): 845.11K **Privately Held**

(G-7666)
NEXTPOINT THERAPEUTICS INC
238 Main St Ste 5 (02142-1099)
PHONE...............................917 208-0865
Detlev Biniszkiewicz, *CEO*
Detlev Biniszkiewicz, *Prin*
Paul Conrad, *Prin*
Ansbert Gadicke, *Prin*
Matt Roden, *Prin*
EMP: 9 EST: 2019
SALES (est): 1.12MM **Privately Held**
Web: www.nextpointtx.com
SIC: 2834 Pills, pharmaceutical

(G-7667)
NOVARTIS CORPORATION
Also Called: Nibr Novartis
181 Massachusetts Ave (02139-4342)
PHONE...............................617 225-0820
EMP: 28
Web: www.novartis.com
SIC: 2834 Pharmaceutical preparations
HQ: Novartis Corporation
1 Health Plz
East Hanover NJ 07936
212 307-1122

(G-7668)
NOVARTIS INSTTTES FOR BMDCAL R (HQ)
Also Called: Nibr
700 Main St (02139-3543)
PHONE...............................617 777-8276
Mark Fishman, *Pr*
Keith Boudreau, *
Christiana Klee, *
▲ EMP: 24 EST: 2002
SQ FT: 1,500
SALES (est): 183.91MM **Privately Held**
Web: www.novartis.com
SIC: 2834 Pharmaceutical preparations
PA: Novartis Ag
Lichtstrasse 35
Basel BS 4056

(G-7669)
NOVARTIS MLCLAR DAGNOSTICS LLC
45 Sidney St (02139-4133)
PHONE...............................617 871-8441
EMP: 20 EST: 2008
SALES (est): 618.4K **Privately Held**
Web: www.novartis.com
SIC: 5047 2834 Diagnostic equipment, medical; Pharmaceutical preparations

(G-7670)
NOVARTIS VCCNES DAGNOSTICS INC
350 Massachusetts Ave Ste 200 (02139-4182)
PHONE...............................617 871-7000
Joerg Reinhardt, *CEO*
EMP: 1092
SALES (corp-wide): 35.31B **Privately Held**
Web: www.novartis.com
SIC: 2834 Pharmaceutical preparations
HQ: Novartis Vaccines And Diagnostics, Inc.
475 Green Oaks Pkwy
Holly Springs NC 27540
617 871-7000

(G-7671)
NOVIRIO PHARMACEUTICALS INC
60 Hampshire (02139-1548)
PHONE...............................617 250-3100
Ansbert Gadicke, *V Ch Bd*
James Egan Senior, *Vice President Business*
George Chao, *Vice President Biostatistics Data Management*
John P Dunphy, *CFO*
Scot M Barry, *VP Mfg*
EMP: 58 EST: 1998
SQ FT: 21,815
SALES (est): 12.33MM
SALES (corp-wide): 59.28B **Publicly Held**
SIC: 2834 8731 Pharmaceutical preparations; Commercial physical research
HQ: Idenix Pharmaceuticals, Inc.
320 Bent St
Cambridge MA 02141
617 995-9800

(G-7672)
NUVALENT INC (PA)
1 Broadway Ste 14 (02142-1187)
PHONE...............................857 357-7000
Anna Protopapas, *Ch Bd*
James R Porter, *Pr*
Alexandra Balcom, *CFO*
Christopher D Turner, *CMO*
Deborah Miller, *CLO*
EMP: 27 EST: 2017
Web: www.nuvalent.com
SIC: 2834 Pharmaceutical preparations

(G-7673)
OFF THE DIAL MEDIA LLC
Also Called: Indie617
36 Bay State Rd Ste 2 (02138-1266)
PHONE...............................617 929-3424
Paul Driscoll, *Pr*
EMP: 16 EST: 2017
SALES (est): 800K **Privately Held**
SIC: 4832 7372 Radio broadcasting stations ; Application computer software

(G-7674)
ON THE BEAT INC
Also Called: American Police Beat
43 Thorndike St Ste 2-4 (02141-1762)
PHONE...............................617 491-8878
Richard Devlin, *Pr*
Cynthia Brown, *Ch*
H James Brown, *Treas*
EMP: 8 EST: 1993
SQ FT: 1,000
SALES (est): 840.17K **Privately Held**
Web: www.apbweb.com
SIC: 2711 Newspapers: publishing only, not printed on site

(G-7675)
ONO PHARMA USA INC
1 Main St (02142-1531)
PHONE...............................617 904-4500
Wataru Kamoshima, *Pr*
David Trexler, *CCO*
EMP: 12 EST: 1998
SALES (est): 11.61MM **Privately Held**
Web: us.ono-pharma.com
SIC: 2834 Pharmaceutical preparations
PA: Ono Pharmaceutical Co., Ltd.
1-8-2, Kyutaromachi, Chuo-Ku
Osaka OSK 541-0

(G-7676)
OPENDATASOFT LLC
185 Alewife Brook Pkwy Ste 210 (02138-1100)

PHONE..........................781 952-0515
Franck Carassus, *Prin*
EMP: 70 **EST:** 2017
SALES (est): 295.02K **Privately Held**
SIC: 7299 7372 Miscellaneous personal
service; Prepackaged software

(G-7677)
ORACLE CORPORATION
Also Called: Oracle
101 Main St Ste 1 (02142-1519)
PHONE..........................617 497-7713
William Crevan, *Owner*
EMP: 19
SALES (corp-wide): 49.95B **Publicly Held**
Web: www.oracle.com
SIC: 7372 Business oriented computer
software
PA: Oracle Corporation
2300 Oracle Way
Austin TX 78741
737 867-1000

(G-7678)
ORACLE OTC SUBSIDIARY LLC
Also Called: Atg
1 Main St Ste 7 (02142-1599)
PHONE..........................617 386-1000
Robert D Burke, *Pr*
Lawrence Joseph Ellison, *
EMP: 545 **EST:** 1991
SQ FT: 59,000
SALES (est): 92.56MM
SALES (corp-wide): 49.95B **Publicly Held**
SIC: 7372 Application computer software
PA: Oracle Corporation
2300 Oracle Way
Austin TX 78741
737 867-1000

(G-7679)
OSMO LABS PBC
750 Main St (02139-3544)
PHONE..........................508 439-4692
Alex Wiltschko, *CEO*
EMP: 11
SALES (est): 1.04MM **Privately Held**
SIC: 2899 Chemical preparations, nec

(G-7680)
PADLOCK THERAPEUTICS INC
Also Called: Padlock Therapeutics
200 Cambridgepark Dr (02140)
P.O. Box 4000 (08543-4000)
PHONE..........................978 381-9601
Michael Gilman, *CEO*
Rajesh Devraj, *CSO*
Samantha Truex, *Chief Business Officer*
EMP: 17 **EST:** 2014
SALES (est): 2.29MM
SALES (corp-wide): 46.16B **Publicly Held**
SIC: 2834 Pharmaceutical preparations
PA: Bristol-Myers Squibb Company
430 E 29th St Fl 14
New York NY 10016
212 546-4000

(G-7681)
PEGASYSTEMS INC (PA)
Also Called: PEGA
1 Main St (02142-1531)
PHONE..........................617 374-9600
Alan Trefler, *Ch Bd*
Kenneth Stillwell, *CFO*
Kerim Akgonul, *CPO*
Efstathios Kouninis, *CAO*
EMP: 972 **EST:** 1983
SALES (est): 1.32B
SALES (corp-wide): 1.32B **Publicly Held**
Web: www.pega.com

SIC: 7379 7371 7372 Computer related
consulting services; Computer software
development; Business oriented computer
software

(G-7682)
PENDAR TECHNOLOGIES LLC (PA)
30 Spinelli Pl (02138-1070)
PHONE..........................617 588-2128
EMP: 10 **EST:** 2011
SALES (est): 10.5MM **Privately Held**
Web: www.pendar.com
SIC: 3845 Electromedical equipment

(G-7683)
PFIZER INC
Also Called: Pfizer
610 Main St (02139-3526)
PHONE..........................617 551-3000
Cynthia Wood, *Prin*
EMP: 14
SALES (corp-wide): 100.33B **Publicly Held**
Web: www.pfizer.com
SIC: 2834 Pharmaceutical preparations
PA: Pfizer Inc.
66 Hudson Blvd E
New York NY 10001
212 733-2323

(G-7684)
PFIZER INC
Also Called: Pfizer
1 Portland St (02139-3528)
PHONE..........................617 674-7436
EMP: 8
SALES (corp-wide): 100.33B **Publicly Held**
Web: www.pfizer.com
SIC: 2834 Pharmaceutical preparations
PA: Pfizer Inc.
66 Hudson Blvd E Fl 20
New York NY 10001
212 733-2323

(G-7685)
PHARMION CORPORATION
200 Cambridgepark Dr (02140-2307)
PHONE..........................857 706-1311
EMP: 20
SALES (corp-wide): 46.16B **Publicly Held**
Web: www.bms.com
SIC: 2834 Pharmaceutical preparations
HQ: Pharmion Corporation
86 Morris Ave
Summit NJ 07901
908 673-9000

(G-7686)
PHILIPS HOLDING USA INC (HQ)
Also Called: Philips Consumer Lifestyle
222 Jacobs St (02141-2296)
PHONE..........................978 687-1501
◆ **EMP:** 587 **EST:** 1995
SQ FT: 100,000
SALES (est): 3.87B
SALES (corp-wide): 18.51B **Privately Held**
Web: usa.philips.com
SIC: 3674 5045 5047 3641 Semiconductors
and related devices; Computers,
peripherals, and software; Medical and
hospital equipment; Electric lamps
PA: Koninklijke Philips N.V.
High Tech Campus 52
Eindhoven NB 5656
853015541

(G-7687)
POSTDOC VENTURES LLC
1668 Massachusetts Ave (02138-1838)
PHONE..........................617 492-3555
Matthew Alan Wallace, *Prin*
EMP: 9 **EST:** 2010
SALES (est): 468.16K **Privately Held**
SIC: 2026 Yogurt

(G-7688)
PRESIDENT AND FELLOWS OF HARVARD COLLEGE (PA)
Also Called: Harvard University
1350 Massachusetts Ave (02138-3846)
PHONE..........................617 496-4873
◆ **EMP:** 9500 **EST:** 1636
SALES (est): 6.1B
SALES (corp-wide): 6.1B **Privately Held**
Web: www.harvarduniversity.com
SIC: 8221 8732 2721 University;
Educational research; Magazines:
publishing and printing

(G-7689)
PRINTING DEPT
795 Massachusetts Ave (02139-3201)
PHONE..........................617 349-4206
Marie Killackey, *Mgr*
EMP: 41 **EST:** 2011
SALES (est): 133.78K **Privately Held**
SIC: 2752 Offset printing

(G-7690)
PRIORITY PRINT
337 Cambridge St (02141-1208)
PHONE..........................617 547-6919
Jeff Klein, *Prin*
EMP: 8 **EST:** 2007
SALES (est): 139.42K **Privately Held**
SIC: 2752 Offset printing

(G-7691)
PTC THERAPEUTICS GT INC
245 First St Ste 1800 (02142-1292)
PHONE..........................781 799-9179
Mark Pykett, *CEO*
Christopher J Silber, *Chief Medical Officer*
EMP: 30 **EST:** 2013
SALES (est): 4.91MM
SALES (corp-wide): 698.8MM **Publicly Held**
SIC: 2834 Drugs acting on the central
nervous system & sense organs
PA: Ptc Therapeutics, Inc.
100 Corporate Ct
South Plainfield NJ 07080
908 222-7000

(G-7692)
RA PHARMACEUTICALS INC (DH)
Also Called: Ra Pharmaceuticals
87 Cambridgepark Dr (02140-2311)
PHONE..........................617 401-4060
EMP: 29 **EST:** 2008
SQ FT: 27,000
SALES (est): 3MM
SALES (corp-wide): 1.04B **Privately Held**
SIC: 2834 Pharmaceutical preparations
HQ: Ucb Holdings, Inc.
1950 Lake Park Dr Se
Smyrna GA 30080
770 970-7500

(G-7693)
RADAR WIND UP CORPORATION (HQ)
30 Kelley St (02138-1314)

PHONE..........................917 488-6050
Meredith Moss, *Pr*
EMP: 11 **EST:** 2010
SALES (est): 2.49MM
SALES (corp-wide): 1.99B **Publicly Held**
Web: www.finomial.com
SIC: 7372 7389 Prepackaged software;
Business Activities at Non-Commercial Site
PA: Sei Investments Company
1 Freedom Valley Dr
Oaks PA 19456
610 676-1000

(G-7694)
READCUBE
25 1st St Ste 104 (02141-1801)
PHONE..........................857 265-4945
Alex Hodgson, *Prin*
EMP: 14 **EST:** 2017
SALES (est): 430.13K **Privately Held**
Web: www.papersapp.com
SIC: 2731 Book publishing

(G-7695)
RELAY THERAPEUTICS INC (PA)
Also Called: RELAY THERAPEUTICS
399 Binney St Fl 2 (02142-1038)
PHONE..........................617 670-8837
Sanjiv K Patel, *Pr*
Donald Bergstrom, *Ex VP*
Thomas Catinazzo, *VP Fin*
EMP: 100 **EST:** 2015
SQ FT: 46,631
SALES (est): 1.38MM
SALES (corp-wide): 1.38MM **Publicly Held**
Web: www.relaytx.com
SIC: 2836 Biological products, except
diagnostic

(G-7696)
RIBON THERAPEUTICS INC
35 Cambridgepark Dr Ste 300 (02140-2325)
PHONE..........................617 914-8700
Prakash Raman, *Pr*
Danielle Knight, *Prin*
Sudha Parasuraman, *CMO*
Paul Brannelly, *CFO*
Victoria Richon, *Bd of Dir*
EMP: 44 **EST:** 2015
SALES (est): 5.63MM **Privately Held**
Web: www.ribontx.com
SIC: 2834 Pharmaceutical preparations

(G-7697)
RING THERAPEUTICS INC (PA)
140 1st St Ste 401 (02141-2109)
PHONE..........................617 218-1549
Tuyen Ong, *CEO*
EMP: 13 **EST:** 2019
SALES (est): 5.28MM
SALES (corp-wide): 5.28MM **Privately Held**
Web: www.ringtx.com
SIC: 2834 Pharmaceutical preparations

(G-7698)
ROBERT BENTLEY INC
Also Called: Bentley Publishers
1734 Massachusetts Ave (02138-1804)
PHONE..........................617 547-4170
Michael Bentley, *CEO*
▲ **EMP:** 26 **EST:** 1950
SQ FT: 10,000
SALES (est): 2.2MM **Privately Held**
Web: www.bentleypublishers.com
SIC: 2731 5192 Books, publishing only;
Books

(G-7699)
ROUNDTOWN INC
45 Prospect St (02139-2402)
PHONE..............................415 425-6891
Adam Dingle, *CEO*
Steven Shwartz, *Prin*
EMP: 8 EST: 2013
SQ FT: 300
SALES (est): 460K **Privately Held**
Web: www.roundtown.com
SIC: 2741 Internet publishing and broadcasting

(G-7700)
SAGE THERAPEUTICS INC (PA)
215 1st St (02142-1213)
PHONE..............................617 299-8380
EMP: 653 EST: 2011
SQ FT: 63,017
SALES (est): 86.45MM **Publicly Held**
Web: www.sagerx.com
SIC: 2834 Pharmaceutical preparations

(G-7701)
SANA BIOTECHNOLOGY INC (PA)
300 Technology Sq (02139-3515)
PHONE..............................202 790-0313
Nathan Hardy, *Pr*
Brian Cuneo, *Sec*
Paul Thurk, *Dir*
EMP: 8 EST: 2018
SALES (est): 4.63MM
SALES (corp-wide): 4.63MM **Privately Held**
Web: www.sana.com
SIC: 2834 Pharmaceutical preparations

(G-7702)
SAND 9 INC
Also Called: Www.sand9.com
1 Kendall Sq Ste B2305 (02139-1594)
P.O. Box 119 (01740-0119)
PHONE..............................617 358-0957
Vincent Graziani, *CEO*
Alex Erhart, *Ex VP*
Paul Hallee, *Sec*
◆ **EMP: 9 EST:** 2007
SQ FT: 1,300
SALES (est): 1.09MM **Privately Held**
Web: www.sand9.com
SIC: 3674 Semiconductors and related devices

(G-7703)
SANOFI PASTEUR BIOLOGICS LLC (HQ)
38 Sidney St Ste 370 (02139-4169)
PHONE..............................617 866-4400
Paul Hudson, *CEO*
Thomas Triomphe, *Ex VP*
EMP: 122 EST: 1990
SQ FT: 50,000
SALES (est): 53.63MM **Privately Held**
SIC: 2834 8731 Pharmaceutical preparations; Biological research
PA: Sanofi
46 Avenue De La Grande Armee
Paris 75017

(G-7704)
SANOFI US SERVICES INC
500 Kendall St Ste 500 (02142-1108)
PHONE..............................617 562-4555
June Strupczewski, *Mgr*
EMP: 112
Web: www.sanofi.us
SIC: 2834 Pharmaceutical preparations
HQ: Sanofi Us Services Inc.
55 Corporate Dr

Bridgewater NJ 08807
800 981-2491

(G-7705)
SANOFI US SERVICES INC
450 Water St (02141-2288)
PHONE..............................800 981-2491
EMP: 42
Web: www.sanofi.com
SIC: 2834 Pharmaceutical preparations
HQ: Sanofi Us Services Inc.
55 Corporate Dr
Bridgewater NJ 08807
800 981-2491

(G-7706)
SAREPTA THERAPEUTICS INC (PA)
Also Called: Sarepta
215 1st St Ste 415 (02142-1213)
PHONE..............................617 274-4000
Douglas S Ingram, *Pr*
M Kathleen Behrens, *Non-Executive Chairman of the Board*
Ian M Estepan, *Ex VP*
Louise Rodino-klapac, *CSO*
Bilal Arif, *Chief Technician*
EMP: 168 EST: 1980
SQ FT: 149,589
SALES (est): 933.01MM
SALES (corp-wide): 933.01MM **Publicly Held**
Web: www.sarepta.com
SIC: 2834 Pharmaceutical preparations

(G-7707)
SCHLUMBERGER TECHNOLOGY CORP
Also Called: Schlumberger-Doll Research
1 Hampshire St Ste 1 (02139-1579)
PHONE..............................617 768-2000
Phillipe Lacour-gayet, *Dir*
EMP: 130
SIC: 1389 1382 Servicing oil and gas wells; Oil and gas exploration services
HQ: Schlumberger Technology Corp
300 Schlumberger Dr
Sugar Land TX 77478
281 285-8500

(G-7708)
SCHOLAR ROCK HOLDING CORP (PA)
301 Binney St Ste 3 (02142-1071)
PHONE..............................857 259-3860
Jay Backstrom, *CEO*
David Hallal, *Ch Bd*
Edward H Myles, *Head OF Business Operations*
Gregory J Carven, *CSO*
Yung H Chyung, *CMO*
EMP: 12 EST: 2012
SALES (est): 33.19MM
SALES (corp-wide): 33.19MM **Publicly Held**
Web: www.scholarrock.com
SIC: 2834 2836 Pharmaceutical preparations; Biological products, except diagnostic

(G-7709)
SEMMA THERAPEUTICS INC (HQ)
Also Called: Vertex Cell Genetic Therapies
100 Technology Sq Fl 3 (02139-3585)
PHONE..............................857 529-6430
Bastiano Sanna, *Pr*
David Lebwohl, *CMO**
David Digiusto, *

Mary Kay Fenton, *
EMP: 20 EST: 2014
SALES (est): 9.02MM **Publicly Held**
Web: www.vrtx.com
SIC: 2834 Pharmaceutical preparations
PA: Vertex Pharmaceuticals Incorporated
50 Northern Ave
Boston MA 02210

(G-7710)
SERES THERAPEUTICS INC (PA)
200 Sidney St Fl 4 (02139-4218)
PHONE..............................617 945-9626
Eric D Shaff, *Pr*
Stephen A Berenson, *
David Arkowitz, *Head Business Development*
David S Ege, *Ex VP*
Thomas J Desrosier, *CLO*
EMP: 64 EST: 2010
SQ FT: 83,396
SALES (est): 7.13MM
SALES (corp-wide): 7.13MM **Publicly Held**
Web: www.serestherapeutics.com
SIC: 2834 Pharmaceutical preparations

(G-7711)
SHINTRON CO INC
Also Called: Shintron Co Interligua Div
144 Rogers St (02142-1024)
PHONE..............................617 491-8701
EMP: 10 EST: 2000
SALES (est): 111.68K **Privately Held**
Web: www.shintron.com.tw
SIC: 3661 Telephone and telegraph apparatus

(G-7712)
SHIRE PHARMACEUTICALS LLC
650 E Kendall St (02142-4201)
PHONE..............................617 588-8800
Jason Booth, *Brnch Mgr*
EMP: 674
Web: www.takeda.com
SIC: 2834 Pharmaceutical preparations
HQ: Shire Pharmaceuticals Llc
300 Shire Way
Lexington MA 02421
617 349-0200

(G-7713)
SHIRE PHARMACEUTICALS LLC
185 Alewife Brook Pkwy (02138-1100)
PHONE..............................781 482-9245
EMP: 674
Web: www.takeda.com
SIC: 2834 Pharmaceutical preparations
HQ: Shire Pharmaceuticals Llc
300 Shire Way
Lexington MA 02421
617 349-0200

(G-7714)
SIGILON THERAPEUTICS INC (HQ)
Also Called: Sigilon Therapeutics
100 Binney St Ste 600 (02142-1096)
PHONE..............................617 336-7540
Rogerio Vivaldi Coelho, *Pr*
Douglas Cole, *Ch Bd*
Glenn Reicin, *CFO*
Deya Corzo, *CMO*
EMP: 99 EST: 2015
SQ FT: 44,118
SALES (est): 12.94MM
SALES (corp-wide): 28.54B **Publicly Held**
Web: www.sigilon.com
SIC: 2834 Pharmaceutical preparations
PA: Eli Lilly And Company
Lilly Corporate Ctr

Indianapolis IN 46285
317 276-2000

(G-7715)
SILVERTHREAD INC
1 Broadway Ste 14 (02142-1187)
PHONE..............................800 674-9366
Daniel Sturtevant, *CEO*
EMP: 7 EST: 2013
SALES (est): 873.89K **Privately Held**
Web: www.silverthreadinc.com
SIC: 7371 7372 8733 8748 Computer software systems analysis and design, custom; Application computer software; Physical research, noncommercial; Systems analysis and engineering consulting services

(G-7716)
SIMON & SCHUSTER INC
Also Called: SIMON & SCHUSTER, INC.
10 Fawcett St Ste 4 (02138-1175)
PHONE..............................617 492-1220
EMP: 75
SALES (corp-wide): 544.79MM **Privately Held**
Web: www.simonandschuster.com
SIC: 2731 Books, publishing only
PA: Simon & Schuster, Llc
1230 Ave Of The Americas
New York NY 10020
212 698-7000

(G-7717)
SKY PUBLISHING CORPORATION
Also Called: Sky & Telescope
90 Sherman St Ste D (02140-3264)
PHONE..............................617 864-7360
EMP: 16 EST: 2007
SALES (est): 1.77MM **Privately Held**
Web: www.skyandtelescope.org
SIC: 2721 Magazines: publishing only, not printed on site

(G-7718)
SL 301B LLC
Also Called: Smartlabs
301 Binney St (02142-1071)
PHONE..............................888 315-9598
Robin Feeney, *VP Acctg*
EMP: 8 EST: 2016
SALES (est): 539.09K **Privately Held**
SIC: 3231 Medical and laboratory glassware: made from purchased glass

(G-7719)
SOCIETY OF ST JOHN THE EVANG
980 Memorial Dr (02138-5717)
PHONE..............................617 876-3037
Pastor Curtis Almquist, *Prin*
Pastor Martin Smith Ssje, *Prin*
EMP: 7 EST: 1870
SQ FT: 29,795
SALES (est): 487.36K **Privately Held**
Web: www.ssje.org
SIC: 8661 2731 Monastery; Books, publishing only

(G-7720)
SSI LIQUIDATING INC
Also Called: Educators Publishing Service
625 Mount Auburn St Ste 4 (02138-4555)
PHONE..............................617 547-6706
Rick Holden, *Pr*
EMP: 11
SALES (corp-wide): 600.83MM **Privately Held**

Web: webmaintenance.schoolspecialty.com
SIC: 2731 2741 Textbooks: publishing only,
not printed on site; Miscellaneous publishing
PA: Ssi Liquidating, Inc.
56 Harrison St
New Rochelle NY 10801
914 235-1075

(G-7721)
**STALLRGENES GREER
HOLDINGS INC**
55 Cambridge Pkwy (02142-1234)
PHONE....................617 588-4900
Richard Russell, *Pr*
Anthony Palombo, *
EMP: 25 **EST:** 2013
SQ FT: 5,500
SALES (est): 2.86MM **Privately Held**
Web: www.stallergenesgreer.com
SIC: 2834 Pharmaceutical preparations

(G-7722)
SUN CATALYTIX CORPORATION
61 Moulton St (02138-1127)
PHONE....................617 374-3797
EMP: 26
SIC: 3629 Electronic generation equipment

(G-7723)
SUNU INC
Also Called: Sunu
245 Main St 2nd Fl (02142-1064)
PHONE....................617 980-9807
Marco Trujillo, *CEO*
Fernando Albertorio, *COO*
EMP: 16 **EST:** 2016
SALES (est): 986.01K **Privately Held**
Web: www.sunu.com
SIC: 3663 Radio and t.v. communications
equipment

(G-7724)
SUPERIOR NUT COMPANY INC
Also Called: Superior
225 Monsignor Obrien Hwy (02141-1249)
P.O. Box 410086 (02141-0001)
PHONE....................800 251-6060
Harry N Hintlian, *Pr*
Justin H Hintlian, *
Lauren Hintlian, *
▲ **EMP:** 40 **EST:** 1933
SQ FT: 80,000
SALES (est): 8.98MM **Privately Held**
Web: www.superiornutstore.com
SIC: 2068 2099 Nuts: dried, dehydrated,
salted or roasted; Peanut butter

(G-7725)
SUPERPEDESTRIAN INC (PA)
84 Hamilton St (02139-4525)
PHONE....................877 678-7518
Assaf Biderman, *CEO*
EMP: 208 **EST:** 2012
SALES (est): 57.27MM
SALES (corp-wide): 57.27MM **Privately
Held**
Web: www.superpedestrian.com
SIC: 3621 3751 7371 7373 Torque motors,
electric; Motor scooters and parts;
Computer software development; Computer
integrated systems design

(G-7726)
**SUPPORTIVE THERAPEUTICS
LLC**
1 Broadway Fl 14 (02142-1187)
PHONE....................860 625-9226
Anthony Garland, *Ch*
Micahel Morin, *CEO*

EMP: 8 **EST:** 2012
SQ FT: 100
SALES (est): 1.01MM **Privately Held**
SIC: 2834 Proprietary drug products

(G-7727)
SUSE LLC
Also Called: Suse Linux
10 Canal Park Ste 200 (02141-2250)
PHONE....................617 613-2000
EMP: 79
SALES (corp-wide): 2.67MM **Privately
Held**
Web: www.suse.com
SIC: 7372 Prepackaged software
HQ: Suse Llc
1221 S Valley Grove Way
Pleasant Grove UT 84062
800 453-1267

(G-7728)
SUSTAINABLE MINDS LLC
1 Bdwy Kendall Sq (02142-1100)
PHONE....................617 401-2269
Terry Swack, *CEO*
Greg Canavera, *Software DESIGN*
EMP: 12 **EST:** 2010
SALES (est): 1.06MM **Privately Held**
Web: www.sustainableminds.com
SIC: 7372 Business oriented computer
software

(G-7729)
SYNLOGIC INC (PA)
Also Called: Synlogic
301 Binney St Ste 3 (02142-1071)
PHONE....................617 401-9975
Aoife Brennan, *Pr*
Peter Barrett, *Ch Bd*
Antoine Awad, *COO*
Michael Jensen, *CFO*
EMP: 31 **EST:** 2007
SALES (est): 1.18MM **Publicly Held**
Web: www.synlogictx.com
SIC: 2834 8731 Pharmaceutical
preparations; Biological research

(G-7730)
TAKEDA BUILDING 35 5
35 Landsdowne St (02139-4232)
PHONE....................617 444-4352
EMP: 7 **EST:** 2017
SALES (est): 372.84K **Privately Held**
SIC: 2834 Pharmaceutical preparations

(G-7731)
**TAKEDA DEV CTR AMERICAS
INC**
Also Called: Tdc Americas
500 Kendall St (02142-1108)
PHONE....................617 349-0200
Nancy Joseph-ridge, *Ch*
Stuart Dollow, *Pr*
John Campbell, *Treas*
Kenneth D Greisman, *Sec*
Patrick Butler, *Asst Tr*
EMP: 549 **EST:** 2003
SALES (est): 126.81MM **Privately Held**
Web: www.takeda.com
SIC: 2834 Pharmaceutical preparations
HQ: Takeda Pharmaceuticals U.S.A., Inc.
95 Hayden Ave
Lexington MA 02421
877 825-3327

(G-7732)
**TAKEDA PHARMACEUTICALS
INC**
35 Landsdowne St (02139-4232)

PHONE....................617 679-7348
Demo Dominique, *Prin*
EMP: 25
SALES (est): 12.67MM **Privately Held**
Web: www.takedaoncology.com
SIC: 2834 Pharmaceutical preparations

(G-7733)
**TAKEDA PHARMACEUTICALS
USA INC**
Also Called: Takeda
350 Massachusetts Ave (02139-4182)
PHONE....................781 733-5208
EMP: 15 **EST:** 2018
SALES (est): 5.61MM **Privately Held**
Web: www.takedaoncology.com
SIC: 2834 Pharmaceutical preparations

(G-7734)
TAKEDA VACCINES INC
40 Landsdowne St (02139-4234)
PHONE....................970 672-4918
Patrick Green, *Prin*
EMP: 84
Web: www.takeda.com
SIC: 2834 Pharmaceutical preparations
HQ: Takeda Vaccines, Inc.
75 Sidney St
Cambridge MA 02139

(G-7735)
TCR2 THERAPEUTICS INC (HQ)
Also Called: Tcr2 Therapeutics
100 Binney St Ste 710 (02142-1096)
PHONE....................617 949-5200
Garry E Menzel, *Pr*
Ansbert Gadicke, *Ch Bd*
Robert Hofmeister, *CSO*
Angela Justice, *CPO*
Alfonso Quintas Cardama, *CMO*
EMP: 91 **EST:** 2015
SALES (corp-wide): 27.15MM **Privately
Held**
Web: www.adaptimmune.com
SIC: 2836 Biological products, except
diagnostic
PA: Adaptimmune Therapeutics Plc
60 Jubilee Avenue Milton Park
Abingdon OXON OX14
123 543-0000

(G-7736)
TECHNOLOGY REVIEW INC
Also Called: Mlt Technology Review
196 Broadway Ste 3 (02139-1949)
PHONE....................617 475-8000
R Bruce Journey, *Pr*
Jason Pontin, *
EMP: 40 **EST:** 2001
SALES (est): 17.6MM
SALES (corp-wide): 4.27B **Privately Held**
Web: www.technologyreview.com
SIC: 2721 8221 Magazines: publishing and
printing; University
PA: Massachusetts Institute Of Technology
77 Massachusetts Ave
Cambridge MA 02139
617 253-1000

(G-7737)
TERADAR INC
501 Massachusetts Ave (02139-4018)
PHONE....................508 433-0269
Matthew Carey, *Pr*
EMP: 28 **EST:** 2021
SALES (est): 2.77MM **Privately Held**
SIC: 3825 Semiconductor test equipment

(G-7738)
TERRAPIN
955 Massachusetts Ave (02139-3233)
PHONE....................508 487-8181
William Glass, *Pr*
EMP: 9 **EST:** 2001
SALES (est): 199.78K **Privately Held**
Web: www.terrapinlogo.com
SIC: 7372 7389 Prepackaged software;
Business services, nec

(G-7739)
TESHIMA INTERNATIONAL CORP
1 Broadway Fl 14 (02142-1100)
PHONE....................617 830-1886
Yukiko Teshima, *Pr*
EMP: 9 **EST:** 2009
SALES (est): 99.05K **Privately Held**
Web: www.teshimaintl.com
SIC: 3498 Tube fabricating (contract
bending and shaping)

(G-7740)
**THESEUS PHARMACEUTICALS
INC (PA)**
Also Called: Theseus
314 Main St Ste 04-200 (02142-1042)
PHONE....................857 400-9491
Iain D Dukes, *Ch Bd*
William C Shakespeare, *Research &
Development*
Bradford D Dahms, *CFO*
Victor M Rivera, *CSO*
EMP: 14 **EST:** 2017
SQ FT: 7,351
Web: www.theseusrx.com
SIC: 2834 8731 Pharmaceutical
preparations; Commercial physical research

(G-7741)
TIBURIO THERAPEUTICS INC
700 Technology Sq Ste 2 (02139-3557)
PHONE....................617 231-6050
EMP: 7 **EST:** 2019
SALES (est): 394.09K **Privately Held**
Web: www.tiburio.com
SIC: 2834 Pharmaceutical preparations

(G-7742)
TOLERX INC
300 Technology Sq Ste 4 (02139-3520)
PHONE....................617 354-8100
Douglas J Ringler, *CEO*
Antonin De Fougerolles, *
Elizabeth Czerepak, *
Wayne T Hockmeyer, *
Stephen Hoffman, *
EMP: 22 **EST:** 2000
SQ FT: 37,000
SALES (est): 1.04MM **Privately Held**
SIC: 2834 Powders, pharmaceutical

(G-7743)
TOOTSIE CHAMBRIDGE PLANT
810 Main St (02139-3588)
PHONE....................617 491-2500
EMP: 7 **EST:** 2010
SALES (est): 85.68K **Privately Held**
SIC: 2064 Candy and other confectionery
products

(G-7744)
TORQUE THERAPEUTICS INC
Also Called: Torque
1 Kendall Sq Bldg 1400 (02139-1675)
PHONE....................617 945-1082
James Mullen, *Ch Bd*
Thomas Andresen, *CSO*
EMP: 25 **EST:** 2016

SALES (est): 4.95MM **Privately Held**
Web: www.repertoire.com
SIC: **8731** 2834 Biotechnical research, commercial; Pharmaceutical preparations

(G-7745)
TYPESAFE INC
1 Brattle Sq (02138-3723)
PHONE..................617 622-2200
EMP: 8 EST: 2011
SALES (est): 146.99K **Privately Held**
SIC: **7372** Prepackaged software

(G-7746)
UCB INC
87 Cambridgepark Dr (02140-2311)
PHONE..................844 599-2273
EMP: 33 EST: 2008
SALES (est): 2.87MM **Privately Held**
Web: www.ucb.com
SIC: **2834** Pharmaceutical preparations

(G-7747)
ULTIVUE INC (PA)
763d Concord Ave (02138-1290)
PHONE..................617 945-2662
Jacques Corriveau, *CEO*
Michelle Giovenelli, *
Richard C Malabre, *
EMP: 45 EST: 2015
SQ FT: 2,000
SALES (est): 6.4MM
SALES (corp-wide): 6.4MM **Privately Held**
Web: biomarker.ultivue.com
SIC: **2835** Diagnostic substances

(G-7748)
UNICA CORPORATION
1 Rogers St (02142-1209)
PHONE..................781 839-8000
EMP: 519
SIC: **7372** Prepackaged software

(G-7749)
VACUUM PROCESS TECHNOLOGY LLC
1 Broadway (02142-1100)
PHONE..................508 732-7200
Ralf Faber, *Pr*
EMP: 35 EST: 1991
SALES (est): 8.63MM **Privately Held**
SIC: **3826** 8711 3827 Analytical optical instruments; Engineering services; Optical instruments and lenses

(G-7750)
VBI VACCINES INC (PA)
Also Called: Vbi
222 3rd St Ste 2241 (02142-1259)
PHONE..................617 830-3031
Jeffrey R Baxter, *Pr*
Steven Gillis, *Ch Bd*
Christopher Mcnulty, *CFO*
David E Anderson, *CSO*
Francisco Diaz-mitoma, *CMO*
EMP: 7 EST: 1965
SQ FT: 3,475
SALES (est): 1.08MM
SALES (corp-wide): 1.08MM **Publicly Held**
Web: www.vbivaccines.com
SIC: **2834** 2836 Pharmaceutical preparations; Vaccines

(G-7751)
VECTOR SOFTWARE USA CORP
Also Called: Vector Itc Group
245 Frst St Rvrview Ii Fl Riverview (02142)
PHONE..................305 332-1703

Fransico Alverez-marino, *Mgr*
EMP: 11 EST: 2016
SALES (est): 609.53K **Privately Held**
SIC: **7372** Prepackaged software
HQ: Softtek Digital Solutions SI
Carretera Corula (Km. 16) 38
Las Rozas De Madrid M 28031

(G-7752)
VERICEL CORPORATION (PA)
64 Sidney St (02139-4170)
P.O. Box 376 (48106-0376)
PHONE..................617 588-5555
Dominick C Colangelo, *Pr*
Robert L Zerbe, *
Joe Mara, *Finance Officer*
Michael Halpin, *COO*
Sean C Flynn, *VP*
EMP: 252 EST: 1989
SQ FT: 57,000
SALES (est): 164.37MM **Publicly Held**
Web: www.vcel.com
SIC: **2836** Biological products, except diagnostic

(G-7753)
VERITAS MEDICINE INC
11 Cambridge Ctr (02142-1400)
PHONE..................617 234-1500
Joseph Avellone, *CEO*
EMP: 14 EST: 1999
SQ FT: 5,000
SALES (est): 344.52K **Privately Held**
SIC: **2741** Miscellaneous publishing

(G-7754)
VERTICA SYSTEMS LLC
150 Cambridgepark Dr (02140-2370)
PHONE..................617 386-4400
EMP: 120 EST: 2005
SALES (est): 40.21MM
SALES (corp-wide): 1.77MM **Privately Held**
Web: www.vertica.com
SIC: **7372** Business oriented computer software
HQ: Micro Focus (Us), Inc.
700 King Farm Blvd # 125
Rockville MD 20850
301 838-5000

(G-7755)
VERVE THERAPEUTICS INC
26 Landsdowne St (02139-4216)
PHONE..................617 603-0070
EMP: 16
SALES (corp-wide): 1.94MM **Publicly Held**
Web: www.vervetx.com
SIC: **2834** Pharmaceutical preparations
PA: Verve Therapeutics, Inc.
500 Technology Sq Ste 1
Cambridge MA 02139
617 603-0070

(G-7756)
VERVE THERAPEUTICS INC (PA)
Also Called: Verve Therapeutics
500 Technology Sq Ste 1 (02139-3521)
PHONE..................617 603-0070
Sekar Kathiresan, *CEO*
Burt Adelman, *Ch Bd*
Andrew Ashe, *Pr*
Andrew Bellinger, *CSO*
Joan Nickerson, *Senior Vice President Human Resources*
EMP: 22 EST: 2018
SALES (est): 1.94MM
SALES (corp-wide): 1.94MM **Publicly Held**

Web: www.vervetx.com
SIC: **2834** Pharmaceutical preparations

(G-7757)
VOR BIOPHARMA INC (PA)
Also Called: VOR BIOPHARMA
100 Cambridgepark Dr Ste 101 (02140-2317)
PHONE..................617 655-6580
Robert Ang, *Pr*
Matthew R Patterson, *Ch Bd*
Nathan Jorgensen, *CFO*
Tirtha Chakraborty, *CSO*
EMP: 133 EST: 2015
SQ FT: 32,798
Web: www.vorbio.com
SIC: **2836** Biological products, except diagnostic

(G-7758)
WALDEN BIOSCIENCES INC
1 Kendall Sq Ste 7102 (02139-1562)
PHONE..................617 794-2733
EMP: 19 EST: 2019
SALES (est): 3.13MM **Privately Held**
SIC: **2834** Pharmaceutical preparations

(G-7759)
WANDERLUST GROUP INC
1035 Cambridge St Ste 30 (02141-1154)
P.O. Box 179 (04032-0179)
PHONE..................617 784-3696
EMP: 25 EST: 2016
SALES (est): 886.29K **Privately Held**
SIC: **7372** Prepackaged software

(G-7760)
WILEX INC
100 Acorn Park Dr Fl 6 (02140-2303)
PHONE..................617 492-3900
Patrick Muracka, *CEO*
Peter Llewellyn Davis, *CEO*
EMP: 10 EST: 2010
SALES (est): 608.93K **Privately Held**
SIC: **2834** Pharmaceutical preparations

(G-7761)
WINDOW BOOK INC
Also Called: Automating Information
300 Franklin St (02139-3708)
P.O. Box 391407 (02139-0015)
PHONE..................617 395-4500
Christopher O'brien, *Pr*
EMP: 87 EST: 1988
SQ FT: 4,200
SALES (est): 12.76MM **Privately Held**
Web: www.windowbook.com
SIC: **7371** 7372 7373 Computer software development; Business oriented computer software; Office computer automation systems integration
HQ: Dmt Solutions Global Corporation
37 Executive Dr
Danbury CT 06810
833 874-0552

(G-7762)
WOOBO INC
198 River St (02139-4426)
PHONE..................630 639-6326
Shen Guo, *Pr*
Feng Tan, *CEO*
EMP: 12 EST: 2015
SALES (est): 480.8K **Privately Held**
Web: www.woobo.io
SIC: **3942** Dolls and stuffed toys

(G-7763)
XAM ONLINE INC (PA)
25 1st St (02141-1802)
PHONE..................781 662-9268
Sharon A Wynne, *Pr*
EMP: 8 EST: 1997
SQ FT: 2,100
SALES (est): 1.18MM
SALES (corp-wide): 1.18MM **Privately Held**
Web: www.xamonline.com
SIC: **2731** Book publishing

(G-7764)
ZYLOTECH
101 Main St Fl 14 (02142-1527)
PHONE..................845 802-3188
Ernie Cormier, *Pr*
EMP: 8 EST: 2018
SALES (est): 437.6K **Privately Held**
SIC: **7372** Prepackaged software

Canton
Norfolk County

(G-7765)
ABBOTT-ACTION INC
Also Called: French Packaging Services
10 Campanelli Cir (02021-2481)
PHONE..................781 702-5710
Brian French V Pres Protective, *Brnch Mgr*
EMP: 22
SALES (corp-wide): 21.46MM **Privately Held**
Web: www.abbottaction.com
SIC: **2449** 4783 Shipping cases and drums, wood: wirebound and plywood; Packing and crating
PA: Abbott-Action, Inc.
3 Venus Way
Attleboro MA 02703
401 722-2100

(G-7766)
AGFA HEALTHCARE CORPORATION
150 Royall St Ste 107 (02021-1054)
PHONE..................978 284-7900
EMP: 88
SALES (corp-wide): 431.66MM **Privately Held**
Web: www.agfahealthcare.com
SIC: **3845** 3823 Electromedical equipment; Absorption analyzers: infrared, x-ray, etc.: industrial
HQ: Agfa Healthcare Corporation
580 Gotham Pkwy
Carlstadt NJ 07072

(G-7767)
AMERICAN WATER SYSTEMS LLC
9 Pequot Way (02021-2305)
PHONE..................781 830-9722
EMP: 17 EST: 1987
SALES (est): 821.91K **Privately Held**
Web: www.americanwatersystems.org
SIC: **3589** 5999 7699 Water purification equipment, household type; Water purification equipment; Industrial equipment services

(G-7768)
AMERICANBIO INC
20 Dan Rd (02021-2879)
PHONE..................508 655-4336
Wayne Gagnon, *CEO*
Vincent Cooney, *Pr*

David Cooney, *VP*
Heidi Fleshman, *VP*
EMP: 10 **EST:** 1977
SQ FT: 6,000
SALES (est): 9.1MM **Privately Held**
Web: www.americanbio.com
SIC: 2819 Chemicals, high purity: refined from technical grade

(G-7769)
APA LLC
4 Campanelli Cir (02021-2481)
PHONE..............................781 986-5900
Alexander Alfieri, *Prin*
EMP: 50 **EST:** 2011
SALES (est): 5.8MM **Privately Held**
Web: www.apav.com
SIC: 3564 Blowing fans: industrial or commercial

(G-7770)
ASD LIGHTING CORP
120 Shawmut Rd (02021-1430)
PHONE..............................781 739-3977
Igor Kozhemiakin, *CEO*
Mikhail Mashkovtcev, *
▲ **EMP:** 38 **EST:** 1999
SALES (est): 8.39MM **Privately Held**
Web: www.asd-lighting.com
SIC: 3646 Ceiling systems, luminous

(G-7771)
ASTREA BIOSEPARATIONS US INC
Also Called: Astrea Bioseparations
960 Turnpike St (02021-2824)
PHONE..............................919 899-9087
Terry Pizzie, *CEO*
Steve Burton, *Pr*
EMP: 11 **EST:** 2020
SALES (est): 941.04K **Privately Held**
SIC: 2834 Pharmaceutical preparations

(G-7772)
AUTHOR REPUTATION PRESS LLC
45 Dan Rd (02021-2869)
PHONE..............................800 220-7660
Michael Kravitz, *Prin*
EMP: 9 **EST:** 2018
SALES (est): 343.01K **Privately Held**
Web: www.authorreputationpress.com
SIC: 2741 Miscellaneous publishing

(G-7773)
BARLETTA FSCHBACH GREEN LINE D
40 Shawmut Rd Ste 200 (02021-1409)
PHONE..............................781 737-1705
Michael Foley, *Prin*
EMP: 10 **EST:** 2018
SALES (est): 792.01K **Privately Held**
SIC: 3589 Water treatment equipment, industrial

(G-7774)
BOYAJIAN INC
144 Will Dr (02021-3704)
PHONE..............................781 828-9966
John S Boyajian, *Pr*
▲ **EMP:** 12 **EST:** 1981
SALES (est): 2.34MM **Privately Held**
Web: www.boyajianinc.com
SIC: 2099 5149 5499 Food preparations, nec; Specialty food items; Gourmet food stores

(G-7775)
CAMIO CUSTOM CABINETRY INC
130 Jackson St Ste 2 (02021-2094)
PHONE..............................781 562-1573
Chris Constantino, *Pr*
Michael J Shea, *VP*
EMP: 11 **EST:** 2011
SQ FT: 11,000
SALES (est): 1.81MM **Privately Held**
Web: www.camiocabinetry.com
SIC: 2434 Wood kitchen cabinets

(G-7776)
CANTON CITIZEN INC
866 Washington St (02021-2587)
P.O. Box 291 (02021-0291)
PHONE..............................781 821-4418
Beth Ericson, *Pr*
EMP: 9 **EST:** 1987
SALES (est): 541.37K **Privately Held**
Web: www.thecantoncitizen.com
SIC: 2711 Newspapers, publishing and printing

(G-7777)
CEACO INC
Also Called: Gamewright
250 Royall St (02021-1058)
PHONE..............................617 926-8080
Nagendra Raina, *CEO*
◆ **EMP:** 48 **EST:** 1987
SALES (est): 8.89MM **Privately Held**
Web: www.gamewright.com
SIC: 3944 Puzzles
HQ: Buffalo Games, Llc
220 James E Casey Dr
Buffalo NY 14206
716 827-8393

(G-7778)
CHASM ADVANCED MATERIALS INC (PA)
480 Neponset St Ste 6 (02021-1971)
PHONE..............................781 821-0443
David Arthur, *Pr*
Robert Praino, *COO*
EMP: 9 **EST:** 2015
SALES (est): 2.55MM
SALES (corp-wide): 2.55MM **Privately Held**
Web: www.chasmtek.com
SIC: 8999 2869 Scientific consulting; Accelerators, rubber processing: cyclic or acyclic

(G-7779)
COPLEY CONTROLS CORPORATION (DH)
20 Dan Rd (02021-2879)
PHONE..............................781 828-8090
Matthew Lorber, *Pr*
Jerry V Klima, *
▲ **EMP:** 276 **EST:** 1978
SQ FT: 104,000
SALES (est): 48.9MM
SALES (corp-wide): 869MM **Privately Held**
Web: www.copleycontrols.com
SIC: 3679 3663 Parametric amplifiers; Radio and t.v. communications equipment
HQ: Analogic Corporation
8 Centennial Dr
Peabody MA 01960
978 326-4000

(G-7780)
COUNTERRA LLC
399 Neponset St Ste 202 (02021-1959)

PHONE..............................781 821-2100
Shaun Weston, *Mgr*
EMP: 10 **EST:** 2013
SQ FT: 2,500
SALES (est): 613.33K **Privately Held**
Web: www.counterra.com
SIC: 2434 3281 Wood kitchen cabinets; Cut stone and stone products

(G-7781)
COX ENGINEERING COMPANY (PA)
35 Industrial Dr (02021-2801)
PHONE..............................781 302-3300
▲ **EMP:** 135 **EST:** 1945
SALES (est): 115.13MM
SALES (corp-wide): 115.13MM **Privately Held**
Web: www.coxengineering.com
SIC: 1711 1761 3585 3444 Mechanical contractor; Sheet metal work, nec; Refrigeration and heating equipment; Sheet metalwork

(G-7782)
DAWSON FORTE HOLDINGS LLC (PA)
40 Shawmut Rd (02021-1409)
PHONE..............................508 651-7910
Andrew Bartmess, *Managing Member*
EMP: 30 **EST:** 2014
SALES (est): 6.75MM
SALES (corp-wide): 6.75MM **Privately Held**
Web: www.dawsonforte.com
SIC: 5611 5621 5632 5199 Clothing, male: everyday, except suits and sportswear; Ready-to-wear apparel, women's; Knitwear, women's; Woolen and worsted yarns

(G-7783)
DEDHAM CABINET SHOP INC
550 Turnpike St (02021-2725)
PHONE..............................781 326-4090
Alfred J Priore Junior, *Pr*
Ronald Priore, *Treas*
EMP: 10 **EST:** 1942
SQ FT: 7,000
SALES (est): 1.85MM **Privately Held**
Web: www.dedhamcabinetshop.com
SIC: 5211 2434 Cabinets, kitchen; Wood kitchen cabinets

(G-7784)
DESCO INDUSTRIES INC
1 Colgate Way (02021-1558)
PHONE..............................781 821-8370
Darryl Allen, *Mgr*
EMP: 26
SALES (corp-wide): 49.98MM **Privately Held**
Web: www.descoindustries.com
SIC: 3629 Static elimination equipment, industrial
PA: Desco Industries, Inc.
3651 Walnut Ave
Chino CA 91710
909 627-8178

(G-7785)
DIREX SYSTEMS CORP
956 Turnpike St (02021-2877)
PHONE..............................339 502-6013
Gabriel Henkin, *CEO*
EMP: 7 **EST:** 1989
SQ FT: 6,000
SALES (est): 2.47MM **Privately Held**
Web: www.direxusa.com
SIC: 3841 Surgical and medical instruments
HQ: Direx Systems Gmbh
Blumenstr. 10d

Wiesbaden HE 65189
80022322322

(G-7786)
DRAPER KNITTING COMPANY INC
28 Draper Ln (02021-1598)
PHONE..............................781 828-0029
Kristin Draper, *Pr*
Scott Draper, *
▲ **EMP:** 40 **EST:** 1984
SQ FT: 130,000
SALES (est): 10.23MM
SALES (corp-wide): 11.68MM **Privately Held**
Web: www.draperknitting.com
SIC: 2297 2257 Nonwoven fabrics; Pile fabrics, circular knit
PA: Draper Brothers Company
1105 N Market St Ste 1300
Wilmington DE
302 777-4726

(G-7787)
DYNASOL INDUSTRIES INC
330 Pine St (02021-3366)
PHONE..............................781 821-8888
▲ **EMP:** 15 **EST:** 1996
SQ FT: 25,000
SALES (est): 2.44MM **Privately Held**
Web: www.dynasolinc.com
SIC: 2842 2841 Polishes and sanitation goods; Soap and other detergents

(G-7788)
EMERGENT BIOSOLUTIONS INC
50 Shawmut Rd (02021-1409)
PHONE..............................781 302-3000
EMP: 12
SALES (corp-wide): 1.12B **Publicly Held**
Web: www.emergentbiosolutions.com
SIC: 2834 Pharmaceutical preparations
PA: Emergent Biosolutions Inc.
400 Professional Dr # 400
Gaithersburg MD 20879
240 631-3200

(G-7789)
ENE SYSTEMS INC (PA)
Also Called: Johnson Contrls Authorized Dlr
480 Neponset St Ste 11d (02021-1970)
PHONE..............................781 828-6770
Lindsay Drisko, *Pr*
EMP: 72 **EST:** 1987
SQ FT: 20,000
SALES (est): 51.09MM **Privately Held**
Web: www.enesystems.com
SIC: 3822 Environmental controls

(G-7790)
FARGANYD INC
112 Will Dr (02021-3704)
PHONE..............................781 575-1700
EMP: 115
SIC: 2752 2796 Offset printing; Platemaking services

(G-7791)
FASTECH INC
18 Washington St Ste 33 (02021-4004)
PHONE..............................781 964-3010
Matthew Fink, *Pr*
▲ **EMP:** 28 **EST:** 2000
SQ FT: 30,000
SALES (est): 2.47MM **Privately Held**
Web: www.fastechinc.com
SIC: 2342 Bras, girdles, and allied garments

(G-7792)
FRESENIUS KABI COMPOUNDING LLC
20 Dan Rd (02021-2879)
PHONE..................224 358-1150
EMP: 35 EST: 2017
SALES (est): 11.02MM
SALES (corp-wide): 42.42B **Privately Held**
SIC: 2834 Pharmaceutical preparations
HQ: Fresenius Kabi Pharmaceuticals
Holding, Llc
3 Corporate Dr
Lake Zurich IL 60047
847 550-2300

(G-7793)
HARBAR LLC
Also Called: Harbar
320 Turnpike St (02021-2703)
PHONE..................781 828-0848
▲ EMP: 174 EST: 1986
SQ FT: 39,000
SALES (est): 23.38MM **Privately Held**
Web: www.harbar.com
SIC: 5461 2099 Retail bakeries; Tortillas, fresh or refrigerated

(G-7794)
HARRIS REBAR
136 Will Dr (02021-3704)
PHONE..................781 575-8999
John Faherty, *Mgr*
EMP: 10 EST: 2018
SALES (est): 150.22K **Privately Held**
Web: www.harrisrebar.com
SIC: 3441 Fabricated structural metal

(G-7795)
HEALTHY LIFE SNACK INC
Also Called: Healthy Life
905 Turnpike St Ste D2 (02021-2833)
PHONE..................781 575-6744
Royce Williams, *Prin*
EMP: 14 EST: 1997
SALES (est): 925.1K **Privately Held**
Web: www.healthylifesnacks.com
SIC: 2671 Paper; coated and laminated packaging

(G-7796)
HENKEL CORPORATION
Henkel Corporation
869 Washington St (02021-2513)
PHONE..................781 737-1400
Joe Debiase, *Mgr*
EMP: 160
SALES (corp-wide): 23.26B **Privately Held**
Web: www.henkel.com
SIC: 2891 2821 Adhesives and sealants; Plastics materials and resins
HQ: Henkel Us Operations Corporation
1 Henkel Way
Rocky Hill CT 06067
860 571-5100

(G-7797)
HOMELAND FUELS COMPANY LLC
40 Shawmut Rd Ste 200 (02021-1409)
PHONE..................781 737-1892
Victor Gatto, *Pr*
Charles Dornbush, *CEO*
Gregory L Benik, *Ex VP*
EMP: 10 EST: 2009
SALES (est): 1.18MM **Privately Held**
Web: www.homelandfuelscompany.com
SIC: 2869 2992 2911 Fuels; Cutting oils, blending: made from purchased materials; Diesel fuels

(G-7798)
HONEYWELL INTERNATIONAL INC
Also Called: Honeywell
65 Shawmut Rd Unit 5 (02021-1461)
PHONE..................781 298-2700
David Cote, *Brnch Mgr*
EMP: 8
SALES (corp-wide): 35.47B **Publicly Held**
Web: www.honeywell.com
SIC: 3724 Aircraft engines and engine parts
PA: Honeywell International Inc.
855 S Mint St
Charlotte NC 28202
704 627-6200

(G-7799)
IDEAL INSTRUMENT CO INC
863 Washington St (02021-2513)
PHONE..................781 828-0881
Renato J Perfetti, *Pr*
Christopher Perfetti, *VP*
John Perfetti, *Treas*
EMP: 11 EST: 1951
SQ FT: 7,000
SALES (est): 1.71MM **Privately Held**
Web: www.idealinstrument.com
SIC: 3599 Machine shop, jobbing and repair

(G-7800)
IET SOLUTIONS LLC (DH)
25 Dan Rd (02021-2817)
PHONE..................818 838-0606
Corry S Homg, *Pr*
EMP: 35 EST: 2003
SQ FT: 7,000
SALES (est): 9.35MM
SALES (corp-wide): 579.13MM **Privately Held**
Web: www.iet-solutions.com
SIC: 7372 7371 Prepackaged software; Computer software systems analysis and design, custom
HQ: Unicom Systems Inc.
15535 San Fernando Missio
Mission Hills CA 91345
818 838-0606

(G-7801)
INTEGER HOLDINGS CORPORATION
Electrochem Industries Div
670 Paramount Dr (02021)
PHONE..................781 830-5800
EMP: 166
SALES (corp-wide): 1.38B **Publicly Held**
Web: www.integer.net
SIC: 3845 3692 3691 Defibrillator; Primary batteries, dry and wet; Storage batteries
PA: Integer Holdings Corporation
5830 Gran Pkwy Ste 1150
Plano TX 75024
214 618-5243

(G-7802)
J L ENTERPRISES INC
Also Called: J L McIntosh
875 Washington St (02021-2513)
PHONE..................781 821-6300
Susan Kelley, *Pr*
EMP: 7 EST: 1877
SALES (est): 371.73K **Privately Held**
Web: www.jlmcintosh.com
SIC: 7336 2759 2675 7389 Graphic arts and related design; Commercial printing, nec; Die-cut paper and board; Laminating service

(G-7803)
JEWELRY SOLUTIONS LLC
Also Called: J R S
448 Turnpike St Ste 2 (02021-2704)
PHONE..................781 821-6100
EMP: 8 EST: 1997
SQ FT: 1,500
SALES (est): 539.28K **Privately Held**
SIC: 3911 Jewelry, precious metal

(G-7804)
KEATING COMMUNICATION GROUP
Also Called: Ke Printing & Graphics
956 Turnpike St (02021-2877)
PHONE..................781 828-9030
EMP: 7 EST: 1994
SQ FT: 6,500
SALES (est): 960.17K **Privately Held**
SIC: 2752 3993 2791 2789 Offset printing; Signs and advertising specialties; Typesetting; Bookbinding and related work

(G-7805)
LENIS INC
Also Called: Leni's Textiles
480 Neponset St Ste 4a (02021-1936)
PHONE..................781 401-3273
Leni Joyce, *Pr*
EMP: 8 EST: 1967
SQ FT: 4,400
SALES (est): 520.84K **Privately Held**
Web: www.leniinc.com
SIC: 2299 Hand woven fabrics

(G-7806)
M8TRIX TECH LLC
Also Called: M8trix Technology
45 Dan Rd (02021-2852)
PHONE..................617 925-7030
John Pisarczyk, *Managing Member*
EMP: 7 EST: 2015
SALES (est): 625.71K **Privately Held**
SIC: 3577 7379 Computer peripheral equipment, nec; Computer related consulting services

(G-7807)
MAJESTIC MARBLE & GRANITE INC
253 Revere St (02021-2920)
PHONE..................781 830-1020
Reza Alemi, *Pr*
EMP: 8 EST: 2002
SQ FT: 10,000
SALES (est): 1.1MM **Privately Held**
Web: www.majesticfabrication.com
SIC: 3281 Granite, cut and shaped

(G-7808)
MASSMICROELECTRONICS LLC
50 Energy Dr Ste 202 (02021-2863)
P.O. Box 231311 (11023-0311)
PHONE..................781 828-6110
EMP: 58 EST: 1999
SQ FT: 8,000
SALES (est): 991.25K **Privately Held**
SIC: 3679 Electronic circuits

(G-7809)
NATIONAL RESOURCE MGT INC (PA)
Also Called: N R M
480 Neponset St Ste 2a (02021-1935)
PHONE..................781 828-8877
Emre Schveighoffer, *Pr*
Emre J Schveighoffer, *
Janelle R Schveighoffer, *

Jim Staley, *
EMP: 25 EST: 1991
SQ FT: 9,000
SALES (est): 14.12MM **Privately Held**
Web: www.nrminc.com
SIC: 3823 8711 8748 Controllers, for process variables, all types; Energy conservation engineering; Energy conservation consultant

(G-7810)
NECI LLC
Also Called: Neci
530 Turnpike St (02021-2761)
PHONE..................781 828-4883
Steve Mccoy, *Managing Member*
Paul Bittrich, *
EMP: 36 EST: 2002
SQ FT: 1,000
SALES (est): 911.39K **Privately Held**
SIC: 2675 2679 Folders, filing, die-cut: made from purchased materials; Paper products, converted, nec

(G-7811)
NEEDHAM ELECTRIC SUPPLY LLC (DH)
Also Called: Nesco
5 Shawmut Rd (02021-1408)
PHONE..................781 828-9494
EMP: 60 EST: 1958
SALES (est): 133.43MM **Publicly Held**
Web: www.needhamelectric.com
SIC: 5063 3648 Electrical supplies, nec; Lighting fixtures, except electric: residential
HQ: Wesco Distribution, Inc.
225 W Station Square Dr # 700
Pittsburgh PA 15219

(G-7812)
NEW VALENCE ROBOTICS CORP
Also Called: NV Bots
480 Neponset St Ste 10c (02021-1970)
PHONE..................857 529-6397
Alfonso Perez, *Pr*
Paul Burke, *CRO*
Christopher Haid, *COO*
Edward Brady, *Dir Fin*
EMP: 9 EST: 2014
SALES (est): 279.41K **Privately Held**
SIC: 2752 Commercial printing, lithographic

(G-7813)
NORFOLK ASPHALT PAVING INC
1010 Turnpike St (02021-2839)
PHONE..................617 293-9775
EMP: 11 EST: 2009
SALES (est): 881.61K **Privately Held**
Web: www.norfolkpavinginc.com
SIC: 2951 Asphalt and asphaltic paving mixtures (not from refineries)

(G-7814)
ORGANOGENESIS HOLDINGS INC (PA)
Also Called: Organogenesis
85 Dan Rd (02021-2810)
PHONE..................781 575-0775
Gary S Gillheeney Senior, *Pr*
Gary S Gillheeney Senior, *Pr*
Antonio S Montecalvo, *VP*
David C Francisco, *CFO*
Patrick Bilbo, *COO*
EMP: 14 EST: 2018
SQ FT: 300,000
SALES (est): 450.89MM
SALES (corp-wide): 450.89MM **Publicly Held**

Web: www.organogenesis.com
SIC: 2834　Pharmaceutical preparations

(G-7815)
ORGANOGENESIS INC (HQ)
85 Dan Rd (02021-2810)
PHONE..............................781 575-0775
Gary S Gillheeney Senior, *CEO*
Timothy M Cunningham, *
Brian Grow, *Chief Commercial Officer*
Patrick Bilbo, *
Howard Walthall, *
▲ EMP: 248 EST: 1985
SALES (est): 173.55MM
SALES (corp-wide): 450.89MM **Publicly Held**
Web: www.organogenesis.com
SIC: 2836　Biological products, except diagnostic
PA: Organogenesis Holdings Inc.
　85 Dan Rd
　Canton MA 02021
　781 575-0775

(G-7816)
OWENS CORNING SALES LLC
Also Called: Owens Corning
P.O. Box 6159 (02021)
PHONE..............................800 438-7465
EMP: 8
SIC: 3296　Mineral wool
HQ: Owens Corning Sales, Llc
　1 Owens Corning Pkwy
　Toledo OH 43659
　419 248-8000

(G-7817)
PAYNE ENGRG FABRICATION CO INC
28 Draper Ln Ste 3 (02021-1694)
P.O. Box 520 (02021-0520)
PHONE..............................781 828-9046
Harry F Payne, *Pr*
Beverly Butterworth, *
Katherine Payne, *
EMP: 32 EST: 1969
SQ FT: 13,500
SALES (est): 2.38MM **Privately Held**
Web: www.payneengineering.net
SIC: 3499 3444 3441 3599　Machine bases, metal; Sheet metalwork; Fabricated structural metal; Machine shop, jobbing and repair

(G-7818)
PEARLCO OF BOSTON INC
Also Called: Saratoga Salad Dressing
5 Whitman Rd (02021-2707)
PHONE..............................781 821-1010
Judith Pearlstein, *Pr*
EMP: 20 EST: 1978
SQ FT: 25,000
SALES (est): 1.97MM **Privately Held**
Web: www.saratogadressings.com
SIC: 2035　Dressings, salad: raw and cooked (except dry mixes)

(G-7819)
PHOENIX ELECTRIC CORP
40 Hudson Rd (02021-1407)
P.O. Box 53 (02137-0053)
PHONE..............................781 821-0200
Christine T Clark, *Ch Bd*
Thomas P Clark, *
Paul Clark, *
Stephen G Simo, *
Philip Smith, *
▲ EMP: 50 EST: 1973
SQ FT: 25,000
SALES (est): 9.85MM **Privately Held**

Web: www.phoenixeleccorp.com
SIC: 3629 5063 3823 3676　Electronic generation equipment; Electrical apparatus and equipment; Process control instruments; Electronic resistors

(G-7820)
PLYMOUTH RUBBER COMPANY LLC
104 Revere St (02021-3070)
PHONE..............................781 828-0220
Maurice Hamilburg, *Prin*
▲ EMP: 15 EST: 2009
SALES (est): 541.72K **Privately Held**
Web: www.plymouthrubber.com
SIC: 3069　Fabricated rubber products, nec

(G-7821)
PODGURSKI WLDG & HVY EQP REPR
Also Called: PODGURSKI WELDING AND HEAVY EQUIPMENT REPAIR
8 Springdale Ave Ste 2 (02021-3281)
PHONE..............................781 830-9901
Christopher Podgurski, *Prin*
EMP: 37
SALES (corp-wide): 335.35K **Privately Held**
Web: www.podgurskicorp.com
SIC: 7692　Welding repair
PA: Podgurski Welding Inc.
　607 East St
　Bridgewater MA 02324
　781 830-9901

(G-7822)
PRODRIVE TECHNOLOGIES INC
15 University Rd Ste A (02021-1434)
PHONE..............................617 475-1617
Pieter Janssen, *CEO*
EMP: 9 EST: 2014
SALES (est): 5.44MM **Privately Held**
Web: www.prodrive-technologies.com
SIC: 3672　Printed circuit boards
HQ: Prodrive Technologies International B.V.
　Science Park Eindhoven 5501
　Son En Breugel NB

(G-7823)
RESEARCH CMPT CONSULTING SVCS (PA)
Also Called: Research Cmpt Cnsulting Servic
960 Turnpike St Foxford Business Center (02021-2824)
PHONE..............................781 821-1221
Kayode I Bright, *Pr*
Daniel N Carney, *VP*
EMP: 8 EST: 1984
SQ FT: 2,500
SALES (est): 1.39MM
SALES (corp-wide): 1.39MM **Privately Held**
SIC: 7372 7374 7375 7376　Prepackaged software; Data processing and preparation; Information retrieval services; Computer facilities management

(G-7824)
SANOFI PASTEUR BIOLOGICS LLC
50 Shawmut Rd (02021-1409)
PHONE..............................781 302-3000
Michael Kishko, *Mgr*
EMP: 79
SIC: 5122 2834　Drugs and drug proprietaries; Pharmaceutical preparations
HQ: Sanofi Pasteur Biologics, Llc
　38 Sidney St Ste 370

Cambridge MA 02139

(G-7825)
SARNAFIL SERVICES INC
100 Dan Rd (02021-2898)
PHONE..............................781 828-5400
EMP: 140 EST: 1988
SQ FT: 60,000
SALES (est): 27.94MM **Privately Held**
Web: usa.sika.com
SIC: 2952 1761　Roofing materials; Roofing contractor
HQ: Sika Corporation
　201 Polito Ave
　Lyndhurst NJ 07071
　201 933-8800

(G-7826)
SCHLAGE LOCK COMPANY LLC
Kryptonite
5 Shawmut Rd (02021-1408)
PHONE..............................781 828-6655
EMP: 8
Web: www.schlage.com
SIC: 3429 5091　Locks or lock sets; Bicycle parts and accessories
HQ: Schlage Lock Company Llc
　11819 N Penn St
　Carmel IN 46032
　317 810-3700

(G-7827)
SEA STREET TECHNOLOGIES INC
779 Washington St Ste 2c (02021-3022)
PHONE..............................617 600-5150
Harley Stowell, *CEO*
Stephen J Ivanoski, *
EMP: 50 EST: 2012
SALES (est): 4.7MM **Privately Held**
Web: www.seastreet.com
SIC: 7372　Prepackaged software

(G-7828)
SHERMAN PRINTING CO INC
9 Kelly Way (02021-2786)
PHONE..............................781 828-8855
Peter W Sherman, *Pr*
James Sherman, *
Ellen Sherman, *
Mike Shields, *
EMP: 25 EST: 1986
SALES (est): 2.58MM **Privately Held**
Web: www.shermanprinting.com
SIC: 2752 2791 2789　Offset printing; Typesetting; Bookbinding and related work

(G-7829)
SHIELD REALTY CALIFORNIA INC (PA)
Also Called: Shield CA
99 University Rd (02021-1431)
PHONE..............................909 628-4707
George P Bates, *Pr*
Todd A Johnston, *
A Bruce Simpson, *
Troy D Wilson, *
Louis A Sgarzi, *
▲ EMP: 41 EST: 1983
SALES (est): 10.02MM
SALES (corp-wide): 10.02MM **Privately Held**
SIC: 2813　Aerosols

(G-7830)
SOLEO HEALTH INC
5 Shawmut Rd Ste 103 (02021-1408)
PHONE..............................781 298-3427
EMP: 22

Web: www.soleohealth.com
SIC: 2834 5912　Druggists' preparations (pharmaceuticals); Drug stores and proprietary stores
HQ: Soleo Health Inc.
　950 Calcon Hook Rd Ste 19
　Sharon Hill PA 19079
　888 244-2340

(G-7831)
SOUTHEAST RAILING CO INC
901 Turnpike St Unit A (02021-2861)
PHONE..............................781 828-7088
Robert De Voe, *Pr*
EMP: 10 EST: 1974
SQ FT: 5,000
SALES (est): 1MM **Privately Held**
SIC: 3446 1799　Railings, banisters, guards, etc: made from metal pipe; Ornamental metal work

(G-7832)
SPECTROWAX CORPORATION (PA)
Also Called: Safeworld International
330 Pine St (02021-3366)
PHONE..............................617 543-0400
Arnold Rosenberg, *Pr*
Arnold H Rosenberg, *
EMP: 60 EST: 1967
SQ FT: 18,000
SALES (est): 4.19MM
SALES (corp-wide): 4.19MM **Privately Held**
SIC: 2841 2842　Soap and other detergents; Specialty cleaning

(G-7833)
TDL INC
Also Called: T D L
550 Turnpike St (02021-2725)
P.O. Box 266 (02021-0266)
PHONE..............................781 828-3366
Tobe Deutschmann Junior, *Pr*
John J Ahearn, *VP*
Ruth Darcy, *Sec*
EMP: 20 EST: 1959
SQ FT: 12,000
SALES (est): 1.69MM **Privately Held**
Web: www.registrar-transfers.com
SIC: 3675 5065　Electronic capacitors; Electronic parts and equipment, nec

(G-7834)
THOMPSON STEEL COMPANY INC
Also Called: Arrow Thompson Metals
120 Royall St (02021-1096)
PHONE..............................781 828-8800
◆ EMP: 250
SIC: 5051 3316　Steel; Strip, steel, cold-rolled, nec: from purchased hot-rolled,

(G-7835)
TRILLIUM BREWING COMPANY LLC (PA)
Also Called: Trillium Brewing
100 Royall St (02021-1048)
PHONE..............................781 298-7126
EMP: 7 EST: 2011
SALES (est): 7.34MM **Privately Held**
Web: www.trilliumbrewing.com
SIC: 2082　Beer (alcoholic beverage)

(G-7836)
UNICOM ENGINEERING INC (HQ)
Also Called: Nei
25 Dan Rd (02021-2817)

PHONE..............781 332-1000
Corry Hong, *Pr*
Lawrence Yelsey, *
▲ EMP: 46 EST: 1999
SQ FT: 52,000
SALES (est): 263.83MM
SALES (corp-wide): 579.13MM **Privately Held**
Web: www.unicomengineering.com
SIC: 3572 7372 Computer storage devices; Business oriented computer software
PA: Unicom Global, Inc.
15535 San Fernando Mssion
Mission Hills CA 91345
818 838-0606

(G-7837)
UNIVERSAL WILDE INC (PA)
135 Will Dr Unit 2 (02021-3771)
PHONE..............781 251-2700
William Fitzgerald, *CEO*
John Sisson, *
Tom Andrade, *
Stephen Payne, *
Anthony Andrade, *
▲ EMP: 150 EST: 2000
SALES (est): 105.95MM **Privately Held**
Web: www.universalwilde.com
SIC: 2752 Offset printing

(G-7838)
UNIVERSAL WILDE INC
Also Called: Acme Printing
135 Will Dr Unit 2 (02021-3771)
PHONE..............978 658-0800
EMP: 101
Web: www.universalwilde.com
SIC: 2752 Offset printing; Typesetting; Bookbinding and related work
PA: Universal Wilde, Inc.
135 Will Dr Unit 2
Canton MA 02021

(G-7839)
VANITY WORLD INC
Also Called: Absolute Marble & Granite
348 Turnpike St Ste 1 (02021-2708)
PHONE..............508 668-1800
George Dolabany, *Pr*
EMP: 11 EST: 2008
SQ FT: 12,000
SALES (est): 485.62K **Privately Held**
Web: www.vanityworld.com
SIC: 3281 2434 Table tops, marble; Vanities, bathroom: wood

(G-7840)
WESTWOOD SYSTEMS INC
Also Called: Newman Associates
80 Hudson Rd Ste 200 (02021-1416)
PHONE..............781 821-1117
Henry Newman Iii, *Pr*
EMP: 10 EST: 1994
SALES (est): 2.49MM **Privately Held**
Web: www.newmanassoc.com
SIC: 3441 Expansion joints (structural shapes), iron or steel

(G-7841)
WIND RIVER SYSTEMS INC
Est
120 Royall St (02021-1028)
PHONE..............781 364-2200
Peter Dawson, *Prin*
EMP: 85
SALES (corp-wide): 17.49B **Privately Held**
Web: www.windriver.com
SIC: 3577 Computer peripheral equipment, nec
HQ: Wind River Systems, Inc.
500 Wind River Way

Alameda CA 94501
510 748-4100

(G-7842)
WOODCRAFT DESIGNERS BLDRS LLC
Also Called: Woodcraft Millwork
45 North St (02021-3338)
PHONE..............508 584-4200
Janice Wasiak, *Managing Member*
Lukasz Wasiak, *
Janice Wasiak, *Pr*
EMP: 39 EST: 2012
SALES (est): 5MM **Privately Held**
Web: www.woodcraftgroup.com
SIC: 2431 Millwork

(G-7843)
WRAPSOL LLC
55 North St Ste 1 (02021-3354)
▲ EMP: 32 EST: 2009
SALES (est): 3.4MM
SALES (corp-wide): 368.51MM **Privately Held**
Web: www.wrapsol.com
SIC: 3699 Electronic training devices
PA: Otter Products, Llc
209 S Meldrum St
Fort Collins CO 80521
855 688-7269

(G-7844)
ZSCHIMMER SCHWARZ INTRPLYMER I (DH)
200 Dan Rd (02021-2843)
PHONE..............781 828-7120
Norwin W Wolff, *Pr*
Norwin W Wolff, *Park Ranger*
Patti Converse, *
Gretchen Fleming, *
Thomas T Martin, *
▼ EMP: 25 EST: 1963
SQ FT: 41,000
SALES (est): 23.23MM
SALES (corp-wide): 865.79MM **Privately Held**
Web: www.zschimmer-schwarz.com
SIC: 2821 Thermoplastic materials
HQ: Zschimmer & Schwarz Gmbh
Max-Schwarz-Str. 3-5
Lahnstein RP
2621120

Carlisle
Middlesex County

(G-7845)
ASSURANCE TECHNOLOGY CORP (PA)
84 South St (01741-1596)
PHONE..............978 369-8848
H Larue Renfroe, *Pr*
Warren Tolman, *
Fredrick A Lund, *
Cosmo Diciaccio, *
William C Place, *
EMP: 80 EST: 1969
SQ FT: 18,000
SALES (est): 89.07MM
SALES (corp-wide): 89.07MM **Privately Held**
Web: www.assurtech.com
SIC: 3629 8711 3761 8748 Power conversion units, a.c. to d.c.: static-electric; Consulting engineer; Space vehicles, complete; Testing services

(G-7846)
QWIKLABS INC
37 Davis Rd (01741-1692)
PHONE..............978 760-0732
Enis Konuk, *Pr*
Nidhi Aggarwal, *Sec*
Kenneth Sauter, *Treas*
EMP: 12 EST: 2012
SALES (est): 360.37K
SALES (corp-wide): 282.84B **Publicly Held**
Web: www.cloudskillsboost.google
SIC: 3652 Prerecorded records and tapes
HQ: Google Llc
1600 Amphitheatre Pkwy
Mountain View CA 94043
650 253-0000

(G-7847)
TRANS MAG CORP
104 Canterbury Ct (01741-1861)
PHONE..............978 458-1487
Ashok Berajawala, *Pr*
EMP: 8 EST: 1979
SALES (est): 941.94K **Privately Held**
Web: www.transmagcorp.com
SIC: 3612 Power transformers, electric

(G-7848)
TRANSCEND AIR CORPORATION
Also Called: Transcend Aero
779 West St (01741-1426)
PHONE..............781 883-4818
Gregory Bruell, *Prin*
Peter Schmidt, *Prin*
EMP: 9 EST: 2017
SALES (est): 957.66K **Privately Held**
Web: www.transcend.aero
SIC: 3721 Aircraft

(G-7849)
UVTECH SYSTEMS INC
335 River Rd (01741-1819)
PHONE..............978 440-7282
EMP: 8 EST: 1994
SALES (est): 783.04K **Privately Held**
Web: www.uvtechsystems.com
SIC: 3589 Commercial cleaning equipment

(G-7850)
VALORA TECHNOLOGIES INC
81 Daniels Ln (01741-1056)
PHONE..............781 229-2265
Sandra E Serkes, *Pr*
Aaron Goodisman, *Treas*
EMP: 15 EST: 2000
SALES (est): 1.55MM **Privately Held**
Web: www.valoratech.com
SIC: 7372 7378 5734 Business oriented computer software; Computer maintenance and repair; Computer and software stores

(G-7851)
WEE FOREST FOLK INC
887 Bedford Rd (01741-1811)
PHONE..............978 369-0286
William R Peterson, *Pr*
Richard E Peterson, *Treas*
Annette Peterson, *Sec*
EMP: 9 EST: 1969
SALES (est): 507.54K **Privately Held**
Web: www.weeforestfolk.com
SIC: 3299 Art goods: plaster of paris, papier mache, and scagliola

---

Carver
Plymouth County

(G-7852)
ACME-SHOREY PRECAST CO INC
334 Tremont St (02330-1714)
PHONE..............508 548-9607
EMP: 7
SALES (corp-wide): 3.44MM **Privately Held**
Web: www.acmeshorey.com
SIC: 3272 Concrete products, precast, nec
PA: Acme-Shorey Precast Co., Inc.
36 Great Western Rd
Harwich MA 02645
508 432-0530

(G-7853)
DECAS CRANBERRY PRODUCTS INC (PA)
4 Old Forge Way Ste 1 (02330-1765)
PHONE..............508 866-8506
Charles B Dillon, *Pr*
Norman R Beauregard, *Treas*
John Decas, *Dir*
Gregory Decas, *Dir*
Cynthia Parola, *Dir*
▼ EMP: 22 EST: 1996
SALES (est): 24.63MM
SALES (corp-wide): 24.63MM **Privately Held**
Web: www.decascranberry.com
SIC: 2034 0171 8611 Dried and dehydrated fruits, vegetables and soup mixes; Cranberry bog; Growers' associations

(G-7854)
FRANCER INDUSTRIES INC
77 Green St (02330-2021)
P.O. Box 890124 (02189-0003)
EMP: 32 EST: 1949
SALES (est): 2.64MM **Privately Held**
Web: www.francer.net
SIC: 3444 5074 Sheet metalwork; Plumbing and hydronic heating supplies

(G-7855)
PEACEFUL MEADOWS ICE CREAM INC (PA)
5 Russell Holmes Way (02330-1258)
P.O. Box 895 (02347-0895)
PHONE..............781 447-3700
Marlene Hogg, *Pr*
Carol Mcsweeney, *VP*
EMP: 10 EST: 1962
SALES (est): 2.01MM
SALES (corp-wide): 2.01MM **Privately Held**
Web: www.peacefulmeadows.com
SIC: 6514 0241 2026 5451 Dwelling operators, except apartments; Dairy farms; Milk processing (pasteurizing, homogenizing, bottling); Milk

(G-7856)
PIECING PUZZLE
1 Hardhill Rd (02330-1003)
PHONE..............508 450-0323
Erica S Mccaffrey, *Prin*
EMP: 7 EST: 2011
SALES (est): 125.48K **Privately Held**
Web: www.piecingthepuzzle.org
SIC: 3944 Puzzles

(G-7857)
PLYMOUTH GRATING LAB INC
5 Commerce Way (02330-1080)
PHONE..............................508 465-2274
Douglas Smith, *Pr*
Eileen Smith, *Sec*
▼ **EMP:** 15 **EST:** 2004
SQ FT: 7,500
SALES (est): 2.45MM **Privately Held**
Web: www.plymouthgrating.com
SIC: 3827 Gratings, diffraction

(G-7858)
TLI GROUP LTD
35 Kennedy Dr (02330-1623)
PHONE..............................508 866-9825
William Coviello, *Pr*
EMP: 10 **EST:** 1999
SQ FT: 2,000
SALES (est): 877.46K **Privately Held**
Web: www.tligroup.com
SIC: 2899 Fire extinguisher charges

Cataumet
Barnstable County

(G-7859)
MOORING SYSTEMS INCORPORATED
1227 Rt 28a (02534-1077)
P.O. Box 413 (02534-0413)
PHONE..............................508 776-0254
James Cappellini, *Pr*
Peter Clay, *Pr*
EMP: 8 **EST:** 1985
SALES (est): 1.02MM **Privately Held**
Web: www.mooringsystems.com
SIC: 3443 3429 3499 Buoys, metal; Marine
hardware; Fire- or burglary-resistive
products

Centerville
Barnstable County

(G-7860)
MINUTEMAN PRESS
Also Called: Minuteman Press
1694 Falmouth Rd (02632-2933)
PHONE..............................508 775-9890
Judy Herring, *Pr*
EMP: 7 **EST:** 2015
SALES (est): 285.97K **Privately Held**
Web: www.minuteman.com
SIC: 2752 Commercial printing, lithographic

Charlestown
Suffolk County

(G-7861)
ATW ELECTRONICS INC
24 Spice St Ste 2 (02129-1312)
PHONE..............................617 304-3579
Jeffrey Spinks, *CEO*
EMP: 12 **EST:** 1991
SQ FT: 1,400
SALES (est): 489.26K **Privately Held**
Web: www.atw-electronics.com
SIC: 3677 Electronic transformers

(G-7862)
BOSTON BOATWORKS LLC
Also Called: Boston Boatworks
333 Terminal St (02129-3901)
PHONE..............................617 561-9111
◆ **EMP:** 40 **EST:** 1996

SALES (est): 10.9MM **Privately Held**
Web: www.bostonboatworks.com
SIC: 3732 Boats, fiberglass: building and
repairing

(G-7863)
BOSTON SAND & GRAVEL COMPANY
40 Bunker Hill Industrial Park (02129-1621)
PHONE..............................617 242-5540
Jomarie Bolen, *Pr*
EMP: 124
SALES (corp-wide): 100.01K **Privately Held**
Web: www.bostonsand.com
SIC: 3273 Ready-mixed concrete
PA: Boston Sand & Gravel Company Inc
100 N Washington St Fl 2
Boston MA 02114
617 227-9000

(G-7864)
BOUNCEPAD NORTH AMERICA INC
50 Terminal St Unit 710 (02129)
PHONE..............................617 804-0110
Tobi Schneidler, *Pr*
EMP: 7 **EST:** 2013
SALES (est): 137.25K **Privately Held**
Web: us.bouncepad.com
SIC: 2678 Tablets and pads

(G-7865)
BROWN PUBLISHING NETWORK INC (PA)
10 City Sq Ste 3 (02129-3740)
PHONE..............................781 547-7600
Marie L Brown, *Pr*
Mark S Brown, *
EMP: 30 **EST:** 1983
SQ FT: 12,000
SALES (est): 3.12MM **Privately Held**
SIC: 2741 2731 Miscellaneous publishing;
Book publishing

(G-7866)
CONFER HEALTH INC
56 Roland St Ste 208 (02129-1223)
PHONE..............................617 433-8810
Mounir Ahmad Koussa, *Pr*
Joshua John Forman, *Treas*
Zhi-yang Tsun, *Sec*
EMP: 9 **EST:** 2015
SALES (est): 578.56K **Privately Held**
Web: www.confer.health
SIC: 2835 In vitro diagnostics

(G-7867)
CROSBY WHISTLE STOP
24 Roland St (02129-1249)
PHONE..............................617 974-7410
James Georgaklis, *Prin*
EMP: 7 **EST:** 2011
SALES (est): 125.08K **Privately Held**
SIC: 3999 Whistles

(G-7868)
DIVERSIFIED INDUSTRIAL SUP LLC
100 Terminal St (02129-1980)
PHONE..............................800 244-3647
Dave Gorman Managing, *Prin*
Richard Callahan Managing, *Prin*
EMP: 10 **EST:** 2011
SALES (est): 681.77K **Privately Held**
SIC: 3052 Fire hose, rubber

(G-7869)
ECOVENT CORP
Also Called: Ecovent
24 Cambridge St Ste 6 (02129-1307)
P.O. Box 729 (01740-0729)
PHONE..............................620 983-6863
Dipul Patel, *CEO*
EMP: 10 **EST:** 2013
SALES (est): 934.23K **Privately Held**
SIC: 3634 Fans, exhaust and ventilating,
electric: household

(G-7870)
EDGE EMBOSSING INC
56 Roland St Ste 211 (02129-1233)
PHONE..............................617 850-2868
Andrew E Kamholz, *CEO*
EMP: 8 **EST:** 2005
SALES (est): 997.6K **Privately Held**
Web: www.edgeprecision.com
SIC: 2759 7389 Embossing on paper;
Business Activities at Non-Commercial Site

(G-7871)
EMBR LABS INC
24 Roland St Ste 1 (02129-1250)
PHONE..............................413 218-0629
Elizabeth Gazda, *CEO*
Matthew Smith, *CSO*
Samuel Shames, *COO*
David Cohen-tanugi, *Dir*
EMP: 16 **EST:** 2014
SALES (est): 2.99MM **Privately Held**
Web: www.embrlabs.com
SIC: 3679 Electronic circuits

(G-7872)
FARMER WILLIES INC
Also Called: Willie's Superbrew
50 Terminal St Bldg 1 (02129-1973)
PHONE..............................401 441-2997
Nico Enriquez, *Pr*
Jason D Halsted, *CFO*
EMP: 7 **EST:** 2014
SALES (est): 550.24K **Privately Held**
SIC: 2095 Roasted coffee

(G-7873)
FOUND ENERGY CO
50 Terminal St Ste 2 (02129-1973)
PHONE..............................201 315-9955
EMP: 10
SALES (est): 548.48K **Privately Held**
SIC: 2813 Hydrogen

(G-7874)
GLOUCESTER BUILDERS INC
92 Arlington Ave (02129-1031)
P.O. Box 290608 (02129-0211)
PHONE..............................617 241-5513
Frank Murphy, *Pr*
Patrick Brady, *VP*
EMP: 20 **EST:** 1985
SQ FT: 7,000
SALES (est): 3.53MM **Privately Held**
Web: www.gloucesterbuilders.com
SIC: 1542 2431 Commercial and office
buildings, renovation and repair; Millwork

(G-7875)
GREENSIGHT INC
529 Main St (02129-1106)
PHONE..............................617 633-4919
James Peverill, *CEO*
Joel Pedlikin, *
Justin Mcclellan, *CFO*
EMP: 45 **EST:** 2015
SALES (est): 7.61MM **Privately Held**
Web: www.greensightag.com

SIC: 3721 3861 8711 8713 Research and
development on aircraft by the manufacturer
; Photo reconnaissance systems; Aviation
and/or aeronautical engineering;
Photogrammetric engineering

(G-7876)
HYDRATION LABS INC (PA)
Also Called: Bevi
529 Main St Ste 304 (02129-1125)
PHONE..............................617 315-4715
Sean Grundy, *CEO*
Elizabeth Becton, *Pr*
Frank Lee, *Sec*
Sean Mcelduff, *VP Fin*
Christopher Lai, *Dir*
EMP: 21 **EST:** 2014
SALES (est): 22.63MM
SALES (corp-wide): 22.63MM **Privately Held**
SIC: 3565 Aerating machines, for beverages

(G-7877)
JOINERY SHOP INC
92 Arlington Ave (02129-1031)
PHONE..............................617 242-4718
EMP: 7 **EST:** 1995
SQ FT: 7,000
SALES (est): 668.84K **Privately Held**
Web: www.thejoineryshop.com
SIC: 2431 Millwork

(G-7878)
LUCIDITY LIGHTS INC (PA)
Also Called: Finally Light Bulb Company
56 Roland St Ste 300 (02129-1233)
PHONE..............................781 995-2405
John Goscha, *Pr*
Albert Roc, *VP*
▲ **EMP:** 26 **EST:** 2010
SALES (est): 8.59MM
SALES (corp-wide): 8.59MM **Privately Held**
Web: www.luciditylights.com
SIC: 3641 5063 Lamps, incandescent
filament, electric; Lighting fixtures

(G-7879)
MATHSOFT CORPORATE HOLDINGS (HQ)
101 Main St (02129-3514)
PHONE..............................617 444-8000
J Christian Randles, *CEO*
EMP: 75 **EST:** 2000
SALES (est): 113.3MM
SALES (corp-wide): 2.1B **Publicly Held**
SIC: 7372 Prepackaged software
PA: Ptc Inc.
121 Seaport Blvd
Boston MA 02210
781 370-5000

(G-7880)
POMEROY & CO INC
18 Spice St Ste 1 (02129-1395)
PHONE..............................617 241-0234
Gregory E Pomeroy, *Pr*
EMP: 35 **EST:** 1989
SALES (est): 3.85MM **Privately Held**
Web: www.pomeroyco.com
SIC: 2431 Woodwork, interior and
ornamental, nec

(G-7881)
RF MCMANUS COMPANY INC
7 Sherman St (02129-1024)
PHONE..............................617 241-8081
EMP: 13 **EST:** 1985
SALES (est): 481.64K **Privately Held**

SIC: 2434 Wood kitchen cabinets

(G-7882)
SMUDGE INK INCORPORATED
50 Terminal St Ste 2 (02129-3632)
PHONE..............................617 242-8228
Katherine Saliba, *Pr*
Deb Bastien, *VP*
EMP: 8 **EST:** 2004
SALES (est): 848.05K **Privately Held**
Web: www.smudgeink.com
SIC: 2759 7334 Screen printing;
Photocopying and duplicating services

(G-7883)
SOLID BIOSCIENCES INC (PA)
Also Called: Solid Biosciences
500 Rutherford Ave Fl 3 (02129-1647)
PHONE..............................617 337-4680
Ilan Ganot, *Pr*
Ian Smith, *Ch Bd*
Joel Schneider, *COO*
Carl Morris, *CSO*
Erin Powers Brennan, *CLO*
EMP: 27 **EST:** 2013
SQ FT: 16,000
SALES (est): 8.09MM
SALES (corp-wide): 8.09MM **Publicly Held**
Web: www.solidbio.com
SIC: 2836 8731 Biological products, except
diagnostic; Biotechnical research,
commercial

(G-7884)
WHITTEMORE-WRIGHT COMPANY INC
62 Alford St (02129-1004)
P.O. Box 290227 (02129-0204)
PHONE..............................617 242-1180
Charles M Hoyt Iii, *Pr*
Karl B Hoyt, *VP*
Charles M Hoyt Iv, *Treas*
Breck Hosmer, *VP*
Freda M Hoyt, *Sec*
◆ **EMP:** 10 **EST:** 1908
SQ FT: 30,000
SALES (est): 2.4MM **Privately Held**
Web: www.whittemore-wright.com
SIC: 2899 Oils and essential oils

Charlton
Worcester County

(G-7885)
ALL GRANITE & MARBLE INC II
379 Worcester Rd (01501-1503)
PHONE..............................508 434-0611
Altramiro Abranches, *Pr*
Alecxandro Santos, *VP*
▲ **EMP:** 8 **EST:** 1999
SALES (est): 1.03MM **Privately Held**
Web: www.allgranite2.com
SIC: 3281 Stone, quarrying and processing
of own stone products

(G-7886)
CRONIN CABINETS - MARINE LLP
164 Sturbridge Rd Ste 20 (01507-5324)
PHONE..............................508 248-7026
John D Cronin Senior, *Pt*
Caroline Cronin, *Pt*
John D Cronin Junior, *Pt*
Cindy Cronin, *Pt*
Tom Cronin, *Pt*
EMP: 8 **EST:** 1962
SQ FT: 6,000

SALES (est): 733.2K **Privately Held**
Web: www.cronincabinets.com
SIC: 2434 Wood kitchen cabinets

(G-7887)
DG MARSHALL ASSOCIATES INC
6 H Putnam Rd (01507-1220)
PHONE..............................508 943-2394
EMP: 24 **EST:** 2007
SALES (est): 3.09MM **Privately Held**
Web: www.dgmarshallassoc.com
SIC: 3535 Conveyors and conveying
equipment

(G-7888)
GHM INDUSTRIES INC (PA)
Also Called: Gessner Company
100 Sturbridge Rd Unit A (01507-5380)
PHONE..............................508 248-3941
Paul Jankovic, *Pr*
James E Phillips, *Treas*
Al Papesy, *VP*
◆ **EMP:** 13 **EST:** 1992
SALES (est): 2.56MM **Privately Held**
Web: www.millerproducts.net
SIC: 3531 Construction machinery

(G-7889)
INCOM INC
Also Called: Manfucturer
294 Southbridge Rd (01507-5238)
PHONE..............................508 909-2200
Anthony M Detarando, *Ch Bd*
Michael A Detarando, *
Darlene Bruch, *
▲ **EMP:** 150 **EST:** 1971
SQ FT: 52,000
SALES (est): 23.72MM **Privately Held**
Web: www.incomusa.com
SIC: 3827 Optical instruments and lenses

(G-7890)
KARL STORZ ENDOVISION INC
91 Carpenter Hill Rd (01507-5274)
PHONE..............................508 248-9011
Karl Storz, *CEO*
Sybill Storz, *
Eric Schmirler, *
EMP: 600 **EST:** 1989
SQ FT: 85,000
SALES (est): 118.41MM
SALES (corp-wide): 2.14B **Privately Held**
Web: www.karlstorz.com
SIC: 3841 Surgical and medical instruments
PA: Karl Storz Se & Co. Kg
Dr.-Karl-Storz-Str. 34
Tuttlingen BW 78532
74617080

(G-7891)
KELTON WOODWORK INC
11b Colicum Dr (01507-1444)
PHONE..............................617 997-7261
Robert Kelly, *Pr*
EMP: 17 **EST:** 2014
SALES (est): 1.2MM **Privately Held**
SIC: 2431 Millwork

(G-7892)
L & P PAPER INC
267 Southbridge Rd (01507-5241)
P.O. Box 775 (06239-0775)
PHONE..............................508 248-3265
Martin Gubb, *Pr*
Ronald Camarra, *
Margaret M Desantis, *
EMP: 60 **EST:** 2003
SALES (est): 9.26MM **Privately Held**
SIC: 2621 Paper mills

(G-7893)
MTD MICRO MOLDING INC
15 Trolley Crossing Rd (01507-1351)
PHONE..............................508 248-0111
Richard J Tully, *CEO*
Dennis Tully, *
EMP: 34 **EST:** 1970
SQ FT: 16,500
SALES (est): 5.49MM **Privately Held**
Web: www.mtdmicromolding.com
SIC: 3544 Special dies and tools

(G-7894)
NORTH AMERICAN TOOL & MCH CORP
278 Southbridge Rd (01507-5237)
P.O. Box 1157 (01585-1157)
PHONE..............................508 248-9862
▲ **EMP:** 10 **EST:** 1993
SQ FT: 5,500
SALES (est): 2.39MM **Privately Held**
Web: www.northamericantool.com
SIC: 3599 Machine shop, jobbing and repair

(G-7895)
SANTACROCE GRAPHICS INC
Also Called: Bennington Sports & Graphic
47 E Baylies Rd (01507-5120)
PHONE..............................802 447-0020
Frank Santacroce, *Pr*
Thomas A Husser, *Pr*
Bernard J Husser, *VP*
Joyce M Husser, *Sec*
EMP: 11 **EST:** 2020
SALES (est): 285.55K **Privately Held**
Web: www.satelliteoffer.net
SIC: 2395 5651 5661 Embroidery and art
needlework; Family clothing stores; Shoe
stores

Chartley
Bristol County

(G-7896)
RELIABLE ELECTRO PLATING INC
Also Called: Reliable Plating
304 W Main St (02712)
P.O. Box 91 (02712-0091)
PHONE..............................508 222-0620
Dale Broadbent, *Pr*
Karen Broadbent, *VP*
EMP: 7 **EST:** 1932
SQ FT: 6,500
SALES (est): 617.32K **Privately Held**
Web: www.reliableelectroplating.com
SIC: 3471 Electroplating of metals or
formed products

Chatham
Barnstable County

(G-7897)
HYORA PUBLICATIONS INC
Also Called: Cape Cod Chronicle
60 Munson Meeting Way Ste C
(02633-1992)
PHONE..............................508 430-2700
Henry C Hyora, *Pr*
Karen Hyora, *VP*
EMP: 16 **EST:** 1965
SALES (est): 1.44MM **Privately Held**
Web: www.capecodchronicle.com
SIC: 2711 Newspapers, publishing and
printing

(G-7898)
MAHI GOLD INC
Also Called: Mahi Gold Outfitters
465 Main St (02633-2459)
PHONE..............................508 348-5487
Michael Gorman, *Pr*
EMP: 13 **EST:** 2013
SALES (est): 1.95MM **Privately Held**
Web: www.mahigold.com
SIC: 5944 2329 5137 Jewelry, precious
stones and precious metals; Men's and
boys' sportswear and athletic clothing;
Women's and children's clothing

(G-7899)
NIXIE SPARKLING WATER INC
149 Cross St (02633-2278)
PHONE..............................617 784-8671
Nicole Dawes, *Managing Member*
EMP: 9 **EST:** 2018
SALES (est): 753.16K **Privately Held**
SIC: 2086 Bottled and canned soft drinks

(G-7900)
PVH CORP
Also Called: Van Heusen
1238 Main St (02633-1861)
PHONE..............................508 945-4063
Kay Janulewicz, *Brnch Mgr*
EMP: 7
SALES (corp-wide): 9.02B **Publicly Held**
Web: www.pvh.com
SIC: 2321 Men's and boys' dress shirts
PA: Pvh Corp.
285 Madison Ave
New York NY 10017
212 381-3500

Chelmsford
Middlesex County

(G-7901)
3M COMPANY
Also Called: 3M
279 Billerica Rd (01824-4180)
PHONE..............................978 256-3911
Brian Nilsson, *Brnch Mgr*
EMP: 29
SQ FT: 65,000
SALES (corp-wide): 34.23B **Publicly Held**
Web: www.3m.com
SIC: 3629 3317 3083 Static elimination
equipment, industrial; Steel pipe and tubes;
Laminated plastics plate and sheet
PA: 3m Company
3m Center
Saint Paul MN 55144
651 733-1110

(G-7902)
ADTRAN NETWORKS NORTH AMER INC
Also Called: Mrv Communications
300 Apollo Dr (01824-3629)
PHONE..............................978 674-6800
EMP: 150
SALES (corp-wide): 1.03B **Publicly Held**
Web: www.adva.com
SIC: 3661 Telephone and telegraph
apparatus
HQ: Adtran Networks North America Inc.
5755 Peachtree Indus Blvd
Norcross GA 30092

(G-7903)
ALARMSAFE INC
6 Omni Way (01824-4187)
PHONE..............................978 658-6717

Phil Stevens, *Pr*
Philip Stevens, *
EMP: 30 **EST:** 1979
SALES (est): 2.29MM **Privately Held**
Web: www.alarmsaf.com
SIC: 3669　Burglar alarm apparatus, electric

(G-7904)
ALM WORKS INC
12 Biltmore Ave　(01824-3202)
PHONE..........................617 600-4369
Ekaterina Malykh, *Prin*
Igor Sereda, *Prin*
Mikhail Babushkin, *Prin*
EMP: 24 **EST:** 2016
SALES (est): 686.34K **Privately Held**
Web: www.almworks.com
SIC: 7372　Business oriented computer
software

(G-7905)
AMERICAN BUSINESS SYSTEMS INC
Also Called: ABS
315 Littleton Rd Unit 1　(01824-3449)
P.O. Box 427　(01922-0427)
PHONE..........................978 250-0335
James Hamilton, *Pr*
James Fiske, *
EMP: 25 **EST:** 1978
SQ FT: 10,000
SALES (est): 2.69MM **Privately Held**
Web: www.abs-software.com
SIC: 7371 7372　Custom computer
programming services; Prepackaged
software

(G-7906)
ANALOG DEVICES FEDERAL LLC (HQ)
20 Alpha Rd　(01824-4123)
PHONE..........................978 250-3373
Vincent Roche, *Pr*
Ray Stata, *
EMP: 300 **EST:** 2015
SALES (est): 131.35MM
SALES (corp-wide): 12.31B **Publicly Held**
SIC: 3674　Semiconductors and related
devices
PA: Analog Devices, Inc.
　1 Analog Way
　Wilmington MA 01887
　781 935-5565

(G-7907)
APPLIED ANALYTICS INC
21 Alpha Rd　(01824-4170)
PHONE..........................978 294-8214
EMP: 25 **EST:** 2010
SALES (est): 4.33MM **Privately Held**
Web: www.aai.solutions
SIC: 3823　Industrial process measurement
equipment

(G-7908)
ARROW INTERNATIONAL LLC
Also Called: Teleflex Medical
16 Elizabeth Dr　(01824-4112)
PHONE..........................978 250-5100
EMP: 100
SALES (corp-wide): 2.79B **Publicly Held**
SIC: 3841　Surgical instruments and
apparatus
HQ: Arrow International Llc
　550 E Swedesford Rd # 400
　Wayne PA 19087
　610 225-6800

(G-7909)
ARROW INTERVENTIONAL INC
Also Called: Teleflex
16 Elizabeth Dr　(01824-4112)
PHONE..........................919 433-4948
EMP: 51 **EST:** 1994
SALES (est): 9.7MM
SALES (corp-wide): 2.79B **Publicly Held**
SIC: 3841 3842　Surgical and medical
instruments; Surgical appliances and
supplies
PA: Teleflex Incorporated
　550 E Swedesford Rd # 400
　Wayne PA 19087
　610 225-6800

(G-7910)
ARTHUR MAPES INC
Also Called: Mrs Nelsons Candy House
292 Chelmsford St　(01824-2403)
PHONE..........................978 256-4061
Arthur Mapes, *Owner*
EMP: 15 **EST:** 1954
SALES (est): 929.79K **Privately Held**
Web: www.mrsnelsonscandyhouse.com
SIC: 5441 2066 2064　Candy; Chocolate and
cocoa products; Candy and other
confectionery products

(G-7911)
ASSEMBLY GUIDANCE SYSTEMS INC
Also Called: Aligned Vision
27 Industrial Ave Unit 4　(01824-3618)
PHONE..........................978 244-1166
Scott W Blake, *Pr*
Robert G Coyne, *Ex VP*
▼ **EMP:** 19 **EST:** 1988
SQ FT: 90,000
SALES (est): 3.87MM **Privately Held**
Web: www.aligned-vision.com
SIC: 3823　Industrial process control
instruments

(G-7912)
ASSURANCE TECHNOLOGY CORP
303 Littleton Rd　(01824-3311)
PHONE..........................978 250-8060
Steven Brassard, *Brnch Mgr*
EMP: 70
SALES (corp-wide): 89.07MM **Privately Held**
Web: www.assurtech.com
SIC: 3629 3663　Power conversion units,
a.c. to d.c.: static-electric; Radio and t.v.
communications equipment
PA: Assurance Technology Corp
　84 South St
　Carlisle MA 01741
　978 369-8848

(G-7913)
ATLAS DEVICES LLC
Also Called: Atlas Devices
21 Alpha Rd Ste B　(01824-4172)
PHONE..........................617 415-1657
Bryan Schmid, *Managing Member*
Nathan Ball, *Managing Member*
EMP: 13 **EST:** 2005
SALES (est): 4.43MM **Privately Held**
Web: www.atlasdevices.com
SIC: 3674 7372 7389　Solid state electronic
devices, nec; Application computer software
; Business services, nec

(G-7914)
AZENTA INC
12 Elizabeth Dr　(01824-4147)

PHONE..........................978 262-2795
Robert Anastasi, *Executive Global
Operation Vice-President*
EMP: 450
Web: www.azenta.com
SIC: 3563 3561 3559　Vacuum pumps,
except laboratory; Pumps and pumping
equipment; Cryogenic machinery, industrial
PA: Azenta, Inc.
　200 Summit Dr Ste 600
　Burlington MA 01803

(G-7915)
BP LOGUE & CO
10 Jean Ave Ste 16　(01824-1740)
PHONE..........................978 251-4433
Bryan Logue, *Pr*
EMP: 10 **EST:** 1993
SALES (est): 1.89MM **Privately Held**
Web: www.bplogue.com
SIC: 1731 1521 7629 3621　General
electrical contractor; New construction,
single-family houses; Generator repair;
Generator sets: gasoline, diesel, or dual-fuel

(G-7916)
BROOKS AUTOMATION US LLC
12 Elizabeth Dr　(01824-4147)
PHONE..........................978 262-4613
EMP: 112
SALES (corp-wide): 25.87MM **Privately Held**
SIC: 3563　Air and gas compressors
HQ: Brooks Automation Us, Llc
　15 Elizabeth Dr
　Chelmsford MA 01824
　978 262-2400

(G-7917)
BROOKS AUTOMATION US LLC (DH)
15 Elizabeth Dr　(01824-4111)
PHONE..........................978 262-2400
David Jarzynka, *CEO*
David Pietrantoni, *
EMP: 7 **EST:** 2021
SALES (est): 25.87MM
SALES (corp-wide): 25.87MM **Privately Held**
SIC: 3674　Semiconductors and related
devices
HQ: Brooks Automation Holding, Llc
　15 Elizabeth Dr
　Chelmsford MA 01824
　978 262-2400

(G-7918)
BROOKS PRECISION MACHINING INC
4 Kidder Rd　(01824-3382)
PHONE..........................978 256-7477
Charles Brooks, *Pr*
Denise M Brooks, *VP*
EMP: 10 **EST:** 1979
SQ FT: 6,000
SALES (est): 1.22MM **Privately Held**
Web: www.brooks-mfg.com
SIC: 3599　Machine shop, jobbing and repair

(G-7919)
BULL DATA SYSTEMS INC
285 Billerica Rd Ste 200　(01824-4174)
PHONE..........................978 294-6000
David Seybold, *CEO*
Eves Blanc, *VP*
Richard Griesbach, *Sec*
Anil Agarwal, *CFO*
EMP: 2200 **EST:** 1989
SQ FT: 12,000
SALES (est): 175.2MM

SALES (corp-wide): 129.21MM **Privately Held**
SIC: 3571 3577 7378　Electronic computers;
Computer peripheral equipment, nec;
Computer maintenance and repair
HQ: Atos It Solutions And Services Inc.
　5920 Wndhven Pkwy Ste 120
　Plano TX 75093
　682 978-8622

(G-7920)
CONCEPTS NREC LLC
285 Billerica Rd Ste 102　(01824-4174)
PHONE..........................781 935-9050
Peter Baldwin, *CEO*
EMP: 18
SALES (corp-wide): 13.02MM **Privately Held**
Web: www.conceptsnrec.com
SIC: 8711 8731 3511　Engineering services;
Commercial physical research; Turbines
and turbine generator sets
PA: Concepts Nrec, Llc
　217 Billings Farm Rd
　White River Junction VT 05001
　802 296-2321

(G-7921)
CUNNINGHAM MACHINE CO INC
35 Hunt Rd　(01824-2601)
PHONE..........................978 256-7541
Wayne Cunningham, *Pr*
Susan Cunningham, *Sec*
EMP: 7 **EST:** 1965
SQ FT: 4,000
SALES (est): 632.79K **Privately Held**
Web: www.cunningham-machine.com
SIC: 3599 3469　Machine shop, jobbing and
repair; Machine parts, stamped or pressed
metal

(G-7922)
DATACON INC
10 Elizabeth Dr Unit 8　(01824-4145)
PHONE..........................781 273-5800
John Marshall, *CEO*
John A Marshall, *
EMP: 45 **EST:** 1971
SQ FT: 50,000
SALES (est): 11.06MM **Privately Held**
Web: www.data-con.com
SIC: 3679　Electronic circuits

(G-7923)
DIELECTRIC SCIENCES INC
88 Turnpike Rd　(01824-3598)
PHONE..........................978 250-1507
▲ **EMP:** 46 **EST:** 1970
SALES (est): 11.53MM **Publicly Held**
Web: www.dielectricsciences.com
SIC: 3643 3357　Current-carrying wiring
services; Nonferrous wiredrawing and
insulating
HQ: Hvt Group Inc
　88 Turnpike Rd
　Chelmsford MA 01824
　978 250-1507

(G-7924)
EDWARDS VACUUM LLC
Also Called: Igc Polycold Systems
15 Elizabeth Dr　(01824-4111)
PHONE..........................978 262-2400
EMP: 72
SALES (corp-wide): 13.47B **Privately Held**
Web: www.edwardsvacuum.com
SIC: 3563　Vacuum (air extraction) systems,
industrial
HQ: Edwards Vacuum Llc
　6416 Inducon Dr W

▲ = Import ▼ = Export
◆ = Import/Export

Sanborn NY 14132
800 848-9800

(G-7925)
EMERGNCY PWR GNRATORS NENG LLC
4 Etta Rd (01824-4733)
PHONE....................978 455-0461
Kristopher M Coleman, *Prin*
EMP: 9 **EST:** 2010
SALES (est): 929.99K **Privately Held**
SIC: 3621 Power generators

(G-7926)
EN-PRO MANAGEMENT INC
269 Mill Rd (01824-4105)
PHONE....................866 352-5433
EMP: 13 **EST:** 2003
SQ FT: 3,100
SALES (est): 191.75K **Privately Held**
Web: www.zoll.com
SIC: 3845 Electromedical equipment

(G-7927)
ENDEAVOR ROBOTIC HOLDINGS INC (DH)
19 Alpha Rd Ste 101 (01824-4124)
PHONE....................978 769-9333
Sean Bielat, *CEO*
Tom Frost, *Pr*
David Adams, *CFO*
Jihfen Lei, *Ex VP*
EMP: 15 **EST:** 2016
SALES (est): 25.34MM
SALES (corp-wide): 5.46B **Publicly Held**
SIC: 3826 Analytical instruments
HQ: Teledyne Flir Defense, Inc.
1024 S Innovation Way
Stillwater OK 74074

(G-7928)
FLEMING & SON CORP
Also Called: Fleming Printing
3 Marigold Ln (01824-4879)
PHONE....................617 623-3047
Gary F Shea, *Pr*
Ed Ryan, *VP*
EMP: 13 **EST:** 1938
SALES (est): 984.8K **Privately Held**
SIC: 2752 Offset printing

(G-7929)
FOUR IN ONE LLC
12 Alpha Rd (01824-4102)
PHONE....................978 250-0751
Gene Lee, *Managing Member*
Jim Lee, *
Jay Lee, *
EMP: 80 **EST:** 2001
SALES (est): 5.05MM **Privately Held**
Web: www.fourinone.com
SIC: 2099 Food preparations, nec

(G-7930)
HARDY DORIC INC
22 Progress Ave (01824-3607)
PHONE....................978 250-1113
Gerald Hardy, *Pr*
Robert Hardy, *VP*
Jeffrey Hardy, *VP*
Sheila M Hardy, *Sec*
EMP: 7 **EST:** 1930
SQ FT: 10,000
SALES (est): 944.4K **Privately Held**
Web: www.hardydoric.com
SIC: 3272 Burial vaults, concrete or precast terrazzo

(G-7931)
HARTE HANKS INC (PA)
Also Called: Harte Hanks
2 Executive Dr Ste 103 (01824-2566)
PHONE....................512 434-1100
Kirk Davis, *CEO*
John H Griffin Junior, *Ch Bd*
Laurilee Kearnes, *VP*
◆ **EMP:** 20 **EST:** 1920
SALES (est): 206.28MM
SALES (corp-wide): 206.28MM **Publicly Held**
Web: www.hartehanks.com
SIC: 7331 7372 Direct mail advertising services; Prepackaged software

(G-7932)
HIGH TECH MACHINISTS INC
177 Riverneck Rd (01824-2926)
PHONE....................978 256-1600
Robert K Moores Junior, *Pr*
▲ **EMP:** 45 **EST:** 1985
SQ FT: 25,000
SALES (est): 7.36MM **Privately Held**
Web: www.hightechmachinists.com
SIC: 3599 Machine shop, jobbing and repair

(G-7933)
HITTITE MICROWAVE LLC (HQ)
2 Elizabeth Dr (01824-4112)
PHONE....................978 250-3343
Rick D Hess, *Pr*
William D Hannabach, *Global Operations Vice President*
Larry W Ward, *
Susan J Dicecco, *
Robert Sweet, *
EMP: 76 **EST:** 1985
SQ FT: 103,000
SALES (est): 68.65MM
SALES (corp-wide): 12.31B **Publicly Held**
Web: www.analog.com
SIC: 3674 Integrated circuits, semiconductor networks, etc.
PA: Analog Devices, Inc.
1 Analog Way
Wilmington MA 01887
781 935-5565

(G-7934)
INFOBIONIC INC
321 Billerica Rd Ste 5 (01824-4100)
PHONE....................978 674-8304
Stuart Long, *CEO*
Dave Maccutcheon, *
Paul Mcewan, *CFO*
EMP: 26 **EST:** 2011
SALES (est): 3.49MM **Privately Held**
Web: www.infobionic.com
SIC: 3845 Electrocardiographs

(G-7935)
KONECRANES INC
Also Called: Crane Pro Services
25 Industrial Ave Ste 1 (01824-3617)
PHONE....................978 256-5525
EMP: 25
Web: www.konecranes.com
SIC: 3536 Hoists, cranes, and monorails
HQ: Konecranes, Inc.
4401 Gateway Blvd
Springfield OH 45502

(G-7936)
LOCKHEED MARTIN CORPORATION
Also Called: Lockheed Martin
16 Maple Rd (01824-3737)
PHONE....................978 256-4113
Joel Naidus, *Pr*

EMP: 22
Web: www.gyrocamsystems.com
SIC: 3812 Search and navigation equipment
PA: Lockheed Martin Corporation
6801 Rockledge Dr
Bethesda MD 20817

(G-7937)
MAGELLAN DIAGNOSTICS INC (HQ)
Also Called: Dionex
22 Alpha Rd (01824-4123)
PHONE....................978 250-7000
Walter Di Giusto, *Pr*
Wayne Matson, *
Herbert H Hooper, *
Peter D Parker, *
Robert J Rosenthal, *
▲ **EMP:** 84 **EST:** 1968
SALES (est): 26.08MM
SALES (corp-wide): 44.91B **Publicly Held**
Web: www.magellandx.com
SIC: 3826 2819 8071 3825 Analytical instruments; Chemicals, reagent grade: refined from technical grade; Testing laboratories; Instruments to measure electricity
PA: Thermo Fisher Scientific Inc.
168 3rd Ave
Waltham MA 02451
781 622-1000

(G-7938)
MERCURY COMMERCIAL ELECTRONICS INC
201 Riverneck Rd (01824-2820)
PHONE....................978 967-1364
EMP: 208
SIC: 3571 3825 Electronic computers; Microwave test equipment

(G-7939)
MINUTEMAN LABORATORIES INC
7a Stuart Rd (01824-4107)
PHONE....................978 263-2632
Jerome Nihen, *Pr*
Jerome Nihen, *Pr*
John Gilmore, *VP*
EMP: 10 **EST:** 1965
SQ FT: 20,000
SALES (est): 182.63K **Privately Held**
SIC: 3826 Spectrometers

(G-7940)
MRV COMMUNICATIONS AMERICAS INC
Also Called: Mrv Commmunications
300 Apollo Dr (01824-3630)
PHONE....................978 674-6800
EMP: 150
SIC: 3661 Telephone and telegraph apparatus

(G-7941)
NEOPRINT INC
11 Alpha Rd (01824-4124)
PHONE....................978 256-9939
EMP: 45
Web: www.neoprintinc.com
SIC: 2752 Offset printing

(G-7942)
ON-SITE ANALYSIS INC (DH)
1 Executive Dr Ste 101 (01824-2564)
PHONE....................561 775-5756
William C Willis, *Pr*
Rose Lynch, *Contrlr*
EMP: 7 **EST:** 1985

SQ FT: 1,862
SALES (est): 9.91MM
SALES (corp-wide): 6.15B **Publicly Held**
SIC: 3826 Analytical instruments
HQ: Spectro Scientific, Inc.
1 Executive Dr Ste 101
Chelmsford MA 01824
978 486-0123

(G-7943)
OSAAP AMERICA LLC
10 Kidder Rd (01824-3375)
PHONE....................877 652-7227
James B Chase, *Pr*
EMP: 10 **EST:** 2015
SALES (est): 1.68MM **Privately Held**
Web: www.osaap.com
SIC: 3086 Packaging and shipping materials, foamed plastics

(G-7944)
PARISI ASSOCIATES LLC
6 Omni Way (01824-4141)
PHONE....................978 667-8700
John M Caputo, *Pr*
EMP: 19 **EST:** 1967
SQ FT: 9,410
SALES (est): 2.49MM **Privately Held**
Web: www.parisiassociatesinc.com
SIC: 3679 Electronic circuits

(G-7945)
PICKERING INTERFACES INC
221 Chelmsford St Ste 6 (01824-2300)
PHONE....................781 897-1710
Keith Moore, *Pr*
Robert Stanonis, *Sec*
EMP: 7 **EST:** 1998
SQ FT: 500
SALES (est): 4.94MM
SALES (corp-wide): 49.09MM **Privately Held**
Web: www.pickeringtest.com
SIC: 3613 3679 Switches, electric power except snap, push button, etc.; Electronic switches
HQ: Pickering Interfaces Limited
10 Davy Road
Clacton-On-Sea CO15

(G-7946)
PORT PLASTICS INC
101 Brick Kiln Rd Ste 13 (01824-3284)
PHONE....................978 259-0002
Jason Askew, *Pr*
David Bradford, *Sec*
Christopher C Chotard, *CFO*
EMP: 9 **EST:** 2011
SALES (est): 1.3MM **Privately Held**
Web: www.portplastics.com
SIC: 2821 Plastics materials and resins

(G-7947)
QORVO INC
2 Executive Dr Ste 400 (01824-2566)
PHONE....................978 770-2158
EMP: 28
SALES (corp-wide): 3.57B **Publicly Held**
Web: www.qorvo.com
SIC: 3674 Semiconductors and related devices
PA: Qorvo, Inc.
7628 Thorndike Rd
Greensboro NC 27409
336 664-1233

(G-7948)
QORVO US INC
Also Called: Qorvo
300 Apollo Dr Ste 1 (01824-3630)

PHONE..................978 467-4290
Robert Bruggeworth, *Pr*
EMP: 27
SALES (corp-wide): 3.57B **Publicly Held**
Web: www.qorvo.com
SIC: 3674 Semiconductors and related
devices
HQ: Qorvo Us, Inc.
2300 Ne Brookwood Pkwy
Hillsboro OR 97124
336 664-1233

(G-7949)
**QUALITY ENGINEERING ASSOC
INC**
Also Called: Q E A
6 Omni Way (01824-4187)
PHONE..................978 528-2034
Ming-kai Tse, *Pr*
Ananna Tse, *Treas*
Karen Mathiasen, *Clerk*
EMP: 7 **EST:** 1987
SALES (est): 882.16K **Privately Held**
Web: www.qea.com
SIC: 3829 8711 Measuring and controlling
devices, nec; Consulting engineer

(G-7950)
QUICK PRINT LTD INC
Also Called: Qpl
27 Industrial Ave Unit 4a (01824-3618)
PHONE..................978 256-1822
Maxine C Derby, *Pr*
Peter Derby, *VP*
EMP: 7 **EST:** 1985
SQ FT: 2,800
SALES (est): 905.16K **Privately Held**
SIC: 2752 3993 Offset printing; Signs and
advertising specialties

(G-7951)
**RED MILL GRAPHICS
INCORPORATED**
14 Alpha Rd (01824-4102)
PHONE..................978 251-4081
Bernie E Gilet, *Pr*
Jim Gilet, *VP*
EMP: 15 **EST:** 2002
SQ FT: 1,000
SALES (est): 2.35MM **Privately Held**
Web: www.redmillgraphics.com
SIC: 2759 7331 Screen printing; Mailing
service

(G-7952)
ROCKWELL AUTOMATION INC
2 Executive Dr (01824-2565)
PHONE..................978 441-9500
Elik Fooks, *VP*
EMP: 57
Web: www.rockwellautomation.com
SIC: 3625 Electric controls and control
accessories, industrial
PA: Rockwell Automation, Inc.
1201 S 2nd St
Milwaukee WI 53204

(G-7953)
S&H ENGINEERING INC
248 Mill Rd Ste 4 (01824-4148)
PHONE..................978 256-7231
Stephen Smith, *Pr*
EMP: 16 **EST:** 1980
SQ FT: 30,000
SALES (est): 970.23K **Privately Held**
Web: www.s-and-h.com
SIC: 3599 Machine shop, jobbing and repair

(G-7954)
**SCHLEIFRING NORTH
AMERICA LLC**
Also Called: Schleifring
222 Mill Rd (01824-4127)
PHONE..................978 677-2500
▲ **EMP:** 12 **EST:** 2000
SQ FT: 7,000
SALES (est): 5.57MM
SALES (corp-wide): 2.14B **Privately Held**
Web: www.schleifring.com
SIC: 3824 Mechanical and
electromechanical counters and devices
HQ: Schleifring Gmbh
Am Hardtanger 10
Furstenfeldbruck BY 82256
81414030

(G-7955)
**SCHOEFFEL INTERNATIONAL
CORP**
Also Called: McPherson
7a Stuart Rd (01824-4107)
PHONE..................978 256-4512
Chris Schoeffel, *CEO*
Dietmar Schoeffel, *
▼ **EMP:** 24 **EST:** 1953
SQ FT: 23,000
SALES (est): 4.7MM **Privately Held**
Web: www.mcphersoninc.com
SIC: 3826 3829 Analytical instruments;
Measuring and controlling devices, nec

(G-7956)
SI-REL INC
Also Called: Vpt RAD
101 Brick Kiln Rd Ste 2 (01824-3284)
PHONE..................978 455-8737
Aridio Sanchez, *Prin*
EMP: 7 **EST:** 2017
SALES (est): 3.06MM **Publicly Held**
SIC: 3724 Aircraft engines and engine parts
PA: Heico Corporation
3000 Taft St
Hollywood FL 33021

(G-7957)
**SILICON TRANSISTOR
CORPORATION**
27 Katrina Rd (01824-2864)
PHONE..................978 256-3321
Stephen Apostolides, *Pr*
Robert Cauldwell, *Treas*
Borick B Frusztajer, *Stockholder*
EMP: 15 **EST:** 1972
SQ FT: 40,000
SALES (est): 189.78K **Privately Held**
SIC: 3674 Transistors

(G-7958)
SKY COMPUTERS INC
27 Industrial Ave Unit 1 (01824-3618)
PHONE..................978 250-2420
Henry Shean, *Pr*
EMP: 15 **EST:** 1980
SQ FT: 10,000
SALES (est): 2.4MM **Privately Held**
Web: www.skycomputers.com
SIC: 3577 Computer peripheral equipment,
nec

(G-7959)
SPECTRO SCIENTIFIC INC (HQ)
1 Executive Dr Ste 101 (01824-2564)
PHONE..................978 486-0123
Brian Mitchell, *Pr*
Carey Ross, *Sec*
▲ **EMP:** 78 **EST:** 1983
SQ FT: 50,000

SALES (est): 38.77MM
SALES (corp-wide): 6.15B **Publicly Held**
Web: www.spectrosci.com
SIC: 5084 3823 3829 3827 Indicating
instruments and accessories; Process
control instruments; Measuring and
controlling devices, nec; Optical
instruments and lenses
PA: Ametek, Inc.
1100 Cassatt Rd
Berwyn PA 19312
610 647-2121

(G-7960)
SUNS INTERNATIONAL LLC
127 Riverneck Rd (01824-2951)
PHONE..................978 349-2329
Fan Ye, *Pr*
Fan Ye, *Managing Member*
Christine Ni, *
▲ **EMP:** 350 **EST:** 2001
SQ FT: 3,000
SALES (est): 22.98MM **Privately Held**
Web: www.suns-usa.com
SIC: 3625 3613 3669 Switches, electric
power; Switchgear and switchgear
accessories, nec; Signaling apparatus,
electric
PA: Shanghai Suns Electric Co., Ltd.
Block 1, Floor 11, East Tower Of Hi-
Tech Wor, No.668, Beijing Ea
Shanghai SH 20000

(G-7961)
SVH SOFTWARE INC
139 Billerica Rd Ste 1 (01824-3634)
PHONE..................978 566-1812
Srinivasa Mandava, *Pr*
EMP: 7 **EST:** 2015
SALES (est): 436.19K **Privately Held**
Web: www.svhsoftware.com
SIC: 7372 7371 Prepackaged software;
Software programming applications

(G-7962)
SYCAMORE NETWORKS INC
220 Mill Rd (01824-4144)
PHONE..................978 250-2900
EMP: 250
Web: www.sycamorenet.com
SIC: 3577 3827 Computer peripheral
equipment, nec; Optical instruments and
apparatus

(G-7963)
TECH RIDGE INC
190 Hunt Rd (01824-3722)
P.O. Box 4001 (01824-0601)
PHONE..................978 256-5741
Stephen Comeau, *Pr*
Gary Comeau, *VP*
EMP: 27 **EST:** 1958
SQ FT: 11,000
SALES (est): 2.46MM **Privately Held**
Web: www.techridge.net
SIC: 3544 3599 Special dies and tools;
Machine shop, jobbing and repair

(G-7964)
**TELEDYNE FLIR UNMNNED
GRUND SY (DH)**
19 Alpha Rd Ste 101 (01824-4124)
PHONE..................978 769-9333
Sean Bielat, *CEO*
Tom Frost, *
Peter Manos, *
David Adams, *
EMP: 52 **EST:** 2016
SQ FT: 20,000
SALES (est): 23.31MM

SALES (corp-wide): 5.46B **Publicly Held**
Web: www.flir.com
SIC: 3569 Robots, assembly line: industrial
and commercial
HQ: Endeavor Robotic Holdings, Inc.
19 Alpha Rd Ste 101
Chelmsford MA 01824
978 769-9333

(G-7965)
THERMO EGS GAUGING LLC
22 Alpha Rd (01824-4123)
PHONE..................978 663-2300
John Sharood, *Pr*
Seth H Hoogasian, *
Richard Murphy, *
Vince Chambers, *
Jack Turpin, *
▲ **EMP:** 120 **EST:** 1983
SQ FT: 39,000
SALES (est): 26.56MM
SALES (corp-wide): 44.91B **Publicly Held**
Web: www.egsgauging.com
SIC: 3823 7699 Process control instruments
; Industrial equipment services
PA: Thermo Fisher Scientific Inc.
168 3rd Ave
Waltham MA 02451
781 622-1000

(G-7966)
**THERMO FISHER SCIENTIFIC
INC**
22 Alpha Rd (01824-4123)
PHONE..................978 250-7000
Patrcia Mcdermott, *Mgr*
EMP: 31
SALES (corp-wide): 44.91B **Publicly Held**
Web: www.thermofisher.com
SIC: 3826 Analytical instruments
PA: Thermo Fisher Scientific Inc.
168 3rd Ave
Waltham MA 02451
781 622-1000

(G-7967)
THERMO ORION INC (HQ)
22 Alpha Rd (01824-4123)
PHONE..................800 225-1480
▲ **EMP:** 50 **EST:** 1995
SALES (est): 75.59MM
SALES (corp-wide): 44.91B **Publicly Held**
SIC: 3826 Analytical instruments
PA: Thermo Fisher Scientific Inc.
168 3rd Ave
Waltham MA 02451
781 622-1000

(G-7968)
**VACUUM PLUS
MANUFACTURING INC**
80 Turnpike Rd (01824-3526)
PHONE..................978 441-3100
David J Rioux, *Pr*
William P Mcgrath, *VP*
EMP: 12 **EST:** 2009
SALES (est): 1.48MM **Privately Held**
Web: www.vacuumplusinc.com
SIC: 3674 Semiconductors and related
devices

(G-7969)
VJ ELECTRONIX INC
19 Alpha Rd (01824-4124)
PHONE..................631 589-8800
Vijay Alreja, *Pr*
Satya Korlipara, *
Kamla Alreja, *
▲ **EMP:** 45 **EST:** 2003
SQ FT: 30,000

▲ = Import ▼ = Export
◆ = Import/Export

SALES (est): 9.92MM **Privately Held**
Web: www.vjelectronix.com
SIC: 3844   X-ray apparatus and tubes

(G-7970)
WADDINGTON NORTH AMERICA INC
Also Called: Wna
6 Stuart Rd (01824-4108)
PHONE.............................978 256-6551
Amber Fox, *Brnch Mgr*
EMP: 182
SALES (corp-wide): 10.97B **Publicly Held**
Web: www.novolex.com
SIC: 3089 3086 3263   Injection molding of plastics; Cups and plates, foamed plastics; Semivitreous table and kitchenware
HQ: Waddington North America, Inc.
50 E Rver Ctr Blvd Ste 65
Covington KY 29550

(G-7971)
ZOLL MEDICAL CORPORATION
11 Alpha Rd (01824-4124)
PHONE.............................978 421-9132
EMP: 37
Web: www.zoll.com
SIC: 3845   Electromedical equipment
HQ: Zoll Medical Corporation
269 Mill Rd
Chelmsford MA 01824
978 421-9655

(G-7972)
ZOLL MEDICAL CORPORATION (HQ)
Also Called: Zoll
269 Mill Rd (01824-4105)
PHONE.............................978 421-9655
Jonathan A Rennert, *CEO*
Richard Packer, *
Elijah White, *
John P Bergeron, *
Aaron Grossman, *
▲ **EMP:** 1180 **EST:** 1980
SQ FT: 221,000
SALES (est): 646.41MM **Privately Held**
Web: www.zoll.com
SIC: 7372 3845   Prepackaged software; Defibrillator
PA: Asahi Kasei Corporation
1-1-2, Yurakucho
Chiyoda-Ku TKY 100-0

(G-7973)
ZOREAN INC
Also Called: Accutronics
10 Elizabeth Dr Ste 3 (01824-4145)
PHONE.............................978 250-9144
Luis M Pedroso, *Dir*
Maria Silva, *
EMP: 50 **EST:** 2003
SQ FT: 31,000
SALES (est): 15.68MM **Privately Held**
Web: www.accutronics.us
SIC: 3699   Electrical equipment and supplies, nec

Chelsea
Suffolk County

(G-7974)
AMERICAN BOLT & NUT CO INC
124 Carter St # 38 (02150-1519)
P.O. Box 6119 (02150-0009)
PHONE.............................617 884-3331
Ralph A Carbone, *Pr*
Priscilla Carbone, *Clerk*

Catherine Mccue, *Dir*
EMP: 8 **EST:** 1931
SQ FT: 8,000
SALES (est): 959.09K **Privately Held**
SIC: 3452   Bolts, metal

(G-7975)
CARBONE SHEET METAL CORP
Also Called: Carbone Metal Fabricator
240 Marginal St (02150-3510)
PHONE.............................617 884-0237
Peter J Carbone, *Pr*
Ann Walsh, *
John H Kelley, *
Eugene Lerman, *
EMP: 45 **EST:** 1986
SQ FT: 50,000
SALES (est): 8.5MM **Privately Held**
Web: www.cmfi.com
SIC: 3444   Sheet metalwork

(G-7976)
CATALENT MASSACHUSETTS LLC
190 Everett Ave (02150-1817)
PHONE.............................617 660-4110
Joe Musiak, *Mgr*
EMP: 13
Web: www.catalent.com
SIC: 2834   Pharmaceutical preparations
HQ: Catalent Massachusetts, Llc
14 Schoolhouse Rd
Somerset NJ 08873
732 537-6200

(G-7977)
CHELSEA CLOCK LLC
101 2nd St (02150-1828)
P.O. Box 1082 (02669-1082)
PHONE.............................617 884-0250
John Kirby Nicholas, *Managing Member*
Bruce Mauch, *
Anastasios Parafestas, *
▲ **EMP:** 35 **EST:** 1897
SQ FT: 27,000
SALES (est): 4.43MM **Privately Held**
Web: www.chelseaclock.com
SIC: 3873   Watches, clocks, watchcases, and parts

(G-7978)
CIVITAS THERAPEUTICS INC
Also Called: Acorda Therapeutics
190 Everett Ave (02150-1817)
PHONE.............................617 884-3004
EMP: 47 **EST:** 2009
SALES (est): 22.93MM **Publicly Held**
Web: www.acorda.com
SIC: 2834   Drugs acting on the central nervous system & sense organs
PA: Acorda Therapeutics, Inc.
2 Blue Hill Plz Ste 1703
Pearl River NY 10965

(G-7979)
COOPER CROUSE-HINDS LLC
Also Called: Wpi-Sarasota Division
222 Williams St (02150-3820)
PHONE.............................617 889-3700
Doug Koenig, *Genl Mgr*
EMP: 25
Web: www.coopercrouse-hinds.com
SIC: 3069 3679   Hard rubber and molded rubber products; Electronic circuits
HQ: Cooper Crouse-Hinds, Llc
1201 Wolf St
Syracuse NY 13208
315 477-7000

(G-7980)
COOPER CROUSE-HINDS LLC
222 Williams St (02150-3820)
P.O. Box 696460 (78269-6460)
PHONE.............................617 889-3700
Joseph Galli, *Genl Mgr*
EMP: 44
Web: www.coopercrouse-hinds.com
SIC: 3699   Electrical equipment and supplies, nec
HQ: Cooper Crouse-Hinds, Llc
1201 Wolf St
Syracuse NY 13208
315 477-7000

(G-7981)
FIRST ELECTRONICS CORPORATION
222 Williams St (02150-3820)
P.O. Box 1 (02150)
PHONE.............................617 288-2430
William Donnellan, *Mgr*
EMP: 83
SALES (corp-wide): 2.8B **Privately Held**
Web: www.feccables.com
SIC: 3679   Harness assemblies, for electronic use: wire or cable
HQ: The First Electronics Corporation
71 Von Hillern St Ste 1
Dorchester MA 02125
617 288-2430

(G-7982)
GARDEN FRESH SALAD CO INC
Also Called: Garden Fresh Salad
15 New England Produce Ctr # 20 (02150-1720)
PHONE.............................617 889-1580
Ismaele D'alleva, *Pr*
Luigi D'alleva, *VP*
Lisa Burke, *
Rita Whitney, *
EMP: 25 **EST:** 1966
SQ FT: 6,000
SALES (est): 10.31MM **Privately Held**
Web: www.gfsalad.com
SIC: 5148 2099   Fruits, fresh; Cole slaw, in bulk

(G-7983)
J B SASH & DOOR COMPANY INC
280 2nd St (02150-1710)
PHONE.............................617 884-8940
TOLL FREE: 800
Richard Bertolami, *Pr*
Ugo Bertolami, *
Salvatore J Bertolami, *
EMP: 32 **EST:** 1940
SALES (est): 5.11MM **Privately Held**
Web: www.jbsash.com
SIC: 2431 5211   Window sashes, wood; Sash, wood or metal

(G-7984)
KAYEM FOODS INC (PA)
75 Arlington St (02150-2365)
PHONE.............................781 933-3115
Ralph O Smith, *Pr*
Peter Monkiewicz, *
Michael Monkiewicz, *
Stephan Monkiewicz, *
▲ **EMP:** 375 **EST:** 1909
SQ FT: 160,000
SALES (est): 260.37K
SALES (corp-wide): 260.37K **Privately Held**
Web: www.kayem.com
SIC: 2011 2013   Meat packing plants; Smoked meats, from purchased meat

(G-7985)
LARIAT BIOSCIENCES INC
39 John St (02150-2124)
PHONE.............................603 244-9657
Jonathan William Larson, *Prin*
EMP: 8 **EST:** 2010
SALES (est): 245.55K **Privately Held**
Web: www.lariatbio.com
SIC: 2836   Biological products, except diagnostic

(G-7986)
LONE STAR HOLDINGS INC (HQ)
180 2nd St (02150-1806)
PHONE.............................781 935-2224
Randall Hicks, *Pr*
EMP: 20 **EST:** 1989
SQ FT: 2,000
SALES (est): 4.67MM **Privately Held**
SIC: 1743 3471   Terrazzo, tile, marble and mosaic work; Plating and polishing
PA: Metalstone Technologies Llc
180 2nd St
Chelsea MA 02150

(G-7987)
NANCY SALES CO INC
Also Called: Nanco
22 Willow St (02150-3506)
P.O. Box 6477 (02150-0013)
PHONE.............................617 884-1700
◆ **EMP:** 100
SIC: 5099 5199 5092 3942   Souvenirs; Gifts and novelties; Toys, nec; Dolls and stuffed toys

(G-7988)
NEW ENGLAND ELC MTR SVC CORP
25 Griffin Way (02150-3377)
PHONE.............................617 884-9200
Leonard F Guerrette, *Ch Bd*
Robert Tilton, *Pr*
EMP: 21 **EST:** 1939
SQ FT: 22,000
SALES (est): 2.84MM **Privately Held**
Web: www.weco-group.com
SIC: 5063 7694   Motors, electric; Electric motor repair

(G-7989)
RSVP PRESS
Also Called: Rsvp
300 Commandants Way Apt 314 (02150-4051)
PHONE.............................917 334-3102
Janet Kim, *Prin*
EMP: 7 **EST:** 2011
SALES (est): 66.32K **Privately Held**
Web: www.rsvpadvertising.com
SIC: 2741   Miscellaneous publishing

(G-7990)
RUBBER RIGHT ROLLERS INC
120 Eastern Ave Ste 206 (02150-3371)
PHONE.............................617 466-1447
Lorraine Ottaviano, *Prin*
EMP: 10 **EST:** 2014
SALES (est): 802.64K **Privately Held**
Web: www.rubberright.com
SIC: 3069   Fabricated rubber products, nec

(G-7991)
RUMAS PALLET WORLD LLC
124 2nd St Ste 2 (02150-1833)
PHONE.............................617 389-8090
Luis E Minnig, *Managing Member*
EMP: 50 **EST:** 2020
SALES (est): 2.71MM **Privately Held**

GEOGRAPHIC

Web: www.rumaspalletworld.com
SIC: 2448 Pallets, wood

(G-7992)
SPRING AIR OHIO LLC
124 2nd St (02150-1833)
PHONE..................................617 884-0041
Michael Brown, *Managing Member*
EMP: 9 EST: 2009
SALES (est): 527.55K **Privately Held**
SIC: 2515 Mattresses, innerspring or box
spring

(G-7993)
STANDARD BOX CO INC
28 Gerrish Ave (02150-2907)
PHONE..................................617 884-4200
H Fella Goldberg, *Pr*
EMP: 10 EST: 1907
SQ FT: 90,000
SALES (est): 227.18K **Privately Held**
SIC: 2657 Folding paperboard boxes

(G-7994)
STEELE CANVAS BASKET CORP
201 Williams St (02150-3805)
P.O. Box 6267 (02150-0995)
PHONE..................................800 541-8929
John Lordan, *Pr*
Sylvia M Lordan, *
▲ EMP: 36 EST: 1921
SQ FT: 24,000
SALES (est): 6.49MM **Privately Held**
Web: www.steelecanvas.com
SIC: 2393 3799 3537 2394 Canvas bags;
Pushcarts; Dollies (hand or power trucks),
industrial,except mining; Canvas and
related products

Cherry Valley
Worcester County

(G-7995)
WOOD ART INCORPORATED
Also Called: Wood Art Exhibit Group
424 Main St Ste 1 (01611-3000)
PHONE..................................508 892-8058
Joseph Loader, *Pr*
William C Tattan, *Sec*
EMP: 8 EST: 1972
SQ FT: 45,000
SALES (est): 465.65K **Privately Held**
Web: www.woodartexhibitgroup.com
SIC: 3993 Signs and advertising specialties

Chester
Hampden County

(G-7996)
BANNISH LUMBER INC
632 Route 20 (01011-9652)
P.O. Box 338 (01011-0338)
PHONE..................................413 354-2279
Harold M Bannish, *Pr*
Marlene Bannish, *Asst Tr*
Matthew Bannish, *VP*
Aaron Bannish, *VP*
EMP: 12 EST: 1932
SQ FT: 12,300
SALES (est): 368.26K **Privately Held**
Web: www.bannishlumber.com
SIC: 2421 2426 Sawmills and planing mills,
general; Hardwood dimension and flooring
mills

Chesterfield
Hampshire County

(G-7997)
CHESTERFIELD PRODUCTS INC
Also Called: Chesterfield Custom
11 Bofat Hill Rd (01012)
PHONE..................................413 296-0066
Frank J Keefe Junior, *Pr*
EMP: 20 EST: 1978
SQ FT: 40,000
SALES (est): 1.83MM **Privately Held**
Web: www.chesterfieldcustom.com
SIC: 3089 7336 3565 2672 Plastics
containers, except foam; Silk screen design
; Packaging machinery; Paper; coated and
laminated, nec

Chestnut Hill
Middlesex County

(G-7998)
CHARBERT INC
Also Called: Charbert Fabrics
830 Boylston St Ste 209 (02467-2502)
PHONE..................................401 364-7751
Bill Maher, *Prin*
▲ EMP: 16 EST: 1986
SALES (est): 387.96K **Privately Held**
SIC: 2258 Warp and flat knit products

(G-7999)
FE KNIGHT INC (PA)
Also Called: Castaldo Proudcts
56 Monadnock Rd (02467-1155)
PHONE..................................508 520-1666
Rona Knight, *VP*
Michael Knight, *Pr*
EMP: 7 EST: 1941
SALES (est): 2.48MM
SALES (corp-wide): 2.48MM **Privately Held**
SIC: 3915 Jewelers' castings

(G-8000)
LIQUIDSKY TECHNOLOGIES INC
321 Heath St (02467-2820)
PHONE..................................857 389-9893
Frank Gangi, *Pr*
EMP: 10 EST: 2013
SALES (est): 982.93K **Privately Held**
SIC: 3694 Battery charging alternators and
generators

(G-8001)
SIMULCONSULT INC
27 Crafts Rd Ste 101 (02467-1823)
PHONE..................................617 566-5383
Lynn Feldman, *CEO*
Michael Segal Ph.d., *Pr*
Harry Hanson Iii, *Sec*
EMP: 7 EST: 1998
SALES (est): 225.48K **Privately Held**
Web: www.simulconsult.com
SIC: 8099 2741 Medical services
organization; Miscellaneous publishing

(G-8002)
TRUSTEES OF BOSTON COLLEGE
Also Called: Center For Work and Family
22 Stone Ave (02467-3953)
PHONE..................................617 552-2844
Brad Harrington, *Ex Dir*
EMP: 10
SALES (corp-wide): 1.02B **Privately Held**
Web: www.bc.edu
SIC: 2741 8221 Technical manual and
paper publishing; College, except junior
PA: Trustees Of Boston College
140 Commonwealth Ave
Chestnut Hill MA 02467
617 552-8000

(G-8003)
WHITE MOUNTAIN CREAMERY INC
Also Called: White Mountain Creamery
19 Commonwealth Ave (02467-1003)
PHONE..................................617 527-8790
Peter Coutos, *Pr*
EMP: 14 EST: 1983
SQ FT: 750
SALES (est): 172.86K **Privately Held**
Web: www.whitemtncreamery.com
SIC: 5812 5451 2024 6794 Ice cream
stands or dairy bars; Ice cream (packaged);
Ice cream and frozen deserts; Franchises,
selling or licensing

Chicopee
Hampden County

(G-8004)
A1 SCREW MACHINE PRODUCTS INC
717 Fuller Rd (01020-3755)
P.O. Box 569 (01021-0569)
PHONE..................................413 594-8939
Steven Fido, *Pr*
Jack Fido, *Treas*
EMP: 16 EST: 1988
SQ FT: 13,000
SALES (est): 1.71MM **Privately Held**
Web: www.a1screwmachine.com
SIC: 3599 3452 Machine shop, jobbing and
repair; Nuts, metal

(G-8005)
AGILENT TECHNOLOGIES INC
300 Griffith Rd (01022-2126)
PHONE..................................413 593-2900
EMP: 35
SALES (corp-wide): 6.83B **Publicly Held**
Web: www.agilent.com
SIC: 3825 Instruments to measure electricity
PA: Agilent Technologies, Inc.
5301 Stevens Creek Blvd
Santa Clara CA 95051
800 227-9770

(G-8006)
AM LITHOGRAPHY CORPORATION
694 Center St Ste 2 (01013-1566)
PHONE..................................413 737-9412
EMP: 113 EST: 1984
SALES (est): 15.89MM **Privately Held**
Web: www.amlitho.com
SIC: 2752 Commercial printing, lithographic

(G-8007)
AMERICAN SPCIALTY GRINDING INC (HQ)
904 Sheridan St (01022-1031)
PHONE..................................413 593-5412
Raymond Fontaine, *Pr*
Richard Duplessie, *VP*
EMP: 20 EST: 1969
SQ FT: 5,800
SALES (est): 5MM **Publicly Held**
SIC: 3541 Grinding machines, metalworking
PA: Msc Industrial Direct Co., Inc.
515 Broadhollow Rd # 1000

Melville NY 11747

(G-8008)
AUTOMATED LOGIC CORPORATION
260 Griffith Rd (01022-2125)
PHONE..................................413 547-6595
Charles Abro, *Prin*
EMP: 12
SALES (corp-wide): 20.42B **Publicly Held**
Web: www.automatedlogic.com
SIC: 3822 Temperature controls, automatic
HQ: Automated Logic Corporation
1150 Roberts Blvd Nw
Kennesaw GA 30144
770 429-3000

(G-8009)
BAXTER SAND & GRAVEL INC
652 Prospect St (01020-3048)
PHONE..................................413 536-3370
Leo E Ouellette, *Pr*
Lorainne Ouellette, *
Lorainne Mrs L Ouellette, *Prin*
EMP: 11 EST: 1967
SQ FT: 300
SALES (est): 285.8K **Privately Held**
Web: www.chicopeeconcrete.com
SIC: 1442 5211 Construction sand mining;
Lumber and other building materials

(G-8010)
BERNARDINOS BAKERY INC (PA)
105 Exchange St (01013-1211)
P.O. Box 180 (01014-0180)
PHONE..................................413 592-1944
Fernando A Goncalves, *Pr*
Manuel A Silva, *
Carlos Albert, *
Alfred Cunha, *
EMP: 58 EST: 1918
SQ FT: 20,000
SALES (est): 4.89MM
SALES (corp-wide): 4.89MM **Privately Held**
Web: www.bernardinosbakeryinc.com
SIC: 2051 Bakery: wholesale or wholesale/
retail combined

(G-8011)
BLTEES INC
Also Called: B L Tees
165 Front St Ste 3 (01013-1261)
PHONE..................................413 594-7547
Bryon Lewis, *Pr*
EMP: 10 EST: 1995
SQ FT: 1,700
SALES (est): 586.93K **Privately Held**
SIC: 2759 Screen printing

(G-8012)
C & C LAMINATION
34 Pajak St (01013-1318)
PHONE..................................413 594-6910
Corol Cataldo, *Pr*
EMP: 7 EST: 1999
SALES (est): 87.98K **Privately Held**
SIC: 3089 Laminating of plastics

(G-8013)
CALLAWAY GOLF COMPANY
Also Called: CALLAWAY GOLF COMPANY
425 Meadow St (01013-2201)
PHONE..................................413 536-1200
David A Laverty, *Brnch Mgr*
EMP: 49
SALES (corp-wide): 4B **Publicly Held**
Web: www.topgolfcallawaybrands.com

▲ = Import ▼ = Export
◆ = Import/Export

SIC: 3949 Sporting and athletic goods, nec
PA: Topgolf Callaway Brands Corp.
2180 Rutherford Rd
Carlsbad CA 92008
760 931-1771

(G-8014)
CARAUSTAR INDUSTRIES INC
70 Better Way (01022-2118)
PHONE..................................413 593-9700
Wayne Kelch, *Mgr*
EMP: 22
SALES (corp-wide): 5.22B **Publicly Held**
Web: www.greif.com
SIC: 2655 Fiber cans, drums, and similar
products
HQ: Caraustar Industries, Inc.
5000 Astell Pwdr Sprng Rd
Austell GA 30106
770 948-3101

(G-8015)
CHICOPEE FOUNDATIONS INC
Also Called: Dispatch Plant
158 New Lombard Rd (01020-4859)
PHONE..................................413 594-4700
Leo Ouette, *Mgr*
EMP: 23
SALES (corp-wide): 5.23MM **Privately
Held**
Web: www.chicopeeconcrete.com
SIC: 3273 1521 Ready-mixed concrete;
Single-family housing construction
PA: Chicopee Foundations, Inc.
652 Prospect St
Chicopee MA 01020
413 536-3370

(G-8016)
**CHICOPEE PROVISION
COMPANY INC**
19 Sitarz Ave (01013-1342)
P.O. Box 7 (01014-0007)
PHONE..................................413 594-4765
TOLL FREE: 800
Tina Vezina, *Pr*
Thomas Bardon, *
Carolyn Donnelly, *
Gary Bernatowicz, *
EMP: 32 EST: 1920
SQ FT: 25,500
SALES (est): 4.72MM **Privately Held**
Web: www.bluesealkielbasa.com
SIC: 2013 5147 2011 Sausages and other
prepared meats; Meats and meat products;
Meat packing plants

(G-8017)
CHUCKS AUTO BODY TOWING
78 West St (01013-1627)
PHONE..................................413 459-4636
Charles Swider, *CEO*
EMP: 9 EST: 1994
SALES (est): 193.13K **Privately Held**
Web: www.chucksautoser.com
SIC: 3559 Special industry machinery, nec

(G-8018)
CITY TIRE CO INC
1385 Memorial Dr (01020-3967)
PHONE..................................413 534-2946
Daniel Greenberg, *Ofcr*
EMP: 20
SALES (corp-wide): 23.19MM **Privately
Held**
Web: www.city-tire.com
SIC: 7534 5531 Tire retreading and repair
shops; Automotive tires
PA: City Tire Co., Inc.
25 Avocado St

Springfield MA 01104
413 737-1419

(G-8019)
**COMMONWEALTH PACKAGING
CORP**
1146 Sheridan St (01022-2101)
P.O. Box 329 (01021-0329)
PHONE..................................413 593-1482
Joseph V Gosselin Junior, *Pr*
EMP: 55 EST: 1977
SQ FT: 90,000
SALES (est): 9.99MM **Privately Held**
Web: www.cartons.com
SIC: 2653 Boxes, corrugated: made from
purchased materials

(G-8020)
**CONVERGENT - PHOTONICS
LLC (DH)**
Also Called: Prima Electro North Amer LLC
711 E Main St (01020-6307)
PHONE..................................413 598-5200
Terry L Vanderwert, *Pr*
▲ EMP: 23 EST: 1984
SQ FT: 88,000
SALES (est): 19.23MM
SALES (corp-wide): 503.36MM **Privately
Held**
Web: convergent.lumibird.com
SIC: 3699 Laser systems and equipment
HQ: Prima Electro Spa
Strada Carignano 48/2
Moncalieri TO 10024
011 989-9800

(G-8021)
**COSTA PRECISION MFG CORP
(PA)**
475 Lombard Rd (01020-4851)
P.O. Box 990 (03743-0990)
PHONE..................................603 542-5229
Richard Zielinski, *Pr*
Richard M Zielinski, *
Martin A Zielinski, *
EMP: 43 EST: 1986
SALES (est): 7.36MM
SALES (corp-wide): 7.36MM **Privately
Held**
Web: www.costaprecision.com
SIC: 3599 3544 Machine shop, jobbing and
repair; Special dies, tools, jigs, and fixtures

(G-8022)
DIAMOND WATER SYSTEMS INC
863 Montgomery St (01013-3823)
PHONE..................................413 536-8186
William Dalton, *Pr*
EMP: 21 EST: 1989
SQ FT: 105,000
SALES (est): 2.3MM **Privately Held**
Web: www.diamondwater.com
SIC: 3589 5113 Water filters and softeners,
household type; Industrial and personal
service paper

(G-8023)
**DIECUTTING TOOLING SVCS
INC (PA)**
680 Meadow St (01013-1824)
P.O. Box 7 (01075-0007)
PHONE..................................413 331-3500
Mark K Lambert, *Pr*
EMP: 9 EST: 1990
SALES (est): 1.05MM
SALES (corp-wide): 1.05MM **Privately
Held**
SIC: 3544 Special dies and tools

(G-8024)
DIELECTRICS INC
300 Burnett Rd (01020-4636)
PHONE..................................413 594-8111
R Jeffrey Bailly, *Pr*
Ronald J Lataille, *Sec*
▲ EMP: 250 EST: 1954
SQ FT: 140,000
SALES (est): 45.34MM
SALES (corp-wide): 353.79MM **Publicly
Held**
Web: www.ufpmedtech.com
SIC: 3081 Vinyl film and sheet
PA: Ufp Technologies, Inc.
100 Hale St
Newburyport MA 01950
978 352-2200

(G-8025)
DISSTON COMPANY
45 Plainfield St (01013-1523)
PHONE..................................800 272-4436
Stephen Chen, *CEO*
Lane Morton, *
Rebecca Zhu, *
Joe Klepadlo Ctrl, *Prin*
▲ EMP: 35 EST: 1984
SALES (est): 10.97MM **Privately Held**
Web: www.disstontools.com
SIC: 5072 3425 Power tools and
accessories; Saw blades, for hand or power
saws

(G-8026)
DOW JONES & COMPANY INC
Also Called: Dow Jones
84 2nd Ave (01020-4625)
PHONE..................................212 416-3858
Rica Woyan, *Dir*
EMP: 20
SALES (corp-wide): 9.88B **Publicly Held**
Web: www.dowjones.com
SIC: 2711 Newspapers, publishing and
printing
HQ: Dow Jones & Company, Inc.
1211 Avenue Of The Americ
New York NY 10036
800 369-5663

(G-8027)
DOW JONES & COMPANY INC
Also Called: Dow Jones
200 Burnett Rd (01020-4615)
P.O. Box 7007 (01021-7007)
PHONE..................................413 598-4000
EMP: 52
SQ FT: 62,000
SALES (corp-wide): 9.88B **Publicly Held**
Web: www.dowjones.com
SIC: 2711 2721 Newspapers: publishing
only, not printed on site; Periodicals
HQ: Dow Jones & Company, Inc.
1211 Avenue Of The Americ
New York NY 10036
800 369-5663

(G-8028)
**DUVAL PRECISION GRINDING
INC**
940 Sheridan St (01022-1031)
PHONE..................................413 593-3060
Malcolm Getz, *CEO*
Ron Parlengas, *Pr*
EMP: 29 EST: 1949
SQ FT: 11,000
SALES (est): 3.26MM **Privately Held**
Web: www.duvalgrinding.com
SIC: 7389 3541 Grinding, precision:
commercial or industrial; Machine tools,
metal cutting type

(G-8029)
EASTERN CHEM-LAC LLC (PA)
Also Called: C&C Ventures
33 Haynes Cir (01020-3712)
PHONE..................................413 592-4191
EMP: 23 EST: 1932
SALES (est): 5.39MM
SALES (corp-wide): 5.39MM **Privately
Held**
SIC: 2851 Lacquer: bases, dopes, thinner

(G-8030)
**EASTERN ETCHING AND MFG
CO**
Also Called: Eastern Etching
35 Lower Grape St (01013-2674)
PHONE..................................413 594-6601
Joseph Lavallee, *CEO*
Joseph Lavallee, *Ch Bd*
John A Lavallee, *
Jay Wallace, *
Joseph Lavallee Junior, *VP*
EMP: 49 EST: 1935
SQ FT: 100,000
SALES (est): 6.29MM **Privately Held**
Web: www.eastern-etching.com
SIC: 3479 3993 2752 2759 Name plates:
engraved, etched, etc.; Name plates:
except engraved, etched, etc.: metal;
Decals, lithographed; Decals: printing, nsk

(G-8031)
ETHOSENERGY TC INC (DH)
1310 Sheridan St (01022-2102)
PHONE..................................802 257-2721
Neil Sigmund, *Pr*
Bryan Joyce, *
◆ EMP: 130 EST: 1994
SALES (est): 58.88MM
SALES (corp-wide): 5.43B **Privately Held**
Web: www.ethosenergy.com
SIC: 3511 3612 4789 Turbines and turbine
generator sets; Power and distribution
transformers; Pipeline terminal facilities,
independently operated
HQ: Ethosenergy Gts Holdings (Us), Llc
3100 S Sam Houston Pkwy E
Houston TX 77047

(G-8032)
FERGUSON ENTERPRISES LLC
1125 Sheridan St (01022-1044)
PHONE..................................413 593-1219
EMP: 7
SALES (corp-wide): 2.67MM **Privately
Held**
Web: www.ferguson.com
SIC: 3494 3432 5074 Valves and pipe
fittings, nec; Plumbing fixture fittings and
trim; Plumbing fittings and supplies
HQ: Ferguson Enterprises, Llc
751 Lakefront Cmns
Newport News VA 23606
757 969-4011

(G-8033)
FLEMING INDUSTRIES INC
Also Called: Iron Duck Division
102 1st Ave (01020-4679)
PHONE..................................413 593-3300
Michael Fleming, *CEO*
A Michael Fleming, *
Michael J Fleming, *
Shela Fleming, *
▲ EMP: 45 EST: 1980
SALES (est): 4.46MM **Privately Held**
Web: www.ironduck.com

SIC: **2393** 3842 2396 Bags and containers, except sleeping bags: textile; Orthopedic appliances; Screen printing on fabric articles

(G-8034)
GARAN ENTERPRISES INC
Also Called: Millies Pierogi
129 Broadway St (01020-2693)
PHONE.................................413 594-4991
Anna Lopuk, *Pr*
Anna Kerigan, *VP*
EMP: 12 EST: 1972
SQ FT: 100,000
SALES (est): 488.07K **Privately Held**
SIC: **2032** Ethnic foods, canned, jarred, etc.

(G-8035)
GUARDAIR CORPORATION
47 Veterans Dr (01022-1062)
PHONE.................................413 594-4400
Thomas C Tremblay, *Pr*
Hardy Hamann, *
Philip C Hanson, *
Ross E Sherbrooke, *
▲ **EMP: 40 EST:** 1943
SQ FT: 6,500
SALES (est): 9.42MM **Privately Held**
Web: www.guardair.com
SIC: **3546** 3492 3052 3563 Guns, pneumatic: chip removal; Fluid power valves and hose fittings; Rubber and plastics hose and beltings; Air and gas compressors

(G-8036)
HOPPE TECHNOLOGIES INC
107 1st Ave (01020-4620)
PHONE.................................413 592-9213
John Brocke, *Pr*
▲ **EMP: 75 EST:** 1941
SQ FT: 40,000
SALES (est): 16.17MM
SALES (corp-wide): 155.26MM **Privately Held**
Web: www.precinmac.com
SIC: **3544** 3545 Special dies and tools; Precision tools, machinists'
PA: Maine Machine Products Company
    79 Prospect Ave
    South Paris ME 04281
    207 743-6344

(G-8037)
IDEAL KITCHENS OF PALMER (PA)
Also Called: Ideal Kitchens
838 Grattan St (01020-1271)
PHONE.................................413 532-2253
EMP: 7 EST: 1990
SQ FT: 1,000
SALES (est): 930.55K **Privately Held**
Web: www.idealkitchens.us
SIC: **2434** Wood kitchen cabinets

(G-8038)
INDUSTRIAL STL BOILER SVCS INC
939 Chicopee St Ste 2 (01013-2893)
PHONE.................................413 532-7788
TOLL FREE: 800
William E O'neil, *Pr*
Gayle Rae, *Treas*
Bill O'neil, *Prin*
▲ **EMP: 23 EST:** 1991
SQ FT: 26,000
SALES (est): 5.11MM **Privately Held**
Web: www.isbservices.com

SIC: **3443** 3531 3441 7699 Fabricated plate work (boiler shop); Snow plow attachments; Fabricated structural metal; Boiler and heating repair services

(G-8039)
INSA INC
35 Center St Ste 1a (01013-2765)
PHONE.................................877 500-4672
Peter Gallagher, *CEO*
EMP: 32 EST: 2018
SALES (est): 8.94MM **Privately Held**
Web: www.insa.com
SIC: **2833** Medicinals and botanicals

(G-8040)
INTERNATIONAL METAL PDTS INC
Also Called: I M P
1165 Montgomery St (01013-3924)
PHONE.................................413 532-2411
Michael Dupuis, *Pr*
Mark Bergeron, *
Michael Hass, *
Gerald Burke, *
▲ **EMP: 41 EST:** 1989
SQ FT: 60,000
SALES (est): 5.42MM **Privately Held**
SIC: **3469** 3496 Stamping metal for the trade ; Miscellaneous fabricated wire products

(G-8041)
JAIN AMERICA FOODS INC
Also Called: Nucedar Mills
1000 Sheridan St (01022-1031)
PHONE.................................413 593-8883
Bruce Worchington, *Opers Mgr*
EMP: 14
Web: www.jainamericas.com
SIC: **2431** Trim, wood
HQ: Jain America Foods, Inc.
    1819 Walcutt Rd Ste 1
    Columbus OH 43228

(G-8042)
KAD MACHINE INC
Also Called: K A D Machine & Tool
28 Holgate Ave (01020-4018)
PHONE.................................413 538-8684
Douglas A Abbey, *Pr*
EMP: 9 EST: 1978
SQ FT: 5,000
SALES (est): 853.69K **Privately Held**
Web: www.kadindustries.com
SIC: **3599** Machine shop, jobbing and repair

(G-8043)
KG PALLET LLC
Also Called: Day Lumber Company
70 Orange St (01013-3842)
PHONE.................................413 536-3511
Jason Kaplan, *Pr*
EMP: 20 EST: 1929
SQ FT: 40,000
SALES (est): 2MM **Privately Held**
Web: www.daylumber.com
SIC: **2448** 2441 Pallets, wood; Boxes, wood

(G-8044)
LAMB KNITTING MACHINE CORP
Also Called: Lamb
66 New Lombard Rd (01020-4899)
PHONE.................................413 592-2501
William Giokas, *Pr*
Andrew Giokas, *DESIGN MANUFACTURING*
Besse F Giokas, *Asst Tr*
EMP: 7 EST: 1931

SQ FT: 12,000
SALES (est): 918.2K **Privately Held**
Web: www.lambkmc.com
SIC: **3552** Knitting machines

(G-8045)
LEO CONCRETE SERVICE INC
652 Prospect St (01020-3048)
PHONE.................................413 536-3370
Leo E Ouelette, *Pr*
Lorraine G Ouelette, *
EMP: 19 EST: 1953
SQ FT: 2,400
SALES (est): 502.07K **Privately Held**
Web: www.chicopeeconcrete.com
SIC: **3273** Ready-mixed concrete

(G-8046)
MAGNAT-FAIRVIEW INC
1102 Sheridan St (01022-1043)
PHONE.................................413 593-5742
▲ **EMP: 65**
Web: www.maxcessintl.com
SIC: **3599** 3554 Machine and other job shop work; Paper industries machinery,

(G-8047)
MERCHANTS METALS LLC
Merchants Metals
390 Burnett Rd (01020-4602)
PHONE.................................413 562-9981
Wayne Theriaque, *Mgr*
EMP: 56
SQ FT: 45,000
SALES (corp-wide): 1.06B **Privately Held**
Web: www.merchantsmetals.com
SIC: **3496** Fencing, made from purchased wire
HQ: Merchants Metals Llc
    3 Ravinia Dr Ste 1750
    Atlanta GA 30346
    770 741-0300

(G-8048)
METAL MEN
280 Ludlow Rd (01020-4488)
PHONE.................................413 533-0513
Walter Rose, *Owner*
EMP: 10 EST: 2002
SALES (est): 1.26MM **Privately Held**
Web: www.the-metalmen.com
SIC: **3444** Sheet metalwork

(G-8049)
MICROTEK INC
2070 Westover Rd (01022-1079)
PHONE.................................413 593-1025
Maria Goncalves, *Pr*
Anne Paradis, *
Diane Lavoie, *
Patricia Behan, *
Rosemary Tarantino, *
EMP: 120 EST: 1982
SQ FT: 24,000
SALES (est): 595.35K **Privately Held**
Web: www.microtek-cables.com
SIC: **3679** 3613 Harness assemblies, for electronic use: wire or cable; Control panels, electric

(G-8050)
MOSHER COMPANY INC
15 Exchange St (01013-1294)
P.O. Box 177 (01014-0177)
PHONE.................................413 598-8341
Jeffrey Templeton, *Pr*
EMP: 10 EST: 1934
SQ FT: 25,000
SALES (est): 2.49MM **Privately Held**
Web: www.mocomfg.com

SIC: **3291** Abrasive products

(G-8051)
NATIONAL VINYL LLC
7 Coburn St (01013-3809)
PHONE.................................413 420-0548
Scott Channell, *Genl Mgr*
Ben Surner, *Managing Member**
EMP: 50 EST: 1984
SQ FT: 100,000
SALES (est): 9.67MM **Privately Held**
Web: www.nationalvinyl.com
SIC: **3089** Windows, plastics

(G-8052)
ONDRICK MATERIALS & RECYCL LLC
22 Industry Rd (01020-3715)
PHONE.................................413 592-2566
Adam J Ondrick, *Managing Member*
EMP: 43 EST: 2014
SALES (est): 22MM **Privately Held**
Web: www.ondrickmr.com
SIC: **1611** 2951 4953 Surfacing and paving; Asphalt paving mixtures and blocks; Recycling, waste materials

(G-8053)
PFE ROLLS INC
Also Called: Perma Flex Engineering
1102 Sheridan St (01022-1043)
PHONE.................................978 544-7803
EMP: 74
SALES (est): 16.94MM
SALES (corp-wide): 333.41MM **Privately Held**
SIC: **3547** Rolling mill machinery
HQ: Webex, Inc.
    1035 Breezewood Ln
    Neenah WI 73114
    920 729-6666

(G-8054)
PIONEER PACKAGING INC (PA)
220 Padgette St (01022-1316)
PHONE.................................413 378-6930
Jeffrey Shinners, *Pr*
Jill Camossi, *
Louise Laflamme, *
EMP: 54 EST: 1946
SQ FT: 92,775
SALES (est): 9.57MM
SALES (corp-wide): 9.57MM **Privately Held**
Web: www.pioneerpackaginginc.com
SIC: **2657** 3089 2671 Folding paperboard boxes; Thermoformed finished plastics products, nec; Paper; coated and laminated packaging

(G-8055)
POLY-PLATING INC
2096 Westover Rd (01022-1055)
PHONE.................................413 593-5477
Edwin Ondrick, *Pr*
Carol Ondrick, *Treas*
Edwin Ondrick Junior, *VP*
Chris Ondrick, *VP*
EMP: 26 EST: 1976
SQ FT: 15,000
SALES (est): 3.31MM **Privately Held**
Web: www.poly-ond.com
SIC: **3471** Electroplating of metals or formed products

(G-8056)
POREX CLEANROOM PRODUCTS INC
Also Called: Essentra Porous Technologies

2255 Westover Rd (01022-1060)
PHONE..............................800 628-8606
Jon Peacock, *CEO*
John Udelhofen, *
Tim Mcarthy, *VP*
◆ **EMP:** 85 **EST:** 1906
SQ FT: 70,000
SALES (est): 50.7MM
SALES (corp-wide): 1.05B **Privately Held**
Web: www.saturix.com
SIC: 2842 Polishes and sanitation goods
PA: Filtration Group Corporation
 1 Tower Ln Ste 900
 Oakbrook Terrace IL 60181
 630 968-1730

(G-8057)
R DUCHARME INC
451 Mckinstry Ave (01020-1101)
PHONE..............................413 534-4516
Dean E Ducharme, *Pr*
EMP: 8 **EST:** 1910
SQ FT: 11,000
SALES (est): 1.23MM **Privately Held**
SIC: 3271 Blocks, concrete or cinder:
 standard

(G-8058)
REPUBLIC IRON WORKS INC
40 Champion Dr (01020-2833)
PHONE..............................413 594-8819
Gary Visconti, *Pr*
EMP: 7 **EST:** 2005
SQ FT: 15,000
SALES (est): 1.41MM **Privately Held**
SIC: 3441 Fabricated structural metal

(G-8059)
**ROGERS GENERAL
MACHINING INC**
181 Ludlow Rd (01020-4477)
PHONE..............................413 532-4673
Steve Guyott, *Pr*
Kenneth Guyott, *VP*
EMP: 10 **EST:** 1972
SQ FT: 8,000
SALES (est): 1MM **Privately Held**
SIC: 3599 Machine shop, jobbing and repair

(G-8060)
SHARON DINETTE INC
118 Dulong Cir (01022-1153)
PHONE..............................413 593-6731
Samuel J Rickless, *Pr*
Marsha Rickless, *Sec*
▲ **EMP:** 11 **EST:** 1898
SQ FT: 18,000
SALES (est): 456.53K **Privately Held**
Web: www.massasoittrading.com
SIC: 2241 Narrow fabric mills

(G-8061)
SIGN TECHNIQUES INC
Also Called: Sign Tech
361 Chicopee St (01013-1746)
P.O. Box 237 (01021-0237)
PHONE..............................413 594-8240
TOLL FREE: 800
Zenon Lemanski, *Pr*
Jane Lemanski, *Treas*
EMP: 11 **EST:** 1987
SQ FT: 3,150
SALES (est): 841.81K **Privately Held**
Web: www.signtechniques.net
SIC: 3993 Electric signs

(G-8062)
**TED ONDRICK COMPANY LLC
(PA)**

58 Industry Rd (01020-3715)
PHONE..............................413 592-2565
EMP: 12 **EST:** 1934
SQ FT: 1,500
SALES (est): 4.38MM
SALES (corp-wide): 4.38MM **Privately
Held**
Web: www.tedondrickco.com
SIC: 2951 1741 1611 4953 Asphalt and
 asphaltic paving mixtures (not from
 refineries); Masonry and other stonework;
 Highway and street paving contractor;
 Recycling, waste materials

(G-8063)
TRAFA PHARMACEUTICAL INC
140 Padgette St Ste D (01022-1309)
PHONE..............................866 998-7232
Shahid Habib, *Pr*
Hamid Habib, *Sec*
Zahid Habib, *Treas*
Tahir Habib, *Dir*
▲ **EMP:** 15 **EST:** 2009
SALES (est): 1.59MM **Privately Held**
Web: www.trafapharma.com
SIC: 2834 Pharmaceutical preparations

(G-8064)
TUNSTALL CORPORATION (PA)
118 Exchange St (01013-1243)
P.O. Box 434 (01101-0434)
PHONE..............................413 594-8695
Timothy P Tunstall, *Pr*
Laura Maspo, *COO*
Ryan Tunstall, *Sec*
▲ **EMP:** 21 **EST:** 1958
SQ FT: 15,000
SALES (est): 4.68MM
SALES (corp-wide): 4.68MM **Privately
Held**
Web: www.tunstall-inc.com
SIC: 3433 Steam heating apparatus

(G-8065)
UFP TECHNOLOGIES INC
300 Burnett Rd (01020-4636)
PHONE..............................800 372-3172
EMP: 25
SALES (est): 2.2MM **Privately Held**
Web: www.ufpmedtech.com
SIC: 3841 Surgical and medical instruments

(G-8066)
UNECO MANUFACTURING INC
330 Fuller Rd (01020-3724)
PHONE..............................413 594-2700
Al Fontana, *Pr*
Walter K Twarowski, *
EMP: 30 **EST:** 1993
SQ FT: 17,000
SALES (est): 2.58MM **Privately Held**
Web: www.unecomfg.com
SIC: 3469 3544 Metal stampings, nec;
 Special dies, tools, jigs, and fixtures

(G-8067)
**US TSUBAKI AUTOMOTIVE LLC
(DH)**
106 Lonczak St (01022-1305)
PHONE..............................413 593-1100
▲ **EMP:** 200 **EST:** 2010
SALES (est): 89.14MM **Privately Held**
Web: www.ustsubaki.com
SIC: 3462 3568 3496 Automotive forgings,
 ferrous: crankshaft, engine, axle, etc.;
 Power transmission equipment, nec;
 Miscellaneous fabricated wire products
HQ: U.S. Tsubaki Holdings, Inc.
 301 E Marquardt Dr
 Wheeling IL 60090
 847 459-9500

(G-8068)
VIANT CHICOPEE INC
Also Called: United Plastics Group
1040 Sheridan St (01022-1043)
PHONE..............................413 612-2100
◆ **EMP:** 200 **EST:** 1961
SALES (est): 48.72MM
SALES (corp-wide): 1.18B **Privately Held**
SIC: 3089 Injection molding of plastics
HQ: Viant Medical, Llc
 2 Hampshire St
 Foxborough MA 02035

(G-8069)
WALL STREET JOURNAL
84 2nd Ave (01020-4625)
PHONE..............................800 369-5663
Richard Zannino, *Prin*
EMP: 40 **EST:** 1994
SALES (est): 315.79K **Privately Held**
SIC: 2711 Newspapers, publishing and
 printing

(G-8070)
WESTFIELD READY-MIX INC
652 Prospect St (01020-3048)
PHONE..............................413 594-4700
Lee Ouellette, *Pr*
EMP: 16 **EST:** 2008
SALES (est): 770.77K **Privately Held**
Web: www.chicopeeconcrete.com
SIC: 3273 Ready-mixed concrete

Chilmark
Dukes County

(G-8071)
**GREY BARN FARM
ENTERPRISES LLC**
22 South Rd (02535-2329)
PHONE..............................508 645-4854
EMP: 8 **EST:** 2014
SALES (est): 501.42K **Privately Held**
Web: www.thegreybarnandfarm.com
SIC: 0241 2022 7389 Dairy farms; Natural
 cheese; Business Activities at Non-
 Commercial Site

Clarksburg
Berkshire County

(G-8072)
**PERIOD LIGHTING FIXTURES
INC**
167 River Rd (01247-2147)
PHONE..............................413 664-7141
Chris Berta, *Treas*
EMP: 10 **EST:** 1972
SQ FT: 6,000
SALES (est): 801.17K **Privately Held**
Web: www.periodlighting.com
SIC: 3645 5961 5063 3648 Residential
 lighting fixtures; Electronic kits and parts,
 mail order; Electrical apparatus and
 equipment; Lighting equipment, nec

(G-8073)
R I BAKER CO INC (PA)
Also Called: Ribco Supply Co
163 River Rd (01247-2147)
P.O. Box 895 (01247-0895)
PHONE..............................413 663-3791
Thomas Pelczynski, *Pr*
Maynard A Hodgdon, *
EMP: 27 **EST:** 1968
SQ FT: 20,000

SALES (est): 4.47MM
SALES (corp-wide): 4.47MM **Privately
Held**
Web: www.ribcosupply.com
SIC: 3599 1711 5074 3441 Machine shop,
 jobbing and repair; Plumbing contractors;
 Plumbing fittings and supplies; Fabricated
 structural metal

(G-8074)
STOREY PUBLISHING LLC (DH)
784 Middle Rd (01247-9634)
PHONE..............................413 346-2100
Pam Art, *Managing Member*
Peter Workman, *
Daniel Reynolds, *
▲ **EMP:** 40 **EST:** 1983
SALES (est): 11.45MM **Privately Held**
Web: www.hachettebookgroup.com
SIC: 2731 5192 5961 Books, publishing only
 ; Books; Catalog and mail-order houses
HQ: Workman Publishing Co. Inc.
 1290 Ave Of The Americas
 New York NY 10104
 212 254-5900

Clinton
Worcester County

(G-8075)
CLINTON BCI INC
179 Woodlawn St (01510-1831)
PHONE..............................978 365-7335
▲ **EMP:** 36
SIC: 2821 Plastics materials and resins

(G-8076)
**DARMANN ABRASIVE
PRODUCTS INC (PA)**
100 Sterling St (01510-1914)
PHONE..............................978 365-4544
◆ **EMP:** 73 **EST:** 1982
SALES (est): 7.97MM
SALES (corp-wide): 7.97MM **Privately
Held**
Web: www.darmann.com
SIC: 3291 Hones

(G-8077)
DUNN & CO INC
75 Green St Ste 1 (01510-3017)
PHONE..............................978 368-8505
Dave Dunn, *Prin*
▼ **EMP:** 125 **EST:** 1976
SQ FT: 250,000
SALES (est): 19.41MM **Privately Held**
Web: www.booktrauma.com
SIC: 2732 Books, printing and binding

(G-8078)
INJECTRONICS CORPORATION
Also Called: Injectronics
1 Union St (01510-2930)
PHONE..............................978 365-1200
▲ **EMP:** 70
Web: www.injectronics.com
SIC: 3089 3083 Injection molding of plastics
 ; Laminated plastics plate and sheet

(G-8079)
JABIL INC
Also Called: Jabil Healthcare
101 Union St (01510-2908)
PHONE..............................978 365-9721
EMP: 44
SALES (corp-wide): 34.7B **Publicly Held**
Web: www.radiusinnovation.com

GEOGRAPHIC

SIC: 3672 Printed circuit boards
PA: Jabil Inc.
10800 Roosevelt Blvd N
Saint Petersburg FL 33716
727 577-9749

(G-8080)
LEGACY PUBLISHING GROUP INC
75 Green St Ste 1 (01510-3017)
P.O. Box 299 (01510-0299)
PHONE..............................800 322-3866
◆ EMP: 20 EST: 1992
SQ FT: 20,000
SALES (est): 3.66MM **Privately Held**
Web: www.shoplegacy.com
SIC: 2741 Miscellaneous publishing

(G-8081)
LIBERTY COMPASSION INC
Also Called: Affinity
179 Brook St (01510-1503)
PHONE..............................978 213-8757
Vincent Giordano, *Pr*
EMP: 50 EST: 2018
SALES (est): 9.5MM
SALES (corp-wide): 1.02B **Privately Held**
Web: www.affinityne.com
SIC: 3999
PA: Green Thumb Industries Inc.
325 W Huron St Ste 700
Chicago IL 60654
312 471-6720

(G-8082)
LLOYD & BOUVIER INC
10 Parker St (01510-1906)
PHONE..............................978 365-5700
Carter F Lloyd, *Pr*
Brian Bouvier, *
Linda D Lloyd, *
◆ EMP: 25 EST: 1990
SALES (est): 9.84MM **Privately Held**
Web: www.lloydbouvier.com
SIC: 5063 3552 Electrical apparatus and equipment; Rope and cordage machines

(G-8083)
MASS BREWING LLC (PA)
Also Called: Sterling Street Brewery
175 Sterling St (01510-1937)
PHONE..............................617 800-7070
EMP: 7 EST: 2021
SALES (est): 62.38K
SALES (corp-wide): 62.38K **Privately Held**
Web: www.sterlingstreetbrewery.com
SIC: 2082 Beer (alcoholic beverage)

(G-8084)
N P MEDICAL INC
101 Union St (01510-2908)
PHONE..............................978 365-9721
Luis J Maseda, *Pr*
◆ EMP: 32 EST: 1982
SQ FT: 2,000
SALES (est): 11.62MM
SALES (corp-wide): 34.7B **Publicly Held**
Web: www.npmedical.com
SIC: 3841 Surgical and medical instruments
HQ: Nypro Inc.
101 Union St
Clinton MA 01510
978 365-9721

(G-8085)
NEVADA HEAT TREATING LLC
Also Called: California Brazing
90 Parker St (01510-1531)
PHONE..............................978 365-4999
Richard T Penros, *Managing Member*

EMP: 29
SALES (corp-wide): 42.04MM **Privately Held**
Web: www.vitessesys.com
SIC: 3599 Machine shop, jobbing and repair
PA: Nevada Heat Treating, Llc
37955 Central Ct Ste D
Newark CA 94560
510 790-2300

(G-8086)
NYPRO HEALTHCARE BAJA INC (DH)
Also Called: Nypro Precision Assemblies
101 Union St (01510-2935)
PHONE..............................619 498-9250
Joe Borden, *Ch*
David Beamer, *
Gregory Hebard, *
▲ EMP: 86 EST: 1993
SQ FT: 60,000
SALES (est): 83.33MM
SALES (corp-wide): 34.7B **Publicly Held**
Web: www.jabil.com
SIC: 3841 3679 Surgical and medical instruments; Electronic circuits
HQ: Nypro Inc.
101 Union St
Clinton MA 01510
978 365-9721

(G-8087)
NYPRO INC (HQ)
Also Called: Clinton Nypro
101 Union St (01510-2935)
PHONE..............................978 365-9721
David Beamer, *Pr*
Robert Katz, *
Gregory Hebard, *
◆ EMP: 1000 EST: 1955
SQ FT: 500,000
SALES (est): 1.92B
SALES (corp-wide): 34.7B **Publicly Held**
Web: www.jabil.com
SIC: 3089 3559 8711 7389 Injection molding of plastics; Robots, molding and forming plastics; Engineering services; Design, commercial and industrial
PA: Jabil Inc.
10800 Roosevelt Blvd N
Saint Petersburg FL 33716
727 577-9749

(G-8088)
NYPRO INC
25 School St (01510-3419)
PHONE..............................978 368-6021
Courtney Ryan, *Brnch Mgr*
EMP: 178
SQ FT: 26,000
SALES (corp-wide): 34.7B **Publicly Held**
Web: www.jabil.com
SIC: 2834 Pharmaceutical preparations
HQ: Nypro Inc.
101 Union St
Clinton MA 01510
978 365-9721

(G-8089)
NYPROMOLD INC (PA)
144 Pleasant St (01510-3416)
PHONE..............................978 365-4547
Robert Katz, *Pr*
John Casali, *
▲ EMP: 100 EST: 1987
SQ FT: 9,000
SALES (est): 25.68MM
SALES (corp-wide): 25.68MM **Privately Held**
Web: www.nypromold.com

SIC: 3089 Injection molding of plastics

(G-8090)
QEP CO INC
179 Brook St (01510-1503)
PHONE..............................978 368-8991
Joseph Kelly, *CEO*
EMP: 9
SALES (corp-wide): 387.6MM **Privately Held**
Web: www.qepcorporate.com
SIC: 3089 Injection molding of plastics
PA: Q.E.P. Co., Inc.
1001 Broken Sound Pkwy Nw A
Boca Raton FL 33487
561 994-5550

(G-8091)
SPECIALTY RESTORATION INC
32 Greeley St (01510-1902)
PHONE..............................978 365-1700
EMP: 9 EST: 1996
SQ FT: 10,000
SALES (est): 992.77K **Privately Held**
Web:
www.centralmasspowdercoating.com
SIC: 3479 Coating of metals and formed products

(G-8092)
STERLING PRECISION INC
99 Lawrence St (01510-1533)
PHONE..............................978 365-4999
Robert Heckman, *Pr*
Richard Lazazzero, *Sec*
EMP: 15 EST: 2021
SALES (est): 3.38MM **Privately Held**
Web: www.vitessesys.com
SIC: 3599 Machine shop, jobbing and repair

(G-8093)
TYCA CORPORATION (PA)
470 Main St (01510-2422)
PHONE..............................978 612-0002
Franklin V Hardy, *Pr*
Mary Ann Castillo, *
▲ EMP: 34 EST: 1978
SQ FT: 26,000
SALES (est): 2.45MM
SALES (corp-wide): 2.45MM **Privately Held**
Web: www.tyca.com
SIC: 2326 3089 2329 2339 Jackets, overall and work; Molding primary plastics; Jackets (suede, leatherette, etc.), sport: men's and boys'; Women's and misses' outerwear, nec

Cohasset
Norfolk County

(G-8094)
COHASSET REDEMPTION INC
166 King St (02025-1392)
PHONE..............................781 383-3100
Thao T Nguyen, *Dir*
EMP: 9 EST: 2015
SALES (est): 516.89K **Privately Held**
Web: www.wickedlocal.com
SIC: 2711 Newspapers, publishing and printing

Colrain
Franklin County

(G-8095)
COLRAIN SAND AND GRAVEL INC

465 Jacksonville Rd (01340-9603)
PHONE..............................413 624-5118
June Butler, *Prin*
EMP: 12 EST: 2013
SALES (est): 66.08K **Privately Held**
Web: www.colrain-ma.gov
SIC: 1442 Construction sand and gravel

(G-8096)
MORRELL METALSMITHS LTD
207 Greenfield Rd (01340-9637)
PHONE..............................413 624-1200
C Leigh Morrell, *Pr*
EMP: 7 EST: 2003
SALES (est): 399.32K **Privately Held**
Web: www.morrellmetalsmiths.com
SIC: 7692 Welding repair

Concord
Middlesex County

(G-8097)
ALPHAGRAPHICS
Also Called: AlphaGraphics
192 Sudbury Rd (01742-3420)
PHONE..............................508 380-8344
EMP: 7 EST: 2017
SALES (est): 236.07K **Privately Held**
Web: www.alphagraphics.com
SIC: 2752 Commercial printing, lithographic

(G-8098)
ANDOR TECHNOLOGY INC
300 Baker Ave Ste 150 (01742-2124)
PHONE..............................978 405-1116
Brian Dutko, *
EMP: 36 EST: 2019
SALES (est): 3.28MM **Privately Held**
Web: andor.oxinst.com
SIC: 3826 Analytical instruments

(G-8099)
ANDOR TECHNOLOGY LTD (DH)
300 Baker Ave Ste 150 (01742-2124)
PHONE..............................860 290-9211
Ain Barkshire, *CEO*
Gary Wilmont, *Pr*
EMP: 12 EST: 1998
SQ FT: 6,000
SALES (est): 11.62MM
SALES (corp-wide): 534.42MM **Privately Held**
Web: andor.oxinst.com
SIC: 3826 Analytical instruments
HQ: Andor Technology Limited
7 Millennium Way Springvale Business Park
Belfast BT12
289 023-7126

(G-8100)
APOGEE IMAGING SYSTEMS INC
300 Baker Ave Ste 150 (01742-2124)
EMP: 19 EST: 1996
SALES (est): 7.07MM
SALES (corp-wide): 534.42MM **Privately Held**
SIC: 3861 7371 Cameras and related equipment; Custom computer programming services
HQ: Andor Technology Limited
7 Millennium Way Springvale Business Park
Belfast BT12
289 023-7126

(G-8101)
APRIORI TECHNOLOGIES INC (PA)
300 Baker Ave Ste 370 (01742-2155)
PHONE..............................978 371-2006
Stephanie A Feraday, *CEO*
Stephanie A Feraday, *Pr*
Arnie Greenfield, *
Scott Carlyle, *
Julie Driscoll, *
EMP: 96 **EST:** 2003
SQ FT: 15,000
SALES (est): 29.34MM
SALES (corp-wide): 29.34MM **Privately Held**
Web: www.apriori.com
SIC: 7372 Prepackaged software

(G-8102)
ARTINIAN GARABET CORPORATION
39 Main St (01742-2560)
PHONE..............................978 371-7110
Garabet Artinian, *Pr*
EMP: 12 **EST:** 1976
SQ FT: 800
SALES (est): 760.46K **Privately Held**
Web: www.artinianjewelry.com
SIC: 3911 5094 5944 Jewelry, precious metal; Jewelry; Jewelry, precious stones and precious metals

(G-8103)
ATLANTIS TECHNOLOGY CORP
1620 Sudbury Rd Ste 1 (01742-5800)
PHONE..............................978 341-0999
Thomas Biggins, *CEO*
EMP: 7 **EST:** 2001
SALES (est): 1.12MM **Privately Held**
Web: www.atlantistech.com
SIC: 7372 Prepackaged software

(G-8104)
B S E INTERNATIONAL CORP
79 Macone Farm Ln (01742-5441)
PHONE..............................781 863-5270
Bryan S Subsick, *Prin*
EMP: 7 **EST:** 2010
SALES (est): 87.95K **Privately Held**
SIC: 3599 Machine shop, jobbing and repair

(G-8105)
BETA BIONICS INC
Also Called: Beta Bionics
300 Baker Ave Ste 301 (01742-2157)
PHONE..............................855 745-3800
Sean Saint, *CEO*
Edward Damiano, *
Edward Raskin, *VP*
Veena Rao, *CCO*
EMP: 42 **EST:** 2015
SALES (est): 4.97MM **Privately Held**
Web: www.betabionics.com
SIC: 3845 Electromedical apparatus

(G-8106)
BLUECATBIO MA INC
Also Called: Bluecatbio
58 Elsinore St (01742-2316)
PHONE..............................978 405-2533
Frank Feist, *Pr*
EMP: 7 **EST:** 2015
SALES (est): 482.2K **Privately Held**
Web: www.bluecatbio.com
SIC: 3821 5963 8711 Laboratory apparatus and furniture; Direct selling establishments; Engineering services

(G-8107)
CALLENSTITCH LLC
52 Domino Dr (01742-2817)
PHONE..............................978 369-9080
EMP: 11 **EST:** 1980
SQ FT: 10,000
SALES (est): 463.3K **Privately Held**
Web: www.callenstitch.com
SIC: 3999 2395 Embroidery kits; Pleating and stitching

(G-8108)
CONCORD TEACAKES ETCETERA INC (PA)
30 Domino Dr Ste 1 (01742-2802)
P.O. Box 1427 (01742-1427)
PHONE..............................978 369-2409
Peter Mahler, *Pr*
Judy Fersch, *
Peter Mahler, *VP*
EMP: 13 **EST:** 1984
SQ FT: 5,300
SALES (est): 2.47MM **Privately Held**
Web: www.concordteacakes.com
SIC: 2051 Bakery: wholesale or wholesale/retail combined

(G-8109)
CONCORD TEACAKES ETCETERA INC
59 Commonwealth Ave (01742-3003)
PHONE..............................978 369-7644
Gery Armsdy, *Mgr*
EMP: 14
Web: www.concordteacakes.com
SIC: 2052 5461 2051 Cookies; Retail bakeries; Cakes, pies, and pastries
PA: Concord Teacakes Etcetera, Inc.
30 Domino Dr Ste 1
Concord MA 01742

(G-8110)
CORPORATE CASUALS LLC
52 Domino Dr (01742-2817)
PHONE..............................978 369-5935
EMP: 18 **EST:** 1978
SQ FT: 10,000
SALES (est): 3.47MM **Privately Held**
Web: www.corporatecasuals.com
SIC: 5136 7389 2339 Sportswear, men's and boys'; Embroidery advertising; Women's and misses' outerwear, nec

(G-8111)
CYBERGRX INC
Also Called: Cyber Global Risk Exchange
33 Bradford St (01742-2986)
PHONE..............................877 929-2374
Frederick Kneip, *CEO*
Jonathan Simkins, *
Bryan Gale, *CPO*
Scott Schneider, *CRO*
Anthony Urbanovich, *
EMP: 170 **EST:** 2015
SALES (est): 46.29MM **Privately Held**
Web: www.cybergrx.com
SIC: 7372 Business oriented computer software

(G-8112)
DELL TECHNOLOGIES INC
777 Virginia Rd (01742-2762)
PHONE..............................781 259-2552
EMP: 35
Web: www.dell.com
SIC: 3571 Computers, digital, analog or hybrid
PA: Dell Technologies Inc.
1 Dell Way
Round Rock TX 78682

(G-8113)
DIVERT INC (PA)
23 Bradford St Ste 3 (01742-2971)
PHONE..............................978 341-5430
Nicholas Whitman, *Pr*
Ryan Begin, *CEO*
Richard Burnes, *Dir*
David Worthen, *Dir*
EMP: 25 **EST:** 2006
SALES (est): 19.98MM
SALES (corp-wide): 19.98MM **Privately Held**
Web: www.divertinc.com
SIC: 4953 2875 Recycling, waste materials; Compost

(G-8114)
DMR PRINT INC (PA)
Also Called: Ambit Creative Group
13 Dover St (01742-5712)
PHONE..............................617 876-3688
David M Reed, *Pr*
Peter Reed, *VP*
Pam Reed, *Sec*
EMP: 26 **EST:** 1992
SALES (est): 4.48MM **Privately Held**
SIC: 2752 2789 2791 Offset printing; Bookbinding and related work; Typesetting

(G-8115)
DONCAR INC
Also Called: Action Unlimited Newspaper
100 Domino Dr 1 (01742-2817)
PHONE..............................978 371-2442
Carol Margraf, *Pr*
EMP: 15 **EST:** 1970
SALES (est): 771.57K **Privately Held**
SIC: 2711 Newspapers: publishing only, not printed on site

(G-8116)
DYNASIL CORPORATION AMERICA (PA)
Also Called: Dynasil
200 Baker Ave Ste 301 (01742-2182)
PHONE..............................617 668-6855
Peter Sulick, *Ch Bd*
Holly A Hicks, *CFO*
▲ **EMP:** 20 **EST:** 1960
SQ FT: 2,868
SALES (est): 43.7MM
SALES (corp-wide): 43.7MM **Privately Held**
Web: www.dynasil.com
SIC: 8731 3827 Commercial physical research; Optical instruments and apparatus

(G-8117)
EVOPOINT BIOSCIENCES USA INC
300 Baker Ave Ste 300 (01742-2124)
PHONE..............................646 750-2661
Jing Qiang, *Dir*
EMP: 7 **EST:** 2018
SALES (est): 195.66K **Privately Held**
SIC: 2834 Pharmaceutical preparations

(G-8118)
GATEHOUSE MEDIA MASS I INC
Also Called: Billerica Minute-Man
150 Baker Ave Ste 101 (01742-2126)
P.O. Box 9191 (01742-9191)
PHONE..............................978 667-2156
Anne Marie Magerman, *Mgr*
EMP: 8
SQ FT: 2,147
SALES (corp-wide): 2.95B **Publicly Held**
Web: www.ghmne.com
SIC: 2711 Newspapers, publishing and printing
HQ: Gatehouse Media Massachusetts I, Inc.
48 Dunham Rd
Beverly MA 01915
585 598-0030

(G-8119)
HAYES PUMP INC (PA)
66 Old Powder Mill Rd I (01742-4696)
PHONE..............................978 369-8800
Eric W Zadravec, *Pr*
Robert L Simonds, *
J Craig Huff Iii, *VP Sls*
Scott Putman, *
Patrick Furnari, *
EMP: 50 **EST:** 1898
SQ FT: 17,000
SALES (est): 57.7MM
SALES (corp-wide): 57.7MM **Privately Held**
Web: www.hayespump.com
SIC: 5084 3561 Pumps and pumping equipment, nec; Pumps and pumping equipment

(G-8120)
HYDROGEN ENERGY CALIFORNIA LLC
30 Monument Sq Ste 235 (01742-1869)
PHONE..............................978 287-9529
James Croyle, *CEO*
Julie Millar, *
Mark Lerdal, *
EMP: 18 **EST:** 2007
SALES (est): 1.62MM
SALES (corp-wide): 2.26MM **Privately Held**
Web: www.homeupgradeplace.com
SIC: 2813 Hydrogen
PA: Scs Energy Llc
30 Monument Sq Ste 235
Concord MA 01742
978 287-0281

(G-8121)
INRIVER TANK & BOAT INC
152 Commonwealth Ave Ste 21 (01742-2990)
PHONE..............................978 287-9534
Julius Pereli, *Pr*
Kendreen Green, *VP*
▲ **EMP:** 8 **EST:** 2013
SALES (est): 990K **Privately Held**
Web: www.littlescullingboat.com
SIC: 3732 Boatbuilding and repairing

(G-8122)
LDR CARE INC
162 Park Ln (01742-1620)
PHONE..............................978 786-5110
Nisreen Bagasra, *Prin*
EMP: 8 **EST:** 2013
SALES (est): 96.37K **Privately Held**
SIC: 3841 Surgical and medical instruments

(G-8123)
LEXIA LEARNING SYSTEMS LLC
300 Baker Ave Ste 320 (01742-2131)
PHONE..............................800 435-3942
Robert Lemire, *Ch Bd*
Nick Kaider, *Pr*
Nancy Johnson, *OK Vice President*
EMP: 37 **EST:** 1984
SQ FT: 6,500
SALES (est): 9.93MM
SALES (corp-wide): 491MM **Privately Held**
Web: www.lexialearning.com

SIC: 7372 Educational computer software
HQ: Rosetta Stone Ltd.
　　135 W Market St
　　Harrisonburg VA 22801

(G-8124)
MANUFACTURERS SERVICES LIMITED
300 Baker Ave (01742-2131)
PHONE..............................617 330-7682
EMP: 47 **EST:** 1994
SQ FT: 16,765
SALES (est): 3.47MM
SALES (corp-wide): 422MM **Privately Held**
SIC: 3571 3577 3572 3661 Electronic computers; Computer peripheral equipment, nec; Computer storage devices; Telephone sets, all types except cellular radio
HQ: Celestica Inc
　　1900-5140 Yonge St
　　Toronto ON M2N 6
　　416 448-5800

(G-8125)
MINUTE-MAN PRINTING CORP
Also Called: Minuteman Press
20 Beharrell St Ste 1 (01742-2987)
P.O. Box 1026 (01742-1026)
PHONE..............................978 369-2808
Robert P Steinman, *Pr*
James D Steinman, *VP*
Maureen Steinman, *Sec*
F David Edes, *Clerk*
EMP: 10 **EST:** 1916
SQ FT: 20,000
SALES (est): 526.61K **Privately Held**
Web: www.mmp1907.com
SIC: 2752 2789 Offset printing; Bookbinding and related work

(G-8126)
MUNICIPAL MARKET ANALYTICS INC (PA)
75 Main St (01742-2503)
PHONE..............................617 968-5906
Thomas G Doe, *Pr*
Timothy R Holler, *COO*
Matt Fabian, *Pt*
Lisa Washburn, *CCO*
Nicholas Sourbis, *Business Development*
EMP: 7 **EST:** 2015
SQ FT: 400
SALES (est): 770.03K
SALES (corp-wide): 770.03K **Privately Held**
Web: www.mma-research.com
SIC: 2721 Trade journals: publishing only, not printed on site

(G-8127)
NATIONAL CON TNKS / FRGUARD JV
82 Tarbell Spring Rd (01742-4023)
PHONE..............................978 505-5533
Robert Barbarisi, *VP*
Thomas Macelhaney, *VP*
EMP: 10 **EST:** 2004
SALES (est): 651.23K **Privately Held**
SIC: 3272 Tanks, concrete

(G-8128)
NATIONAL GRAPE COOP ASSN INC
555 Virginia Rd (01742-2770)
PHONE..............................978 371-1000
Dianna Hammer, *Brnch Mgr*
EMP: 8

SALES (corp-wide): 498.48MM **Privately Held**
Web: www.welchs.com
SIC: 2033 Fruit juices: packaged in cans, jars, etc.
PA: National Grape Co-Operative Association, Inc.
　　71 E Main St
　　Westfield NY 14787
　　716 326-5200

(G-8129)
OMNIPROBE INC
300 Baker Ave Ste 150 (01742-2124)
EMP: 42 **EST:** 1999
SQ FT: 18,000
SALES (est): 2.18MM
SALES (corp-wide): 534.42MM **Privately Held**
SIC: 3826 Analytical instruments
PA: Oxford Instruments Plc
　　Magnetic Resonance
　　Abingdon OXON OX13
　　186 539-3200

(G-8130)
OXFORD INSTRS MSREMENT SYSTEMS
Also Called: Oxford Instruments America
300 Baker Ave Ste 150 (01742-2124)
PHONE..............................978 369-9933
Scott Reiman, *Pr*
Christopher S Fraser, *
James Pollock, *
EMP: 47 **EST:** 1997
SQ FT: 120,000
SALES (est): 4.07MM
SALES (corp-wide): 534.42MM **Privately Held**
Web: www.oxinst.com
SIC: 3829 Measuring and controlling devices, nec
PA: Oxford Instruments Plc
　　Magnetic Resonance
　　Abingdon OXON OX13
　　186 539-3200

(G-8131)
OXFORD INSTRUMENTS AMERICA INC (HQ)
Also Called: Oxford Instruments
300 Baker Ave Ste 150 (01742-2124)
P.O. Box 83136 (01813-3136)
PHONE..............................978 369-9933
Jonathan Flint, *CEO*
William Keating, *
Sarah Harvey, *
▲ **EMP:** 50 **EST:** 1982
SQ FT: 18,000
SALES (est): 48.05MM
SALES (corp-wide): 534.42MM **Privately Held**
Web: www.oxinst.com
SIC: 5049 3829 Scientific instruments; Measuring and controlling devices, nec
PA: Oxford Instruments Plc
　　Magnetic Resonance
　　Abingdon OXON OX13
　　186 539-3200

(G-8132)
REASONS TO BE CHEERFUL
110 Commonwealth Ave (01742-2904)
PHONE..............................978 610-6248
Wade Rubenstein, *Owner*
EMP: 9 **EST:** 2010
SALES (est): 107.23K **Privately Held**
Web: www.cheerful-reasons.com
SIC: 5812 2024 Ice cream stands or dairy bars; Ice cream, bulk

(G-8133)
SPACECLAIM CORPORATION
150 Baker Avenue Ext (01742-2126)
PHONE..............................978 482-2100
Chris Randles, *Pr*
Gregory Stott, *Operations**
Daniel Dean, *Senior Vice President Research & Development**
EMP: 61 **EST:** 2005
SALES (est): 14.77MM
SALES (corp-wide): 2.07B **Publicly Held**
Web: www.ansys.com
SIC: 7372 Prepackaged software
PA: Ansys, Inc.
　　2600 Ansys Dr
　　Canonsburg PA 15317
　　844 462-6797

(G-8134)
STARMET CORPORATION (PA)
2229 Main St (01742-3897)
PHONE..............................978 369-5410
Robert E Quinn, *Ch Bd*
William T Nachtrab, *Technology Vice President*
EMP: 22 **EST:** 1972
SQ FT: 180,000
SALES (est): 7.47MM
SALES (corp-wide): 7.47MM **Privately Held**
Web: www.nmisite.org
SIC: 3399 2819 3841 3483 Powder, metal; Nuclear fuel scrap, reprocessing; Surgical and medical instruments; Forgings, projectile: machined for ammunition over 30 mm.

(G-8135)
TECHNICAL COMMUNICATIONS CORP (PA)
Also Called: Tcc
100 Domino Dr (01742-2817)
PHONE..............................978 287-5100
Carl H Guild Junior, *Ch Bd*
EMP: 21 **EST:** 1960
SALES (est): 1.3MM
SALES (corp-wide): 1.3MM **Publicly Held**
Web: www.tccsecure.com
SIC: 3663 Encryption devices

(G-8136)
TOTH INC (PA)
Also Called: Toth Brand Imaging
86 Baker Avenue Ext Ste 230 (01742-2132)
PHONE..............................617 577-6400
Michael Toth, *Pr*
Susan C Toth, *
Jackie Sharry, *
Richard Hunter Cross Iii, *Sec*
EMP: 30 **EST:** 1985
SQ FT: 14,000
SALES (est): 6.41MM
SALES (corp-wide): 6.41MM **Privately Held**
SIC: 7311 2752 7336 Advertising consultant ; Commercial printing, lithographic; Graphic arts and related design

(G-8137)
TREMEAU PHARMACEUTICALS INC
53 Main St Ste 202 (01742-2531)
PHONE..............................617 485-0250
Bradford C Sippy, *Pr*
Mark Corrigan, *VP*
Ben Enerson, *Sec*
Travis Helm, *Dir*
EMP: 11 **EST:** 2007
SALES (est): 1.03MM **Privately Held**
Web: www.tremeau.com

SIC: 2834 Pharmaceutical preparations

(G-8138)
VIBRAM CORPORATION (HQ)
Also Called: Vibram USA Inc.
9 Damonmill Sq Fl 2 (01742-2858)
PHONE..............................978 318-0000
Michael Gionfriddo, *CEO*
Fabrizio Gamberini, *
Richard Riegel, *
▲ **EMP:** 45 **EST:** 1999
SALES (est): 74.17MM
SALES (corp-wide): 335.14MM **Privately Held**
Web: www.vibram.com
SIC: 3069 3131 5661 Soles, boot or shoe: rubber, composition, or fiber; Body parts, shoe outers; Shoe stores
PA: Vibram Spa
　　Via Cristoforo Colombo 5
　　Albizzate VA 21041
　　033 199-9700

(G-8139)
WELCH FOODS INC A COOPERATIVE
300 Baker Ave Ste 101 (01742-2131)
PHONE..............................978 371-3762
William Hewins, *Brnch Mgr*
EMP: 60
SALES (corp-wide): 498.48MM **Privately Held**
Web: www.welchs.com
SIC: 2033 Canned fruits and specialties
HQ: Welch Foods Inc., A Cooperative
　　575 Virginia Rd
　　Concord MA 01742
　　978 371-1000

(G-8140)
WELCH FOODS INC A COOPERATIVE (HQ)
Also Called: Welch's
575 Virginia Rd (01742-2761)
PHONE..............................978 371-1000
Trevor Bynum, *Pr*
Delisle Flynn, *VP*
Vivian Tseng, *VP*
Lisa Flynn, *Pers/VP*
◆ **EMP:** 275 **EST:** 1972
SQ FT: 60,000
SALES (est): 389.84MM
SALES (corp-wide): 498.48MM **Privately Held**
Web: www.welchs.com
SIC: 2033 2037 Fruit juices: packaged in cans, jars, etc.; Frozen fruits and vegetables
PA: National Grape Co-Operative Association, Inc.
　　71 E Main St
　　Westfield NY 14787
　　716 326-5200

(G-8141)
WILLIAMSON CORPORATION
70 Domino Dr (01742-2893)
PHONE..............................978 369-9607
William R Barron Senior, *Pr*
William Barron Junior, *VP*
EMP: 20 **EST:** 1954
SQ FT: 7,500
SALES (est): 4.89MM **Privately Held**
Web: www.williamsonir.com
SIC: 3826 3823 Analytical instruments; Thermometers, filled system: industrial process type

(G-8142)
WITEC INSTRUMENTS CORP
300 Baker Ave Ste 150 (01742-2124)
PHONE..............................865 690-5550
Joachim Koenen, *Pr*
Vlad Bobrek, *
EMP: 13 **EST:** 2002
SALES (est): 608.7K **Privately Held**
Web: raman.oxinst.com
SIC: 3826 5049 Microscopes, electron and proton; Analytical instruments

Conway
Franklin County

(G-8143)
OESCO INC
Also Called: Orchard Equipment & Supply Co
8 Ashfield Rd (01341-9786)
P.O. Box 540 (01341-0540)
PHONE..............................413 369-4335
Russell A French, *Pr*
▲ **EMP:** 24 **EST:** 1954
SQ FT: 20,000
SALES (est): 3.87MM **Privately Held**
Web: www.oescoinc.com
SIC: 3556 5999 5083 3523 Presses, food: cheese, beet, cider, and sugarcane; Farm machinery, nec; Farm and garden machinery; Farm machinery and equipment

(G-8144)
POPLAR HILL MACHINE INC
2077 Roaring Brook Rd (01341-9767)
PHONE..............................413 369-4252
Michael J Kurkulonis, *Pr*
EMP: 11 **EST:** 2004
SALES (est): 1.96MM **Privately Held**
Web: www.poplarhillmachine.com
SIC: 3599 Machine shop, jobbing and repair

(G-8145)
SANGER EQUIPMENT CORPORATION
Wilder Hill Road (01341)
P.O. Box 201 (01370-0201)
PHONE..............................413 625-8304
Peter R Sanger, *Pr*
▲ **EMP:** 14 **EST:** 1992
SALES (est): 648.32K **Privately Held**
Web: www.sanger.net
SIC: 1442 5084 Construction sand and gravel; Industrial machinery and equipment

Cotuit
Barnstable County

(G-8146)
LUJEAN PRINTING CO INC
4507 Falmouth Rd (02635-2652)
P.O. Box 571 (02655-0571)
PHONE..............................508 428-8700
Michael Lally, *Pr*
EMP: 27 **EST:** 1961
SQ FT: 7,500
SALES (est): 1.29MM **Privately Held**
Web: www.lujeanprintingcompany.com
SIC: 2752 2711 2759 Offset printing; Newspapers, publishing and printing; Commercial printing, nec

Cummington
Hampshire County

(G-8147)
OLD CREAMERY GROCERY STORE
445 Berkshire Trl (01026-9610)
PHONE..............................413 634-5560
Ammy Pulley, *Pt*
Alice Cozzolino, *Pt*
EMP: 8 **EST:** 1977
SALES (est): 733.08K **Privately Held**
Web: www.oldcreamery.coop
SIC: 2043 5921 5541 5411 Cereal breakfast foods; Liquor stores; Filling stations, gasoline; Convenience stores, independent

Dalton
Berkshire County

(G-8148)
BERKSHIRE BRIDGE & IRON CO INC
140 E Housatonic St (01226-1928)
P.O. Box 254 (01227-0254)
PHONE..............................413 684-3182
Dennis Fusini, *Pr*
Carlo Fusini, *Stockholder*
EMP: 21 **EST:** 1965
SQ FT: 20,000
SALES (est): 2.48MM **Privately Held**
Web: www.berkshirebridge.com
SIC: 3441 Fabricated structural metal

(G-8149)
COUNTY CONCRETE CORP (PA)
290 Hubbard Ave (01226)
P.O. Box 1306 (01202-1306)
PHONE..............................413 499-3359
Joseph Kroboth, *Pr*
EMP: 12 **EST:** 1973
SQ FT: 5,000
SALES (est): 2.63MM
SALES (corp-wide): 2.63MM **Privately Held**
Web: www.lisasflowershop.com
SIC: 3272 Concrete products, precast, nec

(G-8150)
CRANE & CO INC (HQ)
Also Called: Crane Currency
30 South St (01226-1797)
Rural Route 30 (01226)
PHONE..............................617 648-3799
Annemarie C Watson, *Pr*
Douglas Prince, *
◆ **EMP:** 269 **EST:** 1922
SQ FT: 700,000
SALES (est): 214.77MM
SALES (corp-wide): 3.37B **Publicly Held**
Web: www.cranecurrency.com
SIC: 2621 Bank note paper
PA: Crane Nxt, Co.
950 Winter St Fl 4
Waltham MA 02451
610 430-2510

(G-8151)
NEENAH TECHNICAL MATERIALS INC (DH)
Ashuelot Park Ii 448 Hubbard Ave (01226)
PHONE..............................678 518-3343
Dennis G Lockyer, *Pr*
James W Hackett Junior, *Sec*
Douglas S Prince, *Treas*
▲ **EMP:** 11 **EST:** 2011
SALES (est): 12.13MM **Publicly Held**
Web: www.cranenonwovens.com
SIC: 2621 5943 2752 Paper mills; Stationery stores; Commercial printing, lithographic
HQ: Neenah, Inc.
3460 Preston Ridge Rd # 6
Alpharetta GA 30005
678 566-6500

(G-8152)
PIERCE MACHINE CO INC (PA)
74 E Housatonic St (01226-1961)
P.O. Box 251 (01227-0251)
PHONE..............................413 684-0056
Mark Busch, *Pr*
J Robert Busch, *
EMP: 25 **EST:** 1920
SQ FT: 13,000
SALES (est): 2.25MM
SALES (corp-wide): 2.25MM **Privately Held**
Web: www.piercemachine.com
SIC: 3599 Machine shop, jobbing and repair

(G-8153)
SAFARILAND LLC
401 South St (01226-1758)
PHONE..............................413 684-3104
Dawn Milesi, *Prin*
EMP: 30
SALES (corp-wide): 457.84MM **Publicly Held**
Web: www.safariland.com
SIC: 3842 3199 Bulletproof vests; Holsters, leather
HQ: Safariland, Llc
13386 International Pkwy
Jacksonville FL 32218
904 741-5400

(G-8154)
SILVER BEAR DISTILLERY LLC
63 Flansburg Ave (01226-1410)
PHONE..............................413 242-4892
B O Peter Sternerup, *Prin*
EMP: 7 **EST:** 2015
SALES (est): 485.87K **Privately Held**
Web: www.silverbeardistillery.com
SIC: 2085 Distilled and blended liquors

(G-8155)
SINICON PLASTICS INC
455 Housatonic St (01226-1836)
P.O. Box 204 (01227-0204)
PHONE..............................413 684-5290
David K Allen, *Pr*
EMP: 29 **EST:** 1968
SQ FT: 35,000
SALES (est): 7.53MM **Privately Held**
Web: www.siniconplastics.com
SIC: 3089 Injection molding of plastics

(G-8156)
STUDLEY PRESS INC
151 E Housatonic St (01226-1929)
P.O. Box 214 (01227-0214)
PHONE..............................413 684-0441
Charles Gillett, *Pr*
Suzanne Salinetti, *
EMP: 10 **EST:** 1938
SQ FT: 20,000
SALES (est): 942.55K **Privately Held**
Web: thestudleypresscom.wordpress.com
SIC: 2752 Offset printing

Danvers
Essex County

(G-8157)
ABIOMED INC (HQ)
Also Called: Abiomed
22 Cherry Hill Dr (01923-2599)
PHONE..............................978 646-1400
Andrew J Greenfield, *Pr*
EMP: 405 **EST:** 1981
SALES (est): 1.03B
SALES (corp-wide): 94.94B **Publicly Held**
Web: www.abiomed.com
SIC: 3845 Electromedical apparatus
PA: Johnson & Johnson
1 Johnson And Johnson Plz
New Brunswick NJ 08933
732 524-0400

(G-8158)
ABIOMED CARDIOVASCULAR INC
22 Cherry Hill Dr (01923-2599)
PHONE..............................978 777-5410
EMP: 86 **EST:** 1982
SQ FT: 24,000
SALES (est): 6.86MM
SALES (corp-wide): 94.94B **Publicly Held**
Web: www.abiomed.com
SIC: 3845 Electromedical equipment
HQ: Abiomed, Inc.
22 Cherry Hill Dr
Danvers MA 01923
978 646-1400

(G-8159)
ABIOMED R&D INC (DH)
22 Cherry Hill Dr (01923-2599)
PHONE..............................978 646-1400
David M Lederman, *Pr*
John P Thero, *
EMP: 11 **EST:** 1993
SQ FT: 80,000
SALES (est): 4.03MM
SALES (corp-wide): 94.94B **Publicly Held**
Web: www.abiomed.com
SIC: 3841 Surgical instruments and apparatus
HQ: Abiomed, Inc.
22 Cherry Hill Dr
Danvers MA 01923
978 646-1400

(G-8160)
ACCUTECH MACHINE INC
370 Andover St (01923-1350)
PHONE..............................978 922-7271
EMP: 14 **EST:** 1996
SALES (est): 472.8K **Privately Held**
Web: www.expiredwixdomain.com
SIC: 3599 Machine shop, jobbing and repair

(G-8161)
ADVANCED ENGINEERING CORP
45 Prince St (01923-1437)
PHONE..............................978 777-7147
Richard F Varney Junior, *Pr*
EMP: 10 **EST:** 1990
SALES (est): 437.29K **Privately Held**
Web: www.advancedeng.com
SIC: 3599 Machine shop, jobbing and repair

(G-8162)
ANDY COLLAZZO
15 Mill St (01923-3367)
PHONE..............................978 539-8962
Andy Collazzo, *Prin*

EMP: 9 **EST:** 2012
SALES (est): 795.49K **Privately Held**
Web: www.ac-mfg.com
SIC: 3519 Jet propulsion engines

(G-8163)
AURORA HEALTHCARE US CORP
8 Electronics Ave Ste 1 (01923-1081)
PHONE..........................978 204-5240
Steven James, *CFO*
EMP: 10 **EST:** 2016
SQ FT: 8,000
SALES (est): 897.13K **Privately Held**
Web: www.auroramri.com
SIC: 3845 Magnetic resonance imaging device, nuclear

(G-8164)
AURORA IMAGING TECHNOLOGY INC (PA)
8 Electronics Ave Ste 1 (01923-1081)
PHONE..........................877 975-7530
Gordon M Olsen, *Ch Bd*
Steven J James, *
▼ **EMP:** 50 **EST:** 1999
SQ FT: 63,179
SALES (est): 9.62MM
SALES (corp-wide): 9.62MM **Privately Held**
Web: www.auroramri.com
SIC: 3841 Diagnostic apparatus, medical

(G-8165)
BABCOCK POWER CAPITAL CORP (HQ)
222 Rosewood Dr Fl 3 (01923-4502)
PHONE..........................978 646-3300
Michael D Leclair, *CEO*
Anthony A Brandano, *CFO*
William J Ferguson Junior, *VP*
Scott Leeman, *Treas*
Earl Mason, *VP*
EMP: 26 **EST:** 1977
SALES (est): 82.05MM
SALES (corp-wide): 509.03MM **Privately Held**
Web: www.babcockpower.com
SIC: 3443 Industrial vessels, tanks, and containers
PA: Babcock Power Inc.
222 Rosewood Dr
Danvers MA 01923
978 646-3300

(G-8166)
BABCOCK POWER INC (PA)
222 Rosewood Dr Fl 3 (01923-4520)
PHONE..........................978 646-3300
Michael D Leclair, *Pr*
Anthony Brandano, *Ex VP*
Nathan Hevrony, *Dir*
Dale Miller, *Dir*
William Sigmon, *Dir*
◆ **EMP:** 9 **EST:** 2002
SALES (est): 509.03MM
SALES (corp-wide): 509.03MM **Privately Held**
Web: www.babcockpower.com
SIC: 3443 3569 3433 Fuel tanks (oil, gas, etc.), metal plate; Generators: steam, liquid oxygen, or nitrogen; Burners, furnaces, boilers, and stokers

(G-8167)
BABCOCK POWER RENEWABLES LLC (HQ)
222 Rosewood Dr Fl 3 (01923-4502)
PHONE..........................978 646-3300

EMP: 39 **EST:** 2021
SALES (est): 10.13MM
SALES (corp-wide): 509.03MM **Privately Held**
SIC: 3443 3433 Fabricated plate work (boiler shop); Heating equipment, except electric
PA: Babcock Power Inc.
222 Rosewood Dr
Danvers MA 01923
978 646-3300

(G-8168)
BACKER HOTWATT INC
16a Electronics Ave (01923-1011)
PHONE..........................978 777-0070
Jamie Holley, *Pr*
EMP: 23 **EST:** 2018
SALES (est): 9MM
SALES (corp-wide): 3.82B **Privately Held**
Web: www.hotwatt.com
SIC: 3585 Heating equipment, complete
PA: Nibe Industrier Ab
Jarnvagsgatan 40
Markaryd 285 3
43373000

(G-8169)
BISCO ENVIRONMENTAL INC
55 Ferncroft Rd Ste 110 (01923-4001)
PHONE..........................508 738-5100
Rich Abrams, *Pr*
Thomas W Gorman, *Sec*
James T Donelan, *Treas*
EMP: 14 **EST:** 2001
SALES (est): 1.39MM **Privately Held**
Web: www.biscoenv.com
SIC: 3559 Ammunition and explosives, loading machinery

(G-8170)
BRADFORD & BIGELOW REALTY LLC
1 Industrial Dr (01923-1039)
PHONE..........................978 777-1200
EMP: 8 **EST:** 2018
SALES (est): 80.61K **Privately Held**
Web: www.bradford-bigelow.com
SIC: 2759 Commercial printing, nec

(G-8171)
BURNELL CONTROLS INC
Also Called: Honeywell Authorized Dealer
153 Andover St Ste 202 (01923-1477)
PHONE..........................978 646-9992
EMP: 33 **EST:** 1994
SQ FT: 3,500
SALES (est): 4.39MM **Privately Held**
Web: www.burnellcontrols.com
SIC: 3822 Temperature controls, automatic

(G-8172)
BURR INDUSTRIES INC
495 Newbury St (01923-1078)
P.O. Box 1771 (02345-1771)
PHONE..........................978 774-2527
Paul Cavanagh, *Pr*
EMP: 8 **EST:** 1964
SQ FT: 7,200
SALES (est): 730.33K **Privately Held**
Web: www.burrindustriesllc.com
SIC: 3599 Machine shop, jobbing and repair

(G-8173)
COMPUMACHINE INC
Also Called: Compumachine
6 Electronics Ave (01923-1008)
PHONE..........................978 777-8440
David H Shaby, *Pr*
Glen M Hartzler, *Sec*

▲ **EMP:** 16 **EST:** 1980
SQ FT: 15,000
SALES (est): 9.59MM **Privately Held**
Web: www.compumachine.com
SIC: 5084 3542 3541 Machine tools and accessories; Machine tools, metal forming type; Machine tools, metal cutting type

(G-8174)
COTTER BROTHERS CORPORATION
8 Southside Rd (01923-1409)
PHONE..........................978 777-5001
Randy Cotter, *Prin*
Timothy Cotter, *
Frank Armstrong, *
Bartholomew P Molloy, *
▼ **EMP:** 43 **EST:** 2003
SQ FT: 25,000
SALES (est): 8.13MM **Privately Held**
Web: www.cotterbrothers.com
SIC: 3559 Pharmaceutical machinery

(G-8175)
COTTER CORPORATION
8 Southside Rd (01923-1409)
PHONE..........................978 774-6777
Louis J Giuliano, *CEO*
EMP: 45 **EST:** 1979
SQ FT: 25,000
SALES (est): 8.32MM
SALES (corp-wide): 2.99B **Publicly Held**
Web: www.cotterbrothers.com
SIC: 3443 Fabricated plate work (boiler shop)
HQ: Itt Llc
1133 Westchester Ave N-100
White Plains NY 10604
914 641-2000

(G-8176)
CUNNINGHAM ENGINEERING INC
9 Electronics Ave (01923-1008)
PHONE..........................978 774-4169
Thomas Cunningham, *Pr*
Katherine Cunningham, *Treas*
EMP: 36 **EST:** 1975
SQ FT: 10,000
SALES (est): 933.06K **Privately Held**
SIC: 3599 Machine shop, jobbing and repair

(G-8177)
D V DIE CUTTING INC
45 Prince St (01923-1474)
PHONE..........................978 777-0300
Richard F Varney, *Pr*
EMP: 28 **EST:** 1964
SQ FT: 14,000
SALES (est): 4.23MM **Privately Held**
Web: www.dvdie.com
SIC: 3053 3544 Gaskets, all materials; Dies and die holders for metal cutting, forming, die casting

(G-8178)
DANVERS HERALD
152 Sylvan St (01923-3558)
PHONE..........................978 774-0505
Cathryn O'hare, *Publisher*
EMP: 7 **EST:** 2011
SALES (est): 122.27K **Privately Held**
Web: www.wickedlocal.com
SIC: 2711 Newspapers, publishing and printing

(G-8179)
DEMAKES ENTERPRISES INC
18 Electronics Ave (01923-1011)

PHONE..........................978 739-1506
EMP: 65
SALES (corp-wide): 47.83MM **Privately Held**
Web: www.oldneighborhoodfoods.com
SIC: 2013 Sausages and other prepared meats
PA: Demakes Enterprises, Inc.
37 Waterhill St
Lynn MA 01905
781 417-1100

(G-8180)
DERMAL PHOTONICS CORPORATION
Also Called: Nira Skin
153 Andover St Ste 111 (01923-1477)
PHONE..........................781 451-1717
David Bean, *CEO*
EMP: 11 **EST:** 2012
SALES (est): 1.42MM **Privately Held**
Web: www.niraskin.com
SIC: 3845 Laser systems and equipment, medical

(G-8181)
DIGITAL ON DEMAND LLC
44 Garden St Ste 3 (01923-1451)
PHONE..........................978 224-7900
Benjamin Adner, *Mgr*
EMP: 8 **EST:** 2020
SALES (est): 339.84K **Privately Held**
Web: www.digitalondemand.com
SIC: 2752 Offset printing

(G-8182)
DILUIGIS INC
41 Popes Ln (01923-1410)
PHONE..........................978 750-9900
Louis J Diluigi Junior, *Pr*
Louis J Diluigi Junior, *Pr*
Kathleen Diluigi, *
Robert Capezzuto, *
Christoper Capezzuto, *
EMP: 100 **EST:** 1988
SQ FT: 18,000
SALES (est): 23.91MM **Privately Held**
Web: www.diluigifoods.com
SIC: 2013 Sausages and related products, from purchased meat

(G-8183)
DIXIE MEDIA LLC
Also Called: Xtelligent Healthcare Media
199 Rosewood Dr Ste 230 (01923-1388)
PHONE..........................508 739-1999
Sean Brooks, *Mgr*
Jason Krantz, *Mgr*
EMP: 25 **EST:** 2012
SALES (est): 4.59MM
SALES (corp-wide): 297.49MM **Publicly Held**
Web: www.xtelligentmedia.com
SIC: 7313 2721 8742 Electronic media advertising representatives; Magazines: publishing only, not printed on site; Marketing consulting services
PA: Techtarget, Inc.
275 Grove St Ste 1150
Auburndale MA 02466
617 431-9200

(G-8184)
EDGIL ASSOCIATES INC
222 Rosewood Dr Unit 210 (01923-4534)
PHONE..........................978 262-9799
Leslie Bernhard, *Prin*
EMP: 11 **EST:** 1984
SALES (est): 253.99K **Privately Held**
Web: www.payway.com

SIC: 7372   Prepackaged software

(G-8185)
EMD MILLIPORE CORPORATION
17 Cherry Hill Dr (01923-2565)
PHONE..................978 762-5100
James Groves, *Brnch Mgr*
EMP: 30
SALES (corp-wide): 23.09B **Privately Held**
Web: www.millipore.com
SIC: 3826   Analytical instruments
HQ: Emd Millipore Corporation
    400 Summit Dr
    Burlington MA 01803
    800 645-5476

(G-8186)
FIRE DEFENSES NEW
ENGLAND LLC
Also Called: Allstate Fire Equipment
44 Garden St Ste 1 (01923-1451)
P.O. Box 1025 (01940-3025)
PHONE..................978 304-1506
EMP: 16
SQ FT: 7,500
SALES (est): 992.41K **Privately Held**
SIC: 3999 7389   Fire extinguishers, portable;
    Fire extinguisher servicing

(G-8187)
FRIEND BOX COMPANY INC
90 High St (01923-3196)
P.O. Box 275 (01923-0475)
PHONE..................978 774-0240
Charles J Fox, *Pr*
EMP: 55 EST: 1884
SQ FT: 40,100
SALES (est): 4.9MM **Privately Held**
Web: www.friendbox.com
SIC: 2653 2652   Boxes, corrugated: made
    from purchased materials; Setup
    paperboard boxes

(G-8188)
G&F PRECISION MOLDING INC
33 Cherry Hill Dr (01923-2579)
PHONE..................978 560-2622
John G Argitis, *Pr*
EMP: 7
SALES (corp-wide): 17.07MM **Privately**
Held
Web: www.gandfprecision.com
SIC: 3089 3544   Injection molding of plastics
    ; Special dies and tools
PA: G&F Precision Molding, Inc.
    709 Main St
    Fiskdale MA 01518
    508 347-9132

(G-8189)
HANNAH ENGINEERING INC
36 Longbow Rd (01923-2099)
P.O. Box 2033 (01923-5033)
PHONE..................978 777-5892
Richard Barker, *Pr*
Richard Barker Junior, *Pr*
EMP: 24 EST: 1972
SALES (est): 887.72K **Privately Held**
SIC: 3599   Machine shop, jobbing and repair

(G-8190)
HILLSIDE ENGINEERING INC
10r Rainbow Ter Ste A (01923-3779)
PHONE..................978 762-6640
Charles Cummings, *Pr*
▼ EMP: 9 EST: 2009
SALES (est): 899.14K **Privately Held**
Web: www.hillsideeng.com

SIC: 3599   Machine shop, jobbing and repair

(G-8191)
HOLDETTE
165 Hobart St (01923-1852)
PHONE..................301 412-3660
Sarah Greisdorf, *CEO*
EMP: 8 EST: 2020
SALES (est): 50K **Privately Held**
Web: www.holdette.com
SIC: 2337   Women's and misses' suits and
    coats

(G-8192)
HONEYWELL DMC SERVICES
LLC
Also Called: Honeywell
199 Rosewood Dr (01923-1398)
PHONE..................978 774-3007
▲ EMP: 410
SIC: 8748 7363 7372   Energy conservation
    consultant; Office help supply service;
    Application computer software

(G-8193)
ILLINOIS TOOL WORKS INC
30 Endicott St (01923-3712)
PHONE..................978 777-1100
Chris Stevens, *VP*
EMP: 145
SALES (corp-wide): 15.93B **Publicly Held**
Web: www.itw.com
SIC: 2891   Adhesives and sealants
PA: Illinois Tool Works Inc.
    155 Harlem Ave
    Glenview IL 60025
    847 724-7500

(G-8194)
ITK CHEMICALS INC
10 Electronics Ave (01923-1011)
PHONE..................978 531-2279
Itamar Tom Kutai, *Pr*
Jeffrey J Krugman, *Treas*
EMP: 12 EST: 1989
SALES (est): 846.44K **Privately Held**
Web: www.solventkleene.com
SIC: 2911 2865   Solvents; Chemical
    indicators

(G-8195)
ITW DEVCON INC
30 Endicott St (01923-3712)
PHONE..................978 777-1100
Chow Yee Chu, *Contrlr*
▲ EMP: 17 EST: 2009
SALES (est): 4.62MM **Privately Held**
Web: www.itwperformancepolymers.com
SIC: 2891   Adhesives

(G-8196)
ITW PERFORMANCE POLYMERS
✪
30 Endicott St (01923-3712)
PHONE..................978 777-1100
EMP: 80 EST: 2023
SALES (est): 3.97MM **Privately Held**
SIC: 2891   Adhesives and sealants

(G-8197)
LABEL HAUS INC
3 Southside Rd Ste B (01923-1695)
PHONE..................978 777-1773
John Mcnally, *Pr*
EMP: 9 EST: 1998
SQ FT: 9,000
SALES (est): 872K **Privately Held**
Web: www.labelhausinc.com

SIC: 2759   Labels and seals: printing, nsk

(G-8198)
LEE ELECTRIC INC
128 Maple St (01923-2061)
PHONE..................978 777-0070
Robert S Lee, *Ch Bd*
William E Lee, *Pr*
Samuel Sayward, *Ex VP*
Robert F Cummings, *Treas*
▼ EMP: 120 EST: 1952
SQ FT: 70,000
SALES (est): 14.48MM **Privately Held**
SIC: 3822   Electric heat proportioning
    controls, modulating controls

(G-8199)
LEICA BIOSYSTEMS
38 Cherry Hill Dr (01923-2575)
PHONE..................978 471-0625
Richard Sidlowski, *Acctg Mgr*
EMP: 58 EST: 2015
SALES (est): 400.71K **Privately Held**
Web: www.leicabiosystems.com
SIC: 3826   Analytical instruments

(G-8200)
M & H ENGINEERING CO INC
183 Newbury St (01923-1090)
PHONE..................978 777-1222
Richard Haley, *Pr*
Michael A Martens, *
Timothy H Martens, *
Andrew J Martens, *
EMP: 40 EST: 1966
SQ FT: 20,000
SALES (est): 5.41MM **Privately Held**
Web: www.mheng.com
SIC: 3599 3544   Machine shop, jobbing and
    repair; Special dies, tools, jigs, and fixtures

(G-8201)
M & M LABEL CO INC
5 Electronics Ave (01923-1008)
PHONE..................781 321-2737
Michael Mccourt, *Pr*
▼ EMP: 9 EST: 1989
SALES (est): 1.72MM **Privately Held**
Web: www.mandmlabel.com
SIC: 2759   Labels and seals: printing, nsk

(G-8202)
M & M SCALE COMPANY INC
Also Called: M&M Label Company
5 Electronics Ave (01923-1008)
PHONE..................781 321-2737
Michael J Mc, *Court*
EMP: 15 EST: 1986
SALES (est): 212.06K **Privately Held**
SIC: 3596 7699   Scales and balances,
    except laboratory; Scale repair service

(G-8203)
MAXAM TIRE NORTH AMERICA
INC (HQ)
300 Rosewood Dr Ste 102 (01923-1389)
PHONE..................844 629-2662
Troy Kline, *CEO*
Radek Costa Sarnicki, *Sec*
Ian Thomas, *Dir*
▲ EMP: 12 EST: 2014
SALES (est): 25.28MM **Privately Held**
Web: www.maxamtirena.com
SIC: 3011   Agricultural tires, pneumatic
PA: Sailun Group Co., Ltd.
    No. 588, Maoshan Road, Huangdao
    District
    Qingdao SD 26602

(G-8204)
MCNEILLY EMS EDUCATORS
INC
125 Liberty St (01923-3325)
P.O. Box 7 (01944-0007)
PHONE..................978 278-3008
James T Mcneilly, *CEO*
EMP: 21 EST: 2010
SALES (est): 1.22MM **Privately Held**
Web: www.mcneillyems.com
SIC: 3999   Education aids, devices and
    supplies

(G-8205)
MEDDATA GROUP LLC
300 Rosewood Dr Ste 250 (01923-4509)
PHONE..................978 887-0039
Melissa Chang, *Prin*
EMP: 18 EST: 2012
SALES (est): 4.27MM **Publicly Held**
Web: www.meddatagroup.com
SIC: 7372   Prepackaged software
PA: Iqvia Holdings Inc.
    2400 Ellis Rd
    Durham NC 27703

(G-8206)
MEDTRNIC INTRVNTNAL
VSCLAR INC
Also Called: Medtronic
37a Cherry Hill Dr (01923-2565)
PHONE..................978 777-0042
Sean Salmon, *Pr*
Philip Albert, *
Bradley Lerman, *
Linda Harty, *
Douglas Hoekstra, *
▲ EMP: 750 EST: 1982
SQ FT: 40,000
SALES (est): 173.73MM **Privately Held**
Web: www.medtronic.com
SIC: 3841   Catheters
HQ: Medtronic, Inc.
    710 Medtronic Pkwy
    Minneapolis MN 55432
    763 514-4000

(G-8207)
MEDTRONIC INC
Also Called: Medtronic
37 Cherry Hill Dr (01923-2565)
PHONE..................978 777-0042
EMP: 17
Web: www.medtronic.com
SIC: 3845 3842 3841   Electromedical
    equipment; Implants, surgical; Blood
    transfusion equipment
HQ: Medtronic, Inc.
    710 Medtronic Pkwy
    Minneapolis MN 55432
    763 514-4000

(G-8208)
MEDTRONIC INC
Also Called: Medtronic
35 Cherry Hill Dr (01923-4393)
PHONE..................978 739-3080
Thomas Nowak, *Mgr*
EMP: 23
Web: www.medtronic.com
SIC: 3845 3842 3841   Electromedical
    equipment; Implants, surgical; Blood
    transfusion equipment
HQ: Medtronic, Inc.
    710 Medtronic Pkwy
    Minneapolis MN 55432
    763 514-4000

(G-8209)
MERCK GROUP
17 Cherry Hill Dr (01923-2565)
PHONE...............................978 762-5280
EMP: 78 EST: 2018
SALES (est): 237.06K **Privately Held**
Web: www.merck.com
SIC: 2834 Pharmaceutical preparations

(G-8210)
MOTION INDUSTRIES INC
Also Called: Axis New England
6 Cherry Hill Dr (01923-2575)
PHONE...............................978 774-7100
EMP: 23
SALES (corp-wide): 22.1B **Publicly Held**
Web: www.axisne.com
SIC: 5085 3625 3823 3671 Bearings; Motor
controls and accessories; Viscosimeters,
industrial process type; Light sensing and
emitting tubes
HQ: Motion Industries, Inc.
1605 Alton Rd
Birmingham AL 35210
205 956-1122

(G-8211)
NEUROLOGICA CORP
14 Electronics Ave (01923-1011)
PHONE...............................978 564-8500
David Webster, COO
Yongkwan Kim, OF*
Hanjo Kim, *
Kwang-bo Choi, Treas
▲ EMP: 90 EST: 2004
SQ FT: 80,000
SALES (est): 33.32MM **Privately Held**
Web: www.neurologica.com
SIC: 3841 Surgical and medical instruments
HQ: Samsung Electronics America, Inc.
85 Challenger Rd
Ridgefield Park NJ 07660
201 229-4000

(G-8212)
NEUTRON THERAPEUTICS LLC
1 Industrial Dr Ste 1 (01923-1039)
PHONE...............................978 777-0846
Noah Smick, CEO
Elizabeth Reczek, CEO
Theodore Smick, CEO
EMP: 23 EST: 2016
SQ FT: 33,000
SALES (est): 3.3MM **Privately Held**
Web: www.neutrontherapeutics.com
SIC: 3845 Ultrasonic scanning devices,
medical

(G-8213)
**NORTH ATLANTIC PCF
SEAFOOD LLC**
Also Called: Naps
8 Treetops Ln (01923-1137)
P.O. Box 2201 (02818-0625)
PHONE...............................401 969-3886
◆ EMP: 10 EST: 2009
SALES (est): 2.53MM **Privately Held**
Web: www.nafisheries.com
SIC: 5199 2092 7389 Bait, fishing; Fresh or
frozen packaged fish; Fish broker

(G-8214)
ORBIT PLASTICS CORP
45 Prince St (01923-1437)
PHONE...............................978 465-5300
Thomas Feid, Pr
Frederick Jackson, Treas
EMP: 22 EST: 1971
SALES (est): 2.29MM **Privately Held**
Web: www.orbitplastics.com

SIC: 3089 Injection molding of plastics

(G-8215)
QUICK MANUFACTURING CO
4 Electronics Ave (01923-1043)
PHONE...............................978 750-4202
Thomas Manolakos, Pr
John Manolakos, VP
EMP: 8 EST: 1993
SQ FT: 6,000
SALES (est): 1.01MM **Privately Held**
Web: www.quickmanufacturing.com
SIC: 3599 Machine shop, jobbing and repair

(G-8216)
**R WALTERS FOODS LTD LBLTY
CO (PA)**
Also Called: Meninno Brothers Gourmet
Foods
144 Pine St (01923-2630)
PHONE...............................978 646-8950
Rick Walters, Managing Member
Richard R Walters, Prin
EMP: 29 EST: 2004
SQ FT: 13,000
SALES (est): 8.35MM
SALES (corp-wide): 8.35MM **Privately
Held**
Web: www.elevation-foods.com
SIC: 2099 Food preparations, nec

(G-8217)
REGIONAL INDUSTRIES INC
301 Newbury St # 332 (01923-1092)
PHONE...............................978 750-8787
Robert Pratt, Pr
Robert K Pratt, *
Monica H Pratt, *
EMP: 9 EST: 1992
SQ FT: 100,000
SALES (est): 753.73K **Privately Held**
Web: www.regionalindustries.com
SIC: 3599 Custom machinery

(G-8218)
**REIFENHAUSER
INCORPORATED**
27 Garden St Ste B (01923-1686)
PHONE...............................847 669-9972
Richard Buddy Dexter Ii, Genl Mgr
John Wise, Merch Mgr
▲ EMP: 9 EST: 1976
SQ FT: 19,132
SALES (est): 2.34MM
SALES (corp-wide): 761.46MM **Privately
Held**
Web: www.reifenhauser.com
SIC: 3559 Plastics working machinery
HQ: Reifenhauser Gmbh & Co. Kg
Maschinenfabrik
Spicher Str. 46
Troisdorf NW 53844
224 123-5100

(G-8219)
SEMINEX CORPORATION
153 Andover St Ste 201 (01923-1477)
PHONE...............................978 326-7700
David Bean, CEO
EMP: 13 EST: 2003
SQ FT: 2,000
SALES (est): 1.29MM **Privately Held**
Web: www.seminex.com
SIC: 3674 Semiconductors and related
devices

(G-8220)
**SMC CORPORATION OF
AMERICA**

99 Rosewood Dr Ste 180 (01923-4537)
PHONE...............................978 767-2328
EMP: 17
Web: www.smcusa.com
SIC: 3625 Relays and industrial controls
HQ: Smc Corporation Of America
10100 Smc Blvd
Noblesville IN 46060
317 899-4440

(G-8221)
SPOTLIGHT LLC
6 Southside Rd (01923-1409)
PHONE...............................978 762-8352
Stacey Cruwys, Prin
EMP: 11 EST: 2010
SALES (est): 126.27K **Privately Held**
Web: www.ne-arc.org
SIC: 3648 Lighting equipment, nec

(G-8222)
STEVEN TEDESCO
Also Called: North Shore Marble & Granite
100 Newbury St Ste A (01923-1042)
P.O. Box 1347 (01940-5347)
PHONE...............................978 777-4070
▲ EMP: 8 EST: 1996
SQ FT: 10,000
SALES (est): 624.36K **Privately Held**
Web: www.nsmarbleandgranite.com
SIC: 3281 Marble, building: cut and shaped

(G-8223)
T D F METAL FINISHING CO INC
9 Electronics Ave (01923-1008)
P.O. Box 8026 (01904-0026)
PHONE...............................978 223-4292
Thomas D Ferrairo, Pr
EMP: 30 EST: 1980
SQ FT: 5,800
SALES (est): 2.27MM **Privately Held**
Web: www.tdfmetalfinishing.com
SIC: 3471 Electroplating of metals or
formed products

(G-8224)
TDF METAL FINISHING CO INC
6 Electronics Ave (01923-1008)
PHONE...............................978 223-4292
Thomas D Ferrairo, Pr
EMP: 13 EST: 2006
SALES (est): 991.06K **Privately Held**
Web: www.tdfmetalfinishing.com
SIC: 3471 Electroplating of metals or
formed products

(G-8225)
**TODD CLARK AND
ASSOCIATES INC**
Also Called: Axis New England
6 Cherry Hill Dr (01923-2575)
PHONE...............................978 774-7100
EMP: 23
SIC: 8711 3625 3823 3671 Consulting
engineer; Motor controls and accessories;
Viscosimeters, industrial process type;
Light sensing and emitting tubes

(G-8226)
TRANS FORM PLASTICS CORP
45 Prince St (01923-1437)
PHONE...............................978 777-1440
P P Varney, Pr
Tom Holloran, *
Richard F Varney Senior Stlk H ldr, Prin
EMP: 25 EST: 1976
SQ FT: 14,000
SALES (est): 4.98MM **Privately Held**
Web: www.transformplastics.com

SIC: 3089 Injection molding of plastics

(G-8227)
TRANSENE COMPANY INC (PA)
10 Electronics Ave (01923-1011)
PHONE...............................978 777-7860
Christopher Christuk, Pr
Martin E Hecht, Pr
▲ EMP: 7 EST: 1962
SQ FT: 16,000
SALES (est): 9.07MM
SALES (corp-wide): 9.07MM **Privately
Held**
Web: www.transene.com
SIC: 2819 3674 3644 2899 Industrial
inorganic chemicals, nec; Semiconductors
and related devices; Noncurrent-carrying
wiring devices; Chemical preparations, nec

(G-8228)
U S MADE CO INC
76 Newbury St (01923-1034)
PHONE...............................978 777-8383
Anthony Bernardo, Pr
Maria Bernardo, *
▲ EMP: 14 EST: 1985
SQ FT: 10,000
SALES (est): 429K **Privately Held**
SIC: 2386 Garments, leather

(G-8229)
WINNING MOVES INC
Also Called: Winning Moves Games
75 Sylvan St Ste C104 (01923-5609)
PHONE...............................978 777-7464
▲ EMP: 16 EST: 1994
SQ FT: 8,000
SALES (est): 2.49MM **Privately Held**
Web: www.winning-moves.com
SIC: 3944 Board games, puzzles, and
models, except electronic

Dartmouth
Bristol County

(G-8230)
**HERITAGE WHARF COMPANY
LLC**
218 Elm St (02748-3420)
PHONE...............................508 990-1011
David J Nolan Junior, Prin
EMP: 8 EST: 2010
SALES (est): 249.02K **Privately Held**
Web: www.southwharf.com
SIC: 3732 Yachts, building and repairing

(G-8231)
**SENSING SYSTEMS
CORPORATION**
7 Commerce Way (02747-1588)
P.O. Box 50180 (02745-0006)
PHONE...............................508 992-0872
Ricardo Bermudez, Pr
EMP: 10 EST: 1990
SQ FT: 9,500
SALES (est): 1.32MM **Privately Held**
Web: www.sensing-systems.com
SIC: 3586 1389 Measuring and dispensing
pumps; Measurement of well flow rates, oil
and gas

(G-8232)
**TROPICAL SMOOTHIE OF
BRISTOL**
14 Eliza Ln (02747-2395)
PHONE...............................508 636-1424
Gilbert M Desousa, Pr

Ana Desousa, *Sec*
EMP: 8 **EST:** 2007
SALES (est): 474.93K **Privately Held**
SIC: 2621 Bristols

(G-8233)
XIPHOS PARTNERS INC
419 Elm St (02748-2244)
PHONE................................508 991-1014
Matthew Sedgwick, *CEO*
EMP: 8 **EST:** 2018
SALES (est): 553.64K **Privately Held**
SIC: 8742 7371 3812 Management
consulting services; Software programming
applications; Defense systems and
equipment

(G-8234)
YANKEE BUILDERS
Also Called: Yankee Builders & Woodworking
1227 Russells Mills Rd (02748-1029)
PHONE................................508 636-8660
Michael Woyciechouski, *Owner*
EMP: 7 **EST:** 1974
SALES (est): 672.22K **Privately Held**
SIC: 1521 2541 New construction, single-
family houses; Cabinets, except
refrigerated: show, display, etc.: wood

Dedham
Norfolk County

(G-8235)
ALIMED INC
297 High St (02026-2898)
P.O. Box 9135 (02027-9135)
PHONE................................781 329-2900
▲ **EMP:** 230 **EST:** 1971
SALES (est): 41.76MM **Privately Held**
Web: www.alimed.com
SIC: 5047 3069 Medical equipment and
supplies; Bags, rubber or rubberized fabric

(G-8236)
ATLANTIC PWR US GP HLDINGS
INC
3 Allied Dr Ste 155 (02026-6101)
PHONE................................617 977-2400
EMP: 8 **EST:** 2014
SALES (est): 233K **Privately Held**
Web: www.atlanticpower.com
SIC: 4911 3621 Generation, electric power;
Power generators

(G-8237)
CANADIAN HILLS WIND LLC
3 Allied Dr Ste 155 (02026-6101)
PHONE................................617 977-2400
EMP: 7 **EST:** 2012
SALES (est): 141.16K **Privately Held**
SIC: 2911 Oils, fuel

(G-8238)
CLARICODE INC
980 Washington St Ste 330 (02026-6797)
PHONE................................781 449-2450
Andrew Needleman, *CEO*
EMP: 21 **EST:** 2003
SALES (est): 2.57MM **Privately Held**
Web: www.claricode.com
SIC: 7371 7372 Computer software
development; Business oriented computer
software

(G-8239)
CLARK HAMMERBEAM
CORPORATION

886 Washington St (02026-6010)
P.O. Box 381 (02027-0381)
PHONE................................781 461-1946
Jim Bardolph, *Pr*
Maria Reichenhall, *Treas*
EMP: 10 **EST:** 1998
SALES (est): 368.76K **Privately Held**
Web: www.fiberwebflashing.com
SIC: 2295 Waterproofing fabrics, except
rubberizing

(G-8240)
CRANE MDSG SYSTEMS INC
Also Called: Streamware
990 Washington St Ste 205 (02026-6717)
PHONE................................781 501-5800
EMP: 9
SALES (corp-wide): 3.37B **Publicly Held**
Web: www.cranepi.com
SIC: 3589 Coffee brewing equipment
HQ: Crane Merchandising Systems. Inc.
2043 Wdlnd Pkwy Ste 102
Saint Louis MO 63146
314 298-3500

(G-8241)
DEDHAM RECYCLED GRAVEL
CO INC
Also Called: Fed
1039 East St (02026-6363)
PHONE................................781 329-1044
Joseph Federico Junior, *Pr*
Al Morteo, *VP*
EMP: 10 **EST:** 2004
SQ FT: 6,600
SALES (est): 2.45MM **Privately Held**
Web: www.recycledgravel.com
SIC: 1442 Gravel mining

(G-8242)
DIVERSIFIED BIOTECH INC
65 Commerce Way (02026-2953)
PHONE................................781 326-6709
Mark L Fins, *Pr*
▲ **EMP:** 10 **EST:** 1984
SQ FT: 10,000
SALES (est): 1.83MM **Privately Held**
Web: www.divbio.com
SIC: 2836 Biological products, except
diagnostic

(G-8243)
FABLEVISION LEARNING LLC
368 Washington St Ste 207 (02026-1868)
P.O. Box 1242 (02027-1242)
PHONE................................781 320-3225
Peter Reynolds, *Managing Member*
EMP: 11 **EST:** 2007
SQ FT: 1,500
SALES (est): 652.26K **Privately Held**
Web: www.fablevisionlearning.com
SIC: 7372 Educational computer software

(G-8244)
GENERAL DYNAMICS MISSION
150 Rustcraft Rd (02026-4534)
PHONE................................781 410-9635
Christopher Marzilli, *Pr*
EMP: 340
SALES (corp-wide): 42.27B **Publicly Held**
Web: www.gdmissionsystems.com
SIC: 3571 Electronic computers
HQ: General Dynamics Mission Systems,
Inc.
12450 Fair Lakes Cir
Fairfax VA 22033
877 449-0600

(G-8245)
IMD SOFT INC (DH)
980-990 Washington St Ste 115 (02026)
PHONE................................781 449-5567
Shahar Sery, *COO*
EMP: 23 **EST:** 1996
SALES (est): 22.34MM
SALES (corp-wide): 6.62B **Privately Held**
Web: www.imd-soft.com
SIC: 7372 Prepackaged software
HQ: N. Harris Computer Corporation
1 Antares Dr Suite 100
Ottawa ON K2E 8
888 847-7747

(G-8246)
MARTIN BENJAMIN
CORPORATION
115 Commerce Way (02026-2994)
P.O. Box 1313 (02027-1313)
PHONE................................781 326-8311
Benjamin Seltzer, *Pr*
Martin Seltzer, *Treas*
▲ **EMP:** 24 **EST:** 1977
SQ FT: 10,000
SALES (est): 2.12MM **Privately Held**
Web: www.hospitalityframes.com
SIC: 3499 Picture frames, metal

(G-8247)
PROFITECT INC (HQ)
Also Called: Profit Ect
3 Allied Dr Ste 220 (02026-6148)
PHONE................................781 290-0009
Guy Yehiav, *CEO*
Amanda Duguay, *CFO*
EMP: 12 **EST:** 2010
SALES (est): 9.84MM
SALES (corp-wide): 5.78B **Publicly Held**
Web: www.profitect.com
SIC: 7372 Business oriented computer
software
PA: Zebra Technologies Corporation
3 Overlook Pt
Lincolnshire IL 60069
847 634-6700

(G-8248)
ROSARIO CABINETS INC
49 Lower East St Ste 2 (02026-2082)
PHONE................................781 329-0639
Rosario Papparazzo, *Pr*
Josephine Papparazzo, *Treas*
▲ **EMP:** 8 **EST:** 1983
SQ FT: 30,000
SALES (est): 833.1K **Privately Held**
Web: www.rosariocabinets.com
SIC: 2434 Wood kitchen cabinets

(G-8249)
SAP PROFESSIONAL JOURNAL
(PA)
Also Called: View, The
20 Carematrix Dr (02026-6149)
PHONE................................781 407-0360
David Penzias, *Pr*
Bonnie Penzias, *
EMP: 60 **EST:** 1991
SALES (est): 4.71MM **Privately Held**
SIC: 2741 Technical manual and paper
publishing

(G-8250)
SKG ASSOCIATES INC
59 Mcdonald St (02026-3914)
PHONE................................781 878-7250
Donald C Brayshaw, *Pr*
Norman Goldberg, *Clerk*
Mark Brayshaw, *VP*

EMP: 7 **EST:** 1966
SALES (est): 678.22K **Privately Held**
SIC: 3469 3544 Stamping metal for the trade
; Special dies and tools

(G-8251)
SME LTD
14 Atkins St (02026-2931)
PHONE................................617 842-4682
EMP: 9 **EST:** 2018
SALES (est): 435.76K **Privately Held**
SIC: 3444 Sheet metalwork

(G-8252)
TERANODE INC
3 Allied Dr Ste 230 (02026-6102)
PHONE................................781 493-6900
Jon Kizner, *VP*
EMP: 7 **EST:** 2011
SALES (est): 102.6K **Privately Held**
Web: www.teranode.com
SIC: 3652 Prerecorded records and tapes

(G-8253)
VALIANTYS AMERICA INC
Also Called: Valiantys
980 Washington St (02026-6704)
PHONE................................781 375-2494
Francois Dussurget, *Pr*
Lucas Dussurget, *VP*
EMP: 18 **EST:** 2017
SALES (est): 1.07MM **Privately Held**
SIC: 7373 7372 Value-added resellers,
computer systems; Business oriented
computer software

(G-8254)
VANTAGE REPORTING INC
Also Called: Vantage Software
3 Allied Dr Ste 303 (02026-6148)
PHONE................................212 750-2256
Gregory J Woolf, *Pr*
EMP: 26 **EST:** 1999
SQ FT: 2,500
SALES (est): 4.5MM **Privately Held**
Web: www.vantage-software.com
SIC: 7372 Business oriented computer
software

(G-8255)
VILLA MACHINE ASSOCIATES
INC
61 Mcdonald St (02026-3914)
PHONE................................781 326-5969
Louis R Villa, *Pr*
EMP: 13 **EST:** 1965
SQ FT: 8,000
SALES (est): 1.47MM **Privately Held**
Web: www.villamachine.com
SIC: 3599 7692 Machine shop, jobbing and
repair; Welding repair

Deerfield
Franklin County

(G-8256)
TREW CORP
901 River Rd (01342-9753)
P.O. Box 395 (01375-0395)
PHONE................................413 773-9798
Mike Smead, *Mgr*
EMP: 13
SALES (corp-wide): 1.17MM **Privately
Held**
SIC: 2951 Asphalt paving mixtures and
blocks
PA: Trew Corp
Amherst Rd

Sunderland MA 01375
413 665-4051

Dennis
Barnstable County

(G-8257)
CAPE COD POLISH COMPANY INC
Also Called: Cape Cod Metal Polsg Cloths
348 Hokum Rock Rd (02638)
P.O. Box 2039 (02638-5039)
PHONE..............................508 385-5099
William Block, *Pr*
EMP: 8 **EST:** 1990
SQ FT: 5,000
SALES (est): 911.35K **Privately Held**
Web: www.capecodpolish.com
SIC: 2842 Polishing preparations and related products

(G-8258)
EAGLE VISION INC
1017 Main St (02638-1518)
P.O. Box 1243 (02638-6243)
PHONE..............................508 385-2283
Donald J Weagle, *Prin*
EMP: 7 **EST:** 2010
SALES (est): 198.22K **Privately Held**
SIC: 3841 Surgical and medical instruments

Dennis Port
Barnstable County

(G-8259)
ALUMINUM PRODUCTS CAPE COD INC (PA)
476 Main St (02639-1319)
P.O. Box 10 (02639-0010)
PHONE..............................508 398-8546
Paul Hunter, *Pr*
EMP: 17 **EST:** 1949
SQ FT: 13,000
SALES (est): 2.35MM
SALES (corp-wide): 2.35MM **Privately Held**
Web: www.apofcc.com
SIC: 1751 1761 5211 3442 Window and door (prefabricated) installation; Gutter and downspout contractor; Windows, storm: wood or metal; Storm doors or windows, metal

(G-8260)
DRIVE-O-RAMA INC
Drive-O-Rama Inc (02639)
P.O. Box 95 (02639-0095)
PHONE..............................508 394-0028
Philip J Baroni, *Ch*
Derrick Sanford, *
Michael Baroni, *
EMP: 9 **EST:** 2016
SQ FT: 47,700
SALES (est): 112.94K **Privately Held**
SIC: 2511 5021 5712 Wood household furniture; Mattresses; Beds and accessories

(G-8261)
FEDELE AND CARTER INC
Also Called: Stage Stop Candy
411 Main St (02639-1308)
PHONE..............................508 394-1791
Amanda Fedele, *Prin*
Joshua Fedele, *Prin*
EMP: 10 **EST:** 2016
SALES (est): 636.14K **Privately Held**

SIC: 5441 2064 Candy; Candy and other confectionery products

(G-8262)
SIGN COMPANY
343 Main St (02639-1309)
P.O. Box 501 (02639-0501)
PHONE..............................508 760-5400
EMP: 10 **EST:** 1996
SALES (est): 301.75K **Privately Held**
Web: www.thesignco.com
SIC: 3993 Signs and advertising specialties

(G-8263)
STAGE STOP CANDY LTD INC
411 Main St (02639-1308)
PHONE..............................508 394-1791
Donna M Hebert, *Pr*
Raymond L Hebert, *Clerk*
Donna M Hebert Prestreas, *Prin*
EMP: 8 **EST:** 1982
SQ FT: 6,100
SALES (est): 888.38K **Privately Held**
Web: www.stagestopcandy.com
SIC: 2064 5441 5145 Candy and other confectionery products; Candy; Candy

Devens
Middlesex County

(G-8264)
ACCELRF CORPORATION
94 Jackson Rd (01434-4011)
PHONE..............................978 391-4009
EMP: 7 **EST:** 2015
SALES (est): 160.28K **Privately Held**
Web: www.accelrf.com
SIC: 3825 Instruments to measure electricity

(G-8265)
ACCUMET ENGINEERING INC
41 Lake George St (01434-4002)
PHONE..............................978 692-6180
Gregory J Sexton, *Pr*
Marie C Sexton, *
June P Beauchesne, *
Bruce N Beauchesne, *
EMP: 34 **EST:** 1979
SALES (est): 5.41MM **Privately Held**
Web: www.accumet.com
SIC: 3599 Machine shop, jobbing and repair

(G-8266)
ACCUMET ENGINEERING CORP
41 Lake George St (01434-4002)
PHONE..............................978 568-8311
Adrian E Schrauwen, *Pr*
EMP: 28 **EST:** 1970
SALES (est): 2.11MM **Privately Held**
Web: www.accumet.com
SIC: 3264 3471 7389 Porcelain electrical supplies; Plating and polishing; Inspection and testing services

(G-8267)
ADAPTIVE OPTICS ASSOCIATES INC
Also Called: Aoa Xinetics
53 Jackson Rd (01434-4026)
PHONE..............................978 391-0000
Mark Ealey, *Mgr*
EMP: 16
Web: www.aoa-supplylink.com
SIC: 3827 Optical instruments and lenses
HQ: Adaptive Optics Associates, Inc.
115 Jackson Rd
Devens MA 01434
978 757-9600

(G-8268)
ADAPTIVE OPTICS ASSOCIATES INC
Also Called: Aoa Xinetics
115 Jackson Rd (01434-4408)
PHONE..............................978 757-9600
Jeffrey Yorsz, *Pr*
EMP: 12
Web: www.aoa-supplylink.com
SIC: 3827 Lenses, optical: all types except ophthalmic
HQ: Adaptive Optics Associates, Inc.
115 Jackson Rd
Devens MA 01434
978 757-9600

(G-8269)
ADAPTIVE OPTICS ASSOCIATES INC (DH)
Also Called: Aoa Xinetics
115 Jackson Rd (01434-4408)
PHONE..............................978 757-9600
Tom Wilson, *Rector*
EMP: 100 **EST:** 1976
SQ FT: 60,000
SALES (est): 38.67MM **Publicly Held**
Web: www.aoa-supplylink.com
SIC: 3827 3695 3861 3577 Lenses, optical: all types except ophthalmic; Optical disks and tape, blank; Cameras, still and motion picture (all types); Computer peripheral equipment, nec
HQ: Northrop Grumman Systems Corporation
2980 Fairview Park Dr
Falls Church VA 22042
703 280-2900

(G-8270)
BIONOSTICS INC
Also Called: Rna Medical Division
7 Jackson Rd (01434-4026)
PHONE..............................978 772-7070
Brenda S Furlow, *Dir*
Micheal Thomas, *
Randy Beard, *
Matthew Rice, *
◆ **EMP:** 143 **EST:** 1981
SQ FT: 45,000
SALES (est): 37.03MM
SALES (corp-wide): 1.14B **Publicly Held**
Web: www.bionostics.com
SIC: 2835 Diagnostic substances
HQ: Research And Diagnostic Systems, Inc.
614 Mckinley Pl Ne
Minneapolis MN 55413
612 379-2956

(G-8271)
BRISTOL-MYERS SQUIBB COMPANY
Also Called: Bristol-Myers Squibb
38 Jackson Rd (01434-4020)
PHONE..............................978 588-6001
Paul Mckenzie, *Mgr*
EMP: 265
SALES (corp-wide): 45.01B **Publicly Held**
Web: www.bms.com
SIC: 2834 Pharmaceutical preparations
PA: Bristol-Myers Squibb Company
430 E 29th St Fl 14
New York NY 10016
212 546-4000

(G-8272)
COMREX CORPORATION
19 Pine Rd (01434-5068)
PHONE..............................978 784-1776
◆ **EMP:** 11 **EST:** 1961

SALES (est): 2.25MM **Privately Held**
Web: www.comrex.com
SIC: 3663 Mobile communication equipment

(G-8273)
INDUSTRIAL PHYSICS PDT INTGRIT
Also Called: Tm Electronics
137 Barnum Rd (01434-3509)
PHONE..............................978 772-0970
Doug Lindemann, *Pr*
EMP: 15 **EST:** 1961
SALES (est): 4.63MM **Privately Held**
SIC: 3829 Measuring and controlling devices, nec

(G-8274)
LADDAWN INC (HQ)
155 Jackson Rd (01434-5614)
PHONE..............................800 446-3639
Owen Richardson, *VP*
▲ **EMP:** 100 **EST:** 1976
SQ FT: 110,000
SALES (est): 100.83MM **Publicly Held**
Web: www.laddawn.com
SIC: 2673 3081 Plastic bags: made from purchased materials; Polyethylene film
PA: Berry Global Group, Inc.
101 Oakley St
Evansville IN 47710

(G-8275)
LEWA PROCESS TECHNOLOGIES INC
Also Called: I P T
8 Charlestown St (01434-4458)
P.O. Box 6820 (01434)
PHONE..............................978 487-1100
EMP: 65
Web: www.intprotech.com
SIC: 3823 8711 Industrial process measurement equipment; Industrial engineers

(G-8276)
LOWELL SUN PUBLISHING COMPANY
78 Barnum Rd (01434-3508)
PHONE..............................978 772-0777
Ken Blanchette, *Brnch Mgr*
EMP: 108
SALES (corp-wide): 1.96B **Privately Held**
Web: www.lowellsun.com
SIC: 2711 Newspapers, publishing and printing
HQ: Lowell Sun Publishing Company
491 Dutton St Ste 2
Lowell MA 01854
978 459-1300

(G-8277)
MAGNEMOTION INC
139 Barnum Rd (01434-3509)
PHONE..............................978 757-9100
EMP: 78 **EST:** 1996
SQ FT: 43,000
SALES (est): 13.11MM **Publicly Held**
Web: www.rockwellautomation.com
SIC: 3535 Unit handling conveying systems
PA: Rockwell Automation, Inc.
1201 S 2nd St
Milwaukee WI 53204

(G-8278)
MASS BREWING LLC
65 Jackson Rd (01434-4026)
PHONE..............................617 800-7070
EMP: 7
SALES (corp-wide): 62.38K **Privately Held**

Web: www.sterlingstreetbrewery.com
SIC: 2082 Beer (alcoholic beverage)
PA: Mass Brewing Llc
    175 Sterling St
    Clinton MA 01510
    617 800-7070

(G-8279)
MAXANT INDUSTRIES INC
58 Barnum Rd (01434-3508)
P.O. Box 454 (01432-0454)
PHONE................................978 772-0576
Valerie Delker, *Pr*
William T Maxant, *Treas*
EMP: 10 EST: 1913
SQ FT: 16,000
SALES (est): 2.25MM **Privately Held**
Web: www.maxantindustries.com
SIC: 3556 3559 Food products machinery;
    Stone working machinery

(G-8280)
MEDIANEWS GROUP INC
78 Barnum Rd (01434-3508)
P.O. Box 362 (01432-0362)
PHONE................................978 772-0777
Becky Pellerin, *Off Mgr*
EMP: 44
SALES (corp-wide): 1.96B **Privately Held**
Web: www.medianewsgroup.com
SIC: 2759 Commercial printing, nec
HQ: Medianews Group, Inc.
    5990 Washington St
    Denver CO 80216

(G-8281)
NEW ENGLAND SHEETS LLC
(PA)
36 Saratoga Blvd (01434-5217)
PHONE................................978 487-2500
Fred Hamilton, *Managing Member*
EMP: 32 EST: 2009
SALES (est): 9.89MM
SALES (corp-wide): 9.89MM **Privately
Held**
Web: www.newenglandsheets.com
SIC: 3444 Sheet metalwork

(G-8282)
NFALL CORP
10 Andrews Pkwy (01434-4017)
PHONE................................978 615-4030
EMP: 26
SALES (corp-wide): 912.94K **Privately
Held**
Web: www.minuteman.com
SIC: 2752 Commercial printing, lithographic
PA: Nfall Corp.
    · 12 Fisher Rd
    Chelmsford MA 01824
    978 615-4030

(G-8283)
NYPRO INC
112 Barnum Rd (01434-3506)
PHONE................................978 784-2006
Brent Bethel, *CEO*
EMP: 471
SALES (corp-wide): 34.7B **Publicly Held**
Web: www.jabil.com
SIC: 3089 Injection molding of plastics
HQ: Nypro Inc.
    101 Union St
    Clinton MA 01510
    978 365-9721

(G-8284)
OX3 CORPORATION
Also Called: Fka Orion Electronics
31 Macarthur Ave (01434-4443)

PHONE................................978 772-1222
Gustav G Widmayer, *Pr*
Dennis Phelan, *Prin*
EMP: 20 EST: 1991
SALES (est): 2.31MM **Privately Held**
Web: www.ox3.com
SIC: 3674 Semiconductors and related
    devices

(G-8285)
PARKER-HANNIFIN
CORPORATION
Also Called: Gas Turbine Fuel Systems Div
14 Robbins Pond Rd (01434-5613)
PHONE................................978 784-1200
Venlenanne Cooazzo, *Brnch Mgr*
EMP: 123
SALES (corp-wide): 19.07B **Publicly Held**
Web: www.parker.com
SIC: 3728 3724 Aircraft parts and
    equipment, nec; Aircraft engines and
    engine parts
PA: Parker-Hannifin Corporation
    6035 Parkland Blvd
    Cleveland OH 44124
    216 896-3000

(G-8286)
ROFIN-BAASEL INC (HQ)
68 Barnum Rd (01434-3508)
PHONE................................978 635-9100
Lou Molnar, *Pr*
Cindy Denis, *
▲ EMP: 30 EST: 1985
SQ FT: 14,500
SALES (est): 27.28MM
SALES (corp-wide): 5.16B **Publicly Held**
SIC: 3699 3953 Laser systems and
    equipment; Marking devices
PA: Coherent Corp.
    375 Saxonburg Blvd
    Saxonburg PA 16056
    724 352-4455

(G-8287)
SMC LTD
18 Independence Dr (01434-5294)
P.O. Box 460 (01564-0460)
PHONE................................978 422-6800
Chetan N Patel, *Pr*
EMP: 80 EST: 1984
SQ FT: 32,000
SALES (est): 24.84MM
SALES (corp-wide): 444.76MM **Privately
Held**
Web: www.smcltd.com
SIC: 3089 Injection molding of plastics
PA: Scientific Molding Corporation, Ltd.
    330 Smc Dr
    Somerset WI 54025
    715 247-3500

(G-8288)
VERANOVA LP (HQ)
Also Called: Pharm Eco Laboratories
25 Patton Rd (01434-3803)
PHONE................................484 581-0149
Mike Riley, *CEO*
Andrew Wesztergom, *CFO*
Victoria Brown, *Chief Human Resource
Officer*
Lucas Sauer-jones, *General Vice President*
Jose Ibietatorremendia, *Sr VP*
▲ EMP: 135 EST: 1972
SQ FT: 160,000
SALES (est): 118.93MM
SALES (corp-wide): 118.93MM **Privately
Held**
Web: www.veranova.com

SIC: 2834 8731 Pharmaceutical
    preparations; Commercial physical research
PA: Veranova Bidco, L.P.
    435 Devon Park Dr Ste 400
    Wayne PA 19087
    610 254-5349

(G-8289)
VULCANFORMS INC
112 Barnum Rd (01434-3506)
PHONE................................781 472-0160
Martin Feldmann, *CEO*
Ghildyal Anupam, *
Maura Ditucci, *
Anupam Ghildyal, *
EMP: 65 EST: 2015
SALES (est): 22.7MM **Privately Held**
Web: www.vulcanforms.com
SIC: 2759 1531 Commercial printing, nec

(G-8290)
YMC AMERICA INC
Also Called: Ymc Process Technologies, Inc.
8 Charlestown St (01434-4458)
PHONE................................978 487-1130
EMP: 46 EST: 2018
SALES (est): 9.52MM **Privately Held**
Web: www.ymcamerica.com
SIC: 3823 Industrial process measurement
    equipment
PA: Ymc Co.,Ltd.
    284, Nishihairudaigocho, Karasuma,
    Gojodoori, Shimogyo-Ku
    Kyoto KYO 600-8

Dighton
Bristol County

(G-8291)
ARMIN INNOVATIVE PRODUCTS
INC
Also Called: Metalgrommets.com
1424 Somerset Ave (02715-1238)
P.O. Box 26 (02715-0026)
PHONE................................508 822-4629
Kenneth Raifman, *Pr*
◆ EMP: 39 EST: 1981
SQ FT: 43,000
SALES (est): 7.98MM **Privately Held**
Web: www.arminip.com
SIC: 2673 Bags: plastic, laminated, and
    coated

(G-8292)
BLACK EARTH TECHNOLOGIES
INC
2575 County St (02715-1606)
PHONE................................508 397-1335
Roger Teixeira, *Prin*
EMP: 8 EST: 2008
SALES (est): 172.05K **Privately Held**
SIC: 3674 Semiconductors and related
    devices

(G-8293)
LINS PROPANE TRUCKS CORP
2281 Cedar St (02715-1009)
PHONE................................508 669-6665
Andrew Johnson, *Pr*
Timothy Johnson, *Dir*
▼ EMP: 18 EST: 1985
SQ FT: 8,000
SALES (est): 3.58MM **Privately Held**
Web: www.linspropanetrucks.com
SIC: 3715 Truck trailers

(G-8294)
QUINTAL BURIAL VAULT INC
3425 Sharps Lot Rd (02715-1417)
PHONE................................508 669-5717
Joseph Quintal, *Owner*
EMP: 13 EST: 1960
SALES (est): 761.78K **Privately Held**
SIC: 3281 3272 5087 4226 Burial vaults,
    stone; Burial vaults, concrete or precast
    terrazzo; Concrete burial vaults and boxes;
    Document and office records storage

Dorchester
Suffolk County

(G-8295)
2 DOGS TREATS LLC
171 Neponset Ave (02122-3343)
PHONE................................617 286-4844
Buttra Christian Sann, *Managing Member*
EMP: 8 EST: 2013
SALES (est): 1.84MM **Privately Held**
Web: www.2dogstreats.com
SIC: 2047 Dog food

(G-8296)
88 ACRES FOODS INC
196 Quincy St Ste 5 (02121-1995)
PHONE................................617 208-8651
Nicole Marie Ledoux, *Brnch Mgr*
EMP: 12
SALES (corp-wide): 5.71MM **Privately
Held**
Web: www.88acres.com
SIC: 2051 Charlotte Russe, bakery product:
    except frozen
PA: 88 Acres Foods, Inc.
    65 Shawmut Rd Unit 6
    Canton MA 02021
    617 208-8651

(G-8297)
BOSTON IRISH REPORTER
Also Called: Dorchester Reporter
150 Mount Vernon St Ste 120 (02125)
PHONE................................617 436-1222
Ed Forry, *Pr*
EMP: 10 EST: 1989
SALES (est): 623.59K **Privately Held**
Web: www.bostonirish.com
SIC: 2711 Newspapers, publishing and
    printing

(G-8298)
DUTCH MAID BAKERY INC
50 Park St Ste 2 (02122-3287)
PHONE................................617 265-5417
▲ EMP: 150 EST: 1978
SALES (est): 15.84MM **Privately Held**
Web: www.dutchmaidbakery.com
SIC: 2053 Cakes, bakery: frozen

(G-8299)
FIRST ELECTRONICS
CORPORATION (DH)
71 Von Hillern St Ste 1 (02125-1193)
PHONE................................617 288-2430
William Donnellan, *Pr*
EMP: 45 EST: 1955
SQ FT: 50,000
SALES (est): 25.18MM
SALES (corp-wide): 1.28B **Privately Held**
Web: www.feccables.com
SIC: 3679 3643 Harness assemblies, for
    electronic use: wire or cable; Current-
    carrying wiring services
HQ: Tpc Wire & Cable Corp.
    9600 Valley View Rd

Macedonia OH 44056

(G-8300)
HASTONE HOMESTONE INC
115 E Cottage St (02125-2622)
PHONE.................................617 784-3284
For Ming Ha, *Pr*
▲ **EMP:** 8 **EST:** 2006
SALES (est): 425.82K **Privately Held**
Web: www.hastonecabinetry.com
SIC: 2434 2499 Wood kitchen cabinets;
Kitchen, bathroom, and household ware:
wood

(G-8301)
VIETAZ INC
Also Called: Caring Pharmacy 2
2288 Dorchester Ave (02124-5622)
PHONE.................................617 322-1933
Christine Phan, *Pr*
EMP: 7 **EST:** 2013
SALES (est): 227.95K **Privately Held**
SIC: 2834 Druggists' preparations
(pharmaceuticals)

Dracut
Middlesex County

(G-8302)
BROX INDUSTRIES INC (PA)
Also Called: Brox
1471 Methuen St (01826-5499)
PHONE.................................978 454-9105
Stephen M Brox, *Pr*
Stephen M Brox, *Pr*
George C Brox, *VP*
Cecilia P Nickerson, *Dir*
Ann-louise Brox, *Dir*
EMP: 60 **EST:** 1982
SQ FT: 3,000
SALES (est): 88.34MM
SALES (corp-wide): 88.34MM **Privately
Held**
Web: www.broxindustries.com
SIC: 1442 1499 1611 1629 Construction
sand mining; Asphalt mining and
bituminous stone quarrying; Highway and
street paving contractor; Land clearing
contractor

(G-8303)
DAKOTA SYSTEMS INC
1057 Bdwy Rd Rte 113 (01826-2807)
PHONE.................................978 275-0600
John M Thomas, *Pr*
EMP: 90 **EST:** 1984
SQ FT: 25,500
SALES (est): 17.73MM **Privately Held**
Web: www.dakotasystems.com
SIC: 3312 Stainless steel

(G-8304)
DE MARI PASTA DIES USA INC
48 Chuck Dr (01826-2613)
PHONE.................................978 454-4099
Mauricio Demari, *Pr*
Gabriella Cannata, *Dir*
▲ **EMP:** 8 **EST:** 1998
SALES (est): 1.42MM **Privately Held**
Web: www.demaripastadies.com
SIC: 3544 Special dies, tools, jigs, and
fixtures

(G-8305)
**ESSEX SILVERLINE
CORPORATION (PA)**
1118 Lakeview Ave (01826-4739)
P.O. Box 40 (01826-0040)

PHONE.................................978 957-2116
Francis Barous, *CEO*
Dennis Barous, *Pr*
▼ **EMP:** 17 **EST:** 1938
SQ FT: 10,000
SALES (est): 4.99MM
SALES (corp-wide): 4.99MM **Privately
Held**
Web: www.essexsilverline.com
SIC: 5085 3589 Abrasives; Floor sanding
machines, commercial

(G-8306)
J & J HEATING & AC INC
Also Called: J & J Heating and AC
17 Arlington St (01826-3952)
PHONE.................................978 454-8197
Edward T Ayotte, *Pr*
EMP: 38 **EST:** 1971
SQ FT: 7,000
SALES (est): 4.49MM **Privately Held**
Web: www.jjheatac.com
SIC: 1711 3444 8711 3585 Warm air
heating and air conditioning contractor;
Sheet metalwork; Heating and ventilation
engineering; Refrigeration and heating
equipment

(G-8307)
MAJILITE CORPORATION
1530 Broadway Rd (01826-2830)
PHONE.................................978 441-6800
Bruce Eben Pindyck, *CEO*
Michael Willwerth, *
◆ **EMP:** 75 **EST:** 1979
SQ FT: 150,000
SALES (est): 19.5MM
SALES (corp-wide): 331.16MM **Privately
Held**
Web: www.majilite.com
SIC: 2295 2261 Coated fabrics, not
rubberized; Finishing plants, cotton
PA: Meridian Industries, Inc.
735 N Water St Ste 630
Milwaukee WI 53202
414 224-0610

(G-8308)
MAJILITE MANUFACTURING INC
1530 Broadway Rd (01826-2830)
PHONE.................................978 441-6800
Michael Willewerth, *Pr*
Douglas J Arnold, *Sec*
Joseph B Tyson, *Sec*
Douglas C Miller, *Treas*
EMP: 25 **EST:** 1979
SQ FT: 100,000
SALES (est): 2.22MM
SALES (corp-wide): 331.16MM **Privately
Held**
Web: www.majilite.com
SIC: 2262 Chemical coating or treating of
manmade broadwoven fabrics
PA: Meridian Industries, Inc.
735 N Water St Ste 630
Milwaukee WI 53202
414 224-0610

(G-8309)
MILL CITY IRON FABRICATORS
479 Textile Ave (01826-4424)
PHONE.................................978 957-6833
Jean R Soucy, *Pr*
EMP: 19 **EST:** 1997
SQ FT: 10,000
SALES (est): 4.66MM **Privately Held**
Web: www.millcityiron.com
SIC: 3449 3441 Miscellaneous metalwork;
Fabricated structural metal

(G-8310)
PJ KEATING COMPANY
2140 Bridge St Route 38 (01826-1432)
PHONE.................................978 454-7878
EMP: 60
SALES (corp-wide): 32.72B **Privately Held**
Web: www.pjkeating.com
SIC: 5032 1611 2951 Stone, crushed or
broken; Surfacing and paving; Asphalt
paving mixtures and blocks
HQ: P.J. Keating Company
998 Reservoir Rd
Lunenburg MA 01462
978 582-5200

(G-8311)
**PORTLAND STONE WARE CO
INC (PA)**
50 Mcgrath Rd (01826-2840)
P.O. Box 670 (01826-0670)
PHONE.................................978 459-7272
TOLL FREE: 800
Donna Morgan, *Pr*
▲ **EMP:** 35 **EST:** 1847
SQ FT: 41,000
SALES (est): 4.54MM
SALES (corp-wide): 4.54MM **Privately
Held**
Web: www.portlandstoneware.com
SIC: 3272 5051 5032 Columns, concrete;
Metals service centers and offices; Building
stone

(G-8312)
SYNTHETIC LABS INC
24 Victory Ln (01826-4643)
PHONE.................................978 957-2919
Edward Hosmer, *Pr*
David Miller, *VP*
Suzanne Hosmer, *Clerk*
EMP: 30 **EST:** 1963
SQ FT: 15,000
SALES (est): 7.35MM **Privately Held**
Web: www.syntecpro.com
SIC: 2841 Soap and other detergents

(G-8313)
**VINTAGE MILLWORK
CORPORATION**
19 School St (01826-4684)
PHONE.................................978 957-1400
Raymond Bullock, *Pr*
Joseph Cusano, *VP*
EMP: 7 **EST:** 2003
SALES (est): 990.99K **Privately Held**
Web: www.vintagemillworkcorp.com
SIC: 2431 Millwork

(G-8314)
WASIK ASSOCIATES INC
29 Diana Ln (01826-1500)
PHONE.................................978 454-9787
Peter T Wasik Junior, *Pr*
EMP: 17 **EST:** 1982
SQ FT: 14,000
SALES (est): 2.42MM **Privately Held**
Web: www.wasik.com
SIC: 3679 7629 Power supplies, all types:
static; Electrical equipment repair, high
voltage

Dudley
Worcester County

(G-8315)
**AMERICAN SUB ASSMBLY
PRDCERS I**

Also Called: ASAP
137 Schofield Ave (01571-6074)
P.O. Box 417 (01570-0417)
PHONE.................................508 949-2320
Douglas Sherblom, *Pr*
EMP: 43 **EST:** 1992
SQ FT: 7,000
SALES (est): 2.38MM **Privately Held**
SIC: 3679 1731 3677 Electronic circuits;
Fire detection and burglar alarm systems
specialization; Electronic transformers

(G-8316)
ANCHOR PLASTICS INC
26 Knollwood Rd (01571-6041)
PHONE.................................508 753-2169
Joseph C Smolen, *Pr*
EMP: 7 **EST:** 1988
SQ FT: 600
SALES (est): 833.46K **Privately Held**
SIC: 3089 Injection molding of plastics

(G-8317)
BONIFACE TOOL & DIE INC
181 Southbridge Rd (01571-6925)
PHONE.................................508 764-3248
Peter Didonato, *Pr*
Angelo Didonato, *
David Didonato, *
▲ **EMP:** 30 **EST:** 1957
SQ FT: 33,000
SALES (est): 3.76MM **Privately Held**
Web: www.bonifacetool.com
SIC: 3544 3599 3728 Special dies, tools,
jigs, and fixtures; Machine shop, jobbing
and repair; Military aircraft equipment and
armament

(G-8318)
**HENKE SASS WOLF AMERICA
INC**
135 Schofield Ave (01571-6029)
PHONE.................................508 671-9300
Peter Decker, *CEO*
Armin Lekitsch, *
Thomas Ziesemer, *
Stefan Knefel, *
Fabian-alexander Muller, *VP Sls*
▲ **EMP:** 100 **EST:** 1991
SQ FT: 32,000
SALES (est): 10.74MM **Privately Held**
Web: www.henkesasswolf.de
SIC: 7699 3845 Optical instrument repair;
Ultrasonic scanning devices, medical
HQ: Henke-Sass, Wolf Gmbh
Keltenstr. 1
Tuttlingen BW 78532
746294660

(G-8319)
I F ENGINEERING CORP
3 Foshay Rd (01571-2600)
P.O. Box 1 (01571-0001)
PHONE.................................860 935-0280
Lee C Foshay, *Pr*
Lois A Foshay, *
EMP: 27 **EST:** 1997
SQ FT: 7,500
SALES (est): 4.74MM **Privately Held**
Web: www.ifengineering.com
SIC: 3669 Signaling apparatus, electric

(G-8320)
**MYRIAD FIBER IMAGING TECH
INC**
56 Southbridge Rd (01571-6923)
PHONE.................................508 949-3000
EMP: 15 **EST:** 1995
SQ FT: 3,500
SALES (est): 2.23MM **Privately Held**

Web: www.myriadfiber.com
SIC: 3845 3229 Endoscopic equipment, electromedical, nec; Fiber optics strands

(G-8321)
RYSZARD A KOKOSINSKI
Also Called: Kokos Machine Co
75 Oxford Ave (01571-5603)
PHONE..................508 943-2700
Ryszard A Kokosinski, *Owner*
EMP: 25 EST: 1980
SQ FT: 20,000
SALES (est): 832.23K Privately Held
Web: www.kokosmachine.com
SIC: 3599 Machine shop, jobbing and repair

(G-8322)
SAND A INDUSTRIES
137 Schofield Ave (01571-6074)
PHONE..................508 943-1178
Tracy Rossik, *Prin*
EMP: 7 EST: 2008
SALES (est): 151.01K Privately Held
SIC: 2399 Fabricated textile products, nec

(G-8323)
SHIELD PACKAGING CO INC
50 Oxford Rd (01571-5609)
PHONE..................508 949-0900
Bruce Simpson, *Brnch Mgr*
EMP: 40
SALES (corp-wide): 45.52MM Privately Held
Web: www.shieldpackaging.com
SIC: 2813 5169 3087 2879 Aerosols; Aerosols; Custom compound purchased resins; Agricultural chemicals, nec
PA: Shield Packaging Co., Inc.
99 University Rd
Canton MA 02021
781 821-0400

(G-8324)
SOUTHBRIDGE TOOL & MFG INC
181 Southbridge Rd (01571-6925)
PHONE..................508 764-6819
Peter Didonato, *Pr*
Angelo Didonato, *
EMP: 30 EST: 1981
SQ FT: 24,000
SALES (est): 4.61MM Privately Held
Web: www.southbridgetool.com
SIC: 3544 Special dies and tools

(G-8325)
STEVENS LINEN ASSOCIATES INC
137 Schofield Ave Ste 5 (01571-6074)
PHONE..................508 943-0813
Gregory C Kline, *Pr*
Carl W Copeland, *
▲ EMP: 29 EST: 1846
SQ FT: 142,000
SALES (est): 1.19MM Privately Held
Web: www.stevenslinen.com
SIC: 2392 2211 2259 2262 Placemats, plastic or textile; Broadwoven fabric mills, cotton; Towels, washcloths, and dishcloths: knit; Finishing plants, manmade

(G-8326)
UNIVERSAL TAG INC
36 Hall Rd (01571-5964)
P.O. Box 1518 (01571-1518)
PHONE..................508 949-2411
Paul J Mandeville, *Pr*
Jeanne L Mandeville, *
A Robert Mandeville, *
EMP: 28 EST: 1927
SQ FT: 28,000

SALES (est): 8.15MM Privately Held
Web: www.universaltag.com
SIC: 2679 2752 Tags, paper (unprinted): made from purchased paper; Offset printing

(G-8327)
WEBCO CHEMICAL CORPORATION
420 W Main St (01571-5936)
PHONE..................508 943-2337
Mark Puliafico, *Pr*
Edward Ruggeri, *
Mark Ruggeri, *
Pat Fulk, *
▲ EMP: 76 EST: 1956
SQ FT: 120,000
SALES (est): 17.51MM Privately Held
Web: www.webco-chemical.com
SIC: 7389 2842 Labeling bottles, cans, cartons, etc.; Cleaning or polishing preparations, nec

---

Dunstable
Middlesex County

(G-8328)
MSR UTILITY
209 Pleasant St (01827-1717)
PHONE..................978 649-0002
Matthew Raymond, *Owner*
EMP: 9 EST: 2013
SALES (est): 682.62K Privately Held
SIC: 1389 Oil and gas field services, nec

Duxbury
Plymouth County

(G-8329)
BRITE-STRIKE TECHNOLOGIES INC
Also Called: Brite Strike Tctcal Illmntion
1145 Franklin St (02332)
PHONE..................781 585-3525
Glenn Bushee, *Pr*
Sarah Bushe, *VP*
EMP: 8 EST: 2006
SQ FT: 14,000
SALES (est): 819.01K Privately Held
Web: www.brite-strike.com
SIC: 3648 Flashlights

(G-8330)
DUXBURY CLIPPER INC
11 S Station St (02332-4534)
P.O. Box 1656 (02331-1656)
PHONE..................781 934-2811
David Cutler, *Pr*
Joshua Cutler, *Prin*
David S Cutler, *Clerk*
EMP: 21 EST: 1950
SQ FT: 1,000
SALES (est): 866.31K Privately Held
Web: www.duxburyclipper.com
SIC: 2711 Newspapers: publishing only, not printed on site

(G-8331)
GCB MEDICAL LLC
Also Called: Gcb Medical Supply
289 Saint George St (02332-3939)
P.O. Box 1194 (02331-1194)
PHONE..................617 699-6715
Kate Bowen, *CEO*
EMP: 10 EST: 2020
SALES (est): 724.94K Privately Held
Web: www.gcbmedicalsupply.com

SIC: 3841 Surgical and medical instruments

(G-8332)
GRIFFIN PUBLISHING CO INC
Also Called: Griffin Report Food Marketing
21 Chestnut St (02332-4419)
P.O. Box 2826 (02331-2826)
PHONE..................781 829-4700
Kevin B Griffin, *Pr*
EMP: 10 EST: 1966
SQ FT: 3,500
SALES (est): 817.29K Privately Held
Web: www.theshelbyreport.com
SIC: 2721 Magazines: publishing only, not printed on site

(G-8333)
PERFORMANCE TEXTILES INC
42 Tremont St Ste 3 (02332-5300)
PHONE..................781 934-7055
EMP: 12
Web: www.perftex.com
SIC: 2211 Broadwoven fabric mills, cotton

East Bridgewater
Plymouth County

(G-8334)
ALLOY CASTINGS CO INC
151 W Union St (02333-1745)
P.O. Box 473 (02333-0473)
PHONE..................508 378-2541
Franklin J Santilli, *Pr*
EMP: 22 EST: 1948
SQ FT: 90,000
SALES (est): 747.63K Privately Held
Web: www.alloycastings.com
SIC: 3366 Copper foundries

(G-8335)
ATLANTIC BROOM SERVICE INC
Also Called: Atlantic Highway Sign Company
600 N Bedford St Ste 300 (02333-1282)
PHONE..................774 226-1300
EMP: 32 EST: 1955
SALES (est): 3.61MM Privately Held
Web: www.atlanticbroom.com
SIC: 3991 3531 3993 Street sweeping brooms, hand or machine; Snow plow attachments; Signs, not made in custom sign painting shops

(G-8336)
CENTCO ARCHITECTURAL MTLS INC
523 Spring St (02333-1802)
PHONE..................508 456-1888
Larry Dale, *Pr*
EMP: 10 EST: 1985
SQ FT: 10,000
SALES (est): 917.3K Privately Held
Web: www.centcometals.com
SIC: 3442 Storm doors or windows, metal

(G-8337)
CHRISTEYNS LAUNDRY TECH LLC
100 Laurel St Ste 120 (02333-1847)
PHONE..................617 203-2169
EMP: 14 EST: 2011
SALES (est): 837.33K Privately Held
SIC: 2841 Soap and other detergents

(G-8338)
CROCETTI OAKDALE PKG CO INC (PA)
Also Called: South Shore Meats

378 Pleasant St (02333-1349)
PHONE..................508 587-0035
Carl F Crocetti, *
Joan A Hurkett, *Sec*
EMP: 12 EST: 1977
SQ FT: 15,000
SALES (est): 5.08MM
SALES (corp-wide): 5.08MM Privately Held
Web: www.crocettis.com
SIC: 2013 2011 Sausages and other prepared meats; Meat packing plants

(G-8339)
D W CLARK INC (PA)
692 N Bedford St (02333-1126)
P.O. Box 448 (02333-0448)
PHONE..................508 378-4014
Jeffrey Burek, *Pr*
Mary Ann Burek, *
EMP: 22 EST: 1902
SQ FT: 12,000
SALES (est): 7.04MM
SALES (corp-wide): 7.04MM Privately Held
Web: www.dwclark.com
SIC: 3325 3369 3366 Steel foundries, nec; Nonferrous foundries, nec; Copper foundries

(G-8340)
FTC ENTERPRISES INC
170 W Union St (02333-1746)
PHONE..................508 378-2799
Patrick Climo, *VP*
Fred Climo Iii, *Pr*
Fred Climo Junior, *Prin*
EMP: 10 EST: 1988
SALES (est): 412.26K Privately Held
Web: www.ftcenterprisesinc.com
SIC: 2299 Batting, wadding, padding and fillings

(G-8341)
JET MACHINED PRODUCTS LLC
221 Highland St (02333-1409)
P.O. Box 577 (02333-0577)
PHONE..................508 378-3200
EMP: 14 EST: 1965
SQ FT: 10,000
SALES (est): 2.5MM Privately Held
Web: www.jetmachprod.com
SIC: 3599 Machine shop, jobbing and repair

(G-8342)
L T TECHNOLOGIES
612 Plymouth St Ste 12 (02333-2057)
PHONE..................508 456-0315
Thomas Belmont, *Pr*
EMP: 7 EST: 2010
SALES (est): 447.06K Privately Held
SIC: 3589 Water treatment equipment, industrial

(G-8343)
MCSTOWE ENGRG & MET PDTS INC
Also Called: McStowe Engrg & Met Pdts Co
548 Spring St (02333-1896)
PHONE..................508 378-7400
Paul Mc Stowe Junior, *Pr*
Evelyn E Mc Stowe, *VP*
Linda Mc Stowe, *VP*
EMP: 15 EST: 1962
SQ FT: 16,000
SALES (est): 961.35K Privately Held
SIC: 3644 3429 3613 Electric outlet, switch, and fuse boxes; Metal fasteners; Control panels, electric

GEOGRAPHIC

(G-8344)

MUELLER CORPORATION
530 Spring St (02333-1834)
PHONE..............................508 456-4500
Mark D Svizzero, *Pr*
Glenn Mueller, *
David A Guadagnoli, *
Robert B Luick, *
▲ EMP: 160 EST: 1955
SQ FT: 20,000
SALES (est): 20.4MM **Privately Held**
Web: www.muellercorp.com
SIC: 3471 Electroplating of metals or
formed products

(G-8345)

**SUPERIOR RAIL AND IR WORKS
INC**
350 West St (02333-1844)
PHONE..............................508 378-4025
Leonard H Ferrara Junior, *Prin*
Leonard H Ferrara Junior, *Prin*
Anthony J Ferrara, *Prin*
EMP: 20 EST: 1960
SQ FT: 14,000
SALES (est): 4.02MM **Privately Held**
Web: www.superiorrail.net
SIC: 1791 3446 3441 Iron work, structural;
Architectural metalwork; Fabricated
structural metal

(G-8346)

THORNDIKE CORPORATION
680 N Bedford St Ste 1 (02333-1292)
P.O. Box 533 (02333-0533)
PHONE..............................508 378-9797
James O Thorndike Iii, *Pr*
Mary Ellen Thorndike, *Treas*
EMP: 12 EST: 1982
SQ FT: 3,500
SALES (est): 2.02MM **Privately Held**
Web: www.thorndikecorp.com
SIC: 3679 Microwave components

(G-8347)

WARE RITE DISTRIBUTORS INC
40 Industrial Dr (02333-1680)
PHONE..............................508 690-2145
Roger Ware, *Pr*
▲ EMP: 100 EST: 1978
SQ FT: 40,000
SALES (est): 23.23MM **Privately Held**
Web: www.warerite.com
SIC: 2821 2541 Plastics materials and resins
; Counter and sink tops

East Dennis
Barnstable County

(G-8348)

**AUBIN EQUIPMENT AND
AUTOMOTIVE**
372 Hokum Rock Rd (02641)
PHONE..............................508 385-3237
John Aubin, *Pr*
EMP: 7 EST: 2013
SALES (est): 120.1K **Privately Held**
SIC: 3524 Lawn and garden tractors and
equipment

East Douglas
Worcester County

(G-8349)

CLASSIC ENVELOPE INC
120 Gilboa St Unit 1 (01516-2275)

PHONE..............................508 731-6747
EMP: 70 EST: 1988
SALES: 19.79MM
SALES (corp-wide): 202.84MM **Privately
Held**
Web: www.supremex.com
SIC: 2677 2759 2752 Envelopes;
Envelopes: printing, nsk; Commercial
printing, lithographic
PA: Supremex Inc
7213 Rue Cordner
Lasalle QC H8N 2
514 595-0555

(G-8350)

EMX CONTROLS INC
Also Called: Flagship Automation
100 Davis St # 1 (01516-2310)
PHONE..............................508 876-9700
Richard W Padovano, *Dir*
Richard W Padovano, *Pr*
Eleanor Padovano Clrk, *Prin*
Allen Stanski, *
EMP: 40 EST: 1963
SALES (est): 4.57MM **Privately Held**
Web: www.emxcontrols.com
SIC: 3625 5084 3613 Electric controls and
control accessories, industrial; Industrial
machine parts; Control panels, electric

(G-8351)

JT MACHINE INC
Also Called: Jt Machine Shop
175 Davis St (01516-2313)
P.O. Box 297 (01516-0297)
PHONE..............................508 476-1508
Ronald Deschene, *Pr*
Steven Deschene, *VP Opers*
Kevin Decshene, *VP Mfg*
EMP: 21 EST: 1975
SQ FT: 15,000
SALES (est): 1.8MM **Privately Held**
Web: www.jtmachineinc.com
SIC: 3541 3599 Machine tool replacement &
repair parts, metal cutting types; Machine
shop, jobbing and repair

(G-8352)

**MONALEX MANUFACTURING
INC**
10 Riedell Rd (01516-2146)
P.O. Box 1195 (01516-1195)
PHONE..............................508 476-1200
EMP: 9 EST: 1992
SQ FT: 3,500
SALES (est): 969.12K **Privately Held**
Web: www.monalexmfg.com
SIC: 7389 3561 Design, commercial and
industrial; Industrial pumps and parts

East Falmouth
Barnstable County

(G-8353)

ACCURATE COMPOSITES LLC
Also Called: Accurate Plastics
33 Technology Park Dr (02536-4442)
PHONE..............................508 457-9097
John R Egan Junior, *CEO*
EMP: 60 EST: 2019
SALES (est): 7.95MM **Privately Held**
Web: www.acculam.com
SIC: 2821 Plastics materials and resins

(G-8354)

ACCURATE PLASTICS INC
33 Technology Park Dr (02536-4442)
PHONE..............................508 457-9097

Joseph Roy, *Mgr*
EMP: 34
SALES (corp-wide): 5MM **Privately Held**
Web: www.acculam.com
SIC: 2821 Plastics materials and resins
PA: Accurate Plastics, Inc.
18 Morris Pl
Yonkers NY 10705
914 476-0700

(G-8355)

**ASSOCIATES OF CAPE COD
INC (PA)**
Also Called: ACC
124 Bernard E Saint Jean (02536-4445)
PHONE..............................508 540-3444
A J Meuse, *Pr*
Alison Skinner, *
▲ EMP: 70 EST: 1974
SQ FT: 80,000
SALES (est): 50.82MM
SALES (corp-wide): 50.82MM **Privately
Held**
Web: www.acciusa.com
SIC: 2835 Diagnostic substances

(G-8356)

**ATLANTIC MBL & GRAN GROUP
INC**
59 Technology Park Dr (02536-4442)
PHONE..............................508 540-9770
Sandoval Pereira, *Dir*
Danffsney P Goncalves, *Pr*
EMP: 7 EST: 2017
SALES (est): 950.04K **Privately Held**
SIC: 3281 1743 Granite, cut and shaped;
Tile installation, ceramic

(G-8357)

BLACKSMITH SHOP FARMS INC
716 Blacksmith Shop Rd (02536-4410)
PHONE..............................508 548-7714
Donn Breivogel, *Pr*
EMP: 7 EST: 1987
SALES (est): 899.28K **Privately Held**
Web: www.blacksmithshopfarms.com
SIC: 4953 2499 5261 5083 Recycling,
waste materials; Mulch, wood and bark;
Retail nurseries and garden stores;
Landscaping equipment

(G-8358)

**DAVIES FAMILY SELECTIONS
INC**
255 Hill And Plain Rd (02536-3978)
PHONE..............................508 317-6024
Ian C Davies, *Pr*
EMP: 7 EST: 2012
SALES (est): 296.07K **Privately Held**
Web: www.vinologicscorp.com
SIC: 2084 Wines

(G-8359)

FALMOUTH READY MIX INC
475 Thomas B Landers Rd (02536-4406)
PHONE..............................508 548-6100
Robert A Moniz, *Pr*
Catherine A Moniz, *Sec*
EMP: 14 EST: 1993
SALES (est): 2.18MM **Privately Held**
Web: www.falmouthreadymix.com
SIC: 3273 Ready-mixed concrete

(G-8360)

FUCCILLO READY MIX INC
548 Thomas B Landers Rd (02536-4414)
PHONE..............................508 540-2821
Valerie Fuccillo, *Pr*
David P Fuccillo, *VP*

EMP: 10 EST: 2003
SALES (est): 1.54MM **Privately Held**
SIC: 3273 Ready-mixed concrete

(G-8361)

**MCLANE RESEARCH LABS INC
(PA)**
121 Bernard E Saint Jean (02536-4444)
PHONE..............................508 495-4000
Susumu Honjo, *Pr*
Harry J Honan, *Sec*
Yuki Honjo, *Pr*
▲ EMP: 7 EST: 1983
SALES (est): 3.61MM
SALES (corp-wide): 3.61MM **Privately
Held**
Web: www.mclanelabs.com
SIC: 3699 8731 Underwater sound
equipment; Commercial research laboratory

(G-8362)

WALPOLE OUTDOORS LLC
958 E Falmouth Hwy (02536-6228)
P.O. Box 28 (02536-0028)
PHONE..............................508 540-0300
Richard Kolbert, *Brnch Mgr*
EMP: 20
SALES (corp-wide): 50.41MM **Privately
Held**
Web: www.walpoleoutdoors.com
SIC: 2499 5211 5712 2452 Fencing, wood;
Fencing; Outdoor and garden furniture;
Prefabricated wood buildings
PA: Walpole Outdoors Llc
255 Patriot Pl
Foxboro MA 02035
508 668-2800

East Freetown
Bristol County

(G-8363)

BRADFORD STEEL CO INC
46 Braley Rd (02717-1100)
P.O. Box 477 (02717-0477)
PHONE..............................508 763-5921
Brian Jackson, *Pr*
Michael Souza, *VP*
EMP: 15 EST: 1977
SQ FT: 2,200
SALES (est): 5.66MM **Privately Held**
Web: www.bradfordsteel.com
SIC: 5051 3441 Steel; Building components,
structural steel

(G-8364)

LPS ENTERPRISES INC
128 Braley Rd Bldg A3 (02717-1147)
P.O. Box 67 (02717-0067)
PHONE..............................508 763-3830
Anthony Little, *Pr*
Linda Veronneau, *
EMP: 26 EST: 1989
SQ FT: 6,000
SALES (est): 3.48MM **Privately Held**
Web: www.calllps.com
SIC: 3524 7349 Snowblowers and throwers,
residential; Building maintenance services,
nec

(G-8365)

**PREFERRED CONCRETE
CORPORATION**
66 Braley Rd (02717-1151)
P.O. Box 539 (02717-0539)
PHONE..............................508 763-5500
Amelia Mcnutt, *Pr*
Antonio Sousa, *VP*

▲ = Import ▼ = Export
◆ = Import/Export

EMP: 17 **EST:** 1999
SALES (est): 2.63MM **Privately Held**
Web: www.preferredconcrete.com
SIC: 3273 Ready-mixed concrete

(G-8366)
REFRESCO BEVERAGES US INC
65 Chace Rd (02717-1128)
PHONE.................................508 763-3515
EMP: 11
Web: www.refresco-na.com
SIC: 2086 Carbonated beverages, nonalcoholic: pkged. in cans, bottles
HQ: Refresco Beverages Us Inc.
 8112 Woodland Center Blvd
 Tampa FL 33614

(G-8367)
TOWN BOOKBINDERY INC
154 County Rd (02717-1219)
P.O. Box 91 (02717-0091)
PHONE.................................508 763-2713
Raymond De Costa, *Pr*
EMP: 50 **EST:** 1964
SQ FT: 2,800
SALES (est): 2.45MM **Privately Held**
SIC: 2789 Binding only: books, pamphlets, magazines, etc.

East Longmeadow
Hampden County

(G-8368)
ALVIN JOHNSON
Also Called: Eba
26 Maple Ct (01028-2737)
P.O. Box 108 (01028-0108)
PHONE.................................413 525-6334
Alvin Johnson, *Owner*
EMP: 8 **EST:** 1978
SQ FT: 2,800
SALES (est): 781.99K **Privately Held**
Web: www.ebametalbelts.com
SIC: 3496 3443 3599 7692 Conveyor belts; Metal parts; Machine shop, jobbing and repair; Welding repair

(G-8369)
AMERICAN SAW & MFG COMPANY INC
Also Called: Lenox
301 Chestnut St (01028-2823)
PHONE.................................413 525-3961
Stephen Davis, *Pr*
Ann Keiser, *
John Davis, *
◆ **EMP:** 218 **EST:** 1996
SALES (est): 73.64MM
SALES (corp-wide): 9.46B **Publicly Held**
Web: www.lenoxsaw.com
SIC: 3545 Machine tool accessories
PA: Newell Brands Inc.
 6655 Pachtree Dunwoody Rd
 Atlanta GA 30328
 770 418-7000

(G-8370)
ARCLIN SURFACES - E LONGMEADOW
Also Called: Arclin
82 Deer Park Dr (01028-3196)
PHONE.................................678 781-5341
Shelia Waters, *CEO*
▲ **EMP:** 18 **EST:** 1993
SALES (est): 1.83MM **Privately Held**
Web: www.arclin.com
SIC: 2672 Paper; coated and laminated, nec

(G-8371)
CARTAMUNDI EAST LONGMEADOW LLC
443 Shaker Rd (01028-3124)
PHONE.................................413 526-2000
Jeffrey Lombard, *CEO*
Eric Defilipi, *
▼ **EMP:** 400 **EST:** 2015
SQ FT: 1,200,000
SALES (est): 95.12MM
SALES (corp-wide): 2.67MM **Privately Held**
Web: www.cartamundi.com
SIC: 3944 3999 Board games, puzzles, and models, except electronic; Novelties, bric-a-brac, and hobby kits
PA: Cartamundi
 Turnovatoren 14, Internal Postal Box 1
 Turnhout 2300
 14420201

(G-8372)
COATING HOUSE INC
15 Benton Dr Ste 14 (01028-3232)
PHONE.................................413 525-3100
EMP: 14 **EST:** 1980
SALES (est): 2.5MM **Privately Held**
Web: www.thecoatinghouse.com
SIC: 5072 2891 Hardware; Adhesives and sealants

(G-8373)
DESIGNING HEALTH INC
302 Benton Dr (01028-3208)
PHONE.................................661 257-1705
Robert M Collett, *CEO*
Bernard Collett, *CEO*
Nate Armstrong, *VP*
◆ **EMP:** 19 **EST:** 1994
SQ FT: 9,000
SALES (est): 837.77K **Privately Held**
SIC: 2833 5961 2048 5499 Vitamins, natural or synthetic: bulk, uncompounded; Pharmaceuticals, mail order; Prepared feeds, nec; Health and dietetic food stores

(G-8374)
DIEBOLT & COMPANY
341 Shaker Rd (01028-3125)
P.O. Box 744 (06371-0744)
PHONE.................................860 434-2222
Mark Diebolt, *CEO*
EMP: 7
SQ FT: 30,000
Web: www.dieboltco.com
SIC: 3491 Industrial valves
PA: Diebolt & Company
 18 Riverview Dr
 Old Lyme CT 06371

(G-8375)
EXCEL DRYER INC
Also Called: Excel Dryer
357 Chestnut St (01028-2742)
P.O. Box 365 (01028-0365)
PHONE.................................413 525-4531
Denis Gagnon, *Pr*
Bruce Bohmer, *
William Gagnon, *
Nancy Gagnon, *
▲ **EMP:** 50 **EST:** 1963
SQ FT: 35,000
SALES (est): 11.3MM **Privately Held**
Web: www.exceldryer.com
SIC: 3699 Electrical equipment and supplies, nec

(G-8376)
GARELCO SALES COMPANY INC
Also Called: New England Lumber & Packaging
42 Maple Ct (01028-2737)
P.O. Box 565 (01028-0565)
PHONE.................................413 525-3316
Walter T Gunn, *Pr*
Carla G Gunn, *Sec*
EMP: 9 **EST:** 1942
SALES (est): 826.91K **Privately Held**
SIC: 2441 2449 2421 Box cleats, wood; Wood containers, nec; Lumber: rough, sawed, or planed

(G-8377)
GENSCOPE INC
18 Deer Park Dr (01028-3196)
P.O. Box 386 (01028-0386)
PHONE.................................413 526-0802
David A Reeves, *Pr*
EMP: 10 **EST:** 1992
SQ FT: 5,000
SALES (est): 917.9K **Privately Held**
Web: www.genscope.com
SIC: 3827 Optical instruments and lenses

(G-8378)
GROUP FOUR TRANSDUCERS INC (PA)
22 Deer Park Dr (01028-3196)
PHONE.................................413 525-2705
▲ **EMP:** 7 **EST:** 1994
SQ FT: 5,000
SALES (est): 5.1MM **Privately Held**
Web: www.groupfourtransducers.com
SIC: 3825 Transducers for volts, amperes, watts, vars, frequency, etc.

(G-8379)
HAMPDEN ENGINEERING CORP
99 Shaker Rd (01028-2762)
P.O. Box 563 (01028-0563)
PHONE.................................413 525-3981
TOLL FREE: 800
John M Flynn, *Pr*
John D Flynn, *
Sheila R Flynn, *CLRK*
Michael J Flynn, *
▲ **EMP:** 85 **EST:** 1954
SQ FT: 50,000
SALES (est): 21.34MM **Privately Held**
Web: www.hampden.com
SIC: 3825 Instruments to measure electricity

(G-8380)
INDUSTRIAL ETCHING INC
Also Called: Northeast Screen Graphics
21 Fisher Ave (01028-1707)
P.O. Box 304 (01028-0304)
PHONE.................................413 525-4110
Dan Major, *Pr*
Paul Major, *Stockholder*
EMP: 13 **EST:** 1958
SQ FT: 17,500
SALES (est): 926.09K **Privately Held**
Web: www.yeuell.com
SIC: 2759 3479 Screen printing; Etching on metals

(G-8381)
JOMA DIAMOND TOOL LLC
46 Baldwin St Ste A (01028-2232)
P.O. Box 68 (01028-0068)
PHONE.................................413 525-0760
John Basiliere, *Pt*
P D Crane, *Pt*
EMP: 10 **EST:** 1984

SQ FT: 2,000
SALES (est): 925.25K **Privately Held**
Web: www.jomadiamondtool.com
SIC: 3545 5085 Diamond cutting tools for turning, boring, burnishing, etc.; Industrial supplies

(G-8382)
JOY & ROBERT CROMWELL
243 Prospect St (01028-2863)
PHONE.................................413 224-1440
Joy Cromwell, *Owner*
Robert Cromwell, *Owner*
EMP: 8 **EST:** 2010
SALES (est): 175.63K **Privately Held**
SIC: 3312 Pipes and tubes

(G-8383)
LM/TARBELL INC
Also Called: Lm76 Linear Motion Bearings
140 Industrial Dr (01028-3102)
P.O. Box 1300 (01028-5300)
PHONE.................................413 525-4166
John W Tarbell, *Pr*
Lesley N Tarbell, *Sec*
◆ **EMP:** 15 **EST:** 1938
SQ FT: 22,500
SALES (est): 3.79MM **Privately Held**
Web: www.lm76.com
SIC: 5085 3568 Bearings; Bearings, bushings, and blocks

(G-8384)
LORI DONUTS INC
Also Called: Dunkin' Donuts
55 Maple St (01028-2745)
PHONE.................................413 526-9944
John Salema, *Mgr*
EMP: 20
Web: www.dunkindonuts.com
SIC: 5461 2051 Doughnuts; Bread, cake, and related products
PA: Lori Donuts, Inc.
 1918 Wilbraham Rd # 1920
 Springfield MA 01129

(G-8385)
MACKENZIE VAULT INC
165 Benton Dr (01028-3214)
P.O. Box 264 (01028-0264)
PHONE.................................413 525-8827
Neil G Mckenzie, *Pr*
EMP: 13 **EST:** 1956
SQ FT: 5,000
SALES (est): 2.09MM **Privately Held**
Web: www.mackenzievault.com
SIC: 3272 Precast terrazzo or concrete products

(G-8386)
MAYBURY ASSOCIATES INC
Also Called: Maybury Material Handling
90 Denslow Rd (01028-3160)
PHONE.................................413 525-4216
EMP: 66 **EST:** 1976
SALES (est): 20.65MM **Privately Held**
Web: www.maybury.com
SIC: 5084 3537 Materials handling machinery; Industrial trucks and tractors

(G-8387)
MCGILL HOSE & COUPLING INC (PA)
Also Called: McGill Hose
45 Industrial D (01028-3162)
P.O. Box 408 (01028-0408)
PHONE.................................413 525-3977
Harry C Mcgill, *Pr*
Alexander Mcgill, *VP*
Ainsley Mcgill, *VP*

Sharon Mcgill, *Sec*
▲ **EMP:** 30 **EST:** 1962
SQ FT: 30,000
SALES (est): 18.27MM
SALES (corp-wide): 18.27MM **Privately Held**
Web: www.mcgillhose.com
SIC: 5085 3492 Hose, belting, and packing; Fluid power valves and hose fittings

(G-8388)
NEWELL BRANDS INC
Also Called: Lenox
301 Chestnut St (01028-2742)
PHONE...............................413 526-5150
Bill Wilder, *Dir*
EMP: 11
SALES (corp-wide): 9.46B **Publicly Held**
Web: www.newellbrands.com
SIC: 3089 Plastics kitchenware, tableware, and houseware
PA: Newell Brands Inc.
6655 Pachtree Dunwoody Rd
Atlanta GA 30328
770 418-7000

(G-8389)
PRECISION FEEDING SYSTEMS INC
45 Deer Park Dr (01028-3198)
P.O. Box 630 (01036-0630)
PHONE...............................413 525-9200
Raymond C Legary, *Pr*
Raymond C Legary, *Pr*
Caroline Bayne, *Mgr*
EMP: 8 **EST:** 1986
SQ FT: 5,000
SALES (est): 950.5K **Privately Held**
SIC: 3569 Assembly machines, non-metalworking

(G-8390)
PROCESS SOLUTIONS INC
198 Benton Dr (01028-3204)
PHONE...............................413 525-5870
Carlton Nappin, *Pr*
▼ **EMP:** 7 **EST:** 1997
SALES (est): 790K **Privately Held**
Web: www.us-fluids.com
SIC: 3861 Photographic processing chemicals

(G-8391)
QUAD/GRAPHICS INC
Springfield Division
245 Benton Dr (01028-3221)
P.O. Box 328 (01028-0328)
PHONE...............................413 525-8552
Len Fitzmaurice, *Brnch Mgr*
EMP: 51
SALES (corp-wide): 3.22B **Publicly Held**
Web: www.quad.com
SIC: 2759 7331 2752 Commercial printing, nec; Direct mail advertising services; Commercial printing, lithographic
PA: Quad/Graphics, Inc.
N61w23044 Harrys Way
Sussex WI 53089
414 566-6000

(G-8392)
RDP MANUFACTURING INC
70 Maple St (01028-2744)
PHONE...............................413 525-7700
▲ **EMP:** 100
SIC: 3433 Heating equipment, except electric

(G-8393)
REMINDER PUBLICATIONS
Also Called: The Childsplay
280 N Main St Ste 1 (01028-1814)
PHONE...............................413 525-3947
Dan Buendo, *Publisher*
Dan Buendo, *Prin*
Barbara Perry, *
EMP: 41 **EST:** 1962
SQ FT: 4,500
SALES (est): 4.61MM **Privately Held**
Web: www.reminderwebdesign.com
SIC: 2711 2791 2741 Newspapers: publishing only, not printed on site; Typesetting; Miscellaneous publishing

(G-8394)
SHAFIIS INC (PA)
Also Called: Tigerpress
50 Industrial Dr (01028-3102)
P.O. Box 215 (01028-0215)
PHONE...............................413 224-2100
Jennifer R Shafii, *CEO*
Reza M Shafii, *
▲ **EMP:** 25 **EST:** 1985
SQ FT: 20,000
SALES (est): 12.41MM
SALES (corp-wide): 12.41MM **Privately Held**
Web: www.tigerpress.com
SIC: 2752 7334 Offset printing; Photocopying and duplicating services

(G-8395)
SPRINGFIELD SPRING CORPORATION (PA)
311 Shaker Rd (01028-3125)
P.O. Box 505 (01028-0505)
PHONE...............................413 525-6837
Norman L Rodriques, *Pr*
Tina Malley, *
EMP: 23 **EST:** 1942
SQ FT: 15,000
SALES (est): 5.79MM
SALES (corp-wide): 5.79MM **Privately Held**
Web: www.springfieldspring.com
SIC: 3469 3495 Stamping metal for the trade; Wire springs

(G-8396)
STREAMLINE PLASTICS CO INC
35 Industrial Dr (01028-3239)
PHONE...............................718 401-4000
Joseph Bartner, *Pr*
Stewart Bartner, *
EMP: 33 **EST:** 1939
SALES (est): 1.11MM **Privately Held**
Web: www.streamlineplasticinc.com
SIC: 3089 Injection molding of plastics

(G-8397)
SUDDEKOR LLC
82 Deer Park Dr (01028-3196)
PHONE...............................413 525-4070
Andrei Scottsman, *Brnch Mgr*
▲ **EMP:** 30
SALES (corp-wide): 246.55MM **Privately Held**
Web: www.surteco.com
SIC: 2672 Paper; coated and laminated, nec
HQ: Suddekor Llc
240 Bowles Rd
Agawam MA 01001
413 821-9000

(G-8398)
TECHNI-PRODUCTS INC
126 Industrial Dr (01028-3102)
P.O. Box 215 (01028-0215)
PHONE...............................413 525-6321
Margery Morehardt, *Pr*
Robert C Morehardt Junior, *VP*
Bruce Morehardt, *
EMP: 25 **EST:** 1962
SQ FT: 33,000
SALES (est): 494.15K **Privately Held**
Web: www.techni-products.com
SIC: 3599 3444 Machine shop, jobbing and repair; Sheet metalwork

(G-8399)
TONER PLASTICS INC
35 Industrial Dr (01028-3240)
PHONE...............................413 789-1300
Steven L Graham, *Pr*
Jean M Graham, *
◆ **EMP:** 35 **EST:** 1990
SQ FT: 120,000
SALES (est): 8.64MM **Privately Held**
Web: www.tonerplastics.com
SIC: 3089 Injection molding of plastics

(G-8400)
VOLO AERO MRO INC
21 Fisher Ave (01028-1707)
P.O. Box 955 (01028-0955)
PHONE...............................413 525-7211
Andrew Walmsley, *Pr*
EMP: 9 **EST:** 2015
SALES (est): 1.1MM **Privately Held**
Web: www.volo-aero.com
SIC: 3599 Machine shop, jobbing and repair

(G-8401)
VULCAN INDUSTRIES INC
16 Deer Park Dr (01028-3196)
P.O. Box 714 (01028-0714)
PHONE...............................413 525-8846
Jan Liao, *Pr*
Joe Reale, *VP*
▲ **EMP:** 7 **EST:** 2006
SALES (est): 607.16K **Privately Held**
Web: www.vulcan-industry.com
SIC: 3562 Casters

(G-8402)
W F YOUNG INCORPORATED (PA)
Also Called: W. F. Young
302 Benton Dr (01028-3210)
PHONE...............................800 628-9653
Tyler F Young, *Pr*
Tyler F Young, *Prin*
Jean Young, *
Adam D Raczkowski, *
◆ **EMP:** 25 **EST:** 1892
SALES (est): 11.09MM
SALES (corp-wide): 11.09MM **Privately Held**
Web: www.wfyoung.com
SIC: 2834 Liniments

East Otis
Berkshire County

(G-8403)
WILLIAMS STONE CO INC
1158 Lee Westfield Rd (01029-4538)
P.O. Box 278 (01029-0278)
PHONE...............................413 269-4544
Edwin C Williams, *Pr*
Charlotte I Williams, *
EMP: 40 **EST:** 1947
SQ FT: 50,000
SALES (est): 4.66MM **Privately Held**
Web: www.williamsstone.com

SIC: 3281 1411 3272 Curbing, granite or stone; Greenstone, dimension-quarrying; Concrete products, nec

East Sandwich
Barnstable County

(G-8404)
CRANE COMPOSITION INC
23 Ploughed Neck Rd (02537-1048)
P.O. Box 208 (02562-0208)
PHONE...............................774 338-5183
Thomas Lewis, *Pr*
Theodore D Dunn, *VP*
EMP: 9 **EST:** 1981
SALES (est): 650K **Privately Held**
SIC: 2791 Typesetting, computer controlled

(G-8405)
ROSE OFFICE CARL
8 Pinecone Dr (02537-1706)
PHONE...............................508 833-8758
Carl Rose, *Owner*
EMP: 7 **EST:** 2011
SALES (est): 79.88K **Privately Held**
SIC: 2951 Asphalt and asphaltic paving mixtures (not from refineries)

East Taunton
Bristol County

(G-8406)
BROUILLETTE HVAC & SHTMTL INC
13 Stevens St (02718-1026)
PHONE...............................508 822-4800
Donald Provencher, *Pr*
Carlton A Caron, *Sec*
EMP: 8 **EST:** 2010
SALES (est): 1.61MM **Privately Held**
Web: www.brouillettehvacinc.com
SIC: 3444 Casings, sheet metal

(G-8407)
J W FISHERS MFG INC
1953 County St (02718-1322)
PHONE...............................508 822-7330
Karen Fisher, *Pr*
Brian Fisher, *COO*
EMP: 11 **EST:** 1963
SALES (est): 1.21MM **Privately Held**
Web: www.jwfishers.com
SIC: 3812 Detection apparatus: electronic/ magnetic field, light/heat

(G-8408)
JORDANS FURNITURE INC (HQ)
450 Revolutionary Dr (02718-1369)
PHONE...............................508 828-4000
Eliot Tatelman, *CEO*
David Stavros, *CFO*
Peter Bolton, *COO*
Joshua Tatelman, *Sec*
Steve Wholley, *Sec*
◆ **EMP:** 600 **EST:** 1918
SQ FT: 800,000
SALES (est): 255.49MM
SALES (corp-wide): 302.09B **Publicly Held**
Web: www.jordans.com
SIC: 5712 2511 5021 Mattresses; Wood bedroom furniture; Dining room furniture
PA: Berkshire Hathaway Inc.
3555 Farnam St Ste 1440
Omaha NE 68131
402 346-1400

▲ = Import ▼ = Export
◆ = Import/Export

(G-8409)
NORWELL MFG CO INC
82 Stevens St (02061-1398)
PHONE.................................508 822-2831
Alan Indursky, *Pr*
Ruth Parr, *
▲ **EMP:** 42 **EST:** 1947
SQ FT: 72,000
SALES (est): 9.06MM **Privately Held**
SIC: 3646 Commercial lighting fixtures

(G-8410)
PANCON CORPORATION (PA)
350 Revolutionary Dr (02718-1368)
PHONE.................................781 297-6000
Mike Kirkman, *CEO*
Ronald Levine, *
▲ **EMP:** 151 **EST:** 2011
SALES (est): 27.84MM
SALES (corp-wide): 27.84MM **Privately
Held**
Web: www.panconcorp.com
SIC: 3613 Switchgear and switchboard
apparatus

(G-8411)
**READERS HARDWOOD SUPPLY
LLC**
250 Cape Hwy Ste 9 (02718-1580)
PHONE.................................508 301-3206
EMP: 10 **EST:** 2020
SALES (est): 679.25K **Privately Held**
Web: www.readershardwoodsupply.com
SIC: 2435 Plywood, hardwood or hardwood
faced

(G-8412)
**SAINT-GOBAIN PRFMCE PLAS
CORP**
250 Revolutionary Dr (02718-1392)
PHONE.................................508 823-7701
EMP: 65
SALES (corp-wide): 397.78MM **Privately
Held**
Web: www.saint-gobain.com
SIC: 3089 Injection molding of plastics
HQ: Saint-Gobain Performance Plastics
Corporation
20 Moores Rd
Malvern PA 19355
440 836-6900

(G-8413)
STRAFELLO PRECAST INC
250 Cape Hwy (02718-1552)
PHONE.................................774 501-2628
EMP: 41
SALES (corp-wide): 224.96K **Privately
Held**
SIC: 3272 Precast terrazzo or concrete
products
PA: Strafello Precast Inc
601 Pleasant St
Stoughton MA

East Templeton
Worcester County

(G-8414)
RAGGED HILL INCORPORATED
Also Called: Graves Concrete
147 Gardner Rd (01438)
P.O. Box 680 (01438-0680)
PHONE.................................978 939-5712
John Fletcher, *Pr*
James Fletcher, *
EMP: 29 **EST:** 1997
SALES (est): 4.96MM **Privately Held**

Web: www.gravesconcrete.com
SIC: 3273 Ready-mixed concrete

(G-8415)
TRELLIS STRUCTURES INC
25 N Main St (01438)
PHONE.................................888 285-4624
David Valcovic, *Pr*
David Valcovic, *Pt*
Patricia Cornell, *Pt*
EMP: 24 **EST:** 1995
SQ FT: 2,500
SALES (est): 770.04K **Privately Held**
Web: www.trellisstructures.com
SIC: 2431 Exterior and ornamental
woodwork and trim

(G-8416)
WJ GRAVES CNSTR CO INC (PA)
192 Depot Rd (01438-1201)
P.O. Box 401 (01438-0401)
PHONE.................................978 939-5568
John L Fletcher, *Pr*
James L Fletcher, *
EMP: 25 **EST:** 1929
SQ FT: 1,056
SALES (est): 9.81MM
SALES (corp-wide): 9.81MM **Privately
Held**
Web: www.wjgraves.com
SIC: 5032 1442 Sand, construction;
Construction sand and gravel

East Walpole
Norfolk County

(G-8417)
**COMMERCIAL GEAR
SPROCKET INC**
618 Washington St (02032-1300)
PHONE.................................508 668-1073
Thomas Shaw, *Pr*
Margaret A Shaw, *Clerk*
EMP: 21 **EST:** 1946
SQ FT: 7,500
SALES (est): 2.01MM **Privately Held**
Web: www.commercialgear.com
SIC: 3566 Gears, power transmission,
except auto

(G-8418)
**HOLLINGSWORTH & VOSE
COMPANY (PA)**
Also Called: H&V
112 Washington St (02032-1098)
PHONE.................................508 850-2000
Josh Ayer, *CEO*
Valentine Hollingsworth Iii, *Ch*
James Noonan, *
◆ **EMP:** 250 **EST:** 1728
SQ FT: 125,000
SALES (est): 584.59MM
SALES (corp-wide): 584.59MM **Privately
Held**
Web: www.hollingsworth-vose.com
SIC: 2621 3053 2297 2499 Filter paper;
Gasket materials; Nonwoven fabrics;
Battery separators, wood

(G-8419)
**HUMAN SYSTEMS
INTEGRATION INC**
153 Washington St Ste 4 (02032-1163)
PHONE.................................508 660-2500
Brian Farrell, *Pr*
David Mcdonad, *Dir Opers*
EMP: 19 **EST:** 2014
SALES (est): 2.58MM **Privately Held**

Web:
www.humansystemsintegration.com
SIC: 3829 Measuring and controlling
devices, nec

(G-8420)
PEGGY LAWTON KITCHENS INC
255 Washington St (02032-1199)
P.O. Box 33 (02032-0033)
PHONE.................................508 668-1215
William Wolf, *Pr*
EMP: 16 **EST:** 1949
SQ FT: 30,000
SALES (est): 1.18MM **Privately Held**
Web: www.plkitchens.com
SIC: 2052 Cookies

(G-8421)
PRIMROSE MEDICAL INC
286 Union St (02032-1037)
PHONE.................................508 660-8688
Fletcher T Longley, *Pr*
Tom Kottelles, *Mgr*
▲ **EMP:** 10 **EST:** 1983
SQ FT: 4,000
SALES (est): 824.48K **Privately Held**
Web: www.primrosemedical.com
SIC: 3841 Surgical and medical instruments

East Wareham
Plymouth County

(G-8422)
FIRESLATE 2 INC
3065 Cranberry Hwy A24 (02538-1325)
P.O. Box 431 (02532-0431)
PHONE.................................508 273-0047
Thomas B Worthen, *Pr*
EMP: 11 **EST:** 1983
SQ FT: 9,000
SALES (est): 293.15K **Privately Held**
SIC: 3272 Concrete products, nec

East Weymouth
Norfolk County

(G-8423)
ADVANCED FRP SYSTEMS INC
20 Mathewson Dr (02189-2346)
PHONE.................................508 927-6915
Russell Esker Giudici, *Pr*
Peter Krukiel, *Dir*
EMP: 7 **EST:** 2015
SALES (est): 900K **Privately Held**
Web: www.advancedfrpsystems.com
SIC: 2822 5198 Ethylene-propylene
rubbers, EPDM polymers; Paints,
varnishes, and supplies

(G-8424)
ALMONT COMPANY INC
Also Called: Boxerbrand
293 Libbey Industrial Pkwy Ste 500
(02189-3112)
PHONE.................................617 269-8244
David E Salk, *Pr*
◆ **EMP:** 24 **EST:** 1985
SALES (est): 4.76MM **Privately Held**
Web: www.boxerbrand.com
SIC: 2392 Bags, laundry: made from
purchased materials

(G-8425)
B G WICKBERG COMPANY INC
30 Woodrock Rd (02189-2336)
PHONE.................................781 335-7800
John Murch, *Pr*

Irene Murch, *Treas*
EMP: 7 **EST:** 1930
SQ FT: 10,000
SALES (est): 441.08K **Privately Held**
Web: www.bgwickberg.com
SIC: 7699 3564 Industrial equipment
services; Purification and dust collection
equipment

(G-8426)
**BATES BROS SEAM-FACE
GRAN CO**
611 Pleasant St (02189-3201)
PHONE.................................781 337-1150
James Bristol, *CEO*
Mary Bristol, *Sec*
EMP: 19 **EST:** 1920
SQ FT: 15,000
SALES (est): 901.26K **Privately Held**
Web: www.jfpriceco.com
SIC: 3281 Stone, quarrying and processing
of own stone products

(G-8427)
BRADY ENTERPRISES INC (PA)
Also Called: Bell's Foods
167 Moore Rd (02189-2332)
P.O. Box 890099 (02189-0002)
PHONE.................................781 340-4571
Kevin Maguire, *Pr*
Mary A Gudolawicz, *Treas*
John J Brady, *Ch Bd*
▲ **EMP:** 80 **EST:** 1964
SQ FT: 160,000
SALES (est): 28.61MM
SALES (corp-wide): 28.61MM **Privately
Held**
Web: www.bradyenterprises.com
SIC: 2099 2087 2842 Seasonings and
spices; Cocktail mixes, nonalcoholic;
Cleaning or polishing preparations, nec

(G-8428)
**CAPITAL INDUSTRIES
CORPORATION**
200 Libbey Industrial Pkwy (02189-3102)
PHONE.................................781 337-9807
Daniel P Buonagurio Junior, *Pr*
Daniel J Murphy, *VP*
EMP: 13 **EST:** 1989
SALES (est): 425.15K **Privately Held**
SIC: 4212 2611 Garbage collection and
transport, no disposal; Pulp mills

(G-8429)
**INDUSTRIAL WOODWORKING
CO INC**
Also Called: Camio Kitchens
143 Moore Rd (02189-2332)
PHONE.................................781 340-7474
Donald Constantino, *Pr*
Robert Constantino, *VP*
EMP: 10 **EST:** 1946
SQ FT: 20,000
SALES (est): 756.35K **Privately Held**
SIC: 2434 Wood kitchen cabinets

(G-8430)
JOHN J CAHILL DISPLAYS INC
293 Libbey Industrial Pkwy (02189-3112)
PHONE.................................617 737-3232
EMP: 9 **EST:** 2016
SALES (est): 189.89K **Privately Held**
Web: www.cahilldisplay.com
SIC: 3993 Signs and advertising specialties

(G-8431)
KENNEDY SHEET METAL INC
1319 Pleasant St (02189-2797)

PHONE..................781 331-7764
James B Kennedy Junior, *Pr*
James B Kennedy Senior, *Pr*
EMP: 14 EST: 1981
SQ FT: 9,000
SALES (est): 972.76K **Privately Held**
SIC: 3444 1711   Sheet metalwork; Plumbing, heating, air-conditioning

(G-8432)
LDG CORPORATION
Also Called: Unique Woodworking
143 Moore Rd (02189-2332)
PHONE..................781 337-7155
EMP: 7 EST: 1995
SQ FT: 5,000
SALES (est): 983.84K **Privately Held**
SIC: 2522   Cabinets, office: except wood

(G-8433)
S M LORUSSO & SONS INC
Also Called: Lorusso-Bristol Stone
611 Pleasant St (02189-3201)
P.O. Box 890144 (02189-0003)
PHONE..................781 337-6770
Bob Bedard, *Mgr*
EMP: 21
SQ FT: 1,991
SALES (corp-wide): 22.19MM **Privately Held**
SIC: 1422   Crushed and broken limestone
PA: S. M. Lorusso & Sons, Inc.
   331 West St
   Walpole MA 02081
   508 668-2600

Eastham
Barnstable County

(G-8434)
HOLE IN ONE
Also Called: Hole In One Donut Shop
4295 Us-6 (02642)
P.O. Box 854 (02651-0854)
PHONE..................508 255-5359
Cindy Bazzano, *Prin*
Gaetano Bazzano, *
EMP: 11 EST: 1989
SQ FT: 5,933
SALES (est): 444.49K **Privately Held**
Web: www.theholecapecod.com
SIC: 2051 5461 5812   Bakery: wholesale or wholesale/retail combined; Doughnuts; Italian restaurant

(G-8435)
RICHARD GAUDREAU ENGRAVING
County Rd (02642)
P.O. Box 354 (02642-0354)
PHONE..................508 240-2940
Richard Gaudreau, *Owner*
EMP: 7 EST: 2002
SALES (est): 114.85K **Privately Held**
SIC: 3479   Metal coating and allied services

(G-8436)
WELLFLEET SHELLFISH CO INC
Also Called: MACS SEAFOOD
137 Holmes Rd (02642-2183)
P.O. Box 1768 (02667-1768)
PHONE..................508 255-5300
Alexander Hay, *Pr*
Macgregor B Hay, *
Samuel Bradford, *
Alexander B Hay, *
EMP: 25 EST: 2006
SALES (est): 457.28K **Privately Held**

Web: www.macsseafood.com
SIC: 2091   Seafood products: packaged in cans, jars, etc.

Easthampton
Hampshire County

(G-8437)
ADHESIVE APPLICATIONS INC (PA)
Also Called: Stik-II Products
41 Oneil St (01027-1103)
P.O. Box 71 (01027-0071)
PHONE..................413 527-7120
Michael Schaefer, *Pr*
Michael Schaefer, *Pr*
Wayne Tangel, *Pr*
▲ **EMP: 45 EST:** 2000
SQ FT: 40,000
SALES (est): 17.62MM **Privately Held**
Web: www.adhesiveapps.com
SIC: 2891   Adhesives

(G-8438)
ADHESIVE TAPES INTL INC
41 Oneil St (01027-1103)
PHONE..................203 792-8279
Dieter Woll, *Pr*
Fred Macaluso, *Treas*
◆ **EMP: 8 EST:** 1987
SALES (est): 762.74K **Privately Held**
SIC: 3842   Adhesive tape and plasters, medicated or non-medicated

(G-8439)
BERRY GLOBAL INC
44 Oneil St (01027-1146)
PHONE..................812 424-2904
EMP: 47
SIC: 3089   Plastics containers, except foam
HQ: Berry Global, Inc.
   101 Oakley St
   Evansville IN 47710

(G-8440)
BERRY PLASTICS CORP
122 Pleasant St (01027-1358)
P.O. Box 567 (01027-0567)
PHONE..................413 529-2183
▲ **EMP: 196 EST:** 2009
SALES (est): 1MM **Privately Held**
SIC: 3089   Plastics containers, except foam

(G-8441)
CHILSONS SHOPS INC
Also Called: Pioneer Shade & Awning
8 Industrial Pkwy (01027-1164)
PHONE..................413 529-8062
TOLL FREE: 800
Edward A Ghareeb, *Pr*
Ernest Ghareeb, *Treas*
David Ghareeb, *VP*
EMP: 20 EST: 1962
SQ FT: 10,000
SALES (est): 2.46MM **Privately Held**
Web: www.chilsonspioneer.com
SIC: 5719 1799 2211   Window furnishings; Drapery track installation; Canvas

(G-8442)
DAILY HAMPSHIRE GAZETTE
72 Main St (01027-2049)
PHONE..................413 527-4000
Louis Groccia, *Pr*
EMP: 7 EST: 2013
SALES (est): 85.18K **Privately Held**
Web: www.gazettenet.com

SIC: 2711   Newspapers, publishing and printing

(G-8443)
DZI
150 Pleasant St Ste 320 (01027-1547)
PHONE..................413 527-4500
Mac Coy, *Prin*
▲ **EMP: 10 EST:** 1999
SALES (est): 891.94K **Privately Held**
Web: www.dzi.com
SIC: 3621   Generators and sets, electric

(G-8444)
EASTHAMPTON MACHINE & TOOL INC
72 Parsons St (01027-1550)
PHONE..................413 527-8770
Christopher Heon, *Pr*
EMP: 9 EST: 1987
SQ FT: 5,000
SALES (est): 907K **Privately Held**
Web: www.easthamptonmachine.com
SIC: 3599   Machine shop, jobbing and repair

(G-8445)
EASTHAMPTON PRECISION MFG
16 Arthur St (01027-1202)
PHONE..................413 527-1650
Jeremy Segal, *Pr*
EMP: 8 EST: 1989
SQ FT: 12,200
SALES (est): 986.98K **Privately Held**
SIC: 3599   Machine shop, jobbing and repair

(G-8446)
GAZETTE PRINTING CO INC
58 Oneil St (01027-1157)
PHONE..................413 527-7700
Mark Goodwyn, *Pr*
EMP: 14 EST: 1874
SQ FT: 8,500
SALES (est): 1.02MM **Privately Held**
Web: www.gazetteprintingcompany.com
SIC: 2752 2759   Offset printing; Letterpress printing

(G-8447)
INFLIGHT CORPORATION
1 Cottage St Unit 39 (01027-1615)
PHONE..................800 853-7505
James La Brash, *Pr*
John Bonin, *Dir*
EMP: 10 EST: 2013
SALES (est): 3.18MM **Privately Held**
Web: www.skuid.com
SIC: 7372   Business oriented computer software
HQ: Skuid, Inc.
   110 Somerville Ave
   Chattanooga TN 37405
   800 515-2535

(G-8448)
JPS ELASTOMERICS CORP
Also Called: Stevens Urethane
412 Main St (01027-1918)
PHONE..................413 779-1200
▲ **EMP:** 145
SIC: 3069   Roofing, membrane rubber

(G-8449)
MACHINEMETRICS INC
116 Pleasant St (01027-2756)
PHONE..................413 341-5747
EMP: 48 EST: 2014
SALES (est): 8.88MM **Privately Held**
Web: www.machinemetrics.com

SIC: 7372   Prepackaged software

(G-8450)
MICHAEL BRISEBOIS
Also Called: Mountainbase Mold & Mfg
6 Industrial Pkwy (01027-1164)
PHONE..................413 527-9590
Michael P Brisebois, *Owner*
EMP: 12 EST: 1996
SQ FT: 3,000
SALES (est): 1.6MM **Privately Held**
SIC: 3545   Tools and accessories for machine tools

(G-8451)
MOUNTAIN BASE MFG LLC
180 Pleasant St Ste 1 (01027-1297)
PHONE..................413 527-9590
Michael P Brisebois, *Prin*
EMP: 9 EST: 2015
SALES (est): 474.57K **Privately Held**
Web: www.mbmmach.com
SIC: 3999   Manufacturing industries, nec

(G-8452)
NATIONAL NONWOVENS INC
180 Pleasant St (01027-1287)
PHONE..................413 527-3445
EMP: 25
SALES (corp-wide): 25.47MM **Privately Held**
Web: www.nationalnonwovens.com
SIC: 2231 2297   Felts, woven: wool, mohair, or similar fibers; Nonwoven fabrics
PA: National Nonwovens Inc.
   110 Pleasant St
   Easthampton MA 01027
   413 527-3445

(G-8453)
NATIONAL NONWOVENS INC (PA)
110 Pleasant St (01027-1342)
P.O. Box 150 (01027-0150)
PHONE..................413 527-3445
Anthony J Centofanti, *Ch Bd*
◆ **EMP: 75 EST:** 1905
SQ FT: 115,000
SALES (est): 25.47MM
SALES (corp-wide): 25.47MM **Privately Held**
Web: www.nationalnonwovens.com
SIC: 2231 2297   Felts, woven: wool, mohair, or similar fibers; Nonwoven fabrics

(G-8454)
NATIONAL NONWOVENS INC
Also Called: Wool Felt Division
27 Mechanic St (01027-1561)
PHONE..................413 527-3445
Ken Piazzo, *Brnch Mgr*
EMP: 25
SALES (corp-wide): 25.47MM **Privately Held**
Web: www.nationalnonwovens.com
SIC: 2299   Felts and felt products
PA: National Nonwovens Inc.
   110 Pleasant St
   Easthampton MA 01027
   413 527-3445

(G-8455)
NORTHAMPTON MACHINE CO INC
Also Called: Baystate Machine Co.
16 Industrial Pkwy (01027-1164)
PHONE..................413 529-2530
Frank Basile, *Pr*
Colleen Basile, *Clerk*

EMP: 22 **EST:** 1975
SQ FT: 10,800
SALES (est): 2.35MM **Privately Held**
Web: www.baystatemachine.com
SIC: 3599 Machine shop, jobbing and repair

(G-8456)
OCTOBER COMPANY INC (PA)
Also Called: Chemetal Division
51 Ferry St (01027-1235)
P.O. Box 71 (01027-0071)
PHONE..............................413 527-9380
Michael Schaefer, *Pr*
David J Podolski, *
Leslie P Schaefer, *Prin*
James Thompson, *
Geoffrey Schaefer, *
▲ **EMP:** 89 **EST:** 1959
SQ FT: 150,000
SALES (est): 21.45MM
SALES (corp-wide): 21.45MM **Privately
Held**
Web: www.octobercompany.com
SIC: 3499 2599 Furniture parts, metal;
Factory furniture and fixtures

(G-8457)
OCTOBER COMPANY INC
Also Called: Chemetal Division
39 Oneil St (01027-1103)
PHONE..............................413 529-0718
EMP: 40
SQ FT: 45,000
SALES (corp-wide): 21.45MM **Privately
Held**
Web: www.octobercompany.com
SIC: 3499 3083 Furniture parts, metal;
Laminated plastics plate and sheet
PA: The October Company Inc
51 Ferry St
Easthampton MA 01027
413 527-9380

(G-8458)
OVERLOOK INDUSTRIES INC
193 Northampton St Ste 2 (01027-1080)
P.O. Box 869 (01027-0869)
PHONE..............................413 527-4344
EMP: 24 **EST:** 1992
SQ FT: 10,000
SALES (est): 2.72MM **Privately Held**
Web: www.ovlk.com
SIC: 3559 Pharmaceutical machinery

(G-8459)
**PHILIPP MANUFACTURING
COMPANY**
19 Ward Ave (01027-2214)
PHONE..............................413 527-4444
Herman R Tauscher, *Pr*
Herman R Tauscher, *Pr*
Elwood W Beebe, *
EMP: 31 **EST:** 1875
SQ FT: 50,000
SALES (est): 1.69MM **Privately Held**
Web: www.philipp-mfg.com
SIC: 3442 Metal doors

(G-8460)
REISER CREATIONS
222 Loudville Rd (01027-9741)
PHONE..............................508 259-5794
EMP: 7 **EST:** 2014
SALES (est): 59.38K **Privately Held**
SIC: 3556 Food products machinery

(G-8461)
ROCK VALLEY TOOL LLC
54 Oneil St (01027-1169)
PHONE..............................413 527-2350

Elizabeth Paquette, *
EMP: 34 **EST:** 1949
SQ FT: 20,000
SALES (est): 4.76MM **Privately Held**
Web: www.rockvalleytool.com
SIC: 3599 Machine shop, jobbing and repair

(G-8462)
SET AMERICAS INC
Also Called: Set Americas
180 Pleasant St Ste 207 (01027-1356)
PHONE..............................413 203-6130
Christopher Bakker, *CEO*
EMP: 7 **EST:** 2018
SALES (est): 1MM **Privately Held**
Web: www.smart-e-tech.us
SIC: 3823 Process control instruments

(G-8463)
TECH180 CORP
Also Called: Tech180 System
180 Pleasant St Ste 211 (01027-1356)
PHONE..............................413 203-6123
Roy Walker, *Prin*
Christopher Bakker, *CEO*
Sarah Robinson, *Admn*
Burt Snober, *Prin*
EMP: 10 **EST:** 2018
SALES (est): 500K **Privately Held**
Web: www.tech180.us
SIC: 3825 5049 5999 Test equipment for
electronic and electric measurement; Bank
equipment and supplies; Electronic parts
and equipment

(G-8464)
YANKEE HILL MACHINE CO INC
412 Main St (01027-1918)
PHONE..............................413 584-1400
James J Graham, *Pr*
Bonita Graham, *
EMP: 85 **EST:** 1951
SQ FT: 38,000
SALES (est): 7.64MM **Privately Held**
Web: www.yhm.net
SIC: 3451 Screw machine products

Edgartown
Dukes County

(G-8465)
**BAD MARTHA FARMERS
BREWERY LLC**
270 Upper Main St (02539-5932)
PHONE..............................978 335-9879
EMP: 14 **EST:** 2013
SALES (est): 118.66K **Privately Held**
Web: www.badmarthabeer.com
SIC: 5813 2082 Bars and lounges; Beer
(alcoholic beverage)

(G-8466)
**INNOVATIVE PUBLISHING
COMPANY**
91 Litchfield Rd (02539-4317)
P.O. Box 980 (02539-0980)
PHONE..............................267 266-8876
Rick Biros, *Managing Member*
EMP: 10 **EST:** 2009
SALES (est): 920.56K **Privately Held**
Web: www.foodsafetytech.com
SIC: 2741 8742 7389 Miscellaneous
publishing; Business planning and
organizing services; Business services, nec

(G-8467)
MICROTRONIC INC
5 Peases Point Rd (02539-7805)
P.O. Box 3359 (02539-3359)
PHONE..............................508 627-8951
Reiner Fenske, *Pr*
EMP: 25 **EST:** 1995
SALES (est): 1.83MM **Privately Held**
Web: www.microtronic.com
SIC: 3674 Semiconductors and related
devices

(G-8468)
VINEYARD GAZETTE LLC (PA)
34 S Summer St (02539-8104)
P.O. Box 66 (02539-0066)
PHONE..............................508 627-4311
Jane Seagraee, *Prin*
EMP: 27 **EST:** 1846
SQ FT: 15,000
SALES (est): 4.67MM
SALES (corp-wide): 4.67MM **Privately
Held**
Web: www.vineyardgazette.com
SIC: 2711 2731 Commercial printing and
newspaper publishing combined; Book
publishing

Erving
Franklin County

(G-8469)
ERVING INDUSTRIES INC (PA)
Also Called: Erving Paper Mills
97 E Main St (01344-9717)
PHONE..............................413 422-2700
Charles B Housen, *Ch Bd*
Morris Housen, *
Marjorie G Housen, *
William Wescott, *
▼ **EMP:** 62 **EST:** 1905
SQ FT: 250,000
SALES (est): 56.62MM
SALES (corp-wide): 56.62MM **Privately
Held**
Web: www.ervingpaper.com
SIC: 2621 2676 Napkin stock, paper;
Sanitary paper products

(G-8470)
ERVING PAPER MILLS INC
97 E Main St (01344-9717)
PHONE..............................413 422-2700
Morris Housen, *Pr*
Charles B Housen, *Ch Bd*
Denis L Emmett, *Treas*
▼ **EMP:** 125 **EST:** 1993
SQ FT: 300,000
SALES (est): 54.5MM
SALES (corp-wide): 56.62MM **Privately
Held**
Web: www.ervingpapermill.com
SIC: 2621 Paper mills
PA: Erving Industries, Inc.
97 E Main St
Erving MA 01344
413 422-2700

(G-8471)
RENOVATORS SUPPLY INC
Also Called: Rensup.com, Old Mill Marketing
1 River St (01344-8903)
PHONE..............................413 423-3300
Claude Jeanloz, *Pr*
◆ **EMP:** 38 **EST:** 1978
SQ FT: 300,000
SALES (est): 4.37MM **Privately Held**
Web: www.rensup.com

SIC: 3429 3645 3646 3432 Builders'
hardware; Residential lighting fixtures;
Commercial lighting fixtures; Plumbing
fixture fittings and trim

Essex
Essex County

(G-8472)
ATLANTIC INDUSTRIAL MODEL
197 Western Ave (01929-1115)
PHONE..............................978 768-4568
EMP: 7 **EST:** 2018
SALES (est): 244.88K **Privately Held**
Web: www.atlanticind.com
SIC: 3599 Machine shop, jobbing and repair

(G-8473)
**ATLANTIC INDUSTRIAL
MODELS LLC**
7 Essex Park Rd (01929-1125)
PHONE..............................978 768-7686
EMP: 22 **EST:** 1980
SQ FT: 5,000
SALES (est): 6.8MM **Privately Held**
Web: www.atlanticind.com
SIC: 3999 3443 Models, general, except toy
; Metal parts

(G-8474)
COLLINS MANUFACTURING INC
239 Western Ave (01929-1189)
PHONE..............................978 768-2553
Robert J Collins, *Pr*
Eleanor A Collins, *Treas*
Kevin T Collins, *Rgnl Mgr*
EMP: 13 **EST:** 1978
SQ FT: 11,000
SALES (est): 2.01MM **Privately Held**
Web: www.collinscnc.com
SIC: 3599 Machine shop, jobbing and repair

(G-8475)
JETO ENGINEERING INC
191 Western Ave (01929-1115)
PHONE..............................978 768-6472
Thomas M Weinburg, *Pr*
▲ **EMP:** 20 **EST:** 1985
SQ FT: 1,600
SALES (est): 746.76K **Privately Held**
Web: www.jetoeng.com
SIC: 3599 Machine shop, jobbing and repair

(G-8476)
JUNGLE INC (PA)
6 Dodge St (01929-1337)
PHONE..............................978 356-7722
▼ **EMP:** 18 **EST:** 1988
SALES (est): 2.39MM
SALES (corp-wide): 2.39MM **Privately
Held**
Web: www.junglestuff.com
SIC: 2759 2395 2754 2393 Screen printing;
Embroidery and art needlework;
Promotional printing, gravure; Canvas bags

(G-8477)
MARBLEHEAD ENGINEERING
7 Essex Park Rd (01929-1125)
PHONE..............................978 432-1386
David Gardner, *Owner*
EMP: 12 **EST:** 1985
SQ FT: 4,800
SALES (est): 473K **Privately Held**
SIC: 3449 8711 7692 3444 Miscellaneous
metalwork; Engineering services; Welding
repair; Sheet metalwork

(G-8478)
MEZZANINE SAFETI-GATES INC
Also Called: Roly Safeti-Gate
174 Western Ave (01929-1110)
PHONE....................978 768-3000
James M Conway, Pr
Aaron Conway, VP
EMP: 7 EST: 1984
SQ FT: 4,500
SALES (est): 820.26K Privately Held
Web: www.mezzgate.com
SIC: 3446 5084 Gates, ornamental metal;
Safety equipment

(G-8479)
QUINN BROS OF ESSEX INC
Also Called: Quinn Brothers
239 Western Ave Ste 1 (01929-1102)
PHONE....................978 768-6929
John Edward Coughlin, Pr
Joseph Paul Coughlin, *
Priscilla M Coughlin, *
EMP: 35 EST: 1994
SQ FT: 80,000
SALES (est): 9.59MM Privately Held
SIC: 1791 3446 3441 Structural steel
erection; Ornamental metalwork;
Fabricated structural metal

(G-8480)
**STEPHEN TERHUNE
WOODWORKING IN**
106 Western Ave (01929-1177)
PHONE....................978 768-0106
William T Carpenter Iii, Pr
EMP: 9 EST: 2005
SALES (est): 203.22K Privately Held
Web: www.stephenterhune.com
SIC: 2431 Millwork

Everett
Middlesex County

(G-8481)
ACS GROUP INC
27 Carter St (02149-2501)
PHONE....................617 381-0822
Mucio M Aquino, Prin
EMP: 25 EST: 2008
SALES (est): 2.4MM Privately Held
Web: www.acsgroupinc.com
SIC: 3621 Electric motor and generator
auxiliary parts

(G-8482)
AP IRON DESIGN INC
40 Crescent St (02149-4636)
PHONE....................617 389-0001
Anthony Pescara, Pr
EMP: 7 EST: 2002
SQ FT: 3,500
SALES (est): 853.27K Privately Held
Web: www.apirondesign.com
SIC: 3446 Architectural metalwork

(G-8483)
BOSTONIAN BODY INC
151 Bow St (02149-3332)
PHONE....................617 944-0985
David Hughes, Pr
David Celata, VP
EMP: 13 EST: 1983
SQ FT: 9,000
SALES (est): 1.96MM Privately Held
Web: www.bostonianbody.com
SIC: 3713 5012 Truck bodies and parts;
Truck bodies

(G-8484)
CUMAR INC
Also Called: Cumar Marble and Granite
69 Norman St Ste 4 (02149-1946)
PHONE....................617 389-7818
TOLL FREE: 800
Angelo Cubi, Pr
◆ EMP: 27 EST: 1992
SQ FT: 25,000
SALES (est): 8.32MM Privately Held
Web: www.cumar.com
SIC: 5032 5999 3281 1411 Marble building
stone; Monuments and tombstones; Cut
stone and stone products; Dimension stone

(G-8485)
DAMPNEY COMPANY INC
85 Paris St (02149-4411)
PHONE....................617 389-2805
Raymond K Pavlik, Pr
Peter Barrett, *
EMP: 25 EST: 1917
SQ FT: 43,000
SALES (est): 9.8MM Privately Held
Web: www.dampney.com
SIC: 2851 Marine paints

(G-8486)
**DATASITE GLOBAL
CORPORATION**
Also Called: Merrill/Daniels
40 Commercial St (02149-5507)
P.O. Box 9171 (02150)
PHONE....................617 389-7900
Ray Goodwin, Prin
EMP: 275
SALES (corp-wide): 463.52MM Privately
Held
Web: www.datasite.com
SIC: 2752 2789 Offset printing; Bookbinding
and related work
PA: Datasite Global Corporation
733 Marquette Ave Ste 600
Minneapolis MN 55402
651 632-4000

(G-8487)
**DUNCAN GALVANIZING
CORPORATION**
Also Called: Hi-Tech Plating
69 Norman St Ste 2 (02149-1946)
PHONE....................617 389-8440
TOLL FREE: 800
Richard L Brooks, Ch Bd
Abby Brooks, Pr
Dan Bever, CFO
EMP: 56 EST: 1912
SQ FT: 62,000
SALES (est): 9.77MM Privately Held
Web: www.duncangalvanizing.com
SIC: 3479 Coating of metals and formed
products

(G-8488)
EVERETT ALUMINUM INC
10 Everett Ave (02149-5902)
PHONE....................617 389-3839
Peter Conti, Pr
Lillian Conti, Clerk
Robert Conti, Dir
EMP: 11 EST: 1957
SALES (est): 796.04K Privately Held
Web: www.everettaluminum.com
SIC: 1761 5211 3444 3442 Siding contractor
; Doors, storm: wood or metal; Sheet
metalwork; Metal doors, sash, and trim

(G-8489)
L & M MACHINE INC
115 Tremont St (02149-1132)
PHONE....................617 294-0378
Ann H Moran, Pr
Richard C Moran, Sec
EMP: 14 EST: 1957
SQ FT: 15,000
SALES (est): 400.09K Privately Held
SIC: 3599 Machine shop, jobbing and repair

(G-8490)
**LILLYS GSTRONOMIA ITALIANA
INC**
Also Called: Lilly's Fresh Pasta
208 Main St (02149-5736)
PHONE....................617 387-9666
Pasqualina D'alelio, Pr
Antonio D'alelio, VP
▲ EMP: 11 EST: 1986
SQ FT: 3,000
SALES (est): 2.56MM Privately Held
Web: www.lillysfreshpasta.com
SIC: 2099 Food preparations, nec

(G-8491)
LIMA FREDY
Also Called: Boston Iron Works
128 Spring St (02149-4505)
PHONE....................781 599-3055
Fredy Lima, Owner
Daniel Dennis, Prin
EMP: 10 EST: 2009
SALES (est): 965.21K Privately Held
Web: www.bostonironworks.com
SIC: 7692 Welding repair

(G-8492)
**M & M GARMENT
MANUFACTURING**
167 Bow St Ste 2 (02149-3339)
PHONE....................617 389-7787
Kim M Phung, Pr
EMP: 7 EST: 1997
SALES (est): 143.38K Privately Held
SIC: 2339 2329 Sportswear, women's;
Men's and boys' sportswear and athletic
clothing

(G-8493)
MARIOS OIL CORP
22 Forest Ave (02149-2622)
P.O. Box 490216 (02149-0009)
PHONE....................617 202-8259
EMP: 9 EST: 2009
SQ FT: 11,000
SALES (est): 592.81K Privately Held
Web: www.mariosoil.com
SIC: 3433 Heaters, swimming pool: oil or
gas

(G-8494)
**MARKET FORGE INDUSTRIES
INC**
35 Garvey St (02149-4403)
PHONE....................617 387-4100
EMP: 8 EST: 2019
SALES (est): 442.75K Privately Held
Web: www.crownsteamgroup.com
SIC: 3999 Manufacturing industries, nec

(G-8495)
**MCLAUGHLIN UPHOLSTERING
CO INC**
1813 Revere Beach Pkwy (02149-5912)
PHONE....................617 389-0761
Kevin Mclaughlin, Pr
EMP: 12 EST: 1889

SQ FT: 16,000
SALES (est): 424.81K Privately Held
Web: www.mclaughlinupholstering.com
SIC: 7641 2512 Furniture upholstery repair;
Upholstered household furniture

(G-8496)
**MUNIZ CUSTOM WOODWORK
INC**
165 Chelsea St (02149-4631)
PHONE....................617 970-3430
Luiz Muniz, Prin
EMP: 7 EST: 2012
SALES (est): 141.27K Privately Held
Web: www.munizcustomwoodwork.com
SIC: 2431 Millwork

(G-8497)
RELIABLE FABRICS INC
Also Called: House of Kobrin
29 Henderson St (02149-2610)
PHONE....................617 387-5321
Charles Schultz, Pr
EMP: 15 EST: 1928
SQ FT: 15,000
SALES (est): 477.26K Privately Held
Web: www.reliablefabrics.com
SIC: 2391 5714 5719 Curtains and draperies
; Draperies; Window furnishings

(G-8498)
RUBBER-RIGHT ROLLERS INC
101 Tileston St (02149-1928)
PHONE....................617 387-6060
Stephen Ottaviano, Pr
EMP: 7 EST: 1925
SQ FT: 5,000
SALES (est): 756.59K Privately Held
Web: www.rubberright.com
SIC: 3069 Medical and laboratory rubber
sundries and related products

(G-8499)
**SALS CLOTHING & FABRIC
RESTOR**
15 Henderson St (02149-2610)
PHONE....................617 387-6726
Sal Barresi, Pr
EMP: 11 EST: 2007
SALES (est): 457.73K Privately Held
Web: www.salsclothingrestoration.com
SIC: 3842 Cosmetic restorations

(G-8500)
**SAMUEL HOLMES
INCORPORATED**
56 Garden St (02149-4513)
PHONE....................617 269-5740
Carl Bruce Bartlett, Pr
Paula Curtin, *
Elizabeth Holmes, *
EMP: 11 EST: 1911
SALES (est): 1.94MM Privately Held
Web: www.samuelholmesinc.com
SIC: 5144 2015 Poultry and poultry products
; Poultry slaughtering and processing

(G-8501)
STATE-LINE GRAPHICS INC
6 Victoria St Ste 109 (02149-3533)
P.O. Box 490587 (02149-0010)
PHONE....................617 389-1200
Arthur F Berardino, Pr
Stephen T Berardino, VP
EMP: 13 EST: 1988
SQ FT: 15,000
SALES (est): 978.11K Privately Held
Web: www.statelinegraphics.com

▲ = Import ▼ = Export
◆ = Import/Export

SIC: 2752 4226 5112 Offset printing; Document and office records storage; Office supplies, nec

(G-8502)
UNIVERSAL SCREENING STUDIO INC
175 Ferry St (02149-5634)
PHONE..............................617 387-1832
Robert Noe, *Pr*
EMP: 8 **EST:** 1985
SQ FT: 10,000
SALES (est): 942.46K **Privately Held**
Web:
www.universalscreeningstudio.com
SIC: 2396 7336 2395 Screen printing on fabric articles; Silk screen design; Embroidery and art needlework

(G-8503)
VELOCITY LLC
120 Tremont St Ste 2 (02149-1148)
PHONE..............................617 389-5452
EMP: 34 **EST:** 1996
SALES (est): 239.05K **Privately Held**
Web: watch.motortrend.com
SIC: 2759 Commercial printing, nec

Fairhaven
Bristol County

(G-8504)
ACUSHNET COMPANY (DH)
333 Bridge St (02719-4900)
P.O. Box 965 (02719-0965)
PHONE..............................508 979-2000
David Maher, *Pr*
Peg Nicholson, *CIO*
◆ **EMP:** 273 **EST:** 1921
SQ FT: 760,000
SALES (est): 1.34B **Publicly Held**
Web: www.titleist.com
SIC: 3949 3149 2381 Balls: baseball, football, basketball, etc.; Athletic shoes, except rubber or plastic; Fabric dress and work gloves
HQ: Acushnet Holdings Corp.
    333 Bridge St
    Fairhaven MA 02719
    800 225-8500

(G-8505)
ACUSHNET HOLDINGS CORP (HQ)
Also Called: Acushnet
333 Bridge St (02719-4905)
PHONE..............................800 225-8500
David Maher, *Pr*
Yoon Soo Yoon, *Ch Bd*
Sean Sullivan, *Ex VP*
Roland Giroux, *CLO*
Brendan Reidy, *CPO*
EMP: 29 **EST:** 1910
SQ FT: 222,720
SALES (est): 2.27B **Publicly Held**
Web: www.acushnetholdingscorp.com
SIC: 3949 Golf equipment
PA: Magnus Holdings Co., Ltd.
    18/F
    Seoul 05340

(G-8506)
ACUSHNET INTERNATIONAL INC (DH)
333 Bridge St (02719-4905)
P.O. Box 965 (02719-0965)
PHONE..............................508 979-2000
Peg Nicholson, *CIO*

▲ **EMP:** 200 **EST:** 1975
SQ FT: 760,000
SALES (est): 121.44MM **Publicly Held**
Web: www.acushnetholdingscorp.com
SIC: 3431 Sinks: enameled iron, cast iron, or pressed metal
HQ: Acushnet Holdings Corp.
    333 Bridge St
    Fairhaven MA 02719
    800 225-8500

(G-8507)
BLW HOLDINGS INC (PA)
Also Called: Brahmin Leather Works
77 Alden Rd (02719-4639)
PHONE..............................508 994-4000
▲ **EMP:** 118 **EST:** 2009
SALES (est): 24.23MM
SALES (corp-wide): 24.23MM **Privately Held**
SIC: 3161 3171 3172 Luggage; Women's handbags and purses; Personal leather goods, nec

(G-8508)
BRAHMIN LEATHER WORKS LLC
77 Alden Rd (02719-4618)
PHONE..............................509 994-4000
Susan Thacker, *Managing Member*
Wendy Goldstein, *CFO*
EMP: 228 **EST:** 2018
SALES (est): 52.48MM
SALES (corp-wide): 11.68B **Publicly Held**
Web: www.brahmin.com
SIC: 3161 3171 3172 Luggage; Women's handbags and purses; Personal leather goods, nec
PA: Markel Group Inc.
    4521 Highwoods Pkwy
    Glen Allen VA 23060
    804 747-0136

(G-8509)
MIKE SHEAS CFFHUSE TRDTNALS IN
37 Winsegansett Ave (02719-1117)
PHONE..............................508 807-5754
Michael J Shea, *Prin*
EMP: 14 **EST:** 2010
SQ FT: 1,800
SALES (est): 426.18K **Privately Held**
Web: www.mikesheascoffee.com
SIC: 5812 2095 5046 5149 Coffee shop; Roasted coffee; Coffee brewing equipment and supplies; Coffee, green or roasted

(G-8510)
MONAGHAN PRINTING COMPANY
59 Alden Rd (02719-4639)
PHONE..............................508 991-8087
Julia Monaghan, *Pr*
EMP: 14 **EST:** 1984
SALES (est): 426.7K **Privately Held**
Web: www.monaghanprinting.com
SIC: 2752 Offset printing

(G-8511)
NEW BEDFORD THREAD CO INC
10 Howland Rd (02719-3453)
P.O. Box 7072 (02742-7072)
PHONE..............................508 996-8584
▲ **EMP:** 35
Web: www.newbedfordthread.com
SIC: 2284 Cotton thread

(G-8512)
NYE LUBRICANTS INC (HQ)
12 Howland Rd (02719-3453)
P.O. Box 8927 (02742-8927)
PHONE..............................508 996-6721
▲ **EMP:** 180 **EST:** 1844
SALES (est): 89.94MM
SALES (corp-wide): 3.54B **Privately Held**
Web: www.nyelubricants.com
SIC: 2992 Oils and greases, blending and compounding
PA: Fuchs Se
    Einsteinstr. 11
    Mannheim BW 68169
    62138020

(G-8513)
RJD WOODWORKING LLC
92 Long Rd (02719-4206)
PHONE..............................508 984-4315
Richard J Desrosiers, *Prin*
EMP: 7 **EST:** 2005
SALES (est): 224.55K **Privately Held**
SIC: 2431 Millwork

(G-8514)
ROLANDS TIRE SERVICE INC (PA)
11 Howland Rd (02719-3440)
P.O. Box D 8 (02719)
PHONE..............................508 997-4501
Michael Bourgault, *Pr*
Michael Bourgault, *Pr*
Charles R Bourgault, *
Lyles R Bourgault, *
▲ **EMP:** 47 **EST:** 1955
SQ FT: 13,600
SALES (est): 8.08MM
SALES (corp-wide): 8.08MM **Privately Held**
Web: www.rolandstire.com
SIC: 5014 7534 5531 Automobile tires and tubes; Tire retreading and repair shops; Automotive tires

(G-8515)
WINDWARD POWER SYSTEMS INC
379 Alden Rd (02719-4451)
PHONE..............................774 992-0059
Nathan Tynan, *Pr*
James Tynan, *VP*
◆ **EMP:** 9 **EST:** 2006
SQ FT: 7,500
SALES (est): 2.14MM **Privately Held**
Web: www.windwardpower.com
SIC: 5551 3492 Marine supplies and equipment; Fluid power valves and hose fittings

Fall River
Bristol County

(G-8516)
A BISMARK COMPANY
Also Called: White Dog Press
5 Probber Ln Ste 1 (02720-1342)
PHONE..............................508 675-2002
Donald Paquette, *Pr*
Diana Paquette, *Sec*
EMP: 7 **EST:** 2002
SQ FT: 24,000
SALES (est): 544.66K **Privately Held**
Web: www.whitedogpress.com
SIC: 2752 Commercial printing, lithographic

(G-8517)
A L ELLIS INC
113 Griffin St Ste 1 (02724-2773)
PHONE..............................508 672-4799
Mike Ellis, *Pr*
Eva D Ellis, *
Robert Fontaine, *
▲ **EMP:** 73 **EST:** 1920
SQ FT: 10,000
SALES (est): 4.45MM **Privately Held**
Web: www.elliscurtain.com
SIC: 2391 Curtains, window: made from purchased materials

(G-8518)
ACCURATE SERVICES INC
Also Called: Accurate Services
951 Broadway Ste 4 (02724-2769)
P.O. Box 6129 (02724-0697)
PHONE..............................508 674-5773
Frank Teixeira, *Pr*
Suzanne Teixeira, *
EMP: 25 **EST:** 1988
SALES (est): 2.64MM **Privately Held**
Web: www.accurateservice.com
SIC: 2674 5137 5136 2369 Shipping and shopping bags or sacks; Women's and children's clothing; Men's and boy's clothing ; Girl's and children's outerwear, nec

(G-8519)
AMERICAN DRYER CORPORATION
88 Currant Rd (02720-4781)
PHONE..............................508 678-9000
Christopher Fitzgerald, *Pr*
Michael Davidson, *CFO*
◆ **EMP:** 230 **EST:** 1965
SQ FT: 300,000
SALES (est): 39.61MM
SALES (corp-wide): 19.72B **Publicly Held**
Web: www.adclaundry.com
SIC: 3582 Dryers, laundry: commercial, including coin-operated
PA: Whirlpool Corporation
    2000 N M 63
    Benton Harbor MI 49022
    269 923-5000

(G-8520)
AMERICAN POWER SOURCE INC (PA)
Also Called: American Players
15 Shaw St (02724-1423)
PHONE..............................508 672-8847
EMP: 15 **EST:** 1994
SQ FT: 2,000
SALES (est): 20.85MM **Privately Held**
Web:
american-power-source-inc3.sbcontract.com
SIC: 2325 2331 Men's and boy's trousers and slacks; Women's and misses' blouses and shirts

(G-8521)
ANDERSON AIRMOTIVE INC
Also Called: Anderson Airmotive Products Co
994 Jefferson St Ste 10 (02721-4823)
PHONE..............................508 646-0950
Matthew Steger, *Pr*
EMP: 19 **EST:** 2019
SALES (est): 2.72MM **Privately Held**
Web: www.andersonairmotive.com
SIC: 3728 3643 Aircraft body and wing assemblies and parts; Ground clamps (electric wiring devices)

(G-8522)
ASHWORTH INTERNATIONAL INC
222 Milliken Blvd Ste 7 (02721-1623)
PHONE..............................508 674-4693
Robert Ashworth Iii, *Dir*
EMP: 15 **EST:** 2002
SALES (est): 301.85K **Privately Held**
SIC: 3086　Plastics foam products

(G-8523)
ATLANTIC LIGHTING INC
231 Commerce Dr (02720-4761)
PHONE..............................508 678-5411
◆ **EMP:** 29 **EST:** 1998
SQ FT: 18,000
SALES (est): 7.49MM **Privately Held**
Web: www.atlantic-lighting.com
SIC: 3646 3645　Commercial lighting fixtures
; Residential lighting fixtures

(G-8524)
BAKER SIGN WORKS INC
75 Ferry St Ste 5 (02721-1111)
PHONE..............................508 674-6600
Linda Baker, *Pr*
EMP: 10 **EST:** 2008
SALES (est): 880.27K **Privately Held**
Web: www.bakersignworks.com
SIC: 3993　Electric signs

(G-8525)
BISZKO CONTRACTING CORP
20 Development St (02721-3246)
PHONE..............................508 679-0518
Alan Biszko, *Pr*
EMP: 43 **EST:** 1975
SALES (est): 5.5MM **Privately Held**
SIC: 1389　Construction, repair, and
dismantling services

(G-8526)
BLOUNT FINE FOODS CORP (PA)
Also Called: Blount Fine Foods
630 Currant Rd (02720-4713)
PHONE..............................774 888-1300
Ted Blount, *Pr*
Nelson Blount Ii, *Pr*
Jonathan Arena, *VP Opers*
Bob Sewall, *VP Sls*
Michael Mistrot, *CFO*
▲ **EMP:** 175 **EST:** 1946
SQ FT: 65,000
SALES (est): 137.55MM
SALES (corp-wide): 137.55MM **Privately
Held**
Web: www.blountfinefoods.com
SIC: 2092 2038　Fresh or frozen packaged
fish; Soups, frozen

(G-8527)
BOLGER AND OHEARN INC
47 Slade St (02724-1347)
P.O. Box 250 (02724-0250)
PHONE..............................508 676-1518
Shaun O'hearn, *Pr*
Kelly O'hearn, *VP*
◆ **EMP:** 25 **EST:** 1946
SQ FT: 2,500
SALES (est): 5.29MM **Privately Held**
Web: www.bolgerohearn.com
SIC: 2899　Chemical preparations, nec

(G-8528)
BORDEN & REMINGTON CORP
Also Called: Borden
63 Water St Ste 1 (02721-1559)
P.O. Box 2573 (02722-2573)
PHONE..............................508 675-0096
TOLL FREE: 800
Daniel Bogan, *Prin*
Robert Bogan, *
Sharon Quinn, *
Susan Canfield, *
Linda Little, *
▲ **EMP:** 40 **EST:** 1837
SQ FT: 100,000
SALES (est): 29.71MM **Privately Held**
Web: www.boremco.com
SIC: 5169 2869　Chemicals, industrial and
heavy; Industrial organic chemicals, nec

(G-8529)
CLEAN PRODUCTS LLC
537 Quequechan St (02721-4004)
PHONE..............................508 676-9355
EMP: 10 **EST:** 2015
SALES (est): 9.76MM **Privately Held**
Web: www.cstsoap.com
SIC: 3089　Automotive parts, plastic

(G-8530)
COMMONWEALTH LIQUID PDTS LLC
537 Quequechan St (02721-4004)
PHONE..............................508 676-9355
Edward Layne, *Managing Member*
EMP: 11 **EST:** 2017
SALES (est): 920.2K **Privately Held**
SIC: 2841　Soap and other detergents

(G-8531)
COMMONWLTH SOAP TOILETRIES INC (PA)
Also Called: CST
537 Quequechan St (02721-4004)
PHONE..............................508 676-9355
▲ **EMP:** 38 **EST:** 1997
SQ FT: 280,000
SALES (est): 17.48MM **Privately Held**
Web: www.cstsoap.com
SIC: 2844 2841　Perfumes, cosmetics and
other toilet preparations; Soap: granulated,
liquid, cake, flaked, or chip

(G-8532)
CORPORATE IMAGE APPAREL INC
Also Called: CIA Ink
596 Airport Rd (02720-4735)
PHONE..............................508 676-3099
Mark N Dumont, *Pr*
Gilbert Lloyd, *
▲ **EMP:** 28 **EST:** 1980
SQ FT: 10,000
SALES (est): 2.1MM **Privately Held**
Web: www.ciainc.com
SIC: 2395 2759　Embroidery products,
except Schiffli machine; Commercial
printing, nec

(G-8533)
DHM THREAD CORPORATION
Also Called: Consolidated Thread Mills
192 Anawan St Ste 301 (02721-1557)
P.O. Box 1107 (02722-1107)
PHONE..............................508 672-0032
Donald Ashton, *Pr*
Sally Mc Cann, *Stockholder*
EMP: 17 **EST:** 1933
SQ FT: 30,000
SALES (est): 2.17MM **Privately Held**
Web: www.consolidatedthreadmills.com
SIC: 2284 2298　Thread from manmade
fibers; Twine, nec

(G-8534)
DOROTHY COXS CANDIES INC
Also Called: Dorothy Cox Chocolates
100 Griffin St (02724-2733)
PHONE..............................774 678-0654
TOLL FREE: 800
Francis J Cox Junior, *Pr*
Geraldine Cox, *Treas*
Francis J Cox Senior, *VP*
EMP: 20 **EST:** 1928
SQ FT: 8,200
SALES (est): 1.7MM **Privately Held**
Web: www.momnpopslollipops.com
SIC: 2064 5441 2066　Candy and other
confectionery products; Candy; Chocolate
and cocoa products

(G-8535)
DURO TEXTILES LLC
110 Chace St (02724-1416)
PHONE..............................508 675-0102
◆ **EMP:** 234
Web: www.duroindustries.com
SIC: 2261 2262　Finishing plants, cotton;
Finishing plants, manmade

(G-8536)
DURO TEXTILES LLC
Duro Textile Printers
206 Globe Mills Ave (02724-1418)
P.O. Box A (02724-0399)
PHONE..............................508 679-0076
FAX: 508 678-1151
EMP: 200
SALES (corp-wide): 90.98MM **Privately
Held**
SIC: 2261 2262　Printing of cotton
broadwoven fabrics; Finishing plants,
manmade
PA: Duro Textiles Llc
110 Chace St
Fall River MA 02724
508 675-0102

(G-8537)
E-I-E-I-O INCORPORATED
502 Bedford St (02720-4855)
PHONE..............................508 324-9311
Karen Golden, *Pr*
Karen Golden, *Pr*
Stephen Oronte, *VP*
Clifford Bail, *Treas*
EMP: 9 **EST:** 1987
SQ FT: 10,000
SALES (est): 1.18MM **Privately Held**
SIC: 2369　Girl's and children's outerwear,
nec

(G-8538)
EASTERN ICE COMPANY INC
281 Commerce Dr (02720-4761)
PHONE..............................508 672-1800
C Joseph Rossi, *Pr*
Joseph Rossi, *Pr*
David Rossi, *VP*
Robert F Clooney, *VP*
Chad J Rossi, *VP*
EMP: 22 **EST:** 1971
SQ FT: 8,000
SALES (est): 4.73MM **Privately Held**
Web: www.easternice.net
SIC: 2097 5999　Manufactured ice; Ice

(G-8539)
EC PIGMENTS USA INC
749 Quequechan St (02721-4004)
P.O. Box 5360 (02723-0407)
PHONE..............................508 676-3481
▲ **EMP:** 120
Web: www.ecpigments.com
SIC: 2865　Color pigments, organic

(G-8540)
ECIN INDUSTRIES INC
Also Called: Harvey Bigelow Designs
1 Ace St Unit 2 (02720-1355)
PHONE..............................508 675-6920
Patricia Macmillen, *Pr*
EMP: 31 **EST:** 1912
SQ FT: 53,000
SALES (est): 2.43MM **Privately Held**
Web: www.ecinindustries.com
SIC: 2515 5712　Mattresses and foundations
; Furniture stores

(G-8541)
EMCO SERVICES INC
37 Slade St (02724-1347)
PHONE..............................508 674-5504
Edward J Mc Namara, *Pr*
EMP: 9 **EST:** 1978
SALES (est): 555.05K **Privately Held**
SIC: 2261 2899　Fire resistance finishing of
cotton broadwoven fabrics; Chemical
preparations, nec

(G-8542)
ERGONOMIC PRODUCTS INC
198 Airport Rd (02720-4770)
PHONE..............................508 636-2263
David J Ahearn, *CEO*
Jennifer Ahearn, *
EMP: 19 **EST:** 2010
SALES (est): 5.16MM **Privately Held**
Web: www.ergonomic-products.com
SIC: 3843　Dental equipment and supplies

(G-8543)
EXEMPLAR LABORATORIES LLC
Also Called: Xemplar Pharmaceuticals
200 Riggenbach Rd (02720-4737)
PHONE..............................508 676-6726
▲ **EMP:** 8 **EST:** 2008
SALES (est): 211.27K **Privately Held**
SIC: 2834　Pharmaceutical preparations

(G-8544)
EXEMPLAR PHARMA LLC
Also Called: Exemplar Pharmaceuticals
927 Currant Rd (02720-4712)
PHONE..............................508 676-6726
Charles R Eck, *Pr*
Abdul Zahir, *VP Opers*
EMP: 37 **EST:** 2008
SQ FT: 10,000
SALES (est): 5.46MM
SALES (corp-wide): 58.05B **Publicly Held**
Web: www.exemplarpharm.com
SIC: 2834　Pharmaceutical preparations
HQ: Allergan, Inc.
1 N Waukegan Rd
North Chicago IL 60064
862 261-7000

(G-8545)
FALL RIVER APPAREL INC
192 Anawan St Ste 201 (02721-1557)
PHONE..............................508 677-1975
Mary Cordeiro, *Owner*
EMP: 7 **EST:** 2002
SALES (est): 496.92K **Privately Held**
Web: www.fallriverapparelinc.com
SIC: 2392 2391 2393 2335　Household
furnishings, nec; Curtains and draperies;
Textile bags; Women's, junior's, and
misses' dresses

(G-8546)
FALL RIVER HAT COMPANY
Also Called: Korber Hats
394 Kilburn St (02724-2214)
PHONE................................508 672-7033
Jason Ouhrabka, *Pr*
▲ **EMP:** 18 **EST:** 2012
SQ FT: 300,000
SALES (est): 1.64MM **Privately Held**
SIC: 2353 Hats and caps, nec

(G-8547)
FALL RIVER MFG CO INC
540 Currant Rd (02720-4711)
PHONE................................508 675-1125
Timothy J Csanadi, *Pr*
John Conte, *
David Monti, *
EMP: 72 **EST:** 1984
SALES (est): 9.4MM **Privately Held**
Web: www.fallrivermfg.com
SIC: 3452 3316 Screws, metal; Cold
finishing of steel shapes

(G-8548)
FALL RIVER MODERN PRTG CO INC
Also Called: Quick Copy
798 Plymouth Ave (02721-1946)
PHONE................................508 673-9421
Raymond Schenck, *Pr*
Rita Schenck, *Treas*
Richard R Schenck, *VP*
Donald R Schenck, *VP*
EMP: 10 **EST:** 1948
SQ FT: 2,000
SALES (est): 426.43K **Privately Held**
Web: www.frmodern.com
SIC: 2752 2759 Offset printing; Letterpress
printing

(G-8549)
FALL RIVER READY-MIX CON LLC
245 Tripp St (02724-2434)
PHONE................................508 675-7540
Stephen A Cardi, *Prin*
EMP: 8 **EST:** 2016
SALES (est): 335.49K **Privately Held**
Web: www.fallriver-readymix.com
SIC: 3273 1611 Ready-mixed concrete;
Guardrail construction, highways

(G-8550)
FALL RIVER TOOL & DIE CO INC
994 Jefferson St Ste 2 (02721-4823)
P.O. Box 4070 (02723-0400)
PHONE................................508 674-4621
TOLL FREE: 800
Joseph Fontaine, *Pr*
Ronald Fontaine, *VP*
David Fontaine, *Clerk*
EMP: 14 **EST:** 1947
SQ FT: 25,000
SALES (est): 1.44MM **Privately Held**
SIC: 3364 3544 3089 Zinc and zinc-base
alloy die-castings; Dies, plastics forming;
Injection molding of plastics

(G-8551)
GATEHOUSE MEDIA LLC
Also Called: Herald News, The
207 Pocasset St (02721-1532)
P.O. Box 3408 (02722-3408)
PHONE................................508 676-8211
Sean Burke, *Brnch Mgr*
EMP: 13
SALES (corp-wide): 2.95B **Publicly Held**
Web: www.heraldnews.com

SIC: 2711 2741 Newspapers, publishing
and printing; Miscellaneous publishing
HQ: Gatehouse Media, Llc
175 Sullys Trl Ste 203
Pittsford NY 14534
585 598-0030

(G-8552)
GEORGE PATTON ASSOCIATES INC
Also Called: Displays2go
81 Commerce Dr (02720-4743)
PHONE................................800 572-2194
◆ **EMP:** 180
Web: www.displays2go.com
SIC: 7389 3993 2821 2542 Design services;
Displays and cutouts, window and lobby;
Plastics materials and resins; Partitions and
fixtures, except wood

(G-8553)
GINSCO INC
1572 President Ave (02720-7148)
PHONE................................508 677-4767
Steven Cohen, *Owner*
EMP: 14
SALES (corp-wide): 1.73MM **Privately Held**
Web: www.newyorkbagel.com
SIC: 2051 Bagels, fresh or frozen
PA: Ginsco, Inc.
1706 President Ave
Fall River MA 02720
508 677-4767

(G-8554)
GINSCO INC (PA)
Also Called: New York Bagel Co
1706 President Ave (02720-7115)
PHONE................................508 677-4767
Steve Ginsberg, *Pr*
Steve Cohen, *VP*
EMP: 14 **EST:** 1988
SQ FT: 2,000
SALES (est): 1.73MM
SALES (corp-wide): 1.73MM **Privately Held**
SIC: 2051 5461 5812 Bagels, fresh or frozen
; Bagels; Delicatessen (eating places)

(G-8555)
GOLD MEDAL BAKERY INC (PA)
21 Penn St (02724-1276)
P.O. Box I (02724-0391)
PHONE................................508 674-5766
Roland S Lecomte, *CEO*
Brian R Lecomte, *
Michele Lecomte Chambers, *
Michael A Keho, *
Florine Lecomte, *
EMP: 450 **EST:** 1912
SQ FT: 410,000
SALES (est): 84.75MM
SALES (corp-wide): 84.75MM **Privately Held**
Web: www.goldmedalbakery.com
SIC: 2051 Bread, all types (white, wheat,
rye, etc); fresh or frozen

(G-8556)
GOOD CLOTHING COMPANY INC
28 Anawan St # 2 (02721-1523)
PHONE................................508 419-6152
Kathryn Hilderbrand, *CEO*
EMP: 18 **EST:** 2015
SALES (est): 961.45K **Privately Held**
Web: www.goodclothingcompany.com

SIC: 5651 2339 2326 Family clothing stores
; Women's and misses' athletic clothing and
sportswear; Men's and boy's work clothing

(G-8557)
GRAPHIX PLUS INC
52 Queen St (02724-1422)
P.O. Box 6180 (02724-0697)
PHONE................................508 677-2122
Christopher Gagnon, *Pr*
Roger Lachapelle, *VP*
EMP: 10 **EST:** 1988
SQ FT: 6,000
SALES (est): 823.75K **Privately Held**
Web: graphix-plus.espwebsite.com
SIC: 2759 Screen printing

(G-8558)
GRIFFIN MANUFACTURING CO INC
502 Bedford St (02720-4855)
P.O. Box 1671 (02722-1671)
PHONE................................508 677-0048
Gene Laudon, *Pr*
Olivia Perry, *Sec*
◆ **EMP:** 29 **EST:** 1991
SQ FT: 60,000
SALES (est): 1.5MM **Privately Held**
Web: www.griffinmanufacturing.com
SIC: 2329 2339 Athletic clothing, except
uniforms: men's, youths' and boys'; Athletic
clothing: women's, misses', and juniors'

(G-8559)
H & S TOOL AND ENGINEERING INC
777 Airport Rd (02720-4724)
PHONE................................508 672-6509
Karl D Hetzler, *Pr*
Robert St Pierre, *
EMP: 25 **EST:** 1980
SQ FT: 25,000
SALES (est): 3.87MM **Privately Held**
Web: www.hstool1.com
SIC: 3599 Machine shop, jobbing and repair

(G-8560)
HEVEATEX CORPORATION
106 Ferry St Ste 1 (02721-1113)
P.O. Box 2573 (02722-2573)
PHONE................................508 675-0181
Paul Valentine, *Pr*
◆ **EMP:** 154 **EST:** 1928
SQ FT: 30,000
SALES (est): 944.42K
SALES (corp-wide): 40.13MM **Privately Held**
SIC: 3069 2822 Reclaimed rubber and
specialty rubber compounds; Synthetic
rubber
PA: Tillotson Corporation
159 Main St
Nashua NH 03060
781 402-1731

(G-8561)
HIGHLANDS LUNCHETTE
Also Called: Highlands Lunchonette
757 Robeson St (02720-5433)
PHONE................................508 674-6206
EMP: 9 **EST:** 1997
SALES (est): 150.04K **Privately Held**
Web: www.highlandluncheonette.com
SIC: 5812 2051 American restaurant;
Doughnuts, except frozen

(G-8562)
JOURNAL REGISTER COMPANY
O Jornal

207 Pocasset St (02721-1532)
PHONE................................508 678-3844
Ric Oliveria, *Mgr*
EMP: 10
SALES (corp-wide): 293.08MM **Privately Held**
Web: www.heraldnews.com
SIC: 2711 Commercial printing and
newspaper publishing combined
PA: Journal Register Company
5 Hanover Sq Fl 25
New York NY 10004
212 257-7212

(G-8563)
JP SAW MFG INC
192 Anawan St (02721-1562)
PHONE................................508 567-0469
EMP: 7 **EST:** 2019
SALES (est): 505.98K **Privately Held**
SIC: 3999 Manufacturing industries, nec

(G-8564)
JS INTERNATIONAL INC (PA)
Also Called: Jsi Quality Cabinetry
485 Commerce Dr (02720-4706)
PHONE................................508 675-4722
Jiam Shen, *Pr*
◆ **EMP:** 47 **EST:** 1997
SQ FT: 125,000
SALES (est): 21.63MM
SALES (corp-wide): 21.63MM **Privately Held**
Web: www.jsicabinetry.com
SIC: 2599 2434 Cabinets, factory; Wood
kitchen cabinets

(G-8565)
KELLSPORT INDUSTRIES INC
22 Boomer St (02720-2714)
PHONE................................508 646-0855
Robert Smith, *Pr*
▲ **EMP:** 35 **EST:** 1974
SALES (est): 3.39MM **Privately Held**
Web: www.kellsport.com
SIC: 2329 2339 Athletic clothing, except
uniforms: men's, youths' and boys'; Athletic
clothing: women's, misses', and juniors'

(G-8566)
KLEAR-VU CORPORATION (PA)
600 Airport Rd (02720-4735)
PHONE................................508 674-5723
Jacob Mintz, *Prin*
Jacob Mintz, *Prin*
Robert W Cooper, *
Denise Smith, *
▲ **EMP:** 99 **EST:** 1936
SQ FT: 100,000
SALES (est): 14.68MM
SALES (corp-wide): 14.68MM **Privately Held**
Web: www.klearvu.com
SIC: 2392 Cushions and pillows

(G-8567)
L3 OCEANSERVER INC (DH)
275 Martine St Ste 103 (02723-1500)
PHONE................................508 678-0550
Robert B Anderson, *Pr*
Jonathan C Crowell, *Treas*
EMP: 13 **EST:** 2003
SQ FT: 6,000
SALES (est): 4.68MM
SALES (corp-wide): 17.06B **Publicly Held**
Web: www.ocean-server.com
SIC: 3731 Shipbuilding and repairing
HQ: L3 Technologies, Inc.
600 3rd Ave Fl 34
New York NY 10016
321 727-9100

(G-8568)

LAVOIE INDUSTRIES LLC
969 Charles St (02724-4202)
PHONE...........................508 542-1062
Paul Lavoie, *Prin*
EMP: 8 **EST:** 2008
SALES (est): 496.16K **Privately Held**
SIC: 3999 Manufacturing industries, nec

(G-8569)

LINCOLN PRESS CO INC
Also Called: Jiffy Print Copy Center
407 Pleasant St (02721-3030)
P.O. Box 904 (02722-0904)
PHONE...........................508 673-3241
Paul Senra, *Pr*
Alan Hutchinson, *Stockholder*
EMP: 16 **EST:** 1934
SQ FT: 14,000
SALES (est): 419.08K **Privately Held**
SIC: 2759 2752 3953 Letterpress printing; Commercial printing, lithographic; Date stamps, hand: rubber or metal

(G-8570)

M P BREWING COMPANY
52 Ferry St (02721-1106)
PHONE...........................508 944-8531
Christopher Martin, *CEO*
EMP: 12 **EST:** 2021
SALES (est): 500.41K **Privately Held**
SIC: 2082 7389 Beer (alcoholic beverage); Business services, nec

(G-8571)

MA INDUSTRIAL FALL RIVER LLC
81 Commerce Dr (02720-4743)
PHONE...........................508 672-5217
EMP: 9 **EST:** 2014
SALES (est): 211.4K **Privately Held**
Web: www.fallrivermfg.com
SIC: 3599 Machine shop, jobbing and repair

(G-8572)

MALLARD PRINTING INC
657 Quarry St Ste 9 (02723-1021)
PHONE...........................508 675-5733
Mario Rodriguez, *Prin*
Robert Lunquest, *Pr*
Jeffrey Marques, *VP*
EMP: 18 **EST:** 1998
SQ FT: 5,000
SALES (est): 2.36MM **Privately Held**
Web: www.mallardprinting.com
SIC: 2752 Offset printing

(G-8573)

MAPLEWOOD MACHINE CO INC
271 Anthony St (02721-3307)
PHONE...........................508 673-6710
Edward Viveiros, *Pr*
Donna Viveiros, *Treas*
EMP: 10 **EST:** 1980
SALES (est): 930.99K **Privately Held**
Web: www.maplewoodmachine.com
SIC: 3599 Machine shop, jobbing and repair

(G-8574)

MARZILLI MACHINE CO
621 S Almond St (02724-1551)
PHONE...........................508 567-4145
James A Marzilli, *Pr*
James Marzilli, *
EMP: 25 **EST:** 2011
SALES (est): 4.03MM **Privately Held**
Web: www.marzmachine.com

SIC: 7699 3448 Industrial machinery and equipment repair; Prefabricated metal components

(G-8575)

MATOUK FACTORY STORE INC
925 Airport Rd (02720-4724)
PHONE...........................508 997-3444
George Matouk, *Pr*
◆ **EMP:** 50 **EST:** 2001
SALES (est): 3.15MM **Privately Held**
Web: www.matouk.com
SIC: 2392 Blankets, comforters and beddings

(G-8576)

MATOUK TEXTILE WORKS INC
925 Airport Rd (02720-4724)
PHONE...........................508 997-3444
George Matouk Junior, *Pr*
George Matouk Senior, *Treas*
EMP: 33 **EST:** 1988
SALES (est): 4.15MM **Privately Held**
Web: www.matouk.com
SIC: 2395 Embroidery products, except Schiffli machine

(G-8577)

MERIDA LLC
1 Currant Rd Ste 1 (02720-4741)
PHONE...........................508 675-6572
Bob Segal, *Brnch Mgr*
EMP: 35
SALES (corp-wide): 7.61MM **Privately Held**
Web: www.meridastudio.com
SIC: 2273 Carpets and rugs
PA: Merida, Llc
1 Design Center Pl # 330
Boston MA 02210
800 345-2200

(G-8578)

MERROW MANUFACTURING LLC (PA)
502 Bedford St Ste 3 (02720-4844)
PHONE...........................508 689-4095
Charlie Merrow, *CEO*
EMP: 300 **EST:** 2017
SALES (est): 24.34MM
SALES (corp-wide): 24.34MM **Privately Held**
Web: www.merrowmfg.com
SIC: 3559 Sewing machines and attachments, industrial, nec

(G-8579)

MERROW SUPERIOR LLC
502 Bedford St (02720-4855)
PHONE...........................212 691-3400
Charles Merrow, *Managing Member*
EMP: 7 **EST:** 2020
SALES (est): 2.14MM **Privately Held**
Web: www.merrow.com
SIC: 3639 Sewing equipment

(G-8580)

MFG MACH CORP
847 Pleasant St (02723-1005)
PHONE...........................774 294-4285
EMP: 8 **EST:** 2018
SALES (est): 484.43K **Privately Held**
Web: www.mfgmachine.com
SIC: 3599 Machine shop, jobbing and repair

(G-8581)

MICRO MAGNETICS INC
617 Airport Rd (02720-4722)
P.O. Box 9366 (02720-0007)

PHONE...........................508 672-4489
Gang Xiao, *Ch*
Gang Xiao, *Ch*
▲ **EMP:** 10 **EST:** 1998
SQ FT: 7,000
SALES (est): 979.41K **Privately Held**
Web: www.micromagnetics.com
SIC: 3674 8731 Semiconductors and related devices; Commercial physical research

(G-8582)

MIKEL INC (PA)
589 Commerce Dr (02720-4757)
PHONE...........................401 846-0052
Kelly Mendell, *Pr*
Brian W Guimond, *Treas*
Charlotte Guimond, *Ch Bd*
Michael Guimond, *Sec*
EMP: 9 **EST:** 1999
SQ FT: 3,000
SALES (est): 24.74MM
SALES (corp-wide): 24.74MM **Privately Held**
Web: www.mikelinc.com
SIC: 3812 Search and navigation equipment

(G-8583)

MILLSTONE MED OUTSOURCING LLC (PA)
580 Commerce Dr (02720-4759)
PHONE...........................508 679-8384
Karl Neuberger, *CEO*
Kelly Lucenti, *
James Dwyer, *
Brian Heath, *
Victoria Hughes, *Quality Vice President**
▲ **EMP:** 130 **EST:** 2004
SQ FT: 26,230
SALES (est): 48.66MM
SALES (corp-wide): 48.66MM **Privately Held**
Web: www.millstonemedical.com
SIC: 2671 2631 Paper, coated or laminated for packaging; Container, packaging, and boxboard

(G-8584)

MIRANDA BROTHERS INC
Also Called: Micheals Provision
317 Lindsey St (02720-1132)
PHONE...........................508 672-0982
Ronnie Miranda, *Pr*
Joe Miranda, *VP*
EMP: 9 **EST:** 1988
SALES (est): 999.3K **Privately Held**
Web: www.michaelsprovision.com
SIC: 2013 Sausages and other prepared meats

(G-8585)

MIW CORP
1205 Bay St (02724-1203)
PHONE...........................508 672-4029
George Malatos, *Pr*
EMP: 25 **EST:** 2009
SQ FT: 18,000
SALES (est): 2.52MM **Privately Held**
Web: www.miwcorporation.com
SIC: 3441 Fabricated structural metal

(G-8586)

NEW ENGLAND ALPACA FIBR POOL I
115 N 7th St (02720-4906)
P.O. Box 1398 (02790-0605)
PHONE...........................508 659-6731
Christopher Riley, *Pr*
EMP: 7 **EST:** 2004
SALES (est): 338.01K **Privately Held**

Web: neafplander.squarespace.com
SIC: 3559 Fiber optics strand coating machinery

(G-8587)

NEW ENGLAND ELCTRPOLISHING INC
Also Called: N E E
220 Shove St (02724-2018)
P.O. Box 845 (02722-0845)
PHONE...........................508 672-6616
Alvin Almedia, *Pr*
EMP: 25 **EST:** 1985
SALES (est): 3.01MM **Privately Held**
Web: www.neelectropolishing.com
SIC: 3471 Electroplating of metals or formed products

(G-8588)

NORTHEAST EQUIPMENT INC
Also Called: Delta Mechanical Seals
44 Probber Ln (02720-1308)
PHONE...........................508 324-0083
Carl C Bjornson, *Pr*
EMP: 19 **EST:** 1995
SALES (est): 798.98K **Privately Held**
Web: www.delta-seals.com
SIC: 3561 3053 Pumps and pumping equipment; Gaskets; packing and sealing devices

(G-8589)

NORTHEAST KNITTING MILLS INC (PA)
69 Alden St (02723-1787)
PHONE...........................508 678-7553
Gary Reitzas, *Pr*
Max Blum, *Pr*
Gary Reitzas, *VP*
Jay Elias, *Treas*
Lois Reitzas, *Clerk*
EMP: 20 **EST:** 1911
SQ FT: 150,000
SALES (est): 4.09MM **Privately Held**
Web: www.neknitting.com
SIC: 2253 5949 2339 Sweaters and sweater coats, knit; Sewing, needlework, and piece goods; Women's and misses' outerwear, nec

(G-8590)

OCM INC
Also Called: Oriental Chow Mein Co
42 8th St (02720-3014)
PHONE...........................508 675-7711
Frederick Wong, *Pr*
Alfred Wong, *Treas*
Nelson Wong, *VP*
EMP: 10 **EST:** 1937
SQ FT: 2,600
SALES (est): 467.59K **Privately Held**
Web: www.ocm-inc.com
SIC: 2098 Noodles (e.g. egg, plain, and water), dry

(G-8591)

OPALALA INC
994 Jefferson St Ste 10 (02721-4823)
PHONE...........................508 646-0950
▲ **EMP:** 19 **EST:** 1994
SQ FT: 10,000
SALES (est): 3.18MM **Privately Held**
SIC: 3728 3643 Aircraft body and wing assemblies and parts; Ground clamps (electric wiring devices)

(G-8592)

ORNAMENTAL IRONWORKS INC
Also Called: Ornamental Ironworks

75 Ferry St Ste 1 (02721-1111)
P.O. Box 158 (02724-0158)
PHONE..............................508 678-0687
Isaac Cordeiro, *Pr*
EMP: 10 **EST**: 1987
SQ FT: 21,000
SALES (est): 473.52K **Privately Held**
SIC: **1799** 3446 3444   Ornamental metal
work; Architectural metalwork; Sheet
metalwork

(G-8593)
PAIVA CORP
Also Called: Express Printing
192 Anawan St Ste 602 (02721-1563)
PHONE..............................508 679-7921
EMP: 7 **EST**: 1996
SQ FT: 3,000
SALES (est): 710K **Privately Held**
SIC: **2759** 2789 2752 2672   Commercial
printing, nec; Bookbinding and related work
; Commercial printing, lithographic; Paper;
coated and laminated, nec

(G-8594)
PARAMOUNT TOOL LLC
473 Pleasant St (02721-3026)
PHONE..............................508 672-0844
Jacqueline Gardikis, *
▲ **EMP**: 25 **EST**: 1981
SQ FT: 25,000
SALES (est): 4.79MM **Privately Held**
Web: www.paramounttool.net
SIC: **3469** 3599   Stamping metal for the trade
; Machine shop, jobbing and repair

(G-8595)
PASCALE INDUSTRIES INC
Ey Technologies
939 Currant Rd (02720-4712)
PHONE..............................508 673-3307
Raymond Pascale, *Genl Mgr*
EMP: 45
Web: www.eytechnologies.com
SIC: **2295**   Plastic coated yarns or fabrics
PA: Pascale Industries, Inc.
4301 Pratt Remmel Rd
Little Rock AR 72206

(G-8596)
**PDK WORLDWIDE ENTPS INC
(PA)**
Also Called: Pdk Worldwide
10 N Main St Ste 3g # 3 (02720-2130)
PHONE..............................508 676-2155
Paul Zheng, *Pr*
Katherine Zheng, *VP*
▲ **EMP**: 20 **EST**: 1995
SQ FT: 50,000
SALES (est): 1.91MM **Privately Held**
SIC: **2392**   Blankets, comforters and
beddings

(G-8597)
PLZ CORP
300 Riggenbach Rd (02720-4738)
PHONE..............................650 543-7600
Will Brown, *Brnch Mgr*
EMP: 107
SALES (corp-wide): 766.3MM **Privately
Held**
Web: www.plzcorp.com
SIC: **2813**   Aerosols
PA: Plz Corp.
2651 Wrrnvlle Rd Stre 300 300 Stre
Downers Grove IL 60515
630 628-3000

(G-8598)
POTTERS PRINTING INC
Also Called: Cambridge Offsett Printing
207 Pocasset St (02721-1532)
PHONE..............................617 547-3161
Kris Potter, *Pr*
Kris Sousa, *Prin*
EMP: 15 **EST**: 1966
SQ FT: 8,000
SALES (est): 2.23MM **Privately Held**
Web: www.cambridgeoffset.com
SIC: **2752** 2759   Offset printing; Textile
printing rolls: engraving

(G-8599)
PRECISION SPORTSWEAR INC
54 Front St Unit 3 (02721-4399)
PHONE..............................508 674-3034
Neal Venancio, *Pr*
EMP: 8 **EST**: 1983
SALES (est): 492.02K **Privately Held**
Web: www.precspts.com
SIC: **2369** 2329   Girl's and children's
outerwear, nec; Men's and boys' athletic
uniforms

(G-8600)
RAMSBOTTOM PRINTING INC
Also Called: RPI Printing
135 Waldron Rd (02720-4723)
PHONE..............................508 730-2220
Scott Ramsbottom, *Pr*
EMP: 33 **EST**: 1967
SQ FT: 12,000
SALES (est): 4.44MM **Privately Held**
Web: www.rpiprinting.net
SIC: **2752** 2791   Offset printing; Typesetting

(G-8601)
RECTORSEAL LLC
1244 Davol St (02720-1108)
PHONE..............................508 673-7561
K Ortler, *Prin*
EMP: 11
SALES (corp-wide): 757.9MM **Publicly
Held**
Web: www.rectorseal.com
SIC: **2891** 2899 2842   Sealing compounds
for pipe threads or joints; Chemical
preparations, nec; Polishes and sanitation
goods
HQ: Rectorseal, Llc
2601 Spenwick Dr
Houston TX 77055
713 263-8001

(G-8602)
**REX CUT PRODUCTS
INCORPORATED**
Also Called: Rex Cut
960 Airport Rd (02720-4799)
PHONE..............................508 678-1985
Claude M Gelinas, *Pr*
James E Carroll, *Prin*
Robert Costa, *Prin*
Maria Prado, *Prin*
Robert J Gauvin, *
▲ **EMP**: 56 **EST**: 1920
SQ FT: 84,000
SALES (est): 8.03MM **Privately Held**
Web: www.rexcut.com
SIC: **3291**   Wheels, abrasive

(G-8603)
RICKS SHEET METAL INC
82 Lea Ln (02721-2385)
PHONE..............................774 488-9576
Eric Christopher Nadich, *Pr*
EMP: 11 **EST**: 2013
SALES (est): 500.25K **Privately Held**

SIC: 3444   Sheet metalwork

(G-8604)
**RIVER FALLS MANUFACTURING
CO**
40 County St (02723-2104)
PHONE..............................508 646-2900
Mark Friedman, *Pr*
Isidore Friedman, *
Paul Friedman, *
William Fuchs, *
EMP: 95 **EST**: 1966
SALES (est): 4.19MM
SALES (corp-wide): 56.79MM **Privately
Held**
Web:
www.controlledtechnicalservices.com
SIC: **2253**   Knit outerwear mills
HQ: Fieldston Clothes, Inc
1407 Broadway Fl 10
New York NY 10018
212 354-8550

(G-8605)
**ROBBINS MANUFACTURING CO
INC**
1200 Airport Rd (02720-4736)
P.O. Box 704 (02722-0704)
PHONE..............................508 675-2555
Barry Robbins, *Pr*
EMP: 50 **EST**: 1970
SQ FT: 90,000
SALES (est): 4.84MM **Privately Held**
Web: www.robbinsmfgfasteners.com
SIC: **3452**   Bolts, metal

(G-8606)
SHERLE WAGNER INTL LLC
1 Lewiston St Unit 2 (02721-4289)
PHONE..............................212 758-3300
Walter Geoffroy, *Brnch Mgr*
EMP: 15
Web: www.sherlewagner.com
SIC: **5023** 3431 3432 3281   Kitchenware;
Metal sanitary ware; Plumbing fixture
fittings and trim; Cut stone and stone
products
PA: Sherle Wagner International Llc
699 Madison Ave Fl 4
New York NY 10065

(G-8607)
SPECTRUM LIGHTING INC
994 Jefferson St Ste 5 (02721-4823)
PHONE..............................508 678-2303
Christopher Roenlin, *Pr*
Jeffrey Fein, *
▲ **EMP**: 100 **EST**: 1993
SALES (est): 32.06MM **Privately Held**
Web: www.speclight.com
SIC: **3646**   Commercial lighting fixtures

(G-8608)
**STAIRWAY MANUFACTURERS
ASSOC**
657 Quarry St Ste 3 (02723-1021)
PHONE..............................508 646-1313
Bill Bivona, *Pr*
EMP: 8 **EST**: 2008
SALES (est): 340.91K **Privately Held**
Web: www.stairways.org
SIC: **3534**   Elevators and moving stairways

(G-8609)
STEWARD PET IMAGING LLC
795 Middle St (02721-1733)
PHONE..............................508 259-8919
Robert E Guyon, *Managing Member*
EMP: 30 **EST**: 2002

SALES (est): 1.52MM **Privately Held**
SIC: **3845**   Position emission tomography
(PET scanner)

(G-8610)
STIRRINGS LLC
Also Called: Stirrings Better Cocktails
1 West St Unit 2 (02720-1336)
PHONE..............................508 324-9800
EMP: 39 **EST**: 2008
SALES (est): 1.7MM
SALES (corp-wide): 21.15B **Privately Held**
Web: www.stirrings.com
SIC: **2085** 2087   Cocktails, alcoholic;
Cocktail mixes, nonalcoholic
HQ: Diageo North America, Inc.
3 World Trade Ctr 175
New York NY 10007
212 202-1800

(G-8611)
**SWAN DYEING AND PRINTING
CORP**
Also Called: Swan Fabrics
372 Stevens St (02721-4934)
PHONE..............................508 674-4611
Michael A Rodriguez, *Pr*
▲ **EMP**: 95 **EST**: 1966
SALES (est): 6.61MM **Privately Held**
Web: b.swanfabrics.com
SIC: **2396**   Fabric printing and stamping

(G-8612)
**SWAN FINISHING COMPANY
INC (PA)**
372 Stevens St (02721-4999)
PHONE..............................508 674-4611
Pat Guerriero, *Pr*
Michael Rodrigues, *
Ralph A Guerriero Junior, *Treas*
▲ **EMP**: 229 **EST**: 1958
SQ FT: 200,000
SALES (est): 12.62MM
SALES (corp-wide): 12.62MM **Privately
Held**
SIC: **2231** 2261 2262   Wool broadwoven
fabrics; Dyeing cotton broadwoven fabrics;
Dyeing: manmade fiber and silk
broadwoven fabrics

(G-8613)
SWIMEX INC
390 Airport Rd (02720-4707)
PHONE..............................508 646-1600
Mark Pearson, *Pr*
Karen Dias, *
Suzanne Vaughan, *
▼ **EMP**: 50 **EST**: 2002
SQ FT: 22,500
SALES (est): 9.34MM **Privately Held**
Web: www.swimex.com
SIC: **3949**   Swimming pools, except plastic

(G-8614)
TECH-ETCH INC
100 Riggenbach Rd (02720-4708)
PHONE..............................508 675-5757
Jorgen Mortenson, *Brnch Mgr*
EMP: 30
SALES (corp-wide): 91.21MM **Privately
Held**
Web: www.techetch.com
SIC: **3357** 3469 3444   Magnet wire,
nonferrous; Metal stampings, nec; Sheet
metalwork
PA: Tech-Etch, Inc.
45 Aldrin Rd
Plymouth MA 02360
508 747-0300

GEOGRAPHIC

(G-8615)
TEKNIKOR AUTOMTN & CONTRLS INC
Also Called: E C S
595 Airport Rd (02720-4702)
PHONE................................508 679-9474
Ken Potvin, *Pr*
Philip J Pelletier, *CEO*
EMP: 16 **EST:** 1989
SALES (est): 4.96MM **Privately Held**
Web: www.teknikor.com
SIC: 3625 3613 3823　Motor control centers; Switchgear and switchboard apparatus; Process control instruments

(G-8616)
TEUFELBERGER FIBER ROPE CORP
Also Called: Teufelberger
848 Airport Rd (02720-4735)
PHONE................................508 678-8200
Christopher T Lavin, *Pr*
Franz Hilber, *
Robert Fontaine, *
◆ **EMP:** 189 **EST:** 1967
SQ FT: 150,000
SALES (est): 23.86MM **Privately Held**
Web: www.neropes.com
SIC: 2298　Cordage and twine

(G-8617)
TRI TEXTILES CORPORATION (PA)
Also Called: Fleecepro
147 Plymouth Ave (02721-4303)
PHONE................................631 420-0011
Andrew Lesser, *Pr*
▲ **EMP:** 8 **EST:** 2001
SALES (est): 941.07K
SALES (corp-wide): 941.07K **Privately Held**
Web: www.fleecepro.com
SIC: 2392 7389　Blankets: made from purchased materials; Textile and apparel services

(G-8618)
TUFTANE EXTRUSION TECH INC
Also Called: Tuftane Eti
96 Wordell St (02721-4311)
PHONE................................978 921-8200
EMP: 10 **EST:** 1995
SQ FT: 13,000
SALES (est): 1.74MM **Privately Held**
Web: www.tuftaneeti.com
SIC: 2821　Plastics materials and resins

(G-8619)
TWEAVE LLC
1450 Brayton Ave (02721-5235)
PHONE................................508 285-6701
EMP: 22 **EST:** 2008
SALES (est): 2.47MM
SALES (corp-wide): 47.66MM **Privately Held**
Web: www.gehring-tricot.com
SIC: 2258　Lace and warp knit fabric mills
PA: Gehring Tricot Corporation
68 Ransom St
Dolgeville NY 13329
315 429-8551

(G-8620)
US BEDDING INC
451 Quarry St (02723-1007)
PHONE................................508 678-6988
David Wayne, *Pr*
▲ **EMP:** 18 **EST:** 2006
SALES (est): 2.39MM **Privately Held**

Web: www.usbeddingonline.com
SIC: 2515 2221 5712　Mattresses and foundations; Bedding, manmade or silk fabric; Bedding and bedsprings

(G-8621)
US PACKAGING SPECIALTIES
117 Tripp St (02724-2423)
PHONE................................508 674-3636
Antonio Oliveira, *Pr*
John Mellow, *VP*
▲ **EMP:** 14 **EST:** 2001
SQ FT: 13,000
SALES (est): 740.44K **Privately Held**
Web: www.militaryfabrication.com
SIC: 3399 7389　Aluminum atomized powder ; Packaging and labeling services

(G-8622)
VANSON LEATHERS INC
951 Broadway Ste 1 (02724-2769)
PHONE................................508 678-2000
Michael Van Der Sleesen, *Pr*
◆ **EMP:** 56 **EST:** 1983
SALES (est): 4.99MM **Privately Held**
Web: www.vansonleathers.com
SIC: 2386　Leather and sheep-lined clothing

(G-8623)
VITAL WOOD PRODUCTS INC
218 Shove St (02724-2068)
P.O. Box 86 (02790-0086)
PHONE................................508 673-7976
EMP: 25 **EST:** 1994
SQ FT: 22,000
SALES (est): 911.28K **Privately Held**
SIC: 2515　Box springs, assembled

(G-8624)
WAKEFIELD ENGINEERING
132 Sykes Rd (02720-4728)
PHONE................................603 417-8310
EMP: 9 **EST:** 2018
SALES (est): 363.8K **Privately Held**
Web: www.wakefieldthermal.com
SIC: 5051 3334　Metals service centers and offices; Primary aluminum

(G-8625)
WALTER A FURMAN CO INC
180 Liberty St (02724-1433)
PHONE................................508 674-7751
Carl Furman, *Pr*
Walter A Furman, *
▲ **EMP:** 75 **EST:** 1954
SQ FT: 35,000
SALES (est): 7.65MM **Privately Held**
Web: www.walterafurman.com
SIC: 2431　Millwork

(G-8626)
WHOLE EARTH HAT CO INC
Also Called: Korber Hats
394 Kilburn St (02724-2214)
P.O. Box 336 (02724-0336)
PHONE................................508 672-7033
EMP: 13 **EST:** 1997
SALES (est): 260.16K **Privately Held**
Web: www.korberhats.com
SIC: 2353　Hats and caps, nec

(G-8627)
XILECTRIC INC
Also Called: Xilectric
151 Martine St Ste 125-1 (02723-1514)
PHONE................................781 247-4567
Steven Weiss, *Pr*
EMP: 7 **EST:** 2012
SALES (est): 739.51K **Privately Held**

Web: www.xilectric.com
SIC: 3691 3825 8731　Storage batteries; Engine electrical test equipment; Commercial research laboratory

Falmouth
Barnstable County

(G-8628)
BEN & BILLS CHOCOLATE EMPORIUM
Also Called: BEN & BILL'S CHOCOLATE EMPORIUM
209 Main St (02540-2749)
PHONE................................508 548-7878
Jeannette Michaud, *Mgr*
EMP: 10
SALES (corp-wide): 1.31MM **Privately Held**
Web: www.benandbillsfalmouth.com
SIC: 2064 5441　Candy and other confectionery products; Candy
PA: Ben & Bill's Chocolate Emporium, Inc.
143 Main St
Northampton MA 01060
413 584-5695

(G-8629)
CELEBRATIONS
210 Main St (02540-2744)
PHONE................................508 457-0530
EMP: 10 **EST:** 1987
SQ FT: 2,940
SALES (est): 239.77K **Privately Held**
SIC: 5947 8999 5943 2759　Gift shop; Calligrapher; Stationery stores; Invitation and stationery printing and engraving

(G-8630)
ENTERPRISE PUBLICATIONS (PA)
Also Called: Falmouth Enterprise
50 Depot Ave (02540-2349)
PHONE................................508 548-4700
Bill Hough, *Pr*
EMP: 35 **EST:** 1929
SQ FT: 7,100
SALES (est): 6.51MM
SALES (corp-wide): 6.51MM **Privately Held**
Web: www.capenews.net
SIC: 2711 2721　Newspapers: publishing only, not printed on site; Periodicals

(G-8631)
FALMOUTH MAR YACHTING CTR INC
Also Called: Falmouth Marine
278 Scranton Ave (02540-3401)
PHONE................................508 548-4600
Vincent Jeffrey, *Pr*
EMP: 10 **EST:** 1939
SQ FT: 50,000
SALES (est): 399.06K **Privately Held**
Web: www.falmouthmarine.com
SIC: 7699 4491 5983 5551　Boat repair; Docks, incl. buildings and facilities: operation and maint.; Fuel oil dealers; Marine supplies, nec

(G-8632)
FOXEES CO INC
419 Palmer Ave Ste 6 (02540-5118)
PHONE................................508 548-8485
Marilyn Fox, *Pr*
Scott Fox, *Treas*
EMP: 27 **EST:** 1990
SQ FT: 1,700

SALES (est): 439K **Privately Held**
Web: www.durangoconcerts.com
SIC: 5812 2051　Coffee shop; Bagels, fresh or frozen

(G-8633)
HOGY LURE COMPANY LLC
15 Simpson Ln (02540-2230)
P.O. Box 570 (02541-0570)
PHONE................................617 699-5157
▲ **EMP:** 8 **EST:** 2008
SALES (est): 953.52K **Privately Held**
Web: www.hogylures.com
SIC: 3949　Lures, fishing: artificial

(G-8634)
KERFOOT TECHNOLOGIES INC
49 Ransom Rd (02540-1655)
PHONE................................508 539-3002
William B Kerfoot, *Pr*
Patricia Kerfoot, *Treas*
EMP: 10 **EST:** 1978
SALES (est): 852.72K **Privately Held**
Web: www.kva-equipment.com
SIC: 3589 3594 3829 8748　Water treatment equipment, industrial; Fluid power pumps; Hydrometers, except industrial process type ; Environmental consultant

(G-8635)
MCKNIGHT MANAGEMENT CO INC (PA)
505 Palmer Ave (02540-2954)
PHONE................................508 540-5051
Robert Mcknight, *Pr*
Martin Miller, *VP*
EMP: 8 **EST:** 1987
SQ FT: 6,000
SALES (est): 1.26MM
SALES (corp-wide): 1.26MM **Privately Held**
SIC: 2721　Magazines: publishing only, not printed on site

Feeding Hills
Hampden County

(G-8636)
NORGAARD MACHINE INC
370 Garden St (01030-2508)
P.O. Box 249 (01030-0249)
PHONE................................413 789-1291
Gerald Norgaard, *Pr*
Geraldine Norgaard, *Mgr*
EMP: 8 **EST:** 1975
SQ FT: 10,000
SALES (est): 862.24K **Privately Held**
Web: www.iiocpa.com
SIC: 3599　Machine shop, jobbing and repair

(G-8637)
WANIEWSKI FARMS INC
409 S Westfield St (01030-2721)
PHONE................................413 786-1182
Matthew Waniewski, *Pr*
EMP: 12 **EST:** 1948
SQ FT: 3,000
SALES (est): 676.02K **Privately Held**
SIC: 2013　Sausages, from purchased meat

Fiskdale
Worcester County

(G-8638)
G&F MEDICAL INC
709 Main St (01518-1304)

▲ = Import ▼ = Export
◆ = Import/Export

PHONE..............................978 560-2622
John J Argitis, *CEO*
David W Argitis, *VP*
Gary Degroat, *CFO*
▲ **EMP:** 22 **EST:** 2007
SQ FT: 14,500
SALES (est): 4.67MM **Privately Held**
Web: www.gandfprecision.com
SIC: 3089 Injection molding of plastics

(G-8639)
G&F PRECISION MOLDING INC (PA)
709 Main St (01518-1304)
PHONE..............................508 347-9132
John G Argitis, *Pr*
John J Argitis, *
▲ **EMP:** 92 **EST:** 1962
SQ FT: 61,000
SALES (est): 17.07MM
SALES (corp-wide): 17.07MM **Privately Held**
Web: www.gandfprecision.com
SIC: 3089 3544 Injection molding of plastics; Special dies and tools

---

Fitchburg
Worcester County

(G-8640)
ADVANCED PRINT TECHNOLOGY INC
Also Called: APT
76 Laurel St (01420-7710)
PHONE..............................978 342-0093
Alvah M Reida, *Pr*
EMP: 7 **EST:** 1984
SQ FT: 4,800
SALES (est): 800.08K **Privately Held**
Web: www.aptshirts.com
SIC: 2396 5136 5137 Screen printing on fabric articles; Men's and boy's clothing; Women's and children's clothing

(G-8641)
ADVANCED VISIBILITY LLC
983 John Fitch Hwy (01420-2693)
PHONE..............................603 660-6033
EMP: 8
SALES (est): 507.13K **Privately Held**
Web: www.glowguard.com
SIC: 2396 Printing and embossing on plastics fabric articles

(G-8642)
ARRHYTHMIA RESEARCH TECHNOLOGY
25 Sawyer Passway (01420-5769)
PHONE..............................978 602-1436
EMP: 18 **EST:** 2019
SALES (est): 723.88K **Privately Held**
Web: www.micronsolutions.com
SIC: 3845 Electromedical equipment

(G-8643)
AVERY DENNISON CORPORATION
Also Called: Avery Dennison Fastener Div
224 Industrial Rd (01420-4634)
PHONE..............................978 353-2100
Gary Buchholz, *Brnch Mgr*
EMP: 220
SQ FT: 40,000
SALES (corp-wide): 9.04B **Publicly Held**
Web: www.averydennison.com
SIC: 2672 Coated paper, except photographic, carbon, or abrasive
PA: Avery Dennison Corporation
8080 Norton Pkwy

Mentor OH 44060
440 534-6000

(G-8644)
BOPKG INC (HQ)
251 Authority Dr (01420-6044)
PHONE..............................978 343-3067
Ward Mclaughlin, *Pr*
William Hodges, *
William Lorenz, *
Jeffrey Coleman, *
▲ **EMP:** 140 **EST:** 1887
SQ FT: 80,000
SALES (est): 47.35MM
SALES (corp-wide): 95.47MM **Privately Held**
Web: www.oliverinc.com
SIC: 2752 2759 2671 2657 Offset printing; Commercial printing, nec; Paper; coated and laminated packaging; Folding paperboard boxes
PA: Oliver Printing & Packaging Co., Llc
1760 Enterprise Pkwy
Twinsburg OH 44087
330 425-7890

(G-8645)
C V TOOL COMPANY INC
12 Baltic Ln Ste 1 (01420-2800)
PHONE..............................978 353-7901
Ken Mattson, *Mgr*
EMP: 18
SALES (corp-wide): 9.64MM **Privately Held**
Web: www.cvtool.com
SIC: 3599 Machine shop, jobbing and repair
PA: C. V. Tool Company, Inc.
44 Robert Porter Rd
Southington CT 06489
978 353-7901

(G-8646)
CADO MANUFACTURING INC
1 Princeton Rd Ste 2 (01420-4638)
PHONE..............................978 343-2989
Claude Chapdelaine, *Pr*
EMP: 10 **EST:** 1990
SQ FT: 16,000
SALES (est): 946.75K **Privately Held**
Web: www.cadocompany.com
SIC: 3089 Injection molding of plastics

(G-8647)
CADO PRODUCTS INC
Also Called: Union Products
1 Princeton Rd Ste 2 (01420-4609)
PHONE..............................978 343-2989
Bruce Zarozny, *Pr*
Claude Chapdelaine, *
EMP: 30 **EST:** 1997
SQ FT: 70,000
SALES (est): 3.73MM **Privately Held**
Web: www.cadocompany.com
SIC: 3089 Injection molding of plastics

(G-8648)
CARAUSTAR INDUSTRIES INC
Also Called: Newark America
100 Newark Ave (01420-4637)
PHONE..............................978 665-2632
Dana Pelletier, *Brnch Mgr*
EMP: 78
SALES (corp-wide): 5.22B **Publicly Held**
Web: www.greif.com
SIC: 2631 Paperboard mills
HQ: Caraustar Industries, Inc.
5000 Astell Pwdr Sprng Rd
Austell GA 30106
770 948-3101

(G-8649)
CORRUGATED PACKAGING INC
215 Cleghorn (01420)
PHONE..............................978 342-6076
Lynn Thornton, *Pr*
Alexander Urquhart, *Treas*
EMP: 14 **EST:** 1983
SQ FT: 35,000
SALES (est): 1.61MM **Privately Held**
Web: www.gbp.com
SIC: 2653 Boxes, corrugated: made from purchased materials

(G-8650)
CRISTY CORPORATION
260 Authority Dr (01420-6097)
PHONE..............................978 343-4330
Donald A Cristy, *Pr*
EMP: 13 **EST:** 1943
SQ FT: 25,000
SALES (est): 483.85K **Privately Held**
Web: www.drygas.com
SIC: 2899 Antifreeze compounds

(G-8651)
CROCKER TECHNICAL PAPERS INC
Also Called: C T P
431 Westminster St (01420-4700)
PHONE..............................978 345-7771
▲ **EMP:** 50
SIC: 2621 Specialty papers

(G-8652)
DENARDO WIRE AND CABLE CO INC
149 Industrial Rd (01420-4654)
P.O. Box 321 (01772-0321)
PHONE..............................978 343-6412
John E Denardo, *Pr*
Nancy Denardo, *VP*
EMP: 22 **EST:** 1979
SQ FT: 40,000
SALES (est): 582.95K **Privately Held**
Web: www.denardowireandcable.com
SIC: 3357 Nonferrous wiredrawing and insulating

(G-8653)
DRS NAVAL POWER SYSTEMS INC
166 Boulder Dr Ste 201 (01420-3168)
PHONE..............................978 343-9719
EMP: 120
SALES (corp-wide): 15.28B **Publicly Held**
Web: www.leonardodrs.com
SIC: 3812 Search and navigation equipment
HQ: Drs Naval Power Systems, Inc
W126n7449 Flint Dr
Menomonee Falls WI 53051
414 875-4314

(G-8654)
FITCHBURG PUBLISHING
808 Main St (01420-5388)
P.O. Box 730 (01420-0007)
PHONE..............................978 343-6911
Karen Fioretti, *Prin*
EMP: 7 **EST:** 2010
SALES (est): 129.71K **Privately Held**
Web: www.fitchburgleominster.net
SIC: 2741 Miscellaneous publishing

(G-8655)
FOAMTECH LLC
1 Nursery Ln (01420-3043)
PHONE..............................978 343-4022
EMP: 16 **EST:** 2007

SALES (est): 2.23MM **Privately Held**
Web: www.foamtechna.com
SIC: 2295 Resin or plastic coated fabrics

(G-8656)
GREAT NORTHERN DUNNAGE LLC
291 Westminster St (01420-3774)
P.O. Box 410543 (32941-0543)
PHONE..............................978 343-2300
Kathleen Rocheleau, *Managing Member*
EMP: 30 **EST:** 2009
SQ FT: 300,000
SALES (est): 4.88MM **Privately Held**
Web: www.gndunnage.com
SIC: 5031 2448 Lumber, plywood, and millwork; Wood pallets and skids

(G-8657)
IMAGE DIAGNOSTICS INC
Also Called: IDI
310 Authority Dr (01420-6047)
PHONE..............................978 829-0009
Remo Rossi, *Pr*
Robert Rudd, *VP*
EMP: 29 **EST:** 1985
SQ FT: 26,000
SALES (est): 15.6MM **Privately Held**
Web: www.imagediagnostics.com
SIC: 5047 3845 Medical equipment and supplies; Laser systems and equipment, medical

(G-8658)
KELLEY WOOD PRODUCTS INC
85 River St (01420-3093)
PHONE..............................978 345-7531
S Michael Kelley, *Pr*
John Kelley, *VP*
Florence I Kelley, *Clerk*
EMP: 18 **EST:** 1972
SQ FT: 17,000
SALES (est): 2.12MM **Privately Held**
Web: www.kelleywoodpro.com
SIC: 2448 2441 Pallets, wood; Boxes, wood

(G-8659)
M-R RESOURCES INC
160 Authority Dr (01420-6045)
PHONE..............................978 345-9010
Jonathan Webb, *CEO*
Jonathan O Webb, *
Robert Crosby, *
EMP: 25 **EST:** 1986
SQ FT: 22,000
SALES (est): 1.55MM **Privately Held**
Web: www.mrr.com
SIC: 3826 5049 5047 3845 Instruments measuring magnetic and electrical properties; Laboratory equipment, except medical or dental; Diagnostic equipment, medical; Electromedical equipment

(G-8660)
MA MFG LLC
Also Called: Peak Manufacturing
325 Authority Dr (01420-6049)
PHONE..............................978 400-9991
EMP: 20 **EST:** 2013
SALES (est): 1.31MM **Privately Held**
SIC: 3599 Machine shop, jobbing and repair

(G-8661)
MAR-LEE COMPANIES INC
Also Called: Mar Lee Companies Tech Ctrs
190 Authority Dr (01420-6045)
PHONE..............................978 343-9600
Al Gravelle, *Mgr*
EMP: 8
SALES (corp-wide): 5.48MM **Privately Held**

Web: www.texen.com
SIC: **3089** Molding primary plastics
HQ: Mar-Lee Companies, Inc.
   180 Authority Dr
   Fitchburg MA 01420
   978 343-9600

(G-8662)
MAR-LEE COMPANIES INC (HQ)
180 Authority Dr (01420-6045)
PHONE..........................978 343-9600
▲ **EMP:** 65 **EST:** 2001
SALES (est): 47.17MM
SALES (corp-wide): 5.48MM **Privately Held**
Web: www.texen.com
SIC: **3544** Forms (molds), for foundry and plastics working machinery
PA: Psb Industries
   4 Allee Du Parmelan
   Epagny Metz Tessy 74370
   450090002

(G-8663)
MEDIANEWS GROUP INC
Also Called: Sentinel and Enterprise
808 Main St (01420-5388)
P.O. Box 730 (01420-0007)
PHONE..........................978 343-6911
EMP: 49
SALES (corp-wide): 1.96B **Privately Held**
Web: www.medianewsgroup.com
SIC: **2711** 2752 Newspapers: publishing only, not printed on site; Commercial printing, lithographic
HQ: Medianews Group, Inc.
   5990 Washington St
   Denver CO 80216

(G-8664)
MERIT MACHINE MFG INC
25 Willow St (01420-7824)
PHONE..........................978 342-7677
Ross Barber, *Pr*
June A Barber, *Sec*
Roger Barber, *VP*
EMP: 10 **EST:** 1945
SQ FT: 12,000
SALES (est): 390.78K **Privately Held**
Web: www.meritmachineinc.com
SIC: **3599** 3541 Machine shop, jobbing and repair; Machine tools, metal cutting type

(G-8665)
MICRON PRODUCTS INC
25 Sawyer Passway (01420-5702)
PHONE..........................978 345-5000
James E Rouse, *Pr*
David Garrison, *
Salvatore Emma Junior, *Pr*
Derek T Welch, *
Mark Laviolette, *
▲ **EMP:** 50 **EST:** 1972
SQ FT: 116,000
SALES (est): 14.89MM
SALES (corp-wide): 17.5MM **Privately Held**
Web: www.micronsolutions.com
SIC: **3089** 3841 Injection molding of plastics; Surgical and medical instruments
PA: Micron Solutions, Inc.
   25 Sawyer Passway
   Fitchburg MA 01420
   978 345-5000

(G-8666)
MICRON SOLUTIONS INC (PA)
25 Sawyer Passway (01420-5769)
PHONE..........................978 345-5000
Salvatore Emma Junior, *Pr*

Andrei Soran, *Ch Bd*
Derek T Welch, *CFO*
EMP: 30 **EST:** 1987
SQ FT: 116,000
SALES (est): 17.5MM
SALES (corp-wide): 17.5MM **Privately Held**
Web: www.micronsolutions.com
SIC: **3845** Electromedical apparatus

(G-8667)
MODU FORM INC (PA)
Also Called: Moduform
172 Industrial Rd (01420-4639)
PHONE..........................978 345-7942
William L Weissman, *Pr*
Thomas C Hurd, *
Joshua Weissman, *
Laura Wade, *Point of Contact*
▼ **EMP:** 75 **EST:** 1976
SQ FT: 100,000
SALES (est): 14.17MM
SALES (corp-wide): 14.17MM **Privately Held**
Web: www.moduform.com
SIC: **2511** 2521 2522 2531 Wood household furniture; Wood office furniture; Office furniture, except wood; Seats, miscellaneous public conveyances

(G-8668)
NEW ENGLAND KEYBOARD INC
Also Called: N E K
1 Princeton Rd Ste 1 (01420-4638)
PHONE..........................978 345-8332
David P Myers, *Pr*
Mark A Yates, *
Philip Myers, *
Mark Yates, *
▲ **EMP:** 50 **EST:** 1985
SQ FT: 16,000
SALES (est): 6.5MM **Privately Held**
Web: www.newenglandkeyboard.com
SIC: **3577** Computer peripheral equipment, nec

(G-8669)
NEW ENGLAND WIRECLOTH CO LLC
123 Kelly Ave (01420-4530)
PHONE..........................978 343-4998
EMP: 9 **EST:** 1999
SALES (est): 931.49K **Privately Held**
SIC: **3496** Woven wire products, nec

(G-8670)
OPCO LABORATORY INC
704 River St (01420-2913)
PHONE..........................978 345-2522
David Maldari, *Pr*
Saverio Maldari, *Ch*
EMP: 20 **EST:** 1976
SQ FT: 10,000
SALES (est): 2.66MM **Privately Held**
Web: www.opcolab.com
SIC: **3827** Lenses, optical: all types except ophthalmic

(G-8671)
P J ALBERT INC
199 Upham St (01420-4594)
P.O. Box 2165 (01420-0013)
PHONE..........................978 345-7828
Jacqueline M Albert, *Pr*
William Wheeler, *
Philip J Albert, *
EMP: 65 **EST:** 1981
SQ FT: 2,800
SALES (est): 5.47MM **Privately Held**
Web: www.pjalbert.com

SIC: **3295** 1611 1771 Pulverized earth; Highway and street paving contractor; Concrete work

(G-8672)
PORTANCE CORP
Also Called: Peak Manufacturing
325 Authority Dr (01420-6049)
PHONE..........................978 400-9991
Peter Mendes, *Pr*
EMP: 13 **EST:** 2016
SALES (est): 510.77K **Privately Held**
SIC: **3599** Machine shop, jobbing and repair

(G-8673)
ROCHELEAU TOOL AND DIE CO INC
Also Called: Rocheleau Blow Molding Systems
117 Indl Rd (01420)
PHONE..........................978 345-1723
Steven Roland Rocheleau, *Pr*
Jeffrey Rocheleau, *
Daniel Rocheleau, *
Lisa Ann Rocheleau, *
◆ **EMP:** 57 **EST:** 1938
SQ FT: 32,000
SALES (est): 9.6MM **Privately Held**
Web: www.rocheleautool.com
SIC: **3559** Plastics working machinery

(G-8674)
SIMONDS INDUSTRIES INTL
135 Intervale Rd (01420-6519)
P.O. Box 500 (01420-0005)
PHONE..........................978 424-0100
Ray Martino, *Pr*
▲ **EMP:** 15 **EST:** 2009
SALES (est): 719.18K **Privately Held**
Web: www.simondsint.com
SIC: **3541** Machine tools, metal cutting type

(G-8675)
SIMONDS INTERNATIONAL LLC (HQ)
135 Intervale Rd (01420-6519)
P.O. Box 600 (01420-0054)
PHONE..........................978 424-0100
Raymond J Martino, *Pr*
Henry J Botticello, *
David P Witman, *
◆ **EMP:** 300 **EST:** 1988
SQ FT: 400,000
SALES (est): 101.98MM
SALES (corp-wide): 206.09MM **Privately Held**
Web: www.simondsint.com
SIC: **3553** Woodworking machinery
PA: Wood Fiber Holdings, Inc.
   139 Intervale Rd
   Fitchburg MA 01420
   800 426-6226

(G-8676)
STEEL-FAB INC
430 Crawford St (01420-6892)
P.O. Box 2145 (01420-0013)
PHONE..........................978 345-1112
Mark W Freeman, *Pr*
Louis Bartolini, *
Sanford L Crane, *
Bernard M Freeman, *
Shelly Cloecchi, *Corporate Secretary*
EMP: 40 **EST:** 1966
SQ FT: 43,000
SALES (est): 9.45MM **Privately Held**
Web: www.steelfabinc.com
SIC: **3443** 3441 Weldments; Dam gates, metal plate

(G-8677)
STEEL-FAB ENGINEERING & SALES
552 Oak Hill Rd (01420-4818)
PHONE..........................978 345-0035
EMP: 7 **EST:** 2017
SALES (est): 109.96K **Privately Held**
Web: www.steelfabinc.com
SIC: **3441** Fabricated structural metal

(G-8678)
SYNTHOMER INC
83 Authority Dr (01420-6018)
PHONE..........................978 342-5831
Dan Slint, *Mgr*
EMP: 123
SQ FT: 23,556
SALES (corp-wide): 2.87B **Privately Held**
Web: www.omnova.com
SIC: **2819** 2821 Industrial inorganic chemicals, nec; Plastics materials and resins
HQ: Synthomer Inc.
   25435 Harvard Rd
   Beachwood OH 44122
   216 682-7000

(G-8679)
UNIVERSAL MCH & DESIGN CORP
323 Princeton Rd (01420-4879)
PHONE..........................978 343-4688
Jess Ouellette, *Owner*
▲ **EMP:** 8 **EST:** 1985
SALES (est): 939.79K **Privately Held**
Web: www.universalmachine.net
SIC: **3599** Machine shop, jobbing and repair

(G-8680)
VINYL TECHNOLOGIES INC
Also Called: Vytek
195 Industrial Rd (01420-4654)
PHONE..........................978 342-9800
Dirk Burrowes, *Pr*
▲ **EMP:** 35 **EST:** 1990
SQ FT: 40,000
SALES (est): 4.94MM **Privately Held**
Web: www.vy-tek.com
SIC: **3599** Machine shop, jobbing and repair

(G-8681)
VISIONSTEP CONSULTING INC
Also Called: Tk Cups-Sorg's
750 Crawford St (01420-6814)
PHONE..........................978 422-1447
EMP: 45 **EST:** 1996
SALES (est): 5.95MM **Privately Held**
Web: www.birchpoint.com
SIC: **2621** 5113 Paper mills; Industrial and personal service paper

(G-8682)
WHITNEY & SON INC
95 Kelly Ave (01420-4520)
PHONE..........................978 343-6353
Daniel M Whitney, *CEO*
Charlie Jones, *Pr*
Janice Whitney, *Dir*
Jason Whitney, *Prin*
Doug Baker, *Prin*
▲ **EMP:** 21 **EST:** 1964
SQ FT: 8,000
SALES (est): 10.62MM **Privately Held**
Web: www.whitneyandson.com
SIC: **3559** 5084 7359 3496 Stone working machinery; Industrial machinery and equipment; Equipment rental and leasing, nec; Miscellaneous fabricated wire products

▲ = Import ▼ = Export
◆ = Import/Export

Florence
Hampshire County

(G-8683)
BI-QEM INC
238 Nonotuck St (01062-2671)
PHONE...................................413 584-2472
Gabriel Munck, *Pr*
Claudio Colombo, *
Linda Haskell, *
Jeanne Mazuch, *
Scott Chisholm, *
◆ **EMP:** 25 **EST:** 1983
SQ FT: 200,000
SALES (est): 12.33MM **Privately Held**
SIC: 2821 Molding compounds, plastics
HQ: Bi-Qem Spa
Via Dante Alighieri 60
Carbonate CO 22070
033 183-6511

(G-8684)
LUCAS FABRICATION INC
Also Called: Tom Raredon Metal Work
30 N Maple St Ste 2 (01062-1360)
PHONE...................................413 586-0941
Tom Raredon, *Pr*
EMP: 12 **EST:** 1978
SALES (est): 400.01K **Privately Held**
Web: www.raredonresources.com
SIC: 2514 Metal household furniture

(G-8685)
PIONEER PRECISION OPTICS INC
296c Nonotuck St (01062-2645)
PHONE...................................413 341-3992
Thomas J Mcgrath, *Prin*
Thomas Mcgrath, *Prin*
EMP: 10 **EST:** 2013
SALES (est): 981.75K **Privately Held**
Web: www.pioneerprecisionoptics.com
SIC: 3827 Optical instruments and lenses

(G-8686)
SHAFT CURRENT SOLUTIONS INC
Also Called: Sohre Turbomachinery
34 N Maple St Ste 7 (01062-1497)
PHONE...................................413 267-0590
Rui Fernandes, *Pr*
Dorothy Fernandes, *VP*
EMP: 9 **EST:** 2019
SALES (est): 942.92K **Privately Held**
Web: www.sohreturbo.com
SIC: 3714 3511 Drive shafts, motor vehicle;
Turbines and turbine generator sets and
parts

(G-8687)
W G FRY CORP
28 Sylvan Ln (01062-9616)
PHONE...................................413 747-2551
Saul Kuhr, *Pr*
EMP: 47 **EST:** 1920
SQ FT: 50,000
SALES (est): 1.11MM **Privately Held**
SIC: 2679 5112 2782 2789 Paper products,
converted, nec; Stationery and office
supplies; Blankbooks and looseleaf binders
; Binding only: books, pamphlets,
magazines, etc.

Foxboro
Norfolk County

(G-8688)
4TELL SOLUTIONS LP
124 Washington St Ste 101 (02035-1368)
PHONE...................................207 828-7900
James Kavanagh, *Pr*
James Fitzgibbons, *CFO*
Robert Slaton, *COO*
EMP: 35 **EST:** 2007
SALES (est): 2.22MM **Privately Held**
SIC: 8742 7372 Business management
consultant; Application computer software

(G-8689)
ACCUTECH PACKAGING INC
Also Called: Accutech
157 Green St (02035-2868)
PHONE...................................508 543-3800
Richard J Madigan Junior, *Pr*
Patrick L Madigan, *General Vice President**
Michael E Keneally, *
▲ **EMP:** 71 **EST:** 1986
SQ FT: 72,000
SALES (est): 28.22MM **Privately Held**
Web: www.accutechpkg.com
SIC: 3089 3544 3565 2674 Thermoformed
finished plastics products, nec; Industrial
molds; Packaging machinery; Bags:
uncoated paper and multiwall

(G-8690)
ACT MANUFACTURING SECURITIES C
124 Washington St Ste 101 (02035-1368)
PHONE...................................508 481-5246
John A Pino, *Prin*
EMP: 7 **EST:** 2003
SALES (est): 180.27K **Privately Held**
SIC: 3999 Manufacturing industries, nec

(G-8691)
AUTO-CHLOR SYSTEM NY CY INC
140 Washington St Ste 1 (02035-1379)
PHONE...................................508 543-6767
Tony Pecci, *COO*
EMP: 189
SALES (corp-wide): 1.07MM **Privately Held**
Web: www.autochlor.com
SIC: 3589 Dishwashing machines,
commercial
PA: Auto-Chlor System Of New York City,
Inc.
450 Ferguson Dr
Mountain View CA 94043
650 967-3085

(G-8692)
CHRISTOPHER-GORDON PUBLISHING
3 Bailey St (02035-2836)
PHONE...................................781 762-5577
EMP: 10
SALES (est): 1.1MM **Privately Held**
Web: www.christopher-gordon.com
SIC: 2731 Books, publishing only

(G-8693)
CONOPCO INC
Also Called: Auto Chlor Systems Co
140 Washington St Ste 1 (02035-1379)
PHONE...................................508 543-6767
Richard Goldstein, *Pr*
EMP: 10

SALES (corp-wide): 62.39B **Privately Held**
Web: www.autoclor.com
SIC: 2844 Perfumes, cosmetics and other
toilet preparations
HQ: Conopco, Inc.
700 Sylvan Ave
Englewood Cliffs NJ 07632
201 894-7760

(G-8694)
DOREL JUVENILE GROUP INC
Also Called: Safety 1st
25 Forbes Blvd Unit 4 (02035-2873)
PHONE...................................800 544-1108
Vincent D Alleva, *Brnch Mgr*
EMP: 176
SALES (corp-wide): 1.57B **Privately Held**
Web: www.doreljuvenile.com
SIC: 3089 3069 3429 3699 Plastics
kitchenware, tableware, and houseware;
Baby pacifiers, rubber; Hardware, nec;
Security devices
HQ: Dorel Juvenile Group, Inc.
2525 State St
Columbus IN 47201
800 457-5276

(G-8695)
DOREL JUVENILE GROUP INC
Also Called: Dorel Design & Development Ctr
25 Forbes Blvd Unit 4 (02035-2873)
PHONE...................................508 216-1800
Dinnie D'alleba, *Genl Mgr*
EMP: 198
SALES (corp-wide): 1.57B **Privately Held**
Web: www.doreljuvenile.com
SIC: 3944 Games, toys, and children's
vehicles
HQ: Dorel Juvenile Group, Inc.
2525 State St
Columbus IN 47201
800 457-5276

(G-8696)
EPIRUS BIOPHARMACEUTICALS INC
124 Washington St Ste 101 (02035-1368)
PHONE...................................617 600-3497
EMP: 33
Web: www.epirusbiopharma.com
SIC: 2834 Pharmaceutical preparations

(G-8697)
GIGANTUM INC
124 Washington St (02035-1368)
PHONE...................................301 960-8012
Jonathan Whitehouse, *Prin*
Dean Kleissas, *Prin*
EMP: 8 **EST:** 2019
SALES (est): 1.03MM **Privately Held**
Web: www.nvidia.com
SIC: 3674 Semiconductors and related
devices

(G-8698)
GUTOR ELECTRONIC AMERICAS LLC ✪
70 Mechanic St (02035-2040)
PHONE...................................713 397-3798
Tierre Vanstoslegatte, *Managing Member*
EMP: 51 **EST:** 2022
SALES (est): 10MM
SALES (corp-wide): 4.43MM **Privately Held**
SIC: 3629 Power conversion units, a.c. to
d.c.: static-electric
PA: Latour Capital Management Sas
104 Avenue Des Champs Elysees
Paris 75008
140623000

(G-8699)
HY9 CORPORATION
124 Washington St Ste 101 (02035-1368)
PHONE...................................508 698-1040
Gary Clarke, *Pr*
Walter Juda, *Ch*
Donald S Bradshaw Junior, *CEO*
Douglas B Holmes, *VP*
Ann H Oppenheimer, *Sec*
EMP: 7 **EST:** 2006
SALES (est): 971.15K **Privately Held**
Web: 618889.shop.ename.com
SIC: 3621 Power generators

(G-8700)
ICONICS INC (HQ)
100 Foxboro Blvd Ste 130 (02035-2883)
▼ **EMP:** 49 **EST:** 1986
SALES (est): 30.47MM **Privately Held**
Web: www.iconics.com
SIC: 7372 7371 Prepackaged software;
Custom computer programming services
PA: Mitsubishi Electric Corporation
2-7-3, Marunouchi
Chiyoda-Ku TKY 100-0

(G-8701)
INDUSTRIAL DEFENDER INC
225 Foxboro Blvd Ste 202 (02035-3062)
PHONE...................................617 675-4206
James Crowey, *CEO*
Phil Dunbar, *
EMP: 68 **EST:** 2019
SALES (est): 30MM **Privately Held**
Web: www.industrialdefender.com
SIC: 7372 Business oriented computer
software

(G-8702)
INTRALIGN HOLDINGS LLC
124 Washington St Ste 101 (02035-1368)
PHONE...................................602 773-8506
Rick Ferreira, *Pr*
Tim Einwechter, *CFO*
Arthur Goodrich, *Ex VP*
Randel Richner, *Executive Advanced
Analytics Vice President*
Kristin Simoens, *Executive Intelligent Care
Design Vice President*
EMP: 8 **EST:** 2012
SALES (est): 141.4K **Privately Held**
SIC: 3841 8742 Surgical and medical
instruments; Hospital and health services
consultant

(G-8703)
JOULE UNLIMITED TECHNOLOGIES INC
124 Washington St Ste 101 (02035-1368)
PHONE...................................781 533-9100
EMP: 100
SIC: 2869 8731 Ethyl alcohol, ethanol;
Biotechnical research, commercial

(G-8704)
JP PLASTICS INC
67 Green St Ste 1 (02035-3824)
PHONE...................................508 203-2420
EMP: 8 **EST:** 1995
SQ FT: 10,000
SALES (est): 603.93K **Privately Held**
Web: www.maltzsales.com
SIC: 5084 3547 Industrial machinery and
equipment; Plate rolling mill machinery

(G-8705)
KRAFT GROUP LLC (PA)
1 Patriot Pl (02035-1374)
PHONE...................................508 384-4230

Jonathan A Kraft, *Pr*
Robert Kraft, *
Michael Quattromani, *
EMP: 147 **EST:** 1995
SALES (est): 910.1MM **Privately Held**
Web: www.thekraftgroup.com
SIC: 2653   Boxes, corrugated: made from
   purchased materials

(G-8706)
LANTOS TECHNOLOGIES INC
Also Called: Lantos Tech
124 Washington St Ste 101 (02035-1368)
PHONE..............................781 443-7633
EMP: 9 **EST:** 2009
SALES (est): 3.12MM **Privately Held**
Web: www.lantostechnologies.com
SIC: 3845   Electromedical equipment

(G-8707)
MASSACHUSETTS ASSN
REALTORS (PA)
Also Called: MAR
18 Washington St (02035-1072)
PHONE..............................781 890-3700
Theresa Hatton, *Ex VP*
Anne Blatz, *Pr*
EMP: 16 **EST:** 1924
SALES (est): 5MM
SALES (corp-wide): 5MM **Privately Held**
Web: www.marealtor.com
SIC: 8611 6531 2721   Real estate board;
   Real estate agents and managers;
   Periodicals

(G-8708)
MICROFIBRES INC
124 Washington St Ste 101 (02035-1368)
PHONE..............................401 725-4883
◆ **EMP:** 1080
SIC: 2221 2295 5131 2262   Upholstery
   fabrics, manmade fiber and silk; Coated
   fabrics, not rubberized; Upholstery fabrics,
   woven; Printing, manmade fiber and silk
   broadwoven fabrics

(G-8709)
N12 TECHNOLOGIES INC
124 Washington St Ste 101 (02035-1368)
PHONE..............................857 259-6622
EMP: 7 **EST:** 2010
SALES (est): 1.55MM **Privately Held**
Web: www.n12technologies.com
SIC: 3624   Fibers, carbon and graphite

(G-8710)
NEW-INDY CONTAINERBOARD
LLC
1 Patriot Pl (02035-1374)
PHONE..............................508 384-4230
EMP: 11 **EST:** 2012
SALES (est): 859.2K **Privately Held**
Web: www.newindycontainerboard.com
SIC: 2653   Corrugated and solid fiber boxes

(G-8711)
OASYS WATER INC
124 Washington St Ste 101 (02035-1368)
PHONE..............................617 963-0450
James Matheson, *Pr*
Bob Muscat, *
Aaron Mandell, *
Edward Freedman, *
Robert Mcginnis, *Bd of Dir*
▲ **EMP:** 39 **EST:** 2009
SALES (est): 4.77MM **Privately Held**
Web: www.oasyswater.com
SIC: 3559   Desalination equipment

(G-8712)
OWNCLOUD INC
124 Washington St Ste 101 (02035-1368)
PHONE..............................617 515-3664
Markus Rex, *CEO*
Matthew Richards, *
Daniel Curtis, *
EMP: 57 **EST:** 2011
SALES (est): 1.54MM **Privately Held**
Web: www.owncloud.com
SIC: 7372   Business oriented computer
   software

(G-8713)
PANDA PLATES INC (PA)
Also Called: Yumble Kids
124 Washington St Ste 101 (02035-1368)
PHONE..............................888 997-6623
Joanna Parker, *Pr*
EMP: 7 **EST:** 2016
SALES (est): 984.47K
SALES (corp-wide): 984.47K **Privately
Held**
Web: www.yumblefoods.com
SIC: 2099   Ready-to-eat meals, salads, and
   sandwiches

(G-8714)
PANDA PLATES INC
Also Called: Yumble
124 Washington St Ste 101 (02035-1368)
PHONE..............................917 848-8777
Hillel David Parker, *Admn*
EMP: 17
SALES (corp-wide): 984.47K **Privately
Held**
Web: www.yumblefoods.com
SIC: 2099   Ready-to-eat meals, salads, and
   sandwiches
PA: Panda Plates Inc.
   124 Washington St Ste 101
   Foxboro MA 02035
   888 997-6623

(G-8715)
QD VISION INC
124 Washington St Ste 101 (02035-1368)
PHONE..............................781 652-7500
EMP: 68
SIC: 3663   Television monitors

(G-8716)
REA-CRAFT PRESS
INCORPORATED
10 Wall St (02035-2914)
P.O. Box 398 (02035-0398)
PHONE..............................508 543-8710
Tom Shannon, *Pr*
Maureen Madden, *VP*
EMP: 13 **EST:** 1937
SQ FT: 13,000
SALES (est): 428K **Privately Held**
Web: www.reacraft.com
SIC: 2752   Offset printing

(G-8717)
RUBIUS THERAPEUTICS
124 Washington St (02035-1368)
PHONE..............................401 349-0818
EMP: 10 **EST:** 2019
SALES (est): 1.74MM **Privately Held**
SIC: 2834   Pharmaceutical preparations

(G-8718)
SCHNEDER ELC SYSTEMS
ARGNTINA
38 Neponset Ave (02035-2037)
PHONE..............................508 543-8750
George Spencer, *Pr*

EMP: 106 **EST:** 1968
SALES: 8.5MM
SALES (corp-wide): 82.05K **Privately Held**
SIC: 3823 8711 8741   Process control
   instruments; Industrial engineers;
   Management services
HQ: Invensys Limited
   2nd Floor
   London SW1E
   870 608-8608

(G-8719)
SCHNEIDER ELC SYSTEMS USA
INC
38 Neponset Ave (02035-2037)
PHONE..............................508 543-8750
Al Luggier, *Genl Mgr*
EMP: 10
SALES (corp-wide): 82.05K **Privately Held**
Web: www.flowfoxboro.com
SIC: 3823 8711 8741   Process control
   instruments; Engineering services;
   Management services
HQ: Schneider Electric Systems Usa, Inc.
   70 Mechanic St
   Foxboro MA 02035
   508 543-8750

(G-8720)
SCHNEIDER ELC SYSTEMS USA
INC
70 Mechanic St (02035-2040)
PHONE..............................508 543-8750
EMP: 10
SALES (corp-wide): 177.91K **Privately
Held**
Web: www.flowfoxboro.com
SIC: 3823 8711   Process control instruments
   ; Industrial engineers
HQ: Schneider Electric Systems Usa, Inc.
   70 Mechanic St
   Foxboro MA 02035
   508 543-8750

(G-8721)
SCHNEIDER ELC SYSTEMS USA
INC (DH)
Also Called: Schneider Electric
70 Mechanic St (02035-2040)
PHONE..............................508 543-8750
Nathalie Marcotte, *Pr*
Brian Dibenedetto, *
Karen Hamilton, *GLOBAL SUPPORT**
Peter Kent, *
▲ **EMP:** 39 **EST:** 1914
SQ FT: 1,175,899
SALES (est): 2.48B
SALES (corp-wide): 82.05K **Privately Held**
Web: www.flowfoxboro.com
SIC: 8711 8741 3823   Industrial engineers;
   Management services; Flow instruments,
   industrial process type
HQ: Invensys Limited
   2nd Floor
   London SW1E
   870 608-8608

(G-8722)
SCHNEIDER ELECTRIC
FOXBORO
38 Neponset Ave (02035-2037)
PHONE..............................508 543-8750
EMP: 500 **EST:** 1981
SALES (est): 52.14MM **Privately Held**
Web: www.se.com
SIC: 3823   Process control instruments

(G-8723)
SCHNEIDER ELECTRIC IT CORP
(DH)
Also Called: A P C M G E
70 Mechanic St (02035-2040)
PHONE..............................508 543-8750
David Johnson, *CEO*
Pankaj Sharma, *
Cyril Helbert, *
Neil Rasmussen, *
◆ **EMP:** 900 **EST:** 1981
SQ FT: 252,000
SALES (est): 1.18B
SALES (corp-wide): 82.05K **Privately Held**
SIC: 3629 3677 7372   Power conversion
   units, a.c. to d.c.: static-electric; Filtration
   devices, electronic; Prepackaged software
HQ: Schneider Electric Industries Sas
   35 Rue Joseph Monier
   Rueil Malmaison 92500
   141297000

(G-8724)
SCHNEIDER ELECTRIC USA INC
Also Called: Schneider Electric
15 Pond Ave (02035-2006)
PHONE..............................508 549-3385
EMP: 20
SALES (corp-wide): 82.05K **Privately Held**
Web: www.se.com
SIC: 3643 3612 3823 3625   Bus bars
   (electrical conductors); Power transformers,
   electric; Controllers, for process variables,
   all types; Relays and industrial controls
HQ: Schneider Electric Usa, Inc.
   1 Boston Pl Ste 2700
   Boston MA 02108
   978 975-9600

(G-8725)
SPACE AGE ACCESSORIES INC
Also Called: Space Age Americana
131 Morse St (02035-5220)
PHONE..............................508 543-3661
Edward Goldman, *Pr*
Stephen Goldman, *
Dennis Brennan, *
EMP: 24 **EST:** 1972
SQ FT: 21,000
SALES (est): 2.99MM **Privately Held**
SIC: 2821 3993   Acrylic resins; Signs and
   advertising specialties

(G-8726)
SUPPLYSCAPE CORPORATION
124 Washington St Ste 101 (02035-1368)
PHONE..............................781 503-7426
Mark O'connell, *Pr*
Shabbir Dahod, *
Gary Vilchick, *CFO*
Peter Spellman, *Sr VP*
Martin Kane, *Dir*
▲ **EMP:** 55 **EST:** 2004
SQ FT: 15,000
SALES (est): 2.99MM **Privately Held**
SIC: 7372   Prepackaged software

(G-8727)
TELTRON ENGINEERING INC
131 Morse St Ste 9 (02035-5200)
PHONE..............................508 543-6600
Ernest Whitaker, *Pr*
Carol Downey, *Admn*
EMP: 15 **EST:** 1967
SQ FT: 25,000
SALES (est): 2.29MM **Privately Held**
Web: www.teltronmetalfab.com
SIC: 3444   Sheet metal specialties, not
   stamped

(G-8728)
THE SENTRY COMPANY
65 Leonard St (02035-1899)
PHONE..............................508 543-5391
Thomas P Crocker, *Pr*
Bristol B Crocker, *Ch Bd*
Janet Vigor, *Sec*
EMP: 9 **EST:** 1921
SALES (est): 696.64K **Privately Held**
Web: www.vakcousa.com
SIC: 3567 Heating units and devices, industrial: electric

(G-8729)
TML MANUFACTURING INC
7 Perry Dr (02035-1024)
PHONE..............................508 264-0494
Michael R Berube Junior, *Dir*
EMP: 8 **EST:** 2015
SALES (est): 438.97K **Privately Held**
SIC: 3999 Manufacturing industries, nec

(G-8730)
VIAMET PHRMCTCALS HOLDINGS LLC
124 Washington St Ste 101 (02035-1368)
PHONE..............................919 467-8539
Robert J Schotzinger, *Pr*
Robert A Ingram, *
Oren J Cohen, *Chief Medical Officer*
Volker Herrmann, *Chief Commercial Officer*
Richard D Katz, *CFO*
EMP: 32 **EST:** 2011
SALES (est): 2.92MM **Privately Held**
SIC: 2834 Pharmaceutical preparations

(G-8731)
WB ENGINEERING INC
Also Called: Presto Lifts
2 Hampshire St (02035-2896)
PHONE..............................508 952-4000
James Cabot, *Pr*
EMP: 38
SALES (corp-wide): 57.73MM **Privately Held**
Web: www.prestolifts.com
SIC: 3537 Industrial trucks and tractors
HQ: W.B. Engineering, Inc.
11 Gray Rd
Falmouth ME 04105
207 878-0700

(G-8732)
WINTHROP PRINTING COMPANY INC
124 Washington St Ste 101 (02035-1368)
PHONE..............................617 268-9660
Roy E Orrall, *Pr*
John Peter Orrall, *
EMP: 21 **EST:** 1916
SQ FT: 5,500
SALES (est): 706.41K **Privately Held**
SIC: 2752 2759 2791 2789 Commercial printing, lithographic; Letterpress printing; Typesetting; Bookbinding and related work

(G-8733)
WOODFORMS INC
131 Morse St Ste 10 (02035-5200)
P.O. Box 69 (02035-0069)
PHONE..............................508 543-9417
Robert O'hare, *Pr*
EMP: 7 **EST:** 1981
SQ FT: 11,000
SALES (est): 611.98K **Privately Held**
Web: www.woodforms.net
SIC: 2511 Wood bedroom furniture

Foxborough
Norfolk County

(G-8734)
CAMBRIDGE HEART INC (PA)
124 Washington St (02035-1368)
PHONE..............................978 654-7600
Ali Haghighi-mood, *Pr*
Vincenzo Licausi, *VP Fin*
EMP: 19 **EST:** 1990
SALES (est): 3.86MM **Privately Held**
Web: www.cambridgeheart.com
SIC: 3841 3845 Diagnostic apparatus, medical; Electromedical equipment

(G-8735)
MICROPORT NAVIBOT INTL LLC
300 Foxboro Blvd (02035-2899)
PHONE..............................774 215-5471
EMP: 30 **EST:** 2020
SALES (est): 2.48MM **Privately Held**
SIC: 3841 Medical instruments and equipment, blood and bone work

(G-8736)
NEW-INDY CNTINERBOARD HOLD LLC (HQ)
1 Patriot Pl (02035-1374)
PHONE..............................508 384-4230
Robert K Kraft, *
▲ **EMP:** 105 **EST:** 2012
SALES (est): 486.22MM
SALES (corp-wide): 679.24MM **Privately Held**
SIC: 2631 Container, packaging, and boxboard
PA: New-Indy Jv Corp.
3500 Porsche Way Ste 150
Ontario CA 91764
909 296-3400

(G-8737)
RED OAK SOURCING LLC
2 Hampshire St Ste 200 (02035-2950)
PHONE..............................401 742-0701
Craig Heneghan, *Pr*
Laird Daniels, *CFO*
EMP: 60 **EST:** 2014
SQ FT: 20,605
SALES (est): 19.77MM
SALES (corp-wide): 322.47B **Publicly Held**
Web: www.redoaksourcing.com
SIC: 2834 Pharmaceutical preparations
PA: Cvs Health Corporation
1 Cvs Dr
Woonsocket RI 02895
401 765-1500

(G-8738)
WORMTOWN BREWERY LLC
Also Called: Foxborough Taproom
250 Patriot Pl (02035-5100)
PHONE..............................774 215-5403
EMP: 11 **EST:** 2020
SALES (est): 55.21K **Privately Held**
Web: www.wormtownbrewery.com
SIC: 5813 2082 Drinking places; Malt beverages

Framingham
Middlesex County

(G-8739)
AB SCIEX SALES LP
Also Called: AB Sciex
500 Old Connecticut Path Bldg B (01701-4574)
PHONE..............................508 383-7700
David Roblin, *COO*
EMP: 72 **EST:** 2014
SALES (est): 11.71MM **Privately Held**
Web: www.sciex.com
SIC: 3826 Analytical instruments

(G-8740)
ALZHEON INC
Also Called: Alzheon
111 Speen St Ste 306 (01701-2090)
PHONE..............................508 861-7709
Martin Tolar, *Pr*
Jean-pierre Garnier, *Ch Bd*
Neil Flanzraich, *V Ch Bd*
Susan Abushakra, *CMO*
John Hey, *CSO*
EMP: 23 **EST:** 2013
SQ FT: 3,317
SALES (est): 2.93MM **Privately Held**
Web: www.alzheon.com
SIC: 2834 Pharmaceutical preparations

(G-8741)
APPLIED BIOSYSTEMS LLC
1455 Concord St Ste 8 (01701-7773)
PHONE..............................508 877-1307
EMP: 12
SALES (corp-wide): 44.91B **Publicly Held**
Web: www.thermofisher.com
SIC: 3826 Analytical instruments
HQ: Applied Biosystems, Llc
5791 Van Allen Way
Carlsbad CA 92008

(G-8742)
BEACON APPLICATION SVCS CORP (PA)
40 Speen St Ste 104 (01701-1898)
PHONE..............................508 663-4433
Daniel P Maude, *Pr*
EMP: 35 **EST:** 1990
SALES (est): 8.72MM **Privately Held**
Web: 140750.group0.sites.hubspot.net
SIC: 7372 8742 5045 Business oriented computer software; Management consulting services; Computers, peripherals, and software

(G-8743)
BERG LLC (HQ)
Also Called: Berg
500 Old Connecticut Path Ste 3 (01701-4574)
PHONE..............................617 588-0083
EMP: 23 **EST:** 2006
SALES (est): 17.91MM
SALES (corp-wide): 17.91MM **Privately Held**
Web: www.berghealth.com
SIC: 2834 Pharmaceutical preparations
PA: Bpg Bio Inc
500 Old Connecticut Path
Framingham MA 01701
617 588-0083

(G-8744)
BLOOM & COMPANY INC
220 Baldwin Ave (01701-2638)
PHONE..............................617 923-1526
Richard Bloom, *Pr*
George Bloom, *VP*
EMP: 12 **EST:** 1955
SALES (est): 490.9K **Privately Held**
Web: www.bloomandcompany.com
SIC: 2391 7389 Curtains, window: made from purchased materials; Interior decorating

(G-8745)
BOSE CORPORATION (PA)
Also Called: Bose Corporate Center
100 The Mountain Rd (01701-8863)
PHONE..............................508 879-7330
Lila Snyder, *CEO*
James Scammon, *Pr*
Robert Maresca, *Dir*
Bryan K Fontaine, *VP*
Mario J Cornacchio, *Treas*
◆ **EMP:** 2000 **EST:** 1964
SQ FT: 900,000
SALES (est): 3.6B
SALES (corp-wide): 3.6B **Privately Held**
Web: www.bose.com
SIC: 5731 3651 High fidelity stereo equipment; Household audio equipment

(G-8746)
BOSE CORPORATION
145 Pennsylvania Ave (01701-8866)
PHONE..............................508 766-1265
James Kostinden, *Brnch Mgr*
EMP: 15
SALES (corp-wide): 3.6B **Privately Held**
Web: www.bose.com
SIC: 3825 3651 Digital test equipment, electronic and electrical circuits; Household audio equipment
PA: Bose Corporation
100 The Mountain Rd
Framingham MA 01701
508 879-7330

(G-8747)
BOSE CORPORATION
1 New York Ave (01701-8860)
PHONE..............................508 879-7330
EMP: 25
SALES (corp-wide): 3.6B **Privately Held**
Web: www.bose.com
SIC: 3651 Household audio and video equipment
PA: Bose Corporation
100 The Mountain Rd
Framingham MA 01701
508 879-7330

(G-8748)
BPG BIO INC (PA) ✪
500 Old Connecticut Path (01701-4574)
PHONE..............................617 588-0083
Niven Narain, *Pr*
EMP: 15 **EST:** 2023
SALES (est): 17.91MM
SALES (corp-wide): 17.91MM **Privately Held**
SIC: 2834 Pharmaceutical preparations

(G-8749)
CCL INDUSTRIES CORPORATION (HQ)
Also Called: CCL Label
161 Worcester Rd Ste 403 (01701-5310)
PHONE..............................508 872-4511
Geoffrey T Martin, *CEO*
Wayne M E Mcleod, *Pr*
Steve Lancaster, *
Bohdan Sirota, *
◆ **EMP:** 85 **EST:** 1982
SALES (est): 1.02B
SALES (corp-wide): 4.75B **Privately Held**
Web: www.ccllabel.com
SIC: 2759 2992 3411 2819 Flexographic printing; Lubricating oils and greases; Aluminum cans; Industrial inorganic chemicals, nec
PA: Ccl Industries Inc.
111 Gordon Baker Rd Suite 801
Toronto ON M2H 3
416 756-8500

(G-8750)
CCL LABEL INC (HQ)
Also Called: CCL Design
161 Worcester Rd Ste 403 (01701-5310)
PHONE..................................508 872-4511
Geoffrey Martin, *Pr*
Sean Washchuk, *
Lalitha Vaidyanathan, *
Mark Mcclendon, *VP*
◆ **EMP: 85 EST:** 1987
SALES (est): 661.3MM
SALES (corp-wide): 4.75B **Privately Held**
Web: www.cclind.com
SIC: 2759 3411 2671 Flexographic printing;
  Aluminum cans; Paper; coated and
  laminated packaging
PA: Ccl Industries Inc.
  111 Gordon Baker Rd Suite 801
  Toronto ON M2H 3
  416 756-8500

(G-8751)
CENTAGE CORPORATION
330 Cochituate Rd Unit 807 (01701-5036)
PHONE..................................800 366-5111
Peter Messana, *CEO*
EMP: 100 **EST:** 2002
SQ FT: 8,000
SALES (est): 17.91MM **Privately Held**
Web: www.centage.com
SIC: 7372 Business oriented computer
  software

(G-8752)
CENTRAL TOOLS INC
1644 Concord St (01701-3531)
PHONE..................................781 893-0095
EMP: 9
SALES (corp-wide): 4.33MM **Privately
Held**
Web: www.centraltools.com
SIC: 3825 3823 Measuring instruments and
  meters, electric; Process control instruments
PA: Central Tools, Inc.
  456 Wellington Ave
  Cranston RI 02910
  401 467-8211

(G-8753)
CREATIVE PLAYTHINGS LTD
(PA)
Also Called: Swingthing
33 Loring Dr (01702-8768)
PHONE..................................508 620-0900
◆ **EMP: 15 EST:** 1976
SALES (est): 13.59MM
SALES (corp-wide): 13.59MM **Privately
Held**
Web: www.creativeplaythings.com
SIC: 3949 5091 5941 Playground equipment
  ; Sporting and recreation goods;
  Playground equipment

(G-8754)
CST OF AMERICA LLC
Also Called: Computer Simulation Technology
492 Old Connecticut Path Ste 500
(01701-4595)
PHONE..................................508 665-4400
David Johns, *Genl Mgr*
Bernhard Wagner, *
EMP: 45 **EST:** 1998
SQ FT: 4,500
SALES (est): 9.69MM **Privately Held**
SIC: 7371 7372 Computer software
  development; Prepackaged software

(G-8755)
DAVID GILBERT
Also Called: D C M Services
10 Olympic St (01701-4528)
PHONE..................................508 879-1507
David Gilbert, *Owner*
EMP: 8 **EST:** 1989
SQ FT: 10,000
SALES (est): 582.09K **Privately Held**
SIC: 3599 7692 Machine shop, jobbing and
  repair; Welding repair

(G-8756)
DEFINITIVE HEALTHCARE
CORP (PA)
492 Old Connecticut Path Ste 401
(01701-4595)
PHONE..................................508 720-4224
Jason Krantz, *Ch Bd*
Richard Booth, *CFO*
David Samuels, *CLO*
Carrie Lazorchak, *CRO*
Kate Shamsuddin, *CPO*
EMP: 535 **EST:** 2021
SALES (est): 222.65MM
SALES (corp-wide): 222.65MM **Publicly
Held**
Web: www.definitivehc.com
SIC: 7372 Prepackaged software

(G-8757)
DETRAPEL INC
92 Blandin Ave Ste H (01702-7072)
PHONE..................................617 514-7778
David Zamarin, *CEO*
David Zamarin, *Managing Member*
Tarek Tabbara, *Prin*
Alec Tolivaisa, *Prin*
EMP: 10 **EST:** 2013
SALES (est): 1.57MM **Privately Held**
Web: www.detrapel.com
SIC: 5231 5198 2842 Paint brushes, rollers,
  sprayers and other supplies; Paints,
  varnishes, and supplies; Disinfectants,
  household or industrial plant

(G-8758)
E E S COMPANIES INC
841 Worcester Rd Ste 503 (01701-5210)
PHONE..................................508 653-6911
Henry P Szretter Junior, *Pr*
June Szretter, *VP*
EMP: 10 **EST:** 1989
SALES (est): 844.04K **Privately Held**
Web: www.eesco.com
SIC: 7373 3571 5734 Systems software
  development services; Electronic computers
  ; Computer and software stores

(G-8759)
E H PUBLISHING INC (PA)
Also Called: Electronic House
111 Speen St Ste 200 (01701-2090)
P.O. Box 989 (01701-0989)
PHONE..................................508 663-1500
Kenneth D Moyes, *Prin*
EMP: 47 **EST:** 1992
SQ FT: 8,000
SALES (est): 9.04MM **Privately Held**
Web: www.ehmedia.com
SIC: 2741 Miscellaneous publishing

(G-8760)
EAST COAST PLASTICS INC
Also Called: East Coast Plastic
763 Waverley St Ste 3 (01702-8564)
PHONE..................................508 429-8080
Michael Bagge, *Pr*
EMP: 7 **EST:** 1947
SQ FT: 6,500

SALES (est): 614.94K **Privately Held**
Web: www.eastcoastplastics.com
SIC: 3479 Coating of metals and formed
  products

(G-8761)
ELBONAIS INCORPORATED
Also Called: AlphaGraphics
1451 Concord St Ste 1 (01701-7782)
PHONE..................................508 626-2318
Harold Noble Junior, *Pr*
EMP: 8 **EST:** 1986
SQ FT: 2,200
SALES (est): 637.12K **Privately Held**
Web: www.alphagraphics.com
SIC: 2752 2791 2789 2759 Commercial
  printing, lithographic; Typesetting;
  Bookbinding and related work; Commercial
  printing, nec

(G-8762)
ELECTRONIC COMPONENTS INC
39 Loring Dr (01702-8768)
PHONE..................................508 881-8399
Richard Nadeau, *Pr*
EMP: 7 **EST:** 2000
SQ FT: 6,000
SALES (est): 3MM **Privately Held**
Web: www.ecompbiz.com
SIC: 3699 Electrical equipment and
  supplies, nec

(G-8763)
FRAMINGHAM WELDING &
ENGINEERING CORPORATION
120 Leland St (01702-5206)
EMP: 50 **EST:** 1945
SALES (est): 4.88MM **Privately Held**
SIC: 3599 3443 7692 Machine shop,
  jobbing and repair; Fabricated plate work
  (boiler shop); Welding repair

(G-8764)
GATEHOUSE MEDIA MASS I INC
Also Called: Framingham Tab
33 New York Ave (01701-8857)
PHONE..................................508 626-4412
Richard Lodge, *Prin*
EMP: 8
SALES (corp-wide): 2.95B **Publicly Held**
Web: www.ghmne.com
SIC: 2711 Newspapers, publishing and
  printing
HQ: Gatehouse Media Massachusetts I, Inc.
  48 Dunham Rd
  Beverly MA 01915
  585 598-0030

(G-8765)
GENZYME CORPORATION
51 New York Ave (01701-8861)
PHONE..................................508 872-8400
EMP: 40
Web: www.sanofi.com
SIC: 2834 Pharmaceutical preparations
HQ: Genzyme Corporation
  450 Water St
  Cambridge MA 02141
  617 252-7500

(G-8766)
GENZYME CORPORATION
76 New York Ave (01701-8859)
PHONE..................................508 872-8400
EMP: 43
Web: www.sanofi.com
SIC: 2834 Pharmaceutical preparations
HQ: Genzyme Corporation
  450 Water St
  Cambridge MA 02141
  617 252-7500

(G-8767)
GENZYME CORPORATION
74 New York Ave (01701-8859)
PHONE..................................508 872-8400
EMP: 45
Web: www.sanofi.com
SIC: 2834 Pharmaceutical preparations
HQ: Genzyme Corporation
  450 Water St
  Cambridge MA 02141
  617 252-7500

(G-8768)
GENZYME CORPORATION
45 New York Ave (01701-8861)
PHONE..................................508 872-8400
EMP: 57
Web: www.sanofi.com
SIC: 2834 Pharmaceutical preparations
HQ: Genzyme Corporation
  450 Water St
  Cambridge MA 02141
  617 252-7500

(G-8769)
GENZYME CORPORATION
68 New York Ave (01701-8859)
PHONE..................................508 872-8400
EMP: 58
Web: www.sanofi.com
SIC: 2834 Pharmaceutical preparations
HQ: Genzyme Corporation
  450 Water St
  Cambridge MA 02141
  617 252-7500

(G-8770)
GENZYME CORPORATION
200 Crossing Blvd (01702-4486)
PHONE..................................508 271-2642
Nick Wan, *Mgr*
EMP: 65
Web: www.sanofi.com
SIC: 2834 Pharmaceutical preparations
HQ: Genzyme Corporation
  450 Water St
  Cambridge MA 02141
  617 252-7500

(G-8771)
GENZYME CORPORATION
80 New York Ave (01701-8859)
PHONE..................................508 370-9690
Jorge Colado, *Prin*
EMP: 80
Web: www.sanofi.com
SIC: 2834 Pharmaceutical preparations
HQ: Genzyme Corporation
  450 Water St
  Cambridge MA 02141
  617 252-7500

(G-8772)
GENZYME CORPORATION
78 New York Ave (01701-8859)
PHONE..................................617 252-7500
Tracie Atkins, *Mgr*
EMP: 93
Web: www.sanofi.com
SIC: 2834 Pharmaceutical preparations
HQ: Genzyme Corporation
  450 Water St
  Cambridge MA 02141
  617 252-7500

(G-8773)
GENZYME CORPORATION
8 New York Ave (01701-8806)
PHONE..................................617 252-7500

William Sibold, *Bmch Mgr*
EMP: 37
Web: www.sanofi.com
SIC: 2834 3842 2836 5122 Pharmaceutical preparations; Surgical appliances and supplies; Biological products, except diagnostic; Drugs, proprietaries, and sundries
HQ: Genzyme Corporation
10 California Ave
Cambridge MA 02141
617 252-7500

(G-8774)
GENZYME CORPORATION
Also Called: Genzyme Therapeutic Products
10 California Ave (01701-8802)
PHONE..................................617 252-7500
EMP: 42
Web: www.sanofi.com
SIC: 2834 8071 Pharmaceutical preparations; Biological laboratory
HQ: Genzyme Corporation
450 Water St
Cambridge MA 02141
617 252-7500

(G-8775)
GREENTREE MARKETING INC
Also Called: Norco
10 Central St (01701-4163)
P.O. Box 3500 (01705-3500)
PHONE..................................508 877-2581
Lee Jensen, *Pr*
EMP: 10 **EST:** 1982
SQ FT: 10,000
SALES (est): 1.09MM **Privately Held**
Web: www.greentreemktg.com
SIC: 2752 Offset printing

(G-8776)
GTC BIOTHERAPEUTICS INC
175 Crossing Blvd Ste 410 (01702-4476)
PHONE..................................508 370-5429
EMP: 42 **EST:** 2019
SALES (est): 975.25K **Privately Held**
SIC: 2834 Pharmaceutical preparations

(G-8777)
HEARTWARE INTERNATIONAL INC (DH)
500 Old Connecticut Path (01701-4574)
PHONE..................................508 739-0950
Douglas Godshall, *Pr*
Larry Knopf, *Sr VP*
Jeffrey Larose, *Ex VP*
Katrin Leadley Md, *Chief Medical Officer*
Peter F Mcaree, *Sr VP*
EMP: 39 **EST:** 2008
SQ FT: 74,000
SALES (est): 167.11MM **Privately Held**
Web: www.heartware.com
SIC: 3841 Surgical instruments and apparatus
HQ: Medtronic, Inc.
710 Medtronic Pkwy
Minneapolis MN 55432
763 514-4000

(G-8778)
ICL IMAGING CORP
Also Called: Icl Eb Luce
51 Mellen St (01702-8522)
PHONE..................................508 872-3280
Larry Capodilupo Iii, *Pr*
EMP: 46 **EST:** 1956
SQ FT: 35,000
SALES (est): 5.84MM **Privately Held**
Web: www.icl-imaging.com

SIC: 7384 7336 2791 2759 Film processing and finishing laboratory; Commercial art and graphic design; Typesetting; Commercial printing, nec

(G-8779)
IDG COMMUNICATIONS INC
Also Called: Idg Brokerage Services
492 Old Connecticut Path (01701-4584)
P.O. Box 9151 (01701-9151)
PHONE..................................508 766-5300
Andrew Sambrook, *Genl Mgr*
EMP: 25
SALES (corp-wide): 8.52B **Publicly Held**
Web: www.idg.com
SIC: 2721 Trade journals: publishing only, not printed on site
HQ: Idg Communications, Inc.
140 Kendrick St Ste A110
Needham MA 02494
508 872-8200

(G-8780)
IDG CORPORATE SALES
3 Speen St 2nd Fl (01701-4679)
PHONE..................................508 875-5000
Patrick J Mcgovern, *Ch*
EMP: 50 **EST:** 2005
SALES (est): 6.48MM
SALES (corp-wide): 8.52B **Publicly Held**
SIC: 2741 Newsletter publishing
HQ: International Data Group, Inc.
140 Kendrick St Bldg B
Needham MA 02494
508 875-5000

(G-8781)
IDG CORPORATE SERVICES GROUP
5 Speen St Ste 5 (01701-4674)
P.O. Box 3 (01704-0003)
PHONE..................................508 875-5000
Deb Goldstein, *Pr*
EMP: 8 **EST:** 1987
SALES (est): 542.7K
SALES (corp-wide): 8.52B **Publicly Held**
SIC: 2721 8732 Magazines: publishing only, not printed on site; Commercial nonphysical research
HQ: Idg Communications, Inc.
140 Kendrick St Ste A110
Needham MA 02494
508 872-8200

(G-8782)
IMPRINT GRAPHICS INC
59 Fountain St Fl 4 (01702-6268)
PHONE..................................508 879-0544
EMP: 10 **EST:** 1992
SQ FT: 5,700
SALES (est): 707.94K **Privately Held**
Web: www.imprintgraphics.com
SIC: 2759 Screen printing

(G-8783)
KAMROWSKI REFINISHING CO INC
Also Called: Kamrowski Metal Refinishing
12 Bradford Rd (01701-7617)
PHONE..................................508 877-0367
TOLL FREE: 800
Richard Kamrowski, *Pr*
Deborah Kamrowski, *Treas*
EMP: 10 **EST:** 1982
SALES (est): 767.46K **Privately Held**
Web: www.drbfacilityservices.com
SIC: 3446 Architectural metalwork

(G-8784)
KINK PIECES OF A DREAM LLC
550 Cochituate Rd Ste 25 (01701-4654)
PHONE..................................508 748-5417
Whitney A Branch, *Pr*
EMP: 12 **EST:** 2013
SALES (est): 497.2K **Privately Held**
SIC: 7389 2273 8999 5999 Interior design services; Art squares: twisted paper, grass, reed, coir, sisal, etc.; Artist; Canvas products

(G-8785)
LFB USA INC (DH)
175 Crossing Blvd Ste 420 (01702-4475)
PHONE..................................508 370-5100
William Gavin, *Pr*
Sean Evans, *
Jeffry Lawrence, *
Harry M Meade, *
Michael Megna, *
EMP: 24 **EST:** 2014
SALES (est): 26.53MM
SALES (corp-wide): 4.23MM **Privately Held**
Web: www.lfb-usa.com
SIC: 8733 2834 Medical research; Pharmaceutical preparations
HQ: Laboratoire Francais Du Fractionnement Et Des Biotechnologies Tour W 19eme Etage
Puteaux 92800

(G-8786)
LIFE TECHNOLOGIES CORPORATION
Applied Biosystems Group
500 Old Connecticut Path Ste 10 (01701-4574)
PHONE..................................508 383-7700
Kevin Tillis, *Mgr*
EMP: 42
SALES (corp-wide): 44.91B **Publicly Held**
Web: www.thermofisher.com
SIC: 3826 Analytical instruments
HQ: Life Technologies Corporation
5781 Van Allen Way
Carlsbad CA 92008
760 603-7200

(G-8787)
LIFELINE SYSTEMS COMPANY (HQ)
Also Called: Lifeline
111 Lawrence St (01702-8156)
PHONE..................................855 600-6127
Ronald Feinstein, *Pr*
Mark G Beucler, *Treas*
Jeffrey Stein, *Sec*
L Dennis Shapiro, *Dir*
▲ **EMP:** 544 **EST:** 1974
SQ FT: 84,000
SALES (est): 208.16MM
SALES (corp-wide): 262.01MM **Privately Held**
Web: www.life-line.com
SIC: 3669 Emergency alarms
PA: Connect America.Com, Llc
3 Bala Plz W Ste 200
Bala Cynwyd PA 19004
800 215-4206

(G-8788)
MASSACHSETTS BREWERS GUILD INC
237 Belknap Rd (01701-4714)
P.O. Box 2096 (01703-2096)
PHONE..................................508 405-9115
Katie Stinchon, *Ex Dir*

EMP: 12 **EST:** 2008
SALES (est): 310.82K **Privately Held**
Web: www.massbrewersguild.org
SIC: 8699 7372 7389 Charitable organization; Prepackaged software; Business services, nec

(G-8789)
MCR LABS LLC
85 Speen St Ste 100 (01701-1902)
PHONE..................................508 872-6666
EMP: 80 **EST:** 2013
SQ FT: 1,200
SALES (est): 9.33MM **Privately Held**
Web: www.mcrlabs.com
SIC: 3999

(G-8790)
MIDDLESEX NEWS
33 New York Ave (01701-8880)
PHONE..................................508 626-3800
Chuck Goodrick, *Prin*
EMP: 8 **EST:** 2010
SALES (est): 178.1K **Privately Held**
SIC: 2711 Commercial printing and newspaper publishing combined

(G-8791)
NEW ENGLAND SAND & GRAV CO INC
Corner Of Danforth St & Birch Rd (01701)
P.O. Box 3248 (01705-3248)
PHONE..................................508 877-2460
Frank Generazio Junior, *Pr*
Richard Generazio, *VP*
EMP: 10 **EST:** 1939
SQ FT: 750
SALES (est): 819.08K **Privately Held**
SIC: 1442 Construction sand and gravel

(G-8792)
NEW ENGLAND WATER HEATER CO
1101 Worcester Rd Ste 2 (01701-5249)
P.O. Box 1485 (01460-4485)
PHONE..................................781 647-7004
Chris Doremus, *Pr*
EMP: 9 **EST:** 2005
SALES (est): 317.77K **Privately Held**
Web: www.newh.net
SIC: 3822 Water heater controls

(G-8793)
ONYX MARBLE & GRANITE LLC
93 Beaver St (01702-7017)
PHONE..................................508 620-0775
EMP: 12 **EST:** 2013
SQ FT: 20,000
SALES (est): 1.42MM **Privately Held**
Web: www.onyxgranite.com
SIC: 1799 3281 Counter top installation; Table tops, marble

(G-8794)
OPUS TELECOM INC
119 Herbert St (01702-8774)
PHONE..................................508 875-4444
Jay L Gainsboro, *Pr*
Barbara Gainsboro, *
EMP: 19 **EST:** 1979
SQ FT: 8,000
SALES (est): 234.56K **Privately Held**
SIC: 3661 Telephones and telephone apparatus

(G-8795)
OVERTONE STUDIO INC
492 Old Connecticut Path # 102 (01701-4584)

PHONE..................774 290-2900
Nick Burt, *Genl Mgr*
EMP: 8 **EST:** 2017
SALES (est): 306.74K **Privately Held**
SIC: 7372 Application computer software

(G-8796)
PACON CORPORATION
79 Main St Ste 202 (01702-2945)
PHONE..................508 370-0780
EMP: 24
SALES (corp-wide): 8.58MM **Privately Held**
Web: www.paconct.com
SIC: 2672 Adhesive papers, labels, or tapes: from purchased material
PA: Pacon Corporation
145 Park Rd
Putnam CT 06260
860 315-9030

(G-8797)
PALL CORPORATION
41 Berkeley Rd (01701-2830)
PHONE..................508 259-5107
EMP: 9
SALES (corp-wide): 31.47B **Publicly Held**
Web: www.pall.com
SIC: 3569 Filters
HQ: Pall Corporation
25 Harbor Park Dr
Port Washington NY 11050
516 484-5400

(G-8798)
PIP FOUNDATION INC
7 Bishop St (01702-8323)
PHONE..................508 757-0103
Bruce Hulme, *Pr*
EMP: 99 **EST:** 2001
SALES (est): 203.27K
SALES (corp-wide): 147.24MM **Privately Held**
Web: www.smoc.org
SIC: 2752 Offset printing
PA: South Middlesex Opportunity Council, Inc.
7 Bishop St
Framingham MA 01702
508 620-2300

(G-8799)
PP MANUFACTURING CORPORATION
Also Called: Ppm
175 Crossing Blvd Ste 200 (01702-4472)
PHONE..................508 766-2700
Pierre Pages, *Pr*
Michel Garaudet, *Treas*
Florence Bambuck, *Sec*
▼ **EMP:** 19 **EST:** 2004
SQ FT: 21,000
SALES (est): 9.16MM
SALES (corp-wide): 426.68MM **Privately Held**
Web: www.aquilabio.com
SIC: 2834 Veterinary pharmaceutical preparations
PA: Virbac
Lid
Carros 06510
492087100

(G-8800)
QBL WINDDOWN LLC
3 Speen St Ste 300 (01701-4664)
PHONE..................617 219-8300
Paul Miller, *CEO*
EMP: 10 **EST:** 2009
SALES (est): 2.49MM **Privately Held**

SIC: 2721 Periodicals

(G-8801)
RACK ATTACK USA LLP
745 Worcester Rd (01701-5204)
PHONE..................508 665-4361
Charlie Carp, *Genl Mgr*
EMP: 9 **EST:** 2001
SALES (est): 1.03MM **Privately Held**
Web: www.rackattack.com
SIC: 2542 Racks, merchandise display or storage: except wood

(G-8802)
REVO BIOLOGICS INC (DH)
175 Crossing Blvd (01702-4475)
PHONE..................508 620-9700
William Heiden, *Pr*
Yann Echelard, *Pr*
John B Green, *Sr VP*
Harry M Meade Ph.d., *Sr VP*
Richard A Scotland, *Senior Vice President Regulatory Affairs*
EMP: 18 **EST:** 2012
SQ FT: 106,793
SALES (est): 48.84MM
SALES (corp-wide): 4.23MM **Privately Held**
Web: www.lfb-usa.com
SIC: 6794 2834 Patent buying, licensing, leasing; Pharmaceutical preparations
HQ: Lfb-Biotechnologies
Za De Courtaboeuf
Les Ulis 91940
169827010

(G-8803)
SANOFI US SERVICES INC
51 New York Ave (01701-8861)
PHONE..................508 424-4485
EMP: 126
Web: www.sanofi.com
SIC: 2834 Pharmaceutical preparations
HQ: Sanofi Us Services Inc.
55 Corporate Dr
Bridgewater NJ 08807
800 981-2491

(G-8804)
SCHEDULING SYSTEMS INC
85 Speen St Ste 300 (01701-1902)
PHONE..................508 620-0390
John Pararas, *Pr*
EMP: 8 **EST:** 1990
SQ FT: 6,000
SALES (est): 984.33K **Privately Held**
Web: www.schedsys.com
SIC: 7372 Application computer software

(G-8805)
SYNER-G BIOPHARMA GROUP LLC (PA)
100 Pennsylvania Ave Ste 300 (01701-8870)
PHONE..................508 460-9700
Prabu Nambiar, *Managing Member*
EMP: 37 **EST:** 2007
SALES (est): 11.58MM
SALES (corp-wide): 11.58MM **Privately Held**
Web: www.synergbiopharma.com
SIC: 2834 Pharmaceutical preparations

(G-8806)
VELOXINT CORPORATION
125 Newbury St Ste 200 (01701-4592)
P.O. Box 436317 (40253-6317)
PHONE..................774 777-3369
Alan Lund, *CEO*
Kevin Mcneely, *COO*

Phoebe Kwan, *CCO*
EMP: 13 **EST:** 2015
SALES (est): 8.7MM
SALES (corp-wide): 10.88MM **Privately Held**
Web: www.veloxint.com
SIC: 3499 7389 Friction material, made from powdered metal; Business Activities at Non-Commercial Site
PA: Unity Aluminum Inc.
9300 Shelbyville Rd # 401
Louisville KY 40222
606 420-4645

(G-8807)
VIVIDO NATURAL LLC (PA)
2 Central St Ste 161 (01701-4186)
PHONE..................617 630-0131
▲ **EMP:** 10 **EST:** 2001
SQ FT: 1,500
SALES (est): 660.02K **Privately Held**
Web: www.vividonatural.com
SIC: 2099 Food preparations, nec

(G-8808)
VIVOX INC
40 Speen St Ste 305 (01701-1898)
PHONE..................508 650-3571
Robert A Seaver, *CEO*
EMP: 41 **EST:** 2005
SALES (est): 7.87MM
SALES (corp-wide): 1.39B **Publicly Held**
Web: www.unity.com
SIC: 3669 Visual communication systems
PA: Unity Software Inc.
30 3rd St
San Francisco CA 94103
415 539-3162

(G-8809)
W B MASON CO INC
1455 Concord St Ste 4a (01701-7773)
PHONE..................888 926-2766
EMP: 67
SALES (corp-wide): 1.01B **Privately Held**
Web: www.wbmason.com
SIC: 5943 5712 2752 Office forms and supplies; Office furniture; Commercial printing, lithographic
PA: W. B. Mason Co., Inc.
59 Centre Street
Brockton MA 02301
508 586-3434

(G-8810)
WALPOLE TIMES INC
1 Speen St Ste 200 (01701-4644)
P.O. Box 388 (02081-0388)
PHONE..................508 668-0243
Kay Macdonald, *Pr*
Kay Mac Donald, *Pr*
EMP: 13 **EST:** 1974
SALES (est): 243.02K **Privately Held**
Web: www.walpoletimes.com
SIC: 2711 Newspapers, publishing and printing

(G-8811)
WAVERLY TOOL RENTAL & SALES CO
Also Called: Out of Business Dec 2019
28 Miller Ave (01702-7205)
PHONE..................508 872-8866
William J Deceased, *Pr*
William J Stucchi, *Pr*
Arthur F Stucchi, *VP*
William E Stucchi, *VP*
Mary I Stucchi, *Treas*
EMP: 13 **EST:** 1957
SALES (est): 776.99K **Privately Held**

Web: waverlytool.stihldealer.net
SIC: 5082 7359 1796 3545 General construction machinery and equipment; Tool rental; Power generating equipment installation; Tools and accessories for machine tools

(G-8812)
XOSOFT INC
100 Staples Dr (01702-4479)
PHONE..................800 225-5224
Leonid Shtilman, *Ch*
Thomas O'connell, *Pr*
Gil Rappaport, *Ex VP*
EMP: 46 **EST:** 1999
SALES (est): 8.55MM
SALES (corp-wide): 35.82B **Publicly Held**
SIC: 3674 Semiconductors and related devices
HQ: Ca, Inc.
520 Madison Ave
New York NY 10022
800 225-5224

Franklin
Norfolk County

(G-8813)
ACCODALE TECHNOLGY INC
124 Grove St (02038-3156)
PHONE..................508 520-1400
Robbie Dhillon, *CEO*
EMP: 11 **EST:** 2015
SALES (est): 268.65K **Privately Held**
Web: www.accoladetechnology.com
SIC: 7372 Prepackaged software

(G-8814)
AIRLOC CORPORATION
42 Hayward St (02038-2153)
PHONE..................508 528-0022
Robert Kucher, *CEO*
Dawn Thayer, *Prin*
EMP: 9 **EST:** 2007
SALES (est): 2.62MM **Privately Held**
Web: www.airloc.com
SIC: 3625 Control equipment, electric
PA: Airloc Ag
Industriestrasse 2
Oetwil Am See ZH 8618

(G-8815)
ALPHA GRAINGER MFG INC
20 Discovery Way (02038-2555)
PHONE..................508 520-4005
Jacob Grainger, *Pr*
Gary Grainger, *
Barbara Grainger, *
▲ **EMP:** 118 **EST:** 1973
SQ FT: 90,000
SALES (est): 24.24MM **Privately Held**
Web: www.agmi.com
SIC: 3451 Screw machine products

(G-8816)
ALTIUM PACKAGING LLC
Franklin Plastics
1253 W Central St (02038-3109)
PHONE..................508 520-8800
Ed Baggie, *Mgr*
EMP: 61
SALES (corp-wide): 15.9B **Publicly Held**
Web: www.altiumpkg.com
SIC: 3089 Plastics containers, except foam
HQ: Altium Packaging Llc
2500 Windy Ridge Pkwy Se # 1400
Atlanta GA 30339
678 742-4600

(G-8817)
ARTHROSURFACE INCORPORATED
28 Forge Pkwy (02038-3247)
PHONE..............................508 520-3003
Steven W Ek, *Pr*
Steve Tallarida, *Ch Bd*
James Lousararian, *VP*
Frank Fedorowicz, *Ex VP*
Lester Fehr, *VP*
EMP: 81 **EST:** 2001
SALES (est): 20.86MM **Publicly Held**
Web: www.anika.com
SIC: 3841 Surgical and medical instruments
PA: Anika Therapeutics, Inc.
32 Wiggins Ave
Bedford MA 01730

(G-8818)
AUTOMATIC PRESS INC
Also Called: Perkins Division
842 Union St Ste 1 (02038-2599)
PHONE..............................508 528-2000
Arthur F St Andre, *Pr*
John E Dronzek, *VP*
Karen E Dronzek, *Clerk*
EMP: 8 **EST:** 1983
SQ FT: 4,200
SALES (est): 405.53K **Privately Held**
SIC: 5999 8741 3542 Business machines and equipment; Management services; Machine tools, metal forming type

(G-8819)
BELLINGHAM METAL WORKS LLC
Also Called: Bellingham Metal Works
101 Jefferson Rd (02038-3388)
PHONE..............................617 519-5958
Robert L Stow, *Managing Member*
EMP: 8 **EST:** 1997
SQ FT: 2,400
SALES (est): 1.01MM **Privately Held**
Web: www.bellinghammetal.com
SIC: 3441 7699 Fabricated structural metal; Boiler repair shop

(G-8820)
BERRY GLOBAL INC
Also Called: Berry Plastics
25 Forge Pkwy (02038-3135)
P.O. Box G (02038-0817)
PHONE..............................508 918-1714
Brendan Fenn, *Mgr*
EMP: 127
Web: www.berryglobal.com
SIC: 3089 Plastics containers, except foam
HQ: Berry Global, Inc.
101 Oakley St
Evansville IN 47710

(G-8821)
BJS WHOLESALE CLUB INC
Also Called: BJ's Wholesale Club
100 Corporate Dr (02038-3184)
PHONE..............................508 553-9889
Ted Kriakidis, *Genl Mgr*
EMP: 70
SALES (corp-wide): 19.32B **Publicly Held**
Web: www.bjs.com
SIC: 5399 4812 5995 7534 Warehouse club stores; Cellular telephone services; Optical goods stores; Tire repair shop
HQ: Bj's Wholesale Club, Inc.
350 Campus Dr
Marlborough MA 01752
774 512-7400

(G-8822)
CARPE DIEM TECHNOLOGIES INC
34 Saxon St (02038-3023)
P.O. Box 189 (02038-0189)
PHONE..............................508 541-2055
John Berg, *Pr*
EMP: 13 **EST:** 2005
SQ FT: 14,000
SALES (est): 2.14MM **Privately Held**
Web: www.carpediemtech.com
SIC: 8731 5084 3559 Commercial physical research; Paper manufacturing machinery; Semiconductor manufacturing machinery

(G-8823)
CLARK-CUTLER-MCDERMOTT COMPANY
Also Called: Airloc Products Division
5 Fisher St (02038-2163)
P.O. Box 269 (02038-0269)
PHONE..............................508 528-1200
▲ **EMP:** 200
Web: www.clarkcutlermcdermott.com
SIC: 2297 2299 Nonwoven fabrics; Acoustic felts

(G-8824)
COHESIVE TECHNOLOGIES INC (HQ)
Also Called: Cohesive Biotechnologies
101 Constitution Blvd Ste G (02038-2587)
PHONE..............................508 528-7989
Peter H Glick, *Pr*
Hubert Quinn, *
▲ **EMP:** 27 **EST:** 1992
SQ FT: 10,000
SALES (est): 9.31MM
SALES (corp-wide): 44.91B **Publicly Held**
SIC: 3826 Liquid chromatographic instruments
PA: Thermo Fisher Scientific Inc.
168 3rd Ave
Waltham MA 02451
781 622-1000

(G-8825)
COLD CHAIN TECHNOLOGIES LLC
Also Called: Massachusetts Thermal Tstg Lab
135 Constitution Blvd (02038-2584)
PHONE..............................508 429-1395
EMP: 15
Web: www.coldchaintech.com
SIC: 3841 Surgical instruments and apparatus
HQ: Cold Chain Technologies, Llc
135 Constitution Blvd
Franklin MA 02038
508 429-1395

(G-8826)
COLD CHAIN TECHNOLOGIES LLC (HQ)
135 Constitution Blvd (02038-2584)
PHONE..............................508 429-1395
Ranjeet Banerjee, *CEO*
Bob Bohne, *
Anthony Rizzo, *CCO*
Dave Walling, *
◆ **EMP:** 75 **EST:** 1967
SQ FT: 96,000
SALES (est): 107.65MM **Privately Held**
Web: www.coldchaintech.com
SIC: 3412 3841 2899 2821 Metal barrels, drums, and pails; Surgical instruments and apparatus; Chemical preparations, nec; Plastics materials and resins
PA: Aurora Capital Partners, L.P.
11611 San Vicente Blvd # 8

Los Angeles CA 90049

(G-8827)
CORE CONCEPTS INC
305 Union St Ste 7 (02038-2480)
PHONE..............................508 528-0070
Stephen C Dunn, *Pr*
Jeanne B Fox, *
EMP: 25 **EST:** 1998
SQ FT: 25,000
SALES (est): 5.74MM **Privately Held**
Web: www.coreconceptsinc.com
SIC: 2631 1541 Container, packaging, and boxboard; Food products manufacturing or packing plant construction

(G-8828)
CUSTOM KTCHENS BY CHMPAGNE INC
170 Grove St (02038-3171)
PHONE..............................508 528-7919
Patricia Champagne, *Treas*
Roland A Champagne, *Pr*
EMP: 16 **EST:** 1984
SQ FT: 15,000
SALES (est): 951.36K **Privately Held**
Web: www.customkitchensfranklin.com
SIC: 2541 2517 2511 2434 Cabinets, except refrigerated: show, display, etc.: wood; Wood television and radio cabinets; Wood household furniture; Wood kitchen cabinets

(G-8829)
DALE MEDICAL PRODUCTS INC (PA)
40 Kenwood Cir Ste 7 (02038-3298)
P.O. Box 1556 (02762-0556)
PHONE..............................800 343-3980
Robert Simpson, *CEO*
Rosanne Tierney, *CFO*
John Brezack, *Dir*
Doug Harper, *Ex VP*
▲ **EMP:** 100 **EST:** 1961
SQ FT: 17,000
SALES (est): 22.82MM
SALES (corp-wide): 22.82MM **Privately Held**
Web: www.dalemed.com
SIC: 5047 3841 Medical equipment and supplies; Surgical and medical instruments

(G-8830)
DANGELO BURIAL VAULTS
30 Raymond St (02038-1829)
PHONE..............................508 528-0385
Nancy Spencer, *Prin*
EMP: 8 **EST:** 2010
SALES (est): 227.45K **Privately Held**
SIC: 3272 Burial vaults, concrete or precast terrazzo

(G-8831)
DYNISCO INSTRUMENTS LLC (HQ)
Also Called: Dj Instruments
38 Forge Pkwy (02038-3134)
PHONE..............................508 541-9400
Brian D Jellison, *Managing Member*
◆ **EMP:** 130 **EST:** 1953
SQ FT: 62,500
SALES (est): 94.01MM
SALES (corp-wide): 223.55MM **Privately Held**
Web: www.dynisco.com
SIC: 3829 5084 3825 3823 Measuring and controlling devices, nec; Industrial machinery and equipment; Instruments to measure electricity; Process control instruments

PA: Indicor, Llc
11605 N Cmnity Hse Rd
Charlotte NC

(G-8832)
DYNISCO LLC (HQ)
Also Called: Dj Instruments
38 Forge Pkwy (02038-3134)
PHONE..............................508 541-3195
EMP: 69 **EST:** 2000
SALES (est): 22.33MM
SALES (corp-wide): 5.37B **Publicly Held**
Web: www.dynisco.com
SIC: 3829 Measuring and controlling devices, nec
PA: Roper Technologies, Inc.
6901 Prof Pkwy E Ste 200
Sarasota FL 34240
941 556-2601

(G-8833)
EATON CORPORATION
165 Grove St Ste 10 (02038-3195)
PHONE..............................508 520-2444
Kevin Finnerty, *Mgr*
EMP: 26
Web: www.dix-eaton.com
SIC: 3613 Switchgear and switchboard apparatus
HQ: Eaton Corporation
1000 Eaton Blvd
Cleveland OH 44122
440 523-5000

(G-8834)
EMC CORPORATION
55 Constitution Blvd (02038-2545)
PHONE..............................800 275-8777
EMP: 50
Web: www.emc.com
SIC: 3572 Computer storage devices
HQ: Emc Corporation
176 South St
Hopkinton MA 01748
508 435-1000

(G-8835)
EMC CORPORATION
50 Constitution Blvd (02038-2531)
P.O. Box 9103 (01748-9103)
PHONE..............................508 435-1000
Kurt Grazewski, *Brnch Mgr*
EMP: 65
Web: www.emc.com
SIC: 3572 Computer storage devices
HQ: Emc Corporation
176 South St
Hopkinton MA 01748
508 435-1000

(G-8836)
EMC CORPORATION
111 Constitution Blvd (02038-2584)
PHONE..............................866 438-3622
EMP: 79
Web: www.emc.com
SIC: 3572 Computer storage devices
HQ: Emc Corporation
176 South St
Hopkinton MA 01748
508 435-1000

(G-8837)
FORM CENTERLESS GRINDING INC
1 Kenwood Cir (02038-3201)
PHONE..............................508 520-0900
Alan Rose, *Ch Bd*
Leo Blair, *Treas*
▲ **EMP:** 10 **EST:** 1968

SQ FT: 28,000
SALES (est): 1.01MM **Privately Held**
SIC: 3599 Grinding castings for the trade

(G-8838)
FRANKLIN PAINT COMPANY INC
259 Cottage St (02038-3006)
PHONE....................................800 486-0304
Lawrence H Boise, *Pr*
Stephen S Schultz, *
Mark S Herbert, *
▲ **EMP:** 26 **EST:** 1947
SQ FT: 45,000
SALES (est): 7.31MM **Privately Held**
Web: www.franklinpaint.com
SIC: 2851 Paints and allied products

(G-8839)
FRANKLIN SHEET METAL WORKS INC
231 Cottage St (02038-3006)
P.O. Box 368 (02038-0368)
PHONE....................................508 528-3600
Fred C Baglioni, *Pr*
Peter C Baglioni, *Treas*
EMP: 9 **EST:** 1953
SQ FT: 12,000
SALES (est): 852.59K **Privately Held**
SIC: 3444 Sheet metalwork

(G-8840)
GARELICK FARMS LLC (DH)
1199 W Central St Ste 1 (02038-3160)
PHONE....................................508 528-9000
Brian J Willey, *Managing Member*
▲ **EMP:** 600 **EST:** 1902
SQ FT: 35,000
SALES (est): 389.79MM **Privately Held**
Web: www.garelickfarms.com
SIC: 2026 Milk processing (pasteurizing, homogenizing, bottling)
HQ: Dean East, Llc
 2900 Bristol Hwy
 Johnson City TN 37601
 423 283-5700

(G-8841)
GLENPHARMER DISTILLERY LLC
860 W Central St (02038-3153)
PHONE....................................508 654-6577
Patrick Downing, *Pr*
Patrick F Downing, *
EMP: 30 **EST:** 2018
SALES (est): 2.96MM **Privately Held**
Web: www.glenpharmer.com
SIC: 3556 Distillery machinery

(G-8842)
HAMILTON STORAGE TECH INC
Biophile
3 Forge Pkwy (02038-3135)
PHONE....................................508 544-7000
Robert Rovingdull, *Mgr*
EMP: 9
Web: www.hamiltoncompany.com
SIC: 3821 Freezers, laboratory
HQ: Hamilton Storage Technologies, Inc.
 3 Forge Pkwy
 Franklin MA 02038
 508 544-7000

(G-8843)
HAMILTON STORAGE TECH INC (DH)
3 Forge Pkwy (02038-3135)
PHONE....................................508 544-7000
Steve T Hamilton, *Pr*
Franklin C Hamilton, *

Chris Jablonski, *
Daniel O Hamilton, *
▲ **EMP:** 50 **EST:** 1982
SQ FT: 15,000
SALES (est): 31.6MM **Privately Held**
Web: www.hamiltoncompany.com
SIC: 3823 Process control instruments
HQ: Hamilton Company
 4970 Energy Way
 Reno NV 89502
 775 858-3000

(G-8844)
JACO INC
140 Constitution Blvd (02038-2544)
PHONE....................................508 553-1000
Del France, *Pr*
Michael Picchi, *
EMP: 112 **EST:** 1972
SQ FT: 94,000
SALES (est): 23.42MM **Privately Held**
Web: www.jacoinc.com
SIC: 3499 Safes and vaults, metal
HQ: Gcx Corporation
 3875 Cypress Dr
 Petaluma CA 94954
 707 773-1100

(G-8845)
JEM ELECTRONICS INC
23 National Dr (02038-0259)
PHONE....................................508 520-3105
John S Mcdonald, *Pr*
▲ **EMP:** 125 **EST:** 1994
SQ FT: 32,000
SALES (est): 49.48MM **Privately Held**
Web: www.jemelectronics.com
SIC: 5065 3679 Electronic parts; Harness assemblies, for electronic use: wire or cable

(G-8846)
JNJ INDUSTRIES INC
290 Beaver St (02038-3022)
PHONE....................................508 553-0529
John J Volpe, *Pr*
Gail Howe, *VP*
▲ **EMP:** 21 **EST:** 1990
SQ FT: 89,000
SALES (est): 1.8MM **Privately Held**
Web: www.high-techconversions.com
SIC: 3672 3555 Printed circuit boards; Printing trades machinery

(G-8847)
K-F LIQUIDATION INC
842 Union St Ste 1 (02038)
PHONE....................................508 528-2000
Arthur St Andre, *Pr*
EMP: 8 **EST:** 2014
SALES (est): 594.14K **Privately Held**
Web: www.kensol-franklinhotstamp.com
SIC: 3599 Custom machinery

(G-8848)
KEEBLER COMPANY
Also Called: Keebler
17 Forge Pkwy (02038-3135)
PHONE....................................508 520-7223
Steve O'sullivan, *Mgr*
EMP: 82
SQ FT: 50,000
SALES (corp-wide): 15.31B **Publicly Held**
Web: www.keebler.com
SIC: 2052 Cookies
HQ: Keebler Company
 1 Kellogg Sq
 Battle Creek MI 49017
 269 961-2000

(G-8849)
KIMBERLY-CLARK CORPORATION
Also Called: Kimberly-Clark
38 Pawn Street Ste 108 (02038)
PHONE....................................508 520-1355
Gerald Gibbs, *Prin*
EMP: 8
SALES (corp-wide): 20.43B **Publicly Held**
Web: www.kimberly-clark.com
SIC: 2621 2676 Sanitary tissue paper; Infant and baby paper products
PA: Kimberly-Clark Corporation
 351 Phelps Dr
 Irving TX 75038
 972 281-1200

(G-8850)
MEDICAL RESEARCH NETWORX
Also Called: Mrn Diagnostics
101 Constitution Blvd (02038-2587)
PHONE....................................508 530-4289
Gregory Chiklis, *CEO*
Robert Mckie, *CEO*
Donald George Morin, *
EMP: 30 **EST:** 2011
SALES (est): 3.93MM **Privately Held**
Web: www.mrndx.com
SIC: 8733 2835 Medical research; Blood derivative diagnostic agents

(G-8851)
MGB US INC
157 Grove St Ste 30 (02038-3193)
PHONE....................................774 415-0060
Veronique Roda, *Pr*
EMP: 10 **EST:** 2008
SQ FT: 15,000
SALES (est): 934.2K **Privately Held**
SIC: 3451 Screw machine products

(G-8852)
MIDSTATEMOLDING LLC
20 Liberty Way Ste D (02038-2577)
PHONE....................................508 520-0011
Steven Devine, *Prin*
EMP: 10 **EST:** 2012
SALES (est): 992.88K **Privately Held**
Web: www.midstatemold.com
SIC: 3089 Injection molding of plastics

(G-8853)
MOSELEY CORPORATION
31 Hayward St Ste A2 (02038-2166)
PHONE....................................508 520-4004
Thomas C Moseley, *Pr*
Thomas C Moseley Junior, *Pr*
EMP: 50 **EST:** 1988
SQ FT: 50,000
SALES (est): 843.2K **Privately Held**
Web: www.moseley.group
SIC: 3799 8748 3444 3441 Pushcarts; Business consulting, nec; Sheet metalwork; Fabricated structural metal

(G-8854)
NEWHOMESALE LLC
Also Called: Nhs Print
363 E Central St Ste 2 (02038-6301)
PHONE....................................508 541-8900
John Marino, *Genl Mgr*
EMP: 13 **EST:** 2002
SQ FT: 2,300
SALES (est): 858.73K **Privately Held**
Web: www.nhsprint.com
SIC: 7313 7331 2711 Printed media advertising representatives; Direct mail advertising services; Commercial printing and newspaper publishing combined

(G-8855)
NEWPORT CORPORATION
Newport Franklin
8 Forge Pkwy Ste 2 (02038-3138)
PHONE....................................508 553-5035
Mike Carta, *Brnch Mgr*
EMP: 67
SALES (corp-wide): 3.55B **Publicly Held**
Web: go.newport.com
SIC: 3827 Optical instruments and lenses
HQ: Newport Corporation
 1791 Deere Ave
 Irvine CA 92606
 949 863-3144

(G-8856)
NISSHA MTLLIZING SOLUTIONS LTD
24 National Dr Forge Park (02038-3245)
PHONE....................................508 541-7700
Paul Van Emmerick, *Pr*
Christophe Van Quickenborne, *Sec*
Martin Raeymakers, *Treas*
Michael Coniglio, *Dir Fin*
Mark Kelly Board, *Prin*
◆ **EMP:** 100 **EST:** 2012
SALES (est): 23.74MM **Privately Held**
Web: www.packle.io
SIC: 2672 Metallic covered paper: made from purchased materials
HQ: Nissha Metallizing Solutions
 Woudstraat 8
 Genk 3600
 89848000

(G-8857)
PRECISION MACHINISTS CO INC
9 Forge Pkwy (02038-3150)
PHONE....................................508 528-2325
Joe Kajano, *Brnch Mgr*
EMP: 12
SALES (corp-wide): 4.84MM **Privately Held**
Web: www.precisionmachinists.net
SIC: 3599 Grinding castings for the trade
PA: Precision Machinists Company Inc.
 299 Littleton Rd
 Chelmsford MA
 978 256-4592

(G-8858)
PRINCTON GAMMA-TECH INSTRS INC
Also Called: P G T
27 Forge Pkwy (02038-3135)
PHONE....................................609 924-7310
Juhani Taskinen, *CEO*
EMP: 21 **EST:** 2005
SQ FT: 26,000
SALES (est): 3.91MM
SALES (corp-wide): 44.91B **Publicly Held**
SIC: 3844 3812 3829 5049 X-ray apparatus and tubes; Search and navigation equipment; Nuclear radiation and testing apparatus; Scientific instruments
PA: Thermo Fisher Scientific Inc.
 168 3rd Ave
 Waltham MA 02451
 781 622-1000

(G-8859)
RJ FOUNTAIN GROUP INC
1376 W Central St Ste 130 (02038-7100)
PHONE....................................508 429-9950
Robert N Jewett, *Pr*
EMP: 15 **EST:** 1976
SQ FT: 12,000
SALES (est): 4.34MM **Privately Held**
Web: www.terracon-solutions.com

SIC: 3089   Plastics and fiberglass tanks

(G-8860)
RPH ENTERPRISES INC
50 Earls Way (02038-1268)
PHONE..................................508 238-3351
Russell P Holmes, *Pr*
Peter J Randall, *
EMP: 55 **EST:** 1979
SQ FT: 15,000
SALES (est): 8.16MM **Privately Held**
SIC: 3841 3842   Surgical instruments and
apparatus; Orthopedic appliances

(G-8861)
RT ENGINEERING
CORPORATION
1 Kenwood Cir (02038-3201)
PHONE..................................800 343-1182
Chadwick Blair, *Pr*
Leo Blair, *
EMP: 43 **EST:** 2006
SALES (est): 17.04MM **Privately Held**
Web: www.rteng.com
SIC: 8711 3559 5063 8748   Mechanical
engineering; Electronic component making
machinery; Motors, electric; Systems
engineering consultant, ex. computer or
professional

(G-8862)
RYPOS INC (PA)
Also Called: Rypos
40 Kenwood Cir Ste 8 (02038-3298)
PHONE..................................508 429-4552
Peter C Bransfield, *Ch*
Klaus J Peter, *Pr*
Donald Simoneau, *CFO*
James Ernstmeyer, *Sec*
▲ **EMP:** 35 **EST:** 1997
SQ FT: 25,000
SALES (est): 7.33MM **Privately Held**
Web: www.rypos.com
SIC: 3569   Filters

(G-8863)
SAYLENT TECHNOLOGIES INC
122 Grove St Ste 300 (02038-2181)
PHONE..................................508 570-2161
EMP: 22 **EST:** 2006
SALES (est): 619.9K **Privately Held**
Web: www.meridianlink.com
SIC: 7372   Prepackaged software

(G-8864)
SPEEDLINE TECHNOLOGIES INC
16 Forge Pkwy (02038-3157)
PHONE..................................508 541-4867
◆ **EMP:** 465
Web: www.itweae.com
SIC: 3565 3569   Packing and wrapping
machinery; Assembly machines, non-
metalworking

(G-8865)
STEEL CONNECTIONS INC
101 Jefferson Rd (02038-3388)
PHONE..................................508 958-5129
Robert L Snow Junior, *Prin*
EMP: 14 **EST:** 2016
SALES (est): 2.15MM **Privately Held**
SIC: 3441   Fabricated structural metal

(G-8866)
TEGRA MEDICAL LLC (HQ)
16 Forge Pkwy (02038-3157)
PHONE..................................508 541-4200
J Mark King, *CEO*
Craig Campbell, *

EMP: 200 **EST:** 2007
SQ FT: 81,000
SALES (est): 118.77MM **Privately Held**
Web: www.tegramedical.com
SIC: 3841   Surgical and medical instruments
PA: Sfs Group Ag
Rosenbergsaustrasse 8
Heerbrugg SG 9435

(G-8867)
THERMO EBERLINE LLC (HQ)
Also Called: Thermo Fisher Scientific
27 Forge Pkwy (02038-3135)
PHONE..................................508 553-1582
Marc N Casper, *CEO*
Rodney Smith, *Pr*
James Neville, *General Vice President*
Molly Smith, *OF CUST SERV*
Joseph Rotunda, *Global Director*
◆ **EMP:** 15 **EST:** 1998
SQ FT: 20,000
SALES (est): 99.14MM
SALES (corp-wide): 44.91B **Publicly Held**
SIC: 3826   Analytical instruments
PA: Thermo Fisher Scientific Inc.
168 3rd Ave
Waltham MA 02451
781 622-1000

(G-8868)
THERMO ENVMTL INSTRS LLC
(HQ)
27 Forge Pkwy (02038-3135)
PHONE..................................508 520-0430
Seth H Hoogasian, *Pr*
Sandra Lambert, *
Brian Fisher, *
Anthony H Smith, *
▲ **EMP:** 145 **EST:** 1980
SQ FT: 30,000
SALES (est): 44.74MM
SALES (corp-wide): 44.91B **Publicly Held**
Web:
www.analyticalinstrumentparts.com
SIC: 3826 3845 3829 3823   Analytical
instruments; Electromedical equipment;
Measuring and controlling devices, nec;
Process control instruments
PA: Thermo Fisher Scientific Inc.
168 3rd Ave
Waltham MA 02451
781 622-1000

(G-8869)
THERMO FISHER SCIENTIFIC
INC
27 Forge Pkwy (02038-3135)
PHONE..................................713 272-0404
James Meier, *Brnch Mgr*
EMP: 225
SALES (corp-wide): 44.91B **Publicly Held**
Web: www.thermofisher.com
SIC: 3826 3821 3721   Analytical instruments
; Laboratory equipment: fume hoods,
distillation racks, etc.; Research and
development on aircraft by the manufacturer
PA: Thermo Fisher Scientific Inc.
168 3rd Ave
Waltham MA 02451
781 622-1000

(G-8870)
THERMO PROCESS
INSTRUMENTS LP
Also Called: Thermo Electron
27 Forge Pkwy (02038-3135)
PHONE..................................508 553-6913
◆ **EMP:** 190 **EST:** 1996
SALES (est): 48.31MM
SALES (corp-wide): 44.91B **Publicly Held**

SIC: 3823 3829   Process control instruments
; Instrumentation for reactor controls,
auxiliary
PA: Thermo Fisher Scientific Inc.
168 3rd Ave
Waltham MA 02451
781 622-1000

(G-8871)
THERMO VISION CORP (HQ)
8 Forge Pkwy Ste 4 (02038-3138)
PHONE..................................508 520-0083
EMP: 24 **EST:** 1995
SALES (est): 15.54MM
SALES (corp-wide): 44.91B **Publicly Held**
Web: www.nailsetcetera.com
SIC: 3827   Optical instruments and lenses
PA: Thermo Fisher Scientific Inc.
168 3rd Ave
Waltham MA 02451
781 622-1000

(G-8872)
THOMSON SERVICE CORP
Also Called: Thomson Group, The
842 Union St Ste 1 (02038-2599)
PHONE..................................508 528-2000
EMP: 15 **EST:** 1992
SALES (est): 170.82K **Privately Held**
Web: www.technicolor.com
SIC: 5962 5084 7629 3554   Merchandising
machine operators; Industrial machinery
and equipment; Electrical repair shops;
Paper industries machinery

(G-8873)
TYCO ADHESIVES
25 Forge Pkwy (02038-3135)
PHONE..................................508 918-1600
Edward Breen, *Prin*
EMP: 7 **EST:** 2011
SALES (est): 113.49K **Privately Held**
SIC: 2891   Adhesives

(G-8874)
WAJA ASSOCIATES INC
38 Forge Pkwy (02038-3134)
PHONE..................................508 543-6050
Don Adams, *Pr*
EMP: 20 **EST:** 1987
SQ FT: 6,000
SALES (est): 1.12MM **Privately Held**
SIC: 3625 8721   Control equipment, electric;
Accounting, auditing, and bookkeeping

(G-8875)
WATERS TECHNOLOGIES CORP
210 Grove St (02038-3119)
PHONE..................................508 482-4807
Kathleen Wright, *Mgr*
EMP: 25
SQ FT: 56,000
Web: www.waters.com
SIC: 3826   Analytical instruments
HQ: Waters Technologies Corporation,
34 Maple St
Milford MA 01757
508 478-2000

(G-8876)
XPRESSION PRINTS INC
31 Hayward St Ste B2 (02038-2179)
PHONE..................................401 413-6930
Dale A Allen, *Prin*
EMP: 8 **EST:** 2010
SALES (est): 517.65K **Privately Held**
Web: www.xpressionprints.com
SIC: 2752   Commercial printing, lithographic

(G-8877)
XTHERA CORPORATION
Also Called: Theracycle
31 Hayward St Ste B1 (02038-2166)
PHONE..................................508 528-3100
▲ **EMP:** 7
SALES (corp-wide): 913.31K **Privately
Held**
Web: www.theracycle.com
SIC: 3949   Exercising cycles
PA: Xthera Corporation
4 Lynn Rd
Needham MA
781 453-8787

Gardner
Worcester County

(G-8878)
ADOLF JANDRIS & SONS INC
202 High St (01440-3632)
PHONE..................................978 632-0089
Dana Morse, *Pr*
Rodney T Moore, *
EMP: 37 **EST:** 1920
SQ FT: 125,000
SALES (est): 4.72MM **Privately Held**
Web: www.ajandris.com
SIC: 3271   Blocks, concrete or cinder:
standard

(G-8879)
AMERICAN SCREW AND
BARRELS INC
60 Linus Allain Ave (01440-2478)
PHONE..................................978 630-1300
Alfonzo Toro, *Pr*
Maria Toro, *Bookkpr*
▲ **EMP:** 12 **EST:** 1983
SQ FT: 6,000
SALES (est): 1.37MM **Privately Held**
Web: www.cfscrew.com
SIC: 3599   Machine shop, jobbing and repair

(G-8880)
BLUE BARN INC
708 Whitney St (01440-3442)
PHONE..................................617 894-6987
Jason Hoynash, *Pr*
EMP: 10 **EST:** 2011
SALES (est): 765.58K **Privately Held**
Web: www.bluebarnbuildsit.com
SIC: 2541   Store and office display cases
and fixtures

(G-8881)
CHAIR CITY MEATS INC
766 W Broadway (01440-2882)
P.O. Box 1051 (01440-6051)
PHONE..................................978 630-1050
Joshua Paddock, *Pr*
Bonnie Paddock, *Treas*
EMP: 16 **EST:** 1992
SALES (est): 284.85K **Privately Held**
Web: www.chaircitymeats.com
SIC: 2013 5421   Sausages and related
products, from purchased meat; Meat
markets, including freezer provisioners

(G-8882)
CONTINENTAL FEED SCREW
INC
60 Linus Allain Ave (01440-2478)
PHONE..................................978 630-1300
EMP: 12 **EST:** 2018
SALES (est): 831.49K **Privately Held**
Web: www.cfscrew.com

SIC: 3599 Machine shop, jobbing and repair

(G-8883)
DATA GUIDE CABLE CORPORATION
Also Called: D G C
232 Sherman St (01440-3000)
PHONE.................................978 632-0900
Donald R Irving, *Pr*
Robert Beardsley, *
Robert Seder J, *
Melissa Irving, *
▲ **EMP:** 93 **EST:** 1984
SQ FT: 45,500
SALES (est): 23.67MM **Privately Held**
Web: www.dataguidecable.com
SIC: 3643 3357 3351 Power line cable;
Nonferrous wiredrawing and insulating;
Copper rolling and drawing

(G-8884)
DENNECREPE CORPORATION
70 Fredette St (01440-3722)
PHONE.................................978 630-8669
EMP: 83 **EST:** 1994
SALES (est): 14.26MM
SALES (corp-wide): 131.46MM **Privately Held**
Web: www.seamanpaper.com
SIC: 2679 2621 Crepe paper or crepe paper
products: purchased material; Paper mills
PA: Seaman Paper Company Of
Massachusetts, Inc.
35 Wilkins Rd
Gardner MA 01440
978 632-1513

(G-8885)
E F INC
88 Suffolk Ln (01440-1760)
PHONE.................................978 630-3800
Michael E Lenihan, *Pr*
Michael T Pappas, *Treas*
EMP: 10 **EST:** 1988
SQ FT: 27,000
SALES (est): 1.61MM **Privately Held**
Web: www.feswiss.com
SIC: 3451 3089 Screw machine products;
Air mattresses, plastics

(G-8886)
FIRST MATE PRTG CONVERTING INC (HQ)
Also Called: Garlock Printing & Converting
164 Fredette St (01440-3722)
PHONE.................................978 630-1028
Peter Garlock, *Pr*
George Jones Iii, *Sec*
Kevin W King, *
Joseph Litchwell, *
James Jones, *
▲ **EMP:** 75 **EST:** 1987
SQ FT: 69,000
SALES (est): 54.36MM
SALES (corp-wide): 131.46MM **Privately Held**
Web: www.garlockprinting.com
SIC: 2759 2679 3554 Flexographic printing;
Paper products, converted, nec; Bag and
envelope making machinery, paper
PA: Seaman Paper Company Of
Massachusetts, Inc.
35 Wilkins Rd
Gardner MA 01440
978 632-1513

(G-8887)
GARDNER SCREW CORPORATION
220 Union St (01440-3446)
PHONE.................................978 632-0850
Curtis A Erickson, *Pr*
Theodore S Cushing, *VP*
Diane Cushing, *Stockholder*
EMP: 10 **EST:** 1923
SQ FT: 16,000
SALES (est): 1.89MM **Privately Held**
Web: www.gardnerscrew.com
SIC: 5072 5085 3469 3452 Miscellaneous
fasteners; Industrial supplies; Metal
stampings, nec; Bolts, nuts, rivets, and
washers

(G-8888)
GP&C OPERATIONS LLC
77 Industrial Rowe (01440-2831)
PHONE.................................978 630-1028
Pete Bugarlock, *Mgr*
EMP: 76
SALES (corp-wide): 28.49MM **Privately Held**
Web: www.garlockprinting.com
SIC: 2759 2679 Flexographic printing;
Paper products, converted, nec
PA: Gp&c Operations, Llc
164 Fredette St
Gardner MA 01440
978 630-1028

(G-8889)
GP&C OPERATIONS LLC (PA)
Also Called: Garlock Printing & Converting
164 Fredette St (01440-3722)
PHONE.................................978 630-1028
Peter Garlock, *Pr*
EMP: 34 **EST:** 2020
SALES (est): 28.49MM
SALES (corp-wide): 28.49MM **Privately Held**
Web: www.garlockprinting.com
SIC: 2671 Paper; coated and laminated
packaging

(G-8890)
GRAPHITE INSULG SYSTEMS INC
36 Lachance St (01440-2476)
PHONE.................................978 630-8988
Vincent Lucchesi, *Pr*
Crystal Lucchesi, *Sec*
EMP: 10 **EST:** 2000
SQ FT: 9,000
SALES (est): 1.32MM **Privately Held**
Web:
www.graphiteinsulatingsystems.com
SIC: 8711 3999 Engineering services;
Heating pads, nonelectric

(G-8891)
INTEGRITY MOLD INC
246 Suffolk Ln (01440-1760)
PHONE.................................978 669-0093
Joseph R Hollenbeck, *Pr*
EMP: 16 **EST:** 2001
SALES (est): 3.29MM **Privately Held**
Web: www.integritymold.com
SIC: 3089 Molding primary plastics

(G-8892)
KE TUBE INC
Also Called: Kirk Eastern Company
79 Wilkins Rd (01440-2833)
PHONE.................................978 630-1436
EMP: 20
SIC: 3317 Pipes, wrought: welded, lock
joint, or heavy riveted

(G-8893)
MACK PROTOTYPE INC
424 Main St (01440-3019)
PHONE.................................978 632-3700
Ric Perry, *Pr*
EMP: 30 **EST:** 1981
SQ FT: 75,000
SALES (est): 9.95MM
SALES (corp-wide): 856.43MM **Privately Held**
Web: www.mackprototype.com
SIC: 3089 3544 3369 Injection molding of
plastics; Special dies, tools, jigs, and
fixtures; Nonferrous foundries, nec
PA: Mack Group, Inc.
608 Warm Brook Rd
Arlington VT 05250
802 375-2511

(G-8894)
MAKI BUILDING CENTERS INC (HQ)
513 Betty Spring Rd (01440-2489)
PHONE.................................978 343-7422
Glenn V Maki, *Pr*
Barry Lafluer, *
Alan Maki, *
Jean Maki, *
Roberta Salo, *
EMP: 40 **EST:** 1949
SALES (est): 22.42MM
SALES (corp-wide): 32.51MM **Privately Held**
Web: www.makicorp.com
SIC: 5231 5211 5251 3354 Paint, glass, and
wallpaper stores; Lumber and other
building materials; Hardware stores;
Aluminum extruded products
PA: Maki Corp.
513 Betty Spring Rd
Gardner MA 01440
978 343-7422

(G-8895)
MAKI CORP (PA)
513 Betty Spring Rd (01440-2489)
PHONE.................................978 343-7422
Glenn V Maki, *Pr*
Steven D Senay, *
EMP: 30 **EST:** 1985
SALES (est): 32.51MM
SALES (corp-wide): 32.51MM **Privately Held**
Web: www.makicorp.com
SIC: 7359 5031 5231 5198 Equipment
rental and leasing, nec; Building materials,
exterior; Paint; Paints

(G-8896)
NEW ENGLAND WOODEN WARE CORP (PA)
205 School St Ste 201 (01440-2781)
PHONE.................................978 632-3600
David Urquhart, *Pr*
Mark S Salisbury, *
Jodi Womble, *
Alexander W Urquhart Iii, *Sec*
▲ **EMP:** 30 **EST:** 1834
SQ FT: 173,000
SALES (est): 22.62MM
SALES (corp-wide): 22.62MM **Privately Held**
Web: www.newwpkg.com
SIC: 3993 2653 Signs and advertising
specialties; Boxes, corrugated: made from
purchased materials

(G-8897)
OLDSIGNSNSTUFFCOM INC
104 E Broadway (01440-3387)
PHONE.................................978 407-6718
Linda F Gutmans, *Prin*
EMP: 14 **EST:** 2012
SALES (est): 473.66K **Privately Held**
SIC: 3993 Signs and advertising specialties

(G-8898)
PRECISION OPTICS CORP INC (PA)
Also Called: Poc
22 E Broadway (01440-7311)
PHONE.................................978 630-1800
Joseph N Forkey, *Pr*
Peter H Woodward, *Ch Bd*
Wayne Coll, *CFO*
Mahesh Lawande, *COO*
EMP: 51 **EST:** 1982
SALES (est): 21.04MM
SALES (corp-wide): 21.04MM **Publicly Held**
Web: www.poci.com
SIC: 3827 3845 Optical instruments and
apparatus; Electromedical equipment

(G-8899)
SEAMAN PAPER COMPANY MASS INC (PA)
Also Called: Seaman Paper Company
35 Wilkins Rd (01440-2833)
P.O. Box 21 (01436-0021)
PHONE.................................978 632-1513
George D Jones Iii, *Pr*
James Jones, *
Joseph F Lichwell, *
Jean Jones Chen, *
◆ **EMP:** 25 **EST:** 1954
SQ FT: 550,000
SALES (est): 131.46MM
SALES (corp-wide): 131.46MM **Privately Held**
Web: www.seamanpaper.com
SIC: 2621 Wrapping paper

(G-8900)
SPECIALIZED PPR CONVERTING INC
21 Industrial Rowe (01440-2831)
PHONE.................................978 632-5524
James B Jones, *Pr*
George D Jones Iii, *Treas*
Mary-elisabeth L Jones, *Sec*
EMP: 24 **EST:** 1996
SQ FT: 50,000
SALES (est): 2.27MM **Privately Held**
Web: www.seamanpaper.com
SIC: 2621 Paper mills

(G-8901)
SPECIALTY WHOLESALE SUP CORP
101 Linus Allain Ave (01440-2483)
PHONE.................................978 632-1472
Jim Le Blanc, *Mgr*
EMP: 37
SALES (corp-wide): 32.51MM **Privately Held**
Web: www.swscorp.net
SIC: 2431 5031 Millwork; Doors and
windows
HQ: Specialty Wholesale Supply Corp.
160 Massachusetts Ave
Lunenburg MA 01462
978 343-7422

(G-8902)
STANDARD CHAIR GARDNER INC
1 S Main St (01440-3343)
PHONE..................978 632-1301
Steven K Ostroff, *Pr*
Melvin Ostroff, *
▼ EMP: 19 EST: 1957
SQ FT: 75,000
SALES (est): 4.48MM Privately Held
Web: www.standardchair.com
SIC: 2511 Chairs, household, except upholstered: wood

(G-8903)
SUPERIOR KITCHEN DESIGNS INC
166 Mill St (01440-3292)
P.O. Box 398 (01440-0398)
PHONE..................978 632-5072
EMP: 11 EST: 1992
SQ FT: 15,952
SALES (est): 621.27K Privately Held
Web: www.superiorkitchens.net
SIC: 2434 2517 Wood kitchen cabinets; Wood television and radio cabinets

Georgetown
Essex County

(G-8904)
A I C INC (PA)
Also Called: Cai Inks
7 Martel Way (01833-2224)
PHONE..................978 352-4510
Vincent Sartorelli, *Pr*
Michael Sartorelli, *Prin*
John Sartorelli, *Prin*
Paul Sartorelli, *Treas*
◆ EMP: 20 EST: 1985
SALES (est): 8.94MM
SALES (corp-wide): 8.94MM Privately Held
Web: www.caiink.com
SIC: 2851 2893 Lacquers, varnishes, enamels, and other coatings; Printing ink

(G-8905)
BLACK DIAMOND MFG & ENGRG INC
8 Searle St (01833-1705)
PHONE..................978 352-6716
▲ EMP: 10 EST: 2010
SALES (est): 685.48K Privately Held
Web: www.santineng.com
SIC: 3089 Thermoformed finished plastics products, nec

(G-8906)
CAMBRIDGEPORT AIR SYSTEMS INC
4 Carleton Dr (01833-2501)
PHONE..................978 465-8481
John S Desmond, *Pr*
David Smith, *
Steve Petro, *
Gerard E Dumont, *
James C Heffernan, *
EMP: 125 EST: 1975
SALES (est): 39.03MM
SALES (corp-wide): 115.13MM Privately Held
Web: www.cambridgeport.net
SIC: 3444 3585 Sheet metalwork; Refrigeration and heating equipment
PA: Cox Engineering Company
35 Industrial Dr
Canton MA 02021
781 302-3300

(G-8907)
COATINGS ADHESIVES INKS
7 Martel Way (01833-2224)
PHONE..................978 352-7273
Vincent Sartorelli, *Owner*
EMP: 10 EST: 2003
SALES (est): 968.82K Privately Held
Web: www.caiink.com
SIC: 2891 2893 2759 Adhesives; Printing ink ; Commercial printing, nec

(G-8908)
EASTERN WOODWORKS LLC
132 Tenney St (01833-1823)
PHONE..................978 352-2005
Steve Greenfield, *Owner*
EMP: 11 EST: 1986
SQ FT: 19,800
SALES (est): 653.41K Privately Held
Web: www.eastern-solid-surface-laminate-countertops.com
SIC: 2434 Wood kitchen cabinets

(G-8909)
METAL TRONICS INC
Also Called: MTI
23 National Ave (01833)
PHONE..................978 659-6960
Peter B Orthwein, *Pr*
▲ EMP: 47 EST: 1967
SQ FT: 20,000
SALES (est): 10.97MM
SALES (corp-wide): 149.03MM Privately Held
Web: www.mmgmfg.com
SIC: 3444 Sheet metal specialties, not stamped
PA: Momentum Manufacturing Group - North, L.L.C.
210 Pierce Rd
Saint Johnsbury VT 05819
802 748-5007

(G-8910)
MOMENTUM MFG GROUP LLC (HQ)
23 National Ave (01833)
PHONE..................978 659-6960
James E Moroney, *CEO*
Matthew Smith, *Sr VP*
Steven Gore, *Sr VP*
Thomas W Mungovan, *CFO*
EMP: 62 EST: 2017
SALES (est): 138.07MM
SALES (corp-wide): 149.03MM Privately Held
Web: www.mmgmfg.com
SIC: 3443 3444 Plate work for the metalworking trade; Sheet metal specialties, not stamped
PA: Momentum Manufacturing Group - North, L.L.C.
210 Pierce Rd
Saint Johnsbury VT 05819
802 748-5007

(G-8911)
PARALLEL SYSTEMS CORP
118 Tenney St (01833-1823)
PHONE..................978 352-7100
EMP: 25 EST: 1991
SQ FT: 3,800
SALES (est): 644.13K Privately Held
Web: www.parsysco.com
SIC: 3577 3821 Computer peripheral equipment, nec; Laboratory apparatus and furniture

(G-8912)
ROLAND GATCHELL
119 Thurlow St (01833-1132)
PHONE..................978 352-6132
Roland Gatchell, *Owner*
EMP: 8 EST: 1997
SALES (est): 355.14K Privately Held
Web: www.rolysworld.com
SIC: 3444 Forming machine work, sheet metal

Gilbertville
Worcester County

(G-8913)
HARDWICK LAMINATORS INC
268 Main St (01031-9604)
P.O. Box 37 (01031-0037)
PHONE..................413 477-6600
Robert T Salem, *Pr*
Ernest L Salem, *Treas*
Richard Salem, *Admn*
David S Salem, *Sec*
EMP: 8 EST: 1966
SQ FT: 12,000
SALES (est): 660K Privately Held
SIC: 2295 Laminating of fabrics

(G-8914)
SHAWN ROBERTS WOODWORKING
830 Lower Rd (01031-9843)
PHONE..................413 477-0060
Shawn Roberts, *Owner*
EMP: 7 EST: 1991
SALES (est): 474.33K Privately Held
SIC: 2431 Millwork

Gill
Franklin County

(G-8915)
PETERMANS BOARDS AND BOWLS INC
61 French King Hwy (01354-9718)
P.O. Box 776 (01376-0776)
PHONE..................413 863-2116
Spencer L Peterman, *Prin*
EMP: 7 EST: 2010
SALES (est): 311.96K Privately Held
Web: www.spencerpeterman.com
SIC: 2499 5023 5719 Woodenware, kitchen and household; Kitchenware; Kitchenware

Gloucester
Essex County

(G-8916)
4TH DIMENSION BIOPROCESS INC
27 Rowley Shr (01930-1143)
PHONE..................978 979-4222
Lynne Frick, *CEO*
EMP: 7 EST: 2019
SALES (est): 148.22K Privately Held
SIC: 2834 Druggists' preparations (pharmaceuticals)

(G-8917)
ACME MERCHANDISE AND AP INC
Also Called: Acme Apparel
46 Blackburn Ctr Ste 47 (01930-2271)
P.O. Box 820 (01931-0820)

PHONE..................978 282-4800
◆ EMP: 27 EST: 1996
SQ FT: 9,000
SALES (est): 4.78MM Privately Held
Web: www.acmeapparel.com
SIC: 2321 2331 Men's and boy's furnishings ; T-shirts and tops, women's: made from purchased materials

(G-8918)
ANCHOR-SEAL INC
54 Great Republic Dr (01930-2277)
PHONE..................978 515-6004
Peter E Spinney, *Pr*
Marjorie Spinney, *Treas*
EMP: 9 EST: 1979
SQ FT: 12,500
SALES (est): 2.73MM Privately Held
Web: www.anchorseal.com
SIC: 2821 Plastics materials and resins

(G-8919)
APPLIED MATERIALS INC
35 Dory Rd (01930-2236)
PHONE..................978 282-2000
EMP: 19
SALES (corp-wide): 26.52B Publicly Held
Web: publish-p33711-e119406.adobeaemcloud.com
SIC: 3559 3674 Semiconductor manufacturing machinery; Semiconductors and related devices
PA: Applied Materials, Inc.
3050 Bowers Ave
Santa Clara CA 95054
408 727-5555

(G-8920)
AVENGER INC
Also Called: Avenger Filter Force
129 Thatcher Rd (01930-1951)
PHONE..................978 356-7311
Russell Morris, *Pr*
Patricia Kavanagh, *Treas*
John Naves, *VP*
EMP: 10 EST: 1983
SALES (est): 1.1MM Privately Held
Web: www.avenger.us
SIC: 3569 Filter elements, fluid, hydraulic line

(G-8921)
AXIAM INC (PA)
90 Blackburn Ctr (01930-2273)
PHONE..................978 281-3550
Donald W Lohin, *Pr*
Morse Barnes-brown Pendleton, *Sec*
EMP: 8 EST: 1983
SALES (est): 2.64MM
SALES (corp-wide): 2.64MM Privately Held
Web: www.axiam.com
SIC: 3825 Measuring instruments and meters, electric

(G-8922)
BAMBOO ROSE LLC (PA)
Also Called: Bamboo Rose Software
17 Rogers St (01930-5038)
PHONE..................978 281-3723
EMP: 141 EST: 2009
SALES (est): 13.32MM Privately Held
Web: www.bamboorose.com
SIC: 7372 Prepackaged software

(G-8923)
BLACK EARTH COMPOST LLC
2 Hillside Rd (01930-4248)
PHONE..................262 227-1067
Conor Solberg Miller, *Managing Member*

GEOGRAPHIC

EMP: 13 EST: 2013
SALES (est): 10.1MM **Privately Held**
Web: www.blackearthcompost.com
SIC: 2875 Compost

(G-8924)
BOMCO INC
125 Gloucester Ave (01930-2294)
PHONE.............................978 283-9000
Michael A Mccarthy, *Pr*
Paul Hubbert, *VP*
Anthony J Bertolino, *Sec*
Leslie Fay Anderson, *Treas*
James H Carangelo, *Dir*
EMP: 108 **EST:** 1958
SQ FT: 46,000
SALES (est): 24.04MM **Privately Held**
Web: www.bomco.com
SIC: 3444 Sheet metalwork

(G-8925)
BR HOLDINGS INC (PA)
Also Called: Bamboo Rose
17 Rogers St Ste 2 (01930-5039)
PHONE.............................978 281-3723
Susan Welch, *CEO*
Jon Baron, *Pr*
Ann Diamante, *CPO*
Tim O'brien, *CFO*
EMP: 177 **EST:** 2001
SQ FT: 25,000
SALES (est): 19.01MM
SALES (corp-wide): 19.01MM **Privately Held**
SIC: 7372 Prepackaged software

(G-8926)
C B FISK INC
21 Kondelin Rd (01930-5108)
PHONE.............................978 283-1909
Virginia Lee Fisk, *Ch Bd*
Steven Dieck, *
David Pike, *
▲ **EMP:** 27 **EST:** 1950
SQ FT: 20,000
SALES (est): 3.59MM **Privately Held**
Web: www.cbfisk.com
SIC: 3931 Pipes, organ

(G-8927)
CAPE POND ICE COMPANY (PA)
Also Called: Bresna Hand Ice
104 Commercial St (01930-5042)
P.O. Box 440 (01931-0440)
PHONE.............................978 283-0174
R Scott Memhard, *Pr*
R Scott Memhard, *Pr*
Richard C Memhard, *Ch Bd*
Laura M Fleming, *Clerk*
Robert Despres, *VP*
EMP: 20 **EST:** 1848
SQ FT: 37,000
SALES (est): 2.39MM
SALES (corp-wide): 2.39MM **Privately Held**
Web: www.capepondice.com
SIC: 2097 Manufactured ice

(G-8928)
CHANGE LOGIC
30 Trask St (01930-2837)
PHONE.............................617 274-8661
Andrew Binns, *Managing Principal*
EMP: 10 **EST:** 2010
SALES (est): 1.35MM **Privately Held**
Web: www.changelogic.com
SIC: 2992 Lubricating oils

(G-8929)
CKG LIMITED
Also Called: Wells Bindery
39 Revere St (01930-1252)
PHONE.............................781 893-2514
Charles Mcginn, *Pr*
Charles Mc Ginn, *Pr*
EMP: 9 **EST:** 1908
SQ FT: 6,000
SALES (est): 460.5K **Privately Held**
SIC: 2789 Binding only: books, pamphlets, magazines, etc.

(G-8930)
COMDEL INC
Also Called: Comdel Rf Power Systems
11 Kondelin Rd (01930-5108)
P.O. Box 157 (08073-0157)
PHONE.............................978 282-0620
EMP: 10
Web: www.xppower.com
SIC: 8711 3674 Engineering services; Semiconductors and related devices

(G-8931)
CUSTOM SEASONINGS INC
12 Heritage Way (01930-2216)
PHONE.............................978 762-6300
Mark D Dellafera, *Pr*
EMP: 23 **EST:** 2002
SQ FT: 35,000
SALES (est): 3.17MM **Privately Held**
Web: www.customseasonings.com
SIC: 2099 Seasonings and spices

(G-8932)
DITUSA CORPORATION
19 Shepherd St (01930-5501)
PHONE.............................978 335-5259
Miguel Peralta Cobo, *Pr*
EMP: 45 **EST:** 2013
SALES (est): 8.92MM **Privately Held**
Web: www.discefa.com
SIC: 2091 Seafood products: packaged in cans, jars, etc.
PA: Discefa Sl.
Poligono Industrial (Espiritu Santo) (Cl Marconi), 131 - 132
Cambre 15650

(G-8933)
EAGLE-TRIBUNE PUBLISHING CO
Also Called: Gloucester Daily Times
36 Whittemore St (01930-2553)
PHONE.............................978 282-0077
Marybeth Callahan, *Mgr*
EMP: 11
SALES (corp-wide): 33.14B **Privately Held**
Web: www.gloucestertimes.com
SIC: 2711 Newspapers, publishing and printing
HQ: Eagle-Tribune Publishing Company
100 Turnpike St
North Andover MA 01845
978 946-2000

(G-8934)
F W BRYCE INC (DH)
8 Pond Rd (01930-1833)
PHONE.............................978 283-7080
Keith Moores, *Pr*
Kazuo Kozakai, *Sec*
Paul Cantrell, *CFO*
◆ **EMP:** 20 **EST:** 1947
SQ FT: 20,000
SALES (est): 22.74MM **Privately Held**
Web: www.fwbryce.com

SIC: 5142 2092 Packaged frozen goods; Seafoods, frozen: prepared
HQ: Nissui Usa, Inc.
15400 Ne 90th St 100
Redmond WA 98052
425 869-1703

(G-8935)
GLOUCESTER ENGINEERING CO INC (DH)
Also Called: G E C
11 Dory Rd (01930-2236)
PHONE.............................978 281-1800
Rick Tattersfield, *CEO*
Bill Schmidt, *
Carl Johnson, *OF OEM DIV*
◆ **EMP:** 16 **EST:** 1961
SQ FT: 165,000
SALES (est): 25.52MM **Privately Held**
SIC: 3559 Plastics working machinery
HQ: Davis-Standard, Llc
1 Extrusion Dr
Pawcatuck CT 06379

(G-8936)
GLOUCESTER ENGINEERING CO INC
18 Sargent St (01930-2875)
PHONE.............................978 515-7008
Bob Snider, *Mgr*
EMP: 22
SIC: 3559 Plastics working machinery
HQ: Gloucester Engineering Co., Inc.
11 Dory Rd
Gloucester MA 01930
978 281-1800

(G-8937)
GLOUCESTER GRAPHICS INC (PA)
19 Pond Rd (01930-1834)
PHONE.............................978 281-4500
P Sean Gibney, *Pr*
Norma Gibney, *VP*
Amber Gibney, *Sec*
EMP: 9 **EST:** 1981
SQ FT: 26,000
SALES (est): 1.68MM
SALES (corp-wide): 1.68MM **Privately Held**
Web: www.gloucestergraphics.com
SIC: 2759 3993 5199 2262 Labels and seals: printing, nsk; Letters for signs, metal; Posters and decals; Screen printing: manmade fiber and silk broadwoven fabrics

(G-8938)
GLOUCESTER TRANSIT MIX INC
45 Emerson Ave (01930-2556)
P.O. Box 1328 (01931-1328)
PHONE.............................978 283-9649
Jeffery Pybus, *Pr*
Robert Pybus, *VP*
Timothy A Pybus, *Treas*
EMP: 8 **EST:** 1994
SALES (est): 606.26K **Privately Held**
Web: www.gloucestertransitmix.com
SIC: 3273 Ready-mixed concrete

(G-8939)
GORTONS INC (DH)
Also Called: Gortons
128 Rogers St (01930-5005)
P.O. Box 361 (01931-0361)
PHONE.............................978 283-3000
Kurtis Hogan, *Pr*
Judson Reis, *
◆ **EMP:** 300 **EST:** 1849
SALES (est): 325.42MM **Privately Held**

Web: www.gortons.com
SIC: 2092 2091 Fresh or frozen packaged fish; Seafood products: packaged in cans, jars, etc.
HQ: Nissui Usa, Inc.
15400 Ne 90th St Ste 100
Redmond WA 98052
425 869-1703

(G-8940)
GP AGGREGATE CORP
19 Pond Rd (01930-1834)
PHONE.............................978 283-5318
Paul M Butman Junior, *Prin*
EMP: 10 **EST:** 2010
SALES (est): 1.31MM **Privately Held**
SIC: 3273 Ready-mixed concrete

(G-8941)
HEFRING INC
Also Called: Hefring Engineering
417 Main St (01930-3006)
PHONE.............................617 938-9544
Atle Lohrmann, *Managing Member*
EMP: 10 **EST:** 1998
SQ FT: 800
SALES (est): 1.09MM **Privately Held**
Web: www.hefringengineering.com
SIC: 3829 Measuring and controlling devices, nec

(G-8942)
J & L WELDING & MACHINE CO
Also Called: J&L
19 Arthur St # 25 (01930-2736)
PHONE.............................978 283-3388
Jeffery Amero, *Pr*
EMP: 25 **EST:** 1984
SQ FT: 11,000
SALES (est): 4.66MM **Privately Held**
Web: www.jlweldingandmachine.com
SIC: 7692 3599 Welding repair; Machine and other job shop work

(G-8943)
MAGMA
11 Pleasant St (01930-5916)
PHONE.............................978 381-3494
EMP: 7 **EST:** 2018
SALES (est): 353.61K **Privately Held**
Web: www.magma.center
SIC: 7372 Prepackaged software

(G-8944)
NATIONAL FISH AND SEAFOOD INC
11-15 Parker St (01930-3017)
PHONE.............................978 282-7880
◆ **EMP:** 253
Web: www.nationalfish.com
SIC: 5146 2092 Fish, frozen, unpackaged; Fresh or frozen packaged fish

(G-8945)
NEW ENGLAND GRUND SLUTIONS LLC
127 Eastern Ave Ste 2 (01930-6511)
PHONE.............................978 203-6277
EMP: 9 **EST:** 2018
SALES (est): 353.34K **Privately Held**
SIC: 2951 Asphalt paving mixtures and blocks

(G-8946)
NICHOLS CANDIES INC
1 Crafts Rd (01930-2135)
PHONE.............................978 283-9850
Barbara Nichols, *Pr*
EMP: 13 **EST:** 1954

SQ FT: 21,500
SALES (est): 1.04MM **Privately Held**
Web: www.nicholscandies.com
SIC: 2064 5441 Candy and other
confectionery products; Confectionery

(G-8947)
NSD SEAFOOD INC (PA)
Also Called: Atlantic Fish & Seafood
159 E Main St (01930-3844)
PHONE..............................978 282-7880
Nick Osgood, *Pr*
David Hynes, *Sec*
Shawn Hynes, *Dir*
EMP: 155 EST: 2019
SQ FT: 170,000
SALES (est): 17.8MM
SALES (corp-wide): 17.8MM **Privately Held**
SIC: 2092 8742 Fresh or frozen fish or
seafood chowders, soups, and stews;
Restaurant and food services consultants

(G-8948)
OCEAN CREST SEAFOOD INC
88 Commercial St (01930-5025)
PHONE..............................978 281-0232
Leonard Parco, *Pr*
EMP: 14 EST: 1967
SQ FT: 10,000
SALES (est): 189.07K **Privately Held**
SIC: 2092 Fresh or frozen packaged fish

(G-8949)
**OCEAN CREST SEAFOODS INC
(PA)**
88 Commercial St (01930-5025)
P.O. Box 1183 (01931-1183)
PHONE..............................978 281-0232
Leonard Parco, *Pr*
Maria Churchill, *
Edward E Mc Collum Junior, *Stockholder*
Ann Molloy, *Stockholder**
Salvatore Parco, *Stockholder**
▲ EMP: 21 EST: 1965
SQ FT: 100,000
SALES (est): 5.63MM
SALES (corp-wide): 5.63MM **Privately Held**
Web: www.neptunesharvest.com
SIC: 2873 5146 2092 2875 Fertilizers:
natural (organic), except compost; Fish,
fresh; Fresh or frozen packaged fish;
Fertilizers, mixing only

(G-8950)
P M S MANUFACTURED PDTS INC
Also Called: PMS Mfg
10 Sadler St (01930-2918)
PHONE..............................978 281-2600
Richard Perruzzi, *Pr*
Dayne Perruzzi, *VP*
EMP: 11 EST: 1960
SQ FT: 10,000
SALES (est): 1.85MM **Privately Held**
Web: www.pmsmetal.com
SIC: 3444 3469 Sheet metalwork; Stamping
metal for the trade

(G-8951)
PARA RESEARCH INC
Also Called: Champlain Software
85 Eastern Ave (01930-1889)
PHONE..............................978 282-1100
Tonia N Molinski, *Pr*
EMP: 8 EST: 1972
SQ FT: 1,000
SALES (est): 406.44K **Privately Held**
Web: www.pararesearch.com

SIC: 7372 7371 Application computer
software; Custom computer programming
services

(G-8952)
PROTEUS INDUSTRIES INC
33 Commercial St (01930-5040)
PHONE..............................978 281-9545
William R Fielding, *CEO*
Stephen Kelleher, *Pr*
Douglas Hall Iii, *Treas*
◆ EMP: 7 EST: 2000
SQ FT: 5,000
SALES (est): 4.63MM
SALES (corp-wide): 626.11MM **Privately Held**
Web: www.kemin.com
SIC: 2824 Protein fibers
PA: Kemin Industries, Inc.
1900 Scott Ave
Des Moines IA 50317
515 559-5100

(G-8953)
QUAYSIDE PUBLISHING GROUP
33 Commercial St (01930-5040)
PHONE..............................978 282-9590
Ken Fund, *Pr*
EMP: 13 EST: 2005
SALES (est): 671.7K
SALES (corp-wide): 92.94MM **Privately Held**
SIC: 2741 Business service newsletters:
publishing and printing
PA: Quarto Group Inc
276 5th Ave Rm 205
New York NY 10001
212 779-0700

(G-8954)
RENBRANDT INC
32 Blackburn Ctr (01930-2270)
PHONE..............................617 445-8910
G Stewart Renner, *CEO*
Raymond Renner, *Pr*
EMP: 16 EST: 1951
SQ FT: 4,500
SALES (est): 1.78MM **Privately Held**
Web: www.renbrandt.com
SIC: 3568 Couplings, shaft: rigid, flexible,
universal joint, etc.

(G-8955)
ROSES OIL SERVICE INC (PA)
Also Called: Rose's Marine Service
375 Main St (01930-3006)
P.O. Box 1346 (01931-1346)
PHONE..............................877 283-3334
Timothy Rose, *Pr*
EMP: 36 EST: 1964
SQ FT: 3,000
SALES (est): 32.82MM
SALES (corp-wide): 32.82MM **Privately Held**
Web: www.rosesmarine.com
SIC: 5172 5551 3429 3599 Fuel oil; Marine
supplies and equipment; Hardware, nec;
Machine shop, jobbing and repair

(G-8956)
RULE INDUSTRIES LLC
1 Kondelin Rd Cape Ann Industrial Pk
(01930-5198)
PHONE..............................978 281-0440
◆ EMP: 200
SIC: 3561 3812 2851 2899 Pumps and
pumping equipment; Nautical instruments;
Marine paints; Chemical preparations, nec

(G-8957)
SANDY BAY MACHINE INC
11 Dory Rd # 2 (01930-2236)
PHONE..............................978 546-1331
EMP: 143 EST: 1978
SALES (est): 2.44MM
SALES (corp-wide): 68.92B **Publicly Held**
Web:
sandybaymachine.bethermalandpower.com
SIC: 3661 7629 Fiber optics
communications equipment;
Telecommunication equipment repair
(except telephones)
HQ: Tsi Group, Inc.
94 Tide Mill Rd
Hampton NH 03842

(G-8958)
SOITEC USA INC (HQ)
2 Blackburn Ctr (01930-2201)
PHONE..............................978 531-2222
Andre Auberton-herve, *CEO*
Andrew Wittkower, *Pr*
EMP: 9 EST: 1992
SQ FT: 1,000
SALES (est): 5.52MM
SALES (corp-wide): 1.1B **Privately Held**
Web: preprod.soitec.com
SIC: 3674 5063 Silicon wafers, chemically
doped; Electrical apparatus and equipment
PA: Soitec
Parc Techno Des Fontaines
Bernin 38190
476927500

(G-8959)
**SONOLITE PLASTICS
CORPORATION**
10 Fernwood Lake Ave (01930-3331)
PHONE..............................978 281-0662
Peter J Lawrence, *Pr*
Jonathan B Lawrence, *Treas*
▲ EMP: 18 EST: 1963
SQ FT: 22,000
SALES (est): 2.49MM **Privately Held**
Web: www.sonoliteplastics.com
SIC: 3089 3542 Injection molding of plastics
; Bending machines

(G-8960)
STRONG GROUP INC (PA)
Also Called: Strong Leather Co
39 Grove St (01930)
P.O. Box 1195 (01931-1195)
PHONE..............................978 281-3300
David A Cutter, *Pr*
Steve Kaity, *
Richard Cutter, *
Richard Lindner, *
Ralph Pino Clrk, *Prin*
▲ EMP: 59 EST: 1932
SQ FT: 53,000
SALES (est): 4.52MM
SALES (corp-wide): 4.52MM **Privately Held**
Web: www.strongbadgecase.com
SIC: 3993 5199 3172 3199 Advertising
novelties; Leather goods, except footwear,
gloves, luggage, belting; Personal leather
goods, nec; Holsters, leather

(G-8961)
SURFARI INC
88 Bass Ave (01930-3119)
PHONE..............................978 283-7873
Christian Del Rosario, *Pr*
Nicole Del Rosario, *Sec*
EMP: 8 EST: 2011
SALES (est): 246.68K **Privately Held**
Web: www.surfcapeann.com

SIC: 3949 Surfboards

(G-8962)
VACUUM TECHNOLOGY INC
15 Great Republic Dr Ste 4 (01930-2343)
PHONE..............................510 333-6562
Yuling Cai, *Pr*
▲ EMP: 7 EST: 2012
SQ FT: 2,700
SALES (est): 730.47K **Privately Held**
Web: www.vti-glovebox.com
SIC: 3564 3821 3826 Air purification
equipment; Evaporation apparatus,
laboratory type; Moisture analyzers

(G-8963)
**VARIAN SEMICDTR EQP ASSOC
INC (HQ)**
Also Called: Applied Materials Varian
35 Dory Rd (01930-2236)
PHONE..............................978 282-2000
Gary E Dickerson, *CEO*
Robert J Halliday, *
Gary J Rosen Ph.d., *VP Engg*
Robert J Perlmutter Ph.d., *IMPLANT BUS
UNITS*
Yong-kil Kim Ph.d., *Ex VP*
◆ EMP: 143 EST: 1999
SALES (est): 598.97MM
SALES (corp-wide): 26.52B **Publicly Held**
SIC: 5065 3674 Semiconductor devices;
Semiconductors and related devices
PA: Applied Materials, Inc.
3050 Bowers Ave
Santa Clara CA 95054
408 727-5555

(G-8964)
VSEA INC
35 Dory Rd (01930-2236)
PHONE..............................978 282-2000
Thomas Baker, *Contrlr*
▲ EMP: 43 EST: 2006
SALES (est): 2.3MM **Privately Held**
SIC: 3674 Semiconductors and related
devices

(G-8965)
XP POWER LLC
Also Called: Xp Comdel
11 Kondelin Rd (01930-5108)
PHONE..............................978 282-0620
Scott Johnson, *Brnch Mgr*
EMP: 59
Web: www.xppower.com
SIC: 3674 8711 Semiconductors and related
devices; Engineering services
HQ: Xp Power Llc
990 Benecia Ave
Sunnyvale CA 95131

Goshen
Hampshire County

(G-8966)
ACCUFAB IRONWORKS INC
82 S Main St (01032-9614)
P.O. Box 328 (01032-0328)
PHONE..............................413 268-7133
EMP: 10 EST: 1995
SQ FT: 5,700
SALES (est): 1.79MM **Privately Held**
SIC: 3441 Fabricated structural metal

(G-8967)
GEORGE D JUDD & SONS LLC
145 Berkshire Trl W (01032-9600)
PHONE..............................413 268-7590

TOLL FREE: 800
Francis Judd, *Managing Member*
EMP: 8 EST: 1938
SALES (est): 1.86MM **Privately Held**
Web: www.originalgoshenstone.com
SIC: 5032 1411   Gravel; Dimension stone

Grafton
Worcester County

(G-8968)
MEDCON BIOLAB
TECHNOLOGIES INC
50 Brigham Hill Rd (01519-1136)
P.O. Box 196 (01519-0196)
PHONE..........................508 839-4203
Virgil F Pichierri, *Pr*
Robert Borgatti, *VP*
John Mccloud, *VP*
Damian Pichierri, *Ex VP*
Laura Pichierri, *Clerk*
EMP: 7 EST: 1987
SQ FT: 3,200
SALES (est): 589.21K **Privately Held**
SIC: 3841   Surgical and medical instruments

(G-8969)
VAN-GO GRAPHICS
94 Fitzpatrick Rd (01519-1095)
PHONE..........................508 865-7300
Robert Vanasse, *Pr*
Michael Goulet, *Treas*
EMP: 7 EST: 1987
SALES (est): 487.13K **Privately Held**
Web: www.vangographics.com
SIC: 2759 2752   Thermography; Commercial
printing, lithographic

Granby
Hampshire County

(G-8970)
C & G MACHINE TOOL CO INC
180 W State St (01033-9463)
PHONE..........................413 467-9556
Omer Gingras Junior, *Pr*
Shirley Gingras, *Sec*
EMP: 16 EST: 1953
SQ FT: 4,000
SALES (est): 474.52K **Privately Held**
Web: www.c-gtool.com
SIC: 3599   Machine shop, jobbing and repair

(G-8971)
INTER-ALL CORPORATION
25 W State St (01033-9467)
PHONE..........................413 467-7181
Gino E Maggi Junior, *Pr*
EMP: 13 EST: 1965
SQ FT: 17,000
SALES (est): 325.81K **Privately Held**
Web: www.inter-all.com
SIC: 2395 2397   Embroidery and art
needlework; Schiffli machine embroideries

Granville
Hampden County

(G-8972)
WACKERBARTH BOX MFG CO
INC
Also Called: Wackerbarth Box Shop
383 Granby Rd (01034-9483)
P.O. Box 257 (01034-0257)
PHONE..........................413 357-8816

James F Wackerbarth, *Pr*
Nancy Petersen, *Treas*
EMP: 16 EST: 1924
SQ FT: 10,000
SALES (est): 485.55K **Privately Held**
SIC: 2448   Pallets, wood

Great Barrington
Berkshire County

(G-8973)
BERKSHIRE CORPORATION
(HQ)
Also Called: Berkshire
21 River St (01230-1330)
PHONE..........................413 528-2602
Whitmore Kelley, *CEO*
Valerie Lorette, *Dir*
James H Bodurtha, *Dir*
Richard M Marotta, *Ex VP*
George Bacigalupo, *Ex VP*
◆ EMP: 30 EST: 1967
SQ FT: 30,000
SALES (est): 32.94MM **Privately Held**
Web: www.berkshire.com
SIC: 2269 2392   Finishing plants, nec;
Household furnishings, nec
PA: Berkshire Singapore Pte. Ltd.
51 Goldhill Plaza
Singapore 30890

(G-8974)
BERKSHIRE PUBLISHING
GROUP LLC
Also Called: Berkshire Reference Works
122 Castle St (01230-1506)
PHONE..........................413 528-0206
EMP: 10 EST: 1995
SALES (est): 953.31K **Privately Held**
Web: www.berkshirepublishing.com
SIC: 2731   Book publishing

(G-8975)
CHAMBERLAIN GROUP LLC
Also Called: Chamberlain Group
934 Main St (01230-2013)
PHONE..........................413 528-7744
EMP: 10 EST: 1999
SQ FT: 2,500
SALES (est): 2.66MM **Privately Held**
Web: www.thecgroup.com
SIC: 3842   Models, anatomical

(G-8976)
IREDALE COSMETICS INC (PA)
Also Called: Jane Iredale
50 Church St (01230-1315)
PHONE..........................413 644-9900
◆ EMP: 97 EST: 1994
SQ FT: 4,000
SALES (est): 56.72MM **Privately Held**
Web: www.janeiredale.com
SIC: 5122 2844   Cosmetics; Cosmetic
preparations

(G-8977)
KWIK-PRINT INC
35 Bridge St (01230-1310)
PHONE..........................413 528-2885
John Raifstanger Junior, *Pr*
Cheryl Raifstanger, *Treas*
EMP: 15 EST: 1973
SQ FT: 2,100
SALES (est): 837.09K **Privately Held**
Web: www.kwikprintinc.com
SIC: 2752   Offset printing

(G-8978)
SOUTHERN BRKSHIRE
SHPPERS GIDE
Also Called: Shoppers Guide
271 Main St Ste 4 (01230-1749)
P.O. Box 89 (01230-0089)
PHONE..........................413 528-0095
Eunice Raifstanger, *Pr*
Robin Hare, *Treas*
John Raifstanger Junior, *Clerk*
EMP: 12 EST: 1968
SALES (est): 857.9K **Privately Held**
Web: www.shoppersguide-inc.com
SIC: 2741 6531 2796 2791   Guides:
publishing only, not printed on site; Real
estate agents and managers; Platemaking
services; Typesetting

(G-8979)
THE ORION SOCIETY INC
Also Called: Orion Magazine
187 Main St (01230-1623)
PHONE..........................413 528-4422
EMP: 13 EST: 1997
SALES (est): 1.11MM **Privately Held**
Web: www.orionmagazine.org
SIC: 2721   Magazines: publishing only, not
printed on site

(G-8980)
WARRIOR TRADING INC
47 Railroad St (01230-1741)
P.O. Box 330 (01230-0330)
PHONE..........................413 591-1100
Ross Cameron, *Pr*
EMP: 34 EST: 2017
SALES (est): 747.08K **Privately Held**
Web: www.warriortrading.com
SIC: 7372   Educational computer software

Greenfield
Franklin County

(G-8981)
APPLIED DYNAMICS
CORPORATION (PA)
38 Butternut St (01301-1379)
P.O. Box 907 (01302-0907)
PHONE..........................413 774-7268
Michael Hogan, *Pr*
David Cunningham, *
EMP: 46 EST: 1987
SQ FT: 26,500
SALES (est): 16.65MM
SALES (corp-wide): 16.65MM **Privately**
Held
Web: www.applied-dynamics.com
SIC: 5063 7694 7629 3625   Motors, electric;
Armature rewinding shops; Electronic
equipment repair; Crane and hoist controls,
including metal mill

(G-8982)
ARGOTEC LLC
Also Called: Argotec, LLC
53 Silvio O Conte Dr (01301-1382)
PHONE..........................413 772-2564
Caio Sedeno, *Brnch Mgr*
EMP: 500
Web: www.argotec.com
SIC: 3081 2821   Plastics film and sheet;
Plastics materials and resins
HQ: Argotec Llc
53 Silvio O Conte Dr
Greenfield MA 01301

(G-8983)
ARGOTEC LLC (HQ)
Also Called: Argotec
53 Silvio O Conte Dr (01301-1382)
PHONE..........................413 772-2564
Jeffrey Kramer, *CEO*
Allison Aden, *VP Fin*
Michel Fievez, *PAPERS*
Daniel Lister, *ADVANCED MATERIALS &*
STRUCTURES
Robert Cardin, *Corporate Controller*
◆ EMP: 201 EST: 1986
SQ FT: 55,000
SALES (est): 163.07MM **Publicly Held**
Web: www.argotec.com
SIC: 3081 2821   Plastics film and sheet;
Plastics materials and resins
PA: Mativ Holdings, Inc.
100 Kimball Pl Ste 600
Alpharetta GA 30009

(G-8984)
ASSOCTION FOR GRVSTONE
STUDIES
278 Main St Ste 209 (01301-3230)
PHONE..........................413 772-0836
Penelope Davis, *Admn*
Tom Malloy, *Pr*
Robert Young, *VP*
EMP: 9 EST: 1977
SALES (est): 138.69K **Privately Held**
Web: www.gravestonestudies.org
SIC: 2741   Business service newsletters:
publishing and printing

(G-8985)
BETE FOG NOZZLE INC (PA)
50 Greenfield St (01301-1378)
PHONE..........................413 772-0846
Matthew Bete, *Ch Bd*
Tom Fitch, *
Dawn Bete, *
Doug Dziadzio, *
Thomas Bassett, *
◆ EMP: 125 EST: 1950
SQ FT: 54,000
SALES (est): 37.32MM
SALES (corp-wide): 37.32MM **Privately**
Held
Web: www.bete.com
SIC: 3499   Nozzles, spray: aerosol, paint, or
insecticide

(G-8986)
CNS OUTDOOR
TECHNOLOGIES LLC
627 Barton Rd (01301-1011)
PHONE..........................413 475-3840
Neville Orsmond, *CEO*
EMP: 21 EST: 2014
SALES (est): 994.76K **Privately Held**
SIC: 3949   Fishing equipment

(G-8987)
COCA-COLA BTLG STHSTERN
NENG I
Coca-Cola
180 Silvio O Conte Dr (01301-1356)
PHONE..........................413 448-8296
TOLL FREE: 800
Randy Markland, *Mgr*
EMP: 28
Web: www.coca-cola.com
SIC: 2086   Bottled and canned soft drinks
HQ: Coca-Cola Bottling Company Of
Southeastern New England, Inc.
150 Waterford Parkway S
Waterford CT 06385
860 443-2816

(G-8988)
COCA-COLA REFRESHMENTS USA INC
Coca-Cola
180 Silvio O Conte Dr (01301-1356)
PHONE...................413 772-2617
John O'neil, *Brnch Mgr*
EMP: 10
SALES (corp-wide): 43B **Publicly Held**
Web: www.coca-cola.com
SIC: 2086 5149 Bottled and canned soft drinks; Groceries and related products, nec
HQ: Coca-Cola Refreshments Usa, Inc.
1 Coca Cola Plz Nw
Atlanta GA 30313
770 989-3000

(G-8989)
DECKER MACHINE WORKS INC
201 Munson St (01301-9605)
P.O. Box 1001 (01330-1001)
PHONE...................413 628-3300
Scott A Decker, *Pr*
Noah Decker, *Genl Mgr*
EMP: 20 **EST:** 1982
SQ FT: 10,000
SALES (est): 2.78MM **Privately Held**
Web: www.deckermachineworks.com
SIC: 3599 Machine shop, jobbing and repair

(G-8990)
DUMONT COMPANY LLC
Also Called: Minute Man Broaches
289 Wells St (01301-1614)
P.O. Box 469 (01302-0469)
PHONE...................413 773-3675
EMP: 16 **EST:** 1946
SQ FT: 12,000
SALES (est): 2.32MM **Privately Held**
Web: www.pilotprecision.com
SIC: 3541 Machine tools, metal cutting type

(G-8991)
FOUR PHANTOMS BREWING CO LLC
33 Forest Ave (01301-1916)
PHONE...................931 247-0315
Lloyd Phillips, *Prin*
EMP: 7 **EST:** 2019
SALES (est): 239.14K **Privately Held**
Web: www.fourphantoms.net
SIC: 5813 2082 Bars and lounges; Beer (alcoholic beverage)

(G-8992)
GREENFIELD INDUSTRIES INC
34 Sanderson St (01301-2715)
PHONE...................413 772-3200
Joe Anzalotti, *Ex Dir*
EMP: 8 **EST:** 2010
SALES (est): 122.67K **Privately Held**
Web: www.gfii.com
SIC: 3999 Manufacturing industries, nec

(G-8993)
HITPOINT INC (PA)
30 Olive St (01301-3318)
P.O. Box 476 (01302-0476)
PHONE...................413 992-6663
Paul Hake, *CEO*
Aaron St John, *
Paul Hake, *Pr*
Steve Victorino, *
EMP: 44 **EST:** 2009
SQ FT: 2,400
SALES (est): 4.81MM
SALES (corp-wide): 4.81MM **Privately Held**
Web: www.hitpointstudios.com

SIC: 3944 Electronic games and toys

(G-8994)
KENNAMETAL INC
34 Sanderson St (01301-2715)
PHONE...................802 626-3331
Mike Kinsman, *Brnch Mgr*
EMP: 74
SALES (corp-wide): 2.08B **Publicly Held**
Web: www.kennametal.com
SIC: 3545 Cutting tools for machine tools
PA: Kennametal Inc.
525 William Penn Pl # 3300
Pittsburgh PA 15219
412 248-8000

(G-8995)
NEW ENGLAND EXPERT TECH CORP
Also Called: Ne - Xt Technologies
15 Greenfield St (01301-1378)
PHONE...................413 773-8200
Steven Capshaw, *Pr*
EMP: 35 **EST:** 1971
SQ FT: 22,000
SALES (est): 6.28MM **Privately Held**
Web: www.ne-xtusa.com
SIC: 3953 5088 Marking devices; Aeronautical equipment and supplies

(G-8996)
NEW ENGLAND NATURAL BAKERS INC
74 Fairview St E (01301-9654)
PHONE...................413 772-2239
EMP: 39 **EST:** 1977
SALES (est): 8.04MM **Privately Held**
Web: www.newenglandnaturalbakers.com
SIC: 2043 Cereal breakfast foods

(G-8997)
NORTHEASTERN METALS LLC
Also Called: Manufacturer
322 Wells St (01301-1628)
PHONE...................800 506-7090
Kyle Provencal, *Pr*
Jonathan P Provencal, *Managing Member*
EMP: 11 **EST:** 2012
SALES (est): 989.08K **Privately Held**
SIC: 3444 Metal ventilating equipment

(G-8998)
REAL PICKLES COPERATIVE INC
Also Called: Real Pickles
311 Wells St (01301-1639)
PHONE...................413 774-2600
Kristin Howard, *Pr*
Catherine Korby, *Clerk*
Gregory Nichols, *Treas*
EMP: 22 **EST:** 2014
SALES (est): 1.2MM **Privately Held**
Web: www.realpickles.com
SIC: 2035 Cucumbers, pickles and pickle salting

(G-8999)
SILVER GREENFIELD INC
Also Called: Lunt Silversmiths
298 Federal St (01301-1971)
PHONE...................413 774-2774
▲ **EMP:** 200
SIC: 3914 3421 3423 Silverware, sterling silver; Table and food cutlery, including butchers'; Knives, agricultural or industrial

(G-9000)
SILVER SCREEN DESIGN INC
324 Wells St Ste 3 (01301-1636)
PHONE...................413 773-1692
Cheryl Termo, *Pr*
John Pollard, *CFO*
EMP: 18 **EST:** 1984
SQ FT: 14,000
SALES (est): 4.56MM **Privately Held**
Web: www.silverscreendesign.com
SIC: 2261 2759 7336 3993 Screen printing of cotton broadwoven fabrics; Screen printing; Graphic arts and related design; Signs and advertising specialties

(G-9001)
SWM
53 Silvio O Conte Dr (01301-1382)
PHONE...................413 772-2564
EMP: 21 **EST:** 2017
SALES (est): 4.57MM **Privately Held**
Web: www.swmintl.com
SIC: 3081 Unsupported plastics film and sheet

(G-9002)
THIN FILM IMAGING TECHNOLOGIES
Also Called: Tfi Technologies
11 Blanker Ln (01301-1111)
PHONE...................413 774-6692
EMP: 10 **EST:** 1995
SALES (est): 775.79K **Privately Held**
Web: www.tfitech.com
SIC: 3827 Optical instruments and lenses

(G-9003)
THOMAS & THOMAS RODMAKERS
627 Barton Rd Ste 1 (01301-1001)
PHONE...................413 475-3840
Tom Dorsey, *Mgr*
▲ **EMP:** 15 **EST:** 1969
SALES (est): 949.7K **Privately Held**
Web: www.thomasandthomas.com
SIC: 3949 5091 5941 Rods and rod parts, fishing; Fishing equipment and supplies; Fishing equipment

(G-9004)
W B MASON CO INC
121 Wells St (01301-2363)
PHONE...................888 926-2766
EMP: 34
SALES (corp-wide): 1.01B **Privately Held**
Web: www.wbmason.com
SIC: 5943 5712 2752 Office forms and supplies; Office furniture; Commercial printing, lithographic
PA: W. B. Mason Co., Inc.
59 Centre Street
Brockton MA 02301
508 586-3434

(G-9005)
WELLS TOOL COMPANY
106 Hope St (01301-3569)
P.O. Box 1531 (01302-1531)
PHONE...................413 773-3465
Phillip Duda, *Pr*
Sandra Duda, *VP*
EMP: 11 **EST:** 1928
SALES (est): 483.39K **Privately Held**
Web: www.wellstool.com
SIC: 3545 Taps, machine tool

(G-9006)
WOOD & WOOD INC
19 Butternut St (01301-1379)

PHONE...................413 772-0889
Van V Wood, *Pr*
Molly L Wood, *
▼ **EMP:** 30 **EST:** 1971
SQ FT: 36,000
SALES (est): 4.04MM **Privately Held**
Web: www.smallcorp.com
SIC: 2542 2499 Fixtures: display, office, or store: except wood; Picture and mirror frames, wood

(G-9007)
WTE RECYCLING INC
75 Southern Ave (01301-3913)
PHONE...................413 772-2200
M Scott Mellen, *Pr*
Nancy C Wrisley, *
Carol Chin Forman, *
EMP: 40 **EST:** 1987
SALES (est): 21.12MM
SALES (corp-wide): 49.98MM **Privately Held**
Web: www.wte.com
SIC: 4953 5093 3341 Recycling, waste materials; Metal scrap and waste materials; Secondary nonferrous metals
PA: Wte Corporation
91 Hartwell Ave
Lexington MA 02421
781 275-6400

Groton
Middlesex County

(G-9008)
CJS WORKSHOP LLC
31 Adams Ave (01450-1241)
PHONE...................323 445-5012
Robert Saunders, *CEO*
Robert Saunders, *Managing Member*
EMP: 30 **EST:** 2021
SALES (est): 1.26MM **Privately Held**
SIC: 7389 7929 3999 2389 Business Activities at Non-Commercial Site; Entertainment service; Puppets and marionettes; Costumes

(G-9009)
EBSNET INC
Also Called: On Time Software
274e Main St (01450-1236)
P.O. Box 819 (01450-0819)
PHONE...................978 448-9000
Sarah Richardson, *Pr*
Tom Vanoudenaren, *VP*
EMP: 8 **EST:** 1987
SQ FT: 1,500
SALES (est): 868.59K **Privately Held**
Web: www.ebsnetinc.com
SIC: 7372 Prepackaged software

(G-9010)
INSCO CORPORATION
Also Called: Insco
412 Main St (01450-1232)
P.O. Box 489 (01450-0489)
PHONE...................978 448-6368
David L Ammen, *Pr*
Gary R Rutherford, *
Edward T Kotowski, *
EMP: 27 **EST:** 1955
SQ FT: 65,000
SALES (est): 4.42MM **Privately Held**
Web: www.inscocorp.com
SIC: 7389 3566 3714 3462 Grinding, precision: commercial or industrial; Gears, power transmission, except auto; Gears, motor vehicle; Iron and steel forgings

(G-9011)
NAVTEC RIGGING SOLUTIONS INC
11 Lakeside Dr (01450-2067)
▲ **EMP:** 22 **EST:** 2012
SALES (est): 488.87K **Privately Held**
Web: www.navtec.net
SIC: 3731 3594 3492 Marine rigging; Fluid power pumps and motors; Control valves, fluid power: hydraulic and pneumatic

Groveland
Essex County

(G-9012)
A W CHESTERTON COMPANY (PA)
Also Called: Chesterton
860 Salem St (01834-1563)
P.O. Box 3351 (02241-3351)
PHONE.................................781 438-7000
Brian O'donnell, *Pr*
Richard Hoyle, *CEO*
Ron Maxwel, *VP*
Joseph Riley, *Sec*
Mary Janet Baird, *Treas*
◆ **EMP:** 45 **EST:** 1884
SQ FT: 65,000
SALES (est): 282.58MM
SALES (corp-wide): 282.58MM **Privately Held**
Web: www.chesterton.com
SIC: 3053 2851 2992 2891 Gaskets, all materials; Epoxy coatings; Lubricating oils; Sealing compounds for pipe threads or joints

(G-9013)
A W CHESTERTON COMPANY
860 Salem St (01834-1563)
P.O. Box 189 (01834-0189)
PHONE.................................781 438-7000
Greg Plakias, *Brnch Mgr*
EMP: 400
SALES (corp-wide): 282.58MM **Privately Held**
Web: www.chesterton.com
SIC: 2819 3561 3053 2992 Industrial inorganic chemicals, nec; Pumps and pumping equipment; Gaskets; packing and sealing devices; Lubricating oils and greases
PA: A. W. Chesterton Company
860 Salem St
Groveland MA 01834
781 438-7000

(G-9014)
ITAL-TECH ENGINEERING CO INC
3 Federal Way (01834-1564)
PHONE.................................978 373-6773
Elvis Di Genova, *Pr*
Giuliana Di Genova, *Treas*
Frank Di Genova, *VP*
Laurie Coma, *Off Mgr*
Marina Digenova, *Dir*
EMP: 13 **EST:** 1976
SQ FT: 12,000
SALES (est): 1.2MM **Privately Held**
Web: www.ital-tech.net
SIC: 3599 Machine shop, jobbing and repair

(G-9015)
ITAL-TECH MACHINED PDTS LLC
3 Federal Way (01834-1564)
PHONE.................................978 373-6773

David Slutz, *Managing Member*
EMP: 16 **EST:** 2017
SQ FT: 12,000
SALES (est): 1.61MM **Privately Held**
Web: www.ital-tech.net
SIC: 3599 Machine shop, jobbing and repair

(G-9016)
UNION MACHINE COMPANY LYNN INC (PA)
6 Federal Way (01834-1564)
PHONE.................................978 521-5100
Eric Harper, *Pr*
Robin Trickett, *
EMP: 39 **EST:** 1954
SQ FT: 25,000
SALES (est): 8.86MM
SALES (corp-wide): 8.86MM **Privately Held**
Web: www.unionmachine.com
SIC: 3599 7692 3728 3724 Machine shop, jobbing and repair; Welding repair; Aircraft parts and equipment, nec; Aircraft engines and engine parts

Hadley
Hampshire County

(G-9017)
ARCHITECTURAL TIMBER MLLWK INC
49 Mount Warner Rd (01035-9674)
P.O. Box 719 (01035-0719)
PHONE.................................413 586-3045
Thomas N Harris, *Pr*
EMP: 19 **EST:** 1986
SQ FT: 7,500
SALES (est): 2.35MM **Privately Held**
Web: www.atimber.com
SIC: 2452 5031 5039 2439 Prefabricated wood buildings; Structural assemblies, prefabricated: wood; Structural assemblies, prefabricated: non-wood; Structural wood members, nec

(G-9018)
HOLLROCK ENGINEERING INC
294 Russell St (01035-9539)
P.O. Box 378 (01035-0378)
PHONE.................................413 586-2256
J Richard Hollrock, *Pr*
Richard H Hollrock Senior, *VP*
▲ **EMP:** 21 **EST:** 1974
SQ FT: 3,000
SALES (est): 780.63K **Privately Held**
Web: www.hollrockgolfrange.com
SIC: 3949 5091 7999 Golf equipment; Golf and skiing equipment and supplies; Golf driving range

(G-9019)
ZEN ART & DESIGN INC
119 Rocky Hill Rd (01035-9598)
PHONE.................................800 215-6010
Will Carswell, *Pr*
EMP: 7 **EST:** 2014
SQ FT: 2,750
SALES (est): 187.39K **Privately Held**
Web: www.zenpuzzles.com
SIC: 3944 Puzzles

Halifax
Plymouth County

(G-9020)
DAVID LEFORT
Also Called: Lefort Fine Furniture

13 Arrowhead Path (02338-1647)
PHONE.................................781 826-9033
David Lefort, *Pr*
EMP: 8 **EST:** 1979
SQ FT: 12,000
SALES (est): 291.93K **Privately Held**
Web: www.lefortfurnituremakers.com
SIC: 2511 2512 Wood household furniture; Upholstered household furniture

(G-9021)
FIBERGLASS BUILDING PDTS INC
546a Plymouth St (02338)
P.O. Box 139 (02338-0139)
PHONE.................................847 650-3045
Edward Mayo, *Pr*
EMP: 11 **EST:** 2015
SALES (est): 238.22K **Privately Held**
Web: www.fiberglasshomes.com
SIC: 3089 5031 Fiberglass doors; Fencing, wood

Hampden
Hampden County

(G-9022)
DEMAREY INSURANCE SOFTWARE
10 Chestnut Hill Rd (01036-9711)
PHONE.................................413 531-3991
Jeffrey S Demarey, *Pr*
EMP: 8 **EST:** 2004
SALES (est): 145.88K **Privately Held**
Web: www.stonewallinsurancegroup.com
SIC: 7372 Prepackaged software

(G-9023)
STAINED GLASS RESOURCES INC (PA)
Also Called: Our Glass
15 Commercial Dr (01036-9673)
PHONE.................................413 566-5053
Fred Shea, *Pr*
EMP: 23 **EST:** 1975
SQ FT: 20,000
SALES (est): 2.3MM
SALES (corp-wide): 2.3MM **Privately Held**
Web: test.stainedglassresources.ourgrnbusiness.com
SIC: 1793 3231 Glass and glazing work; Stained glass: made from purchased glass

Hancock
Berkshire County

(G-9024)
BBMC INC
1 N Main St (01237-9782)
PHONE.................................413 443-3333
EMP: 10 **EST:** 1992
SQ FT: 15,000
SALES (est): 159.97K **Privately Held**
Web: www.forevermugs.com
SIC: 3086 Plastics foam products

(G-9025)
LANSEN MOLD CO INC
1 Main St (01237-9201)
P.O. Box 1481 (01237-1481)
PHONE.................................413 443-5328
Neil C Kristensen Junior, *Pr*
Karen Rosier, *Sec*
EMP: 10 **EST:** 1960
SQ FT: 24,400

SALES (est): 1.93MM **Privately Held**
Web: www.lansenmold.com
SIC: 3089 3544 Injection molding of plastics ; Industrial molds

Hanover
Plymouth County

(G-9026)
BOSTON GAR FLRG & CABINETS LLC
145 Webster St Ste 2 (02339-1228)
PHONE.................................339 788-9580
Benjamin A Bennett, *Prin*
Michael Kenney, *Prin*
EMP: 10 **EST:** 2010
SALES (est): 911.03K **Privately Held**
Web: www.bostongarage.com
SIC: 3429 7359 Cabinet hardware; Garage facility and tool rental

(G-9027)
BUCKLEY ASSOCIATES INC (PA)
Also Called: Buckley Air Products
385 King St (02339-2447)
P.O. Box 1410 (02339-1006)
PHONE.................................781 878-5000
Robert L Buckley Ii, *Pr*
Steven Buckley, *
Thomas Buckley, *
Susan J Mielbye, *
David M Buckley, *
EMP: 60 **EST:** 1970
SQ FT: 55,000
SALES (est): 92.59MM
SALES (corp-wide): 92.59MM **Privately Held**
Web: www.buckleyonline.com
SIC: 5075 3444 Warm air heating equipment and supplies; Ducts, sheet metal

(G-9028)
CRI-TECH INC
85 Winter St (02339-2553)
PHONE.................................781 826-5600
Shigeru Ushijima, *Pr*
Mitsuru Kishine, *
Robert Berg, *
Lisa Strassman, *
▲ **EMP:** 28 **EST:** 2004
SQ FT: 6,600
SALES (est): 11.45MM **Privately Held**
Web: www.critechinc.com
SIC: 3069 Reclaimed rubber and specialty rubber compounds
HQ: Daikin America, Inc.
20 Olympic Dr
Orangeburg NY 10962

(G-9029)
CUSTOM MACHINE & TOOL CO INC
301 Winter St Ste 2 (02339-2581)
P.O. Box 298 (02339-0298)
PHONE.................................781 924-1003
Robert Bennett, *Pr*
EMP: 24 **EST:** 1964
SQ FT: 10,000
SALES (est): 9.7MM **Privately Held**
Web: www.cmtco.com
SIC: 3566 3568 Gears, power transmission, except auto; Sprockets (power transmission equipment)

(G-9030)
ELDRED WHEELER COMPANY
199 Winter St Ste 3 (02339-2597)

PHONE..............................781 924-5067
Eldred Wheeler, *Owner*
EMP: 9 **EST:** 2010
SALES (est): 830.33K **Privately Held**
Web: www.eldredwheeler.com
SIC: 3532 Feeders, ore and aggregate

(G-9031)
EYESAVER INTERNATIONAL INC
Also Called: E S I
348 Circuit St Ste 2 (02339-2143)
PHONE..............................781 829-0808
Steven George, *Pr*
Matthew B Smillie, *
▲ **EMP:** 70 **EST:** 1990
SQ FT: 50,000
SALES (est): 8.18MM **Privately Held**
Web: www.eyesaverinternational.com
SIC: 3599 Custom machinery

(G-9032)
GEM GRAVURE CO INC (PA)
112 School St (02339-2400)
P.O. Box 1158 (02339-1003)
PHONE..............................781 878-0456
David J Gemelli, *Pr*
▲ **EMP:** 65 **EST:** 1952
SQ FT: 30,000
SALES (est): 12.65MM
SALES (corp-wide): 12.65MM **Privately Held**
Web: www.gemgravure.com
SIC: 3555 2893 Presses, gravure; Gravure ink

(G-9033)
GRAPHIC DEVELOPMENTS INC
70 Mayflower Dr (02339-2007)
P.O. Box 1415 (02339-1010)
PHONE..............................781 878-2222
Robert Damon, *Pr*
George E Davis, *
Jay Leach, *
EMP: 44 **EST:** 1973
SQ FT: 13,500
SALES (est): 2.74MM **Privately Held**
Web: www.graphicdevelopments.com
SIC: 2752 Offset printing

(G-9034)
HAPCO INC
353 Circuit St (02339-2018)
PHONE..............................781 826-8801
Robert C Hale, *Pr*
EMP: 35 **EST:** 1970
SQ FT: 27,000
SALES (est): 5MM **Privately Held**
Web: www.hapcoincorporated.com
SIC: 2821 3089 3544 2891 Thermosetting materials; Plastics processing; Special dies, tools, jigs, and fixtures; Adhesives and sealants

(G-9035)
INTESET TECHNOLOGIES LLC
Also Called: Inteset Systems
51 Mill St Ste 21 (02339-1641)
PHONE..............................781 826-1560
James Lloyd, *Pt*
James A Lloyd, *Managing Member*
EMP: 9 **EST:** 2013
SALES (est): 1.04MM **Privately Held**
Web: www.intesettech.com
SIC: 5045 3577 Computers, nec; Computer peripheral equipment, nec

(G-9036)
J & R GRAPHICS INC
155 Webster St Ste L (02339-1229)
PHONE..............................781 871-7577

Richard J Fougere, *Pr*
Janet Fougere, *VP*
EMP: 11 **EST:** 1974
SQ FT: 8,000
SALES (est): 973.4K **Privately Held**
Web: www.jrgraphics.biz
SIC: 2752 Offset printing

(G-9037)
NEW ENGLAND SHRLINES COMPANIES
107 Broadway (02339-2309)
PHONE..............................781 826-0140
Roger Morton, *Pr*
EMP: 10 **EST:** 1974
SALES (est): 973.12K **Privately Held**
Web: www.foreverframewindows.com
SIC: 2431 5031 Millwork; Millwork

(G-9038)
P A LANDERS INC (PA)
351 Winter St (02339-2509)
P.O. Box 217 (02339-0217)
PHONE..............................781 826-8818
David R Prosper, *Pr*
David R Prosper, *CFO*
Joseph R Timmons, *
Louise M Landers, *
John Souza Esq, *Sec*
EMP: 230 **EST:** 1969
SQ FT: 15,000
SALES (est): 50.43MM
SALES (corp-wide): 50.43MM **Privately Held**
Web: www.palanders.com
SIC: 1611 1442 General contractor, highway and street construction; Construction sand and gravel

(G-9039)
P A LANDERS INC
Also Called: Mayflower Sand & Gravel Co
351 Winter St (02339-2509)
P.O. Box 217 (02339-0217)
PHONE..............................508 747-1800
TOLL FREE: 800
EMP: 10
SALES (corp-wide): 50.43MM **Privately Held**
Web: www.palanders.com
SIC: 5211 1794 1799 3273 Lumber and other building materials; Excavation work; Building site preparation; Ready-mixed concrete
PA: P. A. Landers, Inc.
351 Winter St
Hanover MA 02339
781 826-8818

(G-9040)
RECOLOR PAINTS LLC
149 Winter St Ste B (02339-2596)
PHONE..............................833 732-6567
EMP: 13 **EST:** 2009
SALES (est): 1.85MM **Privately Held**
Web: www.recolorpaints.com
SIC: 2851 Paints and paint additives

(G-9041)
RUSTIC MARLIN DESIGNS LLC
389 Columbia Rd Ste 40 (02339-2499)
PHONE..............................508 376-1004
Melanie Oneil, *
EMP: 32 **EST:** 2014
SQ FT: 50,000
SALES (est): 3.97MM **Privately Held**
Web: www.rusticmarlin.com
SIC: 3993 Advertising artwork

(G-9042)
SRC MEDICAL INC
263 Winter St (02339-2557)
PHONE..............................781 826-9100
Roy Clifton Tinkham, *Pr*
Lisa Lynne Raasch, *
EMP: 98 **EST:** 1950
SQ FT: 40,000
SALES (est): 9.8MM **Privately Held**
Web: www.srcmedical.com
SIC: 3089 3069 Injection molding of plastics ; Bulbs, rubber: for atomizers, syringes, medicine droppers

(G-9043)
STANDARD RUBBER PRODUCTS INC
Also Called: S & D Rubber Co Div
64 B St (02339-1891)
P.O. Box 920385 (02492-0005)
PHONE..............................781 878-2626
Patricia Davis, *Pr*
Joseph Davis, *
EMP: 40 **EST:** 1958
SQ FT: 95,000
SALES (est): 5.62MM **Privately Held**
Web: www.standardrubberproducts.com
SIC: 2891 3069 Adhesives and sealants; Hard rubber products, nec

(G-9044)
STOUGHTON STEEL COMPANY INC
347 Circuit St (02339-2036)
PHONE..............................781 826-6496
Andry Lagsdin, *Pr*
Andris Lagsdin, *
Eric Lagsdin, *
Dolores Lagsdin, *
▼ **EMP:** 30 **EST:** 1976
SQ FT: 21,000
SALES (est): 8.24MM **Privately Held**
Web: www.stoughtonsteel.com
SIC: 3531 3441 Construction machinery attachments; Fabricated structural metal

(G-9045)
STURTEVANT INC (PA)
Also Called: Sturtevant Mill Company
348 Circuit St Ste 1 (02339-2143)
PHONE..............................781 829-6501
William S English, *Ch Bd*
W Sturtevant English Junior, *Sec*
Edna English, *
▲ **EMP:** 34 **EST:** 1883
SQ FT: 33,000
SALES (est): 6.93MM
SALES (corp-wide): 6.93MM **Privately Held**
Web: www.sturtevantinc.com
SIC: 3559 Chemical machinery and equipment

(G-9046)
TRIANGLE ENGINEERING INC
6 Industrial Way (02339-2425)
PHONE..............................781 878-1500
Robert N Coultring Junior, *Pr*
Matthew Coultring, *Treas*
Robert Coultring Iii, *Sec*
Jason Coultring, *Frmn Supr*
EMP: 15 **EST:** 1960
SQ FT: 20,000
SALES (est): 4.8MM **Privately Held**
Web: www.trieng.com
SIC: 3443 3829 3498 8711 Fabricated plate work (boiler shop); Physical property testing equipment; Pipe sections, fabricated from purchased pipe; Engineering services

(G-9047)
TRUEX MACHINE CO INC
25 Pond St (02339-1607)
PHONE..............................781 826-6875
Ruth G Flood, *Pr*
Stephen Flood, *VP*
EMP: 9 **EST:** 1977
SQ FT: 6,000
SALES (est): 727.61K **Privately Held**
Web: www.truexmachine.com
SIC: 3599 Machine shop, jobbing and repair

(G-9048)
WEYMOUTH GAS LLC
33 Stockbridge Rd (02339-2547)
PHONE..............................781 826-4327
Jessica Nassif, *Mgr*
EMP: 11 **EST:** 2005
SALES (est): 201.69K **Privately Held**
SIC: 2911 Gases and liquefied petroleum gases

Hanson
Plymouth County

(G-9049)
A A A METALS COMPANY INC
Also Called: Hanson Commerce Center
68 Industrial Blvd 9 (02341-1547)
PHONE..............................781 447-1220
David Ford, *Pr*
EMP: 10 **EST:** 1978
SQ FT: 5,000
SALES (est): 3.19MM **Privately Held**
Web: www.aaa-metals.com
SIC: 5051 3312 Forgings, ferrous; Stainless steel

(G-9050)
BRENNAN MACHINE CO INC
820 Monponsett St (02341-2005)
PHONE..............................781 293-3997
Andrew J Brennan Junior, *Pr*
EMP: 20 **EST:** 1975
SQ FT: 3,200
SALES (est): 2.41MM **Privately Held**
Web: www.brennanmachine.com
SIC: 3599 Machine shop, jobbing and repair

(G-9051)
EASTERN MACHINE & DESIGN CORP
1062 Main St (02341-1521)
P.O. Box 120 (02341-0120)
PHONE..............................781 293-6391
Raymond Holman, *Pr*
James Holman, *VP*
Diane E Holman, *Sec*
EMP: 18 **EST:** 1964
SQ FT: 14,530
SALES (est): 450.62K **Privately Held**
Web: www.emadcorp.com
SIC: 3599 Machine shop, jobbing and repair

(G-9052)
JMC ASSET HOLDINGS INC
162 Industrial Blvd Ste 7 (02341-1538)
PHONE..............................781 447-9264
John Mcgrail, *Pr*
▲ **EMP:** 8 **EST:** 1985
SQ FT: 3,200
SALES (est): 849.16K **Privately Held**
SIC: 3599 Machine shop, jobbing and repair

(G-9053)
MARTIN INTERIORS INC
22 Industrial Blvd Ste G (02341-1548)
PHONE..............................781 447-1022

Phil Martin, *Owner*
EMP: 9 **EST:** 2005
SALES (est): 438.53K **Privately Held**
Web: www.martininteriors1.com
SIC: 2431   Millwork

(G-9054)
MENTON MACHINE CO INC
1299 Main St (02341-1534)
PHONE...................781 293-8394
John Parks, *Pr*
EMP: 7 **EST:** 1990
SQ FT: 9,488
SALES (est): 816.85K **Privately Held**
Web: www.mentonmachinecompany.com
SIC: 3599   Machine shop, jobbing and repair

(G-9055)
PRESIDENT TITANIUM CO INC
243 Franklin St (02341-1535)
P.O. Box 36 (02341-0036)
PHONE...................781 294-0000
Joseph E Leod Mac, *CEO*
Shawn Mac Leod, *Pr*
Joseph A Leod Mac, *VP*
▲ **EMP:** 15 **EST:** 1973
SQ FT: 6,000
SALES (est): 5.27MM **Privately Held**
Web: www.presidenttitanium.com
SIC: 3356 5051   Titanium and titanium alloy
   bars, sheets, strip, etc.; Nonferrous metal
   sheets, bars, rods, etc., nec

(G-9056)
SOUTH SHORE
MANUFACTURING INC
Also Called: Jack's Machine Company
162 Industrial Blvd Ste 2b (02341-1538)
PHONE...................781 447-9264
Patrick Johnson, *Pr*
EMP: 10 **EST:** 2015
SQ FT: 10,000
SALES (est): 1.1MM **Privately Held**
Web:
www.southshoremanufacturing.com
SIC: 3599   Machine shop, jobbing and repair

(G-9057)
WALKER-CLAY INC
211 Station St (02341-1581)
P.O. Box 688 (02341-0688)
PHONE...................781 294-1100
William L Clay, *Pr*
Diana H Clay, *Sec*
Amanda Clay, *VP*
EMP: 14 **EST:** 1956
SQ FT: 15,500
SALES (est): 5.01MM **Privately Held**
Web: www.walker-clay.com
SIC: 5199 2759   Advertising specialties;
   Promotional printing

(G-9058)
WEBSTER PRINTING COMPANY
INC (PA)
1069 W Washington St (02341-1536)
PHONE...................781 447-5484
Ernest W Foster, *CEO*
Ernest W Foster, *Pr*
Mark Diserio, *
EMP: 38 **EST:** 1957
SQ FT: 18,600
SALES (est): 6.98MM
SALES (corp-wide): 6.98MM **Privately
Held**
Web: www.websterprinting.com
SIC: 2752   Offset printing

Hardwick
Hampshire County

(G-9059)
AMERICAN DISPOSABLES INC
2705 Greenwich Rd (01082-9395)
P.O. Box 800 (01082-0800)
PHONE...................413 967-6201
Louis J Despres Junior, *Pr*
▲ **EMP:** 11 **EST:** 1976
SQ FT: 55,000
SALES (est): 495.5K **Privately Held**
Web: www.americandisposables.com
SIC: 2676   Diapers, paper (disposable):
   made from purchased paper

Harvard
Worcester County

(G-9060)
CCO HOLDINGS LLC
289 Ayer Rd (01451-1110)
PHONE...................978 615-1032
EMP: 109
SALES (corp-wide): 54.02B **Publicly Held**
SIC: 4841 3663 3651   Cable television
   services; Radio and t.v. communications
   equipment; Household audio and video
   equipment
HQ: Cco Holdings, Llc
   400 Atlantic St
   Stamford CT 06901
   203 905-7801

(G-9061)
CYBERTOOLS
249 Ayer Rd Ste 302 (01451-1133)
PHONE...................800 894-9206
Mike Wubben Engineering, *Research &
Development*
EMP: 7 **EST:** 1997
SALES (est): 186.25K **Privately Held**
Web: www.cybertoolsforlibraries.com
SIC: 3823   Process control instruments

(G-9062)
ELDERSAFE TECHNOLOGIES
INC
127 Poor Farm Rd (01451-1240)
PHONE...................617 852-3018
EMP: 33
SALES (corp-wide): 194.08K **Privately
Held**
SIC: 3845   Electromedical equipment
PA: Eldersafe Technologies, Inc.
   16192 Coastal Hwy
   Lewes DE 19958
   617 852-3018

(G-9063)
HARVARD PRODUCTS INC
Also Called: Harvard Machinery
325 Ayer Rd Ste A105 (01451-1151)
P.O. Box 338 (01451-0338)
PHONE...................978 772-0309
TOLL FREE: 800
Bryce B Larrabee Junior, *Pr*
EMP: 10 **EST:** 1979
SQ FT: 15,000
SALES (est): 1.14MM **Privately Held**
Web: www.harvardmachinery.com
SIC: 3599 5084   Custom machinery;
   Machine tools and accessories

(G-9064)
HXI LLC
Also Called: Hxi Millimeter Wave Products
12 Lancaster County Rd Ste 1
(01451-1152)
PHONE...................978 772-7774
Thampy Kurian, *Mgr*
Thampy Kurian, *CEO*
Earle Stewart, *Mgr*
EMP: 19 **EST:** 2008
SQ FT: 16,400
SALES (est): 2.95MM
SALES (corp-wide): 35.31MM **Privately
Held**
Web: www.rec-usa.com
SIC: 3812 3679 3663   Antennas, radar or
   communications; Microwave components;
   Microwave communication equipment
HQ: Renaissance Electronics &
   Communications, Llc
   12 Lancaster County Rd
   Harvard MA 01451

(G-9065)
MANCHESTER CORPORATION
280 Ayer Rd (01451-1160)
PHONE...................978 772-2900
Irving B Morrow Junior, *Pr*
EMP: 20 **EST:** 1976
SQ FT: 14,000
SALES (est): 435.98K **Privately Held**
Web: www.mancorp.com
SIC: 8711 3564   Pollution control engineering
   ; Blowers and fans

Harwich
Barnstable County

(G-9066)
ACME-SHOREY PRECAST CO
INC (PA)
Also Called: Shorey Precast Division
36 Great Western Rd (02645-2314)
P.O. Box 1539 (02645-6539)
PHONE...................508 432-0530
John D Our, *Pr*
Christopher W Our, *VP*
Joan A Our, *Treas*
EMP: 10 **EST:** 1974
SQ FT: 1,600
SALES (est): 3.44MM
SALES (corp-wide): 3.44MM **Privately
Held**
Web: www.acmeshorey.com
SIC: 3272 5084   Concrete products, precast,
   nec; Industrial machinery and equipment

(G-9067)
BIG ROCK OYSTER COMPANY
INC
501 Depot St (02645-2309)
PHONE...................774 408-7951
Aaron Brochu, *Prin*
EMP: 7 **EST:** 2007
SALES (est): 299.96K **Privately Held**
Web: www.bigrockoyster.com
SIC: 3089   Plastics boats and other marine
   equipment

(G-9068)
JR CHEMICAL COATINGS LLC
139 Queen Anne Rd (02645-2406)
PHONE...................508 896-3383
EMP: 20
SALES (corp-wide): 352.51K **Privately
Held**
Web: www.washsafe.com

SIC: 3479   Etching and engraving
PA: Jr Chemical Coatings Llc
   400 Tubman Rd
   Brewster MA

(G-9069)
KARLS BOAT SHOP INC
50 Great Western Rd (02645-2314)
PHONE...................508 432-4488
▲ **EMP:** 7 **EST:** 1996
SQ FT: 3,072
SALES (est): 495.62K **Privately Held**
Web: www.karlsboatshop.com
SIC: 3732 5551   Boatbuilding and repairing;
   Boat dealers

Harwich Port
Barnstable County

(G-9070)
ALLEN HARBOR MARINE SVC
INC
335 Lower County Rd (02646-1622)
P.O. Box 445 (02646-0445)
PHONE...................508 432-0353
Rupert Nichols Junior, *Pr*
Rupert Nichols Senior, *Treas*
EMP: 34 **EST:** 1927
SQ FT: 17,920
SALES (est): 3.71MM **Privately Held**
Web: www.allenharbor.com
SIC: 5551 3732 4493   Motor boat dealers;
   Boatbuilding and repairing; Marinas

Hatfield
Hampshire County

(G-9071)
H S GERE & SONS INC
33 Main St (01038-9702)
PHONE...................413 247-5010
EMP: 22
SALES (corp-wide): 96.33MM **Privately
Held**
Web: www.gazettenet.com
SIC: 2711   Newspapers, publishing and
   printing
HQ: H S Gere & Sons, Inc.
   115 Conz St
   Northampton MA
   413 584-5000

(G-9072)
INNOVATIVE DESIGNS & DISP
INC
Also Called: Precision Metal Goods
157 Main St (01038-9759)
PHONE...................413 586-9854
James L Hogan, *Pr*
Michael W Hogan, *VP*
EMP: 13 **EST:** 1993
SQ FT: 117,000
SALES (est): 1.6MM **Privately Held**
Web: www.precisionmetalgoods.com
SIC: 5051 3353   Sheets, metal; Aluminum
   sheet, plate, and foil

(G-9073)
INTER-EGO SYSTEMS INC (PA)
Also Called: Pinnacle Loud Speakers
131 Main St Ste 1 (01038-9786)
PHONE...................516 576-9052
Richard Rothenberg, *Pr*
Michael Rothenberg, *VP*
Marc Rothenberg, *Ch Bd*
▲ **EMP:** 12 **EST:** 1976
SQ FT: 10,000

SALES (est): 1.33MM
SALES (corp-wide): 1.33MM **Privately Held**
SIC: 3651 Speaker systems

Haverhill
Essex County

(G-9074)
ARDEO SYSTEMS INC
17 Parkridge Rd Ste 2 (01835-8511)
PHONE................................978 373-4680
Mark Finocchario, *Pr*
EMP: 8 EST: 2003
SQ FT: 4,000
SALES (est): 976.55K **Privately Held**
Web: www.ardeosystems.com
SIC: 3674 Semiconductors and related devices

(G-9075)
ATC SCREW MACHINE INC
419 River St (01832-5114)
PHONE................................781 939-0725
John J Triggs, *Pr*
Paul Kierce, *Treas*
Petrina Triggs, *Clerk*
EMP: 15 EST: 1988
SQ FT: 5,500
SALES (est): 164.1K **Privately Held**
SIC: 3451 Screw machine products

(G-9076)
BARIL CORPORATION
Also Called: Team Technologies
50 Ward Hill Ave (01835-6929)
PHONE................................978 373-7910
Dan Baril, *CEO*
Ken Kovacs, *
Marshall White, *
▲ EMP: 33 EST: 1986
SQ FT: 25,000
SALES (est): 9.85MM **Privately Held**
Web: www.teamtech.com
SIC: 3544 Special dies and tools
HQ: Team Technologies, Inc.
5949 Commerce Blvd
Morristown TN 37814
423 587-2199

(G-9077)
BATTLE GROUNDS COFFEE CO LLC
Also Called: Battle Grounds Coffee Company
39 Washington St (01832-5523)
PHONE................................978 891-5860
EMP: 10 EST: 2016
SALES (est): 483.41K **Privately Held**
Web: www.battlecoffee.com
SIC: 5812 2095 3589 5046 Cafeteria; Roasted coffee; Coffee brewing equipment; Coffee brewing equipment and supplies

(G-9078)
BAY STATE PALLET CO INC
125 Ward Hill Ave (01835-6928)
PHONE................................978 374-4840
Gary Williams, *Pr*
Donna Williams, *Admn*
EMP: 8 EST: 1979
SQ FT: 30,000
SALES (est): 420.83K **Privately Held**
Web: www.baystatepallet.com
SIC: 2448 Pallets, wood

(G-9079)
BOLD MAKER LLC
45 Wingate St (01832-5736)

PHONE................................978 891-5920
Jason A Matses, *Pr*
EMP: 7 EST: 2016
SALES (est): 272.16K **Privately Held**
Web: www.boldmaker.com
SIC: 2759 Commercial printing, nec

(G-9080)
BOSTON STEEL & MFG CO
89 Newark St (01832-1348)
PHONE................................781 324-3000
David L Burke, *Pr*
Ronald J Burke, *
EMP: 34 EST: 1915
SQ FT: 36,000
SALES (est): 1.72MM **Privately Held**
Web: www.tremcar.com
SIC: 3443 3714 Tanks for tank trucks, metal plate; Motor vehicle parts and accessories

(G-9081)
BRADFORD FINSHG POWDR COAT INC
2 S Grove St (01835-7573)
PHONE................................978 469-9965
Michael Pushee, *Pr*
EMP: 9 EST: 2005
SALES (est): 993.37K **Privately Held**
Web: www.bradfordfinishing.com
SIC: 3471 7389 Finishing, metals or formed products; Finishing services

(G-9082)
BURGETT BROTHERS INCORPORATED
Also Called: Mason & Hamlin
35 Duncan St (01830-4801)
PHONE................................978 374-8888
Kirk A Burgett, *Pr*
Gary Burgett, *
▲ EMP: 50 EST: 1996
SALES (est): 4.04MM **Privately Held**
Web: www.masonhamlin.com
SIC: 3931 Pianos, all types: vertical, grand, spinet, player, etc.

(G-9083)
CABOT COACH BUILDERS INC (PA)
Also Called: Royale Limousines
99 Newark St (01832-1348)
PHONE................................978 374-4530
Cabot B Smith, *Pr*
Macgregor Smith, *
Richard Portors, *
◆ EMP: 50 EST: 1983
SQ FT: 30,000
SALES (est): 9.62MM
SALES (corp-wide): 9.62MM **Privately Held**
Web: www.cabotcoach.com
SIC: 3711 Automobile assembly, including specialty automobiles

(G-9084)
CABOT CORPORATION
Also Called: Cabot
50 Rogers Rd Ste 1 (01835-8038)
PHONE................................978 556-8400
Dirk Sykes, *Mgr*
EMP: 112
SALES (corp-wide): 3.93B **Publicly Held**
Web: www.cabotcorp.com
SIC: 2895 3081 3084 2819 Carbon black; Polyethylene film; Plastics pipe; Silica, amorphous
PA: Cabot Corporation
2 Seaport Ln Ste 1300
Boston MA 02210
617 345-0100

(G-9085)
CHAUCER ACCESSORIES INC
Also Called: Chaucer Leather
143 Essex St Ste 3 (01832-5732)
PHONE................................978 373-1566
Tom Bates, *Pr*
Patricia Goodrich, *VP*
▲ EMP: 9 EST: 1975
SQ FT: 15,000
SALES (est): 482.77K **Privately Held**
Web: www.chaucerleather.com
SIC: 2387 2389 Apparel belts; Suspenders

(G-9086)
CIRCUIT TECHNOLOGY CENTER INC
Also Called: Circuitmedic
22 Parkridge Rd (01835-7278)
PHONE................................978 374-5000
Jeffrey S Ferry, *Pr*
Joanne M Ferry, *Sec*
◆ EMP: 27 EST: 1981
SQ FT: 13,000
SALES (est): 5.16MM **Privately Held**
Web: www.circuitrework.com
SIC: 3672 Printed circuit boards

(G-9087)
COASTAL INDUSTRIES INC
77 Newark St (01832-1399)
PHONE................................978 373-1543
William J Cunningham Senior, *Pr*
EMP: 25 EST: 1973
SQ FT: 47,500
SALES (est): 2.69MM **Privately Held**
Web: www.ciiwindowsanddoors.com
SIC: 3442 Metal doors

(G-9088)
CONVECTRONICS INC
111 Neck Rd (01835-8027)
PHONE................................978 374-7714
Philip G Aberizk Junior, *Pr*
EMP: 24 EST: 1985
SQ FT: 20,000
SALES (est): 2.49MM **Privately Held**
Web: www.convectronics.com
SIC: 3829 3634 Thermocouples; Electric housewares and fans

(G-9089)
CTR ENTERPRISES INC
60 Railroad St Ste 1 (01835-7563)
PHONE................................978 794-2093
Rick Morgano, *Pr*
EMP: 8 EST: 1985
SQ FT: 9,700
SALES (est): 772.97K **Privately Held**
Web: www.ctrenterprises.com
SIC: 3444 Sheet metal specialties, not stamped

(G-9090)
D B S INDUSTRIES INC
Also Called: Diversified Business Systems
144 Hilldale Ave (01832-3830)
PHONE................................978 373-4748
EMP: 52 EST: 1969
SALES (est): 4.05MM **Privately Held**
SIC: 2752 2741 2754 2791 Commercial printing, lithographic; Racing forms and programs: publishing and printing; Forms, business: gravure printing; Photocomposition, for the printing trade

(G-9091)
DELA INCORPORATED (PA)
Also Called: Dela Lamimnation Solutions
175 Ward Hill Ave Ste 1 (01835-6943)

P.O. Box 8235 (01835-0735)
PHONE................................978 372-7783
Charles J Abrams, *Pr*
Steven M Abrams, *
▲ EMP: 34 EST: 1988
SQ FT: 52,400
SALES (est): 8.81MM
SALES (corp-wide): 8.81MM **Privately Held**
Web: www.delaquality.com
SIC: 2295 3089 Laminating of fabrics; Laminating of plastics

(G-9092)
DL TECHNOLOGY LLC
Also Called: DI Technology
216 River St (01832-5211)
PHONE................................978 374-6451
Jeffrey Paul Fugere, *Managing Member*
Donna Lee Fugere, *Prin*
EMP: 22 EST: 1999
SQ FT: 6,500
SALES (est): 4.2MM **Privately Held**
Web: www.dltechnology.com
SIC: 3679 Electronic circuits

(G-9093)
EAGLE-TRIBUNE PUBLISHING CO
Also Called: Haverhill Gazette
181 Merrimack St (01830-6129)
P.O. Box 991 (01831-2499)
PHONE................................978 374-0321
EMP: 11
SALES (corp-wide): 33.14B **Privately Held**
Web: www.hgazette.com
SIC: 2711 7313 Newspapers, publishing and printing; Newspaper advertising representative
HQ: Eagle-Tribune Publishing Company
100 Turnpike St
North Andover MA 01845
978 946-2000

(G-9094)
ENGINERED PRESSURE SYSTEMS INC
Also Called: E P S I
165 Ferry Rd (01835-8017)
PHONE................................978 469-8280
Gary Nelson, *VP*
◆ EMP: 12 EST: 1992
SQ FT: 7,000
SALES (est): 6.76MM
SALES (corp-wide): 13.2MM **Privately Held**
Web: www.epsi-highpressure.com
SIC: 3462 Iron and steel forgings
PA: Engineered Pressure Systems International
Walgoedstraat 19
Temse 9140
37112464

(G-9095)
FTG CIRCUITS HAVERHILL INC
Also Called: Imi, Inc.
140 Hilldale Ave (01832-3830)
PHONE................................978 373-9190
Brad Bourne, *Pr*
EMP: 25 EST: 1971
SQ FT: 33,000
SALES (est): 5.02MM
SALES (corp-wide): 65.73MM **Privately Held**
Web: www.imipcb.com
SIC: 3672 Circuit boards, television and radio printed

HQ: Firan Technology Group (Usa)
Corporation
20750 Marilla St
Chatsworth CA 91311
818 407-4024

(G-9096)
GARE INCORPORATED
165 Rosemont St (01832-1340)
P.O. Box 1686 (01831-2386)
PHONE......................978 373-9131
Thomas L Alaimo Senior, *Ch Bd*
David Alaimo, *
Thomas L Alaimo Junior, *VP Fin*
Gerald Murphy, *
◆ **EMP:** 50 **EST:** 1950
SQ FT: 103,000
SALES (est): 4.94MM **Privately Held**
Web: www.gareceramics.com
SIC: 3269 3544 2851 2821　Pottery household articles, except kitchen articles; Special dies, tools, jigs, and fixtures; Paints and allied products; Plastics materials and resins

(G-9097)
GELPAC POLY USA INC (PA)
60 Fondi Rd (01832-1302)
PHONE......................978 372-3300
Alain Robillard, *Pr*
EMP: 15 **EST:** 2019
SALES (est): 2.56MM
SALES (corp-wide): 2.56MM **Privately Held**
SIC: 2821　Plastics materials and resins

(G-9098)
GOLDEN FLEECE MFG GROUP LLC (DH)
Also Called: Southwick
25 Computer Dr (01832-1236)
PHONE......................978 686-3833
Claudio Del Vecchio, *Pr*
John Martynec, *
Edward J Ponto, *
▲ **EMP:** 470 **EST:** 1929
SALES (est): 103.1MM
SALES (corp-wide): 100.19K **Privately Held**
Web: www.southwick.com
SIC: 2329　Men's and boys' sportswear and athletic clothing
HQ: Bbgi Us, Inc.
1180 Madison Ave
New York NY 10028

(G-9099)
GREENWICH TRIANGLE LLC (DH)
Also Called: Southwick Clothing LLC
25 Computer Dr (01832-1236)
PHONE......................800 634-5312
Robert Bayer, *Managing Member*
Robert Nelson, *
▲ **EMP:** 179 **EST:** 1999
SQ FT: 240,000
SALES (est): 41.66MM
SALES (corp-wide): 100.19K **Privately Held**
SIC: 2311 2325　Suits, men's and boys': made from purchased materials; Slacks, dress: men's, youths', and boys'
HQ: Bbgi Us, Inc.
1180 Madison Ave
New York NY 10028

(G-9100)
HALL MAILING & FULFILLMENT INC
46 Rogers Rd Ste 1 (01835-6959)
PHONE......................978 372-6546
Douglas Hall, *CEO*
Lisa A Hall, *CFO*
◆ **EMP:** 18 **EST:** 2001
SQ FT: 20,000
SALES (est): 2.23MM **Privately Held**
Web: www.hmfprinting.com
SIC: 2752　Offset printing

(G-9101)
HANS KISSLE COMPANY LLC
9 Creek Brook Dr (01832-1548)
PHONE......................978 556-4500
Scott Moffitt, *Pr*
Daniel F Roche Junior, *Pr*
Patrick Roche, *VP*
Tim Sousa, *CFO*
EMP: 140 **EST:** 1984
SQ FT: 110,000
SALES (est): 50.74MM **Privately Held**
Web: www.hanskissle.com
SIC: 2099　Salads, fresh or refrigerated
PA: Mitsui&Co., Ltd.
1-2-1, Otemachi
Chiyoda-Ku TKY 100-0

(G-9102)
HAVERHILL HOUSE PUBLISHING LLC
643 E Broadway (01830-2420)
PHONE......................781 879-3102
John Mcilveen, *Prin*
EMP: 7 **EST:** 2017
SALES (est): 59.23K **Privately Held**
Web: www.haverhillhouse.com
SIC: 2741　Miscellaneous publishing

(G-9103)
HIGH SPEED ROUTING LLC
42 Newark St (01832-1342)
PHONE......................603 527-8027
Mark Bailey, *Prin*
EMP: 10 **EST:** 2010
SALES (est): 562.39K **Privately Held**
Web: www.hsrouting.com
SIC: 3083　Plastics finished products, laminated

(G-9104)
HORSESHOE SUNDAY LLC
506 Amesbury Rd (01830-1703)
PHONE......................978 476-9766
Daniel J Roche, *Prin*
EMP: 7 **EST:** 2016
SALES (est): 294.23K **Privately Held**
SIC: 3462　Horseshoes

(G-9105)
INSIGNIA INCORPORATED
40 Orchard St (01830-5640)
PHONE......................978 372-3721
Matt Rothwell, *Brnch Mgr*
EMP: 22
SQ FT: 8,000
SALES (corp-wide): 8.14MM **Privately Held**
Web: www.thesigncenter.com
SIC: 3993 7389　Electric signs; Lettering service
PA: Insignia, Incorporated
2 Alder Ln
Wilbraham MA 01095
978 372-3721

(G-9106)
JOMA LLC
12 Rogers Rd Ste 1 (01835-6925)
PHONE......................978 374-0034
Joseph J Scott, *Mgr*

EMP: 8 **EST:** 2005
SALES (est): 80.63K **Privately Held**
Web: www.jomadiamondtool.com
SIC: 3599　Machine shop, jobbing and repair

(G-9107)
JOSEPHS GOURMET PASTA COMPANY
262 Primrose St (01830-3930)
PHONE......................978 521-1718
David Zwartendijk, *CEO*
John Birch, *
Ian B Mactaggart, *
▼ **EMP:** 300 **EST:** 2013
SALES (est): 58.56MM
SALES (corp-wide): 84.87MM **Privately Held**
Web: www.josephsgourmetpasta.com
SIC: 2099　Pasta, uncooked: packaged with other ingredients
HQ: Jgps Holdings, Llc
8 Sound Shore Dr Ste 265
Greenwich CT 06830
203 622-1790

(G-9108)
LEIDOS SEC DTCTION AUTOMTN INC
179 Ferry Rd 181 (01835)
PHONE......................781 939-3800
Mark Bush, *Brnch Mgr*
EMP: 10
SIC: 3663　Telemetering equipment, electronic
HQ: Leidos Security Detection & Automation, Inc.
1 Radcliff Rd
Tewksbury MA 01876
781 970-1563

(G-9109)
LIGHTSPEED MFG CO LLC
63 Neck Rd (01835-8025)
PHONE......................978 521-7676
EMP: 15 **EST:** 2003
SALES (est): 2.72MM **Privately Held**
Web: www.lightspeedmfg.com
SIC: 3699　Electric sound equipment

(G-9110)
LUMINA POWER INC
26 Ward Hill Ave (01835-6929)
PHONE......................978 241-8260
Tung Huynh, *Pr*
EMP: 42 **EST:** 2001
SALES (est): 9.08MM **Publicly Held**
Web: www.luminapower.com
SIC: 3699　Electrical equipment and supplies, nec
PA: Heico Corporation
3000 Taft St
Hollywood FL 33021

(G-9111)
LYNX SYSTEM DEVELOPERS INC
179 Ward Hill Ave (01835-6973)
PHONE......................978 556-9780
Douglas J De Angelis, *Pr*
EMP: 20 **EST:** 1991
SALES (est): 4.51MM **Privately Held**
Web: www.finishlynx.com
SIC: 3625　Timing devices, electronic

(G-9112)
MAGELLAN AEROSPACE USA INC (DH)
Also Called: Middleton Aerospace
20 Computer Dr (01832-1236)

PHONE......................978 774-6000
Philip Underwood, *CEO*
▲ **EMP:** 18 **EST:** 1996
SALES (est): 42.44MM
SALES (corp-wide): 569.19MM **Privately Held**
SIC: 3724　Aircraft engines and engine parts
HQ: Magellan Aerospace Limited
3160 Derry Rd E
Mississauga ON L4T 1
905 677-1889

(G-9113)
MAGELLAN AROSPC HAVERHILL INC
Also Called: Middleton Aerospace
20 Computer Dr (01832-1236)
PHONE......................978 774-6000
James S Butyniec, *Pr*
Elena Milantoni, *
John Dekker, *
John Marcello, *
Daniel Chaisson, *
▲ **EMP:** 120 **EST:** 1986
SALES (est): 22.88MM
SALES (corp-wide): 569.19MM **Privately Held**
SIC: 3724　Aircraft engines and engine parts
HQ: Magellan Aerospace Usa, Inc.
20 Computer Dr
Haverhill MA 01832
978 774-6000

(G-9114)
MERRIMAC INDUSTRIAL SALES INC (PA)
111 Neck Rd (01835-8027)
PHONE......................978 372-6006
Philip G Aberizk Junior, *Pr*
Michelle Berube, *Acctg Mgr*
EMP: 27 **EST:** 1978
SQ FT: 50,000
SALES (est): 5.24MM **Privately Held**
Web: www.merrimacindustrial.com
SIC: 5075 5084 5063 3585　Electrical heating equipment; Instruments and control equipment; Lighting fixtures; Compressors for refrigeration and air conditioning equipment

(G-9115)
MERRIMAC INDUSTRIAL SALES INC (PA)
111 Neck Rd (01835-8027)
PHONE......................978 372-6006
Philip G Aberizk Junior, *Prin*
EMP: 35 **EST:** 1947
SQ FT: 50,000
SALES (est): 10.33MM
SALES (corp-wide): 10.33MM **Privately Held**
Web: www.merrimacindustrial.com
SIC: 5084 3443　Heat exchange equipment, industrial; Heat exchangers: coolers (after, inter), condensers, etc.

(G-9116)
MERRIMAC SPOOL AND REEL CO INC
203 Essex St (01832-5595)
PHONE......................978 372-7777
Joseph J Alosky, *Pr*
Beverly Graham, *
EMP: 35 **EST:** 1951
SQ FT: 18,500
SALES (est): 4.62MM **Privately Held**
Web: www.spool.com
SIC: 2655 2675　Spools, fiber: made from purchased material; Die-cut paper and board

▲ = Import ▼ = Export
◆ = Import/Export

(G-9117)

MKS INSTRUMENTS INC
55 Foundation Ave Unit 4 (01835-7291)
PHONE..................978 284-4015
EMP: 13
SALES (corp-wide): 3.55B Publicly Held
Web: www.mks.com
SIC: 3823 Pressure measurement
instruments, industrial
PA: Mks Instruments, Inc.
2 Tech Dr Ste 201
Andover MA 01810
978 645-5500

(G-9118)

MORGAN SCIENTIFIC INC (PA)
151 Essex St Ste 8 (01832-5733)
PHONE..................978 521-4440
Patrick Morgan, CEO
Patrick Morgan Prestreas, Prin
Christina Morgan, Mgr
EMP: 10 EST: 1981
SQ FT: 12,000
SALES (est): 3.5MM
SALES (corp-wide): 3.5MM Privately Held
Web: www.morgansci.com
SIC: 7372 5045 3841 Application computer
software; Computer peripheral equipment;
Diagnostic apparatus, medical

(G-9119)

OLYMPIC ENGINEERING SERVICE
Also Called: Olympic Engineering
65 Avco Rd Unit C (01835-8502)
PHONE..................978 373-2789
EMP: 9 EST: 1994
SQ FT: 2,800
SALES (est): 1.54MM Privately Held
Web: www.olympicengineering.com
SIC: 3599 Machine shop, jobbing and repair

(G-9120)

PARKER-HANNIFIN CORPORATION
Also Called: Filtration & Separation Div
242 Neck Rd (01835-8034)
PHONE..................978 858-0505
Scott Feeman, Brnch Mgr
EMP: 123
SALES (corp-wide): 19.07B Publicly Held
Web: www.parker.com
SIC: 3569 3564 Filters; Blowers and fans
PA: Parker-Hannifin Corporation
6035 Parkland Blvd
Cleveland OH 44124
216 896-3000

(G-9121)

PLASTIC DISTRS FABRICATORS INC
144 Hilldale Ave (01832-3830)
PHONE..................978 374-0300
Mark Abare, Pr
EMP: 40 EST: 1974
SQ FT: 36,000
SALES (est): 8.08MM Privately Held
Web: www.plasticdistributors.com
SIC: 3089 Injection molding of plastics

(G-9122)

PRINT PRO
34 Rogers Rd (01835-6946)
PHONE..................978 914-7619
EMP: 7 EST: 2011
SALES (est): 153.88K Privately Held
Web: www.printprotees.com
SIC: 2752 Commercial printing, lithographic

(G-9123)

PRINTPRO SILKSCREEN CO LLC
233 Neck Rd (01835-8029)
PHONE..................978 556-1695
Derek Coughlin, Managing Member
EMP: 74 EST: 1995
SQ FT: 35,000
SALES (est): 3.73MM Privately Held
Web: www.printprotees.com
SIC: 2759 Screen printing

(G-9124)

R W HATFIELD COMPANY INC (PA)
Also Called: Pro-Line
10 Avco Rd Ste 1 (01835-6997)
PHONE..................978 521-2600
Robert W Hatfield Junior, Pr
Robert Simmons, *
EMP: 46 EST: 1965
SQ FT: 12,500
SALES (est): 8.57MM
SALES (corp-wide): 8.57MM Privately Held
Web: www.1proline.com
SIC: 2522 Office furniture, except wood

(G-9125)

RAPID COATINGS INC
35 Avco Rd (01835-6936)
PHONE..................339 227-6490
George Grom, Pr
EMP: 9 EST: 2020
SALES (est): 598.11K Privately Held
Web: www.rapidcoatingsinc.com
SIC: 3479 Coating of metals and formed
products

(G-9126)

REBARS & MESH INC
111 Avco Rd (01835-6956)
PHONE..................978 374-2244
TOLL FREE: 800
▲ EMP: 20 EST: 1994
SQ FT: 30,000
SALES (est): 4.88MM Privately Held
Web: www.rebarsandmesh.com
SIC: 3449 5211 5051 Bars, concrete
reinforcing: fabricated steel; Lumber and
other building materials; Steel

(G-9127)

REGCO CORPORATION
Also Called: Regenie's All Natural Snacks
46 Rogers Rd (01835-6957)
PHONE..................978 521-4370
Regina A Ragonese, Pr
EMP: 30 EST: 1998
SQ FT: 30,000
SALES (est): 4.95MM Privately Held
Web: www.regenies.com
SIC: 2096 Potato chips and similar snacks

(G-9128)

RUNTAL NORTH AMERICA INC
Also Called: Sterling Hydraulics
187 Neck Rd (01835-8027)
P.O. Box 8278 (01835-0778)
PHONE..................800 526-2621
Hans Peter Zehneder, Ch
Richard Heller, *
▲ EMP: 45 EST: 1980
SQ FT: 53,000
SALES (est): 12.33MM Privately Held
Web: www.runtalnorthamerica.com
SIC: 3567 1711 3433 Radiant heating
systems, industrial process; Plumbing,
heating, air-conditioning; Heating
equipment, except electric
HQ: Zehnder Group Ag
Moortalstrasse 1

GrAnichen AG

(G-9129)

S & F MACHINE CO INC
1405 River St (01832-3599)
PHONE..................978 374-1552
Peter Strozza, Pr
EMP: 10 EST: 1964
SQ FT: 10,000
SALES (est): 828.9K Privately Held
Web: www.sfmachinecompany.com
SIC: 3599 Machine shop, jobbing and repair

(G-9130)

SAFC HITECH INC
1429 Hilldale Ave (01832-1300)
PHONE..................978 374-5200
◆ EMP: 32
SIC: 5169 2869 Chemicals and allied
products, nec; Industrial organic chemicals,
nec

(G-9131)

SPECIALIZED PLATING INC
Also Called: S P I
15 Ward Hill Ave (01835-6998)
PHONE..................978 373-8030
Paul Kelly, Pr
EMP: 20 EST: 1970
SQ FT: 15,000
SALES (est): 1.92MM Privately Held
Web: www.specializedplating.com
SIC: 3471 Electroplating of metals or
formed products

(G-9132)

SPECTRAL EVOLUTION INC
26 Parkridge Rd Ste 1a (01835-8515)
PHONE..................978 687-1833
Dennis Witz, CEO
EMP: 7 EST: 2004
SALES (est): 1.24MM Privately Held
Web: www.spectralevolution.com
SIC: 3826 Analytical instruments

(G-9133)

SPRING HILL MACHINE CO INC
48 Laurier St (01832-1950)
PHONE..................978 374-4461
EMP: 13 EST: 2007
SALES (est): 453.64K Privately Held
Web: www.springhillmachine.com
SIC: 3599 Machine shop, jobbing and repair

(G-9134)

SPRUCE ENVIRONMENTAL TECH INC
Also Called: Radonaway
3 Saber Way (01835-8000)
P.O. Box 8244 (01835-0744)
PHONE..................978 521-0901
Alan Zucchino, Pr
Howie Zidel, *
David Kapturowski, *
Jessica A Zucchino, *
▲ EMP: 55 EST: 1989
SQ FT: 26,000
SALES (est): 23.1MM Privately Held
Web: www.spruce.com
SIC: 3634 3564 Fans, exhaust and
ventilating, electric: household; Blowers
and fans

(G-9135)

TRU CHOCOLATE INC
610 Kenoza St (01830-2331)
PHONE..................855 878-2462
John Cappadona, Pr
EMP: 7 EST: 2017

SALES (est): 695.95K Privately Held
Web: www.tru-chocolate.com
SIC: 2066 Chocolate

(G-9136)

UFP TECHNOLOGIES INC
175 Ward Hill Ave (01835-6960)
PHONE..................978 352-2200
EMP: 10
SALES (corp-wide): 353.79MM Publicly
Held
Web: www.ufpt.com
SIC: 3086 Packaging and shipping
materials, foamed plastics
PA: Ufp Technologies, Inc.
100 Hale St
Newburyport MA 01950
978 352-2200

(G-9137)

ULTRASONIC SYSTEMS INC
135 Ward Hill Ave (01835-8508)
PHONE..................978 521-0095
Drew Erickson, CEO
Stuart Erickson, *
EMP: 25 EST: 1989
SQ FT: 20,000
SALES (est): 5.21MM Privately Held
Web: www.ultraspray.com
SIC: 3479 Coating of metals and formed
products

(G-9138)

UPTITE COMPANY INC
1001 Hilldale Ave (01832-1352)
PHONE..................978 377-0451
Beverly Bergeron, Pr
Cheryl Beshara Mquillian, Treas
Joseph G Beshara Junior, Clerk
EMP: 7 EST: 1974
SQ FT: 5,000
SALES (est): 1.04MM Privately Held
SIC: 2834 Veterinary pharmaceutical
preparations

Hingham
Plymouth County

(G-9139)

AJA INTERNATIONAL INC
72 Sharp St Ste B (02043-4364)
P.O. Box 246 (02060-0246)
PHONE..................781 545-7365
Michael Hale, Pr
William Hale, Pr
Michael R Hale, Sec
James Hannon, Sec
William M Provost, Treas
EMP: 33 EST: 1989
SQ FT: 3,200
SALES (est): 8.25MM Privately Held
Web: www.ajaint.com
SIC: 3829 3821 Measuring and controlling
devices, nec; Laboratory apparatus and
furniture

(G-9140)

ALLBIRDS INC
94 Derby St (02043-4220)
PHONE..................781 208-6094
EMP: 19
SALES (corp-wide): 297.77MM Publicly
Held
Web: www.allbirds.com
SIC: 3143 Men's footwear, except athletic
PA: Allbirds, Inc.
730 Montgomery St
San Francisco CA 94111
628 225-4848

(G-9141)
APPLIED TISSUE TECH LLC
99 Derby St Ste 200 (02043-4216)
PHONE.....................781 366-3848
Michael Broomhead, *CEO*
EMP: 9 **EST:** 2000
SALES (est): 513.49K **Privately Held**
Web: www.appliedtissue.com
SIC: 3841 Surgical and medical instruments

(G-9142)
BARREL HOUSE Z LLC
Also Called: Barrel House
14 Union St (02043-2946)
PHONE.....................617 480-2880
Jason W Morgan, *Brnch Mgr*
EMP: 35
SALES (corp-wide): 1.2MM **Privately Held**
Web: www.barrelhousepub.com
SIC: 2082 5812 Beer (alcoholic beverage);
Eating places
PA: Barrel House Z, Llc
95 Woodrock Rd
Weymouth MA 02189
339 207-7888

(G-9143)
BEANTOWN BEDDING LLC
137 Main St (02043-2506)
PHONE.....................781 608-9915
Kirsten Lambert, *Prin*
EMP: 9 **EST:** 2012
SALES (est): 401.77K **Privately Held**
Web: www.beantownbedding.com
SIC: 2392 Household furnishings, nec

(G-9144)
BRAYTON WILSON COLE CORP
70 Sharp St (02043-4312)
PHONE.....................781 803-6624
David Roffo, *Pr*
Beverly Roffo, *Sec*
EMP: 7 **EST:** 1924
SQ FT: 20,000
SALES (est): 1.67MM **Privately Held**
Web: www.bwcboston.com
SIC: 3446 3441 Ornamental metalwork;
Fabricated structural metal

(G-9145)
**BRIDGESTONE RET
OPERATIONS LLC**
Also Called: Firestone
22 Whiting St (02043-3821)
PHONE.....................781 749-6454
John Puffer, *Mgr*
EMP: 9
Web: www.bridgestoneamericas.com
SIC: 5531 7534 Automotive tires;
Rebuilding and retreading tires
HQ: Bridgestone Retail Operations, Llc
333 E Lake St Ste 300
Bloomingdale IL 60108
630 259-9000

(G-9146)
CASEY & HAYES INC
Also Called: Brede
100 Industrial Park Rd (02043-4313)
P.O. Box E62 (02127-0004)
PHONE.....................617 269-5900
EMP: 200
Web: www.caseyandhayes.com
SIC: 4213 3993 4214 Household goods
transport; Signs and advertising specialties;
Local trucking with storage

(G-9147)
CLANDESTINE KITCHEN LLC
3 Birch Cir (02043-1703)
PHONE.....................415 516-0378
EMP: 7 **EST:** 2018
SALES (est): 561.95K **Privately Held**
Web: www.clandestinekitchen.com
SIC: 2099 2741 Food preparations, nec;
Internet publishing and broadcasting

(G-9148)
DRESCO BELTING CO INC
24 French St (02043-3031)
PHONE.....................781 335-1350
Robert Dresser, *Pr*
Robert Dresser Junior, *Stockholder*
James G Dresser, *Stockholder*
Norman K Dresser, *Stockholder*
EMP: 8 **EST:** 1929
SALES (est): 632.58K **Privately Held**
Web: www.drescobelt.com
SIC: 3052 Rubber belting

(G-9149)
DTM MASSMAN LLC
Also Called: Dtm Packaging & Custom
Automtn
150 Recreation Park Dr Ste 5 (02043-4251)
P.O. Box 308 (02043-0308)
PHONE.....................781 749-1866
Jeffrey Hohn, *Pr*
Kendall Kim Doble, *
Guy Tringale, *
Scott Mackenzie, *
EMP: 30 **EST:** 2019
SALES (est): 6.55MM
SALES (corp-wide): 44.83MM **Privately
Held**
Web: www.dtmpackaging.com
SIC: 3565 Packaging machinery
PA: Massman Automation Designs, Llc
1010 Lake St
Villard MN 56385
320 554-2550

(G-9150)
EAST COAST PRINTING INC
2 Keith Way Ste 5 (02043-4246)
PHONE.....................781 331-5635
Lou Silva, *Pr*
Tony Fontes, *Treas*
EMP: 8 **EST:** 1999
SQ FT: 2,000
SALES (est): 2.4MM **Privately Held**
Web: www.eastcoastpress.com
SIC: 2752 Offset printing

(G-9151)
**INTERCNTNENTAL ENRGY
GROUP LLC**
350 Lincoln St Ste 111 (02043-1578)
PHONE.....................781 749-9800
EMP: 7 **EST:** 1995
SALES (est): 785.2K **Privately Held**
SIC: 4911 2611 Generation, electric power;
Pulp mills

(G-9152)
**MASSA PRODUCTS
CORPORATION**
280 Lincoln St (02043-1796)
PHONE.....................781 749-3120
Donald P Massa, *Pr*
Paul L Hellar, *
Richard M Carpenter, *
Edward G Casey, *
Charles J Humphreys, *
▲ **EMP:** 65 **EST:** 1945
SALES (est): 13.75MM **Privately Held**

Web: www.massa.com
SIC: 3679 3812 3625 Transducers, electrical
; Sonar systems and equipment; Control
equipment, electric

(G-9153)
MEDIAVUE SYSTEMS INC
35 Pond Park Rd Ste 14 (02043-4366)
PHONE.....................781 926-0676
David L Degiorgi, *Pr*
EMP: 25 **EST:** 2016
SALES (est): 2.94MM **Privately Held**
Web: www.mediavuesystems.com
SIC: 3993 7373 Electric signs; Systems
engineering, computer related

(G-9154)
MEDIAVUE SYSTEMS LLC
35 Pond Park Rd Ste 14 (02043-4366)
PHONE.....................781 926-0676
EMP: 20
Web: www.mediavuesystems.com
SIC: 3571 Mainframe computers

(G-9155)
**NEW ENGLAND GEN-CONNECT
LLC**
Also Called: Genconnex
35 Pond Park Rd Ste 11 (02043-4366)
PHONE.....................617 571-6884
Gary A Mook, *Prin*
EMP: 8 **EST:** 2012
SALES (est): 398.13K **Privately Held**
Web: www.genconnex.net
SIC: 3569 3621 Gas generators; Power
generators

(G-9156)
ONEVIEW COMMERCE INC
350 Lincoln St Ste 2400 (02043-1579)
PHONE.....................617 279-0549
EMP: 70 **EST:** 2011
SALES (est): 12.58MM
SALES (corp-wide): 11.62MM **Privately
Held**
Web: www.oneviewcommerce.com
SIC: 7372 7379 Business oriented computer
software; Computer related maintenance
services
PA: Oneview Group Limited
201 Temple Chambers
London EC4Y
163 467-3172

(G-9157)
PREMCO INC
55 Research Rd S Shore Park
(02043-4377)
PHONE.....................781 749-0333
EMP: 65 **EST:** 1965
SALES (est): 15.16MM
SALES (corp-wide): 498.74MM **Publicly
Held**
Web: www.nninc.com
SIC: 3599 Machine shop, jobbing and repair
PA: Nn, Inc.
6210 Ardrey Kell Rd # 600
Charlotte NC 28277
980 264-4300

(G-9158)
RUSSELECTRIC INC
99 Industrial Park Rd (02043-4387)
PHONE.....................781 749-6000
EMP: 422
Web: new.siemens.com
SIC: 3613 Power switching equipment

(G-9159)
SIEMENS INDUSTRY INC
Also Called: Russelectric A Siemens Bus
99 Industrial Park Rd (02043-4306)
PHONE.....................781 749-6000
Daryl D Dulaney, *CEO*
EMP: 422
SALES (corp-wide): 84.48B **Privately Held**
Web: www.siemens.com
SIC: 3613 Power switching equipment
HQ: Siemens Industry, Inc.
100 Technology Dr
Alpharetta GA 30005
847 215-1000

(G-9160)
**SLESAR BROS BREWING CO
INC**
18 Shipyard Dr (02043-1670)
PHONE.....................781 749-2337
EMP: 18
SIC: 2082 Beer (alcoholic beverage)
PA: Slesar Bros. Brewing Company, Inc.
110 Canal St
Boston MA

(G-9161)
**VACUUM TECHNOLOGY ASSOC
INC**
Also Called: Dynavac
110 Industrial Park Rd (02043-4313)
PHONE.....................781 740-8600
Thomas P Foley, *Pr*
Joel Smolka, *
Robert W Schaffer, *
Peter H Kehew, *
EMP: 99 **EST:** 1999
SQ FT: 22,000
SALES (est): 25.49MM **Privately Held**
Web: www.dynavac.com
SIC: 3563 Vacuum (air extraction) systems,
industrial

(G-9162)
VENUS WAFERS INC
Also Called: Venus
100 Research Rd (02043-4345)
PHONE.....................781 740-1002
Luke E Barmakian, *Pr*
Jill Barmakian, *
▲ **EMP:** 26 **EST:** 1933
SQ FT: 56,500
SALES (est): 6MM **Privately Held**
Web: www.venuswafers.com
SIC: 2052 Crackers, dry, nec

(G-9163)
VULCAN COMPANY INC (PA)
Also Called: Vulcan Tool Mfg
51 Sharp St (02043-4311)
P.O. Box 36 (02018-0036)
PHONE.....................781 337-5970
Alexander G Clark, *Pr*
William P Kennedy, *
◆ **EMP:** 55 **EST:** 1890
SQ FT: 50,000
SALES (est): 9.6MM
SALES (corp-wide): 9.6MM **Privately Held**
Web: www.vulcantools.com
SIC: 3546 3545 3531 Power-driven
handtools; Machine tool accessories;
Paving breakers

(G-9164)
WESTON CORPORATION
Also Called: Weston Communications
45 Industrial Park Rd (02043-4357)
PHONE.....................781 749-0936
Alden Weston Senior, *Pr*

Alden Weston Junior, *VP*
John Weston, *VP*
Blanche Weston, *Clerk*
EMP: 21 **EST:** 1959
SQ FT: 7,200
SALES (est): 1.86MM **Privately Held**
Web: www.westongraphics.com
SIC: 2791 7336 7334 Typesetting;
  Commercial art and illustration; Blueprinting
  service

(G-9165)
WESTWOOD MILLS CORP
55 Sharp St Ste 6 (02043-4353)
PHONE.................................781 335-4466
Douglas Laughlin, *Pr*
▲ **EMP:** 11 **EST:** 2004
SALES (est): 647.92K **Privately Held**
Web: www.westwoodmills.com
SIC: 3469 Boxes: tool, lunch, mail, etc.:
  stamped metal

(G-9166)
XACT ROBOTICS INC
75 Sgt William B Terry Dr Ste 200
(02043-1606)
PHONE.................................781 252-9143
EMP: 9 **EST:** 2019
SALES (est): 1.2MM **Privately Held**
Web: www.xactrobotics.com
SIC: 3841 Surgical and medical instruments

Hinsdale
Berkshire County

(G-9167)
WESTERN MASS PENNY SAVER
55 Ashmere Rd (01235-9290)
P.O. Box 2111 (01235-2111)
PHONE.................................413 655-9957
EMP: 7 **EST:** 2018
SALES (est): 107.06K **Privately Held**
Web: www.pioneerpennysaver.com
SIC: 2741 Miscellaneous publishing

Holbrook
Norfolk County

(G-9168)
**ASSOCIATED MKTG SYSTEMS
INC**
2 Kleen Way (02343-1304)
PHONE.................................781 767-9001
James F Mcdonald, *Pr*
John Mc Donald Senior, *Pr*
Jodi Cohen, *Contrlr*
EMP: 21 **EST:** 1980
SALES (est): 3.5MM **Privately Held**
SIC: 2448 7389 Pallets, wood; Business
  services, nec

(G-9169)
**AVON CUSTOM MIXING SVCS
INC**
55 High St (02343-2005)
P.O. Box 187 (02025-0187)
PHONE.................................781 767-0511
Mark Chase, *Pr*
Timothy Nestor, *Marketing*
EMP: 25 **EST:** 1976
SQ FT: 200,000
SALES (est): 494.81K **Privately Held**
SIC: 3069 Custom compounding of rubber
  materials

(G-9170)
**BOSTON STEEL FABRICATORS
INC**
610 South St (02343-1300)
P.O. Box 310 (02343-0310)
PHONE.................................781 767-1540
Barry Brown, *Pr*
Stephen Brown, *VP*
EMP: 9 **EST:** 1956
SQ FT: 22,000
SALES (est): 978.1K **Privately Held**
Web: www.bostonsteelfabricators.com
SIC: 3441 3446 Building components,
  structural steel; Ornamental metalwork

(G-9171)
**DRAPER ELEVATOR CAB CO
INC**
260 Centre St (02343-1074)
PHONE.................................781 961-3146
Diane Giblin, *Prin*
EMP: 11 **EST:** 2006
SALES (est): 1.02MM **Privately Held**
Web: www.draperelevator.com
SIC: 1796 3444 3499 Elevator installation
  and conversion; Sheet metalwork;
  Fabricated metal products, nec

(G-9172)
**DRAPER METAL FABRICATION
INC**
260 Centre St Unit A (02343-1074)
PHONE.................................781 961-3146
EMP: 8 **EST:** 1995
SQ FT: 10,000
SALES (est): 1.67MM **Privately Held**
Web: www.drapermetalfabrication.com
SIC: 3444 Sheet metalwork

(G-9173)
**GRAPHIC FULLFILLMENT &
FINISHING INC**
145 Union St Ste 3 (02343-1463)
PHONE.................................781 727-8845
EMP: 8 **EST:** 1994
SALES (est): 875.88K **Privately Held**
SIC: 2789 Bookbinding and related work

(G-9174)
I G MARSTON COMPANY
Also Called: Igm
8 Mear Rd (02343-1339)
P.O. Box 432 (02343-0432)
PHONE.................................781 767-2894
Evelyn Piercy, *Pr*
Sarah Piercy, *VP*
EMP: 15 **EST:** 1844
SQ FT: 10,000
SALES (est): 2.06MM **Privately Held**
Web: www.igmarston.com
SIC: 3089 3053 Washers, plastics; Gaskets,
  all materials

(G-9175)
**INFRA-RED BLDG & PWR SVC
INC (PA)**
152 Ctr St (02343-1011)
P.O. Box 243 (02322-0243)
PHONE.................................781 767-0888
Thomas C Mc Donald, *Pr*
EMP: 13 **EST:** 1990
SQ FT: 21,000
SALES (est): 7.29MM **Privately Held**
Web: www.infraredbps.com
SIC: 1731 3613 5063 General electrical
  contractor; Control panels, electric;
  Electrical supplies, nec

(G-9176)
JANNEL MANUFACTURING INC
5 Mear Rd (02343-1329)
PHONE.................................781 767-0666
Yves Nahmias, *Pr*
Pyarlai Nanji, *
◆ **EMP:** 35 **EST:** 1979
SQ FT: 60,000
SALES (est): 4.94MM **Privately Held**
Web: www.proampac.com
SIC: 2677 2673 Envelopes; Plastic bags:
  made from purchased materials

(G-9177)
**LANDMARK WINDOW
FASHIONS INC**
5 Mear Rd Ste 4 (02343-1329)
P.O. Box 350 (02343-0350)
PHONE.................................781 767-3535
Harlan Bliss, *Pr*
William J Buckley, *
Judith H Bliss, *
EMP: 27 **EST:** 1992
SQ FT: 12,000
SALES (est): 2.09MM **Privately Held**
SIC: 2591 Blinds vertical

(G-9178)
LANE PRINTING CO INC
Also Called: Lane PRInting& Advertising
210 S Franklin St (02343-1461)
PHONE.................................781 767-4450
Francis P Lane Junior, *Pr*
Carolyn P Lane, *Treas*
EMP: 14 **EST:** 1985
SQ FT: 5,500
SALES (est): 1.03MM **Privately Held**
Web: www.laneprint.com
SIC: 2752 3993 7312 7336 Offset printing;
  Signs and advertising specialties; Outdoor
  advertising services; Creative services to
  advertisers, except writers

(G-9179)
MICA-TRON PRODUCTS CORP
275 Centre St Ste 13 (02343-1079)
PHONE.................................781 767-2163
Paul J Tassinari, *Pr*
Flora Tassinari, *Treas*
EMP: 7 **EST:** 1960
SQ FT: 6,000
SALES (est): 1.53MM **Privately Held**
Web: www.mica-tron.com
SIC: 3599 Machine shop, jobbing and repair

(G-9180)
MICRO WIRE PRODUCTS INC
5 Mear Rd Ste 3 (02343-1329)
P.O. Box 427 (02343-0427)
PHONE.................................508 584-0200
Jeff Weafer, *Pr*
◆ **EMP:** 60 **EST:** 1952
SQ FT: 70,000
SALES (est): 8.25MM **Privately Held**
Web: www.microwire-products.com
SIC: 3496 Miscellaneous fabricated wire
  products

(G-9181)
NEW CAN COMPANY INC (HQ)
1 Mear Rd (02343-1338)
P.O. Box 421 (02343-0421)
PHONE.................................330 928-1191
Ted Bustany, *CEO*
Thomas Houston, *Pr*
Ann Bilodeau, *CFO*
Laufey V Bustany, *Sec*
EMP: 30 **EST:** 1902
SQ FT: 115,000
SALES (est): 10.29MM

SALES (corp-wide): 14.08MM **Privately
Held**
Web: www.newcan.com
SIC: 3469 Perforated metal, stamped
PA: New Can Holdings, Inc.
  1 Mear Rd
  Holbrook MA 02343
  781 767-1650

(G-9182)
NEW CAN HOLDINGS INC (PA)
Also Called: New Can Company
1 Mear Rd (02343-1338)
P.O. Box 421 (02343-0421)
PHONE.................................781 767-1650
Ted Bustany, *CEO*
EMP: 25 **EST:** 1993
SQ FT: 114,000
SALES (est): 14.08MM
SALES (corp-wide): 14.08MM **Privately
Held**
Web: www.newcan.com
SIC: 3317 Steel pipe and tubes

(G-9183)
**OLDCASTLE APG NORTHEAST
INC**
Also Called: Oldcastle North Atlantic
46 Spring St (02343-2019)
PHONE.................................781 506-9473
Steve Getto, *Brnch Mgr*
EMP: 55
SQ FT: 106,000
SALES (corp-wide): 32.72B **Privately Held**
Web: www.oldcastleapg.com
SIC: 3271 3272 Blocks, concrete or cinder:
  standard; Concrete products, nec
HQ: Oldcastle Apg Northeast, Inc.
  13555 Wllngton Ctr Cir St
  Gainesville VA 20155
  703 365-7070

(G-9184)
QUALITY AIR METALS INC
Also Called: Quality Air Metals
283 Centre St Ste B (02343-1075)
PHONE.................................781 986-9967
EMP: 28 **EST:** 1994
SALES (est): 2.52MM **Privately Held**
SIC: 3444 Sheet metalwork

(G-9185)
**SPECTOR METAL PRODUCTS
CO INC**
608 South St (02343-1300)
PHONE.................................781 767-5600
Morris Spector, *Pr*
Steven Spector, *VP*
Brian Spector, *VP*
EMP: 21 **EST:** 1952
SQ FT: 24,000
SALES (est): 2.33MM **Privately Held**
Web: www.spectormetal.com
SIC: 3441 Bridge sections, prefabricated,
  highway

(G-9186)
VATER PERCUSSION INC
270 Centre St Unit D (02343-1073)
PHONE.................................781 767-1877
Ronald Vater, *Pr*
Allan Vater, *
▲ **EMP:** 21 **EST:** 1979
SQ FT: 7,200
SALES (est): 1.68MM **Privately Held**
Web: www.vater.com
SIC: 3931 Drums, parts, and accessories
  (musical instruments)

Holden
Worcester County

(G-9187)
AVIENT COLORANTS USA LLC (HQ)
85 Industrial Dr (01520-1848)
PHONE....................508 829-6321
▲ **EMP:** 50 **EST:** 2015
SALES (est): 822.85MM **Publicly Held**
Web: www.avient.com
SIC: 2819 2869 Industrial inorganic chemicals, nec; Industrial organic chemicals, nec
PA: Avient Corporation
33587 Walker Rd
Avon Lake OH 44012

(G-9188)
DPS PACKAGING LLC
1010 Main St Ste 1 (01520-1237)
PHONE....................508 459-8917
EMP: 8 **EST:** 2015
SALES (est): 993.12K **Privately Held**
SIC: 3599 Flexible metal hose, tubing, and bellows

(G-9189)
GATEHOUSE MEDIA LLC
1105 Main St Ste A (01520-1219)
PHONE....................508 829-5981
EMP: 10
SALES (corp-wide): 2.95B **Publicly Held**
Web: www.gannett.com
SIC: 2711 Newspapers, publishing and printing
HQ: Gatehouse Media, Llc
175 Sullys Trl Ste 203
Pittsford NY 14534
585 598-0030

(G-9190)
HELVETIA LLC
269 Wachusett St (01520-1854)
PHONE....................508 829-7607
EMP: 8 **EST:** 2009
SALES (est): 248.07K **Privately Held**
SIC: 3714 Motor vehicle parts and accessories

(G-9191)
INNER-TITE CORP
110 Industrial Dr (01520-1893)
PHONE....................508 829-6361
George W Davis, *Pr*
Bonnie J Williams, *
▼ **EMP:** 85 **EST:** 1917
SQ FT: 100,000
SALES (est): 18.95MM **Privately Held**
Web: www.inner-tite.com
SIC: 3699 3429 Security devices; Locks or lock sets

(G-9192)
LUMEWAY PRODUCTS INC
800 Main St Ste 205 (01520-1838)
PHONE....................508 829-2112
Jeffrey Summit, *Pr*
EMP: 8 **EST:** 2011
SALES (est): 172.81K **Privately Held**
Web: www.lumeway.com
SIC: 3699 Electrical equipment and supplies, nec

(G-9193)
MASSACHUSETTS BROKEN STONE CO
Also Called: Holden Trap Rock Co
2077 N Main St (01520)
P.O. Box 31 (01520-0031)
PHONE....................508 829-5353
Andrew Forrest, *VP*
EMP: 20
SALES (corp-wide): 4.38MM **Privately Held**
Web: www.massbroken.com
SIC: 2951 Asphalt paving mixtures and blocks
PA: Massachusetts Broken Stone Company
332 Sawyer Hill Rd
Berlin MA 01503
978 838-9999

(G-9194)
PEPSI-COLA BTLG WORCESTER INC (PA)
Also Called: Pepsico
90 Industrial Dr (01520-1898)
PHONE....................508 829-6551
Robert Rauh, *Pr*
Robert W Rauh, *
William T Rauh, *
Marjorie Rauh, *Stockholder*
Richard Rauh, *
EMP: 85 **EST:** 1956
SQ FT: 60,000
SALES (est): 22.65MM
SALES (corp-wide): 22.65MM **Privately Held**
Web: www.pepsiworcester.com
SIC: 2086 Carbonated soft drinks, bottled and canned

(G-9195)
PRISMIC PHARMACEUTICALS INC
650 South Rd (01520-1042)
PHONE....................971 506-6415
Peter Moriarty, *CEO*
Zachary Dutton, *Pr*
EMP: 7 **EST:** 2011
SALES (est): 1.45MM **Privately Held**
SIC: 2834 Pharmaceutical preparations
PA: Fsd Pharma Inc
199 Bay St Suite 400
Toronto ON M5L 1
416 854-8884

(G-9196)
WOODMEISTER MASTER BLDRS INC (PA)
1 Woodmeister Way (01520-3803)
PHONE....................774 345-1000
Theodore B Goodnow, *CEO*
Kim Goodnow, *
Kevin Greene, *
Michael Lizotte, *
◆ **EMP:** 105 **EST:** 1983
SQ FT: 75,000
SALES (est): 65.33MM
SALES (corp-wide): 65.33MM **Privately Held**
Web: www.woodmeister.com
SIC: 1522 2434 2431 1751 Residential construction, nec; Wood kitchen cabinets; Millwork; Cabinet building and installation

Holliston
Middlesex County

(G-9197)
ABBESS INSTRS & SYSTEMS INC
Also Called: Abbess Instruments
75 October Hill Rd (01746-1344)
P.O. Box 498 (01721-0498)
PHONE....................508 429-0002
Geoffrey Zeamer, *Pr*
Michelle Zeamer, *VP*
EMP: 17 **EST:** 1986
SQ FT: 4,000
SALES (est): 4.1MM **Privately Held**
Web: www.abbess.com
SIC: 3829 Measuring and controlling devices, nec

(G-9198)
AMERICAN DURAFILM CO INC
55 Boynton Rd (01746-1460)
P.O. Box 6770 (01746-6770)
PHONE....................508 429-8000
EMP: 21 **EST:** 1956
SALES (est): 7.86MM **Privately Held**
Web: www.americandurafilm.com
SIC: 3479 3081 Coating of metals with plastic or resins; Plastics film and sheet

(G-9199)
AMERICAN RECYCLED MTLS INC
157 Lowland St 165 (01746)
PHONE....................508 429-1455
Michael L Brumber, *Prin*
EMP: 7 **EST:** 2014
SALES (est): 496.84K **Privately Held**
Web: www.materialsrecycled.com
SIC: 4953 3559 Recycling, waste materials; Recycling machinery

(G-9200)
AUTOGEN INC
84 October Hill Rd Ste 5 (01746-1371)
PHONE....................508 429-5965
Robert J Sullivan, *CEO*
Michael Messier, *
Melissa Messier, *
▲ **EMP:** 25 **EST:** 1998
SQ FT: 3,500
SALES (est): 4.17MM **Privately Held**
Web: www.autogen.com
SIC: 3826 Analytical instruments

(G-9201)
AVERY PRODUCTS CORPORATION
89 Cross St (01746-2230)
P.O. Box 5878 (01746-5878)
PHONE....................508 893-1000
Robert A Hederman, *Mgr*
EMP: 150
SALES (corp-wide): 4.75B **Privately Held**
Web: www.avery.com
SIC: 2678 Notebooks: made from purchased paper
HQ: Avery Products Corporation
50 Pointe Dr
Brea CA 92821
714 674-8500

(G-9202)
BAGGE INC
Also Called: East Coast Perfection Coating
150 Kuniholm Dr Ste 4 (01746-1398)
PHONE....................508 429-8080
EMP: 8 **EST:** 1995
SQ FT: 7,000
SALES (est): 903.39K **Privately Held**
SIC: 3479 Coating of metals and formed products

(G-9203)
CADWELL PRODUCTS COMPANY INC
Also Called: Cadwell Company
3 Kuniholm Dr (01746-1376)
PHONE....................508 429-3100
Mindy Murray, *Pr*
Michael Todisco, *VP*
Jim Murray, *Treas*
EMP: 14 **EST:** 1983
SQ FT: 7,000
SALES (est): 2.28MM **Privately Held**
Web: www.cadwellsign.com
SIC: 3993 Signs, not made in custom sign painting shops

(G-9204)
CENTURY-TYWOOD J3 CORP ✪
Also Called: Century-Tywood
79 Lowland St (01746-2030)
PHONE....................508 429-4011
Andrew Slifka, *Pr*
EMP: 11 **EST:** 2022
SALES (est): 1.89MM **Privately Held**
Web: www.century-tywood.com
SIC: 3444 3661 3469 3999 Sheet metalwork; Fiber optics communications equipment; Metal stampings, nec; Manufacturing industries, nec

(G-9205)
CONVANTA HOLLISTON
115 Washington St (01746-1345)
PHONE....................508 429-9750
EMP: 9 **EST:** 2008
SALES (est): 234.71K **Privately Held**
Web: www.hollistonreporter.com
SIC: 2673 Wardrobe bags (closet accessories): from purchased materials

(G-9206)
DIAMOND DIAGNOSTICS INC (PA)
Also Called: Diamond Diagnostics -USA
333 Fiske St (01746-2048)
PHONE....................508 429-0450
◆ **EMP:** 67 **EST:** 1996
SQ FT: 38,000
SALES (est): 13.44MM **Privately Held**
Web: www.diamonddiagnostics.com
SIC: 5047 3841 Diagnostic equipment, medical; Diagnostic apparatus, medical

(G-9207)
DIGILAB GENOMIC SOLUTIONS INC
Also Called: Digilab
84 October Hill Rd Ste 7 (01746-1371)
PHONE....................508 893-3130
David Giddings, *Pr*
Joseph Griffin, *VP*
EMP: 10 **EST:** 2007
SALES (est): 134.86K **Privately Held**
SIC: 3841 Surgical and medical instruments

(G-9208)
EASTMAN PERFORMANCE FILMS LLC
Also Called: Premiumshield
35 Jeffrey Ave (01746-2027)
PHONE....................508 474-6002
David Diminico, *Managing Member*
EMP: 38 **EST:** 2006
SALES (est): 15.26MM **Publicly Held**
Web: www.premiumshield.com
SIC: 5162 2891 2851 Resins; Adhesives; Paints and paint additives
PA: Eastman Chemical Company
200 S Wilcox Dr
Kingsport TN 37660

▲ = Import ▼ = Export
◆ = Import/Export

(G-9209)
ESCO TECHNOLOGIES INC
Also Called: Esco Tool
75 October Hill Rd (01746-1344)
PHONE....................................508 429-4441
Matthew Brennan, *Pr*
Craig Winterseld, *
James Moruzzi, *
▲ **EMP:** 35 **EST:** 1935
SQ FT: 18,000
SALES (est): 4.81MM **Privately Held**
Web: www.escotool.com
SIC: 3545 5085   Cutting tools for machine
tools; Industrial supplies

(G-9210)
FLEXHEAD INDUSTRIES INC
56 Lowland St (01746-2029)
PHONE....................................508 893-9596
John P Williamson, *Pr*
Charles M Cohrs, *Treas*
Daniel S Kelly, *Sec*
▲ **EMP:** 50 **EST:** 1993
SALES (est): 4.76MM **Publicly Held**
SIC: 3569   Sprinkler systems, fire: automatic
PA: Atkore Inc.
16100 Lathrop Ave
Harvey IL 60426

(G-9211)
FLEXHEAD INDUSTRIES
MASSACHUSETTS BUSINESS
TRUST
56 Lowland St (01746-2029)
PHONE....................................508 893-9596
▲ **EMP:** 15
SIC: 3569   Sprinkler systems, fire: automatic

(G-9212)
GENOMIC SOLUTIONS INC
84 October Hill Rd Ste 7 (01746-1371)
PHONE....................................734 975-4800
EMP: 20 **EST:** 1981
SQ FT: 14,500
SALES (est): 2.11MM **Publicly Held**
SIC: 3826   Analytical instruments
PA: Harvard Bioscience, Inc.
84 October Hill Rd Ste 10
Holliston MA 01746

(G-9213)
HARVARD APPARATUS INC
Also Called: Hbio
84 October Hill Rd (01746-1388)
PHONE....................................508 893-8999
David Green, *Pr*
Chane Graziano, *Treas*
▲ **EMP:** 80 **EST:** 1996
SALES (est): 25.58MM **Publicly Held**
Web: www.harvardapparatus.com
SIC: 5049 3841 3561   Scientific instruments;
Surgical and medical instruments; Pumps
and pumping equipment
PA: Harvard Bioscience, Inc.
84 October Hill Rd Ste 10
Holliston MA 01746

(G-9214)
HARVARD APPRTUS RGNRTIVE
TECH (PA)
Also Called: BIOSTAGE
84 October Hill Rd Ste 11 (01746-1371)
PHONE....................................774 233-7300
Jerry He, *CEO*
Saverio Lafrancesca, *CMO*
Thomas Mcnaughton, *CFO*
Hong Yu, *Pr*
Joseph Damasi, *CFO*
EMP: 28 **EST:** 2007

SQ FT: 17,000
Web: www.biostage.com
SIC: 3841   Diagnostic apparatus, medical

(G-9215)
HIGHLAND LABS INC
163 Woodland St (01746-1821)
PHONE....................................508 429-2918
Peter Lewis, *Pr*
EMP: 7 **EST:** 1953
SQ FT: 21,600
SALES (est): 400.59K **Privately Held**
Web: www.highlandlabs.com
SIC: 3999 3559 3841 3596   Soap dispensers
; Paint making machinery; Surgical and
medical instruments; Scales and balances,
except laboratory

(G-9216)
IWAKI AMERICA
INCORPORATED (HQ)
Also Called: Iwaki America
5 Boynton Rd Hopping Brook Park
(01746-1460)
PHONE....................................508 429-1440
John P Miersma, *Pr*
Robert J Dziekiewicz Junior, *Sec*
Shigeru Fujinaka, *
Jeffrey Hadley, *
Dennis Ruis, *
▲ **EMP:** 23 **EST:** 1974
SQ FT: 53,000
SALES (est): 22.88MM **Privately Held**
Web: www.iwakiamerica.com
SIC: 3561 5084 3823 3625   Industrial pumps
and parts; Pumps and pumping equipment,
nec; Controllers, for process variables, all
types; Relays and industrial controls
PA: Iwaki Co., Ltd.
2-6-6, Kandasudacho
Chiyoda-Ku TKY 101-0

(G-9217)
IWAKI PUMPS INC (DH)
5 Boynton Rd (01746-1460)
PHONE....................................508 429-1440
Ronald Yates, *Pr*
Richard Jewett, *Ch Bd*
▲ **EMP:** 20 **EST:** 1989
SQ FT: 30,000
SALES (est): 20.55MM **Privately Held**
Web: www.iwakiamerica.com
SIC: 3561 7699 3674   Industrial pumps and
parts; Pumps and pumping equipment
repair; Semiconductors and related devices
HQ: Iwaki America Incorporated
5 Boynton Rd
Holliston MA 01746
508 429-1440

(G-9218)
JF2 LLC
215 Hopping Brook Rd (01746-1456)
PHONE....................................508 429-1022
John Sallona, *Owner*
EMP: 187
SIC: 3448   Farm and utility buildings
HQ: Jf2, Llc
52 Canco Rd
Portland ME 04103
207 588-3300

(G-9219)
KRAMERS CSTM KITCHENS &
WDWKG
47 October Hill Rd (01746-1758)
PHONE....................................508 429-9007
EMP: 8 **EST:** 2020
SALES (est): 509.35K **Privately Held**
Web: www.kramerskitchens.com

SIC: 2431   Millwork

(G-9220)
LEWA-NIKKISO AMERICA INC
(DH)
132 Hopping Brook Rd (01746-1455)
P.O. Box 6820 (01746-6820)
PHONE....................................508 429-7403
Peter Castellanos, *Pr*
Ray Ruddy, *
◆ **EMP:** 37 **EST:** 1968
SQ FT: 19,000
SALES (est): 45.6MM
SALES (corp-wide): 13.47B **Privately Held**
Web: www.lewa-inc.com
SIC: 5084 3586 3561   Pumps and pumping
equipment, nec; Measuring and dispensing
pumps; Pumps and pumping equipment
HQ: Lewa Gmbh
Ulmer Str. 10
Leonberg BW 71229
7152140

(G-9221)
LISTA INTERNATIONAL
CORPORATION
106 Lowland St (01746-2094)
PHONE....................................508 429-1350
▲ **EMP:** 163
SIC: 2599   Cabinets, factory

(G-9222)
MIANO PRINTING SERVICES INC
Also Called: MPS
89 October Hill Rd (01746-1378)
PHONE....................................617 935-2830
Stephen M Miano, *Pr*
EMP: 11 **EST:** 1985
SALES (est): 454.8K **Privately Held**
Web: www.mpscentral.com
SIC: 2752   Offset printing

(G-9223)
MILLER H C WOOD WORKING
INC
93 Bartzak Dr (01746-1374)
PHONE....................................508 429-4220
Bob De Marre, *Pr*
EMP: 8 **EST:** 1931
SQ FT: 10,000
SALES (est): 911.94K **Privately Held**
SIC: 2431 2434   Doors, wood; Wood kitchen
cabinets

(G-9224)
MOOR METALS INC (PA)
2 Kuniholm Dr Ste 2 (01746-1355)
PHONE....................................508 429-9446
Paul J Maloney, *Pr*
◆ **EMP:** 9 **EST:** 1992
SQ FT: 3,500
SALES (est): 2.36MM **Privately Held**
Web: www.moormetals.com
SIC: 5051 3315   Steel; Wire products,
ferrous/iron: made in wiredrawing plants

(G-9225)
OX PAPER TUBE AND CORE INC
89 October Hill Rd (01746-1378)
PHONE....................................508 879-1141
Edward Santiago, *Mgr*
EMP: 17
Web: www.oxindustries.com
SIC: 2655   Tubes, fiber or paper: made from
purchased material
PA: Ox Paper Tube And Core, Inc.
600 W Elm Ave
Hanover PA 17331

(G-9226)
PAGELL CORPORATION
74 Lowland St (01746-2029)
PHONE....................................508 429-2998
Brett Kane, *Pr*
◆ **EMP:** 45 **EST:** 1961
SQ FT: 72,000
SALES (est): 4.66MM **Privately Held**
Web: www.pagell.com
SIC: 2621   Paper mills

(G-9227)
PEGASUS INC
39 Locust St (01746-1377)
P.O. Box 6160 (01746-6160)
PHONE....................................508 429-2461
Christopher Best, *Pr*
Peter Best, *Treas*
Corine Arnold, *Clerk*
EMP: 8 **EST:** 1956
SQ FT: 5,600
SALES (est): 831.38K **Privately Held**
Web: www.pegasusincmachining.com
SIC: 3599   Machine shop, jobbing and repair

(G-9228)
SE SHIRES INC
260 Hopping Brook Rd (01746-1455)
PHONE....................................508 634-6805
▲ **EMP:** 35 **EST:** 1995
SQ FT: 12,000
SALES (est): 1.79MM **Privately Held**
Web: www.seshires.com
SIC: 3931   Brass instruments and parts

(G-9229)
SILVER LEAF BOOKS LLC
13 Temi Rd (01746-1219)
P.O. Box 6460 (01746-6460)
PHONE....................................781 799-6609
EMP: 7 **EST:** 2003
SALES (est): 246.91K **Privately Held**
Web: www.silverleafbooks.com
SIC: 2731   Books, publishing only

(G-9230)
STANLEY INDUSTRIAL & AUTO
LLC
Also Called: Lista International
106 Lowland St (01746-2031)
PHONE....................................508 429-1350
Donald Brown, *Pr*
EMP: 458
SALES (corp-wide): 16.95B **Publicly Held**
Web: www.listaintl.com
SIC: 2599   Cabinets, factory
HQ: Stanley Industrial & Automotive, Llc
5195 Blazer Pkwy
Dublin OH 43017
614 755-7000

(G-9231)
STARBURST PRTG & GRAPHICS
INC
300 Hopping Brook Rd (01746-3405)
PHONE....................................508 893-0900
Paul Nunez Junior, *Pr*
EMP: 18 **EST:** 1988
SQ FT: 13,000
SALES (est): 2.31MM **Privately Held**
Web: www.starburstprinting.com
SIC: 2752   Offset printing

(G-9232)
TIBERIO MANUFACTURING
CORP
79 Lowland St (01746-2030)
PHONE....................................508 429-4011

Maurice N St Germain, *Pr*
Faith K Tiberio, *
Maurice N St Germain, *VP*
Joan M Currier, *OF BOARD*
EMP: 90 **EST:** 1947
SQ FT: 35,000
SALES (est): 8.36MM **Privately Held**
Web: www.century-tywood.com
SIC: 3452 3469 2392   Washers, metal;
Stamping metal for the trade; Sheets,
fabric: made from purchased materials

(G-9233)
TOLEDO WOODWORKING INC
1246 Highland St (01746-1696)
PHONE.............................508 280-3354
Geovany Toledo, *Pr*
EMP: 9 **EST:** 2014
SALES (est): 22.93K **Privately Held**
SIC: 7299 2434   Home improvement and
renovation contractor agency; Wood
kitchen cabinets

(G-9234)
TOTAL RECOIL MAGNETICS INC
Also Called: Blue Hill Transformer
84 October Hill Rd Ste 6a (01746-1371)
PHONE.............................508 429-9600
EMP: 16 **EST:** 1995
SQ FT: 6,000
SALES (est): 2.16MM **Privately Held**
Web: www.totalrecoilmagnetics.com
SIC: 3612   Power transformers, electric

(G-9235)
TY-WOOD CORPORATION
79 Lowland St (01746-2076)
PHONE.............................508 429-4011
EMP: 30
SIC: 3444 3441   Sheet metalwork;
Fabricated structural metal

(G-9236)
UNION BIOMETRICA INC (PA)
84 October Hill Rd Ste 12 (01746-1371)
PHONE.............................508 893-3115
David Strack, *Pr*
Christopher Bogan, *COO*
EMP: 18 **EST:** 1995
SQ FT: 20,000
SALES (est): 3.55MM **Privately Held**
Web: www.unionbio.com
SIC: 3826   Analytical instruments

(G-9237)
UNIVERSAL WILDE INC
201 Summer St (01746-2258)
P.O. Box 9110 (02062-9110)
PHONE.............................508 429-5515
Evelyn Edmonds, *Pr*
EMP: 101
Web: www.dsguw.com
SIC: 2752   Offset printing
PA: Universal Wilde, Inc.
135 Will Dr Unit 2
Canton MA 02021

(G-9238)
WARD PROCESS INC
Also Called: American Acoustical Products
311 Hopping Brook Rd (01746-1456)
PHONE.............................508 429-1165
Russell S Moody, *Pr*
◆ **EMP:** 55 **EST:** 1963
SQ FT: 80,000
SALES (est): 17.04MM **Privately Held**
Web: www.aapusa.com

SIC: 3081 3296 3229 3086   Polyvinyl film
and sheet; Mineral wool insulation products
; Glass fibers, textile; Plastics foam products

(G-9239)
WARNER INSTRUMENTS
84 October Hill Rd Ste 10 (01746-1371)
PHONE.............................203 776-0664
EMP: 8 **EST:** 2016
SALES (est): 496.9K **Privately Held**
Web: www.warneronline.com
SIC: 3841   Surgical and medical instruments

Holyoke
Hampden County

(G-9240)
A-T SURGICAL MFG CO INC
115 Clemente St (01040-5644)
PHONE.............................413 532-4551
Eugene P Kirejczyk, *Pr*
Eugene P Kirejczyk, *Pr*
Cynthia F Kirejczyk, *
EMP: 7 **EST:** 1938
SQ FT: 10,000
SALES (est): 497.14K **Privately Held**
Web: www.atsmanufacture.com
SIC: 3842   Supports: abdominal, ankle, arch,
kneecap, etc.

(G-9241)
AT SURGICAL COMPANY
Also Called: Ats Manufacturing,
115 Clemente St (01040-5644)
PHONE.............................888 233-4069
Mark E Shoham, *Pr*
▼ **EMP:** 15 **EST:** 2008
SQ FT: 10,000
SALES (est): 845.09K **Privately Held**
Web: www.atsmanufacture.com
SIC: 3842   Braces, orthopedic

(G-9242)
BARCLAY FURNITURE
ASSOCIATES
532 Main St Ste 6 (01040-5598)
PHONE.............................413 536-8084
Michael Hynek, *Pr*
Ronald Hynek, *Treas*
EMP: 8 **EST:** 1952
SQ FT: 16,000
SALES (est): 874.33K **Privately Held**
SIC: 2512   Couches, sofas, and davenports:
upholstered on wood frames

(G-9243)
BAY STATE PLATING INC
18 N Bridge St (01040-5827)
P.O. Box 187 (01041-0187)
PHONE.............................413 533-6927
Timothy Roberts, *Pr*
EMP: 9 **EST:** 1954
SQ FT: 18,000
SALES (est): 1.04MM **Privately Held**
Web: www.rlhelectric.com
SIC: 3559 3471   Metal finishing equipment
for plating, etc.; Electroplating and plating

(G-9244)
BLENDCO SYSTEMS LLC
C.A.R. Products
630 Beaulieu St (01040-5439)
PHONE.............................800 537-7797
Robert Goldenberg, *Mgr*
EMP: 60
SALES (corp-wide): 5.31MM **Privately Held**
Web: www.duboischemicals.com

SIC: 2841 5013 5087 3714   Soap and other
detergents; Automotive supplies; Service
establishment equipment; Motor vehicle
parts and accessories
HQ: Blendco Systems, Llc
1 Pearl Buck Ct
Bristol PA 19007
215 785-3147

(G-9245)
C M S LANDSCAPING
CORPORATION
175 Suffolk St (01040-4152)
PHONE.............................413 533-3300
Robert Camron, *Pr*
EMP: 15 **EST:** 1976
SQ FT: 312
SALES (est): 976.82K **Privately Held**
Web: www.cmslandscaping.com
SIC: 0782 3494   Lawn care services;
Sprinkler systems, field

(G-9246)
CAR GOLD INC
630 Beaulieu St (01040-5439)
PHONE.............................800 537-7797
TOLL FREE: 800
▲ **EMP:** 25
SIC: 2841 5013 5087 3714   Soap and other
detergents; Automotive supplies; Service
establishment equipment; Motor vehicle
parts and accessories

(G-9247)
CITY MACHINE CORPORATION
155 N Canal St (01040-6246)
PHONE.............................413 538-9766
Allan Lukasik, *Pr*
Ovila Pimpare Junior, *VP*
Charles P Burns Iii, *VP*
Patricia Hamel, *Treas*
EMP: 19 **EST:** 1998
SQ FT: 12,200
SALES (est): 972.22K **Privately Held**
Web: www.citymachinecorp.com
SIC: 3599   Machine shop, jobbing and repair

(G-9248)
CONKLIN OFFICE SERVICES
INC (PA)
Also Called: Conklin Office Furniture
75 Appleton St (01040-6427)
PHONE.............................413 315-4924
Francis J Arnold, *Pr*
Rosemary Arnold, *
▲ **EMP:** 23 **EST:** 1981
SALES (est): 10.75MM
SALES (corp-wide): 10.75MM **Privately
Held**
Web: www.conklinoffice.com
SIC: 5712 2522 2541 7641   Office furniture;
Office furniture, except wood; Shelving,
office and store, wood; Reupholstery and
furniture repair

(G-9249)
CUBIT WIRE & CABLE CO INC
164 Race St Ste 100 (01040-5874)
PHONE.............................413 539-9892
EMP: 25
SIC: 3357   Nonferrous wiredrawing and
insulating

(G-9250)
D & S PLATING CO INC
102 Cabot St Ste 6 (01040-6074)
PHONE.............................413 533-7771
Steve M Dupuis, *Pr*
Debbie Dupuis, *VP*

EMP: 19 **EST:** 1984
SQ FT: 6,000
SALES (est): 1.04MM **Privately Held**
Web: www.dsplatingco.com
SIC: 3471   Electroplating of metals or
formed products

(G-9251)
DUPONT PACKAGING INC
68b Winter St # 4 (01040-6409)
PHONE.............................413 552-0048
William Dupont, *Pr*
Marie Helene-forest, *Sec*
EMP: 10 **EST:** 1969
SALES (est): 937.63K **Privately Held**
Web: www.dupontpkg.net
SIC: 3089   Plastics containers, except foam

(G-9252)
EAST BAKING COMPANY INC
104 Whiting Farms Rd (01040-2832)
PHONE.............................413 536-2300
Danny Serra, *CEO*
EMP: 200 **EST:** 2005
SQ FT: 32,000
SALES (est): 18.76MM **Privately Held**
Web: www.eastbaking.com
SIC: 5149 2099   Crackers, cookies, and
bakery products; Peanut butter

(G-9253)
ES SPORTS CORPORATION
47 Jackson St (01040-5512)
P.O. Box 771 (01041-0771)
PHONE.............................413 534-5634
TOLL FREE: 800
Eric Suher, *Pr*
Burton S Resnic, *
Frank Suher, *
▲ **EMP:** 70 **EST:** 1981
SQ FT: 120,000
SALES (est): 3.45MM **Privately Held**
Web: www.essports.com
SIC: 2396 2395   Screen printing on fabric
articles; Embroidery and art needlework

(G-9254)
EUREKA LAB BOOK INC
Also Called: Eureka Blank Book Co
110 Winter St (01040-6411)
P.O. Box 150 (01041-0150)
PHONE.............................413 534-5671
Paul S Hapgood, *Pr*
Ann N Hapgood, *VP*
EMP: 10 **EST:** 1890
SQ FT: 65,000
SALES (est): 1.36MM **Privately Held**
Web: www.eurekalabbook.com
SIC: 2678 2782   Notebooks: made from
purchased paper; Blankbooks

(G-9255)
EXPRESSIVE DESIGN GROUP
INC
49 Garfield St (01040-5407)
PHONE.............................413 315-6296
Robert P Milos, *Pr*
Alan Pearlman, *
John D Conforti, *
◆ **EMP:** 45 **EST:** 2003
SALES (est): 9.4MM **Privately Held**
Web: www.theedg.net
SIC: 2771 2679 5112 5113   Greeting cards;
Gift wrap and novelties, paper; Greeting
cards; Paper, wrapping or coarse, and
products

▲ = Import ▼ = Export
◆ = Import/Export

(G-9256)
GENERAL MACHINE INC
56 Jackson St (01040-5583)
PHONE..............................413 533-5744
Kenneth H Lubold, *Pr*
EMP: 7 **EST:** 1975
SQ FT: 5,500
SALES (est): 527.31K **Privately Held**
SIC: 3599 Machine shop, jobbing and repair

(G-9257)
GREGORY MANUFACTURING INC
Also Called: G M I
102 Cabot St Ste 2 (01040-6074)
PHONE..............................413 536-5432
William Gregory, *Pr*
William J Gregory, *
John W Gregory, *
▲ **EMP:** 70 **EST:** 1982
SQ FT: 50,000
SALES (est): 4.3MM **Privately Held**
SIC: 3841 3089 3081 Surgical and medical
instruments; Plastics processing; Packing
materials, plastics sheet

(G-9258)
HADLEY PRINTING COMPANY INC
58 N Canal St (01040-5880)
PHONE..............................413 536-8517
Christopher Desrosiers, *Pr*
Greg Desrosiers, *
Marc Desrosiers, *
EMP: 30 **EST:** 1944
SQ FT: 30,000
SALES (est): 4.79MM **Privately Held**
Web: www.hadleyprinting.com
SIC: 2752 2759 Offset printing; Letterpress
printing

(G-9259)
HAZEN PAPER COMPANY (PA)
Also Called: Hazen
240 S Water St (01040-5979)
P.O. Box 189 (01041-0189)
PHONE..............................413 538-8204
John H Hazen, *Pr*
John H Hazen, *Pr*
Robert M Sylvester, *
Robert Hazen, *
Peter Connor, *
▲ **EMP:** 195 **EST:** 1925
SQ FT: 200,000
SALES (est): 45.17MM
SALES (corp-wide): 45.17MM **Privately Held**
Web: www.hazen.com
SIC: 2672 3497 Coated paper, except
photographic, carbon, or abrasive; Foil,
laminated to paper or other materials

(G-9260)
HITCHCOCK PRESS INC
8 Hanover St (01040-5412)
P.O. Box 803 (01041-0803)
PHONE..............................413 538-8811
J Guy Gaulin, *Pr*
Geraldine Gaulin, *VP*
EMP: 8 **EST:** 1897
SQ FT: 11,000
SALES (est): 490.9K **Privately Held**
Web: www.hitchcockpress.com
SIC: 2752 2759 Offset printing; Letterpress
printing

(G-9261)
HOLYOKE MACHINE COMPANY
514 Main St (01040-5585)

P.O. Box 988 (01041-0988)
PHONE..............................413 534-5612
James Sagalyn, *Pr*
Raphael Sagalyn, *
Sean Parnell, *Prin*
Jose Cruz, *Prin*
Robert Leighton, *Prin*
▲ **EMP:** 40 **EST:** 1863
SQ FT: 48,000
SALES (est): 4.53MM **Privately Held**
Web: www.holyokemachine.com
SIC: 3554 3552 3599 Paper industries
machinery; Textile machinery; Custom
machinery

(G-9262)
INTERNATIONAL LASER SYSTEMS
Also Called: I L S
362 Race St (01040-5613)
PHONE..............................413 533-4372
EMP: 7 **EST:** 1996
SALES (est): 509.98K **Privately Held**
Web: www.myils.com
SIC: 2759 Engraving, nec

(G-9263)
IVEY INDUSTRIES
15 Main St (01040-5811)
PHONE..............................413 736-6464
Bryan Ivey, *Prin*
EMP: 7 **EST:** 2011
SALES (est): 167.37K **Privately Held**
Web: www.iveyind.com
SIC: 3999 Manufacturing industries, nec

(G-9264)
MANSIR PRINTING LLC
24 Shawmut Ave (01040-2324)
P.O. Box 471 (01041-0471)
PHONE..............................413 536-4250
Todd Collier, *Pt*
EMP: 19 **EST:** 2008
SQ FT: 52,000
SALES (est): 3.94MM **Privately Held**
Web: www.mansirprinting.com
SIC: 2752 Offset printing

(G-9265)
MARCUS COMPANY INC
Also Called: Marcus Printing Co
750 Main St (01040-5391)
PHONE..............................413 534-3303
Ben Marcus, *CEO*
Susan Goldsmith, *
EMP: 42 **EST:** 1930
SQ FT: 30,500
SALES (est): 5MM **Privately Held**
Web: www.marcusprinting.com
SIC: 2752 7334 2791 2789 Offset printing;
Photocopying and duplicating services;
Typesetting; Bookbinding and related work

(G-9266)
MAROX CORPORATION
373 Whitney Ave (01040-2855)
PHONE..............................413 536-1300
Manfred Rosenkranz, *CEO*
Barry H Rosenkranz, *Pr*
Brian M Rosenkranz, *Sec*
EMP: 11 **EST:** 1988
SQ FT: 48,000
SALES (est): 5.78MM
SALES (corp-wide): 1.05B **Privately Held**
Web: www.paragonmedical.com
SIC: 3599 Machine shop, jobbing and repair
HQ: Mw Industries, Inc.
2400 Farrell Rd
Houston TX 28277
800 875-3510

(G-9267)
MAYFIELD PLASTICS INC
75 Whiting Farms Rd (01040-2831)
PHONE..............................508 865-8150
Ronald G Cross, *Pr*
A Gordon Cross, *
Alexander W Samoiloff, *
Sandra Wondolowski, *
Jay Kumar, *Prin*
EMP: 43 **EST:** 1972
SALES (est): 10.42MM
SALES (corp-wide): 25.48MM **Privately Held**
Web: www.universalplastics.com
SIC: 3089 Injection molding of plastics
PA: Universal Plastics Corporation
75 Whiting Farms Rd
Holyoke MA 01040
413 592-4791

(G-9268)
MERIDIAN INDUSTRIAL GROUP LLC
529 S East St (01040-6005)
PHONE..............................413 538-9880
EMP: 23 **EST:** 2009
SALES (est): 3.69MM **Privately Held**
Web: www.meridianindustrialgroup.com
SIC: 3599 Machine shop, jobbing and repair

(G-9269)
NEW ENGLAND ETCHING CO INC
23 Spring St (01040-5794)
PHONE..............................413 532-9482
TOLL FREE: 800
Walter Foerster Junior, *Pr*
▼ **EMP:** 27 **EST:** 1931
SQ FT: 32,500
SALES (est): 2.7MM **Privately Held**
Web: www.newenglandetching.com
SIC: 3479 Etching and engraving

(G-9270)
NEW ENGLAND ULTIMATE FINISHING
709 Main St (01040-5337)
PHONE..............................413 532-7777
Robert A Beaupre, *Pr*
Dale Darosa, *
▲ **EMP:** 32 **EST:** 1979
SQ FT: 30,000
SALES (est): 4.64MM **Privately Held**
Web: www.nefinishing.com
SIC: 2675 2672 Die-cut paper and board;
Paper; coated and laminated, nec

(G-9271)
NORADE INC (DH)
Also Called: Edaron, Inc.
100 Appleton St (01040-6402)
PHONE..............................413 533-7159
Louis Moretti, *Pr*
Alice E Shevlin, *VP*
▲ **EMP:** 19 **EST:** 1974
SQ FT: 225,000
SALES (est): 32.93MM **Privately Held**
Web: us03545870.en.ec21.com
SIC: 3944 Puzzles
HQ: Buffalo Games, Llc
220 James E Casey Dr
Buffalo NY 14206
716 827-8393

(G-9272)
NTP/REPUBLIC CLEAR THRU CORP
Also Called: N T P Republic
475 Canal St (01040-6426)

P.O. Box 2448 (01041-2448)
PHONE..............................413 493-6800
James J Macarthy, *Pr*
James J Mccarthy, *Pr*
Joseph Feigen, *Treas*
▲ **EMP:** 22 **EST:** 1993
SQ FT: 45,000
SALES (est): 916.17K
SALES (corp-wide): 2.75MM **Privately Held**
Web: www.ntprepublic.com
SIC: 3089 Blister or bubble formed
packaging, plastics
PA: Walter Drake Incorporated
85 Sargeant St
Holyoke MA 01040
413 536-5463

(G-9273)
OLD SAN JUAN BAKERY INC
408 High St (01040-4961)
PHONE..............................413 534-5555
Alicia Rosario, *Pr*
Oscar Rosario, *Treas*
EMP: 10 **EST:** 1994
SALES (est): 935.05K **Privately Held**
Web: www.michaelcdonaldson.com
SIC: 2051 Bakery: wholesale or wholesale/
retail combined

(G-9274)
PACKAGE MACHINERY COMPANY INC
80 Commercial St (01040-4704)
PHONE..............................413 315-3801
EMP: 8 **EST:** 1996
SQ FT: 22,000
SALES (est): 1.79MM **Privately Held**
Web: www.packagemachinery.com
SIC: 3565 Packing and wrapping machinery

(G-9275)
R R LEDUC CORP
100 Bobala Rd (01040-9657)
PHONE..............................413 536-4329
Robert R Leduc, *Pr*
Robert R Leduc, *Pr*
Eric Leduc, *
Kerry Leduc, *
Kurt Leduc, *
EMP: 48 **EST:** 1967
SQ FT: 61,000
SALES (est): 9.99MM **Privately Held**
Web: www.rrleduc.com
SIC: 3444 Sheet metalwork

(G-9276)
RELIANCE ELECTRIC SVC CO INC
573 S Canal St (01040-5591)
PHONE..............................413 533-3557
Paul Snopek, *Pr*
EMP: 7 **EST:** 1992
SQ FT: 6,000
SALES (est): 490.47K **Privately Held**
Web: www.relianceelectricservice.com
SIC: 7694 5999 Electric motor repair;
Motors, electric

(G-9277)
RGB INDUSTRIES INC
11 Berkshire St (01040-5418)
PHONE..............................413 536-3100
Ryan L Geeleher, *Pr*
EMP: 7 **EST:** 2004
SALES (est): 140K **Privately Held**
SIC: 3999 Manufacturing industries, nec

(G-9278)
RUWAC INC
54 Winter St (01040-6409)
PHONE...............................413 532-4030
Wolfgang Schloesser, *Pr*
Eric Potorski, *CFO*
Shawn Houle, *Prin*
Kristen Mone, *Prin*
▲ EMP: 19 EST: 1984
SQ FT: 20,000
SALES (est): 5.15MM **Privately Held**
Web: www.ruwac.com
SIC: 3563 Vacuum (air extraction) systems, industrial

(G-9279)
S RALPH CROSS AND SONS INC
75 Whiting Farms Rd (01040-2831)
PHONE...............................508 865-8112
Ronald G Cross, *Pr*
A Gordon Cross, *
Stanley R Cross Junior, *VP*
Sandra E Wondolowski, *
EMP: 24 EST: 1946
SALES (est): 1.26MM **Privately Held**
Web: www.universalplastics.com
SIC: 3544 3543 Industrial molds; Industrial patterns

(G-9280)
SEALED AIR CORPORATION
Packaging Products Div
2030 Homestead Ave Lowr (01040-9765)
PHONE...............................413 534-0231
Dan Mcgonigle, *Brnch Mgr*
EMP: 113
SALES (corp-wide): 5.64B **Publicly Held**
Web: www.sealedair.com
SIC: 3086 5199 2671 Packaging and shipping materials, foamed plastics; Packaging materials; Paper; coated and laminated packaging
PA: Sealed Air Corporation
2415 Cascade Pointe Blvd
Charlotte NC 28208
980 221-3235

(G-9281)
SIGNATURE ENGRV SYSTEMS INC
120 Whiting Farms Rd (01040-2832)
PHONE...............................413 533-7500
Christopher A Parent, *Pr*
James Richmond, *
Eric Parent, *
▲ EMP: 40 EST: 1982
SQ FT: 60,000
SALES (est): 6.87MM **Privately Held**
Web: www.signature-engravers.com
SIC: 3555 Printing trades machinery

(G-9282)
SONOCO PRODUCTS COMPANY
200 S Water St (01040-5979)
PHONE...............................413 536-4546
David Schultz, *Mgr*
EMP: 94
SALES (corp-wide): 7.25B **Publicly Held**
Web: www.sonoco.com
SIC: 2631 2621 Paperboard mills; Paper mills
PA: Sonoco Products Company
1 N 2nd St
Hartsville SC 29550
843 383-7000

(G-9283)
TEBALDI ENTERPRISES INC
Also Called: NAPA Motor Parts
2 Cabot St (01040-6032)

PHONE...............................413 532-3261
Theodore Tebaldi, *Pr*
Lawrence Tebaldi, *Treas*
EMP: 15 EST: 1970
SQ FT: 13,000
SALES (est): 2.41MM **Privately Held**
Web: www.napaonline.com
SIC: 5531 3599 Automotive parts; Machine shop, jobbing and repair

(G-9284)
UNI-PAC INC
Also Called: UNI Pac
150 Middle Water St (01040-5588)
PHONE...............................413 534-5284
George N Leclair, *Pr*
George N Le Clair, *
▲ EMP: 60 EST: 1937
SQ FT: 78,000
SALES (est): 9.17MM **Privately Held**
Web: www.uni-pac.com
SIC: 2652 2657 Setup paperboard boxes; Folding paperboard boxes

(G-9285)
UNITED INNOVATIONS INC
120 Whiting Farms Rd Ste 2 (01040-2812)
PHONE...............................413 533-7500
Christopher A Parent, *Pr*
James Richmond, *Sec*
EMP: 10 EST: 1982
SQ FT: 50,000
SALES (est): 866.3K **Privately Held**
Web: www.united-innovations.com
SIC: 3829 Plotting instruments, drafting and map reading

(G-9286)
UNIVERSAL PLASTICS CORPORATION (PA)
Also Called: Universal Bath Systems
75 Whiting Farms Rd (01040-2831)
PHONE...............................413 592-4791
Joseph Peters, *CEO*
Jay Kumar, *
Sunil Kumar, *
EMP: 25 EST: 1965
SQ FT: 65,000
SALES (est): 25.48MM
SALES (corp-wide): 25.48MM **Privately Held**
Web: www.universalplastics.com
SIC: 3089 Thermoformed finished plastics products, nec

(G-9287)
UNIVERSITY PRODUCTS INC (PA)
517 Main St (01040-5514)
P.O. Box 101 (01041-0101)
PHONE...............................413 532-3372
▲ EMP: 99 EST: 1968
SALES (est): 14.26MM
SALES (corp-wide): 14.26MM **Privately Held**
Web: www.universityproducts.com
SIC: 2675 2782 Library cards, die-cut: from purchased materials; Library binders, looseleaf

(G-9288)
US TSUBAKI POWER TRANSM LLC
821 Main St (01040-5449)
PHONE...............................413 536-1576
Charles Monty, *Genl Mgr*
EMP: 250
SQ FT: 210,000
Web: www.ustsubaki.com

SIC: 3568 Power transmission equipment, nec
HQ: U.S. Tsubaki Power Transmission Llc
301 E Marquardt Dr
Wheeling IL 60090
847 459-9500

(G-9289)
VALLEY ETCHING ENGRV DSIGN INC
Also Called: Fdc Grafixx
120b Whiting Farms Rd (01040-2832)
PHONE...............................413 536-2256
Chris Parent, *Pr*
Lori Dorgan, *Genl Mgr*
EMP: 7 EST: 1935
SQ FT: 12,500
SALES (est): 989.13K
SALES (corp-wide): 96.33MM **Privately Held**
Web: www.valley-etching.com
SIC: 7336 2796 Graphic arts and related design; Platemaking services
PA: Newspapers Of New England, Inc.
1 Monitor Dr
Concord NH 03301
603 224-5301

(G-9290)
WALTER DRAKE INCORPORATED (PA)
85 Sargeant St (01040-5632)
P.O. Box 691 (01041-0691)
PHONE...............................413 536-5463
James J Mc Carthy, *Pr*
Joseph M Feigen, *VP*
EMP: 7 EST: 1959
SQ FT: 70,000
SALES (est): 2.75MM
SALES (corp-wide): 2.75MM **Privately Held**
Web: www.walterdrake.com
SIC: 3089 3081 2671 Blister or bubble formed packaging, plastics; Packing materials, plastics sheet; Paper; coated and laminated packaging

(G-9291)
WESTSIDE FINISHING CO INC
Also Called: Westside Finishing
15 Samosett St (01040-6112)
PHONE...............................413 533-4909
Brian Bell, *Pr*
Jeanne L Bell, *
EMP: 40 EST: 1965
SQ FT: 20,000
SALES (est): 6.26MM **Privately Held**
Web: www.wsfinish.com
SIC: 3479 Coating of metals and formed products

(G-9292)
XENOCS INC
4 Open Square Way Ste L101 (01040-6376)
PHONE...............................413 587-4000
Karsten Joensen, *CEO*
EMP: 12 EST: 2014
SALES (est): 1.94MM **Privately Held**
Web: www.xenocs.com
SIC: 3844 X-ray apparatus and tubes

Hopedale
Worcester County

(G-9293)
AEREO INC
2 Rosenfeld Dr Ste F (01747-2114)

PHONE...............................617 861-8287
EMP: 14 EST: 2010
SALES (est): 756.65K **Privately Held**
Web: www.aereo.com
SIC: 3577 Computer peripheral equipment, nec

(G-9294)
ALGONQUIN INDUSTRIES INC
2 Business Way (01747-1540)
PHONE...............................508 634-3733
EMP: 9
SALES (corp-wide): 12MM **Privately Held**
Web: www.algonquinindustries.com
SIC: 3599 Machine shop, jobbing and repair
PA: Algonquin Industries, Inc.
139 Farm St Ste 1
Bellingham MA 02019
508 966-4600

(G-9295)
COLCORD MACHINE CO INC
2 Rosenfeld Dr Ste G (01747-2114)
PHONE...............................508 634-8840
Robert Bob Colcord, *Pr*
Robert L Colcord, *Pr*
EMP: 10 EST: 1997
SQ FT: 4,000
SALES (est): 376.97K **Privately Held**
SIC: 3599 Machine shop, jobbing and repair

(G-9296)
DC BATES EQUIPMENT CO INC
10 Airport Rd (01747-1529)
P.O. Box 11 (01747-0011)
PHONE...............................508 473-0041
EMP: 23 EST: 1985
SALES (est): 4.39MM **Privately Held**
Web: www.dcbates.com
SIC: 3713 Truck and bus bodies

(G-9297)
FORT HILL SIGN PRODUCTS INC
3b Landing Ln (01747-1531)
PHONE...............................781 321-4320
Paula Dolan, *Clerk*
EMP: 9 EST: 1908
SALES (est): 856.38K **Privately Held**
Web: www.forthillsigns.com
SIC: 3479 3089 3083 3544 Engraving jewelry, silverware, or metal; Engraving of plastics; Laminated plastics plate and sheet ; Special dies and tools

(G-9298)
GREEN MOUNTAIN CHOCLAT CO INC (PA)
1 Rosenfeld Dr (01747-2110)
PHONE...............................508 473-9060
William Campbell, *Pr*
Lisa Campbell, *Sec*
▲ EMP: 8 EST: 1988
SQ FT: 8,000
SALES (est): 2.22MM **Privately Held**
Web: www.greenmountainchocolate.com
SIC: 2066 5947 Chocolate; Gift, novelty, and souvenir shop

(G-9299)
MILFORD MANUFACTURING SVCS LLC
4 Business Way (01747-1540)
PHONE...............................508 478-8544
Jason Price, *Managing Member*
▲ EMP: 37 EST: 1981
SQ FT: 110,000
SALES (est): 1.27MM **Privately Held**

SIC: 3672 7373 3577 3357 Printed circuit boards; Computer integrated systems design; Computer peripheral equipment, nec; Nonferrous wiredrawing and insulating

(G-9300)
PBD PRODUCTIONS LLC
3b Landing Ln (01747-1531)
PHONE..................508 482-9300
EMP: 10 EST: 2010
SALES (est): 948.32K Privately Held
Web: www.partnersbydesignllc.com
SIC: 3446 2541 Architectural metalwork; Cabinets, except refrigerated: show, display, etc.: wood

(G-9301)
REC MANUFACTURING CORP
Also Called: Plastech Molding Solutions
50 Mellen St (01747-1522)
P.O. Box 5959 (01746-5959)
PHONE..................508 634-7999
Robert E Chick Junior, Pr
Stephen M Chick, VP
▼ EMP: 20 EST: 1943
SQ FT: 50,000
SALES (est): 4.98MM Privately Held
Web: www.plastechmolding.com
SIC: 3089 Injection molding of plastics

(G-9302)
ROAR INDUSTRIES INC
2 Rosenfeld Dr Ste A (01747-2114)
PHONE..................508 429-5952
Guile Chip Wood Junior, Pr
EMP: 10 EST: 1983
SALES (est): 1.33MM Privately Held
Web: www.roarindinc.com
SIC: 3444 7692 Sheet metalwork; Welding repair

(G-9303)
ROSENFELD CONCRETE CORP (HQ)
75 Plain St (01747-2100)
P.O. Box 9187 (02114-9187)
PHONE..................508 473-7200
Jeanne-m Boylan, Pr
EMP: 45 EST: 1985
SQ FT: 2,400
SALES (est): 4.46MM
SALES (corp-wide): 100.01K Privately Held
Web: www.rosenfeldconcrete.com
SIC: 3273 1442 Ready-mixed concrete; Construction sand mining
PA: Boston Sand & Gravel Company Inc
100 N Washington St Fl 2
Boston MA 02114
617 227-9000

Hopkinton
Middlesex County

(G-9304)
A123 SYSTEMS LLC
10 Avenue E (01748-2211)
PHONE..................508 497-7200
Phil Mcray, Prin
EMP: 69
Web: www.a123systems.com
SIC: 3691 Storage batteries
HQ: A123 Systems Llc
27101 Cabaret Dr
Novi MI 48377
248 412-9249

(G-9305)
ACBEL (USA) POLYTECH INC
227 South St (01748-2208)
PHONE..................508 625-1768
Jesse Wang, Mgr
EMP: 7
Web: www.acbel.com.tw
SIC: 3572 3571 Computer tape drives and components; Electronic computers
HQ: Acbel (Usa) Polytech, Inc.
251 Dominion Dr Ste 111
Morrisville NC 27560
919 388-4316

(G-9306)
ADAPTIVE SURFACE TECH INC
Also Called: AST
106 South St # 2 (01748-2207)
PHONE..................617 360-7080
David Ward, CEO
Daniel Behr, CEO
EMP: 9 EST: 2014
SALES (est): 1.6MM Privately Held
Web: www.adaptivesurface.tech
SIC: 2899 Chemical preparations, nec

(G-9307)
ARTERIOCYTE MED SYSTEMS INC
Also Called: Isto Biologics
45 South St Ste 3c (01748-2254)
PHONE..................508 395-5998
Donald Brown, CEO
Ganfeng Wu, *
EMP: 102 EST: 2007
SQ FT: 8,000
SALES (est): 28.4MM
SALES (corp-wide): 28.4MM Privately Held
Web: www.istobiologics.com
SIC: 3841 3845 Medical instruments and equipment, blood and bone work; Ultrasonic scanning devices, medical
HQ: Isto Technologies Ii, Llc
45 South St Ste C
Hopkinton MA 01748
888 705-4786

(G-9308)
ATK SPACE SYSTEMS LLC
65 South St Ste 105 (01748-2234)
PHONE..................508 497-9457
EMP: 95
SQ FT: 15,000
Web: www.northropgrumman.com
SIC: 3812 Electronic detection systems (aeronautical)
HQ: Atk Space Systems Llc
6033 Bandini Blvd
Commerce CA 90040
323 722-0222

(G-9309)
BENCO DENTAL
63 South St (01748-2227)
PHONE..................508 435-3000
Chuck Cohen, Pr
EMP: 32 EST: 2005
SALES (est): 399.54K Privately Held
Web: www.hoytlegalllc.com
SIC: 3843 Dental equipment

(G-9310)
CALIPER LIFE SCIENCES INC (DH)
68 Elm St (01748-1668)
PHONE..................203 954-9442
▲ EMP: 200 EST: 1995
SQ FT: 137,000

SALES (est): 133.79MM
SALES (corp-wide): 3.31B Publicly Held
SIC: 3826 Analytical instruments
HQ: Revvity Holdings, Inc.
940 Winter St
Wellesley MA 02481

(G-9311)
CAMBRDGE RES INSTRMNTATION INC
Also Called: C R I
68 Elm St (01748-1602)
PHONE..................781 935-9099
George Abe, Pr
Theodore I Les, *
Peter Miller, *
EMP: 45 EST: 1985
SALES (est): 13.39MM
SALES (corp-wide): 3.31B Publicly Held
Web: www.cri-inc.com
SIC: 3827 8733 8731 Optical instruments and lenses; Scientific research agency; Commercial physical research
HQ: Caliper Life Sciences, Inc.
68 Elm St
Hopkinton MA 01748

(G-9312)
CAMBREX BIO SCIENCE
97 South St (01748-2204)
PHONE..................508 497-0700
EMP: 7 EST: 2019
SALES (est): 310.36K Privately Held
SIC: 2834 Pharmaceutical preparations

(G-9313)
CONTROL TECHNOLOGY CORPORATION (PA)
Also Called: C T C
25 South St (01748-2217)
PHONE..................508 435-9596
Kenneth Crater, Treas
Thomas Schermerhorn, *
F Steven Crater, *
Lenore Tracey, *
EMP: 25 EST: 1975
SQ FT: 15,000
SALES (est): 2.93MM
SALES (corp-wide): 2.93MM Privately Held
Web: www.controltechnologycorp.com
SIC: 3625 Electric controls and control accessories, industrial

(G-9314)
CTS VALPEY CORPORATION (HQ)
75 South St (01748-2204)
PHONE..................508 435-6831
Michael J Ferrantino Junior, Pr
Michael J Kroll, *
Walt Oliwa, *
EMP: 63 EST: 1931
SQ FT: 32,000
SALES (est): 17.29MM
SALES (corp-wide): 586.87MM Publicly Held
Web: www.ctscorp.com
SIC: 3825 3829 Frequency meters: electrical, mechanical, and electronic; Ultrasonic testing equipment
PA: Cts Corporation
4925 Indiana Ave
Lisle IL 60532
630 577-8800

(G-9315)
DIGILAB INC
35 Parkwood Dr (01748-1699)

PHONE..................508 305-2410
Joe Griffin, Pr
Sidney Braginsky, *
EMP: 54 EST: 2004
SALES (est): 6.57MM Privately Held
Web: www.cellularlifesciences.com
SIC: 3821 Laboratory apparatus and furniture

(G-9316)
ELECTRONIC FLUOROCARBONS LLC (PA)
239 South St (01748-2249)
P.O. Box 759 (01748-0759)
PHONE..................508 435-7700
Pavel Perlov, Managing Member
◆ EMP: 48 EST: 2003
SQ FT: 20,000
SALES (est): 25.25MM
SALES (corp-wide): 25.25MM Privately Held
Web: www.efcgases.com
SIC: 2869 Fluorinated hydrocarbon gases

(G-9317)
EMC CORPORATION
117 South St (01748-2206)
PHONE..................508 435-0369
EMP: 10
Web: www.emc.com
SIC: 3572 Computer storage devices
HQ: Emc Corporation
176 South St
Hopkinton MA 01748
508 435-1000

(G-9318)
EMC CORPORATION
80 South St (01748-2205)
PHONE..................800 445-2588
EMP: 10
Web: www.emc.com
SIC: 3572 Computer storage devices
HQ: Emc Corporation
176 South St
Hopkinton MA 01748
508 435-1000

(G-9319)
EMC CORPORATION
171 South St (01748-2222)
PHONE..................508 346-2900
EMP: 50
Web: www.dellemc.com
SIC: 3572 Computer storage devices
HQ: Emc Corporation
176 South St
Hopkinton MA 01748
508 435-1000

(G-9320)
EMC CORPORATION
45 South St (01748-2254)
PHONE..................508 435-2581
EMP: 65
Web: www.emc.com
SIC: 3572 Computer storage devices
HQ: Emc Corporation
176 South St
Hopkinton MA 01748
508 435-1000

(G-9321)
EMC CORPORATION
228 South St Mailstop (01748-2233)
PHONE..................508 249-5883
EMP: 100
Web: www.emc.com

G
E
O
G
R
A
P
H
I
C

SIC: 3572 Computer storage devices
HQ: Emc Corporation
176 South St
Hopkinton MA 01748
508 435-1000

(G-9322)
EMC CORPORATION (HQ)
Also Called: Dell EMC
176 South St (01748-2230)
PHONE..............................508 435-1000
Michael S Dell, *Pr*
David I Goulden, *
Tyler W Johnson, *
Richard J Rothberg, *
Janet B Wright, *
▼ **EMP: 500 EST:** 1979
SQ FT: 1,681,000
SALES (est): 32.44B **Publicly Held**
Web: www.emc.com
SIC: 3572 7372 7371 3577 Computer
storage devices; Prepackaged software;
Custom computer programming services;
Computer peripheral equipment, nec
PA: Dell Technologies Inc.
1 Dell Way
Round Rock TX 78682

(G-9323)
EMC GLOBAL HOLDINGS COMPANY
176 South St (01748-2230)
PHONE..............................508 544-2852
Tyler Wise Johnson Ii, *Trst*
EMP: 51 EST: 2002
SALES (est): 1.93MM **Publicly Held**
SIC: 3572 Computer storage devices
PA: Dell Technologies Inc.
1 Dell Way
Round Rock TX 78682

(G-9324)
EMC INTERNATIONAL HOLDINGS INC
Also Called: Emc2
176 South St (01748-2230)
P.O. Box 9103 (01748-9103)
PHONE..............................508 435-1000
Joseph Tucci, *Pr*
W Paul Fitzgerald, *Sec*
Paul T Dacier, *Dir*
William J Tauber, *Treas*
EMP: 60000 EST: 1986
SQ FT: 205,000
SALES (est): 413.5MM **Publicly Held**
Web: www.emc.com
SIC: 3572 3577 Computer storage devices;
Computer peripheral equipment, nec
HQ: Emc Corporation
176 South St
Hopkinton MA 01748
508 435-1000

(G-9325)
FISHMAN CORPORATION
192 South St (01748-2209)
PHONE..............................508 435-2115
Scott W Beebe, *Pr*
Scott Beebe, *Pr*
Virginia Beebe, *Stockholder*
John J Duffett, *CFO*
▲ **EMP: 17 EST:** 1958
SQ FT: 12,000
SALES (est): 3.8MM **Privately Held**
Web: www.fishmancorp.com
SIC: 3586 Measuring and dispensing pumps

(G-9326)
FLIMP MEDIA
2 Hayden Rowe St Ste 2 (01748-1946)
PHONE..............................508 435-5220
EMP: 53 EST: 2004
SALES (est): 3.74MM **Privately Held**
Web: www.flimp.net
SIC: 7372 Business oriented computer
software

(G-9327)
HOPKINTON MEWS SALES OFFICE
1 Freedom Way (01748-2890)
PHONE..............................508 625-1267
EMP: 8 EST: 2017
SALES (est): 71.09K **Privately Held**
SIC: 2711 Newspapers: publishing only, not
printed on site

(G-9328)
HUTCHINSON AROSPC & INDUST INC
Also Called: Barry Controls
82 South St (01748-2205)
PHONE..............................508 417-7000
Cedric Duclos, *CEO*
EMP: 200
SALES (corp-wide): 7.96B **Publicly Held**
Web: www.hutchinsonai.com
SIC: 3545 Machine tool accessories
HQ: Hutchinson Aerospace & Industry, Inc.
82 South St
Hopkinton MA 01748
508 417-7000

(G-9329)
HUTCHINSON AROSPC & INDUST INC
Vlier
82 South St (01748-2205)
PHONE..............................508 417-7000
Tom Foley, *Genl Mgr*
EMP: 91
SALES (corp-wide): 7.96B **Publicly Held**
Web: www.hutchinsonai.com
SIC: 3699 Electrical equipment and
supplies, nec
HQ: Hutchinson Aerospace & Industry, Inc.
82 South St
Hopkinton MA 01748
508 417-7000

(G-9330)
HUTCHINSON AROSPC & INDUST INC (DH)
82 South St (01748-2205)
PHONE..............................508 417-7000
Julie Holland, *CEO*
Robert Anderson, *DEFENSE & INDUSTRY**
Shano Cristilli, *
Keli Viereck, *
▲ **EMP: 262 EST:** 1943
SALES (est): 103.5MM
SALES (corp-wide): 7.96B **Publicly Held**
Web: www.hutchinsonai.com
SIC: 3714 3061 3724 Shock absorbers,
motor vehicle; Mechanical rubber goods;
Aircraft engines and engine parts
HQ: Hutchinson Corporation
460 Fuller Ave Ne
Grand Rapids MI 49503
616 459-4541

(G-9331)
ILLINOIS TOOL WORKS INC
ITW Electronics Assembly Eqp
35 Parkwood Dr Ste 10 (01748-1727)
PHONE..............................508 520-0083
Charlene Mcneely, *Brnch Mgr*
EMP: 50
SALES (corp-wide): 15.93B **Publicly Held**
Web: www.itw.com
SIC: 3565 3569 Packing and wrapping
machinery; Assembly machines, non-
metalworking
PA: Illinois Tool Works Inc.
155 Harlem Ave
Glenview IL 60025
847 724-7500

(G-9332)
ISILON SYSTEMS LLC
176 South St (01748-2209)
PHONE..............................206 315-7500
EMP: 212
SIC: 3674 Semiconductors and related
devices
HQ: Isilon Systems Llc
505 1st Ave S
Seattle WA 98104
206 315-7500

(G-9333)
IWAVE SOFTWARE LLC
176 South St (01748-2209)
PHONE..............................508 435-7771
EMP: 25 EST: 2003
SALES (est): 7.52MM **Publicly Held**
Web: ma-hopkinton.pacifica.org.au
SIC: 3572 Computer storage devices
HQ: Emc Corporation
176 South St
Hopkinton MA 01748
508 435-1000

(G-9334)
KAMEL PERIPHERALS INC (PA)
88a Elm St Ste 7 (01748-1675)
PHONE..............................508 435-7771
Michael Le Vangie, *Pr*
▲ **EMP: 29 EST:** 1993
SQ FT: 10,000
SALES (est): 2.46MM **Privately Held**
Web: www.kamel-peripherals.com
SIC: 3577 Computer peripheral equipment,
nec

(G-9335)
KENNETH CROSBY CO INC
103 South St (01748-2206)
PHONE..............................508 497-0048
Susan Costa, *Prin*
EMP: 17 EST: 2015
SALES (est): 2.65MM **Privately Held**
Web: www.kennethcrosby.com
SIC: 3625 Industrial electrical relays and
switches

(G-9336)
LYKAN BIOSCIENCE HOLDINGS LLC
Also Called: Roslynct US
97 South St (01748-2204)
PHONE..............................774 341-4200
Anthony Rotunno, *CEO*
Patrick Lucy, *Pr*
Matt Treon, *General Vice President*
Jenifer Wheat, *CCO*
EMP: 18 EST: 2019
SALES (est): 9.75MM **Privately Held**
Web: www.lykanbio.com
SIC: 2834 Pharmaceutical preparations

(G-9337)
NORTHROP GRUMMAN SYSTEMS CORP
Also Called: Aerontics Systems Arspc Strctr
65 South St Ste 105 (01748-2234)
PHONE..............................508 589-6291
Terry Faxon, *Brnch Mgr*
EMP: 15
Web: www.northropgrumman.com
SIC: 3812 Search and navigation equipment
HQ: Northrop Grumman Systems
Corporation
2980 Fairview Park Dr
Falls Church VA 22042
703 280-2900

(G-9338)
OCEAN ORTHOPEDIC SERVICES INC (PA)
45 Oakhurst Rd (01748-2721)
PHONE..............................401 725-5240
John A Murphy, *Pr*
EMP: 11 EST: 1989
SALES (est): 1.02MM **Privately Held**
SIC: 3842 Orthopedic appliances

(G-9339)
PHOSPHOREX LLC
35 Parkwood Dr Ste 210 (01748-1729)
PHONE..............................508 435-9100
Jarlath Keating, *CEO*
Bin Wu, *
EMP: 22 EST: 2005
SALES (est): 4MM **Privately Held**
Web: www.phosphorex.com
SIC: 2834 Pharmaceutical preparations

(G-9340)
PRECISION DIGITAL CORPORATION
233 South St (01748-2208)
PHONE..............................508 655-7300
Jeffrey L Peters, *Pr*
▲ **EMP: 37 EST:** 1969
SQ FT: 9,000
SALES (est): 7.37MM **Privately Held**
Web: www.predig.com
SIC: 3823 Digital displays of process
variables

(G-9341)
PRINT WORKS INC
25 South St Ste 2b (01748-2217)
P.O. Box 157 (01748-0157)
PHONE..............................508 589-4626
Jack O'leary, *Pr*
EMP: 8 EST: 1986
SQ FT: 6,000
SALES (est): 805.36K **Privately Held**
Web: www.onlineprintworks.com
SIC: 2752 Offset printing

(G-9342)
PWB
225 Wood St (01748-1013)
PHONE..............................508 497-3930
John Gray, *Prin*
EMP: 10 EST: 2016
SALES (est): 498.35K **Privately Held**
Web: www.pwbenefits.com
SIC: 3612 Transformers, except electric

(G-9343)
REVVITY INC
Also Called: Perkinelmer
68 Elm St Bldg 2 (01748-1602)
PHONE..............................508 435-9500
EMP: 13
SALES (corp-wide): 3.31B **Publicly Held**
Web: www.perkinelmer.com
SIC: 3826 Analytical instruments
PA: Revvity, Inc.
940 Winter St
Waltham MA 02451
781 663-6900

(G-9344)
SOLECT ENERGY
DEVELOPMENT LLC (PA)
Also Called: Solect
89 Hayden Rowe St Ste E (01748-2507)
PHONE...............................508 598-3511
EMP: 9 EST: 2010
SALES (est): 9.6MM Privately Held
Web: www.solect.com
SIC: 3674 Photovoltaic devices, solid state

(G-9345)
STRYKER CORPORATION
Also Called: Stryker Biotech
35 South St Ste C (01748-2218)
PHONE...............................508 416-5200
Dave Ranker, Brnch Mgr
EMP: 10
SALES (corp-wide): 18.45B Publicly Held
Web: www.stryker.com
SIC: 3841 Medical instruments and
equipment, blood and bone work
PA: Stryker Corporation
2825 Airview Blvd
Portage MI 49002
269 385-2600

(G-9346)
THUREON INC
37 Glen Rd (01748-2344)
PHONE...............................774 249-8110
Darren Smith, Prin
EMP: 12
SALES (est): 654.62K Privately Held
SIC: 3499 Fabricated metal products, nec

(G-9347)
XENOGEN CORPORATION (DH)
68 Elm St (01748-1602)
PHONE...............................508 435-9500
EMP: 79 EST: 1996
SQ FT: 36,000
SALES (est): 28.71MM
SALES (corp-wide): 3.31B Publicly Held
SIC: 3826 Analytical instruments
HQ: Caliper Life Sciences, Inc.
68 Elm St
Hopkinton MA 01748

Hubbardston
Worcester County

(G-9348)
GAS PATH SOLUTIONS LLC
81 Old Boston Tpke (01452-1232)
PHONE...............................978 229-5460
Brian Nason, Pr
Michael Busack, VP
EMP: 12 EST: 2019
SALES (est): 9.7MM Privately Held
Web: www.gaspathsolutions.com
SIC: 3444 Ducts, sheet metal

(G-9349)
WIDE ANGLE MARKETING INC
27d Old Colony Rd (01452-1127)
PHONE...............................978 928-5400
Kraig Kaijala, Pr
EMP: 14 EST: 2003
SALES (est): 714.62K Privately Held
Web: www.wideanglemarketing.com
SIC: 2431 Millwork

Hudson
Middlesex County

(G-9350)
2L INC
4 Kane Industrial Dr (01749-2906)
P.O. Box 105 (01749-0105)
PHONE...............................978 567-8867
Lance Nelson, Pr
EMP: 10 EST: 1998
SALES (est): 1.63MM Privately Held
Web: www.2linc.com
SIC: 3441 3555 Building components,
structural steel; Printing trades machinery

(G-9351)
ADAPTIVE WRELESS
SOLUTIONS LLC
577 Main St Ste 300 (01749-3096)
PHONE...............................978 875-6000
Bruce Thompson, CEO
Philip Hunt, Pr
EMP: 36 EST: 2009
SALES (est): 4.74MM
SALES (corp-wide): 82.05K Privately Held
SIC: 3829 Measuring and controlling
devices, nec
HQ: Schneider Electric Systems Usa, Inc.
70 Mechanic St
Foxboro MA 02035
508 543-8750

(G-9352)
ADVANCED CAM
MANUFACTURING LLC
526 Main St (01749-2909)
PHONE...............................978 562-2825
Stephen Woodworth, Mgr
EMP: 17 EST: 2010
SALES (est): 505.6K Privately Held
SIC: 3999 Manufacturing industries, nec

(G-9353)
ALTERNATE FINISHING INC
15 Kane Industrial Dr (01749-2905)
PHONE...............................978 567-9205
Robert Peterson, Pr
Marie Mungillo, VP
EMP: 7 EST: 2002
SQ FT: 10,000
SALES (est): 911.08K Privately Held
Web: www.alternatefinishing.com
SIC: 3471 Electroplating of metals or
formed products

(G-9354)
ANVER CORPORATION
Also Called: Anver
36 Parmenter Rd (01749-3214)
PHONE...............................978 568-0221
Franck M Vernooy, Pr
Anton J Vernooy, *
Stephen Zaino, *
◆ EMP: 62 EST: 1968
SQ FT: 54,000
SALES (est): 11.26MM Privately Held
Web: www.anver.com
SIC: 3599 5084 3563 Custom machinery;
Industrial machinery and equipment; Air
and gas compressors

(G-9355)
AUCIELLO IRON WORKS INC
560 Main St (01749-2969)
PHONE...............................978 568-8382
Michael A Auciello, Pr
Anthony R Auciello, *
Ralph J Auciello, *
EMP: 25 EST: 1932
SQ FT: 17,000
SALES (est): 3.81MM Privately Held
Web: www.aucielloironworks.com
SIC: 3444 3441 Sheet metalwork; Building
components, structural steel

(G-9356)
BLANK INDUSTRIES LLC
17 Brent Dr (01749-2903)
PHONE...............................855 887-3123
Andrew Blank, CEO
EMP: 30 EST: 2015
SALES (est): 4.11MM Privately Held
Web: www.blankind.com
SIC: 2499 2899 5169 Mulch, wood and bark
; Correction fluid; Salts, industrial

(G-9357)
BORG DESIGN INC
19 Brent Dr (01749-2903)
PHONE...............................978 562-1559
Karl S Borg, Pr
Sharon Borg, Clerk
K Andrew Borg, Ex VP
Brandon Borg, VP
EMP: 15 EST: 1981
SQ FT: 22,000
SALES (est): 3.79MM Privately Held
Web: www.borgdesign.com
SIC: 3599 Machine shop, jobbing and repair

(G-9358)
BOYD COATINGS RESEARCH
CO INC
51 Parmenter Rd (01749-3213)
PHONE...............................978 562-7561
EMP: 100
SIC: 3479 Coating of metals and formed
products

(G-9359)
BUTLER HOME PRODUCTS
LLC (HQ)
Also Called: Cleaner Home Living
2 Cabot Rd Ste 1 (01749-2942)
PHONE...............................508 597-8000
Robert Michelson, CEO
Harris Footer, Pr
Michael Silverman, VP
▲ EMP: 10 EST: 1947
SALES (est): 211.03MM
SALES (corp-wide): 642.04MM Privately
Held
Web: www.cleanerhomeliving.com
SIC: 3991 2392 Brooms; Mops, floor and
dust
PA: Bradshaw International, Inc.
9409 Buffalo Ave
Rancho Cucamonga CA 91730
909 476-3884

(G-9360)
COWBELL TECHNOLOGIES INC
59 Apsley St Unit 11d (01749-1543)
PHONE...............................508 733-1778
EMP: 17
Web: www.morecowbelltech.com
SIC: 5731 7629 3663 Consumer electronic
equipment, nec; Telecommunication
equipment repair (except telephones);
Studio equipment, radio and television
broadcasting
PA: Cowbell Technologies, Inc.
150 E Main St Unit 960
Westborough MA 01581

(G-9361)
D & R PRODUCTS CO INC
455 River Rd (01749-2626)
P.O. Box 718 (01749-0718)
PHONE...............................978 562-4137
Cece Z Newman, Ch Bd
Richard B Newman, *
EMP: 50 EST: 1938
SQ FT: 26,500
SALES (est): 9.73MM Privately Held
Web: www.drproducts.com
SIC: 3545 Precision tools, machinists'

(G-9362)
EDGETECH INSTRUMENTS INC
399 River Rd (01749-2669)
PHONE...............................508 263-5900
Himanshu Patel, Pr
Stephanie Wild, Sec
John Allcott, COO
EMP: 15 EST: 2014
SQ FT: 2,000
SALES (est): 2.74MM Privately Held
Web: www.edgetechinstruments.com
SIC: 3823 Humidity instruments, industrial
process type

(G-9363)
ENERGY RELEASE LLC
14 Brent Dr (01749-2904)
PHONE...............................978 466-9700
EMP: 8 EST: 2008
SALES (est): 192.24K Privately Held
SIC: 3465 Body parts, automobile: stamped
metal

(G-9364)
ENTWISTLE COMPANY LLC (PA)
6 Bigelow St (01749-2697)
PHONE...............................508 481-4000
Wade Knudson, Pr
Fred Astrauskas, *
▲ EMP: 95 EST: 1951
SQ FT: 134,000
SALES (est): 46.02MM
SALES (corp-wide): 46.02MM Privately
Held
Web: www.entwistleco.com
SIC: 3489 3599 3812 3537 Ordnance and
accessories, nec; Catapults; Navigational
systems and instruments; Aircraft loading
hoists

(G-9365)
ENTWISTLE TRUST
6 Bigelow St (01749-2638)
PHONE...............................508 481-4000
Herbert Corkin, CEO
EMP: 160 EST: 2001
SQ FT: 160,000
SALES (est): 12.8MM Privately Held
Web: www.entwistleco.com
SIC: 3549 Wiredrawing and fabricating
machinery and equipment, ex. die

(G-9366)
FABCO MFG INC
Also Called: F M I
14 Bonazzoli Ave (01749-2850)
P.O. Box 340 (01749-0340)
PHONE...............................978 568-8519
Vincent S Natale, Pr
EMP: 35 EST: 1972
SQ FT: 10,000
SALES (est): 4.26MM Privately Held
Web: www.fabcomfg.com
SIC: 3444 Sheet metal specialties, not
stamped

(G-9367)
FLINTEC INC
18 Kane Industrial Dr (01749-2906)
PHONE....................978 562-4548
Jeff Robidoux, *Prin*
Harry Lockery, *
David Weeks, *Dir*
Dale Estey, *Sec*
▲ **EMP:** 30 **EST:** 1988
SQ FT: 13,000
SALES (est): 9.59MM
SALES (corp-wide): 2.58B **Privately Held**
Web: www.flintec.com
SIC: 3679 8731 3825 Transducers, electrical
; Commercial physical research;
Instruments to measure electricity
HQ: Flintec Group Ab
Badhusgatan 12, 2tr
VAsterAs

(G-9368)
FLUOROLITE PLASTICS LLC
555 Main St (01749-2912)
PHONE....................508 788-1200
Ayesha Nawaz, *Pr*
EMP: 7 **EST:** 2019
SALES (est): 1.16MM **Privately Held**
Web: www.fluorolite.com
SIC: 5063 3082 5162 Lighting fittings and
accessories; Unsupported plastics profile
shapes; Plastics materials and basic shapes

(G-9369)
FOURSTAR CONNECTIONS INC
One Robert Bonazzoli Ave (01749)
PHONE....................978 568-9800
EMP: 55 **EST:** 1987
SALES (est): 7.4MM **Privately Held**
Web: www.fourstarconnections.com
SIC: 3679 Harness assemblies, for
electronic use: wire or cable

(G-9370)
GOOGLEPLEX TECHNOLOGIES LLC
43 Broad St Ste A300 (01749-2256)
PHONE....................978 897-0880
Jim C Dowrey, *Managing Member*
EMP: 7 **EST:** 2003
SQ FT: 4,500
SALES (est): 967.99K **Privately Held**
Web: www.googleplextech.com
SIC: 3674 Semiconductors and related
devices

(G-9371)
GRAND IMAGE INC
Also Called: Grand Image
560 Main St Ste 3 (01749-2919)
PHONE....................888 973-2622
Eli Luria, *Pr*
Leah Luria, *VP*
▲ **EMP:** 31 **EST:** 1996
SQ FT: 20,000
SALES (est): 4.46MM **Privately Held**
Web: www.grandimageinc.com
SIC: 3993 Signs and advertising specialties

(G-9372)
HEARTLAND WATER TECHNOLOGY INC
43 Broad St Ste B403 (01749-2556)
PHONE....................603 490-9203
Christopher Beaufait, *Pr*
Casey Cammann, *Prin*
EMP: 16 **EST:** 2016
SALES (est): 3.96MM **Privately Held**
Web: www.heartlandtech.com

SIC: 3589 Water treatment equipment,
industrial

(G-9373)
HUDSON LOCK LLC (PA)
Also Called: Hudson Lock/ESP
81 Apsley St (01749-1593)
PHONE....................978 562-3481
Robert J Sylvia, *Pr*
Gina Melendez, *
▲ **EMP:** 92 **EST:** 1963
SQ FT: 216,000
SALES (est): 24.34MM
SALES (corp-wide): 24.34MM **Privately Held**
Web: www.hudsonlock.com
SIC: 5072 3429 Hardware; Locks or lock
sets

(G-9374)
HUDSON POLY BAG INC
578 Main St (01749-3099)
PHONE....................978 562-7566
TOLL FREE: 800
William J Renwick, *Pr*
Richard D Renwick, *VP*
▼ **EMP:** 14 **EST:** 1965
SQ FT: 17,120
SALES (est): 2.44MM **Privately Held**
Web: www.hudsonpoly.com
SIC: 3081 3949 Polyethylene film; Bags,
rosin

(G-9375)
HYPERTRONICS CORPORATION
Also Called: Hypertac
16 Brent Dr (01749-2978)
PHONE....................978 568-0451
▲ **EMP:** 135
SIC: 3678 Electronic connectors

(G-9376)
INTEGRATECH SOLUTIONS CORP
34b Tower St (01749-1721)
PHONE....................978 567-1000
EMP: 60
SIC: 3399 3672 Metal fasteners; Printed
circuit boards

(G-9377)
INTEL MASSACHUSETTS INC
75 Reed Rd (01749-2895)
P.O. Box 1000 (97123-1000)
PHONE....................978 553-4000
Arvind Sodhani, *Pr*
▲ **EMP:** 900 **EST:** 1997
SALES (est): 105.97MM
SALES (corp-wide): 63.05B **Publicly Held**
Web: www.intel.com
SIC: 3577 Computer peripheral equipment,
nec .
PA: Intel Corporation
2200 Mission College Blvd
Santa Clara CA 95054
408 765-8080

(G-9378)
INTEL NETWORK SYSTEMS INC (HQ)
Also Called: Intel
77 Reed Rd (01749-2809)
PHONE....................978 553-4000
Craig Barrett, *Ch*
EMP: 160 **EST:** 1985
SQ FT: 117,139
SALES (est): 473.88MM
SALES (corp-wide): 54.23B **Publicly Held**
Web: www.intel.com

SIC: 3577 7373 Computer peripheral
equipment, nec; Systems integration
services
PA: Intel Corporation
2200 Mission College Blvd
Santa Clara CA 95054
408 765-8080

(G-9379)
J W MACHINING INC
17 Bonazzoli Ave (01749-2850)
PHONE....................978 562-5611
Charles Bourgeois, *Pr*
Darlene Bourgeois, *Sec*
EMP: 16 **EST:** 1959
SQ FT: 10,000
SALES (est): 409.93K **Privately Held**
Web: www.jwmachining.com
SIC: 3599 Machine shop, jobbing and repair

(G-9380)
KATAHDIN INDUSTRIES INC (PA)
51 Parmenter Rd (01749-3213)
PHONE....................781 329-1420
Tim Cabot, *Pr*
EMP: 45 **EST:** 1964
SQ FT: 30,000
SALES (est): 47.68MM
SALES (corp-wide): 47.68MM **Privately Held**
Web: www.katahdin-inc.com
SIC: 2851 3471 2899 Paints and allied
products; Plating and polishing; Chemical
preparations, nec

(G-9381)
KOROLATH OF NEW ENGLAND INC
Also Called: Korolath
498 River Rd (01749-2621)
PHONE....................978 562-7366
William J Cosgrove, *VP*
EMP: 12
SQ FT: 9,000
SALES (corp-wide): 13.48MM **Privately Held**
SIC: 3089 Injection molding of plastics
HQ: Korolath Of New England, Inc.
310 Salem St
Woburn MA 01801
781 933-6004

(G-9382)
LAKE BOONE ICE CO LLC
710 Main St (01749-3040)
PHONE....................508 755-3099
EMP: 7 **EST:** 2013
SALES (est): 186.64K **Privately Held**
Web: www.lakebooneice.com
SIC: 2097 Manufactured ice

(G-9383)
LAPOINTE HUDSON BROACH CO INC
11 Brent Dr (01749-2903)
PHONE....................978 562-7943
Gary Ezor, *Pr*
▼ **EMP:** 33 **EST:** 1972
SQ FT: 18,040
SALES (est): 2.45MM **Privately Held**
Web: www.pioneerbroach.com
SIC: 3545 Broaches (machine tool
accessories)

(G-9384)
LCI PAPER COMPANY
399 River Rd Ste 3 (01749-2669)
PHONE....................508 281-5088
Karen Armstrong, *Pr*

▲ **EMP:** 17 **EST:** 1995
SALES (est): 2.29MM **Privately Held**
Web: www.lcipaper.com
SIC: 5113 2678 Industrial and personal
service paper; Stationery products

(G-9385)
LINCOLN TOOL & MACHINE CORP
43 Parmenter Rd (01749-3213)
P.O. Box 443 (01749-0443)
PHONE....................508 485-2940
Scott Ferrechia, *VP*
EMP: 30 **EST:** 1980
SQ FT: 34,000
SALES (est): 4.86MM **Privately Held**
Web: www.lincolntool.com
SIC: 3599 Machine shop, jobbing and repair

(G-9386)
LLOYDS WOODWORKING INC
86 River St (01749-2010)
P.O. Box 281 (01749-0281)
PHONE....................978 562-9007
Lloyd P Dubois, *Pr*
Doris E Dubois, *Treas*
EMP: 8 **EST:** 1969
SALES (est): 983.25K **Privately Held**
Web: www.lloydswoodworkinginc.com
SIC: 2431 Millwork

(G-9387)
MACH MACHINE INC
569 Main St (01749-3035)
PHONE....................978 274-5700
EMP: 11 **EST:** 2011
SQ FT: 2,500
SALES (est): 1.45MM **Privately Held**
Web: www.machmachine.com
SIC: 3599 Machine shop, jobbing and repair

(G-9388)
MACHINING FOR ELECTRONICS INC
4 Bigelow St (01749-2638)
P.O. Box 149 (01749-0149)
PHONE....................978 562-7554
Metrophane Zayka, *Pr*
Nicholas Zayka, *Sec*
EMP: 7 **EST:** 1960
SQ FT: 10,000
SALES (est): 493.43K **Privately Held**
Web: www.machiningforelectronics.com
SIC: 3599 Machine shop, jobbing and repair

(G-9389)
MASSACHUSETTS CONTR SUPS INC
Also Called: MCS
71 Parmenter Rd (01749-3213)
PHONE....................978 413-2578
EMP: 9 **EST:** 2016
SALES (est): 818.95K **Privately Held**
Web:
www.massachusettscontractorsupplies.com
SIC: 3272 5039 Concrete products, nec;
Construction materials, nec

(G-9390)
MIDDLESEX RESEARCH MFG CO INC
27 Apsley St (01749-1594)
P.O. Box 444 (01749-0444)
PHONE....................978 562-3697
Douglas Russell, *CEO*
Sara Coldwell, *Sec*
▲ **EMP:** 20 **EST:** 1945
SQ FT: 100,000
SALES (est): 2.29MM **Privately Held**

Web: www.middlesexresearch.com
SIC: **2295** 2891 2261 Coated fabrics, not
rubberized; Laminating compounds;
Flocking of cotton broadwoven fabrics

(G-9391)
MILLIBAR INC
1 Bonazzoli Ave Ste 2 (01749-2849)
PHONE..................................508 488-9870
Brian C Ferri, *Prin*
▲ **EMP: 12 EST:** 2011
SALES (est): 2.37MM **Privately Held**
Web: www.millibar.com
SIC: **3563** Vacuum (air extraction) systems,
industrial

(G-9392)
MOTION TECHNOLOGY INC
1 Bonazzoli Ave (01749-2849)
PHONE..................................508 460-9800
Bill Mcmahon, *Pr*
William Mcmahon, *Pr*
Diane Darling, *
▲ **EMP: 30 EST:** 1990
SALES (est): 4.87MM **Privately Held**
Web: www.mtiproducts.com
SIC: **3589** Commercial cooking and
foodwarming equipment

(G-9393)
MRM SELLER ENTITY LLC
577 Main St Ste 270 (01749-3056)
PHONE..................................978 568-1330
EMP: 13 EST: 2005
SQ FT: 6,500
SALES (est): 2.11MM **Privately Held**
Web: www.centerlinetech-usa.com
SIC: **3599** Machine shop, jobbing and repair

(G-9394)
**MSP DIGITAL MARKETING
MASS INC (HQ)**
Also Called: Tecdocdigital Solutions
399 River Rd (01749-2669)
PHONE..................................978 567-6000
Charles Stine, *Pt*
Roy Grossman, *Pt*
Jonathan Fogel, *
EMP: 24 EST: 1986
SQ FT: 30,000
SALES (est): 6.4MM **Privately Held**
SIC: **8742** 2752 Marketing consulting
services; Commercial printing, lithographic
PA: Msp Digital Marketing Llc
23 Vitti St Ste 201
New Canaan CT 06840

(G-9395)
**NETCO EXTRUDED PLASTICS
INC**
Also Called: New England Tape Co
30 Tower St (01749-1721)
PHONE..................................978 562-3485
Knut Schmiedeknecht, *Pr*
Francis W Murphy, *Sec*
EMP: 20 EST: 1937
SQ FT: 48,000
SALES (est): 9.16MM
SALES (corp-wide): 424.06K **Privately
Held**
Web: www.netcoplastics.com
SIC: **3089** Injection molding of plastics
HQ: Regumed Regulative Medizintechnik
Gmbh
Robert-Koch-Str. 1a
Planegg BY 82152
898546101

(G-9396)
**NORTHPOINT PRINTING SVCS
INC**
18 Bonazzoli Ave (01749-2850)
PHONE..................................781 895-1900
John Allekian, *Pr*
EMP: 12 EST: 2003
SALES (est): 2.39MM **Privately Held**
Web: www.northpointprinting.com
SIC: **2752** Offset printing

(G-9397)
O K ENGINEERING INC
14 Main St Ste 10 (01749-2178)
P.O. Box 788 (01749-0788)
PHONE..................................978 562-1010
James T O'keefe, *Pr*
Dan O' Keefe, *Treas*
EMP: 7 EST: 1968
SALES (est): 603.56K **Privately Held**
Web: www.okengineer.com
SIC: **3559** Electronic component making
machinery

(G-9398)
PATRIOT COATING INC
17 Kane Industrial Dr Ste 2 (01749-2921)
PHONE..................................978 567-9006
Roy Rector, *CEO*
EMP: 7 EST: 2005
SALES (est): 738.46K **Privately Held**
Web: www.patriotcoating.com
SIC: **3479** Painting, coating, and hot dipping

(G-9399)
PATTEN MACHINE INC
299 Central St (01749-1334)
PHONE..................................978 562-9847
Wayne E Cavanagh, *CEO*
EMP: 11 EST: 1977
SQ FT: 5,000
SALES (est): 469.38K **Privately Held**
SIC: **3599** 3069 Machine and other job shop
work; Printers' rolls and blankets: rubber or
rubberized fabric

(G-9400)
**PLASTIC MOLDING MFG INC
(PA)**
34 Tower St (01749-1721)
PHONE..................................978 567-1000
George E Danis, *Prin*
EMP: 24 EST: 2009
SQ FT: 50,000
SALES (est): 49.37MM **Privately Held**
Web: www.plasticmoldingmfg.com
SIC: **3089** Injection molded finished plastics
products, nec

(G-9401)
POLYTEC INC
1 Cabot Rd Ste 102 (01749-2792)
PHONE..................................508 417-1040
Josephine Kamei, *Pr*
EMP: 9
SALES (corp-wide): 89.15MM **Privately
Held**
Web: www.polytec.com
SIC: **3699** 5063 Laser systems and
equipment; Electrical apparatus and
equipment
HQ: Polytec, Inc.
16400 Bake Pkwy Ste 200
Irvine CA 92618
949 943-3033

(G-9402)
**POLYTECH FLTRATION
SYSTEMS INC**

100 Forest Ave (01749-2826)
PHONE..................................978 562-7700
Erik J Andresen, *Pr*
George W Tuttle, *Clerk*
▲ **EMP: 10 EST:** 1990
SALES (est): 994.85K **Privately Held**
Web: www.polytech-filtration.com
SIC: **3569** 5084 Filters, general line:
industrial; Industrial machinery and
equipment

(G-9403)
PRECISION COATING CO INC
Also Called: Boyd Coatings
51 Parmenter Rd (01749-3213)
PHONE..................................978 562-7561
EMP: 50
SALES (corp-wide): 47.68MM **Privately
Held**
Web: www.precisioncoating.com
SIC: **3479** Coating of metals and formed
products
HQ: Precision Coating Co., Inc.
51 Parmenter Rd
Hudson MA 01749
781 329-1420

(G-9404)
**PRECISION COATING CO INC
(HQ)**
51 Parmenter Rd (01749-3213)
PHONE..................................781 329-1420
Robert A Deangelis, *Pr*
Ernest K Anderson Junior, *General Vice
President*
EMP: 40 EST: 1956
SALES (est): 26.71MM
SALES (corp-wide): 47.68MM **Privately
Held**
Web: www.precisioncoating.com
SIC: **3479** 5131 Coating of metals and
formed products; Tape, textile
PA: Katahdin Industries, Inc.
51 Parmenter Rd
Hudson MA 01749
781 329-1420

(G-9405)
**PROVERIS SCIENTIFIC CORP
(PA)**
2 Cabot Rd Ste 5 (01749-2941)
PHONE..................................508 460-8822
EMP: 24 EST: 1995
SQ FT: 7,300
SALES (est): 4.96MM **Privately Held**
Web: www.proveris.com
SIC: **3826** Analytical instruments

(G-9406)
RES-TECH CORPORATION (HQ)
Also Called: Restech Plastic Molding
34 Tower St (01749-1721)
PHONE..................................978 567-1000
George Danis, *Pr*
▲ **EMP: 22 EST:** 1976
SQ FT: 20,000
SALES (est): 49.37MM **Privately Held**
Web: www.plasticmoldingmfg.com
SIC: **3089** 2821 Injection molding of plastics
; Molding compounds, plastics
PA: Plastic Molding Mfg., Inc.
34 Tower St
Hudson MA 01749

(G-9407)
**RESTECH PLASTIC MOLDING
LLC (DH)**
Also Called: Plastic Moulding Manufacturing
34 Tower St (01749-1721)

PHONE..................................978 567-1000
George Danis, *CEO*
EMP: 7 EST: 2012
SALES (est): 14.21MM **Privately Held**
Web: www.restechplastics.com
SIC: **3089** Molding primary plastics
HQ: Res-Tech Corporation
34 Tower St
Hudson MA 01749
978 567-1000

(G-9408)
RGM METALS INC
5 Parmenter Rd (01749-3213)
PHONE..................................978 562-9773
Richard G Mercadante, *Pr*
Karen Mercadante, *Treas*
EMP: 7 EST: 2005
SALES (est): 804.14K **Privately Held**
SIC: **3444** Siding, sheet metal

(G-9409)
SALIGA MACHINE CO INC
10 Bonazzoli Ave (01749-2862)
PHONE..................................978 562-7959
Michael P Saliga, *Pr*
Donald F Saliga, *
Patrick Saliga, *
EMP: 40 EST: 1958
SQ FT: 10,000
SALES (est): 5.04MM **Privately Held**
Web: www.saligamachine.com
SIC: **3599** Machine shop, jobbing and repair

(G-9410)
SCHENCK USA CORP
Also Called: Test Devices By Schenck
571 Main St (01749-3058)
PHONE..................................978 562-6017
David Woodford, *Pr*
EMP: 27
SALES (corp-wide): 4.48B **Privately Held**
Web: www.schenck-usa.com
SIC: **8734** 3829 Testing laboratories;
Fatigue testing machines, industrial:
mechanical
HQ: Schenck Usa Corp.
535 Acorn St
Deer Park NY 11729
631 242-4010

(G-9411)
SCOTIA WOODWORKING
571 Main St (01749-3058)
PHONE..................................978 212-5379
EMP: 8 EST: 2010
SALES (est): 190.18K **Privately Held**
SIC: **2431** Millwork

(G-9412)
**SENKO ADVANCED
COMPONENTS INC (HQ)**
Also Called: Senko America
2 Cabot Rd Ste 103 (01749-2942)
PHONE..................................508 481-9999
Ryosuke Okura, *Pr*
Masahiro Osumi, *
Kazuyoshi Takano, *
▲ **EMP: 26 EST:** 1997
SALES (est): 60.51MM **Privately Held**
Web: www.senko.com
SIC: **3357** Nonferrous wiredrawing and
insulating
PA: Senko Advance Co., Ltd.
2-5-23, Nakagawara
Yokkaichi MIE 510-0

(G-9413)
SMITHS INTRCNNECT AMERICAS INC
16 Brent Dr (01749-2904)
PHONE..............................978 568-0451
Dom Matos, *Pr*
EMP: 135
SALES (corp-wide): 3.83B **Privately Held**
Web: www.smithsinterconnect.com
SIC: 3679 Microwave components
HQ: Smiths Interconnect Americas, Inc.
2001 Ne 46th St
Kansas City MO 64116
913 342-5544

(G-9414)
SP MACHINE INC
Also Called: Tessier Machine Company
526 Main St (01749-2909)
PHONE..............................978 562-2019
Stephen Woodworth, *Pr*
EMP: 20 **EST:** 1979
SQ FT: 5,000
SALES (est): 2.4MM **Privately Held**
Web: www.tessiermachine.com
SIC: 3469 3599 Machine parts, stamped or pressed metal; Machine and other job shop work

(G-9415)
STATIC SOLUTIONS INC (PA)
399 River Rd Ste C1 (01749-2669)
PHONE..............................978 310-7251
▲ **EMP:** 10 **EST:** 1997
SALES (est): 2.43MM **Privately Held**
Web: www.staticsolutions.com
SIC: 3822 3635 Static pressure regulators; Household vacuum cleaners

(G-9416)
STOKES WOODWORKING CO INC (PA)
Also Called: Albert K Stokes
12 Bonazzoli Ave (01749-2849)
PHONE..............................508 481-0414
Albert K Stokes, *Pr*
EMP: 7 **EST:** 1986
SALES (est): 813.31K **Privately Held**
Web: www.stokeswoodworking.com
SIC: 2431 2434 Millwork; Wood kitchen cabinets

(G-9417)
TEST DEVICES INC
571 Main St Ste 2 (01749-3059)
PHONE..............................978 562-6017
EMP: 27
Web: www.testdevices.com
SIC: 3829 8734 Fatigue testing machines, industrial; Testing laboratories

(G-9418)
THE SHARP TOOL CO INC
7 Bonazzoli Ave (01749-2849)
PHONE..............................978 568-9292
Paul J Morette, *Pr*
Leslie Thurmond Morette, *
Paul Michael Morette, *
▲ **EMP:** 28 **EST:** 1968
SQ FT: 12,000
SALES (est): 6.47MM **Privately Held**
Web: www.sharptool.com
SIC: 2819 7699 Carbides; Tool repair services

(G-9419)
THE TYLER CO INC
Also Called: Clark Solutions
10 Brent Dr (01749-2904)
PHONE..............................978 568-3400
Donald A Tyler, *Pr*
◆ **EMP:** 22 **EST:** 1977
SQ FT: 10,000
SALES (est): 4.48MM **Privately Held**
Web: www.clarksol.com
SIC: 5084 3561 Instruments and control equipment; Pumps and pumping equipment

(G-9420)
THERMALOGIC CORPORATION
22 Kane Industrial Dr (01749-2922)
PHONE..............................800 343-4492
John Du Bois Ph.d., *Ch Bd*
Louis Grein, *
EMP: 26 **EST:** 1971
SQ FT: 22,000
SALES (est): 4.71MM **Privately Held**
Web: www.thermalogic.com
SIC: 3829 Temperature sensors, except industrial process and aircraft

(G-9421)
TSI LIQUIDATION INC
8 Kane Industrial Dr (01749-2906)
PHONE..............................978 567-9033
Michael Carrol, *Pr*
Gilbert Wilcox, *
Nathaniel Beale, *
EMP: 25 **EST:** 1988
SALES (est): 2.19MM **Privately Held**
Web: www.telemedsystems.com
SIC: 3841 3845 Surgical and medical instruments; Electromedical equipment

(G-9422)
UNITED STRETCH DESIGN CORP
Also Called: Artcraft
11 Bonazzoli Ave (01749-2849)
PHONE..............................978 562-7781
Manuel P Chaves, *Pr*
Eva Chaves, *
▲ **EMP:** 40 **EST:** 1982
SQ FT: 50,000
SALES (est): 4.99MM **Privately Held**
Web: www.usdcorp.com
SIC: 2241 Elastic narrow fabrics, woven or braided

(G-9423)
USPACK INC
14 Brent Dr (01749-2904)
PHONE..............................978 562-8522
Svet Lana, *Pr*
Svetlana Aptekman, *
EMP: 20 **EST:** 2004
SALES (est): 1.55MM **Privately Held**
Web: www.uspack.net
SIC: 3559 Automotive related machinery

(G-9424)
VISION GVERNMENT SOLUTIONS INC
1 Cabot Rd Ste 100 (01749-2792)
PHONE..............................800 628-1013
Michael Oner, *CEO*
James Rich, *
EMP: 132 **EST:** 2011
SALES (est): 18.42MM **Privately Held**
Web: www.vgsi.com
SIC: 7389 7372 Auction, appraisal, and exchange services; Prepackaged software

(G-9425)
VULCAN INDUSTRIES INC
4 Cabot Rd (01749-2779)
P.O. Box 166 (01749-0166)
PHONE..............................978 562-0003
John H Bandzul, *Pr*
Scott E Bandzul, *Pr*
EMP: 38 **EST:** 1985
SALES (est): 4.47MM **Privately Held**
Web: www.vulcanindustry.com
SIC: 1761 3444 Sheet metal work, nec; Sheet metalwork

(G-9426)
XPONENT GLOBAL INC
Also Called: Netco Extruded Plastics
30 Tower St (01749-1721)
PHONE..............................978 562-3485
Christopher Sullivan, *Pr*
EMP: 23 **EST:** 2016
SALES (est): 2.97MM **Privately Held**
Web: www.xponentglobal.com
SIC: 3089 Extruded finished plastics products, nec

Hull
Plymouth County

(G-9427)
SARRO COHASSET INCORPORATED
Also Called: Red Lion Inn Resort
30 Stoney Beach Rd (02045-3339)
PHONE..............................781 383-1704
Michael Hayes, *Pr*
EMP: 100 **EST:** 1800
SALES (est): 4.51MM **Privately Held**
SIC: 7011 5812 5813 2051 Inns; Eating places; Drinking places; Bread, cake, and related products

Hyannis
Barnstable County

(G-9428)
ABCO TOOL & DIE INC
11 Thornton Dr (02601-1814)
P.O. Box 458 (02601-0458)
PHONE..............................508 771-3225
David B Bourque, *Pr*
EMP: 21 **EST:** 1972
SQ FT: 11,000
SALES (est): 499.37K **Privately Held**
Web: www.abcomolds.com
SIC: 3544 Special dies and tools

(G-9429)
CAPE COD AGGREGATES CORP (PA)
1550 Phinneys Ln (02601)
P.O. Box 517 (02630-0517)
PHONE..............................508 775-3716
Paul Lorusso, *CEO*
Samuel A Lorusso, *Pr*
Antonio J Lorusso Junior, *VP*
Laura L Lorusso, *VP*
Sam Lorusso Junior, *CFO*
EMP: 22 **EST:** 1981
SQ FT: 1,500
SALES (est): 15.61MM
SALES (corp-wide): 15.61MM **Privately Held**
Web: www.capecodagg.com
SIC: 5032 1442 Brick, stone, and related material; Construction sand mining

(G-9430)
CAPE COD POTATO CHIP COMPANY INC
Also Called: Cape Cod
100 Breeds Hill Rd (02601-1886)
P.O. Box 32368 (28232-2368)
PHONE..............................888 881-2447
▼ **EMP:** 141
Web: www.capecodchips.com
SIC: 2096 Potato chips and similar snacks

(G-9431)
CLASSIC KITCHEN DESIGN INC
Also Called: Classic Kitchens & Interiors
127 Airport Rd (02601-1856)
PHONE..............................508 775-3075
EMP: 12 **EST:** 1980
SALES (est): 1.27MM **Privately Held**
Web: www.ckdcapecod.com
SIC: 2434 Wood kitchen cabinets

(G-9432)
CONCORD ELECTRIC SUPPLY LTD
Also Called: Concord Electric Supply
1336 Phinneys Ln (02601-1890)
PHONE..............................774 552-2185
Anthony Bottino, *Brnch Mgr*
EMP: 710
SALES (corp-wide): 719.67K **Privately Held**
SIC: 5063 3699 Electrical supplies, nec; Electrical equipment and supplies, nec
HQ: Concord Electric Supply Limited
2701 Boston Rd Ste 100
Wilbraham MA 01095 .
413 682-0018

(G-9433)
CUSTOM COATINGS
104 Enterprise Rd (02601-2215)
PHONE..............................508 771-8830
Chris Vangelder, *Prin*
EMP: 7 **EST:** 2014
SALES (est): 147.45K **Privately Held**
Web: www.capecodcoatings.com
SIC: 3479 Metal coating and allied services

(G-9434)
DRIVE-O-RAMA INC (PA)
Also Called: Holiday Hill Miniature Golf
270 Communication Way Unit 6 (02601-1883)
PHONE..............................508 771-8100
Philip Baroni, *Pr*
John Pratt, *Ex VP*
▲ **EMP:** 8 **EST:** 1958
SQ FT: 30,000
SALES (est): 12.52MM
SALES (corp-wide): 12.52MM **Privately Held**
SIC: 5712 2511 5947 7999 Unfinished furniture; Wood household furniture; Gift shop; Miniature golf course operation

(G-9435)
EASTWIND COMMUNICATIONS INC
75 Perseverance Way (02601-1816)
PHONE..............................508 862-8600
Anthony Agostinelli, *Pr*
Joseph Norton, *Dir*
EMP: 16 **EST:** 2005
SALES (est): 952.68K **Privately Held**
Web: www.eastwindcom.com
SIC: 3674 Integrated circuits, semiconductor networks, etc.

(G-9436)
EJ JAXTIMER BUILDER INC
48 Rosary Ln (02601-2071)
PHONE..............................508 778-4911
Ernest J Jaxtimer, *Pr*
Ernest John Jaxtimer, *Pr*

EMP: 44 **EST:** 1980
SALES (est): 9.35MM **Privately Held**
Web: www.jaxtimer.com
SIC: 1521 2431   New construction, single-family houses; Millwork

(G-9437)
GATCO INC
Also Called: Folio Associates
297 North St Ste 212 (02601-5133)
PHONE..........................508 815-4910
Paul Rooker, *Pr*
EMP: 11 **EST:** 1961
SALES (est): 391.14K **Privately Held**
Web: www.foliomed.com
SIC: 2741   Directories, nec: publishing only, not printed on site

(G-9438)
HERRING INC
223 Barnstable Rd (02601-2929)
PHONE..........................401 837-3111
Karen Evers, *Prin*
EMP: 8 **EST:** 2016
SALES (est): 240.82K **Privately Held**
SIC: 2752   Commercial printing, lithographic

(G-9439)
INSTANT OFFSET PRESS INC
Also Called: Sunderland Printing
115 Enterprise Rd (02601-2212)
PHONE..........................508 790-1100
Marc Sunderland, *Pr*
Priscilla Sunderland, *Clerk*
Marc Sunderland Presteras, *Prin*
EMP: 10 **EST:** 1984
SQ FT: 6,000
SALES (est): 860.72K **Privately Held**
Web: www.sunderlandprinting.com
SIC: 2752 2759   Offset printing; Commercial printing, nec

(G-9440)
LOCAL MEDIA GROUP INC
Cape Cod Times
319 Main St (02601-4038)
PHONE..........................508 775-1200
Peter Myere, *Mgr*
EMP: 275
SALES (corp-wide): 2.95B **Publicly Held**
Web: www.gannett.com
SIC: 2711   Newspapers, publishing and printing
HQ: Local Media Group, Inc.
90 Crystal Run Rd Ste 310
Middletown NY 10941
845 341-1100

(G-9441)
MINUTEMAN PRESS
223 Barnstable Rd (02601-2929)
PHONE..........................508 778-0220
EMP: 9 **EST:** 2011
SALES (est): 118.34K **Privately Held**
Web: www.minutemanpress.com
SIC: 2752   Commercial printing, lithographic

(G-9442)
ML CUSTOM WOOD WORK INC
105 Ferndoc St Unit Gf (02601-2065)
PHONE..........................508 360-2137
Cezar Lanca, *Pr*
EMP: 9 **EST:** 2016
SALES (est): 567.3K **Privately Held**
Web: www.mlcustomwork.com
SIC: 2431   Millwork

(G-9443)
OTTAWAY NEWSPAPERS
319 Main St (02601-4038)
PHONE..........................508 775-1200
Patrick Purcell, *Prin*
EMP: 20 **EST:** 2010
SALES (est): 146.95K **Privately Held**
SIC: 2711   Newspapers, publishing and printing

(G-9444)
PAIN DAVIGNON II INC
Also Called: Pain Davignon
15 Hinckley Rd Unit C (02601-1948)
PHONE..........................508 771-9771
Toma Stamenkovic, *Pr*
Branislav Stamenkovich, *
EMP: 30 **EST:** 1992
SQ FT: 8,000
SALES (est): 4.23MM **Privately Held**
Web: www.paindavignon.com
SIC: 2051   Bakery: wholesale or wholesale/retail combined

(G-9445)
R F SHEET METAL AND MECH INC
58 Homeport Dr (02601-3605)
P.O. Box 138 (02672-0138)
PHONE..........................508 367-0533
Ryan Fletcher, *Prin*
EMP: 8 **EST:** 2017
SALES (est): 452.73K **Privately Held**
SIC: 3444   Sheet metalwork

(G-9446)
RICCIARDI MARBLE & GRANITE INC
174 Airport Rd (02601-1804)
PHONE..........................508 790-2734
Brian Ricciardi, *Owner*
▲ **EMP:** 9 **EST:** 2001
SALES (est): 950K **Privately Held**
Web: www.ricciardimarble.com
SIC: 3281   Granite, cut and shaped

(G-9447)
ROBERT E GLIDDEN
Also Called: Awning Systems
30 Perseverance Way Ste 3 (02601-8112)
PHONE..........................508 775-6812
Robert E Glidden, *Owner*
Robert Glidden, *Owner*
EMP: 9 **EST:** 1990
SALES (est): 726.46K **Privately Held**
Web: www.awningsystems.net
SIC: 3089   Awnings, fiberglass and plastics combination

(G-9448)
RUSSO WOODWORKING INC
80 Pine Grove Avenue (02601-2525)
PHONE..........................508 428-1772
John Russo, *Brnch Mgr*
EMP: 21
SALES (corp-wide): 190.99K **Privately Held**
SIC: 2431   Millwork
PA: Russo Woodworking Inc.
162 Cinderella Ter
Marstons Mills MA 02648
908 351-2200

(G-9449)
SAVANT SYSTEMS INC (PA)
Also Called: GE Lighting
45 Perseverance Way (02601-1812)
PHONE..........................508 683-2500
Robert Madonna, *CEO*

Tynisha Crews, *Prin*
EMP: 33 **EST:** 2020
SALES (est): 399.47MM
SALES (corp-wide): 399.47MM **Privately Held**
Web: www.savant.com
SIC: 3651   Audio electronic systems

(G-9450)
SENCORP INC
400 Kidds Hill Rd (02601-1850)
PHONE..........................508 771-9400
▲ **EMP:** 150
Web: www.sencorpwhite.com
SIC: 3089 3565   Plastics processing; Packaging machinery

(G-9451)
SENCORPWHITE INC (HQ)
Also Called: Sencorpwhite
400 Kidds Hill Rd (02601-1850)
PHONE..........................508 771-9400
Brian J Urban, *Pr*
Bernard Speckhart, *
Gregory B Meikle, *
◆ **EMP:** 124 **EST:** 2005
SQ FT: 155,000
SALES (est): 49.8MM
SALES (corp-wide): 376.52MM **Privately Held**
Web: www.sencorpwhite.com
SIC: 7373 3572   Systems integration services; Computer auxiliary storage units
PA: Connell Limited Partnership
1 International Pl Fl 31
Boston MA 02110
617 737-2700

(G-9452)
SENCORPWHITE HOLDINGS LLC
400 Kidds Hill Rd (02601-1850)
PHONE..........................508 771-9400
Chris Lingamfelter, *Pr*
EMP: 16 **EST:** 2015
SALES (est): 230.03K **Privately Held**
Web: www.sencorpwhite.com
SIC: 3999   Manufacturing industries, nec

(G-9453)
THREADHEAD INC
Also Called: Advanced Embroidery
38 Plant Rd (02601-1916)
PHONE..........................508 778-6516
Damon E Collins, *Pr*
EMP: 13 **EST:** 1989
SALES (est): 567.32K **Privately Held**
Web: www.advancedembroidery.biz
SIC: 2395   Embroidery products, except Schiffli machine

(G-9454)
TOBY LEARY FINE WDWKG INC
135 Barnstable Rd Ste A (02601-2928)
PHONE..........................508 957-2281
Tober Leary, *Pr*
EMP: 10 **EST:** 2004
SQ FT: 12,000
SALES (est): 491.66K **Privately Held**
Web: www.tobyleary.com
SIC: 2431   Millwork

(G-9455)
VIOLA ASSOCIATES INC
110 Rosary Ln Ste A (02601-2076)
PHONE..........................508 771-3457
John T Viola Junior, *Pr*
EMP: 17 **EST:** 2002
SALES (est): 893.01K **Privately Held**
Web: www.violaassociates.com

SIC: 3432   Lawn hose nozzles and sprinklers

Hyde Park
Suffolk County

(G-9456)
B & J SHEET METAL INC
232 Turtle Pond Pkwy (02136-1222)
PHONE..........................617 590-2295
Robert Gentile, *Prin*
EMP: 8 **EST:** 2013
SALES (est): 466.47K **Privately Held**
Web: www.bandjsheetmetal.com
SIC: 3444   Sheet metalwork

(G-9457)
BOSTON BAGEL INC
101 Sprague St Ste 3 (02136-2385)
PHONE..........................617 364-6900
Bob Boschetto, *Pr*
EMP: 10 **EST:** 1973
SQ FT: 18,000
SALES (est): 469.09K **Privately Held**
Web: www.bostonbaking.com
SIC: 2051   Bagels, fresh or frozen

(G-9458)
BULLETIN NEWSPAPERS INC (PA)
Also Called: West Rxbury / Rslndale Bulltin
695 Truman Hwy Ste 99 (02136-3552)
PHONE..........................617 361-8400
Paul Di Monica, *Pr*
Dennis Cawley, *VP*
EMP: 12 **EST:** 1992
SQ FT: 1,100
SALES (est): 2.47MM **Privately Held**
Web: bulletinnewspapers.weebly.com
SIC: 2711   Newspapers, publishing and printing

(G-9459)
DIANE L IVEY
Also Called: Lady Dye Yarns
1203 River St (02136-2964)
PHONE..........................617 763-9736
Diane L Ivey, *Owner*
EMP: 7 **EST:** 2016
SALES (est): 311.59K **Privately Held**
Web: www.ladydyeyarns.com
SIC: 2269   Dyeing: raw stock, yarn, and narrow fabrics

(G-9460)
FEENEYS FENCE INC
Also Called: Feeney's Welding and Fence Co.
120 Business St Ste 5 (02136-1612)
PHONE..........................617 364-1407
Edward J Feeney Junior, *Pr*
Steven V Furbush, *VP*
EMP: 8 **EST:** 1982
SQ FT: 2,000
SALES (est): 471.89K **Privately Held**
Web: www.feeneysweldingandfence.com
SIC: 7692 1799   Welding repair; Fence construction

(G-9461)
GEBELEIN GROUP INC
Also Called: Orleans Packing
1715 Hyde Park Ave (02136-2457)
PHONE..........................617 361-6611
George Gebelein, *Pr*
◆ **EMP:** 13 **EST:** 1947
SQ FT: 10,000
SALES (est): 3.71MM **Privately Held**
Web: www.orleanspacking.com

SIC: 2033　Fruits and fruit products, in cans, jars, etc.

(G-9462)
MCCREA CAPITAL ADVISORS INC (PA)
Also Called: McCrea's Candies
202 Neponset Valley Pkwy (02136-2410)
PHONE...........................617 276-3388
Jason Mccrea, *Pr*
Catherine Michmerhuizen, *Prin*
EMP: 8 EST: 2010
SALES (est): 1.89MM
SALES (corp-wide): 1.89MM **Privately Held**
Web: www.mccreascandies.com
SIC: 2064　Candy and other confectionery products

(G-9463)
MINUTEMAN PRESS
Also Called: Minuteman Press
1279 Hyde Park Ave (02136-2703)
PHONE...........................617 361-7400
Kamalu L Macphilips, *Prin*
EMP: 8 EST: 2008
SALES (est): 241.16K **Privately Held**
Web: www.minutemanpress.com
SIC: 2752　Commercial printing, lithographic

(G-9464)
MODERN SHOE COMPANY LLC
101 Sprague St Ste 1 (02136-2172)
PHONE...........................617 333-7470
▲ **EMP: 16 EST:** 2005
SQ FT: 14,000
SALES (est): 432.88K **Privately Held**
SIC: 3144 5139　Women's footwear, except athletic; Footwear

(G-9465)
NEW ENGLAND FOUNDATION CO INC (PA)
1 Westinghouse Plz Ste 27 (02136-2075)
PHONE...........................617 361-9750
Patrick A O'neill, *Pr*
Diedra O'neill, *VP*
EMP: 75 EST: 1913
SQ FT: 3,000
SALES (est): 8.75MM
SALES (corp-wide): 8.75MM **Privately Held**
Web: www.nefco.com
SIC: 1771 3448 1794 1781　Foundation and footing contractor; Prefabricated metal buildings and components; Excavation work ; Water well drilling

(G-9466)
ONE MIGHTY MILL LLC
200 Meadow Rd # 115 (02136-2365)
PHONE...........................781 588-0970
Marcos Pacas, *Brnch Mgr*
EMP: 7
SALES (corp-wide): 5.9MM **Privately Held**
Web: www.onemightymill.com
SIC: 2041　Flour and other grain mill products
PA: One Mighty Mill, Llc
　68 Exchange St
　Lynn MA 01901
　781 584-8648

(G-9467)
R R DONNELLEY & SONS COMPANY
65 Sprague St (02136-2061)
PHONE...........................617 360-2000
EMP: 24
SALES (corp-wide): 15B **Privately Held**

Web: www.rrd.com
SIC: 2759　Commercial printing, nec
HQ: R. R. Donnelley & Sons Company
　35 W Wacker Dr
　Chicago IL 60601
　800 782-4892

(G-9468)
XXPRESS AUTO REPAIR SHOP LLC
1318 River St (02136-2122)
P.O. Box 6585 (01746-6585)
PHONE...........................800 591-2068
EMP: 10 EST: 2015
SALES (est): 983.58K **Privately Held**
SIC: 3714 7549 7378　Transmissions, motor vehicle; High performance auto repair and service; Computer peripheral equipment repair and maintenance

Indian Orchard
Hampden County

(G-9469)
42 DESIGN FAB STUDIO INC
34 Front St (01151-1176)
P.O. Box 51942 (01151-5942)
PHONE...........................413 203-4948
EMP: 7 EST: 2011
SALES (est): 776.46K **Privately Held**
Web: www.42designfab.com
SIC: 2599　Furniture and fixtures, nec

(G-9470)
BUTLER METAL FABRICATORS INC
91 Pinevale St (01151-1562)
PHONE...........................413 306-5762
Lisa Brodeur-mcgan, *Prin*
EMP: 26 EST: 2015
SALES (est): 2.94MM **Privately Held**
Web: www.butlermetalinc.com
SIC: 3441　Fabricated structural metal

(G-9471)
CHMURAS BAKERY INC (PA)
12 Pulaski St Ste 14 (01151-2215)
PHONE...........................413 543-2521
Joseph Anselmo, *Pr*
Horacio Salvador, *Treas*
EMP: 19 EST: 1902
SQ FT: 9,000
SALES (est): 767.72K
SALES (corp-wide): 767.72K **Privately Held**
Web: www.chmurasbakery.com
SIC: 5461 5149 2051　Retail bakeries; Bakery products; Bread, cake, and related products

(G-9472)
NIXON COMPANY INCORPORATED
161 Main St (01151-1193)
P.O. Box 51977 (01151-5977)
PHONE...........................413 543-3701
Jonathan Boz Beckian, *Pr*
Deborah Raptopoulos, *
Janice Palukian, *
EMP: 10 EST: 1935
SQ FT: 15,000
SALES (est): 296.77K **Privately Held**
Web: www.nixonawards.com
SIC: 3999 2399 3965 2395　Plaques, picture, laminated; Emblems, badges, and insignia: from purchased materials; Fasteners, buttons, needles, and pins; Pleating and stitching

(G-9473)
ORCHARD TOOL & DIE INC
34 Front St Ste 29 (01151-1148)
PHONE...........................413 433-1233
Alan P Drew, *Prin*
EMP: 8 EST: 2007
SALES (est): 526.47K **Privately Held**
SIC: 3544　Special dies and tools

(G-9474)
SOLUTIA INC
730 Worcester St (01151-1022)
PHONE...........................734 676-4400
Gary Williams, *Brnch Mgr*
EMP: 118
Web: www.eastman.com
SIC: 2821 2824 3231 2819　Plastics materials and resins; Organic fibers, noncellulosic; Products of purchased glass; Industrial inorganic chemicals, nec
HQ: Solutia Inc.
　575 Maryville Centre Dr
　Saint Louis MO 63141
　314 674-1000

(G-9475)
SPRINGFIELD PALLET INC
1819 Page Blvd (01151-1326)
PHONE...........................413 593-0044
Scott Smith, *Mgr*
EMP: 8 EST: 2011
SALES (est): 445.75K **Privately Held**
SIC: 2448　Pallets, wood

(G-9476)
TRUSS ENGINEERING CORPORATION
181 Goodwin St (01151-2112)
P.O. Box 51027 (01151-5027)
PHONE...........................413 543-1298
W Paul Griswold, *Pr*
Joseph Henley, *
EMP: 45 EST: 1961
SQ FT: 33,200
SALES (est): 7.92MM **Privately Held**
Web: www.trussec.com
SIC: 2439　Trusses, wooden roof

Ipswich
Essex County

(G-9477)
ADVANCED PRECISION ENGINEERING INCORPORATED
16 Mitchell Rd (01938-1217)
P.O. Box 549 (01938-0549)
PHONE...........................978 356-7303
EMP: 40 EST: 1985
SALES (est): 8MM **Privately Held**
Web: www.ape10.com
SIC: 3599　Custom machinery

(G-9478)
BODYCOTE THERMAL PROC INC
11 Old Right Rd Ste C (01938-1191)
PHONE...........................978 356-3818
Mike Sakelakos, *Brnch Mgr*
EMP: 40
SALES (corp-wide): 895.27MM **Privately Held**
Web: www.bodycote.com
SIC: 3398　Brazing (hardening) of metal
HQ: Bodycote Thermal Processing, Inc.
　12750 Merit Dr Ste 1400
　Dallas TX 75251
　214 904-2420

(G-9479)
C & C FABRICATING INC
24 Hayward St Ste A (01938-2035)
P.O. Box 542 (01938-0542)
PHONE...........................978 356-9980
Craig Marquis, *Pr*
Roland Mower, *VP*
EMP: 11 EST: 1995
SQ FT: 3,700
SALES (est): 1.79MM **Privately Held**
Web: www.ccfabricating.com
SIC: 3599　Machine shop, jobbing and repair

(G-9480)
COMPANYSTUFFCOM INC
45 S Main St (01938-2321)
PHONE...........................978 282-1525
Steve Lindland, *Pr*
EMP: 7 EST: 2001
SALES (est): 101.43K **Privately Held**
SIC: 2329　Athletic clothing, except uniforms: men's, youths' and boys'

(G-9481)
D AND D MANUFACTURING LLC
49 Mitchell Rd (01938-1218)
EMP: 22 EST: 1998
SQ FT: 9,600
SALES (est): 5.53MM **Privately Held**
SIC: 3599　Machine shop, jobbing and repair

(G-9482)
D J FABRICATORS INC
94 Turnpike Rd (01938-1047)
PHONE...........................978 356-0228
David C Theriault, *Pr*
EMP: 18 EST: 1974
SQ FT: 24,000
SALES (est): 2.32MM **Privately Held**
Web: www.djfabricators.com
SIC: 3444　Sheet metal specialties, not stamped

(G-9483)
DALTON ELECTRIC HEATING CO INC
28 Hayward St (01938-2096)
PHONE...........................978 356-9844
Thomas A Shields, *CEO*
Thomas A Shields, *Pr*
Elliott Whitney, *
Seth Bartlett, *
EMP: 41 EST: 1926
SQ FT: 17,000
SALES (est): 7.14MM **Privately Held**
Web: www.daltonelectric.com
SIC: 3567　Heating units and devices, industrial: electric

(G-9484)
EBINGER BROTHERS LEA CO INC
Also Called: Preston Leather Products
44 Mitchell Rd Ste 1 (01938-1345)
P.O. Box 594 (01938-0594)
PHONE...........................978 356-5701
Christopher Ebinger, *Pr*
▼ **EMP: 11 EST:** 1947
SQ FT: 30,000
SALES (est): 927.08K **Privately Held**
Web:
ebinger-brothers-leather-company-inc-in-ipswich-ma.cityfos.com
SIC: 3199　Equestrian related leather articles

(G-9485)
EBSCO PUBLISHING INC (DH)
Also Called: Ebscohost
10 Estes St (01938-2106)

PHONE..............978 356-6500
Timothy R Collins, *CEO*
Samuel Brooks, *
Allen Powell, *
Doug Jenkins, *CIO**
EMP: 828 **EST:** 1993
SQ FT: 275,000
SALES (est): 165.82MM
SALES (corp-wide): 3.1B **Privately Held**
Web: www.ebsco.com
SIC: 2741 7375 2731 2721 Miscellaneous publishing; Information retrieval services; Book publishing; Periodicals
HQ: Ebsco Information Services, Llc
5724 Highway 280 E
Birmingham AL 35242
205 991-1211

(G-9486)
ESSEX BAY ENGINEERING INC
19 Mitchell Rd (01938-1292)
PHONE..............978 412-9600
John Burroughs, *CEO*
Julia Burroughs, *
Linda Matook, *
John Matook, *
EMP: 49 **EST:** 2003
SQ FT: 24,000
SALES (est): 8.81MM **Privately Held**
Web: www.essexbayengineering.com
SIC: 3599 Machine shop, jobbing and repair

(G-9487)
KC PRECISION MACHINING LLC
23 Old Right Rd Unit 1 (01938-1164)
PHONE..............978 356-8900
James E Moroney, *CEO*
Steven Gore, *COO*
Thomas W Mungovan, *CFO*
Matthew Smith, *Sr VP*
Andrew Curland, *Pr*
EMP: 22 **EST:** 1991
SQ FT: 20,000
SALES (est): 4.01MM
SALES (corp-wide): 149.03MM **Privately Held**
Web: www.mmgmfg.com
SIC: 3599 Machine shop, jobbing and repair
HQ: Momentum Manufacturing Group, Llc
23 National Ave
Georgetown MA 01833
978 659-6960

(G-9488)
KODIAK MACHINING CO INC
20 Hayward St (01938-2044)
P.O. Box 595 (01938-0595)
PHONE..............978 356-9876
Arthur R Gaudet Junior, *Pr*
EMP: 17 **EST:** 1984
SQ FT: 5,000
SALES (est): 1.89MM **Privately Held**
Web: www.kodiakmachine.net
SIC: 3599 Machine shop, jobbing and repair

(G-9489)
LITTLE ENTERPRISES LLC (DH)
31 Locust Rd (01938-1252)
PHONE..............978 356-7422
Scott Little, *Pr*
Steven Lavely, *VP*
EMP: 98 **EST:** 1985
SQ FT: 40,000
SALES (est): 21.78MM
SALES (corp-wide): 149.03MM **Privately Held**
Web: www.mmgmfg.com
SIC: 3599 Machine shop, jobbing and repair
HQ: Momentum Manufacturing Group, Llc
23 National Ave
Georgetown MA 01833
978 659-6960

(G-9490)
MERCURY BREWING & DIST CO INC
23 Hayward St (01938-2074)
PHONE..............978 356-3329
Robert T Martin, *Pr*
EMP: 11 **EST:** 1999
SQ FT: 10,000
SALES (est): 1.09MM **Privately Held**
Web: www.ipswichalebrewery.com
SIC: 2082 2086 Beer (alcoholic beverage); Carbonated beverages, nonalcoholic: pkged. in cans, bottles

(G-9491)
MICRO-MECH INC
33 Turnpike Rd (01938-1048)
P.O. Box 229 (01938-0229)
PHONE..............978 356-2966
Takehiko Hayashi, *Pr*
John E Beaucher, *
Seiji Minoura, *
▲ **EMP:** 48 **EST:** 1976
SALES (est): 9.76MM **Privately Held**
Web: www.micro-mech.com
SIC: 3295 Minerals, ground or treated
HQ: Ibiden U.S.A Corporation
3900 Freedom Cir Ste 130
Santa Clara CA 95054

(G-9492)
NORTH EAST INDUS COATINGS INC
9 Old Right Rd Unit C (01938-1119)
PHONE..............978 356-1200
Glenn Harlow, *Pr*
EMP: 7 **EST:** 2000
SALES (est): 564.74K **Privately Held**
Web: www.necoatings.com
SIC: 3479 Coating of metals and formed products

(G-9493)
OLIVER WELDING & FABG INC
30 Avery St (01938-1211)
PHONE..............978 356-4488
Richard Oliver, *Pr*
▲ **EMP:** 9 **EST:** 1983
SQ FT: 5,000
SALES (est): 980.74K **Privately Held**
Web: www.oliverwelding.com
SIC: 7692 1761 3599 Welding repair; Sheet metal work, nec; Machine shop, jobbing and repair

(G-9494)
PHOENIX VINTNERS LLC
Also Called: Traveling Vineyard
28 Northgate Rd (01938-2633)
PHONE..............877 340-9869
Rick Libby, *Pr*
EMP: 19 **EST:** 2010
SALES (est): 1.18MM **Privately Held**
Web: www.travelingvineyard.com
SIC: 2084 Wines

(G-9495)
PRIVATEER INTERNATIONAL LLC
28 Mitchell Rd (01938-1217)
PHONE..............978 356-0477
Andrew Cabot, *Pr*
▲ **EMP:** 9 **EST:** 2010
SALES (est): 230.84K **Privately Held**
Web: www.privateerrum.com
SIC: 2085 Rum (alcoholic beverage)

(G-9496)
SAN-TRON INC (PA)
4 Turnpike Rd (01938-1024)
PHONE..............978 356-1585
Ronald C Sanders, *Pr*
Kenneth Wayne Sanders, *
Ron Sanders, *
Catherine L Sanders, *
Carl H Sanders, *
▲ **EMP:** 60 **EST:** 1955
SQ FT: 30,000
SALES (est): 16.39MM
SALES (corp-wide): 16.39MM **Privately Held**
Web: www.santron.com
SIC: 3678 3451 3643 Electronic connectors; Screw machine products; Current-carrying wiring services

(G-9497)
SNYDER MACHINE CO INC
30 Avery St (01938-1211)
PHONE..............978 356-4488
Henry R Snyder, *Pr*
▼ **EMP:** 10 **EST:** 1962
SQ FT: 16,000
SALES (est): 243.92K **Privately Held**
Web: www.snydermachine.com
SIC: 3599 3554 Machine shop, jobbing and repair; Paper forming machines

(G-9498)
TRUE NORTH ALE COMPANY LLC
Also Called: True North Ale Company
116 County Rd (01938-2501)
PHONE..............978 312-6473
EMP: 27 **EST:** 2015
SALES (est): 1.76MM **Privately Held**
Web: www.truenorthales.com
SIC: 5812 2082 5921 Eating places; Beer (alcoholic beverage); Beer (packaged)

(G-9499)
VALVES AND CONTROLS US INC
Also Called: Trillium Valves USA
29 Old Right Rd (01938-1119)
PHONE..............978 744-5690
Jeremy Burroughs, *Pr*
Dennis Carder, *
◆ **EMP:** 100 **EST:** 1986
SALES (est): 25.34MM
SALES (corp-wide): 1.72MM **Privately Held**
SIC: 3491 Water works valves
HQ: Trillium Flow Technologies Uk Limited
Britannia House
Elland HX5 9

(G-9500)
XYBOL INTERLYNKS INC
89 Turnpike Rd Ste 204 (01938-1085)
PHONE..............978 356-0750
Mark A Gauthier, *Pr*
Barry Mitchell, *VP*
EMP: 10 **EST:** 2001
SALES (est): 675.74K **Privately Held**
Web: www.xybol.com
SIC: 3678 Electronic connectors

Jamaica Plain
Suffolk County

(G-9501)
GRAPHIC ARTS FINISHERS INC
Also Called: Graphic Arts Finishers
241 Perkins St Unit D201 (02130-4061)
PHONE..............617 241-9292
Morris Greenbaum, *CEO*
Alan Greenbaum, *Pr*
Mark Greenbaum, *VP*
David Greenbaum, *Treas*
Michael Greenbaum, *Dir*
▲ **EMP:** 13 **EST:** 1957
SALES (est): 476.76K **Privately Held**
Web: www.graphicartsfinishers.com
SIC: 2631 Container, packaging, and boxboard

(G-9502)
KENYON WOODWORKING INC
179 Boylston St (02130-4544)
PHONE..............617 524-6883
Dave Kenyon, *Pr*
Jim Kenyon, *Sec*
EMP: 13 **EST:** 1983
SQ FT: 10,000
SALES (est): 901.14K **Privately Held**
Web: www.kenyonwoodworking.com
SIC: 2431 2541 Millwork; Cabinets, lockers, and shelving

(G-9503)
RED SUN PRESS INC
94 Green St (02130-2298)
PHONE..............617 524-6822
Tia Phillips, *Dir*
Eric Johnson, *Treas*
Paul Normandia, *Admn*
Ricardo Huembes, *Pr*
EMP: 15 **EST:** 1976
SQ FT: 10,000
SALES (est): 522.82K **Privately Held**
Web: www.redsunpress.com
SIC: 2752 2621 2732 2791 Offset printing; Book, bond and printing papers; Pamphlets: printing and binding, not published on site; Linotype composition, for the printing trade

(G-9504)
WELD RITE
Also Called: Armor Roll
3371 Washington St (02130-2617)
PHONE..............617 524-9747
Walter Craven, *Owner*
EMP: 9 **EST:** 1970
SQ FT: 10,000
SALES (est): 762.68K **Privately Held**
SIC: 3446 7692 3444 Fire escapes, metal; Welding repair; Sheet metalwork

Kingston
Plymouth County

(G-9505)
CATON CONNECTOR CORP
Also Called: Caton
26 Wapping Rd Ste 1 (02364-1333)
PHONE..............781 585-4315
Daniel Galambos, *Pr*
Tom Ross, *
◆ **EMP:** 32 **EST:** 1973
SQ FT: 50,000
SALES (est): 10.51MM **Privately Held**
Web: www.caton.com
SIC: 3357 3643 Nonferrous wiredrawing and insulating; Current-carrying wiring services

(G-9506)
CLASSIC TRACTOR SERVICES LLC
8b Grove St (02364-1315)
PHONE..............781 585-2050

William E Lyons, *Pr*
EMP: 8 EST: 2006
SALES (est): 1.07MM **Privately Held**
Web: www.classictractorllc.com
SIC: 1442 Construction sand mining

(G-9507)
CRAFT BEER GUILD DISTRG VT LLC (PA)
Also Called: Craft Beer Guild of Vermont
35 Elder Ave (02364-1503)
PHONE......................781 585-5165
Conor Giard, *Managing Member*
EMP: 20 EST: 2010
SALES (est): 2.22MM
SALES (corp-wide): 2.22MM **Privately Held**
Web: www.craftbeerguildsd.com
SIC: 2082 5963 Malt beverages; Bottled water delivery

(G-9508)
JLP MACHINE AND WELDING LLC
10 Winter St (02364-1115)
PHONE......................781 585-1744
Jim Libby, *Managing Member*
EMP: 8 EST: 1998
SQ FT: 6,800
SALES (est): 711.45K **Privately Held**
SIC: 3841 Surgical instruments and apparatus

(G-9509)
KINGSTON ALUMINUM FOUNDRY INC
7 Pembroke St (02364-1108)
PHONE......................781 585-6631
Robert Barbieri Junior, *Pr*
Robert Barbieri Junior, *Pr*
Robert Barbieri Senior, *Dir*
EMP: 7 EST: 1940
SQ FT: 2,500
SALES (est): 622.42K **Privately Held**
SIC: 3363 3364 3365 Aluminum die-castings ; Brass and bronze die-castings; Aluminum foundries

(G-9510)
KINGSTON MANUFACTURING CO INC
3 Pleasant St (02364-2108)
PHONE......................781 585-4476
Joseph T Adamcewicz, *Pr*
Jadwiga E Adamcewicz, *Treas*
EMP: 7 EST: 1977
SQ FT: 1,000
SALES (est): 776.31K **Privately Held**
SIC: 3599 Machine shop, jobbing and repair

(G-9511)
SOUTHEASTERN CONCRETE INC
Also Called: Boston Sand and Gravel
399 Elm St (02364-1805)
P.O. Box 890025 (02189-0001)
PHONE......................617 227-9000
TOLL FREE: 800
Olly Demacedo, *Pr*
Donald Miller, *Clerk*
Dean Boylan, *Treas*
EMP: 10 EST: 1962
SALES (est): 963.75K **Privately Held**
Web:
www.southeasternconcretecorp.com
SIC: 3273 Ready-mixed concrete

(G-9512)
SOUTHEASTERN SAND AND GRAV INC
27 Pine Hill Rd (02364-1883)
PHONE......................781 413-6884
Peter J Opachinski, *Prin*
EMP: 7 EST: 2014
SALES (est): 431.33K **Privately Held**
SIC: 1442 Construction sand and gravel

(G-9513)
TITUS & BEAN GRAPHICS INC
Also Called: Sign-A-Rama
62 Main St Ste 107 (02364-3046)
PHONE......................781 585-1355
Harold Titus, *Pr*
Brenda Titus, *VP*
EMP: 16 EST: 1990
SQ FT: 3,000
SALES (est): 414.81K **Privately Held**
Web: www.signarama.com
SIC: 3993 3953 2752 Signs and advertising specialties; Marking devices; Commercial printing, lithographic

(G-9514)
WE PRINT TODAY LLC
66 Summer St (02364-1469)
PHONE......................781 585-6021
TOLL FREE: 800
EMP: 16 EST: 1980
SQ FT: 8,000
SALES (est): 987.64K **Privately Held**
Web: www.weprinttoday.com
SIC: 2752 2789 7334 Offset printing; Binding and repair of books, magazines, and pamphlets; Photocopying and duplicating services

Lakeville
Plymouth County

(G-9515)
ACCUDYNAMICS LLC
240 Kenneth Welch Dr (02347-1348)
PHONE......................508 946-4545
Michael Mckenna, *Pr*
EMP: 31 EST: 2018
SALES (est): 3.64MM **Privately Held**
Web: www.accudynamics.com
SIC: 3599 Machine shop, jobbing and repair

(G-9516)
COUNTRY PRESS INC
1 Commercial Dr (02347-1661)
P.O. Box 489 (02346-0489)
PHONE......................508 947-4485
Micheal Pintel, *Pr*
EMP: 10 EST: 1967
SQ FT: 15,000
SALES (est): 832.31K **Privately Held**
Web: www.countrypressprinting.com
SIC: 2752 Offset printing

(G-9517)
MAPLE LEAF INDUSTRIES
102 Highland Rd (02347-1829)
PHONE......................508 728-9581
EMP: 7 EST: 2008
SALES (est): 133.31K **Privately Held**
SIC: 3999 Manufacturing industries, nec

(G-9518)
OCEAN SPRAY INTERNATIONAL SLS
1 Ocean Spray Dr (02347-1339)
PHONE......................508 946-1000

EMP: 14 EST: 1995
SALES (est): 7.31MM
SALES (corp-wide): 1.2B **Privately Held**
Web: www.oceanspray.com
SIC: 2033 Canned fruits and specialties
PA: Ocean Spray Cranberries, Inc.
1 Ocean Spray Dr
Middleboro MA 02349
508 946-1000

(G-9519)
OCEAN SPRAY INTL SVCS INC (HQ)
1 Ocean Spray Dr (02347-1339)
PHONE......................508 946-1000
◆ **EMP: 303 EST:** 1995
SALES (est): 219.68MM
SALES (corp-wide): 1.2B **Privately Held**
Web: www.oceanspray.com
SIC: 2034 2033 2037 Fruits, dried or dehydrated, except freeze-dried; Fruits and fruit products, in cans, jars, etc.; Fruit juice concentrates, frozen
PA: Ocean Spray Cranberries, Inc.
1 Ocean Spray Dr
Middleboro MA 02349
508 946-1000

(G-9520)
PIECING PUZZLE INC
11 Riverside Dr (02347-3623)
PHONE......................508 465-0417
EMP: 8 EST: 2020
SALES (est): 497.23K **Privately Held**
Web: www.piecingthepuzzle.org
SIC: 3944 Puzzles

(G-9521)
SPACE BUILDING CORP
8 Harding St Ste 107 (02347-1230)
P.O. Box 283 (02718-0283)
PHONE......................508 947-7277
Robert Di Croce, *Pr*
Robert Di Croce, *Pr*
Carolyn Di Croce, *
EMP: 26 EST: 1951
SQ FT: 300,000
SALES (est): 4.44MM **Privately Held**
Web: www.spacebuildings.com
SIC: 3448 1541 1542 1522 Buildings, portable: prefabricated metal; Prefabricated building erection, industrial; Nonresidential construction, nec; Multi-family dwelling construction, nec

(G-9522)
TODRIN INDUSTRIES INC
305 Kenneth Welch Dr (02347-1373)
PHONE......................508 946-3600
EMP: 15 EST: 1992
SQ FT: 7,500
SALES (est): 4.51MM **Privately Held**
Web: www.todrin.net
SIC: 3444 Sheet metalwork

(G-9523)
WATKA CORPORATION
Also Called: Refrigerated Structures Neng
155 Millenium Cir Ste 104 (02347-1248)
PHONE......................508 946-5555
Jeannette Watka, *Pr*
Gregory Watka, *Treas*
James Connell, *Sec*
EMP: 11 EST: 1990
SQ FT: 8,600
SALES (est): 491.84K **Privately Held**
SIC: 7623 3585 Refrigeration repair service; Refrigeration equipment, complete

Lancaster
Worcester County

(G-9524)
CAROUSEL CABINETS
489 Neck Rd (01523-2275)
P.O. Box 664 (01469-0664)
PHONE......................978 846-8763
David Lamoureux, *Owner*
EMP: 8 EST: 2012
SALES (est): 276.92K **Privately Held**
SIC: 2434 Wood kitchen cabinets

(G-9525)
CE BAIRD CORPORATION
Reliance Engineering
851 Sterling Rd (01523-2915)
PHONE......................978 365-3867
Craig Bovaird, *Bmch Mgr*
EMP: 12
Web: www.beaconmedtech.com
SIC: 3544 Special dies and tools
PA: C.E. Baird Corporation
32 Jungle Rd
Leominster MA 01453

(G-9526)
GOVERNOR SUPPLY CO
Also Called: GSC
22 Hunter Ln (01523-3041)
P.O. Box 111 (01523-0111)
PHONE......................978 870-6888
Gregg O'donnell, *Mng Pt*
Douglas O'donnell, *Pt*
EMP: 7 EST: 2012
SQ FT: 1,000
SALES (est): 1.16MM **Privately Held**
SIC: 3089 Aquarium accessories, plastics

(G-9527)
HORN CORPORATION (PA)
580 Fort Pond Rd (01523-3224)
PHONE......................800 832-7020
Peter Hamilton, *CEO*
Michael Gill, *
David Gomer, *
Edward Gerard Jager, *
EMP: 50 EST: 1992
SQ FT: 100,000
SALES (est): 17.2MM **Privately Held**
SIC: 2653 5113 3086 7389 Boxes, corrugated: made from purchased materials ; Shipping supplies; Packaging and shipping materials, foamed plastics; Packaging and labeling services

(G-9528)
HORN INTERNATIONAL PACKG INC (HQ)
580 Fort Pond Rd (01523-3224)
PHONE......................978 667-8797
David R Gomer, *Pr*
Micheal Gill, *
◆ **EMP: 40 EST:** 1943
SQ FT: 65,000
SALES (est): 17.2MM **Privately Held**
Web: www.perfectdomain.com
SIC: 5085 5199 4225 4213 Crates, except paper; Packaging materials; General warehousing and storage; Trucking, except local
PA: The Horn Corporation
580 Fort Pond Rd
Lancaster MA 01523

(G-9529)
STAINLESS STEEL COATINGS INC

Also Called: Steel-It
835 Sterling Rd (01523-2915)
PHONE..............................978 365-9828
Ivan M Faigen, *CEO*
Michael Faigen, *Pr*
▲ **EMP:** 11 **EST:** 1974
SQ FT: 10,000
SALES (est): 2.84MM **Privately Held**
Web: www.steel-it.com
SIC: 3479 Coating of metals and formed
products

(G-9530)
**STERLING MANUFACTURING
CO INC**
640 Sterling St (01523-1852)
PHONE..............................978 368-8733
John Gravelle, *CEO*
Stanley Bowker, *
Michael Gravelle, *
▲ **EMP:** 57 **EST:** 1967
SQ FT: 35,000
SALES (est): 9.86MM **Privately Held**
Web: www.sterlingmfg.net
SIC: 3089 Injection molding of plastics

(G-9531)
**UNIFIED2 GLOBL PACKG
GROUP LLC**
580 Fort Pond Rd (01523-3224)
PHONE..............................508 865-1155
EMP: 429
SALES (corp-wide): 104MM **Privately
Held**
Web: www.ugpg2.com
SIC: 2441 2448 2653 Nailed wood boxes
and shook; Wood pallets and skids;
Corrugated and solid fiber boxes
PA: Unified2 Global Packaging Group, Llc
223 Wrcster Prvdence Tpke
Sutton MA 01590
508 865-1155

Lanesborough
Berkshire County

(G-9532)
INJECTED SOLUTIONS INC
840 Cheshire Rd (01237-9775)
PHONE..............................413 499-5800
Joseph A Kirchner, *Pr*
Henry Kirchner, *CEO*
Susan Kirchner, *Treas*
▲ **EMP:** 13 **EST:** 2001
SQ FT: 22,000
SALES (est): 2MM **Privately Held**
Web: www.injectedsolutions.com
SIC: 3089 Injection molding of plastics

Lawrence
Essex County

(G-9533)
99DEGREES CUSTOM INC
360 Merrimack St Ste 132 (01843-2162)
PHONE..............................978 655-3362
Brenna N Schneider, *CEO*
▲ **EMP:** 29 **EST:** 2013
SALES (est): 4.64MM **Privately Held**
Web: www.99degreescustom.com
SIC: 3999 Manufacturing industries, nec

(G-9534)
ACE METAL FINISHING INC
Also Called: Ace Metal Finishing
125 Glenn St (01843-1036)
PHONE..............................978 683-2082

Sharon Coskren, *Pr*
James Coskren, *
▲ **EMP:** 21 **EST:** 2008
SQ FT: 5,000
SALES (est): 657.75K **Privately Held**
Web: www.cilinc.com
SIC: 3471 Electroplating of metals or
formed products

(G-9535)
**AERIAL ACOUSTICS
CORPORATION**
15 Union St (01840-1866)
PHONE..............................978 988-1600
Michael Kelly, *Pr*
David Marshall, *VP*
▲ **EMP:** 10 **EST:** 1989
SQ FT: 10,000
SALES (est): 954.25K **Privately Held**
Web: www.aerialacoustics.com
SIC: 3651 5064 Speaker systems; High
fidelity equipment

(G-9536)
**AMERICAN ADHESIVE
COATINGS LLC (PA)**
Also Called: Aacc
12 Osgood St (01843-1828)
P.O. Box 1708 (01842-3708)
PHONE..............................978 688-7400
E A Ted Krug, *Pr*
Gerald Villa, *VP*
Jerry Villa, *VP*
▲ **EMP:** 24 **EST:** 1987
SQ FT: 15,000
SALES (est): 4.93MM
SALES (corp-wide): 4.93MM **Privately
Held**
Web: www.aacchotmelts.com
SIC: 2891 Adhesives

(G-9537)
**ANDOVER ORGAN COMPANY
INC**
560 Broadway (01841-2446)
P.O. Box 36 (01844-0036)
PHONE..............................978 686-9600
Donald H Olson, *Pr*
Ben Mague, *Treas*
EMP: 17 **EST:** 1948
SQ FT: 12,000
SALES (est): 499.48K **Privately Held**
Web: www.andoverorgan.com
SIC: 3931 7699 Organs, all types: pipe,
reed, hand, electronic, etc.; Organ tuning
and repair

(G-9538)
**ARTISAN CHEF
MANUFACTURING LLC (HQ)**
117 Water St (01841-4720)
PHONE..............................978 691-6100
Jospeh P Faro, *Managing Member*
EMP: 15 **EST:** 2019
SALES (est): 16.03MM
SALES (corp-wide): 30.5MM **Privately
Held**
Web: www.artisanmfgco.com
SIC: 2099 2051 Food preparations, nec;
Bread, cake, and related products
PA: Tuscan Brands, Llc
63 Main St
Salem NH 03079
781 365-2800

(G-9539)
ASAHI/AMERICA INC
655 Andover St (01843-1032)
PHONE..............................800 343-3618

Hal Hashimoto, *CEO*
EMP: 7
Web: www.asahi-america.com
SIC: 3084 Plastics pipe
HQ: Asahi/America, Inc.
655 Andover St
Lawrence MA 01843
781 321-5409

(G-9540)
ASAHI/AMERICA INC (HQ)
655 Andover St (01843-1032)
P.O. Box 1108 (01842-2108)
PHONE..............................781 321-5409
Hidetoshi Hal Hashimoto, *C*
Hidetoshi Hal Hashimoto, *CEO*
Harry Aiba, *Pr*
Scott Robichaud, *Ex VP*
Stephen Harrington, *CFO*
◆ **EMP:** 32 **EST:** 1972
SQ FT: 94,000
SALES (est): 29.59MM **Privately Held**
Web: www.asahi-america.com
SIC: 3084 3089 3491 3625 Plastics pipe;
Fittings for pipe, plastics; Industrial valves;
Actuators, industrial
PA: Asahi Yukizai Corporation
2-5955, Nakanosemachi
Nobeoka MYZ 882-0

(G-9541)
BAGEL BOY LLC
485 S Union St (01843-2811)
PHONE..............................978 682-8646
Chaouki M Bouchrouche, *Pr*
▲ **EMP:** 80 **EST:** 1992
SQ FT: 30,000
SALES (est): 24.44MM **Privately Held**
Web: www.crownbakeries.com
SIC: 2051 Bagels, fresh or frozen
PA: Crown Bakeries, Llc
211 Franklin Rd Ste 225
Brentwood TN 37027

(G-9542)
BALLARD AWAY CORPORATION
12 Ballard Way (01843-1044)
P.O. Box 847223 (02284-7223)
PHONE..............................978 689-2800
EMP: 116
SIC: 3069 Rubber hardware

(G-9543)
**BIOPHARM ENGNEERED
SYSTEMS LLC**
421 Merrimack St # 1 (01843-1736)
PHONE..............................978 691-2737
Paul Brouillette, *Pr*
James Nardone, *Eng/Dir*
EMP: 26 **EST:** 2015
SALES (est): 9.22MM **Privately Held**
Web: www.bpesys.com
SIC: 3559 Pharmaceutical machinery

(G-9544)
C Q P BAKERY
19 Blanchard St (01843-1413)
PHONE..............................978 557-5626
Fernando Cafua, *Pt*
Frank Pino, *Pt*
Mike Quinn, *Pt*
EMP: 14 **EST:** 2000
SQ FT: 11,000
SALES (est): 501K **Privately Held**
SIC: 2051 Bakery: wholesale or wholesale/
retail combined

(G-9545)
CAMBRIDGE BRICKHOUSE INC
60 Island St Ste 2 (01840-1835)
PHONE..............................978 725-8001
Yanitzia Canetti, *Pr*
▲ **EMP:** 9 **EST:** 2005
SALES (est): 857.14K **Privately Held**
Web: www.cambridgebh.com
SIC: 2741 Internet publishing and
broadcasting

(G-9546)
**CARDINAL SHOE
CORPORATION**
468 N Canal St Ste 3 (01840-1211)
PHONE..............................978 686-9706
Richard A Bass, *Pr*
Andrew Bass, *VP*
Allan Ornsteen, *VP*
▲ **EMP:** 16 **EST:** 1962
SQ FT: 160,000
SALES (est): 333.91K **Privately Held**
Web: www.cardinalshoe.com
SIC: 3144 4225 Women's footwear, except
athletic; Warehousing, self storage

(G-9547)
CHEMCO CORPORATION
46 Stafford St (01841-2471)
PHONE..............................978 687-9000
Paul Lewis, *Pr*
◆ **EMP:** 24 **EST:** 1978
SALES (est): 977.13K **Privately Held**
Web: www.chemco-usa.com
SIC: 2842 Polishes and sanitation goods

(G-9548)
CIL ELECTROPLATING INC (PA)
Also Called: Ace Metal Finishing
125 Glenn St (01843-1036)
PHONE..............................978 683-2082
James Coskren, *CEO*
EMP: 56 **EST:** 1974
SALES (est): 8.03MM
SALES (corp-wide): 8.03MM **Privately
Held**
Web: www.cilinc.com
SIC: 3471 Electroplating of metals or
formed products

(G-9549)
CIL ELECTROPLATING INC
9 Mill St (01840-1635)
PHONE..............................978 683-2082
EMP: 84
SALES (corp-wide): 8.03MM **Privately
Held**
Web: www.cilinc.com
SIC: 3471 Electroplating of metals or
formed products
PA: C.I.L. Electroplating, Inc.
125 Glenn St
Lawrence MA 01843
978 683-2082

(G-9550)
CIL INC
400 Canal St (01840-1221)
PHONE..............................978 685-8300
James Coskren, *Pr*
EMP: 80 **EST:** 1987
SQ FT: 15,000
SALES (est): 9.62MM **Privately Held**
Web: www.cilinc.com
SIC: 3471 3479 Anodizing (plating) of
metals or formed products; Painting of
metal products

(G-9551)
CLIVUS MULTRUM INC
15 Union St Ste 412 (01840-1867)
PHONE....................978 725-5591
Abby A Rockefeller, *Pr*
Richard Cataldo, *Treas*
▼ **EMP:** 8 **EST:** 1973
SQ FT: 15,000
SALES (est): 907.55K **Privately Held**
Web: www.clivusmultrum.com
SIC: 3261   Plumbing fixtures, vitreous china

(G-9552)
CN CUSTOM CABINETS INC
599 Canal St (01840-1245)
PHONE....................978 300-5531
Eliud O Calderon, *Dir*
Marvin G Calderon, *Pr*
EMP: 10 **EST:** 2007
SALES (est): 475.61K **Privately Held**
Web: www.cncustomcabinets.com
SIC: 2541   Store and office display cases
and fixtures

(G-9553)
COLONY FOODS INC
439 Haverhill St (01841-4324)
PHONE....................978 794-1500
EMP: 24 **EST:** 1965
SALES (est): 24.67MM **Privately Held**
Web: www.colonyfoods.com
SIC: 5147 5143 5141 2621   Meats, fresh;
Cheese; Groceries, general line; Paper mills

(G-9554)
COLUMBIA ASC INC
165 S Broadway Ste167 (01843-1426)
PHONE....................978 683-2205
Marilyn Reilly Cochran, *Pr*
Salvatore Messina, *VP*
EMP: 12 **EST:** 1935
SQ FT: 8,000
SALES (est): 1.79MM **Privately Held**
Web: www.columbiaasc.com
SIC: 3544 2394 7641 3444   Special dies and
tools; Canvas and related products;
Reupholstery and furniture repair; Sheet
metalwork

(G-9555)
CORK TECHNOLOGIES LLC
29 S Canal St Ste 204 (01843-1403)
PHONE....................978 687-9500
Bruce Macomber, *Managing Member*
EMP: 8 **EST:** 2002
SALES (est): 757.56K **Privately Held**
Web: www.corktech.com
SIC: 2499   Cork and cork products

(G-9556)
DELAWARE VALLEY CORP (PA)
500 Broadway (01841-3002)
P.O. Box 987 (01842-1987)
PHONE....................978 688-6995
▲ **EMP:** 14 **EST:** 1953
SALES (est): 8.86MM
SALES (corp-wide): 8.86MM **Privately
Held**
Web:
www.delawarevalleynonwovens.com
SIC: 2297   Nonwoven fabrics

(G-9557)
DIAMOND IRON WORKS INC
109 Blanchard St (01843-1415)
PHONE....................978 794-4640
EMP: 34 **EST:** 1994
SALES (est): 6.96MM **Privately Held**
Web: www.diamondironworks.com

SIC: 3441   Fabricated structural metal

(G-9558)
EAGLE WOODWORKING INC
678 Andover St Ste 1 (01843-1077)
PHONE....................978 681-6194
Christian Kreilkamp, *Pr*
EMP: 10 **EST:** 1973
SQ FT: 15,000
SALES (est): 930.1K **Privately Held**
Web: www.eagledovetaildrawers.com
SIC: 2499 2541   Decorative wood and
woodwork; Cabinets, except refrigerated:
show, display, etc.: wood

(G-9559)
EASTERN PACKAGING INC
283 Lowell St (01840-1097)
PHONE....................978 685-7723
Erik P Curtis, *Pr*
Loreen D Curtis, *
EMP: 60 **EST:** 1955
SQ FT: 85,000
SALES (est): 4.65MM **Privately Held**
Web: www.easternpackinginc.com
SIC: 2821 2673   Polyethylene resins;
Cellophane bags, unprinted: made from
purchased materials

(G-9560)
**EMERSON PRCESS MGT PWR
WTR SLT**
Also Called: Rpp
12 Ballard Way (01843-1044)
PHONE....................978 689-2800
EMP: 29
SALES (corp-wide): 15.16B **Publicly Held**
Web: www.emerson.com
SIC: 3823   Process control instruments
HQ: Emerson Process Management Power
& Water Solutions, Inc.
200 Beta Dr
Pittsburgh PA 15238
412 963-4000

(G-9561)
FIVE STAR PLATING LLC
7a Broadway (01840-1002)
PHONE....................978 655-4081
EMP: 30 **EST:** 2010
SQ FT: 20,000
SALES (est): 4.88MM **Privately Held**
Web: www.fivestarplating.com
SIC: 3471   Electroplating of metals or
formed products
PA: Inoa & Torres Accesorios Y
Suministros De Informatica S.R.L.
Ave Nunez De Caceres No. 22
Santo Domingo

(G-9562)
FLAMETECH STEELS INC
10 Methuen St (01840-1700)
PHONE....................978 686-9518
Samuel F Facella, *Pr*
EMP: 10 **EST:** 1986
SALES (est): 995.96K **Privately Held**
SIC: 3441   Fabricated structural metal

(G-9563)
FLOWSERVE US INC
Also Called: Lawrence Pumps
280 Merrimack St (01843-1787)
PHONE....................978 682-5248
Samuel Barrett, *Brnch Mgr*
EMP: 110
SALES (corp-wide): 3.62B **Publicly Held**
Web: www.flowserve.com

SIC: 3561   Pumps and pumping equipment
HQ: Flowserve Us Inc.
5215 N Ocnnor Blvd Ste 70 Connor
Irving TX 75039
972 443-6500

(G-9564)
GEM GROUP INC (PA)
Also Called: Gemline
9 International Way (01843-1066)
PHONE....................978 691-2000
Jonathan G Isaacson, *CEO*
Frank Carpenito, *
Ronald N Stetler, *
◆ **EMP:** 371 **EST:** 1958
SQ FT: 150,000
SALES (est): 86.59MM
SALES (corp-wide): 86.59MM **Privately
Held**
Web: www.gemline.com
SIC: 7389 2759   Advertising, promotional,
and trade show services; Screen printing

(G-9565)
**GLOBAL CONNECTOR TECH
LTD**
354 Merrimack St Ste 260 (01843-1757)
PHONE....................978 208-1618
Louis Guerra, *Prin*
EMP: 10 **EST:** 2009
SALES (est): 541.87K **Privately Held**
Web: www.gct.co
SIC: 3661   Telephone and telegraph
apparatus

(G-9566)
**HELFRICH BROS BOILER
WORKS INC**
39 Merrimack St (01843-1436)
PHONE....................978 975-2464
Vincent Helfrich, *Pr*
Joseph Helfrich, *
▲ **EMP:** 35 **EST:** 1948
SQ FT: 21,000
SALES (est): 9.73MM **Privately Held**
Web: www.hbbwinc.com
SIC: 3443 1711 1541 3444   Vessels,
process or storage (from boiler shops):
metal plate; Boiler setting contractor;
Renovation, remodeling and repairs:
industrial buildings; Sheet metalwork

(G-9567)
**HELFRICH CONSTRUCTION
SVCS LLC**
39 Merrimack St (01843-1436)
PHONE....................978 683-7244
EMP: 25 **EST:** 2017
SQ FT: 2,000
SALES (est): 1.06MM **Privately Held**
Web: www.hbbwinc.com
SIC: 3443   Flumes, metal plate

(G-9568)
**HIGH-SPEED PROCESS PRTG
CORP**
Also Called: Graphic Litho
130 Shepard St (01843-1026)
PHONE....................978 683-2766
Ralph E Wilbur, *Pr*
Kari Wilbur, *Treas*
Randi Collins, *Contrlr*
EMP: 12 **EST:** 1950
SQ FT: 28,000
SALES (est): 2.24MM **Privately Held**
Web: www.graphiclitho.com
SIC: 2752   Offset printing

(G-9569)
HOOKE LABORATORIES INC
439 S Union St Ste E3 (01843-2837)
PHONE....................617 475-5114
EMP: 99 **EST:** 2007
SALES (est): 11.32MM **Privately Held**
Web: www.hookelabs.com
SIC: 2836   Allergens, allergenic extracts

(G-9570)
IDEAL BOX COMPANY
15 Union St Ste 455 (01840-1866)
PHONE....................978 683-2802
▼ **EMP:** 8 **EST:** 2011
SQ FT: 7,000
SALES (est): 1.03MM **Privately Held**
Web: www.idealboxmakers.com
SIC: 2653   Boxes, corrugated: made from
purchased materials

(G-9571)
JAYBIRD & MAIS INC
360 Merrimack St Ste 20 (01843-1749)
PHONE....................978 686-8659
Scott M Garfield, *Pr*
Norman Mais, *
Stephanie Garfield, *
Jerold Garfield, *
◆ **EMP:** 35 **EST:** 1985
SQ FT: 33,000
SALES (est): 5.06MM **Privately Held**
Web: www.jaybird.com
SIC: 2672   Tape, pressure sensitive: made
from purchased materials

(G-9572)
JGP ENTERPRISES INC
Also Called: Biopharm Engineered Systems
421 Merrimack St # 1 (01843-1736)
PHONE....................978 691-2737
Paul A Brouillette, *Pr*
EMP: 20 **EST:** 2006
SALES (est): 3.81MM **Privately Held**
Web: www.bpesys.com
SIC: 3559   Chemical machinery and
equipment

(G-9573)
KEY POLYMER LLC
17 Shepard St (01843-1023)
PHONE....................978 683-9411
William Newman, *CEO*
Mark Kaluzny, *CFO*
EMP: 40 **EST:** 2021
SQ FT: 170,000
SALES (est): 9.39MM
SALES (corp-wide): 10.13MM **Privately
Held**
Web: www.keypolymer.com
SIC: 2891   Adhesives
PA: Key Polymer Holdings, Llc
17 Shepard St
Lawrence MA 01843
978 683-9411

(G-9574)
**KEY POLYMER HOLDINGS LLC
(PA)**
17 Shepard St (01843-1023)
PHONE....................978 683-9411
William Newman, *CEO*
Mark Kaluzny, *CFO*
EMP: 10 **EST:** 2019
SQ FT: 170,000
SALES (est): 10.13MM
SALES (corp-wide): 10.13MM **Privately
Held**
Web: www.keypolymer.com
SIC: 2891   Adhesives

(G-9575)
LANFORD MANUFACTURING CORP
43 Merrimack St (01843-1463)
PHONE...............................978 557-0240
Mark Mccrill, *Pr*
EMP: 17 **EST:** 1997
SQ FT: 11,000
SALES (est): 938.64K **Privately Held**
Web: www.lmc--inc.com
SIC: 3599 Machine shop, jobbing and repair

(G-9576)
LAPLUME & SONS PRINTING INC
1 Farley St (01843-2614)
PHONE...............................978 683-1009
Ronald Laplume, *Pr*
Ronald La Plume, *
Raymond La Plume, *
Jimmy La Plume, *Stockholder*
EMP: 25 **EST:** 1935
SQ FT: 20,000
SALES (est): 2.36MM **Privately Held**
Web: www.laplumeprinting.com
SIC: 2791 2789 2759 2752 Typesetting; Bookbinding and related work; Commercial printing, nec; Commercial printing, lithographic

(G-9577)
LAWRENCE PUMPS INC
371 Market St (01843-1595)
PHONE...............................978 682-5248
◆ **EMP:** 130
SIC: 3561 Industrial pumps and parts

(G-9578)
LEBLANC ENTERPRISES INC
Also Called: Sawtech
11 Glenn St (01843-1019)
PHONE...............................978 682-5112
William Leblanc, *Pr*
Anne Leblanc, *Contrlr*
EMP: 22 **EST:** 1980
SQ FT: 15,000
SALES (est): 477.17K **Privately Held**
Web: www.sawtech.net
SIC: 7389 3441 Metal cutting services; Fabricated structural metal

(G-9579)
MAINSTREAM GLOBAL INC
91 Glenn St (01843-1036)
PHONE...............................978 682-6767
Juan Yepez, *CEO*
John Borrelli, *
Rafael Rivera, *
Louis E Yepez, *
▲ **EMP:** 42 **EST:** 2000
SQ FT: 7,000
SALES (est): 19.45MM **Privately Held**
Web: www.mainstream-global.com
SIC: 5065 1389 7699 4212 Electronic parts; Testing, measuring, surveying, and analysis services; Professional instrument repair services; Delivery service, vehicular

(G-9580)
MICRO-PRECISION TECH INC (PA)
Also Called: Aerospace Semiconductor
439 S Union St Unit 105 (01843-2837)
PHONE...............................978 688-1299
Adrian Pyke, *CEO*
EMP: 17 **EST:** 1982
SQ FT: 4,357
SALES (est): 4.49MM
SALES (corp-wide): 4.49MM **Privately Held**

Web: www.aerospacesemi.com
SIC: 3672 3674 Printed circuit boards; Semiconductors and related devices

(G-9581)
MICROSEMI CORP-MASSACHUSETTS
Also Called: Microsemi-Lawrence
6 Lake St Ste 1 (01841-3032)
PHONE...............................978 620-2600
EMP: 400
SALES (corp-wide): 8.44B **Publicly Held**
Web: www.microsemi.com
SIC: 3674 Semiconductors and related devices
HQ: Microsemi Corp.- Massachusetts
11861 Western Ave
Garden Grove CA 92841

(G-9582)
MICROSEMI CORP-COLORADO
6 Lake St Ste 1 (01841-3032)
PHONE...............................480 941-6300
James Peterson, *Pr*
Sven Nelson, *
David R Sonksen, *
EMP: 99 **EST:** 1966
SQ FT: 115,000
SALES (est): 31.6MM
SALES (corp-wide): 8.44B **Publicly Held**
Web: www.microsemi.com
SIC: 3674 Semiconductor circuit networks
HQ: Microsemi Corporation
11861 Western Ave
Garden Grove CA 92841
949 380-6100

(G-9583)
MICROSEMI CORPORATION
Also Called: Microsemi-Cdi
6 Lake St Ste 1 (01841-3032)
PHONE...............................781 665-1071
Thomas J Kachel, *Genl Mgr*
EMP: 74
SALES (corp-wide): 8.44B **Publicly Held**
Web: www.microsemi.com
SIC: 3674 Diodes, solid state (germanium, silicon, etc.)
HQ: Microsemi Corporation
11861 Western Ave
Garden Grove CA 92841
949 380-6100

(G-9584)
MICROSEMI NES INC
6 Lake St (01843-3032)
PHONE...............................978 794-1666
George Yencho, *Pr*
Kare Karlsen, *
Douglas Milne, *
EMP: 44 **EST:** 2001
SQ FT: 38,500
SALES (est): 9.81MM
SALES (corp-wide): 8.44B **Publicly Held**
Web: www.microsemi.com
SIC: 3674 Diodes, solid state (germanium, silicon, etc.)
HQ: Microsemi Corporation
11861 Western Ave
Garden Grove CA 92841
949 380-6100

(G-9585)
MKS INSTRUMENTS INC
17 Ballard Way (01843-1045)
PHONE...............................978 975-2350
Onni Wirtanen, *Personnel Representative*
EMP: 10
SALES (corp-wide): 3.55B **Publicly Held**
Web: www.mks.com

SIC: 3829 3825 3823 Measuring and controlling devices, nec; Instruments to measure electricity; Process control instruments
PA: Mks Instruments, Inc.
2 Tech Dr Ste 201
Andover MA 01810
978 645-5500

(G-9586)
NEW BALANCE ATHLETICS INC
5 S Union St (01843-1699)
PHONE...............................978 685-8400
TOLL FREE: 877
John Wilson, *Ex VP*
EMP: 490
SQ FT: 140,000
SALES (corp-wide): 17.22MM **Privately Held**
Web: www.newbalance.com
SIC: 3149 8731 3021 Athletic shoes, except rubber or plastic; Commercial physical research; Rubber and plastics footwear
HQ: New Balance Athletics, Inc.
100 Guest St
Boston MA 02135
617 783-4000

(G-9587)
NEW ENGLAND PRTZEL POPCORN INC
15 Bay State Rd (01841-4701)
PHONE...............................978 687-0342
TOLL FREE: 800
Warren J Sideri Junior, *Pr*
EMP: 7 **EST:** 1982
SQ FT: 13,000
SALES (est): 2.03MM **Privately Held**
Web: www.nepretzel.com
SIC: 2052 2096 2099 Pretzels; Popcorn, already popped (except candy covered); Popcorn, packaged: except already popped

(G-9588)
NEXCELOM BIOSCIENCE LLC (HQ)
360 Merrimack St Ste 47 (01843-2162)
PHONE...............................978 327-5340
Peter Li, *Managing Member*
Peter Y Li, *Managing Member*
Jean Qiu Ph.d., *Managing Member*
EMP: 39 **EST:** 2003
SQ FT: 2,000
SALES (est): 42.88MM
SALES (corp-wide): 3.31B **Publicly Held**
Web: www.revvity.com
SIC: 3821 Laboratory equipment: fume hoods, distillation racks, etc.
PA: Revvity, Inc.
940 Winter St
Waltham MA 02451
781 663-6900

(G-9589)
NORTH AMERICAN CHEMICAL CO
Also Called: Cork Technologies
19 S Canal St Ste 2 (01843-1412)
PHONE...............................978 687-9500
Lance Macomber, *Pr*
Bruce Macomber, *Treas*
EMP: 9 **EST:** 1939
SQ FT: 85,000
SALES (est): 510.83K **Privately Held**
SIC: 3131 Inner parts for shoes

(G-9590)
NORTH AMERICAN COATING SCIENCES INC

12 Osgood St (01843-1828)
P.O. Box 1708 (01842-3708)
PHONE...............................978 691-5622
▲ **EMP:** 9 **EST:** 1994
SALES (est): 871.92K **Privately Held**
SIC: 2891 Adhesives, plastic

(G-9591)
NORTHEAST INDUSTRIAL TECH INC
39 Merrimack St (01843-1436)
PHONE...............................617 360-7220
Thomas Ferraro, *Pr*
EMP: 15 **EST:** 1993
SALES (est): 3.79MM **Privately Held**
Web: www.neind.com
SIC: 3599 Machine shop, jobbing and repair

(G-9592)
NXSTAGE MEDICAL INC (DH)
Also Called: Nxstage
350 Merrimack St (01843-1748)
PHONE...............................978 687-4700
William Valle, *CEO*
EMP: 100 **EST:** 1998
SQ FT: 141,000
SALES (est): 912.69MM
SALES (corp-wide): 20.15B **Privately Held**
Web: www.nxstage.com
SIC: 3845 Dialyzers, electromedical
HQ: Fresenius Medical Care Holdings, Inc.
920 Winter St
Waltham MA 02451

(G-9593)
OBP SURGICAL CORPORATION
360 Merrimack St (01843-1740)
PHONE...............................978 291-6853
Jason Swift, *CEO*
EMP: 12 **EST:** 2021
SALES (est): 1.18MM **Privately Held**
Web: www.obpsurgical.com
SIC: 3841 Surgical and medical instruments

(G-9594)
OPTIMUM SPORTSWEAR INC
34 Groton St Fl 1 (01843-2616)
PHONE...............................978 689-2290
Joseph Comeau, *Pr*
J Peter Como, *VP*
Paul Farnam, *Sec*
EMP: 7 **EST:** 1989
SQ FT: 10,000
SALES (est): 674.75K **Privately Held**
Web: www.optimumsportswear.com
SIC: 2759 5949 Screen printing; Needlework goods and supplies

(G-9595)
RAID INC
439 S Union St Ste 2 (01843-2837)
PHONE...............................978 683-6444
Marc Dizoglio, *Pr*
EMP: 21 **EST:** 1997
SQ FT: 30,000
SALES (est): 5.01MM **Privately Held**
Web: www.raidinc.com
SIC: 3572 Computer storage devices

(G-9596)
SILVER SWEET PRODUCTS CO
Also Called: Silver Sweet Candies Co
522 Essex St (01840-1242)
PHONE...............................978 688-0474
Samuel Silverstein, *Owner*
EMP: 8 **EST:** 1945
SQ FT: 9,000
SALES (est): 478.23K **Privately Held**

SIC: 2064 Candy and other confectionery products

(G-9597)
SIMPSONS INC OF LAWRENCE
Also Called: Simpson Auto & Truck Supply
26 International Way (01843-1064)
PHONE.............................978 683-2417
Mark Simpson, *Pr*
Eleanor Simpson, *Treas*
Gail Davis, *Clerk*
EMP: 10 **EST:** 1953
SQ FT: 14,000
SALES (est): 1.43MM **Privately Held**
Web: www.simpsonstrucksupply.com
SIC: 5013 3599 Truck parts and accessories
; Machine shop, jobbing and repair

(G-9598)
SMALL PLNET COMMUNICATIONS INC
15 Union St Ste 5 (01840-1823)
PHONE.............................978 794-2201
EMP: 8 **EST:** 1994
SQ FT: 1,600
SALES (est): 992.28K **Privately Held**
Web: www.smplanet.com
SIC: 2731 7372 Books, publishing only;
Prepackaged software

(G-9599)
SOLECTRIA RENEWABLES LLC
Also Called: Yaskawa - Solectria Solar
360 Merrimack St Ste 9 (01843-1764)
PHONE.............................978 683-9700
Michael S Knapek, *CEO*
Mark Bernicky, *VP*
Akira Hijikuro, *CFO*
▲ **EMP:** 130 **EST:** 2005
SALES (est): 36.7MM **Privately Held**
Web: www.solectria.com
SIC: 3629 8748 Inverters, nonrotating:
electrical; Systems analysis or design
HQ: Yaskawa America, Inc.
2121 Norman Dr
Waukegan IL 60085
847 887-7000

(G-9600)
SPECTOR TEXTILE PRODUCTS INC (PA)
10 Embankment St Ste 1 (01841-4719)
P.O. Box 315 (01842-0515)
PHONE.............................978 688-3501
TOLL FREE: 800
Howard Spector, *Pr*
Mildred C Spector, *
▲ **EMP:** 31 **EST:** 1934
SQ FT: 12,500
SALES (est): 8.26MM
SALES (corp-wide): 8.26MM **Privately Held**
Web: www.spectortextile.com
SIC: 5099 5093 2394 2326 Safety
equipment and supplies; Waste rags;
Canvas and related products; Men's and
boy's work clothing

(G-9601)
SST COMPONENTS INC (PA)
Also Called: Vpt Components
9 Hampshire St Ste 1 (01840-1326)
PHONE.............................978 670-7300
Joseph Benedetto, *CEO*
Alfred Patane, *Pr*
EMP: 22 **EST:** 1997
SQ FT: 30,000
SALES (est): 4.63MM
SALES (corp-wide): 4.63MM **Privately Held**

Web: www.vptcomponents.com
SIC: 3674 7389 Semiconductors and
related devices; Inspection and testing
services

(G-9602)
TECHPRINT INC
137 Marston St (01841-2201)
PHONE.............................978 975-1245
TOLL FREE: 800
Paul J Durant Junior, *Pr*
Paul J Durant, *Pr*
Mary T Durant, *
Nicole M Smith, *
▲ **EMP:** 75 **EST:** 1974
SQ FT: 35,000
SALES (est): 21.1MM **Privately Held**
Web: www.techprintinc.com
SIC: 2759 2752 Screen printing; Offset
printing

(G-9603)
TERIKA SMITH MINISTRIES CORP
530 Broadway Fl 3 (01841-2446)
P.O. Box 267 (01844-0267)
PHONE.............................978 233-0576
Terika Smith, *Pr*
EMP: 29 **EST:** 2019
SALES (est): 538.41K **Privately Held**
Web: www.terikasmithministries.org
SIC: 8661 8299 2711 7941 Religious
organizations; Schools and educational
services, nec; Newspapers, publishing and
printing; Sports clubs, managers, and
promoters

(G-9604)
TRIPOLI BAKERY INC
106 Common St Ste 6 (01840-1633)
PHONE.............................978 682-7754
Rosario Zappella, *Pr*
Angelo Zappella, *
Steven Zappella, *
EMP: 16 **EST:** 1925
SALES (est): 813.24K **Privately Held**
Web: www.tripolibakery.com
SIC: 2051 5461 Breads, rolls, and buns;
Retail bakeries

(G-9605)
ULTIMATE WINDOWS INC
130 Shepard St (01843-1026)
PHONE.............................978 687-9444
Jack Perrino, *Pr*
EMP: 8
Web: www.ultimatewindowsinc.com
SIC: 5211 1751 3442 1542 Windows, storm:
wood or metal; Window and door
(prefabricated) installation; Screens,
window, metal; Store front construction
PA: Ultimate Windows, Inc.
110 Chelsea St
Everett MA 02149

(G-9606)
UNITED GL TO MET SEALING INC
15 Union St Ste G30 (01840-1823)
PHONE.............................978 327-5880
Richard Darwin, *Pr*
EMP: 12 **EST:** 1974
SQ FT: 6,000
SALES (est): 364.9K **Privately Held**
Web: www.unitedglass.com
SIC: 3599 1799 Machine shop, jobbing and
repair; Coating, caulking, and weather,
water, and fireproofing

(G-9607)
UNITED TOOL & MACHINE CORP (PA)
50 Shepard St (01843-1024)
PHONE.............................978 658-5500
Scott Fallo, *Pr*
EMP: 30 **EST:** 1963
SALES (est): 9.81MM
SALES (corp-wide): 9.81MM **Privately Held**
Web: www.unitedtoolmachine.com
SIC: 3469 3544 3599 Stamping metal for
the trade; Special dies, tools, jigs, and
fixtures; Machine shop, jobbing and repair

(G-9608)
UNITED TOOL & MACHINE CORP
B.G. Peck Company
50 Shepard St (01843-1024)
PHONE.............................978 686-4181
EMP: 26
SALES (corp-wide): 9.81MM **Privately Held**
Web: www.unitedtoolmachine.com
SIC: 3053 3469 Gaskets, all materials;
Metal stampings, nec
PA: United Tool & Machine Corporation
50 Shepard St
Lawrence MA 01843
978 658-5500

(G-9609)
WHITTEMORE COMPANY INC
30 Glenn St (01843-1020)
P.O. Box 3099 (01810-0802)
PHONE.............................978 681-8833
Jeffrey Sheehy, *Pr*
Kathleen Sheehy, *Sec*
▲ **EMP:** 20 **EST:** 1993
SQ FT: 28,000
SALES (est): 8.38MM **Privately Held**
Web: www.whittemoreco.com
SIC: 3295 Perlite, aggregate or expanded

Lee
Berkshire County

(G-9610)
ANDRUS POWER SOLUTIONS INC
Also Called: APS
690 Pleasant St (01238-9323)
PHONE.............................413 243-0043
Dan Andrus, *Pr*
EMP: 10 **EST:** 2003
SQ FT: 2,000
SALES (est): 1.67MM **Privately Held**
Web: www.andruspowersolutions.com
SIC: 3621 1731 Generators and sets,
electric; Electrical work

(G-9611)
BERKSHIRE STERILE MFG LLC
480 Pleasant St (01238-9265)
PHONE.............................413 243-0330
Shawn Kinney, *CEO*
Andrea Wagner, *
Joel Quinones, *CFO*
EMP: 171 **EST:** 2014
SALES (est): 31.33MM
SALES (corp-wide): 2.67MM **Privately Held**
Web:
www.berkshiresterilemanufacturing.com
SIC: 2834 Pharmaceutical preparations
HQ: Sharp Packaging Services, Llc
22-23 Carland Rd
Conshohocken PA 19428
610 395-5800

(G-9612)
BOYD BIOMEDICAL INC (PA)
501 Pleasant St (01238-9322)
P.O. Box 287 (01260-0287)
PHONE.............................413 243-2000
Stephen Boyd, *CEO*
Matthew B Boyd, *
Scott M Hand, *
Cary G Bullock, *
Charles Cooney, *
▲ **EMP:** 47 **EST:** 1979
SQ FT: 76,005
SALES (est): 48.77MM
SALES (corp-wide): 48.77MM **Privately Held**
Web: www.boydbiomedical.com
SIC: 5113 2679 2297 3353 Industrial and
personal service paper; Paper products,
converted, nec; Nonwoven fabrics; Foil,
aluminum

(G-9613)
FOX HOMES INC
225 Housatonic St (01238-1329)
PHONE.............................413 243-1950
Louis Digrigoli, *Pr*
Dave Brown, *VP*
EMP: 16 **EST:** 1984
SQ FT: 1,200
SALES (est): 454.42K **Privately Held**
Web: www.foxmodularhomes.com
SIC: 2452 6552 Modular homes,
prefabricated, wood; Land subdividers and
developers, residential

(G-9614)
LANE CONSTRUCTION CORPORATION
Also Called: Lenox Dale Hot Mix Asp Aggrgat
1 Willow Hill Rd (01238)
P.O. Box 280 (01242-0280)
PHONE.............................413 637-2511
Robert Turner, *Mgr*
EMP: 46
SALES (corp-wide): 7.95B **Privately Held**
Web: www.laneconstruct.com
SIC: 1622 1611 1629 3272 Highway
construction, elevated; Airport runway
construction; Subway construction; Building
materials, except block or brick: concrete
HQ: The Lane Construction Corporation
90 Fieldstone Ct
Cheshire CT 06410
203 235-3351

(G-9615)
LEE TAN ENTERPRISE LLC
265 Greylock St (01238-9483)
PHONE.............................413 243-4717
Sabrina Tan, *Prin*
EMP: 7 **EST:** 2015
SALES (est): 49.74K **Privately Held**
SIC: 2711 Newspapers, publishing and
printing

(G-9616)
LIMELIGHT PRODUCTIONS INC
471 Pleasant St (01238-9322)
PHONE.............................413 243-4950
William Beautyman, *Pr*
EMP: 8 **EST:** 1972
SQ FT: 8,000
SALES (est): 1.42MM **Privately Held**
Web: www.limelightproductions.com
SIC: 7359 5999 2391 1542 Sound and
lighting equipment rental; Theatrical
equipment and supplies; Curtains and
draperies; Commercial and office buildings,
renovation and repair

(G-9617)
PATRIOT ARMRED SYSTEMS HLDG LL
100 Valley St (01238-7701)
PHONE..............................413 637-1060
Thomas Briggs, *Mgr*
Steve Donnally, *
EMP: 60 **EST:** 2018
SALES (est): 2.88MM **Privately Held**
Web: www.pasarmor.com
SIC: 3211 Strengthened or reinforced glass

(G-9618)
PROTECTIVE ARMORED SYSTEMS INC
Also Called: P A S
100 Valley St (01238-7701)
PHONE..............................413 637-1060
▼ **EMP:** 19 **EST:** 1994
SQ FT: 27,000
SALES (est): 467.19K **Privately Held**
Web: www.pasarmored.com
SIC: 3211 3231 Laminated glass; Products of purchased glass

(G-9619)
RAY MURRAY INC (PA)
50 Limestone (01238-9621)
P.O. Box 339 (01238-0339)
PHONE..............................413 243-2164
Michael Hopsicker, *Pr*
▲ **EMP:** 76 **EST:** 1973
SQ FT: 92,000
SALES (est): 87.31MM
SALES (corp-wide): 87.31MM **Privately Held**
Web: www.raymurray.com
SIC: 5084 5085 5075 3631 Propane conversion equipment; Gas equipment, parts and supplies; Warm air heating and air conditioning; Household cooking equipment

Leeds
Hampshire County

(G-9620)
CHAMPLAIN CABLE LEEDS CORPORATION
118 River Rd (01053-9782)
P.O. Box 306 (01053-0306)
PHONE..............................413 584-3853
EMP: 25
SIC: 3357 Nonferrous wiredrawing and insulating

(G-9621)
CHARTPAK INC (HQ)
1 River Rd (01053-9732)
PHONE..............................413 584-5446
Steven W Roth, *Pr*
Robert Rodak, *
◆ **EMP:** 61 **EST:** 1957
SQ FT: 165,000
SALES (est): 28.27MM
SALES (corp-wide): 28.27MM **Privately Held**
Web: www.chartpak.com
SIC: 5999 2782 2672 3952 Artists' supplies and materials; Chart and graph paper, ruled ; Labels (unprinted), gummed: made from purchased materials; Ink, drawing: black and colored
PA: Gpc International, Inc.
510 Broadhollow Rd # 205
Melville NY 11747
631 752-9600

Leicester
Worcester County

(G-9622)
CABLE HARNESS RESOURCES INC
3 Brickyard Rd (01524-1286)
PHONE.................,.....508 892-9495
Phuoc Nguyen, *Pr*
Kim Nguyen, *Mgr*
EMP: 12 **EST:** 2010
SALES (est): 808.42K **Privately Held**
SIC: 3399 Primary metal products

(G-9623)
CULTIVATE LICENSING LLC
Also Called: Cultivate
1794 Main St (01524-1918)
PHONE..............................508 859-8130
Sam Barber, *Pr*
EMP: 16 **EST:** 2019
SALES (est): 2.32MM
SALES (corp-wide): 339.45MM **Privately Held**
SIC: 3999 5999 5993 ; Cannabis store
PA: Cresco Labs, Llc
400 W Erie St Ste 110
Chicago IL 60654
312 929-0993

Lenox
Berkshire County

(G-9624)
16SUR20 MANAGEMENT LLC
Also Called: Seize Sur Vingt
30 Kemble St (01240-2813)
P.O. Box 2280 (01240-5280)
PHONE..............................413 637-5061
EMP: 11 **EST:** 2004
SQ FT: 2,000
SALES (est): 482.25K **Privately Held**
SIC: 2329 2321 2325 Men's and boys' sportswear and athletic clothing; Men's and boy's furnishings; Men's and boy's trousers and slacks
PA: Groupe 16sur20, Llc
30 Kemble St
Lenox MA 01240

(G-9625)
INNOVATIVE TOOLING COMPANY INC
Also Called: I T C
180 Pittsfield Rd (01240-2131)
PHONE..............................413 637-1031
Karl Dastoli, *Pr*
Karl Dastoli, *Pr*
William J Pigott, *VP*
EMP: 10 **EST:** 1983
SQ FT: 7,500
SALES (est): 984.79K **Privately Held**
Web: www.innovativetool.net
SIC: 3544 3089 3599 Industrial molds; Injection molding of plastics; Custom machinery

(G-9626)
LENOX SPECIAL NEEDS
129 West St (01240-2420)
PHONE..............................413 637-5571
EMP: 7 **EST:** 2019
SALES (est): 235.72K **Privately Held**
Web: www.lenoxps.org
SIC: 3585 Refrigeration and heating equipment

(G-9627)
VALMET INC
GL&v Lenox
175 Crystal St (01240)
P.O. Box 846 (01240-0846)
PHONE..............................413 637-2424
Laurent Verreault, *Mgr*
EMP: 220
SALES (corp-wide): 5.27B **Privately Held**
Web: www.valmet.com
SIC: 3554 Paper industries machinery
HQ: Valmet, Inc.
3720 Davinci Ct Ste 300
Norcross GA 30092
770 263-7863

Lenox Dale
Berkshire County

(G-9628)
PATRIOT ARMORED SYSTEMS LLC (PA)
Also Called: Patriot Armor
140 Crystal St (01242-4210)
P.O. Box 400 (01242-0400)
PHONE..............................413 637-1060
EMP: 16 **EST:** 2012
SALES (est): 4.13MM **Privately Held**
Web: www.pasarmor.com
SIC: 3231 Products of purchased glass

Leominster
Worcester County

(G-9629)
175 PIONEER DRIVE LLC
175 Pioneer Dr (01453-3475)
PHONE..............................978 840-1897
Mark Gasbarro, *Prin*
EMP: 9 **EST:** 2013
SALES (est): 516.75K **Privately Held**
Web: www.fmtool.com
SIC: 3089 Injection molding of plastics

(G-9630)
AARON INDUSTRIES CORP
Also Called: Aaron
20 Mohawk Dr Ste 1 (01453-3393)
P.O. Box 607 (01453-0607)
PHONE..............................978 534-6135
Robert G Tocci, *Pr*
Robert M Tocci, *
▲ **EMP:** 30 **EST:** 1983
SQ FT: 20,000
SALES (est): 8.46MM **Privately Held**
Web: www.aaroninc.com
SIC: 3089 Injection molding of plastics

(G-9631)
ACCUCON INCORPORATED
12 Mount Pleasant Ave Ste 100 (01453-5887)
PHONE..............................978 840-0337
John J White, *Pr*
Forrest E Hawes Junior, *VP*
EMP: 9 **EST:** 1984
SQ FT: 3,500
SALES (est): 931.56K **Privately Held**
Web: www.accuconlabels.com
SIC: 2752 2672 Offset printing; Paper, coated and laminated, nec

(G-9632)
ADVANCED PROTOTYPES & MOLDING
Also Called: A P M

21 Howe St (01453-3801)
PHONE..............................978 534-0584
Craig W Powell, *Pr*
Erin Powell, *Sec*
EMP: 8 **EST:** 1981
SQ FT: 5,000
SALES (est): 916K **Privately Held**
Web: www.advancedprototypesandmolding.com
SIC: 3089 3544 Injection molding of plastics ; Forms (molds), for foundry and plastics working machinery

(G-9633)
AFFORDABLE INTR SYSTEMS INC (HQ)
Also Called: A I S
25 Tucker Dr (01453-6501)
PHONE..............................978 562-7500
Bruce Platzman, *Pr*
Arthur Maxwell, *
Steve Savage, *
Bryan Poist, *
◆ **EMP:** 100 **EST:** 1999
SQ FT: 100,000
SALES (est): 144.16MM
SALES (corp-wide): 2.8B **Privately Held**
Web: www.ais-inc.com
SIC: 5712 2522 Office furniture; Benches, office: except wood
PA: Audax Group Limited Partnership
101 Huntington Ave # 2450
Boston MA 02199
617 859-1500

(G-9634)
AIS GROUP HOLDINGS LLC
Also Called: A I S
25 Tucker Dr (01453-6501)
PHONE..............................978 562-7500
◆ **EMP:** 285 **EST:** 2007
SALES (est): 17.59MM **Privately Held**
Web: www.ais-inc.com
SIC: 2522 Panel systems and partitions, office: except wood

(G-9635)
ALLIED RESIN TECHNOLOGIES LLC
Also Called: Garden By Artech
25 Litchfield St (01453-4251)
PHONE..............................978 401-2267
EMP: 15 **EST:** 2014
SALES (est): 2.86MM **Privately Held**
SIC: 2821 Plastics materials and resins

(G-9636)
AMOS GRT-GRT-GRANDDAUGHTER INC
554 Willard St (01453-5923)
P.O. Box 142 (01453-0142)
PHONE..............................413 773-5471
Elizabeth Rugg Grybko, *Pr*
Jonathan Daen, *Dir*
▲ **EMP:** 21 **EST:** 1842
SQ FT: 40,000
SALES (est): 1.88MM **Privately Held**
Web: www.rugg.com
SIC: 3531 3423 Roofing equipment; Garden and farm tools, including shovels

(G-9637)
ART PLASTICS MFG CORP
75 Water St (01453-3218)
PHONE..............................978 537-6640
EMP: 10
SIC: 3089 Injection molded finished plastics products, nec

(G-9638)

BANNER MOLD & DIE CO INC

251 Florence St (01453-4499)
PHONE..............................978 534-6558
James M De Felice, *Pr*
Ralph De Felice, *
EMP: 40 EST: 1946
SQ FT: 46,000
SALES (est): 3.56MM **Privately Held**
Web: www.bannermold.com
SIC: 3544 Forms (molds), for foundry and plastics working machinery

(G-9639)

BAY STATE APPAREL INC

Also Called: Bay State Apparrel
44 Mead St (01453-2966)
PHONE..............................978 534-5810
Brian Whitney, *Prin*
EMP: 8 EST: 1988
SQ FT: 20,000
SALES (est): 1.33MM **Privately Held**
Web: www.baystatesapparel.com
SIC: 7336 2759 2396 Silk screen design; Screen printing; Automotive and apparel trimmings

(G-9640)

BEACON ENGNRED SLTONS - MA LLC

32 Jungle Rd (01453-5273)
PHONE..............................978 466-9591
EMP: 12 EST: 2021
SALES (est): 2.21MM **Privately Held**
SIC: 3089 Injection molding of plastics

(G-9641)

BELDEN INC

Alpha Wire
128 Tolman Ave (01453-1926)
PHONE..............................978 537-8911
Joseph Brown, *Mgr*
EMP: 45
SALES (corp-wide): 2.51B **Publicly Held**
Web: www.belden.com
SIC: 3315 3357 Wire and fabricated wire products; Nonferrous wiredrawing and insulating
PA: Belden Inc.
   1 N Brentwood Blvd Fl 15
   Saint Louis MO 63105
   314 854-8000

(G-9642)

BEVOVATIONS LLC

Also Called: New England Apple Products Co
320 Industrial Rd (01453-1684)
PHONE..............................978 227-5469
Steven D Rowse, *Managing Member*
EMP: 13 EST: 2008
SALES (est): 2.38MM **Privately Held**
Web: www.newenglandapple.com
SIC: 2037 Fruit juices

(G-9643)

BRIDEAU SHTMTL FABRICATION INC

29 Phillips St (01453-4023)
PHONE..............................978 537-3372
David E Brideau, *Pr*
EMP: 29 EST: 1966
SQ FT: 11,000
SALES (est): 1.78MM **Privately Held**
Web: www.brideausheetmetal.com
SIC: 3444 1711 Ducts, sheet metal; Heating and air conditioning contractors

(G-9644)

BROLAN TOOL INC

25 Jytek Rd (01453-5934)
PHONE..............................978 537-0290
Michael F Gasbarro, *Pr*
EMP: 20 EST: 1974
SQ FT: 11,000
SALES (est): 2.49MM **Privately Held**
Web: www.fmtoolanddie.com
SIC: 3544 Special dies and tools

(G-9645)

BWI OF MA LLC

248 Industrial Rd (01453-1642)
PHONE..............................978 534-4065
EMP: 10 EST: 2009
SALES (est): 366.6K **Privately Held**
Web: www.bwi-distribution.com
SIC: 2431 Millwork

(G-9646)

CAMCO MANUFACTURING INC

Also Called: CAMCO MANUFACTURING, INC.
165 Pioneer Dr (01453-3475)
PHONE..............................978 537-6777
Randy Catalucci, *Mgr*
EMP: 54
SALES (corp-wide): 100.88MM **Privately Held**
Web: www.camco.net
SIC: 2899 3085 Antifreeze compounds; Plastics bottles
PA: Camco Manufacturing, Llc
   121 Landmark Dr
   Greensboro NC 27409
   800 334-2004

(G-9647)

CARDINAL COMB & BRUSH MFG CORP

Also Called: Cardinal Comb Mfg
106 Carter St Ste 3 (01453-7303)
PHONE..............................978 537-6330
Anthony J Mazzaferro, *Pr*
Aldo J Mazzaferro Senior, *Treas*
Anna R Mazzaferro, *
EMP: 23 EST: 1969
SQ FT: 54,600
SALES (est): 1.84MM **Privately Held**
Web: www.cardinalcomb.com
SIC: 3991 3089 Brooms and brushes; Injection molded finished plastics products, nec

(G-9648)

CASTLE PLASTICS INC

11 Francis St (01453-4911)
PHONE..............................978 534-6220
Joseph Serafini Junior, *Pr*
EMP: 8 EST: 1940
SQ FT: 10,000
SALES (est): 954.97K **Privately Held**
Web: www.castleplastics.com
SIC: 3089 Injection molded finished plastics products, nec

(G-9649)

CE BAIRD CORPORATION (PA)

Also Called: Reliance Engineering Division
32 Jungle Rd (01453-5273)
PHONE..............................978 368-7250
Craig Bovaird, *Pr*
EMP: 11 EST: 1988
SALES (est): 10.29MM **Privately Held**
Web: www.beaconmedtech.com
SIC: 3089 Injection molding of plastics

(G-9650)

CE BAIRD CORPORATION

Also Called: Reliance Engineering
11 Jytek Rd (01453-5986)
PHONE..............................978 751-8432
EMP: 11
Web: www.beaconmedtech.com
SIC: 3544 Special dies and tools
PA: C.E. Baird Corporation
   32 Jungle Rd
   Leominster MA 01453

(G-9651)

CHRIS PLOOF DESIGNS INC

57 Nashua St (01453-3392)
P.O. Box 786 (01453-0786)
PHONE..............................978 728-4905
Christopher Ploof, *Pr*
EMP: 8 EST: 2013
SALES (est): 234.1K **Privately Held**
Web: www.chrisploof.com
SIC: 7389 3911 Design services; Jewelry apparel

(G-9652)

CHROMA COLOR CORPORATION

50 Francis St (01453-4911)
PHONE..............................978 537-3538
EMP: 48
SALES (corp-wide): 117.78MM **Privately Held**
Web: www.chromacolors.com
SIC: 2821 Plastics materials and resins
PA: Chroma Color Corporation
   3900 W Dayton St
   Mchenry IL 60050
   877 385-8777

(G-9653)

COMEAU CONSULTING INC

Also Called: Albright Silicone
30 Patriots Cir (01453-5967)
PHONE..............................978 466-5870
EMP: 15 EST: 1995
SALES (est): 2.59MM **Privately Held**
Web: www.albrightsilicone.com
SIC: 3089 Injection molding of plastics

(G-9654)

CREATIVE PRINT PRODUCTS INC

243 Whitney St (01453-3222)
PHONE..............................978 534-2030
David J Aronson, *Pr*
EMP: 14 EST: 2001
SQ FT: 2,000
SALES (est): 2.9MM **Privately Held**
Web: www.creativeprintproducts.com
SIC: 2752 Commercial printing, lithographic

(G-9655)

CRH AMERICAS INC

Also Called: Old Materials New England
14 Monument Sq Ste 302 (01453-5766)
PHONE..............................978 840-1176
John Keating, *Pr*
EMP: 292
SALES (corp-wide): 32.72B **Privately Held**
Web: www.crhamericas.com
SIC: 3273 Ready-mixed concrete
HQ: Crh Americas, Inc.
   900 Ashwood Pkwy Ste 600
   Atlanta GA 30338
   770 804-3363

(G-9656)

DAHLICIOUS HOLDINGS LLC

Also Called: Dahlicious

320 Hamilton St Ste 3 (01453-2385)
PHONE..............................978 401-2103
Jaidesh Sethi, *Managing Member*
EMP: 14 EST: 2007
SQ FT: 35,000
SALES (est): 3.29MM **Privately Held**
SIC: 2026 5141 Yogurt; Food brokers

(G-9657)

DAHLICIOUS LLC

320 Hamilton St Ste 3 (01453-2385)
PHONE..............................505 200-0396
EMP: 40 EST: 2016
SALES (est): 3.64MM **Privately Held**
Web: www.dahlicious.com
SIC: 2026 Yogurt

(G-9658)

DIXIE CONSUMER PRODUCTS LLC

149 Hamilton St (01453-2342)
PHONE..............................978 537-4701
EMP: 18
SALES (corp-wide): 36.93B **Privately Held**
SIC: 2621 Paper mills
HQ: Dixie Consumer Products Llc
   133 Peachtree St Ne # 1
   Atlanta GA 30303

(G-9659)

DSM THERMOPLASTICS

29 Fuller St (01453-4225)
PHONE..............................978 537-6484
EMP: 7 EST: 2017
SALES (est): 256.82K **Privately Held**
SIC: 2821 Plastics materials and resins

(G-9660)

E T DUVAL & SONS INC

386 Main St (01453-2937)
P.O. Box 419 (01453-0419)
PHONE..............................978 537-7596
Jeffrey Duval, *Pr*
Francis L Duval, *Prin*
EMP: 8 EST: 1932
SQ FT: 3,200
SALES (est): 931.09K **Privately Held**
Web: www.etduval.com
SIC: 3441 3444 3541 Fabricated structural metal; Sheet metalwork; Machine tools, metal cutting type

(G-9661)

ECLIPSE PRODUCTS INC

60 Commonwealth Cir (01453-2561)
PHONE..............................978 343-8600
Joseph S Pope Junior, *Pr*
Karen Pope, *Treas*
EMP: 10 EST: 1992
SALES (est): 808.41K **Privately Held**
Web: www.eclipseproducts.net
SIC: 3089 Injection molding of plastics

(G-9662)

F & D PLASTICS INC (PA)

Also Called: Fd Plastics
23 Jytek Dr (01453-5984)
PHONE..............................978 668-5140
Darren Rosbury, *Pr*
David Leboeuf, *
Jean Rosbury, *
Chuck Walkovich, *
▲ EMP: 40 EST: 1967
SQ FT: 23,000
SALES (est): 10.01MM
SALES (corp-wide): 10.01MM **Privately Held**
Web: www.fdplastics.com

▲ = Import ▼ = Export
◆ = Import/Export

SIC: **3089** 2851 2816 Molding primary plastics; Paints and allied products; Inorganic pigments

(G-9663)
F & M TOOL & PLASTICS INC
Also Called: Smartware Products
175 Pioneer Dr (01453-3475)
PHONE.................................978 840-1897
Mark Gasbarro, *Pr*
Tim Wendt, *CFO*
▲ **EMP: 260 EST:** 1995
SQ FT: 35,000
SALES (est): 100MM **Privately Held**
Web: www.fmtool.com
SIC: **3089** Injection molding of plastics

(G-9664)
FIRST PLASTICS CORP
Also Called: F P
22 Jytek Rd (01453-5966)
PHONE.................................978 537-0367
Edward Mazzaferro, *Pr*
Aldo J Mazzaferro, *Treas*
Anna R Mazzaferro, *Clerk*
▲ **EMP: 10 EST:** 1952
SQ FT: 33,000
SALES (est): 2.55MM **Privately Held**
Web: www.haddco.com
SIC: **3089** Injection molded finished plastics products, nec

(G-9665)
FOSTA-TEK OPTICS INC (PA)
320 Hamilton St Ste 1 (01453-2371)
PHONE.................................978 534-6511
John Morrison Junior, *Pr*
Karen Olivari, *
James R Leblanc, *
EMP: 89 **EST:** 1991
SQ FT: 113,000
SALES (est): 24.67MM **Privately Held**
Web: www.fostatek.com
SIC: **3851** 3842 Ophthalmic goods; Surgical appliances and supplies

(G-9666)
GEORGIA-PACIFIC LLC
Also Called: Georgia-Pacific
149 Hamilton St (01453-2342)
PHONE.................................978 537-4701
Steve Lambrose, *Brnch Mgr*
EMP: 56
SALES (corp-wide): 36.93B **Privately Held**
Web: www.gp.com
SIC: **2297** 3086 3861 2631 Ribbon, nonwoven (yarn bonded by plastic); Cups and plates, foamed plastics; Film, sensitized motion picture, X-ray, still camera, etc.; Packaging board
HQ: Georgia-Pacific Llc
133 Peachtree St Nw
Atlanta GA 30303
404 652-4000

(G-9667)
GIROUARD TOOL CORP
561 Research Dr (01453-5285)
PHONE.................................978 534-4147
Robert Julius, *Pr*
Lori Julius, *VP*
EMP: 8 **EST:** 2002
SALES (est): 1.47MM **Privately Held**
Web: www.girouardtoolcorp.com
SIC: **2869** Olefins

(G-9668)
GROVE PRODUCTS INC
17 Marguerite Ave Ste 1 (01453-4202)
P.O. Box 240 (01453-0240)
PHONE.................................978 534-5188
David Braune, *Pr*
Simon Braune, *VP*
▼ **EMP: 11 EST:** 1966
SQ FT: 8,000
SALES (est): 4.11MM **Privately Held**
Web: www.groveshims.com
SIC: **3089** Injection molding of plastics

(G-9669)
HEAT TRACE PRODUCTS LLC
233 Florence St (01453-4409)
PHONE.................................978 534-2810
EMP: 20 **EST:** 2004
SQ FT: 30,000
SALES (est): 4.85MM **Privately Held**
Web: www.rscc-heattrace.com
SIC: **3315** Cable, steel: insulated or armored

(G-9670)
IMANOVA PACKAGING
7 New Lancaster Rd (01453-5224)
PHONE.................................978 537-8534
Dave Fischer, *Prin*
EMP: 16 **EST:** 1937
SALES (est): 930.65K **Privately Held**
SIC: **3086** Packaging and shipping materials, foamed plastics

(G-9671)
INNOVATIVE MOLD SOLUTIONS INC
Also Called: I M S
42 Jungle Rd (01453-5208)
PHONE.................................978 840-1503
Paul Boudreau, *Pr*
Richard Cella, *
▲ **EMP: 50 EST:** 1996
SQ FT: 6,000
SALES (est): 9.7MM **Privately Held**
Web: www.urthpact.com
SIC: **3089** Injection molding of plastics

(G-9672)
JAM PLASTICS INC
22 Tucker Dr (01453-6500)
PHONE.................................978 537-2570
J D Mazzaferro Senior, *Pr*
Joseph D Mazzaferro Senior, *Pr*
Joseph D Mazzaferro Junior, *VP*
Matthew Mazzaferro, *VP*
Joseph Mazzaferro, *Pr*
▲ **EMP: 22 EST:** 1973
SQ FT: 32,500
SALES (est): 3.1MM **Privately Held**
Web: www.jam-plastics.com
SIC: **3089** 2752 1799 Injection molding of plastics; Offset and photolithographic printing; Welding on site

(G-9673)
K AND C PLASTICS INC
18 Crawford St (01453-2326)
P.O. Box 781 (01453-0781)
PHONE.................................978 537-0605
Kirt D Wilbur, *Pr*
▲ **EMP: 18 EST:** 1977
SQ FT: 24,000
SALES (est): 999.96K **Privately Held**
Web: www.kandcplastics.com
SIC: **3089** Injection molding of plastics

(G-9674)
KREST PRODUCTS CORP
707 Lancaster St (01453-4545)
P.O. Box 176 (01453-0176)
PHONE.................................978 537-1244
Richard Di Marzio, *Pr*
Pat Di Marzio, *
Esther Di Marzio, *

EMP: 25 EST: 1961
SQ FT: 17,000
SALES (est): 3.48MM **Privately Held**
Web: www.krestcombs.com
SIC: **3089** Combs, plastics

(G-9675)
L & A MOLDING CORPORATION
Also Called: Mid West Colour
50 Francis St (01453-4911)
PHONE.................................978 537-3538
▲ **EMP:** 52
SIC: **2851** Paints and paint additives

(G-9676)
LEAKTITE CORPORATION (DH)
Also Called: Leaktite
40 Francis St (01453-4911)
PHONE.................................978 537-8000
Jay Brooks, *Pr*
Russ Brillon, *
▲ **EMP: 49 EST:** 1965
SQ FT: 100,000
SALES (est): 22.98MM
SALES (corp-wide): 816.52K **Privately Held**
Web: www.leaktite.com
SIC: **3089** 3411 Plastics containers, except foam; Metal cans
HQ: Plastiques Ipl Inc
1155 Boul Rene-Levesque O Bureau 4100
Montreal QC H3B 3
418 789-2880

(G-9677)
LEOMINSTER CHAMPION
285 Central St Ste 202b (01453-6144)
PHONE.................................978 534-6006
Modestino Tropeano, *Treas*
EMP: 10 **EST:** 2011
SALES (est): 191.83K **Privately Held**
Web: www.leominsterhigh.com
SIC: **2711** Commercial printing and newspaper publishing combined

(G-9678)
LEOMINSTER ICE COMPANY INC
Also Called: Leominster Ice & Oil Co
5 Chestnut St (01453-3999)
PHONE.................................978 537-5322
TOLL FREE: 800
Royal F Turner Junior, *Pr*
George E Douglas, *Treas*
Stephen Douglas, *Clerk*
EMP: 7 **EST:** 1923
SQ FT: 2,500
SALES (est): 500.86K **Privately Held**
Web: www.leominstericeandoil.com
SIC: **2097** 5999 Manufactured ice; Ice

(G-9679)
LOCK INSPECTION SYSTEMS INC
98 Adams St Ste 107 (01453-5680)
PHONE.................................978 343-3716
▲ **EMP: 26 EST:** 1986
SALES (est): 2.88MM **Privately Held**
SIC: **3565** Packaging machinery

(G-9680)
M & K INDUSTRIES INC
Also Called: Subcon Technology
177 Florence St (01453-4782)
PHONE.................................978 514-9850
Bimal Patel, *Pr*
Jayshri Patel, *Treas*
▲ **EMP: 25 EST:** 1986
SQ FT: 1,500
SALES (est): 4.79MM **Privately Held**

SIC: **3823** Process control instruments

(G-9681)
MASONITE INTERNATIONAL CORP
248 Industrial Rd (01453-1642)
PHONE.................................978 534-4065
Mark Flynn, *Brnch Mgr*
EMP: 7
SALES (corp-wide): 2.89B **Publicly Held**
Web: www.masonite.com
SIC: **2431** Doors, wood
PA: Masonite International Corporation
1242 E 5th Ave
Tampa FL 33605
813 877-2726

(G-9682)
MAUSER PACKG SOLUTIONS HOLDG
25 Tucker Dr (01453-6501)
PHONE.................................978 728-5000
EMP: 17
Web: www.mauserpackaging.com
SIC: **3089** Buckets, plastics
HQ: Mauser Packaging Solutions Holding Company
8607 Roberts Dr Ste 250
Atlanta GA 30350
770 645-4800

(G-9683)
MEXICHEM SPCALTY COMPOUNDS INC (HQ)
Also Called: Alphagary
170 Pioneer Dr (01453-3474)
PHONE.................................978 537-8071
Gautam Nivart, *Pr*
Mike Funderburg, *
Rick Peiczarka, *
◆ **EMP: 205 EST:** 1992
SQ FT: 130,000
SALES (est): 134.12MM **Privately Held**
Web: www.alphagary.com
SIC: **3087** 2899 Custom compound purchased resins; Chemical preparations, nec
PA: Orbia Advance Corporation, S.A.B. De C.V.
Av. Paseo De La Reforma No. 483
Piso 47
Mexico CMX 06500

(G-9684)
MOHAWK CHICAGO DISTRIBUTION
9 Mohawk Dr (01453-3321)
PHONE.................................781 334-4976
Moe Heon, *Prin*
EMP: 11 **EST:** 2017
SALES (est): 697.29K **Privately Held**
SIC: **3357** Nonferrous wiredrawing and insulating

(G-9685)
NEW ENGLAND FAB MTLS INC
Also Called: Nefm
101 Crawford St (01453-2327)
PHONE.................................978 466-7823
Michael J Boyer, *Pr*
Sally A Boyer, *
EMP: 25 **EST:** 1983
SQ FT: 17,000
SALES (est): 4MM **Privately Held**
Web: www.nefm.com
SIC: **3444** Sheet metal specialties, not stamped

GEOGRAPHIC

(G-9686)

NEW ENGLAND WIRE PRODUCTS INC (PA)
9 Mohawk Dr (01453-3321)
P.O. Box 276 (02493-0002)
PHONE..........................800 254-9473
Charles Peters Junior, *Pr*
Karen Peters, *
EMP: 78 **EST:** 1980
SQ FT: 96,000
SALES (est): 38.98MM
SALES (corp-wide): 38.98MM **Privately Held**
Web: www.displayracks.com
SIC: 3496 3993 2542　Wire cloth and woven wire products; Signs and advertising specialties; Partitions and fixtures, except wood

(G-9687)

NORTHERN PRODUCTS INC
1427 Main St (01453-6612)
PHONE..........................978 840-3383
▲ **EMP:** 10 **EST:** 1993
SALES (est): 1.45MM **Privately Held**
Web: www.glow-sticks.com
SIC: 3089　Injection molding of plastics

(G-9688)

NOVA PACKAGING SYSTEMS INC
Also Called: Imanova
7 New Lancaster Rd (01453-5224)
PHONE..........................978 537-8534
Marco Grassilli, *Pr*
Stewart Harvey, *
▲ **EMP:** 51 **EST:** 2004
SQ FT: 150,000
SALES (est): 8.48MM **Privately Held**
Web: www.ima.it
SIC: 3565　Packing and wrapping machinery
HQ: I.M.A. Industria Macchine Automatiche Spa
　Via Emilia 428-442
　Ozzano Dell'emilia BO 40064
　051 651-4783

(G-9689)

OCEAN AND COMMON INC
Also Called: Acro-Matic Plastics
32 Jungle Rd (01453-5273)
PHONE..........................978 537-4102
Peter Crisci, *Pr*
Vincent Crisci, *
▲ **EMP:** 48 **EST:** 1964
SQ FT: 110,000
SALES (est): 9.47MM **Privately Held**
SIC: 3089 3544　Injection molding of plastics ; Forms (molds), for foundry and plastics working machinery

(G-9690)

OPTOGLO INC
493 Lancaster St (01453-7506)
PHONE..........................978 235-0201
Michael Browne, *Pr*
Kevin Donahue, *Dir*
Joel Bresler, *Dir*
▲ **EMP:** 16 **EST:** 2015
SALES (est): 2.63MM **Privately Held**
Web: www.optoglo.com
SIC: 3648　Lighting fixtures, except electric: residential

(G-9691)

OPTOMISTIC PRODUCTS INC
61 N Main St (01453-5507)
P.O. Box 751 (04078-0751)
PHONE..........................207 865-9181

Frank Langely, *Pr*
EMP: 10 **EST:** 1991
SALES (est): 805.16K **Privately Held**
Web: www.optomisticproducts.com
SIC: 3674　Light emitting diodes

(G-9692)

PATRICIA BARRETT
Also Called: D B Welding
56 Marshall St (01453-2428)
PHONE..........................978 537-0458
EMP: 10 **EST:** 1995
SALES (est): 596.93K **Privately Held**
SIC: 1791 7692　Structural steel erection; Welding repair

(G-9693)

PERIOQ INC
37 Hamilton St Apt 4 (01453-2344)
PHONE..........................978 534-1249
Subhash Gupta, *Prin*
EMP: 9 **EST:** 2009
SALES (est): 138.73K **Privately Held**
SIC: 8021 7389 2833 5499　Dental surgeon; Business services, nec; Vitamins, natural or synthetic: bulk, uncompounded; Health and dietetic food stores

(G-9694)

PFERD INC
30 Jytek Dr (01453-5932)
PHONE..........................978 840-6420
EMP: 21 **EST:** 2020
SALES (est): 406.41K **Privately Held**
Web: us.pferd.com
SIC: 3599　Industrial machinery, nec

(G-9695)

PLANTBASED INNOVATIONS LLC
Also Called: Store Brand Partner
320 Hamilton St Ste 27 (01453-2385)
P.O. Box 320 Hamilton St (01453)
PHONE..........................571 243-4646
Tom Burns, *CEO*
Dharm Khalsa, *
EMP: 37 **EST:** 2019
SALES (est): 12MM **Privately Held**
SIC: 2026　Yogurt

(G-9696)

PLASTICAN INC
196 Industrial Rd (01453-1662)
PHONE..........................978 728-5000
John R Clementi, *Pr*
Kenneth M Roessler, *
Jeffrey O Connell, *
Stephen T Zollo, *
Eva M Kalawski, *
▲ **EMP:** 550 **EST:** 1970
SQ FT: 360,000
SALES (est): 194.19MM **Privately Held**
SIC: 3089 5719　Buckets, plastics; Kitchenware
HQ: Mauser Packaging Solutions Holding Company
　8607 Roberts Dr Ste 250
　Atlanta GA 30350
　770 645-4800

(G-9697)

PROCESS COOLING SYSTEMS INC
800 Research Dr (01453-5274)
PHONE..........................978 537-1996
TOLL FREE: 800
Theodore Rudy, *Pr*
David Doucet, *
David Dufresne, *

EMP: 43 **EST:** 1967
SQ FT: 10,000
SALES (est): 10.32MM **Privately Held**
Web: www.processcooling.net
SIC: 3585 1711　Coolers, milk and water: electric; Process piping contractor

(G-9698)

QG PRINTING CORP
27 Nashua St (01453-3311)
PHONE..........................978 534-8351
Mike Agnew, *Brnch Mgr*
EMP: 22
SALES (corp-wide): 3.22B **Publicly Held**
SIC: 2752　Offset printing
HQ: Qg Printing Corp.
　N61w23044 Harrys Way
　Sussex WI 53089

(G-9699)

QUAD/GRAPHICS INC
Also Called: Quadgraphics
27 Nashua St (01453-3311)
PHONE..........................978 534-8351
Steve Viens, *VP*
EMP: 8
SALES (corp-wide): 3.22B **Publicly Held**
Web: www.quad.com
SIC: 2752　Offset printing
PA: Quad/Graphics, Inc.
　N61w23044 Harrys Way
　Sussex WI 53089
　414 566-6000

(G-9700)

REED & PRINCE MFG CORP
272 Nashua St (01453-3304)
PHONE..........................978 466-6903
James W Richardson, *Pr*
Jane B Richardson, *Sec*
▲ **EMP:** 15 **EST:** 1990
SQ FT: 45,000
SALES (est): 2.16MM **Privately Held**
Web: www.reedandprince.com
SIC: 3452 5085 3965　Screw eyes and hooks ; Fasteners, industrial: nuts, bolts, screws, etc.; Fasteners

(G-9701)

REMEDIATION LOCKWOOD TECH
691 Research Dr (01453-5286)
PHONE..........................404 666-5857
Paul Lockwood, *Pr*
Paul Lockwood, *Managing Member*
Michael Deso, *
EMP: 29 **EST:** 2011
SALES (est): 4.33MM **Privately Held**
Web: www.lrt-llc.net
SIC: 1799 8744 3589　Dewatering; Environmental remediation; Commercial cooking and foodwarming equipment

(G-9702)

RESOURCE COLORS LLC
Also Called: Color Resource Concentrates
517 Lancaster St (01453-7515)
PHONE..........................978 537-3700
EMP: 17 **EST:** 2009
SALES (est): 1.86MM **Privately Held**
Web: www.chromacolors.com
SIC: 2821　Polyvinyl butyral resins

(G-9703)

SIMONDS SAW LLC
Also Called: Simonds Saw - Louisville
435 Lancaster St (01453-4397)
PHONE..........................800 343-1616
Dina Srewart, *Brnch Mgr*
EMP: 23

SALES (corp-wide): 40MM **Privately Held**
Web: www.simondssaw.com
SIC: 3423　Hand and edge tools, nec
PA: Simonds Saw L.L.C.
　435 Lancaster St Ste 211
　Leominster MA 01453
　800 343-1616

(G-9704)

SIMONDS SAW LLC (PA)
Also Called: Simon Holding
435 Lancaster St Ste 211 (01453-4397)
P.O. Box 500 (01420-0005)
PHONE..........................800 343-1616
Raymond Martino, *Pr*
Philip Cochran, *Dir Fin*
▲ **EMP:** 7 **EST:** 2014
SALES (est): 40MM
SALES (corp-wide): 40MM **Privately Held**
Web: www.simondssaw.com
SIC: 3545　Cutting tools for machine tools

(G-9705)

SOIL EXPLORATION CORP (PA)
148 Pioneer Dr (01453-3474)
PHONE..........................978 840-0391
Marilou Bonetti, *Pr*
EMP: 8 **EST:** 1968
SQ FT: 11,000
SALES (est): 2.46MM
SALES (corp-wide): 2.46MM **Privately Held**
Web: www.soilexcorp.com
SIC: 1481 1381　Test boring for nonmetallic minerals; Drilling oil and gas wells

(G-9706)

SPECTRO COATING CORP
Claremont Flock, Div of
107 Scott Dr (01453-3320)
P.O. Box 916 (01453-0916)
PHONE..........................978 534-6191
Rajesh Shah, *Brnch Mgr*
EMP: 13
SALES (corp-wide): 9.16MM **Privately Held**
Web: www.spectrocoating.com
SIC: 2299　Flock (recovered textile fibers)
PA: Spectro Coating Corp.
　68 Main St Unit 916
　Leominster MA 01453
　978 534-1800

(G-9707)

SPECTRO COATING CORP (PA)
68 Main St (01453-7850)
PHONE..........................978 534-1800
Hemendra Shah, *Pr*
Hemendra K Shah, *
Rajesh H Shah, *
◆ **EMP:** 46 **EST:** 1941
SALES (est): 9.16MM
SALES (corp-wide): 9.16MM **Privately Held**
Web: www.spectrocoating.com
SIC: 2299　Flock (recovered textile fibers)

(G-9708)

TEKNOR APEX COMPANY
31 Fuller St (01453-4225)
PHONE..........................978 534-1010
EMP: 21
SALES (corp-wide): 1.03B **Privately Held**
Web: www.teknorapex.com
SIC: 3087　Custom compound purchased resins
PA: Teknor Apex Company
　505 Central Ave
　Pawtucket RI 02861
　401 725-8000

▲ = Import ▼ = Export
◆ = Import/Export

(G-9709)

TEKNOR APEX ELASTOMERS INC

31 Fuller St (01453-4225)
PHONE...................978 466-5344
James E Morrison, *Treas*
Edward T Massoud, *
◆ **EMP:** 67 **EST:** 1991
SQ FT: 1,500
SALES (est): 12.14MM
SALES (corp-wide): 1.03B **Privately Held**
Web: www.teknorapex.com
SIC: 2821 Plastics materials and resins
PA: Teknor Apex Company
     505 Central Ave
     Pawtucket RI 02861
     401 725-8000

(G-9710)

THERMOPLASTICS ENGINEERING CORP

11 Spruce St (01453-3211)
EMP: 12 **EST:** 1986
SALES (est): 1.41MM **Privately Held**
Web: www.thermoplasticseng.com
SIC: 3542 Extruding machines (machine tools), metal

(G-9711)

UNION PAPER & PACKAGING INC

507 Lancaster St (01453-7526)
PHONE...................978 227-5868
Timothy A Spylios, *Pr*
EMP: 8 **EST:** 2020
SALES (est): 326.81K **Privately Held**
SIC: 2621 Packaging paper

(G-9712)

UNITED COMB & NOVELTY CORP (PA)

Also Called: United Plastics
33 Patriots Cir (01453-5967)
P.O. Box 358 (01453-0358)
PHONE...................978 537-2096
Tim Durkin, *CEO*
◆ **EMP:** 60 **EST:** 1977
SQ FT: 175,000
SALES (est): 26.06MM
SALES (corp-wide): 26.06MM **Privately Held**
Web: www.unitedsolutions.net
SIC: 3089 Injection molded finished plastics products, nec

(G-9713)

URTHPACT INNOVATIONS LLC

42 Jungle Rd (01453-5208)
PHONE...................978 847-9747
Paul Boudreau, *Managing Member*
EMP: 13 **EST:** 2013
SALES (est): 2.69MM **Privately Held**
Web: www.urthpact.com
SIC: 3089 Molding primary plastics

(G-9714)

USPACK INC

Also Called: Energy Release
300 Whitney St (01453-3209)
PHONE...................978 466-9700
Bob Waalkes, *CEO*
Alexander Aptekman, *
Dan Byrne, *CRO*
EMP: 35 **EST:** 2004
SQ FT: 12,000
SALES (est): 9.53MM **Privately Held**
Web: www.uspack.net
SIC: 3559 Automotive related machinery

(G-9715)

V&M TOOL & DIE INC

138 Lincoln Ter (01453-4242)
PHONE...................978 534-8814
Mario Ermini, *Owner*
EMP: 10 **EST:** 1995
SALES (est): 115.4K **Privately Held**
Web: www.fmtoolanddie.com
SIC: 3544 Special dies and tools

(G-9716)

WELTON TECHNOLOGY LLC

517 Lancaster St Ste 102 (01453-7517)
PHONE...................978 425-0160
John Welton, *Managing Member*
EMP: 9 **EST:** 2008
SALES (est): 1.4MM **Privately Held**
Web: www.weltontech.com
SIC: 1531 3559
; Semiconductor manufacturing machinery

(G-9717)

WORCESTER TLEGRAM GAZETTE CORP

Also Called: WORCESTER TELEGRAM & GAZETTE CORPORATION
27 Monument Sq (01453-5769)
PHONE...................978 840-0071
Michael Elfland, *Mgr*
EMP: 16
SALES (corp-wide): 2.31B **Publicly Held**
Web: www.telegram.com
SIC: 2711 Newspapers, publishing and printing
HQ: Worcester Telegram & Gazette, Inc.
     100 Front St Fl 20
     Worcester MA 01608
     508 793-9100

Leverett
Franklin County

(G-9718)

LML CONSTRUCTION INC

Also Called: L & F Construction
608 Long Plain Rd (01054-9744)
PHONE...................413 665-3788
Larry La Claire, *Pr*
Carolyn Manley, *Mgr*
EMP: 10 **EST:** 1968
SQ FT: 4,800
SALES (est): 477.57K **Privately Held**
Web: www.landfconstruction.com
SIC: 1794 1771 1611 1711 Excavation and grading, building construction; Driveway contractor; Highway and street paving contractor; Septic system construction

---

Lexington
Middlesex County

(G-9719)

ABLE SOFTWARE CORP (PA)

5 Appletree Ln (02420-2406)
PHONE...................781 862-2804
EMP: 9 **EST:** 1993
SALES (est): 975.37K **Privately Held**
Web: www.ablesw.com
SIC: 7372 7371 Prepackaged software; Custom computer programming services

(G-9720)

ADOLOR CORPORATION

65 Hayden Ave (02421-7994)
PHONE...................781 860-8660
EMP: 268 **EST:** 1993

SQ FT: 80,000
SALES (est): 18.24MM
SALES (corp-wide): 59.28B **Publicly Held**
SIC: 2834 Pharmaceutical preparations
HQ: Cubist Pharmaceuticals Llc
     2000 Galloping Hill Rd
     Kenilworth NJ 07033

(G-9721)

AGENUS INC (PA)

Also Called: Agenus
3 Forbes Rd (02421-7305)
PHONE...................781 674-4400
Garo H Armen, *Ch Bd*
Jennifer S Buell, *Pr*
Steven O'day, *CMO*
Evan D Kearns, *Corporate Secretary*
Christine M Klaskin, *VP Fin*
EMP: 141 **EST:** 1994
SQ FT: 82,000
SALES (est): 98.02MM
SALES (corp-wide): 98.02MM **Publicly Held**
Web: www.agenusbio.com
SIC: 2836 8731 Biological products, except diagnostic; Biological research

(G-9722)

AGILENT TECHNOLOGIES INC

Vacuum Products Division
121 Hartwell Ave (02421-3125)
PHONE...................781 861-7200
Fred Campbell, *Prin*
EMP: 163
SALES (corp-wide): 6.83B **Publicly Held**
Web: www.agilent.com
SIC: 3825 Instruments to measure electricity
PA: Agilent Technologies, Inc.
     5301 Stevens Creek Blvd
     Santa Clara CA 95051
     800 227-9770.

(G-9723)

ALDEYRA THERAPEUTICS INC (PA)

Also Called: Aldeyra Therapeutics
131 Hartwell Ave Ste 320 (02421-3105)
PHONE...................781 761-4904
EMP: 10 **EST:** 2004
SQ FT: 9,351
Web: www.aldeyra.com
SIC: 2834 Pharmaceutical preparations

(G-9724)

ALTIOSTAR NETWORKS INC (PA)

1 Cranberry Hl Ste 203 (02421-7397)
PHONE...................855 709-0701
Ashraf M Dahod, *Pr*
Pierre Kahhale, *
John Delea, *
Anil Sawkar, *
Kuntal Chowdhury, *
▲ **EMP:** 51 **EST:** 2011
SALES (est): 43.88MM
SALES (corp-wide): 43.88MM **Privately Held**
SIC: 5065 3669 Communication equipment; Intercommunication systems, electric

(G-9725)

BACKLIGHT PARENT CORPORATION (PA)

450 Bedford St (02420-1535)
PHONE...................617 665-8844
Benjamin Kaplan, *CEO*
Benjamin Kaplam, *Managing Member*
EMP: 10 **EST:** 2021
SALES (est): 2.69MM

SALES (corp-wide): 2.69MM **Privately Held**
Web: www.backlight.co
SIC: 7372 Prepackaged software

(G-9726)

BAE SYSTEMS INFO ELCTRNIC SYST

Also Called: BAE SYSTEMS INFORMATION AND ELECTRONIC SYSTEMS INTEGRATION INC.
2 Forbes Rd (02421-7306)
PHONE...................603 885-4321
EMP: 131
SALES (corp-wide): 25.59B **Privately Held**
Web: www.baesystems.com
SIC: 3827 3679 3823 3674 Optical instruments and lenses; Electronic circuits; Process control instruments; Semiconductors and related devices
HQ: Bae Systems Information And Electronic Systems Integration Inc.
     65 Spit Brook Rd
     Nashua NH 03060
     603 885-4321

(G-9727)

BCTZ LTD

401 Lowell St (02420-2546)
PHONE...................781 863-0405
Carol R Samson, *Prin*
EMP: 7 **EST:** 2009
SALES (est): 356.85K **Privately Held**
SIC: 3732 Boatbuilding and repairing

(G-9728)

BF SERVICES INC

35 Bedford St Ste 15 (02420-4439)
PHONE...................781 862-9792
Spencer Betts, *Prin*
EMP: 10 **EST:** 2015
SALES (est): 623.03K **Privately Held**
SIC: 3011 Tires and inner tubes

(G-9729)

CENTRA SOFTWARE INC (DH)

430 Bedford St Ste 220 (02420-1527)
PHONE...................781 861-7000
EMP: 92 **EST:** 1995
SQ FT: 49,000
SALES (est): 49.51MM
SALES (corp-wide): 740.92MM **Privately Held**
SIC: 7372 Business oriented computer software
HQ: Saba Software, Inc.
     4120 Dublin Blvd Ste 200
     Dublin CA 94568
     877 722-2101

(G-9730)

COLONIAL TIMES PUBLISHING

805 Massachusetts Ave (02420-3918)
PHONE...................781 274-9997
Jim Shaw, *Owner*
EMP: 10 **EST:** 2004
SALES (est): 395.91K **Privately Held**
Web: www.lexingtontimesmagazine.com
SIC: 2711 Newspapers, publishing and printing

(G-9731)

CONCERT PHARMACEUTICALS INC (HQ)

Also Called: Concert
65 Hayden Ave Ste 3000n (02421-7994)
PHONE...................781 860-0045
Erik Zwicker, *Sec*
EMP: 41 **EST:** 2006

GEOGRAPHIC

SQ FT: 56,000
SALES (est): 32.58MM **Privately Held**
Web: www.sunpharma.com
SIC: 2834   Pharmaceutical preparations
PA: Sun Pharmaceutical Industries Limited
　　Sun House, Plot No. 201 B/1
　　Mumbai MH 40006

(G-9732)
COPIOUS IMAGING LLC
83 Hartwell Ave (02421-3116)
PHONE...............................781 918-6554
William Ross,　*
Michael Kelly,　*
EMP: 50 **EST:** 2017
SALES (est): 14.61MM
SALES (corp-wide): 450.2MM **Privately Held**
Web: www.anduril.com
SIC: 3826   Magnetic resonance imaging apparatus
PA: Anduril Industries, Inc.
　　1400 Anduril
　　Costa Mesa CA 92626
　　949 891-1607

(G-9733)
CPEC LLC
99 Hayden Ave (02421-7998)
PHONE...............................781 861-8444
EMP: 94 **EST:** 2021
SALES (est): 2.31MM **Privately Held**
SIC: 2834   Pharmaceutical preparations
HQ: Endo Pharmaceuticals Solutions Inc.
　　1400 Atwater Dr
　　Malvern PA 19355

(G-9734)
CSA MEDICAL INC
Also Called: Crymed Technologies
131 Hartwell Ave Ste 100 (02421-3105)
PHONE...............................443 921-8053
William H Floyd, *CEO*
Steven E Schaefer, *CFO*
Ellen Sheets, *CMO*
Ian Vawter, *CFO*
EMP: 55 **EST:** 1993
SALES (est): 8.84MM **Privately Held**
Web: www.rejuveair.com
SIC: 3845   Electromedical equipment

(G-9735)
CUBIST PHARMACEUTICALS LLC
65 Hayden Ave (02421-7994)
PHONE...............................781 860-8660
Robert Perez, *COO*
EMP: 100
SALES (corp-wide): 59.28B **Publicly Held**
SIC: 2834   Pharmaceutical preparations
HQ: Cubist Pharmaceuticals Llc
　　2000 Galloping Hill Rd
　　Kenilworth NJ 07033

(G-9736)
CURIS INC (PA)
Also Called: CURIS
128 Spring St Ste 510 (02421-7800)
PHONE...............................617 503-6500
James E Dentzer, *Pr*
Martyn D Greenacre, *Ch Bd*
William Steinkrauss, *CFO*
EMP: 20 **EST:** 2000
SQ FT: 21,772
SALES (est): 10.02MM **Publicly Held**
Web: www.curis.com
SIC: 2834   Pharmaceutical preparations

(G-9737)
CYTEIR THERAPEUTICS INC (PA)
128 Spring St Bldg A (02421-7848)
PHONE...............................857 285-4140
Markus Renschler, *Pr*
Joseph S Zakrzewski, *Ch Bd*
Andrew Gengos, *Chief Business Officer*
Paul Secrist, *CSO*
David Gaiero, *CFO*
EMP: 31 **EST:** 2012
SQ FT: 14,636
Web: www.cyteir.com
SIC: 2834   Pharmaceutical preparations

(G-9738)
DEERWALK INC (HQ)
430 Bedford St Ste 175 (02420-1548)
PHONE...............................781 325-1775
David B Snow Junior, *CEO*
EMP: 103 **EST:** 2009
SALES (est): 6.54K
SALES (corp-wide): 46.63MM **Privately Held**
Web: www.cedargate.com
SIC: 7372 7378   Business oriented computer software; Computer maintenance and repair
PA: Cedar Gate Technologies, Inc.
　　1 Sound Shore Dr Ste 300
　　Greenwich CT 06830
　　203 930-5500

(G-9739)
DICERNA PHARMACEUTICALS INC (HQ)
Also Called: Dicerna
75 Hayden Ave (02421-7979)
PHONE...............................617 621-8097
Bob D Brown, *CSO*
EMP: 234 **EST:** 2006
SQ FT: 91,728
SALES (est): 164.31MM
SALES (corp-wide): 24.71B **Privately Held**
Web: www.novonordisk-us.com
SIC: 2834 2836 8731   Pharmaceutical preparations; Biological products, except diagnostic; Biological research
PA: Novo Nordisk A/S
　　Novo Alle 1
　　Bagsvard 2880
　　44448888

(G-9740)
DOMAIN SURGICAL INC
4 Maguire Rd # 2 (02421-3112)
PHONE...............................801 924-4950
EMP: 30 **EST:** 2010
SALES (est): 1.68MM **Privately Held**
Web: www.omni-guide.com
SIC: 3841   Surgical and medical instruments

(G-9741)
DSM NUTRITIONAL PRODUCTS LLC
60 Westview St (02421-3108)
PHONE...............................781 259-7600
Kevin Madden, *VP*
EMP: 109
Web: www.dsm.com
SIC: 2834   Pharmaceutical preparations
HQ: Dsm Nutritional Products, Llc
　　45 Waterview Blvd
　　Parsippany NJ 07054
　　518 372-5155

(G-9742)
EXCELERGY CORP (PA)
10 Maguire Rd Ste 111 (02421-3110)
PHONE...............................781 274-0420

William Mahoney, *Pr*
Cary G Bullock,　*
Stephen Gregorio, *VP*
Kevin Monagle, *VP*
Vin Mauro, *VP*
EMP: 50 **EST:** 1998
SQ FT: 31,500
SALES (est): 5.49MM
SALES (corp-wide): 5.49MM **Privately Held**
SIC: 7372   Prepackaged software

(G-9743)
FUJIFILM HLTHCARE AMRICAS CORP (DH)
81 Hartwell Ave Ste 300 (02421-3160)
PHONE...............................203 324-2000
Hidetoshi Izawa, *Pr*
Hideru Sato,　*
Steve Lee,　*
Jun Higuchi,　*
Akio Yamamoto,　*
▲ **EMP:** 190 **EST:** 1963
SQ FT: 70,000
SALES (est): 175.14MM **Privately Held**
Web: healthcaresolutions-us.fujifilm.com
SIC: 5047 5043 3861   X-ray film and supplies ; Photographic processing equipment; Photographic equipment and supplies
HQ: Fujifilm Corporation
　　9-7-3, Akasaka
　　Minato-Ku TKY 107-0

(G-9744)
GASWORLD PUBLISHING LLC
Also Called: Cryogas International
5 Militia Dr Ste 16 (02421-4716)
PHONE...............................781 862-0624
Rob Cockerill, *Managing Editor*
Patrick Carlucci, *S&M/Dir*
EMP: 7 **EST:** 2009
SALES (est): 709.12K **Privately Held**
SIC: 2721   Magazines: publishing only, not printed on site
HQ: Gasworld.Com Limited
　　Underground House, Trevissome Park
　　Truro

(G-9745)
GENERAL STEEL PRODUCTS CO INC
16 Russell Rd (02420-2709)
PHONE...............................617 387-5400
George Meltz, *Pr*
EMP: 10 **EST:** 1947
SALES (est): 949.97K **Privately Held**
Web: www.gentexscaffolds.com
SIC: 3441   Fabricated structural metal

(G-9746)
HARTWELL 131 HOLDINGS CORP
131 Hartwell Ave Ste 3 (02421-3105)
PHONE...............................781 328-3220
▼ **EMP:** 48
SIC: 3089   Plastics processing

(G-9747)
HEMANEXT INC
Also Called: Hemanext
99 Hayden Ave Ste 620 (02421-7998)
PHONE...............................240 301-7474
Martin Cannon, *Pr*
Michael Bavonese, *Dir*
Steven Levesque, *Dir*
Doctor Tatsuro Yoshida, *Dir*
Steve Urdahl, *Dir*
EMP: 12 **EST:** 2000
SALES (est): 2.92MM **Privately Held**

Web: www.hemanext.com
SIC: 3841   Surgical and medical instruments

(G-9748)
HIGHTECH AMERCN INDUS LABS INC
Also Called: Hai Labs
320 Massachusetts Ave (02420-4010)
PHONE...............................781 862-9884
▲ **EMP:** 10 **EST:** 1996
SALES (est): 461.59K **Privately Held**
Web: www.hailabs.com
SIC: 3841   Medical instruments and equipment, blood and bone work

(G-9749)
HMK ENTERPRISES INC (PA)
Also Called: Spectrum Management
750 Marrett Rd Ste 401 (02421-7309)
PHONE...............................781 891-6660
Steven Karol, *Ch Bd*
Jane Karol, *Prin*
EMP: 15 **EST:** 1981
SQ FT: 9,500
SALES (est): 19.65MM
SALES (corp-wide): 19.65MM **Privately Held**
Web: www.watermill.com
SIC: 5712 3325 6411   Office furniture; Steel foundries, nec; Insurance agents, brokers, and service

(G-9750)
HOUSTON LONZA INC
4 Hartwell Pl (02421-3122)
PHONE...............................201 316-9200
EMP: 11
Web: www.lonza.com
SIC: 2834   Pharmaceutical preparations
HQ: Houston Lonza Inc
　　14905 Kirby Dr
　　Houston TX 77047

(G-9751)
IN SILICO BIOSCIENCES INC
405 Waltham St (02421-7934)
PHONE...............................781 861-1592
Robert Carr, *Ch*
EMP: 10 **EST:** 1999
SALES (est): 1.07MM **Privately Held**
Web: www.in-silico-biosciences.com
SIC: 8733 2834   Medical research; Druggists' preparations (pharmaceuticals)

(G-9752)
INBALANCE INC
12 Manning St (02421-4346)
PHONE...............................339 223-6636
Thomas Marge, *CEO*
David Hamburger, *Cnslt*
EMP: 7 **EST:** 2020
SALES (est): 293.73K **Privately Held**
Web: www.inbalanceresearch.com
SIC: 7372   Prepackaged software

(G-9753)
INOTEK PHARMACEUTICALS CORP
131 Hartwell Ave Ste 2 (02421-3105)
PHONE...............................781 676-2100
EMP: 14 **EST:** 2018
SALES (est): 850.77K **Privately Held**
Web: www.inotekpharma.com
SIC: 2834   Pharmaceutical preparations

(G-9754)
IVIX TECH INC (PA)
Also Called: Ivix
405 Waltham St Ste 224 (02421-7934)

PHONE..............................702 561-5304
Matan Fattal, *CEO*
Doron Passov, *CPO*
Dana Cass, *VP Mktg*
Dan Volfman, *VP*
EMP: 19 **EST:** 2020
SALES (est): 835.63K
SALES (corp-wide): 835.63K **Privately Held**
SIC: 2741   Internet publishing and broadcasting

(G-9755)
KALEIDO BIOSCIENCES INC (PA)
Also Called: Kaleido
65 Hayden Ave (02421-7994)
PHONE..............................617 674-9000
Dan Menichella, *Pr*
Theo Melas-kyriazi, *Ch Bd*
Johan Van Hylckama Vlieg, *CSO*
Clare Fisher, *Chief Business Officer*
William Duke Junior, *CFO*
EMP: 67 **EST:** 2015
SQ FT: 53,000
SALES (est): 1.1MM
SALES (corp-wide): 1.1MM **Privately Held**
Web: www.kaleido.com
SIC: 2836 8731   Biological products, except diagnostic; Medical research, commercial

(G-9756)
KEROS THERAPEUTICS INC (PA)
Also Called: Keros
1050 Waltham St Ste 302 (02421-8024)
PHONE..............................617 314-6297
Jasbir Seehra, *CEO*
Keith Regnante, *CFO*
Christopher Rovaldi, *COO*
Simon Cooper, *CMO*
EMP: 93 **EST:** 2015
SQ FT: 35,662
Web: www.kerostx.com
SIC: 2834   Pharmaceutical preparations

(G-9757)
KINIKSA PHARMACEUTICALS CORP
100 Hayden Ave Ste 1 (02421-7974)
PHONE..............................781 431-9100
Michael Megna, *Admn*
EMP: 135 **EST:** 2015
SALES (est): 27.93MM **Privately Held**
Web: www.kiniksa.com
SIC: 2834   Pharmaceutical preparations

(G-9758)
LEXINGTON GRAPHICS INC
Also Called: Sir Speedy
76 Bedford St Ste 6 (02420-4640)
PHONE..............................781 863-9510
Ilhami Cinkilic, *Owner*
EMP: 10 **EST:** 1986
SALES (est): 749.69K **Privately Held**
Web: www.lexgraph.com
SIC: 2752   Offset printing

(G-9759)
LOGICBIO THERAPEUTICS INC
65 Hayden Ave Fl 2 (02421-7994)
PHONE..............................617 245-0399
Frederic Chereau, *Pr*
Richard Moscicki, *
Kyle Chiang, *COO*
Cecilia Jones, *CFO*
Mariana Nacht, *CSO*
EMP: 62 **EST:** 2014
SQ FT: 23,901

SALES (est): 5.41MM **Privately Held**
Web: www.logicbio.com
SIC: 2836   Biological products, except diagnostic

(G-9760)
LONZA BIOLOGICS INC
Also Called: Lonza Cell and Gene
4 Hartwell Pl (02421-3122)
PHONE..............................508 435-2331
EMP: 11
SALES (est): 4.04MM **Privately Held**
Web: www.lonza.com
SIC: 2834   Pharmaceutical preparations

(G-9761)
LYNDRA THERAPEUTICS INC
60 Westview St (02421-3108)
PHONE..............................857 201-5314
EMP: 83
SALES (corp-wide): 16.28MM **Privately Held**
Web: www.lyndra.com
SIC: 2834   Pharmaceutical preparations
PA: Lyndra Therapeutics, Inc.
65 Grove St Ste 301
Watertown MA 02472
339 222-6519

(G-9762)
MAC LEAN-FOGG COMPANY
131 Hartwell Ave Ste 3 (02421-3105)
PHONE..............................781 328-3220
EMP: 95
SALES (corp-wide): 1.56B **Privately Held**
SIC: 3089   Plastics processing
PA: Mac Lean-Fogg Company
1000 Allanson Rd
Mundelein IL 60060
847 566-0010

(G-9763)
MILLENNIUM PHARMACEUTICALS INC
45 Hayden Ave # 55 (02421-7956)
PHONE..............................617 679-7000
EMP: 100
Web: www.takedaoncology.com
SIC: 2834   Pharmaceutical preparations
HQ: Millennium Pharmaceuticals, Inc.
40 Landsdowne St
Cambridge MA 02139

(G-9764)
NBD NANOTECHNOLOGIES INC
Also Called: NBD Nano Technologies
99 Hayden Ave Bldg C (02421-7998)
PHONE..............................781 541-4192
Miguel Galvez, *CEO*
Deckard Sorensen, *Pr*
EMP: 12 **EST:** 2012
SQ FT: 4,400
SALES (est): 1.36MM **Privately Held**
Web: www.nbdnano.com
SIC: 2851 2295 3479   Paints and paint additives; Varnished glass and coated fiberglass fabrics; Lacquering of metal products

(G-9765)
NEWPRINT OFFSET INC
405 Waltham St (02421-7934)
PHONE..............................781 891-6002
Anthony Soave, *Pr*
EMP: 13 **EST:** 1981
SALES (est): 391.09K **Privately Held**
Web: www.teachtsp.com
SIC: 2752   Offset printing

(G-9766)
NITROMED INC
125 Spring St (02421-7801)
PHONE..............................781 274-1248
EMP: 9 **EST:** 2019
SALES (est): 438.4K **Privately Held**
SIC: 2834   Pharmaceutical preparations

(G-9767)
NOVO NORDISK INC
Also Called: Novo Nordisk Research Center
33 Hayden Ave (02421-7972)
PHONE..............................463 209-3849
Jacek Mokrosinski, *Senior Scientist*
EMP: 717
SALES (corp-wide): 24.71B **Privately Held**
SIC: 2834   Pharmaceutical preparations
HQ: Novo Nordisk Inc.
800 Scudders Mill Rd
Plainsboro NJ 08536
609 987-5800

(G-9768)
RSA SECURITY LLC
6 Potter Pond (02421-8243)
PHONE..............................781 515-6258
EMP: 18
SALES (corp-wide): 1.44B **Privately Held**
Web: www.rsa.com
SIC: 7372   Prepackaged software
PA: Rsa Security Llc
176 Middlesex Tpke
Bedford MA 01730
800 995-5095

(G-9769)
SARID INC
Also Called: Corporation
66 Middle St (02421-7723)
PHONE..............................781 315-1105
Kathleen Sultan, *Prin*
Javed Sultan, *Ex Dir*
EMP: 7 **EST:** 2008
SALES (est): 244.97K **Privately Held**
Web: www.saridweb.org
SIC: 3589 2611   Sewage and water treatment equipment; Pulp mills, mechanical and recycling processing

(G-9770)
SENSAR MARINE US INC ✪
15 Depot Sq (02420-6358)
PHONE..............................800 910-2150
Austin Bliss, *CEO*
EMP: 15 **EST:** 2022
SALES (est): 656.67K **Privately Held**
Web: www.sensarmarine.com
SIC: 3812   Search and navigation equipment

(G-9771)
SHEMIN NURSERIES INC
Also Called: Shemin Landscape Supply Co
1265 Massachusetts Ave (02420-3825)
PHONE..............................781 861-1111
Pat Grego, *Brnch Mgr*
EMP: 23
SALES (corp-wide): 4.01B **Publicly Held**
SIC: 3531 5193   Construction machinery; Flowers and florists supplies
HQ: Shemin Nurseries, Inc.
42 Old Ridgebury Rd Ste 3
Danbury CT 06810

(G-9772)
SHIRE HUMN GNTIC THERAPIES INC (DH)
Also Called: Shire Pharmaceuticals
300 Shire Way (02421-2101)
PHONE..............................617 349-0200

Doctor Flemming Ornskov, *CEO*
Bill Ciambrone, *
Wayne Eppinger, *
David Pendergast, *
Jonathan Poole, *
EMP: 45 **EST:** 1988
SALES (est): 102.08MM **Privately Held**
Web: www.processonesolutions.com
SIC: 2834   Pharmaceutical preparations
HQ: Shire North American Group Inc.
103 Foulk Rd Ste 202
Wilmington DE 19803
484 595-8800

(G-9773)
SHIRE PHARMACEUTICALS LLC (HQ)
300 Shire Way (02421-2101)
PHONE..............................617 349-0200
James Cavanaugh, *Ch*
Wayne Eppinger, *
John Lee, *
Gary Casto, *
Gwendolyn Niebler, *
EMP: 126 **EST:** 2004
SALES (est): 512.27MM **Privately Held**
SIC: 2834   Pharmaceutical preparations
PA: Takeda Pharmaceutical Company Limited
2-1-1, Nihombashihoncho
Chuo-Ku TKY 103-0

(G-9774)
SHIRE PHARMACEUTICALS LLC
235 Wyman St (02421)
PHONE..............................617 349-0200
EMP: 674
SIC: 2834   Pharmaceutical preparations
HQ: Shire Pharmaceuticals Llc
300 Shire Way
Lexington MA 02421
617 349-0200

(G-9775)
SHIRE US INC (HQ)
Also Called: Shire Pharmaceuticals
300 Shire Way (02421-2101)
PHONE..............................781 482-9222
Flemming Ornskov, *CEO*
Thomas Dittrich, *CFO*
Jason Baranski, *Head US Legal*
▲ **EMP:** 560 **EST:** 1990
SALES (est): 311.32MM **Privately Held**
SIC: 2834   Pharmaceutical preparations
PA: Shire Limited
Block 3 Miesian Plaza
Dublin 2 D02Y7

(G-9776)
SOLAR FIVE LLC
420 Bedford St Ste 335 (02420-1506)
PHONE..............................781 301-7233
EMP: 19 **EST:** 2015
SALES (est): 1.78MM **Privately Held**
Web: www.solarfive.com
SIC: 1711 3674   Solar energy contractor; Solar cells

(G-9777)
SWYMED INCORPORATED
Also Called: Swyme
71 Hancock St (02420-3420)
PHONE..............................855 799-6366
Stefano Migliorisi, *Pr*
Jeffrey Urdan, *COO*
Jan Harmen Witzenburg, *Dir*
EMP: 15 **EST:** 2013
SQ FT: 4,700
SALES (est): 2.46MM **Privately Held**
Web: www.swymed.com

SIC: 4813 7372 Telephone/video communications; Application computer software

(G-9778)
SYNAGEVA BIOPHARMA CORP
33 Hayden Ave (02421-7971)
PHONE..............................781 357-9900
EMP: 282
SIC: 2836 Biological products, except diagnostic

(G-9779)
T2 BIOSYSTEMS INC (PA)
Also Called: T2 Biosystems
101 Hartwell Ave (02421-3125)
PHONE..............................781 761-4646
John Sperzel, *Ch Bd*
John M Sprague, *CFO*
Brett Giffin, *CCO*
Roger Smith, *Sr VP*
Michael Gibbs, *Sr VP*
EMP: 78 **EST:** 2006
SQ FT: 32,000
SALES (est): 22.3MM **Publicly Held**
Web: www.t2biosystems.com
SIC: 3841 2835 Surgical and medical instruments; In vitro diagnostics

(G-9780)
TAKEDA
300 Shire Way (02421-2101)
PHONE..............................781 266-5464
Tansey Helmke, *Prin*
EMP: 77 **EST:** 2019
SALES (est): 9.75MM **Privately Held**
Web: www.takeda.com
SIC: 2834 Pharmaceutical preparations

(G-9781)
TAKEDA MANUFACTURING USA INC
95 Hayden Ave (02421-7942)
PHONE..............................877 825-3327
EMP: 24 **EST:** 2020
SALES (est): 6.88MM **Privately Held**
SIC: 2834 Pharmaceutical preparations
PA: Takeda Pharmaceutical Company Limited
2-1-1, Nihombashihoncho
Chuo-Ku TKY 103-0

(G-9782)
TAKEDA PHARMACEUTICAL CO LTD
200 Shire Way (02421-2001)
PHONE..............................877 872-3700
EMP: 81
Web: www.takeda.com
SIC: 2834 Pharmaceutical preparations
PA: Takeda Pharmaceutical Company Limited
2-1-1, Nihombashihoncho
Chuo-Ku TKY 103-0

(G-9783)
TAKEDA PHARMACEUTICALS USA INC
300 Shire Way (02421-2101)
PHONE..............................617 349-0200
Gerard Michel, *Brnch Mgr*
EMP: 35
Web: jobs.takeda.com
SIC: 2834 Pharmaceutical preparations
HQ: Takeda Pharmaceuticals U.S.A., Inc.
95 Hayden Ave
Lexington MA 02421
877 825-3327

(G-9784)
TAKEDA PHARMACEUTICALS USA INC (HQ)
95 Hayden Ave (02421-7942)
PHONE..............................877 825-3327
Christophe Weber, *Pr*
▲ **EMP:** 558 **EST:** 1998
SALES (est): 1.44B **Privately Held**
Web: www.takeda.com
SIC: 2834 Pharmaceutical preparations
PA: Takeda Pharmaceutical Company Limited
2-1-1, Nihombashihoncho
Chuo-Ku TKY 103-0

(G-9785)
TAKEDA PHRMACEUTICALS AMER INC (DH)
95 Hayden Ave (02421-7942)
PHONE..............................224 554-6500
Douglas Cole, *Pr*
Helen Pring, . *
Kenneth D Greisman, *
Patrick Butler, *
Paul Sundberg, *
EMP: 58 **EST:** 2000
SALES (est): 453.54MM **Privately Held**
Web: www.takeda.com
SIC: 2834 Pharmaceutical preparations
HQ: Takeda Pharmaceuticals U.S.A., Inc.
95 Hayden Ave
Lexington MA 02421
877 825-3327

(G-9786)
TENACITY MEDICAL INC
100 Trade Center (02421)
PHONE..............................617 299-8001
Tim Chaudhry, *Pr*
Bruce Mehler, *VP*
EMP: 7 **EST:** 1975
SQ FT: 4,000
SALES (est): 927.29K
SALES (corp-wide): 158.17MM **Publicly Held**
SIC: 3841 3845 7352 5047 Surgical and medical instruments; Electromedical equipment; Medical equipment rental; Medical equipment and supplies
HQ: Zynex Neurodiagnostics, Inc.
9655 Maroon Cir
Englewood CO 80112

(G-9787)
TEPHA INC (HQ)
99 Hayden Ave Ste 360 (02421-7966)
PHONE..............................781 357-1700
Andrew Joiner, *Pr*
Ian Vawter, *
John Hartnett, *
Said Rizk, *CIO*
EMP: 57 **EST:** 1998
SALES (est): 11.35MM
SALES (corp-wide): 19.37B **Publicly Held**
Web: news.bd.com
SIC: 3841 8731 Surgical and medical instruments; Medical research, commercial
PA: Becton, Dickinson And Company
1 Becton Dr
Franklin Lakes NJ 07417
201 847-6800

(G-9788)
TOMMY HILFIGER FOOTWEAR INC
191 Spring St Fl 4 (02421-8045)
PHONE..............................617 824-6000
EMP: 45
SQ FT: 20,000

SALES (est): 2.12MM
SALES (corp-wide): 2.24B **Publicly Held**
SIC: 3149 Children's footwear, except athletic
HQ: The Stride Rite Corporation
500 Totten Pond Rd Ste 1
Waltham MA 02451
617 824-6000

(G-9789)
TRANSLATE BIO INC (HQ)
Also Called: Translate
29 Hartwell Ave (02421-3102)
PHONE..............................617 945-7361
Ronald C Renaud Junior, *Pr*
Daniel S Lynch, *
Ann Barbier, *CMO*
Paul Burgess, *CLO*
EMP: 50 **EST:** 2011
SALES (est): 138.81MM **Privately Held**
Web: www.sanofi.com
SIC: 2834 Pharmaceutical preparations
PA: Sanofi
46 Avenue De La Grande Armee
Paris 75017

(G-9790)
UNIMACTS MANUFACTURING MX LLC
2 Sedge Rd (02420-1830)
PHONE..............................410 415-6070
EMP: 13 **EST:** 2019
SALES (est): 1.08MM **Privately Held**
SIC: 3599 Machine shop, jobbing and repair
HQ: Unimacts Global, Llc
12333 Sowden Rd Ste B
Houston TX 77080
410 415-6070

(G-9791)
VOYAGER THERAPEUTICS INC (PA)
75 Hayden Ave (02421-7979)
PHONE..............................570 329-6851
Alfred W Sandrock Junior, *CEO*
Michael Higgins, *Ch Bd*
Allison Dorval, *CAO*
Bernard Ravina, *CMO*
Dinah Sah, *CSO*
EMP: 87 **EST:** 2013
SQ FT: 47,493
SALES (est): 40.91MM
SALES (corp-wide): 40.91MM **Publicly Held**
Web: www.voyagertherapeutics.com
SIC: 2836 8731 Biological products, except diagnostic; Biotechnical research, commercial

(G-9792)
VULNCHECK INC
6 Longfellow Rd (02420-1715)
PHONE..............................781 879-6863
Anthony Bettini, *CEO*
Ralph Logan, *Chief Strategy Officer*
EMP: 10 **EST:** 2021
SALES (est): 508.47K **Privately Held**
Web: www.vulncheck.com
SIC: 7372 Prepackaged software

(G-9793)
W R GRACE & CO
Grace Performance Chemicals
91 Hartwell Ave Ste 2 (02421-3125)
PHONE..............................617 876-1400
Richard Williams, *General Vice President*
EMP: 32
SQ FT: 151,000
SALES (corp-wide): 6.27B **Privately Held**
Web: www.grace.com

SIC: 2819 2833 Inorganic metal compounds or salts, nec; Medicinals and botanicals
HQ: W. R. Grace & Co.
7500 Grace Dr
Columbia MD 21044
410 531-4000

Lincoln
Middlesex County

(G-9794)
ADVENT MEDICAL PRODUCTS INC
Also Called: Concord Medical Products
55 Beaver Pond Rd (01773-3308)
PHONE..............................781 272-2813
Randall Fincke, *Pr*
EMP: 9 **EST:** 2010
SALES (est): 238.59K **Privately Held**
SIC: 3069 Medical and laboratory rubber sundries and related products

(G-9795)
ESM SOFTWARE LLC
55 Old Bedford Rd Ste 107 (01773-1125)
P.O. Box 593 (01775-0593)
PHONE..............................781 541-4462
Kent Smack, *Pr*
Julie Warner, *VP Fin*
EMP: 11 **EST:** 2017
SALES (est): 1.51MM **Privately Held**
Web: www.esmgrp.com
SIC: 8742 8299 7372 Marketing consulting services; Educational service, nondegree granting: continuing educ.; Application computer software

(G-9796)
ESM SOFTWARE GROUP INC
55 Old Bedford Rd Ste 107 (01773-1125)
PHONE..............................781 541-4465
EMP: 13
SIC: 8742 8299 7372 Marketing consulting services; Educational service, nondegree granting: continuing educ.; Application computer software

(G-9797)
MCINTIRE BRASS WORKS INC
35 Brooks Rd (01773-1308)
PHONE..............................617 547-1819
Elaine Anthony, *Pr*
Arthur Anthony, *VP*
EMP: 7 **EST:** 1986
SALES (est): 952.26K **Privately Held**
Web: www.slidepole.com
SIC: 3351 3569 Pipe, brass and bronze; Firefighting and related equipment

(G-9798)
MYSTIC VALLEY FOUNDRY INC
35 Brooks Rd (01773-1308)
PHONE..............................617 547-1819
Arthur Anthony, *Pr*
Lara Anthony, *Treas*
EMP: 7 **EST:** 1957
SALES (est): 767.38K **Privately Held**
Web: www.mysticvalleyfoundry.com
SIC: 3366 3363 3365 Castings (except die), nec, bronze; Aluminum die-castings; Aluminum foundries

Littleton
Middlesex County

(G-9799)
ACP WATERJET INC
170 Ayer Rd (01460-1103)
PHONE...................800 951-5127
Carlos Eduardo T Fernandes, *Pr*
EMP: 15 **EST:** 2009
SALES (est): 2.61MM **Privately Held**
Web: www.acpwaterjet.com
SIC: 3541 Machine tools, metal cutting type

(G-9800)
ALPHA TECH PET INC
Also Called: Greenplanet Scientific
25 Porter Rd Ste 210 (01460-1434)
PHONE...................978 486-3690
Shawn Seitz, *Pr*
EMP: 7 **EST:** 1989
SQ FT: 5,676
SALES (est): 927.78K **Privately Held**
Web: www.alphatechpet.com
SIC: 3999 8742 5199 0742 Pet supplies;
Marketing consulting services; Pet supplies;
Veterinary services, specialties

(G-9801)
**ANPESIL DISTRIBUTION
SERVICES LLC**
1 Spectacle Pond Rd (01460-1128)
EMP: 10 **EST:** 2005
SALES (est): 619.79K **Privately Held**
SIC: 2064 Candy and other confectionery
products

(G-9802)
ARLOWE CORPORATION
Also Called: E T M Manufacturing Company
24 Porter Rd (01460-1414)
PHONE...................978 486-9050
Robert L Olney, *Pr*
David Puleo, *VP*
Mike Jancosko, *VP*
EMP: 15 **EST:** 1970
SQ FT: 10,000
SALES (est): 2.07MM **Privately Held**
Web: www.etmmfg.com
SIC: 1761 3599 Sheet metal work, nec;
Machine shop, jobbing and repair

(G-9803)
ARRADIANCE LLC
11a Beaver Brook Rd (01460-6232)
PHONE...................508 202-0593
Michael Trotter, *Managing Member*
Thomas Clay, *Ch Bd*
Jeff Plante, *Bd of Dir*
EMP: 10 **EST:** 2004
SALES (est): 2.01MM **Privately Held**
Web: www.arradiance.com
SIC: 3674 Semiconductors and related
devices

(G-9804)
**ATLANTIC RUBBER COMPANY
INC**
37 Ayer Rd Ste 6 (01460-1034)
P.O. Box 2295 (01460-3295)
PHONE...................800 882-3666
TOLL FREE: 800
William L Carey, *Pr*
William L Carey, *Pr*
Darlene Dowdy, *VP*
Ralph K Lowey, *Sec*
Robert F Mcdermott, *Dir*
▲ **EMP:** 11 **EST:** 1988
SQ FT: 10,000

SALES (est): 958.83K **Privately Held**
Web: www.atlanticrubber.com
SIC: 3053 Gaskets, all materials

(G-9805)
BURK TECHNOLOGY INC
7 Beaver Brook Rd (01460-6232)
PHONE...................978 486-0086
Peter Burk, *Pr*
EMP: 24 **EST:** 1985
SQ FT: 7,600
SALES (est): 4.73MM **Privately Held**
Web: www.burk.com
SIC: 3663 Radio broadcasting and
communications equipment

(G-9806)
CONTROL RESOURCES INC
Also Called: Smartfan
11 Beaver Brook Rd (01460-6232)
PHONE...................978 486-4160
Warren R Kundert, *Ch*
James W Kundert, ***
EMP: 26 **EST:** 1981
SQ FT: 10,000
SALES (est): 4.66MM **Privately Held**
Web: www.controlresources.com
SIC: 3625 3822 3829 3674 Noise control
equipment; Temperature controls, automatic
; Measuring and controlling devices, nec;
Semiconductors and related devices

(G-9807)
CURRICULUM ASSOCIATES LLC
Also Called: Curriculum Associates
1 Distribution Center Cir Ste 200
(01460-6250)
PHONE...................978 313-1276
Sandy Batista, *Mgr*
EMP: 47
SALES (corp-wide): 519.28MM **Privately
Held**
Web: www.curriculumassociates.com
SIC: 2731 Book publishing
PA: Curriculum Associates, Llc
153 Rangeway Rd
North Billerica MA 01862
978 667-8000

(G-9808)
CYGLASS INC
Also Called: Cyglass
305 Foster St Ste 200 (01460-2021)
PHONE...................978 665-0280
Prakash Panjwani, *CEO*
EMP: 55 **EST:** 2000
SQ FT: 9,000
SALES (est): 11.92MM **Privately Held**
Web: www.cyglass.com
SIC: 7372 Prepackaged software
PA: Watchguard Technologies, Inc.
505 5th Ave S Ste 500
Seattle WA 98104

(G-9809)
**DAKIN ROAD INVESTMENTS
INC**
Also Called: P&L Machine
162 Ayer Rd (01460-1149)
PHONE...................978 443-4020
Joe D Croman, *Pr*
Eleanor Ting, *Treas*
EMP: 15 **EST:** 2007
SALES (est): 246.33K **Privately Held**
SIC: 3469 Machine parts, stamped or
pressed metal

(G-9810)
**DAY-AHEAD INSTRUMENTATION
LLC**
410 Great Rd Ste B6 (01460-1272)
PHONE...................978 952-2444
James M Bing, *Prin*
EMP: 9 **EST:** 2006
SALES (est): 505.65K **Privately Held**
Web: www.day-ahead.com
SIC: 3825 Instruments to measure electricity

(G-9811)
**DIAMOND ANTENNA
MICROWAVE CORP**
59 Porter Rd (01460-1479)
PHONE...................978 486-0039
Michael Montemagno, *CEO*
Jeffrey T Gilling, *CEO*
Michael Montemagno, *VP*
EMP: 65 **EST:** 1956
SQ FT: 20,000
SALES (est): 11.55MM **Privately Held**
Web: www.diamondantenna.com
SIC: 3679 Electronic circuits

(G-9812)
DIAMOND-ROLTRAN LLC
59 Porter Rd Ste 2 (01460-1479)
PHONE...................978 486-0039
EMP: 14 **EST:** 2007
SALES (est): 827.18K **Privately Held**
Web: www.diamondroll-ring.com
SIC: 3699 Electrical equipment and
supplies, nec

(G-9813)
EGGROCK INC
265 Foster St (01460-2005)
PHONE...................978 952-8800
EMP: 50
SIC: 2452 Prefabricated wood buildings

(G-9814)
FIBA TECH
53 Ayer Rd (01460-1007)
PHONE...................978 486-0586
Frank F Finn Junior, *Prin*
EMP: 11 **EST:** 2013
SALES (est): 1.03MM **Privately Held**
Web: www.fibatech.com
SIC: 3443 Fabricated plate work (boiler
shop)

(G-9815)
FIBA TECHNOLOGIES INC (PA)
53 Ayer Rd (01460-1007)
PHONE...................508 887-7100
Jack Finn, *CEO*
John F Finn, ***
Frank H Finn Junior, *VP*
Robert Morrison, ***
Stephen K Finn, ***
◆ **EMP:** 269 **EST:** 1984
SQ FT: 45,000
SALES (est): 97.7MM
SALES (corp-wide): 97.7MM **Privately
Held**
Web: www.fibatech.com
SIC: 3443 Reactor containment vessels,
metal plate

(G-9816)
HP INC
Also Called: HP
153 Taylor St (01460-1407)
PHONE...................800 222-5547
EMP: 52
SALES (corp-wide): 53.72B **Publicly Held**
Web: www.hp.com

SIC: 3571 Personal computers
(microcomputers)
PA: Hp Inc.
1501 Page Mill Rd
Palo Alto CA 94304
650 857-1501

(G-9817)
HP INC
Also Called: HP
550 King St (01460-6245)
PHONE...................650 857-1501
Ted Mckie, *Prin*
EMP: 18
SALES (corp-wide): 53.72B **Publicly Held**
Web: www.hp.com
SIC: 3571 Personal computers
(microcomputers)
PA: Hp Inc.
1501 Page Mill Rd
Palo Alto CA 94304
650 857-1501

(G-9818)
IMAGE STREAM MEDICAL INC
1 Monarch Dr Ste 102 (01460-1440)
PHONE...................978 486-8494
Eddie Mitchell, *Pr*
EMP: 90 **EST:** 2002
SQ FT: 32,693
SALES (est): 21.26MM **Privately Held**
SIC: 3669 3841 5047 Visual communication
systems; Diagnostic apparatus, medical;
Surgical equipment and supplies

(G-9819)
INFOR INC
30 Porter Rd (01460-1414)
PHONE...................678 319-8000
EMP: 16 **EST:** 2017
SALES (est): 834.19K **Privately Held**
Web: ma-littleton.pacifica.org.au
SIC: 7372 Prepackaged software

(G-9820)
**INJECTION MOLDING ENTPS
LLC**
20 Harvard Rd (01460-1015)
PHONE...................978 339-4535
EMP: 16 **EST:** 2017
SALES (est): 2.49MM **Privately Held**
SIC: 3089 Injection molding of plastics

(G-9821)
**J P RUTHIER SONS RECYCL
CORP (PA)**
256 Ayer Rd (01460-1010)
PHONE...................978 772-4251
Paul Routhier, *Pr*
EMP: 20 **EST:** 2015
SQ FT: 1,500
SALES (est): 2.37MM
SALES (corp-wide): 2.37MM **Privately
Held**
Web: www.jprouthier.com
SIC: 4212 3559 Local trucking, without
storage; Tire shredding machinery

(G-9822)
JOWA USA INC
59 Porter Rd (01460-1479)
PHONE...................978 486-9800
Per Ola Hogdahl, *Pr*
Berndt Bittner, *Sec*
Jan Seehuusen, *Treas*
▲ **EMP:** 21 **EST:** 1965
SQ FT: 20,000
SALES (est): 6.99MM
SALES (corp-wide): 14.73MM **Privately
Held**

Web: www.jowa-usa.com
SIC: 3823   Process control instruments
HQ: Jowa Ab
     Tulebovagen 104
     KAllered 428 3
     317265400

(G-9823)
KENEXA BRASSRING INC
550 King St (01460-6245)
PHONE..............................781 530-5000
EMP: 250 EST: 1999
SQ FT: 65,000
SALES (est): 41.93MM
SALES (corp-wide): 60.53B Publicly Held
SIC: 7372 7379   Prepackaged software;
   Computer related consulting services
HQ: Kenexa Corporation
     650 E Swedesford Rd # 200
     Wayne PA 19087

(G-9824)
MATERIALS SYSTEMS INC
543 Great Rd (01460-1208)
PHONE..............................978 486-0404
Leslie Bowen, Pr
EMP: 9 EST: 2018
SALES (est): 400.48K Privately Held
Web: www.msitransducers.com
SIC: 3829   Measuring and controlling
   devices, nec

(G-9825)
**MEVION MEDICAL SYSTEMS
INC (PA)**
Also Called: Mevion Medical Systems
300 Foster St Ste 3 (01460-2017)
PHONE..............................978 486-1006
Joseph K Jachinowski, CEO
Mark Jones, *
Bill Alvord, *
Donald Melson, *
Mitchell S Bloom, *
▲ EMP: 148 EST: 2004
SQ FT: 85,000
SALES (est): 108.51MM
SALES (corp-wide): 108.51MM Privately
Held
Web: www.mevion.com
SIC: 3845   Electromedical apparatus

(G-9826)
MSI TRANSDUCERS CORP
543 Great Rd (01460-1208)
PHONE..............................978 486-0404
Matthew Boucher, Pr
Stephen Boucher, Treas
Barbara Dee, Mgr
EMP: 15 EST: 2016
SALES (est): 2.85MM
SALES (corp-wide): 50.61MM Privately
Held
Web: www.msitransducers.com
SIC: 3812   Search and navigation equipment
PA: Airmar Technology Corp.
     35 Meadowbrook Dr
     Milford NH 03055
     603 673-9570

(G-9827)
NASHOBA SECURITY INC
474 Great Rd (01460-1290)
PHONE..............................978 486-8615
Charles E Bell, Pr
Caroline R Armstrong, Treas
EMP: 15 EST: 1976
SQ FT: 27,000
SALES (est): 946.75K Privately Held
Web: www.nsisecurity.com

SIC: 7699 7382 1731 1751   Locksmith shop;
   Security systems services; Fiber optic cable
   installation; Window and door installation
   and erection

(G-9828)
NEW OBJECTIVE INC
295 Foster St # 110 (01460-2022)
PHONE..............................781 933-9560
Gary Valaskovic, Pr
Emily Ehrenfele, VP
EMP: 15 EST: 1997
SALES (est): 3.15MM Privately Held
Web: www.newobjective.com
SIC: 3826   Mass spectrometers

(G-9829)
OCTOSCOPE INC
305 Foster St Ste 104 (01460-2021)
PHONE..............................978 486-3130
Fanny Mlinarsky, CEO
EMP: 11 EST: 2006
SALES (est): 2.4MM Privately Held
Web: www.spirent.com
SIC: 3669   Intercommunication systems,
   electric

(G-9830)
**OPTOMETRICS CORPORATION
(HQ)**
521 Great Rd Ste 1 (01460-1208)
PHONE..............................978 772-1700
Michael J Cumbo, CEO
Laura S Lunardo, *
Gary J Bishop, *
▲ EMP: 50 EST: 2004
SQ FT: 10,000
SALES (est): 11.53MM
SALES (corp-wide): 38.79MM Privately
Held
Web: www.optometrics.com
SIC: 3827   Lenses, optical: all types except
   ophthalmic
PA: Omega Optical Holdings, Llc
     21 Omega Dr
     Brattleboro VT 05301
     802 251-7300

(G-9831)
PATRIOT BEVERAGES LLC
20 Harvard Rd (01460-1015)
PHONE..............................978 486-4900
Dan Gray, Managing Member
EMP: 60 EST: 2016
SALES (est): 45MM Privately Held
SIC: 2086   Bottled and canned soft drinks

(G-9832)
PEAK TECHNOLOGIES LLC
Also Called: Opi
9 Beaver Brook Rd (01460-6232)
PHONE..............................978 393-5900
EMP: 34 EST: 2007
SALES (est): 11.87MM Privately Held
Web: www.opticalphusion.com
SIC: 8731 7372   Computer (hardware)
   development; Prepackaged software

(G-9833)
**PROGRAMMED TEST
SOURCES INC**
Also Called: Pts
9 Beaver Brook Rd (01460-6232)
P.O. Box 517 (01460-0517)
PHONE..............................978 486-3008
EMP: 10 EST: 1975
SALES (est): 1.67MM Privately Held
Web: www.programmedtest.com

SIC: 3825   Test equipment for electronic and
electric measurement

(G-9834)
QBIT SEMICONDUCTOR LTD
1 Monarch Dr Ste 203 (01460-1440)
PHONE..............................351 205-0005
EMP: 9 EST: 2017
SALES (est): 716.57K Privately Held
Web: www.qbitsemi.com
SIC: 3674   Semiconductors and related
   devices

(G-9835)
RESIN TECHNOLOGY LLC (DH)
824 Constitution Ave (01460-1137)
PHONE..............................978 448-6926
◆ EMP: 12 EST: 1996
SALES (est): 22.06MM
SALES (corp-wide): 311.49K Privately
Held
Web: www.emeraude-international.com
SIC: 2821   Plastics materials and resins
HQ: Emeraude International
     Zone Industrielle Pre Luquain
     Montreal La Cluse 01460

(G-9836)
ROBERT J MORAN INC
410 Great Rd (01460-1200)
P.O. Box 592 (01460-0592)
PHONE..............................978 486-4718
Robert J Moran Senior, Pr
EMP: 9 EST: 1974
SQ FT: 7,000
SALES (est): 974.49K Privately Held
Web: www.moranmachineshop.com
SIC: 3599   Machine shop, jobbing and repair

(G-9837)
SAJAWI CORPORATION
Also Called: ETM Manufacturing
24 Porter Rd (01460-1414)
PHONE..............................978 486-9050
Douglas Alan Scheffel, CEO
Elizabeth Scheffel, *
EMP: 25 EST: 2018
SQ FT: 6,000
SALES (est): 3.41MM Privately Held
Web: www.etmmfg.com
SIC: 3441   Fabricated structural metal

(G-9838)
**SMALL WATER SYSTEMS SVCS
LLC**
80 Taylor St (01460-1416)
P.O. Box 2014 (01460-3014)
PHONE..............................978 486-1008
Deborah A Trumbull, Managing Member
EMP: 15 EST: 1995
SALES (est): 2.24MM Privately Held
Web: www.swss.biz
SIC: 1623 3824   Water and sewer line
   construction; Water meters

(G-9839)
SPIRENT COMMUNICATIONS INC
305 Foster St (01460-2021)
PHONE..............................774 463-0281
EMP: 128
SALES (corp-wide): 607.5MM Privately
Held
Web: www.spirent.com
SIC: 3825   Instruments to measure electricity
HQ: Spirent Communications Inc.
     27349 Agoura Rd
     Calabasas CA 91301

(G-9840)
STONE YARD LLC
265 Foster St (01460-2005)
PHONE..............................978 742-9800
◆ EMP: 22 EST: 1999
SQ FT: 7,500
SALES (est): 4.79MM Privately Held
Web: www.stoneyard.com
SIC: 5032 3281   Marble building stone; Cut
   stone and stone products

(G-9841)
STONERIDGE DESIGN INC
Also Called: P & L Machine Company
162 Ayer Rd (01460-1149)
PHONE..............................978 486-9626
Joe Crowman, Pr
Eleanor Ting, Sec
EMP: 18 EST: 1979
SQ FT: 6,000
SALES (est): 1.23MM Privately Held
Web: www.plmachine.com
SIC: 3599   Machine shop, jobbing and repair

(G-9842)
VERYFINE PRODUCTS INC (DH)
Also Called: Veryfine
20 Harvard Rd (01460-1015)
PHONE..............................978 486-0812
William Cyr, Pr
James A Rowse Senior, Ch Bd
Samuel B Rowse, *
Frank Orfanello, *
Steven Rowse, *
EMP: 100 EST: 1865
SQ FT: 52,000
SALES (est): 88.45MM
SALES (corp-wide): 491.93MM Privately
Held
Web: www.veryfine.com
SIC: 2086   Fruit drinks (less than 100%
   juice): packaged in cans, etc.
HQ: Sunny Delight Beverage Co
     10300 Alliance Rd Ste 500
     Blue Ash OH 45242
     513 483-3300

(G-9843)
VISIONQUEST HOLDINGS LLC
305 Foster St Ste 204 (01460-2021)
PHONE..............................978 776-9518
Hjalmar Pompe Van Meerdervoort, Pr
Hjalmar Pompe Van Meerdervoort, CEO
Elizabeth Kent, VP Mktg
Thomas Gill Md, Dir
EMP: 10 EST: 2017
SQ FT: 6,000
SALES (est): 350K Privately Held
SIC: 3841   Surgical and medical instruments

(G-9844)
VITAMIN 1 LLC
256 Ayer Rd (01460-1010)
P.O. Box 399 (01451-0399)
PHONE..............................617 523-9090
Michael Taylor, Prin
EMP: 9 EST: 2015
SALES (est): 1MM Privately Held
Web: www.drinkvitamin1.com
SIC: 2086   Water, natural: packaged in cans,
   bottles, etc.

(G-9845)
**WINCHESTER SYSTEMS INC
(PA)**
305 Foster St Ste 100 (01460-2021)
PHONE..............................781 265-0200
Joel Leider, Chief Executive Officer SPHR
Jerry Namery, *
EMP: 24 EST: 1982

▲ = Import ▼ = Export
◆ = Import/Export

SQ FT: 15,000
SALES (est): 4.71MM
SALES (corp-wide): 4.71MM **Privately Held**
Web: www.winsys.com
SIC: 3572 3577 Computer storage devices; Computer peripheral equipment, nec

(G-9846)
XPHOTONICS LLC
32 Surrey Rd (01460-2258)
PHONE.................................978 952-2568
EMP: 7 EST: 2008
SALES (est): 382.65K **Privately Held**
SIC: 3661 Fiber optics communications equipment

(G-9847)
ZEEVEE INC (PA)
295 Foster St Ste 200 (01460-2022)
PHONE.................................978 467-1395
EMP: 33 EST: 2006
SQ FT: 13,325
SALES (est): 7.67MM **Privately Held**
Web: www.zeevee.com
SIC: 3663 Digital encoders

Longmeadow
Hampden County

(G-9848)
BIG Y FOODS INC
Also Called: Big Y Pharmacy
802 Williams St (01106-2049)
PHONE.................................413 567-6231
Joann Hanks, *Mgr*
EMP: 79
SALES (corp-wide): 1.56B **Privately Held**
Web: www.bigy.com
SIC: 5411 5912 2051 Supermarkets, chain; Drug stores and proprietary stores; Bread, cake, and related products
PA: Big Y Foods, Inc.
2145 Roosevelt Ave
Springfield MA 01104
413 784-0600

(G-9849)
CCO HOLDINGS LLC
400 Longmeadow St (01106-1315)
PHONE.................................413 754-0616
EMP: 109
SALES (corp-wide): 54.02B **Publicly Held**
SIC: 4841 3663 3651 Cable television services; Radio and t.v. communications equipment; Household audio and video equipment
HQ: Cco Holdings, Llc
400 Atlantic St
Stamford CT 06901
203 905-7801

Lowell
Middlesex County

(G-9850)
128 TECHNOLOGY INC (PA)
10 Technology Dr (01851-2728)
PHONE.................................781 203-8400
Andrew Ory, *CEO*
Patrick J Melampy, *
Susan Graham Johnston, *
Boris Kilmnik, *
EMP: 101 EST: 2014
SALES (est): 17.41MM
SALES (corp-wide): 17.41MM **Privately Held**

SIC: 7372 Business oriented computer software

(G-9851)
ADVANCED WOODWORKING TECH LLC
258 W Manchester St (01852-4438)
PHONE.................................978 937-1400
Maria T Marlowe, *Mgr*
EMP: 7 EST: 2005
SALES (est): 136.44K **Privately Held**
SIC: 2431 Millwork

(G-9852)
AIR-MART HEATING & COOLING LLC
225 Stedman St Ste 13 (01851-2784)
PHONE.................................603 821-1416
EMP: 8 EST: 2007
SALES (est): 1.12MM **Privately Held**
Web: www.airmart.org
SIC: 3585 Parts for heating, cooling, and refrigerating equipment

(G-9853)
AMES TEXTILE CORPORATION
Also Called: Gametime Fabrics
710 Chelmsford St (01851-5153)
PHONE.................................978 934-8850
◆ EMP: 100
Web: www.amestextile.com
SIC: 2329 2211 Men's and boys' athletic uniforms; Yarn-dyed fabrics, cotton

(G-9854)
ARLIN MFG CO INC
239 Industrial Ave E (01852-5113)
P.O. Box 222 (01853-0222)
PHONE.................................978 454-9165
John R Mitchell, *Ch Bd*
John R Mitchell Junior, *Pr*
Steve Mitchell, *VP*
Paul R Mitchell, *Sec*
▲ EMP: 15 EST: 1954
SQ FT: 4,500
SALES (est): 2.58MM **Privately Held**
Web: www.arlinmfg.com
SIC: 3081 Polyethylene film

(G-9855)
ARRIS TECHNOLOGY INC
900 Chelmsford St (01851-8100)
PHONE.................................978 614-2900
EMP: 11 EST: 2018
SALES (est): 710.84K **Privately Held**
SIC: 3663 Radio and t.v. communications equipment

(G-9856)
ATLANTIC MICROWAVE CORPORATION
1001 Pawtucket Blvd (01854-1040)
EMP: 140
Web: www.cheltonmicrowave.com
SIC: 3663 Television antennas (transmitting) and ground equipment

(G-9857)
AVCARB LLC
Also Called: Avcarb Material Solutions
2 Indl Ave (01851)
PHONE.................................978 452-8961
Roger Masse, *CEO*
▲ EMP: 64 EST: 2013
SQ FT: 30,000
SALES (est): 24.42MM **Privately Held**
Web: www.avcarb.com

SIC: 3955 2221 Carbon paper and inked ribbons; Broadwoven fabric mills, manmade

(G-9858)
AXIS TECHNOLOGIES INC
39 Wilbur St Ste 2 (01851-5221)
PHONE.................................978 275-9908
Dennis W Gibson, *Pr*
Michael Vapolski, *
EMP: 42 EST: 1986
SALES (est): 6.21MM **Privately Held**
Web: www.axistechnologiesinc.com
SIC: 3599 Machine shop, jobbing and repair

(G-9859)
BALLARD MATERIAL PRODUCTS INC
2 Industrial Ave (01851-5107)
PHONE.................................978 452-8961
▲ EMP: 46
SIC: 2221 Automotive fabrics, manmade fiber

(G-9860)
BASSETT & CASSIDY INC
Also Called: Minuteman Press
1527 Middlesex St Apt 1 (01851-1271)
PHONE.................................978 452-9595
Mark Cassidy, *Pr*
Christopher Bassett, *VP*
EMP: 7 EST: 2009
SQ FT: 2,400
SALES (est): 934.08K **Privately Held**
Web: www.minuteman.com
SIC: 2752 Commercial printing, lithographic

(G-9861)
BAY STATE WIRE & CABLE CO INC
645 Lawrence St Ste 3 (01852-3698)
P.O. Box 1093 (01853-1093)
PHONE.................................978 454-2444
Donald Ranagan Junior, *Pr*
EMP: 30 EST: 1979
SQ FT: 10,000
SALES (est): 9.19MM **Privately Held**
Web: www.baystatewire.com
SIC: 5063 3694 3496 Wire and cable; Engine electrical equipment; Miscellaneous fabricated wire products

(G-9862)
BH MEDIA INC (HQ)
Also Called: Boston Herald
491 Dutton St Ste 1 (01854-4292)
P.O. Box 4004 (01886-0032)
PHONE.................................617 426-3000
Patrick J Purcell, *Pr*
Jeff Magram, *
EMP: 108 EST: 1984
SALES (est): 89.56MM
SALES (corp-wide): 1.96B **Privately Held**
Web: www.bostonherald.com
SIC: 2711 2752 Commercial printing and newspaper publishing combined; Commercial printing, lithographic
PA: Digital First Media, Llc
101 W Colfax Ave Fl 11
Denver CO 80202
303 954-6360

(G-9863)
BOOKTALK EVENT
Also Called: Booktalk
125 Charant Rd (01854-1089)
P.O. Box 170554 (02117-0564)
PHONE.................................952 836-6275
Azanta Thakur, *CEO*
Sally Bremer, *COO*

EMP: 35 EST: 2021
SALES (est): 1.12MM **Privately Held**
Web: www.booktalkevent.com
SIC: 2731 7389 Book clubs: publishing only, not printed on site; Business services, nec

(G-9864)
BRADFORD COATINGS INC
Also Called: Bradford Industries
75 Rogers St (01852-3617)
PHONE.................................978 459-4100
Jay Kumar, *CEO*
Stephen Olsen, *
▲ EMP: 75 EST: 1967
SALES (est): 24.2MM
SALES (corp-wide): 24.2MM **Privately Held**
Web: www.bsct.us
SIC: 2295 Laminating of fabrics
PA: Wembly Enterprises Llc
931 Briarwoods Rd
Franklin Lakes NJ

(G-9865)
BRADY BUSINESS FORMS INC
171 Lincoln St Ste 1 (01852-6021)
P.O. Box 667 (01879-0667)
PHONE.................................978 458-2585
TOLL FREE: 800
Mark Brady, *Pr*
Mark Brady, *Pr*
Lou Ann Brady, *VP*
EMP: 8 EST: 1953
SQ FT: 10,000
SALES (est): 829.32K **Privately Held**
Web: www.bradyprint.com
SIC: 2759 5112 2752 Business forms: printing, nsk; Business forms; Offset printing

(G-9866)
CENTIVE INC
Also Called: Xactly
900 Chelmsford St (01851)
PHONE.................................866 469-2285
EMP: 14 EST: 1997
SQ FT: 11,162
SALES (est): 461.92K
SALES (corp-wide): 140.98MM **Privately Held**
Web: www.centive.com
SIC: 7372 Business oriented computer software
HQ: Xactly Corporation
221 Los Gatos Saratoga Rd
Los Gatos CA 95030
408 977-3132

(G-9867)
CIRTEC MEDICAL CORP
1001 Pawtucket Blvd (01854-1040)
PHONE.................................978 703-6822
Brian Highley, *Brnch Mgr*
EMP: 225
SALES (corp-wide): 200MM **Privately Held**
Web: www.cirtecmed.com
SIC: 3679 Electronic circuits
PA: Cirtec Medical Corp.
9200 Xylon Ave N
Brooklyn Park MN 55445
763 493-8556

(G-9868)
COATING SYSTEMS INC
90 Phoenix Ave (01852-4981)
PHONE.................................978 937-3712
Arthur C Sacco, *Pr*
Linda J Sacco, *
EMP: 54 EST: 1992
SQ FT: 20,000

SALES (est): 6.94MM **Privately Held**
Web: www.coatingsystemsgroup.com
SIC: 3471 Electroplating of metals or formed products

(G-9869)
COBHAM DEFENSE ELECTRONIC SYSTEMS CORPORATION
1001 Pawtucket Blvd (01854-1040)
PHONE.............................978 779-7000
EMP: 2650
SIC: 3812 Antennas, radar or communications

(G-9870)
COBHAM ELECTRONIC SYSTEMS INC
Also Called: Cobham Defense Electronics
1001 Pawtucket Blvd (01854-1040)
PHONE.............................978 442-4700
EMP: 1150
Web:
cobhamelectronicsystemsma.mfgpages.com
SIC: 3812 Search and navigation equipment

(G-9871)
CORTRON INC
59 Technology Dr (01851-2851)
PHONE.............................978 975-5445
Eric Friedrichs, *Pr*
Herman L Kabakoff, *
EMP: 48 **EST:** 1987
SQ FT: 28,000
SALES (est): 10.47MM **Privately Held**
Web: www.cortroninc.com
SIC: 3575 3699 3577 Keyboards, computer, office machine; Electrical equipment and supplies, nec; Computer peripheral equipment, nec

(G-9872)
CSP INC (PA)
Also Called: CSPI
175 Cabot St Ste 210 (01854-3635)
PHONE.............................978 954-5038
Victor Dellovo, *Pr*
C Shelton James, *Ch Bd*
Gary W Levine, *VP Fin*
Michael Newbanks, *CAO*
Gary Southwell, *VP*
EMP: 41 **EST:** 1968
SQ FT: 8,257
SALES (est): 64.65MM
SALES (corp-wide): 64.65MM **Publicly Held**
Web: www.cspi.com
SIC: 3577 7372 7373 Computer peripheral equipment, nec; Prepackaged software; Computer integrated systems design

(G-9873)
D S GRAPHICS INC (PA)
Also Called: D S G
120 Stedman St (01851-2797)
PHONE.............................978 970-1359
Jeffrey F Pallis, *Pr*
James J Pallis, *
Justin R Pallis, *
John P Pallis, *
▲ **EMP:** 159 **EST:** 1974
SQ FT: 140,000
SALES (est): 48.71MM
SALES (corp-wide): 48.71MM **Privately Held**
Web: www.dsguw.com
SIC: 2752 2791 2789 Offset printing; Typesetting; Bookbinding and related work

(G-9874)
DESK TOP SOLUTIONS INC
Also Called: Microprint
70 Industrial Ave E (01852-5110)
PHONE.............................781 890-7500
Brian Solov, *Pr*
EMP: 15 **EST:** 1987
SALES (est): 2.24MM **Privately Held**
Web: www.mprint.com
SIC: 2759 Publication printing

(G-9875)
DIAGNOSYS LLC (PA)
55 Technology Dr Ste 1 (01851-5203)
PHONE.............................978 458-1600
Bruce Doran, *Managing Member*
▲ **EMP:** 21 **EST:** 1996
SALES (est): 4.54MM
SALES (corp-wide): 4.54MM **Privately Held**
Web: www.diagnosysllc.com
SIC: 2836 3845 3841 Biological products, except diagnostic; Electromedical equipment; Surgical and medical instruments

(G-9876)
DISPATCH NEWS
Also Called: Lowell Sun
491 Dutton St (01854-4289)
P.O. Box 4004 (01886-0032)
PHONE.............................978 458-7100
Dean Singleton, *Pr*
EMP: 10 **EST:** 2010
SALES (est): 210.64K **Privately Held**
SIC: 2711 Newspapers, publishing and printing

(G-9877)
ETCHOMATIC INC
179 Old Canal Dr (01851-2849)
PHONE.............................978 656-0011
Peter Loven, *Pr*
Craig S Belson, *Ch*
▲ **EMP:** 12 **EST:** 1957
SQ FT: 15,000
SALES (est): 4.03MM **Privately Held**
Web: www.etchomatic.com
SIC: 5065 3861 Electronic parts and equipment, nec; Plates, photographic (sensitized)

(G-9878)
GENERAL WOODWORKING INC
Also Called: Phoenix Workstations
299 Western Ave (01851-1414)
PHONE.............................978 251-4070
EMP: 40
SALES (corp-wide): 8.13MM **Privately Held**
SIC: 2599 Work benches, factory
PA: General Woodworking, Inc.
105 Pevey St
Lowell MA 01851
978 458-6625

(G-9879)
GENERAL WOODWORKING INC (PA)
Also Called: Phoenix Workstation Division
105 Pevey St (01851-1357)
PHONE.............................978 458-6625
John Thompson, *Pr*
Michael Thompson, *VP*
Dan Thompson, *VP*
Sara A Axon, *Sec*
Judith A Thompson, *Treas*
EMP: 10 **EST:** 1976
SALES (est): 8.53MM
SALES (corp-wide): 8.53MM **Privately Held**

Web: www.genwood.com
SIC: 2599 3083 2541 2431 Work benches, factory; Plastics finished products, laminated; Wood partitions and fixtures; Millwork

(G-9880)
GLOBAL MATERIALS INC
Also Called: Specialty Materials
1449 Middlesex St (01851-1111)
PHONE.............................978 322-1900
Monica Rommel, *CEO*
Monte Treasure, *
▲ **EMP:** 36 **EST:** 2019
SQ FT: 54,000
SALES (est): 6.76MM **Privately Held**
Web: www.specmaterials.com
SIC: 2823 Cellulosic manmade fibers

(G-9881)
GN AUDIO USA INC (DH)
Also Called: G N Netcom Unex
900 Chelmsford St 8th Fl (01851-8100)
PHONE.............................800 826-4656
Toon Bouten, *CEO*
Peter Fox, *
Dean G Kacos, *
Deborah Wenger, *
Anna Johnson, *
▲ **EMP:** 350 **EST:** 1986
SQ FT: 57,000
SALES (est): 84.64MM
SALES (corp-wide): 2.61B **Privately Held**
SIC: 3661 Headsets, telephone
HQ: Gn Audio A/S
Lautrupbjerg 7
Ballerup 2750
45750000

(G-9882)
GRAPHIC PACKAGING INTL LLC
164 Meadowcroft St (01852-5326)
P.O. Box 270 (01853-0270)
PHONE.............................978 459-9328
Christine Tamblingson, *Genl Mgr*
EMP: 483
Web: www.americraft.com
SIC: 2657 Folding paperboard boxes
HQ: Graphic Packaging International, Llc
1500 Riveredge Pkwy # 100
Atlanta GA 30328

(G-9883)
GUTZ LLC
71 Willie St (01854-4125)
PHONE.............................978 805-5001
Lisa A Guidi, *Prin*
EMP: 9 **EST:** 2008
SALES (est): 168.59K **Privately Held**
SIC: 3679 Electronic circuits

(G-9884)
HORSEPOWER TECHNOLOGIES INC
600 Suffolk St Ste 250 (01854-3629)
PHONE.............................844 514-6773
Mouli Ramani, *Pr*
EMP: 50 **EST:** 2017
SALES (est): 2.29MM **Privately Held**
Web: www.horsepowertech.com
SIC: 3841 Veterinarians' instruments and apparatus

(G-9885)
IDEAL TAPE CO INC
Also Called: Ideal Tape Co-A Div Amercn Bil
1400 Middlesex St (01851-1296)
PHONE.............................978 458-6833
Michel Merkx, *Genl Mgr*
◆ **EMP:** 70 **EST:** 1970

SQ FT: 50,000
SALES (est): 19.05MM
SALES (corp-wide): 93.38MM **Privately Held**
Web: www.abitape.com
SIC: 2672 2671 Tape, pressure sensitive: made from purchased materials; Paper; coated and laminated packaging
PA: American Biltrite Inc.
57 River St Ste 302
Wellesley MA 02481
781 237-6655

(G-9886)
IDEAS INC
160 Tanner St (01852-4473)
PHONE.............................978 453-6864
Charles Mc Namara Senior, *Pr*
Patrick Mc Namara, *Sec*
EMP: 9 **EST:** 1969
SQ FT: 25,000
SALES (est): 1.45MM **Privately Held**
Web: www.ideasincfab.com
SIC: 3444 Sheet metal specialties, not stamped

(G-9887)
INSIGHTFULVR
160 Western Ave Unit 114 (01851-1449)
PHONE.............................978 429-7874
Layla Mah, *Prin*
EMP: 9 **EST:** 2016
SALES (est): 159.09K **Privately Held**
Web: www.insightfulvr.com
SIC: 7372 Prepackaged software

(G-9888)
J G MACLELLAN CON CO INC (PA)
180 Phoenix Ave (01852-4931)
PHONE.............................978 458-1223
John G Maclellan Iii, *Pr*
Alexander D Maclellan, *
Ann Maclellan, *
Peter A Maclellan, *
EMP: 60 **EST:** 1965
SQ FT: 1,200
SALES (est): 10.15MM
SALES (corp-wide): 10.15MM **Privately Held**
Web: www.jgmaclellanconcrete.com
SIC: 3273 1442 Ready-mixed concrete; Construction sand and gravel

(G-9889)
KALT INCORPORATED (PA)
Also Called: Photo Etch Technology
71 Willie St (01854-4125)
PHONE.............................978 805-5001
Lisa Guidi, *Pr*
Dan Latessa, *
EMP: 30 **EST:** 1992
SALES (est): 4.73MM
SALES (corp-wide): 4.73MM **Privately Held**
Web: www.stencil.com
SIC: 2631 3953 3672 Stencil board; Marking devices; Printed circuit boards

(G-9890)
KING FISHER CO INC
81 Old Ferry Rd (01854-1907)
PHONE.............................978 596-0214
Frank Carideo, *CEO*
Mario Bulhoes, *
EMP: 25 **EST:** 1967
SQ FT: 25,000
SALES (est): 4.88MM **Privately Held**
Web: www.kfci.com

▲ = Import ▼ = Export
◆ = Import/Export

SIC: **3669** 3569 2899 7371   Fire alarm apparatus, electric; Firefighting apparatus; Fire extinguisher charges; Computer software development

(G-9891)
KING PRINTING COMPANY INC
181 Industrial Ave E (01852-5147)
PHONE..................................978 458-2345
Aditya Chinai, *Pr*
Amita Chinai, *
Siddharth Chinai, *
▲ **EMP:** 80 **EST:** 1981
SALES (est): 14.12MM **Privately Held**
Web: www.kingprinting.com
SIC: **2752**   Offset printing

(G-9892)
KRONOS INTERNATIONAL MGT LLC (DH)
900 Chelmsford St Unit 312 (01851-8312)
PHONE..................................978 250-9800
Alyce Moore, *Mgr*
EMP: 16 **EST:** 2011
SALES (est): 1.51MM
SALES (corp-wide): 1.85B **Privately Held**
Web: www.ukg.com
SIC: **7372**   Business oriented computer software
HQ: Ukg Kronos Systems, Llc
    900 Chelmsford St
    Lowell MA 01851
    978 250-9800

(G-9893)
KRONOS SECURITIES CORPORATION
900 Chelmsford St Unit 312 (01851-8312)
PHONE..................................978 250-9800
Aron J Ain, *Prin*
EMP: 10 **EST:** 2009
SALES (est): 1.28MM
SALES (corp-wide): 1.85B **Privately Held**
Web: www.ukg.com
SIC: **7372**   Business oriented computer software
HQ: Ukg Kronos Systems, Llc
    900 Chelmsford St
    Lowell MA 01851
    978 250-9800

(G-9894)
KRONOS SOLUTIONS INC (DH)
900 Chelmsford St Unit 312 (01851-8312)
PHONE..................................978 805-9971
Aron J Ain, *CEO*
Mark Julien, *CFO*
Deirdre Aubuchon, *COO*
EMP: 21 **EST:** 1996
SQ FT: 20,000
SALES (est): 5.44MM
SALES (corp-wide): 1.85B **Privately Held**
Web: www.ukg.com
SIC: **7372**   Business oriented computer software
HQ: Ukg Kronos Systems, Llc
    900 Chelmsford St
    Lowell MA 01851
    978 250-9800

(G-9895)
KRONOS TECH SYSTEMS LTD PARTNR
900 Chelmsford St (01851-8100)
PHONE..................................978 250-9800
EMP: 37 **EST:** 2002
SALES (est): 10.29MM
SALES (corp-wide): 1.85B **Privately Held**
Web: www.ukg.com

SIC: **7372**   Business oriented computer software
HQ: Ukg Kronos Systems, Llc
    900 Chelmsford St
    Lowell MA 01851
    978 250-9800

(G-9896)
LOWELL SUN PUBLISHING COMPANY (DH)
Also Called: Lowell Sun
491 Dutton St (01854-4294)
PHONE..................................978 459-1300
John Habbe, *CFO*
Mack O Neal, *Prin*
EMP: 134 **EST:** 1878
SQ FT: 55,000
SALES (est): 32.35MM
SALES (corp-wide): 1.96B **Privately Held**
Web: www.lowellsun.com
SIC: **2711**   Newspapers, publishing and printing
HQ: Medianews Group, Inc.
    5990 Washington St
    Denver CO 80216

(G-9897)
MACOM METELICS LLC
Also Called: M/A-Com
100 Chelmsford St (01851-2694)
PHONE..................................978 656-2500
EMP: 106
SALES (est): 46.21MM **Privately Held**
Web: www.macom.com
SIC: **3674**   Wafers (semiconductor devices)

(G-9898)
MACOM TECH SLTONS HOLDINGS INC (PA)
Also Called: MACOM
100 Chelmsford St (01851-2694)
PHONE..................................978 656-2500
EMP: 236 **EST:** 1950
SQ FT: 281,700
SALES (est): 648.41MM **Publicly Held**
Web: www.macom.com
SIC: **3674**   Semiconductors and related devices

(G-9899)
MACOM TECHNOLOGY SOLUTIONS INC
Also Called: Macom
121 Hale St (01851-3311)
PHONE..................................978 656-2500
EMP: 23
Web: www.macom.com
SIC: **3663** 3679   Radio and t.v. communications equipment; Microwave components
HQ: Macom Technology Solutions Inc.
    100 Chelmsford St
    Lowell MA 01851

(G-9900)
MACOM TECHNOLOGY SOLUTIONS INC (HQ)
Also Called: M/A-Com
100 Chelmsford St (01851-2694)
PHONE..................................978 656-2500
Stephen Daly, *CEO*
Robert Dennehy, *Sr VP*
Donghyun Thomas Hwang, *Sr VP*
John Ocampo, *Ch Bd*
John Kober, *CFO*
EMP: 355 **EST:** 2008
SALES (est): 379.18MM **Publicly Held**
Web: www.macom.com

SIC: **3663** 3679 3674   Radio and t.v. communications equipment; Microwave components; Semiconductors and related devices
PA: Macom Technology Solutions
    Holdings, Inc.
    100 Chelmsford St
    Lowell MA 01851

(G-9901)
MAGNA ELEC ROADSCAPE AUTO LLC (HQ)
Also Called: Veoneer Roadscape Auto Inc
1011 Pawtucket Blvd (01854-1040)
PHONE..................................978 656-2500
Seetarama Swamy Kotagiri, *CEO*
EMP: 9 **EST:** 2008
SQ FT: 157,000
SALES (est): 11.27MM
SALES (corp-wide): 37.84B **Privately Held**
SIC: **3694**   Automotive electrical equipment, nec
PA: Magna International Inc
    337 Magna Dr
    Aurora ON L4G 7
    905 726-2462

(G-9902)
MAGNA ELECTRONICS LLC
1001 Pawtucket Blvd (01854-1040)
PHONE..................................978 674-6500
EMP: 205
SALES (corp-wide): 37.84B **Privately Held**
Web: www.veoneer.com
SIC: **3694**   Automotive electrical equipment, nec
HQ: Magna Electronics, Llc
    26360 American Dr
    Southfield MI 48034
    248 223-0600

(G-9903)
MAXIMUS
11 Mill St Ste 2 (01852-3588)
PHONE..................................978 728-8000
Maximus Maximus, *Prin*
EMP: 8 **EST:** 2015
SALES (est): 96.55K **Privately Held**
Web: www.maximusprinting.com
SIC: **2752**   Lithographing on metal

(G-9904)
MCGARVIN ENGINEERING INC
35 Maple St Ste 1 (01852-4561)
PHONE..................................978 454-2741
Bob Skinner, *Pr*
EMP: 10 **EST:** 1969
SQ FT: 10,000
SALES (est): 908.08K **Privately Held**
Web: www.mcgarvin.com
SIC: **3444**   Sheet metal specialties, not stamped

(G-9905)
METELICS CORP
100 Chelmsford St (01851-2620)
PHONE..................................408 737-8197
Randy Cavanaugh, *CFO*
EMP: 29 **EST:** 1978
SALES (est): 289.5K **Privately Held**
SIC: **3674**   Semiconductor circuit networks

(G-9906)
MICROSEMI CORP- MASSACHUSETTS
Also Called: Microsemi-Lowell
75 Technology Dr (01851-2729)
PHONE..................................978 442-5600
John A Caruso, *VP*

EMP: 228
SALES (corp-wide): 8.44B **Publicly Held**
Web: www.microsemi.com
SIC: **3674**   Semiconductors and related devices
HQ: Microsemi Corp.- Massachusetts
    11861 Western Ave
    Garden Grove CA 92841

(G-9907)
MICROSEMI CORPORATION
75 Technology Dr (01851-2729)
PHONE..................................978 442-5637
Dean Morgan, *Brnch Mgr*
EMP: 30
SALES (corp-wide): 8.44B **Publicly Held**
Web: www.microsemi.com
SIC: **3674**   Integrated circuits, semiconductor networks, etc.
HQ: Microsemi Corporation
    11861 Western Ave
    Garden Grove CA 92841
    949 380-6100

(G-9908)
MICROSENSE LLC (HQ)
Also Called: Microsense
205 Industrial Ave E (01852-5113)
PHONE..................................978 843-7670
EMP: 24 **EST:** 2009
SALES (est): 10.56MM
SALES (corp-wide): 10.5B **Publicly Held**
Web: www.microsense.net
SIC: **3829**   Measuring and controlling devices, nec
PA: Kla Corporation
    1 Technology Dr
    Milpitas CA 95035
    408 875-3000

(G-9909)
MOR-WIRE & CABLE INC
50 Newhall St Ste 1 (01852-4166)
P.O. Box 1782 (01853-1782)
PHONE..................................978 453-1782
Michael Morin, *Pr*
Gale Vochum, *Treas*
EMP: 10 **EST:** 1988
SQ FT: 16,000
SALES (est): 981.75K **Privately Held**
Web: www.morwireandcable.com
SIC: **3357**   Building wire and cable, nonferrous

(G-9910)
MOTOROLA MOBILITY LLC
Also Called: Motorola
900 Chelmsford St Ofc 1 (01851-8100)
PHONE..................................978 614-2900
Anthony Zona, *Brnch Mgr*
EMP: 46
Web: www.motorola.com
SIC: **8711** 3357 5999   Designing: ship, boat, machine, and product; Nonferrous wiredrawing and insulating; Communication equipment
HQ: Motorola Mobility Llc
    222 Mdse Mart Plz # 1800
    Chicago IL 60654

(G-9911)
ONLINE MARKETING SOLUTIONS INC
128 Warren St (01852-2284)
PHONE..................................978 937-2363
Keith Caveney, *Mgr*
Keith Caveney, *CEO*
Tj Caveney, *Ex VP*
EMP: 24 **EST:** 2000
SQ FT: 3,000

SALES (est): 464.1K **Privately Held**
SIC: 7372　Application computer software

(G-9912)
OWL STAMP COMPANY INC
Also Called: Owlstamp Visual Solutions
31 1st St　(01850-2501)
PHONE.............................978 452-4541
TOLL FREE: 800
Peter Bergeron, *Pr*
EMP: 8 EST: 1912
SQ FT: 3,000
SALES (est): 994.09K **Privately Held**
Web: www.owlstamp.com
SIC: 2752 7389 3993 7331　Offset printing;
　Engraving service; Signs and advertising
　specialties; Direct mail advertising services

(G-9913)
PHOTO TOOL ENGINEERING INC
Also Called: Pohto Etch Tech
71 Willie St　(01854-4125)
PHONE.............................978 805-5000
Arthur Guidi, *Pr*
Lisa Guidi, *＊*
Roberta Guidi, *＊*
EMP: 18 EST: 1986
SALES (est): 792.34K **Privately Held**
SIC: 3672　Printed circuit boards

(G-9914)
PLENUS GROUP INC
Also Called: Pgi
101 Phoenix Ave　(01852-4930)
PHONE.............................978 970-3832
Joseph Jolly Iii, *Pr*
Stephen Post, *＊*
EMP: 50 EST: 2002
SQ FT: 13,000
SALES (est): 16.54MM **Privately Held**
Web: www.pgifoods.com
SIC: 2038 2035　Soups, frozen; Pickles,
　sauces, and salad dressings

(G-9915)
PRECISE INDUSTRIES INC
639 Lakeview Ave　(01850-1827)
PHONE.............................978 453-8490
Charles Dehney, *Pr*
EMP: 27 EST: 1986
SALES (est): 3.16MM **Privately Held**
Web: www.preciseind.com
SIC: 3444　Sheet metal specialties, not
　stamped

(G-9916)
RAPID MICRO BIOSYSTEMS INC (PA)
1001 Pawtucket Blvd Ste 28　(01854-1040)
PHONE.............................978 349-3200
Robert Spignesi, *Pr*
Jeffrey Schwartz, *＊*
Sean Wirtjes, *CFO*
John Wilson, *COO*
Victoria Vezina, *Chief Human Resources Officer*
▲ EMP: 160 EST: 2006
SQ FT: 52,802
SALES (est): 17.13MM
SALES (corp-wide): 17.13MM **Publicly Held**
Web: www.rapidmicrobio.com
SIC: 3826 2834　Analytical instruments;
　Pharmaceutical preparations

(G-9917)
REDCOAT PUBLISHING
21 8th Ave　(01854-1501)
PHONE.............................978 761-0877
Michelle Rivera, *Prin*

EMP: 19 EST: 2010
SALES (est): 114.6K **Privately Held**
SIC: 2741　Miscellaneous publishing

(G-9918)
REVBIO INC
600 Suffolk St Ste 250　(01854-3629)
PHONE.............................617 460-6675
Brian Hess, *CEO*
Grayson Allen, *CFO*
EMP: 12 EST: 2014
SALES (est): 1.53MM **Privately Held**
Web: www.revbio.com
SIC: 2836　Biological products, except
　diagnostic

(G-9919)
RGC MILLWORK INCORPORATED
175a Old Canal Dr　(01851-2736)
PHONE.............................978 275-9529
Richard P Garofano, *Pr*
EMP: 8 EST: 1986
SALES (est): 2.26MM **Privately Held**
Web: www.rgcmillwork.com
SIC: 2431 2434　Millwork; Wood kitchen
　cabinets

(G-9920)
ROCHE BROS BARREL DRUM CO INC
161 Phoenix Ave　(01852-4998)
PHONE.............................978 454-9135
Michael Roche, *Pr*
Charles Roche, *＊*
EMP: 28 EST: 1920
SALES (est): 1.71MM **Privately Held**
Web: www.rochedrum.com
SIC: 3412　Barrels, shipping: metal

(G-9921)
ROCHE MANUFACTURING INC
161 Phoenix Ave　(01852-4930)
PHONE.............................978 454-9135
Michael Roche, *Pr*
Charles Roche, *Treas*
EMP: 10 EST: 1983
SALES (est): 1.25MM **Privately Held**
SIC: 3412　Barrels, shipping: metal

(G-9922)
RUCKUS WIRELESS INC
Also Called: General Instrs Wrline Networks
900 Chelmsford St　(01851-8100)
PHONE.............................978 614-2900
EMP: 204
Web: www.commscope.com
SIC: 3663　Radio and t.v. communications
　equipment
HQ: Ruckus Wireless, Inc.
　350 W Java Dr
　Sunnyvale CA 94089

(G-9923)
SCANNELL BOILER WORKS
50 Tanner St Ste 1　(01852-4406)
PHONE.............................978 454-5629
Dennis Scannell, *Pr*
John Scannell Junior, *Genl Mgr*
Phillip L Scannell Junior, *Treas*
George Scannell, *VP*
EMP: 10 EST: 1867
SQ FT: 28,000
SALES (est): 220.83K **Privately Held**
SIC: 3443 3441　Boilers: industrial, power, or
　marine; Fabricated structural metal

(G-9924)
SOMERSET INDUSTRIES INC
137 Phoenix Ave　(01852-4930)
PHONE.............................978 667-3355
George Athanadiadis, *Pr*
Paul Athanadiadis, *Genl Mgr*
Andrew D Voyatzakis, *Sec*
◆ EMP: 20 EST: 1946
SQ FT: 20,000
SALES (est): 4.67MM **Privately Held**
Web: www.smrset.com
SIC: 3556　Bakery machinery

(G-9925)
STITCHDX LLC
110 Canal St # 3　(01852-4589)
PHONE.............................617 818-8585
Brian Bolton, *Pr*
EMP: 7 EST: 2017
SALES (est): 270.67K **Privately Held**
Web: www.stitchdx.com
SIC: 2395　Embroidery and art needlework

(G-9926)
T & T ANODIZING INC
Also Called: T & T Anonizing & Indus Spray
35 Maple St　(01852-4565)
PHONE.............................978 454-9631
Joseph Teneriello, *Pr*
Mike Teneriello, *VP*
EMP: 13 EST: 1978
SQ FT: 8,000
SALES (est): 488.34K **Privately Held**
Web: www.ttanodizing.com
SIC: 3471　Electroplating of metals or
　formed products

(G-9927)
T & T ANODIZING INCORPORATED
35 Maple St Ste 8　(01852-4561)
PHONE.............................978 454-9631
Joseph Teneriello, *Pr*
Mike Teneriello, *VP*
Peter Teneriello, *Treas*
Corene Teneriello, *Sec*
EMP: 16 EST: 1981
SALES (est): 951.87K **Privately Held**
Web: www.ttanodizing.com
SIC: 3471　Electroplating of metals or
　formed products

(G-9928)
THOMAS & THOMAS INC
Also Called: Pine Hill Press
207 Industrial Ave E　(01852-5113)
PHONE.............................978 453-7444
Albert J Russo, *Pr*
EMP: 15 EST: 1977
SQ FT: 10,000
SALES (est): 890K **Privately Held**
SIC: 2752 7334　Commercial printing,
　lithographic; Photocopying and duplicating
　services

(G-9929)
TRIVAK INCORPORATED
280 Howard St　(01852-4485)
PHONE.............................978 453-7123
Paul Novak, *Pr*
Richard Novak, *Treas*
EMP: 21 EST: 1973
SQ FT: 12,625
SALES (est): 2.48MM **Privately Held**
SIC: 3599 7692　Machine shop, jobbing and
　repair; Welding repair

(G-9930)
UKG INC (HQ)
Also Called: Ultimate Kronos Group
900 Chelmsford St　(01851-8100)
PHONE.............................978 947-2855
Aron Ain, *CEO*
John Butler, *＊*
Chris Todd, *＊*
EMP: 172 EST: 1990
SQ FT: 305,000
SALES (est): 1.85B
SALES (corp-wide): 1.85B **Privately Held**
Web: www.ukg.com
SIC: 7372　Business oriented computer
　software
PA: Unite Parent Corp.
　2000 Ultimate Way
　Weston FL 33326
　800 432-1729

(G-9931)
UKG KRONOS SYSTEMS LLC (DH)
Also Called: Kronos Incorporated
900 Chelmsford St　(01851-8100)
PHONE.............................978 250-9800
Aron J Ain, *CEO*
Mark S Ain, *Ch Bd*
Christopher R Todd, *＊*
John A Butler, *＊*
James J Kizielewicz, *Senior Vice President Corporate Strategy＊*
◆ EMP: 442 EST: 1977
SQ FT: 400,000
SALES (est): 680.01MM
SALES (corp-wide): 1.85B **Privately Held**
Web: www.ukg.in
SIC: 7372 7373 7371　Business oriented
　computer software; Computer integrated
　systems design; Computer software
　development
HQ: Kronos Acquisition Corporation
　900 Chelmsford St Ste 312
　Lowell MA 01851

(G-9932)
UNWRAPPED INC
95 Rock St Fl 1　(01854-4300)
PHONE.............................978 441-0242
▲ EMP: 85 EST: 1994
SQ FT: 16,000
SALES (est): 9.72MM **Privately Held**
Web: www.unwrappedinc.com
SIC: 2393 2392　Textile bags; Laundry,
　garment and storage bags

(G-9933)
UTZ TECHNOLOGIES INC (PA)
71 Willie St　(01854-4125)
PHONE.............................973 339-1100
Dennis Curtis, *Pr*
Arthur Wein, *＊*
Donald Utz, *＊*
EMP: 30 EST: 1967
SALES (est): 5.62MM
SALES (corp-wide): 5.62MM **Privately Held**
SIC: 3679　Electronic circuits

(G-9934)
VEONEER ROADSCAPE AUTO INC
Also Called: Veoneer Roadscape Lowell
1011 Pawtucket Blvd　(01854-1040)
PHONE.............................978 656-2500
EMP: 8
SALES (corp-wide): 37.84B **Privately Held**
SIC: 3694 4225　Automotive electrical
　equipment, nec; General warehousing

HQ: Magna Electronics Roadscape
Automotive, Llc
1011 Pawtucket Blvd
Lowell MA 01854
978 656-2500

(G-9935)
WATERLAC COATING INC
142 Starr Ave (01852-2914)
PHONE..............................573 885-2506
Edmund Rosa, *Pr*
Phillip Burke, *Genl Mgr*
EMP: 7 **EST:** 1950
SQ FT: 7,000
SALES (est): 695.65K **Privately Held**
SIC: 2851 Lacquers, varnishes, enamels,
and other coatings

(G-9936)
XENITH
672 Suffolk St (01854-3660)
PHONE..............................978 328-5297
EMP: 36 **EST:** 2019
SALES (est): 913.79K **Privately Held**
Web: www.xenith.com
SIC: 3949 Sporting and athletic goods, nec

Ludlow
Hampden County

(G-9937)
**ADVANCED DRAINAGE
SYSTEMS INC**
58 Wyoming St (01056-1096)
PHONE..............................413 589-0515
Dick Navin, *Mgr*
EMP: 381
SALES (corp-wide): 3.07B **Publicly Held**
Web: www.adspipe.com
SIC: 3084 Plastics pipe
PA: Advanced Drainage Systems, Inc.
4640 Trueman Blvd
Hilliard OH 43026
614 658-0050

(G-9938)
**ATLAS COPCO COMPRESSORS
LLC**
Also Called: Atlas Copco
151 Carmelinas Cir (01056-3160)
PHONE..............................413 589-7439
EMP: 8
SALES (corp-wide): 13.47B **Privately Held**
Web: www.atlascopco.com
SIC: 3563 Air and gas compressors
HQ: Atlas Copco Compressors Llc
300 Technology Center Way # 550
Rock Hill SC 29730
866 472-1015

(G-9939)
AUBE PRECISION TOOL CO INC
54 Moody St (01056-1245)
PHONE..............................413 589-9048
Lucien A Aube, *Pr*
Beverly Aube, *VP*
Phil Schuman, *Sec*
EMP: 7 **EST:** 1980
SQ FT: 2,500
SALES (est): 657.84K **Privately Held**
Web: www.aubetool.com
SIC: 3599 3546 Machine shop, jobbing and
repair; Power-driven handtools

(G-9940)
B & R MACHINE INC
305a Moody St Ste A (01056-1246)
PHONE..............................413 589-0246
Gerald A Renaud, *Pr*
EMP: 25 **EST:** 1986
SQ FT: 8,500
SALES (est): 8.54MM **Privately Held**
Web: www.brmachineinc.com
SIC: 3599 Machine shop, jobbing and repair

(G-9941)
**BANAS SAND AND GRAVEL CO
INC**
246 Fuller St (01056-1325)
PHONE..............................413 583-8321
John Banas Junior, *Pr*
James E Banas, *Clerk*
EMP: 24 **EST:** 1931
SQ FT: 8,000
SALES (est): 2.71MM **Privately Held**
SIC: 3273 Ready-mixed concrete

(G-9942)
CHEMI-GRAPHIC INC
340 State St (01056-3439)
P.O. Box 410 (01056-0410)
PHONE..............................413 589-0151
Paul R Pohl, *Pr*
Jason Pohl, *
EMP: 50 **EST:** 1947
SQ FT: 30,000
SALES (est): 9.66MM **Privately Held**
Web: www.chemi-graphic.com
SIC: 3479 2796 Name plates: engraved,
etched, etc.; Platemaking services

(G-9943)
CSW INC (PA)
45 Tyburski Rd (01056-1249)
PHONE..............................413 589-1311
Laura Wright, *Pr*
Gary Jambazian, *Stockholder*
Debra Savreau, *Stockholder*
Ann Moore, *Stockholder*
▲ **EMP:** 92 **EST:** 1936
SQ FT: 35,000
SALES (est): 17.01MM
SALES (corp-wide): 17.01MM **Privately
Held**
Web: www.cswgraphics.com
SIC: 2796 3544 Platemaking services; Dies,
steel rule

(G-9944)
**ELITE METAL FABRICATORS
INC**
100 State St Bldg 203 (01056-3435)
P.O. Box 372 (01056-0372)
PHONE..............................413 547-2588
Ricardo Salvador, *Pr*
EMP: 7 **EST:** 2003
SALES (est): 937.54K **Privately Held**
Web: www.elitemetalfab.com
SIC: 3469 Stamping metal for the trade

(G-9945)
**EMCO TOOL & GAUGE
CORPORATION**
100 State St Bldg 206 (01056-3435)
PHONE..............................413 385-0206
EMP: 8 **EST:** 2007
SALES (est): 254.82K **Privately Held**
Web: www.emcotool.com
SIC: 3599 Machine shop, jobbing and repair

(G-9946)
JAMES AUSTIN COMPANY
Also Called: Kik Consumer Products
203 West Ave (01056-2156)
PHONE..............................413 589-1600
Mark Chevrier, *Brnch Mgr*
EMP: 13

SALES (corp-wide): 2.39B **Privately Held**
Web: www.austinsbleach.com
SIC: 2842 Polishes and sanitation goods
HQ: James Austin Company
115 Downieville Rd
Mars PA 16046
724 625-1535

(G-9947)
KLEEBERG SHEET METAL INC
65 Westover Rd (01056-1298)
PHONE..............................413 589-1854
Dan Kleeberg, *Prin*
Todd Davis, *
Scott Cushman, *Prin*
Dan Bauer, *Prin*
▲ **EMP:** 100 **EST:** 1958
SQ FT: 93,000
SALES (est): 25.02MM **Privately Held**
Web: www.kleeberg.com
SIC: 3444 1711 Sheet metalwork; Plumbing,
heating, air-conditioning

(G-9948)
LEE TOOL CO INC
40 Ravenwood Dr (01056-3311)
P.O. Box 509 (01056-0509)
PHONE..............................413 583-8750
Victor Swist, *Pr*
EMP: 12 **EST:** 1981
SQ FT: 8,700
SALES (est): 1.32MM **Privately Held**
Web: www.leetool.com
SIC: 3545 3469 Precision measuring tools;
Machine parts, stamped or pressed metal

(G-9949)
LOVEJOY LLC
185 West Ave Ste 101 (01056-1737)
PHONE..............................413 737-0281
EMP: 25
SALES (corp-wide): 4.5B **Publicly Held**
Web: www.lovejoy-inc.com
SIC: 3568 Couplings, shaft: rigid, flexible,
universal joint, etc.
HQ: Lovejoy, Llc
2655 Wisconsin Ave
Downers Grove IL 60515
630 852-0500

(G-9950)
LUDLOW TOOL
370 Fuller St (01056-1356)
PHONE..............................413 786-6360
Jason Lucas, *Owner*
EMP: 7 **EST:** 2010
SALES (est): 124.95K **Privately Held**
SIC: 3423 Tools or equipment for use with
sporting arms

(G-9951)
**NEW ENGLAND PALLETS SKIDS
INC**
250 West St (01056-1248)
P.O. Box 342 (01056-0342)
PHONE..............................413 583-6628
Peter S Kawie, *Pr*
EMP: 15 **EST:** 1969
SQ FT: 50,000
SALES (est): 2.44MM **Privately Held**
Web: www.nepallets.com
SIC: 2448 Pallets, wood

(G-9952)
REMSPORT MFG LLC
Also Called: Tr Enabling
566 Holyoke St (01056-1236)
PHONE..............................413 589-1911
Ronald Chiasson, *Managing Member*
EMP: 11 **EST:** 2007

SALES (est): 1.42MM **Privately Held**
Web: www.tr-enabling.com
SIC: 3484 Guns (firearms) or gun parts, 30
mm. and below

(G-9953)
ROMA MARBLE INC
15 Westover Rd (01056-1205)
P.O. Box 685 (01095-0685)
PHONE..............................413 583-5017
John A Ruell, *Pr*
James Steigmeyer, *
▲ **EMP:** 19 **EST:** 1967
SQ FT: 22,600
SALES (est): 398.93K **Privately Held**
SIC: 3088 Bathroom fixtures, plastics

(G-9954)
SPRINGFIELD WIRE INC
100 Moody St Ste 2 (01056-1242)
PHONE..............................413 385-0115
▲ **EMP:** 781
Web: www.springfield-wire.com
SIC: 3634 Heating units, for electric
appliances

(G-9955)
VALMONT INC
Valmont
656 Chapin St (01056-2351)
P.O. Box 421 (01056-0421)
PHONE..............................413 583-8351
M J Mack Junior, *Mgr*
EMP: 18
SQ FT: 8,000
SALES (corp-wide): 3.16MM **Privately
Held**
Web: www.valmont.com
SIC: 2342 Brassieres
PA: Valmont, Inc.
600 3rd Ave Fl 2
New York NY 10016
212 685-1653

(G-9956)
WEST SIDE METAL DOOR CORP
190 Moody St (01056-1230)
PHONE..............................413 589-0945
Dale Croteau, *Prin*
Dale Croteau, *VP*
Gary Barber, *Treas*
EMP: 10 **EST:** 1958
SQ FT: 32,000
SALES (est): 1.52MM **Privately Held**
Web: www.westsidemetaldoor.com
SIC: 3442 Metal doors

(G-9957)
WSMD INC
190 Moody St (01056-1230)
PHONE..............................413 589-0945
Amy Royal, *Pr*
EMP: 8 **EST:** 2018
SALES (est): 897.25K **Privately Held**
SIC: 2431 Millwork

Lunenburg
Worcester County

(G-9958)
ECOLOGICAL FIBERS INC (PA)
40 Pioneer Dr (01462-1699)
PHONE..............................978 537-0003
John Quill, *Pr*
Stephen F Quill, *
Chris White, *
Howard J Hall, *
◆ **EMP:** 65 **EST:** 1972

SQ FT: 72,000
SALES (est): 46.56MM
SALES (corp-wide): 46.56MM **Privately Held**
Web: www.ecofibers.com
SIC: 2621　Paper mills

(G-9959)
POWELL STONE & GRAVEL CO INC (PA)
133 Leominster Shirley Rd (01462-1659)
PHONE.............................978 537-8100
Jeffery Powell, *Pr*
Steven R Powell, *
Lynn A Powell, *
EMP: 50 **EST:** 1984
SQ FT: 2,400
SALES (est): 14.16MM
SALES (corp-wide): 14.16MM **Privately Held**
Web: www.powellstone.com
SIC: 1442　Construction sand and gravel

(G-9960)
S&E SPECIALTY POLYMERS LLC
Also Called: Aurora Plastics
140 Leominster Shirley Rd Ste 100 (01462-1691)
PHONE.............................978 537-8261
Ilia Charlat, *VP*
Jeff Conard, *
▲ **EMP:** 58 **EST:** 2004
SQ FT: 60,000
SALES (est): 19.94MM **Privately Held**
Web: www.auroraplastics.com
SIC: 2821　Plastics materials and resins
HQ: Aurora Plastics, Llc
9280 Jefferson St
Streetsboro OH 44241

Lynn
Essex County

(G-9961)
ACCURATE GRAPHICS INC
26 Alley St (01902-4403)
PHONE.............................781 593-1630
Pappi Bolognese, *Pr*
EMP: 7 **EST:** 2001
SALES (est): 986.37K **Privately Held**
Web: accurategraphics.us.com
SIC: 3993　Signs and advertising specialties

(G-9962)
BARRY MANUFACTURING CO INC
15 Bubier St (01901-1704)
PHONE.............................781 598-1055
▲ **EMP:** 20 **EST:** 1946
SALES (est): 1.62MM **Privately Held**
Web: www.mwcharming.com
SIC: 3149　Children's footwear, except athletic

(G-9963)
BENT WATER BREWING CO
180 Commercial St (01905-3054)
PHONE.............................781 780-9948
EMP: 27 **EST:** 2016
SALES (est): 4.35MM **Privately Held**
Web: www.bentwaterbrewing.com
SIC: 2082　Malt beverages

(G-9964)
BREAKWATER FOODS LLC
82 Sanderson Ave (01902-1974)

P.O. Box 1565 (01944-0865)
PHONE.............................617 335-6475
Andrew Dunbar, *Prin*
EMP: 7 **EST:** 2016
SALES (est): 467.11K **Privately Held**
SIC: 2099　Food preparations, nec

(G-9965)
C L HAUTHAWAY & SONS CORP
Also Called: Hauthane
638 Summer St (01905-2044)
PHONE.............................781 592-6444
John Zermani, *Pr*
Leopoldo Johnson, *
Theodore J Johnson, *
◆ **EMP:** 45 **EST:** 1947
SQ FT: 60,000
SALES (est): 24.21MM
SALES (corp-wide): 24.21MM **Privately Held**
Web: www.hauthaway.com
SIC: 2851 2891　Polyurethane coatings; Adhesives and sealants
PA: L H C Inc
638 Summer St
Lynn MA 01905
781 592-6444

(G-9966)
DART WORLD INC
140 Linwood St Ste 1 (01905-1272)
P.O. Box 845 (01903-1045)
PHONE.............................781 581-6035
Donald Amirault, *Pr*
Mark E Amirault, *
◆ **EMP:** 25 **EST:** 1973
SQ FT: 28,000
SALES (est): 2.34MM **Privately Held**
Web: www.dartworld.com
SIC: 3949　Sporting and athletic goods, nec

(G-9967)
DEMAKES ENTERPRISES INC (PA)
Also Called: Old Neighborhood Foods Div
37 Waterhill St (01905-2134)
PHONE.............................781 417-1100
Thomas L Demakes, *Pr*
John N Demakes, *
◆ **EMP:** 220 **EST:** 1914
SQ FT: 66,000
SALES (est): 47.83MM
SALES (corp-wide): 47.83MM **Privately Held**
Web: www.oldneighborhoodfoods.com
SIC: 2013　Sausages and other prepared meats

(G-9968)
DEMAKES ENTERPRISES INC
34 Riley Way (01905-3036)
PHONE.............................781 586-0212
EMP: 200
SALES (corp-wide): 49.66MM **Privately Held**
SIC: 2013 2011　Sausages and other prepared meats; Meat packing plants
PA: Demakes Enterprises, Inc.
37 Waterhill St
Lynn MA 01905
781 417-1100

(G-9969)
DURKEE-MOWER INC
2 Empire St Corner Columbia St (01902-1815)
P.O. Box 470 (01903-0570)
PHONE.............................781 593-8007
Donald D Durkee, *Pr*
Jonathan Durkee, *

EMP: 24 **EST:** 1919
SQ FT: 33,000
SALES (est): 2.51MM **Privately Held**
Web: www.marshmallowfluff.com
SIC: 2099　Marshmallow creme

(G-9970)
EAST COAST MARBLE & GRAN CORP
142 Lynnfield St (01904-2242)
PHONE.............................781 760-0207
James Maravelias, *Pr*
Bertha Maravelias, *Treas*
EMP: 13 **EST:** 2002
SALES (est): 481.69K **Privately Held**
Web: www.ecmarblegranite.com
SIC: 3281　Table tops, marble

(G-9971)
ERC ACQUISITION INC
Also Called: ERC Wiping Products
19 Bennett St (01905-3059)
PHONE.............................781 593-4000
TOLL FREE: 800
Thomas Friedl, *Pr*
◆ **EMP:** 29 **EST:** 1921
SQ FT: 24,000
SALES (est): 7.06MM **Privately Held**
Web: www.ercwipe.com
SIC: 5087 2392　Cleaning and maintenance equipment and supplies; Towels, dishcloths and dust cloths

(G-9972)
ESSEX ENGINEERING INC
Also Called: Essex Engineering & Mfg Co
20 Day St (01905-3008)
P.O. Box 328 (01905-0628)
PHONE.............................781 595-2114
James S Munro Junior, *Pr*
Robert A Munro, *
Wendy B Munro, *
EMP: 50 **EST:** 1956
SQ FT: 16,000
SALES (est): 7.51MM **Privately Held**
Web: www.essexengineering.com
SIC: 3599 3444　Machine shop, jobbing and repair; Sheet metalwork

(G-9973)
GE AVIATION SYSTEMS LLC
Also Called: GE Aviation
1000 Western Ave (01901)
PHONE.............................513 552-3272
John Burke, *Brnch Mgr*
EMP: 21
SALES (corp-wide): 76.56B **Publicly Held**
Web: www.geaerospace.com
SIC: 3728　Aircraft parts and equipment, nec
HQ: Ge Aviation Systems Llc
1 Aviation Way
Cincinnati OH 45215
937 898-9600

(G-9974)
GENERAL ELECTRIC COMPANY
GE
1000 Western Ave (01910-0002)
PHONE.............................781 594-0100
William Hruves, *Brnch Mgr*
EMP: 603
SALES (corp-wide): 76.56B **Publicly Held**
Web: www.geappliances.com
SIC: 3724　Aircraft engines and engine parts
PA: General Electric Company
1 Financial Ctr Ste 3700
Boston MA 02111
617 443-3000

(G-9975)
GENERAL ELECTRIC COMPANY
GE Edison Works
1000 Western Ave (01905-2690)
PHONE.............................781 594-2218
T Noonan, *Brnch Mgr*
EMP: 2854
SALES (corp-wide): 76.56B **Publicly Held**
Web: www.ge.com
SIC: 3724 3714　Aircraft engines and engine parts; Motor vehicle parts and accessories
PA: General Electric Company
1 Financial Ctr Ste 3700
Boston MA 02111
617 443-3000

(G-9976)
GOODYEAR TIRE & RUBBER COMPANY
Also Called: Goodyear
205 Market St (01901-1515)
PHONE.............................781 598-4500
Bill Logan, *Mgr*
EMP: 10
SALES (corp-wide): 20.8B **Publicly Held**
Web: www.goodyear.com
SIC: 5531 7534　Automotive tires; Tire repair shop
PA: The Goodyear Tire & Rubber Company
200 E Innovation Way
Akron OH 44316
330 796-2121

(G-9977)
H O ZIMMAN INC
152 Lynnway (01902-3491)
PHONE.............................781 598-9230
Josh Zimman, *Owner*
Josh Zimman, *Pr*
Helen Zimman, *Treas*
EMP: 26 **EST:** 1938
SQ FT: 4,000
SALES (est): 6.54MM **Privately Held**
Web: www.hozinc.com
SIC: 2721　Periodicals, publishing and printing

(G-9978)
INVERSANT INC
120 Munroe St Ste 1 (01901-1537)
PHONE.............................617 423-0331
Heidi Hancock, *CEO*
Robert Hildreth, *Ex Dir*
EMP: 15 **EST:** 2009
SALES (est): 1.08MM **Privately Held**
Web: www.inversant.org
SIC: 2869　Fuels

(G-9979)
JET-TECH INCORPORATED
52 Alley St (01902-4403)
PHONE.............................781 599-8685
Michael Bubar, *Pr*
Gary Sauve, *VP*
EMP: 19 **EST:** 1996
SQ FT: 12,000
SALES (est): 781.22K **Privately Held**
Web: red-night-chmn03wheuvk.vapor-farm-d1.com
SIC: 3479　Coating of metals and formed products

(G-9980)
KETTLE CUISINE LLC (PA)
330 Lynnway (01901-1706)
P.O. Box 73 (06096-0073)
PHONE.............................617 409-1100
Liam Mcclennon, *CEO*
Nick Murphy, *Innovation PROCESS*
Lorie Donnelly, *Sr VP*

Tim Adler, *VP*
James Reed, *CFO*
▲ **EMP:** 227 **EST:** 1986
SQ FT: 85,000
SALES (est): 105MM
SALES (corp-wide): 105MM **Privately Held**
Web: www.kettlecuisine.com
SIC: 2032 2035 Soups, except seafood: packaged in cans, jars, etc.; Seasonings and sauces, except tomato and dry

(G-9981)
KETTLE CUISINE HOLDINGS LLC
330 Lynnway Ste 405 (01901-1713)
PHONE..............................617 409-1100
EMP: 125
SIC: 6719 2032 2038 2035 Investment holding companies, except banks; Soups, except seafood: packaged in cans, jars, etc.; Soups, frozen; Seasonings and sauces, except tomato and dry

(G-9982)
L H C INC (PA)
638 Summer St (01905-2044)
PHONE..............................781 592-6444
Leopoldo A Johnson, *Ch*
John Zermani, *Pr*
EMP: 13 **EST:** 1852
SQ FT: 60,000
SALES (est): 24.21MM
SALES (corp-wide): 24.21MM **Privately Held**
SIC: 2891 2851 2821 Adhesives; Coating, air curing; Polyurethane resins

(G-9983)
LUNDYS COMPANY INC
34 Boston St (01904-2537)
PHONE..............................781 595-8639
Charles Lundrigan, *Pr*
Kristin Lee Larson, *Treas*
Carole Lundrigan, *Dir*
EMP: 18 **EST:** 1999
SQ FT: 27,000
SALES (est): 993.43K **Privately Held**
Web: www.lundysiron.com
SIC: 2591 1799 Drapery hardware and window blinds and shades; Ornamental metal work

(G-9984)
LYN-LAD GROUP LTD (PA)
20 Boston St (01904-2527)
P.O. Box 8096 (01904-0096)
PHONE..............................781 598-6010
Susan Kline, *Prin*
Susan Kline, *Treas*
Alan Kline, *Dir*
Roberta Kline, *Dir*
Judy Kline, *Prin*
▲ **EMP:** 29 **EST:** 1981
SQ FT: 50,000
SALES (est): 47.21MM
SALES (corp-wide): 47.21MM **Privately Held**
Web: www.lynnladder.com
SIC: 2499 5082 5251 7359 Ladders, wood; Ladders; Hardware stores; Equipment rental and leasing, nec

(G-9985)
LYNN LADDER SCAFFOLDING CO INC (HQ)
20 Boston St 24 (01904-2527)
P.O. Box 8096 (01904-0096)
PHONE..............................781 598-6010
TOLL FREE: 800

Susan Kline, *CEO*
Alan Kline, *
▲ **EMP:** 61 **EST:** 1946
SQ FT: 50,000
SALES (est): 22.39MM
SALES (corp-wide): 47.21MM **Privately Held**
Web: www.lynnladderandscaffolding.com
SIC: 5082 2499 3499 7359 Ladders; Ladders, wood; Metal ladders; Equipment rental and leasing, nec
PA: Lyn-Lad Group, Ltd.
   20 Boston St
   Lynn MA 01904
   781 598-6010

(G-9986)
LYNN PRODUCTS CO
400 Boston St Ste 1 (01905-1699)
PHONE..............................781 593-2500
Daniel C Cullinane Junior, *Pr*
EMP: 16 **EST:** 1927
SALES (est): 769.4K **Privately Held**
Web: www.lynnmfg.com
SIC: 3823 3255 3825 On-stream gas/liquid analysis instruments, industrial; Clay refractories; Instruments to measure electricity

(G-9987)
NEW ENGLAND BRIDGE PDTS INC
93 Brookline St (01902-1809)
PHONE..............................781 592-2444
John Conti, *Pr*
EMP: 8 **EST:** 1993
SQ FT: 12,000
SALES (est): 821.1K **Privately Held**
SIC: 3441 Fabricated structural metal for bridges

(G-9988)
NORTH SHORE STEEL CO INC (PA)
16 Oakville St (01905-2817)
P.O. Box 330 (01905-0630)
PHONE..............................781 598-1645
Subhash Kakkar, *Pr*
EMP: 25 **EST:** 1954
SQ FT: 40,000
SALES (est): 4.05MM
SALES (corp-wide): 4.05MM **Privately Held**
Web: www.fordsteel.com
SIC: 3441 Fabricated structural metal

(G-9989)
PVK INC
86 Sanderson Ave Ste 130 (01902-1948)
PHONE..............................781 595-7771
Paolo Volpati Kedra, *Pr*
Tessa Edick, *Sec*
▲ **EMP:** 11 **EST:** 1999
SALES (est): 1.14MM **Privately Held**
SIC: 5149 5141 2099 Specialty food items; Groceries, general line; Food preparations, nec

(G-9990)
SAN FRANCISO MARKET
2 Lafayette Park (01902-2412)
PHONE..............................781 780-3731
EMP: 8 **EST:** 2010
SALES (est): 118.99K **Privately Held**
SIC: 3643 Outlets, electric: convenience

(G-9991)
SAVORY CREATIONS INTERNATIONAL
330 Lynnway Ste 401 (01901-1713)
PHONE..............................650 638-1024
Doug Takizawa, *Pr*
Hidemasa Takizawa, *Prin*
▲ **EMP:** 9 **EST:** 2004
SALES (est): 506.86K **Privately Held**
Web: www.kettlecuisine.com
SIC: 2048 Feed concentrates

(G-9992)
THERMO-CRAFT ENGINEERING CORP
701 Western Ave (01905-2297)
PHONE..............................781 599-4023
Ralph E Faia Junior, *Pr*
Ralph E Faia Senior, *Pr*
EMP: 40 **EST:** 1969
SQ FT: 32,000
SALES (est): 9.35MM **Privately Held**
Web: www.thermocraftengineering.com
SIC: 3599 3444 7692 Machine shop, jobbing and repair; Sheet metalwork; Welding repair

(G-9993)
WOODWORKS
23 Mudge St (01902-1215)
PHONE..............................781 596-1563
Shane Craven, *Prin*
EMP: 7 **EST:** 2007
SALES (est): 103.44K **Privately Held**
Web: www.woodworks.org
SIC: 2431 Millwork

Lynnfield
Essex County

(G-9994)
APPLEHILL SYSTEMS INC
130 Summer St (01940-1826)
PHONE..............................781 334-7009
Peter Campbell, *Prin*
EMP: 7 **EST:** 2005
SALES (est): 124.47K **Privately Held**
SIC: 3674 Semiconductors and related devices

(G-9995)
HP HOOD LLC (PA)
Also Called: Hood Reorganization
6 Kimball Ln Ste 400 (01940-2685)
PHONE..............................617 887-3000
TOLL FREE: 800
John A Kaneb, *Managing Member*
Theresa M Bresten, *
◆ **EMP:** 163 **EST:** 1846
SALES (est): 2.21B
SALES (corp-wide): 2.21B **Privately Held**
Web: www.hood.com
SIC: 2024 2022 2026 Ice cream and frozen deserts; Processed cheese; Cream, sweet

(G-9996)
HUMAN CARE SYSTEMS INC
120 Salem St (01940-2639)
PHONE..............................781 587-0414
EMP: 26
SALES (corp-wide): 34.9MM **Privately Held**
Web: www.caremetx.com
SIC: 7372 Prepackaged software
HQ: Human Care Systems, Inc.
   1 Faneuil Hall Sq
   Boston MA 02109
   617 720-7838

(G-9997)
INTELLISENSE SOFTWARE CORP
220 Broadway Ste 102 (01940-2352)
PHONE..............................781 933-8098
Yie He, *Pr*
EMP: 15 **EST:** 2003
SALES (est): 404.51K **Privately Held**
Web: www.intellisense.com
SIC: 3679 3695 Commutators, electronic; Computer software tape and disks: blank, rigid, and floppy

(G-9998)
JOHNSON CONTROLS INC
Also Called: Johnson Controls
39 Salem St (01940-2664)
PHONE..............................781 246-5500
TOLL FREE: 800
Mark Mc Caleaghan, *Mgr*
EMP: 42
Web: www.johnsoncontrols.com
SIC: 3822 Energy cutoff controls, residential or commercial types
HQ: Johnson Controls, Inc.
   5757 N Green Bay Ave
   Milwaukee WI 53209
   920 245-6409

(G-9999)
LS INDUSTRIES INC
28 Durham Dr (01940-1064)
PHONE..............................781 844-8115
EMP: 8 **EST:** 2013
SALES (est): 97K **Privately Held**
Web: www.lsindustries.com
SIC: 3999 Manufacturing industries, nec

Malden
Middlesex County

(G-10000)
ACE-LON CORPORATION
960 Eastern Ave (02148-6090)
P.O. Box 642 (02148-0006)
PHONE..............................781 322-7121
Harry T Gentile, *Pr*
EMP: 29 **EST:** 1952
SQ FT: 40,000
SALES (est): 2.28MM **Privately Held**
Web: www.ace-lon.com
SIC: 2673 Plastic bags: made from purchased materials

(G-10001)
ANDERSON COMPONENT CORPORATION
61 Clinton St (02148-2604)
PHONE..............................781 324-0350
TOLL FREE: 800
John A Anderson Senior, *Pr*
▲ **EMP:** 18 **EST:** 1989
SQ FT: 10,000
SALES (est): 1.49MM **Privately Held**
Web: www.andersoncomp.com
SIC: 3429 Metal fasteners

(G-10002)
AXIOMED LLC
350 Main St 2nd Fl (02148-5089)
PHONE..............................978 232-3990
Ken Yamada, *Pr*
EMP: 10 **EST:** 2014
SALES (est): 689.94K **Privately Held**
Web: www.axiomed.com
SIC: 3841 Surgical and medical instruments

(G-10003)

AXIOMED SPINE CORPORATION (PA)
350 Main St (02148-5089)
PHONE..............................978 232-3990
Patrick A Mcbrayer, *Pr*
James M Kuras, *COO*
Nancy Rubin, *CFO*
EMP: 10 **EST:** 2001
SQ FT: 3,000
SALES (est): 1.33MM
SALES (corp-wide): 1.33MM **Privately Held**
Web: www.axiomed.com
SIC: 3845 Ultrasonic scanning devices, medical

(G-10004)

B-C-D METAL PRODUCTS INC
205 Maplewood St (02148-5913)
P.O. Box 667 (02148-0006)
PHONE..............................781 397-9922
Karin Carlson, *Pr*
Jane Carlson, *
EMP: 30 **EST:** 1935
SQ FT: 13,000
SALES (est): 5.29MM **Privately Held**
Web: www.bcdmetalproducts.com
SIC: 3599 Machine shop, jobbing and repair

(G-10005)

BOSTON LIGHT & SOUND INC (PA)
Also Called: BL&s
420 Pearl St (02148-6697)
PHONE..............................617 787-3131
C Chapin Cutler Junior, *Pr*
Lawrence T Shaw, *Sec*
▲ **EMP:** 14 **EST:** 1981
SALES (est): 5.92MM
SALES (corp-wide): 5.92MM **Privately Held**
Web: www.blsi.com
SIC: 5043 7819 7359 5099 Motion picture equipment; Equipment rental, motion picture; Audio-visual equipment and supply rental; Video and audio equipment

(G-10006)

CALIPER WOODWORKING CORP
49 Clinton St (02148-2604)
PHONE..............................781 322-9760
EMP: 26 **EST:** 1994
SQ FT: 12,000
SALES (est): 1.88MM **Privately Held**
Web: www.caliper-woodworking.com
SIC: 2431 2439 Millwork; Structural wood members, nec

(G-10007)

CIMETRICS INC
376 Washington St Ste 104 (02148-1370)
PHONE..............................617 350-7550
James M Lee, *CEO*
EMP: 60 **EST:** 1989
SQ FT: 11,000
SALES (est): 8.51MM **Privately Held**
Web: www.cimetrics.com
SIC: 3823 Process control instruments

(G-10008)

DEVINCENTIS PRESS INC
988 Eastern Ave (02148-6033)
PHONE..............................781 605-3796
Linsey A Devincentis, *Pr*
Joseph A Devincentis, *Sec*
Rhonda E Devincentis, *Treas*
EMP: 13 **EST:** 2007

SALES (est): 455.88K **Privately Held**
SIC: 2752 Offset printing

(G-10009)

DING FANN ENTERPRISES LLC
960 Eastern Ave (02148-6032)
PHONE..............................781 322-7121
▲ **EMP:** 9 **EST:** 2013
SALES (est): 212.57K **Privately Held**
Web: www.ace-lon.com
SIC: 3599 Machine shop, jobbing and repair

(G-10010)

DISTRIBUTION & CONTROL PRODUCT
730 Eastern Ave (02148-5906)
PHONE..............................781 324-0070
Di Panfilo, *Owner*
EMP: 9 **EST:** 2016
SALES (est): 899K **Privately Held**
Web: distribution-control-products-llc.hub.biz
SIC: 3699 Electrical equipment and supplies, nec

(G-10011)

DORO FOODS INC
Also Called: Dom's Sausage Co
10 Riverside Park (02148-6711)
PHONE..............................781 324-1310
Angelo Botticelli, *Pr*
Lorraine Sellitti, *
EMP: 40 **EST:** 1955
SQ FT: 9,400
SALES (est): 8.73MM **Privately Held**
Web: www.domsausage.com
SIC: 5147 2011 Meats, fresh; Meat packing plants

(G-10012)

EASTERN MDDLSEX PRESS PBLCTONS (PA)
Also Called: Daily News-Mercury
277 Commercial St (02148-6708)
PHONE..............................781 321-8000
Daniel Hogan, *Pr*
EMP: 20 **EST:** 1880
SQ FT: 19,000
SALES (est): 1.5MM
SALES (corp-wide): 1.5MM **Privately Held**
SIC: 2711 Newspapers: publishing only, not printed on site

(G-10013)

ENJET AERO MALDEN LLC
60 Winter St (02148-1426)
PHONE..............................781 321-0366
Bruce Breckenridge, *CEO*
Dana Munick, *
Bruce Munick, *
Christopher Ferraro, *
Kayla Walker, *
▼ **EMP:** 55 **EST:** 1957
SQ FT: 50,000
SALES (est): 11.28MM
SALES (corp-wide): 78.96MM **Privately Held**
Web: www.enjetaero.com
SIC: 3469 Stamping metal for the trade
PA: Enjet Aero, Llc
    9401 Indian Creek Pkwy
    Overland Park KS 66210
    913 717-7396

(G-10014)

F M CALLAHAN AND SON INC
22 Sharon St (02148-5915)
PHONE..............................781 324-5101
Eric W Jacklin, *Pr*

Robert L Hennigar, *
Heather J Hennigar, *
EMP: 60 **EST:** 1942
SALES (est): 7.29MM **Privately Held**
Web: www.fmcallahan.com
SIC: 3471 5031 Electroplating of metals or formed products; Doors, nec

(G-10015)

FURNITURE CONCEPTS
7 Cross St (02148-7620)
PHONE..............................781 324-8668
Kevin Mcmahon, *Owner*
▲ **EMP:** 8 **EST:** 1994
SQ FT: 8,000
SALES (est): 836.26K **Privately Held**
Web: www.furnconcepts.com
SIC: 7641 2531 Upholstery work; Public building and related furniture

(G-10016)

GORILLA GRAPHICS INC (PA)
Also Called: Cambridge Repro Graphics
1236 Eastern Ave Ste 1 (02148-6100)
PHONE..............................617 623-2838
Craig Murphy, *Pr*
EMP: 12 **EST:** 1992
SALES (est): 1MM **Privately Held**
Web: www.cambridgereprographics.com
SIC: 7334 2759 Photocopying and duplicating services; Commercial printing, nec

(G-10017)

KABINET KORNER INC
Also Called: Windsor Architectural Wdwkg
212 Maplewood St (02148-5917)
PHONE..............................781 324-9600
Marshall Mazzarella, *CEO*
Michael Moscaritolo, *CFO*
EMP: 23 **EST:** 1978
SQ FT: 25,000
SALES (est): 1.02MM **Privately Held**
Web: www.windsorwoodworking.com
SIC: 2431 Millwork

(G-10018)

L & J ENTERPRISES INC
67 Maplewood St (02148-4377)
PHONE..............................781 233-1966
Lori A Widener, *Pr*
EMP: 8 **EST:** 2004
SALES (est): 998.97K **Privately Held**
SIC: 3441 Fabricated structural metal

(G-10019)

MEDI - PRINT INC (PA)
Also Called: Print House
200 Maplewood St (02148-5914)
PHONE..............................781 324-4455
Paul T Doucette, *Pr*
Paul T Doucette, *Pr*
A Thomas Cyr, *Treas*
EMP: 19 **EST:** 1980
SQ FT: 10,000
SALES (est): 4.84MM
SALES (corp-wide): 4.84MM **Privately Held**
Web: www.printhouse.com
SIC: 2752 Offset printing

(G-10020)

MYSTIC PARKER PRINTING INC
66 Willow St (02148-5832)
PHONE..............................781 321-4948
Christopher J Towle, *Prin*
EMP: 10 **EST:** 2016
SALES (est): 497.19K **Privately Held**
Web: www.mysticparker.com
SIC: 2752 Offset printing

(G-10021)

PALMER MANUFACTURING CO LLC (DH)
Also Called: P M C
243 Medford St (02148-7383)
P.O. Box K (02148-0008)
PHONE..............................781 321-0480
▲ **EMP:** 145 **EST:** 1965
SQ FT: 63,000
SALES (est): 47.2MM
SALES (corp-wide): 139.19MM **Privately Held**
SIC: 3724 Aircraft engines and engine parts
HQ: Paradigm Precision Holdings, Llc
    404 W Guadalupe Rd
    Tempe AZ 85283

(G-10022)

PARADIGM PRCISION HOLDINGS LLC
243 Medford St (02148-7301)
PHONE..............................781 321-0480
Mike Cowell, *Prin*
EMP: 46
SALES (corp-wide): 139.19MM **Privately Held**
Web: www.pursuitaero.com
SIC: 3462 Iron and steel forgings
HQ: Paradigm Precision Holdings, Llc
    404 W Guadalupe Rd
    Tempe AZ 85283

(G-10023)

PIANTEDOSI BAKING CO INC (PA)
Also Called: Piantedosi
240 Commercial St (02148-6709)
PHONE..............................781 321-3400
Thomas L Piantedosi, *Pr*
Robert J Piantedosi, *
Joseph A Piantedosi, *
◆ **EMP:** 238 **EST:** 1916
SQ FT: 65,000
SALES (est): 28.95MM
SALES (corp-wide): 28.95MM **Privately Held**
Web: www.piantedosi.com
SIC: 2051 5812 Bread, all types (white, wheat, rye, etc); fresh or frozen; Eating places

(G-10024)

QUARTZITE PROCESSING INC
6 Holyoke St (02148-5608)
PHONE..............................781 322-3611
Brian Yanofsky, *Pr*
EMP: 10 **EST:** 1956
SQ FT: 5,000
SALES (est): 1.03MM **Privately Held**
Web: www.quartziteprocessing.com
SIC: 3679 Quartz crystals, for electronic application

(G-10025)

REILY FOODS COMPANY
100 Charles St (02148-6704)
PHONE..............................504 524-6131
David Darragh, *Pr*
EMP: 39
SALES (corp-wide): 358.53MM **Privately Held**
Web: www.reilyproducts.com
SIC: 2099 2095 Tea blending; Coffee, ground: mixed with grain or chicory
HQ: Reily Foods Company
    400 Poydras St Fl 10
    New Orleans LA 70130

(G-10026)
SAMTAN ENGINEERING CORP
127 Wyllis Ave (02148-7525)
PHONE..............................781 322-7880
Philip D Askenazy, *Pr*
Samuel Askenazy, *Pr*
George Laberis, *VP*
Richard B Askenazy, *Treas*
EMP: 30 **EST:** 1963
SQ FT: 30,000
SALES (est): 4.21MM **Privately Held**
Web: www.samtanengineering.com
SIC: 3599 3544 3469 Machine shop,
jobbing and repair; Special dies, tools, jigs,
and fixtures; Metal stampings, nec

(G-10027)
SIGN ART INC
60 Sharon St (02148-5915)
PHONE..............................781 322-3785
Andy Layman, *Pr*
EMP: 13 **EST:** 1991
SQ FT: 4,000
SALES (est): 2.38MM **Privately Held**
Web: www.signartboston.com
SIC: 3993 Signs, not made in custom sign
painting shops

(G-10028)
SPINEFRONTIER INC
350 Main St 2nd Fl (02148-5089)
PHONE..............................978 232-3990
Kingsley Chin, *CEO*
Aditya Humad, *CFO*
Jake Lubinski, *COO*
EMP: 50 **EST:** 2006
SALES (est): 9.21MM **Privately Held**
Web: www.spinefrontier.com
SIC: 3841 Surgical and medical instruments

(G-10029)
SUNSETTER PRODUCTS LTD PARTNR
Also Called: Sunsetter Products
184 Charles St (02148-6714)
PHONE..............................781 321-9600
Jonathan Hershberg, *Pt*
Ido Eilam, *Pt*
Les Snader, *Pt*
◆ **EMP:** 73 **EST:** 2014
SQ FT: 68,000
SALES (est): 27.07MM
SALES (corp-wide): 1.56B **Privately Held**
Web: www.sunsetter.com
SIC: 2394 3446 Awnings, fabric: made from
purchased materials; Flagpoles, metal
PA: Springs Window Fashions, Llc
7549 Graber Rd
Middleton WI 53562
608 836-1011

(G-10030)
VAN STRY DESIGN INC
420 Pearl St Ste 2 (02148-6697)
PHONE..............................781 388-9998
Katherine Van Stry, *Pr*
▲ **EMP:** 50 **EST:** 1975
SQ FT: 20,000
SALES (est): 4.64MM **Privately Held**
Web: www.vanstry.com
SIC: 2542 Partitions and fixtures, except
wood

(G-10031)
VIKING SEAFOODS INC
50 Crystal St (02148-5919)
PHONE..............................781 322-2000
▲ **EMP:** 53

SIC: 2092 Seafoods, frozen: prepared

Manchester
Essex County

(G-10032)
A LYONS & COMPANY INC
40 Beach St Ste 105 (01944-1464)
PHONE..............................978 526-4244
Richard J Sullivan Junior, *Pr*
▲ **EMP:** 17 **EST:** 1933
SQ FT: 2,200
SALES (est): 983.79K **Privately Held**
Web: www.alyons.com
SIC: 2211 Cotton broad woven goods

(G-10033)
NORTHERN LIGHT MAR GROUP INC
Also Called: Manchester Marine
17 Ashland Ave (01944-1402)
P.O. Box 1469 (01944-0855)
PHONE..............................978 526-7911
Edward R Hoyle, *Pr*
Gregory Nulk, *VP*
EMP: 24 **EST:** 1990
SQ FT: 1,500
SALES (est): 1.51MM **Privately Held**
Web: www.manchestermarine.com
SIC: 4499 4493 3732 Boat rental,
commercial; Marinas; Boatbuilding and
repairing

(G-10034)
TOM WATERS GOLF SHOP
Also Called: Golf Shop The
153 School St (01944-1236)
PHONE..............................978 526-7311
Tom Waters, *Owner*
EMP: 7 **EST:** 2009
SALES (est): 401.17K **Privately Held**
SIC: 3949 Golf equipment

Mansfield
Bristol County

(G-10035)
ACCUTECH PACKAGING INC
71 Hampden Rd (02048-1875)
PHONE..............................508 543-3800
EMP: 10 **EST:** 2015
SALES (est): 828.22K **Privately Held**
Web: www.accutechpkg.com
SIC: 3089 Injection molding of plastics

(G-10036)
ACORN MANUFACTURING CO INC
457 School St (02048-2011)
P.O. Box 31 (02048-0031)
PHONE..............................508 339-4500
Eric L Delong, *CEO*
Venessa Delong, *
▲ **EMP:** 37 **EST:** 1937
SQ FT: 34,000
SALES (est): 4.54MM **Privately Held**
Web: www.acornmfg.com
SIC: 3429 3462 Builders' hardware; Iron
and steel forgings

(G-10037)
AMERICAN INSULATED WIRE CORPORATION (HQ)
260 Forbes Blvd (02048-1817)
PHONE..............................508 964-1200
▲ **EMP:** 36 **EST:** 1924

SALES (est): 6.51MM
SALES (corp-wide): 1.7B **Privately Held**
SIC: 3357 Communication wire
PA: Southwire Company, Llc
1 Southwire Dr
Carrollton GA 30119
770 832-4529

(G-10038)
AMERICAN PAPER RECYCLING CORP (PA)
87 Central St Bldg 1 (02048-1309)
PHONE..............................800 422-3220
Kenneth S Golden, *Pr*
Richard Kossack, *
Duke Bates, *
EMP: 25 **EST:** 1908
SQ FT: 2,000
SALES (est): 20.02MM
SALES (corp-wide): 20.02MM **Privately Held**
Web: www.aprcorp.com
SIC: 2611 5093 Pulp manufactured from
waste or recycled paper; Scrap and waste
materials

(G-10039)
BAY STATE ENVELOPE INC (PA)
440 Chauncy St (02048-1133)
PHONE..............................508 337-8900
Diana W Skogseth, *CEO*
Diana Skogseth, *
Russell Frizzell, *
Dave Luongo, *
Brian Hewitt, *
EMP: 33 **EST:** 1987
SQ FT: 24,000
SALES (est): 4.49MM
SALES (corp-wide): 4.49MM **Privately Held**
Web: www.bseprint.com
SIC: 2759 Envelopes: printing, nsk

(G-10040)
CANNAN FUELS
157 Pratt St (02048-1555)
PHONE..............................508 339-3317
Sameh Kanan, *Pr*
EMP: 11 **EST:** 2009
SALES (est): 2.48MM **Privately Held**
SIC: 2869 Fuels

(G-10041)
CHARLES A RICHARDSON INC
330 Otis St (02048-2056)
P.O. Box 29 (02048-0029)
PHONE..............................508 339-8600
Jeffrey Richardson, *Pr*
Edward A Richardson, *VP*
Jeffrey C Richardson, *Pr*
William A Richardson, *VP*
Todd R Richardson, *CFO*
▼ **EMP:** 11 **EST:** 1853
SQ FT: 20,000
SALES (est): 2.02MM **Privately Held**
Web: www.carichardson.com
SIC: 3463 3469 Flange, valve or pipe fitting
forgings, nonferrous; Stamping metal for
the trade

(G-10042)
CONTROLLED ENVMT SYSTEMS LLC (PA)
137 High St (02048-2159)
PHONE..............................508 339-4237
Don Roussinos, *Pr*
EMP: 34 **EST:** 1985
SALES (est): 28.19MM
SALES (corp-wide): 28.19MM **Privately Held**

Web: www.controlledenviro.com
SIC: 3585 1742 1761 3823 Humidifiers and
dehumidifiers; Plastering, drywall, and
insulation; Roofing, siding, and sheetmetal
work; Industrial process control instruments

(G-10043)
COVIDIEN FRANCE HOLDINGS INC
15 Hampshire St (02048-1113)
PHONE..............................508 261-8000
EMP: 8 **EST:** 2011
SALES (est): 937.61K **Privately Held**
SIC: 3841 Surgical and medical instruments
HQ: Covidien Limited
20 Lower Hatch Street
Dublin D02 H

(G-10044)
COVIDIEN LLC
Also Called: Covidien
777 West St (02048-1122)
PHONE..............................508 261-8000
EMP: 12 **EST:** 2010
SALES (est): 379.48K **Privately Held**
Web: www.covidien.com
SIC: 3841 Surgical and medical instruments
PA: Medtronic Public Limited Company
20 Hatch Street Lower
Dublin D02 X

(G-10045)
COVIDIEN LP
777 West St (02048-1122)
P.O. Box 778 (55440-0778)
PHONE..............................508 261-8000
Bryan C Hanson, *Pr*
EMP: 446
Web: www.forcetriad.com
SIC: 3841 Surgical and medical instruments
HQ: Covidien Lp
15 Hampshire St
Mansfield MA 02048
763 514-4000

(G-10046)
COVIDIEN LP (HQ)
Also Called: Covidien
15 Hampshire St (02048-1113)
PHONE..............................763 514-4000
Geoffrey S Martha, *Ch Bd*
◆ **EMP:** 102 **EST:** 1998
SALES (est): 803.88MM **Privately Held**
Web: www.forcetriad.com
SIC: 3842 3841 3845 5122 Surgical
appliances and supplies; Surgical and
medical instruments; Respiratory analysis
equipment, electromedical; Drugs,
proprietaries, and sundries
PA: Medtronic Public Limited Company
20 Hatch Street Lower
Dublin D02 X

(G-10047)
COVIDIEN SALES LLC
15 Hampshire St (02048-1113)
PHONE..............................508 261-8000
Bryan Hanson, *Pr*
Patricia Hitt Duft, *
Stacy Enxing Seng, *
Will Mcguire, *VP*
Robert White, *
EMP: 39 **EST:** 2012
SALES (est): 19.42MM **Privately Held**
SIC: 3841 Surgical and medical instruments
HQ: Covidien Lp
15 Hampshire St
Mansfield MA 02048
763 514-4000

(G-10048)
CROSBY VALVE & GAGE INTL INC
Also Called: Anderson Grnwood Crsby Vlve Ga
55 Cabot Blvd　(02048-1137)
PHONE..............................508 384-3121
Greg Hyland, *Pr*
EMP: 47 **EST:** 1972
SALES (est): 4.14MM
SALES (corp-wide): 15.16B **Publicly Held**
SIC: 3491 5085　Pressure valves and regulators, industrial; Valves and fittings
PA: Emerson Electric Co.
　8000 West Florissant Ave
　Saint Louis MO 63136
　314 553-2000

(G-10049)
DOWNEAST CIDER HOUSE LLC
Also Called: Downeast Cider House
31 Plymouth St Ste 2　(02048-2034)
PHONE..............................650 279-2417
Pat Hopkins, *Mgr*
EMP: 77
SALES (corp-wide): 14.29MM **Privately Held**
Web: www.downeastcider.com
SIC: 2085　Applejack (alcoholic beverage)
PA: Downeast Cider House, Llc
　256 Marginal St Bldg 32
　Boston MA 02128
　857 301-8881

(G-10050)
DRISCOLLS RESTAURANT
Also Called: Devon's Place
535 S Main St　(02048-3105)
PHONE..............................508 261-1574
Mike Di Mascio, *Pr*
EMP: 7 **EST:** 1999
SALES (est): 232.03K **Privately Held**
SIC: 2812 5461　Caustic potash, potassium hydroxide; Bagels

(G-10051)
EMERSON ATMTN SLTONS FNAL CTRL
55 Cabot Blvd　(02048-1137)
PHONE..............................508 594-4411
EMP: 93 **EST:** 2001
SALES (est): 16.3MM
SALES (corp-wide): 15.16B **Publicly Held**
SIC: 3491　Automatic regulating and control valves
PA: Emerson Electric Co.
　8000 West Florissant Ave
　Saint Louis MO 63136
　314 553-2000

(G-10052)
FUTURE FOAM INC
47 Maple St　(02048-1508)
PHONE..............................508 339-0354
EMP: 20
SALES (corp-wide): 495.02MM **Privately Held**
Web: www.futurefoam.com
SIC: 3086　Carpet and rug cushions, foamed plastics
PA: Future Foam, Inc.
　1610 Avenue N
　Council Bluffs IA 51501
　712 323-9122

(G-10053)
GPA GLOBAL US HOLDING INC
774 Norfolk St　(02048-1826)
PHONE..............................800 334-1113
Adam Melton, *CEO*
EMP: 11 **EST:** 2007
SALES (est): 88.17K **Privately Held**
SIC: 2671 5999 2653　Paper; coated and laminated packaging; Packaging materials: boxes, padding, etc.; Corrugated boxes, partitions, display items, sheets, and pad

(G-10054)
HARTMANN INCORPORATED
575 West St Ste 110　(02048-1160)
PHONE..............................508 851-1400
David A Herman, *Pr*
Louis A Fantin, *Sec*
Augustus Griffin, *Dir*
Jerome J Ciszewski, *Dir*
EMP: 9 **EST:** 1997
SALES (est): 163.16K **Privately Held**
SIC: 3161　Wardrobe bags (luggage)

(G-10055)
HILSINGER COMPANY PARENT LLC (PA)
Also Called: Hilco Vision
575 West St　(02048-1152)
P.O. Box 1538　(02762-0538)
PHONE..............................508 699-4406
James Ross Brownlee, *Pr*
Paul Janell Wignall, *
▲ **EMP:** 30 **EST:** 2003
SQ FT: 70,000
SALES (est): 89.4MM
SALES (corp-wide): 89.4MM **Privately Held**
Web: www.hilcovision.com
SIC: 3827 3851　Optical instruments and lenses; Ophthalmic goods

(G-10056)
HL OPERATING LLC (DH)
Also Called: Hartmann
575 West St Ste 110　(02048-1160)
PHONE..............................508 851-1400
◆ **EMP:** 40 **EST:** 2007
SQ FT: 20,000
SALES (est): 25.28MM
SALES (corp-wide): 8.01MM **Privately Held**
SIC: 3161 3172　Wardrobe bags (luggage); Personal leather goods, nec
HQ: Samsonite Llc
　575 West St Ste 110
　Mansfield MA 02048
　508 851-1400

(G-10057)
HUB FOLDING BOX COMPANY INC
Also Called: Plastic Technology Division
774 Norfolk St　(02048-1826)
PHONE..............................508 339-0005
Anthony H Dirico, *Pr*
Anthony H Dirico, *VP*
Jack Dirico, *
Patricia A Silvia, *
Mark A Dirico, *
▲ **EMP:** 315 **EST:** 1918
SQ FT: 275,000
SALES (est): 52.92MM
SALES (corp-wide): 52.92MM **Privately Held**
Web: www.gpaglobal.net
SIC: 2653　Boxes, corrugated: made from purchased materials
PA: Gpa Global Corporation
　3852 Coral Crest Way
　San Ysidro CA 92173
　818 237-9771

(G-10058)
INTEGRA LIFESCIENCES PROD CORP
Also Called: Integra Lifesciences
11 Cabot Blvd　(02048-1137)
PHONE..............................781 971-5682
Peter J Arduini, *Pr*
Glenn G Coleman, *VP*
Jeff Mosebrook, *VP*
EMP: 24 **EST:** 2021
SALES (est): 3.76MM **Publicly Held**
SIC: 3841　Surgical and medical instruments
PA: Integra Lifesciences Holdings Corporation
　1100 Campus Rd
　Princeton NJ 08540

(G-10059)
INTEGRATED DYNAMICS ENGRG INC (HQ)
120 Forbes Blvd Ste 180　(02048-1150)
PHONE..............................781 300-6561
Heidi S Shippell-heiland, *Pr*
Peter Heiland, *
Erik Zantinge, *
EMP: 34 **EST:** 1991
SQ FT: 10,000
SALES (est): 12.93MM
SALES (corp-wide): 3.35B **Privately Held**
Web: www.ideworld.com
SIC: 3829　Measuring and controlling devices, nec
PA: Aalberts N.V.
　Stadsplateau 18
　Utrecht UT
　303079300

(G-10060)
IRONMAN INC
150 Rumford Ave Apt 230　(02048-2166)
PHONE..............................989 386-8975
James Lloyd Hatch, *Prin*
EMP: 9 **EST:** 2012
SALES (est): 431.97K **Privately Held**
SIC: 3441　Fabricated structural metal

(G-10061)
JORDI LABS LLC
200 Gilbert St　(02048-2051)
PHONE..............................508 719-8543
Howard C Jordi, *Pr*
Pamela J Jordi, *Treas*
EMP: 22 **EST:** 1980
SQ FT: 4,800
SALES (est): 11.83MM
SALES (corp-wide): 18.06MM **Privately Held**
Web: www.jordilabs.com
SIC: 2819 8734　Silica gel; Testing laboratories
PA: Regulatory And Quality Solutions Llc
　2790 Mosside Blvd Ste 800
　Monroeville PA 15146
　724 327-0230

(G-10062)
KRAFT HEINZ FOODS COMPANY
Also Called: Kraft Foods
111 Forbes Blvd　(02048-1124)
PHONE..............................508 763-3311
EMP: 100
SALES (corp-wide): 26.27B **Publicly Held**
SIC: 2043　Cereal breakfast foods
HQ: Kraft Heinz Foods Company
　1 Ppg Pl Fl 34
　Pittsburgh PA 15222
　412 456-5700

(G-10063)
LACERTA GROUP INC
Also Called: Lacerta Group, Inc.
50 Suffolk Rd　(02048-1878)
PHONE..............................508 339-3312
EMP: 7
Web: www.lacerta.com
SIC: 3089 3559　Blister or bubble formed packaging, plastics; Plastics working machinery
PA: Lacerta Group, Llc
　360 Forbes Blvd
　Mansfield MA 02048

(G-10064)
LACERTA GROUP LLC (PA)
360 Forbes Blvd　(02048-1806)
PHONE..............................508 339-3312
Paul Young, *CEO*
Denise L Lotfi, *
▲ **EMP:** 163 **EST:** 1993
SQ FT: 47,000
SALES (est): 48.55MM **Privately Held**
Web: www.lacerta.com
SIC: 3089 3559　Blister or bubble formed packaging, plastics; Plastics working machinery

(G-10065)
M & W INDUSTRIES INC
Also Called: Mw Life Sciences - Mansfield
11 Forbes Blvd # 101　(02048-1125)
PHONE..............................508 406-2100
EMP: 10
SALES (est): 480.23K **Privately Held**
SIC: 3841　Surgical and medical instruments

(G-10066)
MD STETSON COMPANY INC
11 Norfolk St Ste 3　(02048-1874)
PHONE..............................781 986-6161
TOLL FREE: 800
Michael J Glass, *Pr*
EMP: 45 **EST:** 1938
SALES (est): 14.85MM
SALES (corp-wide): 1.49B **Privately Held**
Web: www.nextgensupply.com
SIC: 2842 5169 2899 2819　Specialty cleaning; Detergents and soaps, except specialty cleaning; Chemical preparations, nec; Industrial inorganic chemicals, nec
HQ: Next-Gen Supply Group Llc
　11 Norfolk St Ste 3
　Mansfield MA 02048
　774 719-0953

(G-10067)
MULTI-CONCEPT INC
15 Victoria Ln　(02048-1756)
PHONE..............................508 366-7676
Stephen Barker, *Pr*
▲ **EMP:** 14 **EST:** 1992
SALES (est): 1.53MM **Privately Held**
Web: www.multiconceptinc.com
SIC: 5063 3699　Electrical apparatus and equipment; Electrical equipment and supplies, nec

(G-10068)
NATIONAL LUMBER COMPANY LLC (HQ)
Also Called: Do It Best
71 Maple St　(02048-1508)
PHONE..............................508 339-8020
Margie Kaitz Seligman, *CEO*
◆ **EMP:** 200 **EST:** 1934
SQ FT: 100,000
SALES (est): 180.48MM
SALES (corp-wide): 22.73B **Publicly Held**
Web: www.national-lumber.com

SIC: **2431 5231 5251** Millwork; Paint, glass, and wallpaper stores; Hardware stores
PA: Builders Firstsource, Inc.
6031 Connection Dr # 400
Irving TX 75039
214 880-3500

(G-10069)
NELLCOR PURITAN BENNETT LLC (DH)
Also Called: Covidien
15 Hampshire St (02048-1113)
PHONE...................508 261-8000
Philip J Albert, *Mgr*
Martha Ha, *
Jason M Bristow, *
▲ EMP: **300** EST: 1981
SALES (est): 393.7MM **Privately Held**
SIC: **3845 3841** Patient monitoring apparatus, nec; Surgical and medical instruments
HQ: Covidien Lp
15 Hampshire St
Mansfield MA 02048
763 514-4000

(G-10070)
NN INC
Also Called: Bridgemedica
111 Forbes Blvd Ste 101 (02048-1124)
PHONE...................508 406-2100
Warren Veltman, *Brnch Mgr*
EMP: **35**
SALES (corp-wide): 498.74MM **Publicly Held**
Web: www.nninc.com
SIC: **8711 3841** Engineering services; Surgical and medical instruments
PA: Nn, Inc.
6210 Ardrey Kell Rd # 600
Charlotte NC 28277
980 264-4300

(G-10071)
O-D TOOL & CUTTER INC
150 Gilbert St (02048-2001)
P.O. Box 372 (02048-0372)
PHONE...................508 339-7507
EMP: **14** EST: 1959
SALES (est): 2.18MM **Privately Held**
Web: www.odtool.com
SIC: **3599** Machine shop, jobbing and repair

(G-10072)
PROVEN PROCESS MED DVCS INC
110 Forbes Blvd (02048-1145)
PHONE...................508 261-0800
EMP: **67** EST: 1994
SQ FT: 43,000
SALES (est): 14.72MM
SALES (corp-wide): 30.91MM **Privately Held**
SIC: **3845** Electromedical equipment
PA: Nextphase Medical Devices Llc
88 Airport Dr Ste 100
Rochester NH 03867
603 332-8900

(G-10073)
QC INDUSTRIES INC (PA)
Also Called: Qual-Craft
60 Maple St (02048-1876)
P.O. Box 36 (02048-0036)
PHONE...................781 344-1000
Robert P Berish, *Pr*
Norman Katz, *
Myrna Katz, *Stockholder*
▲ EMP: **60** EST: 1953
SQ FT: 55,000

SALES (est): 10.74MM
SALES (corp-wide): 10.74MM **Privately Held**
Web: www.guardianfall.com
SIC: **3429 3471** Builders' hardware; Anodizing (plating) of metals or formed products

(G-10074)
REPJTM LLC
Also Called: Bridgemedica, LLC
111 Forbes Blvd Ste 101 (02048-1124)
PHONE...................508 406-2100
EMP: **35**
SIC: **8711 3841** Engineering services; Diagnostic apparatus, medical

(G-10075)
ROSEMOUNT INC
9 Oxford Rd (02048-1126)
PHONE...................508 261-2928
Gary Gregory, *Mgr*
EMP: **7**
SALES (corp-wide): 15.16B **Publicly Held**
Web: www.rosemount.com
SIC: **3823** Manometers, industrial process type
HQ: Rosemount Inc.
8200 Market Blvd
Chanhassen MN 55317
952 906-8888

(G-10076)
SIGMA SYSTEMS CORP
41 Hampden Rd (02048-1807)
PHONE...................781 688-2354
Robert Stewart, *Pr*
EMP: **23** EST: 1955
SQ FT: 5,000
SALES (est): 2.45MM
SALES (corp-wide): 116.83MM **Publicly Held**
Web: www.intestthermal.com
SIC: **3822** Electric heat proportioning controls, modulating controls
PA: Intest Corporation
804 E Gate Dr Ste 200
Mount Laurel NJ 08054
856 505-8800

(G-10077)
SYSNOVA LLC
5 Boundry Rd (02048-1667)
PHONE...................508 309-9264
EMP: **8** EST: 2008
SALES (est): 180.3K **Privately Held**
SIC: **3699** Security devices

(G-10078)
TELEFLEX INCORPORATED
Also Called: Teleflex
375 Forbes Blvd (02048-1805)
PHONE...................508 964-6021
EMP: **50**
SALES (corp-wide): 2.79B **Publicly Held**
Web: www.teleflex.com
SIC: **3841** Surgical and medical instruments
PA: Teleflex Incorporated
550 E Swedesford Rd # 400
Wayne PA 19087
610 225-6800

(G-10079)
TEMPTRONIC CORPORATION (HQ)
Also Called: Intest Thermal Solutions
41 Hampden Rd (02048-1807)
PHONE...................781 688-2300
James Pelrin, *Pr*
Thomas G Gerendas, *

Edward N Gadsby Junior, *Sec*
Henry A Lyden, *
Hugh T Regan Junior, *VP*
▲ EMP: **45** EST: 1999
SQ FT: 62,000
SALES (est): 25.43MM
SALES (corp-wide): 116.83MM **Publicly Held**
Web: www.intestthermal.com
SIC: **3823** Thermal conductivity instruments, industrial process type
PA: Intest Corporation
804 E Gate Dr Ste 200
Mount Laurel NJ 08054
856 505-8800

(G-10080)
THERMONICS INC
41 Hampden Rd (02048-1807)
PHONE...................408 542-5900
Jim Kufis, *Pr*
EMP: **10** EST: 2013
SALES (est): 1.22MM
SALES (corp-wide): 116.83MM **Publicly Held**
Web: www.intestthermal.com
SIC: **3823** Temperature measurement instruments, industrial
PA: Intest Corporation
804 E Gate Dr Ste 200
Mount Laurel NJ 08054
856 505-8800

(G-10081)
TOUCH BIONICS
35 Hampden Rd (02048-1807)
PHONE...................774 719-2199
Ian Stevens, *CEO*
EMP: **14** EST: 2012
SALES (est): 226.57K **Privately Held**
SIC: **3842** Technical aids for the handicapped

(G-10082)
TRELLEBORG OFFSHORE BOSTON INC
290 Forbes Blvd (02048-1817)
PHONE...................774 719-1400
EMP: **24**
SALES (corp-wide): 4.26B **Privately Held**
SIC: **2819** Industrial inorganic chemicals, nec
HQ: Trelleborg Offshore Boston, Inc.
24 Teed Dr
Randolph MA 02368

(G-10083)
VICTAULIC COMPANY
145 Plymouth St Ste A (02048-2093)
PHONE...................508 406-3220
Kevin Collins, *Brnch Mgr*
EMP: **7**
SALES (corp-wide): 574.15MM **Privately Held**
Web: www.victaulic.com
SIC: **3498** Fabricated pipe and fittings
PA: Victaulic Company
4901 Kesslersville Rd
Easton PA 18040
610 559-3300

Marblehead
Essex County

(G-10084)
BARNEY RABIN COMPANY INC
2 Foss Ter (01945-2509)
PHONE...................781 639-0593

Paul Rabin, *Pr*
Kathy Rabin, *Sec*
EMP: **7** EST: 1933
SQ FT: 5,460
SALES (est): 170.32K **Privately Held**
SIC: **2759** Letterpress printing

(G-10085)
COMMUNITY NEWSPAPER INC
122 Washington St (01945-3590)
PHONE...................781 639-4800
Kris Olson, *Prin*
EMP: **8** EST: 2010
SALES (est): 21.64K **Privately Held**
SIC: **2711** Newspapers, publishing and printing

(G-10086)
CW HOOD YACHTS INC
3 Beacon St Ste 4 (01945-2687)
P.O. Box 443 (01945-0443)
PHONE...................781 631-0192
Chris Hood, *Pr*
Chris Stirling, *VP*
▲ EMP: **8** EST: 1995
SQ FT: 6,600
SALES (est): 878.47K **Privately Held**
Web: www.cwhoodyachts.com
SIC: **3732** Yachts, building and repairing

(G-10087)
HEADWATERS INC
Also Called: Sound Oasis Company
134 Pleasant St (01945-2364)
PHONE...................781 715-6404
◆ EMP: **8** EST: 1993
SQ FT: 750
SALES (est): 1.59MM **Privately Held**
Web: www.airtamer.com
SIC: **3564 3651 3635 3634** Purification and dust collection equipment; Sound reproducing equipment; Household vacuum cleaners; Housewares, excluding cooking appliances and utensils

(G-10088)
HOT TOOLS INCORPORATED
24 Tioga Way (01945-1575)
PHONE...................781 639-1000
Charles F Loutrel Junior, *Pr*
EMP: **19** EST: 1979
SQ FT: 2,000
SALES (est): 221.21K **Privately Held**
Web: www.mmnewman.com
SIC: **3423** Hand and edge tools, nec

(G-10089)
KELLEY AND HALL BOOK PUBLICITY
5 Briar Ln (01945-1753)
PHONE...................617 680-1976
Shana Noyes, *Prin*
EMP: **7** EST: 2007
SALES (est): 59.68K **Privately Held**
Web: www.kelleyandhall.com
SIC: **2741** Miscellaneous publishing

(G-10090)
MARBLEHEAD WEATHER GMTS LLC
Also Called: Proquip USA
100 Hoods Ln Ste U8 (01945-2574)
PHONE...................781 639-1060
Peter Dalton, *CEO*
Edward M Kennedy, *VP Opers*
EMP: **8** EST: 2011
SALES (est): 153.35K **Privately Held**
SIC: **2389** Apparel and accessories, nec

(G-10091)
MM NEWMAN CORPORATION
24 Tioga Way (01945-1575)
P.O. Box 615 (01945-0615)
PHONE..............................781 631-7100
Charles F Loutrel Junior, *Pr*
EMP: 12 **EST:** 1957
SQ FT: 24,000
SALES (est): 2.35MM **Privately Held**
Web: www.mmnewman.com
SIC: 3423 3083   Hand and edge tools, nec;
Laminated plastics plate and sheet

(G-10092)
PEPPERCORN FOOD SERVICE INC
91 Pitman Rd (01945-1441)
PHONE..............................781 639-6035
Emanual Argiros, *Pr*
Ellen Argiros, *
Jim Bouley, *
EMP: 8 **EST:** 1986
SQ FT: 22,000
SALES (est): 493.17K **Privately Held**
SIC: 2053   Pies, bakery; frozen

(G-10093)
RADICAL PLASTICS INC
6 Saturn Rd (01945-1809)
PHONE..............................781 631-7924
Kristin L Taylor, *Prin*
EMP: 7 **EST:** 2019
SALES (est): 205.3K **Privately Held**
Web: www.radical-plastics.com
SIC: 3089   Injection molding of plastics

(G-10094)
RIBCRAFT USA LLC
Also Called: Ribcraft
88 Hoods Ln (01945-2576)
P.O. Box 463 (01945-0463)
PHONE..............................781 639-9065
P Brian Gray, *Pr*
Brian Gray, *
▲ **EMP:** 36 **EST:** 2001
SQ FT: 25,000
SALES (est): 8.35MM **Privately Held**
Web: www.ribcraftusa.com
SIC: 5551 3732   Boat dealers; Boatbuilding
and repairing

(G-10095)
SEVEN SWEETS INC
Also Called: Stowaway Sweets
154 Atlantic Ave (01945-3012)
PHONE..............................781 631-0303
Michael Canniffe, *Pr*
Allycia Canniffe, *VP*
EMP: 10 **EST:** 1928
SQ FT: 3,000
SALES (est): 842.43K **Privately Held**
Web: www.stowawaysweets.com
SIC: 2064 5441   Chewing candy, not
chewing gum; Candy

(G-10096)
STROUD INTERNATIONAL LTD
123 Pleasant St Ste 300 (01945-2381)
PHONE..............................781 631-8806
Nat Greene, *CEO*
EMP: 18 **EST:** 2015
SALES (est): 851.82K **Privately Held**
Web: www.stroudinternational.com
SIC: 1382   Oil and gas exploration services

Marion
Plymouth County

(G-10097)
HARDING SAILS INC
Also Called: Harding Sails Nb
732 Mill St (02738-2209)
PHONE..............................508 748-0334
Graham Quinn, *Pr*
EMP: 10 **EST:** 1965
SQ FT: 5,000
SALES (est): 378.79K **Privately Held**
Web: www.hardingsails.com
SIC: 2394   Sails: made from purchased
materials

(G-10098)
NADCO INTERNATIONAL INC
Also Called: Model Engineering
91 Allens Point Rd (02738-2300)
PHONE..............................781 767-1797
Charles F Nadler Junior, *Pr*
EMP: 9 **EST:** 1958
SALES (est): 982.36K **Privately Held**
SIC: 3599   Machine shop, jobbing and repair

(G-10099)
OVTENE INC
11 Sassamon Trl Ste 221 (02738-2121)
P.O. Box 482 (02738-0009)
PHONE..............................617 852-4828
Alberto Tomasini, *CEO*
Sal Giglia, *Pr*
▼ **EMP:** 40 **EST:** 2017
SQ FT: 2,000
SALES (est): 3.25MM **Privately Held**
SIC: 2671   Plastic film, coated or laminated
for packaging

(G-10100)
SEGUE LLC
163 Front St (02738-1526)
PHONE..............................970 274-9801
Michael S Russo, *Prin*
EMP: 7 **EST:** 2017
SALES (est): 87.15K **Privately Held**
Web: www.segue-mfg.com
SIC: 3599   Machine shop, jobbing and repair

(G-10101)
SPERRY SAILS INC
Also Called: Sperry Sails
11 Marconi Ln (02738-1445)
P.O. Box 215 (02738-0004)
PHONE..............................508 748-2581
Matthew Sperry, *Pr*
Stephen C Sperry, *Treas*
Joan Wing, *Sec*
◆ **EMP:** 9 **EST:** 1980
SQ FT: 4,000
SALES (est): 990.82K **Privately Held**
Web: www.sperrysails.com
SIC: 3732 2394   Boatbuilding and repairing;
Sails: made from purchased materials

(G-10102)
TELEDYNE LECROY INC
Teledyne Test Services
513 Mill St (02738-1549)
PHONE..............................508 748-0103
Roger Masson, *Brnch Mgr*
EMP: 30
SALES (corp-wide): 5.46B **Publicly Held**
Web: www.teledyne-ts.com
SIC: 3829   Measuring and controlling
devices, nec
HQ: Teledyne Lecroy, Inc.
700 Chestnut Ridge Rd

Chestnut Ridge NY 10977
845 425-2000

Marlborough
Middlesex County

(G-10103)
ADCOLE LLC (PA)
669 Forest St (01752-3067)
PHONE..............................508 485-9100
Jeff Walker, *Pr*
Thomas K Macdonald, *ADCOLE AEROSPACE DIVISION**
Peter Hunter, *
Stephen Corrado, *
Douglas Vandenberg, *
◆ **EMP:** 111 **EST:** 1957
SQ FT: 43,000
SALES (est): 21.35MM
SALES (corp-wide): 21.35MM **Privately Held**
Web: www.adcolegage.com
SIC: 3812 3823   Aircraft/aerospace flight
instruments and guidance systems;
Process control instruments

(G-10104)
ADEZA BIOMEDICAL CORP
250 Campus Dr (01752-3020)
PHONE..............................508 263-8390
EMP: 10 **EST:** 2010
SALES (est): 212.8K **Privately Held**
SIC: 3845   Electromedical equipment

(G-10105)
AE RED HOLDINGS LLC (PA)
669 Forest St (01752-3067)
PHONE..............................561 372-7820
Peter Cannito, *CEO*
Andrew Rush, *COO*
Al Tadros, *CGO*
EMP: 10 **EST:** 2020
SALES (est): 72.07MM
SALES (corp-wide): 72.07MM **Privately Held**
SIC: 3764 8711   Space propulsion units and
parts; Engineering services

(G-10106)
ALLEGRO MICROSYSTEMS LLC
100 Crowley Dr (01752-1289)
PHONE..............................508 853-5000
Ravi Vig, *VP Mktg*
EMP: 220
Web: www.allegromicro.com
SIC: 3674   Semiconductors and related
devices
HQ: Allegro Microsystems, Llc
955 Perimeter Rd
Manchester NH 03103

(G-10107)
ALTIUM PACKAGING LP
Also Called: Marlboro Plastics
1 Dangelo Dr (01752-3066)
PHONE..............................508 485-2109
EMP: 29
SALES (corp-wide): 15.9B **Publicly Held**
Web: www.altiumpkg.com
SIC: 3089 3999   Plastics containers, except
foam; Atomizers, toiletry
HQ: Altium Packaging Lp
3101 Towercreek Pkwy Se
Atlanta GA 30339
678 742-4600

(G-10108)
AMERICAN ROBOTICS INC
53 Brigham St Unit 4 (01752-5128)
PHONE..............................617 862-2101
Timothy Tenne, *CEO*
EMP: 25 **EST:** 2012
SQ FT: 1,000
SALES (est): 1.24MM
SALES (corp-wide): 2.13MM **Publicly Held**
Web: www.american-robotics.com
SIC: 3523 3721 3812 7372   Farm machinery
and equipment; Motorized aircraft;
Instrument landing systems (ILS), airborne
or ground; Prepackaged software
PA: Ondas Holdings Inc.
411 Waverly Oaks Rd # 11
Waltham MA 02452
888 350-9994

(G-10109)
ANJEN FINISHING
432 Northboro Road Central (01752-1823)
PHONE..............................508 251-1532
K Scott Wyman, *Prin*
EMP: 10 **EST:** 2011
SALES (est): 444.72K **Privately Held**
Web: www.anjenfinishing.com
SIC: 3479   Coating of metals and formed
products

(G-10110)
APAHOUSER INC
40 Hayes Memorial Dr (01752-1830)
PHONE..............................508 786-0309
EMP: 50 **EST:** 1935
SQ FT: 35,000
SALES (est): 8.54MM **Privately Held**
Web: www.apahouser.com
SIC: 3444   Sheet metal specialties, not
stamped

(G-10111)
ASCO POWER TECHNOLOGIES LP
2 Maple St (01752-2905)
PHONE..............................508 624-0466
George Marrino, *Mgr*
EMP: 88
SALES (corp-wide): 82.05K **Privately Held**
SIC: 3629 3663 3699   Electronic generation
equipment; Radio and t.v. communications
equipment; Electrical equipment and
supplies, nec
HQ: Asco Power Technologies, L.P.
160 Park Ave
Florham Park NJ 07932

(G-10112)
ASPEN SYSTEMS LLC (PA)
24 Saint Martin Dr Ste 3 (01752-3060)
PHONE..............................508 281-5322
Kang P Lee, *Pr*
Glenn Deming, *VP*
EMP: 19 **EST:** 2019
SALES (est): 9.75MM
SALES (corp-wide): 9.75MM **Privately Held**
Web: www.aspensystems.com
SIC: 3585 8734 3291 3339   Refrigeration
and heating equipment; Product testing
laboratories; Abrasive products; Primary
nonferrous metals, nec

(G-10113)
ASSAYQUANT TECHNOLOGIES INC
260 Cedar Hill St (01752-3037)
PHONE..............................774 278-3302

Erik Schaefer, *Pr*
Barbara Imperiali, *Treas*
EMP: 26 **EST:** 2015
SALES (est): 3.94MM **Privately Held**
Web: www.assayquant.com
SIC: 2899 Gelatin: edible, technical,
photographic, or pharmaceutical

(G-10114)
AUTOMATIC SPECIALTIES INC
422 Northboro Road Central (01752-1895)
PHONE.............................508 481-2370
Peter Mongeau, *Pr*
Joseph H Moineau, *Pr*
Beverly S Drohan, *Sec*
EMP: 20 **EST:** 1968
SQ FT: 29,000
SALES (est): 4.97MM **Privately Held**
Web: www.automaticspecialties.com
SIC: 3496 3469 Miscellaneous fabricated
wire products; Metal stampings, nec

(G-10115)
AXCEL PHOTONICS INC
45 Bartlett St (01752-3014)
PHONE.............................508 481-9200
EMP: 28
SIC: 3674 Semiconductor circuit networks

(G-10116)
BIOLUCENT LLC
250 Campus Dr (01752-3020)
PHONE.............................508 263-2900
EMP: 10 **EST:** 2015
SALES (est): 1.6MM
SALES (corp-wide): 4.03B **Publicly Held**
SIC: 3845 3844 Ultrasonic medical
equipment, except cleaning; X-ray
apparatus and tubes
PA: Hologic, Inc.
250 Campus Dr
Marlborough MA 01752
508 263-2900

(G-10117)
BOSTON DOCUMENT SYSTEMS INC (PA)
Also Called: BDS
417 South St Ste 9 (01752-3192)
P.O. Box 753 (01752-0753)
PHONE.............................800 616-8576
Jason Alden, *CEO*
Paula Alden, *Sec*
EMP: 42 **EST:** 2011
SQ FT: 20,000
SALES (est): 11.68MM
SALES (corp-wide): 11.68MM **Privately Held**
Web: www.bdsdoc.com
SIC: 2752 7699 Commercial printing,
lithographic; Photocopy machine repair

(G-10118)
BOSTON SCIENTIFIC CORPORATION
100 Boston Scientific Way (01752-1234)
PHONE.............................508 382-0200
Paul Underwood, *Dir*
EMP: 285
SALES (corp-wide): 12.68B **Publicly Held**
Web: www.bostonscientific.com
SIC: 3841 Surgical and medical instruments
PA: Boston Scientific Corporation
300 Boston Scientific Way
Marlborough MA 01752
508 683-4000

(G-10119)
BOSTON SCIENTIFIC CORPORATION (PA)
Also Called: Boston Scientific
300 Boston Scientific Way (01752-1291)
PHONE.............................508 683-4000
Michael F Mahoney, *Ch Bd*
Daniel Brennan, *Ex VP*
Ian T Meredith, *Global Vice President*
Jodi Euerle Eddy, *INFO DIGITAL*
▲ **EMP:** 1037 **EST:** 1960
SALES (est): 12.68B
SALES (corp-wide): 12.68B **Publicly Held**
Web: www.bostonscientific.com
SIC: 3841 Surgical and medical instruments

(G-10120)
BOSTON SCIENTIFIC FUNDING LLC
Also Called: BOSTON SCIENTIFIC
300 Boston Scientific Way (01752-1291)
PHONE.............................508 683-4000
EMP: 8 **EST:** 2017
SALES (est): 1.18MM
SALES (corp-wide): 12.68B **Publicly Held**
SIC: 3841 Surgical and medical instruments
PA: Boston Scientific Corporation
300 Boston Scientific Way
Marlborough MA 01752
508 683-4000

(G-10121)
BOSTON SCIENTIFIC INTL CORP
300 Boston Scientific Way (01752-1291)
PHONE.............................508 683-4000
EMP: 13 **EST:** 2017
SALES (est): 2.47MM
SALES (corp-wide): 12.68B **Publicly Held**
Web: www.bostonscientific.com
SIC: 3841 Surgical and medical instruments
PA: Boston Scientific Corporation
300 Boston Scientific Way
Marlborough MA 01752
508 683-4000

(G-10122)
BTL INDUSTRIES INC
Also Called: Btl Aesthetics
362 Elm St Ste 5 (01752-4559)
PHONE.............................866 285-1656
Marcel Besse, *Pr*
EMP: 150 **EST:** 2011
SALES (est): 27.42MM
SALES (corp-wide): 111.5MM **Privately Held**
Web: www.btlnet.com
SIC: 3841 Surgical and medical instruments
PA: Btl Medical Technologies S.R.O.
Evropska 423/178
Praha 160 0
602291471

(G-10123)
BUSINESS SYSTEMS INCORPORATED
208 Cedar Hill St (01752-3017)
PHONE.............................508 624-4600
Ben Dennis, *Prin*
EMP: 7 **EST:** 2010
SALES (est): 192.08K **Privately Held**
Web: bsi.us.com
SIC: 7372 Prepackaged software

(G-10124)
BWT PHARMA & BIOTECH INC
417 South St Ste 5 (01752-3192)
PHONE.............................508 485-4291
EMP: 42 **EST:** 2013
SQ FT: 10,500

SALES (est): 14.59MM **Privately Held**
Web: www.bwt-pharma.com
SIC: 2834 Chlorination tablets and kits
(water purification)
HQ: Bwt Pharma & Biotech Limited
Unit 2a Ashbourne Business Park
Ashbourne A84 X

(G-10125)
CAM OFFICE SERVICES INC (PA)
41 Brigham St Unit 2 (01752-5143)
PHONE.............................781 932-9868
Janine O Taylor, *CEO*
Kemo Ceesay, *Pr*
EMP: 12 **EST:** 1989
SALES (est): 2.35MM **Privately Held**
Web: www.camofficeservices.com
SIC: 5044 5112 5712 5021 Copying
equipment; Stationery and office supplies;
Office furniture; Office furniture, nec

(G-10126)
CAMIANT INC (PA)
200 Nickerson Rd Ste 200 (01752-4635)
PHONE.............................508 486-9996
Steve Slattery, *Pr*
Ed Delaney, *VP*
EMP: 14 **EST:** 2003
SQ FT: 25,000
SALES (est): 1.86MM
SALES (corp-wide): 1.86MM **Privately Held**
Web: www.camiant.com
SIC: 3577 Data conversion equipment,
media-to-media: computer

(G-10127)
CANDELA CORPORATION (DH)
Also Called: Syneron Candela
251 Locke Dr (01752-7220)
PHONE.............................508 358-7400
Louis P Scafuri, *Pr*
James C Hsia, *
▲ **EMP:** 150 **EST:** 1970
SALES (est): 102.55MM **Privately Held**
Web: www.candelamedical.com
SIC: 3845 Laser systems and equipment,
medical
HQ: Syneron, Inc.
3 Goodyear Ste A
Irvine CA 92618

(G-10128)
CANDELA MEDICAL INC
251 Locke Dr (01752-7220)
PHONE.............................508 358-7400
Geoffrey Crouse, *CEO*
Steven Dyson, *
Ernest Orticerio, *CFO*
Mary Trout, *CCO*
EMP: 860 **EST:** 2021
SQ FT: 50,000
SALES (est): 62.12MM **Privately Held**
Web: www.candelamedical.com
SIC: 3845 Electromedical equipment

(G-10129)
CARDIOFOCUS INC
Also Called: Cardiofocus
500 Nickerson Rd Ste 500200
(01752-4695)
PHONE.............................508 658-7200
Stephen Sagon, *CEO*
Anjie Roldan, *
Mark Olsen, *
Paul Laviolette, *Ex Ch Bd*
Renny Clark, *
EMP: 25 **EST:** 1999
SQ FT: 13,000
SALES (est): 6.86MM **Privately Held**

Web: www.cardiofocus.com
SIC: 3845 3841 Electromedical equipment;
Catheters

(G-10130)
CARL ZEISS VISION INC
257 Simarano Dr Ste 107 (01752-3086)
PHONE.............................800 327-9735
EMP: 7
SIC: 3827 Optical instruments and lenses
HQ: Carl Zeiss Vision Inc.
1040 Worldwide Blvd
Hebron KY 41048

(G-10131)
CEQUR CORPORATION
Also Called: Cequr
734 Forest St Ste 100 (01752-3032)
PHONE.............................508 486-0010
James Peterson, *CEO*
Eric Milledge, *Ch*
Mike Hassman, *Pr*
Douglas Gunthardt, *Prin*
Mads Dall, *Ex VP*
EMP: 20 **EST:** 2008
SALES (est): 8.63MM **Privately Held**
Web: www.myceqursimplicity.com
SIC: 2833 Medicinals and botanicals
PA: Cequr Sa
Ebenaustrasse 10
Horw LU 6048

(G-10132)
CLARET MEDICAL INC
300 Boston Scientific Way (01752-1291)
PHONE.............................707 528-9300
EMP: 15 **EST:** 2020
SALES (est): 482.05K **Privately Held**
Web: www.bostonscientific.com
SIC: 3841 Surgical and medical instruments

(G-10133)
COMPLETE TECHNOLOGY RESOURCES
2 Mount Royal Ave Ste 350 (01752-1976)
PHONE.............................508 909-5961
Jamie Stafslien, *Pr*
EMP: 10 **EST:** 2010
SQ FT: 2,662
SALES (est): 784.15K **Privately Held**
Web:
www.completetechnologyresources.com
SIC: 7378 7372 Computer and data
processing equipment repair/maintenance;
Application computer software

(G-10134)
COMPREHENSIVE POWER INC
Also Called: CPI
420 Northboro Rd (01752)
PHONE.............................508 460-0010
EMP: 47
Web: www.perfectdomain.com
SIC: 3621 3679 Motors and generators;
Electronic circuits

(G-10135)
CONNORS DESIGN LTD
257 Simarano Dr Ste 105 (01752-3086)
PHONE.............................508 481-1930
Daniel Connors, *Pr*
Sandra Connors, *VP*
EMP: 7 **EST:** 1977
SQ FT: 10,000
SALES (est): 504.09K **Privately Held**
Web: www.connorsdesignltd.com
SIC: 2511 Wood household furniture

(G-10136)
CORERO NETWORK SECURITY INC
293 Boston Post Rd W Ste 310
(01752-4825)
PHONE...............................978 212-1500
Ashley Stephenson, *CEO*
Paul Jones, *VP Engg*
Joao Melo, *VP Opers*
Dave Larson, *COO*
Joe Branca, *Finance*
▲ **EMP:** 46 **EST:** 1997
SALES (est): 13.54MM **Privately Held**
Web: www.corero.com
SIC: 3577   Computer peripheral equipment, nec

(G-10137)
COSMAN MEDICAL LLC
300 Boston Scientific Way (01752-1291)
PHONE...............................781 272-6561
Michael Alan Arnold, *Pr*
EMP: 88 **EST:** 2004
SALES (est): 33.57MM
SALES (corp-wide): 12.68B **Publicly Held**
Web: www.cosmanmedical.com
SIC: 3845 8011   Electrotherapeutic apparatus; Neurosurgeon
HQ: Boston Scientific Neuromodulation Corporation
25155 Rye Canyon Loop
Valencia CA 91355

(G-10138)
COUTURE BRANDS LLC
19 Brigham St Unit 9c (01752-3182)
PHONE...............................512 626-7544
Shane Nassar, *Managing Member*
EMP: 8 **EST:** 2014
SQ FT: 15,000
SALES (est): 685.03K **Privately Held**
Web: www.shopcouturebrands.com
SIC: 3999   Candles

(G-10139)
CREDIT CARD SUPPLIES CORP
Also Called: Sylvesters Sales
105 Bartlett St (01752-3025)
PHONE...............................508 485-4230
Patrick T Daley, *Pr*
Kelly A Barringer, *Sec*
Frederick M Daley Iii, *Treas*
▲ **EMP:** 15 **EST:** 1996
SQ FT: 10,000
SALES (est): 2.38MM **Privately Held**
SIC: 3443   Fabricated plate work (boiler shop)

(G-10140)
CYTYC CORPORATION
445 Simarano Dr (01752-3073)
PHONE...............................508 303-4746
Angela Trabucco, *Admn*
EMP: 21
SALES (corp-wide): 4.03B **Publicly Held**
Web: www.hologic.com
SIC: 3845   Electromedical equipment
HQ: Cytyc Corporation
250 Campus Dr
Marlborough MA 01752

(G-10141)
CYTYC CORPORATION (HQ)
250 Campus Dr (01752-3020)
PHONE...............................508 263-2900
Patrick Sullivan, *Ch Bd*
Daniel J Levangie, *Operations*
A Suzanne Mesner-eltrich, *Sr VP*
Timothy M Adams, *Sr VP*
David P Harding, *Sr VP*

▲ **EMP:** 457 **EST:** 1987
SQ FT: 97,000
SALES (est): 125.4MM
SALES (corp-wide): 4.03B **Publicly Held**
Web: www.hologic.com
SIC: 3845   Electromedical equipment
PA: Hologic, Inc.
250 Campus Dr
Marlborough MA 01752
508 263-2900

(G-10142)
CYTYC SURGICAL PRODUCTS LLC (HQ)
250 Campus Dr (01752-3020)
PHONE...............................508 263-2900
John Griffin, *Pr*
Patricia K Dolan, *
Sarah Rana, *
EMP: 43 **EST:** 2008
SQ FT: 185,740
SALES (est): 35.52MM
SALES (corp-wide): 4.03B **Publicly Held**
Web: www.hologic.com
SIC: 3845   Electromedical equipment
PA: Hologic, Inc.
250 Campus Dr
Marlborough MA 01752
508 263-2900

(G-10143)
DAV-TECH PLATING INC
40 Cedar Hill St (01752-3006)
P.O. Box 836 (01752-0836)
PHONE...............................508 485-8472
David C Mason Junior, *Pr*
Linda C Mason, *
Leanna Goine, *
EMP: 50 **EST:** 1974
SQ FT: 30,000
SALES (est): 8.77MM **Privately Held**
Web: www.dav-techplatinginc.com
SIC: 3471   Electroplating of metals or formed products

(G-10144)
DMT EXPORT INC
85 Hayes Memorial Dr (01752-1892)
PHONE...............................508 481-5944
Christine Miller, *Pr*
EMP: 19 **EST:** 1996
SALES (est): 600.05K
SALES (corp-wide): 193.96MM **Publicly Held**
Web: www.dmtsharp.com
SIC: 3545   Machine tool accessories
HQ: Vogel Capital, Inc.
85 Hayes Memorial Dr
Marlborough MA 01752
508 481-5944

(G-10145)
DOBLE ENGINEERING COMPANY (HQ)
123 Felton St (01752-1999)
PHONE...............................617 926-4900
David B Zabetakis, *Pr*
Lawrence H Nordt, *VP Fin*
Don Angell, *VP*
Julie Crisafulli Brown Sphr, *VP*
Paul Griffin, *VP*
▲ **EMP:** 13 **EST:** 1920
SALES (est): 160.64MM **Publicly Held**
Web: www.doble.com
SIC: 3825 7359 3829 3826   Electrical power measuring equipment; Business machine and electronic equipment rental services; Measuring and controlling devices, nec; Analytical instruments
PA: Esco Technologies Inc.
9900 Clayton Rd Ste A

Saint Louis MO 63124

(G-10146)
DOCUSERVE INC
72 Cedar Hill St Ste B (01752-3040)
PHONE...............................508 786-5820
EMP: 24 **EST:** 1994
SQ FT: 16,000
SALES (est): 2.37MM **Privately Held**
Web: www.docuserve.com
SIC: 2759 2752   Commercial printing, nec; Commercial printing, lithographic

(G-10147)
DOW CHEMICAL COMPANY
Also Called: Dow Chemical
455 Forest St (01752-3001)
PHONE...............................508 229-7676
Pierre Brondeau, *Brnch Mgr*
EMP: 102
SALES (corp-wide): 44.62B **Publicly Held**
Web: www.dow.com
SIC: 2819 2821   Industrial inorganic chemicals, nec; Plastics materials and resins
HQ: The Dow Chemical Company
2211 H H Dow Way
Midland MI 48642
989 636-1000

(G-10148)
ERNEST JOHNSON
Also Called: Ernest Johnson Co
146 Phelps St (01752-2732)
P.O. Box 270 (01752-0270)
PHONE...............................508 259-6727
Ernest Johnson, *Owner*
EMP: 8 **EST:** 1997
SALES (est): 431.61K **Privately Held**
SIC: 3441 2821   Fabricated structural metal; Plastics materials and resins

(G-10149)
EXPERTEK SYSTEMS INC
4 Mount Royal Ave Ste 140 (01752-1961)
PHONE...............................508 624-0006
Kenneth P Mostello, *Pr*
Paul F Sorrento, *VP*
Michelle Maglaty, *CFO*
EMP: 23 **EST:** 1992
SALES (est): 4.6MM **Privately Held**
Web: www.expertek.com
SIC: 7372 7371 7379   Prepackaged software ; Computer software development and applications; Computer related consulting services

(G-10150)
FOREFIELD INC
33 Boston Post Rd W Ste 190
(01752-1870)
PHONE...............................508 630-1100
Brent Delehey, *CEO*
Bill Davenport, *
EMP: 21 **EST:** 1997
SALES (est): 1.87MM **Publicly Held**
Web: www.broadridge.com
SIC: 7371 7372   Computer software development; Business oriented computer software
PA: Broadridge Financial Solutions, Inc.
5 Dakota Dr Ste 300
New Hyde Park NY 11042

(G-10151)
GATEHOUSE MEDIA MASS I INC
Also Called: Southborough Villager
40 Mechanic St (01752-4425)
PHONE...............................508 626-3859
Glenda Hazard, *Mgr*

EMP: 8
SALES (corp-wide): 2.95B **Publicly Held**
Web: www.ghmne.com
SIC: 2711   Newspapers, publishing and printing
HQ: Gatehouse Media Massachusetts I, Inc.
48 Dunham Rd
Beverly MA 01915
585 598-0030

(G-10152)
GE HEALTHCARE INC (HQ)
Also Called: GE Healthcare Life Sciences
251 Locke Dr (01752-7220)
PHONE...............................732 457-8667
Kieran Murphy, *Pr*
Frank Jimenez, *
▲ **EMP:** 340 **EST:** 1968
SALES (est): 2.1B
SALES (corp-wide): 4.71B **Publicly Held**
Web: www.cytivalifesciences.com
SIC: 2833 5122   Medicinals and botanicals; Medicinals and botanicals
PA: Ge Healthcare Technologies Inc.
500 W Monroe St
Chicago IL 60661
833 735-1139

(G-10153)
GLOBAL LF SCNCES SLTONS USA LL
Also Called: GE Healthcare Life Sciences
170 Locke Dr (01752-7217)
PHONE...............................800 526-3593
Joseph M Hogan, *CEO*
EMP: 998
SALES (corp-wide): 31.47B **Publicly Held**
Web: www.cytivalifesciences.com
SIC: 2834   Pharmaceutical preparations
HQ: Global Life Sciences Solutions Usa Llc
100 Results Way
Marlborough MA 01752
800 526-3593

(G-10154)
GOTHAM INK OF NEW ENGLAND INC
Also Called: Gotham Ink In Color
255 E Main St (01752-2631)
PHONE...............................508 485-7911
Paul Freitas, *Brnch Mgr*
EMP: 8
SALES (corp-wide): 45.61MM **Privately Held**
SIC: 2893   Lithographic ink
HQ: Gotham Ink Of New England Inc
10 York Ave
West Caldwell NJ 07006
201 478-5600

(G-10155)
GREENBRIER GAMES LLP
12 Bicknell St (01752-4102)
PHONE...............................978 618-8442
EMP: 9 **EST:** 2012
SALES (est): 464.77K **Privately Held**
Web: secure.greenbriergames.com
SIC: 3944 7389   Electronic games and toys; Business services, nec

(G-10156)
GREGORY ENGINEERING CORP
Also Called: Sylvester Products Division
105 Bartlett St (01752-3025)
P.O. Box 22 (01752-0022)
PHONE...............................508 481-0480
Frederick Daley Junior, *Pr*
Frederick Daley Iii, *Treas*
EMP: 19 **EST:** 1963
SQ FT: 10,000

SALES (est): 765.93K **Privately Held**
SIC: 3443   Fabricated plate work (boiler shop)

(G-10157)
GUIDANT CORPORATION
300 Boston Scientific Way (01752-1291)
PHONE..............................508 683-4000
Michael F Mahoney, *CEO*
Michael Mahoney, *CEO*
EMP: 54 EST: 1994
SALES (est): 6.14MM
SALES (corp-wide): 12.68B **Publicly Held**
Web: www.bostonscientific.com
SIC: 3841   Surgical and medical instruments
PA: Boston Scientific Corporation
250 Boston Scientific Way
Marlborough MA 01752
508 683-4000

(G-10158)
HOLOGIC INC
445 Simarano Dr (01752-3073)
PHONE..............................508 263-2900
Donna Kempskie, *Brnch Mgr*
EMP: 195
SALES (corp-wide): 4.03B **Publicly Held**
Web: www.hologic.com
SIC: 3844   X-ray apparatus and tubes
PA: Hologic, Inc.
250 Campus Dr
Marlborough MA 01752
508 263-2900

(G-10159)
HOLOGIC INC (PA)
Also Called: HOLOGIC
250 Campus Dr (01752-3020)
PHONE..............................508 263-2900
Stephen P Macmillan, *Ch Bd*
Stephen P Macmillan, *Ch Bd*
Karleen M Oberton, *CFO*
Elisabeth A Hellmann, *Senior Vice President Human Resources*
◆ EMP: 996 EST: 1985
SALES (est): 4.03B
SALES (corp-wide): 4.03B **Publicly Held**
Web: www.hologic.com
SIC: 3845 3844 3841   Ultrasonic medical equipment, except cleaning; X-ray apparatus and tubes; Medical instruments and equipment, blood and bone work

(G-10160)
HOLOGIC FOREIGN SALES CORP
250 Campus Dr (01752-3020)
PHONE..............................781 999-7300
EMP: 870 EST: 1989
SALES (est): 195.19MM
SALES (corp-wide): 4.03B **Publicly Held**
Web: www.hologic.com
SIC: 3845   Electromedical equipment
PA: Hologic, Inc.
250 Campus Dr
Marlborough MA 01752
508 263-2900

(G-10161)
HOLOGIC SALES AND SERVICE LLC
250 Campus Dr (01752-3020)
PHONE..............................508 263-2900
John Griffin, *
Marci Lerner, *
Anne Liddy, *
EMP: 500 EST: 2002
SALES (est): 83.99MM
SALES (corp-wide): 4.03B **Publicly Held**
Web: www.hologic.com

SIC: 3845   Electromedical equipment
PA: Hologic, Inc.
250 Campus Dr
Marlborough MA 01752
508 263-2900

(G-10162)
HOLOGRAPHIX LLC
140 Locke Dr Ste A (01752-7206)
PHONE..............................978 562-4474
David Rowe, *Pr*
Donna Rowe, *Sec*
EMP: 10 EST: 2002
SQ FT: 8,300
SALES (est): 1.83MM **Privately Held**
Web: www.holographix.com
SIC: 3827   Optical instruments and lenses

(G-10163)
HONLE UV AMERICA INC
261 Cedar Hill St Ste 5 (01752-3056)
PHONE..............................508 229-7774
EMP: 7 EST: 1995
SQ FT: 6,500
SALES (est): 972.01K **Privately Held**
Web: www.honleuv.com
SIC: 3826   Ultraviolet analytical instruments

(G-10164)
HOTTINGER BRUEL & KJAER INC (DH)
19 Bartlett St (01752-3014)
PHONE..............................508 485-7480
Joe Vorih, *Pr*
Mary Hall, *Treas*
Walter Kneissler, *Sec*
▲ EMP: 98 EST: 1973
SQ FT: 45,000
SALES (est): 92.23MM
SALES (corp-wide): 1.6B **Privately Held**
Web: www.hbm.com
SIC: 3679 7371   Transducers, electrical; Computer software development and applications
HQ: Spectris Inc.
117 Flanders Rd
Westborough MA 01581
508 768-6400

(G-10165)
INTEGRATED DYNAMIC METALS CORP
66 Brigham St Unit A (01752-3137)
P.O. Box 64 (01752-0064)
PHONE..............................508 624-7271
Remi Doiron, *Pr*
Jim Mcnamara, *VP*
EMP: 20 EST: 2004
SQ FT: 20,000
SALES (est): 2.04MM **Privately Held**
Web: www.idm-corp.com
SIC: 3444   Ducts, sheet metal

(G-10166)
INTERLACE MEDICAL INC
250 Campus Dr (01752-3020)
PHONE..............................800 442-9892
▲ EMP: 38 EST: 2005
SQ FT: 6,000
SALES (est): 12.18MM
SALES (corp-wide): 4.03B **Publicly Held**
Web: www.hologic.com
SIC: 5047 3845   Medical equipment and supplies; Ultrasonic scanning devices, medical
PA: Hologic, Inc.
250 Campus Dr
Marlborough MA 01752
508 263-2900

SIC: 3845   Electromedical equipment
PA: Hologic, Inc.
250 Campus Dr
Marlborough MA 01752
508 263-2900

(G-10167)
IPG PHOTONICS CORPORATION
257 Cedar Hill St (01752-3004)
PHONE..............................508 373-1100
EMP: 17
SALES (corp-wide): 1.43B **Publicly Held**
Web: www.ipgphotonics.com
SIC: 3699   Laser systems and equipment
PA: Ipg Photonics Corporation
377 Simarano Dr
Marlborough MA 01752
508 373-1100

(G-10168)
IPG PHOTONICS CORPORATION
259 Cedar Hill St (01752-3004)
PHONE..............................508 506-2812
EMP: 20
SALES (corp-wide): 1.43B **Publicly Held**
Web: www.ipgphotonics.com
SIC: 3699   Laser systems and equipment
PA: Ipg Photonics Corporation
377 Simarano Dr
Marlborough MA 01752
508 373-1100

(G-10169)
IPG PHOTONICS CORPORATION (PA)
Also Called: Ipg
377 Simarano Dr (01752-3096)
PHONE..............................508 373-1100
Eugene A Scherbakov, *CEO*
John Peeler, *Non-Executive Chairman of the Board*
Timothy P Mammen V, *Sr VP*
Angelo P Lopresti, *Sr VP*
Alexander Ovtchinnikov, *Sr VP*
▲ EMP: 440 EST: 1990
SQ FT: 389,800
SALES (est): 1.43B
SALES (corp-wide): 1.43B **Publicly Held**
Web: www.ipgphotonics.com
SIC: 3699 3229 3674   Laser systems and equipment; Fiber optics strands; Semiconductor diodes and rectifiers

(G-10170)
J&J MACHINE COMPANY INC
66b Brigham St (01752-3137)
P.O. Box 702 (01752-0702)
PHONE..............................508 481-8166
Devin Brown, *Pr*
EMP: 10 EST: 1979
SQ FT: 11,000
SALES (est): 1.98MM **Privately Held**
Web: www.jjmachine.com
SIC: 3599   Machine shop, jobbing and repair

(G-10171)
JENTEK SENSORS INC
121 Bartlett St (01752-3025)
PHONE..............................781 642-9666
Neil Goldfine, *Pr*
Jonie Hatem, *Sr VP*
EMP: 15 EST: 1992
SALES (est): 3.02MM **Privately Held**
Web: www.jenteksensors.com
SIC: 3826   Analytical instruments

(G-10172)
JORDAN ENTERPRISES INC
Also Called: Super Dup'r Instant Printing
40 Hudson St Ste B (01752-1266)
PHONE..............................508 481-2948
Robert J Jordan, *Pr*
Joanne Jordan, *Clerk*
Jennifer R Jordan, *VP*
EMP: 10 EST: 1970
SQ FT: 6,000

SALES (est): 961.68K **Privately Held**
SIC: 2752   Offset printing

(G-10173)
K & M ENGINEERING INC
583 Berlin Rd (01752-1131)
PHONE..............................978 235-7923
Michael Marrazzo, *Pr*
Jason Kittredge, *Sec*
EMP: 12 EST: 2013
SQ FT: 3,000
SALES (est): 1.03MM **Privately Held**
Web: www.kandmengineering.com
SIC: 3599   Machine and other job shop work

(G-10174)
KAZ INC (HQ)
400 Donald Lynch Blvd Ste 300 (01752-4733)
PHONE..............................508 490-7000
Jon Kosheff, *Prin*
Mark Simon, *Prin*
Roelof Zeijpveld, *Prin*
Christophe Coudray, *Global CIO*
◆ EMP: 100 EST: 1936
SQ FT: 60,000
SALES (est): 121.94MM **Privately Held**
Web: www.helenoftroy.com
SIC: 8082 2834 5047   Home health care services; Pharmaceutical preparations; Medical and hospital equipment
PA: Helen Of Troy Limited
C/O Conyers Corporate Services (Bermuda) Limited
Hamilton HM 11

(G-10175)
KAZ USA INC
400 Donald Lynch Blvd (01752-4733)
PHONE..............................508 490-7000
▲ EMP: 83 EST: 1989
SALES (est): 30.61MM **Privately Held**
SIC: 3634   Electric housewares and fans
HQ: Kaz, Inc.
400 Donald Lynch Blvd
Marlborough MA 01752
508 490-7000

(G-10176)
KENS FOODS INC (PA)
1 Dangelo Dr (01752-3066)
P.O. Box 849 (01752-0849)
PHONE..............................508 229-1100
Frank A Crowley Iii, *Pr*
James Sutherby, *
Brian L Crowley, *FOOD SERVICES*
Paul Galvani, *
Joseph Shay, *
◆ EMP: 428 EST: 1958
SQ FT: 340,000
SALES (est): 476.41MM
SALES (corp-wide): 476.41MM **Privately Held**
Web: www.kensfoods.com
SIC: 2033   Barbecue sauce: packaged in cans, jars, etc.

(G-10177)
KNM HOLDINGS LLC
Also Called: John Deere Authorized Dealer
410 Forest St Ste 3 (01752-4172)
PHONE..............................508 229-1400
EMP: 8 EST: 2004
SQ FT: 2,000
SALES (est): 1.61MM **Privately Held**
Web: www.asne.com
SIC: 3511 5082   Turbo-generators; Construction and mining machinery

(G-10178)
KTRON INCORPORATED
90 Bartlett St (01752-3013)
PHONE.....................................508 229-0919
Barry Kittredge, *Pr*
Daren Kittredge, *
EMP: 40 **EST:** 2002
SQ FT: 35,500
SALES (est): 5.16MM **Privately Held**
Web: www.ktron-inc.com
SIC: 3549 Metalworking machinery, nec

(G-10179)
KUBOTEK USA INC
2 Mount Royal Ave Ste 500 (01752-1960)
PHONE.....................................508 229-2020
Nakamoto Yoko, *CEO*
Naotake Kakishita, *
Ramgopal Eswaran, *
Tetsuo Kubo, *
EMP: 24 **EST:** 2003
SALES (est): 6.79MM **Privately Held**
Web: www.kubotekkosmos.com
SIC: 7372 7373 Business oriented computer
software; Computer-aided design (CAD)
systems service
PA: Kubotek Corporation
4-3-36, Nakanoshima, Kita-Ku
Osaka OSK 530-0

(G-10180)
LINMEL ASSOCIATES INC
Also Called: Sir Speedy
160 Main St (01752-3865)
PHONE.....................................508 481-6699
Steven Hitner, *Pr*
EMP: 10 **EST:** 1985
SQ FT: 4,000
SALES (est): 1.2MM **Privately Held**
Web: www.sirspeedy.com
SIC: 2752 2796 2791 2789 Commercial
printing, lithographic; Platemaking services;
Typesetting; Bookbinding and related work

(G-10181)
MAGNETIKA/EAST LTD
PARTNERSHIP
34 Saint Martin Dr Ste 11 (01752-3021)
PHONE.....................................508 485-7555
Basil Caloyeras, *Pt*
EMP: 13 **EST:** 1988
SQ FT: 5,000
SALES (est): 1.62MM **Privately Held**
Web: www.magnetika.com
SIC: 3612 Power and distribution
transformers

(G-10182)
MARLBOROUGH FOUNDRY INC
555 Maple St (01752-3268)
PHONE.....................................508 485-2848
Robert L Nye, *Pr*
Joyce Nye, *CFO*
Joyce L Nye-taylor, *VP*
EMP: 21 **EST:** 1954
SQ FT: 44,000
SALES (est): 4.34MM **Privately Held**
Web: www.marlboroughfoundry.com
SIC: 3365 Aluminum and aluminum-based
alloy castings

(G-10183)
MASSACHUSETTS CONTAINER
CORP
300 Cedar Hill St (01752-3036)
PHONE.....................................508 481-1100
Lawrence Perkins, *Ch*
Louis Cerruzi, *
Harry Perkins, *

▲ **EMP:** 114 **EST:** 1963
SALES (est): 26.37MM
SALES (corp-wide): 151.34MM **Privately**
Held
Web: www.unicorr.com
SIC: 2653 Boxes, corrugated: made from
purchased materials
PA: Connecticut Container Corp.
455 Sackett Point Rd
North Haven CT 06473
203 248-2161

(G-10184)
MHQ INC (PA)
Also Called: Mhq Municipal Vehicles
401 Elm St (01752-4566)
PHONE.....................................508 573-2600
Diane Mohieldin, *CEO*
Charles Ribakoff, *
Patricia F Ribakoff, *
EMP: 65 **EST:** 1960
SQ FT: 100,000
SALES (est): 20.18MM **Privately Held**
Web: www.buymchq.com
SIC: 5999 3711 Police supply stores; Patrol
wagons (motor vehicles), assembly of

(G-10185)
MOCANA CORPORATION
225 Cedar Hill St Ste 332 (01752-5900)
PHONE.....................................508 251-5086
EMP: 7 **EST:** 2014
SALES (est): 84.1K **Privately Held**
SIC: 7372 Prepackaged software

(G-10186)
NAVILYST MEDICAL INC
26 Forest St Ste 200 (01752-3068)
PHONE.....................................508 658-7990
Ronald Sparks, *Prin*
EMP: 53 **EST:** 2008
SALES (est): 620.42K **Privately Held**
Web: www.angiodynamics.com
SIC: 3841 Surgical and medical instruments

(G-10187)
NVISION MEDICAL
CORPORATION
100 Boston Scientific Way (01752-1234)
PHONE.....................................408 655-3577
Surbhi Sarna, *CEO*
EMP: 7 **EST:** 2009
SALES (est): 2.62MM
SALES (corp-wide): 12.68B **Publicly Held**
SIC: 3841 7389 Surgical and medical
instruments; Business Activities at Non-
Commercial Site
PA: Boston Scientific Corporation
300 Boston Scientific Way
Marlborough MA 01752
508 683-4000

(G-10188)
O/K MACHINERY CORPORATION
73 Bartlett St (01752-3071)
PHONE.....................................508 303-8286
Owen Kellett, *Pr*
EMP: 24 **EST:** 1982
SQ FT: 25,000
SALES (est): 764.1K **Privately Held**
Web: www.okcorp.com
SIC: 3496 3565 Conveyor belts; Packaging
machinery

(G-10189)
OK DURABLE PACKAGING INC
73 Bartlett St (01752-3071)
PHONE.....................................508 303-8067
Adam Kwiek, *Pr*
EMP: 11 **EST:** 2001

SALES (est): 558.79K **Privately Held**
Web: www.okcorp.com
SIC: 2671 Paper; coated and laminated
packaging

(G-10190)
OMTEC CORP
Also Called: Omtec Ball Transfers
181 Liberty St (01752-4333)
PHONE.....................................508 481-3322
Susan Masciarelli, *Pr*
Camillo Masciarelli, *Pr*
▲ **EMP:** 19 **EST:** 1988
SQ FT: 8,000
SALES (est): 2.43MM **Privately Held**
Web: www.omtec.com
SIC: 3535 5084 Conveyors and conveying
equipment; Industrial machinery and
equipment

(G-10191)
ONDAS HOLDINGS INC
Also Called: American Robotics Inc
53 Brigham St Unit 4 (01752-5128)
PHONE.....................................617 862-2101
Reese Mozer, *Brnch Mgr*
EMP: 25
SALES (corp-wide): 2.13MM **Publicly**
Held
Web: www.ondas.com
SIC: 3523 3721 3812 7372 Farm machinery
and equipment; Motorized aircraft;
Instrument landing systems (ILS), airborne
or ground; Prepackaged software
PA: Ondas Holdings Inc.
411 Waverly Oaks Rd # 11
Waltham MA 02452
888 350-9994

(G-10192)
OPTOS INC
Also Called: Optos North America
500 Nickerson Rd Ste 201 (01752-4637)
PHONE.....................................508 787-1400
Stephane Sallmard, *CEO*
▲ **EMP:** 85 **EST:** 1998
SQ FT: 3,800
SALES (est): 41.45MM **Privately Held**
Web: www.optos.com
SIC: 3827 Optical instruments and lenses
HQ: Optos Public Limited Company
Queensferry House
Dunfermline KY11
138 384-3300

(G-10193)
OXFORD IMMUNOTEC USA INC
293 Boston Post Rd W Ste 210
(01752-4615)
PHONE.....................................833 682-6933
Peter Wrighton-smith, *CEO*
Stefan Linn, *
Richard Altieri, *
EMP: 90 **EST:** 2018
SALES (est): 4.83MM **Privately Held**
Web: www.oxfordimmunotec.com
SIC: 3841 Diagnostic apparatus, medical

(G-10194)
PACTOLUS CMMNCTIONS
SFTWR CORP
200 Nickerson Rd (01752-4635)
P.O. Box 119 (01740-0119)
PHONE.....................................508 616-0900
Paul Blondin, *Ch Bd*
David Horton, *
EMP: 18 **EST:** 1999
SQ FT: 960
SALES (est): 515.35K **Privately Held**

SIC: 7372 Prepackaged software

(G-10195)
PHILIPS HLTHCARE INFRMTICS
INC
Phillips Lifeline Systems
200 Donald Lynch Blvd (01752-4815)
PHONE.....................................508 988-1000
EMP: 19
SALES (corp-wide): 18.51B **Privately Held**
SIC: 3669 Emergency alarms
HQ: Philips Healthcare Informatics, Inc.
4430 Rosewood Dr Ste 200
Pleasanton CA 94588
650 293-2300

(G-10196)
PLATINUM FIRE PRTCTION
SVCS LL (PA)
Also Called: Platinum Fire Protection
34 Saint Martin Dr Ste 12 (01752-3356)
PHONE.....................................508 481-8242
EMP: 30 **EST:** 2010
SALES (est): 10.31MM
SALES (corp-wide): 10.31MM **Privately**
Held
Web: www.platinumfireprotection.com
SIC: 1711 3498 Plumbing, heating, air-
conditioning; Fabricated pipe and fittings

(G-10197)
PRYSM INC
45 Bartlett St Ste 2 (01752-4171)
PHONE.....................................978 405-3091
Monica Vought, *Brnch Mgr*
EMP: 14
Web: www.prysmsystems.com
SIC: 3999 Feathers and feather products
PA: Prysm, Inc.
513 Fairview Way
Milpitas CA 95035

(G-10198)
QUADTECH INC
734 Forest St Ste 500 (01752-3008)
PHONE.....................................978 461-2100
Philip H Harris, *Pr*
EMP: 54 **EST:** 1991
SQ FT: 25,000
SALES (est): 4.41MM **Privately Held**
Web: www.quadtech.com
SIC: 3825 3829 Test equipment for
electronic and electric measurement;
Measuring and controlling devices, nec
HQ: Baldwin Technology Company, Inc.
8027 Forsyth Blvd
Saint Louis MO 63105
314 726-2152

(G-10199)
QUEST DIAGNOSTIC
INCORPORATED
200 Forest St (01752-3023)
PHONE.....................................617 547-8900
Robert E Meehan, *Pr*
EMP: 800 **EST:** 1996
SALES (est): 62.76MM
SALES (corp-wide): 9.88B **Publicly Held**
Web: www.questdiagnostics.com
SIC: 8071 2835 Testing laboratories;
Diagnostic substances
PA: Quest Diagnostics Incorporated
500 Plaza Dr Ste G
Secaucus NJ 07094
973 520-2700

(G-10200)
RAYTHEON COMPANY
Raytheon

1001 Boston Post Rd E (01752-3770)
PHONE...............................978 440-1000
Brian Morrison, *Prin*
EMP: 300
SQ FT: 30,000
SALES (corp-wide): 68.92B **Publicly Held**
Web: www.rtx.com
SIC: 3812 Sonar systems and equipment
HQ: Raytheon Company
870 Winter St
Waltham MA 02451
781 522-3000

(G-10201)
RAYTHEON COMPANY
Raytheon
1001 Boston Post Rd E (01752-3770)
PHONE...............................508 490-1000
Frank S Marchilena, *Brnch Mgr*
EMP: 38
SALES (corp-wide): 67.07B **Publicly Held**
Web: www.rtx.com
SIC: 3812 7371 3728 Sonar systems and equipment; Custom computer programming services; Aircraft parts and equipment, nec
HQ: Raytheon Company
870 Winter St
Waltham MA 02451
781 522-3000

(G-10202)
REPLIGEN CORPORATION
Also Called: Tangenx Technology
111 Locke Dr Ste 100 (01752-7236)
PHONE...............................508 845-6400
John Connors, *Brnch Mgr*
EMP: 41
SALES (corp-wide): 801.54MM **Publicly Held**
Web: www.repligen.com
SIC: 2836 Biological products, except diagnostic
PA: Repligen Corporation
41 Seyon St Ste 100
Waltham MA 02453
781 250-0111

(G-10203)
REWALK ROBOTICS INC (HQ)
200 Donald Lynch Blvd (01752-4815)
PHONE...............................508 251-1154
Larry Jasinski, *CEO*
Mike Lawless, *
EMP: 8 **EST:** 2012
SALES (est): 12.99MM **Privately Held**
Web: www.rewalk.com
SIC: 3842 Surgical appliances and supplies
PA: Rewalk Robotics Ltd
3 Hatnufa
Yokneam Illit 20692

(G-10204)
RILEY POWER INC
Also Called: Riley Pwr A Babcock Pwr Inc Co
26 Forest St Ste 300 (01752-3068)
PHONE...............................508 852-7100
Edward C Dean, *Pr*
Kumar Gopathi, *VP*
William J Ferguson Junior, *Sr VP*
Anthony A Brandano, *Ex VP*
Michael Kelly, *VP*
◆ **EMP:** 320 **EST:** 1913
SQ FT: 120,000
SALES (est): 82.05MM
SALES (corp-wide): 509.03MM **Privately Held**
Web: www.babcockpower.com

SIC: 3569 3443 3433 1711 Generators: steam, liquid oxygen, or nitrogen; Fuel tanks (oil, gas, etc.), metal plate; Burners, furnaces, boilers, and stokers; Boiler maintenance contractor
HQ: Babcock Power Capital Corporation
222 Rosewood Dr Fl 3
Danvers MA 01923
978 646-3300

(G-10205)
ROCKWELL AUTOMATION INC
100 Nickerson Rd Fl 1 (01752-4613)
PHONE...............................508 357-8400
Keith Nosbusch, *Mgr*
EMP: 11
Web: www.rockwellautomation.com
SIC: 3625 Relays and industrial controls
PA: Rockwell Automation, Inc.
1201 S 2nd St
Milwaukee WI 53204

(G-10206)
ROHM HAAS ELECTRONIC MTLS LLC (HQ)
Also Called: Haleos Montgomery Co
455 Forest St (01752-3001)
PHONE...............................508 481-7950
Michael P Heffernan, *
Andrew R Girardi, *
◆ **EMP:** 750 **EST:** 1994
SALES (est): 498.83MM
SALES (corp-wide): 13.02B **Publicly Held**
Web: www.dupont.com
SIC: 2869 2819 Industrial organic chemicals, nec; Industrial inorganic chemicals, nec
PA: Dupont De Nemours, Inc.
974 Centre Rd Bldg 730
Wilmington DE 19805
302 774-3034

(G-10207)
ROHM HAAS ELECTRONIC MTLS LLC
Also Called: Dupont Electronics & Imaging
455 Forest St (01752-3001)
PHONE...............................508 481-7950
EMP: 23
SALES (corp-wide): 13.02B **Publicly Held**
Web: www.dupont.com
SIC: 2879 Agricultural chemicals, nec
HQ: Rohm And Haas Electronic Materials Llc
455 Forest St
Marlborough MA 01752
508 481-7950

(G-10208)
RULAND MANUFACTURING CO INC
6 Hayes Memorial Dr (01752-1830)
PHONE...............................508 485-1000
▲ **EMP:** 50 **EST:** 1937
SALES (est): 16.89MM **Privately Held**
Web: www.ruland.com
SIC: 3568 Couplings, shaft: rigid, flexible, universal joint, etc.

(G-10209)
SEA STAR SEAFOOD CORP
128 Bartlett St (01752-3016)
◆ **EMP:** 45 **EST:** 1983
SALES (est): 4.39MM **Privately Held**
Web: www.seastar.cc
SIC: 2092 5146 Fresh or frozen packaged fish; Fish, frozen, unpackaged

(G-10210)
SEPATON INC
Also Called: Hitachi Protection Platform
400 Nickerson Rd (01752-4717)
PHONE...............................508 490-7900
EMP: 87
SIC: 3572 7371 Computer storage devices; Computer software development

(G-10211)
SPECTRA ANALYSIS INC (PA)
257 Simarano Dr Ste 100 (01752-3070)
PHONE...............................508 281-6232
George J Giansanti Junior, *Pr*
EMP: 9 **EST:** 2005
SALES (est): 1.23MM
SALES (corp-wide): 1.23MM **Privately Held**
Web: www.spectra-analysis.com
SIC: 3826 Analytical instruments

(G-10212)
SPECTRUM MICROWAVE INC
Also Called: API Technologies
400 Nickerson Rd Ste 1 (01752-4717)
PHONE...............................508 485-0336
Walter Gordon, *Mgr*
EMP: 60
Web: www.apitech.com
SIC: 3679 3674 Microwave components; Hybrid integrated circuits
HQ: Spectrum Microwave, Inc.
1900 W College Ave
State College PA 16801
814 272-2700

(G-10213)
SPECTRUM MICROWAVE INC
API Technologies
400 Nickerson Rd Ste 1 (01752-4690)
PHONE...............................508 251-6400
EMP: 178
Web: www.spectrumcontrol.com
SIC: 3679 3812 Microwave components; Search and navigation equipment
HQ: Spectrum Microwave, Inc.
1900 W College Ave
State College PA 16801
814 272-2700

(G-10214)
SPECTRUM MICROWAVE INC
400 Nickerson Rd Ste 1 (01752-4717)
PHONE...............................603 459-1600
EMP: 9 **EST:** 2019
SALES (est): 1.35MM **Privately Held**
Web: www.spectrumcontrol.com
SIC: 3679 Microwave components

(G-10215)
SPIRE METERING TECHNOLOGY LLC
Also Called: Shenitech
34 Saint Martin Dr (01752-3356)
PHONE...............................978 263-7100
Chang Shen, *Managing Member*
▲ **EMP:** 14 **EST:** 2003
SALES (est): 2.08MM **Privately Held**
Web: www.spiremt.com
SIC: 3829 Ultrasonic testing equipment

(G-10216)
SQUARE ROBOT INC
50 Dangelo Dr Ste 5 (01752-3097)
PHONE...............................617 274-8389
EMP: 29 **EST:** 2018
SALES (est): 4.68MM **Privately Held**
Web: www.squarerobots.com

SIC: 8742 3829 Automation and robotics consultant; Measuring and controlling devices, nec

(G-10217)
SUMITOMO PHARMA AMERICA INC (HQ)
Also Called: Sunovion Respiratory Dev
84 Waterford Dr (01752-7010)
PHONE...............................508 481-6700
Myrtle Potter, *CEO*
Nobuhiko Tamura, *
Matthew Dambrosio, *
Antony Loebel, *
Hiroyuki Baba, *
▲ **EMP:** 2100 **EST:** 1984
SQ FT: 192,600
SALES (est): 522.25MM **Privately Held**
Web: us.sumitomo-pharma.com
SIC: 2834 Pharmaceutical preparations
PA: Sumitomo Chemical Company, Limited
2-7-1, Nihombashi
Chuo-Ku TKY 103-0

(G-10218)
SUNDANCE NEWBRIDGE PUBLISHING
33 Boston Post Rd W Ste 440 (01752-1887)
PHONE...............................508 303-1920
Robert Laronga, *Pr*
EMP: 14 **EST:** 1984
SALES (est): 1MM **Privately Held**
Web: www.sundancenewbridge.com
SIC: 5192 2731 Books; Books, publishing only

(G-10219)
SUPERIOR PRINTING INK CO INC
255 E Main St (01752-2631)
PHONE...............................508 481-8250
Bryan Campbell, *Mgr*
EMP: 39
SQ FT: 500
SALES (corp-wide): 45.61MM **Privately Held**
Web: www.superiorink.com
SIC: 2893 Printing ink
PA: Superior Printing Ink Co Inc
10 York Ave
West Caldwell NJ 07006
201 478-5600

(G-10220)
SUROS SURGICAL SYSTEMS INC
250 Campus Dr (01752-3020)
PHONE...............................508 263-2900
Jim Baumgardt, *Ch Bd*
Jim Pearson, *
Richard M Rella, *
Kent Smith, *
Jeff Hanthorn, *
▲ **EMP:** 87 **EST:** 2000
SQ FT: 26,000
SALES (est): 8.95MM
SALES (corp-wide): 4.03B **Publicly Held**
SIC: 3845 Electromedical equipment
PA: Hologic, Inc.
250 Campus Dr
Marlborough MA 01752
508 263-2900

(G-10221)
TARGET THERAPEUTICS INC (HQ)
300 Boston Scientific Way (01752-1291)
PHONE...............................508 683-4000

Michael Mahoney, *Pr*
Gary R Bang, *
Peter M Nicholas, *
Erik T Engelson, *Research & Development*
Abhi Acharya Ph.d., *Quality CLINICAL AFFAIRS*
▼ **EMP: 325 EST:** 1991
SQ FT: 76,000
SALES (est): 111.62MM
SALES (corp-wide): 12.68B **Publicly Held**
SIC: 3841 Surgical instruments and apparatus
PA: Boston Scientific Corporation
　　300 Boston Scientific Way
　　Marlborough MA 01752
　　508 683-4000

(G-10222)
TARPON BIOSYSTEMS INC
197m Boston Post Rd W Ste 273 (01752-1939)
PHONE.....................978 979-4222
Robert A Dishman, *CEO*
Ard A Tijsterman, *Prin*
EMP: 14 EST: 2007
SALES (est): 232.51K **Privately Held**
SIC: 2834 Pharmaceutical preparations

(G-10223)
TASI HOLDINGS INC (PA)
Also Called: Tasi Group
40 Locke Dr Ste B (01752-1145)
PHONE.....................513 202-5182
John Norris, *Pr*
Jack Goffena, *CFO*
EMP: 15 EST: 2003
SALES (est): 286.84MM
SALES (corp-wide): 286.84MM **Privately Held**
Web: www.tasigroup.com
SIC: 3823 3629 Industrial flow and liquid measuring instruments; Electronic generation equipment

(G-10224)
THIRD WAVE TECHNOLOGIES INC (HQ)
250 Campus Dr (01752-3020)
PHONE.....................608 273-8933
Kevin T Conroy, *Pr*
David A Thompson, *Ch Bd*
Maneesh K Arora, *CFO*
Ivan D Trifunovich Ph.d., *Sr VP*
Cindy S Ahn, *Corporate Secretary*
EMP: 44 EST: 2001
SQ FT: 68,000
SALES (est): 55.22MM
SALES (corp-wide): 4.03B **Publicly Held**
SIC: 2835 Diagnostic substances
PA: Hologic, Inc.
　　250 Campus Dr
　　Marlborough MA 01752
　　508 263-2900

(G-10225)
TWENTYFRST CNTURY BCHMCALS INC
Also Called: 21st
260 Cedar Hill St (01752-3037)
PHONE.....................508 303-8222
Jordan Fishman, *Pr*
EMP: 20 EST: 2004
SQ FT: 8,000
SALES (est): 5.48MM **Privately Held**
Web: www.21stcenturybio.com
SIC: 2836 Biological products, except diagnostic

(G-10226)
UNICORR
300 Cedar Hill St (01752-3036)
PHONE.....................508 481-1100
Suzette Bouvier, *Mktg Dir*
EMP: 15 EST: 2018
SALES (est): 1.76MM **Privately Held**
Web: www.unicorr.com
SIC: 2653 Boxes, corrugated: made from purchased materials

(G-10227)
VALERITAS INC
293 Boston Post Rd W Ste 330 (01752-4615)
PHONE.....................908 927-9920
Geoff Jenkins, *Brnch Mgr*
EMP: 20
Web: www.mannkindcorp.com
SIC: 3841 Surgical and medical instruments
HQ: Valeritas, Inc.
　　293 Boston Post Rd W # 330
　　Marlborough MA 01752

(G-10228)
VCE COMPANY LLC
350 Campus Dr (01752-3082)
PHONE.....................831 247-1660
Praveen Akkiraju, *Brnch Mgr*
EMP: 550
Web: www.vce.com
SIC: 3572 Computer storage devices
HQ: Vce Company, Llc
　　1500 N Grnvlle Ave Ste 11
　　Richardson TX 75081

(G-10229)
VERAX BIOMEDICAL INCORPORATED
148 Bartlett St (01752-3016)
PHONE.....................866 948-3729
James Lousararian, *CEO*
Joe Sanders, *VP*
Paul D Mintz, *CMO*
▲ **EMP: 19 EST:** 2001
SALES (est): 4.03MM **Privately Held**
Web: www.veraxbiomedical.com
SIC: 3841 Diagnostic apparatus, medical

(G-10230)
VIASAT INC
300 Nickerson Rd Ste 100 (01752-4639)
PHONE.....................508 229-6500
Henry Debardeleben, *Mgr*
EMP: 15
SALES (corp-wide): 2.56B **Publicly Held**
Web: www.viasat.com
SIC: 3663 Space satellite communications equipment
PA: Viasat, Inc.
　　6155 El Camino Real
　　Carlsbad CA 92009
　　760 476-2200

(G-10231)
VIKING INDUSTRIAL PRODUCTS
3 Brigham St (01752-3140)
PHONE.....................508 481-4600
Aubrey Elms, *Owner*
EMP: 25 EST: 1975
SQ FT: 5,000
SALES (est): 2.19MM **Privately Held**
Web: www.vikingindustrialproducts.com
SIC: 3621 3625 3651 Power generators; Motor controls and accessories; Household audio and video equipment

(G-10232)
VOGEL CAPITAL INC (HQ)
Also Called: Diamond Machining Technology
85 Hayes Memorial Dr (01752-1831)
PHONE.....................508 481-5944
Mark Brandon, *Pr*
EMP: 26 EST: 1976
SQ FT: 28,000
SALES (est): 8.76MM
SALES (corp-wide): 193.96MM **Publicly Held**
Web: www.dmtsharp.com
SIC: 3545 3291 Honing heads; Abrasive products
PA: Acme United Corporation
　　1 Waterview Dr Ste 200
　　Shelton CT 06484
　　203 254-6060

(G-10233)
WAYLAND MILLWORK CORPORATION
344 Boston Post Rd E Ste 1 (01752-3655)
P.O. Box 377 (01752-0377)
PHONE.....................508 485-4172
Paul Ishkanian, *Pr*
Michael Pappas, *Clerk*
EMP: 12 EST: 1959
SQ FT: 12,000
SALES (est): 1.35MM **Privately Held**
Web: www.waylandmillwork.com
SIC: 2431 Millwork

(G-10234)
WEB INDUSTRIES INC (PA)
293 Boston Post Rd W Ste 510 (01752-4609)
PHONE.....................508 898-2988
John Madej, *Pr*
Mark Pihl, *CEO*
Eric Whitman, *COO*
Megan Glidden, *CFO*
▲ **EMP: 7 EST:** 1969
SQ FT: 2,000
SALES (est): 104.33MM
SALES (corp-wide): 104.33MM **Privately Held**
Web: www.webindustries.com
SIC: 2671 2269 5162 3441 Paper, coated or laminated for packaging; Finishing plants, nec; Plastics film; Fabricated structural metal

(G-10235)
WEETABIX CO
300 Nickerson Rd (01752-4694)
PHONE.....................508 683-3600
EMP: 18 EST: 2019
SALES (est): 2.24MM **Privately Held**
Web: www.weetabixusa.com
SIC: 2043 Cereal breakfast foods

(G-10236)
WYEBOT INC
2 Mount Royal Ave Ste 310 (01752-1976)
PHONE.....................508 481-2603
EMP: 47 EST: 2017
SALES (est): 2.83MM **Privately Held**
Web: www.wyebot.com
SIC: 7372 Prepackaged software

(G-10237)
XCELLEREX INC
170 Locke Dr (01752-7217)
PHONE.....................508 480-9235
▲ **EMP: 100**
SIC: 2836 Biological products, except diagnostic

(G-10238)
XTALIC CORPORATION
260 Cedar Hill St Ste 4 (01752-3075)
PHONE.....................508 485-9730
George Thomas Clay, *CEO*
Christopher Hemme, *Treas*
Jeffrey Mccarthy, *Dir*
▲ **EMP: 21 EST:** 2005
SALES (est): 8.63MM **Privately Held**
Web: www.xtalic.com
SIC: 3479 Coating of metals and formed products

Marshfield
Plymouth County

(G-10239)
INVINCIBLE METAL CORP
Also Called: Revered Metal Roofing
1775 Ocean St (02050-4974)
PHONE.....................781 536-4589
Paul Welch, *Pr*
EMP: 11 EST: 2014
SALES (est): 253.43K **Privately Held**
SIC: 3599 Machine shop, jobbing and repair

(G-10240)
KIRWAN SURGICAL PRODUCTS LLC
180 Enterprise Dr (02050-2110)
P.O. Box 427 (02050-0427)
PHONE.....................781 834-9500
▲ **EMP: 100 EST:** 1979
SALES (est): 9.92MM **Privately Held**
Web: www.ksp.com
SIC: 3841 Surgical instruments and apparatus

(G-10241)
LIGHTHOUSE DISTRIBUTORS INC
864 Plain St (02050-2106)
PHONE.....................781 319-9828
Thomas Pena, *Pr*
EMP: 7 EST: 2008
SALES (est): 508.67K **Privately Held**
Web: www.lighthouse-distributors.com
SIC: 5099 5719 3999 Firearms and ammunition, except sporting; Lighting fixtures; Atomizers, toiletry

(G-10242)
NORFOLK CORPORATION
Also Called: Zrc Worldwide
145 Enterprise Dr (02050-2132)
PHONE.....................781 319-0400
Matthew R Steele, *Pr*
Steven P Collins, *VP Sls*
◆ **EMP: 15 EST:** 1978
SQ FT: 31,000
SALES (est): 3.77MM **Privately Held**
Web: www.zrcworldwide.com
SIC: 2851 Coating, air curing

(G-10243)
PERFECTION FENCE CORP (PA)
635 Plain St (02050-2715)
PHONE.....................781 837-3600
Bryan S Skulsky, *Pr*
Todd A Skulsky, *
EMP: 17 EST: 1993
SQ FT: 14,000
SALES (est): 5.57MM **Privately Held**
Web: www.perfectionfence.com
SIC: 1799 2499 3315 3446 Fence construction; Fencing, wood; Chain link fencing; Fences or posts, ornamental iron or steel

(G-10244)
PRECISION ELECTRONICS CORP
Also Called: Percision Electronics
427 Plain St (02050-2788)
PHONE.................................781 834-6677
Jon L Chandler, *Pr*
EMP: 10 **EST:** 1955
SQ FT: 7,500
SALES (est): 932.98K **Privately Held**
SIC: 3677 3621 3612 3548 Transformers power supply, electronic type; Motors and generators; Transformers, except electric; Welding apparatus

(G-10245)
SCITUATE CONCRETE PRODUCTS
120 Clay Pit Rd (02050-2404)
P.O. Box 636 (02050-0636)
PHONE.................................781 837-1747
Richard W Hoffman, *Pr*
William E Hoffman, *
EMP: 58 **EST:** 1971
SQ FT: 10,000
SALES (est): 16.36MM **Privately Held**
Web:
www.scituateconcreteproducts.com
SIC: 3272 Concrete products, precast, nec

(G-10246)
SCITUATE CONCRETE PRODUCTS COR
120 Clay Pit Rd (02050-2404)
PHONE.................................617 837-1747
Justin Hoffman, *Prin*
EMP: 15 **EST:** 2015
SALES (est): 2.26MM **Privately Held**
Web:
www.scituateconcreteproducts.com
SIC: 3272 Concrete products, precast, nec

Marstons Mills
Barnstable County

(G-10247)
CAPE COD BRAIDED RUG CO INC
Also Called: Jhb Enterprises
75 Olde Homestead Dr (02648-1752)
PHONE.................................508 432-3133
Thomas Benton, *Pr*
Nancy Benton, *VP*
EMP: 15 **EST:** 1983
SQ FT: 3,400
SALES (est): 939.27K **Privately Held**
Web: www.capecodbraidedrug.com
SIC: 2273 5713 Rugs, braided and hooked; Rugs

(G-10248)
RUSSO WOODWORKING INC (PA)
162 Cinderella Ter (02648-1011)
PHONE.................................908 351-2200
EMP: 7 **EST:** 2019
SALES (est): 190.99K
SALES (corp-wide): 190.99K **Privately Held**
SIC: 2431 Millwork

Mashpee
Barnstable County

(G-10249)
BIGWOOD CORPORATION
57 Industrial Dr (02649-3405)
PHONE.................................508 477-2220
Jonathan L Bigwood, *Pr*
EMP: 8 **EST:** 1981
SALES (est): 598.45K **Privately Held**
Web: www.bigwoodcorp.com
SIC: 3599 Machine shop, jobbing and repair

(G-10250)
CAPE COD LIFE LLC
Also Called: Cape Cod Life Publications
13 Steeple St Ste 204 (02649-3287)
P.O. Box 1439 (02649-1439)
PHONE.................................508 419-7381
Brian F Shortsleeve, *Pr*
EMP: 15 **EST:** 2004
SALES (est): 2.37MM **Privately Held**
Web: www.capecodlife.com
SIC: 2721 7941 8742 Magazines: publishing only, not printed on site; Stadium event operator services; Management consulting services

(G-10251)
COASTAL-N-COUNTERS INC
92 Industrial Dr (02649-3401)
P.O. Box 2040 (02649-8040)
PHONE.................................508 539-3500
Mark Ducharme, *Pr*
Stacey Ducharme, *Clerk*
EMP: 12 **EST:** 1997
SQ FT: 4,800
SALES (est): 400.32K **Privately Held**
Web: www.coastalncounters.net
SIC: 2434 2514 5031 5211 Wood kitchen cabinets; Kitchen cabinets: metal; Kitchen cabinets; Cabinets, kitchen

(G-10252)
JIFFY LUBE
Also Called: Jiffy Lube
60 Falmouth Rd (02649-2721)
PHONE.................................508 539-8888
Dan Fellows, *Owner*
EMP: 7 **EST:** 2000
SALES (est): 497.67K **Privately Held**
Web: www.jiffylube.com
SIC: 7549 1389 Lubrication service, automotive; Oil and gas field services, nec

(G-10253)
M COHEN AND SONS
20 Joy St (02649-6504)
PHONE.................................774 228-2193
EMP: 7 **EST:** 2012
SALES (est): 139.82K **Privately Held**
Web: www.mcohenandsons.com
SIC: 3446 Architectural metalwork

Mattapan
Suffolk County

(G-10254)
ECONOMY PLUMBING & HTG SUP CO
Also Called: Economy Plumbing
875 Morton St (02126-2453)
PHONE.................................617 433-1200
Claudio Poles, *Pt*
Francesco Poles, *
Livio Poles, *
John Poles, *
▲ **EMP:** 36 **EST:** 1993
SQ FT: 15,000
SALES (est): 48MM **Privately Held**
Web: www.economyplumbing.com
SIC: 5074 3585 5064 Heating equipment (hydronic); Parts for heating, cooling, and refrigerating equipment; Air conditioning appliances

Mattapoisett
Plymouth County

(G-10255)
BROWNELL BOAT STANDS INC
Also Called: Brownell Boatstands
5 Boat Rock Rd (02739-1325)
PHONE.................................508 758-3671
Peter T Kavanaugh, *Managing Member*
▼ **EMP:** 12 **EST:** 1990
SQ FT: 30,000
SALES (est): 3.24MM **Privately Held**
Web: www.boatstands.com
SIC: 3537 Cradles, boat

(G-10256)
DATA INDUSTRIAL CORPORATION
6 County Rd Ste 6 (02739-1585)
PHONE.................................508 758-6390
Norman Bartlett, *Genl Mgr*
Kevin O'brien, *VP Fin*
EMP: 21 **EST:** 1979
SQ FT: 23,000
SALES (est): 999.21K
SALES (corp-wide): 565.57MM **Publicly Held**
Web: www.dataindustrial.com
SIC: 3823 3824 Flow instruments, industrial process type; Fluid meters and counting devices
PA: Badger Meter, Inc.
4545 W Brown Deer Rd
Milwaukee WI 53223
414 355-0400

(G-10257)
DG SERVICE COMPANY INC
23c County Rd (02739-1584)
PHONE.................................508 758-7906
Grace Knox, *Pr*
EMP: 18 **EST:** 1991
SQ FT: 6,500
SALES (est): 3.2MM **Privately Held**
Web: www.dgservicecompany.com
SIC: 3444 1711 Ducts, sheet metal; Mechanical contractor

(G-10258)
JULIUS KOCH USA INC
15 Crooks Way (02739-1215)
PHONE.................................508 995-9565
Lewis M Coco, *Pr*
Richard Gamache, *
Thomas P Kefor, *
Michael J Sitarz, *
▲ **EMP:** 45 **EST:** 1965
SQ FT: 88,000
SALES (est): 2.36MM **Privately Held**
Web: www.jkusa.com
SIC: 2298 2241 Cordage and twine; Narrow fabric mills

Maynard
Middlesex County

(G-10259)
ACACIA COMMUNICATIONS INC (HQ)
Also Called: Acacia
3 Mill And Main Pl Ste 400 (01754-2651)
PHONE.................................978 938-4896
Murugesan Shanmugaraj, *Pr*
Vincent T Roche, *
John F Gavin, *CFO*
Benny P Mikkelsen, *
Christian J Rasmussen, *VP*
EMP: 124 **EST:** 2009
SQ FT: 121,000
SALES (est): 583.45MM
SALES (corp-wide): 57B **Publicly Held**
Web: www.acacia-inc.com
SIC: 3674 8999 Semiconductors and related devices; Communication services
PA: Cisco Systems, Inc.
170 W Tasman Dr
San Jose CA 95134
408 526-4000

(G-10260)
BELARC INC
2 Mill And Main Pl Ste 520 (01754-2672)
PHONE.................................978 461-1100
Gary Newman, *Pr*
Sumin Tchen, *Ch*
EMP: 24 **EST:** 1995
SALES (est): 3.71MM **Privately Held**
Web: www.belarc.com
SIC: 7372 Prepackaged software

(G-10261)
BMF PRECISION INC
Also Called: Boston Micro Fabrication
8 Mill And Main Pl Ste 310 (01754-2668)
PHONE.................................978 637-2050
John Kawola, *Pr*
John Kawola, *Pr*
Mark A Haddad, *
EMP: 25 **EST:** 2019
SALES (est): 6.68MM **Privately Held**
Web: www.bmf3d.com
SIC: 3577 Printers, computer

(G-10262)
EMPIRAMED INC
Also Called: Empiramed
1 Mill And Main Pl Ste 100 (01754-2652)
PHONE.................................978 344-4300
Gregory Erman, *CEO*
Neil Minkoff, *VP*
Cord Awtry, *VP*
EMP: 7 **EST:** 2011
SALES (est): 490.96K **Privately Held**
Web: www.empiramed.com
SIC: 8731 2834 Electronic research; Pharmaceutical preparations

(G-10263)
MYPERFECTGIG INC
1 Clock Tower Pl Ste 200 (01754-2652)
PHONE.................................978 461-6700
W Blair Heavey, *Prin*
EMP: 24 **EST:** 2007
SALES (est): 970.61K **Privately Held**
Web: www.myperfectgig.com
SIC: 7372 Prepackaged software

(G-10264)
PHOTONEX CORPORATION
200 Metrowest Tech Dr (01754-2636)
PHONE.................................978 723-2200

GEOGRAPHIC

Kristin Rauschenbach, *Pr*
Patrick J Scannell Junior, *CFO*
Phil Francisco, *
Curtis R Menyuk, *Chief Scientist**
EMP: 14 **EST:** 1999
SALES (est): 358.68K **Privately Held**
SIC: 3661 Telephone sets, all types except cellular radio

(G-10265)
VERNE Q POWELL FLUTES INC
Also Called: Sonare Winds
3 Mill And Main Pl Ste 130 (01754-2656)
PHONE..................978 461-6111
Francois Kloc, *Pr*
◆ **EMP:** 60 **EST:** 1927
SALES (est): 10.07MM
SALES (corp-wide): 4.94MM **Privately Held**
Web: www.powellflutes.com
SIC: 3931 5099 Flutes and parts; Musical instruments
HQ: Buffet Crampon
5 Rue Maurice Berteaux
Mantes La Ville 78711
130985130

(G-10266)
WILDLIFE ACOUSTICS INC
3 Mill And Main Pl Ste 210 (01754-2657)
PHONE..................978 369-5225
Ian Agranat, *Pr*
EMP: 30 **EST:** 2003
SQ FT: 5,000
SALES (est): 4.83MM **Privately Held**
Web: www.wildlifeacoustics.com
SIC: 3829 Measuring and controlling devices, nec

(G-10267)
XCHANGE IMC LLC
7 Mill And Main Pl Ste 250 (01754-2692)
PHONE..................978 298-2100
Raymond Desabato Junior, *Prin*
EMP: 10 **EST:** 2012
SALES (est): 490.84K
SALES (corp-wide): 3.68B **Publicly Held**
SIC: 3829 3812 Measuring and controlling devices, nec; Navigational systems and instruments
PA: Trimble Inc.
10368 Westmoor Dr
Westminster CO 80021
720 887-6100

(G-10268)
ZLINK INC
141 Parker St Ste 311 (01754-2180)
PHONE..................978 309-3628
Anupam Sachdev, *CEO*
EMP: 75 **EST:** 2017
SQ FT: 2,318
SALES (est): 1.01MM **Privately Held**
Web: www.zlinkcorp.com
SIC: 7374 7371 8712 7372 Data processing and preparation; Custom computer programming services; Architectural services; Prepackaged software

Medfield
Norfolk County

(G-10269)
ATLANTIC PRINTING CO INC
5 Causeway Ln (02052-2301)
PHONE..................781 449-2700
Barry A Feldman, *Pr*
Robert Feldman, *VP Opers*
Stephen Feldman, *VP Sls*

EMP: 10 **EST:** 1926
SQ FT: 10,000
SALES (est): 456.22K **Privately Held**
Web: www.atlanticprinting.com
SIC: 2721 2741 2731 2752 Magazines: publishing and printing; Business service newsletters: publishing and printing; Pamphlets: publishing and printing; Offset printing

(G-10270)
ELECTRIC TIME COMPANY INC
97 West St (02052-1513)
P.O. Box 466 (02052-0466)
PHONE..................508 359-4396
Thomas Erb, *Pr*
▼ **EMP:** 30 **EST:** 1928
SQ FT: 13,000
SALES (est): 4.42MM **Privately Held**
Web: www.electrictime.com
SIC: 3873 Clocks, assembly of

(G-10271)
KINASET THERAPEUTICS INC (PA)
10 Knollwood Rd (02052-2724)
PHONE..................508 858-5810
Robert Clarke, *CEO*
Roger Heerman, *Treas*
Chris Obrien, *CMO*
EMP: 7 **EST:** 2020
SALES (est): 200.47K
SALES (corp-wide): 200.47K **Privately Held**
SIC: 3841 Inhalation therapy equipment

(G-10272)
MILARA INC
71 West St (02052-1513)
PHONE..................508 359-2786
M Sbrodeur, *Owner*
EMP: 9 **EST:** 2017
SALES (est): 107.57K **Privately Held**
Web: www.milarasmt.com
SIC: 2759 Screen printing

(G-10273)
PERKINS BROTHERS CORP
Also Called: Perkins Pre-Coat
358 Main St (02052-2011)
PHONE..................781 858-3031
John E S Perkins, *Pr*
William S C Perkins, *Sec*
EMP: 20 **EST:** 1993
SALES (est): 7.17MM
SALES (corp-wide): 208.79MM **Privately Held**
SIC: 2439 Arches, laminated lumber
PA: Maibec Inc
1984 5e Rue Bureau 202
Levis QC G6W 5
418 659-3323

(G-10274)
PRECISION SENSING DEVICES INC
93 West St Ste D (02052-1556)
PHONE..................508 359-2833
Anthony J Intrieri, *Pr*
Anthony J Intrieri, *Prin*
Mike Sellars, *VP*
EMP: 9 **EST:** 1993
SQ FT: 1,200
SALES (est): 1MM **Privately Held**
Web: www.precisionsensingdevices.com
SIC: 3674 Semiconductors and related devices

(G-10275)
SEA-LAND ENVMTL SVCS INC
18 N Meadows Rd Ste 1 (02052-2334)
PHONE..................508 359-1085
Richard Waterhouse, *Pr*
EMP: 8 **EST:** 2002
SQ FT: 800
SALES (est): 475K **Privately Held**
SIC: 1389 Lease tanks, oil field: erecting, cleaning, and repairing

(G-10276)
STRATGIC CORP ASSSSMENT SYSTEM
14 Hartford St (02052-1412)
PHONE..................508 359-1966
Kim G Davidson, *Pr*
Kathleen Davidson, *Sec*
EMP: 7 **EST:** 1995
SALES (est): 221K **Privately Held**
Web: www.strategicorp.com
SIC: 7372 Prepackaged software

(G-10277)
THOMAS J CRONIN
107 Harding St (02052-1001)
PHONE..................508 510-2328
Thomas J Cronin, *Prin*
EMP: 8 **EST:** 2016
SALES (est): 234.66K **Privately Held**
SIC: 2952 Asphalt felts and coatings

Medford
Middlesex County

(G-10278)
ACCENT BANNER LLC
17 Locust St (02155-5713)
PHONE..................781 391-7300
Aice R Deitrich, *Managing Member*
Derrek Coss, *Managing Member*
EMP: 10 **EST:** 1939
SQ FT: 800
SALES (est): 612K **Privately Held**
Web: www.accentbanner.com
SIC: 2399 5999 5131 Banners, pennants, and flags; Flags; Flags and banners

(G-10279)
ANTHONY MANUFACTURING CO INC
410 Riverside Ave (02155-4916)
PHONE..................781 396-1400
Anthony Fabrizio, *Pr*
EMP: 10 **EST:** 1967
SQ FT: 10,000
SALES (est): 999.23K **Privately Held**
SIC: 2541 2434 Store fixtures, wood; Wood kitchen cabinets

(G-10280)
ARMATRON INTERNATIONAL INC (PA)
Also Called: Flowtron Outdoor Products Div
17 Locust St (02155-5713)
PHONE..................781 321-2300
Charles J Housman, *Pr*
Sal De Yoreo, *
Edward L Housman, .*
▲ **EMP:** 60 **EST:** 1920
SALES (est): 10.93MM
SALES (corp-wide): 10.93MM **Privately Held**
Web: www.flowtron.com
SIC: 3714 3524 3699 Motor vehicle electrical equipment; Lawn and garden equipment; Insect lamps, electric

(G-10281)
BALLHAUS BEV CO LLC
Also Called: Wehl Plant Drops
101 Mystic Ave (02155-4628)
PHONE..................828 302-5837
EMP: 8
SALES (corp-wide): 78.8K **Privately Held**
SIC: 2087 Flavoring extracts and syrups, nec
PA: Ballhaus Bev Co, Llc
110 School St Apt 2
Boston MA 02119
828 302-5837

(G-10282)
CARR-DEE CORP
37 Linden St (02155-4929)
PHONE..................781 391-4500
Arthur Desimone, *Pr*
Henry De Simone, *Clerk*
Arthur De Simone, *Pr*
EMP: 10 **EST:** 1951
SQ FT: 6,000
SALES (est): 999.63K **Privately Held**
SIC: 1481 Test boring for nonmetallic minerals

(G-10283)
CROSS COUNTRY MOTOR CLUB INC (HQ)
Also Called: Ccmc
1 Cabot Rd (02155-5151)
PHONE..................781 393-9300
Dave Ferrick, *CEO*
Michael Saxton, *Pr*
Sidney D Wolk, *Ch*
Peter Necheles, *Sec*
Peggy Ward, *CFO*
EMP: 1450 **EST:** 1972
SQ FT: 77,000
SALES (est): 23.47MM
SALES (corp-wide): 197.83MM **Privately Held**
Web: www.agero.com
SIC: 7549 7372 8741 6331 Road service, automotive; Prepackaged software; Management services; Automobile insurance
PA: Agero, Inc.
400 Rivers Edge Dr
Medford MA 02155
781 393-9300

(G-10284)
FABRIZIO CORPORATION
410 Riverside Ave (02155-4916)
PHONE..................781 396-1400
Anthony Fabrizio Junior, *Pr*
EMP: 20 **EST:** 1993
SQ FT: 18,000
SALES (est): 2.39MM **Privately Held**
Web: www.fabriziocorp.com
SIC: 2511 Wood household furniture

(G-10285)
FRS COMPANY INC
Also Called: Frs Roofing and Gutter Svcs
11 Salem St Ste 12 (02155-3262)
PHONE..................781 322-6252
Zilma Schuab Lima, *Pr*
Moacir Lima, *VP*
EMP: 15 **EST:** 2017
SALES (est): 1.23MM **Privately Held**
Web: www.frsroof.com
SIC: 1761 3444 Roofing contractor; Gutters, sheet metal

(G-10286)
GENERAL ELECTRIC COMPANY
Also Called: GE
3960 Mystic Valley Pkwy (02155-6920)
PHONE..............................781 396-9600
FAX: 781 395-8066
EMP: 8
SQ FT: 14,389
SALES (corp-wide): 123.69B **Publicly Held**
SIC: 7694 Electric motor repair
PA: General Electric Company
41 Farnsworth St
Boston MA 02111
617 443-3000

(G-10287)
GREENLGHT BSCNCES HOLDINGS PBC (PA)
Also Called: Greenlight Biosciences
200 Boston Ave (02155-4243)
PHONE..............................617 616-8188
Andrey J Zarur, *Pr*
Charles L Cooney, *Ch Bd*
Carole Cobb, *COO*
Susan Keefe, *Interim CAO*
Charu Manocha, *CPO*
EMP: 18 **EST:** 2008
SALES (est): 6.78MM
SALES (corp-wide): 6.78MM **Privately Held**
SIC: 2836 Biological products, except diagnostic

(G-10288)
HERB CHAMBERS MEDFORD INC
60 Mystic Ave (02155-4623)
PHONE..............................617 739-6600
David J Rubin, *Prin*
EMP: 10 **EST:** 2018
SALES (est): 451.6K **Privately Held**
SIC: 2833 Drugs and herbs: grading, grinding, and milling

(G-10289)
HOUSING DEVICES INC
407 R Mystic Ave 32b (02155-6329)
PHONE..............................781 395-5200
TOLL FREE: 800
Thomas Richardson, *Pr*
EMP: 10 **EST:** 1977
SQ FT: 6,000
SALES (est): 2.07MM **Privately Held**
Web: www.housingdevices.com
SIC: 3669 Intercommunication systems, electric

(G-10290)
IZON SCIENCE US LIMITED
Also Called: Analytical Instruments
196 Boston Ave Ste 3900 (02155-4296)
PHONE..............................617 945-5936
EMP: 9
Web: www.izon.com
SIC: 3826 Analytical instruments
PA: Izon Science Limited
U C, 8 Homersham Place
Christchurch CAN

(G-10291)
IZON SCIENCE US LLC
196 Boston Ave Ste 3900 (02155-4296)
PHONE..............................617 945-5936
Johannes Van Der Voorn, *CEO*
EMP: 10 **EST:** 2021
SALES (est): 1.04MM **Privately Held**
Web: www.izon.com

SIC: 5047 5049 3826   Medical laboratory equipment; Analytical instruments; Analytical instruments
PA: Izon Science Limited
U C, 8 Homersham Place
Christchurch CAN

(G-10292)
JASON TRUCKS INC
407 Mystic Ave (02155-6339)
PHONE..............................781 396-8300
James Lawrence, *Pr*
Josephine Lawrence, *Treas*
▼ **EMP:** 19 **EST:** 1980
SQ FT: 10,000
SALES (est): 930.24K **Privately Held**
Web: www.jasontrucks.com
SIC: 7623 3715   Air conditioning repair; Demountable cargo containers

(G-10293)
LABTHINK INTERNATIONAL INC
Also Called: Labthink
200 Rivers Edge Dr Ste 1 (02155-5480)
PHONE..............................617 830-2190
Haimo Jiang, *Pr*
Yunzhong Jiang, *Dir*
Craig Primiani, *Ex VP*
EMP: 12 **EST:** 2012
SALES (est): 2.48MM **Privately Held**
Web: www.labthinkinternational.com
SIC: 3826 5084 8071 8748   Instruments measuring thermal properties; Processing and packaging equipment; Testing laboratories; Testing services
PA: Labthink Instruments Co., Ltd.
No.144, Wuyingshan Road, Tianqiao Dist.
Jinan SD 25003

(G-10294)
LACASCIAS BAKERY INC
418 Main St (02155-6286)
PHONE..............................781 395-8612
Fred Moscaritolo, *Pr*
Sonia Moscaritolo, *Clerk*
EMP: 18 **EST:** 1928
SQ FT: 5,000
SALES (est): 440.38K **Privately Held**
Web: www.lacasciasbakery.com
SIC: 5461 5411 2051   Retail bakeries; Delicatessen stores; Bread, all types (white, wheat, rye, etc); fresh or frozen

(G-10295)
MASS-FLEX RESEARCH INC
18 Canal St Ste 3 (02155-3684)
PHONE..............................781 391-3640
Matthew B Hobbs, *Pr*
Evelyn Pierce, *Clerk*
EMP: 9 **EST:** 1973
SQ FT: 7,500
SALES (est): 473.45K **Privately Held**
Web: www.monocoil.com
SIC: 3568 Shafts, flexible

(G-10296)
RIVERSIDE SHTMTL & CONTG INC
15 Reardon Rd 15 (02155-4624)
PHONE..............................781 396-0070
Raymond Magliozzi, *Pr*
Janet Magliozzi, *Corporate Clerk*
EMP: 15 **EST:** 1997
SQ FT: 10,000
SALES (est): 2.27MM **Privately Held**
Web: www.riversidesheetmetal.net
SIC: 3444 Sheet metalwork

(G-10297)
SUPERIOR PRINTING COMPANY INC
Also Called: Superior Promotions
407 Rear Mystic Ave Unit 34a (02155)
PHONE..............................781 391-9090
EMP: 10 **EST:** 1960
SALES (est): 2.04MM **Privately Held**
Web: www.superiorpromo.net
SIC: 5199 2759   Advertising specialties; Commercial printing, nec

(G-10298)
SYRATECH ACQUISITION CORP (HQ)
22 Blake St (02155-4922)
PHONE..............................781 539-0100
Jeffrey Siegel, *Pr*
Ronald Shiftan, *
Robert Mcnally, *VP*
Sara A Shindel, *
Gary Meek, *
◆ **EMP:** 200 **EST:** 2006
SQ FT: 325,000
SALES (est): 101.76MM
SALES (corp-wide): 727.66MM **Publicly Held**
Web: www.lifetimebrands.com
SIC: 3914 3999   Silverware, sterling silver; Christmas tree ornaments, except electrical and glass
PA: Lifetime Brands, Inc.
1000 Stewart Ave
Garden City NY 11530
516 683-6000

(G-10299)
TRAINCROFT INC (PA)
0 Governors Ave Ste 38 (02155-3080)
PHONE..............................781 393-6943
Michael J Tringale, *Managing Member*
EMP: 25 **EST:** 1998
SQ FT: 1,500
SALES (est): 9.63MM
SALES (corp-wide): 9.63MM **Privately Held**
Web: www.traincroft.com
SIC: 7361 3724 7363 8999   Executive placement; Aircraft engines and engine parts; Temporary help service; Technical writing

(G-10300)
TRUSTEES OF TUFTS COLLEGE
Also Called: Tufts Daily
520 Boston Ave (02155-5500)
PHONE..............................617 628-5000
John Di Biaggio, *Pr*
EMP: 7
SALES (corp-wide): 1.43B **Privately Held**
Web: www.tufts.edu
SIC: 2711 8221   Newspapers, publishing and printing; College, except junior
PA: Trustees Of Tufts College
169 Holland St Ste 318
Somerville MA 02144
617 628-5000

Medway
Norfolk County

(G-10301)
ADVANCED SIGNING LLC
4 Industrial Park Rd (02053-1709)
PHONE..............................508 533-9000
William Mc Conaghy, *Managing Member*
Jo Mc Conaghy, *
EMP: 40 **EST:** 1981

SQ FT: 17,000
SALES (est): 5.03MM **Privately Held**
Web: www.poblocki.com
SIC: 3993 Signs and advertising specialties

(G-10302)
AZZ INC
51 Alder St (02053-2291)
PHONE..............................774 854-0700
Sean Noel, *Brnch Mgr*
EMP: 50
SALES (corp-wide): 1.32B **Publicly Held**
Web: www.azz.com
SIC: 3699 Electrical equipment and supplies, nec
PA: Azz Inc.
3100 W 7th St Ste 500
Fort Worth TX 76107
817 810-0095

(G-10303)
BOSTON SPORTS JOURNAL LLC
Also Called: Bostonsportsjournal.com
4 Daniels Rd (02053-6103)
P.O. Box 160 (02053-0160)
PHONE..............................617 306-0166
EMP: 7 **EST:** 2017
SALES (est): 222.92K **Privately Held**
Web: www.bostonsportsjournal.com
SIC: 2741 7389   Internet publishing and broadcasting; Business Activities at Non-Commercial Site

(G-10304)
CYBEX INTERNATIONAL INC
51 Alder St (02053-2291)
PHONE..............................508 533-4167
Paul M Juris, *Ex Dir*
EMP: 250
SIC: 3949 Exercise equipment
HQ: Cybex International, Inc.
1975 24th Ave Sw
Owatonna MN 55060
508 533-4300

(G-10305)
GENERAL DISPLAY INC
6 Industrial Park Rd (02053-1797)
P.O. Box 224 (02053-0224)
PHONE..............................508 533-6676
Arthur Mastrodicasa, *CEO*
Chris Mastrodicasa, *
Glenn Mastrodicasa, *
▲ **EMP:** 19 **EST:** 1958
SQ FT: 85,000
SALES (est): 373.75K **Privately Held**
Web: www.generaldisplay.com
SIC: 3993 Displays and cutouts, window and lobby

(G-10306)
INNOVATIVE COATINGS INC
Also Called: Innovative Coatings,
24 Jayar Rd (02053-1734)
PHONE..............................508 533-6101
George Maravelias, *Pr*
Irene Maravelias, *Clerk*
Robert Buckley, *VP*
EMP: 17 **EST:** 1983
SQ FT: 30,000
SALES (est): 2.2MM **Privately Held**
Web: www.innovativecoatings.com
SIC: 3479 Coating of metals with plastic or resins

(G-10307)
MEDWAY BLOCK CO INC
120 Main St (02053-1801)
P.O. Box 125 (02053-0125)
PHONE..............................508 533-6701

Michael P Pirolli, *Pr*
Robert Pirolli, *Treas*
Peter Hoffman, *Dir*
Susanne Pirolli, *Sec*
EMP: 20 **EST:** 1992
SQ FT: 4,000
SALES (est): 989.4K **Privately Held**
Web: www.medwayblock.com
SIC: 5211 3271 Concrete and cinder block;
  Blocks, concrete or cinder: standard

(G-10308)
MICROGROUP INC
Also Called: All Tube Div
7 Industrial Park Rd (02053-1732)
PHONE......................508 533-4925
William J Bergen, *Pr*
Geoff Holczer, *
EMP: 150 **EST:** 2002
SQ FT: 110,000
SALES (est): 48.87MM **Privately Held**
Web: www.microgroup.com
SIC: 5051 3312 3498 3494 Pipe and tubing,
  steel; Tubes, steel and iron; Fabricated
  pipe and fittings; Valves and pipe fittings,
  nec
HQ: Te Connectivity Corporation
  1050 Westlakes Dr
  Berwyn PA 19312
  610 893-9800

(G-10309)
NRT INC
Also Called: Our Town Publishing
74 Main St Unit 16 (02053-1822)
PHONE......................508 533-4588
Charles Tashjiam, *CEO*
Nicole Renee Tashjian, *Pr*
EMP: 10 **EST:** 1999
SALES (est): 963.13K **Privately Held**
Web: www.ourtownpublishing.com
SIC: 2741 2711 Miscellaneous publishing;
  Newspapers, publishing and printing

(G-10310)
PARAMOUNT INDUSTRIES INC
42 Milford St (02053-1631)
PHONE......................508 533-8480
Robert Parrella, *Pr*
Richard Parrella, *VP*
John Parrella, *Sec*
EMP: 10 **EST:** 1988
SQ FT: 15,000
SALES (est): 853.46K **Privately Held**
Web: www.paramountindustriesinc.com
SIC: 5091 5094 2396 Bowling equipment;
  Trophies; Automotive and apparel trimmings

(G-10311)
PLASTIC MONOFIL CO LTD
Also Called: Green Mountain Knitting
8 Tulip Way (02053-6204)
PHONE......................732 629-7701
William Wilson, *CEO*
▼ **EMP:** 10 **EST:** 1970
SQ FT: 20,000
SALES (est): 1.58MM **Privately Held**
SIC: 3089 Novelties, plastics

Melrose
Middlesex County

(G-10312)
ACKTIFY INC
142 Franklin St (02176-1821)
PHONE......................781 462-3942
David Ingemi, *Prin*
EMP: 20 **EST:** 2017
SALES (est): 552.33K **Privately Held**

Web: www.acktify.com
SIC: 7372 Prepackaged software

(G-10313)
ATLEE DELAWARE INCORPORATED
9 Clinton Rd (02176-4406)
PHONE......................978 681-1003
Gary Bergholtz, *Pr*
William Berkley, *Ch*
EMP: 10 **EST:** 1953
SQ FT: 22,500
SALES (est): 982.94K **Privately Held**
SIC: 3643 3678 3496 Connectors and
  terminals for electrical devices; Electronic
  connectors; Miscellaneous fabricated wire
  products

(G-10314)
CERAMIC TO METAL SEALS INC
78 Stone Pl Ste 4 (02176-6004)
PHONE......................781 665-5002
Nancy Ingemi, *Pr*
EMP: 14 **EST:** 1969
SQ FT: 7,500
SALES (est): 447.22K **Privately Held**
Web: www.ctmseals.com
SIC: 3679 Hermetic seals, for electronic
  equipment

(G-10315)
CHURCHILL CORPORATION
344 Franklin St (02176-1825)
P.O. Box 761038 (02176-0007)
PHONE......................781 665-4700
Marshall W Schermerhorn, *Pr*
Warren Schermerhorn, *
Rhoda H Schermerhorn, *
EMP: 25 **EST:** 1948
SQ FT: 8,000
SALES (est): 4.53MM **Privately Held**
Web: www.atrbox.com
SIC: 3444 Casings, sheet metal

(G-10316)
DORN EQUIPMENT CORP
27 Upham St (02176-3505)
PHONE......................781 662-9300
Matthew Flynn, *Pr*
Alice Flynn, *Treas*
Phylliss Wilson, *Stockholder*
EMP: 15 **EST:** 1939
SQ FT: 17,000
SALES (est): 1.89MM **Privately Held**
Web: www.dornequipment.com
SIC: 2891 3643 Sealants; Electric
  connectors

(G-10317)
NORTH SHORE PRESS INC
6 Eastman Pl Ste 104 (02176-3933)
PHONE......................781 662-6757
Peter Regan, *Owner*
J Peter Regan, *Pr*
Arthur Neuner, *Treas*
EMP: 7 **EST:** 1989
SALES (est): 172.88K **Privately Held**
SIC: 2731 8249 Books, publishing only;
  Real estate and insurance school

(G-10318)
PROMAX SUPPLY LLC
142 Franklin St (02176-1821)
PHONE......................781 620-1602
EMP: 15 **EST:** 2007
SALES (est): 2.05MM **Privately Held**
Web: www.promaxsupply.com
SIC: 2741 Internet publishing and
  broadcasting

(G-10319)
ROWE CONTRACTING CO
90 Woodcrest Dr (02176-3416)
PHONE......................781 620-0052
Warren C Rowe Junior, *Pr*
Warren C Rowe Senior, *Treas*
EMP: 8 **EST:** 1902
SQ FT: 1,000
SALES (est): 599.1K **Privately Held**
SIC: 1481 6531 Mine development,
  nonmetallic minerals; Real estate brokers
  and agents

Mendon
Worcester County

(G-10320)
MD CHEMICALS LLC
6 Dudley Rd (01756-1087)
PHONE......................508 314-9664
Mike Willis, *Brnch Mgr*
EMP: 37
SALES (corp-wide): 994.42K **Privately Held**
Web: www.mdchemicals.net
SIC: 2899 Chemical preparations, nec
PA: Md Chemicals Llc
  120 Jeffrey Ave
  Holliston MA 01746
  508 314-9664

(G-10321)
RRK WALKER INC
22 Park St (01756-1226)
PHONE......................508 541-8100
Robert Walker, *Prin*
EMP: 7 **EST:** 2007
SALES (est): 161.5K **Privately Held**
SIC: 3842 Walkers

(G-10322)
TECHNCAL METAL FABRICATORS INC
134 Uxbridge Rd (01756-1217)
P.O. Box 317 (01756-0317)
PHONE......................508 473-2223
Mike Candela, *Pr*
Joseph Candela, *VP*
Evelyn Candela, *Treas*
EMP: 15 **EST:** 1966
SQ FT: 1,800
SALES (est): 496.35K **Privately Held**
Web: www.techmetalfab.com
SIC: 3444 Sheet metal specialties, not
  stamped

(G-10323)
VISUAL MAGNETICS LTD
1 Emerson St (01756-1273)
PHONE......................508 381-2400
Dayton J Deetz, *Pr*
Sandra L Deetz, *
▲ **EMP:** 30 **EST:** 2011
SALES (est): 4.37MM **Privately Held**
Web: www.visualmagnetics.com
SIC: 2672 Coated paper, except
  photographic, carbon, or abrasive

Merrimac
Essex County

(G-10324)
H I FIVE RENEWABLES
8 Church St (01860-1500)
PHONE......................978 384-8032
Louise Hart, *Ex Dir*

EMP: 7 **EST:** 2012
SALES (est): 133.22K **Privately Held**
SIC: 2869 Fuels

(G-10325)
JAMES F MULLEN CO INC
Also Called: J F M
51 E Main St (01860-2034)
PHONE......................978 346-0045
Robert J Mullen, *Pr*
John P Mullen, *
EMP: 60 **EST:** 1965
SQ FT: 90,000
SALES (est): 8.28MM **Privately Held**
Web: www.jfmullen.com
SIC: 3599 Machine shop, jobbing and repair

(G-10326)
NSD METAL FABRICATION INC
Also Called: James F Mullen Co
51 E Main St (01860-2034)
PHONE......................978 346-0045
Nicholas M Osgood, *Pr*
David N Hynes, *Sec*
EMP: 8 **EST:** 2021
SALES (est): 601.13K **Privately Held**
SIC: 3499 Metal ladders

Methuen
Essex County

(G-10327)
DMJL CONSULTING LLC
145 Milk St (01844-4664)
PHONE......................978 989-0790
John R Loconte, *Prin*
EMP: 12 **EST:** 2003
SALES (est): 446.19K **Privately Held**
SIC: 3273 Ready-mixed concrete

(G-10328)
DUNKIN DONUTS OF METHUEN
Also Called: Dunkin' Donuts
464 Lowell St (01844-2219)
PHONE......................978 681-8123
Judy Faranre, *Mgr*
EMP: 8 **EST:** 1994
SALES (est): 218.71K **Privately Held**
Web: www.dunkindonuts.com
SIC: 5461 2051 Doughnuts; Doughnuts,
  except frozen

(G-10329)
ELECTRONIC ASSEMBLIES MFG INC
Also Called: Conductrf
126 Merrimack St (01844-6109)
PHONE......................978 374-6840
Dean Gammell, *CEO*
Diane Pessinis, *
Denise Shaw, *
Steve Pessinis, *
EMP: 25 **EST:** 1999
SQ FT: 10,000
SALES (est): 3.89MM **Privately Held**
Web: www.conductrf.com
SIC: 3679 3357 5065 5063 Harness
  assemblies, for electronic use: wire or cable
  ; Coaxial cable, nonferrous; Connectors,
  electronic; Control and signal wire and
  cable, including coaxial

(G-10330)
ELEMENT CARE
209 Lawrence St (01844-3849)
PHONE......................978 655-6195
EMP: 7 **EST:** 2019
SALES (est): 268.94K **Privately Held**

Web: www.elementcare.org
SIC: 2819 Elements

(G-10331)
ESSEX RULING & PRINTING CO
Also Called: Essex Printing
154 Haverhill St Ste 2 (01844-3400)
PHONE.................................978 682-2457
Edward Bonaccorsi, *Pr*
Sandra Bonaccorsi, *Sec*
John Bonaccorsi, *VP*
EMP: 9 **EST:** 1941
SALES (est): 684.71K **Privately Held**
Web: www.essexprintingco.com
SIC: 2752 Offset printing

(G-10332)
GOOBY INDUSTRIES CORP
Also Called: Century Box
45 Chase St Ste 45 (01844-3771)
PHONE.................................978 689-0100
Joanna Kagan, *Pr*
David Kagan, *
Mark Kagan, *
Alvin Kagan, *
EMP: 125 **EST:** 1978
SQ FT: 122,000
SALES (est): 21.08MM **Privately Held**
Web: www.centurybox.com
SIC: 2657 Folding paperboard boxes

(G-10333)
H & H ENGINEERING COMPANY INC
Also Called: Mechancal Engrg Met Fbrication
6 Pine St (01844-6818)
PHONE.................................978 682-0567
Joseph P Helfrich Junior, *Pr*
Richard A Helfrich, *Treas*
Mike Helfrich, *VP*
EMP: 15 **EST:** 1975
SQ FT: 12,000
SALES (est): 2.48MM **Privately Held**
Web: www.hhengineers.com
SIC: 3443 Fabricated plate work (boiler shop)

(G-10334)
HOLOGIC INC
14 Aegean Dr Unit A (01844-1557)
PHONE.................................508 263-2900
EMP: 25
SALES (corp-wide): 4.03B **Publicly Held**
Web: www.hologic.com
SIC: 3845 3844 3841 Ultrasonic medical equipment, except cleaning; X-ray apparatus and tubes; Medical instruments and equipment, blood and bone work
PA: Hologic, Inc.
250 Campus Dr
Marlborough MA 01752
508 263-2900

(G-10335)
JOBART INC (PA)
Also Called: New England Outdoor Wood Pdts
37 1/2 Oakland Ave (01844-3741)
PHONE.................................978 689-4414
Joseph Bartolotta, *Pr*
Joseph Bartolotta Senior, *Pr*
Joseph Bartolotta Junior, *VP*
Kathleen Bartolotta, *Treas*
EMP: 15 **EST:** 1969
SQ FT: 13,000
SALES (est): 3.52MM
SALES (corp-wide): 3.52MM **Privately Held**
Web: www.neoutdoor.com

SIC: 2452 5712 Prefabricated wood buildings; Outdoor and garden furniture

(G-10336)
KEVLIN CORPORATION
Also Called: Cobham Sensor Systems
596 Lowell St (01844-2206)
PHONE.................................978 689-8331
EMP: 130
SIC: 3679 3568 Microwave components; Power transmission equipment, nec

(G-10337)
MASS CABINETS INC
99 Cross St (01844-1654)
PHONE.................................978 738-0600
EMP: 20 **EST:** 1989
SQ FT: 20,000
SALES (est): 3.17MM **Privately Held**
Web: www.masscabinetsinc.com
SIC: 2434 Wood kitchen cabinets

(G-10338)
METALCRAFTERS INC
104 Pleasant Valley St (01844-7204)
P.O. Box 729 (01844-0729)
PHONE.................................978 683-7097
▲ **EMP:** 50 **EST:** 1950
SALES (est): 9.74MM **Privately Held**
Web: www.metalcraftersinc.com
SIC: 3444 Sheet metal specialties, not stamped

(G-10339)
MKS INSTRUMENTS INC
Also Called: Mks Astex Products
651 Lowell St (01844-1855)
PHONE.................................978 682-3512
EMP: 50
SALES (corp-wide): 3.55B **Publicly Held**
Web: www.mks.com
SIC: 3823 Pressure measurement instruments, industrial
PA: Mks Instruments, Inc.
2 Tech Dr Ste 201
Andover MA 01810
978 645-5500

(G-10340)
NEW ENGLAND DIE CUTTING INC
Also Called: Nedc Sealing Solutions
96 Milk St (01844-4620)
PHONE.................................978 374-0789
Kimberly L Abare, *Pr*
David G Abare, *
EMP: 27 **EST:** 1982
SQ FT: 71,000
SALES (est): 8.56MM **Privately Held**
Web: www.nedc.com
SIC: 3544 Special dies and tools

(G-10341)
NHV AMERICA INC
100 Griffin Brook Dr (01844-1867)
PHONE.................................978 682-4900
Yaz Hoshi, *Pr*
▲ **EMP:** 43 **EST:** 1988
SALES (est): 910.87K **Privately Held**
Web: www.nissin-nhv.com
SIC: 3699 Atom smasher (particle accelerators)
HQ: Nhv Corporation
47, Umezutakazecho, Ukyo-Ku
Kyoto KYO 615-0

(G-10342)
NORTHERN LIGHTS INC
15 Aegean Dr Ste 4 (01844-1558)

PHONE.................................978 258-7412
EMP: 7 **EST:** 2019
SALES (est): 450.12K **Privately Held**
Web: www.northern-lights.com
SIC: 3621 Motors and generators

(G-10343)
PARLEX
145 Milk St (01844-4699)
PHONE.................................978 946-2500
Christopher John Hasson, *Prin*
▲ **EMP:** 15 **EST:** 2015
SALES (est): 1.04MM **Privately Held**
SIC: 3672 Printed circuit boards

(G-10344)
PROXY MANUFACTURING INC
55 Chase St Ste 7 (01844-3700)
PHONE.................................978 687-3138
Shawn Foy, *Pr*
Kathleen M Dugas, *
EMP: 30 **EST:** 1988
SQ FT: 30,000
SALES (est): 8.3MM **Privately Held**
Web: www.proxyinc.com
SIC: 3672 Printed circuit boards

(G-10345)
THERMATRON ENGINEERING INC
Also Called: Thermatron
687 Lowell St (01844-1869)
PHONE.................................978 687-8844
EMP: 50 **EST:** 1994
SALES (est): 13.9MM **Privately Held**
Web: www.thermatroneng.com
SIC: 3351 3317 3443 Copper and copper alloy pipe and tube; Steel pipe and tubes; Fabricated plate work (boiler shop)

(G-10346)
TORROMEO INDUSTRIES INC (PA)
Also Called: Kingston Materials
33 Old Ferry Rd (01844-4101)
P.O. Box 2308 (01844-1093)
PHONE.................................978 686-5634
TOLL FREE: 800
Henry Torromeo, *Pr*
Bruce Torromeo, *VP*
Charles Gangi, *Treas*
EMP: 18 **EST:** 1958
SQ FT: 11,800
SALES (est): 10.54MM
SALES (corp-wide): 10.54MM **Privately Held**
Web: www.torromeo.com
SIC: 5032 3273 Sand, construction; Ready-mixed concrete

(G-10347)
ULVAC TECHNOLOGIES INC (HQ)
Also Called: ULVAC NORTH AMERICA
401 Griffin Brook Dr (01844-1883)
PHONE.................................978 686-7550
Wayne W Anderson, *Pr*
Dave Sackett, *
▲ **EMP:** 32 **EST:** 1975
SQ FT: 34,000
SALES (est): 24.62MM **Privately Held**
Web: www.ulvac.com
SIC: 5084 5085 3674 3679 Industrial machinery and equipment; Industrial supplies; Semiconductors and related devices; Electronic circuits
PA: Ulvac,Inc.
2500, Hagisono
Chigasaki KNG 253-0

(G-10348)
ADVANCED BLDG COMPONENTS LLC
321 W Grove St (02346-1473)
PHONE.................................508 733-4889
EMP: 11 **EST:** 2016
SALES (est): 5.73MM **Privately Held**
Web: www.advancedbuildingcomponents.com
SIC: 5031 2452 Structural assemblies, prefabricated: wood; Farm and agricultural buildings, prefabricated wood

(G-10349)
AMETEK ARIZONA INSTRUMENT LLC
Also Called: Ametek Brookfield
11 Commerce Blvd (02346-1031)
PHONE.................................508 946-6200
Mick Pearson, *Mgr*
EMP: 180
SALES (corp-wide): 6.15B **Publicly Held**
Web: www.brookfieldengineering.com
SIC: 3823 3824 3825 3621 Process control instruments; Vehicle instruments; Engine electrical test equipment; Motors, electric
HQ: Ametek Arizona Instrument Llc
3375 N Delaware St
Chandler AZ 85225
602 470-1414

(G-10350)
ANDYS MACHINE INC
Also Called: AMI
23 Abbey Ln (02346-3230)
PHONE.................................508 947-1192
Paul E Singley, *Pr*
Charles Gillis, *
EMP: 30 **EST:** 1995
SQ FT: 17,000
SALES (est): 4.53MM **Privately Held**
Web: www.amimachining.com
SIC: 3599 Machine shop, jobbing and repair

(G-10351)
BOUCHER CON FOUNDATION SUPS
80 Cambridge St (02346-4013)
PHONE.................................508 947-4279
Mike Boucher, *Prin*
EMP: 8 **EST:** 2015
SALES (est): 279.75K **Privately Held**
Web: www.boucherformsupply.com
SIC: 3273 Ready-mixed concrete

(G-10352)
BRODER BROS CO
Nes Clothing Div
154 Campanelli Dr (02346-1055)
PHONE.................................508 923-4800
Steve Valeri, *Genl Mgr*
EMP: 157
SALES (corp-wide): 2.19B **Privately Held**
Web: www.alphabroder.com
SIC: 5137 2339 Sportswear, women's and children's; Women's and misses' outerwear, nec
HQ: Broder Bros., Co.
6 Neshaminy Interplex Dr
Feasterville Trevose PA 19053
800 523-4585

(G-10353)

BUTLER AUTOMATIC INC (PA)
41 Leona Dr (02346-1404)
PHONE.....................................508 923-0544
David Johns Ii, *Pr*
Andrew Butler, *
Paul Cleary, *
Mike Mucci, *
▲ **EMP:** 60 **EST:** 1956
SQ FT: 30,000
SALES (est): 15.76MM
SALES (corp-wide): 15.76MM **Privately
Held**
Web: www.butlerautomatic.com
SIC: 3555 3565 3554　Printing trades
machinery; Packaging machinery; Paper
industries machinery

(G-10354)

**BYRNE SAND & GRAVEL CO
INC**
210 Wood St (02346-2853)
PHONE.....................................508 947-0724
Donald Gallant, *Pr*
William L Byrne, *Pr*
Don Gallant, *VP*
Susan Byrne, *Treas*
EMP: 19 **EST:** 1966
SALES (est): 2.19MM **Privately Held**
Web: www.byrnesandandgravel.com
SIC: 3273　Ready-mixed concrete

(G-10355)

CONCENTRIC FABRICATION LLC
7 Coombs St (02346-2409)
PHONE.....................................508 672-4098
Rob Lorenson, *Managing Member*
EMP: 10 **EST:** 2015
SALES (est): 959.65K **Privately Held**
Web: www.concentricfab.com
SIC: 3446 3312　Architectural metalwork;
Rails, steel or iron

(G-10356)

**D & D PRECISION MACHINE CO
INC**
395 Plymouth St (02346-1624)
PHONE.....................................508 946-8010
Dave Demoranville, *Prin*
Dave Demoranville, *Pr*
Joseph Vallatini, *VP*
EMP: 25 **EST:** 2003
SALES (est): 981.29K **Privately Held**
Web: www.ddprecisionmachineinc.com
SIC: 3599　Machine shop, jobbing and repair

(G-10357)

DI-MO MANUFACTURING INC
Also Called: Di MO Tool
35 Harding St (02346-1013)
PHONE.....................................508 947-2200
Albert S Diaz, *Pr*
EMP: 9 **EST:** 1952
SQ FT: 38,000
SALES (est): 936.77K **Privately Held**
Web: www.di-momfg.com
SIC: 3089　Injection molding of plastics

(G-10358)

EPC CORPORATION
Also Called: Enterprise Power Conversion
25 Wareham St (02346-2456)
PHONE.....................................508 923-9503
William Bastiansen, *CEO*
Bastiansen William, *Pr*
Paul Zigouras, *Prin*
EMP: 9 **EST:** 2011
SQ FT: 12,500
SALES (est): 2.5MM **Privately Held**

Web: www.epc-corporation.com
SIC: 3625　Motor controls and accessories

(G-10359)

GORMAN MACHINE CORP
122 E Grove St (02346-2772)
P.O. Box 512 (02346-0512)
PHONE.....................................508 923-9462
Kenneth P Gorman, *Pr*
Daniel Gorman, *Mng Pt*
Diane Sanford, *Treas*
▼ **EMP:** 20 **EST:** 1953
SQ FT: 15,800
SALES (est): 1.85MM **Privately Held**
Web: www.gormanmachine.com
SIC: 3549 5084　Coil winding machines for
springs; Industrial machinery and equipment

(G-10360)

GURUKRUPA I LLC
422 W Grove St (02346-1456)
PHONE.....................................508 947-1080
Narendra H Patel, *Prin*
EMP: 10 **EST:** 2009
SALES (est): 414.3K **Privately Held**
SIC: 7372　Prepackaged software

(G-10361)

HUB TECHNOLOGIES INC
29 Abbey Ln (02346-3230)
P.O. Box 470 (02346-0470)
PHONE.....................................508 947-3513
Stephen Lane, *Pr*
EMP: 32 **EST:** 2003
SQ FT: 59,000
SALES (est): 5.69MM **Privately Held**
SIC: 3316　Cold finishing of steel shapes

(G-10362)

IDEX HEALTH & SCIENCE LLC
Also Called: Sapphire Engineering
16 Leona Dr (02346-1433)
PHONE.....................................774 213-0200
Keith Besse, *Brnch Mgr*
EMP: 120
SALES (corp-wide): 3.18B **Publicly Held**
Web: www.idex-hs.com
SIC: 3821 7389 3231 3264　Laboratory
apparatus and furniture; Grinding,
precision: commercial or industrial;
Products of purchased glass; Porcelain
electrical supplies
HQ: Idex Health & Science Llc
600 Park Ct
Rohnert Park CA 94928
707 588-2000

(G-10363)

LOUIS M GERSON CO INC
Also Called: LOUIS M. GERSON CO., INC
15 Sumner Ave (02346-1535)
PHONE.....................................508 947-4000
Ronald L Gerson, *Brnch Mgr*
EMP: 10
SALES (corp-wide): 22.06MM **Privately
Held**
Web: www.gersonco.com
SIC: 3842　Respiratory protection
equipment, personal
PA: Louis M. Gerson Co., Inc.
16 Commerce Blvd Ste D
Middleboro MA 02346
508 947-4000

(G-10364)

LOUIS M GERSON CO INC (PA)
16 Commerce Blvd Ste D (02346-1085)
PHONE.....................................508 947-4000
Ronald L Gerson, *Ch Bd*
Christopher Nazar, *

◆ **EMP:** 60 **EST:** 1947
SQ FT: 22,500
SALES: 22.06MM
SALES (corp-wide): 22.06MM **Privately
Held**
Web: www.gersonco.com
SIC: 3842　Respiratory protection
equipment, personal

(G-10365)

MALDEN INTL DESIGNS INC
Also Called: Giovanni
19 Cowan Dr (02346-3700)
PHONE.....................................508 946-2270
John Aucello, *Pr*
Ann Aucello, *
◆ **EMP:** 175 **EST:** 1948
SQ FT: 120,000
SALES (est): 16.38MM **Privately Held**
Web: www.malden.com
SIC: 2499 3499　Picture and mirror frames,
wood; Picture frames, metal

(G-10366)

**MASS ENGINEERING & TANK
INC**
29 Abbey Ln (02346-3230)
PHONE.....................................508 947-8669
Carl Horstmann, *Pr*
EMP: 18 **EST:** 1994
SQ FT: 58,000
SALES (est): 742.83K **Privately Held**
Web: www.masstec.com
SIC: 3412 3443　Barrels, shipping: metal;
Fabricated plate work (boiler shop)

(G-10367)

**MASS TANK INSPECTION SVCS
LLC**
29 Abbey Ln (02346-3230)
PHONE.....................................508 923-3445
EMP: 20 **EST:** 2012
SALES (est): 2.62MM **Privately Held**
Web: www.masstankinspection.com
SIC: 3443 7699　Tanks, standard or custom
fabricated: metal plate; Tank and boiler
cleaning service

(G-10368)

MASS TANK SALES CORP
29 Abbey Ln (02346-3230)
PHONE.....................................508 947-8826
Carl Horstmann, *Pr*
EMP: 25 **EST:** 2003
SALES (est): 3.17MM **Privately Held**
Web: www.masstank.com
SIC: 3443　Fabricated plate work (boiler
shop)

(G-10369)

NICHOLAS IERONIMO
459 Wareham St (02346-3421)
PHONE.....................................508 947-5363
Nicholas Ieronimo, *Prin*
EMP: 7 **EST:** 2004
SALES (est): 113.21K **Privately Held**
Web: www.mulchbynick.com
SIC: 5261 2499 5032 3281　Lawn and
garden supplies; Mulch or sawdust
products, wood; Stone, crushed or broken;
Granite, cut and shaped

(G-10370)

OCEAN SPRAY (EUROPE) LTD
1 Ocean Spray Dr (02349-0001)
PHONE.....................................508 946-1000
Andre Chambers, *Pr*
Randy C Papadellis, *CEO*
Charlie Dulany, *Treas*

◆ **EMP:** 10 **EST:** 1986
SALES (est): 4.6MM
SALES (corp-wide): 1.2B **Privately Held**
Web: www.oceanspray.com
SIC: 2033　Fruits: packaged in cans, jars, etc.
PA: Ocean Spray Cranberries, Inc.
1 Ocean Spray Dr
Middleboro MA 02349
508 946-1000

(G-10371)

**OCEAN SPRAY CRANBERRIES
INC (PA)**
Also Called: Ocean Spray Cooperative
1 Ocean Spray Dr (02349-0001)
PHONE.....................................508 946-1000
Tom Hayes, *Pr*
Peter P Dhillon, *
Daniel Cunha, *
Celina Li, *CCO*
◆ **EMP:** 475 **EST:** 1930
SQ FT: 165,000
SALES (est): 1.2B
SALES (corp-wide): 1.2B **Privately Held**
Web: www.oceanspray.com
SIC: 2033 2034 2037　Fruits and fruit
products, in cans, jars, etc.; Fruits, dried or
dehydrated, except freeze-dried; Fruit juice
concentrates, frozen

(G-10372)

**OCEAN SPRAY INTERNATIONAL
INC (HQ)**
1 Ocean Spray Dr (02349-0001)
PHONE.....................................508 946-1000
Thomas P Hayes, *Pr*
Richard A Stamm, *
Richard A Lees, *
◆ **EMP:** 399 **EST:** 1986
SALES (est): 86.78MM
SALES (corp-wide): 1.2B **Privately Held**
Web: www.oceanspray.com
SIC: 2037 2034 2033　Fruit juice
concentrates, frozen; Fruits, dried or
dehydrated, except freeze-dried; Fruits and
fruit products, in cans, jars, etc.
PA: Ocean Spray Cranberries, Inc.
1 Ocean Spray Dr
Middleboro MA 02349
508 946-1000

(G-10373)

PAVESTONE LLC
18 Cowan Dr (02346-3703)
PHONE.....................................508 947-6001
Patricia Perez, *Mgr*
EMP: 100
Web: www.pavestone.com
SIC: 3272　Concrete products, precast, nec
HQ: Pavestone, Llc
5 Concourse Pkwy Ste 1900
Atlanta GA 30328
404 926-3167

(G-10374)

PIECING PUZZLE INC
25 Wareham St Bldg 4 (02346-2456)
PHONE.....................................508 465-0417
Erica S Mccaffrey, *Prin*
EMP: 13 **EST:** 2016
SALES (est): 345.95K **Privately Held**
Web: www.piecingthepuzzle.org
SIC: 3944　Puzzles

(G-10375)

PROGRESS PALLET INC
98 W Grove St (02346-1418)
PHONE.....................................508 923-1930
Paul Shaughnessy, *Pr*
EMP: 25 **EST:** 2002

SQ FT: 30,000
SALES (est): 3.82MM **Privately Held**
Web: www.progresspallet.com
SIC: 2448 Pallets, wood

(G-10376)
QUALITY ENVELOPE & PRINTING CO
Also Called: Quality Envelope
22 Cambridge St Ste H (02346-2090)
PHONE...........................508 947-8878
Arthur Mcdaniels Junior, *Pr*
EMP: 7 **EST:** 1957
SQ FT: 4,000
SALES (est): 551.41K **Privately Held**
Web: www.qenvelopes.com
SIC: 2752 2759 Offset printing; Envelopes: printing, risk

(G-10377)
RV MANUFACTURING INC
20 Harding St (02346-1014)
PHONE...........................508 488-6612
Ronaldo Vieira, *Prin*
EMP: 7 **EST:** 2018
SALES (est): 276.21K **Privately Held**
SIC: 3999 Manufacturing industries, nec

(G-10378)
TECHNICAL POWER SYSTEMS INC
19 Leona Dr (02346-1404)
P.O. Box 606 (60532-0606)
PHONE...........................630 719-1471
Joseph G Giovanatto, *Pr*
Kurt Padera, *VP*
John R Brophy, *VP*
◆ **EMP:** 20 **EST:** 2000
SALES (est): 2.33MM **Privately Held**
Web: valueadd.sager.com
SIC: 3691 3999 Batteries, rechargeable; Barber and beauty shop equipment

(G-10379)
VERTEX FAB & DESIGN LLC
29 Abbey Ln (02346-3230)
PHONE...........................508 947-3513
▲ **EMP:** 20
SIC: 3441 Fabricated structural metal

Middleton
Essex County

(G-10380)
AUTOROLL PRINT TECHNOLOGIES LLC
Also Called: Autoroll Machine
11 River St (01949-2429)
P.O. Box 448 (01985-0548)
PHONE...........................978 777-2160
▲ **EMP:** 21
Web: www.autoroll.net
SIC: 3555 5084 5085 Printing trades machinery; Printing trades machinery, equipment, and supplies; Ink, printer's

(G-10381)
BEN FRANKLIN PRINT CO INC
177 N Main St Ste 611 (01949-1761)
PHONE...........................978 624-7341
Joseph Schulte, *Dir*
EMP: 7 **EST:** 2019
SALES (est): 263.55K **Privately Held**
Web: www.benfranklinprintco.com
SIC: 2752 Commercial printing, lithographic

(G-10382)
BOSTIK INC
211 Boston St (01949-2128)
PHONE...........................978 777-0103
Joseph Denahey, *Brnch Mgr*
EMP: 200
SALES (corp-wide): 125.67MM **Privately Held**
Web: www.bostik.com
SIC: 2891 Adhesives
HQ: Bostik, Inc.
11320 W Watertwn Plnk Rd
Wauwatosa WI 53226
414 774-2250

(G-10383)
FGC PLASMA SOLUTIONS INC
Also Called: Specter Aerospace
11 River St Ste 3 (01949-2429)
PHONE...........................617 999-9078
Felipe Gomez Del Campo, *CEO*
EMP: 35 **EST:** 2014
SQ FT: 80
SALES (est): 5.06MM **Privately Held**
Web: www.specteraerospace.com
SIC: 3728 Aircraft parts and equipment, nec

(G-10384)
H2O CARE INC
18 Lonergan Rd (01949-2402)
PHONE...........................978 777-8330
Mark St Hilaire, *Pr*
Paul Peter Nicolai, *Sec*
EMP: 10 **EST:** 2014
SALES (est): 978.09K **Privately Held**
Web: www.h2ocare.com
SIC: 5999 1711 3589 5074 Water purification equipment; Plumbing contractors; Water filters and softeners, household type; Water purification equipment

(G-10385)
HCPRO INC (HQ)
Also Called: Greeley Company
35 Village Rd Ste 200 (01949-1236)
PHONE...........................781 639-1872
Jennifer Mueller, *Pr*
EMP: 25 **EST:** 1998
SQ FT: 52,000
SALES (est): 24.64MM
SALES (corp-wide): 36.05MM **Privately Held**
Web: www.hcmarketplace.com
SIC: 8742 2741 8331 2721 Hospital and health services consultant; Newsletter publishing; Job training and related services; Periodicals, publishing only
PA: American Health Information Management Association
233 N Michigan Ave Fl 21
Chicago IL 60601
312 233-1100

(G-10386)
INTELLICUT INC
2 De Bush Ave Unit A8 (01949-1679)
PHONE...........................617 417-5236
Knarik Chavushyan, *Pr*
EMP: 10 **EST:** 2015
SALES (est): 456.45K **Privately Held**
Web: www.intellicutinc.com
SIC: 3599 Machine shop, jobbing and repair

(G-10387)
JAY SALEM INC
230 S Main St (01949-3304)
PHONE...........................978 774-4999
EMP: 9 **EST:** 2007
SALES (est): 283.18K **Privately Held**

SIC: 5712 2394 3444 5999 Outdoor and garden furniture; Awnings, fabric: made from purchased materials; Awnings and canopies; Awnings

(G-10388)
LAB FRNTURE INSTLLTONS SLS INC
11 River St Ste 2 (01949-2429)
PHONE...........................978 646-0600
Michael D Hall, *Pr*
Cathleen J Young, *Treas*
Darlene Hall, *Sec*
Gordon R Hall, *VP*
EMP: 15 **EST:** 2000
SQ FT: 12,250
SALES (est): 4.57MM **Privately Held**
Web: www.lab-furniture.com
SIC: 3821 Laboratory furniture

(G-10389)
LISHA & NIRALI FUEL LLC
223 Maple St (01949-2232)
PHONE...........................908 433-6504
Suresh Kumar Patel, *Prin*
EMP: 7 **EST:** 2011
SALES (est): 249.39K **Privately Held**
SIC: 2869 Fuels

(G-10390)
MK SERVICES CORP
194 S Main St (01949-2451)
PHONE...........................978 777-2196
Robert Faia, *Pr*
Lee Quach, *
EMP: 50 **EST:** 2001
SQ FT: 30,000
SALES (est): 9.47MM **Privately Held**
Web: www.mks-corp.com
SIC: 3545 Precision tools, machinists'

(G-10391)
RPT HOLDINGS LLC
30 Log Bridge Rd Bldg 200 (01949-2284)
PHONE...........................877 997-3674
David L Gershaw, *Pr*
▲ **EMP:** 10 **EST:** 2009
SALES (est): 2.3MM **Privately Held**
Web: www.led-llc.com
SIC: 3646 Commercial lighting fixtures

(G-10392)
SALEM METAL INC
177 N Main St (01949-1676)
PHONE...........................978 774-2100
Jason M Vining, *Pr*
James E Vining, *
EMP: 50 **EST:** 1941
SALES (est): 9.63MM **Privately Held**
Web: www.salemmetal.com
SIC: 3444 Sheet metalwork

(G-10393)
SHELPAK PLASTICS INC
339 N Main St (01949-1614)
PHONE...........................781 844-2046
Andrew Sakellarios, *Prin*
EMP: 9 **EST:** 2012
SALES (est): 455.62K **Privately Held**
Web: www.shelpak.com
SIC: 3089 Injection molding of plastics

(G-10394)
SURGICAL TABLES INCORPORATED
2 De Bush Ave Bldg A (01949)
PHONE...........................978 777-4031
Jason Waldo, *Pr*
Matthew Nekoroski, *Treas*

Rob Nekoroski, *Sec*
Christine Cooke, *Dir*
EMP: 12 **EST:** 2004
SQ FT: 1,700
SALES (est): 2.34MM **Privately Held**
Web: www.surgicaltables.com
SIC: 3841 Surgical and medical instruments

(G-10395)
T G G INC
3 Birch Rd (01949-2261)
P.O. Box 366 (01949-0666)
PHONE...........................978 777-5010
Christopher King, *Pr*
EMP: 35 **EST:** 1977
SQ FT: 20,000
SALES (est): 3.37MM **Privately Held**
Web: www.gtgmach.com
SIC: 3599 Machine shop, jobbing and repair

(G-10396)
TOOL TECHNOLOGY INC
3 Ajootian Way Bldg A (01949-2490)
PHONE...........................978 777-5006
Brian Noel, *Pr*
Gregg Noel, *Sec*
▼ **EMP:** 15 **EST:** 1972
SQ FT: 18,000
SALES (est): 2.49MM **Privately Held**
Web: www.tooltechinc.com
SIC: 3545 Measuring tools and machines, machinists' metalworking type

(G-10397)
WATSON BROTHERS INC
6 Birch Rd (01949-2261)
P.O. Box 803 (01949-2803)
PHONE...........................978 774-7677
David Watson, *Pr*
Michael Watson, *CLRK*
EMP: 16 **EST:** 1987
SALES (est): 875.47K **Privately Held**
Web: www.watsonbrothers.com
SIC: 2434 2431 2499 Wood kitchen cabinets; Millwork; Decorative wood and woodwork

Milford
Worcester County

(G-10398)
AU MILFORD LLC
213 Central St (01757-3458)
P.O. Box 929 (28139-0929)
PHONE...........................508 473-1870
▲ **EMP:** 60
SIC: 3069 Rubberized fabrics

(G-10399)
COMARK LLC (HQ)
440 Fortune Blvd (01757-1722)
PHONE...........................508 359-8161
Arthur Ataie, *CEO*
Arthur Ataei, *
Brian Gosselin, *
Pamela Piasecki, *
Rebecca Callinan, *
◆ **EMP:** 47 **EST:** 2013
SQ FT: 25,000
SALES (est): 24.24MM
SALES (corp-wide): 31.65MM **Privately Held**
Web: www.comarkcorp.com
SIC: 3571 Electronic computers
PA: Source Code Midco, Llc
232 Vanderbilt Ave
Norwood MA 02062
781 255-2022

(G-10400)
DILLA ST CORP
130 Cedar St (01757-5117)
PHONE..................................508 478-3419
EMP: 7 **EST:** 2004
SALES (est): 140.03K **Privately Held**
SIC: 3672 Printed circuit boards

(G-10401)
ELENEL INDUSTRIES INC (PA)
Also Called: Photo Fab Engineering
500 Fortune Blvd (01757-1722)
PHONE..................................508 478-2025
William M Lehrer, *Pr*
Betsy Lehrer, *
EMP: 42 **EST:** 1978
SQ FT: 40,000
SALES (est): 11.06MM
SALES (corp-wide): 11.06MM **Privately Held**
Web: www.photofabrication.com
SIC: 3479 Etching on metals

(G-10402)
EMC CORPORATION
5 Technology Dr (01757-3681)
P.O. Box 9103 (01748-9103)
PHONE..................................508 634-2774
EMP: 25
Web: www.emc.com
SIC: 3572 7373 Computer storage devices; Systems engineering, computer related
HQ: Emc Corporation
176 South St
Hopkinton MA 01748
508 435-1000

(G-10403)
GATEHOUSE MEDIA MASS I INC
Also Called: Milford Daily News
197 Main St (01757-2635)
PHONE..................................508 634-7522
Liz Banks, *Pr*
EMP: 10
SALES (corp-wide): 2.95B **Publicly Held**
Web: www.milforddailynews.com
SIC: 2711 Newspapers, publishing and printing
HQ: Gatehouse Media Massachusetts I, Inc.
48 Dunham Rd
Beverly MA 01915
585 598-0030

(G-10404)
MILARA INC
49 Maple St (01757-3650)
PHONE..................................508 533-5322
Krassimir Petkov, *CEO*
Jordan Naydenov, *
▲ **EMP:** 68 **EST:** 1989
SQ FT: 37,000
SALES (est): 12.76MM **Privately Held**
Web: www.milarasmt.com
SIC: 3549 3555 Assembly machines, including robotic; Printing trades machinery

(G-10405)
MILFORD WOODWORKING CO INC
294 West St (01757-1247)
PHONE..................................508 473-2335
Rudolph V Lioce Junior, *Pr*
Susan Lioce, *Clerk*
EMP: 10 **EST:** 1955
SALES (est): 496.49K **Privately Held**
Web: www.milfordwoodworking.com
SIC: 2434 Vanities, bathroom: wood

(G-10406)
MORNSUN AMERICA LLC
13 Country Club Ln (01757)
PHONE..................................978 293-3923
EMP: 8 **EST:** 2008
SALES (est): 87.65K **Privately Held**
Web: www.mornsun-power.com
SIC: 3679 Static power supply converters for electronic applications

(G-10407)
NANMAC CORP
425 Fortune Blvd Ste 206 (01757-1756)
PHONE..................................508 872-4811
Daniel Nanigian, *Pr*
Kim Nanigian, *
EMP: 31 **EST:** 1956
SALES (est): 4.52MM **Privately Held**
Web: www.nanmac.com
SIC: 3829 3822 Thermoccuples; Temperature controls, automatic

(G-10408)
NITTO DENKO AVECIA INC (DH)
125 Fortune Blvd (01757-1746)
PHONE..................................508 532-2500
EMP: 227 **EST:** 1996
SQ FT: 78,000
SALES (est): 95.6MM **Privately Held**
Web: www.avecia.com
SIC: 2833 Medicinals and botanicals
HQ: Nitto Americas, Inc.
400 Frank W Burr Blvd
Teaneck NJ 07666
510 445-5400

(G-10409)
NORTHEAST CHEMICALS INC
11 Princess Pine Ln (01757-1307)
PHONE..................................508 634-6900
EMP: 11
SALES (corp-wide): 4.77MM **Privately Held**
SIC: 2869 Industrial organic chemicals, nec
PA: Northeast Chemicals, Inc.
2 Tower Center Blvd
East Brunswick NJ 08816
508 634-6900

(G-10410)
NOVA SPORTS USA INC
6 Industrial Rd Ste 2 (01757-3594)
PHONE..................................508 473-6540
Robert Righter, *Pr*
Ruth M Righter, *Treas*
◆ **EMP:** 11 **EST:** 1984
SQ FT: 20,000
SALES (est): 3.35MM **Privately Held**
Web: www.novasports.com
SIC: 2891 5941 Sealing compounds, synthetic rubber or plastic; Tennis goods and equipment

(G-10411)
NOYES SHEET METAL
66 Sumner St (01757-1660)
PHONE..................................508 482-9302
Stephen M Noyes, *Owner*
EMP: 16 **EST:** 2010
SALES (est): 1.53MM **Privately Held**
Web: www.noyessheetmetal.com
SIC: 3499 3444 Fabricated metal products, nec; Sheet metalwork

(G-10412)
NUCOR GRATING
55 Sumner St (01757-4601)
P.O. Box 1238 (15090-1238)
PHONE..................................724 934-5320
Tom Clinard, *Pr*
EMP: 16 **EST:** 2017
SALES (est): 4.92MM
SALES (corp-wide): 41.51B **Publicly Held**
SIC: 3446 Gratings, open steel flooring
HQ: Nucor Canada Inc.
1455 Lakeshore Rd Suite 204n
Burlington ON L7S 2
905 634-6868

(G-10413)
PATRIOT WORLDWIDE INC
Also Called: Nanmac
425 Fortune Blvd Ste 206 (01757-1756)
PHONE..................................800 786-4669
Robert Harrington, *Pr*
EMP: 9 **EST:** 2015
SALES (est): 552.09K **Privately Held**
SIC: 3823 Process control instruments

(G-10414)
PHOTOFABRICATION ENGRG INC (HQ)
500 Fortune Blvd (01757-1722)
PHONE..................................508 478-2025
Charles Lehrer, *Pr*
Betsy M Lehrer, *
▲ **EMP:** 42 **EST:** 1967
SQ FT: 40,000
SALES (est): 11.06MM
SALES (corp-wide): 11.06MM **Privately Held**
Web: www.photofabrication.com
SIC: 3599 Machine shop, jobbing and repair
PA: Elenel Industries Inc
500 Fortune Blvd
Milford MA 01757
508 478-2025

(G-10415)
PROJECT PLASMA HOLDINGS CORP
37 Birch St (01757-5501)
PHONE..................................508 244-6400
EMP: 151 **EST:** 2012
SALES (est): 46.98MM
SALES (corp-wide): 17.3MM **Privately Held**
Web: www.seracare.com
SIC: 2836 Biological products, except diagnostic
HQ: Lcp Srls Holdings, Llc
37 Birch St
Milford MA 01757
508 244-6400

(G-10416)
RENALGUARD SOLUTIONS INC (HQ)
Also Called: PLC Medical Systems, Inc.
459 Fortune Blvd (01757-1723)
P.O. Box 707 (01748-0707)
PHONE..................................508 541-8800
Mark Tauscher, *Pr*
Jim Thomasch, *CFO*
Ken Luppi, *VP*
EMP: 12 **EST:** 1981
SQ FT: 23,000
SALES (est): 2.46MM **Publicly Held**
Web: www.renalguard.com
SIC: 3841 Surgical lasers
PA: Viveve Medical, Inc.
345 Inverness Dr S Bldg B
Englewood CO 80112

(G-10417)
RENTSCHLER BIOPHARMA INC
27 Maple St (01757-3650)
PHONE..................................508 282-5800
Ralf Otto, *CEO*
Stefan Rampf, *CFO*
EMP: 58 **EST:** 2006
SALES (est): 19.76MM **Privately Held**
Web: www.rentschler-biopharma.com
SIC: 2834 Pharmaceutical preparations

(G-10418)
SHIRE
27 Maple St (01757-3650)
PHONE..................................508 282-5731
EMP: 13 **EST:** 2018
SALES (est): 230.29K **Privately Held**
SIC: 2834 Pharmaceutical preparations

(G-10419)
SIRA NATURALS INC
13 Commercial Way (01757-3732)
PHONE..................................508 422-0145
EMP: 24 **EST:** 2018
SALES (est): 670.21K **Privately Held**
Web: www.siranaturals.org
SIC: 3999

(G-10420)
THAT CORPORATION (PA)
45 Sumner St (01757-1656)
PHONE..................................508 478-9200
Gary K Hebert, *Dir*
Leslie B Tyler, *
Robert Gertner, *
Arthur S Appel, *
Paul Travaline, *
EMP: 35 **EST:** 1989
SQ FT: 10,000
SALES (est): 7.3MM **Privately Held**
Web: www.thatcorp.com
SIC: 3679 3674 Electronic circuits; Semiconductors and related devices

(G-10421)
THERMO ICE INC (HQ)
Also Called: IEC Centrifuge
450 Fortune Blvd (01757-1722)
▲ **EMP:** 53 **EST:** 1956
SQ FT: 120,000
SALES (est): 21.13MM
SALES (corp-wide): 44.91B **Publicly Held**
SIC: 3826 Analytical instruments
PA: Thermo Fisher Scientific Inc.
168 3rd Ave
Waltham MA 02451
781 622-1000

(G-10422)
UVA LIDKOPING INC
Also Called: Uva Lidkoping
4 Industrial Rd Ste 4 (01757-3589)
PHONE..................................508 634-4301
Bradford Klar, *Pr*
EMP: 8 **EST:** 2010
SALES (est): 2.48MM
SALES (corp-wide): 1.76B **Privately Held**
Web: www.uvalidkoping.com
SIC: 3541 Machine tools, metal cutting type
HQ: Uva LidkOping Ab
Fabriksgatan 2
LidkOping 531 6
51088000

(G-10423)
WATERS ASSOCIATES INC
Also Called: Waters Chromatography Div
34 Maple St (01757-3696)
PHONE..................................508 634-4500
Chancey L Graziano, *Pr*
EMP: 1500 **EST:** 1980
SALES (est): 40.61MM **Privately Held**
SIC: 3826 Chromatographic equipment, laboratory type

(G-10424)
WATERS CORPORATION (PA)
Also Called: Waters
34 Maple St (01757-3696)
PHONE..................................508 478-2000
▲ EMP: 1290 EST: 1958
SALES (est): 2.97B **Publicly Held**
Web: www.waters.com
SIC: 3826 3829 7371 7372
Chromatographic equipment, laboratory
type; Spectrometers, liquid scintillation and
nuclear; Computer software systems
analysis and design, custom; Prepackaged
software

(G-10425)
WATERS TECHNOLOGIES CORP (HQ)
Also Called: Waters
34 Maple St (01757-3696)
P.O. Box Dept Ch 14373 (60055-0001)
PHONE..................................508 478-2000
Christopher J O'connell, *CEO*
John Lynch, *
Mark Beaudouin, *
▲ EMP: 1000 EST: 1994
SQ FT: 500,000
SALES (est): 790.89MM **Publicly Held**
Web: www.waters.com
SIC: 3826 3829 Chromatographic
equipment, laboratory type; Spectrometers,
liquid scintillation and nuclear
PA: Waters Corporation
34 Maple St
Milford MA 01757

Millbury
Worcester County

(G-10426)
ASTRELLA INK
50 Howe Ave Ste 2 (01527-3264)
PHONE..................................508 865-5028
Joe Astrella, *Prin*
EMP: 8 EST: 2014
SALES (est): 207.82K **Privately Held**
SIC: 2759 2395 Screen printing; Embroidery
and art needlework

(G-10427)
BARRDAY CORPORATION
Also Called: Barrday Advanced Mtl Solutions
86 Providence St Bldg 3 (01527-3922)
PHONE..................................508 581-2100
Tony Fiorenzi, *Pr*
▲ EMP: 260 EST: 1982
SQ FT: 55,000
SALES (est): 51.99MM
SALES (corp-wide): 18.34MM **Privately Held**
Web: www.barrday.com
SIC: 2655 2821 Containers, laminated
phenolic and vulcanized fiber; Epoxy resins
PA: Barrday, Inc
181 Groh Ave Suite 201e
Cambridge ON N3C 1
519 621-3620

(G-10428)
BELLHAWK SYSTEMS CORPORATION
2 Jacques Pkwy (01527-1009)
PHONE..................................508 865-8070
Doctor Peter Green, *Pr*
Peter Green, *Pr*
Emily Green, *VP*
EMP: 7 EST: 1989
SALES (est): 712.05K **Privately Held**
Web: www.bellhawk.com
SIC: 7371 7373 7372 Computer software
development; Computer integrated systems
design; Prepackaged software

(G-10429)
CENTRAL MA WATERJET INC
32 Grafton St (01527-3918)
PHONE..................................508 769-4308
Stephen M Haglund, *Prin*
EMP: 7 EST: 2011
SALES (est): 621.21K **Privately Held**
Web: www.centralmawaterjet.com
SIC: 3541 Machine tools, metal cutting type

(G-10430)
CESYL MILLS INC
95 W Main St (01527-1936)
P.O. Box 133 (01527-0133)
PHONE..................................508 865-6129
Mark Aronson, *Pr*
Louise Miller, *
◆ EMP: 65 EST: 1982
SQ FT: 80,000
SALES (est): 9.67MM **Privately Held**
Web: www.cesylmills.com
SIC: 2211 Pile fabrics, cotton

(G-10431)
DEARNLEY BROTHERS INC
190 W Main St (01527-1416)
P.O. Box 186 (01527-0186)
PHONE..................................508 865-2267
David Dearnley, *Pr*
Thomas Dearnley, *
Jeffrey Dearnley, *
John Dearnley, *
EMP: 10 EST: 1952
SQ FT: 16,000
SALES (est): 470.27K **Privately Held**
SIC: 2281 Spinning yarn

(G-10432)
DISCOVER MARBLE & GRANITE INC (PA)
1 Latti Farm Rd (01527-2132)
PHONE..................................877 411-9900
Victor Deoliveira, *Pr*
Christina Deoliveira, *VP*
Laury Deoliveira, *Sec*
◆ EMP: 65 EST: 2001
SALES (est): 15.9MM
SALES (corp-wide): 15.9MM **Privately Held**
Web: www.discovermarble.com
SIC: 1799 3281 Counter top installation; Cut
stone and stone products

(G-10433)
DOSCO SHEET METAL AND MFG INC
6 Grafton St (01527-3918)
PHONE..................................508 865-9998
David Sauer, *Pr*
EMP: 8 EST: 1987
SQ FT: 7,200
SALES (est): 940.18K **Privately Held**
Web: www.doscosheetmetal.com
SIC: 3444 Sheet metal specialties, not
stamped

(G-10434)
G & W FOUNDRY CORP
50 Howe Ave Ste G (01527-3264)
P.O. Box 68 (02769-0068)
PHONE..................................508 581-8719
Richard Bruso, *Pr*
James Bruso, *
EMP: 30 EST: 1974

SQ FT: 60,000
SALES (est): 2.38MM **Privately Held**
Web: www.gwfoundry.com
SIC: 3321 3322 Ductile iron castings;
Malleable iron foundries

(G-10435)
GRANGER LYNCH CORP
Also Called: Northeast Sealcoat
18 Mccracken Rd (01527-1546)
P.O. Box 319 (01527-0319)
PHONE..................................508 756-6244
Stephen P Lynch, *Pr*
William Cabral, *
EMP: 163 EST: 1981
SQ FT: 8,000
SALES (est): 2.22MM
SALES (corp-wide): 52.37MM **Privately Held**
SIC: 2951 2891 Asphalt and asphaltic
paving mixtures (not from refineries);
Sealants
PA: J.H. Lynch & Sons, Inc.
50 Lynch Pl
Cumberland RI 02864
401 333-4300

(G-10436)
GREAT NECK SAW MFRS INC
Also Called: Buck Brothers
100 Riverlin St (01527-4140)
P.O. Box 192 (01527-0192)
PHONE..................................508 865-4482
Gerald K Sortor, *Genl Mgr*
EMP: 75
SQ FT: 42,000
SALES (corp-wide): 83.58MM **Privately Held**
SIC: 3423 3545 3949 Screw drivers, pliers,
chisels, etc. (hand tools); Gauge blocks;
Sporting and athletic goods, nec
PA: Great Neck Tools, Inc.
165 E 2nd St
Mineola NY 11501
516 746-5352

(G-10437)
JEN MFG INC
3 Latti Farm Rd (01527-2132)
P.O. Box 20128 (01602-0128)
PHONE..................................508 753-1076
Gerald Gendron, *Pr*
Jeffrey Gendron, *
▲ EMP: 35 EST: 1956
SQ FT: 62,000
SALES (est): 3.75MM **Privately Held**
Web: www.jenmfg.com
SIC: 3991 3952 Paintbrushes; Lead pencils
and art goods

(G-10438)
JH LYNCH & SONS INC
18 Mccracken Rd (01527-1546)
P.O. Box 319 (01527-0319)
PHONE..................................508 756-6244
Steven P Lynch, *Pr*
EMP: 32
SALES (corp-wide): 48.18MM **Privately Held**
Web: www.jhlynch.com
SIC: 1611 2951 5032 5211 Highway and
street paving contractor; Asphalt and
asphaltic paving mixtures (not from
refineries); Concrete mixtures; Concrete
and cinder block
PA: J.H. Lynch & Sons, Inc.
50 Lynch Pl
Cumberland RI 02864
401 333-4300

(G-10439)
LAURENCE CNDLE MFG CH SUPS INC (PA)
Also Called: Egan Church Supply
10 West St (01527-2608)
PHONE..................................508 865-6061
Andrew Laurence, *Pr*
James F Laurence, *
Joan Laurence, *
EMP: 44 EST: 1973
SQ FT: 4,000
SALES (est): 4.81MM
SALES (corp-wide): 4.81MM **Privately Held**
Web: www.laurencechurchsupplies.com
SIC: 3999 5947 5999 Candles; Gift shop;
Candle shops

(G-10440)
PENNY PINCHERS BREWING CO LLC
75 Elm St (01527-3104)
PHONE..................................774 696-7885
Jason Rondeau, *Prin*
EMP: 13 EST: 2018
SALES (est): 244.23K **Privately Held**
Web: www.pennypinchersbrewing.com
SIC: 5813 2082 Bars and lounges; Malt
beverages

(G-10441)
PRINTGUARD INC
1521 Grafton Rd (01527-4330)
PHONE..................................508 890-8822
Daniel J Rizika, *Pr*
▲ EMP: 12 EST: 1998
SQ FT: 30,000
SALES (est): 1.03MM **Privately Held**
Web: www.printguard.com
SIC: 3231 Reflector glass beads, for
highway signs or reflectors

(G-10442)
RANGER AUTOMATION SYSTEMS INC
9 Railroad Ave (01527-4122)
PHONE..................................508 842-6500
Fidel Ramos, *Pr*
EMP: 35 EST: 1989
SQ FT: 29,500
SALES (est): 8.44MM **Privately Held**
Web: www.rangerautomation.com
SIC: 3559 Robots, molding and forming
plastics

(G-10443)
STELLAR INDUSTRIES CORP
50 Howe Ave (01527-3264)
PHONE..................................508 865-1668
Peter Hoecklin, *Pr*
▲ EMP: 40 EST: 1985
SALES (est): 13.32MM
SALES (corp-wide): 4.51B **Privately Held**
Web: www.stellarind.com
SIC: 3674 3699 Hybrid integrated circuits;
Electrical equipment and supplies, nec
HQ: Trumpf Photonics, Inc.
2601 Route 130
Cranbury NJ 08512
609 925-8200

(G-10444)
UNITED-COUNTY INDUSTRIES CORP
Also Called: County Heat Treat
32 Howe Ave (01527-3211)
P.O. Box 330 (01527-0330)
PHONE..................................508 865-5885
William J Nartowt, *Pr*

Barbara Ann Nartowt, *
Michael D Brockelman, *
Stephen S Dery, *Ql Cn Mgr*
Chris Kania, *Manager*
EMP: 38 **EST:** 1996
SQ FT: 33,000
SALES (est): 5.46MM **Privately Held**
Web: www.countyheattreat.com
SIC: 3398 Brazing (hardening) of metal

(G-10445)
WELD POWER GENERATOR INC
1529 Grafton Rd (01527-4332)
PHONE..............................800 288-6016
Ed Geary, *Prin*
EMP: 11 **EST:** 2016
SALES (est): 420.68K **Privately Held**
Web: www.weldpower.com
SIC: 3621 Power generators

(G-10446)
WYMAN-GORDON COMPANY
1537 Grafton Rd (01527-4300)
PHONE..............................800 343-6070
Jeff Meyers, *Brnch Mgr*
EMP: 474
SALES (corp-wide): 302.09B **Publicly Held**
Web: www.wyman.com
SIC: 3462 Iron and steel forgings
HQ: Wyman-Gordon Company
244 Worcester St
North Grafton MA 01536
508 839-8252

Millers Falls
Franklin County

(G-10447)
DIEMAND EGG FARM INC
Also Called: Diemand Farm
126 Mormon Hollow Rd (01349-1318)
PHONE..............................978 544-3806
Peter Diemand, *Pr*
Anne Diemand, *VP*
Faith Diemand, *Treas*
EMP: 7 **EST:** 1936
SALES (est): 650.34K **Privately Held**
Web: www.thediemandfarm.com
SIC: 0252 0253 5812 5211 Chicken eggs; Turkey farm; Caterers; Lumber products

Millis
Norfolk County

(G-10448)
BALL SLIDES INC
42 Union St (02054-1247)
PHONE..............................508 359-4348
Janet Howie, *Pr*
EMP: 7 **EST:** 1988
SALES (est): 535.51K **Privately Held**
Web: www.ballslides.com
SIC: 3599 Machine shop, jobbing and repair

(G-10449)
COLLT MFG INC
1375 Main St (02054-1450)
PHONE..............................508 376-2525
Liselotte Ward, *Pr*
Lisa Sellers, *
▲ **EMP:** 32 **EST:** 1969
SQ FT: 45,000
SALES (est): 4.95MM **Privately Held**
Web: www.collt.com
SIC: 3479 3469 Coating of metals and formed products; Metal stampings, nec

(G-10450)
RADIO FREQUENCY COMPANY INC
Also Called: Larose Rf Systems
150 Dover Rd (02054-1335)
P.O. Box 158 (02054-0158)
PHONE..............................508 376-9555
Melvyn H Harris, *Ch Bd*
Thomas W James, *
▲ **EMP:** 30 **EST:** 1946
SQ FT: 26,000
SALES (est): 6.53MM **Privately Held**
Web: www.radiofrequency.com
SIC: 3567 Induction heating equipment

Millville
Worcester County

(G-10451)
PINE TREE CONCRETE PDTS INC
151 Lincoln St (01529-160E)
P.O. Box 603 (01529-0603)
PHONE..............................508 883-7072
John Lesperance, *Pr*
Michael Lesperance, *Treas*
EMP: 7 **EST:** 1979
SQ FT: 6,000
SALES (est): 624.4K **Privately Held**
SIC: 3272 Septic tanks, concrete

Milton
Norfolk County

(G-10452)
G H BENT COMPANY
Also Called: Bent's Cookie Factory
7 Pleasant St (02186-4538)
PHONE..............................617 322-9287
Eugene Pierotti, *Pr*
James Pierotti, *VP*
EMP: 60 **EST:** 1801
SQ FT: 15,000
SALES (est): 512.88K **Privately Held**
Web: www.bentscookiefactory.com
SIC: 2052 5812 5461 2051 Crackers, dry, nec; Eating places; Retail bakeries; Bread, cake, and related products

(G-10453)
JOHN MCGILLICUDDY INC
65 Governors Rd (02186-5432)
PHONE..............................617 388-6324
John Mcgillicuddy, *CEO*
EMP: 10 **EST:** 2010
SALES (est): 589.31K **Privately Held**
SIC: 1389 1521 8741 7389 Construction, repair, and dismantling services; General remodeling, single-family houses; Construction management; Business services, nec

(G-10454)
PIG ROCK SAUSAGES LLC
52 Dyer Ave (02186-1512)
PHONE..............................617 851-9422
Arthur Welch, *Brnch Mgr*
EMP: 16
SALES (corp-wide): 257.11K **Privately Held**
Web: www.pigrocksausages.com
SIC: 2013 Sausages and other prepared meats
PA: Pig Rock Sausages Llc
135 Newmarket Sq
Boston MA

Monson
Hampden County

(G-10455)
DIVERSIFIED METALS INC
49 Main St (01057-1392)
P.O. Box 65 (01057-0065)
PHONE..............................413 267-5101
Benjamin Grant, *Pr*
Darlene Salmond, *
Ben Grant, *
Ernest Hamel, *
◆ **EMP:** 79 **EST:** 1978
SQ FT: 15,000
SALES (est): 23.74MM **Privately Held**
Web: www.wieland-diversified.com
SIC: 5051 3599 Steel; Machine shop, jobbing and repair

(G-10456)
SAFE-T-CUT INC
97 Main St (01057-1320)
P.O. Box 466 (01069-0466)
PHONE..............................413 267-9984
Richard Baer Senior, *Pr*
EMP: 10 **EST:** 1969
SQ FT: 5,000
SALES (est): 926.01K **Privately Held**
Web: www.safetcut.com
SIC: 3545 5251 5085 3423 Cutting tools for machine tools; Tools; Tools, nec; Hand and edge tools, nec

(G-10457)
TRELLEBORG CTD SYSTEMS US INC
Also Called: Trellborg Engnered Ctd Fabrics
152 Bethany Rd (01057-9538)
PHONE..............................413 267-4808
Rick Malo, *Mgr*
EMP: 70
SALES (corp-wide): 276.11MM **Privately Held**
SIC: 2295 Coated fabrics, not rubberized
PA: Trelleborg Coated Systems Us, Inc.
715 Railroad Ave
Rutherfordton NC 28139
828 286-9126

Montague
Franklin County

(G-10458)
ARCHITECTURAL COMPONENTS INC
26 N Leverett Rd (01351-9538)
PHONE..............................413 367-9441
Charles Bellingerp, *Pr*
EMP: 10 **EST:** 1979
SQ FT: 8,000
SALES (est): 421.19K **Privately Held**
Web:
www.architecturalcomponentsinc.com
SIC: 2431 Millwork

Montgomery
Hampshire County

(G-10459)
PECKHAM ENTERPRISES LLC
20 Chamberlain Rd (01050-9751)
PHONE..............................413 862-3252
EMP: 9 **EST:** 2011
SALES (est): 48.93K **Privately Held**

SIC: 2951 Asphalt paving mixtures and blocks

Nahant
Essex County

(G-10460)
THE SCHUNDLER COMPANY
10 Central St (01908-1428)
PHONE..............................732 287-2244
▼ **EMP:** 20 **EST:** 1951
SALES (est): 6.4MM
SALES (corp-wide): 253.06K **Privately Held**
Web: www.schundler.com
SIC: 3295 Perlite, aggregate or expanded
PA: Normiska Corporation
15 Suffolk St E
Guelph ON N1H 2
519 780-0955

Nantucket
Nantucket County

(G-10461)
CONCORD ELECTRIC SUPPLY LTD
Also Called: Concord Electric Supply
5 Teasdale Cir (02554-3100)
PHONE..............................774 325-5142
EMP: 710
SALES (corp-wide): 719.67K **Privately Held**
SIC: 5063 3699 Electrical supplies, nec; Electrical equipment and supplies, nec
HQ: Concord Electric Supply Limited
2701 Boston Rd Ste 100
Wilbraham MA 01095
413 682-0018

(G-10462)
E W WINSHIP LTD INC
Also Called: Nantucket Looms
51 Main St (02554-3542)
P.O. Box 1510 (02554-1510)
PHONE..............................508 228-1908
Elizabeth Winship, *Pr*
Betty Browning, *Treas*
▲ **EMP:** 8 **EST:** 1968
SQ FT: 2,000
SALES (est): 1.54MM **Privately Held**
Web: www.nantucketlooms.com
SIC: 2221 5949 2241 2231 Broadwoven fabric mills, manmade; Fabric stores piece goods; Narrow fabric mills; Broadwoven fabric mills, wool

(G-10463)
ERICA WILSON INC (PA)
Also Called: Erica Wilson Needle Works
16 N Liberty St (02554-2140)
PHONE..............................212 348-6196
Erica Wilson Kagan, *Pr*
Vladimir Kagan, *VP*
Vanessa Diserio, *Genl Mgr*
▼ **EMP:** 12 **EST:** 1963
SALES (est): 2.25MM
SALES (corp-wide): 2.25MM **Privately Held**
Web: www.ericawilson.com
SIC: 5949 5961 3999 5092 Needlework goods and supplies; Mail order house, nec; Sewing kits, novelty; Arts and crafts equipment and supplies

(G-10464)
LEMON PRESS MARKET LLC
29 Center St (02554-3687)
PHONE.............................508 228-3800
Darya Afshari, *Prin*
EMP: 8 **EST:** 2015
SALES (est): 536.62K **Privately Held**
Web: www.lemonpressnantucket.com
SIC: 2741 Miscellaneous publishing

(G-10465)
LONGFIN LLC
P.O. Box 427 (02554-0427)
PHONE.............................508 228-4266
Jim Hills, *Managing Member*
EMP: 11 **EST:** 2011
SALES (est): 1.24MM **Privately Held**
SIC: 1442 Construction sand and gravel

(G-10466)
WATER CLOSET LLC
9 Sparks Ave (02554-3952)
PHONE.............................508 228-2828
Megan Turner, *Managing Member*
EMP: 10 **EST:** 2004
SALES (est): 617.52K **Privately Held**
Web: www.nantucketwc.com
SIC: 1799 2434 Kitchen cabinet installation;
Wood kitchen cabinets

Natick
Middlesex County

(G-10467)
ALPS SPORTSWEAR MFG CO INC
5 Commonwealth Rd Ste 1a (01760-1526)
PHONE.............................978 685-5159
Marvin F Axelrod, *Pr*
▲ **EMP:** 15 **EST:** 1931
SQ FT: 50,000
SALES (est): 715.5K **Privately Held**
SIC: 2253 Sweaters and sweater coats, knit

(G-10468)
ALTEC INC
23 Strathmore Rd Ste 2 (01760-2444)
PHONE.............................508 545-8200
Devi Deluca, *CEO*
Carlo J Deluca, *Pr*
EMP: 16 **EST:** 1997
SALES (est): 1.04MM **Privately Held**
Web: www.altec.com
SIC: 3531 Construction machinery

(G-10469)
AMERICAN GIRL BRANDS LLC
1245 Worcester St Ste 109 (01760-1515)
PHONE.............................508 810-3461
EMP: 23
SALES (corp-wide): 5.43B **Publicly Held**
Web: www.americangirl.com
SIC: 5945 2731 Dolls and accessories;
Book publishing
HQ: American Girl Brands, Llc
8400 Fairway Pl
Middleton WI 53562
608 836-4848

(G-10470)
ANACONDA USA INC
154 E Central St (01760-3644)
P.O. Box 358 (02019-0358)
PHONE.............................800 285-5721
Eamon Mcmahon, *Pr*
▲ **EMP:** 16 **EST:** 2009
SALES (est): 2.46MM **Privately Held**
Web: www.anacondaequipment.com

SIC: 3535 Conveyors and conveying
equipment

(G-10471)
BUSEK CO INC
11 Tech Cir (01760-1023)
PHONE.............................508 655-5565
EMP: 50 **EST:** 1985
SALES (est): 24.36MM **Privately Held**
Web: www.busek.com
SIC: 3769 3764 Space vehicle equipment,
nec; Space propulsion units and parts

(G-10472)
COGNEX CORPORATION (PA)
Also Called: Cognex
1 Vision Dr (01760-2077)
PHONE.............................508 650-3000
Robert J Willett, *Pr*
Robert J Shillman, *CCO**
Sheila M Dipalma, *Ex VP*
Carl Gerst, *Ex VP*
Paul D Todgham, *Sr VP*
▲ **EMP:** 400 **EST:** 1981
SQ FT: 100,000
SALES (est): 1.01B
SALES (corp-wide): 1.01B **Publicly Held**
Web: www.cognex.com
SIC: 3823 Process control instruments

(G-10473)
COGNEX EUROPE INC (HQ)
Also Called: Cognex
1 Vision Dr (01760-2083)
PHONE.............................855 426-4639
EMP: 122 **EST:** 2014
SALES (est): 2.34MM
SALES (corp-wide): 1.01B **Publicly Held**
Web: www.cognex.com
SIC: 3823 Process control instruments
PA: Cognex Corporation
1 Vision Dr
Natick MA 01760
508 650-3000

(G-10474)
COGNEX GERMANY INC
Also Called: Cognex
1 Vision Dr (01760-2083)
PHONE.............................508 650-3000
EMP: 58 **EST:** 1992
SALES (est): 4.41MM
SALES (corp-wide): 1.01B **Publicly Held**
Web: www.cognex.com
SIC: 3841 Eye examining instruments and
apparatus
PA: Cognex Corporation
1 Vision Dr
Natick MA 01760
508 650-3000

(G-10475)
COGNEX INTERNATIONAL INC (HQ)
Also Called: Cognex
1 Vision Dr (01760-2083)
PHONE.............................508 650-3000
Robert J Shillman, *Ch*
Robert Willett, ***
Richard A Morin, ***
Patrick A Alias, ***
Theodor Krantz, ***
EMP: 9 **EST:** 1992
SALES (est): 48.17MM
SALES (corp-wide): 1.01B **Publicly Held**
Web: www.cognex.com
SIC: 3823 Computer interface equipment,
for industrial process control
PA: Cognex Corporation
1 Vision Dr

Natick MA 01760
508 650-3000

(G-10476)
DEBCO MACHINE INC
85 North Ave (01760-3556)
PHONE.............................508 655-4469
Daniel E Collari, *Pr*
Helen Donnelly, *Contrlr*
EMP: 10 **EST:** 1974
SQ FT: 10,000
SALES (est): 946.87K **Privately Held**
Web: www.kerrielegend.com
SIC: 3599 Machine shop, jobbing and repair

(G-10477)
DELSYS INC
23 Strathmore Rd Ste 1 (01760-2444)
P.O. Box 1167 (01701-1167)
PHONE.............................508 545-8200
Carlo J De Luca, *Pr*
Devi Bheemappa, *VP Mktg*
Gianluca De Luca, *VP*
EMP: 10 **EST:** 1993
SQ FT: 3,000
SALES (est): 2.01MM **Privately Held**
Web: www.delsys.com
SIC: 3845 Electromedical equipment

(G-10478)
DOGWATCH INC (PA)
10 Michigan Dr (01760-1342)
PHONE.............................508 650-0600
Frederick P King, *Pr*
▲ **EMP:** 7 **EST:** 1990
SQ FT: 10,000
SALES (est): 4.46MM **Privately Held**
Web: www.dogwatch.com
SIC: 3699 0752 1799 Security control
equipment and systems; Animal specialty
services; Fence construction

(G-10479)
EIDOLON CORPORATION
3 Erie Dr (01760-1312)
PHONE.............................781 400-0586
EMP: 8 **EST:** 1984
SQ FT: 5,000
SALES (est): 365.52K **Privately Held**
Web: www.slitlamp.com
SIC: 3827 Lenses, optical: all types except
ophthalmic

(G-10480)
ELECTRIC HYDROGEN CO
1 Strathmore Rd (01760-2418)
PHONE.............................617 546-5710
Raffi Garabedian, *CEO*
Derek Warnick, ***
EMP: 50 **EST:** 2020
SALES (est): 12.01MM **Privately Held**
Web: www.eh2.com
SIC: 2813 Industrial gases

(G-10481)
GENELEC INC
7 Tech Cir (01760-1023)
PHONE.............................508 652-0900
▲ **EMP:** 11 **EST:** 1996
SQ FT: 10,000
SALES (est): 4.85MM
SALES (corp-wide): 65.84MM **Privately Held**
Web: www.genelec.com
SIC: 3651 7629 Loudspeakers,
electrodynamic or magnetic; Electrical
repair shops
PA: Genelec Oy
Olvitie 5
Iisalmi 74100
1783881

(G-10482)
HKD TURBO
15 Mercer Rd (01760-2414)
PHONE.............................508 878-3798
Charles Santry, *Pr*
EMP: 10 **EST:** 2013
SALES (est): 181.73K **Privately Held**
Web: www.hkdsnowmakers.com
SIC: 3585 Refrigeration and heating
equipment

(G-10483)
INVETX INC
22 Strathmore Rd (01760-2453)
PHONE.............................802 233-3103
EMP: 10 **EST:** 2018
SALES (est): 720.59K **Privately Held**
Web: www.invetx.com
SIC: 2834 Pharmaceutical preparations

(G-10484)
KYROMINA OIL CORPORATION
2 Austin Way (01760-2139)
PHONE.............................508 651-8284
Emad Antony, *Pr*
EMP: 7 **EST:** 2015
SALES (est): 249.53K **Privately Held**
SIC: 1311 Crude petroleum production

(G-10485)
MATHWORKS INC
3 Apple Hill Dr (01760-2098)
PHONE.............................508 647-7000
Jack Little, *Pr*
EMP: 900
SALES (corp-wide): 1.3B **Privately Held**
Web: www.mathworks.com
SIC: 7371 3823 8222 Computer software
development; Process control instruments;
Junior colleges
PA: The Mathworks Inc
1 Apple Hill Dr
Natick MA 01760
508 647-7000

(G-10486)
MATHWORKS INC (PA)
1 Apple Hill Dr (01760-2072)
PHONE.............................508 647-7000
Jack Little, *Pr*
Jeanne O'keefe, *Treas*
Steve Bangert, ***
Cleve Moler, ***
Vijay Raghavan, ***
EMP: 900 **EST:** 1984
SQ FT: 260,000
SALES: 1.3B
SALES (corp-wide): 1.3B **Privately Held**
Web: www.mathworks.com
SIC: 7371 3823 8222 Computer software
development; Process control instruments;
Junior colleges

(G-10487)
MCS INDUSTRIES INC
202 N Main St (01760-1133)
PHONE.............................508 651-3755
EMP: 10 **EST:** 2009
SALES (est): 498.33K **Privately Held**
Web: www.mcsindustries.com
SIC: 3999 Manufacturing industries, nec

(G-10488)
NEWTON DISTRIBUTING CO INC
Also Called: Newton
245 W Central St (01760-3774)
P.O. Box 650159 (02465-0159)
PHONE.............................617 969-4002
Catherine Rose Lafave, *Pr*

Lance Lafave, *VP*
EMP: 12 **EST:** 2002
SALES (est): 9.03MM **Privately Held**
Web: www.newtondistributing.com
SIC: 5074 5063 2542   Plumbing and
hydronic heating supplies; Electrical
supplies, nec; Partitions and fixtures,
except wood

(G-10489)
ORGENESIS INC (PA)
27 Strathmore Rd Ofc 5 (01760-2442)
PHONE.................................480 659-6404
Vered Caplan, *Ch Bd*
Neil Reithinger, *CFO*
EMP: 13 **EST:** 2008
SALES (est): 36.02MM **Publicly Held**
Web: www.orgenesis.com
SIC: 2834   Pharmaceutical preparations

(G-10490)
PHILIPS NORTH AMERICA LLC
Also Called: E D A X International Division
12 Michigan Dr (01760-1339)
PHONE.................................508 647-1130
EMP: 67
SALES (corp-wide): 18.51B **Privately Held**
Web: usa.philips.com
SIC: 3826   Analytical instruments
HQ: Philips North America Llc
222 Jacobs St Fl 3
Cambridge MA 02141
617 245-5900

(G-10491)
PIC PHARMACEUTICAL INC
40 Nouvelle Way Unit N947 (01760-6513)
PHONE.................................617 947-3883
Firas Butty, *Prin*
EMP: 8 **EST:** 2016
SALES (est): 212.16K **Privately Held**
SIC: 2834   Pharmaceutical preparations

(G-10492)
PILLAR BIOSCIENCES INC
9 Strathmore Rd (01760-2418)
PHONE.................................781 856-5568
EMP: 85 **EST:** 2016
SALES (est): 5.21MM **Privately Held**
Web: www.pillarbiosci.com
SIC: 2836   Biological products, except
diagnostic

(G-10493)
PPJ LLC (PA)
Also Called: Customic Adjustable Bedz
2 Carsha Dr (01760-5862)
PHONE.................................508 650-3500
◆ **EMP:** 12 **EST:** 2010
SQ FT: 500
SALES (est): 2.51MM
SALES (corp-wide): 2.51MM **Privately
Held**
SIC: 2515   Mattresses and bedsprings

(G-10494)
PRECISION SYSTEMS INC
16 Tech Cir Ste 100 (01760-1038)
PHONE.................................508 655-7010
Charles A Bell, *Pr*
Ann C Bell, *
EMP: 25 **EST:** 1962
SQ FT: 33,000
SALES (est): 2.42MM **Privately Held**
Web: www.precisionsystemsinc.com
SIC: 3841 3826   Surgical and medical
instruments; Analytical instruments

(G-10495)
**REGENOCELL THERAPEUTICS
INC**
16 David Dr (01760-3538)
PHONE.................................508 651-1598
James Frank Mongiardo, *Ch Bd*
James Mongiardo, *Ch Bd*
Joanna C Coogan, *Sec*
▲ **EMP:** 9 **EST:** 2008
SALES (est): 522.7K **Privately Held**
Web: www.regenocell.com
SIC: 2835   Diagnostic substances

(G-10496)
SALISBURY SALES INC
214 N Main St Ste 103 (01760-1131)
PHONE.................................508 907-6610
David S Missle, *Prin*
EMP: 9 **EST:** 2011
SALES (est): 453.19K **Privately Held**
Web: www.salisburysales.com
SIC: 2759   Screen printing

(G-10497)
**SIGMA RESEARCH
BIOCHEMICALS**
1 Strathmore Rd (01760-2418)
PHONE.................................781 237-3828
Frank Wicks, *VP*
EMP: 9
SALES (corp-wide): 23.09B **Privately Held**
Web: www.resbio.com
SIC: 2836 8731   Biological products, except
diagnostic; Commercial physical research
HQ: Sigma Research Biochemicals Inc
3 Strathmore Rd
Natick MA

(G-10498)
SNOW ECONOMICS INC
Also Called: Hkd Snowmakers
15 Mercer Rd (01760-2414)
PHONE.................................508 655-3232
EMP: 7 **EST:** 1992
SALES (est): 1.33MM **Privately Held**
Web: www.snowgun.com
SIC: 3585   Snowmaking machinery

(G-10499)
STRATCOMM INC
Also Called: Strategic Communications
24 Superior Dr Ste 103 (01760-1535)
PHONE.................................508 907-7000
Robert J George, *CEO*
EMP: 170 **EST:** 1978
SQ FT: 8,000
SALES (est): 9.74MM **Privately Held**
Web: www.stratcomminc.com
SIC: 8742 2741 8399   Management
consulting services; Technical manual and
paper publishing; Social service information
exchange

(G-10500)
VINEYARD BRANDS LLC
24 Elmwood Ave (01760-5804)
PHONE.................................508 653-5458
EMP: 10 **EST:** 2018
SALES (est): 66K **Privately Held**
SIC: 2084   Wines

(G-10501)
ZYNO MEDICAL LLC
177 Pine St (01760-1331)
PHONE.................................508 650-2008
Chao Young Lee, *Pr*
Lowell Warner, *VP*
▲ **EMP:** 18 **EST:** 2007
SQ FT: 7,000

SALES (est): 5.27MM **Privately Held**
Web: www.zynomed.com
SIC: 3841   Surgical and medical instruments

Needham
Norfolk County

(G-10502)
ACCUFUND INC
400 Hillside Ave Ste 5 (02494-1226)
PHONE.................................781 433-0233
Peter J Stam, *Pr*
EMP: 9 **EST:** 2001
SQ FT: 1,500
SALES (est): 2.61MM
SALES (corp-wide): 370.24MM **Publicly
Held**
Web: www.accufund.com
SIC: 7372   Business oriented computer
software
PA: I3 Verticals, Inc.
40 Burton Hills Blvd # 415
Nashville TN 37215
615 465-4487

(G-10503)
ACTIFIO FEDERAL INC
105 Cabot St Ste 301e (02494-2801)
PHONE.................................781 795-9182
Ashutosh Ashutosh, *Sec*
John Meyers, *CEO*
EMP: 10 **EST:** 2014
SQ FT: 100
SALES (est): 650.51K **Privately Held**
Web: www.actifio.com
SIC: 7372 7389   Application computer
software; Business Activities at Non-
Commercial Site

(G-10504)
ADAPTIVE NETWORKS INC
123 Highland Ave (02494-3005)
PHONE.................................781 444-4170
Michael B Propp, *Pr*
David Propp, *VP*
EMP: 20 **EST:** 1983
SQ FT: 3,000
SALES (est): 2.34MM **Privately Held**
Web: www.adaptivenetworks.com
SIC: 3663   Radio and t.v. communications
equipment

(G-10505)
ARINSIGHTS LLC
163 Highland Ave # 1038 (02494-3025)
PHONE.................................508 233-3494
Andy Zimmerman, *CEO*
Crystal Golightly, *Customer Service
Operations*
Ed Capps, *Global Sales Vice President*
EMP: 20 **EST:** 2004
SALES (est): 7MM **Privately Held**
Web: www.arinsights.com
SIC: 7372   Publisher's computer software

(G-10506)
BEES MANUFACTURING LLC
40 Wildwood Dr (02492-2736)
PHONE.................................781 400-1280
Mark Leskanic, *Managing Member*
Louis J Quattrucci Junior, *Prin*
EMP: 8 **EST:** 2003
SQ FT: 4,500
SALES (est): 705K **Privately Held**
SIC: 3599   Machine shop, jobbing and repair

(G-10507)
CHILLYBEAR INC (PA)
Also Called: Chillybars Tddy Dog Bntown Brn
6 Brook Rd (02494-2904)
PHONE.................................781 455-6321
Ted Pidcock, *Prin*
Edward P Pidcock, *Pr*
EMP: 13 **EST:** 2000
SQ FT: 5,400
SALES (est): 3.93MM **Privately Held**
SIC: 5651 5699 2261 2396   Unisex clothing
stores; Customized clothing and apparel;
Screen printing of cotton broadwoven
fabrics; Automotive and apparel trimmings

(G-10508)
DIGITAL 128 FIRST AVENUE LLC
128 1st Ave (02494-2805)
PHONE.................................781 726-7736
Maidad Rabina, *Mgr*
EMP: 40 **EST:** 2009
SALES (est): 2.66MM
SALES (corp-wide): 4.69B **Privately Held**
SIC: 3661   Telephone and telegraph
apparatus
HQ: Digital Realty Trust, L.P.
5707 Sw Pkwy Bldg 1
Austin TX 78735
737 281-0101

(G-10509)
ENCORE FIRE PROTECTION ✪
67 4th Ave (02494-2704)
PHONE.................................617 903-3191
EMP: 10 **EST:** 2022
SALES (est): 1.69MM **Privately Held**
Web: www.encorefireprotection.com
SIC: 3569   Firefighting and related equipment

(G-10510)
F W WEBB COMPANY
100 Highland Ave (02494-3006)
PHONE.................................781 247-0300
John Pope, *Brnch Mgr*
EMP: 10
SALES (corp-wide): 1.02B **Privately Held**
Web: www.fwwebb.com
SIC: 5251 5074 5072 3432   Pumps and
pumping equipment; Plumbing fittings and
supplies; Hardware; Plumbing fixture
fittings and trim
PA: F. W. Webb Company
160 Middlesex Tpke
Bedford MA 01730
781 272-6600

(G-10511)
FRENCH PRESS LLC
74 Chapel St (02492-2602)
PHONE.................................781 400-2660
Raji D Spencer, *Pr*
EMP: 10 **EST:** 2015
SALES (est): 418.53K **Privately Held**
Web: www.frenchpressbakery.com
SIC: 2741   Miscellaneous publishing

(G-10512)
HOPE INC
333 Reservoir St (02494-3145)
PHONE.................................781 455-1145
Owen T Rielly, *Pr*
Thomas M Rielly, *
Kimberly Rielly, *
EMP: 30 **EST:** 2021
SALES (est): 2.26MM
SALES (corp-wide): 7.38MM **Privately
Held**

SIC: 5085 5084 3492 Industrial supplies; Hydraulic systems equipment and supplies; Control valves, aircraft: hydraulic and pneumatic
PA: Genalco, Inc.
333 Reservoir St
Needham MA 02494
781 444-9500

(G-10513)
IDG COMMUNICATIONS INC (DH)
140 Kendrick St Bldg B (02494-2742)
P.O. Box 1912 (01701-0112)
PHONE................................508 872-8200
Kumaran Ramanathan, *Pr*
Edward B Bloom, *
John P O'malley, *COO*
Eric Koepele, *CCO**
Brian Stoller, *
EMP: 150 EST: 1964
SQ FT: 5,000
SALES (est): 446.81MM
SALES (corp-wide): 8.52B **Publicly Held**
Web: www.idg.com
SIC: 2721 2731 Trade journals: publishing only, not printed on site; Books, publishing and printing
HQ: International Data Group, Inc.
140 Kendrick St Bldg B
Needham MA 02494
508 875-5000

(G-10514)
INTERNATIONAL DATA GROUP INC (HQ)
Also Called: Executrain
140 Kendrick St Ste C110b (02494-2739)
PHONE................................508 875-5000
Mohamad Ali, *CEO*
Zhiqiang Lu, *Ch*
Edward B Bloom, *CFO*
Margaret Murphy, *Sec*
◆ **EMP: 12 EST:** 1976
SQ FT: 15,000
SALES (est): 835.28MM
SALES (corp-wide): 8.52B **Publicly Held**
Web: www.idginc.com
SIC: 2721 8732 7389 Trade journals: publishing only, not printed on site; Market analysis or research; Trade show arrangement
PA: Blackstone Inc.
345 Park Ave
New York NY 10154
212 583-5000

(G-10515)
JOURNAL OF BONE JINT SRGERY IN
Also Called: JBJS
20 Pickering St Ste 3 (02492-3145)
PHONE................................781 449-9780
Kent Anderson, *CEO*
Richard Gelberman, *
Edward Hanley, *
Peter Stern, *
Stuart Weinstein, *
EMP: 34 EST: 1903
SQ FT: 20,000
SALES (est): 10.08MM **Privately Held**
Web: www.jbjs.org
SIC: 2721 Trade journals: publishing only, not printed on site

(G-10516)
KENEXA COMPENSATION INC (DH)
160 Gould St (02494-2313)
PHONE................................877 971-9171

Donald F Volk, *Pr*
Archie L Jones, *VP*
EMP: 40 EST: 1999
SQ FT: 36,288
SALES (est): 112.47MM
SALES (corp-wide): 60.53B **Publicly Held**
SIC: 7372 Business oriented computer software
HQ: Kenexa Corporation
650 E Swedesford Rd # 200
Wayne PA 19087

(G-10517)
MTP SOFTWARE LLC
145 Rosemary St (02494-3202)
PHONE................................508 353-6221
Frank Cincotta, *Mgr*
EMP: 8 EST: 2005
SALES (est): 121.11K **Privately Held**
SIC: 7372 Business oriented computer software

(G-10518)
PLANT SNACKS LLC
60 Kendrick St Ste 200 (02494-2726)
P.O. Box 920514 (02492-0006)
PHONE................................617 480-6265
Angela Hockman, *CFO*
EMP: 10 EST: 2016
SALES (est): 484.59K **Privately Held**
Web: www.plantsnacks.com
SIC: 2096 Potato chips and other potato-based snacks

(G-10519)
PLATFORMQ EDUCATION INC
100 Crescent Rd Ste 4 (02494-1457)
PHONE................................617 938-6000
Robert Rosenbloom, *Pr*
Hal Garnick, *Prin*
Robert Haber, *Prin*
EMP: 27 EST: 2011
SQ FT: 7,000
SALES (est): 3.75MM **Privately Held**
Web: www.collegeweeklive.com
SIC: 7372 Educational computer software

(G-10520)
SHARKNINJA INC
89 A St Ste 100 (02494-2806)
PHONE................................617 243-0235
Mark Barrocas, *Pr*
Xuning Wang, *
Larry Flynn, *Interim Chief Financial Officer*
Pedro J Lopez-baldrich, *CLO*
Neil Shah, *CCO*
EMP: 2800 EST: 2017
SALES (est): 114.9MM **Privately Held**
SIC: 3639 Major kitchen appliances, except refrigerators and stoves

(G-10521)
SHARKNINJA OPERATING LLC (PA)
89 A St Ste 100 (02494-2806)
PHONE................................617 243-0235
Stan Rosenzweig, *
Brian Seppa, *
Brian Lagarto, *
◆ **EMP: 35 EST:** 2003
SALES (est): 149.33MM
SALES (corp-wide): 149.33MM **Privately Held**
Web: www.sharkninja.com
SIC: 3639 Major kitchen appliances, except refrigerators and stoves

(G-10522)
SILVERLINING HOLDING CORP (PA)
368 Hillside Ave Bsmt (02494-1261)
PHONE................................617 986-4600
EMP: 15 EST: 2010
SQ FT: 3,000
SALES (est): 2.79MM **Privately Held**
Web: www.silverlng.com
SIC: 1542 2851 Commercial and office building, new construction; Undercoatings, paint

(G-10523)
SNOWBOUND SOFTWARE CORPORATION
128 1st Ave (02494-2805)
P.O. Box 834 (02494-0013)
PHONE................................617 607-2000
EMP: 100 EST: 1996
SQ FT: 15,000
SALES (est): 11.49MM **Privately Held**
Web: www.accusoft.com
SIC: 7372 Business oriented computer software

(G-10524)
ST EQUIPMENT & TECHNOLOGY LLC
101 Hampton Ave (02494-2628)
PHONE................................781 972-2319
EMP: 20 EST: 2014
SALES (est): 2.97MM **Privately Held**
Web: www.steqtech.com
SIC: 3569 Liquid automation machinery and equipment

(G-10525)
TECHTRADE INC
935 Great Plain Ave (02492-3031)
PHONE................................781 724-7878
Francis C K Fung, *Pr*
◆ **EMP: 12 EST:** 1997
SQ FT: 2,500
SALES (est): 1.54MM **Privately Held**
Web: www.techtradeinc.com
SIC: 3672 Printed circuit boards

(G-10526)
THINKFLOOD INC
295 Reservoir St (02494-3100)
PHONE................................617 299-2000
Matthew Eagar, *Pr*
Adam Shapiro, *COO*
▲ **EMP: 8 EST:** 2007
SQ FT: 2,500
SALES (est): 704.23K **Privately Held**
SIC: 3571 Electronic computers

(G-10527)
TRUROOTS LLC (PA) ✪
117 Kendrick St Ste 300 (02494-2722)
PHONE................................800 288-3637
Bobby Chacko, *Pr*
Larry Quier, *Sec*
EMP: 31 EST: 2022
SALES (est): 34.66MM
SALES (corp-wide): 34.66MM **Privately Held**
Web: www.truroots.com
SIC: 2099 2032 5153 Rice, uncooked: packaged with other ingredients; Ethnic foods, canned, jarred, etc.; Grains

(G-10528)
VERASTEM INC (PA)
117 Kendrick St Ste 500 (02494-2730)
PHONE................................781 292-4200
Brian Stuglik, *CEO*

Michelle Robertson, *Ch Bd*
Daniel Paterson, *Pr*
Dan Calkins, *CFO*
Mike Crowther Ccbso, *Prin*
EMP: 7 EST: 2010
SQ FT: 27,810
SALES (est): 2.6MM
SALES (corp-wide): 2.6MM **Publicly Held**
Web: www.verastem.com
SIC: 2834 Pharmaceutical preparations

(G-10529)
VITA NEEDLE COMPANY
919 Great Plain Ave (02492-3088)
P.O. Box 920236 (02492-0003)
PHONE................................781 444-1780
Mason N Hartman, *Ch Bd*
Frederick M Hartman, *
▲ **EMP: 30 EST:** 1932
SQ FT: 6,000
SALES (est): 15.8MM **Privately Held**
Web: www.vitaneedle.com
SIC: 5051 3841 3599 3845 Tubing, metal; Hypodermic needles and syringes; Machine and other job shop work; Electromedical equipment

Needham Heights
Norfolk County

(G-10530)
BIG BELLY SOLAR LLC (PA)
150 A St Ste 103 (02494-2824)
P.O. Box 920142 (02492-0002)
PHONE................................888 820-0300
Brian Phillips, *CEO*
Jeff Wakely, *
Thomas Smith, *Worldwide Sales Vice President**
Alex Gamota, *Information Vice President**
◆ **EMP: 42 EST:** 2019
SQ FT: 1,000
SALES (est): 10.81MM
SALES (corp-wide): 10.81MM **Privately Held**
Web: www.bigbelly.com
SIC: 3823 Process control instruments

(G-10531)
BONESUPPORT INC
Also Called: Bonesupport
117 4th Ave (02494-2725)
PHONE................................781 772-1756
Fredrik Lindberg, *CEO*
Offer Nonhoff, *Pr*
EMP: 28 EST: 2007
SALES (est): 5.15MM **Privately Held**
Web: www.bonesupport.com
SIC: 3842 Surgical appliances and supplies

(G-10532)
BOSTON SOFTWARE CORP
189 Reservoir St (02494-3130)
PHONE................................781 449-8585
Tom O'connor, *Pr*
Charles F Walsh, *VP*
EMP: 10 EST: 1995
SALES (est): 1.06MM **Privately Held**
Web: www.bostonsoftware.com
SIC: 7372 6411 Prepackaged software; Insurance agents, brokers, and service

(G-10533)
CANTATA TECHNOLOGY INC (DH)
Also Called: Dialogic
15 Crawford St Ste 201 (02494-2600)
PHONE................................781 449-4100

Timothy L Murray, *CEO*
J C Murphy, *
Paul F Brauneis, *
EMP: 200 **EST:** 1984
SQ FT: 22,000
SALES (est): 32.12MM
SALES (corp-wide): 950.04K **Privately Held**
Web: www.dialogic.com
SIC: 7371 3661 Computer software development; Facsimile equipment
HQ: Eas Holdings Llc
15 Crawford St
Needham Heights MA 02494
781 449-3056

(G-10534)
CELLDEX THERAPEUTICS INC
119 4th Ave (02494-2725)
PHONE..................781 433-0771
EMP: 11
SALES (corp-wide): 2.36MM **Publicly Held**
Web: www.celldex.com
SIC: 2834 Pharmaceutical preparations
PA: Celldex Therapeutics, Inc.
53 Frontage Rd Ste 220
Hampton NJ 08827
908 200-7500

(G-10535)
COCA-COLA BEVS NORTHEAST INC
Also Called: Coca-Cola
9 B St (02494-2701)
PHONE..................978 459-9378
Jeff Polak, *Genl Mgr*
EMP: 27
Web: www.cokenortheast.com
SIC: 2086 Bottled and canned soft drinks
HQ: Coca-Cola Beverages Northeast, Inc.
1 Executive Park Dr # 330
Bedford NH 03110
603 627-7871

(G-10536)
COCA-COLA BTLG STHSTERN NENG I
Also Called: Coca-Cola
9 B St (02494-2701)
P.O. Box 4108 (02101)
PHONE..................781 449-4300
Gary Dumas, *Mgr*
EMP: 18
Web: www.cokenortheast.com
SIC: 2086 2087 Bottled and canned soft drinks; Syrups, nsk
HQ: Coca-Cola Bottling Company Of Southeastern New England, Inc.
150 Waterford Parkway S
Waterford CT 06385
860 443-2816

(G-10537)
COMCAST SPORTSNET NENG LLC
Also Called: NBC Sports Boston
189 B St (02494-2755)
PHONE..................617 630-5000
Christian Wayland, *General MNG*
EMP: 82 **EST:** 2005
SALES (est): 4.9MM **Privately Held**
SIC: 7313 3663 4841 Electronic media advertising representatives; Satellites, communications; Cable television services

(G-10538)
CURAGEN CORPORATION (HQ)
119 4th Ave (02494-2725)

PHONE..................908 200-7500
Anthony S Marucci, *CEO*
Avery W Chip Catlin, *Sr VP*
Elizabeth Crowley, *Sr VP*
Thomas Davis, *Ex VP*
Tibor Keler, *Ex VP*
EMP: 16 **EST:** 1991
SALES (est): 270.74K
SALES (corp-wide): 2.36MM **Publicly Held**
SIC: 2834 Pharmaceutical preparations
PA: Celldex Therapeutics, Inc.
53 Frontage Rd Ste 220
Hampton NJ 08827
908 200-7500

(G-10539)
CXO MEDIA INC (DH)
Also Called: Cxo Media
140 Kendrick St # B (02494-2739)
PHONE..................508 766-5696
Abbie Lundberg, *Sr VP*
Mathew Smith, *
Edward B Bloom, *
Kevin C Krull, *
Bob Hayes, *CSO*
EMP: 138 **EST:** 1975
SALES (est): 27.18MM
SALES (corp-wide): 8.52B **Publicly Held**
SIC: 2791 2721 Typesetting; Trade journals: publishing only, not printed on site
HQ: Idg Communications, Inc.
140 Kendrick St Ste A110
Needham MA 02494
508 872-8200

(G-10540)
D & L ASSOCIATES INC
Also Called: J T C Printing
679 Highland Ave Rear (02494-2221)
PHONE..................781 400-5068
John Luz, *Pr*
EMP: 7 **EST:** 1981
SQ FT: 5,120
SALES (est): 619.12K **Privately Held**
Web: www.jtcprinting.com
SIC: 2752 2791 2789 Offset printing; Typesetting; Bookbinding and related work

(G-10541)
DG INTERNATIONAL HOLDINGS CORP
75 2nd Ave Ste 720 (02494-2826)
PHONE..................781 577-2016
Tim Conley, *COO*
Michael Greiner, *CFO*
EMP: 8 **EST:** 2011
SALES (est): 369.36K **Privately Held**
SIC: 3993 Advertising artwork
HQ: Digital Generation, Inc.
75 2nd Ave Ste 720
Needham Heights MA 02494

(G-10542)
EKRAN SYSTEM INC
60 Kendrick St Ste 201 (02494-2726)
PHONE..................424 242-8838
Oleg Shomonko, *CEO*
Dennis Turpitka, *
Neil Butchart, *
Oleg Shomonko, *CFO*
EMP: 30 **EST:** 2014
SALES (est): 2.32MM **Privately Held**
Web: www.ekransystem.com
SIC: 7372 Prepackaged software

(G-10543)
EURO-PRO HOLDCO LLC
89 A St # 100 (02494-2806)
PHONE..................617 243-0235

EMP: 100 **EST:** 2003
SALES (est): 8.05MM **Privately Held**
SIC: 3639 6719 Major kitchen appliances, except refrigerators and stoves; Investment holding companies, except banks

(G-10544)
FALLON FINE CABINETRY INC
171 Reservoir St (02494-3143)
PHONE..................781 453-6988
Peter Fallon, *Owner*
EMP: 10 **EST:** 2005
SALES (est): 773.6K **Privately Held**
Web: www.falloncustomhomes.com
SIC: 2434 Wood kitchen cabinets

(G-10545)
FAR REACH GRAPHICS INC
Also Called: Fastsigns
15 Kearney Rd (02494-2501)
PHONE..................781 444-4889
Maria Schwede, *Pr*
EMP: 7 **EST:** 1997
SQ FT: 2,000
SALES (est): 863.59K **Privately Held**
Web: www.fastsigns.com
SIC: 3993 Signs and advertising specialties

(G-10546)
FASTSIGNS
Also Called: Fastsigns
15 Kearney Rd (02494-2501)
PHONE..................781 444-4889
FAX: 781 444-8577
EMP: 7
SALES (est): 959.64K **Privately Held**
SIC: 3993 7532 Signs and advertising specialties; Truck painting and lettering

(G-10547)
FAUX DESIGNS INC
46 High St (02494-1530)
PHONE..................617 965-0142
Stacy Landua, *Owner*
EMP: 10 **EST:** 1987
SALES (est): 757.52K **Privately Held**
Web: www.faux-designs.com
SIC: 2759 Stationery: printing, nsk

(G-10548)
FUEL FOR FIRE INC
60 Kendrick St Ste 200 (02494-2726)
PHONE..................508 975-4573
Rob Gilfeather, *Pr*
Mark Neville, *Sls Dir*
Krystle Orlando, *Mktg Dir*
Mary Damkot, *CFO*
EMP: 9 **EST:** 2014
SALES (est): 525.02K **Privately Held**
Web: www.fuelforfire.com
SIC: 2099 Tea blending

(G-10549)
GENERAL DYNMICS MSSION SYSTEMS
77 A St (02494-2806)
PHONE..................954 846-3000
Thomas Turner, *Brnch Mgr*
EMP: 93
SALES (corp-wide): 42.27B **Publicly Held**
Web: www.gdmissionsystems.com
SIC: 3669 Emergency alarms
HQ: General Dynamics Mission Systems, Inc.
12450 Fair Lakes Cir
Fairfax VA 22033
877 449-0600

(G-10550)
HEALTHFLEET INC
163 Highland Ave Ste 1105 (02455-3025)
P.O. Box 550251 (02455-0251)
PHONE..................203 810-5400
Cheryl Morrison Deutsh, *CEO*
William Van Wyck, *
Brent Wilkinson, *
Andy Brooks, *
Anuja Ketan, *
EMP: 61 **EST:** 2009
SALES (est): 5.6MM **Privately Held**
Web: www.healthfleet.com
SIC: 7372 Educational computer software

(G-10551)
MICROWAVE DEVELOPMENT LABS INC
Also Called: M D L
135 Crescent Rd (02494-1483)
P.O. Box 3294 (02241-3294)
PHONE..................781 292-6600
Gordon P Riblet, *Pr*
Bruce K Johnson, *
James J Lynch, *
Douglas Riblet, *
Edward Scollins, *
EMP: 55 **EST:** 1948
SALES (est): 11.97MM **Privately Held**
Web: www.mdllab.com
SIC: 3679 7389 Waveguides and fittings; Design, commercial and industrial

(G-10552)
MIMOCO INC
475 Hillside Ave Ste 1 (02494-1200)
PHONE..................617 783-1100
Evan Blaustein, *Pr*
Dwight Schultheis, *VP*
EMP: 10 **EST:** 2007
SALES (est): 390.12K **Privately Held**
Web: www.mimo-co.com
SIC: 3577 5045 5734 Computer peripheral equipment, nec; Computer peripheral equipment; Computer peripheral equipment

(G-10553)
NETWORK WORLD INC
140 Kendrick St # B (02494-2739)
PHONE..................800 622-1108
Evilee Ebb, *CEO*
EMP: 48 **EST:** 1986
SALES (est): 2.86MM
SALES (corp-wide): 8.52B **Publicly Held**
Web: www.networkworld.com
SIC: 2721 8742 Trade journals: publishing only, not printed on site; Management consulting services
HQ: International Data Group, Inc.
140 Kendrick St Bldg B
Needham MA 02494
508 875-5000

(G-10554)
OPENCLINICA LLC
163 Highland Ave (02494-3025)
PHONE..................617 621-8585
Michael Collins, *CEO*
EMP: 25 **EST:** 2006
SALES (est): 5.23MM **Privately Held**
Web: www.openclinica.com
SIC: 3821 Clinical laboratory instruments, except medical and dental

(G-10555)
PARAMETRIC HOLDINGS INC (HQ)
140 Kendrick St (02494-2739)
PHONE..................781 370-5000

James E Heppelmann, *Pr*
EMP: 25 **EST:** 1989
SALES (est): 8.4MM
SALES (corp-wide): 2.1B **Publicly Held**
SIC: 7372 Prepackaged software
PA: Ptc Inc.
 121 Seaport Blvd
 Boston MA 02210
 781 370-5000

(G-10556)
SERPENTINO STNED LEADED GL INC
21 Highland Cir Ste 6 (02494-3038)
PHONE....................781 449-2074
Maria Serpentino Iriti, *Pr*
Roberto Rosa, *VP*
EMP: 9 **EST:** 1968
SQ FT: 4,200
SALES (est): 935.05K **Privately Held**
Web: www.serpentinostainedglass.com
SIC: 1793 3231 Glass and glazing work;
 Stained glass: made from purchased glass

(G-10557)
SILK TECHNOLOGIES INC
75 2nd Ave Ste 620 (02494-2865)
PHONE....................877 982-2555
EMP: 65 **EST:** 2008
SALES (est): 10.06MM **Privately Held**
Web: www.silk.us
SIC: 3572 Computer storage devices

(G-10558)
STEALTH BIOTHERAPEUTICS INC (HQ)
123 Highland Ave Ste 201 (02494-3005)
PHONE....................617 600-6888
EMP: 14 **EST:** 2007
SALES (est): 30.99MM **Privately Held**
Web: www.stealthbt.com
SIC: 2834 Pharmaceutical preparations
PA: Stealth Biotherapeutics Corp
 C/O: Intertrust Corporate Services
 (Cayman) Limite
 George Town GR CAYMAN

(G-10559)
SUD-CHEMIE PROTECH INC
32 Fremont St Ste 1 (02494-2936)
PHONE....................781 444-5188
Amiram Bar Ilan, *Pr*
Frank Wathan, *
▲ **EMP:** 277 **EST:** 1972
SQ FT: 30,000
SALES (est): 3.88MM
SALES (corp-wide): 51.32MM **Privately Held**
Web: www.clariant.com
SIC: 3822 2819 Incinerator control systems, residential and commercial type; Industrial inorganic chemicals, nec
HQ: Sud-Chemie & Co. Limited Partnership
 1600 W Hill St
 Louisville KY 40210
 502 634-7200

New Bedford
Bristol County

(G-10560)
ACCUSONIC TECHNOLOGIES (DH)
259 Samuel Barnet Blvd Unit 1
(02745-1214)
PHONE....................508 495-6600
▲ **EMP:** 10 **EST:** 1961
SALES (est): 9.24MM

SALES (corp-wide): 3.18B **Publicly Held**
SIC: 3823 3829 3812 Flow instruments, industrial process type; Measuring and controlling devices, nec; Search and navigation equipment
HQ: Ads Llc
 340 The Bridge St Ste 204
 Huntsville AL 35806
 256 430-3366

(G-10561)
ACUSHNET COMPANY
Also Called: Titleist
256 Samuel Barnet Blvd (02745-1215)
P.O. Box 965 (02741-0965)
PHONE....................508 979-2156
Michael Kramer, *Mgr*
EMP: 10
Web: www.titleist.com
SIC: 3949 Shafts, golf club
HQ: Acushnet Company
 333 Bridge St
 Fairhaven MA 02719
 508 979-2000

(G-10562)
ACUSHNET COMPANY
215 Duchaine Blvd (02745-1209)
PHONE....................508 979-2000
Walter Uihlein, *Brnch Mgr*
EMP: 12
Web: www.titleist.com
SIC: 3949 Shafts, golf club
HQ: Acushnet Company
 333 Bridge St
 Fairhaven MA 02719
 508 979-2000

(G-10563)
ACUSHNET COMPANY
Also Called: Titleist & Footjoy Worldwide
700 Belleville Ave (02745-6010)
P.O. Box 965 (02719-0965)
PHONE....................508 979-2000
Jim Arruda, *Mgr*
EMP: 23
Web: www.titleist.com
SIC: 3949 Shafts, golf club
HQ: Acushnet Company
 333 Bridge St
 Fairhaven MA 02719
 508 979-2000

(G-10564)
ACUSHNET RUBBER COMPANY INC
Also Called: Precix
744 Belleville Ave (02745-6010)
PHONE....................508 998-4000
EMP: 400 **EST:** 1997
SQ FT: 120,000
SALES (est): 93.5MM
SALES (corp-wide): 2.06B **Privately Held**
SIC: 3053 3061 2821 Gaskets, all materials; Mechanical rubber goods; Plastics materials and resins
PA: Anhui Zhongding Sealing Parts Co., Ltd.
 Zhongding Industrial Park, Ningguo Economic And Technological De
 Ningguo AH 24230
 563 418-1880

(G-10565)
AEROVOX INCORPORATED
Also Called: Aerovox
167 John Vertente Blvd (02745-1221)
PHONE....................508 994-9661
▲ **EMP:** 1740

SIC: 3629 3675 Capacitors and condensers ; Electronic capacitors

(G-10566)
AFC CABLE SYSTEMS INC
960 Flaherty Dr (02745-1975)
PHONE....................508 998-1131
Bob Pereira, *Brnch Mgr*
EMP: 279
Web: www.atkore.com
SIC: 5085 3599 3444 3429 Industrial supplies; Hose, flexible metallic; Sheet metalwork; Hardware, nec
HQ: Afc Cable Systems, Inc.
 16100 Lathrop Ave
 Harvey IL 60426
 508 998-1131

(G-10567)
ALL SECURITY CO INC
771 Kempton St (02740-2544)
PHONE....................508 993-4271
Paul Wesley, *Pr*
Christine Wesley, *VP*
EMP: 23 **EST:** 1977
SQ FT: 2,652
SALES (est): 2.05MM **Privately Held**
Web: www.allsecuritylocks.com
SIC: 3699 7699 5731 Security devices; Locksmith shop; Video cameras, recorders, and accessories

(G-10568)
AMETEK INC
Also Called: Ametek Aerospace & Defense
50 Welby Rd (02745-1100)
PHONE....................508 998-4335
Susan Curado, *Brnch Mgr*
EMP: 52
SALES (corp-wide): 6.15B **Publicly Held**
Web: www.ametek.com
SIC: 3674 Semiconductors and related devices
PA: Ametek, Inc.
 1100 Cassatt Rd
 Berwyn PA 19312
 610 647-2121

(G-10569)
ART SWISS CORPORATION
1357 E Rodney French Blvd (02744-2124)
PHONE....................508 999-3281
Kenneth Joblon, *Pr*
EMP: 9 **EST:** 1971
SQ FT: 10,000
SALES (est): 186.95K **Privately Held**
SIC: 2759 3555 Textile printing rolls: engraving; Printing trades machinery

(G-10570)
ATI ALLEGHENY LUDLUM INC
Also Called: ATI Flat Rolled Products
1357 E Rodney French Blvd (02744-2124)
PHONE....................508 992-4067
Marissa P Earnest, *Prin*
EMP: 97 **EST:** 2013
SALES (est): 24.47MM **Publicly Held**
Web: www.atimaterials.com
SIC: 3316 Strip, steel, cold-rolled, nec: from purchased hot-rolled,
HQ: Allegheny Ludlum, Llc
 1000 Six Ppg Pl
 Pittsburgh PA 15222
 412 394-2800

(G-10571)
BIG G SEAFOOD INC
48 Antonio Costa Ave (02740-7383)
PHONE....................508 994-5113
EMP: 7 **EST:** 1990

SQ FT: 1,200
SALES (est): 702.72K **Privately Held**
Web: www.biggseafood.com
SIC: 2092 Fresh or frozen packaged fish

(G-10572)
BLUE FLEET WELDING SERVICE
Also Called: Sole Proprietorship
102 Wamsutta St (02740-6822)
PHONE....................508 997-5513
Paul Lenieux, *Owner*
EMP: 7 **EST:** 1986
SQ FT: 3,200
SALES (est): 475.65K **Privately Held**
SIC: 7692 Welding repair

(G-10573)
BRITTANY GLOBAL TECH CORP
1357 E Rodney French Blvd (02744-2124)
PHONE....................508 999-3281
Kenneth Joblon, *Pr*
◆ **EMP:** 89 **EST:** 1939
SQ FT: 400,000
SALES (est): 25.8MM **Privately Held**
Web: www.brittanyusa.com
SIC: 2269 Finishing plants, nec

(G-10574)
BRODEUR MACHINE COMPANY INC
62 Wood St (02745-6248)
PHONE....................508 995-2662
EMP: 45 **EST:** 2011
SALES (est): 10.77MM **Privately Held**
Web: www.brodeurmachine.com
SIC: 3599 Machine shop, jobbing and repair

(G-10575)
BROTHERS ARTISANAL INC
32 William St Unit 1 (02740-6278)
PHONE....................508 938-9161
EMP: 9 **EST:** 2019
SALES (est): 157.33K **Privately Held**
Web: www.brothersartisanal.com
SIC: 2013 Snack sticks, including jerky: from purchased meat

(G-10576)
BUTLER ARCHITECTURAL WDWKG INC
200 Theodore Rice Blvd (02745-1212)
PHONE....................508 985-9980
William D Butler, *Pr*
EMP: 13 **EST:** 2000
SALES (est): 6MM **Privately Held**
Web: www.butlerarchitectural.com
SIC: 2499 Decorative wood and woodwork

(G-10577)
C P BOURG INC (PA)
Also Called: Bourg Collaters System
50 Samuel Barnet Blvd (02745-1285)
PHONE....................508 998-2171
Christian P Bourg, *Pr*
Donald J Schroeder, *
Philippe Lambert Mr, *
Johanne Bourg Thibault, *
James C Donnelly Junior, *Sec*
◆ **EMP:** 50 **EST:** 1976
SQ FT: 36,000
SALES (est): 9.32MM
SALES (corp-wide): 9.32MM **Privately Held**
Web: www.cpbourg.com
SIC: 3579 5044 Duplicating machines; Office equipment

(G-10578)
COATERS INC
305 Nash Rd Unit 1 (02746-1800)
PHONE..................................508 996-5700
Paul Lubin, *Pr*
Simon Lubin, *
Philip Patrick, *
EMP: 8 **EST:** 1934
SQ FT: 245,000
SALES (est): 394.29K **Privately Held**
SIC: 2295 Leather, artificial or imitation

(G-10579)
COPENHGEN OFFSHORE PRTNERS INC
700 Pleasant St (02740-6254)
PHONE..................................508 717-8964
EMP: 23 **EST:** 2018
SALES (est): 13.78MM
SALES (corp-wide): 60.44K **Privately Held**
Web: www.cop.dk
SIC: 1382 Oil and gas exploration services
HQ: Copenhagen Offshore Partners A/S
Amerika Plads 29, Sal St
Kobenhavn O

(G-10580)
CORNELL-DUBILIER ELEC INC
1661 E Rodney French Blvd (02744-2231)
PHONE..................................508 996-8561
Hector Casanova, *Mgr*
EMP: 50
SQ FT: 414,000
SALES (corp-wide): 764.7MM **Publicly Held**
Web: www.cde.com
SIC: 5065 3675 Capacitors, electronic;
Electronic capacitors
HQ: Cornell-Dubilier Electronics, Inc.
140 Technology Pl
Liberty SC 29657
864 843-2277

(G-10581)
CRAFT CORRUGATED BOX INC
4674 Acushnet Ave (02745-4736)
P.O. Box 50070 (02745-0003)
PHONE..................................508 998-2115
Ronald Mardula, *Pr*
EMP: 10 **EST:** 1964
SQ FT: 20,000
SALES (est): 928.29K **Privately Held**
SIC: 2653 Boxes, corrugated: made from purchased materials

(G-10582)
CRYSTAL ICE CO INC
178 Front St (02740-7291)
PHONE..................................508 997-7522
Joseph E Swift, *Pr*
Robert F Swift, *Treas*
EMP: 18 **EST:** 1956
SQ FT: 10,000
SALES (est): 2.46MM **Privately Held**
Web: www.crystaliceco.com
SIC: 2097 Manufactured ice

(G-10583)
D J BASS INC
Also Called: Bass Ready Rooter
84 Bates St (02745-6008)
PHONE..................................508 678-4499
Dennis Bastarache, *Pr*
EMP: 7 **EST:** 1975
SALES (est): 817.37K **Privately Held**
Web: www.bassreddy.com
SIC: 2842 Drain pipe solvents or cleaners

(G-10584)
DAVICO INC
Also Called: Davico Manufacturing
95 Brook St (02746-1782)
PHONE..................................508 998-1150
Raymond Surprenant, *Pr*
▲ **EMP:** 10 **EST:** 1988
SQ FT: 5,000
SALES (est): 1.9MM **Privately Held**
Web: www.davicomfg.com
SIC: 3714 Exhaust systems and parts, motor vehicle

(G-10585)
DESIGN MARK INDUSTRIES INC
Also Called: Design Mark Industries
22 Logan St Unit 1 (02740-7376)
PHONE..................................800 451-3275
John Winzeler Junior, *Pr*
William M Salmons, *
Steve Normandin, *
Spencer L Purinton, *
EMP: 75 **EST:** 2007
SALES (est): 10.51MM
SALES (corp-wide): 19.18MM **Privately Held**
Web: www.design-mark.com
SIC: 2759 3089 3679 Flexographic printing;
Laminating of plastics; Electronic switches
PA: Nfi Corp.
22 Logan St Unit 1
New Bedford MA 02740
508 998-9021

(G-10586)
DION SIGNS AND SERVICE INC
125 Samuel Barnet Blvd (02745-1204)
PHONE..................................401 724-4459
Raymond P Dion, *Pr*
Richard S Dion, *VP*
Rionald M Dion, *VP*
EMP: 10 **EST:** 1988
SALES (est): 2.65MM
SALES (corp-wide): 12.77MM **Privately Held**
Web: www.dionsigns.com
SIC: 3646 7389 Commercial lighting fixtures
; Sign painting and lettering shop
PA: Poyant Signs, Inc.
125 Samuel Barnet Blvd
New Bedford MA 02745
800 544-0961

(G-10587)
DOCKSIDE REPAIRS INC
14 Hervey Tichon Ave (02740-7348)
PHONE..................................508 993-6730
Roy Enoksen, *Pr*
EMP: 28 **EST:** 1971
SQ FT: 1,000
SALES (est): 886.12K **Privately Held**
SIC: 7692 Welding repair

(G-10588)
EDGEWATER MARINE INDS LLC
Also Called: Richardson's Maptech
90 Hatch St Unit 1 (02745-6000)
PHONE..................................508 992-6555
EMP: 19 **EST:** 1998
SALES (est): 1.41MM **Privately Held**
Web: www.richardsonscharts.com
SIC: 2741 7389 Maps: publishing only, not printed on site; Mapmaking services

(G-10589)
EPEC LLC (PA)
176 Samuel Barnet Blvd (02745-1227)
PHONE..................................508 995-5171
Kendall Paradise, *
▲ **EMP:** 80 **EST:** 1952
SQ FT: 60,000
SALES (est): 23.5MM
SALES (corp-wide): 23.5MM **Privately Held**
Web: www.epectec.com
SIC: 3672 Printed circuit boards

(G-10590)
FIBERSPAR LINEPIPE LLC
800 Purchase St Ste 502 (02740-6354)
PHONE..................................281 854-2636
Bonnie Moran, *Brnch Mgr*
EMP: 114
SALES (corp-wide): 7.24B **Publicly Held**
SIC: 3498 Fabricated pipe and fittings
HQ: Fiberspar Linepipe Llc
12239 Fm 529 Rd
Houston TX 77041

(G-10591)
FINICKY PET FOOD INC
68 Blackmer St (02744-2614)
PHONE..................................508 991-8448
William F Schofield Senior, *CEO*
William F Schofield Junior, *Pr*
EMP: 25 **EST:** 1985
SQ FT: 3,000
SALES (est): 4.02MM **Privately Held**
Web: www.finickypetfoods.com
SIC: 2048 Fish food

(G-10592)
FIVE STAR MANUFACTURING INC
163 Samuel Barnet Blvd (02745-1220)
PHONE..................................508 998-1404
David A Cabral, *Pr*
John P Camara, *
Gualter A Massa, *
EMP: 58 **EST:** 2002
SALES (est): 3.56MM **Privately Held**
Web: www.fivestarcompanies.net
SIC: 3841 Surgical and medical instruments

(G-10593)
FIVE STAR SURGICAL INC
Also Called: Five Star Companies
163 Samuel Barnet Blvd (02745-1220)
PHONE..................................508 998-1404
John P Camara, *Pr*
David A Cabral, *
Gualter A Massa, *
EMP: 94 **EST:** 1998
SQ FT: 20,000
SALES (est): 10.63MM **Privately Held**
Web: www.fivestarcompanies.net
SIC: 3841 Surgical instruments and apparatus

(G-10594)
GEC DURHAM INDUSTRIES INC (PA)
255 Samuel Barnet Blvd (02745-1220)
P.O. Box 1101 (65536-1101)
PHONE..................................508 995-2636
J Douglas Russel, *Pr*
George E Carr Stkldr, *Prin*
EMP: 40 **EST:** 1993
SALES (est): 21.16MM **Privately Held**
Web: www.gecdurham.com
SIC: 3612 Transformers, except electric

(G-10595)
GLASSEAL PRODUCTS INC
50 Welby Rd (02745-1100)
PHONE..................................732 370-9100
Ian Mcgavisk, *Pr*
William Hubbard, *
EMP: 40 **EST:** 1956
SALES (est): 4.09MM
SALES (corp-wide): 6.15B **Publicly Held**
SIC: 3643 3679 3471 3812 Connectors and terminals for electrical devices; Hermetic seals, for electronic equipment; Plating of metals or formed products; Search and navigation equipment
HQ: Hcc Industries Leasing, Inc.
4232 Temple City Blvd
Rosemead CA 91770
626 443-8933

(G-10596)
GLOBAL SILICON TECH INC
11 David St (02744-2310)
PHONE..................................508 999-2001
EMP: 14 **EST:** 2019
SALES (est): 2.92MM **Privately Held**
Web: www.gstsilicon.com
SIC: 3674 Semiconductors and related devices

(G-10597)
H LOEB CORPORATION
419 Sawyer St Unit 2 (02746-5605)
PHONE..................................508 996-3745
Geoffrey Faucher, *Pr*
Julius Shaw, *Treas*
▲ **EMP:** 20 **EST:** 1948
SQ FT: 36,000
SALES (est): 4.17MM **Privately Held**
Web: www.hloeb.com
SIC: 3644 3083 2675 Insulators and insulation materials, electrical; Laminated plastics sheets; Die-cut paper and board

(G-10598)
HANNAH BODEN CORP
132 Herman Melville Blvd (02740-7344)
PHONE..................................508 992-3334
Jonathan Williams, *CEO*
EMP: 10 **EST:** 2004
SALES (est): 975.1K **Privately Held**
SIC: 5146 3732 Fish and seafoods; Fishing boats: lobster, crab, oyster, etc.: small

(G-10599)
HCC AEGIS INC (DH)
Also Called: Ametek Aegis
50 Welby Rd (02745-1100)
PHONE..................................508 998-3141
Timothy N Jones, *Pr*
Gregory Myers, *Prin*
William J Burke, *Prin*
Kathryn E Sena, *Prin*
EMP: 237 **EST:** 1987
SQ FT: 95,000
SALES (est): 52.9MM
SALES (corp-wide): 6.15B **Publicly Held**
Web: www.ametekinterconnect.com
SIC: 3674 Microcircuits, integrated (semiconductor)
HQ: Hcc Industries Leasing, Inc.
4232 Temple City Blvd
Rosemead CA 91770
626 443-8933

(G-10600)
HERCULES SLR (US) INC
82 Macarthur Dr (02740-7214)
PHONE..................................508 992-9519
John Reardon, *Genl Mgr*
EMP: 9
SALES (corp-wide): 2.51MM **Privately Held**
Web: www.hercules-slr-us.com
SIC: 3531 5088 5551 Marine related equipment; Marine supplies; Marine supplies and equipment
PA: Hercules Slr (Us) Inc.
44 South St

New Bedford MA 02740
508 993-0010

(G-10601)
HERCULES SLR (US) INC (PA)
44 South St (02740-7221)
PHONE....................................508 993-0010
Christos Giannou, *Pr*
▲ EMP: 10 EST: 2011
SALES (est): 2.39MM
SALES (corp-wide): 2.39MM **Privately Held**
Web: www.hercules-slr-us.com
SIC: 3531 5088 5551 Marine related equipment; Marine supplies; Marine supplies and equipment

(G-10602)
HORACIOS INC
64 John Vertente Blvd (02745-1207)
PHONE....................................508 985-9940
Horacio B Tavares, *Pr*
EMP: 15 EST: 1982
SQ FT: 45,000
SALES (est): 4.67MM **Privately Held**
Web: www.horacios.com
SIC: 7692 Welding repair

(G-10603)
IMAGE SIGNS
126 River Rd (02745-6132)
PHONE....................................774 328-8059
Derek Yates, *Prin*
EMP: 9 EST: 2016
SALES (est): 380.89K **Privately Held**
Web: www.imageprintco.com
SIC: 3993 Electric signs

(G-10604)
INTERNATIONAL PARALLEL MCHS
50 Conduit St (02740-6016)
PHONE....................................508 990-2977
Robin Chang, *Pr*
C T Chang, *Clerk*
EMP: 9 EST: 1980
SQ FT: 107,000
SALES (est): 1MM **Privately Held**
Web: www.ipmiplc.com
SIC: 8731 3571 3823 3625 Computer (hardware) development; Minicomputers; Process control instruments; Relays and industrial controls

(G-10605)
JAZ BRUSH USA INC
Also Called: Jaz USA
59 Tarkiln Pl (02745-1016)
PHONE....................................774 992-7996
David Rodrigues, *Pr*
◆ EMP: 8 EST: 2005
SALES (est): 704.65K **Privately Held**
Web: www.jazsurface.com
SIC: 3991 Brushes, household or industrial

(G-10606)
JOSEPH ABBOUD MFG CORP
689 Belleville Ave (02745-6011)
PHONE....................................508 999-1301
Jose Bahena, *Sr VP*
Leticia Gonzales, *
▲ EMP: 500 EST: 1978
SQ FT: 208,000
SALES (est): 39.59MM
SALES (corp-wide): 2.52B **Privately Held**
Web: www.tailoredbrands.com
SIC: 2311 Suits, men's and boys': made from purchased materials
HQ: The Men's Wearhouse Llc
6380 Rogerdale Rd

Houston TX 77072
281 776-7000

(G-10607)
JP PROGRESSIVE COMM GROUP LLC
Also Called: Reynolds Dewalt
186 Duchaine Blvd (02745-1201)
PHONE....................................800 477-4681
Peter Smith, *Managing Member*
EMP: 9 EST: 2014
SALES (est): 1.54MM **Privately Held**
Web: www.reynoldsdewalt.com
SIC: 7389 2752 Packaging and labeling services; Offset printing

(G-10608)
KASC INC
270 Samuel Barnet Blvd (02745-1219)
PHONE....................................508 985-9898
◆ EMP: 303
Web: www.aheadhq.com
SIC: 2395 Embroidery and art needlework

(G-10609)
KETCHAM SUPPLY CO INC
111 Myrtle St (02740-7029)
PHONE....................................508 997-4787
Heather Ketcham, *Pr*
EMP: 20 EST: 2016
SQ FT: 25,000
SALES (est): 1MM **Privately Held**
Web: www.ketchamsupply.com
SIC: 3429 3496 Animal traps, iron or steel; Traps, animal and fish

(G-10610)
KETCHAM TRAPS
111 Myrtle St (02740-7029)
PHONE....................................508 997-4787
Robert Ketcham, *Owner*
▲ EMP: 7 EST: 1976
SQ FT: 11,000
SALES (est): 573.28K **Privately Held**
Web: www.ketchamsupply.com
SIC: 3429 5199 Marine hardware; Gifts and novelties

(G-10611)
KYLER SEAFOOD INC
Also Called: Kyler's
2 Washburn St (02740-7336)
PHONE....................................508 984-5150
Jeff Nanfelt, *Pr*
Billy Arruda, *
Steve Souza, *
▼ EMP: 100 EST: 1984
SQ FT: 35,000
SALES (est): 16.16MM **Privately Held**
Web: www.kylerseafood.com
SIC: 2092 Seafoods, frozen: prepared

(G-10612)
L & S INDUSTRIES INC (PA)
32 Lambeth St (02745-1003)
P.O. Box 50097 (02745-0004)
PHONE....................................508 995-4654
Jeanne-marie Boylan, *Pr*
Dean Boylan, *VP*
EMP: 23 EST: 1954
SQ FT: 8,400
SALES (est): 2.4MM
SALES (corp-wide): 2.4MM **Privately Held**
Web: www.landsconcrete.com
SIC: 3273 Ready-mixed concrete

(G-10613)
LISBON SAUSAGE CO INC
Also Called: Amaral's

433 S 2nd St (02740-5764)
P.O. Box 2028 (02741-2028)
PHONE....................................508 993-7645
TOLL FREE: 800
Joan Sparrow, *Pr*
◆ EMP: 13 EST: 1928
SQ FT: 1,800
SALES (est): 966.86K
SALES (corp-wide): 2.3MM **Privately Held**
Web: www.medfinefoods.com
SIC: 2013 5147 Sausages, from purchased meat; Meats and meat products
PA: Mediterranean Fine Foods, Llc
433 S 2nd St
New Bedford MA 02740
508 993-7645

(G-10614)
LOCAL MEDIA GROUP INC
Standard Times
25 Elm St (02740-6279)
P.O. Box 5912 (02742-5912)
PHONE....................................508 997-7411
William T Kennedy, *Prin*
EMP: 131
SQ FT: 25,000
SALES (corp-wide): 2.95B **Publicly Held**
Web: www.gannett.com
SIC: 2711 7313 Newspapers: publishing only, not printed on site; Newspaper advertising representative
HQ: Local Media Group, Inc.
90 Crystal Run Rd Ste 310
Middletown NY 10941
845 341-1100

(G-10615)
M & R SCREEN PRINTING INC
95 Rodney French Blvd (02744-1603)
P.O. Box 160 (02717-0160)
PHONE....................................508 996-0419
John B Macaroco, *Pr*
John Macaroco, *
Peter S Russell, *
EMP: 18 EST: 2006
SQ FT: 4,000
SALES (est): 1.5MM **Privately Held**
Web: www.mandrscreenprinting.com
SIC: 2759 Screen printing

(G-10616)
M F FLEY INCRPRTD-NEW BDFORD
Also Called: Foley Fish
77 Wright St (02740-7250)
P.O. Box 1806 (02741-1806)
PHONE....................................508 997-0773
Michael Foley, *Pr*
Linda Foley, *
Peter Barnard Ramsden, *
Laura Foley Ramsden, *
EMP: 40 EST: 1979
SQ FT: 28,053
SALES (est): 9.2MM **Publicly Held**
Web: www.foleyfish.com
SIC: 2092 Fish, fresh: prepared
HQ: M. F. Foley Company
24 W Howell St
Boston MA 02125
508 997-0773

(G-10617)
MANOMET MANUFACTURING INC
194 Riverside Ave (02746-5428)
PHONE....................................508 997-1795
Edward Fitzsimmons, *Pr*
EMP: 8 EST: 2001
SALES (est): 161.57K **Privately Held**

SIC: 3999 Barber and beauty shop equipment

(G-10618)
MAR-LEES SEAFOOD LLC
98 Front St (02740-7262)
P.O. Box 643 (02777-0643)
PHONE....................................508 991-6026
◆ EMP: 200
Web: www.marlees.com
SIC: 2091 Seafood products: packaged in cans, jars, etc.

(G-10619)
MARINE HYDRAULICS INC
256 Herman Melville Blvd (02740-7344)
PHONE....................................508 990-2866
David Chambers, *Pr*
EMP: 10 EST: 1983
SQ FT: 10,000
SALES (est): 2.29MM **Privately Held**
Web: www.marinehydraulicsusa.com
SIC: 5084 3594 Hydraulic systems equipment and supplies; Fluid power pumps and motors

(G-10620)
MARTHAS SEASTREAK VINEYARD LLC
Also Called: New England Fast Ferry
49 State Pier (02740-7254)
PHONE....................................617 896-0293
EMP: 10 EST: 2005
SALES (est): 729.16K **Privately Held**
Web: www.seastreak.com
SIC: 2084 Wines

(G-10621)
MAXIMUM INC
30 Samuel Barnet Blvd (02745-1205)
PHONE....................................508 995-2200
Peter Kilgore, *Pr*
Edward Rogerson, *Treas*
William Rogerson, *Sec*
EMP: 8 EST: 1968
SQ FT: 6,000
SALES (est): 1.95MM
SALES (corp-wide): 18.88MM **Privately Held**
Web: www.maximum-inc.com
SIC: 3829 Meteorological instruments
PA: Imtra Corporation
30 Samuel Barnet Blvd
New Bedford MA 02745
508 995-7000

(G-10622)
MICHAEL ROGOVSKY
244 Bellevue St (02744-1403)
PHONE....................................508 487-3287
EMP: 10
SALES (est): 118.82K **Privately Held**
Web: www.michaelrogovsky.com
SIC: 8999 2851 Artist; Paints: oil or alkyd vehicle or water thinned

(G-10623)
MONTREAL FISHING CORP
13 Centre St Unit 1 (02740-6381)
PHONE....................................508 993-0275
EMP: 7 EST: 2009
SALES (est): 120K **Privately Held**
SIC: 3732 Boatbuilding and repairing

(G-10624)
MORGAN ADVANCED CERAMICS INC
225 Theodore Rice Blvd (02745-1213)
PHONE....................................508 995-1725

John Stang, *Genl Mgr*
EMP: 61
SALES (corp-wide): 1.34B **Privately Held**
Web:
www.morgantechnicalceramics.com
SIC: 2899 3251 Fluxes: brazing, soldering,
galvanizing, and welding; Brick and
structural clay tile
HQ: Morgan Advanced Ceramics, Inc.
2425 Whipple Rd
Hayward CA 94544

(G-10625)
NATIONWIDE TAX & BUSINESS SVCS
5 Dover St Ste 103 (02740-6200)
PHONE...................774 473-8444
Robert Barnes, *Pr*
EMP: 25 **EST:** 2020
SALES (est): 989.46K **Privately Held**
Web: www.thenationwidetax.com
SIC: 7291 8721 2511 7389 Tax return
preparation services; Accounting services,
except auditing; Bookcases, household:
wood

(G-10626)
NERY CORPORATION
Also Called: Coastal McHnery Eqpment
Apprse
700 Pleasant St Ste 330 (02740-6268)
PHONE...................508 990-9800
Kevin Nery, *Pr*
Lory Nery, *Prin*
EMP: 9 **EST:** 1978
SQ FT: 3,500
SALES (est): 888.14K **Privately Held**
Web: www.nerycorp.com
SIC: 7389 3569 6531 Brokers, business:
buying and selling business enterprises;
Assembly machines, non-metalworking;
Real estate agent, commercial

(G-10627)
NEW BEDFORD OCEAN CLUSTER INC
Also Called: NBOC
1213 Purchase St Unit 2 (02740-6694)
PHONE...................508 474-8902
John Bullard, *Pr*
Edward Anthes-washburn, *VP*
EMP: 12 **EST:** 2021
SALES (est): 507.14K **Privately Held**
Web: www.newbedfordoceancluster.org
SIC: 0273 0912 3511 Animal aquaculture;
Finfish; Turbines and turbine generator sets

(G-10628)
NEW BEDFORD SCALE CO INC
144 Francis St (02740-2538)
PHONE...................508 997-6730
TOLL FREE: 800
Jim Stpierre, *Pr*
Gary Pelletier, *Treas*
EMP: 7 **EST:** 1967
SQ FT: 2,200
SALES (est): 860.71K **Privately Held**
Web: www.nbscale.com
SIC: 3596 7699 Industrial scales; Industrial
machinery and equipment repair

(G-10629)
NEW ENGLAND MAR HOLDINGS INC
128 Union St (02740-6389)
PHONE...................508 758-6600
EMP: 24 **EST:** 2011
SALES (est): 1.4MM **Privately Held**

SIC: 2092 Seafoods, fresh: prepared

(G-10630)
NEW ENGLAND PLASTICS CORP
126 Duchaine Blvd (02745-1201)
PHONE...................508 998-3111
Tony Pontes, *Mgr*
EMP: 60
SALES (corp-wide): 13.48MM **Privately
Held**
Web: www.newenglandplastics.com
SIC: 3089 3081 Injection molding of plastics
; Unsupported plastics film and sheet
PA: New England Plastics Corporation
310 Salem St Ste 2
Woburn MA 01801
781 933-6004

(G-10631)
NEWERA SERVICES CORPORATION (PA)
Also Called: Edson Pump Div
146 Duchaine Blvd (02745-1201)
PHONE...................508 995-9711
◆ **EMP:** 25 **EST:** 1859
SALES (est): 9.24MM
SALES (corp-wide): 9.24MM **Privately
Held**
Web: www.edsonintl.com
SIC: 3566 7699 3594 3714 Speed
changers, drives, and gears; Nautical and
navigational instrument repair; Fluid power
pumps; Motor vehicle parts and accessories

(G-10632)
NFI LLC
Also Called: Nameplates For Industry
22 Logan St Unit 1 (02740-7376)
PHONE...................508 998-9021
EMP: 44 **EST:** 1975
SALES (est): 8.04MM **Privately Held**
Web: www.salesandservicestickers.com
SIC: 2759 Commercial printing, nec

(G-10633)
NICHE INC
84 Gifford St (02744-2615)
PHONE...................508 990-4202
Robert Letendre, *Pr*
Roland Letendre, *
Peter Roderick, *
Emily Letendre-ment, *Dir*
Linette Letendre-greilich, *Dir*
▲ **EMP:** 25 **EST:** 1988
SQ FT: 1,000,000
SALES (est): 2.15MM **Privately Held**
Web: www.nicheinc.com
SIC: 2399 Parachutes

(G-10634)
NORTH EAST SILICON TECH INC
11 David St (02744-2310)
PHONE...................508 999-2001
Robert J Weeks, *Pr*
Christopher L Weeks, *
▲ **EMP:** 65 **EST:** 1997
SQ FT: 30,000
SALES (est): 10.38MM **Privately Held**
Web: www.gstsilicon.com
SIC: 3674 Semiconductors and related
devices

(G-10635)
NORTHERN WIND LLC (HQ)
16 Hassey St (02740-7209)
PHONE...................508 997-0727
Kenneth Melanson, *CEO*
Michael Fernandes, *
◆ **EMP:** 65 **EST:** 1987
SQ FT: 12,500

SALES (est): 37.79MM
SALES (corp-wide): 37.79MM **Privately
Held**
Web: www.northernwind.com
SIC: 5146 2092 Seafoods; Fresh or frozen
packaged fish
PA: Atlantic Sustainable Catch
16 Hassey St
New Bedford MA 02740
508 997-0727

(G-10636)
NUTEX INDUSTRIES INC
127 Rodney French Blvd Unit 4
(02744-1623)
P.O. Box 40219 (02744-0016)
PHONE...................508 993-2501
Andrei Klein, *Pr*
EMP: 29 **EST:** 1980
SQ FT: 83,000
SALES (est): 2.11MM **Privately Held**
Web: www.nutexindustries.com
SIC: 2241 Webbing, braids and belting

(G-10637)
OPTICAL LABORATORY INC
14 S 6th St Side (02740-5975)
PHONE...................508 997-9779
Juliette Dube, *Pr*
Dennis Dube, *VP*
Ronald Dube, *Treas*
EMP: 22 **EST:** 1949
SQ FT: 1,600
SALES (est): 1.12MM **Privately Held**
SIC: 3851 7699 3229 Lenses, ophthalmic;
Optical instrument repair; Pressed and
blown glass, nec

(G-10638)
PACKAGING PRODUCTS CORPORATION (PA)
Also Called: Arctic Pack
47 N 2nd St Fl 3 (02740-6205)
PHONE...................508 997-5150
Theodore E Heidenreich Junior, *Ch Bd*
Theodore E Heidenreich Iii, *Pr*
Robert G Heidenreich, *Pr*
James M Graham, *Clerk*
Jane H Heidenreich, *Treas*
◆ **EMP:** 19 **EST:** 1962
SALES (est): 4.25MM
SALES (corp-wide): 4.25MM **Privately
Held**
Web: www.pkgprod.com
SIC: 3081 3086 5199 Packing materials,
plastics sheet; Packaging and shipping
materials, foamed plastics; Packaging
materials

(G-10639)
PLACES TO GO LLC
1 Wamsutta St (02740-7369)
P.O. Box 87081 (02748-0700)
PHONE...................774 202-7756
EMP: 7 **EST:** 2011
SALES (est): 726.83K **Privately Held**
Web: www.placestogosouthcoast.com
SIC: 3799 Carriages, horse drawn

(G-10640)
PLATING TECHNOLOGY INC
Also Called: Star Plating
41 Coffin Ave (02746-2407)
PHONE...................508 996-4006
John S Thompson, *Pr*
William D Roeder, *
EMP: 40 **EST:** 1955
SQ FT: 10,000
SALES (est): 4.29MM **Privately Held**
Web: www.starplatingcompany.com

SIC: 3471 Electroplating of metals or
formed products

(G-10641)
PORTUGUESE TIMES INC
Also Called: Portugues Channel, The
1501 Acushnet Ave (02746-2223)
P.O. Box 61288 (02746-0288)
PHONE...................508 997-3118
Eduardo Lima, *Pr*
EMP: 7 **EST:** 1971
SQ FT: 4,800
SALES (est): 690.35K **Privately Held**
Web: www.portuguesetimes.com
SIC: 7313 2711 Television and radio time
sales; Newspapers, publishing and printing

(G-10642)
POWDER PRO POWDER COATING INC
195 Riverside Ave (02746-2441)
PHONE...................508 991-5999
Antone Salgado, *Owner*
Michael Staab, *Genl Mgr*
EMP: 9 **EST:** 2010
SALES (est): 245.25K **Privately Held**
Web: www.powder-pro.net
SIC: 3479 Coating of metals and formed
products

(G-10643)
POYANT SIGNS INC (PA)
125 Samuel Barnet Blvd (02745-1204)
PHONE...................800 544-0961
TOLL FREE: 800
Leonard M Poyant, *CEO*
Richard Poyant, *
Victor Gonsalves, *
EMP: 48 **EST:** 1938
SQ FT: 50,000
SALES (est): 12.77MM
SALES (corp-wide): 12.77MM **Privately
Held**
Web: www.poyantsigns.com
SIC: 3993 Electric signs

(G-10644)
PROTO XYZ INC
49 Potomska St (02740-5720)
PHONE...................508 525-6363
Michel Fernandes, *CEO*
James G Demello, *Prin*
EMP: 7 **EST:** 2021
SALES (est): 870.37K **Privately Held**
Web: www.protoxyz.com
SIC: 8711 3545 3599 Engineering services;
Precision tools, machinists'; Machine shop,
jobbing and repair

(G-10645)
REYNOLDS D-RAP CORP
186 Duchaine Blvd (02745-1201)
PHONE...................800 477-4681
Peter M Dewalt, *Pr*
Paul Bergeron, *
Diana Baldwin, *
Eric Johnson, *
Jeremiah Coholan, *
▼ **EMP:** 48 **EST:** 1946
SQ FT: 70,000
SALES (est): 4.32MM **Privately Held**
Web: www.reynoldsdewalt.com
SIC: 2752 Offset printing

(G-10646)
RF AERO LLC
Also Called: CD Aero, LLC
167 John Vertente Blvd (02745-1221)
PHONE...................508 910-3500
EMP: 34 **EST:** 2018

SALES (est): 9.98MM
SALES (corp-wide): 764.7MM **Publicly Held**
SIC: **5065** 3675 Electronic parts and equipment, nec; Electronic capacitors
HQ: Cornell-Dubilier Electronics, Inc.
140 Technology Pl
Liberty SC 29657
864 843-2277

(G-10647)
RICHARD CANTWELL WOODWORKING
611 Belleville Ave (02745-5982)
PHONE.................................508 984-7921
William Whitman, *Pr*
EMP: 8 EST: 2012
SALES (est): 254.67K **Privately Held**
SIC: **2431** Millwork

(G-10648)
SCHAEFER MARINE INC
158 Duchaine Blvd., Industrial Park (02745)
PHONE.................................508 995-9511
▲ EMP: 21 EST: 1966
SALES (est): 2.4MM **Privately Held**
Web: www.schaefermarine.com
SIC: **3429** Marine hardware

(G-10649)
SEATRADE INTERNATIONAL CO LLC
10 N Front St (02740-7327)
PHONE.................................774 305-4948
Robert Blais, *CEO*
Paul Lacorazza, *CFO*
Karin Strohbach Barndollar, *Sec*
Teressa Blanchett, *Prin*
◆ EMP: 60 EST: 1981
SQ FT: 16,000
SALES (est): 180MM
SALES (corp-wide): 395.24MM **Privately Held**
Web: www.seatrade-international.com
SIC: **2092** Fish, fresh: prepared
PA: East Coast Seafood Group, Llc
10 N Front St
New Bedford MA 02740
774 305-4948

(G-10650)
SHIP STREET CAPITAL LLC
Also Called: Edson Marine
146 Duchaine Blvd (02745-1201)
PHONE.................................508 995-9711
David Johns Ii, *Mgr*
EMP: 25 EST: 2021
SALES (est): 6MM **Privately Held**
SIC: **3531** Marine related equipment

(G-10651)
STANDARD MODERN COMPANY
186 Duchaine Blvd (02745-1201)
PHONE.................................774 425-3537
EMP: 8
SALES (est): 742.09K **Privately Held**
Web: www.standardmodern.com
SIC: **2752** Offset printing

(G-10652)
STANDARD MODERN COMPANY INC
186 Duchaine Blvd (02745-1201)
PHONE.................................508 586-4300
EMP: 53 EST: 1948
SALES (est): 6.44MM **Privately Held**
Web: www.standardmodern.com
SIC: **2752** Decals, lithographed

(G-10653)
SUNSTAR SPA COVERS INC
305 Nash Rd (02746-5868)
PHONE.................................508 993-5830
Phil Bouthillete, *Mgr*
EMP: 15
SALES (corp-wide): 22.38MM **Privately Held**
SIC: **3999** Hot tub and spa covers
HQ: Sunstar Spa Covers, Inc.
26074 Avenue Hall Ste 13
Valencia CA 91355
858 602-1950

(G-10654)
SYMMETRY MED NEW BEDFORD INC
61 John Vertente Blvd (02745-1202)
PHONE.................................781 447-6661
Karin Gilman, *Pr*
Roger M Burke, *
Frank Difrancesco, *
EMP: 25 EST: 1964
SQ FT: 25,000
SALES (est): 332.61K **Privately Held**
SIC: **3841** 3545 Surgical instruments and apparatus; Cutting tools for machine tools

(G-10655)
SYMMETRY MEDICAL INC
61 John Vertente Blvd (02745-1202)
PHONE.................................508 998-1104
Jay Nunes, *Brnch Mgr*
EMP: 246
SQ FT: 14,000
SALES (corp-wide): 832.81MM **Privately Held**
Web: www.tecomet.com
SIC: **3841** Surgical instruments and apparatus
HQ: Symmetry Medical Inc.
3724 N State Road 15
Warsaw IN 46582

(G-10656)
TONIX PHRMCEUTICALS HOLDG CORP
Also Called: Advanced Development Cente
259 Samuel Barnet Blvd New Bradford Business Park (02745)
PHONE.................................617 908-5040
EMP: 9
Web: www.tonixpharma.com
SIC: **2834** Pharmaceutical preparations
PA: Tonix Pharmaceuticals Holding Corp.
26 Main St
Chatham NJ 07928

(G-10657)
UNDER COVER INC
138 Hatch St (02745-6025)
PHONE.................................508 997-7600
Kelli W Arsenault, *Pr*
Peter C Arsenault, *Treas*
EMP: 10 EST: 2006
SQ FT: 200
SALES (est): 950.68K **Privately Held**
Web: www.undercovernyc.com
SIC: **2393** Textile bags

(G-10658)
VECTRIX LLC
55 Samuel Barnet Blvd (02745-1217)
PHONE.................................508 717-6510
EMP: 7
Web: www.vectrix.com
SIC: **3429** Motor vehicle hardware

(G-10659)
VULPLEX INC
305 Nash Rd (02746-5868)
PHONE.................................508 996-6787
Simon Lubin, *Pr*
Paul Lubin, *
EMP: 14 EST: 1946
SQ FT: 50,000
SALES (est): 244.53K **Privately Held**
SIC: **2295** 2297 2241 Leather, artificial or imitation; Nonwoven fabrics; Narrow fabric mills

(G-10660)
WOOD GEEK INC
685 Orchard St (02744-1017)
PHONE.................................508 858-5282
Frederick A Miller Junior, *Pr*
EMP: 9 EST: 2009
SQ FT: 6,000
SALES (est): 973.52K **Privately Held**
Web: www.newenglandclosetworks.com
SIC: **2511** Storage chests, household: wood

(G-10661)
Y & Z BRISTOL INC
963 Kempton St (02740-1522)
PHONE.................................508 991-7365
Victor Zhang, *Prin*
EMP: 7 EST: 2016
SALES (est): 204.25K **Privately Held**
SIC: **2621** Paper mills

(G-10662)
ZD USA HOLDINGS INC
744 Belleville Ave (02745-6010)
PHONE.................................508 998-4000
David Slutz, *CEO*
EMP: 400 EST: 2012
SALES (est): 19.82MM **Privately Held**
SIC: **3053** Gaskets; packing and sealing devices

New Braintree
Worcester County

(G-10663)
BATCH INC
80 Slein Rd (01531-1602)
P.O. Box 61051 (01116-6051)
PHONE.................................203 948-9212
David Leriche, *Pr*
EMP: 10 EST: 2018
SALES (est): 2.47MM **Privately Held**
Web: www.batchicecream.com
SIC: **3999** Manufacturing industries, nec

New Salem
Franklin County

(G-10664)
HAMILTON ORCHARDS
Also Called: Hamilton Orchards Apple Barn
25 West St (01355-9721)
PHONE.................................978 544-6867
Barbara Hamilton, *Owner*
EMP: 10 EST: 1946
SALES (est): 395.21K **Privately Held**
Web: www.hamiltonorchards.com
SIC: **0175** 0171 5461 2051 Apple orchard; Berry crops; Retail bakeries; Bread, cake, and related products

Newbury
Essex County

(G-10665)
GORDON MARTIN
80 Hanover St (01951-1127)
PHONE.................................351 201-6065
EMP: 9 EST: 2013
SALES (est): 507.77K **Privately Held**
SIC: **3491** Industrial valves

Newburyport
Essex County

(G-10666)
ALFA LAVAL INC
Also Called: Alfa Laval Thermal-Food Ctr
111 Parker St (01950-4011)
PHONE.................................978 465-5777
Craig Martin, *Mgr*
EMP: 87
SQ FT: 15,200
Web: www.alfalaval.com
SIC: **3443** 3556 Heat exchangers: coolers (after, inter), condensers, etc.; Food products machinery
HQ: Alfa Laval Inc.
5400 Intl Trade Dr
Richmond VA 23231
866 253-2528

(G-10667)
ARWOOD MACHINE CORPORATION
Also Called: AMC
95 Parker St Ste 4 (01950-4034)
PHONE.................................978 463-3777
Michael Munday, *Pr*
EMP: 92 EST: 1966
SQ FT: 82,000
SALES (est): 19.3MM **Privately Held**
Web: www.arwoodmachine.com
SIC: **3599** Machine shop, jobbing and repair

(G-10668)
AW AIRFLO INDUSTRIES INC
Also Called: Precision Metal Fabrication
52 Parker St (01950-4056)
PHONE.................................978 465-6260
EMP: 20 EST: 1974
SQ FT: 20,000
SALES (est): 3.81MM **Privately Held**
Web: www.awairflo.com
SIC: **3444** Sheet metal specialties, not stamped

(G-10669)
B & G CABINET
253 Low St Ste 8 (01950-3510)
PHONE.................................978 465-6455
EMP: 14 EST: 1995
SALES (est): 2MM **Privately Held**
Web: www.bgcabinet.com
SIC: **2434** Wood kitchen cabinets

(G-10670)
BERKSHIRE MNUFACTURED PDTS INC
Also Called: Whitcraft Newburyport
116 Parker St (01950-4008)
PHONE.................................978 462-8161
Doug Folsom, *CEO*
Brian Kelly, *
Richard M English, *
Paul J Horton, *
Phillip Krall, *

EMP: 150 **EST:** 1958
SQ FT: 35,000
SALES (est): 22.93MM **Privately Held**
Web: www.pursuitaero.com
SIC: 3469 3599 3544 3471　Metal stampings, nec; Machine shop, jobbing and repair; Special dies, tools, jigs, and fixtures; Plating and polishing

(G-10671)
BIXBY INTERNATIONAL CORP
1 Preble Rd (01950-4042)
PHONE.............................978 462-4100
Daniel S Rocconi, *Pr*
Robert Mc Lellan, *
James Mangan, *
Christopher M Fraser, *
▲ **EMP:** 60 **EST:** 1940
SQ FT: 90,000
SALES (est): 22.28MM **Privately Held**
Web: www.bixbyintl.com
SIC: 3083 3089　Laminated plastics sheets; Extruded finished plastics products, nec

(G-10672)
BRADFORD & BIGELOW INC
3 Perkins Way (01950-4007)
PHONE.............................978 904-3112
John Galligan, *Pr*
Rick Dunn, *
Carmen Frederico, *
Karl Shearer, *
Andrew Benack, *Quality Vice President*
▲ **EMP:** 180 **EST:** 1947
SQ FT: 150,000
SALES (est): 20.17MM **Privately Held**
Web: www.bradford-bigelow.com
SIC: 2752　Offset printing

(G-10673)
BUCKLEGUYCOM LLC
Also Called: Buckleguy
15 Graf Rd (01950-4014)
PHONE.............................978 213-9989
Peter W Harriss, *Managing Member*
EMP: 7 **EST:** 2007
SALES (est): 491.41K **Privately Held**
Web: www.buckleguy.com
SIC: 3965　Buckles and buckle parts

(G-10674)
CAREER PRESS INC (PA)
Also Called: New Page Books
65 Parker St Ste 7 (01950-4600)
PHONE.............................201 848-0310
Ron Fry, *Pr*
◆ **EMP:** 14 **EST:** 1985
SQ FT: 19,000
SALES (est): 2.55MM
SALES (corp-wide): 2.55MM **Privately Held**
Web: www.redwheelweiser.com
SIC: 2731　Books, publishing only

(G-10675)
CARLAT PUBLISHING LLC
2 Prince Pl (01950-2612)
P.O. Box 626 (01950-0726)
PHONE.............................978 499-0583
Jeffrey Ives, *Pr*
EMP: 7 **EST:** 2003
SALES (est): 700.45K **Privately Held**
Web: www.thecarlatreport.com
SIC: 2741　Miscellaneous publishing

(G-10676)
COMDEC INCORPORATED
25 Hale St (01950-3599)
PHONE.............................978 462-3399
Steven A Meredith, *Pr*

Kenneth Harris, *
◆ **EMP:** 31 **EST:** 1982
SQ FT: 48,000
SALES (est): 3.92MM **Privately Held**
Web: www.comdecinc.com
SIC: 2759　Screen printing

(G-10677)
CRYSTAL ENGINEERING CO INC (PA)
2 Stanley Tucker Dr (01950-4039)
PHONE.............................978 465-7007
Michael R Trotta, *Pr*
Arthur J Pappathanasi, *
EMP: 20 **EST:** 1956
SQ FT: 2,600
SALES (est): 4.39MM
SALES (corp-wide): 4.39MM **Privately Held**
Web: www.crystalengineering.com
SIC: 3469 3452　Stamping metal for the trade ; Bolts, nuts, rivets, and washers

(G-10678)
DIANNES FINE DESSERTS INC (PA)
4 Graf Rd (01950-4015)
PHONE.............................800 435-2253
Paul Lapadat, *CEO*
EMP: 190 **EST:** 2012
SQ FT: 90,000
SALES (est): 90.17MM
SALES (corp-wide): 90.17MM **Privately Held**
Web: www.diannesfinedesserts.com
SIC: 2051　Bread, cake, and related products

(G-10679)
DIANNES FINE DESSERTS INC
1 Perry Way (01950-4002)
PHONE.............................978 463-3881
Thomas Lundquist, *CFO*
EMP: 200
SALES (corp-wide): 90.17MM **Privately Held**
Web: www.diannesfinedesserts.com
SIC: 2053　Frozen bakery products, except bread
PA: Dianne's Fine Desserts, Inc.
　4 Graf Rd
　Newburyport MA 01950
　800 435-2253

(G-10680)
EAST CAST WLDG FABRICATION LLC
104 Parker St (01950-4063)
PHONE.............................978 465-2338
Andrew Laurence, *Prin*
Ron April, *Prin*
EMP: 24 **EST:** 2017
SALES (est): 9.98MM **Privately Held**
Web: www.ecweld.com
SIC: 7692　Welding repair

(G-10681)
ELECTRONIC PRODUCTS INDS INC
Also Called: Electronic Products
85 Parker St (01950-4095)
PHONE.............................978 462-8101
Christopher Mosher, *Pr*
EMP: 46 **EST:** 2017
SQ FT: 26,500
SALES (est): 7.06MM **Privately Held**
Web: www.epihermetics.com
SIC: 3674　Semiconductors and related devices

(G-10682)
EPI II INC
Also Called: Industrial Realty Trust
30 Green St (01950-2639)
PHONE.............................978 462-1514
Joseph J Urbanetti, *Pr*
Donald C Griffin, *
EMP: 65 **EST:** 1960
SQ FT: 8,000
SALES (est): 9.29MM **Privately Held**
SIC: 3674　Semiconductors and related devices

(G-10683)
FOILMARK INC (HQ)
Also Called: ITW Shinemark
5 Malcolm Hoyt Dr (01950-4082)
PHONE.............................978 225-8200
Frank J Olsen Junior, *Pr*
Philip Leibel, *
▲ **EMP:** 84 **EST:** 1991
SALES (est): 21.04MM
SALES (corp-wide): 15.93B **Publicly Held**
Web: www.itwshinemark.com
SIC: 3497 3549 3544　Metal foil and leaf; Marking machines, metalworking; Special dies, tools, jigs, and fixtures
PA: Illinois Tool Works Inc.
　155 Harlem Ave
　Glenview IL 60025
　847 724-7500

(G-10684)
FUNCTIONAL COATINGS LLC
13 Malcolm Hoyt Dr (01950-4017)
PHONE.............................978 462-0796
Stephen R Lynch, *Managing Member*
David Lynch, *
▲ **EMP:** 80 **EST:** 1989
SQ FT: 20,000
SALES (est): 8.77MM **Privately Held**
Web: www.tesa.com
SIC: 2891 3554　Adhesives; Paper industries machinery

(G-10685)
GEONAUTICS MANUFACTURING INC
506 Merrimac St (01950-1700)
P.O. Box 230 (01950-0230)
PHONE.............................978 462-7161
Tim Tracy, *Pr*
EMP: 25 **EST:** 1960
SQ FT: 25,000
SALES (est): 418.2K **Privately Held**
Web: www.geonauticsmfg.com
SIC: 3083 3544 3086 3451　Plastics finished products, laminated; Special dies, tools, jigs, and fixtures; Plastics foam products; Screw machine products

(G-10686)
HARBORSIDE PRINTING CO INC
Also Called: Coastal Printing
3 Graf Rd Ste 5 (01950-4601)
PHONE.............................978 462-2026
Micheal R Morin, *Pr*
Walter H Christiansen Junior, *VP*
Doreen Dern, *Sec*
EMP: 12 **EST:** 1984
SALES (est): 577.95K **Privately Held**
Web: www.harborprint.com
SIC: 2752　Offset printing

(G-10687)
HAWTAN LEATHERS LLC
75 Parker St (01950-4000)
PHONE.............................978 465-3791
◆ **EMP:** 105 **EST:** 1975
SALES (est): 3.99MM **Privately Held**

Web: www.hawtanleathermanufacturers.com
SIC: 3111 5199　Leather tanning and finishing; Leather, leather goods, and furs

(G-10688)
HERO COATINGS INC
13 Malcolm Hoyt Dr (01950-4017)
PHONE.............................978 462-0746
Stephen Lynch, *Pr*
David P Lynch, *Sec*
EMP: 9 **EST:** 1968
SQ FT: 20,000
SALES (est): 2.77MM **Privately Held**
Web: www.herocoatings.com
SIC: 2891　Sealants

(G-10689)
IAN MARIE INC
Also Called: Journeyman Press, The
11 Malcolm Hoyt Dr (01950-4017)
PHONE.............................978 463-6742
Dana Thoms, *Pr*
EMP: 40 **EST:** 2014
SALES (est): 9.01MM **Privately Held**
Web: www.jpress.com
SIC: 2741　Miscellaneous publishing

(G-10690)
KEIVER WILLARD-LUMBER CORP
11 Graf Rd 13 (01950-4091)
PHONE.............................978 462-7193
Robert D Keiver, *Pr*
Karl Gray, *
Kevin Barlow, *
Patricia Heintzelman, *
EMP: 71 **EST:** 1953
SALES (est): 9.35MM **Privately Held**
Web: www.keiver-willard.com
SIC: 2431 5031　Millwork; Hardboard

(G-10691)
KLEENLINE LLC
6 Opportunity Way Rear (01950-4043)
PHONE.............................978 463-0827
Jim Laverdiere, *Pr*
Mark W Anderson, *
William M Shult, *
EMP: 55 **EST:** 1987
SALES (est): 27.49MM **Privately Held**
Web: www.kleenline.com
SIC: 3535　Conveyors and conveying equipment
HQ: Pro Mach, Inc.
　50 E Rvrcnter Blvd Ste 18
　Covington KY 41011
　513 831-8778

(G-10692)
KLONE LAB LLC
Also Called: Klone Lab
115a Water St Ste A (01950-3065)
PHONE.............................978 378-3434
Tom Mcgee, *Managing Member*
Brian Seppa, *CFO*
EMP: 17 **EST:** 2016
SALES (est): 8.49MM **Privately Held**
Web: www.klonelab.com
SIC: 3021 7389　Protective footwear, rubber or plastic; Business Activities at Non-Commercial Site

(G-10693)
LABELPRINT AMERICA INC
8 Opportunity Way (01950-4043)
PHONE.............................978 463-4004
Antonio Yemma, *Pr*
Robin Hamilton, *Prin*
Sherri Carnache, *Accounting*

EMP: 29 EST: 2002
SQ FT: 21,000
SALES (est): 2.4MM **Privately Held**
Web: www.inovarpackaging.com
SIC: 2752 Offset printing

(G-10694)
LAKE MANUFACTURING CO INC
6 Opportunity Way (01950-4043)
PHONE..............................978 465-1617
Robert Lake, *Pr*
EMP: 17 EST: 1980
SQ FT: 10,000
SALES (est): 832.3K **Privately Held**
Web: www.lakemfg.com
SIC: 3599 Machine shop, jobbing and repair

(G-10695)
LEAP YEAR PUBLISHING LLC
54 Pleasant St (01950-2606)
PHONE..............................978 688-9900
Enno Tjalsma, *Managing Member*
▲ EMP: 13 EST: 2001
SALES (est): 2.86MM **Privately Held**
Web: www.leapyearbrands.com
SIC: 3944 2754 2741 Puzzles; Stationery:
gravure printing; Miscellaneous publishing

(G-10696)
MACDIARMID LLC
7 Perry Way (01950-4002)
PHONE..............................978 465-3546
David Slutz, *Managing Member*
EMP: 15 EST: 2016
SALES (est): 954.11K **Privately Held**
Web: www.macdmachine.com
SIC: 3599 Machine shop, jobbing and repair

(G-10697)
MACDIARMID MACHINE CORP
7 Perry Way Ste 13 (01950-4002)
PHONE..............................978 465-3546
Scott Macdiarmid, *Pr*
EMP: 10 EST: 1988
SQ FT: 6,000
SALES (est): 841.14K **Privately Held**
Web: www.macdmachine.com
SIC: 3599 Machine shop, jobbing and repair

(G-10698)
**MARK RICHEY WDWKG &
DESIGN INC**
40 Parker St (01950-4092)
PHONE..............................978 499-3800
Mark Richey, *Pr*
Teresa Richey, *
▲ EMP: 79 EST: 1979
SQ FT: 70,000
SALES (est): 18.61MM **Privately Held**
Web: www.markrichey.com
SIC: 2431 Millwork

(G-10699)
MERSEN USA EP CORP (HQ)
Also Called: Mersen
374 Merrimac St (01950-1930)
PHONE..............................978 462-6662
Vadim Radunsky, *Pr*
Dan Balkus, *Treas*
◆ EMP: 80 EST: 1989
SQ FT: 175,000
SALES (est): 95.36MM
SALES (corp-wide): 2.19MM **Privately
Held**
Web: www.mersen.us
SIC: 3443 3315 5051 Heat exchangers,
condensers, and components; Wire and
fabricated wire products; Metals service
centers and offices
PA: Mersen
Tour Trinity

Courbevoie 92400
146915400

(G-10700)
MERSEN USA EV LLC
374 Merrimac St (01950-1930)
PHONE..............................978 518-7648
EMP: 10 EST: 2021
SALES (est): 851.73K **Privately Held**
SIC: 3613 Fuses, electric

(G-10701)
METZYS TAQUERIA LLC
17 55th St (01950-4453)
PHONE..............................978 992-1451
EMP: 15 EST: 2014
SALES (est): 922.75K **Privately Held**
Web: www.metzys.com
SIC: 2599 5812 Food wagons, restaurant;
Mexican restaurant

(G-10702)
MIDDLESEX GENERAL INDS INC
2 New Pasture Rd Ste 7 (01950-4054)
PHONE..............................781 935-8870
Daniel Morin, *Pr*
Adrian L Pyke, *
George W Horn, *
EMP: 35 EST: 1968
SQ FT: 14,000
SALES (est): 3.86MM **Privately Held**
Web: www.midsx.com
SIC: 3825 Semiconductor test equipment

(G-10703)
**MTI-MILLIREN TECHNOLOGIES
INC**
Also Called: Mti-Milliren
2 New Pasture Rd Ste 10 (01950-4054)
PHONE..............................978 465-6064
Bryan T Milliren, *Pr*
EMP: 42 EST: 1990
SQ FT: 25,000
SALES (est): 7.87MM **Privately Held**
Web: www.mti-milliren.com
SIC: 3679 3825 Oscillators; Instruments to
measure electricity

(G-10704)
NETGALLEY LLC (PA)
44 Merrimac St Ste 21 (01950-2580)
PHONE..............................978 465-7755
Jane Lindley, *Dir*
Francis P Toolan Junior, *CEO*
EMP: 15 EST: 2009
SALES (est): 1.42MM
SALES (corp-wide): 1.42MM **Privately
Held**
Web: www.netgalley.com
SIC: 2741 Miscellaneous publishing

(G-10705)
OPPORTUNITY WORKS INC (PA)
Also Called: OPPORTUNITY WORKS
10 Opportunity Way (01950-4043)
P.O. Box 5325 (01835-0325)
PHONE..............................978 462-6144
Jane Harris-fale, *Ex Dir*
Michael Zerigian, *
Pete Falconi, *
Patrick Mccoy, *
Lucien Lacroix, *
EMP: 30 EST: 1974
SQ FT: 120,000
SALES (est): 8.19MM
SALES (corp-wide): 8.19MM **Privately
Held**
Web: www.opportunityworks.org

SIC: 8322 8331 7361 2677 Social services
for the handicapped; Job training and
related services; Employment agencies;
Envelopes

(G-10706)
PACKAGING SPECIALTIES INC
3 Opportunity Way (01950-4044)
PHONE..............................978 462-1300
Gary Swerling, *Pr*
Ray Faneuf, *
Albert Wencl, *
Philip G Ives, *
▲ EMP: 58 EST: 1989
SQ FT: 38,000
SALES (est): 9.51MM **Privately Held**
Web: www.pack-spec.com
SIC: 2621 5199 2657 2652 Packaging paper
; Packaging materials; Folding paperboard
boxes; Setup paperboard boxes

(G-10707)
POLYCARBON INDUSTRIES INC
Also Called: PCI Synthesis
9 Opportunity Way (01950-4044)
PHONE..............................978 462-5555
Jean-pascal Mill, *Pr*
Jeremy S Kandin, *
▲ EMP: 100 EST: 2018
SQ FT: 60,000
SALES (est): 38.38MM
SALES (corp-wide): 20.9MM **Privately
Held**
Web: www.pcisynthesis.com
SIC: 2834 Adrenal pharmaceutical
preparations
PA: Seqens
21 Ecully Parc
Ecully 69130
426991800

(G-10708)
POLYONICS CORPORATION
24 Graf Rd (01950-4015)
PHONE..............................978 462-3600
Thomas F Burke, *Pr*
▲ EMP: 10 EST: 1982
SQ FT: 8,000
SALES (est): 2.66MM **Privately Held**
Web: www.polyonics.com
SIC: 3679 Electronic circuits
PA: Micrometal Technologies, Inc.
5 New Pasture Rd
Newburyport MA 01950

(G-10709)
PRODUCT RESOURCES LLC
4 Mulliken Way (01950-4145)
PHONE..............................978 524-8500
Gerald Mace, *
Carolyn R Libelo, *
John Caruso, *
▲ EMP: 30 EST: 2005
SQ FT: 30,000
SALES (est): 9.28MM **Privately Held**
Web: www.prodres.com
SIC: 3822 3699 8711 8742 Environmental
controls; Electrical equipment and supplies,
nec; Engineering services; Business
planning and organizing services

(G-10710)
QUALITY SOLUTIONS INC (DH)
Also Called: Firebrand Technologies
44 Merrimac St Ste 22 (01950-2580)
PHONE..............................978 465-7755
Francis P Toolan Junior, *Pr*
EMP: 27 EST: 1988
SALES (est): 9.52MM **Privately Held**
Web: www.firebrandtech.com

SIC: 7372 2741 Business oriented computer
software; Business service newsletters:
publishing and printing
HQ: Media Do International, Inc.
12709 Via Terceto
San Diego CA 92130
310 592-3207

(G-10711)
RADAR TECHNOLOGY INC
2 New Pasture Rd (01950-4054)
EMP: 20 EST: 1973
SQ FT: 15,000
SALES (est): 1.69MM **Privately Held**
Web: www.radartechnology.com
SIC: 3812 3625 Radar systems and
equipment; Relays and industrial controls

(G-10712)
REDWHEEL/WEISER LLC (PA)
65 Parker St Ste 7 (01950-4600)
PHONE..............................978 465-0504
▲ EMP: 7 EST: 1926
SQ FT: 2,600
SALES (est): 2.32MM
SALES (corp-wide): 2.32MM **Privately
Held**
Web: www.redwheelweiser.com
SIC: 2731 5192 Books, publishing only;
Books

(G-10713)
RMS MEDIA GROUP INC
21 Middle St (01950-2716)
P.O. Box 788 (01985-2788)
PHONE..............................978 623-8020
Richard Sedler, *CEO*
Richard Sedler, *Pr*
EMP: 20 EST: 2001
SALES (est): 3.94MM **Privately Held**
Web: www.rmsmg.com
SIC: 2721 7311 Magazines: publishing only,
not printed on site; Advertising agencies

(G-10714)
**ROCHESTER ELECTRONICS
LLC**
Also Called: Warehouse
18 Malcolm Hoyt Dr (01950-4018)
PHONE..............................978 462-1248
EMP: 10
SALES (corp-wide): 15MM **Privately Held**
Web: www.rocelec.com
SIC: 3674 Integrated circuits,
semiconductor networks, etc.
PA: Rochester Electronics, Llc
16 Malcolm Hoyt Dr
Newburyport MA 01950
978 462-9332

(G-10715)
**ROCHESTER ELECTRONICS
LLC (PA)**
Also Called: Rochester Electronics
16 Malcolm Hoyt Dr (01950-4018)
PHONE..............................978 462-9332
Curt Gerrish, *CEO*
Patricia Gerrish, *
George Karalias, *
Christopher Gerrish, *
Derick Dezito, *
◆ EMP: 130 EST: 2005
SQ FT: 265,000
SALES (est): 15MM
SALES (corp-wide): 15MM **Privately Held**
Web: www.rocelec.com
SIC: 3674 5065 Integrated circuits,
semiconductor networks, etc.; Electronic
parts

(G-10716)
RUNCO CAPITAL CORPORATION
Also Called: Bishop Audio
25 Storey Ave Ste 3 (01950-1869)
PHONE..........................978 462-0320
EMP: 22
SIC: 3651 Household audio and video equipment
HQ: Runco Capital Corporation
　1195 Nw Compton Way
　Beaverton OR 97006
　510 324-7777

(G-10717)
SPRAY MAINE INC
104 Parker St (01950-4063)
PHONE..........................207 384-2273
Christopher Donahue, *Pr*
John Perrone, *Clerk*
EMP: 14 **EST:** 1974
SALES (est): 620.02K **Privately Held**
SIC: 3479 7336 Lacquering of metal products; Silk screen design

(G-10718)
STREM CHEMICALS INCORPORATED (HQ)
7 Mulliken Way (01950-4019)
PHONE..........................978 499-1600
Michael E Strem, *CEO*
Ephraim Honig, *COO*
Adam B Paton, *Sec*
▲ **EMP:** 92 **EST:** 1964
SQ FT: 29,000
SALES (est): 25.5MM
SALES (corp-wide): 101.73MM **Privately Held**
Web: www.strem.com
SIC: 2819 2869 Industrial inorganic chemicals, nec; Laboratory chemicals, organic
PA: Ascensus Specialties Llc
　2821 Northup Way Ste 275
　Bellevue WA 98004
　425 448-1679

(G-10719)
THE CRICKET SYSTEM INC
Also Called: Visible Good
5 Perkins Way Ste 2 (01950-4504)
PHONE..........................617 905-1420
EMP: 7 **EST:** 2011
SALES (est): 211.56K **Privately Held**
Web: www.visible-good.com
SIC: 3448 Prefabricated metal buildings and components

(G-10720)
THOMAS MACHINE WORKS INC
9 New Pasture Rd (01950-4040)
PHONE..........................978 462-7182
Joseph Casey, *Pr*
EMP: 9 **EST:** 1973
SQ FT: 12,000
SALES (est): 692.86K **Privately Held**
Web: tompotterphotography.pixels.com
SIC: 3545 Machine tool attachments and accessories

(G-10721)
TSHB INC
11 Malcolm Hoyt Dr (01950-4017)
PHONE..........................978 465-8950
Dana Thoms, *Pr*
EMP: 45 **EST:** 1978
SQ FT: 48,000
SALES (est): 3.68MM **Privately Held**
Web: www.jpress.com
SIC: 2752 Offset printing

(G-10722)
UFP TECHNOLOGIES INC (PA)
100 Hale St (01950-3504)
PHONE..........................978 352-2200
R Jeffrey Bailly, *Ch Bd*
Ronald J Lataille, *Sr VP*
Mitchell C Rock, *Sr VP*
EMP: 36 **EST:** 1963
SQ FT: 183,000
SALES (est): 353.79MM
SALES (corp-wide): 353.79MM **Publicly Held**
Web: www.ufpt.com
SIC: 3086 Packaging and shipping materials, foamed plastics

(G-10723)
ULTRACLAD CORPORATION
10 Perry Way (01950-4001)
PHONE..........................978 358-7945
Joseph C Runkle, *Pr*
EMP: 7 **EST:** 1992
SQ FT: 11,000
SALES (est): 797.88K **Privately Held**
SIC: 3544 8731 Special dies and tools; Commercial physical research

(G-10724)
UNION SPECIALTIES INC
3 Malcolm Hoyt Dr (01950-4084)
PHONE..........................978 465-1717
William J Greene, *Pr*
Kevin Rodden, *
John M Sullivan, *
Allyn C Woodward, *
◆ **EMP:** 33 **EST:** 1941
SQ FT: 32,000
SALES (est): 8.37MM **Privately Held**
Web: www.unionspecialtiesinc.com
SIC: 2843 2891 2851 2842 Leather finishing agents; Adhesives and sealants; Paints and allied products; Waxes for wood, leather, and other materials

(G-10725)
VARIAN SEMICDTR EQP ASSOC INC
Also Called: Applied Mtls Vrian Smicdtr Eqp
4 Stanley Tucker Dr (01950-4039)
PHONE..........................978 463-1500
Dave Holbrook, *Mgr*
EMP: 24
SALES (corp-wide): 26.52B **Publicly Held**
SIC: 3559 8249 Semiconductor manufacturing machinery; Vocational schools, nec
HQ: Varian Semiconductor Equipment Associates, Inc.
　35 Dory Rd
　Gloucester MA 01930
　978 282-2000

(G-10726)
VAUNIX TECHNOLOGY CORPORATION
7 New Pasture Rd (01950-4040)
PHONE..........................978 662-7839
Scott Blanchard, *Pr*
Alan Olsen, *Sec*
◆ **EMP:** 15 **EST:** 2005
SQ FT: 7,100
SALES (est): 2.39MM **Privately Held**
Web: www.vaunix.com
SIC: 3825 4813 Digital test equipment, electronic and electrical circuits; Data telephone communications

(G-10727)
WHITCRAFT SCRBOROUGH/ TEMPE LLC
Also Called: Whitcraft Scarborough
116 Parker St (01950-4008)
PHONE..........................763 780-0060
Patrick J Gruetzmacher, *Brnch Mgr*
EMP: 139
SALES (corp-wide): 139.19MM **Privately Held**
SIC: 3728 Aircraft assemblies, subassemblies, and parts, nec
HQ: Whitcraft Scarborough/Tempe Llc
　76 County Rd
　Eastford CT 06242
　860 974-0786

(G-10728)
ZAMPELL REFRACTORIES INC (PA)
Also Called: Zampell
9 Stanley Tucker Dr (01950-4029)
PHONE..........................978 465-0055
James C Zampell, *Pr*
Raymond Flynn, *
Christine Zampell, *
Steve Murphy, *
EMP: 50 **EST:** 1966
SALES (est): 45.44MM
SALES (corp-wide): 45.44MM **Privately Held**
Web: www.zampell.com
SIC: 1711 3255 Heating systems repair and maintenance; Clay refractories

(G-10729)
ZAR TECH
5 Stanley Tucker Dr (01950-4029)
PHONE..........................978 499-5122
James Zampell, *Ch Bd*
Brian Zampell, *CEO*
Stephen J Murphy, *CFO*
Joe Flynn, *VP Opers*
Jason Heath, *OF SAFETY & LOSS CONTROL*
EMP: 10 **EST:** 2018
SALES (est): 734.31K **Privately Held**
Web: www.zartech.com
SIC: 3297 Nonclay refractories

Newton
Middlesex County

(G-10730)
3-D MATRIX INC (HQ)
1234 Chestnut St Ste 2 (02464-1491)
PHONE..........................781 373-9020
Keiji Nagano, *CEO*
Marc Rioult, *Pr*
EMP: 7 **EST:** 2001
SALES (est): 2.72MM **Privately Held**
Web: www.3dmatrix.com
SIC: 2836 Biological products, except diagnostic
PA: 3-D Matrix,Ltd.
　3-2-4, Kojimachi
　Chiyoda-Ku TKY 102-0

(G-10731)
ADOBE INC
275 Washington St Ste 305 (02458-1653)
PHONE..........................617 467-6760
EMP: 67
SALES (corp-wide): 17.61B **Publicly Held**
Web: www.adobe.com
SIC: 7372 Prepackaged software
PA: Adobe Inc.
　345 Park Ave
　San Jose CA 95110
　408 536-6000

(G-10732)
ADVANCE SYSTEMS INC
Also Called: Advance Systems
79a Chapel St (02458-1010)
PHONE..........................888 238-8704
EMP: 10 **EST:** 2010
SALES (est): 588.07K **Privately Held**
Web: www.mitrefinch.com
SIC: 7372 Prepackaged software

(G-10733)
ARGOSY PUBLISHING INC (PA)
Also Called: Argosy
109 Oak St Ste 102 (02464-1493)
PHONE..........................617 527-9999
Andrew Bowditch, *CEO*
Matthew Bowditch, *CFO*
Alex Bilsky, *Sr VP*
EMP: 72 **EST:** 1996
SQ FT: 18,000
SALES (est): 5.55MM
SALES (corp-wide): 5.55MM **Privately Held**
Web: www.visiblebody.com
SIC: 2791 7336 2731 2396 Typesetting; Commercial art and graphic design; Book publishing; Automotive and apparel trimmings

(G-10734)
ARICHELL TECHNOLOGIES INC
55 Border St (02465-2005)
PHONE..........................617 796-9001
▲ **EMP:** 90 **EST:** 1996
SQ FT: 15,000
SALES (est): 4.78MM
SALES (corp-wide): 192.74MM **Privately Held**
SIC: 8731 3491 3823 Electronic research; Industrial valves; Process control instruments
PA: Sloan Valve Company
　10500 Seymour Ave
　Franklin Park IL 60131
　847 671-4300

(G-10735)
ARKLAY S RICHARDS CO INC
72 Winchester St (02461-1720)
PHONE..........................617 527-4385
Lincoln K Richards, *Pr*
▲ **EMP:** 15 **EST:** 1938
SQ FT: 7,000
SALES (est): 804.7K **Privately Held**
Web: www.asrichards.com
SIC: 3823 Thermocouples, industrial process type

(G-10736)
BARCLAY WATER MANAGEMENT INC
55 Chapel St Ste 400 (02458-1075)
PHONE..........................617 926-3400
William J Brett, *Pr*
Joseph Berns, *CFO*
Roland A Dion, *VP*
Joseph J Berns C.p.a., *VP*
Donald Carney Junior, *VP*
EMP: 80 **EST:** 1932
SQ FT: 26,000
SALES (est): 10.12MM
SALES (corp-wide): 23.33MM **Privately Held**
Web: www.barclaywater.com
SIC: 2899 Chemical preparations, nec
PA: Barclay Water Management, Inc.
　55 Chapel St Ste 400

Newton MA
617 926-3400

(G-10737)

BARRETT TECHNOLOGY LLC
320 Nevada St Rear (02460-1435)
PHONE....................................617 252-9000
EMP: 25 EST: 2015
SALES (est): 2.33MM Privately Held
Web: medical.barrett.com
SIC: 3569 8731 3829 Robots, assembly line: industrial and commercial; Commercial physical research; Measuring and controlling devices, nec

(G-10738)

BAYER CORPORATION
45 Industrial Pl (02461-1950)
PHONE....................................617 969-7690
Frank Mckee, Prin
EMP: 28
SALES (corp-wide): 52.7B Privately Held
Web: cropscience.bayer.com
SIC: 2821 Polypropylene resins
HQ: Bayer Corporation
100 Bayer Blvd
Whippany NJ 07981
412 777-2000

(G-10739)

BEACON WELLNESS BRANDS INC (PA)
85 Wells Ave Ste 106 (02459-3298)
PHONE....................................781 449-9500
Lisa Tanzer, CEO
EMP: 13 EST: 2021
SALES (est): 4.68MM
SALES (corp-wide): 4.68MM Privately Held
SIC: 2844 5092 Manicure preparations; Toys, nec

(G-10740)

CALIPER CORPORATION
1172 Beacon St Ste 302 (02461-1149)
PHONE....................................617 527-4700
Howard L Slavin, Pr
EMP: 25 EST: 1983
SQ FT: 10,000
SALES (est): 4.47MM Privately Held
Web: www.caliper.com
SIC: 8742 7372 Management consulting services; Prepackaged software

(G-10741)

CATALYSTSMC INC
Also Called: Beacon Wellness Brands
85 Wells Ave Ste 106 (02459-3298)
PHONE....................................781 449-9500
James M Leventhal, CEO
Maria Warrington, CFO
◆ EMP: 18 EST: 2002
SQ FT: 3,000
SALES (est): 4.68MM
SALES (corp-wide): 4.68MM Privately Held
Web: www.cliodesigns.com
SIC: 2844 5092 Manicure preparations; Toys, nec
PA: Beacon Wellness Brands, Inc.
85 Wells Ave Ste 106
Newton MA 02459
781 449-9500

(G-10742)

CELEROS INC
Also Called: Celeros Separations
1188 Centre St Ste 1 (02459-1556)
PHONE....................................248 478-2800
Scott Coleridge, CEO

Mark Norige, Pr
Kathleen Okolita, Sec
Robert Cutler, COO
EMP: 20 EST: 2004
SQ FT: 17,000
SALES (est): 638.55K Privately Held
Web: www.celerosft.com
SIC: 3559 Chemical machinery and equipment

(G-10743)

CENTERITY SYSTEMS INC
154 Wells Ave Ste 4 (02459-3347)
PHONE....................................339 225-7007
Roi Keren, CEO
Roi Keran, Pr
EMP: 10 EST: 2010
SALES (est): 1.69MM Privately Held
Web: www.centerity.com
SIC: 7371 7372 Computer software development and applications; Prepackaged software
PA: Centerity Ltd
10 Zarchin Alexander
Raanana 43662

(G-10744)

CHEETAH MEDICAL INC (PA)
1320 Centre St Ste 400 (02459-2400)
PHONE....................................617 964-0613
Chris Hutchison, Pr
EMP: 52 EST: 2010
SALES (est): 9.49MM
SALES (corp-wide): 9.49MM Privately Held
SIC: 3841 Medical instruments and equipment, blood and bone work

(G-10745)

CHELSEA INDUSTRIES INC
46a Glen Ave (02459-2066)
PHONE....................................617 232-6060
▲ EMP: 740
SIC: 3535 Conveyors and conveying equipment

(G-10746)

CHESHIRE SOFTWARE INC
1170 Walnut St (02461-1224)
P.O. Box 67487 (02467-0006)
PHONE....................................617 527-4000
Joshua Wright, Pr
EMP: 10 EST: 1990
SALES (est): 801.46K Privately Held
Web: www.cheshire.com
SIC: 7372 Prepackaged software

(G-10747)

COACTIVE TECHNOLOGIES LLC
15 Riverdale Ave Ste 1 (02458-1057)
PHONE....................................617 969-3700
EMP: 125
SIC: 3679 Electronic switches

(G-10748)

CORPORATE RMBURSEMENT SVCS INC
Also Called: C R S
233 Needham St Ste 540 (02464)
PHONE....................................888 312-0788
Gregg Darish, CEO
Anthony Craig Powell, *
Tim Brown, *
EMP: 80 EST: 2004
SALES (est): 1.61MM Privately Held
Web: www.motus.com
SIC: 7374 7372 Data processing and preparation; Business oriented computer software

(G-10749)

COURAGE THERAPEUTICS INC
64 Homer St (02459-1517)
PHONE....................................617 216-9921
Dan Housman, CEO
Fred Mermelstein, Prin *
EMP: 8 EST: 2019
SALES (est): 721.56K Privately Held
Web: www.couragetx.com
SIC: 2834 Pharmaceutical preparations

(G-10750)

CRIMSON UPHOLSTERY COMPANY INC
175 North St Rear (02460-1053)
PHONE....................................617 332-0758
Frank Cucchiara, Pr
Carmen D'aurora, Treas
EMP: 10 EST: 1977
SQ FT: 10,000
SALES (est): 427.65K Privately Held
Web: www.fabric-showroom.com
SIC: 7641 2512 Reupholstery; Upholstered household furniture

(G-10751)

CURREX LLC
Also Called: Currex America
539 Commonwealth Ave (02459-1601)
PHONE....................................206 883-0209
EMP: 7 EST: 2017
SALES (est): 460.98K Privately Held
Web: www.currex.com
SIC: 3714 Motor vehicle parts and accessories

(G-10752)

CYBERARK SOFTWARE INC (HQ)
60 Wells Ave Ste 103 (02459-3257)
PHONE....................................617 965-1544
Udi Mokady, CEO
Chen Bitan, *
Adam Bosnian, *
Alan Bird, *
Suzy Peled-spigelman, VP
EMP: 250 EST: 2000
SQ FT: 1,000
SALES (est): 301.34MM Privately Held
Web: www.cyberark.com
SIC: 7372 Prepackaged software
PA: Cyberark Software Ltd.
9 Hapsagot
Petah Tikva 49510

(G-10753)

DUKE RIVER ENGINEERING CO
Also Called: Duke River Engineering
30 Ossipee Rd (02464-1444)
PHONE....................................617 965-7255
Jeffrey Thumm, Pr
EMP: 7 EST: 1985
SQ FT: 3,000
SALES (est): 860.09K Privately Held
SIC: 3826 Analytical instruments

(G-10754)

EAST BASIN SPORTS INC (PA) ✪
Also Called: Boston Ski Tennis
153 Needham St (02464-1537)
PHONE....................................781 492-2747
Helaine Carroll, Dir
Mike Carroll, Pr
EMP: 50 EST: 2022
SALES (est): 7.44MM
SALES (corp-wide): 7.44MM Privately Held
Web: www.bostonskiandtennis.com

SIC: 3949 7389 Tennis equipment and supplies; Business Activities at Non-Commercial Site

(G-10755)

EMC CORPORATION
95 Wells Ave Ste 160 (02459-3216)
PHONE....................................617 618-3400
Larry Murray, Mgr
EMP: 59
Web: www.emc.com
SIC: 3572 7372 Computer storage devices; Prepackaged software
HQ: Emc Corporation
176 South St
Hopkinton MA 01748
508 435-1000

(G-10756)

FRENDZI INC
275 Grove St (02466)
PHONE....................................617 899-0234
John P Sheehan, CEO
EMP: 10 EST: 2021
SALES (est): 448.24K Privately Held
SIC: 7389 7372 Advertising, promotional, and trade show services; Prepackaged software

(G-10757)

GINGER SOFTWARE INC
128 Chestnut St (02465-2539)
PHONE....................................617 755-0160
EMP: 14 EST: 2007
SALES (est): 585.6K Privately Held
Web: www.gingersoftware.com
SIC: 7372 Application computer software

(G-10758)

GRANDTEN DISTILLING LLC
7 Clinton St (02458-1211)
PHONE....................................484 888-1323
Matthew Nuernberger, Mgr
EMP: 7 EST: 2010
SALES (est): 242K Privately Held
Web: www.grandten.com
SIC: 2085 Distilled and blended liquors

(G-10759)

HID GLOBAL CORPORATION
1320 Centre St Ste 201a (02459-2456)
PHONE....................................617 581-6200
EMP: 21
SALES (corp-wide): 11.51B Privately Held
Web: www.hidglobal.com
SIC: 3825 Radio frequency measuring equipment
HQ: Hid Global Corporation
611 Center Ridge Dr
Austin TX 78753

(G-10760)

HOMEPORTFOLIO INC
Also Called: Building Blocks
288 Walnut St Ste 500 (02460-1994)
PHONE....................................617 559-1197
Dale Williams, Pr
Steven Schneider, *
EMP: 21 EST: 1994
SQ FT: 20,000
SALES (est): 980.32K Privately Held
Web: www.homeportfolio.com
SIC: 7372 7374 7375 Home entertainment computer software; Computer graphics service; Information retrieval services

(G-10761)

INDUSTRIAL VIDEO & CTRL CO LLC

189 Wells Ave Ste 202 (02459)
PHONE...................617 467-3059
Norman Fast, *CEO*
Norman Fast, *Pr*
Bill Richards, *
Gary George, *
▼ **EMP:** 28 **EST:** 2001
SQ FT: 4,000
SALES (est): 5.21MM **Privately Held**
Web: www.ivcco.com
SIC: 3651   Video camera-audio recorders, household use

(G-10762)
INFLAMMASOME
THERAPEUTICS INC
57 Chapel St Ste 100 (02458-1079)
PHONE...................617 331-1071
EMP: 12 **EST:** 2016
SALES (est): 2.23MM **Privately Held**
Web: www.inflam.com
SIC: 2834   Pharmaceutical preparations

(G-10763)
INNOVHEART US INC
55 Chapel St Ste 10 (02458-1095)
PHONE...................858 349-8652
Dong Shin, *Prin*
EMP: 10 **EST:** 2017
SALES (est): 2.3MM **Privately Held**
Web: www.innovheart.com
SIC: 3845   Heart-lung machine

(G-10764)
INTERNATIONAL MARKETING
SPECIALISTS INC
Also Called: IMS
1105 Washington St (02465-2119)
PHONE...................617 965-3400
▲ **EMP:** 15
Web: www.forshrimp.com
SIC: 2092   Seafoods, frozen: prepared

(G-10765)
JOSEPH G PULITANO INSUR
AGCY
Also Called: Advanced Resources Marketing
313 Washington St Ste 225 (02458-1626)
PHONE...................617 783-2622
Joseph Pulitano, *Pr*
Lawrence Pensack, *CFO*
EMP: 10 **EST:** 1983
SQ FT: 30,000
SALES (est): 1.4MM **Privately Held**
Web: www.armltc.com
SIC: 6411 8742 2721   Insurance agents, nec
; Marketing consulting services; Periodicals, publishing only

(G-10766)
KARYOPHARM THERAPEUTICS
INC (PA)
85 Wells Ave Ste 300 (02459-3215)
PHONE...................617 658-0600
Richard Paulson, *Pr*
Tanya Lewis, *REG AFFAIRS STRATEGIC Operations*
Sharon Shacham, *CSO*
Michael Mason, *Sr VP*
Michael Mano, *Sr VP*
EMP: 154 **EST:** 2009
SQ FT: 98,502
SALES (est): 157.07MM
SALES (corp-wide): 157.07MM **Publicly Held**
Web: www.karyopharm.com
SIC: 2834   Pharmaceutical preparations

(G-10767)
KAYAKU ADVANCED
MATERIALS INC
20 Ossipee Rd (02464-1444)
PHONE...................617 965-5511
EMP: 28
Web: www.kayakuam.com
SIC: 2899   Chemical preparations, nec
PA: Kayaku Advanced Materials, Inc.
200 Flanders Rd
Westborough MA 01581

(G-10768)
LIBERTY ENGINEERING INC
26 Farwell St (02460-1071)
PHONE...................617 965-6644
Dennis Chevalier, *Pr*
EMP: 30 **EST:** 1973
SQ FT: 16,000
SALES (est): 5.6MM **Privately Held**
Web: www.libertyenginc.com
SIC: 3672   Printed circuit boards

(G-10769)
LIFE IMAGE INC
Also Called: Lifeimage
300 Washington St Ste 200 (02458-1655)
PHONE...................617 244-8411
Matthew A Michela, *CEO*
Matthew A Michela, *Pr*
Hamid Tabatabaie, *
Janak Joshi, *
Lisa Sanderson, *
EMP: 102 **EST:** 2008
SALES (est): 46.2MM
SALES (corp-wide): 46.14MM **Privately Held**
Web: www.intelerad.com
SIC: 7372   Business oriented computer software
PA: Systemes Medicaux Intelerad Incorporee, Les
12eme-800 Boul De Maisonneuve E
Montreal QC H2L 4
514 931-6222

(G-10770)
NATIONAL LUMBER COMPANY
Also Called: Newton Design Center
15 Needham St (02461-1615)
PHONE...................617 244-8020
TOLL FREE: 800
Rob Golstien, *Mgr*
EMP: 41
SALES (corp-wide): 22.73B **Publicly Held**
Web: www.national-lumber.com
SIC: 5251 2439 5231   Hardware stores; Structural wood members, nec; Paint, glass, and wallpaper stores
HQ: National Lumber Company Llc
71 Maple St
Mansfield MA 02048
508 339-8020

(G-10771)
NEOLANE INC
275 Washington St 3rd Fl (02458-1653)
PHONE...................617 467-6760
EMP: 67
Web: business.adobe.com
SIC: 7372   Prepackaged software

(G-10772)
NEWTON MATERION INC (HQ)
Also Called: H.C. Starck Solutions
45 Industrial Pl (02461-1950)
PHONE...................617 630-5800
Jacob Homiller, *CEO*
Paul A Leblanc, *
Jens Knoell, *

Uli Blankenstein, *CMO* *
◆ **EMP:** 150 **EST:** 1975
SQ FT: 300,000
SALES (est): 147.42MM **Publicly Held**
Web: www.hcstarcksolutions.com
SIC: 3356 3313 3339   Nonferrous rolling and drawing, nec; Electrometallurgical products; Primary nonferrous metals, nec
PA: Materion Corporation
6070 Parkland Blvd
Mayfield Heights OH 44124

(G-10773)
NOVELSAT INC
25 Tanglewood Rd (02459-2849)
PHONE...................617 658-1419
Tuvia Feldman, *Ch*
EMP: 32 **EST:** 2007
SALES (est): 612.33K **Privately Held**
Web: www.novelsat.com
SIC: 3663   Space satellite communications equipment

(G-10774)
PLANNUH INC
150 Gibbs St (02459-1928)
PHONE...................617 965-7393
Peter Mahoney, *Pr*
EMP: 24 **EST:** 2017
SALES (est): 744.88K **Privately Held**
Web: www.planful.com
SIC: 7372   Prepackaged software

(G-10775)
POWER OBJECT INC
123 Ridge Ave (02459-2506)
PHONE...................617 630-5701
Martin Shiu, *Pr*
Martis Shiu, *
EMP: 7 **EST:** 1998
SALES (est): 249.76K **Privately Held**
Web: www.powerobject.com
SIC: 7372   Prepackaged software

(G-10776)
PRIMATOPE THERAPEUTICS
INC
508 Dudley Rd (02459-2809)
PHONE...................617 413-3020
Mike Tepper, *CEO*
EMP: 7 **EST:** 2012
SALES (est): 94.18K **Privately Held**
SIC: 2834   Pharmaceutical preparations

(G-10777)
PROFICIENT SOFTWARE CORP
396 Dedham St (02459-2888)
PHONE...................617 964-3457
Peter M Orkin, *Prin*
EMP: 7 **EST:** 2005
SALES (est): 109.23K **Privately Held**
SIC: 7372   Prepackaged software

(G-10778)
QUANTTUS INC
2 Newton Executive Park Ste 104 (02462-1461)
PHONE...................617 401-2648
Shahid Azim, *CEO*
EMP: 9 **EST:** 2012
SALES (est): 748.94K **Privately Held**
Web: www.quanttus.com
SIC: 3845   Electromedical apparatus

(G-10779)
RED POINT POSITIONING CORP
(PA)
Also Called: Redpoint
313 Washington St (02458-1626)

PHONE...................339 222-0261
◆ **EMP:** 12 **EST:** 2014
SALES (est): 2.67MM
SALES (corp-wide): 2.67MM **Privately Held**
Web: www.redpointpositioning.com
SIC: 8731 7372 7389   Computer (hardware) development; Prepackaged software; Business Activities at Non-Commercial Site

(G-10780)
RELX INC
Also Called: Lexisnexis
313 Washington St Ste 401 (02458-1659)
PHONE...................617 558-4925
EMP: 53
SALES (corp-wide): 10.3B **Privately Held**
Web: www.lexisnexis.com
SIC: 2721   Magazines: publishing only, not printed on site
HQ: Relx Inc.
230 Park Ave Ste 700
New York NY 10169
212 309-8100

(G-10781)
RIG GRIP INCORPORATED
665 Centre St (02458-2341)
PHONE...................800 770-2666
Daniel Weinstein, *Pr*
Sharon Weinstein, *Sec*
Reuben Weinstein, *Treas*
EMP: 7 **EST:** 2014
SALES (est): 604.05K **Privately Held**
Web: www.riggripinc.com
SIC: 2821   Polyesters

(G-10782)
SECOND WIND SYSTEMS INC
Also Called: Second Wind
15 Riverdale Ave (02458-1057)
PHONE...................617 581-6090
Enda Bloomer, *Prin*
EMP: 16 **EST:** 2007
SALES (est): 606.24K **Privately Held**
Web: www.secondwind.com
SIC: 3829   Measuring and controlling devices, nec

(G-10783)
SECOND WIND SYSTEMS INC
Also Called: Second Wind
15 Riverdale Ave (02458-1057)
PHONE...................617 467-1500
▲ **EMP:** 60
SIC: 3829   Measuring and controlling devices, nec

(G-10784)
SHUFRO SECURITY COMPANY
INC
Also Called: Shufro Engineering Labs
1231 Washington St (02460)
P.O. Box 600393 (02460-0004)
PHONE...................617 244-3355
Richard Shufro, *Pr*
EMP: 8 **EST:** 1971
SALES (est): 971.23K **Privately Held**
Web: www.shufro.com
SIC: 3669 1731   Burglar alarm apparatus, electric; Fire detection and burglar alarm systems specialization

(G-10785)
SOFNET TECHNOLOGY INC
5 North St (02460-1123)
PHONE...................857 272-2568
Neeraj Mital, *Pr*
EMP: 10 **EST:** 1997
SQ FT: 1,000

▲ = Import ▼ = Export
◆ = Import/Export

SALES (est): 487.81K **Privately Held**
Web: www.sofnettech.com
SIC: 7372 8748 Prepackaged software;
Systems engineering consultant, ex.
computer or professional

(G-10786)
SPATTER INC
21 Randolph St (02461-1308)
PHONE.................................617 510-0498
Ori Spigelman, *CEO*
Suzy Peled-spigelman, *VP*
Giora Chamizer, *VP*
Yehuda Orr, *Development*
EMP: 8 EST: 2013
SALES (est): 436.36K **Privately Held**
Web: www.spatterit.com
SIC: 7372 Application computer software

(G-10787)
SPIRE SOLAR LLC
2020 Commonwealth Ave Ste 200 (02466)
PHONE.................................617 332-4040
Stephen Hogan, *COO*
EMP: 32 EST: 2016
SQ FT: 250
SALES (est): 5.61MM **Privately Held**
Web: www.eternalsunspire.com
SIC: 3674 Semiconductors and related
devices
HQ: Eternal Sun B.V.
Wolga 11
's-Gravenhage ZH

(G-10788)
STONE TABLET LLC
Also Called: Laborsoft
233 Needham St Ste 514 (02464-1542)
PHONE.................................781 380-8800
David Dorant, *Managing Member*
EMP: 10 EST: 2012
SALES (est): 618.81K **Privately Held**
SIC: 7372 7389 Prepackaged software;
Personal service agents, brokers, and
bureaus

(G-10789)
STUART KARON
Also Called: Spiral Software
248 Park St (02458-2313)
PHONE.................................802 649-1911
Stuart Karon, *Owner*
EMP: 11 EST: 1989
SALES (est): 608.52K **Privately Held**
Web: www.spiralsoftware.com
SIC: 7372 Business oriented computer
software

(G-10790)
SYSAID TECHNOLOGIES INC
128 Chestnut St (02465-2539)
PHONE.................................800 686-7047
Israel Lifshitz, *Ch*
Sarah Lahav, *CEO*
EMP: 20 EST: 2013
SALES (est): 156.54K **Privately Held**
Web: www.sysaid.com
SIC: 7372 Business oriented computer
software

(G-10791)
TRINE PHARMACEUTICALS INC
1 Gateway Ctr (02458-2879)
PHONE.................................617 558-8789
Mark Skaletsky, *Ch Bd*
Timothy Noyes, *COO*
EMP: 12 EST: 1993
SQ FT: 42,000
SALES (est): 252.17K **Privately Held**
Web: www.trinepharma.com

SIC: 2834 Drugs affecting parasitic and
infective diseases

(G-10792)
VAISALA INC
15 Riverdale Ave (02458-1057)
PHONE.................................617 467-1500
EMP: 41
SALES (corp-wide): 534.04MM **Privately
Held**
Web: www.vaisala.com
SIC: 3829 Measuring and controlling
devices, nec
HQ: Vaisala Inc.
194 S Taylor Ave
Louisville CO 80027
303 499-1701

(G-10793)
VBLEARNING LLC
109 Oak St Ste 203 (02464-1493)
PHONE.................................617 527-9999
EMP: 23 EST: 2015
SALES (est): 1.14MM **Privately Held**
SIC: 7372 Educational computer software

(G-10794)
WELLCOIN INC
11 Drumlin Rd (02459-2806)
PHONE.................................617 512-8617
Glenn Laffel, *CEO*
Jp Pollak, *Engr*
Daniela Retelny, *Pdt Mgr*
EMP: 7 EST: 2011
SALES (est): 323.56K **Privately Held**
Web: www.wellcoin.com
SIC: 7372 Application computer software

Newton Upper Falls
Middlesex County

(G-10795)
**SCION MEDICAL
TECHOLOGIES LLC**
90 Oak St # 1 (02464-1439)
PHONE.................................617 455-5186
EMP: 8 EST: 2012
SALES (est): 332.6K **Privately Held**
Web: www.scionmedtech.com
SIC: 3841 Diagnostic apparatus, medical

Newtonville
Middlesex County

(G-10796)
BARRETT TECHNOLOGY INC
320 Nevada St (02460-1435)
PHONE.................................617 252-9000
William Townsend, *Ch Bd*
Burton D.o.s., *COO*
▼ EMP: 20 EST: 1990
SALES (est): 3.47MM **Privately Held**
Web: www.barrett.com
SIC: 8732 3569 Research services, except
laboratory; Robots, assembly line: industrial
and commercial

Norfolk
Norfolk County

(G-10797)
**CAMGER COATINGS SYSTEMS
INC**
364 Main St (02056-1249)
PHONE.................................508 528-5787

Daniel C Iannuzzi, *Pr*
Theresa Iannuzzi, *Stockholder**
Thomas Meisner, *
Debra M Degrazia, *
Brian Falder, *
EMP: 35 EST: 1970
SQ FT: 70,000
SALES (est): 5.15MM **Privately Held**
Web: www.camger.com
SIC: 2851 Lacquer: bases, dopes, thinner

(G-10798)
**GUARDIAN INDUS PDTS INC
MASS**
Also Called: Guardian Industrial
150 Dedham St (02056-1665)
PHONE.................................508 384-0060
Paul Shepard, *Pr*
Marlene A Shepard, *Clerk*
EMP: 8 EST: 1969
SALES (est): 1.05MM **Privately Held**
Web: www.floorfixer.com
SIC: 3081 5169 Floor or wall covering,
unsupported plastics; Chemicals and allied
products, nec

(G-10799)
HAMLIN CABINET CORP
112 Pond St (02056-1610)
PHONE.................................508 384-8371
Roy Hamlin, *Treas*
Brian Hamlin, *Pr*
Kevin Hamlin, *VP*
EMP: 9 EST: 1964
SQ FT: 7,000
SALES (est): 11.57K **Privately Held**
Web: www.hamlincabinetcorp.com
SIC: 2434 Vanities, bathroom: wood

(G-10800)
L J GENTILE & SONS INC
228 Dedham St Rear (02056-1578)
PHONE.................................508 384-5156
Lee Gentile, *Pr*
Lee Gentile, *Pr*
Louis J Gentile, *VP*
EMP: 7 EST: 1973
SQ FT: 6,400
SALES (est): 954.23K **Privately Held**
Web: www.ljgentile.com
SIC: 3272 1794 Concrete products, nec;
Excavation and grading, building
construction

(G-10801)
**LONGWORTH VENTURE
PARTNERS LP (PA)**
17 Chickadee Dr (02056-1740)
PHONE.................................781 663-3600
Paul Margolis, *Sr Pt*
EMP: 9 EST: 1994
SALES (est): 4.88MM
SALES (corp-wide): 4.88MM **Privately
Held**
Web: www.longworth.com
SIC: 7372 6726 Application computer
software; Investment offices, nec

North Adams
Berkshire County

(G-10802)
AIR-TITE HOLDERS INC
1560 Curran Hwy (01247-3900)
P.O. Box 83 (01227-0083)
PHONE.................................413 664-2730
Glenn Therrien, *Pr*
Ann Therrien, *Sec*

▲ EMP: 16 EST: 1980
SQ FT: 27,000
SALES (est): 1.67MM **Privately Held**
Web: www.airtiteholders.com
SIC: 3089 Plastics containers, except foam

(G-10803)
BERKMATICS INC
59 Demond Ave (01247-3240)
P.O. Box 1839 (01247-1839)
PHONE.................................413 664-6152
Douglas Wylde, *Pr*
Russell Wylde, *VP*
Arthur Wylde, *Ch Bd*
Audie Wylde, *VP*
EMP: 10 EST: 1940
SQ FT: 15,000
SALES (est): 982.97K **Privately Held**
Web: www.berkmatics.com
SIC: 3451 Screw machine products

(G-10804)
BOXCAR MEDIA LLC
102 Main St (01247-3402)
PHONE.................................413 663-3384
Osmin F Olivarez, *Managing Member*
Jim Shaker, *
EMP: 11 EST: 2000
SQ FT: 5,000
SALES (est): 540.65K **Privately Held**
Web: www.boxcarmedia.com
SIC: 2741 7372 Telephone and other
directory publishing; Publisher's computer
software

(G-10805)
**CORDMASTER ENGINEERING
CO INC**
Also Called: Cme
1544 Curran Hwy (01247-3900)
PHONE.................................413 664-9371
Bernard J Laroche, *Pr*
Luis Teixeira, *Pr*
Hugh M Daley, *Ex VP*
EMP: 20 EST: 1984
SQ FT: 10,000
SALES (est): 6.19MM **Privately Held**
Web: www.cordmaster.com
SIC: 3643 3613 3625 3699 Current-carrying
wiring services; Switchgear and
switchboard apparatus; Relays and
industrial controls; Electrical equipment and
supplies, nec

(G-10806)
DENAULT INC
Also Called: Deerfield Machine & Tool Co
79 Walden St (01247-3328)
P.O. Box 777 (01247-0777)
PHONE.................................413 664-6771
Alfred Denault, *Pr*
Teresa D Denault, *VP*
EMP: 7 EST: 1978
SQ FT: 5,576
SALES (est): 1.08MM **Privately Held**
Web: www.deerfieldmachineandtool.com
SIC: 3599 Machine shop, jobbing and repair

(G-10807)
**EXCELSIOR PRINTING
COMPANY**
60 Roberts Dr (01247-3254)
P.O. Box 401 (01242-0401)
PHONE.................................413 663-3771
EMP: 60
SIC: 2752 2796 2791 2789 Offset printing;
Platemaking services; Typesetting;
Bookbinding and related work

(G-10808)
GHP MEDIA INC
Also Called: Excelsior Printing
123 Mass Moca Way (01247-2411)
PHONE....................413 663-3771
Joe Lavalla, *Mgr*
EMP: 80
Web: www.ghpmedia.com
SIC: 2752 2796 2791 2789   Offset printing;
Platemaking services; Typesetting;
Bookbinding and related work
PA: Ghp Media Inc.
475 Heffernan Dr
West Haven CT 06516

(G-10809)
J F GRIFFIN PUBLISHING LLC
33 Main St Ste 2 (01247-3410)
PHONE....................413 884-0085
EMP: 14 **EST:** 2004
SALES (est): 2.49MM Privately Held
Web: www.jfgriffin.com
SIC: 2741   Miscellaneous publishing

(G-10810)
LOUIS A GREEN CORP
Also Called: Wicking Products
121 Union St Ste 15 (01247-3526)
PHONE....................781 535-6199
Thomas Kivney, *Pr*
Janet Green, *Treas*
Susan Green, *VP*
◆ **EMP:** 11 **EST:** 1947
SQ FT: 15,000
SALES (est): 2.26MM Privately Held
Web: www.louisagreen.com
SIC: 5199 2241   Woolen and worsted yarns;
Strapping webs

(G-10811)
MORESI & ASSOCIATES DEV
CO LLC
60 Roberts Dr Ste 201 (01247-3256)
PHONE....................413 663-8677
EMP: 13 **EST:** 2014
SALES (est): 1.05MM Privately Held
Web: www.moresiandassociates.com
SIC: 1389   Construction, repair, and
dismantling services

(G-10812)
MORRISON BERKSHIRE INC
865 Church St (01247-4126)
P.O. Box 958 (01247-0958)
PHONE....................413 663-6501
Jim White, *Pr*
Richard Pellerin, *
◆ **EMP:** 29 **EST:** 1983
SQ FT: 130,000
SALES (est): 5.9MM Privately Held
Web: www.morrisonberkshire.com
SIC: 3599   Machine shop, jobbing and repair

(G-10813)
TOG MANUFACTURING
COMPANY INC
1454 S State St (01247-3911)
PHONE....................949 888-7700
Tedd Sellers, *Pr*
Stuart Jones, *
Tracy D Pagliara, *
Raymond K Guba, *
▲ **EMP:** 33 **EST:** 1984
SQ FT: 28,000
SALES (est): 17.08MM
SALES (corp-wide): 16.95B Publicly Held
SIC: 3599   Machine shop, jobbing and repair
PA: Stanley Black & Decker, Inc.
1000 Stanley Dr

New Britain CT 06053
860 225-5111

(G-10814)
TUPELO PRESS INC
60 Roberts Dr Ste 308 (01247-3254)
P.O. Box 1767 (01247-1767)
PHONE....................413 664-9611
Jeffrey E Levine, *CEO*
EMP: 15 **EST:** 2004
SALES (est): 1.21MM Privately Held
Web: www.tupelopress.org
SIC: 8748 2731   Publishing consultant; Book
publishing

North Andover
Essex County

(G-10815)
6K ENERGY LLC
25 Commerce Way Ste 6 (01845-1002)
PHONE....................978 258-1645
EMP: 15 **EST:** 2021
SALES (est): 1.2MM Privately Held
SIC: 3356   Battery metal

(G-10816)
ACE RESIDENTIAL SOLAR LLC
Also Called: Ace Solar
16 High St (01845-2656)
PHONE....................800 223-1462
EMP: 10 **EST:** 2015
SALES (est): 6.4MM Privately Held
Web: www.myacesolar.com
SIC: 4931 4911 1711 3674   Electric and
other services combined; Electric services;
Solar energy contractor; Semiconductors
and related devices

(G-10817)
ADVANCE REPRODUCTIONS
CORP
100 Flagship Dr (01845-6193)
PHONE....................978 685-2911
Thomas J Nigrelli, *Pr*
Paul Nigrelli, *
▼ **EMP:** 70 **EST:** 1945
SQ FT: 37,000
SALES (est): 11.49MM Privately Held
Web: www.advancerepro.com
SIC: 3861   Photographic sensitized goods,
nec

(G-10818)
ANDOVER AUDIO LLC
15 High St (01845-2637)
PHONE....................978 775-3670
▲ **EMP:** 10 **EST:** 2011
SQ FT: 7,000
SALES (est): 1.08MM Privately Held
Web: www.andoveraudio.com
SIC: 3651   Audio electronic systems

(G-10819)
ANDOVER PUBLISHING
COMPANY
Also Called: Andover Townsmen
100 Turnpike St (01845-5033)
P.O. Box 1986 (01810-0186)
PHONE....................978 475-7000
Irving E Rogers Iii, *Pr*
EMP: 17 **EST:** 1950
SQ FT: 5,000
SALES (est): 625.24K Privately Held
Web: www.andovertownsman.com
SIC: 2711   Newspapers: publishing only, not
printed on site

(G-10820)
ARIES SYSTEMS CORPORATION
50 High St Ste 21 (01845-2676)
PHONE....................978 975-7570
Lyndon S Holmes, *Pr*
Kenneth Fogarty, *
Linda Lavelle, *
EMP: 25 **EST:** 1986
SALES (est): 6.1MM
SALES (corp-wide): 10.3B Privately Held
Web: www.ariessys.com
SIC: 7372 7371   Publisher's computer
software; Custom computer programming
services
HQ: Elsevier Inc.
230 Park Ave Fl 7
New York NY 10169
212 309-8100

(G-10821)
BAKE-N-JOY FOODS INC (PA)
351 Willow St (01845-5973)
PHONE....................978 683-1414
EMP: 94 **EST:** 1967
SALES (est): 31.67MM
SALES (corp-wide): 31.67MM Privately
Held
Web: www.bakenjoy.com
SIC: 2053 2045 2051 2038   Frozen bakery
products, except bread; Prepared flour
mixes and doughs; Bread, cake, and
related products; Frozen specialties, nec

(G-10822)
CARRIAGE TOWNE NEWS
100 Turnpike St (01845-5033)
PHONE....................603 642-4499
Al Getler, *Pr*
EMP: 7 **EST:** 1983
SALES (est): 374.75K Privately Held
Web: www.carriagetownenews.com
SIC: 2711   Newspapers: publishing only, not
printed on site

(G-10823)
CENTRAL METAL FINISHING INC
80 Flagship Dr (01845-6106)
PHONE....................978 291-0500
Carol Shibles, *Pr*
EMP: 100 **EST:** 1977
SQ FT: 41,000
SALES (est): 8.95MM Privately Held
Web: www.cenmet.com
SIC: 3471   Anodizing (plating) of metals or
formed products

(G-10824)
COLOR CHANGE
TECHNOLOGY INC
30 Masschstts Ave Ste 306 (01845)
PHONE....................978 377-0050
Charles Pemble, *Treas*
Chris Wyres, *CEO*
EMP: 8 **EST:** 2014
SALES (est): 203.34K Privately Held
SIC: 2816   Inorganic pigments

(G-10825)
COMFORT FOODS INC
25 Commerce Way Ste 5 (01845-1002)
PHONE....................978 557-0009
Michael J Sullivan, *Pr*
Diane M Sullivan, *Stockholder*
Victor Janovich, *Dir*
Stephen J Beattie, *CFO*
▲ **EMP:** 18 **EST:** 1992
SQ FT: 50,000
SALES (est): 9.97MM
SALES (corp-wide): 65.71MM Publicly
Held

Web: www.harmonybaycoffee.com
SIC: 5149 2095   Coffee, green or roasted;
Coffee roasting (except by wholesale
grocers)
PA: Coffee Holding Co., Inc.
3475 Victory Blvd Ste 4
Staten Island NY 10314
718 832-0800

(G-10826)
DOWSLAKE MICROSYSTEMS
CORP
21 High St Ste 306 (01845-2601)
PHONE....................978 691-5700
Dan D Yang, *CEO*
EMP: 9 **EST:** 2000
SALES (est): 394.65K Privately Held
Web: www.dowslakemicro.com
SIC: 3577   Computer peripheral equipment,
nec

(G-10827)
EAGLE-TRIBUNE PUBLISHING
CO
Also Called: Eagle Tribune, The
100 Turnpike St (01845-5033)
P.O. Box 1986 (01810-0186)
PHONE....................978 946-2000
Karen Andreas, *Brnch Mgr*
EMP: 11
SALES (corp-wide): 33.14B Privately Held
Web: www.eagletribune.com
SIC: 2711   Newspapers, publishing and
printing
HQ: Eagle-Tribune Publishing Company
100 Turnpike St
North Andover MA 01845
978 946-2000

(G-10828)
EAGLE-TRIBUNE PUBLISHING
CO (DH)
Also Called: Andover Townsman
100 Turnpike St (01845-5033)
PHONE....................978 946-2000
Al Gepler, *Publisher*
Donna J Barrett, *
Thomas J Lindley Iii, *Sec*
EMP: 200 **EST:** 1940
SQ FT: 100,000
SALES (est): 48.92MM
SALES (corp-wide): 33.14B Privately Held
Web: www.eagletribune.com
SIC: 2711   Newspapers, publishing and
printing
HQ: Newspaper Holding, Inc.
425 Locust St
Johnstown PA 15901
814 532-5102

(G-10829)
EASTPRINT INC
350 Willow St (01845-5997)
PHONE....................978 975-5255
▲ **EMP:** 65 **EST:** 1962
SALES (est): 10.35MM
SALES (corp-wide): 490.36MM Privately
Held
Web: www.ewmfg.com
SIC: 3613   Switchboard apparatus, except
instruments
PA: East West Manufacturing, Llc
4170 Ashford Dnwody Rd St
Brookhaven GA 30319
404 252-9441

(G-10830)
ECRM INCORPORATED (PA)
Also Called: Ecrm Imaging Systems

▲ = Import ▼ = Export
◆ = Import/Export

25 Commerce Way Ste 6 (01845-1002)
P.O. Box 128 (01876-0128)
PHONE..............................978 581-0207
Richard Black, *CEO*
William R Givens, *
Michael Hurton, *
Joe Chevalier, *
Dave Connor, *
▲ **EMP:** 100 **EST:** 1969
SQ FT: 101,786
SALES (est): 10.2MM
SALES (corp-wide): 10.2MM **Privately Held**
Web: www.ecrm.com
SIC: 3555 Printing trades machinery

(G-10831)
FLAGSHIP PRESS INC
150 Flagship Dr (01845-6117)
PHONE..............................978 975-3100
Jeffrey N Poor, *CEO*
Charles N Poor, *
Christopher D Poor, *
Carol A Poor, *
EMP: 129 **EST:** 1950
SQ FT: 63,000
SALES (est): 22.26MM **Privately Held**
Web: www.flagshippress.com
SIC: 2752 2791 2789 Offset printing;
    Typesetting; Bookbinding and related work

(G-10832)
**FLAME LAMINATING
CORPORATION**
2350 Turnpike St Bldg B (01845-6347)
PHONE..............................978 725-9527
Joseph Di Grazia, *Pr*
Eric Digrazia, *Pr*
Joel Digrazia, *Sec*
▲ **EMP:** 15 **EST:** 1979
SQ FT: 40,000
SALES (est): 1.93MM **Privately Held**
Web: www.flamelaminatingcorp.com
SIC: 2295 Laminating of fabrics

(G-10833)
FRESENIUS KABI USA LLC
Also Called: Ivenix
50 High St Ste 50 (01845-2674)
PHONE..............................978 775-8050
John Ducker, *Brnch Mgr*
EMP: 68
SALES (corp-wide): 42.42B **Privately Held**
Web:
publish-p89819-
e783417.adobeaemcloud.com
SIC: 2834 Pharmaceutical preparations
HQ: Fresenius Kabi Usa, Llc
    3 Corporate Dr
    Lake Zurich IL 60047
    847 550-2300

(G-10834)
FROZEN BATTERS INC
Also Called: Bake-N-Joy Foods
351 Willow St (01845-5921)
PHONE..............................508 683-1414
Gary M Ogan, *VP*
Robert M Ogan, *
Jerome Ogan, *
Steven M Weinstein, *
Judith F Ogan, *
EMP: 78 **EST:** 1982
SQ FT: 30,000
SALES (est): 3.25MM **Privately Held**
Web: www.bakenjoy.com
SIC: 2051 Bagels, fresh or frozen

(G-10835)
GARRETTCOM INC
25 Commerce Way Ste 1 (01845-1002)
PHONE..............................978 688-8807
Jahn Shaw, *Brnch Mgr*
EMP: 40
SALES (corp-wide): 2.51B **Publicly Held**
Web: www.belden.com
SIC: 3577 Computer peripheral equipment,
    nec
HQ: Garrettcom, Inc.
    1113 N Main St
    Mooresville NC 28115

(G-10836)
GEFRAN INC (DH)
400 Willow St (01845-5934)
PHONE..............................781 729-5249
Mark Caldwell, *CEO*
Bob Vivier, *
Karston Just, *CSO**
◆ **EMP:** 45 **EST:** 1982
SALES (est): 17.21MM
SALES (corp-wide): 137.6MM **Privately
Held**
Web: www.gefran.com
SIC: 3566 3625 Speed changers, drives,
    and gears; Controls for adjustable speed
    drives
HQ: Gefran Spa
    Via Sebina 74
    Provaglio D'iseo BS 25050

(G-10837)
GEFRAN ISI INC
400 Willow St (01845-5934)
PHONE..............................781 729-0842
Ennio Franceshetti, *Pr*
Mark Caldwell, *VP*
Robert Vivier, *Contrlr*
EMP: 42 **EST:** 1999
SALES (est): 988.65K
SALES (corp-wide): 137.6MM **Privately
Held**
SIC: 3823 3829 Process control instruments
    ; Measuring and controlling devices, nec
HQ: Gefran Spa
    Via Sebina 74
    Provaglio D'iseo BS 25050

(G-10838)
HIPER GLOBAL US LLC (PA)
1616 Osgood St Ste 1001 (01845-1000)
PHONE..............................978 486-0300
James Reinhold, *CEO*
Greg Loycano, *CFO*
Dave Meier, *VP Engg*
EMP: 75 **EST:** 2002
SQ FT: 31,000
SALES (est): 46.63MM
SALES (corp-wide): 46.63MM **Privately
Held**
Web: www.hiper-global.us
SIC: 3571 Electronic computers

(G-10839)
**INFINITE ELECTRONICS INTL
INC**
Also Called: L-Com
50 High St Fl 3 (01845-2661)
PHONE..............................800 341-5266
EMP: 23
SALES (corp-wide): 1.84B **Privately Held**
Web: www.infiniteelectronics.com
SIC: 3678 Electronic connectors
HQ: Infinite Electronics International, Inc.
    17792 Fitch
    Irvine CA 92614
    949 261-1920

(G-10840)
**INTERNTONAL MICRO
PHOTONIX INC**
120 Willow St (01845-5918)
PHONE..............................978 685-3800
Francis S Maldari, *Prin*
EMP: 7 **EST:** 2011
SALES (est): 705.71K **Privately Held**
Web: www.imphotonix.com
SIC: 3661 Fiber optics communications
    equipment

(G-10841)
JAMECO INDUSTRIES INC
815 Chestnut St (01845-6009)
PHONE..............................978 688-1811
EMP: 10 **EST:** 1931
SALES (est): 5.97K **Privately Held**
SIC: 3999 Manufacturing industries, nec

(G-10842)
L-COM INC (DH)
Also Called: L-Com Global Connectivity
50 High St (01845-2674)
PHONE..............................978 682-6936
Terry Jarnigan, *Pr*
Brian Macdonald, *
◆ **EMP:** 90 **EST:** 1983
SALES (est): 102.14MM
SALES (corp-wide): 1.84B **Privately Held**
Web: www.l-com.com
SIC: 3678 3577 3357 Electronic connectors;
    Computer peripheral equipment, nec;
    Nonferrous wiredrawing and insulating
HQ: Infinite Electronics, Inc.
    17792 Fitch
    Irvine CA 92614
    949 261-1920

(G-10843)
LASERCRAZE
1580 Osgood St Ste 2210 (01845-1038)
PHONE..............................978 689-7700
Curt Bellavance, *Ex Dir*
EMP: 7 **EST:** 2010
SALES (est): 184.66K **Privately Held**
Web: www.lasercraze.us
SIC: 2759 Laser printing

(G-10844)
**MICROWAVE ENGINEERING
CORP**
1551 Osgood St (01845-1041)
PHONE..............................978 685-2776
Suzanne Wright, *Pr*
Maurice Aghion, *
Hong Chau, *
Steven Feldman, *
Chris Holman, *COMPONENT**
▲ **EMP:** 80 **EST:** 1984
SQ FT: 60,000
SALES (est): 14.11MM **Privately Held**
Web: www.microwaveeng.com
SIC: 3679 3678 3677 3663 Microwave
    components; Electronic connectors;
    Electronic coils and transformers; Radio
    and t.v. communications equipment

(G-10845)
NORTHEAST SAND & GRAVEL
1637 Osgood St (01845-1021)
PHONE..............................603 213-6133
EMP: 7 **EST:** 2017
SALES (est): 994.89K **Privately Held**
SIC: 1442 Construction sand and gravel

(G-10846)
NORTHEAST STAINLESS INC
2350 Turnpike St Ste 3 (01845-6347)

PHONE..............................781 589-9000
Len Lilley, *Owner*
EMP: 8 **EST:** 2003
SALES (est): 977.6K **Privately Held**
Web: www.nestainless.com
SIC: 7692 Welding repair

(G-10847)
ORION ENTERPRISES INC (HQ)
Also Called: Orion Fittings
1600 Osgood St Ste 2005 (01845-1058)
PHONE..............................913 342-1653
John Mc Coy, *Pr*
Bill Mc Coy, *
James B Mc Coy, *
Joseph Mc Coy, *
Clay Reeder, *
▲ **EMP:** 110 **EST:** 1982
SQ FT: 93,000
SALES (est): 29.24MM
SALES (corp-wide): 1.98B **Publicly Held**
SIC: 3084 5074 3432 3089 Plastics pipe;
    Plumbing and hydronic heating supplies;
    Plumbing fixture fittings and trim; Fittings
    for pipe, plastics
PA: Watts Water Technologies, Inc.
    815 Chestnut St
    North Andover MA 01845
    978 688-1811

(G-10848)
PHILIPS
285 Sutton St (01845-1650)
PHONE..............................978 258-7110
Laurie Fichera, *Pr*
EMP: 18 **EST:** 2010
SALES (est): 630.4K **Privately Held**
Web: usa.philips.com
SIC: 3651 Household audio and video
    equipment

(G-10849)
SOLUSOFT INC
300 Willow St (01845-5910)
PHONE..............................978 375-6021
Kiran Thakrar, *Pr*
Chiman Patel, *Stockholder**
EMP: 23 **EST:** 1994
SQ FT: 20,000
SALES (est): 2.22MM **Privately Held**
Web: www.solu-soft.com
SIC: 7372 7371 Prepackaged software;
    Custom computer programming services

(G-10850)
ST REGIS SPORTSWEAR LTD
3 Ironwood Rd (01845-2126)
PHONE..............................518 725-6767
EMP: 9 **EST:** 1994
SALES (est): 486.62K **Privately Held**
SIC: 2281 Yarn spinning mills

(G-10851)
TECNAU INC (DH)
60 Willow St (01845-5917)
PHONE..............................978 608-0500
Jeff Kerwin, *CEO*
Harold Regan, *
▲ **EMP:** 35 **EST:** 1984
SQ FT: 20,000
SALES (est): 24.71MM
SALES (corp-wide): 56.84MM **Privately
Held**
Web: www.tecnau.com
SIC: 3555 Printing trades machinery
HQ: Tecnau Ab
    Langgatan 21
    Ljungby 341 3
    37225600

(G-10852)
TIDAL COMMUNICATIONS LLC
565 Turnpike St Ste 61 (01845-5936)
PHONE.....................978 687-0900
Chris Faddis, *Pr*
EMP: 9 EST: 2002
SQ FT: 1,200
SALES (est): 997.77K Privately Held
Web: www.tidalcom.com
SIC: 1731 3669 Access control systems
specialization; Intercommunication
systems, electric

(G-10853)
TIMELINX SOFTWARE INC
800 Turnpike St Ste 300 (01845-6156)
PHONE.....................978 296-4090
Mark Engelberg, *Prin*
EMP: 10 EST: 2015
SALES (est): 504.88K Privately Held
Web: www.timelinxsoftware.com
SIC: 7372 Prepackaged software

(G-10854)
TIMELINX SOFTWARE LLC
800 Turnpike St Ste 300 (01845-6156)
PHONE.....................978 662-1171
Jeffrey Gregorec, *Pt*
Jeffrey Gregorec, *Managing Member*
EMP: 9 EST: 2006
SQ FT: 1,000
SALES (est): 1.73MM Privately Held
Web: www.timelinxsoftware.com
SIC: 7373 7372 Systems software
development services; Publisher's
computer software

(G-10855)
**UNITED PLASTIC FABRICATING
INC (PA)**
165 Flagship Dr (01845-6119)
PHONE.....................978 975-4520
F Joseph Lingel, *Pr*
Richard P Mcgonnell, *Dir*
Paul N Romano, *
Bryan R Curley, *
EMP: 100 EST: 1986
SQ FT: 40,000
SALES (est): 41.64MM
SALES (corp-wide): 41.64MM Privately
Held
Web: www.unitedplastic.com
SIC: 3089 3083 Thermoformed finished
plastics products, nec; Laminated plastics
plate and sheet

(G-10856)
UNIVERSAL PHARMA TECH LLC
70 Flagship Dr Ste 3 (01845-6126)
PHONE.....................978 975-7216
Bob Byron, *Genl Mgr*
EMP: 7 EST: 1998
SQ FT: 10,000
SALES (est): 134.09K Privately Held
SIC: 3559 8731 Pharmaceutical machinery;
Chemical laboratory, except testing

(G-10857)
VERANOVA LP
Also Called: Johnson Matthey Phrm Svcs
70 Flagship Dr (01845-6126)
PHONE.....................978 784-5000
EMP: 38
SALES (corp-wide): 118.93MM Privately
Held
Web: www.veranova.com
SIC: 2833 8731 2834 Medicinal chemicals;
Commercial physical research;
Pharmaceutical preparations
HQ: Veranova, L.P.
25 Patton Rd

Devens MA 01434
484 581-0149

(G-10858)
WATTS REGULATOR CO
1600 Osgood St (01845-1048)
PHONE.....................978 688-1811
EMP: 650
SALES (corp-wide): 1.98B Publicly Held
Web: www.watts.com
SIC: 3491 Pressure valves and regulators,
industrial
HQ: Watts Regulator Co.
815 Chestnut St
North Andover MA 01845
978 689-6000

(G-10859)
WATTS REGULATOR CO (HQ)
815 Chestnut St (01845-6098)
PHONE.....................978 689-6000
Andre Dhawan, *Pr*
Robert J Pagano Junior, *Dir*
Shashank Patel, *
Timothy M Macphee, *
Kenneth R Lepage, *
◆ EMP: 230 EST: 1936
SQ FT: 35,000
SALES (est): 498.53MM
SALES (corp-wide): 1.98B Publicly Held
Web: www.watts.com
SIC: 3491 3494 Pressure valves and
regulators, industrial; Plumbing and heating
valves
PA: Watts Water Technologies, Inc.
815 Chestnut St
North Andover MA 01845
978 688-1811

(G-10860)
WATTS SEA TECH INC
815 Chestnut St (01845-6009)
PHONE.....................978 688-1811
◆ EMP: 22 EST: 1995
SQ FT: 40,000
SALES (est): 9.95MM
SALES (corp-wide): 1.98B Publicly Held
Web: www.watts.com
SIC: 5088 3429 3089 Marine crafts and
supplies; Marine hardware; Injection
molding of plastics
PA: Watts Water Technologies, Inc.
815 Chestnut St
North Andover MA 01845
978 688-1811

(G-10861)
**WATTS WATER
TECHNOLOGIES INC (PA)**
Also Called: Watts Water
815 Chestnut St (01845-6009)
PHONE.....................978 688-1811
Robert J Pagano Junior, *Pr*
W Craig Kissel, *
Shashank Patel, *CFO*
Kenneth R Lepage, *Chief Human Resource
Officer*
◆ EMP: 248 EST: 1874
SALES (est): 1.98B
SALES (corp-wide): 1.98B Publicly Held
Web: www.watts.com
SIC: 3494 3491 Plumbing and heating
valves; Pressure valves and regulators,
industrial

(G-10862)
**WHITMAN PRODUCTS
COMPANY INC**
93 Brookview Dr (01845-3252)
PHONE.....................978 975-0502

John Rupp, *Pr*
EMP: 20 EST: 1967
SALES (est): 2.37MM Privately Held
Web: www.whitmanproducts.com
SIC: 3672 Printed circuit boards

North Attleboro
Bristol County

(G-10863)
A G INDUSTRIES INC
75 Chestnut St (02760-2301)
PHONE.....................508 695-4219
Alan Greenleaf, *Pr*
EMP: 7 EST: 1989
SQ FT: 9,340
SALES (est): 798.64K Privately Held
Web: www.agindustriesmass.com
SIC: 3441 Fabricated structural metal

(G-10864)
**ADVANCED METAL CONCEPTS
INC**
385 John L Dietsch Blvd (02763-1031)
PHONE.....................508 695-6400
Anthony Manaeca, *Pr*
Frank Barbieri, *VP*
Charles Breen, *Ofcr*
▲ EMP: 20 EST: 1982
SQ FT: 18,000
SALES (est): 2.15MM Privately Held
SIC: 3364 3369 Nonferrous die-castings
except aluminum; Nonferrous foundries, nec

(G-10865)
ARTCRAFT CO INC
Also Called: Printing
200 John L Dietsch Blvd (02763-1077)
P.O. Box E (02763-0415)
PHONE.....................508 695-4042
John Dumouchel, *CEO*
John R Dumochel, *
▲ EMP: 69 EST: 1939
SQ FT: 45,000
SALES (est): 12.98MM Privately Held
Web: www.artcraft.com
SIC: 2752 Offset printing

(G-10866)
**ASHWORTH ASSOC MFG WHL
JWELERS**
Also Called: Ashworth Awards
41 Richards Ave (02760-1609)
P.O. Box 831 (02761-0831)
PHONE.....................508 695-1900
Daniel Ashworth, *Pr*
▲ EMP: 11 EST: 1965
SQ FT: 6,000
SALES (est): 2.6MM Privately Held
Web: www.ashworthawards.com
SIC: 3961 3911 Costume jewelry, ex.
precious metal and semiprecious stones;
Jewelry, precious metal

(G-10867)
**BARBER ELC ENCLOSURES
MFG INC**
30 Chestnut St (02760-2304)
PHONE.....................508 699-4872
Linda Thibault, *Pr*
EMP: 13 EST: 1915
SALES (est): 1.07MM Privately Held
Web: www.barber-mfg.com
SIC: 3469 Electronic enclosures, stamped
or pressed metal

(G-10868)
BOARDTECH SOLUTIONS INC
322 E Washington St Unit 2 (02760-2370)
PHONE.....................508 643-3684
Dean Duckworth, *Pr*
EMP: 9 EST: 2018
SALES (est): 100.06K Privately Held
Web: www.boardtechsolutions.com
SIC: 3672 Printed circuit boards

(G-10869)
**BORO SAND & STONE CORP
(PA)**
192 Plain St (02760-4124)
PHONE.....................508 699-2911
Thomas P Walsh, *Pr*
EMP: 48 EST: 1945
SQ FT: 3,000
SALES (est): 7.52MM
SALES (corp-wide): 7.52MM Privately
Held
Web: www.borocorp.com
SIC: 3273 5032 Ready-mixed concrete;
Sand, construction

(G-10870)
CLARKIE INDUSTRIES
182 Grant St (02760-2411)
PHONE.....................508 404-0202
EMP: 10 EST: 2010
SALES (est): 147.58K Privately Held
SIC: 2393 Textile bags

(G-10871)
FULLER BOX CO INC (PA)
Also Called: Fuller Box
150 Chestnut St (02760-3205)
P.O. Box 9 (02761-0009)
PHONE.....................508 695-2525
Peter C Fuller, *Pr*
Alvin R Fuller, *
David Whitty, *
Thomas Mercer, *
Jonathan Backner, *
▲ EMP: 100 EST: 1944
SQ FT: 52,000
SALES (est): 21.81MM
SALES (corp-wide): 21.81MM Privately
Held
Web: www.fullerbox.com
SIC: 2675 3172 3086 2657 Cardboard cut-
outs, panels, and foundations: die-cut;
Cases, jewelry; Plastics foam products;
Folding paperboard boxes

(G-10872)
GZSL CORP
90 George Leven Dr (02760-3580)
PHONE.....................508 695-0727
▲ EMP: 21
SIC: 3999 3842 3069 3089 Identification
tags, except paper; Splints, pneumatic and
wood; Boxes, hard rubber; Combs, plastics

(G-10873)
HIGH TECHNOLOGY INC
Also Called: Hti Medical
20 Alice Agnew Dr (02763-1036)
PHONE.....................508 660-2221
Gary Titov, *CEO*
Sergey Titov, *
◆ EMP: 37 EST: 1994
SQ FT: 14,000
SALES (est): 9.9MM Privately Held
Web: www.htmed.com
SIC: 5049 7699 5047 2835 Laboratory
equipment, except medical or dental;
Laboratory instrument repair; Instruments,
surgical and medical; In vitro diagnostics

(G-10874)
HYDROTECH SERVICES INC
38b George Leven Dr (02760-3580)
P.O. Box 928 (85139-0317)
PHONE.................................508 699-5977
Jeffrey Woods, *Pr*
EMP: 10 **EST:** 1998
SALES (est): 433.86K **Privately Held**
Web: www.hydrotechservices.com
SIC: 3589 Water treatment equipment,
industrial

(G-10875)
**IMPROVED CONSUMER
PRODUCTS INC**
100 Towne St (02760-4009)
P.O. Box B (02763-0411)
PHONE.................................508 695-6841
Valerie Paynton, *Pr*
▲ **EMP:** 10 **EST:** 1971
SQ FT: 14,000
SALES (est): 993.55K **Privately Held**
Web: www.chimneycaps.com
SIC: 3444 3498 8711 3494 Ventilators,
sheet metal; Pipe fittings, fabricated from
purchased pipe; Engineering services;
Valves and pipe fittings, nec

(G-10876)
**METALOR TECHNOLOGIES USA
CORP (DH)**
255 John L Dietsch Blvd (02763-1069)
PHONE.................................508 699-8800
Yuxing Shang, *Pr*
Stephen A Chapman, *
Katrina Baptista, *
Jose Camino, *
▲ **EMP:** 30 **EST:** 1988
SQ FT: 35,000
SALES (est): 61.61MM **Privately Held**
SIC: 3339 3341 Gold refining (primary);
Gold smelting and refining (secondary)
HQ: Metalor Technologies International Sa
Route Des Perveuils 8
Marin-Epagnier NE 2074

(G-10877)
**METALOR USA REFINING CORP
(DH)**
Also Called: Metalor
255 John L Dietsch Blvd (02763-1069)
P.O. Box 225 (02761-0225)
PHONE.................................508 699-8800
Antoine Demontmolline, *CFO*
Michael Mooiman, *
Laurence Drummond, *
Todd Kropp, *
Stephen A Chapman, *
▲ **EMP:** 130 **EST:** 1984
SQ FT: 65,000
SALES (est): 41.08MM **Privately Held**
SIC: 3341 3339 2819 Secondary nonferrous
metals; Precious metals; Industrial
inorganic chemicals, nec
HQ: Metalor Technologies Usa Corp
255 John L Dietsch Blvd
North Attleboro MA 02763
508 699-8800

(G-10878)
MINI-SYSTEMS INC (PA)
Also Called: Sunbelt Microelectronics Div
20 David Rd (02760-2102)
P.O. Box 69 (02761-0069)
PHONE.................................508 695-1420
Glen E Robertson, *Pr*
Elaine Ryan, *Sec*
EMP: 75 **EST:** 1968
SQ FT: 17,000

SALES (est): 21.88MM
SALES (corp-wide): 21.88MM **Privately
Held**
Web: www.mini-systemsinc.com
SIC: 3676 3674 3672 3651 Electronic
resistors; Hybrid integrated circuits; Printed
circuit boards; Household audio and video
equipment

(G-10879)
NEEDLETECH PRODUCTS INC
452 John L Dietsch Blvd (02763-1079)
PHONE.................................508 431-4000
Francis J Tarallo, *Pr*
Shirley Stoker, *Ex VP*
EMP: 165 **EST:** 1988
SALES (est): 43.32MM
SALES (corp-wide): 212.5MM **Privately
Held**
Web: www.needletech.com
SIC: 3841 Needles, suture
HQ: Theragenics Corporation
5203 Bristol Indus Way
Buford GA 30518
770 373-7099

(G-10880)
NN INC
Polymetallurgical
262 Broad St (02760-1154)
PHONE.................................508 695-7700
EMP: 33
SALES (corp-wide): 498.74MM **Publicly
Held**
Web: www.nninc.com
SIC: 3562 Ball bearings and parts
PA: Nn, Inc.
6210 Ardrey Kell Rd # 600
Charlotte NC 28277
980 264-4300

(G-10881)
OPTAMARK LLC ✪
865 E Washington St (02760-1873)
PHONE.................................877 888-3878
EMP: 31 **EST:** 2022
SALES (est): 1.18MM **Privately Held**
SIC: 2397 Schiffli machine embroideries

(G-10882)
POLY-TECH DIAMOND CO INC
4 East St (02760-2307)
P.O. Box 6 (02761-0006)
PHONE.................................508 695-3561
Timothy Phipps, *Pr*
EMP: 11 **EST:** 1988
SQ FT: 6,200
SALES (est): 499.23K **Privately Held**
Web: www.polytechdiamond.com
SIC: 3545 Diamond cutting tools for turning,
boring, burnishing, etc.

(G-10883)
POLYMETALLURGICAL LLC
262 Broad St (02760-1154)
PHONE.................................508 695-9312
John Buchan, *Managing Member*
EMP: 61 **EST:** 2006
SALES (est): 6.96MM
SALES (corp-wide): 498.74MM **Publicly
Held**
Web: www.nninc.com
SIC: 1081 Metal mining services
PA: Nn, Inc.
6210 Ardrey Kell Rd # 600
Charlotte NC 28277
980 264-4300

(G-10884)
PORTWEST CORPORATION (PA)
Also Called: Checon
30 Larsen Way (02763-1055)
PHONE.................................508 809-5112
Donald E Conaway, *Ch Bd*
D Allen Conaway, *
Michael R Degrange, *
Patricia G Conaway, *
Susan C Lincoln, *
EMP: 110 **EST:** 1960
SQ FT: 42,000
SALES (est): 23.59MM
SALES (corp-wide): 23.59MM **Privately
Held**
Web: www.checon.com
SIC: 3643 Contacts, electrical

(G-10885)
PREMIER ROLL & TOOL INC
10 Alice Agnew Dr (02763-1099)
PHONE.................................508 695-2551
Maurice Udelson, *Pr*
Keith Udelson, *
Joyce Udelson, *Treas*
EMP: 7 **EST:** 1978
SQ FT: 7,800
SALES (est): 823.38K **Privately Held**
SIC: 3316 3544 Cold finishing of steel
shapes; Special dies, tools, jigs, and fixtures

(G-10886)
S M ENGINEERING CO INC
Also Called: SM Heat Treating
83 Chestnut St (02760-2301)
P.O. Box 948 (02761-0948)
PHONE.................................508 699-4484
Barbara Morin, *VP*
EMP: 15 **EST:** 1954
SQ FT: 30,000
SALES (est): 2.19MM **Privately Held**
Web: www.sm-furnaces.com
SIC: 3567 3398 Industrial furnaces and
ovens; Metal heat treating

(G-10887)
**SIGNET PRODUCTS
CORPORATION**
521 Mount Hope St (02760-2611)
PHONE.................................650 592-3575
Ross A Davies, *Pr*
EMP: 7 **EST:** 2017
SALES (est): 491.72K **Privately Held**
Web: www.signetproducts.com
SIC: 3674 Semiconductors and related
devices

(G-10888)
SRD HOLDINGS INC
211 John L Dietsch Sq (02763-1027)
PHONE.................................508 695-5656
Daniel R Sharples, *Pr*
Helen I Sharples, *Treas*
EMP: 20 **EST:** 1967
SQ FT: 15,000
SALES (est): 2.64MM **Privately Held**
Web: www.sharplesdie.com
SIC: 3544 Special dies and tools

(G-10889)
STAR ENGINEERING INC
1 Vaillancourt Dr (02763-1054)
PHONE.................................508 316-1492
Victor Neagoe, *Pr*
Michael Coleman, *
EMP: 30 **EST:** 1980
SQ FT: 16,000
SALES (est): 4.82MM **Privately Held**
Web: www.starengineeringinc.com

SIC: 3679 8711 Electronic circuits;
Consulting engineer

(G-10890)
SULLIVAN TIRE CO INC
36 George Leven Dr (02760-3580)
PHONE.................................508 695-9920
EMP: 9
SALES (corp-wide): 275.69MM **Privately
Held**
Web: www.sullivantire.com
SIC: 7538 5531 7534 General automotive
repair shops; Automotive tires; Tire repair
shop
HQ: Sullivan Tire Co., Inc.
41 Accord Park Dr
Norwell MA 02061
781 982-1550

(G-10891)
VANTEC LLC
428 Towne St (02760-3407)
PHONE.................................508 726-2830
David Briggs, *Prin*
EMP: 10 **EST:** 2016
SALES (est): 88.48K **Privately Held**
Web: www.vantecinc.com
SIC: 3089 Plastics processing

(G-10892)
WALGREEN CO
Also Called: Walgreens
475 E Washington St (02760-2310)
PHONE.................................781 244-9431
EMP: 11
SALES (corp-wide): 139.08B **Publicly
Held**
Web: www.walgreens.com
SIC: 5912 5999 2771 2759 Drug stores;
Alcoholic beverage making equipment and
supplies; Greeting cards; Commercial
printing, nec
HQ: Walgreen Co.
200 Wilmot Rd
Deerfield IL 60015
800 925-4733

North Billerica
Middlesex County

(G-10893)
**ACCUSEMBLE ELECTRONICS
INC (PA)**
5 Esquire Rd (01862-2522)
PHONE.................................508 254-4538
Deborah Bayley, *Pr*
Clarke Bayley, *VP*
EMP: 8 **EST:** 1979
SQ FT: 12,000
SALES (est): 13.2MM
SALES (corp-wide): 13.2MM **Privately
Held**
Web: www.accusemble.com
SIC: 3672 Printed circuit boards

(G-10894)
AGRIFY CORPORATION (PA)
Also Called: Agrify
76 Treble Cove Rd Ste 3 (01862-2232)
PHONE.................................617 896-5243
Raymond Nobu Chang Junior, *Ch Bd*
Timothy Oakes, *CFO*
David Kessler, *CSO*
Brian Towns, *Ex VP*
EMP: 25 **EST:** 2016
SQ FT: 7,500
SALES (est): 58.26MM
SALES (corp-wide): 58.26MM **Publicly
Held**

Web: www.agrify.com
SIC: 7372 0721 8748 Business oriented computer software; Crop protecting services ; Business consulting, nec

(G-10895)
ALBANO SALES INC
101 Billerica Ave Ste 5-203 (01862-1256)
PHONE.............................978 667-9100
Al Albano, *Pr*
Wallace Rockwell, *Ex VP*
Matthew Vernali, *VP*
Mike Sullivan, *Ex VP*
EMP: 10 **EST:** 1981
SQ FT: 3,960
SALES (est): 1.82MM
SALES (corp-wide): 4.71B **Publicly Held**
SIC: 5141 5143 2038 Food brokers; Dairy products, except dried or canned; Frozen specialties, nec
HQ: Advantage Sales & Marketing Llc
15310 Barranca Pkwy # 100
Irvine CA 92618
949 797-2900

(G-10896)
ALPINE PRECISION LLC
152 Rangeway Rd (01862-2010)
PHONE.............................978 600-0035
EMP: 7
SALES (est): 247.44K **Privately Held**
Web: www.alpineprecisionllc.com
SIC: 3599 Machine shop, jobbing and repair

(G-10897)
ALPINE PRECISION LLC
23 Sullivan Rd (01862-2003)
PHONE.............................978 667-6333
EMP: 10 **EST:** 1985
SQ FT: 6,000
SALES (est): 1.51MM **Privately Held**
Web: www.alpineprecisionllc.com
SIC: 3599 Machine shop, jobbing and repair

(G-10898)
AVED ELECTRONICS LLC
95 Billerica Ave (01862-1231)
PHONE.............................978 453-6393
Ralph P Santosuosso, *Pr*
Deryl Santosuosso, *
▲ **EMP:** 90 **EST:** 1979
SQ FT: 15,000
SALES (est): 32.44MM
SALES (corp-wide): 10.62MM **Privately Held**
Web: www.aved.com
SIC: 3679 Electronic circuits
HQ: Lithion Power Group Ltd
333 7 Ave Sw Suite 970
Calgary AB T2P 2
587 349-5468

(G-10899)
BAKER COMMODITIES INC
Also Called: Corenco Div
134 Billerica Ave (01862-1234)
P.O. Box 132 (01862-0132)
PHONE.............................978 454-8811
TOLL FREE: 800
Joe Huelsman, *Prin*
EMP: 100
SQ FT: 10,000
SALES (corp-wide): 153.63MM **Privately Held**
Web: www.bakercommodities.com
SIC: 2077 2076 2079 Tallow rendering, inedible; Vegetable oil mills, nec; Edible fats and oils
PA: Baker Commodities, Inc.
4020 Bandini Blvd

Vernon CA 90058
323 268-2801

(G-10900)
BNZ MATERIALS INC
400 Iron Horse Park (01862-1616)
PHONE.............................978 663-3401
Richard A Beyer, *Brnch Mgr*
EMP: 105
SALES (corp-wide): 48.8MM **Privately Held**
Web: www.bnzmaterials.com
SIC: 3255 2493 3821 3469 Firebrick, clay; Insulating board, hard pressed; Worktables, laboratory; Architectural panels or parts, porcelain enameled
PA: Bnz Materials, Inc.
6901 S Pierce St Ste 180
Littleton CO 80128
303 978-1199

(G-10901)
BRUCE TECHNOLOGIES INC
23 Esquire Rd (01862-2530)
PHONE.............................978 670-5501
Jong S Whang, *CEO*
Fokko Pentinga, *Pr*
Ong S Whang, *Dir*
Bradley C Anderson, *VP*
▲ **EMP:** 12 **EST:** 2004
SALES (est): 3.36MM
SALES (est): 113.31MM **Publicly Held**
Web: www.brucetechnologiesinc.com
SIC: 5065 3674 3567 Semiconductor devices; Semiconductors and related devices; Industrial furnaces and ovens
PA: Amtech Systems, Inc.
131 S Clark Dr
Tempe AZ 85288
480 967-5146

(G-10902)
BRUNSWICK ENCLOSURE COMPANY
25 Sullivan Rd Ste 6 (01862-2020)
PHONE.............................978 670-1124
Steven Jovellas, *Pr*
EMP: 8 **EST:** 1995
SQ FT: 2,500
SALES (est): 876.17K **Privately Held**
SIC: 3442 Window and door frames

(G-10903)
CRISTEK INTERCONNECTS LLC
95 Billerica Ave (01862-1231)
PHONE.............................978 735-2161
EMP: 8
SALES (corp-wide): 168.44MM **Privately Held**
Web: www.cristek.com
SIC: 3678 Electronic connectors
HQ: Cristek Interconnects, Llc
5395 E Hunter Ave
Anaheim CA 92807
714 696-5200

(G-10904)
CURRICULUM ASSOCIATES LLC (PA)
153 Rangeway Rd (01862-2013)
PHONE.............................978 667-8000
▲ **EMP:** 500 **EST:** 1969
SQ FT: 78,000
SALES (est): 519.28MM
SALES (corp-wide): 519.28MM **Privately Held**
Web: www.curriculumassociates.com

SIC: **2731** 2741 Textbooks: publishing and printing; Business service newsletters: publishing and printing

(G-10905)
DGI COMMUNICATIONS LLC (PA)
Also Called: Dgi Invisuals
101 Billerica Ave Bldg 6-1 (01862-1269)
PHONE.............................781 285-6972
Richard Davisson, *
Mary Gale, *
Stephen Payne, *
EMP: 48 **EST:** 2002
SQ FT: 30,000
SALES (est): 46.42MM
SALES (corp-wide): 46.42MM **Privately Held**
Web: www.dgicommunications.com
SIC: 2759 1731 Business forms: printing, nsk; General electrical contractor

(G-10906)
DIAMOND USA INC (HQ)
85 Rangeway Rd Ste 3 (01862-2105)
PHONE.............................978 256-6544
Erwin Kammerer, *CEO*
Hans Gerber, *Dir*
Lisa Valente, *Treas*
EMP: 18 **EST:** 1992
SQ FT: 10,000
SALES (est): 7.47MM **Privately Held**
Web: www.diausa.com
SIC: 3229 Fiber optics strands
PA: Diamond Sa
Via Dei Patrizi 5
Losone TI 6616

(G-10907)
DIGITAL GRAPHICS INC
101 Billerica Ave Bldg 6 (01862-1271)
PHONE.............................781 270-3670
Jim Dadmun, *Pr*
Bob Novelli, *CFO*
EMP: 8 **EST:** 1994
SQ FT: 15,000
SALES (est): 238.17K **Privately Held**
SIC: 2752 7336 2759 Offset printing; Commercial art and graphic design; Commercial printing, nec

(G-10908)
DL TECH MACHINE INC
144b Rangeway Rd (01862-2010)
P.O. Box 380 (01862-0380)
PHONE.............................978 439-0500
Orlando Velez, *Pr*
EMP: 8 **EST:** 2002
SALES (est): 774.58K **Privately Held**
Web: www.dltechmachine.net
SIC: 3599 Machine shop, jobbing and repair

(G-10909)
E FJELD CO INC
152 Rangeway Rd (01862-2010)
PHONE.............................978 667-1416
Edward Fjeld, *CEO*
Mark B Reynolds, *Pr*
Donald Pascucci, *VP*
Arthur Fraser, *Treas*
Thomas M Fjeld, *Treas*
EMP: 8 **EST:** 1972
SQ FT: 7,000
SALES (est): 962.15K **Privately Held**
Web: www.efjeld.com
SIC: 3826 Microscopes, electron and proton

(G-10910)
ECHOLAB INC
267 Boston Rd Ste 11 (01862-2310)
EMP: 29 **EST:** 2004
SALES (est): 4MM **Privately Held**
Web: www.blackmagicdesign.com
SIC: 3613 Switchgear and switchboard apparatus

(G-10911)
FLIR SYSTEMS-BOSTON INC (DH)
Also Called: Inframetrics
25 Esquire Rd (01862-2501)
PHONE.............................978 901-8000
Andrew C Teich, *CEO*
EMP: 300 **EST:** 1975
SQ FT: 70,000
SALES (est): 119.74MM
SALES (corp-wide): 5.46B **Publicly Held**
Web: www.flir.com
SIC: 3823 3674 3812 Infrared instruments, industrial process type; Infrared sensors, solid state; Infrared object detection equipment
HQ: Teledyne Flir, Llc
27700 Sw Parkway Ave
Wilsonville OR 97070
503 498-3547

(G-10912)
FUNCTIONAL ASSESSMENT TECH INC
Also Called: Fasstech
76 Treble Cove Rd Ste 3 (01862-2232)
PHONE.............................978 663-2800
Lee Brody, *COO*
Stephen Andress, *Sec*
EMP: 11 **EST:** 1996
SQ FT: 12,000
SALES (est): 971.24K **Privately Held**
SIC: 3841 Physiotherapy equipment, electrical
PA: Srs Medical Systems, Inc.
76 Treble Cove Rd Ste 3
North Billerica MA 01862

(G-10913)
GALVANIC APPLIED SCNCES USA IN
101 Billerica Ave Bldg 5ste104 (01862-1271)
PHONE.............................978 848-2701
Helen Cornett, *CEO*
Jack Cotter, *Genl Mgr*
James F Bagley, *Prin*
EMP: 13 **EST:** 1985
SALES (est): 8.65MM
SALES (corp-wide): 15.91MM **Privately Held**
Web: www.galvanic.com
SIC: 3829 Measuring and controlling devices, nec
PA: Galvanic Applied Sciences Inc
7000 Fisher Rd Se
Calgary AB T2H 0
403 252-8470

(G-10914)
GEAR/TRONICS INC
100 Chelmsford Rd (01862-1396)
PHONE.............................781 933-1400
Robert Doherty, *Pr*
EMP: 23 **EST:** 2014
SQ FT: 25,000
SALES (est): 3.89MM **Privately Held**
Web: www.geartronics.com
SIC: 3334 Primary aluminum

(G-10915)
GEAR/TRONICS INDUSTRIES INC
Also Called: X-4 Tool Div
100 Chelmsford Rd (01862-1356)
P.O. Box 376 (01862-0376)
PHONE..................781 933-1400
Richard L Duffy, Pr
Jane Ann Hughes, *
EMP: 53 EST: 1923
SQ FT: 73,000
SALES (est): 5.34MM Privately Held
Web: www.geartronics.com
SIC: 3566 3549 Speed changers, drives, and gears; Wiredrawing and fabricating machinery and equipment, ex. die

(G-10916)
GEM WELDING
12 Republic Rd (01862-2504)
PHONE..................978 362-3873
George Macallister, Pr
EMP: 16 EST: 2015
SALES (est): 992.77K Privately Held
Web: www.gemweldingandmachine.com
SIC: 7692 Welding repair

(G-10917)
GENERAL MANUFACTURING CORP
154 Rangeway Rd (01862-2010)
PHONE..................978 667-5514
Edward Barrett, Pr
EMP: 60 EST: 2001
SQ FT: 12,000
SALES (est): 10.23MM
SALES (corp-wide): 2.67MM Privately Held
Web: www.generalmfgco.com
SIC: 3679 Harness assemblies, for electronic use: wire or cable
HQ: Satys Electric Group
Zone Industrielle
Orgelet 39270

(G-10918)
HYDROCISION INC
267 Boston Rd Ste 28 (01862-2310)
PHONE..................978 474-9300
Alain Tranchemontagne, CEO
Howard Donnelly, *
Kevin Staide, *
Francis Galasso, *
Tom Abert, *
EMP: 30 EST: 1995
SQ FT: 7,500
SALES (est): 4.96MM Privately Held
Web: www.hydrocision.com
SIC: 3841 Surgical instruments and apparatus

(G-10919)
HYDRONICS MANUFACTURING INC
150 Rangeway Rd (01862-2010)
PHONE..................978 528-4335
Joachim Fiedrich, Pr
Marie Fiedrich, Sec
Richard Brockman, CFO
EMP: 7 EST: 2008
SALES (est): 879.91K Privately Held
Web: www.hydronicsmanufacturing.com
SIC: 2426 Flooring, hardwood

(G-10920)
IFS ENTERPRISES LLC
9 Executive Park Dr Ste 200 (01862-1318)
PHONE..................781 369-9500
EMP: 15 EST: 2012

SALES (est): 715.21K Privately Held
Web: www.operix.com
SIC: 7372 Prepackaged software

(G-10921)
INDUSTRIAL FLOOR COVERING INC
148 Rangeway Rd Unit C (01862-2010)
PHONE..................978 362-8655
EMP: 8 EST: 1996
SALES (est): 882.13K Privately Held
SIC: 3996 1752 Hard surface floor coverings, nec; Carpet laying

(G-10922)
KILDER CORPORATION
Also Called: Laminted Plas Dstrs Fbricators
7 Executive Park Dr (01862-1318)
PHONE..................978 663-8800
John Sabatino, Pr
John R Sabatino, *
EMP: 30 EST: 1992
SQ FT: 20,000
SALES (est): 5.17MM Privately Held
Web: www.laminatedplastics.com
SIC: 3082 5162 Unsupported plastics profile shapes; Plastics materials and basic shapes

(G-10923)
LANTHEUS HOLDINGS INC (PA)
Also Called: Lantheus Holdings
331 Treble Cove Rd (01862-2849)
PHONE..................978 671-8001
Mary Anne Heino, Pr
Brian Markison, Non-Executive Chairman of the Board*
Robert J Marshall Junior, CFO
Jean-claude Provost, Interim CMO
Andrea Sabens, CAO
EMP: 612 EST: 1956
SQ FT: 431,000
SALES (est): 935.06MM
SALES (corp-wide): 935.06MM Publicly Held
Web: www.lantheus.com
SIC: 2835 2834 Diagnostic substances; Pharmaceutical preparations

(G-10924)
LANTHEUS MEDICAL IMAGING INC (HQ)
331 Treble Cove Rd Bldg 200-2 (01862-2849)
PHONE..................800 362-2668
Mary Anne Heino, Pr
Robert Marshall Junior, CFO
John Bolla, VP
▲ EMP: 443 EST: 1999
SALES (est): 486.58MM
SALES (corp-wide): 935.06MM Publicly Held
Web: www.lantheus.com
SIC: 2834 3841 Pharmaceutical preparations; Diagnostic apparatus, medical
PA: Lantheus Holdings, Inc.
201 Burlington Rd Ste 1
Bedford MA 01862
978 671-8001

(G-10925)
LANTHEUS MI INTERMEDIATE INC
331 Treble Cove Rd (01862-2849)
PHONE..................978 671-8001
Jeffrey Bailey, Pr
John K Bakewell, CFO
EMP: 519 EST: 2007
SALES (est): 42.26MM Privately Held
Web: www.lantheus.com

SIC: 3841 2834 Diagnostic apparatus, medical; Pharmaceutical preparations

(G-10926)
LEGACY BROADCAST INC
Also Called: Microwave Radio Communications
101 Billerica Ave (01862-1271)
PHONE..................978 330-9300
EMP: 258
SIC: 3663 Microwave communication equipment

(G-10927)
LIQUIGLIDE INC
34 Sullivan Rd (01862-2000)
PHONE..................617 833-8638
EMP: 7 EST: 2012
SALES (est): 393.46K Privately Held
Web: www.liquiglide.com
SIC: 2869 Industrial organic chemicals, nec

(G-10928)
LOUIS C MORIN CO INC
19 Sterling Rd Ste 4 (01862-2524)
PHONE..................978 670-1222
Louis Morin, Pr
EMP: 24 EST: 1964
SALES (est): 553.1K Privately Held
SIC: 3451 Screw machine products

(G-10929)
M C TEST SERVICE INC
Also Called: Mc Assembly
101 Billerica Ave Bldg 7 (01862-1256)
PHONE..................781 218-7550
George Moore, Brnch Mgr
EMP: 219
Web: www.smtc.com
SIC: 3672 Printed circuit boards
HQ: M C Test Service, Inc.
425 North Dr
Melbourne FL 32934
321 253-0541

(G-10930)
MAGELLAN BIOSCIENCES INC (HQ)
101 Billerica Ave Ste 4-2 (01862-1268)
PHONE..................978 856-2345
Amy Winslow, Pr
EMP: 13 EST: 2005
SQ FT: 23,000
SALES (est): 10.13MM
SALES (corp-wide): 333.02MM Privately Held
Web: www.magellanbiosciences.com
SIC: 3826 Analytical instruments
PA: Meridian Bioscience, Inc.
3471 River Hills Dr
Cincinnati OH 45244
513 271-3700

(G-10931)
MAGELLAN DIAGNOSTICS INC
Also Called: Magellan Diagnostics
101 Billerica Ave Ste 4-2 (01862-1268)
PHONE..................978 856-2345
Amy Winslow, Pr
Janine Leblanc, *
Norman Sheppard, *
Itzik Samara, *
Robb Morse, *
EMP: 50 EST: 2004
SQ FT: 23,000
SALES (est): 10.19MM
SALES (corp-wide): 333.02MM Privately Held
Web: www.magellandx.com

SIC: 3826 8071 Analytical instruments; Testing laboratories
HQ: Magellan Biosciences, Inc.
101 Billerica Ave Ste 4-2
North Billerica MA 01862
978 856-2345

(G-10932)
MASS VAC INC
Also Called: Mv Products Division
247 Rangeway Rd (01862-2017)
P.O. Box 359 (01862-0359)
PHONE..................978 667-2393
Herbert R Gatti, Pr
EMP: 30 EST: 1971
SQ FT: 13,100
SALES (est): 4.49MM Privately Held
Web: www.massvac.com
SIC: 3563 7699 5084 3561 Vacuum pumps, except laboratory; Pumps and pumping equipment repair; Pumps and pumping equipment, nec; Pumps and pumping equipment

(G-10933)
MC ASSEMBLY INTERNATIONAL LLC
101 Billerica Ave Bldg 7 (01862-1256)
PHONE..................978 215-9501
EMP: 300
Web: www.smtc.com
SIC: 3672 Printed circuit boards
HQ: Mc Assembly International, Llc
425 North Dr
Melbourne FL 32934

(G-10934)
MEDICAL-TECHNICAL GASES INC
Also Called: Med-Tech
8 Executive Park Dr (01862-1319)
PHONE..................781 395-1946
Ramesh Kapur, Pr
EMP: 25 EST: 1961
SQ FT: 15,000
SALES (est): 993.22K Privately Held
Web: medtech.synergyomni.net
SIC: 3841 Surgical and medical instruments

(G-10935)
METROBLTY OPTICAL SYSTEMS INC
101 Billerica Ave Bldg 7 (01862-1256)
PHONE..................781 255-5300
Alexander Saunders, Pr
Alexander Saunders, CEO
Peter Bennett, Sec
Robert Degan, Ch
▲ EMP: 13 EST: 1981
SQ FT: 40,895
SALES (est): 363.8K Privately Held
SIC: 3577 Computer peripheral equipment, nec

(G-10936)
MFG ELECTRONICS INC
70 Treble Cove Rd Ste 1 (01862-2228)
PHONE..................978 671-5490
Dennis Buchenholz, Pr
Dennis Bubhenholz, Pr
Michael Bubhenholz, Stockholder
Jessica Bubhenholz, Stockholder
EMP: 8 EST: 2004
SALES (est): 1.96MM Privately Held
Web: www.mfge.com
SIC: 3672 Printed circuit boards

(G-10937)
MICROWAVE CMPNNTS SPCLISTS INC
Also Called: MCS
34 Sullivan Rd Ste 10 (01862-2000)
P.O. Box 138 (01865-0138)
PHONE................................978 667-1215
Berardo A Parisse Junior, *Pr*
Berardo A Parisse Junior, *Pr*
Paula Parisse, *Clerk*
EMP: 15 EST: 1968
SQ FT: 5,400
SALES (est): 852.87K **Privately Held**
SIC: 3599 Machine shop, jobbing and repair

(G-10938)
MIKES PRECISION MACHINE INC
14 Hadley St (01862-2605)
PHONE................................978 667-9793
Mike Rosa, *Pr*
EMP: 7 EST: 1998
SQ FT: 1,788
SALES (est): 733.39K **Privately Held**
Web:
www.mikesprecisionmachineinc.com
SIC: 3599 Machine shop, jobbing and repair

(G-10939)
NEXTEK LLC
Also Called: Manufacturer
101 Billerica Ave Bldg 5 (01862-1256)
PHONE................................978 486-0582
▲ **EMP: 20 EST:** 2020
SALES (est): 4.16MM **Privately Held**
Web: www.nextek.com
SIC: 3699 Electrical equipment and supplies, nec

(G-10940)
NISSIN ION EQUIPMENT USA INC
34 Sullivan Rd (01862-2000)
PHONE................................978 362-2590
EMP: 18
Web: www.nissin-ion.com
SIC: 3674 Semiconductors and related devices
HQ: Nissin Ion Equipment Usa, Inc.
8701 N Mopac Expy
Austin TX 78759
512 340-1423

(G-10941)
PACE INDUSTRIES LLC
Cambridge Division
67 Faulkner St (01862-1501)
PHONE................................978 667-8400
EMP: 244
SALES (corp-wide): 682.54MM **Privately Held**
Web: www.paceind.com
SIC: 3363 3364 3365 3369 Aluminum die-castings; Zinc and zinc-base alloy die-castings; Aluminum foundries; Nonferrous foundries, nec
HQ: Pace Industries, Llc
28100 Cabot Dr Ste 200
Novi MI 48377
888 343-2278

(G-10942)
PEAK SCIENTIFIC INC (DH)
19 Sterling Rd Ste 1 (01862-2524)
PHONE................................978 234-4679
Robin Macgeachy, *Pr*
June Macgeachy, *
Joan Murray, *
EMP: 26 EST: 2005

SALES (est): 18.56MM
SALES (corp-wide): 132.22MM **Privately Held**
Web: www.peakscientific.com
SIC: 3621 Motors and generators
HQ: Peak Scientific Instruments Limited
Unit 11
Renfrew PA4 9

(G-10943)
PLASTIC CONCEPTS INC
2 Sterling Rd Unit 2 (01862-2595)
P.O. Box 355 (01821-0355)
PHONE................................978 663-7996
Michael Thompson, *Pr*
EMP: 20 EST: 1989
SQ FT: 15,000
SALES (est): 3.85MM **Privately Held**
Web: www.plastic-concepts.com
SIC: 3089 5162 Plastics hardware and building products; Plastics materials and basic shapes

(G-10944)
PRECISION METAL WORKS INC
100 Rangeway Rd (01862-2133)
PHONE................................978 667-0180
Bruce Martin, *Pr*
Bonnie Martin, *
EMP: 35 EST: 1980
SQ FT: 33,000
SALES (est): 4.83MM **Privately Held**
Web: www.welfab.com
SIC: 3441 7692 3444 Fabricated structural metal; Welding repair; Sheet metalwork

(G-10945)
R F INTEGRATION INC (PA)
85 Rangeway Rd Ste 1 (01862-2105)
PHONE................................978 654-6770
Patrick O'sullivan, *Pr*
Ray Maroney, *OF IC DEVL*
EMP: 8 EST: 1997
SQ FT: 3,200
SALES (est): 2.3MM
SALES (corp-wide): 2.3MM **Privately Held**
Web: www.rfintegration.com
SIC: 3674 Integrated circuits, semiconductor networks, etc.

(G-10946)
RADIO WAVES INC
Also Called: Smith Microwave Company
495 Billerica Ave (01862-1205)
PHONE................................978 459-8800
◆ **EMP:** 40
SIC: 3663 Antennas, transmitting and communications

(G-10947)
RANGEWAY SUPPLY LLC
149 Rangeway Rd (01862-2070)
PHONE................................978 667-8500
Denise L Ploski, *Prin*
EMP: 8 EST: 2015
SALES (est): 968.48K **Privately Held**
Web: www.rangewaysupply.com
SIC: 5032 1411 5211 2499 Granite building stone; Bluestone, dimension-quarrying; Paving stones; Mulch, wood and bark

(G-10948)
RD CONTRACTORS INC
Also Called: R D Fence Co
220 Boston Rd Rte 3a (01862-2309)
PHONE................................978 667-6545
Richard Snydeman, *Pr*
William J Snydeman, *Treas*
EMP: 30 EST: 1973
SQ FT: 2,200

SALES (est): 796.43K **Privately Held**
Web: www.rdfencecompany.com
SIC: 2499 5211 Fencing, wood; Fencing

(G-10949)
REA ASSOCIATES INC
325 Boston Rd (01862-2622)
PHONE................................209 521-2727
Michael Rea, *CEO*
EMP: 8 EST: 1962
SQ FT: 8,000
SALES (est): 788.62K **Privately Held**
SIC: 3679 Microwave components

(G-10950)
REE MACHINE WORKS INC
34 Sullivan Rd Ste 7 (01862-2000)
PHONE................................978 663-9105
Mark Gordon, *Pr*
EMP: 7 EST: 1967
SALES (est): 774.35K **Privately Held**
Web: www.reemachineworks.com
SIC: 3599 Machine shop, jobbing and repair

(G-10951)
ROBERTSON-CHASE FIBERS LLC
16 Esquire Rd Ste 2 (01862-2528)
PHONE................................978 453-2837
Elizabeth Perry, *Managing Member*
▲ **EMP: 9 EST:** 1985
SQ FT: 30,000
SALES (est): 188.9K **Privately Held**
SIC: 2281 Animal fiber yarn, spun

(G-10952)
SEGUE MANUFACTURING SVCS LLC
101 Billerica Ave Bldg 3 (01862-1270)
PHONE................................978 970-1200
Peter Frasso, *CEO*
William Roderick, *VP*
Brian Desmarais, *VP*
Stephanie Lin, *VP*
Chris Brothers, *VP*
▲ **EMP: 100 EST:** 2007
SALES (est): 25.06MM **Privately Held**
Web: www.segue-mfg.com
SIC: 3669 3643 3357 Intercommunication systems, electric; Current-carrying wiring services; Nonferrous wiredrawing and insulating
PA: Lorom Industrial Co., Ltd.
13f-2, No. 78, Anhe Rd., Sec. 2,
Taipei City TAP 10680

(G-10953)
SEMILAB USA LLC
101 Billerica Ave Bldg 5 (01862-1271)
PHONE................................508 647-8400
Han Chang, *Genl Mgr*
EMP: 19
SIC: 3826 Analytical instruments
PA: Semilab Usa Llc
12415 Telecom Dr
Temple Terrace FL 33637

(G-10954)
SEMTECH SOLUTIONS INC
3 Executive Park Dr Ste 1 (01862-1347)
P.O. Box 2155 (01760-0016)
PHONE................................978 663-9822
Mark Reynolds, *CEO*
Gerry O'laughlin, *Pr*
Mark Reynolds, *Pr*
EMP: 20 EST: 2000
SALES (est): 3.05MM **Privately Held**
Web: www.semtechsolutions.com

SIC: 3826 Analytical instruments

(G-10955)
SHAANS PANINI & ROAST BEEF LLC
99 Chelmsford Rd Unit 9rte (01862-1351)
PHONE................................617 230-3166
Harkirat Singh, *Managing Member*
EMP: 11 EST: 2013
SALES (est): 150.82K **Privately Held**
Web:
www.shaanspaniniandroastbeef.com
SIC: 5812 2013 Pizza restaurants; Roast beef, from purchased meat

(G-10956)
SMTC MANUFACTURING
Also Called: Surface Mount Technology Ctr
101 Billerica Ave Bldg 7 (01862-1256)
PHONE................................508 207-6355
EMP: 12 EST: 2020
SALES (est): 1.74MM **Privately Held**
Web: www.smtc.com
SIC: 3999 Manufacturing industries, nec

(G-10957)
SPECIALIZED COATING SVCS LLC
16 Esquire Rd Unit A (01862-2527)
PHONE................................978 362-0346
Abe Ghanbari, *Genl Mgr*
EMP: 23
SALES (corp-wide): 51.51MM **Privately Held**
Web: www.speccoat.com
SIC: 3672 Printed circuit boards
HQ: Specialized Coating Services, Llc
42680 Christy St
Fremont CA 94538
510 226-8700

(G-10958)
SRS MEDICAL SYSTEMS INC (PA)
76 Treble Cove Rd Ste 3 (01862-2232)
PHONE................................978 663-2800
Lee Brody, *CEO*
◆ **EMP: 28 EST:** 1991
SQ FT: 12,500
SALES (est): 7.1MM **Privately Held**
Web: www.srsmedical.com
SIC: 3841 Physiotherapy equipment, electrical

(G-10959)
STANDEX INTERNATIONAL CORP
Spincraft Division
500 Iron Horse Park (01862-1617)
PHONE................................978 667-2771
Rick Paul, *Pr*
EMP: 55
SALES (corp-wide): 741.05MM **Publicly Held**
Web: www.standexetg.com
SIC: 3599 7692 3469 3444 Machine shop, jobbing and repair; Welding repair; Metal stampings, nec; Sheet metalwork
PA: Standex International Corporation
23 Keewaydin Dr Ste 205
Salem NH 03079
603 893-9701

(G-10960)
STATIC CLEAN INTERNATIONAL INC
267 Boston Rd Ste 8 (01862-2310)
PHONE................................781 229-7799
Jim Patterson, *Pr*

Karen Patterson, *Treas*
▲ **EMP:** 10 **EST:** 2003
SQ FT: 3,000
SALES (est): 2.53MM **Privately Held**
Web: www.staticclean.com
SIC: 3699 5065 Electrical equipment and supplies, nec; Electronic parts and equipment, nec

(G-10961)
TELEDYNE FLIR LLC
Also Called: Flir Surveillance
25 Esquire Rd (01862-2501)
PHONE...............................978 901-8000
Jeff Glover, *Crdt Mgr*
EMP: 250
SALES (corp-wide): 5.46B **Publicly Held**
Web: www.flir.com
SIC: 3826 Analytical instruments
HQ: Teledyne Flir, Llc
27700 Sw Parkway Ave
Wilsonville OR 97070
503 498-3547

(G-10962)
TEVTECH LLC
100 Billerica Ave (01862-1234)
PHONE...............................978 667-4557
EMP: 13 **EST:** 1997
SQ FT: 15,000
SALES (est): 3.11MM **Privately Held**
Web: www.tevtechllc.com
SIC: 3567 Vacuum furnaces and ovens

(G-10963)
URSA NAVIGATION SOLUTIONS INC
Also Called: Ursanav
85 Rangeway Rd Ste 3 (01862-2105)
PHONE...............................781 538-5299
Charles Schue, *CEO*
EMP: 25 **EST:** 2004
SQ FT: 9,300
SALES (est): 5.07MM **Privately Held**
Web: www.ursanav.com
SIC: 3812 Navigational systems and instruments

North Brookfield
Worcester County

(G-10964)
VIBRAM CORPORATION (DH)
18 School St (01535-1937)
PHONE...............................508 867-6494
Kevin Donahue, *Ch Bd*
Eric A Rosen, *
James M Barkoskie, *
▲ **EMP:** 238 **EST:** 1916
SQ FT: 33,000
SALES (est): 74.17MM
SALES (corp-wide): 335.14MM **Privately Held**
Web: www.vibram.com
SIC: 3069 5087 Soles, boot or shoe: rubber, composition, or fiber; Boot and shoe cut stock and findings
HQ: Vibram Corporation
9 Damonmill Sq Fl 2
Concord MA 01742
978 318-0000

North Chelmsford
Middlesex County

(G-10965)
BARE BONES SOFTWARE INC
73 Princeton St Ste 206 (01863-1581)
PHONE...............................978 251-0500
Richard M Siegel, *Pr*
Patrick Woolsey, *Treas*
EMP: 10 **EST:** 1993
SQ FT: 1,200
SALES (est): 1.1MM **Privately Held**
Web: www.barebones.com
SIC: 7372 Application computer software

(G-10966)
BOOK-MART PRESS INC
15 Wellman Ave (01863-1334)
PHONE...............................978 251-6000
Gary S Gluckow, *Pr*
Michelle S Gluckow, *
Harriette Gluckow, *
EMP: 18 **EST:** 1977
SQ FT: 80,000
SALES (est): 591.88K **Privately Held**
SIC: 2732 Book printing

(G-10967)
COSMIC SOFTWARE INC
55 Middlesex St Unit 215 (01863-1561)
PHONE...............................978 667-2556
EMP: 11 **EST:** 1994
SALES (est): 529.73K **Privately Held**
Web: www.cosmic-software.com
SIC: 7372 7371 Prepackaged software; Custom computer programming services

(G-10968)
COURIER COMMUNICATIONS LLC (DH)
15 Wellman Ave (01863-1334)
PHONE...............................978 251-6000
EMP: 49 **EST:** 2015
SALES (est): 47.11MM
SALES (corp-wide): 8.23B **Privately Held**
SIC: 2731 Book publishing
HQ: Lsc Communications, Inc.
4101 Winfield Rd
Warrenville IL 60555
773 272-9200

(G-10969)
COURIER COMPANIES INC (PA)
15 Wellman Ave (01863-1334)
PHONE...............................978 251-6000
James F Conway Iii, *Ch Bd*
Robert P Story Junior, *Treas*
F Bierne Lovely Junior, *Clerk*
Peter D Tobin, *Ex VP*
Clarence Strowbridge, *VP*
EMP: 20 **EST:** 1990
SQ FT: 65,000
SALES (est): 3.99MM **Privately Held**
SIC: 2732 5192 Book printing; Books

(G-10970)
COURIER CORPORATION
15 Wellman Ave (01863-1315)
PHONE...............................978 251-6000
EMP: 1576
Web: www.courier.com
SIC: 2732 2731 Book printing; Book publishing

(G-10971)
COURIER INTL HOLDINGS LLC
15 Wellman Ave (01863-1334)
PHONE...............................978 251-6000

EMP: 8 **EST:** 2015
SALES (est): 961.01K
SALES (corp-wide): 15B **Privately Held**
SIC: 2732 Book printing
HQ: R. R. Donnelley & Sons Company
35 W Wacker Dr
Chicago IL 60601
800 782-4892

(G-10972)
COURIER NEW MEDIA INC (PA)
Also Called: Courier Epic
15 Wellman Ave (01863-1334)
PHONE...............................978 251-3945
James F Conway Iii, *Pr*
William Topaz, *VP*
Robert P Story Junior, *Treas*
Lee Cochrane, *Asst Tr*
EMP: 21 **EST:** 1990
SALES (est): 845.21K **Privately Held**
SIC: 2731 2732 Book publishing; Book printing

(G-10973)
COURTSMART DIGITAL SYSTEMS INC
51 Middlesex St Unit 128 (01863-1566)
PHONE...............................978 251-3300
EMP: 32 **EST:** 1997
SALES (est): 4.66MM **Privately Held**
Web: www.courtsmart.com
SIC: 3663 3651 3679 3669 Cameras, television; Household audio and video equipment; Recording and playback apparatus, including phonograph; Visual communication systems

(G-10974)
DATA PLUS INCORPORATED
55 Middlesex St Unit 219 (01863-1570)
PHONE...............................978 888-6300
Bruce Benseler, *Pr*
EMP: 10 **EST:** 1973
SQ FT: 3,282
SALES (est): 1.41MM **Privately Held**
Web: www.dphs.com
SIC: 7372 Prepackaged software

(G-10975)
EXETER ANALYTICAL INC
7 Doris Dr Ste 6a (01863-1237)
PHONE...............................978 251-1411
Paul Brockman, *CEO*
▲ **EMP:** 12 **EST:** 1994
SQ FT: 2,500
SALES (est): 1.79MM **Privately Held**
Web: www.eai1.com
SIC: 3826 Analytical instruments

(G-10976)
FLUIGENT INC
73 Princeton St Ste 310 (01863-1559)
PHONE...............................978 934-5283
Robert P Pelletier, *Pr*
EMP: 16 **EST:** 2014
SALES (est): 651.95K **Privately Held**
Web: www.fluigent.com
SIC: 3625 Relays and industrial controls

(G-10977)
IMAGE SOURCE INC
70 Princeton St Ste 3 (01863-1577)
PHONE...............................978 251-0000
EMP: 10 **EST:** 1992
SALES (est): 938.95K **Privately Held**
Web: www.image-src.com
SIC: 7372 Prepackaged software

(G-10978)
IMPERIAL IMAGE INC
55 Middlesex St (01863-1569)
PHONE...............................978 251-0420
Anthony Demarco, *Pr*
Deborah Boivin, *Treas*
EMP: 11 **EST:** 1991
SQ FT: 10,000
SALES (est): 2.14MM **Privately Held**
Web: www.imperial-image.com
SIC: 2752 2759 Offset printing; Thermography

(G-10979)
JDM COMPANY INC
210 Tyngsboro Rd (01863-1107)
PHONE...............................978 251-1121
Matthew Robbins, *VP*
James Robbins Junior, *Pr*
Dianne Constant, *Sec*
EMP: 8 **EST:** 1990
SQ FT: 9,000
SALES (est): 816.04K **Privately Held**
Web: www.jdmcoinc.com
SIC: 7699 3589 Scientific equipment repair service; Water treatment equipment, industrial

(G-10980)
KELLER PRODUCTS INC
180 Middlesex St (01863-2060)
PHONE...............................978 264-1911
Richard Strauss, *Pr*
Richard Strauss, *Pr*
Jonathan Strauss, *VP*
EMP: 10 **EST:** 1990
SQ FT: 3,500
SALES (est): 1.45MM **Privately Held**
Web: www.kellerfilters.com
SIC: 3589 Water treatment equipment, industrial

(G-10981)
LINEAR TECHNOLOGY LLC
15 Research Pl (01863-2412)
PHONE...............................978 656-4750
Joseph Silk, *Brnch Mgr*
EMP: 7
SQ FT: 29,856
SALES (corp-wide): 12.31B **Publicly Held**
Web: www.analog.com
SIC: 3674 Semiconductors and related devices
HQ: Linear Technology Llc
1630 Mccarthy Blvd
Milpitas CA 95035
408 432-1900

(G-10982)
LSC COMMUNICATIONS INC
Also Called: North Chelmsford Digital
15 Wellman Ave (01863-1334)
PHONE...............................978 251-6000
EMP: 76
SALES (corp-wide): 8.23B **Privately Held**
Web: www.lsccom.com
SIC: 2732 Book printing
HQ: Lsc Communications, Inc.
4101 Winfield Rd
Warrenville IL 60555
773 272-9200

(G-10983)
MAXIM INTEGRATED PRODUCTS INC
8 Technology Dr (01863-2400)
PHONE...............................978 934-7600
Monica Gilbert, *Prin*
EMP: 12
SALES (corp-wide): 12.31B **Publicly Held**

Web: www.analog.com
SIC: 3674 Microcircuits, integrated (semiconductor)
HQ: Maxim Integrated Products, Inc.
160 Rio Robles
San Jose CA 95134
408 601-1000

(G-10984)
MILLENNIUM PLASTICS INC
180 Middlesex St Ste 1 (01863-2060)
PHONE.............................978 372-4822
Steve Fitzgerald, *Pr*
EMP: 10 EST: 1999
SALES (est): 1.72MM **Privately Held**
Web: www.millenniumplasticsllc.com
SIC: 3089 5162 Plastics hardware and building products; Plastics materials and basic shapes

(G-10985)
NONWOVENS INC
100 Wotton St (01863-1336)
P.O. Box 921 (01863-0921)
PHONE.............................978 251-8612
Clifford E Dallmeyer, *Pr*
Margo A Dallmeyer, *VP*
Brian Dallmeyer, *VP*
▲ **EMP: 16 EST:** 1974
SQ FT: 160,000
SALES (est): 2.14MM **Privately Held**
Web: www.nonwovens.com
SIC: 2297 Nonwoven fabrics

(G-10986)
PICKEN PRINTING INC
10 Middlesex St (01863-1783)
P.O. Box 909 (01863-0909)
PHONE.............................978 251-0730
Peter Picken, *Pr*
Lewel Picken, *Clerk*
EMP: 10 EST: 1918
SQ FT: 5,000
SALES (est): 606.92K **Privately Held**
SIC: 2752 2791 2789 Offset printing; Typesetting; Bookbinding and related work

(G-10987)
PLASTIC DESIGN INC
180 Middlesex St Ste 1 (01863-2060)
PHONE.............................978 251-4830
Errol Flynn, *Pr*
Daryl Flynn, *
Kurt Flynn, *
Marilyn Flynn, *
EMP: 30 EST: 1977
SQ FT: 23,000
SALES (est): 6.83MM **Privately Held**
Web: www.plasticdesigninc.com
SIC: 2821 5162 Plastics materials and resins ; Plastics materials and basic shapes

(G-10988)
SCIENTIFIC SOLUTIONS INC
55 Middlesex St Unit 210 (01863-1570)
PHONE.............................978 251-4554
EMP: 10 EST: 1995
SALES (est): 948.28K **Privately Held**
Web: www.ashdowntech.com
SIC: 3827 8731 Optical instruments and lenses; Commercial physical research

(G-10989)
WELCH WELDING AND TRCK EQP INC
Also Called: Welch Welding and Truck Eqp
164 Middlesex St (01863-2028)
PHONE.............................978 251-8726
TOLL FREE: 800
Bradford Welch, *Pr*

EMP: 16 EST: 1977
SQ FT: 6,000
SALES (est): 2.3MM **Privately Held**
Web: www.welchwelding.com
SIC: 7692 3446 3444 Welding repair; Architectural metalwork; Sheet metalwork

North Dartmouth
Bristol County

(G-10990)
CAPE COD CUPOLA CO INC
78 State Rd (02747-2922)
PHONE.............................508 994-2119
John E Bernier Junior, *Pr*
EMP: 12 EST: 1939
SQ FT: 2,100
SALES (est): 1.01MM **Privately Held**
Web: www.capecodcustomcupola.com
SIC: 2431 3443 3599 Ornamental woodwork: cornices, mantels, etc.; Cupolas, metal plate; Weather vanes

(G-10991)
CLARIS VISION LLC
51 State Rd (02747-3319)
PHONE.............................508 994-1400
Marcello Celentano, *CEO*
EMP: 23 EST: 2015
SALES (est): 5.5MM **Privately Held**
Web: www.kocheye.com
SIC: 3851 Eyeglasses, lenses and frames

(G-10992)
DELANO SAW MILL INC
157 Cross Rd (02747-1999)
PHONE.............................508 994-8752
Gerald Delano Junior, *Pr*
EMP: 7 EST: 1961
SALES (est): 497.65K **Privately Held**
SIC: 5211 2421 Lumber and other building materials; Sawmills and planing mills, general

(G-10993)
DEN MAR CORPORATION
1005 Reed Rd (02747-1567)
PHONE.............................508 999-3295
Henry Martin Junior, *Pr*
EMP: 17 EST: 1971
SQ FT: 56,000
SALES (est): 3.51MM **Privately Held**
Web: www.denmar-corp.com
SIC: 3589 Cooking equipment, commercial

(G-10994)
DIEBOLD NIXDORF INCORPORATED
506 State Rd (02747-1802)
PHONE.............................508 984-5936
EMP: 59
SALES (corp-wide): 3.46B **Publicly Held**
Web: www.dieboldnixdorf.com
SIC: 3578 Automatic teller machines (ATM)
PA: Diebold Nixdorf, Incorporated
50 Executive Pkwy
Hudson OH 44236
330 490-4000

(G-10995)
EAST COAST INTERIORS INC
4 Ledgewood Blvd (02747-1229)
PHONE.............................508 995-4200
EMP: 16 EST: 1996
SQ FT: 15,000
SALES (est): 952.07K **Privately Held**
Web: www.eastcoastinteriorsinc.com

SIC: 2431 Interior and ornamental woodwork and trim

(G-10996)
GINSCO INC
Also Called: New York Bagel Co
272 State Rd (02747-4312)
PHONE.............................508 990-3350
Steve Ginsberg, *Owner*
EMP: 10
SALES (corp-wide): 1.73MM **Privately Held**
Web: www.newyorkbagel.com
SIC: 2051 Doughnuts, except frozen
PA: Ginsco, Inc.
1706 President Ave
Fall River MA 02720
508 677-4767

(G-10997)
HARVEY INDUSTRIES INC
Also Called: HARVEY INDUSTRIES, INC.
7 Ledgewood Blvd (02747-1228)
PHONE.............................508 998-9779
William Correia, *Brnch Mgr*
EMP: 150
SALES (corp-wide): 1.2B **Privately Held**
Web: www.harveybp.com
SIC: 2431 Windows and window parts and trim, wood
PA: Harvey Industries, Llc
1400 Main St Fl 3
Waltham MA 02451
800 598-5400

(G-10998)
JC CLOCKS COMPANY INC
9 Ventura Dr (02747-1244)
PHONE.............................508 998-8442
Emanuel Correia, *Pr*
Aguinaldo Correia, *Treas*
EMP: 21 EST: 1980
SQ FT: 9,000
SALES (est): 2.29MM **Privately Held**
Web: www.jcclocks.com
SIC: 2434 2431 2521 Wood kitchen cabinets ; Millwork; Wood office furniture

(G-10999)
MARBUO INC
Also Called: Minuteman Press
634 State Rd Unit E2 (02747-1818)
PHONE.............................508 994-7700
EMP: 12 EST: 2003
SALES (est): 162.77K **Privately Held**
Web: www.minutemanpress.com
SIC: 2752 Commercial printing, lithographic

(G-11000)
PARAMOUNT CORP
Also Called: Oberon Company
375 Faunce Corner Rd Ste E (02747-1258)
PHONE.............................508 999-4442
Jack Hirschmann, *Pr*
EMP: 51 EST: 1978
SALES (est): 11.04MM
SALES (corp-wide): 87.79MM **Privately Held**
Web: www.oberoncompany.com
SIC: 3851 Goggles: sun, safety, industrial, underwater, etc.
PA: Equipement & Outillage Jet Ltee
49 Schooner St
Coquitlam BC V3K 0
604 523-8665

(G-11001)
SAGE PUBLICATIONS INC
285 Old Westport Rd (02747-2356)
PHONE.............................805 499-9774

David Pedro, *Prin*
EMP: 12 EST: 2015
SALES (est): 1.16MM **Privately Held**
SIC: 2731 Book publishing

(G-11002)
STATE ROAD CEMENT BLOCK CO INC
656 State Rd (02747-1894)
PHONE.............................508 993-9473
Richard Bono, *Pr*
Paul Bono, *VP*
EMP: 8 EST: 1947
SQ FT: 3,500
SALES (est): 951.05K **Privately Held**
SIC: 3271 5032 Blocks, concrete or cinder: standard; Masons' materials

North Dighton
Bristol County

(G-11003)
AVILA TEXTILES INC
620 Spring St (02764-1363)
P.O. Box 897 (02764-0881)
PHONE.............................508 828-5882
◆ **EMP: 7 EST:** 1995
SQ FT: 24,000
SALES (est): 997.63K **Privately Held**
Web: www.avilatextiles.com
SIC: 2241 Manmade fiber narrow woven fabrics

(G-11004)
TAUNTON STOVE COMPANY INC
Also Called: Tasco Engineering
490 Somerset Ave Ste 490 (02764-1810)
P.O. Box 198 (02764-0198)
PHONE.............................508 823-0786
Clifford Bodge, *Pr*
Bruce Bodge, *
John F Brady, *
Barbara Bodge, *Stockholder*
▲ **EMP: 34 EST:** 1950
SQ FT: 27,000
SALES (est): 4.16MM **Privately Held**
Web: www.tasco.us
SIC: 3444 3599 3631 3429 Sheet metal specialties, not stamped; Machine shop, jobbing and repair; Stoves, disk; Hardware, nec

(G-11005)
XTREME TUB GRINDING SVCS INC
2450 Chestnut St (02764-1008)
PHONE.............................508 386-6015
Scott Leonard, *Prin*
EMP: 7 EST: 2012
SALES (est): 233.46K **Privately Held**
Web: www.xtremetubgrinding.com
SIC: 3599 Grinding castings for the trade

(G-11006)
ZATEC LLC
620 Spring St (02764-1363)
P.O. Box 588 (02764-0588)
PHONE.............................508 880-3388
▲ **EMP: 50 EST:** 1990
SQ FT: 35,000
SALES (est): 7.62MM **Privately Held**
Web: www.zatecinc.com
SIC: 3081 Plastics film and sheet

North Easton
Bristol County

(G-11007)
AKA MCHLNGELO STRBUILDER LLC
31 Randall St (02356-2236)
PHONE..................508 238-9054
Joshua P Jacobs, *Owner*
EMP: 8 EST: 1984
SALES (est): 179.58K Privately Held
Web: www.akastairs.com
SIC: 2431 Staircases and stairs, wood

(G-11008)
C&J DREAMS INC (PA)
316 Main St (02356-1107)
PHONE..................508 238-6231
Charles Mccarthy, *Pr*
Judith Mccarthy, *Treas*
EMP: 30 EST: 1924
SQ FT: 8,500
SALES (est): 5.04MM
SALES (corp-wide): 5.04MM Privately Held
Web: www.hilliardscandy.com
SIC: 2064 5441 5451 2066 Candy and other confectionery products; Candy; Ice cream (packaged); Chocolate and cocoa products

(G-11009)
DEPOT DONUTS INC
Also Called: Dunkin' Donuts
700 Depot St (02356-2704)
PHONE..................508 230-2888
EMP: 11 EST: 1994
SQ FT: 6,400
SALES (est): 247.75K Privately Held
Web: www.pizzadepoteaston.com
SIC: 5461 2051 Doughnuts; Doughnuts, except frozen

(G-11010)
JOHNSON CONTROLS INC
Also Called: Johnson Controls
28 Main St Bldg 8-7 (02356-1448)
PHONE..................508 238-0536
EMP: 17
Web: www.johnsoncontrols.com
SIC: 2531 Seats, automobile
HQ: Johnson Controls, Inc.
5757 N Green Bay Ave
Milwaukee WI 53209
920 245-6409

(G-11011)
NORTH EASTON MACHINE CO INC
218 Elm St (02356-1115)
P.O. Box 178 (02356-0178)
PHONE..................508 238-6219
Jon Holbrook, *Pr*
Lillian Holbrook, *Treas*
EMP: 18 EST: 1964
SQ FT: 15,000
SALES (est): 3.69MM Privately Held
Web: www.northeastonmachine.com
SIC: 3451 Screw machine products

(G-11012)
PIESCO SPORTING GOODS INC
130 Washington St (02356-1120)
P.O. Box 327 (02356-0327)
PHONE..................508 238-5599
David Piesco, *Pr*
EMP: 12 EST: 1946
SQ FT: 3,000
SALES (est): 2.37MM Privately Held
Web: www.piescosports.com
SIC: 5136 2395 5137 Sportswear, men's and boys'; Art goods for embroidering, stamped: purchased materials; Sportswear, women's and children's

North Falmouth
Barnstable County

(G-11013)
TELEDYNE BENTHOS INC
49 Edgerton Dr (02556-2821)
PHONE..................508 563-1000
◆ EMP: 119
SIC: 3812 Search and navigation equipment

(G-11014)
TELEDYNE INSTRUMENTS INC
Also Called: Teledyne Benthos
49 Edgerton Dr (02556-2821)
PHONE..................508 563-1000
Thomas W Altshuler, *Brnch Mgr*
EMP: 134
SALES (corp-wide): 5.46B Publicly Held
Web: www.teledyne.com
SIC: 3812 Search and navigation equipment
HQ: Teledyne Instruments, Inc.
16830 Chestnut St
City Of Industry CA 91748
626 934-1500

(G-11015)
TELEDYNE INSTRUMENTS INC
Also Called: Teledyne Oceanscience
49 Edgerton Dr (02556-2821)
PHONE..................508 563-1000
Dennis Klahn, *Prin*
EMP: 21
SALES (corp-wide): 5.46B Publicly Held
Web: www.teledyne.com
SIC: 3823 Buoyancy instruments, industrial process type
HQ: Teledyne Instruments, Inc.
16830 Chestnut St
City Of Industry CA 91748
626 934-1500

(G-11016)
TELEDYNE INSTRUMENTS INC
Also Called: Teledyne Webb Research
49 Edgerton Dr (02556-2821)
PHONE..................508 548-2077
EMP: 114
SALES (corp-wide): 5.46B Publicly Held
Web: www.teledyne.com
SIC: 3699 Electrical equipment and supplies, nec
HQ: Teledyne Instruments, Inc.
16830 Chestnut St
City Of Industry CA 91748
626 934-1500

(G-11017)
TELEDYNE INSTRUMENTS INC
Also Called: Teledyne Seabotix
49 Edgerton Dr (02556-2821)
PHONE..................508 563-1000
EMP: 20
SALES (corp-wide): 5.46B Publicly Held
Web: www.teledyne.com
SIC: 3549 Propeller straightening presses
HQ: Teledyne Instruments, Inc.
16830 Chestnut St
City Of Industry CA 91748
626 934-1500

North Grafton
Worcester County

(G-11018)
AFL TELECOMMUNICATIONS LLC
15 Centennial Dr (01536-1860)
PHONE..................508 890-7100
EMP: 14
Web: www.aflglobal.com
SIC: 3357 Nonferrous wiredrawing and insulating
HQ: Afl Telecommunications Llc
170 Ridgeview Center Dr
Duncan SC 29334
864 235-3423

(G-11019)
ALL STEEL FABRICATING INC
84 Creeper Hill Rd (01536-1400)
P.O. Box 597 (01536-0597)
PHONE..................508 839-4471
James Magill, *Pr*
James Magill Junior, *VP Opers*
Kevin H Magill, *
Angela Magill, *
EMP: 30 EST: 1969
SQ FT: 30,000
SALES (est): 5.2MM Privately Held
Web: www.allsteelfab.com
SIC: 3441 3443 Building components, structural steel; Fabricated plate work (boiler shop)

(G-11020)
CCO HOLDINGS LLC
100 Worcester St (01536-1024)
PHONE..................774 293-4026
EMP: 109
SALES (corp-wide): 54.02B Publicly Held
SIC: 4841 3663 3651 Cable television services; Radio and t.v. communications equipment; Household audio and video equipment
HQ: Cco Holdings, Llc
400 Atlantic St
Stamford CT 06901
203 905-7801

(G-11021)
DANCE IT UP INC
Also Called: Sugar Plums
36 N Main St (01536-1553)
PHONE..................508 839-1648
Stephanie Mack, *Pr*
EMP: 16 EST: 1996
SQ FT: 4,300
SALES (est): 959.09K Privately Held
Web: www.danceitup.com
SIC: 5947 3911 3161 5632 Gift shop; Jewelry apparel; Clothing and apparel carrying cases; Dancewear

(G-11022)
DIMITRIA DELIGHTS INC
81 Creeper Hill Rd (01536-1421)
PHONE..................508 839-1638
EMP: 55 EST: 1972
SALES (est): 8.11MM Privately Held
Web: www.dimitriadelights.com
SIC: 2041 2051 2053 2038 Doughs, frozen or refrigerated; Cakes, pies, and pastries; Frozen bakery products, except bread; Frozen specialties, nec

(G-11023)
FDA GROUP LLC
Also Called: FDA Group

3 Bridle Ridge Dr (01536-2204)
PHONE..................413 330-7476
EMP: 36 EST: 2014
SALES (est): 1.96MM Privately Held
Web: www.thefdagroup.com
SIC: 2834 5047 Pharmaceutical preparations; Diagnostic equipment, medical

(G-11024)
LINCOLN PRECISION MACHINING CO
Also Called: Lincoln Hoist
121 Creeper Hill Rd (01536-1437)
P.O. Box 458 (01536-0458)
PHONE..................508 839-2175
David Hallen, *Pr*
Richard Hallen, *
Doris E Hallen, *
▲ EMP: 25 EST: 1945
SQ FT: 20,000
SALES (est): 3.15MM Privately Held
Web: www.lincoln-precision.com
SIC: 3536 Hoists, cranes, and monorails

(G-11025)
PRIMARY COLORS INC
9 Millennium Dr (01536-1862)
PHONE..................508 839-3202
Judy Mickleson, *Pr*
EMP: 24 EST: 1994
SQ FT: 40,000
SALES (est): 6.6MM Privately Held
Web: www.primarycolorsinc.com
SIC: 2821 Plastics materials and resins

(G-11026)
SUNSHINE SIGN COMPANY INC
121 Westboro Rd (01536-1809)
PHONE..................508 839-5588
David R Glispin, *Pr*
Carol Demont, *
Pam Johnson, *
EMP: 130 EST: 1980
SQ FT: 10,000
SALES (est): 9.84MM Privately Held
Web: www.sunshinesign.com
SIC: 3993 Signs and advertising specialties

(G-11027)
VERRILLON INC
15 Centennial Dr (01536-1860)
PHONE..................508 890-7100
Abdel Soufiane Ph.d., *Pr*
Gary Churchill, *
▲ EMP: 68 EST: 2000
SQ FT: 50,000
SALES (est): 22.19MM Privately Held
Web: www.aflglobal.com
SIC: 3357 Nonferrous wiredrawing and insulating
HQ: Afl Telecommunications Llc
170 Ridgeview Center Dr
Duncan SC 29334
864 235-3423

(G-11028)
WASHINGTON MILLS GROUP INC (PA)
20 N Main St (01536-1522)
P.O. Box 428 (01536-0428)
PHONE..................508 839-6511
◆ EMP: 100 EST: 1988
SALES (est): 273.36MM Privately Held
Web: www.washingtonmills.com
SIC: 3291 Abrasive grains

(G-11029)
WASHINGTON MILLS N GRAFTON INC (HQ)
Also Called: Washington Mills
20 N Main St (01536-1522)
P.O. Box 428 (01536-0428)
PHONE....................508 839-6511
Peter H Williams, *Pr*
Nancy E Gates, *
Bruce Vigneaux, *
Alden F L Harris Ii, *Dir*
◆ EMP: 100 EST: 1868
SQ FT: 126,000
SALES (est): 104.83MM Privately Held
Web: www.washingtonmills.com
SIC: 3291   Abrasive grains
PA: Washington Mills Group, Inc.
20 N Main St
North Grafton MA 01536

(G-11030)
WYMAN-GORDON COMPANY (DH)
244 Worcester St (01536-1200)
PHONE....................508 839-8252
Kenneth D Buck, *Pr*
Roger P Becker, *
Roger A Cooke, *
Steven C Blackmore, *
Shawn R Hagel, *
◆ EMP: 400 EST: 1883
SQ FT: 514,000
SALES (est): 581.91MM
SALES (corp-wide): 302.09B Publicly Held
Web: www.pccforgedproducts.com
SIC: 3462 3324 3728 3317   Iron and steel forgings; Aerospace investment castings, ferrous; Aircraft parts and equipment, nec; Pipes, seamless steel
HQ: Precision Castparts Corp.
5885 Meadows Rd Ste 620
Lake Oswego OR 97035
503 946-4800

North Oxford
Worcester County

(G-11031)
CROCKER ARCHITECTURAL SHTMTL
129 Southbridge Rd (01537-1210)
PHONE....................508 987-9900
Christine Crocker Lusignan, *Pr*
David H Crocker, *
Madeline Crocker, *
EMP: 40 EST: 1991
SQ FT: 12,000
SALES (est): 9.84MM Privately Held
Web: www.crockerarchitectural.com
SIC: 3444 1761   Sheet metal specialties, not stamped; Sheet metal work, nec

(G-11032)
CUSTOM CONVYRS FABRICATION INC
140 Southbridge Rd (01537-1168)
P.O. Box 751 (01537-0751)
PHONE....................508 922-0283
Wendell Barnes, *Pr*
EMP: 17 EST: 2007
SALES (est): 1.66MM Privately Held
Web: www.customcandf.com
SIC: 3496   Conveyor belts

(G-11033)
MYRIAD ENGINEERING CO INC
96 Southbridge Rd (01537-1205)
PHONE....................508 731-6416
Dennis Allard, *Pr*
Donna Allard, *VP*
EMP: 15 EST: 1993
SALES (est): 445.53K Privately Held
Web: www.myriadengineering.com
SIC: 3599   Machine shop, jobbing and repair

(G-11034)
STERLING CONCRETE CORP
10 Sterling Way (01537)
P.O. Box 1398 (01564-6398)
PHONE....................978 422-8282
George Defalco, *Pr*
EMP: 10 EST: 2004
SALES (est): 2.05MM Privately Held
Web: www.sterlingconcrete.net
SIC: 3273   Ready-mixed concrete

(G-11035)
SWISS PRECISION PRODUCTS INC (DH)
627 Main St (01537-1305)
PHONE....................508 987-8003
Jay Athanes, *Pr*
EMP: 29 EST: 1961
SQ FT: 15,000
SALES (est): 6.41MM
SALES (corp-wide): 654.23MM Publicly Held
Web: www.swissprpr.com
SIC: 3599 3841 3494   Machine shop, jobbing and repair; Veterinarians' instruments and apparatus; Valves and pipe fittings, nec
HQ: Stratos International, Inc.
299 Johnson Ave Sw
Waseca MN 56093
507 833-8822

North Quincy
Norfolk County

(G-11036)
INDUSTRIAL HEAT TREATING INC
Also Called: I H T
22 Densmore St 26 (02171-1785)
P.O. Box 98 (02171-0002)
PHONE....................617 328-1010
Lynne Davis, *Pr*
EMP: 24 EST: 1942
SQ FT: 48,000
SALES (est): 2.23MM Privately Held
Web: www.indht.com
SIC: 3398   Metal heat treating

North Reading
Middlesex County

(G-11037)
AMAZON ROBOTICS LLC (HQ)
300 Riverpark Dr (01864-2622)
PHONE....................781 221-4640
Michael Mountz, *CEO*
Amy Villeneuve, *
Matt Verminski, *
Joe Quinlivan, *
Benge Ambrogi, *
▲ EMP: 104 EST: 2003
SQ FT: 44,000
SALES (est): 73.47MM Publicly Held
Web: www.kiva-systems.com

SIC: 7373 3535   Systems integration services; Belt conveyor systems, general industrial use
PA: Amazon.Com, Inc.
410 Terry Ave N
Seattle WA 98109

(G-11038)
BOWERS AND WILKINS GROUP
54 Concord St (01864-2602)
PHONE....................978 357-0428
Scott Rundle, *Prin*
EMP: 24 EST: 2010
SALES (est): 2.26MM Privately Held
Web: www.bowerswilkins.com
SIC: 3651 3679   Amplifiers: radio, public address, or musical instrument; Recording heads, speech and musical equipment

(G-11039)
D L MAHER CO
71 Concord St (01864-2601)
PHONE....................781 933-3210
Kevin Maher, *Pr*
J Theodore Morine, *
Robert Maher, *
Peter Maher, *
Edward J Maher, *
EMP: 15 EST: 1941
SQ FT: 2,000
SALES (est): 332.63K Privately Held
Web: www.maherserv.com
SIC: 8748 1381   Business consulting, nec; Drilling water intake wells

(G-11040)
HEFFRON ASPHALT CORP (PA)
Also Called: Heffron Materials
68 Winter St (01864-2203)
P.O. Box 162 (01887-0162)
PHONE....................781 935-1455
Kenneth Heffron, *Dir*
Milton Heffron Senior, *Ch Bd*
Kenneth Heffron, *Pr*
Anna Heffron, *Clerk*
EMP: 7 EST: 1943
SQ FT: 375
SALES (est): 1.24MM
SALES (corp-wide): 1.24MM Privately Held
SIC: 2951 1611 5032   Asphalt and asphaltic paving mixtures (not from refineries); Surfacing and paving; Sand, construction

(G-11041)
IMMEDIA SEMICONDUCTOR INC
Also Called: Blink
100 Riverpark Dr Fl 1 (01864-2649)
PHONE....................978 296-4950
Peter Besen, *CEO*
Don Shulsinger, *VP*
EMP: 15 EST: 2008
SALES (est): 5.43MM Publicly Held
Web: www.blinkforhome.com
SIC: 3674   Semiconductors and related devices
PA: Amazon.Com, Inc.
410 Terry Ave N
Seattle WA 98109

(G-11042)
MASS PRINTING INC
352 Park St Ste 202w (01864-2156)
PHONE....................781 396-1970
Andrew Pallotta, *Pr*
EMP: 7 EST: 1991
SQ FT: 2,000
SALES (est): 1.27MM Privately Held
Web: www.massprinting.com
SIC: 2752   Offset printing

(G-11043)
MAVERICK WORK WEAR INC
Also Called: Brunt Workwear
92 Concord St (01864-2617)
PHONE....................860 944-3776
Eric Girouard, *CEO*
EMP: 39 EST: 2019
SALES (est): 5.22MM Privately Held
Web: www.bruntworkwear.com
SIC: 2326 5699   Work uniforms; Uniforms and work clothing

(G-11044)
MONARCH STONE INC ✪
133 Main St (01864-5002)
PHONE....................978 954-7021
Marcia G Guimaraes, *Dir*
EMP: 7 EST: 2022
SALES (est): 60.01K Privately Held
SIC: 3281   Cut stone and stone products

(G-11045)
REST LLC
3 Bridle Way (01864-1558)
PHONE....................781 788-8113
Barouyr Tchaprazian, *Prin*
EMP: 10 EST: 2009
SALES (est): 474.94K Privately Held
SIC: 3634   Coffee makers, electric: household

(G-11046)
TAKEDA PHARMACEUTICALS USA INC
200 Riverpark Dr (01864-2621)
PHONE....................781 482-1461
EMP: 7 EST: 1998
SALES (est): 91.34K Privately Held
Web: www.takedajobs.com
SIC: 2834   Pharmaceutical preparations

(G-11047)
TERADYNE INC
Also Called: Assembly Test Division
600 Riverpark Dr (01864-2634)
PHONE....................978 370-2700
EMP: 50
SALES (corp-wide): 3.16B Publicly Held
Web: www.teradyne.com
SIC: 3825   Semiconductor test equipment
PA: Teradyne, Inc.
600 Riverpark Dr
North Reading MA 01864
978 370-2700

(G-11048)
TERADYNE INC (PA)
Also Called: Teradyne
600 Riverpark Dr (01864-2634)
PHONE....................978 370-2700
Gregory S Smith, *Pr*
Paul J Tufano, *
Sanjay Mehta, *VP*
Walter G Vahey, *Executive Business Development Vice President*
Charles J Gray, *VP*
▲ EMP: 1320 EST: 1960
SQ FT: 422,000
SALES (est): 3.16B
SALES (corp-wide): 3.16B Publicly Held
Web: www.teradyne.com
SIC: 3825 3643 3674   Semiconductor test equipment; Connectors and terminals for electrical devices; Semiconductors and related devices

(G-11049)
TERADYNE INC
500 Riverpark Dr (01864-2615)

PHONE................................978 370-2700
Rich Homestead, *Mgr*
EMP: 15
SALES (corp-wide): 3.16B **Publicly Held**
Web: www.teradyne.com
SIC: 3825 Test equipment for electronic and
electrical circuits
PA: Teradyne, Inc.
600 Riverpark Dr
North Reading MA 01864
978 370-2700

(G-11050)
TOWN OF NORTH READING
235 North St (01864-1260)
PHONE................................978 664-6027
Martin Tilton, *Brnch Mgr*
EMP: 22
Web: www.northreadingma.gov
SIC: 2721 Periodicals
PA: Town Of North Reading
235 North St Ofc
North Reading MA 01864
978 664-6010

North Truro
Barnstable County

(G-11051)
**TRURO VINEYARDS CAPE COD
LLC**
Also Called: South Hallow Spirits
11 Shore Road Rte 6a (02652)
P.O. Box 834 (02652-0834)
PHONE................................508 487-6200
Dave Roberts, *Managing Member*
▲ **EMP:** 10 **EST:** 1993
SQ FT: 3,200
SALES (est): 2.35MM **Privately Held**
Web: www.trurovineyardsofcapecod.com
SIC: 5182 5921 2084 Wine; Wine; Wines

Northampton
Hampshire County

(G-11052)
**AMHERST WOODWORKING &
SUPPLY INC**
Also Called: Copper Beech Millwork
30 Industrial Dr (01060-3261)
P.O. Box 718 (01061-0718)
PHONE................................413 584-3003
EMP: 40
Web: www.amherstwoodworking.com
SIC: 2431 5211 Millwork; Millwork and
lumber

(G-11053)
**BEN & BLLS CHCLAT
EMPORIUM INC (PA)**
143 Main St (01060-3434)
PHONE................................413 584-5695
Ben Coggins, *Pr*
Robert Koury, *Treas*
EMP: 10 **EST:** 1952
SQ FT: 1,200
SALES (est): 1.31MM
SALES (corp-wide): 1.31MM **Privately
Held**
Web: www.benandbills.com
SIC: 2064 5441 Candy and other
confectionery products; Candy

(G-11054)
**BRIDGESTONE RET
OPERATIONS LLC**

Also Called: Firestone
327 King St (01060-2370)
PHONE................................413 586-1584
Daniel Hamlett, *Mgr*
EMP: 8
Web: www.bridgestoneamericas.com
SIC: 5531 7534 Automotive tires;
Rebuilding and retreading tires
HQ: Bridgestone Retail Operations, Llc
333 E Lake St Ste 300
Bloomingdale IL 60108
630 259-9000

(G-11055)
**COCA-COLA BTLG STHSTERN
NENG I**
Also Called: Coca-Cola
45 Industrial Dr (01060-2394)
PHONE................................413 586-8450
EMP: 32
Web: www.coca-cola.com
SIC: 2086 2033 Bottled and canned soft
drinks; Canned fruits and specialties
HQ: Coca-Cola Bottling Company Of
Southeastern New England, Inc.
150 Waterford Parkway S
Waterford CT 06385
860 443-2816

(G-11056)
**COCA-COLA REFRESHMENTS
USA INC**
Also Called: Coca-Cola
45 Industrial Dr (01060-2394)
PHONE................................413 586-8450
EMP: 73
SALES (corp-wide): 43B **Publicly Held**
Web: www.coca-cola.com
SIC: 2086 2087 Bottled and canned soft
drinks; Concentrates, drink
HQ: Coca-Cola Refreshments Usa, Inc.
1 Coca Cola Plz Nw
Atlanta GA 30313
770 989-3000

(G-11057)
COTTON TREE SERVICE INC
248 Hatfield St (01060-1519)
PHONE................................413 584-9104
TOLL FREE: 800
David J Cotton, *Pr*
David J Cotton, *Pr*
Kim J Cotton, *Clerk*
David Cotton, *Pr*
EMP: 12 **EST:** 1956
SQ FT: 3,000
SALES (est): 779.9K **Privately Held**
Web: www.cottontree.com
SIC: 0782 1794 2411 4959 Landscape
contractors; Excavation work; Wood chips,
produced in the field; Snowplowing

(G-11058)
**COUNCIL ON INTL PUB AFFIRS
INC (PA)**
Also Called: Boot Strap Press
3 Mont View Ave (01060-3320)
PHONE................................212 972-9878
Ward Morehouse, *Pr*
▲ **EMP:** 8 **EST:** 1954
SALES (est): 453.7K
SALES (corp-wide): 453.7K **Privately Held**
SIC: 2731 Books, publishing only

(G-11059)
DIPWELL COMPANY INC
82 Industrial Dr Unit 3 (01060-2389)
PHONE................................413 587-4673
Lynn P Alstadt, *Pr*

Karen Lynn Alstadt, *VP*
Brian Baird, *Treas*
EMP: 8 **EST:** 1946
SALES (est): 506.62K **Privately Held**
Web: www.dipwell.com
SIC: 3914 Stainless steel ware

(G-11060)
**EDWARD ELGAR PUBLISHING
INC**
9 Dewey Ct (01060-3815)
PHONE................................413 584-5551
Edward Elgar, *Pr*
▲ **EMP:** 7 **EST:** 1996
SALES (est): 765.25K **Privately Held**
Web: www.e-elgar.com
SIC: 2731 Books, publishing only

(G-11061)
FARS INC
32 Pleasant St (01060-4158)
PHONE................................413 586-1332
Reza Shafil, *Pr*
Ray Shafie, *VP*
EMP: 20 **EST:** 1985
SQ FT: 2,000
SALES (est): 694.38K **Privately Held**
SIC: 7334 2752 Photocopying and
duplicating services; Offset printing

(G-11062)
FREE PRESS
26 Center St Apt 2 (01060-3027)
PHONE................................413 587-3770
EMP: 7 **EST:** 2018
SALES (est): 107.99K **Privately Held**
Web: www.freepress.net
SIC: 2741 Miscellaneous publishing

(G-11063)
GDMC USA LLC
Also Called: Vomax
296 Nonotuck St Ste 11 (01062-2674)
PHONE................................413 584-0065
Rajiv Singh, *CEO*
EMP: 16 **EST:** 2017
SALES (est): 804.08K **Privately Held**
SIC: 2389 Apparel and accessories, nec

(G-11064)
GE HEALTH CARE
22 Industrial Dr E (01060-2351)
PHONE................................413 586-7720
EMP: 46
SIC: 3821 Calorimeters

(G-11065)
**GLOBAL LF SCNCES SLTONS
USA LL**
22 Industrial Dr E (01060-2351)
PHONE................................413 586-7720
John Brandts, *Brnch Mgr*
EMP: 214
SALES (corp-wide): 31.47B **Publicly Held**
Web: www.cytivalifesciences.com
SIC: 2834 Pharmaceutical preparations
HQ: Global Life Sciences Solutions Usa Llc
100 Results Way
Marlborough MA 01752
800 526-3593

(G-11066)
**HAYDENVILLE WDWKG &
DESIGN INC (PA)**
35 Conz St (01060-3803)
P.O. Box 132 (01373-0132)
PHONE................................413 665-7402
Zinnia Stetson, *CEO*

Lance Hodes, *Pr*
Cory Doubleday, *Pr*
EMP: 8 **EST:** 1982
SQ FT: 3,000
SALES (est): 974.91K **Privately Held**
Web: www.haydenvillewd.com
SIC: 2511 1521 Wood desks, bookcases,
and magazine racks; General remodeling,
single-family houses

(G-11067)
**HIGHLIGHTS FOR CHILDREN
INC**
Also Called: Tinkergarten
9 1/2 Market St (01060-3295)
PHONE................................413 397-2800
EMP: 44
SALES (corp-wide): 109.4MM **Privately
Held**
Web: www.tinkergarten.com
SIC: 2721 Magazines: publishing and
printing
PA: Highlights For Children, Inc.
1800 Watermark Dr
Columbus OH 43215
614 486-0631

(G-11068)
INTERLINK PUBLISHING GROUP
46 Crosby St (01060-1804)
PHONE................................413 582-7054
TOLL FREE: 800
Michel Moushabeck, *Pr*
Ruth Moushabek, *VP*
◆ **EMP:** 27 **EST:** 1982
SQ FT: 10,000
SALES (est): 861.95K **Privately Held**
SIC: 2741 Miscellaneous publishing

(G-11069)
L3 TECHNOLOGIES INC
L3 Keo
50 Prince St (01060-3635)
PHONE................................413 586-2330
Michael Wall, *Brnch Mgr*
EMP: 600
SQ FT: 8,000
SALES (corp-wide): 17.06B **Publicly Held**
Web: www.l3harris.com
SIC: 3621 3625 3827 3812 Motors and
generators; Relays and industrial controls;
Optical instruments and lenses; Search and
navigation equipment
HQ: L3 Technologies, Inc.
600 3rd Ave Fl 34
New York NY 10016
321 727-9100

(G-11070)
MALVERN PANALYTICAL INC
22 Industrial Dr E (01060-2351)
PHONE................................413 586-7720
EMP: 45
SALES (corp-wide): 1.6B **Privately Held**
Web: www.malvernpanalytical.com
SIC: 3826 Analytical instruments
HQ: Malvern Panalytical Inc.
2400 Computer Dr Ste 3
Westborough MA 01581
508 768-6400

(G-11071)
METRICA INTERIOR INC
209 Earle St (01060-3643)
PHONE................................413 587-2750
Bruce Volz, *Pr*
Anthony Clarke, *VP*
EMP: 17 **EST:** 1984
SQ FT: 10,000
SALES (est): 5.01MM **Privately Held**

Web: www.vca-inc.com
SIC: 2531 2431 2517 2511 Public building and related furniture; Millwork; Wood television and radio cabinets; Wood household furniture

(G-11072)
MICROCAL LLC
22 Industrial Dr E (01060-2395)
PHONE.....................413 586-7720
EMP: 10 EST: 2016
SALES (est): 493.54K **Privately Held**
SIC: 3826 Analytical instruments

(G-11073)
MILLITECH INC
29 Industrial Dr E (01060-2351)
PHONE.....................413 582-9620
EMP: 100
Web: www.smithsinterconnect.com
SIC: 4899 3663 3679 Communication signal enhancement network services; Radio and t.v. communications equipment; Microwave components

(G-11074)
PACKAGING CORPORATION AMERICA
Also Called: PCA
525 Mount Tom Rd (01060-4261)
PHONE.....................413 584-6132
Robert Park, Genl Mgr
EMP: 41
SALES (corp-wide): 8.48B **Publicly Held**
Web: www.packagingcorp.com
SIC: 2653 Boxes, corrugated: made from purchased materials
PA: Packaging Corporation Of America
1 N Field Ct
Lake Forest IL 60045
847 482-3000

(G-11075)
PACKAGING CORPORATION AMERICA
Also Called: Pca/Chelmsford 310
525 Mount Tom Rd (01060-4261)
PHONE.....................978 256-4586
Gary Downs, Mgr
EMP: 71
SALES (corp-wide): 8.48B **Publicly Held**
Web: www.packagingcorp.com
SIC: 2653 Boxes, corrugated: made from purchased materials
PA: Packaging Corporation Of America
1 N Field Ct
Lake Forest IL 60045
847 482-3000

(G-11076)
PHILLIPS ENTERPRISES INC
149 Easthampton Rd (01060-4103)
PHONE.....................413 586-5860
William Phillips, Pr
▲ EMP: 18 EST: 1974
SQ FT: 65,000
SALES (est): 4.74MM **Privately Held**
Web: www.phillipsenterprises.com
SIC: 2542 2541 Fixtures: display, office, or store: except wood; Display fixtures, wood

(G-11077)
POINT3 FARMA LLC
48 Round Hill Rd # 23 (01060-2124)
PHONE.....................719 733-3900
Scott Beers, Pr
David Lahar, CFO
Debbie Greve, Sec
EMP: 9 EST: 2018

SALES (est): 479.32K **Privately Held**
SIC: 0191 2834 General farms, primarily crop; Pharmaceutical preparations

(G-11078)
SAINT-GOBAIN CERAMICS PLAS INC
175 Industrial Dr (01060-2326)
PHONE.....................413 586-8167
Terry Thibault, Brnch Mgr
EMP: 181
SALES (corp-wide): 397.78MM **Privately Held**
Web: www.saint-gobain.com
SIC: 3297 Nonclay refractories
HQ: Saint-Gobain Ceramics & Plastics, Inc.
20 Moores Rd
Malvern PA 19355

(G-11079)
SAMSARA
26 Strong Ave (01060-3923)
PHONE.....................413 570-4130
EMP: 9 EST: 2017
SALES (est): 286.2K **Privately Held**
Web: www.samsara.com
SIC: 3577 Computer peripheral equipment, nec

(G-11080)
SMITHS INTERCONNECT INC
29 Industrial Dr E (01060-2351)
PHONE.....................413 582-9620
EMP: 100
SALES (corp-wide): 3.83B **Privately Held**
Web: www.smithsinterconnect.com
SIC: 4899 3663 3679 Communication signal enhancement network services; Radio and t.v. communications equipment; Microwave components
HQ: Smiths Interconnect, Inc.
4726 Eisenhower Blvd
Tampa FL 33634
813 901-7200

(G-11081)
SMJ METAL COMPANY INC
Also Called: Ralph's Blacksmith Shop
36 Smith St (01060-3823)
P.O. Box 897 (01876-0751)
PHONE.....................413 586-3535
Scott Peabody, Pr
Arthur D Grodd, *
EMP: 45 EST: 2004
SQ FT: 5,400
SALES (est): 9.64MM **Privately Held**
Web: www.ralphsblacksmith.com
SIC: 3441 Fabricated structural metal

(G-11082)
TEMP-PRO INCORPORATED
Also Called: Temp-Pro
200 Industrial Dr (01060-2380)
P.O. Box 89 (01061-0089)
PHONE.....................413 584-3165
Rodolfo Jacobson, Pr
Nancy Harding, *
▲ EMP: 41 EST: 1972
SQ FT: 60,000
SALES (est): 8.91MM **Privately Held**
Web: www.temp-pro.com
SIC: 3823 Temperature instruments: industrial process type

(G-11083)
TURNING LEAF CTRS NRTHMPTON LL
261 King St (01060-2361)
PHONE.....................413 204-4749

Stephanie Mcnair, Managing Member
EMP: 7 EST: 2019
SALES (est): 157.84K **Privately Held**
SIC: 3999

(G-11084)
VALLEY ADVOCATE
115 Conz St Ste 2 (01060-4445)
PHONE.....................413 584-0003
Patty Desroche, Prin
EMP: 7 EST: 2008
SALES (est): 133.96K **Privately Held**
Web: www.valleyadvocate.com
SIC: 2711 Commercial printing and newspaper publishing combined

(G-11085)
WALRUS ENTEPRISES LLC
30 Aldrich St (01060-2215)
P.O. Box 1502 (01061-1502)
PHONE.....................413 387-4387
Renato Bartoli, Prin
▲ EMP: 9 EST: 2001
SALES (est): 1.19MM **Privately Held**
Web: www.coloredsmoke.com
SIC: 2865 Dyes and pigments

(G-11086)
WEATHER GUARD INDUSTRIES LLC
36 Smith St (01060-3823)
P.O. Box 897 (01876-0751)
PHONE.....................954 703-0563
Mark Sinclair, Prin
EMP: 8 EST: 2017
SALES (est): 443.75K **Privately Held**
SIC: 3999 Manufacturing industries, nec

(G-11087)
WRIGHT ARCHTECTURAL MLLWK CORP
115 Industrial Dr (01060-2326)
PHONE.....................413 586-3528
Walter K Price, Pr
Michael D Buell, *
EMP: 30 EST: 1989
SQ FT: 20,150
SALES (est): 5.27MM **Privately Held**
Web: www.wrightmw.com
SIC: 2431 Doors, wood

Northborough
Worcester County

(G-11088)
ASPEN AEROGELS INC (PA)
Also Called: Aspen Aerogels
30 Forbes Rd Bldg B (01532-2501)
PHONE.....................508 691-1111
Donald R Young, Pr
William P Noglows, *
Gregg R Landes, STRATEGIC Development
Corby C Whitaker, S&M/VP
EMP: 228 EST: 2001
SQ FT: 51,650
SALES (est): 180.36MM
SALES (corp-wide): 180.36MM **Publicly Held**
Web: www.aerogel.com
SIC: 2899 5033 Insulating compounds; Insulation materials

(G-11089)
ATS CASES INC
172 Otis St Ste 4 (01532-2415)
P.O. Box 723 (01532-0723)
PHONE.....................508 393-9110

Ronald Orlando, Pr
EMP: 8 EST: 1976
SQ FT: 26,000
SALES (est): 1.03MM **Privately Held**
Web: www.atscases.com
SIC: 3161 Cases, carrying, nec

(G-11090)
BEALS & SONS INC
440 Green St (01532-1018)
P.O. Box 1039 (01532-4039)
PHONE.....................508 393-1833
Cindy L Beals, Pr
EMP: 7 EST: 2005
SALES (est): 668.72K **Privately Held**
Web: www.bealsandsons.com
SIC: 3799 Transportation equipment, nec

(G-11091)
BORGWARNER INC
100 Otis St Ste 1 (01532-2438)
PHONE.....................508 281-5500
EMP: 23
SALES (corp-wide): 15.8B **Publicly Held**
Web: www.borgwarner.com
SIC: 3714 Transmissions, motor vehicle
PA: Borgwarner Inc.
3850 Hamlin Rd
Auburn Hills MI 48326
248 754-9200

(G-11092)
BORGWARNER MASSACHUSETTS INC (HQ)
Also Called: Sevcon
100 Otis St (01532-2463)
PHONE.....................508 281-5500
Matthew Boyle, Pr
Paul N Farquhar, VP
▲ EMP: 41 EST: 1987
SALES (est): 33.39MM
SALES (corp-wide): 14.2B **Publicly Held**
Web: www.borgwarner.com
SIC: 3674 3714 Solid state electronic devices, nec; Motor vehicle electrical equipment
PA: Borgwarner Inc.
3850 Hamlin Rd
Auburn Hills MI 48326
248 754-9200

(G-11093)
CAMAR CORP
55 Church St (01532-1439)
PHONE.....................508 845-9263
James A Mercanti, Pr
Barbara Mercanti, Clerk
EMP: 10 EST: 1974
SQ FT: 20,000
SALES (est): 969.86K **Privately Held**
SIC: 3511 Turbines and turbine generator sets

(G-11094)
CRAMARO TARPAULIN SYSTEMS INC
51 Sw Cutoff (01532-2111)
PHONE.....................508 393-3062
David Feitler, Sec
EMP: 9
SQ FT: 3,000
Web: www.cramarotarps.com
SIC: 2394 Tarpaulins, fabric: made from purchased materials
PA: Cramaro Tarpaulin Systems Inc
600 North Dr
Melbourne FL 32934

(G-11095)
EXPANSION OPPORTUNITIES INC
Also Called: Viewpoint Sign & Awning
35 Lyman St Ste 1 (01532-2076)
PHONE.................................508 393-8200
Jeffrey A Kwass, *Pr*
Dave Randa, *
EMP: 48 **EST:** 1994
SQ FT: 18,000
SALES (est): 4.16MM **Privately Held**
SIC: 3993 2394 3444 Signs and advertising specialties; Awnings, fabric: made from purchased materials; Sheet metalwork

(G-11096)
GENZYME CORPORATION
11 Forbes Rd (01532-2501)
PHONE.................................508 351-2699
Robert C Chaves, *Prin*
EMP: 107
Web: www.sanofi.us
SIC: 2834 Pharmaceutical preparations
HQ: Genzyme Corporation
450 Water St
Cambridge MA 02141
617 252-7500

(G-11097)
HOSOKAWA ALPINE AMERICAN INC
455 Whitney St (01532-2503)
PHONE.................................508 655-1123
David Nunes, *Pr*
Robert Hitchins, *VP*
Thomas Valorie, *Sec*
Donald Brophy, *Treas*
▲ **EMP:** 19 **EST:** 2009
SALES (est): 5.94MM **Privately Held**
Web: www.halpine.com
SIC: 3229 Reflectors for lighting equipment, pressed or blown glass
PA: Hosokawa Micron Corporation
1-9, Shodaitajika
Hirakata OSK 573-1

(G-11098)
HOSOKAWA MICRON INTL INC
Also Called: Hosokawa Alpine American Div
455 Whitney St (01532-2503)
PHONE.................................508 655-1123
EMP: 24
Web: www.hmicronpowder.com
SIC: 3559 2393 8711 5044 Chemical machinery and equipment; Textile bags; Pollution control engineering; Copying equipment
HQ: Hosokawa Micron International Inc.
10 Chatham Rd
Summit NJ 07901
908 273-6360

(G-11099)
ID BIMEDICAL CORP NORTHBOROUGH
30 Bearfoot (01532-1514)
PHONE.................................508 351-9333
EMP: 62
SALES (est): 6.61MM **Privately Held**
SIC: 2836 8731 Vaccines; Commercial physical research

(G-11100)
KYRA MEDICAL INC
102 Otis St Ste 1 (01532-2465)
PHONE.................................888 611-5972
Howard Miller, *Pr*
EMP: 8 **EST:** 2016
SALES (est): 500K **Privately Held**

Web: www.kyramedical.com
SIC: 3841 Surgical instruments and apparatus

(G-11101)
LTP CORPORATION (DH)
Also Called: K L X
70 Bearfoot Rd (01532-1514)
P.O. Box 840 (01532-0840)
PHONE.................................508 393-7660
Carey D Rhoten, *Pr*
Jay Hannon, *
Andrew D Myers, *
◆ **EMP:** 75 **EST:** 1933
SQ FT: 60,000
SALES (est): 51.86MM
SALES (corp-wide): 77.79B **Publicly Held**
Web: www.thehopegroup.com
SIC: 5084 3569 3728 3625 Hydraulic systems equipment and supplies; Lubricating equipment; Aircraft parts and equipment, nec; Relays and industrial controls
HQ: Boeing Distribution Services, Inc.
3760 W 108th St Unit 1
Hialeah FL 33018
305 925-2600

(G-11102)
MATEC INSTRUMENT COMPANIES INC (PA)
56 Hudson St (01532-1968)
PHONE.................................508 393-0155
Kenneth Bishop, *Pr*
Kenneth Bishop, *Pr*
David Walling, *
▲ **EMP:** 37 **EST:** 1964
SQ FT: 20,000
SALES (est): 8.85MM
SALES (corp-wide): 8.85MM **Privately Held**
Web: www.matec.com
SIC: 3829 3826 3825 3699 Measuring and controlling devices, nec; Analytical instruments; Instruments to measure electricity; Electrical equipment and supplies, nec

(G-11103)
NEWCORR PACKAGING INC
66 Lyman St (01532-2062)
P.O. Box 29 (01532-0029)
PHONE.................................508 393-9256
Hans Koch, *Pr*
Theodore Romanow, *
▲ **EMP:** 60 **EST:** 1991
SQ FT: 110,000
SALES (est): 22.6MM **Privately Held**
Web: www.newcorrpackaging.com
SIC: 2653 Boxes, corrugated: made from purchased materials

(G-11104)
O R M INC
71 Lyman St Ste 1 (01532-2075)
PHONE.................................508 393-7054
EMP: 10
SIC: 3679 Microwave components

(G-11105)
PALL NORTHBOROUGH (DH)
50 Bearfoot Rd (01532-1551)
P.O. Box 5630 (13045-5630)
PHONE.................................978 263-9888
Eric Krasnoff, *Ch Bd*
John Rozembersky, *VP*
▲ **EMP:** 74 **EST:** 1984
SQ FT: 30,000
SALES (est): 1.73MM
SALES (corp-wide): 31.47B **Publicly Held**

SIC: 3821 3564 Distilling apparatus, laboratory type; Blowers and fans
HQ: Pall Corporation
25 Harbor Park Dr
Port Washington NY 11050
516 484-5400

(G-11106)
POWER SYSTEMS INTEGRITY INC
Also Called: PSI
100 Otis St Ste 6 (01532-2438)
PHONE.................................508 393-1655
Harold Marsden, *Pr*
Aaron Cooledge, *CFO*
EMP: 7 **EST:** 2003
SQ FT: 3,000
SALES (est): 775.6K **Privately Held**
Web: www.psinteg.com
SIC: 3571 3577 3825 3548 Electronic computers; Computer peripheral equipment, nec; Instruments to measure electricity; Arc welders, transformer-rectifier

(G-11107)
SAINT-GOBAIN CERAMICS PLAS INC
9 Goddard Rd (01532-1545)
PHONE.................................508 351-7754
Rakesh Kapoor, *Mgr*
EMP: 285
SALES (corp-wide): 397.78MM **Privately Held**
Web: www.saint-gobain.com
SIC: 2819 Industrial inorganic chemicals, nec
HQ: Saint-Gobain Ceramics & Plastics, Inc.
20 Moores Rd
Malvern PA 19355

(G-11108)
SAINT-GOBAIN CORPORATION
9 Goddard Rd (01532-1545)
PHONE.................................508 351-7112
George M Brown, *Prin*
EMP: 2844
SALES (corp-wide): 397.78MM **Privately Held**
Web:
www.saint-gobain-northamerica.com
SIC: 3269 2891 3221 Laboratory and industrial pottery; Adhesives; Food containers, glass
HQ: Saint-Gobain Corporation
20 Moores Rd
Malvern PA 19355

(G-11109)
STERIS CORPORATION
435 Whitney St (01532-1147)
PHONE.................................508 393-9323
EMP: 54
Web: www.steris.com
SIC: 3841 Surgical and medical instruments
HQ: Steris Corporation
5960 Heisley Rd
Mentor OH 44060
440 354-2600

(G-11110)
SUNDRUM SOLAR INC
Also Called: Mgi Energy
15 Hillside Rd (01532-2401)
PHONE.................................508 740-6256
Michael Intrieri, *CEO*
EMP: 8 **EST:** 2007
SALES (est): 493.99K **Privately Held**
Web: www.sundrumsolar.com
SIC: 3433 Heating equipment, except electric

(G-11111)
TE CONNECTIVITY CORPORATION
Madison Cable
20a Forbes Rd (01532-2501)
PHONE.................................717 592-4299
Chuck Grant, *Brnch Mgr*
EMP: 11
Web: www.te.com
SIC: 3678 3643 Electronic connectors; Current-carrying wiring services
HQ: Te Connectivity Corporation
1050 Westlakes Dr
Berwyn PA 19312
610 893-9800

(G-11112)
TELEFLUENT COMMUNICATIONS INC
104 Otis St Ste 22 (01532-2440)
PHONE.................................508 919-0902
John K Esler, *Pr*
Eric H Karp, *Sec*
EMP: 10 **EST:** 2002
SALES (est): 225.79K **Privately Held**
Web: www.reopromotions.com
SIC: 3645 Garden, patio, walkway and yard lighting fixtures: electric

(G-11113)
TOMANDTIM ENTERPRISES LLC
Also Called: HB Printing
75 W Main St (01532-1880)
P.O. Box 4787 (01704-4787)
PHONE.................................508 380-5550
EMP: 7 **EST:** 1998
SQ FT: 1,800
SALES (est): 535.16K **Privately Held**
Web: www.hbprints.com
SIC: 2759 Commercial printing, nec

(G-11114)
TOOLMEX INDUS SOLUTIONS INC (PA)
Also Called: Toolmex
34 Talbot Rd (01532-2010)
PHONE.................................508 653-8897
Arkadiusz Kielb, *CEO*
Lukas Kielb, *
Michael L Clifford, *
◆ **EMP:** 56 **EST:** 1973
SQ FT: 37,000
SALES (est): 10.4MM
SALES (corp-wide): 10.4MM **Privately Held**
Web: www.toolmex.com
SIC: 3829 3541 5084 3545 Measuring and controlling devices, nec; Machine tools, metal cutting type; Industrial machinery and equipment; Machine tool accessories

(G-11115)
TRANE TECHNOLOGIES COMPANY LLC
Also Called: Ingersoll-Rand
70 Bearfoot Rd (01532-1514)
PHONE.................................781 961-2063
Peter Rhoten, *Mgr*
EMP: 100
Web: www.trane.com
SIC: 3561 Pumps and pumping equipment
HQ: Trane Technologies Company Llc
800 Beaty St Ste E
Davidson NC 28036
704 655-4000

(G-11116)
WOLF ORGANIZATION LLC
Also Called: Wolf Worcester
450 Whitney St (01532-2504)
PHONE..................................508 393-2040
EMP: 77
SALES (corp-wide): 145.69MM Privately Held
Web: www.wolfhomeproducts.com
SIC: 2434 Wood kitchen cabinets
PA: The Wolf Organization Llc
20 W Market St
York PA 17401
717 852-4800

Northbridge
Worcester County

(G-11117)
POLYFOAM LLC
2355 Providence Rd (01534-1085)
PHONE..................................508 234-6323
James Hughes, CEO
EMP: 184 EST: 2020
SALES (est): 54.91MM Publicly Held
Web: www.polyfoamcorp.com
SIC: 3086 Packaging and shipping
materials, foamed plastics
HQ: Foam Fabricators, Inc.
8722 E San Alberto # 200
Scottsdale AZ 85258

(G-11118)
RIVERDALE MILLS
CORPORATION
Also Called: Aquamesh
130 Riverdale St (01534-1381)
P.O. Box 920 (01534-0920)
PHONE..................................508 234-8715
James Knott Senior, Ch Bd
James Knott Junior, Dir
Debra Krikorian, *
◆ EMP: 150 EST: 1979
SQ FT: 392,000
SALES (est): 40.91MM Privately Held
Web: www.riverdale.com
SIC: 3496 3423 Mesh, made from
purchased wire; Hand and edge tools, nec

(G-11119)
TENT CONNECTION INC
Also Called: American Folding Table Mfg
1682 Providence Rd (01534-2208)
PHONE..................................508 234-8746
Paul E Tonry, Pr
Edmond Tonry, Prin
Marie Tonry, Prin
EMP: 9 EST: 1991
SQ FT: 4,000
SALES (est): 583.02K Privately Held
Web: www.tentconnection.com
SIC: 2394 7359 Tents: made from
purchased materials; Tent and tarpaulin
rental

Northfield
Franklin County

(G-11120)
LANE CONSTRUCTION
CORPORATION
216 Mt Hermon Station Rd (01360-9506)
PHONE..................................413 498-5586
Susan Stacey, Mgr
EMP: 62
SALES (corp-wide): 7.95B Privately Held
Web: www.laneconstruct.com

SIC: 1611 3273 2951 1442 General
contractor, highway and street construction;
Ready-mixed concrete; Asphalt paving
mixtures and blocks; Construction sand and
gravel
HQ: The Lane Construction Corporation
90 Fieldstone Ct
Cheshire CT 06410
203 235-3351

(G-11121)
NOTCH MTN SOLAR INC
158 Birnam Rd (01360-9528)
P.O. Box 33 (01360-0033)
PHONE..................................413 498-0018
Michael Humphries, Pr
EMP: 8 EST: 2010
SALES (est): 958K Privately Held
Web: www.michaelhumphries.com
SIC: 2431 Millwork

Norton
Bristol County

(G-11122)
ALNYLAM US INC
20 Commerce Way (02766-3313)
PHONE..................................617 551-8200
EMP: 75
SALES (corp-wide): 1.04B Publicly Held
Web: www.alnylam.com
SIC: 2834 Pharmaceutical preparations
HQ: Alnylam U.S., Inc.
675 W Kendall St
Cambridge MA 02142
617 551-8200

(G-11123)
AXIS-SHIELD POC AS
15 Commerce Way Ste E (02766-3330)
PHONE..................................508 285-4870
John Sperzel, Pr
Steve Grossman, *
EMP: 19 EST: 2005
SALES (est): 675.81K Privately Held
SIC: 2835 Diagnostic substances

(G-11124)
CPS TECHNOLOGIES CORP
111 S Worcester St (02766-2102)
PHONE..................................508 222-0614
Charles Griffith, Pr
Francis J Hughes Junior, Ch Bd
EMP: 104 EST: 1984
SQ FT: 38,000
SALES (est): 26.59MM Privately Held
Web: www.cpstechnologysolutions.com
SIC: 3674 Thermoelectric devices, solid
state

(G-11125)
CREATIVE IMPRINTS INC
Also Called: C I Medical
15 Commerce Way Ste A (02766-3329)
PHONE..................................508 285-7650
Clifford A Garnett, CEO
Marc A Cohen, Pr
▼ EMP: 23 EST: 1985
SQ FT: 20,000
SALES (est): 4.35MM Privately Held
Web: www.cimedical.com
SIC: 2752 5085 Offset printing; Ink, printer's

(G-11126)
DATA TRANSLATION INC (PA)
10 Commerce Way Ste E # F (02766-3321)
PHONE..................................508 481-3700
EMP: 46 EST: 1996

SQ FT: 100,000
SALES (est): 11.41MM Privately Held
Web: www.digilent.com
SIC: 7372 3577 Prepackaged software;
Magnetic ink and optical scanning devices

(G-11127)
FULL CIRCLE PADDING INC
253 Mansfield Ave (02766-1377)
P.O. Box 388 (02766-0388)
PHONE..................................508 285-2500
Charles Rogers Iii, Pr
Colin Rogers, VP
Laura Rogers, Treas
EMP: 13 EST: 1985
SQ FT: 6,000
SALES (est): 775.79K Privately Held
Web: www.fullcirclepadding.com
SIC: 2299 5091 5941 Padding and wadding,
textile; Exercise equipment; Exercise
equipment

(G-11128)
MEASUREMENT COMPUTING
CORP (DH)
10 Commerce Way Ste C1 (02766-3321)
P.O. Box 712604 (19171-2604)
PHONE..................................508 946-5100
Bill Kennedy, VP
▲ EMP: 22 EST: 1989
SALES (est): 9.81MM
SALES (est): 15.16B Publicly Held
Web: www.digilent.com
SIC: 3672 7372 Printed circuit boards;
Application computer software
HQ: National Instruments Corporation
11500 N Mopac Expy
Austin TX 78759
512 683-0100

(G-11129)
MEDICAL DEVICE BUS SVCS INC
15 Commerce Way (02766-3329)
PHONE..................................508 828-2726
EMP: 100
SALES (corp-wide): 94.94B Publicly Held
SIC: 3842 Surgical appliances and supplies
HQ: Medical Device Business Services, Inc.
700 Orthopaedic Dr
Warsaw IN 46582

(G-11130)
NEW ENGLAND
PHTOCONDUCTOR CORP
Also Called: N E P
253 Mansfield Ave (02766-1381)
P.O. Box M (02766-0927)
PHONE..................................508 285-5561
Kara Soares, Pr
Paul M Brennan, Pr
EMP: 22 EST: 1973
SQ FT: 4,500
SALES (est): 870.28K Privately Held
Web: www.nepcorp.com
SIC: 3829 Measuring and controlling
devices, nec

(G-11131)
OUTLAW AUDIO LLC
10b Commerce Way Ste B (02766-3313)
P.O. Box 975 (02334-0975)
PHONE..................................508 286-4110
▲ EMP: 10 EST: 1998
SALES (est): 981.7K Privately Held
Web: www.outlawaudio.com
SIC: 3651 Household audio and video
equipment

(G-11132)
RHEE GOLD COMPANY INC
155 Pine St (02766-3303)
P.O. Box 2150 (02766-0929)
PHONE..................................508 285-6650
Rhee Goldman, Pr
EMP: 10 EST: 1997
SALES (est): 462.25K Privately Held
Web: www.rheegold.com
SIC: 2721 7941 Magazines: publishing and
printing; Stadium event operator services

(G-11133)
ROCHE BROS
SUPERMARKETS LLC
Also Called: Store 111
175 Mansfield Ave Unit 1 (02766-1333)
PHONE..................................508 285-3600
Jim Visconti, Brnch Mgr
EMP: 141
SALES (corp-wide): 283.22MM Privately
Held
Web: www.rochebros.com
SIC: 5411 5992 2051 Supermarkets, chain;
Florists; Bread, cake, and related products
PA: Roche Bros. Supermarkets, Llc
11 Hampshire St
Mansfield MA 02048
781 235-9400

(G-11134)
SIGN BY TOMMORROW
400 Old Colony Rd (02766-2020)
PHONE..................................508 222-1900
David Quin, Owner
EMP: 7 EST: 2014
SALES (est): 335.75K Privately Held
Web: www.signsbytomorrow.com
SIC: 3993 Signs and advertising specialties

(G-11135)
SINCLAIR MANUFACTURING CO
LLC
12 S Worcester St (02766-2012)
P.O. Box 398 (02712-0398)
PHONE..................................508 222-7440
William Hubbard, Pr
EMP: 63 EST: 1943
SQ FT: 50,000
SALES (est): 12.92MM
SALES (corp-wide): 168.44MM Privately
Held
Web: www.hermeticsolutions.com
SIC: 3679 Hermetic seals, for electronic
equipment
HQ: Hermetic Solutions Group Inc.
16 Plains Rd
Essex CT 06426
215 645-9420

(G-11136)
SOUTH SHORE MILLWORK INC
7 Maple St (02766-2605)
PHONE..................................508 226-5500
Jeffrey P Burton, Pr
Susan Burton, *
▼ EMP: 70 EST: 1991
SQ FT: 60,000
SALES (est): 17.15MM Privately Held
Web: www.southshoremillwork.com
SIC: 2431 2499 Millwork; Decorative wood
and woodwork

(G-11137)
VALENTINE TOOL & STAMPING
INC
171 W Main St (02766-1232)
P.O. Box 469 (02766-0469)
PHONE..................................508 285-6911

Charles Valentine Junior, *Pr*
Charles C Valentine Junior, *Pr*
Lawrence Valentine, *VP Engg*
Virginia Welton, *Asst Tr*
EMP: 19 **EST:** 1954
SQ FT: 35,000
SALES (est): 2.33MM **Privately Held**
Web: www.valentinetool.com
SIC: 3469 3861 3542 Stamping metal for the trade; Cameras, still and motion picture (all types); Machine tools, metal forming type

(G-11138)
VW QUALITY COATING
62 Cross St (02766-2319)
PHONE.................................617 963-6503
Joseph Van Wart, *Prin*
EMP: 7 **EST:** 2015
SALES (est): 295.76K **Privately Held**
Web:
www.qualitycoatinghomesolutions.com
SIC: 3479 Metal coating and allied services

Norwell
Plymouth County

(G-11139)
AVEDIS ZILDJIAN CO (PA)
22 Longwater Dr (02061-1612)
PHONE.................................781 871-2200
John Stephans, *CEO*
◆ **EMP:** 130 **EST:** 1623
SQ FT: 66,000
SALES (est): 24.69MM
SALES (corp-wide): 24.69MM **Privately Held**
Web: www.zildjian.com
SIC: 3931 Percussion instruments and parts

(G-11140)
BLACKTRACE INC
156 Norwell Ave (02061-1212)
PHONE.................................617 848-1211
EMP: 8 **EST:** 2010
SALES (est): 2.32MM
SALES (corp-wide): 2.09MM **Privately Held**
Web: www.unchainedlabs.com
SIC: 3821 Calorimeters
HQ: Unchained Labs Royston Ltd.
1 Anglian Business Park
Royston HERTS SG8 5
176 325-2149

(G-11141)
EAST COAST PUBLICATIONS INC (PA)
Also Called: New England Real Estate Jurnl
17 Accord Park Dr Ste 207 (02061-1629)
P.O. Box 55 (02018-0055)
PHONE.................................781 878-4540
TOLL FREE: 800
Thomas Murray, *CEO*
EMP: 19 **EST:** 1963
SQ FT: 8,000
SALES (est): 4.03MM
SALES (corp-wide): 4.03MM **Privately Held**
Web: www.nerej.com
SIC: 2711 6531 2721 Newspapers: publishing only, not printed on site; Real estate agents and managers; Periodicals

(G-11142)
INTENT SOLUTIONS GROUP (PA)
194 Riverside Dr (02061-2238)
PHONE.................................617 909-4714
Robert Rae, *Prin*

EMP: 8 **EST:** 2018
SALES (est): 98.98K
SALES (corp-wide): 98.98K **Privately Held**
Web: www.intentsg.com
SIC: 3652 Prerecorded records and tapes

(G-11143)
MARUHO HTSUJYO INNOVATIONS INC (PA)
55 Accord Park Dr (02061-1665)
PHONE.................................617 653-1617
John F Rousseau Junior, *Pr*
Thomas E Hancock, *VP*
Atsushi Sugita, *Dir*
Ryoai Imai, *Dir*
EMP: 45 **EST:** 2014
SALES (est): 4.8MM
SALES (corp-wide): 4.8MM **Privately Held**
Web: www.mhi-innovations.com
SIC: 3565 3841 Packaging machinery; Surgical and medical instruments

(G-11144)
PARTYLITE WORLDWIDE LLC (DH)
600 Cordwainer Dr Ste 202 (02061-1644)
PHONE.................................888 999-5706
Harry Slatkin, *CEO*
Robert B Goergen Junior, *Pr*
Kathleen Luce C, *Pr*
Dan Chad, *
William Looney, *
◆ **EMP:** 250 **EST:** 2000
SQ FT: 1,000
SALES (est): 306.45MM
SALES (corp-wide): 4.44B **Publicly Held**
SIC: 3999 5961 Candles; Catalog and mail-order houses
HQ: Partylite, Inc.
59 Armstrong Rd
Plymouth MA 02360
203 661-1926

(G-11145)
PETERSON AND NASH INC
846 Main St (02061-2320)
PHONE.................................781 826-9085
Wayne Peterson, *Pr*
Marie Peterson, *
EMP: 7 **EST:** 1939
SQ FT: 11,000
SALES (est): 203.67K **Privately Held**
SIC: 3423 3541 Knives, agricultural or industrial; Machine tools, metal cutting type

(G-11146)
SAFETY-KLEEN SYSTEMS INC (HQ)
Also Called: Safety-Kleen
42 Longwater Dr (02061-1612)
PHONE.................................800 669-5740
Jerry E Correll, *Pr*
Dave Sprinkle, *Executive Oil Re-refining Vice President**
Dave Eckelbarger, *Branch Vice President**
Mark Stone, *CIO**
Chip Duffie, *CCO**
◆ **EMP:** 322 **EST:** 1968
SALES (est): 1.22B
SALES (corp-wide): 5.17B **Publicly Held**
Web: www.safety-kleen.com
SIC: 4953 3559 4212 5172 Recycling, waste materials; Degreasing machines, automotive and industrial; Hazardous waste transport; Petroleum products, nec
PA: Clean Harbors, Inc.
42 Longwater Dr
Norwell MA 02061
781 792-5000

(G-11147)
SULLIVAN INVESTMENT CO INC (PA)
Also Called: Sullivan Tire Co
41 Accord Park Dr (02061-1614)
PHONE.................................781 982-1550
Joseph M Zaccheo, *CFO*
Paul J Sullivan, *
EMP: 50 **EST:** 1979
SQ FT: 6,500
SALES (est): 275.69MM
SALES (corp-wide): 275.69MM **Privately Held**
Web: www.sullivantire.com
SIC: 5531 7534 Automotive tires; Rebuilding and retreading tires

(G-11148)
THE ORIGINAL RANGOON COMPANY INCORPORATED
Also Called: Orc Foods
200 Cordwainer Dr (02061-1671)
PHONE.................................781 596-0070
EMP: 70 **EST:** 1996
SALES (est): 7.5MM **Privately Held**
Web: www.originalrangoon.com
SIC: 2099 Food preparations, nec

(G-11149)
VERSANT ENERGY SERVICES INC (DH)
42 Longwater Dr (02061-1612)
PHONE.................................781 792-5000
EMP: 9 **EST:** 2015
SALES (est): 38.63MM
SALES (corp-wide): 5.17B **Publicly Held**
SIC: 1389 Lease tanks, oil field: erecting, cleaning, and repairing
HQ: Clean Harbors Industrial Services, Inc.
9856 Steelman St
Houston TX 77017

(G-11150)
WEAR-GUARD CORPORATION
Also Called: E T Wright
141 Longwater Dr (02061-1632)
PHONE.................................781 871-4100
▲ **EMP:** 980
SIC: 5699 5961 5661 2385 Uniforms and work clothing; Clothing, mail order (except women's); Men's shoes; Waterproof outerwear

---

Norwood
Norfolk County

(G-11151)
3DEO INC
106 Access Rd Ste 6 (02062-5292)
PHONE.................................781 999-3447
Dale Fried, *CEO*
Charles Devine, *Sec*
EMP: 9 **EST:** 2014
SALES (est): 933.49K **Privately Held**
Web: www.3deo.biz
SIC: 3812 Aircraft/aerospace flight instruments and guidance systems

(G-11152)
3M TOUCH SYSTEMS INC
1 Upland Rd (02062-1568)
PHONE.................................781 386-2770
Paul A Eyers, *Mgr*
EMP: 25
SALES (corp-wide): 34.23B **Publicly Held**
SIC: 3577 Computer peripheral equipment, nec

HQ: 3m Touch Systems, Inc.
3 M Ctr Bldg 2245n40
Saint Paul MN 55144
978 659-9000

(G-11153)
ABSOLUTE METAL FINISHING INC
90 Morse St (02062-4326)
PHONE.................................781 551-8235
Michael Deneen Junior, *Pr*
EMP: 27 **EST:** 1992
SQ FT: 10,000
SALES (est): 4.16MM **Privately Held**
Web: www.absolutemetal.com
SIC: 3471 Electroplating of metals or formed products

(G-11154)
ADINA INC (PA)
90 Kerry Pl Ste 5 (02062-4765)
PHONE.................................781 762-4477
V Zev Rejman, *Pr*
EMP: 20 **EST:** 2001
SQ FT: 11,000
SALES (est): 3.9MM
SALES (corp-wide): 3.9MM **Privately Held**
SIC: 3961 3911 Costume jewelry, ex. precious metal and semiprecious stones; Jewelry, precious metal

(G-11155)
ADMET INC
51 Morgan Dr (02062-5091)
PHONE.................................781 769-0850
Richard Gedney, *Pr*
▲ **EMP:** 7 **EST:** 1989
SALES (est): 2.48MM **Privately Held**
Web: www.admet.com
SIC: 3829 Measuring and controlling devices, nec

(G-11156)
ADVANCED INSTRUMENTS LLC (DH)
2 Technology Way (02062-2630)
PHONE.................................781 320-9000
Byron Selman, *Pr*
Susan Hanlon, *
▲ **EMP:** 46 **EST:** 1973
SQ FT: 55,000
SALES (est): 28.25MM
SALES (corp-wide): 6.03B **Privately Held**
Web: www.aicompanies.com
SIC: 3826 Analytical instruments
HQ: Patricia Industries Inc.
1177 Avenue Of The Americ
New York NY 10036
212 515-9000

(G-11157)
ADVANCED THERMAL SOLUTIONS INC (PA)
89 Access Rd Ste 27 (02062-5234)
PHONE.................................781 769-2800
Kaveh Aza, *Pr*
Kaveh Azar, *
Sharon Koss, *
▲ **EMP:** 38 **EST:** 1989
SQ FT: 15,000
SALES (est): 5.82MM
SALES (corp-wide): 5.82MM **Privately Held**
Web: www.qats.com
SIC: 3823 3829 3826 Thermistors, industrial process type; Measuring and controlling devices, nec; Analytical instruments

---

GEOGRAPHIC

(G-11158)
ALDRICH MARBLE & GRANITE CO
Also Called: Aldrich Stone
83 Morse St Ste 3 (02062-4350)
PHONE..............................781 762-6111
Thomas J Aldrich, *Pr*
Glen Murrey, *VP*
EMP: 8 EST: 1989
SQ FT: 17,000
SALES (est): 410.98K **Privately Held**
Web: www.aldrichstone.com
SIC: 3281 5713 5032   Marble, building: cut and shaped; Floor tile; Marble building stone

(G-11159)
AMERICAD TECHNOLOGY CORP
700 Pleasant St (02062-4632)
P.O. Box 314 (02062-0314)
PHONE..............................781 551-8220
Mark Haslett, *Pr*
Michael Wright, *
EMP: 35 EST: 1993
SQ FT: 19,000
SALES (est): 4.56MM **Privately Held**
Web: www.americadtech.com
SIC: 3089   Injection molding of plastics

(G-11160)
AMERICAN HOLT CORPORATION (PA)
203 Carnegie Row (02062-5000)
PHONE..............................781 440-9993
▲ **EMP: 17 EST:** 1995
SQ FT: 28,000
SALES (est): 11.54MM **Privately Held**
Web: www.americanholt.com
SIC: 5085 3541   Industrial supplies; Drilling machine tools (metal cutting)

(G-11161)
APPLIED PLASTICS CO INC
Also Called: Applied Plastics
25 Endicott St (02062-3006)
P.O. Box 128 (02062-0128)
PHONE..............................781 762-1881
Thomas Barrett, *CEO*
Dave B Ring, *
EMP: 30 EST: 1953
SQ FT: 12,400
SALES (est): 4.37MM **Privately Held**
Web: www.appliedplastics.com
SIC: 3479   Coating of metals with plastic or resins

(G-11162)
APPLIED PLASTICS LLC
25 Endicott St (02062-3006)
PHONE..............................781 762-1881
EMP: 15 EST: 1953
SALES (est): 1.18MM **Privately Held**
Web: www.appliedplastics.com
SIC: 3479   Coating of metals and formed products

(G-11163)
ATLANTIC POLY INC
86 Morse St (02062-4326)
PHONE..............................781 769-4260
John B Maslowski, *Pr*
EMP: 24 EST: 1979
SQ FT: 38,000
SALES (est): 2.5MM **Privately Held**
Web: www.atlanticpoly.com
SIC: 3081 5162   Plastics film and sheet; Plastics materials and basic shapes

(G-11164)
BASCOM-TURNER INSTRUMENTS INC
111 Downey St (02062-2612)
PHONE..............................781 769-9660
A C Makrides, *Pr*
A J Medaglia, *
EMP: 56 EST: 1980
SQ FT: 5,000
SALES (est): 18.62MM
SALES (corp-wide): 18.62MM **Privately Held**
Web: www.bascomturner.com
SIC: 5085 3825 3812   Gas equipment, parts and supplies; Instruments to measure electricity; Search and navigation equipment
PA: Eic Laboratories, Inc.
   111 Downey St
   Norwood MA 02062
   781 769-9450

(G-11165)
BOSTON STONE AND CABINET
165 Lenox St (02062-3491)
PHONE..............................781 352-3623
EMP: 8 EST: 2020
SALES (est): 75.19K **Privately Held**
Web: www.metcabinet.com
SIC: 2434   Wood kitchen cabinets

(G-11166)
BULLETIN NEWSPAPERS INC
661 Washington St Ste 202 (02062-3529)
PHONE..............................617 361-8400
Dennis Cawley, *Prin*
EMP: 7 EST: 2018
SALES (est): 238.86K **Privately Held**
Web: bulletinnewspapers.weebly.com
SIC: 2711   Newspapers, publishing and printing

(G-11167)
BYBLOS INDUSTRIES CORPORATION
1220 Washington St (02062-4006)
PHONE..............................781 727-4764
Joseph G Rouhana, *Prin*
EMP: 8 EST: 2013
SALES (est): 248.96K **Privately Held**
SIC: 3999   Manufacturing industries, nec

(G-11168)
CASTLE ISLAND BREWING CO LLC
31 Astor Ave (02062-5016)
PHONE..............................781 951-2029
Adam Romanow, *Managing Member*
EMP: 40 EST: 2014
SALES (est): 2.55MM **Privately Held**
Web: www.castleislandbeer.com
SIC: 2082   Beer (alcoholic beverage)

(G-11169)
CORBUS PHARMACEUTICALS INC
Also Called: Corbus Pharmaceuticals
500 River Ridge Dr Ste 2 (02062-5045)
PHONE..............................617 963-0100
Yuval Cohen, *CEO*
Edward Monaghan, *VP*
Robert Zurier, *CMO*
Sumner Burstein, *Dir*
Sean Moran, *CFO*
EMP: 9 EST: 2009
SALES (est): 3.72MM **Publicly Held**
Web: www.corbuspharma.com
SIC: 2834   Pharmaceutical preparations
PA: Corbus Pharmaceuticals Holdings, Inc.
   500 River Ridge Dr

Norwood MA 02062
617 963-0100

(G-11170)
CORPORATE PRESS
89 Access Rd Ste 17 (02062-5234)
PHONE..............................781 769-6656
Michael Kadetsky, *Pt*
Steven B Brown, *Pt*
EMP: 10 EST: 1981
SQ FT: 4,500
SALES (est): 895.39K **Privately Held**
SIC: 2752 2741   Offset printing; Miscellaneous publishing

(G-11171)
ECOLAB INC
Also Called: Ecolab
1 Edgewater Dr Ste 210 (02062-4692)
PHONE..............................781 688-2100
Todd Goble, *Genl Mgr*
EMP: 16
SALES (corp-wide): 14.19B **Publicly Held**
Web: www.ecolab.com
SIC: 2841   Detergents, synthetic organic or inorganic alkaline
PA: Ecolab Inc.
   1 Ecolab Pl
   Saint Paul MN 55102
   800 232-6522

(G-11172)
ENTERPRISE NEWSMEDIA LLC
Also Called: Norwood Bulletin
1091 Washington St (02062-4416)
PHONE..............................781 769-5535
EMP: 472
SALES (corp-wide): 3.21B **Publicly Held**
SIC: 2711   Newspapers: publishing only, not printed on site
HQ: Enterprise Newsmedia, Llc
   400 Crown Colony Dr
   Quincy MA 02169
   585 598-0030

(G-11173)
FUEL SOURCE INC
960 Providence Hwy (02062)
PHONE..............................781 469-8449
Ziad Saba, *Prin*
EMP: 8 EST: 2010
SALES (est): 190.72K **Privately Held**
SIC: 2869   Fuels

(G-11174)
FURLONGS CTTAGE CNDIES ICE CRE
1355 Boston Providence Tpke (02062-5055)
PHONE..............................781 762-4124
Gail Ghelfi, *Pr*
Kenneth Thrasher, *VP*
Doris Thrasher, *Sec*
Albert Ghelfi, *Ch*
EMP: 11 EST: 1930
SQ FT: 2,500
SALES (est): 503.44K **Privately Held**
Web: www.furlongscandies.com
SIC: 2064 5441 5812   Candy and other confectionery products; Candy; Soda fountain

(G-11175)
GOLDMAN-KOLBER INC
185 Dean St Ste 204 (02062-4552)
PHONE..............................781 769-6362
David Steinhauer, *Pr*
Susan L Steinhauer, *
EMP: 10 EST: 1919
SQ FT: 3,800

SALES (est): 420.51K **Privately Held**
Web: www.gkjewelry.com
SIC: 3911   Mountings, gold or silver: pens, leather goods, etc.

(G-11176)
HOME MARKET FOODS INC
Also Called: Cooked Perfect
140 Morgan Dr (02062-5076)
PHONE..............................781 948-1500
Wesley L Atamian, *Pr*
Douglas K Atamian, *
EMP: 494 EST: 1995
SQ FT: 85,000
SALES (est): 141.24MM **Privately Held**
Web: www.homemarketfoods.com
SIC: 5147 2013   Meats and meat products; Sausages and other prepared meats

(G-11177)
HORIZON HOUSE PUBLICATIONS INC (PA)
Also Called: Signal Integrity Journal
685 Canton St (02062-2608)
PHONE..............................781 769-9750
William Bazzy, *CEO*
Ivar Anderson Bazzy, *
Jared Bazzy, *
Joan B Egan, *
EMP: 53 EST: 1960
SQ FT: 26,061
SALES (est): 8.58MM
SALES (corp-wide): 8.58MM **Privately Held**
Web: www.horizonhouse.com
SIC: 5192 8748 2721 2731   Books; Telecommunications consultant; Trade journals: publishing only, not printed on site; Books, publishing only

(G-11178)
I & I SLING INC
1400 Boston Providence Tpke Ste 3000 (02062-5044)
P.O. Box 101 (02062-0101)
PHONE..............................781 575-0600
Scott Woodward, *Mgr*
EMP: 20
SALES (corp-wide): 19.76MM **Privately Held**
Web: www.iandisling.com
SIC: 3496   Miscellaneous fabricated wire products
PA: I & I Sling, Inc.
   205 Bridgewater Rd
   Aston PA 19014
   610 485-8500

(G-11179)
ILLINOIS TOOL WORKS INC
Instron A Div III TI Works
825 University Ave (02062-2643)
PHONE..............................781 828-2500
Steve Martindale, *Brnch Mgr*
EMP: 300
SALES (corp-wide): 15.93B **Publicly Held**
Web: www.itw.com
SIC: 3829 3826   Testing equipment: abrasion, shearing strength, etc.; Analytical instruments
PA: Illinois Tool Works Inc.
   155 Harlem Ave
   Glenview IL 60025
   847 724-7500

(G-11180)
INGLESIDE CORPORATION
Also Called: Printmaster
89 Access Rd Ste 17 (02062-5234)
PHONE..............................781 769-6656

Tim Connors, *Pr*
EMP: 9 **EST:** 1985
SQ FT: 1,000
SALES (est): 1.25MM **Privately Held**
Web: printmasteronline.logomall.com
SIC: 2752   Offset printing

(G-11181)
INPHOTONICS INC
111 Downey St (02062-2612)
PHONE..............................781 440-0202
A C Makrides, *Pr*
EMP: 10 **EST:** 1998
SALES (est): 844.56K **Privately Held**
Web: www.inphotonics.com
SIC: 3821   Laboratory equipment: fume
hoods, distillation racks, etc.

(G-11182)
INSIGNIA INCORPORATED
Also Called: Instant Sign Center
1400 Boston Providence Tpke Ste 2500
(02062-5158)
PHONE..............................781 278-0150
Drew Schildwachter, *Brnch Mgr*
EMP: 22
SALES (corp-wide): 8.14MM **Privately
Held**
SIC: 7389 3993   Lettering service; Electric
signs
PA: Insignia, Incorporated
2 Alder Ln
Wilbraham MA 01095
978 372-3721

(G-11183)
INSTITUTE FOR SCIAL CLTRAL
CMM
Also Called: Z Magazine
942 Norwest Dr (02062-1486)
PHONE..............................339 236-1991
Michael Albert, *Pr*
Lydia Sargent, *Sec*
EMP: 7 **EST:** 1988
SALES (est): 48.08K **Privately Held**
Web: www.zmag.org
SIC: 2721   Magazines: publishing only, not
printed on site

(G-11184)
INSTRON JAPAN COMPANY LTD
825 University Ave (02062-2643)
PHONE..............................781 828-2500
EMP: 450 **EST:** 1948
SALES (est): 75.21MM
SALES (corp-wide): 15.93B **Publicly Held**
SIC: 3829   Measuring and controlling
devices, nec
PA: Illinois Tool Works Inc.
155 Harlem Ave
Glenview IL 60025
847 724-7500

(G-11185)
KAMWELD INDUSTRIES INC
Also Called: Norwood
100 Access Rd (02062-5212)
PHONE..............................617 558-7500
Sanjar Azar, *Prin*
EMP: 9 **EST:** 2017
SALES (est): 255.76K **Privately Held**
SIC: 3548 5084   Electric welding equipment;
Instruments and control equipment

(G-11186)
KAMWELD TECHNOLOGIES INC
Also Called: Kam Weld Technologies
90 Access Rd (02062-5237)
PHONE..............................781 762-6922
Kaveh Azar, *Pr*

Sharon Koss, *VP*
EMP: 10 **EST:** 1958
SALES (est): 920.2K **Privately Held**
Web: www.kamweld.com
SIC: 3548   Welding and cutting apparatus
and accessories, nec

(G-11187)
KEIMOS 1988 US INC (PA)
Also Called: U E I
249 Vanderbilt Ave (02062-5033)
PHONE..............................508 921-4590
Shaun Miller, *Pr*
◆ **EMP:** 19 **EST:** 1988
SALES (est): 13.55MM
SALES (corp-wide): 13.55MM **Privately
Held**
Web: www.ueidaq.com
SIC: 3571   Electronic computers

(G-11188)
KELLY CORNED BEEF CO
CHICAGO
Also Called: Kelly Eisenberg
140 Morgan Dr (02062-5013)
PHONE..............................773 588-2882
Howard Eisenberg, *Pr*
Calvin Eisenberg, *Pr*
▼ **EMP:** 12 **EST:** 1929
SALES (est): 1MM **Privately Held**
SIC: 5147 2011   Meats, fresh; Meat packing
plants

(G-11189)
L T X INTERNATIONAL INC
Also Called: LTX Credence
825 University Ave (02062-2643)
PHONE..............................781 461-1000
David Tacelli, *CEO*
Roger W Blethen, *
Mark J Gallenberger, *
David Tacelli, *Pr*
EMP: 100 **EST:** 1976
SALES (est): 29.44MM
SALES (corp-wide): 812.77MM **Publicly
Held**
Web: www.cohu.com
SIC: 3825 7629 7373 3674   Semiconductor
test equipment; Electronic equipment repair
; Computer integrated systems design;
Semiconductors and related devices
HQ: Xcerra Corporation
825 University Ave
Norwood MA 02062
781 461-1000

(G-11190)
LINEAR SINGAPORE HOLDING
LLC
1 Technology Way (02062-2634)
PHONE..............................781 329-4700
EMP: 19 **EST:** 2017
SALES (est): 1.41MM
SALES (corp-wide): 12.31B **Publicly Held**
SIC: 3674   Semiconductors and related
devices
PA: Analog Devices, Inc.
1 Analog Way
Wilmington MA 01887
781 935-5565

(G-11191)
LQC INC
Also Called: Manufacturer
916 Pleasant St Ste 22 (02062-4666)
PHONE..............................617 586-5139
Duy Duc Cu, *Prin*
Thanh Cu, *Pr*
EMP: 8 **EST:** 2016
SALES (est): 2.28MM **Privately Held**

SIC: 5149 2079 2096 2026   Beverages,
except coffee and tea; Oil, hydrogenated:
edible; Potato chips and similar snacks;
Milk drinks, flavored

(G-11192)
MANUFCTRING RESOURCE
GROUP INC
Also Called: Mrg
930 Washington St (02062-3412)
PHONE..............................781 440-9700
Robert Marotto, *Pr*
EMP: 155 **EST:** 1988
SQ FT: 45,000
SALES (est): 56.78MM
SALES (corp-wide): 6.55B **Privately Held**
Web: www.mrg-inc.com
SIC: 3625   Electric controls and control
accessories, industrial
HQ: Electrical Components International,
Inc.
1 Cityplace Dr Ste 450
Saint Louis MO 63141

(G-11193)
MARIMED INC (PA)
10 Oceana Way Ste 2 (02062-2646)
PHONE..............................781 277-0007
EMP: 26 **EST:** 2011
SQ FT: 10,000
SALES (est): 134.01MM **Publicly Held**
Web: www.marimedinc.com
SIC: 2833   Medicinals and botanicals

(G-11194)
MARKWELL MANUFACTURING
CO INC
692 Pleasant St (02062-4632)
PHONE..............................781 769-6610
Samuel Opland, *Pr*
Cyril Rozowsky, *Treas*
◆ **EMP:** 9 **EST:** 1919
SQ FT: 11,500
SALES (est): 1.75MM **Privately Held**
Web: www.markwellusa.com
SIC: 5072 5085 5046 3496   Staples;
Staplers and tackers; Commercial
equipment, nec; Staples, made from
purchased wire

(G-11195)
MEGANUTRA INC (PA)
128 Carnegie Row Ste 107 (02062-5162)
PHONE..............................781 762-9600
Yao Lin, *Pr*
EMP: 7 **EST:** 2013
SALES (est): 470.78K
SALES (corp-wide): 470.78K **Privately
Held**
Web: www.naturesnutra.com
SIC: 2023   Dietary supplements, dairy and
non-dairy based

(G-11196)
MICRON CORPORATION
89 Access Rd Ste 5 (02062-5234)
PHONE..............................781 769-5771
William C Theos, *Pr*
Charles W Theos, *VP*
Eleftheria Theos, *Sec*
James W Theos, *VP Mktg*
EMP: 23 **EST:** 1982
SQ FT: 5,000
SALES (est): 5.47MM **Privately Held**
Web: www.microncorp.com
SIC: 3672   Printed circuit boards

(G-11197)
MULTI-FLOW INDUSTRIES LLC
51 Morgan Dr Ste 1 (02062-5021)
PHONE..............................617 442-7777
EMP: 34
SALES (corp-wide): 237.79MM **Privately
Held**
Web: www.multiflow.net
SIC: 2087   Beverage bases, concentrates,
syrups, powders and mixes
HQ: Multi-Flow Industries, Llc
1434 County Line Rd
Huntingdon Valley PA 19006
215 322-1800

(G-11198)
MYSTIC SCENIC STUDIOS INC
Also Called: Mystic Millwork
293 Lenox St (02062-3462)
PHONE..............................781 440-0914
Jim Ray, *Pr*
James J Fitzgerald, *
Duncan A Maio, *
EMP: 100 **EST:** 1987
SQ FT: 100,000
SALES (est): 20.57MM **Privately Held**
Web: www.mysticscenic.com
SIC: 3999 3993 7389   Theatrical scenery;
Displays and cutouts, window and lobby;
Trade show arrangement

(G-11199)
NEW ENGLAND PARTNERSHIP
INC
Also Called: New England Coffee Company
30 Walpole St (02062-3356)
PHONE..............................800 225-3537
TOLL FREE: 800
James M Kaloyanides, *Prin*
James M Kaloyanides, *Pr*
James P Dostou, *Prin*
John C Kaloyanides, *
Chuck Kozubal, *
▼ **EMP:** 200 **EST:** 1916
SQ FT: 90,000
SALES (est): 50.01MM
SALES (corp-wide): 358.53MM **Privately
Held**
Web: www.newenglandcoffee.com
SIC: 2095 5149   Coffee roasting (except by
wholesale grocers); Coffee and tea
HQ: Reily Foods Company
400 Poydras St Fl 10
New Orleans LA 70130

(G-11200)
NEWPRO DESIGNS INC
90 Kerry Pl Ste 5 (02062-4765)
PHONE..............................781 762-4477
V Zev Rejman, *Pr*
EMP: 35 **EST:** 1986
SQ FT: 11,000
SALES (est): 3.9MM
SALES (corp-wide): 3.9MM **Privately Held**
SIC: 3961 3911   Costume jewelry, ex.
precious metal and semiprecious stones;
Jewelry, precious metal
PA: Adina Inc.
90 Kerry Pl Ste 5
Norwood MA 02062
781 762-4477

(G-11201)
NORWOOD SHEET METAL CORP
744 Boston Providence Tpke Ste 2
(02062-5291)
P.O. Box 309 (02062-0309)
PHONE..............................781 762-0720
Orlando J Germano Junior, *Pr*
EMP: 10 **EST:** 1946

GEOGRAPHIC

SQ FT: 4,800
SALES (est): 642.54K **Privately Held**
SIC: 3444 Sheet metalwork

(G-11202)
OLYMPIC ADHESIVES INC (PA)
670 Canton St (02062-2671)
PHONE..............................800 829-1871
John E Murray, *CEO*
Mark E Corndell, *Pr*
Stephen P Hopkins, *Ex VP*
Paul C Ryan, *VP*
Stephen Corndell, *VP Sls*
◆ **EMP: 47 EST:** 1975
SQ FT: 60,000
SALES (est): 11.03MM
SALES (corp-wide): 11.03MM **Privately Held**
Web: www.olympic-adhesives.com
SIC: 2891 Adhesives

(G-11203)
PULSE NETWORK INC
Also Called: Tpni
10 Oceana Way (02062-2610)
PHONE..............................781 688-8000
Stephen Saber, *Ch Bd*
Nicholas Saber, *Pr*
John Saber, *CIO*
▲ **EMP: 10 EST:** 2011
SQ FT: 10,000
SALES (est): 3MM **Privately Held**
Web: www.tpni.com
SIC: 7372 Application computer software

(G-11204)
PURATOS CORPORATION
83 Morse St (02062-4351)
PHONE..............................781 688-8560
EMP: 7 EST: 2017
SALES (est): 188.69K **Privately Held**
Web: www.puratos.us
SIC: 2099 Food preparations, nec

(G-11205)
RARE BEAUTY BRANDS INC (PA)
Also Called: Patchology
83 Morse Ste 8a (02062-4350)
P.O. Box 383 (01760-0004)
PHONE..............................888 243-0646
Chris Hobson, *Pr*
Marc Shores, *VP*
Kathy St Clair, *VP*
EMP: 18 EST: 2007
SALES (est): 6.39MM
SALES (corp-wide): 6.39MM **Privately Held**
Web: www.rarebeautybrands.com
SIC: 2844 5122 Perfumes, cosmetics and other toilet preparations; Cosmetics, perfumes, and hair products

(G-11206)
REGAL PRESS INCORPORATED (PA)
79 Astor Ave (02062-3461)
P.O. Box 126 (02062-0126)
PHONE..............................781 769-3900
William N Duffey Junior, *Pr*
William N Duffey Iii, *Treas*
▼ **EMP: 120 EST:** 1970
SQ FT: 150,000
SALES (est): 25.05MM
SALES (corp-wide): 25.05MM **Privately Held**
Web: www.regalpress.com

SIC: 2752 2761 2672 2759 Offset printing; Manifold business forms; Paper; coated and laminated, nec; Business forms: printing, nsk

(G-11207)
REMTEC INCORPORATED (PA)
Also Called: TEC Mark Plating
100 Morse St Ste 7 (02062-4679)
PHONE..............................781 762-9191
Brian Buyea, *Pr*
Gerald Karon, *
Nahum Rapoport, *
Mike Hipsman, *
Chuck Ahern, *
EMP: 35 EST: 1990
SQ FT: 15,000
SALES (est): 9.46MM **Privately Held**
Web: www.remtec.com
SIC: 3672 Printed circuit boards

(G-11208)
REST ENSURED MEDICAL INC
661 Pleasant St Ste 99 (02062-4682)
PHONE..............................603 225-2860
EMP: 9 EST: 2009
SALES (est): 202.68K **Privately Held**
SIC: 3841 Surgical and medical instruments

(G-11209)
SOURCE CODE LLC (PA)
Also Called: Thinkmate
232 Vanderbilt Ave (02062-5046)
PHONE..............................781 688-2248
Pamela Piasecki, *CEO*
Arthur Ataie, *
Brian Gosselin, *
Pamela Piasecki, *CFO*
◆ **EMP: 35 EST:** 1992
SQ FT: 15,000
SALES (est): 186.42MM **Privately Held**
Web: www.sourcecode.com
SIC: 5045 3571 Computer peripheral equipment; Electronic computers

(G-11210)
SOURCE CODE MIDCO LLC (PA)
232 Vanderbilt Ave (02062-5046)
PHONE..............................781 255-2022
Brian Gosselin, *
Pamela Piasecki, *
◆ **EMP: 35 EST:** 2018
SALES (est): 31.65MM
SALES (corp-wide): 31.65MM **Privately Held**
Web: www.sourcecode.com
SIC: 6719 5045 3571 Investment holding companies, except banks; Computer peripheral equipment; Electronic computers

(G-11211)
STEEL ART COMPANY INC
189 Dean St (02062-4542)
PHONE..............................617 566-4079
EMP: 70 EST: 1953
SALES (est): 9.24MM **Privately Held**
Web: www.steelartco.com
SIC: 3993 Letters for signs, metal

(G-11212)
SUN COUNTRY FOODS INC (HQ)
1 Edgewater Dr Ste 200 (02062-4669)
P.O. Box 88176 (98138-2176)
PHONE..............................855 824-7645
John Heily, *Pr*
Michael Castle, *Treas*
Michael Morin, *CFO*
Andy Heily, *Dir*
EMP: 7 EST: 2011
SQ FT: 80,000

SALES (est): 1.04MM
SALES (corp-wide): 219MM **Privately Held**
Web: www.suncountryfoodsinc.com
SIC: 2099 Bread crumbs, except made in bakeries
PA: Continental Mills, Inc.
18100 Andover Park W
Tukwila WA 98188
206 816-7000

(G-11213)
TE CONNECTIVITY CORPORATION
63 Nahatan St Ste 100 (02062-5732)
PHONE..............................781 278-5200
Michael Kirkman, *Mgr*
EMP: 10
Web: www.te.com
SIC: 3678 Electronic connectors
HQ: Te Connectivity Corporation
1050 Westlakes Dr
Berwyn PA 19312
610 893-9800

(G-11214)
TE CONNECTIVITY CORPORATION
62 Nahatan St (02062-5717)
PHONE..............................781 278-5273
Al Dadah, *Mgr*
EMP: 11
Web: www.te.com
SIC: 3678 Electronic connectors
HQ: Te Connectivity Corporation
1050 Westlakes Dr
Berwyn PA 19312
610 893-9800

(G-11215)
TEKSCAN INC
333 Boston Providence Tpke (02062-3927)
PHONE..............................617 464-4500
Jeff Ames, *Pr*
Stephen V Jacobs, *
Charles F Malacaria, *
Mark Lowe, *
EMP: 61 EST: 1983
SQ FT: 28,000
SALES (est): 15.26MM
SALES (corp-wide): 25.3MM **Privately Held**
Web: www.tekscan.com
SIC: 3829 Measuring and controlling devices, nec
PA: Artemis Capital Partners, Llc
160 Federal St
Boston MA 02110
857 327-5606

(G-11216)
THE SAVOGRAN COMPANY
259 Lenox St (02062-3463)
P.O. Box 130 (02062-0130)
PHONE..............................781 762-5400
EMP: 49 EST: 1875
SALES (est): 4.52MM **Privately Held**
Web: www.savogran.com
SIC: 2851 5169 Paint removers; Chemicals and allied products, nec

(G-11217)
UNO FOODS INC
44 Industrial Way (02062-4546)
PHONE..............................617 323-9200
George Herz, *Sec*
Louie Psallieas, *CFO*
EMP: 200 EST: 1990
SALES (est): 44.73MM **Privately Held**
Web: www.unos.com

SIC: 2099 Pizza, refrigerated: except frozen
HQ: Uno Restaurant Holdings Corporation
100 Charles Park Rd
Boston MA 02132

(G-11218)
VERSO CORPORATION
100 River Ridge Dr Ste 112 (02062)
PHONE..............................339 788-1343
EMP: 8 EST: 2018
SALES (est): 183.62K **Privately Held**
Web: www.billerud.com
SIC: 2621 Paper mills

(G-11219)
VISTAPRINT
11 Bonney Ln (02062-1208)
PHONE..............................866 614-8002
EMP: 14 EST: 2013
SALES (est): 435.14K **Privately Held**
SIC: 2752 Commercial printing, lithographic

(G-11220)
XCERRA CORPORATION (HQ)
Also Called: Xcerra
825 University Ave (02062-2643)
PHONE..............................781 461-1000
David G Tacelli, *Pr*
Mark J Gallenberger, *
Colin J Savoy, *
EMP: 138 EST: 1976
SQ FT: 56,400
SALES (est): 410.14MM
SALES (corp-wide): 812.77MM **Publicly Held**
Web: www.cohu.com
SIC: 3825 3429 Semiconductor test equipment; Hardware, nec
PA: Cohu, Inc.
12367 Crosthwaite Cir
Poway CA 92064
858 848-8100

Oak Bluffs
Dukes County

(G-11221)
DA ROSAS
Also Called: Martha's Vineyard Printing Co
46 Circuit Ave (02557-6794)
P.O. Box 1668 (02557-1668)
PHONE..............................508 693-0110
Antonio G Da Rosa Iii, *Pr*
Dennis P Da Rosa, *VP*
Lucinda A Da Rosa Barrett, *Treas*
EMP: 24 EST: 1943
SQ FT: 13,000
SALES (est): 952.04K **Privately Held**
SIC: 2752 5943 5112 Offset printing; Office forms and supplies; Office supplies, nec

(G-11222)
MS ORBIS CORPORATION (PA)
Also Called: Moku Artisan Furniture
8 Uncas Ave (02557-7283)
P.O. Box 835 (02557-0835)
PHONE..............................774 330-5323
Slobodan Todorovic, *CEO*
Marina Jurcevic, *Treas*
Goran Udovicic, *COO*
EMP: 9 EST: 2018
SALES (est): 988.71K
SALES (corp-wide): 988.71K **Privately Held**
SIC: 2511 Novelty furniture: wood

Orange
Franklin County

(G-11223)
HEYES FOREST PRODUCTS INC
34 Daniel Shays Highway, Orange
Industrial Park (01364)
PHONE...............................978 544-8801
Fred L Heyes, Pr
EMP: 8 **EST:** 1971
SQ FT: 46,000
SALES (est): 1.03MM **Privately Held**
Web: www.heyesforest.com
SIC: 2421 1629 3553 Lumber: rough,
sawed, or planed; Land clearing contractor;
Sawmill machines

(G-11224)
IMPACT NANO LLC
153 Quabbin Blvd (01364-6413)
PHONE...............................508 380-8423
EMP: 8 **EST:** 2020
SALES (est): 1.12MM **Privately Held**
Web: www.impact-nano.com
SIC: 2833 Organic medicinal chemicals:
bulk, uncompounded

(G-11225)
MBW INCORPORATED
184 Gov Dukakis Dr (01364-2033)
P.O. Box 423 (01364-0423)
PHONE...............................978 544-6462
▲ **EMP:** 140 **EST:** 1993
SQ FT: 30,000
SALES (est): 22.23MM **Privately Held**
Web: www.markbeamish.com
SIC: 2679 Paper products, converted, nec

(G-11226)
**MCI TRANSFORMER
CORPORATION**
Also Called: M C I
25 Blodgett St (01364-1706)
PHONE...............................978 544-8272
Paul Foss, Mgr
EMP: 13
SQ FT: 4,000
SALES (corp-wide): 9.93MM **Privately
Held**
Web: www.mcitransformer.com
SIC: 5065 3677 3612 Transformers,
electronic; Electronic coils and transformers
; Transformers, except electric
PA: Mci Transformer Corporation
411 Manhattan Ave
West Babylon NY
631 587-0510

(G-11227)
**NORTHWEST CONFECTIONS
MASS LLC**
207 Daniel Shays Hwy (01364-2029)
PHONE...............................971 666-8282
Aaron M Morris, CEO
EMP: 7 **EST:** 2019
SALES (est): 260.87K **Privately Held**
SIC: 2064 Candy and other confectionery
products

(G-11228)
PETES TIRE BARNS INC (PA)
Also Called: Pete's Tire Barns
275 E Main St (01364-1291)
PHONE...............................978 544-8811
▲ **EMP:** 55 **EST:** 1968
SALES (est): 87.54MM
SALES (corp-wide): 87.54MM **Privately
Held**

Web: www.petestire.com
SIC: 5531 7534 Automotive tires;
Rebuilding and retreading tires

(G-11229)
**PHA INDUSTRIES
INCORPORATED**
34 R W Moore Ave (01364-6414)
PHONE...............................978 544-8770
Joseph Carbone, Pr
EMP: 13 **EST:** 2005
SALES (est): 2.3MM **Privately Held**
Web: www.phaindustries.com
SIC: 3999 Manufacturing industries, nec

(G-11230)
QUABBIN INC
158 Gov Dukakis Dr (01364-2033)
PHONE...............................978 544-3872
Mark F Leboeuf, Pr
Thomas J Leboeuf, VP
EMP: 17 **EST:** 1986
SQ FT: 33,000
SALES (est): 2.46MM **Privately Held**
Web: www.quabbininc.com
SIC: 3545 3599 Cutting tools for machine
tools; Machine shop, jobbing and repair

(G-11231)
REPLICA WORKS INC
Also Called: Echo Industries
61 R W Moore Ave (01364-6415)
PHONE...............................978 544-7000
Maynard H Southard, Treas
Bret H Bero, Pr
EMP: 20 **EST:** 1987
SQ FT: 25,000
SALES (est): 2.75MM **Privately Held**
Web: www.echoindustries.com
SIC: 3469 3356 3355 3423 Stamping metal
for the trade; Nonferrous rolling and
drawing, nec; Aluminum rolling and
drawing, nec; Hand and edge tools, nec

(G-11232)
**RODNEY HUNT-FONTAINE INC
(HQ)**
46 Mill St (01364-1251)
PHONE...............................978 544-2511
Kerry Gahm, Pr
Howard Lederman, *
Patricia Whaley, *
Robert Kennedy, *
▲ **EMP:** 46 **EST:** 1840
SQ FT: 318,000
SALES (est): 25.26MM
SALES (corp-wide): 443.08MM **Privately
Held**
Web: www.rodneyhunt.com
SIC: 3491 3322 3728 3494 Water works
valves; Malleable iron foundries; Aircraft
parts and equipment, nec; Valves and pipe
fittings, nec
PA: Zurn Llc
3001 W Canal St
Milwaukee WI 53208
877 935-9750

(G-11233)
**SEAMAN PAPER COMPANY
MASS INC**
184 Gov Dukakis Dr (01364-2033)
PHONE...............................978 544-2455
Frank Hogan, Mgr
EMP: 7
SALES (corp-wide): 131.46MM **Privately
Held**
Web: www.seamanpaper.com
SIC: 2621 Tissue paper

PA: Seaman Paper Company Of
Massachusetts, Inc.
35 Wilkins Rd
Gardner MA 01440
978 632-1513

(G-11234)
SISSON ENGINEERING CORP
450 W River St (01364-1429)
PHONE...............................413 498-2840
Cody F Sisson, Pr
Cody Sisson, Pr
Jeanne Sisson, Sec
EMP: 23 **EST:** 1978
SQ FT: 18,000
SALES (est): 3.41MM **Privately Held**
Web: www.sissoncorp.com
SIC: 3599 Machine shop, jobbing and repair

(G-11235)
THOMAS J DOANE
59 Ward Rd (01364-9750)
PHONE...............................978 821-2361
Thomas J Doane, Prin
EMP: 8 **EST:** 2009
SALES (est): 239.7K **Privately Held**
SIC: 2411 Logging

Orleans
Barnstable County

(G-11236)
CAPE COD READY MIX INC
300 Route 6 A (02653-3114)
P.O. Box 399 (02653-0399)
PHONE...............................508 255-4600
Christopher W Our, Pr
Peter Joy, *
EMP: 24 **EST:** 1997
SALES (est): 5.9MM **Privately Held**
Web: www.capecodreadymix.com
SIC: 3273 Ready-mixed concrete

(G-11237)
COMMUNITY OF JESUS INC (PA)
5 Bay View Dr (02653-2206)
P.O. Box 1094 (02653-1094)
PHONE...............................508 255-1094
Betty Pugsley, Pr
Hollis Shackelford, Treas
▲ **EMP:** 22 **EST:** 1960
SALES (est): 10.02MM
SALES (corp-wide): 10.02MM **Privately
Held**
Web: www.communityofjesus.org
SIC: 2731 8661 2721 7819 Books,
publishing and printing; Non-
denominational church; Magazines:
publishing and printing; Editing services,
motion picture production

(G-11238)
HARWICH ORACLE
Also Called: Register, The
5 Namskaket Rd (02653-3202)
PHONE...............................508 247-3200
Mark Skayla, Chief
EMP: 10 **EST:** 2001
SALES (est): 134.29K **Privately Held**
Web: www.wickedlocal.com
SIC: 2711 Newspapers, publishing and
printing

(G-11239)
**HERSEY CLUTCH COMPANY
LLC**
Also Called: Protek-Sure
8 Commerce Dr Ste A (02653-4033)

P.O. Box 328 (02653-0328)
PHONE...............................508 255-2533
Richard Hersey, Owner
EMP: 10 **EST:** 1964
SQ FT: 7,200
SALES (est): 749K **Privately Held**
Web: www.herseyclutch.com
SIC: 3568 3566 Clutches, except vehicular;
Torque converters, except auto

(G-11240)
NAUSET MARINE INC (PA)
45 Rt 6a (02653-2451)
P.O. Box 357 (02653-0357)
PHONE...............................508 255-0777
Todd Walker, Pr
EMP: 45 **EST:** 1961
SQ FT: 75,000
SALES (est): 18.61MM
SALES (corp-wide): 18.61MM **Privately
Held**
Web: www.nausetmarine.com
SIC: 5551 3732 Motor boat dealers;
Boatbuilding and repairing

(G-11241)
OUTDOOR OUTFITTERS INC
Also Called: Goose Hummock Shop
15 Rt 6a (02653-2437)
P.O. Box 57 (02653-0057)
PHONE...............................508 255-0455
Michael Macaskill, Pr
EMP: 20 **EST:** 1946
SQ FT: 12,000
SALES (est): 2.2MM **Privately Held**
Web: www.goosehummockshops.com
SIC: 3949 5091 Fishing tackle, general;
Sporting and recreation goods

(G-11242)
P WILES INC (PA)
Also Called: Agway
20 Lots Hollow Rd (02653-3329)
P.O. Box 1129 (02660-1129)
PHONE...............................508 385-4321
Joshua Wile, Pr
Susan A Wile, Clerk
EMP: 15 **EST:** 1993
SALES (est): 8.64MM **Privately Held**
Web: www.agwaycapecod.com
SIC: 5261 3999 0782 Retail nurseries and
garden stores; Pet supplies; Lawn and
garden services

(G-11243)
TRUE WORDS TORTILLAS INC
136 Rt 6a (02653-3264)
PHONE...............................508 255-3338
EMP: 9 **EST:** 2012
SALES (est): 533.26K **Privately Held**
SIC: 2099 Tortillas, fresh or refrigerated

(G-11244)
W S WALCOTT INC
Also Called: Sir Speedy
180 Hilltop Plz Rte 6a (02653)
PHONE...............................508 240-0882
Thomas Spollen, Pr
Linda Phillips, VP
EMP: 8 **EST:** 1989
SQ FT: 1,600
SALES (est): 724.4K **Privately Held**
Web: www.sirspeedy.com
SIC: 2752 Commercial printing, lithographic

Osterville
Barnstable County

(G-11245)
CROSBY YACHT YARD INC
72 Crosby Cir Ste 1 (02655-2087)
PHONE..........................508 428-6900
Richard Egan Senior, *Pr*
Gregory Egan, *
EMP: 30 EST: 1850
SQ FT: 15,000
SALES (est): 3.71MM **Privately Held**
Web: www.crosbyyacht.com
SIC: 4493 3732 5551 Boat yards, storage
and incidental repair; Boatbuilding and
repairing; Marine supplies, nec

(G-11246)
**SILVA JEWELERS OF
OSTERVILLE**
1112 Main St Ste 1 (02655-1591)
P.O. Box 305 (02655-0305)
PHONE..........................508 428-2872
Richard Silva, *Pr*
Cynthia J Silva, *VP*
EMP: 7 EST: 1982
SQ FT: 1,500
SALES (est): 937.29K **Privately Held**
Web: www.silvajewelers.com
SIC: 5944 7631 3911 7389 Jewelry,
precious stones and precious metals;
Jewelry repair services; Jewelry, precious
metal; Appraisers, except real estate

Oxford
Worcester County

(G-11247)
A B ENGINEERING & CO
Also Called: AB Engineering & Company
3 Old Cudworth Rd (01540-2842)
P.O. Box 690 (01540-0690)
PHONE..........................508 987-0318
Alfred Beland, *Pr*
Alfred E Beland, *Pr*
EMP: 9 EST: 1967
SQ FT: 55,000
SALES (est): 975.45K **Privately Held**
Web: www.ajeceng.com
SIC: 3559 Degreasing machines,
automotive and industrial

(G-11248)
ADVANCE PLASTICS INC
27 Industrial Park Rd E (01540-2858)
P.O. Box 94 (01571-0094)
PHONE..........................508 987-7235
Mark Hattabaugh, *Pr*
EMP: 7 EST: 1989
SQ FT: 4,500
SALES (est): 773.16K **Privately Held**
SIC: 3089 Injection molding of plastics

(G-11249)
BONSAL AMERICAN INC
Old Webster Rd (01540)
PHONE..........................508 987-8188
Michael Carmevele, *Mgr*
EMP: 8
SALES (corp-wide): 32.72B **Privately Held**
SIC: 3531 3272 Mixers, concrete; Concrete
products, nec
HQ: Bonsal American, Inc.
625 Griffith Rd Ste 100
Charlotte NC 28217
704 525-1621

(G-11250)
CHASE CORPORATION
24 Dana Rd (01540-1704)
PHONE..........................508 731-2710
EMP: 9
Web: www.chasecorp.com
SIC: 3644 3479 3672 Insulators and
insulation materials, electrical; Coating
electrodes; Printed circuit boards
HQ: Chase Corporation
375 University Ave
Westwood MA 02090
781 332-0700

(G-11251)
D D J
Also Called: Dunkin' Donuts
17 Sutton Ave (01540-1753)
PHONE..........................508 987-0417
James Carafotes, *Owner*
EMP: 13 EST: 1994
SQ FT: 1,350
SALES (est): 373.14K **Privately Held**
Web: www.dunkindonuts.com
SIC: 5461 2051 Doughnuts; Doughnuts,
except frozen

(G-11252)
DAVID PACKARD COMPANY INC
15 Industrial Park Rd E (01540-2858)
P.O. Box 594 (01540-0594)
PHONE..........................508 987-2998
Kathleen Packard, *Prin*
EMP: 8 EST: 1989
SQ FT: 10,000
SALES (est): 1.18MM **Privately Held**
Web: www.dpcmachining.com
SIC: 3599 Machine shop, jobbing and repair

(G-11253)
FLAGG PALMER PRECAST INC
1 Industrial Park Rd W (01540-2849)
P.O. Box 421 (02668-0421)
PHONE..........................508 987-3400
TOLL FREE: 800
Frank Maki, *Pr*
Tam Toowl, *Sec*
EMP: 9 EST: 1950
SQ FT: 6,000
SALES (est): 807.5K **Privately Held**
Web: www.flaggpalmerprecast.com
SIC: 3272 Burial vaults, concrete or precast
terrazzo

(G-11254)
FX GROUP
2 Hawksley Rd Ste B (01540-2863)
PHONE..........................508 987-1366
▲ EMP: 8
SALES (est): 459.92K **Privately Held**
SIC: 2542 Fixtures: display, office, or store:
except wood

(G-11255)
IPG PHOTONICS CORPORATION
16b Old Webster Rd (01540-2706)
PHONE..........................508 506-2585
EMP: 12
SALES (est): 3.42MM **Privately Held**
Web: www.ipgphotonics.com
SIC: 3699 Laser systems and equipment

(G-11256)
KITCHEN OPTIONS INC
Also Called: Kitchen Options of New England
193 Sutton Ave (01540-1814)
PHONE..........................508 987-3384
Raymond Lentine, *Owner*
EMP: 7 EST: 2007

SALES (est): 868.68K **Privately Held**
Web: www.mykitchenoptions.com
SIC: 2434 Wood kitchen cabinets

(G-11257)
**L & L CONCRETE PRODUCTS
INC**
28 Linwood St (01540-2846)
P.O. Box 516 (01570-0516)
PHONE..........................508 987-8175
Louis A Esposito Junior, *Pr*
Emilia Esposito, *Sec*
EMP: 23 EST: 1940
SQ FT: 6,000
SALES (est): 873.1K **Privately Held**
SIC: 3272 Manhole covers or frames,
concrete

(G-11258)
**LEGGETT & PLATT
INCORPORATED**
Also Called: Oxford Spring 5301
23 Dana Rd (01540-1703)
P.O. Box 719 (01540-0719)
PHONE..........................508 987-8706
Paul Napieralski, *Brnch Mgr*
EMP: 51
SALES (corp-wide): 5.15B **Publicly Held**
Web: www.leggett.com
SIC: 2515 2514 5085 3495 Box springs,
assembled; Frames for box springs or
bedsprings: metal; Springs; Wire springs
PA: Leggett & Platt, Incorporated
1 Leggett Rd
Carthage MO 64836
417 358-8131

(G-11259)
LINE BORE INDUSTRIES INC
3 Harlan Dr (01540-2840)
PHONE..........................508 987-6509
Charles Dickson Junior, *Pr*
Cheryl Dickson, *VP*
Betty Dickson, *Clerk*
EMP: 10 EST: 1989
SQ FT: 8,500
SALES (est): 978.42K **Privately Held**
Web: www.linebore.com
SIC: 3599 Machine shop, jobbing and repair

(G-11260)
LVR INC
2 Hawksley Rd Unit C (01540-2863)
PHONE..........................508 987-2337
Kent Coston, *Mgr*
EMP: 9 EST: 2017
SALES (est): 302.98K **Privately Held**
Web: www.lvrinc.com
SIC: 3297 Nonclay refractories

(G-11261)
**MAKERS TOOL AND MFG CO
LLC**
175 Main St (01540-2504)
PHONE..........................774 633-0658
Paul Mark Johnson, *Pr*
EMP: 12 EST: 2020
SALES (est): 535.77K **Privately Held**
Web: www.makerstm.com
SIC: 3999 8711 Manufacturing industries,
nec; Engineering services

(G-11262)
MATKIM INDUSTRIES INC
Also Called: Matkim
2 Hawksley Rd Ste D (01540-2863)
P.O. Box 168 (01540-0168)
PHONE..........................508 987-3599
Matt Shenker, *Pr*

EMP: 40 EST: 1989
SQ FT: 20,000
SALES (est): 6.97MM **Privately Held**
Web: www.matkim.com
SIC: 3644 Insulators and insulation
materials, electrical

(G-11263)
**S LANE JOHN & SON
INCORPORATED**
Off Clara Barton (01540)
P.O. Box 781 (01537-0781)
PHONE..........................508 987-3959
EMP: 10
SALES (corp-wide): 21.76MM **Privately
Held**
Web: www.jslane.com
SIC: 1422 5032 Crushed and broken
limestone; Stone, crushed or broken
PA: S Lane John & Son Incorporated
311 E Mountain Rd
Westfield MA 01085
413 568-8986

(G-11264)
SWISSTURN/USA INC
21 Dana Rd (01540-1709)
PHONE..........................508 987-6211
Kenneth J Mandile, *Pr*
Diane M Mandile, *
EMP: 55 EST: 1987
SQ FT: 25,000
SALES (est): 9.84MM **Privately Held**
Web: www.swissturn.com
SIC: 3451 Screw machine products

(G-11265)
T & D SPECIALTIES INC
35 Industrial Park Rd E (01540-2858)
P.O. Box 13 (01540-0013)
PHONE..........................508 987-8344
Paul Sirard, *Pr*
Steven Sirard, *VP*
Cherie Sirard, *VP*
▼ EMP: 20 EST: 1972
SQ FT: 8,000
SALES (est): 2.25MM **Privately Held**
Web: www.tdspecialties.net
SIC: 8732 3599 7699 Business research
service; Machine and other job shop work;
Precision instrument repair

(G-11266)
TEC ENGINEERING CORP
Also Called: TEC
31 Town Forest Rd (01540-2868)
PHONE..........................508 987-0231
Maurice Minardi, *Pr*
EMP: 16 EST: 1982
SQ FT: 31,000
SALES (est): 4.78MM **Privately Held**
Web: www.tecautomation.com
SIC: 3535 3559 5084 Conveyors and
conveying equipment; Plastics working
machinery; Conveyor systems

(G-11267)
VENMILL INDUSTRIES INC
36 Town Forest Rd (01540-2839)
PHONE..........................508 363-0410
Michael U Schmidt, *Pr*
Karen L Brady, *Treas*
Peter Tam, *Dir*
Robert Treadwell, *Dir*
Robert Wilkins, *Dir*
▲ EMP: 20 EST: 2002
SALES (est): 4.18MM **Privately Held**
Web: www.venmill.com
SIC: 3651 Household audio and video
equipment

(G-11268)
WEAR-RITE CORP
Cudworth Rd (01540)
P.O. Box 690 (01540-0690)
PHONE...............................508 987-0361
Maureen E Beland, Pr
EMP: 10 **EST:** 1992
SQ FT: 78,000
SALES (est): 198.8K **Privately Held**
SIC: 3599 Machine shop, jobbing and repair

Palmer
Hampden County

(G-11269)
ADAPTAS SOLUTIONS LLC (PA)
9 2nd St (01069-1536)
PHONE...............................413 284-9975
Jay Ray, Pr
Laura Jean Ray, *
Pat Roy Stckhlder, Prin
Patricia Roy, *
Kevin Topor, *
▲ **EMP:** 23 **EST:** 1997
SQ FT: 3,000
SALES (est): 21.75MM
SALES (corp-wide): 21.75MM **Privately Held**
Web: www.adaptas.com
SIC: 3671 Electron tubes

(G-11270)
AMERICAN CABLE ASSEMBLIES INC (PA)
21 Wilbraham St Unit A12 (01069-9526)
PHONE...............................413 283-2515
Sean Kelly, Pr
EMP: 15 **EST:** 2000
SALES (est): 4.42MM **Privately Held**
Web:
www.americancableassemblies.com
SIC: 3357 Nonferrous wiredrawing and insulating

(G-11271)
BLACK BAY VENTURES VI LLC
Also Called: Palmer Foundry
22 Mount Dumplin Rd (01069-1128)
PHONE...............................413 283-2976
Robert Logan, Managing Member
EMP: 10 **EST:** 2009
SALES (est): 887.37K **Privately Held**
Web: www.palmerfoundry.com
SIC: 3365 Aluminum foundries

(G-11272)
CREATIVE MATERIAL TECH LTD
Also Called: Dynamic Coating Solutions
21 Wilbraham St Unit B11 (01069-9685)
PHONE...............................413 284-0000
John C Becker Iv, Pr
Ann M Becker, Sec
EMP: 7 **EST:** 1997
SQ FT: 38,000
SALES (est): 2.34MM **Privately Held**
Web: www.creativematerial.com
SIC: 5031 5211 2851 Building materials, exterior; Lumber and other building materials; Coating, air curing

(G-11273)
DUBLIN STEEL CORPORATION
95 2nd St (01069-1543)
PHONE...............................413 289-1218
Shannon Danylieko, Pr
Donald Duffy, Treas
EMP: 20 **EST:** 1986
SQ FT: 8,400
SALES (est): 4.85MM **Privately Held**
Web: www.dublinsteel.net
SIC: 3441 Building components, structural steel

(G-11274)
ESSITY NORTH AMERICA INC
Also Called: Molnycke
1st St (01069)
P.O. Box 720 (01069-0720)
PHONE...............................413 289-1221
EMP: 416
SALES (corp-wide): 14.89B **Privately Held**
SIC: 2676 Sanitary paper products
HQ: Essity North America Inc.
2929 Arch St Ste 2600
Philadelphia PA 19104

(G-11275)
LIGNETICS NEW ENGLAND INC
21 Wilbraham St Unit B13 (01069-9685)
P.O. Box 532 (03452-0532)
PHONE...............................413 284-1050
Richard Walch, Mgr
EMP: 8
Web: www.lignetics.com
SIC: 2448 Pallets, wood
HQ: Lignetics Of New England, Inc.
1075 E S Boulder Rd
Louisville CO 80027
303 802-5400

(G-11276)
LINDE GAS & EQUIPMENT INC
19 2nd St (01069-1536)
PHONE...............................413 283-9906
Michael Erwin, Brnch Mgr
EMP: 7
Web: www.lindeus.com
SIC: 2813 Industrial gases
HQ: Linde Gas & Equipment Inc.
10 Riverview Dr
Danbury CT 06810
844 445-4633

(G-11277)
MASS DRY ICE CORPORATION (DH)
Also Called: American Dry Ice Corporation
19 2nd St (01069-1536)
P.O. Box 719 (01069-0719)
PHONE...............................413 283-9906
Robert Koerner, Pr
George Koerner, Treas
EMP: 13 **EST:** 1984
SQ FT: 5,600
SALES (est): 9.97MM **Privately Held**
Web: www.americancarbonation.com
SIC: 2097 Manufactured ice
HQ: Linde Gas & Equipment Inc.
10 Riverview Dr
Danbury CT 06810
844 445-4633

(G-11278)
NORTHEAST SEAT COMPANY INC
21 Wilbraham St (01069-9605)
PHONE...............................413 283-6236
Allen Simmons, Prin
EMP: 9 **EST:** 2010
SALES (est): 319.49K **Privately Held**
SIC: 3721 Aircraft

(G-11279)
NOVACEL INC (DH)
Also Called: Novacel
21 3rd St (01069-1542)
PHONE...............................413 283-3468
Laurent Derolez, CEO
David Anderson, *
Richard Karane, *
William Dopp, *
Michael Story, *
◆ **EMP:** 50 **EST:** 1985
SQ FT: 250,000
SALES (est): 46.58MM **Privately Held**
Web: www.novacel-solutions.com
SIC: 2671 Paper, coated or laminated for packaging
HQ: Novacel
27 Rue Du Docteur Emile Bataille
Deville Les Rouen 76250
323839898

(G-11280)
PALMER FOUNDRY INC
22 Mount Dumplin Rd (01069-1128)
P.O. Box 955 (01069-0955)
PHONE...............................413 283-2976
David Logan, CEO
Robert Logan, Pr
Dennis Hayden, VP
EMP: 70 **EST:** 1951
SQ FT: 51,000
SALES (est): 9.7MM **Privately Held**
Web: www.palmerfoundry.com
SIC: 3366 Copper foundries

(G-11281)
PALMER PAVING CORPORATION (PA)
25 Blanchard St (01069-1860)
P.O. Box 47 (01069-0047)
PHONE...............................413 283-8354
TOLL FREE: 800
David Callahan, Pr
Ronald Somers, *
Manuel Perry, *
Janet M Callahan, *
Ronald Bucchi, *
EMP: 30 **EST:** 1955
SQ FT: 4,000
SALES (est): 8.93MM
SALES (corp-wide): 8.93MM **Privately Held**
Web: www.palmerpaving.com
SIC: 1611 2951 Highway and street paving contractor; Asphalt paving mixtures and blocks

(G-11282)
POLYMER CORPORATION
Also Called: Polymer Injection Molding
1 3rd St (01069-1542)
PHONE...............................413 267-5524
James F Ryan, Brnch Mgr
EMP: 38
Web: www.polymercorporation.com
SIC: 3089 Injection molding of plastics
HQ: Polymer Corporation
180 Pleasant St
Rockland MA 02370
781 871-4606

(G-11283)
PROFILES INCORPORATED
7 First St (01069)
P.O. Box 850 (01069-0850)
PHONE...............................413 283-7790
Jeff Buck, Pr
Thomas Allard, *
Dean Kiley, *
▲ **EMP:** 35 **EST:** 1962
SQ FT: 75,000
SALES (est): 9.09MM
SALES (corp-wide): 498.74MM **Publicly Held**
Web: www.nninc.com

(G-11283 continued)
SIC: 3315 3496 Wire, ferrous/iron; Miscellaneous fabricated wire products
PA: Nn, Inc.
6210 Ardrey Kell Rd # 600
Charlotte NC 28277
980 264-4300

(G-11284)
SANDERSON-MACLEOD INCORPORATE
1199 S Main St (01069-1855)
P.O. Box 50 (01069-0050)
PHONE...............................413 283-3481
Eric Sanderson, Pr
Linda Mitchell, *
James Pascale, *
Mark Borsari, *
▲ **EMP:** 115 **EST:** 1961
SQ FT: 84,000
SALES (est): 17.85MM **Privately Held**
Web: www.sandersonmacleod.com
SIC: 3991 3351 3315 2221 Brushes, except paint and varnish; Copper rolling and drawing; Steel wire and related products; Broadwoven fabric mills, manmade

(G-11285)
TMI INDUSTRIES INC
Also Called: Thorndike Mills
25 Ware St (01069-1514)
P.O. Box 968 (01069-0968)
PHONE...............................413 283-9021
Mitchell Garabedian, Pr
Edward Garabedian, *
Anna Garabedian, *
▲ **EMP:** 25 **EST:** 1925
SQ FT: 50,000
SALES (est): 950.13K **Privately Held**
SIC: 2273 7389 5713 Rugs, braided and hooked; Brokers' services; Rugs

(G-11286)
TURLEY PUBLICATIONS INC (PA)
24 Water St (01069-1862)
PHONE...............................800 824-6548
Keith P Turley, Prin
Peter Howard, Prin
Bob Allen, Prin
EMP: 150 **EST:** 1962
SQ FT: 15,000
SALES (est): 21.98MM
SALES (corp-wide): 21.98MM **Privately Held**
Web: newspapers.turley.com
SIC: 2711 2741 Commercial printing and newspaper publishing combined; Miscellaneous publishing

(G-11287)
UNICORE LLC
6 Chamber Rd (01069-9318)
P.O. Box 324 (01069-0324)
PHONE...............................413 284-9995
Robert Yahn Junior, Managing Member
EMP: 20 **EST:** 1999
SQ FT: 20,000
SALES (est): 1.99MM **Privately Held**
SIC: 2821 Molding compounds, plastics

(G-11288)
VARTANIAN CUSTOM CABINETS
10 Second St (Palmer Industrial Park) (01069-1534)
PHONE...............................413 283-3438
Aram P Vartanian, Treas
Aram P Vartanian, CEO
John N Vartanian, Pr
Debra Vartanian, Sec
EMP: 20 **EST:** 1984
SQ FT: 15,000

SALES (est): 2.72MM **Privately Held**
Web: www.vartaniancabinets.com
SIC: 2434 Wood kitchen cabinets

Paxton
Worcester County

(G-11289)
HANDY PAD SUPPLY INC
57 Richards Ave (01612-1100)
PHONE....................508 791-2722
Russell H Tessier, *Pr*
Michael Tessier, *Clerk*
EMP: 12 EST: 1914
SQ FT: 45,000
SALES (est): 939.08K **Privately Held**
SIC: 3842 Dressings, surgical

(G-11290)
NORTHEAST OUTDOORS INC
Also Called: NORTHEAST BIG BUCK CLUB
390 Marshall St (01612-1228)
PHONE....................508 752-8762
Jeffrey E Brown, *Pr*
EMP: 8 EST: 1996
SALES (est): 56.78K **Privately Held**
Web: www.bigbuckclub.com
SIC: 2721 7997 Magazines: publishing and
printing; Gun and hunting clubs

(G-11291)
SPECTRUM PLASTICS GROUP
149 Marshall St (01612-1216)
PHONE....................203 736-5230
EMP: 8 EST: 2018
SALES (est): 244.56K **Privately Held**
Web: www.spectrumplastics.com
SIC: 3089 Injection molding of plastics

Peabody
Essex County

(G-11292)
A & A INDUSTRIES INC
320 Jubilee Dr (01960-4030)
PHONE....................978 977-9660
Aurelian Mardiros, *Pr*
Aurelian Mardiros, *Pr*
Anahid Mardiros, *
Charles Toomajian, *
▲ **EMP: 32 EST:** 1978
SQ FT: 120,000
SALES (est): 5.42MM **Privately Held**
Web: www.aandaindustries.com
SIC: 3599 Machine shop, jobbing and repair

(G-11293)
AES CORPORATION
285 Newbury St Ste 1 (01960-7468)
P.O. Box 2093 (01960-7093)
PHONE....................978 535-7310
Michael Sherman, *CEO*
Gary Shottes, *
Owais Hassan, *
David Kaplan, *
◆ **EMP: 53 EST:** 1974
SQ FT: 26,500
SALES (est): 16.92MM **Privately Held**
Web: www.aes-corp.com
SIC: 3699 7382 Security control equipment
and systems; Burglar alarm maintenance
and monitoring

(G-11294)
**AES INTERNATIONAL
CORPORATION**

285 Newbury St Ste 1 (01960-7468)
P.O. Box 2010 (01960-7010)
PHONE....................978 535-7310
Ann Sherman, *Pr*
Michael Sherman, *VP*
Mark Brandstein, *COO*
Victoria Harker, *CFO*
EMP: 13 EST: 1988
SQ FT: 4,500
SALES (est): 2.38MM **Privately Held**
Web: www.aesintlcorp.com
SIC: 7382 3699 Security systems services;
Security devices

(G-11295)
ALLIANCE LEATHER INC
58 Pulaski St Ste 2 (01960-1829)
PHONE....................978 531-6771
▲ **EMP: 10 EST:** 1996
SQ FT: 4,000
SALES (est): 222.78K **Privately Held**
SIC: 3172 3111 Personal leather goods, nec
; Leather tanning and finishing

(G-11296)
ANALOGIC CORPORATION (HQ)
Also Called: Analogic
8 Centennial Dr (01960-7987)
PHONE....................978 326-4000
Thomas Ripp, *CEO*
Will Rousmaniere, *CFO*
Mervat Faltas, *Sr VP*
Brooks West, *Sr VP*
▲ **EMP: 1000 EST:** 1967
SQ FT: 514,000
SALES (est): 869MM
SALES (corp-wide): 869MM **Privately
Held**
Web: www.analogic.com
SIC: 3825 3812 Instruments to measure
electricity; Search and detection systems
and instruments
PA: Anlg Holding Company, Inc.
8 Centennial Dr
Peabody MA 01960
978 326-4000

(G-11297)
ANALOGIC CORPORATION
Analogic Measurement & Control
8 Centennial Dr (01960-7987)
PHONE....................978 977-3000
Andrew Toth, *Mgr*
EMP: 10
SALES (corp-wide): 869MM **Privately
Held**
Web: www.analogic.com
SIC: 3825 Digital panel meters, electricity
measuring
HQ: Analogic Corporation
8 Centennial Dr
Peabody MA 01960
978 326-4000

(G-11298)
AP PLASTICS LLC
103 Foster St (01960-5933)
PHONE....................800 222-1117
EMP: 15
SALES (est): 891.47K
SALES (corp-wide): 3.51B **Publicly Held**
Web: applastic.ppwd.com
SIC: 2891 Adhesives
PA: H.B. Fuller Company
1200 Willow Lake Blvd
Saint Paul MN 55110
651 236-5900

(G-11299)
BIOPHYSICS PHARMA INC
9 Centennial Dr Unit 102 (01960-7940)
PHONE....................781 608-7738
James Mongiando, *Pr*
Pearl Zhu, *Sr VP*
Laura Stephens, *Sr VP*
John Masiz, *Sec*
EMP: 10 EST: 2018
SALES (est): 1.05MM **Privately Held**
Web: www.b-physics.com
SIC: 2834 Pharmaceutical preparations

(G-11300)
CALENDAR PRESS INC
18 Rainbow Cir (01960-5720)
P.O. Box 191 (01960-0991)
PHONE....................508 531-1860
Catherine Trainor, *Pr*
George Trainor, *
EMP: 30 EST: 1973
SALES (est): 2.08MM **Privately Held**
Web: www.calendarpressinc.com
SIC: 2752 Offset printing

(G-11301)
CARL ZEISS NTS LLC (DH)
Also Called: Llc, Carl Zeiss NTS
1 Corporate Pl Ste 3 (01960-3827)
PHONE....................978 826-1500
▲ **EMP: 87 EST:** 1995
SQ FT: 5,100
SALES (est): 93.24MM **Privately Held**
SIC: 5047 3826 Medical laboratory
equipment; Microscopes, electron and
proton
HQ: Carl Zeiss Ag
Carl-Zeiss-Str. 22
Oberkochen BW 73447
7364200

(G-11302)
COMMUNICATION INK INC
140 Summit St (01960-5156)
P.O. Box 3373 (01961-3373)
PHONE....................978 977-4595
EMP: 25 EST: 1995
SALES (est): 928.7K **Privately Held**
Web: www.communications-ink.net
SIC: 2741 7331 Catalogs: publishing and
printing; Direct mail advertising services

(G-11303)
**CREATIVE PUBLISHING CORP
AMER (PA)**

2 1st Ave Ste 103 (01960-4960)
P.O. Box 6039 (01961-6039)
PHONE....................978 532-5880
Richard H Ayer, *Clrk*
EMP: 39 EST: 1980
SQ FT: 9,000
SALES (est): 2.29MM
SALES (corp-wide): 2.29MM **Privately
Held**
SIC: 2711 7336 2791 Newspapers; Graphic
arts and related design; Typesetting

(G-11304)
CSI KEYBOARDS INC
56 Pulaski St Unit 1 (01960-1830)
PHONE....................978 532-8181
Peter J Castner, *Pr*
▲ **EMP: 36 EST:** 1979
SQ FT: 20,000
SALES (est): 4.92MM **Privately Held**
Web: www.csikeyboards.com

SIC: 3575 3643 3577 Keyboards, computer,
office machine; Current-carrying wiring
services; Computer peripheral equipment,
nec

(G-11305)
DESK TOP GRAPHICS INC (HQ)
Also Called: Spire Express
1 1st Ave (01960-4963)
PHONE....................617 832-1927
Eric Dyer, *Pr*
Isaac Dyer, *Ex VP*
Rick Theder, *Ex VP*
▲ **EMP: 28 EST:** 1988
SQ FT: 80,000
SALES (est): 2.21MM
SALES (corp-wide): 45.5MM **Privately
Held**
Web: www.spireexpress.com
SIC: 2796 2752 7336 7374 Color
separations, for printing; Offset printing;
Commercial art and graphic design;
Computer graphics service
PA: Digipress, Inc.
1 1st Ave Ste 1 # 1
Peabody MA 01960
617 832-1927

(G-11306)
DIGIPRESS INC (PA)
Also Called: Spire
1 1st Ave Ste 1 (01960-4963)
PHONE....................617 832-1927
Eric W Dyer, *Pr*
Rick Theder, *
Isaac C Dyer, *
EMP: 150 EST: 1998
SQ FT: 80,000
SALES (est): 45.5MM
SALES (corp-wide): 45.5MM **Privately
Held**
SIC: 2752 Commercial printing, lithographic

(G-11307)
**DOE & INGLLS MSSCHSTTS
OPRTING**

300 Jubilee Dr # 400 (01960-4068)
PHONE....................781 391-0090
Andrew Finn, *Mgr*
John Sabo, *
Thomas Spencer Todd, *
EMP: 36 EST: 1921
SALES (est): 8.62MM
SALES (corp-wide): 44.91B **Publicly Held**
SIC: 3826 Analytical instruments
HQ: Doe & Ingalls Management, Llc
4813 Emperor Blvd Ste 300
Durham NC 27703

(G-11308)
DUNAJSKI DAIRY INC
Also Called: Pure Country Products
22 Buxton Ln (01960-1702)
PHONE....................978 531-1457
Theodore Dunajski, *Pr*
Christine Dunajski, *Stockholder*
Michael Dunajski, *Stockholder*
Tracy Dunajski, *Off Mgr*
EMP: 8 EST: 1921
SQ FT: 40,000
SALES (est): 572.24K **Privately Held**
Web: www.ddairy.com
SIC: 0241 2033 2086 5149 Milk production;
Fruit juices: fresh; Fruit drinks (less than
100% juice): packaged in cans, etc.; Water,
distilled

(G-11309)
EMTEX INC
Also Called: Emerson Textiles

▲ = Import ▼ = Export
◆ = Import/Export

58 Pulaski St (01960-1800)
PHONE.............................978 907-4500
▲ **EMP:** 15 **EST:** 1985
SALES (est): 4.89MM **Privately Held**
Web: www.emtexglobal.com
SIC: 2241 5131 2295 Trimmings, textile; Piece goods and notions; Laminating of fabrics

(G-11310)
FURNITURE DESIGN SERVICES INC
119 Foster St Bldg 13 (01960-5933)
PHONE.............................978 531-3250
Chris Rice, *Pr*
EMP: 8 **EST:** 2007
SALES (est): 330.31K **Privately Held**
Web: www.furnituredesignservices.com
SIC: 2434 Wood kitchen cabinets

(G-11311)
GOODRICH CORPORATION
Also Called: UTC Aerospace Systems
5th St (01960)
P.O. Box 3369 (01961-3369)
PHONE.............................978 532-2350
Michael Stewart, *Brnch Mgr*
EMP: 35
SALES (corp-wide): 68.92B **Publicly Held**
Web: www.collinsaerospace.com
SIC: 3728 Alighting (landing gear) assemblies, aircraft
HQ: Goodrich Corporation
2730 W Tyvola Rd
Charlotte NC 28217
704 423-7000

(G-11312)
GOT INTERFACE
2 Centennial Dr Ste 310b (01960-0121)
PHONE.............................781 547-5700
Daniel Skiba, *Pr*
EMP: 19 **EST:** 2014
SALES (est): 4.43MM **Privately Held**
Web: www.gotinterface.com
SIC: 3823 Computer interface equipment, for industrial process control

(G-11313)
HENDRICKSON PUBLISHERS LLC
3 Centennial Dr Ste 130 (01960-7931)
P.O. Box 3473 (01961-3473)
PHONE.............................978 532-6546
◆ **EMP:** 25 **EST:** 1980
SALES (est): 1.07MM **Privately Held**
Web: www.hendricksonrose.com
SIC: 2731 Books, publishing only

(G-11314)
HENDRICKSON PUBLISHERS INC
3 Centennial Dr Ste 130 (01960-7931)
P.O. Box 3473 (01961-3473)
PHONE.............................800 358-3111
EMP: 13 **EST:** 2017
SALES (est): 485.5K **Privately Held**
Web: www.hendricksonrose.com
SIC: 2741 Miscellaneous publishing

(G-11315)
HILLER COMPANIES INC
Also Called: Advanced Safety Systems
141 Summit St Ste 2 (01960-5101)
PHONE.............................978 532-5730
EMP: 25
SALES (corp-wide): 179.36MM **Privately Held**
Web: www.advancedsafetysystems.com

SIC: 5063 1731 2899 Fire alarm systems; Fire detection and burglar alarm systems specialization; Chemical preparations, nec
PA: The Hiller Companies, Llc
3751 Joy Springs Dr
Mobile AL 36693
251 661-1275

(G-11316)
HP HOOD LLC
18 Blackstone St (01960-1002)
PHONE.............................978 535-3385
Joseph Hood, *Brnch Mgr*
EMP: 14
SALES (corp-wide): 2.21B **Privately Held**
Web: www.hood.com
SIC: 2026 Fluid milk
PA: Hp Hood Llc
6 Kimball Ln Ste 400
Lynnfield MA 01940
617 887-3000

(G-11317)
IDEAL ELECTRIC CO INC
0 Centennial Dr (01960-7927)
PHONE.............................781 284-2525
Richard Viveiros, *Pr*
Peter Binda, *
EMP: 30 **EST:** 1983
SQ FT: 4,000
SALES (est): 2.39MM **Privately Held**
Web: www.ideal-electric.com
SIC: 1731 3625 General electrical contractor ; Electric controls and control accessories, industrial

(G-11318)
INNOVENT TECHNOLOGIES LLC
6 Centennial Dr (01960-7902)
PHONE.............................978 538-0808
▼ **EMP:** 50 **EST:** 2005
SALES (est): 9.97MM **Privately Held**
Web: www.innoventtech.com
SIC: 3559 Semiconductor manufacturing machinery

(G-11319)
INTERNATIONAL LIGHT TECH INC
Also Called: International Light
10 Technology Dr (01960-7976)
PHONE.............................978 818-6180
Michael Edwards, *Pr*
Robert Harrison, *VP*
◆ **EMP:** 50 **EST:** 1965
SQ FT: 17,000
SALES (est): 14.74MM
SALES (corp-wide): 2.23B **Privately Held**
Web: www.internationallight.com
SIC: 3641 3826 3999 3829 Electric lamps; Analytical instruments; Shades, lamp or candle; Measuring and controlling devices, nec
HQ: Ocean Optics, Inc.
3500 Quadrangle Blvd
Orlando FL 32817

(G-11320)
JEOL USA INC (HQ)
11 Dearborn Rd (01960-3862)
P.O. Box 6043 (01961-6043)
PHONE.............................978 535-5900
Peter Genovese, *Pr*
Robert Pohorenec, *VP*
Masuru Iwatani, *VP*
◆ **EMP:** 120 **EST:** 1962
SQ FT: 30,000
SALES (est): 53.18MM **Privately Held**
Web: www.jeolusa.com

SIC: 3826 Analytical instruments
PA: Jeol Ltd.
3-1-2, Musashino
Akishima TKY 196-0

(G-11321)
JOHN COVEY
Also Called: Covey Engineering
6 Cobb Ave (01960-3610)
P.O. Box 2026 (01960-7026)
PHONE.............................978 535-4681
John Covey, *Owner*
EMP: 10 **EST:** 1968
SQ FT: 3,000
SALES (est): 241.69K **Privately Held**
SIC: 3599 Machine shop, jobbing and repair

(G-11322)
KSG ENTERPRISES INC
Also Called: Finelines
77 Walnut St Ste 8 (01960-5691)
PHONE.............................978 977-7357
Karen S Gilman, *Pr*
EMP: 19 **EST:** 1984
SQ FT: 4,000
SALES (est): 682.78K **Privately Held**
SIC: 2392 2391 Pillows, bed: made from purchased materials; Curtains and draperies

(G-11323)
LASER PROCESS MFG INC
2 Centennial Dr Ste 6 (01960-7911)
PHONE.............................978 531-6003
EMP: 17 **EST:** 1992
SQ FT: 7,000
SALES (est): 434.31K **Privately Held**
Web: www.laserprocessmfg.com
SIC: 3599 Machine shop, jobbing and repair

(G-11324)
LIFOAM INDUSTRIES LLC
Also Called: Lifoam Industries
2 5th St (01960-4916)
PHONE.............................978 278-0008
John Cantlin, *Prin*
EMP: 49
SALES (corp-wide): 1.86B **Privately Held**
Web: www.lifoam.com
SIC: 2821 Plastics materials and resins
HQ: Lifoam Industries, Llc
1303 S Batesville Rd
Greer SC 29650
410 889-1023

(G-11325)
LONGHORN STEEL INC
15 Price Rd (01960-2704)
PHONE.............................978 265-3646
Anthony Dewayne Holmes, *Prin*
EMP: 7 **EST:** 2006
SALES (est): 62.52K **Privately Held**
SIC: 3448 Prefabricated metal buildings and components

(G-11326)
NEW ENGLAND LABEL ✪
10 Centennial Dr (01960-7900)
PHONE.............................978 281-3663
EMP: 8 **EST:** 2022
SALES (est): 305.93K **Privately Held**
Web: www.resourcelabel.com
SIC: 2759 Labels and seals: printing, nsk

(G-11327)
NORTH SHORE LABORATORIES CORP
Also Called: Safety Seals
44 Endicott St (01960-3122)
P.O. Box 568 (01960-7568)

PHONE.............................978 531-5954
Robert A Niconchuk, *Pr*
Susan Pelletier, *Sec*
▲ **EMP:** 11 **EST:** 1964
SALES (est): 984.38K **Privately Held**
Web: www.safetyseal.com
SIC: 3714 7389 Motor vehicle parts and accessories; Business Activities at Non-Commercial Site

(G-11328)
NORTH SHORE NEWS COMPANY INC (PA)
90 Forest St (01960-4135)
PHONE.............................781 592-1300
TOLL FREE: 800
Thomas A Mulkern Senior, *Ch*
Thomas A Mulkern Junior, *CEO*
EMP: 40 **EST:** 1956
SALES (est): 3.19MM
SALES (corp-wide): 3.19MM **Privately Held**
Web: www.mulkern.com
SIC: 2711 Newspapers, publishing and printing

(G-11329)
OXFORD GRAPHICS LLC
10 Centennial Dr (01960-7900)
PHONE.............................978 281-3663
EMP: 11 **EST:** 2014
SALES (est): 974.23K **Privately Held**
Web: www.resourcelabel.com
SIC: 2752 Commercial printing, lithographic
PA: Resource Label Group, Llc
2550 Meridian Blvd # 370
Franklin TN 37067

(G-11330)
PALMER MANUFACTURING CO LLC
Also Called: PALMER MANUFACTURING CO., LLC
1 2nd St Ste 1 (01960-4958)
PHONE.............................781 321-0480
EMP: 11
SALES (corp-wide): 402.2MM **Privately Held**
SIC: 3724 Aircraft engines and engine parts
HQ: Palmer Manufacturing Co., Llc.
243 Medford St
Malden MA 02148
781 321-0480

(G-11331)
PARADIGM PRCISION HOLDINGS LLC
1 2nd St (01960-4957)
PHONE.............................978 278-7100
John Russell, *Brnch Mgr*
EMP: 230
SALES (corp-wide): 402.2MM **Privately Held**
Web: www.paradigmprecision.com
SIC: 3724 Aircraft engines and engine parts
HQ: Paradigm Precision Holdings, Llc
404 W Guadalupe Rd
Tempe AZ 85283

(G-11332)
PFC PUBLICATIONS LLC
8 Ashford Trl Apt 831 (01960-8864)
PHONE.............................508 366-2984
EMP: 7
SALES (est): 266.26K **Privately Held**
SIC: 2741 Miscellaneous publishing

(G-11333)
PINPOINT LASER SYSTEMS INC
56 Pulaski St Unit 5 (01960-1830)
PHONE.....................978 532-8001
Albert M Creighton, *Pr*
EMP: 20 EST: 1992
SQ FT: 5,000
SALES (est): 2.13MM **Privately Held**
Web: www.pinpointlaser.com
SIC: 3821 3829 Laser beam alignment
devices; Measuring and controlling devices,
nec

(G-11334)
PLUS ONE CORPORATION
11 Mason St (01960-5981)
P.O. Box 673 (01960-7673)
PHONE.....................978 532-3700
William H Thorpe Junior, *Pr*
Carol A Cole, *Treas*
EMP: 10 EST: 1967
SQ FT: 10,000
SALES (est): 913.48K **Privately Held**
Web: www.plusonecorp.com
SIC: 3599 Machine shop, jobbing and repair

(G-11335)
**PRATTVILLE MACHINE & TL CO
INC**
240 Jubilee Dr Fl 2 (01960-4062)
PHONE.....................978 538-5229
John Russo, *Pr*
Vincent Spinali, *
Mario Russo, *Stockholder**
EMP: 80 EST: 1967
SQ FT: 48,000
SALES (est): 9.28MM **Privately Held**
Web: www.prattvillemachine.com
SIC: 3599 Machine shop, jobbing and repair

(G-11336)
**PRO TOUCH HOME
IMPROVEMENT INC**
Also Called: Home Improvement
118 Shore Dr (01960-3010)
PHONE.....................617 378-1929
Nilton Dornelas, *Owner*
EMP: 18 EST: 2017
SALES (est): 1.17MM **Privately Held**
SIC: 1389 1521 1442 Construction, repair,
and dismantling services; Single-family
housing construction; Construction sand
and gravel

(G-11337)
**RIVERSIDE ENGINEERING CO
INC**
12 County St (01960-5208)
PHONE.....................978 531-1556
Bruce Madden, *Pr*
EMP: 7 EST: 1977
SQ FT: 3,500
SALES (est): 745.87K **Privately Held**
Web: www.riverside-engineering.org
SIC: 3599 Machine shop, jobbing and repair

(G-11338)
ROCKWELL COLLINS INC
Also Called: Collins Aerospace
1 5th St (01960-4915)
PHONE.....................978 532-2350
EMP: 12
SALES (corp-wide): 68.92B **Publicly Held**
Web: www.rockwellcollins.com
SIC: 3728 Aircraft parts and equipment, nec
HQ: Rockwell Collins, Inc.
400 Collins Rd Ne
Cedar Rapids IA 52498

(G-11339)
ROUSSELOT PEABODY INC
227 Washington St (01960-5423)
PHONE.....................978 573-3700
Larry Jeske, *Pr*
John F Sterling, *Sec*
Stephen Smith, *Treas*
Kathy Olbrich, *Prin*
◆ EMP: 18 EST: 1930
SQ FT: 480,000
SALES (est): 10.76MM
SALES (corp-wide): 6.53B **Publicly Held**
Web: www.rousselot.com
SIC: 2899 Gelatin: edible, technical,
photographic, or pharmaceutical
PA: Darling Ingredients Inc.
5601 N Macarthur Blvd
Irving TX 75038
972 717-0300

(G-11340)
**SHAWMUT ADVERTISING INC
(PA)**
Also Called: Shawmut
310 Jubilee Dr (01960-4030)
PHONE.....................978 762-7500
Dominick C Peluso, *Pr*
Michael Peluso, *
Stacy Peluso Slaney, *
Daniel M Peluso, *
EMP: 40 EST: 1951
SALES (est): 9.88MM
SALES (corp-wide): 9.88MM **Privately
Held**
Web: www.shawmutdelivers.com
SIC: 2752 3823 7331 5199 Offset printing;
Digital displays of process variables; Direct
mail advertising services; Advertising
specialties

(G-11341)
SHAWMUT PRINTING
310 Jubilee Dr (01960-4030)
PHONE.....................978 762-7500
Dom Peluso, *Prin*
▲ EMP: 20 EST: 2011
SALES (est): 2.07MM **Privately Held**
Web: www.shawmutdelivers.com
SIC: 2752 Offset printing

(G-11342)
SPECIALIZED TURNING INC
147 Summit St Ste 7 (01960-5173)
PHONE.....................978 977-0444
Harold E Holm Junior, *Pr*
EMP: 27 EST: 2007
SALES (est): 1.74MM **Privately Held**
Web: www.specializedturning.com
SIC: 3451 Screw machine products

(G-11343)
SPIRE INC
1 1st Ave Ste 1 (01960-4963)
PHONE.....................617 474-8800
Eric W Dyer, *Pr*
Isaac C Dyer, *Dir*
Rick Theder, *Dir*
EMP: 26 EST: 1999
SALES (est): 2.9MM **Privately Held**
Web: www.spire.net
SIC: 2741 Miscellaneous publishing

(G-11344)
STAHL (USA) INC (DH)
13 Corwin St (01960-5107)
PHONE.....................978 968-1382
Huub Van Beijeren, *CEO*
Bram Drexhage, *
◆ EMP: 35 EST: 2001
SQ FT: 6,223,120

SALES (est): 32.56MM **Privately Held**
Web: www.stahl.com
SIC: 2891 Adhesives and sealants
HQ: Stahl Holdings B.V.
Sluisweg 10
Waalwijk NB 5145
416689111

(G-11345)
**SYNVENTIVE MOLDING
SOLUTIONS INC (HQ)**
10 Centennial Dr (01960-7938)
PHONE.....................978 750-8065
EMP: 140 EST: 1983
SALES (est): 55.78MM
SALES (corp-wide): 1.49B **Publicly Held**
Web: www.synventive.com
SIC: 3544 3559 Special dies, tools, jigs, and
fixtures; Plastics working machinery
PA: Barnes Group Inc.
123 Main St
Bristol CT 06010
860 583-7070

(G-11346)
**TECHNICAL MANUFACTURING
CORP (HQ)**
Also Called: Tmcs
15 Centennial Dr (01960-7993)
PHONE.....................978 532-6330
Bruce P Wilson, *Pr*
William J Burke Traes, *Prin*
Robert S Feit, *
Keith J Kowalski, *
▲ EMP: 78 EST: 1979
SQ FT: 50,000
SALES (est): 21.86MM
SALES (corp-wide): 6.15B **Publicly Held**
Web: www.techmfg.com
SIC: 3829 Measuring and controlling
devices, nec
PA: Ametek, Inc.
1100 Cassatt Rd
Berwyn PA 19312
610 647-2121

(G-11347)
**THERMO WAVE
TECHNOLOGIES LLC**
1 Centennial Dr Ste 1 (01960-7920)
PHONE.....................800 733-9615
Ralph Faia, *CEO*
▼ EMP: 8 EST: 2011
SALES (est): 1.24MM **Privately Held**
Web: www.thermowavetech.com
SIC: 3589 Microwave ovens (cooking
equipment), commercial

(G-11348)
**TLC VISION (USA)
CORPORATION**
201 Andover St (01960-1603)
PHONE.....................978 531-4114
EMP: 40
SALES (corp-wide): 1.22B **Privately Held**
Web: www.tlcvision.com
SIC: 2591 Window blinds
HQ: Tlc Vision (Usa) Corporation
16305 Swingley Ridge Rd # 300
Chesterfield MO 63017
636 534-2300

(G-11349)
TRU TECHNOLOGIES INC
245 Lynnfield St (01960-5049)
PHONE.....................978 532-0775
Linda Moulton, *CEO*
EMP: 18 EST: 2008
SALES (est): 271.37K **Privately Held**

SIC: 3679 3812 3643 3678 Microwave
components; Search and navigation
equipment; Current-carrying wiring services
; Electronic connectors

(G-11350)
TUCKER ENGINEERING INC
4 5th St (01960-4916)
PHONE.....................978 532-5900
Donald A Tucker, *Pr*
Tina M Tucker, *
EMP: 38 EST: 1981
SQ FT: 12,000
SALES (est): 5.08MM **Privately Held**
Web: www.tuckereng.com
SIC: 3599 Machine shop, jobbing and repair

(G-11351)
VORTEX INC
4 Dearborn Rd (01960-3804)
PHONE.....................978 535-8721
Vito P Martello, *Pr*
David Allen, *
▲ EMP: 65 EST: 1986
SQ FT: 25,000
SALES (est): 8.49MM **Privately Held**
Web: www.vortexmetal.com
SIC: 3444 3312 Sheet metalwork; Tool and
die steel

(G-11352)
WALNUT 65 HOLDINGS INC (PA)
Also Called: Tannin
65 Walnut St (01960-0075)
P.O. Box 606 (01960-7606)
PHONE.....................978 532-4010
John V Thompson, *Pr*
Thomas A Odonnell Junior, *VP*
Robert W Thompson, *
Rachael M Thompson Clrk, *Prin*
Thomas W Thompson, *
◆ EMP: 30 EST: 1914
SQ FT: 50,000
SALES (est): 23.02MM
SALES (corp-wide): 23.02MM **Privately
Held**
Web: www.tannincorp.com
SIC: 2899 Oil treating compounds

(G-11353)
**WINCHESTER INTERCONNECT
CORP**
Also Called: Winchester Interconnect
245 Lynnfield St (01960-5049)
PHONE.....................978 532-0775
Stephen Eccles, *Genl Mgr*
EMP: 65
SALES (corp-wide): 17.49B **Privately Held**
Web: www.winconn.com
SIC: 3678 Electronic connectors
HQ: Winchester Interconnect Corporation
68 Water St
Norwalk CT 06854

(G-11354)
**WINCHESTER INTERCONNECT
CORP**
Winchester Interconnect
245 Lynnfield St (01960-5049)
PHONE.....................978 532-0775
Stephen Eccles, *Genl Mgr*
EMP: 65
SALES (corp-wide): 17.49B **Privately Held**
Web: www.winconn.com
SIC: 3678 Electronic connectors
HQ: Winchester Interconnect Corporation
68 Water St
Norwalk CT 06854

(G-11355)
WOODMAN PRECISION ENGRG INC
119 Foster St (01960-5933)
PHONE..............................978 538-9544
Chris Ahordini, *Pr*
EMP: 10 **EST:** 1982
SALES (est): 1.43MM **Privately Held**
SIC: 3599 Machine shop, jobbing and repair

Pembroke
Plymouth County

(G-11356)
AB-WEY MACHINE & DIE CO INC
51 School St (02359-3407)
P.O. Box 567 (02341-0567)
PHONE..............................781 294-8031
Anthony Delacono, *Pr*
Raymond J Sylvester, *Clerk*
EMP: 15 **EST:** 1967
SQ FT: 18,000
SALES (est): 2.44MM **Privately Held**
Web: www.abwey-machine.com
SIC: 3599 3542 Machine shop, jobbing and repair; Machine tools, metal forming type

(G-11357)
ANTENNA RESEARCH ASSOC INC
Seavey Engineering
28 Riverside Dr Ste 2 (02359-4947)
PHONE..............................781 829-4740
EMP: 37
SQ FT: 39,850
SALES (corp-wide): 24.47MM **Privately Held**
Web: www.ara-inc.com
SIC: 3663 Antennas, transmitting and communications
PA: Antenna Research Associates, Inc.
8880 Gorman Rd
Laurel MD 20723
301 937-8888

(G-11358)
APPLE MILL HOLDING COMPANY INC
Also Called: Sunrise
720 Washington St (02359-2324)
PHONE..............................781 826-9706
Henry C Appleton, *Pr*
Henry C Appleton, *Pr*
Judith B Appleton, *Sec*
EMP: 11 **EST:** 1976
SQ FT: 20,000
SALES (est): 4.18MM
SALES (corp-wide): 4.18MM **Privately Held**
Web:
sunrisesystems.sunrisesesatech.com
SIC: 3993 3674 Electric signs; Solid state electronic devices, nec
PA: Sunrise Systems Electronics Co. Inc.
720 Washington St
Pembroke MA 02359
781 826-9706

(G-11359)
BELCO FUEL COMPANY INC
38 Mountain Ash Ln (02359-2006)
PHONE..............................781 331-6521
Tony Borrelli, *Prin*
EMP: 7 **EST:** 2010
SALES (est): 241.88K **Privately Held**
SIC: 2869 Fuels

(G-11360)
CHERRY HILL CONSTRUCTION CORP
Also Called: Cherry Hill Pool & Spa
722 Washington St (02359-2324)
P.O. Box 6 (02358-0006)
PHONE..............................781 826-6886
Jim Mcgill, *Pr*
EMP: 7 **EST:** 2002
SQ FT: 3,000
SALES (est): 982.17K **Privately Held**
Web: www.cherryhillpool.com
SIC: 3949 Swimming pools, except plastic

(G-11361)
DATANATIONAL CORPORATION
Also Called: Wti Systems
100 Schoosett St Ste 2a (02359-1875)
PHONE..............................781 826-3400
Robert M Raymond, *Pr*
Joseph E Kaminski Iii, *Pr*
EMP: 22 **EST:** 1976
SQ FT: 2,000
SALES (est): 182.47K **Privately Held**
Web: www.zobrio.com
SIC: 7372 Application computer software

(G-11362)
DIMARK PRECISION MACHINING INC
745 Washington St (02359-2341)
P.O. Box 317 (02358-0317)
PHONE..............................781 447-7990
James Porter, *Pr*
Richard Lawrence, *VP*
John Porter, *Sec*
EMP: 12 **EST:** 1992
SQ FT: 8,500
SALES (est): 605.39K **Privately Held**
Web: www.dimarkprecision.com
SIC: 3599 Machine shop, jobbing and repair

(G-11363)
DIVISION 15 HVAC INC
300 Oak St Ste 930 (02359-1930)
PHONE..............................781 285-3115
Harry Frank Papp Iii, *Pr*
EMP: 32 **EST:** 2008
SALES (est): 3.31MM **Privately Held**
Web: www.division15hvac.com
SIC: 1711 3822 8711 Mechanical contractor; Temperature controls, automatic; Engineering services

(G-11364)
E S RITCHIE & SONS INC
Also Called: Richie Navigation
243 Oak St (02359-1980)
P.O. Box 548 (02359-0548)
PHONE..............................781 826-5131
Jonathan Sherman, *Pr*
EMP: 35 **EST:** 1850
SQ FT: 22,500
SALES (est): 4.52MM **Privately Held**
Web: www.ritchienavigation.com
SIC: 3812 Nautical instruments

(G-11365)
FCI OPHTHALMICS INC
30 Corporate Park Dr Ste 310 (02359-2052)
PHONE..............................781 826-9060
EMP: 7 **EST:** 1996
SALES (est): 1.23MM **Privately Held**
Web: www.fci-ophthalmics.com
SIC: 3841 Surgical and medical instruments
HQ: Carl Zeiss Meditec Ag
Goschwitzer Str. 51-52
Jena TH 07745
36412200

(G-11366)
GLIDECAM INDUSTRIES INC (PA)
125 Church St Ste 90-131 (02359-1991)
PHONE..............................508 577-6261
EMP: 10 **EST:** 1993
SALES (est): 1.31MM **Privately Held**
Web: www.glidecam.com
SIC: 3861 Cameras and related equipment

(G-11367)
HOOD E BENSON LABORATORIES
575 Washington St (02359-2342)
PHONE..............................781 826-7573
Lewis Marten, *Pr*
James Marten, *Treas*
Dennis Creedon, *VP*
EMP: 15 **EST:** 1962
SQ FT: 8,000
SALES (est): 2.59MM **Privately Held**
Web: www.hoodlabs.com
SIC: 8731 3842 Commercial physical research; Prosthetic appliances

(G-11368)
HORNER MILLWORK CORP
55 Corporate Park Dr Ste 1 (02359-1959)
PHONE..............................781 826-7770
Peter D Humphrey, *Brnch Mgr*
EMP: 22
SALES (corp-wide): 25.7MM **Privately Held**
Web: www.hornermillwork.com
SIC: 2431 Millwork
PA: Horner Millwork Corp.
1255 Grand Army Hwy
Somerset MA 02726
508 679-6479

(G-11369)
HOYLU INC
Also Called: Hoylu Boston
50 Corporate Park Dr Ste 270 (02359-1998)
PHONE..............................877 554-6958
EMP: 17
SALES (corp-wide): 5.84MM **Privately Held**
Web: www.hoylu.com
SIC: 7372 Prepackaged software
PA: Hoylu, Inc.
11335 Ne 122nd Way # 105
Kirkland WA 98034
877 554-6958

(G-11370)
HYER INDUSTRIES INC
Also Called: Thayer Scale
91 Schoosett St (02359-1839)
P.O. Box 669 (02359-0669)
PHONE..............................781 826-8101
EMP: 40 **EST:** 1949
SALES (est): 10MM **Privately Held**
Web: www.thayerscale.com
SIC: 3596 Weighing machines and apparatus

(G-11371)
JAMES F STEARNS CO LLP
Also Called: James F Stearns
42 Winter St Ste 35 (02359-4958)
PHONE..............................781 829-0095
James F Stearns Iv, *Pt*
Tania R Cleary, *
Karl J Feitelberg, *
David Scott Sloan, *
EMP: 30 **EST:** 2007
SALES (est): 3.99MM **Privately Held**

SIC: 1791 3441 Iron work, structural; Fabricated structural metal

(G-11372)
JLC-TECH LLC
130 Corporate Park Dr (02359-1910)
PHONE..............................781 826-8162
Silvio Porciatti, *Prin*
▲ **EMP:** 20 **EST:** 2013
SALES (est): 2.67MM **Privately Held**
Web: www.jlc-tech.com
SIC: 3646 Commercial lighting fixtures

(G-11373)
KENT FABRICATIONS INC
171 Mattakeesett St (02359-2547)
PHONE..............................339 244-4533
Raymond A Miller, *Pr*
EMP: 8 **EST:** 2010
SALES (est): 896.26K **Privately Held**
Web: www.kentfabrications.com
SIC: 3441 Fabricated structural metal

(G-11374)
MACKENZIE MACHINE & DESIGN INC
171 Mattakeesett St Ste 2 (02359-2539)
PHONE..............................339 933-8157
Neal Mackenzie, *Pr*
EMP: 19 **EST:** 1959
SQ FT: 5,000
SALES (est): 780.24K **Privately Held**
Web: www.mackenzie-machine.com
SIC: 3599 Machine shop, jobbing and repair

(G-11375)
NORTH RIVER GRAPHICS INC
100 Corporate Park Dr Ste 1730 (02359-4964)
PHONE..............................781 826-6866
Mary Hill, *Pr*
Jeffrey Hill, *Treas*
EMP: 9 **EST:** 2007
SALES (est): 853.39K **Privately Held**
Web: www.northrivergraphics.com
SIC: 2752 Offset printing

(G-11376)
PROTECTOWIRE CO INC
Also Called: Protectowire
60 Washington St (02359-1833)
PHONE..............................781 826-3878
Andrew K Sullivan, *Pr*
Carol M Sullivan, *
Gary P Fields, *
Stephen Joseph Loughlin, *
EMP: 30 **EST:** 1936
SALES (est): 6.55MM **Privately Held**
Web: www.protectowire.com
SIC: 3669 Fire detection systems, electric

(G-11377)
SANDBOX MEDICAL LLC
50 Corporate Park Dr # 750 (02359-1998)
PHONE..............................781 826-6905
EMP: 7 **EST:** 2010
SALES (est): 75.63K **Privately Held**
SIC: 3069 Baby pacifiers, rubber

(G-11378)
TAG GLOBAL SYSTEMS LLC
575 Washington St Ste 1 (02359-2342)
PHONE..............................800 630-4708
EMP: 8 **EST:** 2019
SALES (est): 205.4K **Privately Held**
Web: www.tagglobalsystems.com
SIC: 3571 Electronic computers

(G-11379)
YANKEE TRADER SEAFOOD LTD
1610 Corporate Park (02359)
PHONE..............................781 829-4350
EMP: 12 EST: 1994
SQ FT: 8,800
SALES (est): 2.78MM Privately Held
Web: www.yankeetraderseafood.com
SIC: 2099　Food preparations, nec

Pepperell
Middlesex County

(G-11380)
ALCAMI CAROLINAS CORPORATION
27 Lomar Park (01463-1416)
PHONE..............................910 619-3952
EMP: 7
SALES (corp-wide): 418.48MM Privately Held
Web: www.alcami.com
SIC: 2834 8731 8734　Drugs affecting neoplasms and endrocrine systems; Biological research; Product testing laboratories
HQ: Alcami Carolinas Corporation
　　2320 Scientific Park Dr
　　Wilmington NC 28405

(G-11381)
ALCAMI CAROLINAS CORPORATION
10 Lomar Park Ste 4 (01463-1486)
PHONE..............................910 619-3952
EMP: 7
SALES (corp-wide): 418.48MM Privately Held
Web: www.alcami.com
SIC: 2834 8734 8731　Drugs affecting neoplasms and endrocrine systems; Product testing laboratories; Biological research
HQ: Alcami Carolinas Corporation
　　2320 Scientific Park Dr
　　Wilmington NC 28405

(G-11382)
ALCAMI CAROLINAS CORPORATION
20 Mill St (01463-1669)
PHONE..............................910 619-3952
EMP: 10
SALES (corp-wide): 418.48MM Privately Held
Web: www.alcami.com
SIC: 2834 8734 8731　Drugs affecting neoplasms and endrocrine systems; Product testing laboratories; Biological research
HQ: Alcami Carolinas Corporation
　　2320 Scientific Park Dr
　　Wilmington NC 28405

(G-11383)
ASTRON INC (PA)
Also Called: Circle Wire
21 Lomar Park (01463-1416)
PHONE..............................978 433-9500
David M Abbot, *Ch Bd*
Albert A Polmonari, *
Mark Mathews, *
John H Kellogg, *
EMP: 26 EST: 1906
SQ FT: 28,000
SALES (corp-wide): 6.03MM Privately Held

Web: www.astronstamping.com
SIC: 3469 3452　Stamping metal for the trade; Washers, metal

(G-11384)
HITEC PRODUCTS INC
4 Lomar Park (01463-1416)
PHONE..............................978 772-6963
Vincent P Wnuk, *Pr*
Stephen P Wnuk Junior, *Treas*
EMP: 14 EST: 1985
SALES (est): 2.2MM Privately Held
Web: www.hitecprod.com
SIC: 3829　Measuring and controlling devices, nec

(G-11385)
KEYSTONE PRECISION & ENGRG INC
16 Lomar Park Ste 3 (01463-1449)
PHONE..............................978 433-8484
Anthony Serino, *Pr*
Robert E Stanieich, *VP*
EMP: 20 EST: 1994
SQ FT: 6,300
SALES (est): 2.72MM Privately Held
Web: www.keystoneprec.com
SIC: 3599　Machine shop, jobbing and repair

(G-11386)
KEYSTONE PRECISION INC
16 Lomar Park Ste 3 (01463-1449)
PHONE..............................978 433-8484
Ronald V Long, *Pr*
Ethel Long, *Clerk*
EMP: 9 EST: 1984
SQ FT: 4,300
SALES (est): 2.42MM Privately Held
Web: www.keystoneprec.com
SIC: 3679　Electronic circuits

(G-11387)
PEPPERELL BRAIDING COMPANY INC (PA)
22 Lowell St (01463-1703)
P.O. Box 1487 (01463-3487)
PHONE..............................978 433-2133
William P Slivinski, *Pr*
Thomas J Murray Junior, *VP*
Sandra J Lavalley, *
◆ EMP: 30 EST: 1917
SQ FT: 18,500
SALES (est): 9.43MM
SALES (corp-wide): 9.43MM Privately Held
Web: www.pepperell.com
SIC: 3089 2241 2298　Extruded finished plastics products, nec; Narrow fabric mills; Cordage and twine

Petersham
Worcester County

(G-11388)
COBRA PRECISION MACHINING CORP
57 Birch Dr (01366-9607)
PHONE..............................603 434-8424
David Granquist, *Pr*
EMP: 7 EST: 2013
SALES (est): 833.59K Privately Held
SIC: 3491 3545 3469　Industrial valves; Machine tool accessories; Machine parts, stamped or pressed metal

Pittsfield
Berkshire County

(G-11389)
ADVANCE MACHINE & TOOL INC
50 Greenway St (01201-6604)
PHONE..............................413 499-4900
Michael Wasuk, *Pr*
Alan Pavoni, *VP*
EMP: 10 EST: 2003
SQ FT: 6,000
SALES (est): 989.73K Privately Held
Web: www.advancemachineandtool-inc.com
SIC: 3599　Machine shop, jobbing and repair

(G-11390)
APEX RESOURCE TECHNOLOGIES INC
Also Called: Inanycase
17 Downing Three Park Bldg 1 (01201-4169)
PHONE..............................413 442-1414
John Wolf, *CEO*
Rob Bonatakis, *
▲ EMP: 62 EST: 2002
SQ FT: 12,000
SALES (est): 12.11MM
SALES (corp-wide): 80.44MM Privately Held
Web: www.spectrumplastics.com
SIC: 3089　Injection molding of plastics
PA: Spectrum Plastics Group, Inc.
　　7309 W 27th St
　　Minneapolis MN 55426
　　952 929-3312

(G-11391)
B & G GLASS LLC
Also Called: Berkshire Plate Glass
35 1st St (01201-6211)
PHONE..............................413 442-3113
Harold Boland, *Managing Member*
EMP: 7 EST: 2012
SALES (est): 698.1K Privately Held
Web: www.berkshireplateglass.com
SIC: 1793 3211　Glass and glazing work; Flat glass

(G-11392)
BERKSHIRE CONCRETE CORP (HQ)
550 Cheshire Rd (01201-1823)
P.O. Box 1145 (01202-1145)
PHONE..............................413 443-4734
Perri C Petricca, *Pr*
Basil A Petricca, *
Robert Petricca, *
EMP: 50 EST: 1936
SQ FT: 2,000
SALES (est): 42.87MM
SALES (corp-wide): 143.21MM Privately Held
Web: www.berkshireconcreterepair.com
SIC: 3273 5211 1442　Ready-mixed concrete; Sand and gravel; Construction sand and gravel
PA: Petricca Industries, Inc.
　　550 Cheshire Rd
　　Pittsfield MA 01201
　　413 499-1441

(G-11393)
BERKSHIRE CUSTOM COATING INC
50 Downing Industrial Park (01201-3836)
PHONE..............................413 442-3757

Kevin Ploss, *Pr*
Lorraine Ploss, *Treas*
Doug Smith, *VP*
EMP: 31 EST: 1973
SQ FT: 15,000
SALES (est): 835.33K Privately Held
Web: www.berkshirecustomcoating.net
SIC: 3479　Coating of metals and formed products

(G-11394)
BERKSHIRE PRECISION TOOL LLC
9 Betnr Industrial Dr (01201-7899)
PHONE..............................413 499-3875
EMP: 68 EST: 2003
SALES (est): 9.69MM
SALES (corp-wide): 29.49MM Privately Held
SIC: 3545　Cutting tools for machine tools
PA: Harpoint Holdings, Inc.
　　200 Front St
　　Millersburg PA 17061
　　717 692-2113

(G-11395)
CAVALLERO PLASTICS INC
1250 North St (01201-1541)
PHONE..............................413 443-0925
▲ EMP: 80 EST: 1964
SALES (est): 15.42MM Privately Held
Web: www.cplas.com
SIC: 3089 3544　Injection molding of plastics; Special dies, tools, jigs, and fixtures

(G-11396)
CITY TIRE CO INC
560 Hubbard Ave (01201-3863)
PHONE..............................413 445-5578
Scott Casella, *Mgr*
EMP: 8
SALES (corp-wide): 23.19MM Privately Held
Web: www.city-tire.com
SIC: 5014 5531 7534　Truck tires and tubes; Automotive tires; Tire recapping
PA: City Tire Co., Inc.
　　25 Avocado St
　　Springfield MA 01104
　　413 737-1419

(G-11397)
GENERAL DYNMICS DEF SYSTEMS IN
100 Plastics Ave (01201-3632)
PHONE..............................413 494-1110
Nicholas D Chabraja, *Pr*
▲ EMP: 165 EST: 1996
SALES (est): 19.37MM
SALES (corp-wide): 42.27B Publicly Held
Web: www.gdmissionsystems.com
SIC: 3812 3795 3625　Search and detection systems and instruments; Tanks and tank components; Relays and industrial controls
PA: General Dynamics Corporation
　　11011 Sunset Hills Rd
　　Reston VA 20190
　　703 876-3000

(G-11398)
GENERAL DYNMICS MSSION SYSTEMS
100 Plastics Ave (01201-3632)
PHONE..............................413 494-1110
Gerald Wergland, *Mgr*
EMP: 746
SALES (corp-wide): 42.27B Publicly Held
Web: www.gdmissionsystems.com

SIC: **3669** 3812   Transportation signaling
devices; Search and navigation equipment
HQ: General Dynamics Mission Systems,
Inc.
12450 Fair Lakes Cir
Fairfax VA 22033
877 449-0600

(G-11399)
GRAPHIC IMPACT SIGNS INC
575 Dalton Ave (01201-2908)
PHONE...............................413 499-0382
John Renzi, *Pr*
Nancy Renzi, *
EMP: 30 **EST:** 1951
SQ FT: 17,600
SALES (est): 2.29MM **Privately Held**
Web: www.gisigns.com
SIC: **3993** 1799   Electric signs; Sign
installation and maintenance

(G-11400)
HALLOWELL ENGRG & MFG CORP
Also Called: Hallowell EMC
35 Downing Industrial Park (01201-3811)
PHONE...............................413 445-4263
W Stetson Hallowell, *Pr*
Donna Hallowell, *Clerk*
EMP: 9 **EST:** 1988
SALES (est): 1.23MM **Privately Held**
Web: www.hallowell.com
SIC: **3841**   Anesthesia apparatus

(G-11401)
HI-TECH MOLD & TOOL INC
1 Technology Dr W (01201-8222)
PHONE...............................413 443-9184
William Kristensen, *Pr*
▲ **EMP:** 120 **EST:** 1983
SQ FT: 72,000
SALES (est): 18.44MM **Privately Held**
Web: www.hitechmoldtool.com
SIC: **3089**   Injection molding of plastics

(G-11402)
INTERPRINT INC
101 Central Berkshire Blvd (01201-8511)
PHONE...............................413 443-4733
◆ **EMP:** 120 **EST:** 1983
SALES (est): 38.14MM **Privately Held**
Web: www.interprint.com
SIC: **2754**   Commercial printing, gravure
HQ: Interprint Gmbh
Westring 22
Arnsberg NW 59759
29329500

(G-11403)
JOHNS BUILDING SUPPLY CO INC
891 Crane Ave Ste 1 (01201-1764)
PHONE...............................413 442-7846
William Koziara, *Pr*
EMP: 10 **EST:** 1948
SQ FT: 5,000
SALES (est): 2.21MM **Privately Held**
Web: www.johnsbuildingsupply.com
SIC: **3271** 5211   Blocks, concrete or cinder:
standard; Masonry materials and supplies

(G-11404)
LAKEWOOD INDUSTRIES INC
Also Called: Lakewood Mold
40 Downing Industrial Park (01201-3806)
PHONE...............................413 499-3550
George F Rufo Junior, *Pr*
EMP: 19 **EST:** 1962
SQ FT: 25,000

SALES (est): 386.26K **Privately Held**
SIC: **3089** 3544   Injection molding of plastics
; Special dies, tools, jigs, and fixtures

(G-11405)
LAURIN PUBLISHING CO INC (PA)
Also Called: Photonics Media
100 West St (01201-5779)
P.O. Box 4949 (01202-4949)
PHONE...............................413 499-0514
Thomas F Laurin, *Pr*
Francis Laurin, *
Teddi C Laurin, *
Ralph Cianflone Junior, *Sec*
EMP: 65 **EST:** 1954
SQ FT: 20,000
SALES (est): 20.5MM
SALES (corp-wide): 20.5MM **Privately Held**
Web: www.photonicscorporateguide.com
SIC: **2721** 2741   Trade journals: publishing
only, not printed on site; Miscellaneous
publishing

(G-11406)
LENCO INDUSTRIES INC
Also Called: Lenco Armored Vehicles
10 Betnr Industrial Dr (01201-7831)
PHONE...............................413 443-7359
Leonard W Light, *Pr*
Diane M Light, *
◆ **EMP:** 60 **EST:** 1981
SQ FT: 65,000
SALES (est): 19.51MM **Privately Held**
Web: www.armoredtrucks.com
SIC: **3711**   Cars, armored, assembly of

(G-11407)
LTI SMART GLASS INC
Also Called: LTI Group
14 Federico Dr (01201-5518)
PHONE...............................413 637-5001
Jeff Besse, *Pr*
Jeffrey E Besse, *
John H Martino, *
▲ **EMP:** 100 **EST:** 2003
SQ FT: 100,000
SALES (est): 11.52MM **Privately Held**
Web: www.ltisg.com
SIC: **3211** 3231   Laminated glass; Products
of purchased glass

(G-11408)
MAGNUS MOLDING INC
1995 East St (01201-3850)
PHONE...............................413 443-1192
David Pedrotti, *Pr*
EMP: 26 **EST:** 1985
SQ FT: 20,000
SALES (est): 2.27MM
SALES (corp-wide): 9.44MM **Privately Held**
SIC: **3089** 3544   Injection molding of plastics
; Special dies, tools, jigs, and fixtures
PA: Modern Mold And Tool, Inc.
45 Downing Industrial Par
Pittsfield MA 01201
413 443-1192

(G-11409)
MARLAND MOLD INC
12 Betnr Industrial Dr (01201-7831)
PHONE...............................413 443-4481
EMP: 44
Web: www.marlandmold.com
SIC: **3089**   Injection molding of plastics

(G-11410)
MAX CUFF LLC
34 Churchill St (01201-1209)
P.O. Box 137 (01202-0137)
PHONE...............................413 553-3511
David Hall, *Managing Member*
EMP: 8 **EST:** 2010
SALES (est): 153.88K **Privately Held**
Web: www.maxcuff.com
SIC: **3429**   Handcuffs and leg irons

(G-11411)
MILLERS PETROLEUM SYSTEMS INC
875 Crane Ave (01201-1709)
PHONE...............................413 499-2134
Dennis Miller, *Pr*
EMP: 8 **EST:** 1971
SQ FT: 6,000
SALES (est): 892.86K **Privately Held**
Web: www.millerspetroleum.com
SIC: **3559** 1799   Petroleum refinery
equipment; Service station equipment
installation, maint., and repair

(G-11412)
MODERN MOLD AND TOOL INC (PA)
Also Called: Magnus Molding
45 Downing Industrial Park (01201-3812)
PHONE...............................413 443-1192
David J Pedrotti, *Pr*
John Ciullu, *
EMP: 25 **EST:** 1951
SALES (est): 9.44MM
SALES (corp-wide): 9.44MM **Privately Held**
Web: www.tonerplastics.com
SIC: **3089** 3544   Injection molding of plastics
; Special dies, tools, jigs, and fixtures

(G-11413)
MOLDMASTER ENGINEERING INC
187 Newell St (01201-5465)
P.O. Box 1161 (01202-1161)
PHONE...............................413 442-5793
Thomas F Kushi Junior, *Pr*
Timothy Kushi, *
Kevin B Kushi Clrk, *Sec*
EMP: 40 **EST:** 1945
SQ FT: 30,000
SALES (est): 4.91MM **Privately Held**
Web: www.moldmaster.com
SIC: **3089** 3544   Injection molding of plastics
; Dies, plastics forming

(G-11414)
NEW ENGLAND NEWSPAPERS INC (DH)
Also Called: Town Crier, The
75 S Church St Ste L1 (01201-6140)
PHONE...............................413 447-7311
EMP: 200 **EST:** 1995
SQ FT: 25,000
SALES (est): 70.64MM
SALES (corp-wide): 1.96B **Privately Held**
Web: www.berkshireeagle.com
SIC: **2711**   Newspapers, publishing and
printing
HQ: Medianews Group, Inc.
5990 Washington St
Denver CO 80216

(G-11415)
O W LANDERGREN INC
1500 W Housatonic St (01201-7500)
PHONE...............................413 442-5632
George A Goodrich, *Sec*

Arthur E Goodrich, *
Paul W Polidoro, *
Mark R Pratt, *
▲ **EMP:** 33 **EST:** 1956
SQ FT: 25,000
SALES (est): 2.46MM **Privately Held**
Web: www.owlandergren.com
SIC: **3469** 7692 3599 3441   Spinning metal
for the trade; Welding repair; Machine
shop, jobbing and repair; Fabricated
structural metal

(G-11416)
PEN RO MOLD AND TOOL INC
Also Called: Pen Ro Group
343 Pecks Rd Ste 5 (01201-1352)
PHONE...............................413 499-0464
Rick Arena, *Pr*
▲ **EMP:** 28 **EST:** 1966
SQ FT: 40,000
SALES (est): 2.37MM **Privately Held**
Web: www.pen-ro.com
SIC: **3544** 3089   Industrial molds; Injection
molding of plastics

(G-11417)
PERX LLC
25 Downing Three Park (01201-3881)
P.O. Box 285 (01227-0285)
PHONE...............................413 358-9020
John L Enright, *Pr*
Beverly Enright, *Treas*
EMP: 19 **EST:** 1974
SQ FT: 3,000
SALES (est): 4.88MM
SALES (corp-wide): 2.55MM **Privately Held**
Web: www.perx.com
SIC: **5048** 5995 5047 3851   Ophthalmic
goods; Optical goods stores; Medical and
hospital equipment; Ophthalmic goods
HQ: Essilor Laboratories Of America
Holding Co., Inc.
13555 N Stemmons Fwy
Dallas TX 75234
214 496-4141

(G-11418)
PETRICCA INDUSTRIES INC (PA)
Also Called: Unistress
550 Cheshire Rd (01201-1823)
P.O. Box 1145 (01202-1145)
PHONE...............................413 499-1441
Basil A Petricca, *Ch Bd*
Robert Petricca, *Ex VP*
Perri C Petricca, *Ex VP*
Thomas A Groff, *CFO*
Virginia Petricca, *Sec*
▲ **EMP:** 31 **EST:** 1973
SQ FT: 6,000
SALES (est): 143.21MM
SALES (corp-wide): 143.21MM **Privately Held**
Web: www.unistresscorp.com
SIC: **1611** 1623 3273 3272   General
contractor, highway and street construction;
Sewer line construction; Ready-mixed
concrete; Prestressed concrete products

(G-11419)
PITTSFIELD PLASTICS ENGRG LLC
Also Called: Precision Spools
1510 W Housatonic St (01201-7508)
P.O. Box 1246 (01202-1246)
PHONE...............................413 442-0067
Bruce Dixon, *CEO*
▲ **EMP:** 100 **EST:** 1968
SQ FT: 36,000
SALES (est): 19.28MM **Privately Held**

Web: www.pittsplas.com
SIC: 3089 3544 Injection molding of plastics
  ; Industrial molds

(G-11420)
PITTSFIELD RYE BAKERY INC
1010 South St (01201-8225)
P.O. Box 637 (01202-0637)
PHONE.............................413 443-9141
Arnold Robbins, *Pr*
Linda Robbins, *Sec*
Rick Robbins, *Treas*
EMP: 9 EST: 1937
SQ FT: 3,000
SALES (est): 1.7MM **Privately Held**
Web: www.pittsfieldrye.com
SIC: 2051 Bread, all types (white, wheat,
  rye, etc); fresh or frozen

(G-11421)
**QUALITY PRINTING COMPANY
INC**
3 Federico Dr (01201-5518)
P.O. Box 632 (01202-0632)
PHONE.............................413 442-4166
TOLL FREE: 800
John Di Santis, *Pr*
Robert King, *
Nicholas E Disantis, *
EMP: 51 EST: 1963
SQ FT: 20,000
SALES (est): 4.91MM **Privately Held**
Web: www.qualprint.com
SIC: 2752 Offset printing

(G-11422)
**SABIC INNOVATIVE PLAS US
LLC**
1240 Tyler St Extention (01201)
PHONE.............................413 448-7110
EMP: 258
Web: www.sabic.com
SIC: 2821 Plastics materials and resins
HQ: Sabic Innovative Plastics Us Llc
  2500 Citywest Blvd # 100
  Houston TX 77042

(G-11423)
SAMPCO INC (PA)
56 Downing Pkwy (01201-3882)
PHONE.............................413 442-4043
Michael O Ryan, *Pr*
▲ EMP: 125 EST: 1985
SQ FT: 40,000
SALES (est): 61.98MM **Privately Held**
Web: www.sampco.com
SIC: 2599 7389 Boards: planning, display,
  notice; Design, commercial and industrial

(G-11424)
STAR BASE TECHNOLOGIES INC
343 Pecks Rd (01201-1350)
PHONE.............................413 499-4005
EMP: 50 EST: 1988
SALES (est): 8.64MM **Privately Held**
Web: www.starbasetech.com
SIC: 3544 Industrial molds

(G-11425)
STUART ALLYN CO INC
17 Taconic Park Dr Ste 2 (01201-2682)
P.O. Box 2342 (01202-2342)
PHONE.............................413 443-7306
Stuart A Scace, *Pr*
Allyn Scace, *VP*
Marcia Scace, *Treas*
Peter Gerard, *Sec*
EMP: 7 EST: 1985
SQ FT: 4,000

SALES (est): 970.67K **Privately Held**
Web: www.stuartallyn.com
SIC: 3544 3089 Industrial molds; Injection
  molding of plastics

(G-11426)
UNISTRESS CORP
550 Cheshire Rd (01201-1823)
P.O. Box 1145 (01202-1145)
PHONE.............................413 499-1441
Perri C Petricca, *Pr*
Saul Shenkman, *
Ronald Deangelis, *
Beth Mitchell, *
Michael E Macdonald, *
▲ EMP: 300 EST: 1968
SQ FT: 90,000
SALES (est): 96.2MM
SALES (corp-wide): 143.21MM **Privately
Held**
Web: www.unistresscorp.com
SIC: 3272 Prestressed concrete products
PA: Petricca Industries, Inc.
  550 Cheshire Rd
  Pittsfield MA 01201
  413 499-1441

(G-11427)
WOHRLES FOODS INC (PA)
1619 East St (01201-3857)
P.O. Box 224 (01202-0224)
PHONE.............................413 442-1518
TOLL FREE: 800
Walter Pickwell, *Pr*
Jon Pickwell, *
Barbara Pickwell, *
Lynn Kessler, *
EMP: 35 EST: 1952
SQ FT: 25,000
SALES (est): 4.73MM
SALES (corp-wide): 4.73MM **Privately
Held**
Web: www.wohrlesonline.com
SIC: 2013 5147 5142 5141 Sausages and
  other prepared meats; Meats, fresh;
  Packaged frozen goods; Groceries, general
  line

Plainfield
Hampshire County

(G-11428)
BOOTSTRAP COMPOST INC
470 W Main St (01070-9734)
PHONE.............................617 642-1979
Andrew Brooks, *Prin*
EMP: 12 EST: 2013
SALES (est): 2.44MM **Privately Held**
Web: www.bootstrapcompost.com
SIC: 2875 Compost

Plainville
Norfolk County

(G-11429)
ATCO PLASTICS INC
31 W Bacon St (02762-2418)
PHONE.............................508 695-3573
Ralph P Schlenker, *Pr*
William F Machen, *
▲ EMP: 19 EST: 1955
SQ FT: 40,000
SALES (est): 413.35K **Privately Held**
Web: www.munroefoundation.com
SIC: 3089 3544 Injection molding of plastics
  ; Industrial molds

(G-11430)
**BUILDING ENVELOPE
SYSTEMS LLC**
Also Called: Team Bes
20 High St (02762-1000)
PHONE.............................508 381-0429
Brett Miller, *CEO*
EMP: 60 EST: 2011
SALES (est): 8.49MM **Privately Held**
Web: www.teambes.com
SIC: 3449 Bars, concrete reinforcing:
  fabricated steel

(G-11431)
DESCO ELECTRONICS INC
36 Bacon Sq (02762-2067)
PHONE.............................508 643-1950
Angela Frankudakis, *Pr*
George Hrabushi, *Marketing*
EMP: 20 EST: 1971
SQ FT: 7,100
SALES (est): 809.92K **Privately Held**
Web: www.descoelectronics.com
SIC: 3679 Harness assemblies, for
  electronic use: wire or cable

(G-11432)
ELECTRO-FIX INC
300 South St (02762-1529)
P.O. Box 1775 (02762-0775)
PHONE.............................508 695-0228
Thomas Kade, *Pr*
John Kade, *Treas*
Carl Costa, *Dir*
EMP: 22 EST: 1979
SQ FT: 20,000
SALES (est): 2.36MM **Privately Held**
Web: www.electro-fix.com
SIC: 3825 3829 Test equipment for
  electronic and electrical circuits; Measuring
  and controlling devices, nec

(G-11433)
**GASKIN MANUFACTURING
CORP**
Also Called: Swiss Technology New England
17 Cross St Unit 8 (02762-1531)
PHONE.............................508 695-8949
Shawn Gaskin, *CEO*
EMP: 13 EST: 2000
SALES (est): 1.42MM **Privately Held**
Web: www.swisstechnologiesne.com
SIC: 3599 Machine shop, jobbing and repair

(G-11434)
HMH RELIGIOUS MFG INC
11 Mirimichi St (02762-1710)
PHONE.............................508 699-9464
Alexis Dean, *Pr*
EMP: 7 EST: 2014
SALES (est): 362.41K **Privately Held**
Web: www.hmhreligious.com
SIC: 3999 Candles

(G-11435)
LAKESIDE MANAGEMENT CORP
3 Belcher St (02762-1303)
PHONE.............................508 695-3252
Gerard Lorusso, *Pr*
EMP: 7 EST: 2000
SALES (est): 299.44K **Privately Held**
Web: www.lakeside-management.com
SIC: 1442 Construction sand and gravel

(G-11436)
**LEWICKI & SONS EXCAVATING
INC**
15 Wilmarth Ln (02762-1116)

PHONE.............................508 695-0122
Stan Lewicki, *Pr*
EMP: 8 EST: 1993
SQ FT: 10,000
SALES (est): 994.05K **Privately Held**
Web: www.lewickiandsons.com
SIC: 3531 1542 Plows: construction,
  excavating, and grading; Nonresidential
  construction, nec

(G-11437)
LORUSSO CORP (PA)
320 South St (02762-1529)
PHONE.............................508 668-6520
Gerard C Lorusso, *Pr*
Henry Grill, *
▲ EMP: 50 EST: 1965
SALES (est): 21.46MM
SALES (corp-wide): 21.46MM **Privately
Held**
Web: www.lorussocorp.com
SIC: 2951 1442 3272 Asphalt and asphaltic
  paving mixtures (not from refineries);
  Construction sand mining; Concrete
  products, nec

(G-11438)
MI-BOX SOUTHERN MASS LLC
20 High St (02762-1000)
PHONE.............................774 719-7367
Brett M Miller, *Prin*
EMP: 8 EST: 2019
SALES (est): 541.53K **Privately Held**
Web: www.miboxsouthernmass.com
SIC: 2621 Paper mills

(G-11439)
MINI-SYSTEMS INC
Electronic Package Division
168 E Bacon St (02762-2107)
P.O. Box 1597 (02762-0597)
PHONE.............................508 695-2000
Robert Lemar, *Mgr*
EMP: 42
SALES (corp-wide): 21.88MM **Privately
Held**
Web: www.mini-systemsinc.com
SIC: 3231 3676 3825 3674 Products of
  purchased glass; Electronic resistors;
  Instruments to measure electricity;
  Semiconductors and related devices
PA: Mini-Systems, Inc.
  20 David Rd
  North Attleboro MA 02760
  508 695-1420

(G-11440)
MORSE READY MIX LLC
24 Cross St (02762-1402)
P.O. Box 2189 (02762-0296)
PHONE.............................508 809-4644
Ron Almeita, *Genl Mgr*
EMP: 35 EST: 2005
SALES (est): 3.81MM **Privately Held**
SIC: 3273 Ready-mixed concrete

(G-11441)
**NEW ENGLAND METALFORM
INC**
380 South St (02762-1529)
PHONE.............................508 695-9340
Herman Krobath, *Pr*
Robert Gagliardo, *
EMP: 36 EST: 1990
SQ FT: 16,500
SALES (est): 3.84MM **Privately Held**
Web: www.nemetalform.com
SIC: 3469 3444 Stamping metal for the trade
  ; Sheet metalwork

▲ = Import ▼ = Export
◆ = Import/Export

(G-11442)
SEMCO MACHINE CORP
Also Called: Semco
14 High St (02762-1114)
PHONE..................................508 384-8303
Fred F Holmes, *Pr*
Miriam Holmes, *
EMP: 24 EST: 1989
SALES (est): 2.47MM Privately Held
Web: www.camtrac.com
SIC: 3599 Machine shop, jobbing and repair

(G-11443)
**TITUS ENGRV &
STONESETTING INC**
Also Called: Ledor Jewelry
44 Washington St Unit 1 (02762-5111)
P.O. Box 2369 (02762-0299)
PHONE..................................508 695-6842
Dana L Titus, *Pr*
EMP: 14 EST: 1979
SALES (est): 433.43K Privately Held
Web: www.ledorjewelry.com
SIC: 3479 Engraving jewelry, silverware, or
metal

(G-11444)
TRIAD INC
44 Washington St (02762-5111)
PHONE..................................508 695-2247
Andrew P Harney, *Pr*
Shirley H Harney, *Treas*
Dana Titus, *VP*
EMP: 7 EST: 1969
SQ FT: 3,300
SALES (est): 231.9K Privately Held
Web: www.triadroyalfindings.com
SIC: 7692 3548 Welding repair; Welding
and cutting apparatus and accessories, nec

Plymouth
Plymouth County

(G-11445)
ALL AMERICAN SIGNS INC
Also Called: All American Signs Plus
15 Roberts Rd Ste G (02360-5069)
PHONE..................................508 830-0505
Eric Burke, *Pr*
Steven Holsberg, *Treas*
EMP: 10 EST: 1992
SQ FT: 3,200
SALES (est): 951K Privately Held
Web: www.allamericansignsplus.com
SIC: 7312 3993 Outdoor advertising services
; Signs and advertising specialties

(G-11446)
AMARELLO S MACHINING
8 Meadow Park Rd (02360-5085)
PHONE..................................508 746-8010
Steve Amarello, *Prin*
EMP: 7 EST: 2008
SALES (est): 186.5K Privately Held
SIC: 3599 Machine shop, jobbing and repair

(G-11447)
AUTOMATECH INC (PA)
138 Industrial Park Rd (02360-7243)
PHONE..................................508 830-0088
Tom Schiller, *Pr*
Tom Schiller, *Pr*
Henry Bacher, *Stockholder*
Jack Nedleman, *Stockholder*
EMP: 8 EST: 1994
SQ FT: 12,000
SALES (est): 4.96MM Privately Held
Web: www.automatech.com

SIC: 7372 7379 Prepackaged software;
Computer hardware requirements analysis

(G-11448)
AVWATCH INC
246 S Meadow Rd Ste 55 (02360)
PHONE..................................508 274-7937
Chris Kluckhuhn, *Pr*
EMP: 12 EST: 2008
SALES (est): 2.5MM
SALES (corp-wide): 182.79MM Privately
Held
Web: www.tsc.com
SIC: 3812 Search and navigation equipment
PA: Technology Service Corporation
251 18th St S Ste 705
Arlington VA 22202
703 251-6400

(G-11449)
BASCOM ENVIRONMENTAL CO
7 Pleasant Harbour Rd (02360-7117)
P.O. Box 240683 (02124-0012)
PHONE..................................617 282-9500
Troy Bascom, *Pr*
EMP: 45 EST: 2013
SALES (est): 1.6MM Privately Held
SIC: 1611 3292 1542 1721 General
contractor, highway and street construction;
Insulation, molded asbestos; School
building construction; Residential painting

(G-11450)
BAYONET OCEAN VEHICLES INC
10 Cordage Park Cir Ste 243 (02360-7318)
PHONE..................................802 434-6033
Ben Kinnaman, *CEO*
EMP: 10
SALES (est): 422.76K Privately Held
Web: www.greenseaiq.com
SIC: 3711 Amphibian motor vehicles,
assembly of

(G-11451)
BLADE TECH SYSTEMS INC
Also Called: Flexo Concepts
100 Armstrong Rd Ste 103 (02360-7219)
PHONE..................................508 830-9506
Kevin Mclaughlin, *Pr*
Maria Mclaughlin, *Sec*
▲ EMP: 7 EST: 1988
SQ FT: 5,000
SALES (est): 905.7K Privately Held
SIC: 3555 Printing trade parts and
attachments

(G-11452)
C S H INDUSTRIES INC
15 Appollo 11 Rd (02360-4877)
PHONE..................................508 747-1990
James A Hassan, *Pr*
EMP: 43 EST: 1973
SQ FT: 10,000
SALES (est): 1.01MM Privately Held
Web: www.cshindustries.com
SIC: 3444 Sheet metal specialties, not
stamped

(G-11453)
CAPEWAY WELDING INC
9 Appollo 11 Rd (02360-4866)
PHONE..................................508 747-6666
TOLL FREE: 800
Ronald Peck, *Pr*
Alice Peck, *Clerk*
Douglas Peck, *VP*
EMP: 10 EST: 1969
SQ FT: 16,000
SALES (est): 509.69K Privately Held

SIC: 7692 3599 Welding repair; Machine
shop, jobbing and repair

(G-11454)
CDF CORPORATION (PA)
77 Industrial Park Rd (02360-4868)
PHONE..................................508 747-5858
Joseph J Sullivan Senior, *Prin*
Joseph J Sullivan Senior, *Prin*
Joseph J Sullivan Junior, *Pr*
Marcia I Sullivan, *
Laura Beechwood, *
◆ EMP: 98 EST: 1973
SQ FT: 155,000
SALES (est): 46.34MM
SALES (corp-wide): 46.34MM Privately
Held
Web: www.cdf1.com
SIC: 3089 3081 2821 Plastics containers,
except foam; Unsupported plastics film and
sheet; Plastics materials and resins

(G-11455)
**COOL GEAR INTERNATIONAL
LLC (DH)**
36 Cordage Park Cir (02360-7320)
PHONE..................................508 830-3440
▲ EMP: 35 EST: 1985
SALES (est): 11.86MM
SALES (corp-wide): 2.84B Privately Held
Web: shop.coolgearinc.com
SIC: 3089 Tumblers, plastics
HQ: Igloo Products Corp.
777 Igloo Rd
Katy TX 77494
281 394-6800

(G-11456)
DIECAST CONNECTIONS CO INC
10 Cordage Park Cir Ste 222 (02360-7318)
PHONE..................................413 592-8444
Beth Zastawny, *Pr*
William Gillespie, *
William Douglas Gillespie, *
▲ EMP: 24 EST: 2004
SQ FT: 15,000
SALES (est): 1.1MM Privately Held
Web: www.diecastconnections.com
SIC: 3363 Aluminum die-castings

(G-11457)
**EASTERN INDUSTRIAL PDTS
INC**
3 Collins Ave (02360-4808)
P.O. Box 1150 (02359-1150)
PHONE..................................781 826-9511
Daniel Spurling, *Pr*
EMP: 18 EST: 1983
SALES (est): 2.48MM Privately Held
Web:
www.easternindustrialproducts.com
SIC: 3053 Gaskets; packing and sealing
devices

(G-11458)
**ELECTROPOLISHING SYSTEMS
INC**
24 Aldrin Rd (02360-4804)
PHONE..................................508 830-1717
Alan Ryalls, *Pr*
Jennifer Ryalls, *
EMP: 50 EST: 1995
SQ FT: 40,000
SALES (est): 4.42MM Privately Held
Web: www.electropolishingsystems.com
SIC: 3471 Electroplating of metals or
formed products

(G-11459)
EYE HEALTH SERVICES INC
Also Called: Eye Health Services
146 Industrial Park Rd # 2 (02360-7243)
PHONE..................................508 747-6425
Marti Erbe, *Brnch Mgr*
EMP: 46
SALES (corp-wide): 20.76MM Privately
Held
Web: www.eyehealthservices.com
SIC: 8011 5995 8042 3851 Opthalmologist;
Optical goods stores; Offices and clinics of
optometrists; Ophthalmic goods
PA: Eye Health Services, Inc.
1900 Crown Colony Dr # 301
Quincy MA 02169
617 472-5242

(G-11460)
G & G SILK SCREENING
187 Court St (02360-4004)
PHONE..................................508 830-1075
Joseph Gallant, *Owner*
EMP: 7 EST: 1985
SQ FT: 2,800
SALES (est): 446.75K Privately Held
Web: www.ggsilkscreen.com
SIC: 2759 2395 Screen printing; Emblems,
embroidered

(G-11461)
GATEHOUSE MEDIA MASS I INC
10 Cordage Park Cir Ste 240 (02360-7318)
PHONE..................................781 433-6917
EMP: 334
SALES (corp-wide): 2.95B Publicly Held
Web: www.ghmne.com
SIC: 2711 Commercial printing and
newspaper publishing combined
HQ: Gatehouse Media Massachusetts I, Inc.
48 Dunham Rd
Beverly MA 01915
585 598-0030

(G-11462)
GTC FALCON INC
130 Industrial Park Rd (02360-7243)
PHONE..................................508 746-0200
EMP: 10 EST: 1995
SQ FT: 5,200
SALES (est): 937.97K Privately Held
Web: www.gtcfalcon.com
SIC: 3829 Medical diagnostic systems,
nuclear

(G-11463)
K & J INTERIORS INC
Also Called: K&J Construction
4 Court St (02360-8328)
PHONE..................................508 830-0670
Kevin Craffey, *Pr*
EMP: 100 EST: 1989
SALES (est): 4.77MM Privately Held
SIC: 1742 1761 2431 2439 Drywall; Sheet
metal work, nec; Millwork; Structural wood
members, nec

(G-11464)
**MCGIRR GRAPHICS
INCORPORATED**
19 Richards Rd (02360-4871)
PHONE..................................508 747-6400
James Mcgirr, *Pr*
Graham Mcgirr, *VP*
Harriet J Mcgirr, *Treas*
EMP: 25 EST: 1980
SQ FT: 6,000
SALES (est): 4.59MM Privately Held
Web: www.cranberrygraphics.com

SIC: **2759** 2752 Commercial printing, nec; Offset printing

(G-11465)
METALPRO USA INC
21 Bettencourt Rd (02360-4290)
PHONE...................................508 942-9746
James M Primavera, *Owner*
EMP: 7 **EST:** 2009
SALES (est): 219.39K **Privately Held**
SIC: **3651** Household audio and video equipment

(G-11466)
MICROCUT INC
182 Standish Ave # 2 (02360-4162)
PHONE...................................781 582-8090
Joseph G Dennehy, *Pr*
▼ **EMP:** 7 **EST:** 2001
SALES (est): 949.5K **Privately Held**
Web: www.microcutusa.com
SIC: **3545** End mills

(G-11467)
MICROWAY INC
12 Richards Rd (02360-4846)
P.O. Box 79 (02364-0079)
PHONE...................................508 746-7341
EMP: 15 **EST:** 1982
SALES (est): 4.95MM **Privately Held**
Web: www.microway.com
SIC: **3571** 3577 Computers, digital, analog or hybrid; Computer peripheral equipment, nec

(G-11468)
MINUTEMAN PRINTING
Also Called: Minuteman Press
53 S Meadow Rd (02360-4768)
PHONE...................................508 830-3500
Donald Rust, *Prin*
EMP: 9 **EST:** 2009
SALES (est): 109.56K **Privately Held**
Web: www.minutemanpress.com
SIC: **2752** Commercial printing, lithographic

(G-11469)
NORTHICE
Also Called: North Taste
624 Long Pond Rd (02360-2612)
PHONE...................................781 985-5225
Jerry Levine, *VP*
EMP: 10 **EST:** 2004
SALES (est): 525.94K **Privately Held**
Web: www.northtaste.com
SIC: **2087** Flavoring extracts and syrups, nec

(G-11470)
OLIVERI & ASSOCIATES INC
22 Skipping Stone (02360-3575)
PHONE...................................781 320-9090
Patricia Oliveri, *Pr*
John Oliveri, *VP*
EMP: 7 **EST:** 1992
SALES (est): 891.59K **Privately Held**
Web: www.oliveriprinting.com
SIC: **8742** 2752 Industry specialist consultants; Commercial printing, lithographic

(G-11471)
PARTYLITE INC (HQ)
59 Armstrong Rd (02360-7206)
PHONE...................................203 661-1926
Harry Slatkin, *CEO*
Dan Chad, *
◆ **EMP:** 98 **EST:** 1977
SALES (est): 3.99B

SALES (corp-wide): 4.44B **Publicly Held**
Web: www.partylite.com
SIC: **2023** 3999 3641 5199 Dietary supplements, dairy and non-dairy based; Candles; Electric lamps; Candles
PA: The Carlyle Group Inc
1001 Pennsylvania Ave Nw 220s
Washington DC 20004
202 729-5626

(G-11472)
PILGRIM INNOVATIVE PLAS LLC
127 Industrial Park Rd (02360-7242)
PHONE...................................508 732-0297
Joel Nickerson, *Managing Member*
EMP: 12 **EST:** 1999
SQ FT: 16,400
SALES (est): 2.3MM **Privately Held**
Web: www.pipllc.com
SIC: **3089** Injection molded finished plastics products, nec

(G-11473)
PLYMTRON INDUSTRIES INC
9 Aldrin Rd (02360-4890)
PHONE...................................508 746-1126
Douglas Zimble, *Pr*
Susan Zimble, *Sec*
EMP: 16 **EST:** 1977
SQ FT: 20,000
SALES (est): 1.3MM **Privately Held**
SIC: **3451** Screw machine products

(G-11474)
RICHARDS MICRO-TOOL LLC
Also Called: Cutting Edge Technologies
250 Cherry St (02360-4876)
PHONE...................................508 746-6900
Eli Crotzer, *Pr*
EMP: 40 **EST:** 1961
SQ FT: 25,000
SALES (est): 9.83MM
SALES (corp-wide): 88.16MM **Privately Held**
Web: www.archcuttingtools.com
SIC: **3545** Cutting tools for machine tools
PA: Scp Agp Llc
2600 S Telg Rd Ste 180
Bloomfield Hills MI 48302

(G-11475)
RICHMOND SAND AND GRAVEL INC
70 Minuteman Ln (02360-2105)
PHONE...................................508 224-2231
Jeremiah Richmond, *Pr*
EMP: 7 **EST:** 2005
SALES (est): 938.37K **Privately Held**
Web: www.richmondinc.net
SIC: **1611** 1389 Gravel or dirt road construction; Excavating slush pits and cellars

(G-11476)
S & M FUELS INC
86 Sandwich St (02360-3334)
PHONE...................................508 746-1495
Sameh Kanan, *Prin*
EMP: 11 **EST:** 2015
SALES (est): 594.72K **Privately Held**
SIC: **2869** Fuels

(G-11477)
SEABURY SPLASH INC
10 Cordage Park Cir Ste 212 (02360-7318)
PHONE...................................508 830-3440
◆ **EMP:** 23 **EST:** 1986
SALES (est): 343.61K **Privately Held**

SIC: **3089** Plastics containers, except foam

(G-11478)
SMARTPAK EQUINE LLC (DH)
Also Called: Smartpak
40 Grissom Rd Ste 500 (02360-7251)
PHONE...................................774 773-1100
Paal C Gisholt, *Managing Member*
▲ **EMP:** 100 **EST:** 1999
SQ FT: 65,000
SALES (est): 98.69MM
SALES (corp-wide): 4.58B **Privately Held**
Web: www.smartpakequine.com
SIC: **2048** 5199 5999 Feed supplements; Pet supplies; Pet supplies
HQ: Covetrus North America, Llc
400 Metro Pl N Ste 100
Dublin OH 43017

(G-11479)
SUNCOR STAINLESS INC
70 Armstrong Rd (02360-4807)
PHONE...................................508 732-9191
◆ **EMP:** 80 **EST:** 1991
SALES (est): 22.68MM **Privately Held**
Web: www.suncorstainless.com
SIC: **3462** Iron and steel forgings

(G-11480)
T L EDWARDS INC
300 Cherry St (02360-7217)
PHONE...................................508 732-9148
Terry L Edwards, *Brnch Mgr*
EMP: 13
SALES (corp-wide): 15.1MM **Privately Held**
Web: www.tledwards.net
SIC: **1611** 2951 5032 Highway and street paving contractor; Asphalt and asphaltic paving mixtures (not from refineries); Gravel
PA: T. L. Edwards, Inc.
100 Wales Ave Rear
Avon MA 02322
508 583-2029

(G-11481)
TECH-ETCH INC (PA)
45 Aldrin Rd (02360-4886)
PHONE...................................508 747-0300
George E Keeler, *Pr*
Roy B Whittaker, *
Kiernan P Kearney, *
Richard P Balonis, *
Kevin J Feeney, *
EMP: 360 **EST:** 1964
SQ FT: 120,000
SALES (est): 91.21MM
SALES (corp-wide): 91.21MM **Privately Held**
Web: www.techetch.com
SIC: **3469** 3672 3479 Metal stampings, nec; Printed circuit boards; Etching and engraving

(G-11482)
TECHNOLOGY SERVICE CORPORATION
656 Burke's Way (02360)
PHONE...................................508 275-5113
EMP: 25
SALES (corp-wide): 182.79MM **Privately Held**
Web: www.tsc.com
SIC: **3769** Space vehicle equipment, nec
PA: Technology Service Corporation
251 18th St S Ste 705
Arlington VA 22202
703 251-6400

(G-11483)
TECHNOLOGY SERVICE CORPORATION
246 S Meadow Rd (02360-4790)
PHONE...................................508 275-5113
EMP: 51
SALES (corp-wide): 182.79MM **Privately Held**
Web: www.tsc.com
SIC: **3769** Space vehicle equipment, nec
PA: Technology Service Corporation
251 18th St S Ste 705
Arlington VA 22202
703 251-6400

Plympton
Plymouth County

(G-11484)
FIRST QUALITY METAL PDTS CORP
171 Palmer Rd Ste D (02367-1212)
PHONE...................................781 585-5820
Paul Goyett, *Pr*
EMP: 9 **EST:** 1985
SALES (est): 916.12K **Privately Held**
SIC: **3444** Sheet metalwork

(G-11485)
LITECONTROL CORPORATION
Also Called: Lite Control
65 Spring St (02367-1701)
PHONE...................................781 294-0100
Peter Lau, *Pr*
Katherine Lane, *
Johnathon Murphy, *
Johnathan Del Nero, *
▲ **EMP:** 205 **EST:** 1936
SQ FT: 180,000
SALES (est): 52.75MM
SALES (corp-wide): 1.6B **Privately Held**
Web: www.currentlighting.com
SIC: **3646** Fluorescent lighting fixtures, commercial
PA: Current Lighting Employeeco, Inc.
25825 Science Park Dr # 400
Beachwood OH 44122
216 462-4700

Pocasset
Barnstable County

(G-11486)
FALMOUTH SCIENTIFIC INC (PA)
Also Called: Manufacturer of Goods
33 Jonathan Bourne Dr (02559-1981)
P.O. Box 326 (02559-0326)
PHONE...................................508 564-7640
EMP: 12 **EST:** 1989
SALES (est): 2.56MM **Privately Held**
Web: www.falmouth.com
SIC: **3812** Search and navigation equipment

(G-11487)
GLOBAL INTERCONNECT INC (PA)
11 Jonathan Bourne Dr (02559-4917)
PHONE...................................508 563-6306
◆ **EMP:** 75 **EST:** 1995
SQ FT: 20,000
SALES (est): 14.42MM **Privately Held**
Web: www.globalinterconnect.com
SIC: **3678** 3679 Electronic connectors; Harness assemblies, for electronic use: wire or cable

▲ = Import ▼ = Export
◆ = Import/Export

(G-11488)
HYDROID LLC
1 Henry Dr (02559-1415)
PHONE..................................508 563-6565
EMP: 51 **EST:** 2001
SQ FT: 2,070
SALES (est): 2.42MM **Privately Held**
Web: www.hydroidinc.com
SIC: 3731 Submarine tenders, building and
repairing
HQ: Simrad North America, Inc.
19210 33rd Ave W Ste A
Lynnwood WA 98036

(G-11489)
IMAGE FACTORY
50 Portside Dr (02559-1928)
PHONE..................................508 295-3876
Nancy Sawyer, *Owner*
EMP: 9 **EST:** 2006
SALES (est): 733.98K **Privately Held**
SIC: 2389 2759 5137 5651 Apparel and
accessories, nec; Screen printing; Women's
and children's sportswear and swimsuits;
Family clothing stores

(G-11490)
PAINES PATIO INC
674 Macarthur Blvd (02559-2230)
PHONE..................................508 563-7557
EMP: 7 **EST:** 2011
SALES (est): 73.45K **Privately Held**
Web: www.painespatio.com
SIC: 2511 Wood household furniture

(G-11491)
**POCASSET MACHINE
CORPORATION**
7 Commerce Park Rd (02559-2298)
P.O. Box 3088 (02559-3088)
PHONE..................................508 563-5572
Barry M Kent, *Pr*
Christopher T Kent, *
Victoria J Kent, *
Donna Kent, *
▲ **EMP:** 29 **EST:** 1977
SALES (est): 3.44MM **Privately Held**
Web: www.pocassetmachine.com
SIC: 3469 3599 3061 Machine parts,
stamped or pressed metal; Machine shop,
jobbing and repair; Mechanical rubber
goods

(G-11492)
SHAW WOODWORKING INC
150 Highland Ave (02559)
PHONE..................................508 563-1242
James R Shaw, *Pr*
Vicki Shaw, *VP*
EMP: 7 **EST:** 1981
SQ FT: 3,500
SALES (est): 723.05K **Privately Held**
Web: www.shawwoodworking.com
SIC: 2431 Millwork

(G-11493)
**WIGGIN MEANS PRECAST CO
INC**
79 Barlows Landing Rd (02559-1914)
P.O. Box 1507 (02559-1507)
PHONE..................................508 564-6776
Mark Ricciardi, *Pr*
Brian Ricciardi, *Treas*
EMP: 8 **EST:** 2013
SALES (est): 911.67K **Privately Held**
Web: www.wigginprecast.com
SIC: 3272 Concrete products, precast, nec

(G-11494)
WIGGIN PRECAST CORP
79 Barlows Landing Rd (02559-1914)
P.O. Box 1138 (02559-1138)
PHONE..................................508 564-6776
Daniel Wiggin, *Pr*
EMP: 11 **EST:** 1983
SALES (est): 373.86K **Privately Held**
Web: www.wigginprecast.com
SIC: 3272 Concrete products, precast, nec

Princeton
Worcester County

(G-11495)
LAWRENCE SIGLER
Also Called: Sigler Machine Co
314 Ball Hill Rd (01541-1706)
PHONE..................................510 782-6737
Lawrence J Sigler, *Owner*
EMP: 8 **EST:** 1976
SQ FT: 7,500
SALES (est): 432.25K **Privately Held**
SIC: 3599 3553 3549 Machine shop,
jobbing and repair; Woodworking machinery
; Metalworking machinery, nec

Provincetown
Barnstable County

(G-11496)
PROVINCETOWN BANNER INC
167 Commercial St Ste 2 (02657-2144)
P.O. Box 977 (02657-0977)
PHONE..................................508 487-7400
EMP: 13 **EST:** 1995
SALES (est): 703.04K **Privately Held**
Web: www.wickedlocal.com
SIC: 7383 2711 News correspondents,
independent; Newspapers

(G-11497)
SHOP THERAPY IMPORTS
20 Province Rd (02657-1240)
PHONE..................................508 487-8970
Patti Tronolone, *Owner*
▲ **EMP:** 8 **EST:** 2007
SALES (est): 192.39K **Privately Held**
Web: www.shoptherapy.com
SIC: 2321 2331 2369 5137 Men's and boy's
furnishings; Women's and misses' blouses
and shirts; Girl's and children's outerwear,
nec; Women's and children's clothing

(G-11498)
STELLAR MENUS INC
14 Brewster St (02657-1631)
PHONE..................................617 882-2800
Steven Nicks, *CEO*
EMP: 8
SALES (est): 307.52K **Privately Held**
SIC: 7389 7372 Business Activities at Non-
Commercial Site; Prepackaged software

(G-11499)
TIN CAN ALLEY
269 Commercial St (02657-2201)
PHONE..................................508 487-1648
Larry Hendershot, *Prin*
EMP: 7 **EST:** 2014
SALES (est): 177.57K **Privately Held**
Web: www.tinpanalleytown.com
SIC: 3411 Tin cans

Quincy
Norfolk County

(G-11500)
**ACCELENET BY ITC A DIV
VIASAT**
1250 Hancock St Ste 701n (02169-4335)
PHONE..................................617 773-3369
Bill Sebastian, *Prin*
EMP: 7 **EST:** 2010
SALES (est): 99.66K **Privately Held**
SIC: 3669 Communications equipment, nec

(G-11501)
**ADVANCED MEDIA
CORPORATION**
159 Thomas Burgin Pkwy (02169-4213)
PHONE..................................800 844-0599
▼ **EMP:** 99
SIC: 2721 Magazines: publishing and
printing

(G-11502)
**AMERIDRIVES INTERNATIONAL
LLC**
14 Hayward St (02171-2416)
PHONE..................................617 689-6237
EMP: 17 **EST:** 2009
SALES (est): 1.97MM
SALES (corp-wide): 5.22B **Publicly Held**
SIC: 3568 Power transmission equipment,
nec
HQ: Altra Industrial Motion Corp.
300 Granite St Ste 201
Braintree MA 02184
781 917-0600

(G-11503)
**APPLIED IMAGE
RPROGRAPHICS INC (PA)**
Also Called: Air Graphics
82 Sagamore St (02171-1955)
PHONE..................................617 471-3373
TOLL FREE: 800
Michael Cully, *Pr*
Michael Cully, *Pr*
Kevin Cully, *
Kevin D O'neill, *Dir*
EMP: 19 **EST:** 1987
SQ FT: 7,000
SALES (est): 4.96MM
SALES (corp-wide): 4.96MM **Privately
Held**
Web: www.airgraphics.com
SIC: 2752 Offset printing

(G-11504)
**ATLANTIC AIR PRODUCTS MFG
LLC**
1266 Furnace Brook Pkwy Ste 300
(02169-4758)
PHONE..................................603 410-3900
EMP: 10 **EST:** 2000
SALES (est): 947.27K **Privately Held**
Web: www.atlanticairproducts.com
SIC: 3444 Sheet metal specialties, not
stamped

(G-11505)
**BAY STATE MILLING COMPANY
(PA)**
Also Called: Bay State Milling Co
100 Congress St (02169-0906)
PHONE..................................617 328-4400
Brian Rothwell, *Ch*
Bernard Rothwell Iii, *Ch*
Peter Levangie, *

Peter Banat, *
James Wilmes, *
◆ **EMP:** 40 **EST:** 1960
SQ FT: 35,000
SALES (est): 131.82MM
SALES (corp-wide): 131.82MM **Privately
Held**
Web: www.baystatemilling.com
SIC: 2041 Flour

(G-11506)
**BIOENERGY INTERNATIONAL
LLC**
Also Called: Myri
3 Batterymarch Park Ste 301 (02169-7500)
PHONE..................................617 657-5200
Stephen J Gatto, *Managing Member*
EMP: 10 **EST:** 2005
SALES (est): 783.5K **Privately Held**
Web: www.bioenergyinternational.com
SIC: 2865 Chemical indicators

(G-11507)
**BOSTON SCIENTIFIC
CORPORATION**
Also Called: Customer Fulfillment Center
500 Commander Shea Blvd (02171-1518)
PHONE..................................617 689-6000
Rick Barlow, *Mgr*
EMP: 285
SALES (corp-wide): 12.68B **Publicly Held**
Web: www.bostonscientific.com
SIC: 3841 Surgical and medical instruments
PA: Boston Scientific Corporation
300 Boston Scientific Way
Marlborough MA 01752
508 683-4000

(G-11508)
**BRIDGESTONE RET
OPERATIONS LLC**
Also Called: Firestone
2 School St (02169-6604)
PHONE..................................617 479-3208
Frank Evans, *Mgr*
EMP: 8
Web: www.bridgestoneamericas.com
SIC: 5531 7534 Automotive tires;
Rebuilding and retreading tires
HQ: Bridgestone Retail Operations, Llc
333 E Lake St Ste 300
Bloomingdale IL 60108
630 259-9000

(G-11509)
**DEPENDABLE CLEANERS INC
(PA)**
Also Called: Dependable Launderers & Clrs
320 Quincy Ave (02169-8108)
PHONE..................................617 770-9232
Christa F Hagearty, *Pr*
EMP: 15 **EST:** 1982
SQ FT: 10,000
SALES (est): 11.34MM
SALES (corp-wide): 11.34MM **Privately
Held**
Web: www.dependablecleaners.com
SIC: 7216 7211 2335 Cleaning and dyeing,
except rugs; Power laundries, family and
commercial; Dresses,paper, cut and sewn

(G-11510)
**DIAMOND HRSESHOE DEV
GROUP LLC**
1266 Furnace Brook Pkwy Ste 300
(02169-4758)
PHONE..................................617 755-6100
Leah Vazza, *Prin*
EMP: 7 **EST:** 2013

SALES (est): 325.8K **Privately Held**
SIC: 3462   Horseshoes

(G-11511)
DIVE TECHNOLOGIES INC
258 Willard St (02169-1530)
PHONE.............................339 236-4599
Brian Schimpf, *CEO*
EMP: 9 **EST:** 2018
SQ FT: 4,100
SALES (est): 2.55MM
SALES (corp-wide): 450.2MM **Privately Held**
SIC: 3731   Submersible marine robots, manned or unmanned
PA: Anduril Industries, Inc.
   1400 Anduril
   Costa Mesa CA 92626
   949 891-1607

(G-11512)
DRIGGIN SANDRA DBA EXTRA EXTRA
Also Called: Extra Extra Daily
21 Mayor Thomas J Mcgrath Hwy Ste 405 (02169-5351)
PHONE.............................617 773-6996
Sandra Driggin, *Owner*
EMP: 10 **EST:** 1993
SALES (est): 139.08K **Privately Held**
Web: www.giftaccents.com
SIC: 2711 2741   Newspapers, publishing and printing; Miscellaneous publishing

(G-11513)
EGLEAN INC
Also Called: Eglean.com
1266 Furnace Brook Pkwy (02169-4778)
PHONE.............................617 229-5863
Ray Deck, *Pr*
EMP: 8 **EST:** 2000
SALES (est): 574.08K **Privately Held**
SIC: 2741   Miscellaneous publishing

(G-11514)
EMD MILLIPORE CORPORATION
4 Batterymarch Park Ste 200 (02169-7468)
PHONE.............................800 637-7872
Udit Batra, *Pr*
EMP: 10 **EST:** 2013
SALES (est): 1.11MM **Privately Held**
SIC: 3826   Analytical instruments

(G-11515)
EMD SERONO BIOTECH CENTER INC
4 Batterymarch Park Ste 2 (02169-7468)
PHONE.............................978 294-1100
EMP: 21
SALES (corp-wide): 23.09B **Privately Held**
SIC: 2834   Pharmaceutical preparations
HQ: Emd Serono Biotech Center, Inc.
   1 Technology Pl
   Rockland MA 02370
   800 283-8088

(G-11516)
EXCEL TOOL & DIE CO INC
69 Sumner St (02169-7036)
PHONE.............................617 472-0473
Richard Wicklund, *Pr*
Alan Wicklund, *VP*
EMP: 8 **EST:** 1952
SQ FT: 12,000
SALES (est): 934.62K **Privately Held**
Web: www.exceltool-die.com
SIC: 3469   Stamping metal for the trade

(G-11517)
EYE HEALTH SERVICES INC (PA)
Also Called: Vitreo Retinal Consultants
1900 Crown Colony Dr Ste 301 (02169-0975)
PHONE.............................617 472-5242
Eric Johnson, *Pr*
Robert T Lacey, *
Paul J Watson, *
Admiral Steven Ockey, *Prin*
EMP: 25 **EST:** 1971
SQ FT: 5,000
SALES (est): 20.76MM
SALES (corp-wide): 20.76MM **Privately Held**
Web: www.eyehealthservices.com
SIC: 8011 5995 8042 3851   Opthalmologist; Optical goods stores; Offices and clinics of optometrists; Ophthalmic goods

(G-11518)
FEELEYS COMPANY INC
232 Water St 238 (02169-6539)
PHONE.............................617 773-1711
Stephen A Feeley, *Pr*
James J Feeley Junior, *Pr*
Stephen Feeley, *VP*
Marcia Feeley Dyment, *Clerk*
EMP: 7 **EST:** 1954
SQ FT: 40,000
SALES (est): 700.22K **Privately Held**
Web: www.masspowder.com
SIC: 3479   Coating of metals and formed products

(G-11519)
FNSJ INC
Also Called: Fastsigns
70 Quincy Ave (02169-6769)
PHONE.............................617 302-2882
Frank Meroney, *Pr*
Nicole Marie Meroney, *Dir*
EMP: 13 **EST:** 2015
SALES (est): 662.57K **Privately Held**
Web: www.fastsigns.com
SIC: 3993   Signs and advertising specialties

(G-11520)
FOXROCK GRANITE LLC
100 Newport Ave (02171)
PHONE.............................617 249-8015
Jason T Ward, *Prin*
EMP: 11 **EST:** 2015
SALES (est): 619.3K **Privately Held**
SIC: 3281   Granite, cut and shaped

(G-11521)
GALAXY SOFTWARE INC
200 Falls Blvd Unit B301 (02169-8186)
PHONE.............................617 773-7790
EMP: 7 **EST:** 1994
SALES (est): 465.03K **Privately Held**
Web: www.galaxysoftware.com
SIC: 7372   Application computer software

(G-11522)
GENERAL DYNMICS MSSION SYSTEMS
553 South St (02169-7318)
PHONE.............................617 715-7000
Chris Marzilli, *Pr*
▲ **EMP:** 99 **EST:** 1997
SQ FT: 9,600
SALES (est): 23.85MM
SALES (corp-wide): 39.41B **Publicly Held**
Web: www.gdmissionsystems.com
SIC: 3812   Search and navigation equipment

HQ: General Dynamics Mission Systems, Inc.
   12450 Fair Lakes Cir
   Fairfax VA 22033
   877 449-0600

(G-11523)
INTELLGENT CMPRESSION TECH INC
1250 Hancock St Ste 701n (02169-4335)
PHONE.............................617 773-3369
Michael Slygh, *Pr*
Bob Eastwood, *VP*
George Wilson, *CFO*
Peter Lepeska, *VP*
EMP: 25 **EST:** 1995
SALES (est): 2.42MM
SALES (corp-wide): 2.56B **Publicly Held**
Web: www.ictcompress.com
SIC: 7372   Business oriented computer software
PA: Viasat, Inc.
   6155 El Camino Real
   Carlsbad CA 92009
   760 476-2200

(G-11524)
INTELYCARE INC
Also Called: Intelycare
1250 Hancock St Ste 501n (02169-4486)
PHONE.............................617 971-8344
Ike Nnah, *Prin*
John Shagoury, *Pr*
EMP: 236 **EST:** 2015
SALES (est): 16.34MM **Privately Held**
Web: www.intelycare.com
SIC: 7372   Application computer software

(G-11525)
K IRWIN CONSTRUCTION INC
82 Grove St (02169-1127)
PHONE.............................617 481-2420
Patrick Irwin, *Prin*
EMP: 7 **EST:** 2016
SALES (est): 67.86K **Privately Held**
SIC: 2082   Malt beverages

(G-11526)
LANSEA SYSTTEMS INC
25 Fairmount Way (02169-1922)
PHONE.............................617 877-9773
Henry Dondero, *Pr*
EMP: 7 **EST:** 2015
SALES (est): 121.56K **Privately Held**
Web: www.lanseasystems.com
SIC: 3648   Lighting equipment, nec

(G-11527)
MAKING YOUR MARK INC
121 Liberty St (02169-7639)
PHONE.............................617 479-0999
John Delano, *Pr*
EMP: 7 **EST:** 1991
SQ FT: 4,000
SALES (est): 770.53K **Privately Held**
Web: www.myminc.com
SIC: 3953   Embossing seals and hand stamps

(G-11528)
MEDTHERAPY BIOTECHNOLOGY INC
1250 Hancock St Ste 803n (02169-4331)
PHONE.............................617 938-7082
Bikash Verma, *CEO*
EMP: 50 **EST:** 2018
SALES (est): 2.68MM **Privately Held**

SIC: 8731 2834   Biotechnical research, commercial; Pharmaceutical preparations

(G-11529)
NEW ENGLAND WORLDWIDE EXPORT
Also Called: Interior Design Center
247 Water St (02169-6533)
PHONE.............................617 472-0251
Khamis Sidahmed, *Owner*
EMP: 9 **EST:** 1977
SQ FT: 2,200
SALES (est): 650K **Privately Held**
Web: www.neupholsterysupply.com
SIC: 2211 5714   Upholstery fabrics, cotton; Upholstery materials

(G-11530)
PAUL H MURPHY & CO INC
634 Willard St (02169-7415)
PHONE.............................617 472-7707
Paul H Murphy Senior, *Pr*
EMP: 10 **EST:** 1982
SQ FT: 8,000
SALES (est): 1.17MM **Privately Held**
Web: www.phmurphyandcompany.com
SIC: 2759   Commercial printing, nec

(G-11531)
PRECISION WOODWORKING INC
50 Samoset Ave (02169-2324)
PHONE.............................617 479-7604
John G O'shea, *Prin*
EMP: 7 **EST:** 2008
SALES (est): 187.6K **Privately Held**
SIC: 2431   Millwork

(G-11532)
PRESIDENT PRESS INC
100 Columbia St (02169-7552)
PHONE.............................617 773-1235
John Eckblom, *Pr*
Bert Eckblom, *Sec*
EMP: 10 **EST:** 1934
SQ FT: 7,000
SALES (est): 798.62K **Privately Held**
SIC: 2752   Offset printing

(G-11533)
PUZZLE PIECES LLC
1266 Furnace Brook Pkwy Ste 308 (02169-4758)
PHONE.............................617 481-2304
Megan S Selchan, *Prin*
EMP: 20 **EST:** 2015
SALES (est): 481.41K **Privately Held**
Web: www.puzzlepiecesmass.com
SIC: 3944   Puzzles

(G-11534)
QUINCY ELECTRONICS CO INC
182 Washington St (02169-5508)
PHONE.............................617 471-7700
Peter Jahn, *Pr*
EMP: 7 **EST:** 1962
SQ FT: 5,000
SALES (est): 475.48K **Privately Held**
Web: www.quincyelectronics.com
SIC: 7699 3812 5088   Nautical and navigational instrument repair; Navigational systems and instruments; Navigation equipment and supplies

(G-11535)
QUINCY SUN PUBLISHING CO INC
Also Called: Quincy Sun
1372 Hancock St Ste 102 (02169-5190)
PHONE.............................617 471-3100

▲ = Import ▼ = Export
◆ = Import/Export

Henry W Bosworth Junior, *Pr*
Dorothy Bosworth, *Clerk*
EMP: 10 **EST:** 1968
SQ FT: 3,000
SALES (est) 554.99K **Privately Held**
Web: www.thequincysun.com
SIC: 2711 Newspapers, publishing and printing

(G-11536)
REGGIES OIL COMPANY INC
92-R Franklin St (02169-7825)
PHONE..............................617 471-2095
Joseph Reggiannini, *Pr*
EMP: 14 **EST:** 1950
SQ FT: 400
SALES (est): 2.39MM **Privately Held**
Web: www.reggiesoil.com
SIC: 5983 3494 Fuel oil dealers; Plumbing and heating valves

(G-11537)
RHEINWERK PUBLISHING INC
Also Called: Galileo Press, Inc.
2 Heritage Dr Ste 305 (02171-2165)
PHONE..............................781 228-5070
EMP: 10 **EST:** 2002
SALES (est): 1.54MM
SALES (corp-wide): 250.34MM **Privately Held**
Web: www.sap-press.com
SIC: 2741 Miscellaneous publishing
HQ: Rheinwerk Verlag Gmbh
Rheinwerkallee 4
Bonn NW 53227
228421500

(G-11538)
SAP PRESS
2 Heritage Dr (02171-2165)
PHONE..............................617 481-0448
EMP: 11 **EST:** 2018
SALES (est): 424.65K **Privately Held**
Web: www.sap-press.com
SIC: 2741 Miscellaneous publishing

(G-11539)
STEARNS PERRY & SMITH COMPANY
33 Fayette St Ste 1 (02171-2655)
PHONE..............................617 423-4775
Charles Smith, *Pr*
Ralph Young, *Treas*
Barbara Smith, *Prin*
Paul Smith, *Prin*
EMP: 9 **EST:** 1919
SQ FT: 8,000
SALES (est): 586.52K **Privately Held**
SIC: 7694 Electric motor repair

(G-11540)
STRAN & COMPANY INC (PA)
Also Called: Stran Promotional Solutions
2 Heritage Dr Ste 600 (02171-2168)
PHONE..............................617 822-6950
Andrew C Stranberg, *CEO*
Michael Gallugi, *
Andy J Shape, *
Randolph Birney, *
Robert Trevisani, *
◆ **EMP:** 30 **EST:** 1994
SQ FT: 20,000
SALES (est): 58.95MM
SALES (corp-wide): 58.95MM **Publicly Held**
Web: www.stran.com
SIC: 3999 Advertising display products

(G-11541)
TWIN RIVERS TECH HOLDINGS INC
Also Called: Twin Rivers Technologies U.S.
780 Washington St (02169-7333)
PHONE..............................617 472-9200
Scott Chatlin, *CEO*
EMP: 120 **EST:** 2007
SALES (est): 29.03MM **Privately Held**
Web: www.twinriverstechnologies.com
SIC: 2819 Chemicals, reagent grade: refined from technical grade
HQ: Fgv Holdings Berhad
Level 21 Wisma Fgv
Kuala Lumpur KLP 50350

(G-11542)
TWIN RIVERS TECH LTD PARTNR
Also Called: Twin Rivers Technologies
780 Washington St (02169-7333)
PHONE..............................617 472-9200
Paul Angelico, *Pr*
EMP: 118 **EST:** 2015
SALES (est): 54.23MM **Privately Held**
Web: www.twinriverstechnologies.com
SIC: 2869 Fatty acid esters, aminos, etc.

(G-11543)
TWIN RIVERS TECH MFG CORP
780 Washington St (02169-7333)
PHONE..............................888 929-8780
Dato M E Mavani Abdullah, *Dir*
EMP: 71 **EST:** 1998
SALES (est): 49.27MM **Privately Held**
Web: www.twinriverstechnologies.com
SIC: 2819 Ammonium compounds, except fertilizers, nec
HQ: Fgv Holdings Berhad
Level 21 Wisma Fgv
Kuala Lumpur KLP 50350

(G-11544)
TWIN RIVERS TECHNOLOGIES US INC
Also Called: Twin Rivers Technologies Mfg
780 Washington St (02169-7356)
PHONE..............................617 472-9200
◆ **EMP:** 170
SIC: 2819 Chemicals, reagent grade: refined from technical grade

(G-11545)
WINTER & COMPANY INC
Also Called: Inkspot, The
40 Oval Rd (02170-3813)
PHONE..............................617 773-7605
EMP: 15 **EST:** 2003
SALES (est): 716.8K **Privately Held**
SIC: 7336 2759 7331 Commercial art and graphic design; Commercial printing, nec; Mailing service

Randolph
Norfolk County

(G-11546)
ACCURATE METAL FINISHING LLC
414 South St (02368-5338)
PHONE..............................781 963-7300
Allyn Ryalls Iii, *Pr*
Donna J Derringer, *
EMP: 30 **EST:** 1967
SQ FT: 22,000
SALES (est): 2.62MM **Privately Held**
Web: www.accuratemetalfinishing.com

SIC: 3471 Electroplating of metals or formed products

(G-11547)
ALLOY FABRICATORS NENG INC
39 York Ave (02368-1891)
PHONE..............................781 986-6400
Christian G Dietz, *Pr*
Royal C Mulkern, *Sec*
▼ **EMP:** 14 **EST:** 1973
SQ FT: 15,000
SALES (est): 2.15MM **Privately Held**
Web: www.alloyfabne.com
SIC: 3443 3499 Weldments; Aerosol valves, metal

(G-11548)
AMERICAN RETAIL SVC INC
39 Teed Dr (02368-4201)
PHONE..............................781 885-7369
Candy Rankin, *Owner*
EMP: 8 **EST:** 2018
SALES (est): 77.45K **Privately Held**
Web: www.icssvcs.com
SIC: 3069 Fabricated rubber products, nec

(G-11549)
AUDIOSPECTRUM INC
Also Called: Audio Spectrum
50 Mazzeo Dr (02368-3402)
PHONE..............................781 767-1331
EMP: 22 **EST:** 1994
SALES (est): 4.87MM **Privately Held**
Web: www.audiospectrum.com
SIC: 5961 7389 3999 7359 Record and/or tape (music or video) club, mail order; Promoters of shows and exhibitions; Stage hardware and equipment, except lighting; Sound and lighting equipment rental

(G-11550)
BEW CORP
280 Pond St (02368-2668)
PHONE..............................781 963-0315
Hillary Librot, *Pr*
Michael Figuerado, *Prin*
Doug Allen, *Prin*
Penny Debassio, *Prin*
EMP: 10 **EST:** 1988
SQ FT: 15,000
SALES (est): 791.86K **Privately Held**
Web: www.eliteenvelope.com
SIC: 7389 2752 Printing broker; Commercial printing, lithographic

(G-11551)
BFS PHARMA INC
78 Pacella Park Dr 80 (02368-1757)
PHONE..............................781 767-2020
◆ **EMP:** 15
SIC: 2834 Pharmaceutical preparations

(G-11552)
BREWSTER WALLPAPER LLC
Also Called: Brewster Home Fashions
67 Pacella Park Dr (02368-1755)
PHONE..............................800 366-1700
EMP: 93 **EST:** 2017
SALES (est): 10.96MM
SALES (corp-wide): 26.75MM **Privately Held**
Web: www.brewsterwallcovering.com
SIC: 2679 Wallpaper
PA: 288 Holdings Corporation
67 Pacella Park Dr
Randolph MA 02368
781 963-4800

(G-11553)
CAMBRIDGEPORT
21 Pacella Park Dr (02368-1755)
PHONE..............................781 302-3347
Filip Silipov, *Prin*
EMP: 12 **EST:** 2011
SALES (est): 5.61MM **Privately Held**
Web: www.cambridgeport.net
SIC: 3444 Sheet metalwork

(G-11554)
CURRYS LEATHER SHOP INC
Also Called: Curry's Leather Products
314 High St (02368-1634)
PHONE..............................781 963-0679
Robert Curry, *Pr*
▲ **EMP:** 7 **EST:** 1946
SALES (est): 258.17K **Privately Held**
Web: www.currysleather.com
SIC: 3161 3999 3172 3199 Satchels; Identification tags, except paper; Watch straps, except metal; Holsters, leather

(G-11555)
ECONOCORP INC
72 Pacella Park Dr (02368-1791)
PHONE..............................781 986-7500
Wayne Goldberg, *Pr*
Mark Jacobson, *
Fred Grein, *
◆ **EMP:** 50 **EST:** 1955
SQ FT: 20,000
SALES (est): 16.86MM **Privately Held**
Web: www.econocorp.com
SIC: 3565 Carton packing machines

(G-11556)
ELITE ENVELOPE & GRAPHICS INC
Also Called: Elite Envelope
280 Pond St (02368-2668)
PHONE..............................781 961-1800
David Theriault, *Pr*
Gerard Velona, *Ex VP*
Jerry Velona, *Ex VP*
EMP: 17 **EST:** 2003
SQ FT: 17,000
SALES (est): 2.59MM **Privately Held**
Web: www.eliteenvelope.com
SIC: 7336 2759 Commercial art and graphic design; Commercial printing, nec

(G-11557)
FLEXCON INDUSTRIES INC
300 Pond St (02368-2661)
P.O. Box 782 (02368-0782)
PHONE..............................781 986-2424
George L Simas Junior, *Prin*
George L Simas, *
Thomas J Swan Iii, *Prin*
Joseph E Swan, *Pr*
George Simas, *
◆ **EMP:** 125 **EST:** 1987
SQ FT: 150,000
SALES (est): 45.27MM **Privately Held**
Web: www.flexconind.com
SIC: 3443 Tanks, standard or custom fabricated: metal plate

(G-11558)
FOWLER PRINTING & GRAPHICS INC
Also Called: Fowler Printing and Graphics
132 York Ave (02368-1845)
PHONE..............................781 986-8900
Joanne Brennan, *Pr*
EMP: 14 **EST:** 1963
SQ FT: 16,000
SALES (est): 2.33MM **Privately Held**

GEOGRAPHIC

Web: www.fowlerprinting.com
SIC: 2752 Offset printing

(G-11559)
FRANK I ROUNDS COMPANY (PA)
65 York Ave (02368-1827)
PHONE.............................401 333-5014
W S Ehrenzeller Junior, *Pt*
Deborah Armstead, *Pt*
EMP: 30 **EST:** 1936
SQ FT: 10,000
SALES (est): 24.74MM
SALES (corp-wide): 24.74MM **Privately Held**
Web: www.frankirounds.com
SIC: 5074 3443 5084 Heating equipment (hydronic); Boiler shop products: boilers, smokestacks, steel tanks; Industrial machinery and equipment

(G-11560)
GATEHOUSE MEDIA MASS I INC
Also Called: Wellesley Townsman
15 Pacella Park Dr (02368-1780)
PHONE.............................781 235-4000
Cathy Brauner, *Mgr*
EMP: 125
SALES (corp-wide): 2.95B **Publicly Held**
Web: www.wickedlocal.com
SIC: 2711 Newspapers, publishing and printing
HQ: Gatehouse Media Massachusetts I, Inc.
48 Dunham Rd
Beverly MA 01915
585 598-0030

(G-11561)
GORDON INDUSTRIES INC (PA)
Also Called: Amramp
358 North St (02368-4171)
PHONE.............................857 401-8398
Julian Gordon, *Pr*
EMP: 49 **EST:** 1998
SALES (est): 12.2MM
SALES (corp-wide): 12.2MM **Privately Held**
Web: www.amramp.com
SIC: 3448 6794 Ramps, prefabricated metal ; Franchises, selling or licensing

(G-11562)
HOLBROOK SUN INC
15 Pacella Park Dr # 200 (02368-1780)
PHONE.............................781 767-4000
Greg Rush, *CEO*
Cathy Conley, *Prin*
EMP: 8 **EST:** 1994
SALES (est): 116.14K **Privately Held**
SIC: 2711 Newspapers, publishing and printing

(G-11563)
HORIZON VERT PURE LLC
51 Teed Dr (02368-4201)
P.O. Box 320261 (02132-0003)
PHONE.............................857 236-0904
Maly Sebastien, *Prin*
EMP: 12 **EST:** 2016
SALES (est): 1.45MM **Privately Held**
SIC: 2044 Rice milling

(G-11564)
HORLICK COMPANY INC
91 Pacella Park Dr (02368-1755)
PHONE.............................781 963-0090
William A Nesbitt, *Pr*
Shawn D Hennessey, *VP*
▲ **EMP:** 8 **EST:** 1992
SQ FT: 23,500

SALES (est): 5.08MM
SALES (corp-wide): 5.08MM **Privately Held**
Web: www.horlick.com
SIC: 3621 3625 Motor generator sets; Relays and industrial controls
PA: J E S Inc
4562 Wynn Rd Unit Main
Bellingham WA 98226
360 734-1910

(G-11565)
HYTEX INDUSTRIES INC
Also Called: Hytex Decorative Textiles
67 Pacella Park Dr (02368-1755)
PHONE.............................781 963-4400
Jeremiah J Mcquillen, *Pr*
Alan N Horwitz, *Dir*
Rick Rigazio, *VP Sls*
Veronica Muarray, *Sec*
Joseph H Matzkin, *Sec*
▲ **EMP:** 21 **EST:** 1959
SALES (est): 4.86MM **Privately Held**
Web: www.hytex.com
SIC: 3081 3089 3069 Floor or wall covering, unsupported plastics; Plastics containers, except foam; Medical and laboratory rubber sundries and related products

(G-11566)
INTERFACE ENGINEERING CORP
51 N Main St Ste 1 (02368-4636)
PHONE.............................781 986-2600
Deborah Scanlon, *CEO*
Thomas Scanlon, *Pr*
EMP: 14 **EST:** 1970
SQ FT: 1,400
SALES (est): 162.38K **Privately Held**
SIC: 3674 3679 Modules, solid state; Electronic circuits

(G-11567)
ISTAR PUBLISHING LLC
21 Grove Sq (02368-4027)
PHONE.............................781 885-7724
Maksim Karolinskiy, *Prin*
EMP: 8 **EST:** 2010
SALES (est): 93.1K **Privately Held**
SIC: 2741 Miscellaneous publishing

(G-11568)
MELVILLE CANDY CORPORATION
Also Called: Melville Old Time Candy & Pdts
28 York Ave (02368-1828)
PHONE.............................800 638-8063
Gary Newcomb Melville, *Pr*
Joseph Melville, *Sec*
EMP: 22 **EST:** 1980
SQ FT: 4,000
SALES (est): 9.41MM **Privately Held**
Web: www.melvillecandy.com
SIC: 2064 Candy and other confectionery products

(G-11569)
MYGRANT GLASS COMPANY INC
196 High St (02368-2306)
PHONE.............................781 767-3289
EMP: 13
SALES (corp-wide): 168.98MM **Privately Held**
Web: www.mygrantglass.com
SIC: 5039 3211 Glass construction materials ; Flat glass
PA: Mygrant Glass Company, Inc.
3271 Arden Rd

Hayward CA 94545
510 785-4360

(G-11570)
NEW-COM METAL PDTS GROUP LLC
40c Teed Dr (02368-4225)
PHONE.............................781 767-7520
Seth Rogers, *Pr*
William Puleo, *Pr*
Anthony Puleo, *Sec*
EMP: 20 **EST:** 2008
SQ FT: 21,000
SALES (est): 4.53MM **Privately Held**
Web: www.newcommetal.com
SIC: 3444 Sheet metalwork

(G-11571)
PEARL MEAT PACKING CO INC
27 York Ave (02368-1827)
PHONE.............................781 228-5100
EMP: 42 **EST:** 1944
SALES (est): 4.44MM **Privately Held**
Web: www.pearlmeat.com
SIC: 2013 2011 Sausages and other prepared meats; Meat packing plants

(G-11572)
PROMOUNDS INC (PA)
Also Called: On Deck Sports
15 Pacella Park Dr Ste 240 (02368-1700)
PHONE.............................508 580-6171
Joseph T Murphy, *Pr*
▲ **EMP:** 41 **EST:** 2001
SALES (est): 10.75MM
SALES (corp-wide): 10.75MM **Privately Held**
Web: www.promounds.com
SIC: 3949 Baseball equipment and supplies, general

(G-11573)
RANDOLPH ENGINEERING INC
Also Called: Randolph Sunglasses
26 Thomas Patten Dr (02368-3902)
PHONE.............................781 961-6070
Peter M Waszkiewicz, *CEO*
Richard Waszkiewicz, *
Stanislaw J Zaleski, *
Richard Zaleski, *
▲ **EMP:** 40 **EST:** 1973
SQ FT: 22,000
SALES (est): 9.3MM **Privately Held**
Web: www.randolphusa.com
SIC: 3851 Frames and parts, eyeglass and spectacle

(G-11574)
SAVIN PRODUCTS COMPANY INC
214 High St (02368-1837)
P.O. Box 323 (02368-0323)
PHONE.............................781 961-2743
Margaret Ambrosia, *Pr*
EMP: 22 **EST:** 1921
SQ FT: 10,000
SALES (est): 952.16K **Privately Held**
Web: www.savinproducts.com
SIC: 2842 5169 Cleaning or polishing preparations, nec; Chemicals and allied products, nec

(G-11575)
STACYS PITA CHIP COMPANY INC
1 Posturepedic Dr (02368-4323)
PHONE.............................781 961-2800
◆ **EMP:** 100 **EST:** 1997
SQ FT: 17,500

SALES (est): 18.29MM
SALES (corp-wide): 86.39B **Publicly Held**
SIC: 2096 Potato chips and similar snacks
PA: Pepsico, Inc.
700 Anderson Hill Rd
Purchase NY 10577
914 253-2000

(G-11576)
TALLY TRANSPORTATION LLC
45 North St (02368-4614)
PHONE.............................781 510-2411
EMP: 20 **EST:** 2015
SALES (est): 1.91MM **Privately Held**
Web: www.tallytransportation.com
SIC: 4789 3537 Transportation services, nec ; Trucks, tractors, loaders, carriers, and similar equipment

(G-11577)
TRELLEBORG OFFSHORE BOSTON INC (HQ)
Also Called: Trelleborg Applied Tech
24 Teed Dr (02368-4202)
PHONE.............................781 437-1171
▲ **EMP:** 30 **EST:** 1995
SALES (est): 26.4MM
SALES (corp-wide): 4.26B **Privately Held**
SIC: 2819 3086 Industrial inorganic chemicals, nec; Insulation or cushioning material, foamed plastics
PA: Trelleborg Ab
Johan Kocksgatan 10
Trelleborg 231 4
410670000

(G-11578)
VENT-RITE VALVE CORP (PA)
Also Called: Skidmore Co
300 Pond St (02368-2661)
P.O. Box 783 (02368-0783)
PHONE.............................781 986-2000
Thomas J Swan Junior, *Pr*
Joseph Swan, *
Michael Kennedy, *
▲ **EMP:** 40 **EST:** 1984
SQ FT: 200
SALES (est): 9.59MM
SALES (corp-wide): 9.59MM **Privately Held**
Web: www.emersonswan.com
SIC: 3443 3491 Boiler and boiler shop work; Industrial valves

(G-11579)
WICKED LOCAL
15 Pacella Park Dr (02368-1780)
PHONE.............................781 433-6905
EMP: 9 **EST:** 2019
SALES (est): 492.88K **Privately Held**
Web: www.wickedlocal.com
SIC: 2741 Miscellaneous publishing

(G-11580)
ZIPRINT CENTERS INC
217 N Main St (02368-4635)
PHONE.............................781 963-2250
Scott G Roberts, *Pr*
EMP: 7 **EST:** 1981
SQ FT: 1,800
SALES (est): 785.59K **Privately Held**
Web: www.ziprintcenters.com
SIC: 2752 Offset printing

Raynham
Bristol County

(G-11581)
ARTS INTERNATIONAL WHOLESALE
104 Forge River Pkwy (02767-1465)
PHONE..............................508 822-7181
Arthur Cabral, *Owner*
EMP: 8 **EST:** 2004
SQ FT: 9,980
SALES (est): 429.97K **Privately Held**
Web: www.artsinternationalbakery.com
SIC: 2051 Bread, cake, and related products

(G-11582)
C H BABB CO INC
Also Called: Babbco
445 Paramount Dr (02767-5178)
PHONE..............................508 977-0600
Foran William C, *Pr*
Charles Foran, *
▲ **EMP:** 40 **EST:** 1918
SQ FT: 75,000
SALES (est): 14.59MM **Privately Held**
Web: www.tunnelovens.com
SIC: 3556 Bakery machinery

(G-11583)
CERENOVUS INC
Also Called: Cerenovus, Inc
325 Paramount Dr (02767-5199)
PHONE..............................908 704-4024
EMP: 72
SALES (corp-wide): 94.94B **Publicly Held**
SIC: 3841 Surgical and medical instruments
HQ: Cerenovus, Inc.
   6303 Wtrford Dst Dr Ste 3
   Miami FL 33126

(G-11584)
COMPLETE ENERGY SERVICES CORP
407 South St E Ste A2 (02767-5432)
PHONE..............................833 237-2677
Michael Duffy, *Pr*
Michael D Duffy, *Pr*
Brian Munro, *Sec*
Kevin Munro, *Treas*
EMP: 19 **EST:** 2018
SQ FT: 1,200
SALES (est): 1.1MM **Privately Held**
Web: www.cescorp.com
SIC: 8748 5211 3625 1731 Energy conservation consultant; Insulation and energy conservation products; Electric controls and control accessories, industrial; Lighting contractor

(G-11585)
CONSTRUCTION SOURCE MGT LLC
Also Called: Csourceauto
33 Commercial St (02767-5360)
PHONE..............................508 484-5100
John C Kelly, *Managing Member*
EMP: 19 **EST:** 2014
SALES (est): 12.63MM **Privately Held**
Web: www.constructionsource.com
SIC: 1442 Construction sand and gravel

(G-11586)
DEPUY MITEK LLC
325 Paramount Dr (02767-5199)
PHONE..............................508 880-8100
Ian Lawson, *Pr*
Gregory Maloblocki, *

▲ **EMP:** 398 **EST:** 1991
SALES (est): 85.13MM
SALES (corp-wide): 94.94B **Publicly Held**
SIC: 3841 Surgical and medical instruments
PA: Johnson & Johnson
   1 Johnson And Johnson Plz
   New Brunswick NJ 08933
   732 524-0400

(G-11587)
DEPUY SPINE LLC (HQ)
325 Paramount Dr (02767-5199)
PHONE..............................508 880-8100
Max M Reinhardt, *Pr*
Gregory Maloblocki, *Dir*
Lisa Woodruff, *GOVERNMENT CHANNEL*
▲ **EMP:** 350 **EST:** 1983
SQ FT: 280,000
SALES (est): 213.52MM
SALES (corp-wide): 94.94B **Publicly Held**
SIC: 3842 Implants, surgical
PA: Johnson & Johnson
   1 Johnson And Johnson Plz
   New Brunswick NJ 08933
   732 524-0400

(G-11588)
DEPUY SYNTHES PRODUCTS INC (DH)
Also Called: Cerenovus
325 Paramount Dr (02767-5199)
PHONE..............................508 880-8100
Martin Fitchett, *Pr*
EMP: 18 **EST:** 2013
SALES (est): 56.63MM
SALES (corp-wide): 94.94B **Publicly Held**
SIC: 3841 Surgical and medical instruments
HQ: Depuy Spine, Llc
   325 Paramount Dr
   Raynham MA 02767
   508 880-8100

(G-11589)
ELECTROCHEM SOLUTIONS INC
670 Paramount Dr (02767-5411)
PHONE..............................781 575-0800
Peter Hunkeler, *Mgr*
EMP: 120
SALES (corp-wide): 1.38B **Publicly Held**
Web: www.electrochemsolutions.com
SIC: 3692 5063 5065 Primary batteries, dry and wet; Power transmission equipment, electric; Electronic parts and equipment, nec
HQ: Electrochem Solutions, Inc.
   10000 Wehrle Dr
   Clarence NY 14031

(G-11590)
MAJESTIC MEDICAL INC
44 Commercial St Ste 2 (02767-1306)
PHONE..............................508 824-1944
Norman J Le Maire Iii, *Pr*
EMP: 11 **EST:** 1995
SALES (est): 394.25K **Privately Held**
Web: www.majesticmedical.com
SIC: 3841 7699 Surgical and medical instruments; Surgical instrument repair

(G-11591)
MEDICAL DEVICE BUS SVCS INC
Also Called: Johnson & Johnson
325 Paramount Dr (02767-5199)
PHONE..............................508 880-8100
David Hable, *Brnch Mgr*
EMP: 20
SALES (corp-wide): 94.94B **Publicly Held**
SIC: 3841 Surgical and medical instruments
HQ: Medical Device Business Services, Inc.
   700 Orthopaedic Dr

Warsaw IN 46582

(G-11592)
MEDROBOTICS CORPORATION
475 Paramount Dr (02767-5178)
PHONE..............................508 692-6460
Samuel F Straface, *Pr*
David S Smith, *
Mark A Peters, *CDO**
Kevin P Gilmartin, *
Michael W Gallagher, *
EMP: 32 **EST:** 2010
SALES (est): 4.81MM **Privately Held**
Web: www.medrobotics.com
SIC: 3841 Surgical and medical instruments

(G-11593)
MEGA NA INC
175 Paramount Dr (02767-1065)
PHONE..............................781 784-7684
Lucio De Risi, *CEO*
Daniel Hebda, *
Frank Bernieri, *
Sebastien Rey, *
EMP: 38 **EST:** 2002
SQ FT: 3,422
SALES (est): 9.3MM **Privately Held**
Web: www.mega.com
SIC: 7372 Business oriented computer software
PA: Mega International Srl
   Via Della Spiga 36
   Milano MI

(G-11594)
MODULAR AIR FILTRATION SYSTEMS
450 Richmond St (02767-5301)
PHONE..............................508 823-4900
William Lovenbury, *Pr*
Robert Lovenbury, *Treas*
EMP: 24 **EST:** 1986
SALES (est): 227.12K **Privately Held**
Web: www.nicholssportinggoods.com
SIC: 3677 Filtration devices, electronic

(G-11595)
OMNI LIFE SCIENCE INC (DH)
480 Paramount Dr (02767-1085)
PHONE..............................508 824-2444
Rick Epstein, *CEO*
George B Cipollett, *
David Lorenzi, *
David L Lasalle, *
James V Barrile, *
▲ **EMP:** 35 **EST:** 1980
SQ FT: 12,000
SALES (est): 7.81MM
SALES (corp-wide): 2.67MM **Privately Held**
Web: www.coringroup.com
SIC: 3842 Orthopedic appliances
HQ: Corin Orthopaedics Holdings Limited
   The Corinium Centre
   Cirencester GLOS GL7 1

(G-11596)
RYAN IRON WORKS INC
1830 Bdwy (02767-1967)
P.O. Box 159 (02767-0159)
PHONE..............................508 821-2058
Howard F Shea, *Pr*
John Shea, *
Paul Berube, *
Lawrence W Kelley, *
Charlene Diauto, *
EMP: 50 **EST:** 1918
SQ FT: 65,000
SALES (est): 9.76MM **Privately Held**
Web: www.ryanironworks.net

SIC: 3446 Architectural metalwork

(G-11597)
SUNRISE TECHNOLOGIES INC
370 Paramount Dr Ste 2 (02767-5419)
PHONE..............................508 821-1597
EMP: 17 **EST:** 2017
SALES (est): 2.1MM **Privately Held**
Web: www.sun-tech.biz
SIC: 3699 Photographic control systems, electronic

(G-11598)
SUNRISE TECHNOLOGIES LLC
54 Commercial St Ste 2 (02767-1300)
PHONE..............................508 884-9732
▼ **EMP:** 15 **EST:** 1997
SALES (est): 2.41MM **Privately Held**
Web: www.sun-tech.biz
SIC: 3648 Street lighting fixtures

(G-11599)
TECHNICAL SERVICES INC
263 South St E (02767-5129)
PHONE..............................781 389-8342
Sean Riley, *Prin*
EMP: 10 **EST:** 2016
SALES (est): 144.28K **Privately Held**
Web: www.tsiames.com
SIC: 3672 Printed circuit boards

Reading
Middlesex County

(G-11600)
AUTOCRAFT COLLISION INC
943 Main St (01867-1716)
PHONE..............................781 670-9001
EMP: 7 **EST:** 2019
SALES (est): 224.72K **Privately Held**
Web: www.autocraftcollisioninc.com
SIC: 7534 Tire repair shop

(G-11601)
FRAEN CORPORATION (PA)
Also Called: Fraen
80 New Crossing Rd (01867-3291)
PHONE..............................781 205-5300
Nicholas Scarfo, *CEO*
Nicodemo Scarfo, *CEO*
Peter W Fuller, *Dir*
Anthony L Bolzan, *Sec*
Lynne A Scarfo, *Treas*
◆ **EMP:** 120 **EST:** 1924
SQ FT: 65,000
SALES (est): 23.05MM
SALES (corp-wide): 23.05MM **Privately Held**
Web: www.fraen.com
SIC: 3469 3451 3089 3873 Stamping metal for the trade; Screw machine products; Plastics containers, except foam; Watches, clocks, watchcases, and parts

(G-11602)
HEAD 2 TOE LLC
167 Pleasant St (01867-2759)
P.O. Box 508 (01867-0708)
PHONE..............................781 944-0286
Patricia Griffin, *Pr*
EMP: 10 **EST:** 2001
SALES (est): 506.34K **Privately Held**
SIC: 2842 Wax removers

(G-11603)
MAIN STREET BLANCHARD LLC
505 Main St (01867-3168)
PHONE..............................781 944-4000

James Freeman, *Prin*
EMP: 7 **EST:** 2009
SALES (est): 96.36K **Privately Held**
SIC: 3931 Piano parts and materials, nec

(G-11604)
PGC ACQUISITION LLC
Also Called: Pairpoint Crystal
74 Pleasant St (01867-3018)
P.O. Box 515 (02561-0515)
PHONE...................................508 888-2344
TOLL FREE: 800
Tomas J Fiocco, *Prin*
Tom Fiocco, *Pr*
EMP: 8 **EST:** 1969
SQ FT: 35,000
SALES (est): 209.88K **Privately Held**
Web: www.pairpoint.com
SIC: 3229 5719 5023 5199 Glassware, art
or decorative; Glassware; Glassware;
Glassware, novelty

(G-11605)
READING DIAGNOSTIC CENTER
Also Called: Reading Health Center
20 Pondmeadow Dr Ste 106 (01867-3222)
PHONE...................................781 942-9876
EMP: 10 **EST:** 1994
SALES (est): 399.14K **Privately Held**
Web: www.readingma.gov
SIC: 8071 2711 1629 7359 Medical
laboratories; Newspapers; Tennis court
construction; Stores and yards equipment
rental

(G-11606)
RICHARDSONS ICE CREAM
50 Walkers Brook Dr (01867-3224) ·
PHONE...................................781 944-9121
Chris Richardson, *Prin*
EMP: 8 **EST:** 2005
SALES (est): 250.44K **Privately Held**
Web: www.richardsonsicecream.com
SIC: 2024 5812 Ice cream, bulk; Ice cream
stands or dairy bars

(G-11607)
ROGER A REED INC
Also Called: Reed Wax
167 Pleasant St (01867-2759)
P.O. Box 508 (01867-0708)
PHONE...................................781 944-4640
TOLL FREE: 800
Patricia Griffin, *Pr*
EMP: 13 **EST:** 1939
SALES (est): 952.63K **Privately Held**
Web: www.reedwax.com
SIC: 2842 Waxes for wood, leather, and
other materials

Rehoboth
Bristol County

(G-11608)
FASTSIGNS OF ATTLEBORO
Also Called: Fastsigns
5 Greenwood Dr (02769-2243)
PHONE...................................508 699-6699
Joe Tavares, *Owner*
EMP: 10 **EST:** 2008
SALES (est): 243.29K **Privately Held**
Web: www.fastsigns.com
SIC: 3993 Signs and advertising specialties

(G-11609)
HONEY DEW REHOBETH
317 Tremont St (02769-2707)
PHONE...................................508 431-2784

Steve Provaza, *Owner*
EMP: 10 **EST:** 2001
SALES (est): 230.65K **Privately Held**
Web: www.honeydewdonuts.com
SIC: 5812 2051 Snack shop; Doughnuts,
except frozen

(G-11610)
J & K SALES CO INC
Also Called: Komor Mfg Co
225 Pleasant St (02769-1617)
PHONE...................................508 252-6235
Henry Jablecki, *Ch Bd*
Michael Jablecki, *
Stephen Jablecki, *
Katherine Tardiff, *
Mary Maguire, *
EMP: 7 **EST:** 1946
SQ FT: 110,000
SALES (est): 143.18K **Privately Held**
SIC: 3961 Costume jewelry, ex. precious
metal and semiprecious stones

(G-11611)
NANTUCKET PAVERS INC
71 Fall River Ave (02769-1009)
PHONE...................................508 336-5800
John P Ferreira, *Pr*
▲ **EMP:** 11 **EST:** 1997
SALES (est): 1.4MM **Privately Held**
Web: www.nantucketpavers.com
SIC: 3272 Concrete products, nec

(G-11612)
NEW ENGLAND GRAVEL HAULERS
Also Called: New England Gravel
42 Winthrop St (02769-2606)
PHONE...................................508 922-4518
James Barishian, *Pr*
EMP: 8 **EST:** 2013
SALES (est): 2.5MM **Privately Held**
Web: www.neoutdoorproducts.com
SIC: 1442 Construction sand and gravel

(G-11613)
OLDCASTLE INFRASTRUCTURE INC
Also Called: Rotondo Precast
41 Almeida Rd (02769-1007)
PHONE...................................508 336-7600
Chris Fowler, *Mgr*
EMP: 40
SALES (corp-wide): 32.72B **Privately Held**
Web: www.oldcastleinfrastructure.com
SIC: 3272 1711 Precast terrazzo or
concrete products; Septic system
construction
HQ: Oldcastle Infrastructure, Inc.
7000 Central Pkwy Ste 800
Atlanta GA 30328
770 270-5000

(G-11614)
TRACKCAM LLC
285 Winthrop St Unit 2b (02769-1835)
PHONE...................................508 556-1955
Phillip Hicks, *Mgr*
EMP: 8 **EST:** 2019
SALES (est): 361.97K **Privately Held**
Web: www.gotrackcam.com
SIC: 3663 5731 7389 Global positioning
systems (GPS) equipment; Video cameras
and accessories; Business services, nec

(G-11615)
WAYNES SHEET METAL INC
157 Tremont St (02769-2818)
PHONE...................................508 431-8057

Wayne Gaudreau, *Pr*
Margaret Gardrue, *Treas*
EMP: 7 **EST:** 2000
SALES (est): 600K **Privately Held**
Web: www.waynessheetmetal.net
SIC: 3444 Sheet metalwork

Revere
Suffolk County

(G-11616)
ALTRI JUNK REMOVAL SERVICES ✪
40a Waite St (02151-4641)
PHONE...................................781 629-2500
EMP: 20 **EST:** 2022
SALES (est): 816.59K **Privately Held**
SIC: 2851 Removers and cleaners

(G-11617)
BEST EMBROIDERY
231 Park Ave (02151-5218)
PHONE...................................857 258-0333
Cristian Yepes Mora, *Pr*
EMP: 7 **EST:** 2013
SALES (est): 127.5K **Privately Held**
SIC: 2395 Embroidery and art needlework

(G-11618)
DURANT PRFMCE COATINGS INC
Also Called: Durant Performance Coatings
112 Railroad Ave (02151-4085)
PHONE...................................781 289-1400
Ronald A Yanetti, *Pr*
Marilyn Yanetti, *VP*
Al Losanno, *VP*
EMP: 12 **EST:** 1950
SQ FT: 19,000
SALES (est): 2.19MM **Privately Held**
Web: www.durantcorp.com
SIC: 2851 5231 Paints: oil or alkyd vehicle
or water thinned; Paint

(G-11619)
INDEPENDANT NEWSPAPER GROUP
Also Called: Chelsea Record
385 Broadway Ste 105 (02151-3049)
PHONE...................................781 485-0588
Stephen Quigley, *Pr*
EMP: 10 **EST:** 2001
SALES (est): 441.81K **Privately Held**
Web: www.chelearecord.com
SIC: 2759 2711 Commercial printing, nec;
Newspapers

(G-11620)
INDEPENDENT NEWSPAPER GROUP
Also Called: BEACON HILL TIMES,THE
385 Broadway (02151-3033)
PHONE...................................781 485-0588
EMP: 10 **EST:** 1995
SALES (est): 167.16K **Privately Held**
Web: www.beaconhilltimes.com
SIC: 2711 Newspapers, publishing and
printing

(G-11621)
LA PATISSERIE INC
Also Called: La Patisserie Bakery Cafe
260 Proctor Ave (02151-4924)
PHONE...................................781 729-9441
Stephen Pazyra, *Pr*
Danette Pazyra, *VP*
EMP: 11 **EST:** 1984

SALES (est): 412.11K **Privately Held**
Web: www.lapatisseriecyrillignac.com
SIC: 5461 5149 5812 2052 Cakes; Bakery
products; Eating places; Cookies and
crackers

(G-11622)
NEW ENGLAND CONFECTIONERY COMPANY INC
Also Called: Necco
135 American Legion Hwy (02151-2405)
PHONE...................................781 485-4500
◆ **EMP:** 500
SIC: 2064 2066 Candy and other
confectionery products; Chocolate and
cocoa products

(G-11623)
REVERE INDEPENDENT
385 Broadway Ste 105 (02151-3049)
PHONE...................................781 485-0588
Steven Quigley, *Pt*
EMP: 10 **EST:** 1999
SALES (est): 344.52K **Privately Held**
Web: www.reverejournal.com
SIC: 2711 Newspapers, publishing and
printing

(G-11624)
SWEETHEARTS CANDY CO LLC
135 American Legion Hwy (02151-2405)
P.O. Box 1390 (01940-5390)
PHONE...................................781 485-4500
EMP: 500 **EST:** 2018
SALES (est): 23.53MM **Privately Held**
SIC: 2064 2066 Candy and other
confectionery products; Chocolate and
cocoa products

(G-11625)
WHITMOR COMPANY INC (PA)
15 Whitmore Rd (02151-5916)
P.O. Box 249 (02151-0008)
PHONE...................................781 284-8000
Anthony Pesce, *Pr*
Stephen Stickney, *VP*
EMP: 13 **EST:** 1942
SQ FT: 25,000
SALES (est): 2.84MM
SALES (corp-wide): 2.84MM **Privately Held**
Web: www.whitmorcompany.com
SIC: 3613 5084 Switchboards and parts,
power; Industrial machinery and equipment

Richmond
Berkshire County

(G-11626)
GROVE STREET ENTERPRISES INC
Also Called: Hilltop Orchard
508 Canaan Rd (01254-5116)
P.O. Box 189 (01254-0189)
PHONE...................................413 698-3301
John Vittori, *VP*
Wendy Vittori, *Sec*
EMP: 11 **EST:** 1985
SQ FT: 2,500
SALES (est): 429.37K **Privately Held**
Web: www.hilltoporchards.com
SIC: 2084 Wines

Rochdale
Worcester County

(G-11627)
KEMP TECHNOLOGIES INC
7 Virginia Dr (01542-1201)
PHONE...............................631 418-8407
Dolores Farrell, *Prin*
EMP: 8 EST: 2010
SALES (est): 122.75K **Privately Held**
Web: www.kemptechnologies.com
SIC: 3577 7371 Computer peripheral
equipment, nec; Computer software
development

(G-11628)
MODERN MFG INC WORCESTER
Also Called: Modern Architechtural Glazing
82 Huntoon Memorial Hwy (01542-1307)
PHONE...............................508 791-7151
Richard F Uras, *Pr*
Donna Bolte, *Treas*
EMP: 20 EST: 1952
SALES (est): 4.7MM **Privately Held**
Web: www.modernglazing.com
SIC: 3442 3231 Window and door frames;
Products of purchased glass

(G-11629)
WORCESTER COUNTY WELDING INC
112 Huntoon Memorial Hwy (01542-1307)
P.O. Box 325 (01542-0325)
PHONE...............................508 892-4884
John Daige, *Pr*
EMP: 9 EST: 1980
SALES (est): 2.48MM **Privately Held**
Web: www.wcweld.com
SIC: 1799 7692 3441 Welding on site;
Welding repair; Fabricated structural metal

(G-11630)
WORCESTER TOOL & STAMPING CO
11 Hankey St (01542-1132)
P.O. Box 292 (01542-0292)
PHONE...............................508 892-8194
Stephen P Magnuson, *Pr*
David Magnuson, *
Karen Magnuson, *
EMP: 40 EST: 1913
SQ FT: 50,000
SALES (est): 2.55MM **Privately Held**
SIC: 3429 3469 Hardware, nec; Metal
stampings, nec

Rochester
Plymouth County

(G-11631)
DRS DEVELOPMENT LLC
10 Marion Rd (02770-4123)
PHONE...............................774 271-0533
George B Dornblaser Junior, *Prin*
EMP: 7 EST: 2009
SALES (est): 157.22K **Privately Held**
SIC: 3674 Semiconductors and related
devices

Rockland
Plymouth County

(G-11632)
3M COMPANY
Also Called: 3M

30 Commerce Rd (02370-1053)
PHONE...............................781 871-1400
EMP: 23
SALES (corp-wide): 34.23B **Publicly Held**
Web: www.3m.com
SIC: 2891 Adhesives
PA: 3m Company
3m Center
Saint Paul MN 55144
651 733-1110

(G-11633)
AIRXCHANGE INC
85 Longwater Dr (02370-1093)
PHONE...............................781 871-4816
Donald Steele, *Pr*
Randall E Steele, *
James Connell, *
▲ EMP: 65 EST: 1980
SQ FT: 35,000
SALES (est): 17.23MM **Privately Held**
Web: www.airxchange.com
SIC: 3585 Refrigeration and heating
equipment

(G-11634)
ARBO MACHINE CO INC
45 Union St (02370-1919)
PHONE...............................781 871-3449
Aram Onbashian Junior, *Pr*
EMP: 9 EST: 1963
SQ FT: 3,500
SALES (est): 776.95K **Privately Held**
Web: www.arbomachine.com
SIC: 3599 Machine shop, jobbing and repair

(G-11635)
ARBORWAY METAL FINISHING INC
Also Called: AMF Technologies
401 Vfw Dr (02370-1100)
P.O. Box 537 (02018-0537)
PHONE...............................781 982-0137
Thomas J O'mara, *Pr*
Susan M O'mara, *Clerk*
EMP: 38 EST: 1980
SQ FT: 12,000
SALES (est): 835.18K **Privately Held**
Web: www.amftechnologies.com
SIC: 3471 Electroplating of metals or
formed products

(G-11636)
BENDON GEAR AND MACHINE INC
100 Weymouth St Ste A1 (02370-1145)
PHONE...............................781 878-8100
S George Belezos, *Pr*
Douglas Truessel, *
Christopher P Belezos, *
EMP: 29 EST: 1951
SQ FT: 26,000
SALES (est): 4.48MM **Privately Held**
Web: www.bendongear.com
SIC: 3599 3566 Machine shop, jobbing and
repair; Gears, power transmission, except
auto

(G-11637)
BIO SPHERE MEDICAL INC
1050 Hingham St Fl 1 (02370-1076)
PHONE...............................208 844-5008
Riccardo Pigliucci, *Dir*
EMP: 21 EST: 2017
SALES (est): 789.53K **Privately Held**
SIC: 3841 Surgical and medical instruments

(G-11638)
CAPEWAY PRINTING & COPY CENTER
71 Reservoir Park Dr (02370-1060)
PHONE...............................781 878-1600
TOLL FREE: 800
Jim Grady, *Pr*
EMP: 7 EST: 1976
SALES (est): 570.7K **Privately Held**
SIC: 2752 Offset printing

(G-11639)
CAROLS CANVAS COMPANY INC
273 Weymouth St (02370-1143)
PHONE...............................781 871-8288
EMP: 9 EST: 2019
SALES (est): 274.45K **Privately Held**
Web: www.canvasbycarol.com
SIC: 2211 Canvas

(G-11640)
CLEARWTER TECH CNSLTING WTR SV
Also Called: Www.cwt-Usa.com
83 E Water St (02370-1834)
PHONE...............................781 871-5157
Bill Varney Junior, *Pr*
Michael O'brien, *Sec*
Bill Varney Senior, *Mgr*
EMP: 10 EST: 1994
SQ FT: 10,000
SALES (est): 860K **Privately Held**
Web: www.cwt-usa.com
SIC: 8742 2899 Industry specialist
consultants; Water treating compounds

(G-11641)
CREATIVE SUCCESS ALLIANCE CORP
100 Weymouth St Ste D2 (02370-1145)
PHONE...............................781 878-7114
Tammy Beckwith, *CFO*
David Lindahl, *
EMP: 33 EST: 2011
SALES (est): 2.45MM **Privately Held**
Web: www.creativesuccessalliance.com
SIC: 2741 6099 Newsletter publishing;
Escrow institutions other than real estate

(G-11642)
EMD ACCNTING SLTONS SVCS AMER
1 Technology Pl (02370-1071)
PHONE...............................781 982-9000
EMP: 131 EST: 2010
SALES (est): 2.28MM
SALES (corp-wide): 23.09B **Privately Held**
SIC: 2834 Pharmaceutical preparations
HQ: Emd Serono, Inc.
1 Technology Pl
Rockland MA 02370
781 982-9000

(G-11643)
EMD SERONO INC (DH)
Also Called: EMD Pharmaceuticals
1 Technology Pl (02370-1071)
PHONE...............................781 982-9000
James Hoyes, *Pr*
Ellen Rosenberg, *
Monica Elliot, *
Andrew Suchoff, *
Gary Zieziula, *CCO*
▲ EMP: 625 EST: 1971
SQ FT: 60,000
SALES (est): 214.21MM
SALES (corp-wide): 23.09B **Privately Held**

Web: us.fertility.com
SIC: 2834 Pharmaceutical preparations
HQ: Merck Serono Sa
Zone Industrielle De L'ouriettaz
Aubonne VD 1170

(G-11644)
EMD SERONO BIOTECH CENTER INC (HQ)
1 Technology Pl (02370-1071)
PHONE...............................800 283-8088
James Hoyes, *Pr*
Lisa Costantino, *
Thorsten Eickenhorst, *
Devin Smith, *
Steve Arkinstall, *
EMP: 82 EST: 1992
SALES (est): 23.81MM
SALES (corp-wide): 23.09B **Privately Held**
SIC: 2834 Pharmaceutical preparations
PA: Merck Kg Auf Aktien
Frankfurter Str. 250
Darmstadt HE 64293
6151720

(G-11645)
EMD SERONO HOLDING INC
1 Technology Pl (02370-1071)
PHONE...............................781 982-9000
EMP: 108 EST: 2011
SALES (est): 1.68MM
SALES (corp-wide): 23.09B **Privately Held**
SIC: 2834 Pharmaceutical preparations
HQ: Emd Serono, Inc.
1 Technology Pl
Rockland MA 02370
781 982-9000

(G-11646)
EMD SERONO RES & DEV INST INC (HQ)
Also Called: EMD Serono Research Inst Inc
1 Technology Pl (02370-1071)
PHONE...............................781 982-9000
James Hoyes, *Pr*
Pinchas Gross, *Dir Fin*
Thomas Gunning, *Sec*
Lisa Costantino, *CFO*
Thorsten Eickenhorst, *Sr VP*
EMP: 20 EST: 1989
SALES (est): 22.58MM
SALES (corp-wide): 23.09B **Privately Held**
SIC: 2834 Pharmaceutical preparations
PA: Merck Kg Auf Aktien
Frankfurter Str. 250
Darmstadt HE 64293
6151720

(G-11647)
GTA-NHT INC (HQ)
Also Called: Venture Tape
30 Commerce Rd (02370-1053)
PHONE...............................781 331-5900
Mark Hurowitz, *Pr*
Manuel Pardo, *
M M Dai, *
◆ EMP: 180 EST: 1980
SQ FT: 134,000
SALES (est): 52.14MM
SALES (corp-wide): 34.23B **Publicly Held**
Web: www.venturetape.com
SIC: 2672 3842 2671 2295 Tape, pressure
sensitive: made from purchased materials;
Surgical appliances and supplies; Paper;
coated and laminated packaging; Coated
fabrics, not rubberized
PA: 3m Company
3m Center
Saint Paul MN 55144
651 733-1110

(G-11648)
H H ARNOLD CO INC
529 Liberty St (02370-1239)
P.O. Box 526 (02370-0526)
PHONE.....................781 878-0346
William Arnold, *Pr*
John B Arnold, *
Richard Arnold, *
William G Arnold, *
EMP: 25 **EST:** 1902
SQ FT: 36,000
SALES (est): 2.04MM **Privately Held**
Web: www.hharnold.com
SIC: 3599   Machine shop, jobbing and repair

(G-11649)
LAMITECH
800 Hingham St Ste 200 (02370-1067)
PHONE.....................781 878-7708
Andrew Londergran, *Mgr*
EMP: 11 **EST:** 2002
SALES (est): 479.5K **Privately Held**
Web: www.lamitech.com
SIC: 2631   Cardboard

(G-11650)
MED TECH MACHINE COMPANY INC
100 Weymouth St Ste G2 (02370-1146)
PHONE.....................781 878-2250
John C Schuchert, *Pr*
EMP: 12 **EST:** 1973
SQ FT: 5,500
SALES (est): 1.01MM **Privately Held**
SIC: 3599   Machine shop, jobbing and repair

(G-11651)
MERIT MEDICAL SYSTEMS INC (HQ)
1050 Hingham St Fl 1 (02370-1076)
PHONE.....................781 681-7900
Fred Lampropoulos, *Pr*
Kent Stanger, *CFO*
Martin Stephens, *S&M/VP*
Arlin Nelson, *COO*
EMP: 10 **EST:** 1993
SQ FT: 13,000
SALES (est): 7.64MM
SALES (corp-wide): 1.15B **Publicly Held**
Web: www.merit.com
SIC: 3841   Surgical and medical instruments
PA: Merit Medical Systems, Inc.
1600 W Merit Pkwy
South Jordan UT 84095
801 253-1600

(G-11652)
MONAHAN PRODUCTS LLC (PA)
Also Called: Uppababy
276 Weymouth St (02370-1139)
PHONE.....................844 823-3132
Robert Dennison Monahan, *Managing Member*
◆ **EMP:** 52 **EST:** 2006
SALES (est): 24.36MM **Privately Held**
Web: www.uppababy.com
SIC: 3944   Baby carriages and restraint seats

(G-11653)
NATIONAL COATING CORPORATION
105 Industrial Way (02370-2799)
PHONE.....................781 878-2781
EMP: 8 **EST:** 2018
SALES (est): 729.57K **Privately Held**
Web: www.natcoat.com
SIC: 3441   Fabricated structural metal

(G-11654)
NTT DATA INC
Also Called: NTT Data Inc.
1099 Hingman St (02370-3319)
PHONE.....................877 532-6312
EMP: 20
Web: www.nttdata.com
SIC: 7372   Prepackaged software
HQ: Ntt Data Americas, Inc.
7950 Legacy Dr Ste 1100
Plano TX 75024
800 745-3263

(G-11655)
PARADIGM BIODEVICES INC
800 Hingham St Ste 207s (02370-1079)
P.O. Box 518 (02061-0518)
PHONE.....................781 982-9950
Michael O'neill, *Pr*
Susan O'neill, *Treas*
EMP: 7 **EST:** 1997
SALES (est): 694.95K **Privately Held**
Web: www.paradigmbiodevices.com
SIC: 3841   Diagnostic apparatus, medical

(G-11656)
POLYMER CORPORATION (HQ)
Also Called: Polymer Liquid Resin Casting
180 Pleasant St (02370-1229)
PHONE.....................781 871-4606
Robert Underwood, *CEO*
Robert Underwood, *Pr*
▲ **EMP:** 60 **EST:** 2000
SQ FT: 25,000
SALES (est): 35.87MM **Privately Held**
Web: www.polymercorporation.com
SIC: 3089 5162   Injection molding of plastics
; Plastics resins
PA: North American Fund Iii, Lp
135 S La Salle St # 3225
Chicago IL 60603

(G-11657)
PRESSURE SIGNAL INC
11 Commerce Rd Ste C (02370-1080)
PHONE.....................781 871-5629
John J Mc Sheffrey, *Pr*
Michaella Mc Sheffrey, *
▲ **EMP:** 40 **EST:** 1972
SQ FT: 48,000
SALES (est): 4.83MM **Privately Held**
Web: www.keltrongauges.com
SIC: 3823   Pressure gauges, dial and digital

(G-11658)
PRIOR SCIENTIFIC INC (HQ)
80 Reservoir Park Dr (02370-1062)
PHONE.....................781 878-8442
Thomas Freda, *Prin*
Myles Fielding, *Prin*
Simon Smith, *Prin*
Dennis Doherty, *Prin*
Mark Cherwek, *Prin*
EMP: 16 **EST:** 1991
SQ FT: 9,000
SALES (est): 6.72MM
SALES (corp-wide): 26.92MM **Privately Held**
Web: www.prior.com
SIC: 3827 3829   Optical instruments and apparatus; Measuring and controlling devices, nec
PA: Prior Scientific Instruments Limited
3-4 Wilbraham Road Fielding Industrial Estate
Cambridge CAMBS CB21
122 388-1711

(G-11659)
ROCKLAND EQUIPMENT COMPANY LLC
171 Vfw Dr (02370-1129)
PHONE.....................781 871-4400
EMP: 17 **EST:** 2005
SALES (est): 1.35MM **Privately Held**
SIC: 3531   Construction machinery

(G-11660)
SERONO INC
1 Technology Pl (02370-1071)
PHONE.....................781 681-2137
Dawne Green, *Prin*
EMP: 48 **EST:** 2012
SALES (est): 1.51MM **Privately Held**
SIC: 2834   Pharmaceutical preparations

(G-11661)
SOUTHSTERN MTAL FBRICATORS INC
Air Station Industrial Park (02370)
P.O. Box 362 (02370-0362)
PHONE.....................781 878-1505
Russell J Anderson Iii, *Pr*
Elio D Roffo, *
Ronald Mavilia, *
EMP: 30 **EST:** 1959
SQ FT: 80,000
SALES (est): 2.68MM **Privately Held**
Web: www.southeasternmetal.com
SIC: 3446 3441   Architectural metalwork; Fabricated structural metal

(G-11662)
T & T MACHINE PRODUCTS INC
254 Beech St (02370-2749)
P.O. Box 430 (02370-0430)
PHONE.....................781 878-3861
Anthony F Muscillo, *Pr*
Thomas Brown, *Treas*
EMP: 10 **EST:** 1984
SALES (est): 1.7MM **Privately Held**
Web: www.ttmachineproductsinc.com
SIC: 3643 3229 3841   Electric connectors; Fiber optics strands; Surgical and medical instruments

(G-11663)
UNITED HVAC CO INC
333 Weymouth St (02370-1141)
PHONE.....................781 871-1060
Thomas Scolero, *Pr*
EMP: 20 **EST:** 1991
SALES (est): 4.54MM **Privately Held**
Web: www.united-hvac.com
SIC: 1761 3444   Sheet metal work, nec; Sheet metalwork

(G-11664)
UNIVERSAL WILDE INC
403 Vfw Dr (02370-1170)
PHONE.....................781 251-2700
Shawn Gill, *Brnch Mgr*
EMP: 101
Web: www.universalwilde.com
SIC: 2752   Offset printing
PA: Universal Wilde, Inc.
135 Will Dr Unit 2
Canton MA 02021

(G-11665)
XL TECHNOLOGY SYSTEMS INC
401 Vfw Dr (02370-1176)
PHONE.....................781 982-1220
EMP: 26 **EST:** 1995
SALES (est): 3.47MM **Privately Held**
Web: www.dynavac.com

SIC: 3443   Tank towers, metal plate

Roslindale
Suffolk County

(G-11666)
G R SANDS MONUMENTAL WORKS
3859 Washington St (02131-1220)
PHONE.....................617 522-1001
EMP: 8 **EST:** 1996
SALES (est): 634.86K **Privately Held**
SIC: 5099 3281   Monuments and grave markers; Cut stone and stone products

---

Rowley
Essex County

(G-11667)
ATLANTIC AUTO & TRCK PARTS LLC
Also Called: NAPA
26 Hammond St (01969-1829)
PHONE.....................978 535-6777
Dick Ziemlak, *Pr*
Jeff Clarke, *VP*
EMP: 8 **EST:** 1998
SALES (est): 837.43K **Privately Held**
Web: www.napaonline.com
SIC: 3089 5531   Automotive parts, plastic; Automotive parts

(G-11668)
CAPCO CRANE & HOIST INC
58 Forest Ridge Dr (01969-2143)
PHONE.....................978 948-2998
▲ **EMP:** 24 **EST:** 1995
SQ FT: 12,000
SALES (est): 5.7MM **Privately Held**
Web: www.capcocrane.com
SIC: 3536   Hoists, cranes, and monorails

(G-11669)
CAPCO CRANE & HOIST PARTS INC
58 Forest Ridge Dr (01969-2143)
PHONE.....................978 948-2998
Anthony Caputo Iii, *Prin*
EMP: 8 **EST:** 2015
SALES (est): 105.3K **Privately Held**
Web: www.capcocrane.com
SIC: 3536   Hoists, cranes, and monorails

(G-11670)
CAPONE IRON CORPORATION
20 Turcotte Memorial Dr (01969-1706)
P.O. Box 706 (01969-3706)
PHONE.....................978 948-8000
Stephen J Capone, *Pr*
Gary D Capone, *
EMP: 35 **EST:** 1972
SQ FT: 33,000
SALES (est): 6.78MM **Privately Held**
Web: www.caponeiron.com
SIC: 3441   Fabricated structural metal

(G-11671)
CASSIDY BROS FORGE INC
282 Newburyport Tpke (01969-2009)
PHONE.....................978 948-7303
Maurice Cassidy, *Pr*
Vincent Paul Cassidy, *VP*
Peter Cassidy, *VP*
EMP: 21 **EST:** 1965
SQ FT: 15,000
SALES (est): 1.62MM **Privately Held**

Web: www.cassidybros.com
SIC: 3446 Architectural metalwork

(G-11672)
CHOICE GRAPHICS INC
140 Central St Ste 4 (01969-1327)
PHONE..............................978 948-2789
Jon Keith Harris, *Pr*
Christina Harris, *VP*
EMP: 7 EST: 1995
SQ FT: 2,400
SALES (est): 797.81K **Privately Held**
Web: www.partnerwithchoice.com
SIC: 2752 Offset printing

(G-11673)
DEFIANCE GRAPHICS CORP
140 Central St (01969-1301)
P.O. Box 313 (01969-0783)
PHONE..............................978 948-2789
Paul Tardiff, *Pr*
Beverly Tardiff, *VP*
EMP: 10 EST: 1945
SQ FT: 6,000
SALES (est): 852.4K **Privately Held**
Web: www.partnerwithchoice.com
SIC: 2759 2752 Commercial printing, nec;
Offset printing

(G-11674)
**GENERAL PRODUCTS & GEAR
CORP**
Also Called: GP&g
445 Newburyport Tpke (01969-1728)
PHONE..............................978 948-8146
Quinton Schaffer, *Pr*
EMP: 10 EST: 1952
SALES (est): 973.31K **Privately Held**
Web: www.gpgc.com
SIC: 3599 Machine shop, jobbing and repair

(G-11675)
GRAPE ISLAND INC
41 Railroad Ave (01969-1202)
PHONE..............................978 432-1280
Richard Rousseau, *Pr*
EMP: 7 EST: 2010
SALES (est): 194.59K **Privately Held**
SIC: 0172 2084 Grapes; Wines

(G-11676)
HELICAL SOLUTIONS LLC
428 Newburyport Tpke (01969-1761)
PHONE..............................207 854-5581
EMP: 32 EST: 2017
SALES (est): 1.58MM **Privately Held**
Web: www.harveyperformance.com
SIC: 3599 Machine shop, jobbing and repair

(G-11677)
IPSWICH BAY GLASS CO INC
420 Newburyport Tpke (01969-1725)
P.O. Box 511 (01969-0911)
PHONE..............................978 948-6644
H A Patrican Junior, *Pr*
Brian J Patrican, *
Diane E Patrican, *
▲ EMP: 150 EST: 1969
SQ FT: 85,000
SALES (est): 31.98MM **Privately Held**
Web: www.ibglass.com
SIC: 1793 3312 Glass and glazing work;
Blast furnaces and steel mills

(G-11678)
KNEELAND BROS INC
51 Wethersfield St (01969-1715)
PHONE..............................978 948-3919
Roy D Kneeland, *Pr*

EMP: 10 EST: 1962
SQ FT: 1,000
SALES (est): 451.68K **Privately Held**
SIC: 2091 Canned and cured fish and
seafoods

(G-11679)
**MILACRON MARKETING
COMPANY LLC**
428 Newburyport Tpke (01969-1761)
PHONE..............................978 238-7100
Steven Morris, *Genl Mgr*
EMP: 104
Web: www.milacron.com
SIC: 3089 Injection molding of plastics
HQ: Milacron Marketing Company Llc
4165 Half Acre Rd
Batavia OH 45103

(G-11680)
MOLDED PLASTICS ENGRG INC
58 Kittery Ave (01969-1012)
PHONE..............................978 948-7153
Arthur Corben, *Prin*
EMP: 9 EST: 2008
SALES (est): 65.12K **Privately Held**
Web: www.psimp.com
SIC: 3089 Injection molding of plastics

(G-11681)
MPS PRODUCTS CORP
Also Called: Steel
453 Newburyport Tpke (01969-1728)
PHONE..............................978 817-2144
Michael Pimental, *Pr*
EMP: 10 EST: 2015
SALES (est): 974.31K **Privately Held**
Web: www.mpsproductscorp.com
SIC: 3441 1791 Fabricated structural metal;
Structural steel erection

(G-11682)
NORTHEAST METALS TECH LLC
289 Newburyport Tpke (01969-2008)
PHONE..............................978 948-2633
EMP: 8 EST: 2000
SALES (est): 854.97K **Privately Held**
SIC: 3398 Metal heat treating

(G-11683)
RAMCO MACHINE LLC
27 Turcotte Memorial Dr (01969-1706)
PHONE..............................978 948-3778
Carolyn Jezowski, *
Mike Jezowski, *
Tim Jezowski, *
EMP: 29 EST: 1984
SQ FT: 24,000
SALES (est): 4.29MM **Privately Held**
Web: www.ramcomachine.com
SIC: 3599 Machine and other job shop work

(G-11684)
ROWLEY READY MIX INC
Also Called: Rowley Concrete
84 Central St (01969-1701)
P.O. Box 321 (01969-0771)
PHONE..............................978 948-2544
Downey H Shea Junior, *Pr*
EMP: 15 EST: 1948
SQ FT: 500
SALES (est): 1.27MM **Privately Held**
SIC: 3273 5211 Ready-mixed concrete;
Paving stones

(G-11685)
SPEEDBOARD USA INC
39 Kittery Ave (01969-1014)
PHONE..............................978 884-3900

Robert Blair, *Pr*
EMP: 7 EST: 2011
SALES (est): 100K **Privately Held**
Web: www.speedboardusa.com
SIC: 2493 3644 Hardboard; Raceways

(G-11686)
TOWN COMMON INC
77 Wethersfield St (01969-1713)
PHONE..............................978 948-8696
Marc Malazalli, *Pr*
EMP: 10 EST: 2005
SQ FT: 2,287
SALES (est): 559.04K **Privately Held**
Web: www.thetowncommon.com
SIC: 2711 Newspapers, publishing and
printing

(G-11687)
**WINFREYS OLDE ENGLISH
FDGE INC (PA)**
Also Called: Winfrey's Fudge & Candy
40 Newburyport Tpke Ste 1 (01969-2106)
PHONE..............................978 948-7448
Christine Winfrey, *Pr*
Stuart Winfrey, *Treas*
EMP: 16 EST: 1979
SQ FT: 10,000
SALES (est): 2.48MM
SALES (corp-wide): 2.48MM **Privately
Held**
Web: www.winfreys.com
SIC: 2064 2066 Fudge (candy); Chocolate
and cocoa products

Roxbury
Suffolk County

(G-11688)
CHAND LLC
99 Circuit St (02119-1971)
PHONE..............................310 483-5769
Rashif Tahmid Ahmed, *Prin*
EMP: 8 EST: 2015
SALES (est): 177.85K **Privately Held**
Web: www.chand.com
SIC: 2732 Book printing

(G-11689)
CITY FRESH FOODS INC
Also Called: City Fresh Foods
77 Shirley St (02119-3035)
P.O. Box 255698 (02125-5698)
PHONE..............................617 606-7123
EMP: 80 EST: 1994
SQ FT: 150,000
SALES (est): 11.19MM **Privately Held**
Web: www.cityfresh.com
SIC: 2099 Box lunches, for sale off premises

(G-11690)
CITY FRESH FOODS INC
Also Called: City Fresh Foods
69 Shirley St (02119-3066)
P.O. Box 255698 (02125-5698)
PHONE..............................617 606-7123
Sheldon Lloyd, *CEO*
EMP: 80 EST: 2009
SALES (est): 5.27MM **Privately Held**
Web: www.cityfresh.com
SIC: 2099 Almond pastes

(G-11691)
FUSE BUILDS LLC (PA)
65 Allerton St (02119-2901)
PHONE..............................617 602-4001
Kevin Chin, *Pr*
Marshall Felix, *

Joseph Prates, *
EMP: 40 EST: 2004
SALES (est): 60.95MM
SALES (corp-wide): 60.95MM **Privately
Held**
Web: www.libertycs.com
SIC: 1389 Construction, repair, and
dismantling services

(G-11692)
PAYNE/BOUCHIER INC (PA)
173a Norfolk Ave (02119-3045)
PHONE..............................617 445-4323
Oliver Bouchier, *Pr*
Steve Payne, *
Thomas Payne, *
EMP: 35 EST: 1983
SQ FT: 5,000
SALES (est): 8.76MM **Privately Held**
Web: www.paynebouchier.com
SIC: 1751 2431 2434 Cabinet and finish
carpentry; Millwork; Wood kitchen cabinets

Roxbury Crossing
Suffolk County

(G-11693)
PLACE TAILOR
103 Terrace St Fl 3 (02120-3441)
PHONE..............................617 639-0633
Evan Smith, *Pr*
EMP: 30 EST: 2019
SALES (est): 2.98MM **Privately Held**
Web: www.placetailor.com
SIC: 1389 Construction, repair, and
dismantling services

Russell
Hampden County

(G-11694)
**COUNTRYSIDE WOODCRAFT
LLP**
665 Huntington Rd (01071-9525)
P.O. Box 439 (01071-0439)
PHONE..............................413 862-3276
Jerald Reinford, *Pt*
Ronald Hess, *Pt*
EMP: 14 EST: 2000
SQ FT: 13,580
SALES (est): 439.93K **Privately Held**
SIC: 2511 Wood household furniture

(G-11695)
TEXON USA INC
1190 Huntington Rd (01071-9527)
P.O. Box 609 (01086-0609)
PHONE..............................413 862-3652
◆ EMP: 50
SIC: 2824 Elastomeric fibers

Rutland
Worcester County

(G-11696)
BRIGGS LUMBER PRODUCTS
336 E County Rd (01543-2034)
P.O. Box 203 (01543-0203)
PHONE..............................978 630-4207
Michael A Ball, *Owner*
EMP: 12 EST: 1958
SQ FT: 10,000
SALES (est): 442.09K **Privately Held**
SIC: 2448 Pallets, wood

Sagamore Beach
Barnstable County

(G-11697)
PEPSI-COLA METRO BTLG CO INC
Also Called: Pepsi-Cola
103 State Rd (02562-2415)
PHONE................................508 833-5600
John Baptista, *Mgr*
EMP: 41
SALES (corp-wide): 86.39B **Publicly Held**
Web: www.pepsico.com
SIC: 4226 2086 Special warehousing and storage, nec; Bottled and canned soft drinks
HQ: Pepsi-Cola Metropolitan Bottling Company, Inc.
700 Anderson Hill Rd
Purchase NY 10577
914 767-6000

(G-11698)
SOUTHEASTERN MILLWORK CO INC
150 State Rd (02562-2317)
PHONE................................508 888-6038
Charles S Cooper, *Prin*
EMP: 8 **EST:** 2012
SALES (est): 215.04K **Privately Held**
Web: www.southeasternmillwork.com
SIC: 2431 Millwork

Salem
Essex County

(G-11699)
ACCUPROBE CORPORATION
Also Called: Accuprobe
35 Congress St Ste 201 (01970-7315)
PHONE................................978 745-7878
Madhukar Reddy, *Brnch Mgr*
EMP: 12
SQ FT: 7,000
SALES (corp-wide): 4.06MM **Privately Held**
Web: www.accuprobe.com
SIC: 3674 Semiconductors and related devices
PA: Accuprobe Corporation
5 Eliot Rd
Lexington MA

(G-11700)
AMERICAL SERGICAL COMPANY
45 Congress St (01970-5579)
PHONE................................781 592-7200
Barbara Greenspan, *Treas*
EMP: 7 **EST:** 2015
SALES (est): 503.78K **Privately Held**
Web: www.americansurgical.com
SIC: 3842 Surgical appliances and supplies

(G-11701)
AMERICAN SURGICAL COMPANY LLC
45 Congress St Ste 153 (01970-5998)
PHONE................................781 592-7200
Roger Piasio, *Managing Member*
Shirley Piasio, *
EMP: 40 **EST:** 1985
SQ FT: 11,000
SALES (est): 5.09MM **Privately Held**
Web: www.americansurgical.com

SIC: 3841 3842 Surgical and medical instruments; Surgical appliances and supplies

(G-11702)
ATOMIC CAFE INC (PA)
45 Mason St Ste 1 (01970-2266)
PHONE................................978 910-0489
EMP: 7 **EST:** 2010
SALES (est): 416.81K **Privately Held**
Web: www.atomicafe.com
SIC: 2095 Coffee roasting (except by wholesale grocers)

(G-11703)
BIRCH OUTFITTERS LLC
Also Called: Liv Outdoor
27 Congress St Ste 210 (01970-5523)
PHONE................................978 498-4631
Ronald J Petrucci, *Managing Member*
Ronald A Petrucci, *Managing Member*
EMP: 12 **EST:** 2018
SALES (est): 1.49MM **Privately Held**
Web: www.livoutdoor.com
SIC: 5699 5961 2211 5136 Designers, * apparel; Women's apparel, mail order; Apparel and outerwear fabrics, cotton; Men's and boys' outerwear

(G-11704)
BRISTOL BAY LLC
70 Washington St Ste 310 (01970-3520)
PHONE................................978 744-4272
George C Vernet Iii, *Prin*
EMP: 7 **EST:** 2016
SALES (est): 339.45K **Privately Held**
SIC: 2621 Paper mills

(G-11705)
BRITO ICE LLC
17 Canal St (01970-4881)
PHONE................................978 744-7727
Danny Biega, *Managing Member*
EMP: 10 **EST:** 2019
SALES (est): 800.98K **Privately Held**
Web: www.britoice.com
SIC: 2097 Manufactured ice

(G-11706)
BURNHAM ASSOCIATES INC
14 Franklin St (01970-2504)
PHONE................................978 745-1788
Craig Burnham, *Pr*
Cynthia Burnham, *Clerk*
EMP: 15 **EST:** 1961
SALES (est): 2.18MM **Privately Held**
Web: www.burnhammarine.com
SIC: 3944 1629 Games, toys, and children's vehicles; Marine construction

(G-11707)
CABOT HERITAGE CORPORATION
Also Called: Cabot Market Letter
176 North St (01970-1648)
P.O. Box 2049 (01970-6249)
PHONE................................978 745-5532
Timothy W Lutts, *Pr*
EMP: 20 **EST:** 1970
SQ FT: 2,000
SALES (est): 2.43MM **Privately Held**
Web: www.cabotwealth.com
SIC: 2721 Magazines: publishing only, not printed on site

(G-11708)
CRYSTAL GT SYSTEMS LLC
Also Called: Corporation, Gtat
35 Congress St (01970-5592)

PHONE................................978 745-0088
◆ **EMP:** 15
Web: www.crystalsystems.com
SIC: 8731 3679 3674 3281 Commercial research laboratory; Crystals and crystal assemblies, radio; Semiconductors and related devices; Cut stone and stone products

(G-11709)
DARK MONK LLC
21 Conant St (01970-2662)
PHONE................................978 766-5315
Chad Franklin Bennett, *Prin*
EMP: 7 **EST:** 2015
SALES (est): 152.72K **Privately Held**
Web: www.dark-monk.com
SIC: 3949 Sporting and athletic goods, nec

(G-11710)
DEACON GILES INC
75 Canal St (01970-4886)
PHONE................................781 883-8256
Ian Hunter, *CEO*
Dawn Mcdonald, *Managing Member*
EMP: 7 **EST:** 2015
SALES (est): 619.04K **Privately Held**
Web: www.deacongiles.com
SIC: 2085 Distilled and blended liquors

(G-11711)
DESCHAMPS PRINTING CO INC
Also Called: Deschamps Printing
3 Dodge St (01970-3603)
P.O. Box 127 (01970-0127)
PHONE................................978 744-2152
Henry P Deschamps, *Pr*
Gina Viscusi Deschamps, *Treas*
Thomas J Alexander, *Sec*
EMP: 17 **EST:** 1916
SQ FT: 12,000
SALES (est): 2.07MM **Privately Held**
Web: www.deschampsprinting.com
SIC: 2752 Offset printing

(G-11712)
DOYLE SAILMAKERS INC (PA)
96 Swampscott Rd Ste 8 (01970-7004)
PHONE................................978 740-5950
Robert Doyle, *Pr*
▲ **EMP:** 30 **EST:** 1982
SQ FT: 12,000
SALES (est): 6.35MM
SALES (corp-wide): 6.35MM **Privately Held**
Web: www.doylesails.com
SIC: 2394 Sails: made from purchased materials

(G-11713)
ENDODYNAMIX INC
121 Loring Ave Ste 910 (01970-4491)
PHONE................................978 740-0400
Pavel Menn, *Pr*
EMP: 10 **EST:** 2008
SALES (est): 266.82K
SALES (corp-wide): 1.05B **Publicly Held**
Web: www.endodynamix.com
SIC: 3841 Surgical and medical instruments
PA: Conmed Corporation
11311 Concept Blvd
Largo FL 33773
727 392-6464

(G-11714)
EXCELITAS TECHNOLOGIES CORP
35 Congress St Ste 2021 (01970-7314)
PHONE................................800 775-6786
Jim Roche, *Brnch Mgr*

EMP: 150
SALES (corp-wide): 1.48B **Privately Held**
Web: www.excelitas.com
SIC: 3677 3679 Electronic coils and transformers; Power supplies, all types: static
HQ: Excelitas Technologies Corp.
200 West St Ste 4
Waltham MA 02451

(G-11715)
FOOTPRINT PWR ACQUISITIONS LLC
24 Fort Ave (01970-5623)
PHONE................................978 740-8411
Peter Furniss, *Prin*
EMP: 10 **EST:** 2012
SALES (est): 434.68K **Privately Held**
Web: www.footprintpower.com
SIC: 2752 Commercial printing, lithographic

(G-11716)
G & D TOOL CO INC
12 Proctor St (01970-2117)
PHONE................................978 745-0020
FAX: 978 745-5215
EMP: 10
SQ FT: 4,000
SALES (est): 1.43MM **Privately Held**
Web: www.gdtool.com
SIC: 3545 Precision tools, machinists'

(G-11717)
G&E STEEL FABRICATORS INC
4 Florence St Unit 5 (01970-4884)
PHONE................................978 741-0391
▲ **EMP:** 16 **EST:** 1995
SQ FT: 3,000
SALES (est): 2.16MM **Privately Held**
Web: www.gandesteel.com
SIC: 3441 Fabricated structural metal

(G-11718)
GARDNER MATTRESS CORPORATION (PA)
254 Canal St (01970-4596)
PHONE................................978 744-1810
TOLL FREE: 800
Gardner P Sisk, *Pr*
EMP: 16 **EST:** 1933
SQ FT: 20,000
SALES (est): 2.29MM
SALES (corp-wide): 2.29MM **Privately Held**
Web: www.gardnermattress.com
SIC: 2515 Mattresses, innerspring or box spring

(G-11719)
GILLIANS FOODS INC
45 Congress St Ste 4 (01970-5598)
PHONE................................781 586-0086
Robert W Otolo, *Pr*
Nicholas Sideri, *
Gillian Sideri, *
▲ **EMP:** 30 **EST:** 1996
SQ FT: 30,000
SALES (est): 4.86MM **Privately Held**
Web: www.gilliansfoodsglutenfree.com
SIC: 2099 Food preparations, nec

(G-11720)
H&H PROPELLER AND SHAFT INC
0 Essex St (01970-5246)
PHONE................................800 325-0117
Ralph Faia, *CEO*
EMP: 12 **EST:** 2020
SALES (est): 570.76K **Privately Held**

Web: www.hhprop.com
SIC: 3429 Hardware, nec

(G-11721)
H&H PROPELLER SHOP INC (PA)
0 Essex St (01970-5246)
PHONE...........................978 744-3806
John A Pelletier, *Pr*
Laurence Martin, *
Robert L Telletier, *
William Clemens, *
▲ **EMP:** 38 **EST:** 1951
SALES (est): 5.18MM
SALES (corp-wide): 5.18MM **Privately Held**
Web: www.hhprop.com
SIC: 3714 Motor vehicle parts and accessories

(G-11722)
HAWTHORNE COVE MARINA INC
10 White St (01970-5609)
PHONE...........................978 740-9890
Russell Vickers, *Pr*
Antoinette Vickers, *Sec*
EMP: 8 **EST:** 1992
SQ FT: 2,500
SALES (est): 988.75K **Privately Held**
SIC: 4493 3732 Boat yards, storage and incidental repair; Non-motorized boat, building and repairing

(G-11723)
HENDRICK MANUFACTURING CORP (PA)
32 Commercial St (01970-3917)
PHONE...........................781 631-4400
Daniel P Wiggin, *Pr*
Linda K Wiggin, *CFO*
Jeffrey Grant, *VP*
▲ **EMP:** 19 **EST:** 1952
SQ FT: 10.000
SALES (est): 2.3MM
SALES (corp-wide): 2.3MM **Privately Held**
Web: www.hendrickmanufacturing.com
SIC: 3541 2599 3564 Saws, power (metalworking machinery); Work benches, factory; Dust or fume collecting equipment, industrial

(G-11724)
JEWISH JOURNAL
Also Called: Journal Jewish
121 Loring Ave (01970-4473)
PHONE...........................978 745-4111
Gerald Posner, *Supervisor*
EMP: 10 **EST:** 1976
SALES (est): 892.48K **Privately Held**
Web: www.jewishjournal.org
SIC: 2711 Commercial printing and newspaper publishing combined

(G-11725)
KAISER SYSTEMS INC
Also Called: K S I
35 Congress St Ste 202 (01970-5567)
PHONE...........................978 224-4135
EMP: 99
SIC: 3679 Power supplies, all types: static

(G-11726)
LDR INC
35 Congress St (01970-5529)
PHONE...........................978 825-0020
▲ **EMP:** 44
SIC: 3993 Signs and advertising specialties

(G-11727)
NORTH SHORE JEWISH PRESS LTD
Also Called: Jewish Journal, The
121 Loring Ave (01970-4461)
PHONE...........................978 745-4111
Izzy Adams, *Pr*
EMP: 10 **EST:** 1976
SALES (est): 750.14K **Privately Held**
SIC: 2711 Newspapers: publishing only, not printed on site

(G-11728)
OLSEN & SILK ABRASIVES
35 Congress St (01970-5529)
P.O. Box 8467 (01971-8467)
PHONE...........................978 744-4720
Peter Silk, *Pt*
EMP: 12 **EST:** 1982
SQ FT: 3,000
SALES (est): 1.98MM **Privately Held**
SIC: 3291 Abrasive products

(G-11729)
PAGE STREET PUBLISHING COMPANY
27 Congress St Ste 105 (01970-5577)
PHONE...........................978 594-8758
William Kiester, *Prin*
◆ **EMP:** 13 **EST:** 2011
SALES (est): 996.58K **Privately Held**
Web: www.pagestreetpublishing.com
SIC: 2731 Book publishing

(G-11730)
PLASTILAM INC
14 Proctor St (01970-2117)
P.O. Box 2057 (01970-6257)
PHONE...........................978 745-5563
James Mcguire, *Pr*
Michael Donegan, *VP*
Terry Hardy, *VP*
EMP: 20 **EST:** 1979
SQ FT: 11,000
SALES (est): 488.9K **Privately Held**
Web: www.plastilam.com
SIC: 7389 2752 2759 Laminating service; Offset printing; Screen printing

(G-11731)
POWELL AND MAHONEY LLC
39 Norman St (01970-3357)
PHONE...........................978 745-4332
Mark E Mahoney, *Prin*
EMP: 13 **EST:** 2012
SALES (est): 992.03K **Privately Held**
Web: www.powellandmahoney.com
SIC: 2087 Beverage bases, concentrates, syrups, powders and mixes

(G-11732)
SOUNDOWN CORPORATION (PA)
16 Broadway (01970-2922)
PHONE...........................978 745-7000
◆ **EMP:** 38 **EST:** 1983
SALES (est): 7.25MM
SALES (corp-wide): 7.25MM **Privately Held**
Web: www.soundown.com
SIC: 3296 Acoustical board and tile, mineral wool

(G-11733)
STEEL ROOT INC
16 Front St Ste 202 (01970-3743)
PHONE...........................978 312-7668
Ryan Heidorn, *Pr*

EMP: 19 **EST:** 2016
SALES (est): 2.2MM **Privately Held**
Web: www.c3isit.com
SIC: 3699 Security devices

(G-11734)
THERMAL CIRCUITS INC
1 Technology Way (01970-7000)
PHONE...........................978 745-1162
Anthony A Klein, *Pr*
David M Abbot, *
John H Kellogg, *
▲ **EMP:** 150 **EST:** 1961
SQ FT: 52,000
SALES (est): 21.93MM **Privately Held**
Web: www.thermalcircuits.com
SIC: 3699 3433 3585 Electric sound equipment; Heating equipment, except electric; Refrigeration and heating equipment

(G-11735)
TITAN ADVNCED ENRGY SLTONS INC
35 Congress St Ste 251 (01970-5529)
PHONE...........................561 654-5558
Sean O'day, *CCO*
Shawn Murphy, *CEO*
◆ **EMP:** 16 **EST:** 2016
SALES (est): 1.36MM **Privately Held**
Web: www.titanaes.com
SIC: 3691 Batteries, rechargeable

(G-11736)
TROPICAL PRODUCTS INC
220 Highland Ave (01970-1842)
PHONE...........................978 740-5665
Edward Berman, *Pr*
▲ **EMP:** 45 **EST:** 1992
SQ FT: 50,000
SALES (est): 9.85MM **Privately Held**
Web: www.tropicalproducts.com
SIC: 2844 Face creams or lotions

(G-11737)
UNITED STATES BIOLOGICAL CORP
4 Technology Way (01970-7002)
P.O. Box 261 (01907-0461)
PHONE...........................978 744-0345
EMP: 31 **EST:** 1995
SALES (est): 5.73MM **Privately Held**
Web: www.usbio.net
SIC: 8999 2899 Chemical consultant; Chemical preparations, nec

---

Salisbury
Essex County

(G-11738)
AMERICAN SHEET METAL LLC
4 Fanaras Dr (01952-1443)
PHONE...........................978 578-8360
James Levasseur, *Prin*
EMP: 25 **EST:** 2009
SALES (est): 4.21MM **Privately Held**
Web: www.americansheetmetal.net
SIC: 3444 Sheet metalwork

(G-11739)
ANDOVER HEALTHCARE INC
Also Called: Ovik Health
9 Fanaras Dr (01952-1444)
PHONE...........................978 465-0044
Thomas S Murphy, *CEO*
Paula Cerulli, *Ex Sec*
◆ **EMP:** 260 **EST:** 1976
SQ FT: 50,000

SALES (est): 50.18MM
SALES (corp-wide): 1.69B **Privately Held**
Web: www.milliken.com
SIC: 3841 Surgical and medical instruments
PA: Milliken & Company
920 Milliken Rd
Spartanburg SC 29303
864 503-2020

(G-11740)
CULVER COMPANY LLC
104 Bridge Rd (01952-2410)
PHONE...........................978 463-1700
Francis Culver Junior, *Managing Member*
EMP: 17 **EST:** 1977
SALES (est): 3.31MM **Privately Held**
Web: www.culverco.com
SIC: 2741 Miscellaneous publishing

(G-11741)
EASTERN MASS MACHINED PDTS INC
164 Elm St (01952-1805)
PHONE...........................978 462-9301
Jack E Hillman Senior, *Pr*
Joseph E Faro, *Clerk*
EMP: 13 **EST:** 1975
SQ FT: 2,000
SALES (est): 476.68K **Privately Held**
Web: www.emmpinc.com
SIC: 3599 Machine shop, jobbing and repair

(G-11742)
MEI RIGGING & CRATING LLC
Also Called: Harnum Crane Service
18 Fanaras Dr (01952-1443)
PHONE...........................978 685-7700
Keith Harnum, *Brnch Mgr*
EMP: 12
SALES (corp-wide): 90.03MM **Privately Held**
Web: www.meiriggingcrating.com
SIC: 1796 7359 3537 Machine moving and rigging; Equipment rental and leasing, nec; Cranes, industrial truck
PA: Mei Rigging & Crating, Llc
421 Water Ave Ne Ste 4300
Albany OR 97321
541 704-2764

(G-11743)
NEW ENGLAND STINLESS DISTR LLC
18 Fanaras Dr (01952-1443)
PHONE...........................978 255-4830
EMP: 18 **EST:** 2010
SQ FT: 3,500
SALES (est): 1.9MM **Privately Held**
SIC: 1711 3795 3312 3498 Process piping contractor; Tanks and tank components; Stainless steel; Piping systems for pulp, paper, and chemical industries

(G-11744)
PV ENGINEERING & MFG INC
88 Rabbit Rd (01952-1312)
PHONE...........................978 465-1221
Vicky Vlismas, *Pr*
Peter Vlismas, *VP*
Nicholas Vlismas, *Treas*
EMP: 22 **EST:** 1996
SQ FT: 17,000
SALES (est): 4.25MM **Privately Held**
Web: www.pvengineering.net
SIC: 3599 Machine shop, jobbing and repair

(G-11745)
VAUGHN THERMAL CORPORATION

---

26 Old Elm St (01952-1898)
P.O. Box 5431 (01952-0431)
PHONE......................978 462-6683
Don Flynn, *Prin*
Ian Bratt, *
Jim Leonard, *
Jimmy Valliere Production Sche duler, *Prin*
▲ **EMP:** 40 **EST:** 1988
SALES (est): 9.22MM
SALES (corp-wide): 51.44MM **Privately Held**
Web: www.vaughncorp.com
SIC: 3639 3634 Major kitchen appliances, except refrigerators and stoves; Electric household cooking appliances
PA: The Nudyne Group Llc
  45 Seymour St
  Stratford CT 06615
  203 378-2659

(G-11746)
VYNORIUS PRESTRESS INC
Also Called: Vynorius Companies, The
150 Elm St (01952-1805)
PHONE......................978 462-7765
William Vynorius, *Pr*
Mary Lou Vynorius, *VP*
Micheal Barth, *VP*
Tracy Vynorius Harris, *Treas*
EMP: 10 **EST:** 1970
SALES (est): 1.99MM **Privately Held**
Web: www.vynorius.com
SIC: 3271 Brick, concrete

Sandwich
Barnstable County

(G-11747)
BOSTON SAND & GRAVEL COMPANY
Also Called: Lawrence Ready-Mix
181 Kiahs Way (02563-2823)
P.O. Box 2096 (02563-8096)
PHONE......................508 888-8002
Jack Greeley, *Mgr*
EMP: 10
SALES (corp-wide): 100.01K **Privately Held**
Web: www.bostonsand.com
SIC: 3273 Ready-mixed concrete
PA: Boston Sand & Gravel Company Inc
  100 N Washington St Fl 2
  Boston MA 02114
  617 227-9000

(G-11748)
COCA COLA BTLG CO OF CAPE COD
Also Called: Coca-Cola
370 Route 130 (02563-2302)
P.O. Box 779 (02563-0779)
PHONE......................508 888-0001
John Kayajan, *Pr*
John Kayajan, *Pr*
Stephen Sinclair, *Clerk*
EMP: 75 **EST:** 1939
SQ FT: 75,000
SALES (est): 4.16MM **Privately Held**
Web: www.cokenortheast.com
SIC: 2086 Soft drinks: packaged in cans, bottles, etc.

(G-11749)
COCA-COLA BEVS NORTHEAST INC
Also Called: Coca-Cola
370 Route 130 (02563-2302)
PHONE......................508 888-0001

Gina Devlin, *Brnch Mgr*
EMP: 21
Web: www.cokenortheast.com
SIC: 2086 5149 Bottled and canned soft drinks; Groceries and related products, nec
HQ: Coca-Cola Beverages Northeast, Inc.
  1 Executive Park Dr # 330
  Bedford NH 03110
  603 627-7871

(G-11750)
GONCO INC (PA)
Also Called: Cape Cod Textile
338 Route 130 (02563-2302)
PHONE......................508 833-3900
Stephen D Gonneville, *Pr*
EMP: 12 **EST:** 1987
SQ FT: 8,000
SALES (est): 990.28K
SALES (corp-wide): 990.28K **Privately Held**
Web: www.capecodtextile.com
SIC: 2395 2261 2385 Embroidery products, except Schiffli machine; Screen printing of cotton broadwoven fabrics; Bibs, waterproof: made from purchased materials

(G-11751)
JP LILLIS ENTERPRISES INC (PA)
Also Called: Polar Cap Ice Co
7 Jan Sebastian Dr (02563-2394)
PHONE......................508 888-8394
Joseph P Lillis, *Pr*
Robert White, *Treas*
Philip Castleman, *Sec*
EMP: 15 **EST:** 1986
SQ FT: 12,000
SALES (est): 4.46MM
SALES (corp-wide): 4.46MM **Privately Held**
SIC: 2097 Manufactured ice

(G-11752)
PID ANALYZERS LLC
Also Called: Hnu
2 Washington Cir Ste 4 (02563-2376)
PHONE......................774 413-5281
Jennifer L Driscoll, *Managing Member*
EMP: 10 **EST:** 2003
SALES (est): 1.85MM **Privately Held**
Web: www.hnu.com
SIC: 3823 Analyzers, industrial process type

(G-11753)
TRIPLE CROWN CBNETS MLLWK CORP
12b Jan Sebastian Dr (02563-2395)
PHONE......................508 833-6500
Kevin Fitzpatrick, *Pr*
Wayne Paciocco, *VP*
EMP: 7 **EST:** 2000
SALES (est): 935.68K **Privately Held**
Web: www.triplecrowncabinetandmillwork.com
SIC: 2431 2434 Planing mill, millwork; Wood kitchen cabinets

Saugus
Essex County

(G-11754)
C F G CORPORATION
181 Central St (01906-2031)
P.O. Box 1146 (01906-0346)
PHONE......................781 233-6110
William J Roberts, *Pr*
EMP: 19 **EST:** 1975

SQ FT: 1,000
SALES (est): 205.24K **Privately Held**
SIC: 5085 3568 3451 Industrial supplies; Power transmission equipment, nec; Screw machine products

(G-11755)
COUNTER CULTURE
60 Main St (01906-3353)
PHONE......................781 439-9810
Chris Galvin, *Prin*
EMP: 7 **EST:** 2010
SALES (est): 217.44K **Privately Held**
Web: www.counterculturecoffee.com
SIC: 3131 Counters

(G-11756)
DATTCO SALES & SERVICE
121 Ballard St (01906-1762)
PHONE......................860 229-4878
EMP: 8 **EST:** 2019
SALES (est): 56.14K **Privately Held**
Web: www.dattco.com
SIC: 7539 3713 Automotive repair shops, nec; Truck and bus bodies

(G-11757)
EASTERN METAL INDUSTRIES INC
910 Broadway Rear (01906-3236)
PHONE......................781 231-5220
Gabriel Pasquale, *Pr*
EMP: 10 **EST:** 1987
SQ FT: 14,000
SALES (est): 1.79MM **Privately Held**
Web: www.easternmetalind.com
SIC: 3441 Fabricated structural metal

(G-11758)
GMF ENGINEERING INC
Also Called: Park Press Printers
15 Main St (01906-2347)
PHONE......................781 233-0315
Gebrael M Farhat, *Pr*
EMP: 19 **EST:** 1993
SALES (est): 1.02MM **Privately Held**
Web: www.parkpressprinters.com
SIC: 2752 Offset printing

(G-11759)
HAMILTON ELEVATOR INTERIORS
6 Belair St (01906-3004)
PHONE......................781 233-9540
Glenn Bowie, *Pr*
EMP: 20 **EST:** 2014
SALES (est): 1.96MM **Privately Held**
SIC: 3534 Elevators and equipment

(G-11760)
HOLCIM - NER INC (DH)
1715 Broadway (01906-4703)
PHONE......................781 941-7200
EMP: 48 **EST:** 1949
SALES (est): 54.25MM **Privately Held**
SIC: 2951 3273 1429 1611 Concrete, bituminous; Ready-mixed concrete; Igneus rock, crushed and broken-quarrying; Highway and street paving contractor
HQ: Holcim - Acm Management, Inc.
  8700 W Bryn Mawr Ave
  Chicago IL 60631
  773 372-1000

(G-11761)
HUNTER ASSOCIATES INC
Also Called: Auto Hunter Magazine
92 Walnut St Ste 3 (01906-1949)
P.O. Box 13 (01940-0013)

PHONE......................781 233-9100
Thomas Lemberger, *Pr*
EMP: 10 **EST:** 1973
SQ FT: 4,000
SALES (est): 571.84K **Privately Held**
Web: www.hunterassociates.com
SIC: 2721 Magazines: publishing only, not printed on site

(G-11762)
LAMB & RITCHIE COMPANY INC
90 Broadway (01906-1091)
PHONE......................781 941-2700
David A Ritchie, *Pr*
▲ **EMP:** 40 **EST:** 1872
SQ FT: 86,000
SALES (est): 9.18MM **Privately Held**
Web: www.lambritchie.com
SIC: 3444 Metal roofing and roof drainage equipment

(G-11763)
NEVRON PLASTICS INC
Also Called: Nevron Plastics and Metals
124 Ballard St (01906-1799)
PHONE......................781 233-1310
Thomas Jarosz, *Pr*
EMP: 15 **EST:** 1965
SQ FT: 58,000
SALES (est): 2.5MM **Privately Held**
Web: www.nevronplastics.com
SIC: 3441 3089 Fabricated structural metal; Plastics processing

(G-11764)
PDKD ENTERPRISES INC
Also Called: Kanes Donuts
120 Lincoln Ave (01906-2812)
P.O. Box 992 (01906-0192)
PHONE......................781 233-8499
Paul Delios, *Pr*
Catherine D Panesis, *Treas*
Maria Delios, *Sec*
EMP: 33 **EST:** 1988
SALES (est): 779.68K **Privately Held**
Web: www.kanesdonuts.com
SIC: 5812 2052 Eating places; Bakery products, dry

(G-11765)
RUSSOS INC
329 Main St (01906-3143)
P.O. Box 665 (02148-0006)
PHONE......................781 233-1737
Vincent J Vannah, *CEO*
Joanne Vannah, *Pr*
EMP: 7 **EST:** 1954
SQ FT: 1,200
SALES (est): 382.47K **Privately Held**
Web: www.russoscandy.com
SIC: 2064 2024 5441 5451 Candy and other confectionery products; Ice cream and frozen deserts; Candy; Ice cream (packaged)

(G-11766)
SHARP SERVICES INC
222 Central St (01906-2107)
P.O. Box 1364 (01906-0664)
PHONE......................781 854-3334
Paul Maganbini, *Owner*
EMP: 7 **EST:** 2009
SALES (est): 959.5K **Privately Held**
Web: www.sharpservicesinc.biz
SIC: 3556 Dehydrating equipment, food processing

(G-11767)
W J ROBERTS CO INC
181 Central St (01906-2031)

P.O. Box 1146 (01906-0346)
PHONE..............................781 233-8176
William J Roberts, *Pr*
EMP: 22 **EST:** 1972
SQ FT: 11,011
SALES (est): 946.5K **Privately Held**
Web: www.wjroberts.com
SIC: 3599 3699 3643 3429 Machine shop, jobbing and repair; Electrical equipment and supplies, nec; Current-carrying wiring services; Hardware, nec

Savoy
Berkshire County

(G-11768)
S & S MACHINE AND WELDING INC
128 Windsor Rd (01256-9211)
PHONE..............................413 743-5714
Fred Sawyer, *Pr*
Gwen Deblois, *Sec*
Allen Sawyer, *Prin*
Richard Sawyer, *Prin*
▼ **EMP:** 9 **EST:** 1989
SQ FT: 2,800
SALES (est): 1.47MM **Privately Held**
Web: www.ssmachineandwelding.com
SIC: 3599 Machine shop, jobbing and repair

Scituate
Plymouth County

(G-11769)
RENEWABLE ENERGY SYSTEMS LLC
15 Wigwam Ln (02066-1439)
PHONE..............................781 545-3320
Debra Katz, *Prin*
EMP: 10
SALES (est): 881.21K **Privately Held**
Web: www.ressolar.com
SIC: 3585 Heating equipment, complete

(G-11770)
SAFVE INC
Also Called: Safve
24 Ladds Way (02066-1921)
PHONE..............................781 545-3546
Shirley Young, *Pr*
EMP: 8 **EST:** 2012
SALES (est): 481.23K **Privately Held**
Web: www.safve.org
SIC: 3589 7389 Water filters and softeners, household type; Fund raising organizations

(G-11771)
SALES SOLUTIONS INC
266 Old Oaken Bucket Rd (02066-4403)
PHONE..............................781 588-2703
Steven P Shurdut, *Pr*
EMP: 9 **EST:** 2005
SALES (est): 448.9K **Privately Held**
Web: www.salessol.com
SIC: 8743 2676 2679 Sales promotion; Sanitary paper products; Paper products, converted, nec

(G-11772)
SCITUATE CONCRETE PIPE CORP
1 Buckeye Ln (02066-1924)
P.O. Box 870 (02066-0870)
PHONE..............................781 545-0564
TOLL FREE: 800
William E Hoffman, *Pr*

Richard W Hoffman, *
EMP: 40 **EST:** 1959
SALES (est): 5.56MM **Privately Held**
Web:
www.scituateconcreteproducts.com
SIC: 3272 Concrete products, precast, nec

(G-11773)
UNTOLD BREWING LLC (PA)
6 Old Country Way (02066-3773)
PHONE..............................781 378-0559
Matthew Elder, *Prin*
EMP: 10 **EST:** 2018
SALES (est): 549.02K
SALES (corp-wide): 549.02K **Privately Held**
Web: www.untoldbrewing.com
SIC: 5813 2082 Bars and lounges; Beer (alcoholic beverage)

Seekonk
Bristol County

(G-11774)
AMARAL CUSTOM FABRICATIONS INC
40 Mead St (02771-5913)
PHONE..............................508 336-6681
EMP: 12
Web: www.amaralcf.com
SIC: 3444 Sheet metalwork

(G-11775)
CONSOLIDATED TRUCK & EQP INC
1727 Fall River Ave (02771-2032)
PHONE..............................508 252-3330
Robert S Dias, *Pr*
Robert S Dias, *Pr*
Patricia Dias, *Treas*
EMP: 8 **EST:** 1984
SALES (est): 910.94K **Privately Held**
Web:
www.consolidatedtruckequipment.com
SIC: 5531 5013 5015 3713 Automotive parts; Automotive supplies and parts; Automotive supplies, used: wholesale and retail; Truck bodies and parts

(G-11776)
H & W TEST PRODUCTS INC
58 Industrial Ct (02771-2017)
PHONE..............................508 336-3200
Gordon R Hutton, *Pr*
Steven A Whitcomb, *VP*
EMP: 12 **EST:** 1989
SQ FT: 6,000
SALES (est): 2.14MM **Privately Held**
Web: www.hwtestproducts.com
SIC: 3825 Test equipment for electronic and electrical circuits

(G-11777)
HERSHEY CREAMERY COMPANY
Also Called: Hershey Ice Cream
107 Pond St (02771-3925)
PHONE..............................508 399-8560
TOLL FREE: 800
Anthony Monteleone, *Mgr*
EMP: 10
SQ FT: 2,800
SALES (corp-wide): 154.45MM **Privately Held**
Web: www.hersheyicecream.com
SIC: 5143 2024 Ice cream and ices; Ice cream and frozen deserts
PA: Hershey Creamery Company
301 S Cameron St

Harrisburg PA 17101
717 238-8134

(G-11778)
IPPOLITOS STONE CRAFT INC
Also Called: Ippolito's Stone Craft
1960 Fall River Ave (02771-2037)
PHONE..............................508 336-9616
▲ **EMP:** 10 **EST:** 1993
SQ FT: 6,000
SALES (est): 1.01MM **Privately Held**
Web: www.ippolitosstonecraft.com
SIC: 3281 Building stone products

(G-11779)
KORNER BAGEL PARTNERSHIP
Also Called: Krazy Korner Bagel & Deli
23 Circle Dr (02771-3724)
PHONE..............................508 336-5204
Betty Delude, *Pt*
Richard Coty, *Pt*
EMP: 9 **EST:** 1994
SALES (est): 249.94K **Privately Held**
SIC: 2051 5461 5812 Bagels, fresh or frozen ; Bagels; Eating places

(G-11780)
LITTLE KIDS INC
1015 Newman Ave (02771-4411)
PHONE..............................800 545-5437
James D Engle, *Pr*
Richard Engle, *
Robin Engle, *OF SPECIAL Project**
Sarah Marcotte, *
◆ **EMP:** 54 **EST:** 1989
SQ FT: 74,000
SALES (est): 9.52MM **Privately Held**
Web: www.littlekidsinc.com
SIC: 3089 3944 Cups, plastics, except foam ; Games, toys, and children's vehicles

(G-11781)
MICRO ELECTRONICS INC
1005 Newman Ave (02771-4411)
PHONE..............................508 761-9161
Gary Perrino, *Pr*
EMP: 10 **EST:** 1974
SQ FT: 2,700
SALES (est): 1MM **Privately Held**
Web: www.micro-strip.com
SIC: 3549 Metalworking machinery, nec

(G-11782)
NU CHROME CORP
32 Industrial Ct (02771-2017)
P.O. Box 362 (02771-0362)
PHONE..............................508 557-1418
Don Kemp, *Pr*
EMP: 15 **EST:** 1992
SQ FT: 40,000
SALES (est): 279.24K **Privately Held**
SIC: 3471 Electroplating of metals or formed products

(G-11783)
PHOENIX INC
257 Pine St (02771-2601)
PHONE..............................508 399-7100
Robert C Fuller, *Pr*
Steven Fuller, *
▲ **EMP:** 38 **EST:** 1974
SQ FT: 65,000
SALES (est): 5.81MM **Privately Held**
Web: www.phoenix-inc.com
SIC: 3541 Machine tools, metal cutting type

(G-11784)
QCI INC
Also Called: Qci Engineering

257 Pine St (02771-2601)
PHONE..............................508 399-8983
EMP: 12 **EST:** 1994
SALES (est): 1.67MM **Privately Held**
Web: www.qcieng.com
SIC: 3634 3599 5088 3841 Housewares, excluding cooking appliances and utensils; Machine and other job shop work; Aeronautical equipment and supplies; Surgical and medical instruments

(G-11785)
SEEKONK MANUFACTURING CO INC
Also Called: Seekonk Precision Tools
87 Perrin Ave (02771-4195)
PHONE..............................508 761-8284
Frederick Dobras, *Pr*
Cindy Richard, *Contrlr*
EMP: 21 **EST:** 1941
SQ FT: 40,000
SALES (est): 2.24MM **Privately Held**
Web: www.seekonk.com
SIC: 3423 Hand and edge tools, nec

(G-11786)
TCI AMERICA INC
21 Industrial Ct (02771-2016)
PHONE..............................508 336-6633
Kathleen Hayes, *Pr*
Michael Young, *VP*
Paula Beliveau, *Contrlr*
EMP: 19 **EST:** 1985
SALES (est): 277.15K **Privately Held**
SIC: 2741 7389 Internet publishing and broadcasting; Fund raising organizations

(G-11787)
TCI PRESS INC
21 Industrial Ct (02771-2016)
PHONE..............................508 336-6633
Mark D Hayes, *Pr*
Steve Dicaprio, *
Kathleen M Hayes, *
EMP: 50 **EST:** 1989
SQ FT: 20,000
SALES (est): 4.04MM **Privately Held**
Web: www.tcipress.com
SIC: 2752 Offset printing

(G-11788)
TELCO COMMUNICATIONS INC
Also Called: TCI
21 Industrial Ct (02771-2026)
PHONE..............................508 336-6633
Mark Hayes, *Pr*
Mark Hayes, *Pr*
Kathleen Hayes, *
EMP: 12 **EST:** 1977
SQ FT: 14,000
SALES (est): 468.55K **Privately Held**
SIC: 2721 7389 Periodicals, publishing only; Promoters of shows and exhibitions

(G-11789)
TILLOTSON RUBBER CO INC
1539 Fall River Ave (02771-3748)
PHONE..............................781 402-1731
Grafton Corbett, *Asst Tr*
Frederick Tillotson, *Dir*
EMP: 256 **EST:** 1967
SQ FT: 50,000
SALES (est): 727.42K
SALES (corp-wide): 40.13MM **Privately Held**
SIC: 3842 Gloves, safety
PA: Tillotson Corporation
159 Main St
Nashua NH 03060
781 402-1731

(G-11790)
WRIGHT TRAILERS INC
1825 Fall River Ave (02771-2007)
PHONE.....................508 336-8530
Daniel D Wright, *Pr*
Steven T Wright, *Dir*
Susan M Wright, *Treas*
Jenn C Caron, *Sec*
EMP: 16 **EST:** 1984
SQ FT: 22,000
SALES (est): 1.16MM **Privately Held**
Web: www.wrighttrailers.com
SIC: 3799 7539　Trailers and trailer
　equipment; Trailer repair

Sharon
Norfolk County

(G-11791)
ADVANCED PRINT SOLUTIONS INC
45 Bishop Rd (02067-2408)
PHONE.....................508 655-8434
Benjamin Zibrak, *Pr*
EMP: 10 **EST:** 2005
SALES (est): 654.03K **Privately Held**
SIC: 2752　Commercial printing, lithographic

(G-11792)
BANACEK INVSTGTONS SRCH RECOVE
1075 Providence Hwy (02067-1671)
P.O. Box 6054 (85246-6054)
PHONE.....................781 784-1400
Gene Irwin, *Prin*
EMP: 8 **EST:** 2014
SALES (est): 686.25K **Privately Held**
Web: www.metalbellows.com
SIC: 3599　Industrial machinery, nec

(G-11793)
INDUSTRIAL METAL PDTS CO INC
Also Called: Inmetal
15 Merchant St (02067-1614)
PHONE.....................781 762-3330
Evelyn E Hurlbut, *Pr*
Craig A Perry, *
EMP: 84 **EST:** 1959
SQ FT: 25,000
SALES (est): 17.04MM **Privately Held**
Web: www.inmetal.com
SIC: 3444 3441　Sheet metalwork;
　Fabricated structural metal

(G-11794)
NOVAGENESIS LLC
77 Norwood St (02067-1262)
PHONE.....................781 784-1149
EMP: 10 **EST:** 1993
SQ FT: 1,000
SALES (est): 843.11K **Privately Held**
Web: www.toughandquick.com
SIC: 2844　Perfumes, cosmetics and other
　toilet preparations

(G-11795)
SENIOR OPERATIONS LLC
Also Called: Metal Bellows
1075 Providence Hwy (02067-1671)
PHONE.....................781 784-1400
John Cory, *Dir*
EMP: 200
SQ FT: 70,000
SALES (corp-wide): 1.02B **Privately Held**
Web: www.metalbellows.com

SIC: 3599　Hose, flexible metallic
HQ: Senior Operations Llc
　300 E Devon Ave
　Bartlett IL 60103
　630 372-3500

(G-11796)
TODD & WELD LLP
4 Manns Hill Cres (02067-2267)
PHONE.....................781 784-1026
James Krachey, *Owner*
EMP: 8 **EST:** 2015
SALES (est): 87.94K **Privately Held**
Web: www.toddweld.com
SIC: 7692　Welding repair

Sheffield
Berkshire County

(G-11797)
CUSTOM EXTRUSION INC (HQ)
34 Home Road (01257-2002)
P.O. Box 517 (01257-0517)
PHONE.....................413 229-8748
EMP: 36 **EST:** 1957
SALES (est): 10.62MM
SALES (corp-wide): 295.68MM **Privately Held**
Web: www.pexco.com
SIC: 3089 3083　Plastics processing;
　Laminated plastics plate and sheet
PA: Pexco Llc
　6470 E Johns Xing Ste 430
　Johns Creek GA 30097
　678 990-1523

(G-11798)
PLASKOLITE LLC
113 Silver St (01257-9626)
PHONE.....................800 628-5084
Don Shultz, *Brnch Mgr*
EMP: 40
SALES (corp-wide): 443.48MM **Privately Held**
Web: www.plaskolite.com
SIC: 2821　Plastics materials and resins
PA: Plaskolite, Llc
　400 W Nationwide Blvd # 400
　Columbus OH 43215
　614 294-3281

(G-11799)
PLASKOLITE LLC
Also Called: Sheffield Plastic Division
119 Salisbury Rd (01257-9706)
PHONE.....................800 628-5084
Don Shultz, *Brnch Mgr*
EMP: 120
SALES (corp-wide): 443.48MM **Privately Held**
Web: www.plaskolite.com
SIC: 2821　Plastics materials and resins
PA: Plaskolite, Llc
　400 W Nationwide Blvd # 400
　Columbus OH 43215
　614 294-3281

(G-11800)
PLASKOLITE MASSACHUSETTS LLC
119 Salisbury Rd (01257-9706)
PHONE.....................413 229-8711
Richard J Larkin, *CFO*
EMP: 140 **EST:** 2018
SALES (est): 44.9MM
SALES (corp-wide): 443.48MM **Privately Held**

SIC: 2821　Plastics materials and resins
PA: Plaskolite, Llc
　400 W Nationwide Blvd # 400
　Columbus OH 43215
　614 294-3281

(G-11801)
SHEFFIELD POTTERY INC
995 N Main St Us (01257-9579)
P.O. Box 399 (01257-0399)
PHONE.....................413 229-7700
John Cowen, *Pr*
Patricia Buteux, *
▼ **EMP:** 25 **EST:** 1946
SQ FT: 37,000
SALES (est): 4.7MM **Privately Held**
Web: www.sheffield-pottery.com
SIC: 3269 5719 3999 1459　Stoneware
　pottery products; Cookware, except
　aluminum; Novelties, bric-a-brac, and
　hobby kits; Clays (common) quarrying

Shelburne Falls
Franklin County

(G-11802)
AUCTIONMETHOD LLC
30 Williams St (01370-1018)
P.O. Box 426 (01370-0426)
PHONE.....................413 489-1389
EMP: 8 **EST:** 2012
SALES (est): 479.81K **Privately Held**
Web: www.auctionmethod.com
SIC: 7372　Prepackaged software

(G-11803)
DAVID W WALLACE
Also Called: Bittersweet Herb Farm
635 Mohawk Trl (01370-9775)
PHONE.....................413 625-6523
David W Wallace, *Owner*
▲ **EMP:** 8 **EST:** 1983
SALES (est): 969.34K **Privately Held**
Web:
bittersweet-herb-farm.myshopify.com
SIC: 3999 5961 5947 5499　Novelties, bric-a-
　brac, and hobby kits; Novelty merchandise,
　mail order; Novelties; Spices and herbs

(G-11804)
EDDIES WHEELS INC
140 State St (01370-1020)
PHONE.....................413 625-0033
Leslie Grinnell, *Pr*
▲ **EMP:** 10 **EST:** 2007
SALES (est): 428.64K **Privately Held**
Web: www.eddieswheels.com
SIC: 3842　Braces, elastic

(G-11805)
JOSH SMPSON CNTEMPORARY GL INC
30 Frank Williams Rd (01370-9724)
PHONE.....................413 625-6145
Josiah Simpson, *Pr*
EMP: 10 **EST:** 1970
SQ FT: 6,000
SALES (est): 929.35K **Privately Held**
Web: www.joshsimpsonglass.com
SIC: 3229　Pressed and blown glass, nec

(G-11806)
LAMSON AND GOODNOW LLC
Also Called: Lamson and Goodnow Mfg
45 Conway St (01370-1420)
P.O. Box 846 (01086-0846)
PHONE.....................413 625-0201
Brian J Hayes, *Prin*

▲ **EMP:** 18 **EST:** 2003
SQ FT: 26,000
SALES (est): 792.24K **Privately Held**
Web: lamson.myshopify.com
SIC: 3421 3089 3423　Table and food
　cutlery, including butchers'; Plastics
　kitchenware, tableware, and houseware;
　Hand and edge tools, nec

(G-11807)
LAMSON AND GOODNOW MFG CO
Also Called: Lamsonsharp
45 Conway St (01370-1420)
PHONE.....................413 625-6311
J Ross Anderson, *CEO*
▲ **EMP:** 38 **EST:** 1837
SQ FT: 30,000
SALES (est): 1.77MM **Privately Held**
Web: www.lamsonproducts.com
SIC: 3421 3423　Table cutlery, except with
　handles of metal; Knives, agricultural or
　industrial

(G-11808)
RAE JS
2231 Mohawk Trl (01370-9434)
PHONE.....................413 625-9228
EMP: 12 **EST:** 2018
SALES (est): 1.08MM **Privately Held**
Web: www.jsrae.com
SIC: 7692　Welding repair

(G-11809)
WILLIAM GREEN INC
18 Conway Rd (01370-9772)
P.O. Box 444 (01370-0444)
PHONE.....................413 475-2014
William Green, *Prin*
EMP: 10 **EST:** 2010
SALES (est): 223.38K **Privately Held**
SIC: 2431　Millwork

Sherborn
Middlesex County

(G-11810)
COMPOSITE COMPANY INC
19 Kendall Ave (01770-1321)
PHONE.....................508 651-1681
EMP: 8 **EST:** 1975
SQ FT: 2,000
SALES (est): 958.3K **Privately Held**
Web: www.compositecompanyinc.com
SIC: 7692　Welding repair

(G-11811)
STORMALONG CIDER LLC (PA)
12 Sewall Brook Ln (01770-1423)
PHONE.....................213 280-4533
Shannon Edgar, *Pr*
EMP: 8
SALES (est): 1MM
SALES (corp-wide): 1MM **Privately Held**
SIC: 2084　Wines, brandy, and brandy spirits

Shirley
Middlesex County

(G-11812)
34 TOWER STREET INC
76 Walker Rd (01464-2900)
PHONE.....................978 425-2311
Tom King, *Pr*
Lisa King-schiappa, *VP*
▲ **EMP:** 35 **EST:** 1976

▲ = Import　▼ = Export
◆ = Import/Export

SQ FT: 21,000
SALES (est): 6.07MM **Privately Held**
Web: www.thermofab.com
SIC: 3089 3469 Thermoformed finished
plastics products, nec; Metal stampings, nec

(G-11813)
ALCAMI CAROLINAS CORPORATION
3 Patterson Rd (01464-2907)
PHONE.................910 619-3952
EMP: 7
SALES (corp-wide): 418.48MM **Privately Held**
Web: www.alcami.com
SIC: 2834 8734 8731 Drugs affecting neoplasms and endrocrine systems; Product testing laboratories; Biological research
HQ: Alcami Carolinas Corporation
2320 Scientific Park Dr
Wilmington NC 28405

(G-11814)
ANNIES GLUTEN FREE BAKERY
Also Called: Wholesale Bakery
2 Shaker Rd Ste C205a (01464-2559)
PHONE.................978 425-5385
EMP: 7 **EST:** 2012
SALES (est): 483.07K **Privately Held**
Web: www.anniesgfbakery.com
SIC: 2051 Bakery: wholesale or wholesale/retail combined

(G-11815)
BEMIS ASSOCIATES INC (PA)
Also Called: Bemis
1 Bemis Way (01464-2527)
PHONE.................978 425-6761
Stephen Howard, *CEO*
Michael Johansen, *
◆ **EMP:** 170 **EST:** 1910
SQ FT: 160,000
SALES (est): 136.54MM
SALES (corp-wide): 136.54MM **Privately Held**
Web: www.bemisworldwide.com
SIC: 2891 2851 3479 Adhesives; Lacquers, varnishes, enamels, and other coatings; Painting, coating, and hot dipping

(G-11816)
HERFCO INC
9 Great Rd (01464-2898)
PHONE.................978 772-4758
James K Farnsworth, *Pr*
EMP: 22 **EST:** 1966
SQ FT: 20,500
SALES (est): 2.65MM **Privately Held**
Web: www.herfco.com
SIC: 3444 Sheet metalwork

(G-11817)
IMAGE SOFTWARE SERVICES INC
Also Called: ISS
2 Shaker Rd Ste D103 (01464-2551)
PHONE.................978 425-3600
Jeffrey W Schwarz, *Pr*
EMP: 8 **EST:** 1992
SQ FT: 2,000
SALES (est): 509.59K **Privately Held**
Web: www.issondemand.com
SIC: 2759 2741 3652 Commercial printing, nec; Posters: publishing and printing; Compact laser discs, prerecorded

(G-11818)
JAMESBROOK ENTERPRISES INC
Also Called: Closets By Design
2 Shaker Rd Ste D100 (01464-2565)
PHONE.................978 425-6166
Russell E Smith, *Pr*
EMP: 9 **EST:** 2002
SQ FT: 6,000
SALES (est): 863.28K **Privately Held**
Web: www.closetsbydesign.com
SIC: 5211 2599 7389 Closets, interiors and accessories; Cabinets, factory; Design services

(G-11819)
KCB SOLUTIONS LLC
900 Mount Laurel Cir (01464-2422)
PHONE.................978 425-0400
Ralph Nilsson, *Pr*
EMP: 16 **EST:** 2003
SALES (est): 7.32MM
SALES (corp-wide): 340.38MM **Privately Held**
Web: www.micross.com
SIC: 3674 Semiconductors and related devices
HQ: Chip Supply, Inc.
1810 S Orange Blossom Trl
Apopka FL 32703
407 298-7100

(G-11820)
MCELROY ELECTRONICS CORP
27 Fredonian St # 33 (01464-2836)
P.O. Box 488 (01464-0488)
PHONE.................978 425-4055
John C Mc Elroy Junior, *Pr*
Daniel L Mc Elroy, *VP*
EMP: 10 **EST:** 1957
SQ FT: 7,500
SALES (est): 883.73K **Privately Held**
Web: www.mcelroyelectronics.com
SIC: 3612 Transformers, except electric

(G-11821)
MOBIUS IMAGING LLC
2 Shaker Rd Ste F100 (01464-2535)
PHONE.................978 796-5068
Kevin A Lobo, *Ch Bd*
▲ **EMP:** 84 **EST:** 2008
SQ FT: 30,000
SALES (est): 18.63MM
SALES (corp-wide): 18.45B **Publicly Held**
Web: www.stryker.com
SIC: 3841 Surgical and medical instruments
PA: Stryker Corporation
2825 Airview Blvd
Portage MI 49002
269 385-2600

(G-11822)
POLAR CONTROLS INC
2 Shaker Rd D-205 (01464-2555)
PHONE.................978 425-2233
Adam Cohen, *Pr*
Josh Tang, *VP*
EMP: 8 **EST:** 1999
SQ FT: 5,000
SALES (est): 922.3K **Privately Held**
Web: www.polarcontrols.com
SIC: 3699 Electrical equipment and supplies, nec

(G-11823)
TIER 7 COMMUNICATIONS
41 Holden Rd (01464-2114)
PHONE.................978 425-9543
Thomas Oldfield, *Pr*
EMP: 7 **EST:** 1999

SALES (est): 598.7K **Privately Held**
SIC: 3674 Integrated circuits, semiconductor networks, etc.

(G-11824)
VANCE CABINET & CARPENTRY
2 Shaker Rd (01464-2525)
PHONE.................603 801-5221
Richard Vance, *Owner*
EMP: 7 **EST:** 2001
SALES (est): 134.41K **Privately Held**
SIC: 2499 Decorative wood and woodwork

Shrewsbury
Worcester County

(G-11825)
ADVANCED MICROSENSORS CORP
333 South St Bldg 2 (01545-7807)
PHONE.................508 770-6600
▼ **EMP:** 40
Web: advancedmicrosensors.openfos.com
SIC: 3674 Semiconductors and related devices

(G-11826)
ALTEC INC
10 Fortune Blvd (01545-4389)
PHONE.................508 752-0660
Arnaud Henrard, *Brnch Mgr*
EMP: 63
SALES (corp-wide): 1.21B **Privately Held**
Web: www.altec.com
SIC: 3531 Construction machinery
PA: Altec, Inc.
210 Inverness Center Dr
Birmingham AL 35242
205 991-7733

(G-11827)
ANOMET PRODUCTS INC
830 Boston Tpke (01545-3386)
PHONE.................508 842-0174
Terence Wong, *Pr*
James Wong, *
EMP: 35 **EST:** 1976
SQ FT: 32,000
SALES (est): 3.81MM **Privately Held**
Web: www.anometproducts.com
SIC: 3471 3643 3357 Anodizing (plating) of metals or formed products; Current-carrying wiring services; Nonferrous wiredrawing and insulating

(G-11828)
ATLANTIC VISION INC
810 Boston Tpke Ste 2 (01545-3389)
PHONE.................508 845-8401
Kathleen Mcdonough, *Pr*
▲ **EMP:** 8 **EST:** 1998
SQ FT: 10,000
SALES (est): 970.65K **Privately Held**
Web: www.atlanticvision.com
SIC: 3827 5049 Optical instruments and apparatus; Optical goods

(G-11829)
BOSTON MEDICAL PRODUCTS INC
70 Chestnut St (01545-4101)
PHONE.................508 898-9300
Stuart K Montgomery, *Pr*
Gabriele Meissner, *
Marcus A Eisenhut, *
EMP: 25 **EST:** 1980
SQ FT: 16,000
SALES (est): 5.41MM **Privately Held**

Web: www.bosmed.com
SIC: 3842 5047 Surgical appliances and supplies; Surgical equipment and supplies
PA: Bess Ag
Gustav-Krone-Str. 7
Berlin BE 14167

(G-11830)
DONAHUE INDUSTRIES INC
5 Industrial Dr (01545-5835)
PHONE.................508 845-6501
Judith L Donahue, *Pr*
Walter Laptewicz, *
EMP: 25 **EST:** 1973
SQ FT: 23,000
SALES (est): 2.58MM **Privately Held**
Web: www.donahueindustries.com
SIC: 3421 3452 3089 3541 Cutlery; Nuts, metal; Plastics containers, except foam; Machine tools, metal cutting type

(G-11831)
DUVA DISTRIBUTORS INC
479 Hartford Tpke (01545-4002)
P.O. Box 560 (01545-0560)
PHONE.................508 841-8182
Christopher Duva, *Pr*
EMP: 30 **EST:** 1997
SQ FT: 13,000
SALES (est): 2.73MM **Privately Held**
Web: duva-distributors-inc.hub.biz
SIC: 2051 Bread, cake, and related products

(G-11832)
EMBROIDERY PLACE
10 Broushane Cir (01545-2050)
PHONE.................508 842-5311
Colleen Gardner, *Owner*
EMP: 8 **EST:** 2000
SALES (est): 244.86K **Privately Held**
SIC: 2395 Embroidery and art needlework

(G-11833)
HEBERT CONFECTIONS LLC
Also Called: Hebert's Candy Mansion
574 Hartford Tpke (01545-4048)
EMP: 14 **EST:** 2005
SQ FT: 25,000
SALES (est): 896.2K **Privately Held**
SIC: 5441 2064 Confectionery produced for direct sale on the premises; Candy bars, including chocolate covered bars

(G-11834)
HEBERT RETAIL LLC
Also Called: Hebert Candies
574 Hartford Tpke (01545-4048)
PHONE.................508 845-8051
Sheila Shechtman, *CEO*
Richard Shechtman, *Ex VP*
EMP: 60 **EST:** 1917
SQ FT: 65,000
SALES (est): 13.19MM
SALES (corp-wide): 24.07MM **Privately Held**
Web: www.hebertcandies.com
SIC: 2064 5441 Candy bars, including chocolate covered bars; Candy, nut, and confectionery stores
PA: American Gourmet Group, Llc
574 Hartford Tpke
Shrewsbury MA 01545
860 761-6500

(G-11835)
INDUSTRIAL POLYMERS & CHEM INC (PA)
508 Boston Tpke (01545-5997)
PHONE.................508 845-6112
Susan M Dacey, *CEO*

Robert Desrosiers, *
▲ **EMP:** 19 **EST:** 1959
SQ FT: 35,000
SALES (est): 5.91MM
SALES (corp-wide): 5.91MM **Privately Held**
Web: www.industrial-polymers.com
SIC: 2821   Plastics materials and resins

(G-11836)
JUNIPER NETWORKS INC
74 S Quinsigamond Ave (01545-4266)
P.O. Box 197 (01545-0197)
PHONE.........................508 523-0427
EMP: 11 **EST:** 2018
SALES (est): 331.69K **Privately Held**
Web: www.juniper.net
SIC: 3577   Computer peripheral equipment, nec

(G-11837)
LFR CHASSIS INC
20 Sewall St (01545-1329)
PHONE.........................508 425-3117
Rob Fuller, *Prin*
EMP: 14 **EST:** 2014
SALES (est): 534.63K **Privately Held**
Web: www.tfrdistribution.com
SIC: 3714   Motor vehicle parts and accessories

(G-11838)
MOHAWK FENCE COMPANY INC
185 Oak St (01545-5809)
PHONE.........................508 614-5507
Michael P Obrien, *Prin*
EMP: 7 **EST:** 2019
SALES (est): 248.82K **Privately Held**
Web: www.mohawkfence.com
SIC: 2273   Finishers of tufted carpets and rugs

(G-11839)
MOTOR SERVICE INC
38 Wachusett Ave (01545-1426)
PHONE.........................508 832-6291
Brian Casey, *Pr*
Kevin Casey, *Treas*
EMP: 11 **EST:** 1926
SALES (est): 491.06K **Privately Held**
Web: www.motorserviceinc.org
SIC: 7538 3715   Engine rebuilding: automotive; Truck trailers

(G-11840)
RASA INCORPORATED
Also Called: Spitjack
268 Boston Tpke (01545-2639)
PHONE.........................508 425-3261
Bruce Frankel, *Pr*
EMP: 12 **EST:** 1978
SALES (est): 326.42K **Privately Held**
Web: www.spitjack.com
SIC: 3433   Logs, gas fireplace

(G-11841)
SEAGATE TECHNOLOGY LLC
333 South St (01545-7807)
PHONE.........................508 770-3111
John J Gannon, *Mgr*
EMP: 19
Web: www.seagate.com
SIC: 3572   Computer storage devices
HQ: Seagate Technology Llc
47488 Kato Rd
Fremont CA 94538
800 732-4283

(G-11842)
SUNRISE GROUP USA LLC
85 Commons Dr Unit 403 (01545-4941)
PHONE.........................508 873-1519
Ashan Abeysekara, *CEO*
Ashan Abeysekara, *Managing Member*
EMP: 50 **EST:** 2021
SALES (est): 1.26MM **Privately Held**
SIC: 8243 2258 0182 2211   Software training, computer; Cloth, warp knit; Food crops grown under cover; Print cloths, cotton

(G-11843)
SUPERCON INCORPORATED
830 Boston Tpke (01545-3386)
PHONE.........................508 842-0174
James Wong, *Ch Bd*
Terenci Wong, *
▲ **EMP:** 39 **EST:** 1962
SQ FT: 32,000
SALES (est): 9.27MM **Privately Held**
Web: www.supercon-wire.com
SIC: 3357   Nonferrous wiredrawing and insulating

(G-11844)
TRANE TECHNOLOGIES COMPANY LLC
Also Called: Ingersoll-Rand
908 Boston Tpke (01545-3303)
PHONE.........................508 842-5769
April Dickey, *Mgr*
EMP: 50
Web: www.trane.com
SIC: 3561   Pumps and pumping equipment
HQ: Trane Technologies Company Llc
800 Beaty St Ste E
Davidson NC 28036
704 655-4000

(G-11845)
TRI-STAR PLASTICS CORP (PA)
Also Called: Tristar
906 Boston Tpke (01545-3303)
P.O. Box 3065 (02241-3065)
PHONE.........................508 845-1111
Richard Cedrone, *CEO*
David Mello, *
David Biering, *
Judy Cedrone, *
Adrian Carrera, *
▲ **EMP:** 50 **EST:** 1982
SQ FT: 38,000
SALES (est): 26.16MM
SALES (corp-wide): 26.16MM **Privately Held**
Web: www.tstar.com
SIC: 5162 3082 3081 3599   Plastics products, nec; Tubes, unsupported plastics; Plastics film and sheet; Machine shop, jobbing and repair

(G-11846)
VALMET FLOW CONTROL INC
42 Bowditch Dr (01545-1719)
PHONE.........................508 852-0200
EMP: 21
SALES (corp-wide): 5.27B **Privately Held**
Web: www.valmet.com
SIC: 3592   Valves
HQ: Valmet Flow Control Inc.
44 Bowditch Dr
Shrewsbury MA 01545
508 852-0200

(G-11847)
VALMET FLOW CONTROL INC (HQ)
44 Bowditch Dr (01545-1719)
PHONE.........................508 852-0200
Pasi Laine, *CEO*
Donroy R Ferdinand, *
Katri Hokkanen, *
▲ **EMP:** 104 **EST:** 1997
SALES (est): 156.32MM
SALES (corp-wide): 5.27B **Privately Held**
Web: www.neles.com
SIC: 3592   Valves
PA: Valmet Oyj
Keilasatama 5
Espoo 02150
106720000

(G-11848)
WELD ENGINEERING CO INC
34 Fruit St (01545-3200)
PHONE.........................508 842-2224
Thomas Less, *Pr*
◆ **EMP:** 26 **EST:** 1979
SALES (est): 1.98MM **Privately Held**
Web: www.weldengineering.com
SIC: 3548 5084 3564   Electric welding equipment; Welding machinery and equipment; Air cleaning systems

(G-11849)
WORCESTER SAND AND GRAV CO INC
182 Holden St (01545-5524)
PHONE.........................508 852-1683
Michael A Trotto, *Pr*
Joseph Trotto, *VP*
EMP: 25 **EST:** 1910
SQ FT: 7,500
SALES (est): 2.08MM **Privately Held**
Web:
www.worcestersandandgravelco.com
SIC: 1442   Construction sand and gravel

(G-11850)
ZYCAL BIOCEUTICALS MFG LLC
3 Turning Leaf Cir (01545-5484)
PHONE.........................888 779-9225
Elaine Ann Fankhauser, *Admn*
EMP: 24
SALES (corp-wide): 251.35K **Privately Held**
Web: www.ostinol.com
SIC: 3999   Barber and beauty shop equipment
PA: Zycal Bioceuticals Manufacturing Llc
5a Executive Dr
Toms River NJ 08755
888 779-9225

Somerset
Bristol County

(G-11851)
CONCENTRIC FABRICATION LLC
179 Riverside Ave (02725-2842)
PHONE.........................774 955-5692
Derek Riley, *Prin*
EMP: 8 **EST:** 2014
SALES (est): 1.21MM **Privately Held**
Web: www.concentricfab.com
SIC: 3446   Architectural metalwork

(G-11852)
LENMARINE INC
1 Main St (02726-5631)
PHONE.........................508 678-1234
EMP: 7
SALES (corp-wide): 6.75MM **Privately Held**

Web: www.bristolmarine.com
SIC: 2621   Bristols
PA: Lenmarine, Inc.
99 Poppasquash Rd Ste 1
Bristol RI 02809
401 253-2200

(G-11853)
N FERRARA INC
10 Riverside Ave (02725-2869)
PHONE.........................508 679-2440
Nicola Ferrara, *Pr*
Liana Ferrara, *Clerk*
◆ **EMP:** 10 **EST:** 1981
SQ FT: 20,000
SALES (est): 895.11K **Privately Held**
Web: www.nferrara.com
SIC: 3547 5084   Rolling mill machinery; Metalworking machinery

(G-11854)
NORTH ATLANTIC CORP
Also Called: Namco
1255 Grand Army Hwy (02726-1203)
PHONE.........................508 235-4830
TOLL FREE: 800
Peter Humphrey, *Pr*
Irving D Humphrey, *
I Gary Fox, *
◆ **EMP:** 180 **EST:** 1992
SALES (est): 43.71MM **Privately Held**
Web: www.northatlanticcorp.com
SIC: 5031 2431   Doors, nec; Awnings, blinds and shutters: wood

(G-11855)
SPINDLE CITY PRECIOUS METALS
161 Wilbur Ave (02725-2058)
PHONE.........................508 567-1597
EMP: 8 **EST:** 2012
SALES (est): 232.13K **Privately Held**
SIC: 3339   Precious metals

(G-11856)
TAMER INDUSTRIES INC
Also Called: G. T. Safety Products
185 Riverside Ave (02725-2842)
PHONE.........................508 677-0900
Atwell B Hedly, *Pr*
Jeffrey Hedly, *
EMP: 100 **EST:** 1973
SALES (est): 19.06MM **Privately Held**
Web: www.tamerind.com
SIC: 3444   Metal housings, enclosures, casings, and other containers

(G-11857)
THE DUCLOS CORPORATION
Also Called: Gladding-Hearn Shipbuilding
168 Walker St (02725-2043)
P.O. Box 300 (02726-0300)
PHONE.........................508 676-8596
▲ **EMP:** 100 **EST:** 1955
SALES (est): 10.66MM **Privately Held**
Web: www.gladding-hearn.com
SIC: 8711 3731 3732   Designing: ship, boat, machine, and product; Shipbuilding and repairing; Yachts, building and repairing

---

Somerville
Middlesex County

(G-11858)
943 ENTERETAINMENT CORP ✪
21 Cypress St (02143-2601)
PHONE.........................617 608-6943
Travis Rogers, *CEO*

EMP: 10 EST: 2023
SALES (est): 413.57K Privately Held
SIC: 2741 7389 Internet publishing and broadcasting; Business services, nec

(G-11859)
AB OVO NORTH AMERICA INC
285 Washington St Ste 101 (02143-4068)
PHONE....................617 718-0765
Fred Trompert, CEO
EMP: 9 EST: 2017
SALES (est): 494.1K Privately Held
Web: www.ab-ovo.com
SIC: 7372 Prepackaged software
HQ: Ab Ovo Nederland B.V.
Barbizonlaan 87
Capelle Aan Den Ijssel ZH 2908
102861533

(G-11860)
AMES SAFETY ENVELOPE COMPANY (DH)
Also Called: Ames Color File Div
12 Tyler St (02143-3241)
PHONE....................617 684-1000
Kurt Ramsauer, Pr
Tim Donnhue, *
Robert Ainold, *
Steve Diforge, *
◆ EMP: 16 EST: 1919
SQ FT: 270,000
SALES (est): 49.32MM Privately Held
SIC: 2675 5112 Folders, filing, die-cut: made from purchased materials; Office filing supplies
HQ: Tab Products Co. Llc
605 4th St Apt C
Mayville WI 53050
920 387-3131

(G-11861)
ARCHITECTURAL OPENINGS INC
16 Garfield Ave (02145-2105)
PHONE....................617 776-9223
Stephen Kearns, Pr
▲ EMP: 22 EST: 1987
SQ FT: 10,000
SALES (est): 3.94MM Privately Held
Web: www.archop.com
SIC: 3442 Metal doors, sash, and trim

(G-11862)
AUTONOMOUS MARINE SYSTEMS INC
28 Dane St (02143-3237)
PHONE....................703 348-4778
EMP: 9 EST: 2014
SALES (est): 338.88K Privately Held
Web: www.automarinesys.com
SIC: 3429 Aircraft & marine hardware, inc. pulleys & similar items

(G-11863)
BANKS PUBLICATIONS LLC
519 Somerville Ave (02143-3347)
PHONE....................617 996-2283
Holli Banks, Prin
EMP: 8 EST: 2014
SALES (est): 475.49K Privately Held
Web: www.scoutsomerville.com
SIC: 2741 Miscellaneous publishing

(G-11864)
BLUEBIRD BIO INC (PA)
Also Called: Bluebird
455 Grand Union Blvd (02145-1446)
PHONE....................339 499-9300
EMP: 513 EST: 1992

SQ FT: 72,988
SALES (est): 3.6MM Publicly Held
Web: www.bluebirdbio.com
SIC: 2836 8731 Biological products, except diagnostic; Biotechnical research, commercial

(G-11865)
BRYAN ONCOR INC
141 Powder House Blvd (02144-1613)
PHONE....................617 957-9858
Christopher Adams, CEO
EMP: 7 EST: 2009
SQ FT: 1,000
SALES (est): 875.28K Privately Held
SIC: 2834 Pharmaceutical preparations

(G-11866)
CANDLEWICK PRESS INC
99 Dover St Ste 3 (02144-2816)
PHONE....................617 661-3330
Karen Lotz, Pr
David Heatherwick, *
Hilary Berkman, *
Emily M Marchand, *
▲ EMP: 90 EST: 1991
SQ FT: 28,000
SALES (est): 32.39MM Privately Held
Web: www.candlewick.com
SIC: 2731 Books, publishing only
HQ: Walker Books Limited
87 Vauxhall Walk
London SE11
207 793-0909

(G-11867)
CERVENA BARVA PRESS LLC
294 Highland Ave Apt 2 (02144-3272)
PHONE....................617 764-2229
Gloria J Mindock, Mgr
EMP: 8 EST: 2005
SALES (est): 341.66K Privately Held
Web: www.cervenabarvapress.com
SIC: 2741 Miscellaneous publishing

(G-11868)
DE-ICE TECHNOLOGIES INC
444 Somerville Ave Ste 2 (02143-3260)
PHONE....................857 829-7651
Alexandru Bratianu-badea, CEO
EMP: 11 EST: 2015
SQ FT: 2,000
SALES (est): 1.03MM Privately Held
Web: www.deice.com
SIC: 3634 3812 3429 3728 Space heaters, electric; Aircraft/aerospace flight instruments and guidance systems; Aircraft hardware; Deicing equipment, aircraft

(G-11869)
DMC INC
20 Holland St Ste 408 (02144-2749)
PHONE....................617 758-8517
Frank Riordan, Pr
EMP: 8 EST: 2015
SALES (est): 258.77K Privately Held
Web: www.dmcinfo.com
SIC: 3581 Mechanisms and parts for automatic vending machines

(G-11870)
EVERGAGE INC
212 Elm St Ste 4 (02144-2959)
PHONE....................888 310-0589
Karl Wirth, CEO
Meera Murthy, Chief Strategy Officer*
EMP: 70 EST: 2010
SQ FT: 5,000
SALES (est): 10.55MM
SALES (corp-wide): 31.35B Publicly Held

SIC: 7372 Business oriented computer software
PA: Salesforce, Inc.
415 Mission St Fl 3
San Francisco CA 94105
415 901-7000

(G-11871)
FAT HEN LLC
124 Broadway (02145-3201)
PHONE....................617 764-1412
Daniel Bojorquez, Prin
EMP: 9 EST: 2014
SALES (est): 327.73K Privately Held
Web: www.fathenboston.com
SIC: 3663 Cable television equipment

(G-11872)
FINCH THERAPEUTICS INC
200 Innerbelt Rd Ste 400 (02143-4456)
PHONE....................617 229-6499
Mark Smith, Pr
Andrew Noh, Treas
James Burgess, Dir
EMP: 87 EST: 2016
SALES (est): 9.77MM Privately Held
Web: www.finchtherapeutics.com
SIC: 3844 Therapeutic X-ray apparatus and tubes

(G-11873)
FINCH THERAPEUTICS GROUP INC
Also Called: Finch Therapeutics
200 Innerbelt Rd Ste 400 (02143-4531)
PHONE....................617 229-6499
Mark Smith, CEO
Chris Shumway, *
Gregory D Perry, CFO
Zain Kassam, CMO
Marc Blaustein, COO
EMP: 131 EST: 2014
SQ FT: 36,285
SALES (est): 861K Privately Held
Web: www.finchtherapeutics.com
SIC: 2836 Biological products, except diagnostic

(G-11874)
FLAGRAPHICS INC
30 Alston St (02143-2102)
P.O. Box 108 (02143-0002)
PHONE....................617 776-7549
Antonio G Lafuente, Pr
EMP: 25 EST: 1984
SQ FT: 18,349
SALES (est): 1.44MM Privately Held
Web: www.flagraphics.com
SIC: 2399 3446 2499 3089 Flags, fabric; Flagpoles, metal; Flagpoles, wood; Plastics hardware and building products

(G-11875)
FORMLABS INC (PA)
35 Medford St Ste 201 (02143-4237)
PHONE....................617 932-5227
Max Lobovsky, CEO
Mitchell Kapor, *
Dan Oshaughnessy, *
◆ EMP: 400 EST: 2011
SQ FT: 300
SALES (est): 179.32MM
SALES (corp-wide): 179.32MM Privately Held
Web: www.formlabs.com
SIC: 2759 Commercial printing, nec

(G-11876)
GEOMETRIC INFORMATICS INC
387 Somerville Ave Apt 2 (02143-2951)
P.O. Box 325 (02143-0009)
PHONE....................617 440-1078
Shing-tunt Yau, Pr
Yalin Wang, Prin
Xian Feng, Prin
EMP: 9 EST: 2002
SALES (est): 557.92K Privately Held
Web: www.geometricinformatics.com
SIC: 7372 Business oriented computer software

(G-11877)
GEOORBITAL INC
17 Rev Nazareno Properzi Way (02143-3228)
P.O. Box 252 (02494-0009)
PHONE....................617 651-1102
Michael Burtov, CEO
EMP: 15 EST: 2014
SQ FT: 2,000
SALES (est): 1.7MM Privately Held
Web: www.geoo.com
SIC: 3714 Motor vehicle parts and accessories

(G-11878)
GROVE LABS INC
28 Dane St (02143-3237)
PHONE....................703 608-8178
Gabriel Blanchet, CEO
James Byron, Engr
EMP: 13 EST: 2013
SALES (est): 1.06MM Privately Held
Web: www.grovegrown.com
SIC: 3699 7371 Appliance cords, for household electrical equipment; Computer software development and applications

(G-11879)
HERALDAPI INC
246 Highland Ave Apt 3 (02143-1445)
PHONE....................781 799-1165
Matt Antoszyk, Pr
EMP: 15
SALES (est): 528.69K Privately Held
SIC: 7372 Prepackaged software

(G-11880)
HOME HEATING SERVICES CORP
2 Alpine St (02144-2790)
P.O. Box 207 (02143-0902)
PHONE....................617 625-8255
Peter Dupuis, Owner
EMP: 9 EST: 1950
SALES (est): 746.2K Privately Held
SIC: 1389 Oil and gas field services, nec

(G-11881)
INDEPENDENT FABRICATION INC
86 Joy St Rear (02143-2154)
PHONE....................617 666-3609
EMP: 13 EST: 1995
SQ FT: 3,000
SALES (est): 1.3MM Privately Held
Web: www.ifbikes.com
SIC: 3751 Frames, motorcycle and bicycle

(G-11882)
JAMES A KILEY COMPANY
15 Linwood St (02143-2112)
PHONE....................617 776-0344
John C Kiley, Pr
James Kiley Junior, VP
Timothy Kiley, *

EMP: 45 **EST:** 1890
SQ FT: 40,000
SALES (est): 8.78MM **Privately Held**
Web: www.jakiley.com
SIC: 3713 Truck bodies (motor vehicles)

(G-11883)
LABMINDS INC
285 Washington St Ste 3 (02143-3339)
PHONE..............................844 956-8327
Jeff Caputo, *Pr*
Jochen Klingelhoefer, *VP*
Michal Wozny, *VP*
Ricklef Wohlers, *VP*
EMP: 11 **EST:** 2013
SALES (est): 3.02MM **Privately Held**
Web: www.accroma.com
SIC: 3821 Laboratory equipment: fume
   hoods, distillation racks, etc.

(G-11884)
MAGIQ TECHNOLOGIES INC (PA)
11 Ward St Ste 300 (02143-4214)
PHONE..............................617 661-8300
Bob Gelfond, *CEO*
Steven Bookman, *CFO*
Michael Lagasse, *VP*
Audrius Berzanskis, *COO*
Andrew Hammond, *VP*
▲ **EMP:** 12 **EST:** 1999
SALES (est): 2.08MM
SALES (corp-wide): 2.08MM **Privately
Held**
Web: www.magiqtech.com
SIC: 3699 Security devices

(G-11885)
MANGE LLC
Also Called: Mange
30 Summer St Apt 1 (02143-1986)
PHONE..............................917 880-2104
Christopher Spivak, *Managing Member*
▼ **EMP:** 8 **EST:** 2012
SALES (est): 350.22K **Privately Held**
Web: www.freshfruitvinegars.com
SIC: 2099 5149 Vinegar; Condiments

(G-11886)
MICRO-LEADS INC
255 Elm St Ste 300 (02144-2957)
PHONE..............................617 580-3030
Bryan Mclaughlin, *Pr*
EMP: 16 **EST:** 2014
SALES (est): 3.74MM **Privately Held**
Web: www.micro-leads.com
SIC: 3845 Electromedical equipment

(G-11887)
PERFORMER PUBLICATIONS INC
24 Dane St (02143-3202)
P.O. Box 8385 (02888-0385)
PHONE..............................617 627-9200
William House, *CEO*
EMP: 8 **EST:** 1988
SALES (est): 586.96K **Privately Held**
Web: www.performermag.com
SIC: 2741 Music, sheet: publishing and
   printing

(G-11888)
PETER FORG MANUFACTURING CO
50 Park St (02143-3614)
P.O. Box 433 (02143-0006)
PHONE..............................617 625-0337
Donald Forg, *Pr*
David Forg, *VP*

Nancy Forg Clrk, *Prin*
EMP: 18 **EST:** 1881
SQ FT: 30,000
SALES (est): 2.28MM **Privately Held**
Web: www.peterforg.com
SIC: 3469 Stamping metal for the trade

(G-11889)
PRINCETON PRINTING LLC
260 Elm St (02144-2951)
PHONE..............................617 530-0990
Patricia A Wynn, *Prin*
EMP: 7 **EST:** 2011
SALES (est): 137.94K **Privately Held**
SIC: 2752 Commercial printing, lithographic

(G-11890)
PSG FRAMING INC
130 Broadway (02145-3201)
PHONE..............................617 261-1817
Bernard Pucker, *Pr*
Suzanne Pucker, *Sec*
Archie Agan, *Acctg Mgr*
EMP: 15 **EST:** 1976
SQ FT: 9,800
SALES (est): 489.45K **Privately Held**
Web: www.psgframing.com
SIC: 2499 Picture frame molding, finished

(G-11891)
PUCKER GALLERY INC
Also Called: Psg Framing
130 Broadway Rear (02145-3201)
PHONE..............................617 261-1817
J Watkins, *Mgr*
EMP: 13
SALES (corp-wide): 2.15MM **Privately
Held**
Web: www.puckergallery.com
SIC: 3952 4225 Lead pencils and art goods;
   General warehousing and storage
PA: Pucker Gallery, Inc.
   240 Newbury St Ste 3
   Boston MA 02116
   617 267-9473

(G-11892)
QRSTS LLC
Also Called: R.A.w
561 Windsor St Ste B101 (02143-4144)
PHONE..............................617 625-3335
Peter Rinneg, *Managing Member*
EMP: 8 **EST:** 2004
SALES (est): 497.93K **Privately Held**
Web: www.qrsts.com
SIC: 2759 Screen printing

(G-11893)
RAW RINNIGADE ART WORKS LLC
Also Called: Qrst's
561 Windsor St Ste A301 (02143-4194)
PHONE..............................617 625-3335
Peter Rinnig, *Prin*
Ruth Silverstein, *Prin*
EMP: 8 **EST:** 2001
SALES (est): 494.71K **Privately Held**
Web: www.uncooked.com
SIC: 2759 Screen printing

(G-11894)
REFRAME SYSTEMS INC ✪
444 Somerville Ave (02143-3260)
PHONE..............................781 417-9061
Vikas Enti, *CEO*
Charly Mwangi, *Bd of Dir*
Amy Villeneuve, *Bd of Dir*
EMP: 8 **EST:** 2022
SALES (est): 1.03MM **Privately Held**

SIC: 2452 Modular homes, prefabricated,
   wood

(G-11895)
ROGERS FOAM AUTOMOTIVE CORP
20 Vernon St Ste 1 (02145-3699)
PHONE..............................617 623-3010
William Tee, *Brnch Mgr*
EMP: 10
SALES (corp-wide): 94.68MM **Privately
Held**
Web: www.rogersfoam.com
SIC: 3086 Plastics foam products
HQ: Rogers Foam Automotive Corporation
   501 W Kearsley St
   Flint MI 48503
   810 820-6323

(G-11896)
ROGERS FOAM CORPORATION (PA)
20 Vernon St (02145-3699)
PHONE..............................617 623-3010
David P Marotta, *Pr*
Leonard F Clarkin, *Sec*
Mathew Rogers, *Ch*
Dorothy Rogers, *Sec*
◆ **EMP:** 350 **EST:** 1947
SQ FT: 140,500
SALES (est): 94.68MM
SALES (corp-wide): 94.68MM **Privately
Held**
Web: www.rogersfoam.com
SIC: 3086 Packaging and shipping
   materials, foamed plastics

(G-11897)
SOMERVILLE OFFICE
344 Somerville Ave (02143-2918)
PHONE..............................617 776-0738
Joseph A Curtatone, *Mayor.*
EMP: 9 **EST:** 2006
SALES (est): 337.38K **Privately Held**
Web: www.somervillema.gov
SIC: 2053 Cakes, bakery: frozen

(G-11898)
SOMERVILLE ORNA IR WORKS INC
7 George St (02145-3467)
PHONE..............................617 666-8872
Maria Lorusso, *Pr*
Elio A Lorusso, *Treas*
EMP: 9 **EST:** 1996
SALES (est): 903.12K **Privately Held**
Web: www.somervilleiron.com
SIC: 3446 Fences or posts, ornamental iron
   or steel

(G-11899)
SPARKCHARGE INC
455 Grand Union Blvd Pmb 5 (02145-1446)
PHONE..............................866 906-2330
Joshua Aviv, *CEO*
EMP: 50 **EST:** 2017
SALES (est): 9.94MM **Privately Held**
Web: www.sparkcharge.io
SIC: 3621 Storage battery chargers, motor
   and engine generator type

(G-11900)
TESSERA THERAPEUTICS INC
101 South St Ste 500 (02143-4278)
PHONE..............................860 910-6030
EMP: 73
SALES (corp-wide): 660.57MM **Privately
Held**
Web: www.tesseratherapeutics.com

SIC: 2834 Pharmaceutical preparations
HQ: Tessera Therapeutics, Inc.
   55 Cambridge Pkwy Ste 800
   Cambridge MA 02142
   617 868-1888

(G-11901)
THERMO FISHER
61 Medford St (02143-3421)
PHONE..............................781 325-8726
EMP: 11
SALES (est): 1.19MM **Privately Held**
SIC: 3826 Analytical instruments

(G-11902)
TOC FINISHING CORP
22 Clifton St (02144-2560)
PHONE..............................617 623-3310
Timothy J Harney, *Pr*
EMP: 28 **EST:** 1986
SQ FT: 9,000
SALES (est): 521.84K **Privately Held**
Web: www.tocfinishing.com
SIC: 3599 Machine shop, jobbing and repair

(G-11903)
TOR PROJECT INC
56 Waterhouse St Apt 1 (02144-1872)
PHONE..............................206 512-5312
EMP: 15 **EST:** 2018
SALES (est): 83.6K **Privately Held**
Web: www.torproject.org
SIC: 7372 Prepackaged software

(G-11904)
TRACER TECHNOLOGIES INC
Also Called: Eco Division
20 Assembly Square Dr (02145-1307)
PHONE..............................617 776-6410
Fraser M Walsh, *Pr*
▲ **EMP:** 36 **EST:** 1970
SQ FT: 10,000
SALES (est): 6.61MM **Privately Held**
Web: www.tracerbattery.com
SIC: 3691 8731 Storage batteries; Chemical
   laboratory, except testing

(G-11905)
TRI STAR PRINTING & GRAPHICS
33 Park St (02143-3254)
PHONE..............................617 666-4480
Ping Jiang, *Pr*
EMP: 8 **EST:** 1993
SQ FT: 3,207
SALES (est): 983.01K **Privately Held**
Web: www.tristarprinting.com
SIC: 2752 7334 Offset printing;
   Photocopying and duplicating services

(G-11906)
TRUSTEES OF TUFTS COLLEGE (PA)
Also Called: Tufts University
169 Holland St Ste 318 (02144-2401)
PHONE..............................617 628-5000
Anthony Monaco, *Pr*
James A Stern, *
Sol Gittleman, *
Thomas S Mc Gurty, *
Kathe Cronin, *Human Relations Vice
President*
▲ **EMP:** 300 **EST:** 1852
SALES (est): 1.43B
SALES (corp-wide): 1.43B **Privately Held**
Web: www.tufts.edu
SIC: 8221 2791 2752 University; Typesetting
   ; Commercial printing, lithographic

▲ = Import ▼ = Export
◆ = Import/Export

(G-11907)
TULIP INTERFACES INC (PA)
Also Called: Tulip
77 Middlesex Ave Ste A (02145-1109)
PHONE...................................833 468-8547
Natan Linder, *CEO*
Natan Linder, *Pr*
Rony Kubat, *
EMP: 111 EST: 2013
SALES (est): 14.28MM
SALES (corp-wide): 14.28MM **Privately Held**
Web: www.tulip.co
SIC: 7372 Business oriented computer software

(G-11908)
U-HAUL CO MASS & OHIO INC (DH)
Also Called: U-Haul
151 Linwood St (02143-2196)
PHONE...................................617 625-2789
▲ **EMP: 40 EST:** 1990
SALES (est): 51.36MM
SALES (corp-wide): 5.86B **Publicly Held**
Web: www.uhaul.com
SIC: 3715 7539 7538 7513 Truck trailers; Trailer repair; General truck repair; Truck rental and leasing, no drivers
HQ: U-Haul International, Inc.
2727 N Central Ave
Phoenix AZ 85004
602 263-6011

(G-11909)
VAGRANTS INC
230 Somerville Ave (02143-3406)
PHONE...................................857 400-8870
EMP: 16 EST: 2017
SALES (est): 2.36MM **Privately Held**
Web: www.vagrants.com
SIC: 3572 Computer storage devices

(G-11910)
VIA SCIENCE INC (PA)
49r Day St (02144-2823)
PHONE...................................857 600-2171
Colin Gounden, *CEO*
Katherine Ravanis, *Sr VP*
EMP: 10 EST: 2016
SALES (est): 2.04MM
SALES (corp-wide): 2.04MM **Privately Held**
Web: www.solvewithvia.com
SIC: 7372 Business oriented computer software

(G-11911)
VIDEOIQ INC
450 Artisan Way Ste 200 (02145-1262)
PHONE...................................781 222-3069
Alexander Fernandes, *Ch Bd*
Douglas Marman, *
Michael Gardner, *
Mahesh Saptharishi, *
Stephen Lefkowitz, *
▲ **EMP: 32 EST:** 2007
SQ FT: 10,000
SALES (est): 4.49MM **Privately Held**
Web: www.videoiq.com
SIC: 3699 8731 7382 Security devices; Electronic research; Confinement surveillance systems maintenance and monitoring

(G-11912)
VOXEL8 INC
21 Rev Nazareno Properzi Way Ste N (02143-3222)
PHONE...................................916 396-3714

Jennifer Lewis, *Pr*
EMP: 16 EST: 2014
SALES (est): 2.57MM **Privately Held**
Web: www.kornit.com
SIC: 3577 7371 Printers and plotters; Computer software development and applications

(G-11913)
WATERTOWN PRINTERS INC
21 Mcgrath Hwy Ste 3 (02143-4219)
PHONE...................................781 893-9400
Bradley Geilfuss, *Pr*
John H Geilfuss, *Treas*
Son Hui Geilfuss, *Dir*
EMP: 7 EST: 1983
SQ FT: 6,000
SALES (est): 481.56K **Privately Held**
SIC: 2759 Screen printing

South Barre
Worcester County

(G-11914)
290 INDUSTRIAL STITCHING INC
49 Main St (01074-7728)
P.O. Box 204 (01005-0204)
PHONE...................................978 355-0271
Shoua Her, *Dir*
EMP: 8 EST: 2007
SALES (est): 207.38K **Privately Held**
Web: www.mattsewing.com
SIC: 2395 Hemstitching: for the trade

South Carver
Plymouth County

(G-11915)
REDI-MIX LP
P.O. Box 682 (02366-0682)
PHONE...................................508 295-5111
EMP: 38
SIC: 3273 Ready-mixed concrete
HQ: Redi-Mix Lp
1445 Mac Arthur Dr Ste 13
Carrollton TX 75007
972 242-4550

South Dartmouth
Bristol County

(G-11916)
CONCORDIA CO INC
300 Gulf Rd (02748-1515)
PHONE...................................508 999-1381
Robert Macgregor, *Pr*
EMP: 22 EST: 1926
SQ FT: 30,000
SALES (est): 1.77MM **Privately Held**
Web: www.concordiaboats.com
SIC: 7699 4226 3732 Boat repair; Special warehousing and storage, nec; Boatbuilding and repairing

(G-11917)
MARSHALL MARINE CORPORATION
55 Shipyard Ln (02748-2115)
PHONE...................................508 994-0414
Geoff Marshall, *Pr*
Jo-ann Taylor, *Off Mgr*
▼ **EMP: 16 EST:** 1963
SQ FT: 10,000
SALES (est): 417.83K **Privately Held**
Web: www.marshallcat.com

SIC: 3732 4493 Boats, fiberglass: building and repairing; Boat yards, storage and incidental repair

(G-11918)
P STRAKER LTD
Also Called: Penny Straker Gardens
8 Middle St (02748-3428)
PHONE...................................508 996-4804
Penelope Straker, *Pr*
EMP: 7 EST: 1961
SQ FT: 1,500
SALES (est): 481.87K **Privately Held**
SIC: 2741 5949 Patterns, paper: publishing only, not printed on site; Knitting goods and supplies

(G-11919)
PHOENIX SHEET METAL
53 Cove Rd (02748-2736)
PHONE...................................508 994-4046
Stephen Contois, *Owner*
EMP: 8 EST: 1980
SQ FT: 800
SALES (est): 782.81K **Privately Held**
SIC: 3444 1761 Sheet metalwork; Sheet metal work, nec

South Deerfield
Franklin County

(G-11920)
ATLANTIC FURNITURE INC
5 Industrial Dr W (01373-7324)
P.O. Box 287 (01373-0287)
PHONE...................................413 665-4700
Mark S Valone, *Pr*
Dan Lanchard, *
◆ **EMP: 35 EST:** 1985
SQ FT: 80,000
SALES (est): 8.57MM **Privately Held**
Web: www.afifurnishings.com
SIC: 5712 2511 Furniture stores; Wood household furniture

(G-11921)
BERKSHIRE BREWING COMPANY INC (PA)
12 Railroad St (01373-1034)
P.O. Box 251 (01373-0251)
PHONE...................................413 665-6600
Christopher T Lalli, *Pr*
Gary Bogoff, *Treas*
▲ **EMP: 10 EST:** 1992
SQ FT: 7,000
SALES (est): 4.91MM **Privately Held**
Web: www.berkshire-brewing.com
SIC: 5813 2082 Bars and lounges; Beer (alcoholic beverage)

(G-11922)
CHANNING BETE COMPANY INC (PA)
Also Called: Channing-Bete
1 Community Pl (01373-7328)
P.O. Box 908 (01302-0908)
PHONE...................................413 665-7611
Michael G Bete, *Pr*
Channing L Bete, *
Kim M Canuel, *
Joseph T Bartlett Junior, *Sec*
Channing L Bete Junior, *Dir*
◆ **EMP: 220 EST:** 1936
SALES (est): 47.01MM
SALES (corp-wide): 47.01MM **Privately Held**
Web: www.channingbete.com

SIC: 2731 7812 2732 Pamphlets: publishing and printing; Video tape production; Book printing

(G-11923)
HABITAT POST & BEAM INC
Also Called: Habitat Virtual Village
21 Elm St (01373-1005)
PHONE...................................413 665-4006
Peter D May, *Pr*
Huckle May, *VP*
EMP: 23 EST: 1973
SQ FT: 2,860
SALES (est): 1.44MM **Privately Held**
Web: www.postandbeam.com
SIC: 2452 Modular homes, prefabricated, wood

(G-11924)
HARDIGG INDUSTRIES LLC (HQ)
Also Called: Hardigg Cases
147 N Main St (01373-1026)
P.O. Box 201 (01373-0201)
PHONE...................................413 665-2163
◆ **EMP: 225 EST:** 1954
SALES (est): 62.2MM
SALES (corp-wide): 508.69MM **Privately Held**
Web: hardigg-industries-inc.sbcontract.com
SIC: 3559 3089 3086 8711 Plastics working machinery; Plastics containers, except foam ; Insulation or cushioning material, foamed plastics; Designing: ship, boat, machine, and product
PA: Pelican Products, Inc.
23215 Early Ave
Torrance CA 90505
310 326-4700

(G-11925)
NUCOR HRRIS RBAR NORTHEAST LLC
Also Called: Harris Steel
73 Old State Rd (01373-9758)
P.O. Box 221 (01373-0221)
PHONE...................................413 665-2381
Brian Luippold, *Brnch Mgr*
EMP: 55
SALES (corp-wide): 41.51B **Publicly Held**
Web: www.harrisrebar.com
SIC: 3441 Fabricated structural metal
HQ: Nucor Harris Rebar Northeast Llc
55 Sumner St Ste 1
Milford MA 01757
800 370-0132

(G-11926)
PELICAN PRODUCTS INC
147 N Main St (01373-1026)
PHONE...................................413 665-2163
Mark Case, *Brnch Mgr*
EMP: 25
SALES (corp-wide): 508.69MM **Privately Held**
Web: www.pelican.com
SIC: 3648 Lighting equipment, nec
PA: Pelican Products, Inc.
23215 Early Ave
Torrance CA 90505
310 326-4700

(G-11927)
PILOT PRECISION PRODUCTS LLC
Also Called: Pilot Precision
15 Merrigan Way (01373-1106)
PHONE...................................413 350-5200
EMP: 30 EST: 2016
SALES (est): 2.73MM **Privately Held**

Web: www.pilotprecision.com
SIC: 3545 Broaches (machine tool accessories)

(G-11928)
PRO PEL PLASTECH INC (PA)
378 Long Plain Rd (01373-9642)
P.O. Box 165 (01373-0165)
PHONE..........................413 665-3379
Joseph H Nickerson Iii, *CEO*
Joseph H Nickerson Iv, *Pr*
Marcia L Nickerson, *
EMP: 40 EST: 1984
SQ FT: 32,500
SALES (est): 4.8MM
SALES (corp-wide): 4.8MM **Privately Held**
Web: www.propelplastech.com
SIC: 3089 Injection molding of plastics

(G-11929)
TECHNOMAD ASSOCIATES LLC
37 Harvard St Ste 2 (01373)
PHONE..........................413 665-6704
EMP: 7
Web: www.technomad.com
SIC: 3651 Loudspeakers, electrodynamic or magnetic
PA: Technomad Associates, Llc
   5 Tina Dr
   South Deerfield MA 01373

(G-11930)
WORTHINGTON ASSEMBLY INC
14 Industrial Dr E Unit 2 (01373-7338)
PHONE..........................413 397-8265
Neil C Scanlon, *Pr*
Tom Quinn, *Pt*
Barbara Quinn, *Pt*
Peter Connor, *Sec*
Rafal Dybacki, *CFO*
EMP: 15 EST: 1974
SQ FT: 2,000
SALES (est): 4.6MM **Privately Held**
Web: www.worthingtonassembly.com
SIC: 3672 Printed circuit boards

(G-11931)
YANKEE CANDLE COMPANY INC (DH)
Also Called: Yankee Candle
16 Yankee Candle Way (01373-7325)
P.O. Box 110 (01373-0110)
PHONE..........................413 665-8306
Lisa Mccarthy, *CEO*
James A Perley, *CAO*
◆ EMP: 200 EST: 1969
SQ FT: 90,000
SALES (est): 1.9B
SALES (corp-wide): 9.46B **Publicly Held**
Web: www.yankeecandle.com
SIC: 3999 2899 5999 Candles; Oils and essential oils; Candle shops
HQ: Yankee Holding Corp.
   16 Yankee Candle Way
   South Deerfield MA 01373

(G-11932)
YANKEE CANDLE INVESTMENTS LLC (DH)
16 Yankee Candle Way (01373-7325)
PHONE..........................413 665-8306
EMP: 30 EST: 2011
SALES (est): 371.88MM
SALES (corp-wide): 9.46B **Publicly Held**
SIC: 3999 5999 Candles; Candle shops
HQ: Jarden Llc
   221 River St
   Hoboken NJ 07030

(G-11933)
YANKEE HOLDING CORP (DH)
16 Yankee Candle Way (01373-7325)
PHONE..........................413 665-8306
Craig W Rydin, *Ch Bd*
Lisa K Mccarthy, *VP Fin*
Martha S Lacroix, *Chief Human Resources Officer*
James A Perley, *Ex VP*
Howard Barron, *CIO*
EMP: 100 EST: 2006
SQ FT: 75,000
SALES (est): 1.9B
SALES (corp-wide): 9.46B **Publicly Held**
SIC: 3999 2899 Candles; Oils and essential oils
HQ: Jarden Llc
   221 River St
   Hoboken NJ 07030

(G-11934)
YCC HOLDINGS LLC
16 Yankee Candle Way (01373-7325)
PHONE..........................413 665-8306
Lisa K Mccarthy, *Treas*
EMP: 4935 EST: 2006
SQ FT: 75,000
SALES (est): 2.55MM
SALES (corp-wide): 9.46B **Publicly Held**
SIC: 3999 2899 5999 Candles; Oils and essential oils; Candle shops
HQ: Yankee Candle Investments Llc
   16 Yankee Candle Way
   South Deerfield MA 01373

South Dennis
Barnstable County

(G-11935)
SANDCASTLE PUBLISHING LLC
434 Route 134 Ste A2 (02660-3433)
P.O. Box 1620 (02653-1620)
PHONE..........................508 398-3100
Jeffrey H Heth, *Prin*
EMP: 7 EST: 2010
SALES (est): 235.06K **Privately Held**
SIC: 2741 Miscellaneous publishing

South Easton
Bristol County

(G-11936)
ALLEGION ACCESS TECH LLC
24 Black Brook Rd (02375-1059)
PHONE..........................508 230-2350
EMP: 32
Web: www.stanleyaccess.com
SIC: 3545 Cutting tools for machine tools
HQ: Allegion Access Technologies Llc
   65 Scott Swamp Rd
   Farmington CT 06032

(G-11937)
BEE INTERNATIONAL INC
46 Eastman St Ste 5 (02375-1297)
PHONE..........................508 238-5558
Tal Shechter, *Pr*
Deborah Shechter, *Treas*
▲ EMP: 31 EST: 1998
SQ FT: 3,000
SALES (est): 11.8MM **Privately Held**
Web: www.pion-inc.com
SIC: 3561 5084 Pumps and pumping equipment; Processing and packaging equipment

PA: Bee (Best Emulsifying Equipment) International Ltd.
   Migdal Haemek

(G-11938)
BLUEDROP LLC
24 Norfolk Ave Ste A (02375-1914)
PHONE..........................877 662-7873
Brendan Dickinson, *Pr*
EMP: 10 EST: 2013
SALES (est): 1.3MM **Privately Held**
Web: www.bluedropwater.com
SIC: 7389 3589 7359 5078 Water softener service; Water filters and softeners, household type; Equipment rental and leasing, nec; Drinking water coolers, mechanical

(G-11939)
CASE ASSEMBLY SOLUTIONS INC
Also Called: Treetop
19 Norfolk Ave Ste B (02375-1911)
PHONE..........................508 238-5665
Gregory Cronin, *Pr*
Jay Sullivan, *
Jerome J Sullivan Junior, *Sec*
▲ EMP: 29 EST: 1998
SQ FT: 18,000
SALES (est): 8.47MM **Privately Held**
Web: www.case-assembly.com
SIC: 3672 3679 Printed circuit boards; Electronic circuits

(G-11940)
CONNECTED AUTO SYSTEMS NENG IN
Also Called: Cas of New England
87 Eastman St (02375-6200)
PHONE..........................508 238-5855
John P Jenkins, *Pr*
EMP: 25 EST: 1995
SQ FT: 7,500
SALES (est): 3.91MM **Privately Held**
Web: www.oemtools.com
SIC: 3825 5013 7371 Engine electrical test equipment; Automotive servicing equipment ; Software programming applications

(G-11941)
DEANGELIS IRON WORK INC (PA)
46 Eastman St (02375-1297)
P.O. Box 350 (02375-0350)
PHONE..........................508 238-4310
Richard J Davis Junior, *Pr*
Harry M Dodakian, *VP*
Donald R Jacobs, *Sec*
Christopher S Conne, *Treas*
EMP: 34 EST: 1978
SQ FT: 18,600
SALES (est): 8.44MM
SALES (corp-wide): 8.44MM **Privately Held**
Web: www.deangelisiron.com
SIC: 3446 Gates, ornamental metal

(G-11942)
EASTON SPRINGS CORPORATION
Also Called: Simpson Spring Corp
719 Washington St (02375-1139)
P.O. Box 328 (02375-0328)
PHONE..........................508 238-2741
TOLL FREE: 800
James Bertarelli, *Pr*
EMP: 12 EST: 1892
SQ FT: 80,000
SALES (est): 2.32MM **Privately Held**

Web: www.simpsonspring.com
SIC: 5149 5963 7359 2086 Mineral or spring water bottling; Bottled water delivery; Equipment rental and leasing, nec; Bottled and canned soft drinks

(G-11943)
FORTE TECHNOLOGY INC
58 Norfolk Ave Ste 4 (02375-1940)
PHONE..........................508 297-2363
Patricia R White, *Pr*
▼ EMP: 10 EST: 1956
SQ FT: 7,200
SALES (est): 1.28MM **Privately Held**
Web: www.forte-tec.com
SIC: 3829 Physical property testing equipment

(G-11944)
IBC CORPORATION
27 Belmont St (02375-1103)
PHONE..........................508 238-7941
EMP: 70 EST: 1965
SALES (est): 26.15MM **Privately Held**
Web: www.ibcwire.com
SIC: 3357 3355 Nonferrous wiredrawing and insulating; Aluminum rolling and drawing, nec

(G-11945)
ID GRAPHICS GROUP INC
Also Called: ID Sign Group
9 Bristol Dr (02375-1109)
P.O. Box 506 (02375-0506)
PHONE..........................508 238-8500
Timothy Fisher, *Pr*
Jacquelyn Churchill, *Treas*
EMP: 25 EST: 1967
SQ FT: 6,000
SALES (est): 595.37K **Privately Held**
Web: www.idsg.us
SIC: 3993 3089 2796 Signs, not made in custom sign painting shops; Engraving of plastics; Platemaking services

(G-11946)
INTERNATIONAL COIL INC
Also Called: I C I
8 Norfolk Ave Unit 2 (02375-1156)
P.O. Box 668 (02375-0668)
PHONE..........................508 580-8515
▲ EMP: 9 EST: 1995
SQ FT: 13,000
SALES (est): 859.04K **Privately Held**
Web: www.internationalcoil.com
SIC: 3612 Power and distribution transformers

(G-11947)
LION LABELS INC
15 Hampden Dr (02375-1159)
P.O. Box 820 (02375-0820)
PHONE..........................508 230-8211
TOLL FREE: 800
Michael Berke, *Pr*
Jerome M Berke, *
Tami Decelles, *
Nina Berke, *
EMP: 24 EST: 1966
SQ FT: 29,000
SALES (est): 4.91MM **Privately Held**
Web: www.lionlabels.com
SIC: 2672 2752 Labels (unprinted), gummed: made from purchased materials; Commercial printing, lithographic

(G-11948)
PHARMASOL CORPORATION
1 Norfolk Ave Ste 1 (02375-1900)
PHONE..........................508 238-0105

Marc Badia, *Pr*
Michel Badia, *
Howard Katzen, *
▲ **EMP:** 150 **EST:** 1973
SQ FT: 160,000
SALES (est): 27.18MM **Privately Held**
Web: www.pharmasol.com
SIC: 2834 2844 Pharmaceutical
  preparations; Cosmetic preparations

(G-11949)
POP TOPS COMPANY INC
Also Called: Pop Tops Sportswear
10 Plymouth Dr (02375-1192)
PHONE..........................508 580-2580
James Fine, *Pr*
Susan Fine, *
EMP: 30 **EST:** 1972
SQ FT: 10,000
SALES (est): 4.87MM **Privately Held**
Web: www.poptopssportswear.com
SIC: 2395 2329 2339 Pleating and stitching;
  Men's and boys' sportswear and athletic
  clothing; Women's and misses' athletic
  clothing and sportswear

(G-11950)
**PRESSURE BIOSCIENCES INC
(PA)**
Also Called: Pbi
14 Norfolk Ave (02375-1907)
PHONE..........................508 230-1828
Richard T Schumacher, *Pr*
Jeffrey N Peterson, *Ch Bd*
Richard T Schumacher, *Pr*
Edmund Ting, *Sr VP*
Alexander Lazarev, *CSO*
EMP: 8 **EST:** 1978
SALES (est): 1.73MM
SALES (corp-wide): 1.73MM **Publicly
Held**
Web: www.pressurebiosciences.com
SIC: 3841 Surgical and medical instruments

(G-11951)
**PROFESSIONAL TL GRINDING
INC (PA)**
18 Plymouth Dr (02375-1163)
PHONE..........................508 230-3535
Carmen Tropeano, *Pr*
Ciro Tropeano, *
David Tropeano, *
EMP: 22 **EST:** 1971
SQ FT: 16,000
SALES (est): 4.79MM
SALES (corp-wide): 4.79MM **Privately
Held**
Web: www.ptgspecials.com
SIC: 3541 Machine tools, metal cutting type

(G-11952)
RIVKIND ASSOCIATES INC (PA)
30 Twin Brooks Dr (02375-6206)
PHONE..........................781 269-2415
Melvin Rivkind, *CEO*
Kenneth Rivkind, *Pr*
David Kovner, *VP*
EMP: 19 **EST:** 1966
SQ FT: 15,000
SALES (est): 1.33MM
SALES (corp-wide): 1.33MM **Privately
Held**
Web: www.rivkind.com
SIC: 2752 7331 Offset printing; Direct mail
  advertising services

(G-11953)
SHAROC REALTY INC
Also Called: Solar Seal Company
55 Bristol Dr Ste 1 (02375-1195)

PHONE..........................508 238-0151
▲ **EMP:** 95
SIC: 3211 Insulating glass, sealed units

(G-11954)
TRUCBRUSH CORPORATION
28 Renker Dr (02375-1937)
PHONE..........................877 783-0237
James A Burns, *Pr*
Deborah Babin Katz, *VP*
EMP: 11 **EST:** 2014
SALES (est): 695.61K **Privately Held**
Web: www.trucbrush.com
SIC: 3714 Ice scrapers and window
  brushes, motor vehicle

(G-11955)
VIAMED CORP
15 Plymouth Dr Ste D (02375-1164)
PHONE..........................508 238-0220
Gary Lewis, *Pr*
EMP: 11 **EST:** 1986
SQ FT: 7,500
SALES (est): 838.84K **Privately Held**
Web: www.viamedcorp.com
SIC: 3841 3496 Catheters; Miscellaneous
  fabricated wire products

(G-11956)
WELDING CRAFTSMEN CO INC
63 Norfolk Ave (02375-1190)
PHONE..........................508 230-7878
Paul Raynard, *Pr*
EMP: 15 **EST:** 1977
SQ FT: 16,000
SALES (est): 2.91MM **Privately Held**
Web: www.weldingcraftsmen.com
SIC: 3444 7692 Sheet metalwork; Welding
  repair

South Grafton
Worcester County

(G-11957)
TAURUS TECHNOLOGIES CORP
134 Ferry St (01560-1390)
P.O. Box 231 (01534-0231)
PHONE..........................508 234-6372
▲ **EMP:** 11 **EST:** 1995
SQ FT: 24,000
SALES (est): 2.97MM **Privately Held**
Web: www.huesonwire.com
SIC: 3357 Building wire and cable,
  nonferrous

(G-11958)
TEMP-FLEX LLC
26 Milford Rd (01560-1208)
PHONE..........................508 839-3120
Kris Lower, *
Rick Black, *
Dan Laforest, *
▲ **EMP:** 129 **EST:** 1985
SALES (est): 24.74MM
SALES (corp-wide): 36.93B **Privately Held**
SIC: 3315 3357 Cable, steel: insulated or
  armored; Nonferrous wiredrawing and
  insulating
HQ: Molex, Llc
  2222 Wellington Ct
  Lisle IL 60532
  630 969-4550

South Hadley
Hampshire County

(G-11959)
CANSON INC
21 Industrial Dr (01075-2621)
PHONE..........................413 538-9250
James J Allery, *Pr*
Eric Joan, *
Sonja M Stewart, *
◆ **EMP:** 100 **EST:** 1928
SQ FT: 110,000
SALES (est): 26.12MM **Privately Held**
Web: www.canson-infinity.com
SIC: 2679 5199 Paper products, converted,
  nec; Artists' materials
HQ: Latame 2
  Canson International
  Herouville Saint Clair

(G-11960)
**CLEAN RUN PRODUCTIONS
LLC**
17 Industrial Dr (01075-2621)
PHONE..........................413 532-1389
Pam Green, *Finance*
▲ **EMP:** 10 **EST:** 2001
SALES (est): 1.22MM **Privately Held**
Web: www.cleanrun.com
SIC: 5999 2721 Pet supplies; Magazines:
  publishing only, not printed on site

(G-11961)
EIS WIRE & CABLE INC
775 New Ludlow Rd (01075-2625)
PHONE..........................413 536-0152
Thomas L Depetrillo, *Ch*
Nicholas J Moceri, *
Roy St Andre, *
Armand Mayotte, *
Thomas Quinn, *
EMP: 55 **EST:** 1910
SQ FT: 125,000
SALES (est): 23.65MM **Privately Held**
Web: www.eiswire.com
SIC: 3357 Nonferrous wiredrawing and
  insulating

(G-11962)
GGS CUSTOM METALS INC
Also Called: Gg Inks
785 New Ludlow Rd (01075-2625)
PHONE..........................413 315-4344
Gerry-paul Geoffrion, *Prin*
EMP: 10 **EST:** 2007
SALES (est): 403.47K **Privately Held**
Web: www.gginks.com
SIC: 2752 Commercial printing, lithographic

(G-11963)
JANLYNN CORPORATION
2078 Memorial Dr (01075-3020)
PHONE..........................413 206-0002
▲ **EMP:** 100
Web: www.janlynn.com
SIC: 2395 2339 2396 Art needlework: made
  from purchased materials; Aprons, except
  rubber or plastic: women's, misses', juniors'
  ; Screen printing on fabric articles

(G-11964)
**KNIGHT MACHINE & TOOL CO
INC**
11 Industrial Dr (01075-2621)
PHONE..........................413 532-2507
Gary T O'brien, *Pr*
EMP: 10 **EST:** 1969
SQ FT: 3,500

SALES (est): 1.82MM **Privately Held**
Web: www.knightmachine.net
SIC: 3599 Machine shop, jobbing and repair

(G-11965)
LYMAN CONRAD (PA)
Also Called: American Canvas & Aluminum
228 Lathrop St (01075-3309)
P.O. Box 667 (01086-0667)
PHONE..........................413 538-8200
TOLL FREE: 800
Lyman Conrad, *Owner*
EMP: 13 **EST:** 1974
SQ FT: 4,000
SALES (est): 950.95K
SALES (corp-wide): 950.95K **Privately
Held**
SIC: 2394 3089 3444 7299 Awnings, fabric:
  made from purchased materials; Awnings,
  fiberglass and plastics combination;
  Awnings, sheet metal; Stitching services

(G-11966)
**PUBLISHING COLLABORATIVE
LLC**
475 Hadley St (01075-1049)
PHONE..........................413 538-4170
James D Bothwell, *Prin*
EMP: 7 **EST:** 2017
SALES (est): 94.6K **Privately Held**
Web: www.collaborative.org
SIC: 2741 Miscellaneous publishing

(G-11967)
TECH FAB INC
1 W Main St (01075-2798)
PHONE..........................413 532-9022
W Ken Cordes, *Pr*
EMP: 20 **EST:** 1945
SQ FT: 20,000
SALES (est): 2.31MM **Privately Held**
Web: www.techfabinc.com
SIC: 3469 3444 Metal stampings, nec;
  Metal housings, enclosures, casings, and
  other containers

(G-11968)
YANKEE PRINTING GROUP INC
630 New Ludlow Rd (01075-2669)
PHONE..........................413 532-9513
Harold L Davis Junior, *Pr*
Richard R Davis, *
Kathryn Trudeau, *
EMP: 25 **EST:** 1971
SQ FT: 30,000
SALES (est): 2.45MM **Privately Held**
SIC: 2759 2752 2675 2791 Envelopes:
  printing, nsk; Offset printing; Die-cut paper
  and board; Typesetting

South Hamilton
Essex County

(G-11969)
DANVERSBANK
Also Called: Hamilton Branch
25 Railroad Ave (01982-2218)
PHONE..........................978 468-2243
Marcia Crateau, *Prin*
EMP: 7 **EST:** 2010
SALES (est): 402.88K **Privately Held**
SIC: 3578 Automatic teller machines (ATM)

South Lancaster
Worcester County

(G-11970)
ATLANTIC BOOKBINDERS INC
87 Flagg St (01561)
P.O. Box 1231 (01561-1231)
PHONE....................978 365-4524
David Bruso, Pr
Timothy Paddock, Treas
Susan Bruso, Sec
EMP: 7 **EST:** 1976
SQ FT: 10,000
SALES (est): 433.65K **Privately Held**
SIC: 2789 2782 Bookbinding and repairing:
trade, edition, library, etc.; Blankbooks and
looseleaf binders

(G-11971)
**JAMES MONROE WIRE &
CABLE CORP (PA)**
767 Sterling Rd (01561)
P.O. Box 1203 (01561-1203)
PHONE....................978 368-0131
David Bruso, Pr
John A Mavricos, *
Robert Leger, Prin
William Blair, *
▲ **EMP:** 79 **EST:** 1977
SQ FT: 185,000
SALES (est): 25.56MM
SALES (corp-wide): 25.56MM **Privately
Held**
Web: www.jamesmonroewire.com
SIC: 3315 3357 5063 Cable, steel: insulated
or armored; Coaxial cable, nonferrous; Wire
and cable

South Lee
Berkshire County

(G-11972)
ONYX SPECIALTY PAPERS INC
40 Willow St (01260-7705)
P.O. Box 188 (01260-0188)
PHONE....................413 243-1231
Patricia Begrowicz, Pr
Christopher Mathews, *
◆ **EMP:** 204 **EST:** 2009
SALES (est): 56.26MM **Privately Held**
Web: www.onyxpapers.com
SIC: 2621 Paper mills

South Orleans
Barnstable County

(G-11973)
P B Y A INC
Also Called: Arey's Pond Boat Yard
45 Arey's Ln (02662)
P.O. Box 222 (02662-0222)
PHONE....................508 255-0994
Tony Davis, Pr
Robin Davis, VP
EMP: 8 **EST:** 1966
SQ FT: 6,000
SALES (est): 981.68K **Privately Held**
Web: www.areyspondboatyard.com
SIC: 4493 7699 3732 5551 Boat yards,
storage and incidental repair; Boat repair;
Boatbuilding and repairing; Boat dealers

South Weymouth
Norfolk County

(G-11974)
ALL-WAY SERVICE CORP
1182 Main St (02190-1559)
P.O. Box 367 (02190-0003)
PHONE....................781 335-4533
EMP: 10 **EST:** 1994
SALES (est): 757.19K **Privately Held**
Web: www.allwayservice.com
SIC: 4214 3589 2842 4953 Local trucking
with storage; Garbage disposers and
compactors, commercial; Cleaning or
polishing preparations, nec; Garbage:
collecting, destroying, and processing

(G-11975)
ELERTS CORPORATION
1132 Main St Ste 300 (02190-1511)
PHONE....................781 803-6362
Edward English, CEO
Christopher Russo, VP
EMP: 15 **EST:** 2010
SALES (est): 2.33MM **Privately Held**
Web: www.elerts.com
SIC: 7372 Business oriented computer
software

(G-11976)
FENCE LINES INC
457 Columbian St (02190-1127)
PHONE....................781 331-2121
David J O'neil, Dir
EMP: 13 **EST:** 2019
SALES (est): 1.05MM **Privately Held**
Web: www.fencelines.com
SIC: 3315 Steel wire and related products

(G-11977)
**SBARZOLA CONSTRUCTION
CORP**
1183 Main St (02190-1514)
PHONE....................781 817-6485
Sonia Dahlquist, Pr
Sonia Vizarreta, Pr
EMP: 7 **EST:** 2013
SALES (est): 2.1MM **Privately Held**
Web: www.sbarzolaconstruction.com
SIC: 1542 8742 3272 2951 Commercial and
office building contractors; Construction
project management consultant; Stone,
cast concrete; Asphalt paving mixtures and
blocks

(G-11978)
**STONE DESIGN MARBLE &
GRAN CO**
1235 Main St (02190-1515)
PHONE....................781 331-3000
Hoa Thanh Vu, Pr
▲ **EMP:** 7 **EST:** 2004
SQ FT: 3,080
SALES (est): 795.34K **Privately Held**
SIC: 3281 5032 Marble, building: cut and
shaped; Marble building stone

(G-11979)
**W M GULLIKSEN MFG CO INC
(PA)**
30 Fairway Lndg (02190-4203)
PHONE....................617 323-5750
Chester A Gillis, Pr
EMP: 17 **EST:** 1927
SALES (est): 2.35MM
SALES (corp-wide): 2.35MM **Privately
Held**

SIC: 3089 3544 Molding primary plastics;
Special dies and tools

South Yarmouth
Barnstable County

(G-11980)
**ACME-SHOREY PRECAST CO
INC**
351 Whites Path (02664-1214)
P.O. Box 374 (02556-0374)
PHONE....................508 430-0956
EMP: 8
SALES (corp-wide): 3.44MM **Privately
Held**
Web: www.acmeshorey.com
SIC: 3272 Concrete products, precast, nec
PA: Acme-Shorey Precast Co., Inc.
36 Great Western Rd
Harwich MA 02645
508 432-0530

(G-11981)
**BREWER ELECTRIC &
UTILITIES IN**
110 Old Town House Rd (02664-1661)
PHONE....................508 771-2040
James Riley, Pr
Scott Ventura, Mgr
EMP: 7 **EST:** 2002
SALES (est): 181.32K **Privately Held**
SIC: 3825 1731 Digital panel meters,
electricity measuring; Electrical work

(G-11982)
CAPE COD FENCE CO (PA)
1093 Route 28 (02664-4100)
PHONE....................508 398-6041
Dewitt Davenport, Prin
EMP: 12 **EST:** 1957
SQ FT: 2,000
SALES (est): 2.37MM
SALES (corp-wide): 2.37MM **Privately
Held**
Web: 3631507999.nxcli.net
SIC: 1799 5211 3496 3446 Fence
construction; Fencing; Miscellaneous
fabricated wire products; Architectural
metalwork

(G-11983)
FIRST SAIL GROUP INC
69 Neptune Ln (02664-5161)
PHONE....................425 409-2783
Matthew Garbauskas, Pr
EMP: 9 **EST:** 2016
SALES (est): 760.91K **Privately Held**
SIC: 7389 2759 8742 Design services;
Screen printing; Marketing consulting
services

(G-11984)
**INTERSTATE ALL BATTERY
CENTER**
484 Station Ave (02664-1220)
PHONE....................508 394-9400
Richard Kelley, Prin
EMP: 10 **EST:** 2011
SALES (est): 522.25K **Privately Held**
Web: www.interstatebatteries.com
SIC: 5531 5063 3691 Batteries, automotive
and truck; Batteries; Storage batteries

Southampton
Hampshire County

(G-11985)
GRAPHICS SOURCE CO
18 Pequot Rd (01073-9587)
P.O. Box 51885 (01151-5885)
PHONE....................413 543-0700
Lee Deshais, Owner
EMP: 8 **EST:** 1998
SALES (est): 449.59K **Privately Held**
SIC: 2759 Labels and seals: printing, nsk

(G-11986)
**J&E PRECISION TL HOLDINGS
LLC (PA)**
107 Valley Rd (01073-9589)
PHONE....................413 527-8778
Sean Holly, CEO
James Labrie, VP
Eugene R Labrie, EFGI
Jonathan Labrie, VP
Stephen Cook, VP
EMP: 22 **EST:** 2019
SALES (est): 31.47MM
SALES (corp-wide): 31.47MM **Privately
Held**
Web: www.jeprecision.com
SIC: 3599 Machine shop, jobbing and repair

(G-11987)
J&E PRECISION TOOL LLC
107 Valley Rd (01073-9589)
PHONE....................413 527-8778
EMP: 100 **EST:** 1980
SALES (est): 23.09MM
SALES (corp-wide): 31.47MM **Privately
Held**
Web: www.jeprecision.com
SIC: 3599 Machine shop, jobbing and repair
PA: J&E Precision Tool Holdings, Llc
107 Valley Rd
Southampton MA 01073
413 527-8778

(G-11988)
LYMAN SHEET METAL CO INC
281 College Hwy (01073-9625)
P.O. Box 215 (01073-0215)
PHONE....................413 527-0848
Kevin West, Pr
Myrna West, VP
Glenn West, VP
Keith West, VP
EMP: 7 **EST:** 1894
SQ FT: 2,700
SALES (est): 935.57K **Privately Held**
Web: www.lymansheetmetal.com
SIC: 3444 Sheet metalwork

Southborough
Worcester County

(G-11989)
**ASHLAND CABINET
CORPORATION**
150 Cordaville Rd Ste 100 (01772-1848)
PHONE....................508 303-8100
Matt Di Pilato, Pr
Brian Bush, Treas
EMP: 7 **EST:** 1977
SALES (est): 935.41K **Privately Held**
Web: www.ashlandcabinet.com
SIC: 2434 Wood kitchen cabinets

(G-11990)
BALLARD UNMANNED SYSTEMS INC
153 Northboro Rd Ste 1 (01772-1034)
PHONE.................................508 687-4970
Paul Osenar, *Pr*
Christopher R Schuster, *CFO*
David A Ierardi, *VP*
Phil Robinson, *VP*
Greg Sipriano, *VP*
EMP: 15 **EST:** 2000
SQ FT: 12,000
SALES (est): 10.95MM
SALES (corp-wide): 83.79MM **Privately Held**
SIC: 3629   Electrochemical generators (fuel cells)
PA: Ballard Power Systems Inc
9000 Glenlyon Pky
Burnaby BC V5J 5
604 454-0900

(G-11991)
BLOCK ENGINEERING LLC
132 Turnpike Rd Ste 110 (01772-2129)
PHONE.................................508 480-9643
Petros A Kotidis, *CEO*
Steve Buckley, *Pr*
EMP: 20 **EST:** 2003
SALES (est): 4.43MM **Privately Held**
Web: www.blockeng.com
SIC: 3826   Spectroscopic and other optical properties measuring equip.

(G-11992)
BLOCK MEMS LLC
132 Turnpike Rd Ste 110 (01772-2129)
PHONE.................................508 251-3100
Daniel J Cavicchio Junior, *Managing Member*
EMP: 15 **EST:** 2003
SALES (est): 1.67MM **Privately Held**
Web: www.blockeng.com
SIC: 3824   Mechanical and electromechanical counters and devices

(G-11993)
CABINET DEPOT OUTLET INC
3 Atwood Rd (01772-1901)
PHONE.................................508 485-7777
Thomas P Coder, *Prin*
EMP: 7 **EST:** 2016
SALES (est): 247.42K **Privately Held**
Web: www.cabinetdepotoutlet.com
SIC: 2434   Wood kitchen cabinets

(G-11994)
DEVICE TECHNOLOGIES INC
Also Called: Dti
155 Northboro Rd Ste 8 (01772-1033)
PHONE.................................508 229-2000
Nicholas Petri, *CEO*
Nicholas B Petri, *
◆ **EMP:** 25 **EST:** 1984
SQ FT: 23,000
SALES (est): 4.94MM **Privately Held**
Web: www.devicetech.com
SIC: 3429 3451 3495 3061   Metal fasteners; Screw machine products; Wire springs; Mechanical rubber goods

(G-11995)
GRAPHIC ARTS INSTITUTE OF NENG
Also Called: PRINTING INDUSTRIES OF NEW ENG
5 Crystal Pond Rd (01772-1758)
PHONE.................................508 804-4100
James Tepper, *Pr*

Tim Donohue, *Treas*
Paul Marinelli, *Ch*
EMP: 16 **EST:** 1887
SQ FT: 14,400
SALES (est): 466.48K **Privately Held**
Web: www.pine.org
SIC: 8742 2721   Management consulting services; Periodicals

(G-11996)
GTXCEL INC
144 Turnpike Rd Ste 140 (01772-2121)
PHONE.................................508 804-3092
Peter E Stilson, *CEO*
EMP: 35 **EST:** 2014
SALES (est): 4.52MM **Privately Held**
Web: www.gtxcel.com
SIC: 2741   Miscellaneous publishing

(G-11997)
HONEYWELL INTERNATIONAL INC
Also Called: Honeywell
250 Turnpike Rd (01772-1742)
PHONE.................................508 490-7100
EMP: 114
SALES (corp-wide): 41.8B **Publicly Held**
SIC: 3724   Aircraft engines and engine parts
PA: Honeywell International Inc.
300 S Tryon St
Charlotte NC 28202
973 455-2000

(G-11998)
NANODX INC
Also Called: Nanodiagnostics
144 Turnpike Rd Ste 110 (01772-2138)
PHONE.................................508 599-2400
James Wylie, *Ch Bd*
Sharad Joshi, *Pr*
Brian Mcglynn, *Ex VP*
Stephen Brackett, *Dir*
Robert Mercier, *Dir*
EMP: 21 **EST:** 2010
SALES (est): 3.27MM **Privately Held**
Web: www.biodirection.com
SIC: 3841   Diagnostic apparatus, medical

(G-11999)
NEWMAN ENTERPRISES INC
Also Called: Sign-A-Rama
2 Southville Rd Unit C (01772-4026)
PHONE.................................508 875-7446
Jeffrey H Newman, *Pr*
EMP: 7 **EST:** 2002
SQ FT: 3,000
SALES (est): 484.15K **Privately Held**
Web: www.signarama.com
SIC: 3993   Signs and advertising specialties

(G-12000)
NOVOTECHNIK US INC
155 Northboro Rd Ste 31 (01772-1033)
PHONE.................................508 485-2244
Matt Pietro, *Pr*
EMP: 7 **EST:** 1987
SQ FT: 7,000
SALES (est): 2.17MM
SALES (corp-wide): 35.86MM **Privately Held**
Web: www.novotechnik.com
SIC: 3825   Instruments to measure electricity
PA: Novotechnik Messwertaufnehmer Ohg
Horbstr. 12
Ostfildern BW 73760
711 448-9234

(G-12001)
SEMICONSOFT INC
Also Called: Semiconsoft
83 Pine Hill Rd (01772-1313)
PHONE.................................617 388-6832
Leo Asinovski, *Pr*
EMP: 10 **EST:** 2001
SQ FT: 2,000
SALES (est): 925.86K **Privately Held**
Web: www.semiconsoft.com
SIC: 3829   Measuring and controlling devices, nec

(G-12002)
SENTINEL PROCESS SYSTEMS INC
10 Southville Rd (01772-4029)
PHONE.................................508 624-5577
Joseph Loughren, *Mgr*
EMP: 10
SALES (corp-wide): 14.95MM **Privately Held**
Web: www.sentinelprocess.com
SIC: 5085 3229   Valves and fittings; Tubing, glass
PA: Sentinel Process Systems, Inc.
3265 Sunset Ln
Hatboro PA 19040
215 675-5700

(G-12003)
UPSTART POWER INC
153 Northboro Rd Ste 1 (01772-1034)
PHONE.................................614 877-8278
Paul Osenar, *CEO*
EMP: 40 **EST:** 2017
SALES (est): 5.07MM **Privately Held**
Web: www.upstartpower.com
SIC: 3674   Semiconductors and related devices

(G-12004)
VDC RESEARCH GROUP INC (PA)
144 Turnpike Rd Ste 230 (01772-2122)
PHONE.................................508 653-9000
Mitchell Solomon, *CEO*
Lewis Solomon, *Pr*
EMP: 25 **EST:** 1971
SALES (est): 5.27MM
SALES (corp-wide): 5.27MM **Privately Held**
Web: www.vdcresearch.com
SIC: 2721 8742   Statistical reports (periodicals): publishing only; Management consulting services

(G-12005)
VECTURA INCORPORATED
371 Turnpike Rd Ste 120 (01772-1747)
PHONE.................................508 573-5700
EMP: 9 **EST:** 2010
SALES (est): 254.51K **Privately Held**
SIC: 2834   Pharmaceutical preparations

(G-12006)
WEBCO ENGINEERING INC
155 Northboro Rd Ste 20 (01772-1033)
PHONE.................................508 303-0500
Roger Mc Clelland, *Pr*
Roland Hill, *VP*
EMP: 19 **EST:** 1972
SQ FT: 15,622
SALES (est): 1.8MM **Privately Held**
Web: www.webcoeng.com
SIC: 3554 7699   Paper industries machinery; Industrial machinery and equipment repair

Southbridge
Worcester County

(G-12007)
59 BEECHER STREET LLC
59 Beecher St (01550-2655)
PHONE.................................631 734-6200
Joseph P Marinelli Junior, *Prin*
EMP: 7 **EST:** 2010
SALES (est): 284.53K **Privately Held**
SIC: 2084   Wines

(G-12008)
A & M TOOL & DIE COMPANY INC
Also Called: Saga Packaging Machinery Div
64 Mill St Ste 1 (01550-0017)
PHONE.................................508 764-3241
Alvino Aliberti, *Pr*
Guido Jacques, *
Robert G Caprera, *
Robert Jacques, *
EMP: 50 **EST:** 1948
SQ FT: 250,000
SALES (est): 9.37MM **Privately Held**
SIC: 3544 3565   Jigs and fixtures; Bag opening, filling, and closing machines

(G-12009)
ALLTEC LASER TECHNOLOGY
50 Optical Dr (01550-2584)
PHONE.................................508 765-6666
Jeanine Mcelroy, *Prin*
EMP: 11 **EST:** 2004
SALES (est): 266.8K **Privately Held**
Web: www.fobalaser.com
SIC: 2759   Laser printing

(G-12010)
BERMER PRECISION PRODUCTS LLC
94 Ashland Ave (01550-2804)
PHONE.................................508 764-2521
EMP: 8 **EST:** 2008
SALES (est): 358.68K **Privately Held**
Web: www.bermerprecision.com
SIC: 3599   Machine shop, jobbing and repair

(G-12011)
BERMER TOOL & DIE INC
81 Ashland Ave (01550-2803)
P.O. Box 159 (01550-0159)
PHONE.................................508 764-2521
John Szugda, *Pr*
EMP: 18 **EST:** 1955
SQ FT: 33,000
SALES (est): 1.88MM **Privately Held**
Web: www.bermerprecision.com
SIC: 3544   Dies, plastics forming

(G-12012)
CREATEK-STONE INC
Also Called: Createk
833 Main St Ste 2 (01550-1119)
PHONE.................................888 786-6389
Albert C West Junior, *Pr*
James W Schoepfer, *VP*
▼ **EMP:** 9 **EST:** 1980
SQ FT: 6,700
SALES (est): 973.45K **Privately Held**
Web: www.createkinc.com
SIC: 3999   Lawn ornaments

(G-12013)
DEGREASING DEVICES CO
105 Dresser St (01550-2436)
PHONE.................................508 765-0045

Roderick P Murphy, *Pr*
Jean Murphy, *VP*
▲ **EMP:** 9 **EST:** 1985
SQ FT: 8,000
SALES (est): 717K **Privately Held**
Web: www.degreasingdevices.com
SIC: 3559 3677 3699 5084   Degreasing machines, automotive and industrial; Filtration devices, electronic; Electrical equipment and supplies, nec; Industrial machinery and equipment

(G-12014)
DEXTER-RUSSELL INC
Also Called: Dexter
44 River St (01550-1834)
P.O. Box 983122 (02298-3122)
PHONE...................................508 765-0201
Richard B Hardy, *Ch Bd*
Kevin Clark, *VP*
Thomas B Hardy, *Sec*
Craig M Giguere, *Treas*
▲ **EMP:** 125 **EST:** 1968
SQ FT: 160,000
SALES (est): 31.5MM
SALES (corp-wide): 66.45MM **Privately Held**
Web: www.dexter1818.com
SIC: 3421 3423   Knives: butchers', hunting, pocket, etc.; Knives, agricultural or industrial
PA: Hyde Group, Inc.
54 Eastford Rd
Southbridge MA 01550
800 872-4933

(G-12015)
ELEMENT PRECISION LLC
10 Cabot St (01550-2683)
PHONE...................................774 318-1777
Greg Peter, *Pr*
EMP: 11 **EST:** 2016
SALES (est): 478.85K **Privately Held**
Web: www.elementprecision.com
SIC: 3599   Machine shop, jobbing and repair

(G-12016)
FALL PREVENTION ALARMS INC
186 Hamilton St Apt 1l (01550-1881)
PHONE...................................508 765-5050
EMP: 7 **EST:** 2008
SALES (est): 914.17K **Privately Held**
Web: www.fallpreventionalarms.com
SIC: 3669   Emergency alarms

(G-12017)
FUSED FIBEROPTICS LLC
Also Called: Fused Fiberoptics
79 Golf St (01550-2866)
PHONE...................................508 765-1652
Thomas A Dowling, *Mng Pt*
Robert F Dowling Junior, *Mng Pt*
EMP: 17 **EST:** 1997
SQ FT: 14,000
SALES (est): 777.16K **Privately Held**
Web: www.fusedfiberoptics.com
SIC: 3229   Pressed and blown glass, nec

(G-12018)
HARDLINE HEAT TREATING INC
134 Ashland Ave (01550-2804)
PHONE...................................508 764-6669
Robert Chalue, *Pr*
▲ **EMP:** 30 **EST:** 2004
SALES (est): 4.34MM **Privately Held**
Web: www.hardlineheattreating.com
SIC: 3398   Tempering of metal

(G-12019)
HIGH PURITY NATURAL PDTS LLC
328 Main St Ste 3 (01550-3795)
PHONE...................................508 864-6072
Tom Barrette, *Pr*
EMP: 8 **EST:** 2017
SALES (est): 472.12K **Privately Held**
Web:
www.highpuritynaturalproducts.com
SIC: 3999

(G-12020)
HYDE GROUP INC (PA)
Also Called: Hyde Tools
54 Eastford Rd (01550-3604)
P.O. Box 1875 (01550-1875)
PHONE...................................800 872-4933
Richard M Clemence, *Pr*
Tammy C Rawls, *
Ronald P Carlson, *
◆ **EMP:** 61 **EST:** 1881
SQ FT: 200,000
SALES (est): 66.45MM
SALES (corp-wide): 66.45MM **Privately Held**
Web: www.hydegrp.com
SIC: 3423 5199 3421   Hand and edge tools, nec; Fabrics, yarns, and knit goods; Knives: butchers', hunting, pocket, etc.

(G-12021)
HYDE TOOLS
54 Eastford Rd (01550-3604)
PHONE...................................508 764-4344
Robert Scoble, *Pr*
Joseph Anzalotti, *VP*
Corie Talbot, *VP*
EMP: 11 **EST:** 2007
SALES (est): 430.57K **Privately Held**
Web: www.hydetools.com
SIC: 3423   Hand and edge tools, nec

(G-12022)
INDUSTRIAL TRANSFER & STOR INC
529 Ashland Ave Ste 1 (01550-3197)
P.O. Box 800 (01550-0800)
PHONE...................................508 765-9178
TOLL FREE: 800
Eric Cooley, *Pr*
Carter Cooley, *
Sandra Cooley, *
▲ **EMP:** 42 **EST:** 1984
SALES (est): 8.98MM **Privately Held**
Web: www.industrialtransfer.com
SIC: 1796 1799 3499   Millwright; Rigging and scaffolding; Fire- or burglary-resistive products

(G-12023)
J P MFG INC
13 Lovely St (01550-1799)
PHONE...................................508 764-2538
Gloria Kania, *Pr*
Edmond Kuzdzal, *VP*
EMP: 9 **EST:** 1969
SQ FT: 10,000
SALES (est): 809.91K **Privately Held**
Web: www.jpmfg.com
SIC: 3827   Lenses, optical: all types except ophthalmic

(G-12024)
K & K THERMOFORMING INC
380 Elm St (01550-3028)
PHONE...................................508 764-7700
David A Keller, *Pr*
EMP: 21 **EST:** 1999

SALES (est): 4.01MM **Privately Held**
Web: www.k-kthermoforming.com
SIC: 2671   Plastic film, coated or laminated for packaging

(G-12025)
KOOKLA INC
Also Called: Dunkin' Donuts
386 E Main St (01550-2939)
PHONE...................................508 765-0442
EMP: 10
Web: www.dunkindonuts.com
SIC: 5461 2051   Doughnuts; Doughnuts, except frozen
PA: Kookla, Inc.
120 Main St
Sturbridge MA 01566

(G-12026)
KSEW
100 Central St (01550-3747)
PHONE...................................774 230-4995
Katie Sotar, *Prin*
EMP: 7 **EST:** 2017
SALES (est): 115.96K **Privately Held**
SIC: 3566   Speed changers, drives, and gears

(G-12027)
LAVALLEE MACHINERY INC
831 Main St (01550-1169)
PHONE...................................508 764-2896
David Lavallee, *Pr*
Beverly Lavallee, *Clerk*
EMP: 7 **EST:** 1994
SQ FT: 10,000
SALES (est): 755.62K **Privately Held**
Web: www.metalcraftmachining.com
SIC: 3599   Machine shop, jobbing and repair

(G-12028)
MBI GRAPHICS & PRINTING CORP
97 Worcester St (01550-3409)
P.O. Box 733 (01518-0733)
PHONE...................................508 765-0658
TOLL FREE: 800
Martin Bania, *Pr*
Jane Bania, *VP*
EMP: 10 **EST:** 1985
SQ FT: 3,200
SALES (est): 978.63K **Privately Held**
Web: www.mbigraphics.com
SIC: 2752 5044   Offset printing; Office equipment

(G-12029)
MBS FABRICATION INC (PA)
270 Ashland Ave (01550-3103)
PHONE...................................508 765-0900
Carleton Macgillivray, *Pr*
David Macgillivray, *VP*
Brenda Macgillivray, *Treas*
Carol Macgillivray, *Sec*
EMP: 8 **EST:** 1996
SALES (est): 4.17MM
SALES (corp-wide): 4.17MM **Privately Held**
Web: www.mbsfab.com
SIC: 3441   Fabricated structural metal

(G-12030)
METALOGIC INDUSTRIES LLC
15 Wells St (01550-4503)
PHONE...................................508 461-6787
Thomas Kokosinski, *Managing Member*
EMP: 12 **EST:** 2010
SALES (est): 6.1MM **Privately Held**
Web: www.metalogicind.com

SIC: 3679   Electronic switches

(G-12031)
MID-STATE WELDING INC
150 Commercial Dr (01550-3443)
PHONE...................................508 987-9410
Daniel Seaver, *Pr*
EMP: 15 **EST:** 1997
SALES (est): 2.76MM **Privately Held**
Web: www.midstateweldingma.com
SIC: 3441 1799   Fabricated structural metal; Welding on site

(G-12032)
OPTIMUM TECHNOLOGIES INC
114 Pleasant St (01550-1236)
PHONE...................................508 765-8100
EMP: 10
SQ FT: 5,300
SALES (est): 2.76MM **Privately Held**
Web: www.optech.org
SIC: 3827 8711   Optical instruments and lenses; Designing: ship, boat, machine, and product

(G-12033)
PATRIOT CUSTOM MFG INC
134 Ashland Ave (01550-2804)
PHONE...................................508 764-7342
Christopher R Twine, *Dir*
EMP: 8 **EST:** 2005
SALES (est): 39.69K **Privately Held**
SIC: 3999   Manufacturing industries, nec

(G-12034)
SCHOTT NORTH AMERICA INC
Schott Fiber Optics
122 Charlton St (01550-1914)
PHONE...................................508 765-9744
Donald Miller, *Mgr*
EMP: 291
Web: www.schott.com
SIC: 3229   Fiber optics strands
HQ: Schott North America, Inc.
2 International Dr # 110
Rye Brook NY 10573
914 831-2200

(G-12035)
STONEBRIDGE PRESS INC (PA)
Also Called: Southbridge News
25 Elm St (01550-2647)
P.O. Box 90 (01550-0090)
PHONE...................................508 764-4325
Frank Chilinski, *Pr*
John Coots, *
David S Cutler, *
Ron Tramblay, *
EMP: 50 **EST:** 1995
SALES (est): 5.13MM **Privately Held**
Web: www.stonebridgepress.com
SIC: 2711   Commercial printing and newspaper publishing combined

(G-12036)
SUPERIOR CAKE PRODUCTS INC
94 Ashland Ave (01550-2804)
PHONE...................................508 764-3276
Kevin P Mccafferty, *CEO*
Michael Faucher, *Pr*
Vincent Martelli, *CFO*
Rick Buchanan, *Dir Fin*
Christopher Smith, *VP*
EMP: 70 **EST:** 1937
SQ FT: 80,000
SALES (est): 18.24MM
SALES (corp-wide): 113.58MM **Privately Held**
Web: www.superiorcake.com

556   2024 Harris New England
Manufacturers Directory   ▲ = Import ▼ = Export
◆ = Import/Export

SIC: 2051 Cakes, bakery: except frozen
PA: Sara Lee Frozen Bakery, Llc
1 Tower Ln Ste 500
Oakbrook Terrace IL 60181
630 282-9900

(G-12037)
UNITED LENS COMPANY INC
259 Worcester St (01550-1376)
PHONE..............................508 765-5421
William R Lannon, *CEO*
Paul J Digregorio, *VP*
Denise R Cournoyer, *Treas*
▲ EMP: 150 EST: 1916
SQ FT: 150,000
SALES (est): 24.19MM Privately Held
Web: www.unitedlens.com
SIC: 3827 Optical instruments and lenses

(G-12038)
VOCERO HISPANO
NEWSPAPER INC
44 Hamilton St (01550-3706)
PHONE..............................866 846-6397
EMP: 10 EST: 1990
SALES (est): 832.88K Privately Held
Web: pds845.wixsite.com
SIC: 7311 8742 7313 2711 Advertising
agencies; Marketing consulting services;
Newspaper advertising representative;
Newspapers: publishing only, not printed on
site

Southfield
Berkshire County

(G-12039)
CUESPORT INC
1415 Canaan Southfield Rd (01259-9764)
PHONE..............................413 229-6626
Norman P Stalker, *Pr*
Donna M Stalker, *Treas*
Frederick J Mali, *Stockholder*
EMP: 9 EST: 1963
SALES (est): 454.63K Privately Held
SIC: 3949 Billiard and pool equipment and
supplies, general

Southwick
Hampden County

(G-12040)
AJ PRECISION INC
13 Industrial Rd (01077-9231)
PHONE..............................413 998-3291
Wade Austin, *Prin*
EMP: 8 EST: 2018
SALES (est): 536.63K Privately Held
Web: www.ajprecision.com
SIC: 7699 3599 Repair services, nec;
Machine shop, jobbing and repair

(G-12041)
B & E GROUP LLC
10 Hudson Dr (01077-9546)
P.O. Box 40 (01077-0040)
PHONE..............................413 569-5585
John A Wilander, *Mgr*
EMP: 41 EST: 2006
SALES (est): 375.94K Privately Held
Web: www.beaerospacegroup.com
SIC: 3545 8711 Precision measuring tools;
Engineering services

(G-12042)
B & E TOOL COMPANY INC
Also Called: B&E Precision Arcft Components
10 Hudson Dr (01077-9546)
P.O. Box 40 (01077-0040)
PHONE..............................413 569-5585
Robert Quaglia, *Pr*
Karen Tuleta, *
Charlie Rossetti, *
▲ EMP: 78 EST: 1950
SQ FT: 35,000
SALES (est): 25.34MM
SALES (corp-wide): 666.39MM Privately
Held
Web: www.beaerospacegroup.com
SIC: 3728 Aircraft parts and equipment, nec
HQ: Cadence Aerospace, Llc
3150 E Miraloma Ave
Anaheim CA 92806
949 877-3630

(G-12043)
HITACHI KOKUSAI ELECTRIC
COMARK LLC
Also Called: Comark Communications
104 Feeding Hills Rd (01077-9349)
PHONE..............................413 998-1100
◆ EMP: 64 EST: 1987
SALES (est): 44.06MM Privately Held
Web: www.comarktv.com
SIC: 3663 Television antennas (transmitting)
and ground equipment
HQ: Hitachi Kokusai Electric America, Ltd.
150 Crossways Park Dr
Woodbury NY 11797
516 682-4403

(G-12044)
JULIE CECCHINI
Also Called: Terra Americana
74 Tannery Rd (01077-9770)
PHONE..............................413 562-2042
EMP: 10 EST: 1994
SALES (est): 493.43K Privately Held
Web: terraamericana.wixsite.com
SIC: 2052 Cookies

(G-12045)
SAWMILL PARK
1 Saw Mill Park (01077-9100)
PHONE..............................413 569-3393
Deb Mc Cann, *Prin*
EMP: 7 EST: 2004
SALES (est): 124.06K Privately Held
SIC: 2421 6513 Sawmills and planing mills,
general; Retirement hotel operation

(G-12046)
THOMSON VIDEO NETWORKS
AMERICAS LLC
104 Feeding Hills Rd (01077-9349)
PHONE..............................413 998-1200
EMP: 25
SIC: 3651 Household audio and video
equipment

(G-12047)
TJ BARK MULCH INC
25 Sam West Rd (01077-9734)
P.O. Box 1168 (01077-1168)
PHONE..............................413 569-2400
EMP: 13 EST: 1988
SALES (est): 423.08K Privately Held
Web: www.tjbarkmulch.com
SIC: 2499 Mulch, wood and bark

(G-12048)
TOVA INDUSTRIES INC
Also Called: D & S Manufacturing

10 Hudson Dr (01077-9546)
P.O. Box 1133 (01077-1133)
PHONE..............................413 569-5688
John Wilander, *Pr*
EMP: 15 EST: 1976
SQ FT: 8,000
SALES (est): 2.36MM Privately Held
Web: www.dsmfgtova.com
SIC: 3599 Machine shop, jobbing and repair

(G-12049)
WESTERN MASS RENDERING
CO INC
94 Foster Rd (01077-9522)
PHONE..............................413 569-6265
David Plakias, *Pr*
EMP: 30 EST: 1937
SQ FT: 23,000
SALES (est): 2.63MM Privately Held
Web: www.westernmassrendering.com
SIC: 2077 Rendering

(G-12050)
WESTFIELD GAGE CO INC
34 Hudson Dr (01077-9546)
PHONE..............................413 569-9444
Frederick F Filios, *Dir*
EMP: 18 EST: 1955
SALES (est): 346.21K Privately Held
Web: www.westfieldgage.com
SIC: 3365 Aerospace castings, aluminum

(G-12051)
WGI INC
34 Hudson Dr (01077-9546)
P.O. Box 1130 (01077-1130)
PHONE..............................413 569-9444
Frederick Filios, *Pr*
Theresa Thomas, *
James Filios, *
Rebecca Totti, *
EMP: 135 EST: 1942
SQ FT: 73,000
SALES (est): 30.31MM Privately Held
Web: www.wgi.us
SIC: 3724 3568 3769 3711 Aircraft engines
and engine parts; Power transmission
equipment, nec; Airframe assemblies,
guided missiles; Military motor vehicle
assembly

(G-12052)
WHALLEY PRECISION INC
28 Hudson Dr (01077-9546)
PHONE..............................413 569-1400
John Whalley, *Pr*
David Whalley, *VP*
▲ EMP: 17 EST: 1990
SQ FT: 17,000
SALES (est): 2.34MM Privately Held
Web: www.whalleyprecision.com
SIC: 3599 Machine shop, jobbing and repair

(G-12053)
WHIP CITY TOOL & DIE CORP
813 College Hwy (01077-9690)
P.O. Box 99 (01077-0099)
PHONE..............................413 569-5528
Nathan Kane, *Pr*
Brian M Iserman, *
Nathan A Kane, *
▼ EMP: 24 EST: 1957
SQ FT: 17,500
SALES (est): 3.93MM Privately Held
Web: www.whipcitytool.com
SIC: 3544 Special dies and tools

Spencer
Worcester County

(G-12054)
BLUESHIFT MATERIALS INC
Also Called: Blueshift
5 S Spencer Rd (01562-2629)
PHONE..............................888 350-7586
Timothy Burbey, *Pr*
Neil Mcdonough, *Dir*
Shaun Mcdonough, *Dir*
Garrett Poe, *
▲ EMP: 30 EST: 2013
SALES (est): 4.95MM Privately Held
Web: www.blueshiftmaterials.com
SIC: 2821 Plastics materials and resins

(G-12055)
BOND CONSTRUCTION
CORPORATION
Also Called: Bond Sand Gravel & Asphalt
98 N Spencer Rd (01562-1402)
PHONE..............................508 885-2480
Joseph W Hubacz Junior, *Pr*
Edward S Hubacz, *Treas*
Nancy Mason, *CFO*
Jodie Ann Hubacz, *Dir*
EMP: 15 EST: 1965
SQ FT: 1,800
SALES (est): 2.47MM Privately Held
Web: www.bondsandandgravel.com
SIC: 2951 5211 Asphalt and asphaltic
paving mixtures (not from refineries);
Paving stones

(G-12056)
CISTERCIAN ABBEY SPENCER
INC
Also Called: St Joseph's Abbey
167 N Spencer Rd (01562-1232)
PHONE..............................508 885-8700
Vincent Rogers, *Admn*
Reverend Damian Carr, *Pr*
Kevin White, *
EMP: 45 EST: 1902
SQ FT: 10,000
SALES (est): 10.29MM Privately Held
Web: www.spencerabbey.org
SIC: 2033 2732 8661 8062 Jams, including
imitation: packaged in cans, jars, etc.; Book
printing; Religious organizations; General
medical and surgical hospitals

(G-12057)
DIENES CORPORATION
27 W Main St (01562-2498)
PHONE..............................508 885-6301
William Shea, *Pr*
Kenneth Jaillet, *VP Fin*
▲ EMP: 40 EST: 1977
SQ FT: 34,000
SALES (est): 13.46MM
SALES (corp-wide): 597.4K Privately Held
Web: www.dienesusa.com
SIC: 5084 3545 Industrial machinery and
equipment; Cutting tools for machine tools
HQ: Supe-Dienes Gmbh
Kolner Str. 7
Overath NW 51491
22066050

(G-12058)
FLEXCON COMPANY INC (PA)
Also Called: Flexcon
1 Flexcon Industrial Park (01562-2643)
PHONE..............................508 885-8200
Neil Mcdonough, *CEO*
C Jean Mcdonough, *Treas*

Lavon Winkler, *President ADT North America*＊
Aimee Peacock, ＊
◆ **EMP: 700 EST:** 1960
SQ FT: 30,000
SALES (est): 314.36MM
SALES (corp-wide): 314.36MM **Privately Held**
Web: www.flexcon.com
SIC: 3081 2891   Plastics film and sheet; Adhesives

(G-12059)
FLEXCON INDUSTRIAL LLC (HQ)
1 S Spencer Rd (01562-2643)
PHONE..........................210 798-1900
▲ **EMP:** 65 **EST:** 2011
SALES (est): 26.02MM
SALES (corp-wide): 314.36MM **Privately Held**
Web: www.arloninnovations.com
SIC: 3086   Plastics foam products
PA: Flexcon Company, Inc.
     1 Flexcon Industrial Park
     Spencer MA 01562
     508 885-8200

(G-12060)
GOLDACRE REALTY INC
Also Called: Dairy Queen
291 Main St (01562-1836)
PHONE..........................508 885-2748
Phil Gertsios, *Pr*
Triantan Gertsios, *Pr*
Ilias Gertsios, *VP*
EMP: 16 **EST:** 1948
SQ FT: 2,000
SALES (est): 387.08K **Privately Held**
Web: www.dairyqueen.com
SIC: 5812 2053   Ice cream stands or dairy bars; Cakes, bakery: frozen

(G-12061)
HORIZON FENCE COMPANY INC
66 Thompson Pond Rd (01562-2921)
PHONE..........................774 289-9254
Jamie Riedle, *Dir*
EMP: 7 **EST:** 2021
SALES (est): 279.74K **Privately Held**
Web: www.horizonfencema.com
SIC: 3496   Miscellaneous fabricated wire products

(G-12062)
LEVEILLEE ARCHTCTRAL MLLWK INC
23 S Spencer Rd (01562-2629)
PHONE..........................508 885-9731
Richard J Leveillee, *Pr*
EMP: 10 **EST:** 2009
SALES (est): 1.16MM **Privately Held**
Web: www.levmillwork.com
SIC: 2431   Millwork

(G-12063)
LFB USA INC
300 Charlton Rd (01562-3138)
PHONE..........................508 370-5100
EMP: 8 **EST:** 2014
SALES (est): 508.18K **Privately Held**
Web: www.lfb-usa.com
SIC: 2834   Pharmaceutical preparations

(G-12064)
MERCURY WIRE PRODUCTS INC
Mercury Dr 1 (01562-1999)
PHONE..........................508 885-6363
Robert K Yard, *Pr*

Christopher Yard, ＊
Perry Harrison, ＊
◆ **EMP:** 135 **EST:** 1966
SQ FT: 65,000
SALES (est): 68.98K **Privately Held**
Web: www.mercurywire.com
SIC: 3357   Communication wire

(G-12065)
REVO BIOLOGICS INC
300 Charlton Rd (01562-3138)
PHONE..........................508 370-5451
Greg Lapsky, *Brnch Mgr*
EMP: 30
SALES (corp-wide): 4.23MM **Privately Held**
Web: www.lfb-usa.com
SIC: 2836 6794   Extracts; Patent buying, licensing, leasing
HQ: Revo Biologics, Inc.
     175 Crossing Blvd
     Framingham MA 01702

(G-12066)
SPENCER INDUSTRIAL PAINTING
60 Wire Village Rd (01562-1439)
PHONE..........................508 885-5406
EMP: 8 **EST:** 1971
SQ FT: 2,000
SALES (est): 502.11K **Privately Held**
SIC: 3479   Painting of metal products

Springfield
Hampden County

(G-12067)
A B C GLASS CO INC
Also Called: A B C Glass & Mirror Works
722 Liberty St (01104-2420)
PHONE..........................413 734-4524
Daniel W Roy, *Pr*
EMP: 10 **EST:** 1958
SQ FT: 8,000
SALES (est): 988.25K **Privately Held**
SIC: 1793 5231 5719 3231   Glass and glazing work; Glass; Mirrors; Products of purchased glass

(G-12068)
A G MILLER COMPANY INC
53 Batavia St (01109-3893)
PHONE..........................413 732-9297
Rick Miller, *Pr*
Ernestine A Miller, *Sec*
▲ **EMP:** 43 **EST:** 1914
SQ FT: 40,000
SALES (est): 8.24MM **Privately Held**
Web: www.agmiller.com
SIC: 3444   Sheet metalwork

(G-12069)
ACCENT ON INDUSTRIAL METAL INC
179 Page Blvd (01104-3035)
PHONE..........................413 785-1654
David M Tassinari, *Pr*
EMP: 10 **EST:** 1980
SQ FT: 25,000
SALES (est): 1.91MM **Privately Held**
Web: www.accentindustrial.com
SIC: 3369   Machinery castings, exc. die, nonferrous, exc. alum. copper

(G-12070)
ACE SIGNS INC
477 Cottage St (01104-3290)
P.O. Box 3374 (01101-3374)

PHONE..........................413 739-3814
TOLL FREE: 800
James Carlin Senior, *Pr*
James Carlin Junior, *VP*
Cathy Smith, *Treas*
EMP: 10 **EST:** 1945
SQ FT: 11,000
SALES (est): 936.28K **Privately Held**
Web: www.acesignsinc.com
SIC: 3993   Electric signs

(G-12071)
AEROBOND COMPOSITES LLC
1 Allen St Ste 201 (01108-1953)
P.O. Box 80269 (01138-0269)
PHONE..........................413 734-2224
Albert Altieri, *CEO*
EMP: 30 **EST:** 2019
SQ FT: 4,800
SALES (est): 4.43MM
SALES (corp-wide): 48.44MM **Privately Held**
Web: www.aerobondcorp.com
SIC: 3724 3728   Aircraft engines and engine parts; Aircraft parts and equipment, nec
PA: Whi Global, Llc
     13914 E Admiral Pl Ste A
     Tulsa OK 74116
     855 944-4562

(G-12072)
AGNOLI SIGN COMPANY INC
722 Worthington St (01105-1115)
P.O. Box 1055 (01101-1055)
PHONE..........................413 732-5111
TOLL FREE: 800
Donald G Agnoli, *Pr*
EMP: 20 **EST:** 1930
SQ FT: 20,000
SALES (est): 2.44MM **Privately Held**
Web: www.agnolisign.com
SIC: 3993   Electric signs

(G-12073)
ALTON E GLEASON COMPANY INC (PA)
658 Berkshire Ave (01109-1052)
PHONE..........................413 732-8207
Patrick Gleason, *Pr*
EMP: 15 **EST:** 1941
SQ FT: 1,200
SALES (est): 4.28MM
SALES (corp-wide): 4.28MM **Privately Held**
Web: www.gleasonpaving.net
SIC: 1611 2951   Highway and street paving contractor; Asphalt and asphaltic paving mixtures (not from refineries)

(G-12074)
AMERICAN TIRE SVC & SLS INC
160 Tapley St (01104-2825)
PHONE..........................413 739-5369
Robert Vanzandt, *Pr*
EMP: 7 **EST:** 1982
SQ FT: 3,600
SALES (est): 1.2MM **Privately Held**
Web: www.americantireservice.com
SIC: 5531 7534   Automotive tires; Tire repair shop

(G-12075)
ANDRITZ INC
40 Progress Ave (01104-3231)
PHONE..........................413 733-6603
EMP: 119
SALES (corp-wide): 7.83B **Privately Held**
Web: www.andritz.com

SIC: 3554 8711 7389   Pulp mill machinery; Industrial engineers; Design, commercial and industrial
HQ: Andritz Inc.
     5405 Windward Pkwy 100w
     Alpharetta GA 30004
     770 640-2500

(G-12076)
ASSOCTED ELECTRO-MECHANICS INC
Also Called: Aem
185 Rowland St (01107-1012)
P.O. Box 2650 (01101-2650)
PHONE..........................413 781-4276
Elayne T Lebeau, *Ch Bd*
Roland A Lafrance, ＊
William Mcclellan, *VP*
Janet Lebeau, ＊
Norman R Lebeau, ＊
EMP: 55 **EST:** 1976
SQ FT: 84,000
SALES (est): 20.93MM **Privately Held**
Web: www.aemservices.com
SIC: 5084 5065 7692   Industrial machinery and equipment; Electronic parts and equipment, nec; Welding repair

(G-12077)
ASTENJOHNSON INC
40 Progress Ave (01104-3231)
PHONE..........................413 733-6603
Dan Cappell, *Brnch Mgr*
EMP: 7
SALES (corp-wide): 425.15MM **Privately Held**
Web: www.astenjohnson.com
SIC: 2221   Broadwoven fabric mills, manmade
PA: Astenjohnson, Inc.
     4399 Corporate Rd
     North Charleston SC 29405
     843 747-7800

(G-12078)
ATHLETIC EMBLEM LETTERING INC
Also Called: Hampden Hat & Cap Co Division
189 Taylor St (01105-1747)
PHONE..........................413 733-8151
Michael Godek, *Pr*
EMP: 11 **EST:** 1960
SQ FT: 20,000
SALES (est): 330.7K **Privately Held**
Web: www.athleticemblem.com
SIC: 2399 2353 2395   Emblems, badges, and insignia: from purchased materials; Baseball caps; Emblems, embroidered

(G-12079)
BLUE RHINO OF NE
1709 Page Blvd (01104-1753)
PHONE..........................413 781-3694
Drabik John, *Prin*
EMP: 8 **EST:** 2008
SALES (est): 943.49K **Privately Held**
Web: www.bluerhino.com
SIC: 2911   Liquefied petroleum gases, LPG

(G-12080)
BRIDGESTONE RET OPERATIONS LLC
Also Called: Firestone
1666 Boston Rd (01129-1141)
PHONE..........................413 543-1312
Brian Harrison, *Mgr*
EMP: 10
Web: www.bridgestoneamericas.com

SIC: 5531 7534   Automotive tires;
Rebuilding and retreading tires
HQ: Bridgestone Retail Operations, Llc
333 E Lake St Ste 300
Bloomingdale IL 60108
630 259-9000

(G-12081)
BUSINESS WEST
Also Called: Business West On Line
1441 Main St Ste 604 (01103-1449)
PHONE................................413 781-8600
John Gormally, *Owner*
EMP: 9 **EST:** 1984
SALES (est): 1.93MM **Privately Held**
Web: www.businesswest.com
SIC: 2711   Newspapers, publishing and
printing

(G-12082)
CARL FISHER CO INC
42 Wilcox St (01105-2399)
P.O. Box 2209 (01101-2209)
PHONE................................413 736-3661
Ronald Fisher, *Pr*
Douglas Fisher, *
EMP: 40 **EST:** 1933
SQ FT: 20,000
SALES (est): 4.86MM **Privately Held**
Web: www.carlfisherco.com
SIC: 3441 3444   Fabricated structural metal;
Ducts, sheet metal

(G-12083)
CHICOPEE VISION CENTER INC
Also Called: 16 Acres Optical
1907 Wilbraham Rd (01129-1822)
PHONE................................413 796-7570
William E Dyke Junior, *Pr*
EMP: 9 **EST:** 1984
SALES (est): 367.49K **Privately Held**
Web: www.sixteenacresoptical.com
SIC: 3851   Eyeglasses, lenses and frames

(G-12084)
CITY TIRE CO INC (PA)
Also Called: Amherst Tire
25 Avocado St (01104-3303)
P.O. Box 2469 (01101-2469)
PHONE................................413 737-1419
Peter Greenberg, *Pr*
Jeff Martin, *
Daniel A Greenberg, *
EMP: 26 **EST:** 1945
SQ FT: 55,000
SALES (est): 23.19MM
SALES (corp-wide): 23.19MM **Privately
Held**
Web: www.city-tire.com
SIC: 5531 5014 7534   Automotive tires;
Truck tires and tubes; Tire recapping

(G-12085)
CONDON MFG CO INC
310 Verge St (01129-1197)
PHONE................................413 543-1250
Kenneth Condon, *Pr*
Gregg Condon, *Treas*
Joanne Evans, *Sec*
EMP: 20 **EST:** 1946
SQ FT: 8,100
SALES (est): 937.31K **Privately Held**
Web: www.condonmfg.com
SIC: 3491 3451   Pressure valves and
regulators, industrial; Screw machine
products

(G-12086)
CRRC MA CORPORATION
655 Page Blvd (01104-3013)

PHONE................................617 415-7190
EMP: 169
Web: www.crrcma.com
SIC: 3743   Interurban cars and car
equipment
HQ: Crrc Ma Corporation
108 Myrtle St Ste 3
Quincy MA 02171
617 415-7180

(G-12087)
CRYSTAL BROOK LDSCP CNSTR INC
Also Called: Crystal Brook Decorative Con
52 Hardy St (01129-1107)
P.O. Box 896 (01095-0896)
PHONE................................413 596-0055
Justin Haggerty, *Pr*
EMP: 10 **EST:** 1999
SALES (est): 780.21K **Privately Held**
Web: www.crystalbrooklandscape.com
SIC: 0782 3271   Landscape contractors;
Paving blocks, concrete

(G-12088)
CUMMINS INC
177 Rocus St Ste 1 (01104-3479)
PHONE................................413 737-2659
Danny Leigh, *Brnch Mgr*
EMP: 9
SALES (corp-wide): 34.06B **Publicly Held**
Web: www.cummins.com
SIC: 3519   Internal combustion engines, nec
PA: Cummins Inc.
500 Jackson St
Columbus IN 47201
812 377-5000

(G-12089)
DAVES TRUCK REPAIR INC
1023 Page Blvd (01104-1639)
PHONE................................413 734-8898
David A Proulx, *Pr*
Ron Proulx, *
EMP: 30 **EST:** 1987
SQ FT: 35,000
SALES (est): 4.21MM **Privately Held**
Web: www.davestruckrepairinc.com
SIC: 7538 7539 3714 3715   General truck
repair; Trailer repair; Trailer hitches, motor
vehicle; Truck trailers

(G-12090)
DONCASTERS INC
Storms Forge Division
160 Cottage St (01104-3250)
PHONE................................413 785-1801
David Simm, *Brnch Mgr*
EMP: 90
Web: www.doncasters.com
SIC: 3325 3462   Steel foundries, nec; Iron
and steel forgings
PA: Doncasters Inc.
835 Poquonnock Rd
Groton CT 06340

(G-12091)
DUC-PAC CORPORATION
1125 Page Blvd (01104-1634)
PHONE................................413 525-3302
Carl F Fisher, *Pr*
Rudolph J Fisher, *
Douglas Fisher, *
Ronald Fisher, *
EMP: 35 **EST:** 1955
SALES (est): 4.46MM **Privately Held**
Web: www.ducpac.com
SIC: 3444 3585 3567   Ducts, sheet metal;
Refrigeration and heating equipment;
Industrial furnaces and ovens

(G-12092)
ELECTRO-TERM INC
Also Called: Electro-Term/Hollingsworth
50 Warehouse St (01118-1058)
PHONE................................413 734-6469
Thomas Dancy, *Pr*
Walt Rustic, *
Andrea Gagne, *
Danette Bucci, *
Douglas Dagrin, *
EMP: 74 **EST:** 1977
SQ FT: 48,000
SALES (est): 9.41MM **Privately Held**
Web: www.hollingsworth.com
SIC: 3643 3678   Solderless connectors
(electric wiring devices); Electronic
connectors

(G-12093)
ELY TOOL INC
455 Cottage St (01104-4005)
PHONE................................413 732-2347
Edward L Young, *Pr*
EMP: 34 **EST:** 1978
SQ FT: 10,000
SALES (est): 2.5MM **Privately Held**
Web: www.young-ely.com
SIC: 3599   Machine shop, jobbing and repair

(G-12094)
EMERY DEVELOPMENT LTD
179 Cooley St (01128-1110)
PHONE................................413 782-1990
Radie Bonemery, *Pr*
Anne Bonemery, *Clerk*
EMP: 7 **EST:** 1985
SQ FT: 2,000
SALES (est): 657.51K **Privately Held**
SIC: 6552 1521 1522 1542   Land
subdividers and developers, commercial;
Single-family housing construction;
Residential construction, nec;
Nonresidential construction, nec

(G-12095)
FLAG FABLES INC
113 Vermont St (01108-8149)
PHONE................................413 747-0525
Wendy Diamond, *Pr*
EMP: 20 **EST:** 1985
SALES (est): 1.4MM **Privately Held**
Web: www.flagfables.com
SIC: 2399 5999 5961   Flags, fabric; Decals;
Catalog and mail-order houses

(G-12096)
GRAPHIC EXCELLENCE LLC
Also Called: Sir Speedy
1441 Main St (01103-1406)
PHONE................................413 733-6691
Traci Conners, *Managing Member*
EMP: 7 **EST:** 1973
SQ FT: 3,200
SALES (est): 745.17K **Privately Held**
Web: www.sirspeedy.com
SIC: 2752   Commercial printing, lithographic

(G-12097)
GRASSETTI SALES ASSOCIATES INC
Also Called: Roberts Manufacturing Company
160 Progress Ave (01104-3232)
PHONE................................413 737-2283
Robert A Grassetti, *Pr*
EMP: 9 **EST:** 1975
SALES (est): 930.83K **Privately Held**
SIC: 3599   Machine shop, jobbing and repair

(G-12098)
GWS TOOL HOLDINGS LLC
Also Called: Benchmark Carbide
616 Dwight St (01104-3409)
PHONE................................800 523-8570
Rick Mcintyre, *Brnch Mgr*
EMP: 33
SALES (corp-wide): 11.77B **Privately Held**
Web: www.gwstoolgroup.com
SIC: 2819   Carbides
HQ: Gws Tool Holdings, Llc
595 County Road 448
Tavares FL 32778
352 343-8778

(G-12099)
HARVEY INDUSTRIES LLC
175 Carando Dr (01104-3276)
PHONE................................413 731-7700
EMP: 27
SALES (corp-wide): 1.2B **Privately Held**
Web: www.harveybp.com
SIC: 5033 5031 3442 2431   Roofing, asphalt
and sheet metal; Windows; Storm doors or
windows, metal; Windows, wood
PA: Harvey Industries, Llc
1400 Main St Fl 3
Waltham MA 02451
800 598-5400

(G-12100)
HEDGE HOG INDUSTRIES CORP
86 Princeton St (01109-3427)
PHONE................................413 363-2528
Mike Serricchio, *Prin*
EMP: 10 **EST:** 2014
SALES (est): 479.21K **Privately Held**
SIC: 3999   Manufacturing industries, nec

(G-12101)
HOLYOKE TIRE & AUTO SVC INC
Also Called: Springfield Tire & Auto
435 Dwight St (01103-1311)
PHONE................................413 733-2141
EMP: 7
SALES (corp-wide): 17.48MM **Privately
Held**
Web: www.springfieldtire.net
SIC: 5014 7538 7534 5531   Tires and tubes;
General automotive repair shops; Tire
retreading and repair shops; Auto and
home supply stores
PA: Holyoke Tire & Auto Service, Inc.
1264 Union Street Ext
West Springfield MA 01089
413 533-0600

(G-12102)
HORIZON SHEET METAL INC
109 Cadwell Dr (01104-1705)
PHONE................................413 734-6966
Peggy Grodd, *Pr*
Gerald A Desjardins, *
Philip C Schultz, *
Peggy K Grodd, *
Arthur D Grodd, *
EMP: 55 **EST:** 1985
SQ FT: 45,000
SALES (est): 6.98MM **Privately Held**
Web: www.horizonsmi.com
SIC: 3444   Sheet metal specialties, not
stamped

(G-12103)
HOT MAMAS FOODS INC
134 Avocado St (01104-3306)
P.O. Box 247 (01101-0247)
PHONE................................413 737-6572
Matthew Morse, *CAO*
Matthew Morse, *CAO*

William J Kenealy, *CFO*
EMP: 137 **EST:** 2013
SQ FT: 24,000
SALES (est): 9.13MM **Privately Held**
Web: www.hotmamas.ca
SIC: 2099 Food preparations, nec

(G-12104)
INEOS MELAMINES LLC
Also Called: Ineos
730b Worcester St (01151-1022)
PHONE..............................413 730-3811
◆ **EMP:** 42 **EST:** 2009
SALES (est): 10.02MM
SALES (corp-wide): 929.53K **Privately Held**
Web: www.ineos.com
SIC: 2821 Plastics materials and resins
HQ: Ineos Group Ag
Avenue Des Uttins 3
Rolle VD

(G-12105)
INTEMPO SOFTWARE INC (PA)
191 Chestnut St 5th Fl (01103-1571)
PHONE..............................800 950-2221
Matt Hopp, *Genl Mgr*
EMP: 15 **EST:** 2008
SQ FT: 5,000
SALES (est): 2.29MM
SALES (corp-wide): 2.29MM **Privately Held**
Web: www.intemposoftware.com
SIC: 7372 Prepackaged software

(G-12106)
INTERNTNAL BR-TECH SLTIONS INC (PA)
225 Armory St (01104-2425)
PHONE..............................413 739-2271
Jonathan Waitt, *Pr*
EMP: 7 **EST:** 1993
SQ FT: 5,500
SALES (est): 2.44MM **Privately Held**
SIC: 3699 Security devices

(G-12107)
JOSEPH FREEDMAN CO INC
40 Albany St (01105-1002)
PHONE..............................413 781-4444
John Freedman, *Brnch Mgr*
EMP: 30
SALES (corp-wide): 24.79MM **Privately Held**
Web: www.jfrecycle.com
SIC: 3355 Aluminum rolling and drawing, nec
PA: Joseph Freedman Co., Inc.
115 Stevens St
Springfield MA 01104
888 677-7818

(G-12108)
JOSEPH FREEDMAN CO INC (PA)
115 Stevens St (01104-3120)
PHONE..............................888 677-7818
TOLL FREE: 800
John Freedman, *Pr*
Ernest Gagnon Junior, *VP*
Michael E Freedman, *
Don George, *
EMP: 55 **EST:** 1891
SQ FT: 120,000
SALES (est): 24.79MM
SALES (corp-wide): 24.79MM **Privately Held**
Web: www.jfrecycle.com
SIC: 3355 Aluminum wire and cable

(G-12109)
KIELB WELDING ENTERPRISES INC
Also Called: Advance Welding
150 Brookdale Dr (01104-3208)
PHONE..............................413 734-4544
Kaz Kielb, *Pr*
Christopher Kielb, *VP*
EMP: 10 **EST:** 1978
SQ FT: 10,000
SALES (est): 860.05K **Privately Held**
Web: www.theperfectweld.com
SIC: 7692 Welding repair

(G-12110)
KIRBY CORPORATION
Also Called: Amped-Up Electric Rides
784 Page Blvd (01104-3025)
PHONE..............................413 363-0005
Diane Kirby, *Pr*
EMP: 8 **EST:** 2021
SALES (est): 185.75K **Privately Held**
Web: www.amped-upelectricrides.com
SIC: 3714 Motor vehicle electrical equipment

(G-12111)
LUSTER-ON PRODUCTS INC
54 Waltham Ave (01109-3398)
P.O. Box 90247 (01139-0247)
PHONE..............................413 739-2541
Paul R Lane, *Pr*
Alexander J Price, *Treas*
Catherine P Rogers, *Sec*
▲ **EMP:** 18 **EST:** 1968
SQ FT: 75,000
SALES (est): 4.98MM **Privately Held**
Web: www.luster-on.com
SIC: 5084 8711 3471 Industrial machinery and equipment; Designing: ship, boat, machine, and product; Electroplating and plating

(G-12112)
MANAGE INC
1380 Main St Ste 500 (01103-1646)
PHONE..............................413 593-9128
EMP: 50 **EST:** 1973
SALES (est): 7.53MM **Privately Held**
Web: www.manage-inc.com
SIC: 3663 3679 3357 Light communications equipment; Harness assemblies, for electronic use: wire or cable; Nonferrous wiredrawing and insulating

(G-12113)
MERRIAM-WEBSTER INCORPORATED (DH)
47 Federal St (01105-1230)
P.O. Box 281 (01102-0281)
PHONE..............................413 734-3134
John M Morse, *Pr*
Caryl Schivley, *
Thomas L Coopee, *
Judith G Recke, *
▲ **EMP:** 93 **EST:** 1831
SQ FT: 35,000
SALES (est): 44.97MM
SALES (corp-wide): 2.67MM **Privately Held**
Web: www.merriam-webster.com
SIC: 2731 2741 Books, publishing only; Miscellaneous publishing
HQ: Encyclopaedia Britannica, Inc.
325 N Lasalle St Ste 200
Chicago IL 60654
312 347-7000

(G-12114)
MITCHELL MACHINE INCORPORATED (PA)
224 Hancock St (01109-4399)
P.O. Box 90128 (01139-0128)
PHONE..............................413 739-9693
John Mitchell, *Pr*
Francis Mitchell, *
Frank Mitchell, *
EMP: 15 **EST:** 1924
SQ FT: 30,000
SALES (est): 4.54MM
SALES (corp-wide): 4.54MM **Privately Held**
Web: www.mitchellmachine.com
SIC: 3554 3559 3548 Paper industries machinery; Plastics working machinery; Welding apparatus

(G-12115)
MPINGO MULTI CASTING
146 Chestnut St (01103-1554)
PHONE..............................413 241-2500
EMP: 7 **EST:** 2004
SALES (est): 150.06K **Privately Held**
SIC: 3369 White metal castings (lead, tin, antimony), except die

(G-12116)
NASH MFG & GRINDING SVCS INC
Also Called: Nash Manufacturing
572 Saint James Ave (01109-3832)
P.O. Box 1266 (01041-1266)
PHONE..............................413 301-5416
Matthew Nash, *Pr*
Jan Lee Nash, *VP*
EMP: 11 **EST:** 1996
SQ FT: 2,100
SALES (est): 1.03MM **Privately Held**
Web: www.nashmanufacturing.com
SIC: 3599 Machine shop, jobbing and repair

(G-12117)
NORTHERN TOOL MFG CO INC
170 Progress Ave (01104-3232)
PHONE..............................413 732-5549
George Frigo, *Pr*
Mary Breglio, *Treas*
EMP: 16 **EST:** 1952
SQ FT: 15,000
SALES (est): 2.1MM **Privately Held**
Web: www.northerntoolmfg.com
SIC: 3089 Injection molding of plastics

(G-12118)
NORTHSTAR PULP & PAPER CO INC
89 Guion St (01104-3070)
PHONE..............................413 263-6000
David Goodman, *CEO*
Lori Goodman-novak, *Pr*
Noah Goodman, *
Aaron E Goodman, *
Seth Goodman, *
▲ **EMP:** 51 **EST:** 2003
SALES (est): 22.46MM **Privately Held**
Web: www.northstarpulpandpaper.com
SIC: 4953 2679 Recycling, waste materials; Paperboard products, converted, nec

(G-12119)
NUFORJ LLC
1350 Main St (01103-1628)
PHONE..............................413 530-0349
Rudy Vogel, *Mng Pt*
Donald Deptowicz, *Prin*
EMP: 14 **EST:** 2016
SALES (est): 1.39MM **Privately Held**

Web: www.nuforj.com
SIC: 3599 Crankshafts and camshafts, machining

(G-12120)
ORTIZ TOOL LLC
395 Liberty St (01104-3779)
PHONE..............................413 733-1206
EMP: 8 **EST:** 2019
SALES (est): 454.1K **Privately Held**
Web: www.ortiztool.com
SIC: 3599 Industrial machinery, nec

(G-12121)
PLAN B BURGER LLC
Also Called: Plan B
1000 W Columbus Ave (01105-2518)
PHONE..............................413 285-8296
Denise Wessig, *Genl Mgr*
EMP: 14 **EST:** 2013
SALES (est): 757.13K **Privately Held**
Web: www.burgersbeerbourbon.com
SIC: 5812 2082 Grills (eating places); Beer (alcoholic beverage)

(G-12122)
POLY-METAL FINISHING INC
1 Allen St Ste 218 (01108-1953)
P.O. Box 80049 (01138-0049)
PHONE..............................413 781-4535
Jason Kudelka, *Pr*
Tim Kellogg, *
Ron Tautic, *
EMP: 70 **EST:** 1971
SQ FT: 40,000
SALES (est): 8.62MM **Privately Held**
Web: www.poly-metal.net
SIC: 3471 3479 Anodizing (plating) of metals or formed products; Painting, coating, and hot dipping

(G-12123)
PYS ENTERPRISES INC
616 Dwight St (01104-3409)
PHONE..............................413 732-7470
Alex Semenick, *CEO*
EMP: 47 **EST:** 1982
SQ FT: 6,500
SALES (est): 2.32MM **Privately Held**
Web: www.teamfubu.net
SIC: 3541 Machine tools, metal cutting type

(G-12124)
RAINBOW GRAPHICS INC
267 Allen St (01108-2078)
PHONE..............................413 733-3376
Margaret Lococo, *Pr*
Augustus Lococo, *Treas*
EMP: 11 **EST:** 1975
SQ FT: 2,000
SALES (est): 880K **Privately Held**
Web: www.wilsonhydraulic.com
SIC: 7336 2752 Graphic arts and related design; Offset printing

(G-12125)
REPUBLICAN COMPANY (HQ)
Also Called: Springfield Newspaper
1860 Main St (01103-1073)
PHONE..............................413 788-1000
TOLL FREE: 800
David B Evans, *Pr*
Thomas S Summer, *
Michael Newhouse, *
EMP: 623 **EST:** 1878
SQ FT: 200,000
SALES (est): 91.49MM
SALES (corp-wide): 2.88B **Privately Held**
Web: www.masslive.com

SIC: 2711 Newspapers, publishing and printing
PA: Advance Publications, Inc.
1 World Trade Ctr Fl 43
New York NY 10007
718 981-1234

(G-12126)
ROBERTS & SONS PRINTING INC
1791 Boston Rd (01129-1129)
PHONE.................................413 283-9356
George Roberts, *Pr*
Diana Roberts, *Treas*
Stephen Manning, *Clerk*
Jeffrey Roberts, *VP*
EMP: 7 **EST:** 1980
SALES (est): 950.86K **Privately Held**
Web:
www.robertsandludlowprinting.com
SIC: 2759 2752 Letterpress printing;
Commercial printing, lithographic

(G-12127)
ROYALTY BRDCSTG SVCS & TRNSP
Also Called: Rst
484 White St (01108-3230)
PHONE.................................413 777-7868
Luis Laboy, *Pr*
EMP: 10 **EST:** 2020
SALES (est): 600.97K **Privately Held**
SIC: 3663 Studio equipment, radio and
television broadcasting

(G-12128)
SKIN CATERING INC
1500 Main St., Ste 220 (01115)
PHONE.................................413 349-8199
Leanne Sedlak, *CEO*
EMP: 15 **EST:** 2010
SALES (est): 467.34K **Privately Held**
Web: www.skincatering.com
SIC: 7231 3999 Beauty shops; Barber and
beauty shop equipment

(G-12129)
SMITH & WESSON BRANDS INC (PA)
2100 Roosevelt Ave (01104-1698)
PHONE.................................800 331-0852
Mark P Smith, *Pr*
Robert L Scott, *
Deana L Mcpherson, *Ex VP*
Kevin A Maxwell, *CCO*
Susan J Cupero, *VP Sls*
EMP: 724 **EST:** 1852
SALES (est): 479.24MM
SALES (corp-wide): 479.24MM **Publicly Held**
Web: www.aob.com
SIC: 3482 Small arms ammunition

(G-12130)
SMITHFIELD DIRECT LLC
Carando
20 Carando Dr (01104-3212)
P.O. Box 491 (01102-0491)
PHONE.................................413 781-5620
Donald Kimdle, *Mgr*
EMP: 122
SQ FT: 160,000
Web: carando.sfdbrands.com
SIC: 2013 2011 Sausages, from purchased
meat; Meat packing plants
HQ: Smithfield Direct, Llc
4225 Naperville Rd # 600
Lisle IL 60532

(G-12131)
SMITHFIELD FOODS INC
Also Called: Carando Foods
20 Carando Dr (01104-3212)
P.O. Box 491 (01102-0491)
PHONE.................................413 781-5620
EMP: 60
Web: www.smithfieldfoods.com
SIC: 2011 Meat packing plants
HQ: Smithfield Foods, Inc.
200 Commerce St
Smithfield VA 23430
757 365-3000

(G-12132)
SOLUTIA INC
730 Worcester St (01151-1022)
P.O. Box 51975 (01151-5975)
PHONE.................................413 788-6911
Jack Mayusky, *Brnch Mgr*
EMP: 750
Web: www.eastman.com
SIC: 2821 Plastics materials and resins
HQ: Solutia Inc.
575 Maryville Centre Dr
Saint Louis MO 63141
314 674-1000

(G-12133)
SPRINGBOARD TECHNOLOGY CORPORATION
1 Federal St (01105-1135)
P.O. Box 4776 (01101-4776)
EMP: 75 **EST:** 1993
SALES (est): 6.82MM **Privately Held**
SIC: 3572 3674 Computer tape drives and
components; Modules, solid state

(G-12134)
SPRINGFIELD EYE ASSOCIATES
Also Called: Jackowitz, Mark A MD
3640 Main St Ste 205 (01107-1139)
PHONE.................................413 739-7367
Doctor Mark A Jackowitz Md, *Pr*
Doctor Bredvik, *Prin*
Gregory Faust, *
Doctor Phillip Moraitis, *Pt*
EMP: 27 **EST:** 1959
SALES (est): 4.65MM **Privately Held**
Web: www.springfieldeyeassociates.com
SIC: 8011 2752 Opthalmologist;
Commercial printing, lithographic

(G-12135)
SPRINGFIELD LABEL TAPE CO INC
430 Saint James Ave (01109-3830)
PHONE.................................413 733-6634
Howard Libowitz, *Pr*
Charles Libowitz, *
EMP: 34 **EST:** 1963
SQ FT: 20,000
SALES (est): 4.62MM **Privately Held**
Web: www.springfieldlabel.com
SIC: 2752 Offset printing

(G-12136)
SUPER BRUSH LLC
800 Worcester St (01151-1042)
PHONE.................................413 543-1442
Roger Allen Sheeks, *Managing Member*
EMP: 95 **EST:** 1964
SQ FT: 40,000
SALES (est): 16.56MM **Privately Held**
Web: www.superbrush.com
SIC: 3089 Injection molded finished plastics
products, nec

(G-12137)
TECHNOLOGY DESIGN MFG SVCS LLC
220 Brookdale Dr (01104-3210)
PHONE.................................413 730-4444
EMP: 20 **EST:** 2002
SQ FT: 17,000
SALES (est): 2.18MM **Privately Held**
Web: www.tdmsinc.com
SIC: 3672 Circuit boards, television and
radio printed

(G-12138)
THOMPSON/CENTER ARMS CO INC (HQ)
Also Called: Thompson/Center Arms
2100 Roosevelt Ave (01104-1606)
PHONE.................................800 331-0852
Peter James Debney, *Pr*
William F Spengler, *Ex VP*
◆ **EMP:** 58 **EST:** 1989
SALES (est): 9.83MM
SALES (corp-wide): 479.24MM **Publicly Held**
Web: www.tcarms.com
SIC: 3484 Pistols or pistol parts, 30 mm.
and below
PA: Smith & Wesson Brands, Inc.
2100 Roosevelt Ave
Springfield MA 01104
800 331-0852

(G-12139)
TITEFLEX COMMERCIAL INC
603 Hendee St (01104-3003)
PHONE.................................413 739-5631
William T Smith, *Pr*
Robert M Speer, *Sec*
◆ **EMP:** 46 **EST:** 2011
SQ FT: 110,000
SALES (est): 11.43MM
SALES (corp-wide): 3.83B **Privately Held**
Web: www.titeflex.com
SIC: 3599 3052 Flexible metal hose, tubing,
and bellows; Rubber and plastics hose and
beltings
PA: Smiths Group Plc
4th Floor
London SW1Y
207 004-1600

(G-12140)
TITEFLEX CORPORATION (HQ)
Also Called: Titeflex
603 Hendee St (01104-3034)
PHONE.................................413 739-5631
Pat Mccaffrey, *Pr*
John S Maggi, *Treas*
Patrick Henry, *VP*
▲ **EMP:** 345 **EST:** 1978
SQ FT: 280,000
SALES (est): 141.88MM
SALES (corp-wide): 3.83B **Privately Held**
Web: www.titeflex.com
SIC: 3052 3599 Plastic hose; Hose, flexible
metallic
PA: Smiths Group Plc
4th Floor
London SW1Y
207 004-1600

(G-12141)
TRANE COMERCIAL SYSTEMS
Also Called: Trane
90 Carando Dr (01104-4205)
PHONE.................................413 271-3001
Paul Crawford, *Prin*
EMP: 11 **EST:** 2010
SALES (est): 464.73K **Privately Held**
Web: www.trane.com

SIC: 3585 Refrigeration and heating
equipment

(G-12142)
TRIDENT ALLOYS INC
181 Abbe Ave (01107-1073)
PHONE.................................413 737-1477
James H Galaska, *Pr*
EMP: 26 **EST:** 1979
SQ FT: 27,500
SALES (est): 7.27MM **Privately Held**
Web: www.tridentalloysinc.com
SIC: 3325 3369 Alloy steel castings, except
investment; Nonferrous foundries, nec

(G-12143)
TRIMBOARD INC
Also Called: Trimboard
983 Page Blvd (01104-1636)
PHONE.................................413 886-0142
David Townsend, *Pr*
EMP: 27 **EST:** 2005
SQ FT: 5,000
SALES (est): 3.76MM **Privately Held**
Web: www.trimboard.net
SIC: 2431 Millwork

(G-12144)
TRISEPTAGON LLC
Also Called: Sterling Architectural Mllwk
55 Avocado St (01104-3303)
PHONE.................................413 732-2131
Jeffrey Allen Struck, *Managing Member*
EMP: 10 **EST:** 2020
SALES (est): 1.23MM **Privately Held**
SIC: 3843 5122 Cabinets, dental; Medicine
cabinet sundries

(G-12145)
UNIVERSAL TOOL CO INC
33 Rose Pl (01104-3198)
PHONE.................................413 732-4807
John M Piane Junior, *Pr*
▲ **EMP:** 24 **EST:** 1928
SQ FT: 12,000
SALES (est): 2.14MM **Privately Held**
SIC: 3469 Stamping metal for the trade

(G-12146)
VALLEY ENTERPRISES INC
4 Birnie Ave (01107-1129)
PHONE.................................413 737-0281
Glenn Beauregard, *Genl Mgr*
▲ **EMP:** 35 **EST:** 1935
SQ FT: 30,000
SALES (est): 4.06MM **Privately Held**
Web: www.lovejoy-inc.com
SIC: 3568 Joints, swivel and universal,
except aircraft and auto

(G-12147)
VALLEY PLATING INC
412 Albany St (01105-1049)
PHONE.................................413 788-7375
John Wietecha, *Pr*
Dennis Chaffee, *
EMP: 75 **EST:** 1978
SQ FT: 39,000
SALES (est): 8.49MM **Privately Held**
Web: www.valleyplatinginc.com
SIC: 3471 Electroplating of metals or
formed products

(G-12148)
VIEWS RECORD LABEL LLC
102 E Alvord St (01108-2217)
PHONE.................................413 204-0930
Jorge A Rodriguez Pagan, *Managing Member*

EMP: 10 **EST:** 2021
SALES (est): 100K **Privately Held**
SIC: 3651 Music distribution apparatus

(G-12149)
WASTE MGMT INC
Also Called: Waste Management Recycle Amer
84 Birnie Ave (01107-1129)
PHONE....................413 747-9294
EMP: 18 **EST:** 1994
SALES (est): 8.79MM
SALES (corp-wide): 20.43B **Publicly Held**
Web: www.springfieldmrf.org
SIC: 3559 Recycling machinery
HQ: Waste Management Holdings Inc
800 Capitol St Ste 3000
Houston TX 77002
713 512-6200

(G-12150)
WEB CLOSEOUT
360 El Paso St (01104-2955)
PHONE....................413 222-8302
Mike Sarrage, *Pr*
EMP: 7 **EST:** 2003
SALES (est): 122.53K **Privately Held**
SIC: 2741 Miscellaneous publishing

(G-12151)
WESTROCK CONTAINER LLC
320 Parker St (01129-1026)
P.O. Box 842159 (02284-2159)
PHONE....................413 733-2211
Dan Kazes, *Brnch Mgr*
EMP: 76
SALES (corp-wide): 20.31B **Publicly Held**
Web: www.westrock.com
SIC: 2653 Boxes, corrugated: made from purchased materials
HQ: Westrock Container, Llc
1601 Blairs Ferry Rd Ne
Cedar Rapids IA 52402
319 393-3610

(G-12152)
WESTROCK MWV LLC
Envelope Division
2001 Roosevelt Ave (01104-1657)
P.O. Box 3300 (01102-3300)
PHONE....................413 736-7211
Barry Levenson, *Brnch Mgr*
EMP: 51
SALES (corp-wide): 20.31B **Publicly Held**
Web: www.westrock.com
SIC: 2631 2677 2671 Linerboard; Envelopes ; Paper; coated and laminated packaging
HQ: Westrock Mwv, Llc
3500 45th St Sw
Lanett AL 36863
804 444-1000

(G-12153)
WESTROCK RKT LLC
320 Parker St (01129-1026)
PHONE....................413 543-7300
EMP: 9
SALES (corp-wide): 20.31B **Publicly Held**
Web: www.westrock.com
SIC: 2653 2652 2631 Partitions, solid fiber: made from purchased materials; Filing boxes, paperboard: made from purchased materials; Container board
HQ: Westrock Rkt, Llc
1000 Abernathy Rd Ste 125
Atlanta GA 30328
770 448-2193

Sterling
Worcester County

(G-12154)
ANDERSON POWER PRODUCTS INC (HQ)
13 Pratts Junction Rd (01564-2305)
PHONE....................978 422-3600
James V James, *CEO*
Nick Shkordoff, *
Jeffrey S Burkhardt, *
▲ **EMP:** 99 **EST:** 2001
SALES (est): 29.36K
SALES (corp-wide): 357.25K **Privately Held**
Web: www.andersonpower.com
SIC: 3829 5065 3678 3643 Measuring and controlling devices, nec; Electronic parts and equipment, nec; Electronic connectors; Current-carrying wiring services
PA: Ideal Industries, Inc.
1375 Park Ave
Sycamore IL 60178
815 895-5181

(G-12155)
AZELIS AMERICAS LLC
Monson
100 Leominster Rd (01564-2156)
PHONE....................212 915-8178
Holly Daley, *Mgr*
EMP: 60
Web: www.azelis.com
SIC: 3569 Lubrication machinery, automatic
HQ: Azelis Americas, Llc
33 Riverside Ave Ste 507
Westport CT 06880
203 274-8691

(G-12156)
BILLY HILL TUBS LLC
47 Chocksett Rd (01564-2353)
PHONE....................978 422-8800
Russell H Mason, *Prin*
EMP: 8 **EST:** 2011
SALES (est): 519.67K **Privately Held**
Web: www.hillbillytubs.com
SIC: 3089 Garbage containers, plastics

(G-12157)
BIOMEDICAL POLYMERS INC
Also Called: Bmp Medical
16 Chocksett Rd (01564-2336)
PHONE....................978 632-2555
Michael T Faulkner, *Pr*
John E Fay, *
▲ **EMP:** 60 **EST:** 1978
SALES (est): 14.85MM **Privately Held**
Web: www.bmpmedical.com
SIC: 3089 Injection molding of plastics

(G-12158)
CIDERMILLRUNSTERLINGCOM
15 Waushacum Ave (01564-2823)
PHONE....................978 422-8675
Julia Vera, *Prin*
EMP: 7 **EST:** 2010
SALES (est): 113.21K **Privately Held**
SIC: 2084 Wines, brandy, and brandy spirits

(G-12159)
CONTINENTAL STONE MBL GRAN INC
Also Called: Continental Stone
287 Leominster Rd (01564-2151)
Rural Route 12 (01453)
PHONE....................978 422-8700
Manoel Leite, *Pr*

Norma Soares, *Treas*
▲ **EMP:** 22 **EST:** 2003
SQ FT: 10,000
SALES (est): 3.81MM **Privately Held**
Web: www.continentalstone.com
SIC: 3281 Granite, cut and shaped

(G-12160)
DON-JO MFG INC
70 Pratts Junction Rd (01564-2304)
P.O. Box 929 (01564-0929)
PHONE....................978 422-3377
Timothy E Roy, *Pr*
▲ **EMP:** 50 **EST:** 1980
SQ FT: 37,500
SALES (est): 4.81MM **Privately Held**
Web: www.don-jo.com
SIC: 3999 Barber and beauty shop equipment

(G-12161)
E H PERKINS CONSTRUCTION INC
Also Called: Pandolf-Perkins
194 Worcester Rd (01564-1473)
P.O. Box 1238 (01564-1238)
PHONE....................978 422-3388
TOLL FREE: 800
Charles Darlington, *Mgr*
EMP: 13
SALES (corp-wide): 9.35MM **Privately Held**
Web: www.ehperkins.com
SIC: 5032 3273 1611 1622 Sand, construction; Ready-mixed concrete; Highway and street paving contractor; Bridge construction
PA: E. H. Perkins Construction, Inc.
560 Main St
Wayland MA 01778
978 562-3436

(G-12162)
FAVREAU FORESTRY LLC
109 Chace Hill Rd (01564-1519)
PHONE....................978 706-1038
EMP: 7 **EST:** 1995
SALES (est): 989.41K **Privately Held**
Web: www.favreauforestry.com
SIC: 1629 2411 Land clearing contractor; Logging

(G-12163)
IDEAL INDUSTRIES INC
Anderson Power Products
13 Pratts Junction Rd (01564-2305)
PHONE....................978 422-3600
James A Colony, *Pr*
EMP: 7
SALES (corp-wide): 357.25K **Privately Held**
Web: www.idealindustries.com
SIC: 3829 5065 3678 3643 Measuring and controlling devices, nec; Electronic parts and equipment, nec; Electronic connectors; Current-carrying wiring services
PA: Ideal Industries, Inc.
1375 Park Ave
Sycamore IL 60178
815 895-5181

(G-12164)
KITCHEN ASSOCIATES INC
Also Called: Sterling Surfaces Div
76 Leominster Rd (01564-2114)
PHONE....................978 422-3322
◆ **EMP:** 48 **EST:** 1958
SALES (est): 6.59MM **Privately Held**
Web: www.kitchenassociates.com

SIC: 1751 2599 Cabinet and finish carpentry ; Factory furniture and fixtures

(G-12165)
KYLE EQUIPMENT CO INC
14 Legate Hill Rd (01564-2312)
P.O. Box 658 (01564-0658)
PHONE....................978 422-8448
Charles F Kyle, *Pr*
Sean Kyle, *VP*
EMP: 7 **EST:** 1982
SQ FT: 8,500
SALES (est): 719.43K **Privately Held**
SIC: 3533 Water well drilling equipment

(G-12166)
LEE PLASTICS INC
102 Pratts Junction Rd (01564-2304)
P.O. Box 39 (01564-0039)
PHONE....................978 422-7611
Leo J Montagna Junior, *Pr*
Mary M Wagner, *
▲ **EMP:** 40 **EST:** 1976
SQ FT: 40,000
SALES (est): 8.67MM **Privately Held**
Web: www.leeplastics.com
SIC: 3089 Injection molding of plastics

(G-12167)
MEADOWBROOK ORCHARDS INC
209 Chace Hill Rd (01564-1518)
PHONE....................978 365-7617
David Chandler, *Pr*
Katherine Chandler, *
EMP: 10 **EST:** 1911
SALES (est): 429.07K **Privately Held**
Web: www.meadowbrookorchards.com
SIC: 0175 5461 2051 Apple orchard; Retail bakeries; Bread, cake, and related products

(G-12168)
MILLHAM LLC
2 Northeast Blvd (01564-2338)
PHONE....................978 422-8621
Ladd M Lavallee, *Dir*
EMP: 10 **EST:** 2009
SALES (est): 1.13MM **Publicly Held**
SIC: 3089 Plastics containers, except foam
PA: Berry Global Group, Inc.
101 Oakley St
Evansville IN 47710

(G-12169)
ROEHR TOOL CORP
7 Chocksett Rd (01564-2353)
PHONE....................978 562-4488
Paul Catalanotti, *Pr*
EMP: 43 **EST:** 1964
SALES (est): 43.21K
SALES (corp-wide): 97K **Privately Held**
Web: www.roehrtool.com
SIC: 3543 Foundry cores
PA: Progressive Components International Corporation
235 Industrial Dr
Wauconda IL 60084
847 487-1000

(G-12170)
SIGLER MACHINE CO
3 Northeast Blvd (01564-2339)
PHONE....................978 422-7868
Lawrence Sigler, *Owner*
EMP: 10 **EST:** 2004
SALES (est): 737.36K **Privately Held**
Web: www.siglermachine.com
SIC: 3599 Machine shop, jobbing and repair

(G-12171)
SPACE AGE ELECTRONICS INC (PA)
58 Chocksett Rd (01564-2354)
PHONE............................800 486-1723
Eugene H Mongeau, *Ch*
Susan Snyder, *
Nicole Leadbetter, *
EMP: 25 **EST:** 1963
SQ FT: 75,000
SALES (est): 13.85MM
SALES (corp-wide): 13.85MM **Privately Held**
Web: www.1sae.com
SIC: 3669 Fire alarm apparatus, electric

(G-12172)
WEETABIX COMPANY INC
12 Industrial Dr (01564-2330)
PHONE............................978 422-2905
EMP: 30
SALES (corp-wide): 1.53MM **Privately Held**
Web: www.weetabixusa.com
SIC: 2043 Cereal breakfast foods
HQ: The Weetabix Company Inc
      20802 Kensington Blvd
      Lakeville MN 55044
      978 365-1000

Stoneham
Middlesex County

(G-12173)
ACTION APPAREL INC
100a Maple St (02180-3143)
PHONE............................781 435-2342
Jj Losco, *Mgr*
EMP: 8
SALES (corp-wide): 1.98MM **Privately Held**
Web: www.actionapparelinc.com
SIC: 2261 5137 Screen printing of cotton broadwoven fabrics; Uniforms, women's and children's
PA: Action Apparel, Inc.
      100a Maple St
      Stoneham MA 02180
      781 224-0777

(G-12174)
AMKOR TECHNOLOGY INC
105 Central St Ste 2300 (02180-1206)
PHONE............................781 438-7800
Ron Simon, *CEO*
EMP: 9
SALES (corp-wide): 7.09B **Publicly Held**
Web: www.amkor.com
SIC: 3674 Semiconductors and related devices
PA: Amkor Technology, Inc.
      2045 E Innovation Cir
      Tempe AZ 85284
      480 821-5000

(G-12175)
CARAT SYSTEMS INC
17 Manison St (02180-3133)
PHONE............................781 560-8082
Roy Gat, *CEO*
EMP: 25 **EST:** 2015
SALES (est): 1.43MM **Privately Held**
Web: www.caratsystems.com
SIC: 3915 Diamond cutting and polishing

(G-12176)
EASTERN TOOL CORPORATION
105 High St (02180-1031)

PHONE............................781 395-1472
Joseph Fustolo, *Pr*
EMP: 10 **EST:** 1981
SALES (est): 852.14K **Privately Held**
Web: www.easterntoolsteel.com
SIC: 3599 Machine shop, jobbing and repair

(G-12177)
ERBI BIOSYSTEMS INC
85 Maple St (02180-3197)
PHONE............................617 297-7422
Michael Chiu, *CEO*
Harry Lee, *Pr*
EMP: 8 **EST:** 2006
SALES (est): 1.08MM **Privately Held**
Web: www.sigmaaldrich.com
SIC: 3821 Laboratory apparatus and furniture

(G-12178)
ESCALON DIGITAL SOLUTIONS INC
Also Called: Sonomedescalon
91 Montvale Ave Ste 320 (02180-3649)
PHONE............................610 688-6830
Richard J Depiano, *CEO*
Richard J Depiano Junior, *VP*
Matt Carnevale, *Ex VP*
Robert O'connor, *CFO*
Mark Wallace, *COO*
EMP: 13 **EST:** 2000
SALES (est): 140.16K **Privately Held**
Web: www.sonomedescalon.com
SIC: 3841 Surgical and medical instruments

(G-12179)
HAUFE GROUP
15 Hersam St (02180-2441)
PHONE............................781 376-3737
EMP: 7 **EST:** 2019
SALES (est): 160.57K **Privately Held**
Web: www.haufe.de
SIC: 3714 Motor vehicle parts and accessories

(G-12180)
LAKE INDUSTRIES INC
Also Called: Lake Hvac
41 Pleasant St (02180-3823)
PHONE............................781 438-8814
TOLL FREE: 800
Donna Pariseau, *Prin*
John Pariseau, *Prin*
Eric Pariseau, *Prin*
EMP: 62 **EST:** 1975
SQ FT: 12,000
SALES (est): 24.44MM **Privately Held**
Web: www.lakehvac.com
SIC: 1711 3585 3433 Mechanical contractor; Refrigeration and heating equipment; Heating equipment, except electric

(G-12181)
LITHO-CRAFT INC
74 Maple St (02180-3130)
P.O. Box 728 (01890-4128)
PHONE............................781 729-1789
Andrew W Bosworth, *Pr*
Marie A Bosworth, *Treas*
Karen Bosworth, *Clerk*
EMP: 15 **EST:** 1976
SALES (est): 2.22MM **Privately Held**
Web: www.litho-craft.com
SIC: 2752 Offset printing

(G-12182)
LPI PRINTING AND GRAPHIC INC
Also Called: Ontraget Promotional

18 Spencer St (02180-2616)
PHONE............................781 438-5400
William D Joseph, *Pr*
EMP: 15 **EST:** 1966
SQ FT: 16,000
SALES (est): 461.08K **Privately Held**
Web: www.lpiprinting.com
SIC: 2741 2752 2791 2789 Business service newsletters: publishing and printing; Catalogs, lithographed; Typesetting; Bookbinding and related work

(G-12183)
NORTHEAST MANUFACTURING CO INC
35 Spencer St (02180-2615)
PHONE............................781 438-3022
Chris Lobdell, *Pr*
Patricia Richards, *Stockholder**
EMP: 34 **EST:** 1951
SQ FT: 12,000
SALES (est): 2.18MM **Privately Held**
Web: www.northeastmfg.com
SIC: 3599 Machine shop, jobbing and repair

(G-12184)
PAC MACHINERY GROUP
5 Gigante Dr (02180-3152)
PHONE............................214 724-8523
EMP: 7 **EST:** 2015
SALES (est): 37.66K **Privately Held**
Web: www.pacmachinery.com
SIC: 3565 Packaging machinery

(G-12185)
PHARMCTCAL STRTGIES STFFING LL
477 Main St (02180-2602)
PHONE............................781 835-2300
EMP: 17 **EST:** 2004
SQ FT: 1,700
SALES (est): 4.66MM **Privately Held**
Web: www.medicalrecruitmentstrategies.com
SIC: 2834 Pharmaceutical preparations

(G-12186)
STERLING BUSINESS PRODUCTS INC
Also Called: Sterling Printing
214 Main St (02180-1619)
P.O. Box 845 (02155-0009)
PHONE............................781 481-1234
Payal Malrani, *Pr*
Ricky Malrani, *VP*
EMP: 10 **EST:** 1987
SQ FT: 7,000
SALES (est): 2.13MM **Privately Held**
Web: www.sterlingprinting.com
SIC: 5112 2754 2752 Business forms; Business form and card printing, gravure; Offset printing

(G-12187)
TR3 SOLUTIONS INC
2 Main St Ste 200 (02180-3389)
PHONE............................781 481-0642
Daniel Gallagher, *Managing Member*
EMP: 16 **EST:** 2009
SALES (est): 1.14MM **Privately Held**
Web: www.tr3solutions.com
SIC: 8999 7372 Communication services; Business oriented computer software

(G-12188)
WESCO BUILDING & DESIGN INC
271 Main St Ste G01 (02180-3504)
PHONE............................781 279-0490

Benjamin J Caggiano Junior, *VP*
EMP: 9 **EST:** 1990
SQ FT: 2,000
SALES (est): 343.83K **Privately Held**
SIC: 2431 6552 1542 Millwork; Subdividers and developers, nec; Commercial and office building contractors

(G-12189)
WESCOR LTD (PA)
271 Main St Ste G01 (02180-3504)
PHONE............................781 279-0490
Benjamin J Caggiano Junior, *Pr*
EMP: 7 **EST:** 1989
SQ FT: 2,000
SALES (est): 2.44MM **Privately Held**
Web: www.wescorltd.com
SIC: 2431 6552 1542 Millwork; Subdividers and developers, nec; Commercial and office building contractors

Stoughton
Norfolk County

(G-12190)
ADJECTIVE ART & FRAMING INC
471 Page St Ste 5 (02072-1141)
PHONE............................617 281-4661
EMP: 10 **EST:** 2014
SALES (est): 566.04K **Privately Held**
Web: www.adjframes.com
SIC: 2499 Picture frame molding, finished

(G-12191)
ALBERT BASSE ASSOCIATES INC
175 Campanelli Pkwy (02072-3743)
PHONE............................781 344-3555
Albert Chip Basse, *Pr*
Ellen B Dietz, *
Edwin E Basse, *
Paul L Manning Junior, *VP*
Ronald J Frisch, *
EMP: 45 **EST:** 1928
SQ FT: 30,000
SALES (est): 7.4MM **Privately Held**
Web: www.albertbasse.com
SIC: 2759 Screen printing

(G-12192)
ALCOA GLOBAL FASTENERS INC
Also Called: Alcoa
44 Campanelli Pkwy (02072-3704)
PHONE............................412 553-4545
Carl A Annese Junior, *VP*
▲ **EMP:** 160 **EST:** 1949
SQ FT: 110,000
SALES (est): 11.32MM
SALES (corp-wide): 6.64B **Publicly Held**
SIC: 3542 3452 Riveting machines; Rivets, metal
HQ: Howmet Global Fastening Systems Inc.
      3990a Heritage Oak Ct
      Simi Valley CA 93063
      805 426-2270

(G-12193)
ALPHA CHEMICAL SERVICES INC
Also Called: A C S
46 Morton St (02072-2829)
P.O. Box 431 (02072-0431)
PHONE............................781 344-8688
Elise Dauksevicz, *CEO*
Steven Juckett, *
Mark Juckett, *

Brian Jacobson, *
Peter Jacobson, *
EMP: 35 **EST:** 1969
SQ FT: 34,000
SALES (est): 8.16MM **Privately Held**
Web: www.alphachemical.com
SIC: 2842 2841 Specialty cleaning; Soap and other detergents

(G-12194)
ANGSTROM ADVANCED INC
95 Mill St (02072-1422)
PHONE..................................781 519-4765
Haiming Li, *Pr*
▲ **EMP:** 100 **EST:** 2007
SQ FT: 20,000
SALES (est): 9.56MM **Privately Held**
Web: www.angstromadvancedinc.com
SIC: 3569 3827 Gas generators; Optical instruments and apparatus

(G-12195)
ARTISAN INDUSTRIES INC
44 Campanelli Pkwy (02072-3704)
PHONE..................................781 893-6800
Timothy L Davis, *Pr*
James M Donovan, *
Anthony J Agostino, *
◆ **EMP:** 100 **EST:** 1934
SQ FT: 114,000
SALES (est): 25.33MM **Privately Held**
Web: www.artisanind.com
SIC: 3559 3449 3563 3643 Chemical machinery and equipment; Miscellaneous metalwork; Vacuum pumps, except laboratory; Current-carrying wiring services

(G-12196)
AVO FENCE & SUPPLY INC (PA)
Also Called: Avo Cedar Fences
50 Washington St (02072-1746)
P.O. Box 148 (02072-0148)
PHONE..................................781 341-2963
Andrew M Knott, *Pr*
Ronald Porcaro, *Sec*
EMP: 12 **EST:** 1975
SQ FT: 7,500
SALES (est): 4.79MM
SALES (corp-wide): 4.79MM **Privately Held**
Web: www.avofenceandsupply.com
SIC: 2499 Applicators, wood

(G-12197)
AVON FOOD COMPANY LLC
30 James Massey Ln (02072-5015)
PHONE..................................781 341-4981
EMP: 11 **EST:** 2002
SALES (est): 16.44K **Privately Held**
Web: www.avonfoodco.com
SIC: 2099 Dressings, salad: dry mixes

(G-12198)
BIODELIVERY SCIENCES INTL INC (HQ)
100 Technology Center Dr Ste 300 (02072-4747)
PHONE..................................919 582-9050
Jeffrey Bailey, *CEO*
Peter S Greenleaf, *
Scott M Plesha, *CCO*
John Golubieski, *CFO*
Thomas B Smith, *CMO*
EMP: 25 **EST:** 1997
SALES (est): 166.7MM
SALES (corp-wide): 463.93MM **Publicly Held**
Web: www.bdsi.com
SIC: 2834 Pharmaceutical preparations
PA: Collegium Pharmaceutical, Inc.
100 Technology Center Dr # 300

Stoughton MA 02072
781 713-3699

(G-12199)
BOSWORTH PRINTING CO INC
28 Tosca Dr (02072-1529)
PHONE..................................781 341-2992
EMP: 10 **EST:** 1952
SALES (est): 503.19K **Privately Held**
SIC: 2752 2759 Offset printing; Letterpress printing

(G-12200)
CAMELOT ENTERPRISES INC
213 Turnpike St Ste 1 (02072-3769)
PHONE..................................781 341-9100
Elliot Kaplan, *Pr*
EMP: 12 **EST:** 1982
SQ FT: 15,000
SALES (est): 1.01MM **Privately Held**
Web: www.camelotemb.com
SIC: 2395 Embroidery products, except Schiffli machine

(G-12201)
COLLEGIUM PHARMACEUTICAL INC (PA)
Also Called: Collegium Pharmaceutical
100 Technology Center Dr Ste 300 (02072-4747)
PHONE..................................781 713-3699
Joseph Ciaffoni, *Pr*
Michael T Heffernan, *
Paul J Brannelly, *Ex VP*
Alison B Fleming, *Ex VP*
Scott Dreyer, *CCO*
EMP: 27 **EST:** 2002
SQ FT: 19,335
SALES (est): 463.93MM
SALES (corp-wide): 463.93MM **Publicly Held**
Web: www.collegiumpharma.com
SIC: 2834 Pharmaceutical preparations

(G-12202)
ELECTRNIC SHTMTAL CRFTSMEN INC
120 Central St (02072-1148)
PHONE..................................781 341-3260
Marc Levine, *Pr*
Richard Levine, *
▼ **EMP:** 25 **EST:** 1962
SQ FT: 20,000
SALES (est): 4.5MM **Privately Held**
Web: www.escinc.biz
SIC: 3444 Sheet metalwork

(G-12203)
EXCELERARX CORP
Also Called: Excelera
100 Technology Center Dr Ste 600 (02072-4749)
PHONE..................................612 293-0378
Lorrie A Carr, *CEO*
EMP: 14 **EST:** 2011
SALES (est): 1.54MM **Privately Held**
Web: www.shieldshealthsolutions.com
SIC: 2834 3821 Pharmaceutical preparations; Clinical laboratory instruments, except medical and dental

(G-12204)
F H PETERSON MACHINE CORP
143 South St (02072-3715)
P.O. Box 617 (02072-0617)
PHONE..................................781 341-4930
Stanley B Urban, *Pr*
Wilbur Boss, *
Venus Waterhouse, *

Jill Kaminsky, *
Stanley B Urban, *Treas*
EMP: 60 **EST:** 1957
SQ FT: 28,000
SALES (est): 10.26MM **Privately Held**
Web: www.fhpetersonmachine.com
SIC: 3599 Machine shop, jobbing and repair

(G-12205)
F W WEBB COMPANY
Also Called: Johnson Contrls Authorized Dlr
152 Will Dr (02072)
P.O. Box 380 (02072-0380)
PHONE..................................781 341-1100
FAX: 781 344-6610
EMP: 23
SALES (corp-wide): 1.26B **Privately Held**
SIC: 5074 3494 Plumbing and hydronic heating supplies; Sprinkler systems, field
PA: F. W. Webb Company
160 Middlesex Tpke
Bedford MA 01730
781 272-6600

(G-12206)
FABREEKA INTERNATIONAL INC (DH)
1023 Turnpike St (02072-1156)
P.O. Box 210 (02072-0210)
PHONE..................................781 341-3655
David Raguckas, *Pr*
Joseph Micciche, *Sec*
EMP: 9 **EST:** 2008
SALES (est): 9.91MM
SALES (corp-wide): 1.32B **Privately Held**
Web: www.fabreeka.com
SIC: 5085 3069 3714 3568 Rubber goods, mechanical; Molded rubber products; Motor vehicle parts and accessories; Power transmission equipment, nec
HQ: Fabreeka International Holdings, Inc.
1023 Turnpike St
Stoughton MA 02072
781 341-3655

(G-12207)
FABREEKA INTL HOLDINGS INC (DH)
1023 Turnpike St (02072-1156)
P.O. Box 210 (02072-0210)
PHONE..................................781 341-3655
David Raguckas, *Pr*
Joseph Micciche, *
▲ **EMP:** 40 **EST:** 1918
SQ FT: 34,000
SALES (est): 33.46MM
SALES (corp-wide): 1.32B **Privately Held**
Web: www.fabreeka.com
SIC: 5085 3069 3829 3714 Rubber goods, mechanical; Molded rubber products; Measuring and controlling devices, nec; Motor vehicle parts and accessories
HQ: Stabilus Gmbh
Wallersheimer Weg 100
Koblenz RP 56070
26189000

(G-12208)
FC PHILLIPS INC
471 Washington St (02072-4203)
P.O. Box 780 (02072-0780)
PHONE..................................781 344-9400
Craig R Snow, *Pr*
Brian R Snow, *
Marjorie P Snow, *
EMP: 50 **EST:** 1911
SQ FT: 35,000
SALES (est): 4.78MM **Privately Held**
Web: www.fcphillips.com

SIC: 3451 Screw machine products

(G-12209)
FIRST IMPRESSION PRINTING INC
178 Tosca Dr (02072-1511)
PHONE..................................781 344-8855
Mark Reed, *Pr*
EMP: 7 **EST:** 1998
SQ FT: 5,400
SALES (est): 814.63K **Privately Held**
Web: www.myprinter.us
SIC: 2752 Offset printing

(G-12210)
GLOBE COMPOSITE SOLUTIONS LLC
200 Shuman Ave Ste 100 (02072-3766)
P.O. Box 802292 (64180-2292)
PHONE..................................781 871-3700
Joe Mccadden, *Managing Member*
Carl Forsythe, *
Michael Dyson, *
William Clement, *
EMP: 85 **EST:** 2019
SQ FT: 72,000
SALES (est): 24MM **Publicly Held**
Web: www.globecomposite.com
SIC: 2655 Cans, composite: foil-fiber and other: from purchased fiber
PA: Esco Technologies Inc.
9900 Clayton Rd Ste A
Saint Louis MO 63124

(G-12211)
GLOBE COMPOSITE SOLUTIONS LTD
200 Shuman Ave (02072-3766)
PHONE..................................781 871-3700
Carl Forsythe, *Prin*
EMP: 59
SALES (corp-wide): 11.71MM **Privately Held**
Web: www.globecomposite.com
SIC: 3089 Injection molded finished plastics products, nec
PA: Globe Composite Solutions, Ltd.
4925 Grnvlle Ave Ste 1400
Dallas TX 75206
781 681-6838

(G-12212)
HALMARK SYSTEMS LLC
354 Page St (02072-1104)
P.O. Box 479 (02072-0479)
PHONE..................................781 630-0123
Dawn Reardon, *Pr*
David Crean, *Treas*
◆ **EMP:** 20 **EST:** 1977
SQ FT: 4,000
SALES (est): 1.89MM **Privately Held**
Web: www.horizonpackaging.com
SIC: 5046 2672 2671 Store equipment; Labels (unprinted), gummed: made from purchased materials; Paper; coated and laminated packaging

(G-12213)
HO TOY NOODLES INC (PA)
1490 Central St (02072-4414)
PHONE..................................617 426-0247
Jeffrey Wong, *Pr*
Barry Wong, *Treas*
Gordon Wong, *VP*
▲ **EMP:** 10 **EST:** 1971
SQ FT: 1,000
SALES (est): 1.68MM
SALES (corp-wide): 1.68MM **Privately Held**

▲ = Import ▼ = Export
◆ = Import/Export

SIC: **2098** 2052 Noodles (e.g. egg, plain, and water), dry; Cookies

(G-12214)
HONORCRAFT LLC
Also Called: Honorcraft
292 Page St Ste A (02072-1136)
P.O. Box 506 (02375-0506)
PHONE..................................781 341-0410
Andrew Hopkin, *Pr*
Irene Clenott, *Off Mgr*
EMP: 10 **EST:** 2015
SQ FT: 18,752
SALES (est): 495.48K **Privately Held**
Web: www.honorcraft.com
SIC: 3555 3993 Plates, metal: engravers'; Name plates: except engraved, etched, etc.: metal

(G-12215)
ITW ARK-LES CORPORATION (HQ)
95 Mill St (02072-1422)
P.O. Box 686 (02072-0686)
PHONE..................................781 297-6000
▲ **EMP:** 30 **EST:** 1937
SALES (est): 111.46MM
SALES (corp-wide): 15.93B **Publicly Held**
Web: 2868-us.all.biz
SIC: 3643 3644 Electric switches; Terminal boards
PA: Illinois Tool Works Inc.
155 Harlem Ave
Glenview IL 60025
847 724-7500

(G-12216)
J F WHITE CONTRACTING CO
White Equipmetn Leasing
56 Old Page St (02072-1115)
PHONE..................................781 436-8497
Stephen White, *Pr*
EMP: 137
Web: www.jfwhite.com
SIC: 1622 3443 Bridge, tunnel, and elevated highway construction; Fabricated plate work (boiler shop)
HQ: J. F. White Contracting Company
10 Burr St
Framingham MA 01701
508 879-4700

(G-12217)
KOCHMAN REIDT & HAIGH INC
471 Page St Ste 8 (02072-1141)
PHONE..................................781 573-1500
Paul Reidt, *Pr*
William Kochman, *
James Kochman, *
Alan Haigh, *
EMP: 42 **EST:** 1991
SQ FT: 20,000
SALES (est): 5.34MM **Privately Held**
Web: www.cabinetmakers.com
SIC: 2541 2434 Cabinets, except refrigerated: show, display, etc.: wood; Wood kitchen cabinets

(G-12218)
M & P MACHINE COMPANY INC
Also Called: M & P
1438 Washington St (02072-3381)
PHONE..................................781 344-5888
EMP: 20 **EST:** 1978
SQ FT: 10,500
SALES (est): 790.96K **Privately Held**
SIC: 3089 7336 3599 2542 Plastics processing; Silk screen design; Catapults; Partitions and fixtures, except wood

(G-12219)
MACHINE INCORPORATED
879 Turnpike St (02072-1114)
PHONE..................................781 297-3700
Richard Mileika, *Pr*
EMP: 20 **EST:** 1981
SQ FT: 15,000
SALES (est): 4.53MM **Privately Held**
Web: www.machineinc.com
SIC: 3599 Machine shop, jobbing and repair

(G-12220)
MANDES INC
593 Washington St (02072-4207)
PHONE..................................781 344-6915
George Michaelidis, *Pr*
EMP: 7 **EST:** 2010
SALES (est): 126.72K **Privately Held**
SIC: 3421 Table and food cutlery, including butchers'

(G-12221)
MARVER MED INC
1063 Turnpike St (02072-1160)
P.O. Box 258 (02072-0258)
PHONE..................................781 341-9372
Steven J Tallarida, *Pr*
Jon T Tallarida, *Sec*
Christopher Laplante, *CFO*
EMP: 10 **EST:** 1947
SQ FT: 5,000
SALES (est): 1.68MM **Privately Held**
Web: www.marvermed.com
SIC: 3451 3599 Screw machine products; Machine shop, jobbing and repair

(G-12222)
MASSACHUSETTS BAY TECH INC
Also Called: Mbt
378 Page St Ste 7 (02072-1124)
PHONE..................................781 344-8809
Brian Fallon, *Pr*
Charles Fallon, *VP*
▼ **EMP:** 19 **EST:** 1999
SQ FT: 12,000
SALES (est): 2.42MM **Privately Held**
Web: www.massbaytech.com
SIC: 3674 Semiconductors and related devices

(G-12223)
MATTER SURFACES INC (PA)
179 Campanelli Pkwy (02072-3743)
P.O. Box 839 (02072-0839)
PHONE..................................800 628-7462
Scott Robichaud, *Pr*
Paul Schiffmann, *VP*
John Schiffmann, *VP*
Richard Schiffmann, *VP*
Carl Olson, *VP*
◆ **EMP:** 15 **EST:** 1984
SALES (est): 46.3MM
SALES (corp-wide): 46.3MM **Privately Held**
Web: www.matsinc.com
SIC: 5023 2273 Carpets; Door mats: paper, grass, reed, coir, sisal, jute, rags, etc.

(G-12224)
MESSER LLC
Also Called: Boc Gases
97 Maple St (02072-1105)
PHONE..................................781 341-4575
EMP: 10
SALES (corp-wide): 1.63B **Privately Held**
Web: www.messeramericas.com
SIC: 2813 Oxygen, compressed or liquefied
HQ: Messer Llc
200 Smrst Corp Blvd # 7000

Bridgewater NJ 08807
800 755-9277

(G-12225)
MILANI INDUSTRIES INCORPORATED
61 Marys Way (02072-2227)
PHONE..................................781 344-3377
Patricia Milani, *Prin*
EMP: 7 **EST:** 2004
SALES (est): 151.49K **Privately Held**
SIC: 3999 Manufacturing industries, nec

(G-12226)
NEXT GENERATION VENDING LLC
800 Technology Center Dr Ste 1a (02072-4721)
PHONE..................................781 828-2345
EMP: 505
Web: www.nextgenerationone.com
SIC: 3581 Automatic vending machines

(G-12227)
PARTICLES PLUS INC
31 Tosca Dr Ste 8 (02072-1500)
PHONE..................................781 341-6898
Adam Giandomenico, *Pr*
EMP: 18 **EST:** 2011
SALES (est): 4.71MM **Privately Held**
Web: www.particlesplus.com
SIC: 3826 Analytical instruments

(G-12228)
PRECISION DOOR & WINDOW INC (PA)
466 Sumner St (02072-3418)
PHONE..................................781 344-6900
TOLL FREE: 800
Anthony Distefano, *CEO*
Albert Distefano Senior, *CEO*
EMP: 13 **EST:** 1960
SQ FT: 20,000
SALES (est): 2.43MM
SALES (corp-wide): 2.43MM **Privately Held**
Web:
www.precisiondoorandwindow.com
SIC: 5211 5031 3442 Doors, storm: wood or metal; Doors and windows; Metal doors, sash, and trim

(G-12229)
PRIMO MEDICAL GROUP INC (PA)
75 Mill St (02072-1422)
PHONE..................................781 297-5700
Steven Tallarida, *Ch Bd*
Frank Fedorowicz, *Ex VP*
Jon Tallarida, *Sr VP*
Christopher Laplante, *CFO*
EMP: 140 **EST:** 1953
SQ FT: 70,000
SALES (est): 34.2MM
SALES (corp-wide): 34.2MM **Privately Held**
Web: www.primomedicalgroup.com
SIC: 3841 Surgical and medical instruments

(G-12230)
RO-59 INC
1 Cabot Pl Ste 3 (02072-4606)
PHONE..................................781 341-1222
Ronald Bender, *Pr*
Oscar Levine Ph.d., *VP*
EMP: 9 **EST:** 1983
SQ FT: 3,000
SALES (est): 993.84K **Privately Held**
Web: www.ro59inc.com

SIC: **2899** 2992 Corrosion preventive lubricant; Lubricating oils and greases

(G-12231)
ROADSAFE TRAFFIC SYSTEMS
331 Page St (02072-1172)
PHONE..................................781 436-5006
EMP: 7 **EST:** 2019
SALES (est): 133.1K **Privately Held**
Web: www.roadsafetraffic.com
SIC: 3531 Construction machinery

(G-12232)
S&S INDUSTRIES INC (PA)
1551 Central St (02072-1686)
PHONE..................................914 885-1500
Joseph Horta, *Pr*
Hugo Duarte, *VP*
◆ **EMP:** 15 **EST:** 1946
SQ FT: 10,000
SALES (est): 16.93MM
SALES (corp-wide): 16.93MM **Privately Held**
SIC: 3315 3496 Steel wire and related products; Miscellaneous fabricated wire products

(G-12233)
SAMAR CO INC
220 Cushing St (02072-2341)
PHONE..................................781 297-7264
William J Selby, *Pr*
William Selby, *
Ronald Selby, *
▲ **EMP:** 44 **EST:** 1972
SQ FT: 50,000
SALES (est): 3.71MM **Privately Held**
SIC: 3052 3083 3082 Rubber hose; Laminated plastics plate and sheet; Tubes, unsupported plastics

(G-12234)
SAMS DRAPERY WORKROOM INC
Also Called: Sam's & Son
15 Smyth St (02072-3207)
PHONE..................................617 364-9440
Howard Bernstein, *Pr*
Roberta Bernstein, *Treas*
EMP: 10 **EST:** 1971
SALES (est): 457.5K **Privately Held**
Web: www.samsandson.com
SIC: 2391 Draperies, plastic and textile: from purchased materials

(G-12235)
SICK INC
800 Technology Center Dr Ste 5 (02072-4721)
PHONE..................................781 302-2500
Thomas Weatherby, *Mgr*
EMP: 60
SALES (corp-wide): 2.22B **Privately Held**
Web: www.sick.com
SIC: 3625 3577 3829 3826 Switches, electric power; Optical scanning devices; Measuring and controlling devices, nec; Analytical instruments
HQ: Sick, Inc
6900 W 110th St
Minneapolis MN 55438
952 941-6780

(G-12236)
SICK AUTO IDENT INC (DH)
Also Called: Sick
800 Technology Center Dr Ste 5 (02072-4721)
PHONE..................................781 302-2500
Robert Bauer, *Ch*

Alberto Bertomeu, *Pr*
Hermann Miedel, *Genl Mgr*
EMP: 37 **EST:** 2001
SQ FT: 46,000
SALES (est): 23.05MM
SALES (corp-wide): 2.22B **Privately Held**
SIC: 3625   Relays and industrial controls
HQ: Sick, Inc
   6900 W 110th St
   Minneapolis MN 55438
   952 941-6780

(G-12237)
SKYRAY INSTRUMENT INC
95 Mill St (02072-1422)
PHONE...............................617 202-3879
EMP: 10 **EST:** 2010
SALES (est): 606.01K **Privately Held**
Web: www.skyrayinstrument.com
SIC: 3826   Analytical instruments

(G-12238)
SPOONTIQUES INC
111 Island St (02072-1401)
PHONE...............................781 344-9530
Ken Sawyer, *Pr*
◆ **EMP:** 60 **EST:** 1971
SQ FT: 65,000
SALES (est): 7.61MM **Privately Held**
Web: www.spoontiques.com
SIC: 3499   Novelties and giftware, including
   trophies

(G-12239)
STD MANUFACTURING INC
1063 Turnpike St (02072-1160)
P.O. Box 420 (02072-0420)
PHONE...............................781 828-4400
Steve Tallarida, *Prin*
EMP: 17 **EST:** 2006
SALES (est): 860.47K **Privately Held**
SIC: 3999   Manufacturing industries, nec

(G-12240)
SUPERLATIVE PRINTING INC
4 Cabot Pl Ste 3 (02072-4613)
PHONE...............................781 341-9000
Sally Mong, *Pr*
EMP: 8 **EST:** 1992
SQ FT: 988
SALES (est): 243.89K **Privately Held**
Web: www.superlativeprinting.com
SIC: 2752   Offset printing

(G-12241)
SX INDUSTRIES INC (PA)
1551 Central St (02072-1686)
PHONE...............................781 828-7111
Michael Fink, *Ch Bd*
Stephen Fink, *
▲ **EMP:** 19 **EST:** 1944
SQ FT: 38,000
SALES (est): 6.79MM
SALES (corp-wide): 6.79MM **Privately
Held**
Web: www.sxindustries.com
SIC: 3131 6512 3444 3356   Ornaments, shoe
   ; Commercial and industrial building
   operation; Sheet metalwork; Nonferrous
   rolling and drawing, nec

(G-12242)
**SYNERGY MANUFACTURING
LLC**
1551 Central St (02072-1686)
PHONE...............................781 209-5538
EMP: 9 **EST:** 2008
SALES (est): 303.34K **Privately Held**
Web: www.nylonmetal.com
SIC: 2824   Nylon fibers

(G-12243)
TIMCO CORPORATION
Also Called: Sx Industries
1551 Central St (02072-1686)
P.O. Box 332 (02188-0002)
PHONE...............................781 821-1041
Tim O'hara, *Pr*
▲ **EMP:** 40 **EST:** 2002
SALES (est): 2.57MM **Privately Held**
SIC: 3469   Stamping metal for the trade

Stow
Middlesex County

(G-12244)
BOSE CORPORATION
688 Great Rd (01775-1051)
PHONE...............................508 766-7330
Mario Cornacchio, *Brnch Mgr*
EMP: 23
SALES (corp-wide): 3.6B **Privately Held**
Web: www.bose.com
SIC: 5731 3651   High fidelity stereo
   equipment; Household audio equipment
PA: Bose Corporation
   100 The Mountain Rd
   Framingham MA 01701
   508 879-7330

(G-12245)
CPI RADANT TECH DIV INC (DH)
255 Hudson Rd (01775-1446)
PHONE...............................978 562-3866
Timothy R Smith, *Pr*
Robert A Fickett, *
Joel A Littman, *
EMP: 75 **EST:** 1984
SQ FT: 75,000
SALES (est): 21.43MM **Privately Held**
Web: www.radanttechnologies.com
SIC: 8731 3663 3812   Commercial physical
   research; Antennas, transmitting and
   communications; Antennas, radar or
   communications
HQ: Communications & Power Industries
   Llc
   811 Hansen Way
   Palo Alto CA 94304

(G-12246)
HYDRO-TEST PRODUCTS INC
85 Hudson Rd (01775-1254)
PHONE...............................978 897-4647
Douglas B Sagar, *Pr*
▼ **EMP:** 16 **EST:** 1971
SQ FT: 10,000
SALES (est): 2.34MM **Privately Held**
Web: www.hydro-test.com
SIC: 3548 3949 3999 3569   Gas welding
   equipment; Skin diving equipment, scuba
   type; Fire extinguishers, portable;
   Firefighting apparatus

(G-12247)
RADIUS MEDICAL TECH INC
46 Edson St (01775-1236)
PHONE...............................978 263-4466
Maureen Finlayson, *Pr*
EMP: 10 **EST:** 1991
SALES (est): 377.88K **Privately Held**
SIC: 3841   Surgical and medical instruments

Sturbridge
Worcester County

(G-12248)
ALSCO INDUSTRIES INC
174 Charlton Rd (01566-1505)
PHONE...............................508 347-1199
Allan J Rieser, *CEO*
Stephen M Rieser, *
▲ **EMP:** 70 **EST:** 1990
SQ FT: 65,000
SALES (est): 6.75MM **Privately Held**
Web: www.alscoindustries.com
SIC: 3089 3544   Injection molding of plastics
   ; Special dies, tools, jigs, and fixtures

(G-12249)
ARLAND TOOL & MFG INC (PA)
Also Called: Arland Tool
421 Main St (01566-1055)
P.O. Box 207 (01566-0207)
PHONE...............................508 347-3368
William Gagnon, *Pr*
Gerald Gagnon, *
Keith Gagnon, *
David Gagnon, *
Melissa Baker, *
◆ **EMP:** 85 **EST:** 1950
SQ FT: 80,000
SALES (est): 14.01MM
SALES (corp-wide): 14.01MM **Privately
Held**
Web: www.arland.com
SIC: 3599   Machine shop, jobbing and repair

(G-12250)
**JOURNAL OF ANTQ &
COLLECTIBLES**
Also Called: Brimfield Flemarket.com
46 Hall Rd (01566-1279)
P.O. Box 950 (01566-2950)
PHONE...............................508 347-1960
Jody Young, *Pr*
Joe Michaelik, *CFO*
EMP: 15 **EST:** 2000
SALES (est): 444.23K **Privately Held**
Web: www.journalofantiques.com
SIC: 2759   Publication printing

(G-12251)
KOOKLA INC (PA)
Also Called: Dunkin' Donuts
120 Main St (01566-1276)
P.O. Box 1138 (01566-3138)
PHONE...............................508 347-2623
EMP: 20 **EST:** 1994
SALES (est): 2.04MM **Privately Held**
Web: www.dunkindonuts.com
SIC: 5461 2051 5812   Doughnuts;
   Doughnuts, except frozen; Eating places

(G-12252)
OFS BRIGHTWAVE LLC
50 Hall Rd (01566-1279)
PHONE...............................508 347-2261
Patrice Dubois, *Prin*
EMP: 16 **EST:** 2008
SALES (est): 1.72MM **Privately Held**
Web: www.ofsoptics.com
SIC: 3357   Nonferrous wiredrawing and
   insulating

(G-12253)
OFS FITEL LLC
50 Hall Rd (01566-1299)
PHONE...............................508 347-2261
Debbie Bleanger, *Brnch Mgr*
EMP: 341

Web: www.ofsoptics.com
SIC: 3357   Nonferrous wiredrawing and
   insulating
HQ: Ofs Fitel Llc
   2000 Northeast Expy
   Norcross GA 30071
   888 342-3743

(G-12254)
OPTIM LLC
64 Technology Park Rd (01566-1253)
PHONE...............................508 347-5100
Jeff Barrett, *CEO*
James Haber, *
EMP: 50 **EST:** 1979
SQ FT: 11,000
SALES (est): 12.34MM **Privately Held**
Web: www.optim-llc.com
SIC: 3841   Surgical and medical instruments

(G-12255)
PEGASUS GLASSWORKS INC
66 Technology Park Rd (01566-1253)
P.O. Box 255 (01566-0255)
PHONE...............................508 347-5656
Peter Graves, *Pr*
▲ **EMP:** 10 **EST:** 1997
SQ FT: 15,000
SALES (est): 904.55K **Privately Held**
Web: www.pegasusglassworks.com
SIC: 3231   Products of purchased glass

(G-12256)
PENWELL
Also Called: Editorial Ofc Indtrl Lser Solt
15 Country Hill Rd (01566-1061)
P.O. Box 245 (01566-0245)
PHONE...............................508 347-8245
David Belforte, *Prin*
EMP: 8 **EST:** 1986
SALES (est): 419.96K **Privately Held**
SIC: 2721   Magazines: publishing only, not
   printed on site

(G-12257)
PHOTONIS SCIENTIFIC INC (DH)
Also Called: Photonis Usa, Inc.
660 Main St (01518-1259)
P.O. Box 1159 (01566-3159)
PHONE...............................508 347-4000
Roland Minnier, *Pr*
Bruce Laprade, *
Goossen Boers, *
Bruno Manac'h, *
Jeannine M Bogacki, *
EMP: 17 **EST:** 1999
SALES (est): 23.17MM
SALES (corp-wide): 28.88K **Privately Held**
Web: www.photonis.com
SIC: 3679 3829 3826 3812   Electronic
   circuits; Measuring and controlling devices,
   nec; Analytical instruments; Search and
   navigation equipment
HQ: Photonis Defense, Inc.
   1000 New Holland Ave
   Lancaster PA 17601
   717 295-6000

(G-12258)
**SOUTHBRIDGE SHTMTL
WORKS INC**
441 Main St (01566-1055)
P.O. Box 517 (01566-0517)
PHONE...............................508 347-7800
John Q Colognesi, *Pr*
Louis E Colognesi Junior, *Pr*
Ernest Colognesi, *
Anthony J Colognesi, *
Jesse R Colognesi, *
▲ **EMP:** 50 **EST:** 1959

SQ FT: 60,000
SALES (est): 8.57MM **Privately Held**
Web: www.ssmwusa.com
SIC: 3444 Sheet metal specialties, not stamped

(G-12259)
WOTTON ENTERPRISES INC
Also Called: Securos
21 Main St Ste 1 (01566-1486)
PHONE..............................855 383-7678
Harry Wotton, *Prin*
Harry Wotton, *Prin*
Darroll Wotton, *Treas*
Kristen Wotton, *Clerk*
Alex Vrancich, *Prin*
EMP: 10 EST: 1997
SQ FT: 10,800
SALES (est): 2.42MM **Privately Held**
SIC: 5047 3841 Veterinarians' equipment and supplies; Fixation appliances, internal

Sudbury
Middlesex County

(G-12260)
ATRIUM INNOVATIONS
33 Union Ave (01776-2246)
PHONE..............................978 579-2346
Toni Hand, *Prin*
EMP: 29 EST: 2018
SALES (est): 2.12MM **Privately Held**
SIC: 3841 Muscle exercise apparatus, ophthalmic

(G-12261)
BOSTON DESIGN GUIDE INC
277 Concord Rd (01776-2342)
PHONE..............................978 443-9886
Melanie Kaplan, *Pr*
EMP: 12 EST: 1997
SALES (est): 793.42K **Privately Held**
Web: www.bostondesignguide.com
SIC: 2721 Magazines: publishing only, not printed on site

(G-12262)
CAUSE FOR CHANGE LLC
Also Called: Skineez Skincarewear
359 Boston Post Rd Ste 2 (01776-3053)
PHONE..............................617 571-6990
Michelle Moran, *Managing Member*
EMP: 30 EST: 2014
SQ FT: 1,925
SALES (est): 4.05MM **Privately Held**
SIC: 5137 3842 5199 Women's and children's clothing; Hosiery, support; General merchandise, non-durable

(G-12263)
DELO INDUSTRIAL ADHESIVES LLC
Also Called: Delo Industrial Adhesives
144 North Rd Ste 2650 (01776-1170)
PHONE..............................978 254-5275
Torsten Uske, *Pr*
John Herold, *Managing Member*
EMP: 11 EST: 2007
SALES (est): 2.46MM
SALES (corp-wide): 205.58MM **Privately Held**
Web: www.delo-adhesives.com
SIC: 2891 Adhesives
PA: Delo Industrie Klebstoffe Gmbh & Co. Kgaa
Delo-Allee 1
Windach BY 86949
819399000

(G-12264)
DJ MICROLAMINATES INC
490 Boston Post Rd (01776-3367)
PHONE..............................978 261-3188
Donald W Johnson, *Pr*
EMP: 10 EST: 2017
SALES (est): 829.28K **Privately Held**
Web: www.djmicrolaminates.com
SIC: 2821 Plastics materials and resins

(G-12265)
DPP INC
385 Boston Post Rd (01776-3051)
PHONE..............................978 443-9995
David Pompey, *Pr*
EMP: 7 EST: 2005
SALES (est): 57.88K **Privately Held**
Web: www.amptek.com
SIC: 3826 Analytical instruments

(G-12266)
DRINK MAPLE INC
144 North Rd Ste 1050 (01776-1179)
P.O. Box 1128 (01776-5128)
PHONE..............................978 610-6408
Rose Jeff, *Prin*
EMP: 15 EST: 2015
SALES (est): 1.34MM **Privately Held**
Web: www.drinksimple.com
SIC: 2087 Flavoring extracts and syrups, nec

(G-12267)
GENTUITY LLC
142 North Rd Ste G (01776-1142)
PHONE..............................978 202-4108
David Kolstad, *Managing Member*
Toshiaki Masuda, *Managing Member*
EMP: 47 EST: 2014
SALES (est): 6.15MM **Privately Held**
Web: www.gentuity.com
SIC: 3845 Electromedical equipment

(G-12268)
METHODS 3D INC
65 Union Ave (01776-2277)
PHONE..............................978 443-5388
Paul Johnston, *Contrlr*
EMP: 7 EST: 2014
SALES (est): 211.42K **Privately Held**
Web: www.methodsmachine.com
SIC: 3569 General industrial machinery, nec

(G-12269)
PURE ENCAPSULATIONS LLC
490 Boston Post Rd (01776-3367)
P.O. Box 2398 (16066-1398)
PHONE..............................800 753-2277
Kyle Wesley Bliffert, *Pr*
David Torralbo, *Sec*
Jean Gagnon, *Treas*
EMP: 39 EST: 2004
SALES (est): 13.83MM **Privately Held**
SIC: 5122 2834 Pharmaceuticals; Vitamin, nutrient, and hematinic preparations for human use
HQ: Atrium Innovations Inc.
3500 Boul De Maisonneuve O Bureau 2405
Westmount QC H3Z 3
514 205-6240

(G-12270)
QUALTRE INC (HQ)
Also Called: Panasnic DVC Slutions Lab Mass
144 North Rd Ste 2250 (01776-1162)
PHONE..............................508 658-8360
Edgar Masri, *Pr*

EMP: 23 EST: 2005
SQ FT: 5,500
SALES (est): 5.23MM **Privately Held**
Web: www.qualtre.com
SIC: 3812 Inertial guidance systems
PA: Panasonic Holdings Corporation
1006, Kadoma
Kadoma OSK 571-0

(G-12271)
VIABELLA HOLDINGS LLC
11 Twillingate Rd (01776-5605)
PHONE..............................978 855-8817
Marc W Salkovitz, *Brnch Mgr*
EMP: 80
SALES (corp-wide): 17.46MM **Privately Held**
Web: www.viabella.com
SIC: 2771 Greeting cards
PA: Viabella Holdings, Llc
9 Kendrick Rd
Wareham MA 02571
800 688-9998

(G-12272)
YAMAHA UNFIED CMMNICATIONS INC
144 North Rd Ste 1100 (01776-1180)
PHONE..............................978 610-4040
Tatsuya Uneo, *CEO*
Peter Hemme, *
Martin Bodley, *
▲ EMP: 30 EST: 2005
SALES (est): 10.31MM **Privately Held**
Web: europe.yamaha.com
SIC: 3651 Audio electronic systems
PA: Yamaha Corporation
10-1, Nakazawacho, Chuo-Ku
Hamamatsu SZO 430-0

Sunderland
Franklin County

(G-12273)
DELTA SAND AND GRAVEL INC
562 Amherst Rd (01375-9466)
P.O. Box 395 (01375-0395)
PHONE..............................413 665-4051
Robert H Warner Junior, *Pr*
Craig R Warner, *VP Opers*
Paul H Warner, *Clerk*
EMP: 16 EST: 1928
SALES (est): 668.15K **Privately Held**
Web: www.delta-sand.com
SIC: 5211 1442 Sand and gravel; Construction sand and gravel

(G-12274)
KSE INC
665 Amherst Rd Ste 1 (01375-5911)
P.O. Box 368 (01004-0368)
PHONE..............................413 549-5506
James R Kittrell, *Pr*
G R Kittrell, *VP*
Howard Harris, *Prin*
EMP: 15 EST: 1977
SQ FT: 11,000
SALES (est): 2.38MM **Privately Held**
Web: www.kse-online.com
SIC: 3564 8734 5049 Purification and dust collection equipment; Product testing laboratories; Scientific and engineering equipment and supplies

(G-12275)
SINAUER ASSOCIATES INC
23 Plumtree Rd (01375-9468)
PHONE..............................413 549-4300

Andrew Sinauer, *Pr*
Dean Scudder, *VP*
▲ EMP: 37 EST: 1969
SQ FT: 6,000
SALES (est): 2.24MM
SALES (corp-wide): 28.23MM **Privately Held**
Web: global.oup.com
SIC: 2731 7812 7372 Textbooks: publishing only, not printed on site; Video tape production; Prepackaged software
HQ: Oxford University Press, Llc
198 Madison Ave Fl 8
New York NY 10016
212 726-6000

Sutton
Worcester County

(G-12276)
ATLAS BOX AND CRATING CO INC (PA)
Also Called: Atlas Global Solutions
223 Worcester Providence Tpke (01590-2905)
PHONE..............................508 865-1155
Arthur Mahassel, *Pr*
Lori Mahassel, *Sec*
◆ EMP: 150 EST: 1987
SALES (est): 24.4MM **Privately Held**
SIC: 2441 2448 2653 Boxes, wood; Wood pallets and skids; Corrugated and solid fiber boxes

(G-12277)
B&C CRYOTECH SERVICES INC
12 John Rd (01590-2507)
PHONE..............................508 277-5440
William Cammuso, *CEO*
EMP: 7 EST: 2009
SALES (est): 1.17MM **Privately Held**
Web: www.bccryotech.com
SIC: 5169 7692 Industrial gases; Welding repair

(G-12278)
BELLAONLINE
80 Lincoln Rd (01590-3716)
PHONE..............................508 865-9593
Lisa Shea, *Prin*
EMP: 40 EST: 2010
SALES (est): 388.16K **Privately Held**
Web: www.bellaonline.com
SIC: 2741 Miscellaneous publishing

(G-12279)
CP DAUPHINAIS INC
Also Called: C P Dauphinais Landscape
203 Worcester Providence Tpke (01590-2905)
PHONE..............................508 865-1755
EMP: 32 EST: 1990
SALES (est): 5.7MM **Privately Held**
Web: www.dauphinaisconcrete.com
SIC: 6513 3273 Apartment building operators; Ready-mixed concrete

(G-12280)
ENTEC POLYMERS
166 Stone School Rd (01590-3725)
PHONE..............................508 865-2001
Ken Pen, *Mgr*
EMP: 10 EST: 2007
SALES (est): 210.83K **Privately Held**
Web: www.entecpolymers.com
SIC: 2821 Plastics materials and resins

(G-12281)
I B A INC (PA)
103 Gilmore Dr (01590-2760)
P.O. Box 31 (01527-0031)
PHONE..................................508 865-6911
▲ **EMP:** 35 **EST:** 1946
SALES (est): 18.6MM
SALES (corp-wide): 18.6MM **Privately Held**
Web: www.ibadairy.com
SIC: 5083 5191 3523 Agricultural machinery and equipment; Farm supplies; Dairy equipment (farm), nec

(G-12282)
INDUSOL INC
11 Depot St (01590-3825)
PHONE..................................508 865-9516
John J Connor Junior, *Pr*
John J Connor Ii, *Pr*
John W Baldwin, *
EMP: 25 **EST:** 1950
SQ FT: 120,000
SALES (est): 4.21MM **Privately Held**
Web: www.indusolinc.com
SIC: 2821 2891 Molding compounds, plastics; Adhesives, plastic

(G-12283)
INTERSTATE GASKET COMPANY INC
55 Gilmore Dr (01590-2745)
PHONE..................................508 234-5500
Edward Z Savickas, *Ch Bd*
Edward Z Savickas, *Ch*
John Savickas, *Pr*
Richard Dearborn, *Clerk*
EMP: 21 **EST:** 1963
SQ FT: 12,000
SALES (est): 504.33K **Privately Held**
Web: www.interstatesp.com
SIC: 3053 Gaskets, all materials

(G-12284)
INTERSTATE SPECIALTY PDTS INC
Also Called: Isp
55 Gilmore Dr (01590-2745)
PHONE..................................800 984-1811
John Savickas, *Pr*
▲ **EMP:** 20 **EST:** 1995
SQ FT: 6,000
SALES (est): 4.39MM **Privately Held**
Web: www.interstatesp.com
SIC: 3053 Gaskets, all materials

(G-12285)
J&G (2021) INC
Also Called: Catelli Brothers Family Foods
71 Blackstone St (01590-3824)
PHONE..................................508 865-1101
Anthony Catelli Junior, *Prin*
EMP: 12 **EST:** 2021
SALES (est): 1.32MM **Privately Held**
SIC: 2011 Meat packing plants

(G-12286)
LAMONTAGNE WILBERT BURIAL VLT
9 Main St Ste Ll9 (01590-1660)
P.O. Box 136 (01516-0136)
PHONE..................................508 476-0040
Marie Lamontagne, *Pr*
EMP: 10 **EST:** 2005
SALES (est): 669.39K **Privately Held**
Web: www.lamontagnevault.com
SIC: 3272 Burial vaults, concrete or precast terrazzo

(G-12287)
LANOCO SPECIALTY WIRE PDTS INC
7 John Rd (01590-2509)
PHONE..................................508 865-1500
Thomas O'connor, *Pr*
John Lannon, *VP*
▲ **EMP:** 26 **EST:** 1984
SQ FT: 13,000
SALES (est): 1.85MM **Privately Held**
Web: www.lanoco.com
SIC: 3315 3496 Wire, steel: insulated or armored; Miscellaneous fabricated wire products

(G-12288)
PACKAGE INDUSTRIES INC
Also Called: Package Steel Buildings
15 Harback Rd (01590-2521)
PHONE..................................508 865-5871
Daniel E Moroney, *Pr*
Miriam Sanderson, *
EMP: 45 **EST:** 1962
SQ FT: 100,000
SALES (est): 6.84MM **Privately Held**
Web: www.packagesteelsystem.com
SIC: 3448 Buildings, portable: prefabricated metal

(G-12289)
PACKAGE STEEL SYSTEMS INC
15 Harback Rd (01590-2521)
PHONE..................................508 865-5871
Robert Fisette, *Pr*
Zach Mcayn Iii, *Treas*
EMP: 40 **EST:** 2014
SALES (est): 8.4MM **Privately Held**
Web: www.packagesteelsystem.com
SIC: 3441 Building components, structural steel

(G-12290)
POLYVINYL FILMS INC
38 Providence Rd Ste 2 (01590-3901)
P.O. Box 753 (01590-0753)
PHONE..................................508 865-3558
John W Baldwin, *Pr*
John J Connor Ii, *Prin*
Robert N Baldwin, *
Maria H Connor, *
◆ **EMP:** 95 **EST:** 1954
SALES (est): 21.25MM **Privately Held**
Web: www.stretchtite.com
SIC: 3081 Polyvinyl film and sheet

(G-12291)
SOURCE INTERNATIONAL CORP
17 Gilmore Dr (01590-2745)
PHONE..................................800 722-0474
Eric Mueller, *Pr*
David L Mcglynn, *Dir*
U Karl Mueller, *Dir*
▲ **EMP:** 29 **EST:** 1982
SQ FT: 100,000
SALES (est): 994.58K **Privately Held**
Web: www.sourceseating.com
SIC: 2521 2522 Wood office chairs, benches and stools; Office chairs, benches, and stools, except wood

(G-12292)
TX5877 INC
Also Called: J&G 2021
71 Blackstone St (01590-3824)
PHONE..................................508 865-1101
EMP: 170 **EST:** 1999
SALES (est): 21.41MM **Privately Held**
Web: www.jgfoods.com

SIC: 2011 Meat packing plants

(G-12293)
UNITED MACHINING INC
219 Whitins Rd Ste 5 (01590-2762)
PHONE..................................508 865-3035
Dylan Polseno, *Pr*
EMP: 8 **EST:** 2014
SALES (est): 1.82MM **Privately Held**
Web: www.unitedmachining.us
SIC: 3599 Machine shop, jobbing and repair

(G-12294)
VAILLANCOURT FOLK ART INC
9 Main St Ste 1h (01590-1660)
PHONE..................................508 476-3601
Gary Vaillancourt, *Pr*
Judi Vaillancourt, *
▲ **EMP:** 30 **EST:** 1977
SQ FT: 7,000
SALES (est): 2.36MM **Privately Held**
Web: www.valfa.com
SIC: 3269 3229 5947 Figures: pottery, china, earthenware, and stoneware; Glass furnishings and accessories; Gift shop

(G-12295)
WHITTIER FARMS INC
90 Douglas Rd (01590-1132)
P.O. Box 455 (01590-0455)
PHONE..................................508 865-1096
Wayne Whittier, *Pr*
EMP: 7 **EST:** 1941
SALES (est): 648.44K **Privately Held**
Web: www.whittiers.com
SIC: 0241 2026 5451 Milk production; Milk processing (pasteurizing, homogenizing, bottling); Dairy products stores

(G-12296)
WINDLE INDUSTRIES INC
94 Singletary Ave (01590-1839)
PHONE..................................508 865-5773
Terrence B Windle, *Pr*
EMP: 7 **EST:** 1945
SQ FT: 150,000
SALES (est): 96.18K **Privately Held**
SIC: 2299 2282 Slubs and nubs; Wool yarn: twisting, winding, or spooling

Swampscott
Essex County

(G-12297)
AGGREGATE INDUSTRIES
30 Danvers Rd (01907-1170)
PHONE..................................781 596-4107
EMP: 11 **EST:** 2019
SALES (est): 1.1MM **Privately Held**
SIC: 3273 Ready-mixed concrete

(G-12298)
BEAL MANUFACTURING INC
2 Shelton Rd (01907-2625)
P.O. Box 848 (28098-0848)
PHONE..................................704 824-9961
Giles D Beal Iii, *Pr*
Jennifer Beal, *
▼ **EMP:** 45 **EST:** 1997
SALES (est): 4.97MM **Privately Held**
Web: www.bealmfg.com
SIC: 2281 Knitting yarn, spun

(G-12299)
SWAMPSCOTT FUEL INC
197 Essex St (01907-1150)
PHONE..................................781 592-1065
Richard Elkhoury, *Prin*

EMP: 10 **EST:** 2011
SALES (est): 496.21K **Privately Held**
SIC: 2869 Fuels

(G-12300)
VEEAM SOFTWARE CORPORATION
45 New Ocean St (01907-1840)
PHONE..................................781 592-0752
EMP: 992
Web: www.veeam.com
SIC: 7372 Prepackaged software
PA: Veeam Software Corporation
8800 Lyra Dr Ste 350
Columbus OH 43240

(G-12301)
VOYAGER PHARMACEUTICAL CORP
51 Berkshire St (01907-1965)
PHONE..................................781 592-1945
Patrick S Smith, *Pr*
David J Corcoran, *Ex VP*
Sheldon Goldberg, *Sr VP*
Michael J Giannini, *Business Operations Vice President*
Timothy J Creech, *CAO*
EMP: 10 **EST:** 2001
SQ FT: 34,400
SALES (est): 213.6K **Privately Held**
SIC: 2834 Pharmaceutical preparations

Swansea
Bristol County

(G-12302)
ABS PRINTING INC
837 Pearse Rd (02777-1241)
PHONE..................................401 826-0870
Bruce Demoranville Junior, *Pr*
Melanie Demoranville, *VP*
EMP: 9 **EST:** 1986
SALES (est): 745.28K **Privately Held**
Web: www.absprinting.com
SIC: 2752 7331 Offset printing; Direct mail advertising services

(G-12303)
COMPU-GARD INC
1432 Gar Hwy (02777-4291)
P.O. Box 469 (02777-0469)
PHONE..................................508 679-8845
Peter Leite, *Pr*
EMP: 19 **EST:** 1980
SQ FT: 30,000
SALES (est): 879.55K **Privately Held**
Web: www.compu-gard.com
SIC: 3699 Security devices

(G-12304)
DIEBOLD NIXDORF INCORPORATED
400 Swansea Mall Dr (02777-4114)
PHONE..................................508 646-4378
EMP: 59
SALES (corp-wide): 3.46B **Publicly Held**
Web: www.dieboldnixdorf.com
SIC: 3578 Automatic teller machines (ATM)
PA: Diebold Nixdorf, Incorporated
50 Executive Pkwy
Hudson OH 44236
330 490-4000

(G-12305)
LAWSON HEMPHILL INC
1658 Gar Hwy Ste 5 (02777-3934)
P.O. Box 255 (19707-0255)

PHONE..................508 679-5364
John Sullivan, *Pr*
Patrick Sullivan, *VP*
EMP: 9 **EST:** 2014
SALES (est): 948.79K **Privately Held**
Web: www.lawsonhemphill.com
SIC: 2426 Blanks, wood: textile machinery
accessories

(G-12306)
LOUIE AND TEDS BLACKTOP INC
105 Buffington St (02777-4822)
PHONE..................508 678-4948
Louie Rebello, *Pr*
Deodato F Rebello, *Treas*
EMP: 10 **EST:** 1979
SALES (est): 774.92K **Privately Held**
SIC: 3531 1629 8711 1622 Plows:
construction, excavating, and grading;
Dams, waterways, docks, and other marine
construction; Construction and civil
engineering; Bridge, tunnel, and elevated
highway construction

(G-12307)
N E PUBLISHING GROUP
Also Called: Publishing
1610 Gar Hwy (02777-3947)
P.O. Box 357 (02777-0357)
PHONE..................508 675-8883
Timothy Branco, *Pr*
EMP: 10 **EST:** 1987
SALES (est): 708.31K **Privately Held**
SIC: 2741 Miscellaneous publishing

(G-12308)
NEW ENGLAND RE BULLTIN
Also Called: New England Publishing Group
1610 Gar Hwy (02777-3947)
P.O. Box 357 (02777-0357)
PHONE..................508 675-8884
Tr Brankco, *Pr*
EMP: 10 **EST:** 1987
SALES (est): 878.39K **Privately Held**
Web: www.southcoasttoday.com
SIC: 2721 Periodicals

(G-12309)
P G L INDUSTRIES INC
1432 Gar Hwy (02777-4291)
P.O. Box 469 (02777-0469)
PHONE..................508 679-8845
Peter G Leite, *Pr*
EMP: 25 **EST:** 1980
SQ FT: 20,000
SALES (est): 1.48MM **Privately Held**
Web: www.pglindustries.com
SIC: 3444 Sheet metal specialties, not
stamped

(G-12310)
S AND S CONCRETE FORMS CNSTR
Also Called: S & S Concrete Forms Cnstr
2224 Gar Hwy (02777-3907)
P.O. Box 35 (02777-0035)
PHONE..................508 379-0191
Antonio Sousa, *Pr*
EMP: 7 **EST:** 1986
SQ FT: 3,000
SALES (est): 861.46K **Privately Held**
SIC: 1771 3444 Concrete work; Concrete
forms, sheet metal

(G-12311)
SHAWMUT METAL PRODUCTS INC
Also Called: Shawmut Metal

1914 Gar Hwy (02777-3930)
P.O. Box 543 (02777-0543)
PHONE..................508 379-0803
Kevin Kelly, *Pr*
Francis Kelly Junior, *VP*
EMP: 38 **EST:** 1965
SQ FT: 20,000
SALES (est): 8.51MM **Privately Held**
Web: www.shawmutmetal.com
SIC: 3441 Fabricated structural metal

(G-12312)
STAR PICKLING CORP
941 Wood St (02777-3550)
PHONE..................508 672-8535
Joseph C Castro, *Pr*
Vivian Castro, *VP*
EMP: 12 **EST:** 1956
SQ FT: 34,000
SALES (est): 450.27K **Privately Held**
SIC: 2035 Pickled fruits and vegetables

(G-12313)
TESTING MACHINES INC
1658 Gar Hwy Ste 6 (02777-3934)
PHONE..................302 613-5600
Dean Ross, *Mgr*
EMP: 65
SALES (corp-wide): 12.93MM **Privately
Held**
Web: www.industrialphysics.com
SIC: 3829 5084 Physical property testing
equipment; Measuring and testing
equipment, electrical
PA: Testing Machines, Inc.
40 Mccullough Dr Unit A
New Castle DE 19720
302 613-5600

(G-12314)
TRUE MACHINE CO INC
2222 Gar Hwy (02777-3907)
PHONE..................508 379-0329
Louis Pestana, *Pr*
EMP: 7 **EST:** 1984
SALES (est): 915.6K **Privately Held**
Web: www.true-machine.com
SIC: 3469 3541 7389 Metal stampings, nec;
Milling machines; Grinding, precision:
commercial or industrial

Taunton
Bristol County

(G-12315)
AD-A-DAY COMPANY INC
245 W Water St (02780-4844)
P.O. Box 950 (02780-0950)
PHONE..................508 824-8676
Merrill N Cross, *Pr*
EMP: 41 **EST:** 1944
SQ FT: 75,000
SALES (est): 4.21MM **Privately Held**
Web: www.ad-a-day.com
SIC: 2759 3993 2741 5199 Calendars:
printing, nsk; Signs and advertising
specialties; Miscellaneous publishing;
Advertising specialties

(G-12316)
AIPCO INC
Also Called: American Insulated Panel Co
75 John Hancock Rd (02780-1096)
PHONE..................508 823-7003
TOLL FREE: 800
John J Lynch, *Pr*
Judith Lynch, *
EMP: 35 **EST:** 1985
SQ FT: 35,000

SALES (est): 4.94MM **Privately Held**
Web: www.americaninsulatedpanel.com
SIC: 3585 Refrigeration equipment,
complete

(G-12317)
ARCH LIGHTING GROUP INC
30 Sherwood Dr (02780-3442)
EMP: 28 **EST:** 2002
SALES (est): 3.38MM **Privately Held**
SIC: 3646 Commercial lighting fixtures

(G-12318)
ARGOS CORPORATION
84 Independence Dr (02780-7363)
PHONE..................508 828-5900
John Cicalis, *Pr*
Perry Cicalis, *Treas*
EMP: 10 **EST:** 1998
SQ FT: 13,000
SALES (est): 2.79MM **Privately Held**
Web: www.argosco.com
SIC: 3089 Injection molding of plastics

(G-12319)
AROCAM INC
Also Called: Wegotsoccer
605 Myles Standish Blvd (02780-7331)
PHONE..................508 822-1220
Michael O Connor, *Pr*
EMP: 16 **EST:** 1912
SALES (est): 12.06MM **Privately Held**
Web: www.wegotsoccer.com
SIC: 5941 5661 5611 5621 Soccer supplies;
Footwear, athletic; Clothing, sportswear,
men's and boys'; Women's sportswear

(G-12320)
AUTOMATIC MACHINE PDTS SLS CO
400 Constitution Dr (02780-7360)
P.O. Box 2892 (02763-0899)
PHONE..................508 822-4226
John S Holden Junior, *Ch Bd*
John S Holden Iii, *Pr*
▲ **EMP:** 42 **EST:** 1941
SALES (est): 4.01MM **Privately Held**
Web: www.ampcomp.com
SIC: 3494 3451 Valves and pipe fittings, nec
; Screw machine products

(G-12321)
AUTOMATIC MACHINE PRODUCTS CO
400 Constitution Dr (02780-7360)
P.O. Box 2892 (02763-0899)
PHONE..................508 822-4226
John Holden Iii, *Pr*
Cheryl L Holden, *Sec*
▲ **EMP:** 40 **EST:** 1941
SALES (est): 5.85MM **Privately Held**
Web: www.ampcomp.com
SIC: 3599 Machine shop, jobbing and repair

(G-12322)
B & J MANUFACTURING CORP
Also Called: Bates & Klinke
55 Constitution Dr (02780-1071)
P.O. Box 507 (02035-0507)
PHONE..................508 822-1990
Stephen Benson, *Pr*
Gregory Benson, *
Peter Benson, *Product Vice President* *
EMP: 60 **EST:** 1946
SQ FT: 36,000
SALES (est): 4.65MM **Privately Held**
Web: www.bjmfg.com

SIC: 3499 3471 Giftware, brass goods;
Electroplating of metals or formed products

(G-12323)
BAY STATE CRUCIBLE CO
740 W Water St (02780-5003)
P.O. Box 407 (02780-0407)
PHONE..................508 824-5121
Bradford Tripp, *Pr*
Nancy Tripp, *Sec*
EMP: 21 **EST:** 1907
SQ FT: 55,000
SALES (est): 1.73MM **Privately Held**
Web: www.baystatecrucible.com
SIC: 3255 Clay refractories

(G-12324)
BAYSTATE BUSINESS VENTURES LLC
Also Called: Eastern Laundry Systems
705 Myles Standish Blvd Ste 3
(02780-7300)
PHONE..................508 828-9274
Dave Cabral, *Mgr*
EMP: 15 **EST:** 2014
SALES (est): 1.64MM **Publicly Held**
Web: www.elsequip.com
SIC: 3582 5087 Commercial laundry
equipment; Laundry and dry cleaning
equipment and supplies
PA: Evi Industries, Inc.
4500 Biscayne Blvd # 340
Miami FL 33137

(G-12325)
BBA REMANUFACTURING INC
300 Myles Standish Blvd Ste 8
(02780-5706)
PHONE..................508 822-4490
Chris Swan, *Pr*
EMP: 23 **EST:** 2005
SQ FT: 7,200
SALES (est): 4.65MM **Privately Held**
Web: us.shop.bba-reman.com
SIC: 3694 Automotive electrical equipment,
nec

(G-12326)
CBM INDUSTRIES INC
470 Constitution Dr (02780-7361)
PHONE..................508 821-4555
Christopher Veglas, *Dir*
James B Veglas, *
Christopher C Veglas, *
▲ **EMP:** 45 **EST:** 1981
SQ FT: 40,000
SALES (est): 22.21MM **Privately Held**
Web: www.cbmind.com
SIC: 5065 5085 3599 3679 Electronic parts;
Fasteners and fastening equipment;
Machine and other job shop work;
Antennas, receiving

(G-12327)
CERAMIC PROCESS SYSTEMS
111 Worcester St (02780-2088)
PHONE..................508 222-0614
Grant Bennett, *Prin*
EMP: 9 **EST:** 2007
SALES (est): 245.45K **Privately Held**
SIC: 3674 Semiconductors and related
devices

(G-12328)
CONTROLS FOR AUTOMATION INC
25 Constitution Dr (02780-1071)
PHONE..................508 802-6005
David S Mochi, *Pr*

Dennis Salisbury, *
▲ **EMP:** 25 **EST:** 1970
SQ FT: 25,000
SALES (est): 5.07MM **Privately Held**
Web: www.gocfa.com
SIC: 3492 5084   Control valves, aircraft:
hydraulic and pneumatic; Hydraulic
systems equipment and supplies

(G-12329)
COPY MASTERS INC
106 Oak St Ste 2 (02780-7901)
PHONE..............................508 824-7187
Francisco Leitao, *Pr*
Rachel Leitao, *
EMP: 11 **EST:** 1981
SQ FT: 20,000
SALES (est): 408.54K **Privately Held**
Web: www.cmprint.com
SIC: 2759 2791 2789 2752   Commercial
printing, nec; Typesetting; Bookbinding and
related work; Commercial printing,
lithographic

(G-12330)
D W CLARK INC
36 Allison Ave (02780-6958)
PHONE..............................508 378-4014
EMP: 8
SALES (corp-wide): 7.04MM **Privately
Held**
Web: www.dwclark.com
SIC: 3325 3369 3366   Steel foundries, nec;
Nonferrous foundries, nec; Copper
foundries
PA: D. W. Clark, Inc.
692 N Bedford St
East Bridgewater MA 02333
508 378-4014

(G-12331)
DAVOL/TAUNTON PRINTING INC
330 Winthrop St Ste 3 (02780-7103)
PHONE..............................508 824-4305
John W Leddy, *Pr*
Catherine J Leddy, *Stockholder*
EMP: 11 **EST:** 1858
SQ FT: 14,000
SALES (est): 903.39K **Privately Held**
Web: www.davoltauntonprint.com
SIC: 2752 2759   Offset printing; Letterpress
printing

(G-12332)
DIAL FABRICS CO INC
20 Cushman St (02780-4204)
P.O. Box 590 (02780-0590)
PHONE..............................508 822-5333
Sergio Cardoza, *Pr*
Delfina Cardoza, *Prin*
EMP: 21 **EST:** 1979
SQ FT: 55,000
SALES (est): 279.76K **Privately Held**
SIC: 2241 5949   Elastic narrow fabrics,
woven or braided; Sewing, needlework, and
piece goods

(G-12333)
DIVERSITECH CORPORATION
Also Called: Quick-Sling
391 W Water St (02780-4899)
PHONE..............................800 699-0453
Kelli Johnson, *Brnch Mgr*
EMP: 9
SALES (corp-wide): 265.76MM **Privately
Held**
Web: www.quick-sling.com
SIC: 3272   Concrete products, nec
PA: Diversitech Corporation
3039 Premiere Pkwy # 600

Duluth GA 30097
678 542-3600

(G-12334)
EMD MILLIPORE CORPORATION
530 John Hancock Rd (02780-7379)
PHONE..............................781 533-5754
Joshua Batcoiffe, *Brnch Mgr*
EMP: 57
SALES (corp-wide): 23.09B **Privately Held**
Web: www.millipore.com
SIC: 3826   Spectroscopic and other optical
properties measuring equip.
HQ: Emd Millipore Corporation
400 Summit Dr
Burlington MA 01803
800 645-5476

(G-12335)
ESP SOLUTIONS INC
580 Myles Standish Blvd Ste 1
(02780-1081)
PHONE..............................508 285-0017
David Arnold, *Pr*
EMP: 13 **EST:** 1983
SQ FT: 5,300
SALES (est): 2.49MM **Privately Held**
Web: www.espsolutions.com
SIC: 7336 2678 2284 3961   Silk screen
design; Stationery products; Embroidery
thread; Bracelets, except precious metal

(G-12336)
ESP SOLUTIONS SERVICES LLC
580 Myles Standish Blvd Ste 2
(02780-1081)
PHONE..............................508 285-0017
Matthew Noonan, *Managing Member*
EMP: 8 **EST:** 2015
SQ FT: 22,000
SALES (est): 541.46K **Privately Held**
Web: www.espsolutions.com
SIC: 2395 2396   Embroidery and art
needlework; Screen printing on fabric
articles

(G-12337)
GENERAL DYNAMICS MISSION
400 John Quincy Adams Rd (02780-1083)
PHONE..............................508 880-4000
Jerry Demuro, *Brnch Mgr*
EMP: 1000
SALES (corp-wide): 42.27B **Publicly Held**
Web: www.gdmissionsystems.com
SIC: 3571   Electronic computers
HQ: General Dynamics Mission Systems,
Inc.
12450 Fair Lakes Cir
Fairfax VA 22033
877 449-0600

(G-12338)
GENERAL DYNMICS MSSION
SYSTEMS
20 Constitution Dr (02780-1070)
PHONE..............................508 880-4000
EMP: 11
SALES (corp-wide): 42.27B **Publicly Held**
Web: www.gdmissionsystems.com
SIC: 3661   Telephone and telegraph
apparatus
HQ: General Dynamics Mission Systems,
Inc.
12450 Fair Lakes Cir
Fairfax VA 22033
877 449-0600

(G-12339)
GREEN BROTHERS
FABRICATING (PA)
15 4th St (02780-4812)
PHONE..............................508 880-3608
Joshua Green, *Pr*
Brett Green, *Treas*
EMP: 24 **EST:** 1995
SALES (est): 4.93MM **Privately Held**
Web: www.greenbrothersfabrication.com
SIC: 3444 3699 3443 3469   Sheet metalwork
; Laser welding, drilling, and cutting
equipment; Weldments; Metal stampings,
nec

(G-12340)
HARODITE INDUSTRIES INC
(PA)
66 South St (02780-4357)
PHONE..............................508 824-6961
Michael P Albert, *Ch Bd*
Aaron M Albert, *
David A Albert, *
◆ **EMP:** 37 **EST:** 1930
SQ FT: 200,000
SALES (est): 10MM
SALES (corp-wide): 10MM **Privately Held**
Web: www.harodite.com
SIC: 2221   Lining fabrics, manmade fiber
and silk

(G-12341)
HOWESTEMCO INC
Also Called: Howestemco
130 Dever Dr (02780-7909)
▲ **EMP:** 93 **EST:** 1992
SALES (est): 6.26MM **Privately Held**
Web: www.nninc.com
SIC: 3599   Machine shop, jobbing and repair

(G-12342)
IMPERIAL POOLS INC
90 John Hancock Rd (02780-1047)
PHONE..............................508 339-3830
Ray Tamayo, *Brnch Mgr*
EMP: 15
SALES (corp-wide): 71.38MM **Privately
Held**
Web: www.imperialpools.com
SIC: 3949   Water sports equipment
PA: Imperial Pools, Inc.
33 Wade Rd
Latham NY 12110
518 786-1200

(G-12343)
IQE KC LLC
200 John Hancock Rd (02780-7320)
PHONE..............................508 824-6696
Andrew W Nelson, *
Brian Schoonover, *
EMP: 82 **EST:** 2012
SALES (est): 18.86MM **Privately Held**
Web: www.iqep.com
SIC: 3674   Wafers (semiconductor devices)

(G-12344)
JH WESTERBEKE CORP
150 John Hancock Rd (02780-7319)
PHONE..............................508 823-7677
John H Westerbeke Junior, *Pr*
EMP: 13 **EST:** 1932
SALES (est): 367.04K **Privately Held**
Web: www.westerbeke.com
SIC: 3519   Diesel, semi-diesel, or duel-fuel
engines, including marine

(G-12345)
JMS MANUFACTURING CO INC
Also Called: Bee Fiberglass
22 5th St Ste 8 (02780-7038)
PHONE..............................508 675-1141
Jose Sousa, *Pr*
EMP: 8 **EST:** 1950
SQ FT: 30,000
SALES (est): 159.39K **Privately Held**
SIC: 3089   Plastics processing

(G-12346)
KMS MACHINE WORKS INC
447 Winthrop St (02780-2154)
PHONE..............................508 822-3151
Charles Cronan, *Pr*
Michael Cronan, *VP*
Frances Cronin, *Clerk*
EMP: 19 **EST:** 1980
SQ FT: 7,500
SALES (est): 2.44MM **Privately Held**
Web: www.kmsmachine.com
SIC: 3599   Machine shop, jobbing and repair

(G-12347)
KOPIN CORPORATION
200 John Hancock Rd (02780-7320)
PHONE..............................508 824-6696
Jbor-yeu Tsaur, *Ex VP*
EMP: 50
SQ FT: 21,000
SALES (corp-wide): 47.4MM **Publicly
Held**
Web: www.kopin.com
SIC: 3674   Semiconductors and related
devices
PA: Kopin Corporation
125 North Dr
Westborough MA 01581
508 870-5959

(G-12348)
MAXON PRECISION MOTORS
INC (HQ)
125 Dever Rd (02780-7910)
PHONE..............................508 677-0520
Chris Blake, *Pr*
Greg Hayman, *
◆ **EMP:** 42 **EST:** 1980
SALES (est): 20.34MM **Privately Held**
Web: www.maxongroup.us
SIC: 3625 3566 3621 7694   Relays and
industrial controls; Speed changers, drives,
and gears; Motors and generators;
Armature rewinding shops
PA: Interelectric Ag
Brunigstrasse 220
Sachseln OW 6072

(G-12349)
MCCABE SAND & GRAVEL CO
INC
120 Berkley St (02780-4900)
PHONE..............................508 823-0771
TOLL FREE: 800
Gregory R Keelan, *Pr*
Kelly A Keelan, *Dir*
Jill A Zajac, *Sec*
Kayla Lopes, *Treas*
EMP: 26 **EST:** 1965
SQ FT: 18,000
SALES (est): 768K **Privately Held**
Web: www.tauntongazette.com
SIC: 3273 5032   Ready-mixed concrete;
Sand, construction

(G-12350)
NABSON INC
45 Independence Dr (02780-1090)

PHONE..............617 323-1101
James Calabrese, *Pr*
EMP: 7 **EST:** 1994
SALES (est): 1.23MM **Privately Held**
Web: www.nabson.com
SIC: 3678 5065   Electronic connectors;
Connectors, electronic

(G-12351)
NESTLE
455 John Hancock Rd (02780-7372)
PHONE..............508 828-3954
EMP: 21 **EST:** 2013
SALES (est): 326.39K **Privately Held**
Web: www.nestle.com
SIC: 2038   Frozen specialties, nec

(G-12352)
NEW ENGLAND BOX BEEF COMPANY
Also Called: Oxford Trading Company
305 Myles Standish Blvd (02780-7327)
PHONE..............781 320-3232
Charles Robinson, *Pr*
Steve Brigham, *VP*
Ron Rur, *Pr*
Harrison Carmichael, *Pr*
Steve Lerner, *Contrlr*
EMP: 20 **EST:** 1968
SALES (est): 4.29MM **Privately Held**
Web: www.oxfordbeef.com
SIC: 5147 2011   Meats, fresh; Beef
products, from beef slaughtered on site

(G-12353)
NUMOTION
300 Myles Standish Blvd Ste 2
(02780-7364)
PHONE..............401 681-2153
EMP: 7 **EST:** 2015
SALES (est): 192.95K **Privately Held**
Web: www.numotion.com
SIC: 3842   Wheelchairs

(G-12354)
PARICON TECHNOLOGIES CORP
500 Myles Standish Blvd Ste 2
(02780-1079)
PHONE..............508 823-0876
TOLL FREE: 877
Roger Weiss, *Pr*
EMP: 14 **EST:** 1997
SALES (est): 2.83MM **Privately Held**
Web: www.paricon-tech.com
SIC: 3678 3679   Electronic connectors;
Electronic circuits

(G-12355)
PRIMARY GRAPHICS CORPORATION
Also Called: Primary Graphics
175 W Water St (02780-4844)
PHONE..............781 575-0411
Anthony F Goodwin, *Pr*
Michael Goodwin, *Treas*
James Goodwin, *Sec*
EMP: 17 **EST:** 1996
SQ FT: 10,000
SALES (est): 2.39MM **Privately Held**
Web: www.primarygraphicscorp.com
SIC: 2752   Offset printing

(G-12356)
PROFESSNAL CNTRACT STRLZTION I
Also Called: P C S
40 Myles Standish Blvd (02780-1026)
PHONE..............508 822-5524
Gary Cranston, *Pr*

Marie Cranston, *Clerk*
▲ **EMP:** 10 **EST:** 1990
SQ FT: 33,000
SALES (est): 993.21K **Privately Held**
Web: www.pcsinc.org
SIC: 3841   Surgical and medical instruments

(G-12357)
PRYSMIAN GROUP SPCLTY CBLES LL
761 Warner Blvd (02780-4343)
PHONE..............508 822-0246
Kevin Sullivan, *Admn*
EMP: 200
SIC: 3357   Nonferrous wiredrawing and
insulating
HQ: Prysmian Group Specialty Cables Llc
656 Warner Blvd
Taunton MA 02780
774 501-7600

(G-12358)
PRYSMIAN GROUP SPCLTY CBLES LL (DH)
656 Warner Blvd (02780-4345)
PHONE..............774 501-7600
Kevin Sullivan, *Admn*
EMP: 150 **EST:** 2021
SALES (est): 70.62MM **Privately Held**
SIC: 3357   Building wire and cable,
nonferrous
HQ: Prysmian Cables And Systems Usa,
Llc
4 Tesseneer Dr
Highland Heights KY 41076
859 572-8000

(G-12359)
PRYSMIAN GROUP SPCLTY CBLES LL
Also Called: Draka Cableteq
656 Warner Blvd (02780-4345)
PHONE..............508 822-5444
Kevin Sullivan, *Admn*
EMP: 200
SIC: 3357   Building wire and cable,
nonferrous
HQ: Prysmian Group Specialty Cables Llc
656 Warner Blvd
Taunton MA 02780
774 501-7600

(G-12360)
QG LLC
Worldcolor Taunton Retail
1133 County St (02780-3712)
PHONE..............508 828-4400
Ted Gilly, *Brnch Mgr*
EMP: 320
SALES (corp-wide): 3.22B **Publicly Held**
SIC: 2752   Offset printing
HQ: Qg, Llc
N61w23044 Harrys Way
Sussex WI 53089

(G-12361)
REDI-MIX SERVICES INCORPORATED
490 Winthrop St (02780-2185)
PHONE..............508 823-0771
Joseph Tutsch Junior, *Prin*
EMP: 18 **EST:** 2016
SALES (est): 2.25MM **Privately Held**
Web: www.redimixcolors.com
SIC: 3251 3273 5169   Structural brick and
blocks; Ready-mixed concrete; Sealants

(G-12362)
RENS WELDING & FABRICATING
988 Crane Ave S Ste 1 (02780-7811)
PHONE..............508 828-1702
EMP: 12 **EST:** 1988
SQ FT: 50,000
SALES (est): 2.43MM **Privately Held**
Web: www.renswelding.com
SIC: 7692 3446 3441   Welding repair;
Architectural metalwork; Fabricated
structural metal

(G-12363)
RETRO-FIT TECHNOLOGIES INC
Also Called: Retro-Fit
350 Myles Standish Blvd Ste 202
(02780-7387)
PHONE..............508 478-2222
Timothy M Lawlor, *CEO*
EMP: 30 **EST:** 1980
SALES (est): 17.96MM **Privately Held**
Web: www.retrofit.com
SIC: 5045 5734 7378 3577   Computers,
peripherals, and software; Computer and
software stores; Computer and data
processing equipment repair/maintenance;
Computer peripheral equipment, nec

(G-12364)
RI KNITTING CO INC
20 Cushman St (02780-4204)
PHONE..............508 822-5333
Ronald Fish, *Pr*
Scott Gauvin, *
Bryan Gardner, *
Alicia Lopez, *
EMP: 59 **EST:** 1987
SQ FT: 48,000
SALES (est): 1.08MM **Privately Held**
Web: www.riknitting.com
SIC: 2241   Elastic narrow fabrics, woven or
braided

(G-12365)
S & E FUELS INC
113 Dean St (02780-2717)
P.O. Box 13 (02780-0013)
PHONE..............617 407-9977
Sameh Kanan, *Prin*
EMP: 11 **EST:** 2016
SALES (est): 1.47MM **Privately Held**
SIC: 2869   Fuels

(G-12366)
SAINT-GOBAIN PRFMCE PLAS CORP
700 Warner Blvd (02780-4345)
PHONE..............508 823-7701
Jim Fricks, *Brnch Mgr*
EMP: 128
SALES (corp-wide): 397.78MM **Privately
Held**
Web: www.saint-gobain.com
SIC: 2821   Plastics materials and resins
HQ: Saint-Gobain Performance Plastics
Corporation
20 Moores Rd
Malvern PA 19355
440 836-6900

(G-12367)
SILVER CITY ALUMINUM CORP
Also Called: Silver City
704 W Water St (02780-5078)
PHONE..............508 824-8631
Ronald Xavier, *Pr*
EMP: 60 **EST:** 1990
SQ FT: 45,000
SALES (est): 15.21MM **Privately Held**
Web: www.scaluminum.com

SIC: 3354   Aluminum extruded products

(G-12368)
SMARTCO SERVICES LLC
200 Myles Standish Blvd Ste A
(02780-7371)
PHONE..............508 880-0816
EMP: 31 **EST:** 2005
SQ FT: 250
SALES (est): 1.81MM **Privately Held**
Web: www.oeconnection.com
SIC: 7372   Prepackaged software

(G-12369)
STAR PRINTING CORP
Also Called: Pilgrim Plastics
10 Mozzone Blvd (02780-3751)
PHONE..............508 583-9046
Mark Abrams, *Pr*
Neal Abrams, *
◆ **EMP:** 40 **EST:** 1946
SALES (est): 5.51MM **Privately Held**
Web: www.starprintingcorp.com
SIC: 2752   Offset printing

(G-12370)
TAUNTON
30 Taunton Grn Ste 1 (02780-3243)
P.O. Box 482 (02780-0482)
PHONE..............774 501-2220
EMP: 9 **EST:** 2017
SALES (est): 158.38K **Privately Held**
Web: www.tauntonpilots.org
SIC: 2711   Newspapers, publishing and
printing

(G-12371)
TMLP ERNEST MELLO
10 Benefit St (02780-2696)
PHONE..............508 823-4849
Joseph Blain, *Prin*
EMP: 9 **EST:** 2010
SALES (est): 120K **Privately Held**
Web: www.tmlp.com
SIC: 3648   Strobe lighting systems

(G-12372)
TPH INC
100 Kimberly Rd (02780-2218)
PHONE..............401 431-1791
▲ **EMP:** 35
SIC: 3429 3452   Metal fasteners; Bolts, nuts,
rivets, and washers

(G-12373)
TRIBE MEDITERRANEAN FOODS INC
110 Prince Henry Dr (02780-7385)
P.O. Box 2178 (18703-2178)
PHONE..............419 695-9925
Tom Davis, *CEO*
▲ **EMP:** 85 **EST:** 2008
SQ FT: 70,000
SALES (est): 18.13MM
SALES (corp-wide): 113.55MM **Privately
Held**
SIC: 2099   Food preparations, nec
PA: Lakeview Farms, Llc
1600 Gressel Dr
Delphos OH 45833
419 695-9925

(G-12374)
UNICUS PHARMACEUTICALS LLC (PA)
30 Robert W Boyden Rd Ste 200a
(02780-7833)
PHONE..............508 659-7002
Pinaki Majhi, *CEO*

EMP: 10 **EST:** 2017
SALES (est): 1.5MM
SALES (corp-wide): 1.5MM **Privately Held**
Web: www.unicuspharma.com
SIC: 2834　Pharmaceutical preparations

(G-12375)
V&S TAUNTON GALVANIZING LLC
585 John Hancock Rd　(02780-7336)
PHONE..............................508 828-9499
Brian Miller,　*
EMP: 35 **EST:** 2002
SALES (est): 2.78MM **Privately Held**
Web: www.hotdipgalvanizing.com
SIC: 3479　Galvanizing of iron, steel, or end-formed products

(G-12376)
WATERS TECHNOLOGIES CORP
177 Robert Treat Paine Dr　(02780-7266)
PHONE..............................508 482-5223
Mike Glynn,　*Brnch Mgr*
EMP: 10
SQ FT: 5,000
Web: www.waters.com
SIC: 3826　Chromatographic equipment, laboratory type
HQ: Waters Technologies Corporation,
　　34 Maple St
　　Milford MA 01757
　　508 478-2000

(G-12377)
WESTERBEKE CORPORATION (PA)
150 John Hancock Rd　(02780-7319)
PHONE..............................508 977-4273
John H Westerbeke Junior, *Pr*
Greg Haidemenos,　*
◆ **EMP:** 45 **EST:** 1934
SQ FT: 110,000
SALES (est): 10.35MM
SALES (corp-wide): 10.35MM **Privately Held**
Web: www.westerbeke.com
SIC: 3519　Marine engines

Teaticket
Barnstable County

(G-12378)
CAPE COD WINERY INC
4 Oxbow Rd　(02536-5102)
P.O. Box 401　(02536-0401)
PHONE..............................508 457-5592
Erika Orlandella, *Pr*
Kristina Lazzari, *Pr*
EMP: 10 **EST:** 1994
SALES (est): 975.93K **Privately Held**
Web: www.capecodwinery.com
SIC: 2084　Wines

(G-12379)
PACKAGING DEVICES INC (PA)
61 Homestead Ln　(02536-5715)
P.O. Box 443　(02541-0443)
PHONE..............................508 548-0224
Paul Ronsetti, *Pr*
Charles Alexander, *VP*
Carol Ronsetti, *Sec*
EMP: 19 **EST:** 1972
SALES (est): 1.23MM **Privately Held**
Web: www.packagingdevices.com
SIC: 2671 3565 3544　Thermoplastic coated paper for packaging; Packaging machinery; Special dies, tools, jigs, and fixtures

Templeton
Worcester County

(G-12380)
JBM SERVICES INC
686 Patriots Rd　(01468-1243)
P.O. Box 295　(01468-0295)
PHONE..............................978 939-8004
Teresa Gagne, *Pr*
EMP: 25 **EST:** 1995
SALES (est): 1.08MM **Privately Held**
SIC: 2448　Pallets, wood

(G-12381)
R H LE MIEUR CORP
638 Patriots Rd　(01468-1301)
PHONE..............................978 939-8741
Robert Le Mieur, *Pr*
Edith Lemieur, *Treas*
EMP: 10 **EST:** 1950
SQ FT: 6,000
SALES (est): 259.18K **Privately Held**
Web: www.rhlemieur.com
SIC: 2511　Chairs, household, except upholstered: wood

(G-12382)
SPACE AGE ELECTRONICS INC
283 Baldwinville Rd　(01468-1443)
PHONE..............................978 652-5421
Eugene H Mongeau, *Brnch Mgr*
EMP: 25
SALES (corp-wide): 13.85MM **Privately Held**
Web: www.1sae.com
SIC: 3669　Fire alarm apparatus, electric
PA: Space Age Electronics, Inc.
　　58 Chocksett Rd
　　Sterling MA 01564
　　800 486-1723

Tewksbury
Middlesex County

(G-12383)
ACEINNA INC
3 Highwood Dr Ste 101w　(01876-1158)
PHONE..............................978 965-3200
Yang Zhao, *CEO*
Patricia Niu, *CFO*
Melissa Locastro, *Corporate Secretary*
EMP: 20 **EST:** 2016
SQ FT: 8,799
SALES (est): 3.75MM **Privately Held**
Web: www.aceinna.com
SIC: 3674　Integrated circuits, semiconductor networks, etc.

(G-12384)
ANALYTIK JENA US LLC (DH)
3 Highwood Dr Ste 103e　(01876-1154)
P.O. Box 5015　(91785-5015)
PHONE..............................909 946-3197
Monde Qhobosheane, *CEO*
Chris Griffith, *CFO*
◆ **EMP:** 100 **EST:** 2006
SQ FT: 42,000
SALES (est): 32.56MM **Privately Held**
Web: www.uvp.com
SIC: 3826 3641　Analytical instruments; Ultraviolet lamps
HQ: Analytik Jena Gmbh+Co. Kg
　　Konrad-Zuse-Str. 1
　　Jena TH 07745
　　36417770

(G-12385)
AXYGEN BIOSCIENCE INC
836 North St Bldg 300　(01876-1297)
PHONE..............................978 442-2200
EMP: 17 **EST:** 2008
SALES (est): 778.78K
SALES (corp-wide): 12.59B **Publicly Held**
SIC: 3089　Injection molding of plastics
PA: Corning Incorporated
　　1 Riverfront Plz
　　Corning NY 14831
　　607 974-9000

(G-12386)
BMS PIZZA INC
1475 Main St　(01876-4747)
PHONE..............................978 851-0540
EMP: 10 **EST:** 2016
SALES (est): 1.45MM **Privately Held**
SIC: 2834　Pharmaceutical preparations

(G-12387)
BOSTON RETAIL PRODUCTS INC (PA)
Also Called: Boston Retail
3 Highwood Dr Ste 100w　(01876-1154)
PHONE..............................781 395-7417
Russell J Rubin, *Pr*
Susan L Ward,　*
Victor Martin,　*
Richard J Rubin,　*
Gerald P Hendrick,　*
◆ **EMP:** 60 **EST:** 1968
SALES (est): 24.26MM
SALES (corp-wide): 24.26MM **Privately Held**
Web: www.boston-group.com
SIC: 2542 3446　Office and store showcases and display fixtures; Architectural metalwork

(G-12388)
C & D SIGNS INC
Also Called: Metro Sign & Awning
170 Lorum St　(01876-1700)
PHONE..............................978 851-2424
Brian A Chipman, *Pr*
Corey Fischer,　*
Tom Dunn,　*
EMP: 35 **EST:** 2004
SQ FT: 3,000
SALES (est): 5.67MM **Privately Held**
Web: www.metrosignandawning.com
SIC: 3993　Signs and advertising specialties

(G-12389)
CAMBRIDGE ISOTOPE LABS INC (DH)
Also Called: Cambridge Isotope Labs
3 Highwood Dr　(01876-1148)
PHONE..............................978 749-8000
Cliff Caldwell, *CEO*
Joel C Bradley,　*
Peter E Dodwell,　*
Todd Osiek, *CSO*
▲ **EMP:** 85 **EST:** 1981
SQ FT: 45,000
SALES (est): 76.44MM **Privately Held**
Web: www.isotope.com
SIC: 2869　Industrial organic chemicals, nec
HQ: Otsuka Pharmaceutical Co., Ltd.
　　2-16-4, Konan
　　Minato-Ku TKY 108-0

(G-12390)
COLDWELL BANKER
Also Called: Dewolfe New England RE
1201 Main St Unit 1　(01876-4775)
PHONE..............................978 851-3731
Merit Macintire, *Mgr*

Michelle Oates, *Mgr*
EMP: 10 **EST:** 1994
SALES (est): 199.7K **Privately Held**
Web: www.billmanchenton.com
SIC: 6531 2097　Real estate agent, residential; Manufactured ice

(G-12391)
CORNING INCORPORATED
Also Called: Corning
836 North St Ste 3401　(01876-1296)
PHONE..............................978 442-2200
Lisa Vorst, *Brnch Mgr*
EMP: 50
SALES (corp-wide): 14.19B **Publicly Held**
Web: www.corning.com
SIC: 3826 3821 3231 3229　Analytical instruments; Laboratory apparatus and furniture; Products of purchased glass; Fiber optics strands
PA: Corning Incorporated
　　1 Riverfront Plz
　　Corning NY 14831
　　607 974-9000

(G-12392)
CUSTOM GLASS AND ALUM CO INC
120 Lumber Ln Unit 4　(01876-1489)
PHONE..............................978 640-5800
Rita Curtis, *Pr*
EMP: 8 **EST:** 2006
SALES (est): 714.7K **Privately Held**
SIC: 3211　Construction glass

(G-12393)
DELAWARE VALLEY CORP
600 Woburn St　(01876-3441)
PHONE..............................978 459-6932
Tim Curtis, *Brnch Mgr*
EMP: 30
SALES (corp-wide): 8.86MM **Privately Held**
Web:
www.delawarevalleynonwovens.com
SIC: 2297 3429 2273　Nonwoven fabrics; Hardware, nec; Carpets and rugs
PA: Delaware Valley Corp.
　　500 Broadway
　　Lawrence MA 01841
　　978 688-6995

(G-12394)
DURAFLOW LLC
120 Lumber Ln Unit 15　(01876-1489)
PHONE..............................978 851-7439
EMP: 15 **EST:** 2009
SQ FT: 8,000
SALES (est): 3.29MM **Privately Held**
Web: www.duraflow.biz
SIC: 2899 3589　Water treating compounds; Water filters and softeners, household type

(G-12395)
EAST COAST PAVERS LLC
1777 Main St　(01876-4772)
PHONE..............................508 577-7832
Anthony Morello, *Prin*
EMP: 7 **EST:** 2014
SALES (est): 184.48K **Privately Held**
SIC: 2951　Asphalt paving mixtures and blocks

(G-12396)
EMERALD IRON WORKS INC
662 Clark Rd Ste 1　(01876-1672)
PHONE..............................978 851-3028
Christa Lynne Tomasi, *Pr*
EMP: 11 **EST:** 2008
SALES (est): 646.25K **Privately Held**

SIC: 3312 Blast furnaces and steel mills

(G-12397)
EVOQUA WATER TECHNOLOGIES LLC
558 Clark Rd (01876-1631)
PHONE...................978 863-4600
Malcolm Kinnaird, *Div Pres*
EMP: 50
Web: www.evoqua.com
SIC: 3589 3569 3823 3826 Sewage and water treatment equipment; Filters, general line: industrial; Water quality monitoring and control systems; Water testing apparatus
HQ: Evoqua Water Technologies Llc
    210 6th Ave Ste 3300
    Pittsburgh PA 15222
    724 772-0044

(G-12398)
EVOQUA WATER TECHNOLOGIES LLC
Also Called: Electric Catalytic Pdts Group
558 Clark Rd (01876-1631)
PHONE...................908 851-4250
John Martin, *Mgr*
EMP: 58
Web: www.evoqua.com
SIC: 3589 Water treatment equipment, industrial
HQ: Evoqua Water Technologies Llc
    210 6th Ave Ste 3300
    Pittsburgh PA 15222
    724 772-0044

(G-12399)
EVOQUA WATER TECHNOLOGIES LLC
558 Clark Rd (01876-1631)
PHONE...................978 934-9349
Francis Ferrara, *Brnch Mgr*
EMP: 200
Web: www.evoqua.com
SIC: 3589 Water treatment equipment, industrial
HQ: Evoqua Water Technologies Llc
    210 6th Ave Ste 3300
    Pittsburgh PA 15222
    724 772-0044

(G-12400)
FOUNDRY SPECIALTY COATINGS LLC
200 Pleasant St (01876-2726)
PHONE...................978 518-9990
Michael Roper, *Prin*
EMP: 10 EST: 2017
SALES (est): 897.14K **Privately Held**
Web: www.foundryspecialtycoatings.com
SIC: 3479 Coating of metals and formed products

(G-12401)
HOLT AND BUGBEE COMPANY (PA)
Also Called: Holt & Bugbee
1600 Shawsheen St (01876-1595)
P.O. Box 37 (01876-0037)
PHONE...................978 851-7201
TOLL FREE: 800
Phillip T Pierce, *Pr*
William A Collins, *
Rebecca Pierce, *
Mary Pierce, *
▲ EMP: 122 EST: 1906
SQ FT: 280,000
SALES (est): 41.15MM
SALES (corp-wide): 41.15MM **Privately Held**

Web: www.holtandbugbee.com
SIC: 5031 2431 2421 Lumber: rough, dressed, and finished; Millwork; Sawmills and planing mills, general

(G-12402)
LEIDOS INC
1 Radcliff Rd (01876-1181)
PHONE...................781 221-7627
EMP: 9
Web: www.leidos.com
SIC: 8731 3679 3575 7371 Commercial physical research; Liquid crystal displays (LCD); Cathode ray tube (CRT), computer terminal; Custom computer programming services
HQ: Leidos, Inc.
    1750 Presidents St
    Reston VA 20190
    571 526-6000

(G-12403)
LEIDOS SEC DTCTION AUTOMTN INC
1 Radcliff Rd Ste 300 (01876-1181)
PHONE...................571 526-6000
EMP: 10
SIC: 3812 Search and navigation equipment
HQ: Leidos Security Detection & Automation, Inc.
    1 Radcliff Rd
    Tewksbury MA 01876
    781 970-1563

(G-12404)
LEIDOS SEC DTCTION AUTOMTN INC
1 Radcliff Rd (01876-1181)
PHONE...................781 939-3800
EMP: 11
SIC: 3663 Telemetering equipment, electronic
HQ: Leidos Security Detection & Automation, Inc.
    1 Radcliff Rd
    Tewksbury MA 01876
    781 970-1563

(G-12405)
MARINE POLYMER TECH INC (PA)
159 Lorum St (01876-1716)
PHONE...................781 270-3200
Sergio Finkielsztein, *Pr*
John Vournakis, *
Marco Finkielsztein, *
Eduardo Finkielsztoen, *
EMP: 35 EST: 1992
SQ FT: 40,000
SALES (est): 13.32MM **Privately Held**
Web: www.marinepolymer.com
SIC: 3842 Surgical appliances and supplies

(G-12406)
MARTEL WELDING & SONS INC
500 Woburn St (01876-3443)
PHONE...................978 458-0661
Gerard Martel, *Pr*
Richard Martel, *Treas*
EMP: 10 EST: 1956
SQ FT: 4,500
SALES (est): 1.11MM **Privately Held**
Web: www.martelwelding.com
SIC: 7532 7692 3715 3537 Body shop, trucks; Automotive welding; Truck trailers; Hoppers, end dump

(G-12407)
MATRIX TECHNOLOGIES
2 Radcliff Rd (01876-1182)
PHONE...................603 521-0547
Ann Mahoney, *Mktg Dir*
EMP: 9 EST: 2018
SALES (est): 244.69K **Privately Held**
Web: www.matrixti.com
SIC: 3821 Laboratory apparatus and furniture

(G-12408)
MC10 INC
5 Mark Rd (01876-3229)
PHONE...................617 234-4448
Scott Pomerantz, *Pr*
Carmichael Roberts, *Ch Bd*
Benjamin Schlatka, *VP*
Paul Klingenstein, *Prin*
Sanjay Gupta, *VP*
◆ EMP: 30 EST: 2008
SALES (est): 4.95MM **Privately Held**
Web: www.medidata.com
SIC: 3699 Electrical equipment and supplies, nec

(G-12409)
MEGATECH CORPORATION
525 Woburn St Ste 3 (01876-3432)
PHONE...................978 937-9600
Vahan V Basmajian, *Pr*
Varant Z Basmajian, *VP*
▲ EMP: 16 EST: 1970
SQ FT: 20,000
SALES (est): 3.73MM **Privately Held**
Web: www.megatechcorp.com
SIC: 3999 2741 Education aids, devices and supplies; Technical manual and paper publishing

(G-12410)
MICROSEMI CORPORATION
890 East St Ste 2 (01876-1476)
PHONE...................978 232-3793
EMP: 17
SALES (corp-wide): 8.44B **Publicly Held**
Web: www.microsemi.com
SIC: 3674 Semiconductors and related devices
HQ: Microsemi Corporation
    11861 Western Ave
    Garden Grove CA 92841
    949 380-6100

(G-12411)
MRSI SYSTEMS LLC
554 Clark Rd (01876-1631)
PHONE...................978 667-9449
Michael Chalsen, *Pr*
EMP: 44 EST: 2013
SALES (est): 11.14MM
SALES (corp-wide): 487.97MM **Privately Held**
Web: www.mrsisystems.com
SIC: 3565 Packaging machinery
PA: Mycronic Ab (Publ)
    Nytorpsvagen 9
    TAby 183 7
    86385200

(G-12412)
PINE AND BAKER MFG INC
Also Called: Pine and Baker
166 Lorum St (01876-1700)
PHONE...................978 851-1215
Philip S Baker, *Pr*
EMP: 17 EST: 1939
SQ FT: 22,000
SALES (est): 572.94K **Privately Held**
Web: www.pineandbaker.com

SIC: 3651 2426 2499 Speaker systems; Furniture dimension stock, hardwood; Fencing, wood

(G-12413)
R M PRECISION MACHINE CORP
120 Lumber Ln Unit 7 (01876-1489)
PHONE...................978 640-2900
Richard Macdonald, *Pr*
Heidi Macdonald, *Treas*
EMP: 12 EST: 1991
SQ FT: 1,800
SALES (est): 886.3K **Privately Held**
Web: www.rmprecision.com
SIC: 3599 Machine shop, jobbing and repair

(G-12414)
RAYTHEON SYSTEMS SUPPORT CO (DH)
50 Apple Hill Dr (01876-1140)
PHONE...................978 851-2134
Daniel J Crowley, *Pr*
EMP: 22 EST: 1973
SALES (est): 85.03K
SALES (corp-wide): 67.07B **Publicly Held**
SIC: 3812 Defense systems and equipment
HQ: Raytheon Company
    870 Winter St
    Waltham MA 02451
    781 522-3000

(G-12415)
RYCA INC
1768 Main St Ste 2 (01876-4752)
PHONE...................978 851-3265
Candida M Connors, *Prin*
EMP: 10 EST: 2004
SALES (est): 246.36K **Privately Held**
SIC: 3714 Motor vehicle brake systems and parts

(G-12416)
SMART MODULAR TECHNOLOGIES INC
2 Highwood Dr Ste 101 (01876-1100)
PHONE...................978 221-3513
EMP: 52
SALES (corp-wide): 1.44B **Publicly Held**
Web: www.smartm.com
SIC: 3577 Computer peripheral equipment, nec
HQ: Smart Modular Technologies Inc.
    39870 Eureka Dr
    Newark CA 94560

(G-12417)
SPRING MANUFACTURING CORP
2235 Main St (01876-3029)
P.O. Box 300 (01876-0300)
PHONE...................978 658-7396
Roger A Desmarais, *Pr*
EMP: 11 EST: 1979
SQ FT: 11,000
SALES (est): 1.03MM **Privately Held**
Web: www.springmancorp.com
SIC: 3495 Instrument springs, precision

(G-12418)
STARENT NETWORKS LLC (HQ)
30 International Pl (01876-1144)
PHONE...................978 851-1100
Ashraf M Dahod, *Pr*
Paul J Milbury, *
Kevin F Newman, *General Vice President**
Robert J Kelly, *Manufacturing Operations Vice President**
Pierre G Kahhale, *Worldwide Field Operations Vice President**

EMP: 34 **EST:** 2000
SQ FT: 56,000
SALES (est): 5.61MM
SALES (corp-wide): 57B **Publicly Held**
SIC: 3663 7372 Radio broadcasting and communications equipment; Prepackaged software
PA: Cisco Systems, Inc.
170 W Tasman Dr
San Jose CA 95134
408 526-4000

(G-12419)
STARKWEATHER ENGINEERING INC
1615 Shawsheen St Ste 14 (01876-1551)
PHONE....................978 858-3700
EMP: 10 **EST:** 1986
SQ FT: 4,000
SALES (est): 850.47K **Privately Held**
Web: www.starkweatherengineering.com
SIC: 3441 1799 Fabricated structural metal; Welding on site

(G-12420)
STEPHEN GOULD CORPORATION
30 Commerce Way Ste 1 (01876-1776)
PHONE....................978 851-2500
Ted Vitas, *Mgr*
EMP: 25
SALES (corp-wide): 1.08B **Privately Held**
Web: www.stephengould.com
SIC: 2657 7336 Paperboard backs for blister or skin packages; Package design
PA: Stephen Gould Corporation
5 Giralda Farms
Madison NJ 07940
973 428-1500

(G-12421)
TESSIS PIZZA & ROAST BEEF
910 Andover St Ste 1 (01876-1090)
PHONE....................978 851-8700
EMP: 11 **EST:** 2015
SALES (est): 197.94K **Privately Held**
Web: www.tessispizzatewksbury.com
SIC: 5812 2013 Pizzeria, independent; Roast beef, from purchased meat

(G-12422)
THERMO FISHER SCIENTIFIC INC
2 Radcliff Rd (01876-1182)
PHONE....................781 622-1000
EMP: 56
SALES (corp-wide): 44.91B **Publicly Held**
Web: www.thermofisher.com
SIC: 3826 Analytical instruments
PA: Thermo Fisher Scientific Inc.
168 3rd Ave
Waltham MA 02451
781 622-1000

(G-12423)
THERMO SCNTFIC PRTBLE ANLYTCAL (HQ)
Also Called: Thermo Scientific
2 Radcliff Rd (01876-1182)
PHONE....................978 657-5555
Daryoosh Vakhshoori, *CEO*
Lisa Witte, *
Kevin O'brien, *VP Fin*
Maura Fitzpatrick, *
Doug Kahn, *
▲ **EMP:** 190 **EST:** 2002
SQ FT: 45,000
SALES (est): 55.27MM
SALES (corp-wide): 44.91B **Publicly Held**

Web: portables.thermoscientific.com
SIC: 3826 Analytical instruments
PA: Thermo Fisher Scientific Inc.
168 3rd Ave
Waltham MA 02451
781 622-1000

(G-12424)
V & G IRON WORKS INC
1500 Shawsheen St (01876-1562)
PHONE....................978 851-9191
Virgilio Bancarotta, *Pr*
Rosaria Bancarotta, *Treas*
EMP: 15 **EST:** 1979
SQ FT: 12,000
SALES (est): 2.51MM **Privately Held**
Web: www.vgironworks.com
SIC: 3441 Fabricated structural metal

(G-12425)
VASCA INC (PA)
3 Highwood Dr (01876-1147)
PHONE....................978 640-0431
▲ **EMP:** 42 **EST:** 1996
SALES (est): 2.54MM **Privately Held**
Web: www.vasca.com
SIC: 3845 3841 Dialyzers, electromedical; Surgical and medical instruments

(G-12426)
YANKEE CUSTOM INC (PA)
1271 Main St (01876-2010)
PHONE....................978 851-9024
TOLL FREE: 800
William A Cole, *Pr*
Judith Cole, *VP*
EMP: 13 **EST:** 1973
SQ FT: 8,000
SALES (est): 5.35MM
SALES (corp-wide): 5.35MM **Privately Held**
Web: www.yankeecustomtruck.com
SIC: 5531 3792 Automotive accessories; Pickup covers, canopies or caps

Thorndike
Hampden County

(G-12427)
O C WHITE COMPANY
4226 Church St (01079-7728)
PHONE....................413 289-1751
Richard May Senior, *Pr*
▲ **EMP:** 21 **EST:** 1893
SQ FT: 13,500
SALES (est): 4.99MM **Privately Held**
Web: www.ocwhite.com
SIC: 3646 Commercial lighting fixtures

(G-12428)
THOMAS SCIENTIFIC LLC
4226 Church St (01079-7728)
PHONE....................413 406-6588
EMP: 55
SALES (corp-wide): 100.03MM **Privately Held**
Web: www.thomassci.com
SIC: 3821 Laboratory apparatus and furniture
PA: Thomas Scientific, Llc
1654 High Hill Rd
Swedesboro NJ 08085
800 345-2100

Three Rivers
Hampden County

(G-12429)
MICRO-LITE INC
2039 Bridge St (01080-1203)
P.O. Box 644 (01079-0644)
PHONE....................413 289-1313
▲ **EMP:** 12 **EST:** 1991
SQ FT: 12,500
SALES (est): 1.37MM **Privately Held**
Web: www.tldcontractors.com
SIC: 3648 5063 3821 3646 Lighting equipment, nec; Electrical apparatus and equipment; Laboratory apparatus and furniture; Commercial lighting fixtures

(G-12430)
MILLENNIUM DIE GROUP INC
Also Called: Stan-Allen Co.
2022 Bridge St (01080-1055)
P.O. Box 128 (01080-0128)
PHONE....................413 283-3500
Richard Sweeting, *Pr*
Earl Quinn, *VP*
John Pangetti, *VP*
EMP: 21 **EST:** 1993
SALES (est): 5.33MM **Privately Held**
Web: www.millenniumdie.com
SIC: 3544 Special dies and tools

(G-12431)
MUSTANG MOTORCYCLE PDTS LLC
4 Springfield St Ste 1 (01080-1243)
PHONE....................413 283-6236
Allen L Simmons, *Pr*
▲ **EMP:** 85 **EST:** 1979
SQ FT: 12,000
SALES (est): 6.24MM **Privately Held**
Web: www.mustangseats.com
SIC: 3751 Saddles and seat posts, motorcycle and bicycle

Topsfield
Essex County

(G-12432)
ENGEMENT COMPANY INC
58 Main St Ste 2 (01983-1840)
PHONE....................603 537-2088
Kennth Dzierzek, *Pr*
EMP: 7 **EST:** 1992
SALES (est): 657.08K **Privately Held**
SIC: 3825 7373 Instruments to measure electricity; Computer integrated systems design

(G-12433)
ESSEX COUNTY COOP FARMING ASSN
146 S Main St (01983-1821)
P.O. Box 338 (01983-0438)
PHONE....................978 887-2300
Clifton Elliott, *Pr*
Albert Gebow, *VP*
Paul Novak, *Treas*
John R Ferris, *Sec*
EMP: 16 **EST:** 1917
SQ FT: 10,000
SALES (est): 3.41MM **Privately Held**
Web: www.essexcountycoop.com
SIC: 5999 3524 2326 5251 Feed and farm supply; Lawn and garden equipment; Jackets, overall and work; Builders' hardware

(G-12434)
EVANS INDUSTRIES LLC
249 Boston St (01983-2295)
P.O. Box 169 (01983-0269)
PHONE....................978 887-8561
Kendall Evans, *Pr*
▲ **EMP:** 105 **EST:** 1965
SQ FT: 12,000
SALES (est): 17.42MM
SALES (corp-wide): 149.03MM **Privately Held**
Web: www.mmgmfg.com
SIC: 3599 Machine shop, jobbing and repair
HQ: Momentum Manufacturing Group, Llc
23 National Ave
Georgetown MA 01833
978 659-6960

(G-12435)
FAIRVIEW MACHINE COMPANY INC
Also Called: FMC
427 Boston St (01983-1238)
PHONE....................978 887-2141
Armand F Lauzon Junior, *CEO*
Michael C Moulton, *
Donna Costello, *
EMP: 50 **EST:** 1962
SQ FT: 25,000
SALES (est): 7.79MM **Privately Held**
Web: www.fairviewmachine.us
SIC: 3599 Machine shop, jobbing and repair

(G-12436)
LAWTON TRUCK EQUIPMENT INC
240 Boston St (01983-2221)
PHONE....................978 887-0005
Raymond Lawton, *Pr*
Patricia Lawton, *Sec*
Raymond Lawton, *Treas*
EMP: 11 **EST:** 2013
SALES (est): 178.07K **Privately Held**
Web: www.lawtonwelding.com
SIC: 3711 5531 Motor vehicles and car bodies; Automotive parts

(G-12437)
NEW ENGLAND CARBIDE INC
Also Called: Newcarb
428 Boston St Ste A (01983-1216)
PHONE....................978 887-0313
Eamonn Mcdonnell, *Pr*
Noeleen Mcdonnell, *Dir*
EMP: 10 **EST:** 1941
SQ FT: 10,000
SALES (est): 791.93K **Privately Held**
Web: www.newenglandcarbide.com
SIC: 3545 Cutting tools for machine tools

(G-12438)
STELLANT PST CORP
Hill Engineering
417 Boston St (01983-1218)
PHONE....................978 887-5754
Scott Schneider, *Mgr*
EMP: 12
SALES (corp-wide): 296.08MM **Privately Held**
Web: www.comtechpst.com
SIC: 3663 3613 Microwave communication equipment; Switchgear and switchboard apparatus
HQ: Stellant Pst Corp.
105 Baylis Rd
Melville NY 11747
631 777-8900

(G-12439)
TEKTRON INC
424 Boston St Ste B (01983-1216)
PHONE..................................978 887-0091
Philip Tanzella, *Pr*
Frank V Tanzella, *VP*
Karen Tanzella, *Clerk*
EMP: 10 **EST:** 1986
SQ FT: 6,000
SALES (est): 994.67K **Privately Held**
Web: www.tektroninc.com
SIC: 3613 3545 3625 3599   Control panels,
   electric; Precision measuring tools; Relays
   and industrial controls; Electrical discharge
   machining (EDM)

(G-12440)
TRIREME MANUFACTURING CO INC
245 Boston St (01983-2215)
PHONE..................................978 887-2132
John Tsiplakis, *Pr*
EMP: 21 **EST:** 1985
SQ FT: 13,000
SALES (est): 4.71MM **Privately Held**
SIC: 3511   Turbines and turbine generator
   sets and parts

Townsend
Middlesex County

(G-12441)
NEW ENGLAND BUSINESS SVC INC (HQ)
Also Called: Nebs
12 South St (01469-1302)
PHONE..................................978 448-6111
TOLL FREE: 800
Richard H Rhoads, *Pr*
Paul F Robinson, *
Barbara Baklund, *
▼ **EMP:** 67 **EST:** 1952
SALES (est): 441.82MM
SALES (corp-wide): 2.24B **Publicly Held**
SIC: 2771 5045 2653 3089   Greeting cards;
   Computer software; Corrugated and solid
   fiber boxes; Plastics containers, except
   foam
PA: Deluxe Corporation
   801 Marquette Ave
   Minneapolis MN 55402
   651 483-7111

(G-12442)
STERILITE CORPORATION (PA)
30 Scales Ln (01469-1010)
P.O. Box 8001 (01469-8001)
PHONE..................................978 597-1000
◆ **EMP:** 120 **EST:** 1945
SALES (est): 430.83MM
SALES (corp-wide): 430.83MM **Privately Held**
Web: www.sterilite.com
SIC: 3089 4226   Plastics kitchenware,
   tableware, and houseware; Special
   warehousing and storage, nec

(G-12443)
TLS PRINTING LLC
84 Tyler Rd (01469-1203)
PHONE..................................508 234-2344
EMP: 8 **EST:** 2005
SQ FT: 38,000
SALES (est): 422.08K **Privately Held**
Web: www.tlsprinting.com
SIC: 2752   Commercial printing, lithographic

Turners Falls
Franklin County

(G-12444)
CHARTER NEXT GENERATION INC
18 Industrial Blvd (01376-1608)
PHONE..................................413 863-3171
EMP: 128
SALES (corp-wide): 1.5B **Privately Held**
Web: www.cnginc.com
SIC: 3081   Packing materials, plastics sheet
PA: Charter Next Generation, Inc.
   300 N La Salle Dr # 1575
   Chicago IL 60654
   608 868-5757

(G-12445)
COLD RIVER MINING INC
17 Masonic Ave (01376-2515)
P.O. Box 501 (01376-0501)
PHONE..................................413 863-5445
Rob Houchens, *Pr*
▲ **EMP:** 9 **EST:** 2008
SALES (est): 692.84K **Privately Held**
Web: www.coldrivermining.com
SIC: 3915   Gems, real and imitation:
   preparation for settings

(G-12446)
HASSAY SAVAGE BROACH CO INC
10 Industrial Blvd (01376-1627)
PHONE..................................413 863-9052
▲ **EMP:** 15
Web: www.pilotprecision.com
SIC: 3545   Machine tool attachments and
   accessories

(G-12447)
HEAT FAB INC
130 Industrial Blvd (01376-1607)
PHONE..................................413 863-2242
Jerry Nolan, *CFO*
EMP: 17 **EST:** 2007
SALES (est): 2.46MM **Privately Held**
Web: www.heatfab.com
SIC: 3444 3443 3564   Flues and pipes,
   stove or furnace: sheet metal; Fabricated
   plate work (boiler shop); Blowers and fans

(G-12448)
HILLSIDE PLASTICS INC
Also Called: Sugarhill Containers
262 Millers Falls Rd (01376-1613)
PHONE..................................413 863-2222
Peter M Haas, *Pr*
Alan H Blanker, *
Kathryn L Colby, *
EMP: 202 **EST:** 1967
SQ FT: 47,000
SALES (est): 20.93MM **Privately Held**
SIC: 3089   Plastics containers, except foam
PA: Carr Management, Inc.
   1 Tara Blvd Ste 303
   Nashua NH 03062

(G-12449)
JARVIS WELDING & MFG CO
Also Called: Jarvis Pools & Spas
72 Unity St (01376-2114)
PHONE..................................413 863-9541
Raymond Jarvis, *Pr*
Raymond Jarvis Prestreas, *Prin*
Korinna Fitzpatrick, *VP*
EMP: 9 **EST:** 1926
SQ FT: 3,240
SALES (est): 399.28K **Privately Held**

SIC: 1799 5091 3564   Swimming pool
   construction; Swimming pools, equipment
   and supplies; Blowers and fans

(G-12450)
JUDD WIRE INC (DH)
124 Turnpike Rd (01376-2699)
PHONE..................................800 545-5833
James Koulgeorge, *Pr*
◆ **EMP:** 258 **EST:** 1988
SQ FT: 472,000
SALES (est): 93.39MM **Privately Held**
Web: www.juddwire.com
SIC: 3357   Aircraft wire and cable,
   nonferrous
HQ: Sumitomo Electric U.S.A., Inc.
   21241 S Wstn Ave Ste 120
   Torrance CA 90501
   310 782-0227

(G-12451)
LIGHTLIFE FOODS INC
153 Industrial Blvd (01376-1611)
PHONE..................................413 774-9000
Roy Lubetkin, *Pr*
EMP: 111
SALES (corp-wide): 3.53B **Privately Held**
Web: www.lightlife.com
SIC: 2099   Food preparations, nec
HQ: Lightlife Foods, Inc.
   180 E Park Ave Ofc 1
   Elmhurst IL 60126
   413 774-9000

(G-12452)
MAYHEW STEEL PRODUCTS INC (PA)
Also Called: Mayhew Tools
199 Industrial Blvd (01376-1611)
PHONE..................................413 625-6351
John C Lawless, *Pr*
William S Lawless, *
▲ **EMP:** 10 **EST:** 1856
SQ FT: 28,565
SALES (est): 9.01MM
SALES (corp-wide): 9.01MM **Privately Held**
Web: www.mayhew.com
SIC: 3423   Hammers (hand tools)

(G-12453)
MONTAGUE INDUSTRIES INC
Also Called: Montague Machine Company
15 Rastallis St (01376-8901)
P.O. Box 777 (01376-0777)
PHONE..................................413 863-4301
S Jay Pierce, *CEO*
Judith A Pierce, *
Les Johnston, *
EMP: 26 **EST:** 1908
SQ FT: 52,000
SALES (est): 3.98MM **Privately Held**
Web: www.montaguemachine.com
SIC: 3599 3554   Machine shop, jobbing and
   repair; Pulp mill machinery

(G-12454)
NEFC
85 Avenue A Ste 204 (01376-1153)
PHONE..................................800 360-6332
EMP: 42 **EST:** 2017
SALES (est): 211.83K **Privately Held**
Web: www.nefc.us
SIC: 2731   Book publishing

(G-12455)
SIMONS STAMPS INC
Also Called: Simon's Stamps
320 Avenue A (01376-1826)
P.O. Box 1 (01376-0001)

PHONE..................................413 863-6800
Simon Alciere, *Pr*
EMP: 14 **EST:** 1989
SALES (est): 1.96MM **Privately Held**
Web: www.simonstamp.com
SIC: 3069 5099 5999   Hard rubber and
   molded rubber products; Rubber stamps;
   Rubber stamps

Tyngsboro
Middlesex County

(G-12456)
AXENICS INC
200 Business Park Dr # 30 (01879-1089)
PHONE..................................978 774-9393
Haywood K Schmidt, *Pr*
Chris Coutis, *
Cindy Whiteman, *
EMP: 38 **EST:** 1984
SALES (est): 6.52MM **Privately Held**
Web: www.axenics.com
SIC: 3494   Couplings, except pressure and
   soil pipe

(G-12457)
BP FLY CORPORATION (PA)
Also Called: Beacon Power
65 Middlesex Rd (01879-2041)
PHONE..................................978 649-9114
Barry R Brits, *Pr*
Matthew L Lazarewicz, *VP Engg*
Judith F Judson, *Asset Management Vice
   President*
James M Spiezio, *Sec*
EMP: 75 **EST:** 1997
SQ FT: 103,000
SALES (est): 8.75MM
SALES (corp-wide): 8.75MM **Privately
Held**
Web: www.beaconpower.com
SIC: 3612   Transformers, except electric

(G-12458)
BROADCAST PIX INC
141 Middlesex Rd Ste 1 (01879-2724)
PHONE..................................978 600-1100
Edgar Whittaker, *Ch*
Kenneth Swanton, *
Jack Swanton, *
Russell Whittaker, *
EMP: 30 **EST:** 2002
SALES (est): 4.9MM **Privately Held**
Web: www.broadcastpix.com
SIC: 3861   Motion picture apparatus and
   equipment

(G-12459)
C & C MACHINE INC
78 Progress Ave (01879-1436)
P.O. Box 490 (01879-0490)
PHONE..................................978 649-0285
Ernie Cote, *Pr*
James Cote, *
Paul Hearu, *
EMP: 29 **EST:** 1986
SQ FT: 15,000
SALES (est): 5.63MM **Privately Held**
Web: www.ccmachineusa.com
SIC: 3599   Machine shop, jobbing and repair

(G-12460)
INDUSTRIAL LBLING SYSTEMS CORP
100 Business Park Dr (01879-1071)
PHONE..................................978 649-7004
James J Blouin, *Pr*
Serhat Kotak, *VP*

▼ **EMP:** 20 **EST:** 1994
SQ FT: 10,000
SALES (est): 2.16MM **Privately Held**
Web: www.ils-barcode.com
SIC: 2396 2672 2671 Fabric printing and
  stamping; Adhesive papers, labels, or
  tapes: from purchased material; Paper;
  coated and laminated packaging

(G-12461)
METAL PROCESSING CO INC
75 Westech Dr (01879-2720)
PHONE..................................978 649-1289
Robin Perry, *Pr*
Michael J Perry, *Treas*
◆ **EMP:** 8 **EST:** 1969
SQ FT: 4,000
SALES (est): 744.2K **Privately Held**
Web: www.metproco.com
SIC: 3679 3398 Hermetic seals, for
  electronic equipment; Metal heat treating

(G-12462)
NEW ENGLAND CRANE INC
500 Potash Hill Rd Unit 1 (01879-2748)
PHONE..................................207 782-7353
EMP: 10
SALES (corp-wide): 2.18MM **Privately
Held**
Web: www.newenglandcrane.com
SIC: 3536 Hoists, cranes, and monorails
PA: New England Crane, Inc.
  70 Commercial St
  Lewiston ME 04240
  207 782-7353

(G-12463)
PICONICS INC
26 Cummings Rd (01879-1498)
PHONE..................................978 649-7501
Stephen A Slenker, *Ch Bd*
Stephen A Slenkerr, *
Marie A Slenker, *
▲ **EMP:** 45 **EST:** 1964
SQ FT: 28,000
SALES (est): 5.68MM **Privately Held**
Web: www.piconics.com
SIC: 3674 Integrated circuits,
  semiconductor networks, etc.

(G-12464)
**PRECISION TECHNOLOGIES
INC**
42 Westech Dr (01879-2720)
P.O. Box 610 (01879-0610)
PHONE..................................978 649-8715
Bryan Subsick, *CEO*
Walter Subsick, *
▲ **EMP:** 32 **EST:** 1990
SQ FT: 11,000
SALES (est): 4.99MM **Privately Held**
Web: www.precision-techno.com
SIC: 3599 Machine shop, jobbing and repair

(G-12465)
**SABIC INNOVATIVE PLAS US
LLC**
Also Called: Sabic Polymershapes
65 Middlesex Rd (01879-2041)
PHONE..................................978 772-5900
Amber Fulmer, *Brnch Mgr*
EMP: 25
Web: www.sabic.com
SIC: 2821 Plastics materials and resins
HQ: Sabic Innovative Plastics Us Llc
  2500 Citywest Blvd # 100
  Houston TX 77042

(G-12466)
SZR FUEL LLC
46 Anderson Dr (01879-2453)
PHONE..................................978 649-2409
Simon Raad, *Prin*
EMP: 7 **EST:** 2010
SALES (est): 284.36K **Privately Held**
SIC: 2869 Fuels

(G-12467)
**TESCO ASSOCIATES
INCORPORATED (PA)**
500 Business Park Dr Unit 1 (01879)
PHONE..................................978 649-5527
G Lawrence Thatcher, *Pr*
EMP: 13 **EST:** 1980
SQ FT: 4,800
SALES (est): 2.49MM
SALES (corp-wide): 2.49MM **Privately
Held**
Web: www.tescoassociates.com
SIC: 3842 Implants, surgical

(G-12468)
TOP HALF INC
15 Fairview Ave (01879-1313)
PHONE..................................978 454-5440
Anthony Gordon Junior, *Pr*
EMP: 10 **EST:** 1970
SALES (est): 893.39K **Privately Held**
Web: www.tophalf.com
SIC: 7336 5611 3953 5136 Silk screen
  design; Men's and boys' clothing stores;
  Screens, textile printing; Men's and boy's
  clothing

Upton
Worcester County

(G-12469)
ARISTOCRAT PRODUCTS INC
17 Taft St (01568-1135)
PHONE..................................626 287-4110
Paul Flaherty, *Pr*
EMP: 8 **EST:** 1948
SQ FT: 4,000
SALES (est): 574.82K **Privately Held**
Web: www.aristocratproducts.com
SIC: 2053 Pies, bakery; frozen

(G-12470)
CCO HOLDINGS LLC
9 Walker Dr (01568-1354)
PHONE..................................774 462-6577
EMP: 109
SALES (corp-wide): 54.02B **Publicly Held**
SIC: 4841 3663 3651 Cable television
  services; Radio and t.v. communications
  equipment; Household audio and video
  equipment
HQ: Cco Holdings, Llc
  400 Atlantic St
  Stamford CT 06901
  203 905-7801

(G-12471)
COOK FOREST PRODUCTS INC
Also Called: Cook Company
252 Milford St (01568-1325)
P.O. Box 1129 (01568-6129)
PHONE..................................508 634-3300
Douglas Cook, *Pr*
EMP: 22 **EST:** 1992
SQ FT: 4,000
SALES (est): 2.42MM **Privately Held**
Web: www.cookfpi.com

SIC: 2499 1629 2421 Mulch, wood and bark
  ; Land clearing contractor; Sawmills and
  planing mills, general

(G-12472)
CRAFTECH UPTON
1 Walker Dr (01568-1354)
P.O. Box 122 (01568-0122)
PHONE..................................508 529-4505
Tom Smart, *Pr*
EMP: 12 **EST:** 2016
SALES (est): 934.64K **Privately Held**
Web: www.craftechrestoration.com
SIC: 1521 3563 7217 Repairing fire
  damage, single-family houses; Vacuum (air
  extraction) systems, industrial; Carpet and
  upholstery cleaning

(G-12473)
**LIQUID SOLIDS CONTROL INC
(PA)**
10 Farm St (01568-1665)
P.O. Box 259 (01568-0259)
PHONE..................................508 529-3377
Paul Bonneau, *Pr*
Gordon Vandenburg, *VP*
EMP: 24 **EST:** 1977
SQ FT: 4,000
SALES (est): 2.45MM
SALES (corp-wide): 2.45MM **Privately
Held**
Web: www.liquidsolidscontrol.com
SIC: 5084 3823 7699 Industrial machinery
  and equipment; Refractometers, industrial
  process type; Industrial equipment services

(G-12474)
TATTERSALL MACHINING INC
190 Milford St (01568-1313)
P.O. Box 1019 (01568-6019)
PHONE..................................508 529-2300
EMP: 9 **EST:** 1989
SQ FT: 6,000
SALES (est): 388.6K **Privately Held**
Web: www.tattersallmachining.com
SIC: 3599 Machine shop, jobbing and repair

(G-12475)
**TOWN CRIER PUBLICATIONS
INC**
Also Called: Upton & Mendon Town Crier
48 Mechanic St (01568-1578)
PHONE..................................508 529-7791
EMP: 10 **EST:** 1992
SALES (est): 446.51K **Privately Held**
Web: www.standingstonedesigns.com
SIC: 2711 Newspapers, publishing and
  printing

Uxbridge
Worcester County

(G-12476)
AA WHITE COMPANY
867 Quaker Hwy Unit A (01569-2252)
PHONE..................................508 779-0821
Anna Picard, *CEO*
EMP: 9 **EST:** 1865
SQ FT: 8,000
SALES (est): 369.53K **Privately Held**
Web: www.aawhite.com
SIC: 3953 Marking devices

(G-12477)
**AR-RO ENGINEERING
COMPANY INC**
406 Pond St (01569-2053)

PHONE..................................401 766-6669
Jefferey D Cote, *Pr*
EMP: 10 **EST:** 1969
SALES (est): 862.3K **Privately Held**
SIC: 3544 3545 5085 Industrial molds; Tools
  and accessories for machine tools;
  Industrial supplies

(G-12478)
**EXTREME PROTOCOL
SOLUTIONS INC**
10 River Rd Ste 102e (01569-2259)
PHONE..................................508 278-3600
Roger Gagnon, *CEO*
Roger Gagnon, *Pr*
David Deming, *Stockholder*
Colin Carufel, *VP*
Brent Burkholder, *Sec*
EMP: 7 **EST:** 1999
SQ FT: 4,000
SALES (est): 747.36K **Privately Held**
Web: www.enterprisedataerasure.com
SIC: 7372 Prepackaged software

(G-12479)
FITNESS EM LLC
Also Called: Fitness Em
660 Douglas St (01569-2171)
P.O. Box 422 (01526-0422)
▲ **EMP:** 34 **EST:** 2001
SQ FT: 5,000
SALES (est): 4.65MM **Privately Held**
Web: www.empowerfitness.com
SIC: 3949 5091 5046 Sporting and athletic
  goods, nec; Sporting and recreation goods;
  Commercial equipment, nec

(G-12480)
HEAT-FLO INC
15 Megan Ct (01569-2272)
P.O. Box 612 (01569-0612)
PHONE..................................508 278-2400
George Celorier, *Pr*
◆ **EMP:** 8 **EST:** 1998
SALES (est): 2.52MM **Privately Held**
Web: www.heat-flo.com
SIC: 3585 7389 Heating and air conditioning
  combination units; Business services, nec

(G-12481)
**INDUSTRIAL FOUNDRY
CORPORATION**
Elmdale Rd (01569)
PHONE..................................508 278-5523
Russell Mclean, *Pr*
Keith Mc Lean, *Clerk*
Craig Mc Lean, *Stockholder*
EMP: 9 **EST:** 1961
SQ FT: 12,000
SALES (est): 989.38K **Privately Held**
SIC: 3365 3364 Aluminum foundries; Brass
  and bronze die-castings

(G-12482)
**JOSEPH P STACHURA
COMPANY INC**
435 Quaker Hwy (01569-1602)
PHONE..................................508 278-6525
Joseph P Stachura, *Pr*
▲ **EMP:** 7 **EST:** 1955
SQ FT: 2,230
SALES (est): 435.55K **Privately Held**
Web:
www.stachurawholesalegemstones.com
SIC: 5094 3915 Precious stones (gems), nec
  ; Gems, real and imitation: preparation for
  settings

(G-12483)
L W TANK REPAIR INCORPORATED
Also Called: L W Tank Repair
410 N Main St (01569-1759)
P.O. Box 308 (01538-0308)
PHONE..................................508 234-6000
Brent Wiersma, *Pr*
Leonard J Wiersma, *
Brent Wiersma, *Treas*
EMP: 25 **EST:** 1969
SQ FT: 12,500
SALES (est): 3.45MM **Privately Held**
Web: www.lwtank.com
SIC: 3731 3713 3795   Tankers, building and repairing; Tank truck bodies; Tanks and tank components

(G-12484)
LAMPIN CORPORATION (PA)
38 River Rd (01569-2245)
P.O. Box 327 (01569-0327)
PHONE..................................508 278-2422
William Dibenedetto, *CEO*
John Biagioni, *Pr*
EMP: 19 **EST:** 1982
SQ FT: 22,000
SALES (est): 3.85MM
SALES (corp-wide): 3.85MM **Privately Held**
Web: www.lampin.com
SIC: 3873 3568 3566 3599   Timers for industrial use, clockwork mechanism only; Sprockets (power transmission equipment); Speed changers, drives, and gears; Machine shop, jobbing and repair

(G-12485)
LENZE AMERICAS CORPORATION (DH)
630 Douglas St (01569-2001)
PHONE..................................508 278-9100
Ralph Rosas Iii, *Pr*
Jeffrey L Donaldson, *
David Cybulski, *
Yorc Schmidt, *
Frank Maier, *
▲ **EMP:** 29 **EST:** 2008
SALES (est): 43.47MM
SALES (corp-wide): 8.03MM **Privately Held**
SIC: 3566   Speed changers, drives, and gears
HQ: Lenze Se
   Hans-Lenze-Str. 1
   Aerzen NI 31855
   5154820

(G-12486)
MEDLINE INDUSTRIES LP
81 Campanelli Dr (01569-3168)
PHONE..................................847 949-5500
EMP: 25
SALES (corp-wide): 7.75B **Privately Held**
Web: www.medline.com
SIC: 3841   Clamps, surgical
PA: Medline Industries, Lp
   3 Lakes Dr
   Northfield IL 60093
   847 949-2645

(G-12487)
NATIONWIDE DIE CUTNG SVCS LLC
59 Tyler Dr (01569-1189)
PHONE..................................617 306-6886
David Mussi, *Prin*
EMP: 7 **EST:** 2017
SALES (est): 237.8K **Privately Held**

Web: www.nationwidedcs.com
SIC: 3599   Machine shop, jobbing and repair

(G-12488)
PRECISION ENGINEERING LLC
✪
29 Industrial Dr (01569-2273)
PHONE..................................508 278-5700
Liora K Stone, *Pr*
EMP: 50 **EST:** 2022
SALES (est): 11.29MM **Privately Held**
SIC: 3444   Sheet metal specialties, not stamped
PA: The Heico Companies L L C
   70 W Madison St Ste 5600
   Chicago IL 60602

(G-12489)
PRECISION TAPE & LABEL CO INC
322 West St (01569-2007)
P.O. Box 566 (01569-0566)
PHONE..................................508 278-7700
N Secord-voelllings, *Pr*
Nicolle Secord-voelllings, *Pr*
Deborah Secord, *VP*
EMP: 10 **EST:** 1975
SQ FT: 10,000
SALES (est): 832.84K **Privately Held**
Web: www.precisiontapeandlabel.com
SIC: 2759   Labels and seals: printing, nsk

(G-12490)
THERMAL SEAL INSULATING GL INC
47 Industrial Dr (01569-2273)
PHONE..................................508 278-4243
Ann M Oliveira, *Pr*
EMP: 10 **EST:** 1989
SQ FT: 4,000
SALES (est): 977.52K **Privately Held**
Web: www.thermalseal.net
SIC: 3211   Insulating glass, sealed units

Vineyard Haven
Dukes County

(G-12491)
MARTHAS VINEYARD FURN CO LLC
Also Called: Marthas Vineyard Intr Design
49 Main St (02568-5401)
P.O. Box 2385 (02557-2385)
PHONE..................................508 687-9555
EMP: 7 **EST:** 2007
SALES (est): 1.26MM **Privately Held**
Web: www.mvidesign.com
SIC: 5712 7389 2511 2512   Furniture stores; Interior design services; Wood household furniture; Upholstered household furniture

(G-12492)
MARTHAS VINEYARD TIMES
30 Beach Rd (02568-2601)
P.O. Box 518 (02568-0518)
PHONE..................................508 693-6100
Doug Cabral, *Pr*
EMP: 18 **EST:** 1984
SALES (est): 4.56MM **Privately Held**
Web: www.mvtimes.com
SIC: 2711   Newspapers: publishing only, not printed on site

(G-12493)
MV TIMES CORPORATION
30 Beach Rd (02568-2601)
PHONE..................................508 693-6100

Barbara I Coles, *Prin*
EMP: 15 **EST:** 2016
SALES (est): 552.56K **Privately Held**
Web: www.mvtimes.com
SIC: 2711   Newspapers: publishing only, not printed on site

(G-12494)
NORTH STAR DISTRIBUTORS INC (PA)
294 State Rd (02568-5623)
P.O. Box 10 (02539-0010)
PHONE..................................508 693-2000
Elio Silva, *CEO*
EMP: 45 **EST:** 2015
SALES (est): 4.91MM
SALES (corp-wide): 4.91MM **Privately Held**
SIC: 5411 5812 2051 5499   Grocery stores, independent; Caterers; Cakes, bakery: except frozen; Health foods

(G-12495)
TISBURY PRINTER INC
39 Lagoon Pond Rd (02568-5514)
P.O. Box 1674 (02568-0909)
PHONE..................................508 693-4222
T Christopher Decker, *Pr*
Cornelia Hubbard Decker, *Treas*
EMP: 10 **EST:** 1976
SQ FT: 2,000
SALES (est): 934.25K **Privately Held**
Web: www.tisburyprinter.com
SIC: 2752   Offset printing

Waban
Middlesex County

(G-12496)
IMBELLUS INC
672 Chestnut St (02468-2043)
PHONE..................................203 710-4667
Rebecca Kantar, *CEO*
EMP: 8 **EST:** 2015
SALES (est): 475.76K **Privately Held**
SIC: 7372   Business oriented computer software

(G-12497)
US BIOCHIPS CORP
14 Hillcrest Cir (02468-2205)
PHONE..................................617 504-5502
Robert Genco, *Pr*
EMP: 9 **EST:** 2002
SALES (est): 700K **Privately Held**
SIC: 3845   Ultrasonic scanning devices, medical

Wakefield
Middlesex County

(G-12498)
ALL-CITY SCREEN PRINTING INC
Also Called: T Stop
983 Main St (01880-3927)
PHONE..................................781 665-0000
Rod Faulkner, *Pr*
Nancy Faulkner, *Treas*
EMP: 9 **EST:** 1994
SQ FT: 4,500
SALES (est): 924.08K **Privately Held**
SIC: 2759 2395   Screen printing; Embroidery and art needlework

(G-12499)
AXIAL INDUSTRIES
27 Water St Ste 111 (01880-3038)
PHONE..................................781 224-0421
John Summers, *Mgr*
▲ **EMP:** 7 **EST:** 2005
SALES (est): 93.52K **Privately Held**
SIC: 3999   Barber and beauty shop equipment

(G-12500)
BARNARD DIE INC
Also Called: Barnard Water Jet Cutting
431 Water St Frnt (01880-3516)
PHONE..................................781 246-3117
Douglas Barnard, *Pr*
Gary Barnard, *Treas*
EMP: 10 **EST:** 1976
SQ FT: 4,200
SALES (est): 891.21K **Privately Held**
Web: www.barnarddie.com
SIC: 3544   Dies, steel rule

(G-12501)
BATTEN BROS INC
Also Called: Batten Sign
893 Main St (01880-3999)
PHONE..................................781 245-4800
TOLL FREE: 800
Richard E Batten, *Pr*
EMP: 14 **EST:** 1947
SQ FT: 8,000
SALES (est): 983.94K **Privately Held**
Web: www.battensign.com
SIC: 3993   Electric signs

(G-12502)
BLUE COW SOFTWARE LLC
19 Garden Ln (01880-2030)
PHONE..................................781 245-2583
EMP: 17
SALES (corp-wide): 279.23MM **Publicly Held**
Web: www.bluecowsoftware.com
SIC: 7372   Prepackaged software
HQ: Blue Cow Software, Llc
   35 Village Rd Ste 301
   Middleton MA 01949
   888 499-2583

(G-12503)
BOSTON ACOUSTICS INC (DH)
301 Edgewater Pl Ste 100 (01880-1281)
PHONE..................................978 538-5000
Yvonne Hao, *CEO*
Debra A Ricker, *
Dominic J Golio, *
Charles M Randall, *
David Meisels, *
◆ **EMP:** 83 **EST:** 1979
SALES (est): 31.74MM **Publicly Held**
Web: www.bostonacoustics.com
SIC: 3651   Speaker systems
HQ: Sound United, Llc
   5541 Fermi Ct
   Carlsbad CA 92008

(G-12504)
CARDIOVASCULAR INSTRUMENT CORP
Also Called: Cinco Medical
102 Foundry St (01880-3204)
P.O. Box 188 (01880-0288)
PHONE..................................781 245-7799
A Edward Urkiewicz, *Pr*
Ann Urkiewicz, *VP*
EMP: 12 **EST:** 1964
SQ FT: 20,000
SALES (est): 303.13K **Privately Held**
Web: www.cinco7799.com

SIC: **3845** Electromedical apparatus

(G-12505)
COMMTANK CARES INC
84 New Salem St (01880-1906)
PHONE..............................781 224-1021
Kevin Hoag, *Prin*
EMP: 9 **EST:** 2013
SALES (est): 190.12K **Privately Held**
Web: www.commtank.com
SIC: 1389 Lease tanks, oil field: erecting, cleaning, and repairing

(G-12506)
D S GREENE CO INC
431 Water St (01880-3516)
P.O. Box 239 (01880-0339)
PHONE..............................781 245-2644
Donald S Greene Junior, *Pr*
Helen M Greene, *Clerk*
EMP: 8 **EST:** 1952
SQ FT: 15,000
SALES (est): 778.93K **Privately Held**
Web: www.dsgreene.com
SIC: 3599 Machine shop, jobbing and repair

(G-12507)
DN TANKS INC (PA)
Also Called: Dn Tanks
11 Teal Rd (01880-1223)
PHONE..............................781 246-1133
▼ **EMP:** 61 **EST:** 2010
SALES (est): 200.6MM **Privately Held**
Web: www.dntanks.com
SIC: 3272 Tanks, concrete

(G-12508)
DN TANKS LLC
Also Called: Dn Tanks of Wyoming
11 Teal Rd (01880-1223)
PHONE..............................781 246-1133
Charles Crowley, *Prin*
Jeff Tellier, *Prin*
Willima Crowley, *Prin*
Christina Degroote, *Prin*
Michael Azarela, *Prin*
EMP: 13 **EST:** 2020
SALES (est): 2.27MM **Privately Held**
Web: www.dntanks.com
SIC: 3272 Concrete products, nec

(G-12509)
FASTCAP SYSTEMS CORPORATION (PA)
Also Called: Nanoramic Laboratories
7 Audubon Rd (01880-1256)
PHONE..............................857 403-6031
Eric Kish, *CEO*
John Cooley, *
Benton Kendig, *
Arunas Chesonis, *
Matthew Fenslau, *
EMP: 59 **EST:** 2008
SALES (est): 13.61MM **Privately Held**
Web: www.nanoramic.com
SIC: 3691 Storage batteries

(G-12510)
FITZ MACHINE INC
4 Railroad Ave Ste 5 (01880-3225)
PHONE..............................781 245-5966
Kathleen Fitzgerald, *CEO*
Edward Fitzgerald, *VP Opers*
EMP: 14 **EST:** 1994
SQ FT: 5,000
SALES (est): 2.45MM **Privately Held**
Web: www.fitzmachine.com
SIC: 3599 Machine shop, jobbing and repair

(G-12511)
HIGH VOLTAGE ENGINEERING CORP
401 Edgewater Pl Ste 680 (01880-6228)
PHONE..............................781 224-1001
Philip M Martineau, *CEO*
Laurence S Levy, *VP*
Clifford Press, *Ch Bd*
Joseph Mchugh, *VP Fin*
Charles A Schultz Junior, *CFO*
EMP: 25 **EST:** 1946
SQ FT: 5,350
SALES (est): 790.65K **Privately Held**
Web: www.highvolteng.com
SIC: 3825 3625 3826 3824 Current measuring equipment, nec; Switches, electric power; Analytical instruments; Fluid meters and counting devices

(G-12512)
HIVEC HOLDINGS INC
401 Edgewater Pl Ste 680 (01880-6228)
PHONE..............................781 224-1001
EMP: 8 **EST:** 2005
SALES (est): 154.94K **Privately Held**
SIC: 3825 Current measuring equipment, nec

(G-12513)
HUBCAST INC
500 Edgewater Dr Ste 568 (01880-6222)
P.O. Box 119 (01740-0119)
PHONE..............................877 207-6665
EMP: 25
SIC: 2759 Commercial printing, nec

(G-12514)
JG MACLELLAN
1 New Salem St (01880-1905)
PHONE..............................781 245-7756
John Maclellan, *Owner*
EMP: 8 **EST:** 2007
SALES (est): 220.96K **Privately Held**
Web: www.jgmaclellanconcrete.com
SIC: 3273 Ready-mixed concrete

(G-12515)
MAIN INDUSTRIAL TIRES LTD (PA)
107 Audubon Rd Ste 2 (01880-1245)
PHONE..............................713 676-0251
Terry Lindbergh, *Pr*
▲ **EMP:** 20 **EST:** 1992
SQ FT: 45,000
SALES (est): 16.18MM **Privately Held**
SIC: 3011 Tires and inner tubes

(G-12516)
MAINE INDUSTRIAL TIRE LLC
Also Called: Maine Industrial Tire
107 Audubon Rd Ste 2 (01880-1245)
PHONE..............................781 914-3410
▲ **EMP:** 150
SIC: 3011 Industrial tires, pneumatic

(G-12517)
MAINE RUBBER INTERNATIONAL
Also Called: Maine Tire
107 Audubon Rd Ste 2 (01880-1245)
PHONE..............................877 648-1949
Terry Lindbergh, *CEO*
Ralph Whitney Eo, *Prin*
Ken Hebert, *Treas*
EMP: 337 **EST:** 1951
SQ FT: 8,500
SALES (est): 1.87MM **Privately Held**

(G-12518)
MELETHARB INC
Also Called: Meletharb Homemade Ice Cream
393 Lowell St (01880-1962)
PHONE..............................781 245-4946
Donna Pallatino, *Pr*
EMP: 9 **EST:** 1976
SQ FT: 1,000
SALES (est): 756.65K **Privately Held**
Web: www.meletharbicecream.com
SIC: 5451 2024 Ice cream (packaged); Ice cream, bulk

(G-12519)
METAL IMPROVEMENT COMPANY LLC
Also Called: Curtiss Wright Surface Tech
1 Nablus Rd (01880-1991)
PHONE..............................781 246-3848
Kelly Hoffman, *Brnch Mgr*
EMP: 51
SALES (corp-wide): 2.56B **Publicly Held**
Web: www.curtisswright.com
SIC: 3398 Shot peening (treating steel to reduce fatigue)
HQ: Metal Improvement Company, Llc
80 E Rte 4 Ste 310
Paramus NJ 07652
201 843-7800

(G-12520)
N-ABLE INC (PA)
301 Edgewater Pl Ste 306 (01880-1281)
PHONE..............................781 328-6490
John Pagliuca, *Pr*
William Bock, *Ch Bd*
Tim O'brien, *Ex VP*
Mike Adler, *Technology*
Kathleen Pai, *CPO*
EMP: 28 **EST:** 2020
SALES (est): 371.77MM
SALES (corp-wide): 371.77MM **Publicly Held**
SIC: 7372 Prepackaged software

(G-12521)
NANORAMIC LABORATORIES
7 Audubon Rd (01880-1256)
PHONE..............................857 403-6031
EMP: 15 **EST:** 2019
SALES (est): 12.04MM **Privately Held**
Web: www.nanoramic.com
SIC: 3572 Computer storage devices

(G-12522)
NATGUN CORPORATION
11 Teal Rd (01880-1223)
PHONE..............................781 224-5180
EMP: 11
Web: www.dntanks.com
SIC: 3795 Tanks and tank components

(G-12523)
NORTHEAST PLASTICS INC
5 Del Carmine St (01880-3402)
PHONE..............................781 245-5512
Jean Leach, *Pr*
Robert Shiebler, *VP*
EMP: 19 **EST:** 1980
SQ FT: 9,000
SALES (est): 3.49MM **Privately Held**
Web: www.neplastics.com

SIC: **3089** 3544 Injection molding of plastics ; Special dies, tools, jigs, and fixtures

(G-12524)
OI SELLERS FUND LLC
607 North Ave # 12 (01880-1322)
PHONE..............................781 587-3242
Robert Cohen, *CEO*
EMP: 9 **EST:** 2016
SALES (est): 286.15K **Privately Held**
Web: www.openimplants.com
SIC: 3842 Surgical appliances and supplies

(G-12525)
OPTIKOS CORPORATION
107 Audubon Rd Ste 25 (01880-1245)
PHONE..............................617 354-7557
Stephen D Fantone, *Pr*
Stephen D Fantone, *Pr*
Elizabeth Fantone, *Care Vice President**
Daniel Orband, *
David Imrie, *
EMP: 86 **EST:** 1982
SQ FT: 8,000
SALES (est): 12.44MM **Privately Held**
Web: www.optikos.com
SIC: 3827 7372 8711 3559 Optical instruments and apparatus; Prepackaged software; Engineering services; Semiconductor manufacturing machinery

(G-12526)
PAUL K GUILLOW INC
Also Called: Guillow
40 New Salem St (01880-1979)
P.O. Box 229 (01880-0329)
PHONE..............................781 245-5255
Thomas G Barker, *Pr*
James D Conniff, *
John H Kimball Junior, *Sec*
Alson G Smith, *
▲ **EMP:** 50 **EST:** 1926
SQ FT: 65,475
SALES (est): 4.7MM **Privately Held**
Web: www.guillow.com
SIC: 3944 Airplane models, toy and hobby

(G-12527)
PERSIMMON TECHNOLOGIES CORP
Also Called: Persimmon Tech
200 Harvard Mill Sq Ste 110 (01880-3238)
PHONE..............................781 587-0677
EMP: 11 **EST:** 2010
SQ FT: 12,000
SALES (est): 5.03MM **Privately Held**
Web: www.persimmontech.com
SIC: 3569 Robots, assembly line: industrial and commercial
PA: Sumitomo Heavy Industries, Ltd.
2-1-1, Osaki
Shinagawa-Ku TKY 141-0

(G-12528)
PICIS CLINICAL SOLUTIONS INC (DH)
100 Quannapowitt Pkwy Ste 405 (01880-1319)
PHONE..............................336 397-5336
Jeff Bender, *CEO*
Steve Hammond, *
Adam Bridge, *
Jeff Harvey, *
Lee Smith, *
EMP: 180 **EST:** 1994
SQ FT: 50,000
SALES (est): 125.13MM
SALES (corp-wide): 6.62B **Privately Held**
Web: www.picis.com

SIC: 7372 7371 Prepackaged software; Computer software writing services
HQ: N. Harris Computer Corporation
1 Antares Dr Suite 100
Ottawa ON K2E 8
888 847-7747

(G-12529)
PMWEB INC
1 Pope St (01880-2179)
PHONE...............................617 207-7080
Marc Jaude, *Pr*
Chris Wagner, *
Michael Vernon, *
▲ EMP: 100 EST: 2006
SQ FT: 15,000
SALES (est): 12.52MM Privately Held
Web: www.pmweb.com
SIC: 7372 7371 Business oriented computer software; Custom computer programming services

(G-12530)
PUBLISHERS CRCLTION FLFLLMENT
Also Called: PCF
607 North Ave Ste 18-5 # 2c (01880-1322)
PHONE...............................978 671-1820
Kevin Daley, *VP*
EMP: 119
SALES (corp-wide): 58.04MM Privately Held
Web: www.pcfcorp.com
SIC: 2741 Miscellaneous publishing
PA: Publishers Circulation Fulfillment, Inc.
502 Wshington Ave Ste 500
Towson MD 21204
410 821-8614

(G-12531)
QUICK CLEAN CAR WASH SYSTEMS I (PA)
590 Main St (01880-3350)
P.O. Box 428 (01876-0428)
PHONE...............................781 245-6809
William Mackenzie, *CEO*
Gary Mackenzie, *Pr*
William D Mackenzie, *Pr*
EMP: 12 EST: 1973
SQ FT: 7,500
SALES (est): 1.34MM
SALES (corp-wide): 1.34MM Privately Held
Web: www.quickandclean.com
SIC: 7542 5541 3993 Carwash, automatic; Gasoline service stations; Signs, not made in custom sign painting shops

(G-12532)
SBE VISION INC
1 Albion St Ste 1 (01880-2817)
PHONE...............................612 237-0128
Robert Nierman, *CEO*
Gian Picone, *CFO*
EMP: 14 EST: 2011
SQ FT: 3,000
SALES (est): 1.04MM Privately Held
Web: www.sbe-vision.com
SIC: 7372 Prepackaged software

(G-12533)
SDL XYENTERPRISE LLC (PA)
Also Called: Xyenterprise Henrico Co
201 Edgewater Dr Ste 225 (01880-6216)
PHONE...............................781 756-4400
Dominic Lavelle, *CEO*
Lori Brittain, *
Kevin Keating, *
EMP: 40 EST: 1998
SQ FT: 20,000

SALES (est): 8.43MM
SALES (corp-wide): 8.43MM Privately Held
SIC: 7378 7371 7372 Computer maintenance and repair; Computer software development and applications; Prepackaged software

(G-12534)
SEMIGEAR INC
107 Audubon Rd Ste 2 (01880-1245)
PHONE...............................781 213-3066
Chungslin Lee, *CEO*
Jian Zhang, *Pr*
▲ EMP: 20 EST: 2000
SQ FT: 5,500
SALES (est): 13.49MM Privately Held
Web: www.semigear.com
SIC: 5065 3674 Semiconductor devices; Semiconductors and related devices
PA: Psk Holdings Inc.
48 Samsung 1-Ro 4-Gil
Hwaseong 18449

(G-12535)
SHELMAR INC
Also Called: Banner Glass Shelmar
187 Water St (01880-2527)
P.O. Box 315 (01880-0615)
PHONE...............................781 245-1206
Lawrence Rosenfield, *Pr*
EMP: 14 EST: 1957
SQ FT: 14,000
SALES (est): 659.26K Privately Held
Web: www.bannerglassshelmar.com
SIC: 5211 3442 3431 3231 Windows, storm; wood or metal; Metal doors, sash, and trim; Bathroom fixtures, including sinks; Products of purchased glass

(G-12536)
ST ASSOCIATES INC
1 Teal Rd (01880-1223)
P.O. Box 534 (01880-4534)
EMP: 34 EST: 1967
SALES (est): 4.98MM Privately Held
Web: www.stassoc.com
SIC: 2741 2791 8742 7336 Technical papers: publishing and printing; Typographic composition, for the printing trade; Marketing consulting services; Commercial art and graphic design

(G-12537)
STANDEX INTERNATIONAL CORP
Innovent Standex Engrv Group
107 Audubon Rd Ste 20 (01880-1245)
PHONE...............................978 538-0808
Casper Prong, *Brnch Mgr*
EMP: 74
SALES (corp-wide): 741.05MM Publicly Held
Web: www.standex.com
SIC: 3545 Machine tool accessories
PA: Standex International Corporation
23 Keewaydin Dr Ste 205
Salem NH 03079
603 893-9701

(G-12538)
STREETSCAN INC
605 Salem St (01880-1227)
P.O. Box 2 (01803-0002)
PHONE...............................617 399-8236
Ralf Birken, *CEO*
EMP: 20 EST: 2015
SALES (est): 1.56MM Privately Held
Web: www.streetscan.com

SIC: 7372 7389 Application computer software; Mapmaking services

(G-12539)
THE WAKEFIELD CORPORATION
29 Foundry St (01880-3200)
P.O. Box 151 (01880-0351)
PHONE...............................781 587-1925
EMP: 33 EST: 1904
SALES (est): 2.92MM Privately Held
Web: www.wakefieldhospice.org
SIC: 3469 Machine parts, stamped or pressed metal

(G-12540)
TTS MEXICAN HOLDING COMPANY
401 Edgewater Pl Ste 680 (01880-6228)
PHONE...............................781 224-1001
EMP: 8 EST: 2005
SALES (est): 94.6K Privately Held
SIC: 3825 Current measuring equipment, nec

(G-12541)
VICTOR MICROWAVE INC
38 W Water St (01880-2999)
PHONE...............................781 245-4472
Robert Parks, *Pr*
EMP: 23 EST: 1954
SQ FT: 16,000
SALES (est): 1.05MM Privately Held
Web: www.victormicrowave.com
SIC: 3679 3825 3663 Microwave components; Microwave test equipment; Microwave communication equipment

(G-12542)
WAKEFIELD ITEM COMPANY
Also Called: Wakefield Daily Item
26 Albion St (01880-2803)
PHONE...............................781 245-0080
Robert P Dolbeare, *Pr*
◆ EMP: 23 EST: 1922
SQ FT: 4,000
SALES (est): 975.69K Privately Held
Web: www.localheadlinenews.com
SIC: 2711 2752 Job printing and newspaper publishing combined; Commercial printing, lithographic

(G-12543)
WILLIAM BLANCHARD CO INC
Also Called: Blanchard Awnings
486 Main St (01880-3320)
PHONE...............................781 245-8050
Allen Young, *Pr*
Colin Young, *Treas*
Thomas Young, *Clerk*
EMP: 10 EST: 1915
SQ FT: 6,000
SALES (est): 504.61K Privately Held
Web: www.wmblanchardco.com
SIC: 2394 Awnings, fabric: made from purchased materials

(G-12544)
YOKOHAMA TWS NORTH AMERICA INC
Also Called: Gpx International
107 Audubon Rd Ste 205 (01880-1245)
PHONE...............................781 914-3410
Michael Lewis, *Mgr*
EMP: 8
SALES (corp-wide): 4.26B Privately Held
SIC: 3714 Wheel rims, motor vehicle
HQ: Yokohama Tws North America, Inc.
1501 Exeter Rd
Akron OH 44306

Walpole
Norfolk County

(G-12545)
2IS INC
75 West St (02081-1847)
PHONE...............................508 850-7520
Gary Burchill, *CEO*
Glenn D House, *Senior President*
EMP: 33 EST: 2002
SQ FT: 13,000
SALES (est): 4.37MM Privately Held
Web: www.northropgrumman.com
SIC: 7371 3452 3462 3728 Custom computer programming services; Bolts, nuts, rivets, and washers; Iron and steel forgings; Aircraft parts and equipment, nec

(G-12546)
ACUMENTRICS RUPS LLC
10 Walpole Park S (02081-2523)
PHONE...............................617 932-7877
EMP: 30 EST: 2009
SALES (est): 5.41MM Privately Held
Web: www.acumentrics.com
SIC: 3571 7389 Electronic computers; Air pollution measuring service

(G-12547)
ADLIFE ADVERTISING & GRAPHICS
Also Called: Adlife
470 High Plain St (02081-4250)
PHONE...............................508 668-4109
Eugene Hayward Junior, *Pr*
EMP: 10 EST: 1989
SQ FT: 3,200
SALES (est): 1.43MM Privately Held
SIC: 7311 2752 Advertising consultant; Offset printing

(G-12548)
AINSLIE CORPORATION
88 Peach St (02081-3404)
PHONE...............................781 848-0850
Eric C Sandquist, *Pr*
EMP: 9 EST: 1954
SQ FT: 80,000
SALES (est): 185.94K Privately Held
SIC: 3599 3679 3677 3469 Machine shop, jobbing and repair; Waveguides and fittings ; Filtration devices, electronic; Spinning metal for the trade

(G-12549)
ALADDIN MANUFACTURING CORP
15 Walpole Park S (02081-2560)
PHONE...............................508 660-8913
Joe Blanchard, *Pr*
EMP: 285
Web: www.mohawkind.com
SIC: 2273 Carpets and rugs
HQ: Aladdin Manufacturing Corporation
160 S Industrial Blvd
Calhoun GA 30701
706 629-7721

(G-12550)
ALLEGIANCE FIRE & RESCUE LLC
2181 Providence Hwy (02081-2528)
PHONE...............................800 225-4808
Bill O'connor, *VP*
EMP: 11 EST: 2020
SALES (est): 79.8K Privately Held

G E O G R A P H I C

SIC: **3711**　Fire department vehicles (motor vehicles), assembly of

(G-12551)
ATREX ENERGY INC (PA)
19 Walpole Park S (02081-2570)
PHONE.............................781 461-8251
▲ **EMP:** 42 **EST:** 1994
SQ FT: 40,000
SALES (est): 12.88MM **Privately Held**
Web: www.atrexenergy.com
SIC: **3629** 3612 7372 3677　Power conversion units, a.c. to d.c.: static-electric; Transformers, except electric; Utility computer software; Filtration devices, electronic

(G-12552)
BAKER HUGHES HOLDINGS LLC
1600 Providence Hwy Ste 4 (02081-2551)
PHONE.............................508 668-0400
Tim Davis, *Brnch Mgr*
EMP: 210
SALES (corp-wide): 25.51B **Publicly Held**
Web: www.bhge.com
SIC: **1389**　Oil field services, nec
HQ: Baker Hughes Holdings Llc
　17021 Aldine Westfield Rd
　Houston TX 77073
　713 439-8600

(G-12553)
BOSTON TRAILER MANUFACTURING
1 Production Rd (02081-1310)
PHONE.............................508 668-2242
Roland A Garrant, *Pr*
Rocco Taddeo, *
EMP: 10 **EST:** 1945
SQ FT: 16,000
SALES (est): 416.17K **Privately Held**
SIC: **3715** 7539 7538 3792　Truck trailers; Trailer repair; General truck repair; Travel trailers and campers

(G-12554)
CAPSTAN ATLANTIC
24 Walpole Park S (02081-2541)
PHONE.............................508 660-6001
EMP: 7 **EST:** 2019
SALES (est): 329.91K **Privately Held**
Web: www.capstanatlantic.com
SIC: **3599**　Machine shop, jobbing and repair

(G-12555)
CASTLE GATE INVSTMNTS LTD LBLT
36 Carl Rd (02081-1106)
PHONE.............................617 596-1126
EMP: 8 **EST:** 2018
SALES (est): 358.4K **Privately Held**
SIC: **1041**　Gold ores mining

(G-12556)
CNE MACHINE INC
2000 Main St Ste 4 (02081-1426)
PHONE.............................508 668-4110
Desmond Quinn, *Owner*
EMP: 8 **EST:** 2005
SALES (est): 265.24K **Privately Held**
Web: www.cnemachine.com
SIC: **3599**　Machine shop, jobbing and repair

(G-12557)
CONSUMER HEARING CONS INC
869 Main St Ste 7 (02081-2985)
PHONE.............................866 658-8800
Don Gross, *Mgr*
EMP: 8 **EST:** 1990

SALES (est): 94.85K **Privately Held**
SIC: **3842**　Surgical appliances and supplies

(G-12558)
COUNTRYWIDE NATIONAL SERVICES
220 Norfolk St (02081-1797)
PHONE.............................508 346-3286
EMP: 8 **EST:** 2018
SALES (est): 342.69K **Privately Held**
SIC: **3089** 3315　Fiberglass doors; Fencing made in wiredrawing plants

(G-12559)
GOLD WATER TECHNOLOGY INC
25 Walpole Park S (02081-2522)
P.O. Box 827 (02090-0827)
PHONE.............................781 551-3590
Judy Lo, *Pr*
Frank Lo, *Prd Mgr*
EMP: 9 **EST:** 1992
SALES (est): 700.14K **Privately Held**
Web: www.goldwaterlawfirm.com
SIC: **3944**　Electronic toys

(G-12560)
HEALTHY TRUTH LLC
Also Called: Healthy Truth
87 West St (02081-1874)
PHONE.............................774 256-5800
Bruce Namenson, *Managing Member*
Craig Singer, *Managing Member*
Edmond Poli Iii, *Managing Member*
▲ **EMP:** 20 **EST:** 2013
SQ FT: 12,000
SALES (est): 4.13MM **Privately Held**
Web: www.healthytruth.com
SIC: **5149** 2099　Health foods; Almond pastes

(G-12561)
INKIFY LLC
25 Walpole Park S Ste 8 (02081-2522)
PHONE.............................617 304-6642
Carlos A Lobato, *Prin*
EMP: 10 **EST:** 2016
SALES (est): 409.73K **Privately Held**
Web: www.inkify.com
SIC: **2759**　Screen printing

(G-12562)
INTELLIGENT NETWORK SALES LLC
689 Main St (02081-3717)
PHONE.............................508 446-3646
Stephen Chase, *Prin*
EMP: 11 **EST:** 2010
SALES (est): 570.1K **Privately Held**
Web: www.intelligentnetworksales.com
SIC: **3861**　Photographic equipment and supplies

(G-12563)
INTERNATIONAL FOOD PDTS INC
Also Called: Sabra Foods
454 High Plain St (02081-4250)
PHONE.............................617 594-5955
Pierre Saroufim, *Pr*
Dorothy Saroufim, *Stockholder*
EMP: 7 **EST:** 1998
SQ FT: 5,000
SALES (est): 936.93K **Privately Held**
Web: www.sabrafoods.com
SIC: **2099**　Salads, fresh or refrigerated

(G-12564)
ISLAND OASIS FRZ COCKTAIL INC (HQ)
Also Called: Island Oasis
141 Norfolk St (02081-1765)
P.O. Box 769 (02081-0769)
PHONE.............................508 660-1177
TOLL FREE: 800
J Michael Herbert, *CEO*
Scott A Kumf, *
Christine Guzzi, *
◆ **EMP:** 90 **EST:** 1983
SQ FT: 20,000
SALES (est): 50.65MM **Privately Held**
Web: www.kerryfoodservice.com
SIC: **2099**　Food preparations, nec
PA: Kerry Group Public Limited Company
　Princes Street
　Tralee V92 E

(G-12565)
J & M CABINET SHOP INC
2050 Main St (02081-1413)
PHONE.............................508 660-6660
Morton Balduf, *Pr*
Paul G Patterson, *VP*
EMP: 9 **EST:** 1974
SQ FT: 8,000
SALES (est): 301.99K **Privately Held**
Web: www.creativecabinet.net
SIC: **2434**　Wood kitchen cabinets

(G-12566)
MASS MACHINE INC
24 Walpole Park S Ste 14 (02081-2541)
PHONE.............................781 467-3550
Peter Watson, *Pr*
EMP: 14 **EST:** 2009
SQ FT: 8,000
SALES (est): 1.08MM **Privately Held**
Web: www.massmachine.com
SIC: **3599**　Machine shop, jobbing and repair

(G-12567)
MASSACHUSETTS MCH WORKS INC
24 Walpole Park S Ste 14 (02081-2541)
PHONE.............................781 467-3550
Leroy Seamore, *Pr*
EMP: 16 **EST:** 1977
SALES (est): 520.24K **Privately Held**
SIC: **3599**　Machine shop, jobbing and repair

(G-12568)
MEDICAL MANAGER PCN INC
Also Called: Solion
100 Elm St (02081-1933)
P.O. Box 11348 (02211-0001)
PHONE.............................508 850-3500
Wendy Coutu, *Pr*
EMP: 13 **EST:** 1994
SQ FT: 5,400
SALES (est): 264.95K **Privately Held**
SIC: **5112** 2759 5045 5111　Business forms; Commercial printing, nec; Computers, peripherals, and software; Printing and writing paper

(G-12569)
MICREX CORPORATION
17 Industrial Rd (02081-1304)
PHONE.............................508 660-1900
Richard C Walton, *Ch Bd*
Peter Smith, *VP*
Susan Olsen Ms, *Sec*
▲ **EMP:** 16 **EST:** 1987
SQ FT: 20,000
SALES (est): 2.25MM **Privately Held**
Web: www.micrex.com

SIC: **3554** 3552　Paper industries machinery; Fabric forming machinery and equipment

(G-12570)
NORTH AMRCN FLTRATION MASS INC
Also Called: Mass Transfer Systems
23 Walpole Park S Ste 12 (02081-2559)
PHONE.............................508 660-9016
Dave Painter, *Pr*
Steven Friedman, *VP*
◆ **EMP:** 16 **EST:** 1997
SQ FT: 20,000
SALES (est): 5.69MM **Privately Held**
Web: www.sanborntechnologies.com
SIC: **3589**　Water treatment equipment, industrial
PA: North American Filtration Inc
　Old Augusta Rd Hwy 70
　Denmark SC 29042

(G-12571)
NORTHEAST BUFFINTON GROUP INC
25 Woodruff Rd (02081-3915)
PHONE.............................401 434-1107
Leo Cesareo, *Pr*
Julia Cesareo, *VP*
EMP: 18 **EST:** 1878
SALES (est): 859.82K **Privately Held**
Web: www.buff-mailers.com
SIC: **2657**　Folding paperboard boxes

(G-12572)
PARKER & BAILEY CORP
4 Walpole Park S Ste 2 (02081-2562)
PHONE.............................508 660-0011
Andrew Schultz, *Pr*
William Schultz, *VP*
EMP: 10 **EST:** 2008
SQ FT: 20,000
SALES (est): 2.46MM **Privately Held**
Web: www.parkerbailey.com
SIC: **5169** 2842　Polishes, nec; Cleaning or polishing preparations, nec

(G-12573)
RF VENUE INC
24 Walpole Park S Ste 1 (02081-2541)
PHONE.............................800 795-0817
Christopher Regan, *Pr*
Robert J Crowley, *Treas*
EMP: 7 **EST:** 2014
SQ FT: 25,000
SALES (est): 1.03MM **Privately Held**
Web: www.rfvenue.com
SIC: **3651**　Audio electronic systems

(G-12574)
ROLLS-ROYCE MARINE NORTH AMER (DH)
110 Norfolk St (02081-1704)
PHONE.............................508 668-9610
Don Roussinos, *Pr*
Mary S Sullivan, *
◆ **EMP:** 150 **EST:** 1958
SQ FT: 18,000
SALES (est): 91.11MM
SALES (corp-wide): 16.28B **Privately Held**
Web: www.rolls-royce.com
SIC: **3599** 3446 3429　Propellers, ship and boat: machined; Acoustical suspension systems, metal; Hardware, nec
HQ: Rolls-Royce North America Holdings Inc.
　1900 Reston Metro Plz # 4
　Reston VA 20190
　703 834-1700

(G-12575)
S M LORUSSO & SONS INC (PA)
Also Called: Wrentham Quarry Div
331 West St (02081-1608)
P.O. Box 230 (02081-0230)
PHONE...................................508 668-2600
Antonio J Lorusso Junior, *Pr*
James Lorusso, *
Steve Stafford, *
Joseph Stafford, *
Samuel Lorusso, *
EMP: 30 **EST:** 1938
SQ FT: 4,400
SALES (est): 22.19MM
SALES (corp-wide): 22.19MM **Privately Held**
SIC: 1442 Construction sand mining

(G-12576)
STAN RUBINSTEIN ASSOCIATES INC
24 Walpole Park S Ste 10 (02081-2541)
PHONE...................................508 668-6044
Randy Rubinstein, *Pr*
Eleanor Rubinstein, *Treas*
▲ **EMP:** 15 **EST:** 1962
SQ FT: 15,000
SALES (est): 4.26MM **Privately Held**
Web: www.sra-solder.com
SIC: 5084 3548 3423 Welding machinery and equipment; Welding and cutting apparatus and accessories, nec; Soldering tools

(G-12577)
TOOLING RESEARCH INC
Also Called: Valcom Division
P.O. Box 306 (02081-0306)
PHONE...................................508 668-5583
Stephanie Lopez, *Sec*
EMP: 12
SALES (corp-wide): 2.44MM **Privately Held**
Web: www.tooling-research.com
SIC: 3592 Valves
PA: Tooling Research, Inc.
   81 Diamond St
   Walpole MA 02081
   508 668-1950

(G-12578)
TOOLING RESEARCH INC (PA)
Also Called: Valcom Division
81 Diamond St (02081-3495)
P.O. Box 306 (02081-0306)
PHONE...................................508 668-1950
Milton F Florest, *Pr*
Milton F Florest Junior, *Pr*
Ann E Florest, *VP*
EMP: 12 **EST:** 1983
SQ FT: 15,000
SALES (est): 2.44MM
SALES (corp-wide): 2.44MM **Privately Held**
Web: www.tooling-research.com
SIC: 3555 3565 Printing trades machinery; Packing and wrapping machinery

(G-12579)
ZEA BIOSCIENCES CORP
85 West St Ste 3 (02081-1844)
PHONE...................................508 921-3280
James G Wilson, *CEO*
EMP: 10 **EST:** 2014
SQ FT: 16,000
SALES (est): 1.58MM **Privately Held**
Web: www.zeabio.com
SIC: 2836 Biological products, except diagnostic

Waltham
Middlesex County

(G-12580)
A123 SYSTEMS LLC
200 West St (02451-1121)
PHONE...................................617 778-5700
Kevin Barnett Attorney, *Brnch Mgr*
EMP: 108
Web: www.a123systems.com
SIC: 3691 5063 Storage batteries; Batteries
HQ: A123 Systems Llc
   27101 Cabaret Dr
   Novi MI 48377
   248 412-9249

(G-12581)
ACKLES STEEL AND IRON CO INC
12 Sun St (02453-4102)
P.O. Box 540363 (02454-0363)
PHONE...................................781 893-6818
William Ackles, *Pr*
William P Ackles, *VP*
Richard Ackles, *VP*
Andrew Ackles, *VP*
EMP: 16 **EST:** 1961
SQ FT: 5,500
SALES (est): 1.94MM **Privately Held**
Web: www.acklessteel.com
SIC: 3312 2431 Structural shapes and pilings, steel; Staircases, stairs and railings

(G-12582)
ACTON METAL PROCESSING CORP
41 Athletic Field Rd (02451-4617)
P.O. Box 540671 (02454-0671)
PHONE...................................781 893-5890
Ruppert Flagg, *Pr*
Ruppert Flagg, *Pr*
Todd Walsh, *
EMP: 19 **EST:** 1960
SQ FT: 15,400
SALES (est): 448.46K **Privately Held**
Web: www.actonmetal.com
SIC: 3471 Electroplating of metals or formed products

(G-12583)
ACTRONICS INCORPORATED
166 Bear Hill Rd (02451-1073)
PHONE...................................781 890-7030
Paul Boudreau, *VP*
EMP: 13 **EST:** 1963
SQ FT: 10,000
SALES (est): 2.49MM **Privately Held**
Web: www.actronics.com
SIC: 3724 3728 Aircraft engines and engine parts; Aircraft parts and equipment, nec

(G-12584)
ADNEXUS THERAPEUTICS INC
100 Beaver St (02453-8400)
PHONE...................................781 891-3745
John Mendlein, *CEO*
Frank D Lee, *
Sonia Vora, *
Jeffrey Galik, *
David T Bonk, *
EMP: 30 **EST:** 2002
SALES (est): 14.06MM
SALES (corp-wide): 45.01B **Publicly Held**
SIC: 2834 Pharmaceutical preparations
PA: Bristol-Myers Squibb Company
   430 E 29th St Fl 14
   New York NY 10016
   212 546-4000

(G-12585)
ADOBE INC
1075 Main St (02451-7464)
PHONE...................................408 536-6000
Shantanu Narayen, *CEO*
EMP: 600
SALES (corp-wide): 19.41B **Publicly Held**
Web: www.adobe.com
SIC: 7372 Prepackaged software
PA: Adobe Inc.
   345 Park Ave
   San Jose CA 95110
   408 536-6000

(G-12586)
AERO-SPACE FABRICATORS INC
116 Harvard St (02453-4197)
P.O. Box 540574 (02454-0574)
PHONE...................................781 899-4535
Raymond T Richard, *Pr*
Mark Richard, *VP*
Concetta Richard, *Clerk*
EMP: 8 **EST:** 1965
SQ FT: 6,500
SALES (est): 979.17K **Privately Held**
Web: www.aerospacefabricators.com
SIC: 3444 Sheet metal specialties, not stamped

(G-12587)
ALERE INC (HQ)
51 Sawyer Rd Ste 200 (02453-3448)
PHONE...................................781 647-3900
Christopher Scoggins, *Pr*
▲ **EMP:** 625 **EST:** 1981
SALES (est): 1.5B
SALES (corp-wide): 43.65B **Publicly Held**
Web: www.globalpointofcare.abbott
SIC: 8071 8742 2835 Medical laboratories; Hospital and health services consultant; In vitro diagnostics
PA: Abbott Laboratories
   100 Abbott Park Rd
   Abbott Park IL 60064
   224 667-6100

(G-12588)
ALERE US HOLDINGS LLC
51 Sawyer Rd Ste 200 (02453-3448)
PHONE...................................781 647-3900
EMP: 16 **EST:** 2011
SALES (est): 9.31MM
SALES (corp-wide): 43.65B **Publicly Held**
SIC: 2835 Diagnostic substances
HQ: Alere Inc.
   51 Sawyer Rd Ste 200
   Waltham MA 02453
   781 647-3900

(G-12589)
ALKERMES INC (HQ)
900 Winter St (02451-1449)
PHONE...................................781 609-6000
Richard Pops, *CEO*
Kathryn L Biberstein Senior V Pres Govrelations Public Policy, *Prin*
Gordon G Pugh, *Chief Risk Officer**
Elliot W Ehrich, *Senior Vice President Research & Development**
Anne Giovanoni, *
▲ **EMP:** 42 **EST:** 1987
SALES (est): 418.11MM **Privately Held**
Web: www.alkermes.com
SIC: 2834 8731 Pharmaceutical preparations; Biotechnical research, commercial
PA: Alkermes Public Limited Company
   Connacht House
   Dublin D04 C

(G-12590)
ALKERMES CNTRLLED THERAPEUTICS
Also Called: Acti
852 Winter St (02451-1420)
PHONE...................................877 706-0510
Richard F Pops, *CEO*
Michael A Wall, *Ch Bd*
David Broecker, *Pr*
James M Frates, *VP*
EMP: 283 **EST:** 1987
SQ FT: 90,000
SALES (est): 25.37MM **Privately Held**
Web: www.alkermes.com
SIC: 2834 Pharmaceutical preparations
HQ: Alkermes, Inc.
   900 Winter St
   Waltham MA 02451
   781 609-6000

(G-12591)
ALLOVIR INC (PA)
Also Called: Allovir
1100 Winter St (02451-1427)
PHONE...................................617 433-2605
David Hallal, *Ch Bd*
Vikas Sinha, *Pr*
Ann Leen, *CSO*
Jeroen Van Beek, *CCO*
Brett Hagen, *CAO*
EMP: 19 **EST:** 2013
SQ FT: 2,879
Web: www.allovir.com
SIC: 2836 Biological products, except diagnostic

(G-12592)
APELLIS PHARMACEUTICALS INC (PA)
Also Called: Apellis
100 5th Ave Fl 3 (02451-8727)
PHONE...................................617 977-5700
EMP: 303 **EST:** 2009
SQ FT: 77,818
SALES (est): 75.42MM **Publicly Held**
Web: www.apellis.com
SIC: 2834 Pharmaceutical preparations

(G-12593)
APOGENT HOLDING COMPANY (HQ)
81 Wyman St (02451-1223)
PHONE...................................781 622-1300
Seth H Hoogasian, *Pr*
Anthony H Smith, *Treas*
EMP: 17 **EST:** 2003
SALES (est): 2.09MM
SALES (corp-wide): 44.91B **Publicly Held**
SIC: 3826 Analytical instruments
PA: Thermo Fisher Scientific Inc.
   168 3rd Ave
   Waltham MA 02451
   781 622-1000

(G-12594)
APOGENT TECHNOLOGIES INC
81 Wyman St (02451-1223)
PHONE...................................781 622-1300
Seth H Hoogasian, *Pr*
Anthony Smith, *
EMP: 7200 **EST:** 1987
SALES (est): 207.91MM
SALES (corp-wide): 44.91B **Publicly Held**
SIC: 3229 3843 3821 Scientific glassware; Dental equipment and supplies; Laboratory heating apparatus
HQ: Fisher Scientific International Llc
   81 Wyman St
   Waltham MA 02451

GEOGRAPHIC

(G-12595)
ARDELYX INC
Also Called: Ardelyx
400 5th Ave Ste 210 (02451-8706)
PHONE.................................510 745-1700
Michael Raab, *Pr*
David Mott, *
Justin Renz, *CFO*
Elizabeth Grammer, *Legal*
Robert Blanks, *Regulatory Affairs*
EMP: 86 **EST:** 2007
SQ FT: 12,864
SALES (est): 52.16MM **Privately Held**
Web: www.ardelyx.com
SIC: 2834 8731 Pharmaceutical
preparations; Biotechnical research,
commercial

(G-12596)
ARM INC
100 5th Ave Fl 5 (02451-8727)
PHONE.................................978 264-7300
EMP: 480
SALES (corp-wide): 11.15B **Privately Held**
Web: www.arm.com
SIC: 3674 Semiconductors and related
devices
HQ: Arm, Inc.
120 Rose Orchard Way
San Jose CA 95134

(G-12597)
ATLAS WATER SYSTEMS INC
301 2nd Ave (02451-1122)
PHONE.................................781 373-4700
TOLL FREE: 800
Simon O'leary, *Pr*
Norm Marowitz, *
Cindy Mealy, *
Michael Mccready, *VP*
Mark J St Hilaire, *
▲ **EMP:** 62 **EST:** 1988
SQ FT: 10,000
SALES (est): 22.3MM **Privately Held**
Web: www.h2ocare.com
SIC: 5999 1711 3589 5074 Water
purification equipment; Plumbing
contractors; Water filters and softeners,
household type; Water purification
equipment
HQ: Quench Usa, Inc.
630 Allendale Rd Ste 200
King Of Prussia PA 19406
888 554-2782

(G-12598)
AUTOMEC INC
82 Calvary St (02453-5918)
PHONE.................................781 893-3403
James Ofria, *Pr*
Linda Jones, *Treas*
◆ **EMP:** 24 **EST:** 1971
SALES (est): 3.31MM **Privately Held**
Web: www.automec.com
SIC: 3549 3545 Assembly machines,
including robotic; Machine tool accessories

(G-12599)
AVAVA INC (PA)
275 Second Ave Ste 3 (02451-1159)
PHONE.................................617 912-2680
Jenifer Perry, *Prin*
EMP: 8 **EST:** 2019
SALES (est): 532.06K
SALES (corp-wide): 532.06K **Privately
Held**
Web: www.avavaaesthetics.com
SIC: 2844 Cosmetic preparations

(G-12600)
B456 SYSTEMS INC
200 West St (02451-1121)
PHONE.................................617 778-5700
▲ **EMP:** 1983
SIC: 3691 Storage batteries

(G-12601)
BATTERY VENTURES VI LP
930 Winter St Ste 2500 (02451-1516)
PHONE.................................781 577-1000
Neeraj Agrawal, *Genl Pt*
Michael Brown, *Genl Pt*
Tom Crotty, *Genl Pt*
Sunil Dhaliwal, *Genl Pt*
Cornel Faucher, *Pt*
EMP: 19 **EST:** 1983
SALES (est): 1.92MM **Privately Held**
SIC: 7372 Prepackaged software

(G-12602)
**BBC PRINTING AND PRODUCTS
INC**
21 Hill Rd (02451-1715)
PHONE.................................781 647-4646
Vasken Basmajian, *Pr*
Sheila Basmajian, *Clerk*
EMP: 8 **EST:** 1971
SQ FT: 22,000
SALES (est): 987.04K **Privately Held**
Web: www.bbcprintingproducts.com
SIC: 2679 2759 2752 Paperboard products,
converted, nec; Menus: printing, nsk;
Commercial printing, lithographic

(G-12603)
BEAVER GROUP LLC
411 Waverley Oaks Rd (02452-8448)
PHONE.................................781 647-5775
EMP: 9 **EST:** 1998
SALES (est): 994.43K **Privately Held**
SIC: 3841 Surgical and medical instruments

(G-12604)
BEAVER-VISITEC INTL INC
500 Totten Pond Rd 10 City Pt
(02451-1916)
PHONE.................................781 906-8080
Shevin Korangy, *Pr*
Shervin Korangy, *CSO*
David Murray, *CFO*
▲ **EMP:** 10 **EST:** 1932
SQ FT: 63,000
SALES (est): 8.23MM
SALES (corp-wide): 2.96B **Publicly Held**
Web: www.bvimedical.com
SIC: 3841 3851 Surgical knife blades and
handles; Ophthalmic goods
HQ: Tpg Capital Management, L.P.
301 Commerce St Ste 3300
Fort Worth TX 76102

(G-12605)
BIGTINCAN MOBILE PTY LTD
260 Charles St Ste 101 (02453-3529)
PHONE.................................617 981-7557
Patrick Welch, *CMO*
EMP: 9
Web: www.bigtincan.com
SIC: 7372 Prepackaged software
HQ: Bigtincan Mobile Pty Ltd
Level 8 320 Pitt Street
Sydney NSW 2000

(G-12606)
BIOCYTOGEN BOSTON CORP
300 3rd Ave Fl 6 (02451-7525)
PHONE.................................781 587-3558
Yuelei Shen, *CEO*
EMP: 62 **EST:** 2018
SALES (est): 12.22MM **Privately Held**
Web: www.biocytogen.com
SIC: 2834 Pharmaceutical preparations
PA: Biocytogen Pharmaceuticals (Beijing)
Co., Ltd.
No.12 Courtyard, South Street,
Baocan, Daxing Biomedical Industr
Beijing BJ 10262

(G-12607)
BIOVERATIV INC (HQ)
225 2nd Ave (02451-1122)
PHONE.................................781 663-4400
Olivier Brandicourt, *CEO*
EMP: 66 **EST:** 2016
SQ FT: 125,000
SALES (est): 353.94MM **Privately Held**
Web: www.bioverativ.com
SIC: 2834 Pharmaceutical preparations
PA: Sanofi
46 Avenue De La Grande Armee
Paris 75017

(G-12608)
**BIOVERATIV THERAPEUTICS
INC (DH)**
225 2nd Ave (02451-1122)
PHONE.................................781 663-4400
John G Cox, *CEO*
Garen Bohlin, *
Alan Bitonti, *
EMP: 25 **EST:** 1997
SALES (est): 27.45MM **Privately Held**
SIC: 2834 Pharmaceutical preparations
HQ: Bioverativ Inc.
225 Second Ave
Waltham MA 02451
781 663-4400

(G-12609)
BLUESNAP INC (PA)
800 South St Ste 640 (02453-1492)
PHONE.................................781 790-5013
EMP: 25 **EST:** 2002
SQ FT: 7,000
SALES (est): 41.24MM **Privately Held**
Web: www.bluesnap.com
SIC: 7372 Business oriented computer
software

(G-12610)
BOSTONMOLECULES INC
204 2nd Ave Ste 1 (02451-1126)
PHONE.................................617 651-1016
Ting Fu, *CEO*
EMP: 10 **EST:** 2016
SALES (est): 817.8K **Privately Held**
Web: www.bostonmolecules.com
SIC: 8731 2835 Biotechnical research,
commercial; In vitro diagnostics

(G-12611)
**BOYNTON MACHINE COMPANY
INC**
101 Clematis Ave Ste 6 (02453-7035)
PHONE.................................781 899-9900
Mark Boynton, *Pr*
EMP: 14 **EST:** 1993
SQ FT: 3,000
SALES (est): 493.3K **Privately Held**
Web: www.boyntonmachine.com
SIC: 3599 Machine shop, jobbing and repair

(G-12612)
**BROOKLINE MACHINE
COMPANY INC (PA)**
184 Riverview Ave Ste A (02453-3865)
PHONE.................................617 782-4018
John Whiting, *Ch*
Frank B Whiting, *
Marie F Gargiulo, *
Marie Whiting, *
EMP: 26 **EST:** 1919
SQ FT: 30,000
SALES (est): 10.06MM
SALES (corp-wide): 10.06MM **Privately
Held**
Web: www.brooklinemachine.com
SIC: 3599 Machine shop, jobbing and repair

(G-12613)
BRUNO DIDUCA
Also Called: Alpha Press
57 Harvard St (02453-4280)
PHONE.................................781 894-5300
Bruno Diduca, *Owner*
EMP: 9 **EST:** 1979
SQ FT: 7,000
SALES (est): 432.37K **Privately Held**
SIC: 2752 6531 Offset printing; Real estate
agents and managers

(G-12614)
**BUSINESS FORECAST
SYSTEMS INC**
Also Called: Forecast Pro
465 Waverley Oaks Rd (02452-8495)
PHONE.................................617 484-5050
Eric A Stellwagen, *CEO*
EMP: 12 **EST:** 2020
SALES (est): 518.97K **Privately Held**
Web: www.forecastpro.com
SIC: 7372 Prepackaged software

(G-12615)
BVI MEDICAL INC (PA)
500 Totten Pond Rd Fl 5 (02451-1916)
PHONE.................................866 906-8080
EMP: 34 **EST:** 2010
SALES (est): 46.38MM **Privately Held**
Web: www.bvimedical.com
SIC: 3841 Ophthalmic instruments and
apparatus

(G-12616)
BVSN LLC
Also Called: Broadvision Waltham
255 Bear Hill Rd Ste 3 (02451-1017)
PHONE.................................781 290-0710
Theresa Markiewicz, *Brnch Mgr*
EMP: 10
SIC: 7371 7372 Software programming
applications; Prepackaged software
HQ: Bvsn, Llc
401 Congress Ave Ste 2650
Austin TX 78701

(G-12617)
C & J CLARK AMERICA INC (DH)
Also Called: Bostonian
60 Tower Rd (02451-1022)
PHONE.................................617 964-1222
Gary Champion, *Pr*
Chris Caswell, *
Thomas J White, *
Maureen Grady, *
◆ **EMP:** 330 **EST:** 1825
SALES (est): 443.6MM **Privately Held**
Web: www.clarks.com
SIC: 3143 5139 5661 Boots, dress or
casual: men's; Shoes; Men's shoes
HQ: Clarks Americas Inc.
140 Kendrick St Ste C110
Needham Heights MA 02494

(G-12618)

C & J CLARK LATIN AMERICA
201 Jones Rd Ste 1 (02451-1613)
PHONE..............................617 243-4100
Maureen Grady, *Pr*
Sharon Schuler, *VP*
Don Brady, *VP*
John Mecone, *Sec*
EMP: 28 **EST:** 2014
SALES (est): 6.54MM **Privately Held**
SIC: 5139 3143 5661 Shoes; Boots, dress
or casual: men's; Men's shoes

(G-12619)

C & K COMPONENTS LLC (HQ)
Also Called: C&K Switches
465 Waverley Oaks Rd Ste 400
(02452-8500)
PHONE..............................617 969-3700
Lars Brickenkamp, *CEO*
Cathy Yang, *CFO*
▲ **EMP:** 74 **EST:** 1957
SALES (est): 21.35MM
SALES (corp-wide): 2.51B **Publicly Held**
Web: www.ckswitches.com
SIC: 3678 3679 3613 3643 Electronic
connectors; Electronic switches;
Switchgear and switchboard apparatus;
Current-carrying wiring services
PA: Littelfuse, Inc.
8755 W Higgins Rd Ste 500
Chicago IL 60631
773 628-1000

(G-12620)

CARBON BLACK LLC (DH)
Also Called: Vmware Carbon Black
1100 Winter St Ste 4900 (02451-1427)
PHONE..............................617 393-7400
Patrick Morley, *Pr*
Thomas Hansen, *COO*
Stephen Webber, *Ex VP*
Ryan Polk, *CPO*
Michael Viscuso, *CSO*
EMP: 350 **EST:** 2002
SQ FT: 81,991
SALES (est): 281.91MM
SALES (corp-wide): 35.82B **Publicly Held**
SIC: 7372 Prepackaged software
HQ: Vmware Llc
1320 Ridder Park Dr
San Jose CA 94304
650 427-5000

(G-12621)

CARE INTERNATIONAL EXCH INC
77 4th Ave Ste 5 (02451-7567)
PHONE..............................781 642-5900
Sheila Marcelo, *Prin*
EMP: 52 **EST:** 2012
SALES (est): 2.27MM
SALES (corp-wide): 5.24B **Publicly Held**
SIC: 7372 Prepackaged software
HQ: Care.Com, Inc.
1501 S Mopac Expy Ste 340
Austin TX 78746

(G-12622)

CAZENA INC
1601 Trapelo Rd Ste 205 (02451-7340)
PHONE..............................781 897-6380
Prat Moghe, *CEO*
Daniel Hayes, *
EMP: 30 **EST:** 2013
SQ FT: 7,300
SALES (est): 3.25MM **Privately Held**
Web: www.cloudera.com
SIC: 7372 Business oriented computer
software

(G-12623)

CERNER CORPORATION
Also Called: Cerner DHT
51 Sawyer Rd Ste 600 (02453-3493)
PHONE..............................781 434-2200
EMP: 11
SALES (corp-wide): 49.95B **Publicly Held**
Web: www.cerner.com
SIC: 7372 Business oriented computer
software
HQ: Cerner Corporation
8779 Hillcrest Rd
Kansas City MO 64138
816 221-1024

(G-12624)

CHECKPOINT THERAPEUTICS INC
95 Sawyer Rd Ste 110 (02453-3471)
PHONE..............................781 652-4500
James Oliviero, *CEO*
EMP: 30 **EST:** 2015
SALES (est): 3.03MM **Privately Held**
Web: www.checkpointtx.com
SIC: 2834 Pharmaceutical preparations

(G-12625)

CHIASMA INC
460 Totten Pond Rd Ste 530 (02451-1944)
PHONE..............................617 928-5300
Raj Kannan, *CEO*
David Stack, *Ch Bd*
Mark J Fitzpatrick, *Pr*
William Ludlam, *Sr VP*
Drew Enamait, *CAO*
EMP: 48 **EST:** 2001
SALES (est): 1.11MM
SALES (corp-wide): 2.86B **Privately Held**
Web: www.amrytpharma.com
SIC: 2834 Pharmaceutical preparations
HQ: Amryt Pharmaceuticals Designated
Activity Company
45 Mespil Road
Dublin D04 W

(G-12626)

CIMPRESS USA INCORPORATED
275 Wyman St (02451-1218)
PHONE..............................866 207-4955
Robert Keane, *CEO*
EMP: 15
Web: www.vistaprintcorporate.com
SIC: 2752 Commercial printing, lithographic
HQ: Cimpress Usa Incorporated
170 Data Dr
Waltham MA 02451
781 652-6300

(G-12627)

CIMPRESS USA INCORPORATED (DH)
Also Called: Cimpress
170 Data Dr (02451-2222)
PHONE..............................781 652-6300
Robert Keane, *Pr*
Robert Keane, *CEO*
Wendy Cebula, *
Janet Holian, *
Lawrence Gold, *
▼ **EMP:** 46 **EST:** 1995
SALES (est): 714.98MM **Privately Held**
Web: www.vistaprintcorporate.com
SIC: 2752 Commercial printing, lithographic
HQ: Vistaprint B.V.
Hudsonweg 8
Venlo LI 5928
778507700

(G-12628)

CINCOR PHARMA INC
230 3rd Ave Ste 6 (02451-7542)
PHONE..............................513 800-2585
Marc De Garidel, *Pr*
EMP: 10 **EST:** 2018
SQ FT: 1,161
Web: www.cincor.com
SIC: 2834 Pharmaceutical preparations

(G-12629)

CITIUS PRINTING & GRAPHICS LLC
20 Clematis Ave (02453-7011)
PHONE..............................781 547-5550
EMP: 9 **EST:** 2002
SQ FT: 6,000
SALES (est): 1.73MM **Privately Held**
Web: www.citiusprint.com
SIC: 2752 Offset printing

(G-12630)

CLEARSWIFT CORPORATION
1050 Winter St Ste 1000 (02451-1406)
PHONE..............................781 839-7321
Don Taylor, *CEO*
Robin Haliday, *
Ivan O Sullivan, *
Chak Cheung, *
EMP: 300 **EST:** 1983
SQ FT: 800
SALES (est): 15.69MM **Privately Held**
SIC: 3699 Security devices

(G-12631)

CLEMATIS MACHINE & FIX CO INC
42 Clematis Ave (02453-7013)
P.O. Box 540421 (02454-0421)
PHONE..............................781 894-0777
William Thompson, *Pr*
William Thompson Junior, *VP*
EMP: 20 **EST:** 1945
SQ FT: 5,500
SALES (est): 448.71K **Privately Held**
Web: www.clematismachine.com
SIC: 3599 Machine shop, jobbing and repair

(G-12632)

CLEVER GREEN CABINETS LLC
738 Main St (02451-0616)
PHONE..............................508 963-6776
Jonathan Taylor, *Prin*
EMP: 7 **EST:** 2008
SALES (est): 537.16K **Privately Held**
SIC: 2434 Wood kitchen cabinets

(G-12633)

CMC MATERIALS INC
1050 Winter St (02451-1401)
PHONE..............................781 530-3833
William P Noglows, *Brnch Mgr*
EMP: 12
SALES (corp-wide): 3.28B **Publicly Held**
Web: www.cabotcmp.com
SIC: 2819 Industrial inorganic chemicals,
nec
HQ: Cmc Materials, Inc.
129 Concord Rd
Billerica MA 01821
978 436-6500

(G-12634)

COGENT BIOSCIENCES INC (PA)
Also Called: COGENT BIOSCIENCES
275 Wyman St Fl 3 (02451-1200)
PHONE..............................617 945-5576
Andrew Robbins, *Pr*
Peter Harwin, *Ch Bd*
John Green, *CFO*
Evan Kearns, *CLO*
John Robinson, *CSO*
EMP: 19 **EST:** 2014
SQ FT: 33,500
Web: www.cogentbio.com
SIC: 2834 8731 Pharmaceutical
preparations; Biotechnical research,
commercial

(G-12635)

COHERENT PATH INC
183 Crescent St (02453-3436)
PHONE..............................508 612-4557
James Glover, *CEO*
EMP: 50 **EST:** 2012
SALES (est): 5.89MM
SALES (corp-wide): 68.88MM **Privately Held**
Web: www.movableink.com
SIC: 7372 Prepackaged software
PA: Movable, Inc.
5 Bryant Park Fl 9 Flr 9
New York NY 10018
800 270-6033

(G-12636)

COMMONWLTH VNTR FNDING GROUP I (PA)
391 Totten Pond Rd Ste 402 (02451-2006)
P.O. Box 3009 (01880-0771)
PHONE..............................781 684-0095
EMP: 9 **EST:** 1998
SQ FT: 2,000
SALES (est): 39.96MM **Privately Held**
Web: www.cvfg.com
SIC: 3713 Truck bodies and parts

(G-12637)

COMPUTER CORPORATION AMERICA (HQ)
77 4th Ave Ste 100 (02451-7567)
PHONE..............................781 577-4402
Elizabeth L Klass, *Pr*
EMP: 80 **EST:** 1965
SQ FT: 10,000
SALES (est): 60.77K **Privately Held**
Web: www.rocketsoftware.com
SIC: 7372 Prepackaged software
PA: Rocket Software, Inc.
77 4th Ave Ste 101
Waltham MA 02451

(G-12638)

CONFLUENT SURGICAL INC
101 1st Ave Ste 4 (02451-1160)
PHONE..............................781 839-1700
Amarpreet S Sawhney, *Pr*
EMP: 97 **EST:** 1998
SQ FT: 20,000
SALES (est): 11MM **Publicly Held**
SIC: 3841 8733 Surgical and medical
instruments; Medical research
PA: Integra Lifesciences Holdings
Corporation
1100 Campus Rd
Princeton NJ 08540

(G-12639)

CONSTANT CONTACT INC (DH)
1601 Trapelo Rd Ste 329 (02451-7357)
PHONE..............................781 472-8100
Frank Vella, *CEO*
Michael Pellegrino, *CFO*
David C Bryson, *CLO*
Timothy S Mathews, *CAO*
Laura Goldberg, *CMO*
EMP: 480 **EST:** 2015
SQ FT: 190,000
SALES (est): 282.11MM **Privately Held**

Web: www.constantcontact.com
SIC: 7372 Business oriented computer software
HQ: Newfold Digital Holdings Group, Inc.
10 Corporate Dr Ste 300
Burlington MA 01803
781 852-3200

(G-12640)
CONVERGENT DENTAL INC (PA)
100 5th Ave Fl 1 (02451-8727)
PHONE...............................508 500-5656
Robert Gershon, *CEO*
Mark Collins, *CFO*
Nathan P Monty, *Sec*
EMP: 49 EST: 2011
SALES (est): 13.36MM
SALES (corp-wide): 13.36MM **Privately Held**
Web: www.convergentdental.com
SIC: 3843 Dental equipment and supplies

(G-12641)
COPLEY GLOBAL SERVICES LLC
Also Called: Copley Global
303 Wyman St Ste 300 (02451-1255)
PHONE...............................617 970-9617
Abdul C Q, *Ex Dir*
EMP: 7 EST: 2005
SALES (est): 239.16K **Privately Held**
Web: www.copleymso.com
SIC: 8742 5063 5045 3825 Management consulting services; Electrical apparatus and equipment; Computers, peripherals, and software; Instruments to measure electricity

(G-12642)
CORVIDIA THERAPEUTICS INC
Also Called: Corvidia
35 Gatehouse Dr (02451-1215)
PHONE...............................781 205-4755
Marc De Garidel, *Pr*
EMP: 9 EST: 2014
SALES (est): 3.82MM
SALES (corp-wide): 24.71B **Privately Held**
SIC: 2834 5122 Pharmaceutical preparations; Pharmaceuticals
PA: Novo Nordisk A/S
Novo Alle 1
Bagsvard 2880
44448888

(G-12643)
COUNTEREDGE LLC
108 Clematis Ave Unit 2 (02453-7040)
PHONE...............................781 891-0050
Vincent Pizzi, *Managing Member*
▲ EMP: 10 EST: 2010
SALES (est): 929.1K **Privately Held**
Web: www.counteredge.com
SIC: 3131 Counters

(G-12644)
CRANE NXT CO (PA)
950 Winter St Fl 4 (02451-1424)
PHONE...............................610 430-2510
Aaron W Saak, *Pr*
Richard A Maue, *Ex VP*
Tamara S Polmanteer, *Chief Human Resources Officer*
Anthony M D'iorio, *Ex VP*
Christina Cristiano, *CAO*
EMP: 248 EST: 1855
SALES (est): 3.37B
SALES (corp-wide): 3.37B **Publicly Held**
Web: www.craneco.com

SIC: 3492 3494 3594 3589 Control valves, fluid power: hydraulic and pneumatic; Pipe fittings; Pumps, hydraulic power transfer; Water treatment equipment, industrial

(G-12645)
CREATIVESTAR SOLUTION INC
1601 Trapelo Rd Ste 260 (02451-7349)
P.O. Box 961139 (02196-1139)
PHONE...............................617 326-5308
Jianxin Gao, *Pr*
Dan Xiao, *VP*
EMP: 11 EST: 2013
SALES (est): 1.03MM **Privately Held**
Web: www.cssinco.com
SIC: 7371 7372 Computer software development; Publisher's computer software

(G-12646)
CURIA GLOBAL INC
Also Called: Amri
201 Jones Rd Ste 300 (02451-1618)
PHONE...............................781 672-4530
Elizabeth Jean Sanders, *Brnch Mgr*
EMP: 10
SALES (corp-wide): 927.92MM **Privately Held**
Web: www.curiaglobal.com
SIC: 2833 Medicinals and botanicals
HQ: Curia Global, Inc.
26 Corporate Cir
Albany NY 12203

(G-12647)
DATA ASSOCIATES BUSINESS TRUST
Also Called: Data Associates
280 Bear Hill Rd (02451-1098)
P.O. Box 267 (02493-0006)
▼ EMP: 89 EST: 1968
SQ FT: 16,000
SALES (est): 1.52MM **Privately Held**
SIC: 2759 Promotional printing

(G-12648)
DECIPHERA PHARMACEUTICALS LLC
200 Smith St (02451-0099)
PHONE...............................781 209-6400
Steven Hoerter, *Pr*
Thomas Kelly, *
Christopher J Morl, *Chief Business Officer*
Daniel L Flynn, *CSO*
Oliver Rosen, *CMO*
EMP: 340 EST: 2003
SALES (est): 130.21MM
SALES (corp-wide): 134.04MM **Publicly Held**
Web: www.deciphera.com
SIC: 2834 Drugs acting on the gastrointestinal or genitourinary system
PA: Deciphera Pharmaceuticals, Inc.
200 Smith St
Waltham MA 02451
781 209-6400

(G-12649)
DECIPHERA PHARMACEUTICALS INC (PA)
Also Called: DECIPHERA
200 Smith St (02451-0099)
PHONE...............................781 209-6400
Steven L Hoerter, *Pr*
Ron Squarer, *Ch Bd*
Daniel L Flynn, *CSO*
Thomas P Kelly, *Ex VP*
Kelley Dealhoy, *Chief Business Officer*
EMP: 200 EST: 2003
SQ FT: 82,346

SALES (est): 134.04MM
SALES (corp-wide): 134.04MM **Publicly Held**
Web: www.deciphera.com
SIC: 2834 Pharmaceutical preparations

(G-12650)
DENTSPLY IH INC (HQ)
Also Called: Wellspect Healthcare
590 Lincoln St (02451-2173)
PHONE...............................781 890-6800
Scott A Root, *Pr*
Jim Bailey, *
▲ EMP: 200 EST: 1991
SQ FT: 16,000
SALES (est): 47.66MM
SALES (corp-wide): 3.92B **Publicly Held**
Web: www.wellspect.us
SIC: 3841 Surgical and medical instruments
PA: Dentsply Sirona Inc.
13320 Balntyn Corp Pl
Charlotte NC 28277
844 848-0137

(G-12651)
DESCAL INC
Also Called: Sir Speedy
1275 Main St Ste 1 (02451-1762)
PHONE...............................781 736-9400
Patricia Sands, *Pr*
EMP: 8 EST: 2001
SQ FT: 8,000
SALES (est): 744.35K **Privately Held**
Web: www.sirspeedyprescott.com
SIC: 2752 Offset printing

(G-12652)
DETAIL MILLWORK INC
160 Riverview Ave (02453-3843)
P.O. Box 1559 (01886-4996)
PHONE...............................781 893-2250
Richard Rigoli, *Pr*
EMP: 11 EST: 1989
SQ FT: 4,000
SALES (est): 232.24K **Privately Held**
Web: www.rigolico.com
SIC: 2431 Millwork

(G-12653)
DIGITAL COGNITION TECH INC
210 Bear Hill Rd Ste 301 (02451-1025)
PHONE...............................617 433-1777
Nancy Briefs, *CEO*
Allison Byers, *VP*
Irma Dishnica, *Contrlr*
EMP: 22 EST: 2015
SALES (est): 2.01MM **Privately Held**
Web: www.linushealth.com
SIC: 3841 Diagnostic apparatus, medical

(G-12654)
DOCBOX INC
77 Rumford Ave Ste 4 (02453-3872)
PHONE...............................978 987-2569
Bobby Shah, *CFO*
Tracy Rausch, *Pr*
EMP: 12 EST: 2007
SALES (est): 1.32MM **Privately Held**
Web: www.docboxmed.com
SIC: 3845 Electromedical equipment

(G-12655)
DOVER MICROSYSTEMS INC
203 Crescent St Ste 108 (02453-3420)
P.O. Box 403 (01778-0403)
PHONE...............................781 577-0300
Jothy Rosenberg, *CEO*
EMP: 9 EST: 2017
SQ FT: 2,000
SALES (est): 980.07K **Privately Held**

Web: www.dovermicrosystems.com
SIC: 3674 Integrated circuits, semiconductor networks, etc.

(G-12656)
DYNATRACE INC (PA)
Also Called: Dynatrace
1601 Trapelo Rd Ste 116 (02451-7351)
PHONE...............................781 530-1000
Rick Mcconnell, *CEO*
Jill Ward, *Ch Bd*
Jim Benson, *CFO*
Bernd Greifeneder, *Sr VP*
Daniel Yates, *Corporate Controller*
EMP: 206 EST: 2005
SQ FT: 50,000
SALES (est): 1.16B
SALES (corp-wide): 1.16B **Publicly Held**
Web: www.dynatrace.com
SIC: 7372 Prepackaged software

(G-12657)
DYNATRACE LLC (HQ)
1601 Trapelo Rd Ste 116 (02451-7351)
PHONE...............................781 530-1000
John Van Siclen, *CEO*
Bernd Greifeneder, *
Kevin Burns, *
Laura Malinasky, *
EMP: 200 EST: 2014
SALES (est): 526.71MM
SALES (corp-wide): 1.16B **Publicly Held**
Web: www.dynatrace.com
SIC: 7372 5045 Prepackaged software; Computer software
PA: Dynatrace, Inc.
1601 Trapelo Rd Ste 116
Waltham MA 02451
781 530-1000

(G-12658)
DYNE THERAPEUTICS INC (PA)
Also Called: Dyne Therapeutics
1560 Trapelo Rd (02451-7306)
PHONE...............................781 786-8230
Joshua Brumm, *Pr*
Joshua T Brumm, *Pr*
Jason Rhodes, *Ch Bd*
Susanna High, *COO*
Oxana Beskrovnaya, *CSO*
EMP: 47 EST: 2017
Web: www.dyne-tx.com
SIC: 2834 Pharmaceutical preparations

(G-12659)
EDUCATION DEVELOPMENT CTR INC (PA)
Also Called: E D C
300 5th Ave 2010 (02451-8778)
PHONE...............................617 969-7100
Liesbet Steer, *Pr*
Cheryl Hoffmann-bray, *CCO*
Siobhan Murphy, *
Robert Rotner, *
Rick Defrancisco, *
EMP: 515 EST: 1958
SQ FT: 110,000
SALES (est): 184.79MM
SALES (corp-wide): 184.79MM **Privately Held**
Web: www.edc.org
SIC: 8732 2741 Educational research; Miscellaneous publishing

(G-12660)
ELEVATEBIO BASE CAMP INC
200 Smith St Ste 301 (02451-2242)
PHONE...............................617 433-2600
Bhakti Bhargava, *Sr VP*
EMP: 204 EST: 2018

SALES (est): 30.15MM **Privately Held**
Web: www.elevate.bio
SIC: 8731 2834 Biotechnical research, commercial; Pharmaceutical preparations

(G-12661)
EMD MILLIPORE CORPORATION
300 2nd Ave (02451-1102)
PHONE...............781 533-5858
EMP: 23
SALES (corp-wide): 23.09B **Privately Held**
Web: www.millipore.com
SIC: 3826 Liquid testing apparatus
HQ: Emd Millipore Corporation
400 Summit Dr
Burlington MA 01803
800 645-5476

(G-12662)
ENGENE USA INC
201 Jones Rd (02451-1600)
PHONE...............857 246-8765
EMP: 12 EST: 2018
SALES (est): 555.77K **Privately Held**
Web: www.engene.com
SIC: 7372 Prepackaged software

(G-12663)
ENSEM THERAPEUTICS INC
880 Winter St Ste 1003 (02451-1464)
PHONE...............662 422-2488
Shengfang Jin, Pr
Jeff Kutok, CSO
EMP: 21 EST: 2021
SALES (est): 1.04MM **Privately Held**
SIC: 2834 Pharmaceutical preparations

(G-12664)
ENTASIS THRPUTICS HOLDINGS INC (HQ)
35 Gatehouse Dr (02451-1215)
PHONE...............781 810-0120
Manoussos Perros, Pr
Michael Gutch, Chief Business Officer
David Altarac, CMO
Ruben Tommasi, CSO
EMP: 16 EST: 2018
SQ FT: 20,062
SALES (corp-wide): 331.34MM **Publicly Held**
Web: www.innovivaspecialtytherapeutics.com
SIC: 2834 Pharmaceutical preparations
PA: Innoviva, Inc.
1350 Old Byshore Hwy Ste
Burlingame CA 94010
650 238-9600

(G-12665)
ERIKA OF TEXAS INC
920 Winter St (02451-1521)
PHONE...............956 783-4689
John S Walker, Pr
Jo Ellen Ojeda, *
A Miles Nogelo, *
EMP: 780 EST: 1974
SALES (est): 85.12MM
SALES (corp-wide): 20.15B **Privately Held**
SIC: 3841 Blood transfusion equipment
HQ: Fresenius Medical Care Holdings, Inc.
920 Winter St
Waltham MA 02451

(G-12666)
ESSEMTEC USA LLC
300 5th Ave Ste 10 (02451-8754)
PHONE...............856 218-1131
Willam Timms, Managing Member
William Timms, Managing Member
EMP: 11 EST: 2003

SALES (est): 1.42MM **Privately Held**
Web: www.essemtec.com
SIC: 3672 3089 Printed circuit boards; Injection molding of plastics

(G-12667)
EVEREST HALTHCARE HOLDINGS INC (DH)
920 Winter St (02451-1521)
PHONE...............781 699-9000
EMP: 8 EST: 2011
SALES (est): 25.88MM
SALES (corp-wide): 20.15B **Privately Held**
SIC: 3841 Surgical and medical instruments
HQ: Fresenius Medical Care Holdings, Inc.
920 Winter St
Waltham MA 02451

(G-12668)
EVIDENT SCIENTIFIC INC (PA)
Also Called: Ossa
48 Woerd Ave Ste 105 (02453-3826)
P.O. Box 822196 (19182-2196)
PHONE...............781 419-3900
EMP: 895 EST: 2005
SALES (est): 167.09MM **Privately Held**
SIC: 3829 3826 Measuring and controlling devices, nec; Analytical instruments

(G-12669)
EVOLV TECH HOLDINGS INC (PA)
Also Called: Evolv Technologies
500 Totten Pond Rd Fl 4 (02451-1916)
PHONE...............781 374-8100
Peter George, CEO
Alan Cohen, Ch Bd
Peter Faubert, CFO
Anthony John De Rosa, CRO
Parag Vaish Cdpo, Prin
EMP: 8 EST: 2013
SALES (est): 55.2MM
SALES (corp-wide): 55.2MM **Publicly Held**
Web: www.evolvtechnology.com
SIC: 3577 3812 Computer peripheral equipment, nec; Search and navigation equipment

(G-12670)
EVOLV TECHNOLOGIES INC (HQ)
Also Called: Evolv Technology
500 Totten Pond Rd 4th Fl (02451-1916)
PHONE...............781 374-8100
Peter G George, Pr
Alan Cohen, Ch Bd
Peter Faubert, CFO
Anthony John De Rosa, CRO
EMP: 82 EST: 2013
SQ FT: 15,100
SALES (est): 4.79MM
SALES (corp-wide): 55.2MM **Publicly Held**
Web: www.evolvtechnology.com
SIC: 3577 3812 Computer peripheral equipment, nec; Search and navigation equipment
PA: Evolv Technologies Holdings, Inc.
500 Totten Pond Rd Fl 4
Waltham MA 02451
781 374-8100

(G-12671)
EXCELITAS TECH HOLDG CORP
200 West St Ste E403 (02451-1121)
PHONE...............781 522-5914
EMP: 6500 EST: 2010
SALES (est): 290.68MM **Privately Held**

Web: www.excelitas.com
SIC: 3648 3845 Lighting equipment, nec; Electromedical apparatus
PA: Excelitas Technologies Holdings Llc
200 West St Ste E403
Waltham MA 02451

(G-12672)
EXCELITAS TECH HOLDINGS LLC (PA)
200 West St Ste E403 (02451-1121)
PHONE...............781 522-5900
EMP: 10 EST: 2010
SALES (est): 370.13MM **Privately Held**
Web: www.excelitas.com
SIC: 3648 Lighting equipment, nec

(G-12673)
EXCELITAS TECHNOLOGIES CORP (DH)
200 W St 4th Fl E (02451-1125)
PHONE...............855 382-2677
EMP: 30 EST: 2010
SALES (est): 1.41B
SALES (corp-wide): 1.48B **Privately Held**
Web: www.excelitas.com
SIC: 3674 3827 3648 3679 Semiconductor diodes and rectifiers; Optical instruments and apparatus; Outdoor lighting equipment; Electronic circuits
HQ: Exc Holdings Ii Corp.
666 5th Ave Fl 36
New York NY 10103
212 644-5900

(G-12674)
FABTRON CORPORATION
80 Calvary St (02453-5952)
PHONE...............781 891-4430
Clifford L Derick Junior, Pr
Martha L Derick, *
EMP: 35 EST: 1973
SQ FT: 33,000
SALES (est): 2.46MM **Privately Held**
Web: www.fabtron.net
SIC: 3444 Sheet metal specialties, not stamped

(G-12675)
FISHER SCIENTIFIC INTL LLC (HQ)
81 Wyman St (02451-1223)
PHONE...............781 622-1000
Anthony H Smith, Pr
Jeffrey Jochims, *
Alan Malus, *
Alex Stachtiaris, *
Michael E Dambach, *
◆ EMP: 125 EST: 1902
SQ FT: 25,000
SALES (est): 2.52B
SALES (corp-wide): 44.91B **Publicly Held**
Web: www.thermofisher.com
SIC: 2869 3821 5169 5049 Laboratory chemicals, organic; Laboratory equipment: fume hoods, distillation racks, etc.; Chemicals and allied products, nec; Laboratory equipment, except medical or dental
PA: Thermo Fisher Scientific Inc.
168 3rd Ave
Waltham MA 02451
781 622-1000

(G-12676)
FLUIDFORM INC
283 Bear Hill Rd (02451-1010)
PHONE...............978 287-4698
Michael Graffeo, CEO

Alexander Lenz, Opers Mgr
Adam Feinberg, Prin
EMP: 8 EST: 2018
SALES (est): 1.15MM **Privately Held**
Web: www.fluidform3d.com
SIC: 2759 Commercial printing, nec

(G-12677)
FMS NEW YORK SERVICES LLC (DH)
920 Winter St (02451-1521)
PHONE...............781 699-9000
EMP: 11 EST: 2010
SALES (est): 9.51MM
SALES (corp-wide): 20.15B **Privately Held**
SIC: 3841 Surgical and medical instruments
HQ: Fresenius Medical Care Holdings, Inc.
920 Winter St
Waltham MA 02451

(G-12678)
FORTRESS BIOTECH INC
95 Sawyer Rd Ste 110 (02453-3471)
PHONE...............781 652-4500
EMP: 10
Web: www.fortressbiotech.com
SIC: 2834 Pharmaceutical preparations
PA: Fortress Biotech, Inc.
2 Gansevoort St Fl 9
New York NY 10014

(G-12679)
FRESENIUS MED CARE HLDINGS INC (DH)
Also Called: Fresenius Medical Care N Amer
920 Winter St Ste A (02451-1521)
PHONE...............781 699-9000
◆ EMP: 600 EST: 1988
SQ FT: 200,000
SALES (est): 10.17B
SALES (corp-wide): 20.15B **Privately Held**
Web: www.fmcna.com
SIC: 3841 8092 Surgical and medical instruments; Kidney dialysis centers
HQ: Fresenius Medical Care Gmbh
Else-Kroner-Str. 1
Bad Homburg HE 61352
61726097054

(G-12680)
FRESENIUS MED CARE RNAL THRPIE
920 Winter St Ste A (02451-1521)
PHONE...............781 699-9000
EMP: 9 EST: 2012
SALES (est): 1.2MM
SALES (corp-wide): 20.15B **Privately Held**
Web: www.fmcna.com
SIC: 3841 Hemodialysis apparatus
HQ: Fresenius Medical Care Holdings, Inc.
920 Winter St
Waltham MA 02451

(G-12681)
FRESENIUS MED CARE VNTURES LLC (DH)
920 Winter St Ste A (02451-1521)
PHONE...............781 699-9000
EMP: 17 EST: 2011
SALES (est): 344.87MM
SALES (corp-wide): 20.15B **Privately Held**
Web: www.fmcna.com
SIC: 3841 Surgical and medical instruments
HQ: Fresenius Medical Care Holdings, Inc.
920 Winter St
Waltham MA 02451

(G-12682)

FRESENIUS MED SVCS GROUP LLC

920 Winter St Ste A (02451-1521)
PHONE.....................781 699-9000
Ronald Kuerbitz, *CEO*
William Valle, *Pr*
Angelo Moesslang, *CFO*
Douglas Kott, *Sr VP*
Mark Fawcett, *Sr VP*
EMP: 17 **EST:** 2012
SALES (est): 491.47K
SALES (corp-wide): 20.15B **Privately Held**
Web: www.freseniusmedicalcare.us
SIC: 3841 8092 Surgical and medical instruments; Kidney dialysis centers
HQ: Fresenius Medical Care Holdings, Inc.
920 Winter St
Waltham MA 02451

(G-12683)

FRESENIUS USA INC (DH)

Also Called: Fresenius Medical Care
920 Winter St (02451-1521)
PHONE.....................781 699-4191
Ronald J Kuerbitz, *CEO*
Ben Lipps, *
Heinz Schmidt, *Finance Treasurer**
Scott Walker, *
Mark Costanzo, *
▲ **EMP:** 220 **EST:** 1974
SQ FT: 85,000
SALES (est): 653.8MM
SALES (corp-wide): 20.15B **Privately Held**
Web: www.fmcna.com
SIC: 2834 3841 2835 3842 Intravenous solutions; Hemodialysis apparatus; Blood derivative diagnostic agents; Surgical appliances and supplies
HQ: Fresenius Medical Care Holdings, Inc.
920 Winter St
Waltham MA 02451

(G-12684)

FRESENIUS USA MARKETING INC (DH)

Also Called: Fresenius Rnal Pharmaceuticals
920 Winter St (02451-1521)
PHONE.....................781 699-9000
EMP: 22 **EST:** 2011
SALES (est): 7.4MM
SALES (corp-wide): 20.15B **Privately Held**
Web: www.fmcna.com
SIC: 3841 Surgical and medical instruments
HQ: Fresenius Medical Care Holdings, Inc.
920 Winter St
Waltham MA 02451

(G-12685)

FSWH INTL HOLDINGS LLC (HQ)

168 3rd Ave (02451-7551)
PHONE.....................781 622-1000
EMP: 22 **EST:** 2018
SALES (est): 6.37MM
SALES (corp-wide): 44.91B **Publicly Held**
SIC: 3826 Analytical instruments
PA: Thermo Fisher Scientific Inc.
168 3rd Ave
Waltham MA 02451
781 622-1000

(G-12686)

GENERATION FOUR INC

Also Called: Minuteman Press
713 Main St (02451-0609)
PHONE.....................781 899-3180
John Fantasia, *Pr*
Julie Fantasia, *Prin*
EMP: 8 **EST:** 1977
SQ FT: 3,000

SALES (est): 680.81K **Privately Held**
Web: www.colorconnection.com
SIC: 2752 2791 2789 Commercial printing, lithographic; Typesetting; Bookbinding and related work

(G-12687)

GENZYME CORPORATION

153 2nd Ave (02451-1122)
PHONE.....................781 487-5728
Edmund Sybertz, *CEO*
EMP: 111
Web: www.sanofi.us
SIC: 2834 Pharmaceutical preparations
HQ: Genzyme Corporation
450 Water St
Cambridge MA 02141
617 252-7500

(G-12688)

GRAPHISOFT NORTH AMERICA INC

1601 Trapelo Rd Ste 162 (02451-7332)
PHONE.....................617 485-4219
▲ **EMP:** 35 **EST:** 1989
SALES (est): 4.2MM **Privately Held**
Web: www.graphisoft.com
SIC: 7372 Business oriented computer software

(G-12689)

H & T SPECIALTY CO INC

56 Clematis Ave (02453-7013)
P.O. Box 540185 (02454-0185)
PHONE.....................781 893-3866
Gary Jenks, *Pr*
EMP: 29 **EST:** 1951
SQ FT: 6,400
SALES (est): 2.01MM **Privately Held**
SIC: 3679 3599 Microwave components; Machine and other job shop work

(G-12690)

HARVEST CONSUMER PRODUCTS LLC (PA)

1432 Main St Ste 1 (02451-1652)
PHONE.....................980 444-2000
Christian G Kasper, *Prin*
David Hitchcock, *
Brian Kura, *
David L Day, *
▲ **EMP:** 25 **EST:** 1969
SALES (est): 10.9MM
SALES (corp-wide): 10.9MM **Privately Held**
SIC: 2499 Mulch, wood and bark

(G-12691)

HARVEY INDUSTRIES LLC (PA)

Also Called: Harvey Building Products
1400 Main St Fl 3 (02451-1689)
PHONE.....................800 598-5400
Thomas Bigony, *CEO*
Erik Jarnryd, *
James M Barreira, *
Thomas Russell, *
Vincent Walsh, *
▲ **EMP:** 200 **EST:** 1961
SQ FT: 55,000
SALES (est): 1.2B
SALES (corp-wide): 1.2B **Privately Held**
Web: www.harveybp.com
SIC: 5031 5033 3442 2431 Windows; Roofing, asphalt and sheet metal; Storm doors or windows, metal; Windows, wood

(G-12692)

HEMEDEX INC

564 Main St Ste 300 (02452-5568)

PHONE.....................617 577-1759
Fredrick H Bowman, *CEO*
EMP: 14 **EST:** 2000
SQ FT: 6,500
SALES (est): 2.45MM **Privately Held**
Web: www.hemedex.com
SIC: 3841 Medical instruments and equipment, blood and bone work

(G-12693)

ID123 INC

397 Moody St Ste 202 (02453-0429)
PHONE.....................617 936-0210
Ceorichard Eicher, *CEO*
EMP: 8 **EST:** 2018
SALES (est): 121.28K **Privately Held**
Web: www.id123.io
SIC: 7372 Application computer software

(G-12694)

IDEAL CONCRETE BLOCK CO

232 Lexington St (02452-4612)
PHONE.....................781 894-3200
Sharonanne Ferris, *Prin*
EMP: 35
SALES (corp-wide): 11.42MM **Privately Held**
Web: www.paversbyidealwaltham.com
SIC: 5032 5082 3271 Concrete mixtures; Masonry equipment and supplies; Concrete block and brick
PA: Ideal Concrete Block Co
45 Powers Rd
Westford MA 01886
978 692-3076

(G-12695)

IMAGING W VAREX HOLDINGS INC

940 Winter St (02451-1457)
PHONE.....................781 663-6900
Sunny Sanyal, *CEO*
Clarence Verhoef, *CFO*
Kim Honeysett, *Corporate Secretary*
Chad Holman, *Chief Human Resource Officer*
EMP: 23 **EST:** 1994
SALES (est): 2.05MM
SALES (corp-wide): 893.4MM **Publicly Held**
SIC: 3826 Analytical instruments
PA: Varex Imaging Corporation
1678 S Pioneer Rd
Salt Lake City UT 84104
801 972-5000

(G-12696)

IMMUNOGEN INC (PA)

Also Called: Immunogen
830 Winter St (02451-1477)
PHONE.....................781 895-0600
Mark J Enyedy, *Pr*
Stephen C Mccluski, *Ch Bd*
Lauren White, *Sr VP*
Anna Berkenblit, *CMO*
Stacy Coen, *Chief Business Officer*
EMP: 12 **EST:** 1981
SQ FT: 120,000
SALES (est): 108.78MM
SALES (corp-wide): 108.78MM **Privately Held**
Web: www.immunogen.com
SIC: 2834 Pharmaceutical preparations

(G-12697)

IMPRIVATA INC (HQ)

480 Totten Pond Rd Fl 6 (02451-1908)
PHONE.....................781 674-2700
Gus Malezis, *Pr*
Robert Egan, *

James Carr, *
Sean Kelly, *CMO**
Kelliann Mccabe, *CPO*
EMP: 300 **EST:** 2001
SALES (est): 93.64MM
SALES (corp-wide): 250.58MM **Privately Held**
Web: www.imprivata.com
SIC: 7382 7372 Security systems services; Application computer software
PA: Imprivata Intermediate Holdings, Inc.
10 Maguire Rd Ste 1
Lexington MA 02421
781 674-2700

(G-12698)

INDUSTRIAL BMDCAL SENSORS CORP

Also Called: I B S
1377 Main St (02451-1644)
PHONE.....................781 891-4201
Sanlu Y Chang, *Pr*
Kuo Chang Ph.d., *Treas*
EMP: 10 **EST:** 1975
SQ FT: 5,000
SALES (est): 984.94K **Privately Held**
Web: www.ibs-corp.com
SIC: 3823 3571 3365 Process control instruments; Electronic computers; Aerospace castings, aluminum

(G-12699)

INFINIDAT INC

500 Totten Pond Rd Ste 61 (02451-1924)
PHONE.....................781 907-7585
Phil Bullinger, *CEO*
Boaz Chalamish, *Ofcr*
Alon Rozenshein, *CFO*
Steve Sullivan, *CRO*
EMP: 100 **EST:** 2013
SALES (est): 14.2MM **Privately Held**
Web: www.infinidat.com
SIC: 7371 3572 Computer software development; Computer storage devices
PA: Infinidat Ltd
9 Hamanofim
Herzliya 46725

(G-12700)

INNOV-X SYSTEMS INC

Also Called: Olympus Innov-X
48 Woerd Ave (02453-3824)
P.O. Box 822196 (19182-2196)
PHONE.....................781 938-5005
EMP: 110
Web: www.innovxsys.com
SIC: 3826 Laser scientific and engineering instruments

(G-12701)

INNOVIVA SPCLTY THRPEUTICS INC ✪

35 Gatehouse Dr (02451-1215)
PHONE.....................800 651-3861
Pavel Raifeld Cfa, *CEO*
EMP: 29 **EST:** 2022
SALES (est): 678.97K **Privately Held**
SIC: 2834 Proprietary drug products

(G-12702)

INTERLEUKIN GENETICS INC

135 Beaver St (02452-8453)
PHONE.....................781 398-0700
EMP: 17
Web: www.ilgenetics.com
SIC: 8731 8748 2835 Commercial physical research; Test development and evaluation service; Diagnostic substances

(G-12703)
**INVERNESS MEDICAL -
BIOSTAR INC**
Also Called: Thermo Biostar Inc.
51 Sawyer Rd Ste 200 (02453-3448)
PHONE.....................781 647-3900
EMP: 180 EST: 1983
SALES (est): 10.24MM
SALES (corp-wide): 43.65B **Publicly Held**
SIC: 8731 8733 3841 2835 Commercial
research laboratory; Medical research;
Diagnostic apparatus, medical; Diagnostic
substances
HQ: Alere Inc.
51 Sawyer Rd Ste 200
Waltham MA 02453
781 647-3900

(G-12704)
IPERIA INC
235 Bear Hill Rd Ste 401 (02451-1014)
PHONE.....................781 839-3800
David Jodoin, CEO
Jonathan Ross, *
Arthur Leondires, *
Steve Gardell, *
EMP: 9 EST: 1997
SALES (est): 371.34K **Privately Held**
Web: www.iperia.com
SIC: 7372 Prepackaged software

(G-12705)
JGPG INC
39 Calvary St 2nd Fl (02453-5974)
PHONE.....................781 891-9640
Joseph D Georgianna, Pr
EMP: 10 EST: 1988
SALES (est): 1.56MM **Privately Held**
Web: www.lectroengineering.com
SIC: 3444 Sheet metal specialties, not
stamped

(G-12706)
K2W LLC
Also Called: Onguard
30 Grant St (02453-4202)
PHONE.....................617 818-2613
EMP: 7 EST: 2009
SALES (est): 118.13K **Privately Held**
SIC: 3081 Unsupported plastics film and
sheet

(G-12707)
KELTRON CORPORATION (HQ)
101 1st Ave Ste 4 # A (02451-1160)
PHONE.....................781 894-8710
David S Wilbourn, Pr
Nancy Sullivan, Sec
David S Wilbourn, Treas
EMP: 21 EST: 1961
SQ FT: 18,000
SALES (est): 7.99MM
SALES (corp-wide): 65.76MM **Privately
Held**
Web: www.keltroncorp.com
SIC: 3669 Burglar alarm apparatus, electric
PA: Valcom, Inc.
5614 Hollins Rd
Roanoke VA 24019
540 427-3900

(G-12708)
**LA JOLLA PHARMACEUTICAL
CO (HQ)**
35 Gatehouse Dr Ste E0 (02451-1215)
PHONE.....................617 715-3600
Pavel Raifeld, CEO
Marianne Zhen, CAO
Kevin C Tang, *

Michael Hearne, CFO
Tony Hodges, Chief Medical Officer
EMP: 22 EST: 1989
SQ FT: 7,388
SALES (est): 75.72MM
SALES (corp-wide): 331.34MM **Publicly
Held**
Web: www.lajollapharmaceutical.com
SIC: 8731 2834 Biotechnical research,
commercial; Pharmaceutical preparations
PA: Innoviva, Inc.
1350 Old Byshore Hwy Ste
Burlingame CA 94010
650 238-9600

(G-12709)
LIGHT METAL PLATERS LLC
70 Clematis Ave (02453-7013)
P.O. Box 540150 (02454-0150)
PHONE.....................781 899-8855
Steven Delorey, Pr
Phyllis Gauthier, Treas
▲ EMP: 20 EST: 1960
SQ FT: 7,600
SALES (est): 1.8MM **Privately Held**
Web: www.lightmetalplaters.com
SIC: 3471 3479 7336 2396 Plating of metals
or formed products; Painting of metal
products; Silk screen design; Automotive
and apparel trimmings

(G-12710)
**LOCKHEED MRTIN ADVNCED
ENRGY S**
117 Beaver St (02452-8428)
PHONE.....................972 603-7611
Pete Zarate, Prin
EMP: 7 EST: 2019
SALES (est): 280.65K **Privately Held**
SIC: 3721 Aircraft

(G-12711)
LOGICAL THERAPEUTICS INC
300 Second Ave (02451-1102)
PHONE.....................781 290-0900
Peter A Lankau, CEO
EMP: 12 EST: 2007
SALES (est): 275.85K **Privately Held**
SIC: 2834 Pharmaceutical preparations

(G-12712)
LTPC HOLDINGS INC
30 Clematis Ave (02453-7069)
PHONE.....................781 893-6672
Daniel Leone, Pr
Peter Brown, *
Milagro Leone, *
▲ EMP: 25 EST: 1990
SQ FT: 5,000
SALES (est): 6MM **Privately Held**
Web: www.niche-electronics.com
SIC: 3672 Printed circuit boards

(G-12713)
MANUS BIO INC (HQ)
Also Called: Nutrasweet
43 Foundry Ave (02453-8313)
PHONE.....................617 299-8466
EMP: 23 EST: 2011
SALES (est): 47.3MM **Privately Held**
Web: www.manusbio.com
SIC: 8731 2869 Biotechnical research,
commercial; Sweeteners, synthetic
PA: Bbgi Public Company Limited
2098 Sukhumvit Road
Phra Khanong 10260

(G-12714)
MARIE DEPROFIO
Also Called: Unlimited Plant Care Service
11 Harrington Rd (02452-4720)
PHONE.....................781 894-9793
Marie Deprofio, Owner
EMP: 7 EST: 1984
SALES (est): 461.2K **Privately Held**
SIC: 2431 Interior and ornamental
woodwork and trim

(G-12715)
MARKFORGED INC (HQ)
60 Tower Rd (02451-1022)
PHONE.....................866 496-1805
Shai Terem, Pr
Antonio Rodriguez, *
Ric Fulop, *
John Brenton, *
Assaf Zipori, *
EMP: 150 EST: 2019
SQ FT: 36,000
SALES (est): 98.95MM
SALES (corp-wide): 100.96MM **Publicly
Held**
Web: www.markforged.com
SIC: 3599 Custom machinery
PA: Markforged Holding Corporation
480 Pleasant St
Watertown MA 02472
866 496-1805

(G-12716)
**MASSACHUSETTS MEDICAL
SOCIETY**
Also Called: New England Journal Medicine
108 Clematis Ave Ste E (02453-7040)
PHONE.....................781 434-7950
C Broderick, Brnch Mgr
EMP: 49
SALES (corp-wide): 77.29K **Privately Held**
Web: www.massmed.org
SIC: 8621 2721 Medical field-related
associations; Trade journals: publishing
and printing
PA: Massachusetts Medical Society Inc
860 Winter St
Waltham MA 02451
781 893-4610

(G-12717)
MATERIALISE DENTAL INC
590 Lincoln St (02451-2173)
PHONE.....................443 557-0121
Barbara Sterner, Prin
EMP: 15 EST: 1981
SALES (est): 251.76K **Privately Held**
SIC: 7372 Prepackaged software

(G-12718)
**MDS NXSTAGE CORPORATION
(DH)**
920 Winter St (02451-1521)
PHONE.....................866 697-8243
Jeffrey H Burbank, Pr
Winifred L Swan, Prin
Matthew W Towse, Prin
◆ EMP: 30 EST: 1981
SQ FT: 11,500
SALES (est): 27.71MM
SALES (corp-wide): 20.15B **Privately Held**
SIC: 3841 Hemodialysis apparatus
HQ: Nxstage Medical, Inc.
350 Merrimack St Ste 5
Lawrence MA 01843
978 687-4700

(G-12719)
METALOGIX SOFTWARE CORP
690 Winter St Ste 115 (02451-1233)
PHONE.....................202 609-9100
EMP: 8 EST: 2017
SALES (est): 312.43K **Privately Held**
Web: www.quest.com
SIC: 7372 Prepackaged software

(G-12720)
MINDEDGE INC
271 Waverley Oaks Rd Ste 404
(02452-8469)
PHONE.....................781 250-1805
Jefferson Flanders, CEO
EMP: 60 EST: 1998
SQ FT: 4,000
SALES (est): 5.37MM **Privately Held**
Web: www.mindedge.com
SIC: 7372 Educational computer software

(G-12721)
**MINERVA NRSCNCES SCRITIES
CORP**
1601 Trapelo Rd Ste 284 (02451-7357)
PHONE.....................617 600-7373
Remy Luthringer, Pr
EMP: 8 EST: 2014
SALES (est): 488.33K **Publicly Held**
Web: www.minervaneurosciences.com
SIC: 2834 Pharmaceutical preparations
PA: Minerva Neurosciences, Inc.
1500 District Ave
Burlington MA 01803
617 600-7373

(G-12722)
MJ RESEARCH INC (HQ)
245 Winter St Ste 100 (02451-8709)
PHONE.....................510 724-7000
John D Finney, Pr
Michael J Finney, *
EMP: 150 EST: 1987
SQ FT: 84,000
SALES (est): 99.3MM
SALES (corp-wide): 2.8B **Publicly Held**
SIC: 3826 Analytical instruments
PA: Bio-Rad Laboratories, Inc.
1000 Alfred Nobel Dr
Hercules CA 94547
510 724-7000

(G-12723)
MODALIS THERAPEUTICS INC
43 Foundry Ave (02453-8313)
PHONE.....................617 219-9808
Haruhiko Morita, Pr
Tetsuya Yamagata, *
Hideki Takeda, *
EMP: 30 EST: 2019
SALES (est): 4.68MM **Privately Held**
Web: www.modalistx.com
SIC: 2834 Pharmaceutical preparations

(G-12724)
MODUS MEDIA INC
1601 Trapelo Rd Ste 170 (02451-7353)
PHONE.....................781 663-5000
Terence M Leahy, Ch Bd
Daniel Beck, President Americas*
David Tanner, EUROPE*
W Kendal Southerland, Area President*
Leo S Vannoni, *
EMP: 41 EST: 1997
SALES (est): 1.52MM
SALES (corp-wide): 40.8MM **Publicly
Held**

SIC: **2752** 2789 5045 7371   Commercial printing, lithographic; Bookbinding and related work; Computers, peripherals, and software; Custom computer programming services
PA: Steel Connect, Inc.
590 Madison Ave Fl 32
New York NY 10022
212 520-2300

(G-12725)
MORPHIC HOLDING INC (PA)
Also Called: MORPHIC THERAPEUTIC
35 Gatehouse Dr A2 (02451-1215)
PHONE......................781 996-0955
Praveen P Tipirneni, *Pr*
Gustav Christensen, *Ch Bd*
Marc Schegerin, *CFO*
Peter G Linde, *CMO*
Bruce N Rogers, *CSO*
EMP: 20 EST: 2014
SQ FT: 35,000
SALES (est): 70.81MM
SALES (corp-wide): 70.81MM **Publicly Held**
Web: www.morphictx.com
SIC: **2834**   Pharmaceutical preparations

(G-12726)
MSM PROTEIN TECHNOLOGIES INC
1393 Main St (02451-1632)
PHONE......................781 373-2405
David Kreimer, *CEO*
EMP: 8 EST: 2017
SALES (est): 281.83K **Privately Held**
Web: www.msmprotein.com
SIC: **2834**   Pharmaceutical preparations

(G-12727)
MURAL ONCOLOGY INC ✪
852 Winter St (02451-1439)
PHONE......................617 694-2481
Caroline Leow, *CEO*
Caroline Leow, *Pr*
Blair Jackson, *Pr*
Iain Brown, *Dir*
Ryan Bis Ctrl, *Prin*
EMP: 27 EST: 2023
SALES (est): 388.78K **Privately Held**
Web: www.muraloncology.com
SIC: **2834** 8731   Pharmaceutical preparations; Biotechnical research, commercial
PA: Mural Oncology Public Limited Company
10 Earlsfort Terrace
Dublin

(G-12728)
NABS INC
Also Called: Nabs Bindery
180 Elm St Ste 5 (02453-5334)
PHONE......................781 899-7719
Nuccia Arsenault, *Pr*
Paul Arsenault Traes, *Clerk*
EMP: 20 EST: 1994
SQ FT: 5,500
SALES (est): 535.68K **Privately Held**
Web: www.nabsbindery.com
SIC: **2789**   Binding only: books, pamphlets, magazines, etc.

(G-12729)
NANO DIMENSION USA INC
Also Called: Nano Dimension 3d
300 5th Ave Ste 10 (02451-8754)
P.O. Box 1227 (95052-1227)
PHONE......................650 209-2866
Simon Fried, *Pr*

EMP: 45 EST: 2017
SALES (est): 10.62MM **Privately Held**
Web: www.nano-di.com
SIC: **3672**   Printed circuit boards
PA: Nano Dimension Ltd
2 Ilan Ramon
Ness Ziona 74036

(G-12730)
NANOENTEK INC
220 Bear Hill Rd (02451-1004)
PHONE......................781 472-2559
Woo Chul Jung, *Pr*
EMP: 7
Web: www.nanoentek.com
SIC: **3841**   Diagnostic apparatus, medical
PA: Nanoentek, Inc.
5 Digital-Ro 26-Gil, Guro-Gu
Seoul 08389

(G-12731)
NANOSEMI INC
200 5th Ave Ste 2020 (02451-8733)
PHONE......................781 472-2832
Helen Kim, *Pr*
EMP: 26 EST: 2014
SALES (est): 4.72MM
SALES (corp-wide): 693.26MM **Publicly Held**
Web: www.nanosemitech.com
SIC: **3679**   Electronic circuits
PA: Maxlinear, Inc.
5966 La Place Ct Ste 100
Carlsbad CA 92008
760 692-0711

(G-12732)
NANOSTONE WATER INC
1432 Main St Ste 1 (02451-1621)
PHONE......................781 209-6900
Matt Aheam, *Dir*
Mike Aheam, *
Alan Henderson, *
Steve Kloos, *
Roger Pederson, *
EMP: 148 EST: 2018
SALES (est): 24.92MM **Privately Held**
Web: www.nanostone.com
SIC: **3589**   Water filters and softeners, household type
PA: True North Venture Partners, L.P.
205 N Michigan Ave # 2930
Chicago IL 60601

(G-12733)
NATALIA MARKETING CORP
Also Called: Natalia
170 High St (02453-5914)
PHONE......................781 693-4900
Kathy Apacidis, *Pr*
▲ EMP: 26 EST: 1991
SQ FT: 16,000
SALES (est): 4.54MM **Privately Held**
Web: www.beadchemistry.com
SIC: **5094** 3911 3961   Beads; Jewelry, precious metal; Costume jewelry

(G-12734)
NATIONAL GRID USA SVC CO INC (DH)
170 Data Dr (02451-2222)
PHONE......................800 260-0054
Thomas B King, *Pr*
Vivienne Bracken, *Pr*
Thomas B King, *Prin*
Kenneth D Daly, *Chief Financial Officer HS*
John A Caroselli, *Ex VP*
▲ EMP: 8 EST: 1935
SQ FT: 100,000
SALES (est): 992.39MM

SALES (corp-wide): 26.03B **Privately Held**
Web: www.nationalgridus.com
SIC: **4911** 1311   Generation, electric power; Crude petroleum production
HQ: National Grid Usa
40 Sylvan Rd
Waltham MA 02451

(G-12735)
NETCRACKER TECHNOLOGY CORP (HQ)
Also Called: Netcracker
95 Sawyer Rd University Office Park Iii (02453-3464)
PHONE......................781 419-3300
Andrew Feinberg, *Pr*
Toshio Takahashi, *
Todd Goffman, *
Atsuo Kawamura, *
Gene Gabbard, *
EMP: 199 EST: 1993
SQ FT: 45,000
SALES (est): 291.79MM **Privately Held**
Web: www.netcracker.com
SIC: **7372**   Prepackaged software
PA: Nec Corporation
5-7-1, Shiba
Minato-Ku TKY 108-0

(G-12736)
NETSILICON INC (HQ)
Also Called: Digital Products
411 Waverley Oaks Rd (02452-8448)
PHONE......................781 647-1234
Bruce Berger, *Genl Mgr*
EMP: 60 EST: 1984
SQ FT: 36,000
SALES (est): 24.95MM
SALES (corp-wide): 444.85MM **Publicly Held**
SIC: **5045** 3577   Computer peripheral equipment; Printers, computer
PA: Digi International Inc.
9350 Excelsior Blvd # 700
Hopkins MN 55343
952 912-3444

(G-12737)
NOCION THERAPEUTICS INC
100 Beaver St Ste 301 (02453-8400)
PHONE......................781 812-6176
Admiral Stephanie Gillis, *Prin*
EMP: 7 EST: 2017
SALES (est): 1.19MM **Privately Held**
Web: www.nociontx.com
SIC: **2834**   Pharmaceutical preparations

(G-12738)
NOVA BIOMEDICAL CORPORATION (PA)
200 Prospect St (02453-3465)
PHONE......................781 894-0800
Francis Manganaro, *Pr*
James E Fowler, *
John N Driscoll, *
Luciano A Borrelli, *
▲ EMP: 621 EST: 1976
SQ FT: 220,000
SALES (est): 307.6MM
SALES (corp-wide): 307.6MM **Privately Held**
Web: www.novabiomedical.com
SIC: **2833** 3826   Medicinals and botanicals; Blood testing apparatus

(G-12739)
NOVELL INC
404 Wyman St Ste 500 (02451-1250)
PHONE......................781 464-8000
Jos Almandoz, *CIO*

EMP: 40 EST: 2019
SALES (est): 579.58K **Privately Held**
Web: www.microfocus.com
SIC: **7372**   Prepackaged software

(G-12740)
NUTRASWEET COMPANY
500 Totten Pond Rd Ste 61 (02451-1924)
PHONE......................706 303-5600
William Defer, *Ex VP*
EMP: 197
SALES (corp-wide): 65.09MM **Privately Held**
Web: www.neotame.com
SIC: **2869**   Sweeteners, synthetic
HQ: The Nutrasweet Company
222 Merchandise Mart Plz
Chicago IL 60654
312 873-5000

(G-12741)
OATSYSTEMS INC
309 Waverly Oaks Rd Ste 306 (02452-8443)
PHONE......................781 907-6100
Michael George, *CEO*
Stephen Royal, *
Karl Waldman, *
Bob Lentz, *
Eric Fischer, *
EMP: 65 EST: 2001
SQ FT: 7,500
SALES (est): 7.66MM **Privately Held**
Web: www.oatsystems.com
SIC: **3699**   Security control equipment and systems

(G-12742)
OLD IRONSIDES ENERGY LLC
500 Totten Pond Rd Ste 1 (02451-1927)
PHONE......................617 366-2030
Gregory S Morzano, *Prin*
Sean P O'neill, *Prin*
Daniel A Rioux, *Prin*
David Delmore, *CFO*
EMP: 21 EST: 2013
SALES (est): 19.23MM **Privately Held**
Web: www.oldironsidesenergy.com
SIC: **1389**   Oil field services, nec

(G-12743)
ON TECHNOLOGY CORP (PA)
880 Winter St Bldg 4 (02451-1464)
PHONE......................781 487-3300
Robert L Doretti, *Pr*
Steven R Wasserman, *Finance Treasurer*
EMP: 55 EST: 1985
SQ FT: 23,000
SALES (est): 8.82MM
SALES (corp-wide): 8.82MM **Privately Held**
SIC: **7373** 7371 7372   Computer integrated systems design; Custom computer programming services; Prepackaged software

(G-12744)
ONDAS HOLDINGS INC (PA)
Also Called: Ondas Holdings
411 Waverley Oaks Rd Ste 114 (02452-8448)
PHONE......................888 350-9994
Eric Brock, *Ch Bd*
Yishay Curelaru, *CFO*
Guy Simpson, *COO*
EMP: 11 EST: 2006
SALES (est): 2.13MM
SALES (corp-wide): 2.13MM **Publicly Held**
Web: www.ondas.com

SIC: 3663 7372 Radio broadcasting and communications equipment; Prepackaged software

(G-12745)
ORACLE CORPORATION
Also Called: Oracle
230 3rd Ave (02451-7528)
PHONE.................781 314-8001
Joe Forgione, *Brnch Mgr*
EMP: 34
SALES (corp-wide): 49.95B **Publicly Held**
Web: www.oracle.com
SIC: 7372 Prepackaged software
PA: Oracle Corporation
2300 Oracle Way
Austin TX 78741
737 867-1000

(G-12746)
PALLEON PHARMA INC
266 Second Ave Fl 2 (02451-1166)
PHONE.................857 285-5904
Li Peng, *Prin*
EMP: 43 **EST:** 2015
SALES (est): 9.82MM **Privately Held**
Web: www.palleonpharma.com
SIC: 2834 Pharmaceutical preparations

(G-12747)
PERSPECTA SVCS & SOLUTIONS INC (DH)
Also Called: Qinetiq North America, Inc.
350 2nd Ave Bldg 1 (02451-1104)
PHONE.................781 684-4000
Doctor Andrew Rogers, *Pr*
Jeff Yorsz, *
Doctor Richard Wiesman, *Chief Scientist*
Doug Ounanian, *Operations*
Robert Polutchko, *Strategy Vice President*
EMP: 9 **EST:** 2005
SALES (est): 6.32MM **Privately Held**
SIC: 3812 8731 Defense systems and equipment; Engineering laboratory, except testing
HQ: Qinetiq Us Holdings, Inc.
5885 Trinity Pkwy Ste 130
Centreville VA 20120
202 429-6630

(G-12748)
PHASE FORWARD
880 Winter St (02451-1464)
PHONE.................781 626-1256
EMP: 26 **EST:** 2019
SALES (est): 702.53K **Privately Held**
Web: www.oracle.com
SIC: 8322 7372 7371 Individual and family services; Prepackaged software; Custom computer programming services

(G-12749)
PLATAINE INC
465 Waverley Oaks Rd Ste 420 (02452-8496)
PHONE.................336 905-0900
EMP: 9 **EST:** 2008
SALES (est): 1.21MM **Privately Held**
Web: www.plataine.com
SIC: 7372 Application computer software

(G-12750)
PLATING FOR ELECTRONICS LLC
94 Calvary St (02453-5920)
PHONE.................781 893-2368
EMP: 67 **EST:** 2020
SALES (est): 3.88MM **Privately Held**
Web: www.platingforelectronics.com

SIC: 3471 Electroplating of metals or formed products

(G-12751)
PRAECIS PHARMACEUTICALS INC
830 Winter St Ste 1 (02451-1477)
PHONE.................781 795-4100
EMP: 5085 **EST:** 1993
SQ FT: 65,000
SALES (est): 6.27MM
SALES (corp-wide): 35.31B **Privately Held**
SIC: 2834 Pharmaceutical preparations
HQ: Glaxosmithkline Holdings (Americas) Inc.
1105 N Market St Ste 622
Wilmington DE 19801
302 984-6932

(G-12752)
PRESTIGE CSTM MIRROR & GL INC
182 High St (02453-5914)
PHONE.................781 647-0878
Phillip Wallace, *Pr*
EMP: 13 **EST:** 1989
SALES (est): 954.72K **Privately Held**
Web: www.prestigecmg.com
SIC: 3231 1793 Doors, glass: made from purchased glass; Glass and glazing work

(G-12753)
PRIMARY PDC INC (PA)
1265 Main St (02451-1743)
PHONE.................781 386-2000
John W Loose, *Ch Bd*
▲ **EMP:** 7 **EST:** 1937
SQ FT: 125,000
SALES (est): 1.34MM
SALES (corp-wide): 1.34MM **Privately Held**
SIC: 3861 3827 3695 3577 Photographic equipment and supplies; Lenses, optical: all types except ophthalmic; Video recording tape, blank; Diskette or key-disk equipment

(G-12754)
PTC INC
230 3rd Ave Prospect Place (02451-7528)
PHONE.................617 792-7622
C R Harrison, *Mgr*
EMP: 7
SALES (corp-wide): 2.1B **Publicly Held**
Web: www.ptc.com
SIC: 7372 Prepackaged software
PA: Ptc Inc.
121 Seaport Blvd
Boston MA 02210
781 370-5000

(G-12755)
PYRAMID TECHNICAL CONS INC
135 Beaver St Ste 102 (02452-8463)
PHONE.................781 402-1700
EMP: 15 **EST:** 1986
SALES (est): 2.33MM **Privately Held**
Web: www.ptcusa.com
SIC: 8711 3845 Consulting engineer; Electromedical equipment

(G-12756)
QUEEN SCREW & MFG INC
60 Farwell St (02453-8378)
PHONE.................781 894-8110
Domenic De Julio, *Pr*
Michael De Julio, *
Peter Babigian, *
Gloria Babigian, *Stockholder*
Sandra Vecchio, *Stockholder*

EMP: 55 **EST:** 1966
SQ FT: 13,500
SALES (est): 7.09MM **Privately Held**
Web: www.queenscrew.com
SIC: 3599 Machine shop, jobbing and repair

(G-12757)
R & H COMMUNICATIONS INC (PA)
Also Called: Allegra Print and Imaging
187 Lexington St Ste 4 (02452-4602)
P.O. Box 550146 (02455-0146)
PHONE.................781 893-6221
Ruth Cretella, *Pr*
Henry A Cretella, *Treas*
EMP: 11 **EST:** 1984
SQ FT: 2,100
SALES (est): 1.42MM
SALES (corp-wide): 1.42MM **Privately Held**
Web: www.allegramarketingprint.com
SIC: 2752 7334 2791 2789 Offset printing; Photocopying and duplicating services; Typesetting; Bookbinding and related work

(G-12758)
RAMPAGE SYSTEMS INC
411 Waverley Oaks Rd Ste 138 (02452-8514)
PHONE.................781 891-1001
Thomas Genova, *Pr*
Paul Mccusker, *Treas*
Mitch Bogart, *
EMP: 26 **EST:** 1992
SQ FT: 15,000
SALES (est): 3.06MM **Privately Held**
Web: www.rampageinc.com
SIC: 3577 7371 3575 Computer peripheral equipment, nec; Computer software development; Computer terminals

(G-12759)
RAYTHEON COMPANY (HQ)
Also Called: Raytheon
870 Winter St (02451-1449)
P.O. Box 660425 (75266-0425)
PHONE.................781 522-3000
Gregory J Hayes, *Ch Bd*
Roy A Azevedo, *Pr*
Anthony F O'brien, *VP*
Michael J Wood, *VP*
EMP: 450 **EST:** 1922
SQ FT: 955,967
SALES (est): 29.18MM
SALES (corp-wide): 68.92B **Publicly Held**
Web: www.rtx.com
SIC: 3812 3663 3761 Defense systems and equipment; Space satellite communications equipment; Guided missiles and space vehicles, research and development
PA: Rtx Corporation
1000 Wilson Blvd
Arlington VA 22209
781 522-3000

(G-12760)
RAYTHEON INTERNATIONAL INC (PA)
870 Winter St (02451-1449)
PHONE.................781 522-3000
John D Harris Ii, *CEO*
Thomas A Vecchiolla, *
Robert B Shanks, *
Richard A Goglia, *
EMP: 11 **EST:** 1993
SALES (est): 1.27MM
SALES (corp-wide): 1.27MM **Privately Held**

SIC: 3812 3769 Missile guidance systems and equipment; Airframe assemblies, guided missiles

(G-12761)
RAYTHEON KOREAN SUPPORT CO (DH)
870 Winter St (02451-1449)
PHONE.................339 645-6111
Richard Guzzardi, *Brnch Mgr*
Thomas A Kennedy, *CEO*
EMP: 37 **EST:** 1922
SALES (est): 68.36K
SALES (corp-wide): 68.92B **Publicly Held**
SIC: 3812 3663 3761 Defense systems and equipment; Space satellite communications equipment; Guided missiles and space vehicles, research and development
HQ: Raytheon Company
870 Winter St
Waltham MA 02451
781 522-3000

(G-12762)
RAYTHEON SUTHEAST ASIA SYSTEMS (DH)
Also Called: Raytheon
870 Winter St (02451-1449)
P.O. Box 2030 (01810-0036)
PHONE.................978 470-5000
William Swanson, *CEO*
▲ **EMP:** 32 **EST:** 1980
SALES (est): 23.95MM
SALES (corp-wide): 68.92B **Publicly Held**
Web: www.rtx.com
SIC: 3812 3663 3674 1629 Radar systems and equipment; Marine radio communications equipment; Transistors; Industrial plant construction
HQ: Raytheon Company
870 Winter St
Waltham MA 02451
781 522-3000

(G-12763)
RECYCLED PAPER COMPANY INC
Also Called: Recycled Paper Printing
37 Whitcomb St (02453-8674)
PHONE.................617 737-9911
TOLL FREE: 800
Todd M Truesdale, *Pr*
EMP: 17 **EST:** 1983
SALES (est): 962.05K **Privately Held**
Web: www.recycledpaper.com
SIC: 2752 Offset printing

(G-12764)
REGENACY PHARMACEUTICALS LLC
303 Wyman St Ste 300 (02451-1255)
PHONE.................617 245-1306
Simon S Jones Ph.d., *Pr*
Matthew Jarpe, *
John Rocha, *
David Michelson Md Ccmo, *Prin*
EMP: 50 **EST:** 2017
SALES (est): 6.4MM **Privately Held**
Web: www.regenacy.com
SIC: 2834 Pharmaceutical preparations

(G-12765)
REPLIGEN CORPORATION (PA)
Also Called: Repligen
41 Seyon St Ste 100 (02453-8358)
PHONE.................781 250-0111
Tony J Hunt, *Pr*
Karen A Dawes, *
Jon K Snodgres, *CFO*

Ralf Kuriyel, *Senior Vice President Research & Development*
Olivier Loeillot, *CCO*
EMP: 120 **EST:** 1981
SQ FT: 76,000
SALES (est): 801.54MM
SALES (corp-wide): 801.54MM **Publicly Held**
Web: www.repligen.com
SIC: 2836 Biological products, except diagnostic

(G-12766)
REVULYTICS INC (DH)
Also Called: Revulytics
130 Turner St (02453-8901)
PHONE..................................781 398-3400
Joseph Noonan, *CEO*
Kevin Ball, *VP Fin*
EMP: 26 **EST:** 2006
SALES (est): 12.13MM
SALES (corp-wide): 25.94MM **Privately Held**
Web: www.revenera.com
SIC: 7372 Business oriented computer software
HQ: Flexera Software Llc
300 Park Blvd
Itasca IL 60143

(G-12767)
REVVITY INC (PA)
Also Called: Perkinelmer
940 Winter St (02451-1457)
PHONE..................................781 663-6900
Prahlad R Singh, *Pr*
Alexis P Michas, *Non-Executive Chairman of the Board**
Max Krakowiak, *Sr VP*
Miriame Victor, *CCO*
Joel S Goldberg, *Admn Execs*
▲ **EMP:** 120 **EST:** 1937
SALES (est): 3.31B
SALES (corp-wide): 3.31B **Publicly Held**
Web: www.perkinelmer.com
SIC: 3845 3826 Electromedical equipment; Environmental testing equipment

(G-12768)
REVVITY HEALTH SCIENCES INC (DH)
Also Called: Perkinelmer Hlth Sciences Inc
940 Winter St (02451-1457)
PHONE..................................781 663-6900
Robert F Friel, *Pr*
▲ **EMP:** 100 **EST:** 1997
SQ FT: 25,000
SALES (est): 156.28MM
SALES (corp-wide): 3.31B **Publicly Held**
Web: www.perkinelmer.com
SIC: 3826 Analytical instruments
HQ: Revvity Holdings, Inc.
940 Winter St
Wellesley MA 02481

(G-12769)
REVVITY SIGNALS SOFTWARE INC (DH)
Also Called: P&E Informatics
940 Winter St (02451-1457)
PHONE..................................781 663-6900
Nathanael M Davis, *Pr*
David C Francisco, *Treas*
Drew C Adams, *VP*
Rusty Irving, *VP*
Devendra Deshmukh, *VP*
EMP: 85 **EST:** 1994
SQ FT: 17,000
SALES (est): 22.94MM
SALES (corp-wide): 3.31B **Publicly Held**

Web: www.cambridgesoft.com
SIC: 7373 7372 7371 Systems software development services; Prepackaged software; Custom computer programming services
HQ: Revvity Holdings, Inc.
940 Winter St
Wellesley MA 02481

(G-12770)
RICHARD H BIRD & CO INC
Also Called: Bird Precision
1 Spruce St (02453-4316)
P.O. Box 540569 (02454-0569)
PHONE..................................781 894-0160
Carl J Cunningham, *Pr*
EMP: 39 **EST:** 1913
SQ FT: 12,400
SALES (est): 4.12MM **Privately Held**
Web: www.birdprecision.com
SIC: 3915 Jewel bearings, synthetic

(G-12771)
ROCKET SOFTWARE INC (PA)
77 4th Ave (02451-7565)
PHONE..................................781 577-4323
Andy Youniss, *Pr*
Matt Deres, *CIO**
Barbara Goose, *
Bruce Bowden, *
Alyse Daghelian, *CRO**
EMP: 144 **EST:** 2002
SALES (est): 654.52K **Privately Held**
Web: www.rocketsoftware.com
SIC: 7372 Prepackaged software

(G-12772)
ROCKET SOFTWARE SYSTEMS INC
77 4th Ave (02451-7565)
PHONE..................................248 833-9000
Maureen Huber, *Pr*
Andy Youniss, *
EMP: 35 **EST:** 1995
SALES (est): 21.27K **Privately Held**
Web: www.rocketsoftware.com
SIC: 7371 7372 Computer software development; Prepackaged software
PA: Rocket Software, Inc.
77 4th Ave Ste 101
Waltham MA 02451

(G-12773)
RODIN THERAPEUTICS INC
852 Winter St (02451-1439)
PHONE..................................857 201-2770
Adam J Rosenberg, *CEO*
Martin Jefson, *COO*
Ajim Tamboli, *CFO*
EMP: 8 **EST:** 2013
SALES (est): 2.34MM **Privately Held**
Web: www.alkermes.com
SIC: 2834 Pharmaceutical preparations
PA: Alkermes Public Limited Company
Connacht House
Dublin D04 C

(G-12774)
ROTEK INSTRUMENT CORP
390 Main St (02452-6640)
P.O. Box 540504 (02454-0504)
PHONE..................................781 899-4611
Paul Lualdi, *Pr*
Rose-ann West, *Sec*
EMP: 20 **EST:** 1970
SQ FT: 6,150
SALES (est): 2.19MM **Privately Held**
Web: www.rotek.com

SIC: 3825 3829 Standards and calibration equipment for electrical measuring; Measuring and controlling devices, nec

(G-12775)
RSD AMERICA INC
77 4th Ave Fl 1 (02451-7567)
PHONE..................................201 996-1000
Pierre Van Beneden, *Pr*
Louis Pierre Roger, *VP*
Deborah St Clair, *Sec*
Serge Quiniou, *Treas*
EMP: 18 **EST:** 1983
SALES (est): 3.28MM **Privately Held**
SIC: 5045 7372 7379 Computer software; Prepackaged software; Computer related consulting services

(G-12776)
SAUCONY INC (DH)
Also Called: Hyde Athletic Industries
500 Totten Pond Rd Ste 1 (02451-1927)
PHONE..................................617 824-6000
John H Fisher, *Ch Bd*
John H Fisher, *Ch Bd*
Charles A Gottesman, *Executive Business Development Vice President**
Michael Umana, *
Roger P Deschenes, *CAO**
▲ **EMP:** 125 **EST:** 1912
SQ FT: 141,000
SALES (est): 100.7MM
SALES (corp-wide): 2.68B **Publicly Held**
Web: www.saucony.com
SIC: 3149 3143 3144 2329 Athletic shoes, except rubber or plastic; Men's footwear, except athletic; Women's footwear, except athletic; Men's and boys' sportswear and athletic clothing
HQ: The Stride Rite Corporation
500 Totten Pond Rd Ste 1
Waltham MA 02451
617 824-6000

(G-12777)
SDPD HOLDINGS INC
94 Calvary St (02453-5920)
P.O. Box 540536 (02454-0536)
PHONE..................................781 893-2368
Stephen J Davino, *Pr*
Phillip J Davino, *
Michael A Davino, *
EMP: 44 **EST:** 1958
SQ FT: 19,000
SALES (est): 4.39MM **Privately Held**
Web: www.platingforelectronics.com
SIC: 3471 Electroplating of metals or formed products

(G-12778)
SEQIRUS INC
225 Wyman St (02451-1291)
PHONE..................................617 871-5734
EMP: 262
Web: www.csl.com
SIC: 2836 Biological products, except diagnostic
HQ: Seqirus Inc.
475 Green Oaks Pkwy
Holly Springs NC 27540
919 577-5000

(G-12779)
SILVERSIDE DETECTORS INC
117 Beaver St (02452-8467)
PHONE..................................617 684-5925
Andrew Inglis, *Pr*
Sarah Haig, *Sec*
EMP: 8 **EST:** 2013
SALES (est): 1.12MM **Privately Held**

Web: www.silverside-detectors.com
SIC: 3829 Count rate meters, nuclear radiation

(G-12780)
SMART SOURCE LLC
280 Bear Hill Rd (02451-1009)
PHONE..................................781 890-0110
EMP: 12
SALES (corp-wide): 55MM **Privately Held**
SIC: 2759 Commercial printing, nec
PA: Smart Source, Llc
60 E 42nd St Ste 1060
New York NY 30024
212 764-7200

(G-12781)
SOBI INC (HQ)
77 4th Ave Fl 3 (02451-7567)
PHONE..................................781 786-7370
Duane Barnes, *Pr*
Christine Belin, *Treas*
Guled Adam, *Sec*
EMP: 16 **EST:** 2012
SALES (est): 11.16MM
SALES (corp-wide): 1.79B **Privately Held**
Web: www.sobi.com
SIC: 2834 5122 Drugs acting on the gastrointestinal or genitourinary system; Pharmaceuticals
PA: Swedish Orphan Biovitrum Ab (Publ)
Tomtebodavagen 23a
Solna 171 6
86972000

(G-12782)
STARFISH STORAGE CORPORATION
271 Waverley Oaks Rd Ste 301 (02452-8470)
PHONE..................................781 250-3000
Deena A Berton, *Prin*
Deena Berton, *Pr*
Joseph Hickson Attorney, *Prin*
EMP: 9 **EST:** 2013
SALES (est): 1.21MM **Privately Held**
Web: www.starfishstorage.com
SIC: 7372 Application computer software

(G-12783)
STRIDE RITE CORPORATION (HQ)
Also Called: Stride Rite
500 Totten Pond Rd Ste 1 (02451-1927)
PHONE..................................617 824-6000
Blake W Krueger, *Pr*
Gregg Ribatt, *
Frank A Caruso, *CAO**
Charles W Redepenning Junior, *Sec*
Yusef Akyuz, *CIO**
◆ **EMP:** 400 **EST:** 1919
SQ FT: 148,000
SALES (est): 409.01MM
SALES (corp-wide): 2.68B **Publicly Held**
Web: www.striderite.com
SIC: 5139 5661 3149 Footwear, athletic; Shoe stores; Children's footwear, except athletic
PA: Wolverine World Wide, Inc.
9341 Courtland Dr Ne
Rockford MI 49351
616 866-5500

(G-12784)
SWISS CONCEPT INC
Also Called: Concept Manufacturing Company
77 Felton St (02453-4120)
P.O. Box 6109 (01746-6109)
PHONE..................................781 894-1281
EMP: 8 **EST:** 1990

SQ FT: 3,000
SALES (est): 856.28K Privately Held
SIC: 3599 Machine shop, jobbing and repair

(G-12785)
SYNDAX PHARMACEUTICALS INC (PA)
Also Called: Syndax
35 Gatehouse Dr Bldg D (02451-1215)
PHONE..................................781 419-1400
EMP: 23 EST: 2005
SQ FT: 12,207
Web: www.syndax.com
SIC: 2834 Pharmaceutical preparations

(G-12786)
SYNDAX SECURITIES CORPORATION
35 Gatehouse Dr (02451-1215)
PHONE..................................781 472-2985
Richard P Shea, Prin
EMP: 11 EST: 2017
SALES (est): 1.06MM Publicly Held
Web: www.syndax.com
SIC: 2834 Pharmaceutical preparations
PA: Syndax Pharmaceuticals, Inc.
   35 Gatehouse Dr Fl 3
   Waltham MA 02451

(G-12787)
TACTAI INC
225 Wyman St (02451-1288)
PHONE..................................617 391-7915
Steven Domenikos, CEO
EMP: 10 EST: 2016
SALES (est): 742.98K Privately Held
Web: www.tactai.com
SIC: 7373 7374 7379 7372 Systems
   software development services; Computer
   processing services; Computer related
   consulting services; Application computer
   software

(G-12788)
TALAMAS COMPANY INC
Also Called: Talamas Broadcast Equipment
280 Bear Hill Rd (02451-1009)
PHONE..................................617 928-3437
David Talamas, Pr
Diane Talamas, VP
Christine Talamas, Sec
EMP: 17 EST: 1979
SALES (est): 2.76MM Privately Held
Web: www.talamas.com
SIC: 5999 3663 3669 Theatrical equipment
   and supplies; Radio and t.v.
   communications equipment; Visual
   communication systems

(G-12789)
TECHNICAL PUBLICATIONS INC
Also Called: Tpi Solutions Ink
45 Calvary St (02453-5974)
PHONE..................................781 899-0263
Carrie Grove, Pr
Diana Spurrell, Clerk
EMP: 10 EST: 1962
SQ FT: 8,000
SALES (est): 1.4MM Privately Held
Web: www.tpisolutionsink.com
SIC: 2752 Offset printing

(G-12790)
TECOGEN INC (PA)
Also Called: Tecogen
45 1st Ave (02451-1105)
PHONE..................................781 466-6402
Benjamin M Locke, CEO
Angelina M Galiteva, *

Robert A Panora, Pr
Abinand Rangesh, *
Roger Deschenes, CAO
▲ EMP: 27 EST: 1960
SQ FT: 43,000
SALES (est): 25MM
SALES (corp-wide): 25MM Publicly Held
Web: www.tecogen.com
SIC: 3585 7623 Air conditioning units,
   complete: domestic or industrial; Air
   conditioning repair

(G-12791)
TEGO INC
204 Second Ave Ste 1 (02451-1126)
PHONE..................................781 547-5680
Timothy Butler, CEO
▼ EMP: 9 EST: 2005
SALES (est): 2.3MM Privately Held
Web: www.tegoinc.com
SIC: 3674 Semiconductors and related
   devices

(G-12792)
TELOME INC
1393 Main St (02451-1632)
PHONE..................................617 383-7565
Preston Estep, CEO
EMP: 9 EST: 2011
SQ FT: 3,800
SALES (est): 638.61K Privately Held
Web: www.telome.com
SIC: 2835 In vitro diagnostics

(G-12793)
TESARO INC (HQ)
Also Called: Tesaro
1000 Winter St Ste 3300 (02451-1230)
PHONE..................................339 970-0900
EMP: 63 EST: 2010
SQ FT: 260,000
SALES (est): 229.84MM
SALES (corp-wide): 35.31B Privately Held
Web: www.gsk.com
SIC: 2834 Pharmaceutical preparations
PA: Gsk Plc
   G S K House
   Brentford MIDDX TW8 9
   208 047-5000

(G-12794)
TESARO SECURITIES CORPORATION
1000 Winter St (02451-1436)
PHONE..................................339 970-0900
Gregory Covino, Dir
Mary Lynne Hedley, *
Jerald Korn, *
EMP: 652 EST: 2012
SALES (est): 2.32MM
SALES (corp-wide): 35.31B Privately Held
SIC: 2834 Pharmaceutical preparations
HQ: Tesaro, Inc.
   1000 Winter St Ste 3300
   Waltham MA 02451

(G-12795)
TETRAPHASE PHARMACEUTICALS INC
Also Called: Tetraphase Pharmaceuticals
35 Gatehouse Dr (02451-1215)
PHONE..................................617 715-3600
Pavel Raifeld, CEO
Marianne Zhen, CAO
EMP: 67 EST: 2006
SQ FT: 37,388
SALES (est): 7.38MM
SALES (corp-wide): 331.34MM Publicly
Held
Web: www.lajollapharmaceutical.com

SIC: 2834 2833 Pharmaceutical
   preparations; Antibiotics
HQ: La Jolla Pharmaceutical Company
   35 Gatehouse Dr Ste E0
   Waltham MA 02451

(G-12796)
THEA PHARMA INC
303 Wyman St (02451-1253)
PHONE..................................781 832-3667
Susan Benton, Pr
EMP: 67 EST: 2014
SALES (est): 4.05MM Privately Held
Web: www.theapharmainc.com
SIC: 3851 Ophthalmic goods

(G-12797)
THERMEDETEC INC
Also Called: Thermo Detection
21 Hickory Dr # 4 (02451-1034)
PHONE..................................508 520-0430
Anne Pol, Sr VP
Kenneth Apicerno, *
EMP: 19 EST: 1990
SQ FT: 34,250
SALES (est): 2.27MM
SALES (corp-wide): 44.91B Publicly Held
SIC: 3826 Analytical instruments
PA: Thermo Fisher Scientific Inc.
   168 3rd Ave
   Waltham MA 02451
   781 622-1000

(G-12798)
THERMO ELECTRON F S C INC
81 Wyman St (02451-1223)
PHONE..................................781 622-1000
Marijn Dekkers, Pr
EMP: 200 EST: 1999
SALES (est): 41.67MM
SALES (corp-wide): 44.91B Publicly Held
SIC: 3398 Metal heat treating
PA: Thermo Fisher Scientific Inc.
   168 3rd Ave
   Waltham MA 02451
   781 622-1000

(G-12799)
THERMO FISHER FINCL SVCS INC
168 3rd Ave (02451-7551)
PHONE..................................781 622-1000
Seth H Hoogasian, Pr
Kenneth J Apicerno, *
EMP: 99 EST: 1996
SALES (est): 46.05MM
SALES (corp-wide): 44.91B Publicly Held
SIC: 3826 Analytical instruments
PA: Thermo Fisher Scientific Inc.
   168 3rd Ave
   Waltham MA 02451
   781 622-1000

(G-12800)
THERMO FISHER SCIENTIFIC INC (PA)
Also Called: Thermo Fisher
168 3rd Ave (02451-7551)
PHONE..................................781 622-1000
Marc N Casper, Ch Bd
Michel Lagarde, Ex VP
Gianluca Pettiti, Ex VP
Stephen Williamson, Sr VP
Michael A Boxer, Sr VP
EMP: 210 EST: 1956
SALES (est): 44.91B
SALES (corp-wide): 44.91B Publicly Held
Web: www.thermofisher.com

SIC: 3826 3845 3823 3629 Analytical
   instruments; Electromedical equipment;
   Process control instruments; Electronic
   generation equipment

(G-12801)
THERMO INSTRUMENT SYSTEMS INC
81 Wyman St (02451-1223)
PHONE..................................781 622-1000
Marizn E Dekkers, Pr
EMP: 17 EST: 1986
SALES (est): 668.79K Privately Held
SIC: 3829 Measuring and controlling
   devices, nec

(G-12802)
THERMO POWER CORPORATION
45 1st Ave (02451-1105)
PHONE..................................781 622-1400
Brian D Holt, Ch Bd
J Timothy Corcoran, *
Theo Melas-kyriazi, CFO
Paul F Kelleher, Chief Accounting Officer*
EMP: 1400 EST: 1985
SQ FT: 400,000
SALES (est): 92.55MM
SALES (corp-wide): 44.91B Publicly Held
Web: www.thermopower.com.ph
SIC: 3585 8731 3519 Air conditioning
   equipment, complete; Commercial physical
   research; Internal combustion engines, nec
PA: Thermo Fisher Scientific Inc.
   168 3rd Ave
   Waltham MA 02451
   781 622-1000

(G-12803)
THIRD POLE INC (PA)
Also Called: Third Pole Therapeutics
309 Waverley Oaks Rd Ste 404
(02452-8460)
PHONE..................................908 310-0596
Bill Athenson, CEO
Christopher Miles, *
Philip E Silkoff, CMO*
Elizabeth Holmberg, *
EMP: 19 EST: 2014
SALES (est): 9.59MM
SALES (corp-wide): 9.59MM Privately
Held
Web: www.pole3.com
SIC: 3845 5047 Respiratory analysis
   equipment, electromedical; Electro-medical
   equipment

(G-12804)
THOMSON REUTERS CORPORATION
950 Winter St Ste 1900 (02451-1479)
PHONE..................................781 250-4340
Thomas Tague, Brnch Mgr
EMP: 20
SALES (corp-wide): 10.66B Publicly Held
Web: www.thomsonreuters.com
SIC: 2741 Miscellaneous publishing
HQ: Thomson Reuters Corporation
   333 Bay St
   Toronto ON M5H 2
   416 687-7500

(G-12805)
TOUCH INC
27 Spring St (02451-4431)
PHONE..................................781 894-8133
George Simpson, Pr
Ira S Bernstein, VP
EMP: 15 EST: 1977

SQ FT: 4,000
SALES (est): 474.62K **Privately Held**
Web: www.the-touch.com
SIC: 3911 Jewelry, precious metal

(G-12806)
TRIPCRAFT LLC
15 Fiske Ave (02453-7703)
PHONE.................................781 588-9100
Michael J Murray, *Prin*
EMP: 10 **EST:** 2010
SALES (est): 322.04K **Privately Held**
Web: www.tripcraft.com
SIC: 7372 Prepackaged software

(G-12807)
TSCAN THERAPEUTICS INC
Also Called: Tscan
830 Winter St (02451-1477)
PHONE.................................857 399-9500
Gavin Macbeath, *CSO*
Timothy Barberich, *
Brian Silver, *Sr VP*
William Desmarais, *Chief Business Officer*
EMP: 61 **EST:** 2018
SALES (est): 13.54MM **Privately Held**
Web: www.tscan.com
SIC: 2836 Biological products, except
　　diagnostic

(G-12808)
UPTODATE INC (DH)
230 3rd Ave Ste 1000 (02451-7560)
P.O. Box 412094 (02241-2094)
PHONE.................................781 392-2000
Denise Basow, *VP*
John Pins, *
David A Del Toro, *
Steve M Kerscher, *
Deidra D Gold, *
EMP: 59 **EST:** 1991
SALES (est): 379.18K
SALES (corp-wide): 5.66B **Privately Held**
Web: www.wolterskluwer.com
SIC: 7372 8011 Business oriented computer
　　software; Offices and clinics of medical
　　doctors
HQ: Wolters Kluwer Health, Inc.
　　2001 Market St Ste 5
　　Philadelphia PA 19103
　　215 521-8300

(G-12809)
VALIDATED CLOUD INC (PA)
330 Bear Hill Rd Ste 205 (02451-1093)
PHONE.................................617 849-8650
Joshua Campbell, *Prin*
EMP: 11 **EST:** 2015
SALES (est): 2.54MM **Privately Held**
Web: www.validatedcloud.com
SIC: 7372 Prepackaged software

(G-12810)
VERALTO CORPORATION ✪
225 Wyman St Ste 250 (02451-1289)
PHONE.................................781 755-3655
Jennifer L Honeycutt, *Pr*
EMP: 7 **EST:** 2022
SALES (est): 78.66K **Privately Held**
SIC: 3589 Sewage and water treatment
　　equipment

(G-12811)
VERALTO ENTERPRISE LLC (PA) ✪
225 Wyman St Ste 250 (02451-1289)
PHONE.................................603 860-7300
Jennifer L Honeycutt, *Pr*
Linda Filler, *Ch Bd*
Sameer Ralhan, *Sr VP*

Surekha Trivedi, *STRAT &
SUSTAINABILITY*
Lesley Beneteau, *Senior Vice President
Human Resources*
EMP: 14664 **EST:** 2022
SALES (est): 751.76MM
SALES (corp-wide): 751.76MM **Publicly
Held**
SIC: 3829 Measuring and controlling
　　devices, nec

(G-12812)
VIRTUAL SOFTWARE SYSTEMS INC
130 Black Bear Dr Unit 1315 (02451-0247)
PHONE.................................781 424-4899
John Conway, *CEO*
Lawrence Bennigson, *Ch*
Elizabeth Hight, *Bd of Dir*
EMP: 7 **EST:** 2014
SALES (est): 463.15K **Privately Held**
SIC: 7372 Business oriented computer
　　software

(G-12813)
VISTAPRINT CORP SOLUTIONS INC
Also Called: Vistaprint
275 Wyman St Ste 100 (02451-1218)
PHONE.................................844 347-4162
Jonathan Chevalier, *Pr*
Paul Mcdermott, *VP*
Kathryn Leach, *Sec*
EMP: 22 **EST:** 2015
SALES (est): 1.54MM **Privately Held**
Web: www.vistaprintcorporate.com
SIC: 2752 Promotional printing, lithographic

(G-12814)
VISTERRA INC
275 Second Ave Ste 300 (02451-1159)
PHONE.................................617 498-1070
Brian Pereira, *Pr*
David Oldach, *Chief Medical Officer*
Zachary Shriver, *
Greg Miller, *Chief Business Officer*
Chris Kiefer, *Chief Accounting Officer*
EMP: 42 **EST:** 2007
SALES (est): 11.79MM **Privately Held**
Web: www.visterrainc.com
SIC: 2834 Druggists' preparations
　　(pharmaceuticals)
HQ: Otsuka America, Inc.
　　1 Embarcadero Ctr # 2020
　　San Francisco CA 94111

(G-12815)
WATERMILLPREFERRED PARTNERS LP
800 South St Ste 355 (02453-1457)
PHONE.................................781 790-5045
Steven Karol, *Mng Pt*
EMP: 18 **EST:** 2002
SALES (est): 420.39K **Privately Held**
SIC: 3069 Custom compounding of rubber
　　materials

(G-12816)
WAVEGUIDE CORPORATION
135 Beaver St Ste 310 (02452-8463)
P.O. Box 607 (02456-0607)
PHONE.................................617 892-9700
EMP: 7 **EST:** 2010
SQ FT: 300
SALES (est): 914.33K **Privately Held**
Web: www.waveguidecorp.com
SIC: 3826 Analytical instruments

(G-12817)
WEST ST INTRMDATE HLDINGS CORP (PA)
195 West St (02451-1111)
PHONE.................................781 434-5051
EMP: 69 **EST:** 2017
SALES (est): 2.44B
SALES (corp-wide): 2.44B **Privately Held**
Web: www.parexel.com
SIC: 2834 Pharmaceutical preparations

(G-12818)
WOODEN KIWI PRODUCTIONS LLC
Also Called: Wooden Kiwi
99 Hammond St Rear (02451-3624)
PHONE.................................781 209-2623
EMP: 9 **EST:** 1993
SQ FT: 4,400
SALES (est): 886.94K **Privately Held**
Web: www.woodenkiwi.com
SIC: 7922 1389 7822 Scenery design,
　　theatrical; Construction, repair, and
　　dismantling services; Motion picture and
　　tape distribution

(G-12819)
WORMTOWN ATOMIC PROPULSION
303 Bear Hill Rd (02451-1016)
PHONE.................................781 487-7777
Richard B Livingston, *Pr*
Ellen Livingston, *Treas*
EMP: 13 **EST:** 1999
SQ FT: 15,000
SALES (est): 633.05K **Privately Held**
SIC: 3764 Space propulsion units and parts

(G-12820)
XILIO THERAPEUTICS INC
Also Called: XILIO THERAPEUTICS
828 Winter St Ste 300 (02451-1420)
PHONE.................................617 430-4680
Rene Russo, *Pr*
Paul Clancy, *Ch Bd*
Salvatore Giovine, *CFO*
EMP: 69 **EST:** 2015
SQ FT: 28,000
Web: www.xiliotx.com
SIC: 2834 Pharmaceutical preparations

(G-12821)
ZERO POROSITY CASTING INC
411 Waverley Oaks Rd (02452-8448)
PHONE.................................617 391-0008
Arpine Azizian, *Prin*
EMP: 10 **EST:** 2010
SALES (est): 499.57K **Privately Held**
Web: www.zpcasting.com
SIC: 3911 Jewelry, precious metal

(G-12822)
ZOOM INFORMATION LLC (DH)
275 Wyman St Ste 120 (02451-1218)
PHONE.................................781 693-7500
Derek Schoettle, *CEO*
Paul Boulanger, *
Peter Weyman, *CRO*
Leo Laferriere, *
Seth Low, *
EMP: 31 **EST:** 2000
SALES (est): 32.31MM
SALES (corp-wide): 1.24B **Publicly Held**
Web: www.zoominfo.com
SIC: 2741 Internet publishing and
　　broadcasting
HQ: Zoominfo Holdings Llc
　　805 Broadway St Ste 900
　　Vancouver WA 98660

(G-12823)
ZURICH INSTRUMENTS USA INC
400 5th Ave (02451-8706)
PHONE.................................949 682-5172
Vikrant Mahajam, *VP*
EMP: 10
SALES (est): 741.84K **Privately Held**
SIC: 3825 Digital test equipment, electronic
　　and electrical circuits

Ware
Hampshire County

(G-12824)
AXIS CNC INCORPORATED
39 Gould Rd (01082-9809)
PHONE.................................413 967-6803
Daniel G Larzazs, *Prin*
EMP: 16 **EST:** 2011
SALES (est): 485.63K **Privately Held**
Web: www.axiscncinc.net
SIC: 3599 Machine shop, jobbing and repair

(G-12825)
GILLESPIE CORPORATION
34 Pine St (01082-1567)
P.O. Box 359 (01082-0359)
PHONE.................................413 967-4980
Gary West, *Owner*
Gary West, *Pr*
Mae Dudek, *
Donna S West, *
Linda Kruckas, *
EMP: 25 **EST:** 1923
SQ FT: 18,000
SALES (est): 3.54MM **Privately Held**
Web: www.gillespiecorp.com
SIC: 3534 3536 8711 Elevators and
　　equipment; Hoists, cranes, and monorails;
　　Consulting engineer

(G-12826)
KANZAKI SPECIALTY PAPERS INC (DH)
20 Cummings St (01082-1716)
PHONE.................................413 967-6204
Stephen P Hefner, *Pr*
Stephen Hefner, *
David Gonsalves, *
Joshua Polak, *
Peter Sawosi, *
◆ **EMP:** 205 **EST:** 1986
SQ FT: 300,000
SALES (est): 87.5MM **Privately Held**
Web: www.kanzakiusa.com
SIC: 2621 Paper mills
HQ: Oji Imaging Media Co., Ltd.
　　5-12-8, Ginza
　　Chuo-Ku TKY 104-0

(G-12827)
QUABBIN WIRE & CABLE CO INC (PA)
10 Maple St (01082-1597)
PHONE.................................413 967-6281
Paul Engel, *Pr*
Michael P Angelini, *
George Melnik, *General Vice President*
Tom Russell, *Technology Vice President*
Stacy Gilmour, *
EMP: 72 **EST:** 1975
SQ FT: 140,000
SALES (est): 18.32MM
SALES (corp-wide): 18.32MM **Privately
Held**
Web: www.quabbin.com
SIC: 3643 3357 Current-carrying wiring
　　services; Communication wire

Wareham
Plymouth County

(G-12828)
BEAVER DAM PARTNERS INC
125 Cromesett Rd (02571-7111)
PHONE.............................508 717-9799
Patrick E Lester, *Prin*
EMP: 8 **EST:** 2009
SALES (est): 202.86K **Privately Held**
Web: www.beaverdampartners.com
SIC: 2711 Newspapers

(G-12829)
BEETLE INC
3 Thacher Ln (02571)
PHONE.............................508 295-8585
EMP: 7 **EST:** 1993
SALES (est): 780.39K **Privately Held**
Web: www.beetlecat.com
SIC: 3732 Boats, fiberglass: building and repairing

(G-12830)
CAPE COD GINGER LLC
8 Kendrick Rd (02571-1154)
PHONE.............................508 295-2795
Richard Monroe, *Managing Member*
EMP: 7 **EST:** 2015
SALES (est): 200K **Privately Held**
Web: www.capecodginger.com
SIC: 5149 2087 Beverages, except coffee and tea; Beverage bases, concentrates, syrups, powders and mixes

(G-12831)
CAPE COD IRON CORP
Also Called: Steel Fabrication
2707 Cranberry Hwy (02571-1064)
PHONE.............................508 322-9985
Georges El Khazen, *Pr*
EMP: 15 **EST:** 2019
SALES (est): 1.11MM **Privately Held**
Web: www.capecodiron.com
SIC: 3441 Fabricated structural metal

(G-12832)
CAPE COD SHIPBUILDING CO
7 Narrows Rd (02571-1630)
P.O. Box 152 (02571-0152)
PHONE.............................508 295-3550
Gordon L Goodwin, *Pr*
Wendy Goodwin, *VP*
▼ **EMP:** 25 **EST:** 1899
SQ FT: 20,000
SALES (est): 986.15K **Privately Held**
Web: www.capecodshipbuilding.com
SIC: 3732 4492 4493 Sailboats, building and repairing; Marine towing services; Boat yards, storage and incidental repair

(G-12833)
CATAKI INTERNATIONAL INC
Also Called: Tak Systems
14 Kendrick Rd Ste 5 (02571-5020)
P.O. Box 939 (02538-0939)
PHONE.............................508 295-9630
Michael Diesso, *Pr*
Cheryl Cavacas, *VP*
EMP: 10 **EST:** 1987
SQ FT: 10,000
SALES (est): 460.5K **Privately Held**
Web: www.cataki.com
SIC: 3843 3069 7841 Dental equipment and supplies; Medical sundries, rubber; Video tape rental

(G-12834)
ELECTRO-PREP INC
Also Called: Greenwood Associates
8 Kendrick Rd Ste 1 (02571-1155)
PHONE.............................508 291-2880
Skip Sullivan, *Pr*
Richard Sullivan, *Treas*
Edward S Sullivan, *Treas*
Casey A Sullivan, *Sec*
EMP: 19 **EST:** 1978
SALES (est): 4.96MM **Privately Held**
Web: www.electroprep.com
SIC: 3496 5045 Miscellaneous fabricated wire products; Computers, peripherals, and software

(G-12835)
ERCON INC
7 Kendrick Rd Ste 3 (02571-1066)
P.O. Box 639 (02576-0639)
PHONE.............................508 291-1400
Dennis Ehrreich, *Pr*
EMP: 21 **EST:** 1967
SQ FT: 20,000
SALES (est): 775.61K **Privately Held**
Web: www.erconinc.com
SIC: 8731 3087 8748 Commercial research laboratory; Custom compound purchased resins; Business consulting, nec

(G-12836)
FACTORY FIVE RACING INC
9 Tow Rd (02571-1086)
PHONE.............................508 291-3443
◆ **EMP:** 39 **EST:** 1995
SQ FT: 41,000
SALES (est): 7.99MM **Privately Held**
Web: www.factoryfive.com
SIC: 5013 3714 Automotive supplies and parts; Motor vehicle parts and accessories

(G-12837)
HI-WAY CONCRETE PDTS CO INC
2746 Cranberry Hwy (02571-1042)
PHONE.............................508 295-0834
Richard J Vicino, *CEO*
Francis C Vicino Junior, *VP*
Michael J Vicino, *
Kristine R Monast, *
EMP: 25 **EST:** 1954
SQ FT: 9,600
SALES (est): 4.47MM **Privately Held**
Web: www.hiwayconcrete.com
SIC: 3271 3281 3251 Blocks, concrete or cinder: standard; Cut stone and stone products; Brick and structural clay tile

(G-12838)
HOSTAR MAR TRNSPT SYSTEMS INC
Also Called: Hostar
1 Kendrick Rd (02571-1077)
PHONE.............................508 295-2900
Patricia B Stimson, *Pr*
Dwight S Stimson Iii, *COO*
▼ **EMP:** 16 **EST:** 1986
SQ FT: 28,000
SALES (est): 4.42MM **Privately Held**
Web: www.hostarmarine.com
SIC: 3799 3537 2599 3569 Boat trailers; Platforms, stands, tables, pallets, and similar equipment; Mechanics' dollies; Jacks, hydraulic

(G-12839)
J & J TECHNOLOGIES INC
18 Kendrick Rd (02571-1079)
PHONE.............................508 291-3803
James Ayars, *Pr*
Jim Ayars, *
Jack Mcnally, *VP*
EMP: 70 **EST:** 1999
SQ FT: 30,000
SALES (est): 20MM **Privately Held**
Web: www.jjtech.com
SIC: 3672 Printed circuit boards

(G-12840)
MARIAN HEATH GREETING CARDS LLC
Also Called: Marian Heath
9 Kendrick Rd (02571-1077)
PHONE.............................508 291-0766
▲ **EMP:** 150
SIC: 2771 2679 2678 Greeting cards; Gift wrap, paper: made from purchased material ; Stationery: made from purchased materials

(G-12841)
NAVIONICS INC
Also Called: Navionics Inc
6 Thacher Ln (02571-1076)
PHONE.............................508 291-6000
Giuseppe Carnevali, *Ch Bd*
Bob Moshiri, *
Daniele Palma, *
▲ **EMP:** 27 **EST:** 1989
SALES (est): 11.96MM **Privately Held**
Web: www.navionics.com
SIC: 3812 Navigational systems and instruments
HQ: Garmin Italy Technologies Srl
Via Fondacci 269
Massarosa LU 55054
058 496-1696

(G-12842)
PROJECT RESOURCES INC
16 Kendrick Rd Ste 6 (02571-1067)
PHONE.............................508 295-7444
Carlo Dipersio, *Pr*
Joan Dipersio, *Clerk*
EMP: 14 **EST:** 1987
SQ FT: 7,500
SALES (est): 455.75K **Privately Held**
SIC: 3577 3613 Computer peripheral equipment, nec; Switchgear and switchboard apparatus

(G-12843)
R B MACHINE CO INC
Also Called: Standard Repair Co Division
2701 Cranberry Hwy (02571-1063)
PHONE.............................508 830-0567
Robert Burr, *Pr*
Dorothy Burr, *Treas*
EMP: 7 **EST:** 1979
SALES (est): 945.88K **Privately Held**
SIC: 3599 Machine shop, jobbing and repair

(G-12844)
SOFT-AS-A-GRAPE INC (PA)
328 Marion Rd (02571-1452)
PHONE.............................508 295-9900
Allen R Katzen, *Pr*
Ruth A Katzen, *
▲ **EMP:** 30 **EST:** 1973
SQ FT: 15,000
SALES (est): 9.19MM
SALES (corp-wide): 9.19MM **Privately Held**
Web: www.softasagrape.com
SIC: 5699 5136 5137 2396 T-shirts, custom printed; Sportswear, men's and boys'; Sportswear, women's and children's; Automotive and apparel trimmings

(G-12845)
SOUTHEAST SHELLFISH INC
22 Kendrick Rd (02571-1079)
PHONE.............................508 273-0323
David Gallant, *Pr*
EMP: 10 **EST:** 1998
SQ FT: 3,000
SALES (est): 2.48MM **Privately Held**
Web: www.diggerschoice-seafood.com
SIC: 5146 2092 Seafoods; Fresh or frozen packaged fish

(G-12846)
TREGO INC
5 Little Brook Rd (02571)
P.O. Box 579 (02576-0579)
PHONE.............................508 291-3816
Michael Smead, *Pr*
EMP: 7 **EST:** 1951
SQ FT: 15,500
SALES (est): 946.14K **Privately Held**
Web: www.tregopowerconnectors.com
SIC: 3678 Electronic connectors

(G-12847)
V POWER EQUIPMENT LLC
Also Called: V Power Equipment
297 Charge Pond Rd (02571-1108)
PHONE.............................508 273-7596
EMP: 10 **EST:** 2017
SALES (est): 645.97K **Privately Held**
Web: www.vpowerequipment.com
SIC: 3714 3563 Water pump, motor vehicle; Air and gas compressors

(G-12848)
VIABELLA HOLDINGS LLC (PA)
Also Called: Mhgc
9 Kendrick Rd (02571-1077)
PHONE.............................800 688-9998
Mark Salkovitz, *Pr*
◆ **EMP:** 20 **EST:** 2015
SALES (est): 17.46MM
SALES (corp-wide): 17.46MM **Privately Held**
Web: www.viabella.com
SIC: 2771 2678 Greeting cards; Stationery: made from purchased materials

(G-12849)
VISIONAID INC
11 Kendrick Rd (02571-1077)
P.O. Box 752310 (38175-2310)
PHONE.............................508 295-3300
Daniel Mccarthy, *Pr*
Timothy Flaherty, *
Ken Duffie, *
Calum Maclachlan, *
◆ **EMP:** 48 **EST:** 1943
SQ FT: 34,000
SALES (est): 8.42MM
SALES (corp-wide): 92.52MM **Privately Held**
Web: www.radians.com
SIC: 3851 3842 2834 Goggles: sun, safety, industrial, underwater, etc.; Surgical appliances and supplies; Pharmaceutical preparations
HQ: Radians, Inc.
5305 Distriplex Farms Dr
Memphis TN 38141
901 388-7776

Warren
Worcester County

(G-12850)
COLFAX FLUID HANDLING

82 Bridge St (01083-2144)
P.O. Box 1601 (01083-1601)
PHONE..............................413 436-7711
EMP: 8 EST: 2018
SALES (est): 190.14K **Privately Held**
SIC: 3494 Valves and pipe fittings, nec

(G-12851)
HARDWICK KNITTED FABRIC INC
81 South St (01083-7979)
P.O. Box 367 (01092-0367)
PHONE..............................413 436-7704
David A Persky, *Pr*
EMP: 9 EST: 1970
SQ FT: 100,000
SALES (est): 308.95K **Privately Held**
SIC: 5949 2257 Fabric stores piece goods;
Dyeing and finishing circular knit fabrics

(G-12852)
PORTLAND VALVE LLC (DH)
82 Bridge St (01083-2144)
P.O. Box 5020 (28111-5020)
PHONE..............................704 289-6511
Darryl Mayhorn, *CEO*
▲ **EMP: 39 EST:** 2004
SQ FT: 36,000
SALES (est): 9MM **Publicly Held**
SIC: 3492 3599 3494 Fluid power valves
and hose fittings; Machine shop, jobbing
and repair; Valves and pipe fittings, nec
HQ: Circor International, Inc.
30 Corporate Dr Ste 200
Burlington MA 01803
781 270-1200

(G-12853)
WARREN PUMPS LLC
82 Bridge St (01083-2144)
P.O. Box 5020 (28111-5020)
PHONE..............................413 436-7711
Thomas Spock, *Managing Member*
EMP: 35 EST: 1985
SALES (est): 7.87MM **Publicly Held**
Web: www.warrenpumps.com
SIC: 3561 Industrial pumps and parts
HQ: Circor International, Inc.
30 Corporate Dr Ste 200
Burlington MA 01803
781 270-1200

Watertown
Middlesex County

(G-12854)
A123 SYSTEMS INC
1 Kingsbury Ave (02472-5789)
PHONE..............................617 972-3400
EMP: 18 EST: 2019
SALES (est): 212.98K **Privately Held**
Web: www.a123systems.com
SIC: 3691 Storage batteries

(G-12855)
ADVANCED MECHANICAL TECH INC (PA)
Also Called: Amti
176 Waltham St (02472-4800)
PHONE..............................617 923-4174
Bruce F White, *Pr*
Gary M Blanchard, *
Fred W Ruland, *
Albert Drueding, *
EMP: 31 EST: 1976
SQ FT: 23,000
SALES (est): 4.71MM
SALES (corp-wide): 4.71MM **Privately Held**

Web: www.amti.biz
SIC: 3829 3825 8733 Thermometers and
temperature sensors; Test equipment for
electronic and electric measurement;
Research institute

(G-12856)
ALEKSIA THERAPEUTICS INC
65 Grove St Ste 102 (02472-2826)
PHONE..............................720 918-6610
Andy Phillips, *CEO*
EMP: 7 EST: 2021
SALES (est): 79.8K **Privately Held**
SIC: 2834 Medicines, capsuled or ampuled

(G-12857)
ALPHAGRAPHICS
Also Called: AlphaGraphics
376 Arsenal St (02472-2892)
PHONE..............................617 924-4091
EMP: 10 EST: 2013
SALES (est): 208.64K **Privately Held**
Web: www.alphagraphicswatertown.com
SIC: 2759 2752 Publication printing;
Commercial printing, lithographic

(G-12858)
APPLIED IMAGE RPRGRPHICS OF WT
Also Called: Air Graphics
63 Pleasant St Ste 1 (02472-2386)
PHONE..............................617 924-6060
Michael G Cully, *Pr*
EMP: 9 EST: 1991
SALES (est): 242.14K **Privately Held**
Web: www.airgraphics.com
SIC: 2752 Offset printing

(G-12859)
ARRANTA BIO HOLDINGS LLC (DH)
Also Called: Arranta Bio
650 Pleasant St (02472-2420)
PHONE..............................785 760-3128
Mark Bamforth, *CEO*
EMP: 7 EST: 2019
SALES (est): 7.64MM
SALES (corp-wide): 112.13MM **Privately Held**
Web: www.recipharm.com
SIC: 2834 Druggists' preparations
(pharmaceuticals)
HQ: Recipharm Ab
Vasagatan 10
Stockholm 111 2

(G-12860)
ATLANTIC BATTERY COMPANY INC
Also Called: Mac Battery
309 Main St Rear (02472-2359)
P.O. Box 172 (02471-0172)
PHONE..............................617 924-2868
Keith Migell, *Pr*
EMP: 12 EST: 1934
SQ FT: 50,000
SALES (est): 1.47MM **Privately Held**
Web: www.atlanticbatterycompany.com
SIC: 3691 Storage batteries

(G-12861)
AVANTI BATTERY COMPANY
149 Grove St (02472-2828)
PHONE..............................617 209-9434
Luis Ortiz, *CEO*
EMP: 14 EST: 2021
SALES (est): 1.45MM **Privately Held**
Web: www.donaldsadoway.com

SIC: 3691 Storage batteries

(G-12862)
BAIKAR ASSOCIATION INC (PA)
Also Called: Armenian Mirror-Spectator
755 Mount Auburn St (02472-1509)
PHONE..............................617 924-4420
Artin Arzoumanian, *Pr*
Doctor Armen Demerjian, *Treas*
Doctor Artin Arzoumanian, *Pr*
EMP: 12 EST: 1926
SALES (est): 1.27MM
SALES (corp-wide): 1.27MM **Privately Held**
Web: www.mirrorspectator.com
SIC: 2731 2732 2711 Pamphlets: publishing
only, not printed on site; Book printing;
Newspapers: publishing only, not printed on
site

(G-12863)
BOSTON SCIENTIFIC CORPORATION
Medi-Tech
480 Pleasant St (02472-2463)
PHONE..............................617 972-4000
Peter Nicholas, *Mgr*
EMP: 16
SALES (corp-wide): 12.68B **Publicly Held**
Web: www.bostonscientific.com
SIC: 3841 Surgical and medical instruments
PA: Boston Scientific Corporation
300 Boston Scientific Way
Marlborough MA 01752
508 683-4000

(G-12864)
BRIDGESTONE RET OPERATIONS LLC
Also Called: Firestone
40 Arsenal St (02472-2604)
PHONE..............................617 924-3989
David Baker, *Mgr*
EMP: 10
SQ FT: 7,463
Web: www.bridgestoneamericas.com
SIC: 5531 7534 Automotive tires;
Rebuilding and retreading tires
HQ: Bridgestone Retail Operations, Llc
333 E Lake St Ste 300
Bloomingdale IL 60108
630 259-9000

(G-12865)
C2SENSE INC
480 Arsenal Way # 110 (02472-2895)
PHONE..............................617 651-3991
George Linscott, *CEO*
Jonathan T Mann, *
EMP: 25 EST: 2013
SALES (est): 3.84MM **Privately Held**
Web: www.c2sense.com
SIC: 3829 Measuring and controlling
devices, nec

(G-12866)
C4 THERAPEUTICS INC (PA)
490 Arsenal Way Ste 200 (02472-2988)
PHONE..............................617 231-0700
Andrew J Hirsch, *Pr*
Kendra Adams, *CFO*
Jolie M Siegel, *CLO*
Stewart Fisher, *CSO*
Leonard M J Reyno, *CMO*
EMP: 48 EST: 2015
SQ FT: 45,400
SALES: 31.1MM
SALES (corp-wide): 31.1MM **Publicly Held**
Web: www.c4therapeutics.com

SIC: 2836 8731 Biological products, except
diagnostic; Biological research

(G-12867)
CAPTIVATE BIO LLC
142 Galen St Fl 2 (02472-4510)
PHONE..............................617 607-4017
Tanya M Potcova, *CEO*
EMP: 8 EST: 2020
SALES (est): 588.9K **Privately Held**
Web: www.captivatebio.com
SIC: 2836 2819 Biological products, except
diagnostic; Chemicals, reagent grade:
refined from technical grade

(G-12868)
CARTESIAN THERAPEUTICS INC (PA)
65 Grove St (02472-2826)
PHONE..............................617 923-1400
Carsten Brunn, *Pr*
Carrie S Cox, *Ch Bd*
Lloyd Johnston, *COO*
Blaine Davis, *CFO*
Takashi Kei Kishimoto, *CSO*
EMP: 17 EST: 2007
SQ FT: 25,078
SALES (est): 110.78MM **Publicly Held**
Web: www.selectabio.com
SIC: 2834 Pharmaceutical preparations

(G-12869)
CHARLESBRIDGE PUBLISHING INC (PA)
Also Called: Imagine Publishing
9 Galen St Ste 220 (02472-4520)
PHONE..............................617 926-0329
Brent H Farmer, *Pr*
Donald Robb, *
▲ **EMP: 32 EST:** 1980
SQ FT: 6,000
SALES (est): 6.41MM
SALES (corp-wide): 6.41MM **Privately Held**
Web: www.charlesbridge.com
SIC: 2741 2731 Miscellaneous publishing;
Books, publishing and printing

(G-12870)
DAY ZERO DIAGNOSTICS INC
85 Walnut St Ste 320 (02472-4065)
PHONE..............................857 770-1125
Jong Lee, *CEO*
Jeff Mirviss, *
EMP: 23 EST: 2016
SALES (est): 3.69MM **Privately Held**
Web: www.dayzerodiagnostics.com
SIC: 3826 8071 Analytical instruments;
Medical laboratories

(G-12871)
DISC MEDICINE INC (PA)
321 Arsenal St Ste 101 (02472-5710)
PHONE..............................617 674-9274
John Quisel, *Pr*
Donald Nicholson, *Ex Ch Bd*
Joanne Bryce, *CFO*
William Savage, *CMO*
EMP: 10 EST: 2015
SQ FT: 7,566
Web: www.discmedicine.com
SIC: 2834 8731 Pharmaceutical
preparations; Biological research

(G-12872)
ENANTA PHARMACEUTICALS INC (PA)
Also Called: ENANTA
500 Arsenal St (02472-2806)

PHONE..................617 607-0800
EMP: 80 **EST:** 1995
SQ FT: 49,000
SALES (est): 79.2MM **Publicly Held**
Web: www.enanta.com
SIC: 2834 8731 Pharmaceutical preparations; Biotechnical research, commercial

(G-12873)
EXERGEN CORPORATION
Also Called: Exergen
400 Pleasant St (02472-2691)
PHONE..................617 923-9900
Francesco Pompei, *Pr*
Henry L Anthony, *
Marybeth Pompei, *
William J Coad, *
◆ **EMP:** 84 **EST:** 1980
SQ FT: 37,000
SALES (est): 24.22MM **Privately Held**
Web: www.exergen.com
SIC: 3826 Instruments measuring thermal properties

(G-12874)
EYE PINT PHRMCTCALS SCRTIES CO
400 Pleasant St (02472-2691)
PHONE..................617 926-5000
EMP: 25 **EST:** 2009
SALES (est): 969.03K
SALES (corp-wide): 41.4MM **Publicly Held**
SIC: 3826 Analytical optical instruments
PA: Eyepoint Pharmaceuticals, Inc.
480 Pleasant St Ste B300
Watertown MA 02472
617 926-5000

(G-12875)
EYEPOINT PHARMACEUTICALS INC (PA)
480 Pleasant St Ste B300 (02472-2468)
PHONE..................617 926-5000
Jay S Duker, *CEO*
Nancy Lurker, *Executive Vice Chairman of the Board*
Goran Ando, *Ch Bd*
Jay S Duker, *Pr*
Michael C Pine, *CORP Development*
EMP: 55 **EST:** 1987
SQ FT: 20,240
SALES (est): 41.4MM
SALES (corp-wide): 41.4MM **Publicly Held**
Web: www.eyepointpharma.com
SIC: 3841 3826 Surgical and medical instruments; Analytical instruments

(G-12876)
FASTACHI LTD
598 Mount Auburn St (02472-4124)
PHONE..................617 924-8787
Souren Etyemezian, *Pr*
EMP: 10 **EST:** 1990
SQ FT: 4,000
SALES (est): 963.38K **Privately Held**
Web: www.fastachi.com
SIC: 5441 2068 Candy; Nuts: dried, dehydrated, salted or roasted

(G-12877)
FORMA THERAPEUTICS INC (DH)
Also Called: Forma Therapeutics
300 North Beacon St Ste 501 (02472-5750)
PHONE..................617 679-1970
Frank Lee, *CEO*

Rob Sarisky, *Chief Business Officer**
Peter B Finn, *
Alexis Borisy, *
Simon Campbell, *
EMP: 50 **EST:** 2007
SALES (est): 1.06MM
SALES (corp-wide): 29.08B **Privately Held**
Web: www.novonordisk.com
SIC: 2834 Pharmaceutical preparations
HQ: Forma Therapeutics Holdings, Inc.
300 North Beacon St # 501
Watertown MA 02472
617 679-1970

(G-12878)
FORMA THRAPEUTICS HOLDINGS INC (HQ)
300 North Beacon St Ste 501 (02472-5750)
PHONE..................617 679-1970
Frank D Lee, *Pr*
Peter Wirth, *Ch Bd*
Todd Shegog, *Sr VP*
Mary Wadlinger, *Chief Human Resources Officer*
Jeannette Potts, *Corporate Secretary*
EMP: 10 **EST:** 2011
SQ FT: 93,526
SALES (corp-wide): 29.08B **Privately Held**
SIC: 2836 Biological products, except diagnostic
PA: Novo Nordisk Fonden
Tuborg Havnevej 19
Hellerup 2900
35276600

(G-12879)
HAIRENIK ASSOCIATION INC
80 Bigelow Ave (02472-2012)
PHONE..................617 926-3974
Pearl Teague, *Pr*
EMP: 10 **EST:** 1899
SQ FT: 2,028
SALES (est): 992.52K **Privately Held**
Web: www.hairenik.com
SIC: 2711 Newspapers: publishing only, not printed on site

(G-12880)
HARRINGTON AIR SYSTEMS LLC
80 Rosedale Rd (02472-2234)
PHONE..................781 341-1999
EMP: 13 **EST:** 2013
SALES (est): 2.69MM **Privately Held**
SIC: 3444 1711 Sheet metalwork; Heating and air conditioning contractors

(G-12881)
HOWE PRESS PERKINS SCH FO
175 North Beacon St (02472-2751)
PHONE..................617 924-3434
Luiza Aguiar, *Dir*
EMP: 9 **EST:** 2014
SALES (est): 348.07K **Privately Held**
Web: www.perkins.org
SIC: 2741 Miscellaneous publishing

(G-12882)
INTELLIGENT BUS ENTRMT INC
480 Pleasant St Ste C210 (02472-2596)
PHONE..................617 519-4172
EMP: 8 **EST:** 2011
SALES (est): 138.05K **Privately Held**
SIC: 7372 7379 Business oriented computer software; Online services technology consultants

(G-12883)
ITEOS THERAPEUTICS INC (PA)
Also Called: Iteos Therapeutics
321 Arsenal St Ste 301 (02472-5710)
PHONE..................339 217-0161
Michel Detheux, *CEO*
David L Hallal, *Non-Executive Chairman of the Board*
Matthew Call, *COO*
Matthew Gall, *CAO*
Joanne Jenkins Lager, *CMO*
EMP: 15 **EST:** 2011
SQ FT: 9,068
SALES (est): 267.63MM
SALES (corp-wide): 267.63MM **Publicly Held**
Web: www.iteostherapeutics.com
SIC: 2836 2834 Biological products, except diagnostic; Pharmaceutical preparations

(G-12884)
JOHN K DIETRICH & ASSOC INC
Also Called: Graphx Copy & Printing
33 Warwick Rd (02472-1237)
PHONE..................617 868-4140
Anne Shuhler, *Pr*
John K Dietrich, *VP*
EMP: 8 **EST:** 1983
SALES (est): 419.17K **Privately Held**
Web: www.mykingdompharmacy.com
SIC: 7334 2752 Photocopying and duplicating services; Commercial printing, lithographic

(G-12885)
KYMERA THERAPEUTICS INC (PA)
200 Arsenal Yards Blvd Ste 230 (02472-5041)
PHONE..................857 285-5300
Nello Mainolfi, *Pr*
Bruce Booth, *Ch Bd*
Bruce Jacobs, *CFO*
Jared Gollob, *CMO*
Richard Chesworth, *CSO*
EMP: 49 **EST:** 2015
SQ FT: 34,522
SALES (est): 46.83MM
SALES (corp-wide): 46.83MM **Publicly Held**
Web: www.kymeratx.com
SIC: 2836 Biological products, except diagnostic

(G-12886)
LANDMARK BIO PBLLC
300 North Beacon St (02472-5750)
PHONE..................617 894-8629
Ran Zheng, *CEO*
Kelly O'shea, *Dir Fin*
EMP: 8 **EST:** 2020
SALES (est): 1.05MM **Privately Held**
Web: www.landmarkbio.com
SIC: 8731 2834 Biotechnical research, commercial; Pharmaceutical preparations

(G-12887)
LEANIX INC (DH)
1 Kingsbury Ave (02472-5789)
PHONE..................781 321-6500
Hylton Southey, *Pr*
Joerg Beyer, *CEO*
Francis Baird, *Sec*
EMP: 10 **EST:** 2016
SALES (est): 4.33MM
SALES (corp-wide): 32.06B **Privately Held**
Web: www.leanix.net
SIC: 7371 7372 Computer software systems analysis and design, custom; Prepackaged software

HQ: Leanix Gmbh
Friedrich-Ebert-Allee 37-39
Bonn NW 53113
22828629920

(G-12888)
LYNDRA THERAPEUTICS INC (PA)
65 Grove St Ste 301 (02472-2826)
PHONE..................339 222-6519
Amy Schulman, *CEO*
Eileen Mcguire, *Mgr*
EMP: 14 **EST:** 2015
SALES (est): 16.28MM
SALES (corp-wide): 16.28MM **Privately Held**
Web: www.lyndra.com
SIC: 2834 Pharmaceutical preparations

(G-12889)
LYRA THERAPEUTICS INC
480 Arsenal Way (02472-2891)
PHONE..................617 393-4600
Maria Palasis, *Pr*
Harlan W Waksal, *
Robert Richard, *Research & Development*
Pamela Nelson, *Regulatory Affairs*
Corinne Noyes, *Senior Vice President Commercial*
EMP: 38 **EST:** 2005
SQ FT: 22,343
SALES (est): 1.36MM **Privately Held**
Web: www.lyratherapeutics.com
SIC: 2834 Pharmaceutical preparations

(G-12890)
MARKARIAN ELECTRIC LLC
586 Pleasant St Ste 5 (02472-2678)
PHONE..................617 393-9700
Eric A Markarian, *Prin*
EMP: 7 **EST:** 2010
SALES (est): 1.48MM **Privately Held**
Web: www.me-companies.com
SIC: 3699 1731 Electrical equipment and supplies, nec; Electrical work

(G-12891)
MARKFORGED HOLDING CORPORATION (PA)
480 Pleasant St (02472-2463)
PHONE..................866 496-1805
Shai Terem, *Pr*
Dorit Liberman, *Chief Human Resource Officer*
EMP: 25 **EST:** 2013
SQ FT: 36,000
SALES (est): 100.96MM
SALES (corp-wide): 100.96MM **Publicly Held**
Web: www.markforged.com
SIC: 3577 Printers, computer

(G-12892)
MASART INC ✪
586 Pleasant St (02472-2677)
PHONE..................781 786-8774
Arman Mnatsakanyan, *Pr*
EMP: 14 **EST:** 2023
SALES (est): 575.99K **Privately Held**
SIC: 3537 Trucks: freight, baggage, etc.: industrial, except mining

(G-12893)
MICROCAD TRNING CONSULTING INC (PA)
Also Called: Autodesk Reseller
440 Arsenal St Ste 3 (02472-2898)
PHONE..................617 923-0500
FAX: 617 923-7006

EMP: 10
SQ FT: 2,600
SALES (est): 16MM **Privately Held**
Web: www.microcad3d.com
SIC: 7372 8243 Prepackaged software;
Software training, computer

(G-12894)
MONADNOCK ASSOCIATES INC
(PA)
3 Brook St (02472-2314)
PHONE................................617 924-7032
Stephen Burakoff, *Pr*
Carl Bindman, *Treas*
Mark Perreault, *CFO*
EMP: 10 EST: 2000
SALES (est): 1.13MM
SALES (corp-wide): 1.13MM **Privately Held**
SIC: 7372 6211 Prepackaged software;
Investment bankers

(G-12895)
MONOTONYAI INC
480 Pleasant St Ste A310 (02472-2467)
PHONE................................202 607-8193
EMP: 10 EST: 2019
SALES (est): 2.4MM **Privately Held**
SIC: 7372 Prepackaged software

(G-12896)
NEUMORA THERAPEUTICS INC
(PA)
490 Arsenal Way Ste 200 (02472-2988)
PHONE................................857 760-0900
Henry O Gosebruch, *Pr*
Paul L Berns, *Ex Ch Bd*
Carol Suh, *COO*
Joshua Pinto, *CFO*
Daljit Singh Aurora, *CSO*
EMP: 75 EST: 2019
SQ FT: 30,067
Web: www.neumoratx.com
SIC: 2836 Biological products, except
diagnostic

(G-12897)
NEW ENGLAND FLAG &
BANNER
165 Dexter Ave (02472-4228)
P.O. Box 306 (02471-0306)
PHONE................................617 782-1892
EMP: 16 EST: 2011
SALES (est): 1.28MM **Privately Held**
Web:
www.newenglandflagandbanner.com
SIC: 3993 Signs and advertising specialties

(G-12898)
P & M BRICK & BLOCK INC
213 Arlington St (02472-2004)
PHONE................................617 924-6020
Michael P Pirolli Junior, *Pr*
Robert A Pirolli, *Treas*
John Pirolli, *VP*
Frank K Sheehan, *Clerk*
▲ EMP: 8 EST: 1985
SQ FT: 16,000
SALES (est): 992.11K **Privately Held**
Web: www.pmbrickandblock.com
SIC: 3271 5211 Blocks, concrete or cinder:
standard; Brick

(G-12899)
PERKINS SCHOOL FOR BLIND
175 North Beacon St (02472-2790)
PHONE................................617 924-3434
Steven M Rothstein, *Pr*
C Richard Carlson, *OF THE*

Frederic Clifford, *
EMP: 846 EST: 1829
SQ FT: 400,000
SALES (est): 94.89MM **Privately Held**
Web: www.perkins.org
SIC: 8211 3999 School for physically
handicapped, nec; Education aids, devices
and supplies

(G-12900)
PITON THERAPEUTICS INC
Also Called: Precidiag
313 Pleasant St (02472-2418)
PHONE................................857 327-7666
Nigel Macclancy, *CEO*
Bing Feng, *Dir*
D Kong, *Sec*
EMP: 14 EST: 2015
SALES (est): 4.93MM **Privately Held**
Web: www.precidiag.com
SIC: 2835 Microbiology and virology
diagnostic products

(G-12901)
PULPDENT CORPORATION
80 Oakland St (02472-2202)
P.O. Box 780 (02471-0780)
PHONE................................617 926-6666
Harold Berk, *Pr*
Gale Boyd Export, *Manager*
Kenneth J Berk, *
Frederick Berk, *
Larry Clark, *CLINICAL AFFAIRS*
▲ EMP: 80 EST: 1947
SQ FT: 60,000
SALES (est): 16.09MM **Privately Held**
Web: www.pulpdent.com
SIC: 3843 Dental equipment and supplies

(G-12902)
RADIATION MONITORING DVCS
INC (HQ)
44 Hunt St Ste 2 (02472-4699)
PHONE................................617 668-6800
Kanai Shah, *Pr*
Matthew Dallimore, *
EMP: 29 EST: 1974
SQ FT: 10,000
SALES (est): 20.66MM
SALES (corp-wide): 43.7MM **Privately
Held**
Web: www.rmdinc.com
SIC: 3829 3845 Nuclear radiation and
testing apparatus; Electromedical
equipment
PA: Dynasil Corporation Of America
200 Baker Ave Ste 301
Concord MA 01742
617 668-6855

(G-12903)
RADLO FOODS LLC (PA)
313 Pleasant St Ste 5 (02472-2491)
P.O. Box 3000 (01888-1700)
PHONE................................617 926-7070
David N Radlo, *Managing Member*
Irene Radlo, *Managing Member*
▼ EMP: 7 EST: 1916
SQ FT: 4,000
SALES (est): 4.82MM
SALES (corp-wide): 4.82MM **Privately
Held**
Web: www.radlo.com
SIC: 5144 2015 Eggs; Poultry slaughtering
and processing

(G-12904)
RESPIRATORY MOTION INC
80 Coolidge Hill Rd (02472-5003)
PHONE................................508 954-2706

EMP: 20 EST: 2010
SALES (est): 3.63MM **Privately Held**
Web: www.respiratorymotion.com
SIC: 3845 Electromedical equipment

(G-12905)
RMD INSTRUMENTS CORP
44 Hunt St Ste 2 (02472-4624)
PHONE................................617 668-6900
Gerald Entine, *Pr*
▲ EMP: 13 EST: 2008
SALES (est): 2.49MM **Privately Held**
Web: www.rmdinc.com
SIC: 3829 Measuring and controlling
devices, nec

(G-12906)
ROOTPATH GENOMICS
65 Grove St (02472-2826)
PHONE................................857 209-1060
Xi Chen, *Prin*
EMP: 13 EST: 2018
SALES (est): 3.87MM **Privately Held**
Web: www.rootpath.com
SIC: 2835 Microbiology and virology
diagnostic products

(G-12907)
SIGNWORKS GROUP INC
Also Called: Signworks Group
60 Arsenal St Ste 2 (02472-2659)
PHONE................................617 924-0292
Bernard Lebow, *Pr*
EMP: 18 EST: 1988
SQ FT: 3,000
SALES (est): 973.74K **Privately Held**
Web: www.signworksgroup.com
SIC: 3993 Signs and advertising specialties

(G-12908)
SOCOMEC INC (DH)
9 Galen St Ste 120 (02472-4521)
PHONE................................617 245-0447
▲ EMP: 11 EST: 2008
SQ FT: 15,000
SALES (est): 12.85MM
SALES (corp-wide): 679.07K **Privately
Held**
Web: www.socomec.us
SIC: 3679 5065 3699 Power supplies, all
types: static; Communication equipment;
Electrical equipment and supplies, nec
HQ: Socomec
1 A 4
Benfeld 67230
388574141

(G-12909)
SQZ BIOTECHNOLOGIES
COMPANY (PA)
Also Called: SQZ BIOTECH
200 Arsenal Yards Blvd Fl 2 (02472-5041)
PHONE................................617 758-8672
Howard Bernstein, *Interim Chief Executive
Officer*
Amy W Schulman, *Ch Bd*
Teri Loxam, *CFO*
Oliver Rosen, *CMO*
EMP: 49 EST: 2013
SQ FT: 63,477
SALES (est): 21.48MM
SALES (corp-wide): 21.48MM **Publicly
Held**
Web: www.sqzbiotech.com
SIC: 2836 Biological products, except
diagnostic

(G-12910)
SYBASE INC
400 Talcott Ave Ste 200 (02472-5712)
PHONE................................617 673-1200
EMP: 9 EST: 2017
SALES (est): 331.33K
SALES (corp-wide): 32.06B **Privately Held**
SIC: 3571 Electronic computers
PA: Sap Se
Dietmar-Hopp-Allee 16
Walldorf BW 69190
622 774-7474

(G-12911)
SYNDEXA PHARMACEUTICALS
CORP
480 Arsenal St (02472-2805)
PHONE................................617 607-7283
Teo Uysal, *CEO*
EMP: 11 EST: 2007
SALES (est): 1.2MM **Privately Held**
Web: www.syndexa.com
SIC: 2834 Pharmaceutical preparations

(G-12912)
TARVEDA THERAPEUTICS INC
134 Coolidge Ave (02472-2971)
PHONE................................617 923-4100
Brian Roberts, *Pr*
Jeffrey D Bloss, *CMO*
EMP: 25 EST: 2011
SALES (est): 10.22MM **Privately Held**
Web: www.tarvedatx.com
SIC: 2834 Pharmaceutical preparations

(G-12913)
THERMA-FLOW INC
Also Called: Everhot
191 Arlington St (02472-2003)
P.O. Box 416 (02471-0416)
PHONE................................617 924-3877
Edwin Hill, *Pr*
Robert Suffredini, *
▲ EMP: 25 EST: 1986
SQ FT: 33,000
SALES (est): 4.69MM **Privately Held**
Web: www.tfi-everhot.com
SIC: 3443 3639 Heat exchangers, plate type
; Hot water heaters, household

(G-12914)
THREE TWINS PRODUCTIONS
INC
18 Bridge St (02472-4811)
PHONE................................617 926-0377
EMP: 9 EST: 1994
SQ FT: 3,200
SALES (est): 639.98K **Privately Held**
Web: www.three-twins.com
SIC: 2759 7389 Screen printing; Embroidery
advertising

(G-12915)
TOM SNYDER PRODUCTIONS
INC (HQ)
100 Talcott Ave Ste 6 (02472-5715)
PHONE................................617 600-2145
Stacey Pusey, *Pr Dir*
Rick Abrams, *
EMP: 100 EST: 1980
SQ FT: 14,500
SALES (est): 28.99MM
SALES (corp-wide): 1.7B **Publicly Held**
SIC: 7372 7371 7331 Educational computer
software; Custom computer programming
services; Direct mail advertising services
PA: Scholastic Corporation
557 Broadway Lbby 1
New York NY 10012
212 343-6100

▲ = Import ▼ = Export
◆ = Import/Export

(G-12916)
TRANS METRICS INC (HQ)
180 Dexter Ave (02472-4202)
P.O. Box 9143 (02471-9143)
PHONE..............................617 926-1000
David Reis, *Pr*
Peter Godfrey, *Corporate Vice President*
Brian Hallihan, *VP Fin*
EMP: 15 **EST:** 1975
SQ FT: 100,000
SALES (est): 3.92MM
SALES (corp-wide): 39.4MM **Privately Held**
Web: www.ueonline.com
SIC: 3829 5084 Pressure transducers; Industrial machinery and equipment
PA: United Electric Controls Company
180 Dexter Ave
Watertown MA 02472
617 926-1000

(G-12917)
UNITED ELECTRIC CONTROLS COMPANY (PA)
180 Dexter Ave (02472-4200)
P.O. Box 9143 (02471-9143)
PHONE..............................617 926-1000
EMP: 170 **EST:** 1931
SALES (est): 39.4MM
SALES (corp-wide): 39.4MM **Privately Held**
Web: www.ueonline.com
SIC: 3823 Temperature instruments: industrial process type

(G-12918)
VIA SEPARATIONS INC
165 Dexter Ave (02472-4228)
PHONE..............................781 354-7945
Shreya Dave, *CEO*
Shreya Dave, *Pr*
Brent Keller, *
EMP: 51 **EST:** 2017
SALES (est): 5.24MM **Privately Held**
Web: www.viaseparations.com
SIC: 3624 Carbon and graphite products

(G-12919)
VIGIL NEUROSCIENCE INC (PA)
100 Forge Rd Ste 7 (02472-2265)
PHONE..............................857 254-4445
Ivana Magovcevic-liebisch, *Pr*
Ivanna Magovcevic-liebisch, *Pr*
Bruce Booth, *Ch Bd*
Jennifer Ziolkowski, *CFO*
Spyros Papapetropoulos, *CMO*
EMP: 21 **EST:** 2020
SQ FT: 6,940
Web: www.vigilneuro.com
SIC: 8071 8731 2834 Neurological laboratory; Biological research; Pharmaceutical preparations

(G-12920)
WEREWOLF THERAPEUTICS INC
Also Called: Werewolf Therapeutics
200 Talcott Ave Fl 2 (02472-5705)
PHONE..............................617 952-0555
Daniel J Hicklin, *Pr*
Luke Evnin, *
Reid Leonard, *COO*
Timothy W Trost, *CFO*
Randi Isaacs, *CMO*
EMP: 28 **EST:** 2017
SALES (est): 16.4MM **Privately Held**
Web: www.werewolftx.com
SIC: 2834 8731 Pharmaceutical preparations; Biotechnical research, commercial

(G-12921)
WITRICITY CORPORATION (PA)
Also Called: Witricity
57 Water St (02472-4603)
PHONE..............................617 926-2700
Alex Gruzen, *CEO*
David Schatz, *VP*
Steve Chen, *VP*
Donald R Peck, *CFO*
EMP: 11 **EST:** 2007
SALES (est): 9.23MM
SALES (corp-wide): 9.23MM **Privately Held**
Web: www.witricity.com
SIC: 3559 7389 Electronic component making machinery; Artists' agents and brokers

(G-12922)
ZIKANI THERAPEUTICS INC
480 Arsenal Way Ste 130 (02472-2891)
P.O. Box 3 (02471-0003)
PHONE..............................617 453-9091
Sumit Aggarwal, *Pr*
EMP: 20 **EST:** 2014
SQ FT: 10,000
SALES (est): 2.61MM **Publicly Held**
Web: www.eloxxpharma.com
SIC: 2834 Pharmaceutical preparations
PA: Eloxx Pharmaceuticals, Inc.
480 Arsenal Way Ste 110
Watertown MA 02472
781 577-5300

Wayland
Middlesex County

(G-12923)
CANDELA CORPORATION
530 Boston Post Rd (01778-1833)
PHONE..............................800 733-8550
EMP: 11 **EST:** 1985
SALES (est): 163.66K **Privately Held**
Web: www.candelamedical.com
SIC: 2844 Cosmetic preparations

(G-12924)
CITY PBLCATIONS GREATER BOSTON
18 Lake Shore Dr (01778-4104)
PHONE..............................617 549-7622
Christopher Howard, *Owner*
EMP: 7 **EST:** 2002
SALES (est): 400K **Privately Held**
Web: www.citypubnationwide.com
SIC: 7372 8742 Prepackaged software; Management consulting services

(G-12925)
E H PERKINS CONSTRUCTION INC (PA)
Also Called: Kane-Perkins
560 Main St (01778)
P.O. Box 301 (01749-0301)
PHONE..............................978 562-3436
TOLL FREE: 800
Edward H Perkins, *Pr*
EMP: 25 **EST:** 1967
SQ FT: 8,000
SALES (est): 9.35MM
SALES (corp-wide): 9.35MM **Privately Held**
Web: www.ehperkins.com
SIC: 5032 3273 1611 1622 Sand, construction; Ready-mixed concrete; Highway and street paving contractor; Bridge construction

---

Webster
Worcester County

(G-12926)
HT MACHINE CO INC
15 Town Forest Rd (01570-3112)
PHONE..............................508 949-1105
Steven Leighton, *Pr*
Kathryn J Holden, *Dir*
Thomas L Holden, *Treas*
EMP: 17 **EST:** 1969
SQ FT: 10,000
SALES (est): 2.51MM **Privately Held**
Web: www.htmachine.com
SIC: 3599 Machine shop, jobbing and repair

(G-12927)
INDUSTRIAL PACKAGING SUPPLY INC (PA)
Also Called: Industrial Packaging
5 Cudworth Rd (01570-3102)
PHONE..............................508 499-1600
TOLL FREE: 800
◆ **EMP:** 10 **EST:** 1953
SALES (est): 19.82MM
SALES (corp-wide): 19.82MM **Privately Held**
Web: www.industrialpackaging.com
SIC: 7389 2671 5084 Packaging and labeling services; Plastic film, coated or laminated for packaging; Packaging machinery and equipment

(G-12928)
JEFFCO FIBRES INC (PA)
12 Park St (01570-2888)
P.O. Box 816 (01570-0816)
PHONE..............................508 943-0440
Eric Lonstein, *CEO*
Jeffrey Lonstein, *
Wayne Ushman, *
Blanche Lonstein, *
◆ **EMP:** 146 **EST:** 1971
SQ FT: 200,000
SALES (est): 61.04MM
SALES (corp-wide): 61.04MM **Privately Held**
Web: www.jeffcofibres.com
SIC: 3086 5199 Plastics foam products; Plastics foam

(G-12929)
LELANITE CORPORATION (PA)
1 Cudworth Rd (01570-3102)
P.O. Box 160 (01570-0160)
PHONE..............................508 987-2637
Richard G Perry, *Pr*
Karen Perry, *
EMP: 42 **EST:** 1956
SQ FT: 106,000
SALES (est): 9.62MM
SALES (corp-wide): 9.62MM **Privately Held**
Web: www.ugpg2.com
SIC: 3086 2448 Packaging and shipping materials, foamed plastics; Pallets, wood

(G-12930)
LINX CONSULTING LLC
Also Called: Raymond L Martin
661 S Main St Ste 7 (01570-2280)
PHONE..............................508 461-6333
Raymond Martin, *Managing Member*
EMP: 10 **EST:** 2009
SQ FT: 6,000
SALES (est): 802.85K **Privately Held**
Web: www.linxconsultingllc.com

SIC: 3663 8741 Antennas, transmitting and communications; Management services

(G-12931)
YANKEE SHOPPER
Also Called: Patriot Newspaper
168 Gore Rd (01570-6814)
PHONE..............................508 943-8784
Paul Odonnell, *Owner*
EMP: 10 **EST:** 1975
SALES (est): 893.76K **Privately Held**
Web: www.yankeeshopper.net
SIC: 2711 Newspapers, publishing and printing

(G-12932)
ZMETRA CLARSPAN STRUCTURES LLC
2 Old Worcester Rd (01570-2109)
P.O. Box 218 (01570-0218)
PHONE..............................508 943-0940
Joseph Zmetra, *Prin*
EMP: 7 **EST:** 2014
SQ FT: 45,000
SALES (est): 1.05MM **Privately Held**
Web: www.zmetra.com
SIC: 2394 Tents: made from purchased materials

Wellesley
Norfolk County

(G-12933)
ACLARA SOFTWARE INC
Also Called: Nexus Energyguide
16 Laurel Ave Ste 100 (02481-7531)
PHONE..............................781 283-9160
Harvey Michaels, *CEO*
Martin Flusberg, *
▲ **EMP:** 92 **EST:** 1997
SQ FT: 15,000
SALES (est): 8.24MM **Publicly Held**
Web: www.hubbell.com
SIC: 7372 Prepackaged software
PA: Esco Technologies Inc.
9900 Clayton Rd Ste A
Saint Louis MO 63124

(G-12934)
ALFRESCO SOFTWARE INC (DH)
100 Worcester St Ste 203 (02481-3628)
PHONE..............................888 317-3395
EMP: 80 **EST:** 2002
SALES (est): 90.67MM
SALES (corp-wide): 1.2B **Privately Held**
Web: www.hyland.com
SIC: 7372 Business oriented computer software
HQ: Hyland Software, Inc.
28105 Clemens Rd
Westlake OH 44145

(G-12935)
AMERICAN BILTRITE INC (PA)
57 River St Ste 302 (02481-2097)
PHONE..............................781 237-6655
Roger S Marcus, *Ch Bd*
Richard G Marcus, *Pr*
William M Marcus, *Ex VP*
Howard N Feist Iii, *VP Fin*
◆ **EMP:** 7 **EST:** 1908
SQ FT: 10,000
SALES (est): 93.38MM
SALES (corp-wide): 93.38MM **Privately Held**
Web: www.ambilt.com

SIC: 3069 2672 2241 3961   Rubber floorcoverings/mats and wallcoverings; Paper; coated and laminated, nec; Fabric tapes; Costume novelties

(G-12936)
ARCHITECTURAL KITCHENS INC
310b Washington St (02481-4972)
PHONE....................................781 239-9750
EMP: 8 **EST:** 1996
SQ FT: 1,400
SALES (est): 891.67K **Privately Held**
Web: www.architecturalkitchens.com
SIC: 2434   Wood kitchen cabinets

(G-12937)
AURORA IMAGING TECHNOLOGY INC
165 Worcester St (02481-3615)
PHONE....................................617 522-6900
Elaine Mccarthy, *Mgr*
EMP: 58
SALES (corp-wide): 9.62MM **Privately Held**
Web: www.auroramri.com
SIC: 3555   Printing presses
PA: Aurora Imaging Technology Inc
    8 Electronics Ave Ste 1
    Danvers MA 01923
    877 975-7530

(G-12938)
BLACK INFUSIONS
396 Washington St Ste 264 (02481-6209)
PHONE....................................617 212-1046
Michael Davidson, *Prin*
EMP: 8 **EST:** 2018
SALES (est): 251.86K **Privately Held**
Web: www.blackinfusions.com
SIC: 2085   Distilled and blended liquors

(G-12939)
COLEY PHARMACEUTICAL GROUP INC
93 Worcester St Ste 101 (02481-3630)
PHONE....................................781 431-9000
Robert L Bratzler, *Pr*
Robert L Bratzler Ph.d., *Pr*
Arthur M Krieg Md, *Executive Research & Development Vice President*
Charles H Abdalian Junior, *VP Fin*
Ferdinand E Massari Md, *Senior Vice President Drug Development*
EMP: 73 **EST:** 1997
SQ FT: 18,500
SALES (est): 3.28MM
SALES (corp-wide): 100.33B **Publicly Held**
SIC: 2834   Pharmaceutical preparations
PA: Pfizer Inc.
    66 Hudson Blvd E
    New York NY 10001
    212 733-2323

(G-12940)
EAGLE INVESTMENT SYSTEMS LLC (HQ)
45 William St (02481-4004)
PHONE....................................781 943-2200
EMP: 30 **EST:** 1989
SQ FT: 6,000
SALES (est): 151.93MM
SALES (corp-wide): 19.99B **Publicly Held**
Web: www.eagleinvsys.com

SIC: 6722 6282 8721 7372   Management investment, open-end; Investment advisory service; Accounting services, except auditing; Business oriented computer software
PA: The Bank Of New York Mellon Corporation
    240 E Greenwich St
    New York NY 10007
    212 495-1784

(G-12941)
FLYING KITES
103 Central St Unit G (02482-5710)
P.O. Box 52326 (02205-2326)
PHONE....................................401 575-0009
EMP: 10 **EST:** 2015
SALES (est): 1.9MM **Privately Held**
Web: www.flyingkites.org
SIC: 3944   Kites

(G-12942)
GEMINI INVESTORS V LP (PA)
20 William St Ste 250 (02481-4103)
PHONE....................................781 237-7001
James Goodman, *Mgr*
James Goodman Managing, *Prin*
Jeffrey Newton Managing, *Prin*
David Millet Managing, *Prin*
James Rich Managing, *Prin*
EMP: 35 **EST:** 2010
SALES (est): 25.2MM
SALES (corp-wide): 25.2MM **Privately Held**
Web: www.gemini-investors.com
SIC: 6799 2599   Investors, nec; Work benches, factory

(G-12943)
INFINITE IQ INC
26 Willow St (02481-5613)
PHONE....................................781 710-8696
Jennifer Jordahl, *Prin*
EMP: 10 **EST:** 2009
SALES (est): 517.17K **Privately Held**
Web: www.infiniteiq.com
SIC: 7373 7372 7389   Systems software development services; Application computer software; Business Activities at Non-Commercial Site

(G-12944)
NEMUCORE MED INNOVATIONS INC
Also Called: Nmi
33 Kirkland Cir (02481-4812)
PHONE....................................617 943-9983
Timothy P Coleman, *CEO*
EMP: 9 **EST:** 2008
SALES (est): 916.55K **Privately Held**
Web: www.nemucore.com
SIC: 2834   Pharmaceutical preparations

(G-12945)
PLUMRIVER LLC
94 Edmunds Rd (02481-2940)
PHONE....................................781 431-7477
Henry White, *Brnch Mgr*
EMP: 15
SALES (corp-wide): 325.9MM **Publicly Held**
Web: www.elasticsuite.com
SIC: 7372   Business oriented computer software
HQ: Plumriver Llc
    1246 Charles St
    State College PA 16801
    781 577-9575

(G-12946)
TRI-MASS INC
32 Monadnock Rd (02481-1338)
PHONE....................................781 235-1075
Ellen R Gordon, *Pr*
EMP: 20 **EST:** 1986
SALES (est): 750.56K
SALES (corp-wide): 686.97MM **Publicly Held**
SIC: 2064   Candy and other confectionery products
PA: Tootsie Roll Industries, Inc.
    7401 S Cicero Ave
    Chicago IL 60629
    773 838-3400

(G-12947)
WATSON PRINTING CO INC
Also Called: David Rich Co
118 Cedar St Ste 2 (02481-3596)
PHONE....................................781 237-1336
Andrew T Watson, *Pr*
EMP: 7 **EST:** 1964
SQ FT: 2,000
SALES (est): 600.32K **Privately Held**
Web: www.watsonprinting.com
SIC: 2752   Offset printing

(G-12948)
WESTWELL INCORPORATED (DH)
12 Appian Dr (02481-1309)
PHONE....................................800 753-2277
▼ **EMP:** 99 **EST:** 1992
SALES (est): 48.53MM **Privately Held**
SIC: 2834 5122   Vitamin, nutrient, and hematinic preparations for human use; Pharmaceuticals
HQ: Nestle Holdings, Inc.
    1812 N Moore St Fl 25
    Arlington VA 22209
    703 682-4600

Wellesley Hills
Norfolk County

(G-12949)
AMERICAN OPTICS LIMITED
34 Washington St Ste 230 (02481-1903)
PHONE....................................905 631-5377
Larry Hicks, *Pr*
David Pierce, *CFO*
EMP: 10 **EST:** 1999
SALES (est): 707.7K **Privately Held**
SIC: 3845 3841 5047   Endoscopic equipment, electromedical, nec; Surgical instruments and apparatus; Instruments, surgical and medical

(G-12950)
ATOMERA INCORPORATED
20 Walnut St Ste 8 (02481-2167)
PHONE....................................617 219-0600
Soctt Bibaud, *CEO*
EMP: 9
SALES (corp-wide): 382K **Publicly Held**
Web: www.mearstechnologies.com
SIC: 8711 3674   Electrical or electronic engineering; Semiconductors and related devices
PA: Atomera Incorporated
    750 University Ave # 280
    Los Gatos CA 95032
    408 442-5248

(G-12951)
GLOBAL ADVANCED METALS USA INC (PA)

100 Worcester St Ste 200 (02481-3628)
P.O. Box 1608 (19512-6608)
PHONE....................................781 996-7300
Andrew O'donovan, *CEO*
Steve Krause, *
Glenn Williams, *
James Realbuto, *
EMP: 18 **EST:** 2011
SALES (est): 95.52MM
SALES (corp-wide): 95.52MM **Privately Held**
Web: www.globaladvancedmetals.com
SIC: 3339   Primary nonferrous metals, nec

(G-12952)
LIFE+GEAR INC
Also Called: Pacific Pathway
21 Cushing Rd (02481-2903)
PHONE....................................858 755-2099
Greg Simko, *Prin*
Nicholas Connor, *
Dennis Bertken, *
◆ **EMP:** 10 **EST:** 2005
SQ FT: 6,800
SALES (est): 421.46K **Privately Held**
Web: www.dorcy.com
SIC: 3949 5099   Camping equipment and supplies; Lifesaving and survival equipment (non-medical)

Wellfleet
Barnstable County

(G-12953)
SICKDAY INC
Also Called: Sickday
3 W Main St (02667-7300)
P.O. Box 1072 (02667-1072)
PHONE....................................508 214-4158
Olaf Valli, *Pr*
Angie Valli, *Sec*
EMP: 11 **EST:** 2009
SALES (est): 1.53MM **Privately Held**
Web: www.sickday.cc
SIC: 2329 2339 3949 5136   Men's and boys' sportswear and athletic clothing; Women's and misses' athletic clothing and sportswear ; Water sports equipment; Men's and boys' sportswear and work clothing

West Boxford
Essex County

(G-12954)
STONE HOUSE FARM INC
Also Called: Nason's Stone House Farm
276 Washington St (01885)
P.O. Box 44 (01885-0044)
PHONE....................................978 352-2323
James H Nason, *Pr*
EMP: 8 **EST:** 1955
SQ FT: 1,200
SALES (est): 458.15K **Privately Held**
Web: www.nasonstonehousefarm.com
SIC: 2053 5461   Pies, bakery; frozen; Pies

West Boylston
Worcester County

(G-12955)
C & C METALS ENGINEERING INC
104 Hartwell St (01583-2410)
PHONE....................................508 835-9011
Anthony Conklin, *Pr*
Rick Cobiski Junior, *VP*

Richard J Cobiski Junior, *Dir*
EMP: 34 **EST:** 1988
SQ FT: 14,000
SALES (est): 6.6MM **Privately Held**
Web: www.ccmetalsinc.com
SIC: 3599   Machine shop, jobbing and repair

(G-12956)
CENTRAL COATING TECH INC
Also Called: Central Coating
165 Shrewsbury St (01583-2198)
PHONE......................508 835-6225
James Ambrose, *Pr*
Robert Killion, *
EMP: 80 **EST:** 1970
SQ FT: 35,000
SALES (est): 11.56MM **Privately Held**
Web: www.centralcoating.com
SIC: 3479   Coating of metals and formed products

(G-12957)
CHECKERBOARD LTD
216 W Boylston St (01583-1728)
PHONE......................508 835-2475
EMP: 200
SIC: 2759   Stationery: printing, nsk

(G-12958)
CURTIS INDUSTRIES LLC (PA)
Also Called: Curtis Tractor Cab
70 Hartwell St (01583-2408)
PHONE......................508 853-2200
Ronald Coburn, *Managing Member*
▲ **EMP:** 10 **EST:** 1968
SQ FT: 168,000
SALES (est): 27.08MM
SALES (corp-wide): 27.08MM **Privately Held**
Web: www.curtisindustries.net
SIC: 3713 3714   Truck cabs, for motor vehicles; Motor vehicle parts and accessories

(G-12959)
DAIRY QUEEN
Also Called: Dairy Queen
328 W Boylston St (01583-2341)
PHONE......................508 853-2700
Mick Mouboubis, *Owner*
Erin Mouboubis, *Off Mgr*
EMP: 19 **EST:** 2010
SALES (est): 191.37K **Privately Held**
Web: www.dairyqueen.com
SIC: 5812 2024   Ice cream stands or dairy bars; Ice cream and frozen deserts

(G-12960)
DCI AUTOMATION INC
70 Hartwell St (01583-2408)
PHONE......................508 752-3071
EMP: 100
Web: www.dciautomation.com
SIC: 3559 7373   Semiconductor manufacturing machinery; Computer integrated systems design

(G-12961)
DIAS INFRARED CORP
75 Sterling St (01583-1218)
PHONE......................845 987-8152
Philip Gregor, *CEO*
EMP: 7 **EST:** 2011
SALES (est): 133.97K **Privately Held**
Web: www.dias-infrared.com
SIC: 3823   Temperature measurement instruments, industrial

(G-12962)
EMUGE CORP
1800 Century Dr (01583-2121)
PHONE......................508 595-3600
Robert W Hellinger, *CEO*
Helmut Glimpel, *
Ronald Garmey, *
▲ **EMP:** 50 **EST:** 1984
SQ FT: 5,000
SALES (est): 24.3MM **Privately Held**
Web: www.emuge-franken-group.com
SIC: 5084 3545   Industrial machinery and equipment; Machine tool accessories
HQ: Emuge-Werk Richard Glimpel Gmbh & Co. Kg Fabrik Fur Prazisionswerkzeuge
Nurnberger Str. 96-100
Lauf A.D.Pegnitz BY 91207
91231860

(G-12963)
H O WIRE CO INC
215 Shrewsbury St (01583-2107)
PHONE......................508 243-7177
Rand Daniels Iii, *Pr*
EMP: 11 **EST:** 1977
SALES (est): 204.93K **Privately Held**
SIC: 3471   Plating of metals or formed products

(G-12964)
LOWELL CORPORATION
Also Called: Porter-Ferguson
65 Hartwell St (01583-2407)
PHONE......................508 835-2900
David S Cummings, *Pr*
◆ **EMP:** 32 **EST:** 1869
SQ FT: 34,000
SALES (est): 5.34MM **Privately Held**
Web: www.lowellcorp.com
SIC: 3423   Mechanics' hand tools

(G-12965)
NEW TEK DESIGN GROUP INC
18 Worcester St (01583-1413)
PHONE......................508 835-4544
David Amato, *VP*
Mark Euler, *VP*
EMP: 8 **EST:** 2005
SALES (est): 476.59K **Privately Held**
Web: www.newtekdesigngroup.com
SIC: 2759   Screen printing

West Bridgewater
Plymouth County

(G-12966)
ATLANTIC RES MKTG SYSTEMS INC
Also Called: Arms
230 W Center St (02379-1620)
PHONE......................508 584-7816
Richard E Swan, *Pr*
Sharon Swan, *VP*
EMP: 12 **EST:** 1980
SQ FT: 26,000
SALES (est): 1.4MM **Privately Held**
Web: www.armsmounts.com
SIC: 3827 5961 3429   Optical instruments and lenses; Mail order house, nec; Hardware, nec

(G-12967)
BATH SYSTEMS MASSACHUSETTS INC
25 Turnpike St (02379-1004)
PHONE......................508 521-2700
Brian Cotton, *Prin*

Glenn Cotton, *Pr*
EMP: 8 **EST:** 2014
SALES (est): 167.98K **Privately Held**
SIC: 3443   Liners/lining

(G-12968)
CHEER PACK NORTH AMERICA LLC
Also Called: Cheer Pack North America
1 United Dr (02379-1027)
PHONE......................508 927-7800
▲ **EMP:** 10 **EST:** 2009
SALES (est): 5.78MM
SALES (corp-wide): 46.34MM **Privately Held**
Web: www.cheerpack.com
SIC: 2671 3081 3089   Paper; coated and laminated packaging; Unsupported plastics film and sheet; Plastics containers, except foam
PA: Cdf Corporation
77 Industrial Park Rd
Plymouth MA 02360
508 747-5858

(G-12969)
CLOZEX MEDICAL INC
375 West St (02379-1014)
PHONE......................781 237-1673
Michael Lebner, *Pr*
EMP: 9 **EST:** 2003
SALES (est): 973.49K **Privately Held**
Web: www.clozex.com
SIC: 3845   Ultrasonic scanning devices, medical

(G-12970)
CORY MANUFACTURING INC
343 Manley St (02379-1094)
PHONE......................508 680-2111
Matthew Berk, *Pr*
EMP: 19 **EST:** 2011
SALES (est): 883.23K **Privately Held**
Web: www.purekitchen.com
SIC: 3999   Manufacturing industries, nec

(G-12971)
DC SCAFFOLD INC
400 West St Ste 2 (02379-1095)
PHONE......................508 580-5100
John Degrenier, *Pr*
EMP: 9 **EST:** 1998
SALES (est): 490.77K **Privately Held**
SIC: 3446   Scaffolds, mobile or stationary: metal

(G-12972)
DOUBLE E COMPANY LLC (PA)
Also Called: Web Handling Equipment
319 Manley St (02379-1034)
PHONE......................508 588-8099
◆ **EMP:** 126 **EST:** 1972
SQ FT: 65,000
SALES (est): 42.52MM
SALES (corp-wide): 42.52MM **Privately Held**
Web: www.ee-co.com
SIC: 3545 3568   Chucks: drill, lathe, or magnetic (machine tool accessories); Shafts, flexible

(G-12973)
JIMSAN ENTERPRISES INC
Also Called: Hilliard's Chocolate System
275 E Center St (02379-1813)
PHONE......................508 587-3666
James Bourne, *Pr*
Sandra Bourne, *Clerk*
EMP: 9 **EST:** 1985
SQ FT: 6,000

SALES (est): 1.67MM **Privately Held**
Web: www.hilliardschocolate.com
SIC: 3556   Confectionery machinery

(G-12974)
KOSO AMERICA INC
Also Called: Rexa
4 Manley St (02379-1017)
PHONE......................774 517-5300
▲ **EMP:** 65 **EST:** 1993
SALES (est): 15.7MM **Privately Held**
Web: www.hammeldahl.com
SIC: 3625   Actuators, industrial
HQ: Nihon Koso Co., Ltd.
1-16-7, Nihombashi
Chuo-Ku TKY 103-0

(G-12975)
MOBILE MINI INC
125 Manley St (02379-1001)
PHONE......................508 427-5395
Jared Chernick, *Brnch Mgr*
EMP: 10
SALES (corp-wide): 2.14B **Publicly Held**
Web: www.mobilemini.com
SIC: 3448   Buildings, portable: prefabricated metal
HQ: Mobile Mini, Inc.
4646 E Van Buren St # 400
Phoenix AZ 85008
480 894-6311

(G-12976)
PARKWAY MANUFACTURING CO INC
1 Bert Dr (02379-1059)
PHONE......................508 559-6686
Thomas Accuavatti, *Pr*
Valerie Acciavatti, *Treas*
James E Bailey, *Clerk*
EMP: 7 **EST:** 1987
SQ FT: 1,500
SALES (est): 492.52K **Privately Held**
SIC: 3599   Machine shop, jobbing and repair

(G-12977)
REXA INC
Also Called: Rexa Electraulic Actuation
4 Manley St (02379-1017)
PHONE......................508 584-1199
Takashi Ikegaya, *Pr*
Etsuko Ikegaya, *
Soterios Lalos, *
◆ **EMP:** 99 **EST:** 2013
SQ FT: 48,358
SALES (est): 21.78MM **Privately Held**
Web: www.rexa.com
SIC: 3625   Actuators, industrial
HQ: Nihon Koso Co., Ltd.
1-16-7, Nihombashi
Chuo-Ku TKY 103-0

(G-12978)
SHARP MANUFACTURING INC
415 N Elm St (02379-1119)
PHONE......................508 583-4080
Steven Madonna, *Pr*
Susan Madonna, *Sec*
EMP: 8 **EST:** 2000
SQ FT: 7,500
SALES (est): 990.17K **Privately Held**
Web: www.sharpmanufacturing.com
SIC: 3599   Machine shop, jobbing and repair

(G-12979)
SHAWMUT LLC (PA)
208 Manley St (02379-1044)
PHONE......................508 588-3300
James H Wyner, *CEO*
Justin Wyner, *

GEOGRAPHIC

Giang T H Wyner, *
George Wyner, *
▲ **EMP:** 130 **EST:** 1916
SQ FT: 140,000
SALES (est): 124.29MM
SALES (corp-wide): 124.29MM **Privately Held**
Web: www.shawmutcorporation.com
SIC: 2295 Laminating of fabrics

(G-12980)
SKEW PRODUCTS INCORPORATED
Also Called: Spec Tools
4 Bert Dr Ste 6 (02379-1038)
PHONE..........................508 580-5800
John A Badiali, *Pr*
Cheryl A Badiali, *Sec*
▲ **EMP:** 13 **EST:** 1985
SQ FT: 5,000
SALES (est): 489.46K **Privately Held**
Web: www.spectools.com
SIC: 3423 Screw drivers, pliers, chisels, etc. (hand tools)

(G-12981)
STD MED INC
375 West St (02379-1014)
PHONE..........................781 828-4400
▲ **EMP:** 9 **EST:** 2014
SALES (est): 153.61K **Privately Held**
Web: www.primomedicalgroup.com
SIC: 3999 Manufacturing industries, nec

(G-12982)
STD PRECISION GEAR & INSTR INC
318 Manley St Ste 5 (02379-1087)
PHONE..........................508 580-0035
James Manning, *Pr*
Steven Tallarida, *
Jon T Tallarida, *
EMP: 35 **EST:** 1986
SQ FT: 8,000
SALES (est): 5.03MM **Privately Held**
Web: www.stdgear.com
SIC: 3566 Gears, power transmission, except auto

(G-12983)
SUNBURST ELCTRNIC MFG SLTONS I (PA)
Also Called: Sunburst Ems
70 Pleasant St (02379-1506)
PHONE..........................508 580-1881
Andrew Chase, *Pr*
George Agyare, *
Julie Caulfield, *
Steve Haley, *
Stephen Chase, *
▲ **EMP:** 67 **EST:** 1989
SQ FT: 36,000
SALES (est): 22.86MM **Privately Held**
Web: www.sunburstems.com
SIC: 3672 3679 Printed circuit boards; Harness assemblies, for electronic use: wire or cable

(G-12984)
THOMAS M LEONARD INC
Also Called: Epoch Industries
319 Manley St Ste 301 (02379-1034)
EMP: 7 **EST:** 1988
SALES (est): 918.84K **Privately Held**
SIC: 3555 3554 3599 Printing trades machinery; Paper industries machinery; Custom machinery

(G-12985)
TMH MACHINING & WELDING CORP
124 Turnpike St Ste 15 (02379-1071)
PHONE..........................508 580-6899
EMP: 9 **EST:** 1989
SALES (est): 453.48K **Privately Held**
Web: www.tmhmachine.com
SIC: 3599 Machine shop, jobbing and repair

(G-12986)
TPI INDUSTRIES LLC (HQ)
208 Manley St (02379-1044)
PHONE..........................845 692-2820
John Bowe, *Pr*
▲ **EMP:** 42 **EST:** 1978
SALES (est): 40.17MM
SALES (corp-wide): 96.2MM **Privately Held**
Web: www.shawmutcorporation.com
SIC: 2295 Laminating of fabrics
PA: Shawmut Llc
208 Manley St
West Bridgewater MA 02379
508 588-3300

(G-12987)
US SHEETMETAL INC
420 West St (02379-1072)
P.O. Box 505 (02379-0505)
PHONE..........................508 427-0500
John Martin Neilan, *Pr*
Christina Neilan, *Treas*
EMP: 7 **EST:** 2001
SALES (est): 910.95K **Privately Held**
SIC: 3444 Sheet metalwork

(G-12988)
VISI-FLASH RENTALS EASTERN
31 Pleasant St (02379-1505)
PHONE..........................508 583-9100
Daniel Doyle, *Pr*
Edward Doyle, *
EMP: 25 **EST:** 1964
SQ FT: 15,000
SALES (est): 4.96MM **Privately Held**
Web: www.visi-flash.com
SIC: 1611 7359 3499 5099 Highway and street sign installation; Work zone traffic equipment (flags, cones, barrels, etc.); Barricades, metal; Signs, except electric

(G-12989)
WARWICK FASTENERS
255 Pleasant St (02379-1507)
PHONE..........................401 739-9200
EMP: 8 **EST:** 2019
SALES (est): 261.05K **Privately Held**
Web: www.warwickfasteners.com
SIC: 3965 Fasteners

(G-12990)
WEST BRIDGEWATER FD PANTRY INC
2 Spring St (02379-1296)
PHONE..........................339 987-1684
Calvin Gray, *Pr*
Alma Keane, *Treas*
Patricia Turner, *Dir*
EMP: 8 **EST:** 2012
SQ FT: 1,000
SALES (est): 244.16K **Privately Held**
SIC: 6733 2099 Trusts, except educational, religious, charity: management; Food preparations, nec

West Brookfield
Worcester County

(G-12991)
ARLAND TOOL & MFG INC
45 Freight House Rd (01585-3132)
PHONE..........................508 867-3085
Meliisa Baker, *Brnch Mgr*
EMP: 15
SALES (corp-wide): 14.01MM **Privately Held**
Web: www.arland.com
SIC: 3599 Machine shop, jobbing and repair
PA: Arland Tool & Mfg, Inc.
421 Main St
Sturbridge MA 01566
508 347-3368

(G-12992)
BROOKFIELD WIRE COMPANY INC (HQ)
231 E Main St (01585-2911)
PHONE..........................508 867-6474
Anthony J Defino, *Pr*
Leonard M Defino, *
Francis P Defino, *
▲ **EMP:** 30 **EST:** 1974
SQ FT: 48,000
SALES (est): 17.66MM **Privately Held**
Web: www.brookfieldwire.com
SIC: 3315 3357 Wire, ferrous/iron; Nonferrous wiredrawing and insulating
PA: A.J.D. Holding Co.
2181 Enterprise Pkwy
Twinsburg OH 44087

(G-12993)
CONCRETE BLOCK INSULG SYSTEMS
Also Called: Cbis
25 Freight House Rd (01585-3132)
P.O. Box 1000 (01585-1000)
PHONE..........................508 867-4241
EMP: 22 **EST:** 1992
SQ FT: 60,000
SALES (est): 5.17MM
SALES (corp-wide): 102.89MM **Privately Held**
Web: www.cbisinc.com
SIC: 3086 Plastics foam products
PA: Foam Holdings, Inc.
10 Cadillac Dr Ste 100
Brentwood TN 37027
833 344-3626

(G-12994)
GAVITT WIRE AND CABLE CO INC
62 Central St (01585-3140)
PHONE..........................508 867-6476
Harold R Chesson Iii, *Pr*
Lisa A Baker, *
Michael P Angelini, *
EMP: 54 **EST:** 1923
SQ FT: 60,000
SALES (est): 20.48MM **Privately Held**
Web: www.gavitt.com
SIC: 3357 Nonferrous wiredrawing and insulating

(G-12995)
GREMARCO INDUSTRIES INC
131 E Main St (01585-2909)
P.O. Box 1041 (01585-1041)
PHONE..........................508 867-5244
Gregory L Deotte, *Pr*
Gregory L Deotte, *Pr*
Mary J Deotte, *VP*
▲ **EMP:** 15 **EST:** 1986
SALES (est): 1.01MM **Privately Held**
Web: www.gremarco.com
SIC: 3564 Filters, air: furnaces, air conditioning equipment, etc.

(G-12996)
MRSE INC
Also Called: Massachstts Rebuild Svc Export
192 W Main St (01585-2728)
P.O. Box 827 (01585-0827)
PHONE..........................508 867-5083
Frank Gaumond, *VP*
Steve Mansur, *VP*
EMP: 11 **EST:** 1992
SQ FT: 14,000
SALES (est): 2.51MM **Privately Held**
SIC: 3541 5085 Machine tools, metal cutting type; Industrial tools

(G-12997)
PRECISION WIRE SHAPES INC
11 Long Hill Rd (01585-3108)
P.O. Box 587 (01585-0587)
PHONE..........................508 867-3859
▲ **EMP:** 15 **EST:** 1967
SALES (est): 1.6MM **Privately Held**
Web: www.precisionwireshapes.com
SIC: 3315 Wire products, ferrous/iron: made in wiredrawing plants

(G-12998)
QUIRK WIRE CO INC
Also Called: Wirecraft Products
146 E Main St (01585-2901)
PHONE..........................508 867-3155
Peter Schlichting, *Pr*
Mary A Falardeau, *
▲ **EMP:** 39 **EST:** 1978
SQ FT: 20,000
SALES (est): 8.63MM **Privately Held**
Web: www.quirkwire.com
SIC: 3357 3496 3315 Nonferrous wiredrawing and insulating; Miscellaneous fabricated wire products; Steel wire and related products

West Dennis
Barnstable County

(G-12999)
THREE FINS COF ROASTERS & MERC
581 Main St (02670-2264)
PHONE..........................508 246-5813
Catherine Bieri, *Pr*
EMP: 16 **EST:** 2017
SALES (est): 1.25MM **Privately Held**
Web: www.threefinscoffee.com
SIC: 2095 Coffee roasting (except by wholesale grocers)

West Falmouth
Barnstable County

(G-13000)
ACME PRECAST CO INC
509 Thomas B Landers Rd (02574)
P.O. Box 374 (02556-0374)
PHONE..........................508 548-9607
Walter E Stone, *Pr*
EMP: 14 **EST:** 1954
SQ FT: 1,500
SALES (est): 507.41K **Privately Held**

SIC: 3272 1711 7699 Liquid catch basins, tanks, and covers: concrete; Septic system construction; Waste cleaning services

West Groton
Middlesex County

(G-13001)
CANNER INCORPORATED
Also Called: Carvers' Guild
1 Cannery Row (01472)
P.O. Box 198 (01472-0198)
PHONE..............................978 448-3063
Carl Canner, *Pr*
Carol Canner, *Clerk*
EMP: 15 EST: 1964
SQ FT: 25,000
SALES (est): 441.47K **Privately Held**
Web: www.carversguild.com
SIC: 3231 7641 2426 Mirrored glass; Reupholstery and furniture repair; Hardwood dimension and flooring mills

(G-13002)
HOLLINGSWORTH & VOSE COMPANY
219 Townsend Rd (01472)
P.O. Box 168 (01472-0168)
PHONE..............................978 448-7000
Robert Moore, *Brnch Mgr*
EMP: 250
SALES (corp-wide): 584.59MM **Privately Held**
Web: www.hollingsworth-vose.com
SIC: 2621 Specialty papers
PA: Hollingsworth & Vose Company
112 Washington St
East Walpole MA 02032
508 850-2000

West Hatfield
Hampshire County

(G-13003)
AARON MORIN
140 West St (01088-9500)
PHONE..............................413 247-0550
Aaron Morin, *Prin*
EMP: 8 EST: 2007
SALES (est): 548.89K **Privately Held**
SIC: 3444 Sheet metalwork

(G-13004)
BROCKWAY-SMITH COMPANY
125 Chestnut St (01088-9501)
P.O. Box 159 (01038-0159)
PHONE..............................413 247-9674
Lou Guillette, *Brnch Mgr*
EMP: 192
SALES (corp-wide): 8.39B **Publicly Held**
Web: www.brosco.com
SIC: 2431 5031 Millwork; Millwork
HQ: Brockway-Smith Company
35 Upton Dr Ste 100
Wilmington MA 01887
978 475-7100

(G-13005)
MILL VALLEY MOLDING INC
15 West St (01088-9516)
PHONE..............................413 247-9313
Ralph Healy, *Club President*
Ralph Healy, *Pr*
James K Patenaude, *
EMP: 20 EST: 1986
SQ FT: 11,000
SALES (est): 360.24K **Privately Held**

West Newbury
Essex County

(G-13006)
ANDALUNA ENTERPRISES INC
Also Called: Newbury Port Olive Oil
159 Indian Hill St (01985-2228)
PHONE..............................617 335-3204
Karen Nelson Shernan, *CEO*
EMP: 8 EST: 2015
SALES (est): 558.66K **Privately Held**
SIC: 2079 Olive oil

(G-13007)
B & W PRESS INC
17 Meadowsweet Rd (01985-1844)
PHONE..............................978 352-6100
EMP: 50
Web: www.bwpress.com
SIC: 2677 2752 Envelopes; Commercial printing, lithographic

(G-13008)
ELECTROLYZER CORP
22 Bachelor St (01985-1522)
PHONE..............................978 363-5349
Duane Mayo, *Pr*
Samuel B Coco, *Pr*
Donald Harper, *Ex VP*
Patrick Lucci, *VP*
Barry Galler, *Dir Opers*
EMP: 7 EST: 2005
SQ FT: 1,000
SALES (est): 575.91K **Privately Held**
Web: www.electrolyzercorp.com
SIC: 3556 Food products machinery

West Roxbury
Suffolk County

(G-13009)
ARMSTRONG PHARMACEUTICALS INC (HQ)
423 Lagrange St (02132-3314)
PHONE..............................617 323-7404
Jack Zhang, *CEO*
Mary Luo, *
James Luo, *
▲ EMP: 70 EST: 2001
SALES (est): 24.56MM
SALES (corp-wide): 498.99MM **Publicly Held**
Web: www.primatene.com
SIC: 2834 Pharmaceutical preparations
PA: Amphastar Pharmaceuticals Inc
11570 6th St
Rancho Cucamonga CA 91730
909 980-9484

(G-13010)
ETEC INC
Also Called: Electronic Test Energy Co
25 Worley St (02132-1713)
PHONE..............................617 477-4308
Mark R Ford Junior, *Pr*
Brian Clozzi, *VP Engg*
EMP: 9 EST: 1986
SQ FT: 10,000
SALES (est): 233.61K **Privately Held**
Web: www.etec.bio
SIC: 3825 7389 Semiconductor test equipment; Inspection and testing services

(G-13011)
IET LABS INC
1202 Vfw Pkwy (02132-4208)
PHONE..............................617 969-0804
FAX: 617 969-6604
EMP: 12
SALES (corp-wide): 5.25MM **Privately Held**
SIC: 3825 Test equipment for electronic and electrical circuits
PA: Iet Labs., Inc.
1 Expressway Plz Ste 120
Roslyn Heights NY 11577
516 334-5959

(G-13012)
INKAMAZON LLC
Also Called: Food Bevs Spclty Import Export
841 Lagrange St Unit 7 (02132-2261)
PHONE..............................617 763-4656
Angel Cortavitarte, *CEO*
Angel Cortavitarte, *Managing Member*
EMP: 7 EST: 2011
SALES (est): 261.97K **Privately Held**
Web: www.inkamazon.com
SIC: 2099 Food preparations, nec

West Springfield
Hampden County

(G-13013)
ARCH PARENT INC
1129 Riverdale St (01089-4615)
PHONE..............................413 504-1433
EMP: 12898
SALES (corp-wide): 499.13MM **Privately Held**
SIC: 2752 Commercial printing, lithographic
PA: Arch Parent Inc.
9 W 57th St Fl 31
New York NY 10019
212 796-8500

(G-13014)
ASP FIBERMARK HOLDINGS LLC
70 Front St (01089-3113)
PHONE..............................413 736-4554
EMP: 591
SIC: 2631 2621 2672 Pressboard; Specialty papers; Adhesive papers, labels, or tapes: from purchased material

(G-13015)
ATLAS COPCO COMPRESSORS LLC
92 Interstate Dr (01089-4532)
PHONE..............................413 493-7290
Uew Fefraber, *Mgr*
EMP: 19
SALES (corp-wide): 13.47B **Privately Held**
Web: www.atlascopco.us
SIC: 3563 Air and gas compressors
HQ: Atlas Copco Compressors Llc
300 Technology Center Way # 550
Rock Hill SC 29730
866 472-1015

(G-13016)
AVSON BREWING LLC
89 Baldwin St (01089-3705)
PHONE..............................781 727-5789
EMP: 8 EST: 2018
SALES (est): 565.72K **Privately Held**
SIC: 2082 Beer (alcoholic beverage)

(G-13017)
BART TRUCK EQUIPMENT LLC
358 River St (01089-3632)
PHONE..............................413 737-2766
EMP: 9 EST: 2010
SALES (est): 891.21K **Privately Held**
Web: www.barttruckllc.com
SIC: 3713 Truck and bus bodies

(G-13018)
CONNECTICUT VALLEY BLOCK CO INC
55 Circuit Ave (01089-4012)
TOLL FREE: 800
EMP: 23 EST: 1945
SALES (est): 3.1MM **Privately Held**
SIC: 3271 5032 Blocks, concrete or cinder: standard; Concrete building products

(G-13019)
COVERIS ADVNCED CTNGS MTTHEWS (DH)
69 William Frank Dr (01089-3261)
PHONE..............................413 539-5547
Ed Mccarron, *VP*
◆ EMP: 20 EST: 2002
SQ FT: 3,000
SALES (est): 13.95MM
SALES (corp-wide): 2.15B **Privately Held**
SIC: 2671 2851 Paper; coated and laminated packaging; Paints and allied products
HQ: Transcontinental Ac Uk Ltd.
Ash Road North Wrexham Industrial Estate
Wrexham LL13
197 866-0241

(G-13020)
CYALUME TECHNOLOGIES INC (HQ)
Also Called: Cyalume
96 Windsor St (01089-3528)
PHONE..............................888 858-7881
Jeremy Steinfink, *CEO*
Robert Nobile, *
◆ EMP: 41 EST: 1997
SALES (est): 29.8MM
SALES (corp-wide): 457.84MM **Publicly Held**
Web: www.cyalume.com
SIC: 3648 Lighting equipment, nec
PA: Cadre Holdings, Inc.
13386 International Pkwy
Jacksonville FL 32218
904 787-8243

(G-13021)
DIAMONDHEAD USA INC
622 Union St (01089-4111)
PHONE..............................413 537-4806
John Deluca, *Prin*
EMP: 10 EST: 2013
SALES (est): 479.8K **Privately Held**
Web: www.diamondhead-usa.com
SIC: 3999 Manufacturing industries, nec

(G-13022)
DINN BROS INC (PA)
Also Called: Dinn Bros Trophies & Plaques
221 Interstate Dr (01089-4506)
P.O. Box 111 (01041-0111)
PHONE..............................413 750-3466
TOLL FREE: 800
Paul Dinn, *Pr*
Mary Ellen Dinn, *
▲ EMP: 100 EST: 1956
SALES (est): 9.45MM
SALES (corp-wide): 9.45MM **Privately Held**

SIC: 3089 Injection molding of plastics

GEOGRAPHIC

Web: www.dinntrophy.com
SIC: **5999** 3993　Trophies and plaques;
　Signs and advertising specialties

(G-13023)
ELM INDUSTRIES INC
380 Union St Ste 67 (01089-4123)
P.O. Box 717 (01090-0717)
PHONE...............................413 734-7762
George W Martin, *Pr*
John F Martin, *VP*
Kenneth C Martin, *VP*
EMP: 20 **EST:** 1967
SQ FT: 11,000
SALES (est): 975.79K **Privately Held**
Web: www.elmindustries-usa.com
SIC: **3089**　Injection molding of plastics

(G-13024)
ES COUNTERTOPS LLC
3 Century Way (01089-4235)
PHONE...............................413 732-8128
Benjamin Abel, *Managing Member*
EMP: 8 **EST:** 2017
SALES (est): 746.48K **Privately Held**
Web: www.escountertops.net
SIC: **3281**　Curbing, granite or stone

(G-13025)
FOUNTAIN PLATING COMPANY
LLC
492 Prospect Ave (01089-4596)
PHONE...............................413 781-4651
Nina Fountain, *Pr*
Dexter Fountain, *
EMP: 95 **EST:** 1963
SQ FT: 70,000
SALES (est): 24.32MM
SALES (corp-wide): 138.9MM **Privately
Held**
Web: www.fountain-plating.com
SIC: **3724** 3471　Research and development
　on aircraft engines and parts; Electroplating
　and plating
PA: Valence Surface Technologies Llc
　300 Continental Blvd # 600
　El Segundo CA 90245
　888 540-0878

(G-13026)
FRG PUBLICATIONS
Also Called: Green Publishing
12 Tatham Hill Rd (01089-2127)
PHONE...............................413 734-3411
EMP: 8 **EST:** 1994
SALES (est): 209.28K **Privately Held**
SIC: **2741**　Miscellaneous publishing

(G-13027)
FUEL FIRST ELM INC
173 Elm St (01089-2726)
PHONE...............................413 732-5732
EMP: 9 **EST:** 2010
SALES (est): 442.32K **Privately Held**
SIC: **2869**　Fuels

(G-13028)
FUNCTIONAL INKS INC
150 Front St Ste 2 (01089-3103)
PHONE...............................413 363-0770
Paul Giusto, *Prin*
EMP: 8 **EST:** 2019
SALES (est): 987.95K **Privately Held**
Web: www.functional-inks.com
SIC: **2893**　Printing ink

(G-13029)
HAYDEN CORPORATION
Also Called: Hayden Laser

333 River St (01089-3603)
PHONE...............................413 734-4981
▲ **EMP:** 43 **EST:** 1919
SALES (est): 4.97MM **Privately Held**
Web: www.haydencorp.com
SIC: **3479**　Painting, coating, and hot dipping

(G-13030)
INTELCOAT TECH DGTAL
IMGING HL
69 William Frank Dr (01089-3261)
PHONE...............................413 536-7800
Bob Champigny, *Pr*
EMP: 20 **EST:** 2001
SALES (est): 518.21K **Privately Held**
SIC: **3826**　Magnetic resonance imaging
　apparatus

(G-13031)
INTERNATIONAL BEAM WLDG
CORP
Also Called: International Beam Welding
63 Doty Cir (01089-1395)
PHONE...............................413 781-4368
William B Howe, *Pr*
Carol A Howe, *Clerk*
EMP: 10 **EST:** 1967
SQ FT: 7,000
SALES (est): 954.14K **Privately Held**
Web:
www.internationalbeamwelding.com
SIC: **7692**　Welding repair

(G-13032)
LEISURE TIME CANVAS INC
140 Norman St (01089-5004)
PHONE...............................413 785-5500
TOLL FREE: 800
John Vogel, *Pr*
Phyllis Hard, *VP*
EMP: 7 **EST:** 1982
SQ FT: 70,000
SALES (est): 491.83K **Privately Held**
Web: www.leisuretimecanvas.com
SIC: **2394**　Canvas and related products

(G-13033)
MCLAUGHLIN PAPER CO INC
(PA)
Also Called: Genevieves Gift Wrap Sales Div
61 Progress Ave (01089-3323)
P.O. Box 147 (01090-0147)
PHONE...............................413 732-7485
Daniel J Mc Laughlin, *CEO*
Daniel C Mc Laughlin, *Pr*
Genevieve C Mc Laughlin, *Treas*
▲ **EMP:** 12 **EST:** 1987
SQ FT: 57,000
SALES (est): 10.87MM
SALES (corp-wide): 10.87MM **Privately
Held**
Web: www.mclaughlinpaper.com
SIC: **5113** 2679　Industrial and personal
　service paper; Paper products, converted,
　nec

(G-13034)
MOUNT TOM BOX COMPANY
INC
190 Interstate Dr (01089-4582)
PHONE...............................413 781-5300
David Strauss, *Pr*
EMP: 10 **EST:** 1968
SQ FT: 65,000
SALES (est): 775.31K **Privately Held**
Web: www.keycontainercorp.com
SIC: **2653**　Boxes, corrugated: made from
　purchased materials

(G-13035)
MTI SYSTEMS INC
Also Called: Manufactures Technologies
1111 Elm St Ste 6 (01089-1540)
PHONE...............................413 733-1972
Rene Laviolette, *Pr*
Thomas Charkiewicz, *Pr*
Rene M Laviolette, *VP*
Nancy Olechna, *Treas*
EMP: 10 **EST:** 1982
SALES (est): 1.57MM **Privately Held**
Web: www.mtisystems.com
SIC: **7371** 7372　Computer software
　development; Business oriented computer
　software

(G-13036)
NEENAH NORTHEAST LLC (DH)
70 Front St (01089-3113)
PHONE...............................413 533-0699
Anthony Pd Maclaurin, *CEO*
Craig Thiel, *Corporate Controller*
Matthew Levine, *
Eric Schondorf, *
◆ **EMP:** 110 **EST:** 1993
SALES (est): 101.48MM **Publicly Held**
SIC: **2621**　Paper mills
HQ: Neenah, Inc.
　3460 Preston Ridge Rd # 6
　Alpharetta GA 30005
　678 566-6500

(G-13037)
NEW ENGLAND DOOR CLOSER
INC
694 Union St (01089-4111)
P.O. Box 28 (01090-0028)
PHONE...............................413 733-7889
EMP: 24 **EST:** 1946
SALES (est): 1.32MM **Privately Held**
Web: www.nedoorcloser.com
SIC: **3429**　Door opening and closing
　devices, except electrical

(G-13038)
NORTEK INC
70 Doty Cir (01089-1394)
PHONE...............................413 781-4777
Bianca P Magnani, *Pr*
Sandra M Santinello Clrk, *Prin*
Raymond Santinello, *VP*
EMP: 20 **EST:** 1968
SQ FT: 8,000
SALES (est): 2.29MM **Privately Held**
Web: www.nortekinc.net
SIC: **3545**　Precision tools, machinists'

(G-13039)
OMNIGLOW LLC
865 Memorial Ave Ste 4 (01089-3540)
PHONE...............................413 241-6010
▲ **EMP:** 450
Web: www.windycitynovelties.com
SIC: **2819** 3229 5947　Industrial inorganic
　chemicals, nec; Glass tubes and tubing;
　Gift, novelty, and souvenir shop

(G-13040)
PACKAGE PRINTING COMPANY
INC
33 Myron St (01089-1486)
P.O. Box 378 (01090-0378)
PHONE...............................413 736-2748
James G Barnhart, *Pr*
James G Barnhart, *Pr*
Robert Barnhart, *
▲ **EMP:** 30 **EST:** 1950
SQ FT: 30,000
SALES (est): 4.86MM **Privately Held**

Web: www.pkgprinting.com
SIC: **2671** 2759　Paper, coated or laminated
　for packaging; Bags, plastic: printing, nsk

(G-13041)
PLACON CORPORATION
1227 Union Street Ext (01089-4022)
PHONE...............................413 785-1553
Ed Kadlam, *Genl Mgr*
EMP: 97
SALES (corp-wide): 131.72MM **Privately
Held**
Web: www.placon.com
SIC: **3089**　Injection molding of plastics
PA: Placon Corporation
　6096 Mckee Rd
　Fitchburg WI 53719
　608 271-5634

(G-13042)
PLASTIC PACKAGING
CORPORATION
1227 Union Street Ext (01089-4076)
P.O. Box 548 (01090-0548)
PHONE...............................413 785-1553
EMP: 120
Web: www.placon.com
SIC: **3089**　Injection molded finished plastics
　products, nec

(G-13043)
Q PIN2S BILLIARDS
885 Riverdale St (01089-4612)
PHONE...............................413 285-7971
Dixie Willison, *Prin*
EMP: 7 **EST:** 2011
SALES (est): 106.07K **Privately Held**
SIC: **3452**　Pins

(G-13044)
SULLIVAN PAPER COMPANY
INC (PA)
42 Progress Ave (01089-3313)
P.O. Box 88 (01090-0088)
PHONE...............................413 827-7030
George R Sullivan, *CEO*
Richard Sullivan, *
Mike Sullivan, *
Joe Sullivan, *
Edward Sullivan, *
◆ **EMP:** 165 **EST:** 1939
SQ FT: 30,000
SALES (est): 23.44MM
SALES (corp-wide): 23.44MM **Privately
Held**
Web: www.sullivanpaper.com
SIC: **2621**　Paper mills

(G-13045)
TRANSTULIT LLC
Also Called: Western Mass Compounding Ctr
138 Memorial Ave Ste 40 (01089-4041)
PHONE...............................413 737-2600
Bradley Sprecher, *Managing Member*
EMP: 9 **EST:** 2015
SALES (est): 1.96MM **Privately Held**
Web: www.wmccma.com
SIC: **1541** 2834　Pharmaceutical
　manufacturing plant construction;
　Druggists' preparations (pharmaceuticals)

(G-13046)
TRUE PRECISION INC
17 Allston Ave (01089-3799)
PHONE...............................413 788-4226
Leo R La Flamme, *Pr*
Robert Serre, *VP*
EMP: 22 **EST:** 1968
SQ FT: 2,200

SALES (est): 460.96K **Privately Held**
Web: www.trueprecisionind.com
SIC: 3599 Machine shop, jobbing and repair

(G-13047)
TRUE PRECISION INDUSTRIES INC
17 Allston Ave (01089-3799)
PHONE..................................413 788-4226
Richard Champigny, *Pr*
Michael Belisle, *Treas*
EMP: 14 EST: 2005
SALES (est): 289.37K **Privately Held**
Web: www.trueprecisionind.com
SIC: 3599 Machine shop, jobbing and repair

(G-13048)
UNITED INDUSTRIAL TEX PDTS INC (PA)
321 Main St (01089-3908)
PHONE..................................413 737-0095
Wayne Perry, *Pr*
Keith Perry, *
Joanne Perry, *
EMP: 34 EST: 1952
SQ FT: 10,000
SALES (est): 3.97MM
SALES (corp-wide): 3.97MM **Privately Held**
Web: www.uitprod.com
SIC: 2394 2299 2393 Canvas and related products; Broadwoven fabrics: linen, jute, hemp, and ramie; Textile bags

(G-13049)
VACUUM ENGINEERING INC
857 Elm St (01089-2658)
PHONE..................................413 734-4400
EMP: 8 EST: 1901
SALES (est): 154.99K **Privately Held**
SIC: 3635 Household vacuum cleaners

(G-13050)
VALENTINE PLATING COMPANY INC
155 Allston Ave (01089-3796)
PHONE..................................413 732-0009
Steve Valentino Junior, *Pr*
Anthony Valentino, *
Janet Santinello, *Treas*
EMP: 34 EST: 1965
SALES (est): 2.37MM **Privately Held**
Web: www.valentineplating.com
SIC: 3471 Electroplating of metals or formed products

(G-13051)
VOGFORM TOOL & DIE CO INC
56 Doty Cir (01089-1308)
PHONE..................................413 737-6947
John Vogel, *Pr*
Elizabeth Vogel, *Treas*
EMP: 23 EST: 1965
SQ FT: 9,000
SALES (est): 1.03MM **Privately Held**
SIC: 3544 Special dies and tools

(G-13052)
WEST SPRINGFIELD RECORD INC
516 Main St (01089-3983)
P.O. Box 357 (01090-0357)
PHONE..................................413 736-1587
Marie Coburn, *Pr*
Thomas Coburn, *Editor*
EMP: 7 EST: 1951
SQ FT: 1,500
SALES (est): 490.56K **Privately Held**

SIC: 2711 Newspapers, publishing and printing

(G-13053)
WESTERN BRONZE INC
54 Western Ave (01089-3491)
PHONE..................................413 737-1319
Daniel Kotowitz, *Pr*
Nancy Kotowitz, *Mgr*
EMP: 10 EST: 1946
SQ FT: 12,000
SALES (est): 1.8MM **Privately Held**
Web: www.westernbronze.com
SIC: 3366 Castings (except die), nsk

West Stockbridge
Berkshire County

(G-13054)
MIELKE CONFECTIONS INC
46 W Center Rd (01266-9378)
PHONE..................................413 528-2510
Trent Kinney, *Pr*
EMP: 7 EST: 2020
SALES (est): 514.1K **Privately Held**
SIC: 2066 Chocolate and cocoa products

West Tisbury
Dukes County

(G-13055)
SOUTH MOUNTAIN COMPANY INC
Also Called: Honeywell Authorized Dealer
15 Red Arrow Rd (02575-5444)
P.O. Box 1260 (02575-1260)
PHONE..................................508 693-4850
John Abrams, *Pr*
Deirdre Bohan, *
Peter Ives, *
Siobhan Mullin, *
Gerald Tulis, *
EMP: 34 EST: 1984
SQ FT: 12,500
SALES (est): 9.42MM **Privately Held**
Web: www.southmountain.com
SIC: 1521 8712 2431 2511 New construction, single-family houses; Architectural services; Millwork; Wood household furniture

West Townsend
Middlesex County

(G-13056)
ALBERT E CADRETTE
Also Called: Settle Shop, The
419a Main St (01474-1158)
PHONE..................................978 597-2312
Albert E Cadette, *Owner*
EMP: 10 EST: 1958
SALES (est): 690.71K **Privately Held**
Web: www.thesettleshop.com
SIC: 5712 5947 2511 Furniture stores; Gift shop; Tables, household: wood

West Wareham
Plymouth County

(G-13057)
CALORIQUE LLC
2380 Cranberry Hwy Ste 6 (02576-1229)
PHONE..................................508 291-2000
William D Mccarthy, *Managing Member*

EMP: 14 EST: 2009
SQ FT: 20,000
SALES (est): 2.36MM **Privately Held**
Web: www.calorique.com
SIC: 3567 Radiant heating systems, industrial process

(G-13058)
COSTELLO DISMANTLING CO INC (PA)
15 Cranberry Hwy Unit 1 (02576-1504)
PHONE..................................508 291-2324
Daniel T Costello, *Pr*
Joan Costello, *
John J Hastings, *
EMP: 31 EST: 1985
SQ FT: 2,500
SALES (est): 8.71MM
SALES (corp-wide): 8.71MM **Privately Held**
Web: www.costellodismantling.com
SIC: 1795 8711 3531 5093 Demolition, buildings and other structures; Mechanical engineering; Crane carriers; Scrap and waste materials

(G-13059)
COTTER MACHINE CO INC (PA)
7 Little Brook Rd (02576-1221)
P.O. Box 249 (02576-0249)
PHONE..................................508 291-7400
Gregory Cotter, *Pr*
EMP: 15 EST: 1975
SQ FT: 10,000
SALES (est): 3.28MM
SALES (corp-wide): 3.28MM **Privately Held**
Web: www.cottermachine.com
SIC: 3599 Machine shop, jobbing and repair

(G-13060)
DCAF OF MASSACHUSETTS INC
Also Called: Calorique
2380 Cranberry Hwy (02576-1229)
PHONE..................................508 291-2000
▲ EMP: 14
SIC: 3567 Radiant heating systems, industrial process

(G-13061)
EDGEONE LLC
Edgetech
4 Little Brook Rd (02576-1222)
PHONE..................................508 291-0057
Greg Macearhern, *Brnch Mgr*
EMP: 9
SALES (corp-wide): 20.3MM **Privately Held**
Web: www.edgetech.com
SIC: 3812 Search and navigation equipment
PA: Edgeone Llc
     4 Little Brook Rd
     West Wareham MA 02576
     508 291-0057

(G-13062)
EDGEONE LLC
Also Called: Ore Offshore
4 Little Brook Rd (02576-1222)
P.O. Box 848 (02576-0848)
PHONE..................................508 291-0960
Steven Withrow, *Brnch Mgr*
EMP: 9
SALES (corp-wide): 20.3MM **Privately Held**
Web: www.edgetech.com
SIC: 3812 5049 Sonar systems and equipment; Scientific instruments
PA: Edgeone Llc
     4 Little Brook Rd

West Wareham MA 02576
508 291-0057

(G-13063)
EDGEONE LLC (PA)
Also Called: Edgetech
4 Little Brook Rd (02576-1222)
PHONE..................................508 291-0057
EMP: 15 EST: 1998
SALES (est): 20.3MM
SALES (corp-wide): 20.3MM **Privately Held**
Web: www.edgetech.com
SIC: 8748 3826 Environmental consultant; Analytical instruments

(G-13064)
FIBERSPAR SPOOLABLE PDTS INC (PA)
28 Pattersons Brook Rd (02576-1272)
PHONE..................................508 291-9000
Peter Quigley, *Pr*
▲ EMP: 25 EST: 1989
SQ FT: 5,000
SALES (est): 4.53MM **Privately Held**
SIC: 3084 Plastics pipe

(G-13065)
FRANKLIN FIXTURES INC (PA)
20 Pattersons Brook Rd Ste 4 (02576-1269)
PHONE..................................508 291-1475
James E Baylis, *Pr*
David N Troe, *
EMP: 29 EST: 1975
SQ FT: 45,000
SALES (est): 3.83MM
SALES (corp-wide): 3.83MM **Privately Held**
Web: www.franklinfixtures.com
SIC: 2541 Display fixtures, wood

(G-13066)
JAMES C CANNELL COFFEES INC
Also Called: Jim's Organic Coffee
21 Pattersons Brook Rd Unit E (02576-1217)
PHONE..................................508 295-7009
James C Cannell, *Pr*
EMP: 16 EST: 1996
SQ FT: 3,750
SALES (est): 3.46MM **Privately Held**
Web: www.jimsorganiccoffee.com
SIC: 5149 2095 Coffee, green or roasted; Roasted coffee

(G-13067)
MAKE ARCHTECTURAL METALWORKING
2358 Cranberry Hwy (02576-1208)
PHONE..................................508 273-7603
Paul A Meneses, *Prin*
EMP: 10 EST: 2012
SALES (est): 877.67K **Privately Held**
Web: www.makearchmetal.com
SIC: 3446 Architectural metalwork

(G-13068)
MASTER MILLWORK LLC
55 Charlotte Furnace Rd (02576-1128)
PHONE..................................508 273-0500
Jesse Kirby, *Managing Member*
▲ EMP: 20 EST: 2008
SALES (est): 4.3MM **Privately Held**
Web: www.mastermillwork.com
SIC: 2541 1751 Store and office display cases and fixtures; Cabinet and finish carpentry

GEOGRAPHIC

(G-13069)

MEDICAL PRODUCTS MFG LLC
Also Called: Brunwick Biomedical Tech
4 Little Brook Rd (02576-1222)
PHONE..............................508 291-1830
James E Nichols, *Pr*
Michelle Hatmaker, *Sec*
EMP: 10 EST: 1944
SQ FT: 11,000
SALES (est): 987.93K **Privately Held**
SIC: 3842 3845 Surgical appliances and
supplies; Electromedical equipment

(G-13070)

PREPPY PUPPY INC
2380 Cranberry Hwy Ste 3 (02576-1229)
PHONE..............................508 291-7555
Amy Singelais, *Pr*
EMP: 35 EST: 2007
SALES (est): 3MM **Privately Held**
Web: www.preppypuppytreats.com
SIC: 2047 Dog food

West Yarmouth
Barnstable County

(G-13071)

AUSTINS SPORTSWEAR INC
Also Called: Austin Screenprint
223 Mid Tech Dr (02673-2581)
PHONE..............................508 775-0554
Steven A Austin, *Pr*
▲ **EMP: 14 EST:** 1984
SQ FT: 9,000
SALES (est): 2.14MM **Privately Held**
Web: www.austinsinc.com
SIC: 5136 5137 2759 2395 Sportswear,
men's and boys'; Women's and children's
clothing; Screen printing; Art needlework:
made from purchased materials

(G-13072)

BAXTER INC
Also Called: Baxter Crane & Rigging
10 Bayview St (02673-8203)
PHONE..............................508 775-0375
Jonathan Baxter, *Pr*
▲ **EMP: 13 EST:** 1957
SQ FT: 450
SALES (est): 985.52K **Privately Held**
Web: www.baxtercrane.com
SIC: 7692 7353 5051 Welding repair;
Cranes and aerial lift equipment, rental or
leasing; Steel

(G-13073)

SPINAL TECHNOLOGY LLC (PA)
191 Mid Tech Dr (02673-2581)
PHONE..............................508 775-0990
James Tierney, *Pr*
James Benelli, *
Ariane St Claire, *
EMP: 35 EST: 1991
SQ FT: 18,000
SALES (est): 9.73MM **Privately Held**
Web: www.spinaltech.com
SIC: 3842 Braces, orthopedic

(G-13074)

T-SHIRTS AUTHORITY INC
20 Iyanough Rd (02673-8135)
PHONE..............................774 855-0000
Marlene Madeira Ribeiro, *Prin*
EMP: 8 EST: 2016
SALES (est): 309.57K **Privately Held**
Web: www.capecodpeninsula.com
SIC: 2759 Screen printing

Westborough
Worcester County

(G-13075)

3M TOUCH SYSTEMS INC
115 Flanders Rd (01581-1033)
PHONE..............................508 871-1840
Samuel Thomas, *Brnch Mgr*
EMP: 65
SALES (corp-wide): 34.23B **Publicly Held**
SIC: 3577 Computer peripheral equipment,
nec
HQ: 3m Touch Systems, Inc.
3 M Ctr Bldg 2245n40
Saint Paul MN 55144
978 659-9000

(G-13076)

APEX PRESS INC
122 Turnpike Rd (01581-2854)
PHONE..............................508 366-1110
Sheila A Gendreau, *Pr*
EMP: 13 EST: 1986
SQ FT: 15,600
SALES (est): 226.16K **Privately Held**
SIC: 2759 7334 2752 Commercial printing,
nec; Photocopying and duplicating services
; Offset printing

(G-13077)

ASCEND ELEMENTS INC (PA)
133 Flanders Rd (01581-1031)
PHONE..............................508 936-7701
Michael O'kronley, *Pr*
Eric Gratz, *Sec*
Andrew Aberdale, *Treas*
EMP: 7 EST: 2017
SALES (est): 11.27MM
SALES (corp-wide): 11.27MM **Privately
Held**
Web: www.ascendelements.com
SIC: 3356 Battery metal

(G-13078)

**ASTELLAS INST FOR RGNRTIVE
MDC (HQ)**
9 Technology Dr (01581-1794)
PHONE..............................800 727-7003
Masahide Goto, *Pr*
Edward Myles, *
EMP: 18 EST: 2005
SQ FT: 30,000
SALES (est): 90.78MM **Privately Held**
Web: www.astellascareers.jobs
SIC: 2834 Pharmaceutical preparations
PA: Astellas Pharma Inc.
2-5-1, Nihombashihoncho
Chuo-Ku TKY 103-0

(G-13079)

ATLAS FIBRE LLC
116 Flanders Rd Ste 3000 (01581-1094)
PHONE..............................847 674-1234
EMP: 11 EST: 2020
SALES (est): 5.17MM **Privately Held**
Web: www.atlasfibre.com
SIC: 3083 Thermosetting laminates: rods,
tubes, plates, and sheet

(G-13080)

BAGDON ADVERTISING INC
Also Called: Community Advocate
32 South St (01581-1619)
P.O. Box 1574 (01581-6574)
PHONE..............................508 366-5500
David D Bagdon, *Pr*
EMP: 24 EST: 1977
SQ FT: 3,600
SALES (est): 2.28MM **Privately Held**
Web: www.communityadvocate.com
SIC: 2711 Newspapers, publishing and
printing

(G-13081)

BATTERY RESOURCERS LLC
Also Called: Battery Resourcers
133 Flanders Rd (01581-1031)
PHONE..............................206 948-6325
Eric Gratz, *Managing Member*
Eric Gratz, *Engr*
EMP: 13 EST: 2015
SALES (est): 1.16MM **Privately Held**
Web: www.ascendelements.com
SIC: 3691 Batteries, rechargeable

(G-13082)

BEL POWER INC
2400 Computer Dr (01581-1887)
PHONE..............................508 870-9775
Howard Kaepplein, *Pr*
Bernie Schroter, *VP Engg*
William Ng, *VP Opers*
▲ **EMP: 72 EST:** 1993
SQ FT: 22,000
SALES (est): 8.6MM
SALES (corp-wide): 654.23MM **Publicly
Held**
Web: www.belfuse.com
SIC: 3629 Power conversion units, a.c. to
d.c.: static-electric
PA: Bel Fuse Inc.
206 Van Vorst St
Jersey City NJ 07302
201 432-0463

(G-13083)

**BRITISH TRANSCO CAPITAL
INC**
25 Research Dr (01581-3680)
PHONE..............................781 907-3646
Malcolm C Cooper, *Pr*
EMP: 27 EST: 2006
SALES (est): 1.54MM
SALES (corp-wide): 26.03B **Privately Held**
SIC: 1311 Natural gas production
HQ: National Gas Transmission Plc
National Grid House
Warwick CV34
207 004-3000

(G-13084)

BUSINESS RESOURCES INC
Also Called: Development Resources
8 Lyman St Ste 200 (01581-1487)
PHONE..............................508 433-4600
David Sears, *CEO*
EMP: 10 EST: 1993
SALES (est): 972.19K **Privately Held**
SIC: 2752 Offset printing

(G-13085)

CAMBEX CORPORATION (PA)
115 Flanders Rd (01581-1033)
PHONE..............................508 983-1200
Joseph F Kruy, *Pr*
Joseph F Kruy, *Pr*
Lois P Lehberger, *Clerk*
Les Koch, *VP*
EMP: 10 EST: 1968
SQ FT: 15,000
SALES (est): 5.68MM
SALES (corp-wide): 5.68MM **Privately
Held**
Web: www.cambex.com
SIC: 3572 Computer storage devices

(G-13086)

**CARLSTROM PRESSED METAL
CO INC**
65 Fisher St (01581-1898)
PHONE..............................508 366-4472
David M Carlstrom, *Pr*
EMP: 25 EST: 1950
SQ FT: 45,000
SALES (est): 2.48MM **Privately Held**
Web: www.carlstrompm.com
SIC: 3469 Stamping metal for the trade

(G-13087)

CGIT WESTBORO INC
30 Oak St (01581-3319)
PHONE..............................508 836-4000
Dana Perry, *CFO*
▲ **EMP: 49 EST:** 1999
SQ FT: 36,578
SALES (est): 16.9MM
SALES (corp-wide): 1.32B **Publicly Held**
SIC: 3613 3612 Switchgear and
switchboard apparatus; Transformers,
except electric
PA: Azz Inc.
3100 W 7th St Ste 500
Fort Worth TX 76107
817 810-0095

(G-13088)

**COCA-COLA BTLG STHSTERN
NENG I**
Also Called: Coca-Cola
2 Sassacus Dr (01581-3348)
PHONE..............................508 836-5200
Mike Gillan, *Mgr*
EMP: 52
Web: www.coca-cola.com
SIC: 2086 Bottled and canned soft drinks
HQ: Coca-Cola Bottling Company Of
Southeastern New England, Inc.
150 Waterford Parkway S
Waterford CT 06385
860 443-2816

(G-13089)

COGHLIN COMPANIES INC (PA)
Also Called: Columbia Tech
27 Otis St (01581-3311)
PHONE..............................508 753-2354
James W Coghlin Senior, *CEO*
Christopher J Coghlin, *Pr*
James W Coghlin Junior, *Sec*
Randy Ziffer, *Sr VP*
Madison Finlay, *COO*
EMP: 150 EST: 1986
SQ FT: 61,000
SALES (est): 139.07MM
SALES (corp-wide): 139.07MM **Privately
Held**
Web: www.coghlincompanies.com
SIC: 3672 Printed circuit boards

(G-13090)

**COLD HARBOR BREWING CO
LLC**
66 Otis St (01581-3323)
PHONE..............................508 768-5232
William Oliveira, *Pr*
William Oliveira, *Managing Member*
EMP: 35 EST: 2015
SALES (est): 1.07MM **Privately Held**
Web: www.coldharborbrewing.com
SIC: 5812 2082 Restaurant, family:
independent; Malt beverage products

(G-13091)

**COLUMBIA ELECTRICAL
CONTRS INC**

Also Called: Columbia Tech
27 Otis St Ste 300 (01581-3311)
PHONE...............................508 366-8297
Christopher J Coghlin, *Pr*
James W Coghlin Senior, *Treas*
James W Coghlin Junior, *Sec*
Christopher J Palermo, *
▲ **EMP:** 240 **EST:** 1991
SQ FT: 55,000
SALES (est): 92.86MM
SALES (corp-wide): 139.07MM **Privately
Held**
Web: www.coghlincompanies.com
SIC: 3613 Panel and distribution boards and
other related apparatus
PA: Coghlin Companies, Inc.
27 Otis St
Westborough MA 01581
508 753-2354

(G-13092)
**COMPONENT SOURCES INTL
INC**
121 Flanders Rd (01581-1030)
PHONE...............................508 986-2300
Stephen Doody, *Pr*
Chris Oneill, *CFO*
EMP: 15 **EST:** 1987
SQ FT: 3,000
SALES (est): 3.91MM **Privately Held**
Web: www.compsources.com
SIC: 3541 3678 3643 Machine tool
replacement & repair parts, metal cutting
types; Electronic connectors; Current-
carrying wiring services

(G-13093)
CONMED CORPORATION
134 Flanders Rd (01581-1023)
PHONE...............................508 366-3668
Eugene R Corasanti, *CEO*
EMP: 13
SALES (corp-wide): 1.05B **Publicly Held**
Web: www.conmed.com
SIC: 3841 Surgical and medical instruments
PA: Conmed Corporation
11311 Concept Blvd
Largo FL 33773
727 392-6464

(G-13094)
**COWBELL TECHNOLOGIES INC
(PA)**
150 E Main St Unit 960 (01581-8145)
P.O. Box 960 (01581-5960)
PHONE...............................508 733-1778
EMP: 8 **EST:** 2013
SALES (est): 513.7K **Privately Held**
Web: www.morecowbelltech.com
SIC: 5731 7629 3663 Consumer electronic
equipment, nec; Telecommunication
equipment repair (except telephones);
Studio equipment, radio and television
broadcasting

(G-13095)
CRANE DATA LLC
110 Turnpike Rd Ste 213 (01581-2863)
PHONE...............................508 439-4419
EMP: 12 **EST:** 2006
SQ FT: 3,000
SALES (est): 934.77K **Privately Held**
Web: www.cranedata.com
SIC: 2721 8211 Statistical reports
(periodicals): publishing only; Seminary

(G-13096)
CSI MFG INC
121 Flanders Rd (01581-1030)
PHONE...............................508 986-2300

Stephen Doody, *Pr*
Michael Vinci, *Treas*
EMP: 20 **EST:** 1994
SQ FT: 15,000
SALES (est): 3.33MM **Privately Held**
Web: www.compsources.com
SIC: 3559 Electronic component making
machinery

(G-13097)
CUMBERLAND FARMS INC (DH)
165 Flanders Rd (01581-1000)
PHONE...............................800 225-9702
Carol Tatebaum, *Pr*
Nick Unkovic, *
◆ **EMP:** 330 **EST:** 1938
SQ FT: 30,000
SALES (est): 1.1B
SALES (corp-wide): 377.54K **Privately
Held**
Web: www.cumberlandfarms.com
SIC: 5411 5541 5172 2086 Convenience
stores, chain; Filling stations, gasoline;
Gasoline; Bottled and canned soft drinks
HQ: Eg America, Llc
165 Flanders Rd
Westborough MA 01581
800 225-9702

(G-13098)
DANAFILMS CORP
5 Otis St (01581-3311)
P.O. Box 624 (01581-0624)
PHONE...............................508 366-8884
Dale Brockman, *Pr*
David Young, *VP*
▲ **EMP:** 22 **EST:** 2015
SALES (est): 10.58MM **Privately Held**
Web: www.inteplastef.com
SIC: 3081 Unsupported plastics film and
sheet
PA: Inteplast Group Corporation
9 Peach Tree Hill Rd
Livingston NJ 07039

(G-13099)
**ELECTRI-CORD
MANUFACTURING CO**
133 Flanders Rd (01581-1031)
PHONE...............................508 836-3510
EMP: 8
SALES (corp-wide): 48.19MM **Privately
Held**
Web: www.ecmfg.com
SIC: 3699 Electrical equipment and
supplies, nec
PA: Electri-Cord Manufacturing Co.
312 E Main St
Westfield PA 16950
814 367-2265

(G-13100)
EMSEAL JOINT SYSTEMS LTD
25 Bridle Ln (01581-2603)
PHONE...............................508 836-0280
Lester Hensley, *Pr*
Timothy Fulham, *Treas*
◆ **EMP:** 50 **EST:** 1981
SQ FT: 30,000
SALES (est): 13.85MM **Privately Held**
Web: www.emseal.com
SIC: 3568 2891 3441 3053 Joints and
couplings; Sealants; Fabricated structural
metal; Gaskets; packing and sealing
devices
HQ: Sika Corporation
201 Polito Ave
Lyndhurst NJ 07071
201 933-8800

(G-13101)
**ESOTERIX GENETIC LABS LLC
(HQ)**
Also Called: Integrated Genetics
3400 Computer Dr (01581-1771)
PHONE...............................508 389-6650
P Samuel Eberts Iii, *Managing Member*
William B Hayes, *Managing Member*
EMP: 46 **EST:** 2010
SALES (est): 99.24MM **Publicly Held**
Web: womenshealth.labcorp.com
SIC: 8731 2835 8071 Commercial physical
research; Diagnostic substances; Testing
laboratories
PA: Laboratory Corporation Of America
Holdings
358 S Main St
Burlington NC 27215

(G-13102)
GENZYME CORPORATION
1 Research Dr Ste 200 (01581-3917)
P.O. Box 9322 (01701-9322)
PHONE...............................508 351-2600
EMP: 97
Web: www.sanofi.us
SIC: 2834 Pharmaceutical preparations
HQ: Genzyme Corporation
450 Water St
Cambridge MA 02141
617 252-7500

(G-13103)
GENZYME CORPORATION
Also Called: Genzyme Genetics
3400 Computer Dr (01581-1771)
PHONE...............................508 898-9001
EMP: 106
Web: www.sanofi.com
SIC: 2834 Pharmaceutical preparations
HQ: Genzyme Corporation
450 Water St
Cambridge MA 02141
617 252-7500

(G-13104)
GYRUS ACMI LLC (DH)
Also Called: Olympus Surgical Tech Amer
800 W Park Dr (01581-4003)
PHONE...............................508 804-2600
Roy Davis, *CEO*
Simon Shaw, *
▲ **EMP:** 150 **EST:** 1987
SALES (est): 201.91MM **Privately Held**
Web: medical.olympusamerica.com
SIC: 3841 5047 Surgical and medical
instruments; Medical equipment and
supplies
HQ: Olympus Corporation Of The Americas
3500 Corp Pkwy
Center Valley PA 18034

(G-13105)
HIREZON CORPORATION
Also Called: Interview Exchange
4 Bellows Rd (01581-3329)
P.O. Box 792 (01581-0792)
PHONE...............................508 836-3800
Naray Viswanathan, *Pr*
EMP: 15 **EST:** 2002
SQ FT: 2,859
SALES (est): 2.73MM **Privately Held**
Web: www.hirezon.com
SIC: 7371 7372 Computer software
development and applications; Business
oriented computer software

(G-13106)
HOPKINGTON INDEPENDENT
32 South St (01581-1619)
PHONE...............................508 435-5188
Sarah Duckett, *Pr*
EMP: 8 **EST:** 2000
SALES (est): 720.38K **Privately Held**
Web: www.hopkintonindependent.com
SIC: 2711 Newspapers: publishing only, not
printed on site

(G-13107)
INFOGIX INC
200 Friberg Pkwy Ste 3008 (01581-3998)
PHONE...............................508 366-1400
EMP: 10
SALES (corp-wide): 446.91MM **Privately
Held**
Web: www.precisely.com
SIC: 7372 Prepackaged software
HQ: Infogix, Inc.
1700 District Ave Ste 300
Burlington MA 01803
630 505-1800

(G-13108)
**INFORMA FINANCIAL
INFORMATION INC**
1 Research Dr Ste 400a (01581-3988)
PHONE...............................508 616-5550
EMP: 120
SIC: 2721 Periodicals, publishing only

(G-13109)
INOV-8 INC
290 Turnpike Rd Ste 6-303 (01581-2843)
P.O. Box 1513 (01581-6513)
PHONE...............................508 251-4904
Gordon Baird, *Pr*
▲ **EMP:** 20 **EST:** 2004
SALES (est): 4.62MM **Privately Held**
SIC: 5091 3949 Sporting and recreation
goods; Sporting and athletic goods, nec
PA: Descente,Ltd.
1-2-3, Minatomachi, Naniwa-Ku
Osaka OSK 556-0

(G-13110)
**INTEPLAST ENGINEERED
FILMS INC**
5 Otis St (01581-3311)
PHONE...............................508 366-8884
Lee Seidel Cntrller, *Brnch Mgr*
EMP: 70
Web: www.inteplastef.com
SIC: 2673 Food storage and trash bags
(plastic)
HQ: Inteplast Engineered Films Inc.
2875 Market St Ste 100
Garland TX 75041
800 373-9410

(G-13111)
**J B SAWMILL & LANDCLEARING
INC**
51 Fisher St (01581-1823)
PHONE...............................508 435-6877
EMP: 9 **EST:** 2016
SALES (est): 463.53K **Privately Held**
SIC: 2421 Sawmills and planing mills,
general

(G-13112)
J T GARDNER INC (PA)
Also Called: Curry Printing
190 Turnpike Rd (01581-2806)
PHONE...............................800 540-4993
TOLL FREE: 800

Peter Gardner, *Pr*
Joseph Gardner, *VP*
EMP: 23 **EST:** 1979
SQ FT: 17,000
SALES (est): 7.58MM
SALES (corp-wide): 7.58MM **Privately Held**
Web: www.curryprinting.com
SIC: 2796 2752 2791 2789   Platemaking services; Offset printing; Typesetting; Bookbinding and related work

(G-13113)
KAYAKU ADVANCED MATERIALS INC (PA)
200 Flanders Rd (01581-1040)
PHONE.............................617 965-5511
Jeremiah J Cole Junior, *Pr*
John Ross, *
Jay Cole, *
Peter B Finn, *
Go Mizutano, *
EMP: 30 **EST:** 1993
SALES (est): 29.52MM **Privately Held**
Web: www.kayakuam.com
SIC: 2899 5049   Chemical preparations, nec ; Scientific and engineering equipment and supplies

(G-13114)
KOPIN CORPORATION (PA)
125 North Dr (01581-3341)
PHONE.............................508 870-5959
Michael Murray, *Pr*
John C C Fan, *
Richard A Sneider, *CFO*
EMP: 62 **EST:** 1984
SQ FT: 74,000
SALES (est): 47.4MM
SALES (corp-wide): 47.4MM **Publicly Held**
Web: www.kopin.com
SIC: 3674   Wafers (semiconductor devices)

(G-13115)
KOPIN TARGETING CORPORATION
125 North Dr (01581-3335)
PHONE.............................508 870-5959
Michelle Aucoin, *Prin*
John C C Fan, *Prin*
EMP: 99 **EST:** 2007
SALES (est): 13.75MM
SALES (corp-wide): 47.4MM **Publicly Held**
SIC: 3679   Electronic circuits
PA: Kopin Corporation
125 North Dr
Westborough MA 01581
508 870-5959

(G-13116)
LEHI SHEET METAL CORPORATION
Also Called: Lehi
245 Flanders Rd (01581-1034)
PHONE.............................508 366-8550
Lori Marie Bullen, *CEO*
Darren Bullen, *Pr*
EMP: 21 **EST:** 1978
SQ FT: 50,000
SALES (est): 5.08MM **Privately Held**
Web: www.lehisheetmetal.com
SIC: 3444   Sheet metalwork

(G-13117)
LG ENERGY SOLUTION VERTECH INC (DH)
Also Called: Nec

155 Flanders Rd (01581-1032)
PHONE.............................508 497-7319
Jaehong Park, *CEO*
Wonbeom Lee, *
▲ **EMP:** 35 **EST:** 2014
SALES (est): 28.95MM **Privately Held**
Web: www.lgensol-vt.com
SIC: 3691   Batteries, rechargeable
HQ: Lg Energy Solution, Ltd.
Tower1
Seoul 07335

(G-13118)
MACNEILL ENGINEERING CO INC
1700 W Park Dr Ste 310 (01581-3976)
PHONE.............................508 481-8830
Harris L Macneill, *Pr*
Nancy L Macneill, *
▲ **EMP:** 36 **EST:** 1931
SQ FT: 67,000
SALES (est): 2.14MM **Privately Held**
SIC: 3089 3949 3131 3021   Boot or shoe products, plastics; Sporting and athletic goods, nec; Footwear cut stock; Rubber and plastics footwear

(G-13119)
MB MACHINING INC
245 Flanders Rd (01581-1034)
PHONE.............................508 251-8663
Darren Bullen, *Prin*
EMP: 10 **EST:** 2015
SALES (est): 257.33K **Privately Held**
Web: www.mbmachining.net
SIC: 3599   Machine shop, jobbing and repair

(G-13120)
MICROS SYSTEMS INC
1800 W Park Dr Ste 250 (01581-3927)
PHONE.............................508 655-7500
Lyndon Daniels, *Brnch Mgr*
EMP: 9
SALES (corp-wide): 49.95B **Publicly Held**
Web: www.oracle.com
SIC: 7372   Prepackaged software
HQ: Micros Systems, Inc.
7031 Columbia Gateway Dr
Columbia MD 21046
443 285-6000

(G-13121)
MICROWAVE CMPNENTS SYSTEMS INC
Also Called: MCS
131 Flanders Rd (01581-1031)
PHONE.............................508 466-8400
EMP: 11 **EST:** 1994
SQ FT: 6,700
SALES (est): 1.79MM **Privately Held**
Web: www.mcsproducts.com
SIC: 3679   Microwave components

(G-13122)
MURATA POWER SOLUTIONS INC (DH)
129 Flanders Rd (01581-1030)
PHONE.............................508 339-3000
Stephen Pimpis, *Pr*
Yoshitaka Kotera, *
Helen Coffran, *
Trieu H Tran, *
▲ **EMP:** 111 **EST:** 1987
SALES (est): 93.47MM **Privately Held**
Web: www.murata-ps.com
SIC: 3679 3672 3629 3825   Electronic circuits; Wiring boards; Power conversion units, a.c. to d.c.: static-electric; Volt meters
HQ: Murata Electronics North America, Inc.
2200 Lake Park Dr Se

Smyrna GA 30080
770 436-1300

(G-13123)
NEO TECH
125 Fisher St (01581-3332)
PHONE.............................508 329-6270
EMP: 8 **EST:** 2020
SALES (est): 4.71MM **Privately Held**
Web: www.neotech.com
SIC: 3672   Printed circuit boards

(G-13124)
NOREMAC MANUFACTURING CORP
Also Called: Noremac Manufacturing
62 Hopkinton Rd (01581-2126)
P.O. Box 867 (01581-0867)
PHONE.............................508 366-8822
Janice Connelly, *CEO*
Joseph Connelly, *
EMP: 30 **EST:** 1961
SQ FT: 6,400
SALES (est): 2.17MM **Privately Held**
Web: m.noremacmfgcorp.com
SIC: 3599 7692   Machine shop, jobbing and repair; Welding repair

(G-13125)
ONCORE MANUFACTURING LLC
Also Called: Neotech
125 Fisher St (01581-3332)
PHONE.............................978 737-3640
EMP: 71
SALES (corp-wide): 1.43B **Privately Held**
Web: www.neotech.com
SIC: 8711 3672   Electrical or electronic engineering; Printed circuit boards
HQ: Oncore Manufacturing Llc
9340 Owensmouth Ave
Chatsworth CA 91311

(G-13126)
ONEPIN INC
2200 W Park Dr Ste 440 (01581-3961)
PHONE.............................508 475-1000
Feyzi Celik, *CEO*
Feyzi Celik, *Ch Bd*
Joe Winn, *Dir*
Kenneth Mabbs, *Dir*
David Baum, *Dir*
EMP: 23 **EST:** 2002
SQ FT: 3,200
SALES (est): 12.13MM **Privately Held**
Web: www.onepin.com
SIC: 7372   Application computer software

(G-13127)
PALL CORPORATION
Also Called: Pall Westborough Pal05
20 Walkup Dr (01581-1019)
PHONE.............................508 871-5380
EMP: 364
SALES (corp-wide): 31.47B **Publicly Held**
Web: www.pall.com
SIC: 3569   Filters, general line: industrial
HQ: Pall Corporation
25 Harbor Park Dr
Port Washington NY 11050
516 484-5400

(G-13128)
PANALYTICAL INC
Also Called: Malvern Panalytical
117 Flanders Rd (01581-1042)
PHONE.............................508 647-1100
EMP: 93
SIC: 3844   X-ray apparatus and tubes

(G-13129)
PARATRONIX INC
200 Flanders Rd (01581-1040)
PHONE.............................508 222-8979
Lawrence Habershaw, *Pr*
Eleanor Habershaw, *Treas*
EMP: 18 **EST:** 1981
SQ FT: 9,500
SALES (est): 4.34MM **Privately Held**
Web: www.paratronix.com
SIC: 3479   Coating of metals and formed products
PA: Kayaku Advanced Materials, Inc.
200 Flanders Rd
Westborough MA 01581

(G-13130)
PHARMATRON INC
2400 Computer Dr (01581-1887)
PHONE.............................603 645-6766
EMP: 10 **EST:** 1990
SQ FT: 4,000
SALES (est): 1.25MM **Privately Held**
Web: www.sotax.com
SIC: 3825   Digital test equipment, electronic and electrical circuits

(G-13131)
RUCKUS WIRELESS INC
Also Called: Arris International
8 Technology Dr Ste 200 (01581-1756)
PHONE.............................508 870-1184
Steven S Birer, *Brnch Mgr*
EMP: 220
Web: www.commscope.com
SIC: 3663   Radio and t.v. communications equipment
HQ: Ruckus Wireless Llc
350 W Java Dr
Sunnyvale CA 94089

(G-13132)
SANWA TECHNOLOGIES INC
Also Called: Sanwa Technologies MA
287 Turnpike Rd (01581-2856)
PHONE.............................508 616-9500
Mark Johnson, *Brnch Mgr*
EMP: 20
SALES (corp-wide): 1.03MM **Privately Held**
Web: www.sanwa-tech.com
SIC: 3661   Telephone cords, jacks, adapters, etc.
PA: Sanwa Technologies, Inc.
4012 Preston Rd Ste 200
Plano TX 75093
972 503-3031

(G-13133)
SECURITY ENGINEERED MCHY INC (PA)
Also Called: Security Engineered Machinery
5 Walkup Dr (01581-1054)
P.O. Box 1045 (01581-6045)
PHONE.............................508 366-1488
Andrew Kelleher, *Pr*
Nicholas Cakounes, *
Michael Paciello, *
Leonard Rosen, *
Terry Creek, *
▲ **EMP:** 31 **EST:** 1967
SQ FT: 25,000
SALES (est): 10.15MM
SALES (corp-wide): 10.15MM **Privately Held**
Web: www.semshred.com
SIC: 7389 3589   Document and office record destruction; Shredders, industrial and commercial

▲ = Import ▼ = Export
◆ = Import/Export

(G-13134)
SENSORTECH SYSTEMS INC
Also Called: Sensor Engineering
8 Technology Dr Ste 100 (01581-1756)
PHONE...........................805 981-3735
Colin Hanson, *Pr*
John Fordham, *Sec*
Roger Carlson, *Stockholder*
▲ **EMP:** 12 **EST:** 1983
SALES (est): 2.28MM **Privately Held**
Web: www.kpmanalytics.com
SIC: 3823 3826 3829 Digital displays of
process variables; Analytical instruments;
Measuring and controlling devices, nec

(G-13135)
SICAL
11 Walkup Dr (01581-1018)
PHONE...........................508 898-1800
EMP: 10 **EST:** 2019
SALES (est): 211.16K **Privately Held**
Web: www.si-cal.com
SIC: 2752 Offset printing

(G-13136)
SIMSOFT CORP
1 Butterfield Dr (01581-3947)
PHONE...........................508 366-5451
EMP: 8 **EST:** 1992
SALES (est): 557.41K **Privately Held**
SIC: 7372 Prepackaged software

(G-13137)
SPECTRIS INC (HQ)
117 Flanders Rd (01581-1042)
PHONE...........................508 768-6400
Clive Graeme Watson, *Pr*
Nicholas John Popper, *Sec*
David Goldstein, *Asst Tr*
Lisa A Bauer, *Admn*
EMP: 47 **EST:** 1994
SQ FT: 15,000
SALES (est): 1.37B
SALES (corp-wide): 1.6B **Privately Held**
Web: www.spectris.com
SIC: 3674 3829 3826 3821 Infrared
sensors, solid state; Thermometers and
temperature sensors; Thermal analysis
instruments, laboratory type; Calibration
tapes, for physical testing machines
PA: Spectris Plc
Heritage House
Egham TW20
178 447-0470

(G-13138)
SPOTBUS INC
114 Turnpike Rd Ste 106 (01581-2862)
PHONE...........................774 262-4052
EMP: 8 **EST:** 2020
SALES (est): 77.3K **Privately Held**
Web: www.spotbus.us
SIC: 7372 Prepackaged software

(G-13139)
SYNOPSYS INC
1800 W Park Dr Ste 410 (01581-3926)
PHONE...........................508 870-6500
Mark Kahan, *Mgr*
EMP: 8
SALES (corp-wide): 5.84B **Publicly Held**
Web: www.synopsys.com
SIC: 7372 Application computer software
PA: Synopsys, Inc.
675 Almanor Ave
Sunnyvale CA 94085
650 584-5000

(G-13140)
TOWN OF WESTBOROUGH
238 Turnpike Rd (01581-2812)
PHONE...........................508 366-7615
Christopher Pratt, *Prin*
EMP: 50
SALES (corp-wide): 137.85MM **Privately
Held**
Web: www.westboroughma.gov
SIC: 9199 3589 General government
administration, Local government; Sewage
and water treatment equipment
PA: Town Of Westborough
34 W Main St
Westborough MA 01581
508 871-5100

(G-13141)
**UNITED SITE SERVICES INC
(PA)**
118 Flanders Rd (01581-1035)
PHONE...........................508 594-2655
James E Hyman, *CEO*
Ron Carapezzi, *
Kevin Podmore, *
Ed Simoneau, *
Nancy Pawlowski, *CIO*
EMP: 167 **EST:** 1999
SALES (est): 703MM
SALES (corp-wide): 703MM **Privately
Held**
Web: www.unitedsiteservices.com
SIC: 7359 3315 Portable toilet rental; Fence
gates, posts, and fittings: steel

(G-13142)
UNITY SCIENTIFIC LLC
8 Technology Dr Ste 100 (01581-1756)
PHONE...........................203 740-2999
Joseph Platano, *CEO*
Douglas J Evans, *
EMP: 40 **EST:** 2008
SALES (est): 4.88MM **Privately Held**
Web: www.kpmanalytics.com
SIC: 3826 Analytical instruments

(G-13143)
VIKING SYSTEMS INC
134 Flanders Rd (01581-1023)
PHONE...........................508 366-3668
EMP: 28
SIC: 3845 Electromedical equipment

(G-13144)
**WESTBOROUGH BOOKS INC
(PA)**
Also Called: Westborough Bookseller
24 Lyman St Ste 200 (01581-1483)
PHONE...........................508 366-4292
TOLL FREE: 800
Eugene S Colangelo, *Pr*
Johanna M Maloney, *Sec*
Dona A Colangelo, *Dir*
EMP: 25 **EST:** 1975
SQ FT: 31,000
SALES (est): 4.75MM
SALES (corp-wide): 4.75MM **Privately
Held**
Web: www.tatnuck.com
SIC: 5942 5192 5812 2731 Book stores;
Books; Cafe; Books, publishing only

Westfield
Hampden County

(G-13145)
A & D METAL INC
555 Southampton Rd (01085-1329)

PHONE...........................413 485-7505
Alexander Lewinski, *Pr*
EMP: 13 **EST:** 1987
SQ FT: 24,000
SALES (est): 4.29MM **Privately Held**
Web: www.admetal.com
SIC: 3444 Sheet metal specialties, not
stamped

(G-13146)
ADVANCE MFGCO INC
8 Turnpike Industrial Rd (01085-1645)
P.O. Box 726 (01086-0726)
PHONE...........................413 568-2411
EMP: 200 **EST:** 1961
SALES (est): 50.78MM **Privately Held**
Web: www.advancemfg.com
SIC: 3599 Machine shop, jobbing and repair

(G-13147)
ALLSTATE HOOD & DUCT INC
88 Notre Dame St (01085-1924)
PHONE...........................413 568-4663
Todd Duval, *Pr*
Kimberly Saletnik, *Treas*
EMP: 10 **EST:** 2006
SALES (est): 990.49K **Privately Held**
SIC: 3444 Sheet metal specialties, not
stamped

(G-13148)
**ARCHITECTS OF PACKAGING
INC**
11 Mainline Dr (01085-3313)
PHONE...........................413 568-3187
David H Small, *Pr*
Donald I Small, *Ch*
EMP: 8 **EST:** 1971
SQ FT: 22,000
SALES (est): 968.71K **Privately Held**
Web: www.architectsofpackaging.com
SIC: 3086 7389 Packaging and shipping
materials, foamed plastics; Design,
commercial and industrial

(G-13149)
**ATLAS COPCO COMPRESSORS
LLC**
94 N Elm St Fl 4 (01085-1641)
P.O. Box 431 (01086-0431)
PHONE...........................518 765-3344
Christine Goodreau, *Brnch Mgr*
EMP: 9
SALES (corp-wide): 13.47B **Privately Held**
Web: www.atlascopco.us
SIC: 3563 Air and gas compressors
HQ: Atlas Copco Compressors Llc
300 Technology Center Way # 550
Rock Hill SC 29730
866 472-1015

(G-13150)
**B & D PLLET BLDG INDUS SUP
INC**
Also Called: B & D Pallet Co
997 Western Ave (01085-2527)
P.O. Box 1567 (01086-1567)
PHONE...........................413 568-9624
Richard Oleksak, *Pr*
Elizabeth Oleksak, *VP*
EMP: 13 **EST:** 1971
SQ FT: 18,000
SALES (est): 429.94K **Privately Held**
SIC: 2448 Pallets, wood

(G-13151)
**BEDARD SHEET METAL
COMPANY INC**
123 Medieros Way Ste 2 (01085-1666)

PHONE...........................413 572-3774
Barbara Bedard, *Pr*
EMP: 7 **EST:** 1993
SQ FT: 5,000
SALES (est): 930.16K **Privately Held**
SIC: 3444 Sheet metalwork

(G-13152)
BERN OPTICS INC
579 Southampton Rd (01085-1659)
PHONE...........................413 568-6800
Bernd H O Gottschalk, *Pr*
EMP: 15 **EST:** 1989
SQ FT: 7,500
SALES (est): 966.95K **Privately Held**
Web: www.bernoptics.com
SIC: 3827 Lenses, optical: all types except
ophthalmic

(G-13153)
BLUE TACTICAL LLC
109 Apremont Way (01085-1305)
PHONE...........................413 315-6344
Daniel Bader, *Mgr*
EMP: 15 **EST:** 2021
SALES (est): 1.26MM **Privately Held**
SIC: 3728 Military aircraft equipment and
armament

(G-13154)
**BOULEVARD MACHINE & GEAR
INC**
326 Lockhouse Rd (01085-1237)
PHONE...........................413 788-6466
Susan Kasa, *Pr*
Kazimierz Kasa, *VP*
EMP: 23 **EST:** 1991
SALES (est): 4.58MM **Privately Held**
Web: www.boulevardmachine.com
SIC: 3599 3462 Machine shop, jobbing and
repair; Gears, forged steel

(G-13155)
BROOK POND MACHINING INC
170 Lockhouse Rd Ste 5 (01085-1236)
PHONE...........................413 562-7411
James L Edinger, *Pr*
Lisa J Edinger, *CFO*
EMP: 9 **EST:** 1979
SQ FT: 6,000
SALES (est): 788.31K **Privately Held**
SIC: 3599 Machine shop, jobbing and repair

(G-13156)
CALIBER COMPANY (PA)
Also Called: Savage Arms
100 Springdale Rd (01085-1987)
PHONE...........................413 642-4260
Stephen M Nolan, *Dir*
Scott D Chaplin, *Dir*
Robert Keller, *Dir*
Albert Kasper, *Dir*
Miguel Lopez, *CFO*
EMP: 14 **EST:** 2011
SALES (est): 91.25MM
SALES (corp-wide): 91.25MM **Privately
Held**
Web: www.caliber.com
SIC: 3484 Rifles or rifle parts, 30 mm. and
below

(G-13157)
CASSJACK INDUSTRIES INC
174 Main St (01085-3151)
P.O. Box 310 (01086-0310)
PHONE...........................413 786-1800
John J Patterson, *Prin*
EMP: 9 **EST:** 2015
SALES (est): 398.23K **Privately Held**

SIC: 3999 Manufacturing industries, nec

(G-13158)
CENVEO
63 Hawks Cir (01085-1575)
PHONE..........................203 595-3109
EMP: 7 EST: 2019
SALES (est): 93.11K Privately Held
Web: www.cenveo.com
SIC: 2752 Offset printing

(G-13159)
CIRCUIT SYSTEMS INC (PA)
Also Called: Dicronite Dry Lube
54 Mainline Dr Ste B (01085-3314)
PHONE..........................413 562-5019
Al Rhynard, Pr
William R Henderson, VP
Alyvin Rhynard, Sec
▲ EMP: 13 EST: 1965
SQ FT: 9,500
SALES (est): 1.21MM
SALES (corp-wide): 1.21MM Privately
Held
SIC: 2992 Lubricating oils and greases

(G-13160)
CMI RESTRUCTURING INC
Also Called: Columbia
1 Cycle St (01085-4447)
P.O. Box 1230 (01086-1230)
PHONE..........................413 562-3664
Kenneth W Howard, Pr
Kenneth W Howard, CEO
Bruce R Turcotte, *
Donald A Bieker, *
Ali Salehi, *
◆ EMP: 65 EST: 1877
SQ FT: 300,000
SALES (est): 4.95MM Privately Held
Web: www.columbiamfginc.com
SIC: 2531 5091 School furniture; Bicycles

(G-13161)
**DIAMOND CUSTOM COATINGS
INC**
3 Progress Ave (01085-1687)
PHONE..........................413 562-2734
EMP: 8 EST: 2017
SALES (est): 613.68K Privately Held
Web: www.diamondcoatingsinc.com
SIC: 3479 Coating of metals and formed
products

(G-13162)
DION LABEL PRINTING INC
539 North Rd (01085-9774)
P.O. Box 1507 (01086-1507)
PHONE..........................413 568-3713
John J Dion Junior, Pr
Dave Dion, *
Jane Dion, *
◆ EMP: 82 EST: 1980
SQ FT: 35,000
SALES (est): 12.45MM Privately Held
Web: www.dionlabel.com
SIC: 2679 2752 Tags and labels, paper;
Commercial printing, lithographic

(G-13163)
**ECHELON INDUSTRIES
CORPORATION**
53 Airport Rd (01085-1357)
PHONE..........................413 562-6659
Clayton Jarvis, Pr
EMP: 28 EST: 2016
SALES (est): 2.65MM Privately Held
Web: www.echelon-co.com

SIC: 3721 Motorized aircraft

(G-13164)
EPICENTER
1 Arch Rd (01085-1795)
PHONE..........................413 568-1360
EMP: 47 EST: 2017
SALES (est): 1.18MM Privately Held
Web: www.epicentererp.com
SIC: 7372 Prepackaged software

(G-13165)
ERD METAL INC
323 Lockhouse Rd Ste 1 (01085-1267)
PHONE..........................508 232-3684
Burak Erdogan, Pr
M Kursad Erdogan, Dir
EMP: 10 EST: 2015
SALES (est): 1.93MM Privately Held
Web: www.erdmetal.com
SIC: 5051 3354 Aluminum bars, rods,
ingots, sheets, pipes, plates, etc.;
Aluminum extruded products

(G-13166)
**GENERAL DYNAMICS AVIATION
SVCS**
33 Elise St (01085-1493)
PHONE..........................413 562-5860
Fran Ahern, Brnch Mgr
EMP: 60
SQ FT: 3,200
SALES (corp-wide): 42.27B Publicly Held
SIC: 3721 Aircraft
HQ: General Dynamics Aviation Services
500 Gulfstream Rd
Savannah GA 31408
912 965-7372

(G-13167)
GREEN MEADOW LUMBER INC
994 Western Ave (01085-2581)
P.O. Box 520 (01086-0520)
PHONE..........................413 568-0056
Stephen Oleksak, Pr
Susan Oleksak, *
EMP: 19 EST: 1920
SALES (est): 474.13K Privately Held
Web: www.greenmeadowlumber.com
SIC: 2448 Pallets, wood

(G-13168)
**GTB INNOVATIVE SOLUTIONS
INC**
507 Southampton Rd Ste 1 (01085-1381)
PHONE..........................413 733-0146
Geraldine Cross, Pr
EMP: 10 EST: 2009
SALES (est): 952.43K Privately Held
Web: www.gtbauctions.com
SIC: 3714 Motor vehicle parts and
accessories

(G-13169)
**GULFSTREAM AEROSPACE
CORP**
33 Elise St (01085-1493)
PHONE..........................413 562-5866
David Ebel, Brnch Mgr
EMP: 117
SALES (corp-wide): 42.27B Publicly Held
Web: www.gulfstream.com
SIC: 3721 Aircraft
HQ: Gulfstream Aerospace Corporation
500 Gulfstream Rd
Savannah GA 31408

(G-13170)
H B SMITH COMPANY INC
61 Union St Ste 7 (01085-2476)
PHONE..........................413 568-3148
Walter Pawlowski, Treas
Peter J Stasz, Clerk
EMP: 16 EST: 1853
SQ FT: 120,000
SALES (est): 1.19MM Privately Held
Web: www.hbsmith.com
SIC: 3433 3567 Boilers, low-pressure
heating: steam or hot water; Industrial
furnaces and ovens

(G-13171)
**INDUSTRIAL CUTTING TOOLS
INC**
351 N Elm St (01085-1622)
P.O. Box 548 (01086-0548)
PHONE..........................413 562-2996
Felix Mcgrath, Pr
Jeanne Mc Grath, Treas
Robert Crowley, Clerk
EMP: 8 EST: 1981
SQ FT: 3,000
SALES (est): 570K Privately Held
Web: www.indcuttool.com
SIC: 3545 Cutting tools for machine tools

(G-13172)
INDUSTRIAL PRECISION INC
1014 Southampton Rd (01085-1397)
PHONE..........................413 562-5161
EMP: 45 EST: 1974
SALES (est): 7.46MM Privately Held
Web: www.industrialprecision.com
SIC: 3599 3769 Machine shop, jobbing and
repair; Space vehicle equipment, nec

(G-13173)
**INSTRUMENT TECHNOLOGY
INC**
Also Called: ITI
33 Airport Rd (01085-1357)
P.O. Box 381 (01086-0381)
PHONE..........................413 562-3512
Gregory Carignan, Pr
Jeffrey K Carignan, *
Dawn A Thomas, *
EMP: 50 EST: 1967
SQ FT: 25,000
SALES (est): 9.35MM
SALES (corp-wide): 9.35MM Privately
Held
Web: www.scopes.com
SIC: 3827 Boroscopes
PA: Transom Shields Group, Llc
Wilmington DE

(G-13174)
JARVIS SURGICAL INC
53 Airport Rd (01085-1357)
PHONE..........................413 562-6659
EMP: 20 EST: 1993
SQ FT: 12,000
SALES (est): 7.8MM
SALES (corp-wide): 18.45MM Privately
Held
Web: www.jarvissurgical.com
SIC: 3841 Surgical and medical instruments
PA: Jarvis Group, Inc.
229 Buckingham St
Hartford CT
860 278-2353

(G-13175)
**JOHNCARLO WOODWORKING
INC**
30 Clifton St (01085-3304)

P.O. Box 1385 (01086-1385)
PHONE..........................413 562-4002
Giancarlo Fiordalice, Pr
Peter Fiordalice, Treas
EMP: 13 EST: 1986
SQ FT: 6,000
SALES (est): 389.13K Privately Held
Web: www.pennerkitchens.com
SIC: 2431 Millwork

(G-13176)
JOSEPH MUTO
61 Bowdoin St (01085-4269)
PHONE..........................413 568-3245
Joseph Muto, Prin
EMP: 7 EST: 2009
SALES (est): 214.7K Privately Held
SIC: 2431 Millwork

(G-13177)
JSL ASPHALT INC (PA)
730 E Mountain Rd (01085-1805)
P.O. Box 125 (01086-0125)
PHONE..........................413 568-8986
Harry C Lane, Pr
Mark F Connor, Treas
Jonathan C Lane, Sec
EMP: 12 EST: 2000
SQ FT: 14,000
SALES (est): 4.77MM
SALES (corp-wide): 4.77MM Privately
Held
SIC: 1611 2951 Highway and street paving
contractor; Asphalt and asphaltic paving
mixtures (not from refineries)

(G-13178)
LANDOLFI FOOD CORP
Also Called: Landolfi Food Products
77 Servistar Indus Way (01085-5601)
PHONE..........................609 392-1830
EMP: 16
SIC: 2038 Frozen specialties, nec

(G-13179)
**LONGCAP LAMSON
PRODUCTS LLC**
79 Mainline Dr (01085-3313)
P.O. Box 846 (01086-0846)
PHONE..........................413 642-8135
David Sepavich, VP
EMP: 15 EST: 2016
SALES (est): 772.46K Privately Held
Web: www.lamsonproducts.com
SIC: 3421 Cutlery

(G-13180)
MAINLINE TOOL & GRIND INC
66 Mainline Dr Ste C (01085-3320)
PHONE..........................413 626-9601
James Joly, Prin
EMP: 7 EST: 2017
SALES (est): 282.26K Privately Held
Web: www.mainlinetool.com
SIC: 3541 Machine tools, metal cutting type

(G-13181)
**MANUFACTURING TECH
GROUP INC**
Also Called: M T G
85 Servistar Industrial Way (01085-5601)
PHONE..........................413 562-4337
EMP: 53 EST: 1996
SQ FT: 67,000
SALES (est): 7.61MM Privately Held
Web: www.mtgfab.com
SIC: 3444 Metal housings, enclosures,
casings, and other containers

(G-13182)
MB WESTFIELD INC
Also Called: Midstate Berkshire
109 Apremont Way (01085-1303)
P.O. Box 828 (01086-0828)
PHONE...............................413 568-8676
EMP: 133
Web: www.berkshireindustries.com
SIC: 3724 3661 3674   Aircraft engines and
engine parts; Telephone and telegraph
apparatus; Semiconductor circuit networks

(G-13183)
MESTEK INC
Beacon-Morris Div
260 N Elm St (01085-1614)
PHONE...............................413 568-9571
John E Reed, Pr
EMP: 10
SALES (corp-wide): 689.94MM Privately
Held
Web: www.mestek.com
SIC: 5075 3643 3567   Warm air heating and
air conditioning; Current-carrying wiring
services; Industrial furnaces and ovens
PA: Mestek, Inc.
260 N Elm St
Westfield MA 01085
470 898-4533

(G-13184)
MESTEK INC
Wrens Division
260 N Elm St (01085-1614)
PHONE...............................413 564-5530
Bruce Dewey, Pr
EMP: 87
SALES (corp-wide): 689.94MM Privately
Held
Web: www.mestek.com
SIC: 3569 3585   Filters; Refrigeration and
heating equipment
PA: Mestek, Inc.
260 N Elm St
Westfield MA 01085
470 898-4533

(G-13185)
MESTEK INC
Sterling Radiator/Reed Nat Div
260 N Elm St (01085-1614)
P.O. Box 519 (01086-0519)
PHONE...............................413 568-9571
John E Reed, Brnch Mgr
EMP: 24
SQ FT: 10,000
SALES (corp-wide): 689.94MM Privately
Held
Web: www.mestek.com
SIC: 3433 3444 3822 3549   Radiators,
except electric; Sheet metalwork;
Environmental controls; Metalworking
machinery, nec
PA: Mestek, Inc.
260 N Elm St
Westfield MA 01085
470 898-4533

(G-13186)
MESTEK INC (PA)
Also Called: Dadanco - Mestek
260 N Elm St (01085-1614)
PHONE...............................470 898-4533
Stuart B Reed, CEO
Jim David, VP
✿ EMP: 20 EST: 1898
SQ FT: 200,000
SALES (est): 689.94MM
SALES (corp-wide): 689.94MM Privately
Held

(G-13187)
**MICRO ABRASIVES
CORPORATION**
720 Southampton Rd (01085-1387)
P.O. Box 669 (01086-0669)
PHONE...............................413 562-3641
Doug Stutz, Pr
Michael Keenan, *
✦ EMP: 53 EST: 1957
SQ FT: 125,000
SALES (est): 8.85MM Privately Held
Web: www.microgrit.com
SIC: 3291   Abrasive grains

(G-13188)
MIDAC CORPORATION
6 Coleman Ave (01085-4404)
PHONE...............................413 642-5595
EMP: 11 EST: 1978
SALES (est): 2.32MM Privately Held
SIC: 3826   Infrared analytical instruments

(G-13189)
**MILLENNIUM POWER SERVICES
INC (PA)**
80 Mainline Dr (01085-3314)
PHONE...............................413 562-5332
Michael Pellegrini, Pr
Edward C Schultz, *
Kendall Walsh Ctrl, Prin
EMP: 37 EST: 2000
SQ FT: 6,000
SALES (est): 12.95MM
SALES (corp-wide): 12.95MM Privately
Held
Web: www.millenniumpower.net
SIC: 3491   Industrial valves

(G-13190)
MILLRITE MACHINE INC
587 Southampton Rd (01085-1662)
PHONE...............................413 562-9212
Robert Valcourt, Pr
Susan Valcourt, *
EMP: 30 EST: 1986
SQ FT: 10,000
SALES (est): 4.52MM Privately Held
Web: www.millrite.com
SIC: 3599   Machine shop, jobbing and repair

(G-13191)
MORTON BUILDINGS INC
563 Southampton Rd (01085-1329)
PHONE...............................413 562-7028
Carl Franz, Brnch Mgr
EMP: 10
SQ FT: 5,932
SALES (corp-wide): 213.04MM Privately
Held
Web: www.mortonbuildings.com
SIC: 3448   Prefabricated metal buildings and
components
PA: Morton Buildings, Inc.
252 W Adams St
Morton IL 61550
800 447-7436

(G-13192)
NES WORLDWIDE INC
3 Progress Ave (01085-1687)
PHONE...............................413 562-8000
✦ EMP: 24 EST: 1997

Web: www.mestek.com
SIC: 3585 3634 3549 3542   Heating
equipment, complete; Heating units, electric
(radiant heat): baseboard or wall;
Metalworking machinery, nec; Punching,
shearing, and bending machines

(G-13193)
NU-TRUSS INC
Also Called: Western Mass Truss
52 Steiger Dr (01085-4945)
P.O. Box 2197 (01086-2197)
PHONE...............................413 562-3861
Keith Cressotti, Pr
Robert Bigelow, VP
Peter Howe, Stockholder
EMP: 22 EST: 1997
SALES (est): 984.49K Privately Held
SIC: 2439   Trusses, wooden roof

(G-13194)
**NUCOR HRRIS RBAR
NORTHEAST LLC**
287 Lockhouse Rd (01085-1235)
PHONE...............................413 568-7803
Tom Dechristopher, Mgr
EMP: 33
SALES (corp-wide): 41.51B Publicly Held
Web: www.harrisrebar.com
SIC: 3312 3449 3441   Bar, rod, and wire
products; Bars, concrete reinforcing:
fabricated steel; Fabricated structural metal
HQ: Nucor Harris Rebar Northeast Llc
55 Sumner St Ste 1
Milford MA 01757
800 370-0132

(G-13195)
NUMERIC INC
Also Called: Numeric Machining Company
321 Munger Hill Rd (01085-4575)
PHONE...............................413 732-6544
Joseph Mcgovern, Pr
Joseph Mcgovern Prestreas, Prin
EMP: 10 EST: 1983
SALES (est): 1.39MM Privately Held
Web: www.numericmachining.com
SIC: 3599 8721   Machine shop, jobbing and
repair; Billing and bookkeeping service

(G-13196)
PARAGON MFG INC
61 Union St (01085-2490)
PHONE...............................413 562-7202
Steven P Beals, Pr
Karen L Beals, Pr
EMP: 15 EST: 1989
SQ FT: 8,000
SALES (est): 2.44MM Privately Held
Web: www.paragonmfg.com
SIC: 3599   Machine shop, jobbing and repair

(G-13197)
PEERLESS PRECISION INC
22 Mainline Dr (01085-3314)
PHONE...............................413 562-2359
Larry A Maier, Pr
EMP: 20 EST: 1976
SQ FT: 6,600
SALES (est): 2.56MM Privately Held
Web: www.peerlessprecision.com
SIC: 3599   Machine shop, jobbing and repair

(G-13198)
PG TECHNOLOGIES INC
91 Servistar Industrial Way (01085-5601)
PHONE...............................413 562-1354
Stephen Flint, Pr
▲ EMP: 8 EST: 1992
SALES (est): 880.44K Privately Held
Web: www.pgtechnologiesinc.com

SQ FT: 38,000
SALES (est): 2.08MM Privately Held
Web: www.sage-llc.com
SIC: 3555   Printing presses

(G-13199)
**PILGRIM CANDLE COMPANY
INC (PA)**
36 Union Ave (01085-2444)
PHONE...............................413 562-2635
Joseph Shibley, Pr
Rosemary Pagios, Treas
Donna Shibley, Clerk
▲ EMP: 20 EST: 1992
SQ FT: 20,000
SALES (est): 2.1MM
SALES (corp-wide): 2.1MM Privately Held
Web: www.pilgrimcandle.com
SIC: 3999 5999 5947   Candles; Candle
shops; Gift, novelty, and souvenir shop

(G-13200)
**PIONEER VALLEY MACHINE
LLC**
121 Summit Lock Rd (01085-1586)
PHONE...............................413 204-0358
Marc Dimauro, Managing Member
EMP: 7 EST: 2004
SALES (est): 265.1K Privately Held
Web: www.pvalleymachine.com
SIC: 3599   Machine shop, jobbing and repair

(G-13201)
PROGRESS ENTERPRISES LLC
3 Progress Ave (01085-1687)
PHONE...............................413 562-2736
▲ EMP: 20 EST: 2012
SALES (est): 1.19MM Privately Held
SIC: 3861   Graphic arts plates, sensitized

(G-13202)
**PROLAMINA CORPORATION
(DH)**
132 N Elm St (01085-1604)
P.O. Box 274 (01086-0274)
PHONE...............................413 562-2315
▲ EMP: 14 EST: 1971
SALES (est): 375.69MM
SALES (corp-wide): 208.73K Privately
Held
Web: www.prolamina.com
SIC: 5199 2671   Packaging materials;
Paper, coated or laminated for packaging
HQ: Proampac Holdings Inc.
12025 Tricon Rd
Cincinnati OH 45246
513 671-1777

(G-13203)
ROSELLIS MACHINE & MFG CO
248 Root Rd (01085-9828)
PHONE...............................413 562-4317
Vincent J Roselli, Pr
EMP: 10 EST: 1966
SQ FT: 3,000
SALES (est): 952.83K Privately Held
SIC: 3451 5941   Screw machine products;
Firearms

(G-13204)
**RPM WOOD FINISHES GROUP
INC**
C C I Division
221 Union St (01085-2423)
PHONE...............................413 562-9655
EMP: 100
SALES (corp-wide): 7.26B Publicly Held
Web: wfgpmt.rpmwfg.com

SIC: 7336 3479 2672 3993   Graphic arts and
related design; Name plates: engraved,
etched, etc.; Adhesive papers, labels, or
tapes: from purchased material; Signs and
advertising specialties

SIC: 2851 2893 3479 Lacquers, varnishes, enamels, and other coatings; Printing ink; Coating of metals and formed products
HQ: Rpm Wood Finishes Group, Inc.
　　2220 Us Highway 70 Se # 100
　　Hickory NC 28602
　　828 261-0325

(G-13205)
S LANE JOHN & SON INCORPORATED (PA)
311 E Mountain Rd (01085-1841)
PHONE....................................413 568-8986
Harry C Lane, *Pr*
Arthur F Turton, *Dir*
Jonathan Lane, *Sec*
EMP: 10 EST: 1890
SALES (est): 21.76MM
SALES (corp-wide): 21.76MM **Privately Held**
Web: www.jslane.com
SIC: 1429 1442 Trap rock, crushed and broken-quarrying; Construction sand mining

(G-13206)
SAVAGE ARMS INC (DH)
100 Springdale Rd (01085-1673)
PHONE....................................413 642-4135
Ronald Coburn, *Ch Bd*
Albert F Kasper, *
◆ EMP: 200 EST: 1896
SQ FT: 336,000
SALES (est): 87.77MM
SALES (corp-wide): 91.25MM **Privately Held**
Web: www.savagearms.com
SIC: 3484 Rifles or rifle parts, 30 mm. and below
HQ: Savage Sports Corporation
　　100 Springdale Rd
　　Westfield MA 01085
　　413 568-7001

(G-13207)
SAVAGE RANGE SYSTEMS INC
100 Springdale Rd (01085-1987)
PHONE....................................413 568-7001
▼ EMP: 8 EST: 1995
SQ FT: 336,000
SALES (est): 2.34MM
SALES (corp-wide): 91.25MM **Privately Held**
SIC: 3949 Shooting equipment and supplies, general
HQ: Savage Sports Corporation
　　100 Springdale Rd
　　Westfield MA 01085
　　413 568-7001

(G-13208)
SAVAGE SPORTS CORPORATION (HQ)
100 Springdale Rd (01085-1987)
PHONE....................................413 568-7001
Ronald Coburn, *Ch Bd*
Albert F Kasper, *Pr*
David Pacentini, *CFO*
EMP: 12 EST: 1995
SQ FT: 336,000
SALES (est): 90.11MM
SALES (corp-wide): 91.25MM **Privately Held**
SIC: 3484 Rifles or rifle parts, 30 mm. and below
PA: Caliber Company
　　100 Springdale Rd
　　Westfield MA 01085
　　413 642-4260

(G-13209)
SONICRON SYSTEMS CORPORATION
Also Called: Plastron Company
382 Southampton Rd Ste 102 (01085)
P.O. Box 38 (01086-0038)
PHONE....................................413 562-5218
Ronald V Cecchini, *Pr*
Marcia Cecchini, *Treas*
EMP: 15 EST: 1971
SQ FT: 16,000
SALES (est): 933.34K **Privately Held**
Web: terra-americana.typepad.com
SIC: 3559 3089 3544 Plastics working machinery; Injection molding of plastics; Special dies, tools, jigs, and fixtures

(G-13210)
TELL TOOL INC
Also Called: Cadence Aerospace
35 Turnpike Industrial Rd (01085-1646)
PHONE....................................413 568-1671
David Smith, *Pr*
Charles Fuller, *
Douglas Perrin, *
Robert Morin, *
John O'donnell, *VP*
EMP: 100 EST: 2006
SQ FT: 60,000
SALES (est): 23.41MM
SALES (corp-wide): 666.39MM **Privately Held**
Web: www.cadenceaerospace.com
SIC: 3724 3769 Aircraft engines and engine parts; Space vehicle equipment, nec
HQ: Tell Tool Acquisition Inc.
　　35 Turnpike Industrial Rd
　　Westfield MA 01085
　　413 568-1671

(G-13211)
TELL TOOL ACQUISITION INC (DH)
35 Turnpike Industrial Rd (01085-1646)
PHONE....................................413 568-1671
Scott Ransley, *CEO*
Jeffrey Tobias, *Pr*
Edward Torres, *VP*
EMP: 21 EST: 2006
SALES (est): 28.15MM
SALES (corp-wide): 666.39MM **Privately Held**
SIC: 3724 3769 Aircraft engines and engine parts; Space vehicle equipment, nec
HQ: Cadence Aerospace, Llc
　　3150 E Miraloma Ave
　　Anaheim CA 92806
　　949 877-3630

(G-13212)
TRANSCON TECHNOLOGIES INC
Also Called: E C I
53 Mainline Dr (01085-3313)
P.O. Box 1536 (01086-1536)
PHONE....................................413 562-7684
Pablo A Nyarady, *Pr*
Bob Carrier, *
EMP: 45 EST: 1947
SQ FT: 35,000
SALES (est): 8.7MM **Privately Held**
Web: www.quanticeci.com
SIC: 3677 Coil windings, electronic

(G-13213)
TRANSOM SCOPES INC
Also Called: Instrument Technology
33 Airport Rd (01085-1300)
P.O. Box 381 (01086-0381)

PHONE....................................413 562-3606
Hugh Dorrian, *CEO*
EMP: 37 EST: 2016
SALES (est): 2.43MM **Privately Held**
SIC: 3827 Optical elements and assemblies, except ophthalmic

(G-13214)
UTZ QUALITY FOODS LLC
225 Root Rd (01085-9832)
PHONE....................................413 562-1102
Jeff Dadmun, *Brnch Mgr*
EMP: 7
SALES (corp-wide): 732.3MM **Privately Held**
Web: www.utzsnacks.com
SIC: 2096 Potato chips and similar snacks
PA: Utz Quality Foods, Llc
　　900 High St
　　Hanover PA 17331
　　800 367-7629

(G-13215)
VAN PELT PRECISION INC
66 S Broad St Ste 3 (01085-6401)
PHONE....................................413 527-1204
EMP: 10 EST: 2019
SALES (est): 975.75K **Privately Held**
SIC: 3599 Machine shop, jobbing and repair

(G-13216)
WATERWOOD CORPORATION
77 Servistar Industrial Way (01085-5601)
PHONE....................................413 572-1010
EMP: 8 EST: 2008
SALES (est): 134.56K **Privately Held**
SIC: 2038 Frozen specialties, nec

(G-13217)
WESTEK ARCHITECTURAL WDWKG INC
97 Servistar Industrial Way (01085-5601)
PHONE....................................413 562-6363
Bruce Scheible, *Pr*
James Kotowicz, *Treas*
EMP: 16 EST: 1990
SQ FT: 15,000
SALES (est): 1.94MM **Privately Held**
Web: www.westekaw.com
SIC: 2431 Millwork

(G-13218)
WESTFIELD CONCRETE INC
403 Paper Mill Rd (01085-1735)
PHONE....................................413 562-4814
Ron Dahle, *Pr*
EMP: 9 EST: 1993
SALES (est): 122.94K **Privately Held**
Web: www.chicopeeconcrete.com
SIC: 3273 Ready-mixed concrete

(G-13219)
WESTFIELD ELECTROPLATING CO (PA)
Also Called: Wepco
68 N Elm St (01085-1690)
P.O. Box 298 (01086-0298)
PHONE....................................413 568-3716
Michael P Stolpinski, *Pr*
Jonathan M Stolpinski, *
Kenneth M Curran, *
Lynn M Poulin, *
Edward P Sienkiewcz, *
EMP: 120 EST: 1946
SQ FT: 52,000
SALES (est): 20.64MM
SALES (corp-wide): 20.64MM **Privately Held**
Web: www.westfieldplating.com

SIC: 3471 3479 Electroplating of metals or formed products; Painting of metal products

(G-13220)
WESTFIELD GRINDING WHEEL CO
Also Called: Gaylord, Richard N
135 Apremont Way (01085-1303)
P.O. Box 798 (01086-0798)
PHONE....................................413 568-8634
Edward S Sauers, *Pr*
▲ EMP: 19 EST: 1923
SQ FT: 29,500
SALES (est): 877.67K **Privately Held**
Web: www.westfieldgrinding.com
SIC: 3291 Wheels, grinding: artificial

(G-13221)
WESTFIELD NEWS PUBLISHING INC (DH)
Also Called: Westfield Evening News
64 School St (01085-2835)
PHONE....................................413 562-4181
Lawrence Hebert, *Prin*
Lawrence I Hebert, *
E Carol Mazza, *
Virginia L White, *
EMP: 47 EST: 1988
SQ FT: 14,000
SALES (est): 21.6MM
SALES (corp-wide): 3.93B **Publicly Held**
SIC: 2711 2752 Newspapers, publishing and printing; Commercial printing, lithographic
HQ: Sinclair Television Of Capital District, Inc.
　　1000 Wilson Blvd Ste 2700
　　Arlington VA 22209
　　703 647-8700

(G-13222)
WESTFIELD TOOL & DIE CO INC
55 Arnold St (01085-2888)
P.O. Box 608 (01086-0608)
PHONE....................................413 562-2393
James Janisieski, *Pr*
John Simmitt, *VP*
EMP: 21 EST: 1961
SQ FT: 10,000
SALES (est): 853.18K **Privately Held**
SIC: 3544 3542 Special dies and tools; Machine tools, metal forming type

(G-13223)
WESTFIELD WHIP MFG CO
360 Elm St (01085-2922)
P.O. Box 425 (01086-0425)
PHONE....................................413 568-8244
Carol Ann Martin, *Pr*
Daniel R Seals, *Treas*
EMP: 10 EST: 1947
SQ FT: 15,000
SALES (est): 248.64K **Privately Held**
Web: www.westfieldwhip.com
SIC: 3199 Whips, leather

Westford
Middlesex County

(G-13224)
ARTEL VIDEO SYSTEMS CORP
5b Lyberty Way (01886-3617)
PHONE....................................978 263-5775
Mike Rizzo, *Pr*
Jeff Masucci, *
▼ EMP: 35 EST: 2001
SQ FT: 17,000
SALES (est): 6.49MM **Privately Held**

Web: www.artel.com
SIC: 3663 3651 3661 Radio and t.v. communications equipment; Household audio and video equipment; Telephone and telegraph apparatus

(G-13225)
BERGERON MACHINE LLC ✪
65 Powers Rd (01886-4110)
PHONE...........................978 577-6235
EMP: 32 EST: 2023
SALES (est): 7.25MM
SALES (corp-wide): 13.5MM Privately Held
SIC: 3315 Welded steel wire fabric
PA: Compass Precision, Llc
4600 Westinghouse Blvd
Charlotte NC 28273
704 790-6764

(G-13226)
BISCOM INC
10 Technology Park Dr Ste 102 (01886-3175)
PHONE...........................978 250-1800
S K Ho, Ch
Bill Ho, *
Michael Gayowski, *
Tom Bishop, *
Don Dunning, *
EMP: 67 EST: 1986
SALES (est): 13.64MM Privately Held
Web: www.biscom.com
SIC: 7372 3661 3571 Application computer software; Telephone and telegraph apparatus; Electronic computers

(G-13227)
CARNEGIE COMMUNICATIONS LLC
210 Littleton Rd Ste 100 (01886-3580)
PHONE...........................978 692-5092
Robert Leyburn, *
Deborah Millin, *
Meghan Dalesandro, *
Mark Cunningham, *
EMP: 33 EST: 1980
SALES (est): 7.13MM
SALES (corp-wide): 13.88MM Privately Held
Web: www.carnegiehighered.com
SIC: 2721 7319 7331 7311 Magazines: publishing only, not printed on site; Display advertising service; Direct mail advertising services; Advertising agencies
PA: Carnegie Dartlet Llc
210 Littleton Rd Ste 100
Westford MA 01886
978 692-5092

(G-13228)
CARNEGIE DARTLET LLC (PA)
Also Called: Clarus
210 Littleton Rd Ste 100 (01886-3580)
PHONE...........................978 692-5092
Joseph Moore, CEO
Meghan Dalesandro, COO
Scott Ochander, CMO
Tyler Borders, CIO
EMP: 62 EST: 2017
SALES (est): 13.88MM
SALES (corp-wide): 13.88MM Privately Held
Web: www.carnegiehighered.com
SIC: 2721 7319 7331 7311 Magazines: publishing only, not printed on site; Display advertising service; Direct mail advertising services; Advertising agencies

(G-13229)
CIMCON SOFTWARE LLC (PA)
Also Called: Cimcon Software
234 Littleton Rd Ste 2h (01886-3530)
PHONE...........................978 464-9180
EMP: 63 EST: 1996
SQ FT: 10,000
SALES (est): 8.56MM Privately Held
Web: www.cimcon.com
SIC: 7371 5734 7372 Computer software development; Computer software and accessories; Prepackaged software

(G-13230)
CLARKWORKS MACHINE
496 Groton Rd Ste 5 (01886-1100)
PHONE...........................978 692-2556
Brad Clarke, Owner
EMP: 7 EST: 2004
SALES (est): 109.09K Privately Held
SIC: 3599 Machine shop, jobbing and repair

(G-13231)
COLLINS AEROSPACE
7 Technology Park Dr (01886-3141)
PHONE...........................978 303-6700
EMP: 23
SALES (est): 2.05MM Privately Held
Web: www.collinsaerospace.com
SIC: 3728 Aircraft parts and equipment, nec

(G-13232)
COURIER WESTFORD INC
Also Called: Courier Fulfillment Services
22 Town Farm Rd (01886-2399)
PHONE...........................978 251-6482
EMP: 300
SIC: 2732 2789 Books, printing and binding; Bookbinding and related work

(G-13233)
CYNOSURE LLC (HQ)
Also Called: Smartlipo
5 Carlisle Rd (01886-3601)
PHONE...........................978 256-4200
Todd Tillemans, CEO
▲ EMP: 303 EST: 1991
SQ FT: 150,000
SALES (est): 220.23MM
SALES (corp-wide): 287.73MM Privately Held
Web: www.cynosure.com
SIC: 3845 Laser systems and equipment, medical
PA: Lotus Buyer, Inc.
5 Carlisle Rd
Westford MA 01886
978 256-4200

(G-13234)
DINNER DAILY LLC
26 Colonial Dr (01886-4503)
P.O. Box 678 (01886-0020)
PHONE...........................978 392-5887
Laurin Mills, Managing Member
EMP: 11 EST: 2010
SALES (est): 272.76K Privately Held
Web: www.thedinnerdaily.com
SIC: 2711 7371 7389 Newspapers, publishing and printing; Computer software development and applications; Business Activities at Non-Commercial Site

(G-13235)
ELPAKCO INC (PA)
2 Carl Thompson Rd (01886-1561)
P.O. Box 72 (01886-0003)
PHONE...........................978 392-0400
John S Grant, Pr

▲ EMP: 12 EST: 1984
SQ FT: 10,000
SALES (est): 1.56MM
SALES (corp-wide): 1.56MM Privately Held
Web: www.elpakco.com
SIC: 3678 5065 3674 Electronic connectors; Electronic parts and equipment, nec; Semiconductors and related devices

(G-13236)
FILTEC PRECISION CERAMICS CORP
37 Village View Rd (01886-2359)
PHONE...........................978 204-2288
Wenying Su, Prin
EMP: 7 EST: 2016
SALES (est): 89.15K Privately Held
Web: www.filtec-corp.com
SIC: 3599 Machine shop, jobbing and repair

(G-13237)
FILTER-KLEEN MANUFACTURING CO
3 Broadway St (01886-2147)
P.O. Box 1319 (01886-4719)
PHONE...........................978 692-5137
Chris Franklyn, Pr
Joanne Guilmett, Treas
Janice D Kelley, Clerk
Troy Guilmette, Operations MANAGEMET
EMP: 12 EST: 1984
SALES (est): 466.08K Privately Held
Web: www.filterkleen.net
SIC: 3569 Filters, general line: industrial

(G-13238)
FLETCHER GRANITE LLC (DH)
535 Groton Rd (01886-1146)
P.O. Box 710 (01879-0710)
PHONE...........................978 692-1312
Antonio C Ramos, Managing Member
EMP: 8 EST: 2011
SALES (est): 49.23MM
SALES (corp-wide): 49.23MM Privately Held
Web: www.fletchergranite.com
SIC: 1411 3281 3272 2951 Granite, dimension-quarrying; Cut stone and stone products; Concrete products, nec; Asphalt paving mixtures and blocks
HQ: Georgia Stone Industries Inc.
15 Branch Pike
Smithfield RI 02917
401 232-2040

(G-13239)
GOODRICH CORPORATION
7 Technology Park Dr (01886-3141)
PHONE...........................978 303-6700
EMP: 700
SALES (corp-wide): 68.92B Publicly Held
Web: www.collinsaerospace.com
SIC: 3724 3728 7372 Aircraft engines and engine parts; Aircraft parts and equipment, nec; Prepackaged software
HQ: Goodrich Corporation
2730 W Tyvola Rd
Charlotte NC 28217
704 423-7000

(G-13240)
GOODRICH CORPORATION
9 Technology Park Dr (01886-3141)
PHONE...........................978 303-6700
Marcelo Macri, Brnch Mgr
EMP: 50
SALES (corp-wide): 67.07B Publicly Held
Web: www.collinsaerospace.com

SIC: 3728 Aircraft parts and equipment, nec
HQ: Goodrich Corporation
2730 W Tyvola Rd
Charlotte NC 28217
704 423-7000

(G-13241)
HCI CLEANING PRODUCTS LLC
7 Grassy Ln (01886-6800)
P.O. Box 1145 (01886-0845)
PHONE...........................508 864-5510
Sandy Posa, CEO
Trip Flavin, COO
Mark Kost, CFO
EMP: 16 EST: 2014
SQ FT: 800
SALES (est): 1.87MM Privately Held
Web: www.forceofnatureclean.com
SIC: 2842 Disinfectants, household or industrial plant

(G-13242)
IDEAL CONCRETE BLOCK CO (PA)
Also Called: Pavers By Ideal
45 Powers Rd (01886-4111)
P.O. Box 747 (01886-0023)
PHONE...........................978 692-3076
John V Burgoyne Senior, Pr
Lawrence Nicolai Senior, VP
Joseph Burgoyne Iii, VP
James M Burgoyne, VP
▲ EMP: 10 EST: 1923
SALES (est): 11.42MM
SALES (corp-wide): 11.42MM Privately Held
Web: www.idealconcreteblock.com
SIC: 3271 5032 Blocks, concrete or cinder: standard; Concrete and cinder block

(G-13243)
JUNIPER NETWORKS INC
10 Technology Park Dr (01886-3175)
PHONE...........................978 589-5800
Martin Clague, Brnch Mgr
EMP: 400
Web: www.juniper.net
SIC: 7373 7372 Computer integrated systems design; Prepackaged software
PA: Juniper Networks, Inc.
1133 Innovation Way
Sunnyvale CA 94089

(G-13244)
KADANT INC (PA)
1 Technology Park Dr Ste 210 (01886-3139)
PHONE...........................978 776-2000
Jeffrey L Powell, Pr
Jonathan W Painter, *
Eric T Langevin, Ex VP
Michael J Mckenney, Ex VP
Deborah S Selwood, CAO
▲ EMP: 224 EST: 1991
SQ FT: 18,000
SALES (est): 904.74MM Publicly Held
Web: www.kadant.com
SIC: 3554 3321 2621 Paper industries machinery; Ductile iron castings; Pressed and molded pulp and fiber products

(G-13245)
LAVELLE MACHINE & TOOL CO INC
485 Groton Rd (01886-1149)
P.O. Box 1558 (01886-4996)
PHONE...........................978 692-8825
Edwin Lavelle Junior, Pr
EMP: 35 EST: 1963
SQ FT: 25,000

GEOGRAPHIC

SALES (est): 2.75MM **Privately Held**
Web: www.lavellemachine.com
SIC: 3599 Machine shop, jobbing and repair

(G-13246)
LIGHTLAB IMAGING INC
4 Robbins Rd (01886-4113)
PHONE.....................................978 577-3400
EMP: 283
Web: www.lightlabimaging.com
SIC: 8732 3841 Research services, except laboratory; Catheters

(G-13247)
MACK TECHNOLOGIES INC (HQ)
27 Carlisle Rd (01886-3644)
PHONE.....................................978 392-5500
William Kendall, *Pr*
Jeffrey T Sample, *Dir*
Donald S Kendall Iii, *Dir*
Florence M Belnap, *Sec*
▲ **EMP:** 200 **EST:** 1993
SQ FT: 108,000
SALES (est): 148.91MM
SALES (corp-wide): 856.43MM **Privately Held**
Web: www.macktech.com
SIC: 3577 3571 Computer peripheral equipment, nec; Electronic computers
PA: Mack Group, Inc.
     608 Warm Brook Rd
     Arlington VT 05250
     802 375-2511

(G-13248)
MAM SOFTWARE INC
163 Plain Rd (01886-1831)
PHONE.....................................978 392-0941
EMP: 7 **EST:** 2017
SALES (est): 85.85K **Privately Held**
Web: www.mamsoftware.com
SIC: 7372 Prepackaged software

(G-13249)
MATERION PRCSION OPTICS THIN F (DH)
2 Lyberty Way (01886-3616)
PHONE.....................................978 692-7513
Ian S Tribick, *Pr*
Christopher E Eberhardt, *Sec*
▼ **EMP:** 10 **EST:** 1971
SQ FT: 125,000
SALES (est): 44.5MM **Publicly Held**
SIC: 3827 Optical instruments and lenses
HQ: Materion Advanced Materials Technologies And Services Inc.
     2978 Main St
     Buffalo NY 14214
     800 327-1355

(G-13250)
MAY GRAPHICS & PRINTING INC
Also Called: Ledgeview Printing
359 Littleton Rd (01886-4065)
P.O. Box 724 (01886-0022)
EMP: 8 **EST:** 1993
SQ FT: 3,000
SALES (est): 1.46MM **Privately Held**
Web: www.ledgeviewprinting.com
SIC: 2752 Offset printing

(G-13251)
MILL WORKS
22 Town Farm Rd (01886-2365)
PHONE.....................................978 692-8222
EMP: 7 **EST:** 2017
SALES (est): 239.09K **Privately Held**

Web: www.millworkswestford.com
SIC: 2431 Millwork

(G-13252)
MUFFINS ON MAIN LLC
40 Main St (01886-2552)
PHONE.....................................978 788-4365
EMP: 7 **EST:** 2016
SALES (est): 82.66K **Privately Held**
Web: www.muffinsonmain.com
SIC: 2024 Ice cream and frozen deserts

(G-13253)
NETSCOUT SYSTEMS INC (PA)
Also Called: Netscout
310 Littleton Rd (01886-4105)
PHONE.....................................978 614-4000
Anil K Singhal, *Ch Bd*
Michael Szabados, *
Jean Bua, *CAO*
John W Downing, *Executive Worldwide Sales Vice-President*
▲ **EMP:** 220 **EST:** 1984
SQ FT: 175,000
SALES (est): 914.53MM
SALES (corp-wide): 914.53MM **Publicly Held**
Web: www.netscout.com
SIC: 7373 3577 Systems software development services; Computer peripheral equipment, nec

(G-13254)
NETWORK EQUIPMENT TECH INC (DH)
Also Called: Net.com
4 Technology Park Dr (01886-3140)
PHONE.....................................510 713-7300
David Wagenseller, *Pr*
Karen C Carte, *Acting Vice President*
Frank Slattery, *VP*
Kevin N Isacks, *Chief Development Officer*
Pete Patel, *Global Operations Vice President*
◆ **EMP:** 28 **EST:** 1983
SQ FT: 97,747
SALES (est): 99.16MM
SALES (corp-wide): 819.76MM **Publicly Held**
Web: www.ribboncommunications.com
SIC: 3577 Computer peripheral equipment, nec
HQ: Ribbon Communications Operating Company, Inc.
     6500 Chase Oaks Blvd
     Plano TX 75023
     877 412-8867

(G-13255)
NEW ENGLAND WOODCRAFT INC
70 Main St (01886-2507)
PHONE.....................................413 522-0137
Betsy Pettit, *Prin*
EMP: 8 **EST:** 2016
SALES (est): 87.92K **Privately Held**
Web: www.newenglandwoodcraft.com
SIC: 2512 Upholstered household furniture

(G-13256)
NOKIA OF AMERICA CORPORATION
1 Robbins Rd (01886-4113)
PHONE.....................................978 952-1616
E Newland, *VP*
EMP: 58
SALES (corp-wide): 25.87B **Privately Held**
Web: www.nokia.com

SIC: 3661 Telephone and telegraph apparatus
HQ: Nokia Of America Corporation
     600 Mountain Ave Ste 700
     New Providence NJ 07974

(G-13257)
PRINTING SOLUTIONS INC
6 Carlisle Rd Ste 6 (01886-3619)
PHONE.....................................978 392-9903
Andre Lagasse, *Pr*
Don Lagasse, *Clerk*
EMP: 10 **EST:** 1990
SQ FT: 15,000
SALES (est): 817.94K **Privately Held**
Web: www.printingsolutionsinc.com
SIC: 2752 Offset printing

(G-13258)
RED HAT INC
314 Little 10 Rd (01886)
PHONE.....................................978 392-1000
EMP: 36
SALES (corp-wide): 60.53B **Publicly Held**
Web: www.redhat.com
SIC: 7372 Prepackaged software
HQ: Red Hat, Inc.
     100 E Davie St
     Raleigh NC 27601

(G-13259)
RENESAS ELECTRONICS AMER INC
515 Groton Rd Ste 102 (01886-9809)
PHONE.....................................978 577-6340
EMP: 49
Web: www.renesas.com
SIC: 3674 Integrated circuits, semiconductor networks, etc.
HQ: Renesas Electronics America Inc.
     6024 Silver Creek Vly Rd
     San Jose CA 95138
     408 284-8200

(G-13260)
RIVERMEADOW SOFTWARE INC
319 Littleton Rd Ste 305 (01886-4100)
PHONE.....................................617 448-4990
Partha Ghosh, *Prin*
EMP: 10 **EST:** 2012
SALES (est): 274.74K **Privately Held**
Web: www.rivermeadow.com
SIC: 7372 Prepackaged software

(G-13261)
SECEON INC
238 Littleton Rd Ste 206 (01886-3531)
PHONE.....................................978 923-0040
Chandra S Pandey, *Prin*
Chandra S Pandey, *Pr*
Gary Scott, *Sec*
EMP: 20 **EST:** 2015
SALES (est): 2.34MM **Privately Held**
Web: www.seceon.com
SIC: 7372 Business oriented computer software

(G-13262)
SIEMENS ENERGY INC
20 Villanova Dr (01886-1960)
PHONE.....................................978 577-6413
EMP: 25
SALES (corp-wide): 33.81B **Privately Held**
Web: new.siemens.com
SIC: 3661 Telephones and telephone apparatus
HQ: Siemens Energy, Inc.
     4400 N Alafaya Trl
     Orlando FL 32826
     407 736-2000

(G-13263)
SOFTWARE EXPERTS INC
4 Grey Fox Ln (01886-1913)
PHONE.....................................978 692-5343
Rao Mallik, *Pr*
Rao Mallik, *Prin*
Malliareddy Karra, *Prin*
EMP: 9 **EST:** 1994
SQ FT: 700
SALES (est): 158.12K **Privately Held**
Web: www.softwareexperts.com
SIC: 7372 Prepackaged software

(G-13264)
ST JUDE MEDICAL LLC
4 Robbins Rd (01886-4113)
PHONE.....................................978 577-3400
EMP: 9
SALES (corp-wide): 43.65B **Publicly Held**
Web: www.cardiovascular.abbott
SIC: 3842 Surgical appliances and supplies
HQ: St. Jude Medical, Llc
     1 Saint Jude Medical Dr
     Saint Paul MN 55117
     651 756-2000

(G-13265)
SYMETRICA INC
4 Lyberty Way Ste 1 (01886-3616)
PHONE.....................................508 718-5610
Eric Zanin, *CEO*
Matthew Dallimore Doctor, *Prin*
Gisele Caisse, *Finance CTRL*
EMP: 30 **EST:** 2005
SQ FT: 19,308
SALES (est): 4.53MM **Privately Held**
Web: www.symetrica.com
SIC: 3812 Search and navigation equipment

(G-13266)
VEEAM SOFTWARE
10 Reinsway Cir (01886-3129)
PHONE.....................................978 660-3276
Tom Chevalier, *VP*
EMP: 202 **EST:** 2018
SALES (est): 561.54K **Privately Held**
SIC: 7372 Prepackaged software

(G-13267)
VISONIC INC (HQ)
6 Technology Park Dr # 101 (01886-3140)
PHONE.....................................860 243-0833
▲ **EMP:** 25
SQ FT: 10,000
SALES (est): 8.15MM
SALES (corp-wide): 74.38MM **Privately Held**
Web: www.visonictech.com
SIC: 3669 Emergency alarms
PA: Visonic Limited
     24 Habarzel
     Tel Aviv-Jaffa 43662
     36456789

Westminster
Worcester County

(G-13268)
ADVANCE COATINGS CO (PA)
42 Depot Rd (01473-1219)
P.O. Box 457 (01473-0457)
PHONE.....................................978 874-5921
▲ **EMP:** 18 **EST:** 1939
SALES (est): 4.63MM
SALES (corp-wide): 4.63MM **Privately Held**
Web: www.advancecoatings.com

▲ = Import ▼ = Export
◆ = Import/Export

SIC: 3229 Glass fiber products

(G-13269)
AMERICAN SUPERCONDUCTOR CORP
95 Aubuchon Dr (01473-1470)
PHONE..............................978 842-3000
Daniel Mcgahn, *Prin*
John Kosiba, *Prin*
EMP: 42 **EST:** 1987
SALES (est): 507.21K **Privately Held**
Web: www.amsc.com
SIC: 3674 Semiconductors and related devices

(G-13270)
FITCHBURG WELDING CO INC
4 Depot Rd (01473-1220)
P.O. Box 467 (01473-0467)
PHONE..............................978 874-2911
Paul H Morin, *Pr*
Paul H Morin Junior, *Asst VP*
Norman J Courtemanche, *
▼ **EMP:** 35 **EST:** 1935
SQ FT: 48,000
SALES (est): 8.69MM **Privately Held**
Web: www.fitchweld.com
SIC: 3441 7692 Fabricated structural metal; Welding repair

(G-13271)
ILLINOIS TOOL WORKS INC
Also Called: ITW EF&c US
180 State Rd E (01473-1208)
PHONE..............................978 874-0151
Marcey Miller, *Brnch Mgr*
EMP: 230
SALES (corp-wide): 15.93B **Publicly Held**
Web: www.itw.com
SIC: 3465 3089 Body parts, automobile:. stamped metal; Automotive parts, plastic
PA: Illinois Tool Works Inc.
155 Harlem Ave
Glenview IL 60025
847 724-7500

(G-13272)
MASSACHUSETTS NATURAL FERT INC
65 Bean Porridge Hill Rd (01473-1121)
P.O. Box 363 (01473-0363)
PHONE..............................978 874-0744
William Page Senior, *Pr*
William Page, *Pr*
EMP: 7 **EST:** 1987
SALES (est): 2.28MM **Privately Held**
Web: www.expiredwixdomain.com
SIC: 2875 Compost

(G-13273)
MAYHEW BASQUE PLASTICS LLC
100 Simplex Dr Ste 3 (01473-1482)
PHONE..............................978 537-5219
John C Lawless, *Managing Member*
▲ **EMP:** 16 **EST:** 1972
SQ FT: 30,000
SALES (est): 4.43MM
SALES (corp-wide): 9.01MM **Privately Held**
Web: www.mayhew.com
SIC: 3089 3544 Injection molding of plastics ; Industrial molds
PA: Mayhew Steel Products, Inc.
199 Industrial Blvd
Turners Falls MA 01376
413 625-6351

(G-13274)
MILES KEDEX CO INC
1 Rowtier Rd (01473-1675)
PHONE..............................978 874-1403
Stephen A Muller, *Pr*
Charles A Gelinas Senior, *Sec*
▲ **EMP:** 35 **EST:** 1928
SQ FT: 35,000
SALES (est): 2.67MM **Privately Held**
Web: www.mileskedex.com
SIC: 2295 2631 3172 Leather, artificial or imitation; Leatherboard; Personal leather goods, nec

(G-13275)
MM-APVH ACQUISITION CO LLC (HQ)
Also Called: Seaboard Folding Box Company
100 Simplex Dr (01473-1482)
PHONE..............................978 516-7050
Anik Patel, *Managing Member*
EMP: 11 **EST:** 2021
SALES (est): 45.67MM
SALES (corp-wide): 58.78MM **Privately Held**
Web: www.seaboardbox.com
SIC: 3554 Die cutting and stamping machinery, paper converting
PA: Vidya Brands Group Llc
6032 94th Ct
Kenosha WI 53142
262 960-2173

(G-13276)
RANOR INC
1 Bella Dr (01473-1058)
PHONE..............................978 874-0591
Alexander Shen, *CEO*
Tom Sammons, *
▲ **EMP:** 98 **EST:** 1956
SQ FT: 120,000
SALES (est): 19.87MM **Publicly Held**
Web: www.ranor.com
SIC: 3441 3599 Fabricated structural metal; Machine and other job shop work
PA: Techprecision Corporation
1 Bella Dr
Westminster MA 01473

(G-13277)
SEABOARD FOLDING BOX CO INC
100 Simplex Dr (01473-1482)
P.O. Box 650 (01473-0650)
PHONE..............................978 342-8921
Michael Mazur, *Pr*
Christopher J Gessner, *Sec*
Jerald P Boudreau, *Treas*
William Gentes, *CFO*
EMP: 51 **EST:** 2014
SALES (est): 10.55MM
SALES (corp-wide): 58.78MM **Privately Held**
Web: www.seaboardbox.com
SIC: 2653 Boxes, corrugated: made from purchased materials
PA: Vidya Brands Group Llc
6032 94th Ct
Kenosha WI 53142
262 960-2173

(G-13278)
SIMPLEX TIME RECORDER LLC (DH)
50 Technology Dr (01441-0001)
EMP: 163 **EST:** 1902
SALES (est): 2.1B **Privately Held**
Web: www.simplexfire.com

SIC: 7382 3669 1711 Security systems services; Emergency alarms; Sprinkler contractors
HQ: Simplexgrinnell Holdings Llc
1501 Nw 51st St
Boca Raton FL 33431

(G-13279)
STR GRINNELL GP HOLDING LLC
50 Technology Dr (01441-0001)
PHONE..............................978 731-2500
Jerry R Boggess, *Pr*
EMP: 32 **EST:** 2001
SALES (est): 4.31MM **Privately Held**
SIC: 3579 Time clocks and time recording devices
HQ: Simplex Time Recorder Llc
50 Technology Dr
Westminster MA 01441

(G-13280)
TECHPRECISION CORPORATION (PA)
Also Called: Techprecision
1 Bella Dr (01473-1058)
PHONE..............................978 874-0591
Alexander Shen, *CEO*
Richard S Mcgowan, *Ch Bd*
Barbara M Lilley, *CFO*
▲ **EMP:** 15 **EST:** 1956
SQ FT: 145,000
SALES (est): 31.43MM **Publicly Held**
Web: www.techprecision.com
SIC: 3599 3441 Machine and other job shop work; Fabricated structural metal for ships

(G-13281)
TOWN OF WESTMINSTER
Also Called: Westminster Fire Department
7 South St (01473-1534)
PHONE..............................978 874-2313
EMP: 10
Web: www.westminster-ma.gov
SIC: 3569 Firefighting and related equipment
PA: Town Of Westminster
11 South St
Westminster MA 01473
978 874-7400

(G-13282)
TWIN CITY MACHINING INC
4 Curtis Rd (01473-1221)
P.O. Box 467 (01473-0467)
PHONE..............................978 874-1940
Mark Morin, *Pr*
Paul Morin, *VP*
Brian Morin, *VP*
▲ **EMP:** 9 **EST:** 1998
SALES (est): 663.68K **Privately Held**
Web: www.fitchweld.com
SIC: 3599 Machine shop, jobbing and repair

(G-13283)
ZF ACTIVE SAFETY & ELEC US LLC
Also Called: TRW Fastening Systems
180 State Rd E (01473-1208)
PHONE..............................978 874-0151
Melven Derek, *Brnch Mgr*
EMP: 84
SALES (corp-wide): 144.19K **Privately Held**
SIC: 3714 Motor vehicle parts and accessories
HQ: Zf Active Safety & Electronics Us Llc
12000 Tech Center Dr
Livonia MI 48150

Weston
Middlesex County

(G-13284)
AAM INC
839 Boston Post Rd (02493-1106)
PHONE..............................781 330-9857
EMP: 12 **EST:** 2011
SALES (est): 250.02K **Privately Held**
Web: www.aam.com
SIC: 3714 Motor vehicle parts and accessories

(G-13285)
GROB INC
19 Fairhope Rd (02493-2108)
PHONE..............................617 817-3123
Ellen L Touart Grob, *Prin*
EMP: 7 **EST:** 2011
SALES (est): 161.84K **Privately Held**
Web: www.larrygrobartist.com
SIC: 3541 Machine tools, metal cutting type

(G-13286)
HUMAN CARE SYSTEMS INC
703 Boston Post Rd (02493-1543)
PHONE..............................781 609-2194
EMP: 26
SALES (corp-wide): 34.9MM **Privately Held**
Web: www.caremetx.com
SIC: 7372 Prepackaged software
HQ: Human Care Systems, Inc.
1 Faneuil Hall Sq
Boston MA 02109
617 720-7838

(G-13287)
METALENZ INC
375 Highland St (02493-2624)
PHONE..............................844 770-1300
EMP: 31 **EST:** 2017
SALES (est): 6.82MM **Privately Held**
Web: www.metalenz.com
SIC: 3674 Semiconductors and related devices

(G-13288)
MONSTER TECH
133 Boston Post Rd 15 (02493-2525)
PHONE..............................978 897-0832
Thomasz Schellenberg, *CEO*
EMP: 11 **EST:** 2015
SALES (est): 697.83K **Privately Held**
SIC: 7311 2741 Advertising agencies; Miscellaneous publishing

(G-13289)
PRIME NATIONAL PUBLISHING CORP
Also Called: Journal Emergency Management
470 Boston Post Rd (02493-1576)
PHONE..............................781 899-2702
Eileen F Devito, *Pr*
Richard Devito, *Stockholder*
EMP: 9 **EST:** 1975
SALES (est): 202.85K **Privately Held**
SIC: 2741 Miscellaneous publishing

(G-13290)
SYNOSTICS INC
3 Old Coach Rd (02493-2001)
PHONE..............................781 248-5699
EMP: 7 **EST:** 2010
SALES (est): 459.45K **Privately Held**
SIC: 2834 Pharmaceutical preparations

(G-13291)
TRYXUS INVESTMENT & TRDG INC
Also Called: Titi
253 Highland St (02493-1111)
PHONE..........................800 981-6616
Degang Shao, *CEO*
EMP: 16 EST: 2012
SALES (est): 1.12MM **Privately Held**
Web: www.tryxus.com
SIC: 3589 6799 6351 Asbestos removal
  equipment; Commodity contract trading
  companies; Credit and other financial
  responsibility insurance

Westport
Bristol County

(G-13292)
AMA ENGNRING - SMRTMOVE CNVYOR
683 American Legion Hwy (02790-4103)
PHONE..........................508 636-7740
EMP: 12 EST: 2009
SALES (est): 2.16MM **Privately Held**
Web: www.4smartmove.com
SIC: 3535 Conveyors and conveying
  equipment

(G-13293)
BAKER PARTS INC
Also Called: Bpi
407 Cornell Rd (02790-5016)
P.O. Box 3942 (02790-0299)
PHONE..........................508 878-5436
▼ EMP: 7 EST: 1978
SQ FT: 10,000
SALES (est): 1.74MM **Privately Held**
Web: www.bakerparts.com
SIC: 3556 5084 Ovens, bakery; Industrial
  machinery and equipment

(G-13294)
BUZZARDS BAY BREWING INC
98 Horseneck Rd (02790-1399)
PHONE..........................508 636-2288
Chris Atkinson, *Dir*
Carol Russel, *Treas*
Robert Russel, *Pr*
Tim Coleman, *Dir*
EMP: 9 EST: 1997
SQ FT: 13,251
SALES (est): 934.22K **Privately Held**
Web: www.buzzardsbrew.com
SIC: 2082 5149 Beer (alcoholic beverage);
  Groceries and related products, nec

(G-13295)
DARTMOUTH AWNING CO INC
Also Called: Bji Enterprises
45 Beeden Rd (02790-1162)
PHONE..........................508 636-6838
Brad Gifford, *Pr*
EMP: 7 EST: 1979
SALES (est): 657.14K **Privately Held**
Web: www.dartmouthawning.com
SIC: 2394 5999 Awnings, fabric: made from
  purchased materials; Awnings

(G-13296)
GRATE PRODUCTS LLC
Also Called: Pioneer Basements
31 Sanford Rd (02790-3502)
PHONE..........................800 649-6140
EMP: 33 EST: 2006
SALES (est): 2.65MM **Privately Held**
Web: www.grateproducts.com

SIC: 2899 Waterproofing compounds

(G-13297)
J W I N PROMOTIONAL CORP
Also Called: New England Promotions
767 Main Rd Ste 3 (02790-4398)
PHONE..........................508 636-1993
John Winters, *Pr*
James Winters, *VP*
EMP: 8 EST: 1983
SQ FT: 2,000
SALES (est): 2.44MM **Privately Held**
SIC: 5199 2396 2395 Advertising specialties
  ; Screen printing on fabric articles;
  Embroidery products, except Schiffli
  machine

(G-13298)
JUST UR WAY SCREEN PRINT
248 Briggs Rd (02790-4041)
PHONE..........................508 235-0422
Justin Estrella, *Prin*
EMP: 10 EST: 2011
SALES (est): 238.56K **Privately Held**
Web: taj.trump.com
SIC: 2752 Commercial printing, lithographic

(G-13299)
RALCO ELECTRIC INC
Also Called: Ralco Electric & Generator
101 State Rd (02790-3521)
PHONE..........................508 679-3363
TOLL FREE: 800
Rene Lachapelle Junior, *Pr*
Pamella Lachapelle, *
EMP: 60 EST: 1986
SQ FT: 5,500
SALES (est): 12.02MM **Privately Held**
Web: www.ralcoelectric.com
SIC: 1731 7694 5063 5999 General
  electrical contractor; Electric motor repair;
  Motors, electric; Motors, electric

(G-13300)
WESTPORT RIVERS INC
Also Called: Westport Rivers Vinyrd Winery
417 Hixbridge Rd (02790-1316)
PHONE..........................508 636-3423
Robert Russell, *Pr*
▲ EMP: 15 EST: 1984
SALES (est): 2.49MM **Privately Held**
Web: www.westportrivers.com
SIC: 2084 Wines

(G-13301)
WILLIAM MCCASKIE INC
197 Forge Rd (02790-1141)
PHONE..........................508 636-8845
Andrew J Bolton, *Pr*
David Bolton, *Treas*
▲ EMP: 8 EST: 1953
SQ FT: 28,000
SALES (est): 970.87K **Privately Held**
Web: www.mccaskiereels.com
SIC: 3499 Reels, cable: metal

(G-13302)
ZIBRA CORPORATION
640 American Legion Hwy (02790-4107)
PHONE..........................508 636-6606
Art Mc Kinley, *Pr*
EMP: 10 EST: 1985
SQ FT: 4,200
SALES (est): 2.01MM **Privately Held**
Web: www.zibracorp.com
SIC: 3827 Boroscopes

Westport Point
Bristol County

(G-13303)
F L TRIPP & SONS INC
Cherry & Webb Lane (02791)
P.O. Box 23 (02791-0023)
PHONE..........................508 636-4058
Richard Gemma, *Pr*
Harold F Tripp, *VP*
Russell M Tripp, *Clerk*
EMP: 14 EST: 1922
SQ FT: 3,150
SALES (est): 793.06K **Privately Held**
Web: www.fltripp.com
SIC: 3731 5551 4493 Fishing vessels, large:
  building and repairing; Boat dealers;
  Marinas

Westwood
Norfolk County

(G-13304)
270 UNIVERSITY AVENUE LLC
270 University Ave (02090-2309)
PHONE..........................781 407-0836
Angela Pacini Fiori, *Prin*
EMP: 8 EST: 2005
SALES (est): 109.17K **Privately Held**
SIC: 3281 Stone, quarrying and processing
  of own stone products

(G-13305)
ADE TECHNOLOGIES INC (HQ)
80 Wilson Way (02090-1806)
PHONE..........................781 467-3500
▲ EMP: 70 EST: 1983
SALES (est): 22.57MM
SALES (corp-wide): 9.21B **Publicly Held**
SIC: 3829 3545 Gauging instruments,
  thickness ultrasonic; Machine tool
  accessories
PA: Kla Corporation
  1 Technology Dr
  Milpitas CA 95035
  408 875-3000

(G-13306)
BLACK & DECKER (US) INC
377 University Ave (02090-2300)
PHONE..........................781 329-3407
Tom Celluci, *Mgr*
EMP: 7
SALES (corp-wide): 16.95B **Publicly Held**
Web: www.blackanddecker.com
SIC: 3546 Power-driven handtools
HQ: Black & Decker (U.S.) Inc.
  1000 Stanley Dr
  New Britain CT 06053
  860 225-5111

(G-13307)
CAMBRIDGE SOUNDWORKS INC
Also Called: Warehouse
26 Dartmouth St (02090-2301)
PHONE..........................781 329-2777
Mike Mahoney, *Mgr*
EMP: 24
SIC: 3651 Audio electronic systems
HQ: Cambridge Soundworks, Inc.
  1630 Cimarron Plz
  Stillwater OK 74075
  405 742-6704

(G-13308)
CHASE CORP INC
375 University Ave (02090-2300)
PHONE..........................781 332-0700
Terry Jones, *Prin*
EMP: 11 EST: 2011
SALES (est): 778.93K **Privately Held**
Web: www.chasecorp.com
SIC: 3644 3479 Insulators and insulation
  materials, electrical; Coating electrodes

(G-13309)
CHASE CORPORATION (HQ)
Also Called: Chase
375 University Ave (02090-2300)
PHONE..........................781 332-0700
Adam P Chase, *Pr*
Lance Reisman, *Ch Bd*
Michael J Bourque, *CFO*
Jeffery D Haigh, *Corporate Secretary*
EMP: 8 EST: 1946
SQ FT: 10,000
SALES (est): 404.01MM **Publicly Held**
Web: www.chasecorp.com
SIC: 3644 3479 3672 Insulators and
  insulation materials, electrical; Coating
  electrodes; Printed circuit boards
PA: Kkr & Co. Inc.
  30 Hudson Yards
  New York NY 10001

(G-13310)
CHASE SPECIALITY COATING
375 University Ave (02090-2300)
PHONE..........................781 332-0700
Adam P Chase, *CEO*
EMP: 15 EST: 2016
SALES (est): 1.45MM **Privately Held**
Web: www.chasecorp.com
SIC: 2851 Lacquers, varnishes, enamels,
  and other coatings

(G-13311)
IDE ACQUISITION CORP
377 University Ave (02090-2300)
PHONE..........................781 326-5700
Heidi Heiland, *Prin*
EMP: 9 EST: 2002
SALES (est): 201.07K **Privately Held**
SIC: 3829 Measuring and controlling
  devices, nec

(G-13312)
IDEX MPT INC (HQ)
Also Called: Fitzpatrick Company, The
90 Glacier Dr Ste 1000 (02090-1818)
PHONE..........................630 530-3333
Andrew Milner, *Pr*
◆ EMP: 100 EST: 1912
SALES (est): 23.23MM
SALES (corp-wide): 3.18B **Publicly Held**
Web: www.fitzpatrick-mpt.com
SIC: 3547 Primary rolling mill equipment
PA: Idex Corporation
  3100 Sanders Rd Ste 301
  Northbrook IL 60062
  847 498-7070

(G-13313)
INEOQUEST TECHNOLOGIES INC (HQ)
Also Called: Ineoquest
247 Station Dr Ste Ne2 (02090-2397)
PHONE..........................508 339-2497
Calvin Harrison, *Pr*
Peter Dawson, *Ch Bd*
Steve Sanford, *CFO*
EMP: 35 EST: 2001
SALES (est): 45.56MM
SALES (corp-wide): 122.84MM **Privately Held**

▲ = Import ▼ = Export
◆ = Import/Export

SIC: 3825 Instruments to measure electricity
PA: Telestream, Llc
848 Gold Flat Rd
Nevada City CA 95959
530 470-1300

(G-13314)
MEDICAL INFORMATION TECH INC (PA)
Meditech Cir (02090)
PHONE.................................781 821-3000
Michelle O'connor, *CEO*
A Neil Pappalardo, *
Lawrence A Polimeno, *
Howard Messing, *
Barbara A Manzolillo, *CFO*
EMP: 524 EST: 1969
SALES (est): 493.84MM
SALES (corp-wide): 493.84MM Privately Held
Web: ehr.meditech.com
SIC: 7372 Business oriented computer software

(G-13315)
MICROFLUIDICS INTL CORP
90 Glacier Dr Ste 1000 (02090-1818)
PHONE.................................617 969-5452
James N Little, *Pr*
EMP: 28 EST: 1983
SALES (est): 9.92MM
SALES (corp-wide): 3.18B Publicly Held
Web: www.microfluidics-mpt.com
SIC: 3559 3821 Pharmaceutical machinery; Laboratory apparatus and furniture
PA: Idex Corporation
3100 Sanders Rd Ste 301
Northbrook IL 60062
847 498-7070

(G-13316)
NEPTCO INCORPORATED (DH)
Also Called: Neptco Laminated Tapes Co Inc
295 University Ave (02090-2315)
PHONE.................................401 722-5500
Guy Marini, *CEO*
Ken Feroldi, *
Joel Gruhn, *
Lois Kilsey, *
Frank Conti, *
◆ **EMP: 95 EST: 1955**
SQ FT: 50,000
SALES (est): 82.97MM Publicly Held
Web: www.chasecorp.com
SIC: 3496 3083 2672 Woven wire products, nec; Laminated plastics sheets; Paper; coated and laminated, nec
HQ: Chase Corporation
375 University Ave
Westwood MA 02090
781 332-0700

(G-13317)
ROMANOW INC (DH)
Also Called: Romanow Container
346 University Ave (02090-2309)
PHONE.................................781 320-9200
Theodore Romanow, *Pr*
Dick Romanow, *
Daniel L Romanow, *
Richard C Romanow, *
EMP: 100 EST: 1924
SQ FT: 145,000
SALES (est): 31.22MM
SALES (corp-wide): 838.82MM Privately Held
Web: www.romanowcontainer.com
SIC: 2653 Boxes, corrugated: made from purchased materials
HQ: Supplyone, Inc.
11 Campus Blvd Ste 150

Newtown Square PA 19073
484 582-5005

(G-13318)
SLATTERY BROS INC
697 High St Unit 460 (02090-2555)
PHONE.................................617 269-3025
▲ **EMP: 7 EST: 1928**
SALES (est): 224.06K Privately Held
SIC: 3111 Leather tanning and finishing

(G-13319)
STATSPIN INC
Also Called: Iris Sample Processing
60 Glacier Dr Ste 2000 (02090-1825)
PHONE.................................781 551-0100
▲ **EMP: 50**
SIC: 3841 Surgical and medical instruments

(G-13320)
SUBURBAN SERVICE CORP NORWOOD
Also Called: Suburban Service
16 S West Park (02090-1548)
PHONE.................................781 769-1515
Cynthia Vito, *Pr*
Richard Vito, *VP*
EMP: 18 EST: 1982
SALES (est): 2.22MM Privately Held
SIC: 3585 Heating and air conditioning combination units

(G-13321)
SURGICAL SPECIALTIES CORP (HQ)
Also Called: Angiotech
247 Station Dr Ste Ne1 (02090-2397)
PHONE.................................781 751-1000
Dan Croteau, *CEO*
Victor Diaz, *
Daniel Sutherby, *
EMP: 200 EST: 1996
SQ FT: 22,000
SALES (est): 68.23MM
SALES (corp-wide): 679.11MM Privately Held
Web: www.corza.com
SIC: 3842 3841 Sutures, absorbable and non-absorbable; Needles, suture
PA: Gtcr, Llc
300 N Lasalle Dr Ste 5600
Chicago IL 60654
312 382-2200

(G-13322)
TAPECOAT COMPANY
295 University Ave (02090-2315)
PHONE.................................781 332-0700
Peter R Chase, *Prin*
EMP: 7 EST: 2013
SALES (est): 294.89K Privately Held
Web: www.chasecorp.com
SIC: 2821 Plastics materials and resins

(G-13323)
TRINITY BUILDERS INC (PA)
217 Washington St (02090)
P.O. Box 122 (02090-0122)
PHONE.................................781 780-6168
Sean Sweeney, *Prin*
EMP: 7 EST: 2018
SALES (est): 231.47K
SALES (corp-wide): 231.47K Privately Held
SIC: 1521 1389 1522 New construction, single-family houses; Construction, repair, and dismantling services; Multi-family dwellings, new construction

Weymouth
Norfolk County

(G-13324)
ELECTRO SWITCH CORP
180 King Ave (02188-2927)
PHONE.................................781 607-3306
Bryan Gregory, *Brnch Mgr*
EMP: 175
SALES (corp-wide): 103.82MM Privately Held
Web: www.electroswitch.com
SIC: 3613 3643 3625 3621 Switches, electric power except snap, push button, etc.; Current-carrying wiring services; Relays and industrial controls; Motors and generators
HQ: Electro Switch Corp.
775 Pleasant St Ste 1
Weymouth MA 02189
781 335-1195

(G-13325)
ELECTRO SWITCH CORP
Also Called: Arga Controls
180 King Ave (02188-2927)
PHONE.................................781 335-1195
Bob Pineau, *Pr*
Linda Halsey, *Pr*
EMP: 12 EST: 1970
SALES (est): 1.09MM Privately Held
Web: www.electroswitch.com
SIC: 3823 3829 3625 3613 Process control instruments; Measuring and controlling devices, nec; Relays and industrial controls ; Switchgear and switchboard apparatus

(G-13326)
INFORS USA INC
25 Mathewson Dr (02189-2345)
PHONE.................................781 335-3108
EMP: 17
Web: www.infors-ht.com
SIC: 3821 Laboratory equipment: fume hoods, distillation racks, etc.
HQ: Infors Usa Inc.
9070 Junction Dr Ste D
Annapolis Junction MD 20701
410 792-8007

(G-13327)
INNOVATIVE MEDIA GROUP INC
Also Called: Signature Graphics & Signs
36 Finnell Dr Ste 3 (02188-1106)
PHONE.................................781 335-8773
Kathleen E Ready, *Pr*
Kathleen Ready, *Owner*
Richard Ready, *Treas*
EMP: 12 EST: 1988
SQ FT: 1,800
SALES (est): 497.87K Privately Held
Web: www.fordsign.com
SIC: 3993 Signs, not made in custom sign painting shops

(G-13328)
KEYSTONE ELEV SVC MDRNZTION LL
320 Libbey Industrial Pkwy Ste 800 (02189-3149)
P.O. Box 850460 (02185-0460)
PHONE.................................781 340-3860
Thomas Haggerty, *Prin*
EMP: 8 EST: 2005
SALES (est): 178.01K Privately Held
Web: www.keystoneelevator.com

SIC: 7699 3534 Elevators: inspection, service, and repair; Elevators and equipment

(G-13329)
MFM ENTERPRISES INC
50 Alewife Ln (02189-2662)
PHONE.................................858 571-1358
Michael Mullen, *Owner*
EMP: 9 EST: 1999
SALES (est): 490.59K Privately Held
Web: www.mfmenterprises.com
SIC: 2711 Newspapers

(G-13330)
MOONEYTUNCO INC
Also Called: Merry Christmas From Heaven
65 Mathewson Dr Ste C (02189-2347)
PHONE.................................781 331-4445
John Mooney, *Pr*
EMP: 7
SALES (corp-wide): 1.93MM Privately Held
Web: www.mooneytunco.com
SIC: 3999 5199 Fire extinguishers, portable; Gifts and novelties
PA: Mooneytunco, Inc.
1023 Washington St
Weymouth MA 02189
781 331-5308

(G-13331)
NE STAINLESS STEEL FAB
86 Finnell Dr Ste 23 (02188-1100)
PHONE.................................781 335-0121
Jean Barry, *Genl Mgr*
EMP: 8 EST: 2010
SALES (est): 730K Privately Held
SIC: 3312 Stainless steel

(G-13332)
NMW HOLDING CO INC
250 West St (02188-1112)
PHONE.................................617 269-5650
Mark J Wolff, *Pr*
EMP: 14 EST: 1983
SALES (est): 524.2K Privately Held
Web: www.primesourcefoods.biz
SIC: 2015 Poultry slaughtering and processing

(G-13333)
PYRAMID PRINTING AND ADVG INC
Also Called: Pyramid Printing and Digital
54 Mathewson Dr # 60 (02189-2346)
PHONE.................................781 337-7609
Ronald Ciccolo, *Pr*
EMP: 21 EST: 1976
SQ FT: 15,000
SALES (est): 475.14K Privately Held
SIC: 2791 2752 2789 Typesetting; Offset printing; Bookbinding and related work

(G-13334)
R & S REDCO INC
106 Finnell Dr Ste 24 (02188-1114)
PHONE.................................781 792-1717
John B Swan, *Pr*
George Maclean, *VP*
EMP: 8 EST: 1972
SQ FT: 5,000
SALES (est): 944.55K Privately Held
Web: www.rsredco.com
SIC: 3599 8711 Machine shop, jobbing and repair; Mechanical engineering

(G-13335)
SOUTHEASTERN CONCRETE INC
611 Pleasant St (02189-3201)
P.O. Box 9187 (02114-9187)
PHONE...............................781 848-9390
Dean M Boylan Junior, *Pr*
Jeanne-marie Boylan, *Sec*
EMP: 13 **EST:** 1962
SALES (est): 427.83K **Privately Held**
Web:
www.southeasternconcretecorp.com
SIC: 3273 Ready-mixed concrete

(G-13336)
STAR LITHO INC
360 Libbey Industrial Pkwy (02189-3133)
PHONE...............................781 340-9401
Ernest Chekoulias, *Pr*
Scott Chekoulias, *Treas*
Dorothy Chekoulias, *Clerk*
EMP: 10 **EST:** 1953
SALES (est): 499.17K **Privately Held**
Web: www.star-litho.com
SIC: 2752 Offset printing

(G-13337)
THOMSON REUTERS CORPORATION
805 Pleasant St (02189-2337)
P.O. Box 95118 (02495-0118)
PHONE...............................781 331-6610
EMP: 19
SALES (corp-wide): 10.66B **Publicly Held**
Web: www.thomsonreuters.com
SIC: 2731 Book publishing
HQ: Thomson Reuters Corporation
333 Bay St
Toronto ON M5H 2
416 687-7500

(G-13338)
W OLIVER TRIPP COMPANY (PA)
Also Called: G L Roller Division
86 Finnell Dr Ste 6 (02188-1100)
P.O. Box 316 (02047-0316)
PHONE...............................781 848-1230
TOLL FREE: 800
Gerald L Tripp, *CEO*
Richard W Wennett, *Clerk*
Michael Tripp, *VP*
Michael Sharpe, *Treas*
▲ **EMP:** 30 **EST:** 1945
SQ FT: 20,000
SALES (est): 7.72MM
SALES (corp-wide): 7.72MM **Privately Held**
SIC: 5199 3555 Art goods and supplies;
Printing trade parts and attachments

Whately
Franklin County

(G-13339)
HI TUNES
Also Called: HI Tune Wax
207 River Rd (01093)
P.O. Box 8 (01373-0008)
PHONE...............................435 962-0405
Gregory Carlson, *Owner*
EMP: 10 **EST:** 2013
SQ FT: 1,000
SALES (est): 277.32K **Privately Held**
SIC: 2842 Polishes and sanitation goods

(G-13340)
YANKEE CANDLE COMPANY INC
102 Christian Ln (01093)
PHONE...............................413 665-8306
EMP: 9
SALES (corp-wide): 9.46B **Publicly Held**
Web: www.yankeecandle.com
SIC: 3999 Candles
HQ: The Yankee Candle Company Inc
16 Yankee Candle Way
South Deerfield MA 01373
413 665-8306

Whitinsville
Worcester County

(G-13341)
LOUD AUDIO LLC
Eastern Acoustic Works
1 Main St Ste 1 (01588-2201)
PHONE...............................508 234-6158
Frank Loyko, *Brnch Mgr*
EMP: 212
SALES (corp-wide): 47.88MM **Privately Held**
Web: www.loudaudio.com
SIC: 3651 3663 Loudspeakers,
electrodynamic or magnetic; Radio and t.v.
communications equipment
PA: Loud Audio, Llc
19820 North Creek Pkwy # 201
Bothell WA 98011
425 892-6500

(G-13342)
MURDER HILL LLC (PA) ✪
670 Linwood Ave (01588-2068)
PHONE...............................774 757-4411
Ben Roesch, *Managing Member*
EMP: 7 **EST:** 2023
SALES (est): 97.92K
SALES (corp-wide): 97.92K **Privately Held**
SIC: 5181 2082 5813 Beer and ale; Malt
beverages; Drinking places

(G-13343)
OMNI CONTROL TECHNOLOGY INC
Also Called: Oct
1 Main St Ste 4 (01588-2201)
P.O. Box 444 (01588-0444)
PHONE...............................508 234-9121
Peter J Bedigian, *Prin*
Peter J Bedigian, *Prin*
EMP: 40 **EST:** 1992
SQ FT: 7,500
SALES (est): 11.07MM
SALES (corp-wide): 3.82B **Privately Held**
Web: www.omnicontroltech.com
SIC: 3625 Control equipment, electric
PA: Nibe Industrier Ab
Jarnvagsgatan 40
Markaryd 285 3
43373000

(G-13344)
QUALITY STONE MARBLE INC (PA)
91 Court St (01588-1942)
PHONE...............................774 813-4801
Andre Joaquim Duarte, *Pr*
EMP: 12 **EST:** 2014
SALES (est): 1.23MM
SALES (corp-wide): 1.23MM **Privately Held**
SIC: 2541 1799 Counter and sink tops;
Counter top installation

(G-13345)
RI KNITTING GROUP LLC
1 Main St Ste 10 (01588-2201)
PHONE...............................508 822-5333
EMP: 9 **EST:** 2018
SALES (est): 530.98K **Privately Held**
Web: www.riknitting.com
SIC: 2241 Narrow fabric mills

(G-13346)
TOM BERKOWITZ TRUCKING INC (PA)
279 Douglas Rd (01588-2021)
P.O. Box 90 (01588-0090)
PHONE...............................508 234-2920
Tom Berkowitz, *Pr*
EMP: 21 **EST:** 1981
SALES (est): 2.35MM
SALES (corp-wide): 2.35MM **Privately Held**
Web: www.berkowitztrucking.com
SIC: 3713 5064 Garbage, refuse truck
bodies; Garbage disposals

(G-13347)
WEST END FIREWOOD INC
496 Purgatory Rd (01588-1617)
P.O. Box 464 (01588-0464)
PHONE...............................508 234-4747
Duane Vandenakker, *Pt*
Bruce Vandenakker, *Pt*
EMP: 7 **EST:** 1990
SALES (est): 980.37K **Privately Held**
Web: www.westendfirewood.com
SIC: 5099 5989 2411 Firewood; Wood (fuel)
; Fuel wood harvesting

Whitman
Plymouth County

(G-13348)
COMPUTRON METAL PRODUCTS INC
66 Pond St (02382-2163)
P.O. Box 167 (02382-0167)
PHONE...............................781 447-2265
Russell J Leone, *Pr*
Russell J Leone, *Pr*
Joseph Gillis, *VP*
EMP: 30 **EST:** 1978
SQ FT: 10,000
SALES (est): 787.99K **Privately Held**
Web: www.computronmetal.com
SIC: 3444 Sheet metal specialties, not
stamped

(G-13349)
DIMARK INCORPORATED
Also Called: Precision Machining
205 Commercial St (02382-2401)
P.O. Box 271 (02382-0271)
PHONE...............................781 447-7990
John W Brown, *Pr*
EMP: 26 **EST:** 1979
SALES (est): 2.47MM **Privately Held**
Web: www.dimarkinc.net
SIC: 3444 Sheet metalwork

(G-13350)
TIME-OUT SPORTS INC
Also Called: Timeout Sportswear Promotions
7 Marble St (02382-2458)
P.O. Box 226 (02382-0226)
PHONE...............................781 447-6670
Joseph T Nickley Junior, *Pr*
Patrick Madigan, *VP*
John Nickley, *Clerk*
EMP: 10 **EST:** 1982

SQ FT: 11,000
SALES (est): 2.42MM **Privately Held**
Web: www.timeoutsportswear.com
SIC: 5131 5199 2395 2396 Textiles, woven,
nec; Advertising specialties; Embroidery
products, except Schiffli machine;
Automotive and apparel trimmings

(G-13351)
WATERTOWN ENGINEERING CORP
Also Called: Watertown Cremation Products
1200 Auburn St (02382-1728)
P.O. Box 308 (02382-0308)
PHONE...............................781 857-2555
Domenic Taverna, *Pr*
Mark Donovan, *
▲ **EMP:** 30 **EST:** 1957
SQ FT: 12,000
SALES (est): 2.85MM **Privately Held**
Web: www.watertownengineering.com
SIC: 3442 3272 Moldings and trim, except
automobile: metal; Burial vaults, concrete
or precast terrazzo

(G-13352)
WHITMAN CASTINGS INC (PA)
40 Raynor Ave (02382-2123)
P.O. Box 456 (02382-0456)
PHONE...............................781 447-4417
R Brian Ladner, *Pr*
James T Bruso, *
Ronald Ladner, *
Francis Ladner, *
EMP: 25 **EST:** 1992
SQ FT: 40,000
SALES (est): 2.97MM **Privately Held**
Web: www.whitmancastings.com
SIC: 3321 3542 3369 Gray iron castings,
nec; Machine tools, metal forming type;
Nonferrous foundries, nec

(G-13353)
WHITMAN COMPANY INC
356 South Ave Ste 1 (02382-2062)
PHONE...............................781 447-2422
TOLL FREE: 800
Peter J Lemonias, *Pr*
James P Lemonias, *
EMP: 30 **EST:** 1947
SQ FT: 45,000
SALES (est): 2.3MM **Privately Held**
Web: www.whitman-company.com
SIC: 3471 Electroplating of metals or
formed products

(G-13354)
WHITMAN TOOL & DIE COMPANY INC
72 Raynor Ave (02382-2123)
P.O. Box 248 (02382-0248)
PHONE...............................781 447-0421
Paul Werthen, *VP*
Aly Werthen, *
Thomas Werthen, *
Peter Werthen, *
EMP: 33 **EST:** 1949
SQ FT: 31,000
SALES (est): 4.19MM **Privately Held**
Web: www.whitmantoolanddie.com
SIC: 3469 3544 Stamping metal for the trade
; Special dies and tools

(G-13355)
WHITMAN VAULT INC
1200 Auburn St (02382-1728)
P.O. Box 308 (02382-0308)
PHONE...............................781 857-3031
Mark Donavon, *Pr*
EMP: 9 **EST:** 1989

SALES (est): 180.05K **Privately Held**
Web: www.whitmanburialvault.com
SIC: 3272 Burial vaults, concrete or precast
terrazzo

Wilbraham
Hampden County

(G-13356)
CS-MA LLC (PA)
Also Called: Construction Service
2420 Boston Rd (01095-1106)
P.O. Box 966 (01095-0966)
PHONE..............................413 733-6631
Shaun P Carroll Senior, *Managing Member*
EMP: 49 EST: 2008
SQ FT: 800
SALES (est): 7.31MM
SALES (corp-wide): 7.31MM **Privately
Held**
Web: www.constructionservice-ma.com
SIC: 3273 Ready-mixed concrete

(G-13357)
DAUPHINAIS & SON INC
Also Called: Construction Service Division
2420 Boston Rd (01095-1106)
P.O. Box 966 (01095-0966)
PHONE..............................413 596-3964
Vincent Dauphinais, *Ch Bd*
EMP: 25 EST: 1992
SQ FT: 2,000
SALES (est): 934.87K **Privately Held**
Web: www.jupitermarket.com
SIC: 3273 5211 5032 1741 Ready-mixed
concrete; Sand and gravel; Gravel;
Retaining wall construction

(G-13358)
FLODESIGN SONICS INC
380 Main St (01095-1639)
PHONE..............................413 596-5900
EMP: 20 EST: 2009
SALES (est): 7.79MM
SALES (corp-wide): 23.09B **Privately Held**
Web: www.fdsonics.com
SIC: 3841 Surgical and medical instruments
HQ: Emd Millipore Corporation
400 Summit Dr
Burlington MA 01803
800 645-5476

(G-13359)
FRANK L REED INC
Also Called: Utility Mfg Co
2443 Boston Rd (01095-1105)
P.O. Box 758 (01095-0758)
PHONE..............................413 596-3861
Loring Reed, *Pr*
Jeffrey Reed, *VP Opers*
Jay T Reed, *VP Engg*
▲ EMP: 20 EST: 1930
SQ FT: 40,000
SALES (est): 2.45MM **Privately Held**
Web: www.utilitymfg.com
SIC: 3315 3351 3496 3316 Wire products,
ferrous/iron: made in wiredrawing plants;
Wire, copper and copper alloy;
Miscellaneous fabricated wire products;
Cold finishing of steel shapes

(G-13360)
**FREEZE OPERATIONS HOLDING
CORP (PA)**
1855 Boston Rd (01095-1002)
PHONE..............................413 543-2445
Harshavardhan V Agadi, *Pr*
Robert K Sawyer, *Sr VP*

Steven C Sanchioni, *CFO*
EMP: 2776 EST: 2007
SALES (est): 38.26MM **Privately Held**
Web: www.friendlys.com
SIC: 5812 2024 5143 Restaurant, family:
chain; Ice cream and frozen deserts; Ice
cream and ices

(G-13361)
KEATING-WILBERT VAULT INC
1840 Boston Rd (01095-1001)
PHONE..............................413 543-1226
David A Dumala, *Pr*
EMP: 17 EST: 1976
SQ FT: 2,500
SALES (est): 2.46MM **Privately Held**
Web: www.keatingwilbert.com
SIC: 3272 5087 Burial vaults, concrete or
precast terrazzo; Concrete burial vaults and
boxes

(G-13362)
NORPIN MFG CO INC
2342 Boston Rd (01095-1104)
P.O. Box 1031 (01095-7031)
PHONE..............................413 599-1628
Norman T Pincince, *Pr*
Kenneth Pincince, *VP*
Mark Pincince, *Manager*
EMP: 14 EST: 1956
SQ FT: 33,000
SALES (est): 1.77MM **Privately Held**
Web: www.norpin.com
SIC: 3469 Stamping metal for the trade

(G-13363)
**SAFEHANDS DISTRIBUTION NE
LLC**
Also Called: Manufacturing/Distribution
35 Post Office Park Ste 3505 (01095-1172)
PHONE..............................413 244-1452
Neil Nordstrom, *Pr*
EMP: 15 EST: 2015
SQ FT: 250
SALES (est): 1.59MM **Privately Held**
Web: www.safehands.com
SIC: 5087 2842 Janitors' supplies;
Sanitation preparations, disinfectants and
deodorants

(G-13364)
YANKEE ELECTRICAL MFG CO
600 Main St (01095-1611)
PHONE..............................413 596-8256
Alfred E Carpluk, *Pr*
Dolores Carpluk, *Treas*
Stuart Carpluk, *VP*
Stephen Carpluk, *VP*
EMP: 9 EST: 1983
SQ FT: 30,000
SALES (est): 704.64K **Privately Held**
SIC: 3674 Solid state electronic devices, nec

Williamsburg
Hampshire County

(G-13365)
LASHWAY LOGGING INC
Also Called: Lashway Firewood Co
67 Main St (01096-9404)
P.O. Box 231 (01096-0231)
PHONE..............................413 268-3600
William J Lashway Junior, *Pr*
Lance Lashway, *VP*
Bryan Lashway, *VP*
Lee H Lashway, *Treas*
EMP: 15 EST: 1965
SQ FT: 15,000

SALES (est): 2.26MM **Privately Held**
Web: www.lashway.com
SIC: 2421 2499 2411 Lumber: rough,
sawed, or planed; Mulch, wood and bark;
Logging

Williamstown
Berkshire County

(G-13366)
FERRO CORPORATION
Also Called: Mra Laboratories
34 Holly Ln (01267-2939)
PHONE..............................413 743-3927
Samir G Maher, *Dir Opers*
EMP: 17
SALES (corp-wide): 1.88B **Privately Held**
Web: www.vibrantz.com
SIC: 8731 2865 Commercial physical
research; Dyes and pigments
HQ: Vibrantz Corporation
6060 Parkland Blvd # 250
Mayfield Heights OH 44124
216 875-5600

(G-13367)
**FIDELITY IND ADVSER
NEWSLETTER**
Also Called: Capital Growth Advertising
25 Main St (01267-2601)
P.O. Box 387 (01267-0387)
PHONE..............................413 458-4700
EMP: 20 EST: 1995
SQ FT: 2,000
SALES (est): 1.77MM **Privately Held**
SIC: 2741 Newsletter publishing

(G-13368)
STEINERFILM INC
Also Called: Steinerfilm USA
987 Simonds Rd (01267-2197)
PHONE..............................413 458-9525
Else Steiner, *Pr*
Else Steiner, *Prin*
Arthur Kazanjian, *
Robert C Rives Junior, *Sec*
◆ EMP: 160 EST: 1972
SQ FT: 198,900
SALES (est): 18.39MM **Privately Held**
Web: www.steinerfilm.com
SIC: 3675 Electronic capacitors

Wilmington
Middlesex County

(G-13369)
**ABACO SYSTEMS
TECHNOLOGY CORP**
50 Fordham Rd (01887-2177)
PHONE..............................256 382-8115
Bernie Anger, *Pr*
Alan Dillbero, *Ch Bd*
Bernie Anger, *CEO*
Christopher Lever, *VP*
George Hearn, *Ex VP*
EMP: 51 EST: 1978
SALES (est): 4.94MM
SALES (corp-wide): 6.15B **Publicly Held**
Web: www.abaco.com
SIC: 3571 Electronic computers
HQ: Abaco Systems Limited
Old Tiffield Road Tove Valley
Towcester NORTHANTS NN12

(G-13370)
**ACCELLENT ACQUISITION
CORP**
100 Fordham Rd Bldg C (01887-2168)
PHONE..............................978 570-6900
EMP: 3667
SIC: 3841 3317 3679 3315 Surgical and
medical instruments; Seamless pipes and
tubes; Microwave components; Wire
products, ferrous/iron: made in wiredrawing
plants

(G-13371)
ACCELLENT HOLDINGS CORP
100 Fordham Rd (01887-2168)
PHONE..............................978 570-6900
Ron Sparks, *Pr*
Stewart Fisher, *
EMP: 3667 EST: 2005
SQ FT: 3,000
SALES (est): 104.78MM **Privately Held**
SIC: 3841 3679 3315 3552 Surgical and
medical instruments; Microwave
components; Wire products, ferrous/iron:
made in wiredrawing plants; Dyeing, drying,
and finishing machinery and equipment

(G-13372)
ADA FABRICATORS INC
323 Andover St Ste 3 (01887-1035)
P.O. Box 179 (01862-0179)
PHONE..............................978 262-9900
John P Flaherty, *Pr*
William Scott Ober, *VP*
EMP: 17 EST: 1997
SQ FT: 25,000
SALES (est): 623.08K **Privately Held**
SIC: 3537 1542 Platforms, cargo;
Nonresidential construction, nec

(G-13373)
ADVANCED IMAGING INC
234 Ballardvale St (01887-1054)
PHONE..............................978 658-7776
John Macnamara, *Pr*
EMP: 28 EST: 1988
SQ FT: 20,000
SALES (est): 2.08MM **Privately Held**
Web: www.advimage.com
SIC: 2759 Commercial printing, nec

(G-13374)
**ADVANSOURCE BIOMATERIALS
CORPORATION**
Also Called: Chronoflex
229 Andover St (01887-1088)
PHONE..............................978 657-0075
▲ EMP: 11
Web: us.mitsubishi-chemical.com
SIC: 3841 Surgical and medical instruments

(G-13375)
AGFA CORPORATION
Also Called: AGFA Finance Group
200 Ballardvale St (01887-1074)
PHONE..............................978 658-5600
Raymond A Melillo, *Brnch Mgr*
EMP: 482
SQ FT: 7,500
SALES (corp-wide): 431.66MM **Privately
Held**
Web: www.agfa.com
SIC: 3861 Film, sensitized motion picture, X-
ray, still camera, etc.
HQ: Agfa Corporation
580 Gotham Pkwy
Carlstadt NJ 07072
800 540-2432

GEOGRAPHIC

(G-13376)
ALLCOAT TECHNOLOGY INC
100 Eames St (01887-3371)
PHONE..............................978 988-0880
Michael Lombard, *Pr*
Corine Parigian, *
EMP: 40 **EST:** 2006
SQ FT: 90,000
SALES (est): 9.12MM **Privately Held**
Web: www.allcoattech.com
SIC: 2822 2891 Ethylene-propylene
rubbers, EPDM polymers; Adhesives

(G-13377)
AMETEK INC
Ametek Aerospace & Defense
50 Fordham Rd (01887-2190)
PHONE..............................978 988-4101
EMP: 68
SALES (corp-wide): 6.15B **Publicly Held**
Web: www.ametek.com
SIC: 3621 3829 3825 3812 Motors and
generators; Measuring and controlling
devices, nec; Instruments to measure
electricity; Search and navigation equipment
PA: Ametek, Inc.
1100 Cassatt Rd
Berwyn PA 19312
610 647-2121

(G-13378)
**AMETEK AROSPC PWR
HOLDINGS INC (HQ)**
50 Fordham Rd (01887-2190)
PHONE..............................978 988-4771
Robert S Feit, *Sr VP*
Robert R Mandos, *
John J Molinelli, *
EMP: 83 **EST:** 2006
SALES (est): 116.47MM
SALES (corp-wide): 6.15B **Publicly Held**
Web:
www.ametekaerospaceanddefense.com
SIC: 3812 3724 Aircraft/aerospace flight
instruments and guidance systems; Aircraft
engines and engine parts
PA: Ametek, Inc.
1100 Cassatt Rd
Berwyn PA 19312
610 647-2121

(G-13379)
ANALOG DEVICES INC (PA)
Also Called: ADI
1 Analog Way (01887-2356)
P.O. Box 9106 (02062-9106)
PHONE..............................781 935-5565
Vincent Roche, *Ch Bd*
Richard C Puccio Junior, *Ex VP*
Janene Asgeirsson, *CLO CRO*
Anelise Sacks, *CCO*
Mariya Trickett, *CPO*
◆ **EMP:** 1000 **EST:** 1965
SQ FT: 826,000
SALES (est): 12.31B
SALES (corp-wide): 12.31B **Publicly Held**
Web: www.analog.com
SIC: 3674 Integrated circuits,
semiconductor networks, etc.

(G-13380)
ANALOG DEVICES INTL INC (HQ)
1 Analog Way (01887-2356)
PHONE..............................800 262-5643
Joseph E Mcdonough, *Pr*
EMP: 39 **EST:** 1976
SALES (est): 157.49MM
SALES (corp-wide): 12.31B **Publicly Held**
Web: www.analog.com

SIC: 3674 3825 Semiconductors and
related devices; Test equipment for
electronic and electric measurement
PA: Analog Devices, Inc.
1 Analog Way
Wilmington MA 01887
781 935-5565

(G-13381)
ASCENT AEROSYSTEMS INC
100 Research Dr Ste 3 (01887-4406)
PHONE..............................330 554-6334
Jan Peter Fuchs, *Prin*
EMP: 24 **EST:** 2015
SALES (est): 3.77MM **Privately Held**
Web: www.ascentaerosystems.com
SIC: 3721 Aircraft

(G-13382)
ASTEX PLASMAQUEST INC
90 Industrial Way (01887-4610)
PHONE..............................781 937-6272
John E Spencer, *Prin*
EMP: 7 **EST:** 2010
SALES (est): 137.38K **Privately Held**
SIC: 3674 Semiconductors and related
devices

(G-13383)
ATC TECHNOLOGIES INC
30b Upton Dr (01887-4455)
PHONE..............................781 939-0725
Paul Kierce, *Pr*
Paul C Kierce, *Pr*
John T Kierce, *Sec*
EMP: 20 **EST:** 1997
SQ FT: 10,000
SALES (est): 3.8MM **Privately Held**
Web: www.atctech.us
SIC: 3841 Surgical and medical instruments

(G-13384)
AZORES CORP
16 Jonspin Rd (01887-1093)
PHONE..............................978 253-6200
Elvino M Da Silveira, *Pr*
Steve Gardner, *VP*
Dave Bushong, *Sec*
▲ **EMP:** 14 **EST:** 1999
SQ FT: 10,000
SALES (est): 4.96MM
SALES (corp-wide): 1.01B **Publicly Held**
Web: www.ontoinnovation.com
SIC: 3672 Circuit boards, television and
radio printed
HQ: Rudolph Technologies, Inc.
16 Jonspin Rd
Wilmington MA 01887
978 253-6200

(G-13385)
**AZURITY PHARMACEUTICALS
INC (HQ)**
841 Woburn St (01887-3414)
PHONE..............................800 461-7449
Richard Blackburn, *CEO*
Amit Patel, *
Ronald L Scarboro, *
Neal I Muni, *
Vern Davenport, *
EMP: 13 **EST:** 1998
SALES (est): 55.81MM
SALES (corp-wide): 64.51MM **Privately
Held**
Web: www.azurity.com
SIC: 2834 Pharmaceutical preparations
PA: Novaquest Capital Management Llc
4208 Six Forks Rd Ste 920
Raleigh NC 27609
919 459-8620

(G-13386)
BACK BAY SIGN LLC
65i Industrial Way (01887-3499)
PHONE..............................781 475-1001
EMP: 15 **EST:** 1945
SQ FT: 18,000
SALES (est): 740.57K **Privately Held**
Web: www.backbaysign.com
SIC: 3993 Electric signs

(G-13387)
BACKBAY ROASTERS
10 Jewel Dr (01887-3350)
PHONE..............................844 532-6269
EMP: 7 **EST:** 2018
SALES (est): 152.85K **Privately Held**
SIC: 2095 2087 Roasted coffee; Beverage
bases, concentrates, syrups, powders and
mixes

(G-13388)
**BAUSCH & LOMB
INCORPORATED**
Bausch & Lomb
100 Research Dr Ste 2 (01887-4406)
PHONE..............................978 658-6111
Ruta Subatis, *Mgr*
EMP: 105
SALES (corp-wide): 8.05B **Privately Held**
Web: www.bausch.com
SIC: 3851 Ophthalmic goods
HQ: Bausch & Lomb Incorporated
400 Somerset Corp Blvd
Bridgewater NJ 08807
866 246-8245

(G-13389)
BCG CONNECT LLC
1 Jewel Dr (01887-3385)
PHONE..............................978 528-7999
▲ **EMP:** 25 **EST:** 2003
SALES (est): 6.05MM **Privately Held**
Web: www.bcgconnect.com
SIC: 5963 7389 2759 Direct sales,
telemarketing; Design services;
Commercial printing, nec

(G-13390)
**BEDROCK AUTOMTN
PLATFORMS INC**
Also Called: Bedrock Automation
1 Analog Way (01887-2356)
PHONE..............................781 821-0280
Robert Honor, *Pr*
EMP: 28 **EST:** 2013
SALES (est): 2.39MM **Privately Held**
SIC: 3823 Absorption analyzers: infrared, x-
ray, etc.: industrial

(G-13391)
BENEVENTO ASPHALT CORP
Also Called: Benevento Asphalt
900 Salem St (01887-1236)
P.O. Box 454 (01887-0454)
PHONE..............................978 658-5300
Charles J Benevento, *Pr*
EMP: 10 **EST:** 2001
SALES (est): 5.22MM **Privately Held**
Web: www.beneventocompanies.com
SIC: 1442 Construction sand and gravel

(G-13392)
**BENEVENTO SAND & STONE
CORP**
Also Called: Benevento Asphalt
200 Salem St (01887-1122)
P.O. Box 454 (01887-0454)
PHONE..............................978 658-4762

Charlie Benevento, *Pr*
EMP: 13 **EST:** 1954
SQ FT: 2,000
SALES (est): 5.82MM **Privately Held**
Web: www.beneventocompanies.com
SIC: 1442 Construction sand and gravel

(G-13393)
BIGREP AMERICA INC
50-E Concord St Ste 100 (01887-2357)
PHONE..............................781 281-0569
Frank Marangell, *Pr*
EMP: 150 **EST:** 2016
SALES (est): 10MM **Privately Held**
Web: www.bigrep.com
SIC: 2759 Laser printing

(G-13394)
**BRIDGESTONE RET
OPERATIONS LLC**
Also Called: Firestone
496 Main St (01887-3210)
PHONE..............................978 658-5660
Stephen Burke, *Mgr*
EMP: 8
Web: www.bridgestoneamericas.com
SIC: 5531 7534 Automotive tires;
Rebuilding and retreading tires
HQ: Bridgestone Retail Operations, Llc
333 E Lake St Ste 300
Bloomingdale IL 60108
630 259-9000

(G-13395)
**BROOKS INTERIORS GROUP
INC**
5 Waltham St Ste 3 (01887-2347)
PHONE..............................978 988-1300
William L Engstrom, *Pr*
Denman B Engstrom, *
EMP: 21 **EST:** 1987
SQ FT: 6,000
SALES (est): 892.26K **Privately Held**
Web: www.ltdofficesolutions.com
SIC: 5943 2522 Stationery stores; Panel
systems and partitions, office: except wood

(G-13396)
BURLINGTON MACHINE INC
340b Fordham Rd (01887-2169)
PHONE..............................978 284-6525
John P Haroutunian, *Pr*
EMP: 18 **EST:** 1987
SQ FT: 5,000
SALES (est): 1.67MM **Privately Held**
Web: www.burlingtonmachine.com
SIC: 3451 Screw machine products

(G-13397)
**CARDIOTECH INTERNATIONAL
INC**
229 Andover St (01887-1088)
PHONE..............................978 657-0075
EMP: 10 **EST:** 2019
SALES (est): 511.08K **Privately Held**
Web: us.mitsubishi-chemical.com
SIC: 3842 Surgical appliances and supplies

(G-13398)
COOKES SKATE SUPPLY INC
446 Main St (01887-3209)
PHONE..............................978 657-7586
Scott Cooke, *Pr*
Michael Bedell, *VP*
EMP: 8 **EST:** 1966
SQ FT: 10,000
SALES (est): 974.24K **Privately Held**
Web: www.cookesskatesupply.com

▲ = Import ▼ = Export
◆ = Import/Export

SIC: **3949** 5941   Ice skates, parts and accessories; Skating equipment

(G-13399)
COVESTRO LLC
730 Main St (01887-3366)
PHONE.............................800 458-0014
Jeffrey Brule, *Pr*
EMP: 140
SALES (corp-wide): 18.66B **Privately Held**
Web: www.covestro.com
SIC: **3479** 2851 2821 5162   Coating of metals with plastic or resins; Paints and allied products; Polyethylene resins; Resins
HQ: Covestro Llc
1 Covestro Cir
Pittsburgh PA 15205
412 413-2000

(G-13400)
CURIRX INC
205 Lowell St # 1c (01887-2972)
PHONE.............................978 658-2962
EMP: 25 **EST:** 2008
SALES (est): 5.56MM **Privately Held**
Web: www.curirx.com
SIC: **2834**   Pharmaceutical preparations

(G-13401)
DAGLE ELECTRICAL CNSTR CORP
68 Industrial Way (01887-3434)
PHONE.............................800 379-1459
Maureen Dagle, *Pr*
James Dagle, *
EMP: 100 **EST:** 1997
SALES (est): 24.93MM **Privately Held**
Web: www.deccorp.com
SIC: **1731** 1389   General electrical contractor ; Construction, repair, and dismantling services

(G-13402)
DAILY WOBURN TIMES INC
Also Called: Town Crier
1 Arrow Drive (01887)
PHONE.............................978 658-2346
Stu Neilson, *Genl Mgr*
EMP: 8
SALES (corp-wide): 4.92MM **Privately Held**
SIC: **2711**   Newspapers: publishing only, not printed on site
PA: Daily Woburn Times Inc
1 Arrow Dr Ste 1 # 1
Woburn MA 01801
781 933-3700

(G-13403)
DSM NEORESINS INC
Also Called: DSM Coating Resins
730 Main St (01887-3366)
PHONE.............................800 458-0014
◆ **EMP:** 140
SIC: **3479** 2851 2821 5162   Coating of metals with plastic or resins; Paints and allied products; Polyethylene resins; Resins

(G-13404)
E GS GAUGING INCORPORATED
200 Research Dr (01887-4442)
PHONE.............................978 262-3100
Carter Watson, *Prin*
EMP: 7 **EST:** 2011
SALES (est): 230.31K **Privately Held**
SIC: **3823**   Water quality monitoring and control systems

(G-13405)
ENERGY SCIENCES INC
Also Called: Esi
42 Industrial Way Ste 1 (01887-3471)
PHONE.............................978 694-9000
Tatsuyuki Kawajiri, *CEO*
Richard Danton, *
▲ **EMP:** 50 **EST:** 1971
SQ FT: 52,000
SALES (est): 13.14MM
SALES (corp-wide): 4.44B **Publicly Held**
Web: www.ebeam.com
SIC: **3565**   Packaging machinery
HQ: Iwasaki Denki K.K.
1-1-7, Higashinihombashi
Chuo-Ku TKY 103-0

(G-13406)
ENGELHARD SURFACE TECH
201 Ballardvale St (01887-1013)
PHONE.............................978 658-0032
Jay Walden, *Prin*
EMP: 9 **EST:** 2014
SALES (est): 171.85K **Privately Held**
Web: www.cwst.co.uk
SIC: **3398**   Metal heat treating

(G-13407)
FERRO-CERAMIC GRINDING INC
5 Cornell Pl (01887-2129)
PHONE.............................781 245-1833
EMP: 35 **EST:** 1966
SALES (est): 3.11MM **Privately Held**
Web: www.ferroceramic.com
SIC: **3599**   Machine shop, jobbing and repair

(G-13408)
FRITO-LAY NORTH AMERICA INC
Also Called: Frito-Lay
337 Ballardvale St (01887-1042)
PHONE.............................978 657-8344
Mike Shimansky, *Brnch Mgr*
EMP: 12
SALES (corp-wide): 86.39B **Publicly Held**
Web: www.fritolay.com
SIC: **2096** 5145   Potato chips and similar snacks; Confectionery
HQ: Frito-Lay North America, Inc.
7701 Legacy Dr
Plano TX 75024

(G-13409)
GERRITYSTONE INC
Also Called: Black Bear Granite
100a Eames St (01887-3371)
PHONE.............................781 938-1820
TOLL FREE: 800
▲ **EMP:** 45 **EST:** 1997
SQ FT: 40,000
SALES (est): 10.22MM
SALES (corp-wide): 20.36MM **Privately Held**
Web: www.gerritystone.com
SIC: **1799** 3281   Counter top installation; Cut stone and stone products
PA: Gerrity Enterprises, Incorporated
63b Bedford St
Lakeville MA 02347
617 916-0776

(G-13410)
HEILIND ELECTRONICS INC (PA)
Also Called: Maverick Electronics
58 Jonspin Rd (01887-1068)
P.O. Box 1320 (01887-7020)
PHONE.............................978 657-4870
Robert W Clapp, *CEO*
Hugo Passerelli Ctnrl, *Prin*
▲ **EMP:** 100 **EST:** 1974
SQ FT: 42,000
SALES (est): 591.87MM
SALES (corp-wide): 591.87MM **Privately Held**
Web: www.heilind.com
SIC: **5065** 3679 5063   Electronic parts; Harness assemblies, for electronic use: wire or cable; Hanging and fastening devices, electrical

(G-13411)
HUBBARD-HALL INC
100 Progress Way (01887-3424)
PHONE.............................978 988-0077
Molly Kellogg, *Brnch Mgr*
EMP: 10
SALES (corp-wide): 105.87MM **Privately Held**
Web: www.hubbardhall.com
SIC: **5169** 3471 2899 2842   Chemicals, industrial and heavy; Finishing, metals or formed products; Chemical preparations, nec; Polishes and sanitation goods
PA: Hubbard-Hall Inc.
563 S Leonard St
Waterbury CT 06708
203 756-5521

(G-13412)
IBC ADVANCED ALLOYS INC-BELAC
55 Jonspin Rd (01887-1020)
PHONE.............................978 284-8900
Raymond L White Iii, *Pr*
EMP: 25
SALES (corp-wide): 26.91MM **Privately Held**
Web: www.ibcadvancedalloys.com
SIC: **3599**   Machine shop, jobbing and repair
PA: Ibc Advanced Alloys Corp
1200-570 Granville St
Vancouver BC V6C 3
604 685-6263

(G-13413)
IMPLANT SCIENCES CORP
500 Research Dr Ste 3 (01887-4400)
PHONE.............................978 752-1700
EMP: 25 **EST:** 2018
SALES (est): 799.19K **Privately Held**
Web: www.implantsciences.com
SIC: **3812**   Search and navigation equipment

(G-13414)
INNOVATIVE FOODS INC
Also Called: Good Wives
330 Ballardvale St (01887-1012)
PHONE.............................781 596-0070
EMP: 140
SIC: **2038**   Frozen specialties, nec

(G-13415)
INNOVION CORPORATION
Also Called: Innovion
265 Ballardvale St (01887-1036)
PHONE.............................978 267-4064
EMP: 11
SALES (corp-wide): 5.16B **Publicly Held**
Web: www.ii-vi.com
SIC: **3674**   Semiconductors and related devices
HQ: Innovion Corporation
2121 Zanker Rd
San Jose CA 95131
408 501-9140

(G-13416)
INSPECTROLOGY LLC
35 Upton Dr (01887-1018)
PHONE.............................978 212-3100

Neil Casa, *Managing Member*
Michael J Kessler, *
Paul C Knutrud, *
▲ **EMP:** 24 **EST:** 2008
SALES (est): 7.02MM
SALES (corp-wide): 1.01B **Publicly Held**
Web: www.ontoinnovation.com
SIC: **3825**   Semiconductor test equipment
PA: Onto Innovation Inc.
16 Jonspin Rd
Wilmington MA 01887
978 253-6200

(G-13417)
J & K CABINETS LTD
66 Industrial Way # 68 (01887-3434)
PHONE.............................978 658-1888
Anna Lam, *Pr*
Chiu Fan Lee, *Sec*
▲ **EMP:** 9 **EST:** 2010
SALES (est): 206.51K **Privately Held**
SIC: **2434**   Wood kitchen cabinets

(G-13418)
JG MACHINE CO INC
21b Concord St (01887-2131)
PHONE.............................978 447-5279
John M Graney, *Pr*
EMP: 10 **EST:** 1964
SQ FT: 2,500
SALES (est): 1.01MM **Privately Held**
Web: www.jgmachineco.com
SIC: **3599**   Machine shop, jobbing and repair

(G-13419)
KENTRON TECHNOLOGIES INC
155 West St Ste 10 (01887-6010)
PHONE.............................978 988-9100
EMP: 7 **EST:** 1996
SALES (est): 183.31K **Privately Held**
Web: www.kentrontech.com
SIC: **3577**   Computer peripheral equipment, nec

(G-13420)
KIRKWOOD HOLDINGS INC (PA)
Also Called: Kirkwood Direct
904 Main St (01887-3319)
PHONE.............................978 658-4200
Robert Coppinger, *Pr*
Edward Kelley, *VP*
William Winship Iv, *Treas*
John Cummings, *Sec*
▲ **EMP:** 255 **EST:** 1973
SQ FT: 48,000
SALES (est): 51.43MM
SALES (corp-wide): 51.43MM **Privately Held**
Web: www.kirkwoodus.com
SIC: **2752** 2791 2789 2759   Offset printing; Typesetting; Bookbinding and related work; Commercial printing, nec

(G-13421)
KOVALUS SPRATION SOLUTIONS LLC (PA)
Also Called: Koch Membrane Solutions
850 Main St (01887-3367)
P.O. Box 9133 (02150-9133)
PHONE.............................978 694-7000
Manwinder Singh, *Pr*
David H Koch, *
Philip M Moynihan, *
David Dotson, *
Robert J Gibson Junior, *Dir*
◆ **EMP:** 200 **EST:** 1988
SQ FT: 122,000
SALES (est): 112.86MM
SALES (corp-wide): 112.86MM **Privately Held**

Web: www.kochmembrane.com
SIC: **3569** 3564   Separators for steam, gas, vapor, or air (machinery); Air purification equipment

(G-13422)
L3 TECHNOLOGIES INC
L3 Ssg
65 Jonspin Rd (01887-1020)
PHONE..................978 694-9991
EMP: 150
SALES (corp-wide): 17.06B **Publicly Held**
Web: www.l3harris.com
SIC: 3827   Optical instruments and lenses
HQ: L3 Technologies, Inc.
600 3rd Ave Fl 34
New York NY 10016
321 727-9100

(G-13423)
**LAKE REGION
MANUFACTURING INC (HQ)**
Also Called: Lake Region Medical
100 Fordham Rd Ste 3 (01887-2154)
PHONE..................952 361-2515
Donald J Spence, *Ch Bd*
Joe Fleischhacker, *
EMP: 890 **EST:** 1947
SQ FT: 159,000
SALES (est): 299.07MM
SALES (corp-wide): 1.38B **Publicly Held**
Web: www.lakeregionmanufacturing.com
SIC: 3841 3845   Surgical instruments and apparatus; Electromedical equipment
PA: Integer Holdings Corporation
5830 Gran Pkwy Ste 1150
Plano TX 75024
214 618-5243

(G-13424)
**LAKE REGION MEDICAL INC
(HQ)**
Also Called: Lake Region Medical
100 Fordham Rd Ste 3 (01887-2168)
PHONE..................978 570-6900
Donald J Spence, *Pr*
Richard E Johnson, *Treas*
Ron Honig, *Sec*
▲ **EMP:** 45 **EST:** 2000
SQ FT: 55,000
SALES (est): 585.3MM
SALES (corp-wide): 1.38B **Publicly Held**
Web: www.integer.net
SIC: 3841   Surgical and medical instruments
PA: Integer Holdings Corporation
5830 Gran Pkwy Ste 1150
Plano TX 75024
214 618-5243

(G-13425)
**LARGO CLEAN ENERGY CORP
(HQ)**
500 Research Dr Ste 1 (01887-4400)
PHONE..................978 566-8220
Stephen Prince, *Pr*
Joe Chau, *CEO*
EMP: 40 **EST:** 2020
SALES (est): 16.48MM
SALES (corp-wide): 809.7K **Privately Held**
Web: www.largoinc.com
SIC: 3692   Primary batteries, dry and wet
PA: Largo Canada Limited
100 Adelaide St W Suite 804
Toronto ON M5H 1
416 362-2122

(G-13426)
LOCUS ROBOTICS CORP (PA)
301 Ballardvale St Ste 4 (01887-4405)

PHONE..................844 562-8700
John Hayes, *Ch*
Rick Faulk, *CEO*
Micheal Johnson, *Pr*
Dustin Pederson, *CFO*
EMP: 10 **EST:** 2015
SQ FT: 40,000
SALES (est): 49.71MM
SALES (corp-wide): 49.71MM **Privately Held**
Web: www.locusrobotics.com
SIC: 3569   Robots, assembly line: industrial and commercial

(G-13427)
**LUBRIZOL GLOBAL
MANAGEMENT INC**
Lubrizol
207 Lowell St (01887-2941)
PHONE..................978 642-5051
EMP: 124
SALES (corp-wide): 302.09B **Publicly Held**
Web: www.lubrizol.com
SIC: 2899 5169   Chemical preparations, nec ; Chemicals and allied products, nec
HQ: Lubrizol Global Management, Inc.
9911 Brecksville Rd
Cleveland OH 44141
216 447-5000

(G-13428)
**MEDSOURCE TECH HOLDINGS
LLC (DH)**
100 Fordham Rd Bldg C (01887-2168)
PHONE..................978 570-6900
Richard Effress, *Ch Bd*
Joseph Caffarelli, *Sr VP*
Daniel Croteau, *VP*
Jim Drill, *Marketing*
William J Kullback, *Sr VP*
EMP: 17 **EST:** 1999
SQ FT: 7,000
SALES (est): 168.34MM
SALES (corp-wide): 1.38B **Publicly Held**
SIC: 3841 8711   Surgical and medical instruments; Engineering services
HQ: Accellent Llc
10000 Fordham Rd
Clarence NY 75024
978 570-6900

(G-13429)
**MEDSOURCE TECHNOLOGIES
LLC (DH)**
100 Fordham Rd Ste 1 (01887-2154)
PHONE..................978 570-6900
EMP: 10 **EST:** 1970
SQ FT: 41,000
SALES (est): 55.53MM
SALES (corp-wide): 1.38B **Publicly Held**
SIC: 3841 3842   Surgical and medical instruments; Surgical appliances and supplies
HQ: Medsource Technologies Holdings, Llc
100 Fordham Rd Bldg C
Wilmington MA 01887
978 570-6900

(G-13430)
**METAL IMPROVEMENT
COMPANY LLC**
Also Called: Curtiss-Wright Surface Tech
201 Ballardvale St (01887-1013)
PHONE..................978 658-0032
EMP: 97
SALES (corp-wide): 2.56B **Publicly Held**
Web: www.curtisswright.com
SIC: 3398   Shot peening (treating steel to reduce fatigue)

HQ: Metal Improvement Company, Llc
80 E Rte 4 Ste 310
Paramus NJ 07652
201 843-7800

(G-13431)
METRO GROUP INC
155 West St Ste 3 (01887-3064)
PHONE..................781 932-9911
Michael Flayhive, *Brnch Mgr*
EMP: 15
SALES (corp-wide): 22.94MM **Privately Held**
Web: district.metrogroupinc.com
SIC: 3589   Water treatment equipment, industrial
PA: Metro Group, Inc.
5023 23rd St
Long Island City NY 11101
718 729-7200

(G-13432)
**MITSUBISHI CHEMICAL AMER
INC**
229 Andover St (01887-1088)
PHONE..................978 657-0075
Steve Gregory, *Mgr*
EMP: 11
Web: www.mitsubishichemicalholdings.com
SIC: 3841   Surgical and medical instruments
HQ: Mitsubishi Chemical America, Inc.
9115 Harris Corners Pkwy # 300
Charlotte NC 28269
980 580-2839

(G-13433)
MKS INSTRUMENTS INC
Also Called: M K S Astex Products
90 Industrial Way (01887-4610)
PHONE..................978 284-4000
Paul Loomis, *Genl Mgr*
EMP: 150
SALES (corp-wide): 3.55B **Publicly Held**
Web: www.mks.com
SIC: 3823   Pressure measurement instruments, industrial
PA: Mks Instruments, Inc.
2 Tech Dr Ste 201
Andover MA 01810
978 645-5500

(G-13434)
MKS MSC INC
90 Industrial Way (01887-4610)
PHONE..................978 284-4000
John R Bertucci, *Pr*
EMP: 96 **EST:** 1986
SALES (est): 2.5MM
SALES (corp-wide): 3.55B **Publicly Held**
Web: www.mks.com
SIC: 3823 3491 3494   Pressure measurement instruments, industrial; Pressure valves and regulators, industrial; Valves and pipe fittings, nec
PA: Mks Instruments, Inc.
2 Tech Dr Ste 201
Andover MA 01810
978 645-5500

(G-13435)
**MONKS MANUFACTURING CO
INC**
1 Upton Dr (01887-1018)
PHONE..................978 657-8282
Ian L Monks, *Pr*
Lee Monks, *Clerk*
Terry Monks, *Dir*
EMP: 21 **EST:** 1973
SQ FT: 12,000
SALES (est): 3.42MM **Privately Held**

Web: www.monksmfg.com
SIC: 3599   Machine shop, jobbing and repair

(G-13436)
NATALE CO SAFETYCARE LL
11 Eames St (01887-3313)
PHONE..................781 933-7205
John Natale, *Owner*
EMP: 7 **EST:** 2010
SALES (est): 241.21K **Privately Held**
SIC: 3312   Bars and bar shapes, steel, hot-rolled

(G-13437)
NEU-TOOL DESIGN INC
Also Called: Bio-Mold Division
220 Ballardvale St Ste A (01887-1050)
PHONE..................978 658-5881
John Neuman, *Pr*
EMP: 20 **EST:** 1986
SQ FT: 12,000
SALES (est): 3.04MM **Privately Held**
Web: www.ntmedical.com
SIC: 3089 3544   Injection molding of plastics ; Forms (molds), for foundry and plastics working machinery

(G-13438)
NEUROTHERM INC
Also Called: Precision Medical Engineering
600 Research Dr Ste 1 (01887-4438)
PHONE..................888 655-3500
EMP: 47
Web: www.neurotherm.com
SIC: 3841   Diagnostic apparatus, medical

(G-13439)
NOEVEON INC
207 Lowell St (01887-2941)
PHONE..................978 642-5004
Michael Voltero, *Prin*
▲ **EMP:** 8 **EST:** 2008
SALES (est): 135.07K **Privately Held**
SIC: 3679   Electronic components, nec

(G-13440)
ONTO INNOVATION INC (PA)
Also Called: Onto Innovation
16 Jonspin Rd (01887-1093)
PHONE..................978 253-6200
Michael P Plisinski, *CEO*
Christopher A Seams, *
Mark R Slicer, *CFO*
Ramil Yaldaei, *COO*
Yoon Ah E Oh, *Corporate Secretary*
EMP: 122 **EST:** 1975
SQ FT: 77,500
SALES (est): 1.01B
SALES (corp-wide): 1.01B **Publicly Held**
Web: www.ontoinnovation.com
SIC: 3829   Measuring and controlling devices, nec

(G-13441)
OPHIR OPTICS LLC
Also Called: Ophir
90 Industrial Way (01887-4610)
PHONE..................978 657-6410
Dennis Cope, *Managing Member*
Jeffrey B Coyne, *Managing Member**
Julie Long, *
◆ **EMP:** 98 **EST:** 2002
SQ FT: 38,000
SALES (est): 25.15MM
SALES (corp-wide): 3.55B **Publicly Held**
Web: www.ophiropt.com
SIC: 3827   Optical instruments and apparatus
HQ: Newport Corporation
1791 Deere Ave

Irvine CA 92606
949 863-3144

(G-13442)
OPTO-LINE INTERNATIONAL INC
265 Ballardvale St Ste 3 (01887-1036)
PHONE..............................978 658-7255
John Arnault, *Pr*
John Sumner, *Treas*
EMP: 10 **EST:** 1985
SQ FT: 10,000
SALES (est): 936.96K **Privately Held**
Web: www.opto-line.com
SIC: 3827 Optical instruments and lenses

(G-13443)
OPTRA INC
4 Jacquith Rd (01887-2212)
PHONE..............................978 887-6600
EMP: 16
Web: www.optra.com
SIC: 8731 3827 3829 3826 Electronic research; Optical instruments and apparatus ; Measuring and controlling devices, nec; Analytical instruments

(G-13444)
OSRAM SYLVANIA INC (DH)
Also Called: Osram Sylvania
200 Ballardvale St Ste 305 (01887-1075)
PHONE..............................978 570-3000
Grant Wright, *CEO*
Mark Quinn, *CFO*
◆ **EMP:** 950 **EST:** 1993
SALES (est): 2.01B
SALES (corp-wide): 5B **Privately Held**
Web: www.sylvania-automotive.com
SIC: 3646 3641 3647 3643 Commercial lighting fixtures; Electric lamps; Headlights (fixtures), vehicular; Current-carrying wiring services
HQ: Osram Licht Ag
Marcel-Breuer-Str. 4
Munchen BY 80807
8962130

(G-13445)
PACIFIC PACKAGING PRODUCTS INC (PA)
Also Called: Pacific Global Packaging South
24 Industrial Way (01887-3434)
P.O. Box 697 (01887-0697)
PHONE..............................978 657-9100
David A Varsano, *
Frank D Goldstein, *
Robert H Goldstein, *
David A Varsano, *
Andrew P Goldstein, *
◆ **EMP:** 152 **EST:** 1952
SQ FT: 193,000
SALES (est): 77.02MM
SALES (corp-wide): 77.02MM **Privately Held**
Web: www.pacificpkg.com
SIC: 5199 5084 5162 2671 Packaging materials; Packaging machinery and equipment; Plastics materials and basic shapes; Paper; coated and laminated packaging

(G-13446)
PEPSI-COLA METRO BTLG CO INC
Also Called: Pepsi-Cola
111 Eames St (01887-3323)
PHONE..............................978 661-6150
Stacey Bartlett, *Mgr*
EMP: 98

SALES (corp-wide): 86.39B **Publicly Held**
Web: www.pepsico.com
SIC: 2086 Bottled and canned soft drinks
HQ: Pepsi-Cola Metropolitan Bottling Company, Inc.
700 Anderson Hill Rd
Purchase NY 10577
914 767-6000

(G-13447)
POLYCHROMIX
30 Upton Dr (01887-1017)
PHONE..............................978 284-6000
Brian Mitchell, *Pr*
Stephen Senturia, *Ch Bd*
Micheal Butler, *VP*
Chandra Mouli Ramanai, *VP*
Richard Payne, *VP*
EMP: 16 **EST:** 2000
SQ FT: 4,809
SALES (est): 2.49MM **Privately Held**
SIC: 3827 Optical instruments and apparatus

(G-13448)
PVD PRODUCTS INC
Also Called: Pvd
35 Upton Dr Ste 200 (01887-1018)
PHONE..............................978 694-9455
EMP: 32 **EST:** 1995
SQ FT: 7,500
SALES (est): 11.2MM
SALES (corp-wide): 11.2MM **Privately Held**
Web: www.pvdproducts.com
SIC: 3826 Laser scientific and engineering instruments
PA: High Temperature Superconductors, Inc.
320 N Nopal St
Santa Barbara CA 93103
805 698-0528

(G-13449)
RIGAKU ANALYTICAL DEVICES INC
30 Upton Dr Ste 2 (01887-1017)
PHONE..............................855 785-1064
Yoichi Yokomizo, *COO*
Alicia Kimsey, *
▲ **EMP:** 30 **EST:** 2011
SQ FT: 6,000
SALES (est): 6.45MM **Privately Held**
Web: handhelds.rigaku.com
SIC: 3812 3826 3823 Search and detection systems and instruments; Spectroscopic and other optical properties measuring equip.; Industrial process control instruments
HQ: Rigaku Corporation Of America
9009 New Trails Dr
The Woodlands TX 77381
281 362-2300

(G-13450)
RUDOLPH TECHNOLOGIES INC (HQ)
Also Called: Rudolph Technologies
16 Jonspin Rd (01887-1093)
PHONE..............................978 253-6200
Michael P Plisinski, *CEO*
Srini Vedula, *
Yoon Ah Oh, *VP*
Mark Slicer, *
Ramil Yaldaei, *
EMP: 56 **EST:** 1940
SALES (est): 125.49MM
SALES (corp-wide): 1.01B **Publicly Held**
Web: www.ontoinnovation.com

SIC: 3829 Measuring and controlling devices, nec
PA: Onto Innovation Inc.
16 Jonspin Rd.
Wilmington MA 01887
978 253-6200

(G-13451)
SCREENPRINT/DOW INC
200 Research Dr Ste 6 (01887-4432)
PHONE..............................978 657-7290
Walter T Dowgiallo, *Pr*
John E Morrison, *
Robert Boileau, *
Bill Donovan, *
George Ford, *
EMP: 74 **EST:** 1969
SQ FT: 30,000
SALES (est): 12.99MM **Privately Held**
Web: www.screenprintdow.com
SIC: 2679 Labels, paper: made from purchased material

(G-13452)
SCULLY SIGNAL COMPANY (PA)
Also Called: Scully Data Systems
70 Industrial Way (01887-3479)
PHONE..............................617 692-8600
Katrina Scully Ohl, *Pr*
Robert G Scully, *
James P Maselan, *
▲ **EMP:** 100 **EST:** 1936
SQ FT: 70,000
SALES (est): 24.87MM
SALES (corp-wide): 24.87MM **Privately Held**
Web: www.scully.com
SIC: 3823 3494 7374 3825 Controllers, for process variables, all types; Couplings, except pressure and soil pipe; Data processing and preparation; Instruments to measure electricity

(G-13453)
SMYTH COMPANIES LLC
271 Ballardvale St (01887-1081)
PHONE..............................800 776-1201
Domenic Mancini, *Mgr*
EMP: 50
Web: www.smythco.com
SIC: 2679 Labels, paper: made from purchased material
HQ: Smyth Companies, Llc
1675 Meadowview Rd
Saint Paul MN 55121
651 646-4544

(G-13454)
SONOSYSTEMS N SCHUNK AMER CORP (DH)
250 Andover St (01887-1048)
PHONE..............................978 658-9400
David Norquist, *Pr*
David Da Rin, *
Stefan Trube, *
▲ **EMP:** 31 **EST:** 1986
SQ FT: 15,000
SALES (est): 8.81MM
SALES (corp-wide): 1.3B **Privately Held**
Web: www.schunk-sonosystems.com
SIC: 3699 Welding machines and equipment, ultrasonic
HQ: Schunk Sonosystems Gmbh
Hauptstr. 95
Wettenberg HE 35435
6418030

(G-13455)
SPECTRA MEDICAL DEVICES LLC

299 Ballardvale St Ste 1 (01887-1065)
PHONE..............................978 657-0889
Chad Nikel, *Managing Member*
EMP: 300 **EST:** 2021
SALES (est): 64MM **Privately Held**
Web: www.spectramedical.com
SIC: 3841 Surgical and medical instruments

(G-13456)
SPECTRO ANALYTICAL INSTRUMENTS INC (HQ)
50 Fordham Rd (01887-2177)
P.O. Box 301155 (75303-1155)
PHONE..............................201 642-3000
EMP: 25 **EST:** 1998
SALES (est): 24.2MM
SALES (corp-wide): 6.15B **Publicly Held**
SIC: 3826 Spectroscopic and other optical properties measuring equip.
PA: Ametek, Inc.
1100 Cassatt Rd
Berwyn PA 19312
610 647-2121

(G-13457)
SSG OPTRONICS
65 Jonspin Rd (01887-1020)
PHONE..............................978 694-9991
Dexter Wang, *Pr*
EMP: 7 **EST:** 2013
SALES (est): 274.62K **Privately Held**
SIC: 3812 Search and navigation equipment

(G-13458)
STAFFORD MANUFACTURING CORP (PA)
256 Andover St (01887-1003)
P.O. Box 277 (01864-0277)
PHONE..............................978 657-8000
Arthur Stafford, *Pr*
▲ **EMP:** 39 **EST:** 1975
SQ FT: 30,000
SALES (est): 4.92MM
SALES (corp-wide): 4.92MM **Privately Held**
Web: www.staffordmfg.com
SIC: 3568 Couplings, shaft: rigid, flexible, universal joint, etc.

(G-13459)
STUFFED FOODS LLC
14 Jewel Dr Ste 3 (01887-3361)
PHONE..............................978 203-0370
▲ **EMP:** 47 **EST:** 2010
SALES (est): 5.41MM **Privately Held**
Web: www.stuffed-foods.com
SIC: 2038 Frozen specialties, nec

(G-13460)
SYMBOTIC LLC (HQ)
200 Research Dr (01887-4442)
PHONE..............................978 284-2800
Richard B Cohen, *CEO*
EMP: 175 **EST:** 2007
SALES (est): 349.49MM
SALES (corp-wide): 15.34B **Privately Held**
Web: www.symbotic.com
SIC: 3549 Assembly machines, including robotic
PA: C&S Wholesale Grocers, Llc
7 Corporate Dr
Keene NH 03431
603 354-7000

(G-13461)
T2 BIOSYSTEMS INC
Also Called: T2 Biosystems Manufacturing
231 Andover St (01887-1001)
PHONE..............................978 447-1069

EMP: 40
Web: www.t2biosystems.com
SIC: 8731 3841 Biotechnical research, commercial; Surgical and medical instruments
PA: T2 Biosystems, Inc.
101 Hartwell Ave
Lexington MA 02421

(G-13462)
TECOMET INC
301 Ballardvale St Ste 3 (01887-4405)
PHONE..............................978 642-2400
EMP: 292
SALES (corp-wide): 832.81MM **Privately Held**
Web: www.tecomet.com
SIC: 3841 3324 3365 3369 Diagnostic apparatus, medical; Aerospace investment castings, ferrous; Aerospace castings, aluminum; Aerospace castings, nonferrous; except aluminum
HQ: Tecomet Inc.
115 Eames St
Wilmington MA 01887
978 642-2400

(G-13463)
TECOMET INC (HQ)
Also Called: Tecomet
115 Eames St (01887-3380)
PHONE..............................978 642-2400
Victor Swint, *CEO*
John Connolly, *
Art Burghouwt, *
Dan Howell, *
Vlad Miskovic, *
EMP: 180 **EST:** 1963
SALES (est): 832.81MM
SALES (corp-wide): 832.81MM **Privately Held**
Web: www.tecomet.com
SIC: 3444 3841 Sheet metalwork; Diagnostic apparatus, medical
PA: Tecostar Holdings, Inc.
18 Commerce Way Ste 500
Woburn MA 01801
978 642-2400

(G-13464)
TERADIODE INC
Also Called: Teradiode
30 Upton Dr (01887-1017)
PHONE..............................978 988-1040
Parviz Tayebati, *Pr*
Bien Chann, *VP*
Fred Leonberger, *Dir*
Robin Huang, *VP*
Damon Pender, *CFO*
▲ **EMP:** 75 **EST:** 2009
SQ FT: 35,000
SALES (est): 18.82MM **Privately Held**
Web: na.panasonic.com
SIC: 3699 Laser systems and equipment
PA: Panasonic Holdings Corporation
1006, Kadoma
Kadoma OSK 571-0

(G-13465)
TEXTRON SYSTEMS CORPORATION
201 Lowell St (01887-4113)
PHONE..............................978 657-5111
EMP: 25
SALES (corp-wide): 12.87B **Publicly Held**
Web: www.textronsystems.com
SIC: 3711 3714 3483 Personnel carriers (motor vehicles), assembly of; Motor vehicle body components and frame; Ammunition, except for small arms, nec

HQ: Textron Systems Corporation
124 Industry Ln
Hunt Valley MD 21030
800 655-2616

(G-13466)
TEXTRON SYSTEMS CORPORATION (DH)
Also Called: Textron Defense Systems
201 Lowell St (01887-4113)
PHONE..............................978 657-5111
Ellen Lord, *Pr*
Mary F Lovejoy, *Treas*
Ian Walsh, *CIO*
Jack Cronin, *COO*
▲ **EMP:** 45 **EST:** 1986
SALES (est): 105.08MM
SALES (corp-wide): 12.87B **Publicly Held**
Web: www.textronsystems.com
SIC: 3483 5088 Ammunition components; Transportation equipment and supplies
HQ: Textron Lycoming Corp
40 Westminster St
Providence RI 02903
401 421-2800

(G-13467)
TNEMEC EAST INC
Also Called: Tnemec
11 Upton Dr (01887-1018)
PHONE..............................978 988-9500
TOLL FREE: 800
Harold Righter, *Pr*
Martin E Greenblat, *Clerk*
EMP: 47 **EST:** 1958
SQ FT: 6,000
SALES (est): 448.13K **Privately Held**
Web: www.tnemec.com
SIC: 2851 Paints and allied products

(G-13468)
TOWNSEND WELDING CO INC
815 Woburn St (01887-3414)
PHONE..............................978 657-5189
Carl F Townsend, *Pr*
Edwin Townsend, *Pr*
Edwin J Townsend, *Treas*
EMP: 42 **EST:** 1967
SQ FT: 11,000
SALES (est): 908.61K **Privately Held**
Web: www.twtic.com
SIC: 1711 1799 3312 7692 Mechanical contractor; Welding on site; Blast furnaces and steel mills; Welding repair

(G-13469)
TRACELINK INC (PA)
200 Ballardvale St Ste 100 (01887-1075)
PHONE..............................781 914-4900
Shabbir M Dahod, *Pr*
Mike Mozzer, *
Peter Spellman, *CLOUD*
Lucy Deus, *
Brian Daleiden, *
EMP: 144 **EST:** 2009
SALES (est): 112.85MM
SALES (corp-wide): 112.85MM **Privately Held**
Web: www.tracelink.com
SIC: 7372 Prepackaged software

(G-13470)
TRANE INC
Also Called: Trane
181 Ballardvale St Ste 201 (01887-1191)
PHONE..............................978 737-3900
Jack Borgschulte, *Brnch Mgr*
EMP: 87
Web: www.trane.com

SIC: 3585 Refrigeration and heating equipment
HQ: Trane Inc.
1 Centennial Ave Ste 101
Piscataway NJ 08854
732 652-7100

(G-13471)
TREXEL INC (PA)
Also Called: Axiomatics
100 Research Dr Ste 1 (01887-4406)
PHONE..............................781 932-0202
Levi Kishbaugh, *CEO*
Petr Janik, *
Brent Strawbridge, *
▲ **EMP:** 18 **EST:** 1982
SQ FT: 15,000
SALES (est): 5.83MM
SALES (corp-wide): 5.83MM **Privately Held**
Web: www.trexel.com
SIC: 3089 3086 Injection molding of plastics ; Plastics foam products

(G-13472)
UNIFIRST CORPORATION (PA)
Also Called: Unifirst
68 Jonspin Rd (01887-1086)
PHONE..............................978 658-8888
Steven S Sintros, *Pr*
Raymond C Zemlin, *
Shane O'connor, *Ex VP*
David M Katz, *Executive Sales & Marketing Vice President*
David A Difillippo, *Ofcr*
▲ **EMP:** 325 **EST:** 1936
SALES (est): 2.23B
SALES (corp-wide): 2.23B **Publicly Held**
Web: www.unifirst.com
SIC: 7218 2326 Industrial clothing launderers; Men's and boy's work clothing

(G-13473)
UNIVERSAL COLOR CORP INC
377 Ballardvale St Unit 1 (01887-1042)
PHONE..............................978 658-2300
Kevin T Coneeny, *Pr*
EMP: 14 **EST:** 2005
SALES (est): 2.33MM **Privately Held**
Web: www.universalcolorcorp.com
SIC: 2893 5999 Printing ink; Alcoholic beverage making equipment and supplies

(G-13474)
VIANT AS&O HOLDINGS LLC
100 Fordham Rd (01887-2168)
PHONE..............................866 899-1392
Andrew Fritz, *VP*
EMP: 26 **EST:** 2018
SALES (est): 2.16MM
SALES (corp-wide): 1.18B **Privately Held**
SIC: 3841 Surgical and medical instruments
PA: Viant Medical Holdings, Inc.
2 Hampshire St
Foxborough MA 02035
480 553-6400

(G-13475)
WALPOLE OUTDOORS LLC
168 Lowell St (01887-2974)
PHONE..............................978 658-3373
Steven Schultz, *Brnch Mgr*
EMP: 20
SALES (corp-wide): 50.41MM **Privately Held**
Web: www.walpoleoutdoors.com
SIC: 2499 5712 2452 3448 Fencing, wood; Outdoor and garden furniture; Prefabricated wood buildings; Prefabricated metal buildings and components

PA: Walpole Outdoors Llc
255 Patriot Pl
Foxboro MA 02035
508 668-2800

(G-13476)
WILMINGTON PARTNERS LP
Also Called: Polymer Technology
100 Research Dr Ste 2 (01887-4406)
PHONE..............................978 658-6111
▼ **EMP:** 250 **EST:** 1853
SALES (est): 26.13MM
SALES (corp-wide): 8.05B **Privately Held**
Web: www.ciudadoptica.com
SIC: 3851 2834 Contact lenses; Solutions, pharmaceutical
HQ: Bausch & Lomb Incorporated
400 Somerset Corp Blvd
Bridgewater NJ 08807
866 246-8245

(G-13477)
XENON CORPORATION (PA)
Also Called: Xenon
37 Upton Dr (01887-4453)
PHONE..............................978 661-9033
Louis R Panico, *CEO*
C Richard Panico, *
▲ **EMP:** 26 **EST:** 1964
SQ FT: 7,608
SALES (est): 5.02MM
SALES (corp-wide): 5.02MM **Privately Held**
Web: www.xenoncorp.com
SIC: 3648 Lighting equipment, nec

Winchendon
Worcester County

(G-13478)
BELLECRAFT WOODWORKING CO INC
540 River St (01475-1054)
PHONE..............................978 297-2672
Thomas Belletete, *VP*
Thomas Belletete, *VP*
Andre P Belletete, *Pr*
EMP: 15 **EST:** 1960
SQ FT: 37,500
SALES (est): 474.96K **Privately Held**
Web: www.bellecraft.com
SIC: 2511 Wood household furniture

(G-13479)
F W LOMBARD COMPANY (PA)
246 Lakeview Dr (01475-2319)
P.O. Box 539 (01430-0539)
PHONE..............................978 827-5333
Carl F Mellin Junior, *Pr*
Robert Joyal, *
EMP: 30 **EST:** 1911
SQ FT: 30,000
SALES (est): 2.29MM
SALES (corp-wide): 2.29MM **Privately Held**
Web: www.fwlombard.com
SIC: 2521 Wood office chairs, benches and stools

(G-13480)
MYLEC INC (PA)
37 Commercial Dr (01475-3006)
P.O. Box 500 (01477)
PHONE..............................978 297-0089
Ricky Laperriere, *Pr*
Ricky P Laperriere, *
◆ **EMP:** 60 **EST:** 1970
SQ FT: 140,000

SALES (est): 6.24MM
SALES (corp-wide): 6.24MM **Privately Held**
Web: www.mylec.com
SIC: 3949 Sporting and athletic goods, nec

(G-13481)
RELIABLE
77 Mill St (01475-1120)
PHONE..................978 230-2689
Shane Walker, *Prin*
EMP: 8 EST: 2008
SALES (est): 228.55K Privately Held
Web: www.reliablegokarts.net
SIC: 3559 Anodizing equipment

(G-13482)
SALOOM FURNITURE CO INC
256 Murdock Ave (01475-1127)
PHONE..................800 297-1901
Peter Saloom, *Pr*
Linda Saloom, *
▲ **EMP: 88 EST: 1978**
SQ FT: 80,000
SALES (est): 9.41MM Privately Held
Web: www.saloom.com
SIC: 2511 Tables, household: wood

Winchester
Middlesex County

(G-13483)
CARRIAGE HSE DEVELOPMENTS LLC
253 Swanton St (01890-1938)
PHONE..................339 221-4253
Mario C Covino, *Managing Member*
EMP: 11 EST: 2009
SALES (est): 516.8K Privately Held
SIC: 2541 7389 Counter and sink tops; Design services

(G-13484)
FIRST PRINT INC
109 Cambridge St (01890-3740)
P.O. Box 865 (01890-8165)
PHONE..................781 729-7714
Thomas Accardo, *Pr*
Edna Accardo, *Treas*
EMP: 10 EST: 1983
SALES (est): 427.04K Privately Held
Web: www.firstprintinc.com
SIC: 2396 Screen printing on fabric articles

(G-13485)
LAR PLASTICS LLC
3 Arbor Ln (01890-1650)
PHONE..................617 860-2020
Leonardo Marino, *Managing Member*
Carlos Trostli, *
EMP: 328 EST: 2021
SALES (est): 14.37MM Privately Held
SIC: 3089 5099 Injection molded finished plastics products, nec; Containers: glass, metal or plastic

(G-13486)
LAVO USA LLC ✪
98 Thornberry Rd (01890-3244)
PHONE..................781 600-4123
David Keeney, *Ex Dir*
EMP: 47 EST: 2022
SALES (est): 1.51MM Privately Held
SIC: 3629 Electrical industrial apparatus, nec

(G-13487)
MILLENNIUM PHARMACEUTICALS INC
50 Harvard St (01890-1216)
PHONE..................781 729-7435
Edward Levesque, *Brnch Mgr*
EMP: 85
Web: www.takedaoncology.com
SIC: 2834 Pharmaceutical preparations
HQ: Millennium Pharmaceuticals, Inc.
40 Landsdowne St
Cambridge MA 02139

(G-13488)
MJW MASS INC
Also Called: M P I
37 East St (01890-1155)
P.O. Box 845563 (02284-5563)
PHONE..................781 721-0332
Edward J Alois, *Pr*
James R Hart, *
◆ **EMP: 70 EST: 1986**
SQ FT: 37,500
SALES (est): 21.39MM Privately Held
Web: www.mpirelease.com
SIC: 3089 Plastics processing

(G-13489)
OLYMPIC SYSTEMS CORPORATION
15 Lowell Ave (01890-1194)
PHONE..................781 721-2740
James Putney, *Pr*
Simon Bedigian, *
Peter G Johannsen, *
EMP: 50 EST: 1983
SQ FT: 20,000
SALES (est): 6.17MM Privately Held
Web: www.olympicsystemscorp.com
SIC: 3599 Machine shop, jobbing and repair

(G-13490)
OPEN SESAME PUBLISHING
45 Yale St (01890-2428)
PHONE..................781 856-8142
David Shiang, *Prin*
EMP: 8 EST: 2014
SALES (est): 123.46K Privately Held
SIC: 2741 Miscellaneous publishing

(G-13491)
PHILIP RS SORBET CO INC
Also Called: Frozen Desserts
750 Main St (01890-4310)
PHONE..................781 721-6330
Phili Rotondo, *Pr*
▲ **EMP: 10 EST: 1994**
SQ FT: 3,500
SALES (est): 1.01MM Privately Held
Web: www.icecream-desserts.com
SIC: 2024 Ice cream, bulk

(G-13492)
TECA-PRINT USA CORP
2a Lowell Ave (01890-1130)
PHONE..................781 369-1084
Liam Clancy, *Dir*
Jean-louis Dubuit, *Pr*
EMP: 15 EST: 1989
SQ FT: 13,000
SALES (est): 2.15MM Privately Held
Web: www.tecaprintusa.com
SIC: 3555 Printing trades machinery

(G-13493)
VERIZON NEW YORK INC
Also Called: Verizon
954 Main St (01890-1927)
PHONE..................781 721-5957

Reo R Surran, *Dir*
EMP: 10
SALES (corp-wide): 133.97B Publicly Held
Web: www.verizon.com
SIC: 4813 4812 2741 8721 Local telephone communications; Cellular telephone services; Directories, telephone: publishing only, not printed on site; Billing and bookkeeping service
HQ: Verizon New York Inc.
140 West St
New York NY 10007
212 395-1000

Woburn
Middlesex County

(G-13494)
A & G CENTERLESS GRINDING INC
15 Linscott Rd (01801-2001)
PHONE..................781 281-0007
Guy Agri, *Pr*
EMP: 18 EST: 1978
SQ FT: 20,000
SALES (est): 2.36MM Privately Held
Web: www.agcenterless.com
SIC: 3599 Machine shop, jobbing and repair

(G-13495)
A GROUP INC
Also Called: Pocathane Technologies
76 Holton St (01801-5205)
PHONE..................781 756-3163
Carl Papalano, *Mgr*
EMP: 46
SALES (corp-wide): 4.73MM Privately Held
Web: www.mpirelease.com
SIC: 2621 Specialty papers
PA: A Group, Inc.
37 East St
Winchester MA 01890
781 729-8300

(G-13496)
AA PHARMACEUTICALS INC
470 Wildwood Ave Ste 3 (01801-2082)
PHONE..................617 935-1241
Dongli Chen, *Pr*
EMP: 8 EST: 2009
SALES (est): 154.88K Privately Held
SIC: 2834 Pharmaceutical preparations

(G-13497)
ABPRO CORPORATION
Also Called: Abpro
68 Cummings Park (01801-2124)
PHONE..................617 225-0808
Ian Chan, *Ch Bd*
Eugene Y Chan, *
Benjamin Ha, *
Adam S Mostafa, *CFO*
Gavin Macbeath, *CSO*
EMP: 42 EST: 2007
SQ FT: 15,000
SALES (est): 7.17MM Privately Held
Web: www.abpro.com
SIC: 2834 2835 Pharmaceutical preparations; Diagnostic substances

(G-13498)
ADDEN FURNITURE INC
444 Washington St Ste 206 (01801-1072)
PHONE..................978 454-7848
◆ **EMP: 100**
Web: www.moduform.com

SIC: 2531 Public building and related furniture

(G-13499)
ADVANCED WELDING & DESIGN INC
6 Draper St (01801-4522)
PHONE..................781 938-7644
John Canney, *Pr*
EMP: 16 EST: 1986
SQ FT: 10,000
SALES (est): 2.34MM Privately Held
Web: www.advancedweldinganddesign.com
SIC: 7692 Welding repair

(G-13500)
ADVANDX INC
400 Tradecenter Ste 6990 (01801-7476)
PHONE..................866 376-0009
EMP: 30
SIC: 2835 Diagnostic substances

(G-13501)
ADVISOR PERSPECTIVES INC
10 State St 2nd Fl (01801-6820)
P.O. Box 380 (02420-0004)
PHONE..................781 376-0050
Robert Keith Huebscher, *Pr*
EMP: 21 EST: 2007
SALES (est): 658.82K Privately Held
Web: www.advisorperspectives.com
SIC: 2741 Business service newsletters: publishing and printing

(G-13502)
AERO BRAZING CORPORATION
223 New Boston St (01801-6214)
PHONE..................781 933-7511
Richard G Mizzoni, *Pr*
Nicholas Zajka, *Treas*
Metrophane Zajka, *Sec*
EMP: 10 EST: 1974
SQ FT: 7,000
SALES (est): 454.59K Privately Held
Web: www.aerobrazing.com
SIC: 7692 Brazing

(G-13503)
ALDEN-HAUK INC
215 Salem St Ste G (01801-2078)
PHONE..................781 281-0154
Geno A Impemba Junior, *Pr*
EMP: 12 EST: 1931
SQ FT: 5,500
SALES (est): 1.66MM Privately Held
Web: www.aldenhauk.com
SIC: 2752 Offset printing

(G-13504)
ALIVIA ANALYTICS LLC
400 Tradecenter Ste 5900 (01801-7471)
PHONE..................617 227-5111
Michael Taylor, *Managing Member*
Alex Kormurshoff, *COO*
Kirk Schultz, *CFO*
EMP: 42 EST: 2021
SALES (est): 2.91MM Privately Held
SIC: 7372 Publisher's computer software

(G-13505)
ALIVIA CAPITAL LLC (PA)
Also Called: Alivia Technology
400 Tradecenter Ste 5900 (01801-7471)
PHONE..................781 569-5212
EMP: 8 EST: 2009
SALES (est): 1.77MM Privately Held
Web: www.aliviaanalytics.com

SIC: 7372 Application computer software

(G-13506)
ALMUSNET INC
400 Tradecenter Ste 4900 (01801-7468)
PHONE......................781 933-1846
Kewan Khawaja, *Pr*
EMP: 40 EST: 2016
SALES (est): 500K **Privately Held**
Web: www.almusnet.com
SIC: 7372 Educational computer software
HQ: Techlogix, Inc.
   400 Tradecenter Ste 4900
   Woburn MA 01801
   781 933-1846

(G-13507)
AMERICAN ULT CRYOGENICS INC (PA)
30 Briarwood Rd (01801-1265)
PHONE......................781 491-0888
Thomas Pasakarnis, *Pr*
Thomas Pasakarnis, *Pr*
Zuyu Zhao, *
Scott Azer, *
▲ EMP: 46 EST: 1960
SALES (est): 9.66MM
SALES (corp-wide): 9.66MM **Privately Held**
Web: www.janis.com
SIC: 3826 Analytical instruments

(G-13508)
AMERICAN ULT CRYOGENICS LLC
Also Called: Janisult
30 Briarwood Rd (01801-1265)
PHONE......................781 491-0999
EMP: 21 EST: 2011
SALES (est): 4.86MM
SALES (corp-wide): 9.66MM **Privately Held**
SIC: 3826 Analytical instruments
PA: American Ult Cryogenics, Inc.
   30 Briarwood Rd
   Woburn MA 01801
   781 491-0888

(G-13509)
AMF OPTICAL SOLUTIONS LLC
30 Nashua St Ste 3 (01801-4566)
PHONE......................781 933-6125
Jeff Kenton, *Managing Member*
Robert Lafieniere, *Pr*
Alice M Faiola, *Cnslt*
EMP: 10 EST: 1975
SQ FT: 10,000
SALES (est): 1.06MM **Privately Held**
Web: www.amfoptics.com
SIC: 3827 5049 Lenses, optical: all types
   except ophthalmic; Optical goods

(G-13510)
ANALYTIX BUS SOLUTIONS LLC (PA)
Also Called: Analytix Solutions
800 W Cummings Park Ste 2000
(01801-6351)
PHONE......................781 503-9000
EMP: 9 EST: 2006
SALES (est): 2.54MM
SALES (corp-wide): 2.54MM **Privately Held**
Web: www.analytix.com
SIC: 8721 7372 7373 Accounting, auditing,
   and bookkeeping; Business oriented
   computer software; Computer-aided design
   (CAD) systems service

(G-13511)
ANTHONY INDUSTRIES INC
5r Green St (01801-4392)
PHONE......................781 305-3750
Marc Antetomaso, *Prin*
EMP: 8 EST: 2017
SALES (est): 427.82K **Privately Held**
SIC: 3999 Manufacturing industries, nec

(G-13512)
ARBORJET INC
99 Blueberry Hill Rd (01801-5266)
PHONE......................781 935-9070
Peter Wild, *Pr*
EMP: 27 EST: 2000
SQ FT: 6,000
SALES (est): 7.46MM **Privately Held**
Web: www.arborjet.com
SIC: 3545 Arbors (machine tool accessories)

(G-13513)
ARCAM CAD TO METAL INC
6 Gill St (01801-1721)
PHONE......................781 281-1718
Eric Bert, *Prin*
EMP: 22 EST: 2015
SALES (est): 7.07MM
SALES (corp-wide): 76.56B **Publicly Held**
SIC: 3365 3842 3444 3699 Aerospace
   castings, aluminum; Trusses, orthopedic
   and surgical; Sheet metalwork; Electron
   beam metal cutting, forming or welding
   machines
HQ: Arcam Ab
   Designvagen 2
   MOlnlycke 435 3

(G-13514)
ARCH MED & AROSPC WOBURN LLC ◊
Also Called: M & K Engineering
166 New Boston St (01801-6204)
PHONE......................781 933-1760
Paul Barck, *Pr*
EMP: 52 EST: 2022
SALES (est): 11.15MM
SALES (corp-wide): 50.28MM **Privately Held**
Web: www.mkeng.com
SIC: 3599 Machine shop, jobbing and repair
PA: Arch Medical Solutions Corp.
   25040 Easy St
   Warren MI 48089
   603 760-1554

(G-13515)
ARISTON ENGRAVING & MCH CO INC
56 Dragon Ct (01801-1014)
PHONE......................781 935-2328
Nicholas Pappas, *Pr*
George Geranis, *Genl Mgr*
EMP: 8 EST: 1964
SQ FT: 6,500
SALES (est): 856.56K **Privately Held**
Web: www.aristonengraving.com
SIC: 3479 Etching and engraving

(G-13516)
ASE (US)INC
400 Tradecenter Ste 4950 (01801-7467)
PHONE......................781 305-5900
Chris Langhammer, *Brnch Mgr*
EMP: 7
Web: www.aseglobal.com
SIC: 3674 Integrated circuits,
   semiconductor networks, etc.
HQ: Ase (U.S.)Inc.
   1255 E Arques Ave

   Sunnyvale CA 94085
   408 636-9500

(G-13517)
ASYMCHEM BOSTON CORPORATION
Also Called: Asymchem
10 Gill St Ste J (01801-1721)
PHONE......................781 896-3998
Peng Dai, *Dir*
Xinhui Hu, *Pr*
EMP: 9 EST: 2020
SALES (est): 911.79K **Privately Held**
SIC: 2833 Medicinals and botanicals

(G-13518)
AXIOM MICRODEVICES INC
20 Sylvan Rd (01801-1845)
PHONE......................781 376-3000
Brett Butler, *CEO*
Bruce Warren, *CFO*
David Kang, *VP Engg*
Donald Mcclymont, *VP Mktg*
EMP: 20 EST: 2002
SALES (est): 1.32MM
SALES (corp-wide): 4.77B **Publicly Held**
Web: www.skyworksinc.com
SIC: 3663 Amplifiers, RF power and IF
PA: Skyworks Solutions, Inc.
   5260 California Ave # 100
   Irvine CA 92617
   949 231-3000

(G-13519)
BALYO INC (HQ)
78b Olympia Ave (01801-2057)
PHONE......................781 281-7957
Denis Lussault, *Pr*
EMP: 8 EST: 2013
SQ FT: 14,000
SALES (est): 9.35MM
SALES (corp-wide): 20.91MM **Privately Held**
Web: www.balyo.com
SIC: 3569 Robots, assembly line: industrial
   and commercial
PA: Balyo
   74 Avenue Vladimir Ilitch Lenine
   Arcueil 94110

(G-13520)
BARBOUR STOCKWELL INC
45 6th Rd (01801-1757)
PHONE......................781 933-5200
Kenneth Maillar, *Pr*
Robert Gautlier, *VP*
Anthony Enos, *VP*
▲ EMP: 20 EST: 1858
SQ FT: 20,000
SALES (est): 6.36MM **Privately Held**
Web: www.barbourstockwell.com
SIC: 8734 3829 Product testing laboratories
   ; Testing equipment: abrasion, shearing
   strength, etc.

(G-13521)
BATAVIA BIOSCIENCES INC
300 Tradecenter Ste 6650 (01801-7436)
PHONE......................781 305-3921
EMP: 9 EST: 2010
SALES (est): 12.43MM **Privately Held**
Web: www.bataviabiosciences.com
SIC: 5122 2834 Pharmaceuticals;
   Pharmaceutical preparations
HQ: Batavia Biosciences B.V.
   Zernikedreef 16
   Leiden ZH

(G-13522)
BERGEN PIPE SUPPORTS INC (HQ)
Also Called: Pipe Supports Group
225 Merrimac St (01801-1756)
PHONE......................781 935-9550
Danny Burns, *CEO*
James Bonetti, *
David Lynch, *
Mike Spellman, *
Donald Culkin, *
EMP: 30 EST: 1964
SQ FT: 5,000
SALES (est): 10.22MM
SALES (corp-wide): 881.42MM **Privately Held**
Web: www.pipesupports.com
SIC: 3498 Tube fabricating (contract
   bending and shaping)
PA: Hill & Smith Plc
   Westhaven House
   Solihull W MIDLANDS B90 4
   121 704-7430

(G-13523)
BEYOND SHAKER LLC
124a Cummings Park (01801-2128)
PHONE......................617 461-6608
EMP: 8 EST: 2010
SALES (est): 239.45K **Privately Held**
Web: www.beyondtheshaker.com
SIC: 2099 Seasonings and spices

(G-13524)
BIOFRONTERA INC (HQ)
Also Called: Biofrontera
120 Presidential Way Ste 330 (01801-1182)
PHONE......................781 245-1325
Hermann Lubbert, *Ex Ch Bd*
Erica Monaco, *CFO*
▲ EMP: 16 EST: 1992
SQ FT: 16,128
SALES (est): 28.67MM **Publicly Held**
Web: www.biofrontera-us.com
SIC: 2834 Pharmaceutical preparations
PA: Biofrontera Ag
   Hemmelrather Weg 201
   Leverkusen NW 51377

(G-13525)
BIOSE INDUSTRIE INC
12 Gill St Ste 5700 (01801-1754)
PHONE......................617 460-1842
EMP: 18 EST: 2020
SALES (est): 217.78K **Privately Held**
SIC: 2836 Biological products, except
   diagnostic

(G-13526)
BITFLOW INC
400 W Cummings Park Ste 5050
(01801-6524)
PHONE......................781 932-2900
Avner A Butnaru, *CEO*
Reynold J Dodson, *Pr*
James W Moore, *Legal Advisor*
EMP: 11 EST: 1993
SQ FT: 5,163
SALES (est): 1.94MM **Privately Held**
Web: www.bitflow.com
SIC: 3672 7371 Printed circuit boards;
   Custom computer programming services

(G-13527)
BLACK DIAMOND GROUP INC
Also Called: Work and Tactical Gear
400 Tradecenter Ste 2990 (01801-7459)
PHONE......................781 939-7824
Alan Lunder, *CEO*
Robert Mills, *Pr*

Michael Teixeira, *Ex VP*
▲ **EMP:** 12 **EST:** 2004
SALES (est): 2.28MM **Privately Held**
Web: www.bdboots.com
SIC: 3021 5139   Rubber and plastics footwear; Footwear

(G-13528)
BOMAS MACHINE SPECIALTIES INC
6 Jefferson Ave (01801-4325)
PHONE.............................617 628-3831
Joseph Annese, *Pr*
Mary Annese, *Treas*
Teresea Annese, *Treas*
EMP: 10 **EST:** 1959
SALES (est): 966.84K **Privately Held**
Web: www.bomas.com
SIC: 3851   Lens grinding, except prescription: ophthalmic

(G-13529)
BOSTON AMERICA CORP
55 6th Rd Ste 8 (01801-1746)
PHONE.............................781 933-3535
Matthew Kavet, *Pr*
◆ **EMP:** 15 **EST:** 1995
SALES (est): 2.55MM **Privately Held**
Web: www.bostonamerica.com
SIC: 3499   Novelties and giftware, including trophies

(G-13530)
BOSTON CENTERLESS INC (PA)
11 Presidential Way (01801-1040)
PHONE.............................781 994-5000
Steven Tamasi, *CEO*
Steven Tamasi, *CEO*
Norman C Spector, *
EMP: 80 **EST:** 1958
SQ FT: 45,000
SALES (est): 27.01MM
SALES (corp-wide): 27.01MM **Privately Held**
Web: www.bostoncenterless.com
SIC: 3541 3545   Grinding machines, metalworking; Precision measuring tools

(G-13531)
BOSTON ELCTRMETALLURGICAL CORP (PA)
Also Called: Boston Metal
6c Gill St (01801-1721)
PHONE.............................781 281-7657
Tadeu Carneiro, *Ch*
Antoine Allanore, *Sec*
Bruce Osterling, *Treas*
EMP: 48 **EST:** 2012
SALES (est): 11.01MM
SALES (corp-wide): 11.01MM **Privately Held**
Web: www.bostonmetal.com
SIC: 3312   Electrometallurgical steel

(G-13532)
BOSTON WELDING & DESIGN INC
7 Micro Dr (01801-5701)
PHONE.............................781 932-0035
Robert Diorio, *Pr*
Evelyn Diorio, *Sec*
EMP: 15 **EST:** 1991
SQ FT: 20,000
SALES (est): 2.49MM **Privately Held**
Web: www.bostonwelding.com
SIC: 7692   Welding repair

(G-13533)
BOSTONCOUNTERS LLC
78h Olympia Ave (01801-2057)
PHONE.............................781 281-1622
Jon Mancini, *Managing Member*
Todd Mancini, *Managing Member*
Cleider Marques, *Managing Member*
Scott Mccollem, *Managing Member*
EMP: 9 **EST:** 2013
SALES (est): 989.56K **Privately Held**
Web: www.bostoncounters.com
SIC: 2511 2514   Kitchen and dining room furniture; Metal kitchen and dining room furniture

(G-13534)
BOYD CORPORATION (WOBURN) INC (DH)
55 Dragon Ct (01801-1039)
PHONE.............................781 933-7300
▲ **EMP:** 190 **EST:** 1982
SALES (est): 65.25MM **Privately Held**
Web: www.boydcorp.com
SIC: 3585 3443   Parts for heating, cooling, and refrigerating equipment; Heat exchangers, condensers, and components
HQ: Boyd Corporation
    5960 Inglewood Dr Ste 115
    Pleasanton CA 94588
    209 236-1111

(G-13535)
BRANNEN BROTHERS-FLUTEMAKERS
Also Called: Brannen Flutes
58 Dragon Ct (01801-1014)
PHONE.............................781 935-9522
Bickford W Brannen, *Pr*
Birgitte M Flanders, *Sec*
EMP: 26 **EST:** 1977
SQ FT: 111,000
SALES (est): 5.39MM **Privately Held**
Web: www.brannenflutes.com
SIC: 3931   Flutes and parts

(G-13536)
BRIDGELINE DIGITAL INC (PA)
Also Called: BRIDGELINE DIGITAL
100 Sylvan Rd Ste G700 (01801)
PHONE.............................781 376-5555
Roger Kahn, *Pr*
Joni Kahn, *Ch Bd*
Thomas R Windhausen, *CFO*
EMP: 31 **EST:** 2000
SQ FT: 3,600
SALES (est): 15.88MM
SALES (corp-wide): 15.88MM **Publicly Held**
Web: www.bridgeline.com
SIC: 7372 7371   Prepackaged software; Computer software development

(G-13537)
BUSINESS SIGNS LLC
Also Called: Fastsigns
155a New Boston St (01801-6201)
PHONE.............................781 808-3153
EMP: 9 **EST:** 2019
SALES (est): 472.55K **Privately Held**
Web: www.fastsigns.com
SIC: 3993   Signs and advertising specialties

(G-13538)
CAES MISSION SYSTEMS LLC
Also Called: Herley New England
10 Sonar Dr (01801-5704)
PHONE.............................781 729-9450
Richard Poirier, *Brnch Mgr*
EMP: 125

SALES (corp-wide): 2.44B **Privately Held**
Web: www.ultra.group
SIC: 3679   Microwave components
HQ: Caes Mission Systems Llc
    3061 Industry Dr
    Lancaster PA 17603
    717 397-2777

(G-13539)
CAMBRIDGE POLYMER GROUP INC
100 Sylvan Rd Ste 200 (01801-9700)
PHONE.............................617 629-4400
Stephen Spiegelberg, *Pr*
Gavin Braithwaite, *VP*
EMP: 23 **EST:** 1996
SQ FT: 14,500
SALES (est): 3.42MM **Privately Held**
Web: www.campoly.com
SIC: 2821 8734 8731   Molding compounds, plastics; Testing laboratories; Biotechnical research, commercial

(G-13540)
CARPENTER & PATERSON INC
225 Merrimac St (01801-1756)
PHONE.............................781 935-7036
Dennis Bourrell, *Brnch Mgr*
EMP: 38
SALES (corp-wide): 35.68MM **Privately Held**
Web: www.pipehangers.com
SIC: 3494   Valves and pipe fittings, nec
PA: Carpenter & Paterson, Inc.
    434 Latigue Rd
    Westwego LA 70094
    504 431-7722

(G-13541)
CENTRAL ADMXTURE PHRM SVCS INC
55 6th Rd (01801-1767)
PHONE.............................781 376-0032
Arthur Dahl, *Prin*
EMP: 7
SALES (corp-wide): 2.67MM **Privately Held**
Web: www.capspharmacy.com
SIC: 2834 5122   Pharmaceutical preparations; Pharmaceuticals
HQ: Central Admixture Pharmacy Services, Inc.
    6430 Oak Cyn Ste 200
    Irvine CA 92618

(G-13542)
CLAYTON LLC DBA BLBIRD GRPHIC
Also Called: Bluebird Graphic Solutions
17 Everberg Rd Ste E (01801-1019)
PHONE.............................617 250-8500
EMP: 20 **EST:** 2011
SQ FT: 8,500
SALES (est): 4.66MM **Privately Held**
Web: www.bluebirdgs.com
SIC: 3993 3446 7336   Signs and advertising specialties; Architectural metalwork; Commercial art and graphic design

(G-13543)
COATING APPLICATION TECH
219 New Boston St (01801-6214)
PHONE.............................781 491-0699
Robert R Withee, *CEO*
Joseph W Selbeck, *
EMP: 13 **EST:** 2010
SALES (est): 1.57MM **Privately Held**
Web: www.coatingapplication.com

SIC: 3479   Coating of metals and formed products

(G-13544)
CONANT CONTROLS INC
215 Salem St Ste K (01801-2061)
P.O. Box 310 (02155-0004)
PHONE.............................781 395-2240
Stanley M Lewis, *Pr*
EMP: 20 **EST:** 1946
SQ FT: 15,000
SALES (est): 1.4MM **Privately Held**
Web: www.conantcontrols.com
SIC: 3592 3494 3492 3491   Valves; Valves and pipe fittings, nec; Fluid power valves and hose fittings; Industrial valves

(G-13545)
CONNOLLY PRINTING LLC
17b Gill St (01801-1768)
PHONE.............................781 932-8885
EMP: 15 **EST:** 2007
SALES (est): 1.29MM **Privately Held**
Web: www.connollyprinting.com
SIC: 2752   Offset printing

(G-13546)
CONTINENTAL METAL PDTS CO INC
Also Called: Cmp
35 Olympia Ave (01801-2045)
P.O. Box 2295 (01888-0495)
PHONE.............................781 935-4400
Paul Siegal, *Pr*
Stephen Siegal, *
EMP: 45 **EST:** 1948
SQ FT: 60,000
SALES (est): 5.95MM **Privately Held**
Web: www.continentalmetal.com
SIC: 3842 3589   Surgical appliances and supplies; Cooking equipment, commercial

(G-13547)
CONTINUPRINT INC
247 Salem St (01801-2004)
P.O. Box 2464 (01888-0864)
PHONE.............................781 933-1800
Michael Colameta, *Pr*
Michael Colameta, *Prin*
Theresa Colameta, *Clerk*
EMP: 8 **EST:** 1988
SALES (est): 1.58MM **Privately Held**
Web: www.beyondprinting.com
SIC: 5112 2761   Business forms; Manifold business forms

(G-13548)
CONTINUUS PHARMACEUTICALS INC
25r Olympia Ave (01801-6307)
PHONE.............................781 281-0115
Salvatore Mascia, *Pr*
Bayan Takizawa, *Chief Business Officer*
EMP: 14 **EST:** 2012
SALES (est): 5.4MM **Privately Held**
Web: www.continuuspharma.com
SIC: 2869 8732   Industrial organic chemicals, nec; Business research service

(G-13549)
COVARIS INC
14 Gill St Unit H (01801-1721)
PHONE.............................781 932-3959
James A Laughann, *Pr*
EMP: 40 **EST:** 1999
SQ FT: 90,000
SALES (est): 19.57MM **Privately Held**
Web: www.covarisinc.com

SIC: 3826 Analytical instruments

(G-13550)
COVIDIEN LP
Also Called: Medtronic
12 Gill St Ste 3500 (01801-1782)
PHONE....................................800 962-9888
EMP: 81
Web: www.covidien.com
SIC: 3841 Surgical and medical instruments
HQ: Covidien Lp
15 Hampshire St
Mansfield MA 02048
763 514-4000

(G-13551)
CROWN EQUIPMENT CORPORATION
Also Called: Crown Lift Trucks
2 Presidential Way (01801-1041)
PHONE....................................781 933-3366
Andy Crampton, Brnch Mgr
EMP: 78
SALES (corp-wide): 7.12B Privately Held
Web: www.crown.com
SIC: 3537 Lift trucks, industrial: fork, platform, straddle, etc.
PA: Crown Equipment Corporation
44 S Washington St
New Bremen OH 45869
419 629-2311

(G-13552)
CUSTOM AROSPC COMPONENTS LLC
30 Nashua St Ste 3 (01801-4566)
PHONE....................................781 935-4940
Joanna Dowling, Managing Member
Cosmo Pascuito, *
Michael Pascuito, *
Anna Pascuito, *
Carl Pasciuto, *
▼ EMP: 66 EST: 2008
SQ FT: 42,000
SALES (est): 2.04MM
SALES (corp-wide): 12.65MM Privately Held
Web: www.custommachineinc.com
SIC: 3599 Machine shop, jobbing and repair
PA: The Custom Group Inc
30 Nashua St Ste 3
Woburn MA 01801
781 935-4940

(G-13553)
CUSTOM GROUP CTR FOR MFG TECH
30 Nashua St (01801-4565)
PHONE....................................781 935-4940
EMP: 7 EST: 2008
SALES (est): 39.69K Privately Held
Web: www.customtrainingcenter.com
SIC: 3999 Manufacturing industries, nec

(G-13554)
CUSTOM MACHINE LLC
30 Nashua St Ste 2 (01801-4566)
PHONE....................................781 935-4940
EMP: 15 EST: 2008
SALES (est): 5.37MM
SALES (corp-wide): 12.65MM Privately Held
Web: www.custommachineinc.com
SIC: 3599 Machine shop, jobbing and repair
PA: The Custom Group Inc
30 Nashua St Ste 3
Woburn MA 01801
781 935-4940

(G-13555)
CUSTOM OFFICE FURN BOSTON INC
10 Atlantic Ave Ste 3 (01801-5188)
PHONE....................................781 933-9970
Timothy Mahoney, Pr
EMP: 18 EST: 1992
SQ FT: 15,000
SALES (est): 681.87K Privately Held
SIC: 2521 2522 Desks, office: wood; Desks, office: except wood

(G-13556)
DATA PRINT INC
18 Cranes Ct (01801-5604)
PHONE....................................781 935-3350
Ralph Wooldridge, Pr
Catherine Wooldridge, Clerk
EMP: 10 EST: 1968
SQ FT: 10,000
SALES (est): 1.13MM Privately Held
Web: www.dataprint.net
SIC: 2752 Offset printing

(G-13557)
DG3 GROUP AMERICA INC
Also Called: Dg3 Digital Pubg Solutions
500 W Cummings Park Ste 4500 (01801-6503)
PHONE....................................617 241-5600
EMP: 8
SALES (corp-wide): 76.85MM Privately Held
Web: www.dg3.com
SIC: 7372 Publisher's computer software
HQ: Dg3 Group America, Inc.
100 Burma Rd
Jersey City NJ 07305

(G-13558)
DOUGH CONNECTION CORP
32a Holton St (01801-5205)
PHONE....................................877 693-6844
EMP: 7 EST: 1996
SALES (est): 893.04K Privately Held
Web: www.thedoughconnection.com
SIC: 2045 2099 Pizza doughs, prepared: from purchased flour; Food preparations, nec

(G-13559)
DUPLICATION MANAGEMENT INC
Also Called: D M I
215 Salem St Ste B (01801-2070)
PHONE....................................781 935-7224
Mark Blanchard, Pr
Michael Jenoski, *
EMP: 55 EST: 1988
SQ FT: 15,000
SALES (est): 4.87MM Privately Held
Web: www.dmiprint.com
SIC: 2752 Offset printing

(G-13560)
E V YEUELL INC
Also Called: Yeuell Name Plate & Label
17 Gill St (01801-1768)
PHONE....................................781 933-2984
Thomas W Barry, Pr
Judith A Hall, *
Andrew F Hall Iii, Treas
EMP: 26 EST: 1963
SALES (est): 4.9MM Privately Held
Web: www.yeuell.com
SIC: 2752 3479 3993 2671 Decals, lithographed; Name plates: engraved, etched, etc.; Signs and advertising specialties; Paper; coated and laminated packaging

(G-13561)
EARLYSENSE INC
800 W Cummings Park Ste 6400 (01801-6372)
PHONE....................................781 373-3228
Avner Halperin, Pr
Tim O'malley, Pr
Hadar Ritte, Sec
Todd Barnett, Dir
Karissa Price-rico, COO
EMP: 13 EST: 2010
SALES (est): 5.32MM Privately Held
Web: www.earlysense.com
SIC: 3841 Surgical and medical instruments
PA: Earlysense Ltd
7 Jabotinsky
Ramat Gan 52520

(G-13562)
EAST CAST MCRWAVE SLS DIST LLC
470 Wildwood Ave Ste 4 (01801-2082)
PHONE....................................781 279-0900
Alan Mond, Pr
EMP: 21 EST: 2015
SQ FT: 10,000
SALES (est): 2.88MM
SALES (corp-wide): 154.18MM Privately Held
Web: www.ecmstockroom.com
SIC: 5999 3357 Electronic parts and equipment; Coaxial cable, nonferrous
PA: Powell Electronics, Inc.
200 Commodore Dr
Swedesboro NJ 08085
856 241-8000

(G-13563)
FACTORIAL INC (PA)
19 Presidential Way Ste 103 (01801-1184)
PHONE....................................617 315-9733
Siyu Huang, CEO
EMP: 38 EST: 2019
SALES (est): 5.37MM
SALES (corp-wide): 5.37MM Privately Held
Web: www.factorialenergy.com
SIC: 3691 Storage batteries

(G-13564)
FEV TUTOR INC
Also Called: Fev Tutor
500 W Cummings Park Ste 2700 (01801-6503)
PHONE....................................781 376-6925
Anirudh Baheti, Ch Bd
Jim Tormey, *
Dayashankara Shivalingaiah, *
Greg Deranian, *
EMP: 100 EST: 2002
SALES (est): 10.55MM Privately Held
Web: www.focuscares.com
SIC: 8082 6411 5045 7372 Home health care services; Education services, insurance; Computer software; Educational computer software

(G-13565)
FILTERED AIR SYSTEMS INC
100 Ashburton Ave Ste 3 (01801-1333)
PHONE....................................781 491-0508
Ryan Greene, Pr
Bryan Murphy, Stockholder
▲ EMP: 8 EST: 2004
SQ FT: 7,400
SALES (est): 757.61K Privately Held
Web: www.filteredairsystems.com
SIC: 3589 Vacuum cleaners and sweepers, electric: industrial

(G-13566)
FINE MAGAZINE
9 Fowle St (01801-5101)
PHONE....................................617 721-7372
John Smiroldo, Pr
EMP: 8 EST: 1990
SALES (est): 154.35K Privately Held
Web: www.afamag.com
SIC: 2721 Magazines: publishing only, not printed on site

(G-13567)
FIRST ELECTRIC MOTOR SVC INC
73 Olympia Ave (01801-2022)
PHONE....................................781 491-1100
James F Steenbruggen, Pr
EMP: 40 EST: 1988
SQ FT: 17,000
SALES (est): 9.09MM Privately Held
Web: www.firstelectricmotor.com
SIC: 7694 5999 Electric motor repair; Engine and motor equipment and supplies

(G-13568)
FLUENT TECHNOLOGIES INC
331 Montvale Ave Ste 300 (01801-4670)
PHONE....................................781 939-0900
EMP: 16 EST: 1996
SQ FT: 3,000
SALES (est): 3.38MM Privately Held
Web: www.fluenttech.com
SIC: 2741 Miscellaneous publishing

(G-13569)
FORWARD PHOTONICS LLC
10c Commerce Way (01801-1028)
PHONE....................................978 224-5488
Robin Huang, CEO
EMP: 10 EST: 2016
SALES (est): 1.13MM Privately Held
Web: www.forwardphotonics.com
SIC: 3674 Solid state electronic devices, nec

(G-13570)
FRAEN CORPORATION
324 New Boston St (01801-6211)
PHONE....................................781 937-8825
Charles R Fuller, Pr
EMP: 78
SALES (corp-wide): 23.05MM Privately Held
Web: www.fraen.com
SIC: 3469 Stamping metal for the trade
PA: Fraen Corporation
80 New Crossing Rd
Reading MA 01867
781 205-5300

(G-13571)
FRAEN MACHINING CORPORATION (PA)
Also Called: Swisstronics
324 New Boston St (01801-6211)
PHONE....................................781 205-5400
Peter W Fuller, *
Nicodemo Scarfo, Treas
Charles R Fuller, Clerk
◆ EMP: 56 EST: 1962
SQ FT: 36,000
SALES (est): 7.47MM
SALES (corp-wide): 7.47MM Privately Held
Web: www.fraen.com
SIC: 3599 Machine shop, jobbing and repair

(G-13572)
FUSION OPTIX INC
17 Wheeling Ave (01801-2008)

▲ = Import ▼ = Export
◆ = Import/Export

PHONE...............781 995-0805
Terence Edward Yeo, *CEO*
Terence E Yeo, *CEO*
James Riley, *
▲ **EMP:** 25 **EST:** 2003
SQ FT: 14,000
SALES (est): 5.69MM **Privately Held**
Web: www.fusionoptix.com
SIC: 3089   Injection molding of plastics

(G-13573)
GANGI PRINTING INC
151 Montvale Ave (01801-3647)
P.O. Box 632 (02143-0008)
PHONE...............617 776-6071
Steven Gangi, *CEO*
Susan Gangi, *Pr*
Stephen L Gangi, *COO*
EMP: 11 **EST:** 1975
SALES (est): 879.87K **Privately Held**
Web: www.gangiprinting.com
SIC: 2752   Offset printing

(G-13574)
GENOA SAUSAGE CO INC
14 Industrial Pkwy (01801-1970)
PHONE...............781 933-3115
Romuald Monkiewicz, *Pr*
EMP: 27 **EST:** 1996
SALES (est): 2.33MM
SALES (corp-wide): 260.37K **Privately Held**
SIC: 2011   Meat packing plants
PA: Kayem Foods, Inc.
75 Arlington St
Chelsea MA 02150
781 933-3115

(G-13575)
GOTUIT MEDIA CORP
Also Called: Gotuit Video
400 Tradecenter Ste 3890 (01801-7462)
PHONE...............801 592-5575
Mark Pascarella, *CEO*
EMP: 10 **EST:** 2001
SALES (est): 222.24K **Privately Held**
SIC: 7372   Business oriented computer software

(G-13576)
GRADIANT OSMOTICS INC
130 New Boston St Ste 200 (01801-6276)
PHONE...............781 819-5034
Rick Stover, *Pr*
EMP: 7 **EST:** 2017
SALES (est): 113.86K **Privately Held**
SIC: 3559   Desalination equipment

(G-13577)
GREENE RUBBER COMPANY INC (PA)
20 Cross St (01801-5606)
PHONE...............781 937-9909
John F Connors, *Pr*
Abraham Ponn, *
Richard Ponn, *
David Ponn, *
Beth Connors, *
▲ **EMP:** 99 **EST:** 1931
SQ FT: 85,000
SALES (est): 40.97MM
SALES (corp-wide): 40.97MM **Privately Held**
Web: www.greenerubber.com
SIC: 5085 3053 3061 3052   Gaskets; Gaskets, all materials; Automotive rubber goods (mechanical); Rubber hose

(G-13578)
GREGSTROM CORPORATION
64 Holton St (01801-5288)
P.O. Box 609 (01801-0709)
PHONE...............781 935-6600
Paul J Didonato, *Ch Bd*
Jeffrey Didonato, *
Judy Didonato, *
▲ **EMP:** 75 **EST:** 1946
SALES (est): 9.94MM **Privately Held**
Web: www.gregstrom.com
SIC: 3089   Injection molding of plastics

(G-13579)
HAGER GEOSCIENCE INC
596 Main St (01801-2924)
PHONE...............781 935-8111
Jutta Hager, *Pr*
Mario Carnevale, *VP*
EMP: 8 **EST:** 1993
SQ FT: 2,500
SALES (est): 759.13K **Privately Held**
Web: www.colliergeophysics.com
SIC: 8999 1389 1382   Scientific consulting; Well logging; Geological exploration, oil and gas field

(G-13580)
HANNAFORD & DUMAS CORPORATION
26 Conn St (01801-5662)
PHONE...............781 503-0100
Steve Bryer, *Pr*
Michelle A Hannaford, *
Chuck Duggan, *
EMP: 35 **EST:** 1976
SQ FT: 15,000
SALES (est): 7.94MM **Privately Held**
Web: www.hannaforddumas.com
SIC: 2759   Commercial printing, nec

(G-13581)
HARVEY INDUSTRIES LLC
33 Commonwealth Ave (01801-1009)
PHONE...............781 935-7990
Dave Deveuev, *Brnch Mgr*
EMP: 14
SALES (corp-wide): 1.2B **Privately Held**
Web: www.harveybp.com
SIC: 3442 5033   Storm doors or windows, metal; Insulation materials
PA: Harvey Industries, Llc
1400 Main St Fl 3
Waltham MA 02451
800 598-5400

(G-13582)
HOPEWELL THERAPEUTICS INC
310 W Cummings Park (01801-6335)
PHONE...............781 218-3318
Qiaobing Xu, *CEO*
Thomas Hennessey Junior, *COO*
EMP: 25 **EST:** 2021
SALES (est): 1.25MM **Privately Held**
SIC: 2834   Pharmaceutical preparations

(G-13583)
II-VI PHOTONICS (US) INC (HQ)
Also Called: Aegis Semiconductor Security
78a Olympia Ave (01801-2057)
PHONE...............781 938-1222
Fran Kramer, *Pr*
Jeffrey D Farmer, *
David J Parent, *
Glenn D Bartolini, *
Michael Cahill, *
EMP: 54 **EST:** 1998
SQ FT: 20,000
SALES (est): 15.9MM
SALES (corp-wide): 5.16B **Publicly Held**

Web: www.ii-vi.com
SIC: 3674   Semiconductors and related devices
PA: Coherent Corp.
375 Saxonburg Blvd
Saxonburg PA 16056
724 352-4455

(G-13584)
IMMUNMLECULAR THERAPEUTICS INC
299 Washington St Ste A (01801-2793)
PHONE...............617 356-8170
Nandan Padukone, *Pr*
EMP: 8 **EST:** 2015
SALES (est): 252.03K **Privately Held**
Web: www.imtherapeutics.com
SIC: 8731 2834   Commercial physical research; Pharmaceutical preparations

(G-13585)
INNOVATIONS IN OPTICS INC
10k Gill St (01801-1721)
PHONE...............781 933-4477
EMP: 18 **EST:** 1993
SALES (est): 3.5MM **Privately Held**
Web: www.innovationsinoptics.com
SIC: 3827   Optical instruments and apparatus

(G-13586)
INSCRIBE INC
12 Linscott Rd Ste C (01801-2088)
PHONE...............781 933-3331
Joseph S Sieber, *Pr*
▲ **EMP:** 40 **EST:** 1984
SALES (est): 6.86MM **Privately Held**
Web: www.inscribe.com
SIC: 7371 3555 7372   Computer software development; Printing trades machinery; Prepackaged software

(G-13587)
INTELON OPTICS INC
331 Montvale Ave (01801-4670)
PHONE...............310 804-9392
Lawrence Yoo, *CEO*
Jang Lawrence Yoo, *CEO*
Huong Wu, *Prin*
EMP: 13 **EST:** 2012
SALES (est): 1.28MM **Privately Held**
Web: www.intelon.com
SIC: 3841 7389   Ophthalmic instruments and apparatus; Business Activities at Non-Commercial Site

(G-13588)
INTERNATIONAL SECURITY ASSISTA
Also Called: ISA Group
400 Tradecenter Ste 5900 (01801-7471)
PHONE...............617 590-7942
Peter Taylor, *
Barbara J Auterio, *
EMP: 200 **EST:** 2014
SALES (est): 7.03MM **Privately Held**
Web: www.isagrp.com
SIC: 7381 8742 8331 3484   Detective and armored car services; Management consulting services; Manpower training; Small arms

(G-13589)
INTERNATIONAL STONE INC
10 Ryan Rd (01801-2444)
PHONE...............781 937-3300
◆ **EMP:** 80 **EST:** 1995
SQ FT: 30,000
SALES (est): 10.25MM **Privately Held**

Web: www.internationalstoneinc.com
SIC: 5032 3281 1799   Brick, stone, and related material; Cut stone and stone products; Counter top installation

(G-13590)
INTERSTATE ELEVATOR CORP
21s Olympia Ave (01801-6307)
PHONE...............603 560-3377
Ourania Ahern, *Prin*
EMP: 8 **EST:** 2016
SALES (est): 568.11K **Privately Held**
Web: www.interstateelevators.com
SIC: 3534   Elevators and moving stairways

(G-13591)
INTUVISION INC
10 Tower Office Park Ste 200 (01801-2182)
PHONE...............781 497-1015
Sadiye Guler, *CEO*
EMP: 7 **EST:** 2005
SQ FT: 2,400
SALES (est): 907.92K **Privately Held**
Web: www.intuvisiontech.com
SIC: 7371 7372 8731   Computer software development; Application computer software; Computer (hardware) development

(G-13592)
IX CAMERAS INC
8 Cabot Rd (01801-1190)
PHONE...............617 225-0080
Peter T Carellas, *CEO*
EMP: 10 **EST:** 2016
SALES (est): 629.28K **Privately Held**
Web: www.ix-cameras.com
SIC: 5946 3861   Cameras; Cameras and related equipment

(G-13593)
JOHN G SHELLEY CO INC
20 Cross St (01801-5606)
P.O. Box 81250 (02481-0411)
PHONE...............781 237-0900
TOLL FREE: 877
H Chandler Shelley Junior, *Pr*
John Dutcher, *VP*
▲ **EMP:** 19 **EST:** 1927
SQ FT: 17,500
SALES (est): 3.51MM **Privately Held**
Web: www.johngshelley.com
SIC: 5085 3069 2891 2869   Rubber goods, mechanical; Hard rubber and molded rubber products; Adhesives and sealants; Industrial organic chemicals, nec

(G-13594)
JOHNSON & JOHNSON
600 Unicorn Park Dr # 102 (01801-3343)
PHONE...............781 264-4804
EMP: 8 **EST:** 1958
SALES (est): 115.34K **Privately Held**
SIC: 2834   Pharmaceutical preparations

(G-13595)
JOSEPH PALMER INC
Also Called: Palmer Spring Co
7 Walnut Hill Park (01801-3719)
P.O. Box 229 (01801-0329)
PHONE...............781 376-0130
TOLL FREE: 800
Joseph B Palmer, *Pr*
Clara R Palmer, *Dir*
EMP: 13 **EST:** 1849
SQ FT: 14,000
SALES (est): 989.8K **Privately Held**
Web: www.palmerspringco.com
SIC: 7539 3714   Automotive springs, rebuilding and repair; Motor vehicle parts and accessories

(G-13596)
KEYSTONE PAPER & BOX CO LLC
10 Tower Office Park (01801-2182)
PHONE..............................781 938-3801
EMP: 33
SALES (corp-wide): 110.2MM Privately Held
Web: www.keystonepaperbox.com
SIC: 2652 Setup paperboard boxes
HQ: Keystone Paper & Box Co., Llc
31 Edwin Rd
South Windsor CT 06074
860 291-0027

(G-13597)
KRAFT HEINZ FOODS COMPANY
Also Called: Kraft Foods
1 Hill St (01801-4625)
PHONE..............................781 933-2800
Kathleen Pigott, Mgr
EMP: 99
SALES (corp-wide): 26.48B Publicly Held
Web: www.kraftfoodsgroup.com
SIC: 2022 2013 2095 Processed cheese;
Sausages and other prepared meats;
Coffee roasting (except by wholesale
grocers)
HQ: Kraft Heinz Foods Company
1 Ppg Pl Ste 3400
Pittsburgh PA 15222
412 456-5700

(G-13598)
L K M INDUSTRIES WOBURN
44 6th Rd (01801-1784)
PHONE..............................781 935-9210
Salvi Colucciello, Pr
EMP: 7 EST: 2015
SALES (est): 146.06K Privately Held
Web: www.lkmindustries.com
SIC: 3599 Machine shop, jobbing and repair

(G-13599)
LAMPLIGHTER BREWING CO LLC
Also Called: Lamplighter Brewing Co.
3 Green St (01801-4320)
PHONE..............................617 945-0450
John Hunsicker, Mgr
EMP: 22
SALES (corp-wide): 7.49MM Privately Held
Web: www.lamplighterbrewing.com
SIC: 2082 Beer (alcoholic beverage)
PA: Lamplighter Brewing Co., Llc
284 Broadway
Cambridge MA 02139
207 650-3325

(G-13600)
LASE INNOVATION INC
16 Tower Office Park (01801-2113)
PHONE..............................617 599-0003
Sheldon Kwok, CEO
Lawrence Yoo, Bd of Dir
EMP: 7 EST: 2018
SALES (est): 969.5K Privately Held
Web: www.laseinnovation.com
SIC: 3826 Analytical instruments

(G-13601)
LEAF PHARMACEUTICALS LLC
216 W Cummings Park (01801-6346)
PHONE..............................781 305-4192
Clet Niyikiza, Managing Member
EMP: 20 EST: 2017
SALES (est): 2.58MM Privately Held
Web: www.leafpharmaceuticals.com

SIC: 2834 Pharmaceutical preparations

(G-13602)
LKM INDUSTRIES INC
Also Called: LKM
44 6th Rd Ste 2 (01801-1784)
PHONE..............................781 935-9210
Salvi Colucciello, Pr
Ralph Colucciello, *
William E Nunnelley, *
EMP: 60 EST: 1978
SQ FT: 101,000
SALES (est): 9.5MM Privately Held
Web: www.lkmindustries.com
SIC: 3511 3724 Turbines and turbine
generator sets; Aircraft engines and engine
parts

(G-13603)
LYMOL MEDICAL CORP (PA)
Also Called: Bryan
4 Plympton St (01801-2917)
PHONE..............................781 935-0004
Kim Abrano, CEO
EMP: 9 EST: 1985
SQ FT: 4,000
SALES (est): 1.09MM
SALES (corp-wide): 1.09MM Privately Held
SIC: 3841 Surgical and medical instruments

(G-13604)
LYTRON FS INC
55 Dragon Ct (01801-1039)
PHONE..............................781 933-7300
EMP: 12 EST: 2017
SALES (est): 1.2MM Privately Held
Web: www.boydcorp.com
SIC: 3443 Fabricated plate work (boiler
shop)

(G-13605)
MASCON INC
Also Called: Mascon Medical
5 Commonwealth Ave Unit 3 (01801-1032)
PHONE..............................781 938-5800
John Chen, CEO
James Chen, *
Jeannie Chen, *
◆ EMP: 50 EST: 1981
SQ FT: 18,000
SALES (est): 8.6MM Privately Held
Web: www.mascon.com
SIC: 3324 3812 5084 3484 Aerospace
investment castings, ferrous; Defense
systems and equipment; Safety equipment;
Guns (firearms) or gun parts, 30 mm. and
below

(G-13606)
MASSACHUSETTS ENVELOPE CO INC (PA)
Also Called: Grossman Marketing Group
10 State St Ste 100 (01801-6820)
P.O. Box 100 (02143-0002)
PHONE..............................617 623-8000
TOLL FREE: 800
Ben Grossman, CEO
David Grossman, *
Maureen Mcgoldrick, VP
Douglas Smith, *
Mary Ellen Grossman, *
EMP: 40 EST: 1910
SALES (est): 24.68MM
SALES (corp-wide): 24.68MM Privately Held
Web: www.grossmanmarketing.com
SIC: 2759 5112 8741 7331 Business forms:
printing, nsk; Business forms; Management
services; Mailing service

(G-13607)
MBL INTERNATIONAL CORPORATION (DH)
15a Constitution Way (01801-1024)
PHONE..............................781 939-6964
Tim Lowery, CEO
Michihiro Hayashi, Dir
Melinda Ascher, Dir
Shinobu Kitamura, Treas
Lauren Puglia, Sec
EMP: 12 EST: 2005
SALES (est): 10.21MM Privately Held
Web: www.mblintl.com
SIC: 2834 5122 Pharmaceutical
preparations; Pharmaceuticals
HQ: Medical&Biological Laboratories Co.,
Ltd.
2-11-8, Shibadaimon
Minato-Ku TKY 105-0

(G-13608)
MCALLISTER OPTICAL INC
17d Everberg Rd (01801-1019)
PHONE..............................781 938-0456
Dennis Mcallister, Pr
EMP: 20 EST: 1978
SQ FT: 6,700
SALES (est): 2.1MM Privately Held
Web: www.opticraftinc.com
SIC: 3827 Optical elements and
assemblies, except ophthalmic

(G-13609)
MEDIATEK USA INC
Also Called: Mediatek Woburn
120 Presidential Way (01801-1181)
PHONE..............................781 503-8000
Koh Hung Loh, Prin
EMP: 145
SIC: 3559 3674 Semiconductor
manufacturing machinery; Semiconductors
and related devices
HQ: Mediatek Usa Inc.
2840 Junction Ave
San Jose CA 95134
408 526-1899

(G-13610)
MEDICAMETRIX LLC
500 Unicorn Park Dr (01801-3377)
PHONE..............................617 488-9233
EMP: 8 EST: 2020
SALES (est): 958.05K Privately Held
Web: www.medicametrix.com
SIC: 3841 Medical instruments and
equipment, blood and bone work

(G-13611)
METALCRAFT DOOR CO INC
87 Olympia Ave (01801-2022)
P.O. Box 2391 (01888-0691)
PHONE..............................781 933-2861
David G Long, Pr
David G Long, Pr
Peter Long, Stockholder
EMP: 20 EST: 1980
SQ FT: 14,000
SALES (est): 4.87MM Privately Held
Web: www.metalcraftdoor.com
SIC: 5031 2491 Metal doors, sash and trim;
Wood products, creosoted

(G-13612)
METRO GLASS & METAL LLC
10 Wheeling Ave (01801-6809)
PHONE..............................781 281-0667
Elliot Kracko, Mgr
EMP: 22 EST: 2014
SALES (est): 1.02MM Privately Held

SIC: 3211 Window glass, clear and colored

(G-13613)
MIDAS TECHNOLOGY INC
400 W Cummings Park Ste 6400
(01801-6533)
PHONE..............................781 938-0069
Kenneth D Towl, Pr
David F Barnes, *
George Bloom, *
▼ EMP: 16 EST: 1986
SQ FT: 1,725
SALES (est): 844.42K Privately Held
Web: www.midastechnology.com
SIC: 3679 3599 Electronic circuits; Custom
machinery

(G-13614)
MONOTYPE IMAGING HOLDINGS INC (DH)
Also Called: Monotype
600 Unicorn Park Dr (01801-3343)
PHONE..............................781 970-6000
Ninan Chacko, CEO
Christopher Brooks, Interim Chief Financial
Officer
Benjamin W L Semmes Iii, CRO
Steven R Martin, Ex VP
Janet M Dunlap, Ex VP
EMP: 53 EST: 2005
SQ FT: 42,000
SALES (est): 127.56MM
SALES (corp-wide): 1.88MM Privately
Held
Web: www.monotype.com
SIC: 7371 7372 Custom computer
programming services; Prepackaged
software
HQ: Marvel Parent, Llc
1950 University Ave # 350
East Palo Alto CA 94303
650 321-4910

(G-13615)
MONOTYPE IMAGING INC (DH)
600 Unicorn Park Dr Ste 3f (01801-3343)
PHONE..............................781 970-6000
Ninan Chacko, CEO
Robert Givens, *
▲ EMP: 90 EST: 1897
SQ FT: 25,000
SALES (est): 97.77MM
SALES (corp-wide): 1.88MM Privately
Held
Web: www.fonts.com
SIC: 7372 7371 Prepackaged software;
Custom computer programming services
HQ: Monotype Imaging Holdings Inc.
600 Unicorn Park Dr Ste 4
Woburn MA 01801

(G-13616)
MYRIANT LAKE PROVIDENCE INC
45 Cummings Park (01801-2123)
PHONE..............................617 657-5200
Ralph Tapia, Prin
Sam Chan, *
EMP: 11 EST: 2010
SALES (est): 654.66K Privately Held
SIC: 2869 Industrial organic chemicals, nec

(G-13617)
NAI CRANES LLC
110 Winn St Ste 205 (01801-2800)
PHONE..............................781 897-4100
EMP: 75
Web: www.naicranes.com
SIC: 3536 Cranes, overhead traveling

(G-13618)
NANTERO INC
25b Olympia Ave (01801-6307)
PHONE....................................781 932-5338
Greg Schmergel, *CEO*
Thomas Rueckes, *
Sohrab Kianian, *
Lee Cleveland, *OF DESIGN*
Robert O Lindefjeld, *
EMP: 50 **EST:** 2001
SALES (est): 10.62MM **Privately Held**
Web: www.nantero.com
SIC: 3674 Semiconductors and related
devices

(G-13619)
NAVITAR INDUSTRIES LLC
30 Nashua St (01801-4565)
PHONE....................................781 933-6125
EMP: 7 **EST:** 2017
SALES (est): 163.38K **Privately Held**
Web: www.navitar.com
SIC: 3999 Manufacturing industries, nec

(G-13620)
NENPA
1 Arrow Dr Ste 6 (01801-2252)
PHONE....................................781 281-2053
Linda Conway, *Prin*
EMP: 9 **EST:** 2018
SALES (est): 144.59K **Privately Held**
Web: www.nenpa.com
SIC: 2711 Newspapers, publishing and
printing

(G-13621)
NEUROMETRIX INC (PA)
4b Gill St (01801-1721)
PHONE....................................781 890-9989
EMP: 9 **EST:** 1996
SQ FT: 10,000
SALES (est): 8.26MM **Publicly Held**
Web: www.neurometrix.com
SIC: 3841 Surgical and medical instruments

(G-13622)
**NEW ENGLAND NEWSPPR
PRESS ASSN**
1 Arrow Dr Ste 1 (01801-2252)
PHONE....................................781 281-2053
George Arwady, *Pr*
EMP: 10 **EST:** 2017
SALES (est): 84.03K **Privately Held**
Web: www.nenpa.com
SIC: 2711 Newspapers, publishing and
printing

(G-13623)
**NEW ENGLAND PLASTICS
CORP (PA)**
310 Salem St (01801-2098)
PHONE....................................781 933-6004
Robert Kearin, *Pr*
Michael P Famiglietti, *
John Stewart, *
EMP: 30 **EST:** 1946
SQ FT: 60,000
SALES (est): 13.48MM
SALES (corp-wide): 13.48MM **Privately
Held**
Web: www.newenglandplastics.com
SIC: 3081 3089 Plastics film and sheet;
Thermoformed finished plastics products,
nec

(G-13624)
**NH LEARNING SOLUTIONS
CORP**

600 W Cummings Park Ste 2250
(01801-6369)
PHONE....................................781 224-1113
Andrew Wight, *Brnch Mgr*
EMP: 69
SALES (corp-wide): 7.72MM **Privately
Held**
Web: www.newhorizons.com
SIC: 8211 7372 Specialty education;
Educational computer software
PA: Nh Learning Solutions Corporation
707 Landa St
New Braunfels TX 78130
734 525-1501

(G-13625)
NOVA METRIX LLC
600 Unicorn Park Dr Ste 4 (01801-3343)
PHONE....................................781 897-1200
EMP: 14 **EST:** 2010
SALES (est): 240.56K **Privately Held**
Web: www.novavg.com
SIC: 3826 Analytical instruments

(G-13626)
OPTICRAFT INC
17d Everberg Rd (01801-1019)
PHONE....................................781 938-0456
Dennis Mcallister, *Genl Mgr*
EMP: 18
SALES (corp-wide): 152.93K **Privately
Held**
SIC: 3827 Optical instruments and lenses
PA: Opticraft, Inc.
26 Bull Run
Charlestown NH
603 826-4411

(G-13627)
OPTOWARES INCORPORATED
15 Presidential Way (01801-1040)
PHONE....................................781 427-7106
Wayne Weimer, *Pr*
EMP: 11 **EST:** 2015
SQ FT: 2,000
SALES (est): 3.36MM
SALES (corp-wide): 9.52MM **Privately
Held**
Web: www.optowares.com
SIC: 3699 Electrical equipment and
supplies, nec
PA: Photonwares Corporation
15 Presidential Way
Woburn MA 01801
781 935-1200

(G-13628)
OROGEN THERAPEUTICS INC
✪
Also Called: Orogen
12 Gill St Ste 4200 (01801-1786)
PHONE....................................617 981-2156
Philip Austin, *Pr*
Brett Chevalier, *VP*
EMP: 8 **EST:** 2023
SALES (est): 348.5K **Privately Held**
SIC: 2834 Pharmaceutical preparations

(G-13629)
**PARKER-HANNIFIN
CORPORATION**
Parker Chomerics Division
77 Dragon Ct (01801-1039)
PHONE....................................781 935-4850
EMP: 400
SALES (corp-wide): 19.07B **Publicly Held**
Web: www.parker.com
SIC: 2891 3053 3444 Adhesives and
sealants; Oil seals, asbestos; Sheet
metalwork

PA: Parker-Hannifin Corporation
6035 Parkland Blvd
Cleveland OH 44124
216 896-3000

(G-13630)
**PARKER-HANNIFIN
CORPORATION**
8 Commonwealth Ave (01801-1010)
PHONE....................................781 935-4850
EMP: 9 **EST:** 2018
SALES (est): 457.2K **Privately Held**
SIC: 3053 Gaskets; packing and sealing
devices

(G-13631)
**PARKER-HANNIFIN
CORPORATION**
Also Called: Parker Hannifin Chomerics
70 Dragon Ct (01801-1014)
PHONE....................................781 939-4278
David Hill, *Brnch Mgr*
EMP: 400
SALES (corp-wide): 19.07B **Publicly Held**
Web: www.parker.com
SIC: 3053 8734 Gaskets and sealing
devices; Product testing laboratory, safety
or performance
PA: Parker-Hannifin Corporation
6035 Parkland Blvd
Cleveland OH 44124
216 896-3000

(G-13632)
**PEARL DIE-CUTTING & FINSHG
LLC**
110 Commerce Way Ste E (01801-1098)
PHONE....................................781 721-6900
Steven Rich, *Prin*
EMP: 11 **EST:** 2006
SALES (est): 310.88K **Privately Held**
Web: www.pearldiecutting.com
SIC: 3544 Dies, steel rule

(G-13633)
PERRCO INC
Also Called: Winfield Brooks Company, Inc.
70 Conn St (01801-5662)
PHONE....................................617 933-5300
Winnfield Perry, *Pr*
Keith Perry, *Ex VP*
Dana Perry, *Sls Dir*
▲ **EMP:** 10 **EST:** 1951
SQ FT: 30,000
SALES (est): 1.65MM **Privately Held**
Web: www.winbro.com
SIC: 2842 2992 2891 2851 Cleaning or
polishing preparations, nec; Lubricating oils
and greases; Adhesives and sealants;
Paints and allied products
PA: Flow Grinding Corp.
70 Conn St
Woburn MA 01801

(G-13634)
PETNET SOLUTIONS INC
268 W Cummings Park (01801-6346)
PHONE....................................781 937-3600
Doug Husa, *Brnch Mgr*
EMP: 33
SALES (corp-wide): 84.48B **Privately Held**
Web: www.siemens-healthineers.com
SIC: 2835 Diagnostic substances
HQ: Petnet Solutions, Inc.
810 Innovation Dr
Knoxville TN 37932
865 218-2000

(G-13635)
**PHOTONWARES CORPORATION
(PA)**
15 Presidential Way (01801-1040)
PHONE....................................781 935-1200
Jing Zhao, *CEO*
EMP: 59 **EST:** 2016
SQ FT: 80,000
SALES (est): 9.52MM
SALES (corp-wide): 9.52MM **Privately
Held**
Web: www.agiltron.com
SIC: 3699 Electrical equipment and
supplies, nec

(G-13636)
PHOTOP AEGIS INC
78a Olympia Ave (01801-2057)
PHONE....................................781 904-4000
Jeffrey Palmer, *Pr*
EMP: 7 **EST:** 2015
SALES (est): 264.53K **Privately Held**
SIC: 3555 Photoengraving machines

(G-13637)
PLASMA PEN USA LLC
800 W Cummings Park Ste 5950
(01801-6372)
PHONE....................................855 568-3776
EMP: 10 **EST:** 2019
SALES (est): 2.67MM **Privately Held**
Web: www.plasmaconcepts.com
SIC: 2836 Plasmas

(G-13638)
PLUROMED INC
Also Called: Genzyme
175 New Boston St Ste F (01801-6257)
PHONE....................................781 932-0574
Jean Marie Vogel, *Pr*
James Wilkie, *VP*
Alexander Schwarz, *Sec*
EMP: 22 **EST:** 2003
SALES (est): 1.6MM **Privately Held**
SIC: 2834 Pharmaceutical preparations

(G-13639)
PONN MACHINE CUTTING CO
20 Cross St (01801-5606)
PHONE....................................781 937-3373
Abraham Ponn, *Pr*
Richard Ponn, *Stockholder*
John Connors, *Stockholder*
EMP: 12 **EST:** 1933
SQ FT: 15,000
SALES (est): 1.96MM **Privately Held**
Web: www.ponnmachine.com
SIC: 3599 Machine shop, jobbing and repair

(G-13640)
**PRINT MANAGEMENT
SYSTEMS INC**
26 Conn St (01801-5662)
PHONE....................................781 944-1041
James G Lenox, *Pr*
EMP: 10 **EST:** 1992
SALES (est): 891.03K **Privately Held**
Web: www.gopmsi.com
SIC: 2752 2759 Offset printing;
Thermography

(G-13641)
**PTTGC INNOVATION AMERICA
CORP (HQ)**
45 Cummings Park (01801-2123)
PHONE....................................617 657-5234
Dennis Mccullough, *Pr*
Regina Detore Paglia, *

Mark Shmorhun, *
Byron S Kalogerou, *
Eric Conlin, *
▲ **EMP:** 25 **EST:** 2009
SALES (est): 21.71MM **Privately Held**
Web: www.rampartmovie.com
SIC: 2869 Industrial organic chemicals, nec
PA: Ptt Global Chemical Public Company
Limited
555/1 Vibhavadi Rangsit Road
Chatuchak 10900

(G-13642)
PURE IMAGING
9 Fowle St (01801-5101)
PHONE.............................781 537-6992
EMP: 8
SALES (est): 507.78K **Privately Held**
Web: www.pureimaging.com
SIC: 2796 Color separations, for printing

(G-13643)
QUAD/GRAPHICS INC
Also Called: QUAD/GRAPHICS INC.
110 Commerce Way Ste F (01801-1098)
PHONE.............................781 231-7200
EMP: 151
SALES (corp-wide): 3.22B **Publicly Held**
Web: www.quad.com
SIC: 2752 Offset printing
PA: Quad/Graphics, Inc.
N61w23044 Harrys Way
Sussex WI 53089
414 566-6000

(G-13644)
QUEEN ASSOCIATES INC
Also Called: Twist & Shape/ Revere
2 Banks St (01801-1678)
PHONE.............................781 389-8494
Mark S Queen, Pr
Sheryl Queen, *
EMP: 55 **EST:** 2002
SALES (est): 1.2MM **Privately Held**
SIC: 5812 2024 7389 Pizza restaurants; Ice
cream and ice milk; Business services, nec

(G-13645)
QUEST DRAPE
46 Cummings Park (01801-2123)
PHONE.............................781 859-0300
Lee Dunalp, CEO
Lee Dunalp, Prin
EMP: 7 **EST:** 2015
SALES (est): 185.63K **Privately Held**
SIC: 2391 Curtains and draperies

(G-13646)
**QUEUES ENFORTH
DEVELOPMENT INC**
Also Called: QED
400 Tradecenter Ste 5900 (01801-7471)
PHONE.............................781 870-1100
David Varney, Pr
David D Varney, Pr
EMP: 14 **EST:** 1974
SQ FT: 2,600
SALES (est): 1.29MM
SALES (corp-wide): 100.85MM **Privately
Held**
Web: www.qed.online
SIC: 7372 Prepackaged software
PA: 22nd Century Technologies Inc.
8251 Greensboro Dr # 900
Mc Lean VA 22102
732 537-9191

(G-13647)
RAYTHEON COMPANY
Also Called: Raytheon
235 Presidential Way (01801-1060)
PHONE.............................781 933-1863
Joan Trovato, Mgr
EMP: 132
SALES (corp-wide): 68.92B **Publicly Held**
Web: www.rtx.com
SIC: 3812 Radar systems and equipment
HQ: Raytheon Company
870 Winter St
Waltham MA 02451
781 522-3000

(G-13648)
RAYTHEON COMPANY
Also Called: Raytheon
225 Presidential Way (01801-5143)
PHONE.............................339 645-6000
Rob Weihmayer, Brnch Mgr
EMP: 132
SALES (corp-wide): 68.92B **Publicly Held**
Web: www.rtx.com
SIC: 3812 Sonar systems and equipment
HQ: Raytheon Company
870 Winter St
Waltham MA 02451
781 522-3000

(G-13649)
REPLIMUNE GROUP INC (PA)
500 Unicorn Park Dr Ste 300 (01801-3345)
PHONE.............................781 222-9600
Philip Astley-sparke, CEO
Dieter Weinand, Ch Bd
Robert Coffin, Research & Development
Andrew Schwendenman, CAO
Colin Love, COO
EMP: 102 **EST:** 2015
SQ FT: 18,712
Web: www.replimune.com
SIC: 2836 Biological products, except
diagnostic

(G-13650)
RESIN DESIGNS LLC (DH)
11 State St (01801-2172)
PHONE.............................781 935-3133
Adam P Chase, CEO
EMP: 27 **EST:** 2003
SQ FT: 20,000
SALES (est): 30.29MM **Publicly Held**
Web: www.chasecorp.com
SIC: 2891 Adhesives
HQ: Chase Corporation
375 University Ave
Westwood MA 02090
781 332-0700

(G-13651)
REVELA INC
500 W Cummings Park Ste 2150
(01801-6503)
PHONE.............................716 725-2657
Evan Zhao, CEO
Evan Zhao, Prin
Cindy Le, Prin
Kongyu Zhang, Prin
Avinash Boppana, Prin
EMP: 7 **EST:** 2021
SALES (est): 840.47K **Privately Held**
Web: www.getrevela.com
SIC: 8731 2844 5122 Biotechnical research,
commercial; Cosmetic preparations;
Cosmetics, perfumes, and hair products

(G-13652)
REVOLUTION COOKING LLC
100 Sylvan Rd Ste 100 (01801-1851)

PHONE.............................301 710-0590
EMP: 12
SALES (corp-wide): 2.75MM **Privately
Held**
Web: www.revcook.com
SIC: 3634 Electric household cooking
appliances
PA: Revolution Cooking, Llc
12435 Pk Potmac Ave # 325
Potomac MD 20854
301 710-0590

(G-13653)
RIVINIUS & SONS INC
225 Salem St (01801-2002)
PHONE.............................781 933-5620
Alan Crosbie, Pr
Forrest C Rivinius, Treas
EMP: 25 **EST:** 1953
SQ FT: 5,000
SALES (est): 2.69MM **Privately Held**
Web: www.riviniusandsons.com
SIC: 3312 Rods, iron and steel: made in
steel mills

(G-13654)
RL CONTROLS LLC
2 Gill St (01801-1721)
PHONE.............................781 932-3349
Lena Walsh, Managing Member
EMP: 72 **EST:** 2006
SQ FT: 2,800
SALES (est): 15MM **Privately Held**
Web: www.rlcontrols.com
SIC: 3743 7629 Railroad equipment;
Electrical repair shops

(G-13655)
ROHTSTEIN CORP (PA)
Also Called: Orchard Food Div
70 Olympia Ave (01801-2036)
P.O. Box 2129 (01888-0229)
PHONE.............................781 935-8300
Steven Rohtstein, Pr
▲ **EMP:** 85 **EST:** 1970
SQ FT: 120,000
SALES (est): 57.08MM
SALES (corp-wide): 57.08MM **Privately
Held**
Web: www.rohtstein.com
SIC: 5149 2099 2087 2062 Specialty food
items; Food preparations, nec; Flavoring
extracts and syrups, nec; Cane sugar
refining

(G-13656)
ROSCID TECHNOLOGIES INC
215 Salem St Ste L (01801-2078)
PHONE.............................781 933-4007
Brad Murray, Pr
EMP: 7 **EST:** 2011
SALES (est): 967.52K **Privately Held**
Web: www.roscidtechnologies.com
SIC: 8711 3728 3823 3826 Consulting
engineer; Oxygen systems, aircraft;
Analyzers, industrial process type; Moisture
analyzers

(G-13657)
RUBIX COMPOSITES INC
10 Hancock St (01801-3712)
P.O. Box 3177 (01888-2077)
PHONE.............................781 856-0342
Jonghoon Han, Pr
EMP: 9 **EST:** 2016
SALES (est): 740.9K **Privately Held**
Web: www.rubixcomposites.com
SIC: 3585 Heating equipment, complete

(G-13658)
SAFECOR HEALTH LLC
317 New Boston St # 100 (01801-6231)
PHONE.............................781 933-8780
Laurel Lombardi, Brnch Mgr
EMP: 8
Web: www.safecorhealth.com
SIC: 7389 2834 Packaging and labeling
services; Pharmaceutical preparations
PA: Safecor Health, Llc
4060 Business Park Dr B
Columbus OH 43204

(G-13659)
SAFECOR HEALTH LLC
317 New Boston St Ste 100 (01801-6231)
PHONE.............................781 933-8780
Stephen Fischbach, CEO
Douglas Moore, CFO
Randy Young, Dir Opers
EMP: 21 **EST:** 2008
SALES (est): 4.18MM **Privately Held**
Web: www.safecorhealth.com
SIC: 2834 Pharmaceutical preparations

(G-13660)
SCHNEEBERGER INC (DH)
44 6th Rd Ste 3 (01801-1784)
PHONE.............................781 271-0140
Hans M Schneeberger, CEO
Adrian Fuchser, Ex VP
▲ **EMP:** 9 **EST:** 1985
SQ FT: 8,000
SALES (est): 10.45MM **Privately Held**
Web: www.schneeberger.com
SIC: 3829 Measuring and controlling
devices, nec
HQ: Schneeberger Ag Lineartechnik
St. Urbanstrasse 12
Roggwil BE 4914

(G-13661)
**SCHRIMPF WLDG FABRICATION
INC**
Also Called: Schrimpf Welding
3 Breed Ave Unit J (01801-1372)
PHONE.............................339 298-2311
Christopher Schrimpf, Pr
EMP: 7 **EST:** 2008
SALES (est): 669.27K **Privately Held**
Web: www.schrimpfwelding.com
SIC: 7692 5039 3449 3462 Welding repair;
Air ducts, sheet metal; Miscellaneous
metalwork; Ornamental metal forgings,
ferrous

(G-13662)
SCIAPS INC (PA)
7 Constitution Way Ste 105 (01801-1193)
PHONE.............................339 222-2585
Don Sackett, Pr
Gary Lortie, *
Dave Day, *
EMP: 21 **EST:** 2012
SALES (est): 5.65MM
SALES (corp-wide): 5.65MM **Privately
Held**
Web: www.sciaps.com
SIC: 3826 Analytical instruments

(G-13663)
SENSERA INC
15 Presidential Way (01801-1040)
PHONE.............................978 606-2600
Tim Stucchi, COO
EMP: 12 **EST:** 2001
SALES (est): 4.31MM **Privately Held**
Web: www.senserasystems.com

▲ = Import ▼ = Export
◆ = Import/Export

SIC: **8731** 3674 Biological research; Integrated circuits, semiconductor networks, etc.
PA: Triton Systems, Inc.
330 Billerica Rd Ste 200
Chelmsford MA 01824

(G-13664)
SHEAR COLOR PRINTING INC
30d 6th Rd (01801-1758)
PHONE...............................781 376-9607
Joel Weitzman, *Pr*
Stewart Weitzman, *Sec*
EMP: 23 EST: 1990
SQ FT: 5,500
SALES (est): 3.64MM **Privately Held**
Web: www.shearcolor.com
SIC: **2752** 2754 Offset printing; Color printing: gravure

(G-13665)
SIGN SOLUTIONS UNLIMITED
30 6th Rd (01801-1758)
PHONE...............................781 537-6156
EMP: 9 EST: 2014
SALES (est): 595.92K **Privately Held**
Web: www.wrapsolutions.net
SIC: **3993** Signs and advertising specialties

(G-13666)
SIGNAL COMMUNICATIONS CORP
Also Called: Sigcom
4 Wheeling Ave (01801-2009)
P.O. Box 2588 (01888-1188)
PHONE...............................781 933-0998
Robert Lapham, *Pr*
EMP: 30 EST: 1986
SQ FT: 17,000
SALES (est): 4.97MM
SALES (corp-wide): 25MM **Privately Held**
Web: www.sigcom.com
SIC: **3669** 3661 3644 Emergency alarms; Telephone and telegraph apparatus; Noncurrent-carrying wiring devices
PA: Gulf Industries, Inc.
70393 Bravo St
Covington LA 70433
985 892-6500

(G-13667)
SIGNS TO GO INC
Also Called: Fastsigns
400 W Cummings Park Ste 1975 (01801-6537)
PHONE...............................781 808-3153
Pankaj R Shah, *Pr*
Sunita P Shah, *Treas*
Darshan R Shah, *Clerk*
EMP: 7 EST: 1994
SQ FT: 1,500
SALES (est): 621.55K **Privately Held**
Web: www.fastsigns.com
SIC: **3993** Signs and advertising specialties

(G-13668)
SIRTEX MEDICAL US HOLDINGS INC
Also Called: Sirtex
300 Unicorn Park Dr (01801-3363)
PHONE...............................888 474-7839
Kevin R Smith, *CEO*
Amy Pan, *CFO*
Kevin P Smith, *VP*
EMP: 15 EST: 2006
SALES (est): 2.84MM **Privately Held**
Web: www.sirtex.com
SIC: **2834** Pharmaceutical preparations

(G-13669)
SKYWORKS SOLUTIONS INC
Also Called: Skyworks Luxembourg S.A.R.L.
20 Sylvan Rd (01801-1885)
PHONE...............................781 935-5150
Ken Bushmich, *Mgr*
EMP: 64
SALES (corp-wide): 4.77B **Publicly Held**
Web: www.skyworksinc.com
SIC: **3679** 3674 Electronic circuits; Semiconductors and related devices
PA: Skyworks Solutions, Inc.
5260 California Ave # 100
Irvine CA 92617
949 231-3000

(G-13670)
SOLIDENERGY SYSTEMS LLC
Also Called: SES
35 Cabot Rd (01801-1003)
PHONE...............................617 972-3412
Qichao Hu, *Mgr*
EMP: 65 EST: 2012
SALES (est): 9.28MM **Publicly Held**
Web: www.ses.ai
SIC: **3691** Storage batteries
PA: Ai Ses Corporation
35 Cabot Rd
Woburn MA

(G-13671)
SQDM
100 Tower Office Park Ste M (01801-2187)
PHONE...............................888 993-9674
Eric Borthwick, *Prin*
EMP: 10 EST: 2015
SALES (est): 313.41K **Privately Held**
Web: www.sqdm.com
SIC: **7372** Prepackaged software

(G-13672)
STARLINK NORTH AMERICA INC
100 Sylvan Rd Ste G700 (01801-1817)
PHONE...............................877 823-1566
Mahmoud Nimer, *Prin*
Nedal Othman, *Prin*
Vivek Gupta, *Prin*
EMP: 9 EST: 2017
SALES (est): 292.75K **Privately Held**
SIC: **3674** Computer logic modules

(G-13673)
STONE DECOR GALLERIA INC
10 Ryan Rd (01801-2444)
PHONE...............................781 937-9377
Santino Gamellaro, *Pr*
▲ EMP: 15 EST: 2012
SALES (est): 545.07K **Privately Held**
Web: www.slabware.com
SIC: **3281** 5032 Furniture, cut stone; Granite building stone

(G-13674)
STONE SURFACES INC
275 Salem St Ste 2 (01801-2168)
PHONE...............................781 270-4600
Pierre Rancourt, *Pr*
Dimitrios Kampouris, *Dir*
▲ EMP: 12 EST: 2004
SQ FT: 7,000
SALES (est): 1.66MM **Privately Held**
Web: www.stonesurfacesinc.net
SIC: **3281** Cut stone and stone products

(G-13675)
TECOMET INC
170 New Boston St (01801-6204)
PHONE...............................781 782-6400
EMP: 659

SALES (corp-wide): 832.81MM **Privately Held**
Web: www.tecomet.com
SIC: **3599** 3823 1629 4911 Machine shop, jobbing and repair; Process control instruments; Power plant construction; Generation, electric power
HQ: Tecomet Inc.
115 Eames St
Wilmington MA 01887
978 642-2400

(G-13676)
TECOSTAR HOLDINGS INC (PA)
18 Commerce Way Ste 500 (01801-1051)
PHONE...............................978 642-2400
EMP: 161 EST: 2013
SALES (est): 832.81MM
SALES (corp-wide): 832.81MM **Privately Held**
SIC: **3841** Diagnostic apparatus, medical

(G-13677)
TERADYNE INC
36 Cabot Rd (01801-1004)
PHONE...............................978 370-2700
Edward Hogan, *Brnch Mgr*
EMP: 11
SALES (corp-wide): 3.16B **Publicly Held**
Web: www.teradyne.com
SIC: **3825** 3643 Semiconductor test equipment; Connectors and terminals for electrical devices
PA: Teradyne, Inc.
600 Riverpark Dr
North Reading MA 01864
978 370-2700

(G-13678)
TERRAFUGIA INC
23 Rainin Rd Ste 2 (01801-4689)
PHONE...............................781 491-0812
Chao Jing, *CEO*
Kevin Colburn, *COO*
EMP: 19 EST: 2017
SALES (est): 4.68MM **Privately Held**
Web: www.terrafugia.com
SIC: **3721** Aircraft
PA: Zhejiang Geely Holding Group Co., Ltd.
No.1760, Jiangling Road, Binjiang District
Hangzhou ZJ 31005

(G-13679)
TRILOG GROUP INC
54 Cummings Park Ste 308 (01801-2192)
PHONE...............................781 937-9963
Alex El Homsi, *Pr*
Ghassan El Homsi, *Dir*
EMP: 24 EST: 1999
SQ FT: 2,000
SALES (est): 2.36MM **Privately Held**
Web: www.triloggroup.com
SIC: **7372** Prepackaged software
PA: Trilog Group S A R L
47, Tmarai & Daadas Building, Corniche An Nahr
Beirut

(G-13680)
UNI-GRAPHIC INC
110j Commerce Way (01801-1008)
PHONE...............................781 231-7200
EMP: 151
SIC: **2752** Commercial printing, lithographic

(G-13681)
UNIMED-MIDWEST INC
100 Sylvan Rd Ste 100 (01801-1851)
PHONE...............................800 347-9023

Douglas Manchester, *CEO*
EMP: 7 EST: 2010
SALES (est): 74.42K **Privately Held**
SIC: **2842** Sanitation preparations, disinfectants and deodorants

(G-13682)
VACUUM BARRIER CORPORATION
4 Barten Ln (01801-5601)
P.O. Box 529 (01801-0529)
PHONE...............................781 933-3570
Russell W Blanton, *Pr*
Leonard C Gardner, *
Priya Gopalan, *
David W Tucker, *
James Westra, *
EMP: 40 EST: 1958
SQ FT: 32,000
SALES (est): 9.4MM **Privately Held**
Web: www.vacuumbarrier.com
SIC: **3559** 3812 Cryogenic machinery, industrial; Detection apparatus: electronic/ magnetic field, light/heat

(G-13683)
VAISALA INC
Also Called: Sigmet, Westford Operations
10d Gill St (01801-1721)
PHONE...............................508 574-1163
Richard E Passarelli Junior, *Pr*
Alan D Siggia, *Treas*
EMP: 9 EST: 1982
SALES (est): 5.11MM
SALES (corp-wide): 534.04MM **Privately Held**
Web: www.vaisala.com
SIC: **3829** Measuring and controlling devices, nec
PA: Vaisala Oyj
Vanha Nurmijarventie 21
Vantaa 01670
989491

(G-13684)
VAT INC
500 W Cummings Park Ste 5450 (01801-6503)
PHONE...............................781 537-5402
EMP: 25 EST: 2019
SALES (est): 505.13K **Privately Held**
Web: www.vatvalve.com
SIC: **3599** Industrial machinery, nec

(G-13685)
VICTORIA GOURMET INC
17a Gill St (01801-1788)
PHONE...............................781 935-2100
Victoria Taylor, *Pr*
▲ EMP: 10 EST: 1997
SQ FT: 2,000
SALES (est): 1.63MM **Privately Held**
Web: www.vgourmet.com
SIC: **2099** Food preparations, nec

(G-13686)
VITASOY USA INC
57 Russell St (01801-4707)
PHONE...............................781 430-8988
◆ EMP: 150
Web: www.vitasoy-na.com
SIC: **5149** 2099 Beverages, except coffee and tea; Tofu, except frozen desserts

(G-13687)
WATERTOWN IRONWORKS INC
47 Henshaw St (01801-4668)
PHONE...............................781 491-0229
Luigi D'amico, *Treas*
Vera D'amico, *Clerk*

Anthony Damico, *Pr*
EMP: 21 **EST:** 1979
SQ FT: 6,000
SALES (est): 1.85MM **Privately Held**
Web: www.watertownironworks.com
SIC: 3446   Stairs, fire escapes, balconies, railings, and ladders

(G-13688)
WHOLESALE PRINTING INC
2 Cedar St Ste 2 (01801-6352)
PHONE.............................781 937-3357
John Struthers, *Pr*
Dan Ornae, *VP*
EMP: 11 **EST:** 1987
SQ FT: 1,600
SALES (est): 477.49K **Privately Held**
Web: www.wholesaleprintinginc.com
SIC: 2752   Offset printing

(G-13689)
WOBURN DAILY TIMES INC (PA)
Also Called: Daily Times Chronicle
1 Arrow Dr (01801-2090)
P.O. Box 2433 (01888-0733)
PHONE.............................781 933-3700
Peter Haggerty, *Pr*
Richard P Haggerty,   *
James D Haggerty Iii, *VP*
EMP: 60 **EST:** 1901
SQ FT: 27,500
SALES (est): 4.92MM
SALES (corp-wide): 4.92MM **Privately Held**
SIC: 2711   Newspapers, publishing and printing

(G-13690)
XYLEM WATER SOLUTIONS USA INC
78 Olympia Ave (01801-2057)
PHONE.............................781 935-6515
Brian Mccarthy, *Brnch Mgr*
EMP: 49
Web: www.xylem.com
SIC: 3561   Pumps and pumping equipment
HQ: Xylem Water Solutions U.S.A., Inc.
4828 Parkway Plaza Blvd # 200
Charlotte NC 28217

(G-13691)
YIELD10 BIOSCIENCE INC (PA)
19 Presidential Way (01801-1184)
PHONE.............................617 583-1700
Joseph Shaulson, *Pr*
Oliver P Peoples, *Pr*
Robert L Van Nostrand, *Ch Bd*
Charles B Haaser, *CAO*
Lynne H Brum, *VP*
◆ **EMP:** 24 **EST:** 1992
SQ FT: 22,213
SALES (est): 450K **Publicly Held**
Web: www.yield10bio.com
SIC: 2869   Industrial organic chemicals, nec

(G-13692)
ZNLABS LLC (HQ)
20 Cabot Rd (01801-1332)
PHONE.............................781 897-6966
EMP: 42 **EST:** 2015
SALES (est): 2.42MM
SALES (corp-wide): 8.08B **Publicly Held**
SIC: 2834   Pharmaceutical preparations
PA: Zoetis Inc.
10 Sylvan Way Ste 100
Parsippany NJ 07054
973 822-7000

(G-13693)
ZWITTERCO INC
Also Called: Zwitterco
12 Cabot Rd Ste B (01801-1198)
PHONE.............................301 442-5662
Alex Rappaport, *CEO*
EMP: 31 **EST:** 2018
SALES (est): 2.96MM **Privately Held**
Web: www.zwitterco.com
SIC: 3564 4953   Filters, air: furnaces, air conditioning equipment, etc.; Rubbish collection and disposal

Worcester
Worcester County

(G-13694)
A F AMORELLO & SONS INC
115 Sw Cutoff Ste 1 (01604-2729)
P.O. Box 277 (01613-0277)
PHONE.............................508 791-8778
Joseph A Amorello, *Pr*
Anthony F Amorello Junior, *VP*
James A Amorello,   *
EMP: 40 **EST:** 1914
SQ FT: 10,000
SALES (est): 9.17MM **Privately Held**
Web: www.afamorello.org
SIC: 1611 1623 2951   Highway and street paving contractor; Sewer line construction; Asphalt paving mixtures and blocks

(G-13695)
A SCHULMAN CUSTOM COMPOUNDING NE INC
53 Millbrook St Ste 2 (01606-2817)
PHONE.............................508 756-0002
◆ **EMP:** 140
Web: www.ecmplastics.com
SIC: 2821   Plastics materials and resins

(G-13696)
ABBOTT LABORATORIES
Also Called: Sodexo Abbott Bioresearch
100 Research Dr (01605-4314)
PHONE.............................508 849-2500
Catherine Tripp, *Brnch Mgr*
EMP: 12
SALES (corp-wide): 43.65B **Publicly Held**
Web: www.abbott.com
SIC: 2834   Druggists' preparations (pharmaceuticals)
PA: Abbott Laboratories
100 Abbott Park Rd
Abbott Park IL 60064
224 667-6100

(G-13697)
ADIRONDACK BEVERAGES CORP
1001 Southbridge St (01610-2218)
PHONE.............................800 734-9800
EMP: 11 **EST:** 2015
SALES (est): 951.9K **Privately Held**
SIC: 2086   Soft drinks: packaged in cans, bottles, etc.

(G-13698)
AERO TURBINE COMPONENTS INC
993 Millbury St (01607-2106)
PHONE.............................508 755-2121
Jon Adams, *Pr*
EMP: 9 **EST:** 2003
SQ FT: 4,841
SALES (est): 1.4MM **Privately Held**
Web: www.aeroturbinecomponents.com

SIC: 3724   Turbines, aircraft type

(G-13699)
ANGEL GUARD PRODUCTS INC
120 Goddard Memorial Dr (01603-1260)
PHONE.............................508 791-1073
James Badgio, *Pr*
Fred Cormier, *Pr*
Scot Peterson, *VP*
▲ **EMP:** 9 **EST:** 1989
SQ FT: 7,000
SALES (est): 932.86K **Privately Held**
Web: www.angelguardproducts.com
SIC: 3991 3842 8732   Brooms and brushes; Personal safety equipment; Commercial nonphysical research

(G-13700)
APPLIED PLASTIC TECHNOLOGY INC
169 Fremont St (01603-2352)
PHONE.............................508 752-5924
Jim Morin, *Pr*
Frank Beckerer,   *
Kathy Brady,   *
Randy Guertin,   *
◆ **EMP:** 32 **EST:** 1978
SQ FT: 55,000
SALES (est): 6.71MM **Privately Held**
Web: www.aplastic.com
SIC: 3089   Injection molding of plastics

(G-13701)
B R T INC
Also Called: Toomey's Rent-All Center
240 Salisbury St (01609-1639)
PHONE.............................508 791-2383
TOLL FREE: 800
Daniel S Toomey, *Pr*
EMP: 24 **EST:** 1973
SALES (est): 2.18MM **Privately Held**
Web: www.toomeysrentall.com
SIC: 7359 2389   Rental store, general; Costumes

(G-13702)
BASF BIORESEARCH CORP
100 Research Dr (01605-4314)
PHONE.............................508 849-2500
EMP: 25 **EST:** 1985
SALES (est): 2.18MM
SALES (corp-wide): 43.65B **Publicly Held**
SIC: 8731 2833   Commercial physical research; Medicinals and botanicals
PA: Abbott Laboratories
100 Abbott Park Rd
Abbott Park IL 60064
224 667-6100

(G-13703)
BELDEN INC
Also Called: Telecast Fibr Systems -An Unnc
324 Clark St (01606-1214)
PHONE.............................508 754-4858
Chris D Minico, *Dir*
EMP: 9
SALES (corp-wide): 2.51B **Publicly Held**
Web: www.belden.com
SIC: 3357   Communication wire
PA: Belden Inc.
1 N Brentwood Blvd Fl 15
Saint Louis MO 63105
314 854-8000

(G-13704)
BODYSHOP WORLD BY WAGNER INC
700 Plantation St (01605-2084)
PHONE.............................508 853-0300

Ronald W Wagner, *Pr*
Marsha Wagner, *Clerk*
EMP: 11 **EST:** 1987
SQ FT: 22,000
SALES (est): 482.87K **Privately Held**
SIC: 7532 5531 7534   Body shop, automotive ; Automotive tires; Tire repair shop

(G-13705)
BOSTON ATLANTIC CORP
Also Called: Boston Atlantic Gasket and Rbr
7 Harris Ct (01610-1555)
PHONE.............................508 754-4076
Carl Benander, *Pr*
EMP: 10 **EST:** 1992
SQ FT: 16,000
SALES (est): 360.12K **Privately Held**
Web: www.gasketexpress.com
SIC: 3053 5085   Gaskets, all materials; Gaskets

(G-13706)
CHILMARK ARCHTCTURAL WDWKG LLC
705 Plantation St (01605-2061)
PHONE.............................508 856-9200
EMP: 10 **EST:** 1992
SALES (est): 1.56MM **Privately Held**
Web: www.chilmarkdm.com
SIC: 2431   Woodwork, interior and ornamental, nec

(G-13707)
CITY WELDING & FABRICATION INC
10 Ararat St Ste 1 (01606-3315)
PHONE.............................508 853-6000
Paul Curci, *Pr*
EMP: 21 **EST:** 1998
SQ FT: 1,500
SALES (est): 891.76K **Privately Held**
Web: www.cityweld.com
SIC: 7692   Welding repair

(G-13708)
CLARK MAILING SERVICE INC
41 Jackson St (01608-2293)
PHONE.............................508 752-1953
Robert H Clark Junior, *Pr*
Dorothy Clark,   *
Robert H Clark Senior, *Mgr*
▲ **EMP:** 35 **EST:** 1963
SQ FT: 30,000
SALES (est): 2.09MM **Privately Held**
Web: www.clarkmailing.com
SIC: 7331 2752   Mailing service; Offset printing

(G-13709)
CONTINENTAL WOODCRAFT INC (PA)
Also Called: Continental Consolidated Inds
7 Coppage Dr (01603-1252)
PHONE.............................508 581-9560
Paul Hamlon, *Pr*
EMP: 41 **EST:** 1960
SALES (est): 4.91MM
SALES (corp-wide): 4.91MM **Privately Held**
Web: www.continentalwoodcraft.com
SIC: 2541 2542 2431   Office fixtures, wood; Office and store showcases and display fixtures; Millwork

(G-13710)
COORSTEK INC
Also Called: Coorstek Worcester
5 Norton Dr (01606-2679)
PHONE.............................774 317-2600

EMP: 310
SALES (corp-wide): 1.16B **Privately Held**
Web: www.coorstek.com
SIC: 3264 3053 3081 3082 Porcelain electrical supplies; Gaskets; packing and sealing devices; Unsupported plastics film and sheet; Unsupported plastics profile shapes
HQ: Coorstek, Inc.
14143 Denver West Pkwy # 400
Lakewood CO 80401
303 271-7000

(G-13711)
CREATIVE PACKAGING INC (PA)
175 James St (01603-1024)
PHONE..................508 756-7275
James E Hamilton, *Pr*
Richard M Perlman, *Care Vice President*
EMP: 38 **EST:** 1974
SQ FT: 100,000
SALES (est): 6.73MM
SALES (corp-wide): 6.73MM **Privately Held**
Web: www.creativeus.com
SIC: 2653 Boxes, corrugated: made from purchased materials

(G-13712)
CRYOGENIC INSTITUTE NENG INC
Also Called: Nitrofreeze Cryogenic Services
78 Chilmark St (01604-2834)
PHONE..................508 459-7447
Robin A Rhodes, *Pr*
EMP: 10 **EST:** 2002
SQ FT: 2,000
SALES (est): 1.94MM **Privately Held**
Web: www.nitrofreeze.com
SIC: 7699 8734 3399 5169 Industrial equipment cleaning; Testing laboratories; Cryogenic treatment of metal; Dry ice

(G-13713)
DAVID CLARK COMPANY INC (PA)
Also Called: David Clark
360 Franklin St (01604-4900)
P.O. Box 15054 (01615-0054)
PHONE..................508 756-6216
Robert A Vincent, *Pr*
Darald R Libby, *Ch Bd*
David A Sweet, *VP*
James T Bergin, *VP*
Richard M Urella, *VP*
▲ **EMP:** 215 **EST:** 2006
SQ FT: 277,000
SALES (est): 96.68MM
SALES (corp-wide): 96.68MM **Privately Held**
Web: www.davidclarkcompany.com
SIC: 3663 3842 3841 Radio broadcasting and communications equipment; Clothing, fire resistant and protective; Medical instruments and equipment, blood and bone work

(G-13714)
DAVIS CORP WORCESTER INC (PA)
Also Called: Davis Publications
44 Portland St (01608-2023)
PHONE..................508 754-7201
Wyatt R Wade, *Pr*
Mark W Davis, *Ch*
Jeffrey Davis, *
Thomas Lucci, *CFO*
◆ **EMP:** 24 **EST:** 1856
SQ FT: 85,000
SALES (est): 6.83K

SALES (corp-wide): 6.83K **Privately Held**
Web: www.davisart.com
SIC: 2731 2721 Books, publishing only; Periodicals

(G-13715)
DAVIS PUBLICATIONS INC
Also Called: Davis Art Images
50 Portland St Fl 3 (01608-2013)
PHONE..................508 754-7201
Julian Wade, *Pr*
Julian D Wade, *Pr*
Mark Davis, *Ch Bd*
EMP: 33 **EST:** 1958
SQ FT: 50,000
SALES (est): 4.24MM
SALES (corp-wide): 6.83K **Privately Held**
Web: www.davisart.com
SIC: 2741 Miscellaneous publishing
PA: Davis Corporation Of Worcester, Inc.
44 Portland St
Worcester MA 01608
508 754-7201

(G-13716)
DESIGN CENTERS COM
725 Southbridge St (01610-2916)
PHONE..................800 570-1120
Jamie Rotman, *Pr*
EMP: 10 **EST:** 2010
SALES (est): 226.47K **Privately Held**
SIC: 3674 Semiconductors and related devices

(G-13717)
DKD SOLUTIONS INC
Also Called: Ruby Electric
77 E Worcester St (01604-3648)
PHONE..................508 762-9114
Donald R Juozaitis, *Pr*
EMP: 9 **EST:** 2010
SALES (est): 1.56MM **Privately Held**
Web: www.dkdsolutions.com
SIC: 3621 Motors, electric

(G-13718)
DOCUMENTS ON DEMAND INC
Also Called: AlphaGraphics
184 Main St (01608-1146)
PHONE..................508 793-0956
Raymond H Mantyla Junior, *Pr*
EMP: 11 **EST:** 2006
SALES (est): 1.72MM **Privately Held**
Web: www.alphagraphics.com
SIC: 2752 Commercial printing, lithographic

(G-13719)
DSS CIRCUITS INC
29 Oriental St (01605-4008)
PHONE..................508 852-8061
Wayne Truchsess, *Pr*
EMP: 9 **EST:** 2010
SALES (est): 145.1K **Privately Held**
Web: www.dsscircuits.com
SIC: 3679 Microwave components

(G-13720)
ENAMEL PURE INC
17 Briden St (01605-2662)
PHONE..................508 335-4824
Nathan Monty, *CEO*
Nathan Monty, *Prin*
Charles Dresser, *Prin*
EMP: 12 **EST:** 2020
SALES (est): 564.14K **Privately Held**
Web: www.enamelpure.com
SIC: 3843 Dental equipment

(G-13721)
EVERSON DISTRIBUTING CO INC
Also Called: Treasuretreats
108 Grove St Ste 200 (01605-2651)
PHONE..................413 533-9261
Robert W Everson, *Pr*
▲ **EMP:** 35 **EST:** 1972
SQ FT: 20,000
SALES (est): 6.65MM **Privately Held**
SIC: 5145 4789 4212 2064 Candy; Cargo loading and unloading services; Local trucking, without storage; Candy and other confectionery products

(G-13722)
FASTCAST CONSORTIUM INC
Also Called: Kervick Entreprises
40 Rockdale St (01606-1908)
PHONE..................508 853-4500
Robert Kervick, *Pr*
Paul Kervick, *
EMP: 24 **EST:** 1994
SALES (est): 484.01K **Privately Held**
SIC: 3069 Castings, rubber

(G-13723)
FISHER CONTRACTING CORPORATION
Also Called: Fisher Contracting
11 Webster Pl (01603-1923)
P.O. Box 20039 (01602-0039)
PHONE..................508 421-6989
Charran Fisher, *Pr*
Charran King Fisher, *Pr*
EMP: 8 **EST:** 1998
SALES (est): 984.69K **Privately Held**
Web: www.fishercontracting.us
SIC: 1795 3443 Wrecking and demolition work; Dumpsters, garbage

(G-13724)
FLEX-O-GRAPHIC PRTG PLATE INC
33 Arctic St Ste 4 (01604-4931)
PHONE..................508 752-8100
John Carlson, *Pr*
EMP: 25 **EST:** 1956
SQ FT: 20,000
SALES (est): 2.28MM **Privately Held**
Web: www.flexographics.com
SIC: 3555 Printing trades machinery

(G-13725)
FORM ROLL DIE CORP (PA)
217 Stafford St (01603-1198)
PHONE..................508 755-2010
Mildred Mason, *Pr*
Donna Damuni, *Sec*
Diane Generelli, *Treas*
Marie Mason, *Stockholder*
Richard Mason, *Stockholder*
▼ **EMP:** 18 **EST:** 1961
SQ FT: 14,000
SALES (est): 2.15MM
SALES (corp-wide): 2.15MM **Privately Held**
Web: www.formrolldie.com
SIC: 3545 3542 Machine tool accessories; Knurling machines

(G-13726)
FORM ROLL DIE CORP
Also Called: Stafford Special Tool
88 Webster Pl (01603-1920)
PHONE..................508 755-5302
Richard Mason, *Brnch Mgr*
EMP: 13
SALES (corp-wide): 2.15MM **Privately Held**

Web: www.formrolldie.com
SIC: 3542 3599 Machine tools, metal forming type; Flexible metal hose, tubing, and bellows
PA: Form Roll Die Corp.
217 Stafford St
Worcester MA 01603
508 755-2010

(G-13727)
GASKET EXPRESS INC
7 Harris Ct (01610)
PHONE..................508 754-4076
Dale L Benander, *Pr*
EMP: 7 **EST:** 2016
SALES (est): 229.91K **Privately Held**
Web: www.gasketexpress.com
SIC: 3053 Gaskets, all materials

(G-13728)
GATEHOUSE MEDIA LLC
Also Called: Landmark, The
100 Front St Ste 500 (01608-1440)
PHONE..................508 829-5981
Kirk Davis, *Brnch Mgr*
EMP: 10
SALES (corp-wide): 2.95B **Publicly Held**
Web: www.gannett.com
SIC: 5963 2711 Newspapers, home delivery, not by printers or publishers; Newspapers
HQ: Gatehouse Media, Llc
175 Sullys Trl Ste 203
Pittsford NY 14534
585 598-0030

(G-13729)
GEISEL SOFTWARE INC
67 Millbrook St Ste 520 (01606-2846)
PHONE..................508 853-5310
Brian J Geisel, *Pr*
EMP: 12 **EST:** 2011
SALES (est): 1.18MM **Privately Held**
Web: www.geisel.software
SIC: 7372 Business oriented computer software

(G-13730)
GEM ASSET ACQUISITION LLC
Also Called: Gemseal Pvements Pdts - Boston
110 Blackstone River Rd (01607-1489)
PHONE..................508 419-7710
EMP: 28
SALES (corp-wide): 17.13MM **Privately Held**
SIC: 2951 Asphalt paving mixtures and blocks
PA: Gem Asset Acquisition Llc
1855 Lindbergh St Ste 500
Charlotte NC 28208
704 225-3321

(G-13731)
GENERAL WIRE PRODUCTS INC
425 Shrewsbury St (01604-1638)
PHONE..................508 752-8260
Thomas P Andrews, *Pr*
Thomas P Andrews Junior, *VP*
Beatrice Andrews, *
EMP: 24 **EST:** 1985
SQ FT: 30,000
SALES (est): 4.27MM
SALES (corp-wide): 4.27MM **Privately Held**
Web: www.generalwireproducts.com

GEOGRAPHIC

SIC: 3357 3643 3496 3315 Building wire and cable, nonferrous; Current-carrying wiring services; Miscellaneous fabricated wire products; Steel wire and related products
PA: United Wire & Cable Corporation
425 Shrewsbury St
Worcester MA 01604
508 757-3872

(G-13732)
GINSENG UP CORPORATION
75 E Worcester St (01604-3648)
PHONE.................................508 799-6178
EMP: 7
SALES (corp-wide): 5.79MM **Privately Held**
Web: www.ginsengup.com
SIC: 2086 Soft drinks: packaged in cans, bottles, etc.
PA: Ginseng Up Corporation
16 Plum St
Worcester MA 01604
508 799-6178

(G-13733)
GINSENG UP CORPORATION (PA)
16 Plum St (01604-3600)
PHONE.................................508 799-6178
Sang Kil Han, *Pr*
◆ **EMP:** 8 **EST:** 1981
SQ FT: 1,000
SALES (est): 5.79MM
SALES (corp-wide): 5.79MM **Privately Held**
Web: www.ginsengup.com
SIC: 2086 Soft drinks: packaged in cans, bottles, etc.

(G-13734)
GLACCET CORPORATION
54 Rockdale St Ste 2 (01606-1928)
PHONE.................................508 752-7356
Mark Mccurn, *Pr*
EMP: 25 **EST:** 1976
SQ FT: 13,000
SALES (est): 3.51MM **Privately Held**
Web: www.ninepointswoodworking.com
SIC: 2431 Millwork

(G-13735)
GUERTINS GRAPHICS INC
Also Called: Guertin Graphics & Awards
134 Southbridge St Ste 136 (01608)
PHONE.................................508 754-0200
TOLL FREE: 800
John Guertin, *Pr*
Florence Guertin, *Pr*
EMP: 10 **EST:** 1987
SQ FT: 9,000
SALES (est): 786.43K **Privately Held**
Web: www.guertingraphics.com
SIC: 5699 2759 T-shirts, custom printed; Screen printing

(G-13736)
HAMILTON SIGN & DESIGN INC
545 Sw Cutoff (01607-1766)
PHONE.................................508 459-9731
Ronald S Hamilton, *Prin*
EMP: 8 **EST:** 2013
SALES (est): 485.44K **Privately Held**
SIC: 3993 Signs and advertising specialties

(G-13737)
HMS
94 Hamilton St (01604-2258)
PHONE.................................508 831-8317
Ron Messier, *Prin*

EMP: 8 **EST:** 2016
SALES (est): 57.99K **Privately Held**
Web: patrickobrian.fandom.com
SIC: 2741 Miscellaneous publishing

(G-13738)
HOWARD PRODUCTS INCORPORATED
4 Birchwood Rd (01609-1108)
P.O. Box 2322 (01613-2322)
PHONE.................................508 757-2440
David Hawley, *Pr*
Bradford F Hawley, *Stockholder*
Martha Amy, *VP*
EMP: 16 **EST:** 1948
SALES (est): 2.24MM **Privately Held**
Web: www.nefm.com
SIC: 3444 Sheet metal specialties, not stamped

(G-13739)
IDEAL SHEET METAL CORP
5 Winter St (01604-4119)
P.O. Box 943 (01613-0943)
PHONE.................................508 799-2781
Joseph J Bafaro, *Pr*
Joseph J Bafaro Prestreas, *Prin*
EMP: 10 **EST:** 1950
SALES (est): 302.72K **Privately Held**
Web: www.choylifut.net
SIC: 1711 3444 Warm air heating and air conditioning contractor; Sheet metalwork

(G-13740)
INDEPENENT PLATING CO
35 New St (01605-3324)
PHONE.................................508 756-0301
Charles D Flanagan, *Pr*
EMP: 17 **EST:** 2011
SALES (est): 188.27K **Privately Held**
Web: www.independentplating.com
SIC: 3471 3479 Plating of metals or formed products; Coating of metals with plastic or resins

(G-13741)
INDUSTRIAL PACKAGING SUP INC
150 Industrial Rd (01605)
PHONE.................................978 514-9960
Louise Dizazzo, *Brnch Mgr*
EMP: 19
SALES (corp-wide): 19.82MM **Privately Held**
Web: www.industrialpackaging.com
SIC: 7389 2671 5084 Packaging and labeling services; Plastic film, coated or laminated for packaging; Packaging machinery and equipment
PA: Industrial Packaging Supply, Inc.
5 Cudworth Rd
Webster MA 01570
508 499-1600

(G-13742)
INSIGNIA ATHLETICS LLC
60 Fremont St (01603-2355)
PHONE.................................508 756-3633
Robert J Devaney, *Prin*
EMP: 9 **EST:** 2010
SALES (est): 430.86K **Privately Held**
Web: www.insigniaathletics.com
SIC: 3949 Sporting and athletic goods, nec

(G-13743)
INTERNATIONAL CRMIC ENGRG CORP (PA)
235 Brooks St (01606-3307)
PHONE.................................508 853-4700

Merrill W Higgins, *CEO*
Jonathan Higgins, *
Andrew Higgins, *
EMP: 48 **EST:** 1976
SQ FT: 10,000
SALES (est): 6.78MM
SALES (corp-wide): 6.78MM **Privately Held**
Web: www.internationalceramicengineering.com
SIC: 3299 Ceramic fiber

(G-13744)
JEFFERSON RUBBER WORKS INC
Also Called: Jefferson Rubber Products
17 Coppage Dr (01603-1252)
PHONE.................................508 791-3600
David F Pentland, *Ch Bd*
▲ **EMP:** 100 **EST:** 1975
SQ FT: 30,000
SALES (est): 17.77MM **Privately Held**
Web: www.jeffersonrubber.com
SIC: 3069 3061 Molded rubber products; Mechanical rubber goods

(G-13745)
JOE MILLER INC
333 Sw Cutoff (01604-2713)
PHONE.................................508 753-8581
TOLL FREE: 800
Joseph P Miller, *Pr*
EMP: 10 **EST:** 1957
SQ FT: 3,520
SALES (est): 1.52MM **Privately Held**
Web: www.millerfence.com
SIC: 1799 5211 5031 5039 Fence construction; Fencing; Fencing, wood; Wire fence, gates, and accessories

(G-13746)
JS SALE CORP
Also Called: Foley Marine & Industrial Engs
200 Summer St (01604-4012)
PHONE.................................508 753-2979
Jay W Foley, *Pr*
Jay W Foley, *Pr*
Susan M Foley, *
▼ **EMP:** 25 **EST:** 1916
SQ FT: 20,000
SALES (est): 6.63MM **Privately Held**
Web: www.foleyengines.com
SIC: 5084 3519 Engines and parts, diesel; Internal combustion engines, nec

(G-13747)
KENNEDY DIE CASTINGS INC
15 Coppage Dr Airport Industrial Park (01603)
PHONE.................................508 791-5594
Paul S Kennedy, *Pr*
Robert M Kennedy, *
Joseph C Deliso, *General Vice President*
EMP: 225 **EST:** 1948
SQ FT: 80,000
SALES (est): 22MM **Privately Held**
SIC: 3363 3364 3369 Aluminum die-castings; Zinc and zinc-base alloy die-castings; Nonferrous foundries, nec

(G-13748)
KERVICK FAMILY FOUNDATION INC
40 Rockdale St (01606-1908)
PHONE.................................508 853-4500
Robert B Kervick, *Pr*
Paul J Kervick, *Ch Bd*
Kevin M Kervick, *Ex VP*
Joseph Dynof, *Treas*
Deborah Emmons, *Asst Tr*

EMP: 41 **EST:** 1905
SQ FT: 160,000
SALES (est): 689.75K **Privately Held**
Web: www.komtek.com
SIC: 3462 3463 2752 3324 Iron and steel forgings; Nonferrous forgings; Offset printing ; Commercial investment castings, ferrous

(G-13749)
KINEFAC CORPORATION
Also Called: Kinepower Company Division
156 Goddard Memorial Dr (01603-1262)
PHONE.................................508 754-6901
Noel P Greis, *Pr*
Roger R Bradford, *
Richard J Koral, *
▲ **EMP:** 55 **EST:** 1962
SQ FT: 57,500
SALES (est): 9.94MM **Privately Held**
Web: www.kinefac.com
SIC: 3541 3542 5085 3547 Machine tools, metal cutting type; Machine tools, metal forming type; Industrial supplies; Rolling mill machinery

(G-13750)
KOMTEK FORGE LLC
40 Rockdale St (01606-1908)
PHONE.................................508 853-4500
Brian Powers, *Managing Member*
EMP: 37 **EST:** 2004
SALES (est): 14.09MM
SALES (corp-wide): 127.75MM **Publicly Held**
Web: www.komtek.com
SIC: 3366 Copper foundries
HQ: Cad Enterprises, Inc.
302 N 52nd Ave
Phoenix AZ 85043
602 278-4407

(G-13751)
L & R MANUFACTURING CO INC
340 Tacoma St (01605-4115)
PHONE.................................508 853-0562
Robert M Ritter, *Pr*
John A Erickson Junior, *Clerk*
EMP: 16 **EST:** 1958
SQ FT: 15,000
SALES (est): 1.81MM **Privately Held**
SIC: 3498 Tube fabricating (contract bending and shaping)

(G-13752)
L HARDY COMPANY INC (PA)
17 Mill St (01603-2075)
P.O. Box 30277 (01603-0277)
PHONE.................................508 757-3480
Norman Monks, *Pr*
◆ **EMP:** 22 **EST:** 1854
SQ FT: 30,000
SALES (est): 4MM
SALES (corp-wide): 4MM **Privately Held**
SIC: 3545 Cutting tools for machine tools

(G-13753)
LIGHTING BY HAMMERWORKS (PA)
6 Fremont St (01603-2305)
PHONE.................................508 755-3434
Mark Rocheford, *Pt*
Thomas Sauriol, *Pt*
EMP: 22 **EST:** 1978
SQ FT: 3,700
SALES (est): 809.33K
SALES (corp-wide): 809.33K **Privately Held**
Web: www.hammerworks.com

▲ = Import ▼ = Export
◆ = Import/Export

SIC: **5961** 3648 5719 5063   General merchandise, mail order; Outdoor lighting equipment; Lighting fixtures; Lighting fixtures

(G-13754)
LUTCO BEARINGS INC
Also Called: Lutco
677 Cambridge St Ste 1 (01610-2664)
PHONE.................................508 756-6296
John C Stowe, *Pr*
Steven Noone, *
EMP: 100 EST: 1945
SQ FT: 80,000
SALES (est): 6.06MM **Privately Held**
Web: www.lutco.com
SIC: 3451   Screw machine products

(G-13755)
MADISON CABLE CORPORATION
125 Goddard Memorial Dr (01603-1233)
PHONE.................................800 522-6752
Nicolas Marinelarena, *CFO*
▲ **EMP:** 98 **EST:** 1970
SQ FT: 180,000
SALES (est): 14.6MM **Privately Held**
SIC: 3357 3643 3577   Nonferrous wiredrawing and insulating; Current-carrying wiring services; Computer peripheral equipment, nec
HQ: Te Connectivity Corporation
1050 Westlakes Dr
Berwyn PA 19312
610 893-9800

(G-13756)
MAGMOTOR TECHNOLOGIES INC
Also Called: Magmotor
10 Coppage Dr (01603-1252)
PHONE.................................508 835-4305
Aryan Papoli, *CEO*
▲ **EMP:** 11 **EST:** 1979
SQ FT: 44,000
SALES (est): 2.4MM **Privately Held**
Web: www.magmotor.com
SIC: 3714 3823   Transmissions, motor vehicle; Computer interface equipment, for industrial process control

(G-13757)
MARINE USA INC
200 Sw Cutoff Ste 1 (01604-2796)
PHONE.................................508 791-7116
TOLL FREE: 800
Alice Tsourides, *Pr*
▼ **EMP:** 32 **EST:** 1986
SQ FT: 22,000
SALES (est): 4.84MM **Privately Held**
Web: www.usamarineinc.com
SIC: 5551 7699 3732   Motor boat dealers; Boat repair; Boatbuilding and repairing

(G-13758)
MASSACHSTTS SIGN INSTLLTION CO
Also Called: AlphaGraphics
184 Main St (01608-1146)
PHONE.................................508 793-0956
Michael Hannigan, *Dir*
EMP: 10 **EST:** 2020
SALES (est): 332.56K **Privately Held**
Web: www.alphagraphics.com
SIC: 3993   Signs and advertising specialties

(G-13759)
MICROBIOTIX INC
1 Innovation Dr Ste 120c (01605-4328)

PHONE.................................508 757-2800
Terry Bowlin, *Pr*
George Wright, *Stockholder**
EMP: 25 **EST:** 1998
SQ FT: 10,739
SALES (est): 8.19MM **Privately Held**
Web: www.microbiotix.com
SIC: 2833 8731   Antibiotics; Biotechnical research, commercial

(G-13760)
MINDSCIENCES INC
45 Hickory Dr (01609-1016)
PHONE.................................516 658-2985
EMP: 9 **EST:** 2012
SALES (est): 204.73K **Privately Held**
Web: www.drjud.com
SIC: 3845   Electroencephalographs

(G-13761)
MORGAN ENTERPRISES INC
110 Blackstone River Rd (01607-1489)
P.O. Box 70316 (01607-0316)
PHONE.................................985 377-3216
Dustin Morgan, *Prin*
EMP: 8 **EST:** 2012
SALES (est): 526.88K **Privately Held**
SIC: 2759   Letterpress and screen printing

(G-13762)
MORONEY BODYWORKS INC
20 Eskow Rd (01604-2702)
PHONE.................................508 792-2878
Norman Quinton Junior, *Pr*
Norman Quinton Senior, *Pr*
Norman Quinton, *Treas*
EMP: 14 **EST:** 1985
SQ FT: 20,000
SALES (est): 2.09MM **Privately Held**
Web: www.moroneybody.com
SIC: 5013 3713   Truck parts and accessories ; Truck bodies and parts

(G-13763)
NALEY INC
774 W Boylston St (01606-3041)
PHONE.................................508 579-8378
Jill Wildt, *Prin*
EMP: 9 **EST:** 2005
SALES (est): 343.76K **Privately Held**
SIC: 2752   Commercial printing, lithographic

(G-13764)
NEW ENGLAND SIGN GROUP INC
Also Called: Kay Gee Sign and Graphics Co
14a E Worcester St (01604-3674)
PHONE.................................508 779-0821
Kari Lunden, *Pr*
Michael Hannigan, *General Vice President*
Norm Picard, *General Vice President*
EMP: 9 **EST:** 2015
SALES (est): 485.32K **Privately Held**
SIC: 3993   Signs and advertising specialties

(G-13765)
NEW ENGLAND SUGARS LLC
1120 Millbury St (01607-1415)
PHONE.................................508 792-3801
EMP: 13 **EST:** 2016
SALES (est): 521.75K **Privately Held**
Web: www.sugars.com
SIC: 2061   Powdered cane sugar

(G-13766)
NEW METHOD PLATING CO INC
43 Hammond St (01610-1523)
PHONE.................................508 754-2671
Ralph J Capalbo Junior, *Pr*

EMP: 26 **EST:** 1931
SQ FT: 25,000
SALES (est): 2.2MM **Privately Held**
Web: www.newmethodplating.com
SIC: 3471   Electroplating of metals or formed products

(G-13767)
PADCO INC
19 Wells St (01604-1727)
PHONE.................................508 753-8486
Joseph A Padavano, *Pr*
Carolyn Padavano, *Treas*
EMP: 17 **EST:** 1974
SALES (est): 541.67K **Privately Held**
Web: www.padco-inc.com
SIC: 2431   Millwork

(G-13768)
PATRIOT SEAL COATING
9 Greendale Ave (01606-3263)
PHONE.................................774 386-8531
EMP: 7 **EST:** 2019
SALES (est): 304.99K **Privately Held**
SIC: 2952   Asphalt felts and coatings

(G-13769)
PILGRIM TOOL & DIE CO INC
565 Southbridge St (01610-1727)
P.O. Box 2837 (01613-2837)
PHONE.................................508 753-0190
Robert J Graham Junior, *Pr*
Jean Graham, *Clerk*
Micheal Graham, *VP*
EMP: 7 **EST:** 1969
SQ FT: 5,000
SALES (est): 822.42K **Privately Held**
SIC: 3544   Forms (molds), for foundry and plastics working machinery

(G-13770)
PLASTICS UNLIMITED OF MA INC
55 Millbrook St Ste 5 (01606-2804)
PHONE.................................508 752-7842
TOLL FREE: 800
Marc L Eisenstock, *Pr*
EMP: 7 **EST:** 1974
SQ FT: 9,000
SALES (est): 1.28MM **Privately Held**
SIC: 5162 3084   Plastics sheets and rods; Plastics pipe

(G-13771)
POBCO INC
Also Called: Pobco
99 Hope Ave (01603-2298)
PHONE.................................508 791-6376
Stephen P Johnson, *Pr*
Thomas G Johnson, *VP*
David W Johnson, *VP*
Lisa K Khoury, *Treas*
▼ **EMP:** 20 **EST:** 1929
SQ FT: 20,000
SALES (est): 6.09MM **Privately Held**
Web: www.pobcoplastics.com
SIC: 3089 2499   Bearings, plastics; Bearings, wood

(G-13772)
POLAR CORP (PA)
Also Called: Polar Beverages
1001 Southbridge St (01610-2218)
P.O. Box 15011 (01615-0011)
PHONE.................................508 753-6383
TOLL FREE: 800
Ralph D Crowley Junior, *Pr*
Christopher Crowley, *
Michael J Mulrain, *
▼ **EMP:** 700 **EST:** 1882

SQ FT: 350,000
SALES (est): 533.01MM
SALES (corp-wide): 533.01MM **Privately Held**
Web: www.polarseltzer.com
SIC: 2086 5149   Soft drinks: packaged in cans, bottles, etc.; Soft drinks

(G-13773)
PREMATECH LLC
Also Called: Prematech Advanced Ceramics
160 Goddard Memorial Dr (01603-1260)
PHONE.................................508 791-9549
Mona Lynn Pappafava, *Pr*
Marcy Pappafava, *
James Vazvo, *
EMP: 35 **EST:** 2004
SQ FT: 26,000
SALES (est): 5.58MM **Privately Held**
Web: www.prematechac.com
SIC: 3291   Grinding balls, ceramic

(G-13774)
PREMATECHNOLIGIES LLC
Prematech Advanced Ceramics
160 Goddard Memorial Dr (01603-1260)
PHONE.................................508 791-9549
John Killem, *Managing Member*
EMP: 45
SALES (corp-wide): 2.5MM **Privately Held**
Web: www.prematechac.com
SIC: 3599   Machine shop, jobbing and repair
PA: Prematechnoligies Llc
Garden St
Greensburg PA

(G-13775)
PUNCHPOPS LLC
61 Harvard St Fl 3 (01609-2752)
PHONE.................................508 344-7932
Michael Melkonian, *Prin*
EMP: 7 **EST:** 2018
SALES (est): 370.72K **Privately Held**
Web: www.drinkpunchpops.com
SIC: 2084   Wines

(G-13776)
RAND-WHITNEY CONTAINER LLC
Also Called: Rand Whitney-Greenwood St
2 Rand Whitney Way (01607-1890)
PHONE.................................774 420-2425
EMP: 10
Web: www.randwhitney.com
SIC: 2653   Boxes, corrugated: made from purchased materials
HQ: Rand-Whitney Container Llc
1 Rand Whitney Way
Worcester MA 01607
508 890-7000

(G-13777)
RAND-WHITNEY CONTAINER LLC (DH)
1 Rand Whitney Way (01607-1890)
PHONE.................................508 890-7000
EMP: 175 **EST:** 1967
SQ FT: 300,000
SALES (est): 103.46MM **Privately Held**
Web: www.randwhitney.com
SIC: 2653 2631   Boxes, corrugated: made from purchased materials; Paperboard mills
HQ: Rand-Whitney Group Llc
1 Rand Whitney Way
Worcester MA 01607
508 791-2301

(G-13778)
RAND-WHITNEY GROUP LLC
(HQ)
1 Rand Whitney Way (01607-1890)
PHONE.............................508 791-2301
EMP: 145 EST: 1857
SQ FT: 200,000
SALES (est): 218.78MM Privately Held
Web: www.randwhitney.com
SIC: 2653 2657 2631 Boxes, corrugated:
　made from purchased materials; Folding
　paperboard boxes; Paperboard mills
PA: Kraft Group Llc
　　1 Patriot Pl
　　Foxboro MA 02035

(G-13779)
RAND-WHITNEY INDUSTRIES
LLC
1 Rand Whitney Way (01607-1890)
PHONE.............................508 791-2301
EMP: 30 EST: 1997
SALES (est): 4.02MM Privately Held
Web: www.randwhitney.com
SIC: 2653 Boxes, corrugated: made from
　purchased materials

(G-13780)
RAND-WHITNEY PACKAGING
CORP
150 Grove St (01605-1706)
PHONE.............................508 929-3400
Robert Kraft, Pr
EMP: 60 EST: 2002
SQ FT: 190,000
SALES (est): 9.96MM Privately Held
Web: www.randwhitney.com
SIC: 7389 2631 Packaging and labeling
　services; Container, packaging, and
　boxboard
HQ: Rand-Whitney Group Llc
　　1 Rand Whitney Way
　　Worcester MA 01607
　　508 791-2301

(G-13781)
READY 2 RUN GRAPHICS SIGNS
INC
240 Barber Ave Ste 5 (01606-2479)
PHONE.............................508 459-9977
David Winchester, Pr
EMP: 12 EST: 2013
SALES (est): 961.03K Privately Held
Web: www.ready2rungraphics.com
SIC: 3993 Signs and advertising specialties

(G-13782)
REED MACHINERY INC (PA)
10a New Bond St (01606-2615)
PHONE.............................508 595-9090
James D Flanagan, Pr
Brian Faucher, VP
Steven Copeland, VP
William P Baldino, Sec
Jeffrey T Hoffman, Treas
▲ EMP: 15 EST: 2003
SQ FT: 25,000
SALES (est): 4.92MM
SALES (corp-wide): 4.92MM Privately
Held
Web: www.reed-machinery.com
SIC: 3545 Threading tools (machine tool
　accessories)

(G-13783)
REINFORCED STRUCTURES
FOR ELEC
50 Suffolk St (01604-4091)

PHONE.............................508 754-5316
James Romeo, Pr
Edward Romeo, *
Robert Romeo, *
Wendy Romeo, *
EMP: 16 EST: 1970
SQ FT: 10,000
SALES (est): 431.99K Privately Held
Web: www.reinforcedstructures.com
SIC: 2821 3678 3674 3644 Molding
　compounds, plastics; Electronic connectors
　; Semiconductors and related devices;
　Noncurrent-carrying wiring devices

(G-13784)
ROB ROY FOODS INC
Also Called: Culpepper's Bakery & Cafe
500 Cambridge St Ste 3 (01610-2600)
PHONE.............................508 755-8393
Robert La Pierre, Pr
Roy Samra, VP
Kevin Bonaventura, Treas
Anthony Bonaventura, Clerk
EMP: 8 EST: 1992
SQ FT: 4,800
SALES (est): 212.89K Privately Held
SIC: 5461 5812 2052 2051 Retail bakeries;
　Eating places; Cookies and crackers;
　Bread, cake, and related products

(G-13785)
S I HOWARD GLASS COMPANY
INC
Also Called: Howard S I Glass Co
379 Sw Cutoff (01604-2713)
PHONE.............................508 753-8146
Earl R Farmer Junior, Pr
Jason Perch, *
▲ EMP: 25 EST: 1940
SQ FT: 24,000
SALES (est): 4.07MM Privately Held
Web: www.howardglass.com
SIC: 3827 Binoculars

(G-13786)
SAEILO INC
130 Goddard Memorial Dr (01603-1260)
PHONE.............................508 799-9809
Sam Wada, Mgr
EMP: 35
SALES (corp-wide): 34.71MM Privately
Held
Web: www.saeilo.com
SIC: 3599 Machine shop, jobbing and repair
HQ: Saeilo, Inc.
　　105 Kahr Ave
　　Greeley PA 18425

(G-13787)
SAEILO USA INC
Kahr Arms
130 Goddard Memorial Dr (01603-1260)
PHONE.............................508 795-3919
EMP: 21
Web: www.saeilo.com
SIC: 3484 Small arms
HQ: Saeilo Usa Inc
　　105 Kahr Ave
　　Greeley PA 18425

(G-13788)
SAINT-GOBAIN ABRASIVES INC
(HQ)
Also Called: Bonded Abrasives
1 New Bond St (01606-2614)
P.O. Box 15008 (01615-0008)
PHONE.............................508 795-5000
Laurent Tellier, Pr
Steven Messmer, *
Minas Apelian, *

Glenn Knowlton, *
Robert Panaro, *
◆ EMP: 2500 EST: 1885
SALES (est): 2.16B
SALES (corp-wide): 397.78MM Privately
Held
Web: www.saint-gobain-abrasives.com
SIC: 3291 3559 3545 3297 Wheels, abrasive
　; Concrete products machinery; Diamond
　cutting tools for turning, boring, burnishing,
　etc.; Graphite refractories: carbon bond or
　ceramic bond
PA: Compagnie De Saint-Gobain
　　Tour Saint Gobain
　　Courbevoie 92400

(G-13789)
SAINT-GOBAIN ADFORS AMER
INC
1 New Bond St (01606-2614)
P.O. Box 15008 (01615-0008)
PHONE.............................508 795-2500
EMP: 72
SALES (corp-wide): 397.78MM Privately
Held
Web: www.adfors.com
SIC: 2297 Nonwoven fabrics
HQ: Saint-Gobain Adfors America, Inc.
　　140 John Jmes Adubon Pkwy
　　Buffalo NY 14228
　　716 775-3900

(G-13790)
SAINT-GOBAIN CERAMICS
PLAS INC
Also Called: Saint-Gobain Ceramic Materials
1 New Bond St (01606-2614)
PHONE.............................508 795-5000
Howard Wallar, Mgr
EMP: 85
SALES (corp-wide): 397.78MM Privately
Held
Web:
ceramicsrefractories.saint-gobain.com
SIC: 2819 Industrial inorganic chemicals,
　nec
HQ: Saint-Gobain Ceramics & Plastics, Inc.
　　20 Moores Rd
　　Malvern PA 19355

(G-13791)
SAINT-GOBAIN CERAMICS
PLAS INC
351 Stores St (01606)
PHONE.............................508 795-5000
EMP: 125
SALES (corp-wide): 397.78MM Privately
Held
Web: www.saint-gobain.com
SIC: 2819 Industrial inorganic chemicals,
　nec
HQ: Saint-Gobain Ceramics & Plastics, Inc.
　　20 Moores Rd
　　Malvern PA 19355

(G-13792)
SAINT-GOBAIN PRFMCE PLAS
CORP
717 Plantation St (01605-2039)
PHONE.............................508 852-3072
John Nolan, Mgr
EMP: 129
SALES (corp-wide): 397.78MM Privately
Held
Web: www.saint-gobain.com
SIC: 3089 3053 3357 3496 Thermoformed
　finished plastics products, nec; Gaskets
　and sealing devices; Nonferrous
　wiredrawing and insulating; Cable,
　uninsulated wire: made from purchased wire

HQ: Saint-Gobain Performance Plastics
　　Corporation
　　20 Moores Rd
　　Malvern PA 19355
　　440 836-6900

(G-13793)
SALT & PEPPER
268 Lincoln St Ste B (01605-2110)
PHONE.............................508 755-1113
Ilir Kashari, Pr
EMP: 13 EST: 2014
SALES (est): 93.08K Privately Held
SIC: 5812 2899 Eating places; Salt

(G-13794)
SANCLIFF INC
Also Called: Dykrex Wire Die Machinery Div
97 Temple St (01604-5029)
P.O. Box 2444 (01613-2444)
PHONE.............................508 795-0747
William G Drumm, Pr
EMP: 23 EST: 1967
SQ FT: 23,000
SALES (est): 977.83K Privately Held
Web: www.sancliff.com
SIC: 3544 3699 3559 Special dies and tools
　; Laser systems and equipment; Fiber
　optics strand coating machinery

(G-13795)
SCANDINAVIAN PANEL
SYSTEMS
370 Main St Ste 950 (01608-1770)
P.O. Box 763 (01092-0763)
PHONE.............................774 530-6340
Charles B Robson, Ch Bd
EMP: 12 EST: 2017
SALES (est): 676.57K Privately Held
SIC: 2431 2439 1522 Panel work, wood;
　Timbers, structural: laminated lumber; Multi-
　family dwellings, new construction

(G-13796)
SEALMASTER
110 Blackstone River Rd (01607-1489)
PHONE.............................508 926-8080
EMP: 8 EST: 2019
SALES (est): 643K Privately Held
Web: www.sealmaster.net
SIC: 2951 Asphalt paving mixtures and
　blocks

(G-13797)
SEM-TEC INC
47 Lagrange St (01610-1537)
PHONE.............................508 798-8551
Steven Krosoczka, Treas
Joseph M Krosoczka, *
▲ EMP: 39 EST: 1954
SQ FT: 100,000
SALES (est): 1.37MM Privately Held
Web: www.semtec.biz
SIC: 3399 3494 Steel balls; Valves and pipe
　fittings, nec

(G-13798)
SER LOGISTICS INC
Also Called: Ser Exposition Services
35b New St (01605-3324)
P.O. Box 178 (01760-0178)
PHONE.............................508 757-3397
Bruce R Nable, Ch
Patrick J Fitzpatrick, COO
EMP: 13 EST: 2011
SALES (est): 624.82K Privately Held
SIC: 4213 7389 2759 Household goods
　transport; Decoration service for special
　events; Commercial printing, nec

(G-13799)
SERRATO SIGNS LLC
Also Called: Serrato Signs
15 Dewey St (01609-2909)
PHONE.................................508 756-7004
EMP: 8 EST: 1946
SQ FT: 6,000
SALES (est): 876.61K **Privately Held**
Web: www.serratosigns.com
SIC: 3993 7389 Signs, not made in custom
sign painting shops; Crane and aerial lift
service

(G-13800)
SIDECHANNEL INC
146 Main St Rm 405 (01608-1137)
PHONE.................................508 925-0114
Brian Haugli, *Pr*
Deborah Macconnel, *Ch Bd*
Ryan Polk, *CFO*
EMP: 19 EST: 1953
SALES (est): 4.79MM **Privately Held**
SIC: 7372 Prepackaged software

(G-13801)
SIGNARAMA
Also Called: Sign-A-Rama
545 Sw Cutoff Ste A (01607-1766)
PHONE.................................508 459-9731
Mike Wood, *Prin*
EMP: 7 EST: 2017
SALES (est): 203.25K **Privately Held**
Web: www.signarama.com
SIC: 3993 Signs and advertising specialties

(G-13802)
SJOGREN INDUSTRIES INC
982 Southbridge St (01610-2219)
PHONE.................................508 987-3206
Carl Sjogren, *Prin*
EMP: 18 EST: 2015
SALES (est): 3.52MM **Privately Held**
Web: www.sjogren.com
SIC: 3999 Manufacturing industries, nec

(G-13803)
SLIDEWAYS INC
705 Plantation St Ste 1 (01605-2062)
PHONE.................................508 854-0799
TOLL FREE: 800
▲ EMP: 40 EST: 1994
SQ FT: 9,000
SALES (est): 10.48MM **Privately Held**
Web: www.slideways.com
SIC: 3089 Bearings, plastics

(G-13804)
SPECIAL METALS
CORPORATION
Special Metals Princeton
80 Hermon St (01610-4010)
PHONE.................................270 365-9551
James D Mc Lindon, *VP*
EMP: 96
SALES (corp-wide): 302.09B **Publicly
Held**
Web: www.specialmetals.com
SIC: 5051 3356 3341 Steel; Nonferrous
rolling and drawing, nec; Secondary
nonferrous metals
HQ: Special Metals Corporation
4832 Richmond Rd Ste 100
Warrensville Heights OH 44128
216 755-3030

(G-13805)
ST CYR INC
Also Called: St Cyr Salon Spa
235 Park Ave (01609-1965)

P.O. Box 816 (03846-0816)
PHONE.................................508 752-2222
Robert C Cyr, *Pr*
EMP: 13 EST: 1967
SQ FT: 5,000
SALES (est): 391.11K **Privately Held**
Web: www.stcyrbycarbonneau.com
SIC: 2844 7231 Cosmetic preparations;
Cosmetologist

(G-13806)
ST PIERRE MANUFACTURING
CORP
Also Called: St Pierre Chain & Wire Rope
317 E Mountain St (01606-1298)
PHONE.................................508 853-8010
TOLL FREE: 800
Henry G St Pierre, *Pr*
Edward J St Pierre, *
Russell Bath, *
▲ EMP: 30 EST: 1966
SQ FT: 45,000
SALES (est): 9.48MM **Privately Held**
Web: www.stpierreusa.com
SIC: 3462 3536 3499 5084 Horseshoes;
Hoists; Metal ladders; Hoists

(G-13807)
STANDARD LOCK WASHER &
MFG CO
Also Called: Valve Components Division
1451 Grafton St (01604-2718)
P.O. Box 397 (01613-0397)
PHONE.................................508 757-4508
Alfred E Barry Senior, *Pr*
EMP: 16 EST: 1938
SQ FT: 28,000
SALES (est): 451.42K **Privately Held**
Web: www.stanlok.com
SIC: 3452 5085 Cotter pins, metal;
Fasteners, industrial: nuts, bolts, screws,
etc.

(G-13808)
STANLOK CORPORATION
Also Called: Stanlok
1451 Grafton St (01604-2718)
P.O. Box 2735 (01613-2735)
PHONE.................................508 757-4508
Al Barry, *Pr*
▲ EMP: 14 EST: 1968
SALES (est): 365.86K **Privately Held**
Web: www.stanlok.com
SIC: 3452 Nuts, metal

(G-13809)
TABLE TALK PIES INC
25 Southgate St (01610-1717)
PHONE.................................508 798-8811
Brian Gangi, *Mgr*
EMP: 77
SALES (corp-wide): 64.72MM **Privately
Held**
Web: www.tabletalkpie.com
SIC: 2051 Cakes, pies, and pastries
PA: Table Talk Pies, Inc.
58 Gardner St
Worcester MA 01610
508 438-1556

(G-13810)
TABLE TALK PIES INC (PA)
Also Called: Table Talk Pies
58 Gardner St (01610-2528)
PHONE.................................508 438-1556
Christos Cocaine, *Pr*
Harry Kokkinis, *
▼ EMP: 99 EST: 1995
SALES (est): 64.72MM
SALES (corp-wide): 64.72MM **Privately
Held**

Web: www.tabletalkpie.com
SIC: 2051 Cakes, pies, and pastries

(G-13811)
THERMOPLASTICS COMPANY
INC
24 Woodward St (01610-2942)
PHONE.................................508 754-4668
G Peter Murphy, *Pr*
EMP: 20 EST: 1973
SQ FT: 33,000
SALES (est): 2.48MM **Privately Held**
Web: www.thermoplasticsco.com
SIC: 3559 7699 5084 Plastics working
machinery; Industrial machinery and
equipment repair; Plastic products
machinery

(G-13812)
THOMAS SMITH COMPANY INC
288 Grove St (01605-3934)
PHONE.................................508 792-5000
Paul Granquist, *CEO*
David Granquist, *
EMP: 50 EST: 1854
SQ FT: 50,000
SALES (est): 8.01MM
SALES (corp-wide): 25.46MM **Privately
Held**
SIC: 3469 Stamping metal for the trade
PA: Lutco Inc.
677 Cambridge St Ste 1
Worcester MA 01610
508 756-6296

(G-13813)
TRICAB (USA) INC
15 Coppage Dr (01603-1252)
PHONE.................................508 421-4680
Allan Greenfield, *Pr*
Michael Armstrong, *
▲ EMP: 50 EST: 2008
SALES (est): 25.23MM **Privately Held**
Web: www.tricab.com
SIC: 3357 Nonferrous wiredrawing and
insulating
HQ: Tricab (Australia) Pty Ltd
33 Prohasky St
Port Melbourne VIC 3207

(G-13814)
UMASS MEM MRI IMAGING CTR
LLC
Also Called: Shields Mri At Umass Memorial
214 Shrewsbury St (01604-4629)
PHONE.................................508 756-7300
EMP: 19 EST: 1999
SALES (est): 1.15MM **Privately Held**
Web: www.ummhealth.org
SIC: 3826 8011 Magnetic resonance
imaging apparatus; Offices and clinics of
medical doctors

(G-13815)
UNITED METAL FABRACATORS
INC
1021 Southbridge St (01610-2218)
PHONE.................................508 754-1800
Theodore Polenski Junior, *Pr*
Pat Cirillo, *Treas*
Bob Maska, *Prin*
EMP: 10 EST: 1992
SQ FT: 14,000
SALES (est): 1.34MM **Privately Held**
SIC: 3443 3599 3444 Weldments; Machine
and other job shop work; Metal housings,
enclosures, casings, and other containers

(G-13816)
UNITED PAPER STOCK CO INC
Also Called: United Box Co Division
2 Pullman St (01606-3311)
PHONE.................................401 724-5700
EMP: 33
SIC: 5093 5113 2675 7389 Waste paper;
Corrugated and solid fiber boxes; Die-cut
paper and board; Document and office
record destruction

(G-13817)
US NORTEK INC
4 Famum St (01602-2102)
PHONE.................................774 314-4006
Jose Lazo, *Pr*
EMP: 10 EST: 2012
SALES (est): 587.59K **Privately Held**
SIC: 8711 3569 Engineering services;
Lubricating systems, centralized

(G-13818)
VALKYRIE COMPANY INC
Also Called: Basco Leather Goods
60 Fremont St (01603-2396)
PHONE.................................508 756-3633
James J Devaney, *Pr*
EMP: 20
SALES (corp-wide): 4.75MM **Privately
Held**
Web: www.abasaccessories.com
SIC: 3172 Personal leather goods, nec
PA: The Valkyrie Company Inc
60 Fremont St
Worcester MA 01603
508 756-3633

(G-13819)
VALKYRIE COMPANY INC (PA)
Also Called: Abas Accessories
60 Fremont St (01603-2396)
PHONE.................................508 756-3633
James J Devaney, *Pr*
Marty Nathan, *
▲ EMP: 80 EST: 1969
SQ FT: 118,000
SALES (est): 4.75MM
SALES (corp-wide): 4.75MM **Privately
Held**
Web: www.abasaccessories.com
SIC: 3172 Wallets

(G-13820)
VANGY TOOL COMPANY INC
621 Millbury St (01607-1019)
PHONE.................................508 754-2669
Michael A Ottaviano, *Pr*
Paul T Ottaviano, *VP*
Sandra Mitchell, *Clerk*
EMP: 9 EST: 1956
SQ FT: 9,000
SALES (est): 954.06K **Privately Held**
Web: www.vangytool.com
SIC: 3599 2671 Machine shop, jobbing and
repair; Paper; coated and laminated
packaging

(G-13821)
VELLUMOID INC
54 Rockdale St (01606-1993)
PHONE.................................508 853-2500
Peter A Parseghian, *Pr*
Stephen C Parseghian, *
Robert S Hight, *
James A Dupre, *
▲ EMP: 40 EST: 1900
SQ FT: 100,000
SALES (est): 4.96MM **Privately Held**
Web: www.vellumoid.com

SIC: 3053　Gaskets, all materials

(G-13822)
VICTORY PRODUCTIONS INC
55 Linden St Ste 2 (01609-4612)
PHONE..................................508 755-0051
EMP: 50 EST: 1996
SQ FT: 9,560
SALES (est): 6.01MM Privately Held
Web: www.victoryprd.com
SIC: 2731　Books, publishing only

(G-13823)
VISIMARK INC (PA)
Also Called: Durable Technologies
14a E Worcester St (01604-4989)
P.O. Box 2570 (01613-2570)
PHONE..................................866 344-7721
Kari Lunden, *Pr*
Christopher Podles, *VP*
◆ EMP: 23 EST: 1985
SALES (est): 3.4MM
SALES (corp-wide): 3.4MM Privately Held
Web: www.durable-tech.com
SIC: 3953　Marking devices

(G-13824)
VISION DYNAMICS LLC
799 W Boylston St Ste 1 (01606-3071)
PHONE..................................203 271-1944
Charlie Collins, *CEO*
Scott V Krug, *Pr*
EMP: 7 EST: 1997
SQ FT: 2,000
SALES (est): 793.83K
SALES (corp-wide): 988.88K Privately
Held
Web: www.nelowvision.com
SIC: 3851 8042　Magnifiers (readers and
simple magnifiers); Visual training specialist
optometrist
PA: Let's Go Technology, Inc.
799 W Boylston St Ste 140
Worcester MA 01606
508 853-8200

(G-13825)
VOLTEA INC
1 Parkton Ave (01605-3148)
PHONE..................................510 861-3719
Mark Andelman, *Pr*
Margie Andelman, *Sec*
Lisa Dorward, *Prin*
EMP: 11 EST: 1988
SQ FT: 5,000
SALES (est): 733.69K Privately Held
Web: www.voltea.com
SIC: 7361 3589 8731　Placement agencies;
Water purification equipment, household
type; Biological research

(G-13826)
VYSTAR CORPORATION
Also Called: Vystar
725 Southbridge St (01610-2916)
PHONE..................................508 791-9114
Steven Rotman, *Ch Bd*
Joseph C Allegra Junior, *Ch Bd*
EMP: 84 EST: 2000
SALES (est): 116.53K Privately Held
Web: www.vystarcorp.com
SIC: 3069　Latex, foamed

(G-13827)
W GILLIES TECHNOLOGIES LLC
250 Barber Ave (01606-2495)
P.O. Box 60329 (01606-0329)
PHONE..................................508 852-2502
Mark Spencer, *Ex VP*
Martin Rosenberger, *Ofcr*

▲ EMP: 8 EST: 1997
SALES (est): 950.03K Privately Held
Web: www.wgillies.com
SIC: 2796 3555　Engraving platemaking
services; Printing trades machinery

(G-13828)
WILLIAM-SEVER INC
61 Sever St (01609-2165)
PHONE..................................617 651-2483
Brien Walton, *Prin*
Brien Walton, *Asst Sec*
Timothy Loew, *Ex Dir*
EMP: 10 EST: 2016
SALES (est): 604.15K Privately Held
SIC: 7372　Educational computer software

(G-13829)
WIREFAB INC
75 Blackstone River Rd Bldg 75
(01607-1493)
PHONE..................................508 754-5359
▲ EMP: 35 EST: 1955
SALES (est): 9.29MM Privately Held
Web: www.wirefab.com
SIC: 3496　Miscellaneous fabricated wire
products

(G-13830)
**WORCESTER
MANUFACTURING INC**
Also Called: Worcester Chrome Furniture
35 New St (01605-3324)
PHONE..................................508 756-0301
William Rastley, *Pr*
Michael Nahorniak, *
John Nahorniak, *
Pamela Nahorniak, *
EMP: 45 EST: 1948
SQ FT: 140,000
SALES (est): 9.48MM Privately Held
Web: www.worcestermanufacturing.com
SIC: 3498 3496 3479 3471　Fabricated pipe
and fittings; Miscellaneous fabricated wire
products; Painting, coating, and hot dipping
; Electroplating of metals or formed products

(G-13831)
**WORCESTER TELEGRAM
GAZETTE INC (HQ)**
Also Called: Community Shopper
100 Front St Fl 20 (01608-1425)
PHONE..................................508 793-9100
Bruce Gaultney, *Admn*
EMP: 400 EST: 1999
SQ FT: 150,000
SALES (est): 84.8MM
SALES (corp-wide): 2.31B Publicly Held
Web: www.telegram.com
SIC: 2711　Newspapers, publishing and
printing
PA: The New York Times Company
620 8th Ave
New York NY 10018
212 556-1234

(G-13832)
**WORCESTER TLEGRAM
GAZETTE CORP**
Also Called: Coulter Press
100 Front St (01608-1425)
PHONE..................................978 368-0176
Gary Hutner, *Mgr*
EMP: 16
SALES (corp-wide): 2.31B Publicly Held
Web: www.telegram.com
SIC: 2711　Newspapers, publishing and
printing
HQ: Worcester Telegram & Gazette, Inc.
100 Front St Fl 20

Worcester MA 01608
508 793-9100

(G-13833)
WORMTOWN BREWERY LLC
72 Shrewsbury St Ste 4 (01604-4660)
PHONE..................................774 239-1555
▲ EMP: 15 EST: 2009
SALES (est): 2.33MM Privately Held
Web: www.wormtownbrewery.com
SIC: 5813 2082　Bars and lounges; Ale
(alcoholic beverage)

(G-13834)
WRIGHT LINE LLC (HQ)
Also Called: Eaton Wright Line
160 Gold Star Blvd (01606-2791)
PHONE..................................508 852-4300
Edward D Bednarcik, *CEO*
Joseph White Senior, *VP*
Pete Rumsey, *
Carl Cottuli, *
Steve Bloch, *Governacne Vice President*
◆ EMP: 267 EST: 1934
SQ FT: 241,000
SALES (est): 50.56MM Privately Held
Web: www.wrightline.com
SIC: 3821 3577 2521 2522　Laboratory
apparatus and furniture; Computer
peripheral equipment, nec; Wood office
furniture; Office furniture, except wood
PA: Eaton Corporation Public Limited
Company
30 Pembroke Road
Dublin D04Y0

(G-13835)
WYMAN-GORDON COMPANY
80 Hermon St (01610-4010)
PHONE..................................508 839-8253
Paul Rossi, *Mgr*
EMP: 100
SALES (corp-wide): 302.09B Publicly
Held
Web: www.wyman.com
SIC: 3462 3463　Iron and steel forgings;
Nonferrous forgings
HQ: Wyman-Gordon Company
244 Worcester St
North Grafton MA 01536
508 839-8252

────────────────

Wrentham
Norfolk County

(G-13836)
ALLBIRDS INC
1 Premium Outlet Blvd Ste 475 (02093)
PHONE..................................774 847-1330
EMP: 19
SALES (corp-wide): 297.77MM Publicly
Held
Web: www.allbirds.com
SIC: 3143　Men's footwear, except athletic
PA: Allbirds, Inc.
730 Montgomery St
San Francisco CA 94111
628 225-4848

(G-13837)
BACON INDUSTRIES INC
65 Warren Dr (02093-1003)
PHONE..................................508 384-0780
Wayne Coburn, *Contrlr*
EMP: 12 EST: 1952
SQ FT: 10,000
SALES (est): 556.35K Privately Held
SIC: 2891 3089　Adhesives; Molding primary
plastics

(G-13838)
CAPSTAN ATLANTIC
10 Cushing Dr (02093-1153)
PHONE..................................508 384-3100
Mark Paullin, *Pr*
EMP: 137 EST: 1996
SALES (est): 21.79MM Privately Held
Web: www.capstanatlantic.com
SIC: 3499　Friction material, made from
powdered metal

(G-13839)
CAPSTAN INDUSTRIES INC
10 Cushing Dr (02093-1153)
PHONE..................................508 384-3100
▼ EMP: 250
SIC: 3399　Powder, metal

(G-13840)
EAST COAST FILTER INC
560 Washington St Ste 3 (02093-1697)
PHONE..................................716 649-2326
Kevin Zagrodny, *Prin*
▲ EMP: 8 EST: 2009
SALES (est): 1.16MM Privately Held
Web: www.eastcoastfilter.com
SIC: 3569　Filters

(G-13841)
ER LEWIN INC
25 Cushing Dr (02093-1154)
PHONE..................................508 384-0363
Eric R Lewin, *Pr*
Brian Costello, *
Evan Thomas, *
◆ EMP: 25 EST: 1991
SQ FT: 30,000
SALES (est): 3.7MM Privately Held
SIC: 3442　Window and door frames

(G-13842)
GRAVEL PUBLIC HOUSE
36 South St (02093-1527)
P.O. Box 762 (02093-0762)
PHONE..................................508 384-0888
EMP: 12 EST: 2015
SALES (est): 1.15MM Privately Held
Web: www.meetmeatthegavel.com
SIC: 1442　Construction sand and gravel

(G-13843)
JOHNSON CONTROLS INC
Also Called: Johnson Controls
78 South St (02093-2119)
PHONE..................................508 384-0018
EMP: 40
SIC: 3822 3829　Building services
monitoring controls, automatic; Measuring
and controlling devices, nec
HQ: Johnson Controls Inc
5757 N Green Bay Ave
Milwaukee WI 53209
414 524-1200

(G-13844)
SCHOOL FAMILY MEDIA LLC
Also Called: Pto Today
100 Stonewall Blvd Ste 3 (02093-2207)
PHONE..................................508 384-0394
Brian Cabezud, *Managing Member*
Timothy Sullivan, *
John Driscoll, *
Mike Schoen, *
EMP: 45 EST: 2000
SQ FT: 5,000
SALES (est): 8.6MM Privately Held
Web: www.schoolfamilymedia.com

SIC: 8641 7372 7374   Parent-teachers'
association; Educational computer software
; Data processing service

(G-13845)
**SHAWMUT ENGINEERING
COMPANY**
38 Weber Farm Rd (02093-1955)
PHONE..............................508 850-9500
Kendall Nygren, *Pr*
EMP: 10 EST: 1920
SALES (est): 841.35K **Privately Held**
SIC: 3469   Stamping metal for the trade

Yarmouth Port
Barnstable County

(G-13846)
WENDI C SMITH
Also Called: Harvest of Barnstable
89 Willow St (02675-1753)
PHONE..............................508 362-4595
Wendi C Smith, *Owner*
EMP: 12 EST: 1981
SQ FT: 1,200
SALES (est): 871.89K **Privately Held**
Web: www.harvestofbarnstable.com
SIC: 3999 5992   Novelties: bone, beaded, or
shell; Florists

NEW HAMPSHIRE

Albany
Carroll County

(G-13847)
**ALVIN J COLEMAN & SON INC
(PA)**
9 Nh Route 113 (03818-7443)
PHONE..............................603 447-5936
Calvin J Coleman, *Pr*
P Noah Coleman, *VP*
Curtis Coleman, *VP*
Caroline Coleman, *Sec*
EMP: 18 EST: 1940
SQ FT: 60,000
SALES (est): 33.12MM
SALES (corp-wide): 33.12MM **Privately
Held**
Web: www.ajcoleman.com
SIC: 1542 1794 3273 5032   Commercial and
office building, new construction;
Excavation work; Ready-mixed concrete;
Sand, construction

(G-13848)
ALVIN J COLEMAN & SON INC
Also Called: Coleman Concrete Division
9 Nh Route 113 (03818-7443)
PHONE..............................603 447-3056
Curtis Coleman, *Brnch Mgr*
EMP: 41
SALES (corp-wide): 33.12MM **Privately
Held**
Web: www.ajcoleman.com
SIC: 3273   Ready-mixed concrete
PA: J Coleman Alvin & Son Inc
9 Nh Route 113
Albany NH 03818
603 447-5936

(G-13849)
AMBIX MANUFACTURING INC
1369 Nh Route 16 (03818-7328)
P.O. Box 55 (03836-0055)
PHONE..............................603 452-5247

▲ EMP: 10 EST: 2011
SALES (est): 1.07MM **Privately Held**
Web: www.ambixllc.com
SIC: 3089   Injection molding of plastics

(G-13850)
COLEMAN CONCRETE INC
9 Nh Route 113 (03818-7320)
PHONE..............................603 447-5936
EMP: 38 EST: 2010
SALES (est): 4.97MM **Privately Held**
Web: www.colemanconcrete.com
SIC: 3273   Ready-mixed concrete

Alexandria
Grafton County

(G-13851)
**ALLSTATE POLYETHYLENE
CORP (PA)**
236 Ragged Mountain Hwy (03222-6812)
P.O. Box 480 (03222-0480)
PHONE..............................800 288-7659
Kevin Francis Powers, *Pr*
Joseph Cioffi, *Prin*
EMP: 8 EST: 1990
SALES (est): 3.94MM **Privately Held**
Web: www.paksolutionsusa.com
SIC: 5169 2821   Synthetic resins, rubber,
and plastic materials; Polyethylene resins

Allenstown
Merrimack County

(G-13852)
MANCO LLC
Also Called: Dunkin' Donuts
43 Allenstown Rd Ste 1 (03275-1812)
PHONE..............................603 485-5327
Amie Rooins, *Prin*
EMP: 8 EST: 2004
SALES (est): 51.84K **Privately Held**
Web: www.dunkindonuts.com
SIC: 5461 2051   Doughnuts; Doughnuts,
except frozen

(G-13853)
**MATERIALS RESEARCH FRNCS
INC**
Also Called: M R F
65 Pinewood Rd Unit 2 (03275-2346)
PHONE..............................603 485-2394
▼ EMP: 19
SQ FT: 17,304
SALES (est): 4.64MM **Privately Held**
Web: www.mrf-furnaces.com
SIC: 3821 3567   Laboratory apparatus and
furniture; Vacuum furnaces and ovens

(G-13854)
**NEW HAMPSHIRE OPTICAL CO
INC (PA)**
32 Library St (03275-1704)
PHONE..............................603 268-0741
Dennis Bresslin, *Pr*
Deanna B Bresslin, *
Gary Person, *Stockholder*
EMP: 30 EST: 1981
SQ FT: 9,000
SALES (est): 4.72MM
SALES (corp-wide): 4.72MM **Privately
Held**
Web: www.nhoptical.net
SIC: 5048 3851   Ophthalmic goods;
Ophthalmic goods

(G-13855)
**RECYCLING MECHANICAL
NENG LLC**
44 Ferry St (03275-1622)
PHONE..............................603 268-8028
EMP: 10 EST: 2005
SQ FT: 9,600
SALES (est): 1.75MM **Privately Held**
Web: www.recmech.com
SIC: 3443 7692   Dumpsters, garbage;
Welding repair

Alstead
Cheshire County

(G-13856)
**BASCOM MAPLE FARMS INC
(PA)**
Also Called: Coombs Family Farms
56 Sugar House Rd (03602-4307)
PHONE..............................603 835-2230
Bruce Bascom, *Pr*
David Bascom, *
Kevin Bascom, *
◆ EMP: 65 EST: 1945
SQ FT: 150,000
SALES (est): 31.71MM
SALES (corp-wide): 31.71MM **Privately
Held**
Web: www.bascommaple.com
SIC: 5149 5083 5961 0831   Syrups, except
for fountain use; Agricultural machinery, nec
; Food, mail order; Maple sap gathering

(G-13857)
FULLER MACHINE CO INC
5 Gilsum Mine Rd (03602-3909)
PHONE..............................603 835-6559
Larry Wilson, *Pr*
EMP: 33 EST: 1930
SQ FT: 2,500
SALES (est): 774.84K **Privately Held**
Web: www.fullermachine.com
SIC: 3599   Machine shop, jobbing and repair

(G-13858)
SEMYA CORP (PA)
Also Called: The Stone Depot
53 Duncan Rd (03602-4528)
PHONE..............................802 875-6564
Gregg P Adamovich, *Pr*
EMP: 8 EST: 1995
SALES (est): 2.61MM
SALES (corp-wide): 2.61MM **Privately
Held**
SIC: 1411   Granite, dimension-quarrying

Alton
Belknap County

(G-13859)
HILLSGROVE MACHINE INC
45 Dudley Rd (03809-5215)
P.O. Box 249 (03809-0249)
PHONE..............................603 776-5090
Daniel Hillsgrove, *Pr*
EMP: 10 EST: 1979
SQ FT: 7,000
SALES (est): 972.15K **Privately Held**
Web: www.hillsgrove-machine.com
SIC: 3599   Machine shop, jobbing and repair

Amherst
Hillsborough County

(G-13860)
AEROSAT AVIONICS LLC
Also Called: Aerosat
60 State Route 101a (03031-2213)
PHONE..............................603 943-8680
D Grayson Allen, *Managing Member*
Dennis Ferguson, *
William Mcnary, *VP*
Skip Feher, *
EMP: 75 EST: 2001
SQ FT: 2,000
SALES (est): 2.9MM **Privately Held**
SIC: 3663   Radio and t.v. communications
equipment
PA: As Liquidation I Company Inc.
62 State Route 101a 2b
Amherst NH 03031

(G-13861)
**ALCAMI CAROLINAS
CORPORATION**
2 Howe Dr (03031-2314)
PHONE..............................910 619-3952
EMP: 8
SALES (corp-wide): 418.48MM **Privately
Held**
Web: www.alcami.com
SIC: 2834 8734 8731   Drugs affecting
neoplasms and endrocrine systems;
Product testing laboratories; Biological
research
HQ: Alcami Carolinas Corporation
2320 Scientific Park Dr
Wilmington NC 28405

(G-13862)
**ATLANTIC TURNKEY CONS
CORP**
54 Ponemah Rd (03031-3110)
PHONE..............................603 673-9447
Gary Conley, *Pr*
Laura Casper, *Treas*
Sandra Rowe, *Sec*
EMP: 11 EST: 1985
SQ FT: 2,400
SALES (est): 665.68K **Privately Held**
SIC: 8742 7372   Management consulting
services; Prepackaged software

(G-13863)
CABLE ASSEMBLIES INC
13 Columbia Dr Unit 17 (03031-2358)
PHONE..............................603 889-4090
Mark Britton, *Pr*
Karen Britton, *VP*
EMP: 10 EST: 1972
SQ FT: 3,600
SALES (est): 1.27MM **Privately Held**
Web: www.cableassembliesinc.com
SIC: 3357   Coaxial cable, nonferrous

(G-13864)
CLASSIC SIGNS INC
13 Columbia Dr Unit 16 (03031-2331)
PHONE..............................603 883-0384
TOLL FREE: 800
Paul Tripp, *Pr*
William Mc Namara, *VP*
George Gagnon, *VP*
EMP: 12 EST: 1989
SQ FT: 5,000
SALES (est): 728.59K **Privately Held**
Web: www.classicsignsnh.com
SIC: 3993   Signs, not made in custom sign
painting shops

GEOGRAPHIC

(G-13865)

CONTROLAIR LLC
8 Columbia Dr (03031-2352)
PHONE..............................603 886-9400
▲ **EMP:** 36 **EST:** 1987
SALES (est): 4.94MM **Privately Held**
Web: www.controlair.com
SIC: **3491 5084 3612 3494** Pressure valves and regulators, industrial; Industrial machinery and equipment; Transformers, except electric; Valves and pipe fittings, nec

(G-13866)

DIACOM CORPORATION
5 Howe Dr (03031-2315)
PHONE..............................603 880-1900
Scott Rafferty, *Pr*
▲ **EMP:** 90 **EST:** 1983
SQ FT: 30,000
SALES (est): 18.05MM **Privately Held**
Web: www.diacom.com
SIC: **3069** Molded rubber products

(G-13867)

EAST COAST CONCRETE PDTS LLC
5 Northern Blvd Ste 15 (03031-2325)
PHONE..............................603 883-3042
EMP: 10 **EST:** 2001
SALES (est): 215.47K **Privately Held**
SIC: **3272** Concrete products, precast, nec

(G-13868)

ENVASES USA INC (HQ)
12 Howe Dr (03031-2314)
PHONE..............................603 889-8311
Martin H Beck, *Pr*
▲ **EMP:** 15 **EST:** 1999
SALES (est): 8.82MM **Privately Held**
Web: www.envases.mx
SIC: **3085** Plastics bottles
PA: Envases Universales De Mexico, S.A.P.I. De C.V.
Calz. Guadalupe No. 504
Mexico MEX 54800

(G-13869)

EXOTHERMICS INC
14 Columbia Dr (03031-2304)
PHONE..............................603 821-5660
EMP: 18 **EST:** 1996
SQ FT: 25,400
SALES (est): 13.58MM **Privately Held**
Web: www.exothermicsinc.com
SIC: **3728 3764 8731** Military aircraft equipment and armament; Guided missile and space vehicle engines, research & devel.; Commercial physical research

(G-13870)

FOUNDATION ARMOR LLC
3 Howe Dr Ste 2 (03031-2362)
PHONE..............................866 306-0246
EMP: 15 **EST:** 2012
SQ FT: 10,000
SALES (est): 1.8MM **Privately Held**
Web: www.foundationarmor.com
SIC: **2851** Paints, waterproof

(G-13871)

FREDERICKS PASTRIES (PA)
109 State Route 101a Ste 4 (03031-2291)
PHONE..............................603 882-7725
TOLL FREE: 877
Sue Roberts, *Owner*
EMP: 10 **EST:** 1980
SQ FT: 5,670
SALES (est): 1.05MM
SALES (corp-wide): 1.05MM **Privately Held**

Web: www.pastry.net
SIC: **2051 5149 5461 2064** Bakery: wholesale or wholesale/retail combined; Crackers, cookies, and bakery products; Pastries; Candy and other confectionery products

(G-13872)

GUILD OPTICAL ASSOCIATES INC
Also Called: Guild Optical Associates
11 Columbia Dr Unit 13 (03031-2317)
PHONE..............................603 889-6247
Mark Breda, *Pr*
EMP: 18 **EST:** 1990
SQ FT: 20,000
SALES (est): 1.55MM **Privately Held**
Web: www.guildoptics.com
SIC: **3211 3827** Transparent optical glass, except lenses; Prisms, optical

(G-13873)

JALBERT PRINTING LLC
Also Called: Murroney's Printing
10 Northern Blvd Ste 17 (03031-2337)
PHONE..............................603 623-4677
Benjamin Jalbert, *Managing Member*
EMP: 7 **EST:** 2014
SALES (est): 590.43K **Privately Held**
Web: www.thecopyshop.com
SIC: **7334 2759** Photocopying and duplicating services; Commercial printing, nec

(G-13874)

JMK INC
15 Caldwell Dr (03031-2345)
PHONE..............................603 886-4100
James W Kennedy, *Pr*
Mary Kennedy, *
EMP: 25 **EST:** 1975
SQ FT: 12,000
SALES (est): 3.96MM **Privately Held**
Web: www.jmkfilters.com
SIC: **3677** Filtration devices, electronic

(G-13875)

JR POIRIER TOOL & MACHINE CO
4 Manhattan Dr (03031-2303)
PHONE..............................603 882-9279
Jim Poirier, *Owner*
Jim Poirer, *Owner*
EMP: 12 **EST:** 1981
SQ FT: 10,000
SALES (est): 474.53K **Privately Held**
Web: www.poiriertool.com
SIC: **3599** Machine shop, jobbing and repair

(G-13876)

M&H LIQUIDATING COMPANY LLC
9a Columbia Dr (03031-2306)
PHONE..............................603 889-8320
Bob Hendrickson, *
Patti Stinson, *
Lori Pelletier, *
◆ **EMP:** 80 **EST:** 1972
SQ FT: 98,000
SALES (est): 10.4MM **Privately Held**
Web: www.mmgmfg.com
SIC: **3444** Sheet metal specialties, not stamped

(G-13877)

MARK ALLEN CABINETRY LLC
13 Columbia Dr Unit 3 (03031-2319)
PHONE..............................603 491-7570
EMP: 20

SALES (corp-wide): 427.25K **Privately Held**
Web: www.markallencabinetry.com
SIC: **2434** Wood kitchen cabinets
PA: Mark Allen Cabinetry Llc
232 Route 13
Brookline NH 03033
603 321-3163

(G-13878)

MARMON UTILITY LLC
116 State Route 101a (03031-2265)
PHONE..............................603 673-2040
EMP: 17
SALES (corp-wide): 302.09B **Publicly Held**
Web: www.marmonutility.com
SIC: **3357** Nonferrous wiredrawing and insulating
HQ: Marmon Utility Llc
53 Old Wilton Rd
Milford NH 03055
603 673-2040

(G-13879)

MAXILON LABORATORIES INC
105 State Route 101a Unit 8 (03031-2277)
P.O. Box 850 (03049-0850)
PHONE..............................603 594-9300
EMP: 7 **EST:** 1995
SALES (est): 455.28K **Privately Held**
Web: www.maxilon.com
SIC: **3841** Surgical and medical instruments

(G-13880)

MEMTEC CORPORATION
17 Old Nashua Rd (03031-2844)
PHONE..............................603 893-8080
Dennis P Garboski, *CEO*
EMP: 15 **EST:** 1962
SALES (est): 973.26K **Privately Held**
Web: www.memteccorp.com
SIC: **3572 3845 3823 3812** Tape storage units, computer; Electromedical equipment; Process control instruments; Search and navigation equipment

(G-13881)

MONARCH INTERNATIONAL INC
Also Called: Monarch Instrument
15 Columbia Dr (03031-2305)
PHONE..............................603 883-3390
Kenneth Grabeau, *CEO*
Kenneth Grabeau, *Pr*
Glenn Grabeau, *
Meridith Kosiorek, *
▲ **EMP:** 40 **EST:** 1977
SQ FT: 33,000
SALES (est): 6.6MM **Privately Held**
Web: www.monarchinstrument.com
SIC: **3824 3825 3845 3823** Tachometer, centrifugal; Stroboscopes; Electromedical equipment; Process control instruments

(G-13882)

NH STEEL FABRICATORS
44 Christian Hill Rd (03031-3310)
PHONE..............................603 213-6357
Russell Hilliard, *Prin*
EMP: 8 **EST:** 2016
SALES (est): 98.39K **Privately Held**
Web: www.nhsteelfab.com
SIC: **3441** Fabricated structural metal

(G-13883)

PATIO BARN
272 State Route 101 (03031-1732)
PHONE..............................603 673-2716
Bret Wilson, *Pr*
EMP: 10 **EST:** 1959

SALES (est): 564.33K **Privately Held**
Web: www.thepatiobarn.com
SIC: **2499** Wood products, nec

(G-13884)

POLY-JECT INC
8 Manhattan Dr (03031-2342)
PHONE..............................603 882-6570
TOLL FREE: 800
Steven Thibeault, *Pr*
▲ **EMP:** 37 **EST:** 1983
SQ FT: 26,000
SALES (est): 4.35MM **Privately Held**
Web: www.polyject.com
SIC: **3089** Injection molding of plastics

(G-13885)

PROFESSNAL SFTWR FOR NRSES INC
4 Limbo Ln (03031-1869)
PHONE..............................800 889-7627
EMP: 86 **EST:** 1996
SALES (est): 10.23MM **Privately Held**
Web: www.promedsoftware.com
SIC: **7372** Prepackaged software

(G-13886)

RESIN SYSTEMS CORPORATION
62 State Route 101a Ste 1 (03031-2295)
PHONE..............................603 673-1234
Daniel B Prawdzik Senior, *Pr*
EMP: 53 **EST:** 1954
SQ FT: 15,000
SALES (est): 8.57MM **Privately Held**
Web: www.resinsystems.com
SIC: **2821** Plastics materials and resins

(G-13887)

RME FILTERS INC
98 State Route 101a (03031-2273)
P.O. Box 838 (03031-0838)
PHONE..............................603 595-4573
Roger Martin, *Pr*
Richard A Secor, *VP*
EMP: 10 **EST:** 1991
SQ FT: 1,500
SALES (est): 1.2MM **Privately Held**
Web: www.himado.com
SIC: **3677 5065** Filtration devices, electronic ; Electronic parts and equipment, nec

(G-13888)

RONTEX AMERICA INC
1 Caldwell Dr (03031-2310)
PHONE..............................603 883-5076
Craig Haley, *Pr*
◆ **EMP:** 29 **EST:** 1970
SQ FT: 30,000
SALES (est): 4.7MM **Privately Held**
Web: www.jonesfamilyco.com
SIC: **2297** Nonwoven fabrics

(G-13889)

S & S MACHINE LLC
11 Caldwell Dr Ste 4 (03031-2321)
PHONE..............................603 204-5542
EMP: 12 **EST:** 2011
SALES (est): 837.28K **Privately Held**
Web: www.ssmachinenh.com
SIC: **3599** Machine shop, jobbing and repair

(G-13890)

SOLID EARTH TECHNOLOGIES INC
3 Howe Dr Ste 3 (03031-2348)
PHONE..............................603 882-5319
Matt Stacy, *Pr*
EMP: 7 **EST:** 2003
SALES (est): 803.97K **Privately Held**

Web: www.solidearthtech.com
SIC: **3493** Helical springs, hot wound:
  railroad equip., etc.

(G-13891)
SPECIALTY COATING SYSTEMS
10 Columbia Dr Ste 2 (03031-2341)
PHONE..............................603 883-3339
EMP: 12 EST: 2019
SALES (est): 953.26K **Privately Held**
Web: www.scscoatings.com
SIC: **3479** Coating of metals and formed
  products

(G-13892)
SUMAKE NORTH AMERICA LLC
10 Northern Blvd Ste 13 (03031-2328)
PHONE..............................603 402-2924
EMP: 10 EST: 2014
SALES (est): 451.96K **Privately Held**
Web: www.sumakenorthamerica.com
SIC: **3621** Torque motors, electric

(G-13893)
**ULTRASYSTEMS
ELECTRONICS INC**
Also Called: Usei
13 Columbia Dr Unit 10 (03031-2331)
PHONE..............................603 578-0444
David Jenkins, *Pr*
EMP: 10 EST: 2004
SALES (est): 990.51K **Privately Held**
Web: www.soctester.com
SIC: **3825** Battery testers, electrical

(G-13894)
UNITED SENSOR CORPORATION
3 Northern Blvd (03031-2326)
PHONE..............................603 672-0909
EMP: 10 EST: 1995
SQ FT: 5,000
SALES (est): 987.58K **Privately Held**
Web: www.unitedsensorcorp.com
SIC: **3829** Measuring and controlling
  devices, nec

(G-13895)
**WILLIAMS & HUSSEY MCH CO
INC**
105 State Route 101a Unit 4 (03031-2245)
P.O. Box 1308 (03031-1308)
PHONE..............................603 732-0219
Stephen Carter, *Pr*
EMP: 16 EST: 1987
SQ FT: 10,000
SALES (est): 938.02K **Privately Held**
Web: www.williamsnhussey.com
SIC: **3553** 3541 Woodworking machinery;
  Machine tools, metal cutting type

Antrim
Hillsborough County

(G-13896)
BRAILSFORD & COMPANY INC
15 Elm Ave (03440-3707)
P.O. Box 459 (03440-0459)
PHONE..............................603 588-2880
Robert Drummond, *Pr*
Kr Smith, *Stockholder**
Betsy Drummond, *
EMP: 18 EST: 1944
SQ FT: 7,600
SALES (est): 1.98MM **Privately Held**
Web: www.brailsford.com

SIC: **3699** 3561 3826 3564 Electrical
  equipment and supplies, nec; Industrial
  pumps and parts; Water testing apparatus;
  Blowers and fans

(G-13897)
MAINELINE GRAPHICS LLC
Also Called: Maineline Graphics
1 High St (03440-3401)
P.O. Box 301 (03440-0301)
PHONE..............................603 588-3177
EMP: 7 EST: 1980
SALES (est): 1.19MM **Privately Held**
Web: www.mainelinesigns.com
SIC: **3993** 7336 Signs and advertising
  specialties; Creative services to
  advertisers, except writers

(G-13898)
**RILEY MOUNTAIN PRODUCTS
INC**
Also Called: Artek
10 Water St (03440-3923)
P.O. Box 550 (03440-0550)
PHONE..............................603 588-7234
William A Prokop, *CEO*
EMP: 11 EST: 1995
SQ FT: 6,000
SALES (est): 343.82K **Privately Held**
SIC: **3083** 2499 Plastics finished products,
  laminated; Novelties, wood fiber

Ashland
Grafton County

(G-13899)
ELPAKCO INC
Main St (03217)
PHONE..............................603 968-9950
EMP: 9
SALES (corp-wide): 1.56MM **Privately
Held**
Web: www.elpakco.com
SIC: **3599** Machine shop, jobbing and repair
PA: Elpakco, Inc.
  2 Carl Thompson Rd
  Westford MA 01886
  978 392-0400

(G-13900)
**FREUDENBERG-NOK GENERAL
PARTNR**
Also Called: Fredenberg-Nok Seals Division
125 Main St (03217-4557)
P.O. Box 1269 (03217-1269)
PHONE..............................603 968-7187
EMP: 96
SALES (corp-wide): 12.23B **Privately Held**
Web: www.freudenberg.com
SIC: **3544** 3053 Industrial molds; Gaskets;
  packing and sealing devices
HQ: Freudenberg-Nok General Partnership
  47774 W Anchor Ct
  Plymouth MI 48170
  734 451-0020

(G-13901)
**MONEYSWORTH & BEST USA
INC**
1 Cedar Ln (03217)
P.O. Box 746 (03217-0746)
PHONE..............................603 968-3300
Deborah French, *Pr*
Nora Gulesserian, *
EMP: 35 EST: 2011
SALES (est): 2.57MM **Privately Held**
SIC: **2499** Shoe trees

(G-13902)
**ROCHESTER SHOE TREE CO
INC (PA)**
1 Cedar Ln (03217)
PHONE..............................603 968-3301
Debra French, *Pr*
▲ **EMP: 88 EST:** 1922
SQ FT: 3,000
SALES (est): 9.33MM
SALES (corp-wide): 9.33MM **Privately
Held**
Web: www.rstco.com
SIC: **2842** 2499 Polishes and sanitation
  goods; Shoe trees

Atkinson
Rockingham County

(G-13903)
IMED MFG
20 Waters Edge (03811-2113)
PHONE..............................603 489-5184
EMP: 7 EST: 2015
SALES (est): 428.99K **Privately Held**
SIC: **3999** Manufacturing industries, nec

(G-13904)
**INTERTECH PROCESS
TECHNOLOGY**
3 Commerce Dr Ste 301 (03811-2175)
PHONE..............................603 893-9566
Matthew Grodowski, *Dir*
EMP: 9 EST: 2006
SALES (est): 296.81K **Privately Held**
SIC: **3532** Mineral beneficiation equipment

(G-13905)
NATURALLY UNCOMMON LLC
14 Industrial Way (03811-2194)
PHONE..............................603 458-2209
EMP: 9 EST: 2016
SALES (est): 652.26K **Privately Held**
Web: www.naturallyuncommon.com
SIC: **2844** Perfumes, cosmetics and other
  toilet preparations

Auburn
Rockingham County

(G-13906)
BRI-WELD INDUSTRIES LLC
55 Gold Ledge Ave (03032-3602)
PHONE..............................603 622-9480
EMP: 10 EST: 1985
SQ FT: 8,200
SALES (est): 825.54K **Privately Held**
Web: www.briweld.com
SIC: **7692** 1799 7532 Welding repair;
  Welding on site; Exterior repair services

(G-13907)
**FOREST MANUFACTURING
CORP**
Also Called: Trickett Woodworks Company
8 Grey Point Ave (03032-3630)
PHONE..............................603 647-6991
Paul Trickett, *Pr*
Chris Trickett, *VP*
EMP: 10 EST: 1993
SQ FT: 10,000
SALES (est): 1.2MM **Privately Held**
Web: www.trickettwoodworks.com
SIC: **2431** Millwork

(G-13908)
**GARVIN INDUSTRIES
INCORPORATED**
81 Priscilla Ln (03032-3724)
PHONE..............................603 647-5410
Forrest Garvin, *Pr*
Bertha Garvin, *VP*
EMP: 7 EST: 1983
SQ FT: 10,000
SALES (est): 708.27K **Privately Held**
Web: www.garvinindustriesinc.com
SIC: **3444** Sheet metal specialties, not
  stamped

(G-13909)
INSTALLED BUILDING PDTS LLC
Also Called: Builders Insulation NH
62 King St (03032-3973)
P.O. Box 5111 (03108-5111)
PHONE..............................603 645-1604
Kyle Niemela, *Genl Mgr*
EMP: 355 EST: 2001
SALES (est): 4.62MM
SALES (corp-wide): 2.67B **Publicly Held**
Web:
www.buildersinstalledproductsnh.com
SIC: **1761** 5021 5719 2515 Gutter and
  downspout contractor; Shelving; Fireplace
  equipment and accessories; Foundations
  and platforms
HQ: Installed Building Products Llc
  495 S High St Ste 150
  Columbus OH 43215
  614 221-3399

(G-13910)
K & B ROCK CRUSHING LLC
20 Commercial Ct (03032-3725)
PHONE..............................603 622-1188
EMP: 9 EST: 2001
SQ FT: 45,000
SALES (est): 1.12MM **Privately Held**
SIC: **1422** Crushed and broken limestone

(G-13911)
MORRILL WOODWORKING LLC
38 Westford Dr (03032-3841)
PHONE..............................603 540-3151
Kyle Morrill, *Brnch Mgr*
EMP: 28
SALES (corp-wide): 86.19K **Privately Held**
SIC: **2431** Millwork
PA: Morrill Woodworking, Llc
  100 International Dr
  Portsmouth NH

(G-13912)
SLATE CORPORATION
236 Rockingham Rd (03032-3958)
P.O. Box 357 (03032-0357)
PHONE..............................603 234-5943
Wayne Theodore, *Pr*
EMP: 12 EST: 2017
SALES (est): 511.29K **Privately Held**
Web: www.slatecorporationservices.com
SIC: **1794** 3272 1521 1711 Excavation work
  ; Septic tanks, concrete; Single-family
  housing construction; Septic system
  construction

Barnstead
Belknap County

(G-13913)
BREEZY HILL LUMBER CO
78 Province Rd (03218-4061)
PHONE..............................603 496-8870
Eddie Watson, *Pr*

EMP: 7 EST: 1992
SALES (est): 122.7K **Privately Held**
SIC: 2421 Sawmills and planing mills, general

Barrington
Strafford County

(G-13914)
GOSOLAR NH LLC
232 Calef Hwy Unit 9 (03825)
PHONE..........................603 948-1189
Jake Ottolini, *Managing Member*
EMP: 7 EST: 2015
SALES (est): 243.24K **Privately Held**
Web: www.gosolarnh.net
SIC: 3674 Solar cells

(G-13915)
PBS PLASTICS INC
219 Old Concord Tpke (03825-5155)
PHONE..........................603 868-1717
Andrew Salach, *Pr*
Kurt Bertram, *VP*
EMP: 10 EST: 1992
SQ FT: 10,000
SALES (est): 1.68MM **Privately Held**
Web: www.pbsplastics.com
SIC: 3089 Injection molding of plastics

(G-13916)
QUALITY FABRICATORS LLC
246 Calef Hwy (03825-7233)
P.O. Box 332 (03825-0332)
PHONE..........................603 905-9012
EMP: 8 EST: 2004
SALES (est): 765.35K **Privately Held**
Web: www.qfinh.com
SIC: 3441 Fabricated structural metal

(G-13917)
TURBOCAM INC (PA)
Also Called: Turbocam International
607 Calef Hwy Ste 100 (03825-5539)
PHONE..........................603 905-0200
Marian Noronha, *Pr*
Robert Bujeaud, *
John Bressoud, *
Doug Patteson, *
▲ **EMP:** 179 **EST:** 1985
SQ FT: 32,000
SALES (est): 98.06MM
SALES (corp-wide): 98.06MM **Privately Held**
Web: www.turbocam.com
SIC: 3599 Machine shop, jobbing and repair

Bartlett
Carroll County

(G-13918)
PEG KEARSARGE CO INC
Also Called: Pegco Process Labs
14 Mill St (03812)
PHONE..........................603 374-2341
Paul W Soares, *Pr*
EMP: 7 EST: 1878
SQ FT: 20,000
SALES (est): 515.77K **Privately Held**
Web: www.kearsargepegco.com
SIC: 2843 2499 2842 3471 Finishing agents
; Stoppers and plugs, wood; Polishes and
sanitation goods; Plating and polishing

Bedford
Hillsborough County

(G-13919)
BRISCO GRAPHICS LLC
21 Commerce Park North (03110-7062)
EMP: 12 EST: 2006
SALES (est): 961.09K **Privately Held**
Web: www.briscographics.com
SIC: 2759 Commercial printing, nec

(G-13920)
BROEN-LAB INC
15 Constitution Dr Ste 122 (03110-6042)
PHONE..........................603 310-5089
▲ **EMP:** 11 **EST:** 1997
SQ FT: 7,500
SALES (est): 2.94MM
SALES (corp-wide): 3.35B **Privately Held**
Web: www.broen-lab.com
SIC: 3491 Gas valves and parts, industrial
HQ: Broen A/S
Skovvej 30
Assens 5610
64712095

(G-13921)
CHASE ELECTRIC MOTORS LLC
Also Called: Wright Electric Motors
10 Iron Horse Dr (03110-6825)
PHONE..........................603 669-2565
EMP: 8 EST: 1996
SALES (est): 898.41K **Privately Held**
Web: www.easternia.com
SIC: 7694 7629 5063 5999 Electric motor
repair; Generator repair; Generators;
Motors, electric

(G-13922)
COCA-COLA BEVERAGES NORTHEAST INC (HQ)
Also Called: Coca-Cola
1 Executive Park Dr Ste 330 (03110-6977)
PHONE..........................603 627-7871
▲ **EMP:** 45 **EST:** 1978
SALES (est): 416.39MM **Privately Held**
Web: www.cokenortheast.com
SIC: 2086 Bottled and canned soft drinks
PA: Kirin Holdings Company, Limited
4-10-2, Nakano
Nakano-Ku TKY 164-0

(G-13923)
CRANE PAYMENT SOLUTIONS INC (DH)
1 Bedford Farms Dr Ste 103 (03110-6524)
PHONE..........................603 685-6999
Bradley L Ellis, *Pr*
◆ **EMP:** 56 **EST:** 1974
SALES (est): 3.23MM
SALES (corp-wide): 3.37B **Privately Held**
Web: www.cranepi.com
SIC: 3578 Change making machines
HQ: Redco Corporation
100 1st Stamford Pl
Stamford CT 06902
203 363-7300

(G-13924)
DEBORAH FROST
Also Called: ACS
20 Commerce Park North Ste 106
(03110-6911)
PHONE..........................603 882-3100
Deborah Frost, *Pr*
▲ **EMP:** 10 **EST:** 2004
SALES (est): 553.91K **Privately Held**

SIC: 3661 Telephone station equipment and
parts, wire

(G-13925)
DESIGN BRAND PARTNERS INC
Also Called: Holmris
2 Bedford Farms Dr Ste 108 (03110-6525)
PHONE..........................603 232-3490
Michael Brandt, *Pr*
EMP: 7 EST: 2013
SALES (est): 150.16K **Privately Held**
SIC: 2599 5712 Factory furniture and
fixtures; Furniture stores

(G-13926)
EAGLE TEST SYSTEMS INC
2 Commerce Dr Ste 102 (03110-6803)
PHONE..........................603 624-5757
Edward Aten, *Brnch Mgr*
EMP: 313
SALES (corp-wide): 3.16B **Publicly Held**
SIC: 3825 Instruments to measure electricity
HQ: Eagle Test Systems, Inc.
21440 W Lake Cook Rd
Deer Park IL 60010
847 367-8282

(G-13927)
EYE EXAM 2000
39 S River Rd Ste 1 (03110-6749)
PHONE..........................603 836-5353
Nancy Wolf, *Owner*
EMP: 7 EST: 1982
SALES (est): 532.5K **Privately Held**
SIC: 5995 3841 Contact lenses, prescription
; Eye examining instruments and apparatus

(G-13928)
FEATURE PRODUCTS LTD
34 Rundlett Hill Rd Ste 1 (03110-5824)
PHONE..........................603 669-0800
EMP: 9 EST: 2018
SALES (est): 274.17K **Privately Held**
Web: www.feature-products.com
SIC: 3599 Machine shop, jobbing and repair

(G-13929)
FEDEX OFFICE & PRINT SVCS INC
119 S River Rd Ste 1 (03110-6757)
PHONE..........................603 644-2679
Doug Conway, *Mgr*
EMP: 13
SALES (corp-wide): 90.16B **Publicly Held**
Web: www.fedex.com
SIC: 7334 2791 2789 2759 Photocopying
and duplicating services; Typesetting;
Bookbinding and related work; Commercial
printing, nec
HQ: Fedex Office And Print Services, Inc.
3 Gallria Twr 13155 Noel 3 Galleria
Tower
Dallas TX 75240
800 463-3339

(G-13930)
FERROTEC (USA) CORPORATION
33 Constitution Dr (03110-6000)
PHONE..........................603 472-6800
EMP: 35
Web: www.ferrotec.com
SIC: 3568 3053 Bearings, bushings, and
blocks; Gaskets and sealing devices
HQ: Ferrotec (Usa) Corporation
566 Exchange Ct
Livermore CA 94550
408 964-7700

(G-13931)
GRANITE STATE KTCHENS DSTRS IN
Also Called: Granite State Cabinetry
384 Route 101 (03110-5050)
PHONE..........................603 472-4080
Frank Morris Junior, *VP*
Frank Morris Junior, *VP*
Frank Morris Senior, *President COOC*
EMP: 20 EST: 1992
SQ FT: 4,500
SALES (est): 1.88MM **Privately Held**
Web: www.gscabinetry.com
SIC: 5211 5031 2434 Cabinets, kitchen;
Kitchen cabinets; Wood kitchen cabinets

(G-13932)
HAIGH-FARR INC
43 Harvey Rd (03110-6805)
PHONE..........................603 644-6170
David P Farr, *Pr*
Norene Farr, *CEO*
Richard Brouillette, *CFO*
EMP: 89 EST: 1969
SQ FT: 30,000
SALES (est): 16.84MM **Privately Held**
Web: www.haigh-farr.com
SIC: 3663 8711 8733 Radio broadcasting
and communications equipment; Consulting
engineer; Research institute

(G-13933)
IBIS LLC
Also Called: Miedge
10 Corporate Dr Ste 100 (03110-5956)
PHONE..........................603 471-0951
Mark J Smith, *Managing Member*
Richard Lowner, *Mng Pt*
EMP: 20 EST: 2010
SALES (est): 2.58MM
SALES (corp-wide): 173.77MM **Privately
Held**
Web: www.miedge.biz
SIC: 7372 Business oriented computer
software
PA: Zywave, Inc.
10100 W Innovation Dr # 300
Milwaukee WI 53226
414 454-6100

(G-13934)
INSTY-PRINTS OF BEDFORD INC
Also Called: Insty-Prints
25 S River Rd (03110-6708)
PHONE..........................603 622-3821
Lawrence Goldberg, *Pr*
Lynn Goldberg, *Treas*
EMP: 7 EST: 1986
SQ FT: 1,354
SALES (est): 791.14K **Privately Held**
Web: www.instyprints.com
SIC: 2752 7336 Commercial printing,
lithographic; Graphic arts and related design

(G-13935)
JAMES W MCCLELLAN & ASSOCIATES INC
Also Called: McClellan Automation Systems
70 Tirrell Hill Rd (03110-5210)
PHONE..........................603 644-1247
EMP: 30
SIC: 3569 Assembly machines, non-
metalworking

(G-13936)
JUTRAS SIGNS INC
Also Called: Jutras Signs & Flags
30 Harvey Rd Unit 8 (03110-6818)
PHONE..........................603 622-2344

TOLL FREE: 800
Cathy Champagne, *CEO*
EMP: 13 **EST:** 1946
SQ FT: 18,000
SALES (est): 404.86K **Privately Held**
Web: www.jutrassigns.com
SIC: 3993 1611 Electric signs; Highway signs and guardrails

(G-13937)
KANA SOFTWARE INC
10 Corporate Dr Ste 2206 (03110-5956)
PHONE..................................650 614-8300
EMP: 173
Web: www.verint.com
SIC: 7372 Prepackaged software
HQ: Kana Software, Inc.
175 Broadhollow Rd # 100
Melville NY 11747
650 614-8300

(G-13938)
KENTICO SOFTWARE LLC
15 Constitution Dr Ste 2c (03110-6002)
PHONE..................................866 328-8998
Renata Dutton, *Managing Member*
EMP: 31 **EST:** 2008
SALES (est): 4.39MM **Privately Held**
Web: www.kentico.com
SIC: 7372 Prepackaged software
PA: Kentico Software S.R.O.
Nove Sady 996/25
Brno 602 0

(G-13939)
LESTAT PRODUCTION 81 CORP
Also Called: Lp81 Shirts
3 Executive Park Dr Ste 223 (03110-6918)
PHONE..................................866 557-4478
Rashawn Harrison, *Pr*
EMP: 50 **EST:** 2021
SALES (est): 2.07MM **Privately Held**
Web: www.lp81shirts.com
SIC: 2759 7336 7221 7389 Screen printing; Graphic arts and related design; Photographer, still or video; Business Activities at Non-Commercial Site

(G-13940)
LYOPHILIZATION SVCS NENG INC
Also Called: Lsne
25 Commerce Dr (03110-6835)
PHONE..................................603 668-5763
Myron Dittmer, *Brnch Mgr*
EMP: 20
SALES (corp-wide): 106.73MM **Privately Held**
Web: www.pci.com
SIC: 2836 Biological products, except diagnostic
HQ: Lyophilization Services Of New England, Inc.
1 Sundial Ave Ste 112
Manchester NH 03103
603 626-5763

(G-13941)
LYOPHILIZATION SVCS NENG INC
19 Harvey Rd Unit 7 (03110-6810)
PHONE..................................603 626-9559
Myron Dittmer, *Brnch Mgr*
EMP: 32
SALES (corp-wide): 106.73MM **Privately Held**
Web: www.pci.com
SIC: 2836 Biological products, except diagnostic

HQ: Lyophilization Services Of New England, Inc.
1 Sundial Ave Ste 112
Manchester NH 03103
603 626-5763

(G-13942)
LYOPHILIZATION SVCS NENG INC
29 Harvey Rd (03110-6805)
PHONE..................................603 626-5763
Tom Mcgrath, *VP*
EMP: 20
SALES (corp-wide): 106.73MM **Privately Held**
Web: www.pci.com
SIC: 2836 2834 Biological products, except diagnostic; Pharmaceutical preparations
HQ: Lyophilization Services Of New England, Inc.
1 Sundial Ave Ste 112
Manchester NH 03103
603 626-5763

(G-13943)
LYOPHILIZATION SVCS NENG INC
Also Called: Lsne
7 Commerce Dr (03110-6835)
PHONE..................................603 668-5763
EMP: 25
SALES (corp-wide): 106.73MM **Privately Held**
Web: www.pci.com
SIC: 2836 2834 Biological products, except diagnostic; Pharmaceutical preparations
HQ: Lyophilization Services Of New England, Inc.
1 Sundial Ave Ste 112
Manchester NH 03103
603 626-5763

(G-13944)
MICROELECTRODES INC
40 Harvey Rd (03110-6805)
PHONE..................................603 668-0692
Normand C Hebert, *Pr*
Marc Hebert, *Sec*
EMP: 8 **EST:** 1970
SQ FT: 5,200
SALES (est): 907.65K **Privately Held**
Web: www.microelectrodes.com
SIC: 3826 Analytical instruments

(G-13945)
NAMTEK CORP
116 S River Rd Unit E # 2 (03110)
PHONE..................................603 262-1630
Keith R Turgeon, *Pr*
James A Mcdonald Junior, *VP*
EMP: 22 **EST:** 2006
SQ FT: 6,000
SALES (est): 4.96MM **Privately Held**
Web: www.namtekcorp.com
SIC: 7373 3699 7372 Systems integration services; Security control equipment and systems; Business oriented computer software

(G-13946)
OMEGA SIX SECURITY LLC
1 Hardy Rd Ste 406 (03110-4915)
PHONE..................................888 866-9954
EMP: 11
SALES (corp-wide): 407.45K **Privately Held**
Web: www.omegasixsecurity.com
SIC: 3699 Security devices
PA: Omega Six Security Llc
304 State Route 101

Amherst NH 03031
888 866-9954

(G-13947)
OPTICS 1 INC (DH)
Also Called: Optics 1
2 Cooper Ln (03110-5966)
PHONE..................................603 296-0469
EMP: 16 **EST:** 1987
SQ FT: 15,000
SALES (est): 26.16MM
SALES (corp-wide): 650.78MM **Privately Held**
Web: www.optics1.com
SIC: 3827 Optical instruments and apparatus
HQ: Safran Vectronix Ag
Max Schmidheiny-Strasse 202
Heerbrugg SG 9435

(G-13948)
REDBLACK SOFTWARE LLC (HQ)
1 Bedford Farms Dr Ste 104 (03110-6524)
PHONE..................................603 232-9404
EMP: 25 **EST:** 2020
SALES (est): 4.23MM
SALES (corp-wide): 6.05B **Publicly Held**
Web: www.intelliflo.com
SIC: 7372 Prepackaged software
PA: Invesco, Ltd.
1555 Peachtree St Ne # 18
Atlanta GA 30309
404 892-0896

(G-13949)
SIERRA NEVADA CORPORATION
43 Constitution Dr Ste 202 (03110-6083)
PHONE..................................775 331-0222
EMP: 30
SALES (corp-wide): 2.38B **Privately Held**
Web: www.sncorp.com
SIC: 3812 3728 Search and navigation equipment; Aircraft parts and equipment, nec
PA: Sierra Nevada Corporation
444 Salomon Cir
Sparks NV 89434
775 331-0222

(G-13950)
SPRAYING SYSTEMS CO
174 Route 101 (03110-5417)
P.O. Box 5046 (03108-5046)
PHONE..................................603 471-0505
EMP: 10
SALES (corp-wide): 434.45MM **Privately Held**
Web: www.spray.com
SIC: 3499 Nozzles, spray: aerosol, paint, or insecticide
PA: Spraying Systems Co.
200 W North Ave
Glendale Heights IL 60139
630 665-5000

(G-13951)
TECHNICAL RESEARCH AND MANUFACTURING INC
Also Called: TRM Microwave
280 S River Rd (03110-6822)
PHONE..................................603 627-6000
EMP: 70 **EST:** 1970
SALES (est): 8.25MM **Privately Held**
Web: www.quantictrm.com
SIC: 3679 Microwave components

(G-13952)
VERIZON COMMUNICATIONS INC
Also Called: Verizon
35 Constitution Dr (03110-6089)
PHONE..................................603 472-2090
John Davis, *Mgr*
EMP: 40
SALES (corp-wide): 133.97B **Publicly Held**
Web: www.verizon.com
SIC: 4812 2741 Cellular telephone services; Miscellaneous publishing
PA: Verizon Communications Inc.
1095 Ave Of The Americas
New York NY 10036
212 395-1000

(G-13953)
VISUAL POLYMER TECH LLC
91 Brick Mill Rd (03110-5145)
PHONE..................................603 488-5064
Gregory Caldwell, *Managing Member*
▲ **EMP:** 7 **EST:** 1996
SALES (est): 602.95K **Privately Held**
Web: www.visualpolymer.com
SIC: 2821 Plastics materials and resins

(G-13954)
WHOLISTIC PET ORGANICS LLC
Also Called: Wholistic Pet
341 Route 101 (03110-5104)
PHONE..................................603 472-8300
John Phillips, *Managing Member*
Sarah Phillips, *Mgr*
EMP: 7 **EST:** 2007
SALES (est): 1.01MM **Privately Held**
Web: www.wholisticpetorganics.com
SIC: 2047 2048 Dog and cat food; Feed supplements

(G-13955)
WIRE BELT COMPANY OF AMERICA (PA)
Also Called: Wire Belt Company of America
17 Colby Ct (03110-6426)
PHONE..................................603 644-2500
David Greer, *Pr*
David Maestri, *
F Wade Greer Junior, *Ch*
Robert Greer, *
▲ **EMP:** 49 **EST:** 1947
SQ FT: 35,500
SALES (est): 17.48MM
SALES (corp-wide): 17.48MM **Privately Held**
Web: www.wirebelt.com
SIC: 3496 Conveyor belts

(G-13956)
Z-FLEX (US) INC
20 Commerce Park North (03110-6900)
PHONE..................................603 669-5136
Ian Donnelly, *Pr*
▲ **EMP:** 25 **EST:** 1985
SQ FT: 40,000
SALES (est): 4.84MM
SALES (corp-wide): 49.34MM **Privately Held**
Web: www.z-flex.com
SIC: 3259 Chimney pipe and tops, clay
HQ: Z-Flex Realty, Inc.
20 Commerce Park North # 107
Bedford NH 03110

(G-13957)
Z-FLEX REALTY INC (DH)
20 Commerce Park North Ste 107 (03110-6900)

PHONE...................................603 669-5136
Ian Donnelly, *Pr*
Donald R Stacy, *
EMP: 25 **EST:** 1985
SQ FT: 28,000
SALES (est): 57.71MM
SALES (corp-wide): 49.34MM **Privately Held**
SIC: 5085 3061　Hose, belting, and packing; Mechanical rubber goods
HQ: Flexmaster Canada Limited
　20 East Pearce St Suite 1
　Richmond Hill ON L4B 1
　905 731-9411

Belmont
Belknap County

(G-13958)
AFL TELECOMMUNICATIONS LLC
Also Called: AFL
16 Eastgate Park Dr　(03220-3604)
PHONE...................................603 528-7780
Sean Adam, *Brnch Mgr*
EMP: 33
Web: www.aflglobal.com
SIC: 3357　Nonferrous wiredrawing and insulating
HQ: Afl Telecommunications Llc
　170 Ridgeview Center Dr
　Duncan SC 29334
　864 235-3423

(G-13959)
AVERY DENNISON CORPORATION
Also Called: Avery Dnnson Dgtal Ink Sltions
7 Fruite St Unit 7 # G　(03220-3544)
PHONE...................................603 217-4144
Adam Tourville, *Mgr*
EMP: 32
SALES (corp-wide): 9.04B **Publicly Held**
Web: www.averydennison.com
SIC: 2672　Paper; coated and laminated, nec
PA: Avery Dennison Corporation
　8080 Norton Pkwy
　Mentor OH 44060
　440 534-6000

(G-13960)
CLEARLY BALANCED DAYS LLC
7 Fruite St Unit C　(03220-3544)
P.O. Box 7025　(03307-7025)
PHONE...................................833 223-4040
Tina M White, *Managing Member*
EMP: 7 **EST:** 2017
SALES (est): 453K **Privately Held**
Web: www.clearlybalanceddays.com
SIC: 3999

(G-13961)
COCA-COLA BEVS NORTHEAST INC
Also Called: Coca-Cola
495 Depot St　(03220-4303)
P.O. Box 809　(03220-0809)
PHONE...................................603 267-8834
Donna Merrill, *Brnch Mgr*
EMP: 24
Web: www.cokenortheast.com
SIC: 2086 8741　Bottled and canned soft drinks; Management services
HQ: Coca-Cola Beverages Northeast, Inc.
　1 Executive Park Dr # 330
　Bedford NH 03110
　603 627-7871

(G-13962)
J TOOL INC
23 Fruite St　(03220-3501)
PHONE...................................603 524-5813
Richard Jorgensen, *Pr*
Sandra Jorgensen, *Asst Tr*
EMP: 24 **EST:** 1986
SQ FT: 8,000
SALES (est): 3.96MM **Privately Held**
Web: www.jorgensentool.com
SIC: 3599 3469　Machine shop, jobbing and repair; Metal stampings, nec

(G-13963)
MILPOWER SOURCE INC
Also Called: Milpower Source
7 Field Ln　(03220-4621)
P.O. Box 810　(03220-0810)
PHONE...................................603 267-8865
EMP: 112 **EST:** 1984
SALES (est): 16.27MM **Privately Held**
Web: www.milpower.com
SIC: 3629　Power conversion units, a.c. to d.c.: static-electric

(G-13964)
NEW MODEL INC
Also Called: Contract Support Group
40 Higgins Dr　(03220-4257)
P.O. Box 958　(03220-0958)
PHONE...................................603 267-8225
Sharon Eng, *Pr*
EMP: 31 **EST:** 1988
SQ FT: 20,000
SALES (est): 738.87K **Privately Held**
SIC: 7389 3679　Packaging and labeling services; Electronic circuits

(G-13965)
NORTHEAST TIRE SERVICE INC
174 Daniel Webster Hwy　(03220-3036)
PHONE...................................603 524-7973
Jeff Fortier, *Pr*
John Fortier, *VP*
EMP: 7 **EST:** 1969
SALES (est): 1.49MM **Privately Held**
SIC: 5014 5531 7538 7534　Tires and tubes; Automotive tires; General automotive repair shops; Tire repair shop

(G-13966)
PERSONS CONCRETE
3 Eastgate Park Dr　(03220-3603)
PHONE...................................603 524-4434
Dave Bissonette, *Prin*
EMP: 10 **EST:** 2013
SALES (est): 387.29K **Privately Held**
Web: www.redimixcompanies.com
SIC: 3273　Ready-mixed concrete

(G-13967)
PIKE INDUSTRIES INC (DH)
Also Called: Cooley Ashalt Paving
3 Eastgate Park Dr　(03220-3603)
PHONE...................................603 527-5100
Barry Duffy, *Pr*
Christopher J Madden, *
Douglas Black, *
Michael G O'driscoll, *Dir*
John J Keating, *
▲ **EMP:** 45 **EST:** 1988
SQ FT: 21,000
SALES (est): 187.96MM
SALES (corp-wide): 32.72B **Privately Held**
Web: www.pikeindustries.com
SIC: 1611 2951 3295　General contractor, highway and street construction; Asphalt and asphaltic paving mixtures (not from refineries); Minerals, ground or treated
HQ: Crh Americas, Inc.
　900 Ashwood Pkwy Ste 600

Atlanta GA 30338
770 804-3363

(G-13968)
PROVINCE KILN DRIED FIREWOOD
428 South Rd　(03220-4420)
PHONE...................................603 524-4447
Brian R Hutchins, *Admn*
EMP: 7 **EST:** 2014
SALES (est): 188.71K **Privately Held**
SIC: 3559　Kilns

(G-13969)
REDIMIX COMPANIES INC (DH)
3 Eastgate Park Dr　(03220-3603)
PHONE...................................603 524-4434
Dave Bissonette, *Pr*
EMP: 50 **EST:** 1954
SQ FT: 30,000
SALES (est): 19.29MM
SALES (corp-wide): 32.72B **Privately Held**
Web: www.redimixcompanies.com
SIC: 3273　Ready-mixed concrete
HQ: Crh Americas Materials, Inc.
　900 Ashwood Pkwy Ste 700
　Atlanta GA 30338

(G-13970)
REDIMIX CONCRETE
3 Eastgate Park Dr　(03220-3603)
PHONE...................................603 581-1805
EMP: 14 **EST:** 2011
SALES (est): 586.89K **Privately Held**
Web: www.redimixcompanies.com
SIC: 3273　Ready-mixed concrete

(G-13971)
RIPLEY ODM LLC
Also Called: Odm
171 Daniel Webster Hwy Unit 1　(03220-3053)
PHONE...................................603 524-8350
Greg Grieco, *Dir Fin*
EMP: 11 **EST:** 2002
SQ FT: 3,000
SALES (est): 2.4MM **Privately Held**
Web: www.ripley-tools.com
SIC: 3661　Fiber optics communications equipment

(G-13972)
S & Q PRINTERS INC
88 Elaine Dr　(03220-3411)
P.O. Box 1031　(03086-1031)
PHONE...................................603 654-2888
Linda Lombardo, *Pr*
▼ **EMP:** 7 **EST:** 1983
SALES (est): 467.42K **Privately Held**
Web: www.sqprinters.com
SIC: 2752　Offset printing

(G-13973)
WILCOM INC
73 Daniel Webster Hwy　(03220-3028)
P.O. Box 508　(03247-0508)
PHONE...................................603 524-2622
Dennis Mccarthy, *Pr*
John Helenek, *
▲ **EMP:** 26 **EST:** 1965
SQ FT: 47,000
SALES (est): 3.23MM **Privately Held**
Web: www.wilcominc.com
SIC: 3823 3825　Transmitters of process variables, stand. signal conversion; Test equipment for electronic and electrical circuits

---

Bennington
Hillsborough County

(G-13974)
ANTRIM CONTROLS & SYSTEMS
76 N Bennington Rd　(03442-4500)
PHONE...................................603 588-6297
Jim Bronson, *Prin*
EMP: 8 **EST:** 2005
SALES (est): 430.22K **Privately Held**
SIC: 3625　Electric controls and control accessories, industrial

(G-13975)
DH HARDWICK & SONS INC
301 Francestown Rd　(03442-4320)
P.O. Box 430　(03440-0430)
PHONE...................................603 588-6618
Teresa Hardwick, *Pr*
Teresa Hardwick Presdeint, *Prin*
EMP: 13 **EST:** 1978
SALES (est): 1.4MM **Privately Held**
Web: www.dhhardwick.com
SIC: 2411 1629 5211　Logging camps and contractors; Land clearing contractor; Sand and gravel

(G-13976)
LYONS TNNEY TIMBER HARVSTG INC
14 Switzer Rd　(03442-4403)
PHONE...................................802 384-2620
Adam Lyons, *Admn*
EMP: 9 **EST:** 2015
SALES (est): 446.75K **Privately Held**
SIC: 2411　Logging

(G-13977)
MONADNOCK PAPER MILLS INC (HQ)
117 Antrim Rd　(03442-4205)
PHONE...................................603 588-3311
Richard G Verney, *Pr*
Andrew Manns, *VP*
Gregory H Smith, *Sec*
Lumina Greenway, *Dir*
Geoffrey Verney, *Dir*
▼ **EMP:** 74 **EST:** 1819
SQ FT: 300,000
SALES (est): 48.17MM
SALES (corp-wide): 48.17MM **Privately Held**
Web: www.mpm.com
SIC: 2621 5085　Specialty papers; Boxes, crates, etc., other than paper
PA: Pierce Hill Holdings Llc
　117 Antrim Rd
　Bennington NH 03442
　603 588-3311

Berlin
Coos County

(G-13978)
3D LOGGING CO INC
302 Howard St　(03570-3746)
PHONE...................................603 915-3020
EMP: 8 **EST:** 1990
SALES (est): 214.4K **Privately Held**
SIC: 2411　Logging

(G-13979)
ALPINE MACHINE CO INC
355 Goebel St　(03570-2318)
PHONE...................................603 752-1441
Raymond Labrecque, *Pr*

Dana Legendre, *VP*
Scott Legendre, *Sec*
EMP: 20 **EST:** 1983
SQ FT: 9,000
SALES (est): 497.17K **Privately Held**
Web: www.alpinemachine.com
SIC: 3599 3441 Machine shop, jobbing and repair; Fabricated structural metal

(G-13980)
BFMC LLC
Also Called: Berlin Foundary & Achine Co
489 Goebel St (03570-2338)
P.O. Box 127 (03570-0127)
PHONE...............................603 752-4550
▼ **EMP:** 20 **EST:** 1904
SQ FT: 60,000
SALES (est): 2.01MM **Privately Held**
Web: www.berlinfoundry.com
SIC: 3554 3599 Paper mill machinery: plating, slitting, waxing, etc.; Machine shop, jobbing and repair

(G-13981)
CROSS MACHINE INC
167 Glen Ave (03570-1905)
P.O. Box 529 (03570-0529)
PHONE...............................603 752-6111
Richard Fournier, *Pr*
Lionel Turgeon, *Sec*
EMP: 19 **EST:** 1972
SQ FT: 11,200
SALES (est): 4.6MM **Privately Held**
Web: www.crossmachine.com
SIC: 3441 Fabricated structural metal

(G-13982)
MAYNESBORO INDUSTRIES INC
Also Called: A & B Electronics Co
55 Maynesboro St Ste 1 (03570-3378)
PHONE...............................603 752-3366
Ronald H Goyette, *Pr*
Susan Martin, *CFO*
EMP: 10 **EST:** 1979
SQ FT: 4,500
SALES (est): 2.27MM **Privately Held**
SIC: 5045 3679 Computers, nec; Solenoids for electronic applications

(G-13983)
MOUNTAIN TIRE CORP
15 Industrial Park Dr (03570-3555)
P.O. Box 306 (03570-0306)
PHONE...............................603 752-8473
Melvin Olson, *Pr*
EMP: 17 **EST:** 1987
SQ FT: 7,000
SALES (est): 2.25MM **Privately Held**
Web: www.mountaintirecorp.com
SIC: 5531 7534 5014 Automotive tires; Tire recapping; Truck tires and tubes

(G-13984)
NEW ENGLAND VLTS MONUMENTS LLC
9 Industrial Park Dr (03570-3555)
PHONE...............................603 449-2165
Dana Brouillece, *Managing Member*
EMP: 8 **EST:** 2014
SALES (est): 837.71K **Privately Held**
SIC: 3272 Burial vaults, concrete or precast terrazzo

(G-13985)
RAYS ELECTRIC & GEN CONTG INC
33 Jericho Rd (03570-1315)
P.O. Box 597 (03570-0597)
PHONE...............................603 752-1370

Raymond Binette Senior, *Pr*
Muriel Binette, *VP*
Ray Binette Junior, *VP*
Dennis Binnette, *VP*
Stephen Binette, *VP*
EMP: 32 **EST:** 1960
SQ FT: 6,000
SALES (est): 9.3MM **Privately Held**
Web: www.rayselectricnh.com
SIC: 1731 7694 1711 General electrical contractor; Electric motor repair; Refrigeration contractor

(G-13986)
SMITH & TOWN PRINTERS LLC
42 Main St (03570-2459)
PHONE...............................603 752-2150
Rachel Godbout, *Managing Member*
EMP: 10 **EST:** 1976
SQ FT: 3,500
SALES (est): 825K **Privately Held**
Web: www.smithandtownprinters.com
SIC: 2752 2791 2759 Offset printing; Typesetting; Commercial printing, nec

(G-13987)
WHITE MOUNTAIN LUMBER CO INC
Also Called: Ace Hardware
30 E Milan Rd (03570-3550)
P.O. Box 7 (03570-0007)
PHONE...............................603 752-1000
Barry J Kelley, *Pr*
Mark C Kelley, *
EMP: 50 **EST:** 1945
SQ FT: 100,000
SALES (est): 9.13MM **Privately Held**
Web: www.whitemtnlumber.com
SIC: 5251 2448 5211 2421 Hardware stores ; Pallets, wood; Lumber and other building materials; Sawmills and planing mills, general

Boscawen
Merrimack County

(G-13988)
CHARLES SMITH STEEL LLC
115 N Main St (03303-1106)
PHONE...............................603 753-9844
Charles Smith Junior, *Pr*
EMP: 9 **EST:** 1977
SALES (est): 2.01MM **Privately Held**
SIC: 3441 Fabricated structural metal

(G-13989)
ELEKTRISOLA INCORPORATED (PA)
126 High St (03303-2809)
PHONE...............................603 796-2114
Oliver Schildbach, *CEO*
Detlef Schildbach, *
George P Downing, *
Terry Smith, *
David Dimartino, *
◆ **EMP:** 194 **EST:** 1975
SALES (est): 24.86MM
SALES (corp-wide): 24.86MM **Privately Held**
Web: www.elektrisola.com
SIC: 3496 3357 Miscellaneous fabricated wire products; Magnet wire, nonferrous

(G-13990)
KENTEK CORPORATION (PA)
5 Jarado Way (03303-2603)
PHONE...............................603 223-4900
Thomas Macmullin, *Pr*

EMP: 25 **EST:** 1983
SQ FT: 15,000
SALES (est): 7.58MM
SALES (corp-wide): 7.58MM **Privately Held**
Web: www.kenteklaserstore.com
SIC: 3826 Laser scientific and engineering instruments

(G-13991)
KSD CUSTOM WOOD PRODUCTS INC
102 High St (03303-2602)
PHONE...............................603 796-2951
Kim Doubleday, *Pr*
EMP: 19 **EST:** 1989
SQ FT: 35,000
SALES (est): 2.24MM **Privately Held**
Web: www.ksdcwp.com
SIC: 2431 Doors and door parts and trim, wood

(G-13992)
PAGE BELTING COMPANY INC
104 High St (03303-2602)
PHONE...............................603 796-2463
TOLL FREE: 800
Mark Coen, *Pr*
EMP: 46 **EST:** 1868
SQ FT: 40,000
SALES (est): 2.28MM **Privately Held**
Web: www.pagebelting.com
SIC: 3199 Leather belting and strapping

Bow
Merrimack County

(G-13993)
AUBIN WOODWORKING INC
359 River Rd Ste 15 (03304-3363)
PHONE...............................603 224-5512
EMP: 17 **EST:** 1996
SALES (est): 2.19MM **Privately Held**
Web: www.aubinwoodworking.com
SIC: 1751 2431 5712 Cabinet building and installation; Woodwork, interior and ornamental, nec; Cabinet work, custom

(G-13994)
BOVIE SCREEN PROCESS PRTG INC
4 Northeast Ave (03304-3407)
P.O. Box 720 (03302-0720)
PHONE...............................603 224-0651
David Lee Gintzler, *Pr*
EMP: 50 **EST:** 2015
SQ FT: 31,000
SALES (est): 9.86MM **Privately Held**
Web: www.bovie.com
SIC: 2759 Screen printing

(G-13995)
CAPITOL DISTRIBUTORS INC
510 Hall St (03304-3105)
P.O. Box 1148 (03302-1148)
PHONE...............................603 223-2086
▲ **EMP:** 22 **EST:** 1963
SALES (est): 3.08MM **Privately Held**
SIC: 5181 2082 Beer and other fermented malt liquors; Malt beverages

(G-13996)
ENE SYSTEMS OF NH INC
155 River Rd Unit 10 (03304-3362)
PHONE...............................603 856-0330
Paul O'brien, *Pr*
Richard Olson, *VP*
EMP: 8 **EST:** 2002

SQ FT: 2,600
SALES (est): 2.61MM **Privately Held**
Web: www.enesystemsnh.com
SIC: 3822 Building services monitoring controls, automatic
PA: Ene Systems, Inc.
480 Neponset St Ste 11d
Canton MA 02021

(G-13997)
EVANS PRINTING CO
155 River Rd Unit 15 (03304-3362)
PHONE...............................603 856-8238
John Holman, *CEO*
Robert Holman, *Pr*
EMP: 8 **EST:** 1930
SQ FT: 12,000
SALES (est): 605.13K **Privately Held**
Web: www.evansprint.com
SIC: 2752 2759 Offset printing; Letterpress printing

(G-13998)
GP2 TECHNOLOGIES INC
Also Called: Gp2 Technologies
157 River Rd Unit 18 (03304-3362)
PHONE...............................603 226-0336
Thomas Porat, *Pr*
Gerald Peterson, *VP Opers*
Thurlow Greene, *VP*
EMP: 8 **EST:** 1999
SQ FT: 9,600
SALES (est): 993.43K **Privately Held**
Web: www.gp2tech.com
SIC: 3555 Bookbinding machinery

(G-13999)
GRANITE SHORE POWER LLC
431 River Rd (03304-3351)
PHONE...............................603 634-2299
Neil Mahajan, *Prin*
EMP: 134 **EST:** 2018
SALES (est): 15.83MM
SALES (corp-wide): 8.23B **Privately Held**
Web: www.graniteshorepower.com
SIC: 7353 4911 3714 Heavy construction equipment rental; Distribution, electric power; Motor vehicle parts and accessories
PA: Atlas Holdings, Llc
100 Northfield St
Greenwich CT 06830
203 622-9138

(G-14000)
GS BLODGETT CORPORATION
Also Called: G.S. BLODGETT CORPORATION
509 Route 3a (03304-3102)
P.O. Box 501 (03302-0501)
PHONE...............................603 225-5688
Bob Granger, *Brnch Mgr*
EMP: 92
SALES (corp-wide): 4.03B **Publicly Held**
Web: www.blodgett.com
SIC: 3589 Cooking equipment, commercial
HQ: G.S. Blodgett, Llc
42 Allen Martin Dr
Essex Junction VT 05452
802 860-3700

(G-14001)
HIGH SPEED TECHNOLOGIES INC
1357 Route 3a Unit 9 (03304-4000)
PHONE...............................603 483-0333
EMP: 21 **EST:** 1987
SALES (est): 1.47MM **Privately Held**
Web: www.highspeedtechnologies.com
SIC: 3599 Machine shop, jobbing and repair

(G-14002)
KALWALL CORPORATION
Also Called: Kal-Lite Division
40 River Rd (03304-3313)
PHONE.............................603 224-6881
William Dannhauer, *Prin*
EMP: 150
SALES (corp-wide): 82.99MM **Privately Held**
Web: www.kal-lite.com
SIC: 3089   Panels, building: plastics, nec
PA: Kalwall Corporation
1111 Candia Rd
Manchester NH 03109
603 627-3861

(G-14003)
KELLER PRODUCTS INCORPORATED
38 River Rd (03304-3313)
PHONE.............................603 224-5502
Dustin Shost, *Brnch Mgr*
EMP: 19
SALES (corp-wide): 11.09MM **Privately Held**
Web: www.kellerplastics.com
SIC: 2821 2431   Vinyl resins, nec; Millwork
PA: Keller Products, Incorporated
41 Union St
Manchester NH 03103
603 627-7887

(G-14004)
KENT NUTRITION GROUP INC
Also Called: Kent Nutrition Group Rtlstr
520 Hall St (03304-3105)
PHONE.............................603 225-6661
EMP: 7
SALES (corp-wide): 517.65MM **Privately Held**
Web: www.kentfeeds.com
SIC: 2048   Livestock feeds
HQ: Kent Nutrition Group, Inc.
2905 N Highway 61
Muscatine IA 52761
866 647-1212

(G-14005)
METZGER/MCGUIRE INC
807 Route 3a (03304-4019)
P.O. Box 2217 (03302-2217)
PHONE.............................603 224-6122
Scott C Metzger, *Pr*
Michelle R Mckinnon, *VP*
Craig N Metzger, *VP*
EMP: 20 **EST:** 1969
SQ FT: 6,000
SALES (est): 4.85MM **Privately Held**
Web: www.metzgermcguire.com
SIC: 2821   Plastics materials and resins

(G-14006)
NEW HAMPSHIRE BINDERY INC
81 Dow Rd (03304-3607)
PHONE.............................603 224-0441
Thomas Ives, *Pr*
Suzanne Ives, *VP*
EMP: 10 **EST:** 1934
SQ FT: 13,333
SALES (est): 424.92K **Privately Held**
Web: www.nhbindery.com
SIC: 2789   Binding only: books, pamphlets, magazines, etc.

(G-14007)
PHYTEK INDUSTRIES INC
578 River Rd Unit B (03304-3357)
PHONE.............................603 226-4197
EMP: 13 **EST:** 2016
SALES (est): 492.59K **Privately Held**

Web: www.phytek.net
SIC: 2431   Millwork

(G-14008)
PITCO FRIALATOR INC (HQ)
Also Called: Magic Kitch'n
553 Route 3a (03304-3215)
P.O. Box 501 (03302-0501)
PHONE.............................603 225-6684
Tim Fitzgerald, *CEO*
Martin Lindsay, *Prin*
▲ **EMP:** 310 **EST:** 1918
SQ FT: 100,000
SALES (est): 98.28MM
SALES (corp-wide): 4.03B **Publicly Held**
Web: www.pitco.com
SIC: 3589   Cooking equipment, commercial
PA: The Middleby Corporation
1400 Toastmaster Dr
Elgin IL 60120
847 741-3300

(G-14009)
PLASTECH MACHINING FABRICATION
25 Dunklee Rd (03304-3308)
PHONE.............................603 228-7601
Louis Ferriero, *Pr*
EMP: 10 **EST:** 1997
SQ FT: 7,000
SALES (est): 1.2MM **Privately Held**
Web: www.plastechfab.com
SIC: 3599   Machine shop, jobbing and repair

(G-14010)
RUMFORD STONE INC (PA)
278 River Rd (03304-3354)
PHONE.............................603 224-9876
Thomas Trento, *Pr*
Vince Trento, *VP*
Todd Trento, *VP*
Jacqueline Trento, *Sec*
▲ **EMP:** 17 **EST:** 1995
SALES (est): 16.72MM
SALES (corp-wide): 16.72MM **Privately Held**
Web: www.rumfordstone.com
SIC: 1743 3281   Marble installation, interior; Altars, cut stone

(G-14011)
SUPERIOR ICE CREAM EQP LLC
155 River Rd Unit 9 (03304-3362)
PHONE.............................603 225-4207
Kevin Mccan, *Managing Member*
EMP: 15 **EST:** 2017
SALES (est): 1.2MM **Privately Held**
Web: www.superioricecream.com
SIC: 3556   Ice cream manufacturing machinery

(G-14012)
ULTRAFRYER SYSTEMS INC
553 Route 3a (03304-3215)
P.O. Box 5369 (78201-0369)
PHONE.............................603 225-6684
Edward T Odmark, *Pr*
EMP: 110 **EST:** 2000
SQ FT: 85,000
SALES (est): 19.33MM
SALES (corp-wide): 4.03B **Publicly Held**
Web: www.ultrafryer.com
SIC: 3589   Commercial cooking and foodwarming equipment
PA: The Middleby Corporation
1400 Toastmaster Dr
Elgin IL 60120
847 741-3300

(G-14013)
UNIQUE MECHANICAL SERVICES INC
Also Called: U M S
162 W Main St (03304)
PHONE.............................603 856-0057
Beverly Skillings, *VP*
EMP: 9 **EST:** 1999
SQ FT: 5,000
SALES (est): 2.18MM **Privately Held**
Web: www.umsamerica.com
SIC: 3317   Welded pipe and tubes

(G-14014)
YARRA DESIGN & FABRICATION LLC
Also Called: Concord Awning & Canvas
1 Tallwood Dr (03304-3302)
PHONE.............................603 224-6880
Denise Sandberg, *Pr*
EMP: 13 **EST:** 1919
SQ FT: 6,000
SALES (est): 541.44K **Privately Held**
Web: www.concordawning.com
SIC: 2394 1799   Awnings, fabric: made from purchased materials; Awning installation

(G-14015)
YOUNG FURNITURE MFG INC
161 River Rd (03304-3352)
PHONE.............................603 224-8830
Andrew N Young, *Pr*
Thomas A Young, *
Kenneth E Young, *
Betty Young, *
EMP: 29 **EST:** 1980
SQ FT: 20,000
SALES (est): 979.49K **Privately Held**
Web: www.youngfurituremfg.com
SIC: 2434   Vanities, bathroom: wood

(G-14016)
Z-TECH LLC
56 Dow Rd (03304-3608)
PHONE.............................603 228-1305
◆ **EMP:** 25 **EST:** 2001
SQ FT: 33,000
SALES (est): 8.55MM **Privately Held**
Web: www.zirpro.com
SIC: 2819 2869   Industrial inorganic chemicals, nec; Industrial organic chemicals, nec

---

Bradford
Merrimack County

(G-14017)
MERRIMACK COUNTY CUSTOMS
14 Steele Rd (03221-3314)
PHONE.............................603 938-5855
Jason Allen, *Prin*
EMP: 7 **EST:** 2012
SALES (est): 227.42K **Privately Held**
Web: www.merrimackcountycustoms.com
SIC: 7692   Welding repair

(G-14018)
VALLEY TRANSPORTATION INC (PA)
Also Called: Valley Fire Equipment
2345 State Route 114 (03221-3522)
P.O. Box 453 (03221-0453)
PHONE.............................603 938-2271
Fred Brunnhoelzl Iii, *Pr*
Carol Brunnhoelzl, *VP*
EMP: 8 **EST:** 1974
SQ FT: 20,500

SALES (est): 1.3MM
SALES (corp-wide): 1.3MM **Privately Held**
SIC: 4151 3711   School buses; Fire department vehicles (motor vehicles), assembly of

---

Brentwood
Rockingham County

(G-14019)
ADVANCED CUSTOM CABINETS INC
13 Prescott Rd (03833-6502)
PHONE.............................603 772-6211
Joseph Ready, *Pr*
EMP: 15 **EST:** 1971
SQ FT: 8,600
SALES (est): 445.01K **Privately Held**
Web: www.advancedcustomcabinets.com
SIC: 2541 2434 1751   Cabinets, except refrigerated: show, display, etc.: wood; Wood kitchen cabinets; Carpentry work

(G-14020)
DRA PRECISION MACHINE
424 Commercial Pl Unit 13 Calef Hwy 125 (03833)
PHONE.............................603 734-2139
David R Amato, *Prin*
EMP: 8 **EST:** 2015
SALES (est): 98.89K **Privately Held**
SIC: 3599   Machine shop, jobbing and repair

(G-14021)
FASTRAX SIGNS INC
67 Route 27 (03833-6647)
PHONE.............................603 775-7500
Shawn Nordin, *Pr*
EMP: 7 **EST:** 2006
SALES (est): 340.95K **Privately Held**
Web: www.fastraxsignservice.com
SIC: 3993   Signs and advertising specialties

(G-14022)
HARD CORE SPRAL TUBE WNDERS IN
50 Pine Rd (03833-6509)
PHONE.............................603 775-0230
Carter Soper, *Pr*
Mathew Soper, *VP*
Taylor Soper, *Stockholder*
EMP: 9 **EST:** 1997
SQ FT: 7,500
SALES (est): 2.12MM **Privately Held**
SIC: 2655   Tubes, fiber or paper: made from purchased material

(G-14023)
MTI POLYEXE CORPORATION
50 Pine Rd (03833-6509)
PHONE.............................603 778-1449
EMP: 15 **EST:** 2015
SALES (est): 9.9MM **Privately Held**
Web: www.mtipolyexe.com
SIC: 2821   Silicone resins

(G-14024)
MULTI TECHNOLOGIES INDUSTRIAL LLC
Also Called: M T I
50 Pine Rd (03833-6509)
PHONE.............................603 778-1449
EMP: 32
SIC: 3081   Plastics film and sheet

▲ = Import ▼ = Export
◆ = Import/Export

(G-14025)
NORTHERN ELASTOMERIC INC
Also Called: Nei Advanced Composite Tech
61 Pine Rd (03833-6510)
PHONE...............................603 778-8899
EMP: 94
SIC: 1761 2952 Roofing, siding, and
sheetmetal work; Roofing materials

(G-14026)
OWENS CORNING
61 Pine Rd (03833-6548)
PHONE...............................603 773-4246
EMP: 9
Web: www.owenscorning.com
SIC: 3296 Fiberglass insulation
PA: Owens Corning
1 Owens Corning Pkwy
Toledo OH 43659

(G-14027)
POLYEXE CORPORATION
50 Pine Rd (03833-6509)
PHONE...............................603 778-1143
Thomas J Zickell, Pr
William Thalheirner, VP
Edmund Nangini, Sec
Nat Bockh, Dir
EMP: 25 EST: 1996
SQ FT: 3,500
SALES (est): 860.55K Privately Held
Web: www.mtipolyexe.com
SIC: 2821 Polyethylene resins

(G-14028)
QUIKRETE COMPANIES LLC
44 Pine Rd (03833-6549)
PHONE...............................603 778-2123
Lynn Allen, Mgr
EMP: 40
Web: www.quikrete.com
SIC: 3272 Concrete products, nec
HQ: The Quikrete Companies Llc
5 Concourse Pkwy Ste 1900
Atlanta GA 30328
404 634-9100

(G-14029)
SKAFF CRYOGENICS INC
48 Pine Rd (03833-6509)
PHONE...............................603 775-0350
▲ EMP: 16 EST: 1979
SQ FT: 25,000
SALES (est): 2.77MM Publicly Held
Web: www.chartindustries.com
SIC: 3443 Fabricated plate work (boiler
shop)
HQ: Chart Inc.
407 7th St Nw
New Prague MN 56071
952 758-4484

(G-14030)
**STARKEY WELDING CRANE
SERVICE**
444 Route 125 (03833-6610)
PHONE...............................603 679-2553
Charles A Starkey, Owner
EMP: 7 EST: 1986
SALES (est): 455.29K Privately Held
SIC: 7692 7389 Welding repair; Crane and
aerial lift service

(G-14031)
**SUNRISE FOODS
INCORPORATED**
25 Pine St (03833-2720)
P.O. Box 601 (03833-0601)
PHONE...............................603 772-4420

Kevin Johnston, Pr
EMP: 10 EST: 1992
SQ FT: 12,000
SALES (est): 654.73K Privately Held
SIC: 2087 5143 Flavoring extracts and
syrups, nec; Cheese

(G-14032)
**WAYNE MANUFACTURING INDS
LLC**
13 Prescott Rd (03833-6502)
PHONE...............................978 416-0899
EMP: 12 EST: 2005
SALES (est): 2.06MM Privately Held
Web: www.waynemfgi.com
SIC: 3086 Padding, foamed plastics

(G-14033)
**WORLD WIDE DISTRIBUTION
CORP**
424 Route 125 Unit 7 (03833-6641)
PHONE...............................603 942-6032
EMP: 9 EST: 2017
SALES (est): 701.01K Privately Held
SIC: 2066 Chocolate

Bristol
Grafton County

(G-14034)
**FREUDENBERG-NOK GENERAL
PARTNR**
Also Called: Components Division
450 Pleasant St (03222-3012)
P.O. Box 2001 (03222-2001)
PHONE...............................603 744-0371
Gregory Keenan, Mgr
EMP: 375
SALES (corp-wide): 12.23B Privately Held
Web: www.freudenberg.com
SIC: 2821 Plastics materials and resins
HQ: Freudenberg-Nok General Partnership
47774 W Anchor Ct
Plymouth MI 48170
734 451-0020

(G-14035)
**FREUDENBERG-NOK GENERAL
PARTNR**
Also Called: Bps Division
450 Pleasant St (03222-3012)
P.O. Box 2 (03106-0002)
PHONE...............................603 934-7800
Glenn Anderson, Brnch Mgr
EMP: 145
SALES (corp-wide): 12.23B Privately Held
Web: www.freudenberg.com
SIC: 3053 Gaskets; packing and sealing
devices
HQ: Freudenberg-Nok General Partnership
47774 W Anchor Ct
Plymouth MI 48170
734 451-0020

(G-14036)
GRIST FOR MILL LLC
Also Called: Mill Fudge Factory, The
2 Central St (03222-3134)
PHONE...............................603 744-0405
EMP: 10 EST: 2006
SALES (est): 570.55K Privately Held
Web: www.themillfudgefactory.com
SIC: 2064 7929 5812 Candy and other
confectionery products; Jazz music group
or artist; Coffee shop

(G-14037)
R P WILLIAMS & SONS INC
400 Summer St (03222-3213)
P.O. Box 537 (03222-0537)
PHONE...............................603 744-5446
TOLL FREE: 800
Robert P Williams Iii, Pr
Craig Williams, VP
Douglas J Williams, Treas
Steven N Williams, Sec
EMP: 15 EST: 1947
SQ FT: 10,000
SALES (est): 1.72MM Privately Held
Web: www.rpwilliams.com
SIC: 5211 5031 2421 Home centers;
Lumber: rough, dressed, and finished;
Sawmills and planing mills, general

Brookline
Hillsborough County

(G-14038)
AVERILL HOUSE VINEYARD LLC
21 Averill Rd (03033-2105)
PHONE...............................603 371-2296
Robert Waite, Owner
EMP: 10 EST: 2016
SALES (est): 419.54K Privately Held
Web: www.averillhousevineyard.com
SIC: 2084 Wines

(G-14039)
**GABRIEL BUSINESS GROUP CO
LTD**
Also Called: Construction
52 Laurel Crest Dr (03033-2138)
PHONE...............................877 401-5544
Gabriel Anghel, Pr
EMP: 10 EST: 2014
SALES (est): 829.47K Privately Held
SIC: 8741 5021 1389 1542 Business
management; Office and public building
furniture; Construction, repair, and
dismantling services; Commercial and
office building contractors

(G-14040)
POWELL STONE GRAVEL
89 Route 13 (03033-2502)
PHONE...............................603 673-8100
EMP: 9 EST: 2018
SALES (est): 450.11K Privately Held
Web: www.powellstone.com
SIC: 1442 Construction sand and gravel

(G-14041)
**SUPERIOR STEEL
FABRICATORS INC**
46 Route 13 (03033-2002)
P.O. Box 116 (03033-0116)
PHONE...............................603 673-7509
P Donald Hoard, Pr
Jeffrey Crocker, Sec
EMP: 17 EST: 1992
SQ FT: 10,000
SALES (est): 1.12MM Privately Held
Web: www.superiorsteelnh.com
SIC: 3446 3441 Stairs, staircases, stair
treads: prefabricated metal; Fabricated
structural metal

(G-14042)
VALDE SYSTEMS INC
4 Hobart Hill Rd (03033-2531)
PHONE...............................603 577-1728
Matthew Linder, Pr
▼ EMP: 8 EST: 2003
SALES (est): 690K Privately Held

Web: www.valdesystems.com
SIC: 3823 Process control instruments

Campton
Grafton County

(G-14043)
EVERGREEN EMBROIDERY
239 Riverside Dr (03223-4651)
P.O. Box 1536 (03223-1536)
PHONE...............................603 726-4271
Donna F Minickiello, Pt
Faust Minickiello, Pt
EMP: 10 EST: 1991
SALES (est): 479.47K Privately Held
Web: www.evergreenembroidery.net
SIC: 2395 Embroidery products, except
Schiffli machine

(G-14044)
**GRANITE STATE LOG HOMES
INC (PA)**
Also Called: Lumber Outlet
17 King Rd (03223-4229)
PHONE...............................603 536-4949
TOLL FREE: 800
Debbie Macdonald, Pr
EMP: 12 EST: 1988
SQ FT: 3,000
SALES (est): 1.25MM
SALES (corp-wide): 1.25MM Privately
Held
Web: www.granitestateloghomes.com
SIC: 2452 5211 Log cabins, prefabricated,
wood; Lumber and other building materials

Canaan
Grafton County

(G-14045)
DOWN TO FAB LLC
453 Us Route 4 (03741-7870)
PHONE...............................603 728-8299
David Amos Plumley, Prin
EMP: 8 EST: 2016
SALES (est): 293.02K Privately Held
Web: www.downtofab.com
SIC: 3714 Motor vehicle parts and
accessories

(G-14046)
FC HAMMOND & SON CO INC
Also Called: Hammond Lumber
11 Hammonds Way (03741)
P.O. Box 17 (03741-0017)
PHONE...............................603 523-4353
Fred Hammond, Pr
Tamra Hammond, VP
EMP: 10 EST: 1945
SQ FT: 2,000
SALES (est): 1.01MM Privately Held
Web: www.hammondgrinding.com
SIC: 2421 5031 Sawmills and planing mills,
general; Lumber: rough, dressed, and
finished

(G-14047)
**NUCOR HRRIS RBAR
NORTHEAST LLC**
Also Called: Canaan Division
450 Us Route 4 (03741-7869)
P.O. Box 553 (03741-0553)
PHONE...............................603 632-5222
EMP: 52
SALES (corp-wide): 41.51B Publicly Held
Web: www.harrisrebar.com

GEOGRAPHIC

SIC: **5039** 5051 5211 3449   Prefabricated structures; Steel; Lumber and other building materials; Miscellaneous metalwork
HQ: Nucor Harris Rebar Northeast Llc
   55 Sumner St Ste 1
   Milford MA 01757
   800 370-0132

Candia
Rockingham County

(G-14048)
EASTERN TIME DESIGNS INC
Also Called: Powertronics
   143 Raymond Rd (03034-2133)
   P.O. Box 474 (03034-0474)
   PHONE..............................603 483-5876
Lawrence P Stacy Prestreas, *Prin*
Lawrence P Stacy, *Pr*
Michael St Laurent, *Stockholder*
Steven Liggett, *Stockholder*
EMP: 14 EST: 1979
SQ FT: 2,200
SALES (est): 899.58K **Privately Held**
Web: www.powertronics.com
SIC: **3825**   Test equipment for electronic and electrical circuits

Center Barnstead
Belknap County

(G-14049)
CMD LOGGING
   520 N Barnstead Rd (03225-3947)
   PHONE..............................603 986-5055
EMP: 8 EST: 2014
SALES (est): 483.25K **Privately Held**
SIC: **2411**   Logging

Center Conway
Carroll County

(G-14050)
CERAMCO INC
   1467 E Main St (03813-4169)
   P.O. Box 300 (03813-0300)
   PHONE..............................603 447-2090
Thomas Henriksen, *Pr*
▲ **EMP: 20 EST:** 1982
SQ FT: 10,350
SALES (est): 2.34MM **Privately Held**
Web: www.ceramcoceramics.com
SIC: **3264** 3299   Porcelain electrical supplies ; Ceramic fiber

(G-14051)
EMM PRECISION INC
   619 E Conway Rd (03813-4057)
   P.O. Box 2410 (03818-2410)
   PHONE..............................603 356-8892
EMP: 10 EST: 1994
SQ FT: 8,000
SALES (est): 1.18MM **Privately Held**
Web: www.emmprecision.com
SIC: **3599**   Machine shop, jobbing and repair

(G-14052)
FADDEN CHIPPING & LOGGING INC
Also Called: Fadden Trucking
   1708 E Conway Rd (03813-4007)
   P.O. Box 243 (03818-0243)
   PHONE..............................603 939-2462
Thomas A Fadden, *Pr*
Vicki Graves, *VP*

EMP: 10 EST: 1980
SALES (est): 968.69K **Privately Held**
Web: www.faddenchipping.com
SIC: **2411**   Logging camps and contractors

(G-14053)
GARLAND LUMBER COMPANY INC
   636 E Conway Rd (03813-4004)
   P.O. Box 10 (03813-0010)
   PHONE..............................603 356-5636
Roger L Garland Senior, *Pr*
Roger Garland Junior, *VP*
Jacqueline M Garland, *
EMP: 30 EST: 1975
SQ FT: 2,500
SALES (est): 2.73MM **Privately Held**
Web: www.garlandlumber.net
SIC: **2411** 1794 4959   Logging camps and contractors; Excavation work; Snowplowing

(G-14054)
GARLAND TRANSPORTATION CORP
   636 E Conway Rd (03813-4004)
   PHONE..............................603 356-5636
Roger L Garland Junior, *Admn*
EMP: 8 EST: 2011
SALES (est): 70.75K **Privately Held**
Web: www.garlandlumber.net
SIC: **2411**   Logging camps and contractors

(G-14055)
LUPINE INC
   16 Lupine Ln (03813-4431)
   P.O. Box 1600 (03818-1600)
   PHONE..............................603 356-7371
David Jensen, *Pr*
Scott Badger, *
Valerie Jensen, *
◆ **EMP: 76 EST:** 1991
SQ FT: 25,000
SALES (est): 4.78MM **Privately Held**
Web: www.lupinepet.com
SIC: **3999** 2399   Pet supplies; Horse and pet accessories, textile

Center Harbor
Belknap County

(G-14056)
JUST HIT PRINT LLC
   23 Main St Ste 1c (03226-3623)
   PHONE..............................603 279-5939
EMP: 7 EST: 2018
SALES (est): 447.73K **Privately Held**
Web: store.justhitprint.net
SIC: **2752**   Offset printing

Center Ossipee
Carroll County

(G-14057)
EFFICIENCY PLUS
   49 Leavitt Rd (03814-6326)
   PHONE..............................603 539-8125
Arthur Butland, *Prin*
EMP: 7 EST: 2004
SALES (est): 105.99K **Privately Held**
SIC: **3433**   Heating equipment, except electric

(G-14058)
MITEE-BITE PRODUCTS LLC
   340 Route 16b (03814-6841)
   P.O. Box 430 (03814-0430)

   PHONE..............................603 539-4538
Richard Porter, *Pr*
EMP: 16 EST: 1977
SQ FT: 10,000
SALES (est): 2.41MM **Privately Held**
Web: www.miteebite.com
SIC: **3599**   Machine shop, jobbing and repair

Center Tuftonboro
Carroll County

(G-14059)
NETC LIQUIDATING CORPORATION
   147 Middle Rd (03816-5904)
   PHONE..............................603 569-3100
EMP: 20
SIC: **3599** 3441   Machine and other job shop work; Fabricated structural metal

Charlestown
Sullivan County

(G-14060)
AMERICAN MARINE PRODUCTS INC
   73 Southwest St (03603-4499)
   P.O. Box 1200 (03603-1200)
   PHONE..............................954 782-1400
Richard Prull, *Pr*
◆ **EMP: 11 EST:** 1968
SQ FT: 30,000
SALES (est): 399.73K **Privately Held**
SIC: **3231** 3083 3732   Safety glass: made from purchased glass; Window sheeting, plastics; Boatbuilding and repairing

(G-14061)
DAVID STREETER
Also Called: Meadowbrook Prcsion Shtmtl Fab
   853 River Rd (03603-4163)
   PHONE..............................603 542-6045
David Streeter, *Owner*
EMP: 7 EST: 1974
SQ FT: 3,600
SALES (est): 199.07K **Privately Held**
SIC: **7699** 3444   Industrial tool grinding; Sheet metalwork

(G-14062)
DESIGN STANDARDS CORP
   957 Claremont Rd (03603-4666)
   P.O. Box 1620 (03603-1620)
   PHONE..............................603 826-7744
Eic Crainich, *Prin*
Laurence Crainich, *
▲ **EMP: 72 EST:** 1972
SALES (est): 10.26MM **Privately Held**
Web: www.designstandards.com
SIC: **3841**   Surgical stapling devices

(G-14063)
GKN AEROSPACE NEW ENGLAND INC
   1105 River Rd (03603-4176)
   PHONE..............................603 542-5135
EMP: 72
SALES (corp-wide): 9.07B **Privately Held**
Web: www.gknaerospace.com
SIC: **3724** 3999 3599   Aircraft engines and engine parts; Barber and beauty shop equipment; Machine shop, jobbing and repair
HQ: Gkn Aerospace New England, Inc.
   183 Louis St

Newington CT 06111

(G-14064)
GREENSOURCE FABRICATION LLC (PA)
   81 Ceda Rd Bldg 1 (03603-4597)
   PHONE..............................603 283-9880
George W Whelen Iv, *Managing Member*
EMP: 100 EST: 2017
SALES (est): 10.88MM
SALES (corp-wide): 10.88MM **Privately Held**
Web: www.greensourcefab.com
SIC: **3672**   Printed circuit boards

(G-14065)
NEWPORT SAND & GRAVEL CO INC
Also Called: Carroll Concrete Co
   368 Springfield Rd (03603-4742)
   PHONE..............................603 826-4444
Colin Nelson, *Mgr*
EMP: 8
SALES (corp-wide): 44.7MM **Privately Held**
Web: www.carrollconcrete.com
SIC: **3273**   Ready-mixed concrete
PA: Newport Sand & Gravel Co., Inc.
   8 Reeds Mill Rd
   Newport NH 03773
   603 298-0199

(G-14066)
OPTICAL SOLUTIONS INC
Also Called: OSI
   26 Bull Run (03603-4346)
   PHONE..............................603 826-4411
EMP: 9 EST: 1996
SQ FT: 8,960
SALES (est): 821.27K **Privately Held**
Web: www.opticalsolutionsinc.com
SIC: **3827** 5049   Optical instruments and lenses; Optical goods

(G-14067)
POMPANETTE LLC (PA)
Also Called: Gray Enterprises
   73 Southwest St (03603-4499)
   P.O. Box 1200 (03603-1200)
   PHONE..............................717 569-2300
Richard Truell, *Managing Member*
James H Bailey, *
◆ **EMP: 70 EST:** 1936
SQ FT: 100,000
SALES (est): 24MM
SALES (corp-wide): 24MM **Privately Held**
Web: www.pompanette.com
SIC: **3732**   Boatbuilding and repairing

(G-14068)
RAY-TECH INFRARED CORPORATION
   198 Springfield Rd Ste 198 (03603-4737)
   P.O. Box 1119 (03603-1119)
   PHONE..............................603 826-3030
Wesley Vanvelsor, *Pr*
Judy Forsaith, *Mgr*
EMP: 19 EST: 1989
SQ FT: 12,000
SALES (est): 2.55MM **Privately Held**
Web: www.raytechinfrared.com
SIC: **5082** 3531   Pavers; Road construction and maintenance machinery

(G-14069)
WHELEN ENGINEERING CO
Also Called: Plastics Group of Whelen, The
   99 Ceda Rd (03603-4597)
   PHONE..............................860 526-9504

John Olson, *Pr*
George Whelen Iv, *Ex VP*
▲ **EMP:** 1500 **EST:** 1953
SQ FT: 32,000
SALES (est): 375.21MM
SALES (corp-wide): 488.29MM **Privately Held**
Web: www.whelen.com
SIC: 3544 Industrial molds
PA: Whelen Engineering Company, Inc.
  51 Winthrop Rd
  Chester CT 06412
  860 526-9504

Chatham
Carroll County

(G-14070)
LOG HOUSE DESIGNS INC (PA)
  184 Butter Hill Rd (03813-5302)
  PHONE..............................603 694-3373
  D Kenyon King, *Pr*
  Janice Purslow, *VP*
  EMP: 15 **EST:** 1974
  SQ FT: 6,000
  SALES (est): 1.64MM
  SALES (corp-wide): 1.64MM **Privately Held**
  Web: www.loghousedesignsusa.com
  SIC: 2385 Waterproof outerwear

Chester
Rockingham County

(G-14071)
STONE MACHINE CO INC
  45 E Derry Rd (03036-4318)
  P.O. Box 368 (03036-0368)
  PHONE..............................603 887-4287
  Frank Camillieri, *Pr*
  Malcolm R Stone, *VP*
  EMP: 18 **EST:** 1980
  SQ FT: 8,400
  SALES (est): 1.92MM **Privately Held**
  Web: www.stonemachine.com
  SIC: 3599 7692 Machine shop, jobbing and repair; Welding repair

Chichester
Merrimack County

(G-14072)
BUSINESS SHIRTMASTERS
Also Called: Shirtmasters Screen Printing
  349 Dover Rd (03258-6525)
  PHONE..............................603 798-3787
  Craig Anderson, *Pr*
  Steve Blasko, *VP*
  Craig Anderson, *Prin*
  EMP: 10 **EST:** 1990
  SQ FT: 2,000
  SALES (est): 678.67K **Privately Held**
  Web: www.shirtmasters.com
  SIC: 5136 2759 2396 2395 Sportswear, men's and boys'; Commercial printing, nec; Automotive and apparel trimmings; Pleating and stitching

(G-14073)
HELEKA COMPANIES LLC (PA)
Also Called: Lilac and Finch
  160 Dover Rd Unit 10 (03258-6537)
  P.O. Box 16147 (03106-6147)
  PHONE..............................603 798-3674
  EMP: 7 **EST:** 2015
  SALES (est): 222.84K

SALES (corp-wide): 222.84K **Privately Held**
Web: www.heleka.com
SIC: 2844 Perfumes, cosmetics and other toilet preparations

Claremont
Sullivan County

(G-14074)
ALLWEATHER COATINGS LLC
  29 Old Newport Rd (03743-4352)
  PHONE..............................603 504-4474
  Tanner Nolin, *Prin*
  EMP: 7 **EST:** 2012
  SALES (est): 128.59K **Privately Held**
  SIC: 3479 Metal coating and allied services

(G-14075)
AMERICAN BRUSH COMPANY INC
  112 Industrial Blvd (03743-5123)
  P.O. Box 1490 (03743-1490)
  PHONE..............................603 542-9951
  Allen Benson, *CEO*
  Brent Swenson, *Pr*
  Mark Saji, *VP*
  EMP: 28 **EST:** 1913
  SQ FT: 116,000
  SALES (est): 1.65MM **Privately Held**
  Web: www.linzerproducts.com
  SIC: 3991 Paintbrushes
  HQ: Linzer Products Corp.
    248 Wyandanch Ave
    West Babylon NY 11704
    631 253-3333

(G-14076)
AMPAC HOLDINGS LLC
Also Called: Proampac
  130 Sullivan St (03743-5210)
  PHONE..............................603 542-0411
  Tom Moore, *Brnch Mgr*
  EMP: 65
  SALES (corp-wide): 208.73K **Privately Held**
  Web: www.proampac.com
  SIC: 2621 Kraft paper
  HQ: Ampac Holdings, Llc
    12025 Tricon Rd
    Cincinnati OH 45246
    513 671-1777

(G-14077)
APC PAPER COMPANY INC (DH)
Also Called: APC Paper Group
  130 Sullivan St (03743-5210)
  PHONE..............................603 542-0411
  Greg Tucker, *CEO*
  ▲ **EMP:** 64 **EST:** 1990
  SQ FT: 83,000
  SALES (est): 22.61MM
  SALES (corp-wide): 208.73K **Privately Held**
  Web: www.apcpaper.com
  SIC: 2621 Kraft paper
  HQ: Ampac Holdings, Llc
    12025 Tricon Rd
    Cincinnati OH 45246
    513 671-1777

(G-14078)
BD ENTERPRISES LLC
Also Called: Diversified Precast
  111 Twistback Rd (03743-4541)
  PHONE..............................603 504-6231
  Brian Desmarais, *Managing Member*
  EMP: 7 **EST:** 2021

SALES (est): 210.88K **Privately Held**
SIC: 3272 Concrete products, nec

(G-14079)
BOURDONS INSTITUTIONAL SLS INC
  85 Plains Rd (03743-4527)
  PHONE..............................603 542-8709
  Daniel Desmarais, *Pr*
  Charles Aiken, *
  ▲ **EMP:** 23 **EST:** 1925
  SQ FT: 45,000
  SALES (est): 3.88MM **Privately Held**
  Web: www.bourdons.com
  SIC: 2515 Mattresses, innerspring or box spring

(G-14080)
BUTCHER BLOCK INC
Also Called: North Country Smokehouse
  19 Syd Clarke Dr (03743-5608)
  PHONE..............................800 258-4304
  Michael Satzow, *CEO*
  Aaron Corbett, *Pr*
  EMP: 20 **EST:** 1972
  SQ FT: 15,000
  SALES (est): 5.38MM **Privately Held**
  Web: www.ncsmokehouse.com
  SIC: 2013 5961 Sausages and other prepared meats; Food, mail order

(G-14081)
CANAM BRIDGES US INC
  386 River Rd (03743-5671)
  PHONE..............................603 542-5202
  EMP: 49 **EST:** 2017
  SALES (est): 10.56MM
  SALES (corp-wide): 1.04B **Privately Held**
  Web: www.canambridges.com
  SIC: 3441 5051 Building components, structural steel; Iron and steel (ferrous) products
  PA: Groupe Canam Inc
    11505 1re Av Bureau 500
    Saint-Georges QC G5Y 7
    418 228-8031

(G-14082)
CARBON FELT INC
  98 Plains Rd (03743-4525)
  PHONE..............................603 542-0202
  Zhonglei Jin, *Pr*
  EMP: 10 **EST:** 2018
  SQ FT: 165,000
  SALES (est): 2.16MM **Privately Held**
  SIC: 2299 Felts and felt products

(G-14083)
CASCADED PURCHASE HOLDINGS INC (PA)
Also Called: New Hampshire Industries
  35 Connecticut River Bend Rd (03743)
  PHONE..............................603 448-1090
  ▲ **EMP:** 100 **EST:** 1995
  SQ FT: 42,000
  SALES (est): 19.99MM **Privately Held**
  Web: www.mechanicalmotionparts.com
  SIC: 3429 Pulleys, metal

(G-14084)
CNC NORTH INC
  16 Industrial Blvd (03743-5122)
  P.O. Box 1395 (03743-1395)
  PHONE..............................603 542-3361
  Patrick Joseph Harrington, *Pr*
  Gary Caravella, *VP*
  Robert Hawkins, *Sec*
  ▲ **EMP:** 9 **EST:** 2005
  SALES (est): 1.76MM **Privately Held**

Web: www.cncnorth.com
SIC: 3541 Grinding machines, metalworking

(G-14085)
CONNECTCUT PRCSION CSTINGS INC
  20 Wentworth Pl (03743-4403)
  PHONE..............................603 542-3373
  Ronald Morello Junior, *Pr*
  Ronald Morello Junior, *Pr*
  Annette Morello, *VP*
  EMP: 8 **EST:** 1986
  SQ FT: 8,500
  SALES (est): 2.17MM **Privately Held**
  Web: www.ctprecisioncastings.com
  SIC: 3363 Aluminum die-castings

(G-14086)
CROWN POINT CABINETRY CORP
  462 River Rd (03743-5653)
  P.O. Box 1560 (03743-1560)
  PHONE..............................603 542-1273
  Brian D Stowell, *Pr*
  Rebecca C Stowell, *
  ▼ **EMP:** 97 **EST:** 1982
  SQ FT: 100,000
  SALES (est): 8.78MM **Privately Held**
  Web: www.crown-point.com
  SIC: 2434 Wood kitchen cabinets

(G-14087)
CROWN POINT REALTY CORP INC
  153 Charlestown Rd (03743-5616)
  P.O. Box 1560 (03743-1560)
  PHONE..............................603 543-1208
  Brian Stowell, *Prin*
  Brian Stowell, *Pr*
  Rebecca Stowell, *
  Jeff Stowell, *Stockholder**
  Patricia Paquette, *Stockholder**
  EMP: 25 **EST:** 1978
  SQ FT: 18,200
  SALES (est): 960.14K **Privately Held**
  Web: www.crown-point.com
  SIC: 2517 2434 Wood television and radio cabinets; Vanities, bathroom: wood

(G-14088)
DIVERSIFIED ENTERPRISES-ADT
Also Called: Diversified Enterprises
  101 Mulberry St Ste 2n (03743-2612)
  PHONE..............................603 543-0038
  Russell E Smith, *Owner*
  EMP: 7 **EST:** 1986
  SQ FT: 3,500
  SALES (est): 467.38K **Privately Held**
  Web: www.accudynetest.com
  SIC: 3826 2899 Analytical instruments; Chemical preparations, nec

(G-14089)
EAGLE PUBLICATIONS INC
Also Called: Eagle Times
  45 Crescent St (03743-2220)
  PHONE..............................603 543-3100
  Harry Hartman, *Pr*
  EMP: 24 **EST:** 1914
  SQ FT: 22,500
  SALES (est): 645.37K **Privately Held**
  Web: www.eagletimes.com
  SIC: 2711 2752 Commercial printing and newspaper publishing combined; Commercial printing, lithographic

(G-14090)

GREEN MOUNTAIN METALS OF VT
2 Wentworth Pl (03743-4403)
PHONE.............................603 542-0005
Robert P Morin, *Pr*
Deborah C Morin, *VP*
EMP: 17 **EST:** 1951
SQ FT: 12,000
SALES (est): 420.59M **Privately Held**
SIC: 3599 Machine shop, jobbing and repair

(G-14091)

JARVIS AUTO MACHINE LLC
13 Bowen St (03743-2330)
PHONE.............................603 504-6144
EMP: 16 **EST:** 2010
SALES (est): 1.53MM **Privately Held**
Web: www.jarvismachine.com
SIC: 3599 Machine shop, jobbing and repair

(G-14092)

LAKE MACHINE CO INC
12 Balcom Pl (03743-4400)
P.O. Box 1088 (03743-1088)
PHONE.............................603 542-8884
Edgar Grallert, *Pr*
▲ **EMP:** 10 **EST:** 1958
SQ FT: 5,000
SALES (est): 750.27K **Privately Held**
Web: www.lakemachine.com
SIC: 3599 Machine shop, jobbing and repair

(G-14093)

MATRIX AEROSPACE CORP
421 River Rd (03743-5652)
PHONE.............................603 542-0191
Ed Farris, *Pr*
Thomas A Hillebrand, *
EMP: 65 **EST:** 2003
SQ FT: 7,500
SALES (est): 9.7MM **Privately Held**
Web: www.matrixaero.com
SIC: 3728 Aircraft parts and equipment, nec

(G-14094)

MIKROS TECHNOLOGIES LLC
24 Colonel Ashley Ln (03743-4424)
PHONE.............................603 690-2020
Javier A Valenzuela, *Pr*
▲ **EMP:** 42 **EST:** 1991
SQ FT: 15,000
SALES (est): 6.71MM **Privately Held**
Web: www.mikrostechnologies.com
SIC: 3599 8731 Machine shop, jobbing and repair; Commercial physical research

(G-14095)

NHI MECHANICAL MOTION LLC
35 Connecticut River Bend Rd (03743)
PHONE.............................603 448-1090
EMP: 16 **EST:** 2019
SALES (est): 1.96MM **Privately Held**
SIC: 3568 Pulleys, power transmission

(G-14096)

RALPH L OSGOOD INC
Also Called: Osgood Welding
144 Grissom Ln (03743-5635)
P.O. Box 63 (05030-0063)
PHONE.............................603 543-1703
Kevin Osgood, *Pr*
Ralph Osgood, *Pr*
Janice Osgood, *Treas*
Debbie Osgood, *Sec*
EMP: 18 **EST:** 1976
SALES (est): 969.36K **Privately Held**
Web: www.osgoodwelding.com

SIC: 7692 7538 Welding repair; Truck engine repair, except industrial

(G-14097)

REED TRUCK SERVICES INC
287 Washington St (03743-5516)
P.O. Box 989 (03743-0989)
PHONE.............................603 542-5032
Scott G Reed, *Pr*
EMP: 13 **EST:** 1993
SQ FT: 4,800
SALES (est): 3.29MM **Privately Held**
Web: www.reedtruckservices.com
SIC: 3715 7538 5531 Truck trailers; Truck engine repair, except industrial; Automotive parts

(G-14098)

THERMACUT INC
153 Charlestown Rd (03743-5616)
PHONE.............................603 543-0585
Richard Mann, *Pr*
Richard Mann, *General ENGG*
Kevin Bonneau, *Marketing**
▲ **EMP:** 30 **EST:** 1990
SQ FT: 50,000
SALES (est): 6.08MM
SALES (corp-wide): 430.73MM **Privately Held**
Web: www.thermacut.us
SIC: 3541 Plasma process metal cutting machines
HQ: Thermacut Gmbh
Am Rubgarten 2
Burbach NW 57299
27362949110

(G-14099)

TIMBERPEG EAST INC (PA)
61 Plains Rd (03743-4526)
PHONE.............................603 542-7762
Robert Britton, *Pr*
EMP: 25 **EST:** 1974
SQ FT: 40,000
SALES (est): 4.08MM
SALES (corp-wide): 4.08MM **Privately Held**
Web: www.timberpeg.com
SIC: 2452 1521 Log cabins, prefabricated, wood; Single-family housing construction

(G-14100)

WHS HOMES INC (PA)
Also Called: Timberpeg
61 Plains Rd (03743-4526)
PHONE.............................603 542-5418
EMP: 25 **EST:** 2011
SALES (est): 7.71MM **Privately Held**
Web: www.realloghomes.com
SIC: 2452 Log cabins, prefabricated, wood

(G-14101)

XRAY AEROSPACE CORP
75 Winter St (03743-5054)
PHONE.............................603 254-8051
Allen Farris, *Pr*
EMP: 16 **EST:** 2020
SALES (est): 1.94MM **Privately Held**
SIC: 3324 Aerospace investment castings, ferrous

(G-14102)

YANKEE BARN HOMES INC
61 Plains Rd (03743-4526)
PHONE.............................603 863-4545
Tony Hanslin, *Pr*
Irene Hanslin, *Stockholder**
EMP: 38 **EST:** 1969
SQ FT: 10,000
SALES (est): 6.27MM **Privately Held**

Web: www.yankeebarnhomes.com
SIC: 2452 Prefabricated buildings, wood

Colebrook
Coos County

(G-14103)

COLUMBIA SAND & GRAVEL INC
Rr.3 (03576)
P.O. Box 132 (03576-0132)
PHONE.............................603 237-5729
Lloyd A Drew, *Pr*
EMP: 7 **EST:** 1989
SALES (est): 598.71K **Privately Held**
SIC: 1442 Construction sand and gravel

(G-14104)

D & E SCREW MACHINE PDTS INC
34 Bill Bromage Dr (03576-2016)
P.O. Box 38 (03576-0038)
PHONE.............................508 658-7344
Leslie Ann Eldridge, *Pr*
EMP: 14 **EST:** 2006
SALES (est): 469.12K **Privately Held**
Web: www.descrew.com
SIC: 3451 Screw machine products

(G-14105)

GILLES CHAMPAGNE
Edwards St (03576)
P.O. Box 10 (03576-0010)
PHONE.............................603 237-5272
Gilles Champagne, *Owner*
EMP: 7 **EST:** 1976
SALES (est): 874.49K **Privately Held**
SIC: 2411 Logging camps and contractors

(G-14106)

HEALTHCO INTERNATIONAL LLC
1 Wilderness Rd (03576-3331)
PHONE.............................603 255-3771
Thomas N Tillotson, *Mgr*
▲ **EMP:** 7 **EST:** 2003
SQ FT: 80,000
SALES (est): 224.76K **Privately Held**
Web: www.healthco.net
SIC: 3842 Gloves, safety

(G-14107)

NEWS & SENTINEL INC
6 Bridge St (03576-3033)
P.O. Box 39 (03576-0039)
PHONE.............................603 237-5501
Karen Ladd, *Pr*
Butch Ladd, *Sec*
EMP: 13 **EST:** 1957
SQ FT: 6,000
SALES (est): 461.17K **Privately Held**
Web: www.colbsent.com
SIC: 2711 Commercial printing and newspaper publishing combined

(G-14108)

PREPCO INC
Also Called: Prepco
57 Colby St (03576-3047)
PHONE.............................603 237-4080
Peter Weiner, *Pr*
Peter J Weiner, *Pr*
Hilda Weiner, *VP*
Gary Bergeron, *Quality*
EMP: 9 **EST:** 1988
SALES (est): 627.4K **Privately Held**
Web: www.prepco.com
SIC: 3841 Surgical and medical instruments

(G-14109)

THE GREAT N WOODS ASSOC/ BLIND
23 Gould St (03576-3056)
PHONE.............................603 490-9877
Louis Leon-guerrero, *Pr*
Rick Tillotson, *Sec*
EMP: 9 **EST:** 2014
SALES (est): 446.98K **Privately Held**
SIC: 3842 Radiation shielding aprons, gloves, sheeting, etc.

(G-14110)

W CRAIG WASHBURN
Also Called: C W Timber
45 Diamond Pond Rd (03576-3500)
PHONE.............................603 237-8403
W Craig Washburn, *Owner*
Lisa Washburn, *Bookpr*
EMP: 7 **EST:** 1988
SALES (est): 431.82K **Privately Held**
SIC: 2411 Logging

(G-14111)

WELOG INC
11 Skyline Dr (03576-3649)
PHONE.............................603 237-8277
Malcolm Washburn, *Pr*
Donna Washburn, *Sec*
EMP: 12 **EST:** 1990
SALES (est): 557.53K **Privately Held**
SIC: 2411 1794 Logging camps and contractors; Excavation work

---

Concord
Merrimack County

(G-14112)

ACW PLASTIC PRODUCTS INC
Also Called: Advantage Plastic Products
38 Henniker St (03301-8528)
PHONE.............................603 227-9540
Mark J Krauss, *Pr*
Mark J Krauss, *Prin*
EMP: 18 **EST:** 2019
SALES (est): 2.06MM **Privately Held**
Web: www.app-nh.com
SIC: 3089 Injection molding of plastics

(G-14113)

APP-JWB INC
38 Henniker St (03301-8528)
PHONE.............................603 227-9540
Joel Beaudette, *Prin*
▲ **EMP:** 25 **EST:** 2008
SALES (est): 4.97MM **Privately Held**
Web: www.app-nh.com
SIC: 3089 Injection molding of plastics

(G-14114)

ARGYLE ASSOCIATES INC
Also Called: New Hampshire Print Mail Svcs
30 Terrill Park Dr (03301-5257)
PHONE.............................603 226-4300
EMP: 23 **EST:** 2005
SALES (est): 2.38MM **Privately Held**
Web: www.nhprintmail.com
SIC: 2759 Business forms: printing, nsk

(G-14115)

BITTWARE INC (DH)
Also Called: Bittware Fpga Cmpt Systems
45 S Main St Fl 2 (03301-4800)
PHONE.............................603 226-0404
Jeffry Milrod, *Pr*
Mark Pinkman, *CFO*
Andy Conn, *Mgr*
EMP: 31 **EST:** 1989

▲ = Import ▼ = Export
◆ = Import/Export

SQ FT: 15,000
SALES (est): 10.05MM
SALES (corp-wide): 36.93B **Privately Held**
Web: www.bittware.com
SIC: 3613 Panel and distribution boards and other related apparatus
HQ: Molex, Llc
2222 Wellington Ct
Lisle IL 60532
630 969-4550

(G-14116)
BOYCE HIGHLANDS FURN CO INC
Also Called: Boyce Highland
14 Whitney Rd (03301-1831)
PHONE..............................603 753-1042
John Lentine, *Pr*
Brien Murphy, *
Robert Lowe, *
EMP: 46 **EST:** 1977
SALES (est): 8.44MM **Privately Held**
Web: www.boycehighlands.com
SIC: 2431 Moldings, wood: unfinished and prefinished

(G-14117)
BRIANS MACHINE SHOP LLC
27 Industrial Park Dr Ste 1 (03301-8523)
PHONE..............................603 224-4333
EMP: 7 **EST:** 2007
SALES (est): 748.17K **Privately Held**
Web: www.briansmachineshopllc.com
SIC: 3599 Machine shop, jobbing and repair

(G-14118)
BRIDGE & BYRON INC
Also Called: Bridge Byron Printers
45 S State St (03301-3729)
PHONE..............................603 225-5221
Robert Rainbill, *Pr*
EMP: 8 **EST:** 1926
SQ FT: 5,000
SALES (est): 492.29K **Privately Held**
Web: www.speedyprintingnh.com
SIC: 2752 Offset printing

(G-14119)
CAPITOL DISTRIBUTORS INC
114 Hall St (03301-3425)
P.O. Box 1148 (03302-1148)
PHONE..............................603 224-3348
John Shea, *CEO*
EMP: 7 **EST:** 2011
SALES (est): 200.1K **Privately Held**
SIC: 2082 Beer (alcoholic beverage)

(G-14120)
CAPITOL SCREEN PRTG & EMBRO
276 N State St (03301-3283)
PHONE..............................603 234-7000
Dave Palisi, *Prin*
EMP: 7 **EST:** 2017
SALES (est): 370.31K **Privately Held**
SIC: 2752 Commercial printing, lithographic

(G-14121)
CHARLES LEONARD STEEL SVCS LLC
Also Called: Clss
183 Pembroke Rd (03301-5768)
PHONE..............................603 225-0211
EMP: 13 **EST:** 2010
SALES (est): 2.46MM **Privately Held**
Web:
www.charlesleonardsteelservices.com
SIC: 3441 Fabricated structural metal

(G-14122)
COMPUTYPE INC
Also Called: Identification Concepts
38 Locke Rd Ste 4 (03301-5422)
PHONE..............................603 225-5500
EMP: 8
SALES (corp-wide): 94MM **Privately Held**
Web: www.computype.com
SIC: 2759 3565 2679 Labels and seals: printing, nsk; Labeling machines, industrial; Labels, paper: made from purchased material
PA: Computype, Inc.
2285 County Road C W
Saint Paul MN 55113
651 633-0633

(G-14123)
CONCORD LITHO GROUP LLC (PA)
92 Old Turnpike Rd (03301-7305)
PHONE..............................603 224-1202
Peter Cook, *CEO*
James D Cook, *
Walter Herrick, *
Marlin Kaufman, *
EMP: 190 **EST:** 1958
SQ FT: 210,000
SALES (est): 41.21MM
SALES (corp-wide): 41.21MM **Privately Held**
Web: www.concorddirect.com
SIC: 2752 Offset printing

(G-14124)
CONCORD MONITOR
60 Manor Rd (03303-1900)
PHONE..............................603 224-5301
Wilma M Fournier, *Prin*
EMP: 8 **EST:** 2010
SALES (est): 79.31K **Privately Held**
Web: www.concordmonitor.com
SIC: 2711 Newspapers, publishing and printing

(G-14125)
CONCORD PHOTO ENGRAVING CO INC
12 Commercial St (03301-5031)
P.O. Box 1355 (03302-1355)
PHONE..............................603 225-3681
Peter Otto, *Pr*
Max Otto, *VP*
▲ **EMP:** 10 **EST:** 1932
SQ FT: 3,600
SALES (est): 466.3K **Privately Held**
Web: www.concordengraving.com
SIC: 2759 Commercial printing, nec

(G-14126)
CONCORDIAN LLC
462 Josiah Bartlett Rd (03301-5928)
P.O. Box 297 (03302-0297)
PHONE..............................603 225-5660
Pattu D Kesavan, *Prin*
EMP: 7 **EST:** 2010
SALES (est): 96.56K **Privately Held**
Web: www.concordianonline.com
SIC: 2711 Newspapers, publishing and printing

(G-14127)
CUBIC CORPORATION
54 Regional Dr (03301-8502)
PHONE..............................603 369-5504
EMP: 12
SALES (corp-wide): 1.48B **Privately Held**
Web: www.cubic.com

SIC: 3812 Defense systems and equipment
HQ: Cubic Corporation
9233 Balboa Ave
San Diego CA 92123
858 277-6780

(G-14128)
DB SIGNS LLC
249 Sheep Davis Rd Ste 4 (03301-5797)
PHONE..............................603 225-4081
John A Wolkowski Esq, *Admn*
EMP: 7 **EST:** 2014
SALES (est): 390.71K **Privately Held**
SIC: 3993 Signs and advertising specialties

(G-14129)
EXACOM INC
99 Airport Rd (03301-7301)
PHONE..............................603 228-0706
Helmut Koch, *Pr*
William Haskett, *VP*
Donald Gartrell, *Sec*
EMP: 20 **EST:** 1986
SQ FT: 26,400
SALES (est): 8.52MM **Privately Held**
Web: www.exacom.com
SIC: 3661 1731 Telephone and telegraph apparatus; Communications specialization

(G-14130)
FIBERNEXT LLC
41 Locke Rd (03301-5417)
PHONE..............................603 226-2400
Ryan Irving, *Managing Member*
◆ **EMP:** 20 **EST:** 2003
SQ FT: 8,000
SALES (est): 5.76MM **Privately Held**
Web: www.fibernext.com
SIC: 1731 3229 Fiber optic cable installation ; Fiber optics strands

(G-14131)
GRANITE STATE CANDY SHOPPE LLC (PA)
13 Warren St (03301-4045)
PHONE..............................603 225-2591
EMP: 15 **EST:** 1927
SQ FT: 13,000
SALES (est): 2.44MM
SALES (corp-wide): 2.44MM **Privately Held**
Web:
www.granitestatecandyshoppe.com
SIC: 2064 5145 5149 5441 Candy and other confectionery products; Confectionery; Chocolate; Candy, nut, and confectionery stores

(G-14132)
GRAPHIC PACKAGING INTL LLC
Also Called: Laporte Division
80 Commercial St (03301-5031)
PHONE..............................603 230-5100
Mike Haney, *Brnch Mgr*
EMP: 92
Web: www.graphicpkg.com
SIC: 2631 2652 Container, packaging, and boxboard; Setup paperboard boxes
HQ: Graphic Packaging International, Llc
1500 Riveredge Pkwy # 100
Atlanta GA 30328

(G-14133)
GRAPHIC PACKAGING INTL LLC
Also Called: Smurfit-Stone
80 Commercial St (03301-5031)
PHONE..............................603 230-5100
Jim Stanley, *Brnch Mgr*
EMP: 233
Web: www.graphicpkg.com

SIC: 2631 2657 2652 Folding boxboard; Folding paperboard boxes; Setup paperboard boxes
HQ: Graphic Packaging International, Llc
1500 Riveredge Pkwy # 100
Atlanta GA 30328

(G-14134)
GRAPHIC PACKAGING INTL LLC
Also Called: Southfield Carton
80 Commercial St (03301-5031)
PHONE..............................603 224-2333
Rodney Alexander, *Pr*
EMP: 33
SQ FT: 6,000
Web: www.graphicpkg.com
SIC: 2657 2631 Folding paperboard boxes; Container board
HQ: Graphic Packaging International, Llc
1500 Riveredge Pkwy # 100
Atlanta GA 30328

(G-14135)
H32 DESIGN AND DEVELOPMENT LLC (PA)
Also Called: Advanced Kiosks
134 Hall St Ste F (03301-3470)
P.O. Box 234 (03287-0234)
PHONE..............................603 865-1000
Howard Henry Horn Ii, *Pr*
Tarra Horn, *CFO*
EMP: 8 **EST:** 2000
SALES (est): 2.57MM
SALES (corp-wide): 2.57MM **Privately Held**
Web: www.advancedkiosks.com
SIC: 5045 3577 Computers, peripherals, and software; Computer peripheral equipment, nec

(G-14136)
HOPTO INC (PA)
Also Called: HOPTO
189 N Main St Ste 102 (03301-6601)
PHONE..............................408 688-2674
Jonathon R Skeels, *Interim Chief Financial Officer*
EMP: 7 **EST:** 1996
SQ FT: 1,548
SALES (est): 3.91MM
SALES (corp-wide): 3.91MM **Publicly Held**
SIC: 7372 Application computer software

(G-14137)
HORSESHOE POND PLACE COMMNTY
26 Commercial St (03301-5038)
PHONE..............................603 224-8390
Vera Ippolito, *Prin*
EMP: 7 **EST:** 2011
SALES (est): 112.94K **Privately Held**
SIC: 3462 Horseshoes

(G-14138)
HOYT ELEC INSTR WORKS INC
23 Meter St (03303-1894)
PHONE..............................603 753-6321
Jeffrey Hoyt, *CEO*
Donald E Hall, *
Andrew Hoyt, *
S Michael Trela, *
▲ **EMP:** 40 **EST:** 1904
SQ FT: 30,000
SALES (est): 6.61MM **Privately Held**
Web: www.hoytmeter.com
SIC: 3825 3613 Analog-digital converters, electronic instrumentation type; Switchgear and switchboard apparatus

(G-14139)
LAND AND SEA INC
25 Henniker St (03301-8528)
PHONE.....................................603 226-3966
◆ **EMP:** 55
SIC: 3559 Automotive maintenance
equipment

(G-14140)
LINDE ADVANCED MTL TECH INC
Praxair
146 Pembroke Rd Ste 1 (03301-5706)
PHONE.....................................603 224-9585
Greg Tucker, *Genl Mgr*
EMP: 70
Web: www.linde-amt.com
SIC: 3563 3542 Spraying and dusting
equipment; Plasma jet spray metal forming
machines
HQ: Linde Advanced Material Technologies
Inc.
1500 Polco St
Indianapolis IN 46222
317 240-2500

(G-14141)
LSR SEALCOATING
6 Bicentennial Sq (03301-4058)
PHONE.....................................603 715-4934
David Steadman, *Prin*
EMP: 8 **EST:** 2019
SALES (est): 144.8K **Privately Held**
SIC: 2952 Asphalt felts and coatings

(G-14142)
MACHINE CRAFT COMPANY INC
114 Hall St (03301-3425)
P.O. Box 3665 (03302-3665)
PHONE.....................................603 225-0958
Kim Jennison, *Pr*
Janette Jennison, *Treas*
▲ **EMP:** 15 **EST:** 1980
SQ FT: 10,000
SALES (est): 2.21MM **Privately Held**
Web: www.machinecraftcompany.com
SIC: 3599 Machine shop, jobbing and repair

(G-14143)
MARKET BASKET PRODUCE INC
108 Fort Eddy Rd (03301-7423)
PHONE.....................................603 224-5479
Tom Beakey, *Mgr*
EMP: 83
SALES (corp-wide): 559.48MM **Privately Held**
Web: www.marketbaskethq.com
SIC: 5411 7384 2052 2051 Grocery stores,
chain; Photofinish laboratories; Cookies
and crackers; Bread, cake, and related
products
HQ: Market Basket Produce, Inc.
875 East St
Tewksbury MA 01876
978 851-8000

(G-14144)
MAX COHEN & SONS INC (HQ)
Also Called: Advanced Recycling
25 Sandquist St (03301-3491)
P.O. Box 2410 (03302-2410)
PHONE.....................................603 224-3532
TOLL FREE: 800
Steven Cohen, *Pr*
Dorothy Bickford, *
◆ **EMP:** 25 **EST:** 1957
SQ FT: 68,000
SALES (est): 9.73MM

SALES (corp-wide): 2.88B **Publicly Held**
SIC: 4953 5093 3341 3312 Recycling,
waste materials; Metal scrap and waste
materials; Secondary nonferrous metals;
Blast furnaces and steel mills
PA: Schnitzer Steel Industries, Inc.
299 Sw Clay St Ste 400
Portland OR 97201
503 224-9900

(G-14145)
MELLEN COMPANY INC (PA)
40 Chenell Dr (03301-8544)
PHONE.....................................603 228-2929
Jonathan Y Mellen, *Pr*
Robert H Mellen Junior Senior
Engineering, *Sec*
EMP: 25 **EST:** 1963
SQ FT: 20,000
SALES (est): 4.38MM
SALES (corp-wide): 4.38MM **Privately Held**
Web: www.mellencompany.com
SIC: 3567 Industrial furnaces and ovens

(G-14146)
MINUTEMAN PRESS
93 Storrs St (03301-4835)
PHONE.....................................603 513-4993
EMP: 8 **EST:** 2018
SALES (est): 217.14K **Privately Held**
Web: www.minutemanpress.com
SIC: 2752 Commercial printing, lithographic

(G-14147)
NATURAL PLAYGROUNDS SHOP LLC
10 Pine St (03301-3825)
PHONE.....................................888 290-8405
Ethan King, *CEO*
EMP: 15 **EST:** 2019
SALES (est): 578.38K **Privately Held**
Web: www.naturalplaygroundsstore.com
SIC: 3999 Manufacturing industries, nec

(G-14148)
NEW ENGLAND BRACE CO INC (PA)
2 Greenwood Ave (03301-3927)
PHONE.....................................508 588-6060
TOLL FREE: 800
Paul W Guimond, *Pr*
Karen M Acton, *VP*
EMP: 14 **EST:** 1945
SQ FT: 8,000
SALES (est): 2.78MM
SALES (corp-wide): 2.78MM **Privately Held**
SIC: 3842 Orthopedic appliances

(G-14149)
NEWSPAPERS NEW HAMPSHIRE INC (HQ)
Also Called: Monadnock Ledger
1 Monitor Dr (03301-1834)
P.O. Box 1177 (03302-1177)
PHONE.....................................603 224-5301
George W Wilson, *Pr*
Clark Lyon, *
Geoidi Wilson, *
EMP: 171 **EST:** 1979
SALES (est): 22.29MM
SALES (corp-wide): 96.33MM **Privately Held**
SIC: 2711 Newspapers, publishing and
printing
PA: Newspapers Of New England, Inc.
1 Monitor Dr

Concord NH 03301
603 224-5301

(G-14150)
ONSITE DRUG TESTING NENG
56 Old Suncook Rd Ste 1 (03301-5122)
PHONE.....................................603 226-3858
Kimberly Reid, *Owner*
EMP: 7 **EST:** 2008
SALES (est): 708.02K **Privately Held**
Web: www.drugtestingnh.com
SIC: 2899 Drug testing kits, blood and urine

(G-14151)
PATSYS BUS SALES AND SERVICE
31 Hall St (03301-3415)
PHONE.....................................603 226-2222
Joseph R Alosa, *Pr*
EMP: 10 **EST:** 2002
SALES (est): 821.36K **Privately Held**
Web: www.patsysbussales.com
SIC: 3711 Buses, all types, assembly of

(G-14152)
PRIORITY MACHINE LLC
10 Chenell Dr (03301-8537)
PHONE.....................................603 677-2507
Kristen Stanton, *Prin*
EMP: 7 **EST:** 2015
SALES (est): 137.06K **Privately Held**
Web: www.prioritymachinene.com
SIC: 3599 Machine shop, jobbing and repair

(G-14153)
RAINVILLE PRINTING ENTPS INC
45 S State St (03301-3729)
PHONE.....................................603 225-6649
Robert Rainville, *Pr*
EMP: 11 **EST:** 1998
SALES (est): 347.41K **Privately Held**
SIC: 2752 Commercial printing, lithographic

(G-14154)
RWC LANDSCAPE SERVICES MGT
Also Called: Outside Unlimited
2 Whitney Rd Unit 21 (03301-1844)
P.O. Box 418 (03253-0418)
PHONE.....................................603 279-1411
EMP: 45 **EST:** 2009
SQ FT: 1,500
SALES (est): 3.99MM **Privately Held**
Web: www.outsideunlimited.com
SIC: 0781 3531 Landscape services; Snow
plow attachments

(G-14155)
SAY IT IN STITCHES INC
128 Hall St Ste B (03301-3440)
PHONE.....................................603 224-6470
TOLL FREE: 800
EMP: 9 **EST:** 1991
SQ FT: 6,000
SALES (est): 620.98K **Privately Held**
Web: www.stitchesnh.com
SIC: 2395 2396 5949 2759 Embroidery
products, except Schiffli machine; Screen
printing on fabric articles; Needlework
goods and supplies; Screen printing

(G-14156)
SECURE CARE PRODUCTS LLC
39 Chenell Dr (03301-8545)
PHONE.....................................603 223-0745
Harold Baldwin, *Pr*
Albert Larose, *
Francine Mcneff, *Sec*
Matthew Mckerley, *Dir*

James P Mckerley, *Dir*
▲ **EMP:** 65 **EST:** 1985
SALES (est): 13.31MM **Privately Held**
Web: www.securecare.com
SIC: 3829 Measuring and controlling
devices, nec

(G-14157)
SIMPLY FOOTWEAR UTAH LLC
Also Called: Simply Birkenstock
31 N Main St (03301-4930)
P.O. Box 130 (03256-0130)
PHONE.....................................603 715-2259
EMP: 10 **EST:** 2011
SALES (est): 498.75K **Privately Held**
Web: www.simplybirkenstock.com
SIC: 3021 Protective footwear, rubber or
plastic

(G-14158)
STANDEX ELCTRNIC MAGNETICS INC
Also Called: Agile Magnetics
24 Chenell Dr (03301-8529)
PHONE.....................................800 805-8991
John Meeks, *Pr*
EMP: 80 **EST:** 2020
SALES (est): 15.82MM
SALES (corp-wide): 741.05MM **Publicly Held**
Web: www.standexelectronics.com
SIC: 3612 Power and distribution
transformers
PA: Standex International Corporation
23 Keewaydin Dr Ste 205
Salem NH 03079
603 893-9701

(G-14159)
STATE MILITARY RESERVATION
1 Minuteman Way (03301-5607)
PHONE.....................................603 225-1230
EMP: 8 **EST:** 2008
SALES (est): 83.65K **Privately Held**
SIC: 2711 Newspapers

(G-14160)
STOWE WOODWARD LLC
Also Called: Stowe Woodward Co-Div SW Ind
60 Old Turnpike Rd (03301-5242)
PHONE.....................................603 224-6300
Brian Ridge, *Mgr*
EMP: 36
SALES (corp-wide): 7.83B **Privately Held**
SIC: 3069 Roll coverings, rubber
HQ: Stowe Woodward Llc
8537 Six Forks Rd Ste 300
Raleigh NC 27615

(G-14161)
SWENSON GRANITE COMPANY LLC (DH)
369 N State St (03301-3233)
PHONE.....................................603 225-4322
Robert Pope, *Pr*
▲ **EMP:** 50 **EST:** 1883
SQ FT: 10,000
SALES (est): 63.46MM
SALES (corp-wide): 2.1MM **Privately Held**
Web: www.swensongranite.com
SIC: 3281 1411 Granite, cut and shaped;
Granite, dimension-quarrying
HQ: Polycor Inc
76 Rue Saint-Paul Bureau 100
Quebec QC G1K 3
418 692-4695

(G-14162)
TAFA INCORPORATED (DH)
Also Called: Praxair Surface
146 Pembroke Rd Ste 1 (03301-5735)
PHONE....................................603 224-9585
Tim Moser, *Pr*
▲ **EMP:** 23 **EST:** 1976
SQ FT: 35,625
SALES (est): 25.15MM **Privately Held**
SIC: 3563 3542 Spraying and dusting
equipment; Plasma jet spray metal forming
machines
HQ: Linde Inc.
10 Riverview Dr
Danbury CT 06810
203 837-2000

(G-14163)
TEDDYS TEES INC
248 Sheep Davis Rd Ste 6 (03301-5751)
PHONE....................................603 226-2762
TOLL FREE: 800
Steven Story, *Pr*
Charlene Story, *Sec*
EMP: 8 **EST:** 1982
SALES (est): 634K **Privately Held**
Web: www.teddystees.com
SIC: 2759 Screen printing

(G-14164)
**TOPCON POSITIONING
SYSTEMS INC**
58 Chenell Dr (03301-8547)
PHONE....................................800 421-0125
EMP: 7
Web: www.topconsolutions.com
SIC: 3829 Surveying instruments and
accessories
HQ: Topcon Positioning Systems, Inc.
7400 National Dr
Livermore CA 94550

(G-14165)
TRI-STATE IRON WORKS INC
24 Industrial Park Dr (03301-8512)
PHONE....................................603 228-0020
TOLL FREE: 800
Kenneth Mclaren, *Pr*
EMP: 30 **EST:** 1974
SQ FT: 4,000
SALES (est): 4.46MM **Privately Held**
Web: www.tristateiron.com
SIC: 3441 Fabricated structural metal

(G-14166)
WHITE MOUNTAIN IMAGING
46 Chenell Dr (03301-8538)
PHONE....................................603 228-2630
Rick Mc Donald, *Mgr*
EMP: 41
SALES (corp-wide): 22.78MM **Privately
Held**
Web: www.whitemountainimaging.com
SIC: 3559 5047 Chemical machinery and
equipment; Medical equipment and supplies
PA: White Mountain Imaging
1617 Battle St
Webster NH 03303
603 648-2124

Contoocook
Merrimack County

(G-14167)
BRYANT GROUP INC
Also Called: Military Art China
28 Riverside Dr (03229-3147)
P.O. Box 808 (03229-0808)

PHONE....................................603 746-1166
Matthew Bryant, *Pr*
▲ **EMP:** 12 **EST:** 1967
SQ FT: 8,000
SALES (est): 417.29K **Privately Held**
Web: www.milart.com
SIC: 3999 Military insignia

(G-14168)
CHUCK ROSE INC
100 Chase Farm Rd (03229-2900)
PHONE....................................603 746-2311
Charles Rose, *Prin*
EMP: 20 **EST:** 2007
SALES (est): 919.78K **Privately Held**
SIC: 2411 Logging

(G-14169)
**EXCALIBUR SHELVING
SYSTEMS INC**
292 Burnham Intervale Rd (03229-3300)
P.O. Box 498 (03229-0498)
PHONE....................................603 746-6200
John Herrick, *Pr*
Philip Taub, *
▼ **EMP:** 43 **EST:** 1982
SQ FT: 50,000
SALES (est): 5.66MM **Privately Held**
Web:
www.excaliburshelvingsystems.com
SIC: 2541 Shelving, office and store, wood

(G-14170)
HERRICK MILL WORK INC
290 Burnham Intervale Rd (03229-3300)
P.O. Box 495 (03229-0495)
PHONE....................................603 746-5092
John L Herrick, *Pr*
Joanne Herrick, *
Don Gartrell, *
EMP: 11 **EST:** 1978
SQ FT: 25,000
SALES (est): 232.23K **Privately Held**
SIC: 2441 2541 2499 2435 Box shook, wood
; Shelving, office and store, wood; Reels,
plywood; Hardwood veneer and plywood

(G-14171)
MARKLIN CANDLE DESIGN LLC
Also Called: Marklin Candle Design
28 Riverside Dr (03229-3147)
P.O. Box 182 (03229-0182)
PHONE....................................603 746-2211
Martin G Marklin, *Managing Member*
Martin G Marklin, *Pr*
Christine Marklin, *VP*
EMP: 13 **EST:** 1985
SALES (est): 901.53K **Privately Held**
Web: www.marklincandle.com
SIC: 3999 Candles

(G-14172)
MULTI-WELD SERVICES INC
Also Called: Multi-Weld Services
153 Riverside Dr (03229-3146)
PHONE....................................603 746-4604
Mark Stock, *Pr*
Jacqueline Stock, *VP*
EMP: 10 **EST:** 1986
SQ FT: 4,000
SALES (est): 1.42MM **Privately Held**
Web: www.multi-weld.com
SIC: 7692 Welding repair

(G-14173)
**PROTOTEK DGTAL MFG
CONCORD LLC (PA)**
Also Called: Prototek Manufacturing
244 Burnham Intervale Rd (03229-3300)

PHONE....................................603 746-2001
William Gress, *CEO*
Brian Francoeur, *
◆ **EMP:** 56 **EST:** 1987
SQ FT: 40,000
SALES (est): 23.27MM
SALES (corp-wide): 23.27MM **Privately
Held**
Web: www.prototek.com
SIC: 3444 Sheet metalwork

(G-14174)
**PROTOTEK INTRMDATE
HLDINGS INC**
244 Burnham Intervale Rd (03229-3300)
PHONE....................................800 403-9777
EMP: 12 **EST:** 2020
SALES (est): 535.09K **Privately Held**
Web: www.prototek.com
SIC: 3444 Sheet metalwork

(G-14175)
SKYTRANS MFG LLC
106 Burnham Intervale Rd (03229-3300)
P.O. Box 216 (03229-0216)
PHONE....................................802 230-7783
Jeremy L Pendleton, *Managing Member*
Daniel E Pendleton, *Managing Member*
EMP: 10 **EST:** 2001
SALES (est): 2.43MM **Privately Held**
Web: www.skytrans-mfg.com
SIC: 3599 4119 Amusement park equipment
; Aerial tramways, except amusement or
scenic

(G-14176)
**WHITE MOUNTAIN WOOD
GRINDING**
576 Pine St (03229-3129)
P.O. Box 799 (03244-0799)
PHONE....................................603 455-6931
EMP: 7 **EST:** 2009
SALES (est): 181.41K **Privately Held**
SIC: 3599 Grinding castings for the trade

Conway
Carroll County

(G-14177)
BARN DOOR SCREEN PRINTERS
56 Pleasant St (03818-6151)
PHONE....................................603 447-5369
David C Peterson, *Admn*
EMP: 7 **EST:** 2011
SALES (est): 473.42K **Privately Held**
Web: www.barndoorscreenprinters.com
SIC: 2759 Screen printing

(G-14178)
**CHUCK ROAST EQUIPMENT
INC (PA)**
90 Odell Hill Rd (03818-4401)
P.O. Box 1450 (03818-1450)
PHONE....................................603 447-5492
Charles Henderson, *Pr*
Lloyd Henderson, *Sec*
EMP: 18 **EST:** 1972
SQ FT: 16,000
SALES (est): 1.98MM
SALES (corp-wide): 1.98MM **Privately
Held**
Web: www.chuckroast.com
SIC: 2329 2339 5621 5611 Men's and boys'
sportswear and athletic clothing; Women's
and misses' athletic clothing and sportswear
; Women's sportswear; Clothing,
sportswear, men's and boys'

(G-14179)
GLASS GRAPHICS INC
Also Called: Campus Crystal
56 Pleasant St (03818-6151)
P.O. Box 1199 (03818-1199)
PHONE....................................603 447-1900
David Peterson, *Pr*
Peter Edwards, *
▲ **EMP:** 17 **EST:** 1981
SQ FT: 24,000
SALES (est): 9.13MM **Privately Held**
Web: www.glassgraphics.com
SIC: 5094 5099 5199 7389 Trophies;
Crystal goods; Gifts and novelties;
Engraving service

(G-14180)
**GREEN MTN RIFLE BARREL CO
INC**
Also Called: Green Mountain Custom Barrels
153 W Main St (03818-6143)
P.O. Box 2670 (03818-2670)
PHONE....................................603 447-1095
Holly Nordholm Meanley, *Pr*
▼ **EMP:** 10 **EST:** 1976
SALES (est): 4.63MM
SALES (corp-wide): 93.04MM **Privately
Held**
Web: www.gmriflebarrel.com
SIC: 3484 3482 Rifles or rifle parts, 30 mm.
and below; Cartridge cases for ammunition,
30 mm. and below
HQ: Modern Muzzleloading, Inc.
213 Dennis St
Athens TN 37303
866 518-4181

(G-14181)
**PALMER MACHINE COMPANY
INC**
48 North Rd (03818-6148)
PHONE....................................603 447-2069
Michael J Palmer, *Pr*
EMP: 26 **EST:** 1985
SQ FT: 17,000
SALES (est): 463.13K **Privately Held**
Web: www.palmermachine.com
SIC: 3599 Machine shop, jobbing and repair

(G-14182)
TEE ENTERPRISES
Rte 16 (03818)
P.O. Box 1700 (03818-1700)
PHONE....................................603 447-5662
Carl Thibodeau, *Owner*
EMP: 19 **EST:** 1978
SQ FT: 10,000
SALES (est): 443.93K **Privately Held**
Web: www.teeenterprises.com
SIC: 3599 Machine shop, jobbing and repair

Cornish
Sullivan County

(G-14183)
LARRY DINGEE
Also Called: Dingee Machine Co
195 Nh Route 120 (03745-4316)
P.O. Box 162 (03746-0162)
PHONE....................................603 542-9682
Larry Dingee, *Owner*
EMP: 7 **EST:** 1979
SQ FT: 7,000
SALES (est): 496.05K **Privately Held**

GEOGRAPHIC

SIC: 3711 7532 3714 3713　Fire department vehicles (motor vehicles), assembly of; Body shop, trucks; Motor vehicle parts and accessories; Truck bodies (motor vehicles)

Danbury
Merrimack County

(G-14184)
WALLACE BUILDING PRODUCTS CORP
40 Wallace Ln　(03230-4437)
P.O. Box 194　(03230-0194)
PHONE..............................603 768-5402
John D Tauriello, *Pr*
EMP: 25 **EST:** 2012
SQ FT: 20,000
SALES (est): 5.6MM **Privately Held**
Web: www.wallacebp.com
SIC: 2452　Prefabricated buildings, wood

Danville
Rockingham County

(G-14185)
POST WOODWORKING INC
Also Called: Storage With Style
163 Kingston Rd　(03819-3230)
PHONE..............................603 382-4951
Mark Post, *Pr*
Paul D P Riley Junior, *VP*
Phil Curtin, *
EMP: 25 **EST:** 1975
SQ FT: 4,500
SALES (est): 4.41MM **Privately Held**
Web: www.postwoodworking.com
SIC: 2452　Prefabricated buildings, wood

Deerfield
Rockingham County

(G-14186)
HARRIS OH CABINETMAKER
63 Nottingham Rd　(03037-1532)
PHONE..............................603 781-1315
Owain Harris, *Prin*
EMP: 8 **EST:** 1991
SALES (est): 331.2K **Privately Held**
SIC: 2512　Upholstered household furniture

Deering
Hillsborough County

(G-14187)
CLARK SUMMIT ALPACAS LLC
168 Wolf Hill Rd　(03244-6420)
P.O. Box 1300　(03244-1300)
PHONE..............................603 464-2588
James Lewis, *Prin*
EMP: 7 **EST:** 2008
SALES (est): 185.01K **Privately Held**
Web: www.clarksummitalpacas.com
SIC: 3523　Cattle feeding, handling, and watering equipment

(G-14188)
LIBERTY CYCLE LLC
113 E Deering Rd　(03244-6609)
PHONE..............................603 620-1851
Denis Laliberte, *Prin*
EMP: 8 **EST:** 2013
SALES (est): 54.34K **Privately Held**
SIC: 3732　Boatbuilding and repairing

Derry
Rockingham County

(G-14189)
APPOLO VINEYARDS LLC
49 Lawrence Rd　(03038-4190)
PHONE..............................603 421-6052
EMP: 7 **EST:** 2016
SALES (est): 444.97K **Privately Held**
Web: www.appolovineyards.com
SIC: 2084　Wines

(G-14190)
ATLAS GRAN COUNTERTOP FLR SUP
4 Windham Depot Rd　(03038-4510)
PHONE..............................603 818-8899
Nguyen K Tran, *Prin*
Hung H Tran, *Prin*
EMP: 8 **EST:** 2010
SALES (est): 543.24K **Privately Held**
Web: www.atlascounters.com
SIC: 1752 3281　Floor laying and floor work, nec; Granite, cut and shaped

(G-14191)
DOIRE DISTILLING LLC
1 E Broadway　(03038-2409)
PHONE..............................603 765-4353
Terri Pastori, *Prin*
EMP: 8 **EST:** 2017
SALES (est): 348.39K **Privately Held**
Web: www.cask.life
SIC: 2085　Distilled and blended liquors

(G-14192)
EAGLE-TRIBUNE PUBLISHING CO
Also Called: Derry News
46 W Broadway　(03038-2329)
PHONE..............................603 437-7000
EMP: 11
SALES (corp-wide): 33.14B **Privately Held**
Web: www.eagletribune.com
SIC: 2711　Newspapers, publishing and printing
HQ: Eagle-Tribune Publishing Company
　　100 Turnpike St
　　North Andover MA 01845
　　978 946-2000

(G-14193)
FIREYE INC (DH)
3 Manchester Rd　(03038-3008)
PHONE..............................603 432-4100
Gerald Slocum, *Pr*
John Devine, *
Laura L Martinage, *
Sarah B Fjelstul, *
Alicia Perrault, *
▲ **EMP:** 190 **EST:** 1994
SQ FT: 80,000
SALES (est): 48.58MM
SALES (corp-wide): 22.1B **Publicly Held**
Web: www.fireye.com
SIC: 3669 3842 3812　Fire detection systems, electric; Surgical appliances and supplies; Search and navigation equipment
HQ: Kidde Fire Protection Inc.
　　350 E Union St
　　West Chester PA 19382

(G-14194)
HAWK QUALITY PRODUCTS INC
125 Rockingham Rd　(03038-4153)
P.O. Box 885　(03038-0885)
PHONE..............................603 432-3319
Jeff Hawkes, *Pr*

Betty Hawkes, *Treas*
Randy Hawkes, *VP*
EMP: 26 **EST:** 1977
SQ FT: 10,000
SALES (est): 954.38K **Privately Held**
Web: www.hawkquality.com
SIC: 3599　Machine shop, jobbing and repair

(G-14195)
HUNTSMAN INTERNATIONAL LLC
52 Kendall Pond Rd　(03038-4395)
PHONE..............................603 421-3500
Rhona Watson, *Mgr*
EMP: 8
SALES (corp-wide): 8.02B **Publicly Held**
Web: www.huntsman.com
SIC: 2821　Plastics materials and resins
HQ: Huntsman International Llc
　　10003 Woodloch Forest Dr # 260
　　The Woodlands TX 77380
　　281 719-6000

(G-14196)
INTELITEK INC
18 Tsienneto Rd　(03038-1505)
PHONE..............................800 221-2763
Ido Jerushalmi, *CEO*
Ziv Shpringer, *CFO*
▲ **EMP:** 20 **EST:** 1986
SQ FT: 30,000
SALES (est): 7.55MM **Privately Held**
Web: www.intelitek.com
SIC: 3451　Screw machine products
PA: Robogroup T.E.K. Ltd
　　13 Hamelacha
　　Rosh Haayin 48091

(G-14197)
KARL GSCHWIND MACHINEWORKS LLC
6 Tinkham Ave　(03038-1408)
PHONE..............................603 434-4211
Robert Allen, *Managing Member*
Karl Gschwind, *Pr*
EMP: 22 **EST:** 1964
SQ FT: 5,000
SALES (est): 481.37K **Privately Held**
Web: www.gschwindmachine.com
SIC: 3599　Machine shop, jobbing and repair

(G-14198)
LANTOS TECHNOLOGIES INC
34 Route 111 Ste 8　(03038-4290)
PHONE..............................781 443-7633
Paul Harkness, *CEO*
EMP: 8 **EST:** 2020
SALES (est): 911.62K **Privately Held**
Web: www.lantostechnologies.com
SIC: 3577　Optical scanning devices

(G-14199)
LEFT-TEES DESIGNS BAYOU LLC
Also Called: Left-Tees Designs Bayou
15 W Broadway Ste 2　(03038-2368)
P.O. Box 1055　(03054-1055)
PHONE..............................603 437-6630
EMP: 14 **EST:** 2002
SQ FT: 4,500
SALES (est): 593.08K **Privately Held**
Web: www.left-tees.com
SIC: 2759　Screen printing

(G-14200)
LIQUID BLUE INC
6 Linlew Dr　(03038-3002)
PHONE..............................401 333-6200
Paul Roidoulis, *Pr*

▲ **EMP:** 100 **EST:** 1987
SALES (est): 13.42MM **Privately Held**
Web: www.liquidblue.com
SIC: 2261 2396　Screen printing of cotton broadwoven fabrics; Automotive and apparel trimmings

(G-14201)
MARTEL ELECTRONICS CORP
3 Corporate Park Dr Unit 1　(03038-2281)
PHONE..............................603 434-6033
▲ **EMP:** 29 **EST:** 1983
SALES (est): 9.27MM
SALES (corp-wide): 5.83B **Publicly Held**
Web: www.fluke.com
SIC: 3825 5084　Instruments to measure electricity; Measuring and testing equipment, electrical
HQ: Fluke Corporation
　　6920 Seaway Blvd
　　Everett WA 98203
　　425 347-6100

(G-14202)
MAYBROOK INC
20 A St　(03038-1716)
PHONE..............................603 898-0811
Donald Francis, *Ch Bd*
Katharine Felson, *VP*
Alexander P Felson, *VP*
◆ **EMP:** 15 **EST:** 1975
SALES (est): 481.72K **Privately Held**
Web: www.maybrook.com
SIC: 2844　Cosmetic preparations

(G-14203)
PGC WIRE & CABLE LLC
Also Called: Pgc Wire & Cable
16 Lesley Cir　(03038-4448)
PHONE..............................603 821-7300
EMP: 14 **EST:** 2012
SALES (est): 2.44MM **Privately Held**
Web: www.pgcwirecable.com
SIC: 3679　Electronic circuits

(G-14204)
PICA MFG SOLUTIONS INC (PA)
Also Called: Pica
4 Ash Street Ext Unit 3　(03038-2274)
PHONE..............................603 845-3258
Rich Shevelow, *Pr*
Mark Pare, *
Steven Goldberg, *
▲ **EMP:** 37 **EST:** 2007
SQ FT: 7,000
SALES (est): 7.52MM **Privately Held**
Web: www.picamfg.com
SIC: 3672 3559　Printed circuit boards; Electronic component making machinery

(G-14205)
POLYTITE MANUFACTURING CORP
4 Tinkham Ave　(03038-1446)
PHONE..............................603 952-9327
Steven Robinson, *Prin*
EMP: 7 **EST:** 2018
SALES (est): 72.38K **Privately Held**
SIC: 3999　Manufacturing industries, nec

(G-14206)
PRECISION TOOL & MOLDING LLC
Also Called: Precision Tool and Die
22 Manchester Rd Unit 10　(03038-3032)
PHONE..............................603 437-6685
Michael Driscoll, *Owner*
▼ **EMP:** 17 **EST:** 1995
SALES (est): 4.84MM

SALES (corp-wide): 172.38MM **Privately Held**
SIC: 3089 Injection molding of plastics
HQ: Ctp Carrera, Inc.
600 Depot St
Latrobe PA 15650
724 539-1833

(G-14207)
PURE ELEMENT
8 Birch St (03038-2171)
PHONE..............................603 235-4373
Cindy Osborn, *Prin*
EMP: 8 EST: 2007
SALES (est): 146.77K **Privately Held**
SIC: 2819 Industrial inorganic chemicals, nec

(G-14208)
SPIRAL AIR MANUFACTURING LLC
1 B St (03038-1723)
P.O. Box 395 (03051-0395)
PHONE..............................603 624-6647
David Quintiliani, *Pr*
EMP: 9 EST: 1996
SQ FT: 17,000
SALES (est): 973.26K **Privately Held**
Web: www.spiralair.com
SIC: 3444 Ducts, sheet metal

(G-14209)
STENTECH INC (PA)
Also Called: Advanced Tooling Design
22 Manchester Rd Unit 8b (03038-3066)
PHONE..............................603 505-4470
Brent Nolan, *Pr*
▲ EMP: 52 EST: 1979
SALES (est): 22.72MM
SALES (corp-wide): 22.72MM **Privately Held**
Web: www.stentech.com
SIC: 3629 Electronic generation equipment

(G-14210)
TEKNOR APEX
4 Meadowbrook Rd (03038-4956)
PHONE..............................603 434-3056
Phil Scadding, *Prin*
EMP: 10 EST: 2006
SALES (est): 114.75K **Privately Held**
Web: www.teknorapex.com
SIC: 2821 Plastics materials and resins

(G-14211)
TRI-K INDUSTRIES INC
Also Called: Tri-K
20 A St (03038-1716)
PHONE..............................973 298-8850
Kathy Felson, *Prin*
EMP: 23
Web: www.tri-k.com
SIC: 2834 2844 Adrenal pharmaceutical preparations; Cosmetic preparations
HQ: Tri-K Industries, Inc.
2 Stewart Ct
Denville NJ 07834
973 298-8850

Dover
Strafford County

(G-14212)
7TH SETTLEMENT BREWERY LLC
47 Washington St (03820-3877)
PHONE..............................603 534-5292
EMP: 10 EST: 2011

SALES (est): 241.92K **Privately Held**
Web: www.7thsettlement.com
SIC: 2082 5812 Beer (alcoholic beverage); Restaurant, family: independent

(G-14213)
ACCUTECH MARINE PROPELLER INC
24 Crosby Rd Ste 6 (03820-4395)
PHONE..............................603 617-3626
Larry Kindberg, *Pr*
Larry Kindberg, *Pr*
Gail E Kindberg, *Sec*
Courtney Kindberg, *Treas*
Jason Kindberg, *VP*
EMP: 9 EST: 2001
SQ FT: 2,400
SALES (est): 693.81K **Privately Held**
Web: www.accutechmarine.com
SIC: 7699 5551 3429 3568 Marine propeller repair; Boat dealers; Aircraft & marine hardware, inc. pulleys & similar items; Couplings, shaft: rigid, flexible, universal joint, etc.

(G-14214)
AFFINITY LED LIGHT LLC
Also Called: Affinity Led Lighting
1 Washington St Ste 5121 (03820-3977)
PHONE..............................978 378-5338
Steven Lieber, *Pr*
Steven R Lieber, *Managing Member*
▲ EMP: 16 EST: 2013
SALES (est): 1.35MM **Privately Held**
Web: www.affinityled.com
SIC: 3646 Commercial lighting fixtures

(G-14215)
AGILITY MFG INC
279 Locust St (03820-4009)
PHONE..............................603 742-7339
Michael J Mcgreevy, *Pr*
Thomas J Ferrin, *
▲ EMP: 40 EST: 1987
SQ FT: 25,000
SALES (est): 9.91MM **Privately Held**
Web: www.agilitymfg.com
SIC: 3672 Circuit boards, television and radio printed

(G-14216)
ANDERSON WELDING LLC
3 Dean Dr (03820-5613)
PHONE..............................603 996-6225
Jesse Anderson, *Prin*
EMP: 20 EST: 2016
SALES (est): 403.75K **Privately Held**
Web: www.awcoutilities.com
SIC: 7692 Welding repair

(G-14217)
ATLAS PRCISION MET FABRICATORS
49 Industrial Park (03820-4332)
PHONE..............................603 742-1226
Keith Corbett, *Pr*
EMP: 14 EST: 2005
SALES (est): 330.76K **Privately Held**
Web: www.atlaspmf.com
SIC: 3441 Fabricated structural metal

(G-14218)
BAYHEAD PRODUCTS CORPORATION
173 Crosby Rd (03820-4356)
PHONE..............................603 742-3000
Elissa Moore, *Pr*
Gregory Moore, *
EMP: 25 EST: 1973

SALES (est): 4.9MM **Privately Held**
Web: www.bayheadproducts.com
SIC: 3089 Injection molding of plastics

(G-14219)
C CRAMER & CO INC
Also Called: Cramer Fabrics, Inc.
20 Venture Dr (03820-5912)
PHONE..............................603 742-3838
Hans Cramer, *Pr*
Annette Studebaker, *
Johannes Cramer, *Dir*
Tara Frank, *
◆ EMP: 45 EST: 1993
SQ FT: 60,000
SALES (est): 10.04MM
SALES (corp-wide): 2.67MM **Privately Held**
Web: www.cramerfabrics.com
SIC: 2221 2297 Broadwoven fabric mills, manmade; Nonwoven fabrics
PA: C. Cramer Beteiligungs-Gmbh
Domring 4-10
Warstein NW 59581
2902880

(G-14220)
CALLING ALL CARGO LLC
Also Called: Calling All Cargo Moving Co
69 Venture Dr Unit 4 (03820-5930)
P.O. Box 2034 (03821-2034)
PHONE..............................603 740-1900
Michael Carlton, *Managing Member*
Jessica Smith, *Admn*
EMP: 10 EST: 2007
SQ FT: 2,500
SALES (est): 1.27MM **Privately Held**
Web: www.callingallcargo.com
SIC: 2298 Cargo nets

(G-14221)
CHAUVIN ARNOUX INC (PA)
Also Called: Aemc Instruments
15 Faraday Dr (03820-4383)
PHONE..............................603 749-6434
Winthrop D Smith, *Pr*
▲ EMP: 40 EST: 1982
SALES (est): 12.69MM
SALES (corp-wide): 12.69MM **Privately Held**
Web: www.aemc.com
SIC: 3829 Testing equipment: abrasion, shearing strength, etc.

(G-14222)
CHISLETTS BOATING & DESIGN LLC
35 Industrial Park (03820-4332)
PHONE..............................603 755-6815
EMP: 8 EST: 2007
SALES (est): 380.81K **Privately Held**
Web: www.chislettsboating.com
SIC: 3732 Motorized boat, building and repairing

(G-14223)
COGEBI INC
14 Faraday Dr (03820-4384)
PHONE..............................603 749-6896
Peter Landendinger, *CEO*
Henry Kanter, *Pr*
Michael Chaisson, *Sec*
James Sluss, *Treas*
Stephen M Abba, *Dir*
◆ EMP: 13 EST: 1983
SQ FT: 17,500
SALES (est): 3.38MM **Privately Held**
Web: www.cogebi.com
SIC: 5075 5085 3299 Furnaces, heating: electric; Gaskets; Mica products

(G-14224)
COSTELLO/APRIL DESIGN INC
Also Called: C/A Design
180 Crosby Rd (03820-4334)
PHONE..............................603 749-6755
EMP: 47 EST: 1993
SALES (est): 12.57MM **Privately Held**
Web: www.c-a-design.com
SIC: 3711 3469 Chassis, motor vehicle; Metal stampings, nec
PA: The Heico Companies L L C
70 W Madison St Ste 5600
Chicago IL 60602

(G-14225)
D F RICHARD INC
Also Called: D. F. Richard Energy
124 Broadway (03820-3238)
P.O. Box 669 (03821-0669)
PHONE..............................603 742-2020
Richard Card, *CEO*
Raymond J Richard, *
Robert A Richard, *
Anita S Corain, *
EMP: 60 EST: 1953
SQ FT: 15,000
SALES (est): 8.65MM **Privately Held**
Web: www.dfrichard.com
SIC: 1382 Oil and gas exploration services

(G-14226)
DMI TECHNOLOGY CORP (PA)
Also Called: Dmi Technology
1 Progress Dr (03820-5537)
PHONE..............................603 742-3330
James Elsner, *Pr*
Logan D Delany Junior, *Ch*
John Arico, *VP Fin*
EMP: 18 EST: 1994
SALES (est): 114.25MM **Privately Held**
Web: www.dmitechnology.com
SIC: 3625 3621 Relays and industrial controls; Electric motor and generator parts

(G-14227)
E-CLOTH INC
131 Broadway (03820-3299)
P.O. Box 812 (03840-0812)
PHONE..............................603 765-9367
EMP: 30 EST: 2007
SALES (est): 5.51MM **Privately Held**
Web: us.e-cloth.com
SIC: 2842 5087 2392 2259 Polishing preparations and related products; Cleaning and maintenance equipment and supplies; Towels, dishcloths and dust cloths ; Towels, washcloths, and dishcloths: knit
PA: E-Cloth Limited
3rd Floor
Altrincham WA14

(G-14228)
ELECTROCRAFT NEW HAMPSHIRE INC (DH)
1 Progress Dr (03820-5537)
PHONE..............................603 742-3330
James Elsner, *Pr*
John Arico, *
▲ EMP: 21 EST: 1942
SQ FT: 120,000
SALES (est): 12.99MM **Privately Held**
SIC: 3621 3825 3694 3625 Motors, electric; Instruments to measure electricity; Engine electrical equipment; Relays and industrial controls
HQ: Electrocraft, Inc.
2 Marin Way Ste 3
Stratham NH 03885

(G-14229)
GREEN MOUNTAIN RISK MGT LLC
660 Central Ave Ste 201 (03820-3435)
PHONE..............................802 683-8586
Randal Schaetzke, *Admn*
EMP: 10 **EST:** 2008
SALES (est): 612.04K **Privately Held**
SIC: 3482 Small arms ammunition

(G-14230)
HAMPSHIRE CONTROLS CORP
1 Grove St (03820-3314)
P.O. Box 516 (03821-0516)
PHONE..............................603 749-9424
Dianne Rush, *Pr*
EMP: 12 **EST:** 1976
SQ FT: 7,225
SALES (est): 1.91MM **Privately Held**
Web: www.hampshirecontrols.com
SIC: 3625 3829 3822 Electric controls and
   control accessories, industrial; Measuring
   and controlling devices, nec; Environmental
   controls

(G-14231)
HM MACHINE LLC
5 Faraday Dr (03820-5024)
PHONE..............................603 617-3450
Sarah Hussey, *Prin*
EMP: 7 **EST:** 2007
SALES (est): 619.6K **Privately Held**
SIC: 3599 Machine shop, jobbing and repair

(G-14232)
KAUTEX INC
74 Industrial Park (03820-4332)
PHONE..............................603 743-2431
EMP: 486
SALES (corp-wide): 12.87B **Publicly Held**
Web: www.kautex.com
SIC: 3714 Motor vehicle parts and
   accessories
HQ: Kautex Inc.
   800 Tower Dr Ste 200
   Troy MI 48098
   248 616-5100

(G-14233)
LOXSMITH BAGEL CORPORATION
1 Washington St (03820-3848)
PHONE..............................603 362-9060
Holly Patterson, *Pr*
EMP: 12 **EST:** 2018
SALES (est): 825.68K **Privately Held**
Web: www.loxsmithbagelco.com
SIC: 7371 5461 5812 2051 Computer
   software development and applications;
   Bagels; Restaurant, family: independent;
   Bagels, fresh or frozen

(G-14234)
MF BLOUIN MDSG SOLUTION
27 Production Dr (03820-5917)
PHONE..............................800 394-1632
Kathryn Limric, *Pr*
EMP: 8 **EST:** 2016
SALES (est): 858K **Privately Held**
Web: www.mfblouin.com
SIC: 3446 Bank fixtures, ornamental metal

(G-14235)
MFB HOLDINGS LLC
Also Called: Blouin Display
27 Production Dr (03820-5917)
P.O. Box 10 (03869-0010)
PHONE..............................603 742-0104
David Zoia, *Managing Member*

Adam Zoia, *Managing Member*
▲ **EMP:** 40 **EST:** 1948
SQ FT: 42,000
SALES (est): 4.27MM **Privately Held**
Web: www.mfblouin.com
SIC: 3446 Bank fixtures, ornamental metal

(G-14236)
MJ MURPHY AND SONS INC
4 Granite St (03820-3518)
P.O. Box 395 (03821-0395)
PHONE..............................603 767-4200
TOLL FREE: 800
Thomas Methvin, *Pr*
Ford W Shaw Iii, *VP*
EMP: 25 **EST:** 1921
SQ FT: 17,000
SALES (est): 961.73K **Privately Held**
SIC: 1711 1761 3444 Plumbing, heating, air-
   conditioning; Roofing contractor; Sheet
   metalwork

(G-14237)
NCIEA
31 Mount Vernon St (03820-3007)
P.O. Box 351 (03821-0351)
PHONE..............................603 749-0733
Richard Hill, *Prin*
EMP: 8 **EST:** 2018
SALES (est): 239.14K **Privately Held**
Web: www.nciea.org
SIC: 3841 Surgical and medical instruments

(G-14238)
NEFAB PACKAGING NORTH EAST LLC (PA)
115 Broadway (03820-3217)
PHONE..............................603 343-5750
EMP: 24 **EST:** 2015
SALES (est): 7.9MM
SALES (corp-wide): 7.9MM **Privately Held**
SIC: 2671 Paper; coated and laminated
   packaging

(G-14239)
NEW ENGLAND HOMES INC
277 Locust St (03820-4009)
PHONE..............................603 436-8830
TOLL FREE: 800
Daniel J Donahue, *Pr*
Kathi Mann, *
EMP: 61 **EST:** 1961
SQ FT: 9,000
SALES (est): 2.37MM **Privately Held**
Web: www.newenglandhomes.net
SIC: 2452 Panels and sections,
   prefabricated, wood

(G-14240)
NEW ENGLAND INNOVATIONS CORP
Also Called: North East Products
4 Progress Dr (03820-5450)
PHONE..............................603 742-6247
Philip Sidmore, *Pr*
Evelyn Sidmore, *VP*
EMP: 18 **EST:** 1958
SQ FT: 13,000
SALES (est): 2.41MM **Privately Held**
Web: www.northeastprecisioncnc.com
SIC: 3599 Machine shop, jobbing and repair

(G-14241)
NORTH COUNTRY TRACTOR INC
Also Called: John Deere Authorized Dealer
10 Littleworth Rd (03820-4329)
PHONE..............................603 742-5488
EMP: 17

Web: www.deere.com
SIC: 3524 5082 Lawn and garden equipment
   ; Construction and mining machinery
PA: North Country Tractor, Inc.
   149 Sheep Davis Rd
   Pembroke NH 03275

(G-14242)
NORTH EAST CUTTING DIE CORP
Also Called: North East Cutting Die
29 Industrial Park (03820-4332)
P.O. Box 2238 (03843-2238)
PHONE..............................603 436-8952
Mark Geller, *Pr*
EMP: 23 **EST:** 1962
SQ FT: 10,000
SALES (est): 728.45K **Privately Held**
Web: www.necuttingdie.com
SIC: 3599 3544 Machine shop, jobbing and
   repair; Special dies and tools

(G-14243)
ODYSSEY PRESS INC (PA)
36 Fords Landing Dr (03820-4552)
PHONE..............................603 749-4433
EMP: 46
SQ FT: 23,000
SALES (est): 3.58MM
SALES (corp-wide): 3.58MM **Privately Held**
SIC: 2752 2732 Commercial printing,
   lithographic; Book printing

(G-14244)
PENTAIR RSDNTIAL FLTRATION LLC
Also Called: Fibredyne
47 Crosby Rd (03820-4340)
PHONE..............................603 749-1610
James Donnelly, *Pr*
▲ **EMP:** 442 **EST:** 1979
SALES (est): 2.13MM **Privately Held**
SIC: 3589 Water filters and softeners,
   household type
HQ: Sta-Rite Industries, Llc
   293 S Wright St
   Delavan WI 53115
   888 782-7483

(G-14245)
PROMETHEUS GROUP OF NH LTD
Also Called: Prometheus Group
1 Washington St Ste 3171 (03820-2234)
PHONE..............................800 442-2325
Richard Poore, *Pr*
▲ **EMP:** 10 **EST:** 1990
SQ FT: 3,700
SALES (est): 2.67MM **Privately Held**
Web: www.theprogrp.com
SIC: 3841 Surgical and medical instruments

(G-14246)
Q LLC
110 Venture Dr (03820-5913)
P.O. Box 6860 (03802-6860)
PHONE..............................603 294-0047
EMP: 9 **EST:** 2016
SALES (est): 1.22MM **Privately Held**
Web: www.liveqordie.com
SIC: 3484 Small arms

(G-14247)
RAND-WHITNEY CONTAINER LLC
15 Stonewall Dr (03820-5531)
PHONE..............................603 822-7300
EMP: 46

Web: www.randwhitney.com
SIC: 2653 Boxes, corrugated: made from
   purchased materials
HQ: Rand-Whitney Container Llc
   1 Rand Whitney Way
   Worcester MA 01607
   508 890-7000

(G-14248)
RELYCO SALES INC (PA)
121 Broadway (03820-3252)
P.O. Box 1229 (03821-1229)
PHONE..............................603 742-0999
Michael R Steinberg, *CEO*
Bruce Steinberg, *
Laurie Steinberg, *
Dennis Veilleux Ctrl, *Prin*
EMP: 38 **EST:** 1989
SQ FT: 13,500
SALES (est): 9.72MM
SALES (corp-wide): 9.72MM **Privately Held**
Web: www.relyco.com
SIC: 2759 5112 5044 Laser printing;
   Stationery and office supplies; Office
   equipment

(G-14249)
SEA HAGG DISTILLERY LLC
Also Called: Plaice Cove Spirits
119 Broadway (03820-3217)
PHONE..............................603 343-1717
EMP: 7 **EST:** 2011
SALES (est): 290.41K **Privately Held**
SIC: 2085 Distilled and blended liquors

(G-14250)
SEACOAST REDIMIX CONCRETE LLC (PA)
349 Mast Rd (03820-5518)
PHONE..............................603 742-4441
TOLL FREE: 800
EMP: 18 **EST:** 2000
SQ FT: 1,500
SALES (est): 2.72MM
SALES (corp-wide): 2.72MM **Privately Held**
Web: www.redimixcompanies.com
SIC: 3273 5211 Ready-mixed concrete;
   Concrete and cinder block

(G-14251)
SYNAP INC
Also Called: Synap
77 Fourth St (03820-2900)
PHONE..............................888 572-1150
Shelby Brewer, *Pr*
EMP: 7 **EST:** 2014
SALES (est): 245.71K **Privately Held**
Web: www.synaphealth.com
SIC: 3372 7389 Application computer
   software; Business services, nec

(G-14252)
TFH LIQUIDATION COMPANY LLC
Also Called: Tasker Funeral Home
621 Central Ave (03820-3401)
PHONE..............................603 742-4961
TOLL FREE: 800
Grover L Tasker Senior, *Managing Member*
EMP: 9 **EST:** 1907
SQ FT: 1,500
SALES (est): 231.78K **Privately Held**
Web: www.taskerfuneralservice.com
SIC: 7261 3272 Funeral home; Monuments
   and grave markers, except terrazzo

▲ = Import ▼ = Export
◆ = Import/Export

(G-14253)
TICKED OFF INC
97 Spruce Ln (03820-4542)
PHONE..............................603 742-0925
Richard Hebbard, *Pr*
Mary Hebbard, *VP*
EMP: 8 **EST:** 1994
SALES (est): 987.73K **Privately Held**
Web: www.tickedoff.com
SIC: 2833 3841 Animal based products;
Surgical and medical instruments

(G-14254)
TRADEPORT USA LLC
3 Progress Dr (03820-5450)
PHONE..............................603 692-2900
EMP: 16 **EST:** 2002
SALES (est): 3.63MM **Privately Held**
Web: www.tradeportusa.com
SIC: 5731 3651 Consumer electronic
equipment, nec; Household audio and
video equipment

(G-14255)
**TURBOCAM ENERGY
SOLUTIONS LLC**
5 Faraday Dr (03820-5024)
PHONE..............................603 905-0200
▲ **EMP:** 45 **EST:** 2013
SALES (est): 4.7MM **Privately Held**
Web: www.turbocam.com
SIC: 3398 Metal heat treating

(G-14256)
VIGILANT INCOPORATED
85 Industrial Park (03820-4332)
PHONE..............................603 285-0400
◆ **EMP:** 45 **EST:** 1995
SQ FT: 46,000
SALES (est): 9.64MM **Privately Held**
Web: www.vigilantinc.com
SIC: 2499 Decorative wood and woodwork

(G-14257)
VISHAY HIREL SYSTEMS LLC
140 Crosby Rd (03820-4334)
PHONE..............................603 742-4375
Gary Bates, *Mgr*
EMP: 95
SALES (corp-wide): 3.5B **Publicly Held**
Web: www.vishay.com
SIC: 3677 3612 Electronic transformers;
Transformers, except electric
HQ: Vishay Hirel Systems Llc
7767 Elm Creek Blvd N # 305
Maple Grove MN 55369
952 544-1344

(G-14258)
VX1 CORPORATION
271 Locust St (03820-4072)
PHONE..............................603 742-2888
EMP: 11 **EST:** 2018
SALES (est): 488.93K **Privately Held**
SIC: 3651 Household audio and video
equipment

(G-14259)
VYGON CORPORATION
87 Venture Dr (03820-5914)
PHONE..............................603 743-5988
EMP: 162
Web: www.vygonusa.com
SIC: 5047 3841 Medical equipment and
supplies; Surgical and medical instruments
HQ: Vygon Corporation
2750 Morris Rd Ste A200
Lansdale PA 19446
215 390-2002

(G-14260)
WELCH FLUOROCARBON INC
113 Crosby Rd Ste 10 (03820-4370)
PHONE..............................603 742-0164
Evan Welch, *Pr*
EMP: 30 **EST:** 1984
SQ FT: 7,800
SALES (est): 9.71MM **Privately Held**
Web: www.welchfluorocarbon.com
SIC: 3089 Injection molding of plastics

Dublin
Cheshire County

(G-14261)
HELMERS PUBLISHING INC
Also Called: Desktop Engineering Magazine
1283 Main St (03444-8242)
PHONE..............................603 563-1631
Stephen Robbins, *Pr*
Tom Conlon, *
Donna Mclain, *COO*
EMP: 23 **EST:** 1979
SALES (est): 218.95K **Privately Held**
Web: www.deskeng.com
SIC: 2721 2741 2731 7389 Magazines:
publishing only, not printed on site;
Directories, nec: publishing only, not printed
on site; Books, publishing only; Advertising,
promotional, and trade show services

(G-14262)
**YANKEE PUBLISHING
INCORPORATED (PA)**
Also Called: Yankee Magazine
1121 Main St (03444-8246)
P.O. Box 520 (03444-0520)
PHONE..............................603 563-8111
James Trowbridge, *Pr*
Judson D Hale Senior, *Ch*
Judson D Hale Junior, *VP*
Sherin E Pierce, *
Jody Bugbee, *
EMP: 50 **EST:** 1935
SQ FT: 15,200
SALES (est): 38.1MM
SALES (corp-wide): 38.1MM **Privately
Held**
Web: www.newengland.com
SIC: 2741 Miscellaneous publishing

Dummer
Coos County

(G-14263)
PAT GAGNE LOGGING LLC
236 Ferry Rd (03588-5340)
PHONE..............................603 449-2479
Patrick Gagne, *Prin*
EMP: 8 **EST:** 2017
SALES (est): 348.41K **Privately Held**
SIC: 2411 Logging camps and contractors

Dunbarton
Merrimack County

(G-14264)
GLH SYSTEMS
181 Stark Hwy S (03046-4411)
PHONE..............................603 774-6374
EMP: 7 **EST:** 2017
SALES (est): 33.85K **Privately Held**
Web: www.dataretrieval.com
SIC: 7372 Prepackaged software

(G-14265)
SPORTS VISIO INC
9 Tucker Hill Rd (03046-4621)
PHONE..............................603 774-1339
Jason Syversen, *CEO*
EMP: 15 **EST:** 2021
SALES (est): 528K **Privately Held**
SIC: 7372 7389 Application computer
software; Business Activities at Non-
Commercial Site

Durham
Strafford County

(G-14266)
EHS PUBLISHING
10 Newmarket Rd (03824-2808)
PHONE..............................203 216-5800
EMP: 7
SALES (est): 6.6K **Privately Held**
Web: www.ehspublishing.com
SIC: 2741 Miscellaneous publishing

(G-14267)
PURE SOURCE LLC
291 Durham Point Rd (03824-3419)
PHONE..............................626 442-6784
Phil Dollar, *CEO*
EMP: 12 **EST:** 2016
SALES (est): 666.06K **Privately Held**
SIC: 3471 Electroplating and plating

(G-14268)
UNIVERSITY SYSTEM NH
Also Called: University NH Brewry
34 Sage Way Barton Hall 111 (03824)
PHONE..............................603 659-2825
Cheryl Parker, *Brnch Mgr*
EMP: 43
SALES (corp-wide): 745.73MM **Privately
Held**
Web: www.usnh.edu
SIC: 2082 Malt beverages
PA: University System Of New Hampshire
5 Chenell Dr Ste 301
Concord NH 03301
603 862-1800

East Hampstead
Rockingham County

(G-14269)
ACE MACHINE INC
563 Rte 111 (03826)
P.O. Box 869 (03826-0869)
PHONE..............................603 329-6716
Bruce De Boyes, *Pr*
EMP: 23 **EST:** 1983
SQ FT: 3,800
SALES (est): 481.27K **Privately Held**
Web: www.ace-machine.com
SIC: 3599 Machine shop, jobbing and repair

(G-14270)
CZ MACHINE INC
Also Called: C Z Machine Shop
110 Hunt Rd (03826-8201)
PHONE..............................603 382-4259
Mike Czeremin, *Pr*
Doris Kendal, *Sec*
Rudi Czeremin, *VP*
EMP: 7 **EST:** 1977
SQ FT: 6,000
SALES (est): 494.73K **Privately Held**
SIC: 3599 Machine shop, jobbing and repair

(G-14271)
**RAM PRINTING INCORPORATED
(PA)**
Also Called: Hampstead Copy Center
Rte 111 (03826)
P.O. Box 900 (03826-0900)
PHONE..............................603 382-7045
Walter Zaremba, *Pr*
Buddy Zaremba, *
EMP: 29 **EST:** 1976
SQ FT: 7,000
SALES (est): 8.05MM
SALES (corp-wide): 8.05MM **Privately
Held**
Web: www.theramcompanies.com
SIC: 2752 7334 2791 Offset printing;
Photocopying and duplicating services;
Typesetting

East Kingston
Rockingham County

(G-14272)
**MSM PROTEIN TECHNOLOGIES
INC**
Also Called: Msm Protein Technologies
97 Giles Rd (03827-2009)
PHONE..............................617 504-9548
Tajib A Mirzabekov, *Pr*
David I Kreimer, *Sec*
C Davis Farmer Junior, *Treas*
EMP: 14 **EST:** 2005
SALES (est): 713.49K **Privately Held**
Web: www.msmprotein.com
SIC: 2834 Pharmaceutical preparations

(G-14273)
RSI METAL FABRICATION LLC
213 Haverhill Rd Bldg 9 (03827-2136)
P.O. Box 479 (03827-0479)
PHONE..............................603 382-8367
Joshua Winter, *Mgr*
EMP: 10 **EST:** 2013
SALES (est): 257.88K **Privately Held**
SIC: 3312 Wire products, steel or iron

Enfield
Grafton County

(G-14274)
ENERTGETIC BALTIC MI
80 Baltic St (03748-3162)
P.O. Box 10 (03748-0010)
PHONE..............................603 252-0804
Timothy Taylor, *Pr*
EMP: 8 **EST:** 2005
SALES (est): 145.56K **Privately Held**
SIC: 3699 Outboard motors, electric

(G-14275)
**TK SPORTS AND ASSOCIATES
INC**
Also Called: Bags and Things
100 Whaleback Mountain Rd (03748-4222)
P.O. Box 310 (03748-0310)
PHONE..............................603 442-6770
James C Keane, *Pr*
EMP: 8 **EST:** 1983
SQ FT: 7,000
SALES (est): 398.63K **Privately Held**
Web: www.inkfactoryclothing.com
SIC: 7336 2396 Silk screen design;
Automotive and apparel trimmings

Epping
Rockingham County

(G-14276)
ALEX VAULT CO
25 Molly Way (03042-1926)
PHONE......................603 944-0132
Alex Mpynn, *Prin*
EMP: 8 **EST:** 2006
SALES (est): 174.66K **Privately Held**
SIC: 3272 Burial vaults, concrete or precast terrazzo

(G-14277)
WILLIAMSON ELECTRICAL CO INC
Also Called: Williamson New England
334b Calef Hwy (03042-2325)
PHONE......................617 884-9200
Robert Lee Tilton, *Pr*
Brian Tilton, *
Robert Anthony Tilton, *
Rebecca Tilton, *
EMP: 65 **EST:** 1944
SALES (est): 24.17MM **Privately Held**
Web: www.weco-group.com
SIC: 5063 5084 1731 3561 Motors, electric; Pumps and pumping equipment, nec; Electrical work; Pumps and pumping equipment

Epsom
Merrimack County

(G-14278)
BEAUMAC COMPANY INC
382 Suncook Valley Hwy (03234-4243)
PHONE......................603 736-9321
David W Beaucher, *Pr*
EMP: 30 **EST:** 1967
SQ FT: 23,000
SALES (est): 776.56K **Privately Held**
Web: www.beaumac.com
SIC: 3599 Machine shop, jobbing and repair

(G-14279)
BUCKEYE BLASTING CORPORATION
48 Old Town Road Ext (03234-4538)
PHONE......................603 736-4681
Mark Riedel, *Prin*
EMP: 8 **EST:** 2005
SALES (est): 403.07K **Privately Held**
Web: www.buckeyeblastingcorp.com
SIC: 1629 1081 3532 Rock removal; Metal mining services; Drills and drilling equipment, mining (except oil and gas)

(G-14280)
NEW HMPSHIRE CNTRY CAMPERS LLC
2060 Dover Rd (03234-4134)
PHONE......................802 223-6417
Maria T Dolder, *Prin*
EMP: 9 **EST:** 2017
SALES (est): 386.63K **Privately Held**
Web: www.rvone.com
SIC: 3792 Truck campers (slide-in)

(G-14281)
NEWSTRESS INC
1640 Dover Rd (03234-4417)
P.O. Box 330 (03234-0330)
PHONE......................603 736-9000
Nishan Nahikian, *Pr*
EMP: 31 **EST:** 1972
SQ FT: 22,000
SALES (est): 1.55MM **Privately Held**
Web: www.newstressinc.com
SIC: 3272 Concrete products, precast, nec

(G-14282)
NORTH RIDGE CONTRACTING INC
14 Jug City Rd (03234-4029)
PHONE......................603 942-6104
Eric Cygan, *Pr*
Vin Porcella, *
Eric Cygan, *VP*
EMP: 32 **EST:** 2007
SALES (est): 2.32MM **Privately Held**
Web: www.northridge-contracting.com
SIC: 1795 1799 1446 Demolition, buildings and other structures; Asbestos removal and encapsulation; Molding sand mining

(G-14283)
OXY-GON INDUSTRIES INC
42 Old Route 28 N (03234-4115)
P.O. Box 40 (03234-0040)
PHONE......................603 736-8422
EMP: 22 **EST:** 1988
SALES (est): 5MM **Privately Held**
Web: www.oxy-gon.com
SIC: 3567 Vacuum furnaces and ovens

Exeter
Rockingham County

(G-14284)
BAUER HOCKEY LLC
100 Domain Dr (03833-2996)
PHONE......................603 430-2111
Edward Kinnaly, *CEO*
◆ **EMP:** 665 **EST:** 2017
SQ FT: 67,000
SALES (est): 99.69MM **Privately Held**
Web: www.bauer.com
SIC: 3949 Sporting and athletic goods, nec

(G-14285)
BENTLEY PHARMACEUTICALS INC (HQ)
2 Holland Way (03833-2937)
PHONE......................603 658-6100
James R Murphy, *Ch Bd*
John A Sedor, *Pr*
Michael Mcgovern, *V Ch Bd*
Richard P Lindsay, *VP*
EMP: 112 **EST:** 1974
SQ FT: 15,700
SALES (est): 2.61MM **Privately Held**
SIC: 2834 Drugs acting on the cardiovascular system, except diagnostic
PA: Teva Pharmaceutical Industries Limited
5 Bazel
Petah Tikva 49510

(G-14286)
BLIND TIGER LLP
3 Wright Ln (03833-4726)
PHONE......................603 498-7005
EMP: 7 **EST:** 2019
SALES (est): 234.7K **Privately Held**
SIC: 2591 Window blinds

(G-14287)
COBHAM
Also Called: Cobham Antenna Systems
32 Industrial Dr (03833-4557)
PHONE......................603 418-9786
EMP: 57 **EST:** 2011
SALES (est): 198.54K **Privately Held**

(G-14288)
COBHAM EXETER INC
11 Continental Dr (03833-4564)
PHONE......................714 841-4976
Mike Kahn, *CEO*
David Macy, *
Mike Berberet, *
▲ **EMP:** 45 **EST:** 1981
SALES (est): 9.37MM **Privately Held**
SIC: 3663 Antennas, transmitting and communications
HQ: Frontgrade Technologies Llc
4350 Centennial Blvd
Colorado Springs CO 80907

(G-14289)
CONTINTENTIAL MICROWAVE
32 Industrial Dr (03833-4557)
PHONE......................603 775-5200
EMP: 10 **EST:** 2014
SALES (est): 685.73K **Privately Held**
SIC: 3812 Search and navigation equipment

(G-14290)
CRITICAL CMMNCTONS CNTRLS INST
8 Commerce Way (03833-4588)
EMP: 17 **EST:** 2000
SQ FT: 10,000
SALES (est): 4.7MM **Privately Held**
Web: www.c3i-usa.com
SIC: 3812 5065 Navigational systems and instruments; Security control equipment and systems

(G-14291)
DUTCH OPHTHALMIC USA INC
10 Continental Dr Bldg 1 (03833-7507)
PHONE......................603 778-6929
Gr Vijfvinkel, *Pr*
EMP: 10 **EST:** 1990
SQ FT: 4,500
SALES (est): 2.36MM **Privately Held**
Web: www.dutchophthalmicusa.com
SIC: 3841 Surgical and medical instruments

(G-14292)
FRONTGRADE TECHNOLOGIES INC
11 Continental Dr (03833-4564)
PHONE......................603 775-5200
Mike Elias, *CEO*
Len Anthony, *
Mark Suffoletto, *
EMP: 454 **EST:** 1980
SQ FT: 165,000
SALES (est): 98.65MM **Privately Held**
Web: www.frontgrade.com
SIC: 3812 Search and navigation equipment

(G-14293)
ICA NORTHEAST INC
41 Industrial Dr Ste 1 (03833-4570)
PHONE......................603 773-2386
Mehdi Ali, *Pr*
Jim Laird, *
EMP: 50 **EST:** 1999
SQ FT: 20,000
SALES: 14.87MM
SALES (corp-wide): 12.62B **Publicly Held**
Web: www.icaholdings.com
SIC: 3679 Harness assemblies, for electronic use: wire or cable
PA: Amphenol Corporation
358 Hall Ave
Wallingford CT 06492
203 265-8900

(G-14294)
MANROLAND GOSS WEB SYSTEMS AMR (DH)
22 Industrial Dr (03833-4557)
PHONE......................603 750-6600
Alexander Wassermann, *CEO*
Dirk Rauh, *
Greg Blue, *
Nicole Vinet, *
Heiko Ritscher, *
◆ **EMP:** 500 **EST:** 1994
SALES (est): 112.17MM
SALES (corp-wide): 144.19K **Privately Held**
Web: www.manrolandgossamericas.com
SIC: 3555 7699 Printing presses; Printing trades machinery and equipment repair
HQ: Manroland Goss Web Systems Gmbh
Alois-Senefelder-Allee 1
Augsburg BY 86153
8214240

(G-14295)
MANROLAND WEB SYSTEMS INC
22 Industrial Dr (03833-4557)
PHONE......................630 920-5850
EMP: 12 **EST:** 2019
SALES (est): 2.46MM
SALES (corp-wide): 144.19K **Privately Held**
SIC: 3555 Printing trades machinery
HQ: Manroland Goss Web Systems Gmbh
Alois-Senefelder-Allee 1
Augsburg BY 86153
8214240

(G-14296)
ME AND OLLIES
64 Water St (03833-2431)
PHONE......................603 319-1561
Roger Elkus, *Owner*
EMP: 8 **EST:** 2008
SALES (est): 472.77K **Privately Held**
Web: www.meandollies.com
SIC: 2051 Cakes, bakery: except frozen

(G-14297)
NEW HAMPSHIRE MACHINE PDTS INC
10 Kingston Rd (03833-4320)
P.O. Box 975 (03833-0975)
PHONE......................603 772-4404
Owen Baril, *Ch*
Barbara Michaud, *Pr*
EMP: 8 **EST:** 1975
SQ FT: 5,000
SALES (est): 831.68K **Privately Held**
Web: www.newhampshiremachineproducts.com
SIC: 3451 Screw machine products

(G-14298)
OLD BH INC
100 Domain Dr (03833-4801)
PHONE......................603 430-2111
◆ **EMP:** 423
SIC: 3949 Helmets, athletic

(G-14299)
OSRAM SYLVANIA INC
Also Called: Chemical & Metallurgical Div
131 Portsmouth Ave (03833-2105)
PHONE......................603 772-4331
David Lamprey, *Mgr*
EMP: 357
SALES (corp-wide): 5B **Privately Held**
Web: www.osram.us

SIC: **3641** 3671 3643 3433 Electric lamps;
Electron tubes; Current-carrying wiring
services; Heating equipment, except electric
HQ: Osram Sylvania Inc.
200 Ballardvale St Bldg 2
Wilmington MA 01887
978 570-3000

(G-14300)
PALMER AND SICARD INC
Also Called: Honeywell Authorized Dealer
89 Holland Way (03833-2937)
PHONE.................................603 778-1841
Mark Hodsdon, *CEO*
Mark J Hodsdon, *
EMP: 55 EST: 1954
SQ FT: 15,000
SALES (est): 23.72MM **Privately Held**
Web: www.palmerandsicard.com
SIC: **1711** 3444 Plumbing contractors;
Sheet metalwork

(G-14301)
SIG SAUER INC
12 Industrial Dr (03833-4557)
PHONE.................................603 610-3000
Ron Cohen, *CEO*
EMP: 99
SALES (corp-wide): 355.83K **Privately
Held**
Web: www.sigsauer.com
SIC: **3484** Small arms
HQ: Sig Sauer Inc.
72 Pease Blvd
Newington NH 03801
603 610-3000

(G-14302)
SIG SAUER INC
18 Industrial Dr (03833-4557)
PHONE.................................603 772-2302
EMP: 454
SALES (corp-wide): 355.83K **Privately
Held**
Web: www.sigsauer.com
SIC: **3484** Small arms
HQ: Sig Sauer Inc.
72 Pease Blvd
Newington NH 03801
603 610-3000

(G-14303)
SUSTAINX INC
Also Called: Sustainx
26 Exeter Highland Dr (03833-4566)
PHONE.................................603 601-7800
▲ EMP: 10
Web: www.sustainx.com
SIC: **3691** Storage batteries

(G-14304)
VAPOTHERM INC (PA)
100 Domain Dr Ste 102 (03833-4904)
PHONE.................................603 658-0011
Joseph Army, *Pr*
James Liken, *Ch Bd*
John Landry, *Sr VP*
Gregoire Ramade, *CCO*
▲ EMP: 20 EST: 1993
SQ FT: 95,320
SALES (est): 66.8MM
SALES (corp-wide): 66.8MM **Publicly
Held**
Web: www.vapotherm.com
SIC: **3841** Surgical instruments and
apparatus

(G-14305)
WALL INDUSTRIES INC
37 Industrial Dr Ste 3 (03833-7519)

PHONE.................................603 778-2300
James F Mccann Junior, *Pr*
James M Bunt, *Treas*
Kevin E Mccann, *Sec*
▲ EMP: 45 EST: 1960
SQ FT: 70,000
SALES (est): 10.25MM
SALES (corp-wide): 407.14MM **Privately
Held**
Web: www.wallindustries.com
SIC: **3621** 3612 Frequency converters
(electric generators); Power transformers,
electric
PA: Continental Resources, Inc.
175 Middlesex Tpke Ste 1
Bedford MA 01730
781 275-0850

(G-14306)
WE CORK INC
16 Kingston Rd Unit 6 (03833-4300)
PHONE.................................800 666-2675
Ann Wicander, *Prin*
▲ EMP: 7 EST: 2015
SALES (est): 696.87K **Privately Held**
Web: www.wecork.com
SIC: **2426** Turnings, furniture: wood

Farmington
Strafford County

(G-14307)
ANDREW J FOSS CO LLC
100 Cocheco Rd (03835-3804)
PHONE.................................603 755-2515
John Cardinal, *Pr*
Emmanuel Krasner, *Sec*
EMP: 19 EST: 1963
SQ FT: 20,000
SALES (est): 810.01K **Privately Held**
Web: www.ajfoss.com
SIC: **3272** Septic tanks, concrete

(G-14308)
ARTEMAS INDUSTRIES INC
20 Sarah Greenfield Way (03835-3709)
PHONE.................................603 755-9777
Donald W Cammet, *Pr*
Donald W Cammett, *Pr*
Michelle S Cammett, *Sec*
David Dugal, *VP*
EMP: 7 EST: 1985
SQ FT: 5,000
SALES (est): 673.36K **Privately Held**
Web: www.artemasind.com
SIC: **3599** Machine shop, jobbing and repair

(G-14309)
**ENERGY RESOURCES GROUP
INC (PA)**
Also Called: Erg
23 Commerce Pkwy (03835-4101)
PHONE.................................603 335-2535
Carrie Hurn, *Pr*
Holly A Baron, *
Jennifer Hames, *
Keith B Frisbee, *
▲ EMP: 24 EST: 1984
SQ FT: 1,600,000
SALES (est): 10.05MM
SALES (corp-wide): 10.05MM **Privately
Held**
Web: www.energyresourcesgroup.us
SIC: **3511** Turbines and turbine generator
sets

(G-14310)
KEVIN EMERY
Also Called: Lightlines
1 Wilson St (03835-3429)
PHONE.................................603 433-5784
Doctor Kevin Emery, *Owner*
EMP: 8 EST: 2001
SALES (est): 171.12K **Privately Held**
SIC: **8322** 2731 General counseling services
; Book publishing

(G-14311)
SCHAEFERROLLS INC
Also Called: Paper Mill and Indus Rbr Pdts
23 Plank Industrial Dr (03835-3811)
P.O. Box 697 (03835-0697)
PHONE.................................603 335-1786
John Fisher, *CEO*
Russell Shillaber, *Sec*
Jeanine Lewis, *Treas*
▲ EMP: 22 EST: 1950
SQ FT: 38,000
SALES (est): 4.65MM **Privately Held**
SIC: **3069** Roll coverings, rubber

Fitzwilliam
Cheshire County

(G-14312)
ABTECH INC
126 Rte 12 N (03447)
P.O. Box 509 (03447-0509)
PHONE.................................603 585-7106
Kenneth Abbott, *Pr*
William Abbott, *VP*
EMP: 20 EST: 1998
SALES (est): 4.83MM **Privately Held**
Web: www.abtechmfg.com
SIC: **3599** 3545 Machine shop, jobbing and
repair; Machine tool accessories

(G-14313)
**DUXBURY COMPOSITE
PRODUCTS INC**
57 Creamery Rd (03447-3528)
P.O. Box 429 (03447-0429)
PHONE.................................603 585-9100
Daniel Scheerer, *Pr*
EMP: 21 EST: 2018
SALES (est): 1.36MM **Privately Held**
Web: www.plpcomp.com
SIC: **3296** Mineral wool

(G-14314)
MONADNOCK GRINDING LLC
98 Royalston Rd (03447-3440)
P.O. Box 152 (03447-0152)
PHONE.................................603 585-7275
Darnell Favreau, *Prin*
EMP: 7 EST: 2007
SALES (est): 490.93K **Privately Held**
Web:
monadnock-grinding.webnode.page
SIC: **3599** Grinding castings for the trade

(G-14315)
**PLP COMPOSITE
TECHNOLOGIES**
57 Creamery Rd (03447-3528)
P.O. Box 429 (03447-0429)
PHONE.................................603 585-9100
William Bazley, *Pr*
▲ EMP: 34 EST: 1984
SALES (est): 4.99MM **Privately Held**
Web: www.plpcomp.com
SIC: **3089** 3446 Laminating of plastics;
Architectural metalwork

(G-14316)
TOMMILA BROTHERS INC
487 Nh (03447)
P.O. Box 723 (03464-0723)
PHONE.................................603 242-7774
John W Tommila, *CEO*
Chuck Nolan, *VP*
EMP: 10 EST: 1936
SQ FT: 800
SALES (est): 815.31K **Privately Held**
Web: www.tommilabrothers.com
SIC: **2421** 5211 5031 2431 Sawmills and
planing mills, general; Millwork and lumber;
Millwork; Millwork

(G-14317)
TURN KEY LUMBER INC
Also Called: Turn Key Lumber
179 Nh Route 12 N 179 (03447-3118)
PHONE.................................978 798-1370
Juliano Fernandes, *Pr*
EMP: 200 EST: 2013
SALES (est): 46MM **Privately Held**
Web: www.turnkeylumber.com
SIC: **3272** 5211 2421 Building materials,
except block or brick: concrete; Lumber and
other building materials; Building and
structural materials, wood

Franklin
Merrimack County

(G-14318)
ACME STAPLE COMPANY INC
87 Hill Rd (03235-1108)
PHONE.................................603 934-2320
Richard L Gold, *Pr*
Thomas R Gold, *VP*
Onno Boswinkel, *General Vice President*
▲ EMP: 15 EST: 1982
SQ FT: 44,000
SALES (est): 3.72MM **Privately Held**
Web: www.acmestaple.com
SIC: **3315** 3579 Staples, steel: wire or cut;
Stapling machines (hand or power)

(G-14319)
**BRAPSARDS POWDER
COATING LLC**
52 Thompson Park (03235-1112)
PHONE.................................603 630-4014
Jason Andrew Brassard, *Prin*
EMP: 7 EST: 2018
SALES (est): 52.49K **Privately Held**
Web: www.powdercoatchicago.com
SIC: **3479** Coating of metals and formed
products

(G-14320)
INSULFAB PLASTICS INC
155 N Main St (03235-1026)
PHONE.................................603 934-2770
Charles A Pauwels, *Brnch Mgr*
EMP: 10
SALES (corp-wide): 23.61MM **Privately
Held**
Web: www.insulfab.com
SIC: **3089** Injection molding of plastics
PA: Insulfab Plastics, Inc.
834 Hayne St
Spartanburg SC 29301
864 582-7506

(G-14321)
PCC STRUCTURALS GROTON
PCC Strcturals Alum Operations
35 Industrial Park Dr (03235-2507)
PHONE.................................603 286-4301

EMP: 47
SALES (corp-wide): 302.09B **Publicly Held**
Web: www.pccstructurals.com
SIC: 3324 Aerospace investment castings, ferrous
HQ: Pcc Structurals Groton
    839 Poquonnock Rd
    Groton CT 06340
    860 405-3700

(G-14322)
PERFORMANCE CHEMICALS LLC
Also Called: Performance Chemicals
40 Industrial Park Dr (03235-2507)
P.O. Box 9 (03235-0009)
PHONE.....................603 228-1200
EMP: 10 **EST:** 2002
SALES (est): 2.27MM **Privately Held**
Web: www.perfchem.us
SIC: 2899 Chemical preparations, nec

(G-14323)
WATTS REGULATOR CO
Webster Valve Company
583 S Main St (03235-1559)
PHONE.....................603 934-5110
Kent Sargent, *Genl Mgr*
EMP: 600
SALES (corp-wide): 1.98B **Publicly Held**
Web: www.watts.com
SIC: 3491 3364 3593 Industrial valves; Nonferrous die-castings except aluminum; Fluid power cylinders and actuators
HQ: Watts Regulator Co.
    815 Chestnut St
    North Andover MA 01845
    978 689-6000

(G-14324)
WATTS WATER TECHNOLOGIES INC
583 S Main St (03235-1559)
PHONE.....................603 934-1369
Bryan Anderson, *Prin*
EMP: 21
SALES (corp-wide): 1.98B **Publicly Held**
Web: www.watts.com
SIC: 3491 Industrial valves
PA: Watts Water Technologies, Inc.
    815 Chestnut St
    North Andover MA 01845
    978 688-1811

(G-14325)
WYMAN-GORDON COMPANY
35 Industrial Park Dr (03235-2507)
PHONE.....................603 934-6630
EMP: 282
SALES (corp-wide): 302.09B **Publicly Held**
Web: www.pccforgedproducts.com
SIC: 3363 Aluminum die-castings
HQ: Wyman-Gordon Company
    244 Worcester St
    North Grafton MA 01536
    508 839-8252

Fremont
Rockingham County

(G-14326)
BEST MACHINE INC
79 Beede Hill Rd (03044-3247)
PHONE.....................603 895-4018
Mark Woodman, *Pr*
Cheryl Woodman, *Dir*

EMP: 7 **EST:** 2004
SQ FT: 2,500
SALES (est): 1.18MM **Privately Held**
Web: www.bestmachineinc.com
SIC: 3291 3599 Abrasive products; Machine shop, jobbing and repair

(G-14327)
FREMONT MACHINE & TOOL CO INC
Also Called: FREMONT ENGINEERING
810 Main St (03044-3585)
PHONE.....................603 895-9445
David Lambert, *Pr*
Roland Lambert Junior, *VP*
EMP: 9 **EST:** 1982
SQ FT: 1,400
SALES (est): 781.28K **Privately Held**
SIC: 3541 Machine tool replacement & repair parts, metal cutting types

(G-14328)
ION PHYSICS CORP
373 Main St (03044-3424)
P.O. Box 165 (03044-0165)
PHONE.....................603 895-5100
Helmuti Milde, *Pr*
Charles Salisbury, *VP Engg*
Leslie F Milde, *Treas*
EMP: 8 **EST:** 1958
SQ FT: 3,000
SALES (est): 769.18K **Privately Held**
Web: www.ionphysics.com
SIC: 3825 8731 3621 Instruments to measure electricity; Environmental research ; Motors and generators

(G-14329)
PRECISION DEPANELING MCHS LLC
326 Main St Unit 11 (03044-3440)
PHONE.....................540 248-1381
EMP: 10 **EST:** 2009
SQ FT: 7,000
SALES (est): 1.8MM
SALES (corp-wide): 2.62MM **Privately Held**
SIC: 3544 3549 Special dies, tools, jigs, and fixtures; Metalworking machinery, nec
PA: Precision Placement Machines, Inc.
    326 Main St Unit 11
    Fremont NH 03044
    603 895-5112

(G-14330)
PRECISION PLACEMENT MCHS INC (PA)
326 Main St Unit 11 (03044-3440)
PHONE.....................603 895-5112
Thomas Nisbet, *Pr*
▲ **EMP:** 12 **EST:** 2000
SQ FT: 15,000
SALES (est): 2.62MM
SALES (corp-wide): 2.62MM **Privately Held**
Web: www.goppm.com
SIC: 3672 Printed circuit boards

(G-14331)
RAGNARTECH INC
44 Iron Horse Dr (03044-3575)
PHONE.....................603 244-7575
Anders Ragnarsson, *Pr*
EMP: 15 **EST:** 2020
SALES (est): 1.05MM **Privately Held**
Web: www.ragnartech-inc.com
SIC: 3531 Cranes, nec

(G-14332)
UNITED MCH & TL DESIGN CO INC
18 River Rd (03044)
P.O. Box 168 (03044-0168)
PHONE.....................603 642-3601
Dan Davis, *Pr*
Barbara Lufkin, *
EMP: 35 **EST:** 1972
SQ FT: 28,000
SALES (est): 4.91MM **Privately Held**
SIC: 3599 Machine shop, jobbing and repair

Gilford
Belknap County

(G-14333)
AMG-AWETIS MFG GROUP CORP
18 Colonial Dr (03249-6401)
PHONE.....................603 286-1645
Jeans Frank, *CEO*
Arthur Rabert, *Opers Mgr*
EMP: 10 **EST:** 2014
SALES (est): 1.96MM **Privately Held**
SIC: 3599 Industrial machinery, nec
HQ: Awetis Gmbh
    Dr.-Werner-Freyberg-Str. 7
    Laudenbach BW
    620 180-6390

(G-14334)
CORE ASSEMBLIES INC
21 Meadowbrook Ln Unit 4 (03249-6305)
PHONE.....................603 293-0270
Cory Navoy, *Pr*
EMP: 15 **EST:** 1984
SQ FT: 4,800
SALES (est): 1.83MM **Privately Held**
Web: www.coreassemblies.com
SIC: 3599 3443 3672 Machine and other job shop work; Housings, pressure; Printed circuit boards

(G-14335)
DGF INDSTRIAL INNVTONS GROUP L
Also Called: Dgf Indstrial Innvations Group
25 Waterford Pl (03249-6661)
P.O. Box 7532 (03247-7532)
PHONE.....................603 528-6591
Gisele Lambert, *Pr*
EMP: 15 **EST:** 1989
SALES (est): 2.5MM **Privately Held**
Web: www.dgfindustrial.com
SIC: 3599 7699 3444 3356 Custom machinery; Cash register repair; Sheet metal specialties, not stamped; Nonferrous rolling and drawing, nec

(G-14336)
HARDWATER INDUSTRIES LLC ✪
15 Bramble Ln (03249-7832)
PHONE.....................603 867-9240
EMP: 7 **EST:** 2023
SALES (est): 61.02K **Privately Held**
SIC: 3999 Manufacturing industries, nec

(G-14337)
HOWARD PRECISION INC
Also Called: Hpi
359 Hounsell Ave (03249-6922)
PHONE.....................603 293-8012
Joseph D Howard, *Pr*
Carole Howard, *VP*
EMP: 18 **EST:** 1986

SQ FT: 9,000
SALES (est): 2.67MM **Privately Held**
Web: www.howardprecision.us
SIC: 3599 Machine shop, jobbing and repair

(G-14338)
SPECIAL PROJECTS GROUP LLC
221 Intervale Rd B2 (03249-7435)
P.O. Box 7283 (03247-7283)
PHONE.....................603 391-9700
EMP: 7 **EST:** 2014
SALES (est): 310K **Privately Held**
Web: www.specialprojectsgroupllc.com
SIC: 3732 7532 Boatbuilding and repairing; Top and body repair and paint shops

Gilmanton
Belknap County

(G-14339)
BZGUNZ LLC
22 Stockwell Hill Rd (03237-4949)
PHONE.....................603 491-8019
Ronald W Mercier Ii, *Admn*
EMP: 7 **EST:** 2014
SALES (est): 204.13K **Privately Held**
Web: www.bzgunzllc.com
SIC: 3482 Small arms ammunition

Gilmanton Iron Works
Belknap County

(G-14340)
ANDRADE SEALCOATING LLC
215 Middle Rte (03837-4527)
PHONE.....................603 435-3704
Cindy Andrade, *Admn*
EMP: 11 **EST:** 2019
SALES (est): 904.19K **Privately Held**
Web: www.andradesealcoating.com
SIC: 2952 Asphalt felts and coatings

Gilsum
Cheshire County

(G-14341)
AVOCUS PUBLISHING INC
4 White Brook Rd (03448)
P.O. Box 89 (03448-0089)
PHONE.....................603 357-0236
EMP: 9 **EST:** 1990
SALES (est): 435.28K **Privately Held**
Web: www.avocus.com
SIC: 2731 Books, publishing only

(G-14342)
HAMPSHIRE HIVES LLC
659 Route 10 (03448-7509)
PHONE.....................603 313-0186
John Solomonides, *Prin*
EMP: 7 **EST:** 2020
SALES (est): 75.68K **Privately Held**
Web: www.hampshirehives.com
SIC: 3999 Manufacturing industries, nec

(G-14343)
PHOENIX WOODWORKS INC ✪
42 Nash Corner Rd (03448-7510)
PHONE.....................603 812-6214
Michael Allen Bailey, *Pr*
EMP: 7 **EST:** 2023
SALES (est): 78.66K **Privately Held**
SIC: 2431 Millwork

▲ = Import ▼ = Export
◆ = Import/Export

(G-14344)
WS BADGER COMPANY INC
Also Called: Badger
768 Route 10 (03448-7503)
P.O. Box 58 (03448-0058)
PHONE...................................603 357-2958
▲ **EMP:** 73 **EST:** 1995
SALES (est): 5.01MM **Privately Held**
Web: www.badgerbalm.com
SIC: 2844 Face creams or lotions

(G-14345)
WSBADGER COMPANY INC
768 Route 10 (03448-7503)
P.O. Box 58 (03448-0058)
PHONE...................................603 357-2958
William Whyte, *Pr*
EMP: 73 **EST:** 1996
SALES (est): 5.3MM **Privately Held**
Web: www.badgerbalm.com
SIC: 2844 Perfumes, cosmetics and other
toilet preparations

Goffstown
Hillsborough County

(G-14346)
ACCURATE BRAZING
CORPORATION (HQ)
36 Cote Ave Ste 5 (03045-5261)
PHONE...................................603 945-3750
Steven Francis, *Pr*
Leo Francis, *Treas*
William Francis, *Dir*
EMP: 47 **EST:** 1989
SQ FT: 10,000
SALES (est): 21.11MM
SALES (corp-wide): 3.35B **Privately Held**
Web: www.aalberts-ab.us
SIC: 3398 Brazing (hardening) of metal
PA: Aalberts N.V.
Stadsplateau 18
Utrecht UT
303079300

(G-14347)
DAVID R BURL
56 N Mast St (03045-1712)
PHONE...................................603 235-2661
David R Burl, *Prin*
EMP: 7 **EST:** 2005
SALES (est): 225.05K **Privately Held**
SIC: 2411 Logging

(G-14348)
HAPPY HOUSE AMUSEMENT
INC
70 Depot St (03045-1755)
P.O. Box 120 (03045-0120)
PHONE...................................603 497-4151
TOLL FREE: 800
Raymond Blondeau Senior, *Pr*
▲ **EMP:** 10 **EST:** 1965
SQ FT: 36,000
SALES (est): 441.9K **Privately Held**
Web: www.happyhouseamusements.com
SIC: 3999 7993 5091 Coin-operated
amusement machines; Amusement
machine rental, coin-operated; Billiard
equipment and supplies

(G-14349)
HAWKES MOTORSPORTS LLC
129a S Mast St (03045-6101)
PHONE...................................603 660-9864
EMP: 7 **EST:** 2016
Web: www.hawkestrailer.com

SIC: 3537 Trucks, tractors, loaders, carriers,
and similar equipment

(G-14350)
JOA TOOLS LLC
7 Tyler Dr (03045-2128)
PHONE...................................850 529-3567
Dwight D Sowerby Esq, *Admn*
EMP: 7 **EST:** 2014
SALES (est): 200.36K **Privately Held**
SIC: 3599 Industrial machinery, nec

(G-14351)
JUST COUNTERS
28 Daniel Plummer Rd Ste 3 (03045-2570)
PHONE...................................603 627-2027
John Laughlin, *Owner*
EMP: 7 **EST:** 2007
SALES (est): 188.31K **Privately Held**
SIC: 2541 Counter and sink tops

(G-14352)
NEW HAMPSHIRE STAMPING
CO INC
9 Lance Ln Ste 2 (03045-5263)
PHONE...................................603 641-1234
Robert La Rochelle, *Pr*
Andrew Hill, *
EMP: 25 **EST:** 1992
SQ FT: 15,000
SALES (est): 2.29MM **Privately Held**
Web: www.nhstamping.com
SIC: 3469 3087 3312 Stamping metal for
the trade; Custom compound purchased
resins; Tool and die steel and alloys

(G-14353)
NEW HAMPSHIRE STL
ERECTORS LLC
17 Lamy Dr (03045-5219)
P.O. Box 4226 (03108-4226)
PHONE...................................603 668-3464
Mark A Ginnard, *Pr*
EMP: 35 **EST:** 1981
SQ FT: 20,200
SALES (est): 953.59K **Privately Held**
Web: www.nhsteelfab.com
SIC: 3446 1791 3441 Stairs, staircases,
stair treads: prefabricated metal; Structural
steel erection; Fabricated structural metal

(G-14354)
NEW HMPSHIRE STL
FBRCATORS LLC
17 Lamy Dr (03045-5219)
P.O. Box 4226 (03108-4226)
PHONE...................................603 668-3464
Mark A Ginnard, *Pr*
EMP: 40 **EST:** 1981
SALES (est): 4.89MM **Privately Held**
Web: www.nhsteelfab.com
SIC: 3441 Fabricated structural metal

(G-14355)
NORTHEASTERN SHEET METAL
INC
31 Depot St (03045-1713)
P.O. Box 246 (03045-0246)
PHONE...................................603 497-4166
EMP: 75 **EST:** 1975
SALES (est): 8.72MM **Privately Held**
Web: www.nesmcorp.com
SIC: 3444 1761 Sheet metalwork; Sheet
metal work, nec

(G-14356)
PLASTIC TECHNIQUES INC
27 Springfield Rd (03045-5232)

P.O. Box 250 (03045-0250)
PHONE...................................603 622-5570
Gossett Mc Rae, *CEO*
EMP: 27 **EST:** 1968
SQ FT: 50,000
SALES (est): 3.5MM **Privately Held**
Web: www.buckettruckaccessories.com
SIC: 3089 3646 3535 Injection molding of
plastics; Commercial lighting fixtures;
Conveyors and conveying equipment

Gorham
Coos County

(G-14357)
GORHAM ACQUISITION LLC
Also Called: White Mountain Paper Company
72 Cascade Flt (03581-1015)
PHONE...................................603 342-2000
Price Howard, *CEO*
Evan Behrins, *Pr*
EMP: 29 **EST:** 2021
SALES (est): 2.9MM **Privately Held**
SIC: 2621 Tissue paper

(G-14358)
GORHAM PAPER AND TISSUE
LLC
70 Cascade Flt (03581-1015)
▲ **EMP:** 1980 **EST:** 1852
SALES (est): 7.43MM
SALES (corp-wide): 1.17K **Privately Held**
Web: www.gorhampt.com
SIC: 2621 Uncoated paper
PA: Patriarch Partners, Llc
1 Liberty Plz Rm 3500
New York NY 10006
212 825-0550

(G-14359)
GORHAM SAND & GRAVEL
42 Lancaster Rd (03581-1411)
PHONE...................................603 466-2291
Roger Martin, *Mgr*
EMP: 8 **EST:** 2005
SALES (est): 132.22K **Privately Held**
Web: www.gsgravel.com
SIC: 1442 Construction sand and gravel

(G-14360)
LABONVILLE INC (PA)
504 Main St (03581-4906)
PHONE...................................603 752-4030
Richard Labonville, *Pr*
Armand Labonville, *VP*
Norman Labonville, *Stockholder*
▲ **EMP:** 21 **EST:** 1962
SQ FT: 18,000
SALES (est): 7.92MM
SALES (corp-wide): 7.92MM **Privately
Held**
Web: www.labonville.com
SIC: 5082 5084 5091 3842 Logging
equipment and supplies; Chainsaws;
Sporting and recreation goods; Clothing,
fire resistant and protective

(G-14361)
PIKE INDUSTRIES INC
42 Lancaster Rd (03581-1411)
PHONE...................................603 466-2772
Tim Bradstreet, *Mgr*
EMP: 13
SALES (corp-wide): 32.72B **Privately Held**
Web: www.pikeindustries.com
SIC: 1611 2951 Highway and street paving
contractor; Asphalt paving mixtures and
blocks

HQ: Pike Industries, Inc.
3 Eastgate Park Dr
Belmont NH 03220
603 527-5100

Grantham
Sullivan County

(G-14362)
AXARD LLC
Also Called: Axard
742 Route 114 (03753-3421)
P.O. Box 1677 (03753-1677)
PHONE...................................603 306-7679
Milosz Mitura, *Admn*
EMP: 10 **EST:** 2011
SALES (est): 1.84MM **Privately Held**
SIC: 5049 3545 3999 Precision tools;
Counterbores, metalworking; Coin-operated
amusement machines

(G-14363)
TOPEK LLC
Also Called: Yankee Barn Home
131 Yankee Barn Rd (03753-3243)
PHONE...................................603 863-2400
EMP: 15 **EST:** 2011
SALES (est): 1.55MM **Privately Held**
Web: www.yankeebarnhomes.com
SIC: 2451 Mobile homes, personal or
private use

Greenfield
Hillsborough County

(G-14364)
MONADNOCK PAPER MILLS INC
Also Called: Monadnock Paper Warehouse
231 Forest Rd (03047-4842)
PHONE...................................603 588-8220
Sarah Barrette, *Prin*
EMP: 22
SALES (corp-wide): 48.17MM **Privately
Held**
Web: www.mpm.com
SIC: 2621 Paper mills
HQ: Monadnock Paper Mills, Inc.
117 Antrim Rd
Bennington NH 03442
603 588-3311

Greenland
Rockingham County

(G-14365)
ADVANCED CONCRETE TECH
INC
Also Called: A C T
300 Portsmouth Ave (03840-2220)
PHONE...................................603 431-5661
Max Hoene, *Pr*
◆ **EMP:** 7 **EST:** 1990
SQ FT: 4,000
SALES (est): 2.64MM
SALES (corp-wide): 9.06MM **Privately
Held**
Web: www.concretebiz.com
SIC: 3531 Concrete plants
PA: Wiggert & Co. Gmbh
Wachhausstr. 3b
Karlsruhe BW 76227
721943460

(G-14366)
ARCHIMEDIA ADVANTAGE INC
Also Called: Actuarial Bookstore
69 (03840)
P.O. Box 69 (03840-0069)
PHONE.....................................603 430-1252
William Marella, *Owner*
EMP: 12 **EST:** 1999
SALES (est): 630.52K **Privately Held**
Web: www.actuarialbookstore.com
SIC: 2731   Book publishing

(G-14367)
ARENS STONEWORKS INC
434 Portsmouth Ave (03840-2222)
P.O. Box 550 (03840-0550)
PHONE.....................................603 436-8000
Robert Arens, *CEO*
Amy Ryan, *VP*
EMP: 7 **EST:** 1998
SALES (est): 334.14K **Privately Held**
Web: www.arensstoneworks.com
SIC: 3281   Marble, building: cut and shaped

(G-14368)
COAST TO CAST FF E INSTLLTONS
2 Spring Hill Rd (03840-2600)
PHONE.....................................603 433-0164
Mark St Pierre, *Pr*
Sherry St Pierre, *VP*
▲ **EMP:** 11 **EST:** 1997
SALES (est): 471.4K **Privately Held**
SIC: 2599 1796   Cabinets, factory; Installing building equipment

(G-14369)
NOVEL IRON WORKS INC
250 Ocean Rd (03840-2431)
PHONE.....................................603 436-7950
Hollie Noveletsky, *CEO*
Thomas Heaney, *
Keith Moreau, *
Josh Rosenthal, *
EMP: 110 **EST:** 1956
SQ FT: 120,000
SALES (est): 20.58MM **Privately Held**
Web: www.noveliron.com
SIC: 3441   Building components, structural steel

(G-14370)
PLW INC
Also Called: Zax Signage
8 Autumn Pond Park (03840-2425)
PHONE.....................................603 889-4126
Patrick Walsh, *Pr*
EMP: 10 **EST:** 1956
SALES (est): 535.09K **Privately Held**
Web: www.zaxcorp.com
SIC: 3993   Signs and advertising specialties

(G-14371)
SWEET GRASS FARM INC
Also Called: Sweet Grass Farm
16 Autumn Pond Park (03840-2426)
PHONE.....................................603 766-1651
Deborah Ludington, *Pr*
Debbie Ludington, *Prin*
▲ **EMP:** 8 **EST:** 1996
SQ FT: 2,400
SALES (est): 780.98K **Privately Held**
Web: www.sweetgrassonline.com
SIC: 2841   Soap and other detergents

(G-14372)
WALL SHOTZ
10 Autumn Pond Park (03840-2425)
PHONE.....................................603 431-0900

Jeff A Cutter, *Prin*
EMP: 7 **EST:** 2010
SALES (est): 143.76K **Privately Held**
Web: www.wallshotz.com
SIC: 2752   Offset printing

Greenville
Hillsborough County

(G-14373)
MONADNOCK LAND CLEARING
Also Called: Monadnock Land Clearing & Chip
932 Fitchburg Rd (03048-3340)
P.O. Box 547 (03048-0547)
PHONE.....................................603 878-2803
Hermel Pelletier, *Pr*
Joseph Lyle Brundige, *VP*
EMP: 7 **EST:** 1974
SQ FT: 800
SALES (est): 856.64K **Privately Held**
Web: www.monadnocklandclearing.com
SIC: 2411 1629   Wood chips, produced in the field; Land clearing contractor

(G-14374)
OLD DUTCH MUSTARD CO INC
Also Called: Pilgrim Foods Co
68 Old Wilton Rd (03048-3100)
PHONE.....................................603 878-2100
Charles R Santich, *Ch Bd*
Paul Santich, *
Renate Santich, *
▼ **EMP:** 70 **EST:** 1915
SQ FT: 3,000
SALES (est): 11.38MM **Privately Held**
Web: www.olddutchmustard.com
SIC: 2099 2033 2035   Vinegar; Fruit juices: concentrated, hot pack; Mustard, prepared (wet)

(G-14375)
WILLIAM N LAMARRE CON PDTS INC
87 Adams Hill Rd (03048-3000)
P.O. Box 333 (03048-0333)
PHONE.....................................603 878-1340
TOLL FREE: 800
Jean L Lamarre, *Pr*
Jean L Lamarre, *Pr*
Marie J Joerger, *Sec*
William N Lamarre, *VP*
EMP: 19 **EST:** 1960
SQ FT: 18,500
SALES (est): 3.3MM **Privately Held**
Web: www.lamarreconcrete.com
SIC: 3272   Septic tanks, concrete

(G-14376)
XOR MEDIA INC
32 Mill St (03048-3102)
P.O. Box 391 (03048-0391)
PHONE.....................................603 878-6400
Zheng Gao, *CEO*
EMP: 11 **EST:** 2012
SALES (est): 1.01MM **Privately Held**
Web: www.xor-media.com
SIC: 3577   Computer peripheral equipment, nec

Groveton
Coos County

(G-14377)
NSA INDUSTRIES LLC
Also Called: NSA Industries L.L.C.
48 Mechanic St (03582-4194)

PHONE.....................................802 748-5007
James Moroney, *CEO*
EMP: 100
SALES (corp-wide): 149.03MM **Privately Held**
Web: www.mmgmfg.com
SIC: 3441   Building components, structural steel
PA: Momentum Manufacturing Group - North, L.L.C.
210 Pierce Rd
Saint Johnsbury VT 05819
802 748-5007

(G-14378)
PERRAS LUMBER CO INC
45 Perras Rd (03582)
P.O. Box 129 (03582-0129)
PHONE.....................................603 636-1830
Robert Perras, *Pr*
EMP: 12 **EST:** 1974
SQ FT: 125,000
SALES (est): 455.27K **Privately Held**
SIC: 2421   Sawmills and planing mills, general

(G-14379)
PRIMA AMERICA CORPORATION
248 State St (03582-4036)
P.O. Box 274 (03582-0274)
PHONE.....................................603 631-5407
▲ **EMP:** 12 **EST:** 2010
SALES (est): 506.44K **Privately Held**
SIC: 2911   Petroleum refining

Hampstead
Rockingham County

(G-14380)
ARC ELECTRONICS INC
Also Called: Nedap Light Controls N Amer
16 Peaslee Ct (03841-2185)
PHONE.....................................603 458-2089
Ken B Sturgess, *Pr*
Jamie K Sturgess, *Dir*
▲ **EMP:** 10 **EST:** 2010
SALES (est): 810.6K **Privately Held**
Web: www.arcelectronics.us
SIC: 3648   Lighting equipment, nec

(G-14381)
BARLOW ARCHITECTURAL MLLWK LLC
30 Gigante Dr (03841-2310)
PHONE.....................................603 329-6026
▲ **EMP:** 25 **EST:** 1955
SALES (est): 3.3MM **Privately Held**
Web: www.barlowmillwork.com
SIC: 2499   Decorative wood and woodwork

(G-14382)
DESIGN CONSULTANTS ASSOCIATES
1 Owens Ct (03841-2400)
PHONE.....................................603 329-4541
Martha Richardson, *Pr*
EMP: 13 **EST:** 1982
SQ FT: 7,600
SALES (est): 116.9K **Privately Held**
SIC: 3677 8711   Transformers power supply, electronic type; Electrical or electronic engineering

(G-14383)
JS MACHINE
319 Kent Farm Rd (03841-2412)
PHONE.....................................603 329-3790
EMP: 9 **EST:** 2008

SALES (est): 84.46K **Privately Held**
SIC: 3599   Machine shop, jobbing and repair

(G-14384)
LEUSIN MICROWAVE LLC
6 Gigante Dr (03841-2310)
P.O. Box 894 (03841-0894)
PHONE.....................................603 329-7270
Antoine Assaf, *Mgr*
EMP: 10 **EST:** 2006
SALES (est): 898.1K **Privately Held**
Web: www.leusin.com
SIC: 3825   Microwave test equipment

(G-14385)
M & A ADVNCED DESIGN CNSTR INC (PA)
Also Called: Advanced Design Construction
1 Gigante Dr (03841-2310)
PHONE.....................................603 329-9515
Theresa Allen, *Pr*
Bob Allen, *VP*
EMP: 10 **EST:** 2006
SQ FT: 6,000
SALES (est): 5.14MM **Privately Held**
SIC: 3569 7699   Generators: steam, liquid oxygen, or nitrogen; Industrial machinery and equipment repair

(G-14386)
MEM-CO FITTINGS INC
45 Gigante Dr (03841-2310)
PHONE.....................................603 329-9633
Ray Joseph, *Pr*
EMP: 9 **EST:** 2003
SALES (est): 438.78K **Privately Held**
Web: www.mem-co.com
SIC: 3494   Valves and pipe fittings, nec

(G-14387)
MTL PRINT SOLUTION LLC
50 Bloody Brook Rd (03841-2124)
PHONE.....................................603 479-2998
Mary Lovell, *Mgr*
EMP: 7 **EST:** 2017
SALES (est): 70.51K **Privately Held**
SIC: 2752   Commercial printing, lithographic

(G-14388)
NCAB GROUP USA INC (DH)
10 Starwood Dr (03841-2339)
PHONE.....................................603 329-4551
Peter Kruk, *CEO*
Kelly Davidson, *
▲ **EMP:** 21 **EST:** 2012
SALES (est): 28.36MM
SALES (corp-wide): 424.93MM **Privately Held**
Web: www.ncabgroup.com
SIC: 3672   Circuit boards, television and radio printed
HQ: Ncab Group France
10 B Rue Nicephore Niepce
Villemandeur 45700
218200140

(G-14389)
PF PRO FNSHG SILKSCREENING INC
13 Gigante Dr (03841-2310)
PHONE.....................................603 329-8344
Frances M Beaudry, *Pr*
Richard D Beaudry, *VP*
EMP: 7 **EST:** 1986
SQ FT: 6,000
SALES (est): 491.42K **Privately Held**
Web: www.profinishinginc.com
SIC: 3479 7336   Coating of metals and formed products; Silk screen design

(G-14390)
PRIME POWER INC
1 Owens Ct Ste 1 (03841-2400)
PHONE.............................603 329-4675
EMP: 15 **EST:** 1992
SALES (est): 4.08MM **Privately Held**
Web: www.prime-power.com
SIC: 5065 7389 3699 Electronic parts and
equipment, nec; Design services; Electrical
equipment and supplies, nec

(G-14391)
REDLINE WELDING INC
25 Emmert Dr (03841)
P.O. Box 496 (03841-0496)
PHONE.............................603 489-2266
Richard P Leavitt, *Pr*
Jacqueline Leavitt, *VP*
EMP: 13 **EST:** 2015
SALES (est): 2.5MM **Privately Held**
SIC: 3441 Fabricated structural metal

(G-14392)
RICKS MTORSPORT ELECTRICS INC
48 Gigante Dr (03841-2310)
PHONE.............................603 329-9901
Rick Shaw, *Pr*
Donna Shaw, *VP*
▲ **EMP:** 8 **EST:** 2002
SALES (est): 1.22MM **Privately Held**
Web: www.ricksmotorsportelectrics.com
SIC: 3694 Engine electrical equipment

(G-14393)
SDV SOFTWARE INC
32 Anne Dr (03841-2365)
PHONE.............................603 329-8164
Edward J Valliere, *Prin*
EMP: 7 **EST:** 2009
SALES (est): 122.3K **Privately Held**
SIC: 7372 Prepackaged software

(G-14394)
WDW MACHINE INC
17 Gigante Dr Ste 1 (03841-2403)
PHONE.............................603 329-9604
Wilbur Webster Junior, *Pr*
EMP: 7 **EST:** 2002
SQ FT: 4,000
SALES (est): 841.58K **Privately Held**
Web: www.wdwmachine.com
SIC: 3599 Machine shop, jobbing and repair

(G-14395)
Z THUNDERLINE INC
11 Hazel Dr (03841-2338)
PHONE.............................603 329-4050
Rick Hirsch, *Pr*
Lenst Pierre, *
EMP: 50 **EST:** 1984
SQ FT: 14,000
SALES (est): 15.18MM
SALES (corp-wide): 15.16B **Publicly Held**
Web: www.sensience.com
SIC: 3823 Process control instruments
PA: Emerson Electric Co.
8000 West Florissant Ave
Saint Louis MO 63136
314 553-2000

Hampton
Rockingham County

(G-14396)
ADHESIVE TECHNOLOGIES INC (PA)
Also Called: Ad-Tech
3 Merrill Industrial Dr (03842-1995)
PHONE.............................603 926-1616
Peter S Melendy, *Pr*
Daniel G Smith, *Sec*
◆ **EMP:** 25 **EST:** 1981
SQ FT: 26,000
SALES (est): 11.71MM
SALES (corp-wide): 11.71MM **Privately Held**
Web: www.adhesivetech.com
SIC: 2891 3546 Glue; Power-driven handtools

(G-14397)
AJ NONWOVENS - HAMPTON LLC
Also Called: Foss Performance Materials LLC
11 Merrill Industrial Dr (03842-1972)
PHONE.............................603 929-6000
Bill Cummings, *COO*
Dave Rowell, *Ex VP*
Brenda Szymanowski, *Treas*
EMP: 93 **EST:** 2017
SALES (est): 14.47MM
SALES (corp-wide): 425.15MM **Privately Held**
Web: www.ajnw.com
SIC: 2211 Broadwoven fabric mills, cotton
PA: Astenjohnson, Inc.
4399 Corporate Rd
North Charleston SC 29405
843 747-7800

(G-14398)
AQUATIC SOLUTIONS LLC ✪
45 Lafayette Rd (03842-2600)
PHONE.............................888 704-7665
Connor Lincoln, *Managing Member*
EMP: 8 **EST:** 2023
SALES (est): 412.32K **Privately Held**
SIC: 1799 3589 5999 Swimming pool
construction; Swimming pool filter and
water conditioning systems; Swimming
pools, hot tubs, and sauna equipment and
supplies

(G-14399)
B/E AEROSPACE INC
94 Tide Mill Rd (03842-2705)
PHONE.............................603 926-5700
Amin J Khoury, *Ch Bd*
EMP: 10
SALES (corp-wide): 67.07B **Publicly Held**
Web: www.collinsaerospace.com
SIC: 2531 3728 3647 Seats, aircraft; Aircraft
parts and equipment, nec; Aircraft lighting
fixtures
HQ: B/E Aerospace, Inc.
150 Oak Plaza Blvd # 200
Winston Salem NC 27105
336 747-5000

(G-14400)
BRAZONICS INC (DH)
94 Tide Mill Rd (03842-2705)
PHONE.............................603 758-6237
Mike Mastergeorge, *Pr*
Kenn Bevins, *
EMP: 109 **EST:** 1960
SQ FT: 36,000
SALES (est): 25.34MM
SALES (corp-wide): 68.92B **Publicly Held**
SIC: 3728 Aircraft parts and equipment, nec
HQ: B/E Aerospace, Inc.
150 Oak Plaza Blvd # 200
Winston Salem NC 27105
336 747-5000

(G-14401)
CBMS LLC
6 Fieldstone Cir (03842-1172)
PHONE.............................508 776-2647
Barry Curtis, *Prin*
EMP: 7 **EST:** 2020
SALES (est): 75.68K **Privately Held**
SIC: 3999 Manufacturing industries, nec

(G-14402)
FINESTKIND BREWING LLC
Also Called: Smuttynose Brewing Company
105 Towle Farm Rd (03842-1806)
PHONE.............................603 436-4026
Stephen Kierstead, *CEO*
Brian Walsh, *
EMP: 95 **EST:** 2018
SALES (est): 9.89MM **Privately Held**
Web: www.smuttynose.com
SIC: 2082 5181 5921 Beer (alcoholic
beverage); Beer and other fermented malt
liquors; Beer (packaged)

(G-14403)
INGENVEN FLRPLYMER SLTIONS LLC
70 High St (03842-2207)
PHONE.............................603 601-0877
David P Midgley, *Prin*
EMP: 10 **EST:** 2011
SALES (est): 581.56K **Privately Held**
Web: www.ingeniven.com
SIC: 3449 Custom roll formed products

(G-14404)
IPURA CONSULTING GROUP LLC
8 Mohawk St (03842-1530)
P.O. Box 599 (03843-0599)
PHONE.............................603 294-4002
EMP: 12 **EST:** 2005
SALES (est): 512.1K **Privately Held**
Web: www.ipuraconsulting.com
SIC: 8742 8731 2834 7374 Automation and
robotics consultant; Biotechnical research,
commercial; Pharmaceutical preparations;
Data processing and preparation

(G-14405)
LABELS INC
Also Called: Flex-Print-Labels
10 Merrill Industrial Dr (03842-1979)
PHONE.............................603 929-3088
Robert J Zakian, *VP*
Robert J Zakian, *CEO*
Edward Paquette, *
John Cardellicchio, *
▲ **EMP:** 47 **EST:** 1976
SQ FT: 40,000
SALES (est): 6.64MM **Privately Held**
Web: www.labelsinc.com
SIC: 2759 3565 Labels and seals: printing,
nsk; Packaging machinery

(G-14406)
LIVE FREE OR DIE ALLIANCE
1 Liberty Ln E Ste 100 (03842-1840)
PHONE.............................210 232-8779
EMP: 12 **EST:** 2015
SALES (est): 413.58K **Privately Held**
Web: www.citizenscount.org
SIC: 3544 Special dies and tools

(G-14407)
MIKEL SURFBOARDS LLC
5 Wheaton Lane Ter (03842-2101)
PHONE.............................603 767-7662
Mikel Evans, *Prin*
EMP: 9 **EST:** 2020

SALES (est): 62.4K **Privately Held**
Web: www.mikelsurfboards.com
SIC: 3949 Surfboards

(G-14408)
MIKROLAR INC
7 Scott Rd Ste 5 (03842-1173)
PHONE.............................603 617-2508
Michael Fortier, *Pr*
EMP: 15 **EST:** 2009
SALES (est): 2.66MM **Privately Held**
Web: www.mikrolar.com
SIC: 3569 Filters

(G-14409)
Q A TECHNOLOGY COMPANY INC
110 Towle Farm Rd (03842-1805)
PHONE.............................603 926-1193
Dave Coe, *Pr*
William Beckett, *
EMP: 75 **EST:** 1981
SQ FT: 83,000
SALES (est): 19.56MM **Privately Held**
Web: www.qatech.com
SIC: 3825 3678 3643 Test equipment for
electronic and electrical circuits; Electronic
connectors; Current-carrying wiring services

(G-14410)
RMK BREWERS LLC
836 Lafayette Rd (03842-1248)
PHONE.............................603 601-8196
Miriam Pelletier, *Prin*
EMP: 8 **EST:** 2014
SALES (est): 425.15K **Privately Held**
SIC: 2082 Malt beverages

(G-14411)
ROWE MACHINE CO
Also Called: Rowe Machine
143 N Shore Rd (03842-1463)
PHONE.............................603 926-0029
Marc Rowe, *Owner*
EMP: 10 **EST:** 1976
SQ FT: 6,000
SALES (est): 602.7K **Privately Held**
Web: www.rowemachine.net
SIC: 3599 5571 Machine shop, jobbing and
repair; Motorcycle dealers

(G-14412)
SLEEPNET CORP
5 Merrill Industrial Dr (03842-1980)
PHONE.............................603 758-6600
Thomas Moulton, *CEO*
▲ **EMP:** 24 **EST:** 1990
SQ FT: 15,000
SALES (est): 5.35MM **Privately Held**
Web: www.sleepnetmasks.com
SIC: 3845 Electromedical equipment

(G-14413)
SMUTTYNOSE BREWING COMPANY INC
105 Towle Farm Rd (03842-1806)
PHONE.............................603 436-4026
▲ **EMP:** 66
Web: www.smuttynose.com
SIC: 2082 5181 5921 Beer (alcoholic
beverage); Beer and other fermented malt
liquors; Beer (packaged)

(G-14414)
SPECTRUM CONTROLS INC
112 N Shore Rd (03842-1469)
PHONE.............................603 686-4442
EMP: 8 **EST:** 2018
SALES (est): 82.21K **Privately Held**

GEOGRAPHIC

SIC: 7372   Prepackaged software

(G-14415)
TELEDYNE INSTRUMENTS INC
Also Called: Teledyne D.G. O Brien
1 Lafayette Rd (03842-2626)
PHONE..............................603 474-5571
EMP: 9
SALES (corp-wide): 5.46B **Publicly Held**
Web: www.teledyne.com
SIC: 3823   Flow instruments, industrial
  process type
HQ: Teledyne Instruments, Inc.
  16830 Chestnut St
  City Of Industry CA 91748
  626 934-1500

(G-14416)
TSI GROUP INC (DH)
Also Called: Thermal Solutions
94 Tide Mill Rd (03842-2705)
PHONE..............................603 964-0296
Gregory R Tucker, *CEO*
David K Helms, *CFO*
Dale Jessick, *Ex VP*
EMP: 20 EST: 1999
SQ FT: 3,000
SALES (est): 112.66MM
SALES (corp-wide): 68.92B **Publicly Held**
Web: www.tsigroup.com
SIC: 3599 3398 3443 3444   Machine and
  other job shop work; Brazing (hardening) of
  metal; Fabricated plate work (boiler shop);
  Sheet metalwork
HQ: B/E Aerospace, Inc.
  150 Oak Plaza Blvd # 200
  Winston Salem NC 27105
  336 747-5000

(G-14417)
VISIBLE LIGHT INC
6 Merrill Industrial Dr Unit 11 (03842-1970)
PHONE..............................603 926-6049
Phil Infurna, *Pr*
EMP: 9 EST: 1997
SALES (est): 895.05K **Privately Held**
Web: www.visible-light.net
SIC: 3648   Lighting equipment, nec

Hampton Falls
Rockingham County

(G-14418)
FAVORITE FUELS LLC
1 Crank Rd (03844-2102)
P.O. Box 395 (03844-0395)
PHONE..............................603 967-4889
John Alkire, *Prin*
EMP: 7 EST: 2010
SALES (est): 1.16MM **Privately Held**
Web: www.favoritefuels.com
SIC: 2869   Fuels

(G-14419)
KENSINGTON GROUP INCORPORATED
Also Called: Imagewise
113 Lafayette Rd (03844-2305)
P.O. Box 1080 (03843-1080)
PHONE..............................603 926-6742
Lawrence Crampsey Junior, *Pr*
Eric Lindsay, *VP*
◆ EMP: 14 EST: 1979
SQ FT: 9,000
SALES (est): 1.24MM **Privately Held**
Web: www.imagewisegraphics.com

SIC: 2741 2752 2791 2731   Miscellaneous
  publishing; Offset printing; Typesetting;
  Pamphlets: publishing and printing

Hancock
Hillsborough County

(G-14420)
TELCOR
15 Forest Rd (03449-6111)
P.O. Box 69 (03449-0069)
PHONE..............................603 525-4769
Eric Spitzbarth, *Prin*
EMP: 8 EST: 2007
SALES (est): 214.87K **Privately Held**
SIC: 3844   X-ray apparatus and tubes

Hanover
Grafton County

(G-14421)
DARTMOUTH INC
Also Called: DARTMOUTH, THE
6175 Robinson Hall (03755-3507)
PHONE..............................603 646-2600
Rdex Tejera, *CEO*
EMP: 52 EST: 1939
SALES (est): 277.69K **Privately Held**
Web: www.thedartmouth.com
SIC: 2711   Newspapers: publishing only, not
  printed on site

(G-14422)
DARTMOUTH PRINTING COMPANY (DH)
Also Called: Sheridan New Hampshire
69 Lyme Rd (03755-1293)
PHONE..............................603 643-2220
▲ EMP: 36 EST: 1938
SALES (est): 18.86MM
SALES (corp-wide): 654.01MM **Privately Held**
Web: home.dartmouth.edu
SIC: 2752   Offset printing
HQ: The Sheridan Group Inc
  450 Fame Ave
  Hanover PA 17331

(G-14423)
GILBERTE INTERIORS LLC (PA)
10 Allen St (03755-2079)
PHONE..............................603 643-3727
Aharon A Boghosian, *Pr*
Cheryl Boghosian, *VP*
Gilberte Boghosian, *Treas*
Neil Roth, *Sec*
EMP: 13 EST: 1967
SQ FT: 18,000
SALES (est): 2.47MM
SALES (corp-wide): 2.47MM **Privately Held**
Web: www.gilberteinteriors.com
SIC: 5719 5714 2391 7389   Wicker, rattan,
  or reed home furnishings: Draperies;
  Draperies, plastic and textile: from
  purchased materials; Interior decorating

(G-14424)
HANOVER REVIEW INC
Also Called: Dartmouth Review
8 Webster Ave (03755-1706)
P.O. Box 343 (03755-0343)
PHONE..............................603 643-4370
Stuart Allan, *Pr*
EMP: 9 EST: 1980
SQ FT: 500
SALES (est): 146.82K **Privately Held**

Web: www.dartreview.com
SIC: 8699 2711   Charitable organization;
  Newspapers: publishing only, not printed on
  site

(G-14425)
HONES LLC
12 South St Ste 3 (03755-2163)
PHONE..............................603 643-4223
EMP: 7 EST: 2010
SALES (est): 166.78K **Privately Held**
SIC: 3291   Hones

(G-14426)
HYPERTHERM INC (PA)
Also Called: Hypertherm Associates
21 Great Hollow Rd (03755-3124)
P.O. Box 5010 (03755-5010)
PHONE..............................603 643-3441
Richard W Couch Junior, *Ch Bd*
Evan Smith, *
Cary Chan, *
Barbara Couch, *
Jeffrey Deckrow, *
◆ EMP: 1100 EST: 1968
SQ FT: 155,000
SALES (est): 471.79MM
SALES (corp-wide): 471.79MM **Privately Held**
Web: www.hypertherm.com
SIC: 3541   Machine tools, metal cutting type

(G-14427)
HYPERTHERM INC
1699 Wall St (03755)
P.O. Box 230 (03755-0230)
PHONE..............................716 434-3755
EMP: 10 EST: 2009
SALES (est): 783.96K **Privately Held**
SIC: 3541   Machine tools, metal cutting type

(G-14428)
INDEPENDENT ROWING NEWS INC
53 S Main St Ste 201 (03755-2022)
P.O. Box 831 (03755-0831)
PHONE..............................603 448-5090
Charles Davis, *Publisher*
EMP: 9 EST: 2008
SALES (est): 207.94K **Privately Held**
Web: www.rowingnews.com
SIC: 2711   Newspapers: publishing only, not
  printed on site

(G-14429)
LYME TIMBER COMPANY LP (PA)
23 S Main St Ste 3 (03755-2075)
PHONE..............................603 643-3300
James W Hourdequin, *CEO*
David P Hoffer, *Pr*
EMP: 10 EST: 2008
SALES (est): 4.77MM
SALES (corp-wide): 4.77MM **Privately Held**
Web: www.lymetimber.com
SIC: 2411   Timber, cut at logging camp

(G-14430)
ROBES DANA WOOD CRAFTSMEN (PA)
3 Great Hollow Rd (03755-3122)
PHONE..............................603 643-9355
Caroline Cannon, *Pr*
Caleb J Wood, *VP*
Martha S Robes, *VP*
Gregory R Russell, *VP*
EMP: 20 EST: 1981
SQ FT: 6,000
SALES (est): 1.16MM

SALES (corp-wide): 1.16MM **Privately Held**
SIC: 2426   Furniture dimension stock,
  hardwood

(G-14431)
TRUSTEES OF DARTMOUTH COLLEGE
Also Called: Dartmouth Alumni Magazine
7 Lebanon St Ste 107 (03755-2112)
PHONE..............................603 646-2256
Shawn Plottner, *Dir*
EMP: 9
SALES (corp-wide): 1.39B **Privately Held**
Web: home.dartmouth.edu
SIC: 8221 2721   College, except junior;
  Periodicals
PA: Trustees Of Dartmouth College
  545 Boylston St Ste 900
  Boston MA 02116
  603 646-1110

Harrisville
Cheshire County

(G-14432)
HARRISVILLE DESIGNS INC (PA)
69 Main St Fl 2 (03450-5302)
PHONE..............................603 827-3333
John Colony Iii, *Pr*
▲ EMP: 7 EST: 1971
SQ FT: 6,000
SALES (est): 4.51MM
SALES (corp-wide): 4.51MM **Privately Held**
Web: www.harrisville.com
SIC: 3552 2281 5199 5949   Looms, textile
  machinery; Yarn spinning mills; Yarns, nec;
  Knitting goods and supplies

Henniker
Merrimack County

(G-14433)
BAREFOOT TECHNOLOGIES CORP
41 Liberty Hill Rd (03242-6045)
PHONE..............................603 428-6255
Tom Jin, *Ex Dir*
EMP: 14 EST: 2012
SALES (est): 1.05MM **Privately Held**
Web: www.barefoot.com
SIC: 3652   Prerecorded records and tapes

(G-14434)
GOSS LUMBER CO INC
841 Flanders Rd (03242-6395)
PHONE..............................603 428-3363
Donald Goss Junior, *Pr*
Robert Howard Iii, *Sec*
Lyne Mors, *Off Mgr*
EMP: 9 EST: 1966
SQ FT: 3,360
SALES (est): 801.19K **Privately Held**
Web: www.gosslumber.com
SIC: 2421 5211   Lumber: rough, sawed, or
  planed; Lumber and other building materials

(G-14435)
HERRICK INDUSTRIES INC
54 Main St (03242-3276)
P.O. Box 2089 (03242-2089)
PHONE..............................603 428-3636
David Herrick, *Pr*
Marlo Herrick, *VP*
EMP: 15 EST: 1998
SALES (est): 503.81K **Privately Held**

SIC: **2421** Sawmills and planing mills, general

(G-14436)
HHP INC (PA)
14 Buxton Industrial Dr (03242-3509)
P.O. Box 489 (03242-0489)
PHONE...............................603 428-3298
Ross D'elia, *Pr*
Richard Carrier, *
EMP: 30 EST: 1966
SQ FT: 40,000
SALES (est): 8.87MM
SALES (corp-wide): 8.87MM **Privately Held**
Web: www.hhp-inc.com
SIC: 5031 2421 2448 Lumber: rough, dressed, and finished; Wood chips, produced at mill; Pallets, wood

(G-14437)
HOPKINTON FOR LAND CLARING INC
88 State Shed Rd (03242-3403)
P.O. Box 2089 (03242-2089)
PHONE...............................603 428-8400
David Herrick, *Pr*
Marlo Herrick, *
EMP: 30 EST: 1990
SALES (est): 6MM **Privately Held**
Web: www.hopkintonforestry.com
SIC: 1629 1794 2411 7389 Land clearing contractor; Excavation work; Logging; Business Activities at Non-Commercial Site

(G-14438)
MICHIE CORPORATION
Also Called: Construction Aggregates
173 Buxton Industrial Dr (03242-3559)
P.O. Box 870 (03242-0870)
PHONE...............................603 428-7426
TOLL FREE: 800
Alan Michie, *Pr*
Stuart Michie, *
Pam Michie, *
Donna Michie, *
Pamela Michie, *
EMP: 75 EST: 1974
SQ FT: 7,000
SALES (est): 13.7MM **Privately Held**
Web: www.michiecorp.com
SIC: 3272 3273 1794 1442 Precast terrazzo or concrete products; Ready-mixed concrete ; Excavation work; Sand mining

(G-14439)
N H CENTRAL CONCRETE CORP
4 Bradford Rd (03242-3015)
P.O. Box 840 (03242-0840)
PHONE...............................603 428-7900
Ronald D Goss, *Pr*
Rodney Patenaude, *VP*
Wayne Patenaude, *Sec*
EMP: 19 EST: 1985
SALES (est): 1.07MM **Privately Held**
Web: www.centralnhconcrete.com
SIC: 3273 Ready-mixed concrete

(G-14440)
PAT TRAP INC
632 Western Ave (03242-3491)
PHONE...............................603 428-3396
Stuart Patenaude, *Pr*
Amy Patenaude, *VP*
Katherine Patenaude, *Treas*
▲ **EMP: 9 EST:** 1983
SALES (est): 902.1K **Privately Held**
Web: www.pattrap.com
SIC: 3949 Sporting and athletic goods, nec

Hillsborough
Hillsborough County

(G-14441)
OSRAM SYLVANIA INC
275 W Main St (03244-5233)
PHONE...............................978 750-3900
Jes Munk Hansen, *Pr*
EMP: 310
SALES (corp-wide): 5B **Privately Held**
Web: www.osram.us
SIC: 3641 Electric lamps
HQ: Osram Sylvania Inc.
    200 Ballardvale St Bldg 2
    Wilmington MA 01887
    978 570-3000

(G-14442)
OSRAM SYLVANIA INC
Also Called: Automotive & Miniature Ltg
275 W Main St (03244-5233)
PHONE...............................603 464-7235
Ben Sucy, *Brnch Mgr*
EMP: 300
SQ FT: 135,000
SALES (corp-wide): 5B **Privately Held**
Web: www.sylvania-automotive.com
SIC: 3641 3714 Electric lamps; Motor vehicle parts and accessories
HQ: Osram Sylvania Inc.
    200 Ballardvale St Bldg 2
    Wilmington MA 01887
    978 570-3000

Hinsdale
Cheshire County

(G-14443)
CONTINENTAL CABLE LLC
Also Called: Gbg Industries
253 Monument Rd (03451-2033)
PHONE...............................800 229-5131
Brian Nadeau, *VP*
Gary Preston, *COO*
Alaine Williams, *Contrlr*
◆ **EMP: 56 EST:** 1949
SQ FT: 51,000
SALES (est): 10.79MM
SALES (corp-wide): 44.72MM **Privately Held**
Web: www.continentalcablellc.com
SIC: 3496 3644 3728 Cable, uninsulated wire: made from purchased wire; Noncurrent-carrying wiring devices; Aircraft parts and equipment, nec
PA: Les Cables Ben-Mor Inc
    1105 Rue Lemire
    Saint-Hyacinthe QC J2T 1
    450 778-0022

(G-14444)
HCP PACKAGING USA INC
370 Monument Rd (03451-2040)
PHONE...............................603 256-3141
George Benegger, *Brnch Mgr*
EMP: 150
SALES (corp-wide): 23.77MM **Privately Held**
Web: www.hcppackaging.com
SIC: 3089 Cases, plastics
PA: Hcp Packaging Usa, Inc.
    1 Waterview Dr Ste 102
    Shelton CT 06484
    203 924-2408

(G-14445)
WAHSBURN VAULT COMPANY INC
18 Washburn Way (03451-2487)
PHONE...............................603 256-6891
Jack Ealdwin, *Pr*
EMP: 7 EST: 2007
SALES (est): 879.89K **Privately Held**
Web: www.washburnvault.com
SIC: 3272 Concrete products, nec

Holderness
Grafton County

(G-14446)
AND FAUNA LLC
949 Us Route 3 (03245-5633)
P.O. Box 153 (03245-0153)
PHONE...............................603 968-7490
Sarah K Sniffen, *Mgr*
EMP: 7 EST: 2012
SALES (est): 70.96K **Privately Held**
SIC: 3999 Manufacturing industries, nec

(G-14447)
MEGAPRINT INC
Also Called: Megaprint
1177 New Hampshire Rte 175 (03245-5031)
P.O. Box 87 (03264-0087)
PHONE...............................603 536-2900
EMP: 10 EST: 1994
SQ FT: 4,800
SALES (est): 2.04MM **Privately Held**
Web: www.megaprint.com
SIC: 2752 Offset printing

Hollis
Hillsborough County

(G-14448)
CAPITAL OFFSET CO INC
95 Runnells Bridge Rd (03049-6535)
P.O. Box 2824 (03302-2824)
PHONE...............................603 225-3308
Jay Stewart, *Dir Fin*
EMP: 19 EST: 1936
SQ FT: 10,000
SALES (est): 652.1K **Privately Held**
Web: www.capitaloffset.com
SIC: 2752 Offset printing

(G-14449)
DEVPROTEK INC
4 Clinton Dr (03049-6595)
PHONE...............................603 577-5557
Les Scenna, *Pr*
EMP: 8 EST: 2000
SQ FT: 3,000
SALES (est): 927.39K **Privately Held**
Web: www.devprotek.com
SIC: 3569 Robots, assembly line: industrial and commercial

(G-14450)
DIAMOND CASTING AND MCH CO LLC
95 Proctor Hill Rd (03049-6427)
PHONE...............................603 465-2263
Gerald Letendre, *Pr*
EMP: 45 EST: 1963
SQ FT: 80,000
SALES (est): 5.36MM **Privately Held**
Web: www.diamondcasting.com

SIC: **3363** 3365 3599 3369 Aluminum die-castings; Aluminum and aluminum-based alloy castings; Machine shop, jobbing and repair; Nonferrous foundries, nec

(G-14451)
ENVIRONMENTAL TEST PDTS INC (PA)
29 Shipley Dr (03049-6029)
PHONE...............................603 924-5010
Rob Gual, *Pr*
Eric Peahl, *Sr VP*
Chris Peahl, *COO*
EMP: 7 EST: 2001
SQ FT: 2,000
SALES (est): 988.27K
SALES (corp-wide): 988.27K **Privately Held**
Web: www.etpproducts.com
SIC: 3826 Environmental testing equipment

(G-14452)
INDUSTRIAL CNC LLC
17d Clinton Dr (03049-6595)
PHONE...............................603 320-3484
EMP: 30 EST: 2006
SALES (est): 2.1MM **Privately Held**
Web: www.industrialcnc.com
SIC: 3599 Machine shop, jobbing and repair

(G-14453)
LW HOLDING LC
Also Called: Flextronics Lighting Solution
12 Silver Lake Rd (03049-6259)
PHONE...............................913 851-3000
▲ **EMP: 40 EST:** 2002
SALES (est): 5.92MM **Privately Held**
SIC: 3646 Commercial lighting fixtures

(G-14454)
MICROMATICS MACHINE CO INC
9 Clinton Dr (03049-6595)
PHONE...............................603 889-2115
Anita Brown, *Pr*
EMP: 14 EST: 1973
SQ FT: 20,000
SALES (est): 4.31MM **Privately Held**
Web: www.micromaticsinc.com
SIC: 3599 Machine shop, jobbing and repair

(G-14455)
NEXTMOVE TECHNOLOGIES LLC
1 Kerk St (03049-6442)
PHONE...............................603 654-1280
EMP: 7 EST: 2008
SALES (est): 933.85K **Privately Held**
Web: www.nextmovetech.com
SIC: 3669 Intercommunication systems, electric

(G-14456)
PARKER-HANNIFIN CORPORATION
Parker Precision Fluidics
26 Clinton Dr Ste 103 (03049-6579)
PHONE...............................603 595-1500
Jim Heselton, *Brnch Mgr*
EMP: 150
SALES (corp-wide): 19.07B **Publicly Held**
Web: www.parker.com
SIC: 3823 3492 Fluidic devices, circuits, and systems for process control; Fluid power valves and hose fittings
PA: Parker-Hannifin Corporation
    6035 Parkland Blvd
    Cleveland OH 44124
    216 896-3000

(G-14457)
PNEUCLEUS TECHNOLOGIES LLC
169 Depot Rd (03049-6559)
PHONE...............................603 465-7346
◆ EMP: 7 EST: 2001
SQ FT: 2,000
SALES (est): 563.13K Privately Held
Web: www.pneucleus.com
SIC: 3823 Process control instruments

(G-14458)
PURITAN PRESS INC (PA)
Also Called: Puritan Capital
95 Runnells Bridge Rd (03049-6535)
PHONE...............................603 889-4500
Kurt Peterson, Pr
Michael Ames, *
Jay Stewart, *
Rene Valiquet, *
EMP: 50 EST: 1976
SQ FT: 30,600
SALES (est): 10.06MM
SALES (corp-wide): 10.06MM Privately Held
Web: www.puritanpress.com
SIC: 2752 2759 2791 7331 Offset printing;
  Periodicals: printing, nsk; Typesetting;
  Direct mail advertising services

(G-14459)
ULTRASOURCE INC
22 Clinton Dr (03049-6595)
PHONE...............................603 881-7799
EMP: 100
Web: www.ultrasource.com
SIC: 3674 Thin film circuits

(G-14460)
VALLEY WELDING & FABG INC
261 Proctor Hill Rd (03049-6427)
P.O. Box 894 (03049-0894)
PHONE...............................603 465-3266
Carolyn A Valley, Pr
Larry Valley, VP
Loren J Valley, Pr
EMP: 20 EST: 1975
SQ FT: 15,000
SALES (est): 2.42MM Privately Held
Web: www.valleyweld.com
SIC: 3444 7692 3443 3441 Sheet metalwork
  ; Welding repair; Fabricated plate work
  (boiler shop); Fabricated structural metal

(G-14461)
VISHAY DALE ELECTRONICS LLC
Also Called: Vishay Ultrasource
22 Clinton Dr (03049-6595)
PHONE...............................603 881-7799
EMP: 100
SALES (corp-wide): 3.5B Publicly Held
Web: www.yourthinfilmsource.com
SIC: 3674 Thin film circuits
HQ: Vishay Dale Electronics, Llc
  1122 23rd St
  Columbus NE 68601
  605 665-9301

Hooksett
Merrimack County

(G-14462)
A & G CRANE LLC
7 Craneway (03106-2194)
PHONE...............................603 668-5844
Gregory Evans, Prin
EMP: 8 EST: 2011
SALES (est): 440.39K Privately Held
Web: www.americancranenh.com
SIC: 3531 Cranes, nec

(G-14463)
BURTON WIRE & CABLE LLC
4 Brookside West (03106-2518)
PHONE...............................603 624-2427
Burton A Hyman, Pr
▲ EMP: 12 EST: 1985
SQ FT: 10,000
SALES (est): 11.8MM Privately Held
Web: www.burtonwire.com
SIC: 3357 Nonferrous wiredrawing and
  insulating

(G-14464)
CUSTOM TRUCK ONE SOURCE LP
6 Sutton Cir (03106-2039)
PHONE...............................574 370-2740
EMP: 39
SALES (corp-wide): 1.57B Publicly Held
Web: www.customtruck.com
SIC: 3713 Utility truck bodies
HQ: Custom Truck One Source, L.P.
  7701 E 24 Hwy
  Kansas City MO 64125
  855 931-1852

(G-14465)
GENERAL ELECTRIC COMPANY
Also Called: GE
31 Industrial Park Dr (03106-1851)
PHONE...............................603 666-8300
Raj Pas, Mgr
EMP: 567
SALES (corp-wide): 76.56B Publicly Held
Web: www.geaerospace.com
SIC: 3724 3728 3714 Aircraft engines and
  engine parts; Aircraft parts and equipment,
  nec; Motor vehicle parts and accessories
PA: General Electric Company
  1 Financial Ctr Ste 3700
  Boston MA 02111
  617 443-3000

(G-14466)
LAD WELDING & FABRICATION
5 Lehoux Dr (03106-1836)
PHONE...............................603 228-6617
William Bodah, Pr
EMP: 12 EST: 1986
SALES (est): 1.73MM Privately Held
Web: www.ladwelding.com
SIC: 3444 1799 Sheet metalwork; Welding
  on site

(G-14467)
LEW A CUMMINGS CO INC
Also Called: Cummings Printing Company
4 Peters Brook Dr (03106-1822)
P.O. Box 16495 (03106-6490)
PHONE...............................603 625-6901
John L Cummings, Pr
Norma J Shea, *
EMP: 106 EST: 1959
SQ FT: 84,000
SALES (est): 20.8MM Privately Held
Web: www.cummingsprinting.com
SIC: 2752 Offset printing

(G-14468)
MACY INDUSTRIES INC
5 Lehoux Dr (03106-1836)
PHONE...............................603 623-5568
Nicholas Mercier, CEO
EMP: 40 EST: 1975
SQ FT: 13,875
SALES (est): 7.23MM Privately Held
Web: www.macyindustries.com
SIC: 3444 7699 Sheet metal specialties, not
  stamped; Industrial equipment services

(G-14469)
PREMIER PACKAGING LLC
47 Post Rd (03106-1725)
PHONE...............................603 485-7465
EMP: 8 EST: 2016
SALES (est): 425.16K Privately Held
SIC: 7372 Prepackaged software

(G-14470)
PSI WATER SYSTEMS LLC (PA)
Also Called: Encon Evaporators
1368 Hooksett Rd (03106-1823)
PHONE...............................603 624-5110
EMP: 19 EST: 1993
SALES (est): 8.58MM Privately Held
Web: www.evaporator.com
SIC: 3589 Water treatment equipment,
  industrial

(G-14471)
R G TOMBS DOOR COMPANY INC
38 West River Rd (03106-2624)
PHONE...............................603 624-5040
TOLL FREE: 800
Richard G Tombs, Pr
Darlene Drechsler, VP
Theodore Wadleigh, Sec
EMP: 20 EST: 1978
SQ FT: 21,000
SALES (est): 3.12MM Privately Held
Web: www.rgtombsdoor.com
SIC: 1751 3442 Garage door, installation or
  erection; Garage doors, overhead: metal

(G-14472)
RAN/ALL METAL TECHNOLOGY INC
7a E Point Dr (03106-2019)
P.O. Box 16419 (03106-6419)
PHONE...............................603 668-1907
James Oriani, Pr
Kevin Mullen, VP
▼ EMP: 9 EST: 1983
SQ FT: 12,000
SALES (est): 917.24K Privately Held
Web: www.ranallmetal.com
SIC: 3444 Sheet metal specialties, not
  stamped

(G-14473)
RB GRAPHICS INC
Also Called: Signature Press & Blue Prtg
45 Londonderry Tpke (03106-2046)
P.O. Box 16328 (03106-6328)
PHONE...............................603 624-4025
TOLL FREE: 800
R William Baker, Pr
Susan La Fond, Sec
EMP: 9 EST: 1961
SALES (est): 896.54K Privately Held
SIC: 2752 2759 7334 2789 Offset printing;
  Commercial printing, nec; Blueprinting
  service; Bookbinding and related work

(G-14474)
RIMOL GREENHOUSE SYSTEMS INC
40 Londonderry Tpke Ste 2d (03106-1914)
PHONE...............................603 629-9004
Robert Rimol, Pr
Robert Rimol, Pr
Karen Rimol, VP
Bob Rimol, Pr
EMP: 10 EST: 1994
SQ FT: 6,000
SALES (est): 1.72MM Privately Held
Web: www.rimol.com
SIC: 3448 5191 Greenhouses, prefabricated
  metal; Greenhouse equipment and supplies

(G-14475)
TRI TOWN CABINETRY
1261 Hooksett Rd Ste 3 (03106-1094)
PHONE...............................603 391-9276
Scott Rogers, Prin
EMP: 7 EST: 2010
SALES (est): 230.39K Privately Held
Web: www.tritowncabinetry.com
SIC: 2434 Wood kitchen cabinets

(G-14476)
VIBEZ SUNGLASSES LLC
237 Londonderry Tpke (03106-1990)
PHONE...............................603 818-2207
Reed Mills, Prin
EMP: 9 EST: 2020
SALES (est): 233.23K Privately Held
Web: www.vibezsunglasses.com
SIC: 3851 Eyeglasses, lenses and frames

Hopkinton
Merrimack County

(G-14477)
HMC CORPORATION (PA)
284 Maple St (03229-3339)
PHONE...............................603 746-3399
Peter R Taylor, *
Peter R Taylor, *
◆ EMP: 35 EST: 1952
SQ FT: 30,000
SALES (est): 5.42MM
SALES (corp-wide): 5.42MM Privately Held
Web: www.hmccorp.com
SIC: 3553 5084 Sawmill machines;
  Industrial machinery and equipment

Hudson
Hillsborough County

(G-14478)
603 MANUFACTURING LLC
21 Park Ave (03051-3985)
PHONE...............................603 578-9876
Mark Twaalfhoven, Pr
EMP: 86 EST: 2017
SALES (est): 10.31MM
SALES (corp-wide): 1.28B Privately Held
Web: www.603manufacturing.com
SIC: 3679 Electronic circuits
HQ: Tpc Wire & Cable Corp.
  9600 Valley View Rd
  Macedonia OH 44056

(G-14479)
ADAX MACHINE CO INC
5 Flagstone Dr (03051-4905)
PHONE...............................603 598-6777
Joseph R Williams, Pr
EMP: 20 EST: 1986
SQ FT: 20,000
SALES (est): 2.04MM Privately Held
Web: www.adaxmachine.com
SIC: 3599 Machine shop, jobbing and repair

(G-14480)
ADVANCED FITNES COMPONENTS LLC
17 Hampshire Dr Ste 18 (03051-4940)

PHONE..............603 595-1967
EMP: 8 **EST:** 2001
SALES (est): 247.85K **Privately Held**
Web: www.spinoflex.com
SIC: 3949 Exercise equipment

(G-14481)
AIREX CORPORATION
17 Executive Dr (03051-4914)
PHONE..............603 821-3065
William R Carroll, *Pr*
EMP: 40 **EST:** 1973
SQ FT: 53,000
SALES (est): 4.94MM **Privately Held**
Web: www.airexfilter.com
SIC: 3564 Filters, air: furnaces, air
conditioning equipment, etc.

(G-14482)
AMERICAN FLGGING TRFFIC CTRL I
4 Rebel Rd (03051-3025)
PHONE..............603 890-1154
Joseph Dunlap, *Pr*
Kathleen Mcphee, *VP*
EMP: 100 **EST:** 1995
SQ FT: 6,500
SALES (est): 4.94MM **Privately Held**
Web: www.americanflagging.com
SIC: 7389 3993 Flagging service (traffic
control); Signs and advertising specialties

(G-14483)
AMERICAN IR SOLUTIONS LLC
Also Called: Airs
1 Wall St (03051-3983)
P.O. Box 1509 (03061-1509)
PHONE..............662 626-2477
EMP: 7 **EST:** 2012
SQ FT: 3,000
SALES (est): 1.07MM **Privately Held**
Web: www.go-airs.com
SIC: 3812 Aircraft/aerospace flight
instruments and guidance systems

(G-14484)
APPROVED SHEET METAL LLC
7 Security Dr (03051-5246)
PHONE..............603 883-1510
EMP: 23 **EST:** 2020
SALES (est): 9.28MM **Privately Held**
Web: www.approvedsheetmetal.com
SIC: 3444 Sheet metalwork

(G-14485)
AXE PLAY LLC
142 Lowell Rd Unit 19 (03051-4938)
PHONE..............603 809-9081
Matthew Keller, *Managing Member*
EMP: 8 **EST:** 2020
SALES (est): 46.61K **Privately Held**
Web: www.axe-play.com
SIC: 3423 7999 Axes and hatchets;
Recreation center

(G-14486)
BAE SYSTEMS INFO ELCTRNIC SYST
Also Called: BAE Systems Information And
Electronic Systems Integration Inc.
65 River Rd (03051-5244)
P.O. Box 868 (03061-0868)
PHONE..............603 885-4321
David Logan, *Co-General Manager*
EMP: 1061
SALES (corp-wide): 25.59B **Privately Held**
Web: www.baesystems.com

SIC: 3679 3812 8731 Electronic circuits;
Search and navigation equipment;
Commercial physical research
HQ: Bae Systems Information And
Electronic Systems Integration Inc.
65 Spit Brook Rd
Nashua NH 03060
603 885-4321

(G-14487)
BAE SYSTEMS OASYS LLC
65 River Rd (03051-5244)
PHONE..............603 232-8221
EMP: 65
SIC: 3827 Optical instruments and lenses

(G-14488)
BAY STATE INDUSTRIAL WELDIN
Also Called: Bsiw
10 Flagstone Dr (03051-4904)
PHONE..............603 881-7663
Rick Mccartney, *Pr*
EMP: 30 **EST:** 1992
SQ FT: 25,000
SALES (est): 18.87MM **Privately Held**
Web: www.bsiw.com
SIC: 1541 7692 8711 1799 Industrial
buildings and warehouses; Welding repair;
Structural engineering; Welding on site

(G-14489)
C & M MACHINE PRODUCTS INC
Also Called: C&M Precision Tech
25 Flagstone Dr (03051-4920)
PHONE..............603 594-8100
Paul Villemaire, *CEO*
Daniel Villemaire, *
Robert Rzasa, *
Jeffrey A Zall, *
▲ **EMP:** 90 **EST:** 1979
SQ FT: 100,000
SALES (est): 24.03MM **Privately Held**
Web: www.cmprecisiontech.com
SIC: 3599 Machine shop, jobbing and repair

(G-14490)
CEI FLOWMASTER PRODUCTS LLC
18 Park Ave (03051-3934)
PHONE..............603 880-0094
EMP: 7 **EST:** 2008
SALES (est): 169.75K **Privately Held**
SIC: 3824 Fluid meters and counting devices

(G-14491)
CONCRETE SYSTEMS INC
Also Called: Cleco Manufacturing
14 Park Ave (03051-3934)
PHONE..............603 886-5472
EMP: 60
SALES (corp-wide): 51.02MM **Privately Held**
Web: www.csigroup.com
SIC: 3448 3272 Prefabricated metal
buildings and components; Manhole covers
or frames, concrete
PA: Concrete Systems, Inc.
9 Commercial St
Hudson NH 03051
603 889-4163

(G-14492)
CYCLONES ARENA
20 Constitution Dr (03051-3986)
PHONE..............603 880-4424
Wes Dolloff, *Owner*
EMP: 10 **EST:** 2007
SALES (est): 868.7K **Privately Held**
Web: www.cyclonesarena.com

SIC: 3674 Hall effect devices

(G-14493)
DIEBOLD NIXDORF INCORPORATED
7 Walmart Blvd (03051-5248)
PHONE..............603 577-9519
EMP: 7
SALES (corp-wide): 3.46B **Publicly Held**
Web: www.dieboldnixdorf.com
SIC: 3578 Automatic teller machines (ATM)
PA: Diebold Nixdorf, Incorporated
50 Executive Pkwy
Hudson OH 44236
330 490-4000

(G-14494)
DURO-FIBER CO INC
11 Park Ave (03051-3985)
PHONE..............603 881-4200
John A Hatfield, *Pr*
EMP: 10 **EST:** 1965
SQ FT: 18,000
SALES (est): 442.22K **Privately Held**
Web: www.durofiber.com
SIC: 2221 Fiberglass fabrics

(G-14495)
E PRINT INC
10 Rebel Rd (03051-3025)
PHONE..............603 594-0009
Ben Maurias, *Pr*
Hiltrud Bennett, *Pr*
Debra Maurias, *Sec*
EMP: 8 **EST:** 1999
SQ FT: 3,000
SALES (est): 801.5K **Privately Held**
Web: www.eprintinc.com
SIC: 2752 7336 5199 Offset printing; Art
design services; Advertising specialties

(G-14496)
FLIR MARITIME US INC
110 Lowell Rd (03051-4806)
PHONE..............603 324-7900
Kevin Murphy, *Contrlr*
◆ **EMP:** 45 **EST:** 2001
SALES (est): 23.35MM
SALES (corp-wide): 5.46B **Publicly Held**
Web: www.raymarine.com
SIC: 3812 Radar systems and equipment
HQ: Raymarine Holdings Limited
Marine House
Fareham HANTS PO15
132 924-6700

(G-14497)
FWM INC
11 Friars Dr (03051-4900)
PHONE..............603 578-3366
Michael J Barry, *Pr*
EMP: 37 **EST:** 1975
SQ FT: 50,000
SALES (est): 7.99MM **Privately Held**
Web: www.fwmdocks.com
SIC: 3441 3599 Fabricated structural metal;
Machine shop, jobbing and repair

(G-14498)
G5 INFRARED LLC
12 Executive Dr Unit A (03051-4939)
PHONE..............603 304-5722
EMP: 20 **EST:** 2011
SALES (est): 2.48MM **Privately Held**
Web: www.g5ir.com
SIC: 3827 Optical instruments and lenses

(G-14499)
GILCHRIST METAL FABG CO INC
12 Park Ave (03051-3927)
PHONE..............603 889-2600
John S Gilchrist Junior, *Brnch Mgr*
EMP: 11
SALES (corp-wide): 8.02MM **Privately Held**
Web: www.gmfco.com
SIC: 3441 Fabricated structural metal
PA: Gilchrist Metal Fabricating Co., Inc.
18 Park Ave
Hudson NH 03051
603 889-2600

(G-14500)
GILCHRIST METAL FABG CO INC (PA)
18 Park Ave (03051-3934)
PHONE..............603 889-2600
John S Gilchrist Junior, *Pr*
Paul Shapiro, *
Susan Martin, *
Stuart Gilchrist, *
Jack Gilchrist, *
EMP: 25 **EST:** 1975
SQ FT: 70,000
SALES (est): 8.02MM
SALES (corp-wide): 8.02MM **Privately Held**
Web: www.gmfco.com
SIC: 3443 3444 3441 Fabricated plate work
(boiler shop); Sheet metalwork; Fabricated
structural metal

(G-14501)
GRANITE FORGE LLC
32 Executive Dr (03051-4919)
PHONE..............603 589-9480
Gregory Davis, *CEO*
Gregory L Davis, *Managing Member*
Mel Speidel, *COO*
Patrick Oneill, *Ex VP*
EMP: 13 **EST:** 2018
SALES (est): 1.01MM **Privately Held**
Web: www.granite-forge.com
SIC: 3463 Aircraft forgings, nonferrous

(G-14502)
GRANITE STATE PLASTICS INC
Also Called: Granite State Plastics
37 Executive Dr (03051-4903)
PHONE..............603 669-6715
Steven W Lunder, *Pr*
John B Emory, *
Steven B Getto, *
▲ **EMP:** 35 **EST:** 1969
SQ FT: 25,000
SALES (est): 9.15MM **Privately Held**
Web: www.granitestateplastics.com
SIC: 3089 Injection molding of plastics

(G-14503)
GT ADVANCED TECHNOLOGIES INC (DH)
Also Called: Gtat
5 Wentworth Dr Ste 1 (03051-4929)
PHONE..............603 883-5200
Gregory C Knight, *CEO*
Michele P Rayos, *
▲ **EMP:** 100 **EST:** 2006
SQ FT: 106,000
SALES (est): 96.34MM
SALES (corp-wide): 8.25B **Publicly Held**
Web: www.onsemi.com
SIC: 3674 Photovoltaic devices, solid state
HQ: Semiconductor Components
Industries, Llc
5701 N Pima Rd
Scottsdale AZ 85250
602 244-6600

(G-14504)
GT ADVANCED TECHNOLOGIES LTD
5 Wentworth Dr (03051-4929)
PHONE..............................603 883-5200
EMP: 7
SALES (est): 195.94K Privately Held
SIC: 3674 Semiconductors and related
devices

(G-14505)
GTAT CORPORATION (DH)
5 Wentworth Dr # 1 (03051-4929)
PHONE..............................603 883-5200
Greg Knight, Pr
Michele Rayos, *
▲ EMP: 73 EST: 1994
SALES (est): 49.55MM
SALES (corp-wide): 8.25B Publicly Held
Web: www.gtat.com
SIC: 3674 Photovoltaic devices, solid state
HQ: Gt Advanced Technologies Inc.
5 Wentworth Dr Ste 1
Hudson NH 03051

(G-14506)
HARDRIC LABORATORIES INC
22 Flagstone Dr (03051-4904)
PHONE..............................978 251-1702
Richard Charbonnier, Pr
Peter N Richard, *
EMP: 38 EST: 1957
SALES (est): 4.14MM Privately Held
Web: www.hardric.com
SIC: 3827 3728 3699 3231 Mirrors, optical;
Aircraft parts and equipment, nec; Electrical
equipment and supplies, nec; Products of
purchased glass

(G-14507)
HUDSON QUARRY CORP
Also Called: Hudson Ouarry
6 Candy Ln (03051-3005)
PHONE..............................603 598-0142
TOLL FREE: 800
Michael Genest, Pr
David Genest, VP
EMP: 10 EST: 1988
SQ FT: 7,500
SALES (est): 1.61MM Privately Held
Web: www.hudsonquarry.com
SIC: 5211 5261 5082 3272 Paving stones;
Top soil; Masonry equipment and supplies;
Concrete products, precast, nec

(G-14508)
INCON INC
21 Flagstone Dr (03051-4920)
PHONE..............................603 595-0550
Robert J Butler, CEO
Ted Schultz, *
Steven Camerino, *
EMP: 49 EST: 1988
SQ FT: 32,000
SALES (est): 6.51MM Privately Held
Web: www.inconconnector.com
SIC: 3678 Electronic connectors

(G-14509)
INSIDE TRACK CABLING INC
18 West Rd (03051-3019)
PHONE..............................603 886-8013
EMP: 30 EST: 1992
SQ FT: 88,000
SALES (est): 5.94MM Privately Held
Web: www.insidetrackcabling.com
SIC: 3643 Power line cable

(G-14510)
INTEGRA BIOSCIENCES CORP
22 Friars Dr (03051-4900)
PHONE..............................603 578-5800
EMP: 13 EST: 2018
SALES (est): 5.65MM Privately Held
Web: www.integra-biosciences.com
SIC: 3826 Analytical instruments

(G-14511)
INTEGRA BIOSCIENCES CORP
2 Wentworth Dr (03051-4918)
PHONE..............................603 578-5800
Gary Nelson, Pr
John Stowell, VP
▲ EMP: 15 EST: 2005
SQ FT: 5,000
SALES (est): 12.52MM Privately Held
Web: www.integra-biosciences.com
SIC: 3826 Analytical instruments
HQ: Integra Biosciences Holding Ag
Tardisstrasse 201
Zizers GR 7205

(G-14512)
INTERVALA LLC
33 Constitution Dr (03051-3986)
PHONE..............................603 595-1987
Craig Norton, Mgr
EMP: 88
SALES (corp-wide): 102.7MM Privately
Held
Web: www.intervala.com
SIC: 3672 3679 Printed circuit boards;
Electronic circuits
PA: Intervala, Llc
1001 Tech Dr Ste 1181
Mount Pleasant PA 15666
412 829-4800

(G-14513)
JMD INDUSTRIES INC
1 Park Ave (03051-3928)
PHONE..............................603 882-3198
James M Dedeus, Pr
Janet Dedeus, *
EMP: 40 EST: 1978
SQ FT: 20,000
SALES (est): 5.18MM Privately Held
Web: www.jmd.industries
SIC: 3471 Electroplating of metals or
formed products

(G-14514)
KASE PRINTING INC
13 Hampshire Dr Ste 12 (03051-4948)
PHONE..............................603 883-9223
John Koumantzelis, Pr
Arthur Glatt, *
EMP: 46 EST: 1992
SQ FT: 9,000
SALES (est): 9.27MM Privately Held
Web: www.kaseprinting.com
SIC: 2752 Offset printing

(G-14515)
KELLEY BROS NEW ENGLAND LLC (HQ)
Also Called: Kelley Bros
17 Hampshire Dr Ste 20 (03051-4940)
PHONE..............................603 881-5559
EMP: 13 EST: 2005
SQ FT: 6,000
SALES (est): 10.16MM
SALES (corp-wide): 130MM Privately
Held
Web: www.kelleybros.com
SIC: 2431 Door frames, wood
PA: Kelley Brothers, Llc
317 E Brighton Ave

Syracuse NY 13210
800 856-2550

(G-14516)
KM HOLDING INC
120 Derry Rd (03051-3715)
P.O. Box 240 (03051-0240)
PHONE..............................603 566-2704
Jonathan Kane, Pr
EMP: 17 EST: 1984
SALES (est): 499.31K Privately Held
SIC: 3827 Optical instruments and
apparatus

(G-14517)
KRETETEK INDUSTRIES INC
66b River Rd (03051-5225)
PHONE..............................855 573-8383
Benjamin Moore, Prin
EMP: 15 EST: 2013
SALES (est): 1.29MM Privately Held
Web: www.ghostshield.com
SIC: 2891 Sealants

(G-14518)
KRETETEK INDUSTRIES LLC
66 River Rd (03051-5225)
PHONE..............................603 402-3073
Jessica Moore, Managing Member
EMP: 10 EST: 2016
SALES (est): 767.15K Privately Held
Web: www.ghostshield.com
SIC: 2851 Wood fillers or sealers

(G-14519)
KSARIA CORPORATION
Also Called: Ksaria
6 Wentworth Dr (03051-4918)
PHONE..............................866 457-2742
Anthony Christopher, Pr
Michael A Dipoto, *
EMP: 117 EST: 2000
SALES (est): 23.22MM
SALES (corp-wide): 106.67MM Privately
Held
Web: www.ksaria.com
SIC: 3679 3678 Harness assemblies, for
electronic use: wire or cable; Electronic
connectors
HQ: Ksaria Holding Corporation
6 Wentworth Dr
Hudson NH 03051
866 457-2742

(G-14520)
KSARIA SERVICE CORPORATION
6 Wentworth Dr (03051-4918)
PHONE..............................978 933-0000
Anthony J Christopher, CEO
Michael Dipoto, *
EMP: 40 EST: 2016
SALES (est): 6.62MM Privately Held
Web: www.ksaria.com
SIC: 3731 Shipbuilding and repairing
PA: Ksaria Corporation
6 Wentworth Dr
Hudson NH 03051

(G-14521)
LEPAGE BAKERIES PARK ST LLC
Also Called: Country Kitchen
2 Security Dr (03051-5246)
PHONE..............................603 880-4446
Tim Jackson, Mgr
EMP: 10
SALES (corp-wide): 4.81B Publicly Held

SIC: 2051 Bread, cake, and related products
HQ: Lepage Bakeries Park Street Llc
415 Lisbon St 4
Lewiston ME 04240
207 783-9161

(G-14522)
LIFE IS GOOD RETAIL INC (PA)
15 Hudson Park Dr (03051-3989)
PHONE..............................603 594-6100
Albert Jacobs, CEO
▲ EMP: 55 EST: 1994
SALES (est): 27.04MM
SALES (corp-wide): 27.04MM Privately
Held
Web: www.lifeisgood.com
SIC: 2759 Screen printing

(G-14523)
LIFE IS GOOD WHOLESALE INC
Also Called: Life Is Good Design Center
15 Hudson Park Dr (03051-3989)
PHONE..............................603 594-6100
TOLL FREE: 800
◆ EMP: 100 EST: 1994
SQ FT: 150,000
SALES (est): 750.86K
SALES (corp-wide): 2.55MM Privately
Held
Web: www.lifeisgood.com
SIC: 2261 Screen printing of cotton
broadwoven fabrics
PA: The Life Is Good Company
253 Summer St Fl 1
Boston MA 02210
888 339-2987

(G-14524)
LNX CORPORATION
267 Lowell Rd (03051-4937)
PHONE..............................603 898-6800
EMP: 60
Web: www.mrcy.com
SIC: 3679 Microwave components

(G-14525)
MASIMO SEMICONDUCTOR INC
25 Sagamore Park Rd (03051-4901)
PHONE..............................603 595-8900
Mark P De Raad, Pr
Gerry Hammarth, *
EMP: 26 EST: 2012
SALES (est): 7.14MM Privately Held
Web: www.masimosemiconductor.com
SIC: 3674 Microcircuits, integrated
(semiconductor)

(G-14526)
MATRIX TECHNOLOGIES LLC
Also Called: Thermo Fisher Scientific
22 Friars Dr (03051-4900)
PHONE..............................603 595-0505
▲ EMP: 7172
SIC: 3821 Laboratory equipment: fume
hoods, distillation racks, etc.

(G-14527)
MERCURY SYSTEMS INC
267 Lowell Rd Ste 101 (03051-4937)
PHONE..............................603 883-2900
Kevin Beals, CEO
EMP: 503
SALES (corp-wide): 973.88MM Publicly
Held
Web: www.mrcy.com
SIC: 3672 Printed circuit boards
PA: Mercury Systems, Inc.
50 Minuteman Rd
Andover MA 01810
978 256-1300

▲ = Import ▼ = Export
◆ = Import/Export

(G-14528)
MODERN METAL SOLUTIONS LLC
12 Park Ave (03051-3927)
PHONE.................................603 402-3022
EMP: 11 EST: 2012
SALES (est): 3.8MM Privately Held
Web: www.modern-metal-solutions.com
SIC: 3412 Metal barrels, drums, and pails

(G-14529)
MORGAN ADVANCED CERAMICS INC
4 Park Ave (03051-3927)
PHONE.................................603 598-9122
Jon Stang, *Brnch Mgr*
EMP: 41
SALES (corp-wide): 1.34B Privately Held
Web:
www.morgantechnicalceramics.com
SIC: 3251 Brick and structural clay tile
HQ: Morgan Advanced Ceramics, Inc.
    2425 Whipple Rd
    Hayward CA 94544

(G-14530)
MRPC NORTHEAST LLC
Also Called: Johnson Precision
12 Executive Dr (03051-4939)
PHONE.................................603 880-3616
Greg Riemer, *Managing Member*
▲ EMP: 33 EST: 2001
SALES (est): 11.32MM
SALES (corp-wide): 28MM Privately Held
Web: www.jpi-plastics.com
SIC: 3089 3544 Injection molding of plastics
    ; Forms (molds), for foundry and plastics
    working machinery
PA: Molded Rubber & Plastic Corporation
    13161 W Glendale Ave
    Butler WI 53007
    262 781-7122

(G-14531)
NASHUA FABRICATION CO INC
7 Security Dr (03051-5246)
PHONE.................................603 889-2181
Micheal Bernazani, *Pr*
Henry Bernazani, *VP*
Jane Noyes, *Treas*
Jeffrey H Mazerolle, *Sec*
EMP: 27 EST: 1973
SQ FT: 20,000
SALES (est): 973.83K Privately Held
Web: www.nashuafab.com
SIC: 3444 3713 Sheet metal specialties, not
    stamped; Truck and bus bodies

(G-14532)
NORTHROP GRUMMAN SYSTEMS CORP
6 Chagnon Ln (03051-3432)
PHONE.................................603 886-4270
Linda Philcrantz, *Brnch Mgr*
EMP: 7
Web: www.northropgrumman.com
SIC: 3812 8748 Search and navigation
    equipment; Communications consulting
HQ: Northrop Grumman Systems
    Corporation
    2980 Fairview Park Dr
    Falls Church VA 22042
    703 280-2900

(G-14533)
OMNI COMPONENTS CORP (HQ)
46 River Rd Ste 1 (03051-5239)
PHONE.................................603 882-4467
William Holka, *Pr*

David A Holka, *
Frank Stone, *
Larry Cuneo, *
EMP: 138 EST: 1978
SQ FT: 37,000
SALES (est): 33.39MM
SALES (corp-wide): 138.57MM Privately
Held
Web: www.vantedgemedical.com
SIC: 3451 3599 Screw machine products;
    Machine and other job shop work
PA: Vander-Bend Manufacturing, Inc.
    2701 Orchard Pkwy
    San Jose CA 95134
    408 245-5150

(G-14534)
PARKER-HANNIFIN CORPORATION
Also Called: Chomerics Division
16 Flagstone Dr (03051-4904)
PHONE.................................603 880-4807
David Hill, *Brnch Mgr*
EMP: 187
SQ FT: 25,000
SALES (corp-wide): 19.07B Publicly Held
Web: www.parker.com
SIC: 3479 Coating of metals with plastic or
    resins
PA: Parker-Hannifin Corporation
    6035 Parkland Blvd
    Cleveland OH 44124
    216 896-3000

(G-14535)
PNEUTEK INC
17 Friars Dr Ste D (03051-4926)
PHONE.................................603 883-1660
Harry M Haytayan, *Pr*
◆ EMP: 10 EST: 1974
SQ FT: 45,000
SALES (est): 1.74MM Privately Held
Web: www.pneutek.com
SIC: 3546 Power-driven handtools

(G-14536)
PRINCETON TECHNOLOGY CORP
33 Constitution Dr (03051-3986)
PHONE.................................603 595-1987
EMP: 88
Web: www.princetontech.com
SIC: 3672 3679 Printed circuit boards;
    Electronic circuits

(G-14537)
PROTO PART INC
71 Pine Rd Unit F (03051-5322)
PHONE.................................603 883-6531
Kendall Roche, *Pr*
EMP: 15 EST: 1988
SQ FT: 12,000
SALES (est): 1.47MM Privately Held
Web:
www.production-tooling-and-parts.com
SIC: 3089 Injection molding of plastics

(G-14538)
R S MACHINE INC
315 Derry Rd Ste 11 (03051-3051)
PHONE.................................603 880-3177
Eugene Stahl, *Pr*
Diana Stahl, *VP*
EMP: 8 EST: 1985
SQ FT: 6,000
SALES (est): 770K Privately Held
SIC: 3599 Machine shop, jobbing and repair

(G-14539)
RDF CORPORATION
Also Called: RDF
23 Elm Ave (03051-3224)
PHONE.................................603 882-5195
Naresh Puri, *Pr*
Lea Wang, *
EMP: 69 EST: 1955
SQ FT: 16,000
SALES (est): 11.85MM Privately Held
Web: www.rdfcorp.com
SIC: 3829 Measuring and controlling
    devices, nec

(G-14540)
REEDS FERRY SMALL BUILDINGS
3 Tracy Ln (03051-3031)
PHONE.................................603 883-1362
Timothy G Carleton, *Pr*
Steven Carleton, *
EMP: 62 EST: 1959
SALES (est): 8.82MM Privately Held
Web: www.reedsferry.com
SIC: 2452 Prefabricated buildings, wood

(G-14541)
RF LOGIC LLC
21 Park Ave (03051-3985)
PHONE.................................603 578-9876
Phil Lausier, *Managing Member*
EMP: 43 EST: 1998
SQ FT: 20,000
SALES (est): 7.36MM Privately Held
Web: www.rflogic.net
SIC: 3679 Delay lines

(G-14542)
ROBINSON PRECISION TOOL CORP
315 Derry Rd Ste 15 (03051-3051)
PHONE.................................603 889-1625
Dana Robinson, *Pr*
EMP: 10 EST: 1987
SQ FT: 3,000
SALES (est): 738.31K Privately Held
SIC: 3599 Machine shop, jobbing and repair

(G-14543)
S L CHASSE WELDING & FABG INC
Also Called: SL Chasse Steel
8 Christine Dr (03051-3026)
PHONE.................................603 886-3436
Stephen Chasse, *Pr*
Stephen L Chasse, *
EMP: 60 EST: 1989
SQ FT: 20,000
SALES (est): 32.12MM Privately Held
Web: www.slchassesteelfab.com
SIC: 1799 3446 7692 3441 Welding on site;
    Stairs, staircases, stair treads:
    prefabricated metal; Welding repair;
    Fabricated structural metal

(G-14544)
SCHUL INTERNATIONAL CO LLC
Also Called: Willseal
34 Executive Dr (03051-4919)
PHONE.................................603 889-6872
▲ EMP: 15 EST: 2002
SQ FT: 17,500
SALES (est): 3.06MM
SALES (corp-wide): 7.26B Publicly Held
Web: www.schul.co
SIC: 2891 Epoxy adhesives
HQ: Tremco Cpg Inc.
    3735 Green Rd

Beachwood OH 44122
216 292-5000

(G-14545)
SEMIKRON INC (HQ)
11 Executive Dr (03051-4914)
P.O. Box 66 (03051-0066)
PHONE.................................603 883-8102
Thomas O'reilley, *Pr*
Ronald A Lague, *
▲ EMP: 38 EST: 1975
SQ FT: 54,000
SALES (est): 19.92MM
SALES (corp-wide): 546.2MM Privately
Held
Web: www.semikron-danfoss.com
SIC: 3674 Semiconductors and related
    devices
PA: Semikron International Dr. Fritz Martin
    Gmbh & Co. Kg
    Sigmundstr. 200
    Nurnberg BY 90431
    91165590

(G-14546)
SONIC MANUFACTURING CO INC
35 Sagamore Park Rd (03051-4915)
PHONE.................................603 882-1020
Thomas Glasheen Senior, *Prin*
EMP: 26 EST: 2011
SALES (est): 2.51MM Privately Held
SIC: 3672 Printed circuit boards

(G-14547)
SOUTHEASTERN CONTAINER INC
36 Executive Dr (03051-4942)
P.O. Box 909 (28728-0909)
PHONE.................................603 324-1204
Thomas Francis, *Ch Bd*
EMP: 31
SALES (corp-wide): 319.93MM Privately
Held
Web: www.secontainer.com
SIC: 3085 Plastics bottles
PA: Southeastern Container, Inc.
    1250 Sand Hill Rd
    Enka NC 28728
    828 350-7200

(G-14548)
SPARTON TECHNOLOGY CORP
8 Hampshire Dr (03051-4921)
PHONE.................................603 880-3692
Victor Breton, *Pr*
Steven Breton, *
Michael S Breton, *
▲ EMP: 75 EST: 1972
SQ FT: 80,000
SALES (est): 10.12MM Privately Held
Web: www.sparton.biz
SIC: 3599 3444 Machine shop, jobbing and
    repair; Sheet metalwork

(G-14549)
SUPERIOR SHEET METAL LLC
14 Flagstone Dr (03051-4904)
PHONE.................................866 468-3828
EMP: 22 EST: 2003
SALES (est): 3.72MM Privately Held
Web: www.superiorsm.com
SIC: 3444 Sheet metalwork

(G-14550)
TECHNICAL MACHINE COMPONENTS
4 Security Dr (03051-5246)
PHONE.................................603 880-0444

Kevin Gervais, *Pr*
Gary Mcniff, *Sec*
EMP: 15 **EST:** 1985
SQ FT: 10,000
SALES (est): 381.33K **Privately Held**
Web: www.technicalmachine.com
SIC: 3599 3444　Machine shop, jobbing and repair; Sheet metalwork

(G-14551)
TELEDYNE FLIR LLC
110 Lowell Rd (03051-4806)
PHONE.............................603 324-7783
Lisa West Kerblom, *Brnch Mgr*
EMP: 44
SALES (corp-wide): 5.46B **Publicly Held**
Web: www.infraredtraining.com
SIC: 3826　Analytical instruments
HQ: Teledyne Flir, Llc
　　27700 Sw Parkway Ave
　　Wilsonville OR 97070
　　503 498-3547

(G-14552)
TELEDYNE FLIR COML SYSTEMS INC
110 Lowell Rd (03051-4806)
PHONE.............................603 324-7824
Tom Scanllan, *Brnch Mgr*
EMP: 200
SALES (corp-wide): 5.46B **Publicly Held**
Web: www.flir.com
SIC: 3826　Analytical instruments
HQ: Teledyne Flir Commercial Systems, Inc.
　　6769 Hollister Ave
　　Goleta CA 93117

(G-14553)
TELEDYNE INSTRS LEEMAN LABS
110 Lowell Rd (03051-4806)
PHONE.............................603 521-3299
Peter G Brown, *Genl Mgr*
EMP: 70 **EST:** 2005
SALES (est): 11.63MM
SALES (corp-wide): 5.46B **Publicly Held**
SIC: 3826　Analytical instruments
PA: Teledyne Technologies Inc
　　1049 Camino Dos Rios
　　Thousand Oaks CA 91360
　　805 373-4545

(G-14554)
TELEDYNE INSTRUMENTS INC
Teledyne Tekmar
110 Lowell Rd (03051-4806)
PHONE.............................603 886-8400
EMP: 65
SALES (corp-wide): 5.46B **Publicly Held**
Web: www.teledyne.com
SIC: 3826　Spectrometers
HQ: Teledyne Instruments, Inc.
　　16830 Chestnut St
　　City Of Industry CA 91748
　　626 934-1500

(G-14555)
TELEDYNE TEKMAR COMPANY INC
Also Called: Teledyne Leeman Labs
110 Lowell Rd (03051-4806)
PHONE.............................603 886-8400
EMP: 65
SIC: 3826　Spectrometers

(G-14556)
TNT PRECISION LLC
Also Called: TNT Precision
315 Derry Rd Ste 14 (03051-3051)

PHONE.............................603 595-6813
Dennis Thompson, *Owner*
EMP: 8 **EST:** 2000
SALES (est): 767.97K **Privately Held**
Web: www.tntprecision.com
SIC: 3599　Machine shop, jobbing and repair

(G-14557)
VARITRON TECHNOLOGIES USA INC
Also Called: Varitron Hudson
12 Executive Dr Ste 2 (03051-4939)
PHONE.............................603 577-8855
Michel Farley, *Pr*
Jonathan Saunders, *VP*
EMP: 40 **EST:** 2003
SQ FT: 15,000
SALES (est): 8.7MM **Privately Held**
Web: www.ewmfg.com
SIC: 3672　Printed circuit boards

(G-14558)
VECTRONICS MICROWAVE CORP (PA)
Also Called: Stealth Microwave
267 Lowell Rd # 101 (03051-4937)
PHONE.............................973 244-1040
David Robins, *Prin*
Dave Robbins, *Sr VP*
Donna Hillsgrove, *Sec*
Diane Bourque, *CEO*
Robert Delitta, *Prin*
EMP: 46 **EST:** 1970
SALES (est): 8.55MM
SALES (corp-wide): 8.55MM **Privately Held**
SIC: 3679　Electronic circuits

(G-14559)
W K HILLQUIST INC
Also Called: W. K. Hillquist
37 Executive Dr (03051-4903)
PHONE.............................603 595-7790
Warren K Hillquist, *Pr*
Michael Torpey, *
▲ **EMP:** 50 **EST:** 1969
SQ FT: 36,000
SALES (est): 4.55MM **Privately Held**
Web: www.wkhillquist.com
SIC: 3089　Injection molded finished plastics products, nec

(G-14560)
WIKOFF COLOR CORPORATION
4 Hampshire Dr (03051-4921)
PHONE.............................603 864-6456
Ryan Lomme, *Brnch Mgr*
EMP: 10
SALES (corp-wide): 156.45MM **Privately Held**
Web: www.wikoff.com
SIC: 2893　Printing ink
PA: Wikoff Color Corporation
　　1886 Merritt Rd
　　Fort Mill SC 29715
　　803 548-2210

Intervale
Carroll County

(G-14561)
RAGGED MOUNTAIN EQUIPMENT INC
Also Called: Ragged Mountain Equipment
279 Nh Route 16 And 302 (03845-6338)
P.O. Box 130 (03845-0130)
PHONE.............................603 356-3042
Robert D Nadler, *Pr*

Cort Hansen, *
Kenneth R Cargill, *
EMP: 24 **EST:** 1985
SQ FT: 15,000
SALES (est): 3.37MM **Privately Held**
Web: www.raggedmountain.com
SIC: 5941 3949 5949 5641　Camping and backpacking equipment; Sporting and athletic goods, nec; Fabric, remnants; Children's wear

Jackson
Carroll County

(G-14562)
JACKSON SIGNSMITH
Rte 16 (03846)
P.O. Box 368 (03846-0368)
PHONE.............................603 383-8900
Eben Moss, *Prin*
EMP: 7 **EST:** 2001
SALES (est): 138.8K **Privately Held**
Web: www.islandtimeeleu.com
SIC: 3993　Signs, not made in custom sign painting shops

Jaffrey
Cheshire County

(G-14563)
APOLLO STEEL LLC
35 Maria Dr (03452-5903)
PHONE.............................603 532-1156
EMP: 18
SALES (est): 2.05MM **Privately Held**
Web: www.apollosteelllc.com
SIC: 3441　Fabricated structural metal

(G-14564)
ATLAS PYRVSION ENTRMT GROUP IN (PA)
Also Called: Atlas Advanced Pyrotechnics
136 Old Sharon Rd (03452-5854)
P.O. Box 498 (03452-0498)
PHONE.............................603 532-8324
Stephen Pelkey, *Pr*
Matthew Shea, *VP*
Sarah Bregeron, *Pr*
EMP: 33 **EST:** 2014
SALES (est): 12.75MM
SALES (corp-wide): 12.75MM **Privately Held**
Web: boom.liveevents.com
SIC: 2899　Fireworks

(G-14565)
D D BEAN & SONS CO (PA)
207 Peterborough St (03452-5868)
P.O. Box 348 (03452-0348)
PHONE.............................603 532-8311
TOLL FREE: 800
Delcie David Bean, *Pr*
Mark Crane Bean, *
Christopher Vernon Bean, *
◆ **EMP:** 122 **EST:** 1938
SQ FT: 70,000
SALES (est): 21.95MM
SALES (corp-wide): 21.95MM **Privately Held**
Web: www.ddbean.com
SIC: 3999　Matches and match books

(G-14566)
DAVID R GODINE PUBLISHER INC
426 Nutting Rd (03452-5745)
P.O. Box 450 (03452-0450)

PHONE.............................603 532-4100
David R Godine, *Pr*
EMP: 8
SALES (corp-wide): 2.2MM **Privately Held**
Web: www.godine.com
SIC: 2741　Miscellaneous publishing
PA: David R. Godine, Publisher, Inc.
　　15 Court Sq Ste 320
　　Boston MA 02108
　　617 451-9600

(G-14567)
EMD MILLIPORE CORPORATION
11 Prescott Rd (03452-6636)
PHONE.............................603 532-8711
Grace Mcglynn, *Mgr*
EMP: 400
SALES (corp-wide): 23.09B **Privately Held**
Web: www.millipore.com
SIC: 3826　Analytical instruments
HQ: Emd Millipore Corporation
　　400 Summit Dr
　　Burlington MA 01803
　　800 645-5476

(G-14568)
GRAPHICAST INC
36 Knight St (03452-5833)
P.O. Box 430 (03452-0430)
PHONE.............................603 532-4481
Walter A Zanchuk, *Pr*
Norma Milne, *
▼ **EMP:** 30 **EST:** 1978
SQ FT: 13,200
SALES (est): 4.87MM **Privately Held**
Web: www.graphicast.com
SIC: 3369　Zinc and zinc-base alloy castings, except die-castings

(G-14569)
JOHNSON ABRASIVES CO INC
49 Fitzgerald Dr (03452-6615)
PHONE.............................603 532-4434
Kelly Bye, *CEO*
◆ **EMP:** 30 **EST:** 1971
SQ FT: 4,000
SALES (est): 5.09MM
SALES (corp-wide): 109.59MM **Privately Held**
Web: www.johnsonabrasives.com
SIC: 3291　Abrasive products
HQ: Virginia Abrasives Corporation
　　2851 Service Rd
　　Petersburg VA 23805
　　804 732-0058

(G-14570)
KING MANUFACTURING CO INC
295 Squantum Rd (03452-6654)
PHONE.............................603 532-6455
William Stewart, *Pr*
Donald Stewart, *VP*
Joseph Hoppock, *Sec*
EMP: 17 **EST:** 1955
SQ FT: 25,000
SALES (est): 342.08K **Privately Held**
SIC: 3315　Staples, steel: wire or cut

(G-14571)
LGNTCS OF ENGLAND
141 Old Sharon Rd (03452-5850)
PHONE.............................603 532-4666
Amanda Brosseau, *Prin*
EMP: 17 **EST:** 2018
SALES (est): 879.29K **Privately Held**
SIC: 2448　Pallets, wood

(G-14572)
LIGNETICS NEW ENGLAND INC
415 Squantum Rd (03452-6655)

PHONE..............................603 532-4666
EMP: 30
Web: www.lignetics.com
SIC: 2448 Pallets, wood
HQ: Lignetics Of New England, Inc.
1075 E S Boulder Rd
Louisville CO 80027
303 802-5400

(G-14573)
LIGNETICS NEW ENGLAND INC
141 Old Sharon Rd (03452-5850)
PHONE..............................603 532-4666
Joe Powers, *Manager*
EMP: 15
Web: www.lignetics.com
SIC: 2499 Laundry products, wood
HQ: Lignetics Of New England, Inc.
1075 E S Boulder Rd
Louisville CO 80027
303 802-5400

(G-14574)
MDI EAST INC
81 Turnpike Rd (03452-6669)
PHONE..............................603 532-5656
Thomas Coneys, *Brnch Mgr*
EMP: 35
SALES (corp-wide): 61.99MM Privately Held
Web: www.moldeddevices.com
SIC: 3841 Surgical instruments and apparatus
HQ: Mdi East, Inc.
740 W Knox Rd
Tempe AZ 85284
951 509-6918

(G-14575)
NEW ENGLAND WOOD PELLET LLC
415 Squantum Rd (03452-6655)
P.O. Box 532 (03452-0532)
PHONE..............................603 532-4666
▲ **EMP:** 30
SIC: 2448 Pallets, wood

(G-14576)
PRECISION TEMPERATURE CONTROL
24 Saw Mill Dr (03452-5947)
PHONE..............................603 471-9023
Gene Hennessy, *Pr*
Gene Hennessy Prestreas, *Prin*
Kathleen Hennessy, *VP*
EMP: 9 **EST:** 1985
SALES (est): 980.63K Privately Held
Web: www.precisiontempcontrol.com
SIC: 3585 Refrigeration and heating equipment

(G-14577)
PUZZLE HOUSE
426 Nutting Rd (03452-5745)
P.O. Box 454 (03458-0454)
PHONE..............................603 532-4442
Sarah Kurzon, *Owner*
▲ **EMP:** 10 **EST:** 1972
SALES (est): 399.52K Privately Held
Web: www.puzzlehouse.com
SIC: 3944 Puzzles

(G-14578)
RADENHAUSEN & ONEILL INC
Also Called: R & O
32 Fitzgerald Dr Ste 6 (03452-6616)
P.O. Box 330 (03452-0330)
PHONE..............................603 532-4879
Lou Radenhausen, *Pr*

Brian O'neill, *Sec*
EMP: 40 **EST:** 1983
SQ FT: 1,600
SALES (est): 3.62MM Privately Held
Web: www.rowelding.net
SIC: 1799 7692 Welding on site; Welding repair

(G-14579)
SAVRON GRAPHICS INC (PA)
4 Stratton Rd (03452-6663)
P.O. Box 250 (03452-0250)
PHONE..............................603 532-7726
Gregory R Lawn, *Pr*
Selma Lawn, *VP*
Jeffrey Crocker, *Sec*
EMP: 7 **EST:** 1967
SQ FT: 3,000
SALES (est): 974.92K
SALES (corp-wide): 974.92K Privately Held
Web: www.savron.com
SIC: 2752 5112 Offset printing; Stationery and office supplies

(G-14580)
TELEFLEX INCORPORATED
Teleflex
50 Plantation Dr (03452-6631)
PHONE..............................603 532-7706
Fred Preiss, *VP*
EMP: 73
SALES (corp-wide): 2.79B Publicly Held
Web: www.teleflex.com
SIC: 3599 3841 3083 3082 Flexible metal hose, tubing, and bellows; Surgical and medical instruments; Laminated plastics plate and sheet; Unsupported plastics profile shapes
PA: Teleflex Incorporated
550 E Swedesford Rd # 400
Wayne PA 19087
610 225-6800

(G-14581)
TFX MEDICAL INCORPORATED
50 Plantation Dr (03452-6631)
PHONE..............................603 532-7706
R Ernest Waaser, *Pr*
C Jeffrey Jacobs, *
Cynthia Sharo, *
Kevin K Gordon, *
EMP: 86 **EST:** 1979
SQ FT: 60,000
SALES (est): 9.54MM
SALES (corp-wide): 2.79B Publicly Held
Web: www.teleflexmedicaloem.com
SIC: 3599 3841 3083 3082 Flexible metal hose, tubing, and bellows; Surgical and medical instruments; Laminated plastics plate and sheet; Unsupported plastics profile shapes
PA: Teleflex Incorporated
550 E Swedesford Rd # 400
Wayne PA 19087
610 225-6800

(G-14582)
WEIDNER SERVICES LLC
5 Saw Mill Dr (03452-5946)
P.O. Box 752 (03461-0752)
PHONE..............................603 532-4833
Maureen Reider, *Prin*
EMP: 9 **EST:** 2013
SALES (est): 494.05K Privately Held
Web: www.weidnerservices.com
SIC: 7692 Welding repair

Jefferson
Coos County

(G-14583)
CAMERON SEALCOATING LLC
115 Couture Rd (03583-6714)
PHONE..............................603 586-7945
EMP: 10 **EST:** 2012
SALES (est): 225.81K Privately Held
SIC: 2952 Asphalt felts and coatings

(G-14584)
INGERSON TRANSPORTATION
36 Alderbrook Dr (03583-6533)
PHONE..............................603 586-4335
Douglas Ingerson, *Pt*
Mitchell Ingerson, *Pt*
EMP: 9 **EST:** 1984
SALES (est): 796.2K Privately Held
SIC: 2499 Mulch, wood and bark

(G-14585)
SDS LOGGING INC
180 Presidential Hwy (03583-6730)
PHONE..............................603 586-7098
EMP: 20
SALES (corp-wide): 527.12K Privately Held
SIC: 2411 Logging camps and contractors
PA: S.D.S. Logging, Inc.
Whitefield NH 03598
603 481-0208

(G-14586)
TREELINE TIMBER
11 Nevers Ln (03583-6800)
PHONE..............................603 586-7725
Craig Crukay, *Owner*
EMP: 8 **EST:** 2000
SALES (est): 541.18K Privately Held
SIC: 2411 Logging

(G-14587)
WATERWHEEL BREAKFAST GIFT HSE
1955 Presidential Hwy (03583-6208)
PHONE..............................603 586-4313
Kevin Arakelian, *Owner*
Patricia Arakelian, *Mgr*
EMP: 8 **EST:** 1999
SALES (est): 247.97K Privately Held
Web: www.waterwheelnh.com
SIC: 5812 5947 2099 Restaurant, family: independent; Gift, novelty, and souvenir shop; Food preparations, nec

Keene
Cheshire County

(G-14588)
AMETEK PRECITECH INC (HQ)
44 Black Brook Rd (03431-5044)
PHONE..............................603 357-2510
Bruce P Wilson, *Pr*
Dan Johnson, *
Kathryn E Sena, *
William J Burke, *
Daniel W Lawrence, *
▲ **EMP:** 97 **EST:** 1962
SQ FT: 63,000
SALES (est): 19.54MM
SALES (corp-wide): 6.15B Publicly Held
Web: www.precitech.com

SIC: 3552 3545 3827 3568 Spindles, textile; Precision tools, machinists'; Optical instruments and lenses; Power transmission equipment, nec
PA: Ametek, Inc.
1100 Cassatt Rd
Berwyn PA 19312
610 647-2121

(G-14589)
BEEZE TEES LLC
117 Main St (03431-3775)
PHONE..............................603 357-1400
EMP: 8 **EST:** 2019
SALES (est): 488.97K Privately Held
Web: www.beezetees.com
SIC: 2759 Screen printing

(G-14590)
BELDEN INC
Also Called: Mark Belden
20 Forest St (03431-2946)
PHONE..............................603 359-7355
EMP: 9
SALES (corp-wide): 2.51B Publicly Held
Web: www.belden.com
SIC: 3357 Nonferrous wiredrawing and insulating
PA: Belden Inc.
1 N Brentwood Blvd Fl 15
Saint Louis MO 63105
314 854-8000

(G-14591)
BORTECH CORPORATION
66 Victoria St (03431-4212)
PHONE..............................603 358-4030
Leo White, *Pr*
EMP: 10 **EST:** 2002
SQ FT: 10,000
SALES (est): 1.13MM Privately Held
Web: www.climaxportable.com
SIC: 3548 Welding apparatus

(G-14592)
CONNELL COMMUNICATIONS INC
155 Washington St (03431-3131)
PHONE..............................603 924-7271
T James Connell, *Pr*
EMP: 56 **EST:** 1987
SALES (est): 12.31MM
SALES (corp-wide): 8.52B Publicly Held
SIC: 2721 2741 Trade journals: publishing only, not printed on site; Miscellaneous publishing
HQ: Idg Communications, Inc.
140 Kendrick St Ste A110
Needham MA 02494
508 872-8200

(G-14593)
CONTOUR FINE TOOLING INC
310 Marlboro St Ste 121 (03431-4118)
PHONE..............................603 876-4908
John Smith Ruddick, *Pr*
Jeffrey Tomlin, *VP*
EMP: 9 **EST:** 1987
SQ FT: 3,000
SALES (est): 662.51K Privately Held
Web: www.contour-diamonds.com
SIC: 7699 5049 3827 3545 Optical instrument repair; Optical goods; Optical instruments and lenses; Machine tool accessories

(G-14594)
CORNING INCORPORATED
Corning
69 Island St Ste T (03431-3507)

PHONE..........................603 357-7662
Kevan Taylor, *Brnch Mgr*
EMP: 120
SALES (corp-wide): 14.19B **Publicly Held**
Web: www.corning.com
SIC: 3229   Pressed and blown glass, nec
PA: Corning Incorporated
1 Riverfront Plz
Corning NY 14831
607 974-9000

(G-14595)
DEBRA RIVEST LTD
222 West St Unit 46 (03431-2456)
PHONE..........................603 355-3335
Debra Rivest, *Pr*
EMP: 50 **EST:** 1995
SALES (est): 2.35MM **Privately Held**
Web: www.elmcitybrewing.com
SIC: 5813 5812 2082   Tavern (drinking
places); American restaurant; Beer
(alcoholic beverage)

(G-14596)
E-Z CRETE LLC
502 Winchester St (03431-3918)
PHONE..........................603 313-6462
Brice Raynor, *Prin*
EMP: 14 **EST:** 2009
SALES (est): 726.9K **Privately Held**
SIC: 3272   Concrete products, nec

(G-14597)
**ELECTRONIC IMAGING MTLS
INC**
20 Forge St (03431-5038)
PHONE..........................603 357-1459
Alex Henkel, *Pr*
Heather Bell,   *
Rand Burnett,   *
EMP: 40 **EST:** 1987
SQ FT: 20,000
SALES (est): 6.77MM **Privately Held**
Web: www.barcode-labels.com
SIC: 2759 2672   Labels and seals: printing,
nsk; Adhesive papers, labels, or tapes:
from purchased material

(G-14598)
EVS NEW HAMPSHIRE INC
Also Called: Holden
50 Optical Ave (03431-4319)
PHONE..........................603 352-3000
Scott Berkowitz, *Pr*
Lisa Carlson,   *
EMP: 75 **EST:** 2008
SQ FT: 30,000
SALES (est): 10.15MM
SALES (corp-wide): 21.97MM **Privately
Held**
Web: www.evsmetal.com
SIC: 3444   Sheet metalwork
PA: Electronic Visions Systems Inc
1 Kenner Ct
Riverdale NJ 07457
973 839-4432

(G-14599)
**FILTRINE MANUFACTURING CO
INC**
Also Called: Filtrine
15 Kit St (03431-5911)
PHONE..........................603 352-5500
C Turner Hansel, *Pr*
John Hansel, *Ch*
Peter Hansel, *Pr*
Turner Hansel, *VP*
Charles Hansel, *VP*
▼ **EMP:** 80 **EST:** 1901
SALES (est): 12.94MM **Privately Held**

Web: www.filtrine.com
SIC: 3585 3589   Condensers, refrigeration;
Water purification equipment, household
type

(G-14600)
**GEMINI FIRFIELD
SCREENPRINTING**
Also Called: Gemini Fairfield Screenprint
294 West St Ste 4 (03431-2400)
PHONE..........................603 357-3847
Steve Myre, *Pr*
Ronald Rzasa, *VP*
EMP: 7 **EST:** 1981
SALES (est): 550K **Privately Held**
SIC: 2759   Screen printing

(G-14601)
**GOOCH & HOUSEGO (KEENE)
LLC**
Also Called: G&H Keene
17a Bradco St (03431-3900)
PHONE..........................603 358-5577
Stephanie Diaz, *Managing Member*
EMP: 30 **EST:** 2005
SQ FT: 12,800
SALES (est): 6.46MM
SALES (corp-wide): 187.38MM **Privately
Held**
Web: www.stingrayoptics.com
SIC: 3827   Optical instruments and lenses
PA: Gooch & Housego Plc
Dowlish Ford
Ilminster TA19
146 025-6440

(G-14602)
GS PRECISION LLC-KEENE DIV
18 Bradco St (03431-3996)
PHONE..........................603 355-1166
Claus Knappe, *Ch*
Ray Anderson,   *
Edward Hewey,   *
EMP: 90 **EST:** 1983
SQ FT: 65,000
SALES (est): 17.6MM
SALES (corp-wide): 105.24MM **Privately
Held**
Web: www.gsprecision.com
SIC: 3599   Machine shop, jobbing and repair
PA: G. S. Precision, Inc.
101 John Seitz Dr
Brattleboro VT 05301
802 257-5200

(G-14603)
JANOS TECHNOLOGY INC
55 Black Brook Rd (03431-5044)
PHONE..........................603 757-0070
EMP: 11 **EST:** 2015
SALES (est): 1.64MM **Privately Held**
Web: www.janostech.com
SIC: 3827   Optical instruments and lenses

(G-14604)
JANOS TECHNOLOGY LLC (DH)
55 Black Brook Rd (03431-5044)
PHONE..........................603 757-0070
Marc Trembly, *Pr*
◆ **EMP:** 90 **EST:** 1970
SQ FT: 35,000
SALES (est): 25.26MM
SALES (corp-wide): 5.83B **Publicly Held**
Web: www.janostech.com
SIC: 3827   Lenses, optical: all types except
ophthalmic
HQ: Fluke Electronics Corporation
6920 Seaway Blvd
Everett WA 98203
425 347-6100

(G-14605)
KEEBOWIL INC (PA)
Also Called: Solar Source
353 West St (03431-2442)
P.O. Box 523 (03431-0523)
PHONE..........................603 352-4232
Robert W Therrien, *Pr*
Robert W Therrien, *Pr*
Alex Kossakoski,   *
Beverly G Therrien,   *
EMP: 43 **EST:** 1932
SQ FT: 35,000
SALES (est): 21.74MM
SALES (corp-wide): 21.74MM **Privately
Held**
Web: www.melanson.com
SIC: 3444 1761   Sheet metalwork; Roofing
contractor

(G-14606)
**KEENE PUBLISHING
CORPORATION**
Also Called: Keene Sentinel
60 West St (03431-3373)
P.O. Box 546 (03431-0546)
PHONE..........................603 352-1234
Terrence L Williams, *Pr*
Thomas Ewing, *Dir*
EMP: 100 **EST:** 1992
SQ FT: 22,800
SALES (est): 14.15MM **Privately Held**
Web: www.sentinelsource.com
SIC: 2711   Commercial printing and
newspaper publishing combined

(G-14607)
**MARKEM-IMAJE CORPORATION
(HQ)**
150 Congress St (03431-4307)
P.O. Box 2100 (03431-7100)
PHONE..........................603 352-1130
▲ **EMP:** 500 **EST:** 1928
SALES (est): 413.61MM
SALES (corp-wide): 8.44B **Publicly Held**
Web: www.markem-imaje.com
SIC: 2893   Printing ink
PA: Dover Corporation
3005 Highland Pkwy # 200
Downers Grove IL 60515
630 541-1540

(G-14608)
MILLWORK MASTERS LTD (PA)
69 Island St Ste B (03431-3507)
PHONE..........................603 358-3038
TOLL FREE: 800
EMP: 12 **EST:** 1995
SQ FT: 4,980
SALES (est): 1.19MM **Privately Held**
Web: www.woodburysupply.com
SIC: 2431 5031 5211   Millwork; Lumber,
plywood, and millwork; Door and window
products

(G-14609)
MILTRONICS MFG SVCS INC
95 Krif Rd (03431-4718)
PHONE..........................603 352-3333
Anton M Neary, *Pr*
Elisabeth G R Neary, *Sec*
Matthew W Neary, *Department Director*
Jim Fischer, *VP*
EMP: 15 **EST:** 1989
SQ FT: 10,000
SALES (est): 4.23MM **Privately Held**
Web: www.miltronics.com
SIC: 3679   Electronic circuits

(G-14610)
MOUNTAIN CORPORATION (HQ)
59 Optical Ave (03431-4320)
P.O. Box 125 (33929-0125)
PHONE..........................603 355-2272
Kenny Ballard, *CEO*
Michael Krinsky,   *
▼ **EMP:** 46 **EST:** 1998
SQ FT: 100,000
SALES (est): 7.31MM **Publicly Held**
Web: www.themountain.com
SIC: 2253 5961   T-shirts and tops, knit;
Electronic shopping
PA: Gladstone Investment Corp
1521 Westbranch Dr # 100
Mc Lean VA 22102

(G-14611)
MPB CORPORATION (HQ)
Also Called: Timken Super Precision
7 Optical Ave (03431-4348)
P.O. Box 607 (03431-0607)
PHONE..........................603 352-0310
Erik Paulhardt, *Pr*
Phillip Fracassa,   *
John Ted Mihaila,   *
Scott Scherff,   *
▲ **EMP:** 125 **EST:** 1941
SQ FT: 178,800
SALES (est): 260.14MM
SALES (corp-wide): 4.5B **Publicly Held**
Web: www.timken.com
SIC: 3562 6061   Ball bearings and parts;
Federal credit unions
PA: The Timken Company
4500 Mount Pleasant St Nw
North Canton OH 44720
234 262-3000

(G-14612)
MULTI-MED INC
26 Victoria Ct (03431-4218)
PHONE..........................603 357-8733
Alan Reid, *Pr*
L Ernest Reid,   *
EMP: 15 **EST:** 1988
SALES (est): 780.18K **Privately Held**
Web: www.multimedinc.com
SIC: 3841   Surgical and medical instruments

(G-14613)
NEW HAMPSHIRE FORGE INC
15 Forge St (03431-5037)
P.O. Box 423 (03431-0423)
PHONE..........................603 357-5692
J Robert Hof, *Pr*
Pamela Hof,   *
Stephen Bragdon,   *
Phillip Hof,   *
◆ **EMP:** 25 **EST:** 1980
SQ FT: 5,000
SALES (est): 2.04MM **Privately Held**
Web: www.nhforge.com
SIC: 3462   Iron and steel forgings

(G-14614)
OPTICAL FILTER CORPORATION
Also Called: Corning Netoptix
69 Island St (03431-3507)
PHONE..........................603 357-7662
EMP: 10000 **EST:** 1997
SALES (est): 174.69MM
SALES (corp-wide): 14.19B **Publicly Held**
SIC: 3827 3851 3826   Optical instruments
and lenses; Lens coating, ophthalmic;
Infrared analytical instruments
PA: Corning Incorporated
1 Riverfront Plz
Corning NY 14831
607 974-9000

(G-14615)
POSITIVE NEWS FOR YOU LLC
50 Woodburn St Apt 25 (03431-2508)
PHONE................................802 384-3993
Lee Robert, *Prin*
EMP: 7 **EST:** 2017
SALES (est): 75.13K **Privately Held**
Web: www.positivenewsforyou.com
SIC: 2741 Miscellaneous publishing

(G-14616)
RK PARISI ENTERPRISES INC
Also Called: Posh House
104 Emerald St (03431-3625)
PHONE................................844 438-7674
Robert Parisi, *Pr*
Krysta Parisi, *VP*
EMP: 10 **EST:** 2012
SQ FT: 40,000
SALES (est): 1.3MM **Privately Held**
Web: www.poshhaus.com
SIC: 5961 5063 3469 3431 Furniture and
furnishings, mail order; Lighting fixtures,
residential; Kitchen fixtures and equipment,
porcelain enameled; Bathroom fixtures,
including sinks

(G-14617)
**SAMSON MANUFACTURING
CORP**
32 Optical Ave (03431-4319)
PHONE................................603 355-3903
EMP: 24 **EST:** 2000
SQ FT: 10,000
SALES (est): 4.96MM **Privately Held**
Web: www.samson-mfg.com
SIC: 3469 Machine parts, stamped or
pressed metal

(G-14618)
SHAKOUR PUBLISHERS INC
Also Called: Monadnock Shopper News
445 West St (03431-2448)
P.O. Box 487 (03431-0487)
PHONE................................603 352-5250
Mitchell G Shakour, *Pr*
EMP: 18 **EST:** 1958
SQ FT: 2,000
SALES (est): 518.66K **Privately Held**
Web: www.shoppernews.com
SIC: 2711 Newspapers, publishing and
printing

(G-14619)
SIMS PORTEX INC
10 Bowman Dr (03431-5043)
P.O. Box 724 (03431-0724)
PHONE................................603 352-3812
John Beauregard, *Prin*
EMP: 8 **EST:** 2008
SALES (est): 151.91K **Privately Held**
SIC: 3841 Surgical and medical instruments

(G-14620)
SMITHS MEDICAL ASD INC
Production Ave (03431)
PHONE................................603 352-3812
Thomas Westra, *VP Fin*
EMP: 10
SALES (corp-wide): 2.28B **Publicly Held**
SIC: 3841 Surgical and medical instruments
HQ: Smiths Medical Asd, Inc.
6000 Nathan Ln N
Plymouth MN 55442
763 383-3000

(G-14621)
SMITHS MEDICAL ASD INC
10 Bowman Dr (03431-5036)

PHONE................................603 352-3812
Lynn Ziman, *Prin*
EMP: 65
SALES (corp-wide): 2.28B **Publicly Held**
SIC: 3841 Surgical and medical instruments
HQ: Smiths Medical Asd, Inc.
6000 Nathan Ln N
Plymouth MN 55442
763 383-3000

(G-14622)
SNF FINISHING LLC
32 Optical Ave (03431-4319)
PHONE................................603 355-3903
Scott W Samson, *Admn*
EMP: 8 **EST:** 2014
SALES (est): 317.64K **Privately Held**
Web: www.snffinishing.com
SIC: 3471 Electroplating of metals or
formed products

(G-14623)
SUNSET TOOL INC
58 Optical Ave (03431-4319)
P.O. Box 798 (03431-0798)
PHONE................................603 355-2246
Richard E Hall, *Pr*
Jane Hall, *VP*
EMP: 20 **EST:** 1980
SQ FT: 11,000
SALES (est): 1.67MM **Privately Held**
Web: www.sunsettoolinc.com
SIC: 3544 3469 3599 Special dies and tools
; Stamping metal for the trade; Machine
and other job shop work

(G-14624)
SURRY LICENSING LLC
7 Corporate Dr (03431-5042)
PHONE................................603 354-7000
EMP: 7 **EST:** 2003
SALES (est): 438.02K **Privately Held**
SIC: 2086 Bottled and canned soft drinks

(G-14625)
SWNH FIRE MUTUAL AID RADIO
350 Marlboro St (03431-4373)
PHONE................................603 352-8635
Dale Paquin, *Mgr*
EMP: 9 **EST:** 2007
SALES (est): 236.53K **Privately Held**
Web: www.firemutualaid.com
SIC: 3711 Fire department vehicles (motor
vehicles), assembly of

(G-14626)
**SYNERGY SPORTSWEAR INC
(PA)**
Also Called: Synergy
5 Main St (03431-3710)
PHONE................................603 352-8681
EMP: 8 **EST:** 1996
SQ FT: 8,400
SALES (est): 4.89MM **Privately Held**
Web: www.synergysportswear.com
SIC: 5651 2389 Unisex clothing stores;
Men's miscellaneous accessories

(G-14627)
TECTA AMERICA CORP
Also Called: Melanson Company, The
353 West St (03431-2442)
PHONE................................603 352-4232
EMP: 100
SALES (corp-wide): 823.93MM **Privately
Held**
Web: www.tectaamerica.com
SIC: 1761 3444 Roofing contractor; Sheet
metalwork
PA: Tecta America Corp.
9450 Bryn Mawr Ave

Rosemont IL 60018
847 581-3888

(G-14628)
WHITNEY BROS CO LLC
Also Called: Whitney Learning Materials
93 Railroad St (03431-3742)
P.O. Box 644 (03431-0644)
PHONE................................603 352-2610
David Stabler, *Pr*
Mike Jablonski, *
▲ **EMP:** 40 **EST:** 1904
SQ FT: 83,000
SALES (est): 6.07MM **Privately Held**
Web: www.whitneybros.com
SIC: 2531 2511 School furniture; Children's
wood furniture

Kensington
Rockingham County

(G-14629)
DAN DAILEY INC
Also Called: Dailey-Mc Neil
2 North Rd (03833-5605)
PHONE................................603 778-2303
Daniel Dailey, *Pr*
Linda Mc Neil, *Treas*
EMP: 10 **EST:** 1990
SALES (est): 604.96K **Privately Held**
Web: www.dandailey.com
SIC: 3231 Art glass: made from purchased
glass

(G-14630)
**FANARAS ELC & INDUS
CONTRLS**
89 Amesbury Rd (03833-5620)
PHONE................................603 772-3425
EMP: 7 **EST:** 1983
SQ FT: 2,240
SALES (est): 559.27K **Privately Held**
SIC: 1731 3613 Electrical work; Control
panels, electric

(G-14631)
**VIKING WLDG & FABRICATION
LLC**
Also Called: Viking Welding
243 Amesbury Rd Ste 1 (03833-5703)
PHONE................................603 394-7887
EMP: 8 **EST:** 2003
SALES (est): 1.03MM **Privately Held**
Web: www.vikingwelding.com
SIC: 3441 3732 Fabricated structural metal;
Boatbuilding and repairing

Kingston
Rockingham County

(G-14632)
**ADVANCED FABRICATING
MCHY INC**
65 Route 125 (03848-3533)
P.O. Box 3010 (03826-3010)
PHONE................................603 642-4906
Craig Van Sant, *Pr*
Robert Paul, *VP*
▲ **EMP:** 10 **EST:** 1995
SQ FT: 6,000
SALES (est): 1.07MM **Privately Held**
Web: www.advancedfab.com
SIC: 3599 Machine shop, jobbing and repair

(G-14633)
ARCHANGEL WOODWORKS INC
3 New Boston Rd (03848-3226)
PHONE................................603 347-5345
EMP: 8 **EST:** 2013
SALES (est): 137.45K **Privately Held**
SIC: 2431 Millwork

(G-14634)
**EAST COAST METAL WORKS
CO INC**
21 Route 125 Unit 2 (03848-3593)
PHONE................................603 642-9600
EMP: 7 **EST:** 1980
SALES (est): 927.25K **Privately Held**
Web: www.eastcoastmetalworks.net
SIC: 3441 1799 7692 3444 Fabricated
structural metal; Welding on site; Welding
repair; Sheet metalwork

(G-14635)
**FOREST NORTHLAND
PRODUCTS INC (PA)**
16 Church St (03848-3061)
P.O. Box 369 (03848-0369)
PHONE................................603 642-3665
▼ **EMP:** 30 **EST:** 1970
SALES (est): 13.68MM
SALES (corp-wide): 13.68MM **Privately
Held**
Web: www.northlandforest.com
SIC: 5031 2426 2421 Lumber: rough,
dressed, and finished; Hardwood
dimension and flooring mills; Sawmills and
planing mills, general

(G-14636)
MIKE MURPHY & SONS INC
57 Newton Junction Rd (03848-3524)
P.O. Box 152 (03811-0152)
PHONE................................603 362-4879
Michael Murphy, *Pr*
Pamela Murphy, *Sec*
EMP: 10 **EST:** 1985
SALES (est): 885.07K **Privately Held**
Web: www.mikemurphyandsons.com
SIC: 5983 1389 Fuel oil dealers; Oil field
services, nec

(G-14637)
TORROMEO INDUSTRIES INC
Also Called: Kingston Materials
18 Dorre Rd (03848-3412)
PHONE................................603 642-5564
EMP: 30
SALES (corp-wide): 9.65MM **Privately
Held**
Web: www.torromeo.com
SIC: 3273 5032 Ready-mixed concrete;
Sand, construction
PA: Torromeo Industries, Inc.
33 Old Ferry Rd
Methuen MA 01844
978 686-5634

Laconia
Belknap County

(G-14638)
AAVID CORPORATION
1 Aavid Cir (03246)
PHONE................................603 528-3400
EMP: 3000 **EST:** 1964
SALES (est): 78.19MM **Privately Held**
Web: www.boydcorp.com
SIC: 3679 Electronic circuits

(G-14639)
AAVID LABORATORIES INC
Also Called: Aavid Thermal Div Boyd Corp
1 Aavid Cir (03246)
PHONE.................................603 528-3400
Mitchell Aiello, *CEO*
EMP: 124 EST: 1973
SALES (est): 974.53K
SALES (corp-wide): 19.19MM **Privately Held**
SIC: 3585 Parts for heating, cooling, and refrigerating equipment
PA: The Boyd Corporation
    5832 Ohio St
    Yorba Linda CA 92886
    714 533-2375

(G-14640)
ACARA HOLDINGS LLC
Also Called: Business Card Express
14 Lexington Dr Ste 2 (03246-3946)
P.O. Box 287 (03038-0287)
PHONE.................................603 434-3175
Ronald Hauff, *Owner*
EMP: 17 EST: 1985
SALES (est): 2.19MM **Privately Held**
Web: www.bcecards.com
SIC: 2759 Visiting cards (including business): printing, nsk

(G-14641)
ACCELLENT ENDOSCOPY INC
45 Lexington Dr (03246-2935)
PHONE.................................603 528-1211
Don Spence, *Pr*
EMP: 49 EST: 1970
SQ FT: 40,000
SALES (est): 2.05MM
SALES (corp-wide): 1.38B **Publicly Held**
SIC: 3841 Surgical and medical instruments
HQ: Accellent Llc
    5830 Gran Pkwy Ste 1150
    Plano TX 75024
    978 570-6900

(G-14642)
ACI - PCB INC
254 Court St Ste A (03246-5600)
PHONE.................................603 528-7711
Jeffrey A Holt, *Prin*
EMP: 9 EST: 2012
SALES (est): 227.41K **Privately Held**
Web: www.additive.com
SIC: 3672 Printed circuit boards

(G-14643)
AIREX LLC
98 Paugus Park Rd (03246-2036)
PHONE.................................603 841-2040
Lindsay Badger, *Dir*
▲ EMP: 35 EST: 1950
SALES (est): 5.01MM
SALES (corp-wide): 502.99MM **Publicly Held**
Web: www.airex.com
SIC: 3612 Transformers, except electric
PA: Allient Inc.
    495 Commerce Dr Ste 3
    Amherst NY 14228
    716 242-8634

(G-14644)
AKA TOOL INC
477 Province Rd Ste 1 (03246-1383)
PHONE.................................603 524-1868
Christopher Lemay, *Ex Dir*
Steven Jorgensen, *
EMP: 27 EST: 2006
SALES (est): 2.65MM **Privately Held**
Web: www.akatool.com

SIC: 3599 Machine shop, jobbing and repair

(G-14645)
BARON MACHINE COMPANY INC
40 Primrose Dr S (03246-3927)
PHONE.................................603 524-6800
Kim E Baron, *Pr*
Lee Mattson, *
Jeremy Baron, *
Suzanne Gavarny, *
EMP: 70 EST: 1956
SQ FT: 45,000
SALES (est): 11.71MM **Privately Held**
Web: www.baronmachine.com
SIC: 7692 3599 Welding repair; Machine shop, jobbing and repair

(G-14646)
BELKNAP TIRE CO HOLDINGS INC
670 Union Ave (03246)
PHONE.................................603 524-4517
TOLL FREE: 800
Gregory Bryar, *Pr*
Linda Bryar, *VP*
Lee Mattson, *Sec*
EMP: 18 EST: 1946
SQ FT: 25,000
SALES (est): 906.24K **Privately Held**
Web: www.belknaptire.com
SIC: 7534 5531 5014 7538 Tire recapping; Automotive tires; Tires and tubes; General automotive repair shops

(G-14647)
BODYCOTE THERMAL PROC INC
187 Water St (03246-3351)
PHONE.................................603 524-7886
Dean Huffman, *Genl Mgr*
EMP: 49
SALES (corp-wide): 895.27MM **Privately Held**
Web: www.bodycote.com
SIC: 3398 Metal heat treating
HQ: Bodycote Thermal Processing, Inc.
    12750 Merit Dr Ste 1400
    Dallas TX 75251
    214 904-2420

(G-14648)
BOULIA-GORRELL LUMBER CO LLC
176 Fair St (03246-3322)
PHONE.................................603 524-1300
John A Veazey, *Pr*
Sally Mcgarry, *Treas*
Charles Veazey, *VP*
EMP: 16 EST: 1866
SQ FT: 10,000
SALES (est): 495.37K **Privately Held**
Web: www.bogolumber.com
SIC: 2431 5211 Millwork; Lumber products

(G-14649)
BOYD LACONIA LLC (DH)
1 Aavid Cir (03246)
PHONE.................................603 528-3400
Alan W Wong, *Managing Member*
Sukhvinder Kang,* *
David Wall, *
◆ EMP: 100 EST: 1964
SQ FT: 188,000
SALES (est): 107.08MM **Privately Held**
Web: www.boydcorp.com
SIC: 3679 Electronic circuits
HQ: Boyd Corporation
    5960 Inglewood Dr Ste 115
    Pleasanton CA 94588
    209 236-1111

(G-14650)
CB VENTURES LLC
14 Lexington Dr Ste 2 (03246-3946)
PHONE.................................603 434-3175
David K Fries Esq, *Admn*
EMP: 17 EST: 2011
SALES (est): 970.98K **Privately Held**
SIC: 2759 Visiting cards (including business): printing, nsk

(G-14651)
FRONEK ANCHOR DARLING ENTP
86 Doris Ray Ct (03246-5509)
PHONE.................................603 528-1931
Durga Agrawal, *Pr*
EMP: 10 EST: 2004
SALES (est): 2.54MM
SALES (corp-wide): 114.78MM **Privately Held**
Web: www.pipingtech.com
SIC: 3494 8711 3441 Expansion joints, pipe ; Engineering services; Fabricated structural metal
PA: Piping Technology & Products, Inc.
    3701 Holmes Rd
    Houston TX 77051
    713 731-0030

(G-14652)
HEBERT FOUNDRY & MACHINE INC
Also Called: Hebert Foundry & Machine Co
113 Fair St (03246-3321)
PHONE.................................603 524-2065
Richard Hebert, *Pr*
Donald Hebert, *
Jennifer Hebert, *
EMP: 40 EST: 1950
SQ FT: 60,000
SALES (est): 998.66K
SALES (corp-wide): 3.47MM **Privately Held**
Web: www.hebertfoundry.com
SIC: 3366 Copper foundries
PA: The Hebert Manufacturing Company
    113 Fair St
    Laconia NH 03246
    603 524-2065

(G-14653)
HEBERT MANUFACTURING COMPANY (PA)
113 Fair St (03246-3321)
PHONE.................................603 524-2065
Richard Hebert, *Pr*
Donald Hebert, *VP*
John Lull, *Sec*
EMP: 15 EST: 1912
SQ FT: 52,000
SALES (est): 3.47MM
SALES (corp-wide): 3.47MM **Privately Held**
Web: www.hebertfoundry.com
SIC: 3364 3363 Brass and bronze die-castings; Aluminum die-castings

(G-14654)
KELLERHAUS INC
259 Endicott St N (03246-1736)
P.O. Box 5337 (03247-5337)
PHONE.................................603 366-4466
Dave Allen, *Pr*
EMP: 12 EST: 1906
SQ FT: 1,800
SALES (est): 858.71K **Privately Held**
Web: www.kellerhaus.com

SIC: 2024 2064 5947 Ice cream and frozen deserts; Candy and other confectionery products; Gift shop

(G-14655)
LACONIA MAGNETICS INC
Prescott Hill Rd (03246)
P.O. Box 1457 (03247-1457)
PHONE.................................603 528-2766
Michael Southworth, *Pr*
Debbie Southworth, *
EMP: 18 EST: 1984
SQ FT: 10,000
SALES (est): 2.52MM **Privately Held**
Web: www.laconiamagnetics.com
SIC: 3677 3612 Transformers power supply, electronic type; Transformers, except electric

(G-14656)
LAKE REGION MEDICAL INC
Also Called: Accellent Laconia
45 Lexington Dr (03246-2935)
PHONE.................................603 528-1211
EMP: 25
SALES (corp-wide): 1.38B **Publicly Held**
Web: www.integer.net
SIC: 3841 Surgical and medical instruments
HQ: Lake Region Medical, Inc.
    100 Fordham Rd
    Wilmington MA 01887

(G-14657)
LAKES REGION TUBULAR PDTS INC
Also Called: Scotia Technology
51 Growth Rd (03246-1318)
P.O. Box 1190 (03247-1190)
PHONE.................................603 528-2838
David F Bonisteel, *Pr*
EMP: 47 EST: 1986
SQ FT: 48,000
SALES (est): 16.75MM
SALES (corp-wide): 3.83B **Privately Held**
Web: lakes-region-tubular-products-inc-in-laconia-nh.cityfos.com
SIC: 3728 Aircraft parts and equipment, nec
HQ: United Flexible, Inc.
    815 Forestwood Dr
    Romeoville IL 60446
    815 886-1140

(G-14658)
LEO ALGERS NH ELC MTRS INC
Also Called: New Hampshire Electric Motors
459 Province Rd (03246-1331)
PHONE.................................603 524-3729
TOLL FREE: 800
Thomas Bates, *Pr*
Karen Bates, *Treas*
EMP: 9 EST: 1962
SALES (est): 822.34K **Privately Held**
Web: www.nheminc.com
SIC: 7694 5063 Electric motor repair; Motors, electric

(G-14659)
MILLS INDUSTRIES INC
167 Water St (03246-3351)
P.O. Box 1459 (03247-1459)
PHONE.................................603 528-4217
Michael Mills, *Pr*
EMP: 21 EST: 1972
SQ FT: 30,000
SALES (est): 2.05MM **Privately Held**
Web: www.millsind.com
SIC: 3089 2653 Boxes, plastics; Boxes, corrugated: made from purchased materials

(G-14660)
NEW ENGLAND BOAT & MOTOR INC
28 Center St (03246-3737)
P.O. Box 1283 (03247-1283)
PHONE......................................603 527-9435
Mark Mason, *Pr*
EMP: 7 **EST:** 1985
SQ FT: 12,000
SALES (est): 490.4K **Privately Held**
Web:
www.newenglandboatandmotor.com
SIC: 3732 Boatbuilding and repairing

(G-14661)
NEW HMPSHIRE BALL BEARINGS INC
Astro Division
155 Lexington Dr (03246-2937)
PHONE......................................603 524-0004
Richard Fleczok, *Brnch Mgr*
EMP: 500
Web: www.nhbb.com
SIC: 3562 3366 3312 Ball bearings and parts; Copper foundries; Blast furnaces and steel mills
HQ: New Hampshire Ball Bearings, Inc.
175 Jaffrey Rd
Peterborough NH 03458
603 924-4100

(G-14662)
ORION ENTRANCE CONTROL INC
76a Lexington Dr (03246-2934)
PHONE......................................603 527-4187
Steven Caroselli, *Pr*
EMP: 43 **EST:** 2009
SALES (est): 4.93MM **Privately Held**
Web: www.orioneci.com
SIC: 7382 3699 Security systems services; Door opening and closing devices, electrical

(G-14663)
PIPE SHIELDS INC
86 Doris Ray Ct (03246-5509)
PHONE......................................603 528-1931
EMP: 7 **EST:** 2018
SALES (est): 61.53K **Privately Held**
Web: www.pipeshields.com
SIC: 3441 Fabricated structural metal

(G-14664)
R & J TOOL INC (PA)
945 Scenic Rd (03246-1807)
P.O. Box 712 (03247-0712)
PHONE......................................603 366-4925
Robert Laflamme, *Pr*
EMP: 9 **EST:** 1984
SALES (est): 1.34MM
SALES (corp-wide): 1.34MM **Privately Held**
Web: www.randjtool.com
SIC: 3545 8742 Cutting tools for machine tools; Industrial and labor consulting services

(G-14665)
R & K MACHINE
53 Blaisdell Ave (03246-4405)
PHONE......................................603 528-0221
Melissa A Hil, *Owner*
EMP: 10 **EST:** 2010
SALES (est): 455.75K **Privately Held**
Web: www.rk-machine.com
SIC: 3599 Machine shop, jobbing and repair

(G-14666)
ROGUE SPACE SYSTEMS CORP
131 Lake St (03246-2129)
PHONE......................................603 460-5069
Jeromy Grimmett, *CEO*
Jon Beam, *COO*
Aimee Eller, *Prin*
EMP: 15 **EST:** 2020
SALES (est): 1.2MM **Privately Held**
Web: www.rogue.space
SIC: 3761 Guided missiles and space vehicles

(G-14667)
SAWYERS JEWELRY INC
520 Main St (03246-3450)
P.O. Box 777 (03247-0777)
PHONE......................................603 527-1000
Robert A Sawyer, *Pr*
EMP: 11 **EST:** 1946
SALES (est): 971K **Privately Held**
Web: www.sawyersjewelry.com
SIC: 5944 5947 7631 3911 Jewelry, precious stones and precious metals; Gift shop; Jewelry repair services; Jewel settings and mountings, precious metal

(G-14668)
SCREW-MATIC CORPORATION
Also Called: SMC Aerospace
10 Primrose Dr S (03246-2940)
P.O. Box 1305 (03038-6305)
PHONE......................................603 468-1610
Mark J Mccarthy, *Pr*
Mark J Mc Carthy, *Pr*
John Andrews, *VP*
Barbara J Andrew, *Stockholder*
Sean Andrews, *
EMP: 45 **EST:** 1960
SQ FT: 14,000
SALES (est): 10.01MM
SALES (corp-wide): 105.24MM **Privately Held**
Web: www.smcaerospace.com
SIC: 3728 Aircraft parts and equipment, nec
PA: G. S. Precision, Inc.
101 John Seitz Dr
Brattleboro VT 05301
802 257-5200

(G-14669)
SHAWN DUDEK
Also Called: No Limits Metal Works
334 White Oaks Rd (03246-1936)
PHONE......................................603 387-1859
Shawn Dudek, *Prin*
EMP: 8 **EST:** 2017
SALES (est): 239.94K **Privately Held**
SIC: 7692 Welding repair

(G-14670)
SMITHS TBLAR SYSTMS-LCONIA INC
Also Called: Titeflex Aerospace
93 Lexington Dr (03246-2935)
PHONE......................................603 524-2064
Pat Mccaffrey, *Pr*
William T Smith, *
Robert M Speer, *
Patrick D Mccaffrey, *VP*
Martin Hough, *
▲ **EMP:** 250 **EST:** 1913
SQ FT: 84,000
SALES (est): 46.32MM
SALES (corp-wide): 3.83B **Privately Held**
Web: www.stsaero.com
SIC: 3463 3498 8734 7692 Machinery forgings, nonferrous; Tube fabricating (contract bending and shaping); Testing laboratories; Welding repair

PA: Smiths Group Plc
4th Floor
London SW1Y
207 004-1600

(G-14671)
STAMPING TECHNOLOGIES INC
20 Growtth Rd (03246-1318)
PHONE......................................603 524-5958
Mark St Gelais, *Pr*
Johanna St Gelais, *VP*
EMP: 16 **EST:** 1989
SQ FT: 8,000
SALES (est): 1.77MM **Privately Held**
Web: www.stampingtec.com
SIC: 3469 3312 3544 Stamping metal for the trade; Tool and die steel and alloys; Special dies, tools, jigs, and fixtures

(G-14672)
TYLERGRAPHICS INC
14 Lexington Dr Ste 2 (03246-3946)
P.O. Box 44 (03230-0044)
PHONE......................................603 524-6625
Wade Heberling, *Pr*
EMP: 8 **EST:** 1995
SALES (est): 951.38K **Privately Held**
Web: www.tylergraphics.net
SIC: 2752 Offset printing

(G-14673)
VIANT MEDICAL LLC
45 Lexington Dr (03246-2935)
PHONE......................................603 528-1211
EMP: 97
SALES (corp-wide): 1.18B **Privately Held**
Web: www.viantmedical.com
SIC: 3841 Surgical and medical instruments
HQ: Viant Medical, Llc
2 Hampshire St
Foxborough MA 02035

(G-14674)
ZHONGDING LACONIA INC
Also Called: Cooper Products, Inc.
210 Fair St (03246-3366)
PHONE......................................603 524-3367
Marcio Lima, *CEO*
Eri Tsukino, *
Kathleen Flon Grenier, *
▲ **EMP:** 44 **EST:** 1984
SQ FT: 33,000
SALES (est): 9.45MM
SALES (corp-wide): 2.06B **Privately Held**
Web: www.cooperproducts.com
SIC: 3061 3053 Mechanical rubber goods; Gaskets; packing and sealing devices
HQ: Zhongding Sealing Parts (Usa), Inc.
400 Detroit Ave
Monroe MI 48162
734 241-8870

Lancaster
Coos County

(G-14675)
A B EXCAVATING INC
653 Main St (03584-3612)
PHONE......................................603 788-5110
EMP: 20 **EST:** 1985
SALES (est): 3.69MM **Privately Held**
Web: www.abexcavatinginc.com
SIC: 2411 1611 1623 1629 Logging camps and contractors; Highway and street construction; Water and sewer line construction; Drainage system construction

(G-14676)
CABOT HILL NATURALS LLC
Also Called: Dent Herb Company
62 Bridge St (03584-3102)
PHONE......................................800 747-4372
David C Hill, *Pr*
Tyler Rancourt, *VP*
EMP: 10 **EST:** 2012
SALES (est): 759.15K **Privately Held**
Web: www.dentalherb.com
SIC: 2844 Oral preparations

(G-14677)
MOUNT WASHINGTON VLY MTN EAR
Also Called: Mountain Ear
79 Main St (03584-3027)
PHONE......................................603 447-6336
Ryan Corneau, *Genl Mgr*
Rich Piatt, *Prin*
EMP: 9 **EST:** 1976
SQ FT: 2,000
SALES (est): 620.79K **Privately Held**
SIC: 2711 Newspapers: publishing only, not printed on site

(G-14678)
PAK 2000 INC
16 Page Hill Rd (03584-3618)
PHONE......................................603 569-3700
EMP: 13
SALES (corp-wide): 19.26MM **Privately Held**
Web: www.paksolutionsusa.com
SIC: 2674 2673 2671 Bags: uncoated paper and multiwall; Plastic and pliofilm bags; Paper; coated and laminated packaging
PA: Pak 2000, Inc.
189 Govenor Wentworth Hwy
Mirror Lake NH 03853
603 569-3700

(G-14679)
SOUTHWORTH TIMBERFRAMES INC
Also Called: Garland Mill
273 Garland Rd (03584-3409)
PHONE......................................603 788-2619
Benjamin Southworth, *Pr*
Dana Southworth, *Treas*
EMP: 9 **EST:** 1977
SALES (est): 994.31K **Privately Held**
Web: www.garlandmill.com
SIC: 2439 2452 Timbers, structural: laminated lumber; Prefabricated wood buildings

(G-14680)
TRIVIDIA MFG SOLUTIONS INC (DH)
Also Called: P.J. Noyes
89 Bridge St (03584-3103)
PHONE......................................603 788-2848
Dennis Wogaman, *COO*
Jen Cusick, *
Scott Verner, *
Jason Mondek, *
Dean Sorrentino, *
▲ **EMP:** 103 **EST:** 1868
SQ FT: 35,000
SALES (est): 21.75MM **Privately Held**
Web: www.trividiams.com
SIC: 2834 2844 2048 Pharmaceutical preparations; Perfumes, cosmetics and other toilet preparations; Prepared feeds, nec
HQ: Trividia Health, Inc.
2400 Nw 55th Ct
Fort Lauderdale FL 33309
954 677-8201

(G-14681)
WEYERHAEUSER
149 Main St (03584-3064)
PHONE..........................603 237-1639
EMP: 12 EST: 2019
SALES (est): 582.12K Privately Held
Web: www.weyerhaeuser.com
SIC: 2421 Sawmills and planing mills,
general

Landaff
Grafton County

(G-14682)
STOCKLEY TRUCKING INC
Also Called: Stockley Storage
405 S Main St (03585-5221)
PHONE..........................603 838-2860
EMP: 9 EST: 1991
SALES (est): 878.39K Privately Held
Web: www.stockleytrucking.com
SIC: 2411 Logging

Lebanon
Grafton County

(G-14683)
AVITIDE INC
16 Cavendish Ct Ste 151 (03766-1441)
PHONE..........................603 965-2100
Kevin Isett, CEO
Scott Kennedy, *
Warren Kett, CSO*
EMP: 34 EST: 2012
SALES (est): 6.4MM
SALES (corp-wide): 801.54MM Publicly
Held
Web: www.avitide.com
SIC: 2836 Biological products, except
diagnostic
PA: Repligen Corporation
41 Seyon St Ste 100
Waltham MA 02453
781 250-0111

(G-14684)
BARRE TILE INC
187 Mechanic St (03766-1509)
PHONE..........................802 476-0912
Bill Clark, Mgr
EMP: 10
Web: www.barretile.com
SIC: 3281 5084 5211 Granite, cut and
shaped; Countersinks; Counter tops
PA: Barre Tile, Inc.
889 S Barre Rd
South Barre VT 05670

(G-14685)
BOND OPTICS LLC
76 Etna Rd (03766-1403)
P.O. Box 422 (03766-0422)
PHONE..........................603 448-2300
Chris Degrasse, *
EMP: 50 EST: 1959
SQ FT: 50,000
SALES (est): 5.12MM Privately Held
Web: www.bondoptics.com
SIC: 3827 Lenses, optical: all types except
ophthalmic

(G-14686)
**CONNECTCUT RVER VLY
YLLOW PGES**
103 Hanover St Ste 9 (03766-1098)
PHONE..........................603 727-4700

Shawn Mason, Owner
EMP: 7 EST: 2010
SALES (est): 302.15K Privately Held
SIC: 2741 Telephone and other directory
publishing

(G-14687)
ECO KNIGHT GROUP LLC (PA) ✪
68 Mountain View Dr (03766-1877)
PHONE..........................802 318-8760
EMP: 7 EST: 2022
SALES (est): 461.18K
SALES (corp-wide): 461.18K Privately
Held
SIC: 2842 7389 Sanitation preparations,
disinfectants and deodorants; Business
services, nec

(G-14688)
FRONTIER DESIGN GROUP LLC
31 Old Etna Rd Ste N5 (03766-1933)
PHONE..........................603 448-6283
EMP: 8 EST: 1996
SQ FT: 1,500
SALES (est): 997.65K Privately Held
Web: www.frontierdesign.com
SIC: 3679 Recording and playback
apparatus, including phonograph

(G-14689)
FUJIFILM DIMATIX INC
Also Called: Delaware Dimatix
109 Etna Rd (03766-1467)
PHONE..........................603 443-5300
John Batterton, Pr
EMP: 95
Web: www.dimatix.com
SIC: 3577 Printers, computer
HQ: Fujifilm Dimatix, Inc.
2250 Martin Ave
Santa Clara CA 95050
408 565-9150

(G-14690)
GEOKON INC
48 Spencer St (03766-1363)
PHONE..........................603 448-1562
Anthony Simmonds, *
Charles Chamley, *
Colin Judd, *
◆ EMP: 100 EST: 1979
SQ FT: 25,000
SALES (est): 19.87MM Privately Held
Web: www.geokon.com
SIC: 3829 Vibration meters, analyzers, and
calibrators

(G-14691)
IMAGENE TECHNOLOGY INC
85 Mechanic St (03766-1537)
P.O. Box 667 (03755-0667)
PHONE..........................603 448-9940
Timothy Chow, Ex Dir
EMP: 10 EST: 1987
SQ FT: 2,000
SALES (est): 431.09K Privately Held
Web: www.imagenetechnology.com
SIC: 3841 Diagnostic apparatus, medical

(G-14692)
LANE POVERTY ORCHARD
Also Called: Farnum Hill Sider
98 Poverty Ln (03766-2700)
PHONE..........................603 448-1511
Stephen M Wood, Owner
▲ EMP: 8 EST: 1978
SALES (est): 359.05K Privately Held
Web: www.farnumhillciders.com
SIC: 0175 2099 2084 Apple orchard; Cider,
nonalcoholic; Wines

(G-14693)
LUMINESCENT SYSTEMS INC
Also Called: Luminescent Systems
4 Lucent Dr (03766-1439)
PHONE..........................603 643-7766
Peter J Gundermann, Pr
EMP: 125
SALES (corp-wide): 534.89MM Publicly
Held
Web: www.astronics.com
SIC: 3648 3641 Lighting equipment, nec;
Electric lamps
HQ: Luminescent Systems, Inc.
130 Commerce Way
East Aurora NY 14052
716 655-0800

(G-14694)
MPB CORPORATION
334 Mechanic St (03766)
PHONE..........................603 448-3000
EMP: 514
SALES (corp-wide): 4.5B Publicly Held
Web: www.timken.com
SIC: 3562 Ball and roller bearings
HQ: Mpb Corporation
7 Optical Ave
Keene NH 03431
603 352-0310

(G-14695)
MPB CORPORATION
Also Called: Mpb
336 Mechanic St (03766-2614)
PHONE..........................603 448-3000
Rober Baulman, Genl Mgr
EMP: 514
SALES (corp-wide): 4.5B Publicly Held
Web: www.timken.com
SIC: 3562 3568 Ball bearings and parts;
Power transmission equipment, nec
HQ: Mpb Corporation
7 Optical Ave
Keene NH 03431
603 352-0310

(G-14696)
**NEW ENGLAND INDUSTRIES
INC**
Also Called: Nei Stamping
85 Etna Rd (03766-1466)
PHONE..........................603 448-5330
Michael B Landgraf, Prin
EMP: 42 EST: 1952
SQ FT: 51,000
SALES (est): 7.35MM Privately Held
Web: www.neistamping.com
SIC: 3469 3544 Stamping metal for the trade
; Special dies and tools

(G-14697)
NJM PACKAGING LLC (DH)
Also Called: Njm Packaging
77 Bank St (03766-1771)
PHONE..........................603 448-0300
Michael Lapierre, Pr
James Moretti, CFO
EMP: 10 EST: 1915
SQ FT: 170,000
SALES (est): 5.49MM Privately Held
Web: www.njmpackaging.com
SIC: 3565 Labeling machines, industrial
HQ: Pro Mach, Inc.
50 E Rvrcnter Blvd Ste 18
Covington KY 41011
513 831-8778

(G-14698)
SIGNALQUEST LLC
10 Water St (03766-1630)
PHONE..........................603 448-6266
Whitmore B Kelley Junior, CEO
EMP: 30 EST: 1999
SALES (est): 17MM Privately Held
Web: www.signalquest.com
SIC: 3812 Navigational systems and
instruments

(G-14699)
SIMBEX LLC
10 Water St Ste 410 (03766-1604)
PHONE..........................603 448-2367
EMP: 45 EST: 2000
SQ FT: 60,000
SALES (est): 9.34MM
SALES (corp-wide): 72.63MM Privately
Held
Web: www.simbex.com
SIC: 3949 8711 8731 Protective sporting
equipment; Engineering services;
Commercial physical research
PA: Evome Medical Technologies Inc.
3330 Caminito Daniella
Del Mar CA 92014
800 760-6826

(G-14700)
TOMTOM NORTH AMERICA INC
Also Called: Tomtom
21 Lafayette St (03766-1490)
PHONE..........................978 405-1677
Jocelyn Vigreux, CEO
EMP: 80 EST: 2002
SALES (est): 18.58MM
SALES (corp-wide): 557.04MM Privately
Held
SIC: 5734 3812 Software, business and non-
game; Search and navigation equipment
PA: Tomtom N.V.
De Ruijterkade 154
Amsterdam NH
207575000

(G-14701)
TOMTOM NORTH AMERICA INC
11 Lafayette St (03766-1445)
PHONE..........................603 643-0330
Taco Titulaer, Pr
David Mackenzie, *
Bruce Radloff, *
Michael Mitsock, CMO*
EMP: 636 EST: 1983
SALES (est): 46.88MM
SALES (corp-wide): 557.04MM Privately
Held
SIC: 7371 3823 3812 Computer software
development; Process control instruments;
Search and navigation equipment
PA: Tomtom N.V.
De Ruijterkade 154
Amsterdam NH
207575000

(G-14702)
**TRUSTEES OF DARTMOUTH
COLLEGE**
Also Called: University Press New England
1 Court St Ste 250 (03766-1358)
PHONE..........................603 448-1533
Michael Burton, Dir
EMP: 20
SALES (corp-wide): 1.39B Privately Held
Web: home.dartmouth.edu
SIC: 2731 8221 Book publishing; College,
except junior
PA: Trustees Of Dartmouth College
545 Boylston St Ste 900

Boston MA 02116
603 646-1110

(G-14703)
WHITMAN COMMUNICATIONS INC
10 Water St (03766-1630)
P.O. Box 1156 (03766-4156)
PHONE..................................603 448-2600
Stephen Whitman, *Ch*
Carolyn Whitman, *Stockholder*
EMP: 9 **EST:** 1968
SQ FT: 15,000
SALES (est): 717.56K **Privately Held**
Web: www.whitman.biz
SIC: 2752 2791 Photo-offset printing; Typesetting

Lee
Strafford County

(G-14704)
A & A WHEELER MFG INC
300 Calef Hwy (03861-6353)
PHONE..................................603 659-4446
EMP: 7 **EST:** 1998
SALES (est): 245.41K **Privately Held**
Web: www.aawheelermfg.com
SIC: 2421 Outdoor wood structural products

(G-14705)
FLAG HILL DISTILLERY LLC
297 N River Rd (03861-6213)
PHONE..................................603 659-2949
Frank Walter Reinhold Junior, *Prin*
EMP: 11 **EST:** 2012
SALES (est): 672.59K **Privately Held**
Web: www.flaghill.com
SIC: 2084 Wines

(G-14706)
FLAG HILL WINERY & VINYRD LLC
Also Called: Flag Hill Winery
297 N River Rd (03861-6213)
PHONE..................................603 659-2949
Frank Reinhold Junior, *Pr*
Linda Reinhold, *VP*
EMP: 9 **EST:** 2012
SALES (est): 560.69K **Privately Held**
Web: www.flaghill.com
SIC: 2084 Wines

Lincoln
Grafton County

(G-14707)
VINEYARD AT SEVEN BIRCHES LLC
22 S Mountain Dr (03251-4268)
PHONE..................................603 745-7550
EMP: 7 **EST:** 2016
SALES (est): 111.48K **Privately Held**
Web: www.sevenbirches.com
SIC: 2084 Wines

Lisbon
Grafton County

(G-14708)
DCI INC (PA)
Also Called: DCI Furniture
265 S Main St (03585-6217)
PHONE..................................800 552-8286

Henry A Kober, *Pr*
C Amos Kober, *
Jacob David Kober, *
Chandelle L Whitney, *
◆ **EMP:** 100 **EST:** 1975
SQ FT: 50,000
SALES (est): 38.2MM
SALES (corp-wide): 38.2MM **Privately Held**
Web: www.dcifurn.com
SIC: 2531 5023 Public building and related furniture; Bedspreads

(G-14709)
DESIGN CONTEMPO
265 S Main St (03585-6217)
PHONE..................................603 838-6544
Patrick Bay, *Mktg Dir*
EMP: 10 **EST:** 2018
SALES (est): 461.58K **Privately Held**
Web: www.dcifurn.com
SIC: 2511 Wood household furniture

(G-14710)
NEW ENGLAND WIRE TECH CORP (HQ)
Also Called: New England Wire Technologies
130 N Main St (03585-6603)
P.O. Box 264 (03585-0264)
PHONE..................................603 838-6624
Richard Johns, *Pr*
Wendell W Jesseman, *
Robert Meserve, *
◆ **EMP:** 351 **EST:** 1898
SQ FT: 335,000
SALES (est): 92.66MM
SALES (corp-wide): 131.64MM **Privately Held**
Web: www.newenglandwire.com
SIC: 3496 Miscellaneous fabricated wire products
PA: Mjm Holdings, Inc.
130 N Main St
Lisbon NH 03585
603 838-6624

(G-14711)
WHITE MOUNTAIN INTL LLC (PA)
Also Called: Connors Footwear
20 Whitcher St (03585-6311)
PHONE..................................603 838-6694
Alen Mamrout, *CEO*
Marc Gold, *CFO*
▲ **EMP:** 20 **EST:** 1979
SQ FT: 45,000
SALES (est): 22.86MM
SALES (corp-wide): 22.86MM **Privately Held**
Web: www.whitemountainshoes.com
SIC: 5139 3144 Shoes; Women's footwear, except athletic

Litchfield
Hillsborough County

(G-14712)
BURLODGE USA INC
24 Pearson St (03052-1094)
PHONE..................................336 776-1010
Neil Kirven, *Pr*
▲ **EMP:** 26 **EST:** 1995
SQ FT: 15,000
SALES (est): 2.15MM
SALES (corp-wide): 2.67MM **Privately Held**
Web: www.burlodge.com
SIC: 3556 Food products machinery
HQ: Ali Group North America Corporation
101 Corporate Woods Pkwy

Vernon Hills IL 60061
847 215-6565

(G-14713)
NEW ENGLAND SMALL TUBE CORP
Also Called: Nest
480 Charles Bancroft Hwy Unit 3 (03052-1090)
PHONE..................................603 429-1600
Patrick M Algeo, *Pr*
Jack Algeo, *
Colleen Mary Ellis, *
Kathleen D Algeo, *Stockholder*
EMP: 82 **EST:** 1986
SQ FT: 20,000
SALES (est): 11.11MM **Privately Held**
Web: www.nesmalltube.com
SIC: 3498 5051 3841 Tube fabricating (contract bending and shaping); Metals service centers and offices; Surgical and medical instruments

Littleton
Grafton County

(G-14714)
APPALACHIAN STITCHING CO LLC (PA)
90 Badger St (03561-4111)
PHONE..................................603 444-4422
▲ **EMP:** 21 **EST:** 2002
SQ FT: 20,000
SALES (est): 4.93MM
SALES (corp-wide): 4.93MM **Privately Held**
Web: www.appalachianstitching.com
SIC: 3172 Personal leather goods, nec

(G-14715)
CALEDONIAN RECORD PUBG CO INC
263 Main St (03561-4021)
PHONE..................................603 444-7141
Todd Smith, *Mgr*
EMP: 8
SALES (corp-wide): 4.48MM **Privately Held**
Web: www.caledonianrecord.com
SIC: 2711 Commercial printing and newspaper publishing combined
PA: Caledonian Record Publishing Company, Inc.
190 Federal St
Saint Johnsbury VT 05819
802 748-8121

(G-14716)
DUTCH GOLD HONEY INC
Also Called: McLures Honey & Maple Products
46 N Littleton Rd (03561-3814)
PHONE..................................603 444-6246
Nancy I Gamber, *Pr*
Wm R Gamber Ii, *VP*
EMP: 14 **EST:** 1954
SALES (est): 2.05MM **Privately Held**
Web: www.dutchgoldhoney.com
SIC: 2099 Food preparations, nec

(G-14717)
DUTCH GOLD HONEY INC
Also Called: McLures's Honey & Maple Prdcts
46 N Littleton Rd (03561-3814)
PHONE..................................603 444-6246
Nancy Gamber, *Brnch Mgr*
EMP: 12
SALES (corp-wide): 155.84MM **Privately Held**

Web: www.dutchgoldhoney.com
SIC: 5149 2099 2087 Honey; Food preparations, nec; Flavoring extracts and syrups, nec
PA: Dutch Gold Honey, Inc.
2220 Dutch Gold Dr
Lancaster PA 17601
717 393-1716

(G-14718)
FCI ELECTRICAL-BRUNDY PRODUCTS
150 Burndy Rd (03561-3957)
PHONE..................................603 444-6781
Betsy Babcock, *Prin*
EMP: 7 **EST:** 2010
SALES (est): 94.96K **Privately Held**
SIC: 3643 Current-carrying wiring services

(G-14719)
GENFOOT AMERICA INC
673 Industrial Park Rd (03561-3953)
PHONE..................................603 575-5114
EMP: 100
SALES (corp-wide): 40.54MM **Privately Held**
SIC: 3089 3021 Boot or shoe products, plastics; Rubber and plastics footwear
PA: Genfoot America, Inc
1940 55e Av
Lachine QC H8T 3
514 341-3950

(G-14720)
HARRISON PUBLISHING HOUSE INC
Also Called: Bradford Price Book
995 Industrial Park Rd (03561-3956)
P.O. Box 320 (03561-0320)
PHONE..................................603 444-0820
David F Mcphaul, *Pr*
Willard Martin, *
EMP: 24 **EST:** 1912
SQ FT: 14,000
SALES (est): 2.15MM **Privately Held**
Web: www.harrisonpub.com
SIC: 2721 2752 Trade journals: publishing only, not printed on site; Commercial printing, lithographic

(G-14721)
LITTLETON MILLWORK INC
44 Lafayette Ave (03561-5707)
PHONE..................................603 444-2677
Mitchell Greaves, *Pr*
EMP: 20 **EST:** 1967
SQ FT: 14,000
SALES (est): 2.26MM **Privately Held**
Web: www.littletonmillwork.com
SIC: 2431 Millwork

(G-14722)
SABBOW AND CO INC
Wtc Granite Industries
390 Highland Ave (03561-4232)
PHONE..................................603 444-6724
Rick Hinck, *Brnch Mgr*
EMP: 14
SALES (corp-wide): 23.08MM **Privately Held**
Web: www.phoenixprecast.com
SIC: 3272 Burial vaults, concrete or precast terrazzo
PA: Sabbow And Co., Inc.
77 Regional Dr
Concord NH 03301
603 225-5169

(G-14723)
SHERWIN DODGE PRINTERS INC
365 Union St (03561-5619)
P.O. Box 481 (03561-0481)
PHONE....................................603 444-6552
EMP: 10 **EST:** 1995
SQ FT: 15,000
SALES (est): 992.68K **Privately Held**
Web: www.sherwindodgeprinters.com
SIC: 2752   Offset printing

(G-14724)
TENDER CORPORATION (PA)
Also Called: Adventure Ready Brands
944 Industrial Park Rd (03561-3956)
PHONE....................................603 444-5464
Christopher Heye, *CEO*
Gary Kiedaisch, *
Richard Tuttle, *Pr*
John Gaulin, *VP*
Edward Gorut, *VP*
◆ **EMP:** 91 **EST:** 1973
SALES (est): 25.44MM
SALES (corp-wide): 25.44MM **Privately Held**
Web: www.adventurereadybrands.com
SIC: 2879 2834   Insecticides and pesticides; Dermatologicals

(G-14725)
WHITE MOUNTAIN BIODIESEL LLC
83 Elm St (03561-4706)
PHONE....................................603 444-0335
Wayne W Presby, *Brnch Mgr*
EMP: 8
SALES (corp-wide): 2.05MM **Privately Held**
Web: www.whitemountainbiodiesel.com
SIC: 2911   Diesel fuels
PA: White Mountain Biodiesel Llc
35 Business Park Rd
North Haverhill NH 03774
603 728-7351

Londonderry
Rockingham County

(G-14726)
603 BREWERY LLC
Also Called: 603 Brewery
12 Liberty Dr Unit 7 (03053-2286)
PHONE....................................603 630-7745
▲ **EMP:** 20 **EST:** 2013
SALES (est): 2.18MM **Privately Held**
Web: www.603brewery.com
SIC: 2084   Wines, brandy, and brandy spirits

(G-14727)
ADMIX INC
Also Called: Advanced Mixing Technologies
144 Harvey Rd (03053-7449)
PHONE....................................603 627-2340
Mike Rizzo, *CEO*
Louis Beaudette, *
Tim Dining, *
EMP: 30 **EST:** 1989
SQ FT: 15,000
SALES (est): 10.06MM **Privately Held**
Web: www.admix.com
SIC: 3556 3559 3531   Mixers, commercial, food; Refinery, chemical processing, and similar machinery; Construction machinery

(G-14728)
ADVANTAGE MOLD INC
576 Mammoth Rd Ste 23 (03053-2151)
PHONE....................................603 647-6678
Peter J Matarozzo, *Pr*
Daniel Matarozzo, *VP*
Edward Hall, *VP*
EMP: 8 **EST:** 1997
SQ FT: 6,600
SALES (est): 959.06K **Privately Held**
Web: www.advantagemoldinc.com
SIC: 3089   Injection molding of plastics

(G-14729)
AL CU MET INC
3 Planeview Dr (03053-2307)
PHONE....................................603 432-6220
Mark Richardson, *Pr*
Russell Wilmarth, *
EMP: 45 **EST:** 1975
SQ FT: 35,000
SALES (est): 6.71MM **Privately Held**
Web: www.alcumet.com
SIC: 3369   Castings, except die-castings, precision

(G-14730)
ALLIED ORTHOTIC INC
3 Commercial Ln Ste E (03053-2200)
PHONE....................................603 434-7722
Michael Michaud, *Pr*
Theresa Young, *Off Mgr*
EMP: 7 **EST:** 1987
SQ FT: 4,800
SALES (est): 481.71K **Privately Held**
SIC: 3842   Foot appliances, orthopedic

(G-14731)
ALTIUM PACKAGING LLC
Also Called: Shelburne Plastics
27 Industrial Dr (03053-2009)
PHONE....................................603 624-6055
EMP: 55
SALES (corp-wide): 15.9B **Publicly Held**
Web: www.altiumpkg.com
SIC: 3089   Plastics containers, except foam
HQ: Altium Packaging Llc
2500 Windy Ridge Pkwy Se # 1400
Atlanta GA 30339
678 742-4600

(G-14732)
ARC MAINTENANCE MACHINING
14 Tinker Ave Unit 2 (03053-2030)
PHONE....................................603 626-8046
David Webber, *Pr*
EMP: 8 **EST:** 1992
SQ FT: 11,000
SALES (est): 216.05K **Privately Held**
SIC: 7692   Welding repair

(G-14733)
BOB BEAN COMPANY INC
Also Called: Minuteman Press
44 Nashua Rd Unit 2 (03053-3450)
PHONE....................................603 818-4390
Bob Bean, *Pr*
EMP: 13 **EST:** 2015
SALES (est): 542.33K **Privately Held**
Web: www.minutemanpress.com
SIC: 2752   Commercial printing, lithographic

(G-14734)
CARR TOOL CO LLC
19 Tinker Ave Unit 2 (03053-2031)
PHONE....................................603 669-0177
Donald Carr Junior, *Pr*
Irene Carr, *Treas*
Micheal Carr V Press, *Prin*

EMP: 10 **EST:** 1968
SALES (est): 1.46MM **Privately Held**
Web: www.carrtoolcoinc.com
SIC: 3599   Machine shop, jobbing and repair

(G-14735)
COCA-COLA BEVS NORTHEAST INC
Also Called: Coca-Cola
7 Symmes Dr (03053-2102)
PHONE....................................603 437-3530
Richard Neal, *Brnch Mgr*
EMP: 31
Web: www.coca-cola.com
SIC: 2086 5149   Bottled and canned soft drinks; Soft drinks
HQ: Coca-Cola Beverages Northeast, Inc.
1 Executive Park Dr # 330
Bedford NH 03110
603 627-7871

(G-14736)
CONCRETE SYSTEMS INC
15 Independence Dr (03053-2248)
PHONE....................................603 432-1840
EMP: 10
SALES (corp-wide): 59MM **Privately Held**
Web: www.csigroup.com
SIC: 3272 3448   Concrete products, nec; Prefabricated metal buildings and components
PA: Concrete Systems, Inc.
9 Commercial St
Hudson NH 03051
603 889-4163

(G-14737)
CONEST SOFTWARE SYSTEMS INC
136a Harvey Rd Ste 102 (03053-7403)
P.O. Box 947 (03053-0947)
PHONE....................................603 437-9353
Jim Beaumont, *Pr*
EMP: 30 **EST:** 2012
SALES (est): 2.25MM **Privately Held**
Web: www.conest.com
SIC: 7372   Prepackaged software

(G-14738)
CORPORTION FOR LSER OPTICS RES (PA)
Also Called: Color
95 Mammoth Rd (03053-3819)
PHONE....................................603 430-2023
Masayuki Karakawa, *Pr*
Robert Zielstorff, *CFO*
EMP: 7 **EST:** 1987
SQ FT: 16,000
SALES (est): 1.36MM
SALES (corp-wide): 1.36MM **Privately Held**
Web: www.laser-crylink.com
SIC: 8731 3993 3699 3577   Commercial physical research; Signs and advertising specialties; Electrical equipment and supplies, nec; Computer peripheral equipment, nec

(G-14739)
CRAWFORD SFTWR CONSULTING INC
1e Commons Dr Unit 26 (03053-3478)
PHONE....................................603 537-9630
Steven Carr, *Pr*
Stephanie Carr, *VP*
EMP: 7 **EST:** 2001
SQ FT: 1,000
SALES (est): 17MM **Privately Held**
Web: www.crawford-software.com

SIC: 7372   Business oriented computer software

(G-14740)
CTS CORPORATION
Also Called: CTS Interconnect Systems
34 Londonderry Rd Unit A1 (03053-3351)
PHONE....................................603 421-2546
Mark Baker, *Dir*
EMP: 54
SALES (corp-wide): 586.87MM **Publicly Held**
Web: www.ctscorp.com
SIC: 5065 3577   Electronic parts and equipment, nec; Computer peripheral equipment, nec
PA: Cts Corporation
4925 Indiana Ave
Lisle IL 60532
630 577-8800

(G-14741)
CYTYC CORPORATION
2 E Perimeter Rd (03053-2020)
PHONE....................................603 668-7688
David Batt, *Mgr*
EMP: 21
SALES (corp-wide): 4.03B **Publicly Held**
Web: www.hologic.com
SIC: 3845   Electromedical equipment
HQ: Cytyc Corporation
250 Campus Dr
Marlborough MA 01752

(G-14742)
DAVID D DOUGLAS INC
23 Londonderry Rd Unit 19 (03053-3314)
P.O. Box 1211 (03053-1211)
PHONE....................................603 437-1151
TOLL FREE: 800
EMP: 8 **EST:** 1979
SQ FT: 2,000
SALES (est): 680.87K **Privately Held**
Web: www.douglas-corian.com
SIC: 1799 5031 2541   Counter top installation; Kitchen cabinets; Table or counter tops, plastic laminated

(G-14743)
DONOVAN EQUIPMENT COMPANY INC
6 Enterprise Dr (03053-2158)
PHONE....................................603 669-2250
TOLL FREE: 800
Donald Francis Donovan, *Pr*
John Chakmakas, *
▲ **EMP:** 60 **EST:** 1920
SQ FT: 30,000
SALES (est): 12.53MM **Privately Held**
Web: www.donovancompany.com
SIC: 5013 7538 5012 3713   Truck parts and accessories; General truck repair; Truck bodies; Truck and bus bodies

(G-14744)
DORMAN LOGGING LLC
506 Mammoth Rd (03053-2323)
PHONE....................................603 437-4403
Blaine Thomas Dorman, *Mgr*
EMP: 7 **EST:** 2010
SALES (est): 274.34K **Privately Held**
SIC: 2411   Logging

(G-14745)
EASTERN METALS INC
4 Old Nashua Rd (03053-3616)
P.O. Box 772 (03053-0772)
PHONE....................................603 818-8639
EMP: 38 **EST:** 1987
SALES (est): 3.42MM **Privately Held**

SIC: 3399 1761 Iron ore recovery from open hearth slag; Sheet metal work, nec

(G-14746)
EBNER FURNACES
51 Harvey Rd Unit C (03053-7414)
PHONE...............................603 552-3806
David Dow, *Pr*
▲ EMP: 7 EST: 2012
SALES (est): 157.67K **Privately Held**
SIC: 3567 Industrial furnaces and ovens

(G-14747)
ELECTRONICS FOR IMAGING INC
Also Called: Efi Inkjet Solutions
12 Innovatiion Way (03053-2052)
PHONE...............................603 285-9800
Guy Gecht, *Brnch Mgr*
EMP: 300
SALES (corp-wide): 1.1B **Privately Held**
Web: www.efi.com
SIC: 3955 Print cartridges for laser and other computer printers
HQ: Electronics For Imaging, Inc.
12 Innovatiion Way
Londonderry NH 03053

(G-14748)
ELECTRONICS FOR IMAGING INC (HQ)
Also Called: Fiery
12 Innovatiion Way (03053-2052)
PHONE...............................650 357-3500
Frank Pennisi, *CEO*
Grant Fitz, *
Frank Mallozzi, *CRO*
Scott Schinlever, *
Douglas Edwards, *
▲ EMP: 50 EST: 1988
SALES (est): 1.1B
SALES (corp-wide): 1.1B **Privately Held**
Web: www.efi.com
SIC: 2759 3955 Commercial printing, nec; Print cartridges for laser and other computer printers
PA: East Private Holdings Ii, Llc
6750 Dumbarton Cir
Fremont CA 94555
650 357-3500

(G-14749)
ENVIRO-TOTE INC
15 Industrial Dr (03053-2009)
PHONE...............................603 647-7171
Nancy Sampo, *Pr*
Marilyn J Lee, *
▲ EMP: 38 EST: 1990
SQ FT: 10,500
SALES (est): 4.75MM **Privately Held**
Web: www.enviro-tote.com
SIC: 2393 2394 Bags and containers, except sleeping bags: textile; Canvas and related products

(G-14750)
FELTON INC
7 Burton Dr (03053-7435)
PHONE...............................603 425-0200
Ben Boehm, *CEO*
Daniel Boehm, *
Mark Godfrey, *
▲ EMP: 75 EST: 1842
SQ FT: 75,000
SALES (est): 23.52MM **Privately Held**
Web: www.feltoninc.com
SIC: 3991 3496 3053 Brushes, household or industrial; Miscellaneous fabricated wire products; Gaskets; packing and sealing devices

(G-14751)
FINISHIELD CORP
5 George Ave (03053-2017)
PHONE...............................603 641-2164
Roger Jubinville, *Pr*
Peter Vetri, *
EMP: 19 EST: 1982
SALES (est): 401.14K **Privately Held**
SIC: 3471 Finishing, metals or formed products

(G-14752)
FREUDENBERG-NOK GNRL PRTNRSHP
11 Ricker Ave (03053-2027)
PHONE...............................603 628-7023
EMP: 10
SALES (est): 780.79K **Privately Held**
SIC: 3089 Plastics processing

(G-14753)
HAMPSHIRE FIRE PROTECTION LLC (PA)
8 N Wentworth Ave (03053-7438)
PHONE...............................603 432-8221
Lawrence J Thibodeau, *Pr*
Diane F Thibodeau, *
EMP: 90 EST: 1978
SQ FT: 21,000
SALES (est): 24.36MM
SALES (corp-wide): 24.36MM **Privately Held**
Web: www.hampshirefire.com
SIC: 1711 3999 Fire sprinkler system installation; Fire extinguishers, portable

(G-14754)
HARVEY INDUSTRIES LLC
30 Jacks Bridge Rd (03053-2145)
PHONE...............................603 216-8300
Brian Allaire, *Brnch Mgr*
EMP: 29
SALES (corp-wide): 1.2B **Privately Held**
Web: www.harveybp.com
SIC: 5031 2431 Windows; Door frames, wood
PA: Harvey Industries, Llc
1400 Main St Fl 3
Waltham MA 02451
800 598-5400

(G-14755)
HOLOGIC INC
2 E Perimeter Rd (03053-2020)
PHONE...............................508 263-2900
EMP: 28
SALES (corp-wide): 4.03B **Publicly Held**
Web: www.hologic.com
SIC: 3844 X-ray apparatus and tubes
PA: Hologic, Inc.
250 Campus Dr
Marlborough MA 01752
508 263-2900

(G-14756)
HUBBELL INCORPORATED
7 Aviation Park Dr (03053-2380)
P.O. Box 9507 (03108-9507)
PHONE...............................800 346-4175
Mary Shand, *Brnch Mgr*
EMP: 50
SALES (corp-wide): 5.37B **Publicly Held**
Web: www.hubbell.com
SIC: 3643 5063 Connectors and terminals for electrical devices; Electrical apparatus and equipment
PA: Hubbell Incorporated
40 Waterview Dr
Shelton CT 06484
475 882-4000

(G-14757)
INSULECTRO
8 Akira Way (03053-2037)
PHONE...............................603 629-4403
Kevin Miller, *Mgr*
EMP: 28
SALES (corp-wide): 115.66MM **Privately Held**
Web: www.insulectro.com
SIC: 3672 5065 Printed circuit boards; Electronic parts and equipment, nec
PA: Insulectro
20362 Windrow Dr
Lake Forest CA 92630
949 587-3200

(G-14758)
KLUBER LUBRIC NORTH AMERCIA LP
32 Industrial Dr (03053-2008)
PHONE...............................603 647-4104
EMP: 21 EST: 2009
SALES (est): 2.15MM **Privately Held**
Web: www.klueber.com
SIC: 2992 Lubricating oils

(G-14759)
KLUBER LUBRICATION NORTH AMERI
54 Wentworth Ave (03053-7475)
PHONE...............................603 434-7704
EMP: 8 EST: 2019
SALES (est): 250.06K **Privately Held**
Web: www.klueber.com
SIC: 2992 Lubricating oils and greases

(G-14760)
L3 TECHNOLOGIES INC
Also Called: Integrated Vision Solutions
9 Akira Way (03053-2037)
PHONE...............................603 626-4800
EMP: 1100
SALES (corp-wide): 17.06B **Publicly Held**
SIC: 3827 Optical instruments and lenses
HQ: L3 Technologies, Inc.
600 3rd Ave Fl 34
New York NY 10016
321 727-9100

(G-14761)
LACTALIS US YOGURT INC
Also Called: Stonyfield Organic
10 Burton Dr (03053-7436)
PHONE...............................603 437-4040
◆ EMP: 400 EST: 1982
SALES (est): 94.4MM
SALES (corp-wide): 355.83K **Privately Held**
Web: www.stonyfield.com
SIC: 2026 2024 Yogurt; Yogurt desserts, frozen
HQ: Lactalis International
Tour Orix Tour Orix
Choisy Le Roi 94600

(G-14762)
LASER PROJECTION TECHNOLOGIES INC
8 Delta Dr Unit 9 (03053-2349)
PHONE...............................603 421-0209
▲ EMP: 39
SIC: 3699 Laser systems and equipment

(G-14763)
LIBERTY ENRGY UTLITIES NH CORP (DH)
Also Called: Liberty Utilities
15 Buttrick Rd (03053-3305)
PHONE...............................905 287-2061
Victor Del Vecchio, *Pr*
EMP: 65 EST: 2011
SALES (est): 463.97MM
SALES (corp-wide): 2.77B **Privately Held**
SIC: 1311 Crude petroleum and natural gas
HQ: Liberty Utilities Co.
14920 W Camelback Rd
Litchfield Park AZ 85340
800 782-2506

(G-14764)
LINEAR & METRIC CO
37 Harvey Rd (03053-7412)
P.O. Box 233 (03053-0233)
PHONE...............................603 432-1700
Leonard Galvin Senior, *Owner*
EMP: 20 EST: 1975
SQ FT: 10,000
SALES (est): 2.41MM **Privately Held**
Web: linear-metric-co.hub.biz
SIC: 3599 Machine shop, jobbing and repair

(G-14765)
MACOM TECH SLTONS HOLDINGS INC
Also Called: Cobham Metelics
54 Grenier Field Rd (03053-2046)
PHONE...............................603 641-3800
Francis Kwan, *Genl Mgr*
EMP: 78
Web: www.macom.com
SIC: 3674 Wafers (semiconductor devices)
PA: Macom Technology Solutions Holdings, Inc.
100 Chelmsford St
Lowell MA 01851

(G-14766)
MEDINA PLATING CORP
17 Kestree Dr (03053-4009)
PHONE...............................330 725-4155
EMP: 28 EST: 1962
SALES (est): 2.75MM **Privately Held**
SIC: 3471 Electroplating of metals or formed products

(G-14767)
MEGGITT (NEW HAMPSHIRE) INC
144 Harvey Rd (03053-7449)
PHONE...............................603 669-0940
EMP: 180
SIC: 3728 3679 3823 3829 Aircraft parts and equipment, nec; Electronic switches; Temperature instruments: industrial process type; Fire detector systems, non-electric

(G-14768)
MEGGITT (ORANGE COUNTY) INC
Also Called: Meggitt Sensing Systems
136 Harvey Rd A9 (03053)
PHONE...............................603 657-2603
EMP: 68
SALES (corp-wide): 19.07B **Publicly Held**
SIC: 3829 Vibration meters, analyzers, and calibrators
HQ: Meggitt (Orange County), Inc.
4 Marconi
Irvine CA 92618

(G-14769)
MERECO TECHNOLOGIES GROUP INC (HQ)
8 Ricker Ave (03053-2001)
PHONE...............................401 822-9300
Philip M Papoojian, *COO*
Richard J Land, *

EMP: 28 EST: 1992
SQ FT: 37,000
SALES (est): 10.43MM
SALES (corp-wide): 5.66MM **Privately Held**
Web: www.protavicamerica.com
SIC: 2891 Epoxy adhesives
PA: Protex International
6 Rue Barbes
Levallois Perret 92300
141341400

(G-14770)
METACHEM RESINS CORPORATION
Also Called: Mereco Technologies
8 Ricker Ave (03053-2001)
EMP: 28 EST: 1960
SALES (est): 8.67MM
SALES (corp-wide): 5.66MM **Privately Held**
Web: www.protavicamerica.com
SIC: 2891 Epoxy adhesives
HQ: Mereco Technologies Group, Inc.
8 Ricker Ave
Londonderry NH 03053

(G-14771)
METAL WORKS INC
24 Industrial Dr (03053-2008)
PHONE.............................603 669-6180
Fred Pierce, *Pr*
David Staffiere, *
Thomas Masiero, *
EMP: 80 EST: 1985
SQ FT: 60,000
SALES (est): 17.53MM **Privately Held**
Web: www.metalworks-inc.com
SIC: 3444 Sheet metalwork

(G-14772)
MICRO-METRICS INC
Also Called: Aeroflex Metelics
54 Grenier Field Rd (03053-2046)
P.O. Box 6022 (11803-0622)
PHONE.............................603 641-3800
EMP: 78
SIC: 3674 Diodes, solid state (germanium, silicon, etc.)

(G-14773)
MICRO-TECH PROD MCH CO INC
Also Called: Machine Shop
1 Commercial Ln (03053-2242)
P.O. Box 870 (03038-0870)
PHONE.............................603 434-1743
Thomas Tufts, *Pr*
Shane Tufts, *Treas*
EMP: 7 EST: 1968
SQ FT: 3,000
SALES (est): 867.89K **Privately Held**
Web: www.micro-techproduction.com
SIC: 3599 Machine shop, jobbing and repair

(G-14774)
MOONLIGHT MEADERY LLC
Also Called: Hidden Moon Brewing
23 Londonderry Rd Unit 17 (03053-3314)
PHONE.............................603 216-2162
M Frbrother, *Genl Mgr*
Michael Fairbrother, *Genl Mgr*
EMP: 10 EST: 2012
SALES (est): 900.07K **Privately Held**
Web: www.moonlightmeadery.com
SIC: 2084 Wines

(G-14775)
MTS ASSOCIATES LONDONDERRY LLC

Also Called: Murray's Auto Recycling Center
55 Hall Rd (03053-2306)
PHONE.............................603 425-2562
Edward Dudek, *Genl Mgr*
EMP: 8
SALES (corp-wide): 4.94MM **Privately Held**
Web: www.murraysautorecycling.com
SIC: 3559 Automotive maintenance equipment
PA: Mts Associates Of Londonderry, L.L.C..
15 Cross Rd
Hooksett NH 03106
603 623-7470

(G-14776)
MUSHIELD COMPANY INC
9 Ricker Ave (03053-2027)
P.O. Box 5045 (03108-5045)
PHONE.............................603 666-4433
David Grilli, *Pr*
Robert Joy, *VP*
Jan Provencher, *Sec*
EMP: 20 EST: 1989
SQ FT: 20,000
SALES (est): 6.95MM **Privately Held**
Web: www.mushield.com
SIC: 3559 3398 3469 Separation equipment, magnetic; Metal heat treating; Metal stampings, nec

(G-14777)
NU-CAST INC
29 Grenier Field Rd (03053-2015)
PHONE.............................603 432-1600
D Donald Mc Kitterick, *Pr*
John Bowkett, *
EMP: 39 EST: 1986
SQ FT: 40,000
SALES (est): 7.05MM **Privately Held**
Web: www.nu-cast.com
SIC: 3365 Aluminum and aluminum-based alloy castings

(G-14778)
NUTFIELD PUBLISHING LLC
118 Hardy Rd (03053-2824)
PHONE.............................603 537-2760
EMP: 9 EST: 2003
SALES (est): 656.14K **Privately Held**
Web: www.nutpub.net
SIC: 2741 Miscellaneous publishing

(G-14779)
PRATT & WHITNEY
Also Called: Pratt & Whitney Aircraft Nelc
52 Pettengill Rd (03053-2050)
PHONE.............................800 742-5877
EMP: 10 EST: 2015
SALES (est): 453.23K **Privately Held**
SIC: 3724 Aircraft engines and engine parts

(G-14780)
PROTAVIC AMERICA INC
8 Ricker Ave (03053-2001)
PHONE.............................603 623-8624
EMP: 9 EST: 2007
SALES (est): 5MM
SALES (corp-wide): 5.66MM **Privately Held**
Web: www.protavicamerica.com
SIC: 2295 2891 Resin or plastic coated fabrics; Adhesives
PA: Protex International
6 Rue Barbes
Levallois Perret 92300
141341400

(G-14781)
RAPID FINISHING NORTH
5 George Ave (03053-2017)
PHONE.............................603 641-2164
EMP: 7 EST: 2019
SALES (est): 113.11K **Privately Held**
Web: www.rapidfinishing.com
SIC: 3479 Coating of metals and formed products

(G-14782)
RIDE-AWAY INC (HQ)
Also Called: Mobilityworks
54 Wentworth Ave (03053-7475)
P.O. Box 1150 (03053-1150)
PHONE.............................603 437-4444
Mark Lore, *Pr*
EMP: 40 EST: 1984
SQ FT: 14,000
SALES (est): 21.84MM
SALES (corp-wide): 218.57MM **Privately Held**
Web: www.mobilityworks.com
SIC: 7532 5511 5013 3999 Van conversion; Vans, new and used; Automotive supplies and parts; Wheelchair lifts
PA: Wmk, Llc
4199 Kinross Lakes Pkwy
Richfield OH 44286
234 312-2000

(G-14783)
SEMI-GENERAL INC
Also Called: Semigen
54 Grenier Field Rd (03053-2046)
PHONE.............................603 641-3800
Tim Filteau, *Pr*
EMP: 62 EST: 1994
SALES (est): 8.59MM **Privately Held**
Web: www.semigen.net
SIC: 3674 Semiconductors and related devices
PA: Naprotek, Llc
90 Rose Orchard Way
San Jose CA 95134

(G-14784)
SIS-USA INC
Also Called: SIS Ergo
55 Wentworth Ave (03053-7476)
PHONE.............................603 432-4495
Scott Mcpartlin, *Pr*
◆ **EMP: 15 EST:** 1984
SQ FT: 36,000
SALES (est): 6.39MM
SALES (corp-wide): 61.64K **Privately Held**
Web: www.hatcollective.com
SIC: 2522 Office furniture, except wood
HQ: Midform Holding Aps
Fjordvej 116
Kolding
28356407

(G-14785)
SYAM SOFTWARE INCORPORATED
12 Lantern Ln (03053-3905)
PHONE.............................603 598-9575
Nicholas Thickins, *CEO*
EMP: 10 EST: 2003
SALES (est): 1.22MM **Privately Held**
Web: www.syamsoftware.com
SIC: 7372 Business oriented computer software

(G-14786)
TEXTILES COATED INCORPORATED (PA)
Also Called: Textiles Coated International

6 George Ave (03053-2016)
PHONE.............................603 296-2221
John W Tippett, *CEO*
Stephen Tippett, *
Alina Bobar, *Information Technology*
Claire Howard, *
▲ **EMP: 25 EST:** 1985
SQ FT: 85,000
SALES (est): 45.91MM
SALES (corp-wide): 45.91MM **Privately Held**
Web: www.textilescoated.com
SIC: 2821 2295 3081 2299 Thermosetting materials; Coated fabrics, not rubberized; Plastics film and sheet; Batting, wadding, padding and fillings

(G-14787)
UFP LONDONDERRY LLC ✪
184 Rockingham Rd (03053-2166)
PHONE.............................603 668-4113
Mike Ellerbrook, *Managing Member*
EMP: 26 EST: 2023
SALES (est): 4.5MM
SALES (corp-wide): 9.63B **Publicly Held**
SIC: 3272 Building materials, except block or brick: concrete
HQ: Shawnlee Construction Llc
74a Taunton St
Plainville MA 02762
508 695-8033

(G-14788)
UNI-CAST LLC
11 Industrial Dr (03053-2011)
PHONE.............................603 625-5761
Henri Fine, *Pr*
▲ **EMP: 150 EST:** 1969
SQ FT: 44,000
SALES (est): 22.6MM **Privately Held**
Web: www.uni-cast.com
SIC: 3366 Copper foundries

(G-14789)
VALID MFG INC
16 Vista Ridge Dr Unit 238 (03053-2479)
PHONE.............................603 880-0948
EMP: 10 EST: 2014
SALES (est): 244.55K **Privately Held**
SIC: 3999 Atomizers, toiletry

(G-14790)
VIBRACOUSTIC USA INC
11 Ricker Ave (03053-2027)
PHONE.............................603 413-7262
EMP: 10
SALES (est): 231.06K **Privately Held**
SIC: 3714 Motor vehicle parts and accessories

(G-14791)
WOODWORKS ARCHITECTURAL MLLWK
16 N Wentworth Ave (03053-7438)
PHONE.............................603 432-4050
Gary Bergeron, *Pr*
Ward Blodgett, *
Michele Bergeron, *
James Hatem, *
D Ward Blodgett, *
EMP: 44 EST: 1985
SQ FT: 75,000
SALES (est): 8.11MM **Privately Held**
Web: www.twnh.com
SIC: 2431 Millwork

(G-14792)
WORKPLACE MODULAR SYSTEMS LLC

562 Mammoth Rd (03053-2117)
PHONE....................................603 622-3727
EMP: 45 **EST:** 1950
SALES (est): 11.44MM
SALES (corp-wide): 25.2MM **Privately Held**
Web: www.workplacenh.com
SIC: 2522   Office furniture, except wood
PA: Gemini Investors V, L.P.
   20 William St
   Wellesley MA 02481
   781 237-7001

Loudon
Merrimack County

(G-14793)
BENEVENTO AGGREGATES LLC
528 Route 106 N (03307-1154)
PHONE....................................603 783-4723
Charles J Benevento, *Mgr*
EMP: 10 **EST:** 2019
SALES (est): 358.56K **Privately Held**
Web: www.beneventocompanies.com
SIC: 1442 5032   Construction sand and
   gravel; Aggregate

(G-14794)
CAPITOL FIRE PROTECTION CO INC
Also Called: New England Pipe & Supply Co
141 N Village Rd (03307-0907)
P.O. Box 7839 (03307-7839)
PHONE....................................603 783-4713
Steven R Rattee, *Pr*
Jean Rattee,   *
Susan Leahy,   *
▲ **EMP:** 30 **EST:** 1963
SQ FT: 45,000
SALES (est): 4.33MM **Privately Held**
Web: www.capitolfireprotection.biz
SIC: 1711 5051 3312   Fire sprinkler system
   installation; Pipe and tubing, steel; Blast
   furnaces and steel mills

(G-14795)
CPH PROGRAM & MACHINE TOOL DES
26 Shaker Brook Park (03307-1142)
PHONE....................................603 716-3849
Christopher Hudon, *Admn*
EMP: 15 **EST:** 2013
SALES (est): 436.94K **Privately Held**
Web:
www.cphcncprogramminganddesign.com
SIC: 3599   Machine shop, jobbing and repair

(G-14796)
NORTHERN DESIGN PRECAST INC
51 International Dr (03307-1210)
P.O. Box 7305 (03247-7305)
PHONE....................................603 783-8989
Bradley J Thompson, *Pr*
Lee W Mattson,   *
EMP: 28 **EST:** 1979
SQ FT: 2,500
SALES (est): 4.56MM **Privately Held**
Web: www.ndprecast.com
SIC: 3272 8712 5211   Concrete products,
   precast, nec; Architectural services;
   Masonry materials and supplies

(G-14797)
PENNY PUBLICATIONS LLC
Also Called: Penny Marketing
570 Route 106 N (03307-1127)
PHONE....................................603 783-9998

Chris Devol, *Mgr*
EMP: 25
Web: www.pennypublications.com
SIC: 2741   Miscellaneous publishing
PA: Penny Publications Llc
   6 Prowitt St
   Norwalk CT 06855

(G-14798)
PLAN TECH INC
7031 Shaker Rd Unit J (03307-1111)
PHONE....................................603 783-4767
David Stewart, *Pr*
Alan Cushing, *VP*
Norman Theriault, *VP*
Linda Theriault, *Sec*
EMP: 23 **EST:** 1985
SQ FT: 28,000
SALES (est): 2.52MM **Privately Held**
Web: www.plantech.com
SIC: 3089 2821   Injection molding of plastics
   ; Plastics materials and resins

(G-14799)
PLEASANT VIEW GARDENS INC (PA)
7316 Pleasant St (03307-1616)
PHONE....................................603 435-8361
Henry Huntington, *Pr*
Jeffrey Huntington,   *
▲ **EMP:** 77 **EST:** 1972
SQ FT: 5,200
SALES (est): 23.7MM
SALES (corp-wide): 23.7MM **Privately Held**
Web: www.pwpvg.com
SIC: 0181 3999   Nursery stock, growing of;
   Plants, artificial and preserved

Lyndeborough
Hillsborough County

(G-14800)
JENESCO INC
138 Herrick Rd (03082-5612)
P.O. Box 873 (03055-0873)
PHONE....................................603 673-4830
Ken Brumleve, *Pr*
Maureen Dwyer, *Sec*
EMP: 10 **EST:** 1987
SQ FT: 6,800
SALES (est): 1.05MM **Privately Held**
Web: www.jenesco.com
SIC: 3559 2321 3714 3674   Ozone machines
   ; Men's and boy's furnishings; Automotive
   wiring harness sets; Semiconductors and
   related devices

Madbury
Strafford County

(G-14801)
TAYLOR EGG PRODUCTS INC
Also Called: Taylor Egg Products
242 Littleworth Rd (03823-7547)
PHONE....................................603 742-1050
William Taylor, *Pr*
EMP: 14 **EST:** 1970
SQ FT: 23,000
SALES (est): 1.87MM
SALES (corp-wide): 43.51MM **Privately Held**
SIC: 2015   Eggs, processed: canned
PA: Siegel Egg Co., Llc
   90 Salem Rd Ste 3
   North Billerica MA 01862
   978 528-2000

Madison
Carroll County

(G-14802)
JK LUMBER LLC
71 Marcella Dr Rte 41 (03849)
P.O. Box 224 (03890-0224)
PHONE....................................603 539-4145
Kim R Moore, *Pr*
James T Smith,   *
John Stockhausen,   *
EMP: 55 **EST:** 2003
SALES (est): 8.56MM **Privately Held**
Web: www.hancocklumber.com
SIC: 2421   Sawmills and planing mills,
   general

(G-14803)
MACLEAN PRECISION MCH CO INC
1928 Village Rd (03849-5401)
P.O. Box 70 (03849-0070)
PHONE....................................,603 367-9011
Douglas Folsom, *Pr*
Pauline Maclean,   *
EMP: 42 **EST:** 1970
SQ FT: 12,000
SALES (est): 4.47MM **Privately Held**
Web: www.macleanprecision.com
SIC: 3599   Machine shop, jobbing and repair

Manchester
Hillsborough County

(G-14804)
ACUANT INC
Also Called: Assuretec Systems
200 Perimeter Rd (03103-3360)
PHONE....................................603 641-8443
EMP: 14
Web: www.idology.com
SIC: 7372   Prepackaged software
HQ: Acuant, Inc.
   2018 Powers Ferry Rd Se
   Atlanta GA 30339
   213 867-2625

(G-14805)
ADVANCE CONCRETE FORM INC
Also Called: Advance Form & Supply
241 Pepsi Rd (03109-5320)
PHONE....................................603 669-4496
Bernard Cancel, *Mgr*
EMP: 7
SALES (corp-wide): 6.61MM **Privately Held**
Web: www.advanceconcreteform.com
SIC: 3444   Concrete forms, sheet metal
PA: Advance Concrete Form, Inc.
   5102 Pflaum Rd
   Madison WI 53718
   608 222-8684

(G-14806)
ADVANCED CNC MACHINE INC
722 E Indus Pk Dr Unit 15 (03109-5628)
PHONE....................................603 625-6631
Lane A Fraser, *Pr*
EMP: 10 **EST:** 1988
SQ FT: 1,200
SALES (est): 139.89K **Privately Held**
SIC: 3599   Machine shop, jobbing and repair

(G-14807)
AERO DEFENSE INTERNATIONAL LLC
400 Bedford St Ste 136 (03101-1195)
PHONE....................................603 644-0305
Stephen Adler, *Prin*
EMP: 8 **EST:** 2007
SALES (est): 615.85K **Privately Held**
SIC: 3812   Aircraft/aerospace flight
   instruments and guidance systems

(G-14808)
ALEX & RYAN DESIGN LLC
630 Harvard St # 2 (03103-4414)
PHONE....................................603 518-8650
Alexander Costa, *CEO*
EMP: 13 **EST:** 2014
SALES (est): 508K **Privately Held**
Web: www.anrkydexholsters.com
SIC: 7389 3089 3812 5941   Design services;
   Thermoformed finished plastics products,
   nec; Defense systems and equipment;
   Firearms

(G-14809)
ALLARD NAZARIAN GROUP INC
Also Called: Snow-Nbstedt Pwr
Transmissions
111 Joliette St Ste 9 (03102-3018)
PHONE....................................603 314-0017
Lee Tack, *Brnch Mgr*
EMP: 14
SALES (corp-wide): 38.95MM **Privately Held**
Web: www.granitestatemfg.com
SIC: 3812 3714   Aircraft/aerospace flight
   instruments and guidance systems;
   Transmissions, motor vehicle
PA: Allard Nazarian Group, Inc.
   124 Joliette St
   Manchester NH 03102
   603 668-1900

(G-14810)
ALLARD NAZARIAN GROUP INC (PA)
Also Called: Granite State Manufacturing
124 Joliette St (03102-3017)
PHONE....................................603 668-1900
John R Allard, *CEO*
Michael Allard,   *
David Nazarian,   *
Younes Nazarian,   *
Douglas Thomson,   *
EMP: 118 **EST:** 1938
SQ FT: 73,484
SALES (est): 38.95MM
SALES (corp-wide): 38.95MM **Privately Held**
Web: www.granitestatemfg.com
SIC: 3812 3829 3599 3566   Aircraft/
   aerospace flight instruments and guidance
   systems; Aircraft and motor vehicle
   measurement equipment; Custom
   machinery; Gears, power transmission,
   except auto

(G-14811)
ALLEGRO MICROSYSTEMS INC (HQ)
Also Called: Allegro
955 Perimeter Rd (03103-3353)
PHONE....................................603 626-2300
Ravi Vig, *Pr*
Yoshihiro Suzuki, *Non-Executive Chairman of the Board*
Paul V Walsh Junior, *Sr VP*
Christopher E Brown, *Sr VP*
Michael C Doogue, *Senior Vice President Technology*

EMP: 326 EST: 1984
SQ FT: 120,000
SALES (est): 973.65MM Publicly Held
Web: www.allegromicro.com
SIC: 3674 Semiconductors and related
devices
PA: Sanken Electric Co., Ltd.
3-6-3, Kitano
Niiza STM 352-0

(G-14812)
ALLEGRO MICROSYSTEMS LLC (HQ)
955 Perimeter Rd (03103-3353)
P.O. Box 11155 (02211-1155)
PHONE....................................603 626-2300
Vineet Nargolwala, Pr
Mark A Feragne, *
Andre G Labrecque, *
Yoshihiro Suzuki, *
Steven Miles, *
◆ EMP: 500 EST: 1990
SQ FT: 250,000
SALES (est): 240.66MM Publicly Held
Web: www.allegromicro.com
SIC: 3674 Semiconductors and related
devices
PA: Sanken Electric Co., Ltd.
3-6-3, Kitano
Niiza STM 352-0

(G-14813)
APOGEE COINS PRECIOUS MTLS LLC
P.O. Box 4184 (03108-4184)
PHONE....................................603 391-6417
Brian Whitmore, Prin
EMP: 7 EST: 2011
SALES (est): 226.47K Privately Held
Web: www.apogeecoins.com
SIC: 3339 Precious metals

(G-14814)
ASTRONICS AEROSAT CORPORATION
220 Hackett Hill Rd (03102-8994)
PHONE....................................603 879-0205
Dennis Ferguson, CEO
Matthew Harrah, *
EMP: 100 EST: 2013
SQ FT: 28,500
SALES (est): 21MM
SALES (corp-wide): 534.89MM Publicly
Held
Web: www.astronics.com
SIC: 3669 8711 Intercommunication
systems, electric; Aviation and/or
aeronautical engineering
PA: Astronics Corporation
130 Commerce Way
East Aurora NY 14052
716 805-1599

(G-14815)
AT COMM CORP
150 Dow St Ste 404 (03101-1254)
PHONE....................................603 624-4424
Bob Boyd, Prin
EMP: 12
SALES (corp-wide): 4.83MM Privately
Held
Web: www.atcomm.com
SIC: 3661 8731 Telephone and telegraph
apparatus; Commercial physical research
PA: At Comm Corporation
907 Burkhart Ave
San Leandro CA 94579
650 375-8188

(G-14816)
BAKER GRAPHICS INC
Also Called: Curry Copy and Printing Center
143 Middle St Ste 1 (03101-1978)
PHONE....................................603 625-5427
Sandy Baker, Pr
EMP: 7 EST: 1976
SQ FT: 3,500
SALES (est): 422.64K Privately Held
Web: www.bakergraphicsonline.com
SIC: 2752 7334 Offset printing;
Photocopying and duplicating services

(G-14817)
BANTRY COMPONENTS INC
Also Called: Krl Electronics
160 Bouchard St (03103-3315)
PHONE....................................603 668-3210
Verna Perry, CEO
Verna Perry, CEO
Teresa Churillo, *
EMP: 50 EST: 1969
SQ FT: 17,000
SALES (est): 6.2MM Privately Held
Web: www.krlbantry.com
SIC: 3825 3823 3674 3577 Instruments to
measure electricity; Process control
instruments; Semiconductors and related
devices; Computer peripheral equipment,
nec

(G-14818)
BB PLASTIC FABRICATION
726 East Industrial Park Dr Unit 5
(03109-5600)
PHONE....................................603 622-9882
EMP: 8 EST: 2019
SALES (est): 138.97K Privately Held
Web: www.bbplasticfabrication.com
SIC: 3089 Injection molding of plastics

(G-14819)
BELLMAN JEWELERS INC
1650 Elm St Ste 102 (03101-1251)
PHONE....................................603 625-4653
David H Bellman, Pr
Douglas Sharek, Treas
EMP: 8 EST: 1981
SQ FT: 3,000
SALES (est): 1.5MM Privately Held
Web: www.bellmans.com
SIC: 7389 5944 3911 Appraisers, except
real estate; Jewelry, precious stones and
precious metals; Jewelry apparel

(G-14820)
BOLES ENTERPRISES INC
Also Called: Coloniel Printing
143 Middle St Ste 1 (03101-1978)
PHONE....................................603 622-4282
Curtis M Boles, Pr
Luke O'neill, Prin
EMP: 9 EST: 1973
SQ FT: 4,000
SALES (est): 932.55K Privately Held
Web: www.colonialprintingnh.com
SIC: 2752 7334 Offset printing;
Photocopying and duplicating services

(G-14821)
BRIDGESTONE RET OPERATIONS LLC
Also Called: Firestone
300 Elm St (03101-2701)
PHONE....................................603 668-1123
Ray Steele, Mgr
EMP: 9
Web: www.bridgestoneamericas.com

SIC: 5531 7534 Automotive tires;
Rebuilding and retreading tires
HQ: Bridgestone Retail Operations, Llc
333 E Lake St Ste 300
Bloomingdale IL 60108
630 259-9000

(G-14822)
BURNDY AMERICAS INC (HQ)
47 East Industrial Park Dr (03109-5311)
PHONE....................................603 647-5000
Rodd Ruland, Pr
EMP: 53 EST: 1992
SALES (est): 490.27MM
SALES (corp-wide): 5.37B Publicly Held
Web: www.hubbell.com
SIC: 3643 5063 Current-carrying wiring
services; Electrical apparatus and
equipment
PA: Hubbell Incorporated
40 Waterview Dr
Shelton CT 06484
475 882-4000

(G-14823)
BURNDY AMERICAS INTL HOLDG LLC
47 East Industrial Park Dr (03109-5311)
PHONE....................................603 647-5000
EMP: 598 EST: 2009
SALES (est): 2.29MM
SALES (corp-wide): 5.37B Publicly Held
Web: www.hubbell.com
SIC: 3643 5063 Current-carrying wiring
services; Electrical apparatus and
equipment
HQ: Burndy Americas Inc
47 E Industrial Pk Dr
Manchester NH 03109

(G-14824)
BURNDY LLC (DH)
47 East Industrial Park Dr (03109-5311)
PHONE....................................603 647-5000
Rodd Ruland, Managing Member
Kevin Ryan, *
◆ EMP: 277 EST: 2009
SALES (est): 257.91MM
SALES (corp-wide): 5.37B Publicly Held
Web: www.hubbell.com
SIC: 3643 5063 Connectors and terminals
for electrical devices; Wire and cable
HQ: Burndy Americas Inc
47 E Industrial Pk Dr
Manchester NH 03109

(G-14825)
CABINETS FOR LESS LLC
679 Mast Rd (03102-1417)
PHONE....................................603 935-7551
Zumra Gutierrez, Prin
EMP: 7 EST: 2011
SALES (est): 690.03K Privately Held
Web: www.cabinetsforlessllc.com
SIC: 2434 5211 3253 5023 Wood kitchen
cabinets; Tile, ceramic; Ceramic wall and
floor tile; Wood flooring

(G-14826)
CELLULAR SPECIALTIES INC
670 North Commercial St Ste 202 (03101)
PHONE....................................603 626-6677
◆ EMP: 72
Web: www.westell.com
SIC: 3663 Radio broadcasting and
communications equipment

(G-14827)
CG HOLDINGS LLC (PA)
669 East Industrial Park Dr (03109-5625)
PHONE....................................603 623-3344
Theodore Lorenzetti Junior, Pr
Paul Lorenzetti, *
▲ EMP: 39 EST: 1984
SALES (est): 7.66MM
SALES (corp-wide): 7.66MM Privately
Held
Web: www.corflexglobal.com
SIC: 3842 8011 Orthopedic appliances;
Offices and clinics of medical doctors

(G-14828)
CHUCKLES INC
Also Called: Sukesha
11925 S Willow St (03103-2329)
P.O. Box 5126 (03108-5126)
PHONE....................................603 669-4228
Charles P Frank, Pr
◆ EMP: 25 EST: 1984
SALES (est): 4.77MM Privately Held
Web: www.allnutrient.com
SIC: 2844 Hair preparations, including
shampoos

(G-14829)
CITY OF MANCHESTER
Also Called: Water Treatment Plant
1581 Lake Shore Rd (03109-5707)
PHONE....................................603 624-6482
EMP: 17
Web: www.manchadernh.gov
SIC: 9511 3589 Water control and quality
agency, government; Sewage and water
treatment equipment
PA: City Of Manchester
1 City Hall Plz
Manchester NH 03101
603 624-6460

(G-14830)
CLARIOS LLC
Also Called: Johnson Controls
915 Holt Ave Unit 7 (03109-5606)
PHONE....................................603 222-2400
EMP: 82
SALES (corp-wide): 1.54B Privately Held
Web: www.clarios.com
SIC: 2531 Seats, automobile
HQ: Clarios, Llc
5757 N Green Bay Ave
Milwaukee WI 53209

(G-14831)
CLOUD SOFTWARE GROUP INC
Also Called: Tibco Scribe
150 Dow St (03101-1227)
PHONE....................................603 622-5109
EMP: 105
SALES (corp-wide): 4.38B Privately Held
Web: www.tibco.com
SIC: 7372 Prepackaged software
HQ: Cloud Software Group, Inc.
851 W Cypress Creek Rd
Fort Lauderdale FL 33309

(G-14832)
COBHAM DEF ELECTRONIC SYSTEMS
336 Abby Rd (03103-3363)
PHONE....................................603 518-2716
EMP: 9 EST: 2018
SALES (est): 124.43K Privately Held
SIC: 3812 Search and navigation equipment

(G-14833)
COCA-COLA BEVS NORTHEAST INC
Also Called: Coca-Cola
99 Eddy Rd (03102-3226)
PHONE...............................603 623-6033
Mark Francoeur, *Mgr*
EMP: 27
Web: www.coca-cola.com
SIC: 2086 Bottled and canned soft drinks
HQ: Coca-Cola Beverages Northeast, Inc.
1 Executive Park Dr # 330
Bedford NH 03110
603 627-7871

(G-14834)
CONNEXIENT LLC
33 S Coml St Ste 302 (03101)
P.O. Box 10782 (03110-0782)
PHONE...............................603 669-1300
Mark Green, *CEO*
EMP: 7 EST: 2012
SALES (est): 209.25K Privately Held
SIC: 7372 Application computer software

(G-14835)
CONSTRCTION SMMARY NEW HMPSHR/
734 Chestnut St (03104-3001)
PHONE...............................603 627-8856
Robert Morin, *Pr*
EMP: 9 EST: 1986
SQ FT: 600
SALES (est): 923.51K Privately Held
Web: www.constructionsummary.com
SIC: 2741 2711 Business service
newsletters: publishing and printing;
Newspapers

(G-14836)
COPY EXPRESS LLC
923 Elm St (03101-2003)
PHONE...............................603 625-4960
Janet Heffron, *Managing Member*
Brian Heffron Senior, *Prin*
Brian Heffron Junior, *Prin*
EMP: 8 EST: 1986
SQ FT: 4,500
SALES (est): 889.34K Privately Held
Web: www.copyexpress.com
SIC: 2732 Book printing

(G-14837)
CORFIN INDUSTRIES INC
1050 Perimeter Rd (03103-3355)
PHONE...............................603 893-9900
Donald Tyler, *CEO*
Kent Rosenthal, *
Kevin Svenconis, *
EMP: 80 EST: 1990
SALES (est): 5.32MM Privately Held
Web: www.micross.com
SIC: 3674 Semiconductors and related
devices

(G-14838)
COUNTER PRO INC
210 Lincoln St (03103-5030)
PHONE...............................603 647-2444
Leigh Paulsen, *Pr*
EMP: 15 EST: 1988
SQ FT: 40,000
SALES (est): 1.91MM Privately Held
Web: www.counterproinc.com
SIC: 2434 Wood kitchen cabinets

(G-14839)
CRH AMERICAS MATERIALS INC

1 Sundial Ave Ste 310 (03103-7299)
PHONE...............................603 669-2373
David Bissonnette, *Brnch Mgr*
EMP: 9
SALES (corp-wide): 32.72B Privately Held
Web: www.oldcastlematerials.com
SIC: 3273 Ready-mixed concrete
HQ: Crh Americas Materials, Inc.
900 Ashwood Pkwy Ste 700
Atlanta GA 30338

(G-14840)
DATAXOOM CORP (PA)
25 Sundial Ave Ste 316 (03103-7244)
PHONE...............................510 474-0044
Christopher Hill, *Pr*
Kelley Carr, *Dir*
Scott Goodrich, *Dir*
EMP: 19 EST: 2012
SALES (est): 4.43MM
SALES (corp-wide): 4.43MM Privately
Held
Web: www.dataxoom.com
SIC: 4813 7371 7372 Proprietary online
service networks; Computer software
development and applications; Business
oriented computer software

(G-14841)
DESMARAIS PLASTICS LLC
1 Bouchard St (03103-3313)
PHONE...............................603 669-8523
Michael Desmarais, *Pr*
Gertrude Desmarais, *VP*
Richard Desmarais, *CFO*
Robert Dastin, *Clerk*
EMP: 75 EST: 1971
SQ FT: 155,000
SALES (est): 24.62MM
SALES (corp-wide): 136.37MM Privately
Held
Web: www.newhampshireplastics.com
SIC: 2821 Thermoplastic materials
PA: Grimco, Inc.
11745 Sppngton Brracks Rd
Saint Louis MO 63127
800 542-9941

(G-14842)
DISTILLERY NETWORK INC
21 W Auburn St Ste 30 (03101-2386)
PHONE...............................603 997-6786
Jonathan Zajac, *Pr*
Phillip Le Clerc, *Off Mgr*
EMP: 22 EST: 2015
SQ FT: 3,500
SALES (est): 395.91K Privately Held
Web: www.buyamoonshinestill.com
SIC: 3556 Distillery machinery

(G-14843)
DOUGHVINCI INC
P.O. Box 5084 (03108-5084)
PHONE...............................603 494-8769
Steve Romano, *Owner*
EMP: 8 EST: 2009
SALES (est): 246.81K Privately Held
Web: www.doughvinci.com
SIC: 2051 Bread, cake, and related products

(G-14844)
DR BIRON INCORPORATED (PA)
Also Called: Keystone Press
20 East Industrial Park Dr Unit 2
(03109-5626)
P.O. Box 5433 (03108-5433)
PHONE...............................603 622-5222
Daniel Biron, *Pr*
EMP: 12 EST: 1915
SQ FT: 11,000

SALES (est): 2.92MM
SALES (corp-wide): 2.92MM Privately
Held
Web: www.keystonepress.com
SIC: 2752 Offset printing

(G-14845)
DUNN INDUSTRIES INC
123 Abby Rd (03103-3306)
PHONE...............................603 666-4800
Duane Dunn, *Pr*
EMP: 24 EST: 1987
SQ FT: 16,000
SALES (est): 5.51MM
SALES (corp-wide): 996.3MM Privately
Held
Web: www.tekni-plex.com
SIC: 3089 Injection molding of plastics
PA: Tekni-Plex, Inc.
460 E Swedesford Rd # 300
Wayne PA 19087
484 690-1520

(G-14846)
DUTILE GLINES & HIGGINS INC
850 Perimeter Rd (03103-3324)
PHONE...............................603 622-0452
David Dutile, *Pr*
Robert Glines, *Treas*
EMP: 10 EST: 1985
SALES (est): 1.65MM Privately Held
Web: www.jewellinstruments.com
SIC: 3823 3674 3577 3571 Computer
interface equipment, for industrial process
control; Semiconductors and related devices
; Computer peripheral equipment, nec;
Electronic computers

(G-14847)
EMPIRE SHEETMETAL INC
155 Baker St (03103-6460)
PHONE...............................603 622-4439
Stanley G Ziemba, *Pr*
Beverly A Ziemba, *
Charles I Dunn Clrk, *Prin*
EMP: 29 EST: 1971
SQ FT: 3,000
SALES (est): 2.12MM Privately Held
SIC: 1761 3312 3444 Sheet metal work, nec
; Iron and steel products, hot-rolled; Sheet
metalwork

(G-14848)
FINALLY FREE LLC
55 South Commercial St (03101-2606)
P.O. Box 1390 (03054-1390)
PHONE...............................603 626-4388
Herbert Langer, *Pr*
EMP: 17 EST: 1955
SQ FT: 1,500
SALES (est): 507.58K Privately Held
Web: www.fishercatsparking.com
SIC: 3086 6531 Packaging and shipping
materials, foamed plastics; Real estate
agents and managers

(G-14849)
FREEDS BAKERY LLC
299 Pepsi Rd (03109-5320)
PHONE...............................603 627-7746
EMP: 50
SIC: 2051 Bakery: wholesale or wholesale/
retail combined

(G-14850)
GARAVENTA U S A INC
999 Candia Rd Bldg 2 (03109-5210)
PHONE...............................603 669-6553
James Hunt, *Mgr*
EMP: 19

SALES (corp-wide): 5.95MM Privately
Held
Web: www.garaventalift.com
SIC: 3999 Wheelchair lifts
HQ: Garaventa U S A, Inc.
225 W Depot St
Antioch IL 60002

(G-14851)
GENTEX CORPORATION
645 Harvey Rd Ste 1 (03103-3342)
PHONE...............................603 657-1200
Mark Smith, *Brnch Mgr*
EMP: 180
SQ FT: 10,000
SALES (corp-wide): 95.04MM Privately
Held
Web: www.gentexcorp.com
SIC: 3812 Defense systems and equipment
PA: Gentex Corporation
324 Main St
Simpson PA 18407
570 282-3550

(G-14852)
GNAW INC
391 Oak St (03104-2616)
PHONE...............................603 418-8900
Lisa North, *Prin*
EMP: 9 EST: 2014
SALES (est): 117.38K Privately Held
SIC: 2082 Malt beverages

(G-14853)
GOWANDA RCD LLC
Also Called: Rcd Components
520 East Industrial Park Dr (03109-5327)
PHONE...............................716 532-2234
Don Mcelheny, *Managing Member*
EMP: 201 EST: 2019
SALES (est): 18.76MM
SALES (corp-wide): 32.66MM Privately
Held
Web: www.gowanda.com
SIC: 3677 5065 Electronic coils and
transformers; Electronic parts and
equipment, nec
PA: Gowanda - Gec, Llc
1 Magnetic Pkwy
Gowanda NY 14070
716 532-2234

(G-14854)
GPI NH-T INC
Also Called: Ira Toyota of Manchester
33 Auto Center Rd (03103-3213)
PHONE...............................603 624-1800
Glen Kimball, *Owner*
EMP: 65 EST: 2015
SALES (est): 23.55MM Publicly Held
Web: www.group1auto.com
SIC: 5511 3713 Automobiles, new and used
; Truck bodies and parts
PA: Group 1 Automotive, Inc.
800 Gessner Rd Ste 500
Houston TX 77024

(G-14855)
GRANITE STATE MANUFACTURING
124 Joliette St (03102-3017)
PHONE...............................800 464-7646
EMP: 18 EST: 1992
SALES (est): 1.03MM Privately Held
Web: www.granitestatemfg.com
SIC: 3549 Assembly machines, including
robotic

(G-14856)
GRANITE STATE STAMPS INC
8025 S Willow St Ste 102　(03103-2311)
P.O. Box 5252　(03108-5252)
PHONE..................................603 669-9322
TOLL FREE: 800
R Bruce Hale, *Pr*
Lynn Hale, *VP*
Kelly Hale, *Treas*
EMP: 11 EST: 1967
SQ FT: 5,000
SALES (est): 333.27K **Privately Held**
SIC: 3953 3993　Embossing seals and hand
　stamps; Signs, not made in custom sign
　painting shops

(G-14857)
GTI SPINDLE TECHNOLOGY INC (DH)
33 Zachary Rd　(03109-5639)
PHONE..................................603 669-5993
Tom Hoenig, *Pr*
Tracy Hoenig, *
Franz J Frei, *
Raymond St Onge, *
Eric Huston, *
▲ EMP: 25 EST: 1997
SQ FT: 14,400
SALES (est): 8.75MM
SALES (corp-wide): 730.18MM **Privately Held**
Web: www.gtispindle.com
SIC: 7699 3599　Industrial machinery and
　equipment repair; Machine and other job
　shop work
HQ: Setco Sales Company
　2255 Global Way
　Hebron KY 41048
　513 941-5110

(G-14858)
HELEKA COMPANIES LLC
Also Called: Lilac and Finch
1361 Elm St　(03101-1324)
PHONE..................................303 856-5457
EMP: 10
SALES (corp-wide): 222.84K **Privately Held**
Web: www.heleka.com
SIC: 2844　Perfumes, cosmetics and other
　toilet preparations
PA: Heleka Companies Llc
　160 Dover Rd Unit 10
　Chichester NH 03258
　603 798-3674

(G-14859)
HIPPOPRESS LLC (PA)
Also Called: Qol Publications
195 Mcgregor St Ste 325　(03102-3749)
PHONE..................................603 625-1855
EMP: 30 EST: 2000
SALES (est): 2.34MM
SALES (corp-wide): 2.34MM **Privately Held**
Web: www.hippopress.com
SIC: 2711　Newspapers: publishing only, not
　printed on site

(G-14860)
HUBBELL INCORPORATED
47 East Industrial Park Dr　(03109-5311)
PHONE..................................603 647-5000
Charles Ackerman, *Brnch Mgr*
EMP: 10
SALES (corp-wide): 5.37B **Publicly Held**
Web: www.hubbell.com

SIC: 3643 3678 3694　Connectors and
　terminals for electrical devices; Electronic
　connectors; Automotive electrical
　equipment, nec
PA: Hubbell Incorporated
　40 Waterview Dr
　Shelton CT 06484
　475 882-4000

(G-14861)
IBMNH INC (PA)
850 East Industrial Park Dr Ste 4
(03109-5635)
PHONE..................................603 644-2326
Robert Quagan, *Pr*
Claudia Quagan, *Treas*
Jennifer Bonanno, *Sec*
▲ EMP: 9 EST: 1985
SQ FT: 2,500
SALES (est): 2.2MM
SALES (corp-wide): 2.2MM **Privately Held**
SIC: 3674 6719　Hybrid integrated circuits;
　Personal holding companies, except banks

(G-14862)
IMAGE 4 CONCEPTS INC
Also Called: Exhibitcenter.com
7 Perimeter Rd Ste 10　(03103-3343)
PHONE..................................603 644-0077
TOLL FREE: 800
Jeffrey Baker, *CEO*
EMP: 19 EST: 1987
SQ FT: 8,500
SALES (est): 2.53MM **Privately Held**
Web: www.image4.com
SIC: 7389 8742 2823　Trade show
　arrangement; Marketing consulting services
　; Acetate fibers, triacetate fibers

(G-14863)
INTEGRATED DEICING SVCS LLC (DH)
Also Called: IDS
175 Ammon Dr　(03103-3311)
PHONE..................................603 647-1717
Roger Langille, *Pr*
Mike Svedruzic, *
Mike Grantz, *
EMP: 338 EST: 2002
SQ FT: 1,800
SALES (est): 99.17MM
SALES (corp-wide): 95.21MM **Privately Held**
Web: www.inlandgroup.aero
SIC: 3728 4581　Deicing equipment, aircraft;
　Aircraft servicing and repairing
HQ: Inland Technologies Canada
　Incorporated
　14 Queen St
　Truro NS B2N 2
　902 895-6346

(G-14864)
INTELLIGENT MFG SOLUTONS LLC
645 Harvey Rd　(03103-3323)
PHONE..................................603 296-1160
Raymond Marshall, *Managing Member*
EMP: 40 EST: 2005
SQ FT: 250,000
SALES (est): 20.12MM **Privately Held**
Web: www.imscorp-us.com
SIC: 5065 3672　Electronic parts; Printed
　circuit boards

(G-14865)
ITNH INC
150 Dow St Ste 200a　(03101-1227)
PHONE..................................603 669-6900
Sasson Shemesh, *Pr*

Micheal Terlizzi, *
Jacob Gilon, *
▲ EMP: 25 EST: 2003
SQ FT: 10,000
SALES (est): 4.45MM **Privately Held**
Web: www.itnh.com
SIC: 2752　Offset printing

(G-14866)
J & R LANGLEY CO INC
169 S Main St　(03102-4498)
PHONE..................................603 622-9653
Robert R Schmidt, *Pr*
Kate Roop, *Prin*
EMP: 21 EST: 1949
SQ FT: 10,000
SALES (est): 530.79K **Privately Held**
Web: www.jrlangley.com
SIC: 2391 5719 5023　Draperies, plastic and
　textile: from purchased materials; Venetian
　blinds; Venetian blinds

(G-14867)
JANICE MILLER
Also Called: Jaymill
150 Dow St Ste 4　(03101-1227)
PHONE..................................603 629-9995
Janice Miller, *Pr*
Janice Miller, *Owner*
EMP: 7 EST: 1991
SALES (est): 417.74K **Privately Held**
Web: www.ceojaymil.com
SIC: 2511　Wood household furniture

(G-14868)
JEWELL INSTRUMENTS LLC (PA)
Also Called: Modutec
850 Perimeter Rd　(03103-3324)
PHONE..................................603 669-5121
Carlo I Carluccio, *Managing Member*
Stephen P Morin, *
◆ EMP: 120 EST: 1938
SQ FT: 60,000
SALES (est): 27.45MM
SALES (corp-wide): 27.45MM **Privately Held**
Web: www.jewellinstruments.com
SIC: 3823　Process control instruments

(G-14869)
JP SERCEL ASSOCIATES INC
Also Called: Jpsa
220 Hackett Hill Rd　(03102-8994)
PHONE..................................603 595-7048
EMP: 33 EST: 1994
SQ FT: 35,000
SALES (est): 2.29MM
SALES (corp-wide): 1.43B **Publicly Held**
Web: www.jpsalaser.com
SIC: 3569 3699　Robots, assembly line:
　industrial and commercial; Laser systems
　and equipment
PA: Ipg Photonics Corporation
　377 Simarano Dr
　Marlborough MA 01752
　508 373-1100

(G-14870)
KALWALL CORPORATION (PA)
1111 Candia Rd　(03109-5211)
P.O. Box 237　(03105-0237)
PHONE..................................603 627-3861
Richard Keller, *Pr*
Amelia S Keller, *International Sales Vice President*
Katherine Garfield, *
◆ EMP: 300 EST: 1955
SQ FT: 100,000
SALES (est): 82.99MM

SALES (corp-wide): 82.99MM **Privately Held**
Web: www.kalwall.com
SIC: 3089 3083　Panels, building: plastics,
　nec; Thermoplastics laminates: rods, tubes,
　plates, and sheet

(G-14871)
KELLER PRODUCTS INCORPORATED (PA)
41 Union St　(03103-6319)
P.O. Box 4105　(03108-4105)
PHONE..................................603 627-7887
Richard R Keller, *Ch Bd*
John A Hudson, *Pr*
David W Keller, *VP*
Katherine K Garfield, *Treas*
◆ EMP: 28 EST: 1946
SQ FT: 30,000
SALES (est): 11.09MM
SALES (corp-wide): 11.09MM **Privately Held**
Web: www.kellerplastics.com
SIC: 2435 3089　Plywood, hardwood or
　hardwood faced; Molding primary plastics

(G-14872)
KLARMANN RULINGS INC
1 Perimeter Rd Ste 900　(03103-3367)
P.O. Box 4795　(03108-4795)
PHONE..................................603 424-2401
Christopher Wilmot, *Pr*
Katherine Lawrence, *VP*
Donna Morin, *Treas*
EMP: 11 EST: 1956
SALES (est): 928.3K **Privately Held**
Web: www.reticles.com
SIC: 8734 3231　Calibration and certification;
　Laboratory glassware

(G-14873)
LADESCO INC
150 Dow St　(03101-1241)
PHONE..................................603 623-3772
Wayne Trombly, *Pr*
EMP: 150 EST: 1973
SQ FT: 65,000
SALES (est): 9.07MM **Privately Held**
Web: www.ladescoinc.com
SIC: 3677　Coil windings, electronic

(G-14874)
LAIRD CONNECTIVITY LLC
205 Pinebrook Pl　(03109-4836)
PHONE..................................603 627-7877
Scott Lordo, *CEO*
EMP: 106
SALES (corp-wide): 98.1MM **Privately Held**
Web: www.lairdconnect.com
SIC: 3674　Computer logic modules
PA: Laird Connectivity Llc
　50 S Main St Ste 1100
　Akron OH 44308
　330 434-7929

(G-14875)
LAIRD TECHNOLOGIES INC
205 Pinebrook Pl　(03109-4836)
PHONE..................................603 627-7877
Adam Alevy, *VP*
EMP: 23
SALES (corp-wide): 13.02B **Publicly Held**
Web: www.lairdtech.com
SIC: 3469 3663　Stamping metal for the trade
　; Cellular radio telephone
HQ: Laird Technologies, Inc.
　16401 Swingley Ridge Rd
　Chesterfield MO 63017
　636 898-6000

(G-14876)
LASER GROUP PUBLISHING INC
177 East Industrial Park Dr (03109-5321)
P.O. Box 276 (03061-0276)
PHONE...............................603 880-8909
Jodi Valcourt, *Pr*
EMP: 10 **EST:** 1996
SALES (est): 1.17MM
SALES (corp-wide): 2.28B **Publicly Held**
SIC: 2721 Magazines: publishing only, not printed on site
HQ: Consumer Source Inc.
3585 Engrg Dr Ste 100
Norcross GA 30092

(G-14877)
LYOPHILIZATION SVCS NENG INC (HQ)
Also Called: Lsne
1 Sundial Ave Ste 112 (03103-7209)
PHONE...............................603 626-5763
Matthew J Halvorsen, *Pr*
John Halvorsen, *VP*
Bob Haggerty, *Sr VP*
Joe Hechavarria, *VP*
Aimee Hodge, *VP*
EMP: 17 **EST:** 1996
SQ FT: 10,000
SALES (est): 99.09MM
SALES (corp-wide): 106.73MM **Privately Held**
Web: www.pci.com
SIC: 2836 2834 Biological products, except diagnostic; Pharmaceutical preparations
PA: Packaging Coordinators, Inc.
3001 Red Lion Rd
Philadelphia PA 19114
215 613-3600

(G-14878)
MANUFACTURING SERVICES GROUP
Also Called: M S G
91 Lilac Ct (03103-7761)
PHONE...............................603 883-1022
Raymond Rose, *Pr*
EMP: 12 **EST:** 2000
SALES (est): 1.02MM **Privately Held**
SIC: 3672 Printed circuit boards

(G-14879)
MARMON AEROSPACE & DEFENSE LLC
655 Valley St (03103)
PHONE...............................603 622-3500
EMP: 7 **EST:** 2018
SALES (est): 245.07K **Privately Held**
Web: www.marmon-ad.com
SIC: 3721 Aircraft

(G-14880)
MARMON AEROSPACE & DEFENSE LLC (DH)
Also Called: Rscc Aerospace & Defense
680 Hayward St (03103-4420)
PHONE...............................603 622-3500
Mike Dube, *
▲ **EMP:** 18 **EST:** 2009
SQ FT: 100,000
SALES (est): 25.9MM
SALES (corp-wide): 302.09B **Publicly Held**
Web: www.marmon-ad.com
SIC: 3357 Nonferrous wiredrawing and insulating
HQ: Marmon Energy Services Company
181 W Madison St Ste 3900
Chicago IL 60602
312 372-9500

(G-14881)
MARQUES GUITARS LLC
230 Laval St (03102-2942)
PHONE...............................603 321-4833
Filipe Neri Marques, *Prin*
EMP: 8 **EST:** 2018
SALES (est): 69.64K **Privately Held**
Web: www.martinguitar.com
SIC: 3999 Manufacturing industries, nec

(G-14882)
MCLEAN COMMUNICATIONS LLC
50 Dow St (03101-1211)
PHONE...............................603 624-1442
Sharron Mccarthy, *Pr*
Ernesto Burden, *VP*
EMP: 85 **EST:** 2012
SALES (est): 1.69MM
SALES (corp-wide): 38.1MM **Privately Held**
Web: www.nhmagazine.com
SIC: 2711 Newspapers, publishing and printing
PA: Yankee Publishing Incorporated
1121 Main St
Dublin NH 03444
603 563-8111

(G-14883)
MERRIMACK MANUFACTURING LLC
540 North Commercial St (03101-1122)
PHONE...............................603 206-0200
EMP: 39
SALES (est): 9.6MM **Privately Held**
Web: www.merrimackmanufacturing.com
SIC: 3841 Surgical and medical instruments

(G-14884)
MICHAEL PERRA INC
640 Harvard St Ste 2 (03103-4481)
PHONE...............................603 644-2110
Michael Perra, *Pr*
Randall Mikami, *VP*
EMP: 10 **EST:** 1985
SQ FT: 21,000
SALES (est): 244.68K **Privately Held**
SIC: 2511 Wood household furniture

(G-14885)
MICROFAB INC
180 Zachary Rd Ste 1 (03109-5623)
PHONE...............................603 621-9522
Tim Filteau, *Pr*
EMP: 10 **EST:** 1999
SQ FT: 5,000
SALES (est): 1.16MM **Privately Held**
Web: www.semigen.net
SIC: 3674 Semiconductors and related devices

(G-14886)
MICROSEMI CORPORATION
48 Abby Rd (03103-3314)
PHONE...............................978 232-3793
EMP: 12
SALES (corp-wide): 8.44B **Publicly Held**
Web: www.microsemi.com
SIC: 3674 Semiconductors and related devices
HQ: Microsemi Corporation
11861 Western Ave
Garden Grove CA 92841
949 380-6100

(G-14887)
MICROSS COMPONENTS LLC
Also Called: Corfin Industries
1050 Perimeter Rd Ste 301 (03103-3355)
PHONE...............................603 893-9900
Marshall Blythe, *Managing Member*
Donald Tyler, *Managing Member**
EMP: 154 **EST:** 1991
SQ FT: 25,000
SALES (est): 26.52MM **Privately Held**
Web: www.micross.com
SIC: 3674 Semiconductors and related devices

(G-14888)
MILL CITY IRON
101 Allard Dr (03102-4007)
PHONE...............................603 622-0042
EMP: 9 **EST:** 2011
SALES (est): 108.17K **Privately Held**
Web: www.millcityiron.com
SIC: 3441 Fabricated structural metal

(G-14889)
MINIM INC (PA)
Also Called: Minim
848 Elm St (03101-2100)
PHONE...............................833 966-4646
Jeremy Hitchcock, *Ex Ch Bd*
Nicole Zheng, *CMO*
John Lauten, *COO*
EMP: 36 **EST:** 1977
SQ FT: 2,656
SALES (est): 50.62MM
SALES (corp-wide): 50.62MM **Publicly Held**
Web: www.minim.com
SIC: 3661 3577 Modems; Computer peripheral equipment, nec

(G-14890)
MIRACO INC
102 Maple St (03103-5616)
PHONE...............................603 665-9449
David Bouley, *Pr*
Jonathan Roberts, *
EMP: 35 **EST:** 1987
SQ FT: 18,000
SALES (est): 4.03MM **Privately Held**
Web: www.miracoinc.com
SIC: 7389 5063 3679 3672 Printed circuitry graphic layout; Electronic wire and cable; Harness assemblies, for electronic use: wire or cable; Printed circuit boards

(G-14891)
MITCH ROSEN EXTRAORDINARY GUNL
540 North Commercial St (03101-1122)
PHONE...............................603 647-2971
Mitch Rosen, *Pt*
EMP: 10 **EST:** 1995
SALES (est): 938.53K **Privately Held**
Web: www.mitchrosen.com
SIC: 3199 Equestrian related leather articles

(G-14892)
MKIND INC
Also Called: Right Height Manufacturing
150 Dow St Ste 4 (03101-1258)
PHONE...............................603 493-6882
Diane Kind, *Pr*
Michael Kind, *VP*
EMP: 8 **EST:** 2008
SALES (est): 941.43K **Privately Held**
Web: www.rightheightmfg.com
SIC: 2522 5021 Office furniture, except wood; Office furniture, nec

(G-14893)
MOTORWAY ENGINEERING INC
85 Hancock St (03101-2820)
PHONE...............................603 668-6315

Joseph Johns, *Pr*
EMP: 10 **EST:** 1970
SQ FT: 12,000
SALES (est): 893.79K **Privately Held**
Web: secure.vulcanworks.net
SIC: 3829 3751 Nuclear radiation and testing apparatus; Motorcycles, bicycles and parts

(G-14894)
MSN CORPORATION
Also Called: Budd Foods
431 Somerville St (03103-5129)
PHONE...............................603 623-3528
Leo T Sprecher, *Pr*
Curtis J Marcott, *
EMP: 100 **EST:** 1979
SQ FT: 30,000
SALES (est): 21.56MM **Privately Held**
Web: www.mrsbudds.com
SIC: 2013 2099 Sausages and other prepared meats; Food preparations, nec

(G-14895)
NATIONAL DENTEX LLC
Also Called: Ndx H&O
1050 Perimeter Rd Ste 101 (03103-3318)
P.O. Box 4194 (03108-4194)
PHONE...............................561 537-8301
TOLL FREE: 800
Vicky Rice, *Brnch Mgr*
EMP: 195
SALES (corp-wide): 339.71MM **Privately Held**
Web: www.nationaldentex.com
SIC: 8072 3843 Crown and bridge production; Dental equipment and supplies
HQ: National Dentex, Llc
1701 Military Trl Ste 150
Jupiter FL 33458
800 678-4140

(G-14896)
NATIONAL EMBROIDERY CORP
140 Bouchard St Ste 3 (03103-3359)
P.O. Box 5427 (03108-5427)
PHONE...............................603 647-1995
Russell Hart, *Pr*
EMP: 10 **EST:** 1987
SQ FT: 3,700
SALES (est): 427.08K **Privately Held**
SIC: 7389 2396 2395 Sewing contractor; Automotive and apparel trimmings; Pleating and stitching

(G-14897)
NEW ENGLAND BRAIDING CO INC
610 Gold St (03103-4005)
P.O. Box 4917 (03108-4917)
PHONE...............................603 669-1987
Sally L Champlin, *Pr*
Jeff Zellers, *Sec*
▲ **EMP:** 12 **EST:** 1979
SQ FT: 17,000
SALES (est): 1.87MM **Privately Held**
Web: www.anti-keystone.com
SIC: 3053 Packing materials

(G-14898)
NEW ENGLAND DUPLICATOR INC
8030 S Willow St Unit 108 (03103-2319)
PHONE...............................603 623-6847
TOLL FREE: 800
Gregory Joas, *Pr*
Brian Joas, *VP*
Mark Wheeler, *Prin*
EMP: 9 **EST:** 1981
SQ FT: 7,200

SALES (est): 955.32K **Privately Held**
Web: www.nedupe.com
SIC: 7334 2752 Photocopying and
   duplicating services; Commercial printing,
   lithographic

(G-14899)
NEW HAMPSHIRE GATEWAY
MDSG
1048 Hayward St (03103-2811)
PHONE.................................603 216-7373
Joel Clarke, *Prin*
EMP: 9 EST: 2013
SALES (est): 255.63K **Privately Held**
SIC: 2711 Newspapers, publishing and
   printing

(G-14900)
NEW HAMPSHIRECOM
1662 Elm St Ste 100 (03101-1243)
PHONE.................................603 314-0447
Dan O'brien, *Prin*
EMP: 9 EST: 2011
SALES (est): 188.91K **Privately Held**
Web: www.unionleader.com
SIC: 2711 Newspapers: publishing only, not
   printed on site

(G-14901)
NEXT STEP BNICS PRSTHETICS
INC (PA)
155 Dow St Ste 200 (03101-1299)
PHONE.................................603 668-3831
TOLL FREE: 800
EMP: 18 EST: 1996
SQ FT: 7,500
SALES (est): 4.64MM **Privately Held**
Web:
www.nextstepbionicsandprosthetics.com
SIC: 3842 Prosthetic appliances

(G-14902)
NORTH AMERICAN PLASTICS
LTD
Also Called: Www.naplasticsltd.com
349 East Industrial Park Dr (03109-5313)
PHONE.................................603 644-1660
Mika E Hyvonen, *Pr*
Eero J Hyvonen, *Pr*
Mika E Hyvonen, *VP*
EMP: 27 EST: 1982
SQ FT: 24,500
SALES (est): 1.17MM **Privately Held**
Web: www.naplasticsltd.com
SIC: 3089 Blow molded finished plastics
   products, nec

(G-14903)
NORTH PENN TECHNOLOGY INC
Also Called: Micross Components
1050 Perimeter Rd (03103-3303)
PHONE.................................603 893-9900
Richard Kingeon, *CEO*
EMP: 37 EST: 1987
SQ FT: 22,500
SALES (est): 7.81MM
SALES (corp-wide): 340.38MM **Privately
Held**
Web: www.micross.com
SIC: 3674 Semiconductors and related
   devices
PA: Micross Inc.
   225 Broadhollow Rd # 305
   Melville NY 11747
   407 298-7100

(G-14904)
NORTH TECOM LLC
1120 Bodwell Rd (03109-5802)

PHONE.................................603 851-5165
Wenjing Huang, *Managing Member*
Yuchang Hu, *Managing Member*
EMP: 14 EST: 2016
SIC: 7371 7372 7379 Computer software
   development and applications; Operating
   systems computer software; Computer
   related maintenance services

(G-14905)
NORTHSTAR DIRECT LLC
Also Called: Northstar
249 Gay St (03103-6819)
P.O. Box 4352 (03108-4352)
EMP: 10 EST: 2004
SQ FT: 24,000
SALES (est): 1.02MM **Privately Held**
Web: www.northstardirect.net
SIC: 2759 Screen printing

(G-14906)
NYLON CORPORATION
AMERICA INC
Also Called: N Y C O A
333 Sundial Ave (03103-7216)
PHONE.................................603 627-5150
Gregory Biederman, *Prin*
◆ EMP: 60 EST: 1955
SQ FT: 150,000
SALES (est): 20.42MM
SALES (corp-wide): 30.48MM **Privately
Held**
Web: www.nycoa.com
SIC: 2821 Nylon resins
PA: Metapoint Partners, A Limited
   Partnership
   108 Beach St
   Manchester MA 01944
   978 531-1398

(G-14907)
NYLTECH NORTH AMERICA
333 Sundial Ave (03103-7216)
PHONE.................................603 627-5150
EMP: 7 EST: 2013
SALES (est): 216.68K **Privately Held**
Web: www.nycoa.com
SIC: 2821 Plastics materials and resins

(G-14908)
ORACLE CORPORATION
Also Called: Oracle
150 Dow St Ste 301 (03101-1254)
PHONE.................................603 668-4998
EMP: 44
SALES (corp-wide): 49.95B **Publicly Held**
Web: www.oracle.com
SIC: 7372 Prepackaged software
PA: Oracle Corporation
   2300 Oracle Way
   Austin TX 78741
   737 867-1000

(G-14909)
OVEN POPPERS INC
99 Faltin Dr (03103-5755)
P.O. Box 5741 (03108-5741)
PHONE.................................603 644-3773
EMP: 42
Web: www.ovenpoppers.com
SIC: 2038 2092 Dinners, frozen and
   packaged; Fresh or frozen packaged fish

(G-14910)
PARAGON ELECTRONIC
SYSTEMS
255 Coolidge Ave (03102-3206)
PHONE.................................603 645-7630
Chris Pearson, *Pr*

Jeff Ruthier, *Pr*
EMP: 11 EST: 1999
SQ FT: 3,000
SALES (est): 1.68MM **Privately Held**
Web: www.paragonelect.com
SIC: 3674 Integrated circuits,
   semiconductor networks, etc.

(G-14911)
PEPSI-COLA METRO BTLG CO
INC
Also Called: Pepsi-Cola
127 Pepsi Rd (03109-5305)
PHONE.................................603 625-5764
Dan Loura, *Brnch Mgr*
EMP: 62
SALES (corp-wide): 86.39B **Publicly Held**
Web: www.pepsico.com
SIC: 2086 Carbonated soft drinks, bottled
   and canned
HQ: Pepsi-Cola Metropolitan Bottling
   Company, Inc.
   700 Anderson Hill Rd
   Purchase NY 10577
   914 767-6000

(G-14912)
POLY-VAC INC
Also Called: Symmetry Medical Manufacturing
253 Abby Rd (03103-3333)
PHONE.................................603 647-7822
Barry Parker, *Genl Mgr*
EMP: 170 EST: 1989
SALES (est): 24.51MM
SALES (corp-wide): 832.81MM **Privately
Held**
Web: www.tecomet.com
SIC: 3842 3826 Orthopedic appliances;
   Analytical instruments
HQ: Symmetry Medical Inc.
   3724 N State Road 15
   Warsaw IN 46582

(G-14913)
PRECISION LETTER LLC
396 Pepsi Rd (03109-5303)
PHONE.................................603 625-9625
Robert Elrick, *Pr*
▲ EMP: 18 EST: 1983
SQ FT: 10,000
SALES (est): 2.84MM **Privately Held**
Web: www.precisionletter.com
SIC: 3089 3993 Panels, building: plastics,
   nec; Letters for signs, metal

(G-14914)
PREMIER SEMICONDUCTOR
SVCS LLC (DH)
Also Called: Micross Components
1050 Perimeter Rd Ste 201 (03103-3339)
PHONE.................................267 954-0130
Richard Kingdon, *Managing Member*
Stephen Tang Managing, *Prin*
Victor Vescovo Managing, *Prin*
▲ EMP: 75 EST: 2001
SALES (est): 24.57MM
SALES (corp-wide): 340.38MM **Privately
Held**
Web: www.premiertest.com
SIC: 7371 3674 Custom computer
   programming services; Semiconductors
   and related devices
HQ: Chip Supply, Inc.
   1810 S Orange Blossom Trl
   Apopka FL 32703
   407 298-7100

(G-14915)
PRINTERS SQUARE INC
Also Called: Talient Action Group
105 Faltin Dr (03103-5755)
PHONE.................................603 703-0795
Sean Owen, *Owner*
EMP: 20 EST: 2015
SALES (est): 1.29MM **Privately Held**
Web: www.talientactiongroup.com
SIC: 2752 Offset printing

(G-14916)
PRO DOUGH INC
8030 S Willow St Unit 2-7 (03103-2321)
PHONE.................................603 623-6844
Tim Gyorda, *Pr*
EMP: 7 EST: 1996
SALES (est): 648.08K **Privately Held**
Web: www.prodoughcompany.com
SIC: 2041 5812 Pizza dough, prepared;
   Pizzeria, chain

(G-14917)
PROTERIAL CABLE AMERICA
INC
Performnce Cble Systems Mtls D
900 Holt Ave (03109-5608)
PHONE.................................603 669-4347
EMP: 175
Web: usa.proterial.com
SIC: 3357 Nonferrous wiredrawing and
   insulating
HQ: Proterial Cable America, Inc.
   2 Manhattanville Rd # 301
   Purchase NY 10577
   914 694-9200

(G-14918)
PRYSMIAN CBLES SYSTEMS
USA LLC
Also Called: Manchester, NH Plant
345 Mcgregor St (03102-3222)
PHONE.................................603 668-1620
Tim Grass, *Mgr*
EMP: 77
Web: na.prysmian.com
SIC: 3496 3357 Miscellaneous fabricated
   wire products; Nonferrous wiredrawing and
   insulating
HQ: Prysmian Cables And Systems Usa,
   Llc
   4 Tesseneer Dr
   Highland Heights KY 41076
   859 572-8000

(G-14919)
PURITAN ELECTRONICS INC
920 Candia Rd (03109)
PHONE.................................800 343-8649
EMP: 25 EST: 1980
SALES (est): 4.95MM **Privately Held**
SIC: 3827 3559 Boards: plotting, spotting,
   and gun fire adjustment; Semiconductor
   manufacturing machinery

(G-14920)
RETRIEVE LLC
Also Called: Retrieve Technologies
50 Commercial St Ste 35s (03101-1161)
PHONE.................................603 413-0022
Dave Arnold, *CEO*
John Rogers, *Pr*
EMP: 46 EST: 2003
SALES (est): 567.29K **Privately Held**
SIC: 7372 Business oriented computer
   software

▲ = Import ▼ = Export
◆ = Import/Export

(G-14921)
REVOLUTION FURNISHINGS LLC
Also Called: Cedar Crest Cabinetry
9050 S Willow St (03103-2390)
PHONE.................................603 606-6123
EMP: 8 EST: 2011
SALES (est): 729.1K Privately Held
Web: www.cedarcrestcabinetry.com
SIC: 2434 Wood kitchen cabinets

(G-14922)
ROSALIE GENDRON LLC
289 Pine St (03103-5255)
PHONE.................................603 836-3692
Ronald R Dupont, Prin
EMP: 7 EST: 2010
SALES (est): 166.9K Privately Held
SIC: 2879 Agricultural chemicals, nec

(G-14923)
RSCC WIRE & CABLE LLC
680 Hayward St (03103-4420)
PHONE.................................603 622-3500
Demitri Maistrellis, Pr
EMP: 53
SALES (corp-wide): 302.09B Publicly Held
Web: www.r-scc.com
SIC: 3357 Nonferrous wiredrawing and insulating
HQ: Rscc Wire & Cable Llc
20 Bradley Park Rd
East Granby CT 06026

(G-14924)
SANMINA CORPORATION
140 Abby Rd (03103-3319)
PHONE.................................603 621-1800
David Solisky, Mgr
EMP: 124
Web: www.sanmina.com
SIC: 3672 Printed circuit boards
PA: Sanmina Corporation
2700 N 1st St
San Jose CA 95134

(G-14925)
SANT BANI PRESS INC
60 Buckley Cir Ste 3 (03109-5236)
PHONE.................................603 286-3114
Joseph Gelbard, Pr
Richard Shannon, VP
EMP: 7 EST: 1969
SQ FT: 8,000
SALES (est): 335.04K
SALES (corp-wide): 2.32MM Privately Held
SIC: 2752 Offset printing
PA: Morgan Press, Inc.
60 Buckley Cir Ste 3
Manchester NH
603 624-8660

(G-14926)
SAVVY WORKSHOP
55 South Commercial St (03101-2606)
PHONE.................................603 792-0080
Lisa Landry, Pr
Joseph Landry, VP
EMP: 7 EST: 1998
SQ FT: 2,000
SALES (est): 947.85K Privately Held
Web: www.savvyworkshop.com
SIC: 2759 7336 Screen printing; Commercial art and graphic design

(G-14927)
SEMPER FI POWER SUPPLY INC
21 W Auburn St Ste 29 (03101-2386)

PHONE.................................603 656-9729
David Pitts, Pr
▲ EMP: 9 EST: 1999
SQ FT: 15,000
SALES (est): 311.55K Privately Held
Web: www.semperfipowersupply.com
SIC: 3612 Power transformers, electric

(G-14928)
SEQUEL MED TECH LLC (PA) ✪
50 Commercial St Fl 3 (03101-1100)
PHONE.................................212 883-1007
Alan Lotvin, CEO
EMP: 9 EST: 2023
SALES (est): 515.63K
SALES (corp-wide): 515.63K Privately Held
SIC: 3841 Surgical and medical instruments

(G-14929)
SIGNIFY NORTH AMERICA CORP
386 Commercial St (03101-1108)
PHONE.................................603 645-6061
EMP: 75
Web: www.signify.com
SIC: 3646 Commercial lighting fixtures
HQ: Signify North America Corporation
400 Crossing Blvd Ste 600
Bridgewater NJ 08807
732 563-3000

(G-14930)
SMOOTHIE BUS LLC
85 Faltin Dr Ste 35 (03103-7096)
PHONE.................................603 303-7353
Josh Philbrick, Managing Member
EMP: 15 EST: 2018
SALES (est): 465.69K Privately Held
Web: www.thesmoothiebus.com
SIC: 5812 2033 Frozen yogurt stand; Fruit juices: fresh

(G-14931)
SNAP SITE STUDIOS LLC
Also Called: Keza Media
55 South Commercial St Ste 99 (03101)
PHONE.................................603 782-3395
EMP: 8 EST: 2004
SQ FT: 2,400
SALES (est): 346.36K Privately Held
Web: www.snapsitestudios.com
SIC: 7374 3993 Computer graphics service; Advertising novelties

(G-14932)
SOPHIA INSTITUTE
525 Greeley St (03102-2340)
P.O. Box 5284 (03108-5284)
PHONE.................................603 641-9344
EMP: 10 EST: 2014
SALES (est): 92.35K Privately Held
Web: www.sophiainstitute.com
SIC: 2741 Miscellaneous publishing

(G-14933)
SOUHEGAN MANAGEMENT CORP (PA)
Also Called: Pie Guy, The
99 Faltin Dr (03103-5755)
PHONE.................................603 898-8868
Christopher Burnley, Pr
EMP: 40 EST: 2009
SALES (est): 4.34MM
SALES (corp-wide): 4.34MM Privately Held
Web: www.wileyroadfoods.com
SIC: 2051 Cakes, pies, and pastries

(G-14934)
SOUSA SIGNS LLC
225 East Industrial Park Dr (03109-5311)
PHONE.................................603 622-5067
Thom Sousa, Managing Member
EMP: 12 EST: 1974
SQ FT: 4,000
SALES (est): 909.52K Privately Held
Web: www.sousasigns.com
SIC: 7389 3993 Lettering service; Signs and advertising specialties

(G-14935)
SOUTH MAIN MANCHESTER HOUSING
198 Hanover St (03104-6136)
PHONE.................................603 626-3034
EMP: 8 EST: 2015
SALES (est): 262.92K Privately Held
Web: www.manchesterhousing.org
SIC: 3444 Housings for business machines, sheet metal

(G-14936)
SPECTRUM MONTHLY LLC
Also Called: Spectrum Marketing Companies
95 Eddy Rd Ste 101 (03102-3258)
PHONE.................................603 627-0042
Kevin Lash, CEO
Brian Mikol, *
Ken Hauser, *
EMP: 240 EST: 1991
SQ FT: 27,000
SALES (est): 25.51MM Privately Held
Web: www.spectrummarketing.com
SIC: 7331 2721 3993 Direct mail advertising services; Magazines: publishing and printing ; Signs and advertising specialties

(G-14937)
SUMMIT PACKAGING SYSTEMS LLC (PA)
Also Called: SPS
400 Gay St (03103-6817)
P.O. Box 5304 (03108-5304)
PHONE.................................603 669-5410
Gordon C Gilroy, Pr
Scott N Gilroy, VP
Michael Conway, CFO
◆ EMP: 400 EST: 1975
SQ FT: 200,000
SALES (est): 97.13MM
SALES (corp-wide): 97.13MM Privately Held
Web: www.summitpackagingsystems.com
SIC: 3499 3089 Aerosol valves, metal; Caps, plastics

(G-14938)
SYLVESTER SHEET METAL LLC
451 Pepsi Rd (03109-5317)
PHONE.................................603 624-4586
Michael Sylvester, Pr
Michael R Sylvester, *
Glenn M Sylvester, *
John J Sylvester, *
Margaret Sylvester, *
EMP: 25 EST: 1962
SQ FT: 31,000
SALES (est): 4.79MM Privately Held
Web: www.ssmnh.com
SIC: 1761 3444 Sheet metal work, nec; Sheet metalwork

(G-14939)
SYNERGY SIGNWORKS LLC
880 Candia Rd Unit 1 (03109-5205)
PHONE.................................603 440-3519

EMP: 11 EST: 2016
SALES (est): 593.86K Privately Held
Web: www.synergysignworks.com
SIC: 3993 Signs and advertising specialties

(G-14940)
TEAM EDA INC
1001 Elm St Bsmt 305 (03101-1845)
PHONE.................................603 656-5200
Guy D Haas, Pr
EMP: 7 EST: 2004
SALES (est): 776.58K Privately Held
Web: www.teameda.com
SIC: 7372 Prepackaged software

(G-14941)
TEMCO TOOL COMPANY INC
800 Holt Ave (03109-5601)
P.O. Box 5031 (03108-5031)
PHONE.................................603 622-6989
Norman P Gagne, Pr
Norman Paul Gagne, Pr
Colleen Ann Gagne, *
EMP: 36 EST: 1963
SQ FT: 28,000
SALES (est): 9.54MM Privately Held
Web: www.temcotool.com
SIC: 3544 Special dies and tools

(G-14942)
TEXAS INSTRUMENTS INCORPORATED
Also Called: Texas Instruments
50 Phillippe Cote St Ste 100 (03101-3105)
PHONE.................................603 222-8500
EMP: 7
SALES (corp-wide): 20.03B Publicly Held
Web: www.ti.com
SIC: 3674 Microprocessors
PA: Texas Instruments Incorporated
12500 Ti Blvd
Dallas TX 75243
214 479-3773

(G-14943)
TEXTILES COATED INCORPORATED
200 Bouchard St (03103-3309)
P.O. Box 5768 (03108-5768)
PHONE.................................603 296-2221
John W Tippett, CEO
EMP: 179
SALES (corp-wide): 45.91MM Privately Held
Web: www.textilescoated.com
SIC: 2821 2295 Plastics materials and resins ; Chemically coated and treated fabrics
PA: Textiles Coated, Incorporated
6 George Ave
Londonderry NH 03053
603 296-2221

(G-14944)
THIBCO INC
41 Alpheus St (03104-5706)
PHONE.................................603 623-3011
Gerard L Thibodeau, Pr
EMP: 7 EST: 1989
SALES (est): 246.48K Privately Held
Web: www.thibco.com
SIC: 2431 1751 Millwork; Cabinet and finish carpentry

(G-14945)
TOLLES COMMUNICATIONS CORP
103 Bay St (03104-3007)
PHONE.................................603 627-9500
Irvin Tolles, Pr

EMP: 7 EST: 1991
SQ FT: 1,600
SALES (est): 566.34K **Privately Held**
SIC: 2711 7389 Newspapers, publishing
and printing; Telemarketing services

(G-14946)
TREE CARE INDUSTRY ASSN INC
Also Called: TREE CARE INDUSTRY
ASSOCIATION
670 North Commercial St Ste 201 (03101)
PHONE..................................603 314-5380
David White, *CEO*
Bob Rouse, *
Amy Tetreault, *
Mike Rennie, *
Peter Gerstenberger, *
EMP: 42 **EST:** 1947
SALES (est): 9.38MM **Privately Held**
Web: www.tcia.org
SIC: 8611 2721 Trade associations;
Magazines: publishing only, not printed on
site

(G-14947)
UNION LEADER CORPORATION (PA)
Also Called: New Hampshire Union Leader
100 William Loeb Dr Unit 2 (03109-5627)
P.O. Box 9555 (03108-9555)
PHONE..................................603 668-4321
Joseph W Mcquaid, *Pr*
Joyce Levesque, *
Michael Rhodes, *
George Stachokas, *
Dirk F Ruemenapp, *
EMP: 360 **EST:** 1946
SQ FT: 167,000
SALES (est): 59.85MM
SALES (corp-wide): 59.85MM **Privately Held**
Web: www.unionleader.com
SIC: 2711 Commercial printing and
newspaper publishing combined

(G-14948)
UNITRODE CORPORATION (HQ)
50 Phillippe Cote St Ste 100 (03101-3105)
PHONE..................................603 222-8500
Edward H Browder, *Pr*
Allan R Campbell, *
EMP: 500 **EST:** 1960
SQ FT: 174,400
SALES (est): 132.58MM
SALES (corp-wide): 17.52B **Publicly Held**
Web: www.ti.com
SIC: 3674 Microcircuits, integrated
(semiconductor)
PA: Texas Instruments Incorporated
12500 Ti Blvd
Dallas TX 75243
214 479-3773

(G-14949)
VAN OTIS CHOCOLATES LLC (PA)
Also Called: House of Van Otis
341 Elm St (03101-2708)
PHONE..................................603 627-1611
Dave Quinn, *Managing Member*
EMP: 8 **EST:** 1911
SQ FT: 3,500
SALES (est): 1.3MM
SALES (corp-wide): 1.3MM **Privately Held**
Web: www.vanotis.com
SIC: 5441 2064 Candy; Candy and other
confectionery products

(G-14950)
VELCRO INC (HQ)
Also Called: Velcro
95 Sundial Ave (03103-7230)
P.O. Box 4806 (03108-4806)
PHONE..................................603 669-4880
Alain Zijlstra, *Pr*
A John Holton, *
Robert E Jauron, *
Fraser Cameron, *
◆ **EMP:** 650 **EST:** 1985
SQ FT: 300,000
SALES (est): 603.62MM **Privately Held**
Web: www.velcro.com
SIC: 2241 Fabric tapes
PA: Velcro Industries N.V
C/O Anta Management Advisory
Services N.V
Willemstad

(G-14951)
VELCRO USA INC (DH)
95 Sundial Ave (03103-7230)
PHONE..................................800 225-0180
TOLL FREE: 800
Gabriella Parisse, *Pr*
Boris P Hadshi, *
Benjamin Kaplan, *
Robert E Jauron, *
Peter A Pelletier, *
◆ **EMP:** 800 **EST:** 1967
SQ FT: 400,000
SALES (est): 296.82MM **Privately Held**
Web: www.velcro.com
SIC: 2241 3965 Fabric tapes; Fasteners,
buttons, needles, and pins
HQ: Velcro, Inc.
95 Sundial Ave
Manchester NH 03103

(G-14952)
VIBRAC LLC (PA)
1050 Perimeter Rd #6 (03103-3355)
P.O. Box 840 (03031-0840)
PHONE..................................603 882-6777
Thomas Rogers, *Managing Member*
◆ **EMP:** 8 **EST:** 1960
SQ FT: 10,000
SALES (est): 2.36MM
SALES (corp-wide): 2.36MM **Privately Held**
Web: www.vibrac.com
SIC: 3829 Measuring and controlling
devices, nec

(G-14953)
VICOR CORPORATION
Also Called: Granite Power Technologies
540 North Commercial St Ste 110 (03101)
PHONE..................................603 623-3222
Tom Duff, *Mgr*
EMP: 34
SALES (corp-wide): 399.08MM **Publicly Held**
Web: www.vicorpower.com
SIC: 3629 Electronic generation equipment
PA: Vicor Corporation
25 Frontage Rd
Andover MA 01810
978 470-2900

(G-14954)
VIRTUAL PUBLISHING LLC
103 Bay St (03104-3007)
PHONE..................................603 627-9500
Irv Tolles, *Owner*
EMP: 7 **EST:** 2005
SALES (est): 103.63K **Privately Held**
SIC: 2741 Miscellaneous publishing

(G-14955)
VISION WINE & SPIRITS LLC
540 N Coml St Ste 311 (03101)
PHONE..................................781 278-2000
Dean Williams, *Brnch Mgr*
EMP: 15
SALES (corp-wide): 3.59MM **Privately Held**
SIC: 2084 Wines, brandy, and brandy spirits
PA: Vision Wine & Spirits, Llc
500 John Hancock Rd
Taunton MA 02780
201 297-9170

(G-14956)
VISION WINE & SPIRITS LLC
540 North Commercial St Ste 311 (03101)
PHONE..................................781 278-2000
▲ **EMP:** 795 **EST:** 2010
SALES (est): 220.76K
SALES (corp-wide): 209.3MM **Privately Held**
SIC: 2084 Wines, brandy, and brandy spirits
PA: Martignetti Companies, Llc
500 John Hancock Rd
Taunton MA 02780
781 348-8000

(G-14957)
W B MASON CO INC
8001 S Willow St (03103-2306)
PHONE..................................888 926-2766
EMP: 68
SALES (corp-wide): 1.01B **Privately Held**
Web: www.wbmason.com
SIC: 5943 5712 2752 Office forms and
supplies; Office furniture; Commercial
printing, lithographic
PA: W. B. Mason Co., Inc.
59 Centre Street
Brockton MA 02301
508 586-3434

(G-14958)
WAVELINK LLC
724 East Industrial Park Dr Unit 6
(03109-5629)
P.O. Box 4358 (03108-4358)
PHONE..................................603 606-7489
Norman Gagne, *Managing Member*
▲ **EMP:** 10 **EST:** 2003
SALES (est): 975.92K **Privately Held**
Web: www.wavelinkcable.com
SIC: 3678 Electronic connectors

(G-14959)
WEMBLY NYCOA HOLDINGS LLC
333 Sundial Ave (03103-7216)
PHONE..................................603 627-5150
EMP: 8 **EST:** 2019
SALES (est): 2.77MM **Privately Held**
Web: www.nycoa.com
SIC: 2821 Plastics materials and resins

(G-14960)
WHITE MOUNTAIN DISTILLERY LLC
2072 Elm St (03104-2315)
PHONE..................................603 391-1306
Stefan Windler, *Prin*
EMP: 8 **EST:** 2012
SALES (est): 360.24K **Privately Held**
SIC: 2085 Distilled and blended liquors

(G-14961)
XMA CORPORATION
Also Called: Omni Spectra
7 Perimeter Rd Ste 2 (03103-3343)
PHONE..................................603 222-2256
Marc Smith, *Pr*
Bruce W Cooper, *
Kelley Carr, *
Scott T Goodrich, *
Peter Richard, *
▲ **EMP:** 55 **EST:** 2003
SQ FT: 10,000
SALES (est): 13.13MM
SALES (corp-wide): 12.62B **Publicly Held**
Web: www.xmacorp.com
SIC: 5065 3678 Electronic parts and
equipment, nec; Electronic connectors
PA: Amphenol Corporation
358 Hall Ave
Wallingford CT 06492
203 265-8900

(G-14962)
YOUR OIL TOOLS LLC
652 Hackett Hill Rd (03102-8525)
PHONE..................................701 645-8665
M Steven Kesserling, *Admn*
EMP: 10 **EST:** 2015
SALES (est): 5.18MM **Privately Held**
Web: www.youroiltools.com
SIC: 1311 Crude petroleum and natural gas

Manchester
Merrimack County

(G-14963)
SOUTHERN NEW HAMPSHIRE UNIV
Also Called: Copies Plus Info Booth
2500 N River Rd (03106-1018)
PHONE..................................603 629-4631
Gregg Mazzola, *Prin*
EMP: 7
SALES (corp-wide): 1.3B **Privately Held**
Web: www.snhu.edu
SIC: 8221 2732 University; Books, printing
only
PA: Southern New Hampshire University
2500 N River Rd
Manchester NH 03106
603 668-2211

Marlborough
Cheshire County

(G-14964)
ELECTRONICS AID INC
32 Roxbury Rd (03455-2215)
P.O. Box 325 (03455-0325)
PHONE..................................603 876-4161
Joel Seavey, *Genl Mgr*
Carroll Willson, *VP*
EMP: 9 **EST:** 1985
SQ FT: 5,500
SALES (est): 736.91K **Privately Held**
SIC: 3672 3679 3678 3699 Printed circuit
boards; Harness assemblies, for electronic
use: wire or cable; Electronic connectors;
Electrical equipment and supplies, nec

(G-14965)
PHYSICAL MEASUREMENT TECH INC
4 Ling St (03455-2427)
P.O. Box 400 (03455-0400)
PHONE..................................603 876-9990
EMP: 7 **EST:** 1993
SALES (est): 673.64K **Privately Held**
Web: www.pmtvib.com
SIC: 3825 Instruments to measure electricity

Marlow
Cheshire County

(G-14966)
AUDIO ACCESSORIES INC
Also Called: Audio Line
25 Mill St (03456-6340)
P.O. Box 360 (03456-0360)
PHONE..............................603 446-3335
Mb Hall, *Pr*
David Hall, *
Homer S Bradley Junior, *Sec*
Timothy Symonds, *
▲ **EMP:** 40 **EST:** 1946
SQ FT: 12,000
SALES (est): 3.13MM **Privately Held**
Web: www.patchbays.com
SIC: 3663 Radio and t.v. communications
equipment

Mason
Hillsborough County

(G-14967)
PARKERS MAPLE BARN CORN CRIB
Also Called: Parker's Maple Barn
1316 Brookline Rd (03048-4400)
PHONE..............................603 878-2308
Ronald Roberts, *Owner*
EMP: 606 **EST:** 1970
SQ FT: 9,000
SALES (est): 8.14MM **Privately Held**
Web: www.parkersmaplebarn.com
SIC: 5812 5947 2099 Restaurant, family;
independent; Gift shop; Maple syrup

Meredith
Belknap County

(G-14968)
COMSTOCK INDUSTRIES INC
Foundry Ave (03253)
PHONE..............................603 279-7045
Richard Dwight Comstock Junior, *Pr*
Richard Dwight Comstock, *Junior President*
Kathleen Mae Comstock, *
EMP: 35 **EST:** 1980
SQ FT: 17,400
SALES (est): 4.8MM **Privately Held**
Web: www.comstockindustries.com
SIC: 3599 3089 3544 Machine shop,
jobbing and repair; Molding primary plastics
; Special dies, tools, jigs, and fixtures

(G-14969)
REMCON/NORTH CORPORATION
7-9 Enterprise Ct (03253)
P.O. Box 957 (03253-0957)
PHONE..............................603 279-7091
Marie P Remson, *Pr*
EMP: 57 **EST:** 1966
SQ FT: 31,000
SALES (est): 4.43MM **Privately Held**
Web: www.remcon-north.com
SIC: 3679 Electronic circuits

(G-14970)
SALMON PRESS LLC (PA)
Also Called: Berlyn Reporter
5 Water St (03253-6233)
P.O. Box 729 (03253-0729)
PHONE..............................603 279-4516
John Coots, *Managing Member*
EMP: 15 **EST:** 1999

SALES (est): 4.09MM
SALES (corp-wide): 4.09MM **Privately Held**
Web: www.salmonpress.com
SIC: 2711 Newspapers: publishing only, not
printed on site

Merrimack
Hillsborough County

(G-14971)
ACE WELDING CO INC
715a Daniel Webster Hwy (03054-2713)
P.O. Box 695 (03054-0695)
PHONE..............................603 424-9936
Brian Robinson, *Pr*
Mary Robinson, *
EMP: 28 **EST:** 1945
SQ FT: 4,000
SALES (est): 4.63MM **Privately Held**
Web: www.aceweldingnh.com
SIC: 3441 7692 Fabricated structural metal;
Welding repair

(G-14972)
AMERICAN PPE COMPANY LLC
21 Continental Blvd (03054-4303)
PHONE..............................603 320-5123
John Gargasz, *CEO*
EMP: 20
SALES (est): 1.3MM **Privately Held**
SIC: 3069 Fabricated rubber products, nec

(G-14973)
ATRIUM MEDICAL CORPORATION (HQ)
Also Called: Atrium Medical
40 Continental Blvd (03054-4332)
PHONE..............................973 709-7654
Steve Herweck, *CEO*
Chad Carlton, *
Ted Karwoski, *
Gary P Sufat, *
◆ **EMP:** 275 **EST:** 1981
SQ FT: 135,000
SALES (est): 99.06MM
SALES (corp-wide): 68.03MM **Privately Held**
Web: www.atriummedical.com
SIC: 3842 3841 Surgical appliances and
supplies; Surgical and medical instruments
PA: Getinge Holding B.V. & Co. Kg
Kehler Str. 31
Rastatt BW 76437
72229320

(G-14974)
AVILITE LLC
59 Daniel Webster Hwy Ste 100
(03054-4877)
PHONE..............................603 626-4388
Robert Gamache, *Pr*
Herbert Langer, *VP*
Jan Langer, *Treas*
John Monson, *Sec*
▲ **EMP:** 9 **EST:** 1989
SQ FT: 50,000
SALES (est): 878.05K **Privately Held**
Web: www.avilitecorp.com
SIC: 2821 3312 Polystyrene resins;
Structural and rail mill products

(G-14975)
BAE SYSTEMS INFO ELCTRNIC SYST
Also Called: BAE SYSTEMS INFORMATION
AND ELECTRONIC SYSTEMS
INTEGRATION INC.

144 Daniel Webster Hwy # 24
(03054-4898)
P.O. Box 868 (03061-0868)
PHONE..............................603 885-4321
John Watkins, *Brnch Mgr*
EMP: 294
SALES (corp-wide): 25.59B **Privately Held**
Web: www.baesystems.com
SIC: 3728 3679 Aircraft parts and
equipment, nec; Electronic circuits
HQ: Bae Systems Information And
Electronic Systems Integration Inc.
65 Spit Brook Rd
Nashua NH 03060
603 885-4321

(G-14976)
BAE SYSTEMS INFO ELCTRNIC SYST
Also Called: Bae Systems Information And
Electronic Systems Integration Inc.
130 Daniel Webster Hwy Bldg 15
(03054-4898)
P.O. Box 868 (03061-0868)
PHONE..............................603 885-4321
Cheryl Labombard Paradis, *Brnch Mgr*
EMP: 718
SALES (corp-wide): 25.59B **Privately Held**
Web: www.baesystems.com
SIC: 3812 Search and navigation equipment
HQ: Bae Systems Information And
Electronic Systems Integration Inc.
65 Spit Brook Rd
Nashua NH 03060
603 885-4321

(G-14977)
CIRCUIT TECHNOLOGY LLC
Also Called: Cirtech
6a Continental Blvd (03054-4302)
PHONE..............................603 424-2200
Beverly Parker, *CEO*
Clare O Parker, *
Bradley Parker, *
Ronald Parker, *
EMP: 65 **EST:** 1984
SQ FT: 15,000
SALES (est): 24.82MM
SALES (corp-wide): 357.41MM **Privately Held**
Web: www.circuittec.com
SIC: 3672 Printed circuit boards
PA: Virtex Enterprises, Lp
16310 Bratton Ln Ste 300
Austin TX 78728
512 835-6772

(G-14978)
COLT REFINING INC (PA)
12a Star Dr (03054-4470)
PHONE..............................603 429-9966
Mitch Coughlin, *Prin*
Harvey J Gottlieb, *
Nancy Gottlieb, *
Mitch Coughlin, *Pr*
James J Maher, *
◆ **EMP:** 45 **EST:** 1976
SQ FT: 24,000
SALES (est): 17.65MM
SALES (corp-wide): 17.65MM **Privately Held**
Web: www.coltrefining.com
SIC: 3339 5093 3341 Precious metals;
Scrap and waste materials; Secondary
nonferrous metals

(G-14979)
DATA RADIO MANAGEMENT CO INC
30 Daniel Webster Hwy Ste 9 (03054-4822)

PHONE..............................603 598-1222
Malcolm N Macintyre, *Pr*
Scott Macintyre, *VP*
EMP: 9 **EST:** 1995
SQ FT: 1,200
SALES (est): 940.86K **Privately Held**
Web: www.dataradio.com
SIC: 8748 3663 Communications consulting
; Radio broadcasting and communications
equipment

(G-14980)
EL-OP US INC
220 Daniel Webster Hwy (03054-4898)
PHONE..............................603 889-2500
Michael Rukin, *Ch Bd*
Roger J Sutherland, *
EMP: 115 **EST:** 1989
SQ FT: 351,458
SALES (est): 9MM **Privately Held**
Web: www.elbitamerica.com
SIC: 3812 3629 Search and navigation
equipment; Electrochemical generators
(fuel cells)
HQ: Elbitamerica, Inc.
4700 Marine Creek Pkwy
Fort Worth TX 76179

(G-14981)
GEORGE GORDON ASSOCIATES INC
12 Continental Blvd (03054-4302)
PHONE..............................603 424-5204
Donald R Belanger, *Pr*
Ron Downing, *SALES*
Robert Bisbee, *VP*
EMP: 15 **EST:** 1984
SQ FT: 25,000
SALES (est): 2.43MM **Privately Held**
Web: www.ggapack.com
SIC: 3565 Packaging machinery

(G-14982)
GETINGE GROUP LOGIS AMERI LLC
Also Called: Getinge AB
40 Continental Blvd (03054-4332)
PHONE..............................603 880-1433
Mattias Perjos, *CEO*
EMP: 700 **EST:** 2016
SALES (est): 24.81MM **Privately Held**
SIC: 3841 Surgical and medical instruments

(G-14983)
GT EQUIPMENT HOLDINGS INC
243 Daniel Webster Hwy (03054-4807)
PHONE..............................603 883-5200
Thomas Gutierrez, *Pr*
EMP: 19 **EST:** 2002
SALES (est): 321.52K **Privately Held**
SIC: 3674 Semiconductors and related
devices

(G-14984)
HYDE SPECIALTY PRODUCTS LLC
Also Called: Wen Industries
12 Webb Dr (03054-4803)
PHONE..............................603 883-7400
EMP: 10 **EST:** 1979
SQ FT: 6,000
SALES (est): 1.1MM **Privately Held**
Web: www.gasbuggy.com
SIC: 5084 3443 Industrial machinery and
equipment; Tank towers, metal plate

(G-14985)
INTEGRA BIOSCIENCES CORP
Also Called: Integra Biosciences USA

GEOGRAPHIC

57 Daniel Webster Hwy (03054-4811)
PHONE..........................603 578-5800
EMP: 8
SALES (est): 301.55K **Privately Held**
Web: www.integra-biosciences.com
SIC: 3826   Analytical instruments

(G-14986)
KEYSPIN MANUFACTURING LLC
21 Continental Blvd (03054-4303)
PHONE..........................603 420-8508
Elizabeth Cacciola, *Admn*
EMP: 9 **EST:** 2016
SALES (est): 527.85K **Privately Held**
Web: www.keyspinmfg.com
SIC: 3999   Manufacturing industries, nec

(G-14987)
KMC SYSTEMS INC
220 Daniel Webster Hwy (03054-4898)
PHONE..........................866 742-0442
▲ **EMP:** 100 **EST:** 1995
SQ FT: 160,000
SALES (est): 30.59MM **Privately Held**
Web: www.kmcsystems.com
SIC: 3812 3841 3629   Search and
   navigation equipment; Surgical and medical
   instruments; Electrochemical generators
   (fuel cells)
HQ: Kollsman, Inc.
   220 Daniel Webster Hwy
   Merrimack NH 03054

(G-14988)
KOLLSMAN INC (DH)
220 Daniel Webster Hwy (03054-4837)
P.O. Box 490 (03054-0490)
PHONE..........................603 889-2500
EMP: 520 **EST:** 1930
SQ FT: 348,500
SALES (est): 93.03MM **Privately Held**
Web: www.elbitamerica.com
SIC: 3812 3629   Search and navigation
   equipment; Electrochemical generators
   (fuel cells)
HQ: Elbit Systems Of America, Llc
   4700 Marine Creek Pkwy
   Fort Worth TX 76179

(G-14989)
LIGHTBLOCKS INC
33 Elm St Bldg 6 (03054-6400)
PHONE..........................603 889-1115
Mary Wellington, *Ch Bd*
EMP: 25 **EST:** 1981
SALES (est): 2.46MM **Privately Held**
Web: www.lightblocks.com
SIC: 3299   Architectural sculptures: gypsum,
   clay, papier mache, etc.

(G-14990)
LOCKHEED MARTIN CORPORATION
Also Called: Sanders- A Lockheed Martin Co
144 Daniel Webster Hwy Bldg 26
(03054-4898)
PHONE..........................603 885-5295
Doug Cummings, *Genl Mgr*
EMP: 10
Web: www.gyrocamsystems.com
SIC: 3812   Search and navigation equipment
PA: Lockheed Martin Corporation
   6801 Rockledge Dr
   Bethesda MD 20817

(G-14991)
MACHINED INTEGRATIONS LLC
1507 Columbia Cir (03054-4164)

P.O. Box 396 (03054-0396)
PHONE..........................603 420-8871
Dennis Tetip, *Managing Member*
EMP: 8 **EST:** 2013
SALES (est): 221.26K **Privately Held**
Web: www.machinedintegrations.com
SIC: 3599   Machine shop, jobbing and repair

(G-14992)
MERRIMACK MICRO LLC
76 Jessica Dr (03054-3570)
PHONE..........................603 809-4183
EMP: 7 **EST:** 2007
SALES (est): 224.51K **Privately Held**
Web: www.merrimackmicro.com
SIC: 3672   Printed circuit boards

(G-14993)
MICROSEMBLY LLC
21 Manchester St (03054-4801)
PHONE..........................603 718-8445
Phuong Kent Dang, *Managing Member*
Kent Dangphuong Kent Dang, *Managing
Member*
Deanna Adams, *
Stephanie Luc, *
EMP: 37 **EST:** 2019
SALES (est): 3.5MM **Privately Held**
Web: www.microsembly.com
SIC: 3674   Semiconductors and related
   devices

(G-14994)
NASHUA CORPORATION
Also Called: Nashua Specialty Coated Pdts
59 Daniel Webster Hwy Ste A
(03054-4858)
PHONE..........................603 880-1100
◆ **EMP:** 761
Web: www.nashua.com
SIC: 2672 2754 2679 2621   Thermoplastic
   coated paper: made from purchased
   materials; Tickets: gravure printing; Tags
   and labels, paper; Specialty papers

(G-14995)
NORTHEAST SAND AND GRAVEL LLC
1 Harwich Ct (03054-3456)
P.O. Box 497 (03071-0497)
PHONE..........................603 305-9429
EMP: 7 **EST:** 2012
SALES (est): 306.07K **Privately Held**
Web: www.nesand.com
SIC: 1442   Construction sand and gravel

(G-14996)
OZ HOLDING CORP
11 Continental Blvd Ste 104 (03054-4341)
PHONE..........................603 546-0090
John O'connor, *Pr*
David Zendzian, *VP Engg*
Lisette O'connor, *Sec*
Thomas O'reilly, *Dir*
EMP: 11 **EST:** 1997
SQ FT: 11,800
SALES (est): 2.67MM **Privately Held**
Web: www.oztekcorp.com
SIC: 3829   Measuring and controlling
   devices, nec
PA: Trystar, Llc
   15765 Acorn Trl
   Faribault MN 55021

(G-14997)
PAPERGRAPHICS PRINT & COPY INC
Also Called: Papergraphics
4 John Tyler St Ste A (03054-4800)

PHONE..........................603 880-1835
Frank Lagana, *Pr*
Beatrice B Figler, *VP*
Linda Lagana, *VP*
Robert Figler, *Sec*
EMP: 15 **EST:** 1982
SQ FT: 7,000
SALES (est): 2.42MM **Privately Held**
Web: www.papergraphicsonline.com
SIC: 2752 2759 2679 2621   Offset printing;
   Photocopying and duplicating services;
   Stationery and office supplies

(G-14998)
PJ DIVERSIFIED MACHINING INC
12b Star Dr Ste 3 (03054-4415)
PHONE..........................603 459-8655
Paula Demers, *Prin*
Joanne M Demers, *Prin*
EMP: 8 **EST:** 2015
SQ FT: 2,500
SALES (est): 467.01K **Privately Held**
SIC: 3599   Machine shop, jobbing and repair

(G-14999)
PRODWAYS
316 Daniel Webster Hwy (03054-4102)
PHONE..........................763 568-7966
Alban D'hallium, *CEO*
Yves-marie Hillion, *Treas*
Elizabeth Smith, *Off Mgr*
EMP: 8 **EST:** 2015
SALES (est): 722.95K **Privately Held**
Web: www.prodways.com
SIC: 3555   Printing trades machinery

(G-15000)
RAYTHEON COMPANY
Also Called: Raytheon
59 Daniel Webster Hwy (03054-4858)
PHONE..........................978 313-0201
EMP: 9
SALES (corp-wide): 68.92B **Publicly Held**
Web: www.rtx.com
SIC: 3812 3663 3761   Defense systems and
   equipment; Space satellite communications
   equipment; Guided missiles and space
   vehicles, research and development
HQ: Raytheon Company
   870 Winter St
   Waltham MA 02451
   781 522-3000

(G-15001)
SAINT-GOBAIN PRFMCE PLAS CORP
701 Daniel Webster Hwy (03054-2713)
PHONE..........................603 424-9000
Robert C Ayotte, *CEO*
EMP: 250
SALES (corp-wide): 397.78MM **Privately
Held**
Web: www.saint-gobain.com
SIC: 2821   Plastics materials and resins
HQ: Saint-Gobain Performance Plastics
   Corporation
   20 Moores Rd
   Malvern PA 19355
   440 836-6900

(G-15002)
SIGLAB INDUSTRIES LLC ✪
9 Greenwich Dr (03054-3027)
PHONE..........................603 860-2931
Tyler Signer, *Mgr*
EMP: 7 **EST:** 2023
SALES (est): 61.02K **Privately Held**
SIC: 3999   Manufacturing industries, nec

(G-15003)
SOLIDSCAPE INC
316 Daniel Webster Hwy (03054-4102)
PHONE..........................603 424-0590
▲ **EMP:** 49 **EST:** 1995
SQ FT: 38,678
SALES (est): 9.26MM
SALES (corp-wide): 1.68B **Privately Held**
Web: www.solidscape.com
SIC: 3577   Computer peripheral equipment,
   nec
HQ: Stratasys, Inc.
   7665 Commerce Way
   Eden Prairie MN 55344

(G-15004)
SONESYS LLC
21 Continental Blvd (03054-4303)
PHONE..........................603 423-9000
EMP: 10 **EST:** 2009
SQ FT: 3,000
SALES (est): 1.03MM **Privately Held**
Web: www.sonesys.us
SIC: 3679   Electronic circuits

(G-15005)
SPACE OPTICS RESEARCH LABS LLC
15 Caron St (03054-4428)
PHONE..........................978 250-8640
Sandra Scannell, *Mgr*
EMP: 14 **EST:** 2006
SQ FT: 16,000
SALES (est): 2.03MM **Privately Held**
Web: www.sorl.com
SIC: 3827   Optical instruments and
   apparatus

(G-15006)
SPRAYING SYSTEMS CO
243 Daniel Webster Hwy (03054-4807)
PHONE..........................603 517-1854
Robert Brooks, *Mgr*
EMP: 35
SALES (corp-wide): 434.45MM **Privately
Held**
Web: www.spray.com
SIC: 3499   Nozzles, spray: aerosol, paint, or
   insecticide
PA: Spraying Systems Co.
   200 W North Ave
   Glendale Heights IL 60139
   630 665-5000

(G-15007)
TECH NH INC (PA)
8 Continental Blvd (03054-4302)
P.O. Box 476 (03054-0476)
PHONE..........................603 424-4404
Richard C Grosky, *Pr*
Pamela Young, *
Roger Somers, *
▲ **EMP:** 67 **EST:** 1996
SQ FT: 25,400
SALES (est): 10.54MM
SALES (corp-wide): 10.54MM **Privately
Held**
Web: www.technh.com
SIC: 3089 8711   Injection molded finished
   plastics products, nec; Consulting engineer

Middleton
Carroll County

(G-15008)
MIDDLETON BUILDING SUPPLY (PA)
Also Called: Diprizio Pines Sales

5 Kings Hwy (03887-6217)
PHONE..............................603 473-2210
Lawrence Huot, *Pr*
Harold Lavalley, *
Marcella S Perry, *
Charles Spanos, *
▲ **EMP:** 101 **EST:** 1993
SALES (est): 22.14MM **Privately Held**
Web: www.lavalleys.com
SIC: 5211 5099 2431 2421 Lumber products
; Wood and wood by-products; Millwork;
Sawmills and planing mills, general

Milan
Coos County

(G-15009)
KEL-LOG INC (PA)
743 E Side River Rd (03588-3517)
PHONE..............................603 752-2000
Michael P Kelley, *Pr*
Susan S Kelley, *
Margaret Vien, *
Peter Bornstein, *
EMP: 25 **EST:** 1976
SALES (est): 2.3MM
SALES (corp-wide): 2.3MM **Privately Held**
SIC: 2411 Logging

Milford
Hillsborough County

(G-15010)
AEGIS HOLDINGS LLC
Also Called: Aegis Container
Riverway W (03055)
P.O. Box 257 (03055-0257)
PHONE..............................603 673-8900
EMP: 25 **EST:** 2008
SALES (est): 4.93MM **Privately Held**
Web: www.aegiscontainer.com
SIC: 2653 Boxes, corrugated: made from
purchased materials

(G-15011)
AETNA INSULATED WIRE LLC
53 Old Wilton Rd (03055-3119)
PHONE..............................757 460-3381
Gregory J Smith, *Pr*
Gregory Smith, *
Vincent Victa, *
Robert Webb, *Secretary General**
Jeff Lovett, *
▼ **EMP:** 116 **EST:** 2004
SQ FT: 320,000
SALES (est): 76.47MM
SALES (corp-wide): 302.09B **Publicly
Held**
SIC: 3357 3351 Nonferrous wiredrawing
and insulating; Copper rolling and drawing
HQ: Marmon Holdings, Inc.
181 W Madison St Ste 3900
Chicago IL 60602
312 372-9500

(G-15012)
AIRMAR TECHNOLOGY CORP
40 Meadowbrook Dr (03055)
PHONE..............................603 673-9570
Dee Dee Tower, *Prin*
EMP: 15
SALES (corp-wide): 50.61MM **Privately
Held**
Web: www.airmar.com
SIC: 3825 1541 Transducers for volts,
amperes, watts, vars, frequency, etc.;
Industrial buildings and warehouses
PA: Airmar Technology Corp.
35 Meadowbrook Dr

Milford NH 03055
603 673-9570

(G-15013)
**AIRMAR TECHNOLOGY CORP
(PA)**
35 Meadowbrook Dr (03055-4617)
PHONE..............................603 673-9570
Stephen Boucher, *CEO*
Matthew Boucher, *Pr*
Karl T Krantz, *VP*
Ted Krantz, *Pr*
Ronald Cormier, *CFO*
◆ **EMP:** 260 **EST:** 1981
SQ FT: 75,000
SALES (est): 50.61MM
SALES (corp-wide): 50.61MM **Privately
Held**
Web: www.airmar.com
SIC: 3825 3829 3541 Transducers for volts,
amperes, watts, vars, frequency, etc.;
Measuring and controlling devices, nec;
Machine tools, metal cutting type

(G-15014)
ALENE CANDLES LLC (PA)
Also Called: Alene Candles
51 Scarborough Ln (03055-3117)
PHONE..............................603 673-5050
◆ **EMP:** 196 **EST:** 1995
SQ FT: 75,000
SALES (est): 109.75MM **Privately Held**
Web: www.alene.com
SIC: 3999 Candles

(G-15015)
AMHERST LABEL INC
15 Westchester Dr (03055-3056)
P.O. Box 596 (03055-0596)
PHONE..............................603 673-7849
Nye Hornor, *Pr*
David Sturm, *
EMP: 60 **EST:** 1978
SQ FT: 35,000
SALES (est): 10.16MM **Privately Held**
Web: www.amherstlabel.com
SIC: 2759 Flexographic printing
HQ: Inovar Packaging Group, Llc
9001 Sterling St
Irving TX 75063

(G-15016)
CIRTRONICS CORPORATION
528 Route 13 S Ste 130 (03055-3480)
P.O. Box 130 (03055-0130)
PHONE..............................603 249-9190
Dave Patterson, *Pr*
Robert C Mccray, *Ch*
Gerardine Ferlins, *GOVERNANCE**
George Mandragouras, *
Kevin Longley, *
▲ **EMP:** 135 **EST:** 1979
SQ FT: 170,000
SALES (est): 48.54MM **Privately Held**
Web: www.cirtronics.com
SIC: 3672 Printed circuit boards

(G-15017)
CNI CORP
Also Called: Computer Network Integrators
468 Route 13 S (03055-3488)
PHONE..............................603 249-5075
Jon Dickinson, *Pr*
Robert Howard, *Sec*
Scott Snow, *VP*
EMP: 9 **EST:** 1989
SQ FT: 4,800
SALES (est): 1.41MM **Privately Held**
Web: www.breezeadworkflow.com

SIC: 7372 7371 Publisher's computer
software; Custom computer programming
services

(G-15018)
**CONTROLLED FLUIDICS LLC
(PA)**
18 Hollow Oak Ln (03055-4270)
PHONE..............................603 673-4323
Thomas Rolff, *Managing Member*
EMP: 15 **EST:** 2011
SALES (est): 3.84MM
SALES (corp-wide): 3.84MM **Privately
Held**
Web: www.controlledfluidics.com
SIC: 3599 Machine shop, jobbing and repair

(G-15019)
COORSTEK INC
Also Called: Coorstek Milford
47 Powers St (03055-4928)
PHONE..............................603 673-7560
Dean Croucher, *Brnch Mgr*
EMP: 83
SALES (corp-wide): 1.16B **Privately Held**
Web: www.coorstek.com
SIC: 3264 Porcelain electrical supplies
HQ: Coorstek, Inc.
14143 Denver West Pkwy # 400
Lakewood CO 80401
303 271-7000

(G-15020)
DATRON DYNAMICS INC
115 Emerson Rd (03055-3583)
PHONE..............................603 215-5850
William King, *Pr*
Robert Murphy, *
◆ **EMP:** 40 **EST:** 2000
SQ FT: 10,000
SALES (est): 8.95MM **Privately Held**
Web: www.datron.com
SIC: 3545 3541 Machine tool accessories;
Machine tools, metal cutting: exotic
(explosive, etc.)

(G-15021)
DC TIRE SERVICE INC
6 Prospect St (03055-3724)
PHONE..............................603 673-9211
Darren Courtemarche, *Pr*
John Hyde, *VP*
David Kinney, *VP*
EMP: 9 **EST:** 1990
SQ FT: 20,000
SALES (est): 935.37K **Privately Held**
SIC: 5531 7534 Automotive tires; Tire
retreading and repair shops

(G-15022)
GARDOC INC (DH)
Also Called: Spear Systems
86 Powers St (03055-4927)
PHONE..............................603 673-6400
Randall Spear, *Pr*
EMP: 9 **EST:** 1971
SQ FT: 35,000
SALES (est): 3.78MM
SALES (corp-wide): 6.8B **Privately Held**
SIC: 2672 Labels (unprinted), gummed:
made from purchased materials
HQ: Mcc - Mason W&S
5510 Courseview Dr
Mason OH 45040
513 459-1100

(G-15023)
**GRANITE STATE CONCRETE CO
INC**

408 Elm St (03055-4305)
P.O. Box 185 (03055-0185)
PHONE..............................603 673-3327
John Mac Lellan Iii, *Pr*
EMP: 16 **EST:** 1946
SQ FT: 2,000
SALES (est): 764.22K **Privately Held**
SALES (corp-wide): 10.15MM **Privately
Held**
SIC: 3273 1442 Ready-mixed concrete;
Construction sand and gravel
PA: J. G. Maclellan Concrete Co., Inc.
180 Phoenix Ave
Lowell MA 01852
978 458-1223

(G-15024)
**HAYDON KERK MTION
SLUTIONS INC**
Also Called: Kerk Products Division
56 Meadowbrook Dr (03055-4612)
PHONE..............................603 213-6290
EMP: 80
SALES (corp-wide): 6.15B **Publicly Held**
Web: www.haydonkerkpittman.com
SIC: 3452 Screws, metal
HQ: Haydon Kerk Motion Solutions, Inc.
1500 Meriden Rd
Waterbury CT 06705
203 756-7441

(G-15025)
HI-TECH FABRICATORS INC
10 Scarborough Ln (03055-3117)
PHONE..............................603 672-3766
Paul Bailey, *Pr*
Ann Bailey, *VP*
EMP: 15 **EST:** 1983
SQ FT: 12,000
SALES (est): 2.2MM **Privately Held**
Web: www.hitechfabricators.com
SIC: 3444 Sheet metalwork

(G-15026)
HITCHINER LLC
117 Old Wilton Rd (03055-3134)
PHONE..............................603 672-9630
EMP: 9 **EST:** 2015
SALES (est): 230.25K **Privately Held**
Web: www.hitchiner.com
SIC: 3599 Machine shop, jobbing and repair

(G-15027)
**HITCHINER MANUFACTURING
CO INC (PA)**
594 Elm St (03055-4306)
PHONE..............................603 673-1100
John Morison Iii, *Ch Bd*
John Morison Iii, *Ch*
Timothy Sullivan, *
Michel Petit, *
Scott Biederman, *
◆ **EMP:** 707 **EST:** 1946
SQ FT: 220,000
SALES (est): 223.75MM
SALES (corp-wide): 223.75MM **Privately
Held**
Web: www.hitchiner.com
SIC: 3324 Steel investment foundries

(G-15028)
HOLLIS LINE MACHINE CO INC
128 Old Wilton Rd (03055-3118)
PHONE..............................603 673-1166
John Siergiewicz Junior, *Pr*
▲ **EMP:** 50 **EST:** 1993
SQ FT: 18,000
SALES (est): 5.53MM **Privately Held**
Web: www.hollisline.com

GEOGRAPHIC

SIC: 7692 3567　Welding repair; Industrial furnaces and ovens

(G-15029)
HY-TEN DIE & DEVELOPMENT CORP
Also Called: Hy-Ten Plastics
38 Powers St　(03055-4982)
PHONE...............................603 673-1611
Udo Fritsch, *Ch Bd*
Franz Fritsch, *
EMP: 50 EST: 1961
SQ FT: 35,000
SALES (est): 9.69MM **Privately Held**
Web: www.hy-ten.com
SIC: 3089 3544　Injection molded finished plastics products, nec; Industrial molds

(G-15030)
INNOVAIRRE STUDIOS INC
Also Called: Brickmill Marketing Services
528 Route 13 S Ste 200　(03055-3492)
PHONE...............................603 579-1600
Chad Spannaus, *Pr*
Mark Schulhof, *
Thomas Schulhof, *
Dean Schulhof, *
EMP: 38 EST: 1975
SQ FT: 6,000
SALES (est): 4.68MM
SALES (corp-wide): 4.68MM **Privately Held**
Web: www.innovairre.com
SIC: 7389 7372 8743　Fund raising organizations; Prepackaged software; Promotion service
PA: Rbs International Direct Marketing Llc
2 Executive Campus # 200
Cherry Hill NJ 08002
856 663-2500

(G-15031)
MARMON UTILITY
53 Old Wilton Rd　(03055-3119)
PHONE...............................603 249-1302
EMP: 18
SALES (est): 287.18K **Privately Held**
Web: www.marmonutility.com
SIC: 2298　Ropes and fiber cables

(G-15032)
MARMON UTILITY LLC (DH)
53 Old Wilton Rd　(03055-3119)
PHONE...............................603 673-2040
◆ EMP: 183 EST: 1951
SQ FT: 175,000
SALES (est): 75.96MM
SALES (corp-wide): 302.09B **Publicly Held**
Web: www.marmonutility.com
SIC: 3357　Communication wire
HQ: Marmon Holdings, Inc.
181 W Madison St Ste 3900
Chicago IL 60602
312 372-9500

(G-15033)
METAL CASTING TECHNOLOGY INC
Also Called: M C T
127 Old Wilton Rd　(03055-3120)
PHONE...............................603 673-9720
Paul Mikkola, *Pr*
Ron Cafferty, *Sec*
EMP: 22 EST: 1987
SQ FT: 24,000
SALES (est): 468.09K
SALES (corp-wide): 223.75MM **Privately Held**
Web: www.hitchiner.com

SIC: 8731 3325　Industrial laboratory, except testing; Steel foundries, nec
PA: Hitchiner Manufacturing Co., Inc.
594 Elm St
Milford NH 03055
603 673-1100

(G-15034)
PLASTI-CLIP CORPORATION
Also Called: Precision Design
38 Perry Rd　(03055-4308)
PHONE...............................603 672-1166
Daniel Faneuf, *CEO*
EMP: 10 EST: 1978
SQ FT: 6,800
SALES (est): 945.91K **Privately Held**
Web: www.plasticlip.com
SIC: 3083 3496　Plastics finished products, laminated; Miscellaneous fabricated wire products

(G-15035)
QUADRIGA ART
528 Route 13 S Ste 200　(03055-3492)
P.O. Box 968　(03055-0968)
PHONE...............................603 654-6141
Thomas Schulhof, *CEO*
EMP: 8 EST: 2017
SALES (est): 212.98K **Privately Held**
SIC: 2771　Greeting cards

(G-15036)
SAINT-GOBAIN CERAMICS PLAS INC
Also Called: Saint-Gobain Crystals
33 Powers St　(03055-4928)
PHONE...............................603 673-5831
Jeff Rioux, *Mgr*
EMP: 136
SALES (corp-wide): 397.78MM **Privately Held**
Web: www.saint-gobain.com
SIC: 2819　Industrial inorganic chemicals, nec
HQ: Saint-Gobain Ceramics & Plastics, Inc.
20 Moores Rd
Malvern PA 19355

(G-15037)
SAINT-GOBAIN GLASS CORPORATION
Also Called: Saint-Gobain Igniter Products
47 Powers St　(03055-4928)
PHONE...............................603 673-7560
Dean Croucher, *Brnch Mgr*
EMP: 33
SALES (corp-wide): 397.78MM **Privately Held**
Web: www.saint-gobain.com
SIC: 3674　Semiconductors and related devices
HQ: Saint-Gobain Glass Corporation
20 Moores Rd
Malvern PA 19355
484 595-9430

(G-15038)
SLINKY STAINLESS STEEL
20 Mont Vernon St　(03055-4115)
PHONE...............................603 673-1104
Michael Jones, *Pr*
EMP: 7 EST: 2011
SALES (est): 92.74K **Privately Held**
SIC: 3312　Stainless steel

(G-15039)
TECH RESOURCES INC
Also Called: T R I
1 Meadowbrook Dr　(03055-4619)

PHONE...............................603 673-9000
EMP: 50 EST: 1978
SALES (est): 4.76MM **Privately Held**
Web: www.trimilford.com
SIC: 3699 3825 3083 3577　Electrical equipment and supplies, nec; Instruments to measure electricity; Laminated plastics plate and sheet; Computer peripheral equipment, nec

(G-15040)
THANKSBEN10 LLC
Also Called: Yankee Toy Box
48 Powers St　(03055-4927)
PHONE...............................603 206-5116
Lisa Lynne Zerr, *Managing Member*
EMP: 10 EST: 2011
SALES (est): 2.49MM **Privately Held**
Web: www.yankeetoybox.com
SIC: 5641 2389 5651　Children's wear; Men's miscellaneous accessories; Unisex clothing stores

(G-15041)
TRELLBORG PIPE SALS MLFORD INC
279 Riverway W　(03055)
PHONE...............................603 673-8680
EMP: 55
SALES (corp-wide): 4.26B **Privately Held**
SIC: 3053　Gaskets; packing and sealing devices
HQ: Trelleborg Pipe Seals Milford, Inc.
250 Elm St
Milford NH 03055
800 626-2180

(G-15042)
TRELLBORG PIPE SALS MLFORD INC (DH)
250 Elm St　(03055-4758)
P.O. Box 301　(03055-0301)
PHONE...............................800 626-2180
Randy L Snyder, *Pr*
Robert Peacock, *
◆ EMP: 11 EST: 1996
SQ FT: 66,000
SALES (est): 45.16MM
SALES (corp-wide): 4.26B **Privately Held**
SIC: 3053 3531 3541 3498　Gaskets and sealing devices; Crushers, grinders, and similar equipment; Machine tools, metal cutting type; Fabricated pipe and fittings
HQ: Trelleborg Pipe Seals Lelystad B.V.
Pascallaan 80
Lelystad FL 8218
320267979

(G-15043)
WILKINS LUMBER CO INC
495 Mont Vernon Rd　(03055-4215)
P.O. Box 393　(03031-0393)
PHONE...............................603 673-2545
Tom Wilkins, *Pr*
Sally Wilkins, *VP*
EMP: 9
SQ FT: 5,000
SALES (est): 810.54K **Privately Held**
Web: www.wilkinslumber.com
SIC: 2421 5211　Lumber: rough, sawed, or planed; Planing mill products and lumber

(G-15044)
WIRE WINDERS INC
Also Called: Wire Winders
151 Mont Vernon Rd　(03055-4125)
P.O. Box 187　(03055-0187)
PHONE...............................603 673-1763
Michael Gaudette, *Pr*
EMP: 7 EST: 1991

SQ FT: 6,000
SALES (est): 854.41K **Privately Held**
Web: www.wirewinders.com
SIC: 3677　Coil windings, electronic

Milton
Strafford County

(G-15045)
EASTERN BOATS INC
Also Called: Eastern Boats
31 Industrial Way　(03851-4335)
P.O. Box 1040　(03851-1040)
PHONE...............................603 652-9213
Robert Bourdeau, *Pr*
Cheryl Randall, *
EMP: 37 EST: 1997
SALES (est): 4.59MM **Privately Held**
Web: www.easternboats.com
SIC: 3732 5551　Boats, fiberglass: building and repairing; Boat dealers

(G-15046)
INDEX PACKAGING INC
Also Called: Index Millwork
1055 White Mountain Hwy　(03851-4443)
PHONE...............................603 350-0018
Bruce Lander, *Pr*
William M Lander, *
Constance B Lander, *
Debora Jordan, *Stockholder*
Connie Lander, *
▼ EMP: 160 EST: 1968
SQ FT: 120,000
SALES (est): 23.28MM **Privately Held**
Web: www.indexpackaging.com
SIC: 2449 3086 3412 2441　Wood containers, nec; Plastics foam products; Metal barrels, drums, and pails; Nailed wood boxes and shook

Monroe
Grafton County

(G-15047)
PETE AND GERRYS ORGANICS LLC (PA)
Also Called: Laflamme Farms
140 Buffum Rd　(03771-3114)
PHONE...............................603 638-2827
Jesse Laflamme, *Managing Member*
▲ EMP: 16 EST: 2000
SALES (est): 22.45MM
SALES (corp-wide): 22.45MM **Privately Held**
Web: www.peteandgerrys.com
SIC: 2015　Egg processing

Mont Vernon
Hillsborough County

(G-15048)
PICKUP PATROL LLC
Also Called: Pickup Patrol
2 Wallace Ln　(03057-1117)
PHONE...............................877 394-7774
Maria Edvalson, *CEO*
Eric Edvalson, *Engr*
Daniel Brackett, *Engr*
Candee Noorda, *Mktg Dir*
EMP: 8 EST: 2014
SALES (est): 462.47K **Privately Held**
Web: www.pickuppatrol.net
SIC: 7372　Application computer software

(G-15049)

VODA INDUSTRIES LLC ✪

127 Tarn Rd (03057-5922)
PHONE..................................908 531-8156
EMP: 7 **EST:** 2023
SALES (est): 61.02K **Privately Held**
SIC: 3999   Manufacturing industries, nec

(G-15050)

WILBUR TECHNICAL SERVICES LLC

97 S Main St (03057-1621)
P.O. Box 397 (03057-0397)
PHONE..................................603 880-7100
Nancy Wilbur, *CEO*
EMP: 8 **EST:** 2004
SALES (est): 2.47MM **Privately Held**
Web: www.jjwilbur.com
SIC: 3826   Laser scientific and engineering instruments

Moultonborough
Carroll County

(G-15051)

CG ROXANE LLC

455 Ossipee Park Rd (03254)
P.O. Box 657 (03254-0657)
PHONE..................................603 476-8844
Mark Wiggins, *Mgr*
EMP: 18
Web: www.crystalgeyserplease.com
SIC: 2086 7999   Water, natural: packaged in cans, bottles, etc.; Tourist attraction, commercial
PA: Cg Roxane Llc
1210 S Hwy 395
Olancha CA 93549

(G-15052)

ELAN PUBLISHING COMPANY INC

72 Whittier Hwy Unit 3 (03254-3686)
P.O. Box 683 (03253-0683)
PHONE..................................603 253-6002
Thomas A Power, *CEO*
Sylvia Detscher, *
▼ **EMP:** 10 **EST:** 1972
SQ FT: 20,000
SALES (est): 972.06K **Privately Held**
Web: www.elanpublish.com
SIC: 2741   Miscellaneous publishing

(G-15053)

ELECTRCAL INSTALLATIONS LLC EI

397 Whittier Hwy (03254-3629)
PHONE..................................603 253-4525
James Fritz, *Pr*
Darlene Fritz, *
Edgar D Mc Kean Iii, *Sec*
James P Fritz, *
Charles L Fritz Junior, *VP*
EMP: 30 **EST:** 1987
SQ FT: 2,500
SALES (est): 10.18MM **Privately Held**
Web: www.eii-hq.com
SIC: 3613 1731   Control panels, electric; Electric power systems contractors

Nashua
Hillsborough County

(G-15054)

AKKEN INC

98 Spit Brook Rd Ste 402 (03062-5737)

PHONE..................................866 590-6695
Giridhar Akkineni, *CEO*
EMP: 51 **EST:** 2007
SQ FT: 6,000
SALES (est): 4.56MM **Privately Held**
Web: www.akkencloud.com
SIC: 7372   Business oriented computer software

(G-15055)

AKUMINA INC (PA)

30 Temple St Ste 301 (03060-2414)
PHONE..................................603 318-8269
Ed Rogers, *CEO*
David Maffei, *CRO*
Ali Riaz, *Ch Bd*
John Dibartolomeo, *CFO*
EMP: 23 **EST:** 2014
SALES (est): 2.65MM
SALES (corp-wide): 2.65MM **Privately Held**
Web: www.akumina.com
SIC: 7372   Prepackaged software

(G-15056)

ALACRON INC

71 Spit Brook Rd Ste 200 (03060-5636)
PHONE..................................603 891-2750
Joseph A Sgro, *CEO*
Paul Stanton, *Pr*
EMP: 10 **EST:** 1985
SQ FT: 10,000
SALES (est): 1.31MM **Privately Held**
Web: www.alacron.com
SIC: 3571   Computers, digital, analog or hybrid

(G-15057)

ALLARD NAZARIAN GROUP INC (PA) ✪

Also Called: Granite State Manufacturing
140 Burke St (03060-4742)
PHONE..................................603 320-8755
John R Allard, *CEO*
EMP: 20 **EST:** 2023
SALES (est): 833.76K
SALES (corp-wide): 833.76K **Privately Held**
SIC: 3999   Manufacturing industries, nec

(G-15058)

ALPHA GRPHICS PRNTSHOP OF FTUR

Also Called: AlphaGraphics
97 Main St Ste 1 (03060-2751)
PHONE..................................603 595-1444
Mary Sue Orpin, *Pt*
David Orpin, *Pt*
EMP: 13 **EST:** 1988
SQ FT: 5,500
SALES (est): 668.75K **Privately Held**
Web: www.alphagraphics.com
SIC: 2752 7334   Commercial printing, lithographic; Photocopying and duplicating services

(G-15059)

ALTSCALE CLOUD SERVICES INC

23 Middle Dunstable Rd (03062-2310)
PHONE..................................800 558-5814
Albena Dimitrova, *Pr*
Rossen Dimitrov, *Prin*
Svetlana Stoykova, *Treas*
George Demirev, *Sec*
EMP: 8 **EST:** 2018
SALES (est): 107.35K **Privately Held**
Web: www.altscale.com

SIC: 7372   Prepackaged software

(G-15060)

AMPHENOL CORPORATION

Also Called: Amphenol Printed Circuits
91 Northeastern Blvd (03062-3141)
PHONE..................................603 879-3000
Tom Pursch, *Mgr*
EMP: 400
SALES (corp-wide): 12.62B **Publicly Held**
Web: www.amphenol.com
SIC: 3672   Printed circuit boards
PA: Amphenol Corporation
358 Hall Ave
Wallingford CT 06492
203 265-8900

(G-15061)

AMPHENOL CORPORATION

Amphenol TCS
200 Innovative Way Ste 201 (03062-5740)
PHONE..................................603 879-3000
Carly Carleton, *Brnch Mgr*
EMP: 345
SALES (corp-wide): 12.62B **Publicly Held**
Web: www.amphenol.com
SIC: 3678 3643 3661 3496   Electronic connectors; Connectors and terminals for electrical devices; Fiber optics communications equipment; Cable, uninsulated wire: made from purchased wire
PA: Amphenol Corporation
358 Hall Ave
Wallingford CT 06492
203 265-8900

(G-15062)

AMPHENOL PRINTED CIRCUITS INC (HQ)

Also Called: APC Phno
91 Northeastern Blvd (03062-3141)
PHONE..................................603 324-4500
R Adam Norwitt, *Pr*
Edward C Wetmore, *
Diana G Reardon, *
▲ **EMP:** 93 **EST:** 1976
SQ FT: 50,000
SALES (est): 194.31MM
SALES (corp-wide): 12.62B **Publicly Held**
Web: www.amphenol-apc.com
SIC: 3679 3678 3672 3357   Electronic circuits; Electronic connectors; Printed circuit boards; Nonferrous wiredrawing and insulating
PA: Amphenol Corporation
358 Hall Ave
Wallingford CT 06492
203 265-8900

(G-15063)

ANALOG DEVICES INC

20 Cotton Rd Ste 101 (03063-1262)
PHONE..................................603 883-2430
EMP: 7
SALES (corp-wide): 12.31B **Publicly Held**
Web: www.analog.com
SIC: 3674   Semiconductors and related devices
PA: Analog Devices, Inc.
1 Analog Way
Wilmington MA 01887
781 935-5565

(G-15064)

ARC TECHNOLOGY SOLUTIONS LLC

165 Ledge St Ste 4 (03060-3061)
PHONE..................................603 883-3027
Kenneth Collins, *Managing Member*
EMP: 65 **EST:** 1999

SQ FT: 15,000
SALES (est): 22.23MM **Privately Held**
Web: www.arcserv.com
SIC: 3825 3812 3829 8711   Test equipment for electronic and electric measurement; Acceleration indicators and systems components, aerospace; Aircraft and motor vehicle measurement equipment; Aviation and/or aeronautical engineering

(G-15065)

AUTOVIRT INC

12 Murphy Dr (03062-1903)
PHONE..................................603 546-2900
Josh Klein, *CEO*
EMP: 8 **EST:** 2007
SALES (est): 295.82K **Privately Held**
Web: www.autovirt.com
SIC: 7372   Word processing computer software

(G-15066)

BAE SYSTEMS ELCTRONIC SOLUTION

65 Spit Brook Rd (03060-6909)
PHONE..................................603 885-3653
EMP: 54 **EST:** 2010
SALES (est): 3.37MM **Privately Held**
SIC: 3812   Search and navigation equipment

(G-15067)

BAE SYSTEMS INFO ELCTRNIC SYST

Also Called: BAE SYSTEMS INFORMATION AND ELECTRONIC SYSTEMS INTEGRATION INC.
95 Canal St (03064-2813)
P.O. Box 868 (03061-0868)
PHONE..................................603 885-4321
Joshua Niedzwiecki, *Brnch Mgr*
EMP: 1354
SALES (corp-wide): 25.59B **Privately Held**
Web: www.baesystems.com
SIC: 3812   Search and navigation equipment
HQ: Bae Systems Information And Electronic Systems Integration Inc.
65 Spit Brook Rd
Nashua NH 03060
603 885-4321

(G-15068)

BAE SYSTEMS INFO ELCTRNIC SYST (DH)

65 Spit Brook Rd (03060-6909)
P.O. Box 868 (03061-0868)
PHONE..................................603 885-4321
Terry Crimmins, *CEO*
EMP: 1953 **EST:** 1951
SQ FT: 622,000
SALES (est): 1.48B
SALES (corp-wide): 25.59B **Privately Held**
Web: www.baesystems.com
SIC: 3812   Search and navigation equipment
HQ: Bae Systems, Inc.
2941 Frview Pk Dr Ste 100
Falls Church VA 22042

(G-15069)

BAGEL ALLEY OF NH INC

Also Called: Bagel Alley Baker
1 Eldridge St (03060-3410)
PHONE..................................603 882-9343
Brett Fleckner, *Treas*
Robert Frank, *Pr*
Maryanne Sleckner, *VP*
Marilyn Frank, *Sec*
EMP: 10 **EST:** 1980
SQ FT: 2,000
SALES (est): 490.99K **Privately Held**

SIC: 2051   Bread, cake, and related products

(G-15070)
BENCHMARK ELECTRONICS INC
100 Innovative Way (03062-5748)
PHONE.................................603 879-7000
Gerry Leo, *Brnch Mgr*
EMP: 350
SALES (corp-wide): 2.89B **Publicly Held**
Web: www.bench.com
SIC: 3672   Printed circuit boards
PA: Benchmark Electronics, Inc.
    56 S Rockford Dr
    Tempe AZ 85288
    623 300-7000

(G-15071)
BIGRAPHICS INC
472 Amherst St Unit 18 (03063-1204)
PHONE.................................603 594-8686
Charles Poor, *Pr*
EMP: 9 EST: 2014
SALES (est): 572.26K **Privately Held**
Web: www.bigraphicsinc.com
SIC: 3993   Signs and advertising specialties

(G-15072)
BLUGLASS INC
77 Northeastern Blvd Ste 103 (03062)
PHONE.................................617 869-5150
Brad Siskavich, *Prin*
EMP: 11 EST: 2020
SALES (est): 718.62K **Privately Held**
Web: www.bluglass.com
SIC: 3674   Semiconductors and related
   devices

(G-15073)
BOSTON BILLOWS INC
55 Lake St (03060-4516)
PHONE.................................603 598-1200
Eric Skoug, *Pr*
Kim Igoe, *VP*
EMP: 8 EST: 1998
SALES (est): 479.63K **Privately Held**
Web: www.bostonbillows.com
SIC: 2392   Cushions and pillows

(G-15074)
BRONZE CRAFT CORPORATION
37 Will St (03060-6002)
P.O. Box 788 (03061-0788)
PHONE.................................603 883-7747
Jack Atkinson, *Ch Bd*
James J Bernard, *
James R Lajeunesse, *
Beverly J Coelho, *
Gerald Bell, *
▲ EMP: 60 EST: 1944
SQ FT: 55,000
SALES (est): 9.87MM **Privately Held**
Web: www.bronzecraft.com
SIC: 3365 3366 3429   Aluminum foundries;
   Castings (except die), nec, bronze;
   Hardware, nec

(G-15075)
CAN-ONE (USA) INC ✪
Also Called: Kj Can
141 Burke St (03060-4757)
PHONE.................................860 299-4608
Alvin Widitora, *CEO*
EMP: 10 EST: 2022
SALES (est): 1.02MM **Privately Held**
SIC: 3411   Aluminum cans

(G-15076)
CARIMAN 44 LLC
2 Knights Bridge Dr (03063-8005)
PHONE.................................603 889-5160
EMP: 8 EST: 2015
SALES (est): 408.58K **Privately Held**
SIC: 3599   Industrial machinery, nec

(G-15077)
CARR MANAGEMENT INC (PA)
Also Called: Plastic Industries
1 Tara Blvd Ste 303 (03062-2809)
PHONE.................................603 888-1315
Beth Muscato, *CEO*
Andrew Carr, *Ch Bd*
Robert Pearson, *CFO*
EMP: 12 EST: 2008
SALES (est): 171.7MM **Privately Held**
Web: www.altiumpkg.com
SIC: 3085   Plastics bottles

(G-15078)
CENTORR/VACUUM INDUSTRIES LLC (PA)
55 Northeastern Blvd Unit 2 (03062)
PHONE.................................603 595-7233
William Nareski, *Pr*
Stephen Hewitt, *
David Downs, *
William Murphy, *
EMP: 42 EST: 1962
SQ FT: 40,000
SALES (est): 9.57MM
SALES (corp-wide): 9.57MM **Privately Held**
Web: www.vacuum-furnaces.com
SIC: 3567   Vacuum furnaces and ovens

(G-15079)
CHOPPERS OF NEW ENGLAND
50 Bridge St (03060-3544)
PHONE.................................603 809-4391
John Mansur, *Admn*
EMP: 8 EST: 2012
SALES (est): 277K **Privately Held**
Web: www.choppersofnewengland.com
SIC: 3751   Motorcycles and related parts

(G-15080)
CIRCUIT CONNECT INC
4 State St (03063-1012)
PHONE.................................603 880-7447
Ben Schuler, *CEO*
▲ EMP: 24 EST: 1990
SQ FT: 28,000
SALES (est): 4.97MM
SALES (corp-wide): 57.37MM **Privately Held**
Web: www.circuit-connect.com
SIC: 3672   Circuit boards, television and
   radio printed
PA: Infinitum Electric Inc.
    106 E Old Settlers Blvd D106
    Round Rock TX 78664
    512 633-2842

(G-15081)
CLEAR ALIGN LLC
Clear Align North
24 Simon St (03060-3025)
PHONE.................................603 889-2116
EMP: 15
SALES (corp-wide): 67MM **Privately Held**
Web: www.clearalign.com
SIC: 3827   Optical instruments and lenses
PA: Clear Align Llc
    2550 Blvd Of The Gnrls # 280
    West Norriton PA 19403
    484 956-0510

(G-15082)
COATING SYSTEMS INC
Also Called: Chemical Consolidated Division
55 Crown St (03060-6392)
PHONE.................................603 883-0553
Aram Jeknavorian, *Pr*
Aram A Jeknavorian, *Pr*
Emil Petrasek, *VP*
EMP: 9 EST: 1972
SQ FT: 4,000
SALES (est): 2.11MM **Privately Held**
SIC: 4953 4212 2851 2891   Hazardous
   waste collection and disposal; Hazardous
   waste transport; Coating, air curing;
   Adhesives

(G-15083)
COLONIAL ELECTRONIC MFRS INC
1 Chestnut St Ste 203 (03060-9307)
PHONE.................................603 881-8244
Steven Holzman, *Pr*
Janet Holzman, *
▲ EMP: 45 EST: 1992
SQ FT: 15,000
SALES (est): 8.6MM **Privately Held**
Web: www.ceminc.net
SIC: 3672   Printed circuit boards

(G-15084)
CRANE SECURITY TECH INC
Also Called: Crane Currency
1 Cellu Dr (03063-1008)
PHONE.................................603 881-1860
Stephen P Defalco, *Pr*
Gerald J Gartner, *
Stephen Curdo, *
Jeff Coner, *
Douglas S Prince, *
▲ EMP: 35 EST: 1989
SQ FT: 12,700
SALES (est): 10.74MM
SALES (corp-wide): 3.37B **Publicly Held**
Web: www.cranecurrency.com
SIC: 2621   Paper mills
PA: Crane Nxt, Co.
    950 Winter St Fl 4
    Waltham MA 02451
    610 430-2510

(G-15085)
CRITICAL PRCESS FILTRATION INC (PA)
1 Chestnut St Ste 221 (03060-9306)
PHONE.................................603 595-0140
Kristen Ramalho, *Pr*
Fred Arbogast, *
◆ EMP: 33 EST: 1998
SQ FT: 50,000
SALES (est): 6.43MM
SALES (corp-wide): 6.43MM **Privately Held**
Web: www.criticalprocess.com
SIC: 2834   Pharmaceutical preparations

(G-15086)
CROSBY BAKERY INC
51 E Pearl St (03060-3437)
PHONE.................................603 882-1851
Michael Cummings, *Pr*
Gale Cummings, *VP*
Frances Crosby, *Clerk*
EMP: 10 EST: 1947
SQ FT: 3,000
SALES (est): 488.29K **Privately Held**
Web: www.crosbybakerynh.com
SIC: 5461 2051   Bread; Bread, cake, and
   related products

(G-15087)
DATANOMIX INC
71 Spit Brook Rd # 210 (03060-5747)
PHONE.................................843 885-4639
Greg Mchale, *Pr*
John Joseph, *CEO*
EMP: 24 EST: 2015
SALES (est): 1.15MM **Privately Held**
Web: www.datanomix.io
SIC: 7372   Application computer software

(G-15088)
DDG FABRICATION LLC
29 Crown St (03060-6486)
PHONE.................................603 883-9292
Robert Moncada, *Prin*
EMP: 8 EST: 2002
SALES (est): 665.95K **Privately Held**
SIC: 3444   Sheet metalwork

(G-15089)
DEGREE CONTROLS INC (PA)
Also Called: Degree C
300 Innovative Way Ste 222 (03062-5746)
PHONE.................................603 672-8900
▲ EMP: 50 EST: 1996
SQ FT: 25,000
SALES (est): 13.02MM **Privately Held**
Web: www.degreec.com
SIC: 3823   Process control instruments

(G-15090)
DELTA EDUCATION LLC
Also Called: Cpo Science
80 Northwest Blvd (03060-4067)
P.O. Box 3000 (03061-3000)
PHONE.................................800 258-1302
Steven Korte, *Managing Member*
▲ EMP: 300 EST: 1973
SQ FT: 350,000
SALES (est): 50.9MM
SALES (corp-wide): 600.83MM **Privately Held**
Web: select.schoolspecialty.com
SIC: 3944   Science kits: microscopes,
   chemistry sets, etc.
PA: Ssi Liquidating, Inc.
    56 Harrison St
    New Rochelle NY 10801
    914 235-1075

(G-15091)
DENALI SOFTWARE INC
154 Broad St Ste 1535 (03063-3205)
PHONE.................................603 566-0991
EMP: 22
SALES (corp-wide): 3.56B **Publicly Held**
SIC: 7372   Application computer software
HQ: Denali Software, Inc.
    2655 Seely Ave
    San Jose CA 95134

(G-15092)
DJ SEMICHEM INC
28 Charron Ave (03063-1783)
PHONE.................................603 204-5101
David Jenkins, *Prin*
EMP: 8 EST: 2009
SALES (est): 143.85K **Privately Held**
SIC: 2892   Explosives

(G-15093)
EBIZ TECH LLC
134 Haines St Unit 2 (03060-4094)
PHONE.................................603 233-8481
Aijiao Zhu, *Prin*
EMP: 10 EST: 2020
SALES (est): 75.68K **Privately Held**

SIC: 2741 Miscellaneous publishing

(G-15094)
ELMO MOTION CONTROL INC
42 Technology Way (03060-3245)
PHONE.................................603 821-9979
John Mclaughlin, *CEO*
EMP: 15 EST: 1999
SALES (est): 5.04MM **Privately Held**
Web: www.elmomc.com
SIC: 3625 Relays and industrial controls
PA: Elmo Motion Control Limited
   60 Amal
   Petah Tikva 49513

(G-15095)
ENVIRONMENTAL INTERIORS INC
400 Amherst St Ste 201 (03063-4223)
PHONE.................................603 889-9290
EMP: 40
Web: www.environmentalinteriors.com
SIC: 1742 1542 3446 Acoustical and ceiling work; Custom builders, non-residential; Architectural metalwork

(G-15096)
EVERETT CHARLES TECH LLC
Also Called: APJ Test Consulting
41 Simon St Ste 1b (03060-3091)
PHONE.................................603 882-2621
EMP: 30
SALES (corp-wide): 451.77MM **Publicly Held**
SIC: 3825 Electrical power measuring equipment
HQ: Everett Charles Technologies, Llc
   14570 Meyer Canyon Dr # 100
   Fontana CA 92064
   909 625-5551

(G-15097)
EXCELL SOLUTIONS INC
41 Simon St Ste 1d (03060-3091)
PHONE.................................978 663-6100
EMP: 9 EST: 2010
SALES (est): 1.71MM **Privately Held**
Web: www.excellsol.com
SIC: 3444 Sheet metalwork

(G-15098)
EXPRESS ASSEMBLYPRODUCTS LLC
1 Chestnut St Ste 215 (03060-3383)
PHONE.................................603 424-5590
Michael Dechambeau, *Managing Member*
EMP: 10 EST: 2005
SQ FT: 2,400
SALES (est): 940.96K **Privately Held**
Web: www.expressassembly.com
SIC: 3541 5072 Machine tools, metal cutting type; Power tools and accessories

(G-15099)
EXTECH INSTRUMENTS CORPORATION
9 Townsend W (03063-1233)
PHONE.................................877 439-8324
Gerald W Blakeley Iii, *Pr*
Lucy M Blakeley, *
Scott Pantalone Senior, *Pr*
Elise Pantalone, *
▲ EMP: 79 EST: 1970
SQ FT: 30,000
SALES (est): 25.08MM
SALES (corp-wide): 5.46B **Publicly Held**
Web: www.flir.com

SIC: 3825 3823 3577 Electrical energy measuring equipment; Industrial process measurement equipment; Printers, computer
HQ: Teledyne Flir, Llc
   27700 Sw Parkway Ave
   Wilsonville OR 97070
   503 498-3547

(G-15100)
FERRITE MICROWAVE TECH LLC
104 Perimeter Rd Ste 1 (03063-1332)
PHONE.................................603 881-5234
Peter Tibbetts, *CEO*
Mark Fitzgerald, *OF COMPONENTS SALE**
Stephen King, *
Paul Alton, *
◆ EMP: 45 EST: 1983
SQ FT: 43,700
SALES (est): 10.47MM **Privately Held**
Web: www.ferriteinc.com
SIC: 5065 3575 Electronic parts and equipment, nec; Computer terminals

(G-15101)
FIBER OPTIC HARDWARE
21 Technology Way Ste 485 (03060-3245)
PHONE.................................603 325-4993
George Kyrias, *Prin*
EMP: 11 EST: 2011
SALES (est): 93.98K **Privately Held**
Web: www.fiberopticresale.com
SIC: 3229 Fiber optics strands

(G-15102)
FISHING HOT SPOTS INC
9 Townsend W (03063-1233)
P.O. Box 1167 (54501-1167)
PHONE.................................715 365-5555
George Swierczyski, *Pr*
Cooke Bausmann, *VP*
EMP: 8 EST: 1975
SQ FT: 9,000
SALES (est): 789.87K **Privately Held**
SIC: 2741 2731 Art copy and poster publishing; Book publishing

(G-15103)
GENERAL DYNMICS MSSION SYSTEMS
24 Simon St (03060-3025)
PHONE.................................603 864-6300
EMP: 13
SALES (corp-wide): 39.41B **Publicly Held**
Web: www.gdmissionsystems.com
SIC: 3827 3851 Lenses, optical: all types except ophthalmic; Lens coating, ophthalmic
HQ: General Dynamics Mission Systems, Inc.
   12450 Fair Lakes Cir
   Fairfax VA 22033
   877 449-0600

(G-15104)
GEOPHYSICAL SURVEY SYSTEMS INC (DH)
Also Called: Gssi
40 Simon St (03060-3075)
PHONE.................................603 893-1109
Christopher C Hawekotte, *Pr*
Charles H Still, *
Donald K Walczyk, *
Hiromasa Shima, *
EMP: 76 EST: 1970
SQ FT: 30,000
SALES (est): 22.8MM **Privately Held**
Web: www.geophysical.com
SIC: 3829 Measuring and controlling devices, nec
HQ: Oyo Corporation U.S.A.
   245 N Carmelo Ave Ste 101

   Pasadena CA 91107

(G-15105)
GL&V USA INC
1 Cellu Dr Ste 200 (03063-1008)
PHONE.................................603 882-2711
◆ EMP: 296
Web: www.valmet.com
SIC: 3554 Paper industries machinery

(G-15106)
GORILLA CIRCUITS
207 Main St (03060-2963)
PHONE.................................603 864-0283
EMP: 11
SALES (corp-wide): 54.02MM **Privately Held**
Web: www.gorillacircuits.com
SIC: 3672 Circuit boards, television and radio printed
PA: Gorilla Circuits
   1445 Oakland Rd
   San Jose CA 95112
   408 294-9897

(G-15107)
GRANITE COMMERCIAL RE LLC
30 Temple St Ste 300 (03060-2412)
PHONE.................................603 669-2770
EMP: 16 EST: 2010
SQ FT: 1,300
SALES (est): 1.2MM **Privately Held**
Web: www.granitecre.com
SIC: 8742 6531 2522 Real estate consultant ; Real estate agents and managers; Benches, office: except wood

(G-15108)
GREENERD PRESS & MCH CO LLC (PA)
41 Crown St (03060-6349)
P.O. Box 886 (03061-0886)
PHONE.................................603 889-4101
▲ EMP: 19 EST: 1962
SQ FT: 27,000
SALES (est): 4.87MM
SALES (corp-wide): 4.87MM **Privately Held**
Web: www.greenerd.com
SIC: 3542 Presses: hydraulic and pneumatic, mechanical and manual

(G-15109)
HAMPSHIRE CHEMICAL CORP (DH)
2 E Spit Brook Rd (03060)
PHONE.................................603 888-2320
James Mc Ilvenny, *Pr*
Patrick J Mc Mahon, *Business Director*
Roger R Gaudette, *R&D Dir*
Cheryl Corbett, *Sec*
▼ EMP: 20 EST: 1955
SQ FT: 50,000
SALES (est): 24.27MM
SALES (corp-wide): 44.62B **Publicly Held**
SIC: 2869 2899 2891 2851 Industrial organic chemicals, nec; Chemical preparations, nec; Adhesives and sealants; Paints and allied products
HQ: The Dow Chemical Company
   2211 H H Dow Way
   Midland MI 48642
   989 636-1000

(G-15110)
HIGHLAND TOOL CO INC
20 Simon St (03060-3096)
PHONE.................................603 882-6907
Donald Boulia, *Pr*

   William Boula, *VP*
EMP: 15 EST: 1952
SQ FT: 10,000
SALES (est): 1.75MM **Privately Held**
SIC: 3599 Machine shop, jobbing and repair

(G-15111)
ICAD INC (PA)
Also Called: Icad
98 Spit Brook Rd Ste 100 (03062-5734)
PHONE.................................603 882-5200
Dana Brown, *Ex Ch Bd*
Eric Lonnqvist, *CFO*
▼ EMP: 14 EST: 1984
SQ FT: 11,000
SALES (est): 27.94MM
SALES (corp-wide): 27.94MM **Publicly Held**
Web: www.icadmed.com
SIC: 3841 2834 Surgical instruments and apparatus; Pharmaceutical preparations

(G-15112)
IE CHEMICAL SYSTEMS INC
402 S Main St (03060-5043)
PHONE.................................603 888-4777
EMP: 10 EST: 1994
SQ FT: 1,000
SALES (est): 803.23K **Privately Held**
SIC: 3625 Control equipment, electric

(G-15113)
IMPACT SCIENCE & TECHNOLOGY INC
Also Called: ITT Exelis
85 Northwest Blvd Ste B (03063-4068)
PHONE.................................603 459-2200
EMP: 215
SIC: 8748 3679 7371 Systems engineering consultant, ex. computer or professional; Electronic circuits; Custom computer programming services

(G-15114)
INFOR (US) LLC
Also Called: Infor Restaurant Systems
175 Ledge St Ste 2 (03060-3099)
PHONE.................................678 319-8000
EMP: 23
SALES (corp-wide): 36.93B **Privately Held**
Web: www.infor.com
SIC: 5734 7372 Software, business and non-game; Business oriented computer software
HQ: Infor (Us), Llc
   641 Ave Of The Americas
   New York NY 10011
   866 244-5479

(G-15115)
INNOVATIVE TEST SOLUTIONS LLC
41 Simon St Ste 2f (03060-3091)
PHONE.................................603 288-0280
Donald Chin, *Managing Member*
EMP: 8 EST: 2012
SALES (est): 500K **Privately Held**
Web: www.itestsol.com
SIC: 3825 Test equipment for electronic and electrical circuits

(G-15116)
IPG PHOTONICS CORPORATION
200 Innovative Way Ste 201 (03062-5740)
PHONE.................................603 518-3200
EMP: 10
SALES (corp-wide): 1.43B **Publicly Held**
Web: www.ipgphotonics.com
SIC: 3699 Laser systems and equipment
PA: Ipg Photonics Corporation
   377 Simarano Dr

Marlborough MA 01752
508 373-1100

(G-15117)
JOGLO INC
15 Factory St (03060-3310)
PHONE..........................603 880-4519
John S Chasse, *Prin*
Barbara Klumpp, *Treas*
EMP: 10 EST: 2001
SALES (est): 442.67K Privately Held
SIC: 2759 Commercial printing, nec

(G-15118)
JOHN E BOEING COMPANY INC
169 Daniel Webster Hwy (03060-5256)
PHONE..........................603 897-8000
Donald F Higley, *Pr*
EMP: 11 EST: 2015
SALES (est): 578.06K Privately Held
Web: www.jebconet.com
SIC: 3721 Airplanes, fixed or rotary wing

(G-15119)
JOSEPH A CURA
4q Snow Cir (03062-2919)
PHONE..........................508 254-4624
Joseph Cura, *Prin*
EMP: 7 EST: 2005
SALES (est): 190.58K Privately Held
SIC: 3489 Ordnance and accessories, nec

(G-15120)
K E I INCORPORATED
Also Called: Ike Micro
486 Amherst St (03063-1282)
PHONE..........................978 656-2575
EMP: 110 EST: 1981
SALES (est): 9.7MM Publicly Held
Web: www.ikemicro.com
SIC: 3679 Electronic circuits
HQ: Macom Technology Solutions Inc.
100 Chelmsford St
Lowell MA 01851

(G-15121)
KBACE TECHNOLOGIES INC (HQ)
6 Trafalgar Sq (03063-1988)
PHONE..........................603 821-7000
Mike Peterson, *Pr*
EMP: 70 EST: 1998
SQ FT: 26,000
SALES (est): 30.51MM Publicly Held
SIC: 8742 7372 8249 7371 Business
management consultant; Business oriented
computer software; Business training
services; Custom computer programming
services
PA: Cognizant Technology Solutions
Corporation
300 Frank W Burr Blvd # 36
Teaneck NJ 07666

(G-15122)
KEVIN S BOGHIGIAN
Also Called: Mountain Ridge Pet Supply
141 Canal St Unit 4 (03064-2879)
P.O. Box 3073 (03061-3073)
PHONE..........................603 883-0236
Kevin S Boghigian, *Owner*
EMP: 8 EST: 1986
SALES (est): 454.88K Privately Held
Web: www.greatstatepet.com
SIC: 3999 Pet supplies

(G-15123)
KEYSIGHT TECHNOLOGIES INC
22 Cotton Rd Ste 150 (03063-4219)

PHONE..........................800 829-4444
EMP: 8 EST: 2016
SALES (est): 246.62K Privately Held
SIC: 3825 Instruments to measure electricity

(G-15124)
LAMARRE INDUSTRIES LLC
379 Amherst St (03063-1226)
PHONE..........................603 889-0165
EMP: 8 EST: 2018
SALES (est): 938.4K Privately Held
Web: www.lamarreindustries.com
SIC: 3999 Manufacturing industries, nec

(G-15125)
LASER ADVANTAGE LLC
4 Townsend W Ste 2 (03063-4220)
PHONE..........................603 886-9464
EMP: 13 EST: 2002
SALES (est): 1.9MM Privately Held
Web: www.laser-advantage.com
SIC: 3699 Laser systems and equipment

(G-15126)
LENNARTZ ENTERPRISES LLC
Also Called: Palace Manufacturing Co
41 Simon St Ste 1d (03060-3091)
PHONE..........................978 663-6100
Marie Lennartz, *Managing Member*
EMP: 14 EST: 2005
SALES (est): 1.59MM Privately Held
Web: www.excellsol.com
SIC: 3599 Machine shop, jobbing and repair

(G-15127)
LENRIC CORP
44 Simon St (03060-6011)
PHONE..........................603 886-6772
Leonard Eisen, *CEO*
Cliff Gabay, *
EMP: 24 EST: 1987
SALES (est): 781.82K Privately Held
SIC: 8748 3699 Business consulting, nec;
Laser systems and equipment

(G-15128)
LOCKHEED MARTIN CORPORATION
Also Called: Lockheed Martin
410 Amherst St Ste 200 (03063-1238)
P.O. Box 868 (03061-0868)
PHONE..........................603 885-4321
EMP: 70
Web: www.gyrocamsystems.com
SIC: 3812 Search and navigation equipment
PA: Lockheed Martin Corporation
6801 Rockledge Dr
Bethesda MD 20817

(G-15129)
M & M GLASS BLOWING CO INC
Also Called: M & M Glassblowing
2 Townsend W Ste 11a (03063-1277)
PHONE..........................603 598-8195
Wayne Martin, *Pr*
Susan Martin, *Treas*
EMP: 7 EST: 1988
SQ FT: 2,400
SALES (est): 441.7K Privately Held
Web: www.mmglassblowing.com
SIC: 3229 Pressed and blown glass, nec

(G-15130)
MASS DESIGN INC (PA)
12 Murphy Dr (03062-1935)
PHONE..........................603 886-6460
Anthony Bourassa, *Pr*
Paul Boduch, *
EMP: 53 EST: 1982

SALES (est): 9.09MM
SALES (corp-wide): 9.09MM Privately
Held
Web: www.massdesign.com
SIC: 3672 Printed circuit boards

(G-15131)
MAVRIKIS UPHLSTRING FURN DSGN
45 Lake St (03060-4512)
PHONE..........................603 883-6868
EMP: 7 EST: 1982
SALES (est): 397.91K Privately Held
SIC: 7641 2512 2521 Reupholstery;
Upholstered household furniture; Wood
office furniture

(G-15132)
MCLAUGHLIN OIL CORP (PA)
20 Progress Ave (03062-1924)
PHONE..........................603 882-5500
M Mclaughlin, *VP*
Michael Mclaughlin, *VP*
EMP: 28 EST: 1986
SQ FT: 84,000
SALES (est): 2.35MM Privately Held
Web: www.mclaughlinoilnh.com
SIC: 4214 4213 1389 Household goods
moving and storage, local; Household
goods transport; Construction, repair, and
dismantling services

(G-15133)
MELEXIS INC
43 Pinehurst Ave (03062-3231)
PHONE..........................603 223-2362
EMP: 20 EST: 1993
SALES (est): 4.35MM Privately Held
Web: www.melexis.com
SIC: 3674 Monolithic integrated circuits
(solid state)
PA: Melexis
Rozendaalstraat 12
Ieper 8900

(G-15134)
MEVATEC CORP
65 Spit Brook Rd (03060-6909)
PHONE..........................603 885-4321
Gregory Hallerman, *Ofcr*
EMP: 8 EST: 2014
SALES (est): 444.44K Privately Held
SIC: 3812 Search and navigation equipment

(G-15135)
MINT PRINTWORKS LLC
1 Pine Street Ext Ste 135 (03060-3214)
PHONE..........................603 718-1100
EMP: 8 EST: 2016
SALES (est): 458.01K Privately Held
Web: www.mintprintworks.com
SIC: 2741 Miscellaneous publishing

(G-15136)
MONZITE CORPORATION (HQ)
165 Ledge St (03060-3061)
PHONE..........................617 429-7050
David Robbins, *CEO*
Carl Lueders, *CFO*
▲ EMP: 7 EST: 2013
SQ FT: 7,800
SALES (est): 3.52MM
SALES (corp-wide): 11.14MM Privately
Held
Web: www.monzite.com
SIC: 3679 Microwave components
PA: Omni-Lite Industries Canada Inc
205 5 Ave Sw Ste 1600
Calgary AB T2P 2
403 298-0331

(G-15137)
N KAMENSKE & CO INC
19 Fairhaven Rd (03060-5305)
PHONE..........................603 888-1007
Allan B Silber, *Pr*
Allan B Silber, *Pr*
Kenneth Silber, *VP*
EMP: 9 EST: 1901
SQ FT: 5,000
SALES (est): 789.33K Privately Held
SIC: 3341 Brass smelting and refining
(secondary)

(G-15138)
NASHUA FOUNDRIES INC
5 Foundry St (03060-3412)
P.O. Box 552 (03061-0552)
PHONE..........................603 882-4811
Peter J Lyons, *Pr*
Colleen Dupre, *
EMP: 23 EST: 1863
SQ FT: 40,000
SALES (est): 2.14MM Privately Held
Web: www.nashuafoundries.com
SIC: 3321 Gray iron castings, nec

(G-15139)
NATIONAL ENERGY & LIGHT LLC
14 Celina Ave Unit 9 (03063-1025)
PHONE..........................603 821-9954
Jim Schmidt, *Pr*
EMP: 40 EST: 2013
SALES (est): 13.69MM Privately Held
Web: www.nelcompany.com
SIC: 5063 3646 Lighting fixtures,
commercial and industrial; Commercial
lighting fixtures

(G-15140)
NEXUS TECHNOLOGY INC
78 Northeastern Blvd Ste 2 (03062)
PHONE..........................877 595-8116
Rob Shelsky, *Pr*
EMP: 14 EST: 1991
SALES (est): 2.24MM Privately Held
Web: www.nexustechnology.com
SIC: 3829 Testing equipment: abrasion,
shearing strength, etc.

(G-15141)
NH RAPID MACHINING LLC
22 Charron Ave (03063-1733)
PHONE..........................603 821-5200
James L Jacob Ii, *Managing Member*
EMP: 8 EST: 2009
SQ FT: 300
SALES (est): 2.08MM Privately Held
Web: www.protolabs.com
SIC: 3599 Machine shop, jobbing and repair

(G-15142)
NIM-COR INC
575 Amherst St (03063-1048)
P.O. Box 1026 (54957-1026)
PHONE..........................603 889-2153
▲ EMP: 50
Web: www.drumusic.com
SIC: 3568 Shafts, flexible

(G-15143)
NTP SOFTWARE OF CA INC (PA)
427 Amherst St (03063-1258)
PHONE..........................603 641-6937
Dave Crocker, *Pr*
Bruce Schwartz, *Treas*
EMP: 8 EST: 1996
SALES (est): 1.85MM
SALES (corp-wide): 1.85MM Privately
Held

SIC: **7372** Prepackaged software

(G-15144)
OAKCRAFT PIZZA INC
Also Called: Oakcraft Pizza
2 Cellu Dr Ste 111 (03063-1000)
PHONE.............................603 521-8452
Richard Carvalho, *Prin*
EMP: 13 **EST:** 2020
SALES (est): 520.21K **Privately Held**
SIC: **2099** Food preparations, nec

(G-15145)
OPTIMUM BINDERY SVCS NENG INC
Also Called: Optimum Bindery Services Neng
120 Northeastern Blvd Unit 1 (03062)
PHONE.............................603 886-3889
Frank Frisoni, *Pr*
Joseph Frisoni, *VP*
EMP: 13 **EST:** 1990
SQ FT: 21,000
SALES (est): 458.27K **Privately Held**
Web: www.optimumbindery.com
SIC: **2789** Binding only: books, pamphlets, magazines, etc.

(G-15146)
ORACLE SYSTEMS CORPORATION
Also Called: Oracle
1 Oracle Dr (03062-2833)
PHONE.............................603 897-3000
Michael Fleck, *Prin*
EMP: 28
SALES (corp-wide): 49.95B **Publicly Held**
SIC: **7372 8731 7374** Prepackaged software
; Commercial physical research; Data processing and preparation
HQ: Oracle Systems Corporation
500 Oracle Pkwy
Redwood City CA 94065

(G-15147)
PFEIFFER VACUUM INC (DH)
24 Trafalgar Sq (03063-1988)
PHONE.............................317 328-8492
▲ **EMP:** 35 **EST:** 1995
SQ FT: 24,000
SALES (est): 165.22MM
SALES (corp-wide): 1.72B **Privately Held**
Web: www.pfeiffer-vacuum.com
SIC: **3561** Industrial pumps and parts
HQ: Pfeiffer Vacuum Technology Ag
Berliner Str. 43
ABlar HE 35614
64418020

(G-15148)
PHOENIX SCREEN PRINTING
61 Bridge St (03060-3533)
PHONE.............................603 578-9599
Scott Macconnell, *Pt*
EMP: 15 **EST:** 1997
SALES (est): 964.29K **Privately Held**
Web: www.phoenixnh.com
SIC: **2759** Screen printing

(G-15149)
PLASTIC INDUSTRIES INC (HQ)
1 Tara Blvd (03062-2809)
PHONE.............................603 888-1315
Beth Muscato, *Pr*
▲ **EMP:** 52 **EST:** 1965
SQ FT: 80,000
SALES (est): 85.66MM **Privately Held**
Web: www.altiumpkg.com
SIC: **3089** Injection molding of plastics
PA: Carr Management, Inc.
1 Tara Blvd Ste 303

Nashua NH 03062

(G-15150)
POWDERED METAL TECHNOLOGY CORP
Also Called: Advanced Specialty Metals
76 Northwest Blvd Ste 29-A (03063-4067)
PHONE.............................617 642-4135
Gerald Hoolahan, *CEO*
EMP: 15 **EST:** 2001
SQ FT: 2,000
SALES (est): 229.37K **Privately Held**
SIC: **3399** Powder, metal

(G-15151)
PROTEQ SOLUTIONS LLC
76 Northeastern Blvd Ste 38a (03062)
PHONE.............................603 888-6630
Charles Freihofer, *Managing Member*
EMP: 11 **EST:** 2006
SALES (est): 1.47MM **Privately Held**
Web: www.proteqsolutions.com
SIC: **3829** Ultrasonic testing equipment

(G-15152)
PROTO LABS INC
15 Charron Ave (03063-1734)
PHONE.............................763 479-2679
EMP: 119
SALES (corp-wide): 488.4MM **Publicly Held**
Web: www.protolabs.com
SIC: **3089** Molding primary plastics
PA: Proto Labs, Inc.
5540 Pioneer Creek Dr
Maple Plain MN 55359
763 479-3680

(G-15153)
QMAGIQ LLC
22 Cotton Rd Ste 180 (03063-4219)
PHONE.............................603 821-3092
Mani Sundaram, *Mgr*
Axel Reisenger, *Mgr*
EMP: 7 **EST:** 2003
SQ FT: 2,534
SALES (est): 927.62K **Privately Held**
Web: www.qmagiq.com
SIC: **3674** Integrated circuits, semiconductor networks, etc.

(G-15154)
RAPID FINISHING LLC
43 Simon St (03060-3029)
PHONE.............................603 889-4234
TOLL FREE: 800
Barbara A O'halloran, *Pr*
EMP: 40 **EST:** 1960
SQ FT: 21,000
SALES (est): 4.95MM **Privately Held**
Web: www.rapidfinishing.com
SIC: **3479 7336 2396** Painting of metal products; Silk screen design; Automotive and apparel trimmings

(G-15155)
RAPID GROUP
15 Charron Ave (03063-1734)
PHONE.............................603 821-7300
EMP: 42 **EST:** 2013
SALES (est): 593.28K **Privately Held**
Web: www.protolabs.com
SIC: **3444** Sheet metalwork

(G-15156)
RAPID MANUFACTURING GROUP LLC
Also Called: Rapid Sheet Metal
15a Charron Ave (03063-1734)

PHONE.............................603 686-8980
EMP: 18 **EST:** 2018
SALES (est): 2.92MM
SALES (corp-wide): 488.4MM **Publicly Held**
Web: www.protolabs.com
SIC: **3444** Sheet metalwork
PA: Proto Labs, Inc.
5540 Pioneer Creek Dr
Maple Plain MN 55359
763 479-3680

(G-15157)
REGDOX SOLUTIONS INC
1 Elm St Ste 201 (03060-3325)
PHONE.............................603 589-4830
William L Obrien, *Pr*
Stephen B Stepanek, *
EMP: 100 **EST:** 2007
SALES (est): 11.38MM
SALES (corp-wide): 721.52MM **Privately Held**
Web: www.regdox.com
SIC: **7372** Educational computer software
HQ: Brainloop Ag
Muhldorfstr. 8a
Munchen BY 81671
894446990

(G-15158)
RESEARCH IN MOTION RF INC (HQ)
22 Technology Way Fl 5 (03060-3245)
PHONE.............................603 598-8880
Ralph Pini, *Pr*
James V Di Lorenzo, *Chief Technician**
Warren Weiner, *
James Oakes, *
Tom Lambalot, *
▲ **EMP:** 24 **EST:** 1998
SQ FT: 12,000
SALES (est): 10.28MM
SALES (corp-wide): 656MM **Privately Held**
SIC: **3812 3663** Search and navigation equipment; Antennas, transmitting and communications
PA: Blackberry Limited
2200 University Ave E
Waterloo ON N2K 0
519 888-7465

(G-15159)
RH LABORATORIES INC
1 Tanguay Ave (03063-1711)
PHONE.............................603 459-5900
Benjamin Robinson, *CEO*
Stephen M Robinson, *
Frank Holt, *
EMP: 40 **EST:** 2001
SQ FT: 18,000
SALES (est): 11.85MM **Publicly Held**
Web: www.rh-labs.com
SIC: **3679** Microwave components
PA: Heico Corporation
3000 Taft St
Hollywood FL 33021

(G-15160)
RIPANO STONEWORKS LTD
90 E Hollis St (03060-6370)
P.O. Box 446 (03051-0446)
PHONE.............................603 886-6655
Richard Laliberte, *Pr*
Richard Lucien Laliberte, *
George Larocque, *
Matthew Richard Laliberte, *Prin*
EMP: 22 **EST:** 1986
SQ FT: 32,000
SALES (est): 2.59MM **Privately Held**

Web: www.ripano.com
SIC: **3281 5999 1799** Furniture, cut stone; Monuments and tombstones; Counter top installation

(G-15161)
RIVERBED TECHNOLOGY INC
15 N Southwood Dr (03063-1817)
PHONE.............................603 402-5200
EMP: 7 **EST:** 2019
SALES (est): 149.01K **Privately Held**
Web: www.riverbed.com
SIC: **3577** Computer peripheral equipment, nec

(G-15162)
S M SERVICES INC
14 Progress Ave (03062-1924)
PHONE.............................603 883-3381
Tim Powell, *Prin*
EMP: 9 **EST:** 2006
SALES (est): 211.1K **Privately Held**
SIC: **2299** Textile goods, nec

(G-15163)
SANNER
2 Troy St (03064-1333)
PHONE.............................603 577-9087
Adam Sanner, *Prin*
EMP: 7 **EST:** 2010
SALES (est): 92.59K **Privately Held**
Web: www.sanner-group.com
SIC: **3714** Motor vehicle parts and accessories

(G-15164)
SEAMARK INTERNATIONAL LLC
16 Celina Ave Unit 5 (03063-1037)
PHONE.............................603 546-0100
▲ **EMP:** 18 **EST:** 1999
SQ FT: 6,000
SALES (est): 2.82MM **Privately Held**
Web: www.seamark-int.com
SIC: **3577** Computer peripheral equipment, nec

(G-15165)
SEBABO SOUTH INC
15 Progress Ave (03062-1923)
PHONE.............................603 881-8720
John Sweeney, *Pr*
EMP: 15 **EST:** 1989
SALES (est): 2.33MM **Privately Held**
Web: www.sweeneymetal.com
SIC: **3444** Sheet metal specialties, not stamped

(G-15166)
SEMPCO INC
Also Called: Educational Instrument
51 Lake St Ste 7 (03060-4513)
P.O. Box 3262 (03061-3262)
PHONE.............................603 889-1830
Dongsup Ro, *Pr*
▲ **EMP:** 19 **EST:** 1986
SQ FT: 18,000
SALES (est): 416.53K **Privately Held**
Web: www.sempcoinc.com
SIC: **3944** Board games, puzzles, and models, except electronic

(G-15167)
SKILLSOFT (US) LLC (DH)
300 Innovative Way Ste 201 (03062-5746)
PHONE.............................603 324-3000
Richard Walker, *Pr*
Sarah Hilty, *CLO**
EMP: 130 **EST:** 1997
SQ FT: 68,755

SALES (est): 373MM
SALES (corp-wide): 555.12K Publicly Held
Web: www.skillsoft.com
SIC: 7372　Educational computer software
HQ: Skillsoft Limited
　　　Block 4 Belfield Office Park
　　　Dublin 4 D04 V

(G-15168)
SKILLSOFT CORP
220 Daniel Webster Hwy　(03060-5504)
PHONE..............................603 889-8834
Charles Moran, *Pr*
EMP: 10 EST: 2020
SALES (est): 118.07K Privately Held
Web: www.skillsoft.com
SIC: 7372　Prepackaged software

(G-15169)
SKILLSOFT LTD
300 Innovative Way Ste 201　(03062-5746)
PHONE..............................603 324-3000
EMP: 213 EST: 2011
SALES (est): 28.82MM
SALES (corp-wide): 555.12K Publicly Held
Web: www.skillsoft.com
SIC: 7372　Prepackaged software
HQ: Skillsoft Limited
　　　Block 4 Belfield Office Park
　　　Dublin 4 D04 V

(G-15170)
SOFTECH INC (HQ)
1 Tara Blvd Ste 104　(03062-2809)
PHONE..............................513 942-7100
Joseph P Mullaney, *Pr*
EMP: 25 EST: 1969
SALES (est): 4.87MM Privately Held
Web: www.softech.com
SIC: 7371 7373 7372　Computer software development; Systems integration services; Prepackaged software
PA: Essig Research Inc.
　　　497 Circle Freeway Dr # 236
　　　West Chester OH 45246

(G-15171)
SPANTECH SOFTWARE INC
20 Trafalgar Sq Ste 422　(03063-1996)
PHONE..............................603 589-4044
Steve Comeau, *Brnch Mgr*
EMP: 10
Web: www.spantech.com
SIC: 7379 7372　Computer related consulting services; Prepackaged software
PA: Spantech Software Inc
　　　2864 Nj 27 Ste F
　　　North Brunswick NJ

(G-15172)
SPECIALTY TRUSS INC
12 Mercier Ln　(03062-1606)
PHONE..............................603 886-5523
EMP: 22 EST: 1994
SALES (est): 222.23K Privately Held
SIC: 2439　Trusses, wooden roof

(G-15173)
SPIRE TECHNOLOGY SOLUTIONS LLC
Also Called: Apex Plastics
3 Capitol St　(03063-1003)
PHONE..............................603 594-0005
David Fanning, *Pr*
EMP: 10 EST: 2016
SALES (est): 975.17K Privately Held

SIC: 3643　Current-carrying wiring services

(G-15174)
TAGGART ICE INC
8 Taggart Dr　(03060-5506)
PHONE..............................603 888-4630
Jodie Ruonala, *Pr*
Ronald Ruonala, *VP*
Chris Beagle, *Treas*
EMP: 18 EST: 1945
SQ FT: 12,800
SALES (est): 1.63MM Privately Held
Web: www.taggartice.com
SIC: 2097 5199　Manufactured ice; Ice, manufactured or natural

(G-15175)
TECHFOURFIVE LLC
45 Edgewood Ave　(03064-1455)
PHONE..............................603 438-5760
Christopher Wilkinson, *Prin*
Christopher Wilkinson, *Managing Member*
EMP: 9 EST: 2015
SALES (est): 243.16K Privately Held
Web: www.techfourfive.com
SIC: 7378 7372　Computer maintenance and repair; Application computer software

(G-15176)
TILLOTSON CORPORATION (PA)
159 Main St　(03060-2725)
PHONE..............................781 402-1731
Peter N Tamposi, *Pr*
Thomas S Deans, *Ch Bd*
David K Fries, *Sec*
Ann Walsh, *COO*
◆ **EMP: 10 EST: 1931**
SALES (est): 40.13MM
SALES (corp-wide): 40.13MM Privately Held
SIC: 3069　Rubber coated fabrics and clothing

(G-15177)
TOTAL AIR SUPPLY LLC
171 E Hollis St　(03060-6319)
PHONE..............................603 889-0100
Ben Quintiliani, *Pr*
Sue Quintiliani, *
EMP: 42 EST: 1975
SQ FT: 30,000
SALES (est): 9.87MM Privately Held
Web: www.totalairsupply.com
SIC: 3444 5075　Sheet metalwork; Air conditioning equipment, except room units, nec

(G-15178)
TREASURE TEES
165 Ledge St Ste 6　(03060-3061)
PHONE..............................855 438-8337
EMP: 7 EST: 2014
SALES (est): 620.5K Privately Held
Web: www.treasuretees.com
SIC: 2759　Screen printing

(G-15179)
TWO IN ONE MANUFACTURING INC
51 Lake St Ste 4　(03060-4513)
PHONE..............................603 595-8212
Mui Nguyen, *Pr*
Lee Nguyen, *
EMP: 50 EST: 1990
SQ FT: 13,000
SALES (est): 4.97MM Privately Held
Web: www.2-in-1.com

SIC: 3674 3672 3676 3944　Semiconductor diodes and rectifiers; Printed circuit boards; Electronic resistors; Games, toys, and children's vehicles

(G-15180)
UNIVERSAL ENVMTL TECH INC
Also Called: U E T
87 Technology Way　(03060-3245)
PHONE..............................603 883-9312
Harold Solomon, *Pr*
Sharon Mcmillin, *VP*
EMP: 8 EST: 1990
SQ FT: 1,250
SALES (est): 770.98K Privately Held
SIC: 8711 8712 8742 8744　Engineering services; Architectural services; Management consulting services; Facilities support services

(G-15181)
VALMET INC
1 Cellu Dr Ste 200　(03063-1008)
PHONE..............................603 882-2711
Steven Shartrand, *Brnch Mgr*
EMP: 224
SALES (corp-wide): 5.27B Privately Held
Web: www.valmet.com
SIC: 3554 3826　Pulp mill machinery; Environmental testing equipment
HQ: Valmet, Inc.
　　　3720 Davinci Ct Ste 300
　　　Norcross GA 30092
　　　770 263-7863

(G-15182)
VASCULAR TECHNOLOGY INC
12 Murphy Dr Unit C　(03062-1930)
PHONE..............................603 594-9700
Nilendu Srivastava, *Pr*
David Regan, *
Gary Douglas, *
Megan Thayer, *
EMP: 30 EST: 2007
SQ FT: 9,700
SALES (est): 6.65MM Privately Held
Web: www.vti-online.com
SIC: 3841　Anesthesia apparatus

(G-15183)
VCK BEST MACHINING LLC
4 Townsend W Ste 8　(03063-4220)
PHONE..............................603 880-8858
EMP: 14 EST: 2007
SQ FT: 6,000
SALES (est): 1.8MM Privately Held
Web: www.bestmachining.com
SIC: 3599　Machine shop, jobbing and repair

(G-15184)
W H BAGSHAW CO INC
Also Called: Manufacturing
1 Pine Street Ext Ste 135　(03060-3214)
PHONE..............................603 883-7758
Aaron Bagshaw, *Pr*
Arron Bagshaw, *
Adria Bagshaw, *
EMP: 43 EST: 1900
SQ FT: 100,000
SALES (est): 8.15MM Privately Held
Web: www.whbagshaw.com
SIC: 3965 3451　Pins and needles; Screw machine products

(G-15185)
WAKEFELD THERMAL SOLUTIONS INC (HQ)
Also Called: Wakefield-Vette
120 Northwest Blvd　(03063-4006)
PHONE..............................603 635-2800

Kevin Kreger, *Pr*
James Polakiewicz, *
Dan Bellerose, *
Steve Lawson, *
▲ **EMP: 243 EST: 1993**
SALES (est): 77.66MM Privately Held
Web: www.wakefieldthermal.com
SIC: 3354　Shapes, extruded aluminum, nec
PA: The Heico Companies L L C
　　　70 W Madison St Ste 5600
　　　Chicago IL 60602

(G-15186)
WATER STREET PRINTING LLC
97 Main St　(03060-2751)
PHONE..............................603 595-1444
EMP: 13 EST: 2014
SALES (est): 619.95K Privately Held
SIC: 2752　Offset printing

(G-15187)
WHITE STAR SOFTWARE LLC
131 Daniel Webster Hwy Pmb 440 (03060-5224)
P.O. Box 3058　(03061-3058)
PHONE..............................603 897-0396
Paul Koufalis, *Managing Member*
EMP: 7 EST: 2010
SALES (est): 499.74K Privately Held
Web: www.wss.com
SIC: 7372　Prepackaged software

(G-15188)
WORTHEN INDUSTRIES INC (HQ)
Also Called: Upaco Adhesives
3 E Spit Brook Rd　(03060-5783)
PHONE..............................603 888-5443
David S Worthen, *CEO*
Frederick P Worthen, *
Tim O'neil, *CFO*
◆ **EMP: 75 EST: 1957**
SQ FT: 69,000
SALES (est): 69.97MM
SALES (corp-wide): 69.97MM Privately Held
Web: www.worthenind.com
SIC: 2891　Adhesives
PA: Wf Holdings, Inc.
　　　3 E Spit Brook Rd
　　　Nashua NH 03060
　　　603 888-5443

(G-15189)
WORTHEN INDUSTRIES INC
Also Called: Nylco Division
34 Cellu Dr　(03063-1009)
PHONE..............................603 886-0973
EMP: 34
SALES (corp-wide): 69.97MM Privately Held
Web: www.worthenind.com
SIC: 2891 2295　Adhesives; Coated fabrics, not rubberized
HQ: Worthen Industries, Inc.
　　　3 E Spit Brook Rd
　　　Nashua NH 03060
　　　603 888-5443

(G-15190)
WORTHEN INDUSTRIES INC
Also Called: Nylco
3 E Spit Brook Rd　(03060-5783)
PHONE..............................978 365-6345
Troy Medearos, *Brnch Mgr*
EMP: 50
SQ FT: 45,000
SALES (corp-wide): 69.97MM Privately Held
Web: www.worthenind.com

SIC: 3069 3089 Rubber coated fabrics and
clothing; Plastics processing
HQ: Worthen Industries, Inc.
3 E Spit Brook Rd
Nashua NH 03060
603 888-5443

(G-15191)
XILINX INC
10 Tara Blvd Ste 410 (03062-2800)
PHONE.................................603 891-1096
Jim Ball, *Brnch Mgr*
EMP: 11
SALES (corp-wide): 22.68B **Publicly Held**
Web: www.amd.com
SIC: 3674 Microcircuits, integrated
(semiconductor)
HQ: Xilinx, Inc.
2100 Logic Dr
San Jose CA 95124
408 559-7778

New Boston
Hillsborough County

(G-15192)
LOW IMPACT LOGGING LLC
141 Riverdale Rd (03070-4204)
PHONE.................................603 487-5298
EMP: 8 EST: 2009
SALES (est): 433.27K **Privately Held**
SIC: 2411 Logging camps and contractors

(G-15193)
PROCRAFT CORPORATION
416 River Rd (03070-3703)
P.O. Box 298 (03070-0298)
PHONE.................................603 487-2080
EMP: 24 EST: 1991
SQ FT: 10,000
SALES (est): 2.31MM **Privately Held**
Web: www.procraftcorp.com
SIC: 2431 1751 Doors, wood; Cabinet and
finish carpentry

(G-15194)
RETCOMP INC
2nd New Hampshire Tpke S (03070)
PHONE.................................603 487-5010
Loretta Caterino, *Pr*
Diane Drew, *VP*
EMP: 19 EST: 1990
SQ FT: 2,750
SALES (est): 815.93K **Privately Held**
Web: www.retcomp.com
SIC: 3672 3357 Printed circuit boards;
Nonferrous wiredrawing and insulating

New Hampton
Belknap County

(G-15195)
ALAN T SEELER INC
Also Called: Ats Precision
87 New Hampshire Rte 132n (03256-4103)
P.O. Box 778 (03256-0778)
PHONE.................................603 744-3736
John Seeler, *Pr*
Elizabeth Putnam, *Sec*
EMP: 12 EST: 1973
SQ FT: 5,550
SALES (est): 1.89MM **Privately Held**
Web: www.atsprecision.com
SIC: 3469 3494 Machine parts, stamped or
pressed metal; Valves and pipe fittings, nec

New Ipswich
Hillsborough County

(G-15196)
AIRLINX COMMUNICATIONS INC
111 Old Country Rd (03071-3619)
P.O. Box 253 (03048-0253)
PHONE.................................603 878-1926
Tjalling Hoiska, *Pr*
Elaine Hoiska, *CFO*
EMP: 16 EST: 1997
SQ FT: 10,000
SALES (est): 575.12K **Privately Held**
Web: www.airlinx.com
SIC: 3663 Radio and t.v. communications
equipment

(G-15197)
DAVIS VILLAGE SOLUTIONS LLC
167 Davis Village Rd (03071-3805)
P.O. Box 379 (03071-0379)
PHONE.................................603 878-3662
EMP: 12 EST: 2011
SALES (est): 1.16MM **Privately Held**
Web: www.davisvillagesolutions.com
SIC: 3519 3537 3799 3599 Internal
combustion engines, nec; Truck trailers,
used in plants, docks, terminals, etc.;
Trailers and trailer equipment; Machine and
other job shop work

(G-15198)
KEY INDUSTRIES
65 Turnpike Rd Unit B (03071-3524)
P.O. Box 403 (03071-0403)
PHONE.................................603 369-9634
Matthew Salmonson, *Prin*
EMP: 11 EST: 2017
SALES (est): 473.45K **Privately Held**
Web: www.keyindustries.net
SIC: 3999 Barber and beauty shop
equipment

(G-15199)
NEW ENGLAND WOODWORKERS
P.O. Box 507 (03071-0507)
PHONE.................................603 562-7200
Kevin Winter, *Prin*
EMP: 7 EST: 2010
SALES (est): 159.04K **Privately Held**
Web:
www.newenglandwoodworkers.com
SIC: 2431 Millwork

(G-15200)
VANGUARD MANUFACTURING INC
100 Temple Rd (03071-3439)
PHONE.................................603 878-2083
Frank Koughan, *CEO*
Susan Kline, *Pr*
Duane Boucher, *VP*
▲ EMP: 70 EST: 1969
SQ FT: 94,000
SALES (est): 20.11MM
SALES (corp-wide): 47.21MM **Privately Held**
Web: www.vanguardmanufacturing.com
SIC: 5082 3446 3713 Scaffolding; Scaffolds,
mobile or stationary: metal; Truck and bus
bodies
PA: Lyn-Lad Group, Ltd.
20 Boston St
Lynn MA 01904
781 598-6010

(G-15201)
WARWICK MILLS INC (PA)
Also Called: Turtle Skin
301 Turnpike Rd (03071-3639)
P.O. Box 409 (03071-0409)
PHONE.................................603 291-1000
Charles A Howland, *Pr*
Virginia Houston Howland, *
Gisele Thibault, *
▲ EMP: 85 EST: 1989
SQ FT: 1,000
SALES (est): 25.18MM
SALES (corp-wide): 25.18MM **Privately Held**
Web: www.warwickmills.com
SIC: 2221 Manmade and synthetic
broadwoven fabrics

New London
Merrimack County

(G-15202)
DURGIN AND CROWELL LBR CO INC
231 Fisher Corner Rd (03257-6550)
P.O. Box 160 (03257-0160)
PHONE.................................603 763-2860
Peter Crowell, *Pr*
Arthur Durgin, *
B Manning, *
EMP: 120 EST: 1976
SQ FT: 10,000
SALES (est): 22.53MM **Privately Held**
Web: www.durginandcrowell.com
SIC: 2421 Lumber: rough, sawed, or planed

(G-15203)
ECHO COMMUNICATIONS INC
Also Called: Country Press
59 Pleasant St (03257-5564)
P.O. Box 2300 (03257-2300)
PHONE.................................603 526-6006
TOLL FREE: 800
Katharyn Hoke, *Pr*
Howard Hoke, *VP*
EMP: 20 EST: 1964
SQ FT: 8,000
SALES (est): 2.35MM **Privately Held**
Web: www.echocominc.com
SIC: 2752 7331 2791 2721 Offset printing;
Mailing service; Typesetting; Periodicals

Newbury
Merrimack County

(G-15204)
SUNAPEE DIFFERENCE LLC
Also Called: Mount Sunapee Ski Resort
1398 Route 103 (03255-5943)
P.O. Box 2021 (03255-2021)
PHONE.................................603 763-3500
Diane Mueller, *
EMP: 100 EST: 1998
SALES (est): 20.45MM **Publicly Held**
Web: www.mountsunapee.com
SIC: 7011 3949 Resort hotel; Snow skis
PA: Vail Resorts, Inc.
390 Interlocken Cres # 10
Broomfield CO 80021

Newfields
Rockingham County

(G-15205)
HUTCHINSON SEALING SYSTEMS INC
72 Pease Blvd (03801-6801)

171 Rte 85 (03856-8216)
P.O. Box 169 (03856-0169)
PHONE.................................603 772-3771
Robert Nadeau, *Brnch Mgr*
EMP: 150
SALES (corp-wide): 7.96B **Publicly Held**
Web:
www.hutchinsonsealing-purchasing.com
SIC: 3069 Rubber automotive products
HQ: Hutchinson Sealing Systems, Inc.
3201 Cross Creek Pkwy
Auburn Hills MI 48326
248 375-3720

Newington
Rockingham County

(G-15206)
CELESTICA NEW ENGLAND INC
72 Pease Blvd (03801-6801)
PHONE.................................603 334-3450
Eugene Polistuk, *COO*
Tony Puppi, *FOR CELESTICA CORP*
Jim Kelly, *
EMP: 430 EST: 1997
SALES (est): 74.29MM
SALES (corp-wide): 422MM **Privately Held**
SIC: 3571 Electronic computers
HQ: Celestica International Inc
844 Don Mills Rd
North York ON
416 448-5800

(G-15207)
GEORGIA-PACIFIC LLC
Georgia-Pacific
170 Shattuck Way (03801-7868)
PHONE.................................603 433-8000
James Jenkins, *Brnch Mgr*
EMP: 150
SALES (corp-wide): 36.93B **Privately Held**
Web: www.gp.com
SIC: 3275 Wallboard, gypsum
HQ: Georgia-Pacific Llc
133 Peachtree St Nw
Atlanta GA 30303
404 652-4000

(G-15208)
NEWSSHOP OF PORTSMOUTH LLC
50 Fox Run Rd Ste 55 (03801-2857)
PHONE.................................603 431-5665
Ouellette Chad, *Prin*
EMP: 7 EST: 2007
SALES (est): 240K **Privately Held**
SIC: 3911 Cigar and cigarette accessories

(G-15209)
OWL SEPARATION SYSTEMS LLC
Also Called: Thermo Fisher Scientific
25 Nimble Hill Rd (03801-2760)
PHONE.................................603 559-9297
Stephen Norton, *Pr*
▲ EMP: 91 EST: 1995
SQ FT: 30,000
SALES (est): 18.91MM
SALES (corp-wide): 44.91B **Publicly Held**
SIC: 3826 Analytical instruments
HQ: Fisher Scientific International Llc
81 Wyman St
Waltham MA 02451

(G-15210)
SIG SAUER INC (DH)
72 Pease Blvd (03801-6801)

PHONE..................603 610-3000
Ron Cohen, *Pr*
◆ **EMP:** 245 **EST:** 1853
SQ FT: 400,000
SALES (est): 430.1MM
SALES (corp-wide): 355.83K **Privately Held**
Web: www.sigsauer.com
SIC: 3484 7999　Small arms; Shooting facilities and archery lanes
HQ: Sig Sauer Beteiligungs Gmbh
　　Hollefeldstr. 46
　　Emsdetten NW 48282
　　25722050

(G-15211)
SIG SAUER US HOLDING LP
72 Pease Blvd (03801-6801)
PHONE..................603 610-3000
Ron Cohen, *Mng Pt*
EMP: 12 **EST:** 2015
SALES (est): 830.14K **Privately Held**
Web: www.sigsauer.com
SIC: 3489　Ordnance and accessories, nec

(G-15212)
SPONGE-JET INC (PA)
Also Called: Sponge-Jet
14 Patterson Ln (03801-2806)
PHONE..................603 610-7950
◆ **EMP:** 7 **EST:** 1994
SALES (est): 4.98MM **Privately Held**
Web: www.spongejet.com
SIC: 3589 5084　High pressure cleaning equipment; Cleaning equipment, high pressure, sand or steam

(G-15213)
SUBCOM LLC
120 Shattuck Way (03801-7868)
PHONE..................603 319-5041
Michael Dumont, *Brnch Mgr*
EMP: 60
SALES (corp-wide): 344.32MM **Privately Held**
Web: www.subcom.com
SIC: 3661　Telephone and telegraph apparatus
PA: Subcom, Llc
　　250 Industrial Way W
　　Eatontown NJ 07724
　　732 578-7000

(G-15214)
SUBCOM CABLE SYSTEMS LLC
100 Piscataqua Dr (03801-8002)
PHONE..................603 436-6100
Thomas Aaron, *
Maryann Brereton, *
Patrick Moriarty, *
Thomas Lynch, *
▲ **EMP:** 275 **EST:** 1840
SQ FT: 693,000
SALES (est): 50.7MM
SALES (corp-wide): 344.32MM **Privately Held**
Web: www.subcom.com
SIC: 3357　Fiber optic cable (insulated)
PA: Subcom, Llc
　　250 Industrial Way W
　　Eatontown NJ 07724
　　732 578-7000

(G-15215)
THERMO NESLAB LLC
25 Nimble Hill Rd (03801-2794)
PHONE..................603 436-9444
Mike Aronson, *VP*
Seth H Hoogasian, *Pr*
Mark Sinclair, *Managing Member*

▲ **EMP:** 60 **EST:** 1963
SQ FT: 120,000
SALES (est): 10.27MM
SALES (corp-wide): 44.91B **Publicly Held**
Web: www.marshallscientific.com
SIC: 3826　Analytical instruments
PA: Thermo Fisher Scientific Inc.
　　168 3rd Ave
　　Waltham MA 02451
　　781 622-1000

(G-15216)
WILCOX INDUSTRIES CORP (PA)
25 Piscataqua Dr (03801-7816)
PHONE..................603 431-1331
James Teetzel, *CEO*
Laurie Teetzel, *
EMP: 95 **EST:** 1995
SQ FT: 33,000
SALES (est): 43.54MM
SALES (corp-wide): 43.54MM **Privately Held**
Web: www.wilcoxind.com
SIC: 3699 3827　Electrical equipment and supplies, nec; Optical instruments and apparatus

(G-15217)
WILCOX INDUSTRIES CORP
1 Wilcox Way (03801-3190)
PHONE..................603 431-1331
EMP: 35
SALES (corp-wide): 43.54MM **Privately Held**
Web: www.wilcoxind.com
SIC: 3827 3699　Optical instruments and apparatus; Electrical equipment and supplies, nec
PA: Wilcox Industries Corp.
　　25 Piscataqua Dr
　　Newington NH 03801
　　603 431-1331

Newmarket
Rockingham County

(G-15218)
CHICK TRUCKING INC
Also Called: Newmarket Sand & Gravel
Route 152 (03857)
PHONE..................603 659-3566
William Chick, *Pr*
Barbara Chick, *Treas*
Doug Chick, *Supervisor*
Dwight Chick, *Superintnt*
EMP: 7 **EST:** 1984
SQ FT: 480
SALES (est): 990.87K **Privately Held**
SIC: 1442　Common sand mining

(G-15219)
EIGENLIGHT CORPORATION
13 Water St Apt B (03857-2091)
PHONE..................603 692-9200
EMP: 30 **EST:** 1994
SALES (est): 3.45MM **Privately Held**
Web: www.lumentum.com
SIC: 3674　Semiconductors and related devices

(G-15220)
HAGAN DESIGN AND MACHINE INC
8 Forbes Rd (03857-2059)
PHONE..................603 292-1101
Jonathan Hagan, *Pr*
Paul Hagan, *VP*
EMP: 17 **EST:** 2000

SQ FT: 8,000
SALES (est): 2.24MM **Privately Held**
Web: www.hagandesign.com
SIC: 3599 7539　Electrical discharge machining (EDM); Machine shop, automotive

(G-15221)
INTERNET SYSTEMS CNSORTIUM INC (PA)
60 Exeter Rd Ste 104 (03857-1945)
P.O. Box 360 (03857-0360)
PHONE..................650 423-1300
Jeff Osborn, *Pr*
EMP: 15 **EST:** 2003
SQ FT: 10,000
SALES (est): 5.6MM
SALES (corp-wide): 5.6MM **Privately Held**
Web: www.isc.org
SIC: 7372　Prepackaged software

(G-15222)
PROFILE METAL FORMING INC (HQ)
Also Called: Profile Metal Forming
10 Forbes Rd (03857-2059)
PHONE..................603 659-8323
George Donovan Junior, *CEO*
Norman French, *
EMP: 31 **EST:** 1986
SALES (est): 23.65MM
SALES (corp-wide): 23.65MM **Privately Held**
Web: www.profilemetal.com
SIC: 3444　Sheet metalwork
PA: Profile Holdings, Inc.
　　370 Republic Dr
　　Mc Kenzie TN 38201
　　731 352-5341

(G-15223)
S&H PRECISION MFG CO INC (PA)
Also Called: S & H Precision
10 Forbes Rd (03857-2069)
PHONE..................603 659-8323
George Donovan, *Pr*
Norman French, *
EMP: 34 **EST:** 1965
SALES (est): 2.67MM
SALES (corp-wide): 2.67MM **Privately Held**
SIC: 3444　Sheet metalwork

(G-15224)
SEACOAST MACHINE COMPANY LLC
80a Exeter Rd (03857-2031)
PHONE..................603 659-3404
EMP: 8 **EST:** 1985
SQ FT: 5,700
SALES (est): 701.21K **Privately Held**
Web: www.seacoastmachineco.com
SIC: 3599　Machine shop, jobbing and repair

Newport
Sullivan County

(G-15225)
AMERIFORGE GROUP INC
AF Gloenco
452 Sunapee St (03773-1488)
PHONE..................603 863-1270
Tom Hahnal, *Mgr*
EMP: 38
SALES (corp-wide): 402.12MM **Privately Held**
Web: www.afgholdings.com

SIC: 3469 3599　Machine parts, stamped or pressed metal; Machine and other job shop work
PA: Ameriforge Group Inc.
　　19450 State Highway 249 # 5
　　Houston TX 77070
　　713 393-4200

(G-15226)
CARROLL CONCRETE CO INC
Also Called: Newport Sand and Gravel
8 Reeds Mill Rd (03773-1249)
PHONE..................603 863-1765
Shaun P Carroll, *Pr*
Michael Feeney, *VP*
EMP: 10 **EST:** 1959
SALES (est): 1.43MM **Privately Held**
Web: www.carrollconcrete.com
SIC: 3273　Ready-mixed concrete

(G-15227)
CS-MA INC
8 Reeds Mill Rd (03773-1249)
PHONE..................603 863-1000
EMP: 14 **EST:** 2009
SALES (est): 263.62K **Privately Held**
SIC: 3271 5032 5211　Concrete block and brick; Concrete and cinder building products ; Masonry materials and supplies

(G-15228)
EICHENAUER INC
Also Called: Hartford
292 Sunapee St (03773-1232)
PHONE..................603 863-1454
Donald Campbell, *Pr*
◆ **EMP:** 50 **EST:** 1951
SQ FT: 25,000
SALES (est): 10.15MM
SALES (corp-wide): 1.08MM **Privately Held**
Web: www.eichenauerusa.com
SIC: 3634　Heating units, for electric appliances
PA: Eichenauer Heizelemente Gmbh & Co. Kg
　　Industriestr. 1
　　Hatzenbuhl RP 76770
　　72757020

(G-15229)
LATVA MACHINE LLC
Also Called: Lm
744 John Stark Hwy (03773-2607)
PHONE..................603 863-5155
Mitchell William Latva, *Pr*
EMP: 50 **EST:** 1973
SQ FT: 28,000
SALES (est): 10MM **Privately Held**
Web: www.latva.com
SIC: 3599　Machine shop, jobbing and repair

(G-15230)
LE WEED & SON LLC (PA)
187 S Main St (03773-1817)
P.O. Box 509 (03773-0509)
PHONE..................603 863-1540
EMP: 9 **EST:** 1946
SQ FT: 15,000
SALES (est): 1.3MM
SALES (corp-wide): 1.3MM **Privately Held**
SIC: 3273　Ready-mixed concrete

(G-15231)
M J HARRINGTON & CO INC (PA)
33 Main St (03773-1504)
P.O. Box 427 (03773-0427)
PHONE..................603 863-1662
David Lantz, *Pr*
Louis Elliott, *Sec*

Louise Lantz, *Stockholder*
EMP: 12 **EST:** 1948
SQ FT: 4,000
SALES (est): 1.49MM
SALES (corp-wide): 1.49MM **Privately Held**
Web: www.mjharrington.com
SIC: 5944 3911 Jewelry, precious stones and precious metals; Jewelry apparel

(G-15232)
NEWPORT CONCRETE BLOCK CO
Also Called: L E Weed and Son
187 S Main St (03773-1817)
P.O. Box 509 (03773-0509)
PHONE..............................603 863-1540
Wayne Weed, *Pt*
Diane Bouche, *Pt*
EMP: 10 **EST:** 1950
SALES (est): 944.66K **Privately Held**
SIC: 3273 Ready-mixed concrete

(G-15233)
NEWPORT SAND & GRAVEL CO INC (PA)
Also Called: Carroll Concrete
8 Reeds Mill Rd (03773-1249)
P.O. Box 1000 (03773-1000)
PHONE..............................603 298-0199
Shaun P Carroll Senior, *Pr*
Michael Feeney, *Sec*
Deborah Spear, *Sec*
EMP: 15 **EST:** 1959
SQ FT: 1,620
SALES (est): 44.7MM
SALES (corp-wide): 44.7MM **Privately Held**
Web: www.carrollconcrete.com
SIC: 3273 3297 Ready-mixed concrete; Nonclay refractories

(G-15234)
POLLUTION RESEARCH & DEV CORP (PA)
Also Called: Matrix Air
475 Sunapee St Ste 4 (03773-1490)
PHONE..............................603 863-7553
Tracy Nangeroni, *Pr*
Michael Nangeroni, *VP*
EMP: 9 **EST:** 1983
SQ FT: 20,000
SALES (est): 1.39MM
SALES (corp-wide): 1.39MM **Privately Held**
Web: www.matrixair.com
SIC: 3564 1711 Air purification equipment; Plumbing, heating, air-conditioning

(G-15235)
R D S MACHINE INC (PA)
3 Putnam Rd (03773-3019)
PHONE..............................603 863-4131
Richard Sullivan, *Pr*
Dina Cody, *
EMP: 26 **EST:** 1988
SQ FT: 4,500
SALES (est): 5.58MM
SALES (corp-wide): 5.58MM **Privately Held**
Web: www.rdsmachine.com
SIC: 3599 Machine shop, jobbing and repair

(G-15236)
R FILION MANUFACTURING INC
Also Called: Kasi Infrared
931 John Stark Hwy (03773-2614)
P.O. Box 895 (03743-0895)
PHONE..............................603 865-1893

Roger G Filion Junior, *Pr*
Susan M Filion, *VP*
EMP: 19 **EST:** 2005
SQ FT: 12,000
SALES (est): 2.37MM **Privately Held**
Web: www.kasiinfrared.com
SIC: 3433 5999 Gas infrared heating units; Plumbing and heating supplies

(G-15237)
ROYMAL INC
475 Sunapee St (03773-1490)
P.O. Box 658 (03773-0658)
PHONE..............................603 863-2410
Roy M Malool, *Ch Bd*
Laura Stocker, *
Lorissa Nugisa, *
▲ **EMP:** 25 **EST:** 1962
SQ FT: 20,000
SALES (est): 4.07MM **Privately Held**
Web: www.roymalinc.com
SIC: 2671 2851 Paper; coated and laminated packaging; Paints and allied products

(G-15238)
SF TOOLS LLC
Also Called: Div of Bttnfeld Glcester Engrg
460 Sunapee St (03773-1488)
PHONE..............................603 863-7719
Chuck Milliken, *Mgr*
Richard Thomas, *Mgr*
▲ **EMP:** 13 **EST:** 2020
SALES (est): 3.34MM **Privately Held**
Web: www.shrinkfasttools.com
SIC: 3081 Plastics film and sheet

(G-15239)
STURM RUGER & COMPANY INC
Also Called: Ruger Records Dept
529 Sunapee St (03773-1491)
PHONE..............................603 865-2424
EMP: 409
SALES (corp-wide): 595.84MM **Publicly Held**
Web: www.ruger.com
SIC: 3484 3324 Guns (firearms) or gun parts, 30 mm. and below; Steel investment foundries
PA: Sturm, Ruger & Company, Inc.
1 Lacey Pl
Southport CT 06890
203 259-7843

(G-15240)
STURM RUGER & COMPANY INC
Pine Tree Castings
411 Sunapee St (03773-1542)
PHONE..............................603 863-3300
Adam Kuper, *Brnch Mgr*
EMP: 200
SQ FT: 100,000
SALES (corp-wide): 595.84MM **Publicly Held**
Web: www.ruger.com
SIC: 3484 3341 3324 Pistols or pistol parts, 30 mm. and below; Secondary nonferrous metals; Steel investment foundries
PA: Sturm, Ruger & Company, Inc.
1 Lacey Pl
Southport CT 06890
203 259-7843

(G-15241)
WILTON PRESSED METALS
488 Oak St (03773-3013)
P.O. Box 909 (03773-0909)
PHONE..............................603 863-1488
T A Parssinen, *Pt*

T A Parssinen Iii, *Pt*
EMP: 8 **EST:** 1985
SQ FT: 5,000
SALES (est): 650.88K **Privately Held**
Web: www.wiltonpressedmetals.com
SIC: 3469 Stamping metal for the trade

Newton
Rockingham County

(G-15242)
CONTINENTAL BIOMASS INDUSTRIES
22 Whittier St (03858-3524)
PHONE..............................603 382-0556
Craig Means, *Pr*
EMP: 16 **EST:** 2018
SALES (est): 2.2MM **Privately Held**
Web: www.terex.com
SIC: 3531 Construction machinery

(G-15243)
PRO DESIGN & MANUFACTURING
13 Elm St (03858-4414)
P.O. Box 415 (03859-0415)
PHONE..............................603 819-4131
EMP: 8 **EST:** 1995
SALES (est): 710K **Privately Held**
SIC: 2221 Fiberglass fabrics

(G-15244)
RAGNAR INC
Also Called: CBI
22 Whittier St (03858-3524)
PHONE..............................603 382-0556
◆ **EMP:** 80
SIC: 3999 Hydroponic equipment

(G-15245)
TEREX USA LLC
Also Called: Terex Environmental Equipment
22 Whittier St (03858-3524)
PHONE..............................603 382-0556
Neal Nowick, *Brnch Mgr*
EMP: 90
SALES (corp-wide): 5.15B **Publicly Held**
Web: www.terex.com
SIC: 3531 Construction machinery
HQ: Terex Usa, Llc
45 Glover Ave Ste 4
Norwalk CT 06850
203 222-7170

North Conway
Carroll County

(G-15246)
CATHEDRAL LEDGE DISTILLERY INC
3340 White Mountain Hwy (03860-5189)
PHONE..............................612 386-4829
Christopher J Burk, *Pr*
EMP: 9 **EST:** 2019
SALES (est): 258.82K **Privately Held**
Web: www.cathedralledgedistillery.com
SIC: 2085 Distilled and blended liquors

(G-15247)
COUNTRY NEWS CLUB INC
Also Called: Conway Daily Sun
64 Seavey St (03860-5355)
P.O. Box 1940 (03860-1940)
PHONE..............................603 356-2999
Mark Guerringue, *Pr*
Adam Hirshan, *

EMP: 40 **EST:** 1989
SQ FT: 100,000
SALES (est): 4.85MM **Privately Held**
Web: www.conwaydailysun.com
SIC: 2711 Commercial printing and newspaper publishing combined

(G-15248)
FEDERAL SPICE CORP (PA)
Also Called: Moat Mtn Smoke Hse Brewing Co
3378 White Mountain Hwy (03860-5189)
P.O. Box 1229 (03860-1229)
PHONE..............................603 356-6381
Steve Johnson, *Pt*
EMP: 38 **EST:** 1971
SALES (est): 2.34MM
SALES (corp-wide): 2.34MM **Privately Held**
Web: www.moatmountain.com
SIC: 7011 5812 5084 2082 Inns; Eating places; Brewery products manufacturing machinery, commercial; Malt beverages

(G-15249)
P2K PRINTING LLC
Also Called: Minuteman Press
1305 White Mountain Hwy (03860-5155)
P.O. Box 1830 (03860-1830)
PHONE..............................603 356-2010
EMP: 7 **EST:** 1982
SQ FT: 3,500
SALES (est): 913.95K **Privately Held**
Web: www.minuteman.com
SIC: 2752 7334 7336 4783 Commercial printing, lithographic; Photocopying and duplicating services; Graphic arts and related design; Packing goods for shipping

(G-15250)
VINTNERS CELLAR WINERY
1857 White Mountain Hwy (03860-5158)
P.O. Box 5002 (03860-5002)
PHONE..............................603 356-9463
Yvonne Staples, *Owner*
EMP: 7 **EST:** 2008
SALES (est): 334.99K **Privately Held**
SIC: 2084 Wines

North Hampton
Rockingham County

(G-15251)
H&L INSTRUMENTS LLC
34 Post Rd (03862-2021)
P.O. Box 580 (03862-0580)
PHONE..............................603 964-1818
EMP: 10 **EST:** 1978
SQ FT: 4,000
SALES (est): 896.85K **Privately Held**
Web: www.hlinstruments.com
SIC: 3661 Fiber optics communications equipment

(G-15252)
LOYALTY BUILDERS INC (PA)
155 Lafayette Rd (03862-2464)
PHONE..............................603 610-8800
Peter Moloney, *CEO*
Leslie Parker, *CFO*
EMP: 10 **EST:** 2011
SALES (est): 1.46MM
SALES (corp-wide): 1.46MM **Privately Held**
Web: www.loyaltybuilders.com
SIC: 7372 Prepackaged software

GEOGRAPHIC

North Haverhill
Grafton County

(G-15253)
UVP LIQUIDATION INC
Also Called: Upper Valley Press
446 Benton Rd (03774-4611)
P.O. Box 459 (03774-0459)
PHONE..............................603 787-7000
Philip Hayward, *Pr*
Dennis Devaux, *
Connie Smith, *
EMP: 80 **EST:** 1996
SQ FT: 65,000
SALES (est): 9.49MM **Privately Held**
Web: www.uvpress.com
SIC: 2752 7311 Offset printing; Advertising
agencies

North Sutton
Merrimack County

(G-15254)
LABSPHERE INC
231 Shaker St (03260-5535)
P.O. Box 70 (03260-0070)
PHONE..............................603 927-4266
Scott Gish, *Pr*
James Longacre, *VP*
John Johansen, *VP*
Stephen Brooks, *VP*
Daniel Scharpf, *Dir*
▲ **EMP:** 105 **EST:** 1979
SQ FT: 33,000
SALES (est): 20.11MM
SALES (corp-wide): 2.23B **Privately Held**
Web: www.labsphere.com
SIC: 3826 Analytical instruments
PA: Halma Public Limited Company
Misbourne Court Rectory Way
Amersham BUCKS HP7 0
149 472-1111

(G-15255)
ROWE TIMBER HARVESTING
LLC
1467 Route 114 (03260-5522)
PHONE..............................603 344-0302
Nicholas David Rowe, *Prin*
EMP: 9 **EST:** 2014
SALES (est): 152.72K **Privately Held**
SIC: 2411 Logging

North Swanzey
Cheshire County

(G-15256)
TILCON ARTHUR WHITCOMB
INC (HQ)
28 Old Homestead Hwy (03431-4546)
P.O. Box 747 (03431-0747)
PHONE..............................603 352-0101
Edward Silks, *VP*
EMP: 10 **EST:** 1933
SQ FT: 20,000
SALES (est): 2.56MM **Privately Held**
Web: www.arthurwhitcomb.com
SIC: 3273 1442 3271 5032 Ready-mixed
concrete; Common sand mining; Blocks,
concrete or cinder: standard; Masons'
materials
PA: Allan Block Corporation
7424 W 78th St
Minneapolis MN 55439

North Walpole
Cheshire County

(G-15257)
GREENER FORMULAS LLC
121 Church St (03609-1724)
PHONE..............................888 825-4460
Robert Racine, *Pr*
Mark Ping, *Genl Mgr*
EMP: 7 **EST:** 2008
SALES (est): 473.74K **Privately Held**
SIC: 2841 2844 Soap and other detergents;
Perfumes, cosmetics and other toilet
preparations

(G-15258)
J H DUNNING CORPORATION
Also Called: Vermont Custom Cabinetry
1 Dunning Dr (03609-1112)
PHONE..............................603 445-5591
Todd M Walker, *Pr*
EMP: 27 **EST:** 1906
SQ FT: 3,000
SALES (est): 4.27MM **Privately Held**
Web: www.dunningdisplays.com
SIC: 2441 3993 2541 Boxes, wood; Signs
and advertising specialties; Wood partitions
and fixtures

(G-15259)
KEVIN L WOOLBERT
118 Church St (03609-1719)
PHONE..............................603 445-5222
Kevin Woolbert, *Prin*
EMP: 7 **EST:** 2010
SALES (est): 365.68K **Privately Held**
SIC: 3993 Signs and advertising specialties

(G-15260)
LEN-TEX CORP
Also Called: Len-Tex Wallcoverings
18 Len Tex Ln (03609-1140)
PHONE..............................603 445-2342
Don Lennon, *Pr*
Charles Lennon, *
Richard Lennon, *
◆ **EMP:** 108 **EST:** 1983
SQ FT: 59,000
SALES (est): 20.48MM **Privately Held**
Web: www.lentexwallcoverings.com
SIC: 2679 Wallpaper

(G-15261)
VERMONT CUSTOM WOOD
PRODUCTS
Also Called: Vermont Custom Cabinetry
5 Dunning Dr (03609-1151)
PHONE..............................802 463-9930
Tom Westra, *Pr*
EMP: 12 **EST:** 1982
SALES (est): 522.15K **Privately Held**
SIC: 2511 2434 Desks, household: wood;
Vanities, bathroom: wood

North Woodstock
Grafton County

(G-15262)
SPI LLC
1366 Daniel Webster Hwy (03262-2860)
PHONE..............................603 745-3911
Jon Perry, *CEO*
EMP: 39
SALES (corp-wide): 144.65MM **Privately**
Held
Web: www.spi-co.com

SIC: 3612 3523 Reactor transformers;
Sprayers and spraying machines,
agricultural
PA: Spi Llc
2101 Rexford Rd Ste 300e
Charlotte NC 28211
704 336-9555

Northfield
Belknap County

(G-15263)
CENTURY MAGNETICS
HOLDINGS INC
27 Sargent St (03276-4017)
PHONE..............................603 934-4931
Jim Klingensmith, *Pr*
Richard Osgood, *CFO*
James Klingensmith, *Pr*
EMP: 12 **EST:** 1985
SALES (est): 1.82MM **Privately Held**
Web: www.pctransformer.com
SIC: 3612 Specialty transformers

(G-15264)
EPTAM PLASTICS LTD (PA)
Also Called: Eptam Precision Solutions
2 Riverside Business Park (03276)
PHONE..............................603 286-8009
Mark Kemp, *CEO*
Carl Annese, *
Judson Samuels, *
Mark Jrolf, *
EMP: 183 **EST:** 1982
SQ FT: 62,500
SALES (est): 88.85MM
SALES (corp-wide): 88.85MM **Privately**
Held
Web: www.eptam.com
SIC: 3089 Injection molding of plastics

(G-15265)
FREUDENBERG-NOK GENERAL
PARTNR
6 Axle Dr (03276-4002)
PHONE..............................603 286-1600
EMP: 168
SALES (corp-wide): 12.23B **Privately Held**
Web: www.freudenberg.com
SIC: 2821 3714 3053 3061 Plastics
materials and resins; Motor vehicle parts
and accessories; Gaskets; packing and
sealing devices; Mechanical rubber goods
HQ: Freudenberg-Nok General Partnership
47774 W Anchor Ct
Plymouth MI 48170
734 451-0020

(G-15266)
FREUDENBERG-NOK GENERAL
PARTNR
Also Called: Tooling Tech Center
19 Axle Dr (03276-4001)
PHONE..............................603 286-1600
Bill Kobin, *Mgr*
EMP: 97
SALES (corp-wide): 12.23B **Privately Held**
Web: www.freudenberg.com
SIC: 3053 3714 5013 2821 Gaskets;
packing and sealing devices; Motor vehicle
parts and accessories; Motor vehicle
supplies and new parts; Plastics materials
and resins
HQ: Freudenberg-Nok General Partnership
47774 W Anchor Ct
Plymouth MI 48170
734 451-0020

(G-15267)
PCC STRUCTURALS GROTON
Also Called: PCC Strcturals Alum Operations
24 Granite St (03276-1632)
P.O. Box 188 (03276-0188)
PHONE..............................603 286-4301
Michael Foster, *Mgr*
EMP: 190
SQ FT: 110,000
SALES (corp-wide): 302.09B **Publicly**
Held
Web: www.pccstructurals.com
SIC: 3369 Nonferrous foundries, nec
HQ: Pcc Structurals Groton
839 Poquonnock Rd
Groton CT 06340
860 405-3700

(G-15268)
QUALITY CONTROLS INC
200 Tilton Rd Ste 1 (03276-4415)
PHONE..............................603 286-3321
Edmond C Young, *Pr*
Edmond C Young, *Pr*
Denise Armstrong, *
EMP: 45 **EST:** 1961
SQ FT: 26,000
SALES (est): 4.65MM **Privately Held**
Web: www.qcivalves.com
SIC: 3491 3593 3494 3492 Industrial valves
; Fluid power cylinders and actuators;
Valves and pipe fittings, nec; Fluid power
valves and hose fittings

(G-15269)
TECHNICAL TOOL & DESIGN
LLC
Also Called: Freudenberg-Nok General Partnr
19 Axle Dr (03276-4001)
PHONE..............................603 286-1600
EMP: 142
SIC: 5084 3544 3469 Tool and die makers
equipment; Special dies, tools, jigs, and
fixtures; Metal stampings, nec

(G-15270)
TILTON - NRTHFELD RCRTION
CNCI
61 Summer St (03276-1644)
P.O. Box 262 (03276-0262)
PHONE..............................603 286-8653
Beth Hennesy, *Admn*
EMP: 9 **EST:** 2007
SALES (est): 222.59K **Privately Held**
SIC: 3599 Amusement park equipment

(G-15271)
VERSATILE SUBCONTRACTING
LLC
200 Tilton Rd Unit A (03276-4415)
PHONE..............................603 286-8081
James R Bickford, *Managing Member*
EMP: 8 **EST:** 2001
SALES (est): 641.94K **Privately Held**
Web: www.versatilesubcontracting.com
SIC: 3679 Harness assemblies, for
electronic use: wire or cable

Northwood
Rockingham County

(G-15272)
D R DIMES & CO LTD
49 Dimes Rd (03261-3618)
P.O. Box 308 (03261-0308)
PHONE..............................603 942-8050
Douglas P Dimes, *Pr*

Thomas W Lavigne, *VP*
EMP: 9 **EST:** 1976
SQ FT: 30,000
SALES (est): 358.67K **Privately Held**
Web: www.drdimes.com
SIC: 2511   Wood household furniture

(G-15273)
HARDING METALS INC
42 Harding Dr (03261)
P.O. Box 418 (03261-0418)
PHONE.....................................603 942-5573
Edwin Harding Iii, *Pr*
Joseph Harding, *
▼ **EMP:** 35 **EST:** 1963
SQ FT: 30,000
SALES (est): 5.22MM **Privately Held**
Web: www.hardingmetals.com
SIC: 3339 5093 4953 3341   Precious metals;
Metal scrap and waste materials; Refuse
systems; Secondary nonferrous metals

(G-15274)
**NORTHWOODS BREWING CO
LLC**
1334 1st Nh Tpke (03261-3214)
P.O. Box 255 (03261-0255)
PHONE.....................................603 942-6400
Jeffrey S Fenerty, *Mgr*
EMP: 16 **EST:** 2016
SALES (est): 1.07MM **Privately Held**
Web:
www.northwoodsbrewingcompany.com
SIC: 2082   Beer (alcoholic beverage)

(G-15275)
OSBORNE CONCRETE
148 Old Turnpike Rd (03261-3712)
PHONE.....................................603 231-3604
Matthew Osborne, *Prin*
EMP: 12 **EST:** 2002
SALES (est): 1.13MM **Privately Held**
Web: www.osborneconcrete.com
SIC: 3273   Ready-mixed concrete

Nottingham
Rockingham County

(G-15276)
FERNALD LUMBER INC
Rte 152 (03290)
P.O. Box 450 (03290-0450)
PHONE.....................................603 679-2997
TOLL FREE: 800
James S Fernald, *Pr*
Linda R Fernald, *Treas*
Earl Kalil, *Sec*
EMP: 13 **EST:** 1978
SQ FT: 17,080
SALES (est): 1.3MM **Privately Held**
Web: www.fernaldlumber.com
SIC: 5031 5211 2421   Millwork; Millwork and
lumber; Sawmills and planing mills, general

(G-15277)
REHRIG PACIFIC COMPANY
153 Mitchell Rd (03290-5616)
PHONE.....................................603 490-8722
EMP: 235
Web: www.rehrigpacific.com
SIC: 3089   Plastics processing
HQ: Rehrig Pacific Company
4010 E 26th St
Vernon CA 90058
323 262-5145

(G-15278)
TALCO ENTERPRISES LLC
6 Freeman Hall Rd (03290-6209)
PHONE.....................................603 765-8052
Branden Steven Talon, *Managing Member*
EMP: 15 **EST:** 2007
SALES (est): 2.16MM **Privately Held**
SIC: 3312   Blast furnaces and steel mills

(G-15279)
UAV - AMERICA INC
240 Stage Rd (03290-6205)
P.O. Box 60 (03290-0060)
PHONE.....................................603 389-6364
EMP: 8 **EST:** 2013
SQ FT: 1,800
SALES (est): 168.8K **Privately Held**
Web: www.uavamerica.com
SIC: 3721   Aircraft

Orange
Grafton County

(G-15280)
SCRIBLIOTECH INC
Also Called: Scribl.com
527 Tuttle Hill Rd (03741-5225)
PHONE.....................................603 306-9000
Colin Higbie, *Ch Bd*
EMP: 8
SALES (est): 101.8K **Privately Held**
Web: www.scribl.com
SIC: 8999 8742 2731   Editorial service;
Marketing consulting services; Books,
publishing only

Orford
Grafton County

(G-15281)
**L & M SERVICE CONTRACTORS
LLC**
126 Nh Route 10 (03777-4119)
PHONE.....................................603 359-1956
Larry Morse, *Pr*
Maureen Morse, *Treas*
EMP: 15 **EST:** 1999
SALES (est): 928.34K **Privately Held**
SIC: 1389   Construction, repair, and
dismantling services

Ossipee
Carroll County

(G-15282)
COYOTE MOUNTAIN FARM INC
93 Duncan Lake Rd (03864-7102)
PHONE.....................................603 662-2164
Arthur J Battles, *Pr*
Aj Battles, *Prin*
EMP: 8 **EST:** 2017
SQ FT: 3,500
SALES (est): 177.15K **Privately Held**
Web: www.get-cmfi.com
SIC: 0191 3429 1542   General farms,
primarily crop; Builders' hardware; Custom
builders, non-residential

(G-15283)
TECHNICOIL LLC
775 Route 16 (03864-7167)
PHONE.....................................603 569-3100
Timothy Caravella, *CEO*
EMP: 18 **EST:** 2012
SALES (est): 2.79MM **Privately Held**

Web: www.technicoil.com
SIC: 3677   Electronic coils and transformers

(G-15284)
TRACS INDUSTRIAL COOLERS
790 Route 16 (03864-7166)
PHONE.....................................603 707-2241
Randy Willette, *Prin*
EMP: 7 **EST:** 2011
SALES (est): 124.58K **Privately Held**
Web: www.tracschillers.com
SIC: 3585   Refrigeration and heating
equipment

(G-15285)
TUFPAK INC
Also Called: Spartech
698 Browns Ridge Rd (03864-7354)
PHONE.....................................603 539-4126
John Inks, *CEO*
▲ **EMP:** 25 **EST:** 1976
SQ FT: 3,000
SALES (est): 4.94MM
SALES (corp-wide): 344.31MM **Privately
Held**
Web: www.tufpak.com
SIC: 2673 2677   Plastic bags: made from
purchased materials; Envelopes
PA: Spartech Llc
11650 Lkeside Crossing Ct
Saint Louis MO 63146
314 569-7400

Pelham
Hillsborough County

(G-15286)
AMERICAN FOODS LLC
33 Bridge St (03076-3475)
PHONE.....................................978 682-1855
EMP: 90 **EST:** 1950
SALES (est): 6.59MM **Privately Held**
Web: www.candybreak.com
SIC: 2064   Candy and other confectionery
products

(G-15287)
C K PRODUCTIONS INC
Also Called: Body Rags
60a Pulpit Rock Rd (03076-3339)
PHONE.....................................603 893-5069
Kenneth B Snow, *CEO*
▲ **EMP:** 41 **EST:** 1997
SQ FT: 50,000
SALES (est): 2.66MM **Privately Held**
Web: www.ckproductions.com
SIC: 2759   Screen printing

(G-15288)
**FOLDER-GLR TECHL SVS GRP
LLC**
Also Called: Gluer-TEC
30 Pulpit Rock Rd (03076-3340)
P.O. Box 984 (03076-0984)
PHONE.....................................603 635-7400
EMP: 7 **EST:** 2002
SQ FT: 2,000
SALES (est): 678.88K **Privately Held**
Web: www.gluertec.com
SIC: 3565   Packaging machinery

(G-15289)
HAMMAR & SONS INC
71 Bridge St (03076-3479)
P.O. Box 184 (03076-0184)
PHONE.....................................603 635-2292
Alrick Hammar Junior, *Pr*
Michael Hammar, *Sec*

Mary Hammar, *Treas*
EMP: 15 **EST:** 1955
SQ FT: 20,000
SALES (est): 471.56K **Privately Held**
Web: www.signsnow.com
SIC: 2262 7389   Screen printing: manmade
fiber and silk broadwoven fabrics; Sign
painting and lettering shop

(G-15290)
**INK OUTSIDE BOX
INCORPORATED**
Also Called: Signs Now New Hampshire
71 Bridge St (03076-3479)
P.O. Box 184 (03076-0184)
PHONE.....................................603 635-2292
Charles Raz, *Pr*
Rosemary Raz, *VP*
EMP: 7 **EST:** 2011
SQ FT: 4,480
SALES (est): 933.41K **Privately Held**
Web: www.signsnow.com
SIC: 3993   Signs and advertising specialties

(G-15291)
**JT MANUFACTURING
CORPORATION**
60b Pulpit Rock Rd (03076-3339)
PHONE.....................................603 821-5720
Frank Anastasi, *Pr*
Steve Anastasi, *
EMP: 34 **EST:** 1980
SQ FT: 30,000
SALES (est): 923.14K **Privately Held**
Web: www.jtmanufacturing.com
SIC: 3451   Screw machine products

(G-15292)
**PATRIOT FOUNDRY &
CASTINGS LLC**
20 Herrick Cir (03076-2645)
PHONE.....................................603 934-3919
EMP: 15 **EST:** 2008
SALES (est): 2.14MM
SALES (corp-wide): 5.54MM **Privately
Held**
Web: www.patriotfoundry.com
SIC: 3365   Aluminum foundries
HQ: Ermak Metals, Inc.
1111 S Governors Ave
Dover DE 19904
952 448-2801

(G-15293)
PELHAM PLASTICS INC
42 Dick Tracy Dr (03076-2154)
P.O. Box 997 (03076-0997)
PHONE.....................................603 886-7226
John J Mackey, *Pr*
EMP: 60 **EST:** 1997
SQ FT: 31,000
SALES (est): 9.76MM **Privately Held**
Web: www.pelhamplastics.com
SIC: 3089   Injection molding of plastics

(G-15294)
PHOTOMACHINING INC
4 Industrial Park Dr Unit 40 (03076-2163)
PHONE.....................................603 882-9944
Ronald Schaeffer, *CEO*
John O'connell, *Pr*
EMP: 15 **EST:** 1997
SALES (est): 2.4MM **Privately Held**
Web: www.photomachining.com
SIC: 3599   Machine shop, jobbing and repair

(G-15295)
RAYTHEON COMPANY
Also Called: Raytheon

50 Bush Hill Rd (03076-3000)
PHONE..............................603 635-6800
Richard Desmarais, *Brnch Mgr*
EMP: 14
SALES (corp-wide): 68.92B **Publicly Held**
Web: www.rtx.com
SIC: 3812 Sonar systems and equipment
HQ: Raytheon Company
    870 Winter St
    Waltham MA 02451
    781 522-3000

(G-15296)
ROCKINGHAM SHEET METAL INC
1 Industrial Park Dr Unit 22 (03076-2161)
PHONE..............................603 886-1799
William A Spirdione, *Pr*
Barry M Scotch, *Sec*
Janine Mcloffline, *Mgr*
EMP: 9 **EST:** 1984
SQ FT: 2,500
SALES (est): 628.62K **Privately Held**
Web: www.rockinghamsheetmetal.com
SIC: 3444 Sheet metalwork

(G-15297)
SOUCY INDUSTRIES INC (PA)
5 Dick Tracy Dr (03076-2154)
PHONE..............................603 883-4500
William J Soucy, *Pr*
Brian Allison, *Treas*
EMP: 20 **EST:** 1923
SQ FT: 12,000
SALES (est): 9.08MM
SALES (corp-wide): 9.08MM **Privately Held**
Web: www.soucyindustries.com
SIC: 1542 3441 3446 Nonresidential construction, nec; Fabricated structural metal; Fences or posts, ornamental iron or steel

(G-15298)
SYLRO SALES CORPORATION
Also Called: Sunvent Industries
1 Industrial Park Dr Unit 26 (03076-2161)
PHONE..............................603 595-4556
Lori Joseph, *Pr*
EMP: 8 **EST:** 1956
SQ FT: 7,000
SALES (est): 959.83K **Privately Held**
Web: www.sunventindustries.com
SIC: 3444 Metal ventilating equipment

(G-15299)
UPNOVR INC
31 Pulpit Rock Rd Unit A (03076-3371)
P.O. Box 199 (03076-0199)
PHONE..............................603 625-8639
Alan Cady, *Pr*
▼ **EMP:** 20 **EST:** 2011
SALES (est): 1.68MM **Privately Held**
Web: www.upnovr.com
SIC: 3446 Architectural metalwork

(G-15300)
VETTE THERMAL SOLUTIONS LLC (HQ)
Also Called: Wakefield-Vette
33 Bridge St (03076-3475)
PHONE..............................603 635-2800
George P Dannecker, *Pr*
Matthew Towse, *Sec*
Jack Hillson, *COO*
▲ **EMP:** 10 **EST:** 2012
SALES (est): 28.68MM **Privately Held**
Web: www.wakefieldthermal.com
SIC: 3679 Cryogenic cooling devices for infrared detectors, masers

PA: The Heico Companies L L C
    70 W Madison St Ste 5600
    Chicago IL 60602

Pembroke
Merrimack County

(G-15301)
ABRASIVES & TOOLS NH INC
Also Called: Atnh
49 Sheep Davis Rd (03275-3705)
P.O. Box 1853 (03302-1853)
PHONE..............................603 224-5376
John David Hamilton, *Pr*
Alvin Hamilton, *
Linc Fuller, *
Eric Duquette, *
EMP: 25 **EST:** 1967
SQ FT: 6,000
SALES (est): 11.13MM **Privately Held**
Web: www.atnh.com
SIC: 5085 3545 Abrasives; Cutting tools for machine tools

(G-15302)
ACANA NORTHEAST INC
360 Commerce Way Unit 3 (03275-3718)
PHONE..............................800 922-2629
Hugh Thomas Kane, *CEO*
EMP: 9 **EST:** 2012
SALES (est): 498.69K **Privately Held**
Web: www.acananortheast.com
SIC: 3556 Ice cream manufacturing machinery

(G-15303)
HEAT AND CONTROL INC
339 Commerce Way (03275-3718)
PHONE..............................603 225-5190
Andrew Caridis, *CEO*
Anthony Caridis, *
Suusan Mc Murry, *
EMP: 30 **EST:** 1937
SQ FT: 50,000
SALES (est): 5.22MM
SALES (corp-wide): 347.43MM **Privately Held**
Web: www.heatandcontrol.com
SIC: 5046 7699 3556 Cooking equipment, commercial; Restaurant equipment repair; Food products machinery
HQ: H. & C., Inc.
    21121 Cabot Blvd
    Hayward CA
    510 259-0500

(G-15304)
MASTERMATIC INC
339 Commerce Way (03275-3718)
PHONE..............................603 225-5190
EMP: 8 **EST:** 2019
SALES (est): 153.93K **Privately Held**
Web: www.heatandcontrol.com
SIC: 3556 Food products machinery

(G-15305)
NHRC LLC
415 4th Range Rd (03275-3311)
PHONE..............................603 485-2248
Peter Gialunis, *Prin*
Jeff Gialunis, *Prin*
Rich Cox, *Prin*
Jeff Ottrson, *Prin*
EMP: 10 **EST:** 1996
SALES (est): 846K **Privately Held**
Web: www.nhrc.net
SIC: 3663 Receivers, radio communications

(G-15306)
NORTHEAST INNOVATIONS INC
145 Sheep Davis Rd (03275-3710)
P.O. Box 120 (03302-0120)
PHONE..............................603 226-4000
John Harrison, *Pr*
EMP: 10 **EST:** 1981
SALES (est): 922.85K **Privately Held**
Web: www.neinnovations.com
SIC: 3661 Telephone and telegraph apparatus

(G-15307)
PITCO FRIALATOR INC
Also Called: Pitco
39 Sheep Davis Rd (03275-3705)
PHONE..............................603 225-6684
EMP: 70
SALES (corp-wide): 4.03B **Publicly Held**
Web: www.pitco.com
SIC: 3589 Cooking equipment, commercial
HQ: Pitco Frialator, Inc.
    553 Route 3a
    Bow NH 03304
    603 225-6684

(G-15308)
RAINVILLE PRINTING ENTPS INC
272 Cross Rd (03275-2906)
PHONE..............................603 485-3422
Robert Rainville, *Pr*
EMP: 7 **EST:** 1998
SALES (est): 192.06K **Privately Held**
SIC: 2752 Offset printing

(G-15309)
WS DENNISON CABINETS INC
779 Silver Hills Dr (03275-4402)
PHONE..............................603 224-8434
Wayne George, *Prin*
EMP: 11 **EST:** 2013
SALES (est): 1.06MM **Privately Held**
Web: www.dennisoncabinets.com
SIC: 2434 Wood kitchen cabinets

Penacook
Merrimack County

(G-15310)
FIFE PACKAGING LLC
77 Merrimack St (03303-1710)
PHONE..............................603 753-2669
John D Pfeifle, *Managing Member*
EMP: 8 **EST:** 2009
SALES (est): 970.37K **Privately Held**
Web: www.fifepkg.com
SIC: 2675 Die-cut paper and board

Peterborough
Hillsborough County

(G-15311)
AMERICAN STEEL FABRICATORS INC
590 Hancock Rd (03458-2125)
P.O. Box 185 (03047-0185)
PHONE..............................603 547-6311
Mark S Carter, *Pr*
EMP: 37 **EST:** 1992
SALES (est): 8.53MM **Privately Held**
Web: www.americansteelfab.com
SIC: 3441 Fabricated structural metal

(G-15312)
B & E ENTERPRISES INC
40 Main St (03458-2420)

PHONE..............................603 924-7203
Bill Littles, *Pr*
Elizabeth Littles, *Treas*
EMP: 8 **EST:** 1860
SQ FT: 4,300
SALES (est): 565.31K **Privately Held**
SIC: 5947 2759 5943 Greeting cards; Commercial printing, nec; Office forms and supplies

(G-15313)
CIM INDUSTRIES INC
23 Elm St Ste 2 (03458-1011)
PHONE..............................603 924-9481
Adam Chase, *Pr*
Richard Stephens, *VP Engg*
EMP: 63 **EST:** 1988
SQ FT: 25,000
SALES (est): 7.35MM **Publicly Held**
Web: www.chasecorp.com
SIC: 2899 Waterproofing compounds
HQ: Chase Corporation
    375 University Ave
    Westwood MA 02090
    781 332-0700

(G-15314)
DAHLE NORTH AMERICA INC
49 Vose Farm Rd Suite 100 (03458-2151)
PHONE..............................603 924-0003
Frank Indenkampen, *Pr*
Scott Prokop, *Ex VP*
Roland Nadeau, *Treas*
Bruno Ghibely, *Dir*
▲ **EMP:** 18 **EST:** 1976
SQ FT: 40,000
SALES (est): 9.53MM
SALES (corp-wide): 153.02MM **Privately Held**
Web: www.dahle.com
SIC: 5044 3554 3952 Office equipment; Cutting machines, paper; Easels, artists'
HQ: Dahle Burotechnik Gmbh
    Nikolaus-A.-Otto-Str. 11
    Rodental BY 96472
    956 375-2990

(G-15315)
DS HUNTINGTON CO LLC
9 Vose Farm Rd (03458-2154)
PHONE..............................603 784-5136
David S Huntington, *Admn*
EMP: 8 **EST:** 2014
SALES (est): 195.22K **Privately Held**
Web: www.dshuntingtoncompany.com
SIC: 2431 Millwork

(G-15316)
HMC SOLUTIONS LLC
23 Vine St (03458-2410)
P.O. Box 13453 (72113-0453)
PHONE..............................501 255-0498
EMP: 8 **EST:** 2003
SALES (est): 923.78K **Privately Held**
SIC: 3599 Custom machinery

(G-15317)
LUCCI CORP
Also Called: Northeast Products
375 Jaffrey Rd Ste 7 (03458-1792)
PHONE..............................603 567-4301
Peter Luccisano, *Pr*
▲ **EMP:** 15 **EST:** 1985
SQ FT: 55,000
SALES (est): 2.25MM **Privately Held**
SIC: 2392 2531 Cushions and pillows; Seats, miscellaneous public conveyances

(G-15318)
MICRO BENDS CORP
365 Jaffrey Rd (03458-1729)
PHONE.................................603 924-0022
Craig Rogozinski, *Pr*
Lisa Rogozinski, *Sec*
EMP: 7 **EST:** 1969
SQ FT: 8,400
SALES (est): 720.95K **Privately Held**
Web: www.microbends.com
SIC: 3498 5051 Tube fabricating (contract bending and shaping); Tubing, metal

(G-15319)
MICROSPEC CORPORATION
327 Jaffrey Rd (03458-1729)
PHONE.................................603 924-4300
Timothy W Steele, *CEO*
Diane P Fukuda, *Pr*
▲ **EMP:** 20 **EST:** 1990
SQ FT: 24,000
SALES (est): 6.31MM **Privately Held**
Web: www.microspecorporation.com
SIC: 3356 3357 Nonferrous rolling and drawing, nec; Fiber optic cable (insulated)

(G-15320)
NEW HMPSHIRE BALL BEARINGS INC
Also Called: Hitech Div
175 Jaffrey Rd (03458-1767)
PHONE.................................818 407-9300
Richard Reynells, *Brnch Mgr*
EMP: 50
Web: www.nhbb.com
SIC: 3562 5085 Ball bearings and parts; Industrial supplies
HQ: New Hampshire Ball Bearings, Inc.
175 Jaffrey Rd
Peterborough NH 03458
603 924-4100

(G-15321)
NEWSPAPERS NEW HAMPSHIRE INC
Also Called: Monadnock Ledger
20 Grove St (03458-1470)
P.O. Box 36 (03458-0036)
PHONE.................................603 924-7172
Geordie Wilson, *Mgr*
EMP: 65
SALES (corp-wide): 96.33MM **Privately Held**
Web: www.ledgertranscript.com
SIC: 2711 Newspapers, publishing and printing
HQ: Newspapers Of New Hampshire, Inc.
1 Monitor Dr
Concord NH 03301
603 224-5301

(G-15322)
NUTTIN ORDINARY LLC
49 Vose Farm Rd Ste 120 (03458-2151)
PHONE.................................603 567-7916
EMP: 10 **EST:** 2013
SALES (est): 442.98K **Privately Held**
Web: www.nuttinordinary.com
SIC: 5812 2015 Eating places; Egg processing

(G-15323)
OLD DUBLIN ROAD INC
Also Called: Peterborough Basket Company
130 Grove St (03458-1756)
P.O. Box 120 (03458-0120)
PHONE.................................603 924-3861
Russell Dodds, *Pr*
Joan Dodds, *

Wayne Dodds, *
EMP: 23 **EST:** 1854
SQ FT: 36,000
SALES (est): 908.29K **Privately Held**
Web: www.peterborobasket.com
SIC: 2449 Baskets: fruit and vegetable, round stave, till, etc.

(G-15324)
PETERBORO BASKET COMPANY
130 Grove St (03458-1756)
P.O. Box 120 (03458-0120)
PHONE.................................603 924-3861
Wayne Dodds, *Owner*
EMP: 15 **EST:** 2015
SALES (est): 1.86MM **Privately Held**
Web: www.peterborobasket.com
SIC: 2449 Wood containers, nec

(G-15325)
PETERBORO TOOL COMPANY INC
Upper Union St (03458)
P.O. Box 96 (03468-0096)
PHONE.................................603 924-3034
Kenneth Stockwell, *Pr*
James Poodiack, *VP*
EMP: 27 **EST:** 1972
SQ FT: 8,000
SALES (est): 446.68K **Privately Held**
Web: www.ptool.com
SIC: 3599 Machine shop, jobbing and repair

(G-15326)
PETERBOROUGH TRANSCRIPT
1 Phoenix Mill Ln Unit 100 (03458-1476)
PHONE.................................603 924-3333
Joseph D Cummings, *Owner*
EMP: 10 **EST:** 1960
SALES (est): 321.29K **Privately Held**
SIC: 2711 Newspapers, publishing and printing

(G-15327)
SOFTWARE OUTSIDE INC
369 Summer St (03458-2415)
PHONE.................................603 820-1994
Leo Reading, *Prin*
EMP: 7 **EST:** 2015
SALES (est): 124.26K **Privately Held**
SIC: 7372 Prepackaged software

Pittsburg
Coos County

(G-15328)
JORDAN ASSOCIATES
Also Called: Lancaster Herrald
Rte 145 (03592)
P.O. Box 263 (03576-0263)
PHONE.................................603 246-8998
Charles Jordan, *Owner*
EMP: 10 **EST:** 1990
SALES (est): 499.52K **Privately Held**
Web: www.northernnhmagazine.com
SIC: 2711 7011 Newspapers, publishing and printing; Hotels and motels

(G-15329)
ROY AND LAUREL AMEY INC
Tabor Rd (03592)
PHONE.................................603 538-7767
Roy Amey, *Pr*
EMP: 9 **EST:** 1974
SALES (est): 436.63K **Privately Held**
SIC: 4213 2411 Trucking, except local; Logging

(G-15330)
WARICK MANAGEMENT COMPANY INC
10 Farr Rd (03592-5169)
P.O. Box 339 (03592-0339)
PHONE.................................603 538-7112
Warren Chase, *Pr*
Richard Judd, *Sec*
EMP: 7 **EST:** 1991
SALES (est): 872.59K **Privately Held**
Web: www.cardinalcabins.com
SIC: 2411 Logging

Pittsfield
Merrimack County

(G-15331)
EVER BETTER EATING INC
Also Called: Rustic Crust
5 Main St (03263-3708)
P.O. Box 56 (03263-0056)
PHONE.................................603 435-5119
Bradford S Sterl, *Pr*
▲ **EMP:** 100 **EST:** 1996
SQ FT: 12,000
SALES (est): 23.78MM **Privately Held**
Web: www.rusticcrust.com
SIC: 2045 Prepared flour mixes and doughs

(G-15332)
GLOBE MANUFACTURING CO LLC (DH)
37 Loudon Rd (03263-3604)
PHONE.................................603 435-8323
Robert A Freese, *
EMP: 330 **EST:** 1887
SQ FT: 73,409
SALES (est): 53.26MM
SALES (corp-wide): 1.53B **Publicly Held**
Web: globe.msasafety.com
SIC: 3842 Clothing, fire resistant and protective
HQ: Globe Holding Company, Llc
37 Loudon Rd
Pittsfield NH 03263

(G-15333)
INOFAB LLC
26 Broadway St (03263-3800)
PHONE.................................603 435-5082
EMP: 12 **EST:** 2012
SALES (est): 4.6MM **Privately Held**
Web: www.inofab.com
SIC: 3448 3444 Prefabricated metal buildings and components; Sheet metalwork

(G-15334)
NORTHEAST EARTH MECHANICS LLC
159 Barnstead Rd (03263-3123)
PHONE.................................603 435-7989
James N Locke Ii, *Pr*
Susan A Tiede, *
Tary D Locke, *
EMP: 45 **EST:** 1988
SQ FT: 1,000
SALES (est): 8.05MM **Privately Held**
Web: www.neearth.com
SIC: 1794 1611 1623 1442 Excavation and grading, building construction; General contractor, highway and street construction; Pipeline construction, nsk; Construction sand and gravel

Plaistow
Rockingham County

(G-15335)
AAK POWER SUPPLY CORPORATION
73 Newton Rd Ste 103 Pmb 2 (03865-2424)
PHONE.................................603 382-2222
Patrice Mccolley, *Pr*
EMP: 10 **EST:** 2015
SQ FT: 2,000
SALES (est): 842K **Privately Held**
Web: www.aakpowersupply.com
SIC: 3629 Battery chargers, rectifying or nonrotating

(G-15336)
ASIA DIRECT LLC
91 Main St Ste 14 (03865-3012)
P.O. Box 511 (03865-0511)
PHONE.................................603 382-9485
Paul Marcotte, *Managing Member*
▼ **EMP:** 10 **EST:** 2003
SALES (est): 197.17K **Privately Held**
SIC: 3679 Electronic circuits

(G-15337)
BERUBE TOOL & DIE INC
34 Main St (03865-3050)
P.O. Box 1100 (03865-1100)
PHONE.................................603 382-2224
Roland Berube, *Pr*
Roland Berube, *Pr*
Normand Berube, *Ofcr*
EMP: 7 **EST:** 1989
SQ FT: 7,000
SALES (est): 647.96K **Privately Held**
Web: www.berubetoolanddie.com
SIC: 3544 Special dies and tools

(G-15338)
CAM TECH
129 Newton Rd (03865-2412)
PHONE.................................603 382-2900
EMP: 9 **EST:** 2017
SALES (est): 381.58K **Privately Held**
Web: www.camtch.com
SIC: 3599 Machine shop, jobbing and repair

(G-15339)
CW KELLER & ASSOCIATES LLC
9 Hale Spring Rd (03865-2313)
PHONE.................................603 382-2028
EMP: 73
SALES (est): 18.96MM **Privately Held**
Web: www.cwkeller.com
SIC: 5021 5712 2511 2434 Furniture; Customized furniture and cabinets; Wood household furniture; Wood kitchen cabinets

(G-15340)
ENVIROMART GREEN INDS INC
4 Wilder Dr Ste 7 (03865-4810)
P.O. Box 1770 (03865-1770)
PHONE.................................603 382-8481
George R Adyns, *Pr*
Michael Rosa, *Ofcr*
Richard Patterson, *Ofcr*
EMP: 12 **EST:** 2016
SALES (est): 470.44K **Privately Held**
SIC: 2655 Fiber cans, drums, and containers

(G-15341)
ENVIROMART INDUSTRIES INC
4 Wilder Dr (03865-4810)
P.O. Box 1770 (03865-1770)
PHONE.................................603 378-0154

Brian Hughes, *Genl Mgr*
EMP: 13 **EST:** 2015
SALES (est): 393.74K **Privately Held**
SIC: 3999 Barber and beauty shop equipment

(G-15342)
ENVIRONMENTAL CONTAINER SVCS
Also Called: Enco
4 Wilder Dr Ste 7 (03865-4810)
P.O. Box 1770 (03865-1770)
PHONE..............................603 382-8481
Michael Rosa, *Pr*
Richard Patterson, *VP*
EMP: 7 **EST:** 1994
SQ FT: 7,500
SALES (est): 2.41MM **Privately Held**
SIC: 2655 Fiber cans, drums, and containers
PA: General Environmental Corporation
33 Pine St
Exeter NH 03833

(G-15343)
FAST SIGNS OF PLAISTOW
Also Called: Fastsigns
160 Plaistow Rd Ste 15 (03865-4805)
PHONE..............................603 894-7446
EMP: 10 **EST:** 2018
SALES (est): 467.44K **Privately Held**
Web: www.fastsigns.com
SIC: 3993 Signs and advertising specialties

(G-15344)
FREEDOM TIRE INC (PA)
Also Called: Freedom Auto and Tire
37 Westville Rd (03865-2946)
P.O. Box 1287 (03865-1287)
PHONE..............................603 382-7223
John J Guide, *Pr*
John J Guide, *Dir*
Herbert P Phillips, *Sec*
EMP: 10 **EST:** 1985
SQ FT: 7,000
SALES (est): 2.49MM
SALES (corp-wide): 2.49MM **Privately Held**
Web: www.freedomtirenh.com
SIC: 5531 7534 Truck equipment and parts; Rebuilding and retreading tires

(G-15345)
GRANITE STATE COVER AND CANVAS
144 Main St (03865-3071)
P.O. Box 1217 (03865-1217)
PHONE..............................603 382-5462
David Callahan, *CEO*
Robert Jubinville, *Sec*
EMP: 14 **EST:** 1989
SQ FT: 10,000
SALES (est): 1.86MM **Privately Held**
Web: www.granitestatecover.com
SIC: 2211 Canvas

(G-15346)
H & S MACHINE COMPANY INC
18 Hickory Ridge Dr (03865-2763)
P.O. Box 897 (01842-1797)
PHONE..............................978 686-2321
George D Younker, *Pr*
Gary Schwardenberg, *VP*
EMP: 10 **EST:** 1948
SALES (est): 982.54K **Privately Held**
SIC: 3599 Machine shop, jobbing and repair

(G-15347)
H&H CUSTOM METAL FABG INC
6 Duston Ave (03865-2203)

P.O. Box 457 (03865-0457)
PHONE..............................603 382-2818
Gary Lesiczka, *Pr*
Lesiczka Gary, *Pr*
Laurie Lesiczka, *VP*
EMP: 8 **EST:** 2000
SALES (est): 677.67K **Privately Held**
Web: www.hhcustommetalfab.com
SIC: 3444 Sheet metal specialties, not stamped

(G-15348)
PLAISTOW CABINET CO INC
Also Called: Nmg
56 Newton Rd (03865-2408)
PHONE..............................603 382-1098
Norman Gallant, *Pr*
Michael Gallant, *VP*
EMP: 10 **EST:** 1991
SALES (est): 718.31K **Privately Held**
Web: www.plaistowcabinet.com
SIC: 2434 Wood kitchen cabinets

(G-15349)
QUALITY MACHINE INC
31 Kingston Rd (03865-2215)
PHONE..............................603 382-2334
Gary Cicale, *Pr*
EMP: 9 **EST:** 1993
SALES (est): 393.45K **Privately Held**
Web: www.qualitymachine1.com
SIC: 3599 Machine shop, jobbing and repair

(G-15350)
SCANDIA PLASTICS INC
55 Westville Rd (03865-2946)
P.O. Box 179 (03865-0179)
PHONE..............................603 382-6533
David R Hallett, *Pr*
Leon Boucher, *
▲ **EMP:** 45 **EST:** 1971
SQ FT: 62,000
SALES (est): 10.55MM
SALES (corp-wide): 295.68MM **Privately Held**
Web: www.scandia-nh.com
SIC: 2821 3083 Plastics materials and resins ; Laminated plastics plate and sheet
PA: Pexco Llc
6470 E Johns Xing Ste 430
Johns Creek GA 30097
678 990-1523

(G-15351)
SPARTON BECKWOOD LLC
27 Hale Spring Rd (03865-2314)
P.O. Box 985 (03865-0985)
PHONE..............................603 382-3840
EMP: 75 **EST:** 2013
SALES (est): 22.87MM **Privately Held**
Web: www.spartronics.com
SIC: 3674 3672 Microprocessors; Printed circuit boards
HQ: Sparton Corporation
5612 Johnson Lake Rd
De Leon Springs FL 32130
847 762-5800

(G-15352)
SPARTRONICS PLAISTOW INC
Also Called: Sparton Beckwood
27 Hale Spring Rd (03865-2314)
P.O. Box 985 (03865-0985)
PHONE..............................603 382-3840
Paul Fraipont, *CEO*
Greg Kelble, *
EMP: 27 **EST:** 1990
SALES (est): 9.65MM
SALES (corp-wide): 810.86MM **Privately Held**

Web: www.spartronics.com
SIC: 3625 3699 Relays and industrial controls; Electrical equipment and supplies, nec
HQ: Spartronics, Llc
2333 Reach Rd
Williamsport PA 17701
763 703-4321

(G-15353)
TRU FORM PRECISION MFG LLC
2 Wilder Dr (03865-2121)
PHONE..............................603 974-2552
Thomas Grimes Junior, *Pr*
Kristen Grimes, *
Jaimie Bezanson, *
EMP: 30 **EST:** 1968
SQ FT: 1,500
SALES (est): 10MM **Privately Held**
Web: www.tfpm.com
SIC: 3599 Machine shop, jobbing and repair

Plymouth
Grafton County

(G-15354)
A & M DONUTS INC
Also Called: Dunkin' Donuts
384 Tenney Mountain Hwy (03264-3714)
PHONE..............................603 536-7622
EMP: 20 **EST:** 1989
SALES (est): 966.08K **Privately Held**
Web: www.dunkindonuts.com
SIC: 5461 2051 2052 Doughnuts; Doughnuts, except frozen; Cookies and crackers

(G-15355)
NARRATIVE 1 SOFTWARE LLC
1 Bridge St Ste 301 (03264-1632)
PHONE..............................603 968-2233
EMP: 10 **EST:** 2010
SALES (est): 181.66K **Privately Held**
SIC: 7372 Prepackaged software

Portsmouth
Rockingham County

(G-15356)
ACTIO SOFTWARE CORPORATION
Also Called: Actio
1 Nh Ave Ste 207 (03801-2904)
PHONE..............................603 433-2300
Russ Mccann, *Pr*
Kal Kawar, *
EMP: 80 **EST:** 1998
SQ FT: 8,000
SALES (est): 9.25MM **Privately Held**
Web: www.actio.net
SIC: 8742 8748 7372 7375 Management consulting services; Business consulting, nec; Prepackaged software; Information retrieval services
HQ: Enviance, Inc.
2045 W Grand Ave Ste B
Chicago IL 60612
760 496-0200

(G-15357)
ADVANCED DESIGN & MFG INC
Also Called: A D M
350 Heritage Ave (03801-8641)
PHONE..............................603 430-7573
Ron Raby, *Pr*
Ron Raby, *Pr*
Caren Raby, *

Jeff Clark, *
EMP: 50 **EST:** 1990
SQ FT: 15,000
SALES (est): 9.94MM **Privately Held**
Web: www.advanceddesign.com
SIC: 3679 Harness assemblies, for electronic use: wire or cable

(G-15358)
ALLIED TELESIS INC
Also Called: Allied Telesis
15 Rye St (03801-6829)
PHONE..............................603 334-6058
EMP: 91
Web: www.alliedtelesis.com
SIC: 3577 Computer peripheral equipment, nec
HQ: Allied Telesis, Inc.
10521 19th Ave Se Ste 200
Everett WA 98208
408 519-8700

(G-15359)
ANNABLLES NTRAL ICE CREAM YGUR
49 Ceres St (03801-3727)
PHONE..............................603 436-3400
Lewis Polasky, *Pr*
EMP: 8 **EST:** 1982
SALES (est): 821.34K **Privately Held**
Web: www.annabellesicecream.com
SIC: 5143 5812 2024 Ice cream and ices; Ice cream stands or dairy bars; Ice cream and frozen deserts

(G-15360)
ASC ENGINEERED SOLUTIONS LLC
75 Portsmouth Blvd Ste 210 (03801-4591)
PHONE..............................708 534-1414
EMP: 11
SALES (corp-wide): 344.54MM **Privately Held**
Web: www.asc-es.com
SIC: 3498 Fabricated pipe and fittings
PA: Asc Engineered Solutions, Llc
2001 Spring Rd Ste 300
Oak Brook IL 60523
603 418-2893

(G-15361)
ASCA INC (PA)
112 Corporate Dr Ste 1 (03801-6890)
P.O. Box 1140 (03802-1140)
PHONE..............................603 433-6700
EMP: 34 **EST:** 1993
SQ FT: 4,200
SALES (est): 4.27MM **Privately Held**
Web: www.asca-design.com
SIC: 3446 Architectural metalwork

(G-15362)
AUTOMATED VIDEO INSPTN DVCS
Also Called: Avid
222 International Dr Ste 195 (03801-6817)
PHONE..............................603 559-9700
Mary Sheffer, *Prin*
EMP: 19 **EST:** 2007
SALES (est): 2.06MM **Privately Held**
Web: www.avidvision.com
SIC: 3829 Measuring and controlling devices, nec

(G-15363)
AZEGO TECHNOLOGY SVCS US INC
300 Heritage Ave Unit 1 (03801-5692)
PHONE..............................603 610-0030

EMP: 20
SALES (corp-wide): 7.36MM **Privately Held**
SIC: 3672   Printed circuit boards
PA: Azego Technology Services (Us) Inc.
103 Bauer Dr Ste A
Oakland NJ 07444
201 327-7500

(G-15364)
BAYCORP HOLDINGS LTD (PA)
953 Islington St Ste 22 (03801-4299)
PHONE..............................603 294-4850
Frank W Getman Junior, *Pr*
Anthony M Callendrello, *CDO*
Patrycia T Mitchell, *VP Fin*
Raymond Faust, *COO*
EMP: 13 **EST:** 1996
SQ FT: 3,000
SALES (est): 6MM
SALES (corp-wide): 6MM **Privately Held**
SIC: 2911   Oils, fuel

(G-15365)
BID2WIN SOFTWARE LLC
Also Called: B2w
99 Bow St Ste 500 (03801-3846)
PHONE..............................800 336-3808
Paul J Mckeon Junior, *Pr*
David Flynn, *CFO*
Jeff Russell, *VP*
Bihari Srinivasan, *VP*
Jeff Pankratz, *VP*
EMP: 121 **EST:** 1993
SQ FT: 22,160
SALES (est): 30.51MM
SALES (corp-wide): 3.68B **Publicly Held**
Web: www.b2wsoftware.com
SIC: 7372   Prepackaged software
PA: Trimble Inc.
10368 Westmoor Dr
Westminster CO 80021
720 887-6100

(G-15366)
BOSTON ENVIRONMENTAL LLC
600 State St Ste 7 (03801-4370)
PHONE..............................603 334-1000
EMP: 22 **EST:** 1993
SQ FT: 6,500
SALES (est): 2.05MM **Privately Held**
Web: www.bostonenv.com
SIC: 3443   Tanks, lined: metal plate

(G-15367)
BOTTOMLINE TECHNOLOGIES INC (PA)
325 Corporate Dr (03801-6847)
PHONE..............................603 436-0700
Craig Saks, *CEO*
Joseph L Mullen, *
Richard D Booth, *CFO*
John J Mason, *CIO*
Eric K Morgan, *Global Controller*
EMP: 511 **EST:** 1989
SQ FT: 85,000
SALES (est): 471.4MM **Privately Held**
Web: www.bottomline.com
SIC: 7372   Business oriented computer software

(G-15368)
CC1 INC
170 West Rd Ste 7 (03801-5663)
PHONE..............................603 319-2000
Richard D Lewis, *Pr*
James Lewis, *
Robin Mills, *
EMP: 25 **EST:** 1980
SQ FT: 11,000

SALES (est): 4.99MM **Privately Held**
Web: www.cc1inc.com
SIC: 3555 3829 3651   Printing trades machinery; Measuring and controlling devices, nec; Household audio and video equipment

(G-15369)
CELLGENIX INC
1 Nh Ave Ste 125 (03801-2904)
PHONE..............................603 373-0408
Felicia Rosenthal, *Pr*
Bernd Leistler, *VP*
Udo Nirenberg, *VP*
Till Puschmann, *VP*
Daniel Spatz, *VP*
EMP: 10 **EST:** 2015
SALES (est): 1.96MM **Privately Held**
Web: www.cellgenix.com
SIC: 2834   Medicines, capsuled or ampuled

(G-15370)
CHADWICK & TREFETHEN INC
50 Borthwick Ave (03801-4186)
PHONE..............................603 436-2568
David A Richards, *Ch Bd*
David Bovee, *VP*
Jane Richards, *Clerk*
EMP: 10 **EST:** 1823
SQ FT: 8,000
SALES (est): 899.64K **Privately Held**
Web: www.chadwickreamers.com
SIC: 3545   Machine tool accessories

(G-15371)
CHASCO INC
Also Called: Four Seasons Fence
15 Banfield Rd Unit 6 (03801-5607)
PHONE..............................603 436-2141
Charles Kuehl, *Pr*
EMP: 15 **EST:** 1979
SQ FT: 17,000
SALES (est): 2.24MM **Privately Held**
Web: www.chascoinc.net
SIC: 2499 5211   Fencing, docks, and other outdoor wood structural products; Fencing

(G-15372)
CHI AEROSPACE
44 Durham St (03801-2877)
PHONE..............................603 380-9951
EMP: 13 **EST:** 2017
SALES (est): 239.76K **Privately Held**
Web: www.chiaerospace.com
SIC: 3812 3721   Aircraft/aerospace flight instruments and guidance systems; Nonmotorized and lighter-than-air aircraft

(G-15373)
CISCO BREWERS PORTSMOUTH LLC
Also Called: Cisco Brewers Portsmouth
35 Corporate Dr (03801-2847)
PHONE..............................603 380-7575
Jason Harman, *Managing Member*
EMP: 40 **EST:** 2019
SALES (est): 1.36MM **Privately Held**
Web: www.ciscobrewersportsmouth.com
SIC: 5813 2082   Bars and lounges; Liquors, malt

(G-15374)
COASTAL STYLE LLC
259 Grant Ave (03801-5748)
PHONE..............................603 328-2000
EMP: 8 **EST:** 2008
SALES (est): 99K **Privately Held**
Web: store.turbify.net

SIC: 2299   Rugbacking, jute or other fiber

(G-15375)
CONNECTED OFFICE TECH LLC
933 Us Highway 1 Byp (03801-3553)
PHONE..............................603 380-7333
Brian Barrington, *Prin*
EMP: 15 **EST:** 2017
SALES (est): 1.97MM **Privately Held**
Web: www.connecttheoffice.com
SIC: 2759   Financial note and certificate printing and engraving

(G-15376)
CORE ELASTOMERS LLC
170 West Rd (03801-5663)
PHONE..............................603 319-6912
Stephen H Roberts Esq, *Admn*
▲ **EMP:** 9 **EST:** 2014
SALES (est): 1.01MM **Privately Held**
Web: www.coretpo.com
SIC: 2821   Plastics materials and resins

(G-15377)
CRAFT BEER GUILD LLC
4 Cutts St Unit 4 (03801-3784)
P.O. Box 330 (01923-0530)
PHONE..............................603 319-8508
Mike Bernfeld, *Genl Mgr*
EMP: 47
SALES (corp-wide): 8.95MM **Privately Held**
Web: www.craftbeerguildnh.com
SIC: 5149 2086 2082   Beverages, except coffee and tea; Bottled and canned soft drinks; Beer (alcoholic beverage)
PA: Craft Beer Guild Llc
170 Market St
Everett MA 02149
617 410-3900

(G-15378)
CRAFT BREW ALLIANCE INC
35 Corporate Dr (03801-2847)
PHONE..............................603 430-8600
EMP: 83
SALES (corp-wide): 627.12MM **Privately Held**
Web: www.anheuser-busch.com
SIC: 2082   Ale (alcoholic beverage)
HQ: Craft Brew Alliance, Inc.
929 N Russell St
Portland OR 97227
503 331-7270

(G-15379)
CYGNUS INC
Also Called: Minuteman Press
95 Brewery Ln Unit 16 (03801-4983)
P.O. Box 67 (03869-0067)
PHONE..............................603 431-8989
Jay Gale, *Pr*
Vivian Gale, *VP*
Peter Lieberman, *Clerk*
EMP: 9 **EST:** 1990
SALES (est): 300.79K **Privately Held**
Web: www.minuteman.com
SIC: 2752 2791 2789   Commercial printing, lithographic; Typesetting; Bookbinding and related work

(G-15380)
DZS INC
112 Corporate Dr Ste 1 (03801-6890)
PHONE..............................510 777-7000
Sean Belanger, *Brnch Mgr*
EMP: 15
SALES (corp-wide): 375.69MM **Publicly Held**
Web: www.dzsi.com

SIC: 3577   Data conversion equipment, media-to-media: computer
PA: Dzs Inc.
5700 Tennyson Pkwy # 400
Plano TX 75024
469 327-1531

(G-15381)
EARTH EAGLE BREWINGS LLC
175 High St Apt 6 (03801-3724)
PHONE..............................603 817-2773
Alex Mcdonald, *Ofcr*
EMP: 8 **EST:** 2012
SALES (est): 261.8K **Privately Held**
Web: www.eartheaglebrewings.com
SIC: 2082   Malt beverages

(G-15382)
ENERTRAC INC
100 Market St Unit 302 (03801-3760)
PHONE..............................603 821-0003
EMP: 10 **EST:** 2009
SALES (est): 1.53MM **Privately Held**
Web: www.anova.com
SIC: 3829   Measuring and controlling devices, nec

(G-15383)
EXTRUSION ALTERNATIVES INC
19 Post Rd (03801-5622)
PHONE..............................603 430-9600
Robert Pickett, *Pr*
Melissa Pickett, *
EMP: 30 **EST:** 2002
SALES (est): 4.23MM **Privately Held**
Web: www.exaltcustomtubing.com
SIC: 3841   Surgical and medical instruments

(G-15384)
FLEX LEASING POWER & SVC LLC
112 Corporate Dr (03801-6890)
PHONE..............................603 430-7000
EMP: 34 **EST:** 2012
SALES (est): 5.56MM
SALES (corp-wide): 24.49MM **Privately Held**
Web: www.flexenergy.com
SIC: 3511   Gas turbine generator set units, complete
PA: Flexenergy Green Solutions, Inc.
112 Corporate Dr
Portsmouth NH 03801
603 430-7000

(G-15385)
FLEXENERGY INC
112 Corporate Dr Ste 3 (03801-6890)
PHONE..............................603 430-7000
Mark Schnepel, *Pr*
Wes Kimmel, *
John Alday, *
Chris Dirk, *
EMP: 90 **EST:** 2008
SALES (est): 15.15MM
SALES (corp-wide): 24.49MM **Privately Held**
Web: www.flexenergy.com
SIC: 3511   Gas turbine generator set units, complete
PA: Flexenergy Green Solutions, Inc.
112 Corporate Dr
Portsmouth NH 03801
603 430-7000

(G-15386)
FLEXENERGY ENERGY SYSTEMS INC
112 Corporate Dr Ste 3 (03801-6890)

PHONE...............................877 477-6937
Mark G Schnepel, *CEO*
Wes Kimmel, *CFO*
▲ **EMP: 7 EST**: 2010
SALES (est): 1.94MM
SALES (corp-wide): 24.49MM **Privately
Held**
SIC: 3511   Gas turbine generator set units,
complete
PA: Flexenergy Green Solutions, Inc.
112 Corporate Dr
Portsmouth NH 03801
603 430-7000

(G-15387)
**FLEXENERGY GREEN
SOLUTIONS INC (PA)**
Also Called: Flexenergy
112 Corporate Dr (03801-6890)
PHONE...............................603 430-7000
Mark Schnepel, *Pr*
George Walker, *
Wes Kimmel, *CFO*
Doug Baltzer, *CCO*
EMP: 42 EST: 1996
SALES (est): 22.65MM
SALES (corp-wide): 22.65MM **Privately
Held**
Web: www.flexenergy.com
SIC: 3511   Gas turbine generator set units,
complete

(G-15388)
FLEXENERGY HOLDINGS LLC
30 Nh Ave (03801-2866)
PHONE...............................603 430-7000
Mark Schnepel, *Pr*
EMP: 90 EST: 2013
SALES (est): 5.48MM **Privately Held**
Web: www.flexenergy.com
SIC: 3511   Gas turbine generator set units,
complete

(G-15389)
**FLEXENERGY POWER
SOLUTIONS LLC**
112 Corporate Dr Ste 3 (03801-6890)
PHONE...............................603 430-7000
Thomas Denison, *Managing Member*
Patrick Connelly, *Managing Member*
EMP: 62 EST: 2015
SALES (est): 3.06MM **Privately Held**
Web: www.flexenergy.com
SIC: 3511   Gas turbine generator set units,
complete

(G-15390)
**FOSTERS DAILY DMCRAT
FSTRS SUN**
111 Nh Ave (03801-2864)
PHONE...............................603 431-4888
Elaine Leduc, *Prin*
EMP: 14 EST: 2010
SALES (est): 210.07K **Privately Held**
SIC: 2711   Commercial printing and
newspaper publishing combined

(G-15391)
FRANKLIN EXETER INC
Also Called: Coastal Speedpro
222 International Dr Ste 135 (03801-6817)
PHONE...............................603 836-8590
Michael Enright, *Pr*
EMP: 11 EST: 2013
SALES (est): 1.01MM **Privately Held**
Web: www.speedpro.com
SIC: 7336 2711   Commercial art and graphic
design; Commercial printing and
newspaper publishing combined

(G-15392)
GALVION LTD (HQ)
160 Corporate Dr (03801-6815)
PHONE...............................514 739-4444
Jonathan Blanshay, *Pr*
Craig Baden, *Prin*
EMP: 17 EST: 2019
SALES (est): 24.72MM
SALES (corp-wide): 17.27MM **Privately
Held**
Web: www.galvion.com
SIC: 3842   Personal safety equipment
PA: Galvion Inc
3800 Rue Saint-Patrick Bureau 200
Montreal QC H4E 1
514 739-4444

(G-15393)
GLOBAL LAMINATES INC
Also Called: Coolback
300 Constitution Ave (03801-8609)
PHONE...............................603 373-8323
William F Hurley, *Ch Bd*
Bruce Edward Hurley, *Pr*
▲ **EMP: 10 EST**: 1991
SALES (est): 981.69K **Privately Held**
Web: www.globallaminates.com
SIC: 3083 3497   Laminated plastics sheets;
Copper foil

(G-15394)
GP GYPSUM CORP
170 Shattuck Way (03801-7868)
PHONE...............................603 433-8000
EMP: 9 EST: 2019
SALES (est): 210.78K **Privately Held**
SIC: 3275   Gypsum products

(G-15395)
**GRANITE STATE PLASMA
CUTTING**
Also Called: Granite State Plasma Cutting
10 Pleasant St Ste 400 (03801-4551)
PHONE...............................603 536-4415
EMP: 38 EST: 1995
SQ FT: 60,000
SALES (est): 1.17MM **Privately Held**
SIC: 3441   Fabricated structural metal

(G-15396)
**GREAT RHYTHM BREWING CO
LLC**
105 Bartlett St Ste 4b (03801-7608)
P.O. Box 1624 (03802-1624)
PHONE...............................603 430-9640
Thornton Scott, *CEO*
EMP: 20 EST: 2012
SALES (est): 1.4MM **Privately Held**
Web: www.greatrhythmbrewing.com
SIC: 2082   Malt beverages

(G-15397)
**GREENWOOD PUBLISHING
GROUP INC**
Heinemann Publishing
145 Maplewood Ave Ste 300 (03801-3715)
P.O. Box 528 (03802-0097)
PHONE...............................603 431-7894
Lori Lampert, *Sls Mgr*
EMP: 2615
SALES (corp-wide): 1.05B **Privately Held**
Web: www.hmhpub.com
SIC: 2731   Books, publishing only
HQ: Greenwood Publishing Group, Llc
125 High St
Boston MA 02110
617 351-5000

(G-15398)
**HANSA CONSULT NORTH AMER
LLC (PA)**
200 International Dr Ste 120 (03801-6833)
PHONE...............................603 422-8833
Karl M Overman, *Managing Member*
EMP: 17 EST: 2000
SQ FT: 5,000
SALES (est): 4.51MM
SALES (corp-wide): 4.51MM **Privately
Held**
Web: www.hcna-llc.com
SIC: 3822   Temperature controls, automatic

(G-15399)
**HARMONY METAL PRODUCTS
NORTH INC**
10 Pleasant St Ste 400 (03801-4551)
PHONE...............................603 536-6012
EMP: 42
Web: www.harmonymetal.com
SIC: 3499   Welding tips, heat resistant: metal

(G-15400)
**HAWTHORN CREATIVE GROUP
LLC**
33 Jewell Ct (03801-2036)
PHONE...............................603 610-0533
EMP: 45 EST: 2004
SQ FT: 6,000
SALES (est): 5.58MM **Privately Held**
Web: www.hawthorncreative.com
SIC: 2741   Miscellaneous publishing

(G-15401)
**HIDEAWAYS INTERNATIONAL
INC**
Also Called: Thiel & Associates
767 Islington St Ste 21 (03801-7206)
PHONE...............................603 430-4433
Michael F Thiel, *CEO*
Gail D Richard, *
EMP: 16 EST: 1979
SQ FT: 7,000
SALES (est): 1.63MM **Privately Held**
Web: www.hideaways.com
SIC: 8699 2721 4724 7311   Travel club;
Periodicals; Tourist agency arranging
transport, lodging and car rental;
Advertising agencies

(G-15402)
**HIGGINGBOTHAM
MANAGEMENT CORP**
Also Called: PIP Printing
222 International Dr Ste 140 (03801-6817)
PHONE...............................603 431-0142
Alan Higginbotham, *Pr*
Steven Feld, *Sec*
EMP: 10 EST: 1979
SALES (est): 867.62K **Privately Held**
Web: www.allegramarketingprint.com
SIC: 2752 2796 2791 2789   Offset printing;
Platemaking services; Typesetting;
Bookbinding and related work

(G-15403)
HIGH LINER FOODS USA INC
Fishery Products International
183 International Dr (03801-6836)
PHONE...............................603 818-5555
EMP: 10
SALES (corp-wide): 875.4MM **Privately
Held**
Web: www.highlinerfoods.com
SIC: 2092 5146   Fish, frozen: prepared;
Fish, frozen, unpackaged
HQ: High Liner Foods (Usa) Incorporated
1 Highliner Ave

Portsmouth NH 03801
603 818-5555

(G-15404)
**HIGHLANDS FUEL DELIVERY
LLC (HQ)**
Also Called: Irving Energy Dist & Mktg
190 Commerce Way (03801-3242)
P.O. Box 11013 (04243-9464)
PHONE...............................603 559-8700
Darren Gillis, *Pr*
James Sepanski, *
◆ **EMP: 100 EST**: 1954
SALES (est): 283.99MM
SALES (corp-wide): 354.16MM **Privately
Held**
Web: www.irvingoil.com
SIC: 5172 5541 1389   Gasoline; Filling
stations, gasoline; Construction, repair, and
dismantling services
PA: Irving Oil Investments Corporation
700 Maine Ave
Bangor ME 04401
207 942-7000

(G-15405)
HOME BRANDS LLC
Also Called: Sheds USA
300 Constitution Ave Unit 200
(03801-8609)
PHONE...............................866 616-2685
EMP: 100
Web: www.tuffshed.com
SIC: 2452   Prefabricated buildings, wood

(G-15406)
**HOUGHTON MIFFLIN
HARCOURT CO**
Also Called: Hmh
361 Hanover St (03801-3959)
PHONE...............................630 467-7000
EMP: 170
SALES (corp-wide): 1.05B **Privately Held**
Web: www.heinemann.com
SIC: 3999 2731   Education aids, devices
and supplies; Book publishing
HQ: Houghton Mifflin Harcourt Company
125 High St Ste 900
Boston MA 02110
617 351-5000

(G-15407)
INFINITE IMAGING INC
933 Islington St (03801-4229)
PHONE...............................603 436-3030
William J Hurley, *Prin*
EMP: 19 EST: 2006
SALES (est): 2.27MM **Privately Held**
Web: www.infiniteimaging.com
SIC: 2752   Offset printing

(G-15408)
**INGERSOLL-RAND ENERGY
SYSTEMS CORPORATION**
Also Called: I R Energy Systems
32 Exeter Street (03801-2842)
P.O. Box 940 (28036-0940)
PHONE...............................603 430-7000
EMP: 70
Web: www.ingersollrand.com
SIC: 7389 8742 3724 3443   Design,
commercial and industrial; New products
and services consultants; Turbines, aircraft
type; Heat exchangers, condensers, and
components

(G-15409)
INGU LLC
210 West Rd (03801-5639)

PHONE..................603 770-5969
EMP: 10 **EST:** 2017
SALES (est): 425.94K **Privately Held**
Web: www.inevergup.com
SIC: 3999 Manufacturing industries, nec

(G-15410)
INTERCEPT MEDICAL LLC
Also Called: Laminated Films & Packaging
3560 Lafayette Rd (03801-6073)
PHONE..................800 622-1114
Kieth Donaldson, *Pr*
EMP: 25 **EST:** 2018
SALES (est): 3.65MM **Privately Held**
Web: www.laminatedfilms.com
SIC: 2671 Plastic film, coated or laminated
for packaging

(G-15411)
IONBOND LLC
195 Nh Ave Ste 190 (03801-7836)
PHONE..................603 610-4460
Bernie Janoss, *Mgr*
EMP: 10
Web: www.ionbond.com
SIC: 3479 Coating of metals and formed
products
HQ: Ionbond, Llc
1823 E Whitcomb Ave
Madison Heights MI 48071

(G-15412)
ISHIGAKI USA LTD
280 Heritage Ave Unit J (03801-8619)
PHONE..................603 433-3334
▲ **EMP:** 15 **EST:** 2012
SALES (est): 1.43MM **Privately Held**
Web: www.ishigakiusa.us
SIC: 3559 Refinery, chemical processing,
and similar machinery
PA: Ishigaki Co., Ltd.
1-6-5, Marunouchi
Chiyoda-Ku TKY 100-0

(G-15413)
JULIET MARINE SYSTEMS INC
14 Manchester Sq Ste 275 (03801-7866)
P.O. Box 21974 (03802-1974)
PHONE..................603 319-8412
EMP: 9 **EST:** 2010
SALES (est): 815.41K **Privately Held**
Web: www.julietmarine.com
SIC: 3732 Boatbuilding and repairing

(G-15414)
LABORIE MEDICAL TECHNOLOGIES CORP (HQ)
Also Called: Laborie
180 International Dr (03801-6837)
PHONE..................802 857-1300
▲ **EMP:** 30 **EST:** 1983
SALES (est): 108.16MM
SALES (corp-wide): 22.73MM **Privately Held**
Web: www.laborie.com
SIC: 3841 Surgical and medical instruments
PA: 2941881 Canada Inc
6415 Northwest Dr Unit 11
Mississauga ON L4V 1
905 612-1170

(G-15415)
LANAIR RESEARCH & DEV INC
Also Called: Atco Lanair
521 Shattuck Way (03801-7872)
PHONE..................603 433-6134
David Lancaster, *Pr*
Richard Sorrentino, *VP*
Mary Liz Lancaster, *VP*
Richard Longley, *Prin*

EMP: 9 **EST:** 1996
SQ FT: 5,600
SALES (est): 984.04K **Privately Held**
Web: www.lanairinc.com
SIC: 3728 Aircraft parts and equipment, nec

(G-15416)
LEGACY GLOBAL SPORTS LP
290 Heritage Ave (03801-6874)
PHONE..................603 373-7262
John St Pierre, *Pr*
Travis G Bezio C.p.a., *Operations*
Jason Mitchell C.p.a., *Dir Opers*
EMP: 24 **EST:** 2016
SALES (est): 2.32MM **Privately Held**
Web: www.legacyglobalsports.com
SIC: 2329 2339 Men's and boys' sportswear
and athletic clothing; Sportswear, women's

(G-15417)
LIGHTHOUSE MANUFACTURING LLC
35 Mirona Road Ext (03801-5343)
PHONE..................978 532-5999
Michael E Bean, *Pr*
J Charles Rivers, *
EMP: 46 **EST:** 1974
SQ FT: 21,000
SALES (est): 4.89MM **Privately Held**
Web: www.lighthousemfg.com
SIC: 3599 Machine shop, jobbing and repair

(G-15418)
LOCAL MEDIA GROUP INC
Also Called: Seacoast Newspapers
111 Nh Ave (03801-2864)
P.O. Box 119 (03802-0119)
PHONE..................603 436-1800
John Tabor, *Mgr*
EMP: 775
SALES (corp-wide): 2.95B **Publicly Held**
Web: www.seacoastonline.com
SIC: 2711 Commercial printing and
newspaper publishing combined
HQ: Local Media Group, Inc.
90 Crystal Run Rd Ste 310
Middletown NY 10941
845 341-1100

(G-15419)
LOFTWARE HOLDINGS INC (PA)
249 Corporate Dr (03801-6885)
PHONE..................603 766-3630
Dana Anderson, *Ch*
Eric Anderson, *VP*
Ed Irwin, *VP*
Brian Collin, *Sec*
Robert Oconnor Junior, *CEO*
EMP: 11 **EST:** 2005
SALES (est): 29.62MM **Privately Held**
Web: www.loftware.com
SIC: 7371 7372 Computer software
development; Prepackaged software

(G-15420)
LONZA BIOLOGICS INC
40 Goosebay Dr (03801)
PHONE..................603 610-4696
EMP: 94
Web: www.lonza.com
SIC: 2834 Pharmaceutical preparations
HQ: Lonza Biologics Inc.
101 International Dr
Portsmouth NH 03801
603 610-4500

(G-15421)
LONZA BIOLOGICS INC
101 International Dr (03801-2815)
PHONE..................201 316-9200

EMP: 94
Web: www.lonza.com
SIC: 2834 Pharmaceutical preparations
HQ: Lonza Biologics Inc.
101 International Dr
Portsmouth NH 03801
603 610-4500

(G-15422)
LONZA BIOLOGICS INC (DH)
Also Called: Lonza
101 International Dr (03801-2815)
PHONE..................603 610-4500
Stephan Kutzer, *Pr*
Alexander Hoy, *
Scott Waldman, *
▼ **EMP:** 155 **EST:** 1993
SALES (est): 192.01MM **Privately Held**
Web: www.lonza.com
SIC: 2834 Pharmaceutical preparations
HQ: Lonza Usa Inc.
412 Mount Kemble Ave 200s
Morristown NJ 07960
201 316-9200

(G-15423)
METAVAC LLC
20 Post Rd (03801-5622)
PHONE..................631 207-2344
EMP: 19 **EST:** 1945
SQ FT: 33,000
SALES (est): 2.42MM
SALES (corp-wide): 44.91B **Publicly Held**
SIC: 3826 Analytical instruments
HQ: Fisher Scientific International Llc
81 Wyman St
Waltham MA 02451

(G-15424)
MMIS INC
Also Called: Medispend
100 International Dr Ste 350 (03801-6851)
PHONE..................603 929-5078
EMP: 51 **EST:** 2010
SQ FT: 3,000
SALES (est): 8.11MM **Privately Held**
Web: www.medispend.com
SIC: 8742 7371 7372 Marketing consulting
services; Software programming
applications; Application computer software

(G-15425)
NEW ERIE SCIENTIFIC LLC (DH)
20 Post Rd (03801-5622)
PHONE..................603 430-6859
Stephen K Wiatt, *Ex VP*
◆ **EMP:** 26 **EST:** 1934
SQ FT: 120,000
SALES (est): 5.36MM **Privately Held**
SIC: 3231 3821 3229 3221 Products of
purchased glass; Laboratory apparatus and
furniture; Pressed and blown glass, nec;
Glass containers
HQ: Epredia
20 Post Rd
Portsmouth NH 03801
603 431-8410

(G-15426)
NITROSECURITY INC (DH)
230 Commerce Way Ste 325 (03801-8201)
PHONE..................603 766-8160
Kenneth Levine, *Managing Member*
EMP: 30 **EST:** 1994
SQ FT: 10,000
SALES (est): 23.11MM
SALES (corp-wide): 1.92B **Privately Held**
Web: www.mcafee.com
SIC: 7372 Prepackaged software
HQ: Mcafee, Llc
6220 America Center Dr

San Jose CA 95002

(G-15427)
OI INFUSION SERVICES LLC
111 Nh Ave (03801-2864)
PHONE..................603 319-6224
EMP: 53 **EST:** 2018
SALES (est): 26.32MM **Privately Held**
Web: www.oi-infusion.com
SIC: 1389 Oil consultants

(G-15428)
OMADA TECHNOLOGIES LLC
36 Maplewood Ave (03801-3712)
PHONE..................603 610-8282
EMP: 10 **EST:** 2017
SALES (est): 2.51MM **Privately Held**
Web: www.omadatechnologies.com
SIC: 7372 7373 Prepackaged software;
Value-added resellers, computer systems

(G-15429)
PIKE INDUSTRIES INC
650 Peverly Hill Rd (03801-5383)
PHONE..................603 436-4432
Derrick Hill, *Mgr*
EMP: 9
SALES (corp-wide): 32.72B **Privately Held**
Web: www.pikeindustries.com
SIC: 1611 2951 1442 Highway and street
paving contractor; Asphalt paving mixtures
and blocks; Construction sand and gravel
HQ: Pike Industries, Inc.
3 Eastgate Park Dr
Belmont NH 03220
603 527-5100

(G-15430)
PORT CITY FOODS LLC
Also Called: Port City Pretzels
170 West Rd Ste 10 (03801-5663)
PHONE..................603 436-3001
Suzanne Foley, *CEO*
EMP: 26 **EST:** 2017
SALES (est): 2.02MM **Privately Held**
SIC: 2052 Pretzels

(G-15431)
POWERPLAY MANAGEMENT LLC
Also Called: Infinite Imaging
933 Islington St (03801-4229)
PHONE..................603 436-3030
Christopher Carrier, *Managing Member*
Christopher Oberg, *Managing Member*
EMP: 23 **EST:** 2019
SQ FT: 4,000
SALES (est): 2.33MM **Privately Held**
Web: www.alphagraphics.com
SIC: 2759 8742 3993 5199 Commercial
printing, nec; Marketing consulting services;
Signs and advertising specialties;
Advertising specialties

(G-15432)
RELX INC
361 Hanover St (03801-3959)
PHONE..................603 431-7894
John C Watson, *Prin*
EMP: 12
SALES (corp-wide): 10.3B **Privately Held**
Web: www.relx.com
SIC: 2721 Periodicals
HQ: Relx Inc.
230 Park Ave Ste 700
New York NY 10169
212 309-8100

(G-15433)
RUSSOUND/FMP INC
200 International Dr Ste 155 (03801-6833)
PHONE..................................603 659-5170
Joe Brouillet, *CEO*
Maureen Baldwin, *
Charlie Porritt, *
Eleanor Sexton, *
◆ EMP: 150 EST: 1971
SQ FT: 36,000
SALES (est): 19.96MM Privately Held
Web: www.russound.com
SIC: 3651 5731 3612 Music distribution apparatus; Radio, television, and electronic stores; Transformers, except electric

(G-15434)
SAIL ENERGY LLC
Also Called: Heutz Oil Co.
210 Commerce Way Ste 210 (03801-8203)
PHONE..................................844 301-7245
Dennis O'brien, *Pr*
Gail Mulvihill, *Managing Member*
EMP: 200 EST: 2012
SALES (est): 20.21MM Privately Held
Web: www.sailenergy.com
SIC: 2911 5983 Liquefied petroleum gases, LPG; Fuel oil dealers

(G-15435)
SCARLET ASPEN LLC
Also Called: BUDGET BLINDS
105 Bartlett St (03801-7608)
PHONE..................................603 509-3990
Ian Kaner, *Managing Member*
EMP: 11 EST: 2016
SALES (est): 1.3MM Privately Held
Web: www.budgetblinds.com
SIC: 5719 5963 2591 1799 Window furnishings; Home related products, direct sales; Drapery hardware and window blinds and shades; Drapery track installation

(G-15436)
SEACOAST TECHNOLOGIES INC
222 International Dr Ste 145 (03801-6817)
PHONE..................................603 766-9800
Donald J Larnard Ph.d., *Pr*
EMP: 7 EST: 2000
SALES (est): 452.38K Privately Held
Web: www.seacoastonline.com
SIC: 3841 Surgical and medical instruments

(G-15437)
SINGULRITY ELCTRNIC SYSTEMS IN
300 Heritage Ave Unit 2 (03801-5692)
PHONE..................................603 430-6000
EMP: 8 EST: 1996
SQ FT: 6,000
SALES (est): 665.38K Privately Held
Web: www.singularitysys.com
SIC: 7629 3672 Circuit board repair; Circuit boards, television and radio printed

(G-15438)
SOUTHPORT MANAGEMENT GROUP LLC
Also Called: Sir Speedy
738 Islington St 800 (03801-7217)
PHONE..................................603 433-4664
EMP: 8 EST: 1987
SQ FT: 2,600
SALES (est): 820.69K Privately Held
Web: www.southportprinting.com
SIC: 2752 7334 2791 Offset printing; Photocopying and duplicating services; Typesetting

(G-15439)
SPIRIT ADVISORY LLC
Also Called: Southport Printing Company
738 Islington St Ste C (03801-7217)
PHONE..................................603 433-4664
Peter V Doyle Esq, *Admn*
Joshua Parison, *Pr*
EMP: 7 EST: 2014
SQ FT: 3,092
SALES (est): 485.6K Privately Held
SIC: 2752 Offset printing

(G-15440)
STENHOUSE PUBLISHERS
Also Called: Teachers Publishing Group
282 Corporate Dr Ste 1 (03801-8008)
P.O. Box 18360 (43218-0360)
PHONE..................................207 253-1600
Dan Tobin, *Pr*
EMP: 15 EST: 1993
SALES (est): 2.48MM
SALES (corp-wide): 109.4MM Privately Held
Web: www.stenhouse.com
SIC: 2731 Books, publishing only
PA: Highlights For Children, Inc.
1800 Watermark Dr
Columbus OH 43215
614 486-0631

(G-15441)
TEKON-TECHNICAL CONS INC
110 Corporate Dr Ste 4 (03801-6822)
PHONE..................................603 335-3080
David Reed, *Pr*
Charles A Corlin, *Pr*
EMP: 20 EST: 1968
SALES (est): 2.38MM Privately Held
Web: www.tekontab.com
SIC: 1761 1389 Sheet metal work, nec; Testing, measuring, surveying, and analysis services

(G-15442)
TELEDYNE INSTRUMENTS INC
Also Called: Teledyne D.G. O'Brien
162 Corporate Dr Ste 100 (03801-6815)
PHONE..................................603 474-5571
Patrick Barry, *Brnch Mgr*
EMP: 228
SALES (corp-wide): 5.46B Publicly Held
Web: www.teledyne.com
SIC: 3643 3357 3621 3699 Current-carrying wiring services; Nonferrous wiredrawing and insulating; Torque motors, electric; Electrical equipment and supplies, nec
HQ: Teledyne Instruments, Inc.
16830 Chestnut St
City Of Industry CA 91748
626 934-1500

(G-15443)
THERMO FISHER SCIENTIFIC INC (HQ)
20 Post Rd (03801-5622)
PHONE..................................603 431-8410
EMP: 26 EST: 2015
SALES (est): 17.66MM
SALES (corp-wide): 44.91B Publicly Held
SIC: 3826 Analytical instruments
PA: Thermo Fisher Scientific Inc.
168 3rd Ave
Waltham MA 02451
781 622-1000

(G-15444)
TRAIL-TEX LLC
140 West Rd Ste 2 (03801-5653)
PHONE..................................603 436-6326
▲ EMP: 16

Web: www.merchant-processing.com
SIC: 2231 Apparel and outerwear broadwoven fabrics

(G-15445)
TVC INC
284 Constitution Ave (03801-5616)
P.O. Box 1340 (03802-1340)
PHONE..................................603 431-5251
Linda Tyring, *Pr*
EMP: 15 EST: 1966
SQ FT: 7,000
SALES (est): 2.44MM Privately Held
Web: www.tvcsystems.com
SIC: 3823 Process control instruments

(G-15446)
UNITED STATES DEPT OF NAVY
Also Called: Portsmouth Naval Shipyard
Portsmouth Naval Shipyard Code 1710 (03804)
PHONE..................................207 438-2714
Kevin Mccoy, *Brnch Mgr*
EMP: 110
Web: www.navy.mil
SIC: 3731 9711 Shipbuilding and repairing; Navy
HQ: United States Department Of The Navy
1200 Navy Pentagon
Washington DC 20350

(G-15447)
VERA ROASTING COMPANY
99 Bow St Ste 100e (03801-3995)
PHONE..................................603 969-7970
Mark Galvin, *CEO*
Glen Miller, *Ch Bd*
Chris Matrumalo, *Mktg Dir*
Evan Young, *Dir Fin*
EMP: 7 EST: 2015
SQ FT: 1,100
SALES (est): 498.85K Privately Held
Web: www.veraroasting.com
SIC: 2095 5499 Roasted coffee; Health foods

(G-15448)
VIDARR INC
280 Heritage Ave Unit G (03801-8619)
PHONE..................................877 636-8432
Cliff Byrd, *CEO*
Scott Schonberber, *COO*
Joseph Powers, *Prin*
Gregory Sancoff, *Prin*
EMP: 7 EST: 2019
SALES (est): 1.15MM Privately Held
Web: www.vidarrinc.com
SIC: 2992 3555 3613 7389 Lubricating oils and greases; Printing trade parts and attachments; Distribution cutouts; Business services, nec

(G-15449)
WAGZ INC (PA)
100 Market St Unit 401 (03801-3760)
P.O. Box 741 (03848-0741)
PHONE..................................603 570-6015
Terry Anderton, *Pr*
Chelsi Christensen, *Dir*
Judith Blake, *Dir*
Thomas Mason, *CSO*
EMP: 11 EST: 2015
SALES (est): 1.5MM
SALES (corp-wide): 1.5MM Privately Held
Web: www.wagz.com
SIC: 3571 7389 Electronic computers; Business Activities at Non-Commercial Site

(G-15450)
WOOD WORKS
855 Islington St Ste 123 (03801-4270)
PHONE..................................603 436-3805
TOLL FREE: 800
William Clerk, *Pt*
EMP: 7 EST: 1981
SALES (est): 489.59K Privately Held
Web: www.wmclarke.com
SIC: 2431 Millwork

Raymond
Rockingham County

(G-15451)
BE YOUNEEQ LLC
62 Langford Rd (03077-1704)
PHONE..................................603 244-3933
Raimundas Nutautas, *Managing Member*
EMP: 7 EST: 2015
SALES (est): 218.4K Privately Held
SIC: 2771 Greeting cards

(G-15452)
EXTREME ADHESIVES INC
63 Epping St (03077-2621)
PHONE..................................603 895-4028
Ted Clark, *Pr*
EMP: 8 EST: 1987
SQ FT: 7,500
SALES (est): 4.11MM
SALES (corp-wide): 3.51B Publicly Held
Web: www.hbfuller.com
SIC: 2891 Adhesives
HQ: Royal Adhesives And Sealants Llc
2001 W Washington St
South Bend IN 46628
574 246-5000

(G-15453)
MAGNUM MACHINE INC
1 Infinity Dr (03077-2482)
PHONE..................................603 895-0545
James Creighton, *Pr*
Marvin Travers, *VP*
EMP: 18 EST: 1980
SQ FT: 11,500
SALES (est): 2.12MM Privately Held
Web: www.magnumnh.com
SIC: 3599 Machine shop, jobbing and repair

(G-15454)
NORTHEAST WOODWORKING PDTS INC
24 Old Manchester Rd (03077-2314)
P.O. Box 123 (03077-0123)
PHONE..................................603 895-4271
Richard Dubois, *Pr*
EMP: 18 EST: 2001
SALES (est): 537.12K Privately Held
Web: www.newoodworkingproducts.com
SIC: 2434 Wood kitchen cabinets

(G-15455)
PARKER & HARPER COMPANIES INC (PA)
Also Called: Gemini Valve
2 Otter Ct (03077-2506)
PHONE..................................603 895-4761
Daniel Packard, *Pr*
Ken Madden, *
Harry Millette, *
Dennis F Gorman, *
Daniel M Packard, *
▲ EMP: 70 EST: 1917
SQ FT: 70,000
SALES (est): 13.2MM
SALES (corp-wide): 13.2MM Privately Held

▲ = Import ▼ = Export
◆ = Import/Export

Web: www.geminivalve.com
SIC: 3494 3451 3643 3593 Valves and pipe fittings, nec; Screw machine products; Current-carrying wiring services; Fluid power cylinders and actuators

(G-15456)
ROCHETTE FMLY CSTM WDWKG & REM
2 Prevere Rd (03077-1561)
PHONE.................................603 895-2181
Christopher D Rochette, *Prin*
EMP: 7 EST: 2008
SALES (est): 188.18K **Privately Held**
Web: www.rochettefamilyremodeling.com
SIC: 2431 Millwork

(G-15457)
ROYAL ADHESIVES & SEALANTS LLC
63 Epping St (03077-2621)
PHONE.................................860 788-3380
EMP: 9 EST: 2018
SALES (est): 224.73K **Privately Held**
Web: www.hbfuller.com
SIC: 2891 Adhesives

(G-15458)
SHOOKUS SPECIAL TOOLS INC
11 Center St (03077-2509)
P.O. Box 1027 (03077-1027)
PHONE.................................603 895-1200
Peter John Shookus, *Pr*
Lori C Shookus, *CFO*
EMP: 14 EST: 1985
SQ FT: 16,000
SALES (est): 2.27MM **Privately Held**
Web: www.shookustools.com
SIC: 3312 Tool and die steel

Rindge
Cheshire County

(G-15459)
AMERICAN KEDER INC (PA)
22 Perkins Rd (03461-5412)
P.O. Box 170107 (53217-8011)
PHONE.................................603 899-3233
Thomas Shields, *Pr*
J David Pozerycki, *VP*
Gerhard Meisterjahn, *Stockholder*
Walter Mueller, *Stockholder*
▲ EMP: 8 EST: 2000
SQ FT: 8,000
SALES (est): 873.79K
SALES (corp-wide): 873.79K **Privately Held**
Web: www.keder.com
SIC: 3792 5199 Tent-type camping trailers; Clothes hangers

(G-15460)
LEXINGTON DATA INCORPORATED
316 Main St (03461-5726)
PHONE.................................603 899-5673
James Critser, *Pr*
EMP: 8 EST: 2008
SALES (est): 605.44K **Privately Held**
SIC: 3571 Electronic computers

(G-15461)
TRIUMPH INTERIORS LLC
1090 Nh Rte 119 (03461-9998)
P.O. Box 408 (03461-0408)
PHONE.................................603 899-5184
Rodney Seppala, *Pr*

EMP: 14 EST: 2011
SALES (est): 866.97K **Privately Held**
Web: www.triumphkm.com
SIC: 2434 1799 5211 Wood kitchen cabinets ; Counter top installation; Millwork and lumber

Rochester
Strafford County

(G-15462)
ALBANY ENGNERED COMPOSITES INC
216 Airport Dr (03867-1718)
PHONE.................................603 330-5851
Brian Coffenberry, *Pr*
EMP: 7
SALES (corp-wide): 1.03B **Publicly Held**
Web: www.albint.com
SIC: 2269 Chemical coating or treating of narrow fabrics
HQ: Albany Engineered Composites, Inc.
216 Airport Dr
Rochester NH 03867
603 330-5800

(G-15463)
ALBANY ENGNERED COMPOSITES INC (HQ)
Also Called: Albany Engineered Composites
216 Airport Dr (03867-1718)
P.O. Box 1907 (12201-1907)
PHONE.................................603 330-5800
Joseph G Morone, *CEO*
Brian Coffenberry, *
John B Cozzolino, *
Charles J Silva Junior, *Sec*
James Shea, *
◆ EMP: 120 EST: 1983
SALES (est): 93.84MM
SALES (corp-wide): 1.03B **Publicly Held**
Web: www.albint.com
SIC: 2269 Chemical coating or treating of narrow fabrics
PA: Albany International Corp.
216 Airport Dr
Rochester NH 03867
603 330-5850

(G-15464)
ALBANY INTERNATIONAL CORP (PA)
216 Airport Dr (03867-1718)
P.O. Box 1907 (12201-1907)
PHONE.................................603 330-5850
A William Higgins, *Pr*
John C Standish, *
Stephen M Nolan, *CFO*
Robert A Hansen, *Sr VP*
Charles J Silva Junior, *VP*
EMP: 100 EST: 1895
SALES (est): 1.03B
SALES (corp-wide): 1.03B **Publicly Held**
Web: www.albint.com
SIC: 2221 3496 2399 2899 Paper broadwoven fabrics; Fabrics, woven wire; Belting, fabric: made from purchased materials; Insulating compounds

(G-15465)
AMERICAN BACON BOSTON FELT INC
31 Front St (03868-5823)
PHONE.................................603 332-7000
Wilson Pryne, *Pr*
◆ EMP: 50 EST: 1973
SQ FT: 55,000
SALES (est): 4.8MM **Privately Held**

Web: www.baconfelt.com
SIC: 2299 Felts and felt products

(G-15466)
ASHLAND ELECTRIC PRODUCTS INC
10 Indl Way (03867)
PHONE.................................603 335-1100
Christophe Y Cloitre, *Pr*
Heather Ann Cloitre, *Treas*
EMP: 20 EST: 1953
SQ FT: 10,000
SALES (est): 3.58MM **Privately Held**
Web: www.ashlandelectric.com
SIC: 3621 Motors, electric

(G-15467)
BOSTON SAND & GRAVEL COMPANY
69 N Coast Rd (03868-8628)
PHONE.................................603 330-3999
Don Hayward, *Admn Mgr*
EMP: 100
SALES (corp-wide): 100.01K **Privately Held**
Web: www.bostonsand.com
SIC: 3273 Ready-mixed concrete
PA: Boston Sand & Gravel Company Inc
100 N Washington St Fl 2
Boston MA 02114
617 227-9000

(G-15468)
BRADFORD WHITE CORP
20 Industrial Way (03867-4296)
PHONE.................................603 332-0116
Jason Fifer, *Mktg Mgr*
EMP: 9 EST: 2016
SALES (est): 209.83K **Privately Held**
Web: www.bradfordwhite.com
SIC: 3433 Heating equipment, except electric

(G-15469)
CHICK EMBROIDERY
556 Portland St (03867-2428)
PHONE.................................603 332-5487
Robert Chick, *Prin*
EMP: 9 EST: 2004
SALES (est): 76.14K **Privately Held**
Web: www.chickembroidery.com
SIC: 2395 Embroidery and art needlework

(G-15470)
COLLINS SPORTS CENTER LLC
Also Called: Collins
663 Columbus Ave (03867-3495)
PHONE.................................603 335-1417
Stephen Marcotte, *Pr*
EMP: 7 EST: 1984
SALES (est): 1.73MM **Privately Held**
Web: www.collinssports.net
SIC: 5091 2261 5941 Sporting and recreation goods; Screen printing of cotton broadwoven fabrics; Sporting goods and bicycle shops

(G-15471)
CONTITECH THERMOPOL LLC
35 Industrial Way Ste 204 (03867-6202)
PHONE.................................603 692-6300
Thomas Reichenbach, *Mgr*
EMP: 35
SALES (corp-wide): 40.93B **Privately Held**
Web: www.continental-industry.com
SIC: 3052 2822 Plastic hose; Synthetic rubber
HQ: Contitech Thermopol Llc
9 Interstate Dr

Somersworth NH 03878

(G-15472)
CUSTOM BANNER & GRAPHICS LLC
184 Milton Rd (03868-8712)
PHONE.................................603 332-2067
R Clay Prewitt, *Managing Member*
EMP: 7 EST: 2001
SQ FT: 8,000
SALES (est): 750K **Privately Held**
Web: www.custombanner.com
SIC: 2399 2269 2231 5131 Banners, made from fabric; Dyeing: raw stock, yarn, and narrow fabrics; Dyeing and finishing: wool or similar fibers; Synthetic fabrics, nec

(G-15473)
DESCO INDUSTRIES INC
73 Allen St (03867-1403)
PHONE.................................603 332-0717
Chris Haas, *Mgr*
EMP: 7
SALES (corp-wide): 49.98MM **Privately Held**
Web: www.descoindustries.com
SIC: 3629 Capacitors and condensers
PA: Desco Industries, Inc.
3651 Walnut Ave
Chino CA 91710
909 627-8178

(G-15474)
DMR INDUSTRIES INC
181 Milton Rd (03868-8714)
PHONE.................................603 335-0325
Darrel Robinson, *Pr*
Marie Robinson, *VP*
EMP: 9 EST: 1993
SQ FT: 7,000
SALES (est): 962.3K **Privately Held**
Web: www.dmrindustries.com
SIC: 3599 Machine shop, jobbing and repair

(G-15475)
DOVER FLEXO ELECTRONICS INC
Also Called: D F E
307 Pickering Rd (03867-4631)
PHONE.................................603 332-6150
Kenneth Ekola, *Pr*
Nancy Ekola, *
David Ekola, *OF BRD*
EMP: 35 EST: 1974
SQ FT: 18,000
SALES (est): 9.6MM **Privately Held**
Web: www.dfe.com
SIC: 7629 3823 3825 3625 Electrical equipment repair services; Flow instruments, industrial process type; Instruments to measure electricity; Relays and industrial controls

(G-15476)
FOSTERS DAILY DEMOCRAT
90 N Main St (03867-1925)
PHONE.................................603 332-2200
Scott Peter, *CFO*
EMP: 12 EST: 2019
SALES (est): 139.49K **Privately Held**
Web: www.fosters.com
SIC: 2711 Commercial printing and newspaper publishing combined

(G-15477)
GREAT BAY MANUFACTURING LLC
73 Pickering Rd Ste 101 (03839-4638)
PHONE.................................603 948-1212

Wayne M Trombly Junior, *Managing Member*
EMP: 12 **EST:** 2018
SALES (est): 990.62K **Privately Held**
Web:
great-bay-manufacturing.business.site
SIC: 3679   Electronic circuits

(G-15478)
HUMPHREYS INDUSTRIAL PDTS INC
Also Called: Rubber Group, The
22 Nadeau Dr (03867-4637)
PHONE..............................603 692-5005
Robert Pruyn, *Pr*
Robert Pruyn, *Pr*
Nadine Hayes, *
Peter F Burger, *
▲ **EMP:** 49 **EST:** 1986
SQ FT: 26,500
SALES (est): 13.51MM **Privately Held**
Web: www.rubber-group.com
SIC: 3069   Molded rubber products

(G-15479)
INTEC AUTOMATION INC
6 Industrial Way (03867-4296)
P.O. Box 1653 (03866-1653)
PHONE..............................603 833-9329
Brian Keith Crossan, *Pr*
Corey Margott, *
EMP: 35 **EST:** 1999
SALES (est): 5.43MM **Privately Held**
Web: www.intecautomation.com
SIC: 3599   Custom machinery

(G-15480)
JAEGER USA INC
198 Pickering Rd (03839-4643)
PHONE..............................603 332-5816
John Simmers, *Pr*
Peter Burger, *Sec*
▲ **EMP:** 18 **EST:** 1979
SQ FT: 20,291
SALES (est): 9.3MM
SALES (corp-wide): 2.67MM **Privately Held**
Web: www.jaeger-us.com
SIC: 3199 1799 2295   Boxes, leather; Caulking (construction); Chemically coated and treated fabrics
HQ: Gebruder Jaeger Gmbh
Otto-Hahn-Str. 7
Wuppertal NW 42369
202246560

(G-15481)
JARVIS COMPANY INC (PA)
100 Jarvis Ave (03868-8811)
PHONE..............................603 332-9000
Marshall N Jarvis Ii, *Pr*
EMP: 100 **EST:** 1901
SQ FT: 35,000
SALES (est): 23.2MM
SALES (corp-wide): 23.2MM **Privately Held**
Web: www.jarviscuttingtools.com
SIC: 3541 5084   Machine tools, metal cutting type; Machine tools and accessories

(G-15482)
JARVIS CUTTING TOOLS INC
100 Jarvis Ave (03868-8801)
PHONE..............................603 332-9000
Marshall Jarvis Ii, *Pr*
Scott Graff, *
EMP: 75 **EST:** 1901
SQ FT: 30,000
SALES (est): 8.65MM
SALES (corp-wide): 23.2MM **Privately Held**

Web: www.jarviscuttingtools.com
SIC: 3545   Machine tool accessories
PA: Jarvis Company, Inc.
100 Jarvis Ave
Rochester NH 03868
603 332-9000

(G-15483)
KW THOMPSON TOOL COMPANY INC
Also Called: Thompson Investment Casting
41 Old Dover Rd (03867-3445)
PHONE..............................603 330-8670
Tyler M Stone, *Pr*
Michael B Haley, *
▲ **EMP:** 100 **EST:** 1942
SQ FT: 100,000
SALES (est): 24.76MM **Privately Held**
Web:
www.thompsoninvestmentcastings.com
SIC: 5051 3366 3325 3324   Foundry products; Castings (except die), nec, brass; Alloy steel castings, except investment; Steel investment foundries

(G-15484)
LAARS HEATING SYSTEMS COMPANY
Also Called: Laars
20 Industrial Way (03867-4296)
PHONE..............................603 335-6300
Bob Carnevale, *CEO*
Angelo Sinisi, *VP*
William R Root, *VP*
Steven Bailey, *Prin*
Cynthia Cindiphillips, *Dir*
▲ **EMP:** 165 **EST:** 1960
SQ FT: 100,000
SALES (est): 41.96MM
SALES (corp-wide): 171.25MM **Privately Held**
Web: www.laars.com
SIC: 3443   Fabricated plate work (boiler shop)
PA: Bradford White Corporation
725 Talamore Dr
Ambler PA 19002
215 641-9400

(G-15485)
LDI SOLUTIONS LLC
145 Airport Dr (03867-1705)
PHONE..............................603 436-0077
Joshua Dame, *
◆ **EMP:** 26 **EST:** 2004
SALES (est): 9.41MM **Privately Held**
Web: www.ldisolutions.com
SIC: 5047 2221   Hospital furniture; Upholstery fabrics, manmade fiber and silk

(G-15486)
LIBERTY RESEARCH CO INC (PA)
7 Nadeau Dr (03867-4637)
P.O. Box 160 (48160-0160)
PHONE..............................603 332-2730
Derrick Perkins Junior, *Pr*
EMP: 40 **EST:** 1957
SQ FT: 40,000
SALES (est): 4.93MM
SALES (corp-wide): 4.93MM **Privately Held**
Web: www.expiredwixdomain.com
SIC: 3451   Screw machine products

(G-15487)
NEXTPHASE MEDICAL DEVICES LLC (PA)
Also Called: Meditron Devices

88 Airport Dr (03867-1706)
PHONE..............................201 968-9400
Carlo W Colesanti, *Pr*
James V Divizio, *
▲ **EMP:** 30 **EST:** 1999
SALES (est): 26.47MM
SALES (corp-wide): 26.47MM **Privately Held**
Web: www.nextphasemed.com
SIC: 3841   Surgical and medical instruments

(G-15488)
NEXTPHASE MEDICAL DEVICES LLC
88 Airport Dr (03867-1706)
PHONE..............................603 332-8900
EMP: 100 **EST:** 1995
SQ FT: 23,000
SALES (est): 22.78MM **Privately Held**
Web: www.nextphasemed.com
SIC: 3841   Surgical and medical instruments

(G-15489)
NORTHEASTERN NONWOVENS INC
7 Amarosa Dr Unit 3 (03868-8638)
PHONE..............................603 332-5900
Michael Roche, *Pr*
◆ **EMP:** 17 **EST:** 2005
SQ FT: 50,000
SALES (est): 4.07MM **Privately Held**
Web: www.nenonwovens.com
SIC: 2297   Nonwoven fabrics

(G-15490)
ROCHESTER USA
73 Allen St (03867-1403)
PHONE..............................603 332-0717
EMP: 7 **EST:** 2010
SALES (est): 243.27K **Privately Held**
SIC: 3821   Laboratory measuring apparatus

(G-15491)
ROKON INTERNATIONAL INC
Also Called: Rokon
50 Railroad Ave (03839-5229)
PHONE..............................603 335-3200
Thomas Blais, *Pr*
Bruce Osborne, *Sec*
▲ **EMP:** 10 **EST:** 1985
SQ FT: 15,800
SALES (est): 1.8MM **Privately Held**
Web: www.rokon.com
SIC: 3799   Recreational vehicles

(G-15492)
RP ABRASIVES & MACHINE INC
20 Spaulding Ave Unit 2 (03868-8730)
PHONE..............................603 335-2132
EMP: 12 **EST:** 1996
SALES (est): 1.66MM **Privately Held**
Web: www.rpabrasives.com
SIC: 3291   Abrasive products

(G-15493)
SERVICE EXPERTS LLC
38 Milton Rd (03868-8805)
PHONE..............................603 332-6466
EMP: 10 **EST:** 2019
SALES (est): 205.96K **Privately Held**
Web: www.serviceexperts.com
SIC: 2842 1711   Polishes and sanitation goods; Plumbing, heating, air-conditioning

(G-15494)
SPAULDING COMPOSITES INC (PA)
55 Nadeau Dr (03867-4637)

PHONE..............................603 332-0555
Donnita Rockwell, *CEO*
Douglas R Keslin, *
▲ **EMP:** 70 **EST:** 1873
SQ FT: 100,000
SALES (est): 20.15MM
SALES (corp-wide): 20.15MM **Privately Held**
Web: www.spauldingcom.com
SIC: 2821   Plastics materials and resins

Rollinsford
Strafford County

(G-15495)
JANCO INC (PA)
50 Goodwin Rd (03869-5002)
P.O. Box 857 (03821-0857)
PHONE..............................603 742-0043
Mark P Janetos, *Pr*
Louise Janetos, *
Kenneth H Swanson, *
Luke Janetos, *Stockholder*
Paul Janetos Junior, *Prin*
EMP: 79 **EST:** 1959
SQ FT: 50,000
SALES (est): 13.02MM
SALES (corp-wide): 13.02MM **Privately Held**
Web: www.janco-inc.com
SIC: 3089   Injection molding of plastics

(G-15496)
JANCO ELECTRONICS INC
50 Goodwin Rd (03869-5002)
P.O. Box 1309 (03821-1309)
PHONE..............................603 742-1581
Lewis E Janetos, *Ch Bd*
Rollins L Janetos, *
William Janetos, *
John Bickford, *
John C Bickford, *
EMP: 70 **EST:** 1985
SQ FT: 40,000
SALES (est): 15.63MM **Privately Held**
Web: www.janco-electronics.com
SIC: 3679   Electronic circuits

Rumney
Grafton County

(G-15497)
CUSTOM LOG HOMES
Also Called: Gordon Couresy & Sons
10 Coursey Ln (03266-4200)
PHONE..............................603 786-9082
Gordon Coursey, *Owner*
EMP: 10 **EST:** 1976
SALES (est): 871.34K **Privately Held**
SIC: 1521 2421 2411 1629   New construction, single-family houses; Sawmills and planing mills, general; Logging ; Land clearing contractor

(G-15498)
STONEWALL CABLE INC
126 Hawkensen Dr (03266-3548)
PHONE..............................603 536-1601
Jeffrey Paul Emery, *Pr*
Deborah J Emery, *
Jeffrey P Emery Ii, *Sec*
EMP: 65 **EST:** 1985
SQ FT: 15,000
SALES (est): 8.95MM **Privately Held**
Web: www.stonewallcable.com
SIC: 3357   Communication wire

Rye
Rockingham County

(G-15499)
KELLEY SOLUTIONS INC
Also Called: Kelley Direct Solutions
14 Browns Ct (03870-2615)
PHONE...............................603 431-3881
Lisa Finneral, *Pr*
Shaun Kelly, *Prin*
EMP: 7 EST: 1972
SALES (est): 847.85K **Privately Held**
Web: www.kelleysolutions.com
SIC: 2752 5112 Offset printing; Business
forms

(G-15500)
VERITAS PRESS LTD
271 Harbor Rd (03870-2413)
PHONE...............................603 379-2790
EMP: 9 EST: 2018
SALES (est): 77.7K **Privately Held**
Web: www.veritaspress.com
SIC: 2741 Miscellaneous publishing

Salem
Rockingham County

(G-15501)
**A TTM TECHNOLOGIES
COMPANY**
27 Northwestern Dr (03079-4844)
PHONE...............................603 870-4580
EMP: 9 EST: 2018
SALES (est): 2.04MM **Privately Held**
SIC: 3672 Printed circuit boards

(G-15502)
ADVANCED POLYMERICS INC
32 Hampshire Rd (03079-4204)
PHONE...............................603 328-8177
Stephen Jewitt, *Pr*
Kim Powers, *VP*
EMP: 9 EST: 2015
SQ FT: 3,000
SALES (est): 1.66MM **Privately Held**
Web: www.api-smartcoat.com
SIC: 2851 3479 1799 Coating, air curing;
Coating, rust preventive; Fireproofing
buildings

(G-15503)
ADVANCED PROGRAMS INC
21 Northwestern Dr (03079-4809)
PHONE...............................603 685-6748
EMP: 18
Web: www.advprograms.com
SIC: 3571 Electronic computers
PA: Advanced Programs, Inc.
7125 Riverwood Dr Ste A
Columbia MD 21046

(G-15504)
**ALLEN DATAGRAPH SYSTEMS
INC**
45a Northwestern Dr (03079-4809)
PHONE...............................603 216-6344
James Michael Elliott, *Pr*
Debby Elliott, *
Michael Elliott, *
▼ **EMP: 31 EST:** 1980
SQ FT: 28,000
SALES (est): 4.81MM **Privately Held**
Web: www.allendatagraph.com
SIC: 3577 3826 Computer peripheral
equipment, nec; Analytical instruments

(G-15505)
ANAREN CERAMICS INC
27 Northwestern Dr (03079-4844)
PHONE...............................603 898-2883
Raymond C Simione, *Pr*
EMP: 75 EST: 1985
SQ FT: 20,000
SALES (est): 23.45MM
SALES (corp-wide): 2.5B **Publicly Held**
SIC: 3672 3625 3679 Printed circuit boards;
Resistors and resistor units; Attenuators
HQ: Anaren, Inc.
6635 Kirkville Rd
East Syracuse NY 13057
315 432-8909

(G-15506)
ANDOVER CORPORATION
4 Commercial Dr (03079-2800)
PHONE...............................603 893-6888
John Cotton, *Pr*
▲ **EMP: 49 EST:** 1978
SQ FT: 44,000
SALES (est): 8.98MM **Privately Held**
Web: www.andovercorp.com
SIC: 3827 Optical instruments and
apparatus

(G-15507)
AP EXTRUSION INC
10 Manor Pkwy Ste E (03079-4864)
PHONE...............................603 890-1086
EMP: 14 EST: 1994
SQ FT: 11,000
SALES (est): 2.44MM **Privately Held**
Web: www.apextrusion.com
SIC: 3089 Injection molding of plastics

(G-15508)
APPLI-TEC INC
7 Industrial Way Ste 1 (03079-2817)
PHONE...............................603 685-0500
Timothy W Walsh, *Pr*
Michael Platts, *
EMP: 25 EST: 1984
SQ FT: 20,000
SALES (est): 13.21MM **Privately Held**
Web: www.appli-tec.com
SIC: 5169 2891 Chemicals and allied
products, nec; Adhesives and sealants

(G-15509)
ATLANTIC MICROTOOL
91 Stiles Rd Ste 207 (03079-5804)
PHONE...............................603 898-3212
Neil Robinson, *Prin*
EMP: 7 EST: 2014
SALES (est): 214.8K **Privately Held**
Web: www.atlanticmicrotool.com
SIC: 3544 Special dies and tools

(G-15510)
**BIO-CONCEPT LABORATORIES
INC**
13 Industrial Way (03079-2838)
PHONE...............................603 437-4990
EMP: 20
Web: www.pacelabs.com
SIC: 2879 8731 Insecticides and pesticides;
Medical research, commercial

(G-15511)
CASSIOPAE US INC
224 Main St Ste 3a (03079-3193)
PHONE...............................603 685-3223
EMP: 7 EST: 2019
SALES (est): 81.55K **Privately Held**
SIC: 7372 Prepackaged software

(G-15512)
CHAMBERLAIN COMPANIES INC
14 Delaware Dr (03079-4033)
PHONE...............................603 893-2606
Rebecca Janco, *CEO*
Douglas Fyffe, *
Rebecca R Janco, *
EMP: 36 EST: 1986
SQ FT: 23,000
SALES (est): 4.98MM **Privately Held**
Web: www.chamberlaincompanies.com
SIC: 5712 1751 2431 Customized furniture
and cabinets; Cabinet and finish carpentry;
Interior and ornamental woodwork and trim

(G-15513)
CHART INC
Also Called: Chart Dist & Stor Group
68 Stiles Rd Ste B (03079-2818)
PHONE...............................603 382-6551
Brian Mac Avoy, *Brnch Mgr*
EMP: 69
Web: www.chartindustries.com
SIC: 8711 3443 Petroleum, mining, and
chemical engineers; Fabricated plate work
(boiler shop)
HQ: Chart Inc.
407 7th St Nw
New Prague MN 56071
952 758-4484

(G-15514)
**CHERUBINO SEALCOATING
LMC LLC** ✪
103 Cluff Crossing Rd Apt M1 (03079)
PHONE...............................781 272-1020
John Cherubino, *Mgr*
EMP: 7 EST: 2023
SALES (est): 300.22K **Privately Held**
SIC: 2952 Asphalt felts and coatings

(G-15515)
CHYME
50 Northwestern Dr Ste 11 (03079-4810)
PHONE...............................603 893-7683
Cheryl Tsetsilas, *Prin*
EMP: 7 EST: 2019
SALES (est): 248.01K **Privately Held**
Web: www.chyme.me
SIC: 7372 Prepackaged software

(G-15516)
**COOKING SOLUTIONS GROUP
INC (HQ)**
Also Called: Bki Worldwide
23 Keewaydin Dr Ste 205 (03079-2857)
PHONE...............................603 893-9701
David A Dunbar, *Pr*
EMP: 18 EST: 2018
SALES (est): 911.39K
SALES (corp-wide): 4.03B **Publicly Held**
SIC: 3556 3631 Ovens, bakery; Household
cooking equipment
PA: The Middleby Corporation
1400 Toastmaster Dr
Elgin IL 60120
847 741-3300

(G-15517)
**DATA ELECTRONIC DEVICES
INC**
Also Called: Dataed
32 Northwestern Dr (03079-4810)
PHONE...............................603 893-2047
Victor Giglio, *CEO*
Raul Tejada, *
▲ **EMP: 125 EST:** 1966
SQ FT: 33,000
SALES (est): 53.3MM

SALES (corp-wide): 140.78MM **Privately
Held**
Web: www.emeraldems.com
SIC: 3621 3679 3672 Frequency converters
(electric generators); Electronic circuits;
Printed circuit boards
PA: Megatronics Us Ultimate Holdco Llc
1 Stiles Rd
Salem NH 03079
888 706-0230

(G-15518)
DIALOGIC (US) INC
18 Keewaydin Dr (03079-2839)
PHONE...............................603 890-7240
Mike Chapman, *Prin*
EMP: 47
SALES (corp-wide): 310.68MM **Privately
Held**
Web: www.dialogic.com
SIC: 3661 Telephone and telegraph
apparatus
HQ: Dialogic (Us) Inc.
216 Route 17 North # 301
Rochelle Park NJ 07662

(G-15519)
EDGE VELOCITY CORPORATION
68 Stiles Rd Ste G (03079-2818)
PHONE...............................603 912-5618
Paula Beauregard, *CEO*
Gerald D'avolico Junior, *Sec*
EMP: 8 EST: 2005
SQ FT: 1,700
SALES (est): 1.06MM **Privately Held**
Web: www.edgevelocity.com
SIC: 3663 Mobile communication equipment

(G-15520)
**ENTELLIGENCE COMPUTER
SVCS LLC**
287 Lawrence Rd Unit 1 (03079-4303)
PHONE...............................603 893-4800
George Mazraani, *Pt*
EMP: 9 EST: 2012
SQ FT: 1,200
SALES (est): 650.92K **Privately Held**
SIC: 7373 7372 8748 Office computer
automation systems integration; Business
oriented computer software; Systems
engineering consultant, ex. computer or
professional

(G-15521)
**ENTERASYS NETWORKS INC
(HQ)**
Also Called: Cabletron
9 Northeastern Blvd Ste 300 (03079)
PHONE...............................603 952-5000
Ed Meyercord, *CEO*
Michael Fabiaschi, *
Terry Schmid, *
Chris Crowell, *
Ken Arola, *
▲ **EMP: 60 EST:** 1988
SQ FT: 150,000
SALES (est): 99.68MM **Publicly Held**
Web: www.voteextreme.com
SIC: 3577 7373 3357 5045 Computer
peripheral equipment, nec; Local area
network (LAN) systems integrator;
Communication wire; Computers,
peripherals, and software
PA: Extreme Networks, Inc.
2121 Rdu Center Dr # 300
Morrisville NC 27560

(G-15522)
FABER INDUSTRIES LLC (HQ)
6 Northwestern Dr (03079-4810)
PHONE.....................................603 681-0484
Klaus Faber, *Ch Bd*
David Workman, *CEO*
Brenda Hood, *Contrlr*
▲ **EMP:** 14 **EST:** 1986
SALES (est): 10.98MM
SALES (corp-wide): 10.98MM **Privately Held**
Web: www.faberllc.com
SIC: 2821 Molding compounds, plastics
PA: Faber Family Associates Lpa
6 Northwestern Dr
Salem NH 03079
603 681-0484

(G-15523)
FABER POLIVOL LLC (DH)
6 Northwestern Dr (03079-4810)
PHONE.....................................603 681-0484
David Workman, *CEO*
Klaus Faber, *Pr*
EMP: 9 **EST:** 2006
SALES (est): 8.84MM
SALES (corp-wide): 10.98MM **Privately Held**
SIC: 3089 Injection molding of plastics
HQ: Faber Industries, Llc
6 Northwestern Dr
Salem NH 03079

(G-15524)
FBN PLASTICS INC
338 N Main St (03079-1286)
PHONE.....................................603 894-4326
Richard Bell, *Prin*
EMP: 9 **EST:** 2006
SALES (est): 452.03K **Privately Held**
Web: www.fbnplastics.com
SIC: 3089 Injection molding of plastics

(G-15525)
FIBERKRAFT INC
Also Called: Gates Mectrol, Inc.
3 Industrial Way (03079-2838)
PHONE.....................................603 621-0090
Steven Giles, *Pr*
Norman Giles, *
Patricia A Giles, *
EMP: 25 **EST:** 1971
SQ FT: 20,000
SALES (est): 4.58MM **Privately Held**
Web: www.fiberkraft.com
SIC: 5112 2759 2677 Business forms; Commercial printing, nec; Envelopes

(G-15526)
FIS SYSTEMS INTERNATIONAL LLC
Sungard
9 Northeastern Blvd Ste 400 (03079)
PHONE.....................................603 898-6185
EMP: 11
SALES (corp-wide): 14.53B **Publicly Held**
SIC: 7372 Business oriented computer software
HQ: Fis Systems International Llc
200 Campus Dr
Collegeville PA 19426
484 582-2000

(G-15527)
FIZZ TIME
Also Called: Bomb Cosmetics
11 Industrial Way Bldg C (03079-4840)
P.O. Box 442 (03087-0442)
PHONE.....................................603 870-0000
TOLL FREE: 877
EMP: 10 **EST:** 1999

SQ FT: 10,000
SALES (est): 664.71K **Privately Held**
SIC: 2844 Cosmetic preparations

(G-15528)
FOXX LIFE SCIENCES LLC (PA)
6 Delaware Dr (03079-4072)
PHONE.....................................603 890-3699
EMP: 12 **EST:** 2013
SALES (est): 4.54MM
SALES (corp-wide): 4.54MM **Privately Held**
Web: www.foxxlifesciences.com
SIC: 3085 Plastics bottles

(G-15529)
FRUGAL PRINTER INC
Also Called: Proofing House Press
47a Northwestern Dr (03079-4809)
PHONE.....................................603 894-6333
Matthew Hanna, *Pr*
Charles Miller, *VP*
John Borlaug, *Treas*
Jeff Hanson, *Sec*
EMP: 8 **EST:** 1987
SQ FT: 5,000
SALES (est): 234.51K **Privately Held**
Web: www.proofinghouse.com
SIC: 2752 Offset printing

(G-15530)
G & A MACHINE INC
168 Lawrence Rd (03079-3910)
PHONE.....................................603 894-6965
Michelle Alsup, *Pr*
Michelle Alsup, *Pr*
Lyn Alsup, *Clerk*
EMP: 20 **EST:** 1984
SALES (est): 705.78K **Privately Held**
Web: www.gandamachine.com
SIC: 3599 Machine shop, jobbing and repair

(G-15531)
GATES TPU INC
Also Called: Gates Mectrol, Inc.
9 Northwestern Dr (03079-4809)
PHONE.....................................603 890-1515
Jim Nicols, *CEO*
Ed Griffin Ctrl, *Prin*
John Zimmerman, *
Dave Carroll, *
◆ **EMP:** 50 **EST:** 1990
SQ FT: 25,000
SALES (est): 29.47MM
SALES (corp-wide): 3.57B **Publicly Held**
Web: www.gates.com
SIC: 5169 2821 Chemicals and allied products, nec; Plastics materials and resins
HQ: The Gates Corporation
1144 15th St Ste 1400
Denver CO 80202
303 744-1911

(G-15532)
GELPAC POLY USA INC
7 Raymond Ave Ste D (03079-2935)
PHONE.....................................603 685-8338
Alain Robillard, *Brnch Mgr*
EMP: 28
SALES (corp-wide): 2.56MM **Privately Held**
SIC: 2821 Plastics materials and resins
PA: Gelpac Poly Usa, Inc.
60 Fondi Rd
Haverhill MA 01832
978 372-3300

(G-15533)
GPD OPTOELECTRONICS CORP
7 Manor Pkwy (03079-2842)

PHONE.....................................603 894-6865
Oliver O Ward, *Pr*
Rufus R Ward, *
William Avery, *
EMP: 30 **EST:** 1973
SQ FT: 28,000
SALES (est): 6.44MM **Privately Held**
Web: www.gpd-ir.com
SIC: 3674 Semiconductor diodes and rectifiers

(G-15534)
GUIDEWIRE TECHNOLOGIES INC
26 Keewaydin Dr Ste D (03079-5803)
PHONE.....................................603 894-4399
Douglas Curtis, *Pr*
EMP: 24 **EST:** 1988
SQ FT: 13,000
SALES (est): 1.56MM **Privately Held**
Web: www.guidewiretech.com
SIC: 3829 3827 3496 Measuring and controlling devices, nec; Optical instruments and apparatus; Miscellaneous fabricated wire products

(G-15535)
HADCO CORPORATION (HQ)
12a Manor Pkwy (03079-2841)
PHONE.....................................603 421-3400
Andrew E Lietz, *Pr*
Horace H Irvine Ii, *Ch Bd*
Timothy P Losik, *
◆ **EMP:** 282 **EST:** 1966
SQ FT: 122,750
SALES (est): 365.43MM **Publicly Held**
SIC: 3672 Printed circuit boards
PA: Sanmina Corporation
2700 N 1st St
San Jose CA 95134

(G-15536)
HBN SHOE LLC
395 Main St Ste 6b (03079-2464)
PHONE.....................................603 622-0272
Michael Backler, *Pr*
Michael Backler, *Pr*
Howard Danabberg, *Dir*
Norman Soloway, *Dir*
Brian Hughes, *Ch*
◆ **EMP:** 7 **EST:** 1997
SQ FT: 800
SALES (est): 1.35MM **Privately Held**
Web: www.insolia.com
SIC: 5139 3089 Shoe accessories; Boot or shoe products, plastics

(G-15537)
HRO INC
Also Called: Ham Radio Outlet
224 N Broadway Ste D12 (03079-2145)
PHONE.....................................603 898-3750
Steve Davidson, *Mgr*
EMP: 9
SALES (corp-wide): 22.88MM **Privately Held**
Web: www.hamradio.com
SIC: 5731 3663 Radios, two-way, citizens band, weather, short-wave, etc.; Radio broadcasting and communications equipment
PA: Hro, Inc.
110 Tampico Ste 110 # 110
Walnut Creek CA 94598
925 933-1771

(G-15538)
HUSSMANN CORPORATION
10 Industrial Way (03079-5832)
P.O. Box 1237 (03079-1152)

PHONE.....................................603 893-7770
Scott Hall, *Mgr*
EMP: 34
SQ FT: 40,000
Web: www.hussmann.com
SIC: 5078 7623 3585 Commercial refrigeration equipment; Refrigeration repair service; Refrigeration and heating equipment
HQ: Hussmann Corporation
12999 St Charles Rock Rd
Bridgeton MO 63044
314 291-2000

(G-15539)
KEN-MAR LLC
2 Northwestern Dr (03079-4810)
PHONE.....................................603 898-1268
EMP: 30 **EST:** 1980
SQ FT: 16,000
SALES (est): 2.16MM **Privately Held**
Web: www.ken-mar-psf.com
SIC: 1761 7692 3444 Sheet metal work, nec ; Welding repair; Sheet metalwork

(G-15540)
KLEIN MARINE SYSTEMS INC ✪
11 Klein Dr (03079-1249)
PHONE.....................................603 893-6131
Robert Capps, *Pr*
Robert P Capps, *Pr*
Mike Williams, *Genl Mgr*
▲ **EMP:** 76 **EST:** 2023
SQ FT: 55,000
SALES (est): 15.87MM
SALES (corp-wide): 35.09MM **Publicly Held**
Web: www.mind-technology.com
SIC: 3812 5065 Sonar systems and equipment; Security control equipment and systems
PA: Mind Technology, Inc.
2002 Timberloch Pl # 550
The Woodlands TX 77380
281 353-4475

(G-15541)
KONCERT LLC
7 Stiles Rd Ste 102 (03079-4820)
PHONE.....................................800 955-5040
Latha Soundar, *Managing Member*
Senraj Soundar, *Managing Member**
EMP: 140 **EST:** 2004
SQ FT: 5,000
SALES (est): 10.72MM **Privately Held**
Web: www.koncert.com
SIC: 7372 Business oriented computer software

(G-15542)
LASER LIGHT ENGINES INC
8 Industrial Way Ste C6 (03079-4834)
PHONE.....................................603 952-4550
Doug Darrow, *CEO*
David J Parent, *VP Fin*
EMP: 10 **EST:** 2008
SALES (est): 963.02K **Privately Held**
Web: www.laserlightengines.com
SIC: 3699 Laser systems and equipment

(G-15543)
LONG ISLAND PIPE SUPPLY NH INC
Also Called: Long Island Pipe New Hampshire
50b Northwestern Dr Ste 5 (03079-4810)
PHONE.....................................603 685-3200
Robert Moss, *Pr*
EMP: 8 **EST:** 2006
SALES (est): 230.36K **Privately Held**

SIC: 3498   Fabricated pipe and fittings

(G-15544)
MEGATRNICS US ULTMATE HLDCO LL (PA)
Also Called: Emerald Ems
1 Stiles Rd (03079-4859)
PHONE...............................888 706-0230
Victor Giglio, *CEO*
Raul Tejada, *CFO*
EMP: 26 EST: 2019
SALES (est): 140.78MM
SALES (corp-wide): 140.78MM **Privately Held**
Web: www.emeraldems.com
SIC: 3621 3679 3672   Frequency converters (electric generators); Electronic circuits; Printed circuit boards

(G-15545)
MICRO-PRECISION TECH INC
10 Manor Pkwy Ste C (03079-4864)
PHONE................................603 893-7600
Vic Servello, *Brnch Mgr*
EMP: 20
SALES (corp-wide): 4.49MM **Privately Held**
Web: www.micropt.com
SIC: 3674   Hybrid integrated circuits
PA: Micro-Precision Technologies, Inc.
439 S Union St Unit 105
Lawrence MA 01843
978 688-1299

(G-15546)
MOVERAS LLC
22 Northwestern Dr (03079-4810)
PHONE................................877 866-8372
Bret P Morrison, *Managing Member*
EMP: 14 EST: 2006
SALES (est): 6.21MM **Privately Held**
Web: www.moveras.com
SIC: 3714   Motor vehicle engines and parts

(G-15547)
NATIONAL APERTURE INC
5 Industrial Way Ste 3a (03079-4866)
PHONE................................603 893-7393
George Mauro, *CEO*
William Grenier, *Pr*
Donna Mauro, *Treas*
EMP: 18 EST: 1971
SALES (est): 3.55MM **Privately Held**
Web: www.nationalaperture.com
SIC: 3827 3829   Optical instruments and apparatus; Measuring and controlling devices, nec

(G-15548)
NAZARIAN JEWELERS NH INC (PA)
Also Called: Nazarian Diamonds
203 S Broadway Ste 2 (03079-3377)
PHONE................................603 893-1600
Robert Nazarian, *Pr*
Stephen Nazarian, *VP*
Deborah Nazarian, *Sec*
EMP: 10 EST: 1991
SALES (est): 2.23MM **Privately Held**
Web: www.nazariandiamonds.com
SIC: 5944 3911 7389   Jewelry, precious stones and precious metals; Jewelry, precious metal; Appraisers, except real estate

(G-15549)
NEWDTC LLC
Also Called: Max Pro-Police & Armor
7 Industrial Way Ste 6b (03079-2817)

PHONE................................603 893-0992
▲ EMP: 12 EST: 2004
SQ FT: 15,000
SALES (est): 927.28K
SALES (corp-wide): 34.23B **Publicly Held**
SIC: 8711 3089   Engineering services; Plastics processing
HQ: 3m Technical Ceramics, Inc.
1922 Barranca Pkwy
Irvine CA 92606
949 862-9600

(G-15550)
NORA SYSTEMS INC (DH)
9 Northeastern Blvd (03079-1996)
PHONE................................603 894-1021
Andreas Mueller, *Pr*
◆ EMP: 60 EST: 1986
SQ FT: 100,000
SALES (est): 48.78MM
SALES (corp-wide): 1.3B **Publicly Held**
Web: www.nora.com
SIC: 3069   Flooring, rubber: tile or sheet
HQ: Nora Systems Gmbh
Hohnerweg 2-4
Weinheim BW 69469
620 180-6633

(G-15551)
NORDSON MEDICAL (NH) INC (HQ)
Also Called: Vention Medical
29 Northwestern Dr (03079-4809)
PHONE................................603 327-0600
Dan Croteau, *Pr*
▲ EMP: 102 EST: 1989
SALES (est): 52.81MM
SALES (corp-wide): 2.63B **Publicly Held**
Web: www.nordsonmedical.com
SIC: 3082 3069 3083   Tubes, unsupported plastics; Balloons, advertising and toy: rubber; Laminated plastics plate and sheet
PA: Nordson Corporation
28601 Clemens Rd
Westlake OH 44145
440 892-1580

(G-15552)
NOVIA CORPORATION
1 Northwestern Dr (03079-4809)
PHONE................................603 898-8600
Brad Forsythe, *CEO*
EMP: 40 EST: 2021
SALES (est): 2.89MM **Privately Held**
Web: www.cp-novia.com
SIC: 3444   Sheet metalwork

(G-15553)
ONVIO LLC (PA)
20 Northwestern Dr (03079-4810)
PHONE................................603 685-0404
Bret P Morrison, *Managing Member*
EMP: 19 EST: 2016
SALES (est): 6.44MM
SALES (corp-wide): 6.44MM **Privately Held**
Web: www.onviollc.com
SIC: 3545   Precision measuring tools

(G-15554)
ONVIO SERVO LLC
Also Called: Onvio
20 Northwestern Dr (03079-4810)
PHONE................................603 685-0404
Bret P Morrison, *Managing Member*
David Workman, *
John D Amico, *
▲ EMP: 200 EST: 2004
SQ FT: 20,000
SALES (est): 15.56MM **Privately Held**

Web: www.onviollc.com
SIC: 3566   Reduction gears and gear units for turbines, except auto

(G-15555)
PACE ANLYTICAL LF SCIENCES LLC
13 Industrial Way (03079-2838)
PHONE................................603 437-4990
Frank Tagliaferri, *Brnch Mgr*
EMP: 20
Web: www.pacelabs.com
SIC: 2879 8731   Insecticides and pesticides; Medical research, commercial
HQ: Pace Analytical Life Sciences, Llc
1311 Helmo Ave N
Oakdale MN 55128

(G-15556)
PROFITKEY INTERNATIONAL INC
50 Stiles Rd (03079-2845)
PHONE................................603 898-9800
Randy Keith, *Pr*
EMP: 25 EST: 1979
SALES (est): 3.28MM **Privately Held**
Web: www.profitkey.com
SIC: 7372 7379 7373 7371   Prepackaged software; Computer related consulting services; Value-added resellers, computer systems; Custom computer programming services

(G-15557)
RICOR USA INC
200 Main St Ste 1 (03079-3149)
PHONE................................603 718-8903
EMP: 7 EST: 2011
SALES (est): 956.71K **Privately Held**
Web: www.ricor.com
SIC: 3999   Manufacturing industries, nec

(G-15558)
ROTARY VACUUM PRODUCTS INC
7a Raymond Ave (03079-2949)
PHONE................................603 890-6001
David Mahoney, *CEO*
EMP: 9 EST: 2020
SALES (est): 909.51K **Privately Held**
Web: www.rotaryvac.com
SIC: 3679   Electronic circuits

(G-15559)
SCOTT ELECTRONICS INC (PA)
5 Industrial Way Ste 2d (03079-4886)
PHONE................................603 893-2845
John Metzemaekers, *Pr*
Jacqueline Metzemaekers, *
Cindy Goguen, *
EMP: 66 EST: 1986
SALES (est): 25.29MM
SALES (corp-wide): 25.29MM **Privately Held**
Web: www.scottelec.com
SIC: 3679   Harness assemblies, for electronic use: wire or cable

(G-15560)
SEICA
50a Northwestern Dr (03079-4827)
PHONE................................978 376-7254
EMP: 19 EST: 2018
SALES (est): 237.13K **Privately Held**
Web: www.seica-na.com
SIC: 3672   Printed circuit boards

(G-15561)
SHEERGARD CMPSITE SLUTIONS INC ✿
6 Industrial Way (03079-2837)
PHONE................................954 661-7372
Rajeev Singh, *CEO*
Rajeev Singh, *Pr*
EMP: 30 EST: 2023
SALES (est): 1.21MM **Privately Held**
SIC: 2822   Ethylene-propylene rubbers, EPDM polymers

(G-15562)
SKEYETRAC LLC
70 N Broadway (03079-2102)
PHONE................................603 898-8000
EMP: 10 EST: 2008
SALES (est): 996.74K **Privately Held**
Web: www.skeyetrac.com
SIC: 3812   Search and detection systems and instruments

(G-15563)
STANDEX INTERNATIONAL CORP (PA)
Also Called: Standex
23 Keewaydin Dr Ste 205 (03079-2857)
PHONE................................603 893-9701
David Dunbar, *Ch Bd*
Ademir Sarcevic, *VP*
Alan J Glass, *CLO*
Annemarie Bell, *Chief Human Resources Officer*
Sean Valashinas, *CAO*
EMP: 40 EST: 1955
SALES (est): 741.05MM
SALES (corp-wide): 741.05MM **Publicly Held**
Web: www.standex.com
SIC: 3549 3675 3585   Metalworking machinery, nec; Electronic capacitors; Refrigeration equipment, complete

(G-15564)
STELLAR MANUFACTURING INC
Also Called: Magnetometric Devices
10 Manor Pkwy Ste A (03079-4864)
PHONE................................978 241-9537
David Gecks, *Pr*
Carole Burns, *
EMP: 27 EST: 2004
SALES (est): 4.98MM **Privately Held**
Web: www.stellarmanufacturing.com
SIC: 3679 3672   Electronic circuits; Printed circuit boards

(G-15565)
STOCKERYALE INC
13 Red Roof Ln Ste 200 (03079-4211)
PHONE................................603 893-8778
EMP: 7 EST: 2019
SALES (est): 225.96K **Privately Held**
Web: www.stockeryale.com
SIC: 3674   Semiconductors and related devices

(G-15566)
STROLID INC
1 Stiles Rd (03079-4804)
PHONE................................978 655-8550
Vinnie Micciche, *CEO*
Shawna Behen, *Dir Opers*
Anthony Adamo, *Dir*
Josh Sack, *Dir*
EMP: 12 EST: 2014
SALES (est): 974.02K **Privately Held**
Web: www.strolid.com

SIC: 7372 Business oriented computer software

(G-15567)
TRI-K INDUSTRIES INC
8 Willow St Ste 2 (03079-2185)
PHONE...............................603 898-0811
EMP: 24
Web: www.tri-k.com
SIC: 2834 Pharmaceutical preparations
HQ: Tri-K Industries, Inc.
2 Stewart Ct
Denville NJ 07834
973 298-8850

(G-15568)
TUSCAN BRANDS LLC (PA)
63 Main St (03079-1924)
PHONE...............................781 365-2800
Joseph Faro, *Managing Member*
EMP: 14 **EST:** 2012
SALES (est): 30.5MM
SALES (corp-wide): 30.5MM **Privately Held**
Web: www.tuscanbrands.com
SIC: 2051 2099 Bread, cake, and related products; Food preparations, nec

(G-15569)
UNIVEX CORPORATION
3 Old Rockingham Rd (03079-2140)
PHONE...............................603 893-6191
John Tsiakos, *Pr*
Demitra Papadinis, *Sec*
Timothy Fidgeon, *Dir*
▲ **EMP:** 60 **EST:** 1948
SQ FT: 42,000
SALES (est): 9.24MM **Privately Held**
Web: www.univexcorp.com
SIC: 3556 Food products machinery

(G-15570)
VISIT WEI
43 Northwestern Dr (03079-4809)
PHONE...............................603 893-0900
EMP: 8 **EST:** 2014
SALES (est): 340.11K **Privately Held**
Web: www.wei.com
SIC: 3572 Computer storage devices

(G-15571)
WEATHER SOURCE LLC
1 Stiles Rd Ste 305 (03079-4804)
PHONE...............................844 813-2617
Mark Gibbas, *Prin*
EMP: 14 **EST:** 2015
SALES (est): 995.46K **Privately Held**
Web: www.weathersource.com
SIC: 7372 7374 7375 Prepackaged software ; Data processing service; On-line data base information retrieval

(G-15572)
WILLIS & PHAM LLC
3 Scotts Ter (03079-2471)
PHONE...............................603 893-6029
Ben Willis, *VP*
John Pham, *Pr*
EMP: 9 **EST:** 2000
SALES (est): 154.32K **Privately Held**
SIC: 3672 Circuit boards, television and radio printed

(G-15573)
WITHROW INC
Also Called: Pie Guy The
9 Hemlock Ln (03079-4252)
PHONE...............................603 898-8868
Michael Withrow, *Pr*

Lisa Withrow, *VP*
EMP: 17 **EST:** 2001
SQ FT: 8,000
SALES (est): 942K **Privately Held**
Web: www.wileyroadfoods.com
SIC: 2051 Cakes, pies, and pastries

(G-15574)
XP POWER LLC
45 Northwestern Dr (03079-4809)
PHONE...............................603 894-4420
Ken Peterson, *Brnch Mgr*
EMP: 10
Web: www.xppower.com
SIC: 3679 Electronic loads and power supplies
HQ: Xp Power Llc
455 E Trimble Rd
San Jose CA 95131

Salisbury
Merrimack County

(G-15575)
AG STRUCTURES LLC
96 Old Turnpike Rd (03268-5508)
PHONE...............................603 648-2987
James Mason, *Managing Member*
Lisa Mason, *Managing Member*
EMP: 9 **EST:** 1979
SALES (est): 769.89K **Privately Held**
Web: www.barnstore.com
SIC: 2452 Farm and agricultural buildings, prefabricated wood

(G-15576)
JOHN C WHYTE
43 Mutton Rd (03268-5313)
P.O. Box 1284 (03302-1284)
PHONE...............................603 530-1168
John Whyte, *Prin*
EMP: 7 **EST:** 2014
SALES (est): 214.05K **Privately Held**
SIC: 2411 Logging

Sanbornton
Belknap County

(G-15577)
NUDD CABINETRY
Also Called: Nudd Carpentry
133 March Rd (03269-2009)
PHONE...............................603 286-3160
Walter Nudd, *Prin*
EMP: 10 **EST:** 2016
SALES (est): 367.87K **Privately Held**
Web: www.nuddcabinetry.com
SIC: 2434 Wood kitchen cabinets

Sanbornville
Carroll County

(G-15578)
DALE E CRAWFORD
2453 Lovell Lake Rd (03872-4120)
PHONE...............................603 473-2738
Dale Crawford, *Prin*
EMP: 7 **EST:** 2008
SALES (est): 164.11K **Privately Held**
SIC: 2411 Logging

Sandown
Rockingham County

(G-15579)
DINO SOFTWARE
10 Loggers Ln (03873-2076)
PHONE...............................603 612-0418
Don Weed, *Prin*
EMP: 16 **EST:** 2015
SALES (est): 66.47K **Privately Held**
SIC: 7372 Prepackaged software

(G-15580)
NEXVAC INC (PA)
56 Giordani Ln (03873-2639)
PHONE...............................603 887-0015
Gary J Bouchard, *Pr*
Frank Dibenedetto, *VP Opers*
Peter Diforte, *CFO*
EMP: 11 **EST:** 2002
SQ FT: 1,000
SALES (est): 1.01MM
SALES (corp-wide): 1.01MM **Privately Held**
Web: www.nexvac.com
SIC: 3563 7699 Vacuum pumps, except laboratory; Industrial machinery and equipment repair

(G-15581)
ZORVINO VINEYARDS
226 Main St (03873-2636)
PHONE...............................603 887-8463
James Zanello, *Owner*
EMP: 15 **EST:** 2010
SALES (est): 1.4MM **Privately Held**
Web: www.zorvino.com
SIC: 2084 Wines

Seabrook
Rockingham County

(G-15582)
ADHESIVE ENGINEERING & SUPPLY
15 Batchelder Rd (03874-4402)
P.O. Box 1445 (03077-3445)
PHONE...............................603 895-4028
James Yeames, *Owner*
EMP: 10 **EST:** 2009
SALES (est): 431K **Privately Held**
SIC: 2891 Adhesives

(G-15583)
AERODYNAMICS LLC
Also Called: Aerodynamics Metal Finishing
142 Batchelder Rd (03874-4403)
PHONE...............................603 474-2547
Gregory Burizynski, *CEO*
Gregory Burizynski, *Pr*
John Mcdermott, *Treas*
EMP: 25 **EST:** 1988
SQ FT: 30,000
SALES (est): 4.31MM **Privately Held**
Web: www.aerodynamicsmetalfinishing.com
SIC: 3471 Electroplating of metals or formed products

(G-15584)
BARTON CORPORATION SALISBURY
Also Called: Barton
34 Folly Mill Rd Ste 4 (03874-4053)
P.O. Box 5787 (01952-0787)
PHONE...............................603 760-2669

Kenneth Brown, *Pr*
EMP: 7 **EST:** 1960
SALES (est): 625.96K **Privately Held**
Web: www.bartoncorporation.com
SIC: 2448 Pallets, wood

(G-15585)
BOCRA INDUSTRIES INC
140 Batchelder Rd (03874-4403)
PHONE...............................603 474-3598
Kirk Boswell, *Pr*
Richard Boswell, *Pr*
EMP: 22 **EST:** 1972
SQ FT: 20,000
SALES (est): 1.09MM **Privately Held**
Web: www.bocraindustries.com
SIC: 3545 3544 7692 Precision tools, machinists'; Special dies, tools, jigs, and fixtures; Welding repair

(G-15586)
CHARLES P BLOUIN INC (PA)
203 New Zealand Rd (03874-4117)
P.O. Box 2690 (03874-2690)
PHONE...............................603 474-3400
Joe Cullen, *Pr*
Joseph F Cullen Ii, *Pr*
Joe Cullen, *Pr*
Charles P Blouin Junior, *Ch Bd*
Roger Blouin, *'*
EMP: 125 **EST:** 1933
SQ FT: 40,000
SALES (est): 17.84MM
SALES (corp-wide): 17.84MM **Privately Held**
Web: www.cpblouin.com
SIC: 1711 3444 Warm air heating and air conditioning contractor; Sheet metalwork

(G-15587)
COCA-COLA BEVS NORTHEAST INC
Also Called: Coca-Cola
118 Stard Rd (03874-4199)
PHONE...............................603 926-0404
Don Girard, *Genl Mgr*
EMP: 22
Web: www.cokenortheast.com
SIC: 2086 Bottled and canned soft drinks
HQ: Coca-Cola Beverages Northeast, Inc.
1 Executive Park Dr # 330
Bedford NH 03110
603 627-7871

(G-15588)
COMMUNCTION CMPNENT FLTERS INC (PA)
Also Called: C C F
145 Batchelder Rd (03874-4500)
PHONE...............................603 294-4685
Dennis Nathan, *Pr*
Allen Cohen, *VP*
▲ **EMP:** 8 **EST:** 2006
SALES (est): 635.55K **Privately Held**
SIC: 3663 Radio and t.v. communications equipment

(G-15589)
CXE EQUIPMENT SERVICES LLC
Also Called: Cxe Equipment Services
33 Beckman Lndg (03874-4289)
PHONE...............................603 437-2477
EMP: 8 **EST:** 1997
SQ FT: 10,000
SALES (est): 809.9K **Privately Held**
SIC: 3674 Semiconductors and related devices

(G-15590)
DYNA ROLL INC
146 Batchelder Rd (03874-4403)
PHONE.................................603 474-2547
Cara Burzynski, *Pr*
EMP: 10 **EST:** 2004
SALES (est): 133.69K **Privately Held**
SIC: 3471 Electroplating of metals or formed products

(G-15591)
GESKUS STUDIOS & YRBK PUBG INC
10 Whitaker Way U2 (03874-4166)
PHONE.................................800 948-1120
EMP: 24 **EST:** 2019
SALES (est): 649.75K **Privately Held**
Web: www.wearegeskus.com
SIC: 2741 Miscellaneous publishing

(G-15592)
GLOBAL PALLET & PACKAGING LLC
148 Batchelder Rd (03874-4403)
PHONE.................................603 969-6660
EMP: 8 **EST:** 2004
SALES (est): 695.91K **Privately Held**
SIC: 2448 Pallets, wood

(G-15593)
HPM NH LLC
19 Batchelder Rd (03874-4402)
PHONE.................................603 474-1879
Norman Hurley, *Managing Member*
EMP: 16 **EST:** 1981
SQ FT: 5,200
SALES (est): 2.41MM **Privately Held**
Web: www.hurleyprecision.com
SIC: 3599 Machine shop, jobbing and repair

(G-15594)
INFINITE CREATIVE ENTPS INC (PA)
Also Called: Infinity Massage Chairs
72 Stard Rd (03874-4597)
PHONE.................................603 347-6006
Michael Garceau, *Pr*
James Coppins, *VP*
▲ **EMP:** 20 **EST:** 2004
SQ FT: 5,000
SALES (est): 21.05MM **Privately Held**
Web: www.icesigns.com
SIC: 3634 Massage machines, electric, except for beauty/barber shops

(G-15595)
IPOTEC LLC
35 Woodworkers Way (03874-4327)
PHONE.................................704 991-6978
▲ **EMP:** 13 **EST:** 1992
SQ FT: 5,000
SALES (est): 2.42MM
SALES (corp-wide): 14.02MM **Privately Held**
Web: www.ipotec.com
SIC: 2822 Synthetic rubber
PA: Marco Group, Llc
35 Woodworkers Way
Seabrook NH 03874
603 468-3600

(G-15596)
MARCO GROUP LLC (PA)
Also Called: Marco Rubber
35 Woodworkers Way (03874-4327)
P.O. Box 1150 (03874-1150)
PHONE.................................603 468-3600
Chad Belinsky, *Pr*

▲ **EMP:** 35 **EST:** 1980
SQ FT: 8,260
SALES (est): 14.02MM
SALES (corp-wide): 14.02MM **Privately Held**
Web: www.marcorubber.com
SIC: 5085 3053 Seals, industrial; Gaskets and sealing devices

(G-15597)
MARTIN INTL ENCLOSURES LLC
14 Woodworkers Way (03874-4327)
PHONE.................................603 474-2626
Mike Martin, *Pr*
EMP: 40 **EST:** 1996
SQ FT: 60,000
SALES (est): 8.24MM **Privately Held**
Web: www.martinenclosures.com
SIC: 3444 Metal housings, enclosures, casings, and other containers

(G-15598)
MICROVISION INC (PA)
20 London Ln (03874-4328)
P.O. Box 1651 (03874-1651)
PHONE.................................603 474-5566
Leonard M Kastrilevich, *Pr*
▼ **EMP:** 25 **EST:** 1998
SQ FT: 15,000
SALES (est): 2.6MM
SALES (corp-wide): 2.6MM **Privately Held**
Web: www.dorcglobal.com
SIC: 3829 Medical diagnostic systems, nuclear

(G-15599)
O BRIEN D G INC
1 Chase Park Rd (03874-4191)
PHONE.................................603 474-5571
Dan Beck, *Prin*
EMP: 7 **EST:** 2010
SALES (est): 165.63K **Privately Held**
SIC: 3643 Current-carrying wiring services

(G-15600)
PREMIER RECYCLING EQP INC
239 Walton Rd (03874-4547)
P.O. Box 238 (01833-0338)
PHONE.................................855 223-5859
Carolyn P Mowbray, *Pr*
EMP: 15 **EST:** 2011
SALES (est): 1.42MM **Privately Held**
Web: www.precontainers.com
SIC: 8711 5084 3559 Engineering services; Recycling machinery and equipment; Recycling machinery

(G-15601)
RESIN TECHNOLOGY GROUP LLC
Also Called: Resin Technology Group
167 Batchelder Rd (03874-4402)
PHONE.................................508 230-8070
▲ **EMP:** 63
SIC: 2891 7389 Adhesives; Packaging and labeling services

(G-15602)
RIVERSIDE SPECIALTY FOODS INC
1 Depot Ln (03874-4492)
P.O. Box 458 (03874-0458)
PHONE.................................603 474-5805
George Hannah, *Pr*
EMP: 8 **EST:** 2007
SALES (est): 174.11K **Privately Held**
SIC: 2099 Salads, fresh or refrigerated

(G-15603)
RUGGLES-KLINGEMANN MFG CO
34 Folly Mill Rd Ste 400 (03874-4053)
P.O. Box 1435 (03874-1435)
PHONE.................................603 474-8500
Robert Lord, *Prin*
EMP: 7
SALES (corp-wide): 2.25MM **Privately Held**
Web: www.r-kmfg.com
SIC: 3491 Industrial valves
PA: Ruggles-Klingemann Mfg Co
78 Water St
Beverly MA 01915
978 232-8300

(G-15604)
SCREEN GEMS INC
34 Folly Mill Rd Ste 2 (03874-4053)
P.O. Box 2275 (03874-2275)
PHONE.................................603 474-5353
Andrew P Skaff, *Pr*
William Skaff, *Sec*
EMP: 12 **EST:** 1989
SQ FT: 6,000
SALES (est): 1.39MM **Privately Held**
Web: www.screengemsnh.com
SIC: 2759 Screen printing

(G-15605)
SEABROOK MEDICAL LLC
15 Woodworkers Way (03874-4327)
PHONE.................................603 474-1919
Paul Barck, *Managing Member*
Paul A Barck, *Managing Member**
Joe Oldfield, *
Patrick Spearman, *
EMP: 145 **EST:** 1973
SQ FT: 55,000
SALES (est): 22.52MM
SALES (corp-wide): 88.16MM **Privately Held**
Web: www.archglobalprecision.com
SIC: 3842 Implants, surgical
PA: Scp Agp Llc
2600 S Telg Rd Ste 180
Bloomfield Hills MI 48302

(G-15606)
WILL-MOR MANUFACTURING LLC
153 Batchelder Rd (03874-4500)
PHONE.................................603 474-8971
Robert Rouillard, *Managing Member*
Fran Roman, *
Mike Kelly, *
EMP: 85 **EST:** 2009
SQ FT: 42,000
SALES (est): 12.26MM **Privately Held**
Web: www.will-mor.com
SIC: 3545 7692 3444 Precision tools, machinists'; Welding repair; Sheet metalwork

Silver Lake
Carroll County

(G-15607)
RICHARDSON MFG CO INC
4 High St (03875-5909)
P.O. Box 178 (03875-0178)
PHONE.................................603 367-9018
EMP: 8 **EST:** 1979
SQ FT: 5,000
SALES (est): 857.61K **Privately Held**

SIC: 3949 2339 2369 2329 Sporting and athletic goods, nec; Snow suits: women's, misses', and juniors'; Girl's and children's outerwear, nec; Down-filled clothing: men's and boys'

Somersworth
Strafford County

(G-15608)
ACLARA TECHNOLOGIES LLC
130 Main St (03878-3108)
PHONE.................................603 749-8376
EMP: 92
SALES (corp-wide): 4.95B **Publicly Held**
Web: www.hubbell.com
SIC: 3825 Instruments to measure electricity
HQ: Aclara Technologies Llc
77 West Port Plz Ste 5
Saint Louis MO 63146
314 895-6400

(G-15609)
AERO PRECISION EAST LLC
Also Called: Fall Machine Company, LLC
10 Willand Dr (03878-1400)
PHONE.................................603 750-7100
EMP: 81 **EST:** 1992
SQ FT: 25,000
SALES (est): 20.15MM **Privately Held**
SIC: 3599 Machine shop, jobbing and repair
PA: Aero Precision, Llc
2320 Commerce St
Tacoma WA 98402

(G-15610)
BAM LAB LLC
186 Blackwater Rd (03878-1208)
PHONE.................................603 973-9388
Benjamin Baumann, *Prin*
EMP: 8 **EST:** 2012
SALES (est): 134.85K **Privately Held**
Web: www.thisisbam.com
SIC: 2752 Commercial printing, lithographic

(G-15611)
BLUE DOLPHIN SCREENPRINT INC
22 Canal St Unit 425 (03878-3264)
PHONE.................................603 692-2500
TOLL FREE: 800
Jay J Meyer, *Pr*
Peter Meyer, *
EMP: 38 **EST:** 1989
SQ FT: 11,000
SALES (est): 4.67MM **Privately Held**
Web: www.printedtees.com
SIC: 7389 5699 2395 Apparel designers, commercial; Designers, apparel; Embroidery and art needlework

(G-15612)
COLBY FOOTWEAR INC
364 Route 108 (03878-1589)
PHONE.................................603 332-2283
Matthew H Krassner, *Pr*
Burton S Silberstein, *
EMP: 11 **EST:** 1959
SQ FT: 50,000
SALES (est): 373.8K **Privately Held**
SIC: 3144 Women's footwear, except athletic

(G-15613)
CONPROCO CORP (PA)
Also Called: Conproco
388 High St (03878-1411)
PHONE.................................603 743-5800
Christopher D Brown, *Pr*

Christopher Brown, *Pr*
Paul Kfoury, *Sec*
EMP: 18 **EST:** 1987
SALES (est): 4.95MM
SALES (corp-wide): 4.95MM **Privately Held**
Web: www.conproco.com
SIC: 3255 3272 Mortars, clay refractory; Concrete products, nec

(G-15614)
CONTITECH THERMOPOL LLC
10 Interstate Dr (03878-1209)
PHONE..............................603 692-6300
Thomas Reichenbach, *Mgr*
EMP: 40
SALES (corp-wide): 40.93B **Privately Held**
Web: www.continental-industry.com
SIC: 3052 2822 Plastic hose; Synthetic rubber
HQ: Contitech Thermopol Llc
    9 Interstate Dr
    Somersworth NH 03878

(G-15615)
CONTITECH THERMOPOL LLC (HQ)
9 Interstate Dr (03878-1210)
PHONE..............................603 692-6300
Greg Mc Cloud, *Managing Member*
Edward Cotter, *
Thomas Reichenbach, *
◆ **EMP:** 124 **EST:** 1992
SQ FT: 50,000
SALES (est): 61.87MM
SALES (corp-wide): 40.93B **Privately Held**
Web: www.continental-industry.com
SIC: 3052 2822 Plastic hose; Synthetic rubber
PA: Continental Ag
    Continental-Plaza 1
    Hannover NI 30175
    51193801

(G-15616)
ECO TOUCH INC
Also Called: Eco Touch
22 Canal St Unit 125 (03878-3264)
PHONE..............................603 319-1762
Anne Ruozzi, *CEO*
James Dudra, *CMO*
EMP: 7 **EST:** 2010
SALES (est): 1.25MM **Privately Held**
Web: www.fillingfactory.com
SIC: 3714 Cleaners, air, motor vehicle

(G-15617)
J-PAC LLC (HQ)
Also Called: J-Pac Medical
25 Ctr Rd (03878-2927)
PHONE..............................603 692-9955
Mark Florence, *Pr*
Mark Florence, *CEO*
Michael Dolge, *
EMP: 90 **EST:** 2010
SQ FT: 60,000
SALES (est): 17.71MM
SALES (corp-wide): 17.71MM **Privately Held**
Web: www.lso-inc.com
SIC: 2671 7389 Plastic film, coated or laminated for packaging; Packaging and labeling services
PA: Torque Medical Holdings, Llc
    437 Madison Ave
    New York NY 10022
    212 705-0143

(G-15618)
LABEL TECH LLC
16 Interstate Dr (03878-1236)
PHONE..............................603 692-2005
Patrick Brady, *CEO*
EMP: 110 **EST:** 1985
SQ FT: 38,000
SALES (est): 17.86MM **Privately Held**
Web: www.fortissolutionsgroup.com
SIC: 2754 2672 2671 Labels: gravure printing; Paper; coated and laminated, nec; Paper; coated and laminated packaging
PA: Fortis Solutions Group, Llc
    2505 Hawkeye Ct
    Virginia Beach VA 23452

(G-15619)
OMNI METALS COMPANY INC
14 Interstate Dr (03878-1238)
PHONE..............................603 692-6664
Gregory Merkley, *Pr*
Daniel Merkley, *
EMP: 24 **EST:** 1970
SQ FT: 20,000
SALES (est): 4.53MM **Privately Held**
Web: www.omnimetalsco.com
SIC: 3444 2821 3479 Sheet metal specialties, not stamped; Plastics materials and resins; Coating of metals and formed products

(G-15620)
PATEL BREW LLC
Also Called: Omnium Brewing
460 High St (03878-1012)
PHONE..............................603 602-7455
Jasmin Patel, *Prin*
EMP: 11 **EST:** 2021
SALES (est): 320.93K **Privately Held**
SIC: 2082 Malt beverages

(G-15621)
POPZUP LLC
22 Canal St Unit 358 (03878-3264)
PHONE..............................603 314-8314
EMP: 7 **EST:** 2015
SALES (est): 488.02K **Privately Held**
Web: www.popzup.com
SIC: 2099 Food preparations, nec

(G-15622)
PROFILE PRECISION MACHINE
350 Route 108 Unit 108 (03878-1563)
PHONE..............................603 692-4116
Brian Williams, *Owner*
EMP: 7 **EST:** 2007
SALES (est): 156K **Privately Held**
SIC: 3599 Machine shop, jobbing and repair

(G-15623)
RAYS TOOL & DIE CO INC
Also Called: RTD Technologies
360 Route 108 (03878-1589)
PHONE..............................603 692-5978
Marc Therrien, *Pr*
Raymond A Therrien, *Pr*
EMP: 8 **EST:** 1978
SQ FT: 2,400
SALES (est): 913.69K **Privately Held**
Web: www.rtd-tech.com
SIC: 3544 Special dies and tools

(G-15624)
RED FISH - BLUE FISH DYE WRKS
Also Called: Rfbf Dye Works
145 Green St (03878-2213)
PHONE..............................603 692-3900
EMP: 8 **EST:** 1994

SQ FT: 10,000
SALES (est): 502.12K **Privately Held**
Web: www.rfbfdyeworks.com
SIC: 2253 2759 Dyeing and finishing knit outerwear, excl. hosiery and glove; Commercial printing, nec

(G-15625)
SUMNER PRINTING INC
433 Route 108 (03878-2043)
PHONE..............................603 692-7424
Michael Sumner Davis, *Pr*
Robert Parsons, *
Michael May, *
▲ **EMP:** 40 **EST:** 1990
SQ FT: 24,000
SALES (est): 7.66MM **Privately Held**
Web: www.sumnerprinting.com
SIC: 2752 2759 2676 Offset printing; Commercial printing, nec; Sanitary paper products
HQ: Hoffmaster Group, Inc.
    2920 N Main St
    Oshkosh WI 54901
    920 235-9330

(G-15626)
THERMOPOL INC
13 Interstate Dr (03878-1210)
PHONE..............................603 692-6300
Shlomo Beitner, *Pr*
▲ **EMP:** 8 **EST:** 1992
SALES (est): 334.62K **Privately Held**
SIC: 3536 Hoists, cranes, and monorails

(G-15627)
TRI-STATE SEAFOODS INC
23 Interstate Dr (03878-1210)
PHONE..............................603 692-7201
Jeffrey Jordan, *Pr*
Fung Ly, *
Seng Ly, *
Chin Ly, *
EMP: 16 **EST:** 1985
SQ FT: 20,000
SALES (est): 3.03MM **Privately Held**
SIC: 5146 2092 Seafoods; Fresh or frozen packaged fish

South Acworth
Sullivan County

(G-15628)
R L BALLA INC
338 Beryl Mountain Rd (03607-4615)
P.O. Box 6 (03607)
PHONE..............................603 835-6529
Robert Balla, *Pr*
John Balla, *Treas*
Lyle Balla, *VP*
EMP: 15 **EST:** 1949
SALES (est): 627.48K **Privately Held**
SIC: 2421 1794 Lumber: rough, sawed, or planed; Excavation and grading, building construction

South Hampton
Rockingham County

(G-15629)
NBR DIAMOND TOOL CORP
22 Exeter Rd Unit 2 (03827-3617)
PHONE..............................603 394-2113
Nazareno B Renzi, *Pr*
EMP: 7 **EST:** 1976
SQ FT: 2,000
SALES (est): 465.18K **Privately Held**

SIC: 3542 Machine tools, metal forming type

Spofford
Cheshire County

(G-15630)
THOMAS INSTRUMENTS INC
1453 Route 9 (03462-4256)
P.O. Box 50 (03462-0050)
PHONE..............................603 363-4500
Lynn Thomas, *Pr*
Linda Thomas, *VP*
▲ **EMP:** 7 **EST:** 1988
SQ FT: 20,000
SALES (est): 983.29K **Privately Held**
SIC: 3829 3629 Measuring and controlling devices, nec; Blasting machines, electrical

Stewartstown
Coos County

(G-15631)
KHEOPS INTERNATIONAL INC (PA)
Also Called: Copper Lease
232 Us Route 3 (03576-5104)
P.O. Box 177 (03576-0177)
PHONE..............................603 237-8188
Mary Josee Viallant, *Pr*
Melanie Viallant, *
Mary Gueymard, *
▲ **EMP:** 23 **EST:** 1994
SQ FT: 15,000
SALES (est): 2.68MM **Privately Held**
Web: www.kheopsinternational.com
SIC: 3231 Ornamental glass: cut, engraved or otherwise decorated

Strafford
Strafford County

(G-15632)
SWEETS LOGGING & LAND CLEARIN
13 Scribner Rd (03884-6347)
PHONE..............................603 664-2349
EMP: 7 **EST:** 2009
SALES (est): 492.73K **Privately Held**
Web: sweetslogging.vpweb.com
SIC: 2411 Logging

Stratham
Rockingham County

(G-15633)
AUDIA WOODWORKING
161 Portsmouth Ave (03885-2206)
PHONE..............................603 817-1309
EMP: 10 **EST:** 2008
SALES (est): 85.66K **Privately Held**
SIC: 2431 Millwork

(G-15634)
ELECTROCRAFT INC (HQ)
2 Marin Way Ste 3 (03885-2613)
PHONE..............................855 697-7966
Tom Dalton, *Pr*
John Arico, *
Logan D Delany Junior, *Prin*
▲ **EMP:** 24 **EST:** 2004
SALES (est): 114.25MM **Privately Held**
Web: www.electrocraft.com

▲ = Import ▼ = Export
◆ = Import/Export

SIC: **3625** 3621 Relays and industrial controls; Electric motor and generator parts
PA: Dmi Technology Corp.
1 Progress Dr
Dover NH 03820

(G-15635)
ELECTROCRAFT NEW HAMPSHIRE INC
2 Marin Way Ste 3 (03885-2613)
PHONE..............................740 441-6208
EMP: 40
Web: www.electrocraft.com
SIC: 3621 Motors, electric
HQ: Electrocraft New Hampshire, Inc.
1 Progress Dr
Dover NH 03820
603 742-3330

(G-15636)
ITACONIX CORPORATION
2 Marin Way Ste 1 (03885-2613)
PHONE..............................603 775-4400
John Shaw, *CEO*
Kevin Matthews, *CEO*
John Shaw, *Pr*
Robin Cridland, *CFO*
Laura Denner, *Dir*
EMP: 13 **EST:** 2011
SQ FT: 27,000
SALES (est): 7.05MM
SALES (corp-wide): 5.6MM **Privately Held**
Web: www.itaconix.com
SIC: 2869 Industrial organic chemicals, nec
HQ: Itaconix (U.K.) Limited
1-2 Newtech Square
Deeside

(G-15637)
LINDT & SPRUNGLI (USA) INC (HQ)
1 Fine Chocolate Pl (03885-2592)
P.O. Box 276 (03885-0276)
PHONE..............................603 778-8100
Daniel Studer, *CEO*
◆ **EMP:** 240 **EST:** 1925
SQ FT: 122,000
SALES (est): 483.99MM **Privately Held**
Web: www.lindtusa.com
SIC: 2066 5149 5441 Chocolate; Chocolate; Candy
PA: Chocoladefabriken Lindt & Sprungli Ag
Seestrasse 204
Kilchberg ZH 8802

(G-15638)
M BRAUN INC
14 Marin Way (03885-2578)
PHONE..............................603 773-9333
▲ **EMP:** 57 **EST:** 1994
SALES (est): 18.02MM
SALES (corp-wide): 1.97B **Privately Held**
Web: www.mbraun.com
SIC: 3826 Analytical instruments
HQ: M. Braun Inertgas-Systeme Gmbh
Dieselstr. 31
Garching B. Munchen BY 85748
89326690

(G-15639)
MBRAUN
14 Marin Way (03885-2578)
PHONE..............................603 773-9333
▲ **EMP:** 64
SALES (est): 5.08MM **Privately Held**
Web: www.mbraun.com
SIC: 3845 Laser systems and equipment, medical

(G-15640)
TEN10 PRODUCTS LLC (PA) ✪
22 Wiggin Way (03885-2486)
PHONE..............................603 770-0502
Dean Cousins, *Managing Member*
EMP: 7 **EST:** 2022
SALES (est): 63.47K
SALES (corp-wide): 63.47K **Privately Held**
SIC: 2099 Food preparations, nec

(G-15641)
TIMBERLAND LLC (HQ)
Also Called: Timberland Company, The
200 Domain Dr (03885-2575)
PHONE..............................603 772-9500
Jim Pisani, *
Richard Orourke, *
◆ **EMP:** 500 **EST:** 1978
SQ FT: 246,000
SALES (est): 388.63MM
SALES (corp-wide): 11.61B **Publicly Held**
Web: www.timberland.com
SIC: 3144 2386 2329 2321 Women's footwear, except athletic; Coats and jackets, leather and sheep-lined; Coats (oiled fabric, leatherette, etc.): men's and boys'; Men's and boy's furnishings
PA: V.F. Corporation
1551 Wewatta St
Denver CO 80202
720 778-4000

Sunapee
Sullivan County

(G-15642)
ARLINGTON SAMPLE BOOK CO INC (PA)
100 Fernwood Point Rd (03782-3100)
PHONE..............................603 763-9082
James S Nichol, *Pr*
▲ **EMP:** 14 **EST:** 1971
SQ FT: 56,000
SALES (est): 891.8K
SALES (corp-wide): 891.8K **Privately Held**
SIC: 2399 2621 Book covers, fabric; Wallpaper (hanging paper)

Swanzey
Cheshire County

(G-15643)
E-Z CRETE LLC
126 Monadnock Hwy (03446-2114)
PHONE..............................603 313-6462
Brice Raynor, *Prin*
EMP: 12 **EST:** 2011
SALES (est): 1.05MM **Privately Held**
Web: www.ez-crete.com
SIC: 3272 Concrete products, nec

(G-15644)
MONRO INC
Also Called: Monro Muffler Brake
1042 W Swanzey Rd (03446-3219)
PHONE..............................603 352-7822
EMP: 9
SALES (corp-wide): 1.33B **Publicly Held**
Web: www.monro.com
SIC: 7539 7533 7534 7549 Wheel alignment, automotive; Muffler shop, sale or repair and installation; Tire retreading and repair shops; Emissions testing without repairs, automotive
PA: Monro, Inc.
200 Holleder Pkwy
Rochester NY 14615
585 647-6400

(G-15645)
MOORE NNTECHNOLOGY SYSTEMS LLC (DH)
Also Called: Nanotechsys
230 Old Homestead Hwy (03446-2120)
PHONE..............................603 352-3030
Len Chaloux, *Pr*
Tom Dupell, *
Mitch Schadler, *Managing Member*
Ralph Murray, *
Bob Cassin, *
EMP: 12 **EST:** 1997
SQ FT: 36,000
SALES (est): 23.8MM
SALES (corp-wide): 91.35MM **Privately Held**
Web: www.nanotechsys.com
SIC: 3827 5084 Optical instruments and lenses; Machine tools and accessories
HQ: Moore Tool Company, Inc.
599 Hollister Ave
Bridgeport CT 06607
203 366-3224

(G-15646)
TALBOT HILL HOLDINGS CORP
36 Denman Thompson Hwy (03446-3003)
PHONE..............................603 357-2523
Gary Barnard, *Pr*
EMP: 30 **EST:** 1989
SQ FT: 26,000
SALES (est): 2.68MM **Privately Held**
Web: www.moldproinc.com
SIC: 3544 3089 Industrial molds; Molding primary plastics

Tamworth
Carroll County

(G-15647)
NORTHERN FBRCTION SLUTIONS LLC
235 Ossipee Lake Rd (03886-4530)
PHONE..............................603 539-4333
EMP: 8 **EST:** 2016
SALES (est): 141.2K **Privately Held**
Web: www.northernfabricationsolutions.com
SIC: 3599 Machine shop, jobbing and repair

(G-15648)
OSSIPEE MOUNTAIN LAND CO LLC
844 Whittier Rd (03886)
P.O. Box 599 (03890-0599)
PHONE..............................603 323-7677
Jeffery Coombs, *Managing Member*
EMP: 30 **EST:** 1986
SQ FT: 20,000
SALES (est): 2.74MM **Privately Held**
Web: www.ossipeemountainlandcompany.com
SIC: 2411 5099 Logging camps and contractors; Firewood

(G-15649)
UNISTAR CORPORATION
Junction Of Rtes 25 & 113 East (03886)
P.O. Box 463 (03886-0463)
PHONE..............................603 323-9327
Michael Dionne, *Pr*
EMP: 8 **EST:** 1989
SQ FT: 4,000
SALES (est): 1.01MM **Privately Held**
SIC: 3599 Machine shop, jobbing and repair

(G-15650)
WINDY RIDGE CORPORATION
Also Called: Tamworth Granite
190 Ossipee Mountain Hwy (03886)
P.O. Box 32 (03886-0032)
PHONE..............................603 323-2323
Timothy E Brown, *Pr*
▲ **EMP:** 9 **EST:** 1982
SQ FT: 13,000
SALES (est): 2.3MM **Privately Held**
Web: www.windyridgecorp.com
SIC: 5082 5051 5211 3398 Logging equipment and supplies; Rope, wire (not insulated); Lumber and other building materials; Metal heat treating

Tilton
Belknap County

(G-15651)
ANM DONUTS INC
Also Called: Dunkin' Donuts
65 Laconia Rd (03276-5259)
PHONE..............................603 286-2770
George Gourgiotis, *Pr*
EMP: 25
SALES (corp-wide): 2.35MM **Privately Held**
Web: www.dunkindonuts.com
SIC: 5461 2051 Doughnuts; Doughnuts, except frozen
PA: A.N.M. Donuts, Inc.
541 W Main St
Tilton NH 03276
603 286-8929

(G-15652)
BARCO MANUFACTURING INC
Also Called: Barco Engineering Co
505 W Main St (03276-5014)
PHONE..............................603 286-3324
David Barbuto, *Pr*
EMP: 25 **EST:** 1961
SQ FT: 10,000
SALES (est): 239.89K **Privately Held**
SIC: 3599 3451 Machine shop, jobbing and repair; Screw machine products

(G-15653)
INNOVATIVE PAPER TECH LLC
Also Called: 3M
1 Paper Trail (03276-5250)
P.O. Box 739 (03276-0739)
PHONE..............................603 286-4891
▼ **EMP:** 54 **EST:** 2002
SALES (est): 9.48MM
SALES (corp-wide): 34.23B **Publicly Held**
SIC: 2621 Insulation siding, paper
PA: 3m Company
3m Center
Saint Paul MN 55144
651 733-1110

(G-15654)
JR HINDS CONST SERV
60 Ridge Rd (03276-5810)
PHONE..............................603 496-2344
Jeffrey Rhinds, *Prin*
EMP: 8 **EST:** 2008
SALES (est): 391.22K **Privately Held**
SIC: 3643 Current-carrying wiring services

(G-15655)
NES EMBROIDERY INC
Also Called: Callahan, Robert
100 Autumn Dr (03276-5935)
PHONE..............................603 293-4664
Robert Callahan, *Pr*

▲ **EMP:** 10 **EST:** 1992
SQ FT: 5,000
SALES (est): 223.19K **Privately Held**
Web: www.americanwatertreatment.net
SIC: 2395 2353　Embroidery and art
　needlework; Hats, caps, and millinery

(G-15656)
SEALITE USA LLC
Also Called: Avlite Systems
61 Business Park Dr (03276-5821)
PHONE..............................603 737-1310
▲ **EMP:** 17 **EST:** 2010
SALES (est): 6.28MM
SALES (corp-wide): 1.46B **Publicly Held**
Web: www.sealite.com
SIC: 3812　Search and navigation equipment
HQ: Canvas Sx, Llc
　6325 Ardrey Kell Rd Ste 4
　Charlotte NC 28277
　980 474-3700

(G-15657)
**SPINNAKER CONTRACT MFG
INC**
95 Business Park Dr (03276-5821)
PHONE..............................603 286-4366
Guy Nickerson, *Pr*
Clarke Nickerson, *
▲ **EMP:** 65 **EST:** 1997
SQ FT: 38,000
SALES (est): 24.76MM **Privately Held**
Web: www.spinnakercontract.com
SIC: 3699　Electrical equipment and
　supplies, nec

Troy
Cheshire County

(G-15658)
SURELL ACCESSORIES INC
198 N Main St (03465-2659)
P.O. Box 599 (03465-0599)
PHONE..............................603 242-7784
Darryl Meattey, *Pr*
▲ **EMP:** 16 **EST:** 1979
SQ FT: 4,000
SALES (est): 1.68MM **Privately Held**
Web: www.shopsurell.com
SIC: 2371 2386　Fur goods; Leather and
　sheep-lined clothing

Walpole
Cheshire County

(G-15659)
**BENSON WOODWORKING
COMPANY INC**
Also Called: Benson Woodhomes
6 Blackjack Xing (03608-4801)
PHONE..............................603 756-3600
Tedd Benson, *Pr*
Christine Benson, *
EMP: 80 **EST:** 1974
SQ FT: 12,500
SALES (est): 11.6MM **Privately Held**
Web: www.bensonwood.com
SIC: 2452 2439　Log cabins, prefabricated,
　wood; Timbers, structural: laminated lumber

(G-15660)
CHAMBERLAIN MACHINE LLC
17 Huntington Ln (03608-4214)
PHONE..............................603 756-2560
Robert E Boynton, *Pr*
Scott W Boynton, *
Judith O Boynton, *

◆ **EMP:** 47 **EST:** 1943
SQ FT: 50,000
SALES (est): 9.48MM **Privately Held**
Web: www.chamberlainmachine.com
SIC: 3599　Machine shop, jobbing and repair

(G-15661)
**FRANK W WHITCOMB CNSTR
CORP (PA)**
Also Called: Flw Associates
187 Whitcomb Rd (03608-4124)
P.O. Box 1000 (03608-1000)
PHONE..............................603 445-5555
Frank L Whitcomb, *Pr*
EMP: 10 **EST:** 1940
SQ FT: 10,000
SALES (est): 19.57MM
SALES (corp-wide): 19.57MM **Privately
Held**
SIC: 1611 1442　Resurfacing contractor;
　Gravel mining

(G-15662)
HICKS ENTERPRISES INC
65 Maplewood Cir (03608-4412)
P.O. Box 445 (03608-0445)
PHONE..............................603 756-3671
Randall Hicks, *Pr*
EMP: 31 **EST:** 1947
SQ FT: 12,000
SALES (est): 778.04K **Privately Held**
SIC: 3599　Machine shop, jobbing and repair

(G-15663)
WALPOLE CABINETRY
5 Lambro Ln (03608-4856)
P.O. Box 364 (03603-0364)
PHONE..............................603 826-4100
Thomas Perkins, *Owner*
EMP: 10 **EST:** 2005
SQ FT: 2,000
SALES (est): 730.26K **Privately Held**
Web: www.walpolecabinets.com
SIC: 2434　Wood kitchen cabinets

(G-15664)
WALPOLE CREAMERY LTD
532 Main St (03608-4470)
PHONE..............................603 445-5700
Robert Kasper Junior, *Pr*
EMP: 9 **EST:** 2011
SALES (est): 603K **Privately Held**
Web: www.walpolecreamery.com
SIC: 2024 5451 5963　Ice cream and frozen
　deserts; Ice cream (packaged); Ice cream
　wagon

Warner
Merrimack County

(G-15665)
MADGETECH INC (PA)
Also Called: Madgetech
6 Warner Rd (03278-4435)
PHONE..............................603 456-2011
Norman E Carlson, *Pr*
Suzan M Lehmann, *
▼ **EMP:** 28 **EST:** 1996
SQ FT: 6,400
SALES (est): 10.23MM
SALES (corp-wide): 10.23MM **Privately
Held**
Web: www.madgetech.com
SIC: 3823　Process control instruments

(G-15666)
MENTIS SCIENCES INC
40 Depot St (03278-4226)

PHONE..............................603 624-9197
John J Dignam, *Pr*
EMP: 40 **EST:** 1996
SQ FT: 30,000
SALES (est): 4.43MM **Privately Held**
Web: www.mentissciences.com
SIC: 8731 3769 3764　Commercial physical
　research; Nose cones, guided missiles;
　Guided missile and space vehicle engines,
　research & devel.

(G-15667)
R C BRAYSHAW & CO LLC (PA)
45 Waterloo St (03278-4221)
P.O. Box 91 (03278-0091)
PHONE..............................603 456-3101
Thomas C Brayshaw, *Pr*
EMP: 23 **EST:** 1979
SQ FT: 5,000
SALES (est): 5.16MM
SALES (corp-wide): 5.16MM **Privately
Held**
Web: www.rcbrayshaw.com
SIC: 2752　Offset printing

Weare
Hillsborough County

(G-15668)
BENJAMIN D KNAPP
108 Perkins Pond Rd (03281-5331)
PHONE..............................603 660-8172
Benjamin D Knapp, *Prin*
EMP: 7 **EST:** 2016
SALES (est): 221.54K **Privately Held**
SIC: 2411　Logging

(G-15669)
BIG FOOTE CRUSHING LLC
1225 River Rd (03281-4719)
P.O. Box 4 (03281-0004)
PHONE..............................603 345-0695
EMP: 9 **EST:** 2004
SALES (est): 762.02K **Privately Held**
SIC: 1442　Construction sand and gravel

(G-15670)
BRAZECOM INDUSTRIES LLC
45 B And B Ln (03281-5903)
PHONE..............................603 529-2080
EMP: 9 **EST:** 2006
SQ FT: 9,600
SALES (est): 1.1MM **Privately Held**
Web: www.brazecom.com
SIC: 3398　Metal heat treating

(G-15671)
J C B LEASING INC
14 B And B Ln (03281-5902)
PHONE..............................603 529-7974
Michael Brown, *Pr*
EMP: 13 **EST:** 1971
SQ FT: 50,000
SALES (est): 178.4K **Privately Held**
SIC: 3462 3531 1794　Construction or
　mining equipment forgings, ferrous;
　Backhoes, tractors, cranes, plows, and
　similar equipment; Excavation work

(G-15672)
JMD DUCT FABRICATION LLC
25 Brown Ridge Rd (03281-5003)
PHONE..............................603 235-9314
Dan Cerullo, *Prin*
EMP: 8 **EST:** 2010
SALES (est): 410.21K **Privately Held**
SIC: 3585　Parts for heating, cooling, and
　refrigerating equipment

(G-15673)
TANDEM KROSS LLC
Also Called: Tandemkross
490 S Stark Hwy (03281-5527)
PHONE..............................603 369-7060
EMP: 9 **EST:** 2012
SALES (est): 1.75MM **Privately Held**
Web: www.tandemkross.com
SIC: 3484 5961　Small arms; Fishing,
　hunting and camping equipment and
　supplies: by mail

Webster
Merrimack County

(G-15674)
SANTA CRUZ GUNLOCKS LLC
Also Called: STA Cruz Gun Locks
450 Tyler Rd (03303-7738)
PHONE..............................603 746-7740
Zsuzsa Tanos, *Pt*
Zsuzsa Tanos, *Pr*
▲ **EMP:** 7 **EST:** 1988
SALES (est): 486.3K **Privately Held**
Web: www.santacruzgunlocks.com
SIC: 3949　Cases, gun and rod (sporting
　equipment)

(G-15675)
WHITE MOUNTAIN IMAGING (PA)
1617 Battle St (03303-7319)
P.O. Box 216 (03268-0216)
PHONE..............................603 648-2124
Robert E Knowles, *Pr*
Richard T Donoghue, *VP*
Gary D Donoghue, *VP*
Thomas E Whitman, *Sec*
◆ **EMP:** 14 **EST:** 1981
SQ FT: 12,000
SALES (est): 22.78MM
SALES (corp-wide): 22.78MM **Privately
Held**
Web: www.whitemountainimaging.com
SIC: 5047 3559　Medical equipment and
　supplies; Chemical machinery and
　equipment

Wentworth
Grafton County

(G-15676)
KING FOREST INDUSTRIES INC
Also Called: King Pine Industries
968 Route 25 (03282)
P.O. Box 230 (03282-0230)
PHONE..............................603 764-5711
John King Junior, *Pr*
EMP: 82 **EST:** 1972
SQ FT: 35,000
SALES (est): 12.69MM
SALES (corp-wide): 31.15MM **Privately
Held**
Web: www.kingforest.com
SIC: 2421　Lumber: rough, sawed, or planed
PA: Kennebec Lumber, Co.
　105 S Main St
　Solon ME 04979
　207 643-2110

(G-15677)
PRECISION LUMBER INC
576 Buffalo Rd (03282-3417)
P.O. Box 158 (03282-0158)
PHONE..............................603 764-9450
Joe Robertie, *Pr*
Larry King, *
EMP: 57 **EST:** 1991

SQ FT: 1,800
SALES (est): 4.24MM **Privately Held**
Web: www.lumbernh.com
SIC: 2426 2421 Hardwood dimension and flooring mills; Kiln drying of lumber

West Lebanon
Grafton County

(G-15678)
BLAKTOP INC (PA)
73 Elm St W (03784-2606)
P.O. Box 5243 (03784-5243)
PHONE.................................603 298-8885
Stuart Close, *Pr*
Warren Ames Iii, *VP*
EMP: 24 EST: 1950
SALES (est): 4.51MM
SALES (corp-wide): 4.51MM **Privately Held**
Web: www.blaktop.com
SIC: 1611 2951 Highway and street paving contractor; Asphalt and asphaltic paving mixtures (not from refineries)

(G-15679)
CENTRICUT INC
2 Technology Dr (03784-1671)
PHONE.................................603 298-7849
EMP: 7 EST: 2015
SALES (est): 152.71K **Privately Held**
SIC: 3541 Machine tools, metal cutting type

(G-15680)
CENTRICUT MANUFACTURING LLC
16 Airpark Rd (03784-1674)
PHONE.................................603 298-6191
Patrick Byrne, *Pt*
EMP: 12 EST: 1987
SALES (est): 195.12K **Privately Held**
SIC: 3541 3548 Plasma process metal cutting machines; Welding apparatus

(G-15681)
CRH AMERICAS INC
Also Called: Arthur Whitcomb
35 Glen Rd (03784-1635)
PHONE.................................603 298-5959
Bruce Hazen, *Brnch Mgr*
EMP: 170
SALES (corp-wide): 32.72B **Privately Held**
Web: www.crhamericas.com
SIC: 3273 Ready-mixed concrete
HQ: Crh Americas, Inc.
900 Ashwood Pkwy Ste 600
Atlanta GA 30338
770 804-3363

(G-15682)
DCI TRAINING INC
Also Called: Dciamerica
1 Oak Ridge Rd Ste 8a (03784-3121)
P.O. Box 859 (03755-0859)
PHONE.................................603 643-6066
EMP: 7 EST: 1990
SQ FT: 700
SALES (est): 253.36K **Privately Held**
Web: www.csninc.net
SIC: 8299 8748 7372 Educational services; Educational consultant; Educational computer software

(G-15683)
ELECTRONICS FOR IMAGING INC
Vutek
79 E Wilder Rd Ste 1 (03784-3101)

PHONE.................................603 279-6800
Scott Shinlever, *Mgr*
EMP: 325
SALES (corp-wide): 1.1B **Privately Held**
Web: www.efi.com
SIC: 3555 5734 Printing trades machinery; Computer and software stores
HQ: Electronics For Imaging, Inc.
12 Innovatiion Way
Londonderry NH 03053

(G-15684)
MOTO TASSINARI LLC
2 Technology Dr (03784-1671)
PHONE.................................603 298-6646
Steven Tassinari, *Pr*
Scott Tassinari, *Treas*
Crystal Pringle, *Sec*
▲ EMP: 10 EST: 1995
SALES (est): 1.46MM **Privately Held**
Web: store.mototassinari.com
SIC: 3751 5571 Motorcycles and related parts; Motorcycle dealers

(G-15685)
MOUNTAINOGA LLC
134 Gould Rd (03784-1025)
PHONE.................................857 972-6446
Temitope Sobodu, *Prin*
EMP: 7 EST: 2021
SALES (est): 75.68K **Privately Held**
SIC: 2741 Miscellaneous publishing

(G-15686)
NEWPORT SAND & GRAVEL CO INC
Also Called: Carroll Concrete Co
301 Plainfield Rd (03784-2010)
P.O. Box 5223 (03784-5223)
PHONE.................................603 298-8777
Mark Lafave, *Mgr*
EMP: 10
SALES (corp-wide): 44.7MM **Privately Held**
Web: www.carrollconcrete.com
SIC: 3273 Ready-mixed concrete
PA: Newport Sand & Gravel Co., Inc.
8 Reeds Mill Rd
Newport NH 03773
603 298-0199

(G-15687)
NOVO NORDISK US BIO PROD INC
9 Technology Dr (03784-1673)
PHONE.................................603 298-3169
Peter Gariepy, *VP*
EMP: 175 EST: 2014
SALES (est): 42.35MM
SALES (corp-wide): 24.71B **Privately Held**
SIC: 2834 Pharmaceutical preparations
HQ: Novo Nordisk Inc.
800 Scudders Mill Rd
Plainsboro NJ 08536
609 987-5800

(G-15688)
PROGRESSIVE MANUFACTURING INC
20 Airpark Rd (03784-1740)
PHONE.................................603 298-5778
Patrick E Moynihan, *Pr*
EMP: 11 EST: 1999
SALES (est): 3.18MM **Privately Held**
Web: www.progressive-mfg.com
SIC: 3444 Sheet metalwork

(G-15689)
THERMAL ARC INC
82 Benning St (03784-3405)
PHONE.................................800 462-2782
Paul D Melnuk, *Ch Bd*
David L Dyckman, *
Steven W Fray, *Global Controller*
Patricia S Williams, *VP*
EMP: 84 EST: 1997
SQ FT: 215,000
SALES (est): 2.38MM
SALES (corp-wide): 2.59B **Publicly Held**
SIC: 3699 Electrical welding equipment
HQ: Thermal Dynamics Corporation
82 Benning St
West Lebanon NH 03784
603 298-5711

(G-15690)
THERMAL DYNAMICS CORPORATION (DH)
Also Called: Thermadyne
82 Benning St (03784-3403)
PHONE.................................603 298-5711
Shyam P Kambeyanda, *Pr*
Kevin Johnson, *
◆ EMP: 266 EST: 1917
SQ FT: 156,200
SALES (est): 47.68MM
SALES (corp-wide): 2.59B **Publicly Held**
Web: www.thermal-dynamics.com
SIC: 3541 5084 Plasma process metal cutting machines; Welding machinery and equipment
HQ: Victor Equipment Company
2800 Airport Rd
Denton TX 76207
940 566-2000

(G-15691)
TWIN STATE SAND & GRAV CO INC
73 Elm St W (03784-2606)
P.O. Box 5243 (03784-5243)
PHONE.................................603 298-8705
Warren Ames Iii, *Pr*
Stuart Close, *VP*
EMP: 8 EST: 1945
SALES (est): 2.46MM **Privately Held**
Web: www.twinstatesandandgravel.com
SIC: 1442 Construction sand and gravel

(G-15692)
WOODSTOCK SOAPSTONE CO INC
66 Airpark Rd (03784-1683)
PHONE.................................800 866-4344
Thomas Morrissey, *Prin*
Alan Bush, *VP*
Leonard E Morrissey, *Sec*
▲ EMP: 10 EST: 1978
SALES (est): 1.73MM **Privately Held**
Web: www.woodstove.com
SIC: 3433 1711 Stoves, wood and coal burning; Plumbing, heating, air-conditioning

West Nottingham
Rockingham County

(G-15693)
DYER S DOCKING SYSTEMS CORP
Also Called: Docking Systems
404 Stage Rd (03291-6110)
PHONE.................................603 942-5122
EMP: 11 EST: 1991
SQ FT: 9,500
SALES (est): 387.07K **Privately Held**

SIC: 3448 Docks, prefabricated metal

West Ossipee
Carroll County

(G-15694)
HOBBS TAVERN & BREWING CO LLC
2415 Route 16 (03890-6000)
P.O. Box 539 (03890-0539)
PHONE.................................603 539-2000
Nathan Deyesso, *Mng Pt*
Robert Finneron, *
Charles Fisphbein, *
EMP: 30 EST: 2014
SQ FT: 12,500
SALES (est): 2.12MM **Privately Held**
Web: www.hobbsbeer.com
SIC: 2082 5813 Beer (alcoholic beverage); Tavern (drinking places)

West Swanzey
Cheshire County

(G-15695)
HURRICANE FARM LLC
735 West Swanzey Rd (03469)
P.O. Box 583 (03469-0583)
PHONE.................................603 352-0053
John Parker-hansel Junior, *Pr*
EMP: 20 EST: 1989
SQ FT: 11,000
SALES (est): 4.78MM **Privately Held**
Web: www.turmoilcoolers.com
SIC: 3822 Air conditioning and refrigeration controls

(G-15696)
PORT-O-LITE COMPANY INC
1 Railroad St (03469)
P.O. Box 630 (03469-0630)
PHONE.................................603 352-3205
Peter C Delaney, *Pr*
Marilyn Woods, *VP*
EMP: 10 EST: 1952
SQ FT: 80,000
SALES (est): 884.76K **Privately Held**
Web: www.monadnockmillwork.com
SIC: 2431 Millwork

(G-15697)
RMA MANUFACTURING LLC
Also Called: Turmoil Manufacturing
735 W Swanzey Rd (03469)
P.O. Box 583 (03469-0583)
PHONE.................................603 352-0053
Ray Anderson, *Managing Member*
EMP: 20 EST: 2014
SQ FT: 11,000
SALES (est): 2.37MM **Privately Held**
Web: www.turmoilcoolers.com
SIC: 3822 Air conditioning and refrigeration controls

Westmoreland
Cheshire County

(G-15698)
POLYONICS INC
28 Industrial Park Dr (03467-4430)
PHONE.................................603 352-1415
▲ EMP: 32 EST: 1995
SALES (est): 6.07MM **Privately Held**
Web: www.polyonics.com

G
E
O
G
R
A
P
H
I
C

SIC: 2672 Adhesive papers, labels, or tapes: from purchased material

---

Whitefield
Coos County

(G-15699)
MOUNTAINTOP WOODWORKING LLC
22 Dusty Dr (03598-3310)
PHONE..................603 616-1160
Jason Homan, *Prin*
EMP: 7 **EST:** 2018
SALES (est): 233.25K **Privately Held**
Web: mountaintop-woodworking-llc.business.site
SIC: 2431 Millwork

(G-15700)
PRESBY PLASTICS INC
143 Airport Rd (03598-3427)
PHONE..................603 837-3826
David Presby, *Pr*
EMP: 25 **EST:** 2002
SALES (est): 5.48MM
SALES (corp-wide): 3.07B **Publicly Held**
Web: www.infiltratorwater.com
SIC: 3089 Septic tanks, plastics
PA: Advanced Drainage Systems, Inc.
4640 Trueman Blvd
Hilliard OH 43026
614 658-0050

Wilton
Hillsborough County

(G-15701)
ALUMINUM CASTINGS INC
Also Called: General Machine & Foundry
4 Hampshire Hills Ln (03086-5500)
P.O. Box 420 (03049-0420)
PHONE..................603 654-9695
Robert Paro, *Pr*
Mark Paro, *VP*
EMP: 7 **EST:** 1971
SQ FT: 43,000
SALES (est): 625.89K **Privately Held**
Web: www.diamondcasting.com
SIC: 3599 3544 Machine shop, jobbing and repair; Industrial molds

(G-15702)
API HOLDINGS INC (PA)
19 Stoney Brook Dr (03086-5025)
PHONE..................603 668-2648
Michael Dion, *Pr*
EMP: 7 **EST:** 2015
SALES (est): 2.23MM
SALES (corp-wide): 2.23MM **Privately Held**
Web: www.atlanticprefab.com
SIC: 2439 Trusses, wooden roof

(G-15703)
BURBAK COMPANIES
Also Called: Burbak Plastic
361 Forest Rd (03086-5136)
P.O. Box 669 (03086-0669)
PHONE..................603 654-2291
Jerry Greene, *Pr*
Louis Belanger, *
EMP: 100 **EST:** 1969
SQ FT: 30,000
SALES (est): 18.82MM **Privately Held**
SIC: 3089 3599 Injection molding of plastics ; Machine and other job shop work

(G-15704)
CUTTING TOOL TECHNOLOGIES INC
327 Forest Rd (03086-5135)
P.O. Box 720 (03086-0720)
PHONE..................603 654-2550
Harold F Armstrong, *Pr*
Bruce K Bakaian, *VP*
Linda Bakaian, *Treas*
EMP: 7 **EST:** 1984
SQ FT: 16,000
SALES (est): 886.1K **Privately Held**
Web: www.cuttingtooltech.com
SIC: 3545 Machine tool accessories

(G-15705)
KIMBALL PHYSICS INC
Also Called: K P I
311 Kimball Hill Rd (03086-5715)
PHONE..................603 878-1616
Charles K Crawford, *Pr*
EMP: 40 **EST:** 1969
SQ FT: 30,000
SALES (est): 6.73MM **Privately Held**
Web: www.kimballphysics.com
SIC: 3821 3829 Physics laboratory apparatus, nec; Measuring and controlling devices, nec

(G-15706)
MONADNOCK MOUNTAIN SPRING WATER INC
8 Mansur Rd (03086)
P.O. Box 518 (03086-0518)
PHONE..................603 654-2728
▲ **EMP:** 75 **EST:** 1987
SALES (est): 9.82MM **Privately Held**
Web: www.monadnockspring.com
SIC: 2086 5149 Bottled and canned soft drinks; Water, distilled

(G-15707)
PEP DIRECT LLC
19 Stoney Brook Dr (03086-5025)
PHONE..................603 654-6141
EMP: 100
SIC: 2771 Greeting cards

(G-15708)
ROSENCRNTZ GLDNSTERN BANKNOTES
6 Burns Hill Rd (03086-5006)
P.O. Box 150 (03055-0150)
PHONE..................603 654-6160
Michael Zielie, *Pr*
Sandra Zielie, *VP*
▲ **EMP:** 9 **EST:** 1992
SQ FT: 12,000
SALES (est): 194.2K **Privately Held**
Web: www.promotion-art.com
SIC: 2782 Checkbooks

(G-15709)
SOUHEGAN WOOD PRODUCTS INC
10 Souhegan St (03086-8700)
P.O. Box 120 (03086-0120)
PHONE..................603 654-2311
Randolph A Dunn, *Pr*
Elizabeth M Dunn, *VP*
▼ **EMP:** 18 **EST:** 1955
SQ FT: 30,000
SALES (est): 4.75MM **Privately Held**
Web: www.souheganwood.com
SIC: 2499 2493 Stoppers and plugs, wood; Reconstituted wood products

(G-15710)
SPECIAL HERMETIC PRODUCTS INC
Also Called: S H P
Riverview Mill 39 Souhegan St (03086)
P.O. Box 269 (03086-0269)
PHONE..................603 654-2002
Anthony Desantis, *Pr*
Lori Jensen, *
William C Sullivan, *
EMP: 30 **EST:** 1987
SQ FT: 15,000
SALES (est): 4.99MM **Privately Held**
Web: www.shp-seals.com
SIC: 3679 3678 Hermetic seals, for electronic equipment; Electronic connectors

(G-15711)
UFP SHELF 1 LLC
Also Called: Ufp Site Built, LLC
19 Stoney Brook Dr (03086-5025)
PHONE..................603 824-9690
Mark Beroney, *Pr*
Mike Ellerbrook, *VP*
EMP: 13 **EST:** 2020
SALES (est): 1.72MM
SALES (corp-wide): 9.63B **Publicly Held**
SIC: 3448 Prefabricated metal buildings and components
PA: Ufp Industries, Inc.
2801 E Beltline Ave Ne
Grand Rapids MI 49525
616 364-6161

(G-15712)
WATERWEAR INC
Also Called: H2o Wear
24 Howard St (03086-5424)
P.O. Box 687 (03086-0687)
PHONE..................603 654-5344
Richard P Lovett, *Pr*
▲ **EMP:** 25 **EST:** 1982
SQ FT: 12,000
SALES (est): 2.33MM **Privately Held**
Web: www.h2owear.com
SIC: 2339 2329 Bathing suits: women's, misses', and juniors'; Bathing suits and swimwear: men's and boys'

Winchester
Cheshire County

(G-15713)
2023 HOLDINGS LLC
Also Called: Plumb Pak
75 Plumb Pak Dr (03470-2928)
PHONE..................603 239-6371
Gary Hill, *Mgr*
EMP: 70
SALES (corp-wide): 48.21MM **Privately Held**
Web: www.elliottkieffer.com
SIC: 3432 Plumbing fixture fittings and trim
PA: 2023 Holdings Llc
1170 Main St
Newington CT 06111
603 239-6371

(G-15714)
INNOVATIVE MACHINE & SUP INC
40 Snow Rd (03470-2806)
PHONE..................603 239-8082
Terry Haskins, *Pr*
Sandy Lapointe, *Treas*
EMP: 14 **EST:** 1985
SQ FT: 12,000
SALES (est): 2.18MM **Privately Held**

Web: www.innovative-machine.com
SIC: 3599 Machine shop, jobbing and repair

(G-15715)
NEW HAMPSHIRE NOVELTY LLC (PA)
20 Snow Rd (03470-2806)
PHONE..................413 325-7648
Tina M Smith, *Managing Member*
EMP: 7 **EST:** 2019
SALES (est): 181.88K
SALES (corp-wide): 181.88K **Privately Held**
Web: www.newhampshirenoveltyllc.com
SIC: 3999 Manufacturing industries, nec

(G-15716)
RESURRECTION DEFENSE LLC
71 Richmond Rd (03470-2428)
PHONE..................603 313-1040
Zachary Nutting, *Prin*
EMP: 8 **EST:** 2016
SALES (est): 535.01K **Privately Held**
SIC: 3812 Defense systems and equipment

(G-15717)
TRI-STATE LOGGING LLC
46 Fullam Pond Rd (03470-2107)
PHONE..................603 499-1499
Jill Beaman, *Prin*
EMP: 7 **EST:** 2018
SALES (est): 445.61K **Privately Held**
SIC: 2411 Logging

(G-15718)
WINCHESTER PRECISION TECH LTD
41 Hildreth St (03470-3121)
PHONE..................603 239-6326
Barry A Bordner, *Pr*
Jason Perron, *VP*
▲ **EMP:** 19 **EST:** 1984
SALES (est): 4.92MM **Privately Held**
Web: www.winpretec.com
SIC: 3547 3599 3441 Rolling mill machinery ; Machine and other job shop work; Fabricated structural metal

---

Windham
Rockingham County

(G-15719)
A & R SAWYER CO INC
67 Rockingham Rd (03087-1304)
PHONE..................603 893-5752
Ryan Sawyer, *Pr*
Angela Sawyer, *VP*
Christine Davis, *Treas*
EMP: 7 **EST:** 1989
SQ FT: 20,000
SALES (est): 952.95K **Privately Held**
Web: www.arsawyer.com
SIC: 7389 2752 Printing broker; Commercial printing, lithographic

(G-15720)
AP DLEY CSTM LAMINATING CORP
6 Ledge Rd (03087-1509)
PHONE..................603 437-6666
Arthur P Dailey, *Pr*
EMP: 20 **EST:** 1984
SQ FT: 30,000
SALES (est): 4.76MM **Privately Held**
Web: www.apdailey.com
SIC: 2431 7389 Doors, wood; Laminating service

2024 Harris New England
Manufacturers Directory

▲ = Import ▼ = Export
◆ = Import/Export

(G-15721)
CAMBRIDGE HEART INC
Also Called: Cambridge Heart
7 Searles Rd (03087-1203)
PHONE..............................978 654-7600
Michael Goodine, *Brnch Mgr*
EMP: 12
Web: www.cambridgeheart.com
SIC: 3841 Diagnostic apparatus, medical
PA: Cambridge Heart, Inc.
124 Washington St
Foxborough MA 02035

(G-15722)
CDC ENTERPRISES LLC
3 Lexington Rd Unit 1a (03087-5500)
PHONE..............................603 437-3090
Sal Yebba, *Pr*
Robin Yebba, *VP*
Brian Reese, *VP*
EMP: 7 **EST:** 1988
SQ FT: 16,000
SALES (est): 799.15K **Privately Held**
Web: www.diecutusa.com
SIC: 2759 2675 2789 7389 Embossing on
paper; Die-cut paper and board;
Bookbinding and related work; Packaging
and labeling services

(G-15723)
CENTILLA CORPORATION
11 Bedros St (03087-1653)
PHONE..............................603 658-3881
William Mckone, *Prin*
Ray Southsworth, *Pr*
Susan Southsworth, *Sec*
Bill Mckone, *Dir*
EMP: 10 **EST:** 2005
SQ FT: 6,600
SALES (est): 987K **Privately Held**
Web: www.centilla.net
SIC: 5084 3572 5045 Industrial machinery
and equipment; Computer storage devices;
Computers, peripherals, and software

(G-15724)
CET TECHNOLOGY LLC
27 Roulston Rd A (03087-1286)
PHONE..............................603 894-6100
▲ **EMP:** 11 **EST:** 1987
SQ FT: 12,000
SALES (est): 1.79MM **Privately Held**
Web: www.cettechnology.com
SIC: 3559 Electronic component making
machinery

(G-15725)
**EQUIPMENT TECHNOLOGIES
INC**
Also Called: Eti
15 Cardiff Rd (03087-1262)
PHONE..............................603 548-0875
Jon Pelletier, *Pr*
▲ **EMP:** 17 **EST:** 1984
SALES (est): 2.63MM **Privately Held**
Web: www.equiptech.com
SIC: 3672 Printed circuit boards

(G-15726)
EVERSOLVE LLC
8 Woodvue Rd (03087-2113)
PHONE..............................603 870-9739
EMP: 7 **EST:** 1998
SALES (est): 340.65K **Privately Held**
Web: www.eversolve.com
SIC: 7372 Application computer software

(G-15727)
GILL DESIGN INC
3 Industrial Dr Unit 5 (03087-2014)
PHONE..............................603 890-1237
Joanne Gill, *Pr*
Milton Stewart, *Sec*
EMP: 8 **EST:** 1985
SALES (est): 916.98K **Privately Held**
Web: www.gilldesign.us
SIC: 3679 8711 Electronic circuits;
Engineering services

(G-15728)
HOMEFREE LLC
10 Industrial Dr Unit 11 (03087-2018)
P.O. Box 491 (03087-0491)
PHONE..............................603 898-0172
Jill G Robbins, *Managing Member*
Jill Grobbins, *Managing Member*
EMP: 21 **EST:** 2005
SQ FT: 9,000
SALES (est): 2.44MM **Privately Held**
Web: www.homefreetreats.com
SIC: 2052 Cookies

(G-15729)
**WHARF INDUSTRIES PRINTING
INC**
3 Lexington Rd Unit 2 (03087-5500)
P.O. Box 367 (03087-0367)
PHONE..............................603 421-2566
Michael Comeau, *Pr*
EMP: 21 **EST:** 1979
SALES (est): 656.8K **Privately Held**
Web: www.wharfindustries.com
SIC: 2752 Offset printing

(G-15730)
**WINDHAM WOOD INTERIORS
INC**
7 Marblehead Rd (03087-2335)
PHONE..............................781 932-8572
James Kusch, *Pr*
EMP: 7 **EST:** 1987
SALES (est): 518.55K **Privately Held**
SIC: 2431 Millwork

Wolfeboro
Carroll County

(G-15731)
GI PLASTEK LLC
5 Wickers Dr (03894-4323)
PHONE..............................603 569-5100
Lee Falgous, *
James M Lynam, *
Joel R Carpenter, *
Perry Ashley, *
▲ **EMP:** 435 **EST:** 1978
SALES (est): 24.3MM **Privately Held**
Web: www.psimp.com
SIC: 3089 Injection molded finished plastics
products, nec

(G-15732)
GI PLASTEK LTD PARTNERSHIP
5 Wickers Dr (03894-4323)
PHONE..............................603 569-5100
EMP: 39 **EST:** 1995
SQ FT: 3,000
SALES (est): 996.27K **Privately Held**
Web: www.psimp.com
SIC: 3089 Injection molding of plastics

(G-15733)
GLOBAL FILTRATION SYSTEMS
615 Center St (03894-4815)
P.O. Box 2166 (03894-2166)
PHONE..............................603 651-8777
EMP: 7 **EST:** 2015
SALES (est): 617.82K **Privately Held**
Web: www.globalfiltrationsystems.com
SIC: 3589 Water treatment equipment,
industrial

(G-15734)
**IMAGE AWNINGS
INCORPORATED**
509 S Main St (03894-4458)
PHONE..............................603 569-6680
Eric T Piper, *Pr*
Amy O Piper, *Sec*
EMP: 9 **EST:** 1987
SQ FT: 5,000
SALES (est): 600.07K **Privately Held**
Web: www.imageawnings.com
SIC: 2394 5999 Awnings, fabric: made from
purchased materials; Awnings

(G-15735)
PSI MOLDED PLASTICS NH INC
Also Called: GI Plastek Wolfeboro
5 Wickers Dr (03894-4323)
PHONE..............................603 569-5100
Daniel H Mills, *Pr*
Tad Vaughn, *
Gerry Gajewski, *
Steve So, *
Rick Collopy, *
◆ **EMP:** 95 **EST:** 2009
SALES (est): 4.17MM
SALES (corp-wide): 21.94MM **Privately
Held**
Web: www.psimp.com
SIC: 3089 Injection molding of plastics
PA: Psi Molded Plastics, Inc.
4900 Highway 501
Myrtle Beach SC 29579
843 347-4218

Wolfeboro Falls
Carroll County

(G-15736)
**PANORAMIC PUBLISHING
GROUP LLC**
Also Called: Dinning Out -Main Coast
83 Center St (03896)
P.O. Box 119 (03896-0119)
PHONE..............................603 569-5257
EMP: 10 **EST:** 1984
SALES (est): 538.45K **Privately Held**
Web: www.thelaker.com
SIC: 2711 Newspapers, publishing and
printing

Woodsville
Grafton County

(G-15737)
STEYN SYNDICATION
35 S Court St (03785-1019)
P.O. Box 30 (03785-0030)
PHONE..............................603 359-1683
Mark Steyn, *Prin*
EMP: 8 **EST:** 2012
SALES (est): 277.59K **Privately Held**
SIC: 2741 Miscellaneous publishing

RHODE ISLAND

Ashaway
Washington County

(G-15738)
**ASHAWAY LINE & TWINE MFG
CO**
24 Laurel St (02804-1515)
PHONE..............................401 377-2221
Pamela A Crandall, *Pr*
Steven Crandall, *
Kathryn Crandall, *
▲ **EMP:** 80 **EST:** 1824
SQ FT: 10,000
SALES (est): 7.94MM **Privately Held**
Web: www.ashawayusa.com
SIC: 2298 3949 3842 Cordage: abaca,
sisal, henequen, hemp, jute, or other fiber;
Strings, tennis racket; Sutures, absorbable
and non-absorbable

(G-15739)
EAGLE INDUSTRIES INC
Also Called: Eagle Electric
23 Gray Ln (02804-1205)
PHONE..............................401 596-8111
Daniel Holdridge, *CEO*
Daniel M Holdridge, *
James Holdridge Junior, *VP*
EMP: 35 **EST:** 2002
SQ FT: 13,100
SALES (est): 4.98MM **Privately Held**
Web: www.eagleelectric.com
SIC: 8711 1731 8742 3625 Engineering
services; Electrical work; Automation and
robotics consultant; Controls for adjustable
speed drives

(G-15740)
GREENVILLE READY MIX INC
Skunk Hill Rd (02804)
PHONE..............................401 539-2333
Ron Gendron, *Prin*
EMP: 7 **EST:** 2007
SALES (est): 88.66K **Privately Held**
Web: www.greenvillereadymix.com
SIC: 3273 Ready-mixed concrete

(G-15741)
HI TECH PROFILES INC
401 Main St (02804-1814)
PHONE..............................401 377-2040
Raymond Quinlan, *CEO*
▲ **EMP:** 31 **EST:** 1988
SQ FT: 50,000
SALES (est): 4.97MM **Privately Held**
Web: www.hitechprofiles.com
SIC: 2821 3089 Thermoplastic materials;
Extruded finished plastics products, nec

(G-15742)
HTP MEDS LLC
Also Called: Htp
15 Gray Ln (02804-1209)
PHONE..............................401 315-0654
EMP: 150
Web: usa.proterial.com
SIC: 3061 Medical and surgical rubber
tubing (extruded and lathe-cut)

(G-15743)
L L ROWE COMPANY
15 Gray Ln Ste 108 (02804-1210)
PHONE..............................781 729-7860
▲ **EMP:** 29

SIC: 3679 Electronic circuits

(G-15744)
L3 TECHNOLOGIES INC
Also Called: Chesapeake Sciences - Ashaway
15 Gray Ln Ste 202 (02804-1210)
PHONE.............................401 377-2300
Bill Birtcher, *Brnch Mgr*
EMP: 20
SALES (corp-wide): 17.06B **Publicly Held**
Web: www.l3harris.com
SIC: 3663 Telemetering equipment,
   electronic
HQ: L3 Technologies, Inc.
   600 3rd Ave Fl 34
   New York NY 10016
   321 727-9100

(G-15745)
TE CONNCTVITY PHENIX OPTIX INC
15 Gray Ln Ste 301 (02804-1210)
PHONE.............................401 637-4600
Kevin Rock, *Pr*
EMP: 143 EST: 2014
SQ FT: 15,000
SALES (est): 249.28K **Privately Held**
SIC: 3229 Fiber optics strands
HQ: Te Connectivity Mog Inc.
   501 Oakside Ave
   Redwood City CA 94063
   650 361-5292

Barrington
Bristol County

(G-15746)
BROUILLETTE WOODWORKING CO INC
Also Called: Heartwood Brouillette Building
48 Barrington Ave (02806-2317)
PHONE.............................401 499-4867
Donald Brouillette, *Prin*
EMP: 7 EST: 2004
SALES (est): 54.13K **Privately Held**
SIC: 2431 Millwork

(G-15747)
COVE HAVEN CORP
Also Called: Brewer's Cove Haven Marina
101 Narragansett Ave Unit 2 (02806-1014)
PHONE.............................401 246-1600
J Michael Keyworth, *Mgr*
EMP: 11
SQ FT: 15,000
SALES (corp-wide): 2.2MM **Privately Held**
SIC: 4493 5551 3732 Boat yards, storage
   and incidental repair; Marine supplies, nec;
   Boatbuilding and repairing
PA: The Cove Haven Corp
   155 E Boston Post Rd
   Mamaroneck NY 10543
   914 698-0295

(G-15748)
IMPERIA CORPORATION
306 Rumstick Rd (02806-4935)
PHONE.............................508 894-3000
Edwin S Barton Iii, *Pr*
EMP: 28 EST: 1965
SQ FT: 48,000
SALES (est): 462.36K **Privately Held**
Web: www.pirobase-imperia.com
SIC: 2434 2521 2431 Wood kitchen cabinets
   ; Cabinets, office: wood; Millwork

(G-15749)
RLCP INC
Also Called: Des Printing
262 New Meadow Rd (02806-3703)
PHONE.............................401 461-6560
Richard Holiday, *Pr*
EMP: 9 EST: 2008
SQ FT: 15,000
SALES (est): 183.18K **Privately Held**
SIC: 2759 Commercial printing, nec

(G-15750)
SIMPATICO SOFTWARE SYSTEMS INC
15 Blanding Ave (02806-1310)
PHONE.............................401 246-1358
EMP: 10
SALES (corp-wide): 1.59MM **Privately Held**
Web: www.simpaticosoftware.com
SIC: 7372 Prepackaged software
PA: Simpatico Software Systems, Inc.
   8 Atlantic Crossing
   Barrington RI 02806
   401 558-0001

Bristol
Bristol County

(G-15751)
136 EXPRESS PRINTING INC
Also Called: 136 Express Prtg & Copy Ctr
380 Metacom Ave (02809-5152)
PHONE.............................401 253-0136
Richard Luiz, *Pr*
Lynn Luiz, *VP*
EMP: 8 EST: 1987
SALES (est): 593.65K **Privately Held**
Web: 136expressprinting.wordpress.com
SIC: 2752 Offset printing

(G-15752)
ALDEN YACHTS CORPORATION
Also Called: Alden Yachts Brokerage
99 Poppasquash Rd Unit I (02809-1033)
PHONE.............................401 683-4200
EMP: 23 EST: 1909
SALES (est): 596.79K **Privately Held**
SIC: 3732 4499 7389 4493 Yachts, building
   and repairing; Boat and ship rental and
   leasing, except pleasure; Yacht brokers;
   Marinas

(G-15753)
APPLIED PLASTICS TECH INC
Also Called: Jam Consultant Services
45 Broadcommon Rd (02809-2721)
P.O. Box 45 (02809-0045)
PHONE.............................401 253-0200
Jane Mac Intyre, *Pr*
Andrew K Intyre Mac, *VP*
John Mac Intyre, *
EMP: 35 EST: 1979
SQ FT: 20,000
SALES (est): 2.77MM **Privately Held**
Web: www.ptfeparts.com
SIC: 3089 Injection molding of plastics

(G-15754)
ATLANTIC AUTOMATION GROUP LLC
Also Called: Orbit Motion Systems
19 Broadcommon Rd (02809-2768)
PHONE.............................401 424-1840
Elizabeth M Tanner Esq, *Admn*
EMP: 47
SALES (corp-wide): 539.87K **Privately Held**

SIC: 5084 7694 Industrial machinery and
   equipment; Electric motor repair
PA: Atlantic Automation Group, Llc
   125 Broadcommon Rd
   Bristol RI 02809
   401 213-3320

(G-15755)
BLUE HORSESHOE LLC
114 Aaron Ave (02809-1549)
PHONE.............................401 253-0037
Richard M Kulbieda, *Prin*
EMP: 9 EST: 2015
SALES (est): 116.79K **Privately Held**
SIC: 3462 Horseshoes

(G-15756)
BRISTOL BAGEL WORKS LTD
420 Hope St (02809-1806)
PHONE.............................401 254-1390
EMP: 10 EST: 1994
SALES (est): 495.77K **Privately Held**
Web: www.bristolbagelworks.com
SIC: 5461 2051 Bagels; Bread, cake, and
   related products

(G-15757)
C & C FIBRGLS COMPONENTS INC
75 Ballou Blvd (02809-2729)
PHONE.............................401 254-4342
Joseph Da Ponte, *Pr*
EMP: 14 EST: 1998
SQ FT: 23,000
SALES (est): 2.19MM **Privately Held**
Web: www.ccfci.com
SIC: 3732 Boatbuilding and repairing

(G-15758)
CLEAR CARBON & COMPONENTS INC
108 Tupelo St (02809-2810)
PHONE.............................401 254-5085
Matthew Dunham, *Pr*
EMP: 25 EST: 2004
SQ FT: 13,879
SALES (est): 2.45MM **Privately Held**
Web: www.clearcarbon.com
SIC: 3543 3544 3624 3089 Industrial
   patterns; Industrial molds; Carbon and
   graphite products; Panels, building:
   plastics, nec

(G-15759)
COMPONENT TECHNOLOGIES CORPORA
14 Griswold Ave (02809-2927)
PHONE.............................401 965-2699
Leeds Mitchell, *Owner*
EMP: 7 EST: 2010
SALES (est): 136.42K **Privately Held**
SIC: 3369 Aerospace castings, nonferrous:
   except aluminum

(G-15760)
COMPOSITE ENERGY TECH INC
Also Called: Goetz Composites
52 Ballou Blvd (02809-2728)
PHONE.............................401 253-2670
Chase Hogoboom, *Pr*
EMP: 35 EST: 2010
SQ FT: 38,000
SALES (est): 4.26MM **Privately Held**
Web:
www.compositeenergytechnologies.com
SIC: 3624 Fibers, carbon and graphite

(G-15761)
CUSTOM CENTRIC MACHINING LLC
Also Called: Custom Centric Machining
500 Wood St Ste 21 (02809)
PHONE.............................401 952-1804
Christopher Mello, *Owner*
EMP: 9 EST: 2016
SQ FT: 3,000
SALES (est): 349.31K **Privately Held**
SIC: 3549 Metalworking machinery, nec

(G-15762)
ELEMENT INDUSTRIES INC
Also Called: Gmt Composites
48 Ballou Blvd (02809-2728)
PHONE.............................401 253-8802
Jonathan Craig, *Pr*
▲ EMP: 10 EST: 1984
SQ FT: 12,000
SALES (est): 874.92K **Privately Held**
Web: www.gmtcomposites.com
SIC: 3732 Boats, fiberglass: building and
   repairing

(G-15763)
ERIC GOETZ CUSTOM SAILBOATS
15 Broadcommon Rd (02809-2721)
PHONE.............................401 253-2670
Eric Goetz, *Pr*
◆ EMP: 38 EST: 1975
SQ FT: 18,000
SALES (est): 660.21K **Privately Held**
Web:
www.compositeenergytechnologies.com
SIC: 3732 Yachts, building and repairing

(G-15764)
FAST FORWARD COMPOSITES INC
91 Broadcommon Rd (02809-2701)
PHONE.............................207 350-1773
Tomas Gonzalez Zenoz, *Pr*
EMP: 15 EST: 2015
SALES (est): 786.58K **Privately Held**
Web: www.fastforwardcomposites.com
SIC: 3731 Shipbuilding and repairing

(G-15765)
FORTUNE ROPE & METAL CO INC (PA)
67 Ballou Blvd (02809-2729)
PHONE.............................800 416-6595
▲ EMP: 11 EST: 1996
SQ FT: 15,000
SALES (est): 4.43MM **Privately Held**
Web: www.fortunerope.com
SIC: 3496 Miscellaneous fabricated wire
   products

(G-15766)
GECKO MARINE INC
Also Called: Zim Sailing
33 Broadcommon Rd Ste 1 (02809-2770)
PHONE.............................401 237-6117
Steve Perry, *Pr*
▲ EMP: 13 EST: 2016
SALES (est): 1.95MM **Privately Held**
Web: www.zimsailing.com
SIC: 3732 5551 Boats, fiberglass: building
   and repairing; Marine supplies and
   equipment

(G-15767)
GURIT (USA) INC
Also Called: Gurit Uk
115 Broadcommon Rd (02809-2714)

PHONE..................401 396-5008
Damian Bannister, *Pr*
Lance Hill, *Sls Dir*
▲ **EMP:** 54 **EST:** 2002
SALES (est): 10.24MM **Privately Held**
Web: www.gurit.com
SIC: 2891 Adhesives and sealants
PA: Gurit Holding Ag
    Ebnaterstrasse 79
    Wattwil SG 9630

(G-15768)
HALL INC
Also Called: Hall Spars & Rigging
33 Broadcommon Rd (02809-2721)
PHONE..................401 253-4858
◆ **EMP:** 60
Web: www.hallcomposites.com
SIC: 3365 3732 3535 3354 Masts, cast aluminum; Boatbuilding and repairing; Conveyors and conveying equipment; Aluminum extruded products

(G-15769)
HUESTIS MACHINE CORPORATION
Also Called: Huestis Medical
68 Buttonwood St (02809-3626)
P.O. Box 718 (02809-0718)
PHONE..................401 253-5500
▲ **EMP:** 40 **EST:** 1928
SALES (est): 7.48MM **Privately Held**
Web: www.huestis.com
SIC: 3844 3599 3841 3549 X-ray apparatus and tubes; Machine and other job shop work; Surgical and medical instruments; Metalworking machinery, nec

(G-15770)
JOSEPH A THOMAS LTD
Also Called: Bad Dog Tools
24 Broadcommon Rd (02809-2722)
P.O. Box 851 (02809-0998)
PHONE..................401 253-1330
Joseph Strong, *Pr*
Ann Strong, *VP*
▲ **EMP:** 20 **EST:** 1981
SQ FT: 4,800
SALES (est): 917.03K **Privately Held**
Web: www.baddogtools.com
SIC: 3291 3532 3423 Wheels, abrasive; Drills, bits, and similar equipment; Hand and edge tools, nec

(G-15771)
KINDER INDUSTRIES INC
Also Called: Aquidneck Awning
75 Tupelo St (02809-2843)
PHONE..................401 253-7076
Phillip Kinder, *Pr*
EMP: 12 **EST:** 1995
SALES (est): 1.12MM **Privately Held**
Web: www.kinderindustries.com
SIC: 2211 2394 Canvas; Awnings, fabric: made from purchased materials

(G-15772)
LENMARINE INC (PA)
Also Called: Bristol Marine
99 Poppasquash Rd Ste 1 (02809-1018)
PHONE..................401 253-2200
Andy Tyska, *Pr*
▼ **EMP:** 20 **EST:** 1998
SALES (est): 6.75MM
SALES (corp-wide): 6.75MM **Privately Held**
Web: www.bristolmarine.com
SIC: 3732 4493 Sailboats, building and repairing; Marinas

(G-15773)
LUTHERS REPAIR SHOP INC
Also Called: Luther's Welding
500 Wood St (02809-2342)
PHONE..................401 253-5550
Francis Luther Junior, *Pr*
Debra Luther, *Treas*
Ronald Gamon, *Sec*
EMP: 10 **EST:** 1934
SALES (est): 1.43MM **Privately Held**
Web: www.lutherswelding.com
SIC: 3441 7692 Fabricated structural metal; Welding repair

(G-15774)
M F ENGINEERING COMPANY INC
7 Peter Rd (02809-2621)
P.O. Box 4 (02809-0004)
PHONE..................401 253-6163
Paul Ferreira, *Pr*
EMP: 16 **EST:** 1976
SQ FT: 8,750
SALES (est): 2.4MM **Privately Held**
Web: www.mfeng.com
SIC: 3451 Screw machine products

(G-15775)
MOULDCAM INC
115 Broadcommon Rd (02809-2714)
PHONE..................401 396-5522
John Barnitt, *Pr*
Jamie Mirima, *Stockholder*
▲ **EMP:** 8 **EST:** 2010
SQ FT: 11,000
SALES (est): 683.66K **Privately Held**
Web: www.mouldcam.com
SIC: 3545 Machine tool accessories

(G-15776)
NEW YORK ACCESSORY GROUP INC
Also Called: I Shalom
500 Wood St Ste 21 (02809-2349)
PHONE..................401 245-6096
Allen Ferreira, *Mgr*
EMP: 56
SALES (corp-wide): 9.88MM **Privately Held**
Web: www.nyagroup.com
SIC: 2389 5137 5136 2353 Handkerchiefs, except paper; Women's and children's clothing; Men's and boy's clothing; Hats, caps, and millinery
PA: New York Accessory Group, Inc.
    411 5th Ave Rm 803
    New York NY 10016
    212 532-7911

(G-15777)
PHOENIX-TIMES PUBLISHING CO
Also Called: East Bay Newspapers
1 Bradford St (02809-1906)
P.O. Box 90 (02809-0090)
PHONE..................401 253-6000
Matthew D Hayes, *Pr*
EMP: 70 **EST:** 1930
SQ FT: 16,000
SALES (est): 5.76MM **Privately Held**
Web: www.eastbayri.com
SIC: 2711 Commercial printing and newspaper publishing combined

(G-15778)
RESOLUTE RACING LLC
77 Broadcommon Rd (02809-2730)
PHONE..................401 253-7384
EMP: 10 **EST:** 2019

SALES (est): 177.22K **Privately Held**
Web: www.resoluteracing.com
SIC: 3732 Boatbuilding and repairing

(G-15779)
ROBIN INDUSTRIES INC
Also Called: Robin Rug
125 Thames St (02809-1815)
P.O. Box 656 (02809-0656)
PHONE..................401 253-8350
Russell Karian, *Pr*
Gordon Karian, *
EMP: 23 **EST:** 1962
SQ FT: 100,000
SALES (est): 373.73K **Privately Held**
Web: www.robin-industries.com
SIC: 2273 5713 Rugs, braided and hooked; Floor covering stores

(G-15780)
SEAMLESS NORTH AMERICA
259 Franklin St (02809-3832)
P.O. Box 771 (02809-0999)
PHONE..................401 714-2925
Brad Cerilli, *Mgr*
EMP: 7 **EST:** 2018
SALES (est): 121.86K **Privately Held**
Web: www.sealegs.com
SIC: 3732 Boatbuilding and repairing

(G-15781)
SHANNON BOAT COMPANY INC
Also Called: Shannon Yachts
19 Broadcommon Rd (02809-2768)
PHONE..................401 253-2441
Walter Schulz, *Pr*
Morris Kellogg, *
William Ramos, *
EMP: 21 **EST:** 1975
SQ FT: 23,000
SALES (est): 698.76K **Privately Held**
Web: www.shannonyachts.com
SIC: 3732 Yachts, building and repairing

(G-15782)
THURSTON SAILS INC
112 Tupelo St (02809-2810)
PHONE..................401 254-0970
Steven K Thurston, *Pr*
Edward M Thurston, *VP*
Phyllis Thurston, *Treas*
Neil Thurston, *Sec*
▼ **EMP:** 9 **EST:** 1935
SQ FT: 15,000
SALES (est): 228.83K **Privately Held**
Web: www.thurstonsails.com
SIC: 2394 Sails: made from purchased materials

(G-15783)
TOWN OF BRISTOL
32 Ridge Rd (02809-1358)
PHONE..................401 787-6763
Ginny Hanson, *Prin*
EMP: 10
Web: www.bristolri.gov
SIC: 2621 Bristols
PA: Town Of Bristol
    10 Court St
    Bristol RI 02809
    401 253-7000

(G-15784)
TRI-MACK PLASTICS MFG CORP
55 Broadcommon Rd Ste 1 (02809-2730)
PHONE..................401 253-2140
Edward Mack Junior, *Pr*
Mary Popham, *
Jeff Popham, *
EMP: 83 **EST:** 1974

SALES (est): 20.58MM **Privately Held**
Web: www.trimack.com
SIC: 3089 Injection molding of plastics

(G-15785)
TXV AEROSPACE COMPOSITES LLC
Also Called: Txv Aerospace Composites
55 Broadcommon Rd Unit 2 (02809-2730)
PHONE..................425 785-0883
EMP: 13 **EST:** 2017
SALES (est): 4.3MM
SALES (corp-wide): 400.57MM **Privately Held**
Web: www.txvaero.com
SIC: 2821 Thermoplastic materials
HQ: Victrex Usa, Inc.
    300 Conshohocken State Rd # 120
    Conshohocken PA 19428

(G-15786)
WESTFALL MANUFACTURING CO
15 Broadcommon Rd (02809-2721)
P.O. Box 7 (02809-0007)
PHONE..................401 253-3799
Robert W Glanville, *Pr*
EMP: 10 **EST:** 1986
SQ FT: 10,000
SALES (est): 1.8MM **Privately Held**
Web: www.westfallstaticmixers.com
SIC: 3589 Water treatment equipment, industrial

Central Falls
Providence County

(G-15787)
CENTRAL FLS PLATE & WIN GL CO
Also Called: Central Falls Glass Co
481 Broad St (02863-2808)
PHONE..................401 722-1267
Robert R Lizotte, *Pr*
Kerryann Duquette, *Sec*
EMP: 12 **EST:** 1923
SQ FT: 1,200
SALES (est): 1.41MM **Privately Held**
Web: www.centralfallsglass.com
SIC: 5231 5719 3442 Glass; Mirrors; Store fronts, prefabricated, metal

(G-15788)
FULLER BOX CO INC
Also Called: Fuller Packaging
1152 High St (02863-1506)
P.O. Box 198 (02863-0198)
PHONE..................401 725-4300
EMP: 150
SALES (corp-wide): 21.81MM **Privately Held**
Web: www.fullerbox.com
SIC: 3069 2396 2653 2652 Battery boxes, jars, or parts, hard rubber; Apparel and other linings, except millinery; Corrugated and solid fiber boxes; Setup paperboard boxes
PA: Fuller Box Co., Inc.
    150 Chestnut St
    North Attleboro MA 02760
    508 695-2525

(G-15789)
HOPE-BFFNTON PCKGING GROUP LLC
575 Lonsdale Ave (02863-2414)
P.O. Box 6250 (02863-0624)
PHONE..................401 725-3646

(PA)=Parent Co (HQ)=Headquarters
✿ = New Business established in last 2 years

2024 Harris New England
Manufacturers Directory

725

GEOGRAPHIC

▲ **EMP:** 13 **EST:** 2002
SQ FT: 50,000
SALES (est): 899.96K **Privately Held**
Web: www.h-bpackaging.com
SIC: 2653   Boxes, corrugated: made from
purchased materials

(G-15790)
K&W WEBBING COMPANY
403 Roosevelt Ave (02863-3129)
PHONE..............................401 725-4441
Jerzy Wec, *Pr*
Stanley Wec, *Treas*
EMP: 18 **EST:** 2000
SQ FT: 20,000
SALES (est): 2.28MM **Privately Held**
Web: www.kwwebbing.com
SIC: 2241   Fabric tapes

(G-15791)
LEEDON WEBBING CO INC
86 Tremont St (02863-1439)
PHONE..............................401 722-1043
Robert Mackenzie, *Pr*
▲ **EMP:** 50 **EST:** 1941
SQ FT: 50,000
SALES (est): 5.1MM **Privately Held**
Web: www.leedonwebbing.com
SIC: 2241   Fabric tapes

(G-15792)
MARTIGNETTI COMPANIES RI
Also Called: Martignetti Companies
500 High St (02863-3131)
P.O. Box 1437 (02816-0026)
PHONE..............................401 722-8008
Carmine Martignetti, *Pr*
Carl Martignetti, *
▲ **EMP:** 172 **EST:** 1928
SALES (est): 4.24MM **Privately Held**
SIC: 5182 5181 2086   Liquor; Beer and
other fermented malt liquors; Bottled and
canned soft drinks
PA: Martignetti Corp.
500 John Hancock Rd
Taunton MA 02780

(G-15793)
**MURDOCK WEBBING
COMPANY INC (PA)**
27 Foundry St (02863-2348)
PHONE..............................401 724-3000
Craig Pilgrim, *CEO*
Don A De Angelis, *
Ed Brodeur, *
Vann Cummings, *
▲ **EMP:** 133 **EST:** 1936
SQ FT: 280,000
SALES (est): 23.07MM
SALES (corp-wide): 23.07MM **Privately
Held**
Web: www.murdockwebbing.com
SIC: 2241   Webbing, woven

(G-15794)
OSRAM SYLVANIA INC
Also Called: Glass Technologies Division
1193 Broad St (02863-1502)
PHONE..............................401 723-1378
Steve Sander, *Mgr*
EMP: 245
SQ FT: 50,000
SALES (corp-wide): 5B **Privately Held**
Web: www.sylvania-automotive.com
SIC: 3641 3498 3369   Electric lamps;
Fabricated pipe and fittings; Nonferrous
foundries, nec
HQ: Osram Sylvania Inc.
200 Ballardvale St Bldg 2
Wilmington MA 01887
978 570-3000

(G-15795)
REED GOWDEY COMPANY
Also Called: Gowdey Reed
325 Illinois St (02863-1935)
PHONE..............................401 723-6114
James H Wilson, *Prin*
▲ **EMP:** 7 **EST:** 1834
SQ FT: 6,000
SALES (est): 562.89K **Privately Held**
Web: www.gowdeyreed.com
SIC: 3552   Reeds, loom

(G-15796)
ROSCO MANUFACTURING LLC
Also Called: Rosco Manufacturing
500 High St (02863-3131)
PHONE..............................401 228-0120
Christopher D'angelo, *Pt*
EMP: 30 **EST:** 2009
SALES (est): 5.47MM **Privately Held**
Web: www.roscomanufacturing.com
SIC: 3599   Machine and other job shop work

(G-15797)
STOLBERGER INCORPORATED
Also Called: Wardwell Braiding Co.
1211 High St (02863-1505)
PHONE..............................401 724-8800
▲ **EMP:** 40 **EST:** 1987
SALES (est): 4.75MM **Privately Held**
Web: www.wardwell.com
SIC: 3552   Braiding machines, textile

(G-15798)
TASTEX CORPORATION
467 469 Roosevelt Ave (02863)
PHONE..............................401 727-2900
EMP: 21 **EST:** 1977
SALES (est): 2.49MM **Privately Held**
Web: www.tastexcorp.com
SIC: 2299   Yarns, specialty and novelty

(G-15799)
TOP SHELL LLC
Also Called: Pizza Gourmet
55 Conduit St Unit 1 (02863-1228)
PHONE..............................401 726-7890
Jack Parente, *Managing Member*
EMP: 7 **EST:** 2010
SALES (est): 419.04K **Privately Held**
SIC: 2099   Pizza, refrigerated: except frozen

(G-15800)
**VOGUE INDUSTRIES LTD
PARTNR**
Also Called: Safety Flag Company
82 Hadwin St (02863-1413)
P.O. Box 200 (02863-0200)
PHONE..............................401 722-0900
Norman E Bernson, *Mng Pt*
James Bernason, *
▲ **EMP:** 27 **EST:** 1953
SQ FT: 6,000
SALES (est): 4.12MM **Privately Held**
Web: www.safetyflag.com
SIC: 2399 5084   Banners, pennants, and
flags; Safety equipment

(G-15801)
**WARDWELL BRAIDING
MACHINE COMPANY (PA)**
Also Called: Wardwell Braiding Company
1211 High St (02863-1505)
P.O. Box 237 (02863-0237)
PHONE..............................401 724-8800
▲ **EMP:** 20 **EST:** 1911
SALES (est): 2.51MM
SALES (corp-wide): 2.51MM **Privately
Held**

Web: www.wardwell.com
SIC: 3552 3549   Braiding machines, textile;
Wiredrawing and fabricating machinery and
equipment, ex. die

(G-15802)
WHITTET-HIGGINS COMPANY
33 Higginson Ave (02863-2412)
P.O. Box 8 (02863-0008)
PHONE..............................401 728-0700
Andrew A O Brown, *Pr*
Susan O Brown, *
David A Brown, *
EMP: 50 **EST:** 1968
SQ FT: 38,000
SALES (est): 5.4MM **Privately Held**
Web: www.whittet-higgins.com
SIC: 3568   Power transmission equipment,
nec

Chepachet
Providence County

(G-15803)
CONCRETE PRODUCTS INC
36 Terry Ln (02814-2159)
P.O. Box U (02814-0721)
PHONE..............................401 568-8874
William J Hamill Iii, *Pr*
Avis Hamill, *VP*
EMP: 22 **EST:** 1960
SQ FT: 5,500
SALES (est): 2.17MM **Privately Held**
Web: www.concreteproductsinc.com
SIC: 1771 3272 5211   Concrete work;
Precast terrazzo or concrete products;
Masonry materials and supplies

(G-15804)
FROSTBITE CUPCAKES
230 Chestnut Oak Rd (02814-2145)
PHONE..............................508 801-6706
Leonard Mello, *Prin*
EMP: 7 **EST:** 2013
SALES (est): 268.19K **Privately Held**
SIC: 2051   Bread, cake, and related products

(G-15805)
JOSEF CREATIONS INC (PA)
Also Called: Fairdeal Mfg Co
141 Jackson School House Rd
(02814-1206)
P.O. Box 72796 (02907-0796)
PHONE..............................401 421-4198
Michael R Impagliazzo, *Pr*
Deborah Impagliazzo, *VP*
Joseph Impagliazzo, *Sec*
◆ **EMP:** 24 **EST:** 1952
SQ FT: 48,000
SALES (est): 2.5MM
SALES (corp-wide): 2.5MM **Privately Held**
SIC: 3961 2399 3499 3993   Costume jewelry
; Emblems, badges, and insignia; Novelties
and giftware, including trophies; Signs and
advertising specialties

Coventry
Kent County

(G-15806)
ARNOLD LUMBER CO
Also Called: Seaside Casual Furniture
11 Industrial Dr (02816-8928)
PHONE..............................401 792-0979
Paul Evans, *Brnch Mgr*
EMP: 31
SALES (corp-wide): 189MM **Privately
Held**

Web: www.seasidecasual.com
SIC: 5211 5712 2519   Insulation material,
building; Furniture stores; Lawn and garden
furniture, except wood and metal
PA: Arnold Lumber Co.
251 Fairgrounds Rd
West Kingston RI 02892
401 783-2266

(G-15807)
BARRETTE FABRICATION LLC
46 Capwell Ave (02816-5406)
PHONE..............................401 996-6691
EMP: 15
Web: www.barrettefabrication.com
SIC: 3999   Barrettes
PA: Barrette Fabrication, Llc
1077 Toll Gate Rd
Warwick RI 02886

(G-15808)
CAL CHEMICAL CORPORATION
592 Arnold Rd (02816-4108)
P.O. Box 1452 (02816-0027)
PHONE..............................401 821-0320
Charles Lamendola, *Pr*
Joan Lamendola, *Sec*
▲ **EMP:** 20 **EST:** 1961
SQ FT: 40,000
SALES (est): 3.31MM **Privately Held**
SIC: 2869 2819   Industrial organic
chemicals, nec; Industrial inorganic
chemicals, nec

(G-15809)
CLARIANT CORPORATION
Also Called: Pigments Division
500 Washington St (02816-5469)
PHONE..............................401 823-2000
John Clocke, *Mgr*
EMP: 325
Web: www.clariant.com
SIC: 2865 2869 2819 3699   Dyes and
pigments; Industrial organic chemicals, nec;
Industrial inorganic chemicals, nec; Laser
systems and equipment
HQ: Clariant Corporation
500 E Morehead St Ste 400
Charlotte NC 28202
704 331-7000

(G-15810)
**COLONIAL MACHINE & TOOL
CO INC**
5 Salvas Ave (02816-4128)
PHONE..............................401 826-1883
Linda Masiello, *VP*
Harry Masiello, *
EMP: 40 **EST:** 1962
SQ FT: 31,500
SALES (est): 5.2MM **Privately Held**
Web: www.colonialmachine.com
SIC: 3599   Machine shop, jobbing and repair

(G-15811)
**CONCORDIA MANUFACTURING
LLC**
Also Called: Concordia Fibers
4 Laurel Ave (02816-5323)
PHONE..............................401 828-1100
▲ **EMP:** 70 **EST:** 1920
SALES (est): 8.15MM **Privately Held**
Web: www.concordiafibers.com
SIC: 2299 2281   Yarns, specialty and novelty
; Yarn spinning mills

(G-15812)
CUSTOM IRON WORKS INC
1600 Flat River Rd (02816-8904)

PHONE.................................401 826-3310
Jacqueline Grace, *Pr*
Jackie Grace, *Pr*
Brian Grace, *VP*
EMP: 22 **EST:** 1995
SQ FT: 2,300
SALES (est): 4.78MM **Privately Held**
Web: www.customironworksri.com
SIC: 1796 3446 1799 3441   Installing building equipment; Stairs, staircases, stair treads: prefabricated metal; Fence construction; Fabricated structural metal

(G-15813)
G&G TECHNOLOGIES INC
6 Grandview St (02816-4116)
PHONE.................................401 295-4000
Guenko Guenev, *Pr*
EMP: 10 **EST:** 2001
SQ FT: 8,500
SALES (est): 1.5MM **Privately Held**
Web: www.ggtechnologies.com
SIC: 5122 8742 3826   Pharmaceuticals; Hospital and health services consultant; Chromatographic equipment, laboratory type

(G-15814)
GS RUBBER INDUSTRIES LLC
1 S Main St (02816-5719)
PHONE.................................508 672-0742
Joseph Sarlo, *Owner*
Christine Mongeon, *Prin*
EMP: 10 **EST:** 1993
SALES (est): 995.25K **Privately Held**
Web: www.gsrind.com
SIC: 3069   Air-supported rubber structures

(G-15815)
HAWKINS MACHINE COMPANY INC
374 Hopkins Hill Rd Unit 3 (02816-6498)
P.O. Box 315 (02816-0006)
PHONE.................................401 828-1424
Charles Hawkins, *Pr*
EMP: 21 **EST:** 1950
SQ FT: 7,500
SALES (est): 857.41K **Privately Held**
Web: www.hawkinsmachineco.com
SIC: 3599   Machine shop, jobbing and repair

(G-15816)
LITTLE RHODY MACHINE REPR INC
Also Called: Little Rhody Railings
7 Alice St (02816-7302)
PHONE.................................401 828-1919
Anita Weikman, *Pr*
Anita Weikman Prestreas, *Prin*
EMP: 13 **EST:** 1963
SQ FT: 6,000
SALES (est): 1.58MM **Privately Held**
Web: www.littlerhodyrailings.com
SIC: 3599   Machine shop, jobbing and repair

(G-15817)
NE FINEST LLC
1372 Main St (02816-8436)
PHONE.................................800 215-6640
EMP: 15 **EST:** 2019
SALES (est): 941.27K **Privately Held**
SIC: 2841 2842 2843 2819   Soap and other detergents; Polishes and sanitation goods; Surface active agents; Industrial inorganic chemicals, nec

(G-15818)
NORAMCO COVENTRY LLC
498 Washington St (02816-5467)

PHONE.................................401 623-1174
Lee Karras, *Managing Member*
EMP: 86 **EST:** 2020
SALES (est): 9.13MM **Privately Held**
SIC: 2834   Pharmaceutical preparations

(G-15819)
PURDUE PHARMA LP
498 Washington St (02816-5467)
PHONE.................................203 588-8000
Randy Shamblen, *Prin*
EMP: 15 **EST:** 2016
SALES (est): 1.07MM **Privately Held**
Web: www.purduepharma.com
SIC: 2834   Pharmaceutical preparations

(G-15820)
RESPONSE TECHNOLOGIES LLC
537 Main St (02816-7851)
PHONE.................................401 585-5918
Edmund Bard, *Pr*
EMP: 33 **EST:** 2015
SALES (est): 5.56MM
SALES (corp-wide): 12.87B **Publicly Held**
Web: www.responsetechs.com
SIC: 3089   Plastics and fiberglass tanks
HQ: Bell Textron Inc.
3255 Bell Flight Blvd
Fort Worth TX 76118
817 280-2011

(G-15821)
SOUTHERN NEW ENGLAND WLDG LLC
7 Acorn St (02816-4345)
PHONE.................................401 822-0596
Terry Upton, *Prin*
EMP: 7 **EST:** 2016
SALES (est): 231.29K **Privately Held**
SIC: 7692   Welding repair

(G-15822)
TECHTRAK LLC
2435 Nooseneck Hill Rd Ste A1b (02816)
PHONE.................................401 397-3983
Thomas Mulligan, *Genl Mgr*
EMP: 7 **EST:** 2013
SQ FT: 1,100
SALES (est): 826.2K **Privately Held**
Web: www.techtrakllc.com
SIC: 2834   Pharmaceutical preparations

(G-15823)
THOMAS ENGINEERING
9 Morin Ave (02816-7421)
PHONE.................................401 822-1235
Thomas Laboissonniere, *Pr*
Violette Laboissonniere, *VP*
Gregory Vanasse, *Stockholder*
EMP: 7 **EST:** 1979
SQ FT: 2,400
SALES (est): 884.26K **Privately Held**
Web: www.thomaseng.net
SIC: 3599   Machine shop, jobbing and repair

Cranston
Providence County

(G-15824)
AGITAR TECHNOLOGIES INC
41 Sharpe Dr (02920-4408)
PHONE.................................401 572-3150
EMP: 9 **EST:** 2019
SALES (est): 543.38K **Privately Held**
Web: www.agitar.com
SIC: 7372   Prepackaged software

(G-15825)
AIM PRODUCTS LLC (HQ)
Also Called: Aim Solder
25 Kenney Dr (02920-4443)
PHONE.................................401 463-5605
Herbert Black, *Managing Member*
▲ **EMP:** 25 **EST:** 1988
SALES (est): 101.25MM
SALES (corp-wide): 115.33MM **Privately Held**
Web: www.aimsolder.com
SIC: 5051 3356   Nonferrous metal sheets, bars, rods, etc., nec; Solder: wire, bar, acid core, and rosin core
PA: Aim Metaux & Alliages S.E.C.
9100 Boul Henri-Bourassa E
Montreal-Est QC H1E 2
514 494-2000

(G-15826)
ALERT SOLUTIONS INC
201 Hillside Rd Ste 2 (02920-5667)
P.O. Box 20160 (02920-0942)
PHONE.................................401 427-2100
EMP: 10 **EST:** 2009
SQ FT: 3,000
SALES (est): 2.41MM
SALES (corp-wide): 9.07MM **Privately Held**
SIC: 2741   Internet publishing and broadcasting
PA: Catalyst Investors, L.P.
711 5th Ave Ste 600
New York NY 10022
212 863-4848

(G-15827)
ALL-STATE FABRICATORS LIMITED PARTNERSHIP
1485 Elmwood Ave (02910-3822)
PHONE.................................401 785-3900
EMP: 60
SIC: 1761 3444   Sheet metal work, nec; Sheet metalwork

(G-15828)
ALLESCO INDUSTRIES INC (PA)
15 Amflex Dr (02921-2028)
PHONE.................................401 943-0680
Robert A Rotondo Senior, *Pr*
▲ **EMP:** 12 **EST:** 1999
SALES (est): 40MM
SALES (corp-wide): 40MM **Privately Held**
Web: www.allesco.net
SIC: 3452 5072   Screws, metal; Screws

(G-15829)
ALLIED GROUP LLC (PA)
Also Called: Allied Group, The
25 Amflex Dr (02921-2073)
PHONE.................................401 946-6100
Robert C Clement, *CEO*
EMP: 300 **EST:** 1946
SALES (est): 41.07MM
SALES (corp-wide): 41.07MM **Privately Held**
Web: www.thealliedgrp.com
SIC: 2752   Offset printing

(G-15830)
ALLOY FASTENERS INC (HQ)
15 Amflex Dr (02921-2028)
PHONE.................................401 943-0639
Joseph Smith Junior, *CFO*
Robert Rotondo, *
Chis Rotondo, *
Allen Sharp, *
▲ **EMP:** 25 **EST:** 1971
SQ FT: 69,000
SALES (est): 25.92MM

SALES (corp-wide): 40MM **Privately Held**
Web: www.alloyfasteners.com
SIC: 5072 3452   Screws; Bolts, nuts, rivets, and washers
PA: Allesco Industries, Inc.
15 Amflex Dr
Cranston RI 02921
401 943-0680

(G-15831)
AMERICAN IRON & METAL USA INC (HQ)
Also Called: American Iron & Metal
25 Kenney Dr (02920-4443)
PHONE.................................401 463-5605
Herbert Black, *CEO*
Richard Black, *
Ronald Black, *
◆ **EMP:** 16 **EST:** 1936
SQ FT: 2,500
SALES (est): 225.21MM
SALES (corp-wide): 407.17MM **Privately Held**
Web: www.aimsolder.com
SIC: 3356 8734   Solder: wire, bar, acid core, and rosin core; Product testing laboratories
PA: La Compagnie Americaine De Fer & Metaux Inc
9100 Boul Henri-Bourassa E
Montreal-Est QC H1E 2
514 494-2000

(G-15832)
AMERICAN RING CO INC
Also Called: American Plating
41 Wheatland Ave (02910-4004)
PHONE.................................401 467-4480
Joseph Calandrelli, *Mgr*
EMP: 12
SQ FT: 10,000
SALES (corp-wide): 4.55MM **Privately Held**
Web: www.americanplatingco.com
SIC: 3471   Electroplating of metals or formed products
PA: American Ring Co., Inc.
19 Grosvenor Ave
East Providence RI 02914
401 438-9060

(G-15833)
ANCHOR CONCRETE
30 Budlong Rd (02920-6428)
PHONE.................................401 942-4800
Antonio Pezza, *Sec*
EMP: 16 **EST:** 1923
SQ FT: 15,000
SALES (est): 1.96MM **Privately Held**
Web: www.anchorconcrete.com
SIC: 3271 3272   Blocks, concrete or cinder: standard; Concrete products, nec

(G-15834)
ANTON ENTERPRISES INC
430 Wellington Ave (02910-2935)
PHONE.................................401 781-3120
Donald Antonelli, *Pr*
Michael Antonelli, *VP*
EMP: 12 **EST:** 1976
SQ FT: 1,800
SALES (est): 643.35K **Privately Held**
Web: www.antonenterprise.com
SIC: 3471   Electroplating of metals or formed products

(G-15835)
AUSTRIAN MACHINE CORP
Also Called: A M C Design and Manufacturing
25 Stamp Farm Rd (02921-3401)
PHONE.................................401 946-4090

Marjorie Kern, *Pr*
Kurt Kern, *VP*
David Machado, *Sec*
EMP: 10 **EST:** 1971
SQ FT: 15,000
SALES (est): 2.02MM **Privately Held**
Web: www.amc-dm.com
SIC: 3599　Machine shop, jobbing and repair

(G-15836)
BNR SUPPLIES
18 Gallup Ave (02910-3929)
PHONE..............................401 461-9132
Morris Rush, *Owner*
EMP: 8 **EST:** 1997
SALES (est): 308.62K **Privately Held**
SIC: 3841　Surgical and medical instruments

(G-15837)
BOBBY PINS
2208 Broad St (02905-3349)
PHONE..............................401 461-3400
Bobby Pins, *Prin*
EMP: 7 **EST:** 2011
SALES (est): 134.17K **Privately Held**
Web: www.bobbypinsri.com
SIC: 3452　Pins

(G-15838)
C SJOBERG & SON INC
415 Station St (02910-2996)
P.O. Box 3583 (02910-0583)
PHONE..............................401 461-8220
Clifford W Sjoberg Junior, *Pr*
Timothy Sjoberg, *VP*
Joan Sjoberg, *Sec*
EMP: 14 **EST:** 1946
SQ FT: 7,000
SALES (est): 498.13K **Privately Held**
Web: www.sjoberginc.com
SIC: 3469　Stamping metal for the trade

(G-15839)
CADENCE MFG INC
2080 Plainfield Pike (02921-2012)
P.O. Box 3166 (24402-3166)
PHONE..............................508 746-6082
▲ **EMP:** 30
SIC: 3089　Injection molded finished plastics
products, nec

(G-15840)
CADENCE SCIENCE INC
Also Called: Incisiontech
2080 Plainfield Pike (02921-2012)
PHONE..............................401 942-1031
Peter Harris, *Ch Bd*
Brian Plummer, *
Alan Connor, *
EMP: 200 **EST:** 1947
SQ FT: 18,500
SALES (est): 47.84MM
SALES (corp-wide): 105.16MM **Privately Held**
Web: somdej17.moph.go.th
SIC: 3841　Hypodermic needles and syringes
PA: Cadence, Inc.
9 Technology Dr
Staunton VA 24401
540 248-2200

(G-15841)
CENTRAL TOOLS INC (PA)
Also Called: Moody Tools
456 Wellington Ave (02910-2900)
PHONE..............................401 467-8211
▲ **EMP:** 30 **EST:** 1905
SALES (est): 4.33MM
SALES (corp-wide): 4.33MM **Privately Held**

Web: www.centraltools.com
SIC: 3545 3646 3423 3825　Precision
measuring tools; Fluorescent lighting
fixtures, commercial; Hand and edge tools,
nec; Instruments to measure electricity

(G-15842)
COLE CABINET CO INC
530 Wellington Ave (02910-2950)
PHONE..............................401 467-4343
Gene Orsi, *Pr*
EMP: 10 **EST:** 1974
SQ FT: 5,000
SALES (est): 1.75MM **Privately Held**
Web: www.colecabinets.com
SIC: 2541 5712　Cabinets, except
refrigerated: show, display, etc.: wood;
Cabinet work, custom

(G-15843)
COOLEY INCORPORATED
5 Slater Rd (02920-4458)
PHONE..............................401 721-6374
Naresh Mehta, *Mgr*
EMP: 30
SALES (corp-wide): 93.15MM **Privately
Held**
Web: www.cooleygroup.com
SIC: 2295　Coated fabrics, not rubberized
HQ: Cooley, Incorporated
350 Esten Ave
Pawtucket RI 02860
401 724-9000

(G-15844)
CRANSTON PRINT WORKS
COMPANY (PA)
Also Called: C P W
1381 Cranston St (02920-6739)
P.O. Box 1465 (02816-0028)
PHONE..............................401 943-4800
Frederic Rockefeller Junior, *Pr*
Frederic Rockefeller Junior, *CEO*
Mark Jones, *
James Thorpe, *
◆ **EMP:** 32 **EST:** 1934
SQ FT: 400,000
SALES (est): 86.78MM
SALES (corp-wide): 86.78MM **Privately
Held**
SIC: 2261 2262 2899　Bleaching cotton
broadwoven fabrics; Bleaching: manmade
fiber and silk broadwoven fabrics; Chemical
preparations, nec

(G-15845)
CROSSTOWN PRESS INC
Also Called: Confidential Copy
829 Park Ave (02910-2037)
PHONE..............................401 941-4061
Steven H Levy, *Pr*
Bernard Levy, *Sec*
EMP: 7 **EST:** 1944
SQ FT: 8,000
SALES (est): 396.28K **Privately Held**
Web: www.crosstownpress.com
SIC: 2752　Offset printing

(G-15846)
CX THIN FILMS LLC
1515 Elmwood Ave (02910-3800)
PHONE..............................401 461-5500
EMP: 10 **EST:** 2018
SALES (est): 2.1MM **Privately Held**
Web: www.cxthinfilms.com
SIC: 3676　Electronic resistors

(G-15847)
DEAN MACHINE
INCORPORATED
25 Sharpe Dr Unit 1 (02920-4463)
P.O. Box 806 (02852-0607)
PHONE..............................401 919-5100
David Maynard, *Pr*
Paul Caito, *
EMP: 25 **EST:** 1981
SQ FT: 25,000
SALES (est): 2.43MM **Privately Held**
Web: www.deanmachine.net
SIC: 3599　Machine shop, jobbing and repair

(G-15848)
DELTA-ELECTRO POWER LLC
215 Niantic Ave (02907-3101)
PHONE..............................401 944-8350
Anthony Rapoza Senior, *Pr*
Ernest Rapoza, *
John Rapoza, *
EMP: 25 **EST:** 1993
SQ FT: 7,700
SALES (est): 10.64MM
SALES (corp-wide): 27.48MM **Privately
Held**
Web: www.deltamotor.com
SIC: 7694　Electric motor repair
PA: Rapid Pump & Meter Service
Company Llc
285 Straight St
Paterson NJ 07501
973 345-5600

(G-15849)
DESIGN FABRICATORS INC
72 Stamp Farm Rd (02921-3400)
PHONE..............................401 944-5294
Robin Degraide, *Pr*
Denise Armstrong, *
EMP: 35 **EST:** 1978
SQ FT: 37,500
SALES (est): 5.68MM **Privately Held**
Web: www.designfabricators.com
SIC: 2431　Millwork

(G-15850)
DIFRUSCIA INDUSTRIES INC
Also Called: DFI Tactical Coatings Group
1425 Cranston St (02920-6739)
PHONE..............................401 943-9900
EMP: 27 **EST:** 1991
SQ FT: 29,000
SALES (est): 6.95MM **Privately Held**
Web: www.difruscia.com
SIC: 3479　Coating of metals and formed
products

(G-15851)
DINA INC
357 Dyer Ave (02920-7008)
PHONE..............................401 942-9633
Lois Bordieri, *Pr*
John Bordieri, *VP*
EMP: 8 **EST:** 1972
SQ FT: 1,500
SALES (est): 566.93K **Privately Held**
Web: www.dina-inc.com
SIC: 3961 5944　Costume jewelry, ex.
precious metal and semiprecious stones;
Jewelry stores

(G-15852)
EASTERN SCREW COMPANY
15 Amflex Dr (02921-2028)
PHONE..............................401 943-0680
Robert Rotondo, *Pr*
▲ **EMP:** 125 **EST:** 1963
SQ FT: 42,000
SALES (est): 14.08MM

SALES (corp-wide): 40MM **Privately Held**
Web: www.easternscrew.com
SIC: 3452 5072　Screws, metal; Screws
PA: Allesco Industries, Inc.
15 Amflex Dr
Cranston RI 02921
401 943-0680

(G-15853)
ELECTRO STANDARDS LAB INC
Also Called: Electro Standards Laboratories
36 Western Industrial Dr (02921-3403)
PHONE..............................401 946-1164
Raymond B Sepe, *Pr*
Raymond B Sepe, *Pr*
Michael Sepe, *
Kenneth Sepe, *
Raymond B Sepe Junior, *VP*
EMP: 63 **EST:** 1976
SQ FT: 25,000
SALES (est): 14.2MM **Privately Held**
Web: www.electrostandards.com
SIC: 3577 8731 7373 3661　Computer
peripheral equipment, nec; Engineering
laboratory, except testing; Local area
network (LAN) systems integrator;
Telephone and telegraph apparatus

(G-15854)
ELMWOOD COUNTERTOP INC
50 Webb St (02920-7923)
PHONE..............................401 785-1677
Thomas Roselli, *Pr*
Thomas G Roselli, *Pr*
EMP: 9 **EST:** 1980
SQ FT: 6,000
SALES (est): 929.17K **Privately Held**
Web: www.elmwoodcountertopsinc.com
SIC: 2434　Wood kitchen cabinets

(G-15855)
EMI INDUSTRIES LLC
Also Called: All-State Fabricators
1485 Elmwood Ave (02910-3822)
PHONE..............................401 785-3900
EMP: 60
SALES (corp-wide): 53.36MM **Privately
Held**
Web: www.emiindustries.com
SIC: 1761 3444　Sheet metal work, nec;
Sheet metalwork
PA: Emi Industries, Llc
1316 Tech Blvd
Tampa FL 33619
813 626-3166

(G-15856)
ENERGY MGT & CTRL SVCS INC
Also Called: EMC Services
116 Budlong Rd (02920-6428)
PHONE..............................401 946-1440
James Jones, *Pr*
Wendy Roskowski, *VP*
EMP: 17 **EST:** 1986
SQ FT: 3,200
SALES (est): 2.72MM **Privately Held**
Web: www.emccontrols.net
SIC: 3822 5075 1731　Building services
monitoring controls, automatic; Thermostats
; Electrical work

(G-15857)
EPOXIES INC
Also Called: Epoxies, Etc
21 Starline Way (02921-3407)
PHONE..............................401 946-5564
Michael Harrington, *Pr*
Paul Harrington, *VP*
EMP: 15 **EST:** 2006
SQ FT: 15,000

SALES (est): 1.61MM **Privately Held**
Web: www.epoxies.com
SIC: 2891 2869 Adhesives and sealants;
Industrial organic chemicals, nec

(G-15858)
ESMOND MANUFACTURING CO INC
169 N View Ave (02920-4832)
PHONE................................401 942-9103
Jerry Dionne, *Pr*
EMP: 8 EST: 1992
SQ FT: 6,000
SALES (est): 848.27K **Privately Held**
Web: www.esmondinc.com
SIC: 3451 Screw machine products

(G-15859)
FEDERAL ELECTRONICS INC
75 Stamp Farm Rd (02921-3401)
PHONE................................401 944-6200
Romolo Evangelista, *Pr*
Richard Evangelista, *
Edward Evangelista, *
EMP: 100 EST: 1948
SQ FT: 42,000
SALES (est): 40.51MM **Privately Held**
Web: www.federalelec.com
SIC: 3679 Electronic circuits

(G-15860)
FIELDING MANUFACTURING INC
780 Wellington Ave (02910-2941)
PHONE................................401 461-0400
TOLL FREE: 800
Steven P Fielding, *Pr*
EMP: 84 EST: 1962
SQ FT: 250,000
SALES (est): 8.84MM **Privately Held**
Web: www.fieldingmfg.com
SIC: 3089 3544 3369 3364 Injection
molding of plastics; Special dies, tools, jigs,
and fixtures; Nonferrous foundries, nec;
Nonferrous die-castings except aluminum

(G-15861)
FIELDING MFG - ZINC DCSTING IN
Also Called: Elmwood Manufacturing Inc
780 Wellington Ave (02910-2941)
PHONE................................401 461-0400
Steven P Fielding, *Pr*
EMP: 61 EST: 1962
SQ FT: 26,000
SALES (est): 2.26MM **Privately Held**
Web: www.fieldingmfg.com
SIC: 3545 3364 Tools and accessories for
machine tools; Zinc and zinc-base alloy die-
castings

(G-15862)
FPP HOLDINGS LLC
Also Called: First Point Power
2000 Chapel View Blvd Ste 450
(02920-8416)
PHONE................................401 684-1443
Peter Schieffelin, *CEO*
Stephen Bestwick, *COO*
EMP: 11 EST: 2013
SALES (est): 508.06K **Privately Held**
Web: www.firstpointpower.com
SIC: 3679 Electronic loads and power
supplies

(G-15863)
FRI RESINS HOLDING COMPANY
Also Called: Epoxies, Etc
21 Starline Way (02921-3407)
PHONE................................401 946-5564

Michael Harrington, *Pr*
Paul Harrington, *VP*
▲ EMP: 15 EST: 1987
SQ FT: 20,000
SALES (est): 3.36MM
SALES (corp-wide): 66.34MM **Privately Held**
Web: www.epoxies.com
SIC: 2891 2851 2869 Adhesives; Paints and
allied products; Industrial organic
chemicals, nec
PA: Meridian Adhesives Group Llc
15720 Brixham Hill Ave
Charlotte NC

(G-15864)
GANNON & SCOTT INC (PA)
33 Kenney Dr (02920-4480)
PHONE................................800 556-7296
Christopher W Jones, *Pr*
▲ EMP: 60 EST: 1919
SQ FT: 40,000
SALES (est): 12.5MM
SALES (corp-wide): 12.5MM **Privately Held**
Web: www.gannon-scott.com
SIC: 3341 Secondary nonferrous metals

(G-15865)
GASBARRE PRODUCTS INC
C I Hayes
81 Western Industrial Dr Ste A
(02921-3444)
PHONE................................401 467-5200
Thomas Gasbarre, *Pr*
EMP: 10
SALES (corp-wide): 36.01MM **Privately Held**
Web: www.gasbarre.com
SIC: 3567 3549 3542 Industrial furnaces
and ovens; Metalworking machinery, nec;
Machine tools, metal forming type
PA: Gasbarre Products, Inc.
590 Division St
Du Bois PA 15801
814 371-3015

(G-15866)
GEM LABEL & TAPE COMPANY
73 Whitewood Dr (02920-5918)
PHONE................................401 724-1300
Jim Jalkin, *Pr*
EMP: 10 EST: 1979
SALES (est): 518.45K **Privately Held**
Web: www.gemlabelinc.com
SIC: 2759 Labels and seals: printing, nsk

(G-15867)
GEM-CRAFT INC
1420 Elmwood Ave (02910-3847)
PHONE................................401 854-1200
Ronald Verri, *Pr*
EMP: 9 EST: 1945
SQ FT: 20,000
SALES (est): 405.32K **Privately Held**
Web: www.gem-craft.com
SIC: 3911 Jewelry, precious metal

(G-15868)
GENNARO INC
Also Called: Casinelli Design
81 Western Industrial Dr (02921-3445)
PHONE................................401 632-4100
Steve Casinelli, *Pr*
Beverly Casinelli, *Sec*
▲ EMP: 15 EST: 1983
SALES (est): 2.31MM **Privately Held**
Web: www.gennaroinc.com

SIC: 3961 Costume jewelry, ex. precious
metal and semiprecious stones

(G-15869)
GREAT AMERICAN RECRTL EQP
24 Stafford Ct (02920-4464)
PHONE................................401 463-5587
David Celani, *Pr*
▲ EMP: 14 EST: 1990
SALES (est): 881.22K **Privately Held**
Web: www.greatamericanrec.com
SIC: 3949 Billiard and pool equipment and
supplies, general

(G-15870)
GREEN DEVELOPMENT LLC
Also Called: Bn Logging
2000 Chapel View Blvd Ste 500
(02920-3040)
PHONE................................401 295-4998
Mark Depasquale, *Managing Member*
EMP: 78 EST: 2014
SALES (est): 22.68MM **Privately Held**
Web: www.green-ri.com
SIC: 4911 3621
; Windmills, electric generating

(G-15871)
GRINNELL CABINET MAKERS INC
169 Mill St (02905-1017)
PHONE................................401 781-1080
Scott Grinnell, *Pr*
EMP: 25 EST: 1979
SQ FT: 80,000
SALES (est): 2.21MM **Privately Held**
Web: www.grinnellcabinetmakers.com
SIC: 2431 Millwork

(G-15872)
HENRY A EVERS CORP
1655 Elmwood Ave Ste 34 (02910-4933)
PHONE................................401 781-4767
Anthony J Diorio, *Pr*
EMP: 10 EST: 1898
SALES (est): 781.1K **Privately Held**
Web: www.henryaevers.com
SIC: 3544 Special dies and tools

(G-15873)
HOUSE OF STAINLESS INC
Also Called: Scott Brass
1637 Elmwood Ave (02910-4937)
P.O. Box 17083 (02917-0702)
PHONE................................800 556-3470
Curt Burhoe, *Pr*
Richard Burkhart, *
▲ EMP: 35 EST: 2006
SALES (est): 7.71MM **Privately Held**
SIC: 3351 Strip, copper and copper alloy

(G-15874)
HUDSON LIQUID ASPHALTS INC (PA)
Also Called: Hudson
2000 Chapel View Blvd Ste 380
(02920-3078)
PHONE................................401 274-2200
Tom Hudson, *Owner*
John J Hudson, *
Francis J O'brien, *COO*
Matthew J Gill, *
Tom Hudson, *CEO*
▲ EMP: 70 EST: 1955
SALES (est): 15.57MM
SALES (corp-wide): 15.57MM **Privately Held**
SIC: 2951 Asphalt paving mixtures and
blocks

(G-15875)
HUDSON TERMINAL CORP
Also Called: Hudson Company
2000 Chapel View Blvd Ste 380
(02920-3040)
PHONE................................401 941-0500
Denis Leamy, *Mgr*
EMP: 8
SALES (corp-wide): 2.31MM **Privately Held**
Web: www.hudsoncompanies.com
SIC: 3531 Asphalt plant, including gravel-
mix type
PA: Hudson Terminal Corp.
29 Terminal Rd
Providence RI 02905
401 274-2200

(G-15876)
ID LABEL INC
160 Midway Rd (02920-5707)
PHONE................................508 809-6199
Neil Johnston, *Pr*
EMP: 18
Web: www.idlabelinc.com
SIC: 2759 Commercial printing, nec
PA: Id Label, Inc.
425 Park Ave
Lake Villa IL 60046

(G-15877)
ISELANN - MOSS INDUSTRIES INC
41 Slater Rd (02920-4466)
PHONE................................401 463-5950
Mark Wolstenholme, *Pr*
Gary Mason, *VP*
EMP: 23 EST: 1969
SQ FT: 12,000
SALES (est): 2.72MM **Privately Held**
Web: www.iselann-moss.com
SIC: 3089 Injection molding of plastics

(G-15878)
JJI INTERNATIONAL INC
Also Called: Jolie Jewels
1 Weingeroff Blvd (02910-4009)
P.O. Box 603334 (02906-0734)
PHONE................................401 780-8668
Lisa Weingeroff, *Pr*
▲ EMP: 22 EST: 1990
SALES (est): 1.4MM **Privately Held**
Web: www.jjiinternational.com
SIC: 3911 Jewelry, precious metal

(G-15879)
JOHN HAZEN WHOTE CORPORATION
1160 Cranston St (02920-7335)
PHONE................................401 942-8000
John Hazen White Senior, *Pr*
EMP: 11 EST: 2001
SALES (est): 20K **Privately Held**
Web:
www.thewhitefamilyfoundation.com
SIC: 3585 Heating equipment, complete

(G-15880)
JOHNSON CONTROLS INC
Also Called: Johnson Controls
2 Starline Way Unit 8 (02921-3413)
PHONE................................401 275-2097
James Cotton, *Mgr*
EMP: 16
Web: www.johnsoncontrols.com
SIC: 2531 Seats, automobile
HQ: Johnson Controls, Inc.
5757 N Green Bay Ave
Milwaukee WI 53209
920 245-6409

(G-15881)
JRB ASSOCIATES INC
Also Called: G & A Plating & Polishing Co
2 2nd Ave (02910-4923)
PHONE...............................401 351-8693
Jim Brown, *Pr*
Douglas James, *Genl Mgr*
EMP: 24 EST: 1997
SALES (est): 978.12K Privately Held
Web: www.japlating.com
SIC: 3471 Electroplating of metals or
formed products

(G-15882)
KINGSTON KRAFTS
15 Industrial Rd Unit 2 (02920-6771)
PHONE...............................401 272-0292
EMP: 8 EST: 2017
SALES (est): 721.39K Privately Held
Web: www.kingstonkrafts.com
SIC: 2599 Beds, not household use

(G-15883)
LAVIGNE MANUFACTURING INC
15 Western Industrial Dr (02921-3402)
PHONE...............................401 490-4627
David T Lavigne, *Pr*
Daniel W Lavigne, *
Gerard E Lavigne, *
Robert R Mcdermott, *Stockholder*
EMP: 110 EST: 1989
SQ FT: 35,000
SALES (est): 15.85MM Privately Held
Web: www.lavignemfg.com
SIC: 3599 Machine shop, jobbing and repair

(G-15884)
LEONARD VALVE COMPANY LLC
1360 Elmwood Ave (02910-3824)
PHONE...............................800 222-1208
▲ EMP: 50 EST: 1913
SALES (est): 9.56MM Privately Held
Web: www.leonardvalve.com
SIC: 3494 Plumbing and heating valves

(G-15885)
LINCOLN PACKING CO
7 Industrial Rd (02920-6796)
PHONE...............................401 943-0878
Giovanni A Colagiovanni, *CEO*
Giovanni A Colagiovanni, *Pr*
Vincent Colagiovanni, *VP*
EMP: 103 EST: 1957
SQ FT: 7,000
SALES (est): 2.45MM
SALES (corp-wide): 2.45MM Privately
Held
Web: www.colafoodsllc.com
SIC: 2013 5147 2011 Sausages, from
purchased meat; Meats, fresh; Meat
packing plants
PA: Cola Foods Llc
7 Industrial Rd
Cranston RI 02920
401 943-0878

(G-15886)
LOST ART CULTURED FOODS LLC
Also Called: Keane's Wood-Fired Catering
1850 Broad St Unit 1 (02905-3525)
PHONE...............................401 437-6933
Kaylyn Keane, *Prin*
EMP: 12 EST: 2015
SALES (est): 936.79K Privately Held
SIC: 2035 Vegetables, pickled

(G-15887)
LUCA + DANNI INC
838 Dyer Ave (02920-6714)
PHONE...............................401 275-5337
Alfred Magnanimi, *Pr*
EMP: 25 EST: 2016
SALES (est): 4.62MM Privately Held
Web: www.lucadanni.com
SIC: 3911 3961 Jewelry, precious metal;
Costume jewelry, ex. precious metal and
semiprecious stones

(G-15888)
LUV2BU INC
17 Yard St (02920-2332)
PHONE...............................401 612-9585
EMP: 9 EST: 2016
SALES (est): 391.88K Privately Held
SIC: 3841 Physiotherapy equipment,
electrical

(G-15889)
LV CONTROLS INCORPORATED
1 Starline Way (02921-3447)
PHONE...............................401 228-3937
Joshua Martins, *Prin*
EMP: 8 EST: 2010
SALES (est): 142.8K Privately Held
Web: www.lv-controls.com
SIC: 3625 Relays and industrial controls

(G-15890)
MAG JEWELRY CO INC
838 Dyer Ave (02920-6714)
PHONE...............................401 942-1840
Daniel J Magnanimi, *Pr*
EMP: 40 EST: 1951
SQ FT: 14,000
SALES (est): 2.45MM Privately Held
Web: www.lucadanni.com
SIC: 3911 3961 Jewelry, precious metal;
Costume jewelry, ex. precious metal and
semiprecious stones

(G-15891)
MALCO SAW CO INC
22 Field St (02920-7395)
PHONE...............................401 942-7380
Gregory Livesey, *Pr*
Austin Livesey, *
EMP: 7 EST: 1939
SALES (est): 893.91K Privately Held
Web: www.malcosaw.com
SIC: 3425 3546 3541 Saw blades, for hand
or power saws; Power-driven handtools;
Machine tools, metal cutting type

(G-15892)
MDC SIGNS PRINTING
70 Gansett Ave (02910-2422)
P.O. Box 25449 (02905-0449)
PHONE...............................401 654-5354
EMP: 8 EST: 2019
SALES (est): 475.85K Privately Held
SIC: 2752 Commercial printing, lithographic

(G-15893)
MEARTHANE PRODUCTS LLC (PA)
16 Western Industrial Dr (02921-3405)
PHONE...............................401 946-4400
Kevin C Redmond, *CEO*
◆ EMP: 44 EST: 1965
SQ FT: 38,000
SALES (est): 16.66MM
SALES (corp-wide): 16.66MM Privately
Held
Web: www.mearthane.com

(G-15894)
METRO INC (PA)
Also Called: Metro Home Video
1 Metro Park Dr (02910-4955)
PHONE...............................401 461-2200
Dennis Nichols, *Pr*
EMP: 50 EST: 1986
SQ FT: 52,000
SALES (est): 4.87MM
SALES (corp-wide): 4.87MM Privately
Held
Web: www.metrob2b.com
SIC: 2721 2731 5099 Magazines: publishing
only, not printed on site; Books, publishing
only; Video cassettes, accessories and
supplies

(G-15895)
MILLWORK ONE INC
60 Kenney Dr (02920-4404)
PHONE...............................401 738-6990
John M Adams, *CEO*
John D Fish, *
Michael R Mcnulty Senior, *VP*
▲ EMP: 65 EST: 2002
SQ FT: 45,000
SALES (est): 11.53MM
SALES (corp-wide): 28.81MM Privately
Held
Web: www.millworkone.com
SIC: 2431 Millwork
PA: Wood Bay Products Business Trust Inc
72 Taunton St
Plainville MA 02762
508 695-8033

(G-15896)
MINIATURE CASTING CORPORATION
Also Called: Mini Cast Precision Casting
21 Slater Rd (02920-4467)
PHONE...............................401 463-5090
Robert Piacitelli, *Pr*
Bill Tallman, *Genl Mgr*
EMP: 15 EST: 1962
SALES (est): 2.43MM Privately Held
Web: www.minicast.com
SIC: 3363 Aluminum die-castings

(G-15897)
NAR INDUSTRIES LLC
Also Called: Rbc Epoxy
1 Weingeroff Blvd (02910-4009)
PHONE...............................401 941-3000
EMP: 20 EST: 2019
SALES (est): 2.05MM Privately Held
SIC: 2821 Epoxy resins

(G-15898)
NE STEEL FABRICATORS LLC
1120 Wellington Ave (02910-3730)
P.O. Box 6166 (02940-6166)
PHONE...............................401 785-1234
EMP: 20 EST: 2017
SALES (est): 2.33MM Privately Held
SIC: 1791 3446 3441 3449 Structural steel
erection; Architectural metalwork;
Fabricated structural metal; Miscellaneous
metalwork

(G-15899)
NELIPAK CORPORATION (PA)
Also Called: Nelipak Healthcare Packaging
21 Amflex Dr (02921-2028)
PHONE...............................401 946-2699
Pat Chambliss, *CEO*
Michael Kellly, *
Paul Hogan, *

Kathryn Buono, *
▲ EMP: 29 EST: 1965
SQ FT: 60,000
SALES (est): 42.44MM
SALES (corp-wide): 42.44MM Privately
Held
Web: www.nelipak.com
SIC: 3081 3083 2671 Packing materials,
plastics sheet; Laminated plastics plate and
sheet; Paper; coated and laminated
packaging

(G-15900)
NEWPORT CREAMERY LLC
35 Sockanosset Cross Rd (02920-5535)
P.O. Box 8819 (02920-0819)
PHONE...............................401 946-4000
Nicholas Janikies, *Pr*
Nicholas Janikies, *Pr*
Leslie Rich, *Sec*
EMP: 11 EST: 2001
SALES (est): 1.09MM Privately Held
Web: www.newportcreamery.com
SIC: 2024 2013 5451 Ice cream and frozen
deserts; Prepared beef products, from
purchased beef; Ice cream (packaged)

(G-15901)
NOBLE METALS SERVICES INC
Also Called: Noble Metal Services
10 Ross Simons Dr (02920-4481)
PHONE...............................866 695-4806
Gary Theriault, *CEO*
Kyle Theriault, *Mgr*
Dan Healey, *Mgr*
EMP: 10 EST: 2009
SALES (est): 2.67MM Privately Held
Web: www.noblemetalservices.com
SIC: 3341 Secondary nonferrous metals

(G-15902)
NORTH SAFETY PRODUCTS LLC
Also Called: North Safety Products
2000 Plainfield Pike (02921-2012)
PHONE...............................401 943-4400
◆ EMP: 1050
SIC: 3842 Gloves, safety

(G-15903)
OCEAN STATE TIRE CO INC
51 Worthington Rd (02920-7938)
P.O. Box 8062 (02920-0062)
PHONE...............................401 946-0880
Shirley Perry, *Pr*
Paul Mccarthy Junior, *VP*
Anthony C Ricci Junior, *Sec*
EMP: 26 EST: 1981
SQ FT: 15,000
SALES (est): 4.23MM Privately Held
Web: www.oceanstatetire.com
SIC: 5014 7534 Truck tires and tubes; Tire
repair shop

(G-15904)
PEPSI-COLA METRO BTLG CO INC
Also Called: Pepsi-Cola
1400 Pontiac Ave (02920-4499)
PHONE...............................401 468-3300
TOLL FREE: 800
Trevor Toolson, *Mgr*
EMP: 215
SQ FT: 15,000
SALES (corp-wide): 86.39B Publicly Held
Web: www.pepsico.com
SIC: 2086 Soft drinks: packaged in cans,
bottles, etc.
HQ: Pepsi-Cola Metropolitan Bottling
Company, Inc.
700 Anderson Hill Rd

SIC: 3949 Skates and parts, roller

▲ = Import ▼ = Export
◆ = Import/Export

Purchase NY 10577
914 767-6000

(G-15905)
PRIMARY FLOW SIGNAL INC (PA)
800 Wellington Ave Unit 2 (02910-3732)
P.O. Box 8479 (02920-0479)
PHONE..............................401 461-6366
Bruce Briggs, *Pr*
Dezi G Halmi, *
Jeanne Groccia, *
◆ **EMP:** 80 **EST:** 1981
SQ FT: 72,000
SALES (est): 42.42MM
SALES (corp-wide): 42.42MM **Privately Held**
Web: www.primaryflowsignal.com
SIC: 5084 3823 Instruments and control equipment; Primary elements for process flow measurement

(G-15906)
RBC INDUSTRIES INC
1 Weingeroff Blvd (02910-4009)
PHONE..............................401 941-3000
◆ **EMP:** 73
Web: www.rbcepoxy.com
SIC: 2821 2822 5084 Epoxy resins; Silicone rubbers; Industrial machinery and equipment

(G-15907)
RIHANI PLASTICS INC
14 Suez St (02920-6517)
P.O. Box 8945 (02920-0988)
PHONE..............................401 942-7393
Ghaleb Victor Rihani, *Pr*
EMP: 17 **EST:** 1978
SQ FT: 30,000
SALES (est): 911.1K **Privately Held**
Web: www.rihani.com
SIC: 3089 Injection molding of plastics

(G-15908)
ROLYN INC (PA)
Also Called: Chante
189 Macklin St (02920-6510)
PHONE..............................401 944-0844
Douglas Ricci, *Pr*
Anthony Rendine, *
▲ **EMP:** 30 **EST:** 1963
SQ FT: 15,500
SALES (est): 1.83MM
SALES (corp-wide): 1.83MM **Privately Held**
Web: www.chante.com
SIC: 3911 3961 3915 Jewelry, precious metal; Costume jewelry, ex. precious metal and semiprecious stones; Jewelers' materials and lapidary work

(G-15909)
SCOPE DISPLAY & BOX CO INC (PA)
1840 Cranston St (02920-4139)
PHONE..............................401 942-7150
Victor Wilbert Junior, *Pr*
Stephen Wilbert, *
EMP: 50 **EST:** 1963
SQ FT: 35,000
SALES (est): 4.69MM
SALES (corp-wide): 4.69MM **Privately Held**
Web: www.scopedisplay.com
SIC: 3993 3999 2542 2541 Displays and cutouts, window and lobby; Advertising display products; Partitions and fixtures, except wood; Wood partitions and fixtures

(G-15910)
SIGNATURE CABLE MFG TECH INC
Also Called: Scmt Inc
14 Suez St (02920-6517)
PHONE..............................401 383-1008
Mohamad Zeyad Sasa, *Pr*
EMP: 29 **EST:** 2004
SALES (est): 3.82MM **Privately Held**
Web: www.signaturecable.com
SIC: 5065 3496 Electronic parts; Cable, uninsulated wire: made from purchased wire

(G-15911)
SIR SPEEDY PRINTING INC
Also Called: Sir Speedy
969 Park Ave (02910-3202)
PHONE..............................401 781-5650
Pat Welch, *Pr*
EMP: 24 **EST:** 1987
SQ FT: 3,000
SALES (est): 1.07MM **Privately Held**
Web: www.sirspeedy.com
SIC: 2752 Commercial printing, lithographic

(G-15912)
SPECTRUM THERMAL PROC LLC
818 Wellington Ave (02910-3719)
PHONE..............................401 808-6249
Paul Squizzero, *Managing Member*
EMP: 18 **EST:** 2013
SQ FT: 12,000
SALES (est): 3.2MM **Privately Held**
Web: www.spectrumtp.com
SIC: 3398 Metal heat treating

(G-15913)
STAFFALL INC
1468 Elmwood Ave (02910-3847)
PHONE..............................401 461-5554
Ernest Crivellone, *Pr*
Diane Yingling, *VP*
Clementina Crivellone, *Sec*
EMP: 22 **EST:** 1967
SQ FT: 22,000
SALES (est): 3.5MM **Privately Held**
Web: www.staffall.com
SIC: 3679 Electronic circuits

(G-15914)
STYLECRAFT INC
1510 Pontiac Ave (02920-4488)
PHONE..............................401 463-9944
Neil Berman, *Pr*
▲ **EMP:** 58 **EST:** 1967
SQ FT: 18,000
SALES (est): 4.58MM **Privately Held**
Web: www.stylecraftusa.com
SIC: 3911 3961 Jewelry, precious metal; Costume jewelry, ex. precious metal and semiprecious stones

(G-15915)
SWAROVSKI NORTH AMERICA LTD (DH)
Also Called: Signity Americas
1 Kenney Dr (02920-4403)
PHONE..............................401 463-6400
Daniel Cohen, *Pr*
Stephan Toljan, *
John Simms, *
◆ **EMP:** 650 **EST:** 1955
SQ FT: 179,000
SALES (est): 273.95MM
SALES (corp-wide): 3.33B **Privately Held**
SIC: 3961 5023 3231 Costume jewelry; Glassware; Products of purchased glass
HQ: Swarovski U.S. Holding Limited
1 Kenney Dr

Cranston RI 02920

(G-15916)
SYQWEST INC
30 Kenney Dr (02920-7962)
PHONE..............................401 432-7129
Robert Tarini, *CEO*
Micheal Curran, *
EMP: 50 **EST:** 2003
SQ FT: 53,600
SALES (est): 9.48MM **Privately Held**
Web: www.syqwestinc.com
SIC: 3812 Sonar systems and equipment

(G-15917)
TACO INC (PA)
Also Called: Taco Comfort Solutions
1160 Cranston St (02920-7300)
PHONE..............................401 942-8000
John H White Junior, *Pr*
Glenn Graham, *
Thomas Lawrence, *
Kyle Adamonis, *
Wil Vandewiel, *
◆ **EMP:** 375 **EST:** 1920
SQ FT: 120,000
SALES (est): 158.9MM
SALES (corp-wide): 158.9MM **Privately Held**
Web: www.tacocomfort.com
SIC: 3433 3561 3443 3822 Heating equipment, except electric; Pumps and pumping equipment; Heat exchangers: coolers (after, inter), condensers, etc.; Environmental controls

(G-15918)
TACO INTERNATIONAL LTD
1160 Cranston St (02920-7300)
PHONE..............................401 942-8000
John Hazen White Junior, *Ch*
Cheryl Merchant, *CEO*
Ken Dumas, *CFO*
EMP: 10 **EST:** 2017
SALES (est): 230.65K **Privately Held**
Web: www.tacocomfort.com
SIC: 3561 Pumps and pumping equipment

(G-15919)
TECHNIC INC (PA)
47 Molter St (02910-1011)
P.O. Box 9650 (02940-9650)
PHONE..............................401 781-6100
Hrant Shoushanian, *Pr*
David Weisberg, *
Alfred M Weisberg, *
Scott Carlisle, *
◆ **EMP:** 150 **EST:** 1944
SQ FT: 90,000
SALES (est): 159.53MM
SALES (corp-wide): 159.53MM **Privately Held**
Web: www.technic.com
SIC: 2899 3559 Metal treating compounds; Electroplating machinery and equipment

(G-15920)
TRANS-TEX LLC
Also Called: Trans-Tex
117 Pettaconsett Ave (02920-7916)
PHONE..............................401 331-8483
Phillip Barr, *
▲ **EMP:** 45 **EST:** 1983
SQ FT: 19,000
SALES (est): 7.78MM **Privately Held**
Web: www.trans-texinc.com
SIC: 2672 Adhesive papers, labels, or tapes: from purchased material

(G-15921)
TRI-BRO TOOL CO INC
1370 Elmwood Ave (02910-3889)
PHONE..............................401 781-6323
Thomas Walsh, *Pr*
Edward Walsh, *Prin*
Robert Walsh, *Prin*
Maggie Mullen, *Prin*
EMP: 23 **EST:** 1946
SQ FT: 24,000
SALES (est): 734.12K **Privately Held**
Web: www.tri-bro.com
SIC: 3915 3544 Jewelers' materials and lapidary work; Forms (molds), for foundry and plastics working machinery

(G-15922)
TWO SAINTS INC
81 Western Industrial Dr Ste B (02921-3444)
PHONE..............................401 490-5500
Richard St Angelo, *CEO*
Richard Stangelo, *CEO*
◆ **EMP:** 10 **EST:** 2000
SQ FT: 15,000
SALES (est): 586.67K **Privately Held**
Web: 2-saints-inc.business.site
SIC: 2511 Wood household furniture

(G-15923)
TYCO FIRE PRODUCTS LP
Also Called: Tyco Fire Protection Products
1467 Elmwood Ave (02910-3849)
PHONE..............................401 781-8220
EMP: 24
Web: www.tyco-fire.com
SIC: 3569 Sprinkler systems, fire: automatic
HQ: Tyco Fire Products Lp
1400 Pennbrook Pkwy
Lansdale PA 02910
215 362-0700

(G-15924)
TYCO FIRE PRODUCTS LP (DH)
Also Called: Tyco Fire Sppression Bldg Pdts
1467 Elmwood Ave (02910-3849)
PHONE..............................215 362-0700
Colleen Repplier, *Pt*
Robert Roche, *Pt*
Ryan K Stafford, *Pt*
Melissa Mcclain, *Mgr*
◆ **EMP:** 150 **EST:** 2000
SALES (est): 2B **Privately Held**
Web: www.tyco-fire.com
SIC: 3569 3494 3321 5085 Sprinkler systems, fire: automatic; Valves and pipe fittings, nec; Water pipe, cast iron; Valves and fittings
HQ: Johnson Controls, Inc.
5757 N Green Bay Ave
Milwaukee WI 53209
920 245-6409

(G-15925)
UNCLES OIL COMPANY CORPORATION
1515 Elmwood Ave Ste 3 (02910-3800)
PHONE..............................401 383-0626
Mardiros Tashjian, *Owner*
EMP: 7 **EST:** 2014
SALES (est): 203.17K **Privately Held**
SIC: 1389 Oil field services, nec

(G-15926)
W B MASON CO INC
99 Bald Hill Rd (02920-2640)
PHONE..............................888 926-2766
EMP: 79
SALES (corp-wide): 1.01B **Privately Held**
Web: www.wbmason.com

GEOGRAPHIC

SIC: **5943** 5712 2752   Office forms and
supplies; Office furniture; Commercial
printing, lithographic
PA: W. B. Mason Co., Inc.
59 Centre Street
Brockton MA 02301
508 586-3434

(G-15927)
WEI INC
25 Webb St (02920-7922)
PHONE.............................401 781-3904
Donald Waddington, *Pr*
EMP: 10
SQ FT: 5,000
SALES (corp-wide): 5.78MM **Privately
Held**
SIC: **3625** 3613   Controls for adjustable
speed drives; Control panels, electric
PA: Wei, Inc.
33 Webb St
Cranston RI 02920
401 781-3904

(G-15928)
WEI INC (PA)
33 Webb St (02920-7922)
PHONE.............................401 781-3904
Donald Waddington, *CEO*
John E Waddington, *VP*
Jacqueline Alger, *Sec*
EMP: 20 **EST:** 1956
SALES (est): 5.78MM
SALES (corp-wide): 5.78MM **Privately
Held**
SIC: **3625** 3613 3812 3674   Controls for
adjustable speed drives; Control panels,
electric; Search and navigation equipment;
Semiconductors and related devices

(G-15929)
**WEINGEROFF ENTERPRISES
INC**
Also Called: Jay Strongwater
1 Weingeroff Blvd (02910-4000)
P.O. Box 9988 (02910-0988)
PHONE.............................401 467-2200
▲ **EMP:** 140
Web: www.weingeroff.com
SIC: **3499** 3961   Picture frames, metal;
Costume jewelry, ex. precious metal and
semiprecious stones

(G-15930)
YUSHIN AMERICA INC (HQ)
35 Kenney Dr (02920-4497)
PHONE.............................401 463-1800
▲ **EMP:** 63 **EST:** 1988
SALES (est): 25.68MM **Privately Held**
Web: www.yushinamerica.com
SIC: **5084** 3559   Robots, industrial; Robots,
molding and forming plastics
PA: Yushin Precision Equipment Co., Ltd.
555, Kuzetonoshirocho, Minami-Ku
Kyoto KYO 601-8

Cumberland
Providence County

(G-15931)
ALESIS LP
Also Called: Wavefront Semiconductor
200 Scenic View Dr Ste 201 (02864-1847)
PHONE.............................401 658-4032
▲ **EMP:** 211 **EST:** 2001
SALES (est): 4.94MM
SALES (corp-wide): 5.87MM **Privately
Held**

Web: www.alesis.com
SIC: **3931**   Musical instruments
PA: Inmusic, Llc
200 Scenic View Dr
Cumberland RI 02864
888 800-0681

(G-15932)
AMBER STYLE INC
Also Called: Living Cocoon
3335 Mendon Rd (02864-2166)
PHONE.............................401 405-0089
Ritesh Mathur, *Pr*
EMP: 50 **EST:** 2009
SQ FT: 700
SALES (est): 1.14MM **Privately Held**
SIC: **2299**   Upholstery filling, textile

(G-15933)
BOTTOMLINE TECHNOLOGIES
36 Ridgeland Drive (02864-3102)
PHONE.............................401 954-2200
Bill Walsh, *Prin*
EMP: 10 **EST:** 2017
SALES (est): 418.8K **Privately Held**
Web: www.bottomline.com
SIC: **7372**   Business oriented computer
software

(G-15934)
BP CUSTOM WOODWORKING
500 Mendon Rd (02864-6219)
PHONE.............................401 787-8750
Barry Penta, *Prin*
EMP: 7 **EST:** 2016
SALES (est): 92.25K **Privately Held**
SIC: **2431**   Millwork

(G-15935)
**CRUZ CONSTRUCTION
COMPANY INC**
23 Maple St Ste 6 (02864-8122)
PHONE.............................401 727-3770
Joseph Cruz, *Pr*
Dawn Cruz, *VP*
EMP: 10 **EST:** 1948
SQ FT: 1,000
SALES (est): 1.19MM **Privately Held**
Web: www.cruzconstruction.net
SIC: **2951**   Asphalt paving blocks (not from
refineries)

(G-15936)
**CUMBERLAND FOUNDRY CO
INC**
310 W Wrentham Rd (02864-1005)
PHONE.............................401 658-3300
Albert Lucchetti, *Pr*
Thomas Lucchetti, *
EMP: 38 **EST:** 1949
SQ FT: 70,000
SALES (est): 4.72MM **Privately Held**
Web: www.cumberlandfoundry.com
SIC: **3321**   Gray iron castings, nec

(G-15937)
CUMBERLAND QUARRY CORP
6 Manville Hill Rd (02864-2448)
PHONE.............................401 658-4442
David Walsh, *Prin*
EMP: 11 **EST:** 2010
SALES (est): 503.86K **Privately Held**
Web: www.cumberlandquarry.com
SIC: **3273**   Ready-mixed concrete

(G-15938)
D & B MACHINING INC
53 John St (02864-7713)
PHONE.............................401 726-2347

Rui Duarte, *Pr*
Tony Duarte, *
Alice Duarte, *
Aldora Duarte, *
EMP: 40 **EST:** 1989
SQ FT: 36,000
SALES (est): 4.83MM **Privately Held**
Web: www.dbmachining.com
SIC: **3599**   Machine shop, jobbing and repair

(G-15939)
FIRECRACKER SPORTS LLC
Also Called: Sports Event and Products Co
8 Windsong Rd (02864-2727)
P.O. Box 7905 (02864-0904)
PHONE.............................401 595-0233
Mark Cooke, *Pr*
EMP: 8 **EST:** 2017
SALES (est): 469.32K **Privately Held**
Web: www.firecrackersports.com
SIC: **7941** 5699 7999 3949   Sports field or
stadium operator, promoting sports events;
Sports apparel; Sports instruction, schools
and camps; Baseball, softball, and cricket
sports equipment

(G-15940)
FRED F WALTZ CO INC
58 Silo Dr (02864-3266)
PHONE.............................401 769-4900
Kimberley J Waltz, *Pr*
EMP: 9 **EST:** 2007
SALES (est): 416.81K **Privately Held**
Web: www.waltzco.com
SIC: **2677** 5112 5942 5999   Envelopes;
Envelopes; Books, religious; Religious
goods

(G-15941)
HANNA INSTRUMENTS INC
35 Industrial Rd (02864-4748)
PHONE.............................401 335-3677
EMP: 11
Web: www.hannainst.com
SIC: **3825**   Electrical power measuring
equipment
PA: Hanna Instruments, Inc.
584 Park East Dr
Woonsocket RI 02895

(G-15942)
HERRICK & WHITE LTD
Also Called: Architectural Building Svcs
3 Flat St (02864-2335)
PHONE.............................401 658-0440
Kenneth E Bertram, *Pr*
Steven Brannigan, *
EMP: 100 **EST:** 1977
SQ FT: 50,000
SALES (est): 15.51MM **Privately Held**
Web: www.herrick-white.com
SIC: **2542** 2541 8712   Office and store
showcases and display fixtures; Wood
partitions and fixtures; Architectural services

(G-15943)
**HINDLEY MANUFACTURING CO
INC**
9 Havens St (02864-8200)
P.O. Box 38 (02864-0038)
PHONE.............................401 722-2550
Charles J Hindley, *Pr*
Scott A Hindley, *
Roy A Medeiros, *
▲ **EMP:** 80 **EST:** 1897
SQ FT: 110,000
SALES (est): 9.24MM **Privately Held**
Web: www.hindley.com

SIC: **3496** 3429 3452   Miscellaneous
fabricated wire products; Hardware, nec;
Screw eyes and hooks

(G-15944)
ICE CREAM MACHINE CO
4288 Diamond Hill Rd (02864-1508)
PHONE.............................401 333-5053
Kim Caron, *Owner*
EMP: 10 **EST:** 1977
SALES (est): 944.78K **Privately Held**
Web: www.icecreampie.com
SIC: **2024** 5421   Ice cream, bulk; Freezer
provisioners, meat

(G-15945)
IDS HIGHWAY SAFETY INC
1230 Mendon Rd (02864-4872)
P.O. Box 7604 (02864-0897)
PHONE.............................401 425-2205
Kristen Ray, *CEO*
EMP: 75 **EST:** 2002
SALES (est): 5MM **Privately Held**
Web: www.idshighwaysafety.com
SIC: **3679** 7389   Attenuators; Flagging
service (traffic control)

(G-15946)
**INTERNATIONAL TEXTILE MFG
INC**
30 Meeting St Unit 4 (02864-8355)
P.O. Box 6 (02864-0803)
▲ **EMP:** 9 **EST:** 2004
SQ FT: 35,000
SALES (est): 974.25K **Privately Held**
SIC: **5023** 2273   Rugs; Carpets and rugs

(G-15947)
ION AUDIO LLC (HQ)
Also Called: Ion
200 Scenic View Dr Ste 201 (02864-1847)
PHONE.............................401 658-3743
Jack O'donnell, *Managing Member*
◆ **EMP:** 10 **EST:** 2002
SALES (est): 8.98MM
SALES (corp-wide): 93.76MM **Privately
Held**
Web: www.ionaudio.com
SIC: **5999** 3651   Audio-visual equipment and
supplies; Household audio equipment
PA: Inmusic Brands, Inc.
200 Scenic View Dr # 201
Cumberland RI 02864
401 658-3131

(G-15948)
JH LYNCH & SONS INC (PA)
Also Called: Lynch Companies
50 Lynch Pl (02864-5334)
PHONE.............................401 333-4300
Stephen P Lynch Junior, *Pr*
David C Lynch Senior, *VP*
Frank Aceto, *
Harry E Myers Iii, *VP*
EMP: 80 **EST:** 1942
SQ FT: 65,000
SALES (est): 48.18MM
SALES (corp-wide): 48.18MM **Privately
Held**
Web: www.jhlynch.com
SIC: **1611** 2951   Highway and street paving
contractor; Asphalt and asphaltic paving
mixtures (not from refineries)

(G-15949)
JOHNSON & JOHNSON
Also Called: Johnson & Johnson
1300 Highland Corporate Dr (02864-8714)
PHONE.............................401 762-6751
EMP: 147

SALES (corp-wide): 94.94B **Publicly Held**
Web: www.jnj.com
SIC: 3842 Surgical appliances and supplies
PA: Johnson & Johnson
  1 Johnson And Johnson Plz
  New Brunswick NJ 08933
  732 524-0400

(G-15950)
LKQ PRECIOUS METALS INC
Also Called: MST
290 Curran Rd (02864-7316)
PHONE.................................800 447-1034
EMP: 130 EST: 2012
SALES (est): 21.48MM
SALES (corp-wide): 12.79B **Publicly Held**
Web: www.qml.us
SIC: 2611 Pulp mills, mechanical and
  recycling processing
PA: Lkq Corporation
  500 W Madison St Ste 2800
  Chicago IL 60661
  312 621-1950

(G-15951)
**NEUROTECH
PHARMACEUTICALS INC**
900 Highland Corporate Dr Bldg 1
(02864-7508)
PHONE.................................617 694-5520
EMP: 43 EST: 1995
SALES (est): 2.4MM **Privately Held**
Web:
www.neurotechpharmaceuticals.com
SIC: 2834 Pharmaceutical preparations

(G-15952)
NFA CORP
Hope Global Headquarters
50 Martin St (02864-5335)
PHONE.................................401 333-8990
Lisie Teoto, *CEO*
EMP: 500
SALES (corp-wide): 185.57MM **Privately
Held**
Web: www.hopeglobal.com
SIC: 2221 Textile mills, broadwoven: silk
  and manmade, also glass
PA: Nfa Corp.
  50 Martin St
  Cumberland RI 02864
  401 753-7800

(G-15953)
NFA CORP
Also Called: Novelty Plastics
50 Martin St (02864-5335)
P.O. Box 505807 (02150-5807)
PHONE.................................401 333-8990
Norton Proman, *Brnch Mgr*
EMP: 156
SQ FT: 61,000
SALES (corp-wide): 185.57MM **Privately
Held**
Web: www.hopeglobal.com
SIC: 2241 2631 Narrow fabric mills;
  Paperboard mills
PA: Nfa Corp.
  50 Martin St
  Cumberland RI 02864
  401 753-7800

(G-15954)
NFA CORP
Hope Global Divison of Nfa
50 Martin St (02864-5335)
PHONE.................................401 333-8947
David Casty, *Pr*
EMP: 30
SQ FT: 125,000

SALES (corp-wide): 185.57MM **Privately
Held**
Web: www.hopeglobal.com
SIC: 2241 Webbing, woven
PA: Nfa Corp.
  50 Martin St
  Cumberland RI 02864
  401 753-7800

(G-15955)
NFA CORP
Also Called: Hope Global
50 Martin St (02864-5335)
PHONE.................................401 333-8990
EMP: 400
SALES (corp-wide): 185.57MM **Privately
Held**
Web: www.hopeglobal.com
SIC: 2241 2257 Webbing, woven; Weft knit
  fabric mills
PA: Nfa Corp.
  50 Martin St
  Cumberland RI 02864
  401 753-7800

(G-15956)
NUMARK INTERNATIONAL INC
200 Scenic View Dr (02864-1847)
PHONE.................................954 761-7550
John E O'donnell, *Pr*
EMP: 10 EST: 2009
SALES (est): 1.05MM **Privately Held**
Web: www.numark.com
SIC: 3674 Semiconductors and related
  devices

(G-15957)
OKONITE COMPANY INC
5 Industrial Rd (02864-4714)
PHONE.................................401 333-3500
Brad Detamore, *Genl Mgr*
EMP: 40
SALES (corp-wide): 505.89MM **Privately
Held**
Web: www.okonite.com
SIC: 3357 3743 3661 Nonferrous
  wiredrawing and insulating; Railroad
  equipment; Telephone and telegraph
  apparatus
PA: The Okonite Company Inc
  102 Hilltop Rd
  Ramsey NJ 07446
  201 825-0300

(G-15958)
ONSET DERMATOLOGICS LLC
900 Highland Corporate Dr (02864-1792)
PHONE.................................401 762-2000
EMP: 100
SIC: 2834 Dermatologicals

(G-15959)
PEELED INC
Also Called: Peeled Snacks
30 Martin St Ste 3b1 (02864-5321)
PHONE.................................212 706-2001
Noha Waibsnaider, *Pr*
Cassie Abrams, *Prin*
Dawn Techow, *Prin*
Ian Kelleher, *Prin*
Jessica Aquila, *Prin*
▲ EMP: 12 EST: 2004
SALES (est): 1.01MM **Privately Held**
Web: www.peeledsnacks.com
SIC: 2068 2034 Nuts: dried, dehydrated,
  salted or roasted; Dried and dehydrated
  fruits

(G-15960)
PLASTICS PLUS INC
Also Called: Envision
51 Abbott St Ste 1 (02864-8713)
P.O. Box 7129 (02864-0893)
PHONE.................................401 727-1447
Daniel J Smalley, *Pr*
▲ EMP: 45 EST: 1983
SALES (est): 9.51MM **Privately Held**
Web: www.envisionsolutionsgroup.com
SIC: 3578 2541 Point-of-sale devices; Store
  and office display cases and fixtures

(G-15961)
PREFERRED PRECAST INC
2 Titus St (02864-8396)
PHONE.................................401 475-5560
EMP: 10 EST: 2018
SALES (est): 656.59K **Privately Held**
Web: www.preferredprecast.com
SIC: 3272 Concrete products, nec

(G-15962)
**RHODE ISLAND TEXTILE
COMPANY**
35 Martin St (02864-5361)
P.O. Box 999 (02862-0999)
PHONE.................................401 722-3700
EMP: 145
SALES (corp-wide): 68.39MM **Privately
Held**
SIC: 2241 Shoe laces, except leather
PA: Rhode Island Textile Company
  35 Martin St
  Cumberland RI 02864
  401 722-3700

(G-15963)
**RHODE ISLAND TEXTILE
COMPANY (PA)**
Also Called: South Carolina Elastic
35 Martin St (02864-5361)
PHONE.................................401 722-3700
▲ EMP: 160 EST: 1913
SALES (est): 23.52MM
SALES (corp-wide): 23.52MM **Privately
Held**
Web: www.phenixtextiles.com
SIC: 2241 2298 5999 Shoe laces, except
  leather; Cordage and twine; Pet supplies

(G-15964)
SWISSLINE PRECISION LLC
23 Ashton Park Way Unit A (02864-4841)
PHONE.................................216 362-3814
Mike Chenevert, *Managing Member*
Gerard Hester, *
Donna Ross, *
EMP: 45 EST: 2015
SQ FT: 30,000
SALES (est): 8.56MM **Privately Held**
Web: www.swisslineprecision.com
SIC: 3451 Screw machine products
PA: Kirkwood Holding Inc.
  1239 Rockside Rd
  Cleveland OH 44134

(G-15965)
SWISSLINE PRECISION MFG INC
23 Ashton Park Way Unit A (02864-4841)
PHONE.................................401 333-8888
EMP: 59 EST: 1994
SALES (est): 4.91MM **Privately Held**
Web: www.swisslineprecision.com
SIC: 3599 Machine shop, jobbing and repair

(G-15966)
SWISSLINE PRODUCTS INC
23 Ashton Park Way Unit A (02864-4841)

PHONE.................................401 333-8888
David Chenevert, *Pr*
Raymond Barsalou, *
EMP: 73 EST: 1985
SQ FT: 30,000
SALES (est): 5MM **Privately Held**
SIC: 3599 3769 Machine shop, jobbing and
  repair; Space vehicle equipment, nec

(G-15967)
TEDOR PHARMA INC
400 Highland Corporate Dr (02864-1788)
PHONE.................................401 658-5219
Theodore L Iorio, *Pr*
Laura Iorio, *
Matthew Iorio Special, *Assistant to Vice
President*
▲ EMP: 41 EST: 2001
SQ FT: 40,000
SALES (est): 8.92MM **Privately Held**
Web: www.tedorpharma.com
SIC: 2834 Pharmaceutical preparations

(G-15968)
TEXCEL INC
18 Meeting St (02864-8323)
P.O. Box 6187 (02940-6187)
PHONE.................................401 727-2113
EMP: 15 EST: 1996
SQ FT: 40,000
SALES (est): 1.36MM **Privately Held**
Web: www.texcelindustries.com
SIC: 3552 Textile machinery

(G-15969)
TEXCEL INDUSTRIES INC
18 Meeting St (02864-8323)
P.O. Box 6187 (02940-6187)
PHONE.................................401 727-2113
Joshua Teverow, *Pr*
Jessica Wasserman, *
Ricahrd Wasserman, *
EMP: 25 EST: 2011
SALES (est): 3.06MM **Privately Held**
Web: www.texcelindustries.com
SIC: 2241 Webbing, woven

(G-15970)
TIFFANY & CO
Also Called: Tiffany
300 Maple Ridge Dr (02864-8707)
PHONE.................................212 755-8000
EMP: 215
SALES (corp-wide): 503.87MM **Privately
Held**
Web: www.tiffany.com
SIC: 3915 Diamond cutting and polishing
HQ: Tiffany & Co.
  200 5th Ave Bsmt 2
  New York NY 10010
  212 755-8000

(G-15971)
WEB PRINTING INC
Also Called: B & M Printing
1300 Mendon Rd (02864-4880)
PHONE.................................401 334-3190
EMP: 7 EST: 2019
SALES (est): 92.3K **Privately Held**
Web: www.bmprintingweb.com
SIC: 2752 Offset printing

East Greenwich
Kent County

(G-15972)
ALEX AND ANI LLC (HQ)
Also Called: Alex and Ani

10 Briggs Dr (02818-1555)
PHONE..................................401 633-1486
▼ **EMP: 44 EST:** 2012
SQ FT: 20,000
SALES (est): 91.95MM
SALES (corp-wide): 91.95MM **Privately Held**
Web: www.alexandani.com
SIC: 3915 Jewelry parts, unassembled
PA: A And A Shareholding Co., Llc
　　10 Briggs Dr
　　East Greenwich RI

(G-15973)
BARDON INDUSTRIES INC
Also Called: Bardons Technology
3377 S County Trl Unit 6 (02818-1481)
P.O. Box 1657 (02818-0698)
PHONE..................................401 884-1814
Thomas Lydon, *Pr*
Thomas J Lydon Junior, *Pr*
Eileen A Barry, *VP*
EMP: 13 EST: 1985
SQ FT: 4,000
SALES (est): 1.62MM **Privately Held**
Web: www.bardons.com
SIC: 2899 Water treating compounds

(G-15974)
BLAZING EDITIONS
Also Called: Blazing Editions
42 Ladd St Ste 12 (02818-4358)
P.O. Box 1954 (02818-0636)
PHONE..................................401 885-4329
Alan Blazar, *Pr*
Joseph Blazar, *VP*
EMP: 9 EST: 1984
SALES (est): 940.61K **Privately Held**
Web: www.blazing.com
SIC: 8412 2752 Art gallery; Offset printing

(G-15975)
BOOTHROYD DEWHURST INC
4474 Post Rd (02818-4124)
PHONE..................................401 783-5840
Nicholas Dewhurst, *Pr*
John Gilligan, *Pr*
Nicholaus Dewhurst, *Sec*
EMP: 14 EST: 1985
SQ FT: 3,600
SALES (est): 2.17MM **Privately Held**
Web: www.dfma.com
SIC: 7372 Prepackaged software

(G-15976)
CARA INCORPORATED
620 Main St Apt 12 (02818-3673)
PHONE..................................401 732-6535
Kenneth P O'leary, *Pr*
Gary O'leary, *VP Sls*
Kathy O'leary, *VP Mktg*
Michael Damiani, *VP*
▲ **EMP: 9 EST:** 1983
SALES (est): 1.81MM **Privately Held**
Web: www.caraincorporated.com
SIC: 3069 Medical sundries, rubber

(G-15977)
CHERRY SEMICONDUCTOR CORP
2000 S County Trl (02818-1530)
PHONE..................................401 885-3600
Andrew F Durette, *Prin*
EMP: 12 EST: 2011
SALES (est): 265.06K **Privately Held**
SIC: 3674 Semiconductors and related devices

(G-15978)
CHRONOMATIC INC
1503 S County Trl (02818-1695)
P.O. Box 610 (02818-0610)
PHONE..................................401 884-6361
Ann Marie Dasilva, *CEO*
EMP: 24 EST: 1963
SQ FT: 13,000
SALES (est): 486.16K **Privately Held**
Web: www.chronomaticinc.com
SIC: 3911 3961 Jewelry, precious metal; Costume jewelry

(G-15979)
CLEAN AWAY INC
154 Peirce St (02818-3200)
PHONE..................................860 985-6743
Ann Bobbitt, *CEO*
Dan E Kehoe, *Sec*
EMP: 10 EST: 2012
SALES (est): 207.19K **Privately Held**
SIC: 3732 Boatbuilding and repairing

(G-15980)
DEWETRON INC
2850 S County Trl Unit 1 (02818-1731)
PHONE..................................401 284-3750
Steve Dipalma, *COO*
◆ **EMP: 15 EST:** 1997
SQ FT: 5,000
SALES (est): 7.87MM
SALES (corp-wide): 1.89B **Privately Held**
Web: www.dewetron.com
SIC: 3826 Specific ion measuring instruments
HQ: Dewetron Deutschland Gmbh
　　Fabrikstr. 18
　　Winterbach BW 73650
　　718 126-9810

(G-15981)
EAGLEPICHER TECHNOLOGIES LLC
Also Called: Eaglepicher Yardney Division
2000 S County Trl (02818-1530)
PHONE..................................401 471-6580
EMP: 15
Web: www.eaglepicher.com
SIC: 3691 Storage batteries
PA: Eaglepicher Technologies, Llc
　　1215 W C St
　　Joplin MO 64801

(G-15982)
EAST GREENWICH OIL CO INC
Also Called: Express Oil Co
390 Main St (02818-3606)
PHONE..................................401 884-2454
Steve De Lisle, *Pr*
Joyce De Lisle, *Sec*
EMP: 8 EST: 1898
SQ FT: 1,000
SALES (est): 831.34K **Privately Held**
Web: www.eastgreenwichoil.com
SIC: 7549 1389 Lubrication service, automotive; Servicing oil and gas wells

(G-15983)
EASTERN FOOD INDUSTRIES INC
Also Called: Chef-A-Roni
2832 S County Trl (02818-1742)
PHONE..................................401 884-8798
Henry G Caniglia, *Pr*
Lillian Caniglia, *VP*
EMP: 9 EST: 1960
SALES (est): 525.91K **Privately Held**
Web: www.chefaroni.com

SIC: 5411 5461 2033 Delicatessen stores; Retail bakeries; Spaghetti and other pasta sauce: packaged in cans, jars, etc

(G-15984)
EDWARD F BRIGGS DISPOSAL INC
Carrs Pond Rd (02818)
PHONE..................................401 294-6391
Edward Briggs, *Prin*
EMP: 9 EST: 2005
SALES (est): 380.34K **Privately Held**
SIC: 3089 Garbage containers, plastics

(G-15985)
ENER-TEK INTERNATIONAL INC
2000 S County Trl (02818-1530)
PHONE..................................401 471-6580
Richard M Scibelli, *CEO*
Vincent A Yevoli, *Pr*
Janice T Donovan, *Sec*
EMP: 48 EST: 1974
SALES (est): 1.15MM **Privately Held**
Web: www.ener-tek.com
SIC: 3691 3692 8741 Storage batteries; Primary batteries, dry and wet; Management services
PA: Eaglepicher Technologies, Llc
　　1215 W C St
　　Joplin MO 64801

(G-15986)
FORMEX INC
3305 S County Trl (02818-1477)
PHONE..................................401 885-9800
Edward Shea, *Pr*
EMP: 30 EST: 1991
SALES (est): 1.39MM **Privately Held**
Web: www.formextool.com
SIC: 7692 3544 3599 Welding repair; Special dies, tools, jigs, and fixtures; Machine and other job shop work

(G-15987)
GLOBAL PHOTONIX LLC
2639 S County Trl (02818-1727)
PHONE..................................401 474-8158
Mark A Davis, *Admn*
EMP: 7 EST: 2016
SALES (est): 135.44K **Privately Held**
SIC: 3661 Fiber optics communications equipment

(G-15988)
JOHNSTON BLCKWOOD SLMAKERS INC
1 Division St (02818-3878)
PHONE..................................401 884-4227
Todd Johnston, *Prin*
EMP: 7 EST: 2011
SALES (est): 125.86K **Privately Held**
SIC: 2394 Sails: made from purchased materials

(G-15989)
LINESIDER BREWING COMPANY LLC
1485 S County Trl Ste 201 (02818-1747)
PHONE..................................401 398-7700
Jeremy Ruff, *Managing Member*
EMP: 10 EST: 2018
SQ FT: 4,200
SALES (est): 613.15K **Privately Held**
Web: www.linesiderbrewing.com
SIC: 2082 Beer (alcoholic beverage)

(G-15990)
MARKETPLACE INC CORPORATE
816 Middle Rd (02818-1826)
PHONE..................................401 336-3000
Neil Stamps, *Pr*
Chris Crawford, *VP*
EMP: 18 EST: 1999
SQ FT: 6,800
SALES (est): 3.61MM **Privately Held**
Web: www.tcmpi.com
SIC: 3911 Jewelry, precious metal

(G-15991)
MERIDIAN PRINTING INC
Also Called: Barrington Printing
1538 S County Trl (02818-1627)
PHONE..................................401 885-4882
Robert Nangle, *Pr*
Steven Lee, *
▲ **EMP: 59 EST:** 1975
SQ FT: 30,000
SALES (est): 16.78MM **Privately Held**
Web: www.meridianprinting.com
SIC: 2752 Offset printing

(G-15992)
NIPPON AMERICAN LIMITED
Also Called: Design Research Optics
3 Cedar Rock Mdws (02818-2443)
PHONE..................................401 885-7353
Mikiko Morimura, *Pr*
Bruce Sunderland, *VP*
EMP: 10 EST: 1990
SALES (est): 366.65K **Privately Held**
SIC: 3827 8299 Optical instruments and apparatus; Educational services

(G-15993)
STANLEY FASTENING SYSTEMS LP (HQ)
2 Briggs Dr (02818-1555)
PHONE..................................401 884-2500
Stanley Works, *Mng Pt*
◆ **EMP: 134 EST:** 1996
SALES (est): 26.68MM
SALES (corp-wide): 16.95B **Publicly Held**
SIC: 3399 3579 Staples, nonferrous metal or wire; Stapling machines (hand or power)
PA: Stanley Black & Decker, Inc.
　　1000 Stanley Dr
　　New Britain CT 06053
　　860 225-5111

(G-15994)
TRADEST1
Also Called: Chocolate Delicacies
219 Main St (02818-3704)
P.O. Box 1034 (02818-0964)
PHONE..................................401 884-4949
EMP: 8 EST: 1992
SQ FT: 2,100
SALES (est): 441.47K **Privately Held**
SIC: 5441 5145 2064 Candy; Candy; Candy and other confectionery products

(G-15995)
US EMBLEM LLC
1503 S County Trl (02818-1695)
P.O. Box 722 (02818-0722)
PHONE..................................401 487-4327
Ann Dasilva, *Managing Member*
EMP: 10 EST: 2012
SALES (est): 500K **Privately Held**
SIC: 3911 Jewelry, precious metal

(G-15996)
VOLTSERVER INC (PA)
42 Ladd St (02818-4361)

PHONE..................401 885-8658
Stephen Eaves, *Pr*
Harry D Lowe, *
Charles Garcia, *
David Mayer, *
Halton Peters, *
EMP: 22 **EST:** 2012
SALES (est): 5.84MM
SALES (corp-wide): 5.84MM **Privately Held**
Web: www.voltserver.com
SIC: 3612 Power and distribution transformers

(G-15997)
WATSON MATERIALS
1500 S County Trl (02818-1627)
PHONE..................401 885-0600
EMP: 9 **EST:** 2019
SALES (est): 251.03K **Privately Held**
Web: www.watsonmulch.com
SIC: 2951 Asphalt paving mixtures and blocks

(G-15998)
YARDNEY TECHNICAL PRODUCTS INC
2000 S County Trl (02818-1530)
P.O. Box 47 (64802-0047)
PHONE..................401 471-6580
EMP: 150
Web: www.yardney.com
SIC: 3691 Storage batteries

East Providence
Providence County

(G-15999)
A & H COMPOSITION AND PRTG INC
Also Called: Copy World
5 Almeida Ave (02914-1001)
PHONE..................401 438-1200
Anthony Andrade, *Pr*
EMP: 9 **EST:** 1971
SQ FT: 6,000
SALES (est): 666.5K **Privately Held**
SIC: 2752 2791 2789 Offset printing; Typesetting; Bookbinding and related work

(G-16000)
A B MUNROE DAIRY INC (PA)
151 N Brow St (02914-4415)
PHONE..................401 438-4450
Robert C Armstrong Junior, *Pr*
Elizabeth Armstrong, *
EMP: 75 **EST:** 1881
SQ FT: 120,000
SALES (est): 9.17MM
SALES (corp-wide): 9.17MM **Privately Held**
Web: www.cowtruck.com
SIC: 2026 2038 Milk and cream, except fermented, cultured, and flavored; Frozen specialties, nec

(G-16001)
ADVANCED PRINT TECH LLC
18 Laura St (02914-3805)
PHONE..................401 434-8802
Tony Andrade, *Ofcr*
EMP: 8 **EST:** 1998
SALES (est): 92.3K **Privately Held**
Web: www.aptpressdirect.com
SIC: 2752 Offset printing

(G-16002)
AMERICAN EQUIPMENT & FABG CORP
Also Called: AE&f
100 Water St (02914-5022)
PHONE..................401 438-2626
Charles E Booth Iii, *Pr*
Patrick B Griffin, *VP*
▲ **EMP:** 15 **EST:** 1985
SQ FT: 5,000
SALES (est): 4.95MM **Privately Held**
Web: www.american-equipment.com
SIC: 7353 3531 5082 Heavy construction equipment rental; Construction machinery; General construction machinery and equipment

(G-16003)
AMERICAN RING CO INC (PA)
Also Called: American Accessories Co.
19 Grosvenor Ave (02914-4569)
PHONE..................401 438-9060
Anthony Calandrelli, *Pr*
▲ **EMP:** 14 **EST:** 1973
SQ FT: 56,000
SALES (est): 4.55MM
SALES (corp-wide): 4.55MM **Privately Held**
SIC: 3961 3471 2675 Jewelry apparel, non-precious metals; Electroplating of metals or formed products; Cards, folders, and mats: die-cut

(G-16004)
AMERICAN TROPHY AND SUPPLY INC
110 Russell Ave (02914-3551)
PHONE..................401 438-3060
Kristen Gossler, *Pr*
EMP: 9 **EST:** 1951
SQ FT: 9,000
SALES (est): 843.03K **Privately Held**
Web: www.americantrophy.com
SIC: 3499 2759 3479 Trophies, metal, except silver; Screen printing; Etching and engraving

(G-16005)
ASPEN AEROGELS RI LLC
3 Dexter Rd (02914-2045)
PHONE..................401 432-2612
Donald Young, *Prin*
EMP: 36 **EST:** 2008
SALES (est): 1.89MM
SALES (corp-wide): 180.36MM **Publicly Held**
Web: www.aerogel.com
SIC: 2899 Chemical preparations, nec
PA: Aspen Aerogels, Inc.
30 Forbes Rd Bldg B
Northborough MA 01532
508 691-1111

(G-16006)
BAZAR GROUP INC (PA)
Also Called: Imperial Pearl
795 Waterman Ave (02914-1713)
PHONE..................401 434-2595
Banice C Bazar, *Pr*
▲ **EMP:** 25 **EST:** 1953
SQ FT: 30,000
SALES (est): 21.2MM
SALES (corp-wide): 21.2MM **Privately Held**
Web: www.imperialpearl.com
SIC: 3911 5094 3961 Jewelry, precious metal; Jewelry; Costume jewelry, ex. precious metal and semiprecious stones

(G-16007)
BOYDCO INC (PA)
101 Commercial Way (02914-1024)
PHONE..................401 438-6900
David Speed, *Pr*
Eric Dewhirst, *VP*
Lee Sprague, *VP*
EMP: 13 **EST:** 1972
SQ FT: 16,000
SALES (est): 4.91MM
SALES (corp-wide): 4.91MM **Privately Held**
Web: www.boydcoinc.com
SIC: 3561 Pumps and pumping equipment

(G-16008)
CARLA CORP
Also Called: Nancy B
33 Sutton Ave (02914-3413)
P.O. Box 14192 (02914-0192)
PHONE..................401 438-7070
Ralph Fleming Junior, *Ch Bd*
Brian Fleming, *
Ralph Fleming Iii, *Pr*
EMP: 150 **EST:** 1965
SQ FT: 35,000
SALES (est): 9.36MM **Privately Held**
Web: www.carlacorp.com
SIC: 3911 Jewelry, precious metal

(G-16009)
CONSOLIDATED CONCRETE CORP (PA)
835 Taunton Ave Unit 1 (02914-1600)
PHONE..................401 438-4700
John R Pesce Junior, *Pr*
George Pesce, *VP*
EMP: 9 **EST:** 1957
SQ FT: 6,000
SALES (est): 2.56MM
SALES (corp-wide): 2.56MM **Privately Held**
Web: www.flofill.com
SIC: 3273 Ready-mixed concrete

(G-16010)
CONTRACT FUSION INC
99 Massasoit Ave (02914-2008)
PHONE..................401 438-1298
John Carter Iii, *Pr*
Letitia Carter, *
EMP: 26 **EST:** 1991
SQ FT: 14,000
SALES (est): 2.11MM **Privately Held**
Web: www.contractfusion.com
SIC: 3599 5084 3915 3548 Machine and other job shop work; Welding machinery and equipment; Jewelers' materials and lapidary work; Welding apparatus

(G-16011)
COPY WORLD INC
5 Almeida Ave (02914-1001)
PHONE..................401 438-1200
Anthony Andrade, *Prin*
EMP: 7 **EST:** 2012
SALES (est): 130.18K **Privately Held**
SIC: 2752 Offset printing

(G-16012)
CUSTOM & MILLER BOX COMPANY
25 Almeida Ave (02914-1001)
P.O. Box 2410 (02861-0410)
PHONE..................401 431-9007
EMP: 57 **EST:** 1994
SQ FT: 40,000
SALES (est): 2.44MM
SALES (corp-wide): 27.03MM **Privately Held**

Web: www.keycontainercorp.com
SIC: 2653 Boxes, corrugated: made from purchased materials
PA: Key Container Corporation
21 Campbell St
Pawtucket RI 02861
401 723-2000

(G-16013)
DEXTER ENTERPRISES CORP
Also Called: Dexter Co The
70 Waterman Ave (02914-4410)
PHONE..................401 434-2300
R S Dexter, *Pr*
EMP: 8 **EST:** 2000
SALES (est): 384.03K **Privately Held**
Web: www.freedombuick.com
SIC: 3993 7389 Signs and advertising specialties; Crane and aerial lift service

(G-16014)
DEXTER SIGN CO
Also Called: Dexter Crane Service
70 Waterman Ave (02914-4410)
PHONE..................401 434-1100
Roy S Dexter, *Pr*
Brent Dexter, *VP*
Kirk Dexter, *Treas*
EMP: 15 **EST:** 1945
SQ FT: 25,000
SALES (est): 494.94K **Privately Held**
Web: www.dexterenterprises.com
SIC: 3993 1542 7389 1731 Electric signs; Commercial and office building, new construction; Crane and aerial lift service; General electrical contractor

(G-16015)
EAST PROVIDENCE MOHAWKS
78 Vine St (02914-4317)
PHONE..................401 829-1411
EMP: 7 **EST:** 2015
SALES (est): 62K **Privately Held**
Web: www.epbgc.org
SIC: 2273 Finishers of tufted carpets and rugs

(G-16016)
ENVIRONMENTAL CTRL SYSTEMS INC
Also Called: Aquas Group
41 Commercial Way (02914-1020)
PHONE..................401 437-8612
Nicholas Paolo Junior, *Pr*
EMP: 17 **EST:** 1986
SALES (est): 5.08MM **Privately Held**
Web: www.aquasgroup.com
SIC: 3559 Chemical machinery and equipment

(G-16017)
EVANS CAPACITOR COMPANY LLC
72 Boyd Ave (02914-1202)
PHONE..................401 435-3555
Kevin Perhamus, *CEO*
▼ **EMP:** 50 **EST:** 1996
SQ FT: 5,000
SALES (est): 9.36MM **Privately Held**
Web: www.quanticevans.com
SIC: 3675 Electronic capacitors

(G-16018)
EVANS FINDINGS COMPANY INC
Also Called: Evans Company
33 Eastern Ave (02914-2107)
PHONE..................401 434-5600
Peter T Evans, *Pr*

Missy Galob, *
◆ **EMP:** 46 **EST:** 1945
SQ FT: 30,000
SALES (est): 9.06MM **Privately Held**
Web: www.evanstechnology.com
SIC: 3469 3915 Stamping metal for the trade
; Jewelers' materials and lapidary work

(G-16019)
FERREIRA CONCRETE FORMS INC
7 Tallman Ave (02914-2022)
PHONE..........................401 639-0931
Mariano Ferreira, *Pr*
Sergio Ferreira, *Sec*
EMP: 17 **EST:** 1986
SQ FT: 17,000
SALES (est): 2.08MM **Privately Held**
Web: www.fcfinc.net
SIC: 3273 Ready-mixed concrete

(G-16020)
GLENCORE RECYCLING LLC
80 Commercial Way (02914-1006)
PHONE..........................401 438-9220
Beatrice Tierre, *Mgr*
EMP: 18
SALES (corp-wide): 255.98B **Privately Held**
Web: www.cyberexport.net
SIC: 5084 3341 Recycling machinery and
equipment; Gold smelting and refining
(secondary)
HQ: Glencore Recycling Llc
1695 Monterey Hwy
San Jose CA 95112
408 998-4930

(G-16021)
GRAPHIC INK INCORPORATED
629 Warren Ave (02914-2914)
PHONE..........................401 431-5081
Nelson Silva, *Pr*
Nelson Silvia, *Pr*
Hilda Allienello, *VP*
EMP: 15 **EST:** 1997
SALES (est): 836.32K **Privately Held**
Web: www.graphicinkonline.com
SIC: 2759 Screen printing

(G-16022)
GUIA COMMERCIAL PORTUGUES INC
100 Warren Ave (02914-5137)
P.O. Box 14331 (02914-0331)
PHONE..........................401 438-1740
David Dasilva, *Pr*
EMP: 7 **EST:** 1982
SQ FT: 3,394
SALES (est): 400.56K **Privately Held**
SIC: 2741 Miscellaneous publishing

(G-16023)
IMPERIAL-DELTAH INC
Also Called: Imperial Pearl Syndicate
795 Waterman Ave (02914-1713)
PHONE..........................401 434-2597
Banice Bazar, *Pr*
▲ **EMP:** 100 **EST:** 1958
SALES (est): 9.96MM
SALES (corp-wide): 21.2MM **Privately Held**
SIC: 3911 5094 Jewelry, precious metal;
Jewelry
PA: The Bazar Group Inc
795 Waterman Ave
East Providence RI 02914
401 434-2595

(G-16024)
INTERSTATE ELEC SVCS CORP
20 N Blossom St (02914-2729)
PHONE..........................401 369-7890
John Sloane, *Brnch Mgr*
EMP: 49
SALES (corp-wide): 122.73MM **Privately Held**
Web: www.iesc1.com
SIC: 1731 3531 Electronic controls
installation; Cranes, nec
PA: Interstate Electrical Services
Corporation
70 Treble Cove Rd
North Billerica MA 01862
978 667-5200

(G-16025)
JH LYNCH & SONS INC
835 Taunton Ave (02914-1614)
PHONE..........................401 434-7100
EMP: 11
SALES (corp-wide): 48.18MM **Privately Held**
Web: www.jhlynch.com
SIC: 2951 Asphalt paving mixtures and
blocks
PA: J.H. Lynch & Sons, Inc.
50 Lynch Pl
Cumberland RI 02864
401 333-4300

(G-16026)
JONES SAFETY EQUIPMENT COMPANY
Also Called: Jones & Company
325 Massasoit Ave (02914-2011)
PHONE..........................401 434-4010
Lawrence K Hey, *Pr*
EMP: 7 **EST:** 1940
SQ FT: 5,000
SALES (est): 496.62K **Privately Held**
SIC: 3851 Goggles: sun, safety, industrial,
underwater, etc.

(G-16027)
KEFI DEVELOPMENT INC
Also Called: Dama Jewelry
800 Waterman Ave (02914-1728)
PHONE..........................401 272-6513
Marcos Fountoulakis, *Pr*
Dominic Meloni, *
▲ **EMP:** 30 **EST:** 1977
SALES (est): 4.61MM **Privately Held**
SIC: 3915 3961 Jewelers' findings and
materials; Costume jewelry

(G-16028)
KELLEY METALS CORP
115 Valley St (02914-4423)
PHONE..........................401 434-8795
John Kelly Junior, *Pr*
John Kelley Iii, *VP*
EMP: 10 **EST:** 1951
SQ FT: 12,000
SALES (est): 1.28MM **Privately Held**
SIC: 3341 Secondary nonferrous metals

(G-16029)
LDC INC
Also Called: Fiesta Jewelry
22 First St (02914-5007)
PHONE..........................401 861-4667
Edward N Decristofaro, *Pr*
Jennifer Brousseau, *Ex VP*
▲ **EMP:** 10 **EST:** 1985
SALES (est): 2.46MM **Privately Held**
Web: www.ldcincorporated.com

SIC: 3544 3312 5944 5094 Special dies and
tools; Pipes and tubes; Jewelry stores;
Jewelry

(G-16030)
MATRIX I LLC
Also Called: Pep Micropep
1 Catamore Blvd (02914-1233)
PHONE..........................401 434-3040
John S Harker, *Pr*
Alan M Huffenus, *
EMP: 74 **EST:** 1963
SQ FT: 65,000
SALES (est): 21.95MM
SALES (corp-wide): 433.51MM **Privately Held**
Web: matrix.ioffice.com
SIC: 3089 3544 Injection molding of plastics
; Special dies, tools, jigs, and fixtures
HQ: Precision Engineered Products Llc
110 Frank Mossberg Dr
Attleboro MA 02703

(G-16031)
MOO INC
Also Called: Moo.com
25 Fairmount Ave (02914-1701)
PHONE..........................401 519-7216
Richard Moross, *Pr*
Brian Murphy, *
▲ **EMP:** 80 **EST:** 2009
SQ FT: 18,000
SALES (est): 29.59MM **Privately Held**
Web: www.moo.com
SIC: 2759 Commercial printing, nec
PA: Moo Print Limited
Unit 12
Dagenham RM9 6

(G-16032)
MORRIS TRANSPARENT BOX CO
945 Warren Ave (02914-1423)
PHONE..........................401 438-6116
Alfred T Morris Junior, *Pr*
Joan Morris, *VP*
Ann Morris, *Sec*
EMP: 15 **EST:** 1958
SQ FT: 20,000
SALES (est): 801.85K **Privately Held**
Web: www.billieannplastics.com
SIC: 3089 5162 2671 Boxes, plastics;
Plastics sheets and rods; Paper; coated
and laminated packaging

(G-16033)
NARRAGANSETT BUS FORMS INC
21 Massasoit Ave (02914-4439)
P.O. Box 9448 (02940-9448)
PHONE..........................401 331-2000
TOLL FREE: 800
David Almeida, *CEO*
EMP: 17 **EST:** 1966
SALES (est): 691.79K **Privately Held**
Web:
www.narragansettbusinessforms.com
SIC: 2752 Offset printing

(G-16034)
NORDSON EFD LLC (HQ)
Also Called: E F D
40 Catamore Blvd (02914-1206)
PHONE..........................401 431-7000
Michael F Hilton, *Pr*
Jeff Pembroke, *VP*
David Guiot, *VP*
John J Keane, *Sr VP*
Gregory A Thaxton, *Sr VP*
▲ **EMP:** 212 **EST:** 1963
SQ FT: 115,000

SALES (est): 91.48MM
SALES (corp-wide): 2.63B **Publicly Held**
Web: www.nordson.com
SIC: 3548 3586 3699 Welding apparatus;
Measuring and dispensing pumps;
Electrical equipment and supplies, nec
PA: Nordson Corporation
28601 Clemens Rd
Westlake OH 44145
440 892-1580

(G-16035)
NUMACO PACKAGING LLC
82 Boyd Ave (02914-1202)
PHONE..........................401 438-4952
◆ **EMP:** 10 **EST:** 1988
SQ FT: 40,000
SALES (est): 2MM **Privately Held**
Web: www.numaco.com
SIC: 3172 2652 3999 3545 Cases, jewelry;
Boxes, newsboard, metal edged: made
from purchased materials; Flocking metal
products; Machine tool accessories

(G-16036)
OCEAN STATE CPL INC
40 Jordan St (02914-1214)
PHONE..........................401 431-0153
Robert Mongeon, *Pr*
Guido Petrosinelli, *
Charles Coelho, *
EMP: 110 **EST:** 2005
SQ FT: 30,356
SALES (est): 4.47MM **Privately Held**
Web: www.oceanstatecpl.com
SIC: 2053 Frozen bakery products, except
bread

(G-16037)
PARSONSKELLOGG LLC
Also Called: Driving Impressions
2290 Pawtucket Ave (02914-1710)
PHONE..........................866 602-8398
Thomas Kellogg, *Pr*
Tom Kellogg, *Pr*
Pete Mccormick, *CFO*
EMP: 100 **EST:** 2001
SQ FT: 21,000
SALES (est): 17.12MM **Privately Held**
Web: www.parsonskellogg.com
SIC: 3949 7389 7319 Sporting and athletic
goods, nec; Embroidery advertising;
Display advertising service

(G-16038)
PG IMTECH OF CALIFORN
27 Dexter Rd (02914-2045)
PHONE..........................401 521-2490
Kenneth Shonk, *Admn*
EMP: 7 **EST:** 2014
SALES (est): 150.77K **Privately Held**
SIC: 2851 Paints and allied products

(G-16039)
QUALITY CHAIN & CABLE LLC
70 Commercial Way (02914-1023)
PHONE..........................401 575-8323
EMP: 7 **EST:** 2009
SALES (est): 122.46K **Privately Held**
Web: www.wwewirerope.com
SIC: 3496 Miscellaneous fabricated wire
products

(G-16040)
QUICK FITTING INC
655 Waterman Ave (02914-1712)
P.O. Box 164 (02878-0164)
PHONE..........................401 734-9500
David Crompton, *Pr*
Michael Pappas, *

Frank Kosky, *
▲ **EMP:** 87 **EST:** 2007
SALES (est): 9.04MM **Privately Held**
Web: www.quickfitting.com
SIC: 3432 3643 Plumbing fixture fittings and trim; Connectors and terminals for electrical devices

(G-16041)
READE INTERNATIONAL CORP (PA)
Also Called: Reade Advanced Materials
850 Waterman Ave Ste 4 (02914-1729)
P.O. Box 15039 (02915-0039)
PHONE................................401 433-7000
Charles F Reade Junior, *Pr*
Emily Reade, *VP*
Bethany Satterfield, *VP*
◆ **EMP:** 15 **EST:** 1983
SQ FT: 5,500
SALES (est): 17.82MM
SALES (corp-wide): 17.82MM **Privately Held**
Web: www.reade.com
SIC: 5051 2819 Miscellaneous nonferrous products; Industrial inorganic chemicals, nec

(G-16042)
REGAL COMPONENTS INC
10 Almeida Ave Ste D (02914-1027)
PHONE................................727 299-0800
Fernando Coelho, *Pr*
▲ **EMP:** 10 **EST:** 2005
SALES (est): 877.83K **Privately Held**
Web: www.regalcomps.com
SIC: 3441 Building components, structural steel

(G-16043)
SE MASS DEVLOPMENT LLC
930 Waterman Ave (02914-1337)
PHONE................................401 434-3329
EMP: 10 **EST:** 2009
SALES (est): 170.75K **Privately Held**
SIC: 3613 Switchgear and switchboard apparatus

(G-16044)
SIGNATURE PRINTING INC
Also Called: Copyworld II
5 Almeida Ave (02914-1001)
PHONE................................401 438-1200
Anthony Andrade, *Pr*
EMP: 60 **EST:** 1994
SQ FT: 1,500
SALES (est): 9.06MM **Privately Held**
Web: www.signatureprinters.com
SIC: 2752 Offset printing

(G-16045)
TAHOE JEWELRY INC
20 J Medeiros Way (02914-1022)
PHONE................................401 435-4114
John Medeiros, *Pr*
EMP: 10 **EST:** 1984
SQ FT: 10,000
SALES (est): 674.02K **Privately Held**
Web: www.johnmedeiros.com
SIC: 3911 Jewelry, precious metal

(G-16046)
UP COUNTRY INC
76 Boyd Ave (02914-1202)
PHONE................................401 431-2940
Alice M Nichols, *Pr*
▲ **EMP:** 22 **EST:** 1981
SQ FT: 3,000
SALES (est): 2.23MM **Privately Held**
Web: www.upcountryinc.com

SIC: 3999 0752 Pet supplies; Animal specialty services

(G-16047)
W R COBB COMPANY
Also Called: Cobb/Ballou Findings
800 Waterman Ave (02914-1728)
PHONE................................401 438-7000
Roderick Lichtenfels, *Pr*
Theodore Lichtenfels, *
▲ **EMP:** 150 **EST:** 1877
SQ FT: 30,000
SALES (est): 22.68MM **Privately Held**
Web: www.wrcobb.com
SIC: 3915 Jewelers' findings and materials

(G-16048)
WHETSTONE WORKSHOP LLC
41 Dexter Rd (02914-2045)
PHONE................................401 368-7410
EMP: 7 **EST:** 2011
SQ FT: 7,500
SALES (est): 808.29K **Privately Held**
Web: www.whetstoneworkshop.com
SIC: 3499 Chair frames, metal

(G-16049)
XSTRATA RECYCLING INC
80 Commercial Way (02914-1006)
PHONE................................401 438-9220
▲ **EMP:** 28
SIC: 8731 3341 Industrial laboratory, except testing; Secondary nonferrous metals

Exeter
Washington County

(G-16050)
AARGO ENVIRONMENTAL INC
35 Beechwood Hill Trl (02822-5233)
PHONE................................401 678-6444
Kathryn Johnson-perry, *Pr*
Ronald Perry, *VP*
EMP: 8 **EST:** 2004
SALES (est): 469.16K **Privately Held**
Web: www.aargoenvironmentaltools.com
SIC: 3563 Vacuum (air extraction) systems, industrial

(G-16051)
HARDWOOD DESIGN INC
Also Called: Hardwood Closet Company
24 Dorset Mill Rd (02822-5026)
PHONE................................401 294-2235
William Bivona, *Pr*
Robinson Berry, *VP*
EMP: 27 **EST:** 1982
SQ FT: 12,000
SALES (est): 906.68K **Privately Held**
Web: www.hdistair.com
SIC: 2431 2434 Staircases and stairs, wood ; Wood kitchen cabinets

(G-16052)
HERITAGE CONCRETE CORP
535 South County Trl (02822-3405)
P.O. Box 553 (02822-0505)
PHONE................................401 294-1524
Sharon Courtois, *Pr*
John Courtois, *Treas*
EMP: 10 **EST:** 1992
SQ FT: 2,500
SALES (est): 1.1MM **Privately Held**
Web: www.heritageconcrete.com
SIC: 3273 Ready-mixed concrete

Fiskeville
Providence County

(G-16053)
ARKWRIGHT ADVANCED COATING INC (HQ)
Also Called: Sihl
538 Main St (02823)
P.O. Box 139 (02823-0139)
PHONE................................401 821-1000
Darren Letang, *Pr*
Stephanie Macleod, *
◆ **EMP:** 110 **EST:** 2008
SALES (est): 89.22MM
SALES (corp-wide): 61.87MM **Privately Held**
Web: www.sihlinc.com
SIC: 2679 Paper products, converted, nec
PA: Diatec Holding Spa
Via Cesare Battisti 8
Milano MI 20122

Glendale
Providence County

(G-16054)
BRUIN PLASTICS CO INC
61 Joslin Rd (02826-1633)
P.O. Box 700 (02826-0700)
PHONE................................800 556-7764
Dennis E Angelone, *Pr*
Stephen M Angelone, *
◆ **EMP:** 40 **EST:** 1964
SQ FT: 75,000
SALES (est): 9.59MM **Privately Held**
Web: www.bruinplastics.com
SIC: 3081 Unsupported plastics film and sheet

Greenville
Providence County

(G-16055)
ARTIC TOOL & ENGRG CO LLC
29 Lark Industrial Pkwy (02828-3024)
PHONE................................401 785-2210
John Sousa, *Genl Mgr*
EMP: 27 **EST:** 1969
SQ FT: 10,000
SALES (est): 847.05K
SALES (corp-wide): 436.59MM **Privately Held**
Web: www.cjmco.com
SIC: 3599 3469 7692 Machine shop, jobbing and repair; Metal stampings, nec; Welding repair
HQ: The Carlyle Johnson Machine Company Llc
291 Boston Tpke
Bolton CT 06043

(G-16056)
B-FRESH INC
37 Lark Industrial Pkwy Unit A (02828-3001)
PHONE................................401 349-0001
Robert Thistle, *Prin*
EMP: 7 **EST:** 2008
SALES (est): 264.93K **Privately Held**
Web: www.bfreshgum.com
SIC: 2099 Food preparations, nec

(G-16057)
CAVANAGH COMPANY
Also Called: Cavanagh

610 Putnam Pike (02828-1438)
PHONE................................401 949-4000
Brian Cavanagh, *Pr*
Peter Cavanagh, *Pr*
Helene Cavanagh, *
▲ **EMP:** 50 **EST:** 1941
SQ FT: 25,000
SALES (est): 4.71MM **Privately Held**
Web: www.cavanaghco.com
SIC: 2051 Bread, cake, and related products

(G-16058)
FAF INC (PA)
Also Called: Fashion Accessories First
26 Lark Industrial Pkwy (02828-3009)
PHONE................................401 949-3000
Joellen Fiorenzano, *Pr*
Jason Gale, *
Arthur Fiorenzano, *
Noel Bentley, *
Nancy Landi, *
▲ **EMP:** 69 **EST:** 1975
SQ FT: 22,000
SALES (est): 23.82MM
SALES (corp-wide): 23.82MM **Privately Held**
Web: www.faf.com
SIC: 3911 Jewelry, precious metal

(G-16059)
HB PRECISION PRODUCTS INC
21 Lark Industrial Pkwy Unit A (02828-3026)
P.O. Box 207 (02876-0207)
PHONE................................401 767-4340
Ronald Houle, *CEO*
Raymond Houle, *VP*
EMP: 10 **EST:** 2004
SALES (est): 917.31K **Privately Held**
Web: www.hbprecision.com
SIC: 3599 Machine shop, jobbing and repair

(G-16060)
JUTRAS MANUFACTURING COMPANY
25 Lark Industrial Pkwy (02828-3024)
PHONE................................401 949-8101
EMP: 8 **EST:** 1985
SALES (est): 220K **Privately Held**
SIC: 2431 Ornamental woodwork: cornices, mantels, etc.

(G-16061)
KERISSA CREATIONS INC
15 Lark Industrial Pkwy Unit E (02828-3029)
PHONE................................401 949-5100
Marcus A Senerchia Junior, *Pr*
Sal Scetta, *
▲ **EMP:** 17 **EST:** 1982
SQ FT: 12,000
SALES (est): 622.63K **Privately Held**
SIC: 3911 Jewelry, precious metal

(G-16062)
PAVEMENT WAREHOUSE
11 Calista St (02828-2805)
PHONE................................401 233-3200
Charles Stanley, *Owner*
EMP: 8 **EST:** 2000
SALES (est): 127.73K **Privately Held**
SIC: 2951 Asphalt paving mixtures and blocks

(G-16063)
REGENT CONTROLS INC
29 Lark Industrial Pkwy (02828-3024)
P.O. Box 9546 (06043-9546)
PHONE................................203 732-6200
Lora C Murphy, *Pr*

Lora C Murphy, *Ch Bd*
H Clay Minor, *VP*
EMP: 11 EST: 1947
SQ FT: 9,000
SALES (est): 1.26MM **Privately Held**
Web: www.regentcontrols.com
SIC: 3625 Electric controls and control accessories, industrial

---

Harrisville
Providence County

(G-16064)
ATLAS BARRELL & PALLET INC
Also Called: Atlas Pallet
50 Old Mill St (02830-1617)
PHONE..............................401 568-2900
Earl Handrigan, *Pr*
EMP: 55 EST: 1950
SQ FT: 60,000
SALES (est): 4.78MM **Privately Held**
Web: www.atlaspalletri.com
SIC: 2448 Pallets, wood

(G-16065)
EAGLE MOTORS INC
Also Called: Eagle Motors Victory
172 Chapel St (02830-1349)
PHONE..............................401 568-2580
Robert Depaulo, *Pr*
EMP: 17 EST: 1979
SALES (est): 1.08MM **Privately Held**
Web: www.eaglemotors.com
SIC: 7538 5521 3089 3799 General automotive repair shops; Automobiles, used cars only; Automotive parts, plastic; Snowmobiles

---

Hope Valley
Washington County

(G-16066)
BUICK LLC
Also Called: Beadery Craft Products, The
106 Canonchet Rd (02832-1109)
P.O. Box 178 (02832-0178)
PHONE..............................401 539-2432
Steven Grahm, *Managing Member*
Jack Warren, *
▲ **EMP: 35 EST:** 1932
SQ FT: 28,000
SALES (est): 4.54MM **Privately Held**
Web: www.thebeadery.com
SIC: 3089 Injection molding of plastics

(G-16067)
KAY DEE DESIGNS INC (PA)
177 Skunk Hill Rd (02832-1262)
P.O. Box 448 (02832-0448)
PHONE..............................401 539-2400
Richard S Rakauskas, *Pr*
Charles Donnell, *
◆ **EMP: 29 EST:** 1951
SQ FT: 50,000
SALES (est): 6.52MM **Privately Held**
Web: www.kaydeedesigns.com
SIC: 2269 2261 5023 Linen fabrics: dyeing, finishing, and printing; Screen printing of cotton broadwoven fabrics; Kitchenware

---

Jamestown
Newport County

(G-16068)
AURORA PERFORMANCE PDTS LLC

Also Called: Argus Analyzers
56 Green Ln (02835-1208)
PHONE..............................401 398-2959
EMP: 7 EST: 2005
SALES (est): 786.22K **Privately Held**
SIC: 3825 Battery testers, electrical

(G-16069)
H V HOLLAND INC
Also Called: Holland, H. V. Sheet Metal
79 North Rd (02835-1433)
P.O. Box 335 (02835-0335)
PHONE..............................401 423-0614
Edward N Holland, *Pr*
Sharon G Holland, *Treas*
EMP: 15 EST: 1966
SALES (est): 880.5K **Privately Held**
Web: www.hvholland.com
SIC: 1761 1711 3444 Roofing, siding, and sheetmetal work; Heating and air conditioning contractors; Sheet metalwork

(G-16070)
ISLAND NEWS ENTERPRISE
Also Called: Jamestown Press
45 Narragansett Ave (02835-1150)
PHONE..............................401 423-3200
Jeff Mc Donough, *Pr*
Jeffrey Mcdonough, *Editor*
EMP: 8 EST: 1989
SALES (est): 793.18K **Privately Held**
Web: www.jamestownpress.com
SIC: 2711 Newspapers, publishing and printing

Johnston
Providence County

(G-16071)
1ST CASTING COMPANY
64 Dyerville Ave (02919-4411)
PHONE..............................401 272-0750
Jerry Traficante, *Pr*
EMP: 10 EST: 1980
SQ FT: 4,400
SALES (est): 895.83K **Privately Held**
SIC: 3356 Nonferrous rolling and drawing, nec

(G-16072)
ACCU RX INC
100 Federal Way (02919-4637)
P.O. Box 19223 (02919-0223)
PHONE..............................401 454-2920
Nicholas Masi, *Pr*
Elaine Masi, *
EMP: 50 EST: 1985
SQ FT: 5,000
SALES (est): 9.63MM
SALES (corp-wide): 2.55MM **Privately Held**
SIC: 3851 Lenses, ophthalmic
HQ: Essilor Laboratories Of America, Inc.
13515 N Stemmons Fwy
Dallas TX 75234
972 241-4141

(G-16073)
AG & G INC (PA)
Also Called: Vieste Rosa
21 Mill St (02919-6817)
PHONE..............................401 946-4330
Anthony Giarrusso, *Pr*
Frank Giarrusso, *
Matthew Giarrusso, *
John Giarrusso, *
Angelo Giarrusso, *Retail Vice President**
▲ **EMP: 45 EST:** 1986
SQ FT: 25,000

SALES (est): 2.91MM
SALES (corp-wide): 2.91MM **Privately Held**
Web: www.cristabellejewelry.com
SIC: 3961 Costume jewelry, ex. precious metal and semiprecious stones

(G-16074)
ALVITI LINK - ALL INC
165 Dyerville Ave Unit 1 (02919-4400)
PHONE..............................401 861-6656
Lucille Knight, *Pr*
Thomas C Plunkett, *Prin*
EMP: 7 EST: 2001
SALES (est): 258.63K **Privately Held**
Web: www.alvitilinkall.com
SIC: 3911 Jewelry, precious metal

(G-16075)
AMRING WORLDWIDE INC ✪
Also Called: A & H Mfg. Co.
1 Carding Ln (02919-4621)
PHONE..............................401 943-5040
Anthony A Calandrelli, *CEO*
EMP: 85 EST: 2022
SALES (est): 6.22MM **Privately Held**
SIC: 2653 2671 Display items, corrugated: made from purchased materials; Paper; coated and laminated packaging

(G-16076)
ARDEN JEWELRY MFG CO
Also Called: Joan Imports
10 Industrial Ln (02919-3126)
PHONE..............................401 274-9800
Steven Abrams, *Pr*
▲ **EMP: 26 EST:** 1940
SQ FT: 28,000
SALES (est): 2.26MM **Privately Held**
Web: www.ardenjewelry.com
SIC: 3911 Jewelry, precious metal

(G-16077)
BAFFONIS POULTRY FARM INC
Also Called: Baffoni's Wholesale & Retail
324 Greenville Ave (02919-2620)
PHONE..............................401 231-6315
Donald Baffoni, *Pr*
Arthur Baffoni, *
EMP: 30 EST: 1932
SALES (est): 1.02MM **Privately Held**
Web: www.baffonispoultryfarm.com
SIC: 0251 0252 2015 Broiler, fryer, and roaster chickens; Chicken eggs; Chicken slaughtering and processing

(G-16078)
CASE FUTURE CORP
27 Mill St (02919-6800)
PHONE..............................401 944-0402
Mario Cimarelli, *Pr*
▲ **EMP: 24 EST:** 1990
SQ FT: 25,000
SALES (est): 1.09MM **Privately Held**
Web: dm.epiq11.com
SIC: 3499 Boxes for packing and shipping, metal

(G-16079)
CHEWBARKA INC
165 Dyerville Ave Unit 2 (02919-4400)
PHONE..............................404 464-9911
Frank Ricci Junior, *Pr*
EMP: 11 EST: 2019
SALES (est): 986.58K **Privately Held**
Web: www.chewbarka.com
SIC: 3599 Machine shop, jobbing and repair

(G-16080)
DEMAICH INDUSTRIES INC
70 Mill St (02919-6251)
PHONE..............................401 944-3576
Douglas Hood, *Pr*
Claire Hood, *VP*
EMP: 15 EST: 1980
SQ FT: 10,000
SALES (est): 2.26MM **Privately Held**
Web: www.demaich.com
SIC: 3469 3599 Stamping metal for the trade ; Machine shop, jobbing and repair

(G-16081)
DIG RITE COMPANY INC
572 Central Ave (02919-4711)
PHONE..............................401 862-5895
Morris Maglioli, *Pr*
Tracy Pine, *Prin*
EMP: 10 EST: 2010
SALES (est): 606.21K **Privately Held**
Web: www.digritecompany.com
SIC: 3531 1389 5082 Plows: construction, excavating, and grading; Excavating slush pits and cellars; Excavating machinery and equipment

(G-16082)
DURA-KOTE TECHNOLOGY LTD
2 Industrial Ln (02919-3126)
PHONE..............................401 331-6460
Louis Francazio, *Pr*
Bob Ricci, *VP*
EMP: 10 EST: 1998
SQ FT: 15,000
SALES (est): 933.99K **Privately Held**
SIC: 3471 Electroplating of metals or formed products

(G-16083)
E & M ENTERPRISES LTD
16 Sunnyside Ave (02919-5318)
PHONE..............................401 274-7405
Ernest Motta, *Pr*
Ernest Motta Presvp, *Prin*
EMP: 10 EST: 2000
SQ FT: 9,000
SALES (est): 954.22K **Privately Held**
SIC: 3599 Machine shop, jobbing and repair

(G-16084)
ERM LLC
16 Sunnyside Ave (02919-5318)
PHONE..............................401 934-2544
EMP: 8 EST: 1976
SALES (est): 458.81K **Privately Held**
SIC: 3911 Jewelry, precious metal

(G-16085)
FIRST CARD CO INC
Also Called: First Card Packaging
1 Carding Ln (02919-4621)
PHONE..............................401 434-6140
Anthony Calandrelli, *Pr*
▲ **EMP: 24 EST:** 1981
SALES (est): 2.27MM **Privately Held**
Web: www.firstcardpackaging.com
SIC: 3911 Jewel settings and mountings, precious metal

(G-16086)
FRED RICCI TOOL CO INC
Also Called: Chewbarka's Tags
165 Dyerville Ave Unit 2 (02919-4400)
PHONE..............................401 464-9911
Frank Ricci, *Pr*
◆ **EMP: 10 EST:** 1985
SQ FT: 15,000
SALES (est): 1.63MM **Privately Held**

Web: www.chewbarka.com
SIC: 3599 Machine shop, jobbing and repair

(G-16087)
FUELING SERVICES LLC
Also Called: Worldwide Fueling
141 Shun Pike (02919-4514)
P.O. Box 40098 (02940-0098)
PHONE......................401 764-0711
Mike Horkins, *CEO*
EMP: 16 EST: 2006
SQ FT: 6,000
SALES (est): 1.87MM **Privately Held**
SIC: 3559 Petroleum refinery equipment

(G-16088)
H B WELDING INC
60 Dyerville Ave (02919-4408)
PHONE......................401 727-0323
Helen Bacon, *Pr*
EMP: 35 EST: 1985
SALES (est): 2.21MM **Privately Held**
Web: www.hbwelding.com
SIC: 7692 Welding repair

(G-16089)
INDUSTRIAL & COMMERCIAL
FINSHG
Also Called: Icf
1339 Plainfield St (02919-6813)
PHONE......................401 942-4680
Ronald Patrick, *Pr*
EMP: 8 EST: 1986
SQ FT: 5,000
SALES (est): 945.97K **Privately Held**
SIC: 3479 Coating of metals and formed
   products

(G-16090)
J ARAKELIAN INC
66 Mill St (02919-6251)
PHONE......................401 943-7366
EMP: 15 EST: 1978
SALES (est): 612.58K **Privately Held**
SIC: 3965 3399 3911 3479 Buttons and
   parts; Metal fasteners; Jewelry, precious
   metal; Jewelry enameling

(G-16091)
K ALGER WOODWORKING INC
54 Argonne St (02919-3670)
PHONE......................401 228-5254
Kenneth Alger, *Pr*
EMP: 8 EST: 2011
SALES (est): 209.04K **Privately Held**
Web: www.kalgerwoodworking.com
SIC: 2431 Millwork

(G-16092)
KIMBALL HARDWOODS LLC
83 King St (02919-4019)
PHONE......................401 300-9070
Derek M Kimball, *Mgr*
EMP: 9 EST: 2017
SALES (est): 378.94K **Privately Held**
Web: www.kimballhardwoods.com
SIC: 2421 Sawmills and planing mills,
   general

(G-16093)
LIMAGE INC
Also Called: Avenir
4 Industrial Ln (02919-3126)
PHONE......................401 369-7141
Thomas V Fiore, *Pr*
Patricia A Fiore, *
▲ EMP: 50 EST: 1984
SQ FT: 8,000
SALES (est): 6.11MM **Privately Held**

Web: l-image-johnston.edan.io
SIC: 3911 Jewelry, precious metal

(G-16094)
LOUIS PRESS INC
39 Greenville Ave Apt 1 (02919-4223)
PHONE......................401 351-9229
Louis Perrotta, *Pr*
Thomas Perrotta, *Pr*
EMP: 7 EST: 1948
SQ FT: 1,800
SALES (est): 521.52K **Privately Held**
Web: www.louispress.com
SIC: 2752 Offset printing

(G-16095)
MARTINS SOLDERING
10 Alcazar Ave (02919-4069)
PHONE......................401 521-2280
John Martin, *Owner*
EMP: 7 EST: 1980
SALES (est): 341.79K **Privately Held**
Web: www.todd-brandt.com
SIC: 3911 Jewelry, precious metal

(G-16096)
MODERN MANUFACTURING INC
Also Called: Modern Jewelry
47 Homeland St (02919-5170)
PHONE......................401 944-9230
▲ EMP: 10
SQ FT: 27,000
SALES (est): 1.22MM **Privately Held**
SIC: 3961 Costume jewelry

(G-16097)
MORGAN MILL METALS LLC
25 Morgan Mill Rd (02919-6320)
PHONE......................401 270-9944
EMP: 13 EST: 2010
SQ FT: 5,000
SALES (est): 825.42K **Privately Held**
Web: www.morganmillmetals.com
SIC: 3341 Secondary nonferrous metals

(G-16098)
MORRIS & BROMS LLC
14 Wychwood Pl (02919-2145)
P.O. Box 3727 (02910-0727)
PHONE......................401 781-3134
EMP: 16 EST: 1954
SALES (est): 1.45MM **Privately Held**
Web: www.mearthane.com
SIC: 3469 3444 Stamping metal for the trade
   ; Sheet metalwork

(G-16099)
PAUL KING FOUNDRY INC
92 Allendale Ave (02919-2351)
PHONE......................401 231-3120
Paul Cabanagh, *Pr*
▲ EMP: 9 EST: 2002
SALES (est): 931.14K **Privately Held**
Web: www.paulkingfoundry.com
SIC: 3366 Castings (except die), nsk

(G-16100)
PHE INVESTMENTS LLC
Also Called: Ava Anderson
1 Carding Ln (02919-4621)
PHONE......................401 289-2900
Ava Sprague Anderson, *CEO*
Kimberly Anderson, *
Robert Anderson, *
Bob Manny, *
EMP: 55 EST: 2009
SQ FT: 120,000
SALES (est): 8.58MM **Privately Held**
Web: www.purehaven.com

SIC: 2834 Pharmaceutical preparations

(G-16101)
PROPRINT INCORPORATED
1145 Atwood Ave (02919-4924)
PHONE......................401 944-3855
Ronald De Stefano, *Pr*
Nancy De Stefano, *Sec*
David De Stefano, *VP*
EMP: 18 EST: 1974
SQ FT: 3,000
SALES (est): 412.96K **Privately Held**
SIC: 2752 Offset printing

(G-16102)
RAMTEL CORPORATION
115 Railroad Ave (02919-2441)
PHONE......................401 231-3340
Robert Moio Senior, *Pr*
EMP: 18 EST: 1978
SALES (est): 2.3MM **Privately Held**
Web: www.ramtel.com
SIC: 3661 Telephones and telephone
   apparatus

(G-16103)
RENAISANCE CORNICE
1010 Plainfield St (02919-6771)
PHONE......................401 275-6500
Alysha Mooney, *Prin*
EMP: 9 EST: 2006
SALES (est): 240.68K **Privately Held**
SIC: 3444 Sheet metal specialties, not
   stamped

(G-16104)
RHODE ISLAND CENTERLESS
INC
24 Morgan Mill Rd (02919-6321)
PHONE......................401 942-0403
David Bryan, *Pr*
David Bryan, *Pr*
Joyce Bryan, *Treas*
Martin Bryan, *Stockholder*
Debra Bryan, *Off Mgr*
EMP: 10 EST: 1989
SQ FT: 7,500
SALES (est): 777.35K **Privately Held**
Web: www.ricenterless.com
SIC: 3291 Wheels, grinding: artificial

(G-16105)
RHODE ISLAND PROVISION CO
Also Called: Little Rhody Brand
5 Day St (02919-4301)
PHONE......................401 831-0815
Edward R Robalisky, *Pr*
David Rickett, *VP*
D Robalisky, *Treas*
EMP: 14 EST: 1940
SQ FT: 10,000
SALES (est): 579.13K **Privately Held**
Web: www.littlerhodyhotdogs.com
SIC: 2013 Sausages, from purchased meat

(G-16106)
SBWINSOR CREAMERY LLC
58 Pine Hill Ave (02919-1451)
PHONE......................401 231-5113
Alan K Winsor, *Owner*
EMP: 7 EST: 2013
SALES (est): 164.34K **Privately Held**
SIC: 2021 Creamery butter

(G-16107)
STUPELL INDUSTRIES LTD INC
14 Industrial Ln (02919-3126)
PHONE......................401 831-5640
Robert Stupell, *Pr*

Todd Stupell, *VP*
Patricia Tobin, *Bookkpr*
▲ EMP: 14 EST: 1961
SQ FT: 12,000
SALES (est): 2.22MM **Privately Held**
Web: www.stupellind.com
SIC: 2499 5023 2394 Decorative wood and
   woodwork; Decorative home furnishings
   and supplies; Canvas and related products

(G-16108)
UBIO INC
1603 Plainfield Pike Apt B5 (02919-6274)
PHONE......................401 541-9172
Lucille De Clemente, *Pr*
John De Clemente, *
EMP: 8 EST: 1975
SALES (est): 206.77K **Privately Held**
Web: www.ubio.org
SIC: 3961 Costume jewelry, ex. precious
   metal and semiprecious stones

(G-16109)
UNIQUE PLATING CO
66 Mill St (02919-6251)
PHONE......................401 943-7366
John Arakelian Junior, *Pr*
EMP: 8 EST: 1976
SQ FT: 13,200
SALES (est): 858.68K **Privately Held**
SIC: 3471 Electroplating of metals or
   formed products

(G-16110)
UTILITY SYSTEMS INC
123 King Philip St (02919-4330)
P.O. Box 19120 (02919-0120)
PHONE......................401 351-6681
Henry V Rosciti, *Pr*
EMP: 21 EST: 1995
SALES (est): 981.25K **Privately Held**
SIC: 3713 Utility truck bodies

(G-16111)
VISION INDUSTRIES CORP
43 Hill Top Dr (02919-3083)
PHONE......................401 764-0916
Jason Tammelleo, *Prin*
EMP: 7 EST: 2007
SALES (est): 110K **Privately Held**
SIC: 3999 Manufacturing industries, nec

Kenyon
Washington County

(G-16112)
KENYON INDUSTRIES INC
Also Called: Brookwood Finishing
36 Sherman Ave (02836-1012)
P.O. Box 115 (02875-0115)
PHONE......................401 364-7761
Joanne Bagley, *Pr*
Joseph Trumpetto, *Treas*
◆ EMP: 300 EST: 1989
SQ FT: 330,000
SALES (est): 47.48MM **Privately Held**
Web: www.brookwoodcompanies.com
SIC: 2262 2269 2295 Dyeing: manmade
   fiber and silk broadwoven fabrics; Finishing
   plants, nec; Coated fabrics, not rubberized
HQ: Brookwood Companies Incorporated
   485 Madison Ave Ste 500
   New York NY 10022
   212 551-0100

GEOGRAPHIC

Kingston
Washington County

(G-16113)
KEY GRAPHICS INC
Also Called: Allegra Print & Imaging No 196
7 Caitlin Ct (02881-1841)
PHONE.....................................401 826-2425
Robert E Sweeney Junior, *Pr*
Samantha A Sweeney, *VP*
EMP: 8 **EST:** 1987
SALES (est): 535.92K **Privately Held**
Web: www.allegramarketingprint.com
SIC: 2752   Offset printing

Lincoln
Providence County

(G-16114)
ABAR COLOR LABS NENG INC
Also Called: Screencraft Graphics
9 Powder Hill Rd (02865-4407)
PHONE.....................................401 351-8644
George R Champagne, *Pr*
Stephen Welch, *VP*
Nancy Champagne, *Sec*
Jean Kruzan, *Treas*
EMP: 19 **EST:** 1950
SQ FT: 37,000
SALES (est): 777.25K **Privately Held**
Web: www.screencraftgraphics.com
SIC: 7384 3993   Photofinishing laboratory;
Signs and advertising specialties

(G-16115)
ACCENT DISPLAY CORP
Also Called: Accent Display
11 Dario Dr (02865-4900)
PHONE.....................................401 461-8787
Joseph Coury, *Pr*
Diane Coury, *
▲ **EMP:** 47 **EST:** 1990
SALES (est): 4.07MM **Privately Held**
Web: www.accentdisplay.com
SIC: 3993   Displays and cutouts, window
and lobby

(G-16116)
ACS INDUSTRIES INC (PA)
Also Called: ACS Industries
1 New England Way Unit 1 (02865-4284)
PHONE.....................................401 769-4700
Steven Buckler, *Pr*
Peter Botvin, *
Jeff Buckler, *
Paul Pimentel, *
◆ **EMP:** 50 **EST:** 1939
SQ FT: 20,000
SALES (est): 227.46MM
SALES (corp-wide): 227.46MM **Privately
Held**
Web: www.acsindustries.com
SIC: 3291 3496 3312 3315   Sponges,
scouring: metallic; Mesh, made from
purchased wire; Wire products, steel or iron
; Steel wire and related products

(G-16117)
AF GROUP INC
24 Albion Rd Ste 210 (02865-3747)
PHONE.....................................401 757-3910
John Carroll, *Ch*
Keith Lonergan, *
▼ **EMP:** 150 **EST:** 2013
SALES (est): 9.36MM **Privately Held**
SIC: 3842   Foot appliances, orthopedic

(G-16118)
AMERICAN TOOL COMPANY
623 George Washington Hwy (02865-4245)
PHONE.....................................401 333-0111
Richard P Mc Cally, *Pr*
Diane U Mc Cally, *VP*
EMP: 20 **EST:** 1917
SQ FT: 13,000
SALES (est): 2.36MM **Privately Held**
Web: www.americantoolcompany.com
SIC: 3599   Machine shop, jobbing and repair

(G-16119)
**ANDON ELECTRONICS
CORPORATION**
4 Court Dr (02865-4203)
PHONE.....................................401 333-0388
John Tate, *Pr*
Irene Small, *
EMP: 35 **EST:** 1988
SQ FT: 55,000
SALES (est): 4.28MM **Privately Held**
Web: www.andonelect.com
SIC: 3679 5065   Electronic circuits;
Electronic parts and equipment, nec

(G-16120)
ARTVAC CORPORATION
17 New England Way (02865-4290)
PHONE.....................................401 333-6120
Herbert Mershon, *Pr*
Richard Mayhew, *
Sol Mershon, *Stockholder*
▲ **EMP:** 23 **EST:** 1963
SQ FT: 15,000
SALES (est): 526.64K **Privately Held**
Web: www.artvac.com
SIC: 3499   Giftware, brass goods

(G-16121)
**BATES ABRASIVE PRODUCTS
INC**
Also Called: Marvel Abrasive Products
6 Carol Dr (02865-4402)
PHONE.....................................773 586-8700
Leslie Branch, *Pr*
Barbara Branch, *
▲ **EMP:** 35 **EST:** 1935
SQ FT: 35,000
SALES (est): 922.53K **Privately Held**
SIC: 3291   Abrasive products

(G-16122)
BREEZE PUBLICATIONS INC
Also Called: Valley Breeze
6 Blackstone Valley Pl Ste 204
(02865-1179)
PHONE.....................................401 334-9555
Tom Ward, *Pr*
James Quinn, *
EMP: 34 **EST:** 1996
SQ FT: 8,000
SALES (est): 2.36MM **Privately Held**
Web: www.valleybreeze.com
SIC: 2711   Newspapers, publishing and
printing

(G-16123)
BULLARD ABRASIVES INC
6 Carol Dr (02865-4402)
PHONE.....................................508 366-4300
Craig A Pickell, *CEO*
Richard A Whyte, *
◆ **EMP:** 90 **EST:** 1927
SQ FT: 30,000
SALES (est): 24.06MM **Privately Held**
Web: www.bullardabrasives.com
SIC: 5085 3291   Industrial supplies;
Abrasive products

(G-16124)
**CALISE & SONS BAKERY INC
(PA)**
Also Called: Calise Bakery
2 Quality Dr (02865-4266)
PHONE.....................................401 334-3444
Michael Calise, *Pr*
Robert L Calise, *
Peter Petrocelli, *
▲ **EMP:** 150 **EST:** 1908
SQ FT: 67,000
SALES (est): 43.94MM
SALES (corp-wide): 43.94MM **Privately
Held**
Web: www.calisebakery.com
SIC: 2051   Bread, cake, and related products

(G-16125)
CHEMART COMPANY
11 New England Way (02865-4289)
PHONE.....................................401 333-9200
Richard Beaupre, *CEO*
EMP: 35
SALES (corp-wide): 24.6MM **Privately
Held**
Web: www.chemart.com
SIC: 3479   Etching, photochemical
PA: Chemart Company
15 New England Way
Lincoln RI 02865
401 333-9200

(G-16126)
CHEMART COMPANY (PA)
Also Called: Beacon Design Company
15 New England Way (02865-4252)
PHONE.....................................401 333-9200
David Beaupre, *CEO*
John Leahy, *
▲ **EMP:** 60 **EST:** 1976
SQ FT: 55,000
SALES (est): 24.6MM
SALES (corp-wide): 24.6MM **Privately
Held**
Web: www.chemart.com
SIC: 3479 3471   Etching, photochemical;
Plating and polishing

(G-16127)
CLARIOS LLC
Also Called: Johnson Controls
6 Blackstone Valley Pl Ste 202
(02865-1179)
PHONE.....................................401 235-6700
Bob Steel, *Mgr*
EMP: 30
SALES (corp-wide): 1.54B **Privately Held**
Web: www.clarios.com
SIC: 2531   Seats, automobile
HQ: Clarios, Llc
5757 N Green Bay Ave
Milwaukee WI 53209

(G-16128)
**CONTINENTAL PLAS & PACKG
INC**
Also Called: Continental Plastics
21 Powder Hill Rd (02865-4417)
PHONE.....................................781 932-1115
John F Conley, *Pr*
EMP: 19 **EST:** 2004
SALES (est): 3.19MM **Privately Held**
Web: www.conplastics.com
SIC: 5199 3089   Packaging materials;
Injection molded finished plastics products,
nec

(G-16129)
**CREST MANUFACTURING
COMPANY**
5 Hood Dr (02865-1103)
P.O. Box 368 (02865-0368)
PHONE.....................................401 333-1350
Gary S Hood, *Pr*
Laura Hood, *
EMP: 38 **EST:** 1953
SQ FT: 18,000
SALES (est): 2.38MM **Privately Held**
Web: www.crestmfg.com
SIC: 3677 3469 3829 3823   Coil windings,
electronic; Stamping metal for the trade;
Measuring and controlling devices, nec;
Process control instruments

(G-16130)
DEALERSHIP SOFTWARE LLC
Also Called: Dealership Software
85 Industrial Cir Ste 201 (02865-2640)
P.O. Box 332 (02865-0332)
PHONE.....................................401 305-3740
William Mcauley, *Managing Member*
EMP: 18 **EST:** 2002
SALES (est): 1.89MM **Privately Held**
Web:
www.simplifydealershipsoftware.com
SIC: 7372   Application computer software

(G-16131)
**DENISON PHARMACEUTICALS
LLC**
100 Higginson Ave (02865-2735)
PHONE.....................................401 723-5500
C Douglas Hill, *Brnch Mgr*
EMP: 67
SALES (corp-wide): 42.51MM **Privately
Held**
Web: www.denisonpharmaceuticals.com
SIC: 2834   Pharmaceutical preparations
PA: Denison Pharmaceuticals, Llc
1 Powder Hill Rd
Lincoln RI 02865
401 723-5500

(G-16132)
**DENISON PHARMACEUTICALS
LLC (PA)**
1 Powder Hill Rd (02865-4407)
PHONE.....................................401 723-5500
C Douglas Hill, *Pr*
Brian Ofarrell, *
EMP: 101 **EST:** 1963
SQ FT: 100,000
SALES (est): 42.51MM
SALES (corp-wide): 42.51MM **Privately
Held**
Web: www.denisonpharmaceuticals.com
SIC: 2834   Pharmaceutical preparations

(G-16133)
DISPLAYS BY GARO INC
2 Carol Dr (02865-4402)
PHONE.....................................401 305-3511
Gary Garofano, *Pr*
EMP: 14 **EST:** 1988
SQ FT: 20,000
SALES (est): 1.64MM **Privately Held**
Web: www.garodisplay.info
SIC: 3578   Point-of-sale devices

(G-16134)
DURASTONE CORPORATION
150 Higginson Ave (02865-2705)
PHONE.....................................401 723-7100
Carol Ann Discuillo, *Pr*
Mary Ann Discuillo, *Sec*
Joanne Ciccarilli, *Treas*

▲ = Import ▼ = Export
◆ = Import/Export

Joanne Discuillo, *Treas*
EMP: 17 **EST:** 1991
SALES (est): 2.4MM **Privately Held**
Web: www.durastonecorporation.com
SIC: 3272 8742   Concrete products, precast, nec; Management consulting services

(G-16135)
EVERETT J PRESCOTT INC
Red Head Manufacturing
38 Albion Rd (02865-3707)
PHONE..........................401 333-8588
Jack Blade, *Brnch Mgr*
EMP: 8
SALES (corp-wide): 110.81MM **Privately Held**
Web: www.ejprescott.com
SIC: 3469 3494   Machine parts, stamped or pressed metal; Valves and pipe fittings, nec
PA: Everett J. Prescott, Inc.
32 Prscott St Lbby Hl Bus Libby Hill
Gardiner ME 04345
207 582-2006

(G-16136)
EXAIL DEFENSE SYSTEMS INC
27 Wellington Rd (02865-4411)
PHONE..........................401 475-4400
Edward P Curley Iii, *Pr*
Fabien Napolitano, *Dir*
Christine L Bearse, *Sec*
EMP: 21 **EST:** 2003
SALES (est): 3.27MM **Privately Held**
Web: www.ixblue.com
SIC: 7699 5088 3812   Nautical and navigational instrument repair; Navigation equipment and supplies; Position indicators for aircraft equipment
HQ: Exail
34 Rue De La Croix De Fer
Saint Germain En Laye 78100
130088888

(G-16137)
FINLAY EXT INGREDIENTS USA INC (DH)
Also Called: Autocrat Coffee
10 Blackstone Valley Pl (02865-1145)
PHONE..........................800 288-6272
Michael Snell Junior, *CEO*
Kevin Liddy, *
▲ **EMP:** 70 **EST:** 1895
SQ FT: 54,000
SALES (est): 50.34MM
SALES (corp-wide): 17.24B **Privately Held**
Web: www.finlays.net
SIC: 2095   Coffee extracts
HQ: James Finlay International, Inc.
120 Corporate Dr
Beaver Dam WI
920 887-8146

(G-16138)
GETS LLC
7 Thornwood Dr (02865-4960)
PHONE..........................401 314-5550
Tomasz Sadowski, *Mgr*
EMP: 71
SALES (corp-wide): 238.15K **Privately Held**
SIC: 3677   Electronic coils and transformers
PA: Gets Llc
374 Roosevelt Ave
Pawtucket RI 02860
401 314-5550

(G-16139)
GREYSTONE INCORPORATED
7 Wellington Rd (02865-4411)
PHONE..........................401 333-0444

John Maconi, *CEO*
Everett Fernald, *Pr*
Dave Lippy, *VP*
Norman Chartier, *CFO*
▲ **EMP:** 10 **EST:** 1932
SQ FT: 74,000
SALES (est): 3.95MM **Privately Held**
Web: www.greyst.com
SIC: 6519 3552 3451   Real property lessors, nec; Textile machinery; Screw machine products

(G-16140)
GREYSTONE OF LINCOLN INC (PA)
Also Called: Induplate
7 Wellington Rd (02865-4411)
PHONE..........................401 333-0444
▲ **EMP:** 140 **EST:** 1995
SQ FT: 75,000
SALES (est): 44.47MM **Privately Held**
Web: www.greyst.com
SIC: 3451 3462   Screw machine products; Iron and steel forgings

(G-16141)
HOPE VALLEY INDUSTRIES LLC
Also Called: Hope Valley
13 Powder Hill Rd (02865-4407)
PHONE..........................401 333-3133
EMP: 11 **EST:** 2019
SALES (est): 956.37K **Privately Held**
Web: www.hopevalleyind.com
SIC: 2211   Broadwoven fabric mills, cotton

(G-16142)
J&E HOME PRODUCTS LLC
Also Called: Anne At Home
21 Carrington St Ste 3 (02865-1701)
PHONE..........................401 464-8677
▲ **EMP:** 20 **EST:** 1997
SQ FT: 11,000
SALES (est): 1.69MM **Privately Held**
Web: www.anneathome.net
SIC: 3429   Builders' hardware

(G-16143)
KLITZNER INDUSTRIES INC
Also Called: H.K. Klitzner Company Division
26 Kirkbrae Dr (02865-1019)
PHONE..........................800 621-0161
Alan J Klitzner, *Pr*
Leta Klitzner, *
Henry Riccitelli, *
Dean Klitzner, *
▲ **EMP:** 28 **EST:** 1907
SQ FT: 20,000
SALES (est): 2.06MM **Privately Held**
Web: www.klitzner.com
SIC: 3911 3961   Jewelry, precious metal; Costume jewelry

(G-16144)
LANCE INDUSTRIES INC (PA)
Also Called: Symmetry Products
55 Industrial Cir Ste 3 (02865-2606)
PHONE..........................401 365-6272
Stephen Lancia, *Pr*
▲ **EMP:** 75 **EST:** 1982
SQ FT: 200,000
SALES (est): 8.23MM
SALES (corp-wide): 8.23MM **Privately Held**
Web: www.symmetryproducts.com
SIC: 3086   Packaging and shipping materials, foamed plastics

(G-16145)
MADEIRA ASSET HOLDINGS INC
9 Powder Hill Rd (02865-4407)
P.O. Box 310 (02864-0310)
PHONE..........................401 728-5903
Luis Agrela, *Pr*
Manuel Martins, *Dir Opers*
Peter Lombardi, *Sec*
EMP: 15 **EST:** 1987
SQ FT: 50,000
SALES (est): 2.5MM **Privately Held**
Web: www.rhodyrug.com
SIC: 2273   Rugs, braided and hooked

(G-16146)
MANDEVILLE SIGNS INC
Also Called: Mandeville
676 George Washington Hwy (02865-4229)
PHONE..........................401 334-9100
Thomas Mandeville, *Pr*
James E Mandeville, *
Jeanne Mandeville, *
EMP: 32 **EST:** 1917
SQ FT: 44,000
SALES (est): 4.69MM **Privately Held**
Web: www.mandevillesign.com
SIC: 3993   Electric signs

(G-16147)
MARION MFG CO
Also Called: Marion Drapery Workroom
1 Court Dr (02865-4202)
PHONE..........................401 331-4343
Jorge Medeiros, *Pr*
Maria Teresa Medeiros, *VP*
EMP: 21 **EST:** 1945
SALES (est): 444.98K **Privately Held**
SIC: 2391 5714   Draperies, plastic and textile: from purchased materials; Draperies

(G-16148)
MARVEL ABRASIVES PRODUCTS LLC
6 Carol Dr (02865-4402)
PHONE..........................800 621-0673
Lelsie J Branch, *Pr*
Barbara Branch, *VP*
▲ **EMP:** 10 **EST:** 2011
SALES (est): 263.1K **Privately Held**
SIC: 3291   Abrasive products

(G-16149)
MATERION TECHNICAL MTLS INC
5 Wellington Rd (02865-4411)
PHONE..........................401 333-1700
Al Lubrano, *Pr*
Robert Tavares, *
M C Hasychak, *
▲ **EMP:** 200 **EST:** 1968
SQ FT: 125,000
SALES (est): 50.55MM **Publicly Held**
SIC: 3331 3339 3423   Primary copper smelter products; Nickel refining (primary); Hand and edge tools, nec
PA: Materion Corporation
6070 Parkland Blvd
Mayfield Heights OH 44124

(G-16150)
NIANTIC SEAL INC
Also Called: Niantic Seal Nrtheast Rbr Pdts
17 Powder Hill Rd (02865-4407)
PHONE..........................401 334-6870
Robert Dirienzo, *Pr*
Peter Divoll, *VP Sls*
Philip Rooney, *CFO*
▲ **EMP:** 21 **EST:** 1963

SQ FT: 12,500
SALES (est): 13.04MM
SALES (corp-wide): 496.49MM **Privately Held**
Web: www.inscogroup.com
SIC: 3599 5085   Hose, flexible metallic; Seals, industrial
HQ: Insco Intermediate Holdings, Llc
17 Powder Hill Rd
Lincoln RI 02865

(G-16151)
PRYSMIAN CBLES SYSTEMS USA LLC
Also Called: Lincoln, RI Plant
3 Carol Dr (02865-4401)
PHONE..........................401 333-4848
Michael Brown, *Brnch Mgr*
EMP: 192
SQ FT: 200,000
Web: na.prysmian.com
SIC: 3357   Automotive wire and cable, except ignition sets: nonferrous
HQ: Prysmian Cables And Systems Usa, Llc
4 Tesseneer Dr
Highland Heights KY 41076
859 572-8000

(G-16152)
RADLEY CORPORATION
Also Called: Radley Corp of Grand Rapids
24 Albion Rd (02865-3747)
PHONE..........................616 554-9060
EMP: 23
SALES (corp-wide): 5.68MM **Privately Held**
Web: www.radley.com
SIC: 7371 5045 7372   Computer software development; Computers, peripherals, and software; Prepackaged software
PA: Radley Corporation
23077 Greenfield Rd # 440
Southfield MI 48075
248 559-6858

(G-16153)
SCREENCRAFT TILEWORKS LLC
Also Called: Screencraft
9 Powder Hill Rd (02865-4407)
PHONE..........................401 427-2816
◆ **EMP:** 7 **EST:** 2004
SALES (est): 945.46K **Privately Held**
Web: www.screencraftgifts.com
SIC: 3999   Advertising curtains

(G-16154)
SHEAFFER PEN CORPORATION
Also Called: Sheaffer Pen U.S.
1 Albion Rd Ste 100 (02865-3749)
PHONE..........................319 372-7444
▲ **EMP:** 600
SIC: 3951 5112 3952   Pens and mechanical pencils; Pens and/or pencils; Lead pencils and art goods

(G-16155)
STACKBIN CORPORATION
29 Powder Hill Rd (02865-4424)
PHONE..........................401 333-1600
William A Shaw, *Pr*
Scott A Shaw, *
Roy A Medeiros, *
James Shaw, *Stockholder*
▼ **EMP:** 45 **EST:** 1931
SQ FT: 60,000
SALES (est): 4.87MM **Privately Held**
Web: www.stackbin.com

SIC: 2599 3444 3443 Work benches, factory
; Sheet metalwork; Fabricated plate work
(boiler shop)

(G-16156)
TANURY INDUSTRIES INC
Also Called: Electronic Surface Coatings
6 New England Way (02865-4286)
PHONE.............................800 428-6213
Thomas Tanury, *Ch Bd*
Michael Akkaoui, *
Joseph Akkaoui, *
Patrick Lynch, *
Martin Buckholtz, *
EMP: 200 EST: 1948
SQ FT: 50,000
SALES (est): 24.57MM **Privately Held**
Web: www.tanury.com
SIC: 3471 Electroplating of metals or
formed products

(G-16157)
WILDTREE INC
15 Wellington Rd (02865-4411)
PHONE.............................401 732-1856
Henry Bedford, *CEO*
Mike Gilkenson, *Pr*
Cynthia Johnstone, *Sec*
Ross Murphy, *CFO*
◆ EMP: 80 EST: 1994
SALES (est): 20.81MM
SALES (corp-wide): 20.81MM **Privately
Held**
Web: www.wildtree.com
SIC: 2099 Seasonings and spices
PA: Wildtree Holdings, Llc
15 Wellington Rd
Lincoln RI 02865
401 732-1856

(G-16158)
WORLDWIDE TOOLING LLC
1 Christopher Dr (02865-4946)
PHONE.............................401 334-9806
▲ EMP: 10 EST: 2001
SQ FT: 800
SALES (est): 880.01K **Privately Held**
Web: www.worldwidetooling.com
SIC: 3089 Injection molding of plastics

Little Compton
Newport County

(G-16159)
CASE HARD
56 Indian Rd (02837-2111)
PHONE.............................401 635-8201
Greg Berdan, *CEO*
Norm Paasche, *Pr*
▲ EMP: 7 EST: 2005
SALES (est): 444.25K **Privately Held**
Web: www.hard-case.com
SIC: 3089 Cases, plastics

(G-16160)
**COLEBROOK INTRLCKING
PVERS WLL**
114 Colebrook Rd (02837-2014)
PHONE.............................401 835-6934
Mike W Rocha, *Prin*
EMP: 11 EST: 2010
SALES (est): 480.6K **Privately Held**
Web: www.mikeslawnandgarden.com
SIC: 3531 Pavers

(G-16161)
JAMES L GALLAGHER INC
408 W Main Rd (02837-1119)

PHONE.............................508 758-3102
James L Gallagher, *Pr*
EMP: 13 EST: 1999
SALES (est): 1.02MM **Privately Held**
Web: www.jlgallagher.com
SIC: 3552 Textile machinery

(G-16162)
SAKONNET VINEYARDS LP
162 W Main Rd (02837-1355)
P.O. Box 197 (02837-0197)
PHONE.............................401 635-8486
Earl Samson, *CEO*
Susan Samson, *Mgr*
EMP: 17 EST: 1975
SQ FT: 20,000
SALES (est): 1.24MM **Privately Held**
Web: www.sakonnetwine.com
SIC: 0172 2084 5182 5921 Grapes; Wine
cellars, bonded: engaged in blending wines
; Wine; Wine

Manville
Providence County

(G-16163)
EASTERN DESIGN INC
70 New River Rd (02838-1712)
P.O. Box 104 (02838-0104)
PHONE.............................401 765-0558
Edward Kelleher, *Pr*
Donna Kelleher, *VP*
EMP: 9 EST: 1994
SALES (est): 842.79K **Privately Held**
SIC: 2431 Interior and ornamental
woodwork and trim

(G-16164)
JOSEPH C LA FOND CO INC
340 Old River Rd (02838-1033)
P.O. Box 20 (02838-0020)
PHONE.............................401 769-3744
Dennis Lafond, *Pr*
Micheal Lafond, *VP*
Susan Buckless, *Sec*
EMP: 10 EST: 1947
SQ FT: 9,800
SALES (est): 671.05K **Privately Held**
SIC: 2231 Weaving mill, broadwoven
fabrics: wool or similar fabric

(G-16165)
MICHAEL HEALY DESIGNS INC
Also Called: Healy Plaques
60 New River Rd (02838-1712)
P.O. Box 4 (02838-0004)
PHONE.............................401 597-5900
Michael F Healy, *Pr*
▲ EMP: 8 EST: 1985
SQ FT: 20,000
SALES (est): 1.51MM **Privately Held**
Web: www.michaelhealy.com
SIC: 3366 3365 3999 3961 Bronze foundry,
nec; Aluminum foundries; Plaques, picture,
laminated; Costume jewelry, ex. precious
metal and semiprecious stones

Mapleville
Providence County

(G-16166)
CHARCUTERIE ARTISANS
1000 Danielle Dr (02839-1275)
PHONE.............................401 426-9499
EMP: 12 EST: 2019
SALES (est): 72.38K **Privately Held**

SIC: 3556 Meat, poultry, and seafood
processing machinery

(G-16167)
**DANIELE INTERNATIONAL LLC
(PA)**
Also Called: Daniele
1000 Charcuterie Dr (02839-1275)
P.O. Box 106 (02859-0106)
PHONE.............................401 371-2000
Timothy Shanley, *CEO*
James Langrock, *
◆ EMP: 187 EST: 1975
SQ FT: 400,000
SALES (est): 92.39MM
SALES (corp-wide): 92.39MM **Privately
Held**
Web: www.delducafood.com
SIC: 2013 Sausages and related products,
from purchased meat

(G-16168)
**SANDBERG ENTERPRISES INC
(PA)**
Also Called: Sandberg Machine
806 Broncos Hwy (02839-1214)
P.O. Box 779 (02814-0997)
PHONE.............................401 568-1602
Robert Sandberg Senior, *CEO*
Donald Sandberg, *
EMP: 18 EST: 1969
SALES (est): 2.11MM
SALES (corp-wide): 2.11MM **Privately
Held**
Web: www.sandbergmachine.com
SIC: 3599 Machine shop, jobbing and repair

(G-16169)
STEDAGIO LLC
1000 Danielle Dr (02839-1275)
P.O. Box 106 (02859-0106)
PHONE.............................401 568-6228
▲ EMP: 9 EST: 2002
SALES (est): 990.73K **Privately Held**
SIC: 2013 Sausages and other prepared
meats

Middletown
Newport County

(G-16170)
BRODEN MILLWORKS LLC
185 Oliphant Ln (02842-4665)
PHONE.............................401 846-0271
EMP: 7 EST: 2006
SQ FT: 4,260
SALES (est): 768.96K **Privately Held**
Web: www.brodensupply.com
SIC: 2431 Millwork

(G-16171)
CHEW PUBLISHING INC
190 E Main Rd Ste 3 (02842-4987)
P.O. Box 626 (02840-0006)
PHONE.............................401 808-0648
EMP: 8 EST: 2016
SALES (est): 249.81K **Privately Held**
SIC: 2741 Miscellaneous publishing

(G-16172)
**DOYLE SAILS NEWPORT
PARTNR**
23 Johnny Cake Hill Rd (02842-5635)
PHONE.............................401 849-9400
EMP: 9
SALES (est): 253.34K **Privately Held**

SIC: 2394 Sails: made from purchased
materials

(G-16173)
E FRANCES PAPER INC
114 W Main Rd # 2 (02842-4937)
PHONE.............................857 250-0036
Alison Flippin, *Pr*
Emily Roberts, *Sec*
Jennine Lavndon, *Prin*
EMP: 10 EST: 2018
SALES (est): 281.4K **Privately Held**
Web: www.efrancespaper.com
SIC: 2771 5947 Greeting cards; Gift,
novelty, and souvenir shop

(G-16174)
HOOD SAILMAKERS INC (PA)
23 Johnny Cake Hill Rd (02842-5635)
PHONE.............................401 849-9400
John Woodhouse, *Pr*
John T Woodhouse, *Pr*
◆ EMP: 9 EST: 1950
SQ FT: 20,000
SALES (est): 970.91K
SALES (corp-wide): 970.91K **Privately
Held**
Web: www.quantumsails.com
SIC: 2394 Sails: made from purchased
materials

(G-16175)
IGITT INC
Also Called: New England Woodworking Co
210 Airport Access Rd (02842-7444)
PHONE.............................401 841-5544
EMP: 10 EST: 1980
SQ FT: 6,000
SALES (est): 813.51K **Privately Held**
SIC: 2431 Millwork

(G-16176)
KVH INDUSTRIES INC
75 Enterprise Ctr (02842-5269)
PHONE.............................401 847-3327
Martin A Kits Van Heyningen, *CEO*
EMP: 200
SALES (corp-wide): 138.88MM **Publicly
Held**
Web: www.kvh.com
SIC: 3663 Mobile communication equipment
PA: Kvh Industries, Inc.
50 Enterprise Ctr
Middletown RI 02842
401 847-3327

(G-16177)
KVH INDUSTRIES INC (PA)
50 Enterprise Ctr (02842-5279)
PHONE.............................401 847-3327
Brent C Bruun, *Pr*
Donald W Reilly, *CFO*
Felise B Feingold, *DATA*
Jennifer Baker, *CAO*
◆ EMP: 165 EST: 1978
SQ FT: 75,000
SALES (est): 138.88MM
SALES (corp-wide): 138.88MM **Publicly
Held**
Web: www.kvh.com
SIC: 3663 3812 Mobile communication
equipment; Navigational systems and
instruments

(G-16178)
LEIDOS INC
28 Jacome Way Ste A (02842-5793)
PHONE.............................401 849-8900
Anthony Moraco, *CEO*
EMP: 21

▲ = Import ▼ = Export
◆ = Import/Export

Web: www.leidos.com
SIC: **8731** 7379 8711 7372   Commercial physical research; Computer related consulting services; Engineering services; Prepackaged software
HQ: Leidos, Inc.
1750 Presidents St
Reston VA 20190
571 526-6000

(G-16179)
MCLAUGHLIN RESEARCH CORP
Also Called: MRC
132 Johnny Cake Hill Rd (02842-5675)
P.O. Box 4132 (02842-0132)
PHONE..............................401 849-4010
Warren Blakeley, *Pr*
EMP: 175
SALES (corp-wide): 30.32MM **Privately Held**
Web: www.mrcds.com
SIC: **8711** 7371 8731 3489   Consulting engineer; Custom computer programming services; Commercial physical research; Ordnance and accessories, nec
PA: Mclaughlin Research Corp
130 Eugene Oneill Dr
New London CT 06320
860 447-2298

(G-16180)
NASONS UG INC (PA)
Also Called: Luke Harding U G Nason & Sons
305 Oliphant Ln Unit B (02842-7429)
PHONE..............................401 847-2497
Luke Harding, *Pr*
EMP: 17 **EST:** 1977
SALES (est): 2.38MM
SALES (corp-wide): 2.38MM **Privately Held**
Web: www.ugnasons.com
SIC: **1711** 3444 3585 3433   Warm air heating and air conditioning contractor; Ventilators, sheet metal; Refrigeration and heating equipment; Heating equipment, except electric

(G-16181)
NEWPORT TOOL & DIE INC
1219 Aquidneck Ave (02842-7240)
PHONE..............................401 847-6711
Mark Nardelli, *Pr*
Salvatore Nardelli, *Sec*
EMP: 11 **EST:** 1947
SQ FT: 7,000
SALES (est): 1.04MM **Privately Held**
Web: www.newporttoolanddieinc.com
SIC: **3544** 3599   Special dies and tools; Electrical discharge machining (EDM)

(G-16182)
**NEWPORT VINEYARDS &
WINERY LLC**
Also Called: Newport Vineyards
909 E Main Rd (02842-5529)
PHONE..............................401 848-5161
EMP: 20 **EST:** 1995
SQ FT: 12,000
SALES (est): 5.77MM **Privately Held**
Web: www.newportvineyards.com
SIC: **0722** 2084   Grapes, machine harvesting services; Wines

(G-16183)
**NORTHROP GRUMMAN
SYSTEMS CORP**
88 Silva Ln Ste 3 (02842-7628)
PHONE..............................401 849-6270
Michael Coffey, *Mgr*
EMP: 365

SQ FT: 20,000
Web: www.northropgrumman.com
SIC: **3812** 7374 7373   Search and navigation equipment; Data processing and preparation; Computer integrated systems design
HQ: Northrop Grumman Systems Corporation
2980 Fairview Park Dr
Falls Church VA 22042
703 280-2900

(G-16184)
**RESEARCH ENGINEERING &
MFG INC**
55 Hammarlund Way (02842-5696)
PHONE..............................401 841-8880
Laurie Mandly, *CEO*
EMP: 10 **EST:** 1958
SALES (est): 1.58MM **Privately Held**
Web: www.taptite.com
SIC: **3452**   Screws, metal

(G-16185)
**TELECOM INSTALLATION SVCS
INC**
28 Jacome Way (02842-5793)
PHONE..............................401 258-2095
David Colangelo, *Pr*
▲ **EMP:** 23 **EST:** 2000
SQ FT: 1,500
SALES (est): 800K **Privately Held**
Web:
www.telecominstallationservices.com
SIC: **1731** 5999 3661   Telephone and telephone equipment installation; Telephone equipment and systems; Carrier equipment, telephone or telegraph

---

Narragansett
Washington County

(G-16186)
**ANALYTICAL SERVICES
COMPANY**
Also Called: A S C Scientific
10 Dean Knauss Dr (02882-1142)
PHONE..............................401 792-3537
John Toth, *Pt*
Craig Amerigian, *Pt*
EMP: 9 **EST:** 1983
SQ FT: 1,400
SALES (est): 2.32MM **Privately Held**
Web: www.ascscientific.com
SIC: **5049** 3821 8731   Scientific and engineering equipment and supplies; Laboratory equipment: fume hoods, distillation racks, etc.; Natural resource research

(G-16187)
**CELESTIAL MONITORING CORP
(HQ)**
24 Celestial Dr Ste B (02882-1148)
P.O. Box 410 (02880-0410)
PHONE..............................401 782-1045
Pierre Gouvin, *Pr*
EMP: 28 **EST:** 2003
SQ FT: 3,000
SALES (est): 7.09MM **Privately Held**
Web: www.geo-instruments.com
SIC: **3823** 1731 8711   Pressure measurement instruments, industrial; Access control systems specialization; Structural engineering
PA: Keller Group Plc
2 Kingdom Street
London W2 6B

(G-16188)
DAVES COFFEE LLC (PA)
35 Walts Way (02882-3438)
PHONE..............................800 483-4436
EMP: 19 **EST:** 2005
SALES (est): 2.5MM **Privately Held**
Web: www.davescoffee.com
SIC: **5499** 2095   Coffee; Roasted coffee

(G-16189)
DEWAL INDUSTRIES LLC
15 Ray Trainor Dr (02882-1105)
P.O. Box 372 (02874-0372)
PHONE..............................401 789-9736
Eric Walsh, *Pr*
Warren Diclemente, *
▲ **EMP:** 150 **EST:** 1975
SQ FT: 64,000
SALES (est): 46.86MM
SALES (corp-wide): 971.17MM **Publicly Held**
Web: www.dewal.com
SIC: **2672** 3861 3069 3081   Tape, pressure sensitive: made from purchased materials; Film, sensitized motion picture, X-ray, still camera, etc.; Tape, pressure sensitive: rubber; Unsupported plastics film and sheet
PA: Rogers Corporation
2225 W Chandler Blvd
Chandler AZ 85224
480 917-6000

(G-16190)
EARTEC COMPANY INC
145 Dean Knauss Dr (02882-1141)
PHONE..............................401 789-8700
▲ **EMP:** 10 **EST:** 1994
SALES (est): 467.28K **Privately Held**
Web: www.eartec.com
SIC: **3661**   Telephone and telegraph apparatus

(G-16191)
MIX MARKETING CORP
68 Old Pine Rd (02882-2422)
PHONE..............................401 954-6121
Barbiejo Fratus, *Prin*
EMP: 8 **EST:** 2011
SALES (est): 171.26K **Privately Held**
SIC: **3273**   Ready-mixed concrete

(G-16192)
NGC INC (PA)
Also Called: Town Dock, The
45 State St (02882-5712)
P.O. Box 608 (02882-0608)
PHONE..............................401 789-2200
Ryan G Clark, *Pr*
Jonathan R Huot, *
◆ **EMP:** 93 **EST:** 1980
SQ FT: 37,500
SALES (est): 25.66MM
SALES (corp-wide): 25.66MM **Privately Held**
Web: www.towndock.com
SIC: **5146** 2092   Seafoods; Fresh or frozen packaged fish

(G-16193)
**OCEAN STATE SHELLFISH
COOP LLC**
20 Walts Way (02882-3438)
PHONE..............................401 789-2065
Graham Brawley, *Mng Pt*
EMP: 9 **EST:** 2009
SALES (est): 751.87K **Privately Held**
Web: www.oceanstateoysters.com
SIC: **2092** 0919   Fresh or frozen packaged fish; Oyster shells, dredging

(G-16194)
PORTA PHONE CO INC
Also Called: Porta Phones
145 Dean Knauss Dr (02882-1141)
P.O. Box 560 (02882-0560)
PHONE..............................401 789-8700
John Hooper Junior, *Pr*
Paul Hooper, *
▲ **EMP:** 20 **EST:** 1961
SALES (est): 772.64K **Privately Held**
Web: www.portaphone.com
SIC: **3663**   Radio and t.v. communications equipment

(G-16195)
RHODE ISLAND ENGINE CO INC
Also Called: John Deere Authorized Dealer
79 State St (02882-5712)
P.O. Box 543 (02882-0543)
PHONE..............................401 789-1021
Barry Gallup Junior, *Pr*
▲ **EMP:** 20 **EST:** 1951
SQ FT: 10,000
SALES (est): 2.27MM **Privately Held**
Web: www.riengine.com
SIC: **7699** 3599 5082   Marine engine repair; Machine shop, jobbing and repair; Construction and mining machinery

(G-16196)
**SOUTH PIER FISH COMPANY
INC**
20 Walts Way (02882-3438)
PHONE..............................401 783-6611
Paul Barbera, *Pr*
Peter Barbera, *
EMP: 10 **EST:** 1982
SQ FT: 10,000
SALES (est): 912.94K **Privately Held**
SIC: **5146** 2092   Fish, fresh; Fresh or frozen packaged fish

(G-16197)
STEPHEN C DEMATRICK
201p Gravelly Hill Rd (02879-4707)
PHONE..............................401 789-4712
Stephen C Dematrick, *Prin*
EMP: 9 **EST:** 2006
SALES (est): 227.08K **Privately Held**
SIC: **2431**   Millwork

(G-16198)
TRAWLWORKS INC
30 Walts Way (02882-3438)
P.O. Box 342 (02882-0342)
PHONE..............................401 789-3964
Robert Taber, *Pr*
◆ **EMP:** 10 **EST:** 1979
SQ FT: 12,000
SALES (est): 1.79MM **Privately Held**
Web: www.trawlworks.com
SIC: **5091** 2298 5941   Fishing tackle; Fishing lines, nets, seines: made in cordage or twine mills; Fishing equipment

---

Newport
Newport County

(G-16199)
ALL NIGHT LONG INC
52 Berkeley Ave (02840-3567)
PHONE..............................860 306-3189
Bronya Shillo, *CEO*
EMP: 15 **EST:** 2019
SALES (est): 5.42MM **Privately Held**
Web: www.filemonade.com
SIC: **5182** 2085   Cocktails, alcoholic: premixed; Cocktails, alcoholic

(G-16200)
AMERICAN FOAM TECHNOLOGIES INC
221 3rd St Ste 101 (02840-1088)
PHONE...........................304 497-3000
William Palombo, *Pr*
▼ EMP: 19 EST: 1962
SQ FT: 66,000
SALES (est): 718.53K **Privately Held**
Web: www.americanfoamtech.com
SIC: 2899 Foam charge mixtures

(G-16201)
ANCHOR TOFFEE LLC
8 Bowens Wharf (02840-3005)
PHONE...........................401 619-1044
EMP: 21
SALES (corp-wide): 522.62K **Privately Held**
Web: www.anchortoffee.com
SIC: 5441 2046 Candy; Corn sugars and syrups
PA: Anchor Toffee, Llc
   10 Sims Ave Apt 112
   Providence RI 02909
   401 439-1517

(G-16202)
ARKWEAR INC
Also Called: Bite Ne Live Bait
337 Thames St Unit 1 (02840-6635)
P.O. Box 113 (02840-0100)
PHONE...........................401 846-9903
Jeffrey A Marlowe, *Pr*
Biteme Livebait, *Prin*
▲ EMP: 10 EST: 1992
SQ FT: 300
SALES (est): 742.99K **Privately Held**
SIC: 2759 Screen printing

(G-16203)
ARNOLD ART INC (PA)
Also Called: Arnold Art Store & The Gallery
210 Thames St (02840-6616)
PHONE...........................401 847-2273
William Fox Rommell, *Pr*
Sandy Macdonald, *VP*
EMP: 13 EST: 1870
SQ FT: 3,600
SALES (est): 1.73MM
SALES (corp-wide): 1.73MM **Privately Held**
Web: www.arnoldart.com
SIC: 5999 2741 Art dealers; Art copy: publishing only, not printed on site

(G-16204)
BECKER MANUFACTURING COMPANY
Also Called: Garland Writing Instruments
18 Annandale Rd (02840-3602)
PHONE...........................401 821-1450
Richard Becker, *Pr*
EMP: 8 EST: 2017
SALES (est): 232.18K **Privately Held**
Web: www.garlandpen.com
SIC: 3951 Pens and mechanical pencils

(G-16205)
BEDJET LLC
17 Connell Hwy (02840)
PHONE...........................401 404-5250
Mark Aramli, *CEO*
▲ EMP: 10 EST: 2013
SALES (est): 1.37MM **Privately Held**
Web: www.bedjet.com
SIC: 3634 Personal electrical appliances

(G-16206)
BERTHON USA INC
40 Mary St (02840)
PHONE...........................401 846-8404
Jennifer Stewart, *Prin*
EMP: 14 EST: 2015
SALES (est): 245.47K **Privately Held**
Web: www.berthonusa.com
SIC: 3732 5551 Boatbuilding and repairing; Boat dealers

(G-16207)
BIBO INTERNATIONAL LLC
34 Morton Ave # 2 (02840-4067)
P.O. Box 492 (02840-0492)
PHONE...........................774 232-4248
Altina Lester, *CEO*
Mark Lester, *Managing Member**
EMP: 24 EST: 2011
SALES (est): 1.35MM **Privately Held**
Web: www.bibollc.com
SIC: 2084 Wines, brandy, and brandy spirits

(G-16208)
DEL NERO CLEANERS LLC
11 Farewell St (02840-2951)
PHONE...........................508 679-0999
EMP: 9 EST: 2016
SALES (est): 800K **Privately Held**
Web: www.delnerocleaners.com
SIC: 2842 Drycleaning preparations

(G-16209)
ENDEAVOR SEAFOOD LLC
Also Called: Endeavor Seafood
110 William St (02840-3309)
PHONE...........................401 841-8637
George Souza, *Pr*
Todd Clark, *VP*
Mike Bush, *Treas*
◆ EMP: 7 EST: 2001
SQ FT: 1,500
SALES (est): 2.35MM **Privately Held**
Web: www.endeavorseafood.com
SIC: 2092 5146 8742 Seafoods, frozen: prepared; Fish, frozen, unpackaged; Food and beverage consultant

(G-16210)
FLORLINK INC
Also Called: Florlink
174 Bellevue Ave Ste 316 (02840-3990)
PHONE...........................617 221-2200
Mark Barnes, *CEO*
EMP: 12 EST: 2020
SALES (est): 526.43K **Privately Held**
SIC: 3577 7389 Computer peripheral equipment, nec; Business services, nec

(G-16211)
GUNBOAT
11 Bowler Ln Unit A (02840-7705)
PHONE...........................401 619-1055
Peter Johnstone, *Prin*
EMP: 10 EST: 2016
SALES (est): 324.82K **Privately Held**
Web: www.gunboat.com
SIC: 3732 Boatbuilding and repairing

(G-16212)
IYRS SCHOOL TECH & TRADES
Also Called: Iyrs
449 Thames St Unit 100 (02840-6751)
PHONE...........................401 846-2587
Ruth Taylor, *Pr*
▲ EMP: 46 EST: 1993
SALES (est): 5.18MM **Privately Held**
Web: www.iyrs.edu

SIC: 3732 5551 3731 Yachts, building and repairing; Boat dealers; Shipbuilding and repairing

(G-16213)
J H BREAKELL & COMPANY INC
132 Spring St (02840-6818)
PHONE...........................401 849-3522
James Breakell, *Pr*
Joan Breakeall, *VP*
EMP: 10 EST: 1973
SALES (est): 994.21K **Privately Held**
Web: www.breakell.com
SIC: 3914 3911 5961 Holloware, silver; Jewelry, precious metal; Catalog and mail-order houses

(G-16214)
KAFFEOLOGY INC
359 Thames St Ste D (02840-6638)
PHONE...........................407 722-0922
EMP: 8 EST: 2018
SALES (est): 518.49K **Privately Held**
Web: www.kaffeologycafe.com
SIC: 2024 Ice cream and frozen deserts

(G-16215)
KINDERWAGON COMPANY
5 Gooseberry Rd (02840-4309)
PHONE...........................617 256-7599
Justin L Shull, *Owner*
▲ EMP: 8 EST: 2010
SALES (est): 207.83K **Privately Held**
SIC: 2013 Sausages and other prepared meats

(G-16216)
MASTER KITCHENS CENTER INC
547 Thames St Unit B (02840-6709)
PHONE...........................401 324-7100
Yanira Gonzalez, *Prin*
EMP: 8 EST: 2020
SALES (est): 61.36K **Privately Held**
Web: www.masterkitchenscenter.net
SIC: 2434 Wood kitchen cabinets

(G-16217)
MIGHTY WELL INC
45 Catherine St (02840-2722)
PHONE...........................617 804-1233
Emily Levy, *Pr*
EMP: 8 EST: 2017
SALES (est): 498.9K **Privately Held**
Web: www.mighty-well.com
SIC: 3949 Sporting and athletic goods, nec

(G-16218)
NAIAD INFLATABLES NEWPORT INC
4 Thurston Ave (02840-1760)
P.O. Box 4153 (02842-0153)
▲ EMP: 14 EST: 2003
SQ FT: 6,000
SALES (est): 466.88K **Privately Held**
Web: www.geronimofab.com
SIC: 3732 Boats, fiberglass: building and repairing

(G-16219)
NEWPORT JERKY COMPANY LLC
Also Called: Newport Jerky Company
125 Swinburne Row (02840-6609)
PHONE...........................774 644-2350
EMP: 10 EST: 2014
SALES (est): 794.81K **Privately Held**
Web: www.newportjerkycompany.com

SIC: 2013 Snack sticks, including jerky: from purchased meat

(G-16220)
OLDPORT MARINE SERVICES INC
Also Called: Newport Harbor Shuttle
Sayer's Wharf (02840)
P.O. Box 141 (02840-0002)
PHONE...........................401 847-9109
Michael Muessel, *Pr*
Ronald Ackman, *Treas*
EMP: 14 EST: 1972
SQ FT: 1,200
SALES (est): 584.58K **Privately Held**
Web: www.oldportmarine.com
SIC: 4489 3732 5551 7999 Sightseeing boats; Boats, fiberglass: building and repairing; Outboard motors; Pleasure boat rental

(G-16221)
RHODE ISLAND MONTHLY
22 Bowens Wharf (02840-3005)
PHONE...........................401 649-4898
Sarah Mead, *Sales & Marketing*
EMP: 7 EST: 2018
SALES (est): 216.33K **Privately Held**
Web: www.rimonthly.com
SIC: 2721 Magazines: publishing only, not printed on site

(G-16222)
SEA-BAND INTERNATIONAL INC
580 Thames St # 440 (02840-6741)
PHONE...........................401 841-5900
EMP: 9
SALES (corp-wide): 11.73MM **Privately Held**
Web: www.sea-band.com
SIC: 2834 5122 Pharmaceutical preparations; Drugs and drug proprietaries
PA: Sea-Band Limited
   8 Hawley Road
   Hinckley LEICS LE10
   145 563-9750

(G-16223)
SHORELINK PUBLICATIONS LLC
31 West St (02840-6809)
PHONE...........................413 320-3611
Anne Vandromme-hood, *Prin*
EMP: 8 EST: 2017
SALES (est): 90.52K **Privately Held**
Web: www.yachtinsidersguide.com
SIC: 2741 Miscellaneous publishing

(G-16224)
SIREN MARINE INC
221 3rd St Ste 200 (02840-1088)
PHONE...........................401 619-4774
Jeffrey B Poole, *Pr*
EMP: 10 EST: 2011
SALES (est): 2.47MM **Privately Held**
Web: www.sirenmarine.com
SIC: 3429 Marine hardware
HQ: Yamaha Marine Systems Company, Inc.
   6555 Katella Ave
   Cypress CA 90630
   714 761-7300

(G-16225)
SPARKMAN & STEPHENS LLC (PA)
26 Washington Sq Ste 3 (02840-2947)
PHONE...........................401 847-5449
John Reuter, *CEO*

Brooke Parish, *Ch*
Jason Black, *COO*
Brendan Abbott, *CDO*
EMP: 13 **EST:** 2016
SALES (est): 5K
SALES (corp-wide): 5K **Privately Held**
Web: www.sparkmanstephens.com
SIC: 3732 7389 Yachts, building and repairing; Yacht brokers

(G-16226)
THAMES GLASS INC
139 Old Beach Rd (02840-3358)
PHONE...............................401 846-0576
Matthew Buechner, *Pr*
Adrian Buechner, *VP*
EMP: 10 **EST:** 1981
SQ FT: 950
SALES (est): 733.37K **Privately Held**
Web: www.thamesglass.com
SIC: 3229 Glassware, art or decorative

(G-16227)
VENDOME GUIDE
Also Called: Western Managment Co
28 Pelham St (02840-3048)
P.O. Box 1461 (02840-0901)
PHONE...............................401 849-8025
Barclay Tim Warburton, *Pr*
EMP: 11 **EST:** 1982
SALES (est): 237.17K **Privately Held**
Web: www.wimco.com
SIC: 2721 Periodicals

North Kingstown
Washington County

(G-16228)
AARGO ENVIRONMENTAL INC
376 Dry Bridge Rd Ste A2 (02852-5239)
PHONE...............................401 267-0077
Ronald Perry, *Prin*
EMP: 7 **EST:** 2015
SALES (est): 133.26K **Privately Held**
Web: www.aargoenvironmentaltools.com
SIC: 3541 Grinding machines, metalworking

(G-16229)
AGILENT TECHNOLOGIES INC
250 Smith St (02852-7723)
PHONE...............................800 338-1754
EMP: 52
SALES (corp-wide): 6.83B **Publicly Held**
Web: www.agilent.com
SIC: 3825 2819 2869 3826 Instruments to measure electricity; Industrial inorganic chemicals, nec; Industrial organic chemicals, nec; Analytical instruments
PA: Agilent Technologies, Inc.
5301 Stevens Creek Blvd
Santa Clara CA 95051
800 227-9770

(G-16230)
AMERICAN MUSSEL HARVESTERS INC
165 Tidal Dr (02852-8003)
PHONE...............................401 294-8999
William Silkes, *Pr*
Jane Bugbee, *
Bill Silkes, *
▲ **EMP:** 30 **EST:** 1986
SQ FT: 12,000
SALES (est): 9.6MM **Privately Held**
Web: www.americanmussel.com
SIC: 5146 2092 0273 Seafoods; Seafoods, fresh: prepared; Animal aquaculture

(G-16231)
APPLIED RADAR INC
315 Commerce Park Rd Unit P2
(02852-8421)
PHONE...............................401 295-0062
William H Weedon, *CEO*
EMP: 25 **EST:** 1996
SQ FT: 11,000
SALES (est): 2.37MM **Privately Held**
Web: www.appliedradar.com
SIC: 8711 3663 Electrical or electronic engineering; Microwave communication equipment

(G-16232)
AQUA TRACTION MARINE LLC
376 Dry Bridge Rd Ste F1 (02852-5239)
PHONE...............................320 237-2225
Joshua Clymer, *Brnch Mgr*
EMP: 14
SALES (corp-wide): 259.14K **Privately Held**
Web: www.aquatraction.com
SIC: 3086 Insulation or cushioning material, foamed plastics
PA: Aqua Traction Marine Llc
220 4th Ave S
Saint Cloud MN 56301
320 237-2225

(G-16233)
ASC ENGINEERED SOLUTIONS LLC
Anvil International Eps
160 Frenchtown Rd (02852-1759)
PHONE...............................401 886-3000
Rick Laviottle, *Brnch Mgr*
EMP: 104
SALES (corp-wide): 344.54MM **Privately Held**
Web: www.asc-es.com
SIC: 3498 Fabricated pipe and fittings
PA: Asc Engineered Solutions, Llc
2001 Spring Rd Ste 300
Oak Brook IL 60523
800 301-2701

(G-16234)
BB&S ACQUISITION CORP
Also Called: B B & S Treated Lumber Neng
61 Bonneau Rd (02852-2612)
P.O. Box 982 (02852-0612)
PHONE...............................401 295-3200
EMP: 65 **EST:** 1983
SALES (est): 10.32MM **Privately Held**
Web: www.bbslumber.com
SIC: 2491 Structural lumber and timber, treated wood

(G-16235)
BSM PUMP CORP
Also Called: Brown & Sharpe Pumps
180 Frenchtown Rd (02852-1759)
PHONE...............................401 471-6350
EMP: 19 **EST:** 1992
SQ FT: 55,000
SALES (est): 2.01MM **Privately Held**
Web: www.bsmpump.com
SIC: 3561 Industrial pumps and parts

(G-16236)
CALLICO METALS INC
512 Old Baptist Rd (02852-2532)
PHONE...............................401 398-8238
John E Baldwin, *Pr*
Carol J Baldwin, *Sec*
EMP: 7 **EST:** 2002
SALES (est): 989.87K **Privately Held**
Web: www.osterpewter.com

SIC: 3356 Nonferrous rolling and drawing, nec

(G-16237)
CLEAN WATER VENTURES INC
81 Ocean State Dr (02852-8525)
PHONE...............................858 437-3294
Roy Dibenerdini, *CEO*
EMP: 14 **EST:** 2017
SALES (est): 598.61K **Privately Held**
SIC: 1382 Oil and gas exploration services

(G-16238)
COLONIAL CUTLERY INTL INC
Also Called: Colonial Knife Company
606 Ten Rod Rd (02852-4214)
P.O. Box 110 (02818-0110)
PHONE...............................401 737-0024
Kathryn M Paolantonio, *Pr*
Steven Paolantonio, *
EMP: 23 **EST:** 2002
SQ FT: 40,000
SALES (est): 969.1K **Privately Held**
Web: www.colonialcutlery.com
SIC: 3421 Knife blades and blanks

(G-16239)
COMPLETELY CUSTOM LLC
376 Dry Bridge Rd Ste D1 (02852-5239)
PHONE...............................401 667-0059
Trish Ventura, *Managing Member*
EMP: 8 **EST:** 1992
SQ FT: 4,500
SALES (est): 976.39K **Privately Held**
Web: www.completelycustom.com
SIC: 1751 2541 2434 Cabinet building and installation; Wood partitions and fixtures; Wood kitchen cabinets

(G-16240)
CONSTANT TECHNOLOGIES INC
Also Called: Constant Tech
125 Steamboat Ave Ste 2 (02852-5805)
PHONE...............................800 518-7369
EMP: 30 **EST:** 1982
SALES (est): 7.62MM **Privately Held**
Web: www.constanttech.com
SIC: 3651 2521 2522 2531 Household audio and video equipment; Wood office furniture; Office furniture, except wood; Public building and related furniture

(G-16241)
COOL POLYMERS INC
51 Circuit Dr (02852-7435)
PHONE...............................401 667-7830
▲ **EMP:** 20
SIC: 2822 3823 Ethylene-propylene rubbers, EPDM polymers; Thermal conductivity instruments, industrial process type

(G-16242)
COTO TECHNOLOGY INC
Also Called: Coto Technology USA
66 Whitecap Dr (02852-7450)
PHONE...............................401 943-2686
Jeffrey A Bentley, *Pr*
John H Fitzsimons, *
Larry Blackman, *
Robert R Dyson, *
Mark A Chamberlin, *
EMP: 350 **EST:** 1916
SALES (est): 55.69MM
SALES (corp-wide): 445.67MM **Privately Held**
Web: www.cotorelay.com
SIC: 3625 Relays, electric power
PA: The Dyson-Kissner-Moran Corporation
2515 South Rd Ste 5

Poughkeepsie NY 12601
212 661-4600

(G-16243)
CUSTOM DESIGN INCORPORATED
370 Commerce Park Rd (02852-8419)
PHONE...............................401 294-0200
Raul Dias Junior, *Pr*
Shirley Sibelski, *
Adam Dias, *
EMP: 49 **EST:** 1976
SQ FT: 52,000
SALES (est): 9.78MM **Privately Held**
Web: www.cdiri.com
SIC: 3089 2542 2541 Plastics containers, except foam; Partitions and fixtures, except wood; Display fixtures, wood

(G-16244)
DEVELOPMENT ASSOCIATES INC
300 Old Baptist Rd (02852-2531)
P.O. Box 1040 (02852-0615)
PHONE...............................401 884-1350
Douglas Nannig, *Pr*
Paul Nannig, *VP*
▲ **EMP:** 17 **EST:** 1974
SQ FT: 5,000
SALES (est): 2.37MM **Privately Held**
Web: www.chemline.net
SIC: 3479 2851 2821 Coating of metals with plastic or resins; Paints and allied products; Plastics materials and resins

(G-16245)
DRYVIT SYSTEMS INC (DH)
Also Called: Dryvit
200 Frenchtown Rd (02852-1711)
PHONE...............................401 822-4100
TOLL FREE: 800
Robert Michael Murphy, *Pr*
Dennis Dallman, *
Glenn R Hasman, *
◆ **EMP:** 80 **EST:** 1969
SALES (est): 100.34MM
SALES (corp-wide): 7.26B **Publicly Held**
Web: www.dryvithomes.com
SIC: 2899 Chemical preparations, nec
HQ: Dryvit Holdings, Inc
1 Energy Way
Providence RI 02903

(G-16246)
DURANT TOOL COMPANY INC
Also Called: D.M.I. Manufacturing
200 Circuit Dr (02852-7441)
PHONE...............................401 781-7800
Edward W Bouclin, *Pr*
▲ **EMP:** 31 **EST:** 1975
SALES (est): 2.42MM **Privately Held**
Web: www.durantco.com
SIC: 3542 3549 3545 Presses: hydraulic and pneumatic, mechanical and manual; Metalworking machinery, nec; Machine tool accessories

(G-16247)
EDESIA INC (PA)
550 Romano Vineyard Way (02852-8429)
PHONE...............................401 272-5521
Navyn Salem, *Pr*
Paul Salem, *VP*
Germaine Gurr, *Dir*
Annie Abbruzzese, *Dir*
▲ **EMP:** 70 **EST:** 2007
SQ FT: 70,000
SALES (est): 85.46MM **Privately Held**
Web: www.edesianutrition.org

SIC: 2834 Vitamin, nutrient, and hematinic preparations for human use

(G-16248)

EDESIA ENTERPRISES LLC
550 Romano Vineyard Way (02852-8429)
PHONE..................................401 272-5521
Navyn Salem, *Managing Member*
◆ **EMP:** 70 **EST:** 2009
SQ FT: 70,000
SALES (est): 8.53MM **Privately Held**
Web: www.edesianutrition.org
SIC: 2834 Vitamin, nutrient, and hematinic preparations for human use

(G-16249)

EDESIA INDUSTRIES LLC
550 Romano Vineyard Way (02852-8429)
PHONE..................................401 272-5521
M Kasparian, *Ex Dir*
Peter Craig, *Prin*
EMP: 86 **EST:** 2007
SALES (est): 5.78MM **Privately Held**
Web: www.edesiaindustries.com
SIC: 2099 5149 Peanut butter; Health foods

(G-16250)

ELECTRIC BOAT CORPORATION
Also Called: Quonset Point Facility
165 Dillabur Ave (02852-7542)
PHONE..................................401 268-2410
EMP: 2171
SALES (corp-wide): 42.27B **Publicly Held**
Web: www.gdeb.com
SIC: 3731 8711 Submarines, building and repairing; Engineering services
HQ: Electric Boat Corporation
75 Eastern Point Rd
Groton CT 06340

(G-16251)

EMISSIVE ENERGY CORP
Also Called: Inforce
135 Circuit Dr (02852-7439)
PHONE..................................401 294-2030
Robert Galli, *CEO*
Mark Lehman, *
Al Jacobs, *
▲ **EMP:** 57 **EST:** 1994
SQ FT: 50,000
SALES (est): 8.14MM **Privately Held**
Web: www.inforcelights.com
SIC: 3648 Lighting equipment, nec

(G-16252)

ENGINEERING WLDG & FABG CO INC
120 Old Baptist Rd (02852-1743)
PHONE..................................401 884-1484
William Poole, *Pr*
Dorothy A Poole, *VP*
EMP: 8 **EST:** 1964
SQ FT: 12,000
SALES (est): 1.11MM **Privately Held**
Web: www.engineeringwelding.com
SIC: 1791 3444 3441 Structural steel erection; Sheet metalwork; Fabricated structural metal

(G-16253)

GOLDLINE CONTROLS INC (DH)
61 Whitecap Dr (02852-7444)
PHONE..................................401 583-1100
Gilbert Conover, *Pr*
Douglas Pickard, *
◆ **EMP:** 75 **EST:** 1975
SQ FT: 43,000
SALES (est): 37.74MM
SALES (corp-wide): 1.31B **Publicly Held**

SIC: 3822 Temperature controls, automatic
HQ: Hayward Industries, Inc.
400 Connell Dr Ste 6100
Berkeley Heights NJ 07922
908 351-5400

(G-16254)

HAYWARD INDUSTRIES INC
Also Called: Hayward Industries
61 Whitecap Dr (02852-7444)
PHONE..................................401 583-1150
EMP: 109
SALES (corp-wide): 1.31B **Publicly Held**
Web: www.hayward.com
SIC: 3949 Sporting and athletic goods, nec
HQ: Hayward Industries, Inc.
400 Connell Dr Ste 6100
Berkeley Heights NJ 07922
908 351-5400

(G-16255)

HEXAGON MFG INTELLIGENCE INC (DH)
Also Called: Hexagon Mfg Intelligence
250 Circuit Dr (02852-7441)
PHONE..................................401 886-2000
Angus Taylor, *Pr*
Mark Delaney, *VP*
Collin Webb, *Sec*
◆ **EMP:** 66 **EST:** 2001
SQ FT: 120,000
SALES (est): 256.51MM
SALES (corp-wide): 491.93K **Privately Held**
Web: www.hexagon.com
SIC: 3545 3823 Precision measuring tools; Process control instruments
HQ: Hexagon Holdings, Inc.
250 Circuit Dr
North Kingstown RI 02852
401 886-2000

(G-16256)

HEXAGON MFG INTLLGNCE-MTRLOGY
Also Called: Wilcox Associates
250 Circuit Dr (02852-7441)
PHONE..................................401 886-2000
William Gruber, *Pr*
Kenneth Woodbine, *
Mark Delaney, *
EMP: 94 **EST:** 1990
SALES (est): 12.83MM
SALES (corp-wide): 491.93K **Privately Held**
SIC: 7371 7372 Computer software development; Prepackaged software
HQ: Hexagon Manufacturing Intelligence Management Limited
Cedar House
Cobham KT11
207 068-6555

(G-16257)

HOPE VALLEY INDUSTRIES INC
338 Compass Cir (02852-2620)
PHONE..................................401 667-7780
EMP: 9 **EST:** 2016
SALES (est): 230.69K **Privately Held**
Web: www.hopevalleyind.com
SIC: 3999 Manufacturing industries, nec

(G-16258)

HUTCHISON COMPANY INC
Also Called: Hutchison Company Advg Display
376 Dry Bridge Rd Ste J1 (02852-5239)
PHONE..................................401 294-3503
Euan Hutchison, *Pr*
EMP: 10 **EST:** 1946

SQ FT: 45,000
SALES (est): 946.11K **Privately Held**
Web: www.hutchco.com
SIC: 3861 3993 Printing frames, photographic; Advertising novelties

(G-16259)

ICON INTERNATIONAL INC
500 Callahan Rd (02852-8522)
PHONE..................................401 295-2533
▲ **EMP:** 100
SIC: 3646 3645 Commercial lighting fixtures ; Residential lighting fixtures

(G-16260)

INTERNATIONAL DIOXCIDE INC
Also Called: Dupont Water Technologies
40 Whitecap Dr (02852-7445)
PHONE..................................401 295-8800
Tom Dwyer, *VP*
Arthur Dornbusch, *
Peter Martin, *
Peter Rapin, *
◆ **EMP:** 25 **EST:** 1961
SQ FT: 2,500
SALES (est): 19.53MM
SALES (corp-wide): 900K **Privately Held**
Web: www.idiclo2.com
SIC: 2812 2819 2899 Alkalies and chlorine; Sodium compounds or salts, inorg., ex. refined sod. chloride; Chemical preparations, nec
HQ: Erco (Us) Holdings Inc.
251 Little Falls Dr
Wilmington DE

(G-16261)

J GOODISON COMPANY (PA)
Also Called: J. Goodison Company, Inc.
125 Zarbo Ave (02852-7407)
PHONE..................................401 667-5938
Jack L Goodison, *Pr*
Jamie D Goodison, *Sr VP*
EMP: 21 **EST:** 1998
SQ FT: 2,500
SALES (est): 8.76MM **Privately Held**
Web: www.jgoodison.com
SIC: 7699 3731 1721 Marine engine repair; Tenders, ships: building and repairing; Industrial painting

(G-16262)

JOHNSON BROTHERS RI INC
Also Called: Johnson Brothers Rhode Island
120 Moscrip Ave (02852-8407)
P.O. Box 802 (02852-0607)
PHONE..................................401 583-0050
TOLL FREE: 800
Keith Miranda, *Pr*
▲ **EMP:** 30 **EST:** 1985
SQ FT: 28,000
SALES (est): 2.49MM
SALES (corp-wide): 1.21B **Privately Held**
Web: www.johnsonbrothersofri.com
SIC: 5182 2085 Wine; Bourbon whiskey
PA: Johnson Brothers Liquor Company
1999 Shepard Rd
Saint Paul MN 55116
651 649-5800

(G-16263)

KANE MOTOR CAR CO INC
Also Called: Kanes Atlantic
1028 Boston Neck Rd (02852-7110)
PHONE..................................401 294-4634
Braden B Kane, *Pr*
David A Owens, *VP*
EMP: 9 **EST:** 1969
SQ FT: 3,000
SALES (est): 925.68K **Privately Held**

Web: www.kanemotorcar.com
SIC: 7538 7532 3949 General automotive repair shops; Body shop, automotive; Fishing tackle, general

(G-16264)

KEARNEY-NATIONAL INC
Also Called: Coto Technology
66 Whitecap Dr (02852-7450)
PHONE..................................401 943-2686
Robert R Dyson, *Pr*
EMP: 147
SQ FT: 9,989
SALES (corp-wide): 445.67MM **Privately Held**
Web: www.cotorelay.com
SIC: 3679 3677 3625 3621 Electronic circuits; Electronic coils and transformers; Relays and industrial controls; Motors and generators
HQ: Kearney-National Inc.
565 5th Ave Fl 4
New York NY 10017
212 661-4600

(G-16265)

KENNEDY INCORPORATED
21 Circuit Dr (02852-7435)
PHONE..................................401 295-7800
Steve Kennedy, *Pr*
Steven M Kennedy, *Pr*
EMP: 18 **EST:** 1969
SQ FT: 15,000
SALES (est): 2.34MM **Privately Held**
Web: www.kennedyincorporated.com
SIC: 3714 3911 3961 2395 Motor vehicle parts and accessories; Jewelry, precious metal; Costume jewelry, ex. precious metal and semiprecious stones; Pleating and stitching

(G-16266)

KNIGHT OPTICAL (USA) LLC
1130 Ten Rod Rd Ste D102 (02852-4167)
PHONE..................................401 521-7000
Susan A Keller, *Prin*
EMP: 9 **EST:** 2014
SALES (est): 272.36K **Privately Held**
Web: www.knightoptical.com
SIC: 3827 Optical instruments and lenses

(G-16267)

LIFTBAG USA INC
6946 Post Rd (02852)
P.O. Box 2030 (02852-0655)
PHONE..................................401 884-8801
Richard Fryburg, *Pr*
▲ **EMP:** 15 **EST:** 1977
SALES (est): 2.16MM **Privately Held**
Web: www.subsalve.com
SIC: 3089 2673 Pontoons, nonrigid: plastics ; Bags: plastic, laminated, and coated

(G-16268)

LIGHTSHIP GROUP LLC (PA)
Also Called: Ask Services
606 Ten Rod Rd Unit 6 (02852-4240)
P.O. Box 1470 (02852-0632)
PHONE..................................401 294-3341
Thomas Alexander Mng Mnr, *Prin*
EMP: 20 **EST:** 1998
SALES (est): 7.82MM
SALES (corp-wide): 7.82MM **Privately Held**
Web: www.lightshipgroup.com
SIC: 3444 5551 Sheet metalwork; Marine supplies, nec

▲ = Import ▼ = Export
◆ = Import/Export

(G-16269)
LJM PACKAGING CO INC
330 Romano Vineyard Way (02852-8417)
PHONE..............................401 295-2660
John A Pezza, *Pr*
EMP: 55 EST: 1987
SQ FT: 56,000
SALES (est): 6.91MM **Privately Held**
Web: www.ljmpackaging.com
SIC: 2653 2449   Corrugated and solid fiber
boxes; Wood containers, nec

(G-16270)
LORIMER STUDIOS LLC
35 Brown St (02852-5035)
PHONE..............................401 714-0014
David Elison, *Managing Member*
Chris Paulhus, *Opers Mgr*
EMP: 10 EST: 2016
SALES (est): 978.99K **Privately Held**
Web: www.wickford.com
SIC: 2521   Tables, office: wood

(G-16271)
MEISTER ABRASIVES USA INC
Also Called: Meister Abrasives
201 Circuit Dr (02852-7440)
PHONE..............................401 294-4503
Thomas Meister, *Pr*
Andy Miller, *VP*
Bruce Northrup, *Sec*
▲ EMP: 14 EST: 1988
SQ FT: 15,000
SALES (est): 3.96MM **Privately Held**
Web: www.meister-abrasives.com
SIC: 3291 5085   Abrasive products;
Abrasives
HQ: Meister Abrasives Ag
Industriestrasse 10
Andelfingen ZH 8450

(G-16272)
NEW BRICK DRYVIT SYSTEMS
200 Frenchtown Rd (02852-1711)
PHONE..............................401 822-4100
EMP: 7 EST: 2020
SALES (est): 879.44K **Privately Held**
SIC: 2899   Chemical preparations, nec

(G-16273)
**NEW ENGLAND CSTM
CABINETS LLC**
840 Ten Rod Rd (02852-4227)
PHONE..............................401 667-2572
Mark Rotondi, *Managing Member*
EMP: 7 EST: 2019
SALES (est): 845.15K **Privately Held**
Web:
www.newenglandcustomcabinets.com
SIC: 2434   Wood kitchen cabinets

(G-16274)
NORTH ATLANTIC DIST INC
Also Called: Norad
100 Tidal Dr (02852-8040)
PHONE..............................401 667-7000
Michael Miranda, *Pr*
EMP: 300 EST: 1972
SQ FT: 5,000
SALES (est): 19.88MM **Privately Held**
Web: www.noradinc.com
SIC: 7549 3711 5599   High performance
auto repair and service; Automobile bodies,
passenger car, not including engine, etc.;
Dunebuggies

(G-16275)
**POWER CHAIR RECYCLERS
NENG LLC**

6802 Post Rd (02852-2137)
PHONE..............................401 294-4111
John Perrotti Junior, *CEO*
Andrew Celani, *Opers Mgr*
EMP: 8 EST: 2014
SALES (est): 175.85K **Privately Held**
Web:
www.mobilityequipmentforless.com
SIC: 3842   Wheelchairs

(G-16276)
R & D TECHNOLOGIES INC
60 Romano Vineyard Way Ste 112
(02852-8424)
PHONE..............................401 885-6400
Andrew Coutu, *CEO*
Justin Coutu, *Pr*
Cyndy Moniz, *Pr*
EMP: 25 EST: 2000
SQ FT: 3,000
SALES (est): 4.67MM **Privately Held**
Web: www.rnd-tech.com
SIC: 3555   Printing trades machinery

(G-16277)
RELENTLESS INC
100 Davisville Pier Rd (02852-8011)
PHONE..............................401 295-2585
Richard Goodwin, *Pr*
Glenn Goodwin, *VP*
EMP: 15 EST: 1987
SALES (est): 194.45K **Privately Held**
SIC: 3731   Fishing vessels, large: building
and repairing

(G-16278)
RENAISSANCE SHEET METAL L
8 Fishing Cove Rd (02852-4011)
PHONE..............................401 294-3703
Thomas Ucci, *Prin*
EMP: 7 EST: 2013
SALES (est): 447.74K **Privately Held**
SIC: 3444   Sheet metalwork

(G-16279)
SEIFERT SYSTEMS INC
75 Circuit Dr (02852-7435)
PHONE..............................401 294-6960
Paulo Macedo, *Pr*
Michael Seifert, *VP*
Brian Thomas, *Contrlr*
▲ EMP: 14 EST: 2001
SQ FT: 16,000
SALES (est): 4.53MM
SALES (corp-wide): 355.83K **Privately
Held**
Web: www.seifertinc.com
SIC: 3443   Heat exchangers, condensers,
and components
HQ: Seifert Systems Gmbh
Albert-Einstein-Str. 3
Radevormwald NW 42477
219 568-9940

(G-16280)
SENESCO MARINE LLC
10 Macnaught St (02852-7414)
PHONE..............................401 295-0373
Gayle A Corrigan, *Managing Member*
Michael J Foster, *
▲ EMP: 300 EST: 2006
SALES (est): 51.41MM **Privately Held**
Web: www.senescomarine.com
SIC: 3731   Shipbuilding and repairing
PA: Reinauer Transportation Companies,
Llc
1983 Richmond Ter
Staten Island NY 10302

(G-16281)
STRUCTURAL STONE LLC
285 Smith St (02852-7730)
PHONE..............................401 667-4969
Angela Conte, *Managing Member*
▲ EMP: 22 EST: 2009
SQ FT: 60,000
SALES (est): 2.41MM **Privately Held**
Web: www.structuralstonellc.com
SIC: 3281   Cut stone and stone products

(G-16282)
SUBSALVE USA LLC
51 Circuit Dr (02852-7435)
P.O. Box 2030 (02852-0655)
PHONE..............................401 884-8801
Richard Heath, *CEO*
Richard Fryburg, *Chief Growth Officer*
EMP: 18 EST: 2017
SQ FT: 16,320
SALES (est): 4.69MM
SALES (corp-wide): 24.41MM **Privately
Held**
Web: www.subsalve.com
SIC: 3089 2673   Pontoons, nonrigid: plastics
; Bags: plastic, laminated, and coated
HQ: Performance Inflatables Co., Llc
7975 E Mcclain Dr Ste 201
Scottsdale AZ 85260
602 315-2391

(G-16283)
SUPFINA MACHINE CO INC
181 Circuit Dr (02852-7439)
PHONE..............................401 294-6600
James Lospaluto, *Pr*
Kai Bitter, *
Georg Himmelsbach, *
Christoph Siegel, *
Isabel Grieshaber, *
◆ EMP: 40 EST: 1984
SQ FT: 35,000
SALES (est): 8.51MM
SALES (corp-wide): 1.86MM **Privately
Held**
Web: www.supfina.com
SIC: 3541   Grinding, polishing, buffing,
lapping, and honing machines
HQ: Supfina Grieshaber Gmbh & Co. Kg
Schmelzegrun 7
Wolfach BW 77709
78348660

(G-16284)
**TAYLOR FARMS NEW
ENGLAND INC**
320 Commerce Park Rd (02852-8419)
PHONE..............................877 323-7374
Garth Borman, *Pr*
EMP: 25 EST: 2018
SALES (est): 16.87MM **Privately Held**
SIC: 5148 2035   Vegetables; Pickles,
sauces, and salad dressings
HQ: Taylor Farms Retail, Inc.
150 Main St Ste 300
Salinas CA 93901

(G-16285)
THANK-U COMPANY INC
360 Callahan Rd (02852-7739)
PHONE..............................401 739-3100
John Prete, *Pr*
EMP: 7 EST: 2011
SALES (est): 932.95K **Privately Held**
Web: www.thank-u.com
SIC: 5999 3999   Trophies and plaques;
Plaques, picture, laminated

(G-16286)
**THERMO FISHER SCIENTIFIC
INC**
1130 Ten Rod Rd (02852-4161)
PHONE..............................401 294-1234
Scott Chapin, *Mgr*
EMP: 7
SALES (corp-wide): 44.91B **Publicly Held**
Web: www.thermofisher.com
SIC: 3826   Analytical instruments
PA: Thermo Fisher Scientific Inc.
168 3rd Ave
Waltham MA 02451
781 622-1000

(G-16287)
**TORAY PLASTICS (AMERICA)
INC (DH)**
50 Belver Ave (02852-7520)
PHONE..............................401 294-4511
◆ EMP: 589 EST: 1972
SALES (est): 173.41MM **Privately Held**
Web: www.toraytpa.com
SIC: 3081   Polypropylene film and sheet
HQ: Toray Holding (U.S.A), Inc.
461 5th Ave Fl 9
New York NY 10017
212 697-8150

(G-16288)
TRICO SPECIALTY FILMS LLC
310 Compass Cir (02852-2606)
PHONE..............................401 294-7022
Ed Cote, *Pr*
Richard J Cayer, *Managing Member*
Rick Cayer, *Pr*
EMP: 15 EST: 1990
SQ FT: 40,000
SALES (est): 2.49MM **Privately Held**
Web: www.tricosf.com
SIC: 2821   Plastics materials and resins

(G-16289)
TSCO INC
25 Bonneau Rd (02852-2612)
P.O. Box 839 (02852-0608)
PHONE..............................401 295-0669
Richard Duckworth, *Pr*
Lorraine Duckworth, *VP*
EMP: 14 EST: 1989
SQ FT: 20,200
SALES (est): 644.86K **Privately Held**
Web: www.trussus.com
SIC: 2439 7389 5211   Trusses, wooden roof;
Design services; Flooring, wood

(G-16290)
**ULTRA SCIENTIFIC
INCORPORATED**
250 Smith St (02852-7723)
PHONE..............................800 338-1754
EMP: 49
Web: www.agilent.com
SIC: 8731 2819 2869 3826   Chemical
laboratory, except testing; Industrial
inorganic chemicals, nec; Industrial organic
chemicals, nec; Analytical instruments

(G-16291)
**VETERANS ASSEMBLED ELEC
LLC (PA)**
Also Called: Vae
106 Sea View Ave (02852-6324)
PHONE..............................401 228-6165
Matthew Vargas, *COO*
EMP: 9 EST: 2009
SALES (est): 3.7MM **Privately Held**

SIC: 3629 8711 3674 3679 Electronic generation equipment; Electrical or electronic engineering; Integrated circuits, semiconductor networks, etc.; Electronic circuits

(G-16292)
WALCOTT ASSOCIATES LLC
P.O. Box 24 (02835-0024)
PHONE..........................401 694-0153
Martin W Keen, *Managing Member*
▲ EMP: 10 EST: 2012
SQ FT: 20,000
SALES (est): 216.69K Privately Held
SIC: 2522 2521 2599 Office furniture, except wood; Wood office furniture; Factory furniture and fixtures

North Providence
Providence County

(G-16293)
379 CHARLES RI INC
Also Called: Palmer Industries
862 Charles St Unit 1 (02904-5669)
PHONE..........................401 521-1101
Anthony Baglini, *Pr*
Anthony Palmer, *Pr*
Anne Baglini, *VP*
▲ EMP: 10 EST: 1970
SQ FT: 7,000
SALES (est): 2.43MM Privately Held
SIC: 5251 7699 3446 Hardware stores; General household repair services; Railings, prefabricated metal

(G-16294)
ANATONE JEWELRY CO INC
Also Called: Ocean State Creations
10 Mark Dr (02904-3330)
PHONE..........................401 728-0490
Lillian Anatone, *Pr*
EMP: 8 EST: 1959
SQ FT: 50,000
SALES (est): 181.73K Privately Held
Web: www.registrar-transfers.com
SIC: 3911 Jewelry, precious metal

(G-16295)
APAC TOOL INC
Also Called: Metal Clay Findings
49 Hurdis St (02904-4905)
PHONE..........................401 724-6090
Anthony Squillacci Senior, *COO*
Anthony Squillacci Junior, *Pr*
EMP: 18 EST: 1966
SQ FT: 1,000
SALES (est): 488.44K Privately Held
Web: www.apactool.com
SIC: 3915 5944 Jewelers' findings and materials; Jewelry stores

(G-16296)
ARO INDUSTRIAL FINISHING LLC
1 Warren Ave (02911-2425)
PHONE..........................401 349-4848
Robert Montaquila, *Prin*
EMP: 8 EST: 2018
SALES (est): 458.61K Privately Held
SIC: 3999 Manufacturing industries, nec

(G-16297)
ARO-SAC INC
Also Called: A&M Design
1 Warren Ave (02911-2495)
PHONE..........................401 231-6655
Robert Montaquila, *Pr*

Madeline Montaquila, *
EMP: 50 EST: 1935
SQ FT: 15,000
SALES (est): 4.36MM Privately Held
Web: www.aro-sac.com
SIC: 3915 3469 Jewelers' findings and materials; Metal stampings, nec

(G-16298)
CUSTOM MOLDED PRODUCTS INC
24 Thelma St (02904-4533)
PHONE..........................401 464-9991
Augusto E Campopiano Junior, *Pr*
Augusto E Campopiano Junior, *Pr*
Anita Campopiano, *Sec*
▲ EMP: 8 EST: 1985
SQ FT: 2,700
SALES (est): 873.57K Privately Held
Web: www.cmpri.com
SIC: 3089 Plastics processing

(G-16299)
DOUGLAS WINE & SPIRITS INC
1661 Mineral Spring Ave (02904-4003)
PHONE..........................401 353-6400
Kathy Haronian, *Pr*
John Haronian, *Prin*
EMP: 10 EST: 1995
SQ FT: 4,000
SALES (est): 529.01K Privately Held
Web: www.douglaswine.com
SIC: 2084 8741 Wines; Business management

(G-16300)
DRAPERY HOUSE INC
Also Called: Contrak Drapery Manufacturing
1307 Mineral Spring Ave (02904-4628)
PHONE..........................401 724-3400
Robert Thomas, *Pr*
Christopher Thomas, *Treas*
Albert Thomas, *Sec*
EMP: 20 EST: 1972
SQ FT: 32,000
SALES (est): 2.27MM Privately Held
Web: www.draperyhouseri.com
SIC: 5714 7389 3429 2591 Draperies; Interior decorating; Hardware, nec; Drapery hardware and window blinds and shades

(G-16301)
EASTERN MANUFACTURING COMPANY
9 Humbert St (02911-2783)
PHONE..........................401 231-8330
Anthony Salvatore Junior, *Pr*
Anthony Salvatore Senior, *Treas*
EMP: 15 EST: 1954
SQ FT: 18,000
SALES (est): 2.11MM Privately Held
Web: www.easternmfg.com
SIC: 3469 Stamping metal for the trade

(G-16302)
G TANURY PLATING CO INC
1 Oak Grove Blvd (02911-2608)
PHONE..........................401 232-2330
George Tanury, *CEO*
Joseph L Traficante, *
EMP: 65 EST: 1973
SALES (est): 4.69MM Privately Held
Web: www.gtanuryplating.com
SIC: 3471 Electroplating of metals or formed products

(G-16303)
INDUPLATE INC (PA)
Also Called: Greystone

1 Greystone Ave (02911-1082)
PHONE..........................401 231-5770
John Maconi, *CEO*
Everett Fernald Junior, *Pr*
David Lippy, *
Susan Marie Piccolomini, *
EMP: 100 EST: 1932
SQ FT: 65,000
SALES (est): 24.99MM
SALES (corp-wide): 24.99MM Privately Held
Web: www.induplate.com
SIC: 3471 3398 Chromium plating of metals or formed products; Metal heat treating

(G-16304)
LANCE INDUSTRIES
1119 Douglas Ave (02904-5305)
PHONE..........................401 654-5394
EMP: 8 EST: 2015
SALES (est): 477.62K Privately Held
Web: www.symmetryproducts.com
SIC: 3999 Manufacturing industries, nec

(G-16305)
NEW ANNEX PLATING INC
Also Called: Annex Plating
9 Warren Ave (02911-2425)
PHONE..........................401 349-0911
Robert Silverman, *Pr*
Barry Fishback, *VP*
▲ EMP: 21 EST: 1972
SALES (est): 926.72K Privately Held
SIC: 3471 Electroplating of metals or formed products

(G-16306)
PALMER INDUSTRIES INC
862r Charles St (02904-5643)
PHONE..........................800 398-9676
Anthony Palmer, *Pr*
Anne Palmer, *VP*
▲ EMP: 10 EST: 1985
SALES (est): 187.97K Privately Held
Web: www.sinklegs.com
SIC: 3431 8711 Sinks: enameled iron, cast iron, or pressed metal; Engineering services

(G-16307)
PERRY BLACKBURNE INC
Also Called: Ultimate Promotional Products
330 Woonasquatucket Ave (02911-2720)
PHONE..........................401 231-7200
Edward Paul, *Pr*
◆ EMP: 15 EST: 1952
SQ FT: 30,000
SALES (est): 1.34MM Privately Held
Web: www.perryblackburne.com
SIC: 3089 3172 3961 3496 Novelties, plastics; Personal leather goods, nec; Costume jewelry; Miscellaneous fabricated wire products

(G-16308)
PROVIDENCE CASTING INC
3 Warren Ave (02911-2425)
PHONE..........................401 231-0860
Anthony Bizzacco, *Pr*
Robert Bizzacco, *VP*
David Bizzacco, *Treas*
EMP: 7 EST: 1957
SQ FT: 2,400
SALES (est): 969.69K Privately Held
Web: www.providencecasting.com
SIC: 3369 Castings, except die-castings, precision

(G-16309)
RHODE RUNNER HOMES LLC
40 Rosner Ave (02904-4446)

PHONE..........................401 489-8501
EMP: 7 EST: 2018
SALES (est): 269.77K Privately Held
SIC: 1389 Construction, repair, and dismantling services

(G-16310)
SERVICE TECH INC (PA)
1164 Douglas Ave (02904-5371)
PHONE..........................401 353-3664
Andrew R Bilodeau, *Pr*
▲ EMP: 7 EST: 1989
SQ FT: 22,000
SALES (est): 1.14MM Privately Held
SIC: 3589 Water treatment equipment, industrial

(G-16311)
SUNSHINE MINTING INC
9 Warren Ave (02911-2425)
PHONE..........................401 265-8383
EMP: 7 EST: 2019
SALES (est): 105.67K Privately Held
Web: www.sunshinemint.com
SIC: 3911 Jewelry, precious metal

(G-16312)
TRAINING THRU PLACEMENT INC
Also Called: PANDORA'S PICKLE PRODUCTS
20 Marblehead Ave (02904-4245)
PHONE..........................401 353-0220
Vincent Igliozzi, *Pr*
John Capobianco, *Ex Dir*
Ernest Acciardo, *VP*
EMP: 10 EST: 1976
SQ FT: 2,000
SALES (est): 312.58K Privately Held
Web: www.tsg-training.co.uk
SIC: 8331 5431 3961 2099 Job training services; Fruit stands or markets; Costume jewelry, ex. precious metal and semiprecious stones; Food preparations, nec

(G-16313)
VSG SNACKS INC
50 Hurdis St (02904-4906)
PHONE..........................401 536-1116
Mateo Giraldo, *Prin*
EMP: 10 EST: 2019
SALES (est): 199.29K Privately Held
SIC: 2096 Potato chips and similar snacks

North Scituate
Providence County

(G-16314)
CHOPMIST HILL WOODWORKS LTD
1586 Chopmist Hill Rd (02857-1626)
PHONE..........................401 374-3143
Russell A Greenhalgh, *Prin*
EMP: 8 EST: 2010
SALES (est): 223.8K Privately Held
SIC: 2431 Millwork

(G-16315)
FRANK J NEWMAN & SON INC
200 Rocky Hill Rd (02857-1235)
PHONE..........................401 231-0550
William J Newman, *Pr*
Annette L Amato, *Sec*
EMP: 9 EST: 1948
SALES (est): 980.97K Privately Held
Web: www.fjnewman.com
SIC: 3444 Sheet metalwork

▲ = Import ▼ = Export
◆ = Import/Export

(G-16316)
ROUNDS SERVICE STATION INC
Also Called: Mason's Racing Engines
53 Hartford Ave (02857-1855)
PHONE.............................401 934-9877
Robert Mason, *Pr*
Deborah Mason, *VP*
EMP: 10 **EST:** 1965
SQ FT: 1,800
SALES (est): 1.48MM **Privately Held**
Web: www.masonsautomotive.com
SIC: 5541 7538 3599 Filling stations,
gasoline; General automotive repair shops;
Machine shop, jobbing and repair

(G-16317)
VILLAGE WOODTURNING
39 Carue Dr (02857-1012)
P.O. Box 173 (02857-0173)
PHONE.............................401 647-3091
Matt Davidson, *Prin*
EMP: 7 **EST:** 2008
SALES (est): 170.34K **Privately Held**
Web: www.villagewoodturning.com
SIC: 2431 Millwork

North Smithfield
Providence County

(G-16318)
ATLANTIC FOOTCARE INC
Also Called: Atlantic Footcare
229 Quaker Hwy (02896-7648)
PHONE.............................401 568-4918
Charlie Sipes, *Pr*
Jane Carroll, *
John Conroy, *
Ken Mazer, *
◆ **EMP:** 75 **EST:** 2001
SQ FT: 41,000
SALES (est): 9.51MM
SALES (corp-wide): 9.51MM **Privately Held**
Web: www.prothotics.com
SIC: 3842 Foot appliances, orthopedic
PA: Af International, Inc.
24 Albion Rd Ste 210
Lincoln RI 02865
401 757-3908

(G-16319)
BRIDGESTONE RET OPERATIONS LLC
Also Called: Firestone
22 Dowling Village Blvd (02896-8267)
PHONE.............................401 766-0233
EMP: 11
Web: www.bridgestoneamericas.com
SIC: 5531 7534 Automotive tires; Tire retreading and repair shops
HQ: Bridgestone Retail Operations, Llc
333 E Lake St Ste 300
Bloomingdale IL 60108
630 259-9000

(G-16320)
CAS AMERICA LLC
Also Called: Cas America
20 Providence Pike (02896-8046)
PHONE.............................401 884-8556
EMP: 18 **EST:** 2015
SALES (est): 3.65MM **Privately Held**
Web: www.casamerica.com
SIC: 2431 5031 3999 Millwork; Millwork;
Atomizers, toiletry

(G-16321)
COMTORGAGE CORPORATION
58 Industrial Dr (02896-8033)
P.O. Box 1217 (02876-0896)
PHONE.............................401 765-0900
Pauline Brodeur, *Pr*
EMP: 13 **EST:** 1928
SQ FT: 6,000
SALES (est): 918.6K **Privately Held**
Web: www.comtorgage.com
SIC: 3545 Gauges (machine tool accessories)

(G-16322)
CUSTOM COATINGS INC
22 Steel St (02896-8055)
PHONE.............................401 766-1500
Gerald Casey, *Pr*
EMP: 10 **EST:** 2020
SALES (est): 583.91K **Privately Held**
SIC: 2295 Laminating of fabrics

(G-16323)
G-FORM LLC
1 Tupperware Dr Ste 7 (02896-6815)
PHONE.............................401 769-0994
Richard Fox, *Pr*
EMP: 45 **EST:** 2014
SALES (est): 5.14MM **Privately Held**
Web: www.g-form.com
SIC: 3089 2821 Soles, boot or shoe: plastics
; Plastics materials and resins

(G-16324)
KB SURFACES LLC
Also Called: Closettec
20 Providence Pike (02896-8046)
PHONE.............................401 727-6792
Kenneth Beck, *Managing Member*
EMP: 14 **EST:** 2007
SQ FT: 2,000
SALES (est): 2.14MM **Privately Held**
Web: www.kbsurfaces.com
SIC: 3281 Cut stone and stone products

(G-16325)
KELMEG WOODWORKING
1067 Victory Hwy (02896-7800)
PHONE.............................401 762-3090
EMP: 7 **EST:** 2008
SALES (est): 147.61K **Privately Held**
SIC: 2431 Millwork

(G-16326)
MATERIAL CONCRETE CORP
618 Greenville Rd (02896-9553)
PHONE.............................401 765-0204
EMP: 15 **EST:** 1992
SALES (est): 800.45K **Privately Held**
Web: www.msscorporation.com
SIC: 3273 Ready-mixed concrete

(G-16327)
MTR MACHINING INC
Also Called: Mtr Guns & Ammo
229 Quaker Hwy (02896-7648)
PHONE.............................401 766-0200
Raymond R Houle Senior, *Prin*
EMP: 11 **EST:** 2007
SALES (est): 320.19K **Privately Held**
SIC: 3599 Machine shop, jobbing and repair

(G-16328)
NARRAGANSETT IMAGING USA LLC
51 Industrial Dr (02896-8032)
P.O. Box 278 (02876-0278)
PHONE.............................401 762-3800
William Ulmschneider, *

EMP: 20 **EST:** 2011
SQ FT: 80,000
SALES (est): 2.63MM **Privately Held**
Web: www.nimaging.com
SIC: 3679 3674 3671 Electronic circuits;
Semiconductors and related devices;
Electron tubes

(G-16329)
NATIONAL MARKER COMPANY
100 Providence Pike (02896-8046)
PHONE.............................401 762-9700
Michael Black, *Pr*
◆ **EMP:** 58 **EST:** 1934
SQ FT: 40,800
SALES (est): 14.41MM
SALES (corp-wide): 484.03MM **Privately Held**
Web: www.accuform.com
SIC: 3993 Neon signs
PA: Justrite Manufacturing Company, L.L.C.
3921 Dewitt Ave
Mattoon IL 61938
217 234-7486

(G-16330)
NMC SOLAR LLC
100 Providence Pike (02896-8046)
PHONE.............................401 762-9700
EMP: 14 **EST:** 2016
SALES (est): 994.27K **Privately Held**
Web: www.accuform.com
SIC: 3993 Signs, not made in custom sign painting shops

(G-16331)
PRECISION PRODUCTS
445 Saint Paul St (02896-6865)
PHONE.............................401 766-0200
Raymond R Houle Senior, *Prin*
EMP: 9 **EST:** 2011
SALES (est): 86.64K **Privately Held**
SIC: 3599 Machine shop, jobbing and repair

(G-16332)
R & R MACHINE INDUSTRIES INC
660 Greenville Rd (02896-9553)
P.O. Box 119 (02876-0119)
PHONE.............................401 766-2505
Roland Legare, *Pr*
Elizabeth Legare, *Prin*
Renay Curran, *CFO*
Diane Ranslow, *Sec*
EMP: 17 **EST:** 1980
SALES (est): 2.32MM **Privately Held**
Web: www.rrmachine.com
SIC: 3599 Machine shop, jobbing and repair

(G-16333)
STONE SYSTEMS NEW ENGLAND LLC
9 Steel St (02896-8055)
PHONE.............................401 766-3603
Roberto Contreras, *Pr*
▲ **EMP:** 46 **EST:** 2002
SALES (est): 3.98MM **Privately Held**
SIC: 3281 1799 Granite, cut and shaped;
Counter top installation
HQ: Stone Suppliers, Inc.
13124 Trinity Dr
Stafford TX
281 494-7277

(G-16334)
WRIGHTS DAIRY FARM INC
Also Called: Wright Scoop, The
200 Woonsocket Hill Rd (02896-7128)
PHONE.............................401 767-3014

Edward Wright, *Pr*
Ellen Puccetti, *
Eli Dulude, *
EMP: 30 **EST:** 1900
SALES (est): 2.2MM **Privately Held**
Web: www.wrightsri.com
SIC: 0241 5451 2026 5461 Dairy farms; Milk
; Milk processing (pasteurizing,
homogenizing, bottling); Retail bakeries

Oakland
Providence County

(G-16335)
TOWN OF BURRILLVILLE
Also Called: Burrillville Waste Water
141 Clear River Dr (02858-1037)
P.O. Box 71 (02830-0071)
PHONE.............................401 568-6296
EMP: 8
SALES (corp-wide): 59.81MM **Privately Held**
Web: www.burrillville.org
SIC: 2899 Water treating compounds
PA: Town Of Burrillville
105 Harrisville Main St
Harrisville RI 02830
401 568-9451

Pascoag
Providence County

(G-16336)
DANIELE INC
105 Davis Dr (02859-3507)
P.O. Box 106 (02859-0106)
PHONE.............................401 568-6228
Stefano Dukcevich, *Pr*
▲ **EMP:** 200 **EST:** 2004
SALES (est): 20.14MM **Privately Held**
SIC: 2013 Sausages and other prepared meats

(G-16337)
DANIELE INTERNATIONAL INC
Also Called: Daniele International, Inc.
105 Davis Dr (02859-3507)
PHONE.............................401 568-6228
Stefano Dukcevich, *Pr*
EMP: 170
SALES (corp-wide): 90.97MM **Privately Held**
Web: www.delducafood.com
SIC: 2013 Sausages and related products,
from purchased meat
PA: Daniele International Llc
1000 Charcuterie Dr
Mapleville RI 02839
401 371-2000

(G-16338)
DANIELE INTERNATIONAL INC
Also Called: DANIELE INTERNATIONAL,
INC.
180 Davis Dr (02859-3506)
PHONE.............................401 568-6228
Stefano Dukcevich, *Pr*
EMP: 170
SALES (corp-wide): 90.97MM **Privately Held**
Web: www.delducafood.com
SIC: 2013 Sausages and related products,
from purchased meat
PA: Daniele International Llc
1000 Charcuterie Dr
Mapleville RI 02839
401 371-2000

(G-16339)
LOCKHEED ARCHTCTRAL SLTONS INC
Also Called: Lockheed Archtctural Solutions
925 S Main St (02859-3521)
P.O. Box 166 (02859-0166)
PHONE..............................401 568-3061
TOLL FREE: 800
Michael Kosiver, *Pr*
Michael Botelho, *
Robert Gregoire, *
▲ EMP: 105 EST: 1980
SQ FT: 60,000
SALES (est): 24.45MM **Privately Held**
Web: www.lockheedsolutions.com
SIC: 3442 1751 1542 Screens, window, metal; Window and door installation and erection; Commercial and office buildings, renovation and repair

(G-16340)
S G INC
Also Called: G S I
885 S Main St (02859-3520)
PHONE..............................401 568-1110
Bert Mountford, *Pr*
Martin Murphy, *VP*
Jason Mountford, *Treas*
EMP: 30 EST: 1987
SQ FT: 13,500
SALES (est): 2.43MM **Privately Held**
Web: www.gslabels.com
SIC: 7336 2759 2671 Graphic arts and related design; Flexographic printing; Paper; coated and laminated packaging

(G-16341)
SANDBERG ENTERPRISES INC
Also Called: Machine Shop
806 Broncos Hwy (02859)
PHONE..............................401 568-1602
Robert Sandberg, *Pr*
EMP: 20
SALES (corp-wide): 2.11MM **Privately Held**
Web: www.sandbergmachine.com
SIC: 3599 Machine shop, jobbing and repair
PA: Sandberg Enterprises, Inc.
    806 Broncos Hwy
    Mapleville RI 02839
    401 568-1602

Pawtucket
Providence County

(G-16342)
ABSORBENT SPECIALTY PDTS LLC
30 Hamlet St (02861-2827)
PHONE..............................401 722-1177
Carol Dancer, *Managing Member*
◆ EMP: 14 EST: 2004
SQ FT: 18,400
SALES (est): 3.29MM **Privately Held**
Web: www.absorbsp.com
SIC: 2393 1629 2842 2679 Textile bags; Dam construction; Sweeping compounds, oil or water absorbent, clay or sawdust; Paper products, converted, nec

(G-16343)
ACCENT PLATING COMPANY INC
25 Esten Ave Unit 5 (02860-4826)
PHONE..............................401 722-6306
Robert Mancini, *Pr*
EMP: 16 EST: 1963
SQ FT: 15,000

SALES (est): 616.71K **Privately Held**
Web: www.accentplatingco.com
SIC: 3471 Electroplating of metals or formed products

(G-16344)
AGAR MACHINING & WELDING INC
270 York Ave (02860-5826)
PHONE..............................401 724-2260
George Lanoie, *Pr*
Thomas Mc Gee, *
EMP: 15 EST: 1986
SQ FT: 10,000
SALES (est): 2.29MM **Privately Held**
Web: www.agarmachine.com
SIC: 3599 Machine shop, jobbing and repair

(G-16345)
ALLIANCE PAPER COMPANY INC
33 India St (02860-5521)
PHONE..............................401 722-0295
Jeff Jones, *Pr*
▲ EMP: 25 EST: 2002
SQ FT: 100,000
SALES (est): 5MM **Privately Held**
SIC: 2679 Paper products, converted, nec

(G-16346)
BACKFLIP STUDIOS LLC
1027 Newport Ave (02861-2539)
PHONE..............................720 475-1970
Julian Farrior, *CEO*
Randy Morgan, *
EMP: 35 EST: 2009
SALES (est): 10.55MM
SALES (corp-wide): 5.86B **Publicly Held**
SIC: 7372 Prepackaged software
PA: Hasbro, Inc.
    1027 Newport Ave
    Pawtucket RI 02861
    401 431-8697

(G-16347)
BEC CORP
Also Called: Broadway Tire and Auto Service
588 Brdwy (02860)
PHONE..............................401 725-3535
James Hallenbeck, *Pr*
EMP: 8 EST: 2014
SQ FT: 9,700
SALES (est): 2.03MM **Privately Held**
SIC: 7534 5531 Tire retreading and repair shops; Automotive tires

(G-16348)
BELLA CABINETS INC
296 Beverage Hill Ave (02861-4422)
PHONE..............................401 722-0038
Roy Silva, *Pr*
EMP: 7 EST: 2014
SALES (est): 225.56K **Privately Held**
Web: www.bellacabinetsne.com
SIC: 2434 Wood kitchen cabinets

(G-16349)
BERGER & COMPANY RECYCLING INC
126 Front St (02860-1044)
PHONE..............................401 723-7240
Charles Sinel, *Pr*
Sam Sinel, *VP*
EMP: 17 EST: 1996
SQ FT: 22,250
SALES (est): 2.38MM **Privately Held**
Web: www.bergerrecycling.com
SIC: 2611 Pulp manufactured from waste or recycled paper

(G-16350)
BLISS MANUFACTURING CO INC
50 Bacon St (02860-4535)
P.O. Box 3440 (02861-0900)
PHONE..............................401 729-1690
Francis Bliss Junior, *Pr*
Jane Bliss, *
EMP: 48 EST: 1901
SQ FT: 300,000
SALES (est): 4.7MM **Privately Held**
Web: www.blissmfg.com
SIC: 3961 3911 Rosaries and small religious articles, except precious metal; Jewelry, precious metal

(G-16351)
BMS PLASTICS INC
535 Prospect St (02860-6200)
PHONE..............................401 465-3960
EMP: 15 EST: 2018
SALES (est): 576.06K **Privately Held**
Web: www.bmsplastics.com
SIC: 3089 Injection molding of plastics

(G-16352)
CAMPBELL ENTERPRISES CORP
1 Campbell St (02860-4896)
P.O. Box 2383 (02861-0383)
PHONE..............................401 753-7778
▲ EMP: 45
SIC: 2657 Folding paperboard boxes

(G-16353)
CATANZARO FOOD PRODUCTS INC
Also Called: Rhode Island's Own
203 Concord St Unit 457 (02860-3481)
PHONE..............................401 255-1700
Kristen J Catanzoro, *Pr*
EMP: 8 EST: 2002
SQ FT: 2,200
SALES (est): 752.71K **Privately Held**
Web: www.catanzarofoodproducts.com
SIC: 2052 2033 2051 Cookies and crackers; Spaghetti and other pasta sauce: packaged in cans, jars, etc; Bakery: wholesale or wholesale/retail combined

(G-16354)
CINTAS CORPORATION NO 2
Also Called: Cintas
700 Narragansett Park Dr (02861-4326)
PHONE..............................401 723-7300
EMP: 8
SALES (corp-wide): 8.82B **Publicly Held**
Web: www.cintas.com
SIC: 3842 Clothing, fire resistant and protective
HQ: Cintas Corporation No. 2
    6800 Cintas Blvd
    Mason OH 45040

(G-16355)
CLASSSICK CUSTOM LLC
5 Carpenter St Ste 101 (02860-1785)
PHONE..............................401 475-7288
EMP: 10 EST: 2008
SALES (est): 926.8K **Privately Held**
Web: www.classsick.com
SIC: 2759 7389 Screen printing; Embroidery advertising

(G-16356)
CONRAD-JARVIS CORP
217 Conant St (02860-1801)
P.O. Box 878 (02862-0878)

PHONE..............................401 722-8700
William T Jarvis, *Pr*
George Scoggins, *
Michele Scoggins, *
▲ EMP: 90 EST: 1917
SQ FT: 120,000
SALES (est): 8.63MM **Privately Held**
Web: www.conrad-jarvis.com
SIC: 2241 Narrow fabric mills

(G-16357)
COOLEY INCORPORATED (HQ)
Also Called: Cooley Building Products
350 Esten Ave (02860-7838)
PHONE..............................401 724-9000
Daniel Dwight, *CEO*
Ronald Markovsky, *
◆ EMP: 125 EST: 1926
SQ FT: 300,000
SALES (est): 47.57MM
SALES (corp-wide): 93.15MM **Privately Held**
Web: www.cooleygroup.com
SIC: 2295 3069 2262 Coated fabrics, not rubberized; Roofing, membrane rubber; Screen printing: manmade fiber and silk broadwoven fabrics
PA: Cooley Group Holdings, Inc.
    350 Esten Ave
    Pawtucket RI 02860
    401 724-0510

(G-16358)
COOLEY GROUP HOLDINGS INC (PA)
Also Called: Cooley/Group
350 Esten Ave (02860-7838)
PHONE..............................401 724-0510
Daniel Dwight, *Pr*
Ronald Markovsky, *
P Robert Siener Junior, *Ch*
David Pettey, *
Stephen Siener, *General Vice President**
◆ EMP: 140 EST: 1999
SALES (est): 93.15MM
SALES (corp-wide): 93.15MM **Privately Held**
Web: www.cooleygroup.com
SIC: 5211 3069 6719 Roofing material; Roofing, membrane rubber; Investment holding companies, except banks

(G-16359)
COVE METAL COMPANY INC (PA)
Also Called: Cove Textile Machinery Co
160 Grenville St (02860-4804)
P.O. Box 29 (02901-0029)
PHONE..............................401 724-3500
Charles T Cove, *Pr*
Charles T Cove Prestreas, *Prin*
EMP: 10 EST: 1955
SQ FT: 14,000
SALES (est): 908K
SALES (corp-wide): 908K **Privately Held**
SIC: 3552 3549 Textile machinery; Wiredrawing and fabricating machinery and equipment, ex. die

(G-16360)
CRYSTAL HORD CORPORATION
33 York Ave Ste 45 (02860-6423)
PHONE..............................401 723-2989
Mark Thomas, *CEO*
▲ EMP: 43 EST: 1989
SALES (est): 4.28MM **Privately Held**
Web: www.hordcrystal.com
SIC: 3915 Jewelers' findings and materials

(G-16361)
CRYSTAL STAMPING LLC
Also Called: Worcester Tool & Stamping Co.
51 Charlton Ave (02860-6211)
PHONE..................................401 724-5880
James Dimello, *Pr*
EMP: 10 **EST:** 2014
SALES (est): 769.13K **Privately Held**
SIC: 3469   Stamping metal for the trade

(G-16362)
CSC INC
51 Charlton Ave (02860-6211)
PHONE..................................401 724-5880
James Dimello, *Pr*
Jeffrey Dimello, *VP*
▲ **EMP:** 16 **EST:** 1985
SQ FT: 16,000
SALES (est): 475.3K **Privately Held**
SIC: 3469   Stamping metal for the trade

(G-16363)
D & W TOOL & FINDINGS INC
601 Mineral Spring Ave (02860-3492)
PHONE..................................401 727-3030
Nisim Tzadok, *Pr*
EMP: 15 **EST:** 1945
SALES (est): 811.96K **Privately Held**
Web: www.dw-tool.com
SIC: 3495 3493   Wire springs; Steel springs,
    except wire

(G-16364)
DISCOVERY MINT INC
Also Called: F F J
151 Exchange St (02860-2210)
P.O. Box 620 (02862-0620)
PHONE..................................401 722-6530
F Paul Mooney Junior, *Pr*
Ward K Mooney, *
EMP: 20 **EST:** 1858
SQ FT: 25,000
SALES (est): 685.07K **Privately Held**
Web: www.fullerfindings.com
SIC: 3915 3911   Jewelers' findings and
    materials; Jewelry, precious metal

(G-16365)
DOMINION REBAR COMPANY
30 Lockbridge St (02860-1612)
PHONE..................................401 724-9200
Mark H Mainelli, *Pr*
Roy Jackson, *
John Pursche, *
EMP: 49 **EST:** 1979
SQ FT: 10,000
SALES (est): 778.58K
SALES (corp-wide): 25.54MM **Privately
Held**
SIC: 3449 3441   Fabricated bar joists and
    concrete reinforcing bars; Fabricated
    structural metal
PA: Aetna Bridge Company
    100 Jefferson Blvd # 100
    Warwick RI 02888
    401 728-0400

(G-16366)
ECOLOGICAL FIBERS INC
Also Called: Narragansett Coated Paper
730 York Ave (02861-2846)
P.O. Box 2203 (02861-0203)
PHONE..................................401 725-9700
EMP: 95
SQ FT: 140,000
SALES (corp-wide): 46.56MM **Privately
Held**
Web: www.ecofibers.com
SIC: 2672   Paper; coated and laminated, nec
PA: Ecological Fibers, Inc.
    40 Pioneer Dr

Lunenburg MA 01462
978 537-0003

(G-16367)
**EXCELLENT COFFEE CO INC
(PA)**
Also Called: Downeast Coffee Roasters
259 East Ave (02860-3800)
PHONE..................................401 724-6393
William Kapos, *CEO*
Theodora Kapos, *
EMP: 116 **EST:** 1950
SQ FT: 20,000
SALES (est): 9.62MM
SALES (corp-wide): 9.62MM **Privately
Held**
Web: www.downeastcoffee.com
SIC: 2095 5149   Roasted coffee; Coffee,
    green or roasted

(G-16368)
**FARBER INDUSTRIAL
FABRICATING**
55 Moss St (02860-4543)
PHONE..................................401 725-2492
Ray Auger, *Pr*
Richard Nadeau, *Sec*
Jane Auger, *VP*
EMP: 9 **EST:** 1918
SQ FT: 9,000
SALES (est): 881.46K **Privately Held**
Web: www.farberindustrial.com
SIC: 3441   Building components, structural
    steel

(G-16369)
**FIESTA JEWELRY
CORPORATION**
Also Called: F2nyc
250 East Ave (02860-3802)
PHONE..................................212 564-6847
Carlos Hatch, *Pr*
EMP: 34
SALES (corp-wide): 281.15K **Privately
Held**
Web: www.f2nyc.com
SIC: 3911   Jewelry, precious metal
PA: Fiesta Jewelry Corporation
    8 W 38th St Rm 801
    New York NY 10018
    212 564-6847

(G-16370)
FULLY ROOTED INC
560 Mineral Spring Ave Unit 120
(02860-3363)
PHONE..................................401 429-8768
Angelo R Mollis, *Pr*
EMP: 10 **EST:** 2015
SALES (est): 797.82K **Privately Held**
Web: www.fullyrooted.com
SIC: 2033   Canned fruits and specialties

(G-16371)
HASBRO INC
1011 Newport Ave (02861-2538)
PHONE..................................401 726-2090
Jane Ritson-parsons, *Mgr*
EMP: 8
SALES (corp-wide): 5.86B **Publicly Held**
Web: hasbro.gcs-web.com
SIC: 3944   Games, toys, and children's
    vehicles
PA: Hasbro, Inc.
    1027 Newport Ave
    Pawtucket RI 02861
    401 431-8697

(G-16372)
HASBRO INC
Also Called: Hasbro
200 Narragansett Park Dr (02861-4342)
PHONE..................................401 431-8412
EMP: 54
SALES (corp-wide): 5.86B **Publicly Held**
Web: hasbro.gcs-web.com
SIC: 3944   Games, toys, and children's
    vehicles
PA: Hasbro, Inc.
    1027 Newport Ave
    Pawtucket RI 02861
    401 431-8697

(G-16373)
HASBRO INC (PA)
Also Called: Hasbro
1027 Newport Ave (02861-2500)
P.O. Box 1059 (02862-1059)
PHONE..................................401 431-8697
Christian P Cocks, *CEO*
Richard S Stoddart, *
Michael R Burns, *
Tom Courtney, *GLOBAL*
Tarrant Sibley, *CLO*
▲ **EMP:** 2800 **EST:** 1923
SQ FT: 343,000
SALES (est): 5.86B
SALES (corp-wide): 5.86B **Publicly Held**
Web: hasbro.gcs-web.com
SIC: 3944 3942   Games, toys, and children's
    vehicles; Dolls and stuffed toys

(G-16374)
**HASBRO INTERNATIONAL INC
(HQ)**
1027 Newport Ave (02861-2500)
PHONE..................................401 431-8697
Brian Coldner, *Pr*
Judis A Smith, *
David D Hargreaves, *
EMP: 1000 **EST:** 1974
SQ FT: 343,000
SALES (est): 269.54MM
SALES (corp-wide): 5.86B **Publicly Held**
SIC: 3944   Games, toys, and children's
    vehicles
PA: Hasbro, Inc.
    1027 Newport Ave
    Pawtucket RI 02861
    401 431-8697

(G-16375)
HELLO TOMORROW LLC
1005 Main St Ste 7050 (02860-7802)
PHONE..................................401 727-0070
Leif Askeland, *Mgr*
EMP: 8 **EST:** 2016
SALES (est): 314.74K **Privately Held**
Web: www.hellotomorrowinc.com
SIC: 7372   Prepackaged software

(G-16376)
**INTERNATIONAL PACKAGING
CORPORATION (PA)**
Also Called: Interpak
517 Mineral Spring Ave (02860-3408)
P.O. Box 427 (02862-0427)
PHONE..................................401 724-1600
◆ **EMP:** 599 **EST:** 1957
SALES (est): 47.18MM
SALES (corp-wide): 47.18MM **Privately
Held**
Web: www.interpak.com
SIC: 3499 3089   Boxes for packing and
    shipping, metal; Boxes, plastics

(G-16377)
ISLE BREWERS GUILD LLC
Also Called: BJ's Brewhouse
461 Main St (02860-2913)
PHONE..................................774 766-9186
Devin P Kelly, *Pr*
EMP: 50 **EST:** 2017
SALES (est): 5.43MM **Privately Held**
Web: www.islebrewers.com
SIC: 2082   Malt beverages

(G-16378)
JEBELLA LLC
Also Called: JB Rails and Fabrication
16 Sabin St (02860-1431)
PHONE..................................401 475-1720
EMP: 9 **EST:** 2016
SALES (est): 247.31K **Privately Held**
SIC: 3312   Rails, steel or iron

(G-16379)
JET ELECTRIC MOTOR CO INC
688 School St (02860-5711)
PHONE..................................401 725-9050
Michael Zurowski, *Pr*
Walter M Zurowski, *VP*
Steven Zurowski, *Sec*
EMP: 21 **EST:** 1959
SQ FT: 32,000
SALES (est): 1.13MM **Privately Held**
Web: www.jetelectricmotorcompany.com
SIC: 5063 7694   Motors, electric; Rewinding
    services

(G-16380)
JS PALLET CO INC
60 Lockbridge St (02860-1612)
P.O. Box 1907 (02862-1907)
PHONE..................................401 723-0223
Carlos Da Silva, *Pr*
Joseph Da Silva, *
▲ **EMP:** 18 **EST:** 1966
SALES (est): 903.22K **Privately Held**
Web: www.jspalletinc.com
SIC: 2448   Pallets, wood

(G-16381)
**KEY CONTAINER
CORPORATION (PA)**
21 Campbell St (02861-4005)
P.O. Box 2370 (02861-0370)
PHONE..................................401 723-2000
David Strauss, *Pr*
◆ **EMP:** 128 **EST:** 1960
SQ FT: 150,000
SALES (est): 27.03MM
SALES (corp-wide): 27.03MM **Privately
Held**
Web: www.keycontainercorp.com
SIC: 2653   Boxes, corrugated: made from
    purchased materials

(G-16382)
**LASERVALL NORTH AMERICA
LLC**
Also Called: Lna Laser Technology
136 Newell Ave (02860-4922)
P.O. Box 998 (02862-0998)
PHONE..................................401 724-0076
EMP: 9 **EST:** 2001
SQ FT: 32,000
SALES (est): 1.9MM **Privately Held**
Web: www.lnalaser.com
SIC: 3699   Laser systems and equipment

(G-16383)
MASON BOX COMPANY
517 Mineral Spring Ave (02860-3408)
PHONE..................................800 842-9526

Hugh D Mason, *Treas*
▲ **EMP:** 42 **EST:** 1891
SQ FT: 96,000
SALES (est): 965.42K **Privately Held**
Web: www.masonbox.com
SIC: 2674 2671 2653 2652 Bags: uncoated paper and multiwall; Paper; coated and laminated packaging; Corrugated and solid fiber boxes; Boxes, newsboard, metal edged: made from purchased materials

(G-16384)
MASTERCAST LTD
Also Called: Amcraft
56 Barnes St (02860-4961)
PHONE..............................401 726-3100
David Katseff, *Pr*
EMP: 16 **EST:** 1976
SQ FT: 6,500
SALES (est): 958.63K **Privately Held**
Web: www.mastercast.com
SIC: 3089 3993 Casting of plastics; Signs and advertising specialties

(G-16385)
MATLET GROUP LLC
60 Delta Dr (02860-4556)
PHONE..............................401 834-3007
EMP: 430
Web: www.thematletgroup.com
SIC: 2759 7389 Commercial printing, nec; Packaging and labeling services

(G-16386)
MEL-CO-ED INC
381 Roosevelt Ave (02860-2145)
P.O. Box 1245 (02862-1245)
PHONE..............................401 724-2160
Randolph Sowa, *Pr*
Philip Sowa, *
▲ **EMP:** 35 **EST:** 1946
SQ FT: 40,000
SALES (est): 4.02MM **Privately Held**
Web: www.melcoed.com
SIC: 3999 Badges, metal: policemen, firemen, etc.

(G-16387)
MERCHBRO INC
1005 Main St Unit 8130 (02860-7813)
PHONE..............................866 428-0095
Brent Mulligan, *CEO*
EMP: 15 **EST:** 2015
SALES (est): 909.9K **Privately Held**
Web: www.merchbro.com
SIC: 5961 2759 5699 Electronic shopping; Promotional printing; T-shirts, custom printed

(G-16388)
MM-APVH ACQUISITION CO LLC
1 Campbell St (02860-4896)
PHONE..............................401 753-7778
EMP: 104
SALES (corp-wide): 58.78MM **Privately Held**
Web: www.seaboardbox.com
SIC: 2657 Folding paperboard boxes
HQ: Mm-Apvh Acquisition Company Llc
100 Simplex Dr
Westminster MA 01473
978 516-7050

(G-16389)
MOTIF MAGAZINE
729 Main St (02860-3625)
PHONE..............................401 312-3305
Cheryl Michalski, *Account Representative*
EMP: 17 **EST:** 2020
SALES (est): 466.34K **Privately Held**

Web: www.motifri.com
SIC: 2721 Magazines: publishing only, not printed on site

(G-16390)
MOUNT TOM BOX CO INC
21 Campbell St (02861-4005)
PHONE..............................413 781-5300
Domenic Lapati, *Prin*
EMP: 10 **EST:** 2010
SALES (est): 233.03K **Privately Held**
Web: www.keycontainercorp.com
SIC: 2653 Boxes, corrugated: made from purchased materials

(G-16391)
NESTOR TRAFFIC SYSTEMS INC (PA)
1080 Main St (02860-4847)
PHONE..............................401 714-7781
William Danzell, *Ch Bd*
Nigel Hebborn, *
EMP: 30 **EST:** 1997
SQ FT: 20,000
SALES (est): 14.73MM
SALES (corp-wide): 14.73MM **Privately Held**
SIC: 3669 8748 Traffic signals, electric; Business consulting, nec

(G-16392)
NEW ENGLAND NEWSPAPERS INC
Also Called: Pawtucket Times, The
2 Dexter St Ste 2 (02860-2991)
P.O. Box 307 (02862-0307)
PHONE..............................401 722-4000
Michael Moses, *Mgr*
EMP: 46
SALES (corp-wide): 1.96B **Privately Held**
Web: www.pawtuckettimes.com
SIC: 2711 Newspapers, publishing and printing
HQ: New England Newspapers, Inc.
75 S Church St Ste L1
Pittsfield MA 01201

(G-16393)
NEW ENGLAND OVERSEAS CORP
Also Called: N E O
358 Lowden St (02860-6052)
P.O. Box 16069 (02916-0698)
PHONE..............................401 722-3800
Andrew Davis Jencks, *Pr*
Stephen B Jencks, *VP*
Benjamin Thurston, *Dir*
Suvia Siekman, *Dir*
Sara Lodge, *Dir*
▲ **EMP:** 16 **EST:** 1971
SQ FT: 28,000
SALES (est): 2.01MM **Privately Held**
Web: www.neocorp.com
SIC: 2298 Cordage: abaca, sisal, henequen, hemp, jute, or other fiber

(G-16394)
NEW ENGLAND PAPER TUBE CO INC
200 Conant St (02860-1836)
P.O. Box 186 (02862-0186)
PHONE..............................401 725-2610
Kenneth W Douglas Junior, *Pr*
James Douglas, *
EMP: 21 **EST:** 1907
SQ FT: 250,000
SALES (est): 636.76K **Privately Held**
Web: www.nepapertube.com

SIC: 2655 2675 Tubes, fiber or paper: made from purchased material; Paper die-cutting

(G-16395)
NORTH EAST KNITTING INC
Also Called: Stretchable Solutions
179 Conant St (02860-7204)
PHONE..............................401 727-0500
Rosalie Darosa, *Pr*
Linda Koussa, *
Alexander Darosa, *
Eric Darosa, *
Mike Darosa, *
◆ **EMP:** 105 **EST:** 1986
SQ FT: 120,000
SALES (est): 9.89MM **Privately Held**
Web: www.nekinc.com
SIC: 2241 5949 Elastic narrow fabrics, woven or braided; Fabric stores piece goods

(G-16396)
NUCOR HRRIS RBAR NORTHEAST LLC
30 Lockbridge St (02860-1612)
PHONE..............................401 724-9200
EMP: 60
SALES (corp-wide): 41.51B **Publicly Held**
Web: www.harrisrebar.com
SIC: 3449 Bars, concrete reinforcing: fabricated steel
HQ: Nucor Harris Rebar Northeast Llc
55 Sumner St Ste 1
Milford MA 01757
800 370-0132

(G-16397)
OCEAN STATE AIR LLC
33 Dale St (02860-5512)
PHONE..............................401 722-2447
Stephen Marasa, *Prin*
EMP: 7 **EST:** 2006
SALES (est): 100K **Privately Held**
SIC: 3564 Air cleaning systems

(G-16398)
OPTICAL POLYMERS LAB CORP
200 Weeden St (02860-1804)
PHONE..............................401 722-0710
Cynthia M Donadio, *Pr*
EMP: 10 **EST:** 1992
SQ FT: 15,000
SALES (est): 943.5K **Privately Held**
Web: www.opticalpolymers.com
SIC: 2821 3369 Acrylic resins; Nonferrous foundries, nec

(G-16399)
PACKAGING GRAPHICS LLC
Also Called: Pg
60 Delta Dr (02860-4556)
PHONE..............................401 725-7700
▲ **EMP:** 187
SIC: 2759 Commercial printing, nec

(G-16400)
PAWTUCKET HOT MIX ASPHALT INC
25 Concord St (02860-3423)
PHONE..............................401 722-4488
Nick Hernandez, *Mgr*
David Walsh, *Pr*
EMP: 27 **EST:** 2018
SALES (est): 3.88MM **Privately Held**
Web: www.pawtuckethotmixasphalt.com
SIC: 3273 Ready-mixed concrete

(G-16401)
PET FOOD EXPERTS INC (PA)
175 Main St Unit 2 (02860-4127)

P.O. Box 8 (02862-0008)
PHONE..............................401 721-5593
Michael G Baker, *Pr*
James Alden, *
▲ **EMP:** 168 **EST:** 1989
SQ FT: 220,000
SALES (est): 80.37MM **Privately Held**
Web: www.petfoodexperts.com
SIC: 5199 2047 General merchandise, non-durable; Dog and cat food

(G-16402)
PHILIP MACHINE COMPANY INC
Also Called: Philip Machine
190 York Ave (02860-6449)
PHONE..............................401 353-7383
Kevin Vanier, *Pr*
Lee Sormanti, *Mgr*
EMP: 25 **EST:** 1979
SQ FT: 15,000
SALES (est): 2.16MM **Privately Held**
Web: www.philipmachine.com
SIC: 3312 3469 Wire products, steel or iron; Metal stampings, nec

(G-16403)
PIATEK MACHINE COMPANY INC
25 Monticello Rd (02861-3899)
PHONE..............................401 728-9930
Gail Piatek, *Pr*
EMP: 10 **EST:** 1940
SQ FT: 2,100
SALES (est): 997.58K **Privately Held**
Web: www.piatekmachine.com
SIC: 3599 3541 Machine shop, jobbing and repair; Machine tool replacement & repair parts, metal cutting types

(G-16404)
PRECISION PLSG ORNAMENTALS INC
Also Called: Precision Polishing
601 Mineral Spring Ave Ste 2 (02860-3366)
PHONE..............................401 728-9994
▲ **EMP:** 10 **EST:** 1994
SQ FT: 12,000
SALES (est): 484.53K **Privately Held**
Web: www.precisionpolishinginc.com
SIC: 2842 3965 3471 Polishes and sanitation goods; Fasteners, buttons, needles, and pins; Plating and polishing

(G-16405)
PROVIDENCE BRAID COMPANY
358 Lowden St (02860-6093)
P.O. Box 6211 (02940-6211)
PHONE..............................401 722-2120
Harrison Huntoon, *Pr*
Howard Huntoon Junior, *VP*
Burton Huntoon, *
EMP: 43 **EST:** 1904
SQ FT: 115,000
SALES (est): 4.41MM **Privately Held**
SIC: 2241 Elastic narrow fabrics, woven or braided

(G-16406)
PROVIDENCE METALLIZING CO INC (PA)
51 Fairlawn Ave (02860-2579)
PHONE..............................401 722-5300
Richard Sugarman, *Pr*
Beverly Sugarman, *
Charles Gadon, *
▲ **EMP:** 86 **EST:** 1951
SQ FT: 300,000
SALES (est): 10.91MM
SALES (corp-wide): 10.91MM **Privately Held**

Web: www.providencemetallizing.com
SIC: 3471 3479 Electroplating of metals or formed products; Coating of metals and formed products

(G-16407)
PROVIDENCE YARN COMPANY INC
Also Called: Yarn Outlet , The
50 Division St (02860-5304)
PHONE...............................401 722-5600
Terry Schuster, *Pr*
Andrew Shuster, *Dir*
◆ EMP: 8 EST: 1931
SQ FT: 30,000
SALES (est): 1.05MM Privately Held
Web: www.providenceyarn.com
SIC: 5949 5199 2281 Knitting goods and supplies; Industrial yarns; Yarn spinning mills

(G-16408)
R & D MANUFACTURING CO INC
60 Dunnell Ln (02860-5828)
PHONE...............................401 305-7662
Diane Fontaine, *Pr*
Phillip Montalto, *CEO*
EMP: 29 EST: 2012
SQ FT: 30,000
SALES (est): 2.05MM Privately Held
Web: www.rdmfgonline.com
SIC: 3961 5094 Costume jewelry; Jewelry

(G-16409)
RACECAR JEWELRY CO
Also Called: Badges of America
19 Mendon Ave (02861-2335)
PHONE...............................401 475-5701
Daniel Grandi, *Pr*
James Grandi, *Sec*
EMP: 8 EST: 1999
SALES (est): 800K Privately Held
Web: www.racecarjewelry.com
SIC: 3911 5944 Jewelry apparel; Jewelry stores

(G-16410)
RAG & BONE BINDERY LTD
1088 Main St Frnt 1 (02860-4890)
PHONE...............................401 728-0762
Jason Thompson, *Pr*
Ilira Steinman, *VP*
EMP: 16 EST: 1992
SQ FT: 10,000
SALES (est): 437.85K Privately Held
Web: www.ragandbonebindery.com
SIC: 2789 Binding only: books, pamphlets, magazines, etc.

(G-16411)
RAND-WHITNEY CONTAINER LLC
Southeast Container
455 Narragansett Park Dr (02861-4321)
PHONE...............................401 729-7900
Scott Robertson, *Prin*
EMP: 61
Web: www.randwhitney.com
SIC: 2631 3412 2653 Folding boxboard; Metal barrels, drums, and pails; Corrugated and solid fiber boxes
HQ: Rand-Whitney Container Llc
1 Rand Whitney Way
Worcester MA 01607
508 890-7000

(G-16412)
RIDCO CASTING CO
6 Beverage Hill Ave (02860-6202)

PHONE...............................401 724-0400
Stanley Cohen, *CEO*
Jeffrey A Cohen, *
EMP: 88 EST: 1955
SQ FT: 63,000
SALES (est): 9.48MM Privately Held
Web: www.ridco.com
SIC: 3369 3364 Nonferrous foundries, nec; Zinc and zinc-base alloy die-castings

(G-16413)
ROSE DISPLAYS
500 Narragansett Park Dr (02861-4325)
PHONE...............................978 219-8120
Jeffrey Hastings, *Prin*
EMP: 10 EST: 2017
SALES (est): 220.74K Privately Held
Web: www.rosedisplays.com
SIC: 3993 Signs and advertising specialties

(G-16414)
RTC HOLDINGS INC
Also Called: American Colorized Coins
211 Weeden St (02860-1807)
P.O. Box 3230 (02861-0997)
PHONE...............................401 728-6980
Robert Chito, *Pr*
EMP: 26 EST: 1981
SQ FT: 32,000
SALES (est): 452.17K Privately Held
Web: www.schofieldprinting.com
SIC: 2759 3993 Screen printing; Signs and advertising specialties

(G-16415)
SARGEANT & WILBUR INC
20 Monticello Pl (02861-3500)
P.O. Box 1166 (02862-1166)
PHONE...............................401 726-0013
Michael F Wilbur, *Pr*
Raymond Mc Mahon, *Sec*
Marcia J Wilbur, *Treas*
EMP: 13 EST: 1939
SQ FT: 18,700
SALES (est): 805.84K Privately Held
Web: www.sargeantandwilbur.com
SIC: 3567 Heating units and devices, industrial: electric

(G-16416)
SCARBOROUGH FAIRE INC
Also Called: British Motor Heritage
1151 Main St (02860-4800)
PHONE...............................401 724-4200
Kenneth G Bruce, *Pr*
Cecelia Bruce, *
◆ EMP: 25 EST: 1971
SQ FT: 11,000
SALES (est): 2.38MM Privately Held
Web: scarboroughfaire.4mg.com
SIC: 3089 5013 5531 7311 Automotive parts, plastic; Automotive supplies and parts ; Automotive parts; Advertising agencies

(G-16417)
SPIRIT RECOGNITION INC (PA)
Also Called: University Spirit
639 Central Ave (02861-2056)
P.O. Box 3006 (02861-0506)
PHONE...............................401 722-6400
Robert Marshall, *Pr*
Jill Marshall, *Sec*
EMP: 15 EST: 1978
SALES (est): 2.03MM
SALES (corp-wide): 2.03MM Privately Held
Web: www.spiritrecognition.com

SIC: 5621 5611 3993 2396 Women's sportswear; Clothing, sportswear, men's and boys'; Signs and advertising specialties ; Automotive and apparel trimmings

(G-16418)
STRETCH PRODUCTS CORP
Also Called: H & W Shoe Supplies
392 Pine St (02860-1833)
P.O. Box 1676 (02862-1651)
PHONE...............................401 722-0400
David Sheibley, *Pr*
Abel Pereira, *
EMP: 42 EST: 1985
SQ FT: 85,000
SALES (est): 4.22MM Privately Held
Web: www.stretchproducts.com
SIC: 2241 Narrow fabric mills

(G-16419)
TECHNIC INC
Also Called: Technic Inc Equipment Division
55 Maryland Ave (02860-6278)
PHONE...............................401 781-6100
Tony Guglielmo, *Ex VP*
EMP: 30
SALES (corp-wide): 159.53MM Privately Held
Web: www.technic.com
SIC: 2899 Chemical preparations, nec
PA: Technic, Inc.
47 Molter St
Cranston RI 02910
401 781-6100

(G-16420)
TEKNOR APEX COMPANY (PA)
505 Central Ave (02861-1900)
P.O. Box 2290 (02861-0290)
PHONE...............................401 725-8000
Donald Wiseman, *CEO*
Jonathan D Fain, *
Suresh Swaminathan, *
Paul Morrisroe, *
◆ EMP: 2000 EST: 1924
SQ FT: 500,000
SALES (est): 1.03B
SALES (corp-wide): 1.03B Privately Held
Web: www.teknorapex.com
SIC: 3087 3069 3052 2869 Custom compound purchased resins; Custom compounding of rubber materials; Garden hose, rubber; Plasticizers, organic: cyclic and acyclic

(G-16421)
TEKNOR COLOR COMPANY
Also Called: Teknor Apex Co
505 Central Ave (02861-1945)
PHONE...............................401 725-8000
Tom Lepozsky, *Mgr*
EMP: 23
SALES (corp-wide): 1.03B Privately Held
Web: www.teknorapex.com
SIC: 2865 2851 Dyes and pigments; Paints and allied products
HQ: Teknor Color Company Llc
505 Central Ave
Pawtucket RI 02861

(G-16422)
TEKNOR COLOR COMPANY LLC (HQ)
505 Central Ave (02861-1945)
P.O. Box 2290 (02861-0290)
▲ EMP: 32 EST: 1963
SALES (est): 40.86MM
SALES (corp-wide): 1.03B Privately Held
Web: www.teknorapex.com

SIC: 2821 Plastics materials and resins
PA: Teknor Apex Company
505 Central Ave
Pawtucket RI 02861
401 725-8000

(G-16423)
TEKNOR PRFMCE ELASTOMERS INC
505 Central Ave (02861-1945)
PHONE...............................401 725-8000
James Morrison, *CFO*
EMP: 46 EST: 2000
SALES (est): 4.1MM
SALES (corp-wide): 1.03B Privately Held
Web: www.teknorapex.com
SIC: 2821 Plastics materials and resins
PA: Teknor Apex Company
505 Central Ave
Pawtucket RI 02861
401 725-8000

(G-16424)
TRACEY GEAR INC
Also Called: Tracey Gear & Precision Shaft
740 York Ave (02861-2846)
P.O. Box 2226 (02861-0226)
PHONE...............................401 725-3920
Terrence Tracey, *Pr*
Kevin Tracey, *
Terrence Tracet, *Stockholder*
Douglas Tracey, *
EMP: 25 EST: 1945
SQ FT: 20,000
SALES (est): 3.68MM Privately Held
Web: www.traceygear.com
SIC: 3568 3429 Couplings, shaft: rigid, flexible, universal joint, etc.; Pulleys, metal

(G-16425)
TRACY GLOVER OBJECTS & LTG INC
Also Called: Tracy Glover Studio
59 Blackstone Ave Unit 11 (02860-1071)
PHONE...............................401 724-1100
Tracy Glover, *Prin*
EMP: 7 EST: 2003
SALES (est): 659.9K Privately Held
Web: www.tracygloverstudio.com
SIC: 3399 Primary metal products

(G-16426)
TRUEX INCORPORATED
300 Armistice Blvd (02861-2332)
PHONE...............................401 722-5023
EMP: 52 EST: 1976
SALES (est): 13.09MM
SALES (corp-wide): 1.03B Privately Held
Web: www.truexinc.com
SIC: 3366 3469 Brass foundry, nec; Metal stampings, nec
PA: Teknor Apex Company
505 Central Ave
Pawtucket RI 02861
401 725-8000

(G-16427)
USG SERVICES CORPORATION
1005 Main St Unit 1201 (02860-7804)
PHONE...............................401 644-7098
Lance Jay Robbins, *Pr*
EMP: 8 EST: 2010
SALES (est): 131.97K Privately Held
Web: www.urbansmartgrowth.com
SIC: 3275 Gypsum products

(G-16428)
VAN & COMPANY INC
547 Weeden St (02860-1625)

PHONE...................401 722-9829
Albert P Van Herpe, *Pr*
Robert L Van Herpe, *VP*
▲ EMP: 10 EST: 1958
SQ FT: 22,500
SALES (est): 459.6K **Privately Held**
Web: www.vanandcompany.com
SIC: 3161   Cases, carrying, nec

(G-16429)
VISUAL CREATIONS INC
Also Called: Rose Disp A Div Visual Creat
500 Narragansett Park Dr (02861-4325)
PHONE...................401 588-5151
Jay Long, *Pr*
Douglas Robertson, *
◆ EMP: 108 EST: 2006
SQ FT: 150,000
SALES (est): 20.15MM **Privately Held**
Web: www.rosedisplays.com
SIC: 2541   Store and office display cases
and fixtures

(G-16430)
**WEEDEN STREET ASSOCIATES
LLC**
Also Called: New England Paper Tube
173 Weeden St (02860-2468)
PHONE...................401 725-2610
EMP: 21 EST: 2015
SALES (est): 1.79MM **Privately Held**
SIC: 2621 2655   Kraft paper; Fiber spools,
tubes, and cones

(G-16431)
WHITING & DAVIS LLC
33 York Ave (02860-6423)
PHONE...................508 699-4412
EMP: 11 EST: 2010
SALES (est): 479.38K **Privately Held**
Web: www.whitinganddavis.com
SIC: 3911   Handbags, precious metal

(G-16432)
ZOLL MEDICAL CORPORATION
Also Called: Bio-Detek
525 Narragansett Park Dr (02861-4323)
PHONE...................401 729-1400
Jonathan Rennert, *Bmch Mgr*
EMP: 357
Web: www.zoll.com
SIC: 3845   Electromedical equipment
HQ: Zoll Medical Corporation
269 Mill Rd
Chelmsford MA 01824
978 421-9655

Peace Dale
Washington County

(G-16433)
**FORTERRA PIPE & PRECAST
LLC**
170 Fiore Industrial Dr (02879-2156)
PHONE...................401 782-2600
Richard Williams, *Mgr*
EMP: 9
Web: www.rinkerpipe.com
SIC: 3272   Precast terrazzo or concrete
products
HQ: Forterra Pipe & Precast, Llc
511 E John Carpenter Fwy
Irving TX 75062
469 458-7973

Portsmouth
Newport County

(G-16434)
A2B TRACKING SOLUTIONS INC
207 Highpoint Ave Ste 7 (02871-1387)
PHONE...................401 683-5215
EMP: 20 EST: 1994
SQ FT: 25,000
SALES (est): 3.84MM **Privately Held**
Web: www.a2btracking.com
SIC: 3555 5045 7371   Plates, metal;
engravers'; Computer software; Computer
software development

(G-16435)
ANCHORS AND THREAD LLC
300 Highpoint Ave (02871-1445)
PHONE...................401 248-8645
EMP: 7 EST: 2018
SALES (est): 214.69K **Privately Held**
Web: www.anchorsandthread.com
SIC: 2394   Canvas and related products

(G-16436)
ARAMID RIGGING INC
14 Regatta Way Ste 3 (02871-6167)
PHONE...................401 683-6966
J Alexander C Wadson, *Pr*
EMP: 9 EST: 1991
SALES (est): 760K **Privately Held**
SIC: 3731 5551   Marine rigging; Marine
supplies, nec

(G-16437)
BIOHOLDINGS LTD
45 Highpoint Ave Ste 3 (02871-8600)
PHONE...................401 683-5400
Timothy P Burns, *Pr*
EMP: 17 EST: 1999
SALES (est): 461.8K **Privately Held**
SIC: 3677   Filtration devices, electronic

(G-16438)
BIOPROCESSH2O LLC
45 Highpoint Ave Ste 3 (02871-8600)
PHONE...................401 683-5400
Tim Burns, *Managing Member*
▼ EMP: 22 EST: 2008
SQ FT: 50,000
SALES (est): 4.81MM **Privately Held**
Web: www.bioprocessh2o.com
SIC: 8731 3569   Commercial physical
research; Filters

(G-16439)
BLACK DOG CORPORATION
Also Called: S & S Fabric Products
1 Maritime Dr Ste 3 (02871-6100)
PHONE...................401 683-5858
TOLL FREE: 800
Paul Di Martino, *Pr*
Victoria Di Martino, *VP*
EMP: 22 EST: 1985
SQ FT: 10,000
SALES (est): 3.62MM **Privately Held**
Web: www.ssfabricproducts.com
SIC: 2394 2399 5961   Sails: made from
purchased materials; Sleeping bags;
Fishing, hunting and camping equipment
and supplies: by mail

(G-16440)
**BRAND & OPPENHEIMER CO
INC (PA)**
Also Called: Ocean State Innovations
208 Clock Tower Sq (02871-1397)
PHONE...................401 293-5500

EMP: 30 EST: 1994
SQ FT: 1,200
SALES (est): 22.81MM **Privately Held**
Web: www.osinnovate.com
SIC: 2231 2211 2221   Broadwoven fabric
mills, wool; Poplin, cotton; Parachute fabrics

(G-16441)
BUTLER VALVE & FITTINGS
81 Black Point Ln (02871-5203)
PHONE...................401 849-3833
Keith Macdonald, *Prin*
EMP: 7 EST: 2010
SALES (est): 117.83K **Privately Held**
SIC: 3592   Valves

(G-16442)
C-END LLC
409 Vanderbilt Ln (02871-2342)
PHONE...................610 350-8674
Erik Holling, *CEO*
EMP: 7
SALES (est): 78.66K **Privately Held**
SIC: 2833   Medicinals and botanicals

(G-16443)
**HODGES BADGE COMPANY
INC (PA)**
Also Called: Image Award Ribbons
205 Clock Tower Sq (02871-1397)
PHONE...................401 682-2000
F James Hodges Junior, *Ch Bd*
Frederick J Hodges Iii, *Pr*
Sheila H Hodges, *
Jane Sousa, *
▲ EMP: 99 EST: 1920
SALES (est): 14.99MM
SALES (corp-wide): 14.99MM **Privately
Held**
Web: www.hodgesbadge.com
SIC: 3999 5999   Buttons: Red Cross, union,
identification; Trophies and plaques

(G-16444)
HUNT YACHTS LLC
1909 Alden Lndg (02871-6164)
PHONE...................401 324-4201
Dave Goodman, *Prin*
Peter Van Lancker, *Prin*
◆ EMP: 12 EST: 2013
SQ FT: 36,000
SALES (est): 6.52MM
SALES (corp-wide): 6.52MM **Privately
Held**
Web: www.huntyachts.com
SIC: 3732   Yachts, building and repairing
PA: Scout Partners Llc
712 5th Ave Fl 47
New York NY

(G-16445)
INTERNATIONAL MFG SVCS INC
Also Called: IMS
50 Schoolhouse Ln (02871-2435)
PHONE...................401 683-9700
John J B Silvia Junior, *Pr*
John J B Silva Iii, *VP*
EMP: 46 EST: 1974
SQ FT: 12,000
SALES (est): 6.72MM **Privately Held**
Web: www.ims-resistors.com
SIC: 3679   Electronic circuits

(G-16446)
MC MILLEN YACHTS
1909 Alden Lndg (02871-6164)
PHONE...................401 682-2610
EMP: 14
SALES (corp-wide): 2.11MM **Privately
Held**

Web: www.woodenyachts.com
SIC: 3732   Boatbuilding and repairing
PA: Mc Millen Yachts
1 Bannisters Wharf
Newport RI 02840
401 846-5557

(G-16447)
MESCO CORPORATION
1676 E Main Rd Ste Bay (02871-2447)
P.O. Box 945 (02871-0919)
PHONE...................401 683-2677
Corey Smith, *Pr*
Bill Watson, *Pr*
EMP: 8 EST: 1998
SALES (est): 5.32MM **Privately Held**
Web: www.mescocorp.com
SIC: 3561   Industrial pumps and parts

(G-16448)
MORRIS YACHTS LLC
Also Called: My
1 Little Harbor Lndg Ste 1 (02871-6168)
PHONE...................207 667-2499
Donald Dow, *Prin*
EMP: 8 EST: 2016
SALES (est): 284.78K **Privately Held**
Web: www.morrisyachts.com
SIC: 3732   Boatbuilding and repairing

(G-16449)
**NEW ENGLAND BOATWORKS
INC**
Also Called: East Passage Yachting Center
1 Lagoon Rd Ste 4 (02871-6142)
PHONE...................401 683-4000
Baxter Underwood, *CEO*
Rives Potts, *
◆ EMP: 100 EST: 1988
SQ FT: 55,800
SALES (est): 13.64MM
SALES (corp-wide): 2.97B **Publicly Held**
Web: www.neboatworks.com
SIC: 4493 3732 4213 3429   Boat yards,
storage and incidental repair; Boatbuilding
and repairing; Heavy hauling, nec; Marine
hardware
HQ: Safe Harbor Marinas, Llc
14785 Preston Rd Ste 975
Dallas TX 75254
972 488-1314

(G-16450)
**NEWPORT ELECTRIC
CORPORATION**
200 Highpoint Ave Ste B5 (02871-1356)
PHONE...................401 293-0527
David Aaron Mcmullen, *Pr*
EMP: 15 EST: 2013
SALES (est): 480.93K **Privately Held**
SIC: 3699 1731   Electrical equipment and
supplies, nec; Electrical work

(G-16451)
NIKO US LLC
300 Highpoint Ave Ste 1b (02871-1445)
P.O. Box 855 (02871-0855)
PHONE...................401 683-7525
▲ EMP: 8 EST: 2010
SALES (est): 625.42K **Privately Held**
Web: www.nikotrack.com
SIC: 3535   Overhead conveyor systems

(G-16452)
QUANTUM NEWPORT
Also Called: Quantum Sails Newport
1170 E Main Rd (02871-2309)
PHONE...................401 849-7700
Robert Macmillian, *Prin*

EMP: 8 EST: 2004
SALES (est): 427.26K **Privately Held**
Web: www.quantumsails.com
SIC: 5551 2394 Marine supplies, nec; Sails:
made from purchased materials

(G-16453)
RAYBERN UTILITY SOLUTIONS LLC

125 Power St (02871-4118)
P.O. Box 836 (02871-0836)
PHONE.............................303 775-5041
Ann Ronan, *CEO*
EMP: 7 EST: 2019
SALES (est): 251.39K **Privately Held**
Web: www.raybernsolutions.com
SIC: 7372 8742 Utility computer software;
Public utilities consultant

(G-16454)
RAYTHEON COMPANY

Raytheon
1847 W Main Rd (02871-1087)
PHONE.............................401 847-8000
David Reynhout, *Brnch Mgr*
EMP: 100
SQ FT: 350,000
SALES (corp-wide): 68.92B **Publicly Held**
Web: www.rtx.com
SIC: 3812 3679 3829 3625 Defense
systems and equipment; Electronic circuits;
Measuring and controlling devices, nec;
Relays and industrial controls
HQ: Raytheon Company
870 Winter St
Waltham MA 02451
781 522-3000

(G-16455)
RHODE NORTHSALES ISLAND INC

Also Called: North Sales Rhode Island
1 Maritime Dr Ste 1 (02871-6100)
PHONE.............................401 683-7997
Thomas Widden, *Pr*
EMP: 8 EST: 1974
SQ FT: 14,000
SALES (est): 108.07K **Privately Held**
SIC: 2394 3732 Sails: made from
purchased materials; Boatbuilding and
repairing

(G-16456)
RONSTAN INTERNATIONAL INC

Also Called: Ronstan
1170 E Main Rd Ste 3 (02871-2332)
PHONE.............................401 293-0539
Alistar Murray, *CEO*
Scott West, *Pr*
◆ EMP: 12 EST: 1977
SALES (est): 3.63MM **Privately Held**
Web: www.ronstan.com
SIC: 3429 5088 Aircraft & marine hardware,
inc. pulleys & similar items; Marine supplies
PA: Ronstan International Pty Ltd
19 Park Way
Braeside VIC 3195

(G-16457)
SQUIRREL WORKS LLC

75 Taylor Rd (02871-5416)
PHONE.............................401 247-3000
EMP: 42
SALES (corp-wide): 477.61K **Privately Held**
SIC: 3732 Boatbuilding and repairing
PA: Squirrel Works Llc
342 Compass Cir Unit B4
North Kingstown RI 02852
401 247-3000

(G-16458)
TALARIA COMPANY LLC (PA)

Also Called: Hinckley Company, The
1 Little Harbor Lndg (02871-6168)
PHONE.............................401 683-7100
Ralph Willerd, *Managing Member*
▲ EMP: 14 EST: 1999
SALES (est): 92.75MM
SALES (corp-wide): 92.75MM **Privately Held**
Web: www.hinckleyyachts.com
SIC: 3732 Boatbuilding and repairing

(G-16459)
TALARIA COMPANY LLC

Also Called: Hinckley Co
1 Little Harbor Lndg Ste 1 (02871-6168)
PHONE.............................401 683-7280
Jim Mcmanus, *Pr*
EMP: 91
SALES (corp-wide): 92.75MM **Privately Held**
Web: www.hinckleyyachts.com
SIC: 3732 Boatbuilding and repairing
PA: The Talaria Company Llc
1 Little Harbor Lndg
Portsmouth RI 02871
401 683-7100

(G-16460)
VEMPLOYEE

47 Taylor Rd (02871-5430)
PHONE.............................888 471-1982
Paul Chiumento, *Prin*
EMP: 10 EST: 2015
SALES (est): 232.95K **Privately Held**
Web: www.clariontech.com
SIC: 3296 Mineral wool

(G-16461)
WEISSENFELS USA INC

45 Highpoint Ave Ste 1 (02871-8600)
PHONE.............................401 683-2900
Stephen Lister, *CEO*
◆ EMP: 12 EST: 1995
SALES (est): 137.25K **Privately Held**
Web: www.peerlesschain.com
SIC: 3496 Miscellaneous fabricated wire
products

Providence
Providence County

(G-16462)
A & F PLATING CO INC

45 River Ave (02908-5427)
P.O. Box 28081 (02908-0081)
PHONE.............................401 861-3597
Antonio Alfieri, *Pr*
EMP: 12 EST: 1982
SQ FT: 15,000
SALES (est): 483.77K **Privately Held**
Web: www.afplating.com
SIC: 3471 Electroplating of metals or
formed products

(G-16463)
A & H DUFFY POLSG & FINSHG CO

175 Dupont Dr (02907-3105)
PHONE.............................401 785-9203
Michael D'angelo, *Pr*
Christopher D'angelo, *COO*
EMP: 25 EST: 1941
SQ FT: 10,000
SALES (est): 1.7MM **Privately Held**
Web: www.ahduffy.com

SIC: 3471 Finishing, metals or formed
products

(G-16464)
ADMIRAL PACKAGING INC

Also Called: Admiral Packaging Co.
10 Admiral St (02908-3203)
P.O. Box 6025 (02940-6025)
PHONE.............................401 274-5588
Harley Frank, *Pr*
Herbert Allan, *
John Wilbur, *
▲ EMP: 78 EST: 1956
SQ FT: 200,000
SALES (est): 22.35MM **Privately Held**
Web: www.admiralpkg.com
SIC: 2671 2673 5113 Bread wrappers,
waxed or laminated: purchased material;
Bags: plastic, laminated, and coated;
Disposable plates, cups, napkins, and
eating utensils

(G-16465)
ADOLF MELLER COMPANY (PA)

Also Called: Meller Opti
120 Corliss St (02904-2602)
P.O. Box 6001 (02940-6001)
PHONE.............................800 821-0180
David Lydon, *CEO*
Martha Scott, *
Lindsay Lydon, *
◆ EMP: 32 EST: 1946
SQ FT: 12,000
SALES (est): 7.85MM
SALES (corp-wide): 7.85MM **Privately Held**
Web: www.melleroptics.com
SIC: 3827 Optical instruments and lenses

(G-16466)
AETNA MANUFACTURING COMPANY

Also Called: Aetna Jewelery Mfg
720 Harris Ave (02909-2423)
PHONE.............................401 751-3260
Frank Caliri, *Pr*
EMP: 8 EST: 1954
SQ FT: 6,500
SALES (est): 513.56K **Privately Held**
SIC: 3911 Jewelry, precious metal

(G-16467)
ALLOY HOLDINGS LLC

Also Called: Morvillo Precision Products
160 Niantic Ave (02907-3118)
PHONE.............................401 353-7500
EMP: 100 EST: 1993
SALES (est): 8.88MM **Privately Held**
Web: www.morvilloproducts.com
SIC: 3496 5094 Miscellaneous fabricated
wire products; Precious metals

(G-16468)
ALPHAGRAPHICS

28 Wolcott St (02908-5508)
PHONE.............................401 648-0078
EMP: 7 EST: 2019
SALES (est): 204.34K **Privately Held**
Web: www.alphagraphics.com
SIC: 2752 Commercial printing, lithographic

(G-16469)
AMERICAN ACCESS CARE RI LLC

100 Highland Ave (02906-2740)
PHONE.............................401 277-9729
EMP: 22 EST: 2011
SALES (est): 503.71K **Privately Held**
Web: www.azuravascularcare.com

SIC: 3841 Diagnostic apparatus, medical

(G-16470)
AMERICAN MATHEMATICAL SOCIETY INC (PA)

Also Called: MATHEMATICAL COUNCIL OF
THE AM
201 Charles St (02904-2294)
P.O. Box 6248 (02940-6248)
PHONE.............................401 455-4000
EMP: 140 EST: 1888
SALES (est): 32.82MM
SALES (corp-wide): 32.82MM **Privately Held**
Web: www.ams.org
SIC: 2731 2673 5113 Textbooks: publishing
only, not printed on site; Periodicals,
publishing only; Scientific membership
association

(G-16471)
ANDERA INC

15 Park Row W Ste 200 (02903-1115)
PHONE.............................401 621-7900
Charles Kroll, *CEO*
Jamie Verdi, *
Ying Chen, *
Craig Wilke, *
Chris Burns, *
EMP: 57 EST: 2000
SALES (est): 17.55MM **Privately Held**
SIC: 7372 Business oriented computer
software
PA: Bottomline Technologies, Inc.
325 Corporate Dr Ste 300
Portsmouth NH 03801

(G-16472)
ANGELO DI MARIA INC

395 Admiral St (02908-2560)
P.O. Box 6106 (02940-6106)
PHONE.............................401 274-0100
John Scungio, *Pr*
Theresa Scungio, *
John Scungio Prestreas, *Prin*
EMP: 21 EST: 1928
SQ FT: 17,500
SALES (est): 660.34K **Privately Held**
SIC: 3469 3915 Stamping metal for the trade
; Jewelers' materials and lapidary work

(G-16473)
APPLITEK TECHNOLOGIES CORP

160 Georgia Ave (02905-4423)
PHONE.............................401 467-0007
Bruce Getchell, *Pr*
Nancy Getchell, *VP*
EMP: 9 EST: 1989
SQ FT: 6,000
SALES (est): 934.09K **Privately Held**
Web: www.applitek-usa.com
SIC: 3549 Wiredrawing and fabricating
machinery and equipment, ex. die

(G-16474)
ARISTON USA LLC (HQ)

Also Called: Heat Transfer Products
225 Dyer St Fl 1 (02903-3927)
PHONE.............................508 763-8071
David B Davis, *CEO*
David R Martin, *
▲ EMP: 40 EST: 1983
SQ FT: 35,000
SALES (est): 67.78MM **Privately Held**
Web: www.htproducts.com
SIC: 5084 3443 Heat exchange equipment,
industrial; Heat exchangers, condensers,
and components
PA: Ariston Holding N.V.
Onbekend Nederlands Adre

Onbekend

(G-16475)

ARMBRUST INTERNATIONAL LTD
735 Allens Ave (02905-5412)
PHONE..............................401 781-3300
EMP: 125 **EST:** 1995
SALES (est): 23.15MM **Privately Held**
Web: store.armbrustinternationalinc.com
SIC: 3911 Jewelry, precious metal

(G-16476)

AT CROSS COMPANY LLC (HQ)
295 Promenade St (02908-5720)
PHONE..............................401 333-1200
James D Miranda, *CEO*
Russell Rosnek, *Managing Member*
EMP: 93 **EST:** 2017
SQ FT: 39,536
SALES (est): 21.5MM
SALES (corp-wide): 1.32B **Privately Held**
Web: www.cross.com
SIC: 3951 5112 5943 Fountain pens and
fountain pen desk sets; Pens and/or pencils
; Writing supplies
PA: Transom Capital Group, Llc
10990 Wilshire Blvd # 905
Los Angeles CA 90024
424 293-2818

(G-16477)

ATAMIAN MANUFACTURING CORP
910 Plainfield St (02909-5451)
PHONE..............................401 944-9614
Robert Atamian, *Pr*
James Atamian, *VP*
Mary Atamian, *VP*
EMP: 20 **EST:** 1978
SQ FT: 20,000
SALES (est): 2.48MM **Privately Held**
Web: www.atamianmfg.com
SIC: 3911 3469 Jewelry, precious metal;
Stamping metal for the trade

(G-16478)

ATOM ADHESIVES LLC
1 Acorn St (02903-1028)
P.O. Box 6003 (02887-6003)
PHONE..............................888 522-6742
EMP: 10 **EST:** 2013
SQ FT: 10,000
SALES (est): 1.06MM **Privately Held**
Web: www.atomadhesives.com
SIC: 2891 Adhesives

(G-16479)

AUDETTE GROUP LLC
144 Westminster St Ste 302 (02903-2216)
PHONE..............................401 667-5884
Roland Audette, *Pr*
EMP: 10 **EST:** 2009
SQ FT: 3,600
SALES (est): 454.6K **Privately Held**
Web: www.theaudettegroup.com
SIC: 3449 Bars, concrete reinforcing;
fabricated steel

(G-16480)

AVCO CORPORATION (DH)
40 Westminster St (02903-2525)
PHONE..............................401 421-2800
Richard J Millman, *Prin*
▲ **EMP:** 123 **EST:** 1929
SALES (est): 40.06MM
SALES (corp-wide): 12.87B **Publicly Held**
Web: www.textron.com

SIC: 3728 3724 Aircraft parts and
equipment, nec; Aircraft engines and
engine parts
HQ: Textron Lycoming Corp
40 Westminster St
Providence RI 02903
401 421-2800

(G-16481)

B DEL TORO & SONS INC
393 Harris Ave (02909-1019)
PHONE..............................401 421-5820
Michael Deltoro, *Pr*
Julie Mello, *VP*
Donna Resendes, *Sec*
EMP: 14 **EST:** 1973
SQ FT: 10,000
SALES (est): 2.33MM **Privately Held**
SIC: 5141 5148 2099 2037 Food brokers;
Fresh fruits and vegetables; Food
preparations, nec; Frozen fruits and
vegetables

(G-16482)

BEACON ROCK PROPERTIES INC
Also Called: Blackstone Supply
125 Whipple St Ste 3 (02908-3258)
PHONE..............................401 421-3470
EMP: 60
Web: www.blackstonesupply.com
SIC: 8741 3429 5013 2851 Business
management; Hardware, nec; Automotive
supplies; Paint driers

(G-16483)

BEAUTIFUL DAY
66 Benefit St Fl 1 (02904-2742)
PHONE..............................617 733-9289
Keith Cooper, *Ex Dir*
EMP: 16 **EST:** 2012
SALES (est): 933.11K **Privately Held**
Web: www.beautifuldayri.org
SIC: 2043 Granola and muesli, except bars
and clusters

(G-16484)

BELL HELICOPTER KOREA INC
40 Westminster St (02903-2525)
PHONE..............................401 421-2800
John R Murphey, *Prin*
EMP: 24 **EST:** 2002
SALES (est): 2.47MM
SALES (corp-wide): 12.87B **Publicly Held**
SIC: 3728 Aircraft parts and equipment, nec
PA: Textron Inc.
40 Westminster St
Providence RI 02903
401 421-2800

(G-16485)

BELL HELICOPTER MIAMI INC
40 Westminster St (02903-2525)
PHONE..............................401 421-2800
EMP: 8 **EST:** 2019
SALES (est): 1.43MM
SALES (corp-wide): 12.87B **Publicly Held**
SIC: 3721 Aircraft
PA: Textron Inc.
40 Westminster St
Providence RI 02903
401 421-2800

(G-16486)

BELL TEXTRON RHODE ISLAND INC
Also Called: Bell Helicopter RI Inc
40 Westminster St (02903-2525)
PHONE..............................401 421-2800

James P Runstadler, *Pr*
EMP: 20 **EST:** 2019
SALES (est): 2.33MM
SALES (corp-wide): 12.87B **Publicly Held**
Web: www.textron.com
SIC: 3721 Aircraft
PA: Textron Inc.
40 Westminster St
Providence RI 02903
401 421-2800

(G-16487)

BOLT COFFEE COMPANY LLC
Also Called: Calverley Club
96 Calverley St (02908-5732)
PHONE..............................401 533-6506
EMP: 29 **EST:** 2012
SALES (est): 1.22MM **Privately Held**
Web: www.boltcoffeeco.com
SIC: 5499 2095 Coffee; Roasted coffee

(G-16488)

BOSTON NTRCEUTICAL SCIENCE LLC
1 Turks Head Pl (02903-2219)
PHONE..............................617 848-4560
EMP: 21 **EST:** 2015
SALES (est): 5.28MM **Privately Held**
SIC: 5122 2064 Druggists' sundries, nec;
Cough drops, except pharmaceutical
preparations

(G-16489)

BOSTON PHOENIX INC (PA)
Also Called: 101.7 FM
1 Chestnut St Ste 1 (02903-4155)
PHONE..............................617 536-5390
Stephen M Mindich, *Prin*
Stephen M Mindich Publ, *Prin*
EMP: 82 **EST:** 1966
SQ FT: 19,500
SALES (est): 4.83MM
SALES (corp-wide): 4.83MM **Privately Held**
Web: contests.thephoenix.com
SIC: 2711 Newspapers: publishing only, not
printed on site

(G-16490)

BP INC
Also Called: Bonollos
55 Clarkson St (02908-2609)
PHONE..............................401 274-7900
TOLL FREE: 800
Edward J Mongeon, *Pr*
Kenneth Mongeon, *
Rosamond Mongeon, *
Edward C Mongeon, *Stockholder*
Patricia Mongeon, *Stockholder*
EMP: 45 **EST:** 1968
SQ FT: 26,000
SALES (est): 9.79MM **Privately Held**
Web: www.bonollos.com
SIC: 5147 2013 2011 Meats, fresh;
Sausages and other prepared meats; Meat
packing plants

(G-16491)

BRIDGESTONE RET OPERATIONS LLC
Also Called: Firestone
987 N Main St (02904-5745)
PHONE..............................401 521-6622
Erik Ovando, *Mgr*
EMP: 10
Web: www.bridgestoneamericas.com
SIC: 5531 7534 Automotive tires;
Rebuilding and retreading tires
HQ: Bridgestone Retail Operations, Llc
333 E Lake St Ste 300

Bloomingdale IL 60108
630 259-9000

(G-16492)

BSG HANDCRAFT
Also Called: Bsg
250 Niantic Ave (02907-3120)
PHONE..............................508 636-5154
Gary Lee, *Pr*
▲ **EMP:** 12 **EST:** 2013
SALES (est): 218.18K **Privately Held**
Web: www.bsghandcraft.com
SIC: 3585 Beer dispensing equipment

(G-16493)

CAMBRIDGE SIGNAL TECH INC
Also Called: Sigtech
60 Eddy St Ste 3 (02903-1733)
PHONE..............................401 490-5682
Burke W Mathes Junior, *Pr*
Ronald P Genereux, *VP*
EMP: 10 **EST:** 1990
SQ FT: 2,000
SALES (est): 577K **Privately Held**
SIC: 3651 8711 Audio electronic systems;
Acoustical engineering

(G-16494)

CAPCO PLASTICS INC (PA)
Also Called: C & S Packing Co.
297 Dexter St (02907-2730)
P.O. Box 9591 (02940-9591)
PHONE..............................401 272-3833
Richard Capuano, *Pr*
Bob Arno, *
EMP: 40 **EST:** 1978
SQ FT: 40,000
SALES (est): 9.99MM
SALES (corp-wide): 9.99MM **Privately
Held**
Web: www.capcoplastics.com
SIC: 3089 Blister or bubble formed
packaging, plastics

(G-16495)

CAPCO STEEL ERECTION COMPANY
Also Called: DMC Steel
33 Acorn St Unit 2 (02903-1094)
PHONE..............................401 383-9388
Michael Caparco Senior, *CEO*
Michael J Caparco Junior, *Pr*
John Casale, *VP Sls*
David Michaels, *Prin*
EMP: 18 **EST:** 2009
SQ FT: 5,000
SALES (est): 7.42MM **Privately Held**
Web: www.capcoerectors.com
SIC: 3499 3312 Picture frames, metal; Blast
furnaces and steel mills

(G-16496)

CAPCO STEEL LLC
25 Acorn St Ste 1 (02903-1087)
PHONE..............................401 861-1220
EMP: 100 **EST:** 2005
SALES (est): 8.99MM **Privately Held**
Web: www.capcosteelco.com
SIC: 1791 3441 1799 Structural steel
erection; Fabricated structural metal;
Ornamental metal work

(G-16497)

CARROLL COATINGS COMPANY INC (PA)
150 Ernest (02905-4604)
PHONE..............................401 450-5500
William Rooks, *Pr*
John Rooks, *VP*

EMP: 8 EST: 1982
SQ FT: 5,800
SALES (est): 1.06MM
SALES (corp-wide): 1.06MM **Privately Held**
Web: www.nano-fission.com
SIC: 2851   Coating, air curing

(G-16498)
CATHEDRAL ART METAL CO INC
Also Called: Camco Display & Screen Prtg
25 Manton Ave (02909-3349)
P.O. Box 6146 (02940-6146)
PHONE.............................401 273-7200
Leo Tracey, *Pr*
Julieanne Wade, *
◆ EMP: 45 EST: 1920
SQ FT: 93,300
SALES (est): 6.34MM **Privately Held**
Web: www.abbeyandcagift.com
SIC: 3499   Novelties and specialties, metal

(G-16499)
CJ INTERNATIONAL INC
Also Called: Jewels of Fashion
150 Niantic Ave (02907-3118)
PHONE.............................401 944-4700
▲ EMP: 50 EST: 1911
SALES (est): 744.89K **Privately Held**
SIC: 3911 3961   Jewelry, precious metal;
Costume jewelry, ex. precious metal and
semiprecious stones

(G-16500)
CJF GROUP LTD
Also Called: C J Fox Company
40 Brenton Ave (02906-2415)
PHONE.............................401 421-2000
E Jill Tobak, *Pr*
EMP: 95 EST: 1895
SALES (est): 5.65MM **Privately Held**
SIC: 2652 2679 2672 2621   Setup
paperboard boxes; Tags, paper (unprinted):
made from purchased paper; Labels
(unprinted), gummed: made from
purchased materials; Card paper

(G-16501)
COCA-COLA REFRESHMENTS USA INC
Also Called: Coca-Cola
95 Pleasant Valley Pkwy (02908-5603)
PHONE.............................401 331-1981
Tom Hunt, *Mgr*
EMP: 63
SQ FT: 20,000
SALES (corp-wide): 43B **Publicly Held**
Web: www.coca-cola.com
SIC: 2086 5149   Bottled and canned soft
drinks; Groceries and related products, nec
HQ: Coca-Cola Refreshments Usa, Inc.
    1 Coca Cola Plz Nw
    Atlanta GA 30313
    770 989-3000

(G-16502)
COFFEE EXCHANGE LTD
Also Called: Boston Coffee Exchange
207 Wickenden St (02903-4348)
PHONE.............................401 273-1198
Charles Fishbein, *Pr*
EMP: 18 EST: 1984
SALES (est): 730.73K **Privately Held**
Web: www.thecoffeeexchange.com
SIC: 5499 2095 5812   Coffee; Roasted
coffee; Cafe

(G-16503)
COMPOST PLANT L3C
Also Called: Remix Organics Company
190 Swan St (02905-4821)
PHONE.............................844 741-4653
Leo Pollock, *Managing Member*
EMP: 11 EST: 2013
SALES (est): 1.5MM **Privately Held**
Web: www.compostplant.com
SIC: 2873 4953   Plant foods, mixed: from
plants making nitrog. fertilizers; Recycling,
waste materials

(G-16504)
CONTECH MEDICAL INC
Also Called: Contech Medical
99 Hartford Ave (02909-3366)
PHONE.............................401 351-4890
R Jeffrey Bailly, *Pr*
EMP: 91 EST: 1987
SQ FT: 110,000
SALES (est): 14.14MM
SALES (corp-wide): 353.79MM **Publicly Held**
Web: www.contechmedical.com
SIC: 3841 7389 4783   Surgical and medical
instruments; Packaging and labeling
services; Packing goods for shipping
PA: Ufp Technologies, Inc.
    100 Hale St
    Newburyport MA 01950
    978 352-2200

(G-16505)
CONTEMPO CARD CO INC (PA)
Also Called: Markard Industries
69 Tingley St (02903-1085)
PHONE.............................401 272-4210
Vark Markarian, *Pr*
Lynne A Markarian, *
◆ EMP: 60 EST: 1978
SQ FT: 60,000
SALES (est): 12.08MM
SALES (corp-wide): 12.08MM **Privately Held**
Web: www.contempocard.com
SIC: 2653 2671 2631   Display items,
corrugated: made from purchased materials
; Paper; coated and laminated packaging;
Paperboard mills

(G-16506)
COSTA INC
A.T. Cross Company
295 Promenade St # 1 (02908-5720)
PHONE.............................401 333-1200
Gregory Rogers, *Mgr*
EMP: 25
SALES (corp-wide): 2.55MM **Privately Held**
Web: www.costadelmar.com
SIC: 5112 3951 3851   Stationery and office
supplies; Pens and mechanical pencils;
Glasses, sun or glare
HQ: Costa Inc.
    2361 Mason Ave Ste 100
    Daytona Beach FL 32117
    386 274-4000

(G-16507)
DECOR CRAFT INC
Also Called: DCI
24 Arnold St (02906-1002)
PHONE.............................401 621-2324
Roni Kabessa, *CEO*
▲ EMP: 34 EST: 1990
SALES (est): 4.75MM **Privately Held**
SIC: 3961   Costume jewelry, ex. precious
metal and semiprecious stones

(G-16508)
DIGITAL PRINTING CONCEPTS INC
225 Freeman Pkwy (02906-4649)
PHONE.............................401 751-4953
John P Cummings, *Pr*
EMP: 7 EST: 2003
SALES (est): 152.49K **Privately Held**
Web: www.dpcbarcode.com
SIC: 2752   Offset printing

(G-16509)
DMANELLY EX MULTISERVICES LLC
918 Atwells Ave (02909-3123)
PHONE.............................401 490-2900
Seraapio Inirio, *Admn*
EMP: 8 EST: 2004
SALES (est): 324.7K **Privately Held**
SIC: 2741   Miscellaneous publishing

(G-16510)
E H BENZ CO INC
Also Called: Benz, Edwin H Co
73 Maplehurst Ave (02908-5324)
PHONE.............................401 331-5650
Ted Benz, *Pr*
EMP: 8 EST: 1967
SQ FT: 9,800
SALES (est): 884.22K **Privately Held**
Web: www.benztesters.com
SIC: 3823 7699   Process control instruments
; Mechanical instrument repair

(G-16511)
ECC HOLDINGS INC (HQ)
35 Livingston St (02904-2726)
P.O. Box 6161 (02940-6161)
PHONE.............................401 331-9000
Barry Shepard, *Pr*
◆ EMP: 38 EST: 1928
SQ FT: 19,000
SALES (est): 22.78MM
SALES (corp-wide): 34.93MM **Privately Held**
SIC: 2816 2865   Inorganic pigments; Color
pigments, organic
PA: Organic Dyes And Pigments, Llc
    1 Crownmark Dr
    Lincoln RI 02865
    401 434-3300

(G-16512)
ECO GLOBAL MANUFACTURING LLC
292 Charles St (02904-2240)
PHONE.............................401 331-5129
EMP: 30 EST: 2016
SALES (est): 3.05MM **Privately Held**
Web: www.ecoglobalmfg.com
SIC: 3086 5199   Padding, foamed plastics;
Plastics foam

(G-16513)
ELECTROLIZING INC
20 Houghton St (02904-1014)
PHONE.............................401 861-5900
Greg Jiede, *Brnch Mgr*
EMP: 38
Web: www.electrolizing.com
SIC: 3471 5169   Electroplating of metals or
formed products; Chemicals and allied
products, nec
HQ: Electrolizing Inc
    114 Simonds Ave
    Dekalb IL

(G-16514)
ENDIPREV USA LLC
10 Dorrance St Ste 700 (02903-2014)
PHONE.............................401 519-3600
Andre Ribeiro, *CEO*
EMP: 70 EST: 2017
SALES (est): 4.09MM **Privately Held**
SIC: 3699   Electrical equipment and
supplies, nec

(G-16515)
EPIVAX INC
188 Valley St Ste 424 (02909-2468)
PHONE.............................401 272-2123
Anne De Groot, *CEO*
Anne S Degroot, *
William Martin, *
Daniel Adams, *
EMP: 30 EST: 1998
SALES (est): 8.34MM **Privately Held**
Web: www.epivax.com
SIC: 8322 2836 8731   Individual and family
services; Vaccines; Biological research

(G-16516)
ESPOSITO JEWELRY INC
225 Dupont Dr (02907-3138)
P.O. Box 72777 (02907-0777)
PHONE.............................401 943-1900
Joseph F Esposito, *Pr*
EMP: 10 EST: 1911
SQ FT: 80,000
SALES (est): 605.04K **Privately Held**
Web: www.esposito-jewelry.com
SIC: 3961 3911   Costume jewelry, ex.
precious metal and semiprecious stones;
Jewelry, precious metal

(G-16517)
FASHION ACCENTS LLC (PA)
Also Called: Museum Collection
100 Nashua St (02904-1816)
PHONE.............................401 331-6626
James Coogan, *Pr*
Robert Allen, *
Philip Shockman, *
▲ EMP: 26 EST: 1983
SALES (est): 4.95MM
SALES (corp-wide): 4.95MM **Privately Held**
Web: www.fashionaccents.com
SIC: 3911   Jewelry, precious metal

(G-16518)
FERGUSON PERFORATING COMPANY (DH)
130 Ernest St (02905-4602)
PHONE.............................401 941-8876
Charles Flack, *CEO*
▼ EMP: 100 EST: 1927
SQ FT: 68,000
SALES (est): 47.98MM
SALES (corp-wide): 17.02B **Publicly Held**
Web: www.fergusonperf.com
SIC: 3469 3496 3444   Stamping metal for
the trade; Hardware cloth, woven wire;
Sheet metalwork
HQ: Diamond Manufacturing Company
    243 W Eigth St
    Wyoming PA 18644
    570 693-0300

(G-16519)
FORTHILL RESOURCES LLC
100 Westminster St # 1500 (02903-2394)
PHONE.............................617 849-0768
Kabir Singh, *Managing Member*
EMP: 10 EST: 2019
SALES (est): 100K **Privately Held**

SIC: 1081   Metal mining services

(G-16520)
FOUNTAIN DISPENSERS CO INC
35 Greenwich St (02907-2534)
PHONE.....................401 461-8400
Francis Marceau, *Prin*
EMP: 7 EST: 2010
SALES (est): 106.6K **Privately Held**
SIC: 2087   Flavoring extracts and syrups, nec

(G-16521)
FRANK LOMBARDO AND SONS INC
78 Narragansett Ave (02907-3322)
PHONE.....................401 461-4547
Frank Lombardo, *Pr*
David Lombardo, *VP*
EMP: 10 EST: 1978
SQ FT: 8,800
SALES (est): 958.81K **Privately Held**
SIC: 1711 3444   Warm air heating and air conditioning contractor; Sheet metalwork

(G-16522)
FRESHCO
15 Clarkson St (02908-2609)
PHONE.....................401 351-1911
EMP: 9 EST: 2015
SALES (est): 448.61K **Privately Held**
Web: www.freshco.ca
SIC: 2752   Commercial printing, lithographic

(G-16523)
G-FORM LLC (HQ)
139 Point St (02903-4735)
PHONE.....................401 250-5555
Glenn Giovanucci, *CEO*
Gregory Scorpio,
▲ EMP: 25 EST: 2007
SALES (est): 20MM
SALES (corp-wide): 477.04MM **Privately Held**
Web: www.g-form.com
SIC: 5961 2329 5136   Fitness and sporting goods, mail order; Baseball uniforms: men's, youths', and boys'; Sportswear, men's and boys'
PA: Eldridge Industries, Llc
    600 Steamboat Rd Ste B
    Greenwich CT 06830
    203 298-5308

(G-16524)
GA REL MANUFACTURING COMPANY
564 Manton Ave (02909-5031)
PHONE.....................401 331-5455
Gregory Lang, *VP*
Karen Lang Fusaro, *Sec*
Alicia Lang, *Treas*
EMP: 10 EST: 1948
SQ FT: 20,000
SALES (est): 418.65K **Privately Held**
Web: www.ga-rel.com
SIC: 3479 3544 3999 3444   Etching and engraving; Die sets for metal stamping (presses); Identification badges and insignia ; Sheet metalwork

(G-16525)
GOODWIN-BRADLEY PATTERN CO INC
216 Oxford St (02905-2099)
PHONE.....................401 461-5220
Robert H Goodwin, *Pr*
EMP: 12 EST: 1912
SQ FT: 15,000

SALES (est): 1.79MM **Privately Held**
Web: www.goodwin-bradley.com
SIC: 3544 3543   Industrial molds; Foundry patternmaking

(G-16526)
GOTHAM GREENS PROVIDENCE LLC
Also Called: Gotham Greens
555 Harris Ave (02909-2424)
PHONE.....................401 816-0245
Eric Haley, *Managing Member*
Viraj Puri, *Managing Member*
EMP: 13 EST: 2017
SALES (est): 419.89K **Privately Held**
Web: www.gothamgreens.com
SIC: 2099   Salads, fresh or refrigerated

(G-16527)
GRACO AWARDS MANUFACTURING INC
177 Georgia Ave (02905-4422)
P.O. Box 27 (77377-0027)
PHONE.....................281 255-2161
Tommy G Tucker, *Pr*
EMP: 13 EST: 1981
SQ FT: 3,812
SALES (est): 511.4K **Privately Held**
Web: www.gracoind.com
SIC: 3999 2241   Military insignia; Ribbons, nec

(G-16528)
GRAPHTEC PRESS
40 Russo St (02904-1271)
PHONE.....................727 267-0940
Bob Bridge, *Prin*
EMP: 7 EST: 2017
SALES (est): 58.3K **Privately Held**
SIC: 2741   Miscellaneous publishing

(G-16529)
GRECO BROS INC
1 Greco Ln (02909-2622)
PHONE.....................401 421-9306
Ralph M Greco, *Pr*
David Greco, *VP*
EMP: 24 EST: 1945
SQ FT: 16,000
SALES (est): 498.76K **Privately Held**
Web: www.grecobrothers.com
SIC: 3559   Degreasing machines, automotive and industrial

(G-16530)
HASBRO INC
Also Called: Hasbro
1 Hasbro Pl (02903-1849)
PHONE.....................401 280-2127
EMP: 23
SALES (corp-wide): 5.86B **Publicly Held**
Web: hasbro.gcs-web.com
SIC: 3944   Craft and hobby kits and sets
PA: Hasbro, Inc.
    1027 Newport Ave
    Pawtucket RI 02861
    401 431-8697

(G-16531)
HEIDELBERG MATERIALS US INC
55 Fields Point Dr (02905-5601)
PHONE.....................800 833-4157
EMP: 13
SALES (corp-wide): 21.19B **Privately Held**
Web: www.heidelbergmaterials.us
SIC: 3273   Ready-mixed concrete
HQ: Heidelberg Materials Us, Inc.
    300 E John Carpenter Fwy

Irving TX 75062

(G-16532)
HOGAN & BOLAS
202 King Philip St (02909-5751)
PHONE.....................401 349-2988
Al Desantis, *Owner*
EMP: 7 EST: 2013
SALES (est): 65.07K **Privately Held**
Web: www.hoganandbolas.com
SIC: 3911   Jewelry, precious metal

(G-16533)
HOOK-FAST SPECIALTIES INC
Also Called: United States Badge Company
63 Seymour St (02905-4716)
PHONE.....................401 781-4466
Dan Garriaran, *CEO*
Steven Gorriaran, *Sec*
Daniel Gorriaran, *Pr*
Michael Gorriaran, *Treas*
EMP: 15 EST: 1926
SQ FT: 10,000
SALES (est): 454.2K **Privately Held**
Web: www.hookfast.com
SIC: 2399   Emblems, badges, and insignia: from purchased materials

(G-16534)
HUB-FEDERAL INC
Also Called: Hub & Federal Sign
135 Dean St (02903-1603)
P.O. Box 1 (02901-0001)
PHONE.....................401 421-3400
Frank R Benell Junior, *Pr*
William Benell, *Treas*
EMP: 8 EST: 1938
SQ FT: 10,000
SALES (est): 292.89K **Privately Held**
Web: www.federalsigns.net
SIC: 3993   Electric signs

(G-16535)
HUDSON TERMINAL CORP (PA)
Also Called: Hudson Liquid Asphalts
29 Terminal Rd (02905-5507)
PHONE.....................401 274-2200
Tom Hudson, *CEO*
Francis J Obrien, *Pr*
Edward R Lodge Junior, *Sr VP*
▲ EMP: 13 EST: 1962
SQ FT: 60,000
SALES (est): 2.31MM
SALES (corp-wide): 2.31MM **Privately Held**
Web: www.hudsoncompanies.com
SIC: 3531   Asphalt plant, including gravel-mix type

(G-16536)
HUNGRY GHOST PRESS LLC
60 Valley St Apt 2 (02909-7404)
PHONE.....................978 677-1000
EMP: 9 EST: 2018
SALES (est): 347.09K **Privately Held**
Web: www.hungryghostpress.com
SIC: 2741   Miscellaneous publishing

(G-16537)
IDEAL PLATING & POLSG CO INC
175 Public St (02903-4915)
PHONE.....................401 455-1700
Arnold De Senna, *Pr*
EMP: 16 EST: 1956
SQ FT: 4,500
SALES (est): 740.9K **Privately Held**
Web: www.idealplating.com

SIC: 3471   Electroplating of metals or formed products

(G-16538)
IGT GLOBAL SOLUTIONS CORPORATION (HQ)
Also Called: Igt
10 Memorial Blvd (02903-1160)
P.O. Box 5427 (07054-6427)
PHONE.....................401 392-7077
◆ EMP: 69 EST: 1980
SALES (est): 602.29MM
SALES (corp-wide): 4.22B **Privately Held**
Web: www.igt.com
SIC: 7999 3575 7372 7378   Lottery operation ; Computer terminals; Prepackaged software; Computer and data processing equipment repair/maintenance
PA: International Game Technology Plc
    3rd Floor
    London EC2A

(G-16539)
INDUSTRIOUS SPIRIT COMPANY LLC
1 Sims Ave Unit 103 (02909-1090)
PHONE.....................401 450-9229
Manya K Rubinstein, *Mgr*
EMP: 7 EST: 2018
SALES (est): 233.65K **Privately Held**
Web: www.iscospirits.com
SIC: 2085   Distilled and blended liquors

(G-16540)
INTERNATIONAL CHROMIUM PLTG CO
Also Called: Intrnatl Chromium Plating Co
2 Addison Pl (02909-2498)
PHONE.....................401 421-0205
Linda Fogarty, *Pr*
Joseph Fogarty, *Sec*
Tim Fogarty, *VP*
Jean Fogarty, *Prin*
EMP: 9 EST: 1927
SQ FT: 15,000
SALES (est): 900.25K **Privately Held**
Web: www.icp1927.com
SIC: 3471   Electroplating of metals or formed products

(G-16541)
INTERNATIONAL ETCHING INC
7 Ninigret Ave (02907-3023)
P.O. Box 73150 (02907-0548)
PHONE.....................401 781-6800
Jonathan Zucchi, *Pr*
EMP: 12 EST: 1982
SQ FT: 14,000
SALES (est): 1.92MM **Privately Held**
Web: www.internationaletching.com
SIC: 3479   Etching on metals

(G-16542)
INTERNATIONAL INSIGNIA CORP
1280 Eddy St (02905-4534)
PHONE.....................401 784-0000
Robert K Reaburn, *Pr*
EMP: 60 EST: 1954
SQ FT: 25,000
SALES (est): 4.66MM **Privately Held**
Web: www.internationalinsignia.com
SIC: 3999   Military insignia

(G-16543)
IRA GREEN INC (PA)
Also Called: Brigade Qm Prince George Co
177 Georgia Ave (02905-4422)
PHONE.....................800 663-7487
Michael Mc Allister, *Ch Bd*

▲ = Import ▼ = Export
◆ = Import/Export

Robert D Gilmartin, *
▲ **EMP:** 211 **EST:** 1945
SQ FT: 80,000
SALES (est): 41.61MM
SALES (corp-wide): 41.61MM **Privately Held**
Web: www.iragreen.com
SIC: 3469 3999 5199 2395 Stamping metal for the trade; Identification badges and insignia; General merchandise, non-durable ; Pleating and stitching

(G-16544)
ISLAND PUBLISHING COMPANY
Also Called: Body Mind & Spirit Magazine
255 Hope St (02906-2261)
P.O. Box 1477 (02901-1477)
PHONE.............................401 351-4320
James Valliere, *Pr*
Daniel Serpico, *Sec*
EMP: 12 **EST:** 1982
SQ FT: 4,800
SALES (est): 842.33K **Privately Held**
SIC: 2721 Magazines: publishing and printing

(G-16545)
J CAL INC
Also Called: House of Primavera
1 Baker St (02905-4416)
PHONE.............................401 941-7700
Trice Clancy, *Mgr*
EMP: 67
SALES (corp-wide): 15.23MM **Privately Held**
Web: www.danecraft.com
SIC: 3911 Jewelry, precious metal
PA: J Cal Inc
  1 Baker St
  Providence RI 02905
  401 941-7700

(G-16546)
J CAL INC (PA)
Also Called: Danecraft
1 Baker St (02905-4416)
PHONE.............................401 941-7700
Victor Primavera Iii, *CEO*
Victor Primavera Junior, *Ch Bd*
Robert Soltys, *
Gail Primavera Gesmondi, *
▲ **EMP:** 100 **EST:** 1934
SQ FT: 100,000
SALES (est): 15.23MM
SALES (corp-wide): 15.23MM **Privately Held**
Web: www.danecraft.com
SIC: 3911 5944 3961 Jewelry, precious metal; Jewelry stores; Costume jewelry

(G-16547)
J L ANTHONY & COMPANY
115 Baker St (02905-4502)
P.O. Box 2026 (02905-0026)
PHONE.............................401 467-9700
Mignon Kolb, *CEO*
Alex Kolb, *Pr*
▲ **EMP:** 9 **EST:** 1914
SQ FT: 10,000
SALES (est): 1.69MM **Privately Held**
Web: www.jlanthonyandcompany.com
SIC: 3356 3351 3353 Nonferrous rolling and drawing, nec; Copper rolling and drawing; Aluminum sheet, plate, and foil

(G-16548)
JCM DESIGN & DISPLAY INC
610 Manton Ave (02909-5633)
PHONE.............................401 781-0470
Joseph Martins, *Pr*

EMP: 41 **EST:** 1989
SQ FT: 54,000
SALES (est): 4.84MM **Privately Held**
Web: www.jcmdisplay.com
SIC: 2542 Fixtures: display, office, or store: except wood

(G-16549)
JEWEL CASE CORPORATION
Also Called: Jewel Case
110 Dupont Dr (02907-3181)
PHONE.............................401 943-1400
Therese Eisen, *Pr*
Elisabeth D Slocum, *
▲ **EMP:** 300 **EST:** 1950
SQ FT: 48,000
SALES (est): 22.43MM **Privately Held**
Web: www.jewelcase.com
SIC: 3499 3172 2631 2671 Boxes for packing and shipping, metal; Cases, jewelry ; Cardboard; Paper; coated and laminated packaging

(G-16550)
JOHNSON & WALES UNIVERSITY
Also Called: Male Clerk
333 Harborside Blvd (02905-5202)
PHONE.............................401 598-1824
Kent Reth, *Dir*
EMP: 33
SALES (corp-wide): 366.41MM **Privately Held**
Web: www.jwu.edu
SIC: 7331 2732 7389 Mailing service; Books, printing only; Printers' services: folding, collating, etc.
PA: Johnson & Wales University Inc
  8 Abbott Park Pl
  Providence RI 02903
  401 598-1000

(G-16551)
JUTRAS WOODWORKING CO
103 Dike St (02909-2826)
PHONE.............................401 949-8101
Paul Jutras, *Prin*
EMP: 9 **EST:** 2006
SALES (est): 277.93K **Privately Held**
Web: www.jutraswoodworking.com
SIC: 2431 Millwork

(G-16552)
LEES MANUFACTURING CO INC
160 Niantic Ave (02907-3118)
PHONE.............................401 275-2383
Charles P Morvillo, *Pr*
Todd R Morvillo, *
Vito P Torrisi, *
Sandy Norris, *
EMP: 50 **EST:** 1953
SQ FT: 15,000
SALES (est): 2.51MM **Privately Held**
Web: www.leesmfg.com
SIC: 3911 Jewelry, precious metal

(G-16553)
LMG RHODE ISLAND HOLDINGS INC (HQ)
119 Harris Ave (02902)
PHONE.............................585 598-0030
Garrett J Cummings Attorney, *Prin*
EMP: 17 **EST:** 2014
SALES (est): 93.24MM
SALES (corp-wide): 2.95B **Publicly Held**
SIC: 2711 Commercial printing and newspaper publishing combined
PA: Gannett Co., Inc.
  7950 Jones Branch Dr Fl 8
  Mc Lean VA 22102
  703 854-6000

(G-16554)
LORAC COMPANY INC
Also Called: Lorac Union Tool
97 Johnson St (02905-4518)
PHONE.............................401 781-3330
Richard Carroll, *Pr*
Steve Carroll, *
EMP: 25 **EST:** 1944
SQ FT: 51,000
SALES (est): 947.76K **Privately Held**
Web: www.loracunion.com
SIC: 3915 3469 Jewelers' findings and materials; Metal stampings, nec

(G-16555)
LOTUFF LEATHER
1 Sims Ave Unit 101 (02909-1090)
P.O. Box 28829 (02908-0829)
PHONE.............................888 763-2247
EMP: 9 **EST:** 2012
SALES (est): 210.12K **Privately Held**
Web: www.lotuffleather.com
SIC: 3111 Bag leather

(G-16556)
LUNA PHARMACEUTICALS INC
Also Called: Premama
244 Weybosset St Ste 3 (02903-3732)
PHONE.............................401 383-0299
Dan Aziz, *Pr*
EMP: 9 **EST:** 2014
SALES (est): 339.92K **Privately Held**
Web: www.premamawellness.com
SIC: 2834 Pharmaceutical preparations

(G-16557)
MANISSES CMMNCATIONS GROUP INC
17 University Ave (02906-4121)
PHONE.............................401 273-5221
Fraser Lang, *Pr*
EMP: 25 **EST:** 1984
SQ FT: 6,400
SALES (est): 2.8MM **Privately Held**
Web: www.manisses.com
SIC: 2721 2731 Periodicals, publishing only; Book publishing

(G-16558)
MARS 2000 INC
Also Called: Mars Plastics
45 Troy St (02909-2816)
PHONE.............................401 421-5275
Karl J Krikorian, *Pr*
Claudette Soucy, *
▲ **EMP:** 850 **EST:** 1972
SQ FT: 120,000
SALES (est): 47.62MM **Privately Held**
Web: www.marsplastics.com
SIC: 3089 Injection molding of plastics

(G-16559)
MASTRO LIGHTING MFG CO INC (PA)
555 Elmwood Ave (02907-1810)
PHONE.............................401 467-7700
Albert A Mastrostefano, *Pr*
Patricia Di Matteo, *VP*
Mary Mastrostefano, *Treas*
Donna Kane, *Sec*
Vincent A Mastrostefano, *OF AFFILIATE*
EMP: 8 **EST:** 1965
SQ FT: 10,000
SALES (est): 462.2K
SALES (corp-wide): 462.2K **Privately Held**
Web: www.mastroelectric.com
SIC: 3646 3645 Commercial lighting fixtures ; Residential lighting fixtures

(G-16560)
MATLET GROUP LLC
1 Park Row Ste 300 (02903-1246)
PHONE.............................401 834-3007
John Gaffney, *COO*
EMP: 7 **EST:** 2019
SALES (est): 310.85K **Privately Held**
SIC: 2752 Commercial printing, lithographic

(G-16561)
MCM TECHNOLOGIES INC
175 Dupont Dr (02907-3105)
PHONE.............................401 785-9204
Michael T D'angelo, *Pr*
Chris D'angelo, *VP*
▲ **EMP:** 80 **EST:** 1997
SQ FT: 12,000
SALES (est): 9.84MM **Privately Held**
Web: www.mcmtech.com
SIC: 3399 Metal powders, pastes, and flakes

(G-16562)
ME-92 OPERATIONS INC
10 Houghton St (02904-1014)
PHONE.............................401 831-9200
Kevin Burr, *Genl Mgr*
Nolan Hannan, *
Jacob Meier, *
EMP: 45 **EST:** 1995
SALES (est): 2.08MM **Privately Held**
Web: www.me-92operations.com
SIC: 3479 Coating of metals and formed products

(G-16563)
METALLURGICAL SOLUTIONS INC
85 Aldrich St (02905-1502)
PHONE.............................401 941-2100
John O'meara, *Pr*
Gregory Dexter, *VP*
EMP: 12 **EST:** 1988
SQ FT: 17,000
SALES (est): 2.06MM **Privately Held**
Web: www.met-sol.com
SIC: 3398 8711 Metal heat treating; Consulting engineer

(G-16564)
MH STALLMAN COMPANY INC (PA)
292 Charles St (02904-2240)
PHONE.............................401 331-5129
Milton Stallman, *Ch Bd*
James Stallman, *
▲ **EMP:** 40 **EST:** 1970
SQ FT: 4,000
SALES (est): 5.57MM
SALES (corp-wide): 5.57MM **Privately Held**
Web: www.mhsco.com
SIC: 3086 Padding, foamed plastics

(G-16565)
MILLS COFFEE ROASTING CO
1058 Broad St (02905-1600)
PHONE.............................401 781-7860
TOLL FREE: 888
David Mills, *Pr*
Susan Mills, *VP*
▲ **EMP:** 9 **EST:** 1860
SQ FT: 20,000
SALES (est): 488.24K **Privately Held**
Web: millscoffeeroasting.wordpress.com
SIC: 2095 5149 Coffee roasting (except by wholesale grocers); Coffee and tea

(G-16566)
MODERN INDUSTRIES INC
Also Called: Architectural Interiors Group
242 W Exchange St (02903-1091)
PHONE..........................401 331-8000
Edmund F Capozzi Senior, *Ch Bd*
Edmund F Capozzi Junior, *Pr*
Elizabeth Capozzi, *
EMP: 28 EST: 1932
SQ FT: 70,000
SALES (est): 948.37K **Privately Held**
Web: www.mdcdesignconstruct.com
SIC: 7389 2541 2521 2431 Interior designer
; Store fixtures, wood; Wood office furniture
; Millwork

(G-16567)
MONARCH INDUSTRIES INC
80 Faunce Dr (02906-4801)
P.O. Box 448 (02885-0448)
PHONE..........................401 247-5200
EMP: 100
Web: www.perfectdomain.com
SIC: 2541 2431 Store fixtures, wood;
Millwork

(G-16568)
MONARCH METAL FINISHING CO INC
189 Georgia Ave (02905-4516)
PHONE..........................401 785-3200
Marc E Marandola, *Pr*
Sharon Volpe, *
▲ EMP: 32 EST: 1971
SQ FT: 15,000
SALES (est): 2.41MM **Privately Held**
Web: www.monarchmetfin.com
SIC: 3471 Plating of metals or formed
products

(G-16569)
MOODY MACHINE PRODUCTS INC
141 Carolina Ave (02905-4418)
PHONE..........................401 941-5130
David A Franklin, *Pr*
Robert B Gates, *Sec*
Micheal J Franklin, *Treas*
EMP: 9 EST: 1958
SQ FT: 15,000
SALES (est): 679.32K **Privately Held**
Web: www.moodymachine.com
SIC: 3451 Screw machine products

(G-16570)
MTI FILM LLC (HQ)
Also Called: M T I
209 Angell St (02906-2121)
P.O. Box 2476 (02906-0476)
PHONE..........................401 831-1315
Larry Chernoff, *Managing Member*
EMP: 7 EST: 2000
SALES (est): 5.7MM **Privately Held**
Web: www.mtifilm.com
SIC: 7371 7819 7372 Computer software
development; Film processing, editing, and
titling: motion picture; Prepackaged software
PA: Mathematical Technologies, Llc
105 Medway St
Providence RI 02906

(G-16571)
NARRAGANSETT IMPROVEMENT CO (PA)
223 Allens Ave (02903-4937)
PHONE..........................401 331-0051
John E Everson, *Pr*
Jon Toegemann, *
Dustin J Everson, *

David Carr, *
EMP: 53 EST: 1893
SQ FT: 5,000
SALES (est): 11.81MM
SALES (corp-wide): 11.81MM **Privately Held**
Web: www.nicori.com
SIC: 6552 1611 1794 2951 Subdividers and
developers, nec; Highway and street
construction; Excavation work; Asphalt
paving mixtures and blocks

(G-16572)
NARRAGASETT JEWELRY INC
Also Called: C & J Jewelry
100 Dupont Dr Ste 1 (02907-3102)
PHONE..........................401 944-2200
Gary Jacobsen, *CEO*
Robert Sirhal, *
◆ EMP: 50 EST: 1993
SQ FT: 40,000
SALES (est): 9.82MM **Privately Held**
Web: www.candjjewelry.com
SIC: 3911 Collar/cuff buttons, precious/
semiprecious metal or stone

(G-16573)
NATIONAL GRID USA SVC CO INC
280 Melrose St (02907-2152)
PHONE..........................401 784-7224
Jose Rodrigues, *Pr*
EMP: 700
SALES (corp-wide): 26.03B **Privately Held**
Web: www.nationalgridus.com
SIC: 4911 1311 Distribution, electric power;
Crude petroleum production
HQ: National Grid Usa Service Company,
Inc.
170 Data Dr
Waltham MA 02451
800 260-0054

(G-16574)
NESTOR INC (PA)
42 Oriental St Fl 3 (02908-3238)
PHONE..........................401 274-5345
William B Danzell, *CEO*
Michael C James, *CEO*
Brian M Milette, *CAO*
EMP: 27 EST: 1975
SQ FT: 12,700
SALES (est): 6.65MM
SALES (corp-wide): 6.65MM **Privately Held**
Web: www.nestor.com
SIC: 3669 7373 Pedestrian traffic control
equipment; Turnkey vendors, computer
systems

(G-16575)
NICKEL CORPORAXION
836 Hope St (02906-3744)
PHONE..........................401 351-6555
Mohammed M Islam, *Pr*
EMP: 8 EST: 2010
SALES (est): 243.1K **Privately Held**
SIC: 3356 Nickel

(G-16576)
NU-LUSTRE FINISHING CORP
Also Called: Nu-Lustre
1 Magnolia St (02909-2945)
PHONE..........................401 521-7800
Robert Mansour, *Pr*
Patricia Moran, *
EMP: 21 EST: 1938
SQ FT: 12,500
SALES (est): 450.36K **Privately Held**

SIC: 3471 3841 Polishing, metals or formed
products; Knives, surgical

(G-16577)
OBERLIN LLC
Also Called: Oberlin
186 Union St (02903-3408)
PHONE..........................401 588-8755
EMP: 7 EST: 2015
SALES (est): 268.05K **Privately Held**
Web: www.oberlinrestaurant.com
SIC: 2752 Commercial printing, lithographic

(G-16578)
OCEAN BIOMEDICAL HOLDINGS INC
Also Called: Ocean
55 Claverick St Ste 325 (02903-4144)
PHONE..........................401 444-7375
Elizabeth Ng, *CEO*
Chirinjeev Kathuria, *Ex Ch Bd*
Gurinder Kalra, *CFO*
Jonathan Heller, *CSO*
Inderjote Kathuria, *Chief Strategy Officer*
EMP: 9 EST: 2019
Web: www.oceanbiomedical.com
SIC: 2834 Pharmaceutical preparations
PA: Ocean Biomedical, Inc.
55 Claverick St Ste 325
Providence RI 02903
401 444-7375

(G-16579)
OCEAN STATE BOOK BINDING INC
Also Called: Icopy
225 Dupont Dr (02907-3112)
PHONE..........................401 528-1172
Bruce Boyarsky, *Pr*
EMP: 10 EST: 2000
SQ FT: 2,000
SALES (est): 1.72MM **Privately Held**
Web: www.oceanstatebookbind.com
SIC: 2789 Binding only: books, pamphlets,
magazines, etc.

(G-16580)
OFFICERS EQUIPMENT COMPANY
177 Georgia Ave (02905-4422)
PHONE..........................703 221-1912
William Milona, *VP*
Margaret S Welch, *
▲ EMP: 13 EST: 1946
SQ FT: 3,000
SALES (est): 509.98K **Privately Held**
Web: www.iragreen.com
SIC: 3999 5137 Military insignia; Uniforms,
women's and children's

(G-16581)
OST SERVICES LLC
55 Chapman St (02905-5405)
PHONE..........................401 467-8661
EMP: 162 EST: 2014
SALES (est): 23.14MM
SALES (corp-wide): 144.19K **Privately Held**
Web: www.ostservices.com
SIC: 1389 Pipe testing, oil field service
HQ: Lisega Inc.
370 E Dumplin Valley Rd
Kodak TN 37764
865 940-5200

(G-16582)
PEAK PRINTING INC
Also Called: Minuteman Press
88 Orange St (02903-2856)

PHONE..........................401 351-0500
Karen Fraielli, *Pr*
EMP: 17 EST: 2002
SALES (est): 477.97K **Privately Held**
Web: providence.minutemanpress.com
SIC: 2752 Commercial printing, lithographic

(G-16583)
PETES TIRE BARNS INC
80 Public St (02903-4917)
PHONE..........................401 521-2240
EMP: 8
SALES (corp-wide): 87.54MM **Privately Held**
Web: www.petestire.com
SIC: 7534 5014 5531 Tire retreading and
repair shops; Tires and tubes; Auto and
home supply stores
PA: Pete's Tire Barns, Inc.
275 E Main St
Orange MA 01364
978 544-8811

(G-16584)
PLASTIC SERVICES ENTPS INC
Also Called: Genere Food
100 Niantic Ave Ste 104 (02907-3146)
PHONE..........................401 490-3811
Jose D Genere, *Pr*
Francis Genere, *Sec*
▲ EMP: 10 EST: 2006
SALES (est): 3.65MM **Privately Held**
Web: www.generefoods.com
SIC: 2631 Container, packaging, and
boxboard

(G-16585)
PORTION MEAT ASSOCIATES INC
356 Valley St (02908-5666)
PHONE..........................401 421-2438
Henry Lantagne, *VP*
Garry Marshall, *Treas*
EMP: 16 EST: 1964
SQ FT: 20,000
SALES (est): 2.23MM **Privately Held**
SIC: 2013 5141 Sausages and other
prepared meats; Groceries, general line

(G-16586)
PPOES INC
102 Waterman St (02906-1170)
PHONE..........................401 421-5160
EMP: 9 EST: 2018
SALES (est): 436K **Privately Held**
SIC: 2752 Offset printing

(G-16587)
PREMIUM POULTRY CO
850 Eddy St (02905-4810)
PHONE..........................401 467-3200
TOLL FREE: 800
Chad Verdi, *
EMP: 15 EST: 1996
SALES (est): 308.34K **Privately Held**
SIC: 2015 Poultry slaughtering and
processing

(G-16588)
PROMET MARINE SERVICE CORP
242 Allens Ave (02905-5002)
PHONE..........................401 467-3730
David Cohen, *Pr*
Joel Cohen, *
▲ EMP: 24 EST: 1974
SQ FT: 40,000
SALES (est): 411.19K **Privately Held**
Web: www.rifishermensalliance.com

SIC: 3731 Shipbuilding and repairing

(G-16589)
PROVIDENCE BUSINESS NEWS
400 Westminster St Ste 600 (02903-3222)
PHONE.................................401 273-2201
Roger Bergenheim, *Pr*
EMP: 30 EST: 1986
SALES (est): 4.72MM **Privately Held**
Web: www.pbn.com
SIC: 2711 Newspapers, publishing and
printing

(G-16590)
PROVIDENCE JOURNAL
COMPANY
75 Fountain St (02902-0004)
PHONE.................................401 277-7000
Howard G Sutton, *Pr*
Sandra J Radcliffe, *Executive Vice*
President Finance & Administration
▲ EMP: 445 EST: 1997
SQ FT: 100,000
SALES (est): 93.24MM
SALES (corp-wide): 2.95B **Publicly Held**
Web: www.providencejournal.com
SIC: 2711 Commercial printing and
newspaper publishing combined
HQ: Rhode Lmg Island Holdings Inc
119 Harris Ave
Providence RI 02902
585 598-0030

(G-16591)
PROVIDENCE LABEL & TAG CO
Also Called: Copy-All
315 Harris Ave (02909-1062)
PHONE.................................401 751-6677
Thomas H Moran, *Pr*
EMP: 12 EST: 1972
SQ FT: 22,000
SALES (est): 443.44K **Privately Held**
Web: www.providencelabel.com
SIC: 2754 2672 Invitations: gravure printing;
Labels (unprinted), gummed: made from
purchased materials

(G-16592)
PROVIDENCE MINT INC
1205 Westminster St (02909-1410)
PHONE.................................401 272-7760
Ronald J Medeiros, *Pr*
Anthony Dineo, *
EMP: 26 EST: 1974
SQ FT: 14,000
SALES (est): 568.99K **Privately Held**
Web: www.tpm-usa.net
SIC: 3469 Metal stampings, nec

(G-16593)
PROVIDENCE SPECIALTY PDTS
INC
Also Called: Narragansett Creamery
33 Dearborn St (02909-4101)
P.O. Box 3328 (02909-0328)
PHONE.................................401 272-4979
Ralph N Durante, *Pr*
Mark Federico, *VP*
▲ EMP: 56 EST: 2000
SQ FT: 35,000
SALES (est): 8.97MM **Privately Held**
Web: www.provsp.com
SIC: 2022 Natural cheese

(G-16594)
PROVIDENCE WIRE CREATIONS
INC
498 Kinsley Ave (02909-1020)
PHONE.................................401 490-3227

Doug Robertson, *CEO*
EMP: 11 EST: 1987
SALES (est): 125.18K **Privately Held**
Web: www.providencewire.com
SIC: 3549 Metalworking machinery, nec

(G-16595)
PYRAMID CASE CO INC
Also Called: Embassy Creations
122 Manton Ave (02909-3369)
PHONE.................................401 273-0643
Joseph Caruso, *Pr*
Richard Caruso, *
▲ EMP: 77 EST: 1989
SQ FT: 333,000
SALES (est): 9.23MM **Privately Held**
Web: shop.pyramidcaseco.com
SIC: 3827 Optical instruments and
apparatus

(G-16596)
QUALITY BEEF CO INC
Also Called: Quality Food Company
25 Bath St (02908-4896)
PHONE.................................401 421-5668
William P Catauro Junior, *Pr*
Vincent M Catauro Iii, *VP*
EMP: 40 EST: 1931
SQ FT: 15,000
SALES (est): 28.06MM **Privately Held**
Web: www.qualityfoodcompany.com
SIC: 5147 2013 Meats, fresh; Sausages
and other prepared meats

(G-16597)
QUALITY SPRAYING TECH INC
150 Park Ln (02907-3148)
PHONE.................................401 861-2413
Michael T D'angelo, *Pr*
Christopher D'angelo, *VP*
EMP: 90 EST: 1953
SALES (est): 4.51MM **Privately Held**
Web: www.qualityspray.com
SIC: 3479 Coating of metals and formed
products

(G-16598)
QUALITY STAMPING
1205 Westminster St (02909-1410)
PHONE.................................401 272-7760
Ronald J Medeiros, *Pr*
EMP: 9 EST: 2018
SALES (est): 206.55K **Privately Held**
Web: www.qst-corp.com
SIC: 3469 Stamping metal for the trade

(G-16599)
REED ALLISON GROUP INC
Also Called: P & B Manufacturing
144 Wayland Ave Ste 1 (02906-4370)
PHONE.................................617 846-1237
Barry Cohen, *Ch Bd*
Lawrence Cohen, *
Pauline Cohen, *
▲ EMP: 80 EST: 1955
SALES (est): 7.26MM **Privately Held**
SIC: 3961 3911 2542 3471 Earrings, except
precious metal; Earrings, precious metal;
Fixtures: display, office, or store: except
wood; Electroplating of metals or formed
products

(G-16600)
REGINE PRINTING CO INC
208 Laurel Hill Ave (02909-4517)
PHONE.................................401 943-3404
John V Regine, *Pr*
EMP: 8 EST: 1975
SQ FT: 6,000
SALES (est): 729.91K **Privately Held**

Web: regineprinting.advaria.net
SIC: 2752 2759 Offset printing; Letterpress
printing

(G-16601)
RGT INC
Also Called: Michele Robyn
1 W Exchange St Unit 2304 (02903-1079)
P.O. Box 4860 (02916-0860)
PHONE.................................401 431-5016
Gloria Duchin, *CEO*
Robyn Smalletz, *Pr*
David Duchin, *Vice Chairman*
Theodore Smalletz, *Treas*
Richard Zacks, *Sec*
▲ EMP: 70 EST: 1979
SALES (est): 4.51MM **Privately Held**
Web: www.gloriaduchin.com
SIC: 3999 3961 Christmas tree ornaments,
except electrical and glass; Costume
novelties

(G-16602)
RHODE ISLAND CHEMICAL
CORP
754 Branch Ave (02904-2246)
P.O. Box 9122 (02940-9122)
PHONE.................................401 274-3905
John Tapis, *Pr*
Irma Tapis, *VP*
EMP: 20 EST: 1975
SQ FT: 12,000
SALES (est): 453.23K **Privately Held**
Web: www.chemicalsri.com
SIC: 2841 Detergents, synthetic organic or
inorganic alkaline

(G-16603)
RHODE ISLAND MONTHLY
717 Allens Ave Ste 105 (02905-5442)
PHONE.................................401 649-4800
John J Palumbo, *Pr*
EMP: 28 EST: 1988
SQ FT: 8,000
SALES (est): 3.75MM **Privately Held**
Web: www.rimonthly.com
SIC: 2721 Magazines: publishing only, not
printed on site

(G-16604)
RHODE ISLAND PRECISION CO
25 Dorr St (02908-5310)
P.O. Box 19610 (02919-0610)
PHONE.................................401 421-6661
Keith Hartley, *Pr*
Deena Hartley, *VP*
EMP: 16 EST: 1973
SQ FT: 1,000
SALES (est): 410.15K **Privately Held**
Web: www.rhodeislandprecision.com
SIC: 3451 Screw machine products

(G-16605)
RICHMOND GRAPHIC
PRODUCTS INC
188 Progress Ave (02909-3848)
PHONE.................................401 233-2700
Hugh C Neville, *CEO*
Deloris A Griffee, *Treas*
Wendy Kraunelis, *Pr*
Douglas A Giron, *Sec*
Frank Ragazzo, *VP*
EMP: 19 EST: 1983
SQ FT: 25,000
SALES (est): 649.7K **Privately Held**
SIC: 3552 Silk screens for textile industry

(G-16606)
RJ MANSOUR INC
1 Magnolia St (02909-2945)
PHONE.................................401 521-7800
Robert Mansour, *Pr*
EMP: 13 EST: 1995
SQ FT: 6,500
SALES (est): 390.65K **Privately Held**
SIC: 3841 3999 Surgical and medical
instruments; Novelties, bric-a-brac, and
hobby kits

(G-16607)
ROLAND AND WHYTOCK
COMPANY INC
Also Called: Accu-Machining Corporation
75 Oxford St Ste 202 (02905-4722)
PHONE.................................401 781-1234
William J Roland, *Pr*
William J Roland, *Pr*
EMP: 20 EST: 1909
SQ FT: 12,500
SALES (est): 1.95MM **Privately Held**
Web: www.rolandwhytock.com
SIC: 2499 3915 Tool handles, wood;
Jewelers' materials and lapidary work

(G-16608)
RXVANTAGE INC
225 Dyer St (02903-3927)
PHONE.................................866 464-2157
Daniel Gilman, *CEO*
Gregory Gilman, *
EMP: 35 EST: 2007
SALES (est): 4MM **Privately Held**
Web: www.rxvantage.com
SIC: 7372 Educational computer software

(G-16609)
SALVADORE TOOL & FINDINGS
INC (PA)
Also Called: Fulford Findings
24 Althea St (02907-2802)
PHONE.................................401 331-6000
David Salvadore, *Pr*
Steven Salvadore, *
Amleto Salvadore, *
EMP: 18 EST: 1945
SQ FT: 55,000
SALES (est): 2.67MM
SALES (corp-wide): 2.67MM **Privately**
Held
Web: www.salvadoretool.com
SIC: 3915 3961 3469 Jewelers' findings and
materials; Costume jewelry; Metal
stampings, nec

(G-16610)
SANOIL LLC
Also Called: Colonial Oil
101 Corliss St (02904-2621)
PHONE.................................401 942-5000
Anthony Santoro Senior, *Managing Member*
EMP: 7 EST: 2011
SALES (est): 207.95K **Privately Held**
SIC: 1389 Pipe testing, oil field service

(G-16611)
SIMPLY SAFER PRODUCTS LLC
69 Tingley St (02903-1072)
PHONE.................................401 474-4957
Vark Markarian, *Managing Member*
EMP: 10 EST: 2020
SALES (est): 747.22K **Privately Held**
SIC: 5169 3842 Sanitation preparations;
Personal safety equipment

(G-16612)
SIR SPEEDY
Also Called: Sir Speedy
50 Nashua St (02904-1815)
PHONE...........................401 351-7400
EMP: 7 EST: 2019
SALES (est): 189.4K Privately Held
Web: www.sirspeedy.com
SIC: 2752 Commercial printing, lithographic

(G-16613)
SNOW & STARS CORPORATION
18 Delaine St (02909-2429)
PHONE...........................401 421-4134
Mickey Yasuda, Pr
Shigeki Nakagawa, VP
Nicky Yasuda, Pr
◆ EMP: 12 EST: 1972
SQ FT: 19,000
SALES (est): 957.9K Privately Held
Web: www.snowandstars.com
SIC: 5094 3961 Jewelers' findings;
    Costume jewelry
PA: Nakagawa Corporation
    1-22-16, Asakusabashi
    Taito-Ku TKY 111-0

(G-16614)
SPECTRUM COATINGS LABS INC
Also Called: C. S. Williams Lacquer Company
217 Chapman St (02905-4507)
PHONE...........................401 781-4847
Earl Faria, Pr
EMP: 12 EST: 1973
SQ FT: 7,000
SALES (est): 2.46MM Privately Held
Web: www.spectrumcoatings.us
SIC: 2851 Coating, air curing

(G-16615)
SPROUTEL INC
Also Called: Empath Labs
60 Valley St Apt 29 (02909-7405)
PHONE...........................914 806-6514
Aaron Horowitz, Pr
Aaron Horowitz, Pr
Hannah Chung, Chief Creative Officer
EMP: 7 EST: 2012
SQ FT: 1,100
SALES (est): 502K Privately Held
Web: www.sproutel.com
SIC: 3942 3944 8711 7371 Stuffed toys,
    including animals; Electronic toys; Electrical
    or electronic engineering; Computer
    software systems analysis and design,
    custom

(G-16616)
STEARNS TOOL COMPANY
56 Sprague St (02907-2503)
PHONE...........................401 351-4765
Robert J Stearns, Pr
Robert J Stearns Junior, VP
Scott R Stearns, Treas
Dorothy Stearns, Sec
EMP: 7 EST: 1973
SQ FT: 6,000
SALES (est): 995.05K Privately Held
Web: www.stearnstool.com
SIC: 3544 3554 Special dies and tools;
    Paper industries machinery

(G-16617)
T SARDELLI AND SONS INC
195 Dupont Dr (02907-3105)
PHONE...........................401 429-2144
Paul Sardelli, Prin
EMP: 7 EST: 2010
SALES (est): 136.01K Privately Held

SIC: 3911 Jewelry, precious metal

(G-16618)
TECHNODIC INC
245 Carolina Ave (02905-4505)
PHONE...........................401 467-6660
Stephen Masso, Pr
Steve Masso, VP
EMP: 23 EST: 1963
SQ FT: 6,000
SALES (est): 835.06K Privately Held
Web: www.technodic.com
SIC: 3479 Coating of metals and formed
    products

(G-16619)
TEESPRING INC
3 Davol Sq Ste B300 (02903-4770)
PHONE...........................855 833-7774
Christopher Daft, Prin
EMP: 31
SALES (corp-wide): 13.8MM Privately
Held
Web: www.teespring.com
SIC: 5699 2253 T-shirts, custom printed; T-
    shirts and tops, knit
HQ: Teespring, Inc.
    2430 3rd St
    San Francisco CA 94107
    855 833-7774

(G-16620)
TERCAT TOOL AND DIE CO II INC
31 Delaine St (02909-2430)
P.O. Box 3375 (02909-0375)
PHONE...........................401 421-3371
Joseph Terino Junior, Pr
EMP: 23 EST: 1946
SQ FT: 35,000
SALES (est): 1.48MM Privately Held
Web: www.tercat.com
SIC: 3469 3915 Stamping metal for the trade
    ; Jewelers' materials and lapidary work

(G-16621)
TEXTRON AVIATION RI INC
40 Westminster St (02903-2525)
PHONE...........................401 421-2800
EMP: 10 EST: 2019
SALES (est): 1.25MM
SALES (corp-wide): 12.87B Publicly Held
Web: www.textron.com
SIC: 3721 Aircraft
PA: Textron Inc.
    40 Westminster St
    Providence RI 02903
    401 421-2800

(G-16622)
TEXTRON FLUID AND POWER INC
40 Westminster St (02903-2525)
PHONE...........................401 588-3400
EMP: 13 EST: 2019
SALES (est): 2.5MM
SALES (corp-wide): 12.87B Publicly Held
Web: www.textron.com
SIC: 3721 Aircraft
PA: Textron Inc.
    40 Westminster St
    Providence RI 02903
    401 421-2800

(G-16623)
TEXTRON INC (PA)
Also Called: Textron
40 Westminster St (02903-2525)
PHONE...........................401 421-2800

Scott C Donnelly, Ch Bd
Frank T Connor, Ex VP
Julie G Duffy, Chief Human Resources
Officer
E Robert Lupone, CCO
◆ EMP: 1458 EST: 1923
SALES (est): 12.87B
SALES (corp-wide): 12.87B Publicly Held
Web: www.textron.com
SIC: 3721 3724 3728 3799 Aircraft; Aircraft
    engines and engine parts; Aircraft parts and
    equipment, nec; Recreational vehicles

(G-16624)
TEXTRON LYCOMING CORP (HQ)
40 Westminster St (02903-2525)
PHONE...........................401 421-2800
Mike Kraft, Genl Mgr
Gregg Shimp, *
Jay Mankad, *
Steve Logue, *
Dave Dawes, *
◆ EMP: 45 EST: 1929
SALES (est): 509.83MM
SALES (corp-wide): 12.87B Publicly Held
Web: www.textron.com
SIC: 3728 3724 Aircraft parts and
    equipment, nec; Aircraft engines and
    engine parts
PA: Textron Inc.
    40 Westminster St
    Providence RI 02903
    401 421-2800

(G-16625)
THE ELLIOTT SALES GROUP INC
Also Called: Elliott Group
111 Dupont Dr (02907-3105)
P.O. Box 6344 (02940-6344)
PHONE...........................401 944-0002
◆ EMP: 65
SIC: 2541 2542 3993 Display fixtures, wood
    ; Fixtures: display, office, or store: except
    wood; Signs and advertising specialties

(G-16626)
THERMOSWITCH INTERNATIONAL LTD
25 Reservoir Ave (02907-3348)
PHONE...........................401 467-5550
Louis Shatkin, Pr
▲ EMP: 16 EST: 1997
SQ FT: 55,000
SALES (est): 230.29K Privately Held
SIC: 3643 3822 Electric switches; Switches,
    thermostatic

(G-16627)
TIENDA Y PANADERIA EL QUICHE
1076 Chalkstone Ave (02908-4551)
PHONE...........................401 521-5154
Amidal Mata, Genl Mgr
EMP: 10 EST: 2007
SALES (est): 327.17K Privately Held
SIC: 5461 2051 Retail bakeries; Bakery:
    wholesale or wholesale/retail combined

(G-16628)
TME CO INC
315 Cole Ave (02906-4855)
PHONE...........................860 354-0686
Peter Orenski, Pr
Dan Gorriaran, *
EMP: 10 EST: 1988
SQ FT: 1,500
SALES (est): 351.38K Privately Held
Web: www.tmealf.com

SIC: 2399 3911 Emblems, badges, and
    insignia: from purchased materials; Jewelry,
    precious metal

(G-16629)
TOWER MANUFACTURING CORP
25 Reservoir Ave (02907-3387)
PHONE...........................401 467-7550
Louis Shatkin, Prin
David Shatkin, *
Kenneth L Laliberte, Prin
Victor Aromin, Prin
◆ EMP: 100 EST: 1946
SQ FT: 60,000
SALES (est): 21.86MM Privately Held
Web: www.towermfg.com
SIC: 3643 Electric switches

(G-16630)
TRIMED MEDIA GROUP INC
Also Called: Innovate Healthcare
235 Promenade St Rm 298 (02908-5761)
P.O. Box 245 (02806-0245)
PHONE...........................401 919-5165
Jack Spears, Pr
EMP: 17 EST: 2002
SALES (est): 2.41MM Privately Held
Web: www.innovatehealthcare.com
SIC: 2759 8742 Magazines: printing, nsk;
    Marketing consulting services

(G-16631)
TWO HANDS INC
7 Ninigret Ave (02907-3023)
P.O. Box 73150 (02907-0548)
PHONE...........................401 785-2727
Linda Brunini, Pr
Jonathan Zucchi, VP
EMP: 10 EST: 1992
SQ FT: 3,000
SALES (est): 493.46K Privately Held
Web: www.twohandsinc.com
SIC: 3911 Jewelry, precious metal

(G-16632)
UNITED STATES ASSOCIATES LLC
Also Called: Hamilton Tool
1205 Westminster St (02909-1410)
PHONE...........................401 272-7760
EMP: 10 EST: 2013
SALES (est): 297.31K Privately Held
Web: whitehouse.senate.gov
SIC: 3469 Metal stampings, nec

(G-16633)
UNIVAR SOLUTIONS USA INC
Also Called: Univar USA
175 Terminal Rd (02905-5500)
PHONE...........................518 762-3500
EMP: 24
SALES (corp-wide): 11.48B Privately Held
Web: www.univarsolutions.com
SIC: 5169 2899 Industrial chemicals;
    Chemical preparations, nec
HQ: Univar Solutions Usa Llc
    3075 Highland Pkwy # 200
    Downers Grove IL 60515
    331 777-6000

(G-16634)
UNIVERSAL PLATING CO INC
25 River Ave (02908-5427)
P.O. Box 28579 (02908-0579)
PHONE...........................401 861-3530
Edward A Johnson Senior, Pr
Edward A Johnson Junior, VP
EMP: 8 EST: 1950
SALES (est): 780.4K Privately Held

SIC: **3471** Electroplating of metals or formed products

(G-16635)
UNIVERSAL SPECIALTY AWARDS
1205 Westminster St (02909-1410)
PHONE......................401 272-7760
Paul Roderick, *Owner*
EMP: 8 EST: 2000
SALES (est): 170.38K **Privately Held**
SIC: **2399** Emblems, badges, and insignia

(G-16636)
VENDA RAVIOLI INC
Also Called: Costantino's Venda Ravioli
150 Royal Little Dr (02904-1860)
PHONE......................401 421-9105
Alan Costantino, *Pr*
EMP: 66
SALES (corp-wide): 9.89MM **Privately Held**
Web: www.vendaravioli.com
SIC: **2098** Macaroni products (e.g. alphabets, rings, and shells), dry
PA: Venda Ravioli Inc.
265 Atwells Ave Ste 1
Providence RI 02903
401 421-9105

(G-16637)
VENDA RAVIOLI INC (PA)
Also Called: Costantino's Venda Ravioli
265 Atwells Ave (02903-1584)
PHONE......................401 421-9105
Alan Costantino, *Pr*
▲ EMP: 41 EST: 1940
SALES (est): 9.89MM
SALES (corp-wide): 9.89MM **Privately Held**
Web: www.vendaravioli.com
SIC: **2099** Food preparations, nec

(G-16638)
VERICHEM LABORATORIES INC
90 Narragansett Ave (02907-3358)
PHONE......................401 461-0180
Anthony Di Monte, *Pr*
Steven Pichette, *VP*
Edna Poulin, *Stockholder*
EMP: 8 EST: 1988
SQ FT: 2,000
SALES (est): 1.49MM **Privately Held**
Web: www.verichemlabs.com
SIC: **8734 3829** Testing laboratories; Medical diagnostic systems, nuclear

(G-16639)
VERTEX PHARMACEUTICALS INC
Also Called: Vertex Cell Genetic Therapies
225a Carolina Ave (02905-4505)
PHONE......................857 529-6430
EMP: 14
Web: www.vrtx.com
SIC: **2834 8731** Pharmaceutical preparations; Biotechnical research, commercial
PA: Vertex Pharmaceuticals Incorporated
50 Northern Ave
Boston MA 02210

(G-16640)
VESUVIUS AMERICA INC (DH)
1 Cookson Pl (02903-3248)
◆ EMP: 30 EST: 1978
SALES (est): 623.06MM
SALES (corp-wide): 2.47B **Privately Held**

SIC: **3548 3699 3575 3679** Soldering equipment, except hand soldering irons; Electrical equipment and supplies, nec; Keyboards, computer, office machine; Electronic circuits
HQ: Vesuvius Holdings Limited
165 Fleet Street
London EC4A
207 822-0000

(G-16641)
VISITOR PRINTING COMPANY
Also Called: Providence Visitor
1 Cathedral Sq (02903-3601)
PHONE......................401 272-1010
Rick Snizek, *Prin*
EMP: 17 EST: 1875
SALES (est): 486.27K **Privately Held**
Web: ricatholic.sprintout.com
SIC: **2711** Newspapers

(G-16642)
WALCO ELECTRIC COMPANY
303 Allens Ave (02905-5006)
PHONE......................401 467-6500
Ellis Stoneman Waldman, *Pr*
Martin Tempkin, *
Marc Amato, *
▲ EMP: 100 EST: 1931
SQ FT: 50,000
SALES (est): 19.22MM **Privately Held**
Web: www.walcokip.com
SIC: **7629 3625 5063 5084** Electrical equipment repair services; Control equipment, electric; Electrical apparatus and equipment; Industrial machinery and equipment

(G-16643)
WARWICK POULTRY CO INC
46 Bath St (02908-4848)
PHONE......................401 421-8500
Barbara Rainone, *Pr*
Michael Rainone Senior, *VP*
EMP: 16 EST: 1957
SALES (est): 899.6K **Privately Held**
Web: www.warwickpoultry.com
SIC: **2015** Poultry slaughtering and processing

(G-16644)
WCM LLC
Also Called: Fit & Fresh
23 Acorn St (02903-1066)
PHONE......................401 273-0444
▲ EMP: 36
SIC: **5113 2656** Sanitary food containers; Sanitary food containers

(G-16645)
WELLINGTON MANUFACTURING INC
100 Aldrich St (02905-1504)
PHONE......................401 461-2248
Norman Pettigrew, *Pr*
EMP: 10 EST: 1974
SALES (est): 730K **Privately Held**
SIC: **3451** Screw machine products

(G-16646)
WESTWELL INDUSTRIES INC
Also Called: Surface Coatings Div
26 Plymouth St (02907-2918)
P.O. Box 27039 (02907-0595)
PHONE......................401 467-2992
John Ryan, *Pr*
William A Ryan Junior, *Sec*
EMP: 14 EST: 1975
SQ FT: 6,500
SALES (est): 1.45MM **Privately Held**

Web: www.surfacecoatingsllc.com
SIC: **3471** Electroplating of metals or formed products

(G-16647)
WHITEGATE INTERNATIONAL CORP
Also Called: Whitegate Features Syndicate
71 Faunce Dr (02906-4805)
PHONE......................401 274-2149
Ed Isaac, *Pr*
Steve Corey, *VP*
EMP: 8 EST: 1988
SALES (est): 507.29K **Privately Held**
Web: www.whitegatefeatures.com
SIC: **2711** Newspapers

(G-16648)
WOODWORKING THOMPSON & DESIGN
100 Dupont Dr Ste 2 (02907-3102)
PHONE......................401 369-7999
Ian Thompson, *Pr*
EMP: 8 EST: 2017
SALES (est): 284.87K **Privately Held**
SIC: **2431** Millwork

(G-16649)
WORLD TROPHIES COMPANY INC
Also Called: World Trophies
275 Silver Spring St (02904-2555)
PHONE......................401 272-5846
TOLL FREE: 866
Peter Evangelista, *Pr*
EMP: 18 EST: 1953
SQ FT: 3,000
SALES (est): 984.16K **Privately Held**
Web: www.worldtrophies.com
SIC: **3499** Trophies, metal, except silver

Prudence Island
Bristol County

(G-16650)
ISLAND MOORING SUPPLIES LLC
68 John Oldham Rd (02872-1221)
PHONE......................401 447-5387
EMP: 10 EST: 2006
SALES (est): 589.04K **Privately Held**
Web: www.homanbuoy.com
SIC: **3089** Buoys and floats, plastics

Richmond
Washington County

(G-16651)
RICHMOND SAND & STONE LLC
35 Stilson Rd (02898-1027)
PHONE......................401 539-7770
EMP: 13 EST: 2009
SALES (est): 2MM **Privately Held**
Web: www.richmondsandandstone.com
SIC: **1442** Construction sand and gravel

Riverside
Providence County

(G-16652)
BILL LZTTE ARCHTCTRAL GL ALUM
400 Wampanoag Trl (02915-2210)
PHONE......................401 383-9535

William Lizotte, *Pr*
Cathy Lizotte, *Sec*
EMP: 26 EST: 2003
SALES (est): 4.85MM **Privately Held**
Web: www.lizotteglassri.com
SIC: **3334 1793** Primary aluminum; Glass and glazing work

(G-16653)
CENTURY SHEET METAL INC
19 Maple Ave (02915-5405)
PHONE......................401 433-1380
Charles Patterson Iii, *Pr*
Pamel Paterson, *VP*
EMP: 7 EST: 1976
SQ FT: 3,200
SALES (est): 828.55K **Privately Held**
Web: www.centurysheetmetal.com
SIC: **3444 1711** Roof deck, sheet metal; Heating and air conditioning contractors

(G-16654)
FAIRHAVEN MARINE CORPORATION
Also Called: Bullock Cove Marine
254 Riverside Dr (02915-4837)
PHONE......................401 433-3010
James Ciolino, *Prin*
EMP: 10 EST: 2010
SALES (est): 265.97K **Privately Held**
Web: www.bullockcovemarine.com
SIC: **3732** Boatbuilding and repairing

(G-16655)
FULFORD MANUFACTURING COMPANY (PA)
65 Tripps Ln (02915-3013)
PHONE......................401 431-2000
Anthony Hart, *Pr*
David Bainer, *VP*
EMP: 16 EST: 1889
SQ FT: 25,000
SALES (est): 4.71MM
SALES (corp-wide): 4.71MM **Privately Held**
Web: www.fulfordmfg.com
SIC: **3429 3432 3469 3961** Hardware, nec; Plumbing fixture fittings and trim; Metal stampings, nec; Costume jewelry

(G-16656)
K&M/NORDIC CO INC
5 Tripps Ln (02915-3013)
PHONE......................401 431-9299
Mark Kindberg, *Pr*
▼ EMP: 32 EST: 1965
SQ FT: 32,000
SALES (est): 2.53MM **Privately Held**
Web: www.nordicpromos.com
SIC: **2759** Screen printing

(G-16657)
MATTHEW W ROBINSON
34 Lakeside St (02915-3100)
PHONE......................401 480-3975
Matthew W Robinson, *Prin*
Matthew W Robinson, *Owner*
EMP: 7 EST: 2011
SALES (est): 80K **Privately Held**
SIC: **7999 3949 5941** Scuba and skin diving instruction; Skin diving equipment, scuba type; Skin diving, scuba equipment and supplies

(G-16658)
MONO DIE CUTTING CO INC
7 Hemingway Dr (02915-2225)
PHONE......................401 434-1274
Alfred T Morris Junior, *Pr*

G E O G R A P H I C

EMP: 12 **EST:** 1943
SQ FT: 21,000
SALES (est): 467.28K **Privately Held**
Web: www.monodiecutting.com
SIC: 3544 2752 2675 Special dies and tools
; Commercial printing, lithographic; Die-cut
paper and board

(G-16659)
QUANTIFACTS INC
100 Amaral St Ste 2 (02915-2226)
PHONE..............................401 421-8300
Jack Nichols, *Pr*
EMP: 7 **EST:** 1980
SQ FT: 2,500
SALES (est): 1.15MM **Privately Held**
Web: www.quantifacts.com
SIC: 7372 5734 Business oriented computer
software; Computer and software stores

(G-16660)
TRANE US INC
Also Called: Trane
10 Hemingway Dr (02915-2224)
PHONE..............................617 908-6710
Nick Sluet, *Brnch Mgr*
EMP: 40
Web: www.trane.com
SIC: 3585 Refrigeration and heating
equipment
HQ: Trane U.S. Inc.
800 Beaty St Ste E
Davidson NC 28036
704 655-4000

Rumford
Providence County

(G-16661)
**AMARAL CUSTOM
FABRICATIONS INC**
310 Bourne Ave Ste 5 (02916-3368)
PHONE..............................401 396-5663
EMP: 9 **EST:** 2016
SALES (est): 768.13K **Privately Held**
Web: www.amaralcf.com
SIC: 3441 Fabricated structural metal

(G-16662)
**BEST ENGINEERED SURFC
TECH LLC**
10 New Rd (02916-2071)
PHONE..............................401 724-2230
William Faucett, *Pr*
EMP: 100
Web: www.1stchoicewindsor.com
SIC: 3479 Coating of metals and formed
products
PA: Best Engineered Surface
Technologies, Llc
1820 Avenue A
Kissimmee FL 34758

(G-16663)
BRANCH GRAPHICS INC
Also Called: American Printing
260 Narragansett Park Dr (02916-1049)
PHONE..............................401 861-1830
EMP: 21 **EST:** 1972
SALES (est): 835.7K **Privately Held**
Web: www.apnavitus.com
SIC: 2752 2791 2789 Commercial printing,
lithographic; Typesetting; Bookbinding and
related work

(G-16664)
CAPE COD ICE
1 Noyes Ave Bldg C (02916-3370)
PHONE..............................401 438-4555
David Fernandes, *Prin*
EMP: 42 **EST:** 2013
SALES (est): 3.43MM **Privately Held**
Web: www.capecodice.com
SIC: 2097 Manufactured ice

(G-16665)
COLONIAL MILLS INC
Also Called: Colonial Mills
77 Pawtucket Ave (02916-2422)
PHONE..............................401 724-6279
Don Scarlata, *Ch Bd*
Steve Broman, *
Gregg Scarlata, *
▼ **EMP:** 90 **EST:** 1978
SALES (est): 8.32MM **Privately Held**
Web: www.colonialmills.com
SIC: 2273 Rugs, hand and machine made

(G-16666)
EATON CORPORATION
Also Called: Centurian Mechanical Seals
10 New Rd (02916-2071)
PHONE..............................401 473-2214
Marvin Pelser, *Mgr*
EMP: 28
Web: www.dix-eaton.com
SIC: 5063 3492 Electrical apparatus and
equipment; Control valves, aircraft:
hydraulic and pneumatic
HQ: Eaton Corporation
1000 Eaton Blvd
Cleveland OH 44122
440 523-5000

(G-16667)
FULCRUM SPEEDWORKS LLC
310 Bourne Ave Ste 29 (02916-3381)
PHONE..............................401 524-3953
Dave Clark, *Managing Member*
EMP: 16 **EST:** 2018
SALES (est): 2MM **Privately Held**
Web: www.fulcrumspeedworks.com
SIC: 3732 Hydrofoil boats

(G-16668)
HOMESTEAD BAKING CO
Also Called: Mrs. Kavanaghs English Muffins
145 N Broadway (02916-2801)
PHONE..............................401 434-0551
Peter Vican, *Pr*
Bill Vican, *
William Vican Junior, *VP*
Theona Pascalides, *
Jimmy Amaral, *
EMP: 95 **EST:** 1920
SQ FT: 40,000
SALES (est): 9.75MM **Privately Held**
Web: www.homesteadbaking.com
SIC: 2051 Rolls, bread type: fresh or frozen

(G-16669)
IGUS BEARINGS INC (HQ)
Also Called: Igus, Inc.
257 Ferris Ave (02916-1033)
P.O. Box 14349 (02914-0349)
PHONE..............................800 521-2747
Frank Blase, *Pr*
Carsten Blase, *
Mohammad Salim Shafi, *
◆ **EMP:** 110 **EST:** 1985
SQ FT: 20,000
SALES (est): 96.37MM
SALES (corp-wide): 1.09B **Privately Held**
Web: www.igus.com

SIC: 5063 5085 3679 Wire and cable;
Bearings; Harness assemblies, for
electronic use: wire or cable
PA: Igus Gmbh
Spicher Str. 1a
Koln NW 51147
220396490

(G-16670)
**INTERPLEX ENGINEERED PDTS
INC**
231 Ferris Ave (02916-1033)
PHONE..............................401 434-6543
EMP: 65
SALES (corp-wide): 17.02MM **Privately
Held**
SIC: 3471 Plating and polishing
PA: Interplex Engineered Products, Inc.
54 Venus Way
Attleboro MA 02916
508 399-6810

(G-16671)
**INTERPLEX ENGINEERED PDTS
INC**
231 Ferris Ave (02916-1033)
PHONE..............................508 399-6810
Ronald Labow, *Ch*
Jack Seidler, *CEO*
Bob Hudson, *Pr*
Paul Dickson, *VP*
▲ **EMP:** 108 **EST:** 1992
SQ FT: 125,000
SALES (est): 10.79MM **Privately Held**
Web: www.interplex.com
SIC: 3471 Electroplating of metals or
formed products

(G-16672)
**INTERPLEX INDUSTRIES INC
(DH)**
231 Ferris Ave (02916-1033)
PHONE..............................401 434-6543
Jack Seidler, *CEO*
Belinda Lin Zijun, *CFO*
▲ **EMP:** 12 **EST:** 1981
SQ FT: 40,000
SALES (est): 69.64MM **Privately Held**
Web: www.interplex.com
SIC: 3471 3825 3674 3469 Electroplating of
metals or formed products; Instruments to
measure electricity; Semiconductor circuit
networks; Stamping metal for the trade
HQ: Ennovi Holdings Pte. Ltd.
298 Tiohg Bahru Raod
Singapore 16873

(G-16673)
JUDD PAPER COMPANY
55 Pawtucket Ave Ste H (02916-2429)
PHONE..............................413 534-5661
William C Jolicoeur, *Ch Bd*
Steven D Stanford, *Pr*
EMP: 15 **EST:** 1883
SQ FT: 28,000
SALES (est): 445.28K **Privately Held**
Web: www.signode.com
SIC: 5111 5113 2679 Printing paper;
Industrial and personal service paper;
Paper products, converted, nec

(G-16674)
**LEXINGTON LIGHTING GROUP
LLC**
Also Called: Prismatrix Lighting
181 Narragansett Park Dr (02916-1052)
PHONE..............................860 564-4512
Steven Kaufman, *CEO*
Mike Durkay, *CFO*

EMP: 30 **EST:** 2013
SALES (est): 4.9MM
SALES (corp-wide): 103MM **Privately
Held**
Web: www.vantageltg.com
SIC: 3646 3645 Commercial lighting fixtures
; Residential lighting fixtures
HQ: Fleco Industries, Llc
2055 Luna Rd Ste 142
Carrollton TX 75006
972 247-3171

(G-16675)
PACKAGING CONCEPTS LTD
Also Called: Concept Displays
275 Ferris Ave (02916-1033)
PHONE..............................401 334-0344
EMP: 225
Web: www.pclfixtures.com
SIC: 2542 3089 Cabinets: show, display, or
storage: except wood; Thermoformed
finished plastics products, nec

(G-16676)
**SIGNODE INDUSTRIAL GROUP
LLC**
Multi Wall Packaging
50 Taylor Dr (02916-1030)
PHONE..............................401 438-5203
EMP: 70
SALES (corp-wide): 12.94B **Publicly Held**
Web: www.signode.com
SIC: 2631 2655 2621 Packaging board;
Reels (fiber), textile: made from purchased
material; Packaging paper
HQ: Signode Industrial Group Llc
14025 Riveredge Dr # 500
Tampa FL

(G-16677)
**TEKA INTERCONNECTION
SYSTEMS INC**
231 Ferris Ave (02916-1033)
PHONE..............................401 785-4110
▲ **EMP:** 63 **EST:** 1975
SALES (est): 4.86MM **Privately Held**
SIC: 3678 Electronic connectors

(G-16678)
THE REAL REEL CORPORATION
Also Called: National Packing Supply
50 Taylor Dr (02916-1030)
P.O. Box 4798 (02916-0798)
PHONE..............................401 434-1070
EMP: 550
Web: www.signode.com
SIC: 2631 2655 2621 Packaging board;
Reels (fiber), textile: made from purchased
material; Packaging paper

(G-16679)
THOMSEN ENTERPRISES LLC
Also Called: Thomsen Restaurant Paper Sup
141 Narragansett Park Dr (02916-1052)
P.O. Box 16219 (02916-0695)
PHONE..............................401 431-2190
Edgar B Thomsen Junior, *Managing
Member*
EMP: 71 **EST:** 1951
SQ FT: 29,000
SALES (est): 12.26MM **Privately Held**
Web: www.thomsenfoodservice.com
SIC: 1541 2084 Food products
manufacturing or packing plant construction
; Wine coolers (beverages)

(G-16680)
WINKLER GROUP LTD (PA)
Also Called: Bernardo Manufacturing

▲ = Import ▼ = Export
◆ = Import/Export

54 Taylor Dr (02916-1030)
PHONE.................................401 272-2885
Traci Winkler Maceroni, *CEO*
Norma Winkler, *
Heidi Winkler Loomis, *
▲ EMP: 150 EST: 1963
SQ FT: 43,000
SALES (est): 10.38MM
SALES (corp-wide): 10.38MM **Privately Held**
Web: www.bernardmfg.com
SIC: 3961 Costume jewelry, ex. precious metal and semiprecious stones

(G-16681)
ZOLL MEDICAL CORPORATION
201 Narragansett Park Dr (02916-1043)
PHONE.................................401 729-1400
EMP: 53
Web: www.zoll.com
SIC: 3845 Defibrillator
HQ: Zoll Medical Corporation
269 Mill Rd
Chelmsford MA 01824
978 421-9655

Slatersville
Providence County

(G-16682)
LINDE GAS & EQUIPMENT INC
Also Called: Praxair
21 Steel St (02876)
P.O. Box 67 (02876-0067)
PHONE.................................401 767-3450
Gary Bassett, *Brnch Mgr*
EMP: 52
Web: www.lindeus.com
SIC: 2813 5084 5999 Carbon dioxide; Welding machinery and equipment; Welding supplies
HQ: Linde Gas & Equipment Inc.
10 Riverview Dr
Danbury CT 06810
844 445-4633

(G-16683)
SILGAN DSPNSING SYSTEMS SLTRSV (DH)
110 Graham Dr (02876-1024)
PHONE.................................401 767-2400
Chris Flater, *
EMP: 25 EST: 1957
SALES (est): 39.96MM **Publicly Held**
Web: www.silgandispensing.com
SIC: 3089 Caps, plastics
HQ: Silgan Holdings Llc
4 Landmark Sq Ste 400
Stamford CT 06901
203 975-7110

Smithfield
Providence County

(G-16684)
ACCESSORIES ASSOC INC
500 Washington Hwy (02917-1926)
PHONE.................................401 231-3800
EMP: 8 EST: 2001
SALES (est): 81.18K **Privately Held**
SIC: 3911 5999 Jewelry, precious metal; Sunglasses

(G-16685)
ACTION CONVEYOR TECH INC
Also Called: Conveyor Installation
90 Douglas Pike (02917-2374)

PHONE.................................401 722-2300
Antionio Cipolla, *CEO*
Antonio Cipolla, *Pr*
EMP: 11 EST: 1996
SALES (est): 926.66K **Privately Held**
SIC: 3535 Conveyors and conveying equipment

(G-16686)
ALCOR SCIENTIFIC LLC
20 Thurber Blvd (02917-1884)
PHONE.................................401 737-3774
▲ EMP: 61 EST: 2002
SALES (est): 9.92MM **Privately Held**
Web: www.alcorscientific.com
SIC: 3841 Medical instruments and equipment, blood and bone work

(G-16687)
AMPLEON USA INC
Also Called: Ampleon
310 Washington Hwy Ste 500 (02917)
PHONE.................................401 830-5420
Roger Williams, *CEO*
Frans Van Heesbeen, *VP*
Kevin Gao, *CFO*
Michael Richter, *Sr VP*
EMP: 20 EST: 2015
SQ FT: 20,000
SALES (est): 2.39MM **Privately Held**
SIC: 3674 Semiconductors and related devices

(G-16688)
AUTOMATED INDUSTRIAL MCH INC
Also Called: Aim Joraco
347 Farnum Pike (02917-1205)
PHONE.................................401 232-1710
Andrew Lewis, *Pr*
▼ EMP: 18 EST: 2004
SQ FT: 8,000
SALES (est): 2.01MM **Privately Held**
Web: www.joraco.com
SIC: 3599 Machine shop, jobbing and repair

(G-16689)
BLACKHAWK MACHINE PRODUCTS INC
Also Called: New England Tool Co.
6 Industrial Dr (02917-1502)
P.O. Box 17250 (02917-0723)
PHONE.................................401 232-7563
Joseph A Cilento, *Pr*
Dorothy Cilento, *Stockholder**
Eugene Cilento, *Stockholder**
EMP: 29 EST: 1976
SQ FT: 18,500
SALES (est): 1.87MM **Privately Held**
Web: www.blackhawk-machine.com
SIC: 3451 3663 Screw machine products; Radio and t.v. communications equipment

(G-16690)
BRANCH RIVER PLASTICS INC
15 Thurber Blvd (02917-1859)
PHONE.................................401 232-0270
Robert H Mayo, *Pr*
EMP: 40 EST: 1978
SQ FT: 50,000
SALES (est): 6.9MM **Privately Held**
Web: www.branchriver.com
SIC: 3086 2821 Packaging and shipping materials, foamed plastics; Polystyrene resins

(G-16691)
CHRISHA CREATIONS LTD
7 Industrial Dr S (02917-1530)

P.O. Box 71 (02828-0071)
▲ EMP: 10 EST: 1982
SALES (est): 931.16K **Privately Held**
Web: www.chrisha.com
SIC: 3942 Stuffed toys, including animals

(G-16692)
COOL AIR CREATIONS INC
10 Business Park Dr (02917-1954)
PHONE.................................401 830-5780
David Campbell, *Pr*
EMP: 20 EST: 2005
SALES (est): 3.07MM **Privately Held**
Web: www.morethantees.com
SIC: 2759 2395 Screen printing; Embroidery and art needlework

(G-16693)
D SIMPSON INC
Also Called: Ultra Precision Machining
13 Industrial Dr (02917-1516)
PHONE.................................401 232-3638
Donald Simpson, *Pr*
Linda Simpson, *VP*
EMP: 20 EST: 1978
SQ FT: 6,400
SALES (est): 353.1K **Privately Held**
Web: www.dsimpsoninc.com
SIC: 3599 Machine shop, jobbing and repair

(G-16694)
DAVES FRESH MRKTPLACE MGT INC
371 Putnam Pike Ste 590 (02917-2451)
PHONE.................................401 830-5650
EMP: 25
SALES (corp-wide): 45.77MM **Privately Held**
Web: www.davesmarketplace.com
SIC: 2449 Baskets: fruit and vegetable, round stave, till, etc.
PA: Dave's Fresh Marketplace Management, Inc.
1000 Division St Unit 20
East Greenwich RI 02818
401 885-1191

(G-16695)
DEJANA TRCK UTILITY EQP CO LLC
Also Called: Dejana Truck & Utility Eqp
9 Business Park Dr (02917-1955)
PHONE.................................401 231-9797
Andrew Dejana, *Brnch Mgr*
EMP: 62
SQ FT: 24,650
Web: www.dejana.com
SIC: 3711 5013 3713 Truck and tractor truck assembly; Motor vehicle supplies and new parts; Truck bodies and parts
HQ: Dejana Truck & Utility Equipment Company, Llc
500 Pulaski Rd
Kings Park NY 11754
631 544-9000

(G-16696)
DURASTONE FLEXICORE INC
550 Washington Hwy (02917-1926)
PHONE.................................401 231-4000
Nandy Sarda, *Pr*
Nandy Sarda, *Pr*
Anthony Sarda, *VP*
EMP: 20 EST: 1933
SQ FT: 20,000
SALES (est): 1.8MM **Privately Held**
SIC: 3272 3231 Concrete products, precast, nec; Reflector glass beads, for highway signs or reflectors

(G-16697)
DYCEM CORPORATION (DH)
33 Appian Way (02917-1777)
PHONE.................................401 738-4420
Stewart Cantley, *Pr*
▲ EMP: 20 EST: 2016
SALES (est): 5.52MM
SALES (corp-wide): 53.22MM **Privately Held**
Web: www.dycem.com
SIC: 2426 Flooring, hardwood
HQ: Dycem Limited
Ashley Trading Estate Ashley Parade
Bristol BS2 9

(G-16698)
FGX INTERNATIONAL HOLDINGS LTD (HQ)
500 Washington Hwy (02917-1926)
PHONE.................................401 231-3800
John H Flynn Junior, *Pr*
Anthony Di Paola, *Ex VP*
Steven Crellin, *VP Sls*
Jeffrey J Giguere, *Ex VP*
EMP: 385 EST: 2007
SQ FT: 187,000
SALES (est): 758.63MM
SALES (corp-wide): 2.55MM **Privately Held**
Web: www.fgxi.com
SIC: 3851 5099 Eyeglasses, lenses and frames; Sunglasses
PA: Essilorluxottica
147 Rue De Paris
Charenton Le Pont 94220
149774224

(G-16699)
FGX INTERNATIONAL INC (DH)
Also Called: Fgx International
500 Washington Hwy (02917-1926)
P.O. Box 17417 (02917-0724)
PHONE.................................401 231-3800
Alex Bernhardt, *CEO*
John H Flynn Junior, *Pr*
Steve Crellin, *
Jeffrey J Giguere, *
◆ EMP: 1122 EST: 2004
SQ FT: 193,300
SALES (est): 758.63MM
SALES (corp-wide): 2.55MM **Privately Held**
Web: www.fgxi.com
SIC: 5099 3851 Sunglasses; Eyeglasses, lenses and frames
HQ: Fgx International Holdings Limited
500 Washington Hwy
Smithfield RI 02917

(G-16700)
FIBERGLASS FABRICATORS INC
Also Called: F F I
964 Douglas Pike (02917-1875)
P.O. Box 17068 (02917-0702)
PHONE.................................401 231-3552
Anthony J Capo, *Pr*
EMP: 20 EST: 1978
SQ FT: 23,000
SALES (est): 4.65MM **Privately Held**
Web: www.fibfab.com
SIC: 3443 5999 Tanks, standard or custom fabricated: metal plate; Fiberglass materials, except insulation
PA: Opac, Inc.
964 Douglas Pike
Smithfield RI 02917

(G-16701)
FINE LINE GRAPHICS INC (PA)
Also Called: Fine Line

GEOGRAPHIC

90 Douglas Pike Unit 3 (02917-2374)
P.O. Box 17370 (02917-0724)
PHONE..............................401 349-3300
James Toles, *Pr*
Ronald Beauregard, *
EMP: 50 **EST:** 1991
SQ FT: 20,000
SALES (est): 15.19MM **Privately Held**
Web: www.flgcorp.com
SIC: 3555 7336 Printing plates; Graphic arts
  and related design

(G-16702)
GEORGIA STONE INDUSTRIES INC (HQ)
Also Called: New England Stone Industries
15 Branch Pike (02917-1223)
PHONE..............................401 232-2040
Antonio Ramos, *CEO*
Ann Marie Ramos, *CFO*
EMP: 12 **EST:** 1987
SQ FT: 5,000
SALES (est): 49.23MM
SALES (corp-wide): 49.23MM **Privately Held**
Web: www.granitesofamerica.co
SIC: 1411 Granite dimension stone
PA: New England Stone Industries, Inc.
  15 Branch Pike
  Smithfield RI 02917
  401 232-2040

(G-16703)
GETCHELL & SON INC
950 Douglas Pike (02917-1875)
P.O. Box 17028 (02917-0701)
PHONE..............................401 231-3850
Donald O Jones, *Pr*
EMP: 19 **EST:** 1872
SQ FT: 17,400
SALES (est): 2.33MM **Privately Held**
Web: www.getchell.com
SIC: 3441 Fabricated structural metal

(G-16704)
GLASS AMERICA WINDOW MFG INC
2 Esmond St (02917-3018)
PHONE..............................401 231-6000
Cody Gallagher, *Prin*
EMP: 14 **EST:** 2015
SALES (est): 501.82K **Privately Held**
SIC: 3211 Window glass, clear and colored

(G-16705)
GRANT FOSTER GROUP L P
500 Washington Hwy (02917-1926)
PHONE..............................401 231-4077
Brian Lagarto, *Prin*
▲ **EMP:** 15 **EST:** 1997
SALES (est): 443.96K **Privately Held**
SIC: 3911 5999 Jewelry, precious metal;
  Sunglasses

(G-16706)
GREENVILLE READY MIX
79 Cedar Swamp Rd (02917-2411)
PHONE..............................401 231-3900
EMP: 8 **EST:** 2019
SALES (est): 409.04K **Privately Held**
Web: www.greenvillereadymix.com
SIC: 3273 Ready-mixed concrete

(G-16707)
GROOV-PIN CORPORATION (PA)
331 Farnum Pike (02917-1205)
PHONE..............................770 251-5054
Scot A Jones, *Pr*
Jacqueline Beshar, *

EMP: 60 **EST:** 1926
SQ FT: 18,000
SALES (est): 17.71MM
SALES (corp-wide): 17.71MM **Privately Held**
Web: www.groov-pin.com
SIC: 3452 3429 3451 Bolts, nuts, rivets, and
  washers; Hardware, nec; Screw machine
  products

(G-16708)
HANNA INSTRUMENTS US INC
270 Washington Hwy (02917-1924)
PHONE..............................401 765-7500
Pamela Nardo, *Pr*
▲ **EMP:** 25 **EST:** 2005
SALES (est): 2.21MM **Privately Held**
SIC: 3825 Instruments to measure electricity
PA: Hanna Instruments, Inc.
  584 Park East Dr
  Woonsocket RI 02895

(G-16709)
HENRY GONSALVES CO
35 Thurber Blvd (02917-1838)
PHONE..............................401 231-6700
Henry Gonsalves, *Pr*
◆ **EMP:** 22 **EST:** 1944
SQ FT: 40,000
SALES (est): 9.66MM **Privately Held**
Web: www.gonsalvesfoods.com
SIC: 5149 2092 Groceries and related
  products, nec; Fresh or frozen packaged
  fish

(G-16710)
HIGH PURITY NEW ENGLAND INC (PA)
Also Called: High Purity New England
2 Thurber Blvd (02917-1858)
P.O. Box 6438 (02940-6438)
PHONE..............................401 349-4477
Mark Sitcoske, *Pr*
Patricia D Sitcoske, *VP*
Michael Quesenberry, *CSO*
EMP: 15 **EST:** 2008
SALES (est): 16.45MM
SALES (corp-wide): 16.45MM **Privately Held**
Web: www.hp-ne.com
SIC: 3559 Pharmaceutical machinery

(G-16711)
HIGH PURITY NEW ENGLAND INC
14 Thurber Blvd (02917-1858)
PHONE..............................401 349-4477
EMP: 94
SALES (corp-wide): 16.45MM **Privately Held**
Web: www.hp-ne.com
SIC: 3559 Pharmaceutical machinery
PA: High Purity New England Inc.
  2 Thurber Blvd
  Smithfield RI 02917
  401 349-4477

(G-16712)
HONEYWELL INTERNATIONAL INC
Also Called: Honeywell
10 Thurber Blvd (02917-1858)
PHONE..............................401 757-2560
Jeff Brown, *Sr VP*
EMP: 11
SALES (corp-wide): 35.47B **Publicly Held**
Web: www.honeywell.com
SIC: 3724 Aircraft engines and engine parts
PA: Honeywell International Inc.
  855 S Mint St

Charlotte NC 28202
704 627-6200

(G-16713)
HONEYWELL SAFETY PDTS USA INC
Also Called: North Safety Products
900 Douglas Pike (02917-1879)
PHONE..............................401 757-2249
Enzo Giuliano, *Brnch Mgr*
EMP: 54
SALES (corp-wide): 35.47B **Publicly Held**
Web: www.honeywell.com
SIC: 3842 Gloves, safety
HQ: Honeywell Safety Products Usa, Inc.
  300 S Tryon St Ste 500
  Charlotte NC 28202
  800 430-5490

(G-16714)
HONEYWELL SAFETY PDTS USA INC
Also Called: Bacou-Dalloz Eye & Face Protec
10 Thurber Blvd (02917-1858)
PHONE..............................401 757-2106
Michael Vittoria, *Brnch Mgr*
EMP: 40
SALES (corp-wide): 35.47B **Publicly Held**
Web: www.honeywell.com
SIC: 3851 3842 Protective eyeware;
  Surgical appliances and supplies
HQ: Honeywell Safety Products Usa, Inc.
  300 S Tryon St Ste 500
  Charlotte NC 28202
  800 430-5490

(G-16715)
IGS STORE FIXTURES INC
28 Cedar Swamp Rd Unit 2 (02917-2447)
PHONE..............................978 532-0010
◆ **EMP:** 180 **EST:** 1992
SALES (est): 9.59MM **Privately Held**
SIC: 2541 Wood partitions and fixtures

(G-16716)
INTEGRATED DEVICE TECHNOLOGY
37 Thurber Blvd Unit 103 (02917-1822)
PHONE..............................401 719-1686
Frank Matthew, *Dir*
EMP: 7 **EST:** 2013
SALES (est): 222.51K **Privately Held**
Web: www.renesas.com
SIC: 3674 Semiconductors and related
  devices

(G-16717)
ISLAND WOODS PERFORMANCE INC
Also Called: Music Stand The
1186 Douglas Pike (02917-1220)
PHONE..............................401 349-4644
Brian Farrar, *Owner*
EMP: 9 **EST:** 2008
SALES (est): 277.07K **Privately Held**
Web:
www.islandwoodssnowequipment.com
SIC: 3931 Musical instruments

(G-16718)
JFL ENTERPRISES INC
Also Called: Interntnal Hder Tol/ Crbide Pd
339 Farnum Pike (02917-1205)
PHONE..............................401 231-1020
John F Lombari, *Pr*
▲ **EMP:** 24 **EST:** 1959
SQ FT: 12,000
SALES (est): 1.8MM **Privately Held**
Web: www.archcuttingtools.com

SIC: 3541 Machine tools, metal cutting type

(G-16719)
JORACO INC
Also Called: Toggle-Aire
347 Furnam Pike (02917-1205)
PHONE..............................401 232-1710
John A Orabone, *Pr*
James D Orabone, *VP*
EMP: 20 **EST:** 1947
SQ FT: 6,200
SALES (est): 429.11K **Privately Held**
Web: www.joraco.com
SIC: 3542 3599 Presses: hydraulic and
  pneumatic, mechanical and manual;
  Machine and other job shop work

(G-16720)
K & C INDUSTRIES INC
2 Esmond St (02917-3018)
PHONE..............................508 520-4600
Jeffrey B Klaus, *Pr*
Daniel J Congdon, *VP*
EMP: 18 **EST:** 1994
SALES (est): 2.38MM **Privately Held**
SIC: 3089 Windows, plastics

(G-16721)
LASER FARE INC (PA)
1 Industrial Dr S (02917-1515)
PHONE..............................401 231-4400
Clifford Brockmyre Ii, *Ch Bd*
EMP: 40 **EST:** 1990
SQ FT: 17,000
SALES (est): 5.81MM **Privately Held**
Web: www.lfiinc.com
SIC: 3599 3542 3699 7692 Machine shop,
  jobbing and repair; Mechanical (pneumatic
  or hydraulic) metal forming machines;
  Laser systems and equipment; Welding
  repair

(G-16722)
LFI INC (PA)
1 Ind Dr S (02917-1515)
PHONE..............................401 231-4400
Clifford Brockmyre Iii, *Pr*
Roland Benjamin, *VP*
EMP: 38 **EST:** 2003
SALES (est): 10.11MM
SALES (corp-wide): 10.11MM **Privately Held**
Web: www.lfimedical.com
SIC: 3699 Laser welding, drilling, and
  cutting equipment

(G-16723)
MACHINEX COMPANY INC
350 Washington Hwy (02917-1921)
P.O. Box 345 (02828-0345)
PHONE..............................401 231-3230
Joan Gagnon, *Pr*
Mary Clark, *VP*
EMP: 7 **EST:** 1966
SQ FT: 1,000
SALES (est): 702.43K **Privately Held**
Web: www.machinex.com
SIC: 3599 3451 Machine shop, jobbing and
  repair; Screw machine products

(G-16724)
NORCROSS SAFETY PRODUCTS LLC
Also Called: Honeywell Safety Products
900 Douglas Pike (02917-1879)
PHONE..............................800 430-5490
▲ **EMP:** 2700

SIC: **3842** 3021 3469 Respiratory protection equipment, personal; Shoes, rubber or plastic molded to fabric; Helmets, steel

(G-16725)
ORION RET SVCS & FIXTURING INC
Also Called: Orion Red
270 Jenckes Hill Rd (02917-1953)
PHONE...............................401 334-5000
Kenneth S Musket, *Pr*
Tom Mackay, *
Rick Mcmillan, *Contrlr*
▲ **EMP:** 100 **EST:** 1989
SQ FT: 60,000
SALES (est): 21.85MM **Privately Held**
Web: www.orionred.com
SIC: **2431** 3993 2541 3646 Millwork; Displays and cutouts, window and lobby; Wood partitions and fixtures; Commercial lighting fixtures

(G-16726)
PRECISION TRNED CMPONENTS CORP
Also Called: Sylvestre Screw Machine Co.
331 Farnum Pike (02917-1205)
PHONE...............................401 232-3377
Scot Jones, *Pr*
EMP: 65 **EST:** 1946
SQ FT: 18,000
SALES (est): 11.46MM
SALES (corp-wide): 17.71MM **Privately Held**
Web: www.groov-pin.com
SIC: **3451** 3679 3678 3643 Screw machine products; Microwave components; Electronic connectors; Current-carrying wiring services
PA: Groov-Pin Corporation
331 Farnum Pike
Smithfield RI 02917
770 251-5054

(G-16727)
QUALITY SCREW MACHINE PDTS INC
9 Industrial Dr S (02917-1515)
PHONE...............................401 231-8900
Alan Sparadeo, *Pr*
Francis Sparadeo, *Stockholder*
EMP: 13 **EST:** 1956
SQ FT: 6,500
SALES (est): 241.9K **Privately Held**
SIC: **3451** Screw machine products

(G-16728)
R I FRUIT SYRUP CO
333 Waterman Ave (02917-2524)
PHONE...............................401 231-0040
Walter Vigneau, *Ofcr*
EMP: 8 **EST:** 2020
SALES (est): 262.54K **Privately Held**
Web: www.rifruitandsyrup.com
SIC: **2087** Flavoring extracts and syrups, nec

(G-16729)
RHODE ISLAND FRT SYRUP CO INC
Also Called: Rhode Island Fruit & Syrup
250 Putnam Pike (02917-2702)
P.O. Box 17138 (02917-0722)
PHONE...............................401 231-0040
Christopher Stone, *Pr*
Walter Vigneau, *Sec*
EMP: 23 **EST:** 1948
SQ FT: 5,000
SALES (est): 442K **Privately Held**

Web: www.rifruitandsyrup.com
SIC: **2087** Syrups, flavoring (except drink)

(G-16730)
SPERIAN EYE & FACE PROTECTION INC
10 Thurber Blvd (02917-1858)
PHONE...............................401 232-1200
▲ **EMP:** 145
SIC: **3851** Eyeglasses, lenses and frames

(G-16731)
SPERIAN PROTECTION USA INC (DH)
Also Called: Honeywell Safety Products
900 Douglas Pike (02917-1879)
PHONE...............................401 232-1200
◆ **EMP:** 20 **EST:** 2001
SALES (est): 467.54MM
SALES (corp-wide): 35.47B **Publicly Held**
Web: www.sperianfire.com
SIC: **3851** 3842 2311 7218 Protective eyeware; Ear plugs; Firemen's uniforms: made from purchased materials; Safety glove supply
HQ: Honeywell Safety Products Usa, Inc.
2711 Centerville Rd
Wilmington DE 19808
302 636-5401

(G-16732)
THURSTON MANUFACTURING COMPANY
14 Thurber Blvd (02917-1858)
P.O. Box 17338 (02917-0704)
PHONE...............................401 232-9100
EMP: 45
SIC: **3425** 3545 Saw blades and handsaws; Cutting tools for machine tools

(G-16733)
UVEX SAFETY MANUFACTURING LTD
10 Thurber Blvd (02917-1858)
PHONE...............................401 232-1200
Herve Meillat, *Pr*
EMP: 13 **EST:** 2001
SALES (est): 4MM
SALES (corp-wide): 35.47B **Publicly Held**
SIC: **3851** Protective eyeware
HQ: Honeywell Safety Products Usa, Inc.
300 S Tryon St Ste 500
Charlotte NC 28202
800 430-5490

Tiverton
Newport County

(G-16734)
AGK SOFT
1420 Main Rd (02878-4456)
PHONE...............................401 466-4213
Antoine Karam, *Pr*
EMP: 7 **EST:** 2017
SALES (est): 94.19K **Privately Held**
Web: www.agksoft.com
SIC: **7372** Prepackaged software

(G-16735)
CAPEWAY YARNS INC
209 Horizon Dr (02878-1370)
P.O. Box 432 (02871-0432)
PHONE...............................401 624-1311
Tom Tracy, *Pr*
Alice Nasise, *VP*
EMP: 8 **EST:** 1976
SQ FT: 15,000

SALES (est): 440K **Privately Held**
SIC: **2269** Dyeing: raw stock, yarn, and narrow fabrics

(G-16736)
GIVENS MARINE SURVIVAL SVC CO
550 Main Rd (02878-1350)
PHONE...............................617 441-5400
◆ **EMP:** 10 **EST:** 1995
SALES (est): 1.32MM **Privately Held**
Web: www.givensliferafts.com
SIC: **3069** Life rafts, rubber

(G-16737)
METALWORKS CORPORATION
Also Called: Metal Works
3940 Main Rd (02878-4898)
PHONE...............................401 624-4400
Gary Neville, *Pr*
EMP: 10 **EST:** 1961
SQ FT: 4,500
SALES (est): 423.37K **Privately Held**
Web: www.themetalworkscorp.com
SIC: **1711** 3444 Warm air heating and air conditioning contractor; Sheet metalwork

(G-16738)
STEPHEN PLAUD INC
381 State Ave (02878-1064)
PHONE...............................401 625-5909
Stephen Plaud, *Pr*
Jeffrey Jenkins, *VP*
Susan Plaud, *Sec*
▲ **EMP:** 15 **EST:** 1986
SQ FT: 8,400
SALES (est): 440.41K **Privately Held**
Web: www.stephenplaud.com
SIC: **2511** Wood household furniture

(G-16739)
SUBSURFACE DRLG REMEDIATION CO
5 Mill St (02878-1157)
P.O. Box 3729 (02910-0729)
PHONE...............................401 275-2088
Phil Goldwait, *Pr*
Philip Thornsberry Junior, *VP*
Kimberly Goldthwait, *Mgr*
EMP: 7 **EST:** 1998
SALES (est): 1000K **Privately Held**
SIC: **1381** Service well drilling

Wakefield
Washington County

(G-16740)
DIAGEO LOYAL SPIRITS CORP
Also Called: Loyal Nine
1425 Kingstown Rd (02879-8313)
PHONE...............................401 284-4006
Mike Reppucti, *Pr*
EMP: 8 **EST:** 2010
SALES (est): 991.97K **Privately Held**
Web: www.drinksol.com
SIC: **2085** Distilled and blended liquors

(G-16741)
GEORGE SHERMAN SAND GRAV INC
881 Curtis Corner Rd (02879-1467)
PHONE...............................401 789-6304
Deborah Sherman, *Pr*
Nancy Sherman, *Sec*
Stephen Sherman, *VP*
EMP: 20 **EST:** 1959
SALES (est): 939.04K **Privately Held**

Web: www.shermansandandgravel.com
SIC: **1794** 1442 1623 1799 Excavation and grading, building construction; Construction sand and gravel; Water, sewer, and utility lines; Building site preparation

(G-16742)
M & T MANUFACTURING
30 Hopkins Ln (02879-2163)
PHONE...............................401 789-0472
Burt Strom, *Owner*
EMP: 8 **EST:** 1975
SALES (est): 178.63K **Privately Held**
Web: www.convertibletopguys.com
SIC: **3714** Motor vehicle parts and accessories

(G-16743)
SOUTH COUNTY NEWSPAPER INC
Also Called: South County Independent, The
10 High St Unit H (02879-3144)
PHONE...............................401 789-6000
Albert Sherman, *Pr*
EMP: 10 **EST:** 1995
SALES (est): 228.1K **Privately Held**
SIC: **2711** Newspapers, publishing and printing

(G-16744)
SOUTHERN RI NEWSPAPERS (HQ)
Also Called: Standard Times
187 Main St (02879-3504)
P.O. Box 232 (02880-0232)
PHONE...............................401 789-9744
Lory Hickey, *Contrlr*
Lori Hickey, *
EMP: 30 **EST:** 1946
SQ FT: 8,000
SALES (est): 8.58MM
SALES (corp-wide): 293.08MM **Privately Held**
Web: www.ricentral.com
SIC: **2711** 2791 Newspapers: publishing only, not printed on site; Typesetting
PA: Journal Register Company
5 Hanover Sq Fl 25
New York NY 10004
212 257-7212

(G-16745)
SWEENORS CHOCOLATES INC (PA)
21 Charles St (02879-3621)
PHONE...............................401 783-4433
Brian Sweenor, *Pr*
Lisa Dunham, *VP*
EMP: 20 **EST:** 1935
SQ FT: 1,600
SALES (est): 50.27K
SALES (corp-wide): 50.27K **Privately Held**
Web: www.sweenorschocolates.com
SIC: **2064** 5441 Candy and other confectionery products; Candy

(G-16746)
TASE-RITE CO INC
1211 Kingstown Rd (02879-2441)
PHONE...............................401 783-7300
Wesley C Lessard, *Pr*
Patricia Lessard, *Sec*
Gary Lessard, *VP*
Beth Lessard, *Treas*
EMP: 10 **EST:** 1952
SQ FT: 4,000
SALES (est): 1.65MM **Privately Held**

SIC: 5147 5421 5146 2013 Meats, fresh;
   Meat markets, including freezer provisioners
   ; Seafoods; Sausages and other prepared
   meats

(G-16747)
YANKEE PRIDE FISHERIES INC
81 Point Ave (02879-6015)
PHONE.............................401 783-9647
Christopher Roebuck, *Pr*
EMP: 12 EST: 2005
SALES (est): 620.85K **Privately Held**
SIC: 2092 Fresh or frozen packaged fish

Warren
Bristol County

(G-16748)
AMERICAN ECOTECH LLC
426 Metacom Ave (02885-2711)
PHONE.............................877 247-0403
Laura Brown, *Prin*
EMP: 16 EST: 2020
SALES (est): 750.95K **Privately Held**
Web: www.americanecotech.com
SIC: 3829 Measuring and controlling
   devices, nec

(G-16749)
AMT ACQUISITION INC
Also Called: Applied Machine Technology
5 Greenlawn Ave (02885-2810)
PHONE.............................401 247-1680
Rena Reno, *CEO*
EMP: 28 EST: 1984
SQ FT: 3,200
SALES (est): 963.42K **Privately Held**
Web: www.amtus.cc
SIC: 3469 Machine parts, stamped or
   pressed metal

(G-16750)
ANCHORAGE INC
Also Called: Anchorage Inc-Dyer Boats
57 Miller St (02885-3118)
P.O. Box 403 (02885-0403)
PHONE.............................401 245-3300
Theodore F Jones, *Pr*
Anna V Jones, *Sec*
▼ EMP: 10 EST: 1930
SQ FT: 12,000
SALES (est): 971.69K **Privately Held**
Web: www.dyerboats.com
SIC: 3732 Boats, fiberglass: building and
   repairing

(G-16751)
ASPECTS INC
Also Called: Aspects
245 Child St (02885-2748)
P.O. Box 408 (02885-0408)
PHONE.............................401 247-1854
Barry D Colvin, *Pr*
Trisha A Torres, *VP*
◆ EMP: 20 EST: 1979
SQ FT: 14,320
SALES (est): 1.86MM **Privately Held**
Web: www.hummzinger.com
SIC: 3089 2449 3499 3829 Plastics
   containers, except foam; Containers,
   plywood and veneer wood; Novelties and
   specialties, metal; Measuring and
   controlling devices, nec

(G-16752)
AVTECH SOFTWARE INC (PA)
16 Cutler St (02885-2770)
PHONE.............................401 628-1600

Michael Sigourney, *Pr*
EMP: 17 EST: 2008
SALES (est): 5.71MM **Privately Held**
Web: www.avtech.com
SIC: 3822 7371 7372 Building services
   monitoring controls, automatic; Computer
   software development; Prepackaged
   software

(G-16753)
BARRINGTON MANUFACTURING INC
Also Called: Bmi
8 Rockland Rd (02885-1442)
PHONE.............................401 245-1737
Thomas Louttit, *Pr*
EMP: 9 EST: 1992
SQ FT: 4,000
SALES (est): 218.62K **Privately Held**
Web: www.bmiri.com
SIC: 3961 Costume novelties

(G-16754)
BLOUNT BOATS INC
461 Water St (02885-3929)
PHONE.............................401 245-8300
Marcia Blount, *Pr*
Julie Blount, *
Nancy Blount, *
▲ EMP: 60 EST: 2003
SQ FT: 500,000
SALES (est): 9.54MM **Privately Held**
Web: www.bloutboats.com
SIC: 3732 3731 3441 Boats, fiberglass:
   building and repairing; Shipbuilding and
   repairing; Fabricated structural metal

(G-16755)
BRISTAL CUSHION & ACC LLC
6 Commercial Way (02885-1637)
PHONE.............................401 247-4499
EMP: 7 EST: 2001
SALES (est): 84.53K **Privately Held**
Web: www.bristolcushion.com
SIC: 2392 Boat cushions

(G-16756)
BROWNLIE LAMAR DESIGN GROUP
Also Called: Altamira Lighting
79 Joyce St (02885-3209)
PHONE.............................401 714-9371
Michael Lamar, *Pr*
Gibb Brownlie, *VP*
EMP: 8 EST: 1986
SQ FT: 7,500
SALES (est): 939.51K **Privately Held**
SIC: 3641 3645 Electric lamps; Residential
   lighting fixtures

(G-16757)
DASKO IDENTIFICATION PRODUCTS
Also Called: Dasko Label
1 New Industrial Way Ste 2 (02885-1642)
P.O. Box 546 (02771-0546)
PHONE.............................401 435-6500
Paul Movsesian, *Owner*
EMP: 19 EST: 2000
SALES (est): 1.39MM **Privately Held**
Web: www.daskolabel.com
SIC: 3555 3993 2679 Printing trade parts
   and attachments; Signs and advertising
   specialties; Tags and labels, paper

(G-16758)
HOPE & MAIN
691 Main St (02885-4318)
PHONE.............................401 245-7400

Lisa Raiola, *Pr*
Luca Carnevale, *Ex Dir*
EMP: 8 EST: 2011
SQ FT: 18,000
SALES (est): 1.21MM **Privately Held**
Web: www.makefoodyourbusiness.org
SIC: 3263 8748 Commercial tableware or
   kitchen articles, fine earthenware; Business
   consulting, nec

(G-16759)
JADE ENGINEERED PLASTICS INC
Also Called: Jade
15 New Industrial Way (02885-1621)
PHONE.............................401 253-4440
Steven M Holland, *Pr*
Lee Holland, *
Mark Holland, *
Glen Holland, *Stockholder**
▲ EMP: 78 EST: 1976
SALES (est): 12.05MM **Privately Held**
Web: www.jadeplastics.com
SIC: 3053 3089 Gaskets; packing and
   sealing devices; Molding primary plastics

(G-16760)
MAGNETIC SEAL LLC
365 Market St (02885-2636)
P.O. Box 445 (02885-0445)
PHONE.............................401 247-2800
Robert Garde Junior, *Pr*
Bruce S Place, *
Lyman Colby, *
Thomas Colby, *
EMP: 70 EST: 1954
SQ FT: 20,000
SALES (est): 11.05MM
SALES (corp-wide): 712.54MM **Publicly Held**
Web: www.magseal.com
SIC: 3728 3053 Aircraft parts and
   equipment, nec; Gaskets; packing and
   sealing devices
HQ: Ducommun Labarge Technologies, Inc.
   23301 Wilmington Ave
   Carson CA 90745
   310 513-7200

(G-16761)
O&G STUDIO LLC
Also Called: Warren Chair Works
30 Cutler St (02885-2750)
PHONE.............................520 247-1820
Jonathan Glatt, *Managing Member*
EMP: 25 EST: 2010
SALES (est): 3.43MM **Privately Held**
Web: www.oandgstudio.com
SIC: 2511 Chairs, household, except
   upholstered: wood

(G-16762)
PERFECT EMPANADA LLC
691 Main St (02885-4318)
PHONE.............................508 241-5150
Pablo Mastandrea, *Mgr*
EMP: 14
SALES (corp-wide): 119.35K **Privately Held**
SIC: 2038 2099 Ethnic foods, nec, frozen;
   Ready-to-eat meals, salads, and
   sandwiches
PA: The Perfect Empanada Llc
   8 Blackstone Rd
   Attleboro MA 02703
   508 241-5150

(G-16763)
PLANET ECLIPSE LLC
130 Franklin St Bldg L4 (02885-3540)

PHONE.............................401 247-9061
▲ EMP: 7 EST: 2000
SALES (est): 1.22MM
SALES (corp-wide): 17.76MM **Privately Held**
Web: www.planeteclipse.com
SIC: 3949 5091 Sporting and athletic goods,
   nec; Sporting and recreation goods
HQ: Planet Eclipse Limited
   Acheson Way
   Manchester
   161 872-5572

(G-16764)
PROGRESSIVE DISPLAYS INC
Also Called: Displays For Less
605 Main St (02885-4316)
PHONE.............................401 245-2909
Tara K Thibaudeau, *Pr*
EMP: 10 EST: 2002
SQ FT: 3,200
SALES (est): 218.74K **Privately Held**
Web: www.pop2go.com
SIC: 3993 Signs and advertising specialties

(G-16765)
PUSTERLA US INC
Also Called: Aristocrat Metal Box Company
293 Child St (02885-1907)
P.O. Box 343 (02885-0343)
PHONE.............................401 245-5900
Laura Brodie, *CEO*
▲ EMP: 47 EST: 1885
SQ FT: 55,000
SALES (est): 10.24MM
SALES (corp-wide): 414.21K **Privately Held**
Web: www.pusterlaus.com
SIC: 2653 Boxes, corrugated: made from
   purchased materials
HQ: Pusterla 1880 Spa
   Via Pusterla 4
   Venegono Inferiore VA 21040
   03311665500

(G-16766)
RMB LTD
Also Called: W E C
36 Franklin St (02885-3501)
P.O. Box 86 (02885-0086)
PHONE.............................401 245-3700
EMP: 25 EST: 1962
SALES (est): 6.63MM **Privately Held**
Web: www.warrenelectriccorp.com
SIC: 3567 Industrial furnaces and ovens

(G-16767)
ROYAL DIVERSIFIED PRODUCTS
287 Market St (02885-2637)
P.O. Box 444 (02885-0444)
PHONE.............................401 245-6900
Roger E Ellin, *Pr*
Douglas Johnston, *
Marjorie E Ellin, *
◆ EMP: 20 EST: 1946
SQ FT: 27,000
SALES (est): 1.39MM **Privately Held**
Web: www.royalpins.com
SIC: 3544 3496 Punches, forming and
   stamping; Clips and fasteners, made from
   purchased wire

(G-16768)
SAMSONITE COMPANY STORES LLC
Also Called: Samsonite
95 Main St (02885-4301)
PHONE.............................401 247-3301
Steve Labao, *Mgr*
EMP: 10

SALES (corp-wide): 8.01MM **Privately Held**
SIC: 3161 5137   Luggage; Handbags
HQ: Samsonite Company Stores, Llc
  575 West St Ste 110
  Mansfield MA 02048
  508 851-1400

(G-16769)
TPI INC
Also Called: Tpi Composites
373 Market St Unit B (02885-2681)
P.O. Box 367 (02885-0367)
PHONE...........................401 247-4010
Steven Lockard, *CEO*
Wayne Monie, *
J P Aleskus Junior, *Pr*
James M Mckenzie, *CFO*
Dan Shelton, *
▲ **EMP:** 100 **EST:** 1987
SQ FT: 66,000
SALES (est): 42.82MM
SALES (corp-wide): 1.52B **Publicly Held**
Web: www.tpicomposites.com
SIC: 3083 Laminated plastics plate and
  sheet
PA: Tpi Composites, Inc.
  9200 E Pima Center Pkwy # 250
  Scottsdale AZ 85258
  480 305-8910

(G-16770)
TPI COMPOSITES INC
373 Market St (02885-2681)
PHONE...........................401 247-4010
EMP: 18
SALES (corp-wide): 1.52B **Publicly Held**
Web: www.tpicomposites.com
SIC: 3083 Laminated plastics plate and
  sheet
PA: Tpi Composites, Inc.
  9200 E Pima Center Pkwy # 250
  Scottsdale AZ 85258
  480 305-8910

(G-16771)
WARDS MANUFACTURING LLC
84 Cutler St Unit 7 (02885-2755)
PHONE...........................404 441-0453
Kelly Ward, *Pr*
EMP: 8
SALES (est): 78.66K **Privately Held**
SIC: 3444 Sheet metalwork

(G-16772)
WATERROWER INC
560 Metacom Ave (02885-2839)
PHONE...........................800 852-2210
Peter King, *Prin*
Helaine Knapp, *Prin*
◆ **EMP:** 51 **EST:** 1987
SQ FT: 4,000
SALES (est): 22.35MM **Privately Held**
Web: www.waterrower.com
SIC: 3949 Rowing machines
HQ: Waterrower (Uk) Ltd.
  4 The Valley Centre
  High Wycombe BUCKS HP13

(G-16773)
WATERROWER
INTERNATIONAL LLC
560 Metacom Ave (02885-2839)
PHONE...........................800 852-2210
EMP: 7 **EST:** 2018
SALES (est): 142.08K **Privately Held**
SIC: 3949 Sporting and athletic goods, nec

Warwick
Kent County

(G-16774)
A D& D WLDG & BOILER
WORKS INC
33 Bleachery Ct (02886-1201)
PHONE...........................401 732-5222
Christopher D Riggs, *Pr*
Daniel F Riggs, *VP*
Gungerd A Riggs, *Sec*
EMP: 10 **EST:** 1978
SQ FT: 3,950
SALES (est): 892.44K **Privately Held**
Web: www.ad-n-d.com
SIC: 7699 7692   Boiler repair shop; Welding
  repair

(G-16775)
ACCURATE MOLDED
PRODUCTS INC
Also Called: AMP
459 Warwick Industrial Dr (02886-2460)
PHONE...........................401 739-2400
Howard Devine Junior, *Pr*
Kay Duckworth, *
EMP: 30 **EST:** 1979
SQ FT: 30,000
SALES (est): 4.14MM **Privately Held**
Web: www.accuratemolded.com
SIC: 3089 Injection molding of plastics

(G-16776)
ADVANCED CHEMICAL
COMPANY
105 Bellows St 131 (02888)
PHONE...........................401 785-3434
Gerald A Smith Iii, *Pr*
John Antonacci, *
Michael W Floskis, *
▲ **EMP:** 50 **EST:** 1972
SQ FT: 24,000
SALES (est): 10.74MM **Privately Held**
Web: www.advchem.com
SIC: 2899 3339   Plating compounds;
  Precious metals

(G-16777)
ALDOTECH CORPORATION
Also Called: Aldo
71 Norwood Ave (02888-2320)
PHONE...........................401 467-6100
Heraldo J Gonzalez Junior, *Pr*
EMP: 41 **EST:** 1997
SQ FT: 18,000
SALES (est): 4.99MM **Privately Held**
SIC: 3672 3661   Printed circuit boards;
  Telephone and telegraph apparatus

(G-16778)
AMMEGA US INC
46 Warwick Industrial Dr (02886-2456)
PHONE...........................401 732-8131
Gary Williamson, *Brnch Mgr*
EMP: 8
Web: www.ammeraalbeltechusa.com
SIC: 3496 Miscellaneous fabricated wire
  products
HQ: Ammega Us Inc.
  10431 Midwest Indus Dr
  Saint Louis MO 63132
  314 890-0016

(G-16779)
ANCHORS AWEIGH TOGETHER
LLC ✪
Also Called: Aa Thrifty Sign & Awning

221 Jefferson Blvd (02888-3818)
PHONE...........................401 738-8055
Darrell Lindley, *Pr*
EMP: 45 **EST:** 2022
SALES (est): 3.17MM **Privately Held**
SIC: 2394 3993   Canvas and related
  products; Signs and advertising specialties

(G-16780)
ANTAYA INC
333 Strawberry Field Rd Ste 3
(02886-2459)
PHONE...........................401 941-7050
Stephen C Antaya, *Pr*
Donald Antaya, *
Mary Antaya, *
John Pereira, *
▼ **EMP:** 31 **EST:** 1985
SQ FT: 15,000
SALES (est): 3.87MM **Privately Held**
Web: www.antaya.com
SIC: 3694 Automotive electrical equipment,
  nec

(G-16781)
ANTAYA TECHNOLOGIES CORP
333 Strawberry Field Rd (02886-2476)
PHONE...........................401 921-3197
Jarod Scherer, *Pr*
▲ **EMP:** 225 **EST:** 1998
SQ FT: 25,000
SALES (est): 41.75MM
SALES (corp-wide): 17.49B **Privately Held**
Web: www.antaya.com
SIC: 3694 Automotive electrical equipment,
  nec
HQ: Aptiv Corporation
  5725 Innovation Dr
  Troy MI 48098

(G-16782)
APPONAUG BREWING
COMPANY
334 Knight St Ste 11101 (02886-1283)
PHONE...........................401 681-4321
Tamara Mckenney, *Pr*
EMP: 22 **EST:** 2018
SALES (est): 1.41MM **Privately Held**
Web: www.apponaugbrewing.com
SIC: 5813 2082   Bars and lounges; Beer
  (alcoholic beverage)

(G-16783)
AQUAMOTION INC
Also Called: Manufacturer
88 Jefferson Blvd Ste C (02888-1000)
PHONE...........................401 785-3000
▲ **EMP:** 20 **EST:** 2002
SALES (est): 2.55MM **Privately Held**
Web: www.aquamotionhvac.com
SIC: 3561 Pumps and pumping equipment

(G-16784)
ASTONISH RESULTS LP
300 Metro Center Blvd (02886-1710)
PHONE...........................401 921-6220
David Simas, *Prin*
EMP: 15 **EST:** 2006
SALES (est): 2.79MM **Privately Held**
Web: www.replicadesignerclothes.ru
SIC: 3823 Digital displays of process
  variables

(G-16785)
ATW COMPANIES INC (PA)
125 Metro Center Blvd Ste 3001
(02886-1768)
PHONE...........................401 244-1002
Frederick G Frost Iii, *Ch Bd*
Peter C Frost, *

Caryn E Mitchell, *
Duane Ottolini, *
▲ **EMP:** 70 **EST:** 1886
SQ FT: 64,000
SALES (est): 70.84MM
SALES (corp-wide): 70.84MM **Privately Held**
Web: www.atwcompanies.com
SIC: 3674 3498   Semiconductors and
  related devices; Fabricated pipe and fittings

(G-16786)
BAKER COMMODITIES INC
Also Called: Corenco
4 Riverdale Ct (02886-0507)
PHONE...........................401 821-3003
EMP: 7
SALES (corp-wide): 153.63MM **Privately Held**
Web: www.bakercommodities.com
SIC: 2077 Animal and marine fats and oils
PA: Baker Commodities, Inc.
  4020 Bandini Blvd
  Vernon CA 90058
  323 268-2801

(G-16787)
BARRETTE FABRICATION LLC
(PA)
Also Called: Ocean State Off Road
1077 Toll Gate Rd (02886-0650)
PHONE...........................401 822-0860
Richard A Barrette Iii, *Admn*
EMP: 8 **EST:** 2017
SALES (est): 484.64K **Privately Held**
Web: www.barrettefabrication.com
SIC: 3999 Barrettes

(G-16788)
BARRINGTON ENTERPRISES
LLC
Also Called: Barrington Printing
334 Knight St Ste S1a (02886-1262)
PHONE...........................401 943-8300
EMP: 26 **EST:** 1999
SALES (est): 3.72MM **Privately Held**
SIC: 2752 Offset printing

(G-16789)
BEACON COMMUNICATIONS
INC
Also Called: Pennysaver, The
1944 Warwick Ave (02889-2448)
PHONE...........................401 732-3100
John Howell, *Pr*
Lynne Taylor, *
EMP: 34 **EST:** 1969
SQ FT: 1,500
SALES (est): 2.48MM **Privately Held**
Web: www.cranstononline.com
SIC: 2711 Newspapers, publishing and
  printing

(G-16790)
BENSON NEPTUNE INC (DH)
Also Called: Evoqua Water Technologies
334 Knight St Unit 3100 (02886-5821)
PHONE...........................401 821-7140
Barry Gertz, *Pr*
Michael Burns, *
◆ **EMP:** 51 **EST:** 1956
SALES (est): 19.29MM **Publicly Held**
Web: www.neptunebenson.com
SIC: 3589 Water treatment equipment,
  industrial
HQ: Evoqua Water Technologies Corp.
  210 6th Ave
  Pittsburgh PA 15222
  724 772-0044

(G-16791)
BIOMEDICAL STRUCTURES LLC
60 Commerce Dr (02886-2470)
PHONE.............................401 223-0990
Dean Tulumaris, *Managing Member*
Diane Baxster, *CFO*
▲ **EMP:** 14 **EST:** 2002
SALES (est): 948.73K **Privately Held**
Web: www.confluentmedical.com
SIC: 3841 Medical instruments and
   equipment, blood and bone work
HQ: Ete Medical, Inc.
   242 Humboldt Ct
   Sunnyvale CA

(G-16792)
BPM LLC
33 College Hill Rd Ste 15b (02886-2786)
PHONE.............................401 615-0700
Brian A Bucci, *Admn*
EMP: 7 **EST:** 2016
SALES (est): 434.88K **Privately Held**
SIC: 3599 Industrial machinery, nec

(G-16793)
BRADA MANUFACTURING INC
46 Warwick Industrial Dr (02886-2456)
P.O. Box 7614 (02887-7614)
PHONE.............................401 739-3774
Michael W Hamilton, *Pr*
EMP: 30 **EST:** 1979
SQ FT: 15,000
SALES (est): 4.61MM **Privately Held**
Web: www.bradamfg.com
SIC: 3599 Machine shop, jobbing and repair

(G-16794)
C R BARD INC
100 Crossings Blvd (02886-2850)
P.O. Box 8500 (02920-0500)
PHONE.............................401 825-8300
EMP: 49
SALES (corp-wide): 19.37B **Publicly Held**
Web: www.crbard.com
SIC: 3841 Surgical and medical instruments
HQ: C. R. Bard, Inc.
   1 Becton Dr
   Franklin Lakes NJ 07417
   201 847-6800

(G-16795)
COLONIAL PRINTING INC (PA)
333 Strawberry Field Rd Ste 11
(02886-2459)
PHONE.............................401 691-3400
Richard Herr, *Pr*
Ken Menna, *
Josh Bainton, *
Richard Pulie, *
EMP: 25 **EST:** 2017
SALES (est): 2.91MM
SALES (corp-wide): 2.91MM **Privately
Held**
Web: www.colonialprinting.net
SIC: 2752 Offset printing

(G-16796)
COLUMBUS DOOR COMPANY
1884 Elmwood Ave (02888-1998)
PHONE.............................401 781-7792
TOLL FREE: 800
Joseph Costantino, *Pr*
Ralph Costantino, *
William Costantino, *
Richard Costantino, *
David Costantino, *
EMP: 60 **EST:** 1920
SQ FT: 85,000
SALES (est): 11.87MM **Privately Held**
Web: www.columbusdoor.com

SIC: 5031 5072 3442 2431   Doors, nec;
   Builders' hardware, nec; Metal doors;
   Millwork

(G-16797)
**CONLEY CASTING SUPPLY
CORP (PA)**
Also Called: Tekcast Industries RI
124 Maple St (02886-2188)
PHONE.............................401 461-4710
TOLL FREE: 800
Arthur T Francis, *Pr*
▲ **EMP:** 15 **EST:** 1972
SQ FT: 20,000
SALES (est): 4.35MM
SALES (corp-wide): 4.35MM **Privately
Held**
Web: www.conleycasting.com
SIC: 3544 3559 2822 Forms (molds), for
   foundry and plastics working machinery;
   Jewelers' machines; Synthetic rubber

(G-16798)
COOLIANCE INC (PA)
60 Alhambra Rd Ste 1 (02886-1442)
PHONE.............................401 921-6500
Russell Hall, *Pr*
Russell Hall, *Pr*
Robert F Mazzeo, *VP*
▲ **EMP:** 10 **EST:** 2008
SALES (est): 1.62MM **Privately Held**
Web: www.cooliance.com
SIC: 3679 Electronic circuits

(G-16799)
COTO TECHNOLOGY
171 Service Ave Ste 330 (02886-1015)
PHONE.............................401 943-2686
EMP: 7 **EST:** 2019
SALES (est): 364.43K **Privately Held**
Web: www.cotorelay.com
SIC: 3625 Relays and industrial controls

(G-16800)
**CRITICARE TECHNOLOGIES
INC**
333 Strawberry Field Rd Ste 11
(02886-2459)
PHONE.............................401 667-3837
Thomas Dietiker, *Dir*
EMP: 20 **EST:** 2016
SALES (est): 2.69MM **Privately Held**
Web: www.criticare.com
SIC: 3845 Electromedical equipment

(G-16801)
**CUSTOM BUILT WINDOW MFG
LLC**
80 Meadow St (02886-6909)
PHONE.............................401 738-3800
EMP: 30 **EST:** 2017
SALES (est): 1.95MM **Privately Held**
Web: www.custombuiltri.com
SIC: 3999 Manufacturing industries, nec

(G-16802)
DATA BINDING INC
10 New England Way (02886-6913)
PHONE.............................401 738-7901
Nicholas Picchione Ii, *Pr*
Michael Halperson, *
Ann O Picchione, *
▲ **EMP:** 60 **EST:** 1945
SQ FT: 40,000
SALES (est): 11.09MM **Privately Held**
Web: www.thedomecompanies.com
SIC: 2789 Binding only: books, pamphlets,
   magazines, etc.
PA: Dome Enterprises Trust
   10 New England Way

Warwick RI 02886

(G-16803)
DAVIDON INDUSTRIES INC
Also Called: Davidon Alloys
87 Dewey Ave (02886-2431)
PHONE.............................401 737-8380
Donald Dinuccio, *Pr*
▲ **EMP:** 15 **EST:** 1987
SQ FT: 4,000
SALES (est): 2.26MM **Privately Held**
Web: www.davidonindustries.com
SIC: 3585 Heating equipment, complete

(G-16804)
DAVOL INC (DH)
100 Crossings Blvd (02886-2850)
P.O. Box 1210 (02887-1210)
PHONE.............................401 825-8300
B Kelly, *Pr*
▲ **EMP:** 16 **EST:** 1874
SQ FT: 180,000
SALES (est): 9.16MM
SALES (corp-wide): 19.37B **Publicly Held**
SIC: 3841 Surgical and medical instruments
HQ: Bard Devices, Inc.
   1 Becton Dr
   Franklin Lakes NJ 07417

(G-16805)
**DAYTON SUPERIOR
CORPORATION**
3970 Post Rd (02886-9235)
PHONE.............................401 885-1934
Claudette Harris, *Brnch Mgr*
EMP: 8
SALES (corp-wide): 69.06B **Privately Held**
Web: www.daytonsuperior.com
SIC: 3315 Steel wire and related products
HQ: Dayton Superior Corporation
   1125 Byers Rd
   Miamisburg OH 45342
   937 866-0710

(G-16806)
**DIEBOLD NIXDORF
INCORPORATED**
25 Pace Blvd (02886-4244)
PHONE.............................401 823-8665
EMP: 7
SALES (corp-wide): 3.46B **Publicly Held**
Web: www.dieboldnixdorf.com
SIC: 3578 Automatic teller machines (ATM)
PA: Diebold Nixdorf, Incorporated
   50 Executive Pkwy
   Hudson OH 44236
   330 490-4000

(G-16807)
**DOME ENTERPRISES TRUST
(PA)**
10 New England Way (02886-6904)
P.O. Box 1220 (02887-1220)
PHONE.............................401 738-7900
Nicholas Picchione Ii, *Trst*
EMP: 7 **EST:** 1972
SQ FT: 40,000
SALES (est): 15.55MM **Privately Held**
Web: www.thedomecompanies.com
SIC: 2789 Bookbinding and related work

(G-16808)
**DOME PUBLISHING COMPANY
INC (HQ)**
10 New England Way (02886-6913)
P.O. Box 1220 (02887-1220)
PHONE.............................401 738-7900
Michael Karsay, *CEO*
John S Renza Junior, *Treas*

Denise Deschenes, *
EMP: 21 **EST:** 1947
SQ FT: 50,000
SALES (est): 4.46MM **Privately Held**
Web: www.thedomecompanies.com
SIC: 2789 Binding only: books, pamphlets,
   magazines, etc.
PA: Dome Enterprises Trust
   10 New England Way
   Warwick RI 02886

(G-16809)
DROITCOUR COMPANY
28 Graystone St (02886-1384)
PHONE.............................401 737-4646
Mike Droitcour, *Pr*
Andrew Droitcour, *
EMP: 80 **EST:** 1931
SQ FT: 58,000
SALES (est): 8.14MM **Privately Held**
Web: www.droitcour.com
SIC: 3599 Machine shop, jobbing and repair

(G-16810)
DUNKIN DONUTS
Also Called: Dunkin' Donuts
341 Providence St (02886-0671)
PHONE.............................401 822-2434
EMP: 10 **EST:** 1978
SALES (est): 134.69K **Privately Held**
Web: www.dunkindonuts.com
SIC: 5461 2051 Doughnuts; Bread, cake,
   and related products

(G-16811)
DUR A FLEX MOTOR SPORTS
875 W Shore Rd (02889-2731)
PHONE.............................401 739-0202
Carl Gustafson, *Prin*
EMP: 8 **EST:** 2007
SALES (est): 262.53K **Privately Held**
Web: www.duraflexracing.com
SIC: 3732 Boatbuilding and repairing

(G-16812)
EAGLE TOOL INC
101 Venturi Ave (02888-1540)
PHONE.............................401 421-5105
Edward Iannone, *Pr*
Frank Iannucci, *Sec*
EMP: 17 **EST:** 1940
SALES (est): 558.73K **Privately Held**
Web: www.eagletool.com
SIC: 3915 Jewelers' findings and materials

(G-16813)
**ELITE CUSTOM COMPOUNDING
INC**
303 Kilvert St (02886-1344)
PHONE.............................401 921-2136
EMP: 7 **EST:** 2018
SALES (est): 391.08K **Privately Held**
SIC: 3087 Custom compound purchased
   resins

(G-16814)
ENOW INC
3970 Post Rd (02886-9235)
PHONE.............................401 732-7080
Jeffrey Flath, *Pr*
▲ **EMP:** 12 **EST:** 2011
SALES (est): 1.21MM **Privately Held**
Web: www.enowsystems.com
SIC: 3674 Solar cells

(G-16815)
ETCO INCORPORATED (PA)
Also Called: Etco
25 Bellows St (02888-1501)

PHONE...............................401 467-2400
David Dunn, *Ch*
John Macaluso, *
Steve Segerson, *
John Stiness, *
Afshin Etebar, *
◆ **EMP:** 80 **EST:** 1947
SQ FT: 25,000
SALES (est): 18.83MM
SALES (corp-wide): 18.83MM **Privately
Held**
Web: www.etco.com
SIC: 3469 3061 Stamping metal for the trade
; Appliance rubber goods (mechanical)

(G-16816)
FRANK SHATZ & CO
61 Dewey Ave Ste D (02886-2471)
PHONE...............................401 739-1822
Frank Shatz, *Pr*
Randy Shatz, *VP*
EMP: 23 **EST:** 1959
SQ FT: 20,000
SALES (est): 3.22MM **Privately Held**
Web: www.frankshatzcompany.com
SIC: 2542 Partitions and fixtures, except
wood

(G-16817)
GEIB REFINING CORPORATION
399 Kilvert St (02886-1381)
PHONE...............................401 738-8560
Kenneth Wightman, *Pr*
Gladys Geib, *
Robert Slack, *
Archibald Kenyon, *
James Geib, *
EMP: 28 **EST:** 1979
SQ FT: 15,000
SALES (est): 4.81MM **Privately Held**
Web: www.geibrefining.com
SIC: 3339 Precious metals

(G-16818)
GEPP LLC
Also Called: Go East Promotions
83 Vermont Ave Bldg 3-4 (02888-3054)
PHONE...............................401 808-8004
Mark Mercurio, *Pr*
Brian Richards, *VP*
▲ **EMP:** 11 **EST:** 2011
SALES (est): 695.86K **Privately Held**
SIC: 3993 Advertising novelties

(G-16819)
GLENN INC
300 Jefferson Blvd (02888-3860)
PHONE...............................800 521-0065
Tim Gooling, *Pr*
EMP: 20 **EST:** 1989
SALES (est): 2.36MM **Privately Held**
Web: www.glenncorp.com
SIC: 2911 Nonaromatic chemical products
HQ: Azelis Americas, Llc
33 Riverside Ave Ste 507
Westport CT 06880
203 274-8691

(G-16820)
HERFF JONES LLC
Also Called: Herff Jones - Dieges & Clust
150 Herff Jones Way (02888-1332)
P.O. Box 6500 (02940-6500)
PHONE...............................401 331-1240
Robert Potts, *Managing Member*
EMP: 10
SALES (corp-wide): 2.02B **Privately Held**
Web: www.yearbookdiscoveries.com
SIC: 3911 Rings, finger: precious metal
HQ: Herff Jones, Llc
4501 W 62nd St

Indianapolis IN 46268
317 297-3741

(G-16821)
IMAGE PRINTING & COPYING INC
33 Plan Way Bldg 7 (02886-1013)
PHONE...............................401 737-9311
EMP: 17 **EST:** 1995
SALES (est): 2.11MM **Privately Held**
Web: www.imageprintingri.com
SIC: 2752 Offset printing

(G-16822)
INFINEON TECH AMERICAS CORP
200 Crossings Blvd Ste 100 (02886-2873)
PHONE...............................401 773-7501
Schuellein George, *Dir*
EMP: 7
SALES (corp-wide): 17.72B **Privately Held**
Web: www.infineon.com
SIC: 3674 Semiconductors and related
devices
HQ: Infineon Technologies Americas Corp.
101 N Pacific Coast Hwy
El Segundo CA 90245
310 726-8200

(G-16823)
INTERNATIONAL TECHNOLOGIES INC
Also Called: River Point Station
115 Maple St (02888-2130)
P.O. Box 430 (02818-0430)
PHONE...............................401 467-6907
Ronald Elsdoerfer, *CEO*
◆ **EMP:** 11 **EST:** 1985
SQ FT: 10,000
SALES (est): 123.03K **Privately Held**
Web: www.riverpointstation.com
SIC: 3629 Electronic generation equipment

(G-16824)
IT SYNERGY GROUP LLC
Also Called: Itsg
2980 W Shore Rd (02886-5422)
PHONE...............................866 767-4874
EMP: 10 **EST:** 2019
SALES (est): 659.31K **Privately Held**
SIC: 7379 7373 3572 7376 Computer
related services, nec; Computer integrated
systems design; Computer storage devices;
Computer facilities management

(G-16825)
JADE MANUFACTURING COMPANY INC
132 Meadow St (02886-6909)
PHONE...............................401 737-2400
Donald Boyle Prestreas, *Prin*
Donald Boyle, *Pr*
EMP: 20 **EST:** 1947
SQ FT: 8,000
SALES (est): 2.33MM **Privately Held**
Web: www.jademanufacturing.net
SIC: 3599 Machine shop, jobbing and repair

(G-16826)
JADE MANUFACTURING COMPANY LLC
132 Meadow St (02886-6909)
PHONE...............................401 737-2400
Don Boyle, *Pr*
EMP: 27 **EST:** 2012
SQ FT: 10,000
SALES (est): 137.07K **Privately Held**
Web: www.jademanufacturing.net

SIC: 3365 3599 Aerospace castings,
aluminum; Machine shop, jobbing and repair

(G-16827)
JAY PACKAGING GROUP INC (DH)
Also Called: Jay Printing Company
100 Warwick Industrial Dr (02886-2486)
PHONE...............................401 244-1300
▲ **EMP:** 97 **EST:** 1945
SQ FT: 180,000
SALES (est): 24.51MM **Privately Held**
Web: www.rohrer.com
SIC: 2752 3089 Offset printing;
Thermoformed finished plastics products,
nec
HQ: Rohrer Corporation
717 Seville Rd
Wadsworth OH 44281
330 335-1541

(G-16828)
JOHN CRANE SEALOL INC (DH)
Also Called: Eagle Div
75 Commerce Dr # 101 (02886-2429)
PHONE...............................401 732-0715
Michael Galluccio, *Pr*
▼ **EMP:** 200 **EST:** 1920
SALES (est): 65.95MM
SALES (corp-wide): 3.83B **Privately Held**
SIC: 3053 3492 3599 Gaskets; packing and
sealing devices; Control valves, aircraft:
hydraulic and pneumatic; Bellows,
industrial: metal
HQ: John Crane Inc.
6400 Oakton St
Morton Grove IL 60053
312 605-7800

(G-16829)
JSG HOLDINGS INC
80 Meadow St (02886-6909)
PHONE...............................401 738-3800
TOLL FREE: 888
EMP: 49 **EST:** 1961
SALES (est): 4.68MM **Privately Held**
Web: www.custombuiltri.com
SIC: 3442 Storm doors or windows, metal

(G-16830)
KEARFLEX ENGINEERING COMPANY
66 Cypress St (02888-2119)
PHONE...............................401 781-4900
Thomas Kearney, *Pr*
Keith Kearney, *Treas*
Thomas Stanton, *Stockholder*
EMP: 18 **EST:** 1963
SALES (est): 2.34MM **Privately Held**
Web: www.kearflex.com
SIC: 3812 3829 3625 Aircraft/aerospace
flight instruments and guidance systems;
Pressure and vacuum indicators, aircraft
engine; Relays and industrial controls

(G-16831)
KENNEY MANUFACTURING COMPANY (PA)
1000 Jefferson Blvd (02886-2200)
PHONE...............................401 739-2200
Leslie M Kenney, *Pr*
G D Kenney, *
◆ **EMP:** 500 **EST:** 1914
SQ FT: 300,000
SALES (est): 49.13MM
SALES (corp-wide): 49.13MM **Privately
Held**
Web: www.kenney.com

SIC: 3261 2511 3699 3499 Bathroom
accessories/fittings, vitreous china or
earthenware; Storage chests, household:
wood; Security devices; Magnetic shields,
metal

(G-16832)
LADY ANN CANDIES INC
Also Called: Fruit & Nut House
86 Warwick Industrial Dr Ste 1
(02886-2464)
PHONE...............................401 738-4321
John Burke, *Owner*
EMP: 12 **EST:** 1950
SQ FT: 3,000
SALES (est): 411.59K **Privately Held**
Web: www.candylandmarket.com
SIC: 2064 5441 5961 2066 Candy and other
confectionery products; Candy, nut, and
confectionery stores; Food, mail order;
Chocolate and cocoa products

(G-16833)
LUMETTA INC
33 Minnesota Ave (02888-6010)
PHONE...............................401 691-3994
William Prichett, *Pr*
EMP: 38 **EST:** 1992
SQ FT: 36,000
SALES (est): 8.05MM **Privately Held**
Web: www.lumetta.com
SIC: 3646 Commercial lighting fixtures

(G-16834)
MALEY LASER PROCESSING INC
Also Called: Maley Laser
25 Graystone St (02886-1313)
P.O. Box 81024 (02888-0931)
PHONE...............................303 952-8941
Kurt R Maley, *Pr*
EMP: 15 **EST:** 1987
SQ FT: 44,000
SALES (est): 2.13MM **Privately Held**
Web: www.maleylaser.com
SIC: 3699 3498 Laser welding, drilling, and
cutting equipment; Tube fabricating
(contract bending and shaping)

(G-16835)
MCB INC
289 Kilvert St (02886-1344)
P.O. Box 7229 (02887-7229)
PHONE...............................401 739-7020
Barry Miller, *Pr*
Paul Miller, *VP*
EMP: 18 **EST:** 1949
SQ FT: 50,000
SALES (est): 488.24K **Privately Held**
Web: www.millerbox.net
SIC: 2653 Boxes, corrugated: made from
purchased materials

(G-16836)
MCLEOD OPTICAL COMPANY INC (PA)
50 Jefferson Park Rd (02888-1016)
P.O. Box 6045 (02940-6045)
PHONE...............................401 467-3000
Scott Mcleod, *Pr*
EMP: 50 **EST:** 1922
SQ FT: 12,900
SALES (est): 2.97MM
SALES (corp-wide): 2.97MM **Privately
Held**
Web: www.mcleodoptical.com
SIC: 3851 5048 Lens coating, ophthalmic;
Ophthalmic goods

(G-16837)
MILLARD WIRE COMPANY
Millard Wireland
259 Warwick Industrial Dr (02886-2416)
PHONE...............................401 737-9330
Daniel R La Croix Senior, *Brnch Mgr*
EMP: 17
SALES (corp-wide): 9.76MM **Privately Held**
Web: www.millardwire.com
SIC: 3547 Rolling mill machinery
PA: Millard Wire Company
　449 Warwick Industrial Dr
　Warwick RI 02886
　401 737-9330

(G-16838)
MILLARD WIRE COMPANY (PA)
Also Called: Millard Jewelry Division
449 Warwick Industrial Dr (02886-2460)
PHONE...............................401 737-9330
Daniel R La Croix Senior, *Pr*
Daniel R La Croix Junior, *VP*
Paul Gilgun, *
C J Lacroix, *
Bill Vesey, *
▲ EMP: 43 EST: 1991
SQ FT: 110,000
SALES (est): 9.76MM
SALES (corp-wide): 9.76MM **Privately Held**
Web: www.millardwire.com
SIC: 3547 3351 Rolling mill machinery;
　Copper rolling and drawing

(G-16839)
MODERN PLASTICS
380 Jefferson Blvd Ste A (02886-1356)
PHONE...............................401 732-0415
Rita Cesario, *Mgr*
EMP: 11 EST: 2013
SALES (est): 246.02K **Privately Held**
Web: www.modernplastics.com
SIC: 3089 Injection molding of plastics

(G-16840)
NATIONAL CHAIN COMPANY (PA)
Also Called: Apogee Precision Parts
55 Access Rd (02886-1000)
PHONE...............................401 732-3634
Steven Cipolla, *Pr*
Ralph Cipolla, *
▲ EMP: 99 EST: 1991
SALES (est): 14.53MM
SALES (corp-wide): 14.53MM **Privately Held**
Web: www.natchain.com
SIC: 3911 Jewelry, precious metal

(G-16841)
NEW ENGLAND ORTHOPEDICS INC (PA)
220 Toll Gate Rd Ste A (02886-4418)
PHONE...............................401 739-9838
Joseph Infantolino, *Pr*
Susan Infantolino, *VP*
EMP: 7 EST: 1982
SQ FT: 500
SALES (est): 911.79K
SALES (corp-wide): 911.79K **Privately Held**
Web: www.neortho.com
SIC: 3842 Prosthetic appliances

(G-16842)
PALEO PRODUCTS INC
Also Called: Paleonola
2 Commerce Dr (02886-2470)

P.O. Box 6061 (02940-6061)
PHONE...............................833 476-3733
Dinos A Stamoulis, *Pr*
Dinos A Stamoulis, *Pr*
EMP: 10 EST: 2011
SALES (est): 1.01MM **Privately Held**
Web: www.paleonola.com
SIC: 2064 Granola and muesli, bars and
　clusters

(G-16843)
PARMATECH 3D INC
55 Service Ave (02886-1020)
PHONE...............................401 739-0740
EMP: 7 EST: 2019
SALES (est): 240.45K **Privately Held**
Web: www.atwcompanies.com
SIC: 3599 Machine shop, jobbing and repair

(G-16844)
PEASE & CURREN INCORPORATED
75 Pennsylvania Ave (02888-3028)
PHONE...............................401 738-6449
Francis H Curren Iii, *Pr*
EMP: 40 EST: 1916
SQ FT: 30,000
SALES (est): 8.81MM **Privately Held**
Web: www.peaseandcurren.com
SIC: 3341 Secondary precious metals

(G-16845)
PERRY PAVING
20 Keystone Dr (02889-8519)
PHONE...............................401 732-1730
Joe Perry, *Prin*
EMP: 9 EST: 2002
SALES (est): 122.52K **Privately Held**
Web: www.jperrypaving.com
SIC: 2951 1611 Asphalt paving mixtures
　and blocks; Surfacing and paving

(G-16846)
PMC LIGHTING INC
Also Called: PMC Lighting
100 Gilbane St (02886-6902)
PHONE...............................401 738-7266
Larry Crystal, *Pr*
Arthur Goldstein, *
▲ EMP: 38 EST: 1991
SQ FT: 28,000
SALES (est): 7MM **Privately Held**
Web: www.pmclighting.com
SIC: 3646 Commercial lighting fixtures

(G-16847)
REED SEMICONDUCTOR CORP (PA)
875 Centerville Rd (02886-4381)
PHONE...............................401 886-0857
Wenkai Wu, *CEO*
EMP: 10 EST: 2019
SALES (est): 473.19K
SALES (corp-wide): 473.19K **Privately Held**
Web: www.reedsemi.us
SIC: 3674 Semiconductors and related
　devices

(G-16848)
RENOVA LIGHTING SYSTEMS INC
36 Bellair Ave Unit 4 (02886-2269)
PHONE...............................800 635-6682
▲ EMP: 25 EST: 1999
SQ FT: 20,000
SALES (est): 4.67MM **Privately Held**
Web: www.renova.com

SIC: 3646 Commercial lighting fixtures

(G-16849)
RHODE ISLAND ASSN REALTORS INC (PA)
Also Called: RI Realtors
100 Bignall St (02888-1005)
PHONE...............................401 785-3650
Sally Hersey, *Pr*
Christopher Whitten, *President Elect*
Claudia Chappel, *CFO*
Michael Pereira, *VP*
William Fain, *Treas*
EMP: 9 EST: 1948
SALES (est): 3.5MM
SALES (corp-wide): 3.5MM **Privately Held**
Web: www.rirealtors.org
SIC: 8611 2721 Trade associations;
　Periodicals, publishing only

(G-16850)
RHODE ISLAND NEWSPPR GROUP INC
1944 Warwick Ave (02889-2448)
PHONE...............................401 732-3100
Richard Foisher, *Pr*
EMP: 12 EST: 1971
SALES (est): 223.82K **Privately Held**
Web: www.rinewspapergroup.com
SIC: 2711 Newspapers, publishing and
　printing

(G-16851)
RITEC INC
60 Alhambra Rd Ste 5 (02886-1442)
PHONE...............................401 738-3660
Michael Ragosta, *CEO*
Gary Petersen Ph.d., *Research*
Bruce B Chick, *Ch Bd*
Michael A Ragosta, *VP*
EMP: 8 EST: 1986
SQ FT: 2,800
SALES (est): 899.25K **Privately Held**
Web: www.ritecinc.com
SIC: 3699 Electrical equipment and
　supplies, nec

(G-16852)
RITRONICS INC
Also Called: Hailux Lighting
60 Alhambra Rd Ste 1 (02886-1442)
PHONE...............................401 732-8175
James T Hagan, *Pr*
Russell J Hall, *VP*
Robert F Nazzeo, *Treas*
EMP: 11 EST: 2009
SALES (est): 931.96K **Privately Held**
Web: www.ritronics.com
SIC: 3679 Electronic loads and power
　supplies

(G-16853)
ROBERT BAXTER ASSOCIATES INC
Also Called: Major Findings Div
200 Jefferson Blvd (02888-3826)
PHONE...............................401 739-8222
Robert B Messerlian, *Pr*
Paul Messerlian, *VP*
Gloria Messerlian, *Sec*
EMP: 12 EST: 1963
SQ FT: 6,400
SALES (est): 2.3MM **Privately Held**
Web: www.baxtersjewelry.com
SIC: 5944 3915 Jewelry, precious stones
　and precious metals; Jewelers' findings and
　materials

(G-16854)
ROMANO INVESTMENTS INC
Also Called: Colonial Instant Printing
333 Strawberry Field Rd Ste 11
(02886-2476)
PHONE...............................401 691-3400
Raymond G Menna, *Pr*
Kenneth Menna, *
EMP: 37 EST: 1978
SQ FT: 39,600
SALES (est): 875.68K **Privately Held**
SIC: 2752 Offset printing

(G-16855)
RUSCO STEEL COMPANY
25 Bleachery Ct (02886-1201)
P.O. Box 7630 (02887-7630)
PHONE...............................401 732-0548
Robert S Russell, *Pr*
EMP: 70 EST: 1979
SALES (est): 3.97MM **Privately Held**
SIC: 3449 Fabricated bar joists and
　concrete reinforcing bars

(G-16856)
S & P HEAT TREATING INC
Also Called: S & P Metallurgy Service
16a Dewey Ave (02886-2432)
PHONE...............................401 737-9272
Arvind Patel, *Pr*
Rajul Patel, *VP*
EMP: 13 EST: 1986
SQ FT: 6,000
SALES (est): 1.47MM **Privately Held**
Web: www.spheattreating.com
SIC: 3398 Metal heat treating

(G-16857)
SAINT GERMAIN
675 W Shore Rd (02889-1352)
PHONE...............................401 738-2800
EMP: 7 EST: 2017
SALES (est): 204.84K **Privately Held**
SIC: 2833 Medicinals and botanicals

(G-16858)
SANDSTROM CRBIDE PDTS CORP INC
140 Imera Ave (02886-1435)
PHONE...............................401 739-5220
Jon J Ash, *Pr*
Chris Ash, *Mgr*
EMP: 10 EST: 1941
SQ FT: 4,800
SALES (est): 921.7K **Privately Held**
Web: www.sandstromcarbide.com
SIC: 3599 Machine shop, jobbing and repair

(G-16859)
SCHROFF INC (HQ)
Also Called: Pentair Electronic Packaging
170 Commerce Dr (02886-2430)
PHONE...............................763 204-7700
Beth Wozniak, *CEO*
Sara Zawoyski, *
Jason Stokes, *
Mark Borin, *
▲ EMP: 260 EST: 1982
SQ FT: 100,000
SALES (est): 465.72MM **Privately Held**
Web: schroff.nvent.com
SIC: 3469 7629 Electronic enclosures,
　stamped or pressed metal;
　Telecommunication equipment repair
　(except telephones)
PA: Nvent Electric Public Limited Company
　10 Earlsfort Terrace
　Dublin D02 T

(G-16860)
SCW CORPORATION
Also Called: Day-O-Lite Fluorescent Fixs
126 Chestnut St (02888-2104)
PHONE..............................401 808-6849
Steve Weisman, *Pr*
Cheryl Weisman, *
EMP: 34 **EST:** 1935
SQ FT: 30,000
SALES (est): 9.32MM **Privately Held**
Web: www.dayolite.com
SIC: 3645 3646 Residential lighting fixtures;
  Fluorescent lighting fixtures, commercial

(G-16861)
SES AMERICA INC
21 Quinton St (02888-1420)
PHONE..............................401 232-3370
Philippe Perut, *Pr*
▲ **EMP:** 16 **EST:** 1986
SQ FT: 6,000
SALES (est): 838.92K **Privately Held**
Web: sesa.sunrisesesatech.com
SIC: 5063 3993 Signaling equipment,
  electrical; Electric signs

(G-16862)
SH CONSULTING CO
55 Access Rd Ste 500 (02886-1045)
P.O. Box 66 (02761-0066)
PHONE..............................508 695-6611
Gregory C Smith, *Pr*
EMP: 19 **EST:** 1923
SQ FT: 22,000
SALES (est): 490.44K **Privately Held**
Web: www.natchain.com
SIC: 3496 Woven wire products, nec

(G-16863)
SONCO WORLDWIDE INC
450 Pavilion Ave (02888-6035)
PHONE..............................401 406-3761
Bill King, *Prin*
EMP: 10
SALES (corp-wide): 50.41MM **Privately
Held**
Web: www.sonco.com
SIC: 3315 5039 2421 7359 Steel wire and
  related products; Wire fence, gates, and
  accessories; Snow fence lath; Work zone
  traffic equipment (flags, cones, barrels, etc.)
PA: Sonco Worldwide, Inc.
  9011 E Hampton Dr
  Capitol Heights MD 20743
  240 487-2490

(G-16864)
SQUADLOCKER INC
240 Bald Hill Rd (02886-1126)
PHONE..............................888 885-6253
George Overholser, *CEO*
Gary Goldberg, *Pr*
Frank Tillinghast, *CFO*
Nellie Tillinghast, *Sr VP*
Tiffany Omicioli, *VP*
EMP: 91 **EST:** 2015
SALES (est): 22.85MM **Privately Held**
Web: www.squadlocker.com
SIC: 5136 5137 2396 2759 Men's and boys'
  sportswear and work clothing; Women's
  and children's sportswear and swimsuits;
  Screen printing on fabric articles; Screen
  printing

(G-16865)
**STATE-WIDE MLTPLE LSTING
SVC I**
100 Bignall St (02888-1005)
PHONE..............................401 785-3650
Susan Arnold, *VP*

EMP: 9 **EST:** 1972
SALES (est): 1.5MM
SALES (corp-wide): 3.5MM **Privately Held**
Web: www.riliving.com
SIC: 2721 Trade journals: publishing only,
  not printed on site
PA: Rhode Island Association Of Realtors,
  Inc.
  100 Bignall St
  Warwick RI 02888
  401 785-3650

(G-16866)
SULLIVAN TIRE CO INC
Also Called: Macey's Car Care Center
1102 Jefferson Blvd (02886-2203)
PHONE..............................401 737-5251
Bart Angelio, *Mgr*
EMP: 9
SALES (corp-wide): 275.69MM **Privately
Held**
Web: www.sullivantire.com
SIC: 7538 7534 General automotive repair
  shops; Tire repair shop
HQ: Sullivan Tire Co., Inc.
  41 Accord Park Dr
  Norwell MA 02061
  781 982-1550

(G-16867)
T TECH MACHINE INC
11 Knight St Bldg A (02886-1281)
PHONE..............................401 732-3590
John Ficorilli, *Pr*
EMP: 15 **EST:** 1989
SQ FT: 9,000
SALES (est): 2.25MM **Privately Held**
Web: ttechmachine-1.myfreesites.net
SIC: 3599 Machine shop, jobbing and repair

(G-16868)
TEXTRON INC
566 Airport Rd (02886-2422)
PHONE..............................401 457-2310
EMP: 26
SALES (corp-wide): 12.87B **Publicly Held**
Web: www.textron.com
SIC: 3721 Aircraft
PA: Textron Inc.
  40 Westminster St
  Providence RI 02903
  401 421-2800

(G-16869)
UNETIXS VASCULAR INC
333 Strawberry Field Rd Ste 11
(02886-2459)
PHONE..............................401 583-0089
Peter Moscovita, *Pr*
EMP: 45 **EST:** 1989
SALES (est): 11.16MM **Privately Held**
Web: www.unetixs.com
SIC: 3841 Diagnostic apparatus, medical
PA: Opto Circuits (India) Limited
  Plot No 83, Electronic City
  Bengaluru KA 56010

(G-16870)
VENSYS ENERGY INC
305 Lincoln Ave (02888-3029)
PHONE..............................401 295-0006
Theodore Peters, *Asst Sec*
EMP: 10 **EST:** 2015
SALES (est): 710.1K **Privately Held**
Web: www.vensys.de
SIC: 3714 Motor vehicle parts and
  accessories

(G-16871)
VENTURI INC
101 Venturi Ave (02888-1547)
P.O. Box 8699 (02888-0595)
PHONE..............................401 781-2647
Roger Ferragamo, *Pr*
Joseph Ferragamo Junior, *VP*
EMP: 7 **EST:** 1959
SQ FT: 45,000
SALES (est): 419.87K **Privately Held**
Web: www.unittoolco.com
SIC: 3915 3961 Jewelers' findings and
  materials; Costume jewelry

(G-16872)
VILLAGE GOLDSMITH
Also Called: The Village Goldsmith
55 Access Rd Ste 500 (02886-1045)
PHONE..............................401 944-8404
Steven Cipolla, *Pr*
Alan Witten, *Dir*
EMP: 13 **EST:** 1991
SALES (est): 487.14K **Privately Held**
Web: www.village-goldsmith.com
SIC: 7631 3915 3999 3914 Jewelry repair
  services; Jewelers' materials and lapidary
  work; Models, general, except toy;
  Trophies, nsk

(G-16873)
VISHAY EFI INC
Also Called: Vishay Electro-Film,
111 Gilbane St (02886-6901)
PHONE..............................401 738-9150
EMP: 40
SIC: 3679 3674 3676 3675 Electronic
  circuits; Hybrid integrated circuits;
  Electronic resistors; Electronic capacitors

(G-16874)
VOICESCRIPT TECHNOLOGIES
193 Crestwood Rd (02886-9436)
PHONE..............................401 524-2246
Andrew Levine, *CEO*
Bruce Hrovat, *Pr*
EMP: 20 **EST:** 2017
SALES (est): 615.58K **Privately Held**
Web: www.voicescripttech.com
SIC: 7372 Application computer software

(G-16875)
VR INDUSTRIES INC
333 Strawberry Field Rd Ste 6
(02886-2459)
PHONE..............................401 732-6800
Brian Pestana, *CEO*
Brian Pestana, *Pr*
EMP: 35 **EST:** 1985
SQ FT: 35,000
SALES (est): 7.8MM **Privately Held**
Web: www.vrindustries.com
SIC: 3672 Printed circuit boards

(G-16876)
W L FULLER INC
7 Cypress St (02888-2124)
P.O. Box 8767 (02888-0767)
PHONE..............................401 467-2900
Gary Fuller, *Pr*
Deborah Fuller, *
Lisa Fuller, *
Diane Nobile, *
EMP: 27 **EST:** 1930
SQ FT: 14,000
SALES (est): 1.68MM **Privately Held**
Web: www.wlfuller.com
SIC: 3545 5085 Drills (machine tool
  accessories); Industrial supplies

(G-16877)
**WARWICK ICE CREAM
COMPANY**
743 Bald Hill Rd (02886-0713)
PHONE..............................401 821-8403
TOLL FREE: 800
Gerard Bucci Junior, *Pr*
Thomas Bucci, *VP*
Antonette Bucci, *Sec*
EMP: 22 **EST:** 1932
SQ FT: 25,000
SALES (est): 4.85MM **Privately Held**
Web: www.warwickicecreamco.com
SIC: 2024 Ice cream, bulk

(G-16878)
WEHR INDUSTRIES INC
Also Called: Pin-Line
14 Minnesota Ave (02888-6011)
PHONE..............................401 732-6565
W David Wehr, *Pr*
David A Wehr, *Pr*
▲ **EMP:** 25 **EST:** 1989
SQ FT: 9,000
SALES (est): 931.83K **Privately Held**
Web: www.wehrinc.com
SIC: 3479 3961 3911 Engraving jewelry,
  silverware, or metal; Costume jewelry;
  Jewelry, precious metal

(G-16879)
**WIESNER MANUFACTURING
COMPANY**
Also Called: Wiesner Chain
55 Access Rd Ste 700 (02886-1045)
PHONE..............................401 421-2406
Albert F Wiesner Iii, *Pr*
Wayne W Wiesner, *
EMP: 11 **EST:** 1890
SALES (est): 481.23K **Privately Held**
Web: www.apogeeprecisionparts.com
SIC: 3911 3462 Jewelry, precious metal;
  Iron and steel forgings

(G-16880)
WINTECH INTL CORP - NK
Also Called: National Velour-Nk
36 Bellair Ave (02886-2268)
PHONE..............................401 383-3307
Todd Manouelian, *Pr*
EMP: 12 **EST:** 2016
SALES (est): 1.07MM **Privately Held**
Web: www.nationalvelour.com
SIC: 2671 Paper; coated and laminated
  packaging

West Greenwich
Kent County

(G-16881)
**AMERICAN WELDING COMPANY
INC**
689 Hopkins Hill Rd (02817-2563)
P.O. Box 1429 (02816-0026)
PHONE..............................401 397-9155
EMP: 20 **EST:** 1953
SALES (est): 3.37MM **Privately Held**
Web: www.awsteel.com
SIC: 3441 Fabricated structural metal

(G-16882)
AMGEN INC
40 Technology Way (02817-1712)
PHONE..............................401 392-1200
Blair Sparks, *Mgr*
EMP: 100
SALES (corp-wide): 26.32B **Publicly Held**

GEOGRAPHIC

Web: www.amgen.com
SIC: 2836 8731 2834 Biological products, except diagnostic; Biotechnical research, commercial; Drugs affecting parasitic and infective diseases
PA: Amgen Inc.
1 Amgen Center Dr
Thousand Oaks CA 91320
805 447-1000

(G-16883)
CONNEAUT INDUSTRIES INC
Also Called: Chadwick Yarn Co.
89 Hopkins Hill Rd (02817-1709)
P.O. Box 1425 (02816-0026)
PHONE.................................401 392-1110
Lancelot Banfield, *Pr*
Russell C Kibbe, *
Ross G Banfield, *
John P Santos, *
▲ **EMP:** 55 **EST:** 1930
SQ FT: 50,000
SALES (est): 11.59MM **Privately Held**
Web: www.conneaut.com
SIC: 2282 2241 2281 Winding yarn; Braids, textile; Yarn spinning mills

(G-16884)
CRANSTON PRINT WORKS COMPANY
Also Called: Cranston Trucking
25 Hopkins Hill Rd (02817-1707)
P.O. Box 1445 (02816-0027)
PHONE.................................401 397-2442
EMP: 11
SALES (corp-wide): 86.78MM **Privately Held**
Web: www.cranstontrucking.com
SIC: 2261 2262 Bleaching cotton broadwoven fabrics; Bleaching: manmade fiber and silk broadwoven fabrics
PA: Cranston Print Works Company Inc
1381 Cranston St
Cranston RI 02920
401 943-4800

(G-16885)
IGT GLOBAL SOLUTIONS CORP
55 Technology Way (02817-1711)
PHONE.................................401 392-7025
Gillis Hill, *Prin*
EMP: 40
SALES (corp-wide): 4.22B **Privately Held**
Web: www.igt.com
SIC: 3575 7372 2752 Computer terminals; Prepackaged software; Commercial printing, lithographic
HQ: Igt Global Solutions Corporation
10 Memorial Blvd
Providence RI 02903
401 392-7077

(G-16886)
IMMUNEX RHODE ISLAND CORP
40 Technology Way (02817-1700)
PHONE.................................401 392-1200
▲ **EMP:** 122 **EST:** 1987
SALES (est): 51.31MM
SALES (corp-wide): 26.32B **Publicly Held**
SIC: 2834 Pharmaceutical preparations
PA: Amgen Inc.
1 Amgen Center Dr
Thousand Oaks CA 91320
805 447-1000

(G-16887)
LEAVERS LACE CORPORATION
144 Mishnock Rd (02817-1669)
PHONE.................................401 397-5555
Mark Klauber, *Pr*

Gordon Klauber, *
York Roberts, *
Deborah Ruzzo, *
▲ **EMP:** 25 **EST:** 1975
SQ FT: 12,000
SALES (est): 1.63MM **Privately Held**
Web: leaverslacecorp.ypgs.net
SIC: 2258 Lace, knit, nec

(G-16888)
LK GOODWIN CO INC (PA)
Also Called: F S Industries
20 Technology Way (02817-1710)
PHONE.................................401 781-5526
Kenneth Goodwin, *Pr*
Lester K Goodwin Junior, *Pr*
Carol Goodwin, *Sec*
Jeff Goodwin, *VP*
Hope Goodwin, *Treas*
EMP: 13 **EST:** 1972
SQ FT: 9,000
SALES (est): 20.14MM
SALES (corp-wide): 20.14MM **Privately Held**
Web: www.lkgoodwin.com
SIC: 5084 5046 3312 3069 Materials handling machinery; Shelving, commercial and industrial; Structural shapes and pilings, steel; Air-supported rubber structures

(G-16889)
MP MANUFACTURING INC
136 Mishnock Rd (02817-1669)
PHONE.................................203 915-2235
Joseph Acquarulo, *Pr*
EMP: 7
SALES (est): 497.93K **Privately Held**
SIC: 3999 Manufacturing industries, nec

(G-16890)
PAGE MCLELLAN INC
136 Mishnock Rd (02817-1669)
PHONE.................................401 397-2795
Wayne J Mclellan, *Pr*
Diane Mclellan, *Sec*
EMP: 7 **EST:** 1983
SALES (est): 775.85K **Privately Held**
Web: www.mclellanpageinc.com
SIC: 3599 Machine shop, jobbing and repair

(G-16891)
PORTER MACHINE INC
765 Victory Hwy Unit 1 (02817-2111)
P.O. Box 567 (02816-0010)
PHONE.................................401 397-8889
Earl Porter Junior, *Pr*
EMP: 28 **EST:** 1988
SQ FT: 9,500
SALES (est): 4.28MM **Privately Held**
Web: www.portermachineinc.com
SIC: 3599 Machine shop, jobbing and repair

West Kingston
Washington County

(G-16892)
18TH CENTURY WOODWORKS
272 James Trl (02892-1700)
PHONE.................................401 829-8760
Ray Clidence, *Prin*
EMP: 7 **EST:** 2005
SALES (est): 230.96K **Privately Held**
SIC: 2431 Millwork

(G-16893)
ARNOLD LUMBER CO (PA)
Also Called: Main Street Branch Co , The

251 Fairgrounds Rd (02892-1512)
P.O. Box 217 (02892-0217)
PHONE.................................401 783-2266
Arthur P Arnold, *Ch*
Bruce A Charleson, *
Allison Arnold, *
Betty J Arnold, *
Katherine A Carret, *
◆ **EMP:** 75 **EST:** 1952
SQ FT: 90,000
SALES (est): 189MM
SALES (corp-wide): 189MM **Privately Held**
Web: www.arnoldlumber.com
SIC: 5031 5211 2431 Lumber, plywood, and millwork; Insulation material, building; Staircases, stairs and railings

(G-16894)
MODINE MANUFACTURING COMPANY
604 Liberty Ln (02892-1802)
P.O. Box 308 (02892-0308)
PHONE.................................401 792-1231
Robert Bursley, *Mgr*
EMP: 75
SALES (corp-wide): 2.3B **Publicly Held**
Web: www.modine.com
SIC: 3443 Fabricated plate work (boiler shop)
PA: Modine Manufacturing Company Inc
1500 De Koven Ave
Racine WI 53403
262 636-1200

(G-16895)
NEW ENGLAND WOOD PRODUCTS LLC
535 Liberty Ln (02892-1801)
PHONE.................................401 789-7474
EMP: 8 **EST:** 1996
SALES (est): 886.84K **Privately Held**
Web: www.newp.us
SIC: 2499 Woodenware, kitchen and household

(G-16896)
RHODE ISLAND WIRING SVC INC
567 Liberty Ln (02892-1801)
P.O. Box 434 (02892-0434)
PHONE.................................401 789-1955
John H Pease, *Pr*
Patricia Pease, *VP*
Travis Pease, *VP*
EMP: 8 **EST:** 1976
SQ FT: 24,000
SALES (est): 840.73K **Privately Held**
Web: www.riwire.com
SIC: 3714 Automotive wiring harness sets

(G-16897)
SHAIDZON BEER COMPANY LLC
141 Fairgrounds Rd (02892-1512)
P.O. Box 375 (02892-0375)
PHONE.................................401 314-8730
EMP: 10 **EST:** 2017
SALES (est): 692.63K **Privately Held**
Web: www.shaidzonbeer.com
SIC: 2082 Beer (alcoholic beverage)

West Warwick
Kent County

(G-16898)
ADVANCED INTERCONNECTIONS CORP
5 Energy Way (02893-2389)

PHONE.................................401 823-5200
Michael J Murphy, *Pr*
Jim Murphy, *
EMP: 85 **EST:** 1982
SQ FT: 30,000
SALES (est): 23.09MM **Privately Held**
Web: www.advanced.com
SIC: 5065 3678 Electronic parts and equipment, nec; Electronic connectors

(G-16899)
AMTROL HOLDINGS INC
Also Called: Amtrol
1400 Division Rd (02893-2300)
PHONE.................................401 884-6300
EMP: 1300 **EST:** 1996
SQ FT: 270,000
SALES (est): 87.65MM **Privately Held**
Web: www.amtrol.com
SIC: 3822 3585 3443 Refrigeration controls (pressure); Heating equipment, complete; Tanks, lined: metal plate

(G-16900)
AMTROL INC (DH)
1400 Division Rd (02893-2300)
PHONE.................................401 884-6300
Geoff G Gilmore, *Pr*
Marcus A Rogier, *
Dale T Brinkman, *
◆ **EMP:** 450 **EST:** 1946
SQ FT: 270,000
SALES (est): 328.87MM
SALES (corp-wide): 4.92B **Publicly Held**
Web: www.amtrol.com
SIC: 3443 3585 Industrial vessels, tanks, and containers; Heating equipment, complete
HQ: New Amtrol Holdings, Inc.
1400 Division Rd
West Warwick RI 02893
614 438-3210

(G-16901)
AMTROL INTL INVESTMENTS INC (DH)
1400 Division Rd (02893-2300)
PHONE.................................401 884-6300
Larry T Guillemette, *Pr*
◆ **EMP:** 12 **EST:** 1997
SALES (est): 9.76MM
SALES (corp-wide): 4.92B **Publicly Held**
Web: www.amtrol.com
SIC: 3443 3585 Fabricated plate work (boiler shop); Refrigeration and heating equipment
HQ: Amtrol Inc.
1400 Division Rd
West Warwick RI 02893
401 884-6300

(G-16902)
ASTRONOVA INC (PA)
Also Called: Astronova
600 E Greenwich Ave (02893-7526)
PHONE.................................401 828-4000
Gregory A Woods, *Pr*
David S Smith, *VP*
Michael J Natalizia, *VP*
Stephen M Petrarca, *VP Opers*
Tom Carll, *VP*
EMP: 133 **EST:** 1969
SQ FT: 135,500
SALES (est): 142.53MM
SALES (corp-wide): 142.53MM **Publicly Held**
Web: www.astronovainc.com
SIC: 3577 3829 Printers, computer; Measuring and controlling devices, nec

(G-16903)
ASTRONOVA INC
Quick Label Systems
600 E Greenwich Ave (02893-7526)
PHONE...................................401 828-4000
EMP: 250
SALES (corp-wide): 142.53MM **Publicly Held**
Web: www.astronovainc.com
SIC: 3577 3841 Printers, computer; Diagnostic apparatus, medical
PA: Astronova, Inc.
600 E Greenwich Ave
West Warwick RI 02893
401 828-4000

(G-16904)
AURORA FUEL COMPANY INC
191 Pulaski St (02893-5227)
PHONE...................................401 345-5996
Wayne Johnson, *Prin*
EMP: 9 **EST:** 2009
SALES (est): 1.43MM **Privately Held**
Web: aurorafuel.yolasite.com
SIC: 2869 Fuels

(G-16905)
BATTENFELD OF AMERICA INC
31 James P Murphy Ind Hwy (02893-2382)
PHONE...................................401 823-0700
Wolfgang Meyer, *Prin*
EMP: 11 **EST:** 2010
SALES (est): 169.09K **Privately Held**
SIC: 2992 Lubricating oils and greases

(G-16906)
BESS HOME FASHIONS INC
155 Brookside Ave (02893-3800)
PHONE...................................401 828-0300
Michael Litner, *Pr*
Steven Burke, *
▲ **EMP:** 186 **EST:** 2006
SQ FT: 40,000
SALES (est): 2.21MM **Privately Held**
Web: www.natcohome.com
SIC: 2511 2392 Wood household furniture; Scarves: table, dresser, etc.: from purchased materials
PA: Natco Home Fashions, Inc.
155 Brookside Ave
West Warwick RI 02893

(G-16907)
CHASE MACHINE CO INC
Also Called: Chase Machine & Engineering
324 Washington St (02893-5926)
PHONE...................................401 821-8879
Mike Sutila, *VP*
▲ **EMP:** 35 **EST:** 1955
SQ FT: 10,000
SALES (est): 6.36MM **Privately Held**
Web: www.chasemachine.com
SIC: 3599 Machine shop, jobbing and repair

(G-16908)
GUILL TOOL & ENGRG CO INC
10 Pike St (02893-3647)
PHONE...................................401 822-8186
Roger Guillemette, *CEO*
Glen Guillemette, *
Diane Guillemette, *
Claudette Guillemette, *
EMP: 55 **EST:** 1962
SQ FT: 30,000
SALES (est): 8.76MM **Privately Held**
Web: www.guill.com
SIC: 3544 3494 3599 7692 Special dies and tools; Pipe fittings; Machine and other job shop work; Welding repair

(G-16909)
GUILL TOOL AND ENGRG CO INC
20 Pike St (02893-3600)
PHONE...................................401 828-7600
Diane Guillemette, *VP*
EMP: 14 **EST:** 2015
SALES (est): 649.4K **Privately Held**
Web: www.guill.com
SIC: 3599 Flexible metal hose, tubing, and bellows

(G-16910)
HILCO ATHLETIC & GRAPHICS INC
Also Called: Hilco
55 Greenhill St (02893-1516)
PHONE...................................401 822-1775
Jeffrey Hill, *Pr*
EMP: 10 **EST:** 1993
SQ FT: 8,000
SALES (est): 963.26K **Privately Held**
Web: www.hilcoathletic.com
SIC: 2759 7389 2339 2329 Screen printing; Sewing contractor; Uniforms, athletic: women's, misses', and juniors'; Men's and boys' athletic uniforms

(G-16911)
KENT COUNTY DAILY TIMES
Also Called: Free Times
1353 Main St (02893-3859)
P.O. Box 277 (02893-0277)
PHONE...................................401 789-9744
David Dear, *Prin*
Louis Hockman, *Prin*
EMP: 15 **EST:** 1892
SQ FT: 3,000
SALES (est): 214.38K **Privately Held**
Web: www.ricentral.com
SIC: 2711 Commercial printing and newspaper publishing combined

(G-16912)
NAGEL MACHINE CO INC
27 Wightman St (02893-3425)
PHONE...................................401 827-8962
Dorothy Nagel, *Pr*
Ron Nagel, *VP*
EMP: 7 **EST:** 1999
SQ FT: 2,500
SALES (est): 725.64K **Privately Held**
Web: www.nagelmachine.com
SIC: 3599 Machine shop, jobbing and repair

(G-16913)
NATCO HOME FASHIONS INC
Corona Curtain Mfg
155 Brookside Ave (02893-3800)
PHONE...................................401 828-0300
Christine Bolton, *Brnch Mgr*
EMP: 10
Web: www.natcohome.com
SIC: 2391 2221 Curtains, window: made from purchased materials; Bedspreads, silk and manmade fiber
PA: Natco Home Fashions, Inc.
155 Brookside Ave
West Warwick RI 02893

(G-16914)
NATCO HOME FASHIONS INC
Soft Impressions
155 Brookside Ave (02893-3800)
PHONE...................................401 828-0300
Richard Russo, *Brnch Mgr*
EMP: 10
Web: www.natcohome.com

SIC: 2391 2221 Curtains, window: made from purchased materials; Bedspreads, silk and manmade fiber
PA: Natco Home Fashions, Inc.
155 Brookside Ave
West Warwick RI 02893

(G-16915)
NATCO HOME FASHIONS INC (PA)
Also Called: Best Home Fashions
155 Brookside Ave (02893-3800)
P.O. Box 190 (02893-0190)
PHONE...................................401 828-0300
▲ **EMP:** 10 **EST:** 2006
SALES (est): 31.72MM **Privately Held**
Web: www.natcohome.com
SIC: 2221 2391 Bedspreads, silk and manmade fiber; Curtains, window: made from purchased materials

(G-16916)
NATCO PRODUCTS CORPORATION (PA)
Also Called: Natco
155 Brookside Ave (02893-3800)
P.O. Box 190 (02893-0190)
PHONE...................................401 828-0300
Michael Litner, *Pr*
Robert T Galkin, *
Warren B Galkin, *
Steve Rosenbaum, *
Alan Ross, *
◆ **EMP:** 260 **EST:** 1923
SALES (est): 5.26K
SALES (corp-wide): 5.26K **Privately Held**
Web: www.natcohome.com
SIC: 2273 3996 5023 Carpets, textile fiber; Asphalted-felt-base floor coverings: linoleum, carpet; Rugs

(G-16917)
NEW AMTROL HOLDINGS INC (DH)
1400 Division Rd (02893-2323)
PHONE...................................614 438-3210
John P Mcconnell, *CEO*
EMP: 13 **EST:** 2013
SALES (est): 328.87MM
SALES (corp-wide): 4.92B **Publicly Held**
Web: www.amtrol.com
SIC: 3316 Strip, steel, cold-rolled, nec: from purchased hot-rolled,
HQ: Worthington Steel Of Michigan Inc
11700 Worthington Dr
Taylor MI 48180
734 374-3260

(G-16918)
NEW ENGLAND UNION CO INC
107 Hay St (02893-2512)
P.O. Box 70 (02893-0070)
PHONE...................................401 821-0800
Glen S Petit, *Pr*
Brian L Petit, *
EMP: 45 **EST:** 1934
SQ FT: 6,000
SALES (est): 4.8MM **Privately Held**
Web: www.newenglandunion.com
SIC: 3498 3369 Pipe fittings, fabricated from purchased pipe; Nonferrous foundries, nec

(G-16919)
ORIGINAL BRDFORD SOAP WRKS INC (DH)
Also Called: Bradford Soap Works
200 Providence St (02893-2508)
PHONE...................................401 821-2141
John H Howland, *Ex Ch Bd*

Stuart Benton, *
Jimmy Curran, *
Chris Buckley, *
◆ **EMP:** 300 **EST:** 1876
SQ FT: 300,000
SALES (est): 77.83MM
SALES (corp-wide): 227.55MM **Privately Held**
Web: www.bradfordsoap.com
SIC: 2841 Soap: granulated, liquid, cake, flaked, or chip
HQ: Bradford Soap International, Inc.
200 Providence St
West Warwick RI 02893

(G-16920)
PINGA BAKERY INC
Also Called: Westcott Farm
30 Newell St (02893-1825)
PHONE...................................401 821-8007
Michael Pinga, *Pr*
EMP: 10 **EST:** 1956
SQ FT: 12,000
SALES (est): 779.47K **Privately Held**
SIC: 2051 Bread, all types (white, wheat, rye, etc); fresh or frozen

(G-16921)
PUREVITA LABS LLC
153 James P Murphy Ind Hwy (02893-2382)
PHONE...................................401 258-8968
EMP: 10 **EST:** 2018
SALES (est): 1.08MM **Privately Held**
Web: www.purevitalabs.com
SIC: 2869 7371 Laboratory chemicals, organic; Computer software development and applications

(G-16922)
READ DISPLAY
1600 Division Rd Unit 1 (02893-7575)
PHONE...................................401 889-2139
Edward Forer, *CEO*
EMP: 8 **EST:** 2016
SALES (est): 90.43K **Privately Held**
SIC: 2541 Store and office display cases and fixtures

(G-16923)
STANDARD MILL MACHINERY CORP
1370 Main St Ste C (02893-8818)
P.O. Box 1335 (02893-0701)
PHONE...................................401 822-7871
EMP: 7 **EST:** 1995
SQ FT: 15,000
SALES (est): 500K **Privately Held**
Web: www.standardmillmachinery.com
SIC: 3552 Winders, textile machinery

(G-16924)
UNCAS INTERNATIONAL LLC (PA)
Also Called: Crimzon Rose
1600 Division Rd (02893-7574)
PHONE...................................401 231-0266
Steven Oneil, *
David Porcaro, *
▲ **EMP:** 100 **EST:** 1911
SQ FT: 75,000
SALES (est): 27.74MM
SALES (corp-wide): 27.74MM **Privately Held**
Web: www.uncasinternational.com
SIC: 5094 3911 Jewelry; Jewelry, precious metal

(G-16925)
WEST WARWICK SCREW PDTS CO INC
21 Factory St (02893-3708)
P.O. Box 310 (02893-0310)
PHONE..............................401 821-4729
Steven Materne, *Pr*
Carolyn R Materne, *Asst Tr*
EMP: 9 **EST:** 1945
SQ FT: 7,500
SALES (est): 908.12K **Privately Held**
Web:
www.westwarwickscrewproducts.com
SIC: 3451   Screw machine products

(G-16926)
WEST WARWICK WELDING INC
Also Called: U. S. Tank
970 Main St (02893-3527)
PHONE..............................401 822-8200
Louis Campisani, *Pr*
EMP: 15 **EST:** 1943
SQ FT: 26,000
SALES (est): 4.91MM **Privately Held**
Web: www.westwarwickwelding.com
SIC: 3443 7692   Tanks, standard or custom
fabricated: metal plate; Welding repair

Westerly
Washington County

(G-16927)
AMETEK SCP INC (HQ)
Also Called: Ametek Sea Connect Products
52 Airport Rd (02891-3402)
P.O. Box 2236 (02891-0920)
PHONE..............................401 596-6658
Timothy N Jones, *Pr*
David Sapio, *
▲ **EMP:** 60 **EST:** 1993
SQ FT: 30,000
SALES (est): 24.48MM
SALES (corp-wide): 6.15B **Publicly Held**
Web: www.ametekscp.com
SIC: 3678 3496 3643   Electronic connectors;
Cable, uninsulated wire: made from
purchased wire; Current-carrying wiring
services
PA: Ametek, Inc.
1100 Cassatt Rd
Berwyn PA 19312
610 647-2121

(G-16928)
ARCH PARENT INC
13 Airport Rd (02891-3401)
PHONE..............................401 388-9802
EMP: 12898
SALES (corp-wide): 499.13MM **Privately Held**
SIC: 2752   Commercial printing, lithographic
PA: Arch Parent Inc.
9 W 57th St Fl 31
New York NY 10019
212 796-8500

(G-16929)
CIMINI & ASSOCIATES INC
46 Airport Rd (02891-3402)
PHONE..............................401 348-0388
David Cimini, *Pr*
Janette Cimini, *
EMP: 35 **EST:** 1992
SALES (est): 5.24MM **Privately Held**
Web: www.ciminiandassociates.com
SIC: 5094 3356   Precious metals; Precious
metals

(G-16930)
ERSA INC
83 Tom Harvey Rd (02891-3688)
P.O. Box 3066 (02891-0935)
PHONE..............................401 348-4000
Christopher J Andaloro, *Pr*
EMP: 40 **EST:** 1976
SQ FT: 46,000
SALES (est): 5.05MM **Privately Held**
SIC: 3599 8711 7629   Machine shop,
jobbing and repair; Engineering services;
Electrical repair shops

(G-16931)
GRISWOLD TEXTILE PRINT INC
84 White Rock Rd (02891-1224)
P.O. Box 514 (02891-0514)
PHONE..............................401 596-2784
Linda Lockwood Pers, *Prin*
Paul Bergendahl, *
▲ **EMP:** 12 **EST:** 1937
SQ FT: 15,000
SALES (est): 482.37K **Privately Held**
Web: www.griswoldtextile.com
SIC: 2759   Screen printing

(G-16932)
HAUSER FOODS INC
Also Called: Hauser Chocolatier
59 Tom Harvey Rd (02891-3685)
PHONE..............................401 596-8866
Rudolf Hauser Senior, *VP*
Lucille Hauser, *VP*
Rudolf Hauser Junior, *Pr*
▲ **EMP:** 22 **EST:** 1985
SQ FT: 4,000
SALES (est): 3.8MM **Privately Held**
Web: www.hauserchocolates.com
SIC: 2064 5441   Candy and other
confectionery products; Confectionery
produced for direct sale on the premises

(G-16933)
J & R SENIOR SHEET METAL INC
15 Langworthy Rd (02891-3909)
PHONE..............................401 322-1509
EMP: 7 **EST:** 2016
SALES (est): 339.04K **Privately Held**
SIC: 3444   Sheet metalwork

(G-16934)
JERRYS AT MISQUAMICUT INC
Also Called: Electrnic Vsion Access Sltns/V
39 Canal St (02891-1511)
PHONE..............................401 596-3155
Gerald Swerdlick, *Pr*
Gerald Swerdlick, *Pr*
Sara Swerdlick, *VP*
Catherine J Swerdlick, *Sec*
▲ **EMP:** 23 **EST:** 1981
SQ FT: 10,000
SALES (est): 952.1K **Privately Held**
SIC: 7373 3571   Turnkey vendors, computer
systems; Computers, digital, analog or
hybrid

(G-16935)
MAXSON AUTOMATIC MACHINERY CO (PA)
Also Called: Mamco
70 Airport Rd (02891-3428)
PHONE..............................401 596-0162
Joseph F Matthews, *Pr*
Merton L Matthews, *
Michael J Terranova, *
Edward F Fox Junior, *Contrlr*
EMP: 33 **EST:** 1932
SQ FT: 75,000

SALES (est): 9.26MM
SALES (corp-wide): 9.26MM **Privately Held**
Web: www.maxsonautomatic.com
SIC: 3554 3317   Paper industries machinery;
Steel pipe and tubes

(G-16936)
MMJ BIOPHARMA CULTIVATION INC
1 Crosswind Dr (02891-3679)
PHONE..............................800 586-7863
Elio Mariani, *CEO*
EMP: 10 **EST:** 2021
SALES (est): 750.8K **Privately Held**
Web:
www.mmjbiopharmacultivation.com
SIC: 2834   Pharmaceutical preparations

(G-16937)
MOORE COMPANY
Darlington Fabrics
48 Canal St (02891-1539)
PHONE..............................401 596-0219
Peter Moore, *Brnch Mgr*
EMP: 47
SALES (corp-wide): 81.32MM **Privately Held**
Web: www.themooreco.com
SIC: 2258   Fabric finishing, warp knit
PA: The Moore Company
36 Beach St
Westerly RI 02891
401 596-2816

(G-16938)
MOORE COMPANY (PA)
Also Called: Darlington Fabrics
36 Beach St (02891-2771)
P.O. Box 538 (02891-0538)
PHONE..............................401 596-2816
Alexandra Moore, *Pr*
Dana Barlow, *
Alexandra Moore, *Ex VP*
Janet Robidoux, *
◆ **EMP:** 180 **EST:** 1909
SQ FT: 150,000
SALES (est): 81.32MM
SALES (corp-wide): 81.32MM **Privately Held**
Web: www.themooreco.com
SIC: 2258 2241   Fabric finishing, warp knit;
Manmade fiber narrow woven fabrics

(G-16939)
MOORE COMPANY
Fulflex
36 Beach St (02891-2771)
PHONE..............................401 596-2816
Jon Senior, *Mgr*
EMP: 47
SALES (corp-wide): 81.32MM **Privately Held**
Web: www.themooreco.com
SIC: 2258 2241 3069 3061   Fabric finishing,
warp knit; Manmade fiber narrow woven
fabrics; Tape, pressure sensitive: rubber;
Appliance rubber goods (mechanical)
PA: The Moore Company
36 Beach St
Westerly RI 02891
401 596-2816

(G-16940)
NIDALO F & B LLC
Also Called: Noodle Revolution
87 Oak St (02891-1736)
PHONE..............................401 596-9559
John F Reis Esq, *Prin*
EMP: 8 **EST:** 2016

SALES (est): 346.55K **Privately Held**
Web: www.noodlerev.com
SIC: 2098   Noodles (e.g. egg, plain, and
water), dry

(G-16941)
NORTHEAST LDSCPG TREE SVCS INC
Also Called: Snow Plowing / Landscaping
128 Oak St (02891-1715)
P.O. Box 551 (02804-0006)
PHONE..............................860 405-5274
Antonio Portunato, *Pr*
EMP: 17 **EST:** 2017
SALES (est): 17.45MM **Privately Held**
SIC: 0781 3991   Landscape services; Street
sweeping brooms, hand or machine

(G-16942)
ROL-FLO ENGINEERING INC
85a Tom Harvey Rd (02891-3691)
PHONE..............................401 596-0060
Randall Orlomoski, *Pr*
Richard Orlomoksi, *VP*
EMP: 13 **EST:** 1978
SQ FT: 7,400
SALES (est): 775.44K **Privately Held**
Web: www.rolflo.com
SIC: 3544 3545   Special dies and tools;
Machine tool accessories

(G-16943)
TMC RHODE ISLAND COMPANY INC
36 Beach St (02891-2728)
P.O. Box 538 (02891-0538)
PHONE..............................401 596-2816
Dana Barlow, *Pr*
EMP: 29 **EST:** 2000
SALES (est): 804.67K **Privately Held**
Web: www.themooreco.com
SIC: 3069   Tape, pressure sensitive: rubber

(G-16944)
TOM AND SALLYS HANDMADE CHOCO
59 Tom Harvey Rd (02891-3685)
PHONE..............................800 289-8783
Thomas E Fegley, *Ch*
Sally E Fegley, *Pr*
EMP: 11 **EST:** 1989
SQ FT: 11,000
SALES (est): 1.22MM **Privately Held**
SIC: 2064 5145 5441   Candy and other
confectionery products; Candy; Candy

(G-16945)
US EXTRUDERS INC
87 Tom Harvey Rd (02891-3688)
PHONE..............................401 584-4710
Bill Kramer, *Pr*
EMP: 15 **EST:** 2017
SALES (est): 2.65MM **Privately Held**
Web: www.us-extruders.com
SIC: 3559   Plastics working machinery

Woonsocket
Providence County

(G-16946)
AIDANCE SCIENTIFIC INC
Also Called: Aidance Skncare Tpcal Slutions
184 Burnside Ave (02895-2114)
P.O. Box 2182 (02895-0953)
PHONE..............................401 432-7750
Perry Antelman, *CEO*
Perry Antelman, *Pr*

Ted Gerlach, *
EMP: 57 **EST:** 2004
SALES (est): 9.11MM **Privately Held**
Web: www.aidanceproducts.com
SIC: 2834   Pharmaceutical preparations

(G-16947)
AMAZING MOBILE
1096 Social St (02895-1329)
PHONE..............................401 597-0566
Felix Fernandez, *Prin*
EMP: 9 **EST:** 2013
SALES (est): 73.59K **Privately Held**
SIC: 2821   Plastics materials and resins

(G-16948)
AMERICAN CORD & WEBBING CO INC
Also Called: A C W
88 Century Dr Ste 1 (02895-6172)
PHONE..............................401 762-5500
Mark Krauss, *Pr*
◆ **EMP:** 44 **EST:** 1918
SQ FT: 35,000
SALES (est): 21.34MM **Privately Held**
Web: www.acw1.com
SIC: 5131 2241 3466 3089   Narrow fabrics; Narrow fabric mills; Closures, stamped metal; Closures, plastics

(G-16949)
AXIS MACHINING INC
549 River St (02895-1819)
PHONE..............................401 766-9911
EMP: 7 **EST:** 1996
SQ FT: 3,000
SALES (est): 860.19K **Privately Held**
SIC: 3599   Machine shop, jobbing and repair

(G-16950)
BLACKSTONE MOLDING INC
Also Called: P M I
100 Founders Dr (02895-6154)
PHONE..............................401 765-6700
William Ober, *Pr*
Susan Ober, *VP*
EMP: 23 **EST:** 1979
SQ FT: 30,000
SALES (est): 9.35MM
SALES (corp-wide): 16.66MM **Privately Held**
Web: www.mearthane.com
SIC: 3089   Injection molding of plastics
PA: Mearthane Products, Llc
16 Western Industrial Dr
Cranston RI 02921
401 946-4400

(G-16951)
BOUCKAERT INDUS TEXTILES INC
235 Singleton St (02895-6907)
PHONE..............................401 769-5474
Max Brockle, *CEO*
Rob Dirienzo, *
Tom Bouckaert, *
▲ **EMP:** 43 **EST:** 1988
SQ FT: 60,000
SALES (est): 7.85MM **Privately Held**
Web: www.bitfelt.com
SIC: 2231   Felts, blanketing and upholstery fabrics: wool

(G-16952)
CABINET GALLERY LTD (PA)
Also Called: Cabby Chic
245 Privilege St (02895-1238)
P.O. Box 336 (02895-0781)
PHONE..............................401 762-4300

Roger E Landry, *Pr*
Donna L Landry, *VP*
EMP: 7 **EST:** 1985
SQ FT: 11,000
SALES (est): 4.42MM
SALES (corp-wide): 4.42MM **Privately Held**
Web: www.cabinetgalleryltd.com
SIC: 5211 1799 7389 2541   Cabinets, kitchen ; Kitchen cabinet installation; Design services; Showcases, except refrigerated: wood

(G-16953)
CNC INTERNATIONAL INC
20 Privilege St (02895-1239)
PHONE..............................401 769-6100
Bruce D Moger, *Ch*
EMP: 9 **EST:** 2017
SALES (est): 328.6K **Privately Held**
SIC: 2999   Waxes, petroleum: not produced in petroleum refineries

(G-16954)
CNC INTERNATIONAL LTD PARTNR
20 Privilege St (02895-1239)
P.O. Box 14097 (02914-0097)
PHONE..............................401 769-6100
Bruce Moger, *Pt*
▼ **EMP:** 11 **EST:** 1967
SQ FT: 225,000
SALES (est): 479.87K **Privately Held**
Web: www.karkraftsystems.com
SIC: 2843   Surface active agents

(G-16955)
COSCO LLC
707 Park East Dr (02895-6158)
PHONE..............................401 765-0009
Ann Marie Costantino, *Pr*
David Costantino, *
EMP: 62 **EST:** 1986
SALES (est): 10MM **Privately Held**
Web: www.coscofence.com
SIC: 1799 1611 3444   Fence construction; Guardrail construction, highways; Sheet metalwork

(G-16956)
DIEBOLD NIXDORF INCORPORATED
1919 Diamond Hill Rd (02895-1538)
PHONE..............................401 766-3606
EMP: 7
SALES (corp-wide): 3.46B **Publicly Held**
Web: www.dieboldnixdorf.com
SIC: 3578   Automatic teller machines (ATM)
PA: Diebold Nixdorf, Incorporated
50 Executive Pkwy
Hudson OH 44236
330 490-4000

(G-16957)
DURALECTRA-CHN LLC
Also Called: Precision Coating
1 Shorr Ct (02895-2062)
PHONE..............................401 597-5000
Steven Schaepe, *
John Tetault, *
EMP: 85 **EST:** 2008
SALES (est): 10.93MM
SALES (corp-wide): 47.68MM **Privately Held**
SIC: 3479   Coating of metals and formed products
PA: Katahdin Industries, Inc.
51 Parmenter Rd
Hudson MA 01749
781 329-1420

(G-16958)
EPOXYTECH INC
Also Called: Epoxyset
718 Park East Dr (02895-6159)
P.O. Box 1256 (02895-0826)
PHONE..............................401 726-4500
Sukirtee Patel, *Pr*
Kiran Patel, *VP*
EMP: 20 **EST:** 1998
SQ FT: 23,000
SALES (est): 3.16MM **Privately Held**
Web: www.epoxysetinc.com
SIC: 2821   Thermosetting materials

(G-16959)
FAIRMOUNT FOUNDRY INC
25 2nd Ave (02895-5194)
PHONE..............................401 769-1585
James W De Witt, *Pr*
Jean De Witt, *Sec*
Gerald Dewitt, *VP*
EMP: 27 **EST:** 1917
SQ FT: 30,000
SALES (est): 1.06MM **Privately Held**
Web: www.fairmountfdry.com
SIC: 3321   Gray iron castings, nec

(G-16960)
FRANK B STRUZIK INC
129 Ballou St (02895-5108)
P.O. Box 985 (02895-0910)
PHONE..............................401 766-6880
Frank B Struzik, *Pr*
▲ **EMP:** 10 **EST:** 1956
SQ FT: 14,000
SALES (est): 802.79K **Privately Held**
SIC: 2298   Cord, braided

(G-16961)
FRIENDS FOUNDRY INC
416 Pond St (02895-1220)
PHONE..............................401 769-0160
Normand Vadenais, *Pr*
Paul Vadenais, *Sec*
John Vadenais, *VP*
EMP: 10 **EST:** 1967
SQ FT: 12,000
SALES (est): 990.87K **Privately Held**
SIC: 3366   Copper foundries

(G-16962)
HANNA INSTRUMENTS INC (PA)
584 Park East Dr (02895-6177)
PHONE..............................401 765-7500
Martino Nardo, *Pr*
Anna Maria Nardo, *
Pamela Nardo, *
▲ **EMP:** 40 **EST:** 1986
SQ FT: 26,000
SALES (est): 25.82MM **Privately Held**
Web: www.hannainst.com
SIC: 3825 3845 3826 3823   Electrical power measuring equipment; Electromedical equipment; Analytical instruments; Process control instruments

(G-16963)
HOPE WOODWORKS INC
684 Jillson Ave (02895-5941)
PHONE..............................401 497-7714
EMP: 7 **EST:** 2019
SALES (est): 54.13K **Privately Held**
Web: www.highhopewoodworks.com
SIC: 2431   Millwork

(G-16964)
HYMAN BRICKLE & SON INC (PA)
Also Called: Northwest Woolen Mills

235 Singleton St (02895-6907)
PHONE..............................401 769-0189
Samuel Brickle, *CEO*
Max Brickle, *Pr*
Shannon Mcgrath, *CFO*
Paulette Butler, *Dir*
◆ **EMP:** 15 **EST:** 1931
SQ FT: 120,000
SALES (est): 23.27MM
SALES (corp-wide): 23.27MM **Privately Held**
Web: www.thebricklegroup.com
SIC: 2299 5093   Wool felts, pressed or needle loom; Textile waste

(G-16965)
IMPREGLON INC
Also Called: Aalberts Surface Technologies
222 Goldstein Dr (02895-6174)
PHONE..............................401 766-3353
EMP: 10 **EST:** 2010
SALES (est): 480.37K **Privately Held**
Web: www.aalberts-st.us
SIC: 3559   Metal finishing equipment for plating, etc.

(G-16966)
JCC RESIDUAL LTD
Also Called: Jeweled Cross
811 Park East Dr (02895-6112)
P.O. Box 4910 (02916-0910)
PHONE..............................508 699-4401
James S Brennan Ii, *Pr*
James S Brennan, *
Gary S Beyer, *
▲ **EMP:** 19 **EST:** 1923
SQ FT: 20,000
SALES (est): 544.27K **Privately Held**
SIC: 3961 3911   Costume jewelry; Necklaces, precious metal

(G-16967)
LOST BROTHERS PALLET CORP
333 River St (02895-2933)
P.O. Box 485 (02895-0485)
PHONE..............................401 585-7194
Robert Montero Junior, *Pr*
EMP: 17 **EST:** 2014
SQ FT: 23,000
SALES (est): 2.28MM **Privately Held**
Web: robert-monteiro.squarespace.com
SIC: 2448   Pallets, wood

(G-16968)
LSI INDUSTRIES INC
601 Park East Dr (02895-6158)
PHONE..............................401 766-7446
EMP: 9 **EST:** 2019
SALES (est): 242.41K **Privately Held**
SIC: 3993   Electric signs

(G-16969)
NORTHERN PRODUCTS INC
153 Hamlet Ave (02895-4837)
P.O. Box 1175 (02895-0819)
EMP: 10
SIC: 2819 2891   Chemicals, high purity: refined from technical grade; Adhesives, plastic

(G-16970)
P M RECYCLING
24 E Mill St (02895-8270)
P.O. Box 149 (02895-0780)
PHONE..............................401 765-0330
EMP: 30 **EST:** 1991
SQ FT: 45,000
SALES (est): 7.32MM **Privately Held**
Web: www.pmrecyclingpallets.com

SIC: 4953 2448   Recycling, waste materials;
Pallets, wood

(G-16971)
**PARKINSON MACHINERY &
MANUFACTURING CORP**
Also Called: Marshall & Williams Plastics
100 Goldstein Dr (02895-6169)
PHONE..............................401 762-2100
◆ **EMP:** 110 **EST:** 1879
SALES (est): 10.47MM **Privately Held**
Web: www.parkinsontechnologies.com
SIC: 3089 3542 3552   Plastics processing;
Pressing machines; Winders, textile
machinery

(G-16972)
**PARKINSON TECHNOLOGIES
INC**
Also Called: Parkinson Technologies
100 Goldstein Dr (02895-6169)
PHONE..............................401 762-2100
▲ **EMP:** 100 **EST:** 1993
SALES (est): 16.69MM **Privately Held**
Web: www.parkinsontechnologies.com
SIC: 3089   Plastics processing

(G-16973)
RALCO INDUSTRIES INC (PA)
Also Called: Plastic Group, The
1112 River St (02895-1861)
PHONE..............................401 765-1000
Robert Lebeaux, *Pr*
Michael Rosenthal, *
EMP: 30 **EST:** 1978
SQ FT: 70,000
SALES (est): 14.38MM
SALES (corp-wide): 14.38MM **Privately
Held**
Web: www.plasticsgroup.com
SIC: 2821   Plastics materials and resins

(G-16974)
**SPORTS SYSTEMS CUSTOM
BAGS**
44 Hazel St (02895-1228)
P.O. Box 1225 (02895-0826)
PHONE..............................401 767-3770
Marc Staelen, *Pr*
EMP: 100 **EST:** 1975
SQ FT: 150,000
SALES (est): 3.8MM **Privately Held**
Web: www.sscbags.com
SIC: 3949   Sporting and athletic goods, nec

(G-16975)
SUMMER INFANT INC (HQ)
1275 Park East Dr (02895-6185)
PHONE..............................401 671-6550
Stuart Noyes, *CEO*
▲ **EMP:** 107 **EST:** 1985
SQ FT: 20,200
SALES (est): 143.66MM
SALES (corp-wide): 202.1MM **Privately
Held**
Web: www.kids2.com
SIC: 2514 2399 3842 3261   Juvenile
furniture, household: metal; Infant carriers;
Personal safety equipment; Bathroom
accessories/fittings, vitreous china or
earthenware
PA: Kids2, Llc
3333 Piedmont Rd Ne # 180
Atlanta GA 30305
770 751-0442

(G-16976)
SUMMER INFANT (USA) INC
1275 Park East Dr (02895-6185)

PHONE..............................401 671-6551
▲ **EMP:** 183 **EST:** 2006
SALES (est): 24.67MM
SALES (corp-wide): 202.1MM **Privately
Held**
Web: www.kids2.com
SIC: 2399   Infant carriers
HQ: Summer Infant, Inc.
1275 Park East Dr
Woonsocket RI 02895
401 671-6550

(G-16977)
SUPREME DAIRY FARMS
171 Saint Augustin St (02895-6126)
PHONE..............................401 739-8180
Paul Areson, *Pr*
▲ **EMP:** 10 **EST:** 2006
SQ FT: 15,000
SALES (est): 2.45MM **Privately Held**
Web: www.registrar-transfers.com
SIC: 5141 2022   Groceries, general line;
Cheese; natural and processed

(G-16978)
SURPLUS SOLUTIONS LLC
2010 Diamond Hill Rd (02895-1542)
PHONE..............................401 526-0055
Joseph D'alton, *Pr*
EMP: 15 **EST:** 2006
SQ FT: 137,800
SALES (est): 4.86MM **Privately Held**
Web: www.ssllc.com
SIC: 3821 5047 5122   Laboratory
equipment: fume hoods, distillation racks,
etc.; Medical and hospital equipment;
Pharmaceuticals

(G-16979)
T & T WOODWORKERS INC
500 Pond St (02895-1220)
PHONE..............................401 766-2304
EMP: 12 **EST:** 2019
SALES (est): 354.56K **Privately Held**
Web: www.tandtwoodworkers.com
SIC: 2431   Millwork

(G-16980)
TEAM INC
Also Called: Textile Engineering & Mfg
841 Park East Dr (02895-6112)
P.O. Box 25 (02895-0779)
PHONE..............................401 762-1500
Steve Clarke, *Pr*
Jerry Moore, *VP Mfg*
▲ **EMP:** 22 **EST:** 1995
SQ FT: 30,000
SALES (est): 4.29MM **Privately Held**
Web: www.teamtextiles.com
SIC: 2297 2299 2221 3624   Nonwoven
fabrics; Yarns and thread, made from non-
fabric materials; Manmade and synthetic
broadwoven fabrics; Fibers, carbon and
graphite

(G-16981)
TEX FLOCK INC
200 Founders Dr (02895-6119)
PHONE..............................401 765-2340
Edward T Abramek Junior, *Ch Bd*
◆ **EMP:** 35 **EST:** 1965
SQ FT: 33,000
SALES (est): 4.8MM **Privately Held**
Web: flocktex.godaddysites.com
SIC: 2262 2299 3086 2671   Flock printing:
manmade fiber and silk broadwoven fabrics
; Flock (recovered textile fibers); Plastics
foam products; Paper; coated and
laminated packaging

(G-16982)
**ULTRA FINE SPECIALTY PDTS
LLC**
500 Park East Dr (02895-6148)
PHONE..............................401 488-4987
Jeffrey Peterson, *CEO*
Dennis Gottilla, *CFO*
Michael Hinchion, *CLO*
EMP: 15 **EST:** 2020
SALES (est): 2.92MM
SALES (corp-wide): 8.75MM **Privately
Held**
Web: www.ultrafinepowder.com
SIC: 3399   Metal powders, pastes, and flakes
PA: Novamet Specialty Products
Corporation
1420 Toshiba Dr E
Lebanon TN 37087
615 466-9999

Wyoming
Washington County

(G-16983)
VIBCO INC (PA)
75 Stilson Rd (02898-1027)
P.O. Box 8 (02898-0008)
PHONE..............................401 539-2392
Ted S Wadensten, *Pr*
Karl Wadensten, *
Karl A Wadensten, *
Aina E Wadensten, *
▼ **EMP:** 71 **EST:** 1962
SQ FT: 52,000
SALES (est): 21.7MM
SALES (corp-wide): 21.7MM **Privately
Held**
Web: www.vibco.com
SIC: 3531   Vibrators for concrete
construction

VERMONT

Alburg
Grand Isle County

(G-16984)
UV III SYSTEMS INC
59 Cedarvale Est (05440-9698)
PHONE..............................508 883-4881
Gordon B Knight, *Pr*
Loretta M Knight, *VP*
EMP: 10 **EST:** 1984
SQ FT: 8,000
SALES (est): 596.29K **Privately Held**
Web: www.uv3.com
SIC: 3648   Ultraviolet lamp fixtures

Arlington
Bennington County

(G-16985)
ARLINGTON INDUSTRIES INC
Also Called: Quadra-Tek
2617 Vt Route 7a (05250-8882)
PHONE..............................802 375-6139
John N Haugsrud, *Pr*
EMP: 32 **EST:** 1968
SALES (est): 4.32MM **Privately Held**
Web: www.quadra-tek.com
SIC: 3089   Injection molding of plastics

(G-16986)
ART LICENSING INTL INC
6366 Vt Route 7a (05250-8427)
P.O. Box 2568 (05255-2568)
PHONE..............................802 362-3662
Jack Appelman, *Admn*
EMP: 25 **EST:** 2012
SALES (est): 987.51K **Privately Held**
Web: www.artlicensing.com
SIC: 2741   Miscellaneous publishing

(G-16987)
HBH PRESTAIN INC (PA)
1223 E Arlington Rd (05250-8620)
P.O. Box 1103 (05250-1103)
PHONE..............................802 375-9723
Edward Hawley, *Pr*
Frederick Hawley, *VP*
▲ **EMP:** 35 **EST:** 1988
SQ FT: 20,000
SALES (est): 4.99MM **Privately Held**
SIC: 2491   Wood preserving

(G-16988)
MACK GROUP INC (PA)
608 Warm Brook Rd (05250-8570)
PHONE..............................802 375-2511
Donald S Kendall Iii, *Pr*
Florence Belnap, *
◆ **EMP:** 400 **EST:** 1997
SQ FT: 300,000
SALES (est): 856.43MM
SALES (corp-wide): 856.43MM **Privately
Held**
Web: www.mack.com
SIC: 3089 3577 6719   Injection molding of
plastics; Computer peripheral equipment,
nec; Investment holding companies, except
banks

(G-16989)
MACK MOLDING COMPANY INC
79 E Arlington Rd (05250-8609)
PHONE..............................802 375-0500
Bud Pagliccia, *Brnch Mgr*
EMP: 167
SALES (corp-wide): 856.43MM **Privately
Held**
Web: www.mack.com
SIC: 3089   Injection molding of plastics
HQ: Mack Molding Company, Inc.
608 Warm Brook Rd
Arlington VT 05250
802 375-2511

(G-16990)
**MACK MOLDING COMPANY INC
(HQ)**
608 Warm Brook Rd (05250-8570)
PHONE..............................802 375-2511
Donald S Kendall Iii, *Pr*
Jeffrey Somple, *
◆ **EMP:** 250 **EST:** 1920
SQ FT: 310,000
SALES (est): 476.08MM
SALES (corp-wide): 856.43MM **Privately
Held**
Web: www.mack.com
SIC: 3089 3577   Injection molding of plastics
; Computer peripheral equipment, nec
PA: Mack Group, Inc.
608 Warm Brook Rd
Arlington VT 05250
802 375-2511

(G-16991)
OLD MILL ROAD MEDIA LLC
Also Called: Manchester Life
316 Old Mill Rd (05250-4302)
PHONE..............................802 375-1366

▲ = Import ▼ = Export
◆ = Import/Export

EMP: 16 **EST:** 2019
SALES (est): 1.08MM **Privately Held**
Web: www.oldmillroadmedia.com
SIC: 2721 Magazines: publishing only, not printed on site

(G-16992)
VERMONTS ORGINAL ICE CREAM INC
Also Called: Wilcox Ice Cream
116 Sweet St E (05250)
PHONE.............................802 375-1133
Craig Wilcox, *Pr*
Chris Wilcox, *VP*
EMP: 8 **EST:** 2001
SQ FT: 1,500
SALES (est): 925.98K **Privately Held**
Web: www.wilcox-ice-cream.com
SIC: 5143 2024 Frozen dairy desserts; Ice cream and frozen deserts

Ascutney
Windsor County

(G-16993)
NEIL H DANIELS INC
Also Called: Daniels Construction
4409 Route 5 (05030)
P.O. Box 246 (05030-0246)
PHONE.............................802 674-6323
Mark S Thompson, *Pr*
Peter M Daniels, *
Neil H Daniels, *
EMP: 30 **EST:** 1965
SQ FT: 5,000
SALES (est): 7.64MM **Privately Held**
Web: www.neilhdaniels.com
SIC: 1622 1541 3541 Bridge construction; Industrial buildings, new construction, nec; Machine tools, metal cutting type

Barnard
Windsor County

(G-16994)
MT JOHNSON INC
1567 Mt Hunger Rd (05031)
P.O. Box 884 (05031-0884)
PHONE.............................802 234-6827
Michael Johnson, *Pr*
Timothy Johnson, *VP*
EMP: 7 **EST:** 2013
SALES (est): 532.96K **Privately Held**
SIC: 2411 Logging

Barnet
Caledonia County

(G-16995)
VERMONT MOLD & TOOL CORP
Also Called: Vermont Microtechnologies
4693 Garland HI (05821-9504)
PHONE.............................802 633-2300
John Mullen, *CEO*
EMP: 8 **EST:** 1963
SALES (est): 1.16MM **Privately Held**
Web: www.vermontmicrodrilling.com
SIC: 3544 3825 Special dies and tools; Semiconductor test equipment

Barre
Washington County

(G-16996)
ACCURA PRINTING
80 East Rd (05641-5391)
P.O. Box 529 (05670-0529)
PHONE.............................802 476-4429
Garritt Bresett, *Pr*
Robin Parry, *Sec*
EMP: 10 **EST:** 1987
SQ FT: 6,000
SALES (est): 474.72K **Privately Held**
Web: www.accuraprinting.com
SIC: 2791 2752 Typesetting; Commercial printing, lithographic

(G-16997)
BETH MUELLER INC
Also Called: Beth Mueller Design
13 Pleasant St (05641-3454)
PHONE.............................802 476-3582
Beth Mueller, *Pr*
Philip Morris, *VP*
EMP: 7 **EST:** 1985
SALES (est): 387.59K **Privately Held**
Web: www.bethmueller.com
SIC: 3269 Art and ornamental ware, pottery

(G-16998)
BUTTURA & SONS INC
Also Called: Buttura Gherardi Gran Artisans
109 Boynton St (05641-4905)
P.O. Box 606 (05641-0606)
PHONE.............................802 476-6646
Mark A Gherardi, *Pr*
Paige Lamthi, *
Milton Todd, *
▲ **EMP:** 50 **EST:** 1928
SALES (est): 4.61MM **Privately Held**
Web: www.graniteartisans.com
SIC: 3281 Granite, cut and shaped

(G-16999)
CARROLL CONCRETE CO
379 Granger Rd (05641-5368)
P.O. Box 1000 (03773-1000)
PHONE.............................802 229-0191
EMP: 9 **EST:** 2009
SALES (est): 88.85K **Privately Held**
Web: www.carrollconcrete.com
SIC: 3273 Ready-mixed concrete

(G-17000)
DESSUREAU MACHINES INC
53 Granite St (05641-4139)
P.O. Box 402 (05641-0402)
PHONE.............................802 476-4561
Mark C Dessureau, *Pr*
Arthur J Dessureau, *Prin*
EMP: 19 **EST:** 1940
SQ FT: 15,000
SALES (est): 3.08MM **Privately Held**
Web: www.dessureau.com
SIC: 3599 3291 Machine shop, jobbing and repair; Abrasive products

(G-17001)
GLOUCESTER ASSOCIATES INC
Also Called: DMS Machining & Fabrication
10 Transport Dr # 1 (05641-4937)
PHONE.............................802 479-1088
Byrom Atwood, *Pr*
Charles Atwood, *
Diane Atwood, *
EMP: 35 **EST:** 1991
SQ FT: 60,000
SALES (est): 4.05MM **Privately Held**
Web: www.dmsmachine.com
SIC: 3599 3444 7692 Custom machinery; Sheet metalwork; Welding repair

(G-17002)
GRANITE IMPORTERS INC (PA)
Also Called: Granite Importers Transport
16 S Vine St (05641-4032)
P.O. Box 712 (05641-0712)
PHONE.............................802 476-5812
Bruce Colgan, *VP*
Sandra Colgan, *Pr*
▲ **EMP:** 23 **EST:** 1971
SQ FT: 30,000
SALES (est): 2.39MM
SALES (corp-wide): 2.39MM **Privately Held**
Web: www.graniteimporters.com
SIC: 3281 Cut stone and stone products

(G-17003)
GRANITE INDUSTRIES VERMONT INC
Also Called: Giv
Vanneti Place (05641)
P.O. Box 537 (05641-0537)
PHONE.............................800 451-3236
Jeffrey Martell, *Pr*
Forrest Rouelle, *
◆ **EMP:** 52 **EST:** 1971
SQ FT: 47,000
SALES (est): 9.95MM
SALES (corp-wide): 2.1MM **Privately Held**
Web: www.granitevermont.com
SIC: 3281 Granite, cut and shaped
HQ: Polycor Stone Corporation
200 Georgia Marble Ln
Tate GA 30177

(G-17004)
H P HOOD-BOOTH BROTHERS DAIRY
219 Allen St (05641-5433)
PHONE.............................802 476-6605
Norman Booth, *Pr*
Thomas Booth, *
Marcell Booth, *
EMP: 10
SQ FT: 60,000
SALES (est): 919.09K **Privately Held**
SIC: 5143 2026 Milk and cream, fluid; Fluid milk

(G-17005)
HILLSIDE SOLID SURFACES
Also Called: Hillside Stone Product
37 Gable Pl (05641)
P.O. Box 134 (05641-0134)
PHONE.............................802 479-2508
Randy Carbonneau, *Pr*
Sarah Summerley, *VP*
EMP: 10 **EST:** 1949
SQ FT: 12,200
SALES (est): 1.16MM **Privately Held**
Web: www.hillsidestone.com
SIC: 3281 Granite, cut and shaped

(G-17006)
HOULE BROS GRANITE CO INC
25 S Front St (05641-2530)
PHONE.............................802 476-6825
Charles J Houle, *Pr*
Roger Houle, *VP*
EMP: 14 **EST:** 1956
SQ FT: 32,537
SALES (est): 2.44MM **Privately Held**
Web: www.houlebrothers.com
SIC: 1411 Dimension stone

(G-17007)
HUTCHINS ROOFING COMPANY INC
Also Called: Lbh Jr
17 W Second St (05641-2510)
P.O. Box 948 (05641-0948)
PHONE.............................802 476-5591
TOLL FREE: 800
Lloyd Hutchins Junior, *Pr*
Nancy Hutchins, *VP*
EMP: 11 **EST:** 1993
SALES (est): 481.21K **Privately Held**
Web: www.hutchinsroofing.com
SIC: 1761 3444 Roofing contractor; Sheet metalwork

(G-17008)
IDRY LLC
29 Pitman Rd (05641-8943)
PHONE.............................800 406-1887
EMP: 9 **EST:** 2018
SALES (est): 1.06MM **Privately Held**
Web: www.idrywood.com
SIC: 2431 Millwork

(G-17009)
INTERNATIONAL STONE PRODUCTS (PA)
21 Metro Way (05641-4478)
PHONE.............................802 476-6636
John Dernavich, *Pr*
Rodney Dernavich, *
Paul Dernavich, *
Dorothy R Dernavich, *
EMP: 75 **EST:** 1937
SQ FT: 100,000
SALES (est): 4.76MM
SALES (corp-wide): 4.76MM **Privately Held**
SIC: 3281 1411 Monuments, cut stone (not finishing or lettering only); Dimension stone

(G-17010)
JET SERVICE ENVELOPE CO INC (PA)
Also Called: Fortune Marketing
80 East Rd (05641-5391)
PHONE.............................802 229-9335
Jeffrey Blow, *Pr*
EMP: 8 **EST:** 1915
SQ FT: 14,000
SALES (est): 1.43MM
SALES (corp-wide): 1.43MM **Privately Held**
Web: www.jetservice-envelope.com
SIC: 2759 Envelopes: printing, nsk

(G-17011)
JOES CSTM MFG QLTY MMRALS INC
874 E Barre Rd (05641-9017)
PHONE.............................800 787-4004
Gerard Perreault, *CEO*
EMP: 7 **EST:** 2008
SALES (est): 91.37K **Privately Held**
Web: www.joescustomman.com
SIC: 3272 Floor slabs and tiles, precast concrete

(G-17012)
L BROWN AND SONS PRINTING INC
14 Jefferson St # 20 (05641-4249)
PHONE.............................802 476-3164
Lawrence Brown, *Pr*
Diane Brown, *
EMP: 32 **EST:** 1988
SQ FT: 22,000

SALES (est): 2.34MM **Privately Held**
Web: www.lbrownandsonsprinting.com
SIC: 2752 7331 2791 2789 Offset printing;
Mailing service; Typesetting; Bookbinding
and related work

(G-17013)
MEMORIAL SANDBLAST INC
15 Blackwell St (05641-4052)
P.O. Box 582 (05641-0582)
PHONE..............................802 476-7086
John M Pelkey, *Pr*
Robert Pelkey, *VP*
Sharon Pelkey, *Treas*
Brynn Pelkey, *Sec*
EMP: 8 EST: 1989
SALES (est): 862.91K **Privately Held**
Web: www.cochrans-monuments.com
SIC: 3281 Curbing, granite or stone

(G-17014)
OLD ROUTE TWO SPIRITS INC
Also Called: Quiver Spirits
69 Pitman Rd (05641-8920)
P.O. Box 205 (05649-0205)
PHONE..............................802 424-4864
Ryan Dumperth, *Pr*
Adam Overbay, *VP*
Jennifer West, *Sec*
EMP: 10 EST: 2016
SALES (est): 225.69K **Privately Held**
Web: www.johnfitchdistilling.com
SIC: 2085 Distilled and blended liquors

(G-17015)
PEPIN GRANITE COMPANY INC
58 Granite St (05641-4142)
P.O. Box 566 (05641-0566)
PHONE..............................802 476-6103
John Pepin, *Pr*
Scott Pepin, *Treas*
EMP: 16 EST: 1962
SALES (est): 807.73K **Privately Held**
Web: www.pepingranite.rocks
SIC: 3281 Monuments, cut stone (not
finishing or lettering only)

(G-17016)
SPRUCE MOUNTIAN GRANITES INC
84 Pitman Rd (05641-8933)
P.O. Box 427 (05641-0427)
PHONE..............................802 476-7474
Paul Bagalio Ii, *CEO*
EMP: 30 EST: 1999
SALES (est): 2.69MM **Privately Held**
Web: www.sprucemountaingranites.com
SIC: 3281 Granite, cut and shaped

(G-17017)
SPRUCE MTN GRNTES CSTM SNDBLAS
84 Pitman Rd (05641-8933)
P.O. Box 427 (05641-0427)
PHONE..............................802 476-7474
Paul A Bagalio, *Prin*
EMP: 13 EST: 2012
SALES (est): 554.61K **Privately Held**
SIC: 3281 Granite, cut and shaped

(G-17018)
SRG INC
Also Called: Carboncraft
37 Gable Pl (05641-4137)
PHONE..............................802 479-2508
Sarah Somerville, *VP*
Sarah Somerville, *VP*
EMP: 8 EST: 1954
SALES (est): 243.39K **Privately Held**

Web: www.hillsidestone.com
SIC: 2411 Stumping for turpentine or
powder manufacturing

(G-17019)
SWENSON GRANITE COMPANY LLC
Anderson-Friberg Division
54 Willey St (05641-2500)
P.O. Box 626 (05641-0626)
PHONE..............................802 476-7021
EMP: 9
SALES (corp-wide): 2.1MM **Privately Held**
Web: www.swensongranite.com
SIC: 3281 5999 Monuments, cut stone (not
finishing or lettering only); Monuments and
tombstones
HQ: Swenson Granite Company Llc
369 N State St
Concord NH 03301
603 225-4322

(G-17020)
TA UPDATE INC (PA)
Also Called: Country Courier
47 N Main St Ste 200 (05641-4168)
PHONE..............................802 479-4040
Robert J Mitchell, *Pr*
R John Mitchell, *
EMP: 90 EST: 1964
SQ FT: 18,000
SALES (est): 7.51MM
SALES (corp-wide): 7.51MM **Privately Held**
Web: www.timesargus.com
SIC: 2711 Commercial printing and
newspaper publishing combined

(G-17021)
TRIEX LLC
Also Called: Filabot
81 Parker Rd (05641-9116)
PHONE..............................802 505-6772
EMP: 9 EST: 2013
SQ FT: 700
SALES (est): 2.42MM **Privately Held**
Web: www.filabot.com
SIC: 5084 8731 3559 8742 Recycling
machinery and equipment; Commercial
research laboratory; Recycling machinery;
Automation and robotics consultant

(G-17022)
TROW & HOLDEN CO INC
45 S Main St Ste 57 (05641-4880)
P.O. Box 475 (05641-0475)
PHONE..............................802 476-7221
Norman Akley, *Pr*
Lauren Lamorte, *VP*
EMP: 27 EST: 1890
SQ FT: 22,000
SALES (est): 1.56MM **Privately Held**
Web: www.trowandholden.com
SIC: 3559 3545 3398 Stone working
machinery; Cutting tools for machine tools;
Brazing (hardening) of metal

(G-17023)
VERMONT STONE ART LLC
21 Metro Way Ste 1 (05641-4478)
PHONE..............................802 238-1498
EMP: 7 EST: 2017
SALES (est): 236.17K **Privately Held**
Web: www.vermontstone.art
SIC: 3281 Cut stone and stone products

(G-17024)
VILLAGE CANNERY VERMONT INC
Also Called: Vermont Village Applesauce
698 S Barre Rd (05641-8108)
PHONE..............................207 351-2713
EMP: 40 EST: 1995
SQ FT: 20,000
SALES (est): 7.45MM **Privately Held**
SIC: 2033 Canned fruits and specialties

(G-17025)
WORKSAFE TRAFFIC CTRL INDS INC (PA)
Also Called: Always On Time Signs & Design
115 Industrial Ln (05641-5432)
PHONE..............................802 223-8948
Deborah Ricker, *Pr*
Debra Ricker, *Pr*
Lorena Laprade, *Treas*
EMP: 8 EST: 1991
SQ FT: 4,000
SALES (est): 1.64MM **Privately Held**
Web: www.worksafetci.com
SIC: 3669 1611 5084 Transportation
signaling devices; General contractor;
highway and street construction; Industrial
machinery and equipment

(G-17026)
WORLD PUBLICATIONS INC
Also Called: World, The
403 Us Route 302 (05641-2272)
PHONE..............................802 479-2582
Gary Hass, *Prin*
Deborah Phillips, *VP*
EMP: 24 EST: 1971
SALES (est): 3.11MM **Privately Held**
Web: www.vt-world.com
SIC: 2711 Newspapers, publishing and
printing

Barton
Orleans County

(G-17027)
CHRONICLE INC
Also Called: Chronicle, The
133 Water (05822-8814)
P.O. Box 660 (05822-0660)
PHONE..............................802 525-3531
Christopher Braithwaite, *Pr*
EMP: 15 EST: 1974
SALES (est): 516.77K **Privately Held**
Web: www.bartonchronicle.com
SIC: 2711 Newspapers, publishing and
printing

Bellows Falls
Windham County

(G-17028)
APPLIED BOLTING TECH PDTS LLC
1413 Rockingham Rd (05101-3314)
PHONE..............................802 460-3100
Kristyn J Wallace, *Pr*
Wayne Wallace, *VP*
Brenda Wallace, *Sec*
John Cavanah, *Dir*
James Cavanah, *Dir*
EMP: 22 EST: 1986
SQ FT: 13,900
SALES (est): 4.66MM **Privately Held**
Web: www.appliedbolting.com
SIC: 8711 3452 Consulting engineer; Bolts,
nuts, rivets, and washers

(G-17029)
CHROMA TECHNOLOGY CORP
10 Imtec Ln (05101-3119)
PHONE..............................802 428-2500
Newell Lessell, *CEO*
Newell Leffell, *
Paul Millman, *
Willem Auer, *
▼ EMP: 172 EST: 1991
SQ FT: 28,800
SALES (est): 58.48MM **Privately Held**
Web: www.chroma.com
SIC: 3827 Optical elements and
assemblies, except ophthalmic

(G-17030)
PJF TRUCKING & LOGGING LLC
35 Schoolbus Depot Rd (05101-3154)
PHONE..............................802 463-3343
Paul J Furgat, *Prin*
EMP: 8 EST: 2001
SALES (est): 496.24K **Privately Held**
SIC: 2411 Logging camps and contractors

(G-17031)
SONNAX INDUSTRIES INC ✪
1 Automatic Dr (05101-4000)
PHONE..............................802 463-0240
EMP: 8 EST: 2022
SALES (est): 69.33K **Privately Held**
Web: www.sonnax.com
SIC: 3714 Motor vehicle parts and
accessories

(G-17032)
SONNAX TRANSMISSION COMPANY (DH)
Also Called: Sonnax
2 Imtec Ln (05101-3119)
P.O. Box 440 (05101-0440)
PHONE..............................802 463-9722
Klynt Baker, *Pr*
Marie S Wiese, *
◆ EMP: 91 EST: 1978
SALES (est): 47.57MM
SALES (corp-wide): 302.09B **Publicly Held**
Web: www.sonnax.com
SIC: 3714 Transmission housings or parts,
motor vehicle
HQ: Marmon Holdings, Inc.
181 W Madison St Ste 3900
Chicago IL 60602
312 372-9500

(G-17033)
WHITNEY BLAKE COMPANY (PA)
Also Called: Interconnect
20 Industrial Dr (05101-3122)
P.O. Box 579 (05101-0579)
PHONE..............................800 323-0479
Sheldon Scott, *Pr*
Michael Laross, *
David Jankowski, *
EMP: 100 EST: 1985
SQ FT: 65,000
SALES (est): 48.85MM
SALES (corp-wide): 48.85MM **Privately Held**
Web: www.wblake.com
SIC: 5051 3643 3542 Wire, nec; Cord
connectors, electric; Elastic membrane
metal forming machines

Belvidere Center
Lamoille County

(G-17034)
GREEN MTN MAPLE SUG REF CO INC
Also Called: Northern VT Cnsld Pure Mple Pr
204 Boarding House Hill Rd (05442-9627)
P.O. Box 82 (05492-0082)
PHONE..............................802 644-2625
Joseph Russo Junior, *Pr*
Robert B Chimilseski, *Sec*
EMP: 10 **EST:** 1991
SALES (est): 436.42K **Privately Held**
Web: www.vermontpuremaplesyrup.com
SIC: 2099 Maple syrup

Bennington
Bennington County

(G-17035)
ABACUS AUTOMATION INC
264 Shields Dr (05201-8307)
PHONE..............................802 442-3662
Donald S Alvarado, *Pr*
Richard G Zens, *
EMP: 30 **EST:** 1985
SQ FT: 8,000
SALES (est): 6.5MM **Privately Held**
Web: www.abacusautomation.com
SIC: 3599 3549 Custom machinery;
Metalworking machinery, nec

(G-17036)
BENNINGTON POTTERS INC (PA)
Also Called: Potters Yard Brasserie
324 County St (05201-1902)
P.O. Box 199 (05201-0199)
PHONE..............................800 205-8033
Paul Silberman, *Pr*
David Gil, *
Sheela Harden, *
Gloria Gil, *
▲ **EMP:** 50 **EST:** 1948
SQ FT: 30,000
SALES (est): 4.75MM
SALES (corp-wide): 4.75MM **Privately Held**
Web: www.benningtonpotters.com
SIC: 3269 5023 5812 Stoneware pottery
products; Pottery; Eating places

(G-17037)
BENNINGTON SHRIFF GLC SLAR LLC
811 Us Route 7 S (05201-9388)
PHONE..............................802 233-3370
EMP: 7 **EST:** 2016
SALES (est): 197.9K **Privately Held**
Web: www.benningtonsheriff.org
SIC: 2711 Newspapers

(G-17038)
CATAMOUNT GLASSWARE CO INC
Also Called: Vermont Glass Factory & Dg
309 County St (05201-1901)
PHONE..............................802 442-5438
Alan Karyo, *Pr*
Irene Volpi, *VP*
Adam Volpi, *VP*
▲ **EMP:** 23 **EST:** 1979
SQ FT: 18,000
SALES (est): 817.27K **Privately Held**
Web: www.catamountglass.com

SIC: 3229 Cooking utensils, glass or glass
ceramic

(G-17039)
EDGEWELL PER CARE BRANDS LLC
401 Gage St (05201-2515)
PHONE..............................802 442-5551
William G Wright, *Mgr*
EMP: 32
SALES (corp-wide): 2.25B **Publicly Held**
Web: www.edgewell.com
SIC: 3691 Storage batteries
HQ: Edgewell Personal Care Brands, Llc
6 Research Dr
Shelton CT 06484
203 944-5500

(G-17040)
HEMMINGS MOTOR NEWS INC
222 Main St (05201-2103)
P.O. Box 100 (05201-0100)
PHONE..............................802 442-3101
Jim Menneto, *
Whitney Shaw, *
Kirk Shaw, *VP*
▲ **EMP:** 777 **EST:** 2002
SALES (est): 9.93MM
SALES (corp-wide): 2.88B **Privately Held**
Web: www.hemmings.com
SIC: 2721 5961 5947 5541 Magazines:
publishing only, not printed on site; Novelty
merchandise, mail order; Novelties; Filling
stations, gasoline
HQ: American City Business Journals, Inc.
120 W Morehead St Ste 400
Charlotte NC 28202
704 973-1000

(G-17041)
INKSPOT PRESS
736 Main St (05201-2633)
PHONE..............................802 447-1768
Margaret Price, *Pr*
Michael Carver, *Prin*
EMP: 29 **EST:** 1980
SQ FT: 9,000
SALES (est): 352.58K **Privately Held**
Web: www.inkspotpress.com
SIC: 2752 Offset printing

(G-17042)
JBM SHERMAN CARMEL INC
14 Morse Rd (05201-1639)
PHONE..............................802 442-5115
Jeffrey Thomayer, *Pr*
Benny Danino, *
Meir Shani, *
Lior Sherman, *
▲ **EMP:** 45 **EST:** 2008
SQ FT: 42,000
SALES (est): 8.11MM **Privately Held**
Web: www.jbm-usa.com
SIC: 3714 Motor vehicle parts and
accessories

(G-17043)
K & E PLASTICS INC
141 Morse Rd (05201-1661)
PHONE..............................802 375-0011
Eric Broderson, *Pr*
Kurt Broderson, *
Patricia Broderson, *
EMP: 24 **EST:** 1966
SQ FT: 12,500
SALES (est): 3.29MM **Privately Held**
Web: www.keplastics.com
SIC: 3089 Injection molding of plastics

(G-17044)
K H CORRUGATED CASE COPR
473 Bowen Rd (05201-2757)
PHONE..............................802 442-5455
EMP: 7 **EST:** 2017
SALES (est): 106.47K **Privately Held**
Web: www.unicorr.com
SIC: 2653 Boxes, corrugated: made from
purchased materials

(G-17045)
K&H GROUP INC
Also Called: Vermont Container Corp
473 Bowen Rd (05201-2757)
PHONE..............................802 442-5455
Charles Pious, *Mgr*
EMP: 245
SALES (corp-wide): 142MM **Privately Held**
Web: www.unicorr.com
SIC: 2653 5113 Boxes, corrugated: made
from purchased materials; Bags, paper and
disposable plastic
HQ: K&H Group, Inc.
330 Lake Osiris Rd
Walden NY 12586
845 778-3555

(G-17046)
KAMAN COMPOSITES - VERMONT INC
25 Performance Dr (05201-1947)
PHONE..............................802 442-9964
James C Larwood Junior, *Pr*
Christopher Simmons, *KAMAN AEROSYSTEMS*
Alphonse J Lariviere Junior, *KAMAN COMPOSITE STRUCTURES*
Michael Lafleur, *KAMAN COMPOSITE STRUCTURES*
Robert D Starr, *
◆ **EMP:** 188 **EST:** 1979
SQ FT: 82,000
SALES (est): 24.02MM
SALES (corp-wide): 687.96MM **Publicly Held**
Web: www.kaman.com
SIC: 3083 Laminated plastics plate and
sheet
HQ: Kaman Aerospace Group, Inc.
1332 Blue Hills Ave
Bloomfield CT 06002

(G-17047)
L & G FABRICATORS INC
137 Harwood Hill Rd (05201-1641)
P.O. Box 1016 (05201-1016)
PHONE..............................802 447-0965
Leo Gauthier, *Pr*
Mona Gauthier, *VP*
David Mccutcheon, *Sec*
EMP: 10 **EST:** 1979
SQ FT: 20,000
SALES (est): 860.96K **Privately Held**
Web: www.lgfabricatorsinc.com
SIC: 3441 3433 Fabricated structural metal;
Stoves, wood and coal burning

(G-17048)
LAUZON MACHINE AND ENGRG INC
Also Called: Lauzon's Machine & Engineering
757 Main St (05201-3600)
P.O. Box 406 (05201-0406)
PHONE..............................802 442-3116
Steve Gallant, *Pr*
Eugene Lauzon, *VP*
Wanda Provensal, *Sec*
EMP: 21 **EST:** 1957
SQ FT: 38,748

SALES (est): 410.26K **Privately Held**
Web: www.lawzo.com
SIC: 3599 Machine shop, jobbing and repair

(G-17049)
MAHAR EXCAVATING & LOGGING
592 Coleville Rd (05201-8879)
PHONE..............................802 442-2954
Michael Mahar, *Prin*
EMP: 8 **EST:** 2001
SALES (est): 363.6K **Privately Held**
SIC: 2411 Logging camps and contractors

(G-17050)
MAINSTREAM INC (PA)
Also Called: Panache
1003 Monument Ave (05201-9233)
PHONE..............................802 442-8859
Nancy Woltman, *Pr*
Kristopher Woltman, *VP*
EMP: 13 **EST:** 1985
SQ FT: 7,600
SALES (est): 1.03MM
SALES (corp-wide): 1.03MM **Privately Held**
SIC: 5621 2771 3961 2511 Boutiques;
Greeting cards; Costume jewelry; Dining
room furniture: wood

(G-17051)
MCGILL AIRFLOW LLC
452 Harwood Hill Rd (05201-8807)
PHONE..............................802 442-1900
David Mcnelly, *Brnch Mgr*
EMP: 7
SALES (corp-wide): 126.17MM **Privately Held**
Web: www.mcgillairflow.com
SIC: 3444 Ducts, sheet metal
HQ: Mcgill Airflow Llc
1 Mission Park
Groveport OH 43125
614 829-1200

(G-17052)
MONUMENT INDUSTRIES INC
159 Phyllis Ln (05201-1663)
P.O. Box 617 (05201-0617)
PHONE..............................802 442-8187
Lawrence W Amos, *Pr*
Jay L Whitten, *VP*
EMP: 22 **EST:** 1968
SQ FT: 24,000
SALES (est): 1.61MM **Privately Held**
Web: www.idsinteractive.com
SIC: 2673 Plastic bags: made from
purchased materials

(G-17053)
NORTH EASTERN PUBLISHING CO
Also Called: Bennington Banner
425 Main St (05201-2141)
PHONE..............................802 447-7567
EMP: 78 **EST:** 1995
SQ FT: 10,000
SALES (est): 491.35K
SALES (corp-wide): 1.96B **Privately Held**
Web: www.benningtonbanner.com
SIC: 2711 7313 Newspapers: publishing
only, not printed on site; Newspaper
advertising representative
HQ: New England Newspapers, Inc.
75 S Church St Ste L1
Pittsfield MA 01201

(G-17054)
NSK STEERING SYSTEMS AMER INC
Also Called: Nssa, Bennington Plant
110 Shields Dr (05201-8309)
PHONE...............................802 442-5448
Michael Allan, *Manager*
EMP: 353
SIC: 3714   Steering mechanisms, motor vehicle
HQ: Nsk Steering Systems America, Inc.
4200 Goss Rd
Ann Arbor MI 48105
734 913-7500

(G-17055)
PORTA-BRACE INC
Also Called: K & H Products
160 Benmont Ave Ste 11 (05201-1926)
P.O. Box 246 (05201-0246)
PHONE...............................802 442-8171
Gregg Haythorn, *Pr*
Thomas S Stark, *
▲ **EMP:** 16 **EST:** 1974
SQ FT: 1,000
SALES (est): 2.4MM **Privately Held**
Web: www.portabrace.com
SIC: 3161   Camera carrying bags

(G-17056)
R JOHN WRIGHT DOLLS INC
2402 West Rd (05201-9811)
PHONE...............................802 447-7072
R John Wright, *Pr*
Susan D Wright, *
▲ **EMP:** 10 **EST:** 1976
SQ FT: 6,000
SALES (est): 788.22K **Privately Held**
Web: www.rjohnwright.com
SIC: 3942 5945   Dolls, except stuffed toy animals; Hobby, toy, and game shops

(G-17057)
VISHAY INTERTECHNOLOGY INC
Also Called: Vishay Tansitor
2813 West Rd (05201-9812)
PHONE...............................802 440-8571
EMP: 14
SALES (corp-wide): 3.5B **Publicly Held**
Web: www.vishay.com
SIC: 3677   Electronic coils and transformers
PA: Vishay Intertechnology, Inc.
63 Lancaster Ave
Malvern PA 19355
610 644-1300

Benson
Rutland County

(G-17058)
NORM BROWN LOGGING
240 Hulett Hill Rd (05743-9439)
PHONE...............................802 537-4474
Norman Brown, *Prin*
EMP: 7 **EST:** 2010
SALES (est): 290.61K **Privately Held**
SIC: 2411   Logging camps and contractors

(G-17059)
ORWELL SAND & GRAVEL
1200 Park Hill Rd (05743-9894)
PHONE...............................802 345-6028
Bob Shaw, *Prin*
EMP: 9 **EST:** 2004
SALES (est): 467.5K **Privately Held**
SIC: 1442   Construction sand and gravel

Bethel
Windsor County

(G-17060)
NOLATO GW INC (HQ)
239 Pleasant St (05032-9762)
P.O. Box 56 (05032-0056)
PHONE...............................802 234-9941
Brenan Riehl, *Pr*
Thomas Johansen, *VP*
Frederic Riehl, *Dir*
▲ **EMP:** 410 **EST:** 1955
SQ FT: 200,000
SALES (est): 135.47MM
SALES (corp-wide): 1.03B **Privately Held**
SIC: 3089 3544   Injection molding of plastics ; Industrial molds
PA: Nolato Ab
Nolatovagen 32
Torekov 269 7
431442290

Bradford
Orange County

(G-17061)
COHASA PUBLISHING INC
Also Called: Journal Opinion
Rte 5 (05033)
P.O. Box 378 (05033-0378)
PHONE...............................802 222-5281
Connie Sanville, *Pr*
EMP: 8 **EST:** 1967
SALES (est): 581.83K **Privately Held**
Web: www.jonews.com
SIC: 2711   Newspapers: publishing only, not printed on site

(G-17062)
GREENWOOD MILL INC
599 Goose Green Rd (05033-9742)
P.O. Box 1348 (05851-1348)
PHONE...............................802 626-0800
Bruno Couture, *CEO*
EMP: 10 **EST:** 1999
SALES (est): 807.72K **Privately Held**
Web: www.ceogreenwoodmills.com
SIC: 2421   Sawmills and planing mills, general

(G-17063)
JOURNAL OPINION INC
48 Main St (05033-9274)
P.O. Box 378 (05033-0378)
PHONE...............................802 222-5281
Robert F Huminski, *Pr*
EMP: 20 **EST:** 1865
SALES (est): 417.3K **Privately Held**
Web: www.jonews.com
SIC: 2711   Job printing and newspaper publishing combined

(G-17064)
STEPHENS PRECISION INC
293 Industrial Dr (05033-9221)
PHONE...............................802 222-9600
Franklin Stephens, *Pr*
Ann Stephens, *Sec*
EMP: 16 **EST:** 1981
SQ FT: 8,000
SALES (est): 2.42MM **Privately Held**
Web: www.stephensprecision.com
SIC: 3599   Machine shop, jobbing and repair

(G-17065)
VILLAGE INDUSTRIAL POWER INC
330 Industrial Dr (05033-9306)
PHONE...............................802 522-8584
Felicity Lodge, *CEO*
Carl N Bielenberg, *Stockholder*
EMP: 10 **EST:** 2015
SALES (est): 973.84K **Privately Held**
Web: www.villageindustrialpower.com
SIC: 3511   Steam engines

Brandon
Rutland County

(G-17066)
HAYES RECYCLED PALLETS INC
16 Maple St (05733-1004)
PHONE...............................802 247-4620
Ronald Hayes, *Pr*
Randy Hayes, *VP*
Lynn Hayes, *Sec*
Carolyn Hayes, *Treas*
Ricky Hayes, *VP*
EMP: 8 **EST:** 1983
SQ FT: 10,000
SALES (est): 232.2K **Privately Held**
SIC: 2448   Pallets, wood

(G-17067)
IDEAL POWDER COATING INC
218 Jones Dr (05733-8221)
PHONE...............................802 345-7532
Al Jackson, *Owner*
EMP: 7 **EST:** 2015
SALES (est): 93.14K **Privately Held**
SIC: 3479   Painting of metal products

(G-17068)
MCKERNON GROUP INC
381 New Rd (05733-8362)
PHONE...............................802 247-8500
John Mc Kernon, *Pr*
Kevin Birchmore, *
EMP: 70 **EST:** 1995
SQ FT: 60,000
SALES (est): 18.76MM **Privately Held**
Web: www.mckernongroup.com
SIC: 1521 7389 3444 1799   New construction, single-family houses; Interior design services; Concrete forms, sheet metal; Kitchen and bathroom remodeling

(G-17069)
NESHOBE WOOD PRODUCTS INC
56 Pearl St (05733-1022)
PHONE...............................802 247-3805
Ralph Ethier, *Pr*
Francine Ethier, *Owner*
EMP: 10 **EST:** 1998
SALES (est): 839.42K **Privately Held**
SIC: 2493   Reconstituted wood products

(G-17070)
NEW ENGLAND WOODCRAFT INC
Also Called: Thor's Elegance
481 North St (05733-9509)
P.O. Box 165 (05745-0165)
PHONE...............................802 247-8211
Charles Thurston, *CEO*
Gary Marini, *
Peter Osborne, *
◆ **EMP:** 130 **EST:** 1977
SQ FT: 65,000

SALES (est): 25.69MM **Privately Held**
Web: www.newenglandwoodcraft.com
SIC: 2512 2511 2531 2521   Upholstered household furniture; Wood household furniture; Public building and related furniture; Wood office furniture

(G-17071)
VERMONT HARD CIDER COMPANY LLC
Also Called: Green Mountain Beverage
1 Tubbs Ave (05733)
PHONE...............................802 385-3656
Walter Scott, *Managing Member*
EMP: 58
SALES (corp-wide): 37.41MM **Privately Held**
Web: www.gmbeverage.com
SIC: 2085   Distilled and blended liquors
HQ: Vermont Hard Cider Company, Llc
1321 Exchange St
Middlebury VT 05753
802 388-0700

Brattleboro
Windham County

(G-17072)
AGAINST GRN GOURMET FOODS LLC
22 Browne Ct Unit 119 (05301-4428)
P.O. Box 225 (05302-0225)
PHONE...............................802 258-3838
Nancy Cain, *Managing Member*
EMP: 8 **EST:** 2005
SALES (est): 1.05MM **Privately Held**
Web: www.againstthegraingourmet.com
SIC: 2051   Bakery: wholesale or wholesale/retail combined

(G-17073)
ASHE AMERICA INC
Also Called: Ashe Converting Equipment
23 Marlboro Rd (05301-9708)
PHONE...............................802 254-0200
John O M Godbold, *Pr*
James Godbold, *
Barbara M Godbold, *
Guy F Carrington, *
◆ **EMP:** 20 **EST:** 2003
SQ FT: 1,000
SALES (est): 484.85K **Privately Held**
Web: www.ashe.co.uk
SIC: 3554 5084   Paper industries machinery; Paper, sawmill, and woodworking machinery

(G-17074)
BACK ROADS FOOD CO LLC
Also Called: Back Roads Granola
74 Cotton Mill Hl Unit A110 (05301-7701)
PHONE...............................802 579-1135
Peter Vogel, *Prin*
Marjorie Virginia Vogel, *Prin*
EMP: 11 **EST:** 2012
SALES (est): 1.01MM **Privately Held**
Web: www.backroadsgranola.com
SIC: 5141 2043   Groceries, general line; Cereal breakfast foods

(G-17075)
BRATTLEBORO KILN DRY & MILLING
1103 Vernon St (05301-5104)
PHONE...............................802 254-4528
Dominic Cersosimo, *Pr*
Richard Elkins, *
Michael Elkins, *
Lawrin Crispe, *

▲ = Import ▼ = Export
◆ = Import/Export

EMP: 15 **EST:** 1954
SQ FT: 300,000
SALES (est): 222.49K **Privately Held**
SIC: 2421 2431 Sawmills and planing mills, general; Millwork

(G-17076)
BUILDINGGREEN INC
Also Called: Environmental Building News
122 Birge St Ste 30 (05301-6703)
PHONE..............................802 257-7300
Nadav Malin, *Pr*
Jerelyn Wilson, *Prin*
EMP: 23 **EST:** 1988
SQ FT: 4,000
SALES (est): 3.71MM **Privately Held**
Web: www.buildinggreen.com
SIC: 8999 2721 Technical writing; Trade journals: publishing only, not printed on site

(G-17077)
C E BRADLEY LABORATORIES INC (PA)
Also Called: Flo-Matic
56 Bennett Dr (05301-5105)
P.O. Box 8238 (05304-8238)
PHONE..............................802 257-7971
Hisham R Kanaan, *Ch Bd*
Robert Rowinski, *
Edward Rochford, *
Stephen R Phillips, *
▲ **EMP:** 50 **EST:** 1939
SALES (est): 11.81MM
SALES (corp-wide): 11.81MM **Privately Held**
Web: www.cebradley.com
SIC: 2851 2869 Lacquers, varnishes, enamels, and other coatings; Industrial organic chemicals, nec

(G-17078)
CARLTON NEWTON CORPORATION LLC
Also Called: New England Sales Team
55 Marlboro Rd Ste 7 (05301-9782)
PHONE..............................802 579-1413
Jeffrey Carlton Newton, *Prin*
EMP: 9 **EST:** 2019
SALES (est): 467.99K **Privately Held**
SIC: 2434 Wood kitchen cabinets

(G-17079)
CAVE MANUFACTURING INC
Also Called: Bradford Machine
22 Browne Ct Unit 104 (05301-5406)
PHONE..............................802 257-9253
Jim Hayssen, *Pr*
EMP: 30 **EST:** 1980
SQ FT: 12,000
SALES (est): 4.84MM **Privately Held**
Web: www.bradfordmachine.com
SIC: 3599 7692 Machine shop, jobbing and repair; Welding repair

(G-17080)
CERSOSIMO INDUSTRIES INC (PA)
439 West River Road Route 30 (05301-9088)
P.O. Box 1800 (05302-1800)
PHONE..............................802 254-4500
Michael Cersosimo, *Pr*
Dominic Cersosimo, *Treas*
Jeffrey Morse, *VP*
Peter Boemig, *VP*
Neil Dawson, *VP*
EMP: 76 **EST:** 1996
SQ FT: 4,000
SALES (est): 4.81MM

SALES (corp-wide): 4.81MM **Privately Held**
Web: www.cersosimorealestate.com
SIC: 6531 8711 1611 1442 Real estate agents and managers; Engineering services ; Highway and street construction; Construction sand and gravel

(G-17081)
CERSOSIMO LUMBER COMPANY INC (PA)
Also Called: Hardwick Dry Kilns
1103 Vernon St (05301-5110)
PHONE..............................802 254-4508
Dominic A Butch, *Ch*
Michael A Cersosimo, *
Neil Dawson, *
John Caveney, *
Jeffrey Hardy, *
◆ **EMP:** 115 **EST:** 1947
SALES (est): 46.86MM
SALES (corp-wide): 46.86MM **Privately Held**
Web: www.cersosimolumber.com
SIC: 2421 Lumber: rough, sawed, or planed

(G-17082)
DOSA KITCHEN LLC
Also Called: Dosa Kitchen
209 Austine Dr (05301-7223)
PHONE..............................802 246-7592
Nash Patel, *Prin*
EMP: 8 **EST:** 2014
SALES (est): 328.71K **Privately Held**
Web: www.ledaskitchen.com
SIC: 5812 2099 Indian/Pakistan restaurant; Food preparations, nec

(G-17083)
G S P COATINGS INC
101 John Seitz Dr (05301-3642)
PHONE..............................802 257-5858
Norman Schneeberger, *Pr*
David Sprague, *VP*
David Henry, *Sec*
EMP: 26 **EST:** 2002
SQ FT: 2,400
SALES (est): 964.05K **Privately Held**
Web: www.gspcoatings.com
SIC: 3479 Coating of metals and formed products

(G-17084)
G S PRECISION INC (PA)
101 John Seitz Dr (05301-3642)
PHONE..............................802 257-5200
Matt O'connell, *CEO*
John Hanley, *
Dennis Elwood, *
Raymond Schneeberger, *
Bryan Mcelwee, *Dir*
◆ **EMP:** 315 **EST:** 1958
SQ FT: 102,000
SALES (est): 105.24MM
SALES (corp-wide): 105.24MM **Privately Held**
Web: www.gsprecision.com
SIC: 3599 Machine shop, jobbing and repair

(G-17085)
GARWARE FULFLEX USA INC
Also Called: Fulflex
32 Justin Holden Dr (05301-7050)
PHONE..............................802 257-5256
Donald Venice, *Brnch Mgr*
EMP: 128
SALES (corp-wide): 75MM **Privately Held**
Web: www.fulflex.com

SIC: 2258 2241 3069 3061 Fabric finishing, warp knit; Manmade fiber narrow woven fabrics; Tape, pressure sensitive: rubber; Appliance rubber goods (mechanical)
PA: Garware Fulflex Usa Inc.
1695 Nw 110th Ave Ste 301
Miami FL 33172
305 436-8915

(G-17086)
HERMIT THRUSH BREWERY LLC (PA)
Also Called: Hermit Thrush Brewery
29 High St Apt 101c (05301-3083)
PHONE..............................585 781-0617
Christopher Gagne, *Prin*
EMP: 7 **EST:** 2014
SALES (est): 976.73K
SALES (corp-wide): 976.73K **Privately Held**
Web: www.hermitthrushbrewery.com
SIC: 2082 Malt beverages

(G-17087)
HOWARD PRINTING INC
Also Called: New England Showcase
14 Noahs Ln (05301-4463)
P.O. Box 996 (05302-0996)
PHONE..............................802 254-3550
Gregory Howard, *Pr*
EMP: 8 **EST:** 1991
SALES (est): 998.17K **Privately Held**
Web: www.howardprintinginc.com
SIC: 2752 Offset printing

(G-17088)
HUMAN RIGHTS DEFENSE CENTER
1013 Lucerne Ave (05303)
PHONE..............................802 257-1342
Paul Wright, *Dir*
EMP: 7 **EST:** 2011
SALES (est): 55.4K **Privately Held**
Web: www.humanrightsdefensecenter.org
SIC: 2741 Miscellaneous publishing

(G-17089)
JACK TARMY LUMBER CO INC
1077 Putney Rd (05301-9050)
P.O. Box 131 (05302-0131)
PHONE..............................802 257-0427
Mark Tarmy, *Pr*
Jonathan Bump, *Sec*
EMP: 12 **EST:** 1965
SQ FT: 10,000
SALES (est): 784.17K **Privately Held**
SIC: 5031 2426 2421 Lumber: rough, dressed, and finished; Hardwood dimension and flooring mills; Sawmills and planing mills, general

(G-17090)
JOHN PENFIELD LTD
Also Called: Brattleboro Tire
558 Putney Rd (05301-9055)
PHONE..............................802 254-5411
John Penfield, *Prin*
Mary Jane Penfield, *Pr*
Bob Shatley, *General MGE*
EMP: 7 **EST:** 1985
SALES (est): 930.28K **Privately Held**
Web: www.brattleborotire.com
SIC: 7534 Tire repair shop

(G-17091)
JOUVE OF NORTH AMERICA INC (DH)
70 Landmark Hill Dr (05301-9102)

P.O. Box 1338 (05302-1338)
PHONE..............................802 254-6073
Emmanuel Benoit, *CEO*
EMP: 73 **EST:** 1999
SALES (est): 16.29MM
SALES (corp-wide): 20.11MM **Privately Held**
SIC: 2721 Periodicals, publishing and printing
HQ: Luminess
561 Rue De Saint Leonard
Mayenne 53100
144765440

(G-17092)
KOLLMORGEN CORPORATION
343 John Seitz Dr (05301-3660)
PHONE..............................802 258-3020
FAX: 802 254-2959
EMP: 25
SALES (corp-wide): 6.22B **Publicly Held**
SIC: 3545 Machine tool accessories
HQ: Kollmorgen Corporation
203a W Rock Rd
Radford VA 24141
540 633-3545

(G-17093)
LEADER DIST SYSTEMS INC
1566 Putney Rd (05301-9497)
P.O. Box 8285 (05304-8285)
PHONE..............................802 254-6093
John Leader, *Pr*
Shaun M Leary, *
William M Mccarty, *Sec*
EMP: 65 **EST:** 2018
SALES (est): 5.11MM **Privately Held**
Web: www.pepsibrattleboro.com
SIC: 2086 Carbonated soft drinks, bottled and canned

(G-17094)
LONG FALLS PAPERBOARD LLC
161 Wellington Rd (05301-7052)
PHONE..............................802 257-0365
Ben Rankin, *Managing Member*
▼ **EMP:** 104 **EST:** 2018
SALES (est): 26MM **Privately Held**
Web: www.longfallspaperboard.com
SIC: 2631 Paperboard mills

(G-17095)
MCNEILLS MANUFACTURING
22 Browne Ct (05301-4487)
PHONE..............................802 246-1171
EMP: 7 **EST:** 2007
SALES (est): 496.35K **Privately Held**
SIC: 3999 Manufacturing industries, nec

(G-17096)
NEW CHAPTER INC (HQ)
Also Called: New Charter Distribution
90 Technology Dr (05301-9180)
PHONE..............................800 543-7279
Larry Allgaier, *CEO*
Paul Schulick, *Vice Chairman* *
Tom Newmark, *
Mark Gavin, *
Ruth B Austin, *
EMP: 219 **EST:** 1986
SQ FT: 93,406
SALES (est): 99.37MM
SALES (corp-wide): 82.01B **Publicly Held**
Web: www.newchapter.com
SIC: 2834 Vitamin preparations
PA: The Procter & Gamble Company
1 Procter And Gamble Plz
Cincinnati OH 45202
513 983-1100

(G-17097)
NEW ENGLAND NEWSPAPERS INC
Also Called: Brattleboro Reformer
62 Black Mountain Rd (05301-9241)
P.O. Box 802 (05302-0802)
PHONE..............................802 254-2311
Edward Woods, *Brnch Mgr*
EMP: 49
SALES (corp-wide): 1.96B **Privately Held**
Web: www.berkshireeagle.com
SIC: 2711 Newspapers, publishing and printing
HQ: New England Newspapers, Inc.
75 S Church St Ste L1
Pittsfield MA 01201

(G-17098)
OMEGA OPTICAL HOLDINGS LLC (PA)
21 Omega Dr (05301-4444)
PHONE..............................802 251-7300
Michael J Cumbo, *CEO*
Justin Turner, *Ex VP*
Mike Ransford, *Ex VP*
EMP: 13 **EST:** 2019
SALES (est): 38.79MM
SALES (corp-wide): 38.79MM **Privately Held**
Web: www.omegafilters.com
SIC: 3827 Optical instruments and lenses

(G-17099)
PEPSI COLA BOTTLING CO
1566 Putney Rd (05301-9497)
P.O. Box 8285 (05304-8285)
PHONE..............................802 254-6093
John Leader, *Ch Bd*
Shaun M Leary, *
EMP: 10 **EST:** 1999
SALES (est): 385.71K **Privately Held**
Web: www.pepsico.com
SIC: 2086 Carbonated soft drinks, bottled and canned

(G-17100)
STRATFORD PUBLISHING SERVICES
70 Landmark Hill Dr (05301-9102)
P.O. Box 1338 (05302-1338)
PHONE..............................802 254-6073
James E Bristol, *Pr*
EMP: 9 **EST:** 1997
SQ FT: 8,000
SALES (est): 241.03K **Privately Held**
SIC: 2731 2791 Book publishing; Typesetting

(G-17101)
THE STORYMATIC CORP
Also Called: Storymatic Studios
74 Cotton Mill Hl Unit A300 (05301-7701)
P.O. Box 2504 (05303-2504)
PHONE..............................917 842-9932
EMP: 7 **EST:** 2014
SALES (est): 246.64K **Privately Held**
Web: www.thestorymatic.com
SIC: 2741 Miscellaneous publishing

(G-17102)
VERMONT CIRCUITS INC
76 Technology Dr (05301-9486)
P.O. Box 1890 (05302-1890)
PHONE..............................802 257-4571
EMP: 90
SIC: 3672 Printed circuit boards

(G-17103)
VERMONT CULINARY ISLANDS LLC
Also Called: Vermont Islands Kitchens Bars
22 Browne Ct Unit 115 (05301-4488)
PHONE..............................802 387-8591
EMP: 10 **EST:** 1998
SQ FT: 6,000
SALES (est): 907.89K **Privately Held**
Web: www.vermontislands.com
SIC: 3639 Major kitchen appliances, except refrigerators and stoves

(G-17104)
VERMONT CULINARY ISLANDS LLC
Also Called: Vermont Islands
22 Browne Ct Unit 115 (05301-4488)
PHONE..............................802 246-2277
Tom Meyer, *Managing Member*
EMP: 10 **EST:** 1999
SALES (est): 992.28K **Privately Held**
Web: www.vermontislands.com
SIC: 2511 2599 Buffets (furniture); Carts, restaurant equipment

(G-17105)
W & MB INC
74 Cotton Mill Hl Unit A108 (05301-7701)
PHONE..............................802 257-1935
Willy Buhlmann, *Pr*
EMP: 17 **EST:** 1990
SQ FT: 3,200
SALES (est): 594.95K **Privately Held**
Web: www.swissp.org
SIC: 3599 Machine shop, jobbing and repair

(G-17106)
W B MASON CO INC
447 Canal St (05301-6619)
PHONE..............................888 926-2766
EMP: 34
SALES (corp-wide): 1.01B **Privately Held**
Web: www.wbmason.com
SIC: 5943 5712 2752 Office forms and supplies; Office furniture; Commercial printing, lithographic
PA: W. B. Mason Co., Inc.
59 Centre Street
Brockton MA 02301
508 586-3434

(G-17107)
WASHBURN VAULT COMPANY INC
795 Meadowbrook Rd (05301-4402)
PHONE..............................802 254-9150
John Baldwin, *Pr*
Dorothy Baldwin, *VP*
Linda Baldwin, *VP*
EMP: 8 **EST:** 1942
SQ FT: 3,435
SALES (est): 967.33K **Privately Held**
Web: www.washburnvault.com
SIC: 3272 5032 Burial vaults, concrete or precast terrazzo; Concrete building products

(G-17108)
WESTINGHOUSE ELECTRIC CO LLC
49 Bennett Dr (05301-5100)
PHONE..............................802 254-9353
EMP: 45
Web: www.westinghousenuclear.com
SIC: 8711 3699 3651 3625 Designing: ship, boat, machine, and product; Electrical equipment and supplies, nec; Household audio and video equipment; Relays and industrial controls

HQ: Westinghouse Electric Company Llc
1000 Wstnghuse Dr Ste 572
Cranberry Township PA 16066
412 374-2020

(G-17109)
WHETSTONE STN REST BREWRY LLC (PA)
Also Called: Whetstone Beer
36 Bridge St (05301-3301)
PHONE..............................802 490-2354
EMP: 30 **EST:** 2012
SALES (est): 1.14MM
SALES (corp-wide): 1.14MM **Privately Held**
Web: www.whetstonebeer.com
SIC: 5812 2082 American restaurant; Malt beverages

(G-17110)
ZEPHYR DESIGNS LTD
129 Main St (05301-3061)
PHONE..............................802 254-2788
Robert W Clements, *Pr*
John Clements, *VP*
EMP: 8 **EST:** 1972
SQ FT: 3,000
SALES (est): 621.61K **Privately Held**
Web: www.zephyrdesignsvt.com
SIC: 2499 5999 Picture and mirror frames, wood; Artists' supplies and materials

---

Bridgewater
Windsor County

(G-17111)
CHARLES SHCKLTON MRNDA THMAS L
Also Called: Shackletonthomas
102 Mill Rd (05034-9801)
P.O. Box 48 (05034-0048)
PHONE..............................802 672-5175
Charles R Shackleton, *Pr*
Miranda Shackleton, *VP*
EMP: 20 **EST:** 1987
SQ FT: 18,000
SALES (est): 962.96K **Privately Held**
Web: www.shackletonthomas.com
SIC: 2511 Bed frames, except water bed frames; wood

Bristol
Addison County

(G-17112)
A JOHNSON CO
106 Andrew Johnson Dr (05443-4478)
PHONE..............................802 453-4884
Kenneth D Johnson, *Pt*
Kenneth D Johnson, *Pr*
David F Johnson, *Pt*
Carolyn J Sayre, *Pt*
William R Sayre, *Pt*
◆ **EMP:** 55 **EST:** 1906
SQ FT: 3,000
SALES (est): 4.99MM **Privately Held**
Web: www.vermontlumber.com
SIC: 2421 5031 5211 0851 Lumber: rough, sawed, or planed; Lumber: rough, dressed, and finished; Lumber products; Forest management services

(G-17113)
AUTUMN HARP INC
61 Pine St (05443-1043)
P.O. Box 267 (05443-0267)
PHONE..............................802 453-4807

EMP: 20 **EST:** 2017
SALES (est): 1.44MM **Privately Held**
Web: www.autumnharp.com
SIC: 2844 Perfumes, cosmetics and other toilet preparations

(G-17114)
BB&C WHOLESALE LLC (PA)
Also Called: Bristol Bakery & Cafe
61 Pine St (05443-1043)
PHONE..............................802 453-7708
Kevin Harper, *Prin*
EMP: 11 **EST:** 2013
SQ FT: 2,700
SALES (est): 4.77MM
SALES (corp-wide): 4.77MM **Privately Held**
SIC: 5149 2051 Bakery products; Bakery: wholesale or wholesale/retail combined

(G-17115)
BROWNS CERTIFIED WELDING INC
275 S 116 Rd (05443-5090)
PHONE..............................802 453-3351
Craig W Brown, *Pr*
Kim Chamberlin, *VP*
EMP: 10 **EST:** 1977
SQ FT: 8,000
SALES (est): 961.09K **Privately Held**
Web: www.brownswelding.com
SIC: 3441 7692 Fabricated structural metal; Welding repair

Brownsville
Windsor County

(G-17116)
BUTCHER & PANTRY LLC
871 Route 44 (05037-9602)
P.O. Box 544 (05037-0544)
PHONE..............................315 396-6464
EMP: 11 **EST:** 2017
SALES (est): 2.19MM **Privately Held**
Web: www.butcherandpantry.com
SIC: 2011 Meat by-products, from meat slaughtered on site

Burlington
Chittenden County

(G-17117)
AMERICAS GRDENING RESOURCE INC (PA)
Also Called: Gardener's Supply Company
128 Intervale Rd (05401-2804)
PHONE..............................802 660-3500
Jim Feinson, *CEO*
Cindy Turcot, *
William Raap, *
Max Harris, *CMO*
Gina Bernadet, *
◆ **EMP:** 108 **EST:** 1989
SQ FT: 50,000
SALES (est): 78.33MM
SALES (corp-wide): 78.33MM **Privately Held**
Web: www.gardeners.com
SIC: 5961 5191 5261 3423 Mail order house, nec; Garden supplies; Garden supplies and tools, nec; Hand and edge tools, nec

(G-17118)
AO GLASS LLC
Also Called: Arentzen Ohlander Glass
29 Ledge Rd (05401-4140)

PHONE....................802 735-5016
Rich Arentzen, *Managing Member*
EMP: 24 **EST:** 2012
SALES (est): 1.5MM **Privately Held**
Web: www.aoglass.com
SIC: 3229   Barware

(G-17119)
AUGMENTUS GROUP LLC
Also Called: Augmentus Ltd Co
57 Loomis St # 3 (05401-8507)
◆ **EMP:** 10 **EST:** 2005
SALES (est): 748.33K **Privately Held**
SIC: 2819 2869 2879   Industrial inorganic
chemicals, nec; Industrial organic
chemicals, nec; Agricultural chemicals, nec

(G-17120)
BIXLER UNIVERSITY
Also Called: Bixler's
227 Main St (05401-8321)
PHONE....................888 361-4558
EMP: 14 **EST:** 2018
SALES (est): 868.83K **Privately Held**
Web: www.bixlers.com
SIC: 3911   Jewelry, precious metal

(G-17121)
BOGNER OF AMERICA INC (PA)
128 Lakeside Ave Ste 302 (05401-5190)
PHONE....................802 451-4417
Willy Bogner, *Ch Bd*
Peter Born, *
Constantine Brandstetter, *
▲ **EMP:** 30 **EST:** 1972
SQ FT: 85,000
SALES (est): 9.07MM
SALES (corp-wide): 9.07MM **Privately
Held**
Web: www.bogner.com
SIC: 2329 2339   Men's and boys' sportswear
and athletic clothing; Sportswear, women's

(G-17122)
BRUNSWICK SQUARE LLC
Also Called: Element Real Estate
208 Flynn Ave (05401-5429)
PHONE....................802 497-2575
EMP: 9 **EST:** 2019
SALES (est): 942.35K **Privately Held**
SIC: 2819   Elements

(G-17123)
BURTON CORPORATION (PA)
Also Called: Riding Enhancement Designs
180 Queen City Park Rd (05401-5935)
PHONE....................800 881-3138
Donna Carpenter, *Ch Bd*
John Lacy, *
Mike Reesr, *
Philippe Gouzes, *
◆ **EMP:** 534 **EST:** 1978
SQ FT: 70,000
SALES (est): 244.17MM
SALES (corp-wide): 244.17MM **Privately
Held**
Web: www.burton.com
SIC: 3949   Snow skiing equipment and
supplies, except skis

(G-17124)
**CHAMPLAIN CHOCOLATE
COMPANY (PA)**
Also Called: Lake Champlain Chocolates
750 Pine St (05401-4923)
PHONE....................800 465-5909
James S Lampman, *Pr*
Anne Lampman, *
John Kingston, *
▲ **EMP:** 75 **EST:** 1983

SQ FT: 24,808
SALES (est): 15.53MM
SALES (corp-wide): 15.53MM **Privately
Held**
Web:
www.lakechamplainchocolates.com
SIC: 5441 2066   Candy; Chocolate bars,
solid

(G-17125)
CHAMPLAIN INDUSTRIES INC
17 Oak St (05401-2812)
P.O. Box 821 (05402-0821)
PHONE....................802 651-0708
Christopher Mason, *CEO*
EMP: 10 **EST:** 2000
SALES (est): 2.46MM **Privately Held**
Web: www.champlain.edu
SIC: 1522 3999   Hotel/motel and multi-family
home construction; Barber and beauty shop
equipment

(G-17126)
CITIZEN CIDER LLC
180 Flynn Ave (05401-5423)
PHONE....................802 288-0576
Samantha Quinn, *Mgr*
EMP: 7
SALES (corp-wide): 2.64MM **Privately
Held**
Web: www.citizencider.com
SIC: 2084   Wines, brandy, and brandy spirits
PA: Citizen Cider, Llc
316 Pine St Ste 114
Burlington VT 05401
802 448-3278

(G-17127)
CITIZEN CIDER LLC (PA)
316 Pine St Ste 114 (05401-4740)
PHONE....................802 448-3278
Justin Heilenbach, *Prin*
EMP: 8 **EST:** 2016
SALES (est): 2.64MM
SALES (corp-wide): 2.64MM **Privately
Held**
Web: www.citizencider.com
SIC: 2084   Neutral spirits, fruit

(G-17128)
CORNELL ONLINE LLC
Also Called: April Cornell
131 Battery St (05401-5208)
PHONE....................802 448-3281
April Cornell, *Managing Member*
EMP: 49 **EST:** 2006
SALES (est): 2.41MM **Privately Held**
Web: www.aprilcornell.com
SIC: 2299 5137   Apparel filling: cotton
waste, kapok, and related material;
Women's and children's clothing

(G-17129)
CRICKET RADIO LLC
260 Battery St (05401-3201)
PHONE....................802 825-8368
EMP: 8 **EST:** 2011
SALES (est): 449.46K **Privately Held**
Web: www.cricketradiointeriors.com
SIC: 2599   Hotel furniture

(G-17130)
DA CAPO PUBLISHING INC
Also Called: Seven Days Newspaper
255 S Champlain St Ste 5 (05401-7703)
P.O. Box 1164 (05402-1164)
PHONE....................802 864-5684
EMP: 49 **EST:** 1995
SALES (est): 6.47MM **Privately Held**
Web: www.sevendaysvt.com

SIC: 2711   Newspapers, publishing and
printing

(G-17131)
DRAKER LABORATORIES INC
431 Pine St Ste 114 (05401-4726)
PHONE....................802 922-1162
EMP: 61
Web: www.drakerenergy.com
SIC: 3825   Energy measuring equipment,
electrical

(G-17132)
EATING WELL INC
Also Called: Eatingwell Media Group
50 Lakeside Ave (05401-5483)
PHONE....................802 425-5700
Thomas P Witschi, *CEO*
Richard Mccormick, *Sec*
EMP: 43 **EST:** 2002
SALES (est): 1.97MM
SALES (corp-wide): 3.68B **Publicly Held**
Web: www.eatingwell.com
SIC: 2721   Magazines: publishing only, not
printed on site
HQ: Hawkeye Acquisition, Inc.
1716 Locust St
Des Moines IA 50309
515 284-3000

(G-17133)
EDLUND COMPANY LLC
319 Queen City Park Rd (05401-5933)
P.O. Box 929 (05402-0929)
PHONE....................802 862-9661
◆ **EMP:** 97 **EST:** 2010
SALES (est): 19.86MM
SALES (corp-wide): 2.67MM **Privately
Held**
Web: www.edlundco.com
SIC: 3423 3556 3596   Can openers, not
electric; Slicers, commercial, food; Scales
and balances, except laboratory
HQ: Ali Holding Srl
Via Piero Gobetti 2/A
Cernusco Sul Naviglio MI 20063
029 219-9292

(G-17134)
FARADAY INC
Also Called: Faraday
431 Pine St Ste 113 (05401-5095)
PHONE....................802 658-2034
Thomas Bryenton, *Prin*
EMP: 25 **EST:** 2016
SALES (est): 2.68MM **Privately Held**
Web: www.faraday.ai
SIC: 7372   Business oriented computer
software

(G-17135)
FIRST STEP PRINT SHOP LLC
115 North St (05401-5126)
P.O. Box 311 (05489-0311)
PHONE....................802 899-2708
Robert Martelle, *Managing Member*
Mary Martelle, *Managing Member*
EMP: 7 **EST:** 1992
SALES (est): 489.14K **Privately Held**
Web: www.firststepprintshop.com
SIC: 2752 5112 7334   Photolithographic
printing; Photocopying supplies;
Photocopying and duplicating services

(G-17136)
FOAM BREWERS LLC
Also Called: House of Fermentology
112 Lake St (05401-5284)
PHONE....................802 399-2511
Robert Grim, *Prin*

EMP: 19 **EST:** 2015
SALES (est): 5.18MM **Privately Held**
Web: www.foambrewers.com
SIC: 5813 2082   Bars and lounges; Beer
(alcoholic beverage)

(G-17137)
GENERAL DYNAMICS CORP
266 Queen City Park Rd (05401-5934)
PHONE....................703 876-3631
EMP: 14 **EST:** 2018
SALES (est): 244.34K **Privately Held**
SIC: 3484   Small arms

(G-17138)
GORILLA BARS INC
Also Called: Garuka Bars
336 N Winooski Ave (05401-3616)
PHONE....................802 309-4997
Mike Rosenberg, *Pr*
Mike Rosenberg, *Prin*
EMP: 7 **EST:** 2011
SALES (est): 574.8K **Privately Held**
SIC: 2064   Granola and muesli, bars and
clusters

(G-17139)
**INNOVTIVE GRDNING
SLUTIONS INC**
Also Called: Gardener's Supply
128 Intervale Rd (05401-2804)
PHONE....................888 560-1037
Cindy Turcot, *Pr*
Richard Harris, *
EMP: 250 **EST:** 1996
SALES (est): 7.76MM **Privately Held**
Web: www.gardeners.com
SIC: 5261 3423   Garden supplies and tools,
nec; Garden and farm tools, including
shovels

(G-17140)
JRS CORP
134 Church St (05401-8401)
PHONE....................802 310-5253
Joshua Markle, *Prin*
EMP: 15 **EST:** 2010
SALES (est): 650K **Privately Held**
SIC: 2599   Bar, restaurant and cafeteria
furniture

(G-17141)
LAKE CHAMPLAIN TRNSP CO
Lake Industries Div
King Street Dock (05401)
PHONE....................802 660-3495
EMP: 58
SALES (corp-wide): 16.98MM **Privately
Held**
Web: www.ferries.com
SIC: 3731 5947   Ferryboats, building and
repairing; Gift shop
PA: Lake Champlain Transportation
Company
1 King St
Burlington VT 05401
802 864-9804

(G-17142)
MAMAVA INC
180 Battery St Ste 210 (05401-5334)
PHONE....................802 347-2111
Sascha Mayer, *CEO*
Sascha Mayer, *Prin*
Elizabeth Adams, *
EMP: 42 **EST:** 2013
SALES (est): 5.39MM **Privately Held**
Web: www.mamava.com

SIC: 2542 2599   Pallet racks: except wood;
Factory furniture and fixtures

(G-17143)
MARVELL GVRNMENT
SOLUTIONS LLC
128 Lakeside Ave Ste 403 (05401-4939)
PHONE..................................845 245-8066
Kimberley Kelly, *Managing Member*
Kevin O'buckley, *Managing Member*
EMP: 50 EST: 2018
SALES (est): 9.1MM
SALES (corp-wide): 5.92B **Publicly Held**
Web: www.marvell.com
SIC: 5065 3674   Semiconductor devices;
Semiconductors and related devices
HQ: Marvell Semiconductor, Inc.
5488 Marvell Ln
Santa Clara CA 95054

(G-17144)
MCHOLBE-NOONAN
CORPORATION
Also Called: Vermont Pub Brewry Burlington
144 College St (05401-8416)
PHONE..................................802 865-0500
Greg Noonan, *Pr*
Robert Beaupre, *
Gregory Donlin, *
Elise Pecor, *
EMP: 8 EST: 1988
SQ FT: 5,000
SALES (est): 449.26K **Privately Held**
Web: www.vermontbrewery.com
SIC: 2082 5813 5812   Beer (alcoholic
beverage); Bar (drinking places); Eating
places

(G-17145)
MFI CORP
44 Lakeside Ave (05401-5404)
PHONE..................................802 658-6600
Steve Spittle, *Pr*
EMP: 94 EST: 1896
SALES (est): 3.23MM
SALES (corp-wide): 4.03B **Publicly Held**
SIC: 3556   Food products machinery
PA: The Middleby Corporation
1400 Toastmaster Dr
Elgin IL 60120
847 741-3300

(G-17146)
NOTABLI INC
209 College St Ste 3w (05401-8394)
PHONE..................................802 448-0810
Thomas O' Leary, *CEO*
EMP: 10 EST: 2012
SQ FT: 35,000
SALES (est): 1.05MM
SALES (corp-wide): 1.05MM **Privately
Held**
Web: www.notabli.com
SIC: 7372   Application computer software
PA: Parent Company Applications, Inc.
20 Hillside Cir
Essex Junction VT 05452
802 233-3612

(G-17147)
NU CHOCOLAT LLC
180 Battery St Ste 110 (05401-5334)
PHONE..................................802 735-7770
EMP: 12 EST: 2017
SALES (est): 747.66K **Privately Held**
Web: www.nuchocolat.com
SIC: 5441 2064   Confectionery; Candy bars,
including chocolate covered bars

(G-17148)
OHMD INC
50 Lakeside Ave (05401-5402)
P.O. Box 8022 (05402-8022)
PHONE..................................802 578-6369
Ethan Bechtel, *CEO*
Nate Bechtel, *
EMP: 50 EST: 2016
SQ FT: 400
SALES (est): 2.98MM **Privately Held**
Web: www.ohmd.com
SIC: 7372   Business oriented computer
software

(G-17149)
OVR TECH LLC
Also Called: Ovr Technology
50 Lakeside Ave Unit 750 (05401-6023)
PHONE..................................802 391-4172
Aaron Wisniewski, *CEO*
Sam Wisniewski, *CFO*
EMP: 9 EST: 2018
SALES (est): 529.22K **Privately Held**
Web: www.ovrtechnology.com
SIC: 7379 3577   Online services technology
consultants; Computer peripheral
equipment, nec

(G-17150)
PEARL STREET BEVERAGE INC
Also Called: Pearl Street Pipe & Beverage
240 Pearl St (05401-8532)
PHONE..................................802 658-1574
John Dubie, *Pr*
EMP: 10 EST: 1983
SQ FT: 6,500
SALES (est): 1.34MM **Privately Held**
Web: www.pearlstreetbeverage.com
SIC: 5921 5411 2086   Beer (packaged);
Grocery stores, independent; Bottled and
canned soft drinks

(G-17151)
PIEMATRIX INC
Also Called: Piematrix
106 Main St (05401-8484)
PHONE..................................802 318-4891
Paul Dandurand, *CEO*
EMP: 10 EST: 2006
SALES (est): 830.7K **Privately Held**
Web: www.pie.me
SIC: 7372   Prepackaged software

(G-17152)
PROSPECT PRESS LLC
47 Prospect Pkwy (05401-4147)
PHONE..................................802 862-6717
Andy Golub, *Owner*
EMP: 7 EST: 2017
SALES (est): 192.6K **Privately Held**
Web: www.prospectpressvt.com
SIC: 2741   Miscellaneous publishing

(G-17153)
QUEEN CITY PRINTERS INC
Also Called: Battery Graphics
701 Pine St (05401-4941)
P.O. Box 756 (05402-0756)
PHONE..................................802 864-4566
TOLL FREE: 800
Alan R Schillhammer, *Pr*
EMP: 35 EST: 1951
SQ FT: 25,000
SALES (est): 2.37MM **Privately Held**
Web: www.qcpinc.com
SIC: 2752 2791 2789   Offset printing;
Typesetting; Bookbinding and related work

(G-17154)
QUEEN DOG LLC
Also Called: Great Harvest Bread
382 Pine St (05401-4776)
PHONE..................................802 660-2733
Christopher Brown, *Managing Member*
EMP: 18 EST: 2018
SALES (est): 1.02MM **Privately Held**
Web: www.greatharvest.com
SIC: 5461 2051   Bread; Bakery: wholesale
or wholesale/retail combined

(G-17155)
RED CORP
180 Queen City Park Rd (05401-5935)
PHONE..................................802 862-4500
EMP: 31 EST: 1997
SALES (est): 5.33MM
SALES (corp-wide): 244.17MM **Privately
Held**
Web: www.burton.com
SIC: 3949   Snow skiing equipment and
supplies, except skis
PA: The Burton Corporation
180 Queen City Park Rd
Burlington VT 05401
802 862-4500

(G-17156)
RHINO FOODS INC (PA)
Also Called: Rhino
179 Queen City Park Rd (05401-5932)
PHONE..................................802 862-0252
Ted Castle, *Pr*
Edward W Castle, *
Anne Castle, *
Jayne R Magnant, *
EMP: 126 EST: 1981
SALES (est): 47.73MM
SALES (corp-wide): 47.73MM **Privately
Held**
Web: www.rhinofoods.com
SIC: 2045 2024   Doughs, frozen or
refrigerated: from purchased flour; Ice
cream and ice milk

(G-17157)
RINGMASTER SOFTWARE CORP
70 S Winooski Ave Ste 1w (05401-3969)
PHONE..................................802 383-1050
EMP: 10 EST: 2020
SALES (est): 322.73K **Privately Held**
Web: www.ringmastersw.com
SIC: 7372   Prepackaged software

(G-17158)
SELECT DESIGN LTD
Also Called: Apparel Marketing Associates
208 Flynn Ave Ste 1a (05401-5420)
PHONE..................................802 864-9075
◆ **EMP: 75 EST:** 1987
SALES (est): 18.03MM **Privately Held**
Web: www.selectdesign.com
SIC: 8742 3999 7389   Marketing consulting
services; Barber and beauty shop
equipment; Packaging and labeling services

(G-17159)
SEVENTH GENERATION INC
(DH)
Also Called: SEVENTH GENERATION
60 Lake St Ste 3n (05401-5307)
PHONE..................................802 658-3773
John Replogle, *Pr*
Maureen Usifer, *
▲ **EMP: 143 EST:** 1985
SALES (est): 270.21K
SALES (corp-wide): 62.39B **Privately Held**
Web: www.seventhgeneration.com

SIC: 2676 5162 5169 5122   Infant and baby
paper products; Plastics products, nec;
Chemicals and allied products, nec; Drugs,
proprietaries, and sundries
HQ: Unilever United States, Inc.
800 Sylvan Ave
Englewood Cliffs NJ 07632
201 735-9661

(G-17160)
SPEEDER & EARLS INC
Also Called: Speeder & Earl's
412 Pine St (05401-4779)
PHONE..................................802 660-3996
Jessica Workman, *Pr*
Jeannie Vento, *Pr*
Jessica Workman, *VP*
EMP: 16 EST: 1993
SQ FT: 2,300
SALES (est): 1.33MM **Privately Held**
Web: www.speederandearls.com
SIC: 5499 5961 5812 2095   Coffee; Catalog
sales; Coffee shop; Roasted coffee

(G-17161)
THIRD PLACE INC
Also Called: American Fltbread - Brlngton H
115 Saint Paul St (05401-8411)
PHONE..................................802 861-2999
Rob Downy, *Prin*
EMP: 23 EST: 2004
SALES (est): 2.54MM **Privately Held**
Web: www.zerogravitybeer.com
SIC: 2082   Malt beverages

(G-17162)
TOPAZ LEGAL INC
29 Church St Ste 303 (05401-4433)
P.O. Box 730 (05453-0730)
PHONE..................................802 540-2504
Christopher Ryan Kave, *Pr*
EMP: 44 EST: 2007
SALES (est): 5.13MM **Privately Held**
Web: www.auroranorth.com
SIC: 7372   Business oriented computer
software

(G-17163)
UVM PRINT MAIL CENTER
85 S Prospect St (05401-3433)
PHONE..................................802 656-8149
EMP: 40 EST: 2018
SALES (est): 906.4K **Privately Held**
Web: www.uvm.edu
SIC: 2752   Commercial printing, lithographic

(G-17164)
YANKEE MEDICAL INC (DH)
276 North Ave (05401-2900)
P.O. Box 276 (05402-0276)
PHONE..................................802 863-4591
Scott Wells, *Pr*
EMP: 18 EST: 1975
SQ FT: 16,000
SALES (est): 3.38MM
SALES (corp-wide): 1.03B **Privately Held**
Web: www.yankeemedical.com
SIC: 5999 3842 5047 3999   Orthopedic and
prosthesis applications; Orthopedic
appliances; Hospital equipment and
furniture; Wheelchair lifts
HQ: The University Of Vermont Health
Network Ventures Inc
111 Colchester Ave
Burlington VT 05401
802 847-0000

(G-17165)
YOUNG WRITERS PROJECT INC
47 Maple St Ste 216 (05401-4956)

PHONE..................802 324-9537
John Canning, *Prin*
EMP: 15 **EST:** 2009
SALES (est): 123.93K **Privately Held**
Web: www.youngwritersproject.org
SIC: 2711 Newspapers, publishing and printing

Cabot
Washington County

(G-17166)
WOODBELLY PIZZA LLC (PA)
34 Lagune Rd (05647)
PHONE..................802 552-3476
EMP: 9 **EST:** 2014
SQ FT: 21,000
SALES (est): 336.93K
SALES (corp-wide): 336.93K **Privately Held**
Web: woodbelly.square.site
SIC: 5812 2038 Pizza restaurants; Pizza, frozen

Calais
Washington County

(G-17167)
DAILY GARDENER
2930 Dugar Brook Rd (05648-7585)
P.O. Box 13 (05648-0013)
PHONE..................802 223-7851
Peter Burke, *Prin*
EMP: 7 **EST:** 2010
SALES (est): 109.08K **Privately Held**
Web: www.thedailygardener.com
SIC: 2711 Newspapers, publishing and printing

Cambridge
Chittenden County

(G-17168)
SOGLE PROPERTY LLC
Also Called: Cave Moose Farm
189 Glenn Dr (05444-4510)
PHONE..................802 849-7943
Eric Sorkin, *Managing Member*
EMP: 20 **EST:** 2000
SALES (est): 4.1MM **Privately Held**
SIC: 5149 5963 1799 0161 Sugar, honey, molasses, and syrups; Food services, direct sales; Fence construction; Lettuce and leaf vegetable farms

Canaan
Essex County

(G-17169)
RICHARD MRCHSSULT DBA BNGTSON
240 Gale St (05903-9507)
PHONE..................802 266-9666
Richard M Marchesseault, *Pr*
EMP: 8 **EST:** 2017
SALES (est): 450.75K **Privately Held**
SIC: 3544 Special dies and tools

(G-17170)
STEPHANE INKEL INC
279 Rt 114 (05903)
P.O. Box 111 (05903-0111)
PHONE..................603 331-3296
Stephane Inkel, *Prin*

Adrien Inkel, *Prin*
EMP: 9 **EST:** 2005
SALES (est): 247.55K **Privately Held**
SIC: 2411 Logging

Castleton
Rutland County

(G-17171)
BROWNS QUARRIED SLATE PDTS INC
2504 S Street Ext (05735-9359)
PHONE..................802 468-2297
Charles W Brown, *Prin*
EMP: 14 **EST:** 2009
SALES (est): 989.9K **Privately Held**
SIC: 3281 Slate products

(G-17172)
HUBBARDTON FORGE LLC
Also Called: Hubbardton Forge
154 Route 30 S (05735-9521)
P.O. Box 827 (05735-0827)
PHONE..................802 468-3090
Bob Dillon, *CEO*
◆ **EMP:** 225 **EST:** 1974
SQ FT: 117,000
SALES (est): 41.15MM **Privately Held**
Web: www.hubbardtonforge.com
SIC: 3645 5063 3446 Residential lighting fixtures; Lighting fixtures; Architectural metalwork

(G-17173)
MCCUE MEMORIAL CO INC
Also Called: Rmg Stone Products
680 E Hubbardton Rd (05735-9735)
P.O. Box 807 (05735-0807)
PHONE..................802 468-5636
John Socinski, *Pr*
David Socinski, *VP*
Janet Socinski, *Sec*
EMP: 27 **EST:** 1910
SQ FT: 12,000
SALES (est): 2.14MM **Privately Held**
Web: www.rmgstone.com
SIC: 5211 5999 5032 5099 Masonry materials and supplies; Monuments, finished to custom order; Marble building stone; Monuments and grave markers

Center Rutland
Rutland County

(G-17174)
GAWET MARBLE & GRANITE INC (PA)
805 Business Route 4 (05736-9639)
P.O. Box 219 (05736-0219)
PHONE..................802 773-8868
Philip Gawet, *Pr*
EMP: 9 **EST:** 1919
SQ FT: 6,000
SALES (est): 2.3MM
SALES (corp-wide): 2.3MM **Privately Held**
Web: www.gawetmarble.com
SIC: 5999 3281 Monuments and tombstones ; Granite, cut and shaped

Charlotte
Chittenden County

(G-17175)
COUNTRY HOME PRODUCTS INC

Also Called: C H P Marketing Services
823 Ferry Rd (05445-9092)
P.O. Box 25 (05491-0025)
PHONE..................802 771-7202
Julia Gilbert, *Mgr*
EMP: 40
Web: www.drpower.com
SIC: 5961 8743 3524 3523 Mail order house, nec; Sales promotion; Lawn and garden equipment; Farm machinery and equipment
HQ: Country Home Products, Inc.
800 Hinesburg Rd
South Burlington VT 05403
802 877-1200

(G-17176)
DARLINGS BOATWORKS INC
821 Ferry Rd (05445-9092)
P.O. Box 32 (05445-0032)
PHONE..................802 425-2004
George Darling, *Pr*
EMP: 7 **EST:** 1978
SALES (est): 671.22K **Privately Held**
Web: www.darlingsboatworks.com
SIC: 3732 Boatbuilding and repairing

(G-17177)
EVAN WEBSTER INK LLC
442 Lewis Creek Rd (05445-9154)
PHONE..................802 222-0344
Evan Webster, *Brnch Mgr*
EMP: 15
SALES (corp-wide): 100.17K **Privately Held**
Web: www.websterink.com
SIC: 2752 Commercial printing, lithographic
PA: Evan Webster Ink, Llc
34 Sage Ct Ste 1
Shelburne VT

Chelsea
Orange County

(G-17178)
HEB MANUFACTURING COMPANY INC
67 Vt Rte 110 (05038-9078)
P.O. Box 188 (05038-0188)
PHONE..................802 685-4821
Bonnie Kennedy, *Pr*
Howard Parker, *
EMP: 40 **EST:** 1957
SQ FT: 35,000
SALES (est): 5.29MM **Privately Held**
Web: www.hebmfg.com
SIC: 3469 3315 Stamping metal for the trade ; Wire products, ferrous/iron: made in wiredrawing plants

(G-17179)
VERMONT WIREFORM INC
Rt. 110 (05038)
P.O. Box 248 (05038-0248)
PHONE..................802 889-3200
Richard Colby, *Pr*
Karen Colby, *Sec*
EMP: 15 **EST:** 1979
SQ FT: 20,000
SALES (est): 2.41MM **Privately Held**
Web: www.vermontwireform.com
SIC: 3496 Miscellaneous fabricated wire products

Chester
Windsor County

(G-17180)
DREWS LLC (HQ)
Also Called: Drew's All Natural
926 Vt Route 103 S (05143-8461)
PHONE..................802 875-1184
William Aubrey, *
EMP: 8 **EST:** 1994
SQ FT: 7,000
SALES (est): 7.72MM
SALES (corp-wide): 21.24MM **Privately Held**
Web: www.drewsorganics.com
SIC: 2035 2099 Dressings, salad: raw and cooked (except dry mixes); Dips, except cheese and sour cream based
PA: Schlotterbeck & Foss, Llc
3 Ledgeview Dr
Westbrook ME 04092
207 772-4666

(G-17181)
MULHOLLAND WLDG & FABRICATION
Also Called: Mulholland Wldg & Fabrication
81 Gold River Ext (05143-0017)
P.O. Box 468 (05143-0468)
PHONE..................802 875-5500
Tucker Mulholland, *Dir*
EMP: 11 **EST:** 2012
SALES (est): 563.8K **Privately Held**
Web: www.vtwelding.com
SIC: 7692 Welding repair

(G-17182)
P AND L TRUCKING
31 Toma Rd (05143)
P.O. Box 993 (05143-0993)
PHONE..................802 875-2819
Palmer Goodrich Ii, *Owner*
Palmer H Goodrich Ii, *Owner*
EMP: 8 **EST:** 1977
SALES (est): 660K **Privately Held**
SIC: 2411 4212 Logging camps and contractors; Timber trucking, local

(G-17183)
SEMYA CORP
4333 Vt Route 103 N (05143-8407)
PHONE..................802 875-6564
Greg P Adamovich, *Pr*
EMP: 23
SALES (corp-wide): 2.61MM **Privately Held**
SIC: 1411 Granite dimension stone
PA: Semya Corp.
53 Duncan Rd
Alstead NH 03602
802 875-6564

(G-17184)
VERMONT FURN HARDWOODS INC
Also Called: Vermont Hardwoods
386 Depot St (05143-9342)
P.O. Box 769 (05143-0769)
PHONE..................802 875-2550
David Waldmann, *Pr*
Rebecca Waldmann, *VP*
EMP: 30 **EST:** 1979
SQ FT: 27,000
SALES (est): 1.99MM **Privately Held**
Web: www.vermonthardwoods.com
SIC: 2431 Millwork

GEOGRAPHIC

Colchester
Chittenden County

(G-17185)
ALKEN INC
Also Called: Polhemus
40 Hercules Dr (05446-5835)
P.O. Box 560 (05446-0560)
PHONE.................................802 655-3159
Allan G Rodgers, *CEO*
Allan G Rodgers Junior, *Pr*
David Wood, *
▲ **EMP:** 25 **EST:** 1970
SQ FT: 18,000
SALES (est): 4.31MM **Privately Held**
Web: www.polhemus.com
SIC: 3577 3829　Computer peripheral
equipment, nec; Weather tracking
equipment

(G-17186)
BAKERS DOZEN INC
Also Called: Baker's Dozen Bakery
70 Roosevelt Hwy Ste 2 (05446-5934)
PHONE.................................802 879-4001
Mike Le Blanc, *Pr*
EMP: 10 **EST:** 1969
SQ FT: 5,000
SALES (est): 244.99K **Privately Held**
SIC: 2051　Bread, cake, and related products

(G-17187)
**CHAMPLAIN CABLE
CORPORATION (PA)**
Also Called: Champlain Cable
175 Hercules Dr (05446-5951)
PHONE.................................802 654-4200
▲ **EMP:** 130 **EST:** 1955
SALES (est): 106.24MM
SALES (corp-wide): 106.24MM **Privately
Held**
Web: www.champcable.com
SIC: 3357　Nonferrous wiredrawing and
insulating

(G-17188)
DELLAMORE ENTERPRISES INC
Also Called: Dell'amore Pasta Sauce
948 Hercules Dr Ste 1 (05446-5926)
P.O. Box 974 (05446-0974)
PHONE.................................802 655-6264
Frank Dell'amore, *Pr*
Lorene Spagnuolo Dell'amore, *VP*
EMP: 7 **EST:** 1986
SQ FT: 4,000
SALES (est): 948.73K **Privately Held**
Web: www.dellamore.com
SIC: 2033　Spaghetti and other pasta sauce:
packaged in cans, jars, etc

(G-17189)
DJS TREE SERVICE & LOG INC
Also Called: Dj's Tree Service and Ldscpg
65 Colchester Point Rd (05446-8160)
PHONE.................................802 655-0264
James Myers, *Pr*
Lisa Myers, *Sec*
EMP: 15 **EST:** 1975
SQ FT: 9,600
SALES (est): 2.42MM **Privately Held**
Web: www.djstree.com
SIC: 0782 0783 4959 2411　Landscape
contractors; Ornamental shrub and tree
services; Snowplowing; Logging

(G-17190)
FAB-TECH INC
Also Called: Psp

480 Hercules Dr Ste 2 (05446-5948)
PHONE.................................802 655-8800
▲ **EMP:** 130 **EST:** 1987
SALES (est): 21.69MM **Privately Held**
Web: www.fabtechinc.com
SIC: 3444　Sheet metalwork

(G-17191)
**FRANK W WHITCOMB CNSTR
CORP**
115 Whitcomb St (05446)
P.O. Box 155 (05404-0155)
PHONE.................................802 655-1270
Frank L Whitcomb, *Brnch Mgr*
EMP: 100
SALES (corp-wide): 19.57MM **Privately
Held**
SIC: 1771 1442　Concrete work;
Construction sand and gravel
PA: Frank W. Whitcomb Construction
Corporation
187 Whitcomb Rd
Walpole NH 03608
603 445-5555

(G-17192)
GARLIC PRESS INC
Also Called: Pop Color
614 Macrae Rd (05446-6827)
PHONE.................................802 864-0670
Michael Swaidner, *Pr*
Carol Mac Donald, *VP*
EMP: 10 **EST:** 1984
SALES (est): 496.18K **Privately Held**
Web: www.popcolorvt.com
SIC: 2741 7336　Guides: publishing only, not
printed on site; Graphic arts and related
design

(G-17193)
GRATE IDEAS OF AMERICA LLC
63 Marina Loop (05446-4488)
PHONE.................................844 292-6044
Charles J Wobby, *Dir*
▼ **EMP:** 8 **EST:** 2010
SALES (est): 412.55K **Privately Held**
Web: www.grate-ideas.com
SIC: 3429　Fireplace equipment, hardware:
andirons, grates, screens

(G-17194)
HAYWARD TYLER INC (DH)
480 Roosevelt Hwy (05446-1594)
P.O. Box 680 (05446-0680)
PHONE.................................802 655-4444
Vince Conte, *Pr*
Bonnie Hale, *
Mark Kelley, *
Stephen Casale, *
▲ **EMP:** 41 **EST:** 1970
SQ FT: 40,000
SALES (est): 25.64MM
SALES (corp-wide): 89.29MM **Privately
Held**
Web: www.haywardtyler.com
SIC: 3561 7699 3621　Industrial pumps and
parts; Pumps and pumping equipment
repair; Motors and generators
HQ: Hayward Tyler Group Limited
1 Kimpton Road
Luton BEDS LU1 3

(G-17195)
**HAZELETT STRIP-CASTING
CORP (HQ)**
135 W Lakeshore Dr (05446-9753)
P.O. Box 600 (05446-0600)
PHONE.................................802 863-6376
▲ **EMP:** 147 **EST:** 1956
SALES (est): 49.85MM **Privately Held**

Web: www.hazelett.com
SIC: 3559　Foundry, smelting, refining, and
similar machinery
PA: Stave Island Limited Partnership
135 W Lakeshore Dr
Colchester VT 05446

(G-17196)
**HUMBLE SCREEN PRINTING
LLC**
1610 Troy Ave (05446-3122)
PHONE.................................802 399-5400
Jerome Mariano, *Prin*
EMP: 7 **EST:** 2010
SALES (est): 290.38K **Privately Held**
Web: www.humblescreenprinting.com
SIC: 2759　Screen printing

(G-17197)
LARCOLINE INC (PA)
Also Called: Minuteman Press
113 Acorn Ln Ste 2 (05446-5947)
PHONE.................................802 864-5440
Jon Cunningham, *Pr*
EMP: 12 **EST:** 1998
SALES (est): 2.07MM
SALES (corp-wide): 2.07MM **Privately
Held**
Web: www.minuteman.com
SIC: 2752　Commercial printing, lithographic

(G-17198)
**OMNI MEASUREMENT
SYSTEMS INC**
Also Called: Omni Medical Systems
808 Hercules Dr (05446-5839)
PHONE.................................802 497-2253
Mark Harvie, *Pr*
EMP: 40 **EST:** 1998
SQ FT: 29,000
SALES (est): 3.95MM **Privately Held**
Web: www.omni-defense.com
SIC: 3612 3825 3699　Ballasts for lighting
fixtures; Analog-digital converters,
electronic instrumentation type; Electrical
equipment and supplies, nec

(G-17199)
PBL INCORPORATED
Also Called: Ace Castings
158 Brentwood Dr Ste 2 (05446-7994)
PHONE.................................802 893-0111
Phillip R Lux, *Pr*
EMP: 11 **EST:** 2000
SQ FT: 80,200
SALES (est): 319.89K **Privately Held**
Web: www.acecastings.com
SIC: 3911 3561 3841　Jewelry, precious
metal; Industrial pumps and parts; Surgical
and medical instruments

(G-17200)
**PRCESS CRITICAL SYSTEMS
GROUP**
Also Called: Sequel Industrial Products Inc
480 Hercules Dr (05446-7917)
PHONE.................................802 448-5860
Jim Howard, *Pr*
W Scot Fine, *Ex VP*
Michael Baranski, *VP*
Jake Conner, *VP*
EMP: 12 **EST:** 2012
SALES (est): 2.63MM
SALES (corp-wide): 242.12K **Privately
Held**
Web: www.cpsgrp.com
SIC: 3498　Fabricated pipe and fittings
HQ: Critical Process Systems Group, Inc.
11789 W Executive Dr

Boise ID 83713
802 448-5860

(G-17201)
RETTIG USA INC
948 Hercules Dr (05446-5926)
P.O. Box 1460 (05495-1460)
PHONE.................................802 654-7500
Luc Cardinaels, *Prin*
▲ **EMP:** 7 **EST:** 1992
SALES (est): 163.69K **Privately Held**
Web: www.purmogroup.com
SIC: 3567　Industrial furnaces and ovens

(G-17202)
SHELBURNE LIMESTONE CORP
1975 Route 7 S (05446)
PHONE.................................802 878-2656
Trampas Demers, *Pr*
EMP: 14
SALES (corp-wide): 22.21MM **Privately
Held**
SIC: 1429　Igneus rock, crushed and broken-
quarrying
PA: Shelburne Limestone Corp
1949 Main St
Colchester VT 05446
802 878-2656

(G-17203)
**SHELBURNE LIMESTONE CORP
(PA)**
Also Called: So. Wallingford Limestone
1949 Main St (05446-7652)
P.O. Box 359 (05453-0359)
PHONE.................................802 878-2656
Trampas Demers, *Pr*
Dennis Demers, *VP*
Trampas Dremers, *Pr*
Kathleen Demers, *Sec*
EMP: 13 **EST:** 1964
SQ FT: 19,000
SALES (est): 22.21MM
SALES (corp-wide): 22.21MM **Privately
Held**
SIC: 5191 5032 1422　Limestone, agricultural
; Stone, crushed or broken; Crushed and
broken limestone

(G-17204)
SYSTEMS & SOFTWARE INC
401 Watertower Cir (05446-1912)
PHONE.................................802 655-4400
EMP: 44
SALES (corp-wide): 6.62B **Privately Held**
Web: www.ssivt.com
SIC: 7372　Prepackaged software
HQ: Systems & Software, Inc.
10 E Allen St
Winooski VT 05404
802 865-1170

(G-17205)
TROY MINERALS INC
Also Called: Florence Crushed Stone
312 Village Dr (05446-7212)
P.O. Box 47 (05446-0047)
PHONE.................................802 878-5103
Michael Chmielewski, *Owner*
EMP: 9 **EST:** 1994
SQ FT: 1,000
SALES (est): 1.21MM **Privately Held**
SIC: 1499 3281　Talc mining; Slate products

(G-17206)
**VERMONT NUT FREE CHOCLAT
INC**
146 Brentwood Dr (05446-7976)
PHONE.................................802 372-4654

▲ = Import ▼ = Export
◆ = Import/Export

Gail Elvidge, *Pr*
Mark T Elvidge, *VP*
EMP: 10 EST: 1998
SALES (est): 1.46MM **Privately Held**
Web: www.vermontnutfree.com
SIC: 2066 5947 Chocolate and cocoa
products; Gift, novelty, and souvenir shop

(G-17207)
VIANOR INC (HQ)
1945 Main St (05446-7652)
P.O. Box 624 (05453-0624)
PHONE.............................802 864-7108
Jason Phelps, *Pr*
Jason Desjardin, *Treas*
EMP: 47 EST: 2008
SALES (est): 9.35MM **Privately Held**
SIC: 5531 7534 Automotive tires; Tire repair
shop
PA: Nokian Renkaat Oyj
Pirkkalaistie 7
Nokia 37100

(G-17208)
VISIBLE
ELECTROPHYSIOLOGY LLC
Also Called: Visible Ep
197 Moonlight Rdg (05446-7797)
P.O. Box 73 (05404-0073)
PHONE.............................802 847-4539
EMP: 10 EST: 2012
SALES (est): 254.1K **Privately Held**
Web: www.visibleep.com
SIC: 7372 Prepackaged software

Cuttingsville
Rutland County

(G-17209)
PVF MAPLE LLC
1368 Lincoln Hill Rd (05738-9482)
PHONE.............................802 492-3364
Neal Sharrow, *Prin*
EMP: 7 EST: 2014
SALES (est): 285.35K **Privately Held**
Web: www.pvfmaplellc.com
SIC: 2099 Maple syrup

Danby
Rutland County

(G-17210)
VERMONT STORE FIXTURE
CORPORATION (PA)
1566 Us Route 7 (05739-9623)
PHONE.............................802 293-5126
EMP: 70 EST: 1978
SALES (est): 9.95MM
SALES (corp-wide): 9.95MM **Privately
Held**
Web: www.vsfc.com
SIC: 2541 2542 Store fixtures, wood;
Partitions and fixtures, except wood

Derby
Orleans County

(G-17211)
LOUIS GARNEAU USA INC
Also Called: Garneau USA Outlet
3916 Us Route 5 (05829-9846)
P.O. Box 1460 (05829-5460)
PHONE.............................802 334-5885
Louis Garneau, *Pr*
▲ **EMP: 70 EST:** 1988

SQ FT: 11,000
SALES (est): 10.29MM
SALES (corp-wide): 79.6MM **Privately
Held**
Web: www.garneau.com
SIC: 2339 2329 Sportswear, women's;
Men's and boys' sportswear and athletic
clothing
PA: Louis Garneau Sports Inc
30 Rue Des Grands-Lacs
Saint-Augustin-De-Desmaures QC
G3A 2
418 878-4135

(G-17212)
NORTH COUNTRY
ENGINEERING INC
106 John Taplin Rd (05829-9778)
PHONE.............................802 766-5396
Jean S Clark, *Pr*
Tammy Benoit, *
EMP: 35 EST: 1963
SQ FT: 12,000
SALES (est): 3.12MM **Privately Held**
Web: www.northcountryeng.com
SIC: 3599 6512 7692 Machine shop,
jobbing and repair; Commercial and
industrial building operation; Welding repair

Derby Line
Orleans County

(G-17213)
TIVOLY INC
434 Baxter Ave (05830-8901)
PHONE.............................802 873-3106
Mark Tivoly, *Pr*
Noel Talagrand, *
Jean Michele Tivoly, *
Janice Lamoureux, *
▲ **EMP: 113 EST:** 1988
SQ FT: 160,000
SALES (est): 24.44MM
SALES (corp-wide): 281.89K **Privately
Held**
Web: www.tivoly.com
SIC: 3545 Machine tool accessories
HQ: Tivoly
266 Route Porte De Tarentaise
Tours En Savoie 73790
479895959

Dorset
Bennington County

(G-17214)
J K ADAMS COMPANY INC
Also Called: Kitchen Store, The
1430 Route 30 (05251-9720)
PHONE.............................802 362-2303
Adam Sigel, *CEO*
Bill Eyre, *
Edgar C Campbell, *
John Rodrigues, *
Robert W Allen, *
▲ **EMP: 40 EST:** 1944
SQ FT: 45,000
SALES (est): 6.84MM **Privately Held**
Web: www.jkadams.com
SIC: 2499 5719 Woodenware, kitchen and
household; Kitchenware

East Barre
Washington County

(G-17215)
VERMONT FLANNEL CO (PA)
128 Mill St (05649-3070)
P.O. Box 220 (05649-0220)
PHONE.............................802 476-5226
Mark Baker, *Pr*
Linda Baker, *
▲ **EMP: 12 EST:** 1991
SALES (est): 9.98MM **Privately Held**
Web: www.vermontflannel.com
SIC: 5137 5136 2369 2339 Uniforms,
women's and children's; Work clothing,
men's and boys'; Girl's and children's
outerwear, nec; Women's and misses'
outerwear, nec

East Dummerston
Windham County

(G-17216)
GREEN MOUNTAIN SPINNERY
INC
7 Brickyard Ln (05346-9752)
P.O. Box 568 (05346-0568)
PHONE.............................802 387-4528
David Ritchie, *Pr*
Clare Wilson, *VP*
Elizabeth Mills, *Sec*
EMP: 9 EST: 1981
SQ FT: 2,200
SALES (est): 409.78K **Privately Held**
Web: www.spinnery.com
SIC: 2281 5949 Wool yarn, spun; Knitting
goods and supplies

(G-17217)
SOUNDVIEW VERMONT
HOLDINGS LLC
67 Kathan Meadow Rd (05346-9704)
PHONE.............................802 387-5571
EMP: 136 EST: 2013
SALES (est): 41.08MM
SALES (corp-wide): 467.08MM **Privately
Held**
SIC: 2621 Napkin stock, paper
HQ: Marcal Manufacturing, Llc
1 Market St
Elmwood Park NJ 07407

East Randolph
Orange County

(G-17218)
KAD MODELS & PROTOTYPES
INC
313 Vt Route 14 S (05041)
P.O. Box 282 (05041-0282)
PHONE.............................510 229-8764
Brian Kippen, *Pr*
John Dove, *Pr*
Brian Kippen, *VP*
EMP: 11 EST: 2012
SALES (est): 1.01MM **Privately Held**
Web: www.kadmodels.com
SIC: 3599 Machine shop, jobbing and repair

East Ryegate
Caledonia County

(G-17219)
YS ENTERPRISES INC
Also Called: Y'S Enterprises
201 Eastwood Ln (05042-3013)
P.O. Box 364 (05042-0364)
PHONE.............................802 238-0902
EMP: 8 EST: 2013
SALES (est): 243.04K **Privately Held**
Web: www.y-sent.com
SIC: 8742 3548 Industrial consultant;
Welding apparatus

Enosburg Falls
Franklin County

(G-17220)
BENJAMIN K LEPESQUEUR
799 Pudvah Hill Rd (05450-4506)
PHONE.............................802 933-5500
Benjamin K Lepesqueur, *Prin*
EMP: 7 EST: 2014
SALES (est): 174.6K **Privately Held**
SIC: 2411 Wooden logs

(G-17221)
COLD HOLLOW PRECISION INC
154 Butternut Hollow Rd (05450-5733)
P.O. Box 218 (05450-0218)
PHONE.............................802 933-5542
EMP: 9 EST: 1993
SQ FT: 10,000
SALES (est): 800.51K **Privately Held**
SIC: 3469 Machine parts, stamped or
pressed metal

(G-17222)
COUNTY COURIER INC
342 Main St (05450-6008)
P.O. Box 398 (05450-0398)
PHONE.............................802 933-4375
Ed Shamy, *CEO*
EMP: 8 EST: 1949
SALES (est): 222.88K **Privately Held**
Web: www.countycourier.net
SIC: 2711 Job printing and newspaper
publishing combined

(G-17223)
FRANKLIN FOODS INC (DH)
68 East St (05450-6189)
P.O. Box 486 (05450-0486)
PHONE.............................802 933-4338
EMP: 48 EST: 1899
SALES (est): 47.7MM
SALES (corp-wide): 2.29B **Privately Held**
Web: www.franklinfoods.com
SIC: 2022 Natural cheese
HQ: Franklin Foods Holdings, Inc.
2500 N Military Trl # 320
Boca Raton FL 33431
561 638-7864

(G-17224)
SNOWSHOE POND MPLE
SGRWRKS LLC
431 Barnes Rd (05450-5833)
PHONE.............................802 777-9676
George Saig, *Admn*
EMP: 8 EST: 2009
SALES (est): 489.78K **Privately Held**
SIC: 3949 Snowshoes

Essex
Chittenden County

(G-17225)
PREAVA INC
22 Essex Way Unit 8203 (05451-2314)
PHONE.................................202 935-1566
Michael Caha, *CEO*
EMP: 7 **EST:** 2020
SALES (est): 279.15K **Privately Held**
Web: www.preava.com
SIC: 7372 Prepackaged software

Essex Junction
Chittenden County

(G-17226)
ASK-INTTAG LLC
Also Called: Paragon ID USA
1000 River St Bldg 966 (05452-4201)
P.O. Box 169 (05453-0169)
PHONE.................................802 288-7210
EMP: 35 **EST:** 2008
SALES (est): 5.08MM
SALES (corp-wide): 2.12MM **Privately Held**
SIC: 3999 Identification tags, except paper
HQ: Paragon Id
Allee Des Aubepins
Argent Sur Sauldre 18410

(G-17227)
AUTUMN-HARP INC
26 Thompson Dr (05452-3405)
PHONE.................................802 857-4600
David Logan, *CEO*
Hillary Burrows, *
John Logan, *
▲ **EMP:** 250 **EST:** 1977
SALES (est): 50.62MM **Privately Held**
Web: www.autumnharp.com
SIC: 2844 Perfumes, cosmetics and other
toilet preparations

(G-17228)
BIOMEDIC APPLIANCES INC
Also Called: Super-Tech Prosthetics
8a Ewing Pl (05452-2821)
PHONE.................................802 878-0930
Deborah Lowe, *Pr*
Susan Thomas, *VP*
EMP: 9 **EST:** 1982
SQ FT: 2,300
SALES (est): 1.05MM **Privately Held**
Web: www.biomedicappliances.com
SIC: 5999 3842 Orthopedic and prosthesis
applications; Prosthetic appliances

(G-17229)
BROWNS RIVER BINDERY INC
Also Called: Browns Rver Rec Prsrvtion Svcs
1 Allen Martin Dr (05452-3403)
P.O. Box 8501 (05451-8501)
PHONE.................................802 878-3335
Charles Remmey, *Pr*
Janet Remmey, *Sec*
Marianne Holzer, *VP*
EMP: 15 **EST:** 1974
SQ FT: 8,000
SALES (est): 990.13K
SALES (corp-wide): 11.14MM **Privately Held**
SIC: 2789 Bookbinding and repairing: trade,
edition, library, etc.
PA: Kofile Products, Inc.
6480 Enduro Dr
Washington MO 63090
636 239-0140

(G-17230)
CATAMOUNT NORTH CABINETRY LLC
Also Called: Simpson Cabinetry
15 Corporate Dr (05452-4434)
PHONE.................................802 264-9009
Andrew Cabrera, *Prin*
Elizabeth Cabrera, *Prin*
EMP: 10 **EST:** 2015
SALES (est): 565.4K **Privately Held**
Web: www.simpsoncabinetry.com
SIC: 2434 Vanities, bathroom: wood

(G-17231)
COOKING SOLUTIONS GROUP INC
Also Called: Bki Worldwide
42 Allen Martin Dr (05452-3400)
PHONE.................................864 963-3471
EMP: 160
SALES (corp-wide): 4.03B **Publicly Held**
SIC: 3556 3631 Ovens, bakery; Household
cooking equipment
HQ: Cooking Solutions Group, Inc.
23 Keewaydin Dr Ste 205
Salem NH 03079
603 893-9701

(G-17232)
COOPER LIGHTING INC
Also Called: Cooper Controls
16 Perkins Dr (05452-3858)
PHONE.................................800 767-3674
Neil Scrimshire, *Pr*
EMP: 21 **EST:** 1982
SQ FT: 15,000
SALES (est): 2.19MM **Privately Held**
Web: www.cooperlighting.com
SIC: 3648 3646 3643 3625 Lighting
equipment, nec; Commercial lighting fixtures
; Current-carrying wiring services; Control
equipment, electric
HQ: Cooper Industries Unlimited Company
41a Drury Street
Dublin D02 C

(G-17233)
GALVION BALLISTICS LTD
7 Corporate Dr (05452-4434)
PHONE.................................802 334-2774
Jonathan Blanshay, *Pr*
EMP: 99 **EST:** 2012
SALES (est): 4.21MM
SALES (corp-wide): 17.27MM **Privately Held**
Web: www.galvion.com
SIC: 3851 5084 5065 Protective eyeware;
Safety equipment; Electronic parts and
equipment, nec
HQ: Galvion Ltd.
160 Corporate Dr
Portsmouth NH 03801
514 739-4444

(G-17234)
GLOBALFOUNDRIES US 2 LLC
Also Called: Global Foundries
1000 River St (05452-4201)
PHONE.................................408 462-4452
Tyler Tassin, *Mgr*
EMP: 2700
Web: www.gf.com
SIC: 3674 Semiconductors and related
devices
HQ: Globalfoundries U.S. 2 Llc
2070 Route 52
Hopewell Junction NY 12533
512 457-3900

(G-17235)
GORDINI USA INC (PA)
Also Called: Drop
67 Allen Martin Dr (05452)
P.O. Box 8440 (05451-8440)
PHONE.................................802 879-5211
David Gellis, *Pr*
Philip Gellis, *Pr*
Kevin Holmes-henry, *CFO*
▲ **EMP:** 84 **EST:** 1977
SQ FT: 50,000
SALES (est): 10.11MM
SALES (corp-wide): 10.11MM **Privately Held**
Web: www.gordini.com
SIC: 3949 Sporting and athletic goods, nec

(G-17236)
GS BLODGETT LLC (HQ)
Also Called: Blodgett Oven Company, The
42 Allen Martin Dr (05452-3400)
PHONE.................................802 860-3700
Selim A Bassoul, *Managing Member*
Timothy J Fitzgerald, *
Martin Lindsay, *
◆ **EMP:** 150 **EST:** 1848
SQ FT: 200,000
SALES (est): 93.99MM
SALES (corp-wide): 4.03B **Publicly Held**
Web: www.blodgett.com
SIC: 3631 3589 Household cooking
equipment; Cooking equipment, commercial
PA: The Middleby Corporation
1400 Toastmaster Dr
Elgin IL 60120
847 741-3300

(G-17237)
GS BLODGETT CORPORATION
Blodgett Combi
42 Allen Martin Dr (05452-3400)
PHONE.................................802 860-3700
EMP: 92
SALES (corp-wide): 4.03B **Publicly Held**
Web: www.blodgett.com
SIC: 3589 Cooking equipment, commercial
HQ: G.S. Blodgett, Llc
42 Allen Martin Dr
Essex Junction VT 05452
802 860-3700

(G-17238)
KEURIG DR PEPPER INC
5 New England Dr (05452-2824)
PHONE.................................802 288-6022
EMP: 18
Web: www.keurigdrpepper.com
SIC: 2086 Soft drinks: packaged in cans,
bottles, etc.
PA: Keurig Dr Pepper Inc.
53 South Ave
Burlington MA 01803

(G-17239)
LAMELL LUMBER CORPORATION
82a Jericho Rd (05452-2799)
PHONE.................................802 878-2475
Ronald R Lamell Senior, *Pr*
Ronald R Lamell Senior, *Prin*
Ronald R Lamell Junior, *VP*
Sheila Lamell, *
EMP: 32 **EST:** 1964
SQ FT: 6,200
SALES (est): 4.52MM **Privately Held**
Web: www.breakingboards.com
SIC: 2421 Lumber: rough, sawed, or planed

(G-17240)
MESSER LLC
Ibm Plant (05452)
PHONE.................................802 878-6339
EMP: 24
SALES (corp-wide): 1.63B **Privately Held**
Web: www.messeramericas.com
SIC: 2813 Industrial gases
HQ: Messer Llc
200 Smrst Corp Blvd # 7000
Bridgewater NJ 08807
800 755-9277

(G-17241)
MICRO WIRE TRANSM SYSTEMS INC
8 Ewing Pl (05452-2821)
PHONE.................................802 876-7901
Brendan Barden, *Dir*
Hwang Chang-soon, *Dir*
Richard Kim, *Dir*
EMP: 13 **EST:** 2011
SALES (est): 3.04MM **Privately Held**
Web: www.mwtscorp.com
SIC: 3315 Cable, steel: insulated or armored

(G-17242)
OFFSET HOUSE INC
Also Called: Catamount Color
89 Sandhill Rd (05452-3909)
P.O. Box 8329 (05451-8329)
PHONE.................................802 878-4440
John P Mc Grath, *Pr*
John Carp, *
Richard B Ronson, *
EMP: 150 **EST:** 1970
SQ FT: 65,000
SALES (est): 13.16MM **Privately Held**
Web: www.catamountcolor.com
SIC: 7331 2752 2796 2791 Mailing service;
Offset printing; Platemaking services;
Typesetting

(G-17243)
RAJ COMMUNICATIONS LTD
Also Called: Ladd Research Industries
3 Ewing Pl (05452-2821)
PHONE.................................802 658-4961
John Arnott, *Ch*
Jd Arnott, *Pr*
Rita Arnott, *VP*
EMP: 20 **EST:** 1950
SALES (est): 1.33MM **Privately Held**
Web: www.laddresearch.com
SIC: 3826 5049 3845 3841 Microscopes,
electron and proton; Laboratory equipment,
except medical or dental; Electromedical
equipment; Surgical and medical
instruments

(G-17244)
RECTRAC LLC
Also Called: Vermont Systems
12 Market Pl (05452-2939)
PHONE.................................802 879-6993
Randy Eckels, *CEO*
Scott Strong, *
EMP: 87 **EST:** 1985
SQ FT: 6,000
SALES (est): 21.96MM **Privately Held**
Web: www.vermontsystems.com
SIC: 7372 7371 5045 Business oriented
computer software; Custom computer
programming services; Computers, nec
PA: Clubessential, Llc
9987 Carver Rd Ste 230
Blue Ash OH 45242

790   2024 Harris New England
Manufacturers Directory   ▲ = Import ▼ = Export
◆ = Import/Export

(G-17245)
REVISION MILITARY LTD (PA)
7 Corporate Dr (05452-4434)
PHONE...............................802 879-7002
Amy Coyne, *CEO*
Amy Coyne, *Pr*
Karan Rai, *
William Cantalupo, *
Jonathon Wainer, *
▲ **EMP:** 125 **EST:** 2004
SQ FT: 45,000
SALES (est): 78.03MM
SALES (corp-wide): 78.03MM **Privately Held**
Web: www.revisionmilitary.com
SIC: 3851 Protective eyeware

(G-17246)
SHEET METAL DESIGN
3 Corporate Dr (05452-4434)
PHONE...............................802 288-9700
EMP: 7
SALES (est): 567.57K **Privately Held**
SIC: 3444 Sheet metal specialties, not stamped

(G-17247)
STANDEX INTERNATIONAL CORP
Also Called: Bki Worldwide
42 Allen Martin Dr (05452-3400)
P.O. Box 80400 (29680-0040)
PHONE...............................864 963-3471
Roger Fix, *CEO*
EMP: 14
SALES (corp-wide): 741.05MM **Publicly Held**
Web: www.standex.com
SIC: 2599 3585 2721 Restaurant furniture, wood or metal; Refrigeration equipment, complete; Periodicals, publishing and printing
PA: Standex International Corporation
23 Keewaydin Dr Ste 205
Salem NH 03079
603 893-9701

(G-17248)
TWIN STATE SIGNS INC
Also Called: Twin State Signs
14 Gauthier Dr (05452-2825)
P.O. Box 8206 (05451-8206)
PHONE...............................802 872-8949
TOLL FREE: 800
Mary Denault, *Pr*
Raymond Denault, *Sec*
EMP: 9 **EST:** 1985
SALES (est): 1.02MM **Privately Held**
Web: www.sbsigns.net
SIC: 3993 1799 7389 Letters for signs, metal ; Sign installation and maintenance; Sign painting and lettering shop

(G-17249)
WELLSKY HUMN SOCIAL SVCS CORP
25 New England Dr (05452-2899)
PHONE...............................802 316-3000
Joe Sander, *Brnch Mgr*
EMP: 54
SALES (corp-wide): 351.62K **Privately Held**
Web: www.wellsky.com
SIC: 7371 7372 Computer software development; Prepackaged software
HQ: Wellsky Human & Social Services Corporation
11700 Plaza America Dr # 100
Reston VA 20190

Fair Haven
Rutland County

(G-17250)
CAMARA SLATE PRODUCTS INC
963 S Main St (05743-4435)
P.O. Box 8 (05743-0008)
PHONE...............................802 265-3200
▲ **EMP:** 23 **EST:** 1964
SALES (est): 2.38MM **Privately Held**
Web: www.camaraslate.com
SIC: 3281 Slate products

(G-17251)
K V SBARDELLA SLATE INC
105 Colvin Rd (05743-1270)
P.O. Box 127 (05743-0127)
PHONE...............................802 265-9955
Karl V Sbardella, *Pr*
Donna Sbardella, *Ex VP*
▲ **EMP:** 9 **EST:** 1987
SALES (est): 847.03K **Privately Held**
Web: www.sbardellaslate.com
SIC: 1761 3441 Roofing contractor; Building components, structural steel

(G-17252)
VERMONT STRUCTURAL SLATE CO (PA)
3 Prospect St (05743-1219)
PHONE...............................802 265-4933
Craig E Markcrow, *Pr*
W E Markcrow, *
Donna J Fortier, *
Eloise Wemette, *
▼ **EMP:** 50 **EST:** 1866
SQ FT: 1,500
SALES (est): 9.27MM
SALES (corp-wide): 9.27MM **Privately Held**
Web: www.vermontstructuralslate.com
SIC: 3281 2952 Slate products; Asphalt felts and coatings

(G-17253)
VERMONT UNFDING GREEN SLATE IN (PA)
963 S Main St (05743-4435)
P.O. Box 8 (05743-0008)
PHONE...............................802 265-3200
David Camara Junior, *Pr*
David Camara Senior, *VP*
EMP: 19 **EST:** 1986
SQ FT: 8,000
SALES (est): 2.42MM
SALES (corp-wide): 2.42MM **Privately Held**
Web: www.vermontstructuralslate.com
SIC: 3281 Slate products

Fairfax
Chittenden County

(G-17254)
APEX SEALING INC
Also Called: Like Nu Electric Motor Service
164 Yankee Park Rd (05454-5448)
PHONE...............................802 524-7100
Gregory Campbell, *Pr*
EMP: 10 **EST:** 2004
SQ FT: 9,000
SALES (est): 2.29MM **Privately Held**
Web: www.apexsealing.com

SIC: 5085 5084 7699 3621 Seals, industrial; Water pumps (industrial); Pumps and pumping equipment repair; Motors and generators

(G-17255)
BARIATRIX NUTRITION CORP
Also Called: Snackergy
308 Industrial Park Rd (05454-4414)
PHONE...............................802 527-2500
Thomas Egger, *Pr*
Rod Egger, *
▲ **EMP:** 33 **EST:** 1982
SQ FT: 30,000
SALES (est): 9.73MM
SALES (corp-wide): 13.21MM **Privately Held**
Web: www.bariatrix.com
SIC: 2023 Dietary supplements, dairy and non-dairy based
PA: Bariatrix Nutrition Inc.
4905 Rue Fairway
Lachine QC H8T 1
514 633-7455

(G-17256)
BUYERS DIGEST PRESS INC
57 Yankee Park Rd (05454-5515)
P.O. Box 10 (05402-0010)
PHONE...............................802 893-4214
Jim Carey, *Pr*
EMP: 14 **EST:** 1973
SQ FT: 12,000
SALES (est): 356.68K **Privately Held**
SIC: 2752 Offset printing

(G-17257)
CENTURY INTERNATIONAL ARMS INC
Also Called: Century Warehouse Office
236 Bryce Blvd (05454-5529)
PHONE...............................802 527-1252
Ken Dargan, *Mgr*
EMP: 80
Web: www.centuryarms.com
SIC: 5099 5091 3484 Firearms and ammunition, except sporting; Sporting and recreation goods; Small arms
PA: Century International Arms, Inc.
430 S Congress Ave Ste 1
Delray Beach FL 33445

(G-17258)
GANNETT RIVER STATES PUBG CORP
Also Called: Buyers Digest
57 Yankee Park Rd (05454-5515)
PHONE...............................802 893-4214
Allen Messier, *Mgr*
EMP: 25
SALES (corp-wide): 2.95B **Publicly Held**
Web: www.gannett.com
SIC: 2711 Newspapers, publishing and printing
HQ: Gannett River States Publishing Corporation
7950 Jones Branch Dr
Mc Lean VA 22102
703 284-6000

(G-17259)
HARRISON CONCRETE CNSTR INC
1803 Skunk Hill Rd (05454-5565)
P.O. Box 2098 (05468-2098)
PHONE...............................802 849-6688
Kevin J Harrison, *Prin*
James Harrison, *
Janet Harrison, *

Kathy Rabtoy, *Prin*
EMP: 49 **EST:** 1968
SALES (est): 5.02MM **Privately Held**
Web: www.harrisonconcreteinc.com
SIC: 3273 Ready-mixed concrete

(G-17260)
HARRISON REDI-MIX CORP
1803 Skunk Hill Rd (05454-5565)
P.O. Box 2098 (05468-2098)
PHONE...............................802 849-6688
James Harrison, *Pr*
Janet Harrison, *VP*
EMP: 37 **EST:** 2002
SALES (est): 1.24MM **Privately Held**
Web: www.harrisonredimix.com
SIC: 3273 Ready-mixed concrete

(G-17261)
LIQUID MEASUREMENT SYSTEMS INC
Also Called: LMS
141 Morse Dr (05454-4448)
P.O. Box 2070 (05468-2070)
PHONE...............................802 528-8100
George Lamphere, *Pr*
David A Lamphere, *
Elizabeth Lamphere, *
▼ **EMP:** 43 **EST:** 1991
SQ FT: 22,000
SALES (est): 6.04MM **Privately Held**
Web: www.liquidmeasurement.com
SIC: 3728 3812 Aircraft parts and equipment, nec; Aircraft/aerospace flight instruments and guidance systems

(G-17262)
MED ASSOCIATES INC (PA)
Also Called: Computer Store Northern VT
166 Industrial Park Rd (05454-4452)
P.O. Box 319 (05478-0319)
PHONE...............................802 527-2343
Bridget Garibay, *Pr*
Joaquin P Aja, *
Jane Zurn, *
EMP: 72 **EST:** 1971
SQ FT: 20,000
SALES (est): 14.61MM
SALES (corp-wide): 14.61MM **Privately Held**
Web: www.med-associates.com
SIC: 3826 Analytical instruments

(G-17263)
RUNAMOK MAPLE LLC
Also Called: Runamok
293 Fletcher Rd (05454-9768)
PHONE...............................802 849-7943
EMP: 26 **EST:** 2017
SQ FT: 55,000
SALES (est): 5.58MM **Privately Held**
Web: www.runamokmaple.com
SIC: 2099 5149 2087 2064 Maple syrup; Specialty food items; Flavoring extracts and syrups, nec; Candy and other confectionery products

(G-17264)
VERMONT INDEXABLE TOOLING INC
331b Bryce Blvd (05454-5578)
PHONE...............................802 752-2002
EMP: 9 **EST:** 1993
SQ FT: 10,000
SALES (est): 805.82K **Privately Held**
Web: www.vermontindexable.com
SIC: 3599 1799 3441 Machine shop, jobbing and repair; Welding on site; Fabricated structural metal

(G-17265)
YANKEE CORPORATION
125 Yankee Park Rd (05454-5547)
PHONE......................................802 527-0177
James E Bryce, *Pr*
James L Bryce, *
EMP: 65 **EST:** 1980
SQ FT: 20,000
SALES (est): 5.08MM **Privately Held**
Web: www.yankeereamer.com
SIC: 3541 3545 Machine tools, metal cutting
  type; Machine tool accessories

Fairfield
Franklin County

(G-17266)
EVERWIDENINGCIRCLESCOM
LLC
1364 Castle Rd (05455-5492)
PHONE......................................802 524-3757
Lynda Ulrich, *Prin*
EMP: 8 **EST:** 2014
SALES (est): 166.1K **Privately Held**
Web: www.goodness-exchange.com
SIC: 2741 Miscellaneous publishing

Fairlee
Orange County

(G-17267)
BRITTON LUMBER COMPANY
INC (PA)
7 Ely Rd (05045-9789)
P.O. Box 389 (05045-0389)
PHONE......................................802 333-4388
Robert E Moses, *Pr*
▲ **EMP:** 41 **EST:** 1946
SQ FT: 2,200
SALES (est): 24.18MM
SALES (corp-wide): 24.18MM **Privately
Held**
Web: www.brittonlumber.com
SIC: 5033 2421 5031 Roofing and siding
  materials; Sawmills and planing mills,
  general; Lumber: rough, dressed, and
  finished

Ferrisburgh
Addison County

(G-17268)
DOCK DOCTORS LLC
Also Called: Dock Doctors, The
19 Little Otter Ln (05456-9651)
PHONE......................................802 877-6756
Jeff Provost, *Managing Member*
EMP: 35 **EST:** 2010
SQ FT: 20,000
SALES (est): 5.8MM **Privately Held**
Web: www.thedockdoctors.com
SIC: 2511 3999 4491 5088 Wood
  household furniture; Dock equipment and
  supplies, industrial; Docks, incl. buildings
  and facilities: operation and maint.; Marine
  crafts and supplies

(G-17269)
VT LVSTK SLGTR & PROC CO
76 Depot Rd (05456-9692)
PHONE......................................802 877-3421
EMP: 10 **EST:** 2007
SALES (est): 839.12K **Privately Held**
Web: www.vermontmeat.com

SIC: 2011 Meat packing plants

Florence
Rutland County

(G-17270)
MYSTIC MOUNTAIN MAPLES
LLC
1888 Fire Hill Rd (05744)
PHONE......................................802 524-6163
EMP: 19
SALES (corp-wide): 139.45K **Privately
Held**
SIC: 2099 Maple syrup
PA: Mystic Mountain Maples, Llc
  77 Rock Island Rd
  Saint Albans VT 05478
  802 524-6163

(G-17271)
OMYA
206 Omya W (05744)
PHONE......................................802 770-7537
EMP: 46 **EST:** 2013
SALES (est): 6.83MM **Privately Held**
Web: www.omya.com
SIC: 2819 Industrial inorganic chemicals,
  nec

(G-17272)
OMYA INC
Also Called: Verpol Plant
206 Omya W Whipple Hollow Rd (05744)
PHONE......................................802 459-3311
EMP: 15
Web: www.omya.com
SIC: 2819 Calcium compounds and salts,
  inorganic, nec
HQ: Omya Inc.
  9987 Carver Rd Ste 300
  Blue Ash OH 45242
  513 387-4600

(G-17273)
TROY MINERALS INC
Also Called: Florence Crushed Stone
180 Fire Hill Rd (05744)
PHONE......................................802 878-5103
Michael P Chmielewski, *Pr*
EMP: 15 **EST:** 2014
SALES (est): 438.78K **Privately Held**
Web: www.florencecrushedstone.com
SIC: 1411 Dimension stone

Forest Dale
Rutland County

(G-17274)
TUCEL INDUSTRIES INC
2014 Forest Dale Rd (05745)
PHONE......................................802 247-6824
John C Lewis Junior, *Pr*
Joanne Raleigh, *VP*
▲ **EMP:** 11 **EST:** 1970
SALES (est): 323.35K **Privately Held**
Web: www.tucel.com
SIC: 3991 Brooms

Grafton
Windham County

(G-17275)
WINDHAM FOUNDATION INC
(PA)
Also Called: Grafton Fund, The

225 Townshend Rd (05146-9817)
P.O. Box 70 (05146-0070)
PHONE......................................802 843-2211
Robert Allen, *Pr*
Dan Normado, *VP*
Paula Johnson, *Sec*
Robert Donald, *CFO*
EMP: 15 **EST:** 1963
SQ FT: 90,000
SALES (est): 11.08MM
SALES (corp-wide): 11.08MM **Privately
Held**
Web: www.windham-foundation.org
SIC: 7011 2022 5947 Motels; Cheese;
  natural and processed; Gift shop

Graniteville
Washington County

(G-17276)
NORTH EAST MATERIALS
GROUP LLC
751 Graniteville Rd (05654-8024)
P.O. Box 231 (98354-0231)
PHONE......................................802 479-7004
L P Hughes, *Managing Member*
EMP: 10 **EST:** 2009
SALES (est): 1.32MM **Privately Held**
Web: www.northeastmg.com
SIC: 1499 Gemstone and industrial
  diamond mining

(G-17277)
ROCK OF AGES CORPORATION
(DH)
Also Called: Granite Industries of Vermont
560 Graniteville Rd (05654-8001)
PHONE......................................802 476-3115
Robert Pope, *Pr*
Donald Labonte, *Pr*
Laura A Plude, *VP*
◆ **EMP:** 130 **EST:** 1885
SALES (est): 40.75MM
SALES (corp-wide): 2.1MM **Privately Held**
Web: www.rockofages.com
SIC: 3281 Granite, cut and shaped
HQ: Swenson Granite Company Llc
  369 N State St
  Concord NH 03301
  603 225-4322

Groton
Caledonia County

(G-17278)
GROTON TIMBERWORKS INC
2126 Scott Hwy (05046-5617)
PHONE......................................802 584-4446
Nathan Puffer, *Owner*
EMP: 8 **EST:** 1992
SALES (est): 694.22K **Privately Held**
Web: www.grotontimberworks.com
SIC: 2452 Log cabins, prefabricated, wood

(G-17279)
VMT LLC
300 Field Rd (05046-9681)
PHONE......................................802 592-3146
EMP: 24
SALES (corp-wide): 1.11MM **Privately
Held**
Web: www.vermontmold.com
SIC: 3544 Special dies and tools
PA: Vmt, Llc
  477 W Main St
  Barnet VT 05821
  802 633-3900

Guilford
Windham County

(G-17280)
COMMONWEALTH DAIRY LLC
Also Called: Green Mountain Creamery
66 Pauls Rd (05301-3658)
PHONE......................................802 251-2300
▲ **EMP:** 100 **EST:** 2009
SALES (est): 47.28MM
SALES (corp-wide): 355.83K **Privately
Held**
Web: www.commonwealthdairy.com
SIC: 5149 2026 Dairy products, dried or
  canned; Acidophilus milk
HQ: Lactalis American Group, Inc.
  2376 S Park Ave
  Buffalo NY 14220
  716 823-6262

(G-17281)
KERBER FARMS LUMBER
COMPANY
3489 Coolidge Hwy (05301-8698)
PHONE......................................802 451-6920
EMP: 8 **EST:** 1979
SALES (est): 216.06K **Privately Held**
Web: www.kerberlumber.com
SIC: 2421 Sawmills and planing mills,
  general

(G-17282)
WH PROPERTY SERVICE LLC
287 Locust Hill Rd (05301-8079)
PHONE......................................802 257-8566
EMP: 12 **EST:** 2018
SALES (est): 100K **Privately Held**
SIC: 2099 Maple syrup

Hardwick
Caledonia County

(G-17283)
GREEN MOUNTAIN CBD INC
273 Kate Brook Rd (05843-9443)
PHONE......................................802 595-3258
Alejandro Bergad, *Pr*
EMP: 7 **EST:** 2016
SALES (est): 430.93K
SALES (corp-wide): 4.92MM **Privately
Held**
SIC: 3999
PA: Skyview Naturals Pbc
  180 Battery St Ste 250
  Burlington VT 05401
  802 495-0795

(G-17284)
HARDWICK GAZETTE PRINT
SHOP
Also Called: Hardwick Gazette Newspaper
42 S Main St (05843-7067)
P.O. Box 367 (05843-0367)
PHONE......................................802 472-6521
EMP: 7 **EST:** 1986
SALES (est): 460.06K **Privately Held**
Web: www.hardwickgazette.com
SIC: 2711 Newspapers, publishing and
  printing

(G-17285)
VERMONT SOY LLC
Also Called: Vermont Soy
180 Junction Rd (05843-6051)
P.O. Box 401 (05843-0401)
PHONE......................................802 472-8500

EMP: 9 EST: 1997
SALES (est): 832.13K Privately Held
Web: www.vermontsoy.com
SIC: 2099 Food preparations, nec

Hartland
Windsor County

(G-17286)
DARWIN A LEWIS INC
Also Called: Lewis Bible Bindery
243 Densmore Hill Rd (05048-8105)
PHONE.............................802 457-4521
Darwin A Lewis, Pr
Robert F Lewis Junior, VP
Karen Lewis, Sec
▲ EMP: 7 EST: 1907
SQ FT: 30,000
SALES (est): 320K Privately Held
SIC: 2789 Bookbinding and related work

(G-17287)
**PRECISION CUTTER GRINDING
INC**
Also Called: Pcg Machine Shop
7 Ferry Rd (05048)
P.O. Box 248 (05048-0248)
PHONE.............................802 436-2039
Todd Hood, Pr
EMP: 9 EST: 1987
SALES (est): 823.03K Privately Held
Web: www.pcgmachineshop.com
SIC: 3599 7389 Machine shop, jobbing and
repair; Business Activities at Non-
Commercial Site

Highgate Center
Franklin County

(G-17288)
DUHAMEL FAMILY FARM LLC
107 Franklin Rd (05459-4167)
PHONE.............................802 868-4954
James Duhamel, Managing Member
Holly Duhamel, Managing Member
EMP: 8 EST: 2014
SALES (est): 858.65K Privately Held
SIC: 2026 Fluid milk

(G-17289)
**GREEN MOUNTAIN FOREST
PRODUCTS**
962 Morey Rd (05459)
P.O. Box 162 (05459-0162)
PHONE.............................802 868-2306
Brian Rowell, Pr
Willard Rowell Senior, VP
Rolande Fortin, Sec
EMP: 14 EST: 1979
SQ FT: 6,000
SALES (est): 395.59K Privately Held
SIC: 2421 Wood chips, produced at mill

Hinesburg
Chittenden County

(G-17290)
DC ENTERPRIZES INC
Also Called: Coffee Enterprises
110 Riggs Rd # B (05461-4453)
PHONE.............................802 865-4480
Daniel Cox, Pr
Daniel C Cox, Pr
EMP: 10 EST: 1992
SQ FT: 8,920

SALES (est): 924.23K Privately Held
Web: www.coffeeenterprises.com
SIC: 5812 7389 8742 1389 Eating places;
Coffee service; Manufacturing management
consultant; Testing, measuring, surveying,
and analysis services

(G-17291)
GIROUX BODY SHOP INC
10370 Route 116 (05461-9163)
PHONE.............................802 482-2162
Victor Giroux, Pr
Steve Giroux, VP
Robert Giroux, Treas
David Giroux, Sec
EMP: 10 EST: 1923
SQ FT: 95,000
SALES (est): 672.34K Privately Held
SIC: 7692 7532 Welding repair; Body shop,
automotive

(G-17292)
**GREENRANGE FURNITURE
COMPANY**
Also Called: Cotswold Furniture Makers
2778 Shelburne Falls Rd (05461-9781)
PHONE.............................802 747-8564
EMP: 7 EST: 1995
SQ FT: 8,000
SALES (est): 841.58K Privately Held
SIC: 2511 Wood household furniture

(G-17293)
HINESBURG RECORD INC
327 Charlotte Rd (05461-9228)
P.O. Box 304 (05461-0304)
PHONE.............................802 482-2350
June Giroux, Prin
EMP: 10 EST: 1990
SALES (est): 438.8K Privately Held
Web: www.hinesburgrecord.org
SIC: 2711 8699 Newspapers: publishing
only, not printed on site; Charitable
organization

(G-17294)
**HINESBURG SAND & GRAVEL
CO INC**
Also Called: O'Casey Trucking
14818 Route 116 (05461-6103)
PHONE.............................802 482-2335
Tim Casey, Pr
Tim Cassey, *
EMP: 25 EST: 1947
SQ FT: 5,000
SALES (est): 2.38MM Privately Held
Web: www.hbpavt.com
SIC: 5032 4212 1442 Sand, construction;
Local trucking, without storage;
Construction sand and gravel

(G-17295)
**IROQUOIS MANUFACTURING
COMPANY**
695 Richmond Rd (05461-8932)
PHONE.............................802 482-2155
Howard Lyman, Pr
Tod Lyman, *
Garret Lyman, *
▲ EMP: 25 EST: 1963
SQ FT: 80,000
SALES (est): 4.97MM Privately Held
Web: www.iroquoismfg.com
SIC: 7532 3713 Body shop, trucks; Truck
bodies (motor vehicles)

(G-17296)
**NESTECH MACHINE SYSTEMS
INC**

223 Commerce St (05461-4491)
P.O. Box 462 (05461-0462)
PHONE.............................802 482-4575
▼ EMP: 8 EST: 1989
SQ FT: 28,000
SALES (est): 830.03K Privately Held
Web: www.nesms.com
SIC: 3565 Packaging machinery

(G-17297)
NRG SYSTEMS INC
Also Called: Renewable NRG Systems
110 Riggs Rd (05461-4453)
P.O. Box 802848 (64180-2848)
PHONE.............................802 482-2255
EMP: 113 EST: 1985
SALES (est): 25.94MM Publicly Held
Web: www.nrgsystems.com
SIC: 3829 3823 Geophysical and
meteorological testing equipment; Process
control instruments
PA: Esco Technologies Inc.
9900 Clayton Rd Ste A
Saint Louis MO 63124

(G-17298)
SENIX CORPORATION
Also Called: Senix
10516 Route 116 Ste 300 (05461-8505)
PHONE.............................802 489-7300
Doug Boehm, Pr
Patricia Ogilvie, Sec
EMP: 14 EST: 1990
SQ FT: 6,300
SALES (est): 2.35MM Privately Held
Web: www.senix.com
SIC: 3829 Measuring and controlling
devices, nec

Hyde Park
Lamoille County

(G-17299)
**CUSTOM MTAL FABRICATORS
VT LLC**
327 Ferry St (05655-9540)
PHONE.............................802 888-0033
David Vilord, Managing Member
EMP: 7 EST: 2004
SALES (est): 759.2K Privately Held
Web: www.cmfofvt.com
SIC: 3441 Fabricated structural metal

(G-17300)
LIGHT LOGIC INC
Also Called: House of Troy
902 Silver Ridge Rd (05655-9396)
PHONE.............................802 888-7984
Malcolm Tripp, CEO
William S Brown, *
◆ EMP: 35 EST: 1960
SQ FT: 32,000
SALES (est): 3.03MM Privately Held
Web: www.houseoftroy.com
SIC: 3645 Residential lighting fixtures

Hydeville
Rutland County

(G-17301)
**CAM DVLPMENT MCRO
CMPNENTS INC**
84 Blissville Rd (05750)
P.O. Box 177 (05750-0177)
PHONE.............................802 265-3240
Stephen Corbett, Pr
Derek Corbett, Ofcr

Lawrence Corbett, VP
EMP: 10 EST: 1960
SQ FT: 6,500
SALES (est): 1.54MM Privately Held
Web: www.camdevelopment.net
SIC: 3599 Machine shop, jobbing and repair

Irasburg
Orleans County

(G-17302)
M PIETTE & SONS LUMBER INC
6 Seminole Ln (05845)
PHONE.............................802 754-8876
Louie Piette, Pr
Dennis Piette, VP
EMP: 14 EST: 1981
SALES (est): 994.37K Privately Held
Web: www.piettelumber.com
SIC: 2421 5211 Lumber: rough, sawed, or
planed; Planing mill products and lumber

(G-17303)
WESTWOOD FENCES INC
5975 Vt Route 14 (05845)
PHONE.............................802 754-8486
Robert G Miltner, Owner
EMP: 10 EST: 1947
SALES (est): 477.17K Privately Held
Web: www.westwoodfence.com
SIC: 1799 3496 Fence construction;
Miscellaneous fabricated wire products

Island Pond
Essex County

(G-17304)
**COMMUNITY APOSTOLIC
ORDER INC (PA)**
Also Called: Parchment Press
Cross St & Main St (05846)
PHONE.............................802 723-4452
Daniel Brosseau, Pr
Guy Brosseau, *
William Johnson, *
John Post, *
EMP: 18 EST: 1978
SQ FT: 3,000
SALES (est): 673.25K
SALES (corp-wide): 673.25K Privately
Held
SIC: 8661 5712 2511 1522 Religious
organizations; Furniture stores; Wood
household furniture; Multi-family dwellings,
new construction

(G-17305)
SWEET TREE HOLDINGS 1 LLC
Also Called: Maple Guild
One Sweet Tree Ln (05846)
P.O. Box 137 (05846-0137)
PHONE.............................802 723-6753
Michael Argyelan, CFO
EMP: 37 EST: 2015
SALES (est): 4.88MM Privately Held
Web: www.sweettreeholdings.com
SIC: 2099 Maple syrup

Jeffersonville
Lamoille County

(G-17306)
**HEIGHT LAND PUBLICATIONS
LTD**
Also Called: Alpinist Magazine

60 Main St (05464-2101)
PHONE................................802 644-6606
Adam Howard, *Prin*
EMP: 9 **EST:** 2003
SALES (est): 470.43K **Privately Held**
Web: www.holpublications.com
SIC: 2741 Miscellaneous publishing

(G-17307)
**SMUGGLERS NOTCH
DISTILLERY LLC**
5087 Route 15 (05464)
PHONE................................860 670-1838
EMP: 8
SALES (corp-wide): 1.3MM **Privately Held**
Web: www.smugglersnotchdistillery.com
SIC: 2085 Distilled and blended liquors
PA: Smugglers' Notch Distillery, Llc
276 Main St
Cambridge VT

Jericho
Chittenden County

(G-17308)
PALMER LANE MAPLE LLC
19 Old Pump Rd (05465-2000)
PHONE................................802 899-8199
EMP: 7 **EST:** 2019
SALES (est): 359.45K **Privately Held**
Web:
palmerlanemaple.mybigcommerce.com
SIC: 2099 Maple syrup

Johnson
Lamoille County

(G-17309)
MANCHESTER LUMBER INC
66 River Rd E (05656-9521)
P.O. Box 304 (05656-0304)
PHONE................................802 635-2315
Alan E Manchester, *Pr*
Carroll J Manchester, *VP*
EMP: 10
SALES (est): 439.69K **Privately Held**
SIC: 2421 5031 Sawmills and planing mills,
general; Lumber, plywood, and millwork

(G-17310)
**VERMONT MAPLE SUGAR CO
INC**
Also Called: Butternut Mountain Farm
29 Clay Hl (05656-9280)
PHONE................................802 888-3491
David Marvin, *Pr*
Lucy Marvin, *Treas*
EMP: 7 **EST:** 1972
SALES (est): 451.92K **Privately Held**
SIC: 2099 Maple syrup

(G-17311)
**VERMONT MAPLE SUGAR CO
INC**
Also Called: Butternut Mountain Farm
31 Main St (05656)
P.O. Box 381 (05656-0381)
PHONE................................802 635-7483
Lucy Marvin, *Mgr*
EMP: 145
SALES (corp-wide): 21.64MM **Privately
Held**
Web: www.marvinscountrystore.com
SIC: 2099 Maple syrup
PA: Sugar Vermont Maple Company Inc
37 Industrial Park Dr

Morrisville VT 05661
802 888-3491

(G-17312)
WOOL ADVISOR LLC
51 Lower Main St E (05656)
P.O. Box 612 (05656-0612)
PHONE................................802 635-2271
Stacy Manosh, *Managing Member*
Stacy B Manosh, *Managing Member*
EMP: 15 **EST:** 1842
SQ FT: 30,000
SALES (est): 991.16K **Privately Held**
Web: www.johnsonwoolenmills.com
SIC: 2231 5651 2339 Apparel and
outerwear broadwoven fabrics; Family
clothing stores; Women's and misses'
outerwear, nec

Killington
Rutland County

(G-17313)
**OUTER LIMITS PUBLISHING
LLC**
Also Called: Mountain Times, The
5465 Rte 4 (05751)
P.O. Box 183 (05751-0183)
PHONE................................802 422-2399
Polly Lynn, *Managing Member*
EMP: 10 **EST:** 1971
SQ FT: 3,500
SALES (est): 842.37K **Privately Held**
Web: www.mountaintimes.info
SIC: 2711 8721 Newspapers: publishing
only, not printed on site; Billing and
bookkeeping service

Ludlow
Windsor County

(G-17314)
**BUILT RITE MANUFACTURING
INC**
750 E Hill Rd (05149-9621)
PHONE................................802 228-7293
John R Smith, *Pr*
Jeremy Smith, *VP*
EMP: 10 **EST:** 1996
SQ FT: 8,000
SALES (est): 1MM **Privately Held**
SIC: 3531 Log splitters

(G-17315)
MAGRIS TALC USA INC
73 E Hill Rd (05149-9798)
PHONE................................802 228-6400
EMP: 40
SALES (corp-wide): 1.39B **Privately Held**
Web: www.magrispm.com
SIC: 1499 Talc mining
HQ: Magris Talc Usa, Inc.
767 Old Yellowstone Trl
Three Forks MT 59752
406 285-5300

Lunenburg
Essex County

(G-17316)
AUNT SADIES INC
108 S Lunenburg Rd (05906-9314)
PHONE................................802 892-5267
Brian Schnetzer, *Pr*
Gary Briggs, *Treas*

EMP: 10 **EST:** 1998
SQ FT: 1,800
SALES (est): 851.32K **Privately Held**
Web: www.auntsadiesonline.com
SIC: 3999 Candles

Lyndonville
Caledonia County

(G-17317)
CALKINS ROCK PRODUCTS INC
Also Called: Calkins Sand & Gravel
34 Calkins Dr (05851)
P.O. Box 82 (05851-0082)
PHONE................................802 626-5755
Paul R Calkins, *Pr*
Kevin Calkins, *VP*
Karen Martell, *Sec*
Rita Calkins, *Treas*
EMP: 8 **EST:** 1956
SQ FT: 8,200
SALES (est): 847.22K **Privately Held**
SIC: 1442 Construction sand and gravel

(G-17318)
JENNE MACHINE LLC
Also Called: Jenne Machine Shop
180 Commercial Ln (05851-4518)
P.O. Box 158 (05850-0158)
PHONE................................802 626-1106
Larry Petreault, *Pr*
Larry Petrault, *Prin*
EMP: 15 **EST:** 1968
SQ FT: 8,000
SALES (est): 1.98MM **Privately Held**
Web: www.jennemachine.com
SIC: 3599 Machine shop, jobbing and repair

(G-17319)
P & L RIENDEAU INC
1640 Sutton Rd (05851-9674)
PHONE................................802 626-9302
EMP: 7 **EST:** 2019
SALES (est): 435.58K **Privately Held**
Web: www.plriendeau.com
SIC: 2411 Logging

(G-17320)
**PRECISION COMPOSITES VT
LLC**
630 Gilman Rd (05851-8311)
P.O. Box 134 (05850-0134)
PHONE................................802 626-5900
EMP: 25 **EST:** 2007
SQ FT: 24,000
SALES (est): 2.11MM **Privately Held**
Web: www.pcovt.com
SIC: 2655 3089 Cans, composite: foil-fiber
and other: from purchased fiber;
Thermoformed finished plastics products,
nec

(G-17321)
**VERMONT AEROSPACE
MANUFACTURING INC**
966 Industrial Pkway (05851)
P.O. Box 1148 (05851-1148)
PHONE................................802 748-8705
EMP: 210
Web: www.vtaerospace.com
SIC: 1761 3728 3599 Sheet metal work, nec
; Aircraft parts and equipment, nec;
Machine shop, jobbing and repair

(G-17322)
VERMONTS ORIGINAL LLC
Also Called: Bag Balm
91 Williams St (05851)

P.O. Box 145 (05851-0145)
PHONE................................802 626-3610
James Kelly, *CEO*
EMP: 8 **EST:** 2014
SALES (est): 1.53MM **Privately Held**
Web: www.bagbalm.com
SIC: 2834 Ointments

Manchester
Bennington County

(G-17323)
DIAGEO NORTH AMERICA INC
Also Called: Equinox Resort Associates
3567 Main St (05254-4132)
P.O. Box 46 (05254-0046)
PHONE................................802 362-4700
Gary Thulander, *Mgr*
EMP: 82
SALES (corp-wide): 21.15B **Privately Held**
Web: www.equinoxresort.com
SIC: 2085 Distilled and blended liquors
HQ: Diageo North America, Inc.
3 World Trade Ctr 175
New York NY 10007
212 202-1800

(G-17324)
ORVIS COMPANY INC
4180 Main St (05254-4182)
PHONE................................802 362-3750
EMP: 36
SALES (corp-wide): 485.62MM **Privately
Held**
Web: www.orvis.com
SIC: 5961 5941 3949 Catalog sales;
Sporting goods and bicycle shops; Fishing
tackle, general
PA: The Orvis Company Inc
178 Conservation Way
Sunderland VT 05250
802 362-3622

(G-17325)
WHALE WATER SYSTEMS INC
Also Called: Mumster Engineering
91 Manchester Valley Rd Bldg E (05254)
PHONE................................802 367-1091
Jennifer Stearnf, *Mgr*
▲ **EMP:** 10 **EST:** 2007
SALES (est): 504.33K **Privately Held**
SIC: 3561 Pumps and pumping equipment

Manchester Center
Bennington County

(G-17326)
**APPLEJACK ART PARTNERS
INC**
Also Called: Rose Selavy Vermont
450 Applejack Rd (05255)
PHONE................................802 362-3662
Jack P Appleman, *Pr*
James Meserve, *Pr*
Jim Giller, *VP*
◆ **EMP:** 24 **EST:** 1996
SALES (est): 2.26MM **Privately Held**
SIC: 5999 6794 2741 Art dealers; Copyright
buying and licensing; Art copy and poster
publishing

(G-17327)
**BATTENKILL
COMMUNICATIONS LLP**
Also Called: Brew Your Own
5515 Main St (05255-9482)
PHONE................................802 362-3981

Bradford L Ring, *Pt*
Kathleen J Ring, *Pt*
EMP: 7 **EST:** 1999
SQ FT: 1,000
SALES (est): 835.98K **Privately Held**
Web: www.byo.com
SIC: 2721 Magazines: publishing and printing

(G-17328)
FUDGE FACTORY INC
Also Called: Mother Myricks
4367 Main St (05255)
P.O. Box 1142 (05255-1142)
PHONE...................................888 669-7425
Jacqueline Baker, *Pr*
Ronald Mancini, *VP*
EMP: 16 **EST:** 1977
SQ FT: 2,500
SALES (est): 1.08MM **Privately Held**
Web: www.mothermyricks.com
SIC: 2064 2051 5441 5461 Candy and other confectionery products; Bread, cake, and related products; Candy; Retail bakeries

(G-17329)
HERSAM ACORN NEWSPAPERS LLC
Also Called: Vermont News Guide
Rte 7 (05255)
PHONE...................................802 362-3535
Dave Honan, *Brnch Mgr*
EMP: 8
SALES (corp-wide): 9.7MM **Privately Held**
SIC: 2711 Newspapers: publishing only, not printed on site
PA: Hersam Acorn Newspapers, Llc
16 Bailey Ave
Ridgefield CT 06877
203 438-6000

(G-17330)
RK MILES INC (PA)
Also Called: Benjamin Moore Authorized Ret
618 Depot St (05255-9807)
P.O. Box 1125 (05255-1125)
PHONE...................................802 362-1952
Josiah E Miles, *Pr*
Ray Pinkos, *
Brenda Monego, *
EMP: 140 **EST:** 1940
SQ FT: 50,000
SALES (est): 36.13MM
SALES (corp-wide): 36.13MM **Privately Held**
Web: www.rkmiles.com
SIC: 5211 7389 2431 5231 Lumber and other building materials; Interior decorating; Millwork; Paint, glass, and wallpaper stores

(G-17331)
SMALL BATCH ORGANICS LLC
53b Manchester Valley Rd (05255-8801)
P.O. Box 1054 (05255-1054)
PHONE...................................802 367-1054
Lindsay Martin, *Managing Member*
Jack Desario, *Managing Member*
EMP: 10 **EST:** 2014
SQ FT: 2,000
SALES (est): 1.62MM **Privately Held**
Web: www.smallbatchgranola.com
SIC: 2043 2064 Granola and muesli, except bars and clusters; Granola and muesli, bars and clusters

(G-17332)
WCW INC (PA)
Also Called: Natural Form Medical
450 Natural Form Way (05255)
P.O. Box 2225 (05255-2225)

PHONE...................................802 362-8053
Jeff Wilkinson, *Pr*
John C Wilkinson, *Prin*
Jean Wilkinson, *Prin*
◆ **EMP:** 63 **EST:** 2011
SALES (est): 11.78MM
SALES (corp-wide): 11.78MM **Privately Held**
Web: www.naturalform.com
SIC: 2515 5712 Mattresses and bedsprings; Beds and accessories

Marshfield
Washington County

(G-17333)
CARTER MACHINE INC
360 Pattys Xing (05658-7043)
PHONE...................................802 426-3501
Brian Carter, *Pr*
Thomas Carter, *VP*
EMP: 7 **EST:** 1978
SQ FT: 5,500
SALES (est): 719.74K **Privately Held**
Web: www.cartermachineinc.com
SIC: 3599 Machine shop, jobbing and repair

Middlebury
Addison County

(G-17334)
7 SOUTH SANDWICH COMPANY LLC
1396 Route 7 S Ste 4 (05753-2061)
PHONE...................................802 388-3354
EMP: 8 **EST:** 2017
SALES (est): 436.62K **Privately Held**
Web: www.7southsandwich.com
SIC: 2599 Food wagons, restaurant

(G-17335)
ADDISON PRESS INC
Also Called: Addison Independent
58 Maple St (05753-1276)
P.O. Box 31 (05753-0031)
PHONE...................................802 388-4944
Angelo Lynn, *Pr*
EMP: 30 **EST:** 1946
SALES (est): 1.9MM **Privately Held**
Web: www.addisonindependent.com
SIC: 2711 Newspapers: publishing only, not printed on site

(G-17336)
AQUA VITEA LLC
Also Called: Aqua Vitea Kombucha
153 Pond Ln (05753-1190)
PHONE...................................802 453-8590
EMP: 17 **EST:** 2016
SALES (est): 3.17MM **Privately Held**
Web: www.aquavitea.com
SIC: 2086 Soft drinks: packaged in cans, bottles, etc.

(G-17337)
BEAU TIES OF VERMONT LLC
69 Industrial Ave (05753-1129)
PHONE...................................802 388-0108
William E Kenerson, *Pr*
Deborah Venman, *
EMP: 27 **EST:** 1992
SQ FT: 6,000
SALES (est): 2.43MM **Privately Held**
Web: www.beautiesltd.com
SIC: 5961 2323 Mail order house, nec; Men's and boy's neckwear

(G-17338)
BEES WRAP LLC
383 Exchange St (05753-1195)
P.O. Box 1016 (05753-5016)
PHONE...................................802 643-2132
Sarah Kaeck, *Managing Member*
EMP: 22 **EST:** 2012
SQ FT: 6,000
SALES (est): 3.14MM **Privately Held**
Web: www.beeswrap.com
SIC: 2429 5113 Wrappers, excelsior; Sanitary food containers

(G-17339)
BTL HOLDINGS LLC
Also Called: Beau Ties Limited of Vermont
69 Industrial Ave (05753-1129)
PHONE...................................917 596-3660
EMP: 25 **EST:** 2000
SALES (est): 841.55K **Privately Held**
Web: www.beautiesltd.com
SIC: 2323 Men's and boy's neckwear

(G-17340)
CANOPY TIMBER ALTERNATIVES INC
30 Grist Mill Rd (05753-4478)
P.O. Box 463 (05740-0463)
PHONE...................................802 388-1548
John Anderson, *Prin*
EMP: 11 **EST:** 2007
SALES (est): 491.26K **Privately Held**
Web: www.canopyta.com
SIC: 2411 Logging camps and contractors

(G-17341)
CHAMPLAIN CONSTRUCTION CO INC
Also Called: Bear Dog Enterprises
1050 Route 7 S (05753-8990)
PHONE...................................802 388-2652
James Danyow, *Pr*
Larry Danyow, *VP*
John Danyow, *Sec*
EMP: 11 **EST:** 1975
SALES (est): 1.68MM **Privately Held**
Web: www.champlainconstruction.com
SIC: 3531 1794 Grapples: rock, wood, etc.; Excavation work

(G-17342)
CONNOR HOMES LLC
1741 Route 7 S (05753-8424)
PHONE...................................802 382-9082
EMP: 70
SALES (est): 12.63MM **Privately Held**
Web: www.connorhomes.com
SIC: 2452 Prefabricated wood buildings

(G-17343)
FEED COMMODITIES INTL INC (HQ)
47 Feed Mill Ln (05753-4496)
PHONE...................................800 639-3191
James K Bushey, *Pr*
Germain Bourdeau, *
Remi Bourdeau, *
Craig Newton, *
EMP: 40 **EST:** 2003
SALES (est): 24.42MM
SALES (corp-wide): 24.42MM **Privately Held**
Web: www.feedcommodities.com
SIC: 5153 2048 Grains; Prepared feeds, nec
PA: Bourdeaus & Bushey, Inc.
88 Seymour St
Middlebury VT 05753
802 388-7000

(G-17344)
JOSEPH P CARRARA & SONS INC
Also Called: JP Carrara & Sons
2464 Case St (05753-9190)
P.O. Box 1000 (05753-5000)
PHONE...................................802 388-6363
Paul J Carrara, *Pr*
EMP: 80
SALES (corp-wide): 18.43MM **Privately Held**
Web: www.jpcarrara.com
SIC: 3273 3272 Ready-mixed concrete; Concrete products, nec
PA: Joseph P. Carrara & Sons, Inc.
167 N Shrewsbury Rd
North Clarendon VT 05759
802 775-2301

(G-17345)
KE USA INC
Durasol Awnings
38b Pond Ln (05753-1189)
PHONE...................................802 388-7309
Craig Dowden, *Mgr*
EMP: 49
SALES (corp-wide): 140.66MM **Privately Held**
Web: www.keoutdoordesign.com
SIC: 3444 2394 Awnings and canopies; Canvas and related products
HQ: Ke Usa, Inc.
445 Bellvale Rd
Chester NY 10918
845 610-1100

(G-17346)
MAPLE LANDMARK INC
Also Called: Maple Landmark Woodcraft
1297 Exchange St (05753-1187)
PHONE...................................802 388-0627
Michael Rainville, *Pr*
Jill Rainville, *
EMP: 24 **EST:** 1979
SQ FT: 15,000
SALES (est): 4.52MM **Privately Held**
Web: www.maplelandmark.com
SIC: 3944 Games, toys, and children's vehicles

(G-17347)
NOPS METAL WORKS
1479 Route 7 S (05753-8803)
PHONE...................................802 382-9300
Louis Nop, *Pr*
EMP: 10 **EST:** 2017
SALES (est): 987.17K **Privately Held**
Web: www.nopsmetalworks.com
SIC: 3441 Fabricated structural metal

(G-17348)
PRESS FORWARD INC
228 Maple St Ste 31b (05753-1605)
PHONE...................................802 989-4383
EMP: 8 **EST:** 2019
SALES (est): 158.01K **Privately Held**
Web: www.pressforwardpr.com
SIC: 2741 Miscellaneous publishing

(G-17349)
VERMONT COUNTRY SOAP CORP
Also Called: Vermont Soap
183 Industrial Ave Ste 1 (05753-1621)
PHONE...................................802 388-4302
Larry Plesent, *Pr*
◆ **EMP:** 25 **EST:** 1992
SQ FT: 9,200
SALES (est): 4.81MM **Privately Held**

Web: www.vermontsoap.com
SIC: 2841 Soap: granulated, liquid, cake, flaked, or chip

(G-17350)
VERMONT HARD CIDER COMPANY LLC (HQ)
Also Called: Green Mountain Beverages
1321 Exchange St (05753-1477)
PHONE..............................802 388-0700
Benjamin Calvi, *Prin*
◆ **EMP:** 27 **EST:** 2003
SQ FT: 62,500
SALES (est): 37.41MM
SALES (corp-wide): 37.41MM **Privately Held**
Web: www.gmbeverage.com
SIC: 2085 Distilled and blended liquors
PA: Northeast Drinks Group Llc
1321 Exchange St
Middlebury VT 05753
802 388-0700

(G-17351)
XAGD INC
Also Called: App Gap
88 Mainelli Rd Ste 1 (05753-1453)
PHONE..............................802 989-7359
Lars Hubbard, *Prin*
EMP: 7 **EST:** 2011
SALES (est): 373.1K **Privately Held**
Web: www.appalachiangap.com
SIC: 2085 Distilled and blended liquors

Middlesex
Washington County

(G-17352)
MCCULLOUGH CRUSHING INC (PA)
548 Mccullough Hill Rd (05602-8488)
PHONE..............................802 223-5693
Frederick Mccullough, *Pr*
Scott Mccullough, *VP*
EMP: 35 **EST:** 1967
SQ FT: 3,500
SALES (est): 5.51MM
SALES (corp-wide): 5.51MM **Privately Held**
Web: www.mcculloughcrushing.com
SIC: 1423 Crushed and broken granite

Milton
Chittenden County

(G-17353)
ADVANCED MACHINE AND TL CO INC
Also Called: A M T
63 Gonyeau Rd Ste B (05468-3200)
P.O. Box 802 (05468-0802)
PHONE..............................802 893-6322
James Monahan Junior, *Pr*
EMP: 15 **EST:** 1982
SQ FT: 8,000
SALES (est): 2.25MM **Privately Held**
Web:
www.advancedmachineandtool.com
SIC: 3599 Machine shop, jobbing and repair

(G-17354)
AMERICAS GRDENING RESOURCE INC
Also Called: Gardener's Supply Co
947 Route 7 S (05468-3822)
P.O. Box 586 (05468-0586)

EMP: 151
SALES (corp-wide): 78.33MM Privately Held
Web: www.gardeners.com
SIC: 5961 5191 5261 3423 Mail order house, nec; Farm supplies; Retail nurseries and garden stores; Hand and edge tools, nec
PA: America's Gardening Resource, Inc.
128 Intervale Rd
Burlington VT 05401
802 660-3500

(G-17355)
CAMP PRECAST CONCRETE PRODUCTS INC
78 Precast Rd (05468-3231)
PHONE..............................802 893-2401
EMP: 30 **EST:** 1976
SALES (est): 5.09MM **Privately Held**
Web: www.campprecast.com
SIC: 3272 Concrete products, precast, nec

(G-17356)
CHAMPLAIN DOOR COMPANY INC
4182 Highbridge Rd (05468)
P.O. Box 2129 (05468-2129)
PHONE..............................802 524-7595
TOLL FREE: 800
Michael Bechard, *Pr*
George Harwood, *Sec*
EMP: 11 **EST:** 1990
SQ FT: 4,000
SALES (est): 964.8K **Privately Held**
Web: www.champlaindoor.com
SIC: 5211 3699 Garage doors, sale and installation; Door opening and closing devices, electrical

(G-17357)
CYR LUMBER INC
215 Poor Farm Rd (05468-3575)
PHONE..............................802 893-4448
Norman L Cyr, *Pr*
Jean-paul Cyr, *VP*
Margaret Cyr, *Sec*
EMP: 17 **EST:** 1973
SQ FT: 10,000
SALES (est): 1.88MM **Privately Held**
Web: www.cyrlumber.com
SIC: 2421 Sawmills and planing mills, general

(G-17358)
GENFOOT AMERICA LLC
Also Called: Genfoot America Inc.
33 Catamount Dr (05468-3236)
PHONE..............................802 893-4280
Richard G Cook, *CEO*
Irwin Kastner, *VP*
Steven Cook, *Ex VP*
Norman Cook, *Ex VP*
David Hallgren, *VP*
▲ **EMP:** 12 **EST:** 1987
SQ FT: 75,000
SALES (est): 2.51MM
SALES (corp-wide): 40.54MM **Privately Held**
SIC: 3021 Rubber and plastics footwear
PA: Genfoot America, Inc
1940 55e Av
Lachine QC H8T 3
514 341-3950

(G-17359)
GRAY ROCK CONCRETE
54 W Milton Rd (05468-3299)
PHONE..............................802 379-5393

EMP: 10 EST: 2013
SALES (est): 726.55K Privately Held
SIC: 3273 Ready-mixed concrete

(G-17360)
INDUSTRIAL MARKING SYSTEMS CORP
Also Called: Bertek Systems
107 Catamount Dr Unit C (05468-3335)
PHONE..............................802 752-3170
EMP: 70
SIC: 2752 Commercial printing, lithographic

(G-17361)
LANCE SMITH INC
Also Called: Vermont Sportscar
85 Gonyeau Rd (05468-3232)
PHONE..............................802 655-3354
◆ **EMP:** 55 **EST:** 1990
SQ FT: 72,000
SALES (est): 10.78MM **Privately Held**
Web: www.vtcar.com
SIC: 5531 3711 7539 Speed shops, including race car supplies; Cars, armored, assembly of; Automotive repair shops, nec

(G-17362)
MILTON VERMONT SHEET METAL INC
Also Called: Tri-Angle Metal Fab
103 Gonyeau Rd (05468-3296)
PHONE..............................802 893-1581
Yancy D Martell, *Pr*
Martin D Martell, *
Marvin A Martell, *Stockholder**
EMP: 64 **EST:** 1972
SQ FT: 40,000
SALES (est): 8.58MM **Privately Held**
Web: www.trianglemetalfab.com
SIC: 3599 3444 3441 1799 Machine shop, jobbing and repair; Sheet metalwork; Fabricated structural metal; Welding on site

(G-17363)
PBM NUTRITIONALS LLC (DH)
Also Called: Perrigo Nutritionals
147 Industrial Park Rd (05468)
PHONE..............................802 527-0521
Joseph C Papa, *CEO*
▲ **EMP:** 109 **EST:** 1981
SQ FT: 218,600
SALES (est): 57.2MM **Privately Held**
Web: www.perrigo.com
SIC: 2834 Pharmaceutical preparations
HQ: Perrigo Company
430 Monroe Ave Nw
Grand Rapids MI 49503
269 673-8451

(G-17364)
SOMALABS INC
Also Called: Doctors Designs
308 Industrial Park Rd (05468)
PHONE..............................802 355-3000
EMP: 10 **EST:** 2010
SALES (est): 392.76K **Privately Held**
SIC: 2834 Pharmaceutical preparations

(G-17365)
US MAILING SYSTEMS INC
15 Catamount Dr (05468-3236)
PHONE..............................802 891-1020
Anthony Villianti Junior, *Pr*
EMP: 13 **EST:** 1984
SQ FT: 15,000
SALES (est): 155.31K **Privately Held**
Web: www.villanti.com
SIC: 2752 Offset printing

(G-17366)
VERMONT CHRISTMAS COMPANY
Also Called: Bridge Building Images
24 Clapper Rd (05468-3216)
P.O. Box 1048 (05402-1048)
PHONE..............................802 893-1670
William Flynn, *Pr*
Andrew E Kelly, *Sec*
▲ **EMP:** 8 **EST:** 1983
SQ FT: 18,000
SALES (est): 1.25MM **Privately Held**
Web: www.vermontchristmasco.com
SIC: 2754 2771 5961 3944 Cards, except greeting: gravure printing; Greeting cards; Catalog and mail-order houses; Board games, puzzles, and models, except electronic

(G-17367)
VILLANTI & SONS PRINTERS INC
Also Called: Villanti Printers
15 Catamount Dr (05468-3236)
PHONE..............................802 864-0723
Jon Villanti, *CEO*
Jay Anthony Villanti, *
Kevin Crook, *
EMP: 60 **EST:** 1972
SALES (est): 8.28MM **Privately Held**
Web: www.villanti.com
SIC: 2752 7331 2789 2791 Offset printing; Direct mail advertising services; Bookbinding and related work; Typesetting

Montgomery Center
Franklin County

(G-17368)
BUMWRAPS INC (PA)
578 Vt Route 242 (05471-5106)
PHONE..............................802 326-4080
Todd G Alix, *Pr*
Myra Alix, *Sec*
▼ **EMP:** 9 **EST:** 1986
SQ FT: 10,000
SALES (est): 976.9K
SALES (corp-wide): 976.9K **Privately Held**
Web: www.bumwraps.com
SIC: 2395 2759 Embroidery products, except Schiffli machine; Screen printing

(G-17369)
WAY OUT WAX INC
Also Called: Candle Cabin, The
68 Puffer Rd (05471-5100)
PHONE..............................802 730-8069
EMP: 15 **EST:** 1994
SALES (est): 2.07MM **Privately Held**
Web: www.wayoutwax.com
SIC: 3999 Candles

Montpelier
Washington County

(G-17370)
CALEDONIA SPIRITS INC
Also Called: Caledonia Spirits
116 Gin Ln (05602-3848)
PHONE..............................802 472-8000
Todd Hardie, *Pr*
Ryan Christiansen, *
EMP: 25 **EST:** 2009
SALES (est): 6.55MM **Privately Held**
Web: www.caledoniaspirits.com
SIC: 5182 2084 Wine and distilled beverages; Wines

(G-17371)
CCO HOLDINGS LLC
89 Main St (05602-3168)
PHONE.................................802 778-0497
EMP: 109
SALES (corp-wide): 54.02B **Publicly Held**
SIC: 4841 3663 3651 Cable television
services; Radio and t.v. communications
equipment; Household audio and video
equipment
HQ: Cco Holdings, Llc
400 Atlantic St
Stamford CT 06901
203 905-7801

(G-17372)
HYZER INDUSTRIES
108 Main St (05602-2906)
PHONE.................................802 223-8277
Scott Kerner, *Prin*
EMP: 8 EST: 2009
SALES (est): 250.14K **Privately Held**
SIC: 3999 Manufacturing industries, nec

(G-17373)
**MONTPELIER GRANITE WORKS
INC**
65 Granite Shed Ln (05602-3677)
P.O. Box 9 (05601-0009)
PHONE.................................802 223-2581
Michelle Parker, *Pr*
▼ EMP: 14 EST: 1925
SQ FT: 8,400
SALES (est): 483.39K **Privately Held**
Web: www.montpeliergraniteworks.com
SIC: 3281 Monuments, cut stone (not
finishing or lettering only)

(G-17374)
REAL GOOD TOYS INC
Also Called: Diamond Deans Dollhouse Co
22 Gallison Hill Rd Unit 1 (05602-4319)
PHONE.................................802 479-2217
James Abrams, *Pr*
Christine Abrams, *VP*
▲ EMP: 8 EST: 1979
SQ FT: 25,000
SALES (est): 1MM **Privately Held**
Web: www.realgoodtoys.com
SIC: 3944 Dollhouses and furniture

(G-17375)
THE LEAHY PRESS INC
Also Called: Northlight Studio Press
79 River St (05602-3757)
P.O. Box 428 (05601-0428)
PHONE.................................802 223-2100
TOLL FREE: 800
Ronald Kowalkowski, *Pr*
EMP: 22 EST: 1969
SQ FT: 12,000
SALES (est): 2.12MM **Privately Held**
Web: www.leahypress.com
SIC: 2752 2759 2677 Offset printing;
Commercial printing, nec; Envelopes

(G-17376)
**VERMONT EVAPORATOR
COMPANY LLC (PA)**
Also Called: Vermont Evaporator
157 Pioneer Ctr Ste 1 (05602-3746)
PHONE.................................802 522-8499
Kate Whelley Mccabe, *CEO*
EMP: 9 EST: 2015
SALES (est): 971.53K
SALES (corp-wide): 971.53K **Privately
Held**
Web: www.vtevap.com

SIC: 3556 Dehydrating equipment, food
processing

(G-17377)
**VERMONT JOURNALISM
TRUST LTD**
Also Called: VTDIGGER.ORG
97 State St Ste 1 (05602-3219)
PHONE.................................802 225-6224
Anne Galloway, *Ex Dir*
EMP: 12 EST: 2009
SALES (est): 2.77MM **Privately Held**
Web: www.vtdigger.org
SIC: 2721 Trade journals: publishing and
printing

(G-17378)
VIANOR INC
375 River St (05602-8300)
PHONE.................................802 223-1747
EMP: 32
SIC: 7534 Tire repair shop
HQ: Vianor, Inc.
1945 Main St
Colchester VT 05446
802 864-7108

(G-17379)
WHISTLEKICK LLC
2030 Jones Brook Rd (05602-8375)
PHONE.................................802 225-6676
EMP: 10 EST: 2013
SALES (est): 456.89K **Privately Held**
Web: www.whistlekick.com
SIC: 3949 Sporting and athletic goods, nec

Morrisville
Lamoille County

(G-17380)
BROSSEAU FUELS LLC
2148 Cadys Falls Rd (05661-4430)
PHONE.................................802 888-9209
James P Brosseau, *Prin*
EMP: 7 EST: 2007
SALES (est): 152.91K **Privately Held**
SIC: 2869 Fuels

(G-17381)
CONCEPT2 INC (PA)
105 Industrial Park Dr (05661-8532)
PHONE.................................802 888-7971
Richard Dreissigacker, *Pr*
Peter Dreissigacker, *
Bari Dreissigacker, *
Linda Markin, *
◆ EMP: 44 EST: 1979
SQ FT: 52,000
SALES (est): 22.47MM
SALES (corp-wide): 22.47MM **Privately
Held**
Web: www.concept2.com
SIC: 2499 3949 Oars and paddles, wood;
Rowing machines

(G-17382)
**GREEN MOUNTAIN DISTILLERS
LLC**
Also Called: Green Mountain Beerworks
2919 Laporte Rd (05661-8310)
PHONE.................................802 498-4848
Timothy Danahy, *Prin*
EMP: 7 EST: 2016
SALES (est): 342.38K **Privately Held**
Web: www.greendistillers.com
SIC: 2085 Distilled and blended liquors

(G-17383)
H A MANOSH CORP
120 Northgate Plz Ste A (05661-8747)
PHONE.................................802 888-5722
Howard A Manosh, *Pr*
Nick Manosh, *
Robert Parsons, *
EMP: 85 EST: 1958
SQ FT: 22,000
SALES (est): 3.59MM **Privately Held**
Web: www.manosh.com
SIC: 1794 1781 1442 Excavation and
grading, building construction; Water well
drilling; Construction sand and gravel

(G-17384)
LEOS SMALL ENGINES INC
541 Vt Route 15 E (05661-9065)
PHONE.................................802 888-7247
Michael Paritz, *Pr*
Joni Paritz, *Sec*
EMP: 10 EST: 1969
SQ FT: 3,000
SALES (est): 949.17K **Privately Held**
Web: www.leossmallengines.com
SIC: 5261 5084 3546 Lawnmowers and
tractors; Engines, gasoline; Saws and
sawing equipment

(G-17385)
LOST NATION BREWING LLC
Also Called: Lost Nation Brewing
87 Old Creamery Rd (05661-6152)
PHONE.................................802 851-8041
EMP: 12 EST: 2012
SALES (est): 912.14K **Privately Held**
Web: www.lostnationbrewing.com
SIC: 2082 5813 5812 Beer (alcoholic
beverage); Bar (drinking places); Eating
places

(G-17386)
**MANUFACTURING SOLUTIONS
INC**
Also Called: Little Pttys Lawn Cr/Demoliton
153 Stafford Ave (05661-8515)
PHONE.................................802 888-3289
Garrett Hirchak, *Pr*
Beth Salvis, *
▲ EMP: 50 EST: 1996
SALES (est): 23.42MM **Privately Held**
Web: www.msivt.com
SIC: 3949 Rowing machines

(G-17387)
NA MANOSH INC
120 Northgate Plz Ste B (05661-8747)
PHONE.................................802 888-5722
Nick Manosh, *Pr*
Andrea Jones, *
EMP: 36 EST: 2015
SALES (est): 4.67MM **Privately Held**
Web: www.manosh.com
SIC: 1381 Drilling water intake wells

(G-17388)
**S & A TROMBLEY
CORPORATION**
Also Called: Lwi Metalworks
76 Houle Ave (05661-8543)
PHONE.................................802 888-2394
Steve Trombley, *Pr*
Lois Trombley, *
Andrea Trombley, *
EMP: 25 EST: 1969
SALES (est): 3.17MM **Privately Held**
Web: www.lwiweld.com

SIC: 3446 3441 3499 3599 Architectural
metalwork; Fabricated structural metal;
Metal household articles; Machine shop,
jobbing and repair

(G-17389)
STERLING TECHNOLOGIES INC
320 Wilkins St (05661-6098)
P.O. Box 728 (05661-0728)
PHONE.................................802 888-4753
Jeffrey Walker, *Pr*
Michael Boudreau, *VP*
EMP: 7 EST: 2005
SQ FT: 10,000
SALES (est): 652.23K **Privately Held**
Web: www.sterlingtechnologiesvt.com
SIC: 3599 Machine shop, jobbing and repair

(G-17390)
STERLING TECHNOLOGIES INC
251 Harrel St (05661-8742)
PHONE.................................802 363-6883
Michael Boudreau, *Ex Dir*
EMP: 15 EST: 2016
SALES (est): 471.91K **Privately Held**
Web: www.sterlingtechnologiesvt.com
SIC: 3599 Machine shop, jobbing and repair

(G-17391)
**VERMONT MAPLE SUGAR CO
INC (PA)**
Also Called: Butternut Mountain Farm
37 Industrial Park Dr (05661-8533)
PHONE.................................802 888-3491
David Marvin, *Pr*
John Kingston, *
Lucy Marvin, *
EMP: 40 EST: 1981
SQ FT: 50,000
SALES (est): 21.64MM
SALES (corp-wide): 21.64MM **Privately
Held**
Web: www.butternutmountainfarm.com
SIC: 2099 Maple syrup

(G-17392)
VIANOR INC
13 Vt Route 15 E (05661-8587)
PHONE.................................802 888-7961
EMP: 32
SIC: 7534 Tire repair shop
HQ: Vianor, Inc.
1945 Main St
Colchester VT 05446
802 864-7108

(G-17393)
WASHBURN COMPANY INC
Also Called: Vermont Originals
320 Wilkins St (05661-6098)
PHONE.................................802 888-3032
Edward Washburn, *CEO*
Jane Washburn, *Pr*
▲ EMP: 12 EST: 2004
SQ FT: 5,000
SALES (est): 233.88K **Privately Held**
Web: www.turtlefur.com
SIC: 2353 Hats, caps, and millinery

New Haven
Addison County

(G-17394)
**PHOENIX FEEDS AND NTRTN
INC (PA)**
Also Called: Kimball Bakery Feeds
5482 Ethan Allen Hwy (05472-1113)
P.O. Box 36 (05472-0036)

GEOGRAPHIC

PHONE.....................802 453-6684
Craig H Newton, *Pr*
David Santos, *VP*
Kathryn W Newton, *VP*
Nicole L Elithorpe, *Sec*
EMP: 25 EST: 2001
SALES (est): 14.75MM
SALES (corp-wide): 14.75MM **Privately Held**
Web: www.phoenixfeeds.net
SIC: 2048 Cereal-, grain-, and seed-based feeds

(G-17395)
PHOENIX FEEDS ORGANIX LLC
5482 Ethan Allen Hwy (05472-1113)
P.O. Box 36 (05472-0036)
PHONE.....................802 453-6684
David Santos, *Pr*
EMP: 50 EST: 2019
SALES (est): 2.53MM **Privately Held**
Web: www.phoenixfeeds.net
SIC: 2048 Livestock feeds

(G-17396)
STARK MOUNTAIN WOODWORKS CO
Also Called: Stark Mountain Woodworking Co
359 South St (05472-4064)
PHONE.....................802 453-5549
Walter Hellier, *Pr*
Louis Dupont, *VP*
EMP: 10 EST: 1992
SALES (est): 1.13MM **Privately Held**
Web: www.starkmountain.com
SIC: 2431 Millwork

Newport
Orleans County

(G-17397)
CALKINS SAND & GRAVEL INC
3258 Vt Route 14 N (05855-8604)
PHONE.....................802 334-8418
Criss Martel, *Mgr*
EMP: 17
SALES (corp-wide): 2.6MM **Privately Held**
SIC: 1442 Construction sand and gravel
PA: Calkins Sand & Gravel, Inc.
　Rr 5
　Lyndonville VT 05851
　802 626-5755

(G-17398)
CODET-NEWPORT CORPORATION (HQ)
Also Called: Big Bill
294 Crawford Rd (05855-9502)
P.O. Box 440 (05855-0440)
PHONE.....................802 334-5811
Vincent Audet, *Pr*
Gilbert Audet, *Pr*
Stephen Audet, *VP*
Robert H Audet, *Sec*
Gobin Audet, *Sec*
▲ **EMP: 10 EST:** 1990
SALES (est): 8.73MM
SALES (corp-wide): 66.33MM **Privately Held**
Web: www.bigbill.com
SIC: 2326 3021　Men's and boy's work clothing; Protective footwear, rubber or plastic
PA: Codet Inc
　49 Rue Maple
　Coaticook QC J1A 1
　866 946-8764

(G-17399)
COLUMBIA FOREST PRODUCTS INC
Indian Head Division
115 Columbia Way (05855-5496)
P.O. Box 605 (05855-0605)
PHONE.....................802 334-6711
Theodore N Jewett, *VP*
EMP: 193
SALES (corp-wide): 494.11K **Privately Held**
Web: cfp.venveodev.com
SIC: 2435 2426　Hardwood veneer and plywood; Hardwood dimension and flooring mills
PA: Columbia Forest Products, Inc.
　7900 Mccloud Rd Ste 200
　Greensboro NC 27409
　336 605-0429

(G-17400)
METAL-FLEX WELDED BELLOWS INC
149 Lakemont Rd (05855-9453)
PHONE.....................802 334-5550
Barrie W Hume, *Pr*
Gwen Hume, *
EMP: 36 EST: 1981
SQ FT: 13,000
SALES (est): 5.13MM **Privately Held**
Web: www.metalflexbellows.com
SIC: 3599 Bellows, industrial: metal

(G-17401)
NEVTEC LTD
Also Called: Nevtec
33 Airport Rd (05855-4519)
PHONE.....................802 334-7800
Leonard Griffes, *Pr*
Roderick Davis, *VP*
Beulah Griffes, *Treas*
Donald Griffes, *Sec*
Gary Hosford, *VP*
EMP: 10 EST: 1971
SQ FT: 4,000
SALES (est): 1.45MM **Privately Held**
Web: www.nevtecltd.com
SIC: 1711 3444　Mechanical contractor; Hoods, range: sheet metal

(G-17402)
NEWPORT FURNITURE PARTS CORP
Also Called: Newport Rocking Chair Center
450 Main St (05855-5535)
PHONE.....................802 334-5428
Laurent Daigneault, *Pr*
David Laforce, *
▲ **EMP: 75 EST:** 1963
SQ FT: 100,000
SALES (est): 9.66MM **Privately Held**
Web: www.builtbynewport.com
SIC: 2431 Millwork

(G-17403)
NEWPORT SAND & GRAVEL CO INC
Also Called: Carroll Concrete Co
2014 Alderbrook Rd (05855-9006)
PHONE.....................802 334-2000
Shaun P Carroll Senior, *Mgr*
EMP: 10
SALES (corp-wide): 44.7MM **Privately Held**
Web: www.carrollconcrete.com
SIC: 3273 Ready-mixed concrete
PA: Newport Sand & Gravel Co., Inc.
　8 Reeds Mill Rd
　Newport NH 03773
　603 298-0199

(G-17404)
POULIN GRAIN INC (PA)
Also Called: Whitman's Feed Store
24 Railroad Sq (05855-2205)
PHONE.....................802 334-6731
EMP: 51 EST: 1970
SALES (est): 31.51MM
SALES (corp-wide): 31.51MM **Privately Held**
Web: www.poulingrain.com
SIC: 2048 5153　Prepared feeds, nec; Grain and field beans

(G-17405)
QUIRION LUC
Also Called: Vermont Olde Tyme Kettle Corn
495 Memphremagog Vw (05855-4926)
PHONE.....................802 673-8386
Luc Quirion, *Owner*
EMP: 7
SALES (corp-wide): 957.33K **Privately Held**
Web:
www.vermontoldetymekettlecorn.com
SIC: 2064 Candy and other confectionery products
PA: Luc Quirion
　96 Western Ave
　Newport VT 05855
　802 673-8386

(G-17406)
QUIRION LUC (PA)
Also Called: Vermont Olde Tyme Kettle Corn
96 Western Ave (05855-8006)
PHONE.....................802 673-8386
Luc Quirion, *Owner*
EMP: 8 EST: 2010
SQ FT: 7,000
SALES (est): 957.33K
SALES (corp-wide): 957.33K **Privately Held**
Web:
www.vermontoldetymekettlecorn.com
SIC: 2064 5145 5441　Popcorn balls or other treated popcorn products; Popcorn and supplies; Popcorn, including caramel corn

(G-17407)
VERMONT HERITAGE DISTRS INC
Also Called: Vermont Heritage Spring Water
98 Johns River Dr (05855-9836)
PHONE.....................802 334-6503
Daniel Martin, *Pr*
Renee Martin, *VP*
EMP: 7 EST: 2007
SQ FT: 3,500
SALES (est): 1MM **Privately Held**
Web: www.vtheritage.com
SIC: 4731 2086　Freight forwarding; Mineral water, carbonated: packaged in cans, bottles, etc.

Newport Center
Orleans County

(G-17408)
VERMONT CENTER WREATHS INC
Also Called: Makers Natural Green Wreaths
44 Kimberly Ln (05857-9432)
P.O. Box 38 (05857-0038)
PHONE.....................802 334-6432
Michael Sicard, *Pr*
Paulette Sicard, *
EMP: 7 EST: 1988
SALES (est): 396.34K **Privately Held**

Web: www.vermontcenterwreaths.com
SIC: 3999 Wreaths, artificial

North Bennington
Bennington County

(G-17409)
MOUNTAIN MOZZARELLA LLC
Also Called: Maple Brook Farm
441 Water St (05257-4420)
PHONE.....................802 440-9950
Michael Scheps, *Managing Member*
Johann Englert, *Prin*
EMP: 50 EST: 2004
SALES (est): 7.19MM **Privately Held**
Web: www.maplebrookvt.com
SIC: 2022 Processed cheese

(G-17410)
NATIONAL HANGER COMPANY INC
Also Called: National Store Supply
276 Water St (05257-4437)
PHONE.....................800 426-4377
Michele Pilcher, *Pr*
Eric Erthein, *
Marcella Erthein, *
James Erthein, *Stockholder*
◆ **EMP: 92 EST:** 1925
SQ FT: 200,000
SALES (est): 16.37MM **Privately Held**
Web: www.nahanco.com
SIC: 3089 Clothes hangers, plastics

(G-17411)
POULIN GRAIN INC
Also Called: Whitman's Feed Store
1873 Vt Route 67 E (05257-8103)
PHONE.....................802 681-1605
Scott Birch, *Brnch Mgr*
EMP: 20
SALES (corp-wide): 31.51MM **Privately Held**
Web: www.poulingrain.com
SIC: 2048 Livestock feeds
PA: Poulin Grain, Inc.
　24 Railroad Sq
　Newport VT 05855
　802 334-6731

(G-17412)
STERLING GUN DRILLS INC
Also Called: Drillmasters of Vermont
940 Water St (05257-9810)
P.O. Box 806 (05257-0806)
PHONE.....................802 442-3525
EMP: 22 EST: 1994
SQ FT: 10,000
SALES (est): 899.97K **Privately Held**
Web: www.sterlinggundrills.com
SIC: 3545 Cutting tools for machine tools

North Clarendon
Rutland County

(G-17413)
CHARLES E TUTTLE CO INC (DH)
Also Called: Tuttle Publishing
364 Innovation Dr (05759-9436)
PHONE.....................802 773-8930
Eric Oey, *Pr*
Michael Sargent, *
◆ **EMP: 35 EST:** 1832
SQ FT: 72,000
SALES (est): 6.59MM **Privately Held**
Web: www.tuttlepublishing.com

▲ = Import　▼ = Export
◆ = Import/Export

SIC: 2731 Books, publishing only
HQ: Periplus Editions (Hk) Limited
   Rm 1005 10/F Far East Finance Ctr
   Admiralty HK

(G-17414)
ISOVOLTA INC
Also Called: Isovolta/Us Samica
477 Windcrest Rd (05759-9517)
PHONE................................802 775-5528
Heinz Riedler, *Pr*
John Roberts, *
Johnnes Mensporss, *
Jody Lafaso, *
Robert S Pratt, *
▲ EMP: 35 EST: 1999
SQ FT: 50,000
SALES (est): 11.83MM
SALES (corp-wide): 1.16B Privately Held
Web: www.isovolta.com
SIC: 3644 3295 Insulators and insulation
   materials, electrical; Minerals, ground or
   treated
HQ: Isovolta Ag
   Iz NO-Sud, StraBe 3/Objekt 1
   Wiener Neudorf 2355
   595950

(G-17415)
**JOSEPH P CARRARA & SONS
INC (PA)**
Also Called: Carrara
167 N Shrewsbury Rd (05759-9507)
P.O. Box 60 (05759-0060)
PHONE................................802 775-2301
Paul J Carrara, *Pr*
Robert Carrara, *
Christine M Carrara, *
▲ EMP: 40 EST: 1935
SQ FT: 20,500
SALES (est): 18.43MM
SALES (corp-wide): 18.43MM Privately
Held
Web: www.jpcarrara.com
SIC: 3272 3273 1442 1771 Prestressed
   concrete products; Ready-mixed concrete;
   Sand mining; Foundation and footing
   contractor

(G-17416)
KNIGHT INDUSTRIES INC
Also Called: Knight Kitchens
20 Innovation Dr (05759-8802)
P.O. Box 66 (05759-0066)
PHONE................................802 773-8777
▼ EMP: 28 EST: 1982
SQ FT: 36,000
SALES (est): 2.48MM Privately Held
Web: www.knightkitchens.com
SIC: 2434 Vanities, bathroom: wood

(G-17417)
MILL RIVER LUMBER LTD
2639 Middle Rd (05759-4413)
P.O. Box 100 (05759-0100)
PHONE................................802 775-0032
Michael C Roberts, *Pr*
Fred Burnett, *
Harry Robbins, *
Peter Buckley, *
Frank Cecot, *
EMP: 55 EST: 1983
SQ FT: 2,800
SALES (est): 5.55MM Privately Held
Web: www.millriverlumber.com
SIC: 2421 5191 5261 5211 Lumber: rough,
   sawed, or planed; Garden supplies; Garden
   supplies and tools, nec; Lumber and other
   building materials

(G-17418)
**VERMONT WOOD PELLET CO
LLC**
1105 Vt Route 7b Central (05759-9508)
PHONE................................802 747-1093
Chris Brooks, *CEO*
Katheryn Adams, *Managing Member*
EMP: 24 EST: 2009
SALES (est): 2.04MM Privately Held
Web: 35e.678.myftpupload.com
SIC: 2499 Applicators, wood

North Ferrisburgh
Addison County

(G-17419)
BOWLES CORPORATION
Also Called: U.S. Environmental Services
445 Longpoint Rd (05473-7089)
PHONE................................802 425-3447
David Bowles, *Pr*
Carol Bowles, *VP*
EMP: 12 EST: 1983
SQ FT: 6,000
SALES (est): 2.23MM Privately Held
Web: www.bowlescorp.com
SIC: 3829 Measuring and controlling
   devices, nec

North Hartland
Windsor County

(G-17420)
**NORTH HARTLAND TOOL CORP
(PA)**
Also Called: Carl Associates
14 Evarts Rd (05052-9719)
P.O. Box 38 (05052-0038)
PHONE................................802 295-3196
John M Mullen, *Pr*
Carol J Mullen, *
EMP: 76 EST: 1957
SQ FT: 15,500
SALES (est): 8.66MM
SALES (corp-wide): 8.66MM Privately
Held
Web: www.nhtool.com
SIC: 3544 Special dies and tools

North Springfield
Windsor County

(G-17421)
**GURNEY BROTHERS
CONSTRUCTION**
19 Gurney Rd (05150-9750)
PHONE................................802 886-2210
Daniel Gurney, *Pr*
EMP: 29 EST: 1957
SQ FT: 3,000
SALES (est): 2.92MM Privately Held
Web: www.gurneybros.com
SIC: 1794 1442 Excavation and grading,
   building construction; Construction sand
   and gravel

(G-17422)
IVEK CORP (PA)
10 Fairbanks Rd (05150-9743)
PHONE................................802 886-2238
Tracey Tanny, *Pr*
Mark N Tanny, *
Michael F Hanley, *
John Mcdonald, *Dir*
EMP: 102 EST: 1979

SQ FT: 31,000
SALES (est): 27.51MM
SALES (corp-wide): 27.51MM Privately
Held
Web: www.ivek.com
SIC: 3561 Industrial pumps and parts

(G-17423)
JELD-WEN INC
Also Called: Jeld-Wen Doors
36 Precision Dr Ste 130 (05150-9706)
PHONE................................802 886-1728
Wen Jeld, *Brnch Mgr*
EMP: 247
Web: www.jeld-wen.com
SIC: 2431 Doors, wood
HQ: Jeld-Wen, Inc.
   2645 Silver Crescent Dr
   Charlotte NC 28273
   800 535-3936

(G-17424)
**SPRINGFIELD FENCE COMPANY
INC**
Also Called: Springfield Fence
50 Route 106 (05150-9747)
P.O. Box 10 (05150-0010)
PHONE................................802 886-2221
Jeffrey W Blauw, *Pr*
Deborah S Blauw, *VP*
E Clifton Shute, *Treas*
EMP: 15 EST: 1968
SQ FT: 13,000
SALES (est): 2.52MM Privately Held
Web: www.springfieldfencevt.com
SIC: 5211 1799 1611 5039 Fencing; Fence
   construction; Guardrail construction,
   highways; Wire fence, gates, and
   accessories

(G-17425)
SPRINGFIELD PRINTING CORP
Also Called: Spc Marcom Studio
19 Precision Dr (05150-9778)
PHONE................................802 886-2201
Mark Sanderson, *Pr*
Bruce Sanderson, *Marketing*
Barbara J Sanderson, *
EMP: 34 EST: 1878
SQ FT: 25,000
SALES (est): 4.94MM Privately Held
Web: www.springfieldprinting.com
SIC: 2752 Offset printing

(G-17426)
VERMONT PACKINGHOUSE LLC
25 Fairbanks Rd (05150-9743)
PHONE................................802 886-8688
Doctor Arion Thiboumery, *Mng Pt*
EMP: 15 EST: 2013
SQ FT: 22,000
SALES (est): 2.91MM Privately Held
Web: www.vermontpackinghouse.com
SIC: 2011 5147 Meat packing plants; Lard

(G-17427)
VERMONT TIMBER WORKS INC
16 Fairbanks Rd (05150-9743)
PHONE................................802 886-1917
FAX: 802 886-6188
EMP: 19
SALES (est): 2MM Privately Held
Web: www.vermonttimberworks.com
SIC: 2491 1521 Structural lumber and
   timber, treated wood; Single-family housing
   construction

North Troy
Orleans County

(G-17428)
**APPALCHIAN ENGINEERED
FLRG INC**
105 Industrial Park Dr (05859)
PHONE................................802 988-1073
Jean Leduc, *Pr*
Gordon Duplain, *VP*
EMP: 18 EST: 2011
SQ FT: 26,000
SALES (est): 6.36MM
SALES (corp-wide): 19.24MM Privately
Held
Web: www.appalachianflooring.com
SIC: 2426 Flooring, hardwood
PA: Planchers Des Appalaches Ltee
   454 Rue De La Riviere
   Cowansville QC J2K 3
   450 266-3999

(G-17429)
JAY MOUNTAIN MAPLES LLC
962 N Jay Rd (05859-9472)
PHONE................................802 988-4086
Breht Grenier, *Owner*
EMP: 7 EST: 2013
SALES (est): 249.17K Privately Held
Web: www.adirondackalmanack.com
SIC: 2099 Maple syrup

(G-17430)
PROLENS INC
47 Main St (05859-9563)
P.O. Box 204 (05859-0204)
PHONE................................802 988-1018
Dominicque Alain, *Pr*
EMP: 7
SALES (corp-wide): 489.64K Privately
Held
Web: www.prolens.com
SIC: 3851 Ophthalmic goods
PA: Prolens Inc
   28 Daniel Plummer Rd # 5
   Goffstown NH 03045
   603 487-1019

Northfield
Washington County

(G-17431)
BARRY T CHOUINARD INC (HQ)
Also Called: Comfort Colors Dyehouse
127 N Main St (05663-6836)
P.O. Box 230 (05663-0230)
PHONE................................802 485-8600
▲ EMP: 20 EST: 1978
SALES (est): 5.6MM
SALES (corp-wide): 3.24B Privately Held
SIC: 2321 2361 2331 Men's and boys' dress
   shirts; T-shirts and tops: girls', children's,
   and infants'; T-shirts and tops, women's:
   made from purchased materials
PA: Les Vetements De Sport Gildan Inc
   600 Boul De Maisonneuve O 33eme
   Etage
   Montreal QC H3A 3
   514 735-2023

(G-17432)
**CABOT HOSIERY MILLS INC
(PA)**
Also Called: Darn Tough Vermont
364 Whetstone Dr (05663-6469)
P.O. Box 307 (05663-0307)
PHONE................................802 485-6066

Marc Cabot, *Pr*
Ric Cabot, *
Michael Lavin, *
◆ **EMP: 84 EST:** 1978
SQ FT: 50,000
SALES (est): 30.84MM
SALES (corp-wide): 30.84MM **Privately Held**
Web: www.darntough.com
SIC: 5137 5136 2252 2251 Hosiery: women's, children's, and infants'; Hosiery, men's and boys'; Hosiery, nec; Women's hosiery, except socks

(G-17433)
NATWORKS INC
454 S Main St (05663-5690)
PHONE.............................802 485-6818
Chris Bradley, *Pr*
Andrew Bothfield, *VP*
EMP: 10 **EST:** 1998
SALES (est): 523.33K **Privately Held**
Web: www.natworks-inc.com
SIC: 7372 7371 Prepackaged software; Custom computer programming services

(G-17434)
S W GRANITE INC
331 Central St (05663-5679)
PHONE.............................713 933-0501
Scott Wright, *Owner*
EMP: 7 **EST:** 2009
SALES (est): 66.29K **Privately Held**
SIC: 3281 Cut stone and stone products

(G-17435)
WALL GOLDFINGER FURNITURE
168 N Main St (05663-6835)
PHONE.............................802 278-5823
Mark Richey, *Prin*
EMP: 24 **EST:** 2019
SALES (est): 211.39K **Privately Held**
Web: www.wallgoldfinger.com
SIC: 2431 Millwork

(G-17436)
WALLGOLDFINGER INC
706 Garvey Hill Rd (05663-6760)
PHONE.............................802 483-4200
John C Wall, *Pr*
Mike Spencer, *
Anne Gould, *
EMP: 45 **EST:** 1971
SALES (est): 8.17MM **Privately Held**
Web: www.wallgoldfinger.com
SIC: 2431 Millwork

Norwich
Windsor County

(G-17437)
CORE VALUE SOFTWARE
316 Main St (05055-4428)
PHONE.............................802 473-3147
George Sandmann, *Pr*
EMP: 10 **EST:** 2008
SALES (est): 749.68K **Privately Held**
Web: www.corevalueforadvisors.com
SIC: 7372 Prepackaged software

Orleans
Orleans County

(G-17438)
KIMTEK CORPORATION
326 Industrial Park Ln (05860-9423)
PHONE.............................802 754-9000

Kimball Johnson, *Pr*
EMP: 8 **EST:** 1984
SQ FT: 4,000
SALES (est): 986.39K **Privately Held**
Web: www.kimtekresearch.com
SIC: 3444 Sheet metalwork

(G-17439)
VERMONT BEEF JERKY CO
348 Industrial Park Ln (05860-9423)
PHONE.............................802 754-9412
Wayne Leiberum, *Pt*
William Perkins, *Pt*
EMP: 12 **EST:** 1989
SQ FT: 6,000
SALES (est): 707.19K **Privately Held**
Web: www.rosiesbeefjerky.com
SIC: 2013 Sausages and other prepared meats

(G-17440)
VILLAGE OF ORLEANS
Also Called: INCOPORATED VILLGE OF ORLEAN
1 Memorial Sq (05860-1215)
PHONE.............................802 754-8584
John Morley, *Mgr*
Shelia Martin, *Treas*
Marilyn Prue, *Off Mgr*
EMP: 8 **EST:** 2006
SALES (est): 903.95K **Privately Held**
SIC: 3679 Electronic loads and power supplies

Pawlet
Rutland County

(G-17441)
MATT WAITE EXCAVATION INC
Also Called: Kelco Concrete
236 Milaura Rd (05761-4417)
P.O. Box 288 (05761-0288)
PHONE.............................802 325-3668
Kellie Baker-waite, *Pr*
Matt Waite, *VP*
EMP: 14 **EST:** 1987
SQ FT: 1,000
SALES (est): 474.04K **Privately Held**
SIC: 1794 3273 Excavation work; Ready-mixed concrete

Perkinsville
Windsor County

(G-17442)
SHEEHAN & SONS LUMBER
251 Stoughton Pond Rd (05151-9688)
PHONE.............................802 263-5545
EMP: 7 **EST:** 1990
SALES (est): 458.15K **Privately Held**
SIC: 2421 4212 Sawmills and planing mills, general; Local trucking, without storage

(G-17443)
WILLIAMS & CO MINING INC
Also Called: Vermont Soapstone
248 Stoughton Pond Rd (05151-9695)
PHONE.............................802 263-5404
Glenn Bowman, *Pr*
Gail Bowman, *VP*
EMP: 17 **EST:** 1967
SQ FT: 6,000
SALES (est): 494.56K **Privately Held**
Web: www.vermontsoapstone.com
SIC: 3281 1499 Household articles, except furniture: cut stone; Soapstone mining

Pittsford
Rutland County

(G-17444)
KEITHS II SPORTS LTD
Also Called: Keith II Sporting Goods
3892 Us Route 7 (05763-9291)
P.O. Box 757 (05702-0757)
PHONE.............................802 483-6050
Daniel Keith, *Pr*
Judith O Keith, *
EMP: 17 **EST:** 1964
SQ FT: 3,000
SALES (est): 755.48K **Privately Held**
SIC: 5091 5941 2396 5949 Sporting and recreation goods; Sporting goods and bicycle shops; Screen printing on fabric articles; Needlework goods and supplies

(G-17445)
MARCELL OIL COMPANY INC
740 Us Route 7 (05763-9566)
PHONE.............................802 775-5050
EMP: 12 **EST:** 2016
SALES (est): 979.41K **Privately Held**
SIC: 1311 Crude petroleum production

(G-17446)
VERMONT VERDE ANTIQUE INTL
2561 Sugar Hollow Rd (05763-9891)
PHONE.............................802 767-4421
Dorando Cavallacci, *Pr*
Mike Solari, *Genl Mgr*
▲ **EMP:** 8 **EST:** 1993
SALES (est): 894.32K **Privately Held**
Web: www.vtverde.com
SIC: 1411 Calcareous tufa, dimension-quarrying

Poultney
Rutland County

(G-17447)
FIRST LIGHT TECHNOLOGIES INC
212 Ideal Way (05764-1052)
PHONE.............................802 287-4195
▲ **EMP:** 85 **EST:** 1994
SQ FT: 25,000
SALES (est): 9.2MM **Privately Held**
Web: www.firstlightusa.com
SIC: 3641 Ultraviolet lamps

(G-17448)
GREENSTONE SLATE COMPANY INC
Also Called: Qsi
325 Upper Rd (05764)
P.O. Box 134 (05764-0134)
PHONE.............................802 287-4333
Richard Hill, *Pr*
Jonathan R Hill, *
◆ **EMP:** 25 **EST:** 1991
SALES (est): 3.45MM **Privately Held**
Web: www.greenstoneslate.com
SIC: 3281 Cut stone and stone products

(G-17449)
QUARRY SLATE INDUSTRIES INC
Also Called: Briar Hill
325 Upper Rd (05764)
P.O. Box 197 (05764-0197)
PHONE.............................802 287-9701
John Hill, *Pr*

Edward Valavyka, *
EMP: 23 **EST:** 1955
SQ FT: 14,000
SALES (est): 1.43MM **Privately Held**
Web: www.greenstoneslate.com
SIC: 2952 1411 Asphalt felts and coatings; Slate, dimension-quarrying

(G-17450)
RUPE SLATE CO INC
54 New Boston Rd (05764-9752)
PHONE.............................802 287-9692
Richard Rupe, *Pr*
Admiral Nancy A Rute, *Sec*
EMP: 7 **EST:** 1985
SALES (est): 381.48K **Privately Held**
Web: www.rupeslatecompany.com
SIC: 3259 Roofing tile, clay

(G-17451)
SOUTH POULTNEY SLATE
376 York St (05764-1023)
PHONE.............................802 287-9278
Frances Hayes, *Owner*
EMP: 7 **EST:** 1998
SALES (est): 673.25K **Privately Held**
SIC: 1411 Slate, dimension-quarrying

(G-17452)
TARAN BROS INC
Also Called: Fair Haven Slate
2522 Vt Route 30 N (05764-9685)
PHONE.............................802 287-9308
Stephen Taran, *Pr*
EMP: 7
SALES (corp-wide): 2.42MM **Privately Held**
SIC: 1411 Argillite, dimension-quarrying
PA: Taran Bros Inc
  Rr 30
  Poultney VT 05764
  802 287-5853

(G-17453)
TARAN BROS INC (PA)
Also Called: Red Slate Quarry
Rte 30 (05764)
PHONE.............................802 287-5853
Stephen M Taran, *Pr*
Gretel Taran, *Sec*
Joseph Taran, *VP*
Barbara Taran, *Sec*
EMP: 20 **EST:** 1930
SALES (est): 2.42MM
SALES (corp-wide): 2.42MM **Privately Held**
SIC: 1411 Slate, dimension-quarrying

(G-17454)
VEMAS CORPORATION
61 Beaman St (05764-1004)
PHONE.............................802 287-4100
EMP: 36
SIC: 3672 3679 Printed circuit boards; Harness assemblies, for electronic use: wire or cable

Pownal
Bennington County

(G-17455)
N W P INC
Also Called: Northeast Wood Products
171 Church St (05261-2003)
PHONE.............................802 442-4749
Robert L Kobelia, *Pr*
Robert Kobelia, *Pr*
Kristena Kobelia, *Treas*

EMP: 9 **EST:** 1946
SALES (est): 750K **Privately Held**
SIC: 2421 5031 2426 Sawmills and planing
mills, general; Lumber: rough, dressed, and
finished; Hardwood dimension and flooring
mills

Proctor
Rutland County

(G-17456)
CARRIS FINANCIAL CORP (PA)
Also Called: Carris Community of Companies
49 Main St (05765-1178)
PHONE..............................802 773-9111
Alberto Aguilar, *CEO*
William Carris, *Ch Bd*
David Fitz-gerald, *VP*
Harold Stotland, *VP*
David Sunderland, *VP*
▲ **EMP:** 15 **EST:** 1990
SALES (est): 94.64MM **Privately Held**
Web: www.carris.com
SIC: 2499 3499 3089 Spools, reels, and
pulleys: wood; Reels, cable: metal; Plastics
hardware and building products

(G-17457)
CARRIS REELS INC (HQ)
Also Called: Carris Plastics
49 Main St (05765-1178)
PHONE..............................802 773-9111
Alberto Aguilar, *Pr*
William Carris, *
David Fitz-gerald, *VP*
David Sunderland, *
Kathy Brytowski, *
▲ **EMP:** 25 **EST:** 1951
SQ FT: 10,531
SALES (est): 76.97MM **Privately Held**
Web: www.carris.com
SIC: 2499 3499 3089 2655 Spools, reels,
and pulleys: wood; Reels, cable: metal;
Plastics hardware and building products;
Tubes, fiber or paper: made from
purchased material
PA: Carris Financial Corp.
49 Main St
Proctor VT 05765

(G-17458)
O M Y A INC
62 Main St (05765-1177)
PHONE..............................802 499-8131
EMP: 28 **EST:** 2015
SALES (est): 3.5MM **Privately Held**
SIC: 2819 Industrial inorganic chemicals,
nec

(G-17459)
OMYA INC
39 Main St (05765-1178)
PHONE..............................802 459-3311
EMP: 28
Web: www.omya.com
SIC: 2819 Calcium compounds and salts,
inorganic, nec
HQ: Omya Inc.
9987 Carver Rd Ste 300
Blue Ash OH 45242
513 387-4600

(G-17460)
PROCTOR GAS INC
2 Market St (05765-1031)
PHONE..............................802 459-3340
TOLL FREE: 877
Judith Taranovich, *Ex Dir*
Judith Taranovich, *Sec*

EMP: 25 **EST:** 1934
SQ FT: 3,200
SALES (est): 1.67MM **Privately Held**
Web: www.proctorgas.com
SIC: 5984 5722 2911 Propane gas, bottled;
Household appliance stores; Petroleum
refining

Proctorsville
Windsor County

(G-17461)
GILCRIS ENTERPRISES INC
Also Called: Proctor Piper Log Homes
283 Peaceful Valley Rd (05153-9751)
PHONE..............................802 226-7764
Richard Gilcris, *Pr*
Wayne Gilcris, *VP*
EMP: 10 **EST:** 1971
SQ FT: 30,000
SALES (est): 663.09K **Privately Held**
SIC: 2421 2452 Sawmills and planing mills,
general; Log cabins, prefabricated, wood

Quechee
Windsor County

(G-17462)
FAT HAT CLOTHING CO
Also Called: Expresso To Go
1 Quechee Main St (05059-3052)
P.O. Box 863 (05059-0863)
PHONE..............................802 296-6646
Joan Ecker, *Pr*
Allen Malcolm, *Sec*
EMP: 13 **EST:** 1979
SQ FT: 9,000
SALES (est): 474.75K **Privately Held**
Web: www.fathat.com
SIC: 2339 2353 2329 Women's and misses'
jackets and coats, except sportswear; Hats,
caps, and millinery; Men's and boys'
leather, wool and down-filled outerwear

(G-17463)
SIMON PEARCE (US) INC
Also Called: Pearce, Simon Restaurant
Main Street (05059)
P.O. Box 799 (05059-0799)
PHONE..............................802 295-2711
Lisa Soule, *Brnch Mgr*
EMP: 21
SALES (corp-wide): 49.22MM **Privately
Held**
Web: www.simonpearce.com
SIC: 5812 3559 3229 Eating places; Glass
making machinery: blowing, molding,
forming, etc.; Pressed and blown glass, nec
PA: Simon Pearce (U.S.), Inc.
109 Park Rd
Windsor VT 05089
802 674-6280

(G-17464)
WHISPER HILLS
5573 Woodstock Rd (05059)
P.O. Box 11 (05049-0011)
PHONE..............................802 296-7627
Randy Cysyk, *Pr*
EMP: 7 **EST:** 2009
SALES (est): 470.84K **Privately Held**
Web: www.whisperhill.com
SIC: 2841 Soap: granulated, liquid, cake,
flaked, or chip

Randolph
Orange County

(G-17465)
4382412 CANADA INC
Also Called: Illumination Devices
44 Hull St Ste D (05060-1276)
PHONE..............................802 225-5911
Jennifer Bauers, *Dir Fin*
EMP: 13
SALES (corp-wide): 6.71MM **Privately
Held**
SIC: 3674 Light emitting diodes
PA: 4382412 Canada Inc.
11650 Elbow Dr Sw
Calgary AB T2W 1

(G-17466)
AADCO MEDICAL INC
2279 Vt Route 66 (05060-4406)
P.O. Box 410 (05060-0410)
PHONE..............................802 728-3400
Robert Marchione, *Pr*
Anthony Skidmore, *
◆ **EMP:** 64 **EST:** 1985
SQ FT: 20,000
SALES (est): 15.13MM **Privately Held**
Web: www.aadcomed.com
SIC: 3844 3842 5047 X-ray apparatus and
tubes; Surgical appliances and supplies; X-
ray machines and tubes

(G-17467)
**APPLIED RESEARCH ASSOC
INC**
Also Called: Vertek
250 Beanville Rd (05060-9301)
PHONE..............................802 728-4588
David Timian, *Genl Mgr*
EMP: 45
SALES (corp-wide): 418.64MM **Privately
Held**
Web: www.ara.com
SIC: 8731 3829 8711 Engineering
laboratory, except testing; Measuring and
controlling devices, nec; Civil engineering
HQ: Applied Research Associates, Inc.
4300 San Mateo Blvd Ne
Albuquerque NM 87110
505 883-3636

(G-17468)
FREEDOM FOODS LLC
300 Beanville Rd (05060-9400)
P.O. Box 211 (05060-0211)
PHONE..............................802 728-0070
▲ **EMP:** 10 **EST:** 2008
SALES (est): 1.04MM **Privately Held**
Web: www.freedom-foods.com
SIC: 2099 Almond pastes

(G-17469)
HERALD OF RANDOLPH
30 Pleasant St (05060-1156)
P.O. Box 309 (05060-0309)
PHONE..............................802 728-3232
M D Drysdale, *Owner*
EMP: 14 **EST:** 1874
SALES (est): 422.47K **Privately Held**
Web: www.ourherald.com
SIC: 2711 Commercial printing and
newspaper publishing combined

(G-17470)
LEDDYNAMICS INC
Also Called: Ledsupply
296 Beanville Rd (05060-9301)
P.O. Box 444 (05060-0444)

PHONE..............................802 728-4533
William Mcgrath, *Pr*
◆ **EMP:** 75 **EST:** 2000
SQ FT: 18,000
SALES (est): 15.5MM **Privately Held**
Web: www.leddynamics.com
SIC: 3674 Light emitting diodes

(G-17471)
NEW ENGLAND PRECISION INC
281 Beanville Rd (05060-9300)
PHONE..............................800 293-4112
Bruce Uryase, *Pr*
Joseph Holland, *CFO*
EMP: 75 **EST:** 1993
SQ FT: 80,000
SALES (est): 11.24MM **Privately Held**
Web: www.newenglandprecision.com
SIC: 3469 3364 3366 Stamping metal for
the trade; Nonferrous die-castings except
aluminum; Copper foundries

(G-17472)
**ONE-PULL SLTONS WIRE
CABLE LLC**
Also Called: Quik-Pull
44 Hull St Ste 2 (05060-1264)
PHONE..............................833 663-7855
EMP: 60 **EST:** 2018
SALES (est): 4.29MM **Privately Held**
Web: www.onepullwire.com
SIC: 3496 Miscellaneous fabricated wire
products

(G-17473)
PORTER MUSIC BOX CO INC
Also Called: Greystone Gift Shop
79 Sunset Hill Rd (05060-9288)
P.O. Box 424 (05060-0424)
PHONE..............................802 728-9694
Dwight Porter, *Pr*
Mary Porter, *VP*
▲ **EMP:** 7 **EST:** 1974
SALES (est): 503.91K **Privately Held**
Web: www.portermusicbox.com
SIC: 3652 3999 Magnetic tape (audio):
prerecorded; Music boxes

(G-17474)
**VERMONT HEMP PROCESSING
INC**
Also Called: Vhp
44 Hull St Ste 6 (05060-1264)
PHONE..............................802 565-8025
Beaudon Spaulding, *Dir*
EMP: 10 **EST:** 2019
SALES (est): 503.9K **Privately Held**
SIC: 2299 Hemp yarn, thread, roving, and
textiles

Richford
Franklin County

(G-17475)
KENT NUTRITION GROUP INC
1 Webster St (05476-7624)
PHONE..............................802 848-7718
Gary Lumbra, *Brnch Mgr*
EMP: 12
SALES (corp-wide): 517.65MM **Privately
Held**
Web: www.kentfeeds.com
SIC: 2048 Livestock feeds
HQ: Kent Nutrition Group, Inc.
2905 N Highway 61
Muscatine IA 52761
866 647-1212

(G-17476)
STAIRS UNLIMITED INC
484 Hardwood Hill Rd (05476-9647)
P.O. Box 267 (05476-0267)
PHONE..............................802 848-7030
EMP: 7 EST: 1993
SQ FT: 23,000
SALES (est): 751.96K **Privately Held**
SIC: **3441** Joists, open web steel: long-span
series

(G-17477)
TWO BROTHERS MAPLE LLC
214 Max Rd (05476-9546)
PHONE..............................802 848-7042
EMP: 7 EST: 2011
SALES (est): 204.59K **Privately Held**
Web: www.twobrothersmaple.com
SIC: **2099** Maple syrup

Richmond
Chittenden County

(G-17478)
ARMACH ROBOTICS INC
10 E Main St (05477-7741)
PHONE..............................802 434-6080
Benjamin Kinnaman, *Prin*
EMP: 10 EST: 2021
SALES (est): 570.73K **Privately Held**
SIC: **3731** Submersible marine robots,
manned or unmanned

(G-17479)
**HARRINGTONS IN VERMONT
INC (PA)**
Also Called: Harrington's of Vermont
210 E Main St (05477-9825)
P.O. Box 288 (05477-0288)
PHONE..............................802 434-7535
Peter Klinkenberg, *Pr*
R B Klinkenberg, *VP*
Joyce Klinkenberg, *Sec*
EMP: 10 EST: 1887
SQ FT: 5,000
SALES (est): 8.52MM
SALES (corp-wide): 8.52MM **Privately
Held**
Web: www.harringtonham.com
SIC: **2013** 5947 2053 2052 Ham, smoked:
from purchased meat; Novelties; Frozen
bakery products, except bread; Cookies
and crackers

(G-17480)
MAPLE WIND FARM INC
1149 E Main St (05477-9661)
PHONE..............................802 434-7257
Bruce Hennessey, *Pr*
Beth Whiting, *VP*
EMP: 9 EST: 2001
SALES (est): 473.03K **Privately Held**
Web: www.maplewindfarm.com
SIC: **0291** 0252 2015 Livestock farm,
general; Chicken eggs; Chicken
slaughtering and processing

(G-17481)
PORTFOLIO SOFTWARE INC
1 Millet St (05477-9492)
P.O. Box 1010 (05477-1010)
PHONE..............................802 434-4000
Jeff Elghanayan, *Pr*
▼ EMP: 11 EST: 1988
SQ FT: 2,200
SALES (est): 792.69K **Privately Held**

SIC: **3695** 2621 5734 5943 Computer
software tape and disks: blank, rigid, and
floppy; Paper mills; Computer tapes; Office
forms and supplies

(G-17482)
**Z M WEAPONS HIGH
PERFORMANCE**
Also Called: Airtight Ink
1958 Wes White Hl (05477-7766)
PHONE..............................802 777-8964
Allen Zitta, *Owner*
EMP: 8 EST: 1989
SQ FT: 11,000
SALES (est): 390.04K **Privately Held**
SIC: **3484** Guns (firearms) or gun parts, 30
mm. and below

Riverton
Washington County

(G-17483)
RIVERTON MEMORIAL INC
Also Called: Riverton Memorial Company
2074 Rte #12 (05663-6533)
P.O. Box 284 (05664-0284)
PHONE..............................802 485-3371
Ernest Lavigne Junior, *Pr*
Jacqueline Miller, *Sec*
Arthur Miller, *Treas*
EMP: 26 EST: 1963
SALES (est): 777.38K **Privately Held**
Web: www.riverton-nj.com
SIC: **3281** Monuments, cut stone (not
finishing or lettering only)

Rochester
Windsor County

(G-17484)
ADVANCED ILLUMINATION INC
440 State Garage Rd (05767-9739)
P.O. Box 237 (05767-0237)
PHONE..............................802 767-3830
▲ EMP: 22 EST: 1993
SQ FT: 12,000
SALES (est): 5.99MM **Privately Held**
Web: www.advancedillumination.com
SIC: **3559** Semiconductor manufacturing
machinery

(G-17485)
**INNER TRADITIONS
INTERNATIONAL (PA)**
Also Called: Bera Company
1 Park St (05767)
P.O. Box 388 (05767-0388)
PHONE..............................802 767-3174
Ehud Sperling, *Pr*
Julius Sperling, *
Pat Harvey, *
▲ EMP: 33 EST: 1975
SQ FT: 2,000
SALES (est): 5.46MM
SALES (corp-wide): 5.46MM **Privately
Held**
Web: www.innertraditions.com
SIC: **2731** Books, publishing only

(G-17486)
LCS CONTROLS INC
1678 Vt Route 100 S (05767-9503)
P.O. Box 286 (05767-0286)
PHONE..............................802 767-3128
Thomas Allen, *Pr*
Donald Crickard, *VP*
Lucia Perry, *Sec*

EMP: 7 EST: 1983
SQ FT: 7,500
SALES (est): 1.43MM **Privately Held**
Web: www.lcscontrols.com
SIC: **3663** Telemetering equipment,
electronic

(G-17487)
OATMEAL STUDIOS INC
Town Rd 35 (05767)
P.O. Box 410 (01242-0410)
PHONE..............................802 967-8014
Joseph Massimino, *Pr*
Helene Lehrer Massimino, *VP*
▼ EMP: 13 EST: 1978
SQ FT: 22,000
SALES (est): 247.58K **Privately Held**
Web: www.oatmealstudios.com
SIC: **2771** 2678 7336 Greeting cards; Desk
pads, paper: made from purchased
materials; Graphic arts and related design

Rutland
Rutland County

(G-17488)
ACCORDANT ENERGY LLC
225 S Main St Ste 2 (05701-4791)
PHONE..............................802 772-7368
Lawrence M Clark Junior, *CEO*
EMP: 9 EST: 2011
SALES (est): 248.97K **Privately Held**
Web: www.accordantenergy.com
SIC: **2869** Fuels

(G-17489)
ANN CLARK LTD
Also Called: American Cookie Cutter
453 Quality Ln (05701-4992)
PHONE..............................802 773-7886
EMP: 20 EST: 1993
SQ FT: 10,000
SALES (est): 7.17MM **Privately Held**
Web: www.annclark.com
SIC: **5149** 5046 5199 3469 Bakery products
; Bakery equipment and supplies; Gifts and
novelties; Utensils, household: metal,
except cast

(G-17490)
BODYCOTE SURFACE TECH INC
112 Quality Ln (05701-4745)
PHONE..............................802 773-4278
Robert Ellison, *Brnch Mgr*
EMP: 45
SALES (corp-wide): 895.27MM **Privately
Held**
Web: www.bodycote.com
SIC: **3398** Metal heat treating
HQ: Bodycote Surface Technology, Inc.
8118 Corp Way Ste 201
Mason OH 45040
513 770-4922

(G-17491)
BRUNSWICK PUBLISHING LLC
77 Grove St Ste 102 (05701-3403)
PHONE..............................802 747-6121
EMP: 7 EST: 2007
SALES (est): 86.92K **Privately Held**
SIC: **2741** Newsletter publishing

(G-17492)
**COCA-COLA BTLG STHSTERN
NENG I**
Coca-Cola
30 Quality Ln (05701-4920)
PHONE..............................802 773-2768

EMP: 7 EST: 1983
SALES (est): 1.43MM **Privately Held**
Susan Roddy, *Mgr*
EMP: 19
Web: www.coca-cola.com
SIC: **4225** 2086 Miniwarehouse,
warehousing; Bottled and canned soft drinks
HQ: Coca-Cola Bottling Company Of
Southeastern New England, Inc.
150 Waterford Parkway S
Waterford CT 06385
860 443-2816

(G-17493)
**CREATIVE MARKETING
SERVICES**
Also Called: Rutland Business Journal
27 Wales St (05701-4027)
PHONE..............................802 775-9500
Richard Rohe, *Pr*
Lillian Rohe, *VP*
EMP: 10 EST: 1981
SQ FT: 1,543
SALES (est): 615.77K **Privately Held**
Web: www.rutlandherald.com
SIC: **2711** Newspapers, publishing and
printing

(G-17494)
**EARTH WASTE SYSTEMS INC
(PA)**
49 Wales St (05701-4028)
P.O. Box 68 (05702-0068)
PHONE..............................802 775-7722
Kevin Elnicki, *Pr*
Jeff Elnicki, *
Stephanie Elnicki, *
Jon S Readnour, *
EMP: 25 EST: 1991
SALES (est): 4.74MM **Privately Held**
Web: www.earthwasteandmetal.com
SIC: **4953** 5093 3341 1795 Recycling,
waste materials; Metal scrap and waste
materials; Secondary nonferrous metals;
Wrecking and demolition work

(G-17495)
EASTVIEW ASSOCIATES INC
Also Called: Sam's Good News
162 N Main St Ste 8 (05701-3024)
PHONE..............................802 773-4040
Samuel Gorrusso, *Pr*
Samuel Gorrusso, *Mgr*
EMP: 7 EST: 2001
SALES (est): 236.73K **Privately Held**
Web: www.samsgoodnews.com
SIC: **2711** Newspapers, publishing and
printing

(G-17496)
EDWARD GROUP INC
Also Called: Quickprint of Rutland , The
194 Seward Rd (05701-4973)
P.O. Box 110 (05702-0110)
PHONE..............................802 775-1029
Mark Lawrence, *Pr*
Patricia Lawrence, *VP*
EMP: 10 EST: 2002
SALES (est): 570.85K **Privately Held**
SIC: **2752** Offset printing

(G-17497)
GENERAL ELECTRIC COMPANY
Also Called: GE
210 Columbian Ave (05701-2799)
PHONE..............................802 775-9842
Doug Folsom, *Brnch Mgr*
EMP: 1400
SALES (corp-wide): 76.56B **Publicly Held**
Web: www.lmwindpower.com

SIC: 3724 3714 Aircraft engines and engine parts; Motor vehicle parts and accessories
PA: General Electric Company
1 Financial Ctr Ste 3700
Boston MA 02111
617 443-3000

(G-17498)
GRAPHIC EDGE LLC
Also Called: Keith's Sports Ltd II
155 Seward Rd (05701-4739)
P.O. Box 757 (05702-0757)
PHONE................................802 855-8840
Pat Venteicher, *Brnch Mgr*
EMP: 60
SALES (corp-wide): 156.07MM **Privately Held**
Web: www.game-one.com
SIC: 2759 Screen printing
HQ: The Graphic Edge Llc
743 E Us Highway 30
Carroll IA 51401

(G-17499)
INITIAL IDEAS INC
378 Quality Ln (05701-4919)
PHONE................................802 775-1685
Peter Louras, *Brnch Mgr*
EMP: 7
SALES (corp-wide): 941.5K **Privately Held**
Web: www.initialideasvt.com
SIC: 2499 Trophy bases, wood
PA: Initial Ideas, Inc.
142 West St
Rutland VT 05701
802 773-6310

(G-17500)
INITIAL IDEAS INC (PA)
142 West St (05701-2860)
P.O. Box 186 (05702-0186)
PHONE................................802 773-6310
Peter Louras, *Pr*
EMP: 9 **EST:** 1982
SQ FT: 6,000
SALES (est): 941.5K
SALES (corp-wide): 941.5K **Privately Held**
Web: www.initialideasvt.com
SIC: 2395 Embroidery products, except Schiffli machine

(G-17501)
KALOW TECHNOLOGIES LLC
155 Seward Rd (05701-4739)
PHONE................................802 775-4633
Paul Van Huis, *Pr*
Ron Coleman, *Dir*
▲ **EMP:** 61 **EST:** 1986
SALES (est): 14.27MM **Privately Held**
Web: www.kalowtech.com
SIC: 3569 Assembly machines, non-metalworking

(G-17502)
KEEBOWIL INC
126 Spruce St (05701-4420)
P.O. Box 237 (05702-0237)
PHONE................................802 775-3572
Richard L Sharon, *Mgr*
EMP: 19
SALES (corp-wide): 21.74MM **Privately Held**
Web: www.melanson.com
SIC: 3444 Sheet metalwork
PA: Keebowil, Inc.
353 West St
Keene NH 03431
603 352-4232

(G-17503)
MARIAH GROUP LLC
92 Park St (05701-5079)
PHONE................................802 747-4000
Doug Babbitt, *VP*
Doug Babbitt, *Ex VP*
EMP: 10 **EST:** 2009
SALES (est): 425.05K **Privately Held**
SIC: 2435 Hardwood veneer and plywood

(G-17504)
Q-SEAL LLC
92 Park St (05701-5079)
PHONE................................802 773-1228
EMP: 7 **EST:** 2018
SALES (est): 301.61K **Privately Held**
Web: www.questech.com
SIC: 3281 Cut stone and stone products

(G-17505)
QUESTECH CORPORATION (PA)
Also Called: Questech Metals
92 Park St (05701-5079)
PHONE................................802 773-1228
Barry Culkin, *Pr*
Roger Questel, *Sec*
Gary Marmer, *VP*
Peter Schelle, *VP*
Paul Laderoute, *CFO*
EMP: 20 **EST:** 1989
SQ FT: 20,000
SALES (est): 15.07MM **Privately Held**
Web: www.questech.com
SIC: 3089 Plastics containers, except foam

(G-17506)
ROYAL GROUP INC (PA)
Also Called: Royal Technologies
150 Woodstock Ave (05701-3656)
PHONE................................802 773-3313
TOLL FREE: 800
Lee Accavallo, *Pr*
James Dick, *Corporate Secretary*
EMP: 20 **EST:** 1934
SQ FT: 5,400
SALES (est): 9.12MM
SALES (corp-wide): 9.12MM **Privately Held**
Web: www.royalvt.com
SIC: 5087 5063 3669 5999 Locksmith equipment and supplies; Electric alarms and signaling equipment; Intercommunication systems, electric; Vaults and safes

(G-17507)
RUTLAND FIRE CLAY CO (PA)
Also Called: Rutland Products
8 Madison St (05701-5001)
PHONE................................802 775-5519
▼ **EMP:** 19 **EST:** 1883
SALES (est): 4.67MM
SALES (corp-wide): 4.67MM **Privately Held**
SIC: 2891 Adhesives and sealants

(G-17508)
RUTLAND PLYWOOD CORP
92 Park St (05701-3856)
PHONE................................802 747-4000
Jack Barrett, *CEO*
EMP: 7 **EST:** 2014
SALES (est): 1.2MM **Privately Held**
Web: www.rutply.com
SIC: 2435 Plywood, hardwood or hardwood faced

(G-17509)
RUTLAND PLYWOOD CORP
92 Park St (05701-3856)
P.O. Box 6180 (05702-6180)
PHONE................................802 747-4000
▲ **EMP:** 250
SIC: 2435 2426 2421 Plywood, hardwood or hardwood faced; Hardwood dimension and flooring mills; Sawmills and planing mills, general

(G-17510)
STRATABOND CO INC
92 Park St (05701-5079)
PHONE................................802 747-4000
John M Barrett, *Acctg Mgr*
EMP: 11 **EST:** 2017
SALES (est): 385.11K **Privately Held**
SIC: 2435 Hardwood veneer and plywood

(G-17511)
T M SERVICES INC
Also Called: Midas Muffler
Route 4 East Woodstock Avenue (05701)
PHONE................................802 775-2948
Francis J Trombetta, *Pr*
Joseph Merone, *VP*
EMP: 25 **EST:** 1976
SQ FT: 5,000
SALES (est): 494.43K **Privately Held**
Web: www.midas.com
SIC: 7533 7539 3714 7549 Muffler shop, sale or repair and installation; Wheel alignment, automotive; Hydraulic fluid power pumps, for auto steering mechanism ; Automotive maintenance services

(G-17512)
TUTTLE LAW PRINT INC
Also Called: Tuttle Printing & Engraving
414 Quality Ln # 453 (05701-4999)
P.O. Box 110 (05702-0110)
PHONE................................802 773-9171
Deva M Bolgioni, *Ch Bd*
Joanne M Cillo, *
R Joseph O'rourke, *Clerk*
EMP: 62 **EST:** 1912
SQ FT: 34,000
SALES (est): 9.9MM **Privately Held**
Web: www.tuttleprinting.com
SIC: 2752 2791 2759 Offset printing; Typesetting; Commercial printing, nec

(G-17513)
UNILEVER BESTFOODS NORTH AMER
Also Called: Bouyea-Fassetts
69 Park St (05701-4708)
PHONE................................802 775-4986
Phil Beudin, *Mgr*
EMP: 8
SALES (corp-wide): 62.39B **Privately Held**
Web: www.unileverusa.com
SIC: 2051 Bakery: wholesale or wholesale/retail combined
HQ: Unilever Bestfoods North America
800 Sylvan Ave
Englewood Cliffs NJ 07632
800 697-7887

(G-17514)
VERMONT QUARRIES CORP
1591 Us Route 4 (05701-6605)
PHONE................................802 775-1065
Fabrizio Ponzanelli, *Pr*
Luca Mannolini, *
Vincenzo Maucchelli, *
◆ **EMP:** 30 **EST:** 1894
SQ FT: 1,300
SALES (est): 4.66MM **Privately Held**

Web: www.vermontdanbymarble.com
SIC: 1411 5032 Marble, dimension-quarrying ; Marble building stone

Saint Albans
Franklin County

(G-17515)
AS HUDAK LUMBER
24 Beverly Ct (05478-1732)
PHONE................................802 527-9802
EMP: 8 **EST:** 2017
SALES (est): 224.23K **Privately Held**
Web: www.ashudaklumber.com
SIC: 2411 Logging

(G-17516)
BARRY CALLEBAUT USA LLC
400 Industrial Park Rd (05478-1875)
PHONE................................802 524-9711
EMP: 183
Web: www.barry-callebaut.com
SIC: 2066 Chocolate
HQ: Barry Callebaut U.S.A. Llc
600 W Chicago Ave Ste 860
Chicago IL 60654

(G-17517)
BOURBEAU AGGREGATE LLC
1881 Sheldon Rd (05478-8082)
PHONE................................802 309-4699
Alan Bourbeau, *Mgr*
EMP: 7 **EST:** 2019
SALES (est): 493.54K **Privately Held**
Web: www.bourbeau-aggregate.com
SIC: 3273 Ready-mixed concrete

(G-17518)
CHAMPLAIN VALLEY EQUIPMENT INC
Also Called: Kubota Authorized Dealer
7 Franklin Park W (05478-2369)
PHONE................................802 524-6782
Jason Bessete, *Mgr*
EMP: 8
SALES (corp-wide): 21.81MM **Privately Held**
Web: www.kubotausa.com
SIC: 5999 5261 5083 3546 Farm equipment and supplies; Lawn and garden equipment; Farm and garden machinery; Saws and sawing equipment
PA: Champlain Valley Equipment, Inc.
453 Exchange St
Middlebury VT 05753
802 388-4967

(G-17519)
CITY FEED AND LUMBER CO INC (PA)
Also Called: Village Home Center
44 Lower Newton St (05478-1907)
PHONE................................802 524-2136
Gerald Belisle, *Pr*
Kris Bullock, *
Donald Wells, *
Jeffrey Lamphere, *
EMP: 26 **EST:** 1968
SQ FT: 14,000
SALES (est): 15.92MM
SALES (corp-wide): 15.92MM **Privately Held**
Web: www.sticksandstuff.com
SIC: 5211 2434 Lumber products; Wood kitchen cabinets

GEOGRAPHIC

(G-17520)
CO OP CREAMERY
140 Federal St (05478-2015)
PHONE.....................802 524-6581
EMP: 10 EST: 2001
SALES (est): 451K **Privately Held**
SIC: 2021 Creamery butter

(G-17521)
EDGEWELL PER CARE BRANDS LLC
75 Swanton Rd (05478-2614)
PHONE.....................802 524-2151
Javad Mirtanah, *Mgr*
EMP: 20
SALES (corp-wide): 2.25B **Publicly Held**
Web: www.edgewell.com
SIC: 3421 Razor blades and razors
HQ: Edgewell Personal Care Brands, Llc
    6 Research Dr
    Shelton CT 06484
    203 944-5500

(G-17522)
FINISH SOLUTIONS LLC
75 Swanton Rd (05478-2614)
P.O. Box 1159 (05478-1159)
PHONE.....................802 540-0326
Adam Routhier, *Managing Member*
Adam Routhier, *Pt*
EMP: 8 EST: 2006
SALES (est): 620.46K **Privately Held**
SIC: 3471 Sand blasting of metal parts

(G-17523)
MPRP INC
Also Called: J C Image
88 Walnut St (05478-2145)
PHONE.....................802 527-1557
EMP: 9 EST: 1991
SQ FT: 4,000
SALES (est): 778.46K **Privately Held**
Web: www.jcimage.com
SIC: 2395 Embroidery products, except Schiffli machine

(G-17524)
MYLAN TECHNOLOGIES INC
700 Ind Park Rd (05478-1889)
PHONE.....................802 527-7792
EMP: 13
SALES (corp-wide): 16.26B **Publicly Held**
SIC: 2834 Dermatologicals
HQ: Mylan Technologies, Inc.
    110 Lake St
    Saint Albans VT 05478
    802 527-7792

(G-17525)
MYLAN TECHNOLOGIES INC (HQ)
110 Lake St (05478-2287)
PHONE.....................802 527-7792
Harry Korman, *Pr*
David Kennedy, *
Kristin A Kolesar, *
Brian Byala, *
Matthew Erick, *
◆ EMP: 237 EST: 1992
SQ FT: 100,000
SALES (est): 114.83MM
SALES (corp-wide): 16.26B **Publicly Held**
SIC: 2834 2833 2675 2891 Dermatologicals
; Medicinals and botanicals; Die-cut paper and board; Adhesives
PA: Viatris Inc.
    1000 Mylan Blvd
    Canonsburg PA 15317
    724 514-1800

(G-17526)
NOURISH LLC
Also Called: Nourish Deli & Bakery
112 N Main St Ste 5 (05478-1768)
PHONE.....................802 782-0012
EMP: 9 EST: 2020
SALES (est): 267.46K **Privately Held**
Web: www.nourishwholesale.com
SIC: 5812 2099 Eating places; Food preparations, nec

(G-17527)
OROURKE MEDIA GROUP LLC (PA)
Also Called: Messenger Marketing
281 N Main St (05478-2503)
PHONE.....................802 524-9771
Jim O'rourke, *CEO*
EMP: 10 EST: 2018
SALES (est): 14.29MM
SALES (corp-wide): 14.29MM **Privately Held**
Web: www.orourkemediagroup.com
SIC: 2711 Newspapers, publishing and printing

(G-17528)
OUTFITTERS INC CORPORATE
Also Called: Corporate Outfitters
12 Champlain Cmns (05478-1563)
P.O. Box 386 (05481-0386)
PHONE.....................802 527-0204
Jack Bliss, *Pr*
William T Counos, *Sec*
EMP: 7 EST: 1980
SQ FT: 4,500
SALES (est): 1.54MM **Privately Held**
Web: www.corporateoutfitters.com
SIC: 5136 5137 2395 Sportswear, men's and boys'; Sportswear, women's and children's; Art needlework: made from purchased materials

(G-17529)
QST INC
Also Called: Q S T
300 Industrial Park Rd (05478-1899)
PHONE.....................802 524-7704
James E Morrison, *
▲ EMP: 33 EST: 1991
SQ FT: 42,000
SALES (est): 1.06MM
SALES (corp-wide): 1.03B **Privately Held**
Web: www.ceoqsttpe.com
SIC: 2821 5169 2822 Molding compounds, plastics; Synthetic resins, rubber, and plastic materials; Synthetic rubber
PA: Teknor Apex Company
    505 Central Ave
    Pawtucket RI 02861
    401 725-8000

(G-17530)
REA INC
Also Called: Beverage Mart
211 Lake St Ste 5 (05478-2286)
PHONE.....................802 527-7437
Ross E Arsenault, *Pr*
EMP: 17 EST: 1976
SQ FT: 5,000
SALES (est): 454.27K **Privately Held**
SIC: 5921 5499 2086 Beer (packaged); Soft drinks; Bottled and canned soft drinks

(G-17531)
ST ALBANS COOPERATIVE CREAMERY INC
140 Federal St (05478-2000)
PHONE.....................802 524-9366

EMP: 70
Web: www.creameryandsupply.com
SIC: 2026 2023 Fluid milk; Dried milk

(G-17532)
ST ALBANS CREAMERY LLC
Also Called: St. Albans Creamery
138 Federal St (05478-2015)
PHONE.....................802 524-9366
Leon Berthiaume, *CEO*
EMP: 23 EST: 2019
SALES (est): 7.94MM **Privately Held**
Web: www.creameryandsupply.com
SIC: 2026 2023 Fluid milk; Dried milk

(G-17533)
SUPERIOR TCHNCAL CERAMICS CORP (HQ)
Also Called: Superior Technical Ceramics
600 Industrial Park Rd (05478-1877)
PHONE.....................802 527-7726
Eric D Ashleman, *CEO*
▲ EMP: 138 EST: 1978
SQ FT: 123,500
SALES (est): 58.95MM
SALES (corp-wide): 3.18B **Publicly Held**
Web: www.ceramics.net
SIC: 3644 3264 3724 3769 Insulators and insulation materials, electrical; Porcelain electrical supplies; Aircraft engines and engine parts; Guided missile and space vehicle parts and aux. equip., R&D
PA: Idex Corporation
    3100 Sanders Rd Ste 301
    Northbrook IL 60062
    847 498-7070

(G-17534)
TEKNOR APEX CO
300 Industrial Park Rd (05478-1899)
PHONE.....................802 524-7704
Paul Burke, *Prin*
▼ EMP: 15 EST: 2011
SALES (est): 801.04K **Privately Held**
Web: www.teknorapex.com
SIC: 3089 Plastics products, nec

(G-17535)
TROY MICRO FIVE INC
79 Walnut St (05478-2144)
PHONE.....................802 524-0076
Gabriel Paquett, *Mgr*
EMP: 9
SALES (corp-wide): 9.21MM **Privately Held**
SIC: 2833 Vitamins, natural or synthetic: bulk, uncompounded
PA: Troy Micro Five, Inc.
    53 E Main St
    North Troy VT 05859
    802 988-4474

(G-17536)
VERMONT PUBLISHING COMANY
Also Called: St Albans Messenger
281 N Main St (05478-2503)
P.O. Box 1250 (05478-1250)
PHONE.....................802 524-9771
Emerson Lynn, *Pr*
EMP: 39 EST: 1861
SQ FT: 12,000
SALES (est): 2.75MM **Privately Held**
Web: www.samessenger.com
SIC: 2711 2752 2741 Newspapers, publishing and printing; Offset printing; Shopping news: publishing and printing

Saint Johnsbury
Caledonia County

(G-17537)
4SMARTPRO LLC
Also Called: Smartpro
599 Farmer Dr (05819-1454)
PHONE.....................802 745-8797
Festus Smart, *Prin*
EMP: 10 EST: 2016
SALES (est): 77.54K **Privately Held**
SIC: 7349 7699 4581 3569 Building and office cleaning services; Brick cleaning; Aircraft cleaning and janitorial service; Blast cleaning equipment, dustless

(G-17538)
A VIEW OF VERMONT LLC
1632 Memorial Dr (05819-4528)
P.O. Box 279 (05851-0279)
PHONE.....................802 748-0880
Jack Papin, *Owner*
EMP: 8 EST: 2009
SALES (est): 121.39K **Privately Held**
SIC: 2273 Carpets and rugs

(G-17539)
CALEDONIA INC (PA)
Also Called: Calco
2878 Vt Route 18 (05819-9714)
P.O. Box 631 (05819-0631)
PHONE.....................802 748-2319
Ken Wood, *Pr*
Betsy Forgin, *Sec*
James Wilkins, *VP*
EMP: 12 EST: 1947
SQ FT: 15,000
SALES (est): 1.82MM
SALES (corp-wide): 1.82MM **Privately Held**
Web: www.caledoniadistrict.org
SIC: 3272 Concrete products, precast, nec

(G-17540)
CALEDONIAN RECORD PUBG CO INC (PA)
Also Called: Caledonian-Record
190 Federal St (05819-5616)
P.O. Box 8 (05819-0008)
PHONE.....................802 748-8121
Mark Smith, *Pr*
EMP: 51 EST: 1837
SQ FT: 8,000
SALES (est): 4.48MM
SALES (corp-wide): 4.48MM **Privately Held**
Web: www.caledonianrecord.com
SIC: 2711 7375 Newspapers, publishing and printing; Information retrieval services

(G-17541)
CLASSIC DSGNS BY MTTHEW BRAK I
84 Central St Ste 104 (05819-2329)
PHONE.....................802 748-6062
Matthew Burak, *Pr*
Mark Desrochers, *VP*
EMP: 25 EST: 1979
SALES (est): 5.96MM **Privately Held**
Web: www.tablelegs.com
SIC: 5021 5961 2431 2426 Household furniture; Furniture and furnishings, mail order; Millwork; Hardwood dimension and flooring mills

(G-17542)
LYNDON WOODWORKING INC (PA)
Also Called: Lyndon Furniture
1135 Industrial Pkwy (05819-8980)
P.O. Box 45 (05849-0045)
PHONE.................................802 748-0100
David Allard, *Pr*
Judy Allard, *
EMP: 50 **EST:** 1978
SQ FT: 10,000
SALES (est): 9.46MM
SALES (corp-wide): 9.46MM **Privately Held**
Web: www.lyndon.com
SIC: 2511 2499 Wood household furniture; Spools, reels, and pulleys: wood

(G-17543)
MAPLE GROVE FARMS VERMONT INC (HQ)
1052 Portland St (05819-2041)
PHONE.................................802 748-5141
David L Wenner, *Pr*
David H Burke, *
Robert C Cantwell, *
▲ **EMP:** 100 **EST:** 1915
SQ FT: 250,000
SALES (est): 20.68MM
SALES (corp-wide): 2.16B **Publicly Held**
Web: www.maplegrove.com
SIC: 2099 2035 2045 2087 Maple syrup; Pickles, sauces, and salad dressings; Pancake mixes, prepared: from purchased flour; Flavoring extracts and syrups, nec
PA: B&G Foods, Inc.
4 Gatehall Dr Ste 110
Parsippany NJ 07054
973 401-6500

(G-17544)
MITI MANUFACTURING CO INC
2176 Portland St (05819-8971)
PHONE.................................802 424-1671
EMP: 11 **EST:** 2019
SALES (est): 608.5K **Privately Held**
Web: www.mitico.com
SIC: 3999 Manufacturing industries, nec

(G-17545)
MOMENTUM MFG GROUP - N LLC (PA)
Also Called: Carts Vermont
210 Pierce Rd (05819-8343)
P.O. Box 54 (05851-0054)
PHONE.................................802 748-5007
James Moroney, *CEO*
Matt Smith, *
Ed Stanley, *
Jeff Fraser, *
▲ **EMP:** 163 **EST:** 1982
SQ FT: 170,000
SALES (est): 149.03MM
SALES (corp-wide): 149.03MM **Privately Held**
Web: www.mmgmfg.com
SIC: 3444 1799 1796 Sheet metal specialties, not stamped; Coating of metal structures at construction site; Machinery installation

(G-17546)
NORTH EAST PRECISION INC
3606 Memorial Dr (05819-8777)
PHONE.................................802 748-1440
Bruce Benoit, *Pr*
Douglas John, *
Alan Brink, *
EMP: 57 **EST:** 1990

SQ FT: 43,000
SALES (est): 6.58MM **Privately Held**
Web: www.neprecision.net
SIC: 3599 Machine shop, jobbing and repair

(G-17547)
VERMONT AEROSPACE INDS LLC
966 Industrial Pkwy (05819)
P.O. Box 1148 (05851-1148)
PHONE.................................802 748-8705
Leonard M Levie, *Pr*
EMP: 80 **EST:** 2016
SQ FT: 40,000
SALES (est): 9.09MM **Privately Held**
Web: www.vtaerospace.com
SIC: 3599 Machine shop, jobbing and repair

(G-17548)
WEIDMANN ELECTRICAL TECHNOLOGY INC (DH)
Also Called: Ehv-Weidmann Industries
1 Gordon Mills Way (05819-8925)
P.O. Box 903 (05819-0903)
PHONE.................................802 748-8106
▲ **EMP:** 300 **EST:** 1877
SALES (est): 86.65MM
SALES (corp-wide): 47.49MM **Privately Held**
Web: www.weidmann-electrical.com
SIC: 3644 Insulators and insulation materials, electrical
HQ: Weidmann Tecnologia Electrica De Mexico, S.A. De C.V.
Carr. Libre Profesor Oscar Flores Tapia No. 304
Arteaga COA 25350

Shaftsbury
Bennington County

(G-17549)
DAILEY PRECAST LLC (HQ)
Also Called: Florida Mega Mix
295 Airport Rd (05262-9693)
P.O. Box 200 (05262-0200)
PHONE.................................802 442-4418
John R Peckham, *CEO*
Joseph Wildermuth, *
Richard E Antes, *
▲ **EMP:** 65 **EST:** 1954
SQ FT: 7,000
SALES (est): 22.71MM
SALES (corp-wide): 173.39MM **Privately Held**
Web: www.daileyprecast.com
SIC: 5211 1794 3273 5032 Sand and gravel ; Excavation work; Ready-mixed concrete; Brick, stone, and related material
PA: Peckham Industries, Inc.
172 Prospect Hill Rd
Brewster NY 10509
914 949-2000

(G-17550)
LEO D BERNSTEIN & SONS INC
Also Called: Bernstein Display
372 Vt Route 67 E (05262-9425)
PHONE.................................802 442-8029
Anthony Tripoli, *Brnch Mgr*
EMP: 72
SALES (corp-wide): 16.94MM **Privately Held**
Web: www.bernsteindisplay.com
SIC: 3999 2541 5046 7389 Forms: display, dress, and show; Store and office display cases and fixtures; Store fixtures; Design services
PA: Leo D. Bernstein & Sons Inc.
151 W 25th St Frnt 1

New York NY 10001
212 337-9578

(G-17551)
LEO D BERNSTEIN AND SONS INC
Also Called: Berstein Display
372 Vt Route 67 E (05262-9425)
PHONE.................................212 337-9578
Roger Friedman, *Pr*
Michelle Bernstein, *
Edmond Bernstein, *
◆ **EMP:** 21 **EST:** 2004
SQ FT: 200,000
SALES (est): 2.02MM **Privately Held**
SIC: 3999 2295 Mannequins; Waxing of cloth

(G-17552)
PECKHAM INDUSTRIES INC
295 Airport Rd (05262-9693)
PHONE.................................802 442-4418
Jacinda Hill Plant, *Clerk*
EMP: 12 **EST:** 2009
SALES (est): 328.49K **Privately Held**
Web: www.peckham.com
SIC: 2951 Asphalt paving mixtures and blocks

(G-17553)
T & M ENTERPRISES INC
251 Church St (05262)
P.O. Box 410 (05262-0410)
PHONE.................................802 447-0601
Thomas T Paquin, *Pr*
Martha Paquin, *Sec*
EMP: 9 **EST:** 1984
SQ FT: 30,000
SALES (est): 1.65MM **Privately Held**
Web: www.tandmplastics.com
SIC: 3089 Injection molding of plastics

(G-17554)
WATSON WHEELER CIDER LLC (PA) ✪
4322 East Rd (05262-9786)
PHONE.................................435 602-9042
EMP: 9 **EST:** 2022
SALES (est): 61.02K
SALES (corp-wide): 61.02K **Privately Held**
SIC: 2086 Bottled and canned soft drinks

Sharon
Windsor County

(G-17555)
GENERAL ABRASIVES INC
Back River Rd (05065)
P.O. Box 9 (05065-0009)
PHONE.................................802 763-7264
Natascha Niffka, *Pr*
Natascha N Niffka, *Pr*
Jurgen Niffka, *Sec*
Eric Janson, *Clerk*
▲ **EMP:** 10 **EST:** 1993
SQ FT: 15,000
SALES (est): 941.41K **Privately Held**
Web: www.generalabrasives.com
SIC: 3291 Coated abrasive products

Shelburne
Chittenden County

(G-17556)
ASCENSION TECHNOLOGY CORP

Also Called: Ascension
120 Graham Way Ste 130 (05482-7217)
P.O. Box 527 (05402-0527)
PHONE.................................802 893-6657
Ernest B Blood, *Pr*
John T Scully Junior, *VP*
EMP: 26 **EST:** 1985
SQ FT: 20,000
SALES (est): 5.21MM
SALES (corp-wide): 5.37B **Publicly Held**
SIC: 3841 Diagnostic apparatus, medical
PA: Roper Technologies, Inc.
6901 Prof Pkwy E Ste 200
Sarasota FL 34240
941 556-2601

(G-17557)
FIDDLEHEAD BREWING COMPANY LLC
31 Sage Ct (05482-1100)
PHONE.................................802 489-5090
EMP: 19 **EST:** 2017
SALES (est): 9.57MM **Privately Held**
Web: www.fiddleheadbrewing.com
SIC: 5181 2082 Beer and ale; Malt beverages

(G-17558)
HIBERNATION HOLDING CO INC (PA)
Also Called: Vermont Teddy Bear Company
6655 Shelburne Rd (05482-7274)
P.O. Box 965 (05482-0965)
PHONE.................................802 985-3001
John Gilbert, *Pr*
EMP: 175 **EST:** 2005
SALES (est): 49.48MM **Privately Held**
Web: www.vermontteddybear.com
SIC: 3942 5961 Stuffed toys, including animals; Toys and games (including dolls and models), mail order

(G-17559)
NPC PROCESSING INC
97 Executive Dr (05482-6476)
PHONE.................................802 660-0496
EMP: 25 **EST:** 1995
SALES (est): 9.71MM **Privately Held**
Web: www.npcprocessing.com
SIC: 2015 2011 2013 Chicken, processed: fresh; Beef products, from beef slaughtered on site; Sausages and other prepared meats

(G-17560)
SECURE PNT INC
135 Pond Rd (05482-7067)
PHONE.................................201 401-4207
Harold J Raveche, *Ch Bd*
George Cheng, *Dir*
John Coburn, *Dir*
Lance Lord, *Dir*
Robert Cleave, *Dir*
EMP: 7 **EST:** 2021
SALES (est): 286.02K **Privately Held**
SIC: 3663 Radio and t.v. communications equipment

(G-17561)
SHELBURNE CORPORATION (PA)
6221 Shelburne Rd (05482-7147)
P.O. Box 158 (05482-0158)
PHONE.................................802 985-3321
Mark H Snelling, *Pr*
Diane Snelling, *Dir*
Jacqueling Snelling, *Dir*
Andrew Snelling, *Sec*
EMP: 15 **EST:** 1981

SQ FT: 70,000
SALES (est): 2.66MM
SALES (corp-wide): 2.66MM **Privately Held**
Web: www.shelburnevt.org
SIC: 3469 Metal stampings, nec

(G-17562)
SHELBURNE FARMS
Also Called: Shelburne Farms Market Garden
1611 Harbor Rd (05482-7671)
PHONE..............................802 985-8498
Alexander S Webb, *Pr*
Jessica Perrault, *'*
EMP: 100 **EST:** 1972
SQ FT: 130,000
SALES (est): 9.39MM **Privately Held**
Web: www.shelburnefarms.org
SIC: 8299 8399 2022 Educational services;
  Fund raising organization, non-fee basis;
  Cheese; natural and processed

(G-17563)
**VERMONT TEDDY BEAR CO
INC (HQ)**
Also Called: Pajama Gram Company
6655 Shelburne Rd (05482-6910)
P.O. Box 965 (05482-0965)
PHONE..............................802 985-3001
William Shouldice Iv, *Pr*
John F Gilbert, *'*
Sarah Pribram, *'*
Robert Stetzel, *'*
Scott Smith, *'*
▲ **EMP:** 110 **EST:** 1981
SALES (est): 48MM **Privately Held**
Web: www.vermontteddybear.com
SIC: 3942 5961 5699 Stuffed toys, including
  animals; Toys and games (including dolls
  and models), mail order; Customized
  clothing and apparel
PA: Hibernation Holding Company, Inc.
  6655 Shelburne Rd
  Shelburne VT 05482

(G-17564)
**VERMONT TORTILLA COMPANY
LLC**
Also Called: Epicerie Azur
22 Sage Ct (05482-1100)
PHONE..............................802 399-2223
EMP: 8 **EST:** 2014
SALES (est): 289.05K **Privately Held**
Web: www.vttortillaco.com
SIC: 2099 Tortillas, fresh or refrigerated

(G-17565)
WIND RIDGE PUBLISHING
Also Called: Shelburne News
233 Falls Rd (05482-7554)
PHONE..............................802 985-3091
Holly Bartlett, *Pr*
EMP: 12 **EST:** 1996
SALES (est): 292.51K **Privately Held**
Web: www.windridgepublishing.com
SIC: 2711 2741 Newspapers; Miscellaneous
  publishing

Sheldon Springs
Franklin County

(G-17566)
WESTROCK CP LLC
Also Called: Rock-Tenn Missisquoi Mill
369 Mill St (05485)
P.O. Box 98 (05485-0098)
PHONE..............................802 933-7733
Chris Ham-ellis, *Brnch Mgr*

EMP: 146
SALES (corp-wide): 20.31B **Publicly Held**
Web: www.westrock.com
SIC: 2631 2611 Paperboard mills; Pulp mills
HQ: Westrock Cp, Llc
  1000 Abernathy Rd Ste 125
  Atlanta GA 30328

Shoreham
Addison County

(G-17567)
**GOAMERICAGO BEVERAGES
LLC**
2139 Quiet Valley Rd (05770-9710)
PHONE..............................802 897-7700
Raj Bhakta, *CO*
EMP: 8 **EST:** 2010
SALES (est): 2.04MM **Privately Held**
Web: www.whistlepigwhiskey.com
SIC: 2085 Rye whiskey
PA: Whistlepig, Llc
  2139 Quiet Valley Rd
  Shoreham VT 05770

(G-17568)
WHISTLEPIG LLC (PA)
2139 Quiet Valley Rd (05770-9710)
PHONE..............................802 897-7700
EMP: 7 **EST:** 2010
SALES (est): 3.52MM **Privately Held**
Web: www.whistlepigwhiskey.com
SIC: 2085 Rye whiskey

South Burlington
Chittenden County

(G-17569)
ALTIUM PACKAGING LLC
Also Called: Shelburne Plastics
8 Harbor View Rd (05403-7850)
PHONE..............................802 658-6588
Gene Torvend, *Brnch Mgr*
EMP: 47
SALES (corp-wide): 15.9B **Publicly Held**
Web: www.altiumpkg.com
SIC: 3089 Plastics containers, except foam
HQ: Altium Packaging Llc
  2500 Windy Ridge Pkwy Se # 1400
  Atlanta GA 30339
  678 742-4600

(G-17570)
AVIATRON INC
25 Customs Dr (05403-6067)
PHONE..............................802 865-9318
Todd Callender, *Ex Dir*
EMP: 28 **EST:** 1990
SALES (est): 6.55MM **Publicly Held**
Web: www.aviatron.com
SIC: 3679 Electronic circuits
PA: Heico Corporation
  3000 Taft St
  Hollywood FL 33021

(G-17571)
**BEN & JERRYS HOMEMADE INC
(HQ)**
Also Called: Ben & Jerry's Ice Cream
530 Community Dr Ste 1 (05403-6650)
PHONE..............................802 846-1500
▲ **EMP:** 200 **EST:** 1977
SALES (est): 250.31MM
SALES (corp-wide): 62.39B **Privately Held**
Web: www.benjerry.com

SIC: 2024 5812 6794 Ice cream, packaged:
  molded, on sticks, etc.; Ice cream stands or
  dairy bars; Franchises, selling or licensing
PA: Unilever Plc
  Unilever House
  London EC4Y
  207 572-1202

(G-17572)
BETA TECHNOLOGIES INC
1150 Airport Dr Ste 101 (05403-6000)
PHONE..............................802 281-3623
Kyle Clark, *CEO*
EMP: 45 **EST:** 2018
SALES (est): 10.59MM **Privately Held**
Web: www.beta.team
SIC: 3721 Aircraft

(G-17573)
**BIRNN CHOCOLATES
VERMONT INC**
102 Kimball Ave Ste 4 (05403-6800)
PHONE..............................802 860-1047
H Jeffrey Birnn, *Pr*
William M Birnn, *VP*
▲ **EMP:** 18 **EST:** 1915
SQ FT: 18,000
SALES (est): 4.14MM **Privately Held**
Web: www.birnn.com
SIC: 2066 5149 Chocolate and cocoa
  products; Chocolate

(G-17574)
BOUTIN/MCQUISTON INC (PA)
Also Called: Vermont Business Magazine
365 Dorset St (05403-6210)
PHONE..............................802 863-8038
John Boutin, *Pr*
Tim Mcquiston, *Prin*
EMP: 10 **EST:** 1989
SQ FT: 2,000
SALES (est): 4.89MM **Privately Held**
Web: www.vermontbiz.com
SIC: 2721 Magazines: publishing only, not
  printed on site

(G-17575)
BULLROCK SOLAR LLC
228 Aviation Ave Ste 200 (05403-6029)
PHONE..............................802 985-1460
EMP: 15 **EST:** 2018
SQ FT: 5,000
SALES (est): 1.16MM **Privately Held**
Web: www.bullrockcorp.com
SIC: 3433 Solar heaters and collectors

(G-17576)
CBD EVENTS LLC
35 Hummingbird Ln (05403-4447)
PHONE..............................802 310-8810
EMP: 8 **EST:** 2018
SALES (est): 402.71K **Privately Held**
Web: www.cateringbydale.com
SIC: 3999

(G-17577)
**DYNAPOWER COMPANY LLC
(DH)**
85 Meadowland Dr (05403-4401)
PHONE..............................802 860-7200
Adam Knudsen, *Genl Mgr*
John Owens, *'*
▲ **EMP:** 99 **EST:** 1963
SQ FT: 150,000
SALES (est): 47.57MM
SALES (corp-wide): 4.03B **Privately Held**
Web: www.dynapower.com

SIC: 3613 3612 3677 3625 Switchgear and
  switchboard apparatus; Specialty
  transformers; Electronic coils and
  transformers; Relays and industrial controls
HQ: Sensata Technologies, Inc.
  529 Pleasant St
  Attleboro MA 02703

(G-17578)
FASTSIGNS - 490101
Also Called: Fastsigns
1335 Shelburne Rd (05403-7714)
PHONE..............................802 238-1247
EMP: 9 **EST:** 2019
SALES (est): 391.82K **Privately Held**
Web: www.fastsigns.com
SIC: 3993 Signs and advertising specialties

(G-17579)
GERMANI INC
1930 Williston Rd (05403-6007)
PHONE..............................802 862-3653
Lori Germani, *Prin*
EMP: 9 **EST:** 2006
SALES (est): 199.26K **Privately Held**
Web: www.pourhousevt.com
SIC: 3421 Table and food cutlery, including
  butchers'

(G-17580)
INSTRUMART LLC (HQ)
35 Green Mountain Dr (05403-7824)
PHONE..............................802 863-0085
Brian Leffler, *Pr*
Peter S Erly, *Sec*
◆ **EMP:** 49 **EST:** 1988
SQ FT: 14,400
SALES (est): 25.85MM
SALES (corp-wide): 496.49MM **Privately
Held**
Web: www.instrumart.com
SIC: 3823 Process control instruments
PA: Ffi Holdings Iii Corp
  3915 Shopton Rd
  Charlotte NC 28217
  800 690-3650

(G-17581)
ISYSTEMS LLC (HQ)
800 Hinesburg Rd (05403-7607)
P.O. Box 706 (05453-0706)
PHONE..............................802 655-8347
Michael Trahan, *Managing Member*
David Meagher, *Pr*
Ca Carol Ann Mcgregor, *CIO*
EMP: 17 **EST:** 1998
SALES (est): 12.49MM
SALES (corp-wide): 95.83MM **Publicly
Held**
Web: www.asuresoftware.com
SIC: 7372 Prepackaged software
PA: Asure Software, Inc.
  405 Colorado St Ste 1800
  Austin TX 78701
  512 437-2700

(G-17582)
KLINGERS BREAD COMPANY
10 Farrell St Ste 4 (05403-6371)
PHONE..............................802 860-6322
David L Klingebiel, *Pr*
Judith L Klingebiel, *'*
Edward R Klingebiel, *'*
Kevin Durnsteel, *'*
EMP: 45 **EST:** 1993
SQ FT: 3,500
SALES (est): 5.34MM **Privately Held**
Web: www.klingersbread.com

SIC: **5149** 5461 5812 2051   Bakery products
; Retail bakeries; Cafe; Bread, cake, and
related products

(G-17583)

LANE PRESS INC

Also Called: Lane Press
87 Meadowland Dr (05403-7605)
P.O. Box 130 (05402-0130)
PHONE..............................877 300-5933
Philip M Drumheller, *Pr*
Bob Morris, *Pers/VP*
Robert Morris, *VP*
Joseph C Duwan, *Sec*
William Gentes, *Treas*
▲ **EMP:** 200 **EST:** 1904
SALES (est): 41.19MM **Privately Held**
Web: www.lanepress.com
SIC: 2752   Offset printing

(G-17584)

LOCKHEED MARTIN CORPORATION

45 Nco Dr (05403)
PHONE..............................802 503-8699
Christopher Clinger, *Prin*
EMP: 14 **EST:** 1996
SALES (est): 131.63K **Privately Held**
Web: www.lockheedmartinjobs.com
SIC: 3721   Aircraft

(G-17585)

MACH 7 TECHNOLOGIES INC

120 Kimball Ave Ste 210 (05403-6837)
P.O. Box 586 (05402-0586)
PHONE..............................802 861-7745
Michael Lampron, *CEO*
Dyan O'herne, *CFO*
David Madaffri, *COO*
EMP: 61 **EST:** 2008
SQ FT: 2,100
SALES (est): 11.23MM **Privately Held**
Web: www.mach7t.com
SIC: 7372   Prepackaged software
HQ: Mach7 Technologies Pte. Ltd.
28 Sin Ming Lane
Singapore 57397

(G-17586)

NATIONAL CHMNEY SPPLY-VRMONT I

Also Called: National Chimney
3 Green Tree Dr (05403-6025)
PHONE..............................802 861-2217
Darin Bibeau, *Pr*
Martin Fuller, ***
Thomas G Dragon, ***
EMP: 88 **EST:** 2000
SALES (est): 8.96MM **Privately Held**
Web: www.nationalchimney.com
SIC: 3317   Steel pipe and tubes

(G-17587)

ONLOGIC INC

Also Called: Logic Supply
35 Thompson St (05403-4475)
PHONE..............................802 861-2300
Roland Groeneveld, *CEO*
Roland Groeneveld, *Pr*
Lisa Baril-groeneveld, *VP*
Sean Larkin, ***
◆ **EMP:** 155 **EST:** 2003
SQ FT: 15,000
SALES (est): 54.65MM **Privately Held**
Web: www.onlogic.com
SIC: 3571 5045   Electronic computers;
Computers, peripherals, and software

(G-17588)

OTHER PAPER

1340 Williston Rd Ste 201 (05403-6469)
P.O. Box 2032 (05407-2032)
PHONE..............................802 864-6670
George Chamberland, *Prin*
EMP: 9 **EST:** 2005
SALES (est): 114.68K **Privately Held**
Web: www.vtcng.com
SIC: 2711   Commercial printing and
newspaper publishing combined

(G-17589)

PAW PRINTS PRESS INC

Also Called: Paw Print Offset/Digital
12 Gregory Dr Ste 8 (05403-6058)
PHONE..............................802 865-2872
EMP: 10 **EST:** 1990
SQ FT: 4,800
SALES (est): 990.24K **Privately Held**
Web: www.paw-prints.com
SIC: 2759 2789 7331   Commercial printing,
nec; Bookbinding and repairing: trade,
edition, library, etc.; Mailing service

(G-17590)

PG ADAMS INC

1215 Airport Pkwy (05403-5805)
PHONE..............................802 862-8664
Paul G Adams, *Pr*
Ashley Adams, *VP*
EMP: 23 **EST:** 1968
SQ FT: 13,000
SALES (est): 851.15K **Privately Held**
Web: www.pgadams.com
SIC: 7692 3441   Welding repair; Fabricated
structural metal

(G-17591)

PIONEER MOTORS AND DRIVES INC

30 Berard Dr Unit 6 (05403-5809)
PHONE..............................802 651-0114
Douglas Hoffman, *Pr*
Thea C Robson, *Sec*
Larisa Hoffman, *Treas*
Douglas A Hoffman, *Dir*
Evan Hoffman, *Dir*
EMP: 10 **EST:** 2001
SALES (est): 920.28K **Privately Held**
Web: www.pioneerdrives.com
SIC: 7694   Electric motor repair

(G-17592)

PLASTIC TECHNOLOGIES MD INC

Also Called: Shelburne Plastics
8 Arbor Rd (05403)
PHONE..............................802 658-6588
Gene Torvend, *Pr*
John Mayer, *CFO*
EMP: 8 **EST:** 2013
SALES (est): 189.46K **Privately Held**
SIC: 3085   Plastics bottles

(G-17593)

PLASTIC TECHNOLOGIES NY LLC

Also Called: Shelborne Plastics
8 Harbor View Rd (05403-7850)
PHONE..............................802 658-6588
Gene Tovend, *Pr*
John Mayer, *CFO*
EMP: 12 **EST:** 2009
SALES (est): 171.21K **Privately Held**
SIC: 3085   Plastics bottles

(G-17594)

PLASTIC TECHNOLOGIES OF VERMONT INC

Also Called: Shelburne Plastics
8 Harbor View Rd (05403-7850)
PHONE..............................802 658-6588
EMP: 94
SIC: 3085   Plastics bottles

(G-17595)

POPULATION MEDIA CENTER INC

Also Called: ENTERTAINMENT EDUCATION
INSTIT
30 Kimball Ave Ste 206 (05403-6825)
P.O. Box 547 (05482-0547)
PHONE..............................802 985-8156
William Ryerson, *Pr*
EMP: 33 **EST:** 1998
SALES (est): 9.45MM **Privately Held**
Web: www.populationmedia.org
SIC: 2836 8732   Biological products, except
diagnostic; Commercial nonphysical
research

(G-17596)

PRATT & WHITNEY ENG SVCS INC

Also Called: Pratt & Whitney
15 Eagle Dr (05403-6037)
PHONE..............................802 658-2208
Bill Burdet, *Mgr*
EMP: 45
SALES (corp-wide): 68.92B **Publicly Held**
Web: www.prattwhitney.com
SIC: 3724   Aircraft engines and engine parts
HQ: Pratt & Whitney Engine Services, Inc.
1525 Midway Park Rd
Bridgeport WV 26330
304 842-5421

(G-17597)

PROM SOFTWARE INC

150 Dorset St Ste 294 (05403-6256)
PHONE..............................802 862-7500
William Symmes, *Pr*
EMP: 10 **EST:** 1976
SQ FT: 7,000
SALES (est): 725.07K **Privately Held**
SIC: 3679 7371   Electronic circuits;
Computer software writing services

(G-17598)

SENTAR INC

Also Called: Selection Unlimited
102 Kimball Ave Ste 2 (05403-6800)
PHONE..............................802 861-6004
Ric Lashway, *Pr*
Derrick W Senior, ***
Randal F Senior, ***
▲ **EMP:** 63 **EST:** 1983
SQ FT: 12,000
SALES (est): 2.26MM **Privately Held**
Web: www.selectionunlimited.com
SIC: 2066   Chocolate and cocoa products

(G-17599)

SPRING FILL

1775 Williston Rd Ste 250 (05403-6491)
PHONE..............................802 846-5900
David Kline, *Pr*
EMP: 10 **EST:** 1984
SALES (est): 946.76K **Privately Held**
Web: www.spring-fill.com
SIC: 3086   Packaging and shipping
materials, foamed plastics

(G-17600)

STEP AHEAD INNOVATIONS INC

Also Called: Mindstream
54 Royal Dr (05403-4482)
PHONE..............................802 233-0211
James Clark, *Prin*
Brian Degen, *Prin*
Giuseppe Detrucci, *OF CHEMICAL
Research*
EMP: 10 **EST:** 2012
SALES (est): 918.23K **Privately Held**
Web: www.diycraftsy.com
SIC: 3823   Liquid analysis instruments,
industrial process type

(G-17601)

STICKY BRND CREATIVE GROUP LLC

66 Bowdoin St (05403-8800)
PHONE..............................609 731-0288
Michael Rist, *CEO*
EMP: 12 **EST:** 2019
SALES (est): 725.14K **Privately Held**
SIC: 2621   Printing paper

(G-17602)

SUNNY SKY PRODUCTS LLC

Also Called: Nectar Cappuccino Group
102 Kimball Ave Ste 1 (05403-6800)
P.O. Box 868 (05468-0868)
PHONE..............................802 861-6004
EMP: 35
SALES (corp-wide): 65.73MM **Privately
Held**
Web: www.sunnyskyproducts.com
SIC: 2066   Chocolate and cocoa products
PA: Sunny Sky Products, Llc
11747 Windfern Rd Ste 100
Houston TX 77064
713 683-9399

(G-17603)

SUPER-TEMP WIRE & CABLE INC

104 Bowdoin St (05403-8021)
PHONE..............................802 655-4211
EMP: 23 **EST:** 1995
SQ FT: 10,000
SALES (est): 2.37MM **Privately Held**
Web: www.super-temp.com
SIC: 3357   Nonferrous wiredrawing and
insulating

(G-17604)

TOP SHOP INC

87 Ethan Allen Dr (05403-5857)
P.O. Box 9493 (05407-9493)
PHONE..............................802 658-1351
Bruce Bouchard, *Pr*
Michelle Bouchard, *Sec*
EMP: 10 **EST:** 1983
SQ FT: 6,000
SALES (est): 973.76K **Privately Held**
SIC: 2542 2541   Counters or counter display
cases, except wood; Counters or counter
display cases, wood

(G-17605)

TRIDYNE PROCESS SYSTEMS INC

80 Allen Rd (05403-7801)
PHONE..............................802 863-6873
Suzette Wijetunga, *Pr*
EMP: 9 **EST:** 2011
SALES (est): 656.94K **Privately Held**
Web: www.tridyne.com
SIC: 3596   Scales and balances, except
laboratory

(G-17606)
TWO GO DRYCLEANING INC
1233 Shelburne Rd Ste 190 (05403-7733)
PHONE.............................802 658-9469
William Obrien, *Prin*
EMP: 20 EST: 2016
SALES (est): 1.22MM Privately Held
SIC: 3582 Ironers, commercial laundry and
drycleaning

(G-17607)
W B MASON CO INC
68 Nesti Dr (05403-7767)
PHONE.............................888 926-2766
EMP: 34
SALES (corp-wide): 1.01B Privately Held
Web: www.wbmason.com
SIC: 5943 5712 2752 Office forms and
supplies; Office furniture; Commercial
printing, lithographic
PA: W. B. Mason Co., Inc.
59 Centre Street
Brockton MA 02301
508 586-3434

(G-17608)
**YELLOW SIGN COMMERCIAL
INC**
18 Dover St (05403-6757)
P.O. Box 4010 (05406-4010)
PHONE.............................802 324-8500
Peter Yee, *Prin*
EMP: 7 EST: 2012
SALES (est): 257.14K Privately Held
Web: www.yellowsigncommercial.com
SIC: 3993 Signs and advertising specialties

South Hero
Grand Isle County

(G-17609)
PHOENIX WIRE INC
31 Tracy Rd (05486-4508)
P.O. Box 186 (05486-0186)
PHONE.............................802 372-4561
Horace W Corbin Junior, *Pr*
Thomas Parizo, *VP*
Sylvia Corbin, *Sec*
EMP: 8 EST: 1970
SQ FT: 10,000
SALES (est): 750.45K Privately Held
Web: www.phoenixwireinc.com
SIC: 3357 Nonferrous wiredrawing and
insulating

(G-17610)
SNOW FARM WINERY
190 W Shore Rd (05486-4617)
PHONE.............................802 372-9463
EMP: 10 EST: 1996
SALES (est): 736.65K Privately Held
Web: www.snowfarm.com
SIC: 2084 Wines

South Londonderry
Windham County

(G-17611)
**LONDONDERRY INDUSTRIAL
PK INC**
Also Called: Vermont Cottage Shop
170 Winhall Station Rd (05155-9235)
PHONE.............................802 297-3760
Domenic Mangano, *Pr*
EMP: 50 EST: 1995
SALES (est): 9.42MM Privately Held

Web: www.jamaicacottageshop.com
SIC: 2452 3272 Log cabins, prefabricated,
wood; Housing components, prefabricated
concrete

South Royalton
Windsor County

(G-17612)
NOLATO GW INC
272 Waterman Rd (05068-5115)
PHONE.............................802 763-2194
Ben Riehl, *Pr*
EMP: 100
SALES (corp-wide): 1.03B Privately Held
SIC: 3089 Injection molding of plastics
HQ: Nolato Gw, Inc.
239 Pleasant St
Bethel VT 05032
802 234-9941

South Ryegate
Caledonia County

(G-17613)
CHIEF LOGGING & CNSTR INC
2494 Stone Rd (05069-8993)
PHONE.............................802 584-3868
Clark S Bogie, *Pr*
EMP: 14 EST: 1999
SALES (est): 628.96K Privately Held
SIC: 2411 Logging camps and contractors

(G-17614)
GANDIN BROTHERS INC
87 Stoneshed Rd (05069-4415)
P.O. Box 155 (05069-0155)
PHONE.............................802 584-3521
Gaylord J Gandin, *Pr*
Judith Gandin, *Sec*
EMP: 16 EST: 1915
SQ FT: 3,500
SALES (est): 465.28K Privately Held
SIC: 3281 Granite, cut and shaped

South Woodstock
Windsor County

(G-17615)
KENDLE ENTERPRISES
Also Called: Kedron Sugar Makers
109 Kendle Rd (05071)
P.O. Box 111 (05071-0111)
PHONE.............................802 457-3015
Paul C Kendall, *Pr*
EMP: 10 EST: 1976
SALES (est): 509.54K Privately Held
Web: www.kedron.com
SIC: 2099 Maple syrup

Springfield
Windsor County

(G-17616)
ARTISAN SURFACES INC
200 Clinton St (05156-3306)
P.O. Box 377 (05156-0377)
PHONE.............................802 885-8677
Raymond C St Gelais, *Clerk*
EMP: 26 EST: 2012
SALES (est): 2.48MM Privately Held
Web: www.artisansurfacesinc.com
SIC: 2541 Counter and sink tops

(G-17617)
**CROWN POINT EXCAVATION
LLC**
890 Chester Rd (05156-9488)
P.O. Box 656 (05143-0656)
PHONE.............................802 291-4817
EMP: 16 EST: 2007
SALES (est): 1.25MM Privately Held
SIC: 1794 1081 Excavation work; Metal
mining exploration and development
services

(G-17618)
IMAGE TEK MFG INC
Also Called: Imagetek Manufacturing
280 Clinton St (05156-3308)
PHONE.............................802 885-6208
Michael Hathaway, *Pr*
George Norfleet, *
Loreen Billings, *
EMP: 40 EST: 1994
SQ FT: 33,000
SALES (est): 6.21MM Privately Held
Web: www.wblake.com
SIC: 3672 3679 3577 2679 Printed circuit
boards; Harness assemblies, for electronic
use: wire or cable; Computer peripheral
equipment, nec; Tags and labels, paper

(G-17619)
J & L METROLOGY INC
Also Called: J & L
280 Clinton St (05156-3308)
PHONE.............................802 885-8291
Peter Klepp, *Pr*
Nathalie Klepp, *
EMP: 25 EST: 2009
SALES (est): 4.71MM Privately Held
Web: www.jlmetrology.com
SIC: 3827 Optical instruments and lenses

(G-17620)
LOVEJOY TOOL COMPANY INC
133 Main St (05156-3509)
P.O. Box 949 (05156-0949)
PHONE.............................802 885-2194
Douglas Priestley, *Pr*
Nancy Lindsay, *
Richard Hopkins, *
Warren Garfield, *
EMP: 48 EST: 1917
SQ FT: 36,000
SALES (est): 8.03MM Privately Held
Web: www.lovejoytool.com
SIC: 3545 Milling cutters

(G-17621)
N B C SOLID SURFACES INC
200 Clinton St (05156-3306)
PHONE.............................802 885-8677
Donald Hinkley, *Pr*
Mike Filipiak, *CFO*
EMP: 9 EST: 1986
SQ FT: 7,000
SALES (est): 1.04MM Privately Held
Web: www.toprevenuegate.com
SIC: 2541 Counter and sink tops

(G-17622)
**VERMONT MACHINE TOOL
CORP**
Also Called: Vermont Machine Tool
65 Pearl St (05156-3041)
PHONE.............................802 885-5161
▲ EMP: 10
Web: www.021hiko.com
SIC: 3542 5084 Rebuilt machine tools,
metal forming types; Industrial machinery
and equipment

(G-17623)
**VERMONT PRECISION
MACHINE SVCS**
Also Called: V P M S
280 Clinton St (05156-3308)
P.O. Box 10 (05156-0010)
PHONE.............................802 885-8291
EMP: 9 EST: 1995
SQ FT: 15,000
SALES (est): 974.85K Privately Held
Web: www.jlmetrology.com
SIC: 3827 Optical comparators

St George
Chittenden County

(G-17624)
VERMONT WARE INC
157 Barber Rd # A (05495-8015)
PHONE.............................802 482-4426
Dale Dawson, *Pr*
Tyler Dawson, *VP*
Elizabeth Dawson, *Sec*
EMP: 7 EST: 1963
SQ FT: 36,000
SALES (est): 610K Privately Held
Web: www.vermontware.com
SIC: 3524 3479 Lawn and garden equipment
; Coating of metals and formed products

Starksboro
Addison County

(G-17625)
**ACER HOLDINGS
STARKSBORO INC**
Also Called: Foam Laminates of Vermont
22 Varney Hill Rd (05487-4417)
P.O. Box 100 (05461-0100)
PHONE.............................802 453-4438
EMP: 15 EST: 2011
SALES (est): 3.15MM Privately Held
Web: www.vermontframes.com
SIC: 2452 2439 7353 Panels and sections,
prefabricated, wood; Structural wood
members, nec; Cranes and aerial lift
equipment, rental or leasing

(G-17626)
**MARU LTD DBA GREENLEAF
METALS**
1022 Mason HI N (05487-7233)
PHONE.............................802 985-5200
Linda Snelling, *Ex Dir*
EMP: 8 EST: 2016
SALES (est): 192.78K Privately Held
SIC: 3312 Bar, rod, and wire products

(G-17627)
MORTISE AND TENON LLC
22 Varney Hill Rd (05487-4417)
PHONE.............................802 643-2227
EMP: 26
SALES (est): 1.05MM Privately Held
SIC: 2452 Prefabricated wood buildings

Stockbridge
Windsor County

(G-17628)
ADVANCED ANIMATIONS
Also Called: Advanced Exhibits
534 Vt Route 107 (05772-6803)
P.O. Box 34 (05772-0034)

▲ = Import ▼ = Export
◆ = Import/Export

PHONE..............................802 746-8974
Peggy Toth, *Pr*
Robert Crean, *
Thomas W Marquis, *
▲ **EMP:** 25 **EST:** 1966
SQ FT: 48,000
SALES (est): 2.4MM **Privately Held**
Web: www.advancedanimations.com
SIC: 3999 Theatrical scenery

Stowe
Lamoille County

(G-17629)
ALCHEMY BREWING STOWE LLC
Also Called: Alchemist Stowe, The
100 Cottage Club Rd (05672-4139)
PHONE..............................802 882-8165
EMP: 12 **EST:** 2012
SALES (est): 485.21K **Privately Held**
Web: www.alchemistbeer.com
SIC: 2082 Beer (alcoholic beverage)

(G-17630)
DALE E PERCY INC
269 Weeks Hill Rd (05672-5245)
PHONE..............................802 253-8503
Dana T Percy, *Pr*
Peter Percy, *VP*
EMP: 10 **EST:** 1950
SQ FT: 15,000
SALES (est): 2.17MM **Privately Held**
Web: www.dalepercyinc.com
SIC: 1442 1794 Construction sand and
gravel; Excavation work

(G-17631)
FORSAKE INC
219 Wood Rd (05672-4501)
P.O. Box 1074 (14127-8074)
PHONE..............................585 576-6358
Jacob Anderson, *CEO*
EMP: 7 **EST:** 2013
SALES (est): 221.06K **Privately Held**
Web: www.forsake.com
SIC: 5139 2329 Footwear, athletic; Men's
and boys' sportswear and athletic clothing

(G-17632)
LITTLE RVER HTGLASS STUDIO INC
Also Called: Little River Hot Glass Studio
593 Moscow Rd (05672-5113)
P.O. Box 1504 (05672-1504)
PHONE..............................802 253-0889
Michael Trimpol, *Pr*
EMP: 7 **EST:** 1995
SQ FT: 1,500
SALES (est): 619.94K **Privately Held**
Web: www.littleriverhotglass.com
SIC: 3229 5947 Pressed and blown glass,
nec; Gift, novelty, and souvenir shop

(G-17633)
X PRESS IN STOWE INC
73 Pond St (05672-5356)
P.O. Box 1441 (05672-1441)
PHONE..............................802 253-9788
Douglas Nerber, *Pr*
EMP: 7 **EST:** 1985
SQ FT: 2,500
SALES (est): 499.41K **Privately Held**
Web: www.thexpressink.com
SIC: 2752 Offset printing

Strafford
Orange County

(G-17634)
EBWS LLC
Also Called: Strafford Organic Creamery
61 Rockbottom Rd (05072-9726)
PHONE..............................802 765-4180
EMP: 7 **EST:** 2001
SALES (est): 692.85K **Privately Held**
Web: www.straffordcreamery.com
SIC: 2026 Fluid milk

Sunderland
Bennington County

(G-17635)
THE ORVIS COMPANY INC (PA)
Also Called: Orvis Sporting Traditions
178 Conservation Way (05250-4465)
PHONE..............................802 362-3622
◆ **EMP:** 260 **EST:** 1856
SALES (est): 485.62MM
SALES (corp-wide): 485.62MM **Privately Held**
Web: www.orvis.com
SIC: 5961 5941 3949 Catalog sales;
Sporting goods and bicycle shops; Fishing
tackle, general

Swanton
Franklin County

(G-17636)
CARGILL INCORPORATED
Also Called: Cargill
149 Jonergin Dr (05488-1368)
P.O. Box 250 (05488-0250)
PHONE..............................802 868-3232
Mike Fornier, *Brnch Mgr*
EMP: 8
SALES (corp-wide): 176.74B **Privately Held**
Web: www.cargill.com
SIC: 5191 2048 Animal feeds; Prepared
feeds, nec
PA: Cargill, Incorporated
15407 Mcginty Rd W
Wayzata MN 55391
800 227-4455

(G-17637)
GREEN MOUNTAIN KNITTING INC
Also Called: Qmd Medical
25 Jonergin Dr (05488-1311)
PHONE..............................800 361-1190
Jeffrey Abyoub, *Pr*
Calvert Kogan, *
Martin Kogan, *
▲ **EMP:** 25 **EST:** 1999
SALES (est): 3.13MM **Privately Held**
Web: www.calkogroup.com
SIC: 2221 Specialty broadwoven fabrics,
including twisted weaves

(G-17638)
NEWPORT SAND & GRAVEL CO INC
1st St (05488)
P.O. Box 158 (05488-0158)
PHONE..............................802 868-4119
Bob Carrel, *Mgr*
EMP: 9
SALES (corp-wide): 44.7MM **Privately Held**

Web: www.carrollconcrete.com
SIC: 3273 Ready-mixed concrete
PA: Newport Sand & Gravel Co., Inc.
8 Reeds Mill Rd
Newport NH 03773
603 298-0199

(G-17639)
PLUMROSE USA INC
14 Jonergin Dr (05488-1312)
PHONE..............................802 868-7314
Dave Schanzer, *CEO*
EMP: 51
Web: www.jbsfoodsgroup.com
SIC: 2013 Sausages and other prepared
meats
HQ: Plumrose Usa, Inc.
651 W Washington Blvd # 304
Chicago IL 60661

(G-17640)
POULIN GRAIN INC
24 Depot St (05488-1348)
PHONE..............................802 868-3323
Krista Rowe, *Mgr*
EMP: 34
SALES (corp-wide): 31.51MM **Privately Held**
Web: www.poulingrain.com
SIC: 2048 5153 Prepared feeds, nec; Grain
and field beans
PA: Poulin Grain, Inc.
24 Railroad Sq
Newport VT 05855
802 334-6731

(G-17641)
RAYMOND GADUES INC
Also Called: Ray's Extrusion Dies Tubing Co
Route78 East (05488)
P.O. Box 385 (05478-0385)
PHONE..............................802 868-2033
Kevin R Gadue, *Pr*
Lori A Kennison, *
EMP: 25 **EST:** 1960
SQ FT: 22,500
SALES (est): 2.57MM **Privately Held**
Web: www.raysdiesandtubing.com
SIC: 3544 3498 5051 Extrusion dies;
Fabricated pipe and fittings; Tubing, metal

(G-17642)
SHELBURNE LIMESTONE CORP
Also Called: Shelburne Limestone
30 Jewett St (05488-1416)
P.O. Box 170 (05488-0170)
PHONE..............................802 868-3357
Michael Duso, *Mgr*
EMP: 22
SALES (corp-wide): 22.21MM **Privately Held**
SIC: 5032 1422 Limestone; Crushed and
broken limestone
PA: Shelburne Limestone Corp
1949 Main St
Colchester VT 05446
802 878-2656

(G-17643)
SWAN VALLEY CHEESE VERMONT LLC
11 Jonergin Dr (05488-1311)
PHONE..............................802 868-7181
▲ **EMP:** 7 **EST:** 2010
SALES (est): 473.75K **Privately Held**
SIC: 2022 Natural cheese

(G-17644)
VERIZON
Also Called: Verizon
12 York St (05488-1337)
PHONE..............................802 879-4954
EMP: 8 **EST:** 2009
SALES (est): 125.19K **Privately Held**
SIC: 7319 2741 Distribution of advertising
material or sample services; Telephone and
other directory publishing

(G-17645)
VERMONT PRECISION TOOLS INC (PA)
Also Called: Vermont Gage
10 Precision Ln (05488-4447)
P.O. Box 182 (05488-0182)
PHONE..............................802 868-4246
Monica Greene, *Pr*
Richard Paquette, *
Joseph J Cahill, *
▲ **EMP:** 125 **EST:** 1968
SQ FT: 90,000
SALES (est): 26.46MM
SALES (corp-wide): 26.46MM **Privately Held**
Web: www.vermontgage.com
SIC: 3545 3823 Precision tools, machinists';
Process control instruments

(G-17646)
VERMONT THREAD GAGE LLC
Also Called: Vermont Gage
10 Precision Ln (05488-4447)
P.O. Box 182 (05488-0182)
PHONE..............................802 868-4246
Monica Greene, *Pr*
EMP: 16 **EST:** 2000
SALES (est): 864.75K **Privately Held**
Web: www.vermontgage.com
SIC: 3545 Machine tool accessories

Taftsville
Windsor County

(G-17647)
ANDREW PEARCE BOWLS LLC
59 Us Route 4 (05073-9700)
PHONE..............................802 356-4632
Andrew Pearce, *CEO*
EMP: 20 **EST:** 2011
SALES (est): 1.18MM **Privately Held**
Web: www.andrewpearcebowls.com
SIC: 2499 Food handling and processing
products, wood

Tinmouth
Rutland County

(G-17648)
LARRY G CARABEAU
Also Called: Windsong Farm
59a East Rd (05773-1105)
PHONE..............................802 446-3123
Larry Carabeau, *Owner*
EMP: 8 **EST:** 1975
SALES (est): 499.3K **Privately Held**
SIC: 0241 2099 0722 Dairy farms; Sugar,
industrial maple; Corn, machine harvesting
services

Topsham
Orange County

(G-17649)
INKJETMALLCOM LTD
17 Powder Spring Rd (05076-3004)
PHONE..............................802 439-3127
EMP: 8 **EST:** 2010
SALES (est): 241.98K **Privately Held**
Web: shop.inkjetmall.com
SIC: 2752 Commercial printing, lithographic

Townshend
Windham County

(G-17650)
CREST STUDIOS
Also Called: Robert Dugrenier Associates
1096 Vt Route 30 (05353-9725)
PHONE..............................802 365-4200
Robert Dugrenier, *Owner*
EMP: 7 **EST:** 1990
SALES (est): 306.41K **Privately Held**
Web: www.dugrenier.com
SIC: 3229 Glassware, art or decorative

Tunbridge
Orange County

(G-17651)
ANICHINI INC
Also Called: Anichini Linea Casa
4 Larkin Rd (05077-9765)
P.O. Box 67 (05077-0067)
PHONE..............................802 889-9430
Susan Dollenmaier, *CEO*
Martha Dollenmaier, *Pr*
◆ **EMP:** 44 **EST:** 1986
SQ FT: 2,400
SALES (est): 9.46MM **Privately Held**
Web: www.anichini.com
SIC: 5023 2392 Linens and towels;
Household furnishings, nec

(G-17652)
CUTTER & LOCKE INC (PA)
Also Called: Historical Publications
234 Monarch Hill Rd (05077-9626)
PHONE..............................802 889-3500
EMP: 8 **EST:** 1986
SALES (est): 1.41MM **Privately Held**
SIC: 2711 Newspapers, publishing and
printing

(G-17653)
E I J INC
Also Called: Iron Horse Standing Seam Roofg
467 Vt Route 110 (05077-9703)
P.O. Box 165 (05077-0165)
PHONE..............................802 889-3432
John Kinnarney, *Pr*
Jennifer Bettis, *Sec*
EMP: 16 **EST:** 1992
SQ FT: 3,600
SALES (est): 885.92K **Privately Held**
SIC: 3442 Garage doors, overhead: metal

Underhill
Chittenden County

(G-17654)
ABBA FUELS INC
1018 Vt Route 15 (05489-9337)
P.O. Box 5212 (05453-5212)
PHONE..............................802 878-8095
Kevin Whitten, *Prin*
EMP: 7 **EST:** 2009
SALES (est): 161.15K **Privately Held**
Web: www.abbafuels.com
SIC: 2869 Fuels

Vergennes
Addison County

(G-17655)
802 PRINT LLC
61 Main St (05491-1113)
PHONE..............................802 598-0967
Gregory Lutton, *Mgr*
EMP: 7 **EST:** 2017
SALES (est): 418.21K **Privately Held**
Web: www.print802.com
SIC: 2752 Commercial printing, lithographic

(G-17656)
BF GOODRICH AERSPCE AIRCRFT IN
100 Panton Rd (05491-1008)
PHONE..............................802 877-2911
David Gitlin, *Pr*
EMP: 8 **EST:** 2014
SALES (est): 641.64K **Privately Held**
SIC: 3812 3721 Aircraft/aerospace flight
instruments and guidance systems;
Nonmotorized and lighter-than-air aircraft

(G-17657)
COLLINS AEROSPACE
Also Called: UTC Aerospace Systems
100 Panton Rd (05491-1008)
PHONE..............................802 877-4000
EMP: 74 **EST:** 2019
SALES (est): 7.16MM **Privately Held**
Web: www.collinsaerospace.com
SIC: 3728 Aircraft parts and equipment, nec

(G-17658)
NECSEL INTLLCTUAL PROPERTY INC
Also Called: Necsel Ip
101 Panton Rd Ste 1 (05491-1073)
PHONE..............................802 877-6432
Joel Melnick, *Brnch Mgr*
EMP: 20
Web: www.ushio.com
SIC: 3679 Electronic circuits
HQ: Necsel Intellectual Property, Inc.
801 Ames Ave
Milpitas CA 95035

(G-17659)
SHACKSBURY HOLDINGS INC
75 Meigs Rd (05491-8905)
PHONE..............................802 458-0530
EMP: 20 **EST:** 2013
SALES (est): 2.21MM **Privately Held**
Web: www.shacksbury.com
SIC: 2084 Wines

(G-17660)
SIMMONDS PRECISION PDTS INC
SIMMONDS PRECISION PRODUCTS, INC.
100 Panton Rd (05491-1008)
PHONE..............................802 877-2911
Gary Loftus, *Brnch Mgr*
EMP: 17
SALES (corp-wide): 68.92B **Publicly Held**
SIC: 3728 Aircraft parts and equipment, nec
HQ: Simmonds Precision Products Inc
100 Panton Rd

Vergennes VT 05491
802 877-4000

(G-17661)
SIMMONDS PRECISION PRODUCTS (DH)
Also Called: Goodrich Snsors Intgrted Syste
100 Panton Rd (05491-1008)
PHONE..............................802 877-4000
Justin Robert Keppy, *CEO*
Paul V Cappiello, *
Vincent Lichtenberger, *
Michael G Mcauley, *Treas*
EMP: 650 **EST:** 1941
SQ FT: 211,000
SALES (est): 134.32MM
SALES (corp-wide): 68.92B **Publicly Held**
SIC: 3829 3694 3724 3728 Aircraft and
motor vehicle measurement equipment;
Ignition systems, high frequency; Aircraft
engines and engine parts; Aircraft parts and
equipment, nec
HQ: Goodrich Corporation
2730 W Tyvola Rd
Charlotte NC 28217
704 423-7000

(G-17662)
THOMANN STEEL LLC
1006 Nortontown Rd (05491-8806)
PHONE..............................802 462-3066
EMP: 7 **EST:** 2019
SALES (est): 346.34K **Privately Held**
SIC: 3441 Fabricated structural metal

Waitsfield
Washington County

(G-17663)
BERING TECHNOLOGY INC
5086 Main St (05673-6310)
PHONE..............................408 364-6500
Leung C Lok, *CEO*
EMP: 9 **EST:** 2009
SALES (est): 128.82K **Privately Held**
Web: www.bering.com
SIC: 3589 Service industry machinery, nec

(G-17664)
CABOT CREAMERY COOPERATIVE INC
Also Called: Cabot Creamery
193 Home Farm Way (05673-7512)
PHONE..............................888 792-2268
Richard Stammer, *Pr*
Margaret Bertolino, *
Paul P Johnston, *
EMP: 300 **EST:** 1919
SALES (est): 94.3MM
SALES (corp-wide): 305.86MM **Privately Held**
Web: www.cabotcheese.coop
SIC: 2022 5143 5451 Natural cheese;
Cheese; Butter
PA: Agri-Mark, Inc.
40 Shattuck Rd Ste 301
Andover MA 01810
978 552-5500

(G-17665)
CITY BOY LOGS LLC
612 Mansfield Rd (05673-7406)
PHONE..............................802 496-4372
EMP: 7 **EST:** 2016
SALES (est): 86.52K **Privately Held**
Web: www.valleyreporter.com
SIC: 2711 Newspapers: publishing only, not
printed on site

(G-17666)
DIFFRACTION LTD
193 Home Farm Way 2 (05673-7512)
PHONE..............................802 496-6640
Robert Kogut, *Mgr*
Robert Kogut, *Genl Mgr*
EMP: 9 **EST:** 1989
SALES (est): 986.05K **Privately Held**
SIC: 8731 3827 Commercial research
laboratory; Sighting and fire control
equipment, optical

(G-17667)
VALLEY REPORTER INCORPORATED
5222 Main St Ste 2 (05673-4445)
P.O. Box 119 (05673-0119)
PHONE..............................802 496-3607
Patricia Clark, *Pr*
Lisa Loomis, *Editor*
EMP: 8 **EST:** 1982
SALES (est): 535.3K **Privately Held**
Web: www.valleyreporter.com
SIC: 2711 Newspapers: publishing only, not
printed on site

(G-17668)
WILLIAM H MOORE INC
Also Called: Moore Design Builders
6971 Main St Ste 1 (05673-6223)
P.O. Box 1092 (05673-1092)
PHONE..............................802 496-3595
William H Moore, *Pr*
Mary Campbell Moore, *ON*
EMP: 8 **EST:** 1988
SQ FT: 225
SALES (est): 1.14MM **Privately Held**
SIC: 1521 8712 1542 2452 New
construction, single-family houses;
Architectural services; Commercial and
office buildings, renovation and repair; Log
cabins, prefabricated, wood

(G-17669)
WOOD & WOOD INC
Also Called: Wood & Wood Sign Systems
98 Carroll Rd (05673-4408)
PHONE..............................802 496-3000
Richard Potter, *Pr*
EMP: 8 **EST:** 1972
SALES (est): 983.68K **Privately Held**
Web: www.woodandwoodsigns.com
SIC: 2499 3952 3993 Signboards, wood;
Frames for artists' canvases; Signs and
advertising specialties

Wallingford
Rutland County

(G-17670)
AMES COMPANIES INC
82 Creek Rd (05773)
P.O. Box 249 (05773-0249)
PHONE..............................802 446-2601
EMP: 21
SALES (corp-wide): 2.69B **Publicly Held**
Web: www.homebyames.com
SIC: 3423 Hand and edge tools, nec
HQ: The Ames Companies Inc
13485 Veterans Way # 200
Orlando FL 32827

Warren
Washington County

(G-17671)
COLD SPRINGS SPIRITS LLC
Also Called: Mad River Distillers
156 Cold Springs Farm Rd (05674-9453)
PHONE.................................802 496-6973
John Egan, *Prin*
EMP: 9 **EST:** 2016
SALES (est): 282.71K **Privately Held**
SIC: 2085 Distilled and blended liquors

(G-17672)
MAD RIVER DISTILLERS
156 Cold Springs Farm Rd (05674-9453)
PHONE.................................802 496-6973
Alex Hilton, *Pr*
▲ **EMP:** 7 **EST:** 2013
SALES (est): 277.39K **Privately Held**
Web: www.madriverdistillers.com
SIC: 2085 Distilled and blended liquors

Waterbury
Washington County

(G-17673)
CYPRESS WOODWORKS LLC
150 Stuart Ln (05676-8808)
PHONE.................................802 338-0538
Alexander Mckenzie, *Pr*
EMP: 7 **EST:** 2017
SALES (est): 260.8K **Privately Held**
Web: www.cypresswoodworksvt.com
SIC: 2431 Millwork

(G-17674)
DARTMOUTH JOURNAL SERVICES INC
Also Called: Sheridan Journal Services
5 Pilgrim Park Rd Ste 5 (05676-1735)
PHONE.................................802 244-1457
Garry Kittredge, *Pr*
EMP: 25 **EST:** 2002
SALES (est): 4.72MM
SALES (corp-wide): 653.94MM **Privately Held**
SIC: 2721 Magazines: publishing only, not printed on site
HQ: The Sheridan Group Inc
450 Fame Ave
Hanover PA 17331

(G-17675)
KEURIG GREEN MOUNTAIN INC (DH)
Also Called: Green Mtn Cof Cafe Visitor Ctr
1 Rotarian Pl (05676-1582)
PHONE.................................877 879-2326
TOLL FREE: 800
Robert Gamgort, *Ch*
Peter Leemputt, *
◆ **EMP:** 58 **EST:** 1993
SALES (est): 1B **Publicly Held**
Web: www.keurigdrpepper.com
SIC: 2095 5499 Coffee extracts; Coffee
HQ: Maple Parent Holdings Corp.
33 Coffee Ln
Waterbury VT 05676
802 244-5621

(G-17676)
NEUDORFER INC
Also Called: Neudorfer Tables
183 Crossett Hl (05676-9408)
P.O. Box 501 (05676-0501)
PHONE.................................802 244-5338
Robert Neudorfer, *Pr*
Kathy Dean, *VP*
Joshua Neudorfer, *Sec*
EMP: 10 **EST:** 1974
SALES (est): 840.85K **Privately Held**
Web: www.neudorfer.com
SIC: 2511 Wood household furniture

(G-17677)
SOF HOLDINGS INC
40 Foundry St Ste 1a (05676-1554)
PHONE.................................802 244-7644
Sunja Yi Hayden, *Pr*
David Hayden, *VP*
EMP: 8 **EST:** 1992
SQ FT: 2,500
SALES (est): 800K **Privately Held**
Web: www.sunjaskimchi.com
SIC: 2099 Food preparations, nec

(G-17678)
T S S INC
Also Called: Super Thin Saws
80 Commercial Dr Ste 5 (05676-8957)
PHONE.................................802 244-8101
John Schultz, *Pr*
Robert D Bisbee, *VP*
Roland D Strom, *VP*
EMP: 21 **EST:** 1977
SQ FT: 10,000
SALES (est): 2.42MM **Privately Held**
Web: www.superthinsaws.com
SIC: 3425 7699 Saw blades and handsaws; Knife, saw and tool sharpening and repair

(G-17679)
WORKWISE LLC
121 S Pinnacle Ridge Rd (05676-4430)
PHONE.................................802 881-8178
EMP: 14 **EST:** 2011
SALES (est): 176.24K **Privately Held**
Web: www.work-wise.com
SIC: 7372 Business oriented computer software

Waterbury Center
Washington County

(G-17680)
COLD HOLLOW CIDER MILL INC
3600 Waterbury-Stowe Rd (05677-8020)
P.O. Box 420 (05677-0420)
PHONE.................................802 244-8771
Paul Brown, *Pr*
Gayle Brown, *VP*
EMP: 22 **EST:** 1974
SQ FT: 15,000
SALES (est): 8.27MM **Privately Held**
Web: www.coldhollow.com
SIC: 5149 5961 2033 5499 Juices; Mail order house, nec; Marmalade: packaged in cans, jars, etc.; Juices, fruit or vegetable

(G-17681)
IVY COMPUTER INC
Also Called: Trash Flow
2933 Waterbury-Stowe Rd # 1 (05677-7030)
PHONE.................................802 244-7880
George C Pierce, *Pr*
Jeff Kilgore, *Corporate Secretary*
EMP: 10 **EST:** 1986
SALES (est): 1.98MM **Privately Held**
Web: www.ivycomputer.com
SIC: 7371 7372 7373 Computer software development; Prepackaged software; Turnkey vendors, computer systems

Waterville
Lamoille County

(G-17682)
COSTA ENTERPRISES LTD CO
2953 Vt Route 109 (05492-9601)
P.O. Box 8 (05492-0008)
PHONE.................................802 644-6782
Allison M Costa, *Owner*
EMP: 7 **EST:** 2009
SALES (est): 439.19K **Privately Held**
SIC: 2879 Insecticides and pesticides

Websterville
Washington County

(G-17683)
ADAMS GRANITE CO INC
Also Called: North Barre Granite
58 Pitman Rd (05678)
P.O. Box 126 (05641-0126)
PHONE.................................802 476-5281
Kerry Zorzi, *Pr*
Carole Cecchini, *
▲ **EMP:** 60 **EST:** 1934
SQ FT: 70,000
SALES (est): 4.88MM **Privately Held**
Web: www.adamsgranite.org
SIC: 3281 1411 Granite, cut and shaped; Dimension stone

(G-17684)
HIGHLAND SUGARWORKS INC
Also Called: Highland Sugarworks
49 Parker Rd (05678)
P.O. Box 58 (05678-0058)
PHONE.................................802 479-1747
James E Macisaac, *Pr*
Judy Macisaac, *VP*
Deborah L Frimodig, *Sec*
▲ **EMP:** 18 **EST:** 1987
SQ FT: 20,000
SALES (est): 1.78MM **Privately Held**
Web: www.highlandsugarworks.com
SIC: 2099 5149 Maple syrup; Sugar, honey, molasses, and syrups

(G-17685)
VERMONT CREAMERY LLC
40 Pitman Rd (05678)
P.O. Box 95 (05678-0095)
PHONE.................................802 479-9371
Adeline Druart, *Pr*
Matthew Reese, *Contrlr*
▲ **EMP:** 29 **EST:** 1984
SALES (est): 11.23MM
SALES (corp-wide): 2.89B **Privately Held**
Web: www.vermontcreamery.com
SIC: 2022 Natural cheese
PA: Land O'lakes, Inc.
4001 Lexington Ave N
Arden Hills MN 55126
651 375-2222

Wells River
Orange County

(G-17686)
BREAD & CHOCOLATE INC
Also Called: Moose Mountain Food Co.
1538 Industrial Park (05081-9806)
P.O. Box 692 (05081-0692)
PHONE.................................802 429-2920
Jonathan Rutstein, *Pr*
Wolf Gang Leibmann, *Ex VP*
Fran Rutstein, *Sec*
▲ **EMP:** 8 **EST:** 1984
SQ FT: 9,600
SALES (est): 826.67K **Privately Held**
Web: www.breadandchocolatevt.com
SIC: 2099 5499 Food preparations, nec; Gourmet food stores

(G-17687)
GREEN MOUNTAIN MONOGRAM INC
Also Called: Top Dead Center Apparel
14 Creamery St (05081-3001)
P.O. Box 753 (05081-0753)
PHONE.................................802 757-2553
Gene R Eastman, *Pr*
EMP: 20 **EST:** 1987
SALES (est): 939.93K **Privately Held**
Web: www.greenmountainmonogram.com
SIC: 2395 Embroidery and art needlework

(G-17688)
SILLYCOW FARMS LLC
293 Industrial Park (05081-9816)
P.O. Box 692 (05081-0692)
PHONE.................................802 429-2920
William Burnham, *Managing Member*
EMP: 20 **EST:** 2015
SALES (est): 1.51MM **Privately Held**
Web: www.sillycowfarms.com
SIC: 2066 Instant cocoa

West Dover
Windham County

(G-17689)
BROWN COUNTRY SERVICES LLC
131 Vt Route 100 (05356)
P.O. Box 127 (05356-0127)
PHONE.................................802 464-5200
Robert Fisher Esq, *Admn*
EMP: 9 **EST:** 2006
SALES (est): 497.14K **Privately Held**
SIC: 2842 Specialty cleaning

(G-17690)
GW SKI INC
Also Called: First Trax Sports Shop
5 Mountain Park Plz (05356-8800)
PHONE.................................802 464-3464
John Grush, *CEO*
EMP: 13 **EST:** 2010
SALES (est): 689.26K **Privately Held**
Web: www.firsttraxsportsshop.com
SIC: 3949 5091 Snow skiing equipment and supplies, except skis; Golf and skiing equipment and supplies

West Pawlet
Rutland County

(G-17691)
J & G HADEKA SLATE FLRG INC
773 Briar Hill Rd (05775-9664)
PHONE.................................802 265-3351
Gary Hadeka, *Pr*
John Hadeka, *VP*
Anne Hadeka, *Sec*
EMP: 8 **EST:** 1984
SALES (est): 568.62K **Privately Held**
SIC: 3281 Slate products

(G-17692)
NEWMONT SLATE CO INC (PA)
720 Vt Route 149 (05775-9792)

PHONE..............................802 645-0203
John M Williams, *Pr*
David Bean, *
EMP: 26 **EST:** 1990
SQ FT: 24,000
SALES (est): 4.33MM **Privately Held**
Web: www.newmontslate.com
SIC: 3281 2952 Stone, quarrying and processing of own stone products; Asphalt felts and coatings

(G-17693)
REAL VERMONT ROOFING SLATE
720 Vt Route 149 (05775-9792)
PHONE..............................802 884-8091
John M Williams, *Prin*
EMP: 8 **EST:** 2007
SALES (est): 112.19K **Privately Held**
SIC: 3444 Roof deck, sheet metal

West Rupert
Bennington County

(G-17694)
AUTHENTIC DESIGNS INC
Also Called: Bast Road Collection
154 Mill Rd (05776-9716)
PHONE..............................802 394-7715
Daniel Krauss, *Pr*
▼ **EMP:** 10 **EST:** 1972
SALES (est): 1.42MM **Privately Held**
Web: www.authenticdesigns.com
SIC: 3645 3646 Residential lighting fixtures; Commercial lighting fixtures

West Rutland
Rutland County

(G-17695)
H HIRSCHMANN LTD
Also Called: Hirschmann Windows and Doors
467 Sheldon Ave (05777-9394)
PHONE..............................802 438-4447
Rolf Hirschmann, *Pr*
Ursula Hirschmann, *Sec*
▲ **EMP:** 18 **EST:** 1982
SALES (est): 2.37MM **Privately Held**
Web: www.hhirschmannltd.com
SIC: 2431 5211 5031 Doors, wood; Door and window products; Doors and windows

(G-17696)
NEUTRAL ZONE LLC
738 Rutland Rd (05777-4421)
PHONE..............................802 989-3133
Jessica Cameron, *Prin*
EMP: 11 **EST:** 2019
SALES (est): 338.37K **Privately Held**
Web: www.neutralzone.net
SIC: 2711 Newspapers

(G-17697)
VERMONT JUVENILE FURN MFG INC
Also Called: Pet Gear
192 Sheldon Ave (05777-9615)
P.O. Box 99 (05777-0099)
PHONE..............................802 438-2231
Scott Jakubowski, *VP*
Todd Jakubowski, *Ex Sec*
Chris Jakubowski, *VP*
▲ **EMP:** 10 **EST:** 1934
SQ FT: 86,000
SALES (est): 952.57K **Privately Held**
Web: www.petgearinc.com
SIC: 3999 Pet supplies

West Topsham
Orange County

(G-17698)
LIMLAWS PULPWOOD INC
Also Called: Limo Chipping and Land Query
261 Vt Route 25 (05086-9741)
PHONE..............................802 439-3503
Bruce E Limlaw, *Pr*
Ruth Limlaw, *Sec*
EMP: 26 **EST:** 1987
SQ FT: 500
SALES (est): 1.27MM **Privately Held**
SIC: 2631 Chip board

Westfield
Orleans County

(G-17699)
ROZELLE INC
4260 Loop Rd (05874-9729)
P.O. Box 70 (05874-0070)
PHONE..............................802 744-2270
Marielle Demuth, *Pr*
Matthias Brittain, *
Gene Besaw, *
EMP: 27 **EST:** 1968
SQ FT: 22,000
SALES (est): 2.45MM **Privately Held**
Web: www.rozelle.com
SIC: 2844 Cosmetic preparations

Westminster
Windham County

(G-17700)
C E MAPLE LLC
663 Bemis Hill Rd (05158)
PHONE..............................802 387-5944
Felicity Ladd, *Brnch Mgr*
EMP: 20
SALES (corp-wide): 226.16K **Privately Held**
SIC: 2099 Maple syrup
PA: C E Maple, Llc
30 Coop Hill Rd
Putney VT

(G-17701)
GREEN MOUNTAIN GAZEBO
237 Kimball Hill Rd (05158)
P.O. Box 80 (05154-0080)
PHONE..............................802 869-1212
Dennis Gilkenson, *Owner*
EMP: 8 **EST:** 2002
SALES (est): 498.66K **Privately Held**
Web: www.greenmountaingazebo.com
SIC: 2542 Stands, merchandise display: except wood

Westminster Station
Windham County

(G-17702)
BURTCO INC
Also Called: Ferrex Industries
185 Rte 123 (05159)
P.O. Box 40 (05159-0040)
PHONE..............................802 722-3358
Stanton N Scott, *Pr*
George W Nostrand, *Sec*
EMP: 10 **EST:** 1973
SQ FT: 25,000
SALES (est): 1.32MM **Privately Held**

SIC: 2911 3443 3446 Fractionation products of crude petroleum, hydrocarbons, nec; Metal parts; Guards, made from pipe

Weybridge
Addison County

(G-17703)
MONUMENT FARMS INC
2107 James Rd (05753-9525)
PHONE..............................802 545-2119
Robert James, *Pr*
Jonathan Rooney V, *Plant Mgr*
Peter James, *
EMP: 39 **EST:** 1930
SQ FT: 3,000
SALES (est): 1.54MM **Privately Held**
Web: www.monumentfarms.com
SIC: 0241 2026 5143 5451 Dairy farms; Milk processing (pasteurizing, homogenizing, bottling); Milk; Dairy products stores

White River Junction
Windsor County

(G-17704)
BLUE MOON FOODS INC
Also Called: Blue Moon Sorbet
568 N Main St Ste 1 (05001-7222)
P.O. Box 874 (05059-0874)
PHONE..............................802 295-1165
John Donaldson, *Pr*
Pamela Frantz, *VP*
EMP: 7 **EST:** 1995
SQ FT: 600
SALES (est): 618.92K **Privately Held**
Web: www.bluemoonsorbet.com
SIC: 2024 Sorbets, non-dairy based

(G-17705)
CHELSEA GREEN PUBLISHING CO
Also Called: Invisible Universe
85 N Main St Ste 120 (05001-7135)
P.O. Box 4529 (05001-4529)
PHONE..............................802 295-6300
Margaret Baldwin Junior, *Pr*
Ian Baldwin, *VP*
▲ **EMP:** 20 **EST:** 1984
SQ FT: 1,800
SALES (est): 3.85MM **Privately Held**
Web: www.chelseagreen.com
SIC: 2731 Books, publishing only

(G-17706)
CONCEPTS ETI INC
Also Called: Concepts Nrec
217 Billings Farm Rd (05001-9486)
PHONE..............................802 296-2321
David Japikse, *CEO*
Harold A Keiling, *
Daniel V Hinch, *
▲ **EMP:** 100 **EST:** 2015
SQ FT: 20,000
SALES (est): 8.78MM **Privately Held**
Web: www.conceptsnrec.com
SIC: 7372 Prepackaged software

(G-17707)
CONCEPTS NREC LLC (PA)
217 Billings Farm Rd (05001-9486)
PHONE..............................802 296-2321
David Japikse, *CEO*
EMP: 60 **EST:** 2015
SALES (est): 13.02MM
SALES (corp-wide): 13.02MM **Privately Held**

Web: www.conceptsnrec.com
SIC: 7372 3511 Prepackaged software; Turbines and turbine generator sets and parts

(G-17708)
IBEX OUTDOOR CLOTHING LLC
132 Ballardvale Dr (05001-7008)
PHONE..............................802 359-4239
Ted Manning, *CEO*
John Fernsell, *
Tina Bourgeois, *
▲ **EMP:** 25 **EST:** 1997
SQ FT: 7,000
SALES (est): 7.43MM
SALES (corp-wide): 46.8MM **Privately Held**
SIC: 2321 Sport shirts, men's and boys': from purchased materials
PA: North Castle Partners, L.L.C.
183 E Putnam Ave
Greenwich CT 06830
203 485-0216

(G-17709)
NOMAD COMMUNICATIONS INC
2456 Christian St Ste 101 (05001-9856)
P.O. Box 1036 (05055-1036)
PHONE..............................802 649-1995
Alexander Khan, *Pr*
▲ **EMP:** 10 **EST:** 1978
SALES (est): 1MM **Privately Held**
Web: www.nomadcommunications.com
SIC: 7319 5137 5632 5611 Transit advertising services; Sweaters, women's and children's; Knitwear, women's; Men's and boys' clothing stores

(G-17710)
TOWN OF HARTFORD
Also Called: Fire Dept
812 Va Cutoff Rd (05001-9777)
PHONE..............................802 295-9425
Steven Locke, *Chief*
EMP: 20
Web: www.hartford-vt.org
SIC: 3711 Fire department vehicles (motor vehicles), assembly of
PA: Town Of Hartford
171 Bridge St
White River Junction VT 05001
802 295-9353

Whiting
Addison County

(G-17711)
TATAS NATURAL ALCHEMY LLC
Also Called: Tata Harper Labratory
1136 Wooster Rd (05778-9712)
PHONE..............................802 462-3958
Graciela Guzman, *Managing Member*
EMP: 96
SALES (corp-wide): 24.42MM **Privately Held**
Web: www.tataharperskincare.com
SIC: 2844 Perfumes, cosmetics and other toilet preparations
PA: Tata's Natural Alchemy, Llc
1135 Wooster Rd
Whiting VT 05778
802 462-3814

(G-17712)
TATAS NATURAL ALCHEMY LLC (PA)
Also Called: Tata Harper Skincare
1135 Wooster Rd (05778-9727)

PHONE..................802 462-3814
Henry Harper, *
Blake Perlman, *
▲ EMP: 50 EST: 2007
SQ FT: 2,000
SALES (est): 24.42MM
SALES (corp-wide): 24.42MM **Privately Held**
Web: www.tataharperskincare.com
SIC: 2844 Cosmetic preparations

Whitingham
Windham County

(G-17713)
SAWYER BENTWOOD INC
247 Maple Dr (05361-9749)
PHONE..................802 368-2357
George Campo, *Pr*
EMP: 25 EST: 1801
SQ FT: 10,000
SALES (est): 2.04MM **Privately Held**
Web: www.sawyerbentwood.com
SIC: 2511 Chairs, Bentwood

Wilder
Windsor County

(G-17714)
DATAMANN INC
Also Called: Computer Connection
1994 Hartford Ave (05088-3013)
P.O. Box 1930 (05088-1930)
PHONE..................802 295-6600
John E Mann, *Pr*
Bill Mann, *
Kathy Reagan, *
EMP: 30 EST: 1975
SQ FT: 15,000
SALES (est): 4.64MM **Privately Held**
Web: www.datamann.com
SIC: 7374 7372 7371 Data processing
   service; Publisher's computer software;
   Computer software development

(G-17715)
**STAVE PUZZLES
INCORPORATED**
Also Called: Weight Wizards
163 Olcott Dr (05088)
P.O. Box 329 (05055-0329)
PHONE..................802 295-5200
Steve Richardson, *Pr*
Martha Richardson, *Treas*
EMP: 15 EST: 1974
SQ FT: 3,500
SALES (est): 767.58K **Privately Held**
Web: www.stavepuzzles.com
SIC: 3944 Puzzles

(G-17716)
**VERMOD HIGH PRFMCE
MNFCTRED HS**
Also Called: Vermod Homes
2677 Rt 5 (05088)
P.O. Box 566 (05088-0566)
PHONE..................802 295-0042
EMP: 9 EST: 2013
SQ FT: 20,000
SALES (est): 429.15K **Privately Held**
Web: www.vermodhomes.com
SIC: 1521 2452 Single-family housing
   construction; Modular homes,
   prefabricated, wood

Williamstown
Orange County

(G-17717)
PROGRESSIVE PLASTICS INC
Also Called: P P I
85 Industry St (05679-9819)
P.O. Box 435 (05679-0435)
PHONE..................802 433-1563
Hank Buermann, *Pr*
◆ EMP: 37 EST: 1989
SQ FT: 12,000
SALES (est): 4.92MM **Privately Held**
Web: www.hyperkinetics.org
SIC: 3089 Injection molding of plastics

(G-17718)
STILLWATER GRAPHICS INC
71 Depot St (05679-9126)
PHONE..................802 433-9898
TOLL FREE: 800
John Rhodes, *Pr*
Dana Laplant, *VP*
EMP: 13 EST: 1994
SQ FT: 6,000
SALES (est): 943.6K **Privately Held**
Web: aegir.deliduka.com
SIC: 2752 7336 2791 Offset printing;
   Graphic arts and related design; Typesetting

Williston
Chittenden County

(G-17719)
89 NORTH INC
Also Called: 89 North
20 Winter Sport Ln Ste 135 (05495-8146)
PHONE..................802 881-0302
Newell Lessel, *CEO*
Carl Padula, *CFO*
Jeff Clark, *Sec*
Jill James, *Treas*
EMP: 13 EST: 2009
SQ FT: 2,700
SALES (est): 2.44MM **Privately Held**
Web: www.89north.com
SIC: 3827 Optical instruments and lenses

(G-17720)
A DROP OF JOY LLC
166 Boyer Cir (05495-9561)
P.O. Box 1137 (05477-1137)
PHONE..................802 598-6419
Joshua A Pfeil, *Brnch Mgr*
EMP: 27
SALES (corp-wide): 484.86K **Privately
Held**
Web: www.adropofjoy.com
SIC: 2013 Canned meats (except baby
   food), from purchased meat
PA: A Drop Of Joy, Llc
   170 Boyer Cir
   Williston VT 05495
   802 598-6419

(G-17721)
ALLEARTH RENEWABLES INC
Also Called: Allearth Renewables
94 Harvest Ln (05495-8997)
PHONE..................802 872-9600
David Blittersdorf, *Pr*
Doug Goldsmith, *
Joyce Dicianna, *
Christie Hutchins, *
EMP: 26 EST: 2005
SALES (est): 9.48MM **Privately Held**
Web: www.allearthrenewables.com

SIC: 3674 5211 Solar cells; Energy
   conservation products

(G-17722)
ASTENJOHNSON INC
Also Called: Johnson Filaments
192 Industrial Ave (05495-9820)
PHONE..................802 658-2040
Teresa Renaud, *Mgr*
EMP: 70
SALES (corp-wide): 425.15MM **Privately
Held**
Web: www.astenjohnson.com
SIC: 3089 3496 3081 2221 Monofilaments,
   nontextile; Miscellaneous fabricated wire
   products; Unsupported plastics film and
   sheet; Broadwoven fabric mills, manmade
PA: Astenjohnson, Inc.
   4399 Corporate Rd
   North Charleston SC 29405
   843 747-7800

(G-17723)
BAKER COMMODITIES INC
354 Avenue B (05495-7149)
PHONE..................802 658-0721
David King, *Mgr*
EMP: 7
SALES (corp-wide): 153.63MM **Privately
Held**
Web: www.bakercommodities.com
SIC: 2077 Animal and marine fats and oils
PA: Baker Commodities, Inc.
   4020 Bandini Blvd
   Vernon CA 90058
   323 268-2801

(G-17724)
**BUSINESS FINANCIAL PUBG
LLC**
380 Hurricane Ln Ste 202 (05495-2085)
PHONE..................802 865-9886
Ian Wyatt, *Prin*
EMP: 7 EST: 2010
SALES (est): 89.24K **Privately Held**
SIC: 2741 Miscellaneous publishing

(G-17725)
**CHAMPLAIN CHOCOLATE
COMPANY**
Also Called: Lake Champlain Chocolates
290 Boyer Cir (05495-8931)
PHONE..................802 864-1808
EMP: 53
SALES (corp-wide): 15.53MM **Privately
Held**
Web:
www.lakechamplainchocolates.com
SIC: 5441 2066 Candy; Chocolate bars,
   solid
PA: Champlain Chocolate Company Inc
   750 Pine St
   Burlington VT 05401
   800 465-5909

(G-17726)
DAL-TILE CORPORATION
Also Called: DAL-TILE CORPORATION
44 Miller Ln Ste 20 (05495-7513)
PHONE..................802 951-2030
Tim Phoenix, *Mgr*
EMP: 10
Web: locations.daltile.com
SIC: 5032 3253 Ceramic wall and floor tile,
   nec; Ceramic wall and floor tile
HQ: Dal-Tile, Llc
   7834 C F Hawn Fwy
   Dallas TX 75217
   214 398-1411

(G-17727)
DIGITAL PRESS PRINTERS LLC
Also Called: Print Tech
128 Commerce St (05495-8126)
PHONE..................802 863-5579
EMP: 9 EST: 1972
SQ FT: 6,000
SALES (est): 462.9K **Privately Held**
Web: www.printtechvt.com
SIC: 2752 7334 Offset printing;
   Photocopying and duplicating services

(G-17728)
DOLLIVER CORPORATION
Also Called: Vermont Plastic Specialties
209 Blair Park Rd (05495-7434)
P.O. Box 483 (05495-0483)
PHONE..................802 879-0072
TOLL FREE: 800
Richard Dolliver, *Pr*
EMP: 8 EST: 1976
SQ FT: 15,000
SALES (est): 862.06K **Privately Held**
Web: www.vermontplastics.com
SIC: 3089 Molding primary plastics

(G-17729)
FLEX-A-SEAL INC
291 Hurricane Ln Ste 101 (05495-2074)
PHONE..................802 878-8307
Hank Slauson, *Pr*
Kim Simmons, *
Debbie Safford, *
Steve Pontbriand, *
▲ EMP: 50 EST: 1983
SALES (est): 23.74MM **Privately Held**
Web: www.flexseal.com
SIC: 5085 3053 Seals, industrial; Gaskets
   and sealing devices

(G-17730)
**FLEXASEAL ENGNRED SALS
SYSTEMS**
Also Called: Flexaseal
291 Hurricane Ln (05495-2074)
PHONE..................800 426-3594
EMP: 150
Web: www.flexaseal.com
SIC: 3053 Gaskets; packing and sealing
   devices

(G-17731)
FOODSCIENCE LLC (HQ)
Also Called: Davinci Laboratories
929 Harvest Ln (05495-4416)
PHONE..................800 451-5190
Sharon Rossi, *CEO*
Bryan Fortier, *
Patricia Wunsch, *CAO*
▲ EMP: 174 EST: 1973
SQ FT: 75,000
SALES (est): 79.56MM
SALES (corp-wide): 3.48B **Privately Held**
Web: www.davincilabs.com
SIC: 2834 5122 Vitamin, nutrient, and
   hematinic preparations for human use;
   Vitamins and minerals
PA: Wind Point Partners, L.P.
   676 N Michigan Ave # 3700
   Chicago IL 60611
   312 255-4800

(G-17732)
**GDS MANUFACTURING
COMPANY**
Also Called: Kemtuff
32 Boyer Cir (05495-8932)
P.O. Box 663 (05495-0663)
PHONE..................802 862-7610

G
E
O
G
R
A
P
H
I
C

Gary Riggs, *Pr*
Tim Wissell, *VP*
EMP: 7 **EST:** 1990
SQ FT: 16,000
SALES (est) 635.14K **Privately Held**
Web: www.kemtuff.com
SIC: 3479 Coating of metals with plastic or resins

(G-17733)
GENERAL DYNAMICS OTS CAL INC
Also Called: Gd-Ots Williston
326 Ibm Rd Bldg 862 (05495-7999)
PHONE..............................802 662-7000
Steve Elgin, *Mgr*
EMP: 262
SALES (corp-wide): 42.27B **Publicly Held**
Web: www.gd-ots.com
SIC: 3728 7382 3812 Military aircraft equipment and armament; Protective devices, security; Search and navigation equipment
HQ: General Dynamics-Ots, Inc.
100 Carillon Pkwy Ste 100 # 100
Saint Petersburg FL 33716
727 578-8100

(G-17734)
GORDONS WINDOW DECOR INC (PA)
Also Called: Gordons Window Decor Centl VT
8 Leroy Rd (05495-8965)
PHONE..............................802 655-7777
Gordon Clements, *Pr*
Dianne Clements, *Sec*
EMP: 12 **EST:** 1986
SQ FT: 7,000
SALES (est): 2.35MM
SALES (corp-wide): 2.35MM **Privately Held**
Web: www.gordonswindowdecor.com
SIC: 2591 2211 5023 2391 Blinds vertical; Draperies and drapery fabrics, cotton; Window furnishings; Curtains and draperies

(G-17735)
HONEYWELL INTERNATIONAL INC
Also Called: Honeywell
203 Cornerstone Dr (05495-4035)
PHONE..............................877 841-2840
Scott Bellows, *Mgr*
EMP: 7
SALES (corp-wide): 35.47B **Publicly Held**
Web: www.honeywell.com
SIC: 3724 Aircraft engines and engine parts
PA: Honeywell International Inc.
855 S Mint St
Charlotte NC 28202
704 627-6200

(G-17736)
KE USA INC
Also Called: Otter Creek Awning
19 Echo Pl (05495-9374)
PHONE..............................802 864-3009
TOLL FREE: 888
Todd Warren, *Pr*
EMP: 49
SALES (corp-wide): 140.66MM **Privately Held**
Web: www.ottercreekawnings.com
SIC: 2394 5999 Canopies, fabric: made from purchased materials; Awnings
HQ: Ke Usa, Inc.
445 Bellvale Rd
Chester NY 10918
845 610-1100

(G-17737)
KP BUILDING PRODUCTS INC
402 Boyer Cir (05495-8924)
PHONE..............................866 850-4447
Lionel Dubrofsky, *Pr*
Tami Dubrofsky, *
EMP: 87 **EST:** 2005
SALES (est): 2.21MM
SALES (corp-wide): 397.78MM **Privately Held**
SIC: 3089 5033 Siding, plastics; Roofing, siding, and insulation
HQ: Kaycan Ltd.
402 Boyer Cir
Williston VT 05495

(G-17738)
LANCASTER IMAGEWORKS INC
Also Called: Pure Energy Apothecary
60 Lyman Dr (05495-9621)
PHONE..............................802 399-2418
Dawn Lancaster, *Prin*
EMP: 11 **EST:** 2006
SALES (est): 302.27K **Privately Held**
Web: www.pureenergyvt.com
SIC: 2844 Perfumes, cosmetics and other toilet preparations

(G-17739)
LIMOGE & SONS GARAGE DOORS INC
Also Called: Limoge & Sons Garage Doors
136 James Brown Dr (05495-7388)
PHONE..............................802 878-4338
Rick Limoge, *Pr*
Mike O'grady, *Prin*
EMP: 10 **EST:** 1969
SQ FT: 4,500
SALES (est): 897.34K **Privately Held**
Web: www.limogegaragedoors.com
SIC: 5211 7699 3699 Garage doors, sale and installation; Garage door repair; Door opening and closing devices, electrical

(G-17740)
MCCLURE NEWSPAPERS INC
Also Called: Burlington Free Press
426 Industrial Ave Ste 160 (05495-4448)
P.O. Box 10 (05402-0010)
PHONE..............................802 863-3441
James M Carey, *Pr*
EMP: 220 **EST:** 1827
SALES (est): 29.03MM
SALES (corp-wide): 2.95B **Publicly Held**
SIC: 2711 2796 2791 2752 Newspapers, publishing and printing; Platemaking services; Typesetting; Commercial printing, lithographic
HQ: Gannett Satellite Information Network, Llc
7950 Jones Branch Dr
Mc Lean VA 22102
703 854-6000

(G-17741)
NEHP INC
1193 S Brownell Rd Ste 35 (05495-7416)
PHONE..............................802 652-1444
Adam Tarr, *CEO*
Russ Walton, *
Julie Spaniel, *
Robin Morris, *
EMP: 55 **EST:** 2000
SQ FT: 15,000
SALES (est): 11.12MM **Privately Held**
Web: www.nehp.com
SIC: 3674 Semiconductors and related devices

(G-17742)
NEW ENGLAND SUPPLY INC (PA)
Also Called: New England Chimney Supply
34 Commerce St (05495-8125)
PHONE..............................802 858-4577
Pierre Simard, *Pr*
Claudette Simard, *
EMP: 80 **EST:** 2010
SALES (est): 8.57MM
SALES (corp-wide): 8.57MM **Privately Held**
Web: www.newenglandchimneysupply.com
SIC: 3444 1791 1741 Flues and pipes, stove or furnace: sheet metal; Smoke stacks, steel: installation and maintenance; Chimney construction and maintenance

(G-17743)
NORTHEASTERN HTG VENT AC CORP
Also Called: Northeastern Heating & Vent
32 Boyer Cir (05495-8932)
PHONE..............................802 865-8008
Gary Riggs, *Pr*
EMP: 17 **EST:** 1978
SQ FT: 18,500
SALES (est): 736.5K **Privately Held**
SIC: 1711 3444 Mechanical contractor; Sheet metalwork

(G-17744)
PIKE INDUSTRIES INC
346 Avenue A (05495-7505)
P.O. Box 2224 (05495-2224)
PHONE..............................802 658-0453
Jay Perkins, *Mgr*
EMP: 9
SALES (corp-wide): 32.72B **Privately Held**
Web: www.pikeindustries.com
SIC: 1611 2951 General contractor, highway and street construction; Asphalt paving mixtures and blocks
HQ: Pike Industries, Inc.
3 Eastgate Park Dr
Belmont NH 03220
603 527-5100

(G-17745)
PRE-TECH PLASTICS INC (PA)
Also Called: Pre-Tech Plastic
209 Blair Park Rd (05495-7434)
P.O. Box 1086 (05495-1086)
PHONE..............................802 879-9441
EMP: 38 **EST:** 1985
SALES (est): 9.92MM
SALES (corp-wide): 9.92MM **Privately Held**
Web: www.pretechmachining.com
SIC: 3821 7692 3599 Laboratory apparatus and furniture; Welding repair; Machine and other job shop work

(G-17746)
PURMO GROUP USA INC
Also Called: Myson
45 Krupp Dr (05495-8911)
P.O. Box 1460 (05495-1460)
PHONE..............................802 654-7500
▲ **EMP:** 11 **EST:** 1977
SQ FT: 17,500
SALES (est): 2.39MM **Privately Held**
Web: www.mysoncomfort.com
SIC: 3567 Induction heating equipment

(G-17747)
S D IRELAND CON CNSTR CORP
Also Called: SD Ireland Companies

193 Industrial Ave (05495-8133)
P.O. Box 2286 (05407-2286)
PHONE..............................802 863-6222
Scott D Ireland, *CEO*
Stephen D Ireland, *
Andrew Marks, *
▲ **EMP:** 225 **EST:** 1974
SQ FT: 7,000
SALES (est): 49.69MM **Privately Held**
Web: www.sdireland.com
SIC: 1771 3273 Concrete work; Ready-mixed concrete

(G-17748)
SATHORN CORPORATION
581 Industrial Ave (05495-7129)
PHONE..............................802 860-2121
Bertrand Blazy, *CEO*
Bertran Blazy, *Pr*
EMP: 20 **EST:** 2012
SALES (est): 2.33MM **Privately Held**
Web: www.sathorncorporation.com
SIC: 3728 3599 Aircraft parts and equipment, nec; Machine shop, jobbing and repair

(G-17749)
SUPERMEDIA LLC
Also Called: Bell Atlantic Yellow Pages
34 Blair Park Rd (05495-7991)
PHONE..............................802 878-2336
EMP: 18
SALES (corp-wide): 1.81B **Privately Held**
SIC: 2741 Telephone and other directory publishing
HQ: Supermedia Llc
2200 W Airfield Dr
Dfw Airport TX 75261
972 453-7000

(G-17750)
TRANE COMPANY
177 Leroy Rd (05495-8909)
PHONE..............................802 864-3816
Brian Frary, *Mgr*
EMP: 7
Web: www.trane.com
SIC: 3585 5722 Refrigeration and heating equipment; Air conditioning room units, self-contained
HQ: The Trane Company
3600 Pammel Creek Rd
La Crosse WI 54601
608 787-2000

(G-17751)
VELAN VALVE CORP (DH)
94 Avenue C (05495-9732)
PHONE..............................802 863-2561
T Velan, *CEO*
A K Velan, *
I Velan, *
W Maar, *
V Apostolescu, *Quality Assurance Vice President*
◆ **EMP:** 83 **EST:** 1956
SQ FT: 153,000
SALES (est): 48.36MM
SALES (corp-wide): 437.82MM **Privately Held**
Web: www.velan.com
SIC: 5085 3491 Valves and fittings; Industrial valves
HQ: Velan Inc
7007 Ch De La Cote-De-Liesse
Saint-Laurent QC H4T 1
514 748-7743

▲ = Import ▼ = Export
◆ = Import/Export

(G-17752)
VERMONT ENGINE SERVICE INC
Also Called: Dixie Chopper of Vermont
16 Krupp Dr (05495-8929)
P.O. Box 513 (05495-0513)
PHONE................................802 863-2326
Robert Twomely, *Pr*
Harold Riley Junior, *VP*
Dean Thibodeau, *Sec*
EMP: 8 **EST:** 1985
SQ FT: 8,000
SALES (est): 731.54K **Privately Held**
Web: www.vermontengine.com
SIC: 7539 3599 Machine shop, automotive; Machine shop, jobbing and repair

(G-17753)
WILLISTON PUBG PROMOTIONS LLC
Also Called: Vermont Maturity
181 Wildflower Cir (05495-9390)
P.O. Box 1158 (05495-1158)
PHONE................................802 872-9000
EMP: 11 **EST:** 1985
SQ FT: 4,000
SALES (est): 802.24K **Privately Held**
Web: www.willistonpublishing.com
SIC: 2711 Newspapers, publishing and printing

Wilmington
Windham County

(G-17754)
INTELLIHOME OF VERMONT L L C
18 Coldbrook Rd (05363-9624)
P.O. Box 851 (05363-0851)
PHONE................................802 464-2499
EMP: 10 **EST:** 2001
SALES (est): 804.67K **Privately Held**
SIC: 3644 Fish wire (electrical wiring tool)

(G-17755)
JOHN MCLEOD LTD (PA)
Also Called: Snow Mountain Jwly & Graphics
111 W Main St (05363-9759)
P.O. Box 338 (05363-0338)
PHONE................................802 464-8175
John Mcleod, *Pr*
EMP: 20 **EST:** 1968
SQ FT: 13,500
SALES (est): 2.45MM
SALES (corp-wide): 2.45MM **Privately Held**
Web: www.vermontbowl.com
SIC: 2499 Woodenware, kitchen and household

(G-17756)
VERMONT MEDIA CORP
Also Called: Deerfield Valley News
797 Vt Route 100 N (05363-7919)
P.O. Box 310 (05356-0310)
PHONE................................802 464-5757
Randy Capitani, *Pr*
Vicki Capitani, *VP*
EMP: 24 **EST:** 1975
SALES (est): 2.26MM **Privately Held**
Web: www.dvalnews.com
SIC: 2711 Newspapers, publishing and printing

Windsor
Windsor County

(G-17757)
ASCUTNEY METAL PRODUCTS INC
2637 Us Route 5 N (05089-9723)
PHONE................................802 674-6721
Jeffery Koel, *Pr*
EMP: 15 **EST:** 1979
SQ FT: 15,000
SALES (est): 2.63MM
SALES (corp-wide): 65.55MM **Privately Held**
SIC: 3599 Machine and other job shop work
HQ: Spirol International Corporation
30 Rock Ave
Danielson CT 06239
860 774-8571

(G-17758)
FELLOWS CORPORATION
7 Everett Ln (05089-1444)
PHONE................................802 674-6500
EMP: 36 **EST:** 1896
SQ FT: 372,000
SALES (est): 1.59MM **Privately Held**
Web: www.fellowscorp.com
SIC: 3541 5084 Gear cutting and finishing machines; Industrial machinery and equipment

(G-17759)
LEBANON SCREW PRODUCTS INC
39 Park Rd (05089-4401)
P.O. Box 379 (05048-0379)
PHONE................................802 674-6347
David L Teffner, *Pr*
EMP: 10 **EST:** 1977
SALES (est): 989.7K **Privately Held**
Web: www.lsp-vt.com
SIC: 3451 Screw machine products

(G-17760)
MBBC VERMONT LLC
Also Called: Harpoon Brewery
336 Ruth Carney Dr (05089-9419)
PHONE................................802 674-5491
EMP: 26 **EST:** 1984
SQ FT: 10,000
SALES (est): 1.45MM
SALES (corp-wide): 49.92MM **Privately Held**
Web: www.harpoonbrewery.com
SIC: 2082 5921 Beer (alcoholic beverage); Beer (packaged)
PA: Mass. Bay Brewing Company, Inc.
306 Northern Ave
Boston MA 02210
617 574-9551

(G-17761)
PURCHASING INVENTORY CONS INC
Also Called: P I C
1706 Brook Rd (05089-9314)
PHONE................................802 674-2620
Francis Hurlburt, *Pr*
Gloria Hurlburt, *VP*
EMP: 12 **EST:** 1984
SQ FT: 9,500
SALES (est): 479.41K **Privately Held**
SIC: 3672 7379 Printed circuit boards; Computer related consulting services

(G-17762)
SIMON PEARCE (US) INC (PA)
Also Called: Simon Pearce Glass and Pottery
109 Park Rd (05089-4440)
PHONE................................802 674-6280
Clayton Adams, *CEO*
Patricia Mcdonnell-pearce, *Sec*
◆ **EMP:** 164 **EST:** 1981
SQ FT: 81,000
SALES (est): 49.22MM
SALES (corp-wide): 49.22MM **Privately Held**
Web: www.simonpearce.com
SIC: 3269 5719 5812 5949 Pottery household articles, except kitchen articles; Glassware; Ethnic food restaurants; Fabric stores piece goods

(G-17763)
SIMON PEARCE US INC
Also Called: Simon Pearce PA
109 Park Rd (05089-4440)
P.O. Box 1 (05089-0001)
PHONE................................802 674-6280
Rick Mickmasters, *Mgr*
EMP: 29
SALES (corp-wide): 49.22MM **Privately Held**
Web: www.simonpearce.com
SIC: 3229 Glass furnishings and accessories
PA: Simon Pearce (U.S.), Inc.
109 Park Rd
Windsor VT 05089
802 674-6280

(G-17764)
WILLEY EARTHMOVING CORP
Also Called: Willey Construction
1335 Hunt Rd (05089-9407)
PHONE................................802 674-2500
Desmond Willey, *Pr*
EMP: 8 **EST:** 1978
SALES (est): 980.46K **Privately Held**
SIC: 1794 2411 Excavation work; Logging camps and contractors

Winooski
Chittenden County

(G-17765)
AGILENT TECHNOLOGIES INC
100 Tigan St (05404-1356)
PHONE................................802 861-8597
Steve Mitchell, *Mgr*
EMP: 13
SALES (corp-wide): 6.83B **Publicly Held**
Web: www.agilent.com
SIC: 3826 7372 Gas testing apparatus; Prepackaged software
PA: Agilent Technologies, Inc.
5301 Stevens Creek Blvd
Santa Clara CA 95051
800 227-9770

(G-17766)
BIOTEK INSTRUMENTS INC
15 Tigan St (05404-1411)
PHONE................................802 655-4040
Briar Alpert, *Pr*
EMP: 7
SALES (corp-wide): 6.83B **Publicly Held**
Web: www.agilent.com
SIC: 3825 Instruments to measure electricity
HQ: Biotek Instruments, Inc.
100 Tigan St
Winooski VT 05404
802 655-4040

(G-17767)
BIOTEK INSTRUMENTS INC (HQ)
Also Called: Biotek
100 Tigan St (05404-1356)
P.O. Box 998 (05404-0998)
PHONE................................802 655-4040
Briar Alpert, *Pr*
Jamie Alpert, *
▲ **EMP:** 221 **EST:** 1968
SQ FT: 30,600
SALES (est): 67.61MM
SALES (corp-wide): 6.83B **Publicly Held**
Web: www.agilent.com
SIC: 3826 3841 Analytical instruments; Surgical and medical instruments
PA: Agilent Technologies, Inc.
5301 Stevens Creek Blvd
Santa Clara CA 95051
800 227-9770

(G-17768)
PRECI-MANUFACTURING INC
400 Weaver St (05404-1391)
PHONE................................802 655-2414
▲ **EMP:** 65 **EST:** 1977
SALES (est): 5MM **Privately Held**
Web: www.preci.com
SIC: 3577 3728 3841 3545 Computer peripheral equipment, nec; Aircraft parts and equipment, nec; Surgical and medical instruments; Machine tool accessories

(G-17769)
TWINCRAFT INC (PA)
Also Called: Twincraft Soap
2 Tigan St (05404-1326)
PHONE................................802 655-2200
Peter Asch, *Pr*
Richard Asch, *
Jim Howard, *
Joe Braun, *MFTG* *
Micheal Ly, *
▲ **EMP:** 176 **EST:** 1977
SALES (est): 48.33MM
SALES (corp-wide): 48.33MM **Privately Held**
Web: www.twincraft.com
SIC: 2841 7389 Soap and other detergents; Business services, nec

(G-17770)
VERMONT FURNITURE DESIGNS INC
4 Tigan St (05404-1326)
P.O. Box 4533 (05406-4533)
PHONE................................802 655-6568
Arthur Weitzenfeld, *Pr*
Sherry Smith, *
Shirley Adams, *
EMP: 18 **EST:** 1970
SQ FT: 35,000
SALES (est): 1.06MM **Privately Held**
Web: www.vermontfurnituredesigns.com
SIC: 2511 Wood household furniture

(G-17771)
VHV COMPANY (PA)
Also Called: Quality Air Control
16 Tigan St Ste A (05404-1326)
PHONE................................802 655-8805
David Brown, *Pr*
Charlie Spence, *
Kenneth Brown, *
Tim Potvin, *
Mike Voghell, *
▲ **EMP:** 128 **EST:** 1949
SQ FT: 27,500
SALES (est): 44.06MM
SALES (corp-wide): 44.06MM **Privately Held**

(PA)=Parent Co (HQ)=Headquarters
✪ = New Business established in last 2 years

2024 Harris New England
Manufacturers Directory

815

GEOGRAPHIC

Web: www.vhv.com
SIC: 1711 1761 1541 3444 Mechanical contractor; Sheet metal work, nec; Industrial buildings and warehouses; Sheet metalwork

(G-17772)
WHITESIDE HOLDINGS INC
Also Called: C L O V
11 Tigan St (05404-1327)
P.O. Box 9342 (05404)
PHONE...............................802 655-7654
TOLL FREE: 800
Dwane L Wall, *Pr*
Frederic T W Wall, *Sec*
EMP: 40 **EST:** 1969
SQ FT: 15,000
SALES (est): 5.47MM **Privately Held**
Web: www.clov.com
SIC: 2752 Offset printing

Wolcott
Lamoille County

(G-17773)
BELLAVANCE WELDING LLC
Also Called: United Steel
5471 Vt Rte 15 (05680-4159)
PHONE...............................802 793-9327
EMP: 7 **EST:** 2019
SALES (est): 201.33K **Privately Held**
SIC: 7692 Welding repair

(G-17774)
FOSTER INDUSTRIES INC
75 Cal Foster Dr (05680-4476)
PHONE...............................802 472-6147
Patricia Foster, *Pr*
Amy Sayers, *VP*
EMP: 15 **EST:** 1983
SQ FT: 7,000
SALES (est): 656.13K **Privately Held**
Web: www.fosterind.com
SIC: 3484 Pistols or pistol parts, 30 mm. and below

(G-17775)
HOLTON FAMILY MAPLE ✪
651 Morey Hill Rd (05680-4339)
PHONE...............................802 888-5183
David Holton, *Prin*
EMP: 7 **EST:** 2022
SALES (est): 78.66K **Privately Held**
SIC: 2099 Maple syrup

Woodstock
Windsor County

(G-17776)
LONGHILL PARTNERS INC (PA)
Also Called: Antoinette Leonard Associates
4 Sunset Farms (05091-1155)
P.O. Box 237 (05091-0237)
PHONE...............................802 457-4000
Stuart M Matlins, *Ch*
Emily Wichland V, *EDTRL*
Amy Wilson, *
Antoinette Leonard Matlins, *
▲ **EMP:** 26 **EST:** 1974
SQ FT: 4,000
SALES (est): 2.27MM
SALES (corp-wide): 2.27MM **Privately Held**
Web: www.longhillpartners.com
SIC: 2731 Books, publishing only

(G-17777)
REPIPER US INC
448 Woodstock Rd (05091-9759)
PHONE...............................802 230-5703
Patrik Brandt, *Pr*
Jesper Stockfors, *Dir*
EMP: 7 **EST:** 2018
SALES (est): 264.66K **Privately Held**
Web: www.repiper.com
SIC: 3429 Clamps, couplings, nozzles, and other metal hose fittings

(G-17778)
SUGARBUSH FARM INC
Also Called: Sugarbush Farm
591 Sugarbush Farm Rd (05091-8089)
PHONE...............................802 457-1757
Elizabeth Betsy Luce, *Pr*
Jeffery M Luce, *VP*
Lawerence Luce, *Treas*
Keery Mcnally, *Sec*
EMP: 7 **EST:** 1944
SQ FT: 8,000
SALES (est): 614.05K **Privately Held**
Web: www.sugarbushfarm.com
SIC: 2099 2022 5961 Maple syrup; Natural cheese; Cheese, mail order

(G-17779)
VERMONT STANDARD INC
23 Elm St (05091-1035)
P.O. Box 88 (05091-0088)
PHONE...............................802 457-1313
Philip Camp, *Pr*
Dan Cotter, *Publisher*
EMP: 10 **EST:** 1853
SALES (est): 854.71K **Privately Held**
Web: www.thevermontstandard.com
SIC: 2711 Newspapers: publishing only, not printed on site

(G-17780)
WILD APPLE GRAPHICS LTD
Also Called: Wild Apple
43 Lincoln Corners Way Ste 102
(05091-4057)
PHONE...............................802 457-3003
John Chester, *Pr*
Laurie Chester, *
EMP: 40 **EST:** 1990
SALES (est): 5.39MM **Privately Held**
Web: www.wildapple.com
SIC: 2741 Posters: publishing only, not printed on site

Worcester
Washington County

(G-17781)
GARDENMATS
374 Calais Rd (05682-9611)
PHONE...............................802 498-3314
Peter Comart, *Pr*
EMP: 7 **EST:** 2011
SALES (est): 197.84K **Privately Held**
Web: www.gardenmats.com
SIC: 5072 3423 Garden tools, hand; Garden and farm tools, including shovels

(G-17782)
STELLAR LASERS LLC
46 Worcester Village Rd (05682-9685)
PHONE...............................802 299-5411
Lillian Weisbart, *Prin*
EMP: 8 **EST:** 2011
SALES (est): 258.45K **Privately Held**
SIC: 3841 Surgical and medical instruments

SIC INDEX

Standard Industrial Classification Alphabetical Index

SIC

SIC NO	PRODUCT	SIC NO	PRODUCT	SIC NO	PRODUCT

3641 Electric lamps
4911 Electric services
5063 Electrical apparatus and equipment
5064 Electrical appliances, television and radio
3699 Electrical equipment and supplies, nec
3629 Electrical industrial apparatus
7629 Electrical repair shops
1731 Electrical work
3845 Electromedical equipment
3313 Electrometallurgical products
3671 Electron tubes
3675 Electronic capacitors
3677 Electronic coils and transformers
3679 Electronic components, nec
3571 Electronic computers
3678 Electronic connectors
5065 Electronic parts and equipment, nec
3676 Electronic resistors
8211 Elementary and secondary schools
3534 Elevators and moving stairways
7361 Employment agencies
3694 Engine electrical equipment
8711 Engineering services
7929 Entertainers and entertainment groups
2677 Envelopes
3822 Environmental controls
7359 Equipment rental and leasing, nec
1794 Excavation work
2892 Explosives

F

2381 Fabric dress and work gloves
3499 Fabricated metal products, nec
3498 Fabricated pipe and fittings
3443 Fabricated plate work (boiler shop)
3069 Fabricated rubber products, nec
3441 Fabricated structural metal
2399 Fabricated textile products, nec
8744 Facilities support services
5651 Family clothing stores
5083 Farm and garden machinery
3523 Farm machinery and equipment
5191 Farm supplies
5159 Farm-product raw materials, nec
3965 Fasteners, buttons, needles, and pins
6061 Federal credit unions
2875 Fertilizers, mixing only
2655 Fiber cans, drums, and similar products
0912 Finfish
2261 Finishing plants, cotton
2262 Finishing plants, manmade
2269 Finishing plants, nec
6331 Fire, marine, and casualty insurance
5146 Fish and seafoods
3211 Flat glass
2087 Flavoring extracts and syrups, nec
5713 Floor covering stores
1752 Floor laying and floor work, nec
5992 Florists
2041 Flour and other grain mill products
5193 Flowers and florists supplies
3824 Fluid meters and counting devices
2026 Fluid milk
3593 Fluid power cylinders and actuators
3594 Fluid power pumps and motors
3492 Fluid power valves and hose fittings
2657 Folding paperboard boxes
0182 Food crops grown under cover
2099 Food preparations, nec
3556 Food products machinery
5139 Footwear
3131 Footwear cut stock
3149 Footwear, except rubber, nec
0831 Forest products
0851 Forestry services
4731 Freight transportation arrangement
5148 Fresh fruits and vegetables
2092 Fresh or frozen packaged fish
2053 Frozen bakery products, except bread
2037 Frozen fruits and vegetables
2038 Frozen specialties, nec
5431 Fruit and vegetable markets

5989 Fuel dealers, nec
5983 Fuel oil dealers
6099 Functions related to depository banking
7261 Funeral service and crematories
2371 Fur goods
5021 Furniture
2599 Furniture and fixtures, nec
5712 Furniture stores

G

3944 Games, toys, and children's vehicles
3053 Gaskets; packing and sealing devices
5541 Gasoline service stations
7538 General automotive repair shops
0291 General farms, primarily animals
0191 General farms, primarily crop
9199 General government, nec
3569 General industrial machinery,
0219 General livestock, nec
8062 General medical and surgical hospitals
4225 General warehousing and storage
5947 Gift, novelty, and souvenir shop
2361 Girl's and children's dresses, blouses
2369 Girl's and children's outerwear, nec
1793 Glass and glazing work
3221 Glass containers
1041 Gold ores
5153 Grain and field beans
0172 Grapes
3321 Gray and ductile iron foundries
2771 Greeting cards
5149 Groceries and related products, nec
5141 Groceries, general line
5411 Grocery stores
3761 Guided missiles and space vehicles
3275 Gypsum products

H

3423 Hand and edge tools, nec
3996 Hard surface floor coverings, nec
5072 Hardware
5251 Hardware stores
3429 Hardware, nec
2426 Hardwood dimension and flooring mills
2435 Hardwood veneer and plywood
2353 Hats, caps, and millinery
8099 Health and allied services, nec
3433 Heating equipment, except electric
7353 Heavy construction equipment rental
1629 Heavy construction, nec
7363 Help supply services
1611 Highway and street construction
5945 Hobby, toy, and game shops
3536 Hoists, cranes, and monorails
6719 Holding companies, nec
8082 Home health care services
5023 Homefurnishings
2252 Hosiery, nec
6324 Hospital and medical service plans
7011 Hotels and motels
5722 Household appliance stores
3639 Household appliances, nec
3651 Household audio and video equipment
3631 Household cooking equipment
2392 Household furnishings, nec
2519 Household furniture, nec
3632 Household refrigerators and freezers
3635 Household vacuum cleaners

I

2024 Ice cream and frozen deserts
8322 Individual and family services
5113 Industrial and personal service paper
1541 Industrial buildings and warehouses
3567 Industrial furnaces and ovens
2813 Industrial gases
2819 Industrial inorganic chemicals, nec
7218 Industrial launderers
5084 Industrial machinery and equipment
3599 Industrial machinery, nec
2869 Industrial organic chemicals, nec
3543 Industrial patterns

1446 Industrial sand
5085 Industrial supplies
3537 Industrial trucks and tractors
3491 Industrial valves
7375 Information retrieval services
2816 Inorganic pigments
1796 Installing building equipment
3825 Instruments to measure electricity
6411 Insurance agents, brokers, and service
3519 Internal combustion engines, nec
6282 Investment advice
6726 Investment offices, nec
6799 Investors, nec
3462 Iron and steel forgings
1011 Iron ores

J

3915 Jewelers' materials and lapidary work
5094 Jewelry and precious stones
5944 Jewelry stores
3911 Jewelry, precious metal
8331 Job training and related services
8222 Junior colleges

K

1455 Kaolin and ball clay
8092 Kidney dialysis centers
2253 Knit outerwear mills
2259 Knitting mills, nec

L

3821 Laboratory apparatus and furniture
2258 Lace and warp knit fabric mills
3083 Laminated plastics plate and sheet
0781 Landscape counseling and planning
3524 Lawn and garden equipment
0782 Lawn and garden services
3952 Lead pencils and art goods
2386 Leather and sheep-lined clothing
3199 Leather goods, nec
3111 Leather tanning and finishing
8111 Legal services
3648 Lighting equipment, nec
3274 Lime
7213 Linen supply
5984 Liquefied petroleum gas dealers
5921 Liquor stores
4119 Local passenger transportation, nec
4214 Local trucking with storage
4212 Local trucking, without storage
2411 Logging
2992 Lubricating oils and greases
3161 Luggage
5948 Luggage and leather goods stores
5211 Lumber and other building materials
5031 Lumber, plywood, and millwork

M

2098 Macaroni and spaghetti
3545 Machine tool accessories
3541 Machine tools, metal cutting type
3542 Machine tools, metal forming type
3695 Magnetic and optical recording media
3322 Malleable iron foundries
2083 Malt
2082 Malt beverages
8742 Management consulting services
6722 Management investment, open-ended
8741 Management services
2761 Manifold business forms
2097 Manufactured ice
3999 Manufacturing industries, nec
4493 Marinas
4491 Marine cargo handling
3953 Marking devices
1741 Masonry and other stonework
2515 Mattresses and bedsprings
3829 Measuring and controlling devices, nec
3586 Measuring and dispensing pumps
5421 Meat and fish markets
2011 Meat packing plants
5147 Meats and meat products

SIC NO	PRODUCT
3061	Mechanical rubber goods
5047	Medical and hospital equipment
7352	Medical equipment rental
8071	Medical laboratories
2833	Medicinals and botanicals
8699	Membership organizations, nec
7997	Membership sports and recreation clubs
5136	Men's and boy's clothing
2329	Men's and boy's clothing, nec
2321	Men's and boy's furnishings
2323	Men's and boy's neckwear
2311	Men's and boy's suits and coats
2325	Men's and boy's trousers and slacks
2322	Men's and boy's underwear and nightwear
2326	Men's and boy's work clothing
5611	Men's and boys' clothing stores
3143	Men's footwear, except athletic
5962	Merchandising machine operators
3412	Metal barrels, drums, and pails
3411	Metal cans
3479	Metal coating and allied services
3442	Metal doors, sash, and trim
3497	Metal foil and leaf
3398	Metal heat treating
2514	Metal household furniture
1081	Metal mining services
3431	Metal sanitary ware
3469	Metal stampings, nec
5051	Metals service centers and offices
3549	Metalworking machinery, nec
2431	Millwork
3296	Mineral wool
3295	Minerals, ground or treated
3532	Mining machinery
5699	Miscellaneous apparel and accessories
6159	Miscellaneous business credit
3496	Miscellaneous fabricated wire products
5499	Miscellaneous food stores
5399	Miscellaneous general merchandise
5719	Miscellaneous homefurnishings
0919	Miscellaneous marine products
3449	Miscellaneous metalwork
1499	Miscellaneous nonmetallic mining
7299	Miscellaneous personal services
2741	Miscellaneous publishing
5999	Miscellaneous retail stores, nec
2451	Mobile homes
7822	Motion picture and tape distribution
7812	Motion picture and video production
3716	Motor homes
3714	Motor vehicle parts and accessories
5015	Motor vehicle parts, used
5013	Motor vehicle supplies and new parts
3711	Motor vehicles and car bodies
5571	Motorcycle dealers
3751	Motorcycles, bicycles, and parts
3621	Motors and generators
8412	Museums and art galleries
3931	Musical instruments

N

SIC NO	PRODUCT
2441	Nailed wood boxes and shook
2241	Narrow fabric mills
9711	National security
1321	Natural gas liquids
5511	New and used car dealers
7383	News syndicates
2711	Newspapers
2873	Nitrogenous fertilizers
3297	Nonclay refractories
8733	Noncommercial research organizations
3644	Noncurrent-carrying wiring devices
5199	Nondurable goods, nec
3364	Nonferrous die-castings except aluminum
3463	Nonferrous forgings
3369	Nonferrous foundries, nec
3356	Nonferrous rolling and drawing, nec
3357	Nonferrous wiredrawing and insulating
3299	Nonmetallic mineral products,
1481	Nonmetallic mineral services
6512	Nonresidential building operators
1542	Nonresidential construction, nec

SIC NO	PRODUCT
2297	Nonwoven fabrics

O

SIC NO	PRODUCT
5044	Office equipment
2522	Office furniture, except wood
3579	Office machines, nec
8041	Offices and clinics of chiropractors
8021	Offices and clinics of dentists
8011	Offices and clinics of medical doctors
8042	Offices and clinics of optometrists
8049	Offices of health practitioner
1382	Oil and gas exploration services
3533	Oil and gas field machinery
1389	Oil and gas field services, nec
1531	Operative builders
3851	Ophthalmic goods
5048	Ophthalmic goods
5995	Optical goods stores
3827	Optical instruments and lenses
3489	Ordnance and accessories, nec
2824	Organic fibers, noncellulosic
0181	Ornamental nursery products
0783	Ornamental shrub and tree services
7312	Outdoor advertising services

P

SIC NO	PRODUCT
5142	Packaged frozen goods
3565	Packaging machinery
4783	Packing and crating
5231	Paint, glass, and wallpaper stores
1721	Painting and paper hanging
2851	Paints and allied products
5198	Paints, varnishes, and supplies
3554	Paper industries machinery
2621	Paper mills
2671	Paper; coated and laminated packaging
2672	Paper; coated and laminated, nec
2631	Paperboard mills
2542	Partitions and fixtures, except wood
7514	Passenger car rental
6794	Patent owners and lessors
3951	Pens and mechanical pencils
2721	Periodicals
6141	Personal credit institutions
3172	Personal leather goods, nec
2999	Petroleum and coal products, nec
5172	Petroleum products, nec
2911	Petroleum refining
2834	Pharmaceutical preparations
7334	Photocopying and duplicating services
7384	Photofinish laboratories
3861	Photographic equipment and supplies
5043	Photographic equipment and supplies
7221	Photographic studios, portrait
2035	Pickles, sauces, and salad dressings
5131	Piece goods and notions
1742	Plastering, drywall, and insulation
3085	Plastics bottles
3086	Plastics foam products
5162	Plastics materials and basic shapes
2821	Plastics materials and resins
3084	Plastics pipe
3088	Plastics plumbing fixtures
3089	Plastics products, nec
2796	Platemaking services
3471	Plating and polishing
2395	Pleating and stitching
5074	Plumbing and hydronic heating supplies
3432	Plumbing fixture fittings and trim
1711	Plumbing, heating, air-conditioning
2842	Polishes and sanitation goods
3264	Porcelain electrical supplies
1474	Potash, soda, and borate minerals
2096	Potato chips and similar snacks
3269	Pottery products, nec
5144	Poultry and poultry products
0254	Poultry hatcheries
2015	Poultry slaughtering and processing
7211	Power laundries, family and commercial
3568	Power transmission equipment, nec
3546	Power-driven handtools
3448	Prefabricated metal buildings

SIC NO	PRODUCT
2452	Prefabricated wood buildings
7372	Prepackaged software
2048	Prepared feeds, nec
2045	Prepared flour mixes and doughs
3652	Prerecorded records and tapes
3229	Pressed and blown glass, nec
3334	Primary aluminum
3692	Primary batteries, dry and wet
3331	Primary copper
3399	Primary metal products
3339	Primary nonferrous metals, nec
3672	Printed circuit boards
5111	Printing and writing paper
2893	Printing ink
3555	Printing trades machinery
3823	Process control instruments
3231	Products of purchased glass
5049	Professional equipment, nec
8621	Professional organizations
2531	Public building and related furniture
7992	Public golf courses
8743	Public relations services
2611	Pulp mills
3561	Pumps and pumping equipment

R

SIC NO	PRODUCT
3663	Radio and t.v. communications equipment
7622	Radio and television repair
4832	Radio broadcasting stations
5731	Radio, television, and electronic stores
7313	Radio, television, publisher representatives
4812	Radiotelephone communication
3743	Railroad equipment
2061	Raw cane sugar
3273	Ready-mixed concrete
6531	Real estate agents and managers
6798	Real estate investment trusts
6519	Real property lessors, nec
2493	Reconstituted wood products
5561	Recreational vehicle dealers
4222	Refrigerated warehousing and storage
3585	Refrigeration and heating equipment
5078	Refrigeration equipment and supplies
7623	Refrigeration service and repair
4953	Refuse systems
9621	Regulation, administration of transportation
3625	Relays and industrial controls
8661	Religious organizations
7699	Repair services, nec
1522	Residential construction, nec
3645	Residential lighting fixtures
5461	Retail bakeries
5261	Retail nurseries and garden stores
7641	Reupholstery and furniture repair
2044	Rice milling
2095	Roasted coffee
2384	Robes and dressing gowns
3547	Rolling mill machinery
5033	Roofing, siding, and insulation
1761	Roofing, siding, and sheetmetal work
3021	Rubber and plastics footwear
3052	Rubber and plastics hose and beltings

S

SIC NO	PRODUCT
2068	Salted and roasted nuts and seeds
2656	Sanitary food containers
2676	Sanitary paper products
4959	Sanitary services, nec
2013	Sausages and other prepared meats
3425	Saw blades and handsaws
2421	Sawmills and planing mills, general
3596	Scales and balances, except laboratory
2397	Schiffli machine embroideries
4151	School buses
8299	Schools and educational services
5093	Scrap and waste materials
3451	Screw machine products
3812	Search and navigation equipment
3341	Secondary nonferrous metals
7338	Secretarial and court reporting
6211	Security brokers and dealers
7382	Security systems services

S I C

SIC NO	PRODUCT
3674	Semiconductors and related devices
3263	Semivitreous table and kitchenware
5087	Service establishment equipment
3589	Service industry machinery, nec
7819	Services allied to motion pictures
8999	Services, nec
2652	Setup paperboard boxes
5949	Sewing, needlework, and piece goods
3444	Sheet metalwork
3731	Shipbuilding and repairing
5661	Shoe stores
6153	Short-term business credit
3993	Signs and advertising specialties
3914	Silverware and plated ware
1521	Single-family housing construction
3484	Small arms
3482	Small arms ammunition
2841	Soap and other detergents
8399	Social services, nec
0711	Soil preparation services
3764	Space propulsion units and parts
3769	Space vehicle equipment, nec
3544	Special dies, tools, jigs, and fixtures
3559	Special industry machinery, nec
2429	Special product sawmills, nec
1799	Special trade contractors, nec
4226	Special warehousing and storage, nec
3566	Speed changers, drives, and gears
3949	Sporting and athletic goods, nec
5091	Sporting and recreation goods
5941	Sporting goods and bicycle shops
7941	Sports clubs, managers, and promoters
5112	Stationery and office supplies
2678	Stationery products
5943	Stationery stores
4961	Steam and air-conditioning supply
3325	Steel foundries, nec
3324	Steel investment foundries
3317	Steel pipe and tubes
3493	Steel springs, except wire
3315	Steel wire and related products
3691	Storage batteries
3259	Structural clay products, nec
1791	Structural steel erection
2439	Structural wood members, nec
6552	Subdividers and developers, nec
6351	Surety insurance
2843	Surface active agents
3841	Surgical and medical instruments
3842	Surgical appliances and supplies
8713	Surveying services
3613	Switchgear and switchboard apparatus
2822	Synthetic rubber

SIC NO	PRODUCT
	T
3795	Tanks and tank components
7291	Tax return preparation services
4822	Telegraph and other communications
3661	Telephone and telegraph apparatus
4813	Telephone communication, except radio
4833	Television broadcasting stations
1743	Terrazzo, tile, marble, mosaic work
8734	Testing laboratories
2393	Textile bags
2299	Textile goods, nec
3552	Textile machinery
7922	Theatrical producers and services
2284	Thread mills
2282	Throwing and winding mills
2296	Tire cord and fabrics
7534	Tire retreading and repair shops
3011	Tires and inner tubes
5014	Tires and tubes
5194	Tobacco and tobacco products
2141	Tobacco stemming and redrying
5993	Tobacco stores and stands
2844	Toilet preparations
7532	Top and body repair and paint shops
4492	Towing and tugboat service
5092	Toys and hobby goods and supplies
3612	Transformers, except electric
5088	Transportation equipment and supplies
3799	Transportation equipment, nec
4789	Transportation services, nec
4724	Travel agencies
3792	Travel trailers and campers
3713	Truck and bus bodies
7513	Truck rental and leasing, without drivers
3715	Truck trailers
4231	Trucking terminal facilities
4213	Trucking, except local
6733	Trusts, nec
6732	Trusts: educational, religious, etc.
3511	Turbines and turbine generator sets
0253	Turkeys and turkey eggs
2791	Typesetting
	U
3081	Unsupported plastics film and sheet
3082	Unsupported plastics profile shapes
2512	Upholstered household furniture
5521	Used car dealers
5932	Used merchandise stores
	V
3494	Valves and pipe fittings, nec
2076	Vegetable oil mills, nec

SIC NO	PRODUCT
0161	Vegetables and melons
3647	Vehicular lighting equipment
0741	Veterinary services for livestock
0742	Veterinary services, specialties
7841	Video tape rental
3261	Vitreous plumbing fixtures
8249	Vocational schools, nec
	W
5075	Warm air heating and air conditioning
7631	Watch, clock, and jewelry repair
3873	Watches, clocks, watchcases, and parts
4489	Water passenger transportation
4941	Water supply
4499	Water transportation services, nec
1781	Water well drilling
1623	Water, sewer, and utility lines
2385	Waterproof outerwear
2257	Weft knit fabric mills
3548	Welding apparatus
7692	Welding repair
2046	Wet corn milling
5182	Wine and distilled beverages
2084	Wines, brandy, and brandy spirits
3495	Wire springs
5632	Women's accessory and specialty stores
5137	Women's and children's clothing
2341	Women's and children's underwear
2331	Women's and misses' blouses and shirts
2339	Women's and misses' outerwear, nec
2337	Women's and misses' suits and coats
5621	Women's clothing stores
3144	Women's footwear, except athletic
3171	Women's handbags and purses
2251	Women's hosiery, except socks
2335	Women's, junior's, and misses' dresses
2449	Wood containers, nec
2511	Wood household furniture
2434	Wood kitchen cabinets
2521	Wood office furniture
2448	Wood pallets and skids
2541	Wood partitions and fixtures
2491	Wood preserving
2499	Wood products, nec
2517	Wood television and radio cabinets
3553	Woodworking machinery
1795	Wrecking and demolition work
	X
3844	X-ray apparatus and tubes
	Y
2281	Yarn spinning mills

SIC INDEX

Standard Industrial Classification Numerical Index

SIC NO	PRODUCT

01 agricultural production - crops

0119 Cash grains, nec
0161 Vegetables and melons
0171 Berry crops
0172 Grapes
0175 Deciduous tree fruits
0181 Ornamental nursery products
0182 Food crops grown under cover
0191 General farms, primarily crop

02 agricultural production - livestock and animal specialties

0219 General livestock, nec
0241 Dairy farms
0251 Broiler, fryer, and roaster chickens
0252 Chicken eggs
0253 Turkeys and turkey eggs
0254 Poultry hatcheries
0273 Animal aquaculture
0291 General farms, primarily animals

07 agricultural services

0711 Soil preparation services
0721 Crop planting and protection
0722 Crop harvesting
0723 Crop preparation services for market
0741 Veterinary services for livestock
0742 Veterinary services, specialties
0752 Animal specialty services
0781 Landscape counseling and planning
0782 Lawn and garden services
0783 Ornamental shrub and tree services

08 forestry

0831 Forest products
0851 Forestry services

09 fishing, hunting and trapping

0912 Finfish
0919 Miscellaneous marine products

10 metal mining

1011 Iron ores
1021 Copper ores
1041 Gold ores
1081 Metal mining services

12 coal mining

1221 Bituminous coal and lignite-surface mining
1222 Bituminous coal-underground mining
1231 Anthracite mining
1241 Coal mining services

13 oil and gas extraction

1311 Crude petroleum and natural gas
1321 Natural gas liquids
1381 Drilling oil and gas wells
1382 Oil and gas exploration services
1389 Oil and gas field services, nec

14 mining and quarrying of nonmetallic minerals, except fuels

1411 Dimension stone
1422 Crushed and broken limestone
1423 Crushed and broken granite
1429 Crushed and broken stone, nec
1442 Construction sand and gravel
1446 Industrial sand
1455 Kaolin and ball clay
1459 Clay and related minerals, nec
1474 Potash, soda, and borate minerals
1481 Nonmetallic mineral services
1499 Miscellaneous nonmetallic mining

15 construction - general contractors & operative builders

1521 Single-family housing construction
1522 Residential construction, nec
1531 Operative builders
1541 Industrial buildings and warehouses
1542 Nonresidential construction, nec

16 heamy construction, except building construction, contractor

1611 Highway and street construction
1622 Bridge, tunnel, and elevated highway
1623 Water, sewer, and utility lines
1629 Heavy construction, nec

17 construction - special trade contractors

1711 Plumbing, heating, air-conditioning
1721 Painting and paper hanging
1731 Electrical work
1741 Masonry and other stonework
1742 Plastering, drywall, and insulation
1743 Terrazzo, tile, marble, mosaic work
1751 Carpentry work
1752 Floor laying and floor work, nec
1761 Roofing, siding, and sheetmetal work
1771 Concrete work
1781 Water well drilling
1791 Structural steel erection
1793 Glass and glazing work
1794 Excavation work
1795 Wrecking and demolition work
1796 Installing building equipment
1799 Special trade contractors, nec

20 food and kindred products

2011 Meat packing plants
2013 Sausages and other prepared meats
2015 Poultry slaughtering and processing
2021 Creamery butter
2022 Cheese; natural and processed
2023 Dry, condensed, evaporated products
2024 Ice cream and frozen deserts
2026 Fluid milk
2032 Canned specialties
2033 Canned fruits and specialties
2034 Dehydrated fruits, vegetables, soups
2035 Pickles, sauces, and salad dressings
2037 Frozen fruits and vegetables
2038 Frozen specialties, nec
2041 Flour and other grain mill products
2043 Cereal breakfast foods
2044 Rice milling
2045 Prepared flour mixes and doughs
2046 Wet corn milling
2047 Dog and cat food
2048 Prepared feeds, nec
2051 Bread, cake, and related products
2052 Cookies and crackers
2053 Frozen bakery products, except bread
2061 Raw cane sugar
2062 Cane sugar refining
2063 Beet sugar
2064 Candy and other confectionery products
2066 Chocolate and cocoa products
2068 Salted and roasted nuts and seeds
2076 Vegetable oil mills, nec
2077 Animal and marine fats and oils
2079 Edible fats and oils
2082 Malt beverages
2083 Malt
2084 Wines, brandy, and brandy spirits
2085 Distilled and blended liquors
2086 Bottled and canned soft drinks
2087 Flavoring extracts and syrups, nec
2091 Canned and cured fish and seafoods

2092 Fresh or frozen packaged fish
2095 Roasted coffee
2096 Potato chips and similar snacks
2097 Manufactured ice
2098 Macaroni and spaghetti
2099 Food preparations, nec

21 tobacco products

2111 Cigarettes
2121 Cigars
2131 Chewing and smoking tobacco
2141 Tobacco stemming and redrying

22 textile mill products

2211 Broadwoven fabric mills, cotton
2221 Broadwoven fabric mills, manmade
2231 Broadwoven fabric mills, wool
2241 Narrow fabric mills
2251 Women's hosiery, except socks
2252 Hosiery, nec
2253 Knit outerwear mills
2257 Weft knit fabric mills
2258 Lace and warp knit fabric mills
2259 Knitting mills, nec
2261 Finishing plants, cotton
2262 Finishing plants, manmade
2269 Finishing plants, nec
2273 Carpets and rugs
2281 Yarn spinning mills
2282 Throwing and winding mills
2284 Thread mills
2295 Coated fabrics, not rubberized
2296 Tire cord and fabrics
2297 Nonwoven fabrics
2298 Cordage and twine
2299 Textile goods, nec

23 apparel, finished products from fabrics & similar materials

2311 Men's and boy's suits and coats
2321 Men's and boy's furnishings
2322 Men's and boy's underwear and nightwear
2323 Men's and boy's neckwear
2325 Men's and boy's trousers and slacks
2326 Men's and boy's work clothing
2329 Men's and boy's clothing, nec
2331 Women's and misses' blouses and shirts
2335 Women's, junior's, and misses' dresses
2337 Women's and misses' suits and coats
2339 Women's and misses' outerwear, nec
2341 Women's and children's underwear
2342 Bras, girdles, and allied garments
2353 Hats, caps, and millinery
2361 Girl's and children's dresses, blouses
2369 Girl's and children's outerwear, nec
2371 Fur goods
2381 Fabric dress and work gloves
2384 Robes and dressing gowns
2385 Waterproof outerwear
2386 Leather and sheep-lined clothing
2387 Apparel belts
2389 Apparel and accessories, nec
2391 Curtains and draperies
2392 Household furnishings, nec
2393 Textile bags
2394 Canvas and related products
2395 Pleating and stitching
2396 Automotive and apparel trimmings
2397 Schiffli machine embroideries
2399 Fabricated textile products, nec

24 lumber and wood products, except furniture

2411 Logging
2421 Sawmills and planing mills, general
2426 Hardwood dimension and flooring mills

SIC NO	PRODUCT
2429	Special product sawmills, nec
2431	Millwork
2434	Wood kitchen cabinets
2435	Hardwood veneer and plywood
2439	Structural wood members, nec
2441	Nailed wood boxes and shook
2448	Wood pallets and skids
2449	Wood containers, nec
2451	Mobile homes
2452	Prefabricated wood buildings
2491	Wood preserving
2493	Reconstituted wood products
2499	Wood products, nec

25 furniture and fixtures

SIC NO	PRODUCT
2511	Wood household furniture
2512	Upholstered household furniture
2514	Metal household furniture
2515	Mattresses and bedsprings
2517	Wood television and radio cabinets
2519	Household furniture, nec
2521	Wood office furniture
2522	Office furniture, except wood
2531	Public building and related furniture
2541	Wood partitions and fixtures
2542	Partitions and fixtures, except wood
2591	Drapery hardware and blinds and shades
2599	Furniture and fixtures, nec

26 paper and allied products

SIC NO	PRODUCT
2611	Pulp mills
2621	Paper mills
2631	Paperboard mills
2652	Setup paperboard boxes
2653	Corrugated and solid fiber boxes
2655	Fiber cans, drums, and similar products
2656	Sanitary food containers
2657	Folding paperboard boxes
2671	Paper; coated and laminated packaging
2672	Paper; coated and laminated, nec
2673	Bags: plastic, laminated, and coated
2674	Bags: uncoated paper and multiwall
2675	Die-cut paper and board
2676	Sanitary paper products
2677	Envelopes
2678	Stationery products
2679	Converted paper products, nec

27 printing, publishing and allied industries

SIC NO	PRODUCT
2711	Newspapers
2721	Periodicals
2731	Book publishing
2732	Book printing
2741	Miscellaneous publishing
2752	Commercial printing, lithographic
2754	Commercial printing, gravure
2759	Commercial printing, nec
2761	Manifold business forms
2771	Greeting cards
2782	Blankbooks and looseleaf binders
2789	Bookbinding and related work
2791	Typesetting
2796	Platemaking services

28 chemicals and allied products

SIC NO	PRODUCT
2812	Alkalies and chlorine
2813	Industrial gases
2816	Inorganic pigments
2819	Industrial inorganic chemicals, nec
2821	Plastics materials and resins
2822	Synthetic rubber
2823	Cellulosic manmade fibers
2824	Organic fibers, noncellulosic
2833	Medicinals and botanicals
2834	Pharmaceutical preparations
2835	Diagnostic substances
2836	Biological products, except diagnostic
2841	Soap and other detergents
2842	Polishes and sanitation goods
2843	Surface active agents
2844	Toilet preparations
2851	Paints and allied products

SIC NO	PRODUCT
2865	Cyclic crudes and intermediates
2869	Industrial organic chemicals, nec
2873	Nitrogenous fertilizers
2875	Fertilizers, mixing only
2879	Agricultural chemicals, nec
2891	Adhesives and sealants
2892	Explosives
2893	Printing ink
2895	Carbon black
2899	Chemical preparations, nec

29 petroleum refining and related industries

SIC NO	PRODUCT
2911	Petroleum refining
2951	Asphalt paving mixtures and blocks
2952	Asphalt felts and coatings
2992	Lubricating oils and greases
2999	Petroleum and coal products, nec

30 rubber and miscellaneous plastic products

SIC NO	PRODUCT
3011	Tires and inner tubes
3021	Rubber and plastics footwear
3052	Rubber and plastics hose and beltings
3053	Gaskets; packing and sealing devices
3061	Mechanical rubber goods
3069	Fabricated rubber products, nec
3081	Unsupported plastics film and sheet
3082	Unsupported plastics profile shapes
3083	Laminated plastics plate and sheet
3084	Plastics pipe
3085	Plastics bottles
3086	Plastics foam products
3087	Custom compound purchased resins
3088	Plastics plumbing fixtures
3089	Plastics products, nec

31 leather and leather products

SIC NO	PRODUCT
3111	Leather tanning and finishing
3131	Footwear cut stock
3143	Men's footwear, except athletic
3144	Women's footwear, except athletic
3149	Footwear, except rubber, nec
3161	Luggage
3171	Women's handbags and purses
3172	Personal leather goods, nec
3199	Leather goods, nec

32 stone, clay, glass, and concrete products

SIC NO	PRODUCT
3211	Flat glass
3221	Glass containers
3229	Pressed and blown glass, nec
3231	Products of purchased glass
3241	Cement, hydraulic
3251	Brick and structural clay tile
3253	Ceramic wall and floor tile
3255	Clay refractories
3259	Structural clay products, nec
3261	Vitreous plumbing fixtures
3263	Semivitreous table and kitchenware
3264	Porcelain electrical supplies
3269	Pottery products, nec
3271	Concrete block and brick
3272	Concrete products, nec
3273	Ready-mixed concrete
3274	Lime
3275	Gypsum products
3281	Cut stone and stone products
3291	Abrasive products
3292	Asbestos products
3295	Minerals, ground or treated
3296	Mineral wool
3297	Nonclay refractories
3299	Nonmetallic mineral products,

33 primary metal industries

SIC NO	PRODUCT
3312	Blast furnaces and steel mills
3313	Electrometallurgical products
3315	Steel wire and related products
3316	Cold finishing of steel shapes
3317	Steel pipe and tubes
3321	Gray and ductile iron foundries
3322	Malleable iron foundries
3324	Steel investment foundries

SIC NO	PRODUCT
3325	Steel foundries, nec
3331	Primary copper
3334	Primary aluminum
3339	Primary nonferrous metals, nec
3341	Secondary nonferrous metals
3351	Copper rolling and drawing
3353	Aluminum sheet, plate, and foil
3354	Aluminum extruded products
3355	Aluminum rolling and drawing, nec
3356	Nonferrous rolling and drawing, nec
3357	Nonferrous wiredrawing and insulating
3363	Aluminum die-castings
3364	Nonferrous die-castings except aluminum
3365	Aluminum foundries
3366	Copper foundries
3369	Nonferrous foundries, nec
3398	Metal heat treating
3399	Primary metal products

34 fabricated metal products

SIC NO	PRODUCT
3411	Metal cans
3412	Metal barrels, drums, and pails
3421	Cutlery
3423	Hand and edge tools, nec
3425	Saw blades and handsaws
3429	Hardware, nec
3431	Metal sanitary ware
3432	Plumbing fixture fittings and trim
3433	Heating equipment, except electric
3441	Fabricated structural metal
3442	Metal doors, sash, and trim
3443	Fabricated plate work (boiler shop)
3444	Sheet metalwork
3446	Architectural metalwork
3448	Prefabricated metal buildings
3449	Miscellaneous metalwork
3451	Screw machine products
3452	Bolts, nuts, rivets, and washers
3462	Iron and steel forgings
3463	Nonferrous forgings
3465	Automotive stampings
3466	Crowns and closures
3469	Metal stampings, nec
3471	Plating and polishing
3479	Metal coating and allied services
3482	Small arms ammunition
3483	Ammunition, except for small arms, nec
3484	Small arms
3489	Ordnance and accessories, nec
3491	Industrial valves
3492	Fluid power valves and hose fittings
3493	Steel springs, except wire
3494	Valves and pipe fittings, nec
3495	Wire springs
3496	Miscellaneous fabricated wire products
3497	Metal foil and leaf
3498	Fabricated pipe and fittings
3499	Fabricated metal products, nec

35 industrial and commercial machinery and computer equipment

SIC NO	PRODUCT
3511	Turbines and turbine generator sets
3519	Internal combustion engines, nec
3523	Farm machinery and equipment
3524	Lawn and garden equipment
3531	Construction machinery
3532	Mining machinery
3533	Oil and gas field machinery
3534	Elevators and moving stairways
3535	Conveyors and conveying equipment
3536	Hoists, cranes, and monorails
3537	Industrial trucks and tractors
3541	Machine tools, metal cutting type
3542	Machine tools, metal forming type
3543	Industrial patterns
3544	Special dies, tools, jigs, and fixtures
3545	Machine tool accessories
3546	Power-driven handtools
3547	Rolling mill machinery
3548	Welding apparatus
3549	Metalworking machinery, nec
3552	Textile machinery

SIC NO	PRODUCT

3553 Woodworking machinery
3554 Paper industries machinery
3555 Printing trades machinery
3556 Food products machinery
3559 Special industry machinery, nec
3561 Pumps and pumping equipment
3562 Ball and roller bearings
3563 Air and gas compressors
3564 Blowers and fans
3565 Packaging machinery
3566 Speed changers, drives, and gears
3567 Industrial furnaces and ovens
3568 Power transmission equipment, nec
3569 General industrial machinery,
3571 Electronic computers
3572 Computer storage devices
3575 Computer terminals
3577 Computer peripheral equipment, nec
3578 Calculating and accounting equipment
3579 Office machines, nec
3581 Automatic vending machines
3582 Commercial laundry equipment
3585 Refrigeration and heating equipment
3586 Measuring and dispensing pumps
3589 Service industry machinery, nec
3592 Carburetors, pistons, rings, valves
3593 Fluid power cylinders and actuators
3594 Fluid power pumps and motors
3596 Scales and balances, except laboratory
3599 Industrial machinery, nec

36 electronic & other electrical equipment & components

3612 Transformers, except electric
3613 Switchgear and switchboard apparatus
3621 Motors and generators
3624 Carbon and graphite products
3625 Relays and industrial controls
3629 Electrical industrial apparatus
3631 Household cooking equipment
3632 Household refrigerators and freezers
3634 Electric housewares and fans
3635 Household vacuum cleaners
3639 Household appliances, nec
3641 Electric lamps
3643 Current-carrying wiring devices
3644 Noncurrent-carrying wiring devices
3645 Residential lighting fixtures
3646 Commercial lighting fixtures
3647 Vehicular lighting equipment
3648 Lighting equipment, nec
3651 Household audio and video equipment
3652 Prerecorded records and tapes
3661 Telephone and telegraph apparatus
3663 Radio and t.v. communications equipment
3669 Communications equipment, nec
3671 Electron tubes
3672 Printed circuit boards
3674 Semiconductors and related devices
3675 Electronic capacitors
3676 Electronic resistors
3677 Electronic coils and transformers
3678 Electronic connectors
3679 Electronic components, nec
3691 Storage batteries
3692 Primary batteries, dry and wet
3694 Engine electrical equipment
3695 Magnetic and optical recording media
3699 Electrical equipment and supplies, nec

37 transportation equipment

3711 Motor vehicles and car bodies
3713 Truck and bus bodies
3714 Motor vehicle parts and accessories
3715 Truck trailers
3716 Motor homes
3721 Aircraft
3724 Aircraft engines and engine parts
3728 Aircraft parts and equipment, nec
3731 Shipbuilding and repairing
3732 Boatbuilding and repairing
3743 Railroad equipment
3751 Motorcycles, bicycles, and parts

3761 Guided missiles and space vehicles
3764 Space propulsion units and parts
3769 Space vehicle equipment, nec
3792 Travel trailers and campers
3795 Tanks and tank components
3799 Transportation equipment, nec

38 measuring, photographic, medical, & optical goods, & clocks

3812 Search and navigation equipment
3821 Laboratory apparatus and furniture
3822 Environmental controls
3823 Process control instruments
3824 Fluid meters and counting devices
3825 Instruments to measure electricity
3826 Analytical instruments
3827 Optical instruments and lenses
3829 Measuring and controlling devices, nec
3841 Surgical and medical instruments
3842 Surgical appliances and supplies
3843 Dental equipment and supplies
3844 X-ray apparatus and tubes
3845 Electromedical equipment
3851 Ophthalmic goods
3861 Photographic equipment and supplies
3873 Watches, clocks, watchcases, and parts

39 miscellaneous manufacturing industries

3911 Jewelry, precious metal
3914 Silverware and plated ware
3915 Jewelers' materials and lapidary work
3931 Musical instruments
3942 Dolls and stuffed toys
3944 Games, toys, and children's vehicles
3949 Sporting and athletic goods, nec
3951 Pens and mechanical pencils
3952 Lead pencils and art goods
3953 Marking devices
3955 Carbon paper and inked ribbons
3961 Costume jewelry
3965 Fasteners, buttons, needles, and pins
3991 Brooms and brushes
3993 Signs and advertising specialties
3996 Hard surface floor coverings, nec
3999 Manufacturing industries, nec

41 local & suburban transit & interurban highway transportation

4119 Local passenger transportation, nec
4151 School buses

42 motor freight transportation

4212 Local trucking, without storage
4213 Trucking, except local
4214 Local trucking with storage
4215 Courier services, except by air
4222 Refrigerated warehousing and storage
4225 General warehousing and storage
4226 Special warehousing and storage, nec
4231 Trucking terminal facilities

44 water transportation

4424 Deep sea domestic transportation of freight
4489 Water passenger transportation
4491 Marine cargo handling
4492 Towing and tugboat service
4493 Marinas
4499 Water transportation services, nec

45 transportation by air

4581 Airports, flying fields, and services

47 transportation services

4724 Travel agencies
4731 Freight transportation arrangement
4783 Packing and crating
4789 Transportation services, nec

48 communications

4812 Radiotelephone communication
4813 Telephone communication, except radio
4822 Telegraph and other communications

4832 Radio broadcasting stations
4833 Television broadcasting stations
4841 Cable and other pay television services
4899 Communication services, nec

49 electric, gas and sanitary services

4911 Electric services
4931 Electric and other services combined
4941 Water supply
4953 Refuse systems
4959 Sanitary services, nec
4961 Steam and air-conditioning supply

50 wholesale trade - durable goods

5012 Automobiles and other motor vehicles
5013 Motor vehicle supplies and new parts
5014 Tires and tubes
5015 Motor vehicle parts, used
5021 Furniture
5023 Homefurnishings
5031 Lumber, plywood, and millwork
5032 Brick, stone, and related material
5033 Roofing, siding, and insulation
5039 Construction materials, nec
5043 Photographic equipment and supplies
5044 Office equipment
5045 Computers, peripherals, and software
5046 Commercial equipment, nec
5047 Medical and hospital equipment
5048 Ophthalmic goods
5049 Professional equipment, nec
5051 Metals service centers and offices
5052 Coal and other minerals and ores
5063 Electrical apparatus and equipment
5064 Electrical appliances, television and radio
5065 Electronic parts and equipment, nec
5072 Hardware
5074 Plumbing and hydronic heating supplies
5075 Warm air heating and air conditioning
5078 Refrigeration equipment and supplies
5082 Construction and mining machinery
5083 Farm and garden machinery
5084 Industrial machinery and equipment
5085 Industrial supplies
5087 Service establishment equipment
5088 Transportation equipment and supplies
5091 Sporting and recreation goods
5092 Toys and hobby goods and supplies
5093 Scrap and waste materials
5094 Jewelry and precious stones
5099 Durable goods, nec

51 wholesale trade - nondurable goods

5111 Printing and writing paper
5112 Stationery and office supplies
5113 Industrial and personal service paper
5122 Drugs, proprietaries, and sundries
5131 Piece goods and notions
5136 Men's and boy's clothing
5137 Women's and children's clothing
5139 Footwear
5141 Groceries, general line
5142 Packaged frozen goods
5143 Dairy products, except dried or canned
5144 Poultry and poultry products
5145 Confectionery
5146 Fish and seafoods
5147 Meats and meat products
5148 Fresh fruits and vegetables
5149 Groceries and related products, nec
5153 Grain and field beans
5159 Farm-product raw materials, nec
5162 Plastics materials and basic shapes
5169 Chemicals and allied products, nec
5172 Petroleum products, nec
5181 Beer and ale
5182 Wine and distilled beverages
5191 Farm supplies
5192 Books, periodicals, and newspapers
5193 Flowers and florists supplies
5194 Tobacco and tobacco products
5198 Paints, varnishes, and supplies

**S
I
C**

SIC NO	PRODUCT

5199 Nondurable goods, nec

52 building materials, hardware, garden supplies & mobile homes

5211 Lumber and other building materials
5231 Paint, glass, and wallpaper stores
5251 Hardware stores
5261 Retail nurseries and garden stores

53 general merchandise stores

5311 Department stores
5399 Miscellaneous general merchandise

54 food stores

5411 Grocery stores
5421 Meat and fish markets
5431 Fruit and vegetable markets
5441 Candy, nut, and confectionery stores
5451 Dairy products stores
5461 Retail bakeries
5499 Miscellaneous food stores

55 automotive dealers and gasoline service stations

5511 New and used car dealers
5521 Used car dealers
5531 Auto and home supply stores
5541 Gasoline service stations
5551 Boat dealers
5561 Recreational vehicle dealers
5571 Motorcycle dealers
5599 Automotive dealers, nec

56 apparel and accessory stores

5611 Men's and boys' clothing stores
5621 Women's clothing stores
5632 Women's accessory and specialty stores
5641 Children's and infants' wear stores
5651 Family clothing stores
5661 Shoe stores
5699 Miscellaneous apparel and accessories

57 home furniture, furnishings and equipment stores

5712 Furniture stores
5713 Floor covering stores
5714 Drapery and upholstery stores
5719 Miscellaneous homefurnishings
5722 Household appliance stores
5731 Radio, television, and electronic stores
5734 Computer and software stores

58 eating and drinking places

5812 Eating places
5813 Drinking places

59 miscellaneous retail

5912 Drug stores and proprietary stores
5921 Liquor stores
5932 Used merchandise stores
5941 Sporting goods and bicycle shops
5942 Book stores
5943 Stationery stores
5944 Jewelry stores
5945 Hobby, toy, and game shops
5946 Camera and photographic supply stores
5947 Gift, novelty, and souvenir shop
5948 Luggage and leather goods stores
5949 Sewing, needlework, and piece goods
5961 Catalog and mail-order houses
5962 Merchandising machine operators
5963 Direct selling establishments
5983 Fuel oil dealers
5984 Liquefied petroleum gas dealers
5989 Fuel dealers, nec
5992 Florists
5993 Tobacco stores and stands
5995 Optical goods stores
5999 Miscellaneous retail stores, nec

60 depository institutions

6061 Federal credit unions
6099 Functions related to depository banking

61 nondepository credit institutions

6141 Personal credit institutions
6153 Short-term business credit
6159 Miscellaneous business credit

62 security & commodity brokers, dealers, exchanges & services

6211 Security brokers and dealers
6221 Commodity contracts brokers, dealers
6282 Investment advice

63 insurance carriers

6321 Accident and health insurance
6324 Hospital and medical service plans
6331 Fire, marine, and casualty insurance
6351 Surety insurance

64 insurance agents, brokers and service

6411 Insurance agents, brokers, and service

65 real estate

6512 Nonresidential building operators
6513 Apartment building operators
6514 Dwelling operators, except apartments
6519 Real property lessors, nec
6531 Real estate agents and managers
6552 Subdividers and developers, nec

67 holding and other investment offices

6712 Bank holding companies
6719 Holding companies, nec
6722 Management investment, open-ended
6726 Investment offices, nec
6732 Trusts: educational, religious, etc.
6733 Trusts, nec
6794 Patent owners and lessors
6798 Real estate investment trusts
6799 Investors, nec

70 hotels, rooming houses, camps, and other lodging places

7011 Hotels and motels

72 personal services

7211 Power laundries, family and commercial
7213 Linen supply
7216 Drycleaning plants, except rugs
7217 Carpet and upholstery cleaning
7218 Industrial launderers
7221 Photographic studios, portrait
7231 Beauty shops
7261 Funeral service and crematories
7291 Tax return preparation services
7299 Miscellaneous personal services

73 business services

7311 Advertising agencies
7312 Outdoor advertising services
7313 Radio, television, publisher representatives
7319 Advertising, nec
7331 Direct mail advertising services
7334 Photocopying and duplicating services
7335 Commercial photography
7336 Commercial art and graphic design
7338 Secretarial and court reporting
7342 Disinfecting and pest control services
7349 Building maintenance services, nec
7352 Medical equipment rental
7353 Heavy construction equipment rental
7359 Equipment rental and leasing, nec
7361 Employment agencies
7363 Help supply services
7371 Custom computer programming services
7372 Prepackaged software
7373 Computer integrated systems design
7374 Data processing and preparation
7375 Information retrieval services
7376 Computer facilities management
7378 Computer maintenance and repair
7379 Computer related services, nec
7381 Detective and armored car services
7382 Security systems services

7383 News syndicates
7384 Photofinish laboratories
7389 Business services, nec

75 automotive repair, services and parking

7513 Truck rental and leasing, without drivers
7514 Passenger car rental
7532 Top and body repair and paint shops
7533 Auto exhaust system repair shops
7534 Tire retreading and repair shops
7536 Automotive glass replacement shops
7537 Automotive transmission repair shops
7538 General automotive repair shops
7539 Automotive repair shops, nec
7542 Carwashes
7549 Automotive services, nec

76 miscellaneous repair services

7622 Radio and television repair
7623 Refrigeration service and repair
7629 Electrical repair shops
7631 Watch, clock, and jewelry repair
7641 Reupholstery and furniture repair
7692 Welding repair
7694 Armature rewinding shops
7699 Repair services, nec

78 motion pictures

7812 Motion picture and video production
7819 Services allied to motion pictures
7822 Motion picture and tape distribution
7841 Video tape rental

79 amusement and recreation services

7911 Dance studios, schools, and halls
7922 Theatrical producers and services
7929 Entertainers and entertainment groups
7933 Bowling centers
7941 Sports clubs, managers, and promoters
7992 Public golf courses
7993 Coin-operated amusement devices
7997 Membership sports and recreation clubs
7999 Amusement and recreation, nec

80 health services

8011 Offices and clinics of medical doctors
8021 Offices and clinics of dentists
8041 Offices and clinics of chiropractors
8042 Offices and clinics of optometrists
8049 Offices of health practitioner
8062 General medical and surgical hospitals
8071 Medical laboratories
8072 Dental laboratories
8082 Home health care services
8092 Kidney dialysis centers
8099 Health and allied services, nec

81 legal services

8111 Legal services

82 educational services

8211 Elementary and secondary schools
8221 Colleges and universities
8222 Junior colleges
8243 Data processing schools
8249 Vocational schools, nec
8299 Schools and educational services

83 social services

8322 Individual and family services
8331 Job training and related services
8399 Social services, nec

84 museums, art galleries and botanical and zoological gardens

8412 Museums and art galleries

86 membership organizations

8611 Business associations
8621 Professional organizations
8641 Civic and social associations
8661 Religious organizations

SIC NO	PRODUCT

8699 Membership organizations, nec

87 engineering, accounting, research, and management services

8711 Engineering services
8712 Architectural services
8713 Surveying services
8721 Accounting, auditing, and bookkeeping
8731 Commercial physical research
8732 Commercial nonphysical research
8733 Noncommercial research organizations
8734 Testing laboratories
8741 Management services

SIC NO	PRODUCT

8742 Management consulting services
8743 Public relations services
8744 Facilities support services
8748 Business consulting, nec

89 services, not elsewhere classified

8999 Services, nec

91 executive, legislative & general government, except finance

9199 General government, nec

SIC NO	PRODUCT

92 justice, public order and safety

9223 Correctional institutions

95 administration of environmental quality and housing programs

9511 Air, water, and solid waste management

96 administration of economic programs

9621 Regulation, administration of transportation

97 national security and international affairs

9711 National security

S
I
C

	CITY	ST	EMP	PHONE	ENTRY#
3089 Plastic Products, NEC					
Lees Indl Prdts Co	Albany	NY	A	518 699-3333	23054
Molded Plastics Co	Canton	OH	C	913 771-1117	27566
National Gadget Mfg (HQ)	Kansas City	KS	A	913 999-7777	39167

4-digit SIC number & description

Designates this location as a headquarters

Employment codes
A = over 500 employees
B = 251-500, C = 101-250
D = 51-100, E = 20-50
F = 10-19, G = 1-9

Geographic Section entry number where full company information appears

Business phone

See footnotes for symbols and codes identification.

- The SIC codes in this section are from the latest Standard Industrial Classification manual published by the U.S. Government's Office of Management and Budget. For more information regarding SICs, see the Explanatory Notes.
- Companies may be listed under multiple classifications.

	CITY	ST	EMP	PHONE	ENTRY#
01 AGRICULTURAL PRODUCTION - CROPS					
0119 Cash grains, nec					
Eagle Ship Management LLC (HQ)	Stamford	CT	C	203 276-8100	3340
0161 Vegetables and melons					
Sogle Property LLC	Cambridge	VT	E	802 849-7943	17168
0171 Berry crops					
Decas Cranberry Products Inc (PA)	Carver	MA	E	508 866-8506	7853
Hamilton Orchards	New Salem	MA	F	978 544-6867	10664
Jasper Wyman & Son	Deblois	ME	F	207 638-2201	4721
0172 Grapes					
Grape Island Inc	Rowley	MA	G	978 432-1280	11675
Sakonnet Vineyards LP	Little Compton	RI	F	401 635-8486	16162
0175 Deciduous tree fruits					
Lyman Farm Incorporated (PA)	Middlefield	CT	C	860 349-1793	1725
Hamilton Orchards	New Salem	MA	F	978 544-6867	10664
Meadowbrook Orchards Inc	Sterling	MA	F	978 365-7617	12167
Lane Poverty Orchard	Lebanon	NH	G	603 448-1511	14692
0181 Ornamental nursery products					
Pleasant View Gardens Inc (PA)	Loudon	NH	D	603 435-8361	14799
0182 Food crops grown under cover					
Freight Farms Inc	Boston	MA	E	877 687-4326	6748
Sunrise Group USA LLC	Shrewsbury	MA	E	508 873-1519	11842
0191 General farms, primarily crop					
Macristy Industries Inc (PA)	Newington	CT	F	860 225-4637	2305
Point3 Farma LLC	Northampton	MA	G	719 733-3900	11077
Haymart LLC	Patten	ME	G	207 528-2058	5153
Lucerne Farms	Fort Fairfield	ME	E	207 488-2520	4785
Springworks Farm Maine Inc	Lisbon	ME	F	207 407-4207	5017
Coyote Mountain Farm Inc	Ossipee	NH	G	603 662-2164	15282
02 AGRICULTURAL PRODUCTION - LIVESTOCK AND ANIMAL SPECIALTIES					
0219 General livestock, nec					
Idexx Laboratories Inc (PA)	Westbrook	ME	A	207 556-0300	5631
0241 Dairy farms					
Willard J Stearns & Sons Inc	Storrs Mansfield	CT	E	860 423-9289	3513
Dunajski Dairy Inc	Peabody	MA	G	978 531-1457	11308
Grey Barn Farm Enterprises LLC	Chilmark	MA	G	508 645-4854	8071
Peaceful Meadows Ice Cream Inc (PA)	Carver	MA	F	781 447-3700	7855
Whittier Farms Inc	Sutton	MA	G	508 865-1096	12295
Wrights Dairy Farm Inc	North Smithfield	RI	E	401 767-3014	16334
Larry G Carabeau	Tinmouth	VT	G	802 446-3123	17648
Monument Farms Inc	Weybridge	VT	E	802 545-2119	17703

	CITY	ST	EMP	PHONE	ENTRY#
0251 Broiler, fryer, and roaster chickens					
Baffonis Poultry Farm Inc	Johnston	RI	E	401 231-6315	16077
0252 Chicken eggs					
Avian Vaccine Services LLC (PA)	Norwich	CT	D	860 889-1389	2602
Moark LLC (HQ)	North Franklin	CT	E	951 332-3300	2383
Diemand Egg Farm Inc	Millers Falls	MA	G	978 544-3806	10447
Baffonis Poultry Farm Inc	Johnston	RI	E	401 231-6315	16077
Maple Wind Farm Inc	Richmond	VT	G	802 434-7257	17480
0253 Turkeys and turkey eggs					
Diemand Egg Farm Inc	Millers Falls	MA	G	978 544-3806	10447
0254 Poultry hatcheries					
Spear Farms Inc	Nobleboro	ME	E	207 832-4488	5101
0273 Animal aquaculture					
New Bedford Ocean Cluster Inc	New Bedford	MA	F	508 474-8902	10627
Sea & Reef Aquaculture LLC	Franklin	ME	F	207 422-2422	4796
American Mussel Harvesters Inc	North Kingstown	RI	E	401 294-8999	16230
0291 General farms, primarily animals					
Maple Wind Farm Inc	Richmond	VT	G	802 434-7257	17480
07 AGRICULTURAL SERVICES					
0711 Soil preparation services					
Brown Construction Inc	Houlton	ME	F	207 532-0910	4898
Earl W Gerrish & Sons	Brownville	ME	F	207 965-2171	4637
0721 Crop planting and protection					
Edi Landscape LLC	Hartford	CT	F	860 216-6871	1477
Agrify Corporation (PA)	North Billerica	MA	E	617 896-5243	10894
0722 Crop harvesting					
Up North Corp	Fort Kent	ME	F	207 834-6178	4795
Newport Vineyards & Winery LLC	Middletown	RI	E	401 848-5161	16182
Larry G Carabeau	Tinmouth	VT	G	802 446-3123	17648
0723 Crop preparation services for market					
Mantrose-Haeuser Co Inc (HQ)	Westport	CT	E	203 454-1800	4182
Natureseal Inc	Westport	CT	F	203 454-1800	4189
Maine Grains Inc	Skowhegan	ME	E	207 474-8001	5471
0741 Veterinary services for livestock					
Idexx Laboratories Inc (PA)	Westbrook	ME	A	207 556-0300	5631
0742 Veterinary services, specialties					
Alpha Tech Pet Inc	Littleton	MA	G	978 486-3690	9800
Massachstts Soc For Prvntion C (PA)	Boston	MA	C	617 522-7282	6872
Covetrus North America LLC (PA)	Portland	ME	C	888 280-2221	5202
0752 Animal specialty services					
Dogwatch Inc (PA)	Natick	MA	G	508 650-0600	10478
Up Country Inc	East Providence	RI	E	401 431-2940	16046

	CITY	ST	EMP	PHONE	ENTRY#

0781 Landscape counseling and planning

	CITY	ST	EMP	PHONE	ENTRY#
E B Asphalt & Landscaping LLC	Oakdale	CT	F	860 639-1921	2621
Edi Landscape LLC	Hartford	CT	F	860 216-6871	1477
Front Line Apparel Group LLC	Hebron	CT	F	860 859-3524	1527
Hayes Services LLC	East Lyme	CT	E	860 739-2273	1059
Royalty Consulting LLC	Rocky Hill	CT	F	800 474-5157	2934
Roberts Ldscp Design & Cnstr	Barnstable	MA	F	508 364-4878	6201
Rwc Landscape Services MGT	Concord	NH	E	603 279-1411	14154
Northeast Ldscpg Tree Svcs Inc	Westerly	RI	F	860 405-5274	16941

0782 Lawn and garden services

	CITY	ST	EMP	PHONE	ENTRY#
Cw Solutions LLC	New Britain	CT	D	860 229-7700	2018
Davis Tree & Logging LLC	Danbury	CT	F	203 938-2153	728
Mist Hill Property Maint LLC	Brookfield	CT	F	203 648-7434	530
C M S Landscaping Corporation	Holyoke	MA	F	413 533-3300	9245
Cotton Tree Service Inc	Northampton	MA	F	413 584-9104	11057
Crystal Brook Ldscp Cnstr Inc	Springfield	MA	F	413 596-0055	12087
P Wiles Inc (PA)	Orleans	MA	F	508 385-4321	11242
Northern Turf Prfessionals Inc	Brunswick	ME	F	207 522-8598	4652
Sports Fields Inc	Monmouth	ME	F	207 933-3547	5072
Djs Tree Service & Log Inc	Colchester	VT	F	802 655-0264	17189

0783 Ornamental shrub and tree services

	CITY	ST	EMP	PHONE	ENTRY#
Davis Tree & Logging LLC	Danbury	CT	F	203 938-2153	728
Edi Landscape LLC	Hartford	CT	F	860 216-6871	1477
Royalty Consulting LLC	Rocky Hill	CT	F	800 474-5157	2934
Cotton Tree Service Inc	Northampton	MA	F	413 584-9104	11057
York Woods Tree Service LLC	Eliot	ME	F	207 703-0150	4752
Djs Tree Service & Log Inc	Colchester	VT	F	802 655-0264	17189

08 FORESTRY

0831 Forest products

	CITY	ST	EMP	PHONE	ENTRY#
Edmond Roy & Sons Inc	Jackman	ME	G	877 425-8491	4910
Bascom Maple Farms Inc (PA)	Alstead	NH	D	603 835-2230	13856

0851 Forestry services

	CITY	ST	EMP	PHONE	ENTRY#
Edmond Roy & Sons Inc	Jackman	ME	G	877 425-8491	4910
James W Sewall Company	Bangor	ME	G	207 817-5410	4506
James W Sewall Company (PA)	Old Town	ME	E	207 827-4456	5125
Voisine Bros Inc (PA)	New Canada	ME	G	207 231-0220	5082
A Johnson Co	Bristol	VT	D	802 453-4884	17112

09 FISHING, HUNTING AND TRAPPING

0912 Finfish

	CITY	ST	EMP	PHONE	ENTRY#
New Bedford Ocean Cluster Inc	New Bedford	MA	F	508 474-8902	10627

0919 Miscellaneous marine products

	CITY	ST	EMP	PHONE	ENTRY#
Brooks Inc (PA)	Thomaston	ME	E	207 354-8763	5542
Ocean Approved Inc	Biddeford	ME	G	207 701-1576	4580
Ocean State Shellfish Coop LLC	Narragansett	RI	G	401 789-2065	16193

10 METAL MINING

1011 Iron ores

	CITY	ST	EMP	PHONE	ENTRY#
Farrel Corporation (DH)	Ansonia	CT	D	203 736-5500	14

1021 Copper ores

	CITY	ST	EMP	PHONE	ENTRY#
Quantum Discoveries Inc	Boston	MA	G	857 272-9998	6989

1041 Gold ores

	CITY	ST	EMP	PHONE	ENTRY#
Castle Gate Invstmnts Ltd Lblt	Walpole	MA	G	617 596-1126	12555

1081 Metal mining services

	CITY	ST	EMP	PHONE	ENTRY#
Liberty Mtals Min Holdings LLC	Boston	MA	F	617 654-4374	6857
Polymetallurgical LLC	North Attleboro	MA	D	508 695-9312	10883
Buckeye Blasting Corporation	Epsom	NH	G	603 736-4681	14279
Forthill Resources LLC	Providence	RI	F	617 849-0768	16519
Crown Point Excavation LLC	Springfield	VT	F	802 291-4817	17617

12 COAL MINING

1221 Bituminous coal and lignite-surface mining

	CITY	ST	EMP	PHONE	ENTRY#
Cloud Peak Energy Inc (PA)	Westport	CT	D	307 687-6000	4161
Eagle Ship Management LLC (HQ)	Stamford	CT	C	203 276-8100	3340
Wexford Capital LP (PA)	Greenwich	CT	G	203 862-7000	1361

1222 Bituminous coal-underground mining

	CITY	ST	EMP	PHONE	ENTRY#
American Metals Coal Intl Inc (HQ)	Greenwich	CT	F	203 625-9200	1311
Wexford Capital LP (PA)	Greenwich	CT	G	203 862-7000	1361

1231 Anthracite mining

	CITY	ST	EMP	PHONE	ENTRY#
Hartford Fire Equipment	Plainville	CT	F	860 747-2757	2763

1241 Coal mining services

	CITY	ST	EMP	PHONE	ENTRY#
Tronox LLC (PA)	Stamford	CT	F	203 705-3800	3487

13 OIL AND GAS EXTRACTION

1311 Crude petroleum and natural gas

	CITY	ST	EMP	PHONE	ENTRY#
Berq Rng Holdings Usa LLC (PA)	Greenwich	CT	F	412 656-8863	1317
CCI Robinsons Bend LLC	Stamford	CT	E	203 564-8571	3306
Direct Energy Inc (HQ)	Stamford	CT	E	800 260-0300	3338
El Paso Prod Oil Gas Texas LP	Hartford	CT	E	860 293-1990	1478
Frc Founders Corporation (PA)	Stamford	CT	E	203 661-6601	3348
Louis Dreyfus Holdg Co US LLC (HQ)	Wilton	CT	B	203 761-2000	4242
Northern Tier Energy LLC (DH)	Ridgefield	CT	F	203 244-6550	2903
Promise Propane Llc	Newington	CT	G	860 685-0676	2319
British Transco Capital Inc	Westborough	MA	E	781 907-3646	13083
Kyromina Oil Corporation	Natick	MA	G	508 651-8284	10484
National Grid USA Svc Co Inc (DH)	Waltham	MA	G	800 260-0054	12734
Poweroptions Inc	Boston	MA	G	617 737-8480	6973
Maine Natural Gas Corporation	Brunswick	ME	F	207 729-0420	4648
Revision Heat LLC	Hampden	ME	F	207 221-5677	4867
Liberty Enrgy Utilities NH Corp (DH)	Londonderry	NH	D	905 287-2061	14763
Your Oil Tools LLC	Manchester	NH	F	701 645-8665	14962
National Grid USA Svc Co Inc	Providence	RI	A	401 784-7224	16573
Marcell Oil Company Inc	Pittsford	VT	F	802 775-5050	17445

1321 Natural gas liquids

	CITY	ST	EMP	PHONE	ENTRY#
Eagle Ship Management LLC (HQ)	Stamford	CT	C	203 276-8100	3340
Six One Cmmodities US Trdg LLC	Stamford	CT	E	203 409-2079	3461
World Energy LLC	Boston	MA	B	617 889-7300	7132

1381 Drilling oil and gas wells

	CITY	ST	EMP	PHONE	ENTRY#
Directional Technologies Inc	Wallingford	CT	G	203 294-9200	3801
Eows Midland Inc	Stamford	CT	F	203 358-5705	3343
Sterling Gas Drlg Fund 1982 LP	Stamford	CT	G	203 358-5700	3474
Total Drilling Supply LLC	Thompson	CT	F	860 923-1091	3653
D L Maher Co	North Reading	MA	F	781 933-3210	11039
New England Foundation Co Inc (PA)	Hyde Park	MA	D	617 361-9750	9465
Soil Exploration Corp (PA)	Leominster	MA	F	978 840-0391	9705
Subsurface Drlg Remediation Co	Tiverton	RI	G	401 275-2088	16739
NA Manosh Inc	Morrisville	VT	E	802 888-5722	17387

1382 Oil and gas exploration services

	CITY	ST	EMP	PHONE	ENTRY#
Ace Energy LLC	Broad Brook	CT	F	860 623-3308	507
Economy Energy LLC	Westport	CT	G	203 227-5181	4167
El Paso Prod Oil Gas Texas LP	Hartford	CT	E	860 293-1990	1478
Equinor Pipelines LLC	Stamford	CT	C	203 978-6900	3344
Equinor US Holdings Inc (DH)	Stamford	CT	C	203 978-6900	3345
Geosonics Inc	Cheshire	CT	F	203 271-2504	595
Moab Oil Inc	Norwalk	CT	F	203 857-6622	2539
Seismic Monitoring Svcs LLC	Danielson	CT	G	860 753-6363	841
Copenhgen Offshore Prtners Inc	New Bedford	MA	E	508 717-8964	10579
Hager Geoscience Inc	Woburn	MA	G	781 935-8111	13579
Hess Oil	Brockton	MA	F	508 587-8325	7283
Nuvera Fuel Cells LLC (HQ)	Billerica	MA	C	617 245-7500	6465
Quantum Discoveries Inc	Boston	MA	G	857 272-9998	6989
Republic Midstream Mktg LLC	Boston	MA	F	617 531-6300	7005
Schlumberger Technology Corp	Cambridge	MA	F	617 768-2000	7707
Stroud International Ltd	Marblehead	MA	F	781 631-8806	10096
Woods Hole Group Inc (DH)	Bourne	MA	E	301 925-4411	7143
Hunting Dearborn Inc	Fryeburg	ME	C	207 935-2171	4809
James W Sewall Company	Bangor	ME	G	207 817-5410	4506
James W Sewall Company (PA)	Old Town	ME	E	207 827-4456	5125
D F Richard Inc	Dover	NH	D	603 742-2020	14225
Clean Water Ventures Inc	North Kingstown	RI	F	858 437-3294	16237

1389 Oil and gas field services, nec

	CITY	ST	EMP	PHONE	ENTRY#
Acuren Inspection Inc (HQ)	Danbury	CT	A	203 702-8740	704
Acuren Inspection Inc	Greenwich	CT	D	203 869-6734	1310
Alliance Energy LLC	New Haven	CT	C	203 933-2511	2114
Anz Petroleum Inc	New Milford	CT	F	860 261-4798	2238
Buffalo Gulf Cast Trminals LLC	Greenwich	CT	E	203 930-3802	1323
Buon Appetito From Italy LLC	New London	CT	G	860 437-3668	2223
Frc Founders Corporation (PA)	Stamford	CT	E	203 661-6601	3348
Icon Capital Management LLC	Greenwich	CT	G	203 542-7792	1335

	CITY	ST	EMP	PHONE	ENTRY#
Innovative Environmental LLC	Colchester	CT	F	860 871-7582	660
J & M Plumbing & Cnstr LLC	Norwich	CT	G	860 319-3082	2608
Kafa Group LLC	Bridgeport	CT	G	475 275-0090	338
Kolmar Americas	Norwalk	CT	G	203 840-5337	2524
Loanworks Servicing LLC	Shelton	CT	F	203 402-7304	3029
Longview Holding Corporation (HQ)	Greenwich	CT	G	203 869-6734	1339
My Slide Lines LLC	Norwalk	CT	F	203 324-1642	2540
National Default Servicing LLC	Meriden	CT	D	858 300-0700	1679
Northeast Companies Inc (PA)	Meriden	CT	F	203 630-9675	1680
Reac Ready LLC	Wethersfield	CT	G	860 550-5049	4213
Right of Way Solutions LLC	Salem	CT	G	860 917-0608	2945
Rockwood Service Corporation (PA)	Greenwich	CT	G	203 869-6734	1348
Royalty Consulting LLC	Rocky Hill	CT	F	800 474-5157	2934
Sigma Tankers Inc	Norwalk	CT	E		2573
Tri State Maintenance Svcs LLC	North Haven	CT	F	203 691-1343	2440
USA Builders Inc	Deep River	CT	G	843 321-9618	887
Verbio North America LLC (PA)	Stamford	CT	E	866 306-4777	3491
Weatherford International LLC	Wallingford	CT	E	203 294-0190	3875
Arclight Enrgy Prtners Fund VI (PA)	Boston	MA	E	617 531-6300	6557
Baker Hughes Holdings LLC	Walpole	MA	C	508 668-0400	12552
Biszko Contracting Corp	Fall River	MA	E	508 679-0518	8525
Bostonian Clg Restoration Inc	Braintree	MA	F	781 356-3303	7170
Commtank Cares Inc	Wakefield	MA	G	781 224-1021	12505
Dagle Electrical Cnstr Corp	Wilmington	MA	D	800 379-1459	13401
Digital Stream Energy Inc	Boston	MA	G	310 488-2743	6697
Fuse Builds LLC (PA)	Roxbury	MA	E	617 602-4001	11691
Hager Geoscience Inc	Woburn	MA	F	781 935-8111	13579
Home Heating Services Corp	Somerville	MA	F	617 625-8255	11880
Jiffy Lube	Mashpee	MA	G	508 539-8888	10252
John McGillicuddy Inc	Milton	MA	F	617 388-6324	10453
Labthink International Inc	Medford	MA	F	617 830-2190	10293
Mainstream Global Inc	Lawrence	MA	E	978 682-6767	9579
Moresi & Associates Dev Co LLC	North Adams	MA	F	413 663-8677	10811
Msr Utility	Dunstable	MA	G	978 649-0002	8328
Mutual Oil Leasing Co Inc	Brockton	MA	F	508 583-5777	7299
Old Ironsides Energy LLC	Waltham	MA	E	617 366-2030	12742
Place Tailor	Roxbury Crossing	MA	F	617 639-0633	11693
Platinum Investments Ltd	Brookline	MA	F	617 731-2447	7325
Port Oil Corp	Bedford	MA	F	617 926-3500	6253
Pro Touch Home Improvement Inc	Peabody	MA	F	617 378-1929	11336
Richmond Sand and Gravel Inc	Plymouth	MA	F	508 224-2231	11475
Schlumberger Technology Corp	Cambridge	MA	C	617 768-2000	7707
Sea-Land Envmtl Svcs Inc	Medfield	MA	G	508 359-1085	10275
Sensing Systems Corporation	Dartmouth	MA	F	508 992-0872	8231
Trinity Builders Inc (PA)	Westwood	MA	F	781 780-6168	13323
Versant Energy Services Inc (DH)	Norwell	MA	G	781 792-5000	11149
Wooden Kiwi Productions LLC	Waltham	MA	G	781 209-2623	12818
Copp Excavating Inc	Durham	ME	F	207 926-4988	4732
Wireless Construction Inc	Standish	ME	E	207 642-5751	5530
Gabriel Business Group Co Ltd	Brookline	NH	F	877 401-5544	14039
Highlands Fuel Delivery LLC (HQ)	Portsmouth	NH	D	603 559-8700	15404
L & M Service Contractors LLC	Orford	NH	F	603 359-1956	15281
McLaughlin Oil Corp (PA)	Nashua	NH	E	603 882-5500	15132
Mike Murphy & Sons Inc	Kingston	NH	F	603 362-4879	14636
Oi Infusion Services LLC	Portsmouth	NH	D	603 319-6224	15427
Tekon-Technical Cons Inc	Portsmouth	NH	E	603 335-3080	15441
Dig Rite Company Inc	Johnston	RI	F	401 862-5895	16081
East Greenwich Oil Co Inc	East Greenwich	RI	G	401 884-2454	15982
Ost Services LLC	Providence	RI	C	401 467-8661	16581
Rhode Runner Homes LLC	North Providence	RI	F	401 489-8501	16309
Sanoil LLC	Providence	RI	G	401 942-5000	16610
Uncles Oil Company Corporation	Cranston	RI	G	401 383-0626	15925
DC Enterprizes Inc	Hinesburg	VT	F	802 865-4480	17290

14 MINING AND QUARRYING OF NONMETALLIC MINERALS, EXCEPT FUELS

1411 Dimension stone

	CITY	ST	EMP	PHONE	ENTRY#
Armetta LLC	Middletown	CT	F	860 788-2369	1736
Coccomo Brothers Drilling LLC	Berlin	CT	F	860 828-1632	60
Connecticut Stone Supplies Inc (PA)	Milford	CT	D	203 882-1000	1814
Infinity Stone Inc	Waterbury	CT	F	203 575-9484	3922
Julian Materials LLC (PA)	Fairfield	CT	F	203 416-5308	1192
LH Gault & Son Incorporated	Westport	CT	D	203 227-5181	4180
Midwood Quarry and Cnstr Inc (PA)	East Hartford	CT	F	860 289-1414	1006
Mildred Coppola (PA)	Stamford	CT	F	203 967-9300	3411
Stony Creek Quarry Corporation	Branford	CT	G	203 483-3904	280
Cumar Inc	Everett	MA	E	617 389-7818	8484
Fletcher Granite LLC (DH)	Westford	MA	F	978 692-1312	13238
George D Judd & Sons LLC	Goshen	MA	G	413 268-7590	8967
Rangeway Supply LLC	North Billerica	MA	G	978 667-8500	10947

	CITY	ST	EMP	PHONE	ENTRY#
Williams Stone Co Inc	East Otis	MA	E	413 269-4544	8403
Semya Corp (PA)	Alstead	NH	G	802 875-6564	13858
Swenson Granite Company LLC (DH)	Concord	NH	E	603 225-4322	14161
Georgia Stone Industries Inc (HQ)	Smithfield	RI	F	401 232-2040	16702
Adams Granite Co Inc	Websterville	VT	D	802 476-5281	17683
Houle Bros Granite Co Inc	Barre	VT	F	802 476-6825	17006
International Stone Products (PA)	Barre	VT	D	802 476-6636	17009
McCue Memorial Co Inc	Castleton	VT	E	802 468-5636	17173
Quarry Slate Industries Inc	Poultney	VT	E	802 287-9701	17449
Semya Corp	Chester	VT	E	802 875-6564	17183
South Poultney Slate	Poultney	VT	G	802 287-9278	17451
Taran Bros Inc	Poultney	VT	F	802 287-9308	17452
Taran Bros Inc (PA)	Poultney	VT	F	802 287-5853	17453
Troy Minerals Inc	Florence	VT	F	802 878-5103	17273
Vermont Quarries Corp	Rutland	VT	F	802 775-1065	17514
Vermont Verde Antique Intl	Pittsford	VT	G	802 767-4421	17446

1422 Crushed and broken limestone

	CITY	ST	EMP	PHONE	ENTRY#
Allyndale Corporation	East Canaan	CT	E	860 824-7959	921
Specialty Minerals Inc	Canaan	CT	F	860 824-5435	557
S Lane John & Son Incorporated	Oxford	MA	F	508 987-3959	11263
S M Lorusso & Sons Inc	East Weymouth	MA	E	781 337-6770	8433
Specialty Minerals Inc	Adams	MA	C	413 743-0591	5775
Dragon Products Company LLC (DH)	Biddeford	ME	F	207 594-5555	4560
Dragon Products Company LLC	Thomaston	ME	E	207 594-5555	5544
K & B Rock Crushing LLC	Auburn	NH	G	603 622-1188	13910
Shelburne Limestone Corp (PA)	Colchester	VT	F	802 878-2656	17203
Shelburne Limestone Corp	Swanton	VT	E	802 868-3357	17642

1423 Crushed and broken granite

	CITY	ST	EMP	PHONE	ENTRY#
Skyline Quarry LLC	Stafford Springs	CT	F	860 875-3580	3259
McCullough Crushing Inc (PA)	Middlesex	VT	E	802 223-5693	17352

1429 Crushed and broken stone, nec

	CITY	ST	EMP	PHONE	ENTRY#
Galasso Materials LLC	East Granby	CT	C	860 527-1825	934
Nu-Stone Mfg & Distrg LLC	Sterling	CT	G	860 564-6555	3503
Holcim - Ner Inc (DH)	Saugus	MA	E	781 941-7200	11760
Isp Freetown Fine Chem Inc	Assonet	MA	D	508 672-0634	5974
Massachusetts Broken Stone Co (PA)	Berlin	MA	E	978 838-9999	6319
R J McDonald Inc	Barre	MA	F	978 355-6649	6203
S Lane John & Son Incorporated (PA)	Westfield	MA	F	413 568-8986	13205
Shelburne Limestone Corp	Colchester	VT	F	802 878-2656	17202

1442 Construction sand and gravel

	CITY	ST	EMP	PHONE	ENTRY#
Adelman Sand & Gravel Inc	Bozrah	CT	F	860 889-3394	226
Brennan Realty LLC (PA)	Shelton	CT	C	203 929-6314	2987
Dan Beard Inc	Shelton	CT	E	203 924-4346	2996
Desiato Sand & Gravel Corp	Storrs Mansfield	CT	E	860 429-6479	3512
Galasso Materials LLC	East Granby	CT	C	860 527-1825	934
Garf Trucking Inc	Windsor	CT	G	860 558-8487	4277
Kobyluck Sand and Gravel Inc	Waterford	CT	F	860 444-9600	3992
Midwood Quarry and Cnstr Inc (PA)	East Hartford	CT	F	860 289-1414	1006
Monroe Recycl & Aggregates LLC	Monroe	CT	G	203 644-7748	1917
O & G Industries Inc	Stamford	CT	D	203 323-1111	3422
Rawson Development Inc	Putnam	CT	F	860 928-4536	2872
Skyline Quarry LLC	Stafford Springs	CT	F	860 875-3580	3259
Thomas Keegan & Sons Inc	Wallingford	CT	F	203 239-9248	3862
Tradebe Treatment and Recycling Northeast LLC (DH)	Meriden	CT			D
203 238-8102	1710				
Tronox LLC (PA)	Stamford	CT	F	203 705-3800	3487
Valley Sand & Gravel Corp	North Haven	CT	F	203 562-3192	2443
Attleboro Sand & Gravel Corp	Attleboro	MA	F	508 222-2870	5995
B R S Inc	Bridgewater	MA	E	508 697-5448	7221
Baxter Sand & Gravel Inc	Chicopee	MA	F	413 536-3370	8009
Benevento Asphalt Corp	Wilmington	MA	F	978 658-5300	13391
Benevento Sand & Stone Corp	Wilmington	MA	F	978 658-4762	13392
Berkshire Concrete Corp (HQ)	Pittsfield	MA	E	413 443-4734	11392
Boston Sand & Gravel Company (PA)	Boston	MA	E	617 227-9000	6616
Brox Industries Inc (PA)	Dracut	MA	D	978 454-9105	8302
Cape Cod Aggregates Corp (PA)	Hyannis	MA	E	508 775-3716	9429
Classic Tractor Services LLC	Kingston	MA	G	781 585-2050	9506
Colrain Sand and Gravel Inc	Colrain	MA	F	413 624-5118	8095
Construction Source MGT LLC	Raynham	MA	F	508 484-5100	11585
Dedham Recycled Gravel Co Inc	Dedham	MA	F	781 329-1044	8241
Delta Sand and Gravel Inc	Sunderland	MA	F	413 665-4051	12273
Gravel Public House	Wrentham	MA	F	508 384-0888	13842
J G Maclellan Con Co Inc (PA)	Lowell	MA	D	978 458-1223	9888
Lakeside Management Corp	Plainville	MA	G	508 695-3252	11435
Lane Construction Corporation	Northfield	MA	D	413 498-5586	11120
Lml Construction Inc	Leverett	MA	F	413 665-3788	9718
Longfin LLC	Nantucket	MA	F	508 228-4266	10465
Lorusso Corp (PA)	Plainville	MA	E	508 668-6520	11437
New England Gravel Haulers	Rehoboth	MA	G	508 922-4518	11612

S I C

	CITY	ST	EMP	PHONE	ENTRY#
New England Sand & Grav Co Inc	Framingham	MA	F	508 877-2460	8791
Northeast Sand & Gravel	North Andover	MA	G	603 213-6133	10845
P A Landers Inc (PA)	Hanover	MA	C	781 826-8818	9038
P A Landers Inc	Hanover	MA	F	508 747-1800	9039
Petricca Industries Inc (PA)	Pittsfield	MA	E	413 499-1441	11418
Powell Stone & Gravel Co Inc (PA)	Lunenburg	MA	F	978 537-8100	9959
Pro Touch Home Improvement Inc	Peabody	MA	F	617 378-1929	11336
Rosenfeld Concrete Corp (HQ)	Hopedale	MA	E	508 473-7200	9303
S Lane John & Son Incorporated (PA)	Westfield	MA	E	413 568-8986	13205
S M Lorusso & Sons Inc	Boston	MA	F	617 323-6380	7019
S M Lorusso & Sons Inc (PA)	Walpole	MA	E	508 668-2600	12575
Sanger Equipment Corporation	Conway	MA	F	413 625-8304	8145
Southeastern Sand and Grav Inc	Kingston	MA	G	781 413-6884	9512
Varney Bros Sand & Gravel Inc	Bellingham	MA	F	508 966-1313	6302
WJ Graves Cnstr Co Inc (PA)	East Templeton	MA	E	978 939-5568	8416
Worcester Sand and Grav Co Inc	Shrewsbury	MA	E	508 852-1683	11849
Dayton Sand & Gravel Inc	Dayton	ME	D	207 499-2306	4720
Dragon Products Company LLC (DH)	Biddeford	ME	E	207 594-5555	4560
Dragon Products Company LLC	Thomaston	ME	E	207 594-5555	5544
Earl W Gerrish & Sons	Brownville	ME	F	207 965-2171	4637
F R Carroll Inc	Limerick	ME	F	207 793-8615	5001
Hanley Construction Inc	Bristol	ME	F	207 677-2207	4630
Hermon Sand & Gravel LLC	Hermon	ME	F	207 848-5977	4883
Hughes Brothers Inc	Hampden	ME	F	207 659-3417	4864
J and L Sand	Lyman	ME	G	207 499-2545	5029
K W Aggregates	Denmark	ME	G	207 452-8888	4723
Lane Construction Corporation	Bangor	ME	B	207 945-0850	4508
McQuade Tidd Industries	Houlton	ME	E	207 532-2675	4901
P & K Sand and Gravel Inc	Naples	ME	E	207 693-6765	5081
State Sand & Gravel Co Inc	Belfast	ME	F	207 338-4070	4538
Sunny Side Land Holdings LLC	Presque Isle	ME	F	207 768-1020	5310
A B Excavating Inc	Lancaster	NH	F	603 788-5110	14675
Benevento Aggregates LLC	Loudon	NH	F	603 783-4723	14793
Big Foote Crushing LLC	Weare	NH	G	603 345-0695	15669
Chick Trucking Inc	Newmarket	NH	F	603 659-3566	15218
Columbia Sand & Gravel Inc	Colebrook	NH	F	603 237-5729	14103
Frank W Whitcomb Cnstr Corp (PA)	Walpole	NH	F	603 445-5555	15661
Gorham Sand & Gravel Inc	Gorham	NH	G	603 466-2291	14359
Granite State Concrete Co Inc	Milford	NH	F	603 673-3327	15023
Michie Corporation	Henniker	NH	D	603 428-7426	14438
Northeast Earth Mechanics LLC	Pittsfield	NH	E	603 435-7989	15334
Northeast Sand and Gravel LLC	Merrimack	NH	G	603 305-9429	14995
Pike Industries Inc	Portsmouth	NH	G	603 436-4432	15429
Powell Stone Gravel	Brookline	NH	G	603 673-8100	14040
Tilcor Arthur Whitcomb Inc (HQ)	North Swanzey	NH	F	603 352-0101	15256
Twin State Sand & Grav Co Inc	West Lebanon	NH	G	603 298-8705	15691
George Sherman Sand Grav Inc	Wakefield	RI	E	401 789-6304	16741
Richmond Sand & Stone LLC	Richmond	RI	F	401 539-7770	16651
Calkins Rock Products Inc	Lyndonville	VT	G	802 626-5755	17317
Calkins Sand & Gravel Inc	Newport	VT	F	802 334-8418	17397
Cersosimo Industries Inc (PA)	Brattleboro	VT	D	802 254-4500	17080
Dale E Percy Inc	Stowe	VT	F	802 253-8503	17630
Frank W Whitcomb Cnstr Corp	Colchester	VT	D	802 655-1270	17191
Gurney Brothers Construction	North Springfield	VT	E	802 886-2210	17421
H A Manosh Corp	Morrisville	VT	D	802 888-5722	17383
Hinesburg Sand & Gravel Co Inc	Hinesburg	VT	E	802 482-2335	17294
Joseph P Carrara & Sons Inc (PA)	North Clarendon	VT	E	802 775-2301	17415
Orwell Sand & Gravel	Benson	VT	G	802 345-6028	17059

1446 Industrial sand

	CITY	ST	EMP	PHONE	ENTRY#
Covia Finance Company LLC	New Canaan	CT	D	203 966-8880	2079
Covia Specialty Minerals Inc	New Canaan	CT	E	203 966-8880	2080
Unimin Texas Co Ltd (HQ)	New Canaan	CT	F	203 966-8880	2090
Unimin Wisconsin Eqp Corp	New Canaan	CT	E	203 966-8880	2091
Unisil Corporation	New Canaan	CT	E	203 966-8880	2092
Harold Macquinn Incorporated (PA)	Hancock	ME	E	207 667-4654	4869
North Ridge Contracting Inc	Epsom	NH	E	603 942-6104	14282

1455 Kaolin and ball clay

	CITY	ST	EMP	PHONE	ENTRY#
JM Huber Corporation	Millinocket	ME	E	207 723-9291	5065

1459 Clay and related minerals, nec

	CITY	ST	EMP	PHONE	ENTRY#
RT Vanderbilt Holding Co Inc (PA)	Norwalk	CT	F	203 295-2141	2568
Vanderbilt Minerals LLC (HQ)	Norwalk	CT	E	203 295-2140	2590
Sheffield Pottery Inc	Sheffield	MA	E	413 229-7700	11801

1474 Potash, soda, and borate minerals

	CITY	ST	EMP	PHONE	ENTRY#
American Natural Soda Ash Corp (PA)	Westport	CT	E	203 226-9056	4156

1481 Nonmetallic mineral services

	CITY	ST	EMP	PHONE	ENTRY#
Haynes Aggrgtes - Deep Rver LL	Oxford	CT	G	203 888-8100	2697
Carr-Dee Corp	Medford	MA	F	781 391-4500	10282
Rowe Contracting Co	Melrose	MA	G	781 620-0052	10319

	CITY	ST	EMP	PHONE	ENTRY#
Soil Exploration Corp (PA)	Leominster	MA	G	978 840-0391	9705

1499 Miscellaneous nonmetallic mining

	CITY	ST	EMP	PHONE	ENTRY#
Galasso Materials LLC	East Granby	CT	C	860 527-1825	934
RT Vanderbilt Holding Co Inc (PA)	Norwalk	CT	F	203 295-2141	2568
Brox Industries Inc (PA)	Dracut	MA	D	978 454-9105	8302
Sun Gro Horticulture Dist Inc	Agawam	MA	E	800 732-8667	5811
Sun Gro Horticulture Dist Inc	Agawam	MA	D	864 224-7989	5812
Magris Talc Usa Inc	Ludlow	VT	E	802 228-6400	17315
North East Materials Group LLC	Graniteville	VT	F	802 479-7004	17276
Troy Minerals Inc	Colchester	VT	G	802 878-5103	17205
Williams & Co Mining Inc	Perkinsville	VT	F	802 263-5404	17443

15 CONSTRUCTION - GENERAL CONTRACTORS & OPERATIVE BUILDERS

1521 Single-family housing construction

	CITY	ST	EMP	PHONE	ENTRY#
American Building Systems Inc	Bristol	CT	G	860 589-0215	395
Central Construction Inds LLC	Putnam	CT	E	860 963-8902	2848
Coastal Exteriors LLC	Wallingford	CT	F	203 626-5396	3790
Country Carpenters Inc	Hebron	CT	G	860 228-2276	1526
Country Log Homes Inc	Goshen	CT	F	413 229-8084	1302
Deschenes & Cooper Architectur	Pawcatuck	CT	G	860 599-2481	2719
Eastern Electric Cnstr Co	Harwinton	CT	F	860 485-1100	1519
Hanford Cabinet & Wdwkg Co Inc	Old Saybrook	CT	G	860 388-5055	2650
Richard Riggio and Sons Inc	Ivoryton	CT	F	860 767-0812	1532
Trigila Construction Inc	Berlin	CT	F	860 828-8444	89
Acton Woodworks Inc	Acton	MA	G	978 263-0222	5732
Bostonian Clg Restoration Inc	Braintree	MA	F	781 356-3303	7170
BP Logue & Co	Chelmsford	MA	F	978 251-4433	7915
Chicopee Foundations Inc	Chicopee	MA	E	413 594-4700	8015
Craftech Upton	Upton	MA	F	508 529-4505	12472
EJ Jaxtimer Builder Inc	Hyannis	MA	E	508 778-4911	9436
Emery Development Ltd	Springfield	MA	G	413 782-1990	12094
Haydenville Wdwkg & Design Inc (PA)	Northampton	MA	F	413 665-7402	11066
John McGillicuddy Inc	Milton	MA	F	617 388-6324	10453
Pro Touch Home Improvement Inc	Peabody	MA	F	617 378-1929	11336
South Mountain Company Inc	West Tisbury	MA	E	508 693-4343	13055
Trinity Builders Inc (PA)	Westwood	MA	F	781 780-6168	13323
Yankee Builders	Dartmouth	MA	G	508 636-8660	8234
C A Construction Inc	Gouldsboro	ME	G	207 422-3493	4838
Harold Macquinn Incorporated (PA)	Hancock	ME	E	207 667-4654	4869
Integrity Composites LLC	Biddeford	ME	F	207 571-0743	4571
Schiavi Homes LLC	Oxford	ME	E	207 539-9600	5149
Tozier Group Inc	Falmouth	ME	F	207 838-7939	4774
Wlhc Inc (PA)	Houlton	ME	E	207 532-6531	4906
Custom Log Homes	Rumney	NH	F	603 786-9082	15497
Slate Corporation	Auburn	NH	F	603 234-5943	13912
Timberpeg East Inc (PA)	Claremont	NH	E	603 542-7762	14099
McKernon Group Inc	Brandon	VT	D	802 247-8500	17068
Vermod High Prfmce Mnfctred Hs	Wilder	VT	G	802 295-0042	17716
Vermont Timber Works Inc	North Springfield	VT	F	802 886-1917	17427
William H Moore Inc	Waitsfield	VT	G	802 496-3595	17668

1522 Residential construction, nec

	CITY	ST	EMP	PHONE	ENTRY#
Coastal Exteriors LLC	Wallingford	CT	F	203 626-5396	3790
Emery Development Ltd	Springfield	MA	G	413 782-1990	12094
Scandinavian Panel Systems	Worcester	MA	F	774 530-6340	13795
Space Building Corp	Lakeville	MA	E	508 947-7277	9521
Trinity Builders Inc (PA)	Westwood	MA	F	781 780-6168	13323
Woodmeister Master Bldrs Inc (PA)	Holden	MA	C	774 345-1000	9196
Davis Zac Fine Woodworking	New Gloucester	ME	G	207 926-4710	5084
Ecocor LLC	Searsmont	ME	E	207 342-2085	5449
Champlain Industries Inc	Burlington	VT	F	802 651-0708	17125
Community Apostolic Order Inc (PA)	Island Pond	VT	F	802 723-4452	17304

1531 Operative builders

	CITY	ST	EMP	PHONE	ENTRY#
Vulcanforms Inc	Devens	MA	D	781 472-0160	8289
Welton Technology LLC	Leominster	MA	G	978 425-0160	9716

1541 Industrial buildings and warehouses

	CITY	ST	EMP	PHONE	ENTRY#
Feman Steel LLC	Bloomfield	CT	F	860 982-6393	164
Kafa Group LLC	Bridgeport	CT	G	475 275-0090	338
Masas Usa Inc	East Haven	CT	E	305 603-8868	1045
O & G Industries Inc (PA)	Torrington	CT	D	860 489-9261	3689
Pds Engineering & Construction	Bloomfield	CT	E	860 242-8586	201
Core Concepts Inc	Franklin	MA	E	508 528-0070	8827
Flo Chemical Corp	Ashburnham	MA	F	978 827-5101	5952
Helfrich Bros Boiler Works Inc	Lawrence	MA	E	978 975-2464	9566
Space Building Corp	Lakeville	MA	E	508 947-7277	9521
Transtulit LLC	West Springfield	MA	G	413 737-2600	13045

Company	CITY	ST	EMP	PHONE	ENTRY#
Harold Macquinn Incorporated (PA)	Hancock	ME	E	207 667-4654	4869
Lander Group LLC	Greenville	ME	F	207 974-3104	4850
Sheridan Corporation (HQ)	Fairfield	ME	E	207 453-9311	4765
Airmar Technology Corp	Milford	NH	F	603 673-9570	15012
Bay State Industrial Weldin	Hudson	NH	E	603 881-7663	14488
Ne Steel Fabricators LLC	Cranston	RI	E	401 785-1234	15898
Thomsen Enterprises LLC	Rumford	RI	D	401 431-2190	16679
Neil H Daniels Inc	Ascutney	VT	E	802 674-6323	16993
Vhv Company (PA)	Winooski	VT	C	802 655-8805	17771

1542 Nonresidential construction, nec

Company	CITY	ST	EMP	PHONE	ENTRY#
American Marketing Intl LLC	Clinton	CT	E	860 669-4100	635
Brennan Realty LLC (PA)	Shelton	CT	C	203 929-6314	2987
Central Construction Inds LLC	Putnam	CT	E	860 963-8902	2848
Kafa Group LLC	Bridgeport	CT	G	475 275-0090	338
Musano Inc	Wolcott	CT	E	203 879-4651	4369
O & G Industries Inc	Beacon Falls	CT	F	203 729-4529	45
O & G Industries Inc	Bridgeport	CT	B	203 366-4586	354
O & G Industries Inc	Danbury	CT	E	203 748-5694	791
O & G Industries Inc	New Milford	CT	E	860 354-4438	2258
O & G Industries Inc	Southbury	CT	E	203 263-2195	3197
O & G Industries Inc	Stamford	CT	D	203 323-1111	3422
O & G Industries Inc (PA)	Torrington	CT	D	860 489-9261	3689
Pds Engineering & Construction	Bloomfield	CT	E	860 242-8586	201
Windham Materials LLC (PA)	Willimantic	CT	E	860 456-4111	4222
Acton Woodworks Inc	Acton	MA	G	978 263-0222	5732
Ada Fabricators Inc	Wilmington	MA	F	978 262-9900	13372
Bascom Environmental Co	Plymouth	MA	E	617 282-9500	11449
Emery Development Ltd	Springfield	MA	G	413 782-1990	12094
Gloucester Builders Inc	Charlestown	MA	E	617 241-5513	7874
Lewicki & Sons Excavating Inc	Plainville	MA	G	508 695-0122	11436
Limelight Productions Inc	Lee	MA	G	413 243-4950	9616
Sbarzola Construction Corp	South Weymouth	MA	G	781 817-6485	11977
Silverlining Holding Corp (PA)	Needham	MA	F	617 986-4400	10522
Space Building Corp	Lakeville	MA	E	508 947-7277	9521
Ultimate Windows Inc	Lawrence	MA	G	978 687-9444	9605
Wesco Building & Design Inc	Stoneham	MA	E	781 279-0490	12188
Wescor Ltd (PA)	Stoneham	MA	G	781 279-0490	12189
Harold Macquinn Incorporated (PA)	Hancock	ME	E	207 667-4654	4869
Lander Group LLC	Greenville	ME	F	207 974-3104	4850
M & H Logging LLC	Rangeley	ME	E	207 864-5617	5312
Sheridan Corporation (HQ)	Fairfield	ME	E	207 453-9311	4765
Alvin J Coleman & Son Inc (PA)	Albany	NH	F	603 447-5936	13847
Coyote Mountain Farm Inc	Ossipee	NH	G	603 662-2164	15282
Environmental Interiors Inc	Nashua	NH	E	603 889-9290	15095
Gabriel Business Group Co Ltd	Brookline	NH	F	877 401-5544	14039
Soucy Industries Inc (PA)	Pelham	NH	E	603 883-4500	15297
Dexter Sign Co	East Providence	RI	F	401 434-1100	16014
Lockheed Archtctral Sltons Inc	Pascoag	RI	C	401 568-3061	16339
McKernon Group Inc	Brandon	VT	D	802 247-8500	17068
William H Moore Inc	Waitsfield	VT	G	802 496-3595	17668

16 HEAMY CONSTRUCTION, EXCEPT BUILDING CONSTRUCTION, CONTRACTOR

1611 Highway and street construction

Company	CITY	ST	EMP	PHONE	ENTRY#
Atlas Industrial Services LLC	Branford	CT	E	203 315-4538	237
Lane Construction Corporation (DH)	Cheshire	CT	C	203 235-3351	603
Lane Industries Incorporated (DH)	Cheshire	CT	G	203 235-3351	604
Laydon Industries LLC (PA)	New Haven	CT	E	203 562-7283	2169
O & G Industries Inc (PA)	Torrington	CT	D	860 489-9261	3689
Tilcon Connecticut Inc (DH)	New Britain	CT	D	860 224-6010	2072
Tilcon Inc (DH)	Newington	CT	B	860 223-3651	2328
Westchester Industries Inc	Greenwich	CT	F	203 661-0055	1360
A F Amorello & Sons Inc	Worcester	MA	E	508 791-8778	13694
Aerial Wireless Services LLC	Bellingham	MA	D	508 657-1213	6282
Alton E Gleason Company Inc (PA)	Springfield	MA	F	413 732-8207	12073
Bascom Environmental Co	Plymouth	MA	E	617 282-9500	11449
Brox Industries Inc (PA)	Dracut	MA	D	978 454-9105	8302
E H Perkins Construction Inc	Sterling	MA	F	978 422-3388	12161
E H Perkins Construction Inc (PA)	Wayland	MA	E	978 562-3436	12925
Fall River Ready-Mix Con LLC	Fall River	MA	G	508 675-7540	8549
Heffron Asphalt Corp (PA)	North Reading	MA	G	781 935-1455	11040
Holcim - Ner Inc (DH)	Saugus	MA	E	781 941-7200	11760
JH Lynch & Sons Inc	Millbury	MA	E	508 756-6244	10438
Jsl Asphalt Inc (PA)	Westfield	MA	F	413 568-8986	13177
Lane Construction Corporation	Lee	MA	E	413 637-2511	9614
Lane Construction Corporation	Northfield	MA	D	413 498-5586	11120
Lml Construction Inc	Leverett	MA	F	413 665-3788	9718
Ondrick Materials & Recycl LLC	Chicopee	MA	E	413 592-2566	8052
P A Landers Inc (PA)	Hanover	MA	C	781 826-8818	9038

Company	CITY	ST	EMP	PHONE	ENTRY#
P J Albert Inc	Fitchburg	MA	D	978 345-7828	8671
Palmer Paving Corporation (PA)	Palmer	MA	E	413 283-8354	11281
Petricca Industries Inc (PA)	Pittsfield	MA	E	413 499-1441	11418
PJ Keating Company	Dracut	MA	D	978 454-7878	8310
Richmond Sand and Gravel Inc	Plymouth	MA	G	508 224-2231	11475
T L Edwards Inc	Plymouth	MA	F	508 732-9148	11480
Ted Ondrick Company LLC (PA)	Chicopee	MA	F	413 592-2565	8062
Visi-Flash Rentals Eastern	West Bridgewater	MA	E	508 583-9100	12988
Wells Development L L C	Arlington	MA	G	781 727-5560	5950
Brown Construction Inc	Houlton	ME	E	207 532-0910	4898
Bruce A Manzer Inc	Farmington	ME	E	207 696-5881	4777
County Concrete & Cnstr Co	Columbia Falls	ME	E	207 483-4409	4698
Harold Macquinn Incorporated (PA)	Hancock	ME	E	207 667-4654	4869
Lane Construction Corporation	Bangor	ME	B	207 945-0850	4508
Lane Construction Corporation	Presque Isle	ME	F	207 764-4137	5301
M & H Logging LLC	Rangeley	ME	E	207 864-5617	5312
Pike Industries Inc	Wells	ME	F	207 676-9973	5604
R A Thomas Logging Inc	Guilford	ME	G	207 876-2722	4858
Shaw Brothers Construction Inc (PA)	Gorham	ME	C	207 839-2552	4835
A B Excavating Inc	Lancaster	NH	E	603 788-5110	14675
Blaktop Inc (PA)	West Lebanon	NH	E	603 298-8885	15678
Frank W Whitcomb Cnstr Corp (PA)	Walpole	NH	F	603 445-5555	15661
Jutras Signs Inc	Bedford	NH	F	603 622-2344	13936
Northeast Earth Mechanics LLC	Pittsfield	NH	E	603 435-7989	15334
Pike Industries Inc (DH)	Belmont	NH	E	603 527-5100	13967
Pike Industries Inc	Gorham	NH	E	603 466-2772	14361
Pike Industries Inc	Portsmouth	NH	G	603 436-4432	15429
Cosco LLC	Woonsocket	RI	E	401 765-0009	16955
George Sherman Sand Grav Inc	Wakefield	RI	E	401 789-6304	16741
JH Lynch & Sons Inc (PA)	Cumberland	RI	D	401 333-4300	15948
Narragansett Improvement Co (PA)	Providence	RI	D	401 331-0051	16571
Perry Paving	Warwick	RI	G	401 732-1730	16845
Cersosimo Industries Inc (PA)	Brattleboro	VT	E	802 254-4500	17080
Pike Industries Inc	Williston	VT	G	802 658-0453	17744
Springfield Fence Company Inc	North Springfield	VT	F	802 886-2221	17424
Worksafe Traffic Ctrl Inds Inc (PA)	Barre	VT	G	802 223-8948	17025

1622 Bridge, tunnel, and elevated highway

Company	CITY	ST	EMP	PHONE	ENTRY#
Lane Construction Corporation (DH)	Cheshire	CT	C	203 235-3351	603
Lane Industries Incorporated (DH)	Cheshire	CT	G	203 235-3351	604
E H Perkins Construction Inc	Sterling	MA	F	978 422-3388	12161
E H Perkins Construction Inc	Wayland	MA	E	978 562-3436	12925
J F White Contracting Co	Stoughton	MA	C	781 436-8497	12216
Lane Construction Corporation	Lee	MA	E	413 637-2511	9614
Louie and Teds Blacktop Inc	Swansea	MA	F	508 678-4948	12306
Neil H Daniels Inc	Ascutney	VT	E	802 674-6323	16993

1623 Water, sewer, and utility lines

Company	CITY	ST	EMP	PHONE	ENTRY#
Brennan Realty LLC (PA)	Shelton	CT	C	203 929-6314	2987
O & G Industries Inc (PA)	Torrington	CT	D	860 489-9261	3689
A F Amorello & Sons Inc	Worcester	MA	E	508 791-8778	13694
Petricca Industries Inc (PA)	Pittsfield	MA	E	413 499-1441	11418
R J McDonald Inc	Barre	MA	F	978 355-6649	6203
Small Water Systems Svcs LLC	Littleton	MA	F	978 486-1008	9838
Harold Macquinn Incorporated (PA)	Hancock	ME	E	207 667-4654	4869
Shaw Brothers Construction Inc (PA)	Gorham	ME	C	207 839-2552	4835
A B Excavating Inc	Lancaster	NH	E	603 788-5110	14675
Northeast Earth Mechanics LLC	Pittsfield	NH	E	603 435-7989	15334
Williamson Electrical Co Inc	Epping	NH	D	617 884-9200	14277
George Sherman Sand Grav Inc	Wakefield	RI	E	401 789-6304	16741

1629 Heavy construction, nec

Company	CITY	ST	EMP	PHONE	ENTRY#
Apcompower Inc (PA)	Windsor	CT	E	860 688-1911	4260
Lane Construction Corporation (DH)	Cheshire	CT	C	203 235-3351	603
Lane Industries Incorporated (DH)	Cheshire	CT	G	203 235-3351	604
LH Gault & Son Incorporated	Westport	CT	D	203 227-5181	4180
Veolia Es Tchncal Slutions LLC	Danbury	CT	F	203 748-9116	832
Brox Industries Inc (PA)	Dracut	MA	D	978 454-9105	8302
Burnham Associates Inc	Salem	MA	E	978 745-1788	11706
Chas G Allen Realty LLC	Barre	MA	D	978 355-2911	6202
Cook Forest Products Inc	Upton	MA	E	508 634-3300	12471
Favreau Forestry LLC	Sterling	MA	G	978 706-1038	12162
Heyes Forest Products Inc	Orange	MA	E	978 544-8801	11223
Lane Construction Corporation	Lee	MA	E	413 637-2511	9614
Louie and Teds Blacktop Inc	Swansea	MA	F	508 678-4948	12306
Onyx Environmental Svcs LLC (DH)	Boston	MA	E	617 849-6600	6936
Raytheon Sutheast Asia Systems (DH)	Waltham	MA	E	978 470-5000	12762
Reading Diagnostic Center	Reading	MA	F	781 942-9876	11605
Tecomet Inc	Woburn	MA	A	781 782-6400	13675
Comprehensive Land Tech Inc	South China	ME	E	207 445-3151	5485
Lander Group LLC	Greenville	ME	F	207 974-3104	4850
Robert W Libby	Porter	ME	G	207 625-8285	5169
Wireless Construction Inc	Standish	ME	E	207 642-5751	5530

SIC

	CITY	ST	EMP	PHONE	ENTRY#
York Woods Tree Service LLC	Eliot	ME	F	207 703-0150	4752
A B Excavating Inc	Lancaster	NH	E	603 788-5110	14675
Buckeye Blasting Corporation	Epsom	NH	G	603 736-4681	14279
Custom Log Homes	Rumney	NH	F	603 786-9082	15497
DH Hardwick & Sons Inc	Bennington	NH	F	603 588-6618	13975
Hopkinton For Land Claring Inc	Henniker	NH	F	603 428-8400	14437
Monadnock Land Clearing	Greenville	NH	G	603 878-2803	14373
Absorbent Specialty Pdts LLC	Pawtucket	RI	F	401 722-1177	16342
Dock Doctors LLC	Ferrisburgh	VT	E	802 877-6756	17268

17 CONSTRUCTION - SPECIAL TRADE CONTRACTORS

1711 Plumbing, heating, air-conditioning

	CITY	ST	EMP	PHONE	ENTRY#
Allstate Fire Systems LLC	Middletown	CT	E	860 246-7711	1734
Atlantic Vent & Eqp Co Inc	Cromwell	CT	E	860 635-1300	687
CBS Contractors Inc	Ansonia	CT	F	203 734-8015	10
Connectcut Boiler Repr Mfg Inc	West Hartford	CT	E	860 953-9117	4054
Dependable Energy Incorporated	Prospect	CT	G	203 758-5831	2833
East Coast Sheet Metal LLC	Litchfield	CT	F	860 283-1126	1556
Innovative Environmental LLC	Colchester	CT	F	860 871-7582	660
J & B Service Company LLC	Bethel	CT	G	203 743-9357	122
J & M Plumbing & Cnstr LLC	Norwich	CT	E	860 319-3082	2608
L & L Mechanical LLC	Goshen	CT	F	860 491-4007	1303
Link Mechanical Services Inc	New Britain	CT	E	860 826-5880	2038
M & O Corporation	Bridgeport	CT	E	203 367-4292	345
McVac Environmental Svcs Inc	New Haven	CT	E	203 497-1960	2173
Sshc Inc	Westbrook	CT	F	860 399-5434	4143
Ace Residential Solar LLC	North Andover	MA	F	800 223-1462	10816
Acme Precast Co Inc	West Falmouth	MA	F	508 548-9607	13000
Atlas Water Systems Inc	Waltham	MA	D	781 373-4700	12597
Brideau Shtmtl Fabrication Inc	Leominster	MA	E	978 537-3372	9643
Cape Light Compact	Barnstable	MA	F	508 375-6703	6199
Cox Engineering Company (PA)	Canton	MA	C	781 302-3300	7781
Dg Service Company Inc	Mattapoisett	MA	F	508 758-7906	10257
Division 15 Hvac Inc	Pembroke	MA	E	781 285-3115	11363
H2o Care Inc	Middleton	MA	F	978 777-8330	10384
Harrington Air Systems LLC	Watertown	MA	F	781 341-1999	12880
Helfrich Bros Boiler Works Inc	Lawrence	MA	E	978 975-2464	9566
Ideal Sheet Metal Corp	Worcester	MA	F	508 799-2781	13739
J & J Heating & AC Inc	Dracut	MA	F	978 454-8197	8306
Kennedy Sheet Metal Inc	East Weymouth	MA	F	781 331-7764	8431
Kleeberg Sheet Metal Inc	Ludlow	MA	D	413 589-1854	9947
Lake Industries Inc	Stoneham	MA	D	781 438-8814	12180
Le Bel Inc	Abington	MA	E	781 878-7279	5725
Leon Eg Company Inc	Boston	MA	E	617 482-8383	6856
Lml Construction Inc	Leverett	MA	F	413 665-3788	9718
New England Stinless Distr LLC	Salisbury	MA	F	978 255-4830	11743
Oldcastle Infrastructure Inc	Rehoboth	MA	E	508 336-7600	11613
Piping Systems Inc	Assonet	MA	E	508 644-2221	5976
Platinum Fire Prtction Svcs LL (PA)	Marlborough	MA	E	508 481-8242	10196
Process Cooling Systems Inc	Leominster	MA	F	978 537-1996	9697
R I Baker Co Inc (PA)	Clarksburg	MA	E	413 663-3791	8073
R J McDonald Inc	Barre	MA	F	978 355-6649	6203
Riley Power Inc	Marlborough	MA	B	508 852-7100	10204
Runtal North America Inc	Haverhill	MA	E	800 526-2621	9128
Simplex Time Recorder LLC (DH)	Westminster	MA	C		13278
Solar Five LLC	Lexington	MA	F	781 301-7233	9776
South Mountain Company Inc	West Tisbury	MA	F	508 693-4850	13055
Townsend Welding Co Inc	Wilmington	MA	F	978 657-5189	13468
Zampell Refractories Inc (PA)	Newburyport	MA	E	978 465-0055	10728
DSM Metal Fabrication Inc	Biddeford	ME	F	207 282-6740	4561
Earl W Gerrish & Sons	Brownville	ME	F	207 965-2171	4637
Fastco Fabrication Inc	Lincoln	ME	F	207 794-3030	5007
Parker-Hannifin Corporation	Kittery	ME	D	207 439-9511	4938
Tigpro Inc	Portland	ME	G	207 878-1190	5282
Wardwell Piping Inc	Windham	ME	F	207 892-0034	5674
Capitol Fire Protection Co Inc	Loudon	NH	E	603 783-4713	14794
Charles P Blouin Inc (PA)	Seabrook	NH	C	603 474-3400	15586
Hampshire Fire Protection LLC (PA)	Londonderry	NH	D	603 432-8221	14753
MJ Murphy and Sons Inc	Dover	NH	F	603 767-4200	14236
Palmer and Sicard Inc	Exeter	NH	D	603 778-1841	14300
Pollution Research & Dev Corp (PA)	Newport	NH	G	603 863-7553	15234
Rays Electric & Gen Contg Inc	Berlin	NH	F	603 752-1370	13985
Service Experts LLC	Rochester	NH	F	603 332-6466	15493
Slate Corporation	Auburn	NH	F	603 234-5943	13912
Woodstock Soapstone Co Inc	West Lebanon	NH	F	800 866-4344	15692
Century Sheet Metal Inc	Riverside	RI	G	401 433-1380	16653
Eagle Industries Inc	Ashaway	RI	F	401 596-8111	15739
Frank Lombardo and Sons Inc	Providence	RI	F	401 461-4547	16521
H V Holland Inc	Jamestown	RI	F	401 423-0614	16069
Metalworks Corporation	Tiverton	RI	F	401 624-4400	16737
Nasons Ug Inc (PA)	Middletown	RI	F	401 847-2497	16180

	CITY	ST	EMP	PHONE	ENTRY#
Nevtec Ltd	Newport	VT	F	802 334-7800	17401
Northeastern Htg Vent AC Corp	Williston	VT	F	802 865-8008	17743
Vhv Company (PA)	Winooski	VT	C	802 655-8805	17771

1721 Painting and paper hanging

	CITY	ST	EMP	PHONE	ENTRY#
Bond Painting Company Inc	Old Greenwich	CT	E	212 944-0070	2630
John Canning & Co Ltd	Cheshire	CT	E	203 272-9868	602
Bascom Environmental Co	Plymouth	MA	E	617 282-9500	11449
Roadsafe Traffic Systems Inc	Avon	MA	D	508 580-6700	6160
Gabriel Business Group Co Ltd	Brookline	NH	F	877 401-5544	14039
J Goodison Company (PA)	North Kingstown	RI	E	401 667-5938	16261

1731 Electrical work

	CITY	ST	EMP	PHONE	ENTRY#
Ac/DC Industrial Electric LLC	Bozrah	CT	G	860 886-2232	225
Command Corporation	East Granby	CT	E	800 851-6012	930
E-J Electric T & D LLC	Wallingford	CT	D	203 626-9625	3803
Eastern Electric Cnstr Co	Harwinton	CT	G	860 485-1100	1519
Eastside Electric Inc	Harwinton	CT	F	860 485-0700	1520
Interstate Elec Svcs Corp	Windsor	CT	E	860 243-5644	4284
Mercury Cabling Systems LLC	Stratford	CT	E	203 378-9008	3556
On Line Building Systems LLC	Danbury	CT	G	203 798-1194	792
Right of Way Solutions LLC	Salem	CT	G	860 917-0608	2945
Tri State Maintenance Svcs LLC	North Haven	CT	E	203 691-1343	2440
TT Trade Group LLC (PA)	Bethel	CT	F	800 354-4502	137
Ward Leonard Operating LLC (DH)	Thomaston	CT	E	860 283-5801	3643
Ward Lonard Houma Holdings LLC	Thomaston	CT	D	860 283-5801	3644
Aerial Wireless Services LLC	Bellingham	MA	D	508 657-1213	6282
American Sub Assmbly Prdcers I	Dudley	MA	E	508 949-2320	8315
Andrus Power Solutions Inc	Lee	MA	F	413 243-0043	9610
Atrex Energy Inc (PA)	Walpole	MA	E	781 461-8251	12551
BP Logue & Co	Chelmsford	MA	F	978 251-4433	7915
Brewer Electric & Utilities In	South Yarmouth	MA	G	508 771-2040	11981
Citiworks Corp	Attleboro	MA	F	508 761-7400	6004
Complete Energy Services Corp	Raynham	MA	F	833 237-2677	11584
Dagle Electrical Cnstr Corp	Wilmington	MA	D	800 379-1459	13401
Dgi Communications LLC (PA)	North Billerica	MA	E	781 285-6972	10905
Giner Elx Sub LLC	Auburndale	MA	E	781 392-0300	6134
Hiller Companies Inc	Peabody	MA	E	978 532-5730	11315
Ideal Electric Co Inc	Peabody	MA	E	781 284-2525	11317
Infra-Red Bldg & Pwr Svc Inc (PA)	Holbrook	MA	F	781 767-0888	9175
L T X International Inc	Norwood	MA	D	781 461-1000	11189
Leon Eg Company Inc	Boston	MA	E	617 482-8383	6856
M & S Electrical Contrs LLC	Brockton	MA	G	781 389-4465	7293
Markarian Electric LLC	Watertown	MA	G	617 393-9700	12890
Nashoba Security Inc	Littleton	MA	F	978 486-8615	9827
Nedap Inc	Burlington	MA	F	844 876-3327	7396
Ralco Electric Inc	Westport	MA	D	508 679-3363	13299
Shufro Security Company Inc	Newton	MA	F	617 244-3355	10784
Tidal Communications LLC	North Andover	MA	F	978 687-0900	10852
Whyte Electric LLC	Braintree	MA	G	781 348-6239	7213
Tyler Technologies Inc	Bangor	ME	F	207 947-4494	4517
Electrcal Installations LLC Ei	Moultonborough	NH	F	603 253-4525	15053
Exacom Inc	Concord	NH	E	603 228-0706	14129
Fanaras Elc & Indus Contrls	Kensington	NH	G	603 772-3425	14630
Fibernext LLC	Concord	NH	E	603 226-2400	14130
Rays Electric & Gen Contg Inc	Berlin	NH	F	603 752-1370	13985
Williamson Electrical Co Inc	Epping	NH	D	617 884-9200	14277
Celestial Monitoring Corp (HQ)	Narragansett	RI	E	401 782-1045	16187
Dexter Sign Co	East Providence	RI	F	401 434-1100	16014
Eagle Industries Inc	Ashaway	RI	F	401 596-8111	15739
Energy MGT & Ctrl Svcs Inc	Cranston	RI	F	401 946-1440	15856
Interstate Elec Svcs Corp	East Providence	RI	F	401 369-7890	16024
Newport Electric Corporation	Portsmouth	RI	F	401 293-0527	16450
Telecom Installation Svcs Inc	Middletown	RI	E	401 258-2095	16185

1741 Masonry and other stonework

	CITY	ST	EMP	PHONE	ENTRY#
Connecticut Basement Systems Inc	Seymour	CT	C	203 881-5090	2959
John Canning & Co Ltd	Cheshire	CT	E	203 272-9868	602
Dauphinais & Son Inc	Wilbraham	MA	E	413 596-3964	13357
Ted Ondrick Company LLC (PA)	Chicopee	MA	F	413 592-2565	8062
Freshwater Stone & Brickwork	Orland	ME	E	207 469-6331	5132
Maine Stove & Chimney LLC	Sanford	ME	G	207 324-4440	5399
North American Supaflu Systems	Scarborough	ME	F	207 883-1155	5441
Hudson Quarry Corp	Hudson	NH	F	603 598-0142	14507
New England Supply Inc (PA)	Williston	VT	D	802 858-4577	17742

1742 Plastering, drywall, and insulation

	CITY	ST	EMP	PHONE	ENTRY#
Ecologic Energy Solutions LLC	Stamford	CT	D	203 889-0505	3342
Controlled Envmt Systems LLC (PA)	Mansfield	MA	E	508 339-4237	10042
K & J Interiors Inc	Plymouth	MA	D	508 830-0670	11463
Zampell Refractories Inc	Auburn	ME	F	207 786-2400	4465
Environmental Interiors Inc	Nashua	NH	E	603 889-9290	15095
Gabriel Business Group Co Ltd	Brookline	NH	F	877 401-5544	14039

	CITY	ST	EMP	PHONE	ENTRY#
1743 Terrazzo, tile, marble, mosaic work					
Joseph Cohn Son Tile Trazo LLC	North Haven	CT	G	203 772-2420	2420
New England Stone Inc	Milford	CT	F	203 876-8606	1853
Atlantic MBL & Gran Group Inc	East Falmouth	MA	G	508 540-9770	8356
Bostonian Clg Restoration Inc	Braintree	MA	F	781 356-3303	7170
Lone Star Holdings Inc (HQ)	Chelsea	MA	E	781 935-2224	7986
Louis W Mian Incorporated (PA)	Boston	MA	F	617 241-7900	6863
Morningstar Marble & Gran Inc	Topsham	ME	F	207 725-7309	5551
Rumford Stone Inc (PA)	Bow	NH	F	603 224-9876	14010
1751 Carpentry work					
A Plus Exterior LLC	Milford	CT	F	203 516-1729	1792
Agw Clssic Hardwood Floors LLC	Westbrook	CT	G	203 640-3106	4135
All-Time Manufacturing Co Inc	Montville	CT	F	860 848-9258	1926
Custom Cft Ktchens By Rzio Bro	Monroe	CT	F	203 268-0271	1912
Hallmark Woodworkers Inc	Bridgeport	CT	F	203 730-0535	327
Pemac Construction	Oakdale	CT	F	860 437-0007	2623
S J Pappas Inc	Meriden	CT	G	203 237-7701	1695
Stanley Black & Decker Inc	Farmington	CT	F	860 677-2861	1248
Aluminum Products Cape Cod Inc (PA)	Dennis Port	MA	F	508 398-8546	8259
Kitchen Associates Inc	Sterling	MA	E	978 422-3322	12164
Master Millwork LLC	West Wareham	MA	E	508 273-0500	13068
Nashoba Security Inc	Littleton	MA	F	978 486-8615	9827
Payne/Bouchier Inc (PA)	Roxbury	MA	F	617 445-4323	11692
Ultimate Windows Inc	Lawrence	MA	G	978 687-9444	9605
Woodmeister Master Bldrs Inc (PA)	Holden	MA	C	774 345-1000	9196
Ambassador Woodworks Inc	Walpole	ME	G	916 858-1092	5580
Bagala Window Works	Westbrook	ME	G	207 887-9231	5616
Brown Construction Inc	Houlton	ME	F	207 532-0910	4898
Overhead Door Co Bangor Inc	Hermon	ME	F	207 848-7200	4888
R G Eaton Woodworks Inc	Westbrook	ME	G	207 883-3398	5644
Advanced Custom Cabinets Inc	Brentwood	NH	F	603 772-6211	14019
Aubin Woodworking Inc	Bow	NH	F	603 224-5512	13993
Chamberlain Companies Inc	Salem	NH	E	603 893-2606	15512
Procraft Corporation	New Boston	NH	E	603 487-2080	15193
R G Tombs Door Company Inc	Hooksett	NH	E	603 624-5040	14471
Thibco Inc	Manchester	NH	G	603 623-3011	14944
Completely Custom LLC	North Kingstown	RI	G	401 667-0059	16239
Lockheed Archtctral Sltons Inc	Pascoag	RI	C	401 568-3061	16339
1752 Floor laying and floor work, nec					
Agw Clssic Hardwood Floors LLC	Westbrook	CT	G	203 640-3106	4135
Bostonian Clg Restoration Inc	Braintree	MA	F	781 356-3303	7170
Industrial Floor Covering Inc	North Billerica	MA	G	978 362-8655	10921
Proknee Corp	Whitefield	ME	E	207 549-5018	5656
Atlas Gran Countertop Flr Sup	Derry	NH	G	603 818-8899	14190
1761 Roofing, siding, and sheetmetal work					
A Plus Exterior LLC	Milford	CT	F	203 516-1729	1792
American Building Systems Inc	Bristol	CT	G	860 589-0215	395
Clarke International Bus Inc	Middletown	CT	E	860 632-1149	1743
Coastal Exteriors LLC	Wallingford	CT	F	203 626-5396	3790
Fabtron Incorporated	Plainville	CT	G	860 410-1801	2759
General Sheet Metal Works Inc	Bridgeport	CT	F	203 333-6111	324
Jhs Restoration Inc	South Windsor	CT	F	860 757-3870	3159
Redco Audio Inc	Monroe	CT	F	203 502-7600	1920
Savetime Corporation	Bridgeport	CT	F	203 382-2991	368
Tech-Air Incorporated	Uncasville	CT	E	860 848-1287	3744
The Petit Tool Co	Thomaston	CT	E	860 283-9626	3636
Aluminum Products Cape Cod Inc (PA)	Dennis Port	MA	F	508 398-8546	8259
Arlowe Corporation	Littleton	MA	F	978 486-9050	9802
Controlled Envmt Systems LLC (PA)	Mansfield	MA	E	508 339-4237	10042
Cox Engineering Company (PA)	Canton	MA	C	781 302-3300	7781
Crocker Architectural Shtmtl	North Oxford	MA	E	508 987-9900	11031
Everett Aluminum Inc	Everett	MA	F	617 389-3839	8488
Frs Company Inc	Medford	MA	F	781 322-6252	10285
K & J Interiors Inc	Plymouth	MA	D	508 830-0670	11463
Oliver Welding & Fabg Inc	Ipswich	MA	G	978 356-4488	9493
Phoenix Sheet Metal	South Dartmouth	MA	G	508 994-4046	11919
Sarnafil Services Inc	Canton	MA	C	781 828-5400	7825
United Hvac Co Inc	Rockland	MA	E	781 871-1060	11663
Vulcan Industries Inc	Hudson	MA	C	978 562-0003	9425
Hahnel Bros Co (PA)	Lewiston	ME	C	207 784-6477	4963
N E Tech-Air Inc	Scarborough	ME	C	207 347-7577	5439
Eastern Metals Inc	Londonderry	NH	E	603 818-8639	14745
Empire Sheetmetal Inc	Manchester	NH	E	603 622-4439	14847
Installed Building Pdts LLC	Auburn	NH	B	603 645-1604	13909
Keebowil Inc (PA)	Keene	NH	E	603 352-4232	14605
Ken-Mar LLC	Salem	NH	E	603 898-1268	15539
MJ Murphy and Sons Inc	Dover	NH	E	603 767-4200	14236
Northeastern Sheet Metal Inc	Goffstown	NH	D	603 497-4166	14355
Northern Elastomeric Inc	Brentwood	NH	D	603 778-8899	14025

	CITY	ST	EMP	PHONE	ENTRY#
Sylvester Sheet Metal LLC	Manchester	NH	E	603 624-4586	14938
Tecta America Corp	Keene	NH	D	603 352-4232	14627
Tekon-Technical Cons Inc	Portsmouth	NH	E	603 335-3080	15441
All-State Fabricators Limited Partnership	Cranston	RI	D	401 785-3900	15827
EMI Industries LLC	Cranston	RI	D	401 785-3900	15855
H V Holland Inc	Jamestown	RI	D	401 423-0614	16069
Hutchins Roofing Company Inc	Barre	VT	F	802 476-5591	17007
K V Sbardella Slate Inc	Fair Haven	VT	G	802 265-9955	17251
Vermont Aerospace Manufacturing Inc	Lyndonville	VT	E	802 748-8705	17321
Vhv Company (PA)	Winooski	VT	C	802 655-8805	17771
1771 Concrete work					
A Aiudi & Sons LLC (PA)	Plainville	CT	G	860 747-5534	2742
A Plus Exterior LLC	Milford	CT	F	203 516-1729	1792
Alliance Carpet Cushion Co (HQ)	Torrington	CT	D	860 489-4273	3667
Connecticut Basement Systems Inc	Seymour	CT	C	203 881-5090	2959
Coreslab Structures Conn Inc	Thomaston	CT	D	860 283-8281	3617
O & G Industries Inc	Bridgeport	CT	B	203 366-4586	354
Thomas Keegan & Sons Inc	Wallingford	CT	F	203 239-9248	3862
Valley Sand & Gravel Corp	North Haven	CT	F	203 562-3192	2443
Bostonian Clg Restoration Inc	Braintree	MA	F	781 356-3303	7170
Ecpi Inc	Bolton	MA	F	774 823-6368	6496
J G Maclellan Con Co Inc	Amesbury	MA	F	978 458-1223	5839
Lml Construction Inc	Leverett	MA	F	413 665-3788	9718
Louie and Teds Blacktop Inc	Swansea	MA	F	508 678-4948	12306
New England Foundation Co Inc (PA)	Hyde Park	MA	D	617 361-9750	9465
P J Albert Inc	Fitchburg	MA	D	978 345-7828	8671
S and S Concrete Forms Cnstr	Swansea	MA	F	508 379-0191	12310
F R Carroll Inc	Limerick	ME	E	207 793-8615	5001
Sandelin Foundation Inc	Topsham	ME	F	207 725-7004	5552
Concrete Products Inc	Chepachet	RI	F	401 568-8874	15803
Frank W Whitcomb Cnstr Corp	Colchester	VT	D	802 655-1270	17191
Joseph P Carrara & Sons Inc (PA)	North Clarendon	VT	E	802 775-2301	17415
S D Ireland Con Cnstr Corp	Williston	VT	C	802 863-6222	17747
1781 Water well drilling					
New England Foundation Co Inc (PA)	Hyde Park	MA	D	617 361-9750	9465
H A Manosh Corp	Morrisville	VT	D	802 888-5722	17383
1791 Structural steel erection					
All Phase Steel Works LLC	New Haven	CT	F	203 375-8881	2113
Berlin Steel Construction Co (PA)	Kensington	CT	E	860 828-3531	1538
Engineered Building Pdts Inc	Bloomfield	CT	E	860 243-1110	161
General Wldg & Fabrication Inc	Watertown	CT	E	860 274-9668	4014
George H Olson Steel Company	Stratford	CT	F	203 375-5656	3541
Jwc Steel Co LLC	Hartford	CT	E	860 296-5517	1489
Steeltech Building Pdts Inc	South Windsor	CT	D	860 290-8930	3184
United Steel Inc	East Hartford	CT	C	860 289-2323	1032
James F Stearns Co LLP	Pembroke	MA	E	781 829-0095	11371
MPS Products Corp	Rowley	MA	E	978 817-2144	11681
Patricia Barrett	Leominster	MA	E	978 537-0458	9692
Quinn Bros of Essex Inc	Essex	MA	E	978 768-6929	8479
Schrimpf Wldg Fabrication Inc	Woburn	MA	E	339 298-2311	13661
Superior Rail and Ir Works Inc	East Bridgewater	MA	E	508 378-4025	8345
Topper & Griggs Group LLC	Agawam	MA	E	860 747-5737	5813
James A McBrady Inc	Scarborough	ME	E	207 883-4176	5435
New Hampshire Stl Erectors LLC	Goffstown	NH	E	603 668-3464	14353
S L Chasse Welding & Fabg Inc	Hudson	NH	D	603 886-3436	14543
Capco Steel LLC	Providence	RI	E	401 861-1220	16496
Engineering Wldg & Fabg Co Inc	North Kingstown	RI	E	401 884-1484	16252
Ne Steel Fabricators LLC	Cranston	RI	E	401 785-1234	15898
New England Supply Inc (PA)	Williston	VT	D	802 858-4577	17742
1793 Glass and glazing work					
Capitol Glass Company Inc	West Hartford	CT	F	860 236-1936	4050
Kensington GL & Frmng Co Inc	Berlin	CT	F	860 828-9428	73
Liberty Glass and Met Inds Inc	North Grosvenordale	CT	E	860 923-3623	2384
A B C Glass Co Inc	Springfield	MA	F	413 734-4524	12067
B & G Glass LLC	Pittsfield	MA	G	413 442-3113	11391
Contract Glass Service Inc	Billerica	MA	E	978 262-1323	6429
Fbne LLC	Boston	MA	F	617 571-6443	6733
Ipswich Bay Glass Co Inc	Rowley	MA	C	978 948-6644	11677
Prestige Cstm Mirror & GL Inc	Waltham	MA	F	781 647-0878	12752
Serpentine Stned Leaded GL Inc	Needham Heights	MA	G	781 449-2074	10556
Stained Glass Resources Inc (PA)	Hampden	MA	E	413 566-5053	9023
Bill Lztte Archtctral GL Alum	Riverside	RI	E	401 383-9535	16652
1794 Excavation work					
Core Site Services LLC	New Haven	CT	G	475 227-9026	2140
Desiato Sand & Gravel Corp	Storrs Mansfield	CT	E	860 429-6479	3512
DR Charles Envmtl Cnstr LLC	Monroe	CT	G	203 445-0412	1913
HI Stone & Son Inc	Southbury	CT	E	203 264-8656	3195

Employee Codes: A=Over 500 employees, B=251-500   2024 Harris New England   833
C=101-250, D=51-100, E=20-50, F=10-19, G=1-9   Manufacturers Directory

SIC

	CITY	ST	EMP	PHONE	ENTRY#
Mist Hill Property Maint LLC	Brookfield	CT	F	203 648-7434	530
O & G Industries Inc	Bridgeport	CT	B	203 366-4586	354
Thomas Keegan & Sons Inc	Wallingford	CT	F	203 239-9248	3862
Brox Industries Inc (PA)	Dracut	MA	D	978 454-9105	8302
Cotton Tree Service Inc	Northampton	MA	F	413 584-9104	11057
E W Sykes General Contractors	Athol	MA	E	978 249-7655	5978
L J Gentile & Sons Inc	Norfolk	MA	G	508 384-5156	10800
Lml Construction Inc	Leverett	MA	F	413 665-3788	9718
New England Foundation Co Inc (PA)	Hyde Park	MA	D	617 361-9750	9465
P A Landers Inc	Hanover	MA	F	508 747-1800	9039
R J McDonald Inc	Barre	MA	F	978 355-6649	6203
Brown Construction Inc	Houlton	ME	F	207 532-0910	4898
FC Work & Sons Incorporated	Jackson	ME	F	207 722-3206	4912
Ferraiolo Construction Inc	Rockland	ME	E	207 594-9840	5327
Hanley Construction Inc	Bristol	ME	F	207 677-2207	4630
Hanscom Construction Inc	Marshfield	ME	F	207 255-8067	5046
Hughes Brothers Inc	Hampden	ME	E	207 659-3417	4864
John Khiel III Log Chpping Inc	Denmark	ME	E	207 452-2157	4722
P & K Sand and Gravel Inc	Naples	ME	E	207 693-6765	5081
Robert McBreairty Jr Sons Inc	Saint Francis	ME	F	207 834-3257	5388
Shaw Brothers Construction Inc (PA)	Gorham	ME	C	207 839-2552	4835
Alvin J Coleman & Son Inc (PA)	Albany	NH	F	603 447-5936	13847
Garland Lumber Company Inc	Center Conway	NH	E	603 356-5636	14053
Hopkinton For Land Claring Inc	Henniker	NH	F	603 428-8400	14437
J C B Leasing Inc	Weare	NH	F	603 529-7974	15671
Michie Corporation	Henniker	NH	D	603 428-7426	14438
Northeast Earth Mechanics LLC	Pittsfield	NH	F	603 435-7989	15334
R L Balla Inc	South Acworth	NH	F	603 835-6529	15628
Slate Corporation	Auburn	NH	F	603 234-5943	13912
Welog Inc	Colebrook	NH	F	603 237-8277	14111
George Sherman Sand Grav Inc	Wakefield	RI	F	401 789-6304	16741
Narragansett Improvement Co (PA)	Providence	RI	D	401 331-0051	16571
Champlain Construction Co Inc	Middlebury	VT	F	802 388-2652	17341
Crown Point Excavation LLC	Springfield	VT	F	802 291-4817	17617
Dailey Precast LLC (HQ)	Shaftsbury	VT	D	802 442-4418	17549
Dale E Percy Inc	Stowe	VT	F	802 253-8503	17630
Gurney Brothers Construction	North Springfield	VT	E	802 886-2210	17421
H A Manosh Corp	Morrisville	VT	D	802 888-5722	17383
Matt Waite Excavation Inc	Pawlet	VT	F	802 325-3668	17441
Willey Earthmoving Corp	Windsor	VT	G	802 674-2500	17764

1795 Wrecking and demolition work

	CITY	ST	EMP	PHONE	ENTRY#
Laydon Industries LLC (PA)	New Haven	CT	E	203 562-7283	2169
Costello Dismantling Co Inc (PA)	West Wareham	MA	E	508 291-2324	13058
Fisher Contracting Corporation	Worcester	MA	G	508 421-6989	13723
Brown Construction Inc	Houlton	ME	F	207 532-0910	4898
North Ridge Contracting Inc	Epsom	NH	E	603 942-6104	14282
Earth Waste Systems Inc (PA)	Rutland	VT	E	802 775-7722	17494

1796 Installing building equipment

	CITY	ST	EMP	PHONE	ENTRY#
Atlantic Eqp Installers Inc	Wallingford	CT	E	203 284-0402	3777
Bay State Elevator Company Inc	Bloomfield	CT	F	860 243-9030	150
Otis Elevator Company	Bloomfield	CT	B	860 242-3632	198
Otis Elevator Company (HQ)	Farmington	CT	C	860 674-3000	1235
Stevenson Group Corporation	Harwinton	CT	F	860 689-0011	1524
Bay State Elevator Company Inc (HQ)	Agawam	MA	E	413 786-7000	5779
Chas G Allen Realty LLC	Barre	MA	D	978 355-2911	6202
Draper Elevator Cab Co Inc	Holbrook	MA	F	781 961-3146	9171
Industrial Transfer & Stor Inc	Southbridge	MA	E	508 765-9178	12022
MEI Rigging & Crating LLC	Salisbury	MA	F	978 685-7700	11742
Nashoba Security Inc	Littleton	MA	F	978 486-8615	9827
Waverly Tool Rental & Sales Co	Framingham	MA	F	508 872-8866	8811
Coast To Cast Ff E Instlltons	Greenland	NH	F	603 433-0164	14368
Custom Iron Works Inc	Coventry	RI	E	401 826-3310	15812
Momentum Mfg Group - N LLC (PA)	Saint Johnsbury	VT	C	802 748-5007	17545

1799 Special trade contractors, nec

	CITY	ST	EMP	PHONE	ENTRY#
Adamsahern Sign Solutions Inc	Hartford	CT	F	860 523-8835	1467
Alloy Welding & Mfg Co Inc	Bristol	CT	F	860 582-3638	394
Arnio Welding LLC	Central Village	CT	F	860 564-7696	565
Bender Management Inc	Norwalk	CT	E	203 847-3865	2471
Connecticut Basement Systems Inc	Seymour	CT	C	203 881-5090	2959
Core Site Services LLC	New Haven	CT	G	475 227-9026	2140
Custom Cft Ktchens By Rzio Bro	Monroe	CT	F	203 268-0271	1912
Feman Steel LLC	Bloomfield	CT	F	860 982-6393	164
Fitzgerald-Norwalk Awng Co Inc	Norwalk	CT	G	203 847-5858	2501
Foleys Pump Service Inc	Danbury	CT	E	203 792-2236	747
Garden Iron LLC	Westbrook	CT	G	860 767-9917	4138
Innovative Environmental LLC	Colchester	CT	F	860 871-7582	660
Innovative Fusion Inc	Naugatuck	CT	E	203 729-3873	1965
J & M Plumbing & Cnstr LLC	Norwich	CT	G	860 319-3082	2608
New England Stone Inc	Milford	CT	F	203 876-8606	1853
Nvi Weld Technology LLC	Waterbury	CT	G	203 707-0587	3953

	CITY	ST	EMP	PHONE	ENTRY#
Show Motion Inc	Milford	CT	E	203 866-1866	1884
Singer Company Inc	Waterford	CT	F	860 439-1234	3995
Veolia Es Tchncal Slutions LLC	Danbury	CT	F	203 748-9116	832
Wad Inc	East Berlin	CT	F	860 828-3331	920
Bells Powder Coating Inc	Attleboro Falls	MA	F	508 643-2222	6079
Bmac Inc	Ayer	MA	E	978 772-3310	6175
Cape Cod Fence Co (PA)	South Yarmouth	MA	F	508 398-6041	11982
Chilsons Shops Inc	Easthampton	MA	E	413 529-8062	8441
Citiworks Corp	Attleboro	MA	F	508 761-7400	6004
Discover Marble & Granite Inc (PA)	Millbury	MA	D	877 411-9900	10432
Dogwatch Inc (PA)	Natick	MA	G	508 650-0600	10478
Feeneys Fence Inc	Hyde Park	MA	F	617 364-1407	9460
Gerritystone Inc	Wilmington	MA	E	781 938-1820	13409
Graphic Impact Signs Inc	Pittsfield	MA	E	413 499-0382	11399
Industrial Transfer & Stor Inc	Southbridge	MA	E	508 765-9178	12022
International Stone Inc	Woburn	MA	D	781 937-3300	13589
Jam Plastics Inc	Leominster	MA	F	978 537-2570	9672
Jarvis Welding & Mfg Co	Turners Falls	MA	G	413 863-9541	12449
Joe Miller Inc	Worcester	MA	F	508 753-8581	13745
Lundys Company Inc	Lynn	MA	F	781 595-8639	9983
Mid-State Welding Inc	Southbridge	MA	F	508 987-9410	12031
Millers Petroleum Systems Inc	Pittsfield	MA	G	413 499-2134	11411
On-Sight Insight	Boston	MA	G	617 502-5985	6931
Onyx Environmental Svcs LLC (DH)	Boston	MA	F	617 849-6600	6936
Onyx Marble & Granite LLC	Framingham	MA	F	508 620-0775	8793
Ornamental Ironworks Inc	Fall River	MA	F	508 678-0687	8592
P A Landers Inc	Hanover	MA	F	508 747-1800	9039
Perfection Fence Corp (PA)	Marshfield	MA	F	781 837-3600	10243
Quality Stone Marble Inc (PA)	Whitinsville	MA	F	774 813-4801	13344
Remediation Lockwood Tech	Leominster	MA	F	404 666-5857	9701
Southeast Railing Co Inc	Canton	MA	F	781 828-7088	7831
Speedy Sign-A-Rama USA	Braintree	MA	G	781 849-1181	7203
Starkweather Engineering Inc	Tewksbury	MA	F	978 858-3700	12419
Townsend Welding Co Inc	Wilmington	MA	F	978 657-5189	13468
United GL To Met Sealing Inc	Lawrence	MA	F	978 327-5880	9606
Water Closet LLC	Nantucket	MA	F	508 228-2828	10466
Worcester County Welding Inc	Rochdale	MA	G	508 892-4884	11629
Alan S Bolster	Brewer	ME	F	207 989-7943	4608
Anchor Corporation	Kennebunk	ME	F	207 985-6018	4920
Bailey Sign Inc	Westbrook	ME	E	207 774-2843	5617
Sign Services Inc	Stetson	ME	F	207 296-2400	5531
Sunny Side Land Holdings LLC	Presque Isle	ME	F	207 768-1020	5310
Advanced Polymerics Inc	Salem	NH	G	603 328-8177	15502
Aquatic Solutions LLC	Hampton	NH	G	888 704-7665	14398
Bay State Industrial Weldin	Hudson	NH	F	603 881-7663	14488
Bri-Weld Industries LLC	Auburn	NH	F	603 622-9480	13906
David D Douglas Inc	Londonderry	NH	G	603 437-1151	14742
East Coast Metal Works Co Inc	Kingston	NH	G	603 642-9600	14634
Jaeger Usa Inc	Rochester	NH	F	603 332-5816	15480
LAD Welding & Fabrication	Hooksett	NH	F	603 228-6617	14466
North Ridge Contracting Inc	Epsom	NH	E	603 942-6104	14282
Radenhausen & ONeill Inc	Jaffrey	NH	F	603 532-4879	14578
Ripano Stoneworks Ltd	Nashua	NH	F	603 886-6655	15160
S L Chasse Welding & Fabg Inc	Hudson	NH	D	603 886-3436	14543
Scarlet Aspen LLC	Portsmouth	NH	F	603 509-3990	15435
Triumph Interiors LLC	Rindge	NH	F	603 899-5184	15461
Yarra Design & Fabrication LLC	Bow	NH	F	603 224-6880	14014
Cabinet Gallery Ltd (PA)	Woonsocket	RI	G	401 762-4300	16952
Capco Steel LLC	Providence	RI	D	401 861-1220	16496
Cosco LLC	Woonsocket	RI	D	401 765-0009	16955
Custom Iron Works Inc	Coventry	RI	E	401 826-3310	15812
George Sherman Sand Grav Inc	Wakefield	RI	E	401 789-6304	16741
Stone Systems New England LLC	North Smithfield	RI	E	401 766-3603	16333
McKernon Group Inc	Brandon	VT	D	802 247-8500	17068
Milton Vermont Sheet Metal Inc	Milton	VT	F	802 893-1581	17362
Momentum Mfg Group - N LLC (PA)	Saint Johnsbury	VT	C	802 748-5007	17545
Sogle Property LLC	Cambridge	VT	F	802 849-7943	17168
Springfield Fence Company Inc	North Springfield	VT	F	802 886-2221	17424
Twin State Signs Inc	Essex Junction	VT	G	802 872-8949	17248
Vermont Indexable Tooling Inc	Fairfax	VT	G	802 752-2002	17264
Westwood Fences Inc	Irasburg	VT	F	802 754-8486	17303

20 FOOD AND KINDRED PRODUCTS

2011 Meat packing plants

	CITY	ST	EMP	PHONE	ENTRY#
Grote & Weigel Inc (PA)	Bloomfield	CT	E	860 242-8528	166
Jbs Aves Ltda	Stamford	CT	F	203 357-5920	3390
Manchester Packing Company Inc	Manchester	CT	D	860 646-5000	1616
Martin Rosols Inc	New Britain	CT	E	860 223-2707	2040
New England Meat Packing LLC	Stafford Springs	CT	F	860 684-3505	3258
Salem Prime Cuts Incorporated	Salem	CT	F	860 859-0741	2946
Boston Brisket Company Inc	Beverly	MA	F	617 442-8814	6335

	CITY	ST	EMP	PHONE	ENTRY#
Cambridge Packing Co Inc	Boston	MA	D	617 464-6000	6635
Chicopee Provision Company Inc	Chicopee	MA	E	413 594-4765	8016
Crocetti Oakdale Pkg Co Inc (PA)	East Bridgewater	MA	F	508 587-0035	8338
Demakes Enterprises Inc	Lynn	MA	C	781 586-0212	9968
DOro Foods Inc	Malden	MA	E	781 324-1310	10011
Genoa Sausage Co Inc	Woburn	MA	E	781 933-3115	13574
J&G (2021) Inc	Sutton	MA	F	508 865-1101	12285
Kayem Foods Inc (PA)	Chelsea	MA	B	781 933-3115	7984
Kelly Corned Beef Co Chicago	Norwood	MA	F	773 588-2882	11188
Mutual Beef Co Inc	Boston	MA	F	617 442-3238	6899
New England Box Beef Company	Taunton	MA	E	781 320-3232	12352
Pearl Meat Packing Co Inc	Randolph	MA	E	781 228-5100	11571
Robbins Beef Co Inc	Boston	MA	F	617 269-1826	7010
Smithfield Direct LLC	Springfield	MA	C	413 781-5620	12130
Smithfield Foods Inc	Springfield	MA	D	413 781-5620	12131
Tx5877 Inc	Sutton	MA	C	508 865-1101	12292
William & Co Foods Inc	Boston	MA	E	617 442-2112	7124
Spear Farms Inc	Nobleboro	ME	E	207 832-4488	5101
Bp Inc	Providence	RI	F	401 274-7900	16490
Lincoln Packing Co	Cranston	RI	C	401 943-0878	15885
Butcher & Pantry LLC	Brownsville	VT	F	315 396-6464	17116
Npc Processing Inc	Shelburne	VT	E	802 660-0496	17559
Vermont Packinghouse LLC	North Springfield	VT	F	802 886-8688	17426
VT LVSTK SLGTR & PROC CO	Ferrisburgh	VT	F	802 877-3421	17269

2013 Sausages and other prepared meats

	CITY	ST	EMP	PHONE	ENTRY#
Baretta Provision Inc	East Berlin	CT	F	860 828-0802	908
Grote & Weigel Inc (PA)	Bloomfield	CT	E	860 242-8528	166
Hummel Bros Inc	New Haven	CT	D	203 787-4113	2161
Longhini LLC	New Haven	CT	E	203 624-7110	2170
Manchester Packing Company Inc	Manchester	CT	D	860 646-5000	1616
Martin Rosols Inc	New Britain	CT	E	860 223-2707	2040
Mittys LLC	Bloomfield	CT	E	516 297-9219	193
Newington Meat Center	Newington	CT	G	860 666-3431	2310
Norpaco Inc	Middletown	CT	E	860 632-2299	1768
Provisionaire & Co LLC	Westport	CT	E	646 681-8600	4193
Brothers Artisanal Inc	New Bedford	MA	G	508 938-9161	10575
Carando Gourmet Foods Corp (PA)	Agawam	MA	E	413 737-0183	5784
Chair City Meats Inc	Gardner	MA	F	978 630-1050	8881
Chicopee Provision Company Inc	Chicopee	MA	E	413 594-4765	8016
Crocetti Oakdale Pkg Co Inc (PA)	East Bridgewater	MA	F	508 587-0035	8338
Demakes Enterprises Inc	Danvers	MA	D	978 739-1506	8179
Demakes Enterprises Inc (PA)	Lynn	MA	C	781 417-1100	9967
Demakes Enterprises Inc	Lynn	MA	C	781 586-0212	9968
Diluigis Inc	Danvers	MA	D	978 750-9900	8182
Home Market Foods Inc	Norwood	MA	B	781 948-1500	11176
Kayem Foods Inc (PA)	Chelsea	MA	B	781 933-3115	7984
Kraft Heinz Foods Company	Woburn	MA	D	781 933-2800	13597
Lisbon Sausage Co Inc	New Bedford	MA	F	508 993-7645	10613
Miranda Brothers Inc	Fall River	MA	G	508 672-0982	8584
Pearl Meat Packing Co Inc	Randolph	MA	E	781 228-5100	11571
Pig Rock Sausages LLC	Milton	MA	F	617 851-9422	10454
Shaans Panini & Roast Beef LLC	North Billerica	MA	F	617 230-3166	10955
Smithfield Direct LLC	Springfield	MA	C	413 781-5620	12130
Tessis Pizza & Roast Beef	Tewksbury	MA	F	978 851-8700	12421
Waniewski Farms Inc	Feeding Hills	MA	F	413 786-1182	8637
Wohrles Foods Inc (PA)	Pittsfield	MA	E	413 442-1518	11427
Angostura International Ltd	Auburn	ME	F	207 786-3200	4419
Butcher Block Inc	Claremont	NH	E	800 258-4304	14080
Msn Corporation	Manchester	NH	D	603 623-3528	14894
Bp Inc	Providence	RI	F	401 274-7900	16490
Daniele Inc	Pascoag	RI	C	401 568-6228	16336
Daniele International Inc	Pascoag	RI	C	401 568-6228	16337
Daniele International Inc	Pascoag	RI	C	401 568-6228	16338
Daniele International LLC (PA)	Mapleville	RI	C	401 371-2000	16167
Kinderwagon Company	Newport	RI	G	617 256-7599	16215
Lincoln Packing Co	Cranston	RI	C	401 943-0878	15885
Newport Creamery LLC	Cranston	RI	F	401 946-4000	15900
Newport Jerky Company LLC	Newport	RI	F	774 644-2350	16219
Portion Meat Associates Inc	Providence	RI	F	401 421-2438	16585
Quality Beef Co Inc	Providence	RI	F	401 421-5668	16596
Rhode Island Provision Co	Johnston	RI	F	401 831-0815	16105
Stedagio LLC	Mapleville	RI	G	401 568-6228	16169
Tase-Rite Co Inc	Wakefield	RI	F	401 783-7300	16746
A Drop of Joy LLC	Williston	VT	E	802 598-6419	17720
Harringtons In Vermont Inc (PA)	Richmond	VT	F	802 434-7535	17479
Npc Processing Inc	Shelburne	VT	E	802 660-0496	17559
Plumrose Usa Inc	Swanton	VT	D	802 868-7314	17639
Vermont Beef Jerky Co	Orleans	VT	F	802 754-9412	17439

2015 Poultry slaughtering and processing

	CITY	ST	EMP	PHONE	ENTRY#
Carls Boned Chicken Inc	New Haven	CT	E	203 777-9048	2135
Moark LLC (HQ)	North Franklin	CT	E	951 332-3300	2383

	CITY	ST	EMP	PHONE	ENTRY#
Waybest Foods Inc	South Windsor	CT	G		3189
Nmw Holding Co Inc	Weymouth	MA	F	617 269-5650	13332
Radlo Foods LLC (PA)	Watertown	MA	G	617 926-7070	12903
Samuel Holmes Incorporated	Everett	MA	F	617 269-5740	8500
Somerville Live Poultry Co Inc	Boston	MA	G	617 547-9191	7045
Willow Tree Poultry Farm Inc	Attleboro	MA	D	508 222-2479	6077
Advancepierre Foods Inc	Portland	ME	A	207 541-2800	5175
Barber Foods LLC	Portland	ME	A	207 772-1934	5182
Barber Foods LLC (DH)	Portland	ME	E	207 482-5500	5183
Nuttin Ordinary LLC	Peterborough	NH	F	603 567-7916	15322
Pete and Gerrys Organics LLC (PA)	Monroe	NH	F	603 638-2827	15047
Taylor Egg Products Inc	Madbury	NH	F	603 742-1050	14801
Baffonis Poultry Farm Inc	Johnston	RI	F	401 231-6315	16077
Premium Poultry Co	Providence	RI	F	401 467-3200	16587
Warwick Poultry Co Inc	Providence	RI	F	401 421-8500	16643
Maple Wind Farm Inc	Richmond	VT	G	802 434-7257	17480
Npc Processing Inc	Shelburne	VT	E	802 660-0496	17559

2021 Creamery butter

	CITY	ST	EMP	PHONE	ENTRY#
Arista Industries Inc (PA)	Wilton	CT	E	203 761-1009	4230
Grass Roots Creamery	Granby	CT	G	860 653-6303	1306
Casco Bay Butter Company Inc	Westbrook	ME	G	207 712-9148	5620
SBwinsor Creamery LLC	Johnston	RI	G	401 231-5113	16106
Co Op Creamery	Saint Albans	VT	F	802 524-6581	17520

2022 Cheese; natural and processed

	CITY	ST	EMP	PHONE	ENTRY#
Calabro Cheese Corporation	East Haven	CT	D	203 469-1311	1038
Elm City Cheese Company Inc	Hamden	CT	F	203 865-5768	1424
Mozzicato Fmly Investments LLC	Wethersfield	CT	F	860 296-0426	4212
Ndr Liuzzi Inc	Hamden	CT	E	203 287-8477	1445
Spread Cheese Co LLC	Middletown	CT	G	203 982-1674	1784
Agri-Mark Inc (PA)	Andover	MA	G	978 552-5500	5869
Grey Barn Farm Enterprises LLC	Chilmark	MA	G	508 645-4854	8071
HP Hood LLC (PA)	Lynnfield	MA	C	617 887-3000	9995
Kraft Heinz Foods Company	Woburn	MA	D	781 933-2800	13597
Pineland Farms Dairy Company	Bangor	ME	F	207 922-4036	4514
Tillamook County Creamery Assn	Portland	ME	G	503 815-1300	5283
Providence Specialty Pdts Inc	Providence	RI	D	401 272-4979	16593
Supreme Dairy Farms	Woonsocket	RI	F	401 739-8180	16977
Cabot Creamery Cooperative Inc	Waitsfield	VT	B	888 792-2268	17664
Franklin Foods Inc (DH)	Enosburg Falls	VT	E	802 933-4338	17223
Mountain Mozzarella LLC	North Bennington	VT	E	802 440-9950	17409
Shelburne Farms	Shelburne	VT	D	802 985-8498	17562
Sugarbush Farm Inc	Woodstock	VT	G	802 457-1757	17778
Swan Valley Cheese Vermont LLC	Swanton	VT	G	802 868-7181	17643
Vermont Creamery LLC	Websterville	VT	E	802 479-9371	17685
Windham Foundation Inc (PA)	Grafton	VT	F	802 843-2211	17275

2023 Dry, condensed, evaporated products

	CITY	ST	EMP	PHONE	ENTRY#
Bactana Corp	Farmington	CT	G	203 716-1230	1208
Culture Fresh Foods Inc	Naugatuck	CT	F	203 632-8433	1955
Healthy Mom LLC	Hamden	CT	F	855 588-6242	1430
Herbalife Distributor	Bristol	CT	G	860 584-9721	453
Inner Armour Black LLC	Berlin	CT	G	860 656-7720	71
Natures First Inc (PA)	Orange	CT	F	203 795-8400	2678
Nestle Usa Inc	Pomfret Center	CT	D	860 928-0082	2813
Unipharm Inc	Waterbury	CT	E	203 528-3230	3978
Ajinomoto Cambrooke Inc (DH)	Ayer	MA	E	508 782-2300	6170
Meganutra Inc (PA)	Norwood	MA	G	781 762-9600	11195
On The Edge Nutrition Llc	Boston	MA	G	617 752-4056	6930
Partylite (HQ)	Plymouth	MA	D	203 661-1926	11471
Native Maine Operations Inc	Westbrook	ME	E	207 856-1100	5640
Pineland Farms Dairy Company	Bangor	ME	F	207 922-4036	4514
Bariatrix Nutrition Corp	Fairfax	VT	E	802 527-2500	17255
St Albans Cooperative Creamery Inc	Saint Albans	VT	D	802 524-9366	17531
St Albans Creamery LLC	Saint Albans	VT	E	802 524-9366	17532

2024 Ice cream and frozen deserts

	CITY	ST	EMP	PHONE	ENTRY#
Big Dipper Ice Cream Fctry Inc	Prospect	CT	F	203 758-3200	2830
Bucks Spumoni Company Inc	Milford	CT	F	203 874-2007	1804
Cold Stone Creamery	Clinton	CT	G	860 669-7025	639
Gelato Giuliana LLC	New Haven	CT	F	203 772-0607	2154
Greg Robbins and Associates	Branford	CT	G	888 699-8876	262
HP Hood LLC	Suffield	CT	C	860 623-4435	3591
J Foster Ice Cream	Simsbury	CT	D	860 651-1499	3092
Michaels Dairy Inc	New London	CT	E	860 443-7617	2230
Mozzicato Pastry & Bake Sp Inc	Hartford	CT	E	860 296-0426	1495
Pralines Inc	Wallingford	CT	F	203 284-8847	3838
Pralines of Plainville	Plainville	CT	G	860 410-1151	2778
Reeds Inc	Norwalk	CT	E	800 997-3337	2563
Royal Ice Cream Company Inc (PA)	Manchester	CT	F	860 649-5358	1632
Salem Vly Farms Ice Cream Inc	Salem	CT	F	860 859-2980	2947
Smoothie King	Waterford	CT	F	860 574-9382	3996

S I C

	CITY	ST	EMP	PHONE	ENTRY#
Soft Serve CT LLC	Bridgeport	CT	F	203 367-3000	373
295 Tremont Inc	Attleboro	MA	D	508 222-2884	5985
Berry Twist	Boston	MA	G	857 362-7455	6589
Dairy Queen	West Boylston	MA	F	508 853-2700	12959
Foodberry Inc	Boston	MA	G	617 491-6600	6743
Freeze Operations Holding Corp **(PA)**	Wilbraham	MA	A	413 543-2445	13360
Hershey Creamery Company	Seekonk	MA	F	508 399-8560	11777
HP Hood LLC **(PA)**	Lynnfield	MA	C	617 887-3000	9995
Meletharb Inc	Wakefield	MA	F	781 245-4946	12518
Mixx Frozen Yogurt Inc **(PA)**	Allston	MA	F	617 782-6499	5824
Muffins On Main LLC	Westford	MA	G	978 788-4365	13252
Peaceful Meadows Ice Cream Inc **(PA)**	Carver	MA	F	781 447-3700	7855
Philip RS Sorbet Co Inc	Winchester	MA	F	781 721-6330	13491
Puritan Ice Cream Boston Inc	Boston	MA	G	617 524-3580	6986
Queen Associates Inc	Woburn	MA	D	781 389-8494	13644
Reasons To Be Cheerful	Concord	MA	G	978 610-6248	8132
Rescor Inc **(PA)**	Boston	MA	F	617 723-3635	7006
Richardsons Ice Cream	Reading	MA	G	781 944-9121	11606
Russos Inc	Saugus	MA	G	781 233-1737	11765
White Mountain Creamery Inc	Chestnut Hill	MA	F	617 527-8790	8003
Franks Bake Shop Inc	Bangor	ME	G	207 947-4594	4502
Gelato Fiasco Inc	Portland	ME	G	207 607-4002	5218
Mount Desert Island Ice Cream	Bar Harbor	ME	F	207 460-5515	4523
Protein Holdings Inc **(PA)**	Portland	ME	F	207 771-0965	5263
Round Top Ice Cream Inc	Damariscotta	ME	F	207 563-5307	4717
Shains	Sanford	ME	D	207 324-1449	5415
Annables Ntral Ice Cream Ygur	Portsmouth	NH	G	603 436-3400	15359
Kellerhaus Inc	Laconia	NH	F	603 366-4466	14654
Lactalis US Yogurt Inc	Londonderry	NH	B	603 437-4040	14761
Walpole Creamery Ltd	Walpole	NH	G	603 445-5700	15664
Ice Cream Machine Co	Cumberland	RI	F	401 333-5053	15944
Kaffeology Inc	Newport	RI	G	407 722-0922	16214
Newport Creamery LLC	Cranston	RI	F	401 946-4000	15900
Warwick Ice Cream Company	Warwick	RI	E	401 821-8403	16877
Ben & Jerrys Homemade Inc **(HQ)**	South Burlington	VT	F	802 846-1500	17571
Blue Moon Foods Inc 17704	White River Junction	VT	G	802 295-1165	
Rhino Foods Inc **(PA)**	Burlington	VT	C	802 862-0252	17156
Vermonts Orignal Ice Cream Inc	Arlington	VT	G	802 375-1133	16992

2026 Fluid milk

	CITY	ST	EMP	PHONE	ENTRY#
Guida-Seibert Dairy Company **(HQ)**	New Britain	CT	C	800 832-8929	2028
Peachwave of Watertown	Watertown	CT	G	203 942-4949	4023
The Yofarm Company	Naugatuck	CT	D	203 720-0000	1990
Willard J Stearns & Sons Inc	Storrs Mansfield	CT	E	860 423-9289	3513
295 Tremont Inc	Attleboro	MA	D	508 222-2884	5985
Agri-Mark Inc **(PA)**	Andover	MA	D	978 552-5500	5869
Brighams Inc **(HQ)**	Arlington	MA	F	800 242-2423	5939
Cumberland Farms Inc **(DH)**	Westborough	MA	B	800 225-9702	13097
Dahlicious Holdings LLC	Leominster	MA	F	978 401-2103	9656
Dahlicious LLC	Leominster	MA	E	505 200-0396	9657
Garelick Farms LLC **(DH)**	Franklin	MA	A	508 528-9000	8840
HP Hood LLC **(PA)**	Lynnfield	MA	C	617 887-3000	9995
HP Hood LLC	Peabody	MA	F	978 535-3385	11316
Johnsons Food Products Corp	Boston	MA	F	617 265-3400	6830
Lqc Inc	Norwood	MA	G	617 586-5139	11191
Peaceful Meadows Ice Cream Inc **(PA)**	Carver	MA	F	781 447-3700	7855
Plantbased Innovations LLC	Leominster	MA	E	571 243-4646	9695
Postdoc Ventures LLC	Cambridge	MA	G	617 492-3555	7687
Whittier Farms Inc	Sutton	MA	G	508 865-1096	12295
Yoway LLC	Brookline	MA	E	617 505-5158	7327
Houlton Farms Dairy Inc **(PA)**	Houlton	ME	F	207 532-3170	4900
Oakhurst Dairy **(HQ)**	Portland	ME	C	207 772-7468	5253
Protein Holdings Inc **(PA)**	Portland	ME	F	207 771-0965	5263
Thors Skyr LLC	Portland	ME	F	315 955-9418	5281
Lactalis US Yogurt Inc	Londonderry	NH	B	603 437-4040	14761
A B Munroe Dairy Inc **(PA)**	East Providence	RI	D	401 438-4450	16000
Wrights Dairy Farm Inc	North Smithfield	RI	F	401 767-3014	16334
Commonwealth Dairy LLC	Guilford	VT	D	802 251-2300	17280
Duhamel Family Farm LLC	Highgate Center	VT	G	802 868-4954	17288
Ebws LLC	Strafford	VT	G	802 765-4180	17634
H P Hood-Booth Brothers Dairy	Barre	VT	F	802 476-6605	17004
Monument Farms Inc	Weybridge	VT	E	802 545-2119	17703
St Albans Cooperative Creamery Inc	Saint Albans	VT	D	802 524-9366	17531
St Albans Creamery LLC	Saint Albans	VT	E	802 524-9366	17532

2032 Canned specialties

	CITY	ST	EMP	PHONE	ENTRY#
D & M Packing LLC	Waterbury	CT	E	203 591-8986	3903
Garan Enterprises Inc	Chicopee	MA	F	413 594-4991	8034
Kettle Cuisine LLC **(PA)**	Lynn	MA	C	617 409-1100	9980
Kettle Cuisine Holdings LLC	Lynn	MA	C	617 409-1100	9981
Royal Food Import Corporation	Boston	MA	F	617 482-3826	7016
TruRoots LLC **(PA)**	Needham	MA	E	800 288-3637	10527

	CITY	ST	EMP	PHONE	ENTRY#
Good To-Go LLC	Kittery	ME	F	207 451-9060	4935
Sams Italian Foods Inc **(PA)**	Lewiston	ME	F	207 782-9145	4991
Stonewall Kitchen LLC **(PA)**	York	ME	C	207 351-2713	5717

2033 Canned fruits and specialties

	CITY	ST	EMP	PHONE	ENTRY#
Cosmos Food Products Inc	West Haven	CT	E	800 942-6766	4099
Guida-Seibert Dairy Company **(HQ)**	New Britain	CT	C	800 832-8929	2028
Kraft Heinz Foods Company	Waterbury	CT	G	203 597-9109	3929
Mutti USA Inc	Danbury	CT	F	844 664-2630	789
Natural Country Farms Inc	Ellington	CT	C	860 872-8346	1112
Onofrios Ultimate Foods Inc	New Haven	CT	F	203 469-4014	2181
Ragozzino Foods Inc **(PA)**	Meriden	CT	F	203 238-2553	1691
Sabatino North America LLC **(PA)**	West Haven	CT	D	718 328-4120	4122
Sewickley LLC	Greenwich	CT	G	203 661-2511	1351
Cistercian Abbey Spencer Inc	Spencer	MA	E	508 885-8700	12056
Coca-Cola Btlg Sthstern Neng I	Northampton	MA	E	413 586-8450	11055
Dunajski Dairy Inc	Peabody	MA	G	978 531-1457	11308
Gebelein Group Inc	Hyde Park	MA	F	617 361-6611	9461
Jugos	Boston	MA	G	617 418-9879	6834
Kens Foods Inc **(PA)**	Marlborough	MA	B	508 229-1100	10176
National Grape Coop Assn Inc	Concord	MA	G	978 371-1000	8128
Ocean Spray (europe) Ltd	Middleboro	MA	F	508 946-1000	10370
Ocean Spray Cranberries Inc **(PA)**	Middleboro	MA	B	508 946-1000	10371
Ocean Spray International Inc **(HQ)**	Middleboro	MA	B	508 946-1000	10372
Ocean Spray International Sls	Lakeville	MA	F	508 946-1000	9518
Ocean Spray Intl Svcs Inc **(HQ)**	Lakeville	MA	B	508 946-1000	9519
Odwalla Inc	Brookline	MA	E	336 877-1634	7322
Rek Inc	Amesbury	MA	G	978 388-1826	5850
Rohtstein Corp **(PA)**	Woburn	MA	D	781 935-8300	13655
Spinelli Ravioli Mfg Co Inc	Boston	MA	F	617 567-1992	7053
Welch Foods Inc A Cooperative	Concord	MA	A	978 371-3762	8139
Welch Foods Inc A Cooperative **(HQ)**	Concord	MA	B	978 371-1000	8140
B&G Foods Inc	Portland	ME	C	207 772-8341	5180
Cherryfield Foods Inc **(DH)**	Cherryfield	ME	F	207 546-7573	4688
Jarden LLC	East Wilton	ME	F	207 645-2574	4741
Jasper Wyman & Son	Cherryfield	ME	F	207 546-3381	4689
Jasper Wyman & Son	Cherryfield	ME	E	207 546-3381	4690
Jasper Wyman & Son	Deblois	ME	F	207 638-2201	4721
Maine Homestead Inc	Lyman	ME	F	207 344-9274	5030
Maine Wild Blueberry Company	Machias	ME	D	207 255-8364	5032
Maine Wild Blueberry Company **(DH)**	Machias	ME	D	207 255-8364	5033
McCain Foods Usa Inc	Easton	ME	C	207 488-2561	4743
Pembertons Food Inc	Gray	ME	G	207 657-6446	4843
Stonewall Kitchen LLC **(PA)**	York	ME	C	207 351-2713	5717
Old Dutch Mustard Co Inc	Greenville	NH	D	603 878-2100	14374
Smoothie Bus LLC	Manchester	NH	F	603 303-7353	14930
B Del Toro & Sons Inc	Providence	RI	F	401 421-5820	16481
Catanzaro Food Products Inc	Pawtucket	RI	G	401 255-1700	16353
Eastern Food Industries Inc	East Greenwich	RI	G	401 884-8798	15983
Fully Rooted Inc	Pawtucket	RI	F	401 429-8768	16370
Cold Hollow Cider Mill Inc	Waterbury Center	VT	E	802 244-8771	17680
Dellamore Enterprises Inc	Colchester	VT	G	802 655-6264	17188
Village Cannery Vermont Inc	Barre	VT	E	207 351-2713	17024

2034 Dehydrated fruits, vegetables, soups

	CITY	ST	EMP	PHONE	ENTRY#
Arcade Industries Inc	Auburn	MA	F	508 832-6300	6103
Decas Cranberry Products Inc **(PA)**	Carver	MA	E	508 866-8506	7853
Ocean Spray Cranberries Inc **(PA)**	Middleboro	MA	B	508 946-1000	10371
Ocean Spray International Inc **(HQ)**	Middleboro	MA	B	508 946-1000	10372
Ocean Spray Intl Svcs Inc **(HQ)**	Lakeville	MA	B	508 946-1000	9519
Maine Coast Sea Vegetables Inc	Hancock	ME	E	207 412-0094	4871
Maine Wild Blueberry Company	Machias	ME	D	207 255-8364	5032
Oceans Balance	Biddeford	ME	G	207 370-4874	4581
Peeled Inc	Cumberland	RI	F	212 706-2001	15959

2035 Pickles, sauces, and salad dressings

	CITY	ST	EMP	PHONE	ENTRY#
Kerry R Wood	Westport	CT	G	203 221-7780	4177
Newmans Own Inc **(PA)**	Westport	CT	F	203 222-0136	4190
Norpaco Inc	Middletown	CT	D	860 632-2299	1768
Onofrios Ultimate Foods Inc	New Haven	CT	F	203 469-4014	2181
Kettle Cuisine LLC **(PA)**	Lynn	MA	C	617 409-1100	9980
Kettle Cuisine Holdings LLC	Lynn	MA	C	617 409-1100	9981
Pearlco of Boston Inc	Canton	MA	E	781 821-1010	7818
Plenus Group Inc	Lowell	MA	E	978 970-3832	9914
Real Pickles Cooperative Inc	Greenfield	MA	E	413 774-2600	8998
Rek Inc	Amesbury	MA	G	978 388-1826	5850
Star Pickling Corp	Swansea	MA	F	508 672-8535	12312
J W Raye & Co Inc	Eastport	ME	F	207 853-4451	4745
Stonewall Kitchen LLC **(PA)**	York	ME	C	207 351-2713	5717
World Harbors LLC	Auburn	ME	C	207 786-3200	4464
Old Dutch Mustard Co Inc	Greenville	NH	D	603 878-2100	14374
Lost Art Cultured Foods LLC	Cranston	RI	F	401 437-6933	15886
Taylor Farms New England Inc	North Kingstown	RI	E	877 323-7374	16284

	CITY	ST	EMP	PHONE	ENTRY#
Drews LLC (HQ)	Chester	VT	G	802 875-1184	17180
Maple Grove Farms Vermont Inc (HQ)	Saint Johnsbury	VT	D	802 748-5141	17543

2037 Frozen fruits and vegetables

	CITY	ST	EMP	PHONE	ENTRY#
Natureseal Inc	Westport	CT	F	203 454-1800	4189
Bevovations LLC	Leominster	MA	F	978 227-5469	9642
Ocean Spray Cranberries Inc (PA)	Middleboro	MA	B	508 946-1000	10371
Ocean Spray International (HQ)	Middleboro	MA	B	508 946-1000	10372
Ocean Spray Intl Svcs Inc (HQ)	Lakeville	MA	B	508 946-1000	9519
Welch Foods Inc A Cooperative (HQ)	Concord	MA	B	978 371-1000	8140
Allens Blueberry Freezer Inc (HQ)	Ellsworth	ME	E	207 667-5561	4753
Coastal Blueberry Service Inc (PA)	Hancock	ME	F	207 667-9750	4868
G M Allen & Son	Orland	ME	G	207 469-7060	5133
Jasper Wyman & Son	Hancock	ME	G	207 546-3381	4870
Jasper Wyman & Son	Jonesboro	ME	G	207 546-3381	4919
Maine Wild Blueberry Company	Machias	ME	D	207 255-8364	5032
Maine Wild Blueberry Company (DH)	Machias	ME	D	207 255-8364	5033
McCain Foods Usa Inc	Easton	ME	C	207 488-2561	4743
McCain Foods Usa Inc	Easton	ME	F	207 488-2561	4744
Merrill Blueberry Farms Inc	Hancock	ME	F	207 667-2541	4872
Penobscot McCrum LLC	Washburn	ME	C	207 338-4360	5587
Purbeck Isle Inc (PA)	Augusta	ME	E	207 623-5119	4479
B Del Toro & Sons Inc	Providence	RI	F	401 421-5820	16481

2038 Frozen specialties, nec

	CITY	ST	EMP	PHONE	ENTRY#
CP Foods LLC	South Windsor	CT	C	860 436-4042	3134
Ragozzino Foods Inc (PA)	Meriden	CT	F	203 238-2553	1691
Villarina Pasta & Fine Foods (PA)	Danbury	CT	G	203 917-4463	833
Albano Sales Inc	North Billerica	MA	F	978 667-9100	10895
Bake-N-Joy Foods Inc (PA)	North Andover	MA	D	978 683-1414	10821
Blount Fine Foods Corp (PA)	Fall River	MA	C	774 888-1300	8526
Chinamerica Fd Manufacture Inc	Boston	MA	F	617 426-1818	6652
Dimitria Delights Inc	North Grafton	MA	D	508 839-1638	11022
Euro International Ltd	Boston	MA	F	617 670-2265	6720
Innovative Foods Inc	Wilmington	MA	C	781 596-0070	13414
Kettle Cuisine Holdings LLC	Lynn	MA	C	617 409-1100	9981
Landolfi Food Corp	Westfield	MA	F	609 392-1830	13178
Nestle	Taunton	MA	F	508 828-3954	12351
Paramount South Boston	Boston	MA	F	617 269-9999	6953
Perfect Empanada LLC (PA)	Attleboro	MA	G	508 241-5150	6047
Plenus Group Inc	Lowell	MA	F	978 970-3832	9914
Rosemathree Inc	Boston	MA	E		7014
Stuffed Foods LLC	Wilmington	MA	E	978 203-0370	13459
Waterwood Corporation	Westfield	MA	G	413 572-1010	13216
Bafs Inc (PA)	Bangor	ME	F	207 942-5226	4489
Barber Foods LLC	Portland	ME	A	207 772-1934	5182
McCain Foods Usa Inc	Easton	ME	C	207 488-2561	4743
Ocean Approved Inc	Biddeford	ME	G	207 701-1576	4580
Orono House of Pizza	Orono	ME	F	207 866-5505	5135
Slab LLC	Portland	ME	E	207 245-3088	5273
Oven Poppers Inc	Manchester	NH	E	603 644-3773	14909
A B Munroe Dairy Inc (PA)	East Providence	RI	D	401 438-4450	16000
Perfect Empanada LLC	Warren	RI	F	508 241-5150	16762
Woodbelly Pizza LLC (PA)	Cabot	VT	G	802 552-3476	17166

2041 Flour and other grain mill products

	CITY	ST	EMP	PHONE	ENTRY#
ADM Group LLC	New Milford	CT	G	860 354-3208	2237
Central Conn Cooperative Farme	South Windsor	CT	E	860 649-4523	3127
Bay State Milling Company (PA)	Quincy	MA	E	617 328-4400	11505
Dimitria Delights Inc	North Grafton	MA	D	508 839-1638	11022
One Mighty Mill LLC	Hyde Park	MA	G	781 588-0970	9466
Rohtstein Corp (PA)	Woburn	MA	D	781 935-8300	13655
Itllbe LLC	Scarborough	ME	G	207 730-7301	5434
Maine Grains Inc	Skowhegan	ME	E	207 474-8001	5471
Pro Dough Inc	Manchester	NH	G	603 623-6844	14916

2043 Cereal breakfast foods

	CITY	ST	EMP	PHONE	ENTRY#
Munk Pack Inc	Stamford	CT	F	203 769-5005	3414
Kraft Heinz Foods Company	Mansfield	MA	D	508 763-3311	10062
New England Natural Bakers Inc	Greenfield	MA	E	413 772-2239	8996
Old Creamery Grocery Store	Cummington	MA	G	413 634-5560	8147
Weetabix Co	Marlborough	MA	F	508 683-3600	10235
Weetabix Company Inc	Sterling	MA	E	978 422-2905	12172
Grandy Organics LLC (PA)	Hiram	ME	E	207 935-7415	4890
Beautiful Day	Providence	RI	F	617 733-9289	16483
Back Roads Food Co LLC	Brattleboro	VT	F	802 579-1135	17074
Small Batch Organics LLC	Manchester Center	VT	F	802 367-1054	17331

2044 Rice milling

	CITY	ST	EMP	PHONE	ENTRY#
Horizon Vert Pure LLC	Randolph	MA	F	857 236-0904	11563

2045 Prepared flour mixes and doughs

	CITY	ST	EMP	PHONE	ENTRY#
Nummy LLC	West Hartford	CT	G	608 801-9850	4075
Watson LLC (DH)	West Haven	CT	E	203 932-3000	4132
Bake-N-Joy Foods Inc (PA)	North Andover	MA	D	978 683-1414	10821
Concord Foods LLC (PA)	Brockton	MA	C	508 580-1700	7269
Dough Connection Corp	Woburn	MA	G	877 693-6844	13558
Raaga Go LLC	Bedford	MA	G	505 983-5555	6255
Wilevco Inc	Billerica	MA	E	978 667-0400	6491
Good Crust LLC	Canaan	ME	G	207 522-4872	4669
Ever Better Eating Inc	Pittsfield	NH	G	603 435-5119	15331
Maple Grove Farms Vermont Inc (HQ)	Saint Johnsbury	VT	D	802 748-5141	17543
Rhino Foods Inc (PA)	Burlington	VT	C	802 862-0252	17156

2046 Wet corn milling

	CITY	ST	EMP	PHONE	ENTRY#
A E Staley Manufacturing Co	Houlton	ME	G	207 532-9523	4895
Ingredion Incorporated	Fort Fairfield	ME	E	207 472-1250	4784
Primary Pdts Ingrdnts Amrcas L	Houlton	ME	E	207 532-9523	4904
Anchor Toffee LLC	Newport	RI	E	401 619-1044	16201

2047 Dog and cat food

	CITY	ST	EMP	PHONE	ENTRY#
Blue Buffalo Company Ltd (DH)	Wilton	CT	D	203 762-9751	4233
Bravo LLC	Vernon	CT	F	860 896-1899	3752
Canidae LLC	Stamford	CT	D	475 208-1789	3301
Joy Food Company	Darien	CT	G	917 549-6240	850
2 Dogs Treats LLC	Dorchester	MA	G	617 286-4844	8295
Channel Fish Co Inc	Boston	MA	G	617 569-3200	6648
Polka Dog Designs LLC (PA)	Boston	MA	G	617 338-5155	6968
Polka Dog Designs LLC	Boston	MA	F	617 307-6733	6969
Preppy Puppy Inc	West Wareham	MA	E	508 291-7555	13070
Wellness Pet LLC (PA)	Burlington	MA	D	877 869-2971	7448
Wholistic Pet Organics LLC	Bedford	NH	G	603 472-8300	13954
Pet Food Experts Inc (PA)	Pawtucket	RI	C	401 721-5593	16401

2048 Prepared feeds, nec

	CITY	ST	EMP	PHONE	ENTRY#
Bactana Corp	Farmington	CT	G	203 716-1230	1208
Blue Buffalo Pet Products Inc (HQ)	Wilton	CT	E	203 762-9751	4234
H J Baker & Bro Inc	Westport	CT	B	203 682-9200	4171
H J Baker & Brother Inc	Shelton	CT	F	501 664-4870	3011
HJ Baker & Bro LLC (PA)	Shelton	CT	F	203 682-9200	3014
HJ Baker International Inc	Shelton	CT	F	203 682-9200	3015
Kent Nutrition Group Inc	Litchfield	CT	G	860 482-7116	1558
Moark LLC (HQ)	North Franklin	CT	E	951 332-3300	2383
Source Inc (PA)	North Branford	CT	G	203 488-6400	2375
Channel Fish Co Inc	Boston	MA	G	617 569-3200	6648
Designing Health Inc	East Longmeadow	MA	F	661 257-1705	8373
Finicky Pet Food Inc	New Bedford	MA	E	508 991-8448	10591
Savory Creations International	Lynn	MA	G	650 638-1024	9991
Smartpak Equine LLC (DH)	Plymouth	MA	C	774 773-1100	11478
Atlantic Laboratories Inc	Waldoboro	ME	D	207 832-5376	5574
Offshore Marine Outfitters	York	ME	G	207 363-8862	5715
Rawz Natural Pet Food (PA)	Cape Neddick	ME	F	207 363-0684	4672
Kent Nutrition Group Inc	Bow	NH	G	603 225-6661	14004
Trividia Mfg Solutions Inc (DH)	Lancaster	NH	C	603 788-2848	14680
Wholistic Pet Organics LLC	Bedford	NH	G	603 472-8300	13954
Cargill Incorporated	Swanton	VT	F	802 868-3232	17636
Feed Commodities Intl Inc (HQ)	Middlebury	VT	G	800 639-3191	17343
Kent Nutrition Group Inc	Richford	VT	F	802 848-7718	17475
Phoenix Feeds and Nutrtn Inc (PA)	New Haven	VT	F	802 453-6684	17394
Phoenix Feeds Organix LLC	New Haven	VT	F	802 453-6684	17395
Poulin Grain Inc	North Bennington	VT	E	802 681-1605	17411
Poulin Grain Inc	Swanton	VT	E	802 868-3323	17640
Poulin Grain Inc (PA)	Newport	VT	D	802 334-6731	17404

2051 Bread, cake, and related products

	CITY	ST	EMP	PHONE	ENTRY#
Amoun Pita & Distribution LLC	South Windsor	CT	F	866 239-9990	3114
Apicellas Bakery Inc	New Haven	CT	E	203 865-6204	2116
Beldotti Bakeries LLC	Stamford	CT	F	203 348-9029	3293
Cheshire Cml LLC	Cheshire	CT	E	203 238-3482	579
DAndrea Corporation (PA)	West Haven	CT	G	203 932-6000	4101
Daybrake Donuts Inc	Bridgeport	CT	G	203 368-4962	314
Katona Bakery LLC	Fairfield	CT	E	203 337-5349	1193
Lupis Incorporated	New Haven	CT	F	203 562-9491	2172
Masscom Distribute Cpl	South Windsor	CT	D	860 882-0717	3162
Milite Bakery	Wolcott	CT	G	203 753-9451	4368
Modern Pastry Shop Inc	Hartford	CT	G	860 296-7628	1494
Mozzicato Pastry & Bake Sp Inc	Hartford	CT	E	860 296-0426	1495
Northeast Foods Inc	Dayville	CT	D	860 779-1117	864
Perkatory Productions LLC	Middletown	CT	G	860 894-6040	1770
Realejo Donuts Inc	Portland	CT	F	860 342-5120	2822
Stella DOro Biscuit Co Inc	Greenwich	CT	C	718 549-3700	1353
Stonehouse Fine Cakes	Meriden	CT	F	203 235-5091	1702
Superior Bakery Inc	North Grosvenordale	CT	E		860 923-9555
2387					
Watson LLC (DH)	West Haven	CT	E	203 932-3000	4132
Whole Donut	Enfield	CT	F	860 745-3041	1159

	CITY	ST	EMP	PHONE	ENTRY#
88 Acres Foods Inc	Dorchester	MA	F	617 208-8651	8296
Abp Corporation **(PA)**	Boston	MA	C	617 423-0629	6505
Annies Gluten Free Bakery	Shirley	MA	G	978 425-5385	11814
Artisan Chef Manufacturing LLC **(HQ)**	Lawrence	MA	F	978 691-6100	9538
Arts International Wholesale	Raynham	MA	F	508 822-7181	11581
Atkins Fruit Bowl Inc	Amherst	MA	C	413 253-9528	5859
Bagel Boy LLC	Lawrence	MA	D	978 682-8646	9541
Bagel Works Inc	Amherst	MA	F	413 835-0561	5860
Bake-N-Joy Foods Inc **(PA)**	North Andover	MA	D	978 683-1414	10821
Bakery To Go Inc	Boston	MA	G	617 482-1015	6582
Begum Brands Corporation	Boston	MA	E	617 269-8400	6588
Bernardinos Bakery Inc **(PA)**	Chicopee	MA	D	413 592-1944	8010
Big Y Foods Inc	Longmeadow	MA	A	413 567-6231	9848
Boston Bagel Inc	Hyde Park	MA	F	617 364-6900	9457
Boston Food Cooperative **(PA)**	Cambridge	MA	C	617 661-1580	7520
C Q P Bakery	Lawrence	MA	F	978 557-5626	9544
Chmuras Bakery Inc **(PA)**	Indian Orchard	MA	F	413 543-2521	9471
Concord Teacakes Etcetera Inc **(PA)**	Concord	MA	F	978 369-2409	8108
Concord Teacakes Etcetera Inc	Concord	MA	F	978 369-7644	8109
Cumberland Farms Inc **(DH)**	Westborough	MA	B	800 225-9702	13097
D D J	Oxford	MA	F	508 987-0417	11251
Depot Donuts Inc	North Easton	MA	F	508 230-2888	11009
Diannes Fine Desserts Inc **(PA)**	Newburyport	MA	C	800 435-2253	10678
Dimitria Delights Inc	North Grafton	MA	D	508 839-1638	11022
Dunkin Donuts of Methuen	Methuen	MA	G	978 681-8123	10328
Duva Distributors Inc	Shrewsbury	MA	E	508 841-8182	11831
Elie Baking Corporation	Brockton	MA	F	508 584-4890	7276
Forge Baking Company Inc	Arlington	MA	G	617 764-5365	5941
Foxees Co Inc	Falmouth	MA	E	508 548-8485	8632
Frozen Batters Inc	North Andover	MA	D	508 683-1414	10834
G H Bent Company	Milton	MA	D	617 322-9287	10452
Ginsco Inc	Fall River	MA	F	508 677-4767	8553
Ginsco Inc **(PA)**	Fall River	MA	F	508 677-4767	8554
Ginsco Inc	North Dartmouth	MA	F	508 990-9533	10996
Gold Medal Bakery Inc **(PA)**	Fall River	MA	B	508 674-5766	8555
Hamilton Orchards	New Salem	MA	F	978 544-6867	10664
Highlands Lunchette	Fall River	MA	G	508 674-6206	8561
Ho Yuen Bakery Inc	Boston	MA	E	617 426-8320	6790
Hole In One	Eastham	MA	F	508 255-5359	8434
Honey Dew Rehobeth	Rehoboth	MA	F	508 431-2784	11609
Iggys Bread Ltd **(PA)**	Cambridge	MA	D	617 491-7600	7610
Kookla Inc	Southbridge	MA	F	508 765-0442	12025
Kookla Inc **(PA)**	Sturbridge	MA	E	508 347-2623	12251
Korner Bagel Partnership	Seekonk	MA	G	508 336-5204	11779
La Patisserie Inc	Revere	MA	F	781 729-9441	11621
Lacascias Bakery Inc	Medford	MA	F	781 395-8612	10294
Lori Donuts Inc	East Longmeadow	MA	E	413 526-9944	8384
Meadowbrook Orchards Inc	Sterling	MA	F	978 365-7617	12167
Montilio Baking Co Inc	Brockton	MA	D	508 894-8855	7297
North Star Distributors Inc **(PA)**	Vineyard Haven	MA	F	508 693-2000	12494
Old San Juan Bakery Inc	Holyoke	MA	F	413 534-5555	9273
Olivenation LLC **(PA)**	Avon	MA	E	781 551-1469	6156
Pain DAvignon II Inc	Hyannis	MA	E	508 771-9771	9444
Piantedosi Baking Co Inc **(PA)**	Malden	MA	C	781 321-3400	10023
Pittsfield Rye Bakery Inc	Pittsfield	MA	G	413 443-9141	11420
Rob Roy Foods Inc	Worcester	MA	G	508 755-8393	13784
Roche Bros Supermarkets LLC	Norton	MA	C	508 285-3600	11133
Sarro Cohasset Incorporated	Hull	MA	D	781 383-1704	9427
Spinelli Ravioli Mfg Co Inc	Boston	MA	E	617 567-1992	7053
Superior Baking Co Inc	Brockton	MA	E	508 586-6601	7310
Superior Cake Products Inc	Southbridge	MA	D	508 764-3276	12036
Table Talk Pies Inc	Worcester	MA	D	508 798-8811	13809
Table Talk Pies Inc **(PA)**	Worcester	MA	D	508 438-1556	13810
Tripoli Bakery Inc	Lawrence	MA	F	978 682-7754	9604
B&G Foods Inc	Portland	ME	C	207 772-8341	5180
Betty Reez Whoopiez	Freeport	ME	G	207 865-1735	4797
C J Cranam Inc	Oxford	ME	E	207 739-1016	5142
Cape Whpie Mnes Grmet Whpie Pl	South Portland	ME	F	207 799-9207	5493
Donut Hole Inc	Buxton	ME	F	207 929-5060	4662
Dunkin Donuts **(PA)**	Auburn	ME	E	207 783-0408	4427
Holy Donut Inc	Portland	ME	E	207 761-7775	5223
Italian Bakery Products Co	Lewiston	ME	F	207 782-8312	4967
Lepage Bakeries Inc	Auburn	ME	A	207 783-9161	4440
Lepage Bakeries Park St LLC	Auburn	ME	F	207 783-9161	4441
Lepage Bakeries Park St LLC **(HQ)**	Lewiston	ME	F	207 783-9161	4971
Lepage Bakeries Park St LLC	Lewiston	ME	D	207 783-9161	4972
Mary Breen & Company Inc	Wells	ME	G	207 646-4227	5602
Mathews Bakery Inc	Westbrook	ME	F	207 793-9647	5637
Natural Selection Inc	Brunswick	ME	E	207 725-6287	4651
Tm and Tm Inc	Livermore Falls	ME	F	207 897-3442	5026
Tonys Donut Shop	Portland	ME	G	207 772-2727	5285
Wpf Liquidating Co Inc **(PA)**	York	ME	D	207 363-0612	5719
A & M Donuts Inc	Plymouth	NH	E	603 536-7622	15354
ANM Donuts Inc	Tilton	NH	E	603 286-2770	15651
Bagel Alley of NH Inc	Nashua	NH	F	603 882-9343	15069
Crosby Bakery Inc	Nashua	NH	F	603 882-1851	15086
Doughnutn Inc	Manchester	NH	G	603 494-8769	14843
Fredericks Pastries **(PA)**	Amherst	NH	F	603 882-7725	13871
Freeds Bakery LLC	Manchester	NH	E	603 627-7746	14849
Lepage Bakeries Park St LLC	Hudson	NH	F	603 880-4446	14521
Loxsmith Bagel Corporation	Dover	NH	F	603 362-9060	14233
Manco LLC	Allenstown	NH	G	603 485-5327	13852
Market Basket Produce Inc	Concord	NH	D	603 224-5479	14143
ME and Ollies	Exeter	NH	F	603 319-1561	14296
Souhegan Management Corp **(PA)**	Manchester	NH	E	603 898-8868	14933
Tuscan Brands LLC **(PA)**	Salem	NH	F	781 365-2800	15568
Withrow Inc	Salem	NH	F	603 898-8868	15573
Bristol Bagel Works Ltd	Bristol	RI	F	401 254-1390	15756
Calise & Sons Bakery Inc **(PA)**	Lincoln	RI	C	401 334-3444	16124
Catanzaro Food Products Inc	Pawtucket	RI	G	401 255-1700	16353
Cavanagh Company	Greenville	RI	E	401 949-4000	16057
Dunkin Donuts	Warwick	RI	F	401 822-2434	16810
Frostbite Cupcakes	Chepachet	RI	G	508 801-6706	15804
Homestead Baking Co	Rumford	RI	D	401 434-0551	16668
Pinga Bakery Inc	West Warwick	RI	F	401 821-8007	16920
Tienda Y Panaderia El Quiche	Providence	RI	F	401 521-5154	16627
Wrights Dairy Farm Inc	North Smithfield	RI	E	401 767-3014	16334
Against Grn Gourmet Foods LLC	Brattleboro	VT	G	802 258-3838	17072
Bakers Dozen Inc	Colchester	VT	F	802 879-4001	17186
BB&c Wholesale LLC **(PA)**	Bristol	VT	F	802 453-7708	17114
Fudge Factory Inc	Manchester Center	VT	F	888 669-7425	17328
Harringtons In Vermont Inc **(PA)**	Richmond	VT	F	802 434-7535	17479
Klingers Bread Company	South Burlington	VT	F	802 860-6322	17582
Queen Dog LLC	Burlington	VT	F	802 660-2733	17154
Unilever Bestfoods North Amer	Rutland	VT	G	802 775-4986	17513

2052 Cookies and crackers

	CITY	ST	EMP	PHONE	ENTRY#
Bagelman III Inc	Danbury	CT	F	203 792-0030	711
Beldotti Bakeries LLC	Stamford	CT	F	203 348-9029	3293
Bob The Baker LLC	Brookfield	CT	F	203 775-1032	510
Cherise Cpl LLC	Meriden	CT	G	203 238-3482	1660
Modern Pastry Shop Inc	Hartford	CT	G	860 296-7628	1494
Mozzicato Pastry & Bake Sp Inc	Hartford	CT	E	860 296-0426	1495
Stella DOro Biscuit Co Inc	Greenwich	CT	C	718 549-3700	1353
Boston Chipyard The Inc	Boston	MA	F	617 742-9537	6607
Boston Food Cooperative **(PA)**	Cambridge	MA	C	617 661-1580	7520
Concord Teacakes Etcetera Inc	Concord	MA	F	978 369-7644	8109
G H Bent Company	Milton	MA	D	617 322-9287	10452
Ho Toy Noodles Inc **(PA)**	Stoughton	MA	F	617 426-0247	12213
Julie Cecchini	Southwick	MA	F	413 562-2042	12044
Keebler Company	Franklin	MA	D	508 520-7223	8848
La Patisserie Inc	Revere	MA	F	781 729-9441	11621
New England Prtzel Popcorn Inc	Lawrence	MA	G	978 687-0342	9587
PDKD Enterprises Inc	Saugus	MA	E	781 233-8499	11764
Peggy Lawton Kitchens Inc	East Walpole	MA	F	508 668-1215	8420
Rob Roy Foods Inc	Worcester	MA	G	508 755-8393	13784
Swissbakers Inc	Boston	MA	F	781 354-6989	7066
Tatte Holdings LLC	Boston	MA	C	617 577-1111	7070
Venus Wafers Inc	Hingham	MA	F	781 740-1002	9162
Moms Organic Munchies Inc	Freeport	ME	G	207 869-4078	4802
A & M Donuts Inc	Plymouth	NH	E	603 536-7622	15354
Homefree Inc	Windham	NH	G	603 898-0172	15728
Market Basket Produce Inc	Concord	NH	D	603 224-5479	14143
Port City Foods LLC	Portsmouth	NH	E	603 436-3001	15430
Catanzaro Food Products Inc	Pawtucket	RI	G	401 255-1700	16353
Harringtons In Vermont Inc **(PA)**	Richmond	VT	F	802 434-7535	17479

2053 Frozen bakery products, except bread

	CITY	ST	EMP	PHONE	ENTRY#
Rich Products Corporation	New Britain	CT	F	866 737-8884	2057
Aristocrat Products Inc	Upton	MA	F	626 287-4110	12469
Bake-N-Joy Foods Inc **(PA)**	North Andover	MA	D	978 683-1414	10821
Diannes Fine Desserts Inc	Newburyport	MA	C	978 463-3881	10679
Dimitria Delights Inc	North Grafton	MA	D	508 839-1638	11022
Dutch Maid Bakery Inc	Dorchester	MA	C	617 265-5417	8298
Goldacre Realty Inc	Spencer	MA	F	508 885-2748	12060
New England Country Pies LLC	Acton	MA	F	781 596-0176	5759
Peppercorn Food Service Inc	Marblehead	MA	G	781 639-6035	10092
Somerville Office	Somerville	MA	F	617 776-0738	11897
Stone House Farm Inc	West Boxford	MA	G	978 352-2323	12954
C J Cranam Inc	Oxford	ME	E	207 739-1016	5142
Ocean State Cpl Inc	East Providence	RI	C	401 431-0153	16036
Harringtons In Vermont Inc **(PA)**	Richmond	VT	F	802 434-7535	17479

2061 Raw cane sugar

	CITY	ST	EMP	PHONE	ENTRY#
New England Sugars LLC	Worcester	MA	F	508 792-3801	13765

	CITY	ST	EMP	PHONE	ENTRY#

2062 Cane sugar refining

	CITY	ST	EMP	PHONE	ENTRY#
CSC Sugar LLC (PA)	Westport	CT	E	203 846-5610	4163
Rohtstein Corp (PA)	Woburn	MA	D	781 935-8300	13655

2063 Beet sugar

	CITY	ST	EMP	PHONE	ENTRY#
CSC Sugar LLC (PA)	Westport	CT	E	203 846-5610	4163

2064 Candy and other confectionery products

	CITY	ST	EMP	PHONE	ENTRY#
Bridgewater Chocolate LLC	Brookfield	CT	G	203 775-2286	513
Fascias Chocolates Inc	Waterbury	CT	F	203 753-0515	3912
Mantrose-Haeuser Co Inc (HQ)	Westport	CT	E	203 454-1800	4182
Munsons Candy Kitchen Inc (PA)	Bolton	CT	E	860 649-4332	221
Pez Candy Inc (HQ)	Orange	CT	D	203 795-0531	2680
Pez Manufacturing Corp	Orange	CT	D	203 795-0531	2681
Reeds Inc	Norwalk	CT	E	800 997-3337	2563
Thompson Brands LLC	Meriden	CT	D	203 235-2541	1708
Thompson Candy Company	Meriden	CT	D	203 235-2541	1709
Anpesil Distribution Services LLC	Littleton	MA	F		9801
Arthur Mapes Inc	Chelmsford	MA	F	978 256-4061	7910
Bay Colony Associates (PA)	Boston	MA	G	617 287-9100	6584
Ben & Bills Chocolate Emporium	Falmouth	MA	F	508 548-7878	8628
Ben & Blls Chclat Emporium Inc (PA)	Northampton	MA	F	413 584-5695	11053
C&J Dreams Inc (PA)	North Easton	MA	E	508 238-6231	11008
Cambridge Brands Mfg Inc	Cambridge	MA	C	617 491-2500	7527
Dorothy Coxs Candies Inc	Fall River	MA	E	774 678-0654	8534
Everson Distributing Co Inc	Worcester	MA	E	413 533-9261	13721
Fedele and Carter Inc	Dennis Port	MA	F	508 394-1791	8261
Flo Chemical Corp	Ashburnham	MA	F	978 827-5101	5952
Furlongs Cttage Cndies Ice Cre	Norwood	MA	F	781 762-4124	11174
Hebert Confections LLC	Shrewsbury	MA	F		11833
Hebert Retail LLC	Shrewsbury	MA	D	508 845-8051	11834
McCrea Capital Advisors Inc (PA)	Hyde Park	MA	G	617 276-3388	9462
Melville Candy Corporation	Randolph	MA	E	800 638-8063	11568
New England Confectionery Company Inc 781 485-4500	Revere 11622	MA			B
Nichols Candies Inc	Gloucester	MA	F	978 283-9850	8946
Northwest Confections Mass LLC	Orange	MA	G	971 666-8282	11227
Phillips Candy House Inc	Boston	MA	E	617 282-2090	6965
Russos Inc	Saugus	MA	G	781 233-1737	11765
Seven Sweets Inc	Marblehead	MA	F	781 631-0303	10095
Silver Sweet Products Co	Lawrence	MA	G	978 688-0474	9596
Stage Stop Candy Ltd Inc	Dennis Port	MA	G	508 394-1791	8263
Sweethearts Candy Co LLC	Revere	MA	B	781 485-4500	11624
Tootsie Chambridge Plant	Cambridge	MA	C	617 491-2500	7743
Tri-Mass Inc	Wellesley	MA	E	781 235-1075	12946
Winfreys Olde English Fdge Inc (PA)	Rowley	MA	F	978 948-7448	11687
Bixby & Co LLC	Rockland	ME	G	207 691-1778	5323
Harbor Candy Shop Inc	Ogunquit	ME	F	207 646-8078	5123
Len Libbys Inc	Scarborough	ME	F	207 883-4897	5437
Wilburs ME Choclat Confections	Freeport	ME	F	207 865-4071	4805
American Foods LLC	Pelham	NH	D	978 682-1855	15286
Fredericks Pastries (PA)	Amherst	NH	F	603 882-7725	13871
Granite State Candy Shoppe LLC (PA)	Concord	NH	F	603 225-2591	14131
Grist For Mill LLC	Bristol	NH	F	603 744-0405	14036
Kellerhaus Inc	Laconia	NH	F	603 366-4466	14654
Van Otis Chocolates LLC (PA)	Manchester	NH	G	603 627-1611	14949
Boston Ntrceutical Science LLC	Providence	RI	E	617 848-4560	16488
Hauser Foods Inc	Westerly	RI	F	401 596-8866	16932
Lady Ann Candies Inc	Warwick	RI	F	401 738-4321	16832
Paleo Products Inc	Warwick	RI	F	833 476-3733	16842
Sweenors Chocolates Inc (PA)	Wakefield	RI	F	401 783-4433	16745
Tom and Sallys Handmade Choco	Westerly	RI	F	800 289-8783	16944
Tradest1	East Greenwich	RI	G	401 884-4949	15994
Fudge Factory Inc	Manchester Center	VT	F	888 669-7425	17328
Gorilla Bars Inc	Burlington	VT	G	802 309-4997	17138
Maple Grove Farms Vermont Inc (HQ)	Saint Johnsbury	VT	D	802 748-5141	17543
Nu Chocolat LLC	Burlington	VT	F	802 735-7770	17147
Quirion Luc	Newport	VT	G	802 673-8386	17405
Quirion Luc (PA)	Newport	VT	G	802 673-8386	17406
Runamok Maple LLC	Fairfax	VT	E	802 849-7943	17263
Small Batch Organics LLC	Manchester Center	VT	F	802 367-1054	17331

2066 Chocolate and cocoa products

	CITY	ST	EMP	PHONE	ENTRY#
Mantrose-Haeuser Co Inc (HQ)	Westport	CT	E	203 454-1800	4182
Munsons Candy Kitchen Inc (PA)	Bolton	CT	E	860 649-4332	221
Thompson Brands LLC	Meriden	CT	D	203 235-2541	1708
Arthur Mapes Inc	Chelmsford	MA	F	978 256-4061	7910
Bb Walpole Liquidation NH Inc	Cambridge	MA	G	617 491-4340	7499
C&J Dreams Inc (PA)	North Easton	MA	E	508 238-6231	11008
Cambridge Brands Mfg Inc	Cambridge	MA	C	617 491-2500	7527
Dorothy Coxs Candies Inc	Fall River	MA	E	774 678-0654	8534
Green Mountain Choclat Co Inc (PA)	Hopedale	MA	G	508 473-9060	9298

	CITY	ST	EMP	PHONE	ENTRY#
Jedwards International Inc	Braintree	MA	G	617 340-9461	7190
Jedwards International Inc (PA)	Braintree	MA	E	617 340-9461	7191
Jedwards International Inc	Bridgewater	MA	G	617 340-9461	7233
LA Burdick Boston LLC	Boston	MA	G	617 303-0113	6850
Mielke Confections Inc	West Stockbridge	MA	G	413 528-2510	13054
New England Confectionery Company Inc 781 485-4500	Revere 11622	MA			B
Phillips Candy House Inc	Boston	MA	E	617 282-2090	6965
Russos Inc	Saugus	MA	G	781 233-1737	11765
Sweethearts Candy Co LLC	Revere	MA	B	781 485-4500	11624
Tru Chocolate Inc	Haverhill	MA	G	855 878-2462	9135
Winfreys Olde English Fdge Inc (PA)	Rowley	MA	F	978 948-7448	11687
Bixby & Co LLC	Rockland	ME	G	207 691-1778	5323
Harbor Candy Shop Inc	Ogunquit	ME	F	207 646-8078	5123
Lindt & Sprungli (usa) Inc (HQ)	Stratham	NH	C	603 778-8100	15637
World Wide Distribution Corp	Brentwood	NH	G	603 942-6032	14033
Lady Ann Candies Inc	Warwick	RI	F	401 738-4321	16832
Barry Callebaut USA LLC	Saint Albans	VT	C	802 524-9711	17516
Birnn Chocolates Vermont Inc	South Burlington	VT	F	802 860-1047	17573
Champlain Chocolate Company (PA)	Burlington	VT	D	800 465-5909	17124
Champlain Chocolate Company	Williston	VT	D	802 864-1808	17725
Sentar Inc	South Burlington	VT	D	802 861-6004	17598
Sillycow Farms Llc	Wells River	VT	E	802 429-2920	17688
Sunny Sky Products LLC	South Burlington	VT	E	802 861-6004	17602
Vermont Nut Free Choclat Inc	Colchester	VT	F	802 372-4654	17206

2068 Salted and roasted nuts and seeds

	CITY	ST	EMP	PHONE	ENTRY#
Wizards Nuts Holdings LLC (PA)	Greenwich	CT	D	708 483-1315	1362
Arcade Industries Inc	Auburn	MA	F	508 832-6300	6103
Fastachi Ltd	Watertown	MA	F	617 924-8787	12876
Superior Nut Company Inc	Cambridge	MA	E	800 251-6060	7724
Peeled Inc	Cumberland	RI	F	212 706-2001	15959

2076 Vegetable oil mills, nec

	CITY	ST	EMP	PHONE	ENTRY#
Baker Commodities Inc	North Billerica	MA	D	978 454-8811	10899

2077 Animal and marine fats and oils

	CITY	ST	EMP	PHONE	ENTRY#
Baker Commodities Inc	North Billerica	MA	D	978 454-8811	10899
Western Mass Rendering Co Inc	Southwick	MA	E	413 569-6265	12049
Baker Commodities Inc	Warwick	RI	G	401 821-3003	16786
Baker Commodities Inc	Williston	VT	G	802 658-0721	17723

2079 Edible fats and oils

	CITY	ST	EMP	PHONE	ENTRY#
Arista Industries Inc (PA)	Wilton	CT	E	203 761-1009	4230
Olive Capizzano Oils & Vinegar	Pawcatuck	CT	G	860 495-2187	2724
Olive Oil Factory LLC	Waterbury	CT	E	203 437-8286	3956
Andaluna Enterprises Inc	West Newbury	MA	G	617 335-3204	13006
Baker Commodities Inc	North Billerica	MA	D	978 454-8811	10899
Catania-Spagna Corporation	Ayer	MA	E	978 772-7900	6177
Lqc Inc	Norwood	MA	G	617 586-5139	11191

2082 Malt beverages

	CITY	ST	EMP	PHONE	ENTRY#
Beerd Brewing Co LLC (PA)	Stonington	CT	E	860 857-1014	3507
Black Pond Brews	Dayville	CT	G	860 207-5295	858
Brewery Legitimus LLC	New Hartford	CT	F	860 810-8894	2099
Diageo Investment Corporation	Stamford	CT	E	203 229-2100	3337
East Rock Brewing Company LLC (PA)	New Haven	CT	G	203 530-3484	2147
Kent Falls Brewing Company	Kent	CT	G	860 398-9645	1542
Lock It Down Inc	Stamford	CT	G	203 313-6454	3403
Masas Usa Inc	East Haven	CT	E	305 603-8868	1045
PH Production CT LLC	South Windsor	CT	G	860 205-0942	3171
Swagnificent Ent LLC	Bridgeport	CT	G	203 449-0124	378
Thimble Island Brewing Company	Branford	CT	E	203 208-2827	282
Amherst Brewing Co Inc	Amherst	MA	E	413 253-4400	5856
Atlas Distributing Inc	Auburn	MA	G	508 791-6221	6106
Avson Brewing LLC	West Springfield	MA	G	781 727-5789	13016
Bad Martha Farmers Brewery LLC	Edgartown	MA	F	978 335-9879	8465
Barrel House Z LLC	Hingham	MA	E	617 480-2880	9142
Bent Water Brewing Co	Lynn	MA	E	781 780-9948	9963
Berkshire Brewing Company Inc (PA)	South Deerfield	MA	F	413 665-6600	11921
Boston Beer Company Inc	Boston	MA	F	617 368-5080	6602
Boston Beer Company Inc (PA)	Boston	MA	A	617 368-5000	6603
Boston Beer Corporation (DH)	Boston	MA	C	617 368-5000	6604
Brockton Beer Company LLC	Brockton	MA	G	508 521-9711	7263
Buzzards Bay Brewing Inc	Westport	MA	G	508 636-2288	13294
Cambridge Brewing Co Inc	Cambridge	MA	E	617 494-1994	7528
Castle Island Brewing Co LLC	Norwood	MA	E	781 951-2029	11168
Cold Harbor Brewing Co LLC	Westborough	MA	E	508 768-5232	13090
Common Crossing Inc	Berkley	MA	G	508 822-8225	6314
Craft Beer Guild Distrg VT LLC (PA)	Kingston	MA	G	781 585-5165	9507
Dorchester Beer Holdings LLC	Boston	MA	F	617 869-7092	6698
Downeast Cider House LLC (PA)	Boston	MA	G	857 301-8881	6700
Essex County Brewing Co LLC	Boxford	MA	G	978 587-2254	7160

	CITY	ST	EMP	PHONE	ENTRY#
Four Phantoms Brewing Co LLC	Greenfield	MA	G	931 247-0315	8991
Harpoon Distributing Co Inc	Boston	MA	F	617 574-9551	6781
John Harvards Brewhouse Llc	Braintree	MA	B	508 875-2337	7192
K Irwin Construction Inc	Quincy	MA	G	617 481-2420	11525
Lamplighter Brewing Co LLC	Cambridge	MA	E	617 945-2743	7628
Lamplighter Brewing Co LLC (PA)	Cambridge	MA	E	207 650-3325	7629
Lamplighter Brewing Co LLC	Woburn	MA	E	617 945-0450	13599
Life Force Beverages LLC	Boston	MA	G	551 265-9482	6858
M P Brewing Company	Fall River	MA	F	508 944-8531	8570
Mass Bay Brewing Company Inc (PA)	Boston	MA	C	617 574-9551	6870
Mass Brewing LLC (PA)	Clinton	MA	G	617 800-7070	8083
Mass Brewing LLC	Devens	MA	G	617 800-7070	8278
Massachusetts Bev Aliance LLC	Bellingham	MA	F	617 701-6238	6294
Mercury Brewing & Dist Co Inc	Ipswich	MA	F	978 356-3329	9490
Murder Hill LLC (PA)	Whitinsville	MA	G	774 757-4411	13342
Penny Pinchers Brewing Co LLC	Millbury	MA	F	774 696-7885	10440
Plan B Burger LLC	Springfield	MA	F	413 285-8296	12121
Slesar Bros Brewing Co Inc	Boston	MA	F	978 745-2337	7040
Slesar Bros Brewing Co Inc	Hingham	MA	F	781 749-2337	9160
Sunday River Brewing Co Inc	Boston	MA	G	207 824-4253	7064
Trillium Brewing Company LLC (PA)	Canton	MA	G	781 298-7126	7835
True North Ale Company LLC	Ipswich	MA	E	978 312-6473	9498
Turtle Swamp Brewing LLC	Boston	MA	F	617 314-2952	7089
Untold Brewing LLC (PA)	Scituate	MA	F	781 378-0559	11773
Wormtown Brewery LLC	Foxborough	MA	F	774 215-5403	8738
Wormtown Brewery LLC	Worcester	MA	F	774 239-1555	13833
Ashleigh Inc (PA)	Kennebunk	ME	E	207 967-4311	4921
Belleflower Brewing Co LLC	Portland	ME	F	617 365-9536	5186
Brays Brewing Company	Naples	ME	E	207 693-6806	5079
Definitive Brewing Company LLC	Portland	ME	F	207 446-4746	5207
First Mile Brewing Co LLC	Fort Kent	ME	G	207 231-4579	4788
Foundation Brewing Company	Portland	ME	F	207 370-8187	5217
Maine Beer Company LLC	Freeport	ME	E	207 221-5711	4801
Nonesuch River Brewing LLC	Scarborough	ME	E	207 219-8948	5440
Orange Bike Brewing Co	Portland	ME	F	207 391-4343	5254
Rising Tide Brewing Co LLC	Portland	ME	F	207 370-2337	5265
Saco River Brewing LLC	Fryeburg	ME	F	207 256-3028	4810
Sacred Profane LLC	Biddeford	ME	G	508 259-3052	4587
Sebago Brewing Company (PA)	Gorham	ME	E	207 856-2537	4834
Trinken Brewing Co LLC	West Bath	ME	G	207 389-6360	5609
York Harbor Brewing Company	Kittery	ME	F	207 703-8060	4941
7th Settlement Brewery LLC	Dover	NH	E	603 534-5292	14212
Capitol Distributors Inc	Bow	NH	F	603 223-2086	13995
Capitol Distributors Inc	Concord	NH	G	603 224-3348	14119
Cisco Brewers Portsmouth LLC	Portsmouth	NH	E	603 380-7575	15373
Craft Beer Guild LLC	Portsmouth	NH	E	603 319-8508	15377
Craft Brew Alliance Inc	Portsmouth	NH	D	603 430-8600	15378
Debra Rivest Ltd	Keene	NH	E	603 355-3335	14595
Earth Eagle Brewings LLC	Portsmouth	NH	E	603 817-2773	15381
Federal Spice Corp (PA)	North Conway	NH	E	603 356-6381	15248
Finestkind Brewing LLC	Hampton	NH	D	603 436-4026	14402
Gnaw Inc	Manchester	NH	E	603 418-8900	14852
Great Rhythm Brewing Co LLC	Portsmouth	NH	E	603 430-9640	15396
Hobbs Tavern & Brewing Co LLC	West Ossipee	NH	E	603 539-2000	15694
Northwoods Brewing Co LLC	Northwood	NH	F	603 942-6400	15274
Patel Brew LLC	Somersworth	NH	F	603 602-7455	15620
Rmk Brewers LLC	Hampton	NH	G	603 601-8196	14410
Smuttynose Brewing Company Inc	Hampton	NH	D	603 436-4026	14413
University System NH	Durham	NH	E	603 659-2825	14268
Apponaug Brewing Company	Warwick	RI	E	401 681-4321	16782
Isle Brewers Guild LLC	Pawtucket	RI	E	774 766-9186	16377
Linesider Brewing Company LLC	East Greenwich	RI	F	401 398-7700	15989
Shaidzon Beer Company LLC	West Kingston	RI	F	401 314-8730	16897
Alchemy Brewing Stowe LLC	Stowe	VT	F	802 882-8165	17629
Fiddlehead Brewing Company LLC	Shelburne	VT	F	802 489-5090	17557
Foam Brewers LLC	Burlington	VT	F	802 399-2511	17136
Hermit Thrush Brewery LLC (PA)	Brattleboro	VT	G	585 781-0617	17086
Lost Nation Brewing LLC	Morrisville	VT	F	802 851-8041	17385
Mbbc Vermont LLC	Windsor	VT	E	802 674-5491	17760
McHolbe-Noonan Corporation	Burlington	VT	G	802 865-0500	17144
Third Place Inc	Burlington	VT	E	802 861-2999	17161
Whetstone Stn Rest Brewry LLC (PA)	Brattleboro	VT	E	802 490-2354	17109

2083 Malt

	CITY	ST	EMP	PHONE	ENTRY#
Blue Ox Malthouse LLC	Lisbon Falls	ME	F	207 649-0018	5019

2084 Wines, brandy, and brandy spirits

	CITY	ST	EMP	PHONE	ENTRY#
Brooke Taylor Farm LLC (PA)	Woodstock	CT	G	860 974-1263	4391
Donelan Fmly Wine Cellars LLC	Ridgefield	CT	G	707 591-0782	2896
Hawk Ridge Winery LLC	Watertown	CT	G	860 274-7440	4015
Highland Imports LLC	Fairfield	CT	E	203 538-6818	1188
Land of Nod Winery LLC	East Canaan	CT	G	860 824-5225	922
Sharpe Hill Vineyard Inc	Pomfret	CT	F	860 974-3549	2811

	CITY	ST	EMP	PHONE	ENTRY#
Stonington Vineyards Inc	Groton	CT	G	860 535-1222	1380
Sunset Meadow Farm LLC	Goshen	CT	F	860 201-4654	1304
Twelve Percent LLC	North Haven	CT	F	203 745-3983	2441
UST LLC	Stamford	CT	A	203 817-3000	3489
59 Beecher Street LLC	Southbridge	MA	G	631 734-6200	12007
A&G Vineyard Inc	Attleboro	MA	G	508 226-4483	5988
Archer Roose Inc	Boston	MA	F	646 283-4152	6556
Cape Cod Winery Inc	Teaticket	MA	F	508 457-5592	12378
Cidermillrunsterlingcom	Sterling	MA	G	978 422-8675	12158
City Winery Boston LLC	Boston	MA	E	617 933-8047	6658
Davies Family Selections Inc	East Falmouth	MA	G	508 317-6024	8358
Grape Island Inc	Rowley	MA	G	978 432-1280	11675
Grove Street Enterprises Inc	Richmond	MA	F	413 698-3301	11626
Hirsch Retail Store Inc	Acton	MA	G	978 621-4634	5753
Marthas Seastreak Vineyard LLC	New Bedford	MA	F	617 896-0293	10620
Marzae LLC	Acton	MA	F	630 915-0352	5758
Marzae LLC (PA)	Bedford	MA	G	619 915-0352	6238
Nashoba Valley Spirits Limited	Bolton	MA	E	978 779-5521	6498
Oak Barrel Imports LLC	Beverly	MA	G	617 286-2524	6369
Phoenix Vintners LLC	Ipswich	MA	F	877 340-9869	9494
Punchpops LLC	Worcester	MA	F	508 344-7932	13775
Stormalong Cider LLC (PA)	Sherborn	MA	G	213 280-4533	11811
Tremont Street Lq Group Inc (PA)	Boston	MA	F	617 262-0379	7085
Truro Vineyards Cape Cod LLC	North Truro	MA	F	508 487-6200	11051
Vineyard Brands	Brighton	MA	G	617 901-3597	7246
Vineyard Brands LLC	Natick	MA	F	508 653-5458	10500
Westport Rivers Inc	Westport	MA	F	508 636-3423	13300
Blue Barn LLC	Scarborough	ME	G	207 536-8002	5426
Blue Lobster Wine Company	Portland	ME	F	207 671-1154	5189
Cellars	Bar Harbor	ME	G	207 288-3907	4522
Maine Craft Distilling LLC	Portland	ME	F	207 798-2528	5240
Mr Boston Brands LLC (HQ)	Lewiston	ME	F	207 783-1433	4978
Sweetgrass Farm Winery & Dist	Portland	ME	G	207 761-8446	5278
603 Brewery LLC	Londonderry	NH	E	603 630-7745	14726
Appolo Vineyards LLC	Derry	NH	F	603 421-6052	14189
Averill House Vineyard LLC	Brookline	NH	F	603 371-2296	14038
Flag Hill Distillery LLC	Lee	NH	F	603 659-2949	14705
Flag Hill Winery & Vinyrd LLC	Lee	NH	F	603 659-2949	14706
Lane Poverty Orchard	Lebanon	NH	G	603 448-1511	14692
Moonlight Meadery LLC	Londonderry	NH	F	603 216-2162	14774
Vineyard At Seven Birches LLC	Lincoln	NH	F	603 745-7550	14707
Vintners Cellar Winery	North Conway	NH	G	603 356-9463	15250
Vision Wine & Spirits LLC	Manchester	NH	F	781 278-2000	14955
Vision Wine & Spirits LLC	Manchester	NH	A	781 278-2000	14956
Zorvino Vineyards	Sandown	NH	F	603 887-8463	15581
Bibo International LLC	Newport	RI	E	774 232-4248	16207
Douglas Wine & Spirits Inc	North Providence	RI	F	401 353-6400	16299
Newport Vineyards & Winery LLC	Middletown	RI	E	401 848-5161	16182
Sakonnet Vineyards LP	Little Compton	RI	F	401 635-8486	16162
Thomsen Enterprises LLC	Rumford	RI	D	401 431-2190	16679
Caledonia Spirits Inc	Montpelier	VT	E	802 472-8000	17370
Citizen Cider LLC	Burlington	VT	G	802 288-0576	17126
Citizen Cider LLC (PA)	Burlington	VT	G	802 448-3278	17127
Shacksbury Holdings Inc	Vergennes	VT	E	802 458-0530	17659
Snow Farm Winery	South Hero	VT	F	802 372-9463	17610

2085 Distilled and blended liquors

	CITY	ST	EMP	PHONE	ENTRY#
American Distilling Inc (PA)	East Hampton	CT	D	860 267-4444	959
Krystal Inc LLC	Granby	CT	G	860 844-1267	1307
Litchfield Distillery	Litchfield	CT	G	860 361-6503	1559
Waypoint Distillery	Bloomfield	CT	G	860 519-5390	216
Black Infusions	Wellesley	MA	G	617 212-1046	12938
Cisco Brwers Dstlrs Vntners Sp	Boston	MA	E	508 325-5929	6656
Deacon Giles Inc	Salem	MA	G	781 883-8256	11710
Downeast Cider House LLC (PA)	Boston	MA	G	857 301-8881	6700
Downeast Cider House LLC	Mansfield	MA	D	650 279-2417	10049
Granden Distilling LLC	Newton	MA	G	484 888-1323	10758
Gt Spirits Inc	Boston	MA	E	617 276-5209	6777
Privateer International LLC	Ipswich	MA	G	978 356-0477	9495
Silver Bear Distillery LLC	Dalton	MA	G	413 242-4892	8154
Stirrings LLC	Fall River	MA	E	508 324-9800	8610
Viva Beverages Inc	Boston	MA	F	617 712-3488	7108
Lu-Dz LLC	Newcastle	ME	G	207 563-2669	5094
Milne Spirit Works LLC	Portland	ME	G	207 536-0592	5245
Mr Boston Brands LLC (HQ)	Lewiston	ME	F	207 783-1433	4978
Stroudwater Distillery	Portland	ME	F	207 272-7327	5276
White Rock Distilleries Inc	Lewiston	ME	C	207 783-1433	4997
Wiggly Bridge Distilleries LLC	York	ME	E	207 363-9322	5718
Cathedral Ledge Distillery Inc	North Conway	NH	G	612 386-4829	15246
Doire Distilling LLC	Derry	NH	G	603 765-4353	14191
Sea Hagg Distillery LLC	Dover	NH	G	603 343-1717	14249
White Mountain Distillery LLC	Manchester	NH	G	603 391-1306	14960
All Night Long Inc	Newport	RI	F	860 306-3189	16199

	CITY	ST	EMP	PHONE	ENTRY#
Diageo Loyal Spirits Corp	Wakefield	RI	G	401 284-4006	16740
Industrious Spirit Company LLC	Providence	RI	G	401 450-9229	16539
Johnson Brothers RI Inc	North Kingstown	RI	E	401 583-0050	16262
Cold Springs Spirits LLC	Warren	VT	G	802 496-6973	17671
Diageo North America Inc	Manchester	VT	D	802 362-4700	17323
Goamericago Beverages LLC	Shoreham	VT	G	802 897-7700	17567
Green Mountain Distillers LLC	Morrisville	VT	G	802 498-4848	17382
Mad River Distillers	Warren	VT	G	802 496-6973	17672
Old Route Two Spirits Inc	Barre	VT	F	802 424-4864	17014
Smugglers Notch Distillery LLC	Jeffersonville	VT	G	860 670-1838	17307
Vermont Hard Cider Company LLC	Brandon	VT	D	802 385-3656	17071
Vermont Hard Cider Company LLC **(HQ)**	Middlebury	VT	E	802 388-0700	17350
Whistlepig LLC **(PA)**	Shoreham	VT	G	802 897-7700	17568
Xagd Inc	Middlebury	VT	G	802 989-7359	17351

2086 Bottled and canned soft drinks

	CITY	ST	EMP	PHONE	ENTRY#
Als Beverage Company Inc	East Windsor	CT	E	860 627-7003	1065
B & E Juices Inc	Bridgeport	CT	E	203 333-1802	299
Bluetriton Brands Inc	Stamford	CT	F	203 531-4100	3295
Bluetriton Brands Inc **(HQ)**	Stamford	CT	B	888 747-7437	3296
Castle Beverages Inc	Ansonia	CT	G	203 732-0883	9
Castle Seltzer Inc	Derby	CT	G	203 736-6887	888
Cell Nique	Weston	CT	G	888 417-9343	4148
Coca-Cola Bevs Northeast Inc	East Hartford	CT	E	860 895-5100	981
Coca-Cola Bevs Northeast Inc	South Windsor	CT	E	800 241-2653	3131
Coca-Cola Bottling Company of Southeastern New England Inc **(DH)**	Waterford	CT	F	860 443-2816	3987
Coca-Cola Btlg Sthstern Neng I	East Hartford	CT	F	860 569-0037	982
Crystal Rock Holdings Inc	Watertown	CT	B	860 945-0661	4006
Crystal Rock Spring Water Co	Watertown	CT	B	860 945-0661	4007
Ds Services of America Inc	Watertown	CT	B	860 945-0661	4009
Foxon Park Beverages Inc	East Haven	CT	G	203 467-7874	1042
G & G Beverage Distributors	Yalesville	CT	E	203 949-6220	4397
Harvest Hill Holdings LLC **(PA)**	Stamford	CT	F	203 914-1620	3367
Light Rock Spring Water Co	Danbury	CT	F	203 743-2251	771
Miami Bay Beverage Company LLC	Guilford	CT	F	203 453-0090	1400
Natural Country Farms Inc	Ellington	CT	C	860 872-8346	1112
New England Beverages LLC	Branford	CT	G	203 208-4517	273
Newmans Own Inc **(PA)**	Westport	CT	F	203 222-0136	4190
Niagara Bottling LLC	Bloomfield	CT	G	909 226-7353	196
Pepsi Cola Bottling Co Bristol	Southington	CT	E	860 628-8200	3228
Pepsi-Cola Btlg Worcester Inc	Dayville	CT	E	860 774-4007	865
Pepsi-Cola Metro Btlg Co Inc	Stratford	CT	E	203 375-2484	3566
Pepsi-Cola Metro Btlg Co Inc	Uncasville	CT	E	860 848-1231	3743
Pepsi-Cola Metro Btlg Co Inc	Windsor	CT	D	860 688-6281	4294
Pepsico	New Haven	CT	E	203 974-8912	2183
Reeds Inc	Norwalk	CT	E	800 997-3337	2563
Sigg Switzerland (usa) Inc	Stamford	CT	F	203 321-1232	3456
Sweet Leaf Tea Company **(DH)**	Stamford	CT	F	203 863-0263	3475
Adirondack Beverages Corp	Worcester	MA	F	800 734-9800	13697
Coca Cola Btlg Co of Cape Cod	Sandwich	MA	D	508 888-0001	11748
Coca-Cola Bevs Northeast Inc	Needham Heights	MA	E	978 459-9378	10535
Coca-Cola Bevs Northeast Inc	Sandwich	MA	E	508 888-0001	11749
Coca-Cola Btlg Sthstern Neng I	Greenfield	MA	E	413 448-8296	8987
Coca-Cola Btlg Sthstern Neng I	Needham Heights	MA	F	781 449-4300	10536
Coca-Cola Btlg Sthstern Neng I	Northampton	MA	E	413 586-8450	11055
Coca-Cola Btlg Sthstern Neng I	Westborough	MA	D	508 836-5200	13088
Coca-Cola Refreshments USA Inc	Greenfield	MA	F	413 772-2617	8988
Coca-Cola Refreshments USA Inc	Northampton	MA	D	413 586-8450	11056
Cumberland Farms Inc **(DH)**	Westborough	MA	B	800 225-9702	13097
Dunajski Dairy Inc	Peabody	MA	G	978 531-1457	11308
Easton Springs Corporation	South Easton	MA	F	508 238-2741	11942
Epic Enterprises Inc	Ayer	MA	D	978 772-2340	6182
Ginseng Up Corporation	Worcester	MA	G	508 799-6178	13732
Ginseng Up Corporation **(PA)**	Worcester	MA	G	508 799-6178	13733
Keurig Dr Pepper Inc **(PA)**	Burlington	MA	D	781 418-7000	7384
Keurig Green Mountain Inc	Burlington	MA	D	781 246-3466	7385
Mercury Brewing & Dist Co Inc	Ipswich	MA	F	978 356-3329	9490
Nixie Sparkling Water Inc	Chatham	MA	G	617 784-8671	7899
Northeast Hot-Fill Co-Op Inc	Ayer	MA	E	978 772-9287	6189
Patriot Beverages LLC	Littleton	MA	D	978 486-4900	9831
Pepsi-Cola Btlg Worcester Inc **(PA)**	Holden	MA	D	508 829-6551	9194
Pepsi-Cola Metro Btlg Co Inc	Sagamore Beach	MA	E	508 833-5600	11697
Pepsi-Cola Metro Btlg Co Inc	Wilmington	MA	D	978 661-6150	13446
Pepsico	Boston	MA	G	857 233-2421	6963
Polar Corp **(PA)**	Worcester	MA	A	508 753-6383	13772
Refresco Beverages US Inc	East Freetown	MA	F	508 763-3515	8366
Tropical Paradise Inc	Bedford	MA	F	781 357-1210	6275
Veryfine Products Inc **(DH)**	Littleton	MA	D	978 486-0812	9842
Vitamin 1 LLC	Littleton	MA	G	617 523-9090	9844
Auburn Spring Water Company **(PA)**	Auburn	ME	G	207 782-1521	4422
Bluetriton Brands Inc	Poland Spring	ME	C	207 998-4315	5163
Coca-Cola Bevs Northeast Inc	Presque Isle	ME	E	207 764-4481	5298
Coca-Cola Bevs Northeast Inc	South Portland	ME	E	207 773-5505	5495
Dr Pepper Bottling Co Portland	Portland	ME	F	207 773-4258	5211
Farmington Coca Cola Btlg Dstr	Farmington	ME	F	207 778-4733	4779
Maine Beverage Association	South Portland	ME	F	207 773-5505	5507
Northeast Merchandising Corp	Skowhegan	ME	E	207 474-3321	5476
Pepsi Cola Bottling Aroostook	Presque Isle	ME	F	207 760-3000	5309
Pepsi-Cola Metro Btlg Co Inc	Auburn	ME	E	207 784-5791	4452
Pepsi-Cola Metro Btlg Co Inc	Hampden	ME	E	207 973-2217	4865
Cg Roxane LLC	Moultonborough	NH	F	603 476-8844	15051
Coca-Cola Beverages Northeast Inc **(HQ)**	Bedford	NH	F	603 627-7871	13922
Coca-Cola Bevs Northeast Inc	Belmont	NH	E	603 267-8834	13961
Coca-Cola Bevs Northeast Inc	Londonderry	NH	E	603 437-3530	14735
Coca-Cola Bevs Northeast Inc	Manchester	NH	E	603 623-6033	14833
Coca-Cola Bevs Northeast Inc	Seabrook	NH	E	603 926-0404	15587
Craft Beer Guild LLC	Portsmouth	NH	E	603 319-8508	15377
Monadnock Mountain Spring Water Inc	Wilton	NH	D	603 654-2728	15706
Pepsi-Cola Metro Btlg Co Inc	Manchester	NH	D	603 625-5764	14911
Surry Licensing LLC	Keene	NH	G	603 354-7000	14624
Coca-Cola Refreshments USA Inc	Providence	RI	D	401 331-1981	16501
Martignetti Companies RI	Central Falls	RI	C	401 722-8008	15792
Pepsi-Cola Metro Btlg Co Inc	Cranston	RI	C	401 468-3300	15904
Aqua Vitea LLC	Middlebury	VT	F	802 453-8590	17336
Coca-Cola Btlg Sthstern Neng I	Rutland	VT	F	802 773-2768	17492
Keurig Dr Pepper Inc	Essex Junction	VT	F	802 288-6022	17238
Leader Dist Systems Inc	Brattleboro	VT	D	802 254-6093	17093
Pearl Street Beverage Inc	Burlington	VT	F	802 658-1574	17150
Pepsi Cola Bottling Co	Brattleboro	VT	F	802 254-6093	17099
Rea Inc	Saint Albans	VT	F	802 527-7437	17530
Vermont Heritage Distrs Inc	Newport	VT	G	802 334-6503	17407
Watson Wheeler Cider LLC **(PA)**	Shaftsbury	VT	G	435 602-9042	17554

2087 Flavoring extracts and syrups, nec

	CITY	ST	EMP	PHONE	ENTRY#
America Extract Corporation	East Hampton	CT	F	860 267-4444	958
American Distilling Inc **(PA)**	East Hampton	CT	D	860 267-4444	959
Brookside Flvors Ingrdents LLC **(HQ)**	Stamford	CT	G	203 595-4520	3297
Carrubba Incorporated	Monroe	CT	D	203 878-0605	1908
Herbasway Laboratories LLC	Wallingford	CT	F	203 269-6991	3812
Jmf Group LLC	East Windsor	CT	D	860 627-7003	1077
Osf Flavors Inc **(PA)**	Windsor	CT	F	860 298-8350	4293
Target Flavors Inc	Brookfield	CT	F	203 775-4727	539
Transatlantic Bubbles LLC	Woodbridge	CT	G	203 464-0051	4383
Watson LLC **(DH)**	West Haven	CT	E	203 932-3000	4132
Backbay Roasters	Wilmington	MA	G	844 532-6269	13387
Ballhaus Bev Co LLC	Medford	MA	G	828 302-5837	10281
Brady Enterprises Inc **(PA)**	East Weymouth	MA	D	781 340-4571	8427
Brighams Inc **(HQ)**	Arlington	MA	F	800 242-2423	5939
Cape Cod Ginger LLC	Wareham	MA	G	508 295-2795	12830
Coca-Cola Btlg Sthstern Neng I	Needham Heights	MA	F	781 449-4300	10536
Coca-Cola Refreshments USA Inc	Northampton	MA	D	413 586-8450	11056
Drink Maple Inc	Sudbury	MA	F	978 610-6408	12266
Keurig Dr Pepper Inc **(PA)**	Burlington	MA	D	781 418-7000	7384
Mrp Trading Innovations LLC	Beverly	MA	F	978 762-3900	6367
Multi-Flow Industries LLC	Norwood	MA	E	617 442-7777	11197
Northice	Plymouth	MA	F	781 985-5225	11469
Powell and Mahoney LLC	Salem	MA	F	978 745-4332	11731
Rohtstein Corp **(PA)**	Woburn	MA	D	781 935-8300	13655
Stirrings LLC	Fall River	MA	E	508 324-9800	8610
B&G Foods Inc	Portland	ME	C	207 772-8341	5180
Bev-Tech Inc	Eliot	ME	F	207 439-8061	4749
Fizz LLC	Portland	ME	E	207 887-9618	5216
FMC Corporation	Rockland	ME	D	207 594-3200	5329
Dutch Gold Honey Inc	Littleton	NH	F	603 444-6246	14717
Sunrise Foods Incorporated	Brentwood	NH	F	603 772-4420	14031
Fountain Dispensers Co Inc	Providence	RI	G	401 461-8400	16520
R I Fruit Syrup Co	Smithfield	RI	G	401 231-0040	16728
Rhode Island Frt Syrup Co Inc	Smithfield	RI	E	401 231-0040	16729
Maple Grove Farms Vermont Inc **(HQ)**	Saint Johnsbury	VT	D	802 748-5141	17543
Runamok Maple LLC	Fairfax	VT	E	802 849-7943	17263

2091 Canned and cured fish and seafoods

	CITY	ST	EMP	PHONE	ENTRY#
Boston Smoked Fish Company LLC	Boston	MA	F	617 819-5476	6619
Ditusa Corporation	Gloucester	MA	E	978 335-5259	8932
Gortons Inc **(DH)**	Gloucester	MA	B	978 283-3000	8939
Iqbal Shaheen	Boston	MA	G	857 415-7585	6817
Kneeland Bros Inc	Rowley	MA	F	978 948-3919	11678
Mar-Lees Seafood LLC	New Bedford	MA	C	508 991-6026	10618
Spence & Co Ltd	Brockton	MA	E	508 427-5577	7308
Wellfleet Shellfish Co Inc	Eastham	MA	E	508 255-5300	8436
Browne Trading Co	Portland	ME	E	207 766-2402	5194
Carver Shellfish Inc	Beals	ME	E	207 497-2261	4532
Cherry Point Products Inc	Milbridge	ME	F	207 546-0930	5060
Community Shellfish Co LLC	Bremen	ME	E	207 529-2700	4607
Flame Grilling Products Inc	Waldoboro	ME	F	800 724-5510	5576

	CITY	ST	EMP	PHONE	ENTRY#
L Ray Packing Company	Milbridge	ME	G	207 546-2355	5062
Looks Gourmet Food Co Inc (HQ)	Machias	ME	F	207 259-3341	5031
Mowi Ducktrap LLC	Belfast	ME	D	207 338-6280	4536
Mowi Ducktrap LLC	Belfast	ME	C	207 338-6280	4537
P S Holding Company Inc	South Portland	ME	C	207 799-9290	5510
Wild Ocean Aquaculture LLC	Portland	ME	F	207 458-6288	5289

2092 Fresh or frozen packaged fish

	CITY	ST	EMP	PHONE	ENTRY#
Essex LLC	Branford	CT	G	602 374-1890	253
Big G Seafood Inc	New Bedford	MA	G	508 994-5113	10571
Blount Fine Foods Corp (PA)	Fall River	MA	C	774 888-1300	8526
Channel Fish Co Inc	Boston	MA	D	617 569-3200	6648
F W Bryce Inc (DH)	Gloucester	MA	F	978 283-7080	8934
Georges Bank LLC	Boston	MA	F	617 423-3474	6756
Gortons Inc (DH)	Gloucester	MA	B	978 283-3000	8939
International Marketing Specialists Inc	Newton	MA	F	617 965-3400	10764
Jordan Bros Seafood Co Inc	Boston	MA	F	508 583-9797	6831
Kyler Seafood Inc	New Bedford	MA	D	508 984-5150	10611
M F Fley Incrprtd-New Bdford	New Bedford	MA	E	508 997-0773	10616
National Fish and Seafood Inc	Gloucester	MA	B	978 282-7880	8944
New England Mar Holdings Inc	New Bedford	MA	F	508 758-6600	10629
North Atlantic PCF Seafood LLC	Danvers	MA	F	401 969-3886	8213
North Coast Sea-Foods Corp (PA)	Boston	MA	C	617 345-4400	6925
Northern Wind LLC (HQ)	New Bedford	MA	F	508 997-0727	10635
Nsd Seafood Inc (PA)	Gloucester	MA	C	978 282-7880	8947
Ocean Crest Seafood Inc	Gloucester	MA	F	978 281-0232	8948
Ocean Crest Seafoods Inc (PA)	Gloucester	MA	F	978 281-0232	8949
Sea Star Seafood Corp	Marlborough	MA	E		10209
Seatrade International Co LLC	New Bedford	MA	D	774 305-4948	10649
Southeast Shellfish Inc	Wareham	MA	F	508 273-0323	12845
Spence & Co Ltd	Brockton	MA	E	508 427-5577	7308
Viking Seafoods Inc	Malden	MA	D	781 322-2000	10031
Bristol Seafood LLC (HQ)	Portland	ME	F	207 761-4251	5192
Bristol Seafood Holdings Inc (PA)	Portland	ME	D	207 761-4251	5193
Carver Shellfish Inc	Beals	ME	E	207 497-2261	4532
Inland Fresh Sfood Corp Amer I	South Portland	ME	F	207 546-7591	5506
Isf Trading Inc	Portland	ME	C	207 879-1575	5228
Maine Coast Nordic	Machiasport	ME	F	207 255-6714	5035
Maine Seafood Ventures LLC	Saco	ME	G	207 303-0165	5372
Mowi Ducktrap LLC	Belfast	ME	C	207 338-6280	4537
North Atlantic Inc	Portland	ME	G	207 774-6025	5252
Sea & Reef Aquaculture LLC	Franklin	ME	F	207 422-2422	4796
Stern Seafood Inc	Scarborough	ME	G	207 303-8466	5443
US Oceans LLC	Rockland	ME	F	207 596-3603	5344
High Liner Foods USA Inc	Portsmouth	NH	F	603 818-5555	15403
Oven Poppers Inc	Manchester	NH	F	603 644-3773	14909
Tri-State Seafoods Inc	Somersworth	NH	F	603 692-7201	15627
American Mussel Harvesters Inc	North Kingstown	RI	E	401 294-8999	16230
Endeavor Seafood LLC	Newport	RI	G	841 841-8637	16209
Henry Gonsalves Co	Smithfield	RI	E	401 231-6700	16709
Ngc Inc (PA)	Narragansett	RI	D	401 789-2200	16192
Ocean State Shellfish Coop LLC	Narragansett	RI	G	401 789-2065	16193
South Pier Fish Company Inc	Narragansett	RI	F	401 783-6611	16196
Yankee Pride Fisheries Inc	Wakefield	RI	F	401 783-9647	16747

2095 Roasted coffee

	CITY	ST	EMP	PHONE	ENTRY#
Als Beverage Company Inc	East Windsor	CT	E	860 627-7003	1065
Masas Usa Inc	East Haven	CT	E	305 603-8868	1045
Oasis Coffee Corp	Norwalk	CT	G	203 847-0554	2547
Omar Coffee Company	Newington	CT	E	860 667-8889	2312
Riseandshine Corporation (PA)	Stamford	CT	F	917 599-7541	3449
Saccuzzo Company Inc	Newington	CT	G	860 665-1101	2323
Tm Ward Co Connecticut LLC	Norwalk	CT	G	203 866-9203	2584
Atomic Cafe Inc (PA)	Salem	MA	F	978 910-0489	11702
Backbay Roasters	Wilmington	MA	G	844 532-6269	13387
Battle Grounds Coffee Co LLC	Haverhill	MA	F	978 891-5860	9077
Comfort Foods Inc	North Andover	MA	F	978 557-0009	10825
Farmer Willies Inc	Charlestown	MA	F	401 441-2997	7872
George Howell Coffee Co LLC	Acton	MA	F	978 635-9033	5748
James C Cannell Coffees Inc	West Wareham	MA	F	508 295-7009	13066
Kraft Heinz Foods Company	Woburn	MA	D	781 933-2800	13597
Mike Sheas Cffhuse Trdtnals In	Fairhaven	MA	F	508 807-5754	8509
New England Partnership Inc	Norwood	MA	C	800 225-3537	11199
Reily Foods Company	Malden	MA	E	504 524-6131	10025
Three Fins Cof Roasters & Merc	West Dennis	MA	F	508 246-5813	12999
Coffee By Design Inc (PA)	Portland	ME	G	207 879-2233	5200
Kerry Inc	Portland	ME	E	207 775-7060	5231
Vera Roasting Company	Portsmouth	NH	G	603 969-7970	15447
Bolt Coffee Company LLC	Providence	RI	G	401 533-6506	16487
Coffee Exchange Ltd	Providence	RI	F	401 273-1198	16502
Daves Coffee LLC (PA)	Narragansett	RI	F	800 483-4436	16188
Excellent Coffee Co Inc (PA)	Pawtucket	RI	C	401 724-6393	16367
Finlay EXT Ingredients USA Inc (DH)	Lincoln	RI	D	800 288-6272	16137

	CITY	ST	EMP	PHONE	ENTRY#
Mills Coffee Roasting Co	Providence	RI	G	401 781-7860	16565
Keurig Green Mountain Inc (DH)	Waterbury	VT	D	877 879-2326	17675
Speeder & Earls Inc	Burlington	VT	F	802 660-3996	17160

2096 Potato chips and similar snacks

	CITY	ST	EMP	PHONE	ENTRY#
Mediterranean Snack Fd Co LLC	Stamford	CT	F	973 402-2644	3410
Old Lyme Gourmet Company	Deep River	CT	E	860 434-7347	879
Rose Sisters Brands Inc	Bridgeport	CT	F	475 999-8115	366
Cape Cod Potato Chip Company Inc	Hyannis	MA	C	888 881-2447	9430
Frito-Lay North America Inc	Wilmington	MA	F	978 657-8344	13408
Lqc Inc	Norwood	MA	G	617 586-5139	11191
New England Prtzel Popcorn Inc	Lawrence	MA	G	978 687-0342	9587
New England Tortilla Inc	Boston	MA	E	617 889-6462	6917
Plant Snacks LLC	Needham	MA	F	617 480-6265	10518
Regco Corporation	Haverhill	MA	E	978 521-1463	9127
Stacys Pita Chip Company Inc	Randolph	MA	D	781 961-2800	11575
Utz Quality Foods LLC	Westfield	MA	G	413 562-1102	13214
Vintage Maine Kitchen LLC	Pownal	ME	G	207 317-2536	5294
Vsg Snacks Inc	North Providence	RI	F	401 536-1116	16313

2097 Manufactured ice

	CITY	ST	EMP	PHONE	ENTRY#
Grotto Always Inc	Waterbury	CT	F	203 754-0295	3915
Twenty-Five Commerce Inc	Norwalk	CT	G	203 866-0540	2588
Vaporizer LLC	Moosup	CT	E	860 564-7225	1931
Brito Ice LLC	Salem	MA	F	978 744-7727	11705
Cape Pond Ice Company (PA)	Gloucester	MA	E	978 283-0174	8927
Coldwell Banker	Tewksbury	MA	F	978 851-3731	12390
Crystal Ice Co Inc	New Bedford	MA	F	508 997-7522	10582
Eastern Ice Company Inc	Fall River	MA	E	508 672-1800	8538
JP Lillis Enterprises Inc (PA)	Sandwich	MA	F	508 888-8394	11751
Lake Boone Ice Co LLC	Hudson	MA	G	508 755-3099	9382
Leominster Ice Company Inc	Leominster	MA	G	978 537-5322	9678
Mass Dry Ice Corporation (DH)	Palmer	MA	F	413 283-9906	11277
Getchell Bros Inc (PA)	Brewer	ME	E	800 949-4423	4613
Getchell Bros Inc	Sanford	ME	E	207 490-0809	5397
Taggart Ice Inc	Nashua	NH	F	603 888-4630	15174
Cape Cod Ice	Rumford	RI	E	401 438-4555	16664

2098 Macaroni and spaghetti

	CITY	ST	EMP	PHONE	ENTRY#
Buitoni Food Company (PA)	Stamford	CT	E	475 210-0128	3298
Grotto Always Inc	Waterbury	CT	F	203 754-0295	3915
Mecha Noodle Bar	New Haven	CT	G	203 691-9671	2174
Oasis Coffee Corp	Norwalk	CT	G	203 847-0554	2547
Villarina Pasta & Fine Foods (PA)	Danbury	CT	G	203 917-4463	833
Chinese Spaghetti Factory Inc	Boston	MA	F	617 445-7714	6653
Ho Toy Noodles Inc (PA)	Stoughton	MA	F	617 426-0247	12213
Ocm Inc	Fall River	MA	F	508 675-7711	8590
Spinelli Ravioli Mfg Co Inc	Boston	MA	E	617 567-1992	7053
Zenna Noodle Bar	Brookline	MA	G	781 883-8624	7328
Umami Noodle	Bangor	ME	F	207 947-9991	4518
Nidalo F & B LLC	Westerly	RI	G	401 596-9559	16940
Venda Ravioli Inc	Providence	RI	D	401 421-9105	16636

2099 Food preparations, nec

	CITY	ST	EMP	PHONE	ENTRY#
Aleias Gluten Free Foods LLC	Branford	CT	E	203 488-5556	233
Atlantic Street Capitl MGT LLC (PA)	Stamford	CT	E	203 428-3158	3289
Cofco Americas Resources Corp (HQ)	Stamford	CT	F	203 658-2820	3316
Country Pure Foods Inc	Ellington	CT	C	330 753-2293	1103
Cw Solutions LLC	New Britain	CT	D	860 229-7700	2018
Dp Foods L L C	Cheshire	CT	D	203 271-6212	588
First Chance Inc	Middletown	CT	F	860 346-3663	1747
Gracies Kitchens Inc	New Haven	CT	F	203 773-0795	2156
Herbasway Laboratories LLC	Wallingford	CT	F	203 269-6991	3812
Hummel Bros Inc	New Haven	CT	D	203 787-4113	2161
If Not Now When Inc	Groton	CT	G	860 445-5276	1373
International Provisions Inc	Hamden	CT	E		1433
JKL Specialty Foods Inc	Stamford	CT	F	203 541-3990	3392
Kerry R Wood	Westport	CT	G	203 221-7780	4177
Lesser Evil	Danbury	CT	G	203 529-3555	769
Lyman Farm Incorporated (PA)	Middlefield	CT	C	860 349-1793	1725
Maple Craft Foods LLC	Sandy Hook	CT	G	203 913-7066	2952
Mozzicato Pastry & Bake Sp Inc	Hartford	CT	C	860 296-0426	1495
Nuovo Pasta Productions Ltd	Stratford	CT	C	203 380-4090	3561
Paridise Foods LLC	Milford	CT	G	203 283-3903	1863
Pasta Vita Inc	Old Saybrook	CT	G	860 395-1452	2658
Peeled Snacks Inc	Lyme	CT	F	773 372-3223	1560
Pepperidge Farm Incorporated (HQ)	Norwalk	CT	A	203 846-7000	2556
Premiere Packg Partners LLC	Waterbury	CT	E	203 694-0003	3964
Salsa Fresca New Haven	New Haven	CT	G	301 675-6226	2193
Severance Foods Inc	Hartford	CT	E	860 724-7063	1506
Source Inc (PA)	North Branford	CT	G	203 488-6400	2375
Too Sweets LLC	Waterbury	CT	G	203 578-6493	3973
Trio Community Meals LLC	Bridgeport	CT	F	203 336-8407	380

	CITY	ST	EMP	PHONE	ENTRY#
Uncle Wileys Inc	Fairfield	CT	F	203 256-9313	1202
Unilever Ascc AG	Shelton	CT	B	203 381-2482	3073
Vinegar Syndrome LLC	Bridgeport	CT	G	475 731-1778	384
Yosi Kosher Catering LLC	Windsor	CT	F	860 688-6677	4316
A To Z Foods Inc	Arlington	MA	G	781 413-0221	5937
Artisan Chef Manufacturing LLC (HQ)	Lawrence	MA	F	978 691-6100	9538
Avon Food Company LLC	Stoughton	MA	F	781 341-4981	12197
Beyond Shaker LLC	Woburn	MA	G	617 461-6608	13523
Boston Salads and Provs Inc	Boston	MA	F	617 541-9054	6614
Boston Salads and Provs Inc (PA)	Boston	MA	E	617 307-6340	6615
Boyajian Inc	Canton	MA	F	781 828-9966	7774
Brady Enterprises Inc (PA)	East Weymouth	MA	D	781 340-4571	8427
Breakwater Foods LLC	Lynn	MA	G	617 335-6475	9964
Chang Shing Tofu Inc	Cambridge	MA	G	617 868-8878	7537
Cherrybrook Kitchen LLC	Burlington	MA	G	781 272-0400	7347
Chew LLC	Boston	MA	E	617 945-1868	6650
Chinamerica Fd Manufacture Inc	Boston	MA	F	617 426-1818	6652
City Fresh Foods Inc	Roxbury	MA	D	617 606-7123	11689
City Fresh Foods Inc	Roxbury	MA	D	617 606-7123	11690
Clandestine Kitchen LLC	Hingham	MA	G	415 516-0378	9147
Concord Foods LLC (PA)	Brockton	MA	C	508 580-1700	7269
Custom Blends LLC	Brockton	MA	F	508 583-2995	7272
Custom Seasonings Inc	Gloucester	MA	E	978 762-6300	8931
Dough Connection Corp	Woburn	MA	G	877 693-6844	13558
Durkee-Mower Inc	Lynn	MA	E	781 593-8007	9969
East Baking Company Inc	Holyoke	MA	C	413 536-2300	9252
Four In One LLC	Chelmsford	MA	D	978 250-0751	7929
Fuel For Fire Inc	Needham Heights	MA	G	508 975-4573	10548
Garden Fresh Salad Co Inc	Chelsea	MA	E	617 889-1580	7982
Gillians Foods Inc	Salem	MA	C	781 586-0086	11719
Hans Kissle Company LLC	Haverhill	MA	C	978 556-4500	9101
Harbar LLC	Canton	MA	C	781 828-0848	7793
Healthy Truth LLC	Walpole	MA	E	774 256-5800	12560
Hot Mamas Foods Inc	Springfield	MA	C	413 737-6572	12103
Inkamazon LLC	West Roxbury	MA	G	617 763-4656	13012
International Food Pdts Inc	Walpole	MA	G	617 594-5955	12563
Island Oasis Frz Cocktail Inc (HQ)	Walpole	MA	D	508 660-1177	12564
Josephs Gourmet Pasta Company	Haverhill	MA	B	978 521-1718	9107
Lightlife Foods Inc	Turners Falls	MA	C	413 774-9000	12451
Lillys Gstronomia Italiana Inc	Everett	MA	F	617 387-9666	8490
Longrun LLC	Belmont	MA	F	617 758-8674	6307
Mange LLC	Somerville	MA	G	917 880-2104	11885
Nasoya Foods Usa LLC	Ayer	MA	C	978 772-6880	6187
New England Prtzel Popcorn Inc	Lawrence	MA	G	978 687-0342	9587
Panda Plates Inc (PA)	Foxboro	MA	G	888 997-6623	8713
Panda Plates Inc	Foxboro	MA	F	917 848-8777	8714
Pasta Bene Inc	Brockton	MA	F	508 583-1515	7300
Perfect Empanada LLC (PA)	Attleboro	MA	G	508 241-5150	6047
Puratos Corporation	Norwood	MA	G	781 688-8560	11204
Pvk Inc	Lynn	MA	F	781 595-7771	9989
R Walters Foods Ltd Lblty Co (PA)	Danvers	MA	E	978 646-8950	8216
Reily Foods Company	Malden	MA	E	504 524-6131	10025
Richelieu Foods Inc (DH)	Braintree	MA	E	781 786-6800	7199
Rohtstein Corp (PA)	Woburn	MA	D	781 935-8300	13655
Shire City Herbals Inc	Berkshire	MA	F	413 344-4740	6317
Sun Country Foods Inc (HQ)	Norwood	MA	G	855 824-7645	11212
Superior Nut Company Inc	Cambridge	MA	E	800 251-6060	7724
The Original Rangoon Company Incorporated	Norwell	MA			D
781 596-0070	11148				
Tribe Mediterranean Foods Inc	Taunton	MA	D	419 695-9925	12373
True Words Tortillas Inc	Orleans	MA	G	508 255-3338	11243
TruRoots LLC (PA)	Needham	MA	E	800 288-3637	10527
United Foods Incorporated (PA)	Boston	MA	G	617 482-9879	7093
Uno Foods Inc	Norwood	MA	C	617 323-9200	11217
Victoria Gourmet Inc	Woburn	MA	F	781 935-2100	13685
Vitasoy USA Inc	Woburn	MA	C	781 430-8988	13686
Vivido Natural LLC (PA)	Framingham	MA	F	617 630-0131	8807
West Bridgewater Fd Pantry Inc	West Bridgewater	MA	G	339 987-1684	12990
Yankee Trader Seafood Ltd	Pembroke	MA	F	781 829-4350	11379
Cherry Point Products Inc	Milbridge	ME	F	207 546-0930	5060
Coffee By Design Inc (PA)	Portland	ME	G	207 879-2233	5200
Heiwa Tofu Inc	Rockport	ME	G	207 236-8638	5350
Kjpl Restaurants Inc	Greene	ME	F	207 577-1728	4846
Mizkan Americas Inc	Auburn	ME	E	207 786-3200	4445
Modernist Pantry LLC	Eliot	ME	G	207 200-3817	4750
R & N Inc	Unity	ME	G	207 948-2613	5567
Sisters Salsa Inc	Blue Hill	ME	G	207 374-2170	4596
Springworks Farm Maine LLC	Lisbon	ME	F	207 407-4207	5017
Bascom Maple Farms Inc (PA)	Alstead	NH	D	603 835-2230	13856
Dutch Gold Honey Inc	Littleton	NH	F	603 444-6246	14716
Dutch Gold Honey Inc	Littleton	NH	F	603 444-6246	14717
Lane Poverty Orchard	Lebanon	NH	G	603 448-1511	14692
Msn Corporation	Manchester	NH	D	603 623-3528	14894
Oakcraft Pizza Inc	Nashua	NH	F	603 521-8452	15144
Old Dutch Mustard Co Inc	Greenville	NH	D	603 878-2100	14374
Parkers Maple Barn Corn Crib	Mason	NH	A	603 878-2308	14967
Popzup LLC	Somersworth	NH	G	603 314-8314	15621
Riverside Specialty Foods Inc	Seabrook	NH	G	603 474-5805	15602
Ten10 Products LLC (PA)	Stratham	NH	G	603 770-0502	15640
Tuscan Brands LLC (PA)	Salem	NH	F	781 365-2800	15568
Waterwheel Breakfast Gift Hse	Jefferson	NH	G	603 586-4313	14587
B Del Toro & Sons Inc	Providence	RI	F	401 421-5820	16481
B-Fresh Inc	Greenville	RI	G	401 349-0001	16056
Edesia Industries LLC	North Kingstown	RI	D	401 272-5521	16249
Gotham Greens Providence LLC	Providence	RI	F	401 816-0245	16526
Perfect Empanada LLC	Warren	RI	F	508 241-5150	16762
Top Shell LLC	Central Falls	RI	G	401 726-7890	15799
Training Thru Placement Inc	North Providence	RI	F	401 353-0220	16312
Venda Ravioli Inc (PA)	Providence	RI	E	401 421-9105	16637
Wildtree Inc	Lincoln	RI	D	401 732-1856	16157
Bread & Chocolate Inc	Wells River	VT	G	802 429-2920	17686
C E Maple LLC	Westminster	VT	E	802 387-5944	17700
Dosa Kitchen LLC	Brattleboro	VT	G	802 246-7592	17082
Drews LLC (HQ)	Chester	VT	G	802 875-1184	17180
Freedom Foods LLC	Randolph	VT	G	802 728-0070	17468
Green Mtn Maple Sug Ref Co Inc	Belvidere Center	VT	F	802 644-2625	17034
Highland Sugarworks Inc	Websterville	VT	F	802 479-1747	17684
Holton Family Maple	Wolcott	VT	G	802 888-5183	17775
Jay Mountain Maples LLC	North Troy	VT	G	802 988-4086	17429
Kendle Enterprises	South Woodstock	VT	F	802 457-3015	17615
Larry G Carabeau	Tinmouth	VT	G	802 446-3123	17648
Maple Grove Farms Vermont Inc (HQ)	Saint Johnsbury	VT	D	802 748-5141	17543
Mystic Mountain Maples LLC	Florence	VT	F	802 524-6163	17270
Nourish Llc	Saint Albans	VT	G	802 782-0012	17526
Palmer Lane Maple LLC	Jericho	VT	G	802 899-8199	17308
Pvf Maple LLC	Cuttingsville	VT	G	802 492-3364	17209
Runamok Maple LLC	Fairfax	VT	E	802 849-7943	17263
SOF Holdings Inc	Waterbury	VT	G	802 244-7644	17677
Sogle Property LLC	Cambridge	VT	E	802 849-7943	17168
Sugarbush Farm Inc	Woodstock	VT	G	802 457-1757	17778
Sweet Tree Holdings 1 LLC	Island Pond	VT	E	802 723-6753	17305
Two Brothers Maple LLC	Richford	VT	G	802 848-7042	17477
Vermont Maple Sugar Co Inc	Johnson	VT	G	802 888-3491	17310
Vermont Maple Sugar Co Inc	Johnson	VT	C	802 635-7483	17311
Vermont Maple Sugar Co Inc (PA)	Morrisville	VT	E	802 888-3491	17391
Vermont Soy LLC	Hardwick	VT	G	802 472-8500	17285
Vermont Tortilla Company LLC	Shelburne	VT	G	802 399-2223	17564
Wh Property Service LLC	Guilford	VT	F	802 257-8566	17282

21 TOBACCO PRODUCTS

2111 Cigarettes

	CITY	ST	EMP	PHONE	ENTRY#
Consumer Product Distrs LLC	Stratford	CT	G	203 378-2193	3531
Philip Morris Intl Inc (PA)	Stamford	CT	A	203 905-2410	3432
Smokey Mountain Chew Inc	Darien	CT	F	203 304-9200	855

2121 Cigars

	CITY	ST	EMP	PHONE	ENTRY#
F D Grave & Son Inc	North Haven	CT	G	203 239-9394	2411
Foundation Cigar Company LLC	Ellington	CT	G	203 738-9377	1108

2131 Chewing and smoking tobacco

	CITY	ST	EMP	PHONE	ENTRY#
Hay Island Holding Corporation (PA)	Darien	CT	C	203 656-8000	847
Nordic American Smokeless Inc	Danbury	CT	F	203 207-9977	790
Nuway Tobacco Company	South Windsor	CT	D	860 289-6414	3167
UST LLC	Stamford	CT	A	203 817-3000	3489

2141 Tobacco stemming and redrying

	CITY	ST	EMP	PHONE	ENTRY#
UST	Greenwich	CT	E	203 661-1100	1359

22 TEXTILE MILL PRODUCTS

2211 Broadwoven fabric mills, cotton

	CITY	ST	EMP	PHONE	ENTRY#
Bond Painting Company Inc	Old Greenwich	CT	E	212 944-0070	2630
D&R Marine Upholstery & Canvas	Rocky Hill	CT	G	860 989-9646	2921
Dimension-Polyant Inc	Putnam	CT	E	860 928-8314	2853
Dune Denim LLC	Bethel	CT	G	203 241-5409	109
North Sails Group LLC (DH)	Bridgeport	CT	D	203 874-7548	353
Z-Medica LLC	Wallingford	CT	D	203 294-0000	3876
Zimmer & Rohde Ltd (DH)	Stamford	CT	F	203 327-1400	3498
A B E Enterprises LLC	Bedford	MA	D	781 271-0000	6204
A Lyons & Company Inc	Manchester	MA	F	978 526-4244	10032
Ames Textile Corporation	Lowell	MA	D	978 934-8800	9853
Birch Outfitters LLC	Salem	MA	F	978 498-4631	11703
Brand & Oppenheimer Co Inc	Bedford	MA	E	781 271-0000	6216

	CITY	ST	EMP	PHONE	ENTRY#
Carols Canvas Company Inc	Rockland	MA	G	781 871-8288	11639
Cesyl Mills Inc	Millbury	MA	D	508 865-6129	10430
Chilsons Shops Inc	Easthampton	MA	E	413 529-8062	8441
Contract Decor Intl Inc	Brockton	MA	D	508 587-7000	7270
Dawson Forte Holdings LLC **(PA)**	Canton	MA	E	508 651-7910	7782
E W Winship Ltd Inc	Nantucket	MA	G	508 228-1908	10462
New England Worldwide Export	Quincy	MA	G	617 472-0251	11529
Performance Textiles Inc	Duxbury	MA	F	781 934-7055	8333
Stevens Linen Associates Inc	Dudley	MA	E	508 943-0813	8325
Sunrise Group USA LLC	Shrewsbury	MA	E	508 873-1519	11842
Textile Waste Supply LLC	Boston	MA	E	617 241-8100	7076
Alfreds Uphlstring Cstm Fbrcti	Alfred	ME	F	207 536-5565	4402
C B P Corp **(PA)**	Arundel	ME	E	207 985-9767	4409
Insulsafe Textiles Inc	Lewiston	ME	E	207 782-7011	4966
Maine Heritage Weavers	Monmouth	ME	E	207 933-2605	5071
Maine Woolens LLC	Brunswick	ME	E	207 725-7900	4649
Miller Industries Inc	Lisbon Falls	ME	B	207 353-4371	5023
Aj Nonwovens - Hampton LLC	Hampton	NH	D	603 929-6000	14397
E-Cloth Inc	Dover	NH	E	603 765-9367	14227
Granite State Cover and Canvas	Plaistow	NH	F	603 382-5462	15345
Brand & Oppenheimer Co Inc **(PA)**	Portsmouth	RI	E	401 293-5500	16440
Hope Valley Industries LLC	Lincoln	RI	F	401 333-3133	16141
Kinder Industries Inc	Bristol	RI	F	401 253-7076	15771
Gordons Window Decor Inc **(PA)**	Williston	VT	F	802 655-7777	17734

2221 Broadwoven fabric mills, manmade

	CITY	ST	EMP	PHONE	ENTRY#
Claremont Sales Corporation	Durham	CT	E	860 349-4499	898
Deer Creek Fabrics Inc	Stamford	CT	G	203 964-0922	3336
Deitsch Plastic Company Inc	West Haven	CT	D	203 934-6601	4102
Dimension-Polyant Inc	Putnam	CT	E	860 928-8314	2853
Swift Textile Metalizing LLC **(HQ)**	Bloomfield	CT	D	860 243-1122	211
A B E Enterprises LLC	Bedford	MA	D	781 271-0000	6204
Astenjohnson Inc	Springfield	MA	G	413 733-6603	12077
Avcarb LLC	Lowell	MA	D	978 452-8961	9857
Ballard Material Products Inc	Lowell	MA	E	978 452-8961	9859
Brand & Oppenheimer Co Inc	Bedford	MA	E	781 271-0000	6216
E W Winship Ltd Inc	Nantucket	MA	G	508 228-1908	10462
Harodite Industries Inc **(PA)**	Taunton	MA	E	508 824-6961	12340
Microfibres Inc	Foxboro	MA	A	401 725-4883	8708
Sanderson-Macleod Incorporate	Palmer	MA	C	413 283-3481	11284
Steele Canvas Basket Corp	Chelsea	MA	E	800 541-8929	7994
US Bedding Inc	Fall River	MA	E	508 678-6988	8620
Auburn Manufacturing Inc **(PA)**	Mechanic Falls	ME	E	207 345-8271	5049
Ocv Fabrics Us Inc	Brunswick	ME	D	207 729-7792	4653
Albany International Corp **(PA)**	Rochester	NH	D	603 330-5850	15464
C Cramer & Co Inc	Dover	NH	E	603 742-3838	14219
Duro-Fiber Co Inc	Hudson	NH	F	603 881-4200	14494
LDI Solutions LLC	Rochester	NH	E	603 436-0077	15485
Pro Design & Manufacturing	Newton	NH	G	603 819-4131	15243
Warwick Mills Inc **(PA)**	New Ipswich	NH	E	603 291-1000	15201
Brand & Oppenheimer Co Inc **(PA)**	Portsmouth	RI	E	401 293-5500	16440
Natco Home Fashions Inc	West Warwick	RI	F	401 828-0300	16913
Natco Home Fashions Inc	West Warwick	RI	F	401 828-0300	16914
Natco Home Fashions Inc **(PA)**	West Warwick	RI	F	401 828-0300	16915
Nfa Corp	Cumberland	RI	B	401 333-8990	15952
TEAM INC	Woonsocket	RI	E	401 762-1500	16980
Astenjohnson Inc	Williston	VT	D	802 658-2040	17722
Green Mountain Knitting Inc	Swanton	VT	E	800 361-1190	17637

2231 Broadwoven fabric mills, wool

	CITY	ST	EMP	PHONE	ENTRY#
E W Winship Ltd Inc	Nantucket	MA	G	508 228-1908	10462
National Nonwovens Inc	Easthampton	MA	E	413 527-3445	8452
National Nonwovens Inc **(PA)**	Easthampton	MA	D	413 527-3445	8453
Swan Finishing Company Inc **(PA)**	Fall River	MA	C	508 674-4611	8612
Maine Alpaca Experience LLC	Unity	ME	E	207 356-4146	5566
Ramblers Way Farm Inc **(PA)**	Kennebunk	ME	G	207 467-8118	4928
U S Felt Company Inc	Sanford	ME	E	207 324-0063	5416
Custom Banner & Graphics LLC	Rochester	NH	D	603 332-2067	15472
Trail-Tex LLC	Portsmouth	NH	F	603 436-6326	15444
Bouckaert Indus Textiles Inc	Woonsocket	RI	E	401 769-5474	16951
Brand & Oppenheimer Co Inc **(PA)**	Portsmouth	RI	E	401 293-5500	16440
Joseph C La Fond Co Inc	Manville	RI	F	401 769-3744	16164
Wool Advisor LLC	Johnson	VT	F	802 635-2271	17312

2241 Narrow fabric mills

	CITY	ST	EMP	PHONE	ENTRY#
H-O Products Corporation	Winsted	CT	E	860 379-9875	4346
American Biltrite Inc **(PA)**	Wellesley	MA	G	781 237-6655	12935
Avila Textiles Inc	North Dighton	MA	G	508 828-5882	11003
Dial Fabrics Co Inc	Taunton	MA	E	508 822-5333	12332
E W Winship Ltd Inc	Nantucket	MA	G	508 228-1908	10462
Emtex Inc	Peabody	MA	F	978 907-4500	11309
Gta-Nht Inc **(HQ)**	Rockland	MA	C	781 331-5900	11647
Julius Koch USA Inc	Mattapoisett	MA	E	508 995-9565	10258

	CITY	ST	EMP	PHONE	ENTRY#
Louis A Green Corp	North Adams	MA	F	781 535-6199	10810
MM Reif Ltd	Boston	MA	D	617 442-9500	6890
Nutex Industries Inc	New Bedford	MA	E	508 993-2501	10636
Pepperell Braiding Company Inc **(PA)**	Pepperell	MA	E	978 433-2133	11387
RI Knitting Co Inc	Taunton	MA	D	508 822-5333	12364
RI Knitting Group LLC	Whitinsville	MA	G	508 822-5333	13345
Sharon Dinette Inc	Chicopee	MA	F	413 593-6731	8060
United Stretch Design Corp	Hudson	MA	F	978 562-7781	9422
Vulplex Inc	New Bedford	MA	F	508 996-6787	10659
Auburn Manufacturing Inc **(PA)**	Mechanic Falls	ME	E	207 345-8271	5049
Bell Manufacturing Co	Lewiston	ME	E	207 784-2961	4953
Sml Inc	Lewiston	ME	D	207 784-2961	4993
Velcro Inc **(HQ)**	Manchester	NH	A	603 669-4880	14950
Velcro USA Inc **(DH)**	Manchester	NH	A	800 225-0180	14951
American Cord & Webbing Co Inc	Woonsocket	RI	E	401 762-5500	16948
Conneaut Industries Inc	West Greenwich	RI	D	401 392-1110	16883
Conrad-Jarvis Corp	Pawtucket	RI	D	401 722-8700	16356
Graco Awards Manufacturing Inc	Providence	RI	F	281 255-2161	16527
K&W Webbing Company	Central Falls	RI	E	401 725-4441	15790
Leedon Webbing Co Inc	Central Falls	RI	E	401 722-1043	15791
Moore Company **(PA)**	Westerly	RI	C	401 596-2816	16938
Moore Company	Westerly	RI	C	401 596-2816	16939
Murdock Webbing Company Inc **(PA)**	Central Falls	RI	C	401 724-3000	15793
Nfa Corp	Cumberland	RI	C	401 333-8990	15953
Nfa Corp	Cumberland	RI	E	401 333-8947	15954
Nfa Corp	Cumberland	RI	B	401 333-8990	15955
North East Knitting Inc	Pawtucket	RI	C	401 727-0500	16395
Providence Braid Company	Pawtucket	RI	E	401 722-2120	16405
Rhode Island Textile Company	Cumberland	RI	C	401 722-3700	15962
Rhode Island Textile Company **(PA)**	Cumberland	RI	C	401 722-3700	15963
Stretch Products Corp	Pawtucket	RI	E	401 722-0400	16418
Texcel Industries Inc	Cumberland	RI	E	401 727-2113	15969
Garware Fulflex USA Inc	Brattleboro	VT	C	802 257-5256	17085

2251 Women's hosiery, except socks

	CITY	ST	EMP	PHONE	ENTRY#
Cabot Hosiery Mills Inc **(PA)**	Northfield	VT	D	802 485-6066	17432

2252 Hosiery, nec

	CITY	ST	EMP	PHONE	ENTRY#
Sock Shack	Portland	ME	G	207 805-1348	5274
Cabot Hosiery Mills Inc **(PA)**	Northfield	VT	D	802 485-6066	17432

2253 Knit outerwear mills

	CITY	ST	EMP	PHONE	ENTRY#
Alps Sportswear Mfg Co Inc	Natick	MA	F	978 685-5159	10467
Birch Outfitters LLC	Salem	MA	F	978 498-4631	11703
Northeast Knitting Mills Inc **(PA)**	Fall River	MA	E	508 678-7553	8589
River Falls Manufacturing Co	Fall River	MA	D	508 646-2900	8604
Mountain Corporation **(HQ)**	Keene	NH	E	603 355-2272	14610
Red Fish - Blue Fish Dye Wrks	Somersworth	NH	G	603 692-3900	15624
Teespring Inc	Providence	RI	E	855 833-7774	16619
Nomad Communications Inc	White River Junction	VT	F	802 649-1995	17709

2257 Weft knit fabric mills

	CITY	ST	EMP	PHONE	ENTRY#
Swift Textile Metalizing LLC **(HQ)**	Bloomfield	CT	D	860 243-1122	211
Draper Knitting Company Inc	Canton	MA	E	781 828-0029	7786
Hardwick Knitted Fabric Inc	Warren	MA	G	413 436-7704	12851
Nfa Corp	Cumberland	RI	B	401 333-8990	15955

2258 Lace and warp knit fabric mills

	CITY	ST	EMP	PHONE	ENTRY#
Barcia LLC	Bridgeport	CT	F	203 367-1010	300
Charbert Inc	Chestnut Hill	MA	F	401 364-7751	7998
Elloit Wright Workroom Inc	Boston	MA	F	617 542-3605	6712
Sunrise Group USA LLC	Shrewsbury	MA	E	508 873-1519	11842
Tweave LLC	Fall River	MA	E	508 285-6701	8619
Leavers Lace Corporation	West Greenwich	RI	E	401 397-5555	16887
Moore Company	Westerly	RI	E	401 596-0219	16937
Moore Company **(PA)**	Westerly	RI	C	401 596-2816	16938
Moore Company	Westerly	RI	C	401 596-2816	16939
Garware Fulflex USA Inc	Brattleboro	VT	C	802 257-5256	17085

2259 Knitting mills, nec

	CITY	ST	EMP	PHONE	ENTRY#
Stevens Linen Associates Inc	Dudley	MA	E	508 943-0813	8325
E-Cloth Inc	Dover	NH	E	603 765-9367	14227

2261 Finishing plants, cotton

	CITY	ST	EMP	PHONE	ENTRY#
Amerbelle Textiles LLC	Vernon Rockville	CT	D		3759
A B E Enterprises LLC	Bedford	MA	D	781 271-0000	6204
Action Apparel Inc	Stoneham	MA	F	781 435-2342	12173
Brand & Oppenheimer Co Inc	Bedford	MA	E	781 271-0000	6216
Chillybear Inc **(PA)**	Needham	MA	F	781 455-6321	10507
Color-Tex International Inc	Boston	MA	C	617 269-8020	6663
Duro Textiles LLC	Fall River	MA	C	508 675-0102	8535
Duro Textiles LLC	Fall River	MA	C	508 679-0076	8536

	CITY	ST	EMP	PHONE	ENTRY#
Emco Services Inc	Fall River	MA	G	508 674-5504	8541
Gonco Inc (PA)	Sandwich	MA	F	508 833-3900	11750
Majilite Corporation	Dracut	MA	D	978 441-6800	8307
Middlesex Research Mfg Co Inc	Hudson	MA	E	978 562-3697	9390
Silver Screen Design Inc	Greenfield	MA	F	413 773-1692	9000
Starensier Inc (PA)	Byfield	MA	E	978 462-7311	7459
Swan Finishing Company Inc (PA)	Fall River	MA	C	508 674-4611	8612
Tyca Corporation (PA)	Clinton	MA	E	978 612-0002	8093
Collins Sports Center LLC	Rochester	NH	G	603 335-1417	15470
Life Is Good Wholesale Inc	Hudson	NH	D	603 594-6100	14523
Liquid Blue Inc	Derry	NH	D	401 333-6200	14200
Cranston Print Works Company (PA)	Cranston	RI	E	401 943-4800	15844
Cranston Print Works Company	West Greenwich	RI	F	401 397-2442	16884
KAY DEE DESIGNS INC (PA)	Hope Valley	RI	E	401 539-2400	16067

2262 Finishing plants, manmade

	CITY	ST	EMP	PHONE	ENTRY#
Tees & More LLC	Hartford	CT	G	860 244-2224	1513
Duro Textiles LLC	Fall River	MA	C	508 675-0102	8535
Duro Textiles LLC	Fall River	MA	C	508 679-0076	8536
Gloucester Graphics Inc (PA)	Gloucester	MA	G	978 281-4500	8937
Majilite Manufacturing Inc	Dracut	MA	E	978 441-6800	8308
Microfibres Inc	Foxboro	MA	A	401 725-4883	8708
Starensier Inc (PA)	Byfield	MA	E	978 462-7311	7459
Stevens Linen Associates Inc	Dudley	MA	E	508 943-0813	8325
Swan Finishing Company Inc (PA)	Fall River	MA	C	508 674-4611	8612
Auburn Manufacturing Inc	Mechanic Falls	ME	D	207 345-8271	5048
Auburn Manufacturing Inc (PA)	Mechanic Falls	ME	E	207 345-8271	5049
Hammar & Sons Inc	Pelham	NH	F	603 635-2292	15289
Cooley Incorporated (HQ)	Pawtucket	RI	C	401 724-9000	16357
Cranston Print Works Company (PA)	Cranston	RI	E	401 943-4800	15844
Cranston Print Works Company	West Greenwich	RI	F	401 397-2442	16884
Kenyon Industries Inc	Kenyon	RI	B	401 364-7761	16112
Tex Flock Inc	Woonsocket	RI	E	401 765-2340	16981

2269 Finishing plants, nec

	CITY	ST	EMP	PHONE	ENTRY#
Brookwood Laminating Inc	Wauregan	CT	D	860 774-5001	4039
Gorilla Graphics Inc	Middletown	CT	F	860 704-8208	1748
Grand Embroidery Inc	Oxford	CT	E	203 888-7484	2695
Berkshire Corporation (HQ)	Great Barrington	MA	E	413 528-2602	8973
Brittany Global Tech Corp	New Bedford	MA	D	508 999-3281	10573
Diane L Ivey	Hyde Park	MA	G	617 763-9736	9459
Stevens Linen Associates Inc	Dudley	MA	E	508 943-0813	8325
Web Industries Inc (PA)	Marlborough	MA	G	508 898-2988	10234
Seacolors	Washington	ME	G	207 845-2587	5588
Albany Engnered Composites Inc	Rochester	NH	G	603 330-5851	15462
Albany Engnered Composites Inc (HQ)	Rochester	NH	C	603 330-5800	15463
Custom Banner & Graphics LLC	Rochester	NH	G	603 332-2067	15472
Capeway Yarns Inc	Tiverton	RI	G	401 624-1311	16735
KAY DEE DESIGNS INC (PA)	Hope Valley	RI	E	401 539-2400	16067
Kenyon Industries Inc	Kenyon	RI	B	401 364-7761	16112

2273 Carpets and rugs

	CITY	ST	EMP	PHONE	ENTRY#
0 Mohawk LLC	Cos Cob	CT	G	203 622-7180	673
Alliance Carpet Cushion Co (HQ)	Torrington	CT	D	860 489-4273	3667
Apricot Home LLC	Greenwich	CT	G	203 552-1791	1312
Connecticut Clean Room Corp	Bristol	CT	E	860 589-0049	430
Elizabeth Eakins Inc	Norwalk	CT	E	203 831-9347	2496
Ethan Allen Retail Inc (HQ)	Danbury	CT	B	203 743-8000	741
Joseph Cohn Son Tile Trazo LLC	North Haven	CT	G	203 772-2420	2420
New Haven Companies Inc	East Haven	CT	F	203 469-6421	1048
Aladdin Manufacturing Corp	Walpole	MA	B	508 660-8913	12549
Cape Cod Braided Rug Co Inc	Marstons Mills	MA	F	508 432-3133	10247
Delaware Valley Corp	Tewksbury	MA	E	978 459-6932	12393
Julie Industries Inc (PA)	Andover	MA	G	978 276-0820	5890
Kink Pieces of A Dream LLC	Framingham	MA	F	508 748-5417	8784
Matter Surfaces Inc (PA)	Stoughton	MA	F	800 628-7462	12223
Merida LLC	Fall River	MA	E	508 675-6572	8577
Merida Meridian Inc	Boston	MA	E	617 464-5400	6885
Mohawk Fence Company Inc	Shrewsbury	MA	G	508 614-5507	11838
Stevens Linen Associates Inc	Dudley	MA	E	508 943-0813	8325
TMI Industries Inc	Palmer	MA	E	413 283-9021	11285
Flemish Master Weavers Inc	Sanford	ME	C	207 324-6600	5396
Colonial Mills Inc	Rumford	RI	D	401 724-6279	16665
East Providence Mohawks	East Providence	RI	G	401 829-1411	16015
International Textile Mfg Inc	Cumberland	RI	G		15946
Madeira Asset Holdings Inc	Lincoln	RI	F	401 728-5903	16145
Natco Products Corporation (PA)	West Warwick	RI	B	401 828-0300	16916
Robin Industries Inc	Bristol	RI	E	401 253-8350	15779
A View of Vermont LLC	Saint Johnsbury	VT	G	802 748-0880	17538

2281 Yarn spinning mills

	CITY	ST	EMP	PHONE	ENTRY#
Beal Manufacturing Inc	Swampscott	MA	E	704 824-9961	12298
Dearnley Brothers Inc	Millbury	MA	F	508 865-2267	10431
Robertson-Chase Fibers LLC	North Billerica	MA	G	978 453-2837	10951
St Regis Sportswear Ltd	North Andover	MA	G	518 725-6767	10850
Family Yarns Inc	Etna	ME	G	207 269-3852	4763
Jagger Brothers	Springvale	ME	E	207 324-5622	5520
Quince & Company Inc	Saco	ME	E	207 210-6630	5378
Worsted Spinning Neng LLC	Springvale	ME	G	207 324-5622	5523
Harrisville Designs Inc (PA)	Harrisville	NH	G	603 827-3333	14432
Concordia Manufacturing LLC	Coventry	RI	D	401 828-1100	15811
Conneaut Industries Inc	West Greenwich	RI	D	401 392-1110	16883
Providence Yarn Company Inc	Pawtucket	RI	E	401 722-5600	16407
Green Mountain Spinnery Inc	East Dummerston	VT	G	802 387-4528	17216

2282 Throwing and winding mills

	CITY	ST	EMP	PHONE	ENTRY#
Archerdx Inc	Beverly	MA	F	978 232-3570	6325
Windle Industries Inc	Sutton	MA	G	508 865-5773	12296
Miller Industries Inc	Lisbon Falls	ME	B	207 353-4371	5023
Conneaut Industries Inc	West Greenwich	RI	D	401 392-1110	16883

2284 Thread mills

	CITY	ST	EMP	PHONE	ENTRY#
New Bedford Thread Company	New London	CT	F	860 333-6700	2231
Dhm Thread Corporation	Fall River	MA	F	508 672-0032	8533
ESP Solutions Inc	Taunton	MA	F	508 285-0017	12335
New Bedford Thread Co Inc	Fairhaven	MA	F	508 996-8584	8511
Hilco Athletic & Graphics Inc	West Warwick	RI	F	401 822-1775	16910

2295 Coated fabrics, not rubberized

	CITY	ST	EMP	PHONE	ENTRY#
Brookwood Laminating Inc	Wauregan	CT	D	860 774-5001	4039
Defender Industries Inc	Waterford	CT	C	860 701-3400	3989
Deitsch Plastic Company Inc	West Haven	CT	D	203 934-6601	4102
Swift Textile Metalizing LLC (HQ)	Bloomfield	CT	D	860 243-1122	211
Trelleborg Ctd Systems US Inc	New Haven	CT	C	203 468-0342	2212
Boston Materials Inc	Billerica	MA	F	617 306-2396	6411
Bradford Coatings Inc	Lowell	MA	D	978 459-4100	9864
Clark Hammerbeam Corporation	Dedham	MA	F	781 461-1946	8239
Coaters Inc	New Bedford	MA	F	508 996-5700	10578
Dela Incorporated (PA)	Haverhill	MA	E	978 372-7783	9091
Emtex Inc	Peabody	MA	F	978 907-4500	11309
Flame Laminating Corporation	North Andover	MA	F	978 725-9527	10832
Foamtech LLC	Fitchburg	MA	F	978 343-4022	8655
Gentex Corporation	Boston	MA	F	617 670-3547	6755
Gta-Nht Inc (HQ)	Rockland	MA	F	781 331-5900	11647
Haartz Corporation	Acton	MA	E	978 264-2607	5750
Haartz Corporation (PA)	Acton	MA	B	978 264-2600	5751
Hardwick Laminators Inc	Gilbertville	MA	G	413 477-6600	8913
Majilite Corporation	Dracut	MA	D	978 441-6800	8307
Microfibres Inc	Foxboro	MA	A	401 725-4883	8708
Middlesex Research Mfg Co Inc	Hudson	MA	E	978 562-3697	9390
Miles Kedex Co Inc	Westminster	MA	E	978 874-1403	13274
NBD Nanotechnologies Inc	Lexington	MA	F	781 541-4192	9764
Pascale Industries Inc	Fall River	MA	E	508 673-3307	8595
Shawmut LLC (PA)	West Bridgewater	MA	C	508 588-3300	12979
Starensier Inc (PA)	Byfield	MA	E	978 462-7311	7459
Tpi Industries LLC (HQ)	West Bridgewater	MA	E	845 692-2820	12986
Trelleborg Ctd Systems US Inc	Monson	MA	D	413 267-4808	10457
Vulplex Inc	New Bedford	MA	F	508 996-6787	10659
Auburn Manufacturing Inc (PA)	Mechanic Falls	ME	E	207 345-8271	5049
Jaeger Usa Inc	Rochester	NH	F	603 332-5816	15480
Protavic America Inc	Londonderry	NH	G	603 623-8624	14780
Textiles Coated Incorporated (PA)	Londonderry	NH	F	603 296-2221	14786
Textiles Coated Incorporated	Manchester	NH	C	603 296-2221	14943
Worthen Industries Inc	Nashua	NH	B	603 886-0973	15189
Cooley Incorporated	Cranston	RI	F	401 721-6374	15843
Cooley Incorporated (HQ)	Pawtucket	RI	C	401 724-9000	16357
Custom Coatings Inc	North Smithfield	RI	F	401 766-1500	16322
Kenyon Industries Inc	Kenyon	RI	B	401 364-7761	16112
Tex Flock Inc	Woonsocket	RI	E	401 765-2340	16981
Leo D Bernstein and Sons Inc	Shaftsbury	VT	E	212 337-9578	17551

2296 Tire cord and fabrics

	CITY	ST	EMP	PHONE	ENTRY#
United Abrasives Inc (PA)	North Windham	CT	B	860 456-7131	2451
Alvin Johnson	East Longmeadow	MA	G	413 525-6334	8368

2297 Nonwoven fabrics

	CITY	ST	EMP	PHONE	ENTRY#
Bethune Nonwovens Inc	East Windsor	CT	C	860 386-8001	1067
Lydall Thermal/Acoustical Inc	Glastonbury	CT	E	860 646-1233	1288
New England Nonwovens LLC	West Haven	CT	F	203 891-0851	4116
Suominen US Holding Inc (HQ)	East Windsor	CT	E	860 386-8001	1087
Swift Textile Metalizing LLC (HQ)	Bloomfield	CT	D	860 243-1122	211
Windsor Locks Nonwovens Inc (DH)	East Windsor	CT	F	860 292-5600	1090
Xamax Industries Inc	Seymour	CT	E	203 888-7200	2976
Boyd Biomedical Inc (PA)	Lee	MA	E	413 243-2000	9612
Clark-Cutler-Mcdermott Company	Franklin	MA	C	508 528-1200	8823
Delaware Valley Corp (PA)	Lawrence	MA	F	978 688-6995	9556

S I C

	CITY	ST	EMP	PHONE	ENTRY#
Delaware Valley Corp	Tewksbury	MA	E	978 459-6932	12393
Draper Knitting Company Inc	Canton	MA	E	781 828-0029	7786
Georgia-Pacific LLC	Leominster	MA	D	978 537-4701	9666
Hollingsworth & Vose Company (PA)	East Walpole	MA	C	508 850-2000	8418
National Nonwovens Inc	Easthampton	MA	E	413 527-3445	8452
National Nonwovens Inc (PA)	Easthampton	MA	D	413 527-3445	8453
Nonwovens Inc	North Chelmsford	MA	F	978 251-8612	10985
Saint-Gobain Adfors Amer Inc	Worcester	MA	D	508 795-2500	13789
Vulplex Inc	New Bedford	MA	E	508 996-6787	10659
Insulsafe Textiles Inc	Lewiston	ME	E	207 782-7011	4966
C Cramer & Co Inc	Dover	NH	E	603 742-3838	14219
Northeastern Nonwovens Inc	Rochester	NH	F	603 332-5900	15489
Rontex America Inc	Amherst	NH	F	603 883-5076	13888
TEAM INC	Woonsocket	RI	E	401 762-1500	16980

2298 Cordage and twine

	CITY	ST	EMP	PHONE	ENTRY#
Brownell & Company Inc (PA)	Moodus	CT	F	860 873-8625	1929
Detotec North America Inc	Sterling	CT	G	860 564-1012	3500
East Shore Wire Rope Rgging Su	North Haven	CT	F	203 469-5204	2407
International Cordage East Ltd (PA)	Colchester	CT	E	860 537-1414	661
Loos & Co Inc (PA)	Pomfret	CT	B	860 928-7981	2809
Comprehensive Identification Products Inc	Burlington	MA			C
781 229-8780					7354
Dhm Thread Corporation	Fall River	MA	F	508 672-0032	8533
Julius Koch USA Inc	Mattapoisett	MA	E	508 995-9565	10258
Pepperell Braiding Company Inc (PA)	Pepperell	MA	E	978 433-2133	11387
Photonic Systems Inc	Billerica	MA	F	978 670-4990	6471
Ropes Wealth Advisors LLC	Boston	MA	E	617 951-7217	7013
Tauten Inc	Beverly	MA	G	978 961-3272	6386
Teufelberger Fiber Rope Corp	Fall River	MA	C	508 678-8200	8616
Advanced Indus Solutions Inc	Waldoboro	ME	E	207 832-0569	5573
Auburn Manufacturing Inc (PA)	Mechanic Falls	ME	E	207 345-8271	5049
David Bird LLC	Waldoboro	ME	F	207 832-0569	5575
Orion Ropeworks Inc (HQ)	Winslow	ME	F	207 877-2224	5687
Spurwink Cordage Inc	Biddeford	ME	G	207 284-5894	4589
Sterling Rope Company Inc	Biddeford	ME	G	800 788-7673	4590
Yale Cordage Inc	Saco	ME	D	207 282-3396	5383
Calling All Cargo LLC	Dover	NH	F	603 740-1900	14220
Marmon Utility	Milford	NH	F	603 249-1302	15031
Two In One Manufacturing Inc	Nashua	NH	E	603 595-8212	15179
American Cord & Webbing Co Inc	Woonsocket	RI	E	401 762-5500	16948
Ashaway Line & Twine Mfg Co	Ashaway	RI	D	401 377-2221	15738
Frank B Struzik Inc	Woonsocket	RI	F	401 766-6880	16960
New England Overseas Corp	Pawtucket	RI	F	401 722-3800	16393
Rhode Island Textile Company (PA)	Cumberland	RI	C	401 722-3700	15963
Trawlworks Inc	Narragansett	RI	F	401 789-3964	16198

2299 Textile goods, nec

	CITY	ST	EMP	PHONE	ENTRY#
A&P Coat Apron & Linen Sup LLC	Hartford	CT	D	914 840-3200	1466
Engineered Fibers Tech LLC	Shelton	CT	F	203 922-1810	3005
Joel Gorkowski Inc	Milford	CT	F	203 877-3896	1841
New Haven Companies Inc	East Haven	CT	F	203 469-6421	1048
Clark-Cutler-Mcdermott Company	Franklin	MA	C	508 528-1200	8823
FTC Enterprises Inc	East Bridgewater	MA	F	508 378-2799	8340
Full Circle Padding Inc	Norton	MA	F	508 285-2500	11127
Lenis Inc	Canton	MA	G	781 401-3273	7805
National Nonwovens Inc	Easthampton	MA	E	413 527-3445	8454
Spectro Coating Corp	Leominster	MA	F	978 534-6191	9706
Spectro Coating Corp (PA)	Leominster	MA	E	978 534-1800	9707
United Industrial Tex Pdts Inc (PA)	West Springfield	MA	E	413 737-0095	13048
Windle Industries Inc	Sutton	MA	G	508 865-5773	12296
Best Felts Liquidation Corp	Thomaston	ME	F	207 596-0566	5541
Fiber Materials Inc (DH)	Biddeford	ME	C	207 282-5911	4564
Kws Inc	Waldoboro	ME	F	207 832-5095	5577
Maine Balsam Fir Prodcts	West Paris	ME	F	207 674-5090	5612
Sea Bags LLC (PA)	Portland	ME	F	207 780-0744	5268
American Bacon Boston Felt Inc	Rochester	NH	E	603 332-7000	15465
Carbon Felt Inc	Claremont	NH	F	603 542-0202	14082
Coastal Style LLC	Portsmouth	NH	G	603 328-2000	15374
S M Services Inc	Nashua	NH	G	603 883-3381	15162
Textiles Coated Incorporated (PA)	Londonderry	NH	E	603 296-2221	14786
Amber Style Inc	Cumberland	RI	F	401 405-0089	15932
Concordia Manufacturing LLC	Coventry	RI	D	401 828-1100	15811
Hyman Brickle & Son Inc (PA)	Woonsocket	RI	F	401 769-0189	16964
Tastex Corporation	Central Falls	RI	E	401 727-2900	15798
TEAM INC	Woonsocket	RI	E	401 762-1500	16980
Tex Flock Inc	Woonsocket	RI	E	401 765-2340	16981
Cornell Online LLC	Burlington	VT	E	802 448-3281	17128
Vermont Hemp Processing Inc	Randolph	VT	F	802 565-8025	17474

23 APPAREL, FINISHED PRODUCTS FROM FABRICS & SIMILAR MATERIALS

2311 Men's and boy's suits and coats

	CITY	ST	EMP	PHONE	ENTRY#
Burlington Coat Fctry Whse Cor	Danbury	CT	E	203 748-8583	718
Front Line Apparel Group LLC	Hebron	CT	F	860 859-3524	1527
Greenwich Triangle LLC (DH)	Haverhill	MA	C	800 634-5312	9099
Joseph Abboud Mfg Corp	New Bedford	MA	B	508 999-1301	10606
Neptune Garment Company	Boston	MA	B	617 482-3980	6909
Sterlingwear of Boston Inc (PA)	Boston	MA	C	617 567-2100	7061
Sperian Protection Usa Inc (DH)	Smithfield	RI	E	401 232-1200	16731
Squadlocker Inc	Warwick	RI	D	888 885-6253	16864

2321 Men's and boy's furnishings

	CITY	ST	EMP	PHONE	ENTRY#
MB Sport LLC (PA)	New Canaan	CT	E	203 966-1985	2082
16sur20 Management LLC	Lenox	MA	F	413 637-5061	9624
Acme Merchandise and AP Inc	Gloucester	MA	F	978 282-4800	8917
New Balance Athletics Inc (HQ)	Boston	MA	B	617 783-4000	6913
Pvh Corp	Chatham	MA	G	508 945-4063	7900
Shop Therapy Imports	Provincetown	MA	F	508 487-8970	11497
Imeldas Fabrics & Designs	New Sharon	ME	G	207 778-0665	5090
Jenesco Inc	Lyndeborough	NH	F	603 673-4830	14800
Timberland LLC (HQ)	Stratham	NH	B	603 772-9500	15641
Barry T Chouinard Inc (HQ)	Northfield	VT	E	802 485-8600	17431
Ibex Outdoor Clothing LLC	White River Junction	VT	E	802 359-4239	17708

2322 Men's and boy's underwear and nightwear

	CITY	ST	EMP	PHONE	ENTRY#
L L Bean Inc	Brunswick	ME	F	207 725-0300	4647

2323 Men's and boy's neckwear

	CITY	ST	EMP	PHONE	ENTRY#
Skurge of Sea LLC	Norwich	CT	G	860 887-7679	2617
New York Accessory Group Inc	Bristol	RI	D	401 245-6096	15776
Beau Ties of Vermont LLC	Middlebury	VT	E	802 388-0108	17337
Btl Holdings LLC	Middlebury	VT	E	917 596-3660	17339

2325 Men's and boy's trousers and slacks

	CITY	ST	EMP	PHONE	ENTRY#
16sur20 Management LLC	Lenox	MA	F	413 637-5061	9624
American Power Source Inc (PA)	Fall River	MA	F	508 672-8847	8520
Greenwich Triangle LLC (DH)	Haverhill	MA	C	800 634-5312	9099
Guess Inc	Braintree	MA	E	781 843-3147	7185
Timberland LLC (HQ)	Stratham	NH	B	603 772-9500	15641

2326 Men's and boy's work clothing

	CITY	ST	EMP	PHONE	ENTRY#
Childrens Medical Group (PA)	Bloomfield	CT	E	860 242-8330	155
Sewn In America Inc (PA)	Ridgefield	CT	D	203 438-9149	2907
Essex County Coop Farming Assn	Topsfield	MA	F	978 887-2300	12433
Good Clothing Company Inc	Fall River	MA	F	508 419-6152	8556
Maverick Work Wear Inc	North Reading	MA	E	860 944-3776	11043
Salk Company Inc	Allston	MA	F	617 782-4030	5825
Spector Textile Products Inc (PA)	Lawrence	MA	E	978 688-3501	9600
Tyca Corporation (PA)	Clinton	MA	E	978 612-0002	8093
Unifirst Corporation (PA)	Wilmington	MA	B	978 658-8888	13472
W D C Holdings Inc	Attleboro	MA	E	508 699-4412	6073
Tempshield LLC	Trenton	ME	F	207 667-9696	5559
Labonville Inc (PA)	Gorham	NH	E	603 752-4030	14360
Codet-Newport Corporation (HQ)	Newport	VT	F	802 334-5811	17398

2329 Men's and boy's clothing, nec

	CITY	ST	EMP	PHONE	ENTRY#
Cycling Sports Group Inc (HQ)	Wilton	CT	D	203 845-8300	4238
Del Arbour LLC	Milford	CT	F	203 882-8501	1817
Everest Isles LLC	Wallingford	CT	G	203 561-5128	3804
Gima LLC	Hartford	CT	F	860 296-4441	1483
Scharf and Breit Inc	Redding	CT	F	516 282-0287	2883
16sur20 Management LLC	Lenox	MA	F	413 637-5061	9624
Ames Textile Corporation	Lowell	MA	D	978 934-8850	9853
Companystuffcom Inc	Ipswich	MA	G	978 282-1525	9480
Golden Fleece Mfg Group LLC (DH)	Haverhill	MA	B	978 686-3833	9098
Griffin Manufacturing Co Inc	Fall River	MA	E	508 677-0048	8558
Kellsport Industries Inc	Fall River	MA	E	508 646-0855	8565
M & M Garment Manufacturing	Everett	MA	G	617 389-7787	8492
Mahi Gold Inc	Chatham	MA	F	508 348-5487	7898
New Balance Athletics Inc (HQ)	Boston	MA	B	617 783-4000	6913
Pop Tops Company Inc	South Easton	MA	E	508 580-2580	11949
Precision Sportswear Inc	Fall River	MA	G	508 674-3034	8599
Reebok International Ltd LLC (HQ)	Boston	MA	B	781 401-5000	7002
Saucony (DH)	Waltham	MA	E	617 824-6000	12776
Sickday Inc	Wellfleet	MA	F	508 214-4158	12953
Tracksmith Corporation (PA)	Boston	MA	G	781 235-0037	7083
Tyca Corporation (PA)	Clinton	MA	E	978 612-0002	8093

	CITY	ST	EMP	PHONE	ENTRY#
Creative Apparel Assoc LLC	Belmont	ME	B	207 342-2814	4543
Rodco Enterprises	Lewiston	ME	F	207 786-2931	4990
Chuck Roast Equipment Inc **(PA)**	Conway	NH	F	603 447-5492	14178
Legacy Global Sports LP	Portsmouth	NH	E	603 373-7262	15416
Richardson Mfg Co Inc	Silver Lake	NH	F	603 367-9018	15607
Timberland LLC **(HQ)**	Stratham	NH	B	603 772-9500	15641
Waterwear Inc	Wilton	NH	E	603 654-5344	15712
G-Form LLC **(HQ)**	Providence	RI	E	401 250-5555	16523
Hilco Athletic & Graphics Inc	West Warwick	RI	F	401 822-1775	16910
Squadlocker Inc	Warwick	RI	D	888 885-6253	16864
Bogner of America Inc **(PA)**	Burlington	VT	E	802 451-4417	17121
Fat Hat Clothing Co	Quechee	VT	F	802 296-6646	17462
Forsake Inc	Stowe	VT	G	585 576-6358	17631
Louis Garneau USA Inc	Derby	VT	D	802 334-5885	17211

2331 Women's and misses' blouses and shirts

	CITY	ST	EMP	PHONE	ENTRY#
Fyc Apparel Group LLC	East Haven	CT	E	203 466-6525	1043
Fyc Apparel Group LLC **(PA)**	Branford	CT	D	203 481-2420	260
Acme Merchandise and AP Inc	Gloucester	MA	E	978 282-4800	8917
American Power Source **(PA)**	Fall River	MA	F	508 672-8847	8520
Shop Therapy Imports	Provincetown	MA	G	508 487-8970	11497
B Peachee Inc	Biddeford	ME	G	207 602-6262	4555
Imeldas Fabrics & Designs	New Sharon	ME	G	207 778-0665	5090
Barry T Chouinard Inc **(HQ)**	Northfield	VT	E	802 485-8600	17431

2335 Women's, junior's, and misses' dresses

	CITY	ST	EMP	PHONE	ENTRY#
Fyc Apparel Group LLC **(PA)**	Branford	CT	D	203 481-2420	260
Dependable Cleaners Inc **(PA)**	Quincy	MA	F	617 770-9232	11509
Fall River Apparel Inc	Fall River	MA	G	508 677-1975	8545
Musette Bridal Inc	Boston	MA	E	617 424-1070	6898
Priscilla of Boston Inc	Boston	MA	F	857 366-4109	6981

2337 Women's and misses' suits and coats

	CITY	ST	EMP	PHONE	ENTRY#
Fyc Apparel Group LLC **(PA)**	Branford	CT	D	203 481-2420	260
MB Sport LLC **(PA)**	New Canaan	CT	E	203 966-1985	2082
Blauer Manufacturing Co Inc **(PA)**	Boston	MA	E	800 225-6715	6597
Holdette	Danvers	MA	G	301 412-3660	8191
Sara Campbell Ltd **(PA)**	Boston	MA	C	617 423-3134	7025
Sterlingwear of Boston Inc **(PA)**	Boston	MA	C	617 567-2100	7061

2339 Women's and misses' outerwear, nec

	CITY	ST	EMP	PHONE	ENTRY#
Del Arbour LLC	Milford	CT	F	203 882-8501	1817
Imerchandise LLC	Centerbrook	CT	E	860 581-8700	562
Accurate Services Inc	Fall River	MA	E	508 674-5773	8518
Broder Bros Co	Middleboro	MA	C	508 923-4800	10352
Corporate Casuals LLC	Concord	MA	F	978 369-5935	8110
Good Clothing Company Inc	Fall River	MA	F	508 419-6152	8556
Griffin Manufacturing Co Inc	Fall River	MA	E	508 677-0048	8558
Janlynn Corporation	South Hadley	MA	D	413 206-0002	11963
Kellsport Industries Inc	Fall River	MA	E	508 646-0855	8565
M & M Garment Manufacturing	Everett	MA	G	617 389-7787	8492
New Balance Athletics Inc **(HQ)**	Boston	MA	B	617 783-4000	6913
Northeast Knitting Mills Inc **(PA)**	Fall River	MA	F	508 678-7553	8589
Pop Tops Company Inc	South Easton	MA	E	508 580-2580	11949
Reebok International Ltd LLC **(HQ)**	Boston	MA	B	781 401-5000	7002
Saucony Inc **(DH)**	Waltham	MA	C	617 824-6000	12776
Sickday Inc	Wellfleet	MA	E	508 214-4158	12953
Tracksmith Corporation **(PA)**	Boston	MA	G	781 235-0037	7083
Tyca Corporation **(PA)**	Clinton	MA	E	978 612-0002	8093
Creative Apparel Assoc LLC	Belmont	ME	B	207 342-2814	4543
Chuck Roast Equipment Inc **(PA)**	Conway	NH	F	603 447-5492	14178
Legacy Global Sports LP	Portsmouth	NH	E	603 373-7262	15416
Richardson Mfg Co Inc	Silver Lake	NH	G	603 367-9018	15607
Waterwear Inc	Wilton	NH	E	603 654-5344	15712
Hilco Athletic & Graphics Inc	West Warwick	RI	F	401 822-1775	16910
Bogner of America Inc **(PA)**	Burlington	VT	E	802 451-4417	17121
Fat Hat Clothing Co	Quechee	VT	F	802 296-6646	17462
Louis Garneau USA Inc	Derby	VT	D	802 334-5885	17211
Vermont Flannel Co **(PA)**	East Barre	VT	F	802 476-5226	17215
Wool Advisor LLC	Johnson	VT	F	802 635-2271	17312

2341 Women's and children's underwear

	CITY	ST	EMP	PHONE	ENTRY#
Dayleen Intimates Inc	Brookfield	CT	F	914 969-5900	516
L L Bean Inc	Brunswick	ME	F	207 725-0300	4647

2342 Bras, girdles, and allied garments

	CITY	ST	EMP	PHONE	ENTRY#
Donghia Inc	Milford	CT	C	800 366-4442	1818
Fastech Inc	Canton	MA	E	781 964-3010	7791
Valmont Inc	Ludlow	MA	F	413 583-8351	9955

2353 Hats, caps, and millinery

	CITY	ST	EMP	PHONE	ENTRY#
Barker Advg Specialty Co Inc **(PA)**	Cheshire	CT	D	203 272-2222	575
Hat Attack Inc **(PA)**	Stamford	CT	E	718 994-1000	3368

	CITY	ST	EMP	PHONE	ENTRY#
Indigo Coast Inc	Kent	CT	G	860 592-0088	1541
Manup LLC	Norwalk	CT	G	203 588-9861	2533
Athletic Emblem Lettering Inc	Springfield	MA	F	413 733-8151	12078
Fall River Hat Company	Fall River	MA	F	508 672-7033	8546
Whole Earth Hat Co Inc	Fall River	MA	F	508 672-7033	8626
DVE Manufacturing Inc	Lewiston	ME	F	207 783-9895	4957
Nes Embroidery Inc	Tilton	NH	F	603 293-4664	15655
New York Accessory Group Inc	Bristol	RI	D	401 245-6096	15776
Fat Hat Clothing Co	Quechee	VT	F	802 296-6646	17462
Washburn Company Inc	Morrisville	VT	F	802 888-3032	17393

2361 Girl's and children's dresses, blouses

	CITY	ST	EMP	PHONE	ENTRY#
Classic Prep Childrenswear Inc	Norwalk	CT	G	203 286-6204	2483
Barry T Chouinard Inc **(HQ)**	Northfield	VT	E	802 485-8600	17431

2369 Girl's and children's outerwear, nec

	CITY	ST	EMP	PHONE	ENTRY#
Accurate Services Inc	Fall River	MA	E	508 674-5773	8518
E-I-E-I-o Incorporated	Fall River	MA	G	508 324-9311	8537
Precision Sportswear Inc	Fall River	MA	G	508 674-3034	8599
Shop Therapy Imports	Provincetown	MA	G	508 487-8970	11497
Imeldas Fabrics & Designs	New Sharon	ME	G	207 778-0665	5090
Richardson Mfg Co Inc	Silver Lake	NH	G	603 367-9018	15607
Vermont Flannel Co **(PA)**	East Barre	VT	F	802 476-5226	17215

2371 Fur goods

	CITY	ST	EMP	PHONE	ENTRY#
Surell Accessories Inc	Troy	NH	F	603 242-7784	15658

2381 Fabric dress and work gloves

	CITY	ST	EMP	PHONE	ENTRY#
Acushnet Company **(DH)**	Fairhaven	MA	B	508 979-2000	8504

2384 Robes and dressing gowns

	CITY	ST	EMP	PHONE	ENTRY#
Graduation Solutions LLC	Greenwich	CT	E	914 934-5991	1332
L L Bean Inc	Brunswick	ME	F	207 725-0300	4647

2385 Waterproof outerwear

	CITY	ST	EMP	PHONE	ENTRY#
Gonco Inc **(PA)**	Sandwich	MA	F	508 833-3900	11750
Mr Idea Inc	Attleboro	MA	E	508 222-0155	6039
Neptune Garment Company	Boston	MA	D	617 482-3980	6909
Sterlingwear of Boston Inc **(PA)**	Boston	MA	C	617 567-2100	7061
Wear-Guard Corporation	Norwell	MA	A	781 871-4100	11150
Log House Designs Inc **(PA)**	Chatham	NH	F	603 694-3373	14070

2386 Leather and sheep-lined clothing

	CITY	ST	EMP	PHONE	ENTRY#
U S Made Co Inc	Danvers	MA	F	978 777-8383	8228
Vanson Leathers Inc	Fall River	MA	D	508 678-2000	8622
Surell Accessories Inc	Troy	NH	F	603 242-7784	15658
Timberland LLC **(HQ)**	Stratham	NH	B	603 772-9500	15641

2387 Apparel belts

	CITY	ST	EMP	PHONE	ENTRY#
Dooney & Bourke Inc **(HQ)**	Norwalk	CT	E	203 853-7515	2492
Karen Callan Designs Inc	Greenwich	CT	G	203 762-9914	1336
Chaucer Accessories Inc	Haverhill	MA	G	978 373-1566	9085
Highland Belts & Fine Lea Gds	Brewer	ME	F	207 989-2597	4614

2389 Apparel and accessories, nec

	CITY	ST	EMP	PHONE	ENTRY#
Bondi Band LLC	Simsbury	CT	F	207 576-4191	3084
Realhub Inc	Darien	CT	F	650 461-9210	854
Robert Miller Associates LLC	Weston	CT	F	718 392-1640	4152
B R T Inc	Worcester	MA	E	508 791-2383	13701
Chaucer Accessories Inc	Haverhill	MA	G	978 373-1566	9085
CJS Workshop LLC	Groton	MA	E	323 445-5012	9008
Gdmc USA LLC	Northampton	MA	F	413 584-0065	11063
Image Factory	Pocasset	MA	G	508 295-3876	11489
Marbleheadweather Gmts LLC	Marblehead	MA	G	781 639-1060	10090
CM Almy & Son Inc	Pittsfield	ME	C	207 487-3232	5159
Highland Belts & Fine Lea Gds	Brewer	ME	F	207 989-2597	4614
Ntension Corp	Hermon	ME	E	207 848-7700	4887
Portland Dry Goods Inc	Portland	ME	G	207 699-5575	5258
Synergy Sportswear Inc **(PA)**	Keene	NH	F	603 352-8681	14626
Thanksben10 LLC	Milford	NH	F	603 206-5116	15040
New York Accessory Group Inc	Bristol	RI	D	401 245-6096	15776

2391 Curtains and draperies

	CITY	ST	EMP	PHONE	ENTRY#
Decorator Services Inc	Bridgeport	CT	G	203 384-8144	315
Draperies Intrors Grenwich LLC	Cos Cob	CT	G	203 489-3010	677
R L Fisher Inc	Hartford	CT	F	860 951-8110	1503
Thomas W Raftery Inc	Hartford	CT	E	860 278-9870	1514
Yard Stick Decore	Bridgeport	CT	F	203 330-0360	388
A L Ellis Inc	Fall River	MA	D	508 672-4799	8517
Bloom & Company Inc	Framingham	MA	F	617 923-1526	8744
Dra-Cor Industries Inc	Brockton	MA	E	508 580-3770	7273
Fall River Apparel Inc	Fall River	MA	G	508 677-1975	8545
Ksg Enterprises Inc	Peabody	MA	F	978 977-7357	11322

SIC

	CITY	ST	EMP	PHONE	ENTRY#
Limelight Productions Inc	Lee	MA	G	413 243-4950	9616
Quest Drape	Woburn	MA	G	781 859-0300	13645
Reliable Fabrics Inc	Everett	MA	F	617 387-5321	8497
Sams Drapery Workroom Inc	Stoughton	MA	F	617 364-9440	12234
United Curtain Co Inc **(PA)**	Avon	MA	E	508 588-4100	6166
Dirigo Stitching Inc	Skowhegan	ME	E	207 474-8421	5466
Gilberte Interiors LLC **(PA)**	Hanover	NH	F	603 643-3727	14423
J & R Langley Co Inc	Manchester	NH	E	603 622-9653	14866
Marion Mfg Co	Lincoln	RI	E	401 331-4343	16147
Natco Home Fashions Inc	West Warwick	RI	G	401 828-0300	16913
Natco Home Fashions Inc	West Warwick	RI	F	401 828-0300	16914
Natco Home Fashions Inc **(PA)**	West Warwick	RI	F	401 828-0300	16915
Gordons Window Decor Inc **(PA)**	Williston	VT	F	802 655-7777	17734

2392 Household furnishings, nec

	CITY	ST	EMP	PHONE	ENTRY#
Dodson Boatyard LLC	Stonington	CT	E	860 535-1507	3508
Hills Point Industries LLC **(PA)**	Westport	CT	F	800 807-8579	4173
Patricia Spratt For Home LLC	Old Lyme	CT	F	860 434-9291	2644
R L Fisher Inc	Hartford	CT	E	860 951-8110	1503
Talalay Global Inc **(DH)**	Shelton	CT	F.	203 924-0700	3067
Thomas W Raftery Inc	Hartford	CT	E	860 278-9870	1514
Almont Company Inc	East Weymouth	MA	E	617 269-8244	8424
Beantown Bedding LLC	Hingham	MA	G	781 608-9915	9143
Berkshire Corporation **(HQ)**	Great Barrington	MA	F	413 528-2602	8973
Butler Home Products LLC **(HQ)**	Hudson	MA	F	508 597-8000	9359
Emotionrx Inc	Cambridge	MA	F	617 500-5976	7561
ERC Acquisition Inc	Lynn	MA	E	781 593-4000	9971
Fall River Apparel Inc	Fall River	MA	E	508 677-1975	8545
Klear-Vu Corporation **(PA)**	Fall River	MA	D	508 674-5723	8566
Ksg Enterprises Inc	Peabody	MA	F	978 977-7357	11322
Matouk Factory Store Inc	Fall River	MA	E	508 997-3444	8575
PDk Worldwide Entps Inc **(PA)**	Fall River	MA	E	508 676-2155	8596
Stevens Linen Associates Inc	Dudley	MA	E	508 943-0813	8325
Therapedic of New England LLC	Brockton	MA	F	508 559-9944	7311
Tiberio Manufacturing Corp	Holliston	MA	G	508 429-4011	9232
Tri Textiles Corporation **(PA)**	Fall River	MA	G	631 420-0011	8617
Unwrapped Inc	Lowell	MA	D	978 441-0242	9932
Dirigo Stitching Inc	Skowhegan	ME	E	207 474-8421	5466
Goodwill Industries Nthrn Neng **(PA)**	Gorham	ME	D	207 774-6323	4820
Maine Balsam Fir Prodcts	West Paris	ME	F	207 674-5090	5612
Two Rivers Pet Products Inc	Turner	ME	E	207 225-3965	5565
Boston Billows Inc	Nashua	NH	G	603 598-1200	15073
E-Cloth Inc	Dover	NH	E	603 765-9367	14227
Lucci Corp	Peterborough	NH	F	603 567-4301	15317
Bess Home Fashions Inc	West Warwick	RI	C	401 828-0300	16906
Bristal Cushion & ACC LLC	Warren	RI	F	401 247-4499	16755
Moore Company	Westerly	RI	E	401 596-2816	16939
Anichini Inc	Tunbridge	VT	E	802 889-9430	17651
Garware Fulflex USA Inc	Brattleboro	VT	C	802 257-5256	17085

2393 Textile bags

	CITY	ST	EMP	PHONE	ENTRY#
Dow Cover Company Incorporated	New Haven	CT	D	203 469-5394	2144
Clarkie Industries	North Attleboro	MA	F	508 404-0202	10870
Fall River Apparel Inc	Fall River	MA	G	508 677-1975	8545
Fleming Industries Inc	Chicopee	MA	E	413 593-3300	8033
Hosokawa Micron Intl Inc	Northborough	MA	E	508 655-1123	11098
Jungle Inc **(PA)**	Essex	MA	F	978 356-7722	8476
MM Reif Ltd	Boston	MA	D	617 442-9500	6890
Steele Canvas Basket Corp	Chelsea	MA	E	800 541-8929	7994
Under Cover Inc	New Bedford	MA	F	508 997-7600	10657
United Industrial Tex Pdts Inc **(PA)**	West Springfield	MA	E	413 737-0095	13048
Unwrapped Inc	Lowell	MA	D	978 441-0242	9932
Byer Manufacturing Company	Bernard	ME	E	207 866-2171	4547
C B P Corp **(PA)**	Arundel	ME	F	207 985-9767	4409
Lapoint Industries Inc **(PA)**	Auburn	ME	D	207 777-3100	4439
Rodco Enterprises	Lewiston	ME	F	207 786-2931	4990
Enviro-Tote Inc	Londonderry	NH	E	603 647-7171	14749
Absorbent Specialty Pdts LLC	Pawtucket	RI	F	401 722-1177	16342

2394 Canvas and related products

	CITY	ST	EMP	PHONE	ENTRY#
3333 LLC	Manchester	CT	G	860 643-1384	1579
American Sign Inc	New Haven	CT	E	203 624-2991	2115
Arrow Shed LLC	Watertown	CT	F	800 560-8383	4002
Commercial Sewing Inc	Torrington	CT	C	860 482-5509	3675
Custom Covers LLC	Clinton	CT	G	860 669-4169	641
Defender Industries Inc	Waterford	CT	E	860 701-3400	3989
Dimension-Polyant Inc	Putnam	CT	E	860 928-8314	2853
Eastern Awning Systems Inc	Watertown	CT	F	860 274-9218	4011
Fitzgerald-Norwalk Awng Co Inc	Norwalk	CT	G	203 847-5858	2501
New Haven Companies Inc	East Haven	CT	F	203 469-6421	1048
North Sails Group LLC **(DH)**	Bridgeport	CT	D	203 874-7548	353
Shelterlogic Corp **(HQ)**	Watertown	CT	E	860 945-6442	4028
Slogic Holding Corp **(PA)**	New Canaan	CT	F	203 966-2800	2086

	CITY	ST	EMP	PHONE	ENTRY#
Soapstone Media Inc	Ellington	CT	F	860 749-0455	1116
Toff Industry Inc	Milldale	CT	G	860 378-0532	1903
Topside Canvas & Uphl Inc	Westbrook	CT	G	860 399-4845	4144
W H Preuss Sons Incorporated	Bolton	CT	G	860 643-9492	224
Columbia ASC Inc	Lawrence	MA	F	978 683-2205	9554
Cramaro Tarpaulin Systems Inc	Northborough	MA	G	508 393-3062	11094
Dartmouth Awning Co Inc	Westport	MA	G	508 636-6838	13295
Doyle Sailmakers Inc **(PA)**	Salem	MA	E	978 740-5950	11712
Expansion Opportunities Inc	Northborough	MA	A	508 393-8200	11095
Harding Sails Inc	Marion	MA	F	508 748-0334	10097
Harry Miller Co LLC	Boston	MA	F	617 427-2300	6782
Harry Miller Co LLC **(PA)**	Boston	MA	E	617 427-2300	6783
Jay Salem Inc	Middleton	MA	G	978 774-4999	10387
Leisure Time Canvas Inc	West Springfield	MA	G	413 785-5500	13032
Lyman Conrad **(PA)**	South Hadley	MA	F	413 538-8200	11965
MM Reif Ltd	Boston	MA	D	617 442-9500	6890
Signs By J Inc	Boston	MA	G	617 825-9855	7037
Spector Textile Products Inc **(PA)**	Lawrence	MA	E	978 688-3501	9600
Sperry Sails Inc	Marion	MA	E	508 748-2581	10101
Steele Canvas Basket Corp	Chelsea	MA	E	800 541-8929	7994
Sunsetter Products Ltd Partnr	Malden	MA	D	781 321-9600	10029
Tent Connection Inc	Northbridge	MA	G	508 234-8746	11119
United Industrial Tex Pdts Inc **(PA)**	West Springfield	MA	E	413 737-0095	13048
William Blanchard Co Inc	Wakefield	MA	F	781 245-8050	12543
Zmetra Clarspan Structures LLC	Webster	MA	G	508 943-0940	12932
Byer Manufacturing Company	Bernard	ME	E	207 866-2171	4547
C B P Corp **(PA)**	Arundel	ME	F	207 985-9767	4409
Canvasworks Inc	Kennebunk	ME	G	207 985-2419	4923
Collabric	Veazie	ME	F	207 945-5095	5570
Custom Canvas & Upholstery LLC	Bridgton	ME	F	207 241-8518	4627
Leavitt & Parris Inc	Portland	ME	F	207 797-0100	5233
Lewiston-Auburn Tent & Awng Co	Lewiston	ME	G	207 784-7353	4974
Maine Bay Canvas Inc	Portland	ME	F	207 878-8888	5237
Enviro-Tote Inc	Londonderry	NH	E	603 647-7171	14749
Image Awnings Incorporated	Wolfeboro	NH	G	603 569-6680	15734
Yarra Design & Fabrication LLC	Bow	NH	F	603 224-6880	14014
Anchors and Thread LLC	Portsmouth	RI	G	401 248-8645	16435
Anchors Aweigh Together LLC	Warwick	RI	F	401 738-8055	16779
Black Dog Corporation	Portsmouth	RI	E	401 683-5858	16439
Doyle Sails Newport Partnr	Middletown	RI	G	401 849-9400	16172
Hood Sailmakers Inc **(PA)**	Middletown	RI	G	401 849-9400	16174
Johnston Blckwood Slmakers Inc	East Greenwich	RI	G	401 884-4227	15988
Kinder Industries Inc	Bristol	RI	F	401 253-7076	15771
Quantum Newport	Portsmouth	RI	G	401 849-7700	16452
Rhode Northsales Island Inc	Portsmouth	RI	G	401 683-7997	16455
Stupell Industries Ltd Inc	Johnston	RI	F	401 831-5640	16107
Thurston Sails Inc	Bristol	RI	G	401 254-0970	15782
Ke Usa Inc	Middlebury	VT	E	802 388-7309	17345
Ke Usa Inc	Williston	VT	E	802 864-3009	17736

2395 Pleating and stitching

	CITY	ST	EMP	PHONE	ENTRY#
Al-Lynn Sales LLC	Shelton	CT	G	203 922-7840	2979
Expert Embroidery LLC	Wallingford	CT	G	203 269-9675	3805
Grand Embroidery Inc	Oxford	CT	F	203 888-7484	2695
Guidera Marketing Services	Pawcatuck	CT	F	860 599-8880	2721
HJ Hoffman Company	Norwalk	CT	G	203 853-7740	2514
Hot Tops LLC	Shelton	CT	F	203 926-2067	3016
Nitch To Stitch LLC	Brookfield	CT	G	203 948-9921	531
Pj Specialties	Willington	CT	F	860 429-7626	4226
R F H Company Inc	Norwalk	CT	F	203 853-2863	2561
TSS & A Inc	Prospect	CT	F	203 758-6303	2844
Zuse Inc	Branford	CT	D	203 458-3295	287
290 Industrial Stitching Inc	South Barre	MA	G	978 355-0271	11914
47 Brand LLC	Boston	MA	F	617 437-1384	6501
All-City Screen Printing Inc	Wakefield	MA	G	781 665-0000	12498
Arocam Inc	Taunton	MA	F	508 822-1220	12319
Astrella Ink	Millbury	MA	F	508 865-5028	10426
Athletic Emblem Lettering Inc	Springfield	MA	F	413 733-8151	12078
Austins Sportswear Inc	West Yarmouth	MA	F	508 775-0554	13071
Avon Cstm EMB & Screenprinting	Avon	MA	G	781 341-4663	6143
Best Embroidery	Revere	MA	G	857 258-0333	11617
Callenstitch LLC	Concord	MA	F	978 369-9080	8107
Camelot Enterprises Inc	Stoughton	MA	F	781 341-9100	12200
Chillybear Inc **(PA)**	Needham	MA	F	781 455-6321	10507
Corporate Image Apparel Inc	Fall River	MA	E	508 676-3099	8532
Embroidery Place	Shrewsbury	MA	G	508 842-5311	11832
Es Sports Corporation	Holyoke	MA	D	413 534-5634	9253
ESP Solutions Services LLC	Taunton	MA	G	508 285-0017	12336
G & G Silk Screening	Plymouth	MA	G	508 830-1075	11460
Gonco Inc **(PA)**	Sandwich	MA	F	508 833-3900	11750
Inter-All Corporation	Granby	MA	F	413 467-7181	8971
J W I N Promotional Corp	Westport	MA	G	508 636-1993	13297
Janlynn Corporation	South Hadley	MA	D	413 206-0002	11963

	CITY	ST	EMP	PHONE	ENTRY#
Jungle Inc (PA)	Essex	MA	F	978 356-7722	8476
Kasc Inc	New Bedford	MA	B	508 985-9898	10608
Matouk Textile Works Inc	Fall River	MA	E	508 997-3444	8576
Nixon Company Incorporated	Indian Orchard	MA	F	413 543-3701	9472
Piesco Sporting Goods Inc	North Easton	MA	F	508 238-5599	11012
Pop Tops Company Inc	South Easton	MA	E	508 580-2580	11949
Red Derby Incorporated Embrdry	Beverly	MA	G	978 927-4838	6378
Santacroce Graphics Inc	Charlton	MA	F	802 447-0020	7895
Silver Screen Design Inc	Greenfield	MA	F	413 773-1692	9000
Stitchdx LLC	Lowell	MA	G	617 818-8585	9925
Threadhead Inc	Hyannis	MA	F	508 778-6516	9453
Time-Out Sports Inc	Whitman	MA	F	781 447-6670	13350
Universal Screening Studio Inc	Everett	MA	G	617 387-1832	8502
Wear-Guard Corporation	Norwell	MA	A	781 871-4100	11150
BBH Apparel	Boothbay Harbor	ME	F	207 633-0601	4601
D R Designs Inc	Manchester	ME	F	207 622-3303	5044
Rodco Enterprises	Lewiston	ME	F	207 786-2931	4990
Winter People Inc	Cumberland Center	ME	E	207 865-6636	4711
Woodland Studios Inc	Ellsworth	ME	F	207 667-3286	4761
Blue Dolphin Screenprint Inc	Somersworth	NH	E	603 692-2500	15611
Business Shirtmasters	Chichester	NH	F	603 798-3787	14072
Chick Embroidery	Rochester	NH	G	603 332-5487	15469
Evergreen Embroidery	Campton	NH	F	603 726-4271	14043
National Embroidery Corp	Manchester	NH	F	603 647-1995	14896
Nes Embroidery Inc	Tilton	NH	F	603 293-4664	15655
Say It In Stitches Inc	Concord	NH	G	603 224-6470	14155
Cool Air Creations Inc	Smithfield	RI	E	401 830-5780	16692
GA Rel Manufacturing Company	Providence	RI	F	401 331-5455	16524
Ira Green Inc (PA)	Providence	RI	C	800 663-7487	16543
Kennedy Incorporated	North Kingstown	RI	F	401 295-7800	16265
Spirit Recognition Inc (PA)	Pawtucket	RI	F	401 722-6400	16417
Bumwraps Inc (PA)	Montgomery Center	VT	G	802 326-4080	17368
Green Mountain Monogram Inc	Wells River	VT	E	802 757-2553	17687
Initial Ideas Inc (PA)	Rutland	VT	G	802 773-6310	17500
Mprp Inc	Saint Albans	VT	G	802 527-1557	17523
Outfitters Inc Corporate	Saint Albans	VT	G	802 527-0204	17528

2396 Automotive and apparel trimmings

	CITY	ST	EMP	PHONE	ENTRY#
Advanced Graphics Incorporated	Stratford	CT	E	203 378-0471	3515
Allied Printing Services Inc (PA)	Manchester	CT	B	860 643-1101	1584
Bennettsville Holdings LLC	Hebron	CT	F	860 444-9400	1525
Hot Tops LLC	Shelton	CT	F	203 926-2067	3016
Jornik Manufacturing Corp	Stamford	CT	F	203 969-0500	3393
Kinamor Incorporated	Wallingford	CT	E	203 269-0380	3824
Michael Zoppa	South Windsor	CT	G	860 289-5881	3165
Nicks Enterprises Inc (PA)	Hamden	CT	F	203 287-9990	1447
Project Graphics Inc	Woodbury	CT	E	802 488-8789	4388
Quality Name Plate Inc	East Glastonbury	CT	D	860 633-9495	923
R F H Company Inc	Norwalk	CT	F	203 853-2863	2561
Sam & Ty LLC (PA)	Norwalk	CT	F	212 840-1871	2569
Systematic Automation Inc	Farmington	CT	E	310 218-3361	1249
T-Shirts Etc Inc	Glastonbury	CT	G	860 657-3551	1298
The Romatic Manufacturing Company	Southbury	CT	C	203 264-8203	3199
Universal Printing Svcs Inc	West Haven	CT	E	203 934-4275	4131
Zuse Inc	Branford	CT	D	203 458-3295	287
A B E Enterprises LLC	Bedford	MA	D	781 271-0000	6204
Advanced Print Technology Inc	Fitchburg	MA	G	978 342-0093	8640
Advanced Visibility LLC	Fitchburg	MA	D	603 660-6033	8641
Argosy Publishing Inc (PA)	Newton	MA	D	617 527-9999	10733
Bay State Apparel Inc	Leominster	MA	G	978 534-5810	9639
Brand & Oppenheimer Co Inc	Bedford	MA	F	781 271-0000	6216
Chillybear Inc (PA)	Needham	MA	F	781 455-6321	10507
Color-Tex International Inc	Boston	MA	C	617 269-8020	6663
E V Yeuell Inc	Woburn	MA	E	781 933-2984	13560
Es Sports Corporation	Holyoke	MA	E	413 534-5634	9253
ESP Solutions Services LLC	Taunton	MA	G	508 285-0017	12336
Excelsior Printing Company	North Adams	MA	D	413 663-3771	10807
First Print Inc	Winchester	MA	F	781 729-7714	13484
Fleming Industries Inc	Chicopee	MA	E	413 593-3300	8033
George H Dean Co	Braintree	MA	D	781 544-3782	7184
Ghp Media Inc	North Adams	MA	D	413 663-3771	10808
Gloucester Graphics Inc (PA)	Gloucester	MA	G	978 281-4500	8937
Industrial Lbling Systems Corp	Tyngsboro	MA	F	978 649-7004	12460
J W I N Promotional Corp	Westport	MA	G	508 636-1993	13297
Janlynn Corporation	South Hadley	MA	D	413 206-0002	11963
Light Metal Platers LLC	Waltham	MA	F	781 899-8855	12709
M & P Machine Company Inc	Stoughton	MA	E	781 344-5888	12218
Paramount Industries Inc	Medway	MA	F	508 533-8480	10310
Priscilla of Boston Inc	Boston	MA	F	857 366-4109	6981
Silver Screen Design Inc	Greenfield	MA	F	413 773-1692	9000
Soft-As-A-grape Inc (PA)	Wareham	MA	E	508 295-9900	12844

	CITY	ST	EMP	PHONE	ENTRY#
Specialty Manufacturing Inc	Amesbury	MA	F	978 388-1601	5853
Swan Dyeing and Printing Corp	Fall River	MA	D	508 674-4611	8611
Time-Out Sports Inc	Whitman	MA	F	781 447-6670	13350
Universal Screening Studio Inc	Everett	MA	G	617 387-1832	8502
Wear-Guard Corporation	Norwell	MA	A	781 871-4100	11150
Atlantic Sportswear Inc	Portland	ME	E	207 797-5028	5178
DVE Manufacturing Inc	Lewiston	ME	G	207 783-9895	4957
Liberty Graphics Inc	Liberty	ME	F	207 589-4596	4999
Tranztape LLC	Appleton	ME	G	207 785-2467	4406
Winter People Inc.	Cumberland Center	ME	E	207 865-6636	4711
Business Shirtmasters	Chichester	NH	F	603 798-3787	14072
Liquid Blue Inc	Derry	NH	D	401 333-6200	14200
National Embroidery Corp	Manchester	NH	F	603 647-1995	14896
Rapid Finishing LLC	Nashua	NH	E	603 889-4234	15154
Say It In Stitches Inc	Concord	NH	G	603 224-6470	14155
Tk Sports and Associates Inc	Enfield	NH	G	603 442-6770	14275
Fuller Box Co Inc	Central Falls	RI	C	401 725-4300	15788
Spirit Recognition Inc (PA)	Pawtucket	RI	F	401 722-6400	16417
Squadlocker Inc	Warwick	RI	F	888 885-6253	16864
Keiths II Sports Ltd	Pittsford	VT	F	802 483-6050	17444

2397 Schiffli machine embroideries

	CITY	ST	EMP	PHONE	ENTRY#
Inter-All Corporation	Granby	MA	F	413 467-7181	8971
Optamark LLC	North Attleboro	MA	E	877 888-3878	10881

2399 Fabricated textile products, nec

	CITY	ST	EMP	PHONE	ENTRY#
Airborne Industries Inc	Branford	CT	F	203 315-0200	232
DS Sewing Inc	New Haven	CT	F	203 773-1344	2145
Flagman of America LLC	Avon	CT	G	860 678-0275	24
Kemper Manufacturing Corp	West Haven	CT	E	203 934-1600	4109
Puppy Hugger	Greenwich	CT	G	203 661-4858	1345
Soapstone Media Inc	Ellington	CT	F	860 749-0455	1116
Accent Banner LLC	Medford	MA	F	781 391-7300	10278
Athletic Emblem Lettering Inc	Springfield	MA	F	413 733-8151	12078
Faverco Inc	Boston	MA	G	617 247-1440	6732
Flag Fables Inc	Springfield	MA	E	413 747-0525	12095
Flagraphics Inc	Somerville	MA	E	617 776-7549	11874
Lane Printing Co Inc	Holbrook	MA	F	781 767-4450	9178
Niche Inc	New Bedford	MA	E	508 990-4202	10633
Nixon Company Incorporated	Indian Orchard	MA	F	413 543-3701	9472
Ouellette Industries Inc	Attleboro Falls	MA	G	508 695-0964	6093
Sand A Industries	Dudley	MA	G	508 943-1178	8322
VH Blackinton & Co Inc	Attleboro Falls	MA	C	508 699-4436	6096
Allen Manufacturing Inc	Lewiston	ME	F	207 333-3385	4950
Bailey Sign Inc	Westbrook	ME	E	207 774-2843	5617
Erin Flett	Gorham	ME	G	207 887-9253	4819
Albany International Corp (PA)	Rochester	NH	D	603 330-5850	15464
Arlington Sample Book Co Inc (PA)	Sunapee	NH	F	603 763-9082	15642
Custom Banner & Graphics LLC	Rochester	NH	G	603 332-2067	15472
Lupine Inc	Center Conway	NH	D	603 356-7371	14055
Black Dog Corporation	Portsmouth	RI	E	401 683-5858	16439
Hook-Fast Specialties Inc	Providence	RI	F	401 781-4466	16533
Josef Creations Inc (PA)	Chepachet	RI	F	401 421-4198	15805
Summer Infant Inc (HQ)	Woonsocket	RI	C	401 671-6550	16975
Summer Infant (usa) Inc	Woonsocket	RI	C	401 671-6551	16976
Tme Co Inc	Providence	RI	G	860 354-0686	16628
Universal Specialty Awards	Providence	RI	G	401 272-7760	16635
Vogue Industries Ltd Partnr	Central Falls	RI	E	401 722-0900	15800

24 LUMBER AND WOOD PRODUCTS, EXCEPT FURNITURE

2411 Logging

	CITY	ST	EMP	PHONE	ENTRY#
C & C Logging	Windsor	CT	G	860 683-0071	4263
Davis Tree & Logging LLC	Danbury	CT	F	203 938-2153	728
Fowler D J Log Land Clearing	Coventry	CT	G	860 742-5842	679
Witkowsky John	North Branford	CT	G	203 483-0152	2380
Brightman Corporation	Assonet	MA	F	508 644-2620	5972
Cotton Tree Service Inc	Northampton	MA	F	413 584-9104	11057
Favreau Forestry LLC	Sterling	MA	G	978 706-1038	12162
Gmo Threshold Logging LLC	Boston	MA	G	617 330-7500	6765
Gmo Thrshold Tmber Hldings LLC	Boston	MA	G	617 330-7500	6766
Lashway Logging Inc	Williamsburg	MA	F	413 268-3600	13365
Noble Tree LLC	Boxford	MA	G	978 590-5011	7161
Roberts Brothers Lumber Co Inc	Ashfield	MA	F	413 628-3333	5955
Thomas J Doane	Orange	MA	F	978 821-2361	11235
West End Firewood Inc	Whitinsville	MA	G	508 234-4747	13347
Ambrose G McCarthy Jr	Skowhegan	ME	G	207 474-8837	5462
Andrew Irish Logging	Peru	ME	F	207 562-8839	5155
Ashley & Harmon Logging Inc	East Machias	ME	F	207 259-2043	4739

Employee Codes: A=Over 500 employees, B=251-500
C=101-250, D=51-100, E=20-50, F=10-19, G=1-9   2024 Harris New England
Manufacturers Directory   849

	CITY	ST	EMP	PHONE	ENTRY#
Ben Savage Logging Inc	Sebec	ME	G	207 735-6699	5456
BP Logging	Saint Francis	ME	G	207 398-4457	5387
Chipping & Logging	Porter	ME	G	207 625-4056	5165
Chopper One Inc	Eagle Lake	ME	G	207 444-5476	4734
Clinton G Bradbury Inc	Rumford	ME	G	207 562-8014	5355
D R Logging Inc	Fort Kent	ME	G	207 316-6434	4786
Darrell C McGuire & Sons Inc	Houlton	ME	F	207 532-0511	4899
Davis Forestry Products Inc	Danforth	ME	F	207 448-2625	4718
Delaite Trucking Inc	Chester	ME	G	207 794-6844	4692
E J Carrier Inc	Jackman	ME	E	207 668-4457	4909
Edmond Roy & Sons Inc	Jackman	ME	G	877 425-8491	4910
Ellen McLaughlin	Medway	ME	G	207 746-3398	5055
Eric T Vannah	Brunswick	ME	G	207 631-2475	4645
Eugene Corson	Sumner	ME	G	207 446-6489	5538
Everett McCabe	Bridgton	ME	G	207 890-9174	4628
Farmington Chipping Entp Inc	Farmington	ME	G	207 778-4888	4778
Forest Chester Products Inc	Lincoln	ME	E	207 794-2303	5008
G V Logging Inc	Fort Kent	ME	G	207 231-1003	4789
Gary M Pomeroy Logging Inc	Hermon	ME	F	207 848-3171	4882
H Arthur York Logging Inc (PA)	Medway	ME	F	207 746-5883	5056
H Arthur York Logging Inc	Medway	ME	F	207 746-5912	5057
Hanington Bros Inc	Macwahoc Plt	ME	F	207 765-2681	5036
Hanington Timberlands	Wytopitlock	ME	F	207 456-7003	5701
Hanscom Construction Inc	Marshfield	ME	G	207 255-8067	5046
Haymart LLC	Patten	ME	G	207 528-2058	5153
Herbert C Haynes Inc (PA)	Winn	ME	E	207 736-3412	5678
Herbert L Hardy & Son Inc	Smyrna Mills	ME	G	207 757-8550	5480
Highland Farms Logging LLC	Cornish	ME	F	207 239-2977	4705
J & M Logging Inc	Sidney	ME	G	207 622-6353	5459
Jackman Lumber Inc (PA)	Jackman	ME	E	207 668-4407	4911
John Khiel III Log Chpping Inc	Denmark	ME	G	207 452-2157	4722
Johnny H Castonguay	Livermore	ME	G	207 897-5945	5024
K B Logging Inc	Smyrna Mills	ME	F	207 757-8818	5481
Kevin S Hawes	Belgrade	ME	G	207 495-3412	4541
L E Taylor and Sons Inc	Porter	ME	G	207 625-4056	5166
Lyle Guptill	East Machias	ME	F	207 255-4130	4740
M & H Logging LLC	Rangeley	ME	E	207 864-5617	5312
M B Eastman Logging Inc	Parsonsfield	ME	G	207 625-8020	5151
M H Humphrey & Sons Inc	Parsonsfield	ME	F	207 625-4965	5152
Madtown Logging LLC	Madawaska	ME	G	207 728-6260	5038
Maine Custom Woodlands LLC	Durham	ME	F	207 353-9020	4733
Mw Trucking and Logging Inc	Norway	ME	F	207 890-3592	5117
Nadeau Logging Inc	Fort Kent	ME	F	207 834-6338	4791
Nicols Brothers Inc	Rumford	ME	G	207 364-7032	5361
Nicols Brothers Logging Inc	Mexico	ME	F	207 364-8685	5058
Norman White Inc	Shapleigh	ME	G	207 636-1636	5458
Olson S Logging LLC	Canaan	ME	G	207 474-8835	4670
Pelletier & Pelletier	Fort Kent	ME	F	207 834-2296	4792
Perleys Logging Inc	Ashland	ME	G	207 227-0513	4413
PFC Logging Inc	Danforth	ME	G	207 448-7998	4719
Pride Manufacturing Co LLC (PA)	Burnham	ME	C	207 487-3322	4661
Pride Manufacturing Co LLC	Guilford	ME	E	207 876-2719	4855
R A Thomas Logging Inc	Guilford	ME	G	207 876-2722	4858
R C McLucas Trucking Inc	Porter	ME	E	207 625-8915	5168
Regan S Pingree	Phillips	ME	F	207 639-5706	5157
Robert McBreairty Jr Sons	Fort Kent	ME	G	207 834-3257	4793
Robert McBreairty Jr Sons Inc	Saint Francis	ME	F	207 834-3257	5388
Robert W Libby	Porter	ME	G	207 625-8285	5169
Robert W Libby & Sons Inc	Porter	ME	G	207 284-3668	5170
Roland H Tyler Logging Inc	Dixfield	ME	G	207 562-7282	4728
Savage & Savage Logging Inc	Patten	ME	G	207 528-2974	5154
SDR Logging Inc	Sebec	ME	E	207 564-8534	5457
SF Madden Inc	Greenbush	ME	G	207 852-2525	4845
Stephen F Madden	Cardville	ME	G	207 827-5737	4673
Syl-Ver Logging Inc	Allagash	ME	G	207 398-3158	4404
T R Dillon Logging Inc (PA)	Madison	ME	F	207 696-8137	5043
T Raymond Forest Products Inc	Lee	ME	F	207 738-2313	4946
Terrence L Hayford	Hartford	ME	G	207 357-0142	4877
Thomas Logging & Forestry Inc	Guilford	ME	G	207 876-2722	4859
Thompson Trucking Inc	Lincoln	ME	F	207 794-6101	5014
Tracy J Morrison	Harmony	ME	G	207 683-2371	4874
Tracy L Gordon	Strong	ME	G	207 684-4462	5537
Trees Ltd A Partnr Consisting	Sidney	ME	G	207 547-3168	5461
Up North Corp	Fort Kent	ME	F	207 834-6178	4795
Voisine Bros Inc (PA)	New Canada	ME	G	207 231-0220	5082
WA Logging LLC	Hodgdon	ME	G	207 694-2921	4892
Western Maine Timberlands Inc	Fryeburg	ME	F	207 925-1138	4811
Willard S Hanington & Son Inc	Reed Plt	ME	F	207 456-7511	5319
William A Day Jr & Sons Inc	Porter	ME	G	207 625-8181	5173
3d Logging Co Inc	Berlin	NH	G	603 915-3020	13978
A B Excavating Inc	Lancaster	NH	E	603 788-5110	14675
Benjamin D Knapp	Weare	NH	G	603 660-8172	15668
Chuck Rose Inc	Contoocook	NH	E	603 746-2311	14168
Cmd Logging	Center Barnstead	NH	G	603 986-5055	14049
Custom Log Homes	Rumney	NH	F	603 786-9082	15497
Dale E Crawford	Sanbornville	NH	G	603 473-2738	15578
David R Burl	Goffstown	NH	G	603 235-2661	14347
DH Hardwick & Sons Inc	Bennington	NH	F	603 588-6618	13975
Dorman Logging LLC	Londonderry	NH	G	603 437-4403	14744
Fadden Chipping & Logging Inc	Center Conway	NH	F	603 939-2462	14052
Garland Lumber Company Inc	Center Conway	NH	E	603 356-5636	14053
Garland Transportation Corp	Center Conway	NH	E	603 356-5636	14054
Gilles Champagne	Colebrook	NH	G	603 237-5272	14105
Hopkinton For Land Claring Inc	Henniker	NH	E	603 428-8400	14437
John C Whyte	Salisbury	NH	G	603 530-1168	15576
Kel-Log Inc (PA)	Milan	NH	E	603 752-2000	15009
Low Impact Logging LLC	New Boston	NH	G	603 487-5298	15192
Lyme Timber Company LP (PA)	Hanover	NH	F	603 643-3300	14429
Lyons Tnney Timber Harvstg Inc	Bennington	NH	E	802 384-2620	13976
Monadnock Land Clearing	Greenville	NH	G	603 878-2803	14373
Ossipee Mountain Land Co LLC	Tamworth	NH	E	603 323-7677	15648
Pat Gagne Logging LLC	Dummer	NH	G	603 449-2479	14263
Rowe Timber Harvesting LLC	North Sutton	NH	G	603 344-0302	15255
Roy and Laurel Amey Inc	Pittsburg	NH	G	603 538-7767	15329
SDS Logging Inc	Jefferson	NH	E	603 586-7098	14585
Stockley Trucking Inc	Landaff	NH	G	603 838-2860	14682
Sweets Logging & Land Clearin	Strafford	NH	G	603 664-2349	15632
Treeline Timber	Jefferson	NH	G	603 586-7725	14586
Tri-State Logging LLC	Winchester	NH	G	603 499-1499	15717
W Craig Washburn	Colebrook	NH	G	603 237-8403	14110
Warick Company Inc	Pittsburg	NH	G	603 538-7112	15330
Welog Inc	Colebrook	NH	F	603 237-8277	14111
AS Hudak Logging	Saint Albans	VT	G	802 527-9802	17515
Benjamin K Lepesqueur	Enosburg Falls	VT	G	802 933-5500	17220
Canopy Timber Alternatives Inc	Middlebury	VT	F	802 388-1548	17340
Chief Logging & Cnstr Inc	South Ryegate	VT	F	802 584-3868	17613
Djs Tree Service & Log Inc	Colchester	VT	F	802 655-0264	17189
Mahar Excavating & Logging	Bennington	VT	G	802 442-2954	17049
Mt Johnson Inc	Barnard	VT	G	802 234-6827	16994
Norm Brown Logging	Benson	VT	G	802 537-4474	17058
P & L Riendeau Inc	Lyndonville	VT	G	802 626-9302	17319
P and L Trucking	Chester	VT	G	802 875-2819	17182
Pjf Trucking & Logging LLC	Bellows Falls	VT	G	802 463-3343	17030
Srg Inc	Barre	VT	G	802 479-2508	17018
Stephane Inkel Inc	Canaan	VT	G	603 331-3296	17170
Willey Earthmoving Corp	Windsor	VT	G	802 674-2500	17764

2421 Sawmills and planing mills, general

	CITY	ST	EMP	PHONE	ENTRY#
Burell Bros Inc	Hampton	CT	G	860 455-9681	1464
E R Hinman & Sons Inc	Burlington	CT	G	860 673-9170	548
Ensign-Bckford Rnwble Enrgies	Simsbury	CT	G	860 843-2000	3088
Eylward Timber Co	Wallingford	CT	G	203 265-4276	3806
Hardwood Lumber Manufacturing	Scotland	CT	B	860 423-2447	2953
Hmtx Industries LLC (PA)	Norwalk	CT	G	203 299-3100	2515
Hull Forest Products Inc	Pomfret Center	CT	E	860 974-0127	2812
Jordan Saw Mill LLC	Sterling	CT	F	860 774-0247	3501
Parker Septic LLC	Somers	CT	G	860 749-8220	3099
Scotland Hardwoods LLC	Scotland	CT	E	860 423-1233	2954
Tallon Lumber Inc	Canaan	CT	E	860 824-0733	558
Tronox Incorporated (DH)	Stamford	CT	C	203 705-3800	3486
Bannish Lumber Inc	Chester	MA	F	413 354-2279	7996
Chocorua Valley Lumber Company	Bellingham	MA	F	508 883-6878	6288
Cook Forest Products Inc	Upton	MA	E	508 634-3300	12471
Delano Saw Mill Inc	North Dartmouth	MA	G	508 994-8752	10992
Garelco Sales Company Inc	East Longmeadow	MA	G	413 525-3316	8376
Gingras Lumber Inc	Ashley Falls	MA	G	413 229-2182	5970
Heyes Forest Products Inc	Orange	MA	G	978 544-8801	11223
Holt and Bugbee Company (PA)	Tewksbury	MA	C	978 851-7201	12401
J B Sawmill & Landclearing Inc	Westborough	MA	G	508 435-6877	13111
Lashway Logging Inc	Williamsburg	MA	F	413 268-3600	13365
Rex Lumber Company (PA)	Acton	MA	D	800 343-0567	5762
Roberts Brothers Lumber Co Inc	Ashfield	MA	F	413 628-3333	5955
Sawmill Park	Southwick	MA	G	413 569-3393	12045
A W Chaffee	Clinton	ME	E	207 426-8568	4697
Barrett Made (PA)	Portland	ME	E	207 650-6500	5184
Boundary Co	Moose River	ME	D	207 668-4193	5076
Carrier Chipping Inc	Skowhegan	ME	G	207 858-4277	5464
Cousineau Wood Products ME LLC	North Anson	ME	E	207 635-4445	5104
Daaquam Lumber Maine Inc (HQ)	Masardis	ME	C	207 435-6401	5047
Deweys Lumber LLC	Liberty	ME	G	207 589-4126	4998
Dimension Lumber	Peru	ME	G	207 897-9973	5156
Downeast Concepts Inc	Yarmouth	ME	G	207 846-3726	5703
Forest Chester Products Inc	Lincoln	ME	E	207 794-2303	5008
Fulghum Fibres Inc	Baileyville	ME	G	207 427-6560	4483
Georgia-Pacific LLC	Baileyville	ME	G	207 427-4077	4484
Gerrity Company Incorporated	Leeds	ME	E	207 933-2804	4948

	CITY	ST	EMP	PHONE	ENTRY#
Hammond Lumber Company (PA)	Belgrade	ME	C	207 495-3303	4540
Hillside Lumber Company Inc	Westbrook	ME	E	207 839-2575	5629
Irving Woodlands LLC (HQ)	St John Plt	ME	E	207 834-5767	5525
Jackman Lumber Inc (PA)	Jackman	ME	E	207 668-4407	4911
Jz Inc	Casco	ME	G	207 655-7520	4681
K B Logging Inc	Smyrna Mills	ME	F	207 757-8818	5481
Keith A Gilpatrick	Richmond	ME	G	207 737-4286	5321
Kevlaur Industries Inc	Van Buren	ME	E	207 868-2761	5569
Linkletter & Sons Inc	Athens	ME	E	207 654-2301	4414
Lovell Lumber Company	Lovell	ME	E	207 925-6455	5027
Maine Cedar Specialty Products	Ludlow	ME	G	207 532-4034	5028
Maine Woods Company LLC	Portage	ME	F	207 435-4393	5164
Maschino & Sons Lumber Co Inc	New Gloucester	ME	E	207 926-4288	5086
Melvin L Yoder	Corinna	ME	F	207 278-3539	4702
Moose River Lumber Company Inc	Dover Foxcroft	ME	D	207 668-4426	4729
N C Hunt Inc	Damariscotta	ME	E	207 563-8503	4716
N C Hunt Inc (PA)	Jefferson	ME	E	207 549-0922	4918
New England Building Materials LLC	Sanford	ME	B	207 324-3350	5401
Oxford Timber Inc	Oxford	ME	F	207 539-9656	5148
Parent Lumber Company Inc	Mechanic Falls	ME	G	207 998-2322	5053
Phinney Lumber Co	Gorham	ME	E	207 839-3336	4829
Pleasant River Lumber Company (PA)	Dover Foxcroft	ME	E	207 564-8520	4731
Pleasant River Lumber Company	Enfield	ME	G	207 403-1507	4762
Prl Hancock LLC	Hancock	ME	E	207 564-8520	4873
R E Lowell Lumber Co Inc	Buckfield	ME	E	207 336-2901	4658
Robbins Lumber Inc (PA)	Searsmont	ME	C	207 342-5221	5450
Robbins Lumber E Baldwin LLC	East Baldwin	ME	E	207 625-3286	4735
Robert W Libby	Porter	ME	F	207 625-8285	5169
S W Collins	Lincoln	ME	E	207 794-6113	5013
Sebasticook Lumber LLC	Saint Albans	ME	G	207 660-1360	5386
Stratton Lumber Inc (HQ)	Stratton	ME	E	207 246-4500	5535
Wood-Mizer Holdings Inc	Chesterville	ME	F	207 645-2072	4695
Yates Lumber Inc	Lee	ME	F	207 738-2331	4947
A & A Wheeler Mfg Inc	Lee	NH	G	603 659-4446	14704
Breezy Hill Lumber Co	Barnstead	NH	F	603 496-8870	13913
Custom Log Homes	Rumney	NH	F	603 786-9082	15497
Durgin and Crowell Lbr Co Inc	New London	NH	C	603 763-2860	15202
FC Hammond & Son Co Inc	Canaan	NH	F	603 523-4353	14046
Fernald Lumber Inc	Nottingham	NH	F	603 679-2997	15276
Forest Northland Products Inc (PA)	Kingston	NH	E	603 642-3665	14635
Goss Lumber Co Inc	Henniker	NH	G	603 428-3363	14434
Herrick Industries Inc	Henniker	NH	F	603 428-3636	14435
Hhp Inc (PA)	Henniker	NH	E	603 428-3298	14436
Jk Lumber LLC	Madison	NH	D	603 539-4145	14802
King Forest Industries Inc	Wentworth	NH	F	603 764-5711	15676
Middleton Building Supply (PA)	Middleton	NH	C	603 473-2210	15008
Perras Lumber Co Inc	Groveton	NH	F	603 636-1830	14378
Precision Lumber Inc	Wentworth	NH	D	603 764-9450	15677
R L Balla Inc	South Acworth	NH	F	603 835-6529	15628
R P Williams & Sons Inc	Bristol	NH	F	603 744-5446	14037
Tommila Brothers Inc	Fitzwilliam	NH	F	603 242-7774	14316
Turn Key Lumber Inc	Fitzwilliam	NH	C	978 749-1370	14317
Weyerhaeuser	Lancaster	NH	F	603 237-1639	14681
White Mountain Lumber Co Inc	Berlin	NH	E	603 752-1000	13987
Wilkins Lumber Co Inc	Milford	NH	G	603 673-2545	15043
Kimball Hardwoods LLC	Johnston	RI	E	401 300-9070	16092
Sonco Worldwide Inc	Warwick	RI	F	401 406-3761	16863
A Johnson Co	Bristol	VT	D	802 453-4884	17112
Brattleboro Kiln Dry & Milling	Brattleboro	VT	F	802 254-4528	17075
Britton Lumber Company Inc (PA)	Fairlee	VT	F	802 333-4388	17267
Carris Reels Inc (HQ)	Proctor	VT	E	802 773-9111	17457
Cersosimo Lumber Company Inc (PA)	Brattleboro	VT	C	802 254-4508	17081
Cyr Lumber Inc	Milton	VT	F	802 893-4448	17357
Gilcris Enterprises Inc	Proctorsville	VT	F	802 226-7764	17461
Green Mountain Forest Products	Highgate Center	VT	F	802 868-2306	17289
Greenwood Mill Inc	Bradford	VT	F	802 626-0800	17062
Jack Tarmy Lumber Co Inc	Brattleboro	VT	F	802 257-0427	17089
Kerber Farms Lumber Company	Guilford	VT	G	802 451-6920	17281
Lamell Lumber Corporation	Essex Junction	VT	E	802 878-2475	17239
M Piette & Sons Lumber Inc	Irasburg	VT	F	802 754-8876	17302
Manchester Lumber Inc	Johnson	VT	F	802 635-2315	17309
Mill River Lumber Ltd	North Clarendon	VT	D	802 775-0032	17417
N W P Inc	Pownal	VT	G	802 442-4749	17455
Rutland Plywood Corp	Rutland	VT	C	802 747-4000	17509
Sheehan & Sons Lumber	Perkinsville	VT	G	802 263-5545	17442

2426 Hardwood dimension and flooring mills

	CITY	ST	EMP	PHONE	ENTRY#
Conway Hardwood Products LLC	Gaylordsville	CT	E	860 355-4030	1264
E R Hinman & Sons Inc	Burlington	CT	G	860 673-9170	548
Hull Forest Products Inc	Pomfret Center	CT	E	860 974-0127	2812
Rossi Group LLC (PA)	Cromwell	CT	F	860 632-3505	695
Tallon Lumber Inc	Canaan	CT	E	860 824-0733	558
Architectural Timber Mllwk Inc	Hadley	MA	F	413 586-3045	9017

	CITY	ST	EMP	PHONE	ENTRY#
Bannish Lumber Inc	Chester	MA	F	413 354-2279	7996
Canner Incorporated	West Groton	MA	F	978 448-3063	13001
Hydronics Manufacturing Inc	North Billerica	MA	G	978 528-4335	10919
Lawson Hemphill Inc	Swansea	MA	G	508 679-5364	12305
Pine and Baker Mfg Inc	Tewksbury	MA	F	978 851-1215	12412
Roberts Brothers Lumber Co Inc	Ashfield	MA	F	413 628-3333	5955
Stiles & Hart Brick Company	Bridgewater	MA	E	508 697-6928	7238
Universal Hardwood Flooring	Boston	MA	G	617 783-2307	7094
Bear Paw Lumber Corp (PA)	Fryeburg	ME	F	207 935-3052	4807
Columbia Forest Products Inc	Presque Isle	ME	C	207 760-3800	5299
Elkins & Co Inc	Boothbay	ME	F	207 633-0109	4597
Ernest R Palmer Lumber Co Inc	Sangerville	ME	E	207 876-2725	5419
K B Logging Inc	Smyrna Mills	ME	F	207 757-8818	5481
Kelly Lumber Sales Inc	Old Town	ME	G	207 435-4950	5128
Lovell Lumber Company	Lovell	ME	E	207 925-6455	5027
Moosewood Millworks LLC	Ashland	ME	F	207 435-4950	4411
Pride Manufacturing Co LLC	Guilford	ME	E	207 876-2719	4855
S W Collins	Lincoln	ME	E	207 794-6113	5013
Turning Acquisitions LLC	Buckfield	ME	E	207 336-2400	4659
Vic Firth Manufacturing Inc	Newport	ME	E	207 368-4358	5099
York-Cmbrland Assn For Hndcppe (PA)	Portland	ME	E	207 879-1140	5292
Forest Northland Products Inc (PA)	Kingston	NH	E	603 642-3665	14635
Precision Lumber Inc	Wentworth	NH	D	603 764-9450	15677
Robes Dana Wood Craftsmen (PA)	Hanover	NH	E	603 643-9355	14430
Tommila Brothers Inc	Fitzwilliam	NH	F	603 242-7774	14316
We Cork Inc	Exeter	NH	G	800 666-2675	14306
Dycem Corporation (DH)	Smithfield	RI	E	401 738-4420	16697
A Johnson Co	Bristol	VT	F	802 453-4884	17112
Appalchian Engineered Flrg Inc	North Troy	VT	F	802 988-1073	17428
Classic Dsgns By Mtthew Brak I	Saint Johnsbury	VT	F	802 748-6062	17541
Columbia Forest Products Inc	Newport	VT	C	802 334-6711	17399
Jack Tarmy Lumber Co Inc	Brattleboro	VT	F	802 257-0427	17089
N W P Inc	Pownal	VT	G	802 442-4749	17455
Rutland Plywood Corp	Rutland	VT	C	802 747-4000	17509

2429 Special product sawmills, nec

	CITY	ST	EMP	PHONE	ENTRY#
Bonito Manufacturing Inc	North Haven	CT	D	203 234-8786	2394
Bees Wrap LLC	Middlebury	VT	E	802 643-2132	17338

2431 Millwork

	CITY	ST	EMP	PHONE	ENTRY#
77 Mattatuck Heights LLC	Waterbury	CT	G	203 597-9338	3878
A-1 Stairs & Rails Llc	Danbury	CT	G	203 792-7367	700
American Wood Products	North Haven	CT	G	203 248-4433	2391
Anderson Stair & Railing	North Haven	CT	F	203 288-0117	2392
Anvil CT LLP	Oxford	CT	F	860 619-0589	2685
Atlantic Woodcraft Inc	Enfield	CT	F	860 749-4887	1121
Bergan Architectural Wdwkg Inc	Middletown	CT	E	860 346-0869	1739
Byrne Woodworking Inc	Bridgeport	CT	G	203 953-3205	308
Century Woodworking Inc	Pleasant Valley	CT	F	860 379-7538	2800
Chapman Lumber Inc	Thomaston	CT	E	860 283-6213	3616
CJS Millwork Inc	Stamford	CT	F	203 708-0080	3314
Cleary Millwork Company Inc	Rocky Hill	CT	F	800 486-7600	2918
Colonial Wood Products Inc	West Haven	CT	G	203 932-9003	4097
Colonial Woodworking Inc	Stamford	CT	E	203 866-5844	3317
Connecticut Carpentry LLC	Meriden	CT	F	203 639-8585	1661
Connecticut Millwork Inc	Vernon	CT	F	860 875-2860	3753
Conway Hardwood Products LLC	Gaylordsville	CT	E	860 355-4030	1264
Curtiss Woodworking Inc	Prospect	CT	D	203 527-9305	2832
Custom Design Woodworks LLC	Old Lyme	CT	G	860 434-0515	2639
Daniel F Crapa	New Fairfield	CT	G	203 746-5706	2095
Deane Inc	Stamford	CT	E	203 327-7008	3335
Deschenes & Cooper Architectur	Pawcatuck	CT	G	860 599-2481	2719
Dlz Architectural Mill Work	Hartford	CT	G	860 883-7562	1476
Dooney Woodworks LLC (PA)	Cos Cob	CT	G	203 340-9770	676
Dooney Woodworks LLC	Greenwich	CT	F	203 869-5457	1328
Eco Millwork LLC	Newington	CT	F	860 266-5744	2288
Fairfield Woodworks LLC	Stratford	CT	F	203 380-9842	3535
Fcmii Inc	Bethany	CT	F	203 393-9751	93
Ferraro Custom Woodwork LLC	Milford	CT	F	203 876-1280	1828
General Wldg & Fabrication Inc	Watertown	CT	E	860 274-9668	4014
Good Earth Millwork LLC	Westport	CT	G	203 226-7958	4170
Greenwich Fine Woodwork LLC	Norwalk	CT	F	203 987-0001	2510
Hallmark Woodworkers Inc	Bridgeport	CT	F	203 730-0535	327
Harris Enterprise Corp	Manchester	CT	E	860 649-4663	1600
Highland Woodworking LLC	Prospect	CT	F	203 758-6625	2835
Industrial Sales Corp (PA)	Westport	CT	F	203 227-5988	4175
Jawor Lumber Inc	Wallingford	CT	F	203 269-4431	3822
Joshua Friedman & Co LLC	New London	CT	F	860 439-1637	2229
Kingsland Company	Norfolk	CT	G	860 542-6981	2360
Legacy Woodworking LLC	Middlebury	CT	G	203 592-8807	1716
Legere Group Ltd	Avon	CT	D	860 674-0392	29
Leos Kitchen and Stair Corp	New Britain	CT	G	860 225-7363	2037
Luckey LLC	New Haven	CT	F	203 747-5270	2171

SIC

	CITY	ST	EMP	PHONE	ENTRY#
Madigan Millworks Inc	Unionville	CT	G	860 673-7601	3749
Marc Woodworks LLC	Hamden	CT	G	203 281-4700	1438
Maurer & Shepherd Joyners	Glastonbury	CT	F	860 633-2383	1289
McKinnon Design LLC	Plainville	CT	G	860 677-7371	2773
Naugatuck Stair Company Inc	Naugatuck	CT	F	203 729-7134	1976
Nci Woodworking LLC LLC	Fairfield	CT	G	203 391-1614	1195
New England Cabinet Co	New Britain	CT	E	860 225-8645	2046
New England Stair Company Inc	Shelton	CT	E	203 924-0606	3038
Nichols Woodworking LLC	Washington Depot	CT	E	860 350-4223	3877
Orion Manufacturing LLC	Mystic	CT	E	203 572-2921	1941
Paco Assensio Woodworking LLC	Norwalk	CT	G	203 536-2608	2550
Petrunti Design & Wdwkg LLC	West Hartford	CT	G	860 953-5332	4078
Porta Door Co	Seymour	CT	E	203 888-6191	2967
Proctor Woodworks LLC	Essex	CT	G	860 767-9881	1170
Quality Stairs Inc	Bridgeport	CT	F	203 367-8390	364
Robert L Lovallo	Stamford	CT	G	203 324-6655	3450
Sanders Archtectural Wdwkg LLC	Berlin	CT	G	860 682-5607	84
Schuco USA Lllp (HQ)	Newington	CT	E	860 666-0505	2324
Shelbrack Woodworking	Simsbury	CT	G	860 431-5028	3096
Shuttercraft Inc	Madison	CT	G	203 245-2608	1571
Sorrento Fine Woodwork LLC	Wallingford	CT	F	203 741-9263	3850
Stately Stair Co Inc	Naugatuck	CT	E	203 575-1966	1987
Summit Stair Inc	Bethel	CT	F	203 778-2251	135
Walston Inc	Guilford	CT	G	203 453-5929	1409
Wesconn Stairs Inc	Danbury	CT	G	203 792-7367	836
West Hrtford Stirs Cbinets Inc	Newington	CT	D	860 953-9151	2334
White Dog Woodworking LLC	Torrington	CT	F	860 482-3776	3707
Whq Woodworks LLC	Oakville	CT	G	203 756-3011	2629
Zavarella Woodworking Inc	Newington	CT	G	860 666-6969	2335
Ackles Steel and Iron Co Inc	Waltham	MA	F	781 893-6818	12581
Advanced Woodworking Tech LLC	Lowell	MA	G	978 937-1400	9851
AKa McHIngelo Strbuilder LLC	North Easton	MA	G	508 238-9054	11007
Allen Woodworking LLC	Bellingham	MA	G	617 306-6479	6284
Amherst Woodworking & Supply Inc	Northampton	MA	E	413 584-3003	11052
Architectural Components Inc	Montague	MA	G	413 367-9441	10458
Architectural Timber Mllwk Inc	Hadley	MA	F	413 586-3045	9017
Boston Area Door Company	Bridgewater	MA	G	508 857-4722	7224
Brockway-Smith Company	West Hatfield	MA	C	413 247-9674	13004
Bwi of MA LLC	Leominster	MA	F	978 534-4065	9645
Caliper Woodworking Corp	Malden	MA	E	781 322-9760	10006
Cape Cod Cupola Co Inc	North Dartmouth	MA	F	508 994-2119	10990
Cape Cod Lumber Co Inc	Abington	MA	C	781 878-0715	5722
Charles River Door Works	Blackstone	MA	G	617 828-3946	6493
Chilmark Archtctural Wdwkg LLC	Worcester	MA	F	508 856-9200	13706
Continental Woodcraft Inc (PA)	Worcester	MA	E	508 581-9560	13709
Detail Millwork Inc	Waltham	MA	F	781 893-2250	12652
Dixon Bros Millwork Inc	Abington	MA	G	781 261-9962	5724
East Coast Interiors Inc	North Dartmouth	MA	F	508 995-4200	10995
EJ Jaxtimer Builder Inc	Hyannis	MA	E	508 778-4911	9436
General Woodworking Inc (PA)	Lowell	MA	F	978 458-6625	9879
Glaccet Corporation	Worcester	MA	E	508 752-7356	13734
Glenns Gardening & Woodworking	Boston	MA	G	617 548-7977	6763
Gloucester Builders Inc	Charlestown	MA	F	617 241-5513	7874
Harvey Industries Inc	North Dartmouth	MA	C	508 998-9779	10997
Harvey Industries LLC	Springfield	MA	E	413 731-7700	12099
Harvey Industries (PA)	Waltham	MA	C	800 598-5400	12691
Hawkes & Huberdeau Wdwkg Inc	Amesbury	MA	F	978 388-7747	5836
Holt and Bugbee Company (PA)	Tewksbury	MA	C	978 851-7201	12401
Horner Millwork Corp	Pembroke	MA	E	781 826-7770	11368
Island Pond Industries Inc	Agawam	MA	F	413 732-6625	5796
J B Sash & Door Company Inc	Chelsea	MA	E	617 884-8940	7983
Jain America Foods Inc	Chicopee	MA	F	413 593-8883	8041
JC Clocks Company Inc	North Dartmouth	MA	E	508 998-8442	10998
Johncarlo Woodworking Inc	Westfield	MA	F	413 562-4002	13175
Joinery Shop Inc	Charlestown	MA	G	617 242-4718	7877
Joseph Muto	Westfield	MA	G	413 568-3245	13176
K & J Interiors Inc	Plymouth	MA	D	508 830-0670	11463
Kabinet Korner Inc	Malden	MA	E	781 324-9600	10017
Keiver Willard-Lumber Corp	Newburyport	MA	D	978 462-7193	10690
Kelton Woodwork Inc	Charlton	MA	F	617 997-7261	7891
Kenyon Woodworking Inc	Jamaica Plain	MA	F	617 524-6883	9502
Kramers Cstm Kitchens & Wdwkg	Holliston	MA	G	508 429-9007	9219
Leveillee Archtctral Mllwk Inc	Spencer	MA	F	508 885-9731	12062
Lloyds Woodworking Inc	Hudson	MA	G	978 562-9007	9386
Maki Corp (PA)	Gardner	MA	E	978 343-7422	8895
Marie Deprofio	Waltham	MA	G	781 894-9793	12714
Mark Richey Wdwkg & Design Inc	Newburyport	MA	D	978 499-3800	10698
Martin Interiors Inc	Hanson	MA	G	781 447-1022	9053
Masonation International Corp	Leominster	MA	G	978 534-4065	9681
Meridian Custom Wdwkg Inc	Brockton	MA	G	508 587-4400	7295
Metrica Interior Inc	Northampton	MA	F	413 587-2750	11071
Mill Works	Westford	MA	G	978 692-8222	13251
Miller H C Wood Working Inc	Holliston	MA	G	508 429-4220	9223
ML Custom Wood Work Inc	Hyannis	MA	G	508 360-2137	9442
Muniz Custom Woodwork Inc	Everett	MA	G	617 970-3430	8496
National Lumber Company LLC (HQ)	Mansfield	MA	C	508 339-8020	10068
New England Shrlines Companies	Hanover	MA	F	781 826-0140	9037
Newpro Operating LLC	Bellingham	MA	F	781 933-4100	6298
North Atlantic Corp	Somerset	MA	C	508 235-4830	11854
Notch Mtn Solar Inc	Northfield	MA	G	413 498-0018	11121
Olde Bostonian	Boston	MA	F	617 282-9300	6928
Padco Inc	Worcester	MA	F	508 753-8486	13767
Payne/Bouchier Inc (PA)	Roxbury	MA	E	617 445-4323	11692
Pomeroy & Co Inc	Charlestown	MA	E	617 241-0234	7880
Precision Woodworking Inc	Quincy	MA	G	617 479-7604	11531
Rex Lumber Company (PA)	Acton	MA	D	800 343-0567	5762
Rgc Millwork Incorporated	Lowell	MA	G	978 275-9529	9919
Richard Cantwell Woodworking	New Bedford	MA	G	508 984-7921	10647
Rjd Woodworking LLC	Fairhaven	MA	G	508 984-4315	8513
Russo Woodworking Inc	Hyannis	MA	E	508 428-1772	9448
Russo Woodworking Inc (PA)	Marstons Mills	MA	G	908 351-2200	10248
Sb Development Corp	Acton	MA	F	978 263-2744	5764
Scandinavian Panel Systems	Worcester	MA	F	774 530-6340	13795
Scotia Woodworking	Hudson	MA	G	978 212-5379	9411
Shaw Woodworking Inc	Pocasset	MA	G	508 563-1242	11492
Shawn Roberts Woodworking	Gilbertville	MA	G	413 477-0060	8914
South Mountain Company Inc	West Tisbury	MA	E	508 693-4850	13055
South Shore Millwork Inc	Norton	MA	D	508 226-5500	11136
Southeastern Millwork Co Inc	Sagamore Beach	MA	G	508 888-6038	11698
Southeastern Millwork Inc	Bourne	MA	G	508 888-6038	7142
Specialty Wholesale Sup Corp	Gardner	MA	E	978 632-1472	8901
Stephen Terhune Woodworking In	Essex	MA	G	978 768-0106	8480
Stokes Woodworking Co Inc (PA)	Hudson	MA	G	508 481-0414	9416
Tall Guy Woodworking Inc	Boston	MA	G	617 901-2166	7068
Thl-Nortek Investors LLC (PA)	Boston	MA	D	617 227-1050	7077
Toby Leary Fine Wdwkg Inc	Hyannis	MA	F	508 957-2281	9454
Trellis Structures Inc	East Templeton	MA	E	888 285-4624	8415
Trimboard Inc	Springfield	MA	E	413 886-0142	12143
Triple Crown Cbnets Mllwk Corp	Sandwich	MA	G	508 833-6500	11753
Vintage Millwork Corporation	Dracut	MA	G	978 957-1400	8313
VT Industries Inc	Amesbury	MA	E	978 388-3792	5854
Walter A Furman Co Inc	Fall River	MA	D	508 674-7751	8625
Watson Brothers Inc	Middleton	MA	F	978 774-7677	10397
Wayland Millwork Corporation	Marlborough	MA	F	508 485-4172	10233
Wesco Building & Design Inc	Stoneham	MA	G	781 279-0490	12188
Wescor Ltd (PA)	Stoneham	MA	G	781 279-0490	12189
Westek Architectural Wdwkg Inc	Westfield	MA	F	413 562-6363	13217
Wide Angle Marketing Inc	Hubbardston	MA	F	978 928-5400	9349
William Green Inc	Shelburne Falls	MA	G	413 475-2014	11809
Woodcraft Designers Bldrs LLC	Canton	MA	E	508 584-4200	7842
Woodmeister Master Bldrs Inc (PA)	Holden	MA	C	774 345-1000	9196
Woodworks	Lynn	MA	E	781 596-1563	9993
Wright Archtectural Mllwk Corp	Northampton	MA	E	413 586-3528	11087
Wsmd Inc	Ludlow	MA	G	413 589-0945	9957
Alfreds Uphlstring Cstm Fbrcti	Alfred	ME	F	207 536-5565	4402
Bangor Millwork & Supply Inc (PA)	Bangor	ME	F	207 947-6019	4491
Coastal Woodworking Inc	Nobleboro	ME	E	207 563-1072	5100
Georgia-Pacific LLC	Baileyville	ME	G	207 427-4077	4484
Harvey Industries Inc	Augusta	ME	F	207 629-3737	4472
Jk Custom Woodworking LLC	South Bristol	ME	F	207 644-1127	5483
L M C Light Iron Inc	Limerick	ME	F	207 793-9957	5002
Little Harbor Window Co Inc	Berwick	ME	E	207 698-1332	4550
Mathews Brothers Company (PA)	Belfast	ME	C	207 338-3360	4535
Mousam Valley Millwork	Springvale	ME	E	207 324-2951	5521
New England Woodworks	Springvale	ME	G	207 324-6343	5522
Northeast Mill Work Inc	Casco	ME	G	207 655-1202	4682
Pond Cove Millwork Inc	Saco	ME	F	207 773-6819	5376
Pre-Hung Doors Inc	Auburn	ME	F	207 783-3881	4455
Precision Millwork Inc	Cumberland Foreside	ME	G	207 761-3997	4713
Quarter Point Woodworking LLC (PA)	New Gloucester	ME	G	207 926-1032	5088
Quarter Point Woodworking LLC	Windham	ME	F	207 892-7022	5667
R G Eaton Woodworks Inc	Westbrook	ME	G	207 883-3398	5644
Saco Bay Millwork Co	Buxton	ME	G	207 929-8400	4664
Unique Spiral Stairs Inc	Albion	ME	G	207 437-2415	4401
Windham Millwork Inc	Windham	ME	D	207 892-3238	5675
Zoulamis Fine Woodworking	Gardiner	ME	G	207 449-1680	4813
AP Dley Cstm Laminating Corp	Windham	NH	E	603 437-6666	15720
Archangel Woodworks Inc	Kingston	NH	G	603 347-5345	14633
Aubin Woodworking Inc	Bow	NH	F	603 224-5512	13993
Audia Woodworking	Stratham	NH	F	603 817-1309	15633
Boulia-Gorrell Lumber Co LLC	Laconia	NH	F	603 524-1300	14648
Boyce Highlands Furn Co Inc	Concord	NH	E	603 753-1042	14116
Chamberlain Companies Inc	Salem	NH	E	603 893-2606	15512
Cw Keller & Associates LLC	Plaistow	NH	D	603 382-2028	15339
Ds Huntington Co LLC	Peterborough	NH	G	603 784-5136	15315

	CITY	ST	EMP	PHONE	ENTRY#
Forest Manufacturing Corp	Auburn	NH	F	603 647-6991	13907
Harvey Industries LLC	Londonderry	NH	E	603 216-8300	14754
Herrick Mill Work Inc	Contoocook	NH	F	603 746-5092	14170
Index Packaging Inc	Milton	NH	C	603 350-0018	15046
Keller Products Incorporated	Bow	NH	F	603 224-5502	14003
Kelley Bros New England LLC (HQ)	Hudson	NH	F	603 881-5559	14515
KSD Custom Wood Products Inc	Boscawen	NH	F	603 796-2951	13991
Littleton Millwork Inc	Littleton	NH	E	603 444-2677	14721
Middleton Building Supply (PA)	Middleton	NH	C	603 473-2210	15008
Millwork Masters Ltd (PA)	Keene	NH	F	603 358-3038	14608
Morrill Woodworking LLC	Auburn	NH	E	603 540-3151	13911
Mountaintop Woodworking LLC	Whitefield	NH	G	603 616-1160	15699
New England Woodworkers	New Ipswich	NH	G	603 562-7200	15199
Phoenix Woodworks Inc	Gilsum	NH	G	603 812-6214	14343
Phytek Industries Inc	Bow	NH	F	603 226-4197	14007
Port-O-Lite Company Inc	West Swanzey	NH	G	603 352-3205	15696
Procraft Corporation	New Boston	NH	E	603 487-2080	15193
Rochette Fmly Cstm Wdwkg & REM	Raymond	NH	G	603 895-2181	15456
Thibco Inc	Manchester	NH	G	603 623-3011	14944
Tommila Brothers Inc	Fitzwilliam	NH	F	603 242-7774	14316
Windham Wood Interiors Inc	Windham	NH	G	781 932-8572	15730
Wood Works	Portsmouth	NH	G	603 436-3805	15450
Woodworks Architectural Mllwk	Londonderry	NH	G	603 432-4050	14791
18th Century Woodworks	West Kingston	RI	G	401 829-8760	16892
Arnold Lumber Co (PA)	West Kingston	RI	D	401 783-2266	16893
BP Custom Woodworking	Cumberland	RI	F	401 787-8750	15934
Broden Millworks LLC	Middletown	RI	G	401 846-0271	16170
Brouillette Woodworking Co Inc	Barrington	RI	G	401 499-4867	15746
Cas America LLC	North Smithfield	RI	F	401 884-8556	16320
Chopmist Hill Woodworks Ltd	North Scituate	RI	F	401 374-3143	16314
Columbus Door Company	Warwick	RI	D	401 781-7792	16796
Constant Technologies Inc	North Kingstown	RI	E	800 518-7369	16240
Design Fabricators Inc	Cranston	RI	E	401 944-5294	15849
Eastern Design Inc	Manville	RI	F	401 765-0558	16163
Grinnell Cabinet Makers Inc	Cranston	RI	E	401 781-1080	15871
Hardwood Design Inc	Exeter	RI	E	401 294-2235	16051
Hope Woodworks Inc	Woonsocket	RI	F	401 497-7714	16963
Igitt Inc	Middletown	RI	F	401 841-5544	16175
Imperia Corporation	Barrington	RI	E	508 894-3000	15748
Jutras Manufacturing Company	Greenville	RI	G	401 949-8101	16060
Jutras Woodworking Co	Providence	RI	G	401 949-8101	16551
K Alger Woodworking Inc	Johnston	RI	G	401 228-5254	16091
Kelmeg Woodworking	North Smithfield	RI	G	401 762-3090	16325
Millwork One Inc	Cranston	RI	D	401 738-6990	15895
Modern Industries Inc	Providence	RI	G	401 331-8000	16566
Monarch Industries Inc	Providence	RI	D	401 247-5200	16567
Orion Ret Svcs & Fixturing Inc	Smithfield	RI	D	401 334-5000	16725
Stephen C Dematrick	Narragansett	RI	G	401 789-4712	16197
T & T Woodworkers Inc	Woonsocket	RI	F	401 766-2304	16979
Village Woodturning	North Scituate	RI	G	401 647-3091	16317
Woodworking Thompson & Design	Providence	RI	G	401 369-7999	16648
Brattleboro Kiln Dry & Milling	Brattleboro	VT	F	802 254-4528	17075
Classic Dsgns By Mtthew Brak I	Saint Johnsbury	VT	F	802 748-6062	17541
Cypress Woodworks LLC	Waterbury	VT	G	802 338-0538	17673
H Hirschmann Ltd	West Rutland	VT	F	802 438-4447	17695
Idry LLC	Barre	VT	G	800 406-1887	17008
Jeld-Wen Inc	North Springfield	VT	C	802 886-1728	17423
Newport Furniture Parts Corp	Newport	VT	D	802 334-5428	17402
RK Miles Inc (PA)	Manchester Center	VT	C	802 362-1952	17330
Stark Mountain Woodworks Co	New Haven	VT	F	802 453-5549	17396
Vermont Furn Hardwoods Inc	Chester	VT	E	802 875-2550	17184
Wall Goldfinger Furniture	Northfield	VT	E	802 278-5823	17435
Wallgoldfinger Inc	Northfield	VT	E	802 483-4200	17436

2434 Wood kitchen cabinets

	CITY	ST	EMP	PHONE	ENTRY#
B & L Finishing Shop Inc	Bristol	CT	G	860 583-1164	400
Belmont Corporation	Bristol	CT	G	860 589-5700	413
Bergan Architectural Wdwkg Inc	Middletown	CT	E	860 346-0869	1739
Bonito Manufacturing Inc	North Haven	CT	D	203 234-8786	2394
Brunarhans Inc	Woodstock	CT	G	860 928-0887	4392
Cabinet Harward Specialti	West Hartford	CT	G	860 231-1192	4049
Cabinets To Go LLC	Wallingford	CT	E	800 222-4638	3785
Captivating Kitchens	West Hartford	CT	G	860 236-6500	4051
Chris Cross LLC	Stratford	CT	F	203 386-8426	3526
Christopher Peacock Home LLC	Norwalk	CT	F	203 388-4022	2481
Christopoulos Designs Inc	Bridgeport	CT	F	203 576-1110	311
Connecticut Solid Surface LLC	Canton	CT	E	860 410-9800	559
Conway Hardwood Products LLC	Gaylordsville	CT	E	860 355-4030	1264
Custom Furniture & Design LLC	Litchfield	CT	G	860 567-3519	1555
Cyr Woodworking Inc	Newington	CT	G	860 232-1991	2284
Domestic Kitchens Inc	Fairfield	CT	E	203 368-1651	1181
European Woodcraft LLC	Norwalk	CT	G	203 847-6195	2498
Focal Metals	Bethel	CT	G	203 743-4443	115
Greenhaven Cabinetry Mllwk LLC	Stonington	CT	G	860 535-1106	3509
Hanford Cabinet & Wdwkg Co Inc	Old Saybrook	CT	G	860 388-5055	2650
Heartwood Cabinetry	Marlborough	CT	G	860 295-0304	1643
Hemingway Custom Cabinetry LLC	Bridgeport	CT	E	203 382-0300	328
John June Custom Cabinetry LLC	Bridgeport	CT	G	203 334-1720	336
Kingswood Kitchens Co Inc	Danbury	CT	D	203 792-8700	767
Kitchen Cab Resurfacing LLC	Bridgeport	CT	F	203 334-2857	340
Kitchen Living LLC	East Hampton	CT	G	860 819-5847	964
Legere Group Ltd	Avon	CT	D	860 674-0392	29
Leos Kitchen and Stair Corp	New Britain	CT	F	860 225-7363	2037
Martin Cabinet Inc	Bristol	CT	F	860 747-5769	464
Martin Cabinet Inc (PA)	Plainville	CT	E	860 747-5769	2772
Milton & Goose LLC	Stamford	CT	F	203 539-1073	3412
Porta Door Co	Seymour	CT	E	203 888-6191	2967
Prestige Remodeling LLC	Bridgeport	CT	F	203 386-8426	362
Robert L Lovallo	Stamford	CT	G	203 324-6655	3450
Royal Woodcraft Inc	Ansonia	CT	F	203 847-3461	19
S J Pappas Inc	Meriden	CT	G	203 237-7701	1695
Specialty Shop Inc	Manchester	CT	F	860 647-1477	1637
Statham Woodwork	Norwalk	CT	G	203 831-0629	2574
Sterling Custom Cabinetry LLC	Bridgeport	CT	F	203 335-5151	375
Stm Imp and Exp Corp	Plainfield	CT	G	973 450-5110	2740
Viking Kitchens Cabinets LLC (PA)	New Britain	CT	E	860 223-7101	2074
West Hrtford Stirs Cbinets Inc	Newington	CT	G	860 953-9151	2334
Anthony Manufacturing Co Inc	Medford	MA	F	781 396-1400	10279
Architectural Kitchens Inc	Wellesley	MA	F	781 239-9750	12936
Ashland Cabinet Corporation	Southborough	MA	B	508 303-8100	11989
B & G Cabinet	Newburyport	MA	F	978 465-6455	10669
Boston Stone and Cabinet	Norwood	MA	F	781 352-3623	11165
Cabinet Depot Outlet Inc	Southborough	MA	F	508 485-7777	11993
Camio Custom Cabinetry Inc	Canton	MA	F	781 562-1573	7775
Carousel Cabinets	Lancaster	MA	F	978 846-8763	9524
Classic Kitchen Design Inc	Hyannis	MA	F	508 775-3075	9431
Clever Green Cabinets LLC	Waltham	MA	F	508 963-6776	12632
Coastal-N-Counters Inc	Mashpee	MA	F	508 539-3500	10251
Counterra LLC	Canton	MA	F	781 821-2100	7780
Cronin Cabinets - Marine LLP	Charlton	MA	G	508 248-7026	7886
Custom Ktchens By Chmpagne Inc	Franklin	MA	F	508 528-7919	8828
Dedham Cabinet Shop Inc	Canton	MA	F	781 326-4090	7783
Dixon Bros Millwork Inc	Abington	MA	G	781 261-9962	5724
Eastern Woodworks Llc	Georgetown	MA	F	978 352-2005	8908
Fallon Fine Cabinetry Inc	Needham Heights	MA	G	781 453-6988	10544
Fort Point Cabinet Makers LLC	Boston	MA	G	617 338-9487	6745
Furniture Design Services Inc	Peabody	MA	G	978 531-3250	11310
Hamlin Cabinet Corp	Norfolk	MA	E	508 384-8371	10799
Hastone Homestone Inc	Dorchester	MA	G	617 784-3284	8300
Ideal Kitchens of Palmer (PA)	Chicopee	MA	G	413 532-2253	8037
Industrial Woodworking Co Inc	East Weymouth	MA	F	781 340-7474	8429
Irvings Home Center Inc	Brockton	MA	G	508 583-4421	7285
J & K Cabinets Ltd	Wilmington	MA	G	978 658-1888	13417
J & M Cabinet Shop Inc	Walpole	MA	G	508 660-6660	12565
JC Clocks Company Inc	North Dartmouth	MA	E	508 998-8442	10998
JS International Inc (PA)	Fall River	MA	E	508 675-4722	8564
Kitchen Options Inc	Oxford	MA	G	508 987-3384	11256
Kochman Reidt & Haigh Inc	Stoughton	MA	E	781 573-1500	12217
Mass Cabinets Inc	Methuen	MA	E	978 738-0600	10337
Milford Woodworking Co Inc	Milford	MA	F	508 473-2335	10405
Miller H C Wood Working Inc	Holliston	MA	G	508 429-4220	9223
Northast Cab Cntrtop Dstrs Inc	Braintree	MA	F	617 296-2100	7197
Payne/Bouchier Inc (PA)	Roxbury	MA	F	617 445-4323	11692
RF McManus Company Inc	Charlestown	MA	F	617 241-8081	7881
Rgc Millwork Incorporated	Lowell	MA	G	978 275-9529	9919
Rosario Cabinets Inc	Dedham	MA	G	781 329-0639	8248
Scandia Kitchens Inc	Bellingham	MA	A	508 966-0300	6300
Star Kitchen Cabinets Inc	Avon	MA	E	508 510-3123	6162
Stokes Woodworking Co Inc (PA)	Hudson	MA	G	508 481-0414	9416
Superior Kitchen Designs Inc	Gardner	MA	F	978 632-5072	8903
Toledo Woodworking Inc	Holliston	MA	G	508 280-3354	9233
Triple Crown Cbnets Mllwk Corp	Sandwich	MA	G	508 833-6500	11753
Vanity World Inc	Canton	MA	F	508 668-1800	7839
Vartanian Custom Cabinets	Palmer	MA	E	413 283-3438	11288
Water Closet LLC	Nantucket	MA	G	508 228-2828	10466
Watson Brothers Inc	Middleton	MA	F	978 774-7677	10397
Wells Development L L C	Arlington	MA	G	781 727-5560	5950
Wolf Organization LLC	Northborough	MA	D	508 393-2040	11116
Woodmeister Master Bldrs Inc (PA)	Holden	MA	G	774 345-1000	9196
Black Cove Cabinetry	Scarborough	ME	G	207 883-8901	5425
Directions To Maine Dovetail	Westbrook	ME	G	207 829-2759	5625
Kennebec Cabinetry Inc	Bath	ME	F	207 442-0813	4527
Kennebec Company	Bath	ME	F	207 443-2131	4528
Lawrence Parson	Brownfield	ME	G	207 935-3737	4636
Naheks Inc	Hermon	ME	F	207 848-7770	4886
R G Eaton Woodworks Inc	Westbrook	ME	G	207 883-3398	5644

	CITY	ST	EMP	PHONE	ENTRY#
Trico Millworks Inc	Limington	ME	E	207 637-2711	5006
Advanced Custom Cabinets Inc	Brentwood	NH	F	603 772-6211	14019
Cabinets For Less LLC	Manchester	NH	G	603 935-7551	14825
Counter Pro Inc	Manchester	NH	F	603 647-2444	14838
Crown Point Cabinetry Corp	Claremont	NH	D	603 542-1273	14086
Crown Point Realty Corp Inc	Claremont	NH	D	603 543-1208	14087
Cw Keller & Associates LLC	Plaistow	NH	D	603 382-2028	15339
Granite State Ktchens Dstrs In	Bedford	NH	E	603 472-4080	13931
Mark Allen Cabinetry LLC	Amherst	NH	F	603 491-7570	13877
Northeast Woodworking Pdts Inc	Raymond	NH	F	603 895-4271	15454
Nudd Cabinetry	Sanbornton	NH	F	603 286-3160	15577
Plaistow Cabinet Co Inc	Plaistow	NH	F	603 382-1098	15348
Revolution Furnishings LLC	Manchester	NH	G	603 606-6123	14921
Tri Town Cabinetry	Hooksett	NH	G	603 391-9276	14475
Triumph Interiors LLC	Rindge	NH	F	603 899-5184	15461
Vermont Custom Wood Products	North Walpole	NH	F	802 463-9930	15261
Walpole Cabinetry	Walpole	NH	F	603 826-4100	15663
Ws Dennison Cabinets Inc	Pembroke	NH	F	603 224-8434	15309
Young Furniture Mfg Inc	Bow	NH	E	603 224-8830	14015
Bella Cabinets Inc	Pawtucket	RI	G	401 722-0038	16348
Completely Custom LLC	North Kingstown	RI	G	401 667-0059	16239
Elmwood Countertop Inc	Cranston	RI	G	401 785-1677	15854
Hardwood Design Inc	Exeter	RI	E	401 294-2235	16051
Imperia Corporation	Barrington	RI	F	508 894-3000	15748
Master Kitchens Center Inc	Newport	RI	G	401 324-7100	16216
New England Cstm Cabinets LLC	North Kingstown	RI	G	401 667-2572	16273
Carlton Newton Corporation LLC	Brattleboro	VT	G	802 579-1413	17078
Catamount North Cabinetry LLC	Essex Junction	VT	F	802 264-9009	17230
City Feed and Lumber Co Inc **(PA)**	Saint Albans	VT	E	802 524-2136	17519
Knight Industries Inc	North Clarendon	VT	E	802 773-8777	17416

2435 Hardwood veneer and plywood

	CITY	ST	EMP	PHONE	ENTRY#
Bergan Architectural Wdwkg Inc	Middletown	CT	E	860 346-0869	1739
Bernhard Thmas Bldg Systems LL	Southport	CT	F	203 925-0414	3243
Readers Hardwood Supply LLC	East Taunton	MA	F	508 301-3206	8411
Bear Paw Lumber Corp **(PA)**	Fryeburg	ME	F	207 935-3052	4807
Columbia Forest Products Inc	Presque Isle	ME	C	207 760-3800	5299
Herrick Mill Work Inc	Contoocook	NH	F	603 746-5092	14170
Keller Products Incorporated **(PA)**	Manchester	NH	E	603 627-7887	14871
Columbia Forest Products Inc	Newport	VT	C	802 334-6711	17399
Mariah Group LLC	Rutland	VT	F	802 747-4000	17503
Rutland Plywood Corp	Rutland	VT	G	802 747-4000	17508
Rutland Plywood Corp	Rutland	VT	F	802 747-4000	17509
Springfield Fence Company Inc	North Springfield	VT	F	802 886-2221	17424
Stratabond Co Inc	Rutland	VT	F	802 747-4000	17510

2439 Structural wood members, nec

	CITY	ST	EMP	PHONE	ENTRY#
Bernhard Thmas Bldg Systems LL	Southport	CT	F	203 925-0414	3243
Country Carpenters Inc	Hebron	CT	G	860 228-2276	1526
Eastern Co **(PA)**	Shelton	CT	E	203 729-2255	3001
International Framers LLC	Naugatuck	CT	E	203 723-4564	1966
Truss Manufacturing Inc	Newington	CT	F	860 665-0000	2329
Architectural Timber Mllwk Inc	Hadley	MA	E	413 586-3045	9017
Caliper Woodworking Corp	Malden	MA	E	781 322-9760	10006
K & J Interiors Inc	Plymouth	MA	D	508 830-0670	11463
National Lumber Company	Newton	MA	E	617 244-8020	10770
Nu-Truss Inc	Westfield	MA	E	413 562-3861	13193
Perkins Brothers Corp	Medfield	MA	E	781 858-3031	10273
Scandinavian Panel Systems	Worcester	MA	F	774 530-6340	13795
Truss Engineering Corporation	Indian Orchard	MA	E	413 543-1298	9476
Aroostook Trusses Inc	Presque Isle	ME	E	207 768-5817	5297
Soyaz	Fairfield	ME	E	207 453-4911	4766
T and P Lumber Inc **(PA)**	Orrington	ME	E	207 825-3317	5139
API Holdings Inc **(PA)**	Wilton	NH	E	603 668-2648	15702
Benson Woodworking Company Inc	Walpole	NH	D	603 756-3600	15659
Southworth Timberframes Inc	Lancaster	NH	G	603 788-2619	14679
Specialty Truss Inc	Nashua	NH	E	603 886-5523	15172
Tsco Inc	North Kingstown	RI	F	401 295-0669	16289
Acer Holdings Starksboro Inc	Starksboro	VT	F	802 453-4438	17625

2441 Nailed wood boxes and shook

	CITY	ST	EMP	PHONE	ENTRY#
Champlin-Packrite Inc	Manchester	CT	E	860 559-6373	1589
Colonial Wood Products Inc	West Haven	CT	G	203 932-9003	4097
Merco Inc	Ellington	CT	E	860 871-1888	1110
Vermont Pallet and Skid Sp Inc	Norwich	CT	G	860 822-6949	2618
Westwood Products Inc	Winsted	CT	F	860 379-9401	4358
Atlas Box and Crating Co Inc **(PA)**	Sutton	MA	C	508 865-1155	12276
Garelco Sales Company Inc	East Longmeadow	MA	G	413 525-3316	8376
Horn International Packg Inc **(HQ)**	Lancaster	MA	E	978 667-8797	9528
Kelley Wood Products Inc	Fitchburg	MA	F	978 345-7531	8658
KG Pallet LLC	Chicopee	MA	E	413 536-3511	8043
Nefab Packaging North East LLC	Bellingham	MA	E	800 258-4692	6297
Unified2 Globl Packg Group LLC	Lancaster	MA	B	508 865-1155	9531

	CITY	ST	EMP	PHONE	ENTRY#
Herrick Mill Work Inc	Contoocook	NH	F	603 746-5092	14170
Index Packaging Inc	Milton	NH	C	603 350-0018	15046
J H Dunning Corporation	North Walpole	NH	E	603 445-5591	15258

2448 Wood pallets and skids

	CITY	ST	EMP	PHONE	ENTRY#
Central Pallet & Box Co LLC	New Britain	CT	F	860 224-4416	2011
HI-Tech Packaging Inc	Stratford	CT	E	203 378-2700	3547
Industrial Pallet LLC	Eastford	CT	F	860 974-0093	1091
JJ Box Co Inc	Bridgeport	CT	G	203 367-1211	335
R & R Pallet Corp	Cheshire	CT	F	203 272-2784	612
Southern Conn Pallet Co Inc	Wallingford	CT	G	203 265-1313	3851
Vermont Pallet and Skid Sp Inc	Norwich	CT	G	860 822-6949	2618
Westwood Products Inc	Winsted	CT	F	860 379-9401	4358
A1 Pallets Inc	Berlin	MA	G	978 838-2720	6318
Associated Mktg Systems Inc	Holbrook	MA	F	781 767-9001	9168
Atlas Box and Crating Co Inc **(PA)**	Sutton	MA	C	508 865-1155	12276
B & D Pllet Bldg Indus Sup Inc	Westfield	MA	F	413 568-9624	13150
Bay State Pallet Co Inc	Haverhill	MA	G	978 374-4840	9078
Briggs Lumber Products	Rutland	MA	F	978 630-4207	11696
Great Northern Dunnage LLC	Fitchburg	MA	F	978 343-2300	8656
Green Meadow Lumber Inc	Westfield	MA	F	413 568-0056	13167
Horn International Packg Inc **(HQ)**	Lancaster	MA	E	978 667-8797	9528
Jbm Services Inc	Templeton	MA	E	978 939-8004	12380
Kelley Wood Products Inc	Fitchburg	MA	F	978 345-7531	8658
KG Pallet LLC	Chicopee	MA	E	413 536-3511	8043
Lelanite Corporation **(PA)**	Webster	MA	E	508 987-2637	12929
Lignetics New England Inc	Palmer	MA	G	413 284-1050	11275
Nefab Packaging North East LLC	Bellingham	MA	E	800 258-4692	6297
New England Pallets Skids Inc	Ludlow	MA	F	413 583-6628	9951
Peco Pallet	Brighton	MA	E	845 642-2780	7243
Progress Pallet Inc	Middleboro	MA	F	508 923-1930	10375
Rumas Pallet World LLC	Chelsea	MA	E	617 389-8090	7991
Springfield Pallet Inc	Indian Orchard	MA	G	413 593-0044	9475
Unified2 Globl Packg Group LLC	Lancaster	MA	B	508 865-1155	9531
Wackerbarth Box Mfg Co Inc	Granville	MA	F	413 357-8816	8972
B&T Pallet Recycling Inc	Lewiston	ME	G	207 784-9048	4952
Chep	Scarborough	ME	G	207 883-0244	5428
Gerrity Company Incorporated	Leeds	ME	E	207 933-2804	4948
Barton Corporation Salisbury	Seabrook	NH	G	603 760-2669	15584
Global Pallet & Packaging LLC	Seabrook	NH	G	603 969-6660	15592
Hhp Inc **(PA)**	Henniker	NH	E	603 428-3298	14436
Lgntcs of England	Jaffrey	NH	E	603 532-4666	14571
Lignetics New England Inc	Jaffrey	NH	E	603 532-4666	14572
New England Wood Pellet LLC	Jaffrey	NH	E	603 532-4666	14575
White Mountain Lumber Co Inc	Berlin	NH	F	603 752-1000	13987
Atlas Barrell & Pallet Inc	Harrisville	RI	D	401 568-2900	16064
Js Pallet Co Inc	Pawtucket	RI	F	401 723-0223	16380
Lost Brothers Pallet Corp	Woonsocket	RI	F	401 585-7194	16967
P M Recycling	Woonsocket	RI	F	401 765-0330	16970
Carris Reels Inc **(HQ)**	Proctor	VT	E	802 773-9111	17457
Hayes Recycled Pallets Inc	Brandon	VT	G	802 247-4620	17066

2449 Wood containers, nec

	CITY	ST	EMP	PHONE	ENTRY#
Champlin-Packrite Inc	Manchester	CT	E	860 559-6373	1589
Pith Products LLC	Ashford	CT	F	860 487-4859	21
Vermont Pallet and Skid Sp Inc	Norwich	CT	G	860 822-6949	2618
Westwood Products Inc	Winsted	CT	F	860 379-9401	4358
Woodfree Crating Systems Inc	Waterbury	CT	F	203 759-1799	3985
Abbott-Action Inc	Canton	MA	E	781 702-5710	7765
Garelco Sales Company Inc	East Longmeadow	MA	G	413 525-3316	8376
Nefab Packaging North East LLC	Bellingham	MA	E	800 258-4692	6297
E G W Bradbury Enterprises Inc	Bridgewater	ME	F	207 429-8141	4625
M & S Enterprises Inc	Brewer	ME	F	207 989-0077	4617
Index Packaging Inc	Milton	NH	C	603 350-0018	15046
Old Dublin Road Inc	Peterborough	NH	E	603 924-3861	15323
Peterboro Basket Company	Peterborough	NH	F	603 924-3861	15324
Aspects Inc	Warren	RI	E	401 247-1854	16751
Daves Fresh Mrktplace MGT Inc	Smithfield	RI	E	401 830-5650	16694
Ljm Packaging Co Inc	North Kingstown	RI	D	401 295-2660	16269

2451 Mobile homes

	CITY	ST	EMP	PHONE	ENTRY#
Champion Enterprises Inc	Storrs	CT	G	860 429-3537	3510
Royal Business Group Inc	Boston	MA	C	617 542-4100	7015
Knickerbocker Group Inc	Boothbay	ME	D	207 541-9333	4598
Tiny Homes of Maine LLC	Houlton	ME	E	207 619-4108	4905
Topek LLC	Grantham	NH	F	603 863-2400	14363

2452 Prefabricated wood buildings

	CITY	ST	EMP	PHONE	ENTRY#
American Prefab Wood Pdts Co	Bloomfield	CT	F	860 242-5468	145
Carefree Building Co Inc **(PA)**	Colchester	CT	F	860 267-7600	655
Country Carpenters Inc	Hebron	CT	G	860 228-2276	1526
Country Log Homes Inc	Goshen	CT	F	413 229-8084	1302
Trigila Construction Inc	Berlin	CT	F	860 828-8444	89

	CITY	ST	EMP	PHONE	ENTRY#
Walpole Outdoors LLC	Ridgefield	CT	E	508 668-2800	2909
Advanced Bldg Components LLC	Middleboro	MA	F	508 733-4889	10348
Architectural Timber Mllwk Inc	Hadley	MA	F	413 586-3045	9017
Eggrock Inc	Littleton	MA	E	978 952-8800	9813
Emery Development Ltd	Springfield	MA	G	413 782-1990	12094
Fox Homes Inc	Lee	MA	F	413 243-1950	9613
Habitat Post & Beam Inc	South Deerfield	MA	E	413 665-4006	11923
Jobart Inc (PA)	Methuen	MA	F	978 689-4414	10335
Marvic Inc	Auburn	MA	E	508 798-2600	6119
Reframe Systems Inc	Somerville	MA	G	781 417-9061	11894
Royal Business Group Inc	Boston	MA	C	617 542-4100	7015
Walpole Outdoors LLC	East Falmouth	MA	E	508 540-0300	8362
Walpole Outdoors LLC	Wilmington	MA	E	978 658-3373	13475
C A Construction Inc	Gouldsboro	ME	G	207 422-3493	4838
Ecocor LLC	Searsmont	ME	E	207 342-2085	5449
Excel Homes of Maine LLC	Oxford	ME	C	207 539-8883	5143
G + O Logic LLC	Belfast	ME	E	413 588-8079	4534
Katahdin Forest Products Co (PA)	Oakfield	ME	D	800 845-4533	5119
Kbs Builders Inc	South Paris	ME	E	207 739-2400	5488
Leland Boggs II	Warren	ME	G	207 273-2610	5583
Modular Fun I Inc	South Paris	ME	C	207 739-2400	5490
Moosehead Country Log Homes	Greenville	ME	G	207 695-3730	4851
Moosehead Wood Components Inc	Greenville Junction	ME	F	207 695-3730	4852
New England Rent To Own LLC	Chelsea	ME	G	207 399-6181	4687
Northeast Structures Barns LLC	Porter	ME	G	207 512-0503	5167
Schiavi Homes LLC	Oxford	ME	E	207 539-9600	5149
Walpole Outdoors LLC	Chester	ME	E	207 794-2248	4694
Wlhc Inc (PA)	Houlton	ME	G	207 532-6531	4906
AG Structures LLC	Salisbury	NH	G	603 648-2987	15575
Benson Woodworking Company Inc	Walpole	NH	G	603 756-3600	15659
Granite State Log Homes Inc (PA)	Campton	NH	F	603 536-4949	14044
Home Brands LLC	Portsmouth	NH	D	866 616-2685	15405
New England Homes Inc	Dover	NH	D	603 436-8830	14239
Post Woodworking Inc	Danville	NH	E	603 382-4951	14185
Reeds Ferry Small Buildings	Hudson	NH	D	603 883-1362	14540
Southworth Timberframes Inc	Lancaster	NH	G	603 788-2619	14679
Timberpeg East Inc (PA)	Claremont	NH	E	603 542-7762	14099
Wallace Building Products Corp	Danbury	NH	E	603 768-5402	14184
Whs Homes Inc (PA)	Claremont	NH	E	603 542-5418	14100
Yankee Barn Homes Inc	Claremont	NH	E	603 863-4545	14102
Acer Holdings Starksboro Inc	Starksboro	VT	E	802 453-4438	17625
Connor Homes Inc	Middlebury	VT	D	802 382-9082	17342
Gilcris Enterprises Inc	Proctorsville	VT	F	802 226-7764	17461
Groton Timberworks Inc	Groton	VT	G	802 584-4446	17278
Londonderry Industrial Pk Inc	South Londonderry	VT	E	802 297-3760	17611
Mortise and Tenon LLC	Starksboro	VT	E	802 643-2227	17627
Vermod High Prfmce Mnfctred Hs	Wilder	VT	G	802 295-0042	17716
William H Moore Inc	Waitsfield	VT	G	802 496-3595	17668

2491 Wood preserving

	CITY	ST	EMP	PHONE	ENTRY#
Amerifix LLC	West Haven	CT	G	203 931-7290	4094
Bridgwell Rsurces Holdings LLC (HQ)	Greenwich	CT	E	203 622-9138	1322
Country Carpenters Inc	Hebron	CT	E	860 228-2276	1526
Metalcraft Door Co Inc	Woburn	MA	E	781 933-2861	13611
Northeast Treaters Inc (HQ)	Belchertown	MA	F	413 323-7811	6281
Integrity Composites LLC	Biddeford	ME	E	207 571-0743	4571
Maine Wood Treaters Inc	Mechanic Falls	ME	E	207 345-8411	5052
Oxford Timber Inc	Oxford	ME	F	207 539-9656	5148
University of Maine System	Orono	ME	F	207 581-2843	5138
BB&s Acquisition Corp	North Kingstown	RI	D	401 295-3200	16234
Hbh Prestain Inc (PA)	Arlington	VT	E	802 375-9723	16987
Vermont Timber Works Inc	North Springfield	VT	F	802 886-1917	17427

2493 Reconstituted wood products

	CITY	ST	EMP	PHONE	ENTRY#
Panolam Industries Intl Inc (PA)	Shelton	CT	E	203 925-1556	3045
Bnz Materials Inc	North Billerica	MA	C	978 663-3401	10900
Speedboard Usa Inc	Rowley	MA	G	978 884-3900	11685
Huber Engineered Woods LLC	Easton	ME	D	207 488-6700	4742
Saunders At Locke Mills LLC	Greenwood	ME	G	207 875-2853	4853
Souhegan Wood Products Inc	Wilton	NH	F	603 654-2311	15709
Neshobe Wood Products Inc	Brandon	VT	F	802 247-3805	17069

2499 Wood products, nec

	CITY	ST	EMP	PHONE	ENTRY#
Acme United Corporation (PA)	Shelton	CT	D	203 254-6060	2978
Agw Clssic Hardwood Floors LLC	Westbrook	CT	G	203 640-3106	4135
Anne Queen Woodworking	Naugatuck	CT	F	203 720-1781	1948
Bender Management Inc	Norwalk	CT	E	203 847-3865	2471
Brass City Tile Designs LLC	Waterbury	CT	G	203 597-8764	3892
Carris Reels Connecticut Inc	Enfield	CT	D	860 749-8308	1122
Church Hill Classics Ltd	Monroe	CT	D	800 477-9005	1909
DR Charles Envmtl Cnstr LLC	Monroe	CT	G	203 445-0412	1913
Eastwoods Arms LLC	Guilford	CT	G	203 615-3476	1393
Elm City Manufacturing LLC	North Haven	CT	F	203 248-1969	2409

	CITY	ST	EMP	PHONE	ENTRY#
Essex Wood Products Inc	Colchester	CT	F	860 537-3451	658
European Woodcraft LLC	Norwalk	CT	G	203 847-6195	2498
Harris Enterprise Corp	Manchester	CT	E	860 649-4663	1600
Hmtx Industries LLC (PA)	Norwalk	CT	G	203 299-3100	2515
Kensington GL & Frmng Co Inc	Berlin	CT	F	860 828-9428	73
La Pietra Thinstone of CT LLC	Seymour	CT	F	203 948-3756	2963
Legere Group Ltd	Avon	CT	D	860 674-0392	29
Mc Cann Bros Inc	Monroe	CT	F	203 335-8630	1916
Natures Harvest LLC	Bethany	CT	F	203 758-3725	96
Pleasant Valley Fence Co Inc	Pleasant Valley	CT	G	860 379-0088	2803
Too Sweets LLC	Waterbury	CT	G	203 578-6493	3973
Vacca Architectural Wdwkg LLC	Pawcatuck	CT	G	860 599-3677	2727
Walpole Outdoors LLC	Ridgefield	CT	E	508 668-2800	2909
Wood Services LLC	Greenwich	CT	G	203 983-5752	1363
Adjective Art & Framing Inc	Stoughton	MA	F	617 281-4661	12190
April Twenty One Corporation	Billerica	MA	G	978 667-8472	6405
Avo Fence & Supply Inc (PA)	Stoughton	MA	F	781 341-2963	12196
Blacksmith Shop Farms Inc	East Falmouth	MA	G	508 548-7714	8357
Blank Industries LLC	Hudson	MA	E	855 887-3123	9356
Butler Architectural Wdwkg Inc	New Bedford	MA	F	508 985-9980	10576
Cook Forest Products Inc	Upton	MA	E	508 634-3300	12471
Cork Technologies LLC	Lawrence	MA	G	978 687-9500	9555
Eagle Woodworking Inc	Lawrence	MA	F	978 681-6194	9558
Flagraphics Inc	Somerville	MA	E	617 776-7549	11874
Harvest Consumer Products LLC (PA)	Waltham	MA	E	980 444-2000	12690
Hastone Homestone Inc	Dorchester	MA	G	617 784-3284	8300
Hollingsworth & Vose Company (PA)	East Walpole	MA	C	508 850-2000	8418
Jones & Vining Incorporated (PA)	Brockton	MA	F	508 232-7470	7287
Lashway Logging Inc	Williamsburg	MA	F	413 268-3600	13365
Lyn-Lad Group Ltd (PA)	Lynn	MA	E	781 598-6010	9984
Lynn Ladder Scaffolding Co Inc (HQ)	Lynn	MA	D	781 598-6010	9985
Malden Intl Designs Inc	Middleboro	MA	C	508 946-2270	10365
Nicholas Ieronimo	Middleboro	MA	G	508 947-5363	10369
Perfection Fence Corp (PA)	Marshfield	MA	F	781 837-3600	10243
Petermans Boards and Bowls Inc	Gill	MA	G	413 863-2116	8915
Pine and Baker Mfg Inc	Tewksbury	MA	F	978 851-1215	12412
Pobco Inc	Worcester	MA	E	508 791-6376	13771
Psg Framing Inc	Somerville	MA	F	617 261-1817	11890
Rangeway Supply LLC	North Billerica	MA	G	978 667-8500	10947
RD Contractors Inc	North Billerica	MA	E	978 667-6545	10948
Reliable Fnce C/Wstern Div Inc	Ashland	MA	F	508 877-1200	5966
South Shore Millwork Inc	Norton	MA	E	508 226-5500	11136
TJ Bark Mulch Inc	Southwick	MA	F	413 569-2400	12047
Vance Cabinet & Carpentry	Shirley	MA	G	603 801-5221	11824
Walpole Outdoors LLC	East Falmouth	MA	E	508 540-0300	8362
Walpole Outdoors LLC	Wilmington	MA	E	978 658-3373	13475
Watson Brothers Inc	Middleton	MA	F	978 774-7677	10397
Wood & Wood Inc	Greenfield	MA	E	413 772-0889	9006
Aroostook Woodsmiths	Saint Agatha	ME	E	207 728-7100	5385
Bagala Window Works	Westbrook	ME	G	207 887-9231	5616
Coastal Woodworking Inc	Nobleboro	ME	E	207 563-1072	5100
Comprehensive Land Tech Inc	South China	ME	E	207 445-3151	5485
Cousineau Wood Products ME LLC	North Anson	ME	E	207 635-4445	5104
Davis Zac Fine Woodworking	New Gloucester	ME	G	207 926-4710	5084
Federal Program Integrators LLC	Indian Island	ME	F		4907
Frontier Forge Inc	Kingfield	ME	F	207 265-2151	4933
Frost Cedar Products Inc	North Anson	ME	E	207 566-5912	5105
Hardwood Products Company LLC	Guilford	ME	E	207 876-3312	4854
Jsi Store Fixtures Inc (HQ)	Milo	ME	C	207 943-5203	5070
Kangas Inc	North Anson	ME	G	207 635-3745	5106
Katahdin Forest Products Co (PA)	Oakfield	ME	D	800 845-4533	5119
Kevlaur Industries Inc	Van Buren	ME	E	207 868-2761	5569
Lignetics of Maine Inc	Strong	ME	F	207 684-3457	5536
Lucerne Farms	Fort Fairfield	ME	E	207 488-2520	4785
Maine Heritage Timber LLC	Millinocket	ME	E	207 723-9200	5066
Maine Turnpike Authority	Cumberland Center	ME	D	207 829-4531	4709
Maine Wood Turning Inc	New Vineyard	ME	G	207 652-2320	5091
Maine Woods Pellet Company LLC	Athens	ME	E	207 654-2237	4415
Peavey Manufacturing Company	Eddington	ME	E	207 843-7861	4746
Puritan Medical Pdts Co I LP	Guilford	ME	B	207 876-3311	4856
S P Holt Corporation	Orono	ME	G	207 866-4867	5136
Turning Acquisitions LLC	Buckfield	ME	F	207 336-2400	4659
Walpole Outdoors LLC	Chester	ME	E	207 794-2248	4694
Woodex Bearing Company Inc	Georgetown	ME	F	207 371-2210	4815
Woodlab LLC	Portland	ME	G	207 536-7542	5291
York Woods Tree Service LLC	Eliot	ME	F	207 703-0150	4752
Barlow Architectural Mllwk LLC	Hampstead	NH	E	603 329-6026	14381
Chasco Inc	Portsmouth	NH	F	603 436-2141	15371
Herrick Mill Work Inc	Contoocook	NH	F	603 746-5092	14170
Ingerson Transportation	Jefferson	NH	G	603 586-4335	14584
Lignetics New England Inc	Jaffrey	NH	F	603 532-4666	14573
Moneysworth & Best USA Inc	Ashland	NH	E	603 968-3301	13901

SIC

	CITY	ST	EMP	PHONE	ENTRY#
Patio Barn	Amherst	NH	F	603 673-2716	13883
Peg Kearsarge Co Inc	Bartlett	NH	G	603 374-2341	13918
Riley Mountain Products Inc	Antrim	NH	F	603 588-7234	13898
Rochester Shoe Tree Co Inc (PA)	Ashland	NH	D	603 968-3301	13902
Souhegan Wood Products Inc	Wilton	NH	F	603 654-2311	15709
Vigilant Incoporated	Dover	NH	E	603 285-0400	14256
Moore Company	Westerly	RI	E	401 596-2816	16939
New England Wood Products LLC	West Kingston	RI	G	401 789-7474	16895
Roland and Whytock Company Inc	Providence	RI	E	401 781-1234	16607
Stupell Industries Ltd Inc	Johnston	RI	F	401 831-5640	16107
Andrew Pearce Bowls LLC	Taftsville	VT	E	802 356-4632	17647
Carris Financial Corp (PA)	Proctor	VT	F	802 773-9111	17456
Carris Reels Inc (HQ)	Proctor	VT	E	802 773-9111	17457
Concept2 Inc (PA)	Morrisville	VT	E	802 888-7971	17381
Garware Fulflex USA Inc	Brattleboro	VT	C	802 257-5256	17085
Initial Ideas Inc	Rutland	VT	G	802 775-1685	17499
J K Adams Company Inc	Dorset	VT	E	802 362-2303	17214
John McLeod Ltd (PA)	Wilmington	VT	E	802 464-8175	17755
Lyndon Woodworking Inc (PA)	Saint Johnsbury	VT	E	802 748-0100	17542
Vermont Wood Pellet Co LLC	North Clarendon	VT	E	802 747-1093	17418
Wood & Wood Inc	Waitsfield	VT	E	802 496-3000	17669
Zephyr Designs Ltd	Brattleboro	VT	G	802 254-2788	17110

25 FURNITURE AND FIXTURES

2511 Wood household furniture

	CITY	ST	EMP	PHONE	ENTRY#
Andre Furniture Industries LLC	South Windsor	CT	G	860 528-8826	3115
Baldwin Lawn Furniture LLC	Middletown	CT	F	860 347-1306	1738
Bonito Manufacturing Inc	North Haven	CT	D	203 234-8786	2394
Carefree Building Co Inc (PA)	Colchester	CT	F	860 267-7600	655
Christopoulos Designs Inc	Bridgeport	CT	F	203 576-1110	311
Connecticut Solid Surface LLC	Canton	CT	E	860 410-9800	559
Custom Furniture & Design LLC	Litchfield	CT	F	860 567-3519	1555
Ethan Allen Interiors Inc (PA)	Danbury	CT	C	203 743-8000	740
European Woodcraft LLC	Norwalk	CT	G	203 847-6195	2498
Finishing Touch Woodcraft	Canton	CT	G	860 916-2642	561
Future Classics USA LLC (PA)	Roxbury	CT	F	860 838-4688	2944
Ian Ingersoll Cabinetmaker	West Cornwall	CT	F	860 672-6334	4044
L & L Capital Partners LLC	Wilton	CT	F	203 834-6222	4241
Madigan Millworks Inc	Unionville	CT	G	860 673-7601	3749
Salamander Designs Ltd	Bloomfield	CT	E	860 761-9500	209
Stowed LLC (PA)	Westport	CT	G	203 346-5687	4197
Tudor House Furniture Co Inc	Hamden	CT	F	203 288-8451	1461
Walpole Outdoors LLC	Ridgefield	CT	E	508 668-2800	2909
Woodworkers Heaven Inc	Bridgeport	CT	F	203 333-2778	386
Abcrosby & Company Inc	Ashburnham	MA	G	978 827-6064	5951
Acton Woodworks Inc	Acton	MA	G	978 263-0222	5732
Albert E Cadrette	West Townsend	MA	F	978 597-2312	13056
Atlantic Furniture Inc	South Deerfield	MA	E	413 665-4700	11920
Bellecraft Woodworking Co Inc	Winchendon	MA	F	978 297-2672	13478
Bostoncounters LLC	Woburn	MA	G	781 281-1622	13533
Connors Design Ltd	Marlborough	MA	G	508 481-1930	10135
Countryside Woodcraft LLP	Russell	MA	F	413 862-3276	11694
Custom Ktchens By Chmpagne Inc	Franklin	MA	F	508 528-7919	8828
David Lefort	Halifax	MA	G	781 826-9033	9020
Drive-O-Rama Inc (PA)	Hyannis	MA	G	508 771-8100	9434
Drive-O-Rama Inc	Dennis Port	MA	G	508 394-0028	8260
Fabrizio Corporation	Medford	MA	E	781 396-1400	10284
Grace Lee Designs Shilling	Cambridge	MA	G	617 661-7090	7593
Haydenville Wdwkg & Design Inc (PA)	Northampton	MA	G	413 665-7402	11066
Jordans Furniture Inc (HQ)	East Taunton	MA	A	508 828-4000	8408
Marthas Vineyard Furn Co LLC	Vineyard Haven	MA	G	508 687-9555	12491
Metrica Interior Inc	Northampton	MA	F	413 587-2750	11071
Modu Form Inc (PA)	Fitchburg	MA	D	978 345-7942	8667
Ms Orbis Corporation (PA)	Oak Bluffs	MA	G	774 330-5323	11222
Nationwide Tax & Business Svcs	New Bedford	MA	E	774 473-8444	10625
Paines Patio Inc	Pocasset	MA	F	508 563-7557	11490
R H Le Mieur Corp	Templeton	MA	F	978 939-8741	12381
Salem Village Craftsmen Inc (PA)	Ashburnham	MA	F	833 827-7267	5953
Saloom Furniture Co Inc	Winchendon	MA	D	800 297-1901	13482
South Mountain Company Inc	West Tisbury	MA	G	508 693-4850	13055
Standard Chair Gardner Inc	Gardner	MA	F	978 632-1301	8902
Walpole Outdoors LLC	East Falmouth	MA	E	508 540-0300	8362
Walpole Outdoors LLC	Wilmington	MA	F	978 658-3373	13475
Wood Geek Inc	New Bedford	MA	G	508 858-5282	10660
Woodforms Inc	Foxboro	MA	G	508 543-9417	8733
Ambassador Woodworks Inc	Walpole	ME	G	916 958-1092	5580
Anchor Corporation	Kennebunk	ME	E	207 985-6018	4920
Burger-Roy Inc	Madison	ME	E	207 696-3978	5041
Byer Manufacturing Company	Bernard	ME	E	207 866-2171	4547
Cedarworks of Maine Inc (PA)	Rockport	ME	E	207 596-1010	5345
Imagineering Inc	Rockland	ME	F	207 596-6483	5333

	CITY	ST	EMP	PHONE	ENTRY#
Jackson Caldwell	Oxford	ME	G	207 539-2325	5146
Maine Bunk Beds LLC	Buxton	ME	F	207 929-4499	4663
Richardson-Allen Inc	Biddeford	ME	G	207 284-8402	4585
Shed Happens Inc (PA)	Saco	ME	F	207 494-7546	5379
Walpole Outdoors LLC	Chester	ME	E	207 794-2248	4694
Waterworks	Bangor	ME	E	207 941-8306	4521
York-Cmbrland Assn For Hndcppe (PA)	Portland	ME	E	207 879-1140	5292
Cw Keller & Associates LLC	Plaistow	NH	D	603 382-2028	15339
D R Dimes & Co Ltd	Northwood	NH	F	603 942-8050	15272
Design Contempo	Lisbon	NH	F	603 838-6544	14709
Janice Miller	Manchester	NH	G	603 629-9995	14867
Michael Perra Inc	Manchester	NH	F	603 644-2110	14884
Vermont Custom Wood Products	North Walpole	NH	F	802 463-9930	15261
Whitney Bros Co LLC	Keene	NH	E	603 352-2610	14628
Bess Home Fashions Inc	West Warwick	RI	C	401 828-0300	16906
Kenney Manufacturing Company (PA)	Warwick	RI	B	401 739-2200	16831
O&G Studio LLC	Warren	RI	F	520 247-1820	16761
Stephen Plaud Inc	Tiverton	RI	F	401 625-5909	16738
Two Saints Inc	Cranston	RI	F	401 490-5500	15922
Charles Shcklton Mrnda Thmas L	Bridgewater	VT	E	802 672-5175	17111
Community Apostolic Order Inc (PA)	Island Pond	VT	F	802 723-4452	17304
Dock Doctors LLC	Ferrisburgh	VT	E	802 877-6756	17268
Greenrange Furniture Company	Hinesburg	VT	G	802 747-8564	17292
Lyndon Woodworking Inc (PA)	Saint Johnsbury	VT	E	802 748-0100	17542
Mainstream Inc (PA)	Bennington	VT	F	802 442-8859	17050
Neudorfer Inc	Waterbury	VT	F	802 244-5338	17676
New England Woodcraft Inc	Brandon	VT	C	802 247-8211	17070
Sawyer Bentwood Inc	Whitingham	VT	E	802 368-2357	17713
Vermont Culinary Islands LLC	Brattleboro	VT	F	802 246-2277	17104
Vermont Furniture Designs Inc	Winooski	VT	F	802 655-6568	17770

2512 Upholstered household furniture

	CITY	ST	EMP	PHONE	ENTRY#
Cerrito Furniture Inds Inc	Branford	CT	F	203 481-2580	244
Ethan Allen Interiors Inc (PA)	Danbury	CT	C	203 743-8000	740
Tudor House Furniture Co Inc	Hamden	CT	F	203 288-8451	1461
Barclay Furniture Associates	Holyoke	MA	G	413 536-8084	9242
Copley Furniture Company Inc	Boston	MA	G	617 566-1000	6668
Crimson Upholstery Company Inc	Newton	MA	G	617 332-0758	10750
David Lefort	Halifax	MA	G	781 826-9033	9020
Grace Lee Designs Shilling	Cambridge	MA	G	617 661-7090	7593
Marthas Vineyard Furn Co LLC	Vineyard Haven	MA	G	508 687-9555	12491
McLaughlin Upholstering Co Inc	Everett	MA	F	617 389-0761	8495
New England Woodcraft Inc	Westford	MA	G	413 522-0137	13255
Twin Cy Upholstering Mat Inc	Braintree	MA	F	781 843-1780	7210
Alfreds Uphlstring Cstm Fbrcti	Alfred	ME	F	207 536-5565	4402
Custom Canvas & Upholstery LLC	Bridgton	ME	E	207 241-8518	4627
Jackson Caldwell	Oxford	ME	G	207 539-2325	5146
Harris OH Cabinetmaker	Deerfield	NH	G	603 781-1315	14186
Mavrikis Uphlstring Furn Dsign	Nashua	NH	G	603 883-6868	15131
New England Woodcraft Inc	Brandon	VT	C	802 247-8211	17070

2514 Metal household furniture

	CITY	ST	EMP	PHONE	ENTRY#
CT Acquisitions LLC	Wallingford	CT	E	888 441-0537	3797
Durham Manufacturing Company (PA)	Durham	CT	D	860 349-3427	899
Salamander Designs Ltd	Bloomfield	CT	E	860 761-9500	209
Southern Almnum Intrmdte Hldin	New Canaan	CT	C	870 234-8660	2087
Bostoncounters LLC	Woburn	MA	G	781 281-1622	13533
Coastal-N-Counters Inc	Mashpee	MA	F	508 539-3500	10251
Edigene Inc	Cambridge	MA	F	617 682-5731	7554
Leggett & Platt Incorporated	Oxford	MA	D	508 987-8706	11258
Lucas Fabrication Inc	Florence	MA	F	413 586-0941	8684
Summer Infant Inc (HQ)	Woonsocket	RI	C	401 671-6550	16975

2515 Mattresses and bedsprings

	CITY	ST	EMP	PHONE	ENTRY#
A&S Innersprings Usa LLC	Windsor	CT	F	860 298-0401	4249
Blue Bell Mattress Company LLC (HQ)	East Windsor	CT	E	860 292-6372	1068
Leggett & Platt Incorporated	Middletown	CT	F	860 635-8811	1758
Subinas USA LLC	Windsor	CT	F	860 298-0401	4305
Symbol Mattress Neng Inc	Dayville	CT	B	860 779-3112	869
Ecin Industries Inc	Fall River	MA	E	508 675-6920	8540
Gardner Mattress Corporation (PA)	Salem	MA	F	978 744-1810	11718
Leggett & Platt Incorporated	Oxford	MA	D	508 987-8706	11258
Ppj LLC (PA)	Natick	MA	F	508 650-3500	10493
Restmore Inc	Brockton	MA	D	508 559-9944	7302
Spring Air Ohio LLC	Chelsea	MA	G	617 884-0041	7992
Therapedic of New England LLC	Brockton	MA	F	508 559-9944	7311
Twin Cy Upholstering Mat Inc	Braintree	MA	F	781 843-1780	7210
US Bedding Inc	Fall River	MA	F	508 678-6988	8620
Vital Wood Products Inc	Fall River	MA	E	508 673-7976	8623
Portland Mattress Makers (PA)	Biddeford	ME	F	207 282-9583	4582
Bourdons Institutional Sls Inc	Claremont	NH	E	603 542-8709	14079
Installed Building Pdts LLC	Auburn	NH	B	603 645-1604	13909
Wcw Inc (PA)	Manchester Center	VT	D	802 362-8053	17332

	CITY	ST	EMP	PHONE	ENTRY#

2517 Wood television and radio cabinets

	CITY	ST	EMP	PHONE	ENTRY#
Belmont Corporation	Bristol	CT	E	860 589-5700	413
Christopoulos Designs Inc	Bridgeport	CT	F	203 576-1110	311
European Woodcraft LLC	Norwalk	CT	G	203 847-6195	2498
Custom Ktchens By Chmpagne Inc	Franklin	MA	F	508 528-7919	8828
Metrica Interior Inc	Northampton	MA	F	413 587-2750	11071
Superior Kitchen Designs Inc	Gardner	MA	F	978 632-5072	8903
Crown Point Realty Corp Inc	Claremont	NH	E	603 543-1208	14087

2519 Household furniture, nec

	CITY	ST	EMP	PHONE	ENTRY#
Lovesac Company (PA)	Stamford	CT	D	888 636-1223	3404
Weston Presidio MGT Co Inc (PA)	Boston	MA	E	617 988-2500	7118
Arnold Lumber Co	Coventry	RI	E	401 792-0979	15806

2521 Wood office furniture

	CITY	ST	EMP	PHONE	ENTRY#
Belmont Corporation	Bristol	CT	E	860 589-5700	413
Bergan Architectural Wdwkg Inc	Middletown	CT	E	860 346-0869	1739
Bloomfield Wood & Melamine Inc	Bloomfield	CT	F	860 243-3226	153
Bold Wood Interiors LLC	New Haven	CT	F	203 907-4077	2131
CFI Millwork Inc	Manchester	CT	F	860 643-7580	1588
Conco Wood Working Inc	West Haven	CT	G	203 934-9665	4098
Cyr Woodworking Inc	Newington	CT	F	860 232-1991	2284
Gregory Woodworks LLC	Bethel	CT	G	203 794-0726	118
Lesro Industries Inc	Bloomfield	CT	D	800 275-7545	189
Neiss Corp	Vernon	CT	F	860 872-8528	3755
Professional Trades Netwrk LLC	Watertown	CT	G	860 567-0173	4026
S J Pappas Inc	Meriden	CT	G	203 237-7701	1695
Salamander Designs Ltd	Bloomfield	CT	E	860 761-9500	209
Stm Imp and Exp Corp	Plainfield	CT	G	973 450-5110	2740
CAM Office Services Inc (PA)	Marlborough	MA	F	781 932-9868	10125
Custom Office Furn Boston Inc	Woburn	MA	F	781 933-9970	13555
F W Lombard Company (PA)	Winchendon	MA	E	978 827-5333	13479
Gill Metal Fab Inc	Brockton	MA	E	508 580-4445	7281
JC Clocks Company Inc	North Dartmouth	MA	E	508 998-8442	10998
Modu Form Inc (PA)	Fitchburg	MA	D	978 345-7942	8667
Officeworks Inc (PA)	Burlington	MA	F	781 270-9000	7403
Source International Corp	Sutton	MA	E	800 722-0474	12291
Wright Line LLC (HQ)	Worcester	MA	B	508 852-4300	13834
Mavrikis Uphlstring Furn Dsign	Nashua	NH	F	603 883-6868	15131
Constant Technologies Inc	North Kingstown	RI	E	800 518-7369	16240
Imperia Corporation	Barrington	RI	E	508 894-3000	15748
Lorimer Studios LLC	North Kingstown	RI	F	401 714-0014	16270
Modern Industries Inc	Providence	RI	E	401 331-8000	16566
Walcott Associates LLC	North Kingstown	RI	F	401 694-0153	16292
New England Woodcraft Inc	Brandon	VT	C	802 247-8211	17070

2522 Office furniture, except wood

	CITY	ST	EMP	PHONE	ENTRY#
Bonito Manufacturing Inc	North Haven	CT	D	203 234-8786	2394
Conco Wood Working Inc	West Haven	CT	G	203 934-9665	4098
Durham Manufacturing Company (PA)	Durham	CT	D	860 349-3427	899
Nutmeg Architectural Wdwrk Inc	Stamford	CT	F	203 325-4434	3420
One & Co Inc	Norwich	CT	G	860 892-5180	2614
Static Safe Products Company	Cornwall Bridge	CT	F	203 937-6391	672
Willco Sales & Service Inc (PA)	Stratford	CT	F	203 366-3895	3584
Affordable Intr Systems Inc (HQ)	Leominster	MA	D	978 562-7500	9633
Ais Group Holdings LLC	Leominster	MA	B	978 562-7500	9634
Brooks Interiors Group Inc	Wilmington	MA	E	978 988-1300	13395
Conklin Office Services Inc (PA)	Holyoke	MA	E	413 315-4924	9248
Custom Office Furn Boston Inc	Woburn	MA	F	781 933-9970	13555
Krueger International Inc	Boston	MA	G	617 542-4043	6847
Ldg Corporation	East Weymouth	MA	G	781 337-7155	8432
Modu Form Inc (PA)	Fitchburg	MA	D	978 345-7942	8667
Officeworks Inc (PA)	Burlington	MA	F	781 270-9000	7403
Production Basics Inc	Billerica	MA	E	617 926-8100	6473
R W Hatfield Company Inc (PA)	Haverhill	MA	F	978 521-2600	9124
Source International Corp	Sutton	MA	E	800 722-0474	12291
Wright Line LLC (HQ)	Worcester	MA	B	508 852-4300	13834
Granite Commercial RE LLC	Nashua	NH	F	603 669-2770	15107
Mkind Inc	Manchester	NH	G	603 493-6882	14892
SIS-USA Inc	Londonderry	NH	G	603 432-4495	14784
Workplace Modular Systems LLC	Londonderry	NH	E	603 622-3727	14792
Constant Technologies Inc	North Kingstown	RI	E	800 518-7369	16240
Walcott Associates LLC	North Kingstown	RI	F	401 694-0153	16292

2531 Public building and related furniture

	CITY	ST	EMP	PHONE	ENTRY#
Bouncyband LLC	Glastonbury	CT	G	860 916-9978	1271
Franklin Products Inc (PA)	Torrington	CT	E	860 482-0266	3681
Johnson Controls Inc	Ledyard	CT	F	860 886-9021	1552
Johnson Controls Inc	Meriden	CT	F	678 297-4040	1670
Johnson Controls Inc	Rocky Hill	CT	F	860 571-3300	2930
Torrington Distributors Inc (PA)	Torrington	CT	E	860 482-4464	3701
Adden Furniture Inc	Woburn	MA	D	978 454-7848	13498

	CITY	ST	EMP	PHONE	ENTRY#
CMI Restructuring Inc	Westfield	MA	D	413 562-3664	13160
Furniture Concepts	Malden	MA	G	781 324-8668	10015
Johnson Controls Inc	Boston	MA	F	617 424-6601	6828
Johnson Controls Inc	Boston	MA	F	617 992-2073	6829
Johnson Controls Inc	North Easton	MA	F	508 238-0536	11010
Metrica Interior Inc	Northampton	MA	F	413 587-2750	11071
Modu Form Inc (PA)	Fitchburg	MA	D	978 345-7942	8667
Production Basics Inc	Billerica	MA	E	617 926-8100	6473
Clarios LLC	Portland	ME	D	603 222-2400	5199
Hussey Corporation (PA)	North Berwick	ME	B	207 676-2271	5108
Hussey Seating Company	North Berwick	ME	B	207 676-2271	5109
B/E Aerospace Inc	Hampton	NH	F	603 926-5700	14399
Clarios LLC	Manchester	NH	D	603 222-2400	14830
Dci Inc (PA)	Lisbon	NH	D	800 552-8286	14708
Lucci Corp	Peterborough	NH	F	603 567-4301	15317
Whitney Bros Co LLC	Keene	NH	E	603 352-2610	14628
Clarios LLC	Lincoln	RI	F	401 235-6700	16127
Constant Technologies Inc	North Kingstown	RI	E	800 518-7369	16240
Johnson Controls Inc	Cranston	RI	F	401 275-2097	15880
New England Woodcraft Inc	Brandon	VT	C	802 247-8211	17070

2541 Wood partitions and fixtures

	CITY	ST	EMP	PHONE	ENTRY#
C Mather Company Inc	South Windsor	CT	G	860 528-5667	3124
Capitol Glass Company Inc	West Hartford	CT	F	860 236-1936	4050
Creative Dimensions Inc	Cheshire	CT	E	203 250-6500	584
Custom Cft Ktchens By Rzio Bro	Monroe	CT	F	203 268-0271	1912
Formatron Ltd	Farmington	CT	E	860 676-0227	1220
Gregory Woodworks LLC	Bethel	CT	G	203 794-0726	118
Leos Kitchen and Stair Corp	New Britain	CT	G	860 225-7363	2037
McKinnon Design LLC	Plainville	CT	G	860 677-7371	2773
Mildred Coppola (PA)	Stamford	CT	F	203 967-9300	3411
New England Cabinet Co	New Britain	CT	E	860 225-8645	2046
One & Co Inc	Norwich	CT	G	860 892-5180	2614
Pemac Construction	Oakdale	CT	F	860 437-0007	2623
Pro Counters New England LLC	Ansonia	CT	G	203 347-8663	17
Robert L Lovallo	Stamford	CT	G	203 324-6655	3450
Specialty Shop Inc	Manchester	CT	G	860 647-1477	1637
Stevenson Group Corporation	Harwinton	CT	F	860 689-0011	1524
Viking Kitchen Cabinets LLC (PA)	New Britain	CT	F	860 223-7101	2074
Anthony Manufacturing Co Inc	Medford	MA	F	781 396-1400	10279
B&B Micro Manufacturing Inc	Adams	MA	E	413 281-9431	5771
Blue Barn Inc	Gardner	MA	F	617 894-6987	8880
Boston Fabrications	Attleboro	MA	F	781 762-9185	5997
Cape Cod Lumber Co Inc	Abington	MA	C	781 878-0715	5722
Carriage Hse Developments LLC	Winchester	MA	F	339 221-4253	13483
CN Custom Cabinets Inc	Lawrence	MA	F	978 300-5531	9552
Conklin Office Services Inc (PA)	Holyoke	MA	E	413 315-4924	9248
Continental Woodcraft Inc (PA)	Worcester	MA	E	508 581-9560	13709
Custom Ktchens By Chmpagne Inc	Franklin	MA	F	508 528-7919	8828
Eagle Woodworking Inc	Lawrence	MA	F	978 681-6194	9558
Franklin Fixtures Inc (PA)	West Wareham	MA	E	508 291-1475	13065
General Woodworking Inc (PA)	Lowell	MA	F	978 458-6625	9879
Jules A Gourdeau Inc	Beverly	MA	F	978 922-0102	6358
Kenyon Woodworking Inc	Jamaica Plain	MA	F	617 524-6883	9502
Kochman Reidt & Haigh Inc	Stoughton	MA	E	781 573-1500	12217
Master Millwork LLC	West Wareham	MA	E	508 273-0500	13068
Pbd Productions LLC	Hopedale	MA	F	508 482-9300	9300
Phillips Enterprises Inc	Northampton	MA	F	413 586-5860	11076
Quality Stone Marble Inc (PA)	Whitinsville	MA	F	774 813-4801	13344
VT Industries Inc	Amesbury	MA	F	978 388-3792	5854
Ware Rite Distributors Inc	East Bridgewater	MA	D	508 690-2145	8347
Yankee Builders	Dartmouth	MA	G	508 636-8660	8234
Bangor Millwork & Supply Inc	Portland	ME	G	207 878-8548	5181
E G W Bradbury Enterprises Inc	Bridgewater	ME	F	207 429-8141	4625
Jsi Store Fixtures Inc (HQ)	Milo	ME	C	207 943-5203	5070
K & D Millworks Inc	Windham	ME	E	207 892-5188	5663
Portland Stone Works Inc	Portland	ME	G	207 878-6832	5261
Tozier Group Inc	Falmouth	ME	E	207 838-7939	4774
Advanced Custom Cabinets Inc	Brentwood	NH	F	603 772-6211	14019
David D Douglas Inc	Londonderry	NH	G	603 437-1151	14742
Excalibur Shelving Systems Inc	Contoocook	NH	E	603 746-6200	14169
Herrick Mill Work Inc	Contoocook	NH	F	603 746-5092	14170
J H Dunning Corporation	North Walpole	NH	E	603 445-5591	15258
Just Counters	Goffstown	NH	G	603 627-2027	14351
Cabinet Gallery Ltd (PA)	Woonsocket	RI	G	401 762-4300	16952
Cole Cabinet Co Inc	Cranston	RI	E	401 467-4343	15842
Completely Custom LLC	North Kingstown	RI	G	401 667-0059	16239
Custom Design Incorporated	North Kingstown	RI	E	401 294-0200	16243
Herrick & White Ltd	Cumberland	RI	D	401 658-0440	15942
Igs Store Fixtures Inc	Smithfield	RI	C	978 532-0010	16715
Kenney Manufacturing Company (PA)	Warwick	RI	B	401 739-2200	16831
Modern Industries Inc	Providence	RI	E	401 331-8000	16566
Monarch Industries Inc	Providence	RI	D	401 247-5200	16567

SIC

	CITY	ST	EMP	PHONE	ENTRY#
Orion Ret Svcs & Fixturing Inc	Smithfield	RI	D	401 334-5000	16725
Plastics Plus Inc	Cumberland	RI	E	401 727-1447	15960
Read Display	West Warwick	RI	G	401 889-2139	16922
Scope Display & Box Co Inc **(PA)**	Cranston	RI	E	401 942-7150	15909
The Elliott Sales Group Inc	Providence	RI	C	401 944-0002	16625
Visual Creations Inc	Pawtucket	RI	D	401 588-5151	16429
Artisan Surfaces Inc	Springfield	VT	E	802 885-8677	17616
Leo D Bernstein & Sons Inc	Shaftsbury	VT	D	802 442-8029	17550
N B C Solid Surfaces Inc	Springfield	VT	E	802 885-8677	17621
Top Shop Inc	South Burlington	VT	F	802 658-1351	17604
Vermont Store Fixture Corporation **(PA)**	Danby	VT	D	802 293-5126	17210

2542 Partitions and fixtures, except wood

	CITY	ST	EMP	PHONE	ENTRY#
American Building Systems Inc	Bristol	CT	G	860 589-0215	395
Ardent Inc **(PA)**	East Hartford	CT	F	860 528-6000	971
Bethel Mail Service	Bethel	CT	F	203 730-1399	100
Bull Metal Products Inc	Middletown	CT	E	860 346-9691	1742
C Mather Company Inc	South Windsor	CT	G	860 528-5667	3124
Di-Cor Industries Inc	Bristol	CT	E	860 585-5583	436
Displaycraft Inc	Plainville	CT	E	860 747-9110	2754
Durham Manufacturing Company **(PA)**	Durham	CT	D	860 349-3427	899
In Store Experience Inc	Westport	CT	E	203 221-4777	4174
Mitchell-Bate Company	Waterbury	CT	E	203 233-0862	3946
Musano Inc	Wolcott	CT	E	203 879-4651	4369
PCL Fixtures Inc	East Hartford	CT	E	401 334-4646	1009
Pemac Construction	Oakdale	CT	F	860 437-0007	2623
Platt-Labonia of N Haven Inc	North Haven	CT	D	203 239-5681	2431
Richard Riggio and Sons Inc	Ivoryton	CT	E	860 767-0812	1532
Bmac Inc	Ayer	MA	E	978 772-3310	6175
Boston Retail Products Inc **(PA)**	Tewksbury	MA	D	781 395-7417	12387
Continental Woodcraft Inc **(PA)**	Worcester	MA	E	508 581-9560	13709
Fx Group	Oxford	MA	G	508 987-1366	11254
George Patton Associates Inc	Fall River	MA	C	800 572-2194	8552
M & P Machine Company Inc	Stoughton	MA	E	781 344-5888	12218
New England Wire Products Inc **(PA)**	Leominster	MA	D	800 254-9473	9686
Newton Distributing Co Inc	Natick	MA	F	617 969-4002	10488
Phillips Enterprises Inc	Northampton	MA	F	413 586-5860	11076
Rack Attack USA LLP	Framingham	MA	G	508 665-4361	8801
Van Stry Design Inc	Malden	MA	E	781 388-9998	10030
Wood & Wood Inc	Greenfield	MA	E	413 772-0889	9006
E G W Bradbury Enterprises Inc	Bridgewater	ME	F	207 429-8141	4625
Jsi Store Fixtures Inc **(HQ)**	Milo	ME	C	207 943-5203	5070
Kardex Remstar LLC **(HQ)**	Westbrook	ME	E	207 854-1861	5633
Stainless Fdsrvice Eqp Mfg Inc	Limestone	ME	F	207 227-7747	5005
Starc Systems Inc	Brunswick	ME	D	844 596-1784	4655
Custom Design Incorporated	North Kingstown	RI	E	401 294-0200	16243
Frank Shatz & Co	Warwick	RI	E	401 739-1822	16816
Herrick & White Ltd	Cumberland	RI	D	401 658-0440	15942
JCM Design & Display Inc	Providence	RI	E	401 781-0470	16548
Packaging Concepts Ltd	Rumford	RI	C	401 334-0344	16675
Reed Allison Group Inc	Providence	RI	D	617 846-1237	16599
Scope Display & Box Co Inc **(PA)**	Cranston	RI	E	401 942-7150	15909
The Elliott Sales Group Inc	Providence	RI	C	401 944-0002	16625
Green Mountain Gazebo	Westminster	VT	G	802 869-1212	17701
Mamava Inc	Burlington	VT	E	802 347-2111	17142
Top Shop Inc	South Burlington	VT	F	802 658-1351	17604
Vermont Store Fixture Corporation **(PA)**	Danby	VT	D	802 293-5126	17210

2591 Drapery hardware and blinds and shades

	CITY	ST	EMP	PHONE	ENTRY#
Ahlstrom Nonwovens LLC **(DH)**	Windsor Locks	CT	B	860 654-8300	4318
Arrow Win Shade Mfg of Mrden I	Wethersfield	CT	G	860 563-4035	4202
Decorator Services Inc	Bridgeport	CT	G	203 384-8144	315
King Industries	Waterbury	CT	F	203 527-7380	3928
R & M Associates Inc	Glastonbury	CT	G	860 633-0721	1296
Rolease Acmeda Inc **(HQ)**	Stamford	CT	D	203 964-1573	3451
Roto-Frank of America Inc	Chester	CT	C	860 526-4996	631
Thomas W Raftery Inc	Hartford	CT	E	860 278-9870	1514
Vertical Retail Solutions LLC	Andover	CT	A	860 742-6464	3
Vertical Ventures Intl LLC	Weston	CT	G	203 227-1364	4155
Cdi LLC A Valley Forge Co	Brockton	MA	C	508 587-7000	7266
Landmark Window Fashions Inc	Holbrook	MA	E	781 767-3535	9177
Lundys Company Inc	Lynn	MA	F	781 595-8639	9983
Merida Meridian Inc	Boston	MA	E	617 464-5400	6885
TLC Vision (usa) Corporation	Peabody	MA	E	978 531-4114	11348
Vertical & Mini Blind Factory	Agawam	MA	G	413 789-2343	5815
Blind Pig Tavern	Gardiner	ME	G	207 592-0776	4812
Mums Cheesecake	York	ME	G	207 351-8543	5714
Blind Tiger LLP	Exeter	NH	G	603 498-7005	14286
Scarlet Aspen LLC	Portsmouth	NH	F	603 509-3990	15435
Drapery House Inc	North Providence	RI	E	401 724-3400	16300
Kenney Manufacturing Company **(PA)**	Warwick	RI	B	401 739-2200	16831
Gordons Window Decor Inc **(PA)**	Williston	VT	F	802 655-7777	17734

2599 Furniture and fixtures, nec

	CITY	ST	EMP	PHONE	ENTRY#
Creole Jos LLC	Glastonbury	CT	F	203 893-2875	1276
Curtiss Woodworking Inc	Prospect	CT	D	203 527-9305	2832
General Seating Solutions LLC	South Windsor	CT	F	860 242-3307	3149
Liberty Garage Inc	Danbury	CT	G	203 778-0222	770
Thorme Wall Inc	Bridgeport	CT	F	203 583-2305	379
Triple Play Sports	Watertown	CT	F	860 417-2877	4033
42 Design Fab Studio Inc	Indian Orchard	MA	G	413 203-4948	9469
Gemini Investors V LP **(PA)**	Wellesley	MA	E	781 237-7001	12942
General Woodworking Inc	Lowell	MA	G	978 251-4070	9878
General Woodworking Inc **(PA)**	Lowell	MA	F	978 458-6625	9879
Hendrick Manufacturing Corp **(PA)**	Salem	MA	F	781 631-4400	11723
Hostar Mar Trnspt Systems Inc	Wareham	MA	F	508 295-2900	12838
Jamesbrook Enterprises Inc	Shirley	MA	G	978 425-6166	11818
JS International Inc **(PA)**	Fall River	MA	E	508 675-4722	8564
Kitchen Associates Inc	Sterling	MA	E	978 422-3322	12164
Lista International Corporation	Holliston	MA	C	508 429-1350	9221
Meitu	Auburndale	MA	G	781 898-7655	6137
Metzys Taqueria LLC	Newburyport	MA	F	978 992-1451	10701
October Company Inc **(PA)**	Easthampton	MA	C	413 527-9380	8456
Sampco Inc **(PA)**	Pittsfield	MA	C	413 442-4043	11423
Stanley Industrial & Auto LLC	Holliston	MA	B	508 429-1350	9230
Quarry Tap Room LLC	Hallowell	ME	G	207 213-6173	4862
Coast To Cast Ff E Instlltons	Greenland	NH	F	603 433-0164	14368
Design Brand Partners Inc	Bedford	NH	A	603 232-3490	13925
Kingston Krafts	Cranston	RI	G	401 272-0292	15882
Stackbin Corporation	Lincoln	RI	E	401 333-1600	16155
Walcott Associates LLC	North Kingstown	RI	F	401 694-0153	16292
7 South Sandwich Company LLC	Middlebury	VT	E	802 388-3354	17334
Cricket Radio LLC	Burlington	VT	G	802 825-8368	17129
JRS Corp	Burlington	VT	F	802 310-5253	17140
Mamava Inc	Burlington	VT	E	802 347-2111	17142
Standex International Corp	Essex Junction	VT	A	864 963-3471	17247
Vermont Culinary Islands LLC	Brattleboro	VT	F	802 246-2277	17104

26 PAPER AND ALLIED PRODUCTS

2611 Pulp mills

	CITY	ST	EMP	PHONE	ENTRY#
City Carting Inc	Stamford	CT	D	888 413-3344	3313
Freepoint Eco-Systems LLC	Stamford	CT	F	203 542-6000	3350
ITT Industries Holdings Inc **(DH)**	Stamford	CT	C	914 641-2000	3389
Willimantic Waste Paper Co Inc **(HQ)**	Willimantic	CT	C	860 423-4527	4221
American Paper Recycling Corp **(PA)**	Mansfield	MA	E	800 422-3220	10038
Capital Industries Corporation	East Weymouth	MA	F	781 337-9807	8428
Intercntnental Enrgy Group LLC	Hingham	MA	G	781 749-9800	9151
Sarid Inc	Lexington	MA	G	781 315-1105	9769
United Paper Stock Co Inc	Worcester	MA	E	401 724-5700	13816
Casella Recycling LLC **(HQ)**	Scarborough	ME	E	207 883-4600	5427
Georgia-Pacific LLC	Baileyville	ME	E	207 427-4077	4484
ND Otm LLC	Old Town	ME	C	207 401-2879	5129
ND Paper Inc	Rumford	ME	B	207 364-4521	5359
Robbins Lumber Inc **(PA)**	Searsmont	ME	C	207 342-5221	5450
Woodland Pulp LLC **(PA)**	Baileyville	ME	B	207 427-3311	4486
Berger & Company Recycling Inc	Pawtucket	RI	F	401 723-7240	16349
Lkq Precious Metals Inc	Cumberland	RI	C	800 447-1034	15950
Westrock Cp LLC	Sheldon Springs	VT	C	802 933-7733	17566

2621 Paper mills

	CITY	ST	EMP	PHONE	ENTRY#
Ahlstrom USA Inc **(DH)**	Windsor Locks	CT	B	860 654-8300	4319
Ahlstrom-Munksjo Nonwovens LLC	Windsor Locks	CT	F	860 654-8300	4320
Ahlstrom-Munksjo Paper Inc	Windsor Locks	CT	F	860 654-8300	4321
Barker Advg Specialty Co Inc **(PA)**	Cheshire	CT	D	203 272-2222	575
Bear Island Paper Company LLC	Greenwich	CT	F	203 661-3344	1316
Brant Industries Inc **(PA)**	Greenwich	CT	F	203 661-3344	1320
Brant Paper Inc	Greenwich	CT	F	203 661-3344	1321
Bristol Adult Resource Ctr Inc	Bristol	CT	D	860 583-8721	418
Bristol Hospitality LLC	Bristol	CT	G	860 589-7766	419
Bristol Rtary Schlrship Fund I	Bristol	CT	G	860 314-1871	422
Cellu Tissue Corporation	East Hartford	CT	A	860 289-7496	979
Dunn Paper Holdings Inc	East Hartford	CT	C	860 289-7496	987
Dunn Paper LLC	East Hartford	CT	D	860 466-4141	988
Hexcelpack LLC	Bristol	CT	G	855 439-2351	454
International Paper Company	Putnam	CT	C	860 928-7901	2861
Kimberly-Clark Corporation	New Milford	CT	D	860 210-1602	2250
Mafcote International Inc **(HQ)**	Norwalk	CT	E	203 644-1200	2532
Mega Sound and Light LLC	Danbury	CT	G	203 743-4200	784
Miami Wabash Paper LLC **(HQ)**	Norwalk	CT	E	203 847-8500	2537
Royal Consumer Products LLC **(HQ)**	Norwalk	CT	E	203 847-8500	2567
Simkins Industries Inc	New Haven	CT	F	203 787-7171	2199
UST LLC	Stamford	CT	A	203 817-3000	3489
Xamax Industries Inc	Seymour	CT	E	203 888-7200	2976

	CITY	ST	EMP	PHONE	ENTRY#
A Group Inc	Woburn	MA	E	781 756-3163	13495
Asp Fibermark Holdings LLC	West Springfield	MA	A	413 736-4554	13014
Boston Paper Board Corp	Boston	MA	F	617 666-1154	6612
Bristol Bay LLC	Salem	MA	G	978 744-4272	11704
Colony Foods Inc	Lawrence	MA	F	978 794-1500	9553
Crane & Co Inc (HQ)	Dalton	MA	B	617 648-3799	8150
Crocker Technical Papers Inc	Fitchburg	MA	E	978 345-7771	8651
Dennecrepe Corporation	Gardner	MA	D	978 630-8669	8884
Dixie Consumer Products LLC	Leominster	MA	F	978 537-4701	9658
Ecological Fibers Inc (PA)	Lunenburg	MA	D	978 537-0003	9958
Erving Industries Inc (PA)	Erving	MA	D	413 422-2700	8469
Erving Paper Mills Inc	Erving	MA	C	413 422-2700	8470
Fortifiber LLC	Attleboro	MA	E	508 222-3500	6018
Georgia-Pacific LLC	Leominster	MA	D	978 537-4701	9666
Hollingsworth & Vose Company (PA)	East Walpole	MA	C	508 850-2000	8418
Hollingsworth & Vose Company	West Groton	MA	C	978 448-7000	13002
Kadant Inc (PA)	Westford	MA	C	978 776-2000	13244
Kanzaki Specialty Papers Inc (DH)	Ware	MA	C	413 967-6204	12826
Kimberly-Clark Corporation	Franklin	MA	G	508 520-1355	8849
L & P Paper Inc	Charlton	MA	D	508 248-3265	7892
Lenmarine Inc	Somerset	MA	G	508 678-1234	11852
Mi-Box Southern Mass LLC	Plainville	MA	G	774 719-7367	11438
Neenah Northeast LLC (DH)	West Springfield	MA	C	413 533-0699	13036
Neenah Technical Materials Inc (DH)	Dalton	MA	F	678 518-3343	8151
Onyx Specialty Papers Inc	South Lee	MA	C	413 243-1231	11972
Packaging Specialties Inc	Newburyport	MA	D	978 462-1300	10706
Pagell Corporation	Holliston	MA	E	508 429-2998	9226
Red Sun Press Inc	Jamaica Plain	MA	F	617 524-6822	9503
SDW Holdings Corporation	Boston	MA	A	617 423-5400	7028
Seaman Paper Company Mass Inc	Baldwinville	MA	D	978 939-5356	6198
Seaman Paper Company Mass Inc (PA)	Gardner	MA	E	978 632-1513	8899
Seaman Paper Company Mass Inc	Orange	MA	G	978 544-2455	11233
Sonoco Products Company	Holyoke	MA	D	413 536-4546	9282
Southworth Company	Agawam	MA	C	413 789-1200	5807
Specialized Ppr Converting Inc	Gardner	MA	E	978 632-5524	8900
Sullivan Paper Company Inc (PA)	West Springfield	MA	C	413 827-7030	13044
Tropical Smoothie of Bristol	Dartmouth	MA	G	508 636-1424	8232
Union Paper & Packaging Inc	Leominster	MA	G	978 227-5868	9711
Verso Corporation	Norwood	MA	G	339 788-1343	11218
Visionstep Consulting Inc	Fitchburg	MA	E	978 422-1447	8681
Y & Z Bristol Inc	New Bedford	MA	G	508 991-7365	10661
Cascades Auburn Fiber Inc	Auburn	ME	E	207 753-5300	4423
Chinetco	Waterville	ME	G	207 873-3351	5594
Domtar Paper Company LLC	Baileyville	ME	C	207 427-6400	4482
Georgia-Pacific LLC	Baileyville	ME	G	207 427-4077	4484
International Paper Company	Auburn	ME	D	207 784-4051	4438
Lincoln Paper and Tissue LLC	Lincoln	ME	B	207 794-0600	5011
Madison Upm	Madison	ME	C	207 696-3307	5042
ND Paper Inc	Old Town	ME	C	207 401-2920	5130
ND Paper LLC	Rumford	ME	A	207 364-4521	5360
Pixelle Androscoggin LLC (HQ)	Jay	ME	D	207 897-3431	4914
Pixelle Spcialty Solutions LLC	Jay	ME	B	207 897-3431	4915
Presumpscot Water Power Co	Westbrook	ME	D	207 856-4000	5643
Sappi Fine Paper Tech Ctr	Westbrook	ME	E	207 239-6071	5645
Sappi North America Inc	Skowhegan	ME	D	207 858-4201	5477
Sappi North America Inc	Skowhegan	ME	A	207 238-3000	5478
Sappi North America Inc	South Portland	ME	D	207 854-7000	5513
Sappi North America Inc	Westbrook	ME	B	207 856-4000	5646
Sappi North America Inc	Westbrook	ME	C	207 856-4911	5647
Tissue Plus LLC	Bangor	ME	F	978 524-0550	4516
Twin Rivers Paper Company Corp	Madawaska	ME	A	207 523-2350	5039
Twin Rivers Paper Company LLC (PA)	Madawaska	ME	E	207 728-3321	5040
Verso Paper Holding LLC	Jay	ME	A	207 897-3431	4917
Ampac Holdings LLC	Claremont	NH	D	603 542-0411	14076
APC Paper Company Inc (DH)	Claremont	NH	D	603 542-0411	14077
Arlington Sample Book Co Inc (PA)	Sunapee	NH	F	603 763-9082	15642
Crane Security Tech Inc	Nashua	NH	E	603 881-1860	15084
Gorham Acquisition LLC	Gorham	NH	E	603 342-2000	14357
Gorham Paper and Tissue LLC	Gorham	NH	A		14358
Innovative Paper Tech LLC	Tilton	NH	D	603 286-4891	15653
Monadnock Paper Mills Inc (HQ)	Bennington	NH	D	603 588-3311	13977
Monadnock Paper Mills Inc	Greenfield	NH	E	603 588-8220	14364
Nashua Corporation	Merrimack	NH	A	603 880-1100	14994
Cjf Group Ltd	Providence	RI	D	401 421-2000	16500
Signode Industrial Group LLC	Rumford	RI	A	401 438-5203	16676
The Real Reel Corporation	Rumford	RI	A	401 434-1070	16678
Town of Bristol	Bristol	RI	F	401 787-6763	15783
Weeden Street Associates LLC	Pawtucket	RI	E	401 725-2610	16430
Portfolio Software Inc	Richmond	VT	F	802 434-4000	17481
Soundview Vermont Holdings LLC	East Dummerston	VT	C	802 387-5571	17217
Sticky Brnd Creative Group LLC	South Burlington	VT	F	609 731-0288	17601

2631 Paperboard mills

	CITY	ST	EMP	PHONE	ENTRY#
Connecticut Container Corp (PA)	North Haven	CT	C	203 248-2161	2399
Fluted Partition Inc (PA)	Bridgeport	CT	C	203 368-2548	322
Fusion Paperboard Connecticut LLC	Versailles	CT	C	888 283-3617	3764
Fusion Paperboard US Inc	Versailles	CT	C	859 586-1100	3765
Hamden Packaging Inc	Hamden	CT	E	203 288-0200	1428
Keystone Paper & Box Co LLC (HQ)	South Windsor	CT	F	860 291-0027	3160
Mafcote Inc (PA)	Norwalk	CT	E	203 847-8500	2530
Metsa Board Americas Corp	Norwalk	CT	D	203 229-0037	2536
Pact Inc	Watertown	CT	F	203 759-1799	4022
Rand-Whtney Cntnrbard Ltd Prtn	Montville	CT	C	860 848-1900	1928
Rice Packaging Inc	Ellington	CT	D	860 870-7057	1113
Russell Partition Co Inc	North Haven	CT	G	203 239-5749	2434
Schrafel Pprbd Converting Corp	West Haven	CT	E	203 931-1700	4124
Simkins Industries Inc	New Haven	CT	F	203 787-7171	2199
Asp Fibermark Holdings LLC	West Springfield	MA	A	413 736-4554	13014
Caraustar Industries Inc	Fitchburg	MA	D	978 665-2632	8648
Core Concepts Inc	Franklin	MA	E	508 528-0070	8827
Danvers Industrial Packg Corp	Beverly	MA	E	978 777-0020	6344
Georgia-Pacific LLC	Leominster	MA	D	978 537-4701	9666
Graphic Arts Finishers Inc	Jamaica Plain	MA	F	617 241-9292	9501
Kalt Incorporated (PA)	Lowell	MA	E	978 805-5001	9889
Lamitech	Rockland	MA	F	781 878-7708	11649
Miles Kedex Co Inc	Westminster	MA	E	978 874-1403	13274
Millstone Med Outsourcing LLC (PA)	Fall River	MA	C	508 679-8384	8583
N3k Informatik Inc	Boston	MA	F	617 289-9282	6901
New-Indy Cntinerboard Hold LLC (HQ)	Foxborough	MA	C	508 384-4230	8736
Northast Dcment Cnsrvtion Ctr	Andover	MA	E	978 470-1010	5901
Rand-Whitney Container LLC (DH)	Worcester	MA	A	508 890-7000	13777
Rand-Whitney Group LLC (HQ)	Worcester	MA	A	508 791-2301	13778
Rand-Whitney Packaging Corp	Worcester	MA	D	508 929-3400	13780
Sonoco Products Company	Holyoke	MA	D	413 536-4546	9282
Westrock Mwv LLC	Springfield	MA	A	413 736-7211	12152
Westrock Rkt LLC	Springfield	MA	G	413 543-7300	12153
Georgia-Pacific LLC	Baileyville	ME	A	207 427-4077	4484
Graphic Packaging Intl LLC	Concord	NH	D	603 230-5100	14132
Graphic Packaging Intl LLC	Concord	NH	C	603 230-5100	14133
Graphic Packaging Intl LLC	Concord	NH	E	603 224-2333	14134
Contempo Card Co Inc (PA)	Providence	RI	D	401 272-4210	16505
Jewel Case Corporation	Providence	RI	B	401 943-1400	16549
Nfa Corp	Cumberland	RI	C	401 333-8990	15953
Plastic Services Entps Inc	Providence	RI	F	401 490-3811	16584
Rand-Whitney Container LLC	Pawtucket	RI	D	401 729-7900	16411
Signode Industrial Group LLC	Rumford	RI	A	401 438-5203	16676
The Real Reel Corporation	Rumford	RI	A	401 434-1070	16678
Limlaws Pulpwood Inc	West Topsham	VT	E	802 439-3503	17698
Long Falls Paperboard LLC	Brattleboro	VT	B	802 257-0365	17094
Westrock Cp LLC	Sheldon Springs	VT	C	802 933-7733	17566

2652 Setup paperboard boxes

	CITY	ST	EMP	PHONE	ENTRY#
Agi-Shorewood Group Us LLC	Stamford	CT	A	203 324-4839	3275
Fusion Paperboard Connecticut LLC	Versailles	CT	C	888 283-3617	3764
Hudson Paper Company (PA)	Stratford	CT	E	203 378-8759	3548
Rice Packaging Inc	Ellington	CT	D	860 870-7057	1113
Rondo America Incorporated	Naugatuck	CT	C	203 723-5831	1985
Friend Box Company Inc	Danvers	MA	D	978 774-0240	8187
Keystone Paper & Box Co LLC	Woburn	MA	E	781 938-3801	13596
Packaging Specialties Inc	Newburyport	MA	D	978 462-1300	10706
UNI-Pac Inc	Holyoke	MA	D	413 534-5284	9284
Westrock Rkt LLC	Springfield	MA	G	413 543-7300	12153
Volk Enterprises Corporation	Biddeford	ME	D	207 282-6151	4594
Graphic Packaging Intl LLC	Concord	NH	D	603 230-5100	14132
Graphic Packaging Intl LLC	Concord	NH	C	603 230-5100	14133
Cjf Group Ltd	Providence	RI	D	401 421-2000	16500
Fuller Box Co Inc	Central Falls	RI	C	401 725-4300	15788
Mason Box Company	Pawtucket	RI	E	800 842-9526	16383
Numaco Packaging LLC	East Providence	RI	F	401 438-4952	16035

2653 Corrugated and solid fiber boxes

	CITY	ST	EMP	PHONE	ENTRY#
AP Disposition LLC	Norwich	CT	F	860 889-1344	2601
Cascades Holding US Inc	Newtown	CT	D	718 340-2136	2336
Champlin-Packrite Inc	Manchester	CT	E	860 559-6373	1589
Colonial Corrugated Pdts Inc	Waterbury	CT	D	203 597-1707	3899
Connecticut Container Corp (PA)	North Haven	CT	C	203 248-2161	2399
Danbury Square Box Company	Danbury	CT	E	203 744-4611	727
Fluted Partition Inc	Bridgeport	CT	D	203 334-3500	321
Fluted Partition Inc (PA)	Bridgeport	CT	C	203 368-2548	322
Fortis Solutions Group LLC	Ellington	CT	E	860 872-6311	1107
General Packaging Products Inc	Norwalk	CT	G	203 846-1340	2505
HI-Tech Packaging Inc	Stratford	CT	E	203 378-2700	3547
Holm Corrugated Container Inc	Southington	CT	D	860 628-5559	3216
Jackson Corrugated Cont Corp	Essex	CT	F	860 767-3373	1168

	CITY	ST	EMP	PHONE	ENTRY#
Merco Inc	Ellington	CT	E	860 871-1888	1110
Merrill Industries LLC	Ellington	CT	E	860 871-1888	1111
Nutmeg Container Corporation (HQ)	Putnam	CT	D	860 963-6727	2867
R & R Corrugated Container Inc	Bristol	CT	D	860 584-1194	488
Rand-Whitney Container LLC	Waterbury	CT	E	203 597-1707	3965
Rand-Whitney Group LLC	Newtown	CT	E	203 426-5871	2345
Rand-Whitney Recycling LLC	Montville	CT	D	860 848-1900	1927
Rice Packaging Inc	Ellington	CT	D	860 870-7057	1113
Russell Partition Co Inc	North Haven	CT	G	203 239-5749	2434
Windham Container Corporation	Putnam	CT	F	860 928-7934	2879
Abbott-Action Inc (PA)	Attleboro	MA	E	401 722-2100	5990
Atlas Box and Crating Co Inc (PA)	Sutton	MA	C	508 865-1155	12276
Big Foot Moving & Storage Inc	Acton	MA	E	781 488-3090	5740
Commonwealth Packaging Corp	Chicopee	MA	D	413 593-1482	8019
Corrugated Packaging Inc	Fitchburg	MA	F	978 342-6076	8649
Corrugated Stitcher Service	Berkley	MA	G	508 823-2844	6315
Craft Corrugated Box Inc	New Bedford	MA	F	508 998-2115	10581
Creative Packaging Inc (PA)	Worcester	MA	E	508 756-7275	13711
E Ink Corporation	Billerica	MA	D	617 499-6000	6437
Friend Box Company Inc	Danvers	MA	F	978 774-0240	8187
GPA Global US Holding Inc	Mansfield	MA	F	800 334-1113	10053
Horn Corporation (PA)	Lancaster	MA	E	800 832-7020	9527
Hub Folding Box Company Inc	Mansfield	MA	B	508 339-0005	10057
Ideal Box Company	Lawrence	MA	E	978 683-2802	9570
Kraft Group LLC (PA)	Foxboro	MA	C	508 384-4230	8705
Massachusetts Container Corp	Marlborough	MA	C	508 481-1100	10183
Mount Tom Box Company Inc	West Springfield	MA	F	413 781-5300	13034
New England Business Svc Inc (HQ)	Townsend	MA	D	978 448-6111	12441
New England Wooden Ware Corp (PA)	Gardner	MA	E	978 632-3600	8896
New-Indy Containerboard LLC	Foxboro	MA	F	508 384-4230	8710
Newcorr Packaging Inc	Northborough	MA	D	508 393-9256	11103
Pacific Packaging Products Inc (PA)	Wilmington	MA	C	978 657-9100	13445
Packaging Corporation America	Northampton	MA	E	413 584-6132	11074
Packaging Corporation America	Northampton	MA	D	978 256-4586	11075
Rand-Whitney Container LLC	Worcester	MA	D	774 420-2425	13776
Rand-Whitney Container LLC (DH)	Worcester	MA	C	508 890-7000	13777
Rand-Whitney Group LLC (HQ)	Worcester	MA	C	508 791-2301	13778
Rand-Whitney Industries LLC	Worcester	MA	E	508 791-2301	13779
Romanow Inc (DH)	Westwood	MA	D	781 320-9200	13317
Seaboard Folding Box Co Inc	Westminster	MA	D	978 342-8921	13277
Triple P Packg & Ppr Pdts Inc	Brockton	MA	D	508 588-0444	7313
Unicorr	Marlborough	MA	F	508 481-1100	10226
Unified2 Globl Packg Group LLC	Lancaster	MA	B	508 865-1155	9531
Westrock - Southern Cont LLC	Boston	MA	E	978 772-5050	7120
Westrock Container LLC	Springfield	MA	D	413 733-2211	12151
Westrock Rkt LLC	Springfield	MA	D	413 543-7300	12153
Ship-Pac Corp	Portland	ME	G	207 797-7444	5270
Volk Packaging Corporation	Biddeford	ME	D	207 282-6151	4594
Westrock	Scarborough	ME	F	770 448-2193	5447
Aegis Holdings LLC	Milford	NH	E	603 673-8900	15010
Mills Industries Inc	Laconia	NH	E	603 528-4217	14659
Rand-Whitney Container LLC	Dover	NH	E	603 822-7300	14247
Amring Worldwide Inc	Johnston	RI	D	401 943-5040	16075
Contempo Card Co Inc (PA)	Providence	RI	D	401 272-4210	16505
Custom & Miller Box Company	East Providence	RI	D	401 431-9007	16012
Fuller Box Co Inc	Central Falls	RI	C	401 725-4300	15788
Hope-Bffnton Pckging Group LLC	Central Falls	RI	F	401 725-3646	15789
Key Container Corporation (PA)	Pawtucket	RI	C	401 723-2000	16381
Ljm Packaging Co Inc	North Kingstown	RI	D	401 295-2660	16269
Mason Box Company	Pawtucket	RI	F	800 842-9526	16383
MCB Inc	Warwick	RI	F	401 739-7020	16835
Mount Tom Box Co Inc	Pawtucket	RI	F	413 781-5300	16390
Pusterla Us Inc	Warren	RI	E	401 245-5900	16765
Rand-Whitney Container LLC	Pawtucket	RI	E	401 729-7900	16411
K H Corrugated Case Copr	Bennington	VT	G	802 442-5455	17044
K&H Group Inc	Bennington	VT	C	802 442-5455	17045

2655 Fiber cans, drums, and similar products

	CITY	ST	EMP	PHONE	ENTRY#
Greif Inc	Windsor Locks	CT	D	740 549-6000	4327
Barrday Corporation	Millbury	MA	B	508 581-2100	10427
CA J&L Enterprises Inc	Avon	MA	E	781 963-6666	6146
Caraustar Industries Inc	Chicopee	MA	E	413 593-9700	8014
Globe Composite Solutions LLC	Stoughton	MA	D	781 871-3700	12210
Merrimac Spool and Reel Co Inc	Haverhill	MA	E	978 372-7777	9116
Ox Paper Tube and Core Inc	Holliston	MA	F	508 879-1141	9225
Replica Works Inc	Orange	MA	E	978 544-7000	11231
Lapoint Industries Inc (PA)	Auburn	ME	D	207 777-3100	4439
Tex-Tech Industries Inc	North Monmouth	ME	E	336 992-7435	5115
Enviromart Green Inds Inc	Plaistow	NH	E	603 382-8481	15340
Environmental Container Svcs	Plaistow	NH	G	603 382-8481	15342
Hard Core Sprsl Tube Wnders In	Brentwood	NH	G	603 775-0230	14022
New England Paper Tube Co Inc	Pawtucket	RI	E	401 725-2610	16394
Signode Industrial Group LLC	Rumford	RI	D	401 438-5203	16676

	CITY	ST	EMP	PHONE	ENTRY#
The Real Reel Corporation	Rumford	RI	A	401 434-1070	16678
Weeden Street Associates LLC	Pawtucket	RI	E	401 725-2610	16430
Carris Reels Inc (HQ)	Proctor	VT	E	802 773-9111	17457
Precision Composites VT LLC	Lyndonville	VT	E	802 626-5900	17320

2656 Sanitary food containers

	CITY	ST	EMP	PHONE	ENTRY#
Wcm LLC	Providence	RI	E	401 273-0444	16644

2657 Folding paperboard boxes

	CITY	ST	EMP	PHONE	ENTRY#
Agi-Shorewood Group Us LLC	Stamford	CT	A	203 324-4839	3275
Curtis Corporation A Del Corp	Sandy Hook	CT	C	203 426-5861	2949
Curtis Packaging Corporation	Sandy Hook	CT	C	203 426-5861	2950
Fusion Paperboard US Inc	Versailles	CT	C	859 586-1100	3765
Hamden Packaging Inc	Hamden	CT	E	203 288-0200	1428
Keystone Paper & Box Co LLC (HQ)	South Windsor	CT	F	860 291-0027	3160
Mafcote Inc (PA)	Norwalk	CT	E	203 847-8500	2530
Rice Packaging Inc	Ellington	CT	D	860 870-7057	1113
Accutech Packaging Inc	Foxboro	MA	D	508 543-3800	8689
Bopkg Inc (HQ)	Fitchburg	MA	C	978 343-3067	8644
Fuller Box Co Inc (PA)	North Attleboro	MA	D	508 695-2525	10871
Gooby Industries Corp	Methuen	MA	C	978 689-0130	10332
Graphic Packaging Intl LLC	Lowell	MA	B	978 459-9328	9882
Northeast Buffinton Group LLC	Walpole	MA	F	401 434-1107	12571
Packaging Specialties Inc	Newburyport	MA	D	978 462-1300	10706
Pioneer Packaging Inc (PA)	Chicopee	MA	D	413 378-6930	8054
Rand-Whitney Group LLC (HQ)	Worcester	MA	C	508 791-2301	13778
Standard Box Co Inc	Chelsea	MA	F	617 884-4200	7993
Stephen Gould Corporation	Tewksbury	MA	E	978 851-2500	12420
UNI-Pac Inc	Holyoke	MA	D	413 534-5284	9284
Volk Packaging Corporation	Biddeford	ME	D	207 282-6151	4594
Graphic Packaging Intl LLC	Concord	NH	C	603 230-5100	14133
Graphic Packaging Intl LLC	Concord	NH	E	603 224-2333	14134
Campbell Enterprises Corp	Pawtucket	RI	E	401 753-7778	16352
Mm-Apvh Acquisition Co LLC	Pawtucket	RI	E	401 753-7778	16388
Numaco Packaging LLC	East Providence	RI	F	401 438-4952	16035

2671 Paper; coated and laminated packaging

	CITY	ST	EMP	PHONE	ENTRY#
Agi-Shorewood Group Us LLC	Stamford	CT	A	203 324-4839	3275
Amgraph	Lisbon	CT	G	860 822-2000	1554
Amgraph Packaging Inc (PA)	Baltic	CT	D	860 822-2000	37
Ansel Label and Packaging Corp	Trumbull	CT	E	203 452-0311	3711
Atlas Agi Holdings LLC	Greenwich	CT	A	203 622-9138	1315
Biomerics LLC	Monroe	CT	D	203 268-7238	1906
Bollore Inc	Dayville	CT	D	860 774-2930	859
CCL Label Inc	Shelton	CT	E	203 926-1253	2990
Flagship Converters Inc	Danbury	CT	D	203 792-0034	746
Fluted Partition Inc (PA)	Bridgeport	CT	C	203 368-2548	322
Fortis Solutions Group LLC	Ellington	CT	E	860 872-6311	1107
General Packaging Products Inc	Norwalk	CT	G	203 846-1340	2505
Identification Products Corp	Bridgeport	CT	D	203 334-5959	331
Identification Products Corp (PA)	Shelton	CT	E	203 334-5959	3019
Koster Keunen LLC (PA)	Watertown	CT	E	860 945-3333	4018
Mafcote Inc (PA)	Norwalk	CT	E	203 847-8500	2530
Northeast Laser Engraving Inc	Monroe	CT	E	203 268-7238	1918
Packaging and Crating Tech LLC	Watertown	CT	E	203 759-1799	4021
Packedge Inc	Westport	CT	E	203 288-0200	4192
Penmar Industries Inc	Stratford	CT	F	203 853-4868	3565
Polymer Films Inc	West Haven	CT	E	203 932-3000	4119
Polymeric Converting LLC	Enfield	CT	E	860 623-1335	1142
Quality Name Plate Inc	East Glastonbury	CT	D	860 633-9495	923
Rol-Vac Limited Partnership	Dayville	CT	F	860 928-9929	868
Sealed Air Corporation	Danbury	CT	C	203 791-3597	814
Sonoco Prtective Solutions Inc	Putnam	CT	D	860 928-7795	2875
Windham Container Corporation	Putnam	CT	F	860 928-7934	2879
Bopkg Inc (HQ)	Fitchburg	MA	C	978 343-3067	8644
CCL Label Inc (HQ)	Framingham	MA	D	508 872-4511	8750
Cheer Pack North America LLC	West Bridgewater	MA	F	508 927-7800	12968
Comprehensive Identification Products Inc	Burlington	MA	C		7354
781 229-8780					
Coveris Advnced Ctngs Mtthews (DH)	West Springfield	MA	E	413 539-5547	13019
E V Yeuell Inc	Woburn	MA	E	781 933-2940	13560
Fortifiber LLC	Attleboro	MA	E	508 222-3500	6018
GP&c Operations LLC (PA)	Gardner	MA	E	978 630-1028	8889
GPA Global US Holding Inc	Mansfield	MA	F	800 334-1113	10053
Gta-Nht Inc (HQ)	Rockland	MA	C	781 331-5900	11647
Halmark Systems LLC	Stoughton	MA	E	781 630-0123	12212
Healthy Life Snack Inc	Canton	MA	F	781 575-6744	7795
Ideal Tape Co Inc	Lowell	MA	D	978 458-6833	9885
Industrial Lbling Systems Corp	Tyngsboro	MA	E	978 649-7004	12460
Industrial Packaging Sup Inc	Worcester	MA	F	978 514-9960	13741
Industrial Packaging Supply Inc (PA)	Webster	MA	F	508 499-1600	12927
K & K Thermoforming Inc	Southbridge	MA	E	508 764-7700	12024
Millstone Med Outsourcing LLC (PA)	Fall River	MA	C	508 679-8384	8583

	CITY	ST	EMP	PHONE	ENTRY#
Novacel Inc **(DH)**	Palmer	MA	E	413 283-3468	11279
OK Durable Packaging Inc	Marlborough	MA	F	508 303-8067	10189
Opsec Security Inc	Boston	MA	G	617 226-3000	6941
Ovtene Inc	Marion	MA	E	617 852-4828	10099
Pacific Packaging Products Inc **(PA)**	Wilmington	MA	C	978 657-9100	13445
Package Printing Company Inc	West Springfield	MA	E	413 736-2748	13040
Packaging Devices Inc **(PA)**	Teaticket	MA	F	508 548-0224	12379
Pioneer Packaging Inc **(PA)**	Chicopee	MA	D	413 378-6930	8054
Prolamina Corporation **(DH)**	Westfield	MA	F	413 562-2315	13202
Sealed Air Corporation	Holyoke	MA	C	413 534-0231	9280
Stickamayka Packaging Inc	Andover	MA	E	978 474-1930	5926
Vangy Tool Company Inc	Worcester	MA	G	508 754-2669	13820
Walter Drake Incorporated **(PA)**	Holyoke	MA	F	413 536-5463	9290
Web Industries Inc **(PA)**	Marlborough	MA	G	508 898-2988	10234
Westrock Mwv LLC	Springfield	MA	D	413 736-7211	12152
Huhtamaki Inc	Lewiston	ME	E	207 795-6000	4964
Kullson Engineered Tech Inc	Lewiston	ME	E	207 576-9808	4969
Pure-Stat Technologies Inc	Lewiston	ME	E	207 795-6000	4987
Transcendia Inc	Lewiston	ME	E	207 786-4790	4994
Verso Paper Holding LLC	Jay	ME	A	207 897-3431	4917
Intercept Medical LLC	Portsmouth	NH	E	800 622-1114	15410
J-Pac LLC **(HQ)**	Somersworth	NH	D	603 692-9955	15617
Label Tech LLC	Somersworth	NH	C	603 692-2005	15618
Nefab Packaging North East LLC **(PA)**	Dover	NH	D	603 343-5750	14238
Pak 2000 Inc	Lancaster	NH	F	603 569-3700	14678
Roymal Inc	Newport	NH	E	603 863-2410	15237
Admiral Packaging Inc	Providence	RI	D	401 274-5588	16464
Amring Worldwide Inc	Johnston	RI	D	401 943-5040	16075
Contempo Card Co Inc **(PA)**	Providence	RI	D	401 272-4210	16505
Jewel Case Corporation	Providence	RI	B	401 943-1400	16549
Mason Box Company	Pawtucket	RI	E	800 842-9526	16383
Morris Transparent Box Co	East Providence	RI	F	401 438-6116	16032
Nelipak Corporation **(PA)**	Cranston	RI	E	401 946-2699	15899
S G Inc	Pascoag	RI	E	401 568-1110	16340
Tex Flock Inc	Woonsocket	RI	E	401 765-2340	16981
Wintech Intl Corp - Nk	Warwick	RI	F	401 383-3307	16880

2672 Paper; coated and laminated, nec

	CITY	ST	EMP	PHONE	ENTRY#
Beiersdorf North America Inc **(DH)**	Stamford	CT	F	203 563-5800	3292
Copy Cats Inc	New London	CT	F	860 442-8424	2225
Design Label Manufacturing Inc	Old Lyme	CT	E	860 739-6266	2640
H-O Products Corporation	Winsted	CT	E	860 379-9875	4346
Illinois Tool Works Inc	Manchester	CT	C	860 646-8153	1605
Markal Finishing Co Inc	Bridgeport	CT	E	203 384-8219	346
Scapa Holdings Inc **(DH)**	Windsor	CT	D	860 688-8000	4298
Securemark Decal Corp	Trumbull	CT	D	203 333-5503	3732
Specialty Printing LLC **(PA)**	Windsor	CT	D	860 623-8870	4300
The E J Davis Company	North Haven	CT	E	203 239-5391	2439
The Gilman Brothers Company	Gilman	CT	D	860 889-8444	1268
Accucon Incorporated	Leominster	MA	G	978 840-0337	9631
American Biltrite Inc **(PA)**	Wellesley	MA	G	781 237-6655	12935
Arclin Surfaces - E Longmeadow	East Longmeadow	MA	F	678 781-5341	8370
Asp Fibermark Holdings LLC	West Springfield	MA	A	413 736-4554	13014
Avery Dennison Corporation	Fitchburg	MA	C	978 353-2100	8643
Chartpak Inc **(HQ)**	Leeds	MA	D	413 584-5446	9621
Chesterfield Products Inc	Chesterfield	MA	E	413 296-0066	7997
Fortifiber LLC	Attleboro	MA	E	508 222-3500	6018
Gta-Nht Inc **(HQ)**	Rockland	MA	C	781 331-5900	11647
Halmark Systems LLC	Stoughton	MA	E	781 630-0123	12212
Hazen Paper Company **(PA)**	Holyoke	MA	C	413 538-8204	9259
Ideal Tape Co Inc	Lowell	MA	D	978 458-6833	9885
Industrial Lbling Systems Corp	Tyngsboro	MA	E	978 649-7004	12460
Jaybird & Mais Inc	Lawrence	MA	E	978 686-8659	9571
Lion Labels Inc	South Easton	MA	E	508 230-8211	11947
Neptco Incorporated **(DH)**	Westwood	MA	D	401 722-5500	13316
New England Ultimate Finishing	Holyoke	MA	E	413 532-7777	9270
Nissha Mtllizing Solutions Ltd	Franklin	MA	D	508 541-7700	8856
Pacon Corporation	Framingham	MA	E	508 370-0780	8796
Paiva Corp	Fall River	MA	G	508 679-7921	8593
Pg Technologies Inc	Westfield	MA	G	413 562-1354	13198
Regal Press Incorporated **(PA)**	Norwood	MA	C	781 769-3900	11206
Shawsheen Rubber Co Inc	Andover	MA	D	978 470-1760	5918
Suddekor LLC **(DH)**	Agawam	MA	E	413 821-9000	5808
Suddekor LLC	East Longmeadow	MA	E	413 525-4070	8397
Tekni-Plex Inc	Ashland	MA	E	508 881-2440	5569
Visual Magnetics Ltd	Mendon	MA	E	508 381-2400	10323
Sappi North America Inc	Skowhegan	ME	A	207 238-3000	5478
Sappi North America Inc	South Portland	ME	D	207 854-7000	5513
Sappi North America Inc	Westbrook	ME	C	207 856-4911	5647
Verso Paper Holding LLC	Jay	ME	A	207 897-3431	4917
Avery Dennison Corporation	Belmont	NH	E	603 217-4144	13959
Electronic Imaging Mtls Inc	Keene	NH	E	603 357-1459	14597
Gardoc Inc **(DH)**	Milford	NH	G	603 673-6400	15022

	CITY	ST	EMP	PHONE	ENTRY#
Label Tech LLC	Somersworth	NH	C	603 692-2005	15618
Nashua Corporation	Merrimack	NH	A	603 880-1100	14994
Polyonics Inc	Westmoreland	NH	E	603 352-1415	15698
Cjf Group Ltd	Providence	RI	D	401 421-2000	16500
Dewal Industries LLC	Narragansett	RI	C	401 789-9736	16189
Ecological Fibers Inc	Pawtucket	RI	D	401 725-9700	16366
Providence Label & Tag Co	Providence	RI	F	401 751-6677	16591
Trans-Tex LLC	Cranston	RI	E	401 331-8483	15920

2673 Bags: plastic, laminated, and coated

	CITY	ST	EMP	PHONE	ENTRY#
Amgraph Packaging Inc **(PA)**	Baltic	CT	D	860 822-2000	37
Fortune Plastics Inc	Old Saybrook	CT	B	800 243-0306	2648
Ace-Lon Corporation	Malden	MA	E	781 322-7121	10000
Armin Innovative Products Inc	Dighton	MA	E	508 822-4629	8291
Convanta Holliston	Holliston	MA	E	508 429-9750	9205
Eastern Packaging Inc	Lawrence	MA	D	978 685-7723	9559
Inteplast Engineered Films Inc	Westborough	MA	D	508 366-8884	13110
Jannel Manufacturing Inc	Holbrook	MA	E	781 767-0666	9176
Laddawn Inc **(HQ)**	Devens	MA	A	800 446-3639	8274
Northeast Packaging Co **(PA)**	Presque Isle	ME	E	207 764-6271	5305
Pak 2000 Inc	Lancaster	NH	F	603 569-3700	14678
Tufpak Inc	Ossipee	NH	E	603 539-4126	15285
Admiral Packaging Inc	Providence	RI	D	401 274-5588	16464
Liftbag Usa Inc	North Kingstown	RI	F	401 884-8801	16267
Subsalve USA LLC	North Kingstown	RI	F	401 884-8801	16282
Monument Industries Inc	Bennington	VT	E	802 442-8187	17052

2674 Bags: uncoated paper and multiwall

	CITY	ST	EMP	PHONE	ENTRY#
Duro Hilex Poly LLC	Meriden	CT	D	203 639-7070	1665
Hudson Paper Company **(PA)**	Stratford	CT	E	203 378-8759	3548
Mettler Packaging LLC	Southington	CT	G	860 628-6193	3222
Accurate Services Inc	Fall River	MA	D	508 674-5773	8518
Accutech Packaging Inc	Foxboro	MA	D	508 543-3800	8689
Maine Potato Growers Inc	Caribou	ME	F	207 764-3131	4676
Northeast Packaging Co **(PA)**	Presque Isle	ME	E	207 764-6271	5305
Sappi North America Inc	Skowhegan	ME	A	207 238-3000	5478
Sappi North America Inc	South Portland	ME	D	207 854-7000	5513
Sappi North America Inc	Westbrook	ME	C	207 856-4911	5647
Pak 2000 Inc	Lancaster	NH	F	603 569-3700	14678
Mason Box Company	Pawtucket	RI	E	800 842-9526	16383

2675 Die-cut paper and board

	CITY	ST	EMP	PHONE	ENTRY#
C & T Print Finishing Inc	South Windsor	CT	F	860 282-0616	3123
Hamden Packaging Inc	Hamden	CT	E	203 288-0200	1428
Liftline Capital LLC	Old Saybrook	CT	F	860 395-0150	2654
Martin Printing Inc	North Haven	CT	E	203 239-7991	2423
Walker Products Incorporated	Glastonbury	CT	F	860 659-3781	1301
Ames Safety Envelope Company **(DH)**	Somerville	MA	F	617 684-1000	11860
Fuller Box Co Inc **(PA)**	North Attleboro	MA	D	508 695-2525	10871
H Loeb Corporation	New Bedford	MA	E	508 996-3745	10597
J L Enterprises Inc	Canton	MA	G	781 821-6300	7802
Merrimac Spool and Reel Co Inc	Haverhill	MA	E	978 372-7777	9116
Neci LLC	Canton	MA	E	781 828-4883	7810
New England Ultimate Finishing	Holyoke	MA	E	413 532-7777	9270
United Paper Stock Co Inc	Worcester	MA	E	401 724-5700	13816
University Products Inc **(PA)**	Holyoke	MA	D	413 532-3372	9287
Winthrop Printing Company Inc	Foxboro	MA	F	617 268-9660	8732
Yankee Printing Group Inc	South Hadley	MA	E	413 532-9513	11968
Tissue Plus LLC	Bangor	ME	F	978 524-0550	4516
Cdc Enterprises Llc	Windham	NH	G	603 437-3090	15722
Fife Packaging LLC	Penacook	NH	E	603 753-2669	15310
American Ring Co Inc **(PA)**	East Providence	RI	F	401 438-9060	16003
Mono Die Cutting Co Inc	Riverside	RI	F	401 434-1274	16658
New England Paper Tube Co Inc	Pawtucket	RI	E	401 725-2610	16394
Mylan Technologies Inc **(HQ)**	Saint Albans	VT	C	802 527-7792	17525

2676 Sanitary paper products

	CITY	ST	EMP	PHONE	ENTRY#
Aci Industries Converting Ltd	Stamford	CT	F	740 368-4166	3271
Capricorn Investors II LP	Greenwich	CT	E	203 861-6600	1325
Cellu Tissue Corporation	East Hartford	CT	A	860 289-7496	979
Edgewell Per Care Brands LLC **(HQ)**	Shelton	CT	B	203 944-5500	3002
Edgewell Personal Care Company **(PA)**	Shelton	CT	E	203 944-5500	3003
Kimberly-Clark Corporation	New Milford	CT	D	860 210-1602	2250
Playtex Products LLC **(HQ)**	Shelton	CT	D	203 944-5500	3050
Soundview Paper Mills LLC **(DH)**	Greenwich	CT	F	201 796-4000	1352
American Disposables Inc	Hardwick	MA	F	413 967-6201	9059
Erving Industries Inc **(PA)**	Erving	MA	D	413 422-2700	8469
Essity North America Inc	Palmer	MA	B	413 289-1221	11274
Kimberly-Clark Corporation	Franklin	MA	A	508 520-1355	8849
Sales Solutions Inc	Scituate	MA	G	781 588-2703	11771
Sumner Printing Inc	Somersworth	NH	E	603 692-7424	15625
Seventh Generation Inc **(DH)**	Burlington	VT	C	802 658-3773	17159

SIC

2677 Envelopes

	CITY	ST	EMP	PHONE	ENTRY#
Cenveo Corporation	Stamford	CT	A	303 790-8023	3307
Cenveo Enterprises Inc (PA)	Stamford	CT	D	203 595-3000	3308
Cenveo Worldwide Limited (DH)	Stamford	CT	E	203 595-3000	3309
Cwl Enterprises Inc (HQ)	Stamford	CT	F	303 790-8023	3332
Accutech Packaging Inc	Foxboro	MA	D	508 543-3800	8689
American Prtg & Envelope Inc	Auburn	MA	E	508 832-6100	6102
B & W Press Inc	West Newbury	MA	E	978 352-6100	13007
Classic Envelope Inc	East Douglas	MA	D	508 731-6747	8349
Jannel Manufacturing Inc	Holbrook	MA	E	781 767-0666	9176
Opportunity Works Inc (PA)	Newburyport	MA	E	978 462-6144	10705
Sheppard Envelope Company Inc	Auburn	MA	E	508 791-5588	6125
Westrock Mwv LLC	Springfield	MA	D	413 736-7211	12152
Worcester Envelope Company	Auburn	MA	C	508 832-5394	6128
Fiberkraft Inc	Salem	NH	G	603 621-0090	15525
Tufpak Inc	Ossipee	NH	E	603 539-4126	15285
Fred F Waltz Co Inc	Cumberland	RI	G	401 769-4900	15940
The Leahy Press Inc	Montpelier	VT	E	802 223-2100	17375

2678 Stationery products

	CITY	ST	EMP	PHONE	ENTRY#
Connecticut Clean Room Corp	Bristol	CT	E	860 589-0049	430
Panagrafix Inc	West Haven	CT	E	203 691-5529	4118
Professional Mktg Svcs Inc	Stratford	CT	F	203 610-6222	3568
Avery Products Corporation	Holliston	MA	C	508 893-1000	9201
Bouncepad North America Inc	Charlestown	MA	G	617 804-0110	7864
ESP Solutions Inc	Taunton	MA	F	508 285-0017	12335
Eureka Lab Book Inc	Holyoke	MA	F	413 534-5671	9254
Great Northern Industries Inc (PA)	Boston	MA	C	617 262-4314	6771
LCI Paper Company	Hudson	MA	F	508 281-5088	9384
Marian Heath Greeting Cards LLC	Wareham	MA	C	508 291-0766	12840
Viabella Holdings LLC (PA)	Wareham	MA	E	800 688-9998	12848
Downeast Concepts Inc	Yarmouth	ME	E	207 846-3726	5703
William Arthur Inc	West Kennebunk	ME	D	413 684-2600	5611
Oatmeal Studios Inc	Rochester	VT	F	802 967-8014	17487

2679 Converted paper products, nec

	CITY	ST	EMP	PHONE	ENTRY#
Ampd Air Quality Services LLC	Hamden	CT	G	203 387-1709	1411
Biomerics LLC	Monroe	CT	D	203 268-7238	1906
Cenveo Enterprises Inc (PA)	Stamford	CT	D	203 595-3000	3308
Cenveo Worldwide Limited (DH)	Stamford	CT	E	203 595-3000	3309
Costa Packaging LLC	South Windsor	CT	F	860 282-2535	3133
Cwl Enterprises Inc (HQ)	Stamford	CT	F	303 790-8023	3332
Dietzgen Corporation	West Haven	CT	F	813 849-4334	4104
George Schmitt & Co Inc (PA)	Guilford	CT	E	203 453-4334	1394
Hamden Packaging Inc	Hamden	CT	E	203 288-0200	1428
Henlay Co	Cheshire	CT	G	908 795-1007	598
Mafcote Inc (PA)	Norwalk	CT	E	203 847-8500	2530
Mercantile Development Inc	Shelton	CT	E	203 922-8880	3030
Northeast Laser Engraving Inc	Monroe	CT	E	203 268-7238	1918
Park City Packaging Inc	Stratford	CT	E	203 378-7384	3564
Royal Consumer Products LLC (HQ)	Norwalk	CT	E	203 847-8500	2567
Schrafel Pprbd Converting Corp	West Haven	CT	E	203 931-1700	4124
Specialty Printing LLC (PA)	Windsor	CT	D	860 623-8870	4300
Surys Inc	Trumbull	CT	C	203 333-5503	3734
Tudor Converted Products Inc (PA)	Danbury	CT	F	203 304-1875	828
Valley Container Inc	Bridgeport	CT	E	203 368-6546	383
BBC Printing and Products Inc	Waltham	MA	G	781 647-4646	12602
Boyd Biomedical Inc (PA)	Lee	MA	E	413 243-2000	9612
Brewster Wallpaper LLC	Randolph	MA	D	800 366-1700	11552
Canson Inc	South Hadley	MA	D	413 538-9250	11959
D B S Industries Inc	Haverhill	MA	D	978 373-4748	9090
Dennecrepe Corporation	Gardner	MA	D	978 630-8669	8884
Dion Label Printing Inc	Westfield	MA	D	413 568-3713	13162
Expressive Design Group Inc	Holyoke	MA	E	413 315-6296	9255
First Mate Prtg Converting Inc (HQ)	Gardner	MA	D	978 630-1028	8886
Folia Materials Inc	Bedford	MA	G	315 559-2135	6227
GP&c Operations LLC	Gardner	MA	D	978 630-1028	8888
Marian Heath Greeting Cards LLC	Wareham	MA	C	508 291-0766	12840
Mbw Incorporated	Orange	MA	C	978 544-6462	11225
McLaughlin Paper Co Inc (PA)	West Springfield	MA	F	413 732-7485	13033
Neci LLC	Canton	MA	E	781 828-4883	7810
Northstar Pulp & Paper Co Inc	Springfield	MA	D	413 263-6000	12118
Sales Solutions Inc	Scituate	MA	G	781 588-2703	11771
Sappi NA Finance LLC	Boston	MA	G	617 423-5439	7024
Screenprint/Dow Inc	Wilmington	MA	D	978 657-7290	13451
Smyth Companies LLC	Wilmington	MA	E	800 776-1201	13453
Universal Tag Inc	Dudley	MA	E	508 949-2411	8326
W G Fry Corp	Florence	MA	E	413 747-2551	8687
Westrock - Southern Cont LLC	Boston	MA	E	978 772-5050	7120
Sappi North America Inc	Skowhegan	ME	A	207 238-3000	5478
Sappi North America Inc	South Portland	ME	D	207 854-7000	5513
Sappi North America Inc	Westbrook	ME	C	207 856-4911	5647

	CITY	ST	EMP	PHONE	ENTRY#
Computype Inc	Concord	NH	G	603 225-5500	14122
Len-Tex Corp	North Walpole	NH	C	603 445-2342	15260
Nashua Corporation	Merrimack	NH	A	603 880-1100	14994
Absorbent Specialty Pdts LLC	Pawtucket	RI	F	401 722-1177	16342
Alliance Paper Company Inc	Pawtucket	RI	F	401 722-0295	16345
Arkwright Advanced Coating Inc (HQ)	Fiskeville	RI	C	401 821-1000	16053
Cjf Group Ltd	Providence	RI	D	401 421-2000	16500
Dasko Identification Products	Warren	RI	F	401 435-6500	16757
Judd Paper Company	Rumford	RI	F	413 534-5661	16673
Image Tek Mfg Inc	Springfield	VT	E	802 885-6208	17618

27 PRINTING, PUBLISHING AND ALLIED INDUSTRIES

2711 Newspapers

	CITY	ST	EMP	PHONE	ENTRY#
21st Century Fox America Inc	Wilton	CT	G	203 563-6600	4228
Advisor	North Haven	CT	G	203 239-4121	2388
American-Republican Inc (PA)	Waterbury	CT	C	203 574-3636	3884
Bargain News Free Clssfied Adv	Stratford	CT	F	203 377-3000	3518
Bristol Press	Torrington	CT	D	860 584-0501	3673
C S M S-I P A	North Haven	CT	G	203 562-7228	2397
Capital Cities Communications	New Haven	CT	G	203 784-8800	2133
Central Conn Cmmunications LLC	New Britain	CT	D	860 225-4601	2010
Chase Media Group	Newtown	CT	F	914 962-3871	2337
Chronicle Printing Company	Willimantic	CT	E	860 423-8466	4217
Comms At Mill River	Hamden	CT	G	203 287-0082	1418
Day Publishing Company (HQ)	New London	CT	B	860 701-4200	2226
Gamut Publishing	Hartford	CT	G	860 296-6128	1482
Gatehouse Media LLC	Norwich	CT	D	860 886-0106	2606
Glastonbury Citizen Inc	Glastonbury	CT	F	860 633-4691	1231
Green Manor Corporation (PA)	Manchester	CT	B	860 643-8111	1599
Greenwich Sentinel	Greenwich	CT	G	203 883-1430	1333
Greenwich Time	Stamford	CT	G	203 253-2922	3359
Hampton Gazette Inc	Hampton	CT	G	860 455-0160	1465
Hartford Courant Company LLC	Avon	CT	G	860 678-1330	26
Hartford Courant Company LLC (DH)	Hartford	CT	A	860 241-6200	1486
Hersam Acorn Cmnty Pubg LLC (HQ)	Ridgefield	CT	G	203 438-6544	2898
Hersam Acorn Cmnty Pubg LLC	Trumbull	CT	F	203 261-2548	3722
Hersam Acorn Newspapers LLC (PA)	Ridgefield	CT	F	203 438-6000	2899
Hispanic Communications LLC	Stamford	CT	G	203 674-6793	3377
Journal Publishing Company Inc	Manchester	CT	A	860 646-0500	1608
Lakeville Journal Company LLC (PA)	Lakeville	CT	E	860 435-9873	1547
Life Publications	West Hartford	CT	F	860 953-0444	4069
Medianews Group Inc	Norwalk	CT	F	203 333-0161	2535
Middlbury Bee-Intelligencer-Ct	Middlebury	CT	G	203 577-6800	1717
Minuteman Newspaper (PA)	Westport	CT	E	203 226-8877	4185
My Citizens News	Waterbury	CT	F	203 729-2228	3947
New Canaan News	Norwalk	CT	G	203 842-2582	2544
New Canaan Sports LLC	New Canaan	CT	G	866 629-2453	2084
New Haven Register LLC	New Haven	CT	A	203 789-5200	2179
News 12 Connecticut LLC	Norwalk	CT	E	203 849-1321	2545
Newspaper Space Buyers LLC	Stamford	CT	G	203 967-6452	3417
NRG Connecticut LLC	Hartford	CT	F	860 231-2424	1497
Printed Communications	South Windsor	CT	G	860 436-9619	3175
Record-Journal Newspaper (PA)	Meriden	CT	C	203 235-1661	1692
Register Citizen Publishing	Torrington	CT	C	860 489-3121	3693
Reminder Broadcaster	Glastonbury	CT	F	860 875-3366	1297
Rmi Inc	Vernon Rockville	CT	C	860 875-3366	3761
Second Wind Media Limited	New Haven	CT	F	203 781-3480	2197
Shore Publishing LLC	Madison	CT	E	203 245-1877	1570
Southern Conn Newspapers Inc	Stamford	CT	B	203 964-2200	3466
Thats Great News LLC	Wallingford	CT	E	203 649-4900	3860
The Bee Publishing Company (PA)	Newtown	CT	E	203 426-8036	2351
Thomson Reuters Risk MGT Inc	Stamford	CT	F	203 539-8000	3482
Thomson Reuters US LLC (DH)	Stamford	CT	D	203 539-8000	3483
Times Community News Group	New London	CT	F	860 437-1150	2235
Tradewinds	Beacon Falls	CT	G	203 723-6966	46
True Publishing Company	Wallingford	CT	F	203 272-5316	3870
Valley Publishing Company Inc	Derby	CT	F	203 735-6696	893
Westport Summit 7 LLC	Westport	CT	G	917 370-2244	4201
Wicks Business Information LLC (PA)	Shelton	CT	F	203 334-2002	3078
Yale University	New Haven	CT	A	203 432-2880	2221
Alberto Vasallo Jr	Boston	MA	G	617 522-5060	6530
Amherst College Public Affairs	Amherst	MA	F	413 542-2321	5857
Andover Publishing Company	North Andover	MA	F	978 475-7000	10819
Asian American Civic Assn Inc (PA)	Boston	MA	E	617 426-9492	6560
Bagdon Advertising Inc	Westborough	MA	E	508 366-5500	13080
Baikar Association Inc (PA)	Watertown	MA	F	617 924-4420	12862
Beaver Dam Partners Inc	Wareham	MA	G	508 717-9799	12828
Beverly Citizen	Beverly	MA	G	978 927-2777	6332
Bh Media Inc (HQ)	Lowell	MA	C	617 426-3000	9862
Boston Business Journal Inc	Boston	MA	B	617 330-1000	6605
Boston Globe LLC	Boston	MA	A	617 929-2684	6608

	CITY	ST	EMP	PHONE	ENTRY#		CITY	ST	EMP	PHONE	ENTRY#
Boston Globe Mdia Partners LLC	Boston	MA	B	617 929-2000	6609	New England Newsppr Press Assn	Woburn	MA	F	781 281-2053	13622
Boston Irish Reporter	Dorchester	MA	F	617 436-1222	8297	Newhomesale LLC	Franklin	MA	F	508 541-8900	8854
Boston Korean	Allston	MA	G	617 254-4654	5820	North Shore Jewish Press Ltd	Salem	MA	F	978 745-4111	11727
Boston Legion LLC	Boston	MA	F	508 718-8912	6610	North Shore News Company Inc (PA)	Peabody	MA	E	781 592-1300	11328
Boston Neighborhood News Inc	Boston	MA	G	617 436-1222	6611	Nrt Inc	Medway	MA	F	508 533-4588	10309
Bostoncom LLC	Boston	MA	G	617 929-8593	6620	On The Beat Inc	Cambridge	MA	F	617 491-8878	7674
Bulletin Newspapers Inc (PA)	Hyde Park	MA	F	617 361-8400	9458	Ottaway Newspapers	Hyannis	MA	E	508 775-1200	9443
Bulletin Newspapers Inc	Norwood	MA	F	617 361-8400	11166	Portuguese Times Inc	New Bedford	MA	G	508 997-3118	10641
Business West	Springfield	MA	G	413 781-8600	12081	Provincetown Banner Inc	Provincetown	MA	F	508 487-7400	11496
Canton Citizen Inc	Canton	MA	G	781 821-4418	7776	Quincy Sun Publishing Co Inc	Quincy	MA	F	617 471-3100	11535
Caribe Cmmnctons Pblctions Inc	Boston	MA	E	617 522-5060	6638	Reading Diagnostic Center	Reading	MA	F	781 942-9876	11605
Carriage Towne News	North Andover	MA	G	603 642-4499	10822	Reminder Publications	East Longmeadow	MA	E	413 525-3947	8393
Christian Science Pubg Soc (PA)	Boston	MA	B	617 450-2000	6655	Republican Company (HQ)	Springfield	MA	A	413 788-1000	12125
Cohasset Redemption Inc	Cohasset	MA	G	781 383-3100	8094	Revere Independent	Revere	MA	F	781 485-0588	11623
Colonial Times Publishing	Lexington	MA	F	781 274-9997	9730	Salem News Archives	Beverly	MA	G	978 922-8303	6381
Community Newspaper Inc	Marblehead	MA	F	781 639-4800	10085	South Boston Today	Boston	MA	G	617 268-4032	7048
Creative Publishing Corp Amer (PA)	Peabody	MA	E	978 532-5880	11303	Stonebridge Press Inc (PA)	Southbridge	MA	E	508 764-4325	12035
Daily Hampshire Gazette	Easthampton	MA	G	413 527-4000	8442	Streetwise Media Inc	Boston	MA	C	857 265-3269	7063
Daily Woburn Times Inc	Wilmington	MA	G	978 658-2346	13402	Taunton	Taunton	MA	G	774 501-2220	12370
Danvers Herald	Danvers	MA	G	978 774-0505	8178	Terika Smith Ministries Corp	Lawrence	MA	G	978 233-0576	9603
Dig Publishing LLC	Boston	MA	F	617 426-8942	6694	Town Common Inc	Rowley	MA	F	978 948-8696	11686
Digboston	Boston	MA	F	617 426-8942	6695	Town Crier Publications Inc	Upton	MA	F	508 529-7791	12475
Dinner Daily LLC	Westford	MA	F	978 392-5887	13234	Trustees of Tufts College	Medford	MA	G	617 628-5000	10300
Dispatch News	Lowell	MA	F	978 458-7100	9876	Turley Publications Inc (PA)	Palmer	MA	C	800 824-6548	11286
Doncar Inc	Concord	MA	F	978 371-2442	8115	United Communications Corp	Attleboro	MA	C	508 222-7000	6071
Dow Jones & Company Inc	Chicopee	MA	E	212 416-3858	8026	Valley Advocate	Northampton	MA	G	413 584-0003	11084
Dow Jones & Company Inc	Chicopee	MA	D	413 598-4000	8027	Vineyard Gazette LLC (PA)	Edgartown	MA	E	508 627-4311	8468
Driggin Sandra DBA Extra Extra	Quincy	MA	F	617 773-6996	11512	Vocero Hispano Newspaper Inc	Southbridge	MA	F	866 846-6397	12038
Duxbury Clipper Inc	Duxbury	MA	E	781 934-2811	8330	Wakefield Item Company	Wakefield	MA	E	781 245-0080	12542
Eagle-Tribune Publishing Co	Gloucester	MA	F	978 282-0077	8933	Wall Street Journal	Chicopee	MA	E	800 369-5663	8069
Eagle-Tribune Publishing Co	Haverhill	MA	F	978 374-0321	9093	Walpole Times Inc	Framingham	MA	F	508 668-0243	8810
Eagle-Tribune Publishing Co	North Andover	MA	F	978 946-2000	10827	West Springfield Record Inc	West Springfield	MA	G	413 736-1587	13052
Eagle-Tribune Publishing Co (DH)	North Andover	MA	C	978 946-2000	10828	Westfield News Publishing Inc (DH)	Westfield	MA	E	413 562-4181	13221
East Coast Publications (PA)	Norwell	MA	F	781 878-4540	11141	Woburn Daily Times Inc	Woburn	MA	D	781 933-3700	13689
Eastern Mddlsex Press Pblctions (PA)	Malden	MA	F	781 321-8000	10012	Worcester Telegram Gazette Inc (HQ)	Worcester	MA	B	508 793-9100	13831
Enterprise Newsmedia LLC	Norwood	MA	B	781 769-5535	11172	Worcester Tlegram Gazette Corp	Leominster	MA	F	978 840-0071	9717
Enterprise Publications (PA)	Falmouth	MA	E	508 548-4700	8630	Worcester Tlegram Gazette Corp	Worcester	MA	F	978 368-0176	13832
Fig City News Inc	Auburndale	MA	G	617 610-1093	6133	Yankee Shopper	Webster	MA	F	508 943-8784	12931
Gatehouse Media LLC	Fall River	MA	F	508 676-8211	8551	Bald Hill Reach Inc	Ellsworth	ME	D	207 667-2576	4754
Gatehouse Media LLC	Holden	MA	F	508 829-5981	9189	Bangor Publishing Company (PA)	Bangor	ME	C	207 990-8000	4493
Gatehouse Media LLC	Worcester	MA	F	508 829-5981	13728	Bangor Publishing Company	Ellsworth	ME	G	207 667-9393	4755
Gatehouse Media Mass I Inc (HQ)	Beverly	MA	A	585 598-0030	6350	Beacon Press Inc	Biddeford	ME	F	207 282-1535	4557
Gatehouse Media Mass I Inc	Concord	MA	G	978 667-2156	8118	Blethen Maine Newspapers Inc	Portland	ME	F	207 791-6650	5188
Gatehouse Media Mass I Inc	Framingham	MA	G	508 626-4412	8764	Bottle King Redemption Center	Newcastle	ME	G	207 563-1520	5092
Gatehouse Media Mass I Inc	Marlborough	MA	G	508 626-3859	10151	Bridgton News Corporation	Bridgton	ME	F	207 647-2851	4626
Gatehouse Media Mass I Inc	Milford	MA	F	508 634-7522	10403	Brunswick Publishing LLC	Brunswick	ME	F	207 729-3311	4643
Gatehouse Media Mass I Inc	Plymouth	MA	B	781 433-6917	11461	Central Maine Morning Sentinel	Waterville	ME	E	207 873-3341	5593
Gatehouse Media Mass I Inc	Randolph	MA	C	781 235-4000	11560	Citizen Printers Incorporated	Albany Twp	ME	G	207 824-2444	4400
H S Gere & Sons Inc	Hatfield	MA	E	413 247-5010	9071	Edge Media Group	Bangor	ME	F	207 942-2901	4498
Hairenik Association Inc	Watertown	MA	F	617 926-3974	12879	Fiddlehead Focus	Fort Kent	ME	G	207 316-2243	4787
Harvard Independent Inc	Cambridge	MA	E	617 495-3682	7601	Forecaster Publishing Inc	South Portland	ME	E	207 781-3661	5503
Harwich Oracle	Orleans	MA	F	508 247-3200	11238	Franklin Group	Farmington	ME	E	207 778-2075	4780
Holbrook Sun Inc	Randolph	MA	G	781 767-4000	11562	Free Press Inc	Rockland	ME	F	207 594-4408	5330
Hopkington Independent	Westborough	MA	G	508 435-5188	13106	Gorham Times Inc	Gorham	ME	G	207 839-8390	4821
Hopkinton Mews Sales Office	Hopkinton	MA	G	508 625-1267	9327	James Newspapers Inc (PA)	Norway	ME	E	207 743-7011	5116
Hyora Publications Inc	Chatham	MA	F	508 430-2700	7897	Lewiston Daily Sun (PA)	Lewiston	ME	C	207 784-3555	4973
Independant Newspaper Group	Revere	MA	F	508 485-0588	11619	Lincoln County Publishing Co	Newcastle	ME	E	207 563-3171	5093
Independent Newspaper Group	Revere	MA	F	781 485-0588	11620	Lincoln News	Lincoln	ME	G	207 794-6532	5010
Jewish Advocate Pubg Corp	Boston	MA	F	617 523-6232	6823	Maine Antique Digest Inc	Waldoboro	ME	F	207 832-7534	5578
Jewish Advocate Religious	Boston	MA	F	617 227-8200	6824	Maine Visual	Portland	ME	G	207 553-0798	5243
Jewish Journal	Salem	MA	F	978 745-4111	11724	Maine-OK Enterprises Inc	Boothbay Harbor	ME	F	207 633-4620	4602
Journal Register Company	Fall River	MA	F	508 678-3844	8562	Mainely Media	Biddeford	ME	E	207 282-4337	4576
Lawyers Weekly LLC (PA)	Boston	MA	D	617 451-7300	6853	Mainely Newspapers Inc	Biddeford	ME	E	207 282-4337	4577
Lee Tan Enterprise LLC	Lee	MA	G	413 243-4717	9615	Mount Desert Islander	Ellsworth	ME	E	207 288-0556	4759
Leominster Champion	Leominster	MA	F	978 534-6006	9677	Mtm Oldco Inc (PA)	Portland	ME	B	207 791-6650	5247
Local Media Group Inc	Hyannis	MA	B	508 775-1200	9440	Northeast Publishing Company	Caribou	ME	G	207 496-3251	4677
Local Media Group Inc	New Bedford	MA	C	508 997-7411	10614	Northeast Publishing Company	Dover Foxcroft	ME	G	207 564-8355	4730
Lowell Sun Publishing Company	Ayer	MA	C	978 433-6685	6185	Northeast Publishing Company	Houlton	ME	G	207 532-2281	4903
Lowell Sun Publishing Company	Devens	MA	C	978 772-0777	8276	Northeast Publishing Company	Presque Isle	ME	G	207 768-5431	5306
Lowell Sun Publishing Company (DH)	Lowell	MA	C	978 459-1300	9896	Northeast Publishing Company (HQ)	Presque Isle	ME	D	207 764-4471	5307
Lujean Printing Co Inc	Cotuit	MA	E	508 428-8700	8146	Northwoods Publications LLC	West Enfield	ME	F	207 732-4880	5610
Marthas Vineyard Times	Vineyard Haven	MA	F	508 693-6100	12492	Penobscot Bay Press (PA)	Stonington	ME	F	207 367-2200	5534
Martins News Shop	Boston	MA	G	617 267-1334	6869	RH Rosenfield Co	Sanford	ME	E	207 324-1798	5410
Massachusetts Institute Tech	Cambridge	MA	G	617 253-7183	7638	Rolling Thunder Press Inc	Newport	ME	G	207 368-2028	5098
Massachusetts Port Authority	Boston	MA	G	617 561-9300	6875	Seattle News Company	Augusta	ME	C	207 623-3811	4480
Mastv / El Planeta LLC	Boston	MA	F	617 379-0210	6878	Shoreline Publications	Wells	ME	F	207 646-8448	5605
Medianews Group Inc	Fitchburg	MA	E	978 343-6911	8663	Sunrise Guide LLC	Portland	ME	G	207 221-3450	5277
Mfm Enterprises Inc	Weymouth	MA	G	858 571-1358	13329	Turner Publishing Inc	Turner	ME	F	207 225-2076	5564
Middlesex News	Framingham	MA	G	508 626-3800	8790	Twin City Times	Auburn	ME	G	207 795-5017	4462
Mv Times Corporation	Vineyard Haven	MA	F	508 693-6100	12493	York County Coast Star Inc	Kennebunk	ME	G	207 985-5901	4931
Ne Media Group Inc (PA)	Boston	MA	D	617 929-2000	6906	Caledonian Record Pubg Co Inc	Littleton	NH	G	603 444-7141	14715
Nenpa	Woburn	MA	G	781 281-2053	13620	Concord Monitor	Concord	NH	G	603 224-5301	14124
New England Newspapers Inc (DH)	Pittsfield	MA	C	413 447-7311	11414	Concordian LLC	Concord	NH	G	603 225-5660	14126

SIC

	CITY	ST	EMP	PHONE	ENTRY#
Constrction Smmary New Hmpshr/	Manchester	NH	G	603 627-8856	14835
Country News Club Inc	North Conway	NH	E	603 356-2999	15247
Dartmouth Inc	Hanover	NH	D	603 646-2600	14421
Eagle Publications Inc	Claremont	NH	E	603 543-3100	14089
Eagle-Tribune Publishing Co	Derry	NH	F	603 437-7000	14192
Fosters Daily Democrat	Rochester	NH	F	603 332-2200	15476
Fosters Daily Dmcrat Fstrs Sun	Portsmouth	NH	F	603 431-4888	15390
Franklin Exeter Inc	Portsmouth	NH	F	603 836-8590	15391
Hanover Review Inc	Hanover	NH	F	603 643-4370	14424
Hippopress LLC (PA)	Manchester	NH	E	603 625-1855	14859
Independent Rowing News Inc	Hanover	NH	G	603 448-5090	14428
Jordan Associates	Pittsburg	NH	F	603 246-8998	15328
Keene Publishing Corporation	Keene	NH	D	603 352-1234	14606
Local Media Group Inc	Portsmouth	NH	A	603 436-1800	15418
McLean Communications LLC	Manchester	NH	D	603 624-1442	14882
Mount Washington Vly Mtn Ear	Lancaster	NH	G	603 447-6336	14677
New Hampshire Gateway Mdsg	Manchester	NH	G	603 216-7373	14899
New Hampshirecom	Manchester	NH	G	603 314-0447	14900
News & Sentinel Inc	Colebrook	NH	F	603 237-5501	14107
Newspapers New Hampshire Inc (HQ)	Concord	NH	C	603 224-5301	14149
Newspapers New Hampshire Inc	Peterborough	NH	D	603 924-7172	15321
Panoramic Publishing Group LLC	Wolfeboro Falls	NH	F	603 569-5257	15736
Peterborough Transcript	Peterborough	NH	F	603 924-3333	15326
Salmon Press LLC (PA)	Meredith	NH	F	603 279-4516	14970
Shakour Publishers Inc	Keene	NH	F	603 352-5250	14618
State Military Reservation	Concord	NH	G	603 225-1230	14159
Tolles Communications Corp	Manchester	NH	G	603 627-9500	14945
Union Leader Corporation (PA)	Manchester	NH	B	603 668-4321	14947
Beacon Communications Inc	Warwick	RI	E	401 732-3100	16789
Boston Phoenix Inc (PA)	Providence	RI	D	617 536-5390	16489
Breeze Publications Inc	Lincoln	RI	E	401 334-9555	16122
Island News Enterprise	Jamestown	RI	F	401 423-3200	16070
Kent County Daily Times	West Warwick	RI	F	401 789-9744	16911
Lmg Rhode Island Holdings Inc (HQ)	Providence	RI	F	585 598-0030	16553
New England Newspapers Inc	Pawtucket	RI	F	401 722-4000	16392
Phoenix-Times Publishing Co	Bristol	RI	D	401 253-6000	15777
Providence Business News	Providence	RI	E	401 273-2201	16589
Providence Journal Company	Providence	RI	B	401 277-7000	16590
Rhode Island Newsppr Group Inc	Warwick	RI	E	401 732-3100	16850
South County Newspaper Inc	Wakefield	RI	F	401 789-6000	16743
Southern RI Newspapers (HQ)	Wakefield	RI	E	401 789-9744	16744
Visitor Printing Company	Providence	RI	F	401 272-1010	16641
Whitegate International Corp	Providence	RI	G	401 274-2149	16647
Addison Press Inc	Middlebury	VT	E	802 388-4944	17335
Bennington Shriff GLC Slar LLC	Bennington	VT	G	802 233-3370	17037
Caledonian Record Pubg Co Inc (PA)	Saint Johnsbury	VT	D	802 748-8121	17540
Chronicle Inc	Barton	VT	F	802 525-3531	17027
City Boy Logs LLC	Waitsfield	VT	G	802 496-4372	17665
Cohasa Publishing Inc	Bradford	VT	G	802 222-5281	17061
County Courier Inc	Enosburg Falls	VT	G	802 933-4375	17222
Creative Marketing Services	Rutland	VT	F	802 775-9500	17493
Cutter & Locke Inc (PA)	Tunbridge	VT	G	802 889-3500	17652
Da Capo Publishing Inc	Burlington	VT	E	802 864-5684	17130
Daily Gardener	Calais	VT	G	802 223-7851	17167
Eastview Associates Inc	Rutland	VT	G	802 773-4040	17495
Gannett River States Pubg Corp	Fairfax	VT	E	802 893-4214	17258
Hardwick Gazette Print Shop	Hardwick	VT	F	802 472-6521	17284
Herald of Randolph	Randolph	VT	F	802 728-3232	17469
Hersam Acorn Newspapers LLC	Manchester Center	VT	G	802 362-3535	17329
Hinesburg Record Inc	Hinesburg	VT	F	802 482-2350	17293
Journal Opinion Inc	Bradford	VT	E	802 222-5281	17063
McClure Newspapers Inc	Williston	VT	C	802 863-3441	17740
Neutral Zone LLC	West Rutland	VT	F	802 989-3133	17696
New England Newspapers Inc	Brattleboro	VT	F	802 254-2311	17097
North Eastern Publishing Co	Bennington	VT	D	802 447-7567	17053
ORourke Media Group LLC (PA)	Saint Albans	VT	F	802 524-9771	17527
Other Paper	South Burlington	VT	G	802 864-6670	17588
Outer Limits Publishing LLC	Killington	VT	F	802 422-2399	17313
Ta Update Inc (PA)	Barre	VT	D	802 479-4040	17020
Valley Reporter Incorporated	Waitsfield	VT	G	802 496-3607	17667
Vermont Media Corp	Wilmington	VT	E	802 464-5557	17756
Vermont Publishing Comany	Saint Albans	VT	F	802 524-9771	17536
Vermont Standard Inc	Woodstock	VT	F	802 457-1313	17779
Williston Pubg Promotions LLC	Williston	VT	F	802 872-9000	17753
Wind Ridge Publishing	Shelburne	VT	E	802 985-3091	17565
World Publications Inc	Barre	VT	F	802 479-2582	17026
Young Writers Project Inc	Burlington	VT	F	802 324-9537	17165

2721 Periodicals

	CITY	ST	EMP	PHONE	ENTRY#
A Guideposts Church Corp (PA)	Danbury	CT	C	203 749-0203	699
Air Age Inc	Wilton	CT	E	203 431-9000	4229
American Library Association	Middletown	CT	F	860 347-6933	1735
Asset International Inc	Greenwich	CT	E	203 629-5014	1314

	CITY	ST	EMP	PHONE	ENTRY#
Bargain News Free Clssfied Adv	Stratford	CT	F	203 377-3000	3518
Belvoir Publications Inc (PA)	Norwalk	CT	E	203 857-3100	2470
Bff Holdings Inc (HQ)	Old Saybrook	CT	C	860 510-0100	2645
Business Journals Inc	Norwalk	CT	D	203 853-6015	2478
Chief Executive Group LLC (PA)	Stamford	CT	E	785 832-0303	3310
Chief Executive Group LP (PA)	Stamford	CT	G	203 930-2700	3311
Comicana Inc	Stamford	CT	G	203 968-0748	3318
Connecticut Forest Pk Assn Inc	Rockfall	CT	F	860 346-2372	2913
Connecticut Parent Magazine	Madison	CT	F	203 483-1700	1561
DCA Business Media LLC	Westport	CT	F	203 227-1699	4164
Domino Media Group Inc	Westport	CT	F	877 223-7844	4165
Dulce Domum LLC	Norwalk	CT	E	203 227-1400	2493
Fairfield County Look LLC	Greenwich	CT	G	203 869-0077	1329
Financial Accnting Foundation (PA)	Norwalk	CT	C	203 847-0700	2500
Gamut Publishing	Hartford	CT	G	860 296-6128	1482
Gracenote Media Services LLC	Wilton	CT	F	518 223-1993	4240
Granta USA Ltd	Danbury	CT	F	440 207-6051	753
Ibnr LLC	Farmington	CT	F	860 676-8600	1222
Informa Business Media Inc	Stamford	CT	C	203 358-9900	3383
Informa Tech Holdings LLC	Darien	CT	F	203 662-6501	849
International Mktg Strategies	Stamford	CT	F	203 406-0106	3384
Jumo Health Usa Inc (PA)	New Haven	CT	E	646 895-9379	2164
Kids Discover LLC	Westport	CT	F	212 677-4457	4178
Legal Affairs Inc	Hamden	CT	G	203 865-2520	1437
Limra International Inc (PA)	Windsor	CT	E	860 688-3358	4287
Lmt Communications Inc	Newtown	CT	E	203 426-4568	2339
Maplegate Media Group Inc	Danbury	CT	F	203 826-7557	782
Maritime Activity Reports (PA)	Easton	CT	F	212 477-6700	1096
Moffly Publications Inc	Westport	CT	E	203 222-0600	4187
National Shting Spt Fndtion In	Shelton	CT	D	203 426-1320	3036
Natural Nutmeg LLC	Avon	CT	G	860 206-9500	32
Overseas Ministries Study Ctr	New Haven	CT	F	203 624-6672	2182
Penny Marketing Ltd Partnr (PA)	Norwalk	CT	E	203 866-6688	2553
Penny Press Inc (PA)	Norwalk	CT	C	203 866-6688	2554
Racing Times	Wallingford	CT	G	203 298-2899	3845
Red 7 Media LLC (HQ)	Norwalk	CT	E	203 853-2474	2562
Relocation Information Svc Inc	Norwalk	CT	F	203 855-1234	2564
Relx Inc	Norwalk	CT	A	203 840-4800	2565
Rgl Inc	Meriden	CT	F	860 653-7254	1693
Savage Latina Magazine LLC	Derby	CT	G	800 260-3525	892
Scholastic Library Pubg Inc (HQ)	Danbury	CT	A	203 797-3500	812
Show Management Associates LLC	Norwalk	CT	D	203 939-9901	2572
Society Plastics Engineers Inc (PA)	Danbury	CT	E	203 740-5422	819
Sumner Communications Inc	Shelton	CT	E	203 748-2050	3066
Taunton Inc	Newtown	CT	A	203 426-8171	2349
Taunton Press Inc	Newtown	CT	C	203 426-8171	2350
The Taunton Press Inc (PA)	Newtown	CT	C	203 426-8171	2352
This Old House Ventures LLC	Stamford	CT	E	475 209-8665	3481
Urban Exposition LLC (DH)	Shelton	CT	E	203 242-8717	3074
Vance Publishing Corporation	Hartford	CT	C	847 634-2600	1516
Wicks Business Information LLC (PA)	Shelton	CT	F	203 334-2002	3078
Windhover Information Inc (DH)	Norwalk	CT	E	203 838-4401	2597
Wire Association Intl Inc (PA)	Madison	CT	F	203 453-2777	1577
Wire Journal Inc	Madison	CT	F	203 453-2777	1578
Woolworks International Ltd	Stamford	CT	F	203 661-7076	3496
World Wrestling Entrmt LLC (DH)	Stamford	CT	F	203 352-8600	3497
Yale Alumni Publications Inc	New Haven	CT	G	203 432-0645	2216
Yale University	New Haven	CT	E	203 764-4333	2218
Yale University (PA)	New Haven	CT	E	203 432-2550	2219
Zackin Publications Inc	Oxford	CT	E	203 262-4670	2715
73-75 Magazine Street LLC	Allston	MA	G	617 787-1913	5818
Abry Partners V L P	Boston	MA	A	617 859-2959	6506
Advanced Media Corporation	Quincy	MA	D	800 844-0599	11501
Advanstar Communications Inc	Burlington	MA	F	339 298-4200	7332
American Mteorological Soc Inc (PA)	Boston	MA	D	617 227-2425	6541
American Soc Law Mdcine Ethics	Boston	MA	G	617 262-4990	6542
Archaeological Institute Amer	Boston	MA	F	617 353-9361	6555
Atlantic Printing Co Inc	Medfield	MA	F	781 449-2700	10269
Biodata Inc	Cambridge	MA	F	512 593-5521	7510
Boston Design Guide Inc	Sudbury	MA	F	978 443-9886	12261
BV Investment Partners LP (PA)	Boston	MA	F	617 224-0057	6629
Cabot Heritage Corporation	Salem	MA	E	978 745-5532	11707
Cape Cod Life LLC	Mashpee	MA	F	508 419-7381	10250
Carnegie Communications LLC	Westford	MA	F	978 692-5092	13227
Carnegie Dartlet LLC (PA)	Westford	MA	F	978 692-5092	13228
Cell Press Inc	Cambridge	MA	C	617 397-2800	7534
Cerulli Associates Inc (PA)	Boston	MA	E	617 437-0084	6647
Christian Science Pubg Soc (PA)	Boston	MA	B	617 450-2000	6655
Clean Run Productions LLC	South Hadley	MA	F	413 532-1389	11960
Community of Jesus Inc (PA)	Orleans	MA	E	508 255-1094	11237
Conquest Business Media Inc	Beverly	MA	E	978 299-1200	6341
Crane Data LLC	Westborough	MA	F	508 439-4419	13095
Cxo Media Inc (DH)	Needham Heights	MA	C	508 766-5696	10539

	CITY	ST	EMP	PHONE	ENTRY#
Davis Corp Worcester Inc (PA)	Worcester	MA	E	508 754-7201	13714
Diacritech Inc	Boston	MA	F	617 236-7500	6692
Dixie Media LLC	Danvers	MA	E	508 739-1999	8183
Dow Jones & Company Inc	Chicopee	MA	D	413 598-4000	8027
East Coast Publications Inc (PA)	Norwell	MA	F	781 878-4540	11141
Ebsco Publishing Inc (DH)	Ipswich	MA	A	978 356-6500	9485
Enterprise Publications (PA)	Falmouth	MA	E	508 548-4700	8630
Family Education Network Inc	Boston	MA	E	617 671-3435	6730
Fine Magazine	Woburn	MA	G	617 721-7372	13566
Forced Exposure Inc	Arlington	MA	E	781 321-0320	5940
Foundtion For Dmcracy In Ukrin	Cambridge	MA	G	617 496-8816	7574
Free Software Foundation Inc	Boston	MA	F	617 542-5942	6747
Gasworld Publishing LLC	Lexington	MA	G	781 862-0624	9744
Graphic Arts Institute of Neng	Southborough	MA	F	508 804-4100	11995
Griffin Publishing Co Inc	Duxbury	MA	F	781 829-4700	8332
H O Zimman Inc	Lynn	MA	E	781 598-9230	9977
Harvard Bus Schl Pubg Corp (HQ)	Brighton	MA	C	617 783-7400	7241
Harvard Lampoon Inc	Cambridge	MA	E	617 495-7801	7602
Harvard Magazine Inc	Cambridge	MA	E	617 495-5746	7603
Hcpro Inc (HQ)	Middleton	MA	E	781 639-1872	10385
Highlights For Children Inc	Northampton	MA	E	413 397-2800	11067
Horizon House Publications Inc (PA)	Norwood	MA	D	781 769-9750	11177
Horn Book Inc	Boston	MA	F	617 278-0225	6791
Hunter Associates Inc	Saugus	MA	F	781 233-9100	11761
Idg	Boston	MA	E	508 875-5000	6802
Idg Communications Inc	Framingham	MA	E	508 766-5300	8779
Idg Communications Inc (DH)	Needham	MA	C	508 872-8200	10513
Idg Corporate Services Group	Framingham	MA	G	508 875-5000	8781
Informa Financial Information Inc	Westborough	MA	C	508 616-5550	13108
Institute For Applied Ntwrk SE	Boston	MA	E	617 399-8100	6814
Institute For Scial Cltral Cmm	Norwood	MA	G	339 236-1991	11183
International Data Group Inc (HQ)	Needham	MA	F	508 875-5000	10514
Joseph G Pulitano Insur Agcy	Newton	MA	F	617 783-2622	10765
Journal of Bone Jint Srgery In	Needham	MA	E	781 449-9780	10515
Just Publications	Brookline	MA	G	617 739-5878	7319
Laurin Publishing Co Inc (PA)	Pittsfield	MA	D	413 499-0514	11405
Liberty Publishing Inc	Beverly	MA	F	978 777-8200	6362
Massachstts Soc For Prvntion C (PA)	Boston	MA	C	617 522-7282	6872
Massachusetts Assn Realtors (PA)	Foxboro	MA	F	781 890-3700	8707
Massachusetts Institute Tech	Cambridge	MA	C	617 253-5646	7637
Massachusetts Medical Society	Boston	MA	E	617 734-9800	6874
Massachusetts Medical Society	Waltham	MA	E	781 434-7950	12716
Massachusetts Review Inc	Amherst	MA	G	413 545-2689	5862
McKnight Management Co Inc (PA)	Falmouth	MA	G	508 540-5051	8635
Municipal Market Analytics Inc (PA)	Concord	MA	F	617 968-5906	8126
National Braille Press Inc	Boston	MA	D	617 425-2400	6903
Network World Inc	Needham Heights	MA	E	800 622-1108	10553
New Beverage Publications Inc	Boston	MA	G	617 598-1900	6914
New England RE Bulltin	Swansea	MA	F	508 675-8884	12308
New Generation Research Inc	Boston	MA	F	617 573-9550	6918
Northeast Outdoors Inc	Paxton	MA	G	508 752-8762	11290
Penwell	Sturbridge	MA	G	508 347-8245	12256
President and Fellows of Harvard College (PA) 617 496-4873	Cambridge 7688	MA			A
President Fllows Hrvard Cllege	Boston	MA	C	617 495-5581	6976
Qbl Winddown LLC	Framingham	MA	F	617 219-8300	8800
Relx Inc	Newton	MA	D	617 558-4925	10780
Rhee Gold Company Inc	Norton	MA	F	508 285-6650	11132
RMS Media Group Inc	Newburyport	MA	E	978 623-8020	10713
Sky Publishing Corporation	Cambridge	MA	E	617 864-7360	7717
Smarter Travel Media LLC	Boston	MA	C	617 886-5555	7041
Technology Review Inc	Cambridge	MA	E	617 475-8000	7736
Telco Communications Inc	Seekonk	MA	F	508 336-6633	11788
The Orion Society Inc	Great Barrington	MA	F	413 528-4422	8979
The Pohly Company	Brewster	MA	F	617 451-1700	7217
Town of North Reading	North Reading	MA	E	978 664-6027	11050
Transitions Abroad Pubg Inc	Amherst	MA	G	413 992-6486	5865
Vdc Research Group Inc (PA)	Southborough	MA	E	508 653-9000	12004
Wilmington Compliance Week	Boston	MA	G	617 570-8600	7126
Wilmington Compliance Week Inc	Boston	MA	E	888 519-9200	7127
Casco Bay Sbstnce Abuse Rsrces	Portland	ME	F	207 773-7993	5196
D E Enterprise Inc	Rockport	ME	E	207 594-9544	5346
Diversified Communications (HQ)	Portland	ME	E	207 842-5500	5209
Down East Enterprise Inc	Rockport	ME	E	207 594-9544	5348
Maine Antique Digest Inc	Waldoboro	ME	F	207 832-7534	5578
Navigator Publishing LLC	Portland	ME	E	207 822-4350	5249
Portland Monthly Inc	Portland	ME	G	207 775-4339	5259
Taproot	Portland	ME	G	802 472-1617	5280
Trueline Publishing LLC	Portland	ME	F	207 510-4099	5286
United Publications Inc	Yarmouth	ME	E	207 846-0600	5709
Woodenboat Publications Inc	Brooklin	ME	E	207 359-4651	4635
Connell Communications Inc	Keene	NH	D	603 924-7271	14592
Echo Communications Inc	New London	NH	E	603 526-6006	15203
Harrison Publishing House Inc	Littleton	NH	E	603 444-0820	14720
Helmers Publishing Inc	Dublin	NH	E	603 563-1631	14261
Hideaways International Inc	Portsmouth	NH	F	603 430-4433	15401
Laser Group Publishing Inc	Manchester	NH	F	603 880-8909	14876
Relx Inc	Portsmouth	NH	F	603 431-7894	15432
Spectrum Monthly LLC	Manchester	NH	C	603 627-0042	14936
Tree Care Industry Assn Inc	Manchester	NH	E	603 314-5380	14946
Trustees of Dartmouth College	Hanover	NH	G	603 646-2256	14431
American Mathematical Society Inc (PA)	Providence	RI	C	401 455-4000	16470
Island Publishing Company	Providence	RI	F	401 351-4320	16544
Manisses Cmmncations Group Inc	Providence	RI	E	401 273-5221	16557
Metro Inc (PA)	Cranston	RI	E	401 461-2200	15894
Motif Magazine	Pawtucket	RI	F	401 312-3305	16389
Rhode Island Assn Realtors Inc (PA)	Warwick	RI	G	401 785-3650	16849
Rhode Island Monthly	Newport	RI	G	401 649-4898	16221
Rhode Island Monthly	Providence	RI	E	401 649-4800	16603
State-Wide Mltple Lsting Svc I	Warwick	RI	G	401 785-3650	16865
Vendome Guide	Newport	RI	F	401 849-8025	16227
Battenkill Communications LLP	Manchester Center	VT	G	802 362-3981	17327
Boutin/Mcquiston Inc (PA)	South Burlington	VT	F	802 863-8038	17574
Buildinggreen Inc	Brattleboro	VT	F	802 257-7300	17076
Dartmouth Journal Services Inc	Waterbury	VT	E	802 244-1457	17674
Eating Well Inc	Burlington	VT	E	802 425-5700	17132
Hemmings Motor News Inc	Bennington	VT	A	802 442-3101	17040
Jouve of North America Inc (DH)	Brattleboro	VT	D	802 254-6073	17091
Old Mill Road Media LLC	Arlington	VT	F	802 375-1366	16991
Standex International Corp	Essex Junction	VT	F	864 963-3471	17247
Vermont Journalism Trust Ltd	Montpelier	VT	F	802 225-6224	17377

2731 Book publishing

	CITY	ST	EMP	PHONE	ENTRY#
A Guideposts Church Corp (PA)	Danbury	CT	C	203 749-0203	699
Air Age Inc	Wilton	CT	E	203 431-9000	4229
Belvoir Media Group LLC	Norwalk	CT	G	203 857-3100	2469
Bff Holdings Inc (HQ)	Old Saybrook	CT	C	860 510-0100	2645
Comicana Inc	Stamford	CT	G	203 968-0748	3318
Cortina Learning Intl Inc (PA)	Wilton	CT	F	800 245-2145	4237
Creative Media Applications	Weston	CT	G	203 226-0544	4149
Early Advantage LLC	Fairfield	CT	F	203 259-6480	1182
Forecast International Inc	Sandy Hook	CT	E	203 426-0800	2951
Gamut Publishing	Hartford	CT	G	860 296-6128	1482
Greenwich Workshop Inc (PA)	Seymour	CT	E	203 881-3336	2961
Grolier Telemarketing Inc	Danbury	CT	E	203 797-3500	754
Informa Tech Holdings LLC	Darien	CT	F	203 662-6501	849
Jumo Health Usa Inc (PA)	New Haven	CT	E	646 895-9319	2164
Kirchoff Wohlberg Inc	Madison	CT	F	212 644-2020	1562
Life Study Fllwship Foundation	Darien	CT	G	203 655-1436	851
Mystic Seaport Museum Inc	Mystic	CT	B	860 572-0711	1940
Rgl Inc	Meriden	CT	F	860 653-7254	1693
Rothstein Associates Inc	Brookfield	CT	G	203 740-7400	538
Sasc LLC	Greenwich	CT	F	203 846-2274	1349
Scholastic Inc (DH)	Danbury	CT	D	212 343-6100	811
Scholastic Library Pubg Inc (HQ)	Danbury	CT	A	203 797-3500	812
Society Plastics Engineers Inc (PA)	Danbury	CT	E	203 740-5422	819
Tantor Media Incorporated	Old Saybrook	CT	C	860 395-1155	2664
Taunton Inc	Newtown	CT	A	203 426-8171	2349
The Taunton Press Inc (PA)	Newtown	CT	C	203 426-8171	2352
Toby Press LLC	New Milford	CT	F	203 830-8508	2261
Weekly Reader Corp	Stamford	CT	F	203 705-3500	3493
Wesleyan University	Middletown	CT	G	860 685-2980	1790
Windhover Information Inc (DH)	Norwalk	CT	E	203 838-4401	2597
Yale University	New Haven	CT	E	203 764-4333	2218
Yale University (PA)	New Haven	CT	E	203 432-2550	2219
Abry Partners V L P	Boston	MA	A	617 859-2959	6506
Addison-Wesley	Boston	MA	E	617 848-6300	6515
American Girl Brands LLC	Natick	MA	E	508 810-3461	10469
Americas Test Kitchen Limited Partnership 617 232-1000	Boston 6544	MA			C
Argosy Publishing Inc (PA)	Newton	MA	D	617 527-9999	10733
Atlantic Printing Co Inc	Medfield	MA	F	781 449-2700	10269
Baikar Association Inc (PA)	Watertown	MA	F	617 924-4420	12862
Berkshire Publishing Group LLC	Great Barrington	MA	F	413 528-0206	8974
Booktalk Event	Lowell	MA	F	952 836-6275	9863
Brill Usa Inc	Boston	MA	F	617 263-2323	6624
Brown Publishing Network Inc (PA)	Charlestown	MA	F	781 547-7600	7865
Candlewick Press Inc	Somerville	MA	D	617 661-3330	11866
Career Press Inc (PA)	Newburyport	MA	F	201 848-0310	10674
Cengage Learning Inc	Boston	MA	F	518 348-2300	6645
Channing Bete Company Inc (PA)	South Deerfield	MA	C	413 665-7611	11922
Charlesbridge Publishing Inc (PA)	Watertown	MA	F	617 926-0329	12869
Cheng & Tsui Co Inc	Boston	MA	F	617 988-2400	6649
Christopher-Gordon Publishing	Foxboro	MA	F	781 762-5577	8692
Community of Jesus Inc (PA)	Orleans	MA	E	508 255-1094	11237
Council On Intl Pub Affairs Inc (PA)	Northampton	MA	G	212 972-9878	11058

SIC

	CITY	ST	EMP	PHONE	ENTRY#
Courier Communications LLC **(DH)**	North Chelmsford	MA	E	978 251-6000	10968
Courier Corporation	North Chelmsford	MA	A	978 251-6000	10970
Courier New Media Inc **(PA)**	North Chelmsford	MA	E	978 251-3945	10972
Curriculum Associates LLC	Littleton	MA	E	978 313-1276	9807
Curriculum Associates LLC **(PA)**	North Billerica	MA	B	978 667-8000	10904
Davis Corp Worcester Inc **(PA)**	Worcester	MA	E	508 754-7201	13714
Diacritech Inc	Boston	MA	F	617 236-7500	6692
Ebsco Publishing Inc **(DH)**	Ipswich	MA	A	978 356-6500	9485
Edward Elgar Publishing Inc	Northampton	MA	G	413 584-5551	11060
Flatworld	Boston	MA	E	781 974-9927	6740
Greenwood Publishing Group LLC **(DH)**	Boston	MA	G	617 351-5000	6772
Harvard Bus Schl Pubg Corp **(HQ)**	Brighton	MA	C	617 783-7400	7241
Harvard Bus Schl Stdnt Assn In	Boston	MA	D	617 495-6812	6784
Hendrickson Publishers LLC	Peabody	MA	E	978 532-6546	11313
HM Publishing Corp	Boston	MA	A	617 251-5000	6788
Hmh Publishers LLC **(DH)**	Boston	MA	F	617 351-5000	6789
Horizon House Publications Inc **(PA)**	Norwood	MA	D	781 769-9750	11177
Houghton Mfflin Hrcurt Fndtion	Boston	MA	F	617 351-5000	6792
Houghton Mfflin Hrcurt Pbls In **(DH)**	Boston	MA	A	617 351-5000	6793
Houghton Mifflin LLC	Boston	MA	D	617 351-5000	6794
Houghton Mifflin Co Intl Inc	Boston	MA	A	617 351-5000	6795
Houghton Mifflin Harcourt Co **(HQ)**	Boston	MA	D	617 351-5000	6796
Houghton Mifflin Harcourt Pubg **(DH)**	Boston	MA	A	425 351-5000	6797
Houghton Mifflin Holding Company Inc	Boston	MA	A	617 351-5000	6798
Human Resource Dev Press **(PA)**	Belchertown	MA	E	413 253-3488	6280
Idg Communications Inc **(DH)**	Needham	MA	C	508 872-8200	10513
Institute For Fgn Plicy Analis **(PA)**	Cambridge	MA	E	617 492-2116	7615
Macmillan Publishing Group LLC	Boston	MA	D	646 307-5617	6867
Massachstts Cntning Lgal Edcat	Boston	MA	E	617 482-2205	6871
Merriam-Webster Incorporated **(DH)**	Springfield	MA	D	413 734-3134	12113
National Braille Press Inc	Boston	MA	E	617 425-2400	6903
Nefc	Turners Falls	MA	E	800 360-6332	12454
North Shore Press Inc	Melrose	MA	G	781 662-6757	10317
Nsight Inc	Andover	MA	E	781 273-6300	5902
OReilly Media Inc	Boston	MA	C	617 354-5800	6944
Page Street Publishing Company	Salem	MA	F	978 594-8758	11729
Pearson Education Inc	Boston	MA	E	617 848-6000	6958
Pearson Education Holdings Inc	Boston	MA	A	617 671-2000	6959
Quarto Pubg Group USA Inc	Beverly	MA	E	978 282-9590	6374
Quayside Publishing Group	Beverly	MA	G	978 282-9590	6376
Readcube	Cambridge	MA	F	857 265-4945	7694
Redwheel/Weiser LLC **(PA)**	Newburyport	MA	G	978 465-0504	10712
Robert Bentley Inc	Cambridge	MA	E	617 547-4170	7698
Sage Publications Inc	North Dartmouth	MA	F	805 499-9774	11001
Scholastic Corporation	Allston	MA	G	617 924-3846	5826
Scienceopen Inc	Burlington	MA	G	781 222-5200	7424
Silver Leaf Books LLC	Holliston	MA	G	781 799-6609	9229
Simon & Schuster Inc	Cambridge	MA	D	617 492-1220	7716
Sinauer Associates Inc	Sunderland	MA	E	413 549-4300	12275
Small Plnet Communications Inc	Lawrence	MA	E	978 794-2201	9598
Society of St John The Evang	Cambridge	MA	G	617 876-3037	7719
Ssi Liquidating Inc	Cambridge	MA	F	617 547-6706	7720
Storey Publishing LLC **(DH)**	Clarksburg	MA	F	413 346-2100	8074
Sundance Newbridge Publishing	Marlborough	MA	F	508 303-1920	10218
Thomson Reuters Corporation	Weymouth	MA	F	781 331-6610	13337
Transitions Abroad Pubg Inc	Amherst	MA	G	413 992-6486	5865
Tupelo Press Inc	North Adams	MA	F	413 664-9611	10814
Unitarian Universalist Assn **(PA)**	Boston	MA	C	617 742-2100	7092
Victory Productions Inc	Worcester	MA	E	508 755-0051	13822
Vineyard Gazette LLC **(PA)**	Edgartown	MA	E	508 627-4311	8468
Wellesley Information Svcs LLC	Boston	MA	E	781 407-9013	7116
Westborough Books Inc **(PA)**	Westborough	MA	E	508 366-4292	13144
Xam Online Inc **(PA)**	Cambridge	MA	G	781 662-9268	7763
D E Enterprise Inc	Rockport	ME	E	207 594-9544	5346
Garmin International Inc	Yarmouth	ME	B	800 561-5105	5704
Island Institute	Rockland	ME	E	207 594-9209	5334
Mathemtics Problem Solving LLC	South Portland	ME	D	207 772-2846	5508
Penobscot Bay Press **(PA)**	Stonington	ME	F	207 367-2200	5534
Solon Ctr For RES & Publishig	Solon	ME	F	207 319-4727	5482
Wayside Publishing	Freeport	ME	F	888 302-2519	4804
Archimedia Advantage Inc	Greenland	NH	F	603 431-7894	14366
Avocus Publishing Inc	Gilsum	NH	G	603 357-0236	14341
Fishing Hot Spots Inc	Nashua	NH	G	715 365-5555	15102
Greenwood Publishing Group Inc	Portsmouth	NH	A	603 431-7894	15397
Helmers Publishing Inc	Dublin	NH	E	603 563-1631	14261
Houghton Mifflin Harcourt Co	Portsmouth	NH	C	630 467-7000	15406
Kensington Group Incorporated	Hampton Falls	NH	F	603 926-6742	14419
Kevin Emery	Farmington	NH	G	603 433-5784	14310
Scribliotech Inc	Orange	NH	G	603 306-9000	15280
Stenhouse Publishers	Portsmouth	NH	F	207 253-1600	15440
Trustees of Dartmouth College	Lebanon	NH	E	603 448-1533	14702
American Mathematical Society Inc **(PA)**	Providence	RI	C	401 455-4000	16470
Manisses Cmmncations Group Inc	Providence	RI	E	401 273-5221	16557
Metro Inc **(PA)**	Cranston	RI	E	401 461-2200	15894
Charles E Tuttle Co Inc **(DH)**	North Clarendon	VT	E	802 773-8930	17413
Chelsea Green Publishing Co	White River Junction	VT	E	802 295-6300	17705
Inner Traditions International **(PA)**	Rochester	VT	E	802 767-3174	17485
Longhill Partners Inc **(PA)**	Woodstock	VT	E	802 457-4000	17776
Stratford Publishing Services	Brattleboro	VT	G	802 254-6073	17100

2732 Book printing

	CITY	ST	EMP	PHONE	ENTRY#
Landmark Print Inc	Stamford	CT	D	800 499-3808	3396
Baikar Association Inc **(PA)**	Watertown	MA	F	617 924-4420	12862
Book-Mart Press Inc	North Chelmsford	MA	F	978 251-6000	10966
Chand LLC	Roxbury	MA	G	310 483-5769	11688
Channing Bete Company Inc **(PA)**	South Deerfield	MA	C	413 665-7611	11922
Cistercian Abbey Spencer Inc	Spencer	MA	E	508 885-8700	12056
Courier Companies Inc **(PA)**	North Chelmsford	MA	E	978 251-6000	10969
Courier Corporation	North Chelmsford	MA	A	978 251-6000	10970
Courier Intl Holdings LLC	North Chelmsford	MA	G	978 251-6000	10971
Courier New Media Inc **(PA)**	North Chelmsford	MA	E	978 251-3945	10972
Courier Westford Inc	Westford	MA	B	978 251-6482	13232
Dunn & Co Inc	Clinton	MA	C	978 368-8505	8077
Lsc Communications Inc	North Chelmsford	MA	D	978 251-6000	10982
Quarto Pubg Group USA Inc	Beverly	MA	E	425 827-7120	6375
Red Sun Press Inc	Jamaica Plain	MA	F	617 524-6822	9503
Center Point Inc	Knox	ME	E	207 568-3717	4943
Mathemtics Problem Solving LLC	South Portland	ME	D	207 772-2846	5508
The Dingley Press Inc **(PA)**	Lisbon	ME	C	207 353-1500	5018
Copy Express LLC	Manchester	NH	G	603 625-4960	14836
Kensington Group Incorporated	Hampton Falls	NH	F	603 926-6742	14419
Odyssey Press Inc **(PA)**	Dover	NH	E	603 749-4433	14243
Southern New Hampshire Univ	Manchester	NH	G	603 629-4631	14963
Johnson & Wales University	Providence	RI	E	401 598-1824	16550

2741 Miscellaneous publishing

	CITY	ST	EMP	PHONE	ENTRY#
Arcat Inc	Fairfield	CT	G	203 929-9444	1176
Barker Advg Specialty Co Inc **(PA)**	Cheshire	CT	D	203 272-2222	575
Bayard Inc **(DH)**	New London	CT	F	860 437-3012	2222
Begell House Inc	Danbury	CT	F	203 456-6161	714
Bff Holdings Inc **(HQ)**	Old Saybrook	CT	C	860 510-0100	2645
Booktriblifecom LLC	Westport	CT	F	203 226-0199	4159
Bristol Press	Bristol	CT	F	860 845-8686	421
Broadcastmed LLC **(PA)**	Farmington	CT	F	860 953-2900	1210
Business Journals Inc	Norwalk	CT	D	203 853-6015	2478
Chicken Soup For Soul LLC	Cos Cob	CT	E	203 861-4000	674
Chicken Soup For Soul Prdctons **(PA)**	Cos Cob	CT	F	855 398-0443	675
Chief Executive Group LLC **(PA)**	Stamford	CT	E	785 832-0303	3310
Childrens Health Market Inc	Wilton	CT	G	203 762-2938	4236
Connectcut Hspnic Yellow Pages	Hartford	CT	F	860 560-8713	1475
Cortelyou Inc	Norwalk	CT	D	203 847-2000	2487
DCA Business Media LLC	Westport	CT	F	203 227-1699	4164
Directory Assistants Inc	Avon	CT	F	860 633-0122	23
Executive Greetings Inc **(HQ)**	New Hartford	CT	B	860 379-9911	2100
Graphics Press LLC	Cheshire	CT	G	203 272-9187	596
Heavy Inc	Westport	CT	F	646 806-2113	4172
Industrial Press Inc	Norwalk	CT	F	888 528-7852	2517
Informa Tech Holdings LLC	Darien	CT	F	203 662-6501	849
Jacoby	Weston	CT	F	203 227-2220	4150
Learntoprogramtv Incorporated	Bridgeport	CT	F	860 840-7090	344
Life Study Fllwship Foundation	Darien	CT	G	203 655-1436	851
Little Tokyo Express Inc	Milford	CT	G	203 878-8814	1846
Merrill Anderson Company Inc	Stratford	CT	E	203 377-4996	3557
Minuteman Press	Trumbull	CT	G	203 261-8318	3725
Mowmedia LLC	Stamford	CT	G	203 240-6466	3413
Nancy Larson Publishers Inc	Old Lyme	CT	E	860 434-0800	2643
National Publisher Svcs LLC	Shelton	CT	F	917 902-9590	3035
National Publishing Co Inc	Westport	CT	E	203 221-2300	4188
National Shting Spt Fndtion In	Shelton	CT	D	203 426-1320	3036
Partner In Publishing LLC	Glastonbury	CT	F	860 430-9440	1292
Penny Press Inc	Milford	CT	E	203 866-6688	1864
Penny Publications LLC	Milford	CT	E	203 866-6688	1865
Penny Publications LLC **(PA)**	Norwalk	CT	E	203 866-6688	2555
Portfolio Arts Group Ltd	Norwalk	CT	F	203 847-2000	2559
Powerphone Inc	Madison	CT	E	203 245-8911	1566
Rare Reminder Incorporated	Rocky Hill	CT	E	860 563-9386	2933
Relocation Information Svc Inc	Norwalk	CT	F	203 855-1234	2564
Rgl Inc	Meriden	CT	F	860 653-7254	1693
Scholastic Inc **(DH)**	Danbury	CT	D	212 343-6100	811
Science Fction Fntsy Wrters AM	Enfield	CT	F	860 698-0536	1146
Senior Network Inc	Stamford	CT	F	203 969-2700	3455
Sfwa	Enfield	CT	F	508 320-5293	1149
Shiller and Company Inc	Wilton	CT	F	203 210-5208	4247
Shop Smart Central Inc	Newtown	CT	G	914 962-3871	2346
Shopper-Turnpike Corporation	Putnam	CT	F	860 928-3040	2874

	CITY	ST	EMP	PHONE	ENTRY#		CITY	ST	EMP	PHONE	ENTRY#
Skull Kingdom Entrmt LLC	Ledyard	CT	G	262 804-8193	1553	Lets Go Inc	Cambridge	MA	A	617 495-9659	7631
Southern Neng Telecom Corp (HQ)	New Haven	CT	B	203 771-5200	2203	Liberty Publishing Inc	Beverly	MA	F	978 777-8200	6362
Stamford Capital Group Inc (PA)	Stamford	CT	F	800 977-7837	3469	LPI Printing and Graphic Inc	Stoneham	MA	F	781 438-5400	12182
Thomson Reuters Corporation	East Haven	CT	E	203 466-5055	1054	Megatech Corporation	Tewksbury	MA	F	978 937-9600	12409
Times Publishing LLC	Middlefield	CT	G	860 349-8532	1730	Merriam-Webster Incorporated (DH)	Springfield	MA	D	413 734-3134	12113
Triple B Media LLC	Cheshire	CT	F	917 710-2222	620	Monster Tech	Weston	MA	F	978 897-0832	13288
US Games Systems Inc	Stamford	CT	E	800 544-2637	3488	Monteferro Press	Ashland	MA	G	508 944-8587	5962
Versimedia	Norwalk	CT	E	203 604-8094	2592	Myjove Corporation	Cambridge	MA	D	617 945-9051	7658
Yale University	New Haven	CT	E	203 764-4333	2218	Mystockplancom Inc	Brookline	MA	F	617 734-1979	7321
Yale University (PA)	New Haven	CT	E	203 432-2550	2219	N E Publishing Group	Swansea	MA	F	508 675-8883	12307
943 Enteretainment Corp	Somerville	MA	F	617 608-6943	11858	Netgalley LLC (PA)	Newburyport	MA	F	978 465-7755	10704
Ad-A-Day Company Inc	Taunton	MA	E	508 824-8676	12315	Nrt Inc	Medway	MA	F	508 533-4588	10309
Advisor Perspectives Inc	Woburn	MA	E	781 376-0050	13501	Open Sesame Publishing	Winchester	MA	F	781 856-8142	13490
Amesbury Community Televi	Amesbury	MA	G	978 388-5900	5827	OReilly Media Inc	Boston	MA	C	617 354-5800	6944
Assoction For Grvstone Studies	Greenfield	MA	G	413 772-0836	8984	P Straker Ltd	South Dartmouth	MA	E	508 996-4804	11918
Atlantic Acm	Boston	MA	F	617 720-3700	6574	Paraclete Press Inc (HQ)	Brewster	MA	E	508 255-4685	7216
Atlantic Printing Co Inc	Medfield	MA	F	781 449-2700	10269	Pearson Custom Publishing	Boston	MA	F	781 248-2721	6957
Author Reputation Press LLC	Canton	MA	G	800 220-7660	7772	Pearson Education Inc	Boston	MA	E	617 848-6000	6958
Banks Publications LLC	Somerville	MA	F	617 996-2283	11863	Pearson Learning Solutions	Boston	MA	F	617 671-3253	6960
Bellaonline	Sutton	MA	E	508 865-9593	12278	Performer Publications Inc	Somerville	MA	G	617 627-9200	11887
Boston Academic Publishing	Boston	MA	G	617 851-8655	6601	PFC Publications LLC	Peabody	MA	G	508 366-2984	11332
Boston Sports Journal LLC	Medway	MA	G	617 306-0166	10303	Press Ganey Associates Inc	Boston	MA	F	781 295-5000	6977
Boxcar Media LLC	North Adams	MA	F	413 663-3363	10804	Prime National Publishing Corp	Weston	MA	F	781 899-2702	13289
Brown Publishing Network Inc (PA)	Charlestown	MA	E	781 547-7600	7865	Promax Supply LLC	Melrose	MA	F	781 620-1602	10318
Brumberg Publications Inc	Brookline	MA	F	617 734-1979	7317	Publishers Crcltion Flfllment	Wakefield	MA	C	978 671-1820	12530
Cambridge Brickhouse Inc	Lawrence	MA	G	978 725-8001	9545	Publishing Collaborative LLC	South Hadley	MA	G	413 538-4170	11966
Cambridgeeditors	Cambridge	MA	F	617 876-2855	7531	Publishing Solutions Group	Burlington	MA	F	781 552-5568	7415
Carlat Publishing LLC	Newburyport	MA	G	978 499-0583	10675	Quality Solutions Inc (DH)	Newburyport	MA	E	978 465-7755	10710
Catapult Sports Inc (HQ)	Boston	MA	E	978 447-5220	6642	Quayside Publishing Group	Beverly	MA	G	978 282-9590	6376
Cervena Barva Press LLC	Somerville	MA	G	617 764-2229	11867	Quayside Publishing Group	Gloucester	MA	F	978 282-9590	8953
Charlesbridge Publishing Inc (PA)	Watertown	MA	E	617 926-0329	12869	Redcoat Publishing	Lowell	MA	F	978 761-0877	9917
Clandestine Kitchen LLC	Hingham	MA	G	415 516-0378	9147	Reminder Publications	East Longmeadow MA		E	413 525-3947	8393
Communication Ink Inc	Peabody	MA	E	978 977-4595	11302	Rheinwerk Publishing Inc	Quincy	MA	F	781 228-5070	11537
Corporate Press	Norwood	MA	F	781 769-6656	11170	Roundtown Inc	Cambridge	MA	F	415 425-6891	7699
Creative Success Alliance Corp	Rockland	MA	E	781 878-7114	11641	Rsvp Press	Chelsea	MA	G	917 334-3102	7989
Culver Company LLC	Salisbury	MA	F	978 463-1700	11740	Saferecipes LLC (PA)	Arlington	MA	G	617 448-6085	5946
Curriculum Associates LLC (PA)	North Billerica	MA	B	978 667-8000	10904	Sandcastle Publishing LLC	South Dennis	MA	G	508 398-3100	11935
D B S Industries Inc	Haverhill	MA	D	978 373-4748	9090	Sap Press	Quincy	MA	F	617 481-0448	11538
Davis Publications Inc	Worcester	MA	E	508 754-7201	13715	Sap Professional Journal (PA)	Dedham	MA	D	781 407-0360	8249
Diacritech Inc	Boston	MA	F	617 236-7500	6692	Shambhala Publications	Boston	MA	G	617 424-0030	7035
Dissertation Editor LLC	Cambridge	MA	F	857 600-2241	7551	Simulconsult Inc	Chestnut Hill	MA	G	617 566-5383	8001
Driggin Sandra DBA Extra Extra	Quincy	MA	F	617 773-6996	11512	Snyk Inc (HQ)	Boston	MA	D	786 506-2615	7042
E H Publishing Inc (PA)	Framingham	MA	E	508 663-1500	8759	Southern Brkshire Shppers Gide	Great Barrington	MA	F	413 528-0095	8978
Earthlink	Acton	MA	G	508 735-1508	5744	Spire Inc	Peabody	MA	E	617 474-8800	11343
Ebsco Publishing Inc (DH)	Ipswich	MA	A	978 356-6500	9485	SRC Publishing Inc	Auburn	MA	G	508 749-3212	6126
Edgewater Marine Inds LLC	New Bedford	MA	F	508 992-6555	10588	Ssi Liquidating Inc	Cambridge	MA	F	617 547-6706	7720
Education Development Ctr Inc (PA)	Waltham	MA	A	617 969-7100	12659	St Associates Inc	Wakefield	MA	E		12536
Eglean Inc	Quincy	MA	G	617 229-5863	11513	Standard Publishing Corp (PA)	Boston	MA	F	617 457-0600	7058
Elsevier Inc	Cambridge	MA	D	781 663-5200	7560	Stratcomm Inc	Natick	MA	C	508 907-7000	10499
Fidelity Ind Advser Newsletter	Williamstown	MA	E	413 458-4700	13367	Supermedia LLC	Braintree	MA	F	781 849-7670	7205
First Ch of Chrst Scntist In B (PA)	Boston	MA	E	617 450-2000	6736	TCI America Inc	Seekonk	MA	F	508 336-6633	11786
Fitchburg Publishing	Fitchburg	MA	F	978 343-6911	8654	Thomson Reuters Corporation	Waltham	MA	E	781 250-4340	12804
Fluent Technologies Inc	Woburn	MA	F	978 939-0900	13568	Trustees of Boston College	Chestnut Hill	MA	F	617 552-2844	8002
Free Press	Northampton	MA	G	413 587-3770	11062	Turley Publications Inc (PA)	Palmer	MA	C	800 824-6548	11286
French Press LLC	Needham	MA	F	781 400-2660	10511	Veritas Medicine Inc	Cambridge	MA	F	617 234-1500	7753
Frg Publications	West Springfield	MA	G	413 734-3411	13026	Verizon New York Inc	Winchester	MA	F	781 721-5957	13493
Gatco Inc	Hyannis	MA	F	508 815-4910	9437	Walter De Gruyter Inc	Boston	MA	G	857 284-7073	7112
Gatehouse Media LLC	Fall River	MA	F	508 676-8211	8551	Web Closeout	Springfield	MA	G	413 222-8302	12150
Groupglobalnet Corp	Boston	MA	G	857 212-4012	6775	Western Mass Penny Saver	Hinsdale	MA	G	413 655-9957	9167
Gtxcel Inc	Southborough	MA	E	508 804-3092	11996	Wicked Local	Randolph	MA	G	781 433-6905	11579
Harvard Bus Schl Pubg Corp (HQ)	Brighton	MA	C	617 783-7400	7241	Zoom Information LLC (DH)	Waltham	MA	E	781 693-7500	12822
Harvard Independent Inc	Cambridge	MA	E	617 495-3682	7601	Bobguide Publishing	Old Town	ME	G	207 827-3782	5124
Haverhill House Publishing LLC	Haverhill	MA	G	781 879-3102	9102	Center Point Inc	Knox	ME	E	207 568-3717	4943
Hcpro Inc (HQ)	Middleton	MA	E	781 639-1872	10385	Central Street Corporation	Bangor	ME	G	207 947-8049	4495
Hendrickson Publishers Inc	Peabody	MA	F	800 358-3111	11314	Direct Display Publishing Co	Bath	ME	G	207 443-4800	4526
HMS	Worcester	MA	G	508 831-8317	13737	Eztousecom Directories	Bangor	ME	G	207 974-3171	4500
Howe Press Perkins Sch Fo	Watertown	MA	F	617 924-3434	12881	Garmin International Inc	Yarmouth	ME	B	800 561-5105	5704
Ian Marie Inc	Newburyport	MA	E	978 463-6742	10689	Journal Publishing Company	Portland	ME	C	800 873-1272	5229
Idg Corporate Sales	Framingham	MA	E	508 875-5000	8780	Mead Papers Group	Rumford	ME	G	207 369-2390	5358
Idg News Service	Boston	MA	E	617 423-9030	6803	Redden Publishing Co LLC	Rockport	ME	G	207 236-0767	5351
Image Software Services Inc	Shirley	MA	G	978 425-3600	11817	Rich Associates Incorporated	Kennebunk	ME	G	207 985-5999	4929
Innovative Publishing Company	Edgartown	MA	F	267 266-8876	8466	Sellers Publishing Inc	South Portland	ME	D	207 772-6833	5514
Interlink Publishing Group	Northampton	MA	E	413 582-7054	11068	Supermedia LLC	South Portland	ME	F	207 828-6100	5515
Ione Press Inc	Boston	MA	E	617 236-1935	6816	Tower Publishing Co (PA)	Standish	ME	F	207 642-5400	5529
Istar Publishing LLC	Randolph	MA	G	781 885-7724	11567	Town of Gorham (PA)	Gorham	ME	E	207 222-1610	4836
Ivix Tech Inc (PA)	Lexington	MA	F	702 561-5304	9754	Connectcut Rver Vly Yllow Pges	Lebanon	NH	G	603 727-4700	14686
J F Griffin Publishing LLC	North Adams	MA	F	413 884-0085	10809	Connell Communications Inc	Keene	NH	D	603 924-7271	14592
Jones & Bartlett Learning LLC (PA)	Burlington	MA	C	978 443-5000	7382	Constrction Smmary New Hmpshr/	Manchester	NH	G	603 627-8856	14835
Kelley and Hall Book Publicity	Marblehead	MA	F	617 680-1976	10089	David R Godine Publisher Inc	Jaffrey	NH	G	603 532-4100	14566
Laurin Publishing Co Inc (PA)	Pittsfield	MA	D	413 499-0514	11405	Ebiz Tech LLC	Nashua	NH	F	603 233-8481	15093
Leap Year Publishing LLC	Newburyport	MA	F	978 688-9900	10695	Ehs Publishing	Durham	NH	G	203 216-5800	14266
Legacy Publishing Group Inc	Clinton	MA	E	800 322-3866	8080	Elan Publishing Company Inc	Moultonborough	NH	F	603 253-6002	15052
Lemon Press Market LLC	Nantucket	MA	G	508 228-3800	10464	Fishing Hot Spots Inc	Nashua	NH	G	715 365-5555	15102

Company	City	ST	EMP	PHONE	ENTRY#
Geskus Studios & Yrbk Pubg Inc	Seabrook	NH	E	800 948-1120	15591
Hawthorn Creative Group LLC	Portsmouth	NH	E	603 610-0533	15400
Helmers Publishing Inc	Dublin	NH	E	603 563-1631	14261
Kensington Group Incorporated	Hampton Falls	NH	F	603 926-6742	14419
Mint Printworks LLC	Nashua	NH	G	603 718-1100	15135
Mountainoga LLC	West Lebanon	NH	G	857 972-6446	15685
Nutfield Publishing LLC	Londonderry	NH	G	603 537-2760	14778
Penny Publications LLC	Loudon	NH	E	603 783-9998	14797
Positive News For You LLC	Keene	NH	G	802 384-3993	14615
Sophia Institute	Manchester	NH	F	603 641-9344	14932
Steyn Syndication	Woodsville	NH	G	603 359-1683	15737
Veritas Press Ltd	Rye	*NH	G	603 379-2790	15500
Verizon Communications Inc	Bedford	NH	F	603 472-2090	13952
Virtual Publishing LLC	Manchester	NH	G	603 627-9500	14954
Yankee Publishing Incorporated (PA)	Dublin	NH	E	603 563-8111	14262
Alert Solutions Inc	Cranston	RI	F	401 427-2100	15826
Arnold Art Inc (PA)	Newport	RI	F	401 847-2273	16203
Chew Publishing Inc	Middletown	RI	G	401 808-0648	16171
DManelly Ex Multiservices LLC	Providence	RI	G	401 490-2900	16509
Graphtec Press	Providence	RI	G	727 267-0940	16528
Guia Commercial Portugues Inc	East Providence	RI	G	401 438-1740	16022
Hungry Ghost Press LLC	Providence	RI	G	978 677-1000	16536
Shorelink Publications LLC	Newport	RI	G	413 320-3611	16223
Applejack Art Partners Inc	Manchester Center	VT		802 362-3662	17326
Art Licensing Intl Inc	Arlington	VT	E	802 362-3662	16986
Brunswick Publishing LLC	Rutland	VT	G	802 747-6121	17491
Business Financial Pubg LLC	Williston	VT	G	802 865-9886	17724
Everwideningcirclescom LLC	Fairfield	VT	G	802 524-3757	17266
Garlic Press Inc	Colchester	VT	F	802 864-0670	17192
Height Land Publications Ltd	Jeffersonville	VT	G	802 644-6606	17306
Human Rights Defense Center	Brattleboro	VT	G	802 257-1342	17088
Press Forward Inc	Middlebury	VT	G	802 989-4383	17348
Prospect Press LLC	Burlington	VT	G	802 862-6717	17152
Supermedia LLC	Williston	VT	F	802 878-2336	17749
The Storymatic Corp	Brattleboro	VT		917 842-9932	17101
Verizon	Swanton	VT	G	802 879-4954	17644
Vermont Publishing Comany	Saint Albans	VT	E	802 524-9771	17536
Wild Apple Graphics Ltd	Woodstock	VT	E	802 457-3003	17780
Wind Ridge Publishing	Shelburne	VT	F	802 985-3091	17565

2752 Commercial printing, lithographic

Company	City	ST	EMP	PHONE	ENTRY#
ABC Printing Inc	East Haven	CT	F	203 468-1245	1034
Action Letter Inc (PA)	Stamford	CT	F	203 323-2466	3273
Adkins Printing Company	New Britain	CT	F	800 228-9745	1997
Advanced Printing Services Inc	Bristol	CT	E	860 583-1906	393
Alliance Graphics Inc	Newington	CT	F	860 666-7992	2270
Allied Printing Services Inc (PA)	Manchester	CT	B	860 643-1101	1584
AlphaGraphics	Stamford	CT	G	203 847-8884	3278
American-Republican Inc (PA)	Waterbury	CT	C	203 574-3636	3884
Amgraph Packaging Inc (PA)	Baltic	CT	D	860 822-2000	37
Appels Prtg & Mailing Bur Inc	Hartford	CT	F	860 522-8189	1470
Arcat Inc	Fairfield	CT	G	203 929-9444	1176
Arch Parent Inc	Willimantic	CT	A	860 336-4856	4216
Arga Prsnlzed Dcment Solutions	New Haven	CT	F	203 401-3650	2117
Automated Mailing Services LLC	Cheshire	CT	G	203 439-2763	574
Baker Graphics Corporation	Westport	CT	F	203 226-6928	4157
Bardell Printing Corp	East Haven	CT	G	203 469-2441	1037
Barile Printers LLC	New Britain	CT	F	860 224-0127	2007
Better Lists Incorporated	Stamford	CT	E	203 324-4171	3294
Brescias Printing Services Inc	East Hartford	CT	G	860 528-4254	976
Briarwood Printing Company Inc	Plainville	CT	F	860 747-6805	2749
Brody Printing Company Inc	Bridgeport	CT	F	203 384-9313	306
Business Cards Tomorrow Inc	Naugatuck	CT	E	203 723-5858	1950
Byrne Group Inc	Waterbury	CT	F	203 573-0100	3894
Cadmus	Stamford	CT		203 595-3000	3300
Cag Imaging LLC	Norwich	CT	G	860 887-0836	2603
Cannelli Printing Co Inc	West Haven	CT	G	203 932-1719	4096
Capitol Printing Co Inc	Hartford	CT	G	860 522-1547	1473
Cenveo Corporation	Stamford	CT	A	303 790-8023	3307
Chase Graphics Inc	Putnam	CT	F	860 315-9006	2849
Clarity Output Solutions LLC	Stratford	CT	D	800 414-1624	3527
Classic Label Inc	Woodbridge	CT	G	203 389-3535	4378
Craftsmen Printing Group Inc	Stamford	CT	G	203 327-2817	3324
Cricket Press Inc	West Hartford	CT	F	860 521-9279	4055
Custom Printing & Copy Inc (PA)	Enfield	CT	F	860 290-6890	1127
Cyberchrome Inc	Branford	CT	E	203 488-9594	246
Data Management Incorporated	Unionville	CT	E	860 677-8586	3748
Data-Graphics Inc	Newington	CT	D	860 667-0435	2285
Derosa Printing Company Inc	Manchester	CT	E	860 646-1698	1592
Digitaldruker Inc	Oxford	CT	F	203 888-6001	2693
Diversified Prtg Solutions Inc	Danbury	CT	G	203 826-7198	732
Docuprint & Imaging Inc	New Haven	CT	G	203 776-6000	2143
E & A Enterprises Inc	Wallingford	CT	G	203 250-8050	3802

Company	City	ST	EMP	PHONE	ENTRY#
E R Hitchcock Company	New Britain	CT	E	860 229-2024	2024
Ellington Printery Inc	Ellington	CT	G	860 875-3310	1105
Elm Press Incorporated	Terryville	CT	E	860 583-3600	3601
Evergreen Printing	Stamford	CT	G	203 323-4717	3347
Fairfield Marketing Group Inc (PA)	Easton	CT	F	203 261-0884	1095
Fine Print New England Inc	Newington	CT	G	860 953-0660	2293
Flow Resources Inc (HQ)	Newington	CT	E	860 666-1200	2294
Franklin Impressions Inc	Norwich	CT	F	860 887-1661	2605
Furci Communications Inc	Stamford	CT	E	203 961-1800	3353
Fusion Paperboard US Inc	Versailles	CT	C	859 586-1100	3765
Gateway Digital Inc	Norwalk	CT	F	203 853-4929	2503
Ghp Media Inc (PA)	West Haven	CT	D	203 479-7500	4107
Goodcopy Printing Center Inc	New Haven	CT	E	203 624-0194	2155
Goulet Enterprises Inc	Pleasant Valley	CT	F	860 379-0793	2801
Graphic Image Inc	Milford	CT	E	203 877-8787	1830
Gulemo Inc	Willimantic	CT	G	860 456-1151	4218
Hartford Business Supply Inc	Hartford	CT	E	860 233-2138	1485
Herff Jones LLC	Bethlehem	CT	G	203 266-7170	143
Herff Jones LLC	Stratford	CT	F	203 368-9344	3546
High Ridge Copy Inc	Stamford	CT	F	203 329-1889	3376
Ideal Printing Co Incorporated	New Haven	CT	G	203 777-7626	2162
Imperial Grphic Cmmnctions Inc	Milford	CT	E	203 650-3478	1837
Impression Point Inc	Stamford	CT	G	203 353-8800	3382
Inform Inc	Shelton	CT	G	203 924-9929	3020
Integrity Graphics Inc	Simsbury	CT	C	800 343-1248	3091
J & T Printing LLC	Wethersfield	CT	F	860 529-4628	4206
Joseph Merritt & Company Inc	Danbury	CT	F	203 743-6734	762
Joseph Merritt & Company Inc (PA)	Hartford	CT	E	860 296-2500	1488
Jupiter Communications LLC	West Haven	CT	F	475 238-7082	4108
Keno Graphic Services Inc	Shelton	CT	E	203 925-7722	3026
Kingsley Printing Assoc LLC	Stratford	CT	G	203 345-6046	3552
Kool Ink LLC	Bloomfield	CT	F	860 242-0303	186
Kramer Printing Company Inc	West Haven	CT	F	203 933-5416	4110
L P Macadams Company Inc	Bridgeport	CT	D	203 366-3647	342
Landmark Print Inc	Stamford	CT	D	800 499-3808	3396
Lebon Press Incorporated	West Hartford	CT	E	860 278-6355	4066
Leejay Industries LLC	Norwalk	CT	E	203 847-3660	2526
Liberty Screen Print Co LLC	Beacon Falls	CT	E	203 632-5449	41
Lithographics Inc	Farmington	CT	E	860 678-1660	1229
Macdermid Incorporated (HQ)	Waterbury	CT	C	203 575-5700	3933
Maple Print Services Inc	Jewett City	CT	G	860 381-5470	1536
Martin Printing Inc	North Haven	CT	E	203 239-7991	2423
Massachusetts Envelope Co Inc	Hartford	CT	F	860 727-9100	1492
Matthews Printing Co	Wallingford	CT	F	203 265-0363	3830
Mdf Systems Inc	Bristol	CT	D	860 584-4750	466
Middletown Printing Co Inc	Middletown	CT	F	860 347-5700	1765
Minit Print Inc	New Haven	CT	G	203 776-6000	2175
Minute Man Press	Hamden	CT	G	203 891-6251	1443
Minuteman Land Services Inc	Norwalk	CT	G	203 854-4949	2538
Minuteman Press	Avon	CT	G	860 674-8700	31
Minuteman Press	Danbury	CT	G	973 748-7160	787
Minuteman Press	Manchester	CT	G	860 646-0601	1618
Minuteman Press	Trumbull	CT	G	203 261-8318	3725
Minuteman Press	Wethersfield	CT	F	860 529-4628	4211
Minuteman Press of Bristol	Bristol	CT	F	860 589-1100	469
Minuteman Press of Danbury	Danbury	CT	G	203 743-6755	788
Mosaic Prtg Signage Mktg Svcs	Branford	CT	G	203 483-4598	272
Muir Envelope Plus Inc	Newington	CT	F	860 953-6847	2307
New Fairfield Press Inc	New Fairfield	CT	F	203 746-2700	2096
New Haven Register LLC	New Haven	CT	A	203 789-5200	2179
Norwich Printing Company Inc	Norwich	CT	F	860 887-7468	2611
Oddo Print Shop Inc	Torrington	CT	G	860 489-6585	3690
P C I Group	Stamford	CT	F	203 327-0410	3425
Paladin Commercial Prtrs LLC	West Hartford	CT	F	860 953-4900	4077
Panagrafix Inc (PA)	Milford	CT	F	203 878-7412	1862
Paul Dewitt	Danbury	CT	G	203 792-5610	795
Paw Print Pantry LLC (PA)	East Lyme	CT	G	860 447-8442	1060
Phoenix Press Inc	New Haven	CT	G	203 865-5555	2186
Play-It Productions Inc	Colchester	CT	F	212 695-6530	663
Preferred Printing Co Inc	Trumbull	CT	E		3728
Print B2b LLC	Bethel	CT	F	203 744-5435	132
Printer Techs LLC	Stamford	CT	G	203 322-1160	3437
Professional Graphics Inc	Norwalk	CT	F	203 846-4291	2560
Project Graphics Inc	Woodbury	CT	E	802 488-8789	4388
Prospect Printing LLC	Prospect	CT	F	203 758-6007	2841
Protopac Inc	Watertown	CT	G	860 274-6796	4027
Pyne-Davidson Company	Hartford	CT	E	860 522-9106	1501
Qg Printing IL LLC	Enfield	CT	D	860 741-0150	1145
Rare Reminder Incorporated	Rocky Hill	CT	E	860 563-9386	2933
Record-Journal Newspaper (PA)	Meriden	CT	C	203 235-1661	1692
Richard E Personette	Middletown	CT	F	860 344-9001	1778
Rmi Inc	Vernon Rockville	CT	C	860 875-3366	3761
Savin Rock Printing	West Haven	CT	G	203 500-1577	4123

	CITY	ST	EMP	PHONE	ENTRY#
Southbury Printing Centre Inc	Southbury	CT	G	203 264-0102	3198
Specialty Printing LLC	East Windsor	CT	F	860 654-1850	1086
Spectrum Press	East Haven	CT	F	203 878-9090	1051
Spm Management Inc	Shelton	CT	F	203 847-1112	3065
Stratis Visuals LLC (PA)	Torrington	CT	E	860 482-1208	3697
Tech-Repro Inc	Stamford	CT	F	203 348-8884	3478
Technical Reproductions Inc	Norwalk	CT	F	203 849-9100	2575
Technique Printers Inc	Clinton	CT	G	860 669-2516	651
Tfac LLC	New Haven	CT	G	203 776-6000	2208
The Hartford Press Inc	Newington	CT	E	860 296-3588	2327
Toto LLC	New Haven	CT	F	203 776-6000	2210
Transmonde USa Inc	North Branford	CT	D	203 484-1528	2377
Trumbull Printing Inc	Trumbull	CT	C	203 261-2548	3735
Turnstone Inc	Greenwich	CT	F	203 625-0000	1358
Universal Printing Svcs Inc	West Haven	CT	E	203 934-4275	4131
Universal Prtg Miling Svcs Inc	Fairfield	CT	F	203 330-0611	1203
US Games Systems Inc	Stamford	CT	E	800 544-2637	3488
Value Print Incorporated	Wallingford	CT	G	203 265-1371	3873
W B Mason Co Inc	East Windsor	CT	D	888 926-2766	1089
W B Mason Co Inc	Norwalk	CT	F	888 926-2766	2593
W B Mason Co Inc	Norwich	CT	C	888 926-2766	2619
Westrock Commercial LLC	Stamford	CT	G	203 595-3130	3494
Wethersfield Printing Co Inc	Rocky Hill	CT	F	860 721-8236	2941
World Color (usa) Holding Company	North Haven	CT	A	203 288-2468	2445
Yale New Haven Hlth Svcs Corp	New Haven	CT	A	203 688-2100	2217
Youngs Communications Inc	Middletown	CT	F	860 347-8569	1791
A Bismark Company	Fall River	MA	G	508 675-2002	8516
ABS Printing Inc	Swansea	MA	G	401 826-0870	12302
Accucon Incorporated	Leominster	MA	G	978 840-0337	9631
Adlife Advertising & Graphics	Walpole	MA	F	508 668-4109	12547
Advanced Print Solutions Inc	Sharon	MA	G	508 655-8434	11791
Alden-Hauk Inc	Woburn	MA	F	781 281-0154	13503
AlphaGraphics	Concord	MA	G	508 380-8344	8097
AlphaGraphics	Watertown	MA	F	617 924-4091	12857
AM Lithography Corporation	Chicopee	MA	C	413 737-9412	8006
American Prtg & Envelope Inc	Auburn	MA	E	508 832-6100	6102
Andover Printing Inc	Andover	MA	F	978 475-4945	5870
Andrew T Johnson Company Inc (PA)	Boston	MA	F	617 742-1610	6548
Apex Press Inc	Westborough	MA	F	508 366-1110	13076
Applied Image Rprgrphics of Wt	Watertown	MA	G	617 924-6060	12858
Applied Image Rprographics Inc (PA)	Quincy	MA	F	617 471-3373	11503
Arch Parent Inc	West Springfield	MA	A	413 504-1433	13013
Artcraft Co Inc	North Attleboro	MA	D	508 695-4042	10865
Atlantic Printing Co Inc	Medfield	MA	F	781 449-2700	10269
B & W Press Inc	West Newbury	MA	E	978 352-6100	13007
Bassett & Cassidy Inc	Lowell	MA	G	978 452-9595	9860
Bassette Printers LLC	Belchertown	MA	E	413 781-7140	6278
BBC Printing and Products Inc	Waltham	MA	G	781 647-4646	12602
Belmont Printing Company	Belmont	MA	G	617 484-0833	6304
Ben Franklin Print Co Inc	Middleton	MA	G	978 624-7341	10381
Bew Corp	Randolph	MA	F	781 963-0315	11550
Bh Media Inc (HQ)	Lowell	MA	C	617 426-3000	9862
Bopkg Inc (HQ)	Fitchburg	MA	C	978 343-3067	8644
Boston Business Printing Inc	Boston	MA	F	617 482-7955	6606
Boston Document Systems Inc (PA)	Marlborough	MA	E	800 616-8576	10117
Boston Print Specialists LLC	Boston	MA	G	617 742-9585	6613
Bosworth Printing Co Inc	Stoughton	MA	F	781 341-2992	12199
Bradford & Bigelow Inc	Newburyport	MA	C	978 904-3112	10672
Brady Business Forms Inc	Lowell	MA	G	978 458-2585	9865
Braintree Printing Inc	Braintree	MA	E	781 848-5300	7171
Bridgewater Prtg Copy Ctr LLC	Bridgewater	MA	G	508 697-5227	7225
Bruno Diduca	Waltham	MA	G	781 894-5300	12613
Business Resources Inc	Westborough	MA	F	508 433-4600	13084
Calendar Press Inc	Peabody	MA	E	508 531-1860	11300
Capeway Printing & Copy Center	Rockland	MA	G	781 878-1600	11638
Cenveo	Westfield	MA	G	203 595-3109	13158
Choice Graphics Inc	Rowley	MA	G	978 948-2789	11672
Cimpress USA Incorporated	Waltham	MA	F	866 207-4955	12626
Cimpress USA Incorporated (DH)	Waltham	MA	E	781 652-6300	12627
Citius Printing & Graphics LLC	Waltham	MA	G	781 547-5550	12629
City of Boston	Boston	MA	C	617 635-3700	6657
Clark Mailing Service Inc	Worcester	MA	E	508 752-1953	13708
Classic Envelope Inc	East Douglas	MA	D	508 731-6747	8349
Colonial Lithograph Inc	Attleboro	MA	F	508 222-1832	6006
Connolly Printing LLC	Woburn	MA	F	781 932-8885	13545
Copy Cop The Digital Printing Company LLC	Boston	MA			E
617 267-8899	6669				
Copy Masters Inc	Taunton	MA	F	508 824-7187	12329
Corporate Press	Norwood	MA	F	781 769-6656	11170
Country Press Inc	Lakeville	MA	F	508 947-4485	9516
Creamer Associates Inc	Cambridge	MA	G	617 374-6000	7544
Creative Imprints Inc	Norton	MA	E	508 285-7650	11125
Creative Print Products Inc	Leominster	MA	F	978 534-2030	9654
D & L Associates Inc	Needham Heights	MA	G	781 400-5068	10540
D B S Industries Inc	Haverhill	MA	D	978 373-4748	9090
D S Graphics Inc (PA)	Lowell	MA	C	978 970-1359	9873
Da Rosas	Oak Bluffs	MA	E	508 693-0110	11221
Data Print Inc	Woburn	MA	F	781 935-3350	13556
Datasite Global Corporation	Everett	MA	B	617 389-7900	8486
Davol/Taunton Printing Inc	Taunton	MA	F	508 824-4305	12331
Defiance Graphics Corp	Rowley	MA	F	978 948-2789	11673
Descal Inc	Waltham	MA	F	781 736-9400	12651
Deschamps Printing Co Inc	Salem	MA	F	978 744-2152	11711
Desk Top Graphics Inc (HQ)	Peabody	MA	E	617 832-1927	11305
Devincentis Press Inc	Malden	MA	F	781 663-3796	10008
Digipress Inc (PA)	Peabody	MA	C	617 832-1927	11306
Digital Graphics Inc	North Billerica	MA	G	781 270-3670	10907
Digital On Demand LLC	Danvers	MA	G	978 224-7900	8181
Dion Label Printing Inc	Westfield	MA	D	413 568-3713	13162
Dmr Print Inc (PA)	Concord	MA	F	617 876-3688	8114
Documents On Demand Inc	Worcester	MA	F	508 793-0956	13718
Docuserve Inc	Marlborough	MA	F	508 786-5820	10146
Duplication Management Inc	Woburn	MA	D	781 935-7224	13559
E V Yeuell Inc	Woburn	MA	F	781 933-2984	13560
East Coast Printing Inc	Hingham	MA	G	781 331-5635	9150
Eastern Etching and Mfg Co	Chicopee	MA	E	413 594-6601	8030
Elbonais Incorporated	Framingham	MA	G	508 626-2318	8761
Enon Copy Inc (PA)	Beverly	MA	G	978 927-8757	6346
Essex Ruling & Printing Co	Methuen	MA	G	978 682-2457	10331
Excelsior Printing Company	North Adams	MA	D	413 663-3771	10807
Fall River Modern Prtg Co Inc	Fall River	MA	F	508 673-9421	8548
Farganyd Inc	Canton	MA	C	781 575-1700	7790
Fars Inc	Northampton	MA	E	413 586-1332	11061
Fasprint Inc (PA)	Brockton	MA	F	508 588-9961	7278
Fenway Cmmunications Group Inc	Boston	MA	E	617 226-1900	6734
First Impression Printing Inc	Stoughton	MA	G	781 344-8855	12209
Flagship Press Inc	North Andover	MA	C	978 975-3100	10831
Fleming & Son Corp	Chelmsford	MA	F	617 623-3047	7928
Footprint Pwr Acquisitions LLC	Salem	MA	F	978 740-8411	11715
Fowler Printing & Graphics Inc	Randolph	MA	F	781 986-8900	11558
Freedom Digital Printing LLC	Ashland	MA	F	508 881-6940	5959
Gangi Printing Inc	Woburn	MA	F	617 776-6071	13573
Gazette Printing Co Inc	Easthampton	MA	F	413 527-7700	8446
Generation Four Inc	Waltham	MA	G	781 899-3180	12686
George H Dean Co	Braintree	MA	D	781 544-3782	7184
Ggs Custom Metals Inc	South Hadley	MA	F	413 315-4344	11962
Ghp Media Inc	North Adams	MA	D	413 663-3771	10808
Gmf Engineering Inc	Saugus	MA	F	781 233-0315	11758
Graphic Developments Inc	Hanover	MA	E	781 878-2222	9033
Graphic Excellence LLC	Springfield	MA	G	413 733-6691	12096
Greentree Marketing Inc	Framingham	MA	F	508 877-2581	8775
Hadley Printing Company Inc	Holyoke	MA	E	413 536-8517	9258
Hall Mailing & Fulfillment Inc	Haverhill	MA	F	978 372-6546	9100
Harborside Printing Co Inc	Newburyport	MA	F	978 462-2026	10686
Herring Inc	Hyannis	MA	B	401 837-3111	9438
High-Speed Process Prtg Corp	Lawrence	MA	F	978 683-2766	9568
Hitchcock Press Inc	Holyoke	MA	G	413 538-8811	9260
Ils Business Services Inc	Agawam	MA	G	413 789-4555	5793
Imperial Image Inc	North Chelmsford	MA	F	978 251-0420	10978
Ingleside Corporation	Norwood	MA	F	781 769-6656	11180
Inkstone Inc	Brockton	MA	F	508 587-5200	7284
Instant Offset Press Inc	Hyannis	MA	F	508 790-1100	9439
J & R Graphics Inc	Hanover	MA	F	781 871-7577	9036
J T Gardner Inc (PA)	Westborough	MA	E	800 540-4993	13112
J&S Business Products Inc	Ayer	MA	G	877 425-4049	6183
Jam Plastics Inc	Leominster	MA	F	978 537-2570	9672
John K Dietrich & Assoc Inc	Watertown	MA	E	617 868-4140	12884
John P Pow Company Inc	Boston	MA	E	617 269-6040	6827
Jordan Enterprises Inc	Marlborough	MA	F	508 481-2948	10172
JP Progressive Comm Group LLC	New Bedford	MA	G	800 477-4681	10607
Just Ur Way Screen Print	Westport	MA	F	508 235-0422	13298
Keating Communication Group	Canton	MA	G	781 828-9030	7804
Kervick Family Foundation Inc	Worcester	MA	E	508 853-4500	13748
King Printing Company Inc	Lowell	MA	D	978 458-2345	9891
Kirkwood Holdings Inc (PA)	Wilmington	MA	B	978 658-4200	13420
Kwik-Print Inc	Great Barrington	MA	F	413 528-2885	8977
Labelprint America Inc	Newburyport	MA	E	978 463-4004	10693
Lane Printing Co Inc	Holbrook	MA	F	781 767-4450	9178
Laplume & Sons Printing Inc	Lawrence	MA	E	978 683-1009	9576
Lexington Graphics Inc	Lexington	MA	F	781 863-9510	9758
Liberty Printing Inc	Brockton	MA	G	508 586-6810	7291
Lincoln Press Co Inc	Fall River	MA	F	508 673-3241	8569
Linmel Associates Inc	Marlborough	MA	F	508 481-6699	10180
Lion Labels Inc	South Easton	MA	E	508 230-8211	11947
Litho-Craft Inc	Stoneham	MA	F	781 729-1789	12181
LPI Printing and Graphic Inc	Stoneham	MA	F	781 438-5400	12182

	CITY	ST	EMP	PHONE	ENTRY#
Lujean Printing Co Inc	Cotuit	MA	E	508 428-8700	8146
M & C Press Inc	Cambridge	MA	F	617 354-2584	7636
Mallard Printing Inc	Fall River	MA	F	508 675-5733	8572
Mansir Printing LLC	Holyoke	MA	F	413 536-4250	9264
Marbuo Inc	North Dartmouth	MA	F	508 994-7700	10999
Marcus Company Inc	Holyoke	MA	E	413 534-3303	9265
Mass Printing Inc	North Reading	MA	G	781 396-1970	11042
Massachusetts Repro Ltd	Boston	MA	F	617 227-2237	6876
Maximus	Lowell	MA	G	978 728-8000	9903
May Graphics & Printing Inc	Westford	MA	G		13250
MBI Graphics & Printing Corp	Southbridge	MA	F	508 765-0658	12028
McGirr Graphics Incorporated	Plymouth	MA	E	508 747-6400	11464
Medi - Print Inc (PA)	Malden	MA	E	781 324-4455	10019
Medianews Group Inc	Fitchburg	MA	E	978 343-6911	8663
Miano Printing Services Inc	Holliston	MA	F	617 935-2830	9222
Miles Press Inc	Auburn	MA	F	508 752-6430	6120
Milk Street Press Inc	Boston	MA	F	617 742-7900	6888
Millennium Press Inc	Agawam	MA	E	413 821-0028	5801
Minute-Man Printing Corp	Concord	MA	F	978 369-2808	8125
Minuteman Press	Burlington	MA	G	781 273-1155	7394
Minuteman Press	Centerville	MA	G	508 775-9890	7860
Minuteman Press	Hyannis	MA	G	508 778-0220	9441
Minuteman Press	Hyde Park	MA	G	617 361-7400	9463
Minuteman Printing	Plymouth	MA	G	508 830-3500	11468
Modus Media Inc	Waltham	MA	E	781 663-5000	12724
Monaghan Printing Company	Fairhaven	MA	F	508 991-8087	8510
MSP Digital Marketing Mass Inc (HQ)	Hudson	MA	F	978 567-6000	9394
Mystic Parker Printing Inc	Malden	MA	F	781 321-4948	10020
Naley Inc	Worcester	MA	G	508 579-8378	13763
Neenah Technical Materials Inc (DH)	Dalton	MA	F	678 518-3343	8151
Neoprint Inc	Chelmsford	MA	F	978 256-9939	7941
New England Mktg & Prtg Inc	Attleboro	MA	E	917 582-1029	6042
New Valence Robotics Corp	Canton	MA	G	857 529-6397	7812
Newprint Offset Inc	Lexington	MA	F	781 891-6002	9765
Nfall Corp	Devens	MA	E	978 615-4030	8282
North River Graphics Inc	Pembroke	MA	G	781 826-6866	11375
Northpoint Printing Svcs Inc	Hudson	MA	F	781 895-1900	9396
Oliveri & Associates Inc	Plymouth	MA	F	781 320-9090	11470
Owl Stamp Company Inc	Lowell	MA	G	978 452-4541	9912
Oxford Graphics LLC	Peabody	MA	F	978 281-3663	11329
Paiva Corp	Fall River	MA	G	508 679-7921	8593
Picken Printing Inc	North Chelmsford	MA	F	978 251-0730	10986
PIP Foundation Inc	Framingham	MA	D	508 757-0103	8798
Plastilam Inc	Salem	MA	E	978 745-5563	11730
Potters Printing Inc	Fall River	MA	F	617 547-3161	8598
President Press Inc	Quincy	MA	F	617 773-1235	11532
Pressed For Time Printing Inc	Boston	MA	F	617 267-4113	6978
Pretty Instant LLC	Boston	MA	F	888 551-6765	6979
Primary Graphics Corporation	Taunton	MA	F	781 575-0411	12355
Princeton Printing LLC	Somerville	MA	G	617 530-0990	11889
Print Management Systems Inc	Woburn	MA	F	781 944-1041	13640
Print Pro	Haverhill	MA	G	978 914-7619	9122
Print Synergy Solutions LLC	Brockton	MA	F	508 587-5200	7301
Print Works Inc	Hopkinton	MA	G	508 589-4626	9341
Printing Dept	Cambridge	MA	E	617 349-4206	7689
Printing Solutions Inc	Westford	MA	F	978 392-9903	13257
Priority Print	Cambridge	MA	G	617 547-6919	7690
Pyramid Printing and Advg Inc	Weymouth	MA	E	781 337-7609	13333
Qg LLC	Taunton	MA	B	508 828-4400	12360
Qg Printing Corp	Leominster	MA	G	978 534-8351	9698
Quad/Graphics Inc	East Longmeadow	MA	D	413 525-8552	8391
Quad/Graphics Inc	Leominster	MA	G	978 534-8351	9699
Quad/Graphics Inc	Woburn	MA	C	781 231-7200	13643
Quality Envelope & Printing Co	Middleboro	MA	F	508 947-8878	10376
Quality Printing Company Inc	Pittsfield	MA	D	413 442-4166	11421
Quick Print Ltd Inc	Chelmsford	MA	G	978 256-1822	7950
R & H Communications Inc (PA)	Waltham	MA	F	781 893-6221	12757
Rainbow Graphics Inc	Springfield	MA	F	413 733-3376	12124
Ramsbottom Printing Inc	Fall River	MA	E	508 730-2220	8600
REA-Craft Press Incorporated	Foxboro	MA	F	508 543-8710	8716
Recycled Paper Company Inc	Waltham	MA	F	617 737-9911	12763
Red Sun Press Inc	Jamaica Plain	MA	F	617 524-6822	9503
Regal Press Incorporated (PA)	Norwood	MA	C	781 769-3900	11206
Reynolds D-Rap Corp	New Bedford	MA	E	800 447-4681	10645
Rhode Island Mktg & Prtg Inc	Attleboro	MA	E	917 582-1029	6054
Rivkind Associates Inc (PA)	South Easton	MA	F	781 269-2415	11952
Roberts & Sons Printing Inc	Springfield	MA	G	413 283-9356	12126
Royal Label Co Inc	Boston	MA	F	617 825-6050	7017
Seventy Nine N Main St Prtg	Andover	MA	G	978 475-4945	5917
Shafiis Inc (PA)	East Longmeadow	MA	E	413 224-2100	8394
Shawmut Advertising Inc (PA)	Peabody	MA	E	978 762-7500	11340
Shawmut Printing	Peabody	MA	E	978 762-7500	11341
Shear Color Printing Inc	Woburn	MA	E	781 376-9607	13664
Sherman Printing Co Inc	Canton	MA	E	781 828-8855	7828
Sical	Westborough	MA	F	508 898-1800	13135
Sir Speedy	Braintree	MA	G	781 848-0990	7202
Springfield Eye Associates	Springfield	MA	E	413 739-7367	12134
Springfield Label Tape Co Inc	Springfield	MA	E	413 733-6634	12135
Standard Modern Company	New Bedford	MA	G	774 425-3537	10651
Standard Modern Company Inc	New Bedford	MA	D	508 586-4300	10652
Star Litho Inc	Weymouth	MA	F	781 340-9401	13336
Star Printing Corp	Taunton	MA	E	508 583-9046	12369
Starburst Prtg & Graphics Inc	Holliston	MA	F	508 893-0900	9231
State-Line Graphics Inc	Everett	MA	F	617 389-1200	8501
Sterling Business Products Inc	Stoneham	MA	F	781 481-1234	12186
Stickamayka Packaging Inc	Andover	MA	E	978 474-1930	5926
Studley Press Inc	Dalton	MA	F	413 684-0441	8156
Superlative Printing Inc	Stoughton	MA	G	781 341-9000	12240
Taylor Communications Inc	Avon	MA	F	508 584-0102	6164
TCI Press Inc	Seekonk	MA	E	508 336-6633	11787
Technical Publications Inc	Waltham	MA	F	781 899-0263	12789
Techprint Inc	Lawrence	MA	D	978 975-1245	9602
Thomas & Thomas Inc	Lowell	MA	F	978 453-7444	9928
Tisbury Printer Inc	Vineyard Haven	MA	F	508 693-4222	12495
Titus & Bean Graphics Inc	Kingston	MA	F	781 585-1355	9513
Tls Printing LLC	Townsend	MA	E	508 234-2344	12443
Toth Inc (PA)	Concord	MA	E	617 577-6400	8136
Tri Star Printing & Graphics	Somerville	MA	G	617 666-4480	11905
Trustees of Tufts College (PA)	Somerville	MA	B	617 628-5000	11906
Tshb Inc	Newburyport	MA	E	978 465-8950	10721
Uni-Graphic Inc	Woburn	MA	C	781 231-7200	13680
Universal Tag Inc	Dudley	MA	E	508 949-2411	8326
Universal Wilde Inc (PA)	Canton	MA	C	781 251-2700	7837
Universal Wilde Inc	Canton	MA	C	978 658-0800	7838
Universal Wilde Inc	Holliston	MA	C	508 429-5515	9237
Universal Wilde Inc	Rockland	MA	C	781 251-2700	11664
Van-Go Graphics	Grafton	MA	G	508 865-7300	8969
Vistaprint	Norwood	MA	F	866 614-8002	11219
Vistaprint Corp Solutions Inc	Waltham	MA	E	844 347-4162	12813
W B Mason Co Inc	Framingham	MA	D	888 926-2766	8809
W B Mason Co Inc	Greenfield	MA	E	888 926-2766	9004
W S Walcott Inc	Orleans	MA	G	508 240-0882	11244
Wakefield Item Company	Wakefield	MA	E	781 245-0080	12542
Watson Printing Co Inc	Wellesley	MA	G	781 237-1336	12947
We Print Today LLC	Kingston	MA	F	781 585-6021	9514
Webster Printing Company Inc (PA)	Hanson	MA	E	781 447-5484	9058
Westfield News Publishing Inc (DH)	Westfield	MA	E	413 562-4181	13221
Westrex International Inc	Boston	MA	F	617 254-1200	7119
Wholesale Printing Inc	Woburn	MA	F	781 937-3357	13688
Winthrop Printing Company Inc	Foxboro	MA	E	617 268-9660	8732
Xpression Prints Inc	Franklin	MA	G	401 413-6930	8876
Yankee Printing Group Inc	South Hadley	MA	E	413 532-9513	11968
Ziprint Centers Inc	Randolph	MA	G	781 963-2250	11580
Alliance Printers LLC	Brunswick	ME	G	207 504-8200	4639
Arch Parent Inc	Connor Twp	ME	A	207 492-5414	4700
Armstrong Family Inds Inc	Hermon	ME	E	207 848-7300	4880
Artco Offset Inc	Augusta	ME	E	781 830-7900	4467
Bromar	Skowhegan	ME	G	207 474-3784	5463
Central Street Corporation	Bangor	ME	F	207 947-8049	4495
Checksforlesscom	Portland	ME	F	800 245-5775	5198
Coastal Business Center Inc	Wiscasset	ME	G	207 882-7197	5697
Copy Center (PA)	Winthrop	ME	F	207 623-1452	5691
County Qwik Print Inc	Caribou	ME	F	207 492-0360	4674
Curry Printing & Copy Center	Portland	ME	F	207 772-5897	5203
Cybercopy Inc	Westbrook	ME	G	207 775-2679	5623
Dale Rand Printing Inc	Portland	ME	G	207 773-8198	5204
Davic Inc	Portland	ME	G	207 774-0093	5206
Dingley Press Inc	Lewiston	ME	C	207 782-1529	4956
Dj Printing Inc	South Portland	ME	G	207 773-0439	5498
Downeast Graphics & Prtg Inc	Ellsworth	ME	F	207 667-5582	4757
E I Printing Co	Portland	ME	F	207 797-4838	5213
Evergreen Custom Printing Inc	Auburn	ME	G	207 782-2327	4430
First Choice Printing Inc	Lisbon Falls	ME	G	207 353-8006	5020
Full Court Press	Westbrook	ME	F	207 464-0002	5626
Furbush Roberts Prtg Co Inc	Bangor	ME	G	207 945-9409	4503
Geiger Bros (PA)	Lewiston	ME	B	207 755-2000	4962
Jiffy Print Inc	Bangor	ME	G	207 947-4490	4507
JS McCarthy Co Inc (PA)	Augusta	ME	D	207 622-6241	4473
L H Thompson Inc	Brewer	ME	F	207 989-3280	4615
Letter Systems Inc (PA)	Augusta	ME	C	207 622-7126	4475
Lincoln County Publishing Co	Newcastle	ME	E	207 563-3171	5093
Minuteman Press	Denmark	ME	G	207 517-5355	4724
Minuteman Press of Saco	Saco	ME	G	207 282-6480	5374
Mpx	Portland	ME	D	207 774-6116	5246
Nemi Publishing Inc	Farmington	ME	E	207 778-4801	4782
Northeast Publishing Company	Dover Foxcroft	ME	G	207 564-8355	4730

Company	CITY	ST	EMP	PHONE	ENTRY#
Penmor Lithographers Inc	Lewiston	ME	E	207 784-1341	4984
Portland Printing Group	Portland	ME	G	207 347-5700	5260
Print-Mail of Maine Inc	Portland	ME	F	207 878-8000	5262
Printemscom	Sanford	ME	G	207 490-5118	5406
Pyramid Checks & Printing	Portland	ME	D	207 878-9832	5264
Quality Copy Inc	Hallowell	ME	G	207 622-7447	4861
R N Haskins Printing Inc	Sidney	ME	F	207 465-2155	5460
RH Rosenfield Co	Sanford	ME	E	207 324-1798	5410
Sheridan Me Inc	Lisbon	ME	G	207 353-1500	5016
Snowman Group	Hermon	ME	E	207 848-7300	4889
The Dingley Press Inc **(PA)**	Lisbon	ME	C	207 353-1500	5018
Time4printing Inc	Windham	ME	F	207 838-1496	5672
W B Mason Co Inc	Augusta	ME	E	888 926-2766	4481
W B Mason Co Inc	Bangor	ME	E	888 926-2766	4520
W B Mason Co Inc	Portland	ME	E	888 926-2766	5288
Waterfront Graphics & Prtg LLC	South Portland	ME	G	207 799-3519	5517
A & R Sawyer Co Inc	Windham	NH	G	603 893-5752	15719
Alpha Grphics Prntshop of Ftur	Nashua	NH	F	603 595-1444	15058
Baker Graphics Inc	Manchester	NH	G	603 625-5427	14816
Bam Lab LLC	Somersworth	NH	G	603 973-9388	15610
Bob Bean Company Inc	Londonderry	NH	F	603 818-4390	14733
Boles Enterprises Inc	Manchester	NH	G	603 622-4282	14820
Bridge & Byron Inc	Concord	NH	G	603 225-5221	14118
Capital Offset Co Inc	Hollis	NH	F	603 225-3308	14448
Capitol Screen Prtg & Embro	Concord	NH	G	603 234-7000	14120
Concord Litho Group LLC **(PA)**	Concord	NH	C	603 224-1202	14123
Cygnus Inc	Portsmouth	NH	G	603 431-8989	15379
Dartmouth Printing Company **(DH)**	Hanover	NH	E	603 643-2220	14422
Dr Biron Incorporated **(PA)**	Manchester	NH	F	603 622-5222	14844
E Print Inc	Hudson	NH	G	603 594-0009	14495
Eagle Publications Inc	Claremont	NH	E	603 543-3100	14089
Echo Communications Inc	New London	NH	E	603 526-6006	15203
Evans Printing Co	Bow	NH	G	603 856-8238	13997
Frugal Printer Inc	Salem	NH	G	603 894-6333	15529
Harrison Publishing House Inc	Littleton	NH	E	603 444-0820	14720
Higgingbotham Management Corp	Portsmouth	NH	F	603 431-0142	15402
Infinite Imaging Inc	Portsmouth	NH	F	603 436-3030	15407
Insty-Prints of Bedford Inc	Bedford	NH	G	603 622-3821	13934
Itnh Inc	Manchester	NH	E	603 669-6900	14865
Just Hit Print LLC	Center Harbor	NH	G	603 279-5939	14056
Kase Printing Inc	Hudson	NH	F	603 883-9223	14514
Kelley Solutions Inc	Rye	NH	G	603 431-3881	15499
Kensington Group Incorporated	Hampton Falls	NH	F	603 926-6742	14419
Lew A Cummings Co Inc	Hooksett	NH	C	603 625-6901	14467
Megaprint Inc	Holderness	NH	F	603 536-2900	14447
Minuteman Press	Concord	NH	G	603 513-4993	14146
Mtl Print Solution LLC	Hampstead	NH	G	603 479-2998	14387
New England Duplicator Inc	Manchester	NH	G	603 623-6847	14898
Odyssey Press Inc **(PA)**	Dover	NH	E	603 749-4433	14243
P2k Printing LLC	North Conway	NH	G	603 356-2010	15249
Papergraphics Print & Copy Inc	Merrimack	NH	F	603 880-1835	14997
Printers Square Inc	Manchester	NH	E	603 703-0795	14915
Puritan Press Inc **(PA)**	Hollis	NH	E	603 889-4500	14458
R C Brayshaw & Co LLC **(PA)**	Warner	NH	E	603 456-3101	15667
Rainville Printing Entps Inc	Concord	NH	F	603 225-6649	14153
Rainville Printing Entps Inc	Pembroke	NH	G	603 485-3422	15308
Ram Printing Incorporated **(PA)**	East Hampstead	NH	E	603 382-7045	14271
RB Graphics Inc	Hooksett	NH	G	603 624-4025	14473
S & Q Printers Inc	Belmont	NH	G	603 654-2888	13972
Sant Bani Press Inc	Manchester	NH	G	603 286-3114	14925
Savron Graphics Inc **(PA)**	Jaffrey	NH	G	603 532-7726	14579
Sherwin Dodge Printers Inc	Littleton	NH	F	603 444-6552	14723
Smith & Town Printers LLC	Berlin	NH	F	603 752-2150	13986
Southport Management Group LLC	Portsmouth	NH	G	603 433-4664	15438
Spirit Advisory LLC	Portsmouth	NH	G	603 433-4664	15439
Sumner Printing Inc	Somersworth	NH	E	603 692-7424	15625
Tylergraphics Inc	Laconia	NH	G	603 524-6625	14672
Uvp Liquidation Inc	North Haverhill	NH	D	603 787-7000	15253
W B Mason Co Inc	Manchester	NH	D	888 926-2766	14957
Wall Shotz	Greenland	NH	G	603 431-0900	14372
Water Street Printing LLC	Nashua	NH	F	603 595-1444	15186
Wharf Industries Printing Inc	Windham	NH	E	603 421-2566	15729
Whitman Communications Inc	Lebanon	NH	G	603 448-2600	14703
136 Express Printing Inc	Bristol	RI	G	401 253-0136	15751
A & H Composition and Prtg Inc	East Providence	RI	G	401 438-1200	15999
Advanced Print Tech LLC	East Providence	RI	G	401 434-8802	16001
Allied Group LLC **(PA)**	Cranston	RI	B	401 946-6100	15829
AlphaGraphics	Providence	RI	G	401 648-0078	16468
Arch Parent Inc	Westerly	RI	A	401 388-9802	16928
Barrington Enterprises LLC	Warwick	RI	E	401 943-8300	16788
Blazing Editions	East Greenwich	RI	G	401 885-4329	15974
Branch Graphics Inc	Rumford	RI	E	401 861-1830	16663
Colonial Printing Inc **(PA)**	Warwick	RI	E	401 691-3400	16795

Company	CITY	ST	EMP	PHONE	ENTRY#
Copy World Inc	East Providence	RI	G	401 438-1200	16011
Crosstown Press Inc	Cranston	RI	G	401 941-4061	15845
Digital Printing Concepts Inc	Providence	RI	G	401 751-4953	16508
Freshco	Providence	RI	G	401 351-1911	16522
Igt Global Solutions Corp	West Greenwich	RI	E	401 392-7025	16885
Igt Global Solutions Corporation **(HQ)**	Providence	RI	D	401 392-7077	16538
Image Printing & Copying Inc	Warwick	RI	F	401 737-9311	16821
Jay Packaging Group Inc **(DH)**	Warwick	RI	D	401 244-1300	16827
Key Graphics Inc	Kingston	RI	G	401 826-2425	16113
Louis Press Inc	Johnston	RI	G	401 351-9229	16094
Matlet Group LLC	Providence	RI	G	401 834-3007	16560
Mdc Signs Printing	Cranston	RI	G	401 654-5354	15892
Meridian Printing Inc	East Greenwich	RI	D	401 885-4882	15991
Mono Die Cutting Co Inc	Riverside	RI	F	401 434-1274	16658
Narragansett Bus Forms Inc	East Providence	RI	F	401 331-2000	16033
Oberlin LLC	Providence	RI	G	401 588-8755	16577
Peak Printing Inc	Providence	RI	F	401 351-0500	16582
Ppoes Inc	Providence	RI	G	401 421-5160	16586
Proprint Incorporated	Johnston	RI	F	401 944-3855	16101
Regine Printing Co Inc	Providence	RI	G	401 943-3404	16600
Romano Investments Inc	Warwick	RI	E	401 691-3400	16854
Signature Printing Inc	East Providence	RI	D	401 438-1200	16044
Sir Speedy	Providence	RI	G	401 351-7400	16612
Sir Speedy Printing Inc	Cranston	RI	E	401 781-5650	15911
W B Mason Co Inc	Cranston	RI	D	888 926-2766	15926
WEB Printing Inc	Cumberland	RI	G	401 334-3190	15971
802 Print LLC	Vergennes	VT	G	802 598-0967	17655
Accura Printing	Barre	VT	G	802 476-4429	16996
Buyers Digest Press Inc	Fairfax	VT	F	802 893-4214	17256
Community Apostolic Order Inc **(PA)**	Island Pond	VT	F	802 723-4452	17304
Digital Press Printers LLC	Williston	VT	F	802 863-5579	17727
Edward Group Inc	Rutland	VT	F	802 775-1029	17496
Evan Webster Ink LLC	Charlotte	VT	F	802 222-0344	17177
First Step Print Shop LLC	Burlington	VT	G	802 899-2708	17555
Howard Printing Inc	Brattleboro	VT	E	802 254-3550	17087
Industrial Marking Systems Corp	Milton	VT	D	802 752-3170	17360
Inkjetmallcom Ltd	Topsham	VT	G	802 439-3127	17649
Inkspot Press	Bennington	VT	E	802 447-1768	17041
L Brown and Sons Printing Inc	Barre	VT	E	802 476-3164	17012
Lane Press Inc	South Burlington	VT	C	877 300-5933	17583
Larcoline Inc **(PA)**	Colchester	VT	F	802 864-5440	17197
McClure Newspapers Inc	Williston	VT	C	802 863-3441	17740
Offset House Inc	Essex Junction	VT	C	802 878-4440	17242
Queen City Printers Inc	Burlington	VT	E	802 864-4566	17153
Springfield Printing Corp	North Springfield	VT	E	802 886-2201	17425
Stillwater Graphics Inc	Williamstown	VT	F	802 433-9898	17718
The Leahy Press Inc	Montpelier	VT	E	802 223-2100	17375
Tuttle Law Print Inc	Rutland	VT	D	802 773-9171	17512
US Mailing Systems Inc	Milton	VT	E	802 891-1020	17365
Uvm Print Mail Center	Burlington	VT	E	802 656-8149	17163
Vermont Publishing Comany	Saint Albans	VT	E	802 524-9771	17536
Villanti & Sons Printers Inc	Milton	VT	D	802 864-0723	17367
W B Mason Co Inc	Brattleboro	VT	E	888 926-2766	17106
W B Mason Co Inc	South Burlington	VT	E	888 926-2766	17607
Whiteside Holdings Inc	Winooski	VT	E	802 655-7654	17772
X Press In Stowe Inc	Stowe	VT	G	802 253-9788	17633

2754 Commercial printing, gravure

Company	CITY	ST	EMP	PHONE	ENTRY#
Brook & Whittle Limited **(PA)**	Guilford	CT	B	203 483-5602	1388
Brook & Whittle Limited	North Branford	CT	F	203 483-5602	2361
Massachusetts Envelope Co Inc	Hartford	CT	F	860 727-9100	1492
Schmitt Realty Holdings Inc	Branford	CT	F	203 488-3252	275
World Color (usa) Holding Company	North Haven	CT	A	203 288-2468	2445
D B S Industries Inc	Haverhill	MA	D	978 373-4748	9090
Interprint Inc	Pittsfield	MA	C	413 443-4733	11402
Jungle Inc **(PA)**	Essex	MA	F	978 356-7722	8476
Laplume & Sons Printing Inc	Lawrence	MA	F	978 683-1009	9576
Leap Year Publishing LLC	Newburyport	MA	F	978 688-9900	10695
Shear Color Printing Inc	Woburn	MA	E	781 376-9607	13664
Stat Products Inc	Ashland	MA	E	508 881-8022	5967
Sterling Business Products Inc	Stoneham	MA	F	781 481-1234	12186
Label Tech LLC	Somersworth	NH	C	603 692-2005	15618
Nashua Corporation	Merrimack	NH	A	603 880-1100	14994
Providence Label & Tag Co	Providence	RI	F	401 751-6677	16591
Vermont Christmas Company	Milton	VT	G	802 893-1670	17366

2759 Commercial printing, nec

Company	CITY	ST	EMP	PHONE	ENTRY#
A To A Studio Solutions Ltd	Stamford	CT	F	203 388-9050	3267
Advanced Graphics Incorporated	Stratford	CT	E	203 378-0471	3515
Allied Printing Services Inc **(PA)**	Manchester	CT	B	860 643-1101	1584
Amgraph Packaging Inc **(PA)**	Baltic	CT	D	860 822-2000	37
Ansel Label and Packaging Corp	Trumbull	CT	E	203 452-0311	3711
Baron Technology Inc	Milford	CT	F	203 452-0515	1800

Employee Codes: A=Over 500 employees, B=251-500
C=101-250, D=51-100, E=20-50, F=10-19, G=1-9   2024 Harris New England
Manufacturers Directory   871

SIC

Company	CITY	ST	EMP	PHONE	ENTRY#
Beekley Corporation (PA)	Bristol	CT	D	860 583-4700	411
Better Lists Incorporated	Stamford	CT	E	203 324-4171	3294
Boltprintingcom	Brookfield	CT	G	203 885-0571	511
Broadrdge Cstmer Cmmnctons E L (PA)	South Windsor	CT	E	860 290-7000	3122
Brook & Whittle Limited (PA)	Guilford	CT	B	203 483-5602	1388
Brook & Whittle Limited	North Branford	CT	F	203 483-5602	2361
Cannelli Printing Co Inc	West Haven	CT	G	203 932-1719	4096
CCL Industries Corporation	Shelton	CT	A	203 926-1253	2989
CCL Label Inc	Shelton	CT	A	203 926-1253	2990
Cenveo Corporation	Stamford	CT	A	303 790-8023	3307
Colorgraphix LLC	Oxford	CT	G	203 264-5212	2690
Copy Cats Inc	New London	CT	F	860 442-8424	2225
Critical Scrn Printg & EMB	Waterford	CT	G	860 443-4327	3988
Custom Tees Plus	New Haven	CT	G	203 752-1071	2142
Custom TS n More LLC	Ridgefield	CT	G	203 438-1592	2894
Design Label Manufacturing Inc	Old Lyme	CT	E	860 739-6266	2640
E Cook Associates Inc	Watertown	CT	F	860 283-9849	4010
Eastwood Printing Inc	Wethersfield	CT	F	860 529-6673	4204
Electrocal Inc	Manchester	CT	C	860 646-8153	1595
Elm Press Incorporated	Terryville	CT	E	860 583-3600	3601
Envelopes & More Inc	Newington	CT	F	860 286-7570	2292
Executive Greetings Inc (HQ)	New Hartford	CT	B	860 379-9911	2100
Fairfield Marketing Group Inc (PA)	Easton	CT	F	203 261-0884	1095
Fresh Ink LLC	West Hartford	CT	F	860 656-7013	4061
Fusion Paperboard US Inc	Versailles	CT	C	859 586-1100	3765
Gateway Digital Inc	Norwalk	CT	F	203 853-4929	2503
George Schmitt & Co Inc (PA)	Guilford	CT	E	203 453-4334	1394
Hamden Packaging Inc	Hamden	CT	E	203 288-0200	1428
Ideal Printing Co Incorporated	New Haven	CT	G	203 777-7626	2162
Identification Products Corp	Bridgeport	CT	F	203 334-5969	331
Identification Products Corp (PA)	Shelton	CT	E	203 334-5969	3019
Imperial Grphic Cmmnctions Inc	Milford	CT	E	203 650-3478	1837
Integrated Print Solutions Inc	Bridgeport	CT	F	203 330-0200	332
Kool Ink LLC	Bloomfield	CT	F	860 242-0303	186
Kramer Printing Company Inc	West Haven	CT	F	203 933-5416	4110
L P Macadams Company Inc	Bridgeport	CT	D	203 366-3647	342
Liberty Screen Print Co LLC	Beacon Falls	CT	F	203 632-5449	41
Lorenco Industries Inc	Bethel	CT	F	203 743-6962	127
Mallace Industries Corp	Bloomfield	CT	F	800 521-0194	191
Martin Printing Inc	North Haven	CT	E	203 239-7991	2423
Matthews Printing Co	Wallingford	CT	F	203 265-0363	3830
McWeeney Marketing Group Inc	Orange	CT	G	203 891-8100	2677
Mlk Business Forms Inc	New Haven	CT	F	203 624-6304	2176
Muir Envelope Plus Inc	Newington	CT	F	860 953-6847	2307
Multiprints Inc	Meriden	CT	G	203 235-4409	1678
National Graphics Inc	North Branford	CT	B	203 481-2351	2370
New Fairfield Press Inc	New Fairfield	CT	F	203 746-2700	2096
O Berk Company Neng LLC	West Haven	CT	F	203 932-8000	4117
Omega Engineering Inc (DH)	Norwalk	CT	C	203 359-1660	2549
Online River LLC	Westport	CT	F	203 801-5900	4191
Paul Dewitt	Danbury	CT	G	203 792-5610	795
Phocuswright Inc (HQ)	Sherman	CT	F	860 350-4084	3082
Planes Road Associates LLC	Essex	CT	F	860 469-3200	1169
Popcorn Movie Poster Co LLC	East Hartford	CT	F	860 610-0000	1012
Practical Automation Inc (HQ)	Milford	CT	D	203 882-5640	1867
PRC Synergy Corp	Bridgeport	CT	B	203 331-9100	360
Print Promowear LLC	Stamford	CT	G	203 504-2858	3436
Privateer LLC	Old Saybrook	CT	F	860 526-1838	2661
Quality Name Plate Inc	East Glastonbury	CT	D	860 633-9495	923
Queen Graphics Printworks Inc	West Haven	CT	F	203 464-7337	4120
Rankin Textile Printing Inc	Danbury	CT	G	203 743-1317	803
Richard E Personette	Middletown	CT	F	860 344-9001	1778
Robinson Tape & Label Inc	Branford	CT	E	203 481-5581	274
Roto-Die Company Inc	East Windsor	CT	F	860 292-7030	1084
Saint Vincent De Paul Place	Norwich	CT	F	860 889-7374	2615
Saybrook Press Incorporated	Guilford	CT	F	203 458-3637	1406
Schmitt Realty Holdings Inc (PA)	Guilford	CT	D	203 453-4334	1407
Schmitt Realty Holdings Inc	Guilford	CT	F	203 453-4334	1408
Screen Tek Printing Co Inc	Hamden	CT	G	203 248-6248	1454
Specialty Printing LLC (PA)	Windsor	CT	D	860 623-8870	4300
Stratis Visuals LLC (PA)	Torrington	CT	E	860 482-1208	3697
Surys Inc	Trumbull	CT	C	203 333-5503	3734
Tex Elm Inc	East Haddam	CT	G	860 873-9715	956
The Hoffman Press Incorporated	New Haven	CT	F	203 865-0818	2209
Universal Printing Svcs Inc	West Haven	CT	F	203 934-4275	4131
UPS Authorized Retailer	Fairfield	CT	G	203 256-9991	1205
Vision Designs LLC	Brookfield	CT	F	203 778-9898	543
Wallingford Prtg Bus Forms Inc	Branford	CT	F	203 481-1911	286
Xtreme Designs LLC	East Haven	CT	F	203 773-9303	1057
Yale University	New Haven	CT	E	203 737-1244	2220
A W McMullen Co Inc	Brockton	MA	F	508 583-2072	7251
Ad-A-Day Company Inc	Taunton	MA	E	508 824-8676	12315
Advanced Imaging Inc	Wilmington	MA	E	978 658-7776	13373
Albert Basse Associates Inc	Stoughton	MA	E	781 344-3555	12191
All-City Screen Printing Inc	Wakefield	MA	G	781 665-0000	12498
Alltec Laser Technology	Southbridge	MA	F	508 765-6666	12009
AlphaGraphics	Watertown	MA	F	617 924-4091	12857
Apex Press Inc	Westborough	MA	F	508 366-1110	13076
Applied Graphics Inc	Amesbury	MA	E	978 241-5300	5828
Art Swiss Corporation	New Bedford	MA	G	508 999-3281	10569
Astrella Ink	Millbury	MA	G	508 865-5028	10426
Austins Sportswear Inc	West Yarmouth	MA	F	508 775-0554	13071
Avon Cstm EMB & Screenprinting	Avon	MA	G	781 341-4663	6143
Barney Rabin Company Inc	Marblehead	MA	G	781 639-0593	10084
Bay State Apparel Inc	Leominster	MA	G	978 534-5810	9639
Bay State Envelope Inc (PA)	Mansfield	MA	E	508 337-8900	10039
BBC Printing and Products Inc	Waltham	MA	G	781 647-4646	12602
Bcg Connect LLC	Wilmington	MA	E	978 528-7999	13389
Belmont Printing Company	Belmont	MA	G	617 484-0833	6304
Bigrep America Inc	Wilmington	MA	C	781 281-0569	13393
Bltees Inc	Chicopee	MA	F	413 594-7547	8011
Bold Maker LLC	Haverhill	MA	G	978 891-5920	9079
Bopkg Inc (HQ)	Fitchburg	MA	C	978 343-3067	8644
Bosworth Printing Co Inc	Stoughton	MA	F	781 341-2992	12199
Bradford & Bigelow Realty LLC	Danvers	MA	G	978 777-1200	8170
Brady Business Forms Inc	Lowell	MA	G	978 458-2585	9865
CCL Industries Corporation (HQ)	Framingham	MA	D	508 872-4511	8749
CCL Label Inc (HQ)	Framingham	MA	D	508 872-4511	8750
Celebrations	Falmouth	MA	F	508 457-0530	8629
Checkerboard Ltd	West Boylston	MA	C	508 835-2475	12957
Classic Envelope Inc	East Douglas	MA	D	508 731-6747	8349
Coatings Adhesives Inks	Georgetown	MA	F	978 352-7273	8907
Comdec Incorporated	Newburyport	MA	E	978 462-3399	10676
Computer Imprntble Lbel System	Burlington	MA	F	877 512-8763	7355
Copy Masters Inc	Taunton	MA	F	508 824-7187	12329
Corporate Image Apparel Inc	Fall River	MA	E	508 676-3099	8532
Crane Currency Us LLC	Boston	MA	F	617 648-3710	6674
Customink LLC	Braintree	MA	F	781 205-4035	7177
Data Associates Business Trust	Waltham	MA	D		12647
Davol/Taunton Printing Inc	Taunton	MA	F	508 824-4305	12331
Defiance Graphics Corp	Rowley	MA	F	978 948-2789	11673
Design Mark Industries Inc	New Bedford	MA	D	800 451-3275	10585
Desk Top Graphics Inc (HQ)	Peabody	MA	E	617 832-1927	11305
Desk Top Solutions Inc	Lowell	MA	F	781 890-7500	9874
Dgi Communications LLC (PA)	North Billerica	MA	E	781 285-6972	10905
Digital Graphics Inc	North Billerica	MA	G	781 270-3670	10907
Docuserve Inc	Marlborough	MA	E	508 786-5820	10146
Eastern Etching and Mfg Co	Chicopee	MA	E	413 594-6601	8030
Edge Embossing Inc	Charlestown	MA	F	617 850-2868	7870
Elbonais Incorporated	Framingham	MA	G	508 626-2318	8761
Elite Envelope & Graphics Inc	Randolph	MA	F	781 961-1800	11556
Excelsior Printing Company	North Adams	MA	D	413 663-3771	10807
Fall River Modern Prtg Co Inc	Fall River	MA	F	508 673-9421	8548
Faux Designs Inc	Needham Heights	MA	F	617 965-0142	10547
First Mate Prtg Converting Inc (HQ)	Gardner	MA	D	978 630-1028	8886
First Sail Group Inc	South Yarmouth	MA	G	425 409-2783	11983
Flashprint Graphics Inc	Cambridge	MA	G	617 492-7767	7570
Fluidform Inc	Waltham	MA	F	978 287-4698	12676
Formlabs Inc (PA)	Somerville	MA	B	617 932-5227	11875
G & G Silk Screening	Plymouth	MA	G	508 830-1075	11460
Gazette Printing Co Inc	Easthampton	MA	F	413 527-7700	8446
Gem Group Inc (PA)	Lawrence	MA	B	978 691-2000	9564
Ghp Media Inc	North Adams	MA	D	413 663-3771	10808
Gloucester Graphics Inc (PA)	Gloucester	MA	G	978 281-4500	8937
Gorilla Graphics Inc (PA)	Malden	MA	F	617 623-2838	10016
GP&c Operations LLC	Gardner	MA	D	978 630-1028	8888
Graphics Source Co	Southampton	MA	G	413 543-0700	11985
Graphix Plus Inc	Fall River	MA	F	508 677-2122	8557
Guertins Graphics Inc	Worcester	MA	F	508 754-0200	13735
Hadley Printing Company Inc	Holyoke	MA	E	413 536-8517	9258
Hannaford & Dumas Corporation	Woburn	MA	E	781 503-0100	13580
Harvard Debate Incorporated	Cambridge	MA	G	617 876-5003	7600
Hercules Press	Boston	MA	G	617 323-1950	6786
Hitchcock Press Inc	Holyoke	MA	G	413 538-8911	9260
Hubcast Inc	Wakefield	MA	E	877 207-6665	12513
Icl Imaging Corp	Framingham	MA	E	508 872-3280	8778
Image Factory	Pocasset	MA	G	508 295-3876	11489
Image Software Services Inc	Shirley	MA	G	978 425-3600	11817
Imperial Image Inc	North Chelmsford	MA	F	978 251-0420	10978
Imprint Graphics Inc	Framingham	MA	F	508 879-0544	8782
Independant Newspaper Group	Revere	MA	F	781 485-0588	11619
Industrial Etching Inc	East Longmeadow	MA	F	413 525-4110	8380
Inkify LLC	Walpole	MA	F	617 304-6642	12561
Instant Offset Press Inc	Hyannis	MA	F	508 790-1100	9439
International Laser Systems	Holyoke	MA	G	413 533-4372	9262
J L Enterprises Inc	Canton	MA	G	781 821-6300	7802

	CITY	ST	EMP	PHONE	ENTRY#
John Brown US LLC	Boston	MA	F	617 449-4354	6826
John Karl Dietrich & Assoc	Cambridge	MA	G	617 868-4140	7619
Journal of Antq & Collectibles	Sturbridge	MA	F	508 347-1960	12250
Julesan Inc	Boston	MA	F	617 437-6860	6835
Jungle Inc **(PA)**	Essex	MA	F	978 356-7722	8476
Kirkwood Holdings Inc **(PA)**	Wilmington	MA	B	978 658-4200	13420
Label Haus Inc	Danvers	MA	G	978 777-1773	8197
Laplume & Sons Printing Inc	Lawrence	MA	E	978 683-1009	9576
Lasercraze	North Andover	MA	G	978 689-7700	10843
Liberty Printing Co Inc	Brockton	MA	G	508 586-6810	7291
Lincoln Press Co Inc	Fall River	MA	F	508 673-3241	8569
Lujean Printing Co Inc	Cotuit	MA	E	508 428-8700	8146
M & M Label Co Inc	Danvers	MA	G	781 321-2737	8201
M & R Screen Printing Inc	New Bedford	MA	F	508 996-0419	10615
Massachusetts Envelope Co Inc **(PA)**	Woburn	MA	E	617 623-8000	13606
Mc Embossing Inc	Attleboro Falls	MA	G	781 821-3088	6090
McGirr Graphics Incorporated	Plymouth	MA	E	508 747-6400	11464
Medianews Group Inc	Devens	MA	E	978 772-0777	8280
Medical Manager Pcn Inc	Walpole	MA	F	508 850-3500	12568
Merrill Corp	Andover	MA	F	978 725-3700	5897
Milara Inc	Medfield	MA	G	508 359-2786	10272
Moonlight Ltd	Brockton	MA	G	508 584-0094	7298
Morgan Enterprises Inc	Worcester	MA	G	985 377-3216	13761
New England Art Publishers Inc	Abington	MA	C	781 878-5151	5726
New England Business Svc Inc **(HQ)**	Townsend	MA	D	978 448-6111	12441
New England Label	Peabody	MA	G	978 281-3663	11326
New Tek Design Group Inc	West Boylston	MA	G	508 835-4544	12965
Nfi LLC	New Bedford	MA	E	508 998-9021	10632
Optimum Sportswear Inc	Lawrence	MA	G	978 689-2290	9594
Package Printing Company Inc	West Springfield	MA	E	413 736-2740	13040
Paiva Corp	Fall River	MA	G	508 679-7921	8593
Paul H Murphy & Co Inc	Quincy	MA	F	617 472-7707	11530
Plastilam Inc	Salem	MA	E	978 745-5563	11730
Potters Printing Inc	Fall River	MA	F	617 547-3161	8598
Precision Tape & Label Co Inc	Uxbridge	MA	F	508 278-7700	12489
Print Management Systems Inc	Woburn	MA	F	781 944-1041	13640
Printpro Silkscreen Co LLC	Haverhill	MA	D	978 556-1695	9123
Qrsts LLC	Somerville	MA	F	617 625-3335	11892
Quad/Graphics Inc	East Longmeadow	MA	D	413 525-8552	8391
Quality Envelope & Printing Co	Middleboro	MA	G	508 947-8878	10376
R R Donnelley & Sons Company	Boston	MA	D	617 345-4300	6992
R R Donnelley & Sons Company	Hyde Park	MA	E	617 360-2000	9467
RAw Rinnigade Art Works LLC	Somerville	MA	G	617 625-3335	11893
Red Mill Graphics Incorporated	Chelmsford	MA	F	978 251-4081	7951
Regal Press Incorporated **(PA)**	Norwood	MA	C	781 769-3900	11206
Roberts & Sons Printing Inc	Springfield	MA	F	413 283-9356	12126
Salisbury Sales Inc	Natick	MA	G	508 907-6610	10496
Ser Logistics Inc	Worcester	MA	F	508 757-3397	13798
Silver Screen Design Inc	Greenfield	MA	F	413 773-1692	9000
Smart Source LLC	Waltham	MA	F	781 890-0110	12780
Smudge Ink Incorporated	Charlestown	MA	G	617 242-8228	7882
Specialty Manufacturing Inc	Amesbury	MA	F	978 388-1601	5853
Stickamayka Packaging Inc	Andover	MA	E	978 474-1930	5926
Superior Printing Company Inc	Medford	MA	F	781 391-9090	10297
T-Shirts Authority Inc	West Yarmouth	MA	F	774 855-0000	13074
Taylor Communications Inc	Avon	MA	F	508 584-0102	6164
Techprint Inc	Lawrence	MA	D	978 975-1245	9602
Tekni-Plex Inc	Ashland	MA	E	508 881-2440	5968
Three Twins Productions Inc	Watertown	MA	G	617 926-0377	12914
Tomandtim Enterprises LLC	Northborough	MA	G	508 380-5550	11113
Van-Go Graphics	Grafton	MA	G	508 865-7300	8969
Velocity LLC	Everett	MA	E	617 389-5452	8503
Vulcanforms Inc	Devens	MA	D	781 472-0160	8289
Walgreen Co	North Attleboro	MA	F	781 244-9431	10892
Walker-Clay Inc	Hanson	MA	F	781 294-1100	9057
Washington ABC Imaging Inc	Boston	MA	F	857 753-4241	7114
Watertown Printers Inc	Somerville	MA	F	781 893-9400	11913
Winter & Company Inc	Quincy	MA	F	617 773-7605	11545
Winthrop Printing Company Inc	Foxboro	MA	E	617 268-9660	8732
Yankee Printing Group Inc	South Hadley	MA	E	413 532-9513	11968
320 Ink LLC	Westbrook	ME	G	207 835-0038	5613
Action Screen Printing	Lewiston	ME	G	207 795-7786	4954
Allen Screen Printing	Scarborough	ME	E	207 510-6800	5422
Allen Uniforms Inc	South Portland	ME	G	207 775-7364	5491
Armstrong Family Inds Inc	Hermon	ME	G	207 848-7300	4880
Artforms **(PA)**	Brunswick	ME	G	800 828-8518	4640
Atlantic Sportswear Inc	Portland	ME	E	207 797-5028	5178
Bangor Ltr Sp & Color Copy Ctr	Bangor	ME	G	207 945-9311	4490
Bell Manufacturing Co	Lewiston	ME	G	207 784-2961	4953
Blue Sky Inc	Portland	ME	G	207 772-0073	5190
Creative Digital Imaging	Bangor	ME	E	207 973-0500	4496
D R Designs Inc	Manchester	ME	G	207 622-3303	5044
Downeast Graphics & Prtg Inc	Ellsworth	ME	F	207 667-5582	4757
Erin Murphy	Windham	ME	G	928 525-2056	5660
Evergreen Custom Printing Inc	Auburn	ME	G	207 782-2327	4430
Gossamer Press	Benton	ME	G	207 827-9881	4545
Identity Group Holdings Corp	Brunswick	ME	E	207 510-6800	4646
Island Approaches	Sunset	ME	F	207 348-2459	5539
James Newspapers Inc	Rumford	ME	G	207 364-7893	5357
JS McCarthy Co Inc **(PA)**	Augusta	ME	D	207 622-6241	4473
Liberty Graphics Inc	Liberty	ME	F	207 589-4596	4999
Lts Inc	Portland	ME	E	207 774-1104	5234
Maine Poly Aquisition Corp	Greene	ME	G	207 946-7000	4847
Mathemtics Problem Solving LLC	South Portland	ME	D	207 772-2846	5508
Northeast Publishing Company	Dover Foxcroft	ME	G	207 564-8355	4730
Northeast Publishing Company	Presque Isle	ME	G	207 764-4471	5308
Penobscot Bay Press **(PA)**	Stonington	ME	F	207 367-2200	5534
Print Bangor	Bangor	ME	G	207 947-8049	4515
Shoreline Publications	Wells	ME	F	207 646-8448	5605
Synergy Printing	Kittery Point	ME	G	207 703-2782	4942
T J Ryan LLC	Brewer	ME	F	207 989-7183	4620
Tomateto Publications Inc	Cornville	ME	G	207 474-6300	4707
Trems Inc	Rockland	ME	G	207 596-6989	5343
W S Emerson Company Inc **(PA)**	Brewer	ME	E	207 989-3410	4623
Waterfront Graphics & Prtg LLC	South Portland	ME	G	207 799-3519	5517
Woodland Studios Inc	Ellsworth	ME	F	207 667-3286	4761
Xtreme Screen & Sportswear LLC	Westbrook	ME	F	207 857-9200	5654
Acara Holdings LLC	Laconia	NH	F	603 434-3175	14640
Amherst Label Inc	Milford	NH	D	603 673-7849	15015
Argyle Associates Inc	Concord	NH	E	603 226-4300	14114
B & E Enterprises Inc	Peterborough	NH	F	603 924-7203	15312
Barn Door Screen Printers	Conway	NH	G	603 447-5369	14177
Beeze Tees LLC	Keene	NH	G	603 357-1400	14589
Bovie Screen Process Prtg Inc	Bow	NH	G	603 224-0651	13994
Brisco Graphics LLC	Bedford	NH	F		13919
Business Shirtmasters	Chichester	NH	F	603 798-3787	14072
C K Productions	Pelham	NH	K	603 893-5069	15287
CB Ventures LLC	Laconia	NH	F	603 434-3175	14650
Cdc Enterprises Llc	Windham	NH	G	603 437-3090	15722
Computype Inc	Concord	NH	G	603 225-5500	14122
Concord Photo Engraving Co Inc	Concord	NH	F	603 225-3681	14125
Connected Office Tech LLC	Portsmouth	NH	F	603 380-7333	15375
Electronic Imaging Mtls Inc	Keene	NH	E	603 357-1459	14597
Electronics For Imaging Inc **(HQ)**	Londonderry	NH	E	650 357-3500	14748
Evans Printing Co	Bow	NH	G	603 856-8238	13997
Fedex Office & Print Svcs Inc	Bedford	NH	G	603 644-2679	13929
Fiberkraft Inc	Salem	NH	E	603 621-0090	15525
Gemini Firfield Screenprinting	Keene	NH	G	603 357-3847	14600
Jalbert Printing LLC	Amherst	NH	G	603 623-4677	13873
Joglo Inc	Nashua	NH	F	603 880-4519	15117
Labels Inc	Hampton	NH	E	603 929-3088	14405
Left-Tees Designs Bayou LLC	Derry	NH	G	603 437-6630	14199
Lestat Production 81 Corp	Bedford	NH	E	866 557-4478	13939
Life Is Good Retail Inc **(PA)**	Hudson	NH	D	603 594-6100	14522
Northstar Direct LLC	Manchester	NH	F		14905
Phoenix Screen Printing	Nashua	NH	F	603 578-9599	15148
Powerplay Management LLC	Portsmouth	NH	E	603 436-3030	15431
Puritan Press Inc **(PA)**	Hollis	NH	E	603 889-4500	14458
RB Graphics Inc	Hooksett	NH	G	603 624-4025	14473
Red Fish - Blue Fish Dye Wrks	Somersworth	NH	G	603 692-3900	15624
Relyco Sales Inc **(PA)**	Dover	NH	E	603 742-0999	14248
Savvy Workshop	Manchester	NH	G	603 792-0080	14926
Say It In Stitches Inc	Concord	NH	G	603 224-6470	14155
Screen Gems Inc	Seabrook	NH	F	603 474-5353	15604
Smith & Town Printers LLC	Berlin	NH	F	603 752-2150	13986
Sumner Printing Inc	Somersworth	NH	E	603 692-7424	15625
Teddys Tees Inc	Concord	NH	G	603 226-2762	14163
Treasure Tees	Nashua	NH	G	855 438-8337	15178
American Trophy and Supply Inc	East Providence	RI	G	401 438-3060	16004
Arkwear Inc	Newport	RI	F	846 846-9903	16202
Classsick Custom LLC	Pawtucket	RI	F	401 475-7288	16355
Cool Air Creations Inc	Smithfield	RI	E	401 830-5780	16692
Gem Label & Tape Company	Cranston	RI	F	401 724-1300	15866
Graphic Inds Incorporated	East Providence	RI	F	401 431-5081	16021
Griswold Textile Print Inc	Westerly	RI	F	401 596-2784	16931
Hilco Athletic & Graphics Inc	West Warwick	RI	F	401 822-1775	16910
ID Label Inc	Cranston	RI	F	508 809-6199	15876
K&M/Nordic Co Inc	Riverside	RI	G	401 431-9299	16656
Matlet Group LLC	Pawtucket	RI	B	401 834-3007	16385
Merchbro Inc	Pawtucket	RI	F	866 428-0095	16387
Moo Inc	East Providence	RI	D	401 519-7216	16031
Packaging Graphics LLC	Pawtucket	RI	C	401 725-7700	16399
Regine Printing Co Inc	Providence	RI	F	401 943-3404	16600
Rlcp Inc	Barrington	RI	G	401 461-6560	15749
RTC Holdings Inc	Pawtucket	RI	E	401 728-6980	16414
S G Inc	Pascoag	RI	E	401 568-1110	16340

Employee Codes: A=Over 500 employees, B=251-500
C=101-250, D=51-100, E=20-50, F=10-19, G=1-9   2024 Harris New England
Manufacturers Directory   873

	CITY	ST	EMP	PHONE	ENTRY#
Squadlocker Inc	Warwick	RI	D	888 885-6253	16864
Trimed Media Group Inc	Providence	RI	F	401 919-5165	16630
Bumwraps Inc (PA)	Montgomery Center	VT	G	802 326-4080	17368
Graphic Edge LLC	Rutland	VT	D	802 855-8840	17498
Humble Screen Printing Llc	Colchester	VT	G	802 399-5400	17196
Jet Service Envelope Co Inc (PA)	Barre	VT	G	802 229-9335	17010
Keiths II Sports Ltd	Pittsford	VT	F	802 483-6050	17444
Paw Prints Press Inc	South Burlington	VT	F	802 865-2872	17589
The Leahy Press Inc	Montpelier	VT	E	802 223-2100	17375
Tuttle Law Print Inc	Rutland	VT	D	802 773-9171	17512

2761 Manifold business forms

	CITY	ST	EMP	PHONE	ENTRY#
Beekley Corporation (PA)	Bristol	CT	D	860 583-4700	411
Federal Business Products Inc	Torrington	CT	E	860 482-6231	3680
Mlk Business Forms Inc	New Haven	CT	F	203 624-6304	2176
Taylor Communications Inc	East Hartford	CT	F	860 875-0731	1026
Wallingford Prtg Bus Forms Inc	Branford	CT	F	203 481-1911	286
Belmont Printing Company	Belmont	MA	G	617 484-0833	6304
BFI Print Communications Inc (PA)	Boston	MA	E	781 447-1199	6591
Continuprint Inc	Woburn	MA	F	781 933-1800	13547
D B S Industries Inc	Haverhill	MA	D	978 373-4748	9090
Full Circle Technologies Inc	Boston	MA	E	617 722-0100	6749
George H Dean Co	Braintree	MA	F	781 544-3782	7184
Regal Press Incorporated (PA)	Norwood	MA	C	781 769-3900	11206
Stat Products Inc	Ashland	MA	E	508 881-8022	5967
Taylor Communications Inc	Avon	MA	F	508 584-0102	6164
Taylor Communications Inc	Braintree	MA	F	781 843-0250	7208
Wise Business Forms Inc	Portland	ME	C	207 774-6560	5290

2771 Greeting cards

	CITY	ST	EMP	PHONE	ENTRY#
Anothercreationbymichele	Stamford	CT	G	203 322-4277	3282
Caspari Inc (PA)	Seymour	CT	F	203 888-1100	2957
Olympia Sales Inc	Enfield	CT	D	860 749-0751	1140
Expressive Design Group Inc	Holyoke	MA	F	413 315-6296	9255
Lovepop Inc (PA)	Boston	MA	G	888 687-9589	6864
Marian Heath Greeting Cards LLC	Wareham	MA	C	508 291-0766	12840
New England Art Publishers Inc	Abington	MA	C	781 878-5151	5726
New England Business Svc Inc (HQ)	Townsend	MA	D	978 448-6111	12441
Viabella Holdings LLC	Sudbury	MA	D	978 855-8817	12271
Viabella Holdings LLC (PA)	Wareham	MA	E	800 688-9998	12848
Walgreen Co	North Attleboro	MA	F	781 244-9431	10892
Borealis Press Inc	Blue Hill	ME	G	800 669-6845	4595
Renaissance Greeting Cards Inc	Sanford	ME	E	207 324-4153	5409
William Arthur Inc	West Kennebunk	ME	D	413 684-2600	5611
Be Youneeq LLC	Raymond	NH	F	603 244-3933	15451
Pep Direct LLC	Wilton	NH	D	603 654-6141	15707
Quadriga Art	Milford	NH	G	603 654-6141	15035
E Frances Paper Inc	Middletown	RI	F	857 250-0036	16173
Mainstream Inc (PA)	Bennington	VT	F	802 442-8859	17050
Oatmeal Studios Inc	Rochester	VT	F	802 967-8014	17487
Vermont Christmas Company	Milton	VT	G	802 893-1670	17366

2782 Blankbooks and looseleaf binders

	CITY	ST	EMP	PHONE	ENTRY#
Data Management Incorporated	Unionville	CT	E	860 677-8586	3748
Mbsw Inc	West Hartford	CT	F	860 243-0303	4071
Scrapbook Clubhouse	Westbrook	CT	F	860 399-4443	4142
Yolanda Dubose Records and	West Haven	CT	F	203 823-6699	4134
Atlantic Bookbinders Inc	South Lancaster	MA	G	978 365-4524	11970
Chartpak Inc (HQ)	Leeds	MA	D	413 584-5446	9621
Eureka Lab Book Inc	Holyoke	MA	E	413 534-5671	9254
Nettwerk Music Group LLC	Cambridge	MA	E	617 497-8200	7662
University Products Inc (PA)	Holyoke	MA	D	413 532-3372	9287
W G Fry Corp	Florence	MA	E	413 747-2551	8687
Gallery Leather Direct Inc	Trenton	ME	E	207 667-9474	5554
Geiger Bros (PA)	Lewiston	ME	B	207 755-2000	4962
Nashua Corporation	Merrimack	NH	A	603 880-1100	14994
Rosencrntz Gldnstern Banknotes	Wilton	NH	G	603 654-6160	15708

2789 Bookbinding and related work

	CITY	ST	EMP	PHONE	ENTRY#
Adkins Printing Company	New Britain	CT	F	800 228-9745	1997
Allied Printing Services Inc (PA)	Manchester	CT	B	860 643-1101	1584
Chapin Packaging LLC	Darien	CT	G	203 202-2747	846
Connecticut Valley Bindery	New Britain	CT	E	860 229-7637	2013
E R Hitchcock Company	New Britain	CT	E	860 229-2024	2024
Elm Press Incorporated	Terryville	CT	E	860 583-3600	3601
Imperial Grphic Cmmnctions Inc	Milford	CT	E	203 650-3478	1837
Joseph Merritt & Company Inc	Danbury	CT	G	203 743-6734	762
Kool Ink LLC	Bloomfield	CT	F	860 242-0303	186
Leejay Industries LLC	Norwalk	CT	E	203 847-3660	2526
Norwich Printing Company Inc	Norwich	CT	F	860 887-7468	2611
Paul Dewitt	Danbury	CT	G	203 792-5610	795
Phoenix Press Inc	New Haven	CT	E	203 865-5555	2186

	CITY	ST	EMP	PHONE	ENTRY#
Richard E Personette	Middletown	CT	F	860 344-9001	1778
Saybrook Press Incorporated	Guilford	CT	G	203 458-3637	1406
STP Bindery Services Inc	East Hartford	CT	F	860 528-1430	1023
Tech-Repro Inc	Stamford	CT	F	203 348-8884	3478
Universal Printing Svcs Inc	West Haven	CT	E	203 934-4275	4131
Acme Bookbinding Company Inc	Billerica	MA	D	617 242-1100	6396
American Prtg & Envelope Inc	Auburn	MA	E	508 832-6100	6102
Andrew T Johnson Company Inc (PA)	Boston	MA	F	617 742-1610	6548
Atlantic Bookbinders Inc	South Lancaster	MA	G	978 365-4524	11970
Belmont Printing Company	Belmont	MA	G	617 484-0833	6304
Bridgeport Nat Bindery Inc	Agawam	MA	D	413 789-1981	5782
Ckg Limited	Gloucester	MA	F	781 893-2514	8929
Copy Cop The Digital Printing Company LLC	Boston	MA	E	617 267-8899	6669
Copy Masters Inc	Taunton	MA	F	508 824-7187	12329
Courier Westford Inc	Westford	MA	B	978 251-6482	13232
D & L Associates Inc	Needham Heights	MA	G	781 400-5068	10540
D S Graphics Inc (PA)	Lowell	MA	C	978 970-1359	9873
Datasite Global Corporation	Everett	MA	B	617 389-7900	8486
Dmr Print Inc (PA)	Concord	MA	F	617 876-3688	8114
Elbonais Incorporated	Framingham	MA	G	508 626-2318	8761
Excelsior Printing Company	North Adams	MA	D	413 663-3771	10807
Flagship Press Inc	North Andover	MA	F	978 975-3100	10831
Generation Four Inc	Waltham	MA	G	781 899-3180	12686
Ghp Media Inc	North Adams	MA	D	413 663-3771	10808
Graphic Fullfillment & Finishing Inc	Holbrook	MA	G	781 727-8845	9173
Hf Group LLC	Billerica	MA	C	617 242-1100	6449
J T Gardner Inc (PA)	Westborough	MA	E	800 540-4993	13112
Keating Communication Group	Canton	MA	G	781 828-9030	7804
Kirkwood Holdings Inc (PA)	Wilmington	MA	B	978 658-4200	13420
Laplume & Sons Printing Inc	Lawrence	MA	D	978 683-1009	9576
Linmel Associates Inc	Marlborough	MA	F	508 481-6699	10180
LPI Printing and Graphic Inc	Stoneham	MA	F	781 438-5400	12182
Marcus Company Inc	Holyoke	MA	F	413 315-6296	9265
Massachusetts Repro Ltd	Boston	MA	F	617 227-2237	6876
Miles Press Inc	Auburn	MA	F	508 752-6430	6120
Minute-Man Printing Corp	Concord	MA	F	978 369-2808	8125
Modus Media Inc	Waltham	MA	E	781 663-5000	12724
Nabs Inc	Waltham	MA	E	781 899-7719	12728
Northast Dcment Cnsrvtion Ctr	Andover	MA	E	978 470-1010	5901
Paiva Corp	Fall River	MA	G	508 679-7921	8593
Picken Printing Inc	North Chelmsford	MA	F	978 251-0730	10986
Pyramid Printing and Advg Inc	Weymouth	MA	E	781 337-7609	13333
R & H Communications Inc (PA)	Waltham	MA	F	781 893-6221	12757
Sherman Printing Co Inc	Canton	MA	F	781 828-8855	7828
Superior Bindery Inc	Braintree	MA	C	781 303-0022	7204
Town Bookbindery Inc	East Freetown	MA	E	508 763-2713	8367
Universal Wilde Inc	Canton	MA	C	978 658-0800	7838
W G Fry Corp	Florence	MA	E	413 747-2551	8687
We Print Today LLC	Kingston	MA	F	781 585-6021	9514
Winthrop Printing Company Inc	Foxboro	MA	E	617 268-9660	8732
Yankee Printing Group Inc	South Hadley	MA	E	413 532-9513	11968
Davic Inc	Portland	ME	G	207 774-0093	5206
Geiger Bros (PA)	Lewiston	ME	B	207 755-2000	4962
JS McCarthy Co Inc (PA)	Augusta	ME	D	207 622-6241	4473
Penmor Lithographers Inc	Lewiston	ME	F	207 784-1341	4984
The Dingley Press Inc (PA)	Lisbon	ME	C	207 353-1500	5018
Cdc Enterprises Llc	Windham	NH	G	603 437-3090	15722
Cygnus Inc	Portsmouth	NH	G	603 431-8989	15379
Fedex Office & Print Svcs Inc	Bedford	NH	F	603 644-2679	13929
Higginbotham Management Corp	Portsmouth	NH	F	603 431-0142	15402
New Hampshire Bindery Inc	Bow	NH	F	603 224-0441	14006
Optimum Bindery Svcs Neng Inc	Nashua	NH	F	603 886-3889	15145
RB Graphics Inc	Hooksett	NH	F	603 624-4025	14473
A & H Composition and Prtg Inc	East Providence	RI	G	401 438-1200	15999
Branch Graphics Inc	Rumford	RI	E	401 861-1830	16663
Data Binding Inc	Warwick	RI	D	401 738-7901	16802
Dome Enterprises Trust (PA)	Warwick	RI	E	401 738-7900	16807
Dome Publishing Company Inc (HQ)	Warwick	RI	E	401 738-7900	16808
Ocean State Book Binding Inc	Providence	RI	F	401 528-1172	16579
Rag & Bone Bindery Ltd	Pawtucket	RI	F	401 728-0762	16410
Browns River Bindery Inc	Essex Junction	VT	F	802 878-3335	17229
Darwin A Lewis Inc	Hartland	VT	G	802 457-4521	17286
L Brown and Sons Printing Inc	Barre	VT	E	802 476-3164	17012
Paw Prints Press Inc	South Burlington	VT	F	802 865-2872	17589
Queen City Printers Inc	Burlington	VT	E	802 864-4566	17153
Villanti & Sons Printers Inc	Milton	VT	D	802 864-0723	17367

2791 Typesetting

	CITY	ST	EMP	PHONE	ENTRY#
A To A Studio Solutions Ltd	Stamford	CT	F	203 388-9050	3267
Action Letter Inc (PA)	Stamford	CT	E	203 323-2466	3273
Allied Printing Services Inc (PA)	Manchester	CT	B	860 643-1101	1584
Appels Prtg & Mailing Bur Inc	Hartford	CT	F	860 522-8189	1470

	CITY	ST	EMP	PHONE	ENTRY#
Brescias Printing Services Inc	East Hartford	CT	G	860 528-4254	976
E R Hitchcock Company	New Britain	CT	E	860 229-2024	2024
Elm Press Incorporated	Terryville	CT	E	860 583-3600	3601
Fairfield Marketing Group Inc (PA)	Easton	CT	F	203 261-0884	1095
Gateway Digital Inc	Norwalk	CT	F	203 853-4929	2503
Hedges & Hedges Ltd	Wethersfield	CT	G	860 257-3170	4205
Image Processing	Guilford	CT	G	203 488-3252	1397
Jupiter Communications LLC	West Haven	CT	F	475 238-7082	4108
Kool Ink LLC	Bloomfield	CT	F	860 242-0303	186
Lettering Inc of New York (PA)	Stamford	CT	E	203 329-7759	3400
Oddo Print Shop Inc	Torrington	CT	G	860 489-6585	3690
Paul Dewitt	Danbury	CT	G	203 792-5610	795
Phoenix Press Inc	New Haven	CT	E	203 865-5555	2186
Professional Graphics Inc	Norwalk	CT	F	203 846-4291	2560
Richard E Personette	Middletown	CT	F	860 344-9001	1778
Saybrook Press Incorporated	Guilford	CT	G	203 458-3637	1406
Tech-Repro Inc	Stamford	CT	F	203 348-8884	3478
Universal Printing Svcs Inc	West Haven	CT	E	203 934-4275	4131
Westchster Bk/Rnsford Type Inc	Danbury	CT	E	203 791-0080	837
Allison Advertising Inc	Boston	MA	F	617 368-6800	6537
American Prtg & Envelope Inc	Auburn	MA	E	508 832-6100	6102
Andrew T Johnson Company Inc (PA)	Boston	MA	F	617 742-1610	6548
Argosy Publishing Inc (PA)	Newton	MA	D	617 527-9999	10733
Belmont Printing Company	Belmont	MA	G	617 484-0833	6304
Copy Masters Inc	Taunton	MA	F	508 824-7187	12329
Crane Composition Inc	East Sandwich	MA	G	774 338-5183	8404
Creative Publishing Corp Amer (PA)	Peabody	MA	E	978 532-5880	11303
Cxo Media Inc (DH)	Needham Heights	MA	C	508 766-5696	10539
D & L Associates Inc	Needham Heights	MA	G	781 400-5068	10540
D B S Industries Inc	Haverhill	MA	D	978 373-4940	9090
D S Graphics Inc (PA)	Lowell	MA	C	978 970-1359	9873
Desk Top Graphics Inc (HQ)	Peabody	MA	E	617 832-1927	11305
Dmr Print Inc (PA)	Concord	MA	F	617 876-3688	8114
Elbonais Incorporated	Framingham	MA	G	508 626-2318	8761
Excelsior Printing Company	North Adams	MA	D	413 663-3771	10807
Fasprint Inc (PA)	Brockton	MA	F	508 588-9961	7278
Flagship Press Inc	North Andover	MA	C	978 975-3100	10831
Generation Four Inc	Waltham	MA	G	781 899-3180	12686
Ghp Media Inc	North Adams	MA	D	413 663-3771	10808
Icl Imaging Corp	Framingham	MA	E	508 872-3280	8778
J T Gardner Inc (PA)	Westborough	MA	E	800 540-4993	13112
John Karl Dietrich & Assoc	Cambridge	MA	G	617 868-4140	7619
Keating Communication Group	Canton	MA	G	781 828-9030	7804
Kirkwood Holdings Inc (PA)	Wilmington	MA	B	978 658-4200	13420
Laplume & Sons Printing Inc	Lawrence	MA	D	978 683-1009	9576
Linmel Associates Inc	Marlborough	MA	F	508 481-6699	10180
LPI Printing and Graphic Inc	Stoneham	MA	F	781 438-5400	12182
Marcus Company Inc	Holyoke	MA	F	413 534-3303	9265
Massachusetts Repro Ltd	Boston	MA	F	617 227-2237	6876
National Reprographics Inc	Boston	MA	F	857 383-3700	6904
Picken Printing Inc	North Chelmsford	MA	F	978 251-0730	10986
Pyramid Printing and Advg Inc	Weymouth	MA	E	781 337-7609	13333
R & H Communications Inc (PA)	Waltham	MA	E	781 893-6221	12757
Ramsbottom Printing Inc	Fall River	MA	E	508 730-2220	8600
Red Sun Press Inc	Jamaica Plain	MA	F	617 524-6822	9503
Reminder Publications	East Longmeadow	MA	E	413 525-3947	8393
Sherman Printing Co Inc	Canton	MA	E	781 828-8855	7828
Southern Brkshre Shppers Gide	Great Barrington	MA	F	413 528-0095	8978
St Associates Inc	Wakefield	MA	E		12536
Teletypesetting Company Inc	Boston	MA	F	617 542-6220	7073
Trustees of Tufts College (PA)	Somerville	MA	B	617 628-5000	11906
Universal Wilde Inc	Canton	MA	C	978 658-0800	7838
Weston Corporation	Hingham	MA	E	781 749-0936	9164
Winthrop Printing Company Inc	Foxboro	MA	E	617 268-9660	8732
Yankee Printing Group Inc	South Hadley	MA	E	413 532-9513	11968
Davic Inc	Portland	ME	G	207 774-0093	5206
JS McCarthy Co Inc (PA)	Augusta	ME	D	207 622-6241	4473
Laserwords Maine	Lewiston	ME	F	207 782-9595	4970
Cygnus Inc	Portsmouth	NH	G	603 431-8989	15379
Echo Communications Inc	New London	NH	E	603 526-6006	15203
Fedex Office & Print Svcs Inc	Bedford	NH	F	603 644-2679	13929
Higgingbotham Management Corp	Portsmouth	NH	F	603 431-0142	15402
Kensington Group Incorporated	Hampton Falls	NH	F	603 926-6742	14419
Puritan Press Inc (PA)	Hollis	NH	E	603 889-4500	14458
Ram Printing Incorporated (PA)	East Hampstead	NH	E	603 382-7045	14271
Smith & Town Printers LLC	Berlin	NH	F	603 752-2150	13986
Southport Management Group LLC	Portsmouth	NH	G	603 433-4664	15438
Whitman Communications Inc	Lebanon	NH	D	603 448-2600	14703
A & H Composition and Prtg Inc	East Providence	RI	G	401 438-1200	15999
Branch Graphics Inc	Rumford	RI	E	401 861-1830	16663
Southern RI Newspapers (HQ)	Wakefield	RI	E	401 789-9744	16744
Accura Printing	Barre	VT	F	802 476-4429	16996
L Brown and Sons Printing Inc	Barre	VT	E	802 476-3164	17012
McClure Newspapers Inc	Williston	VT	C	802 863-3441	17740
Offset House Inc	Essex Junction	VT	C	802 878-4440	17242
Queen City Printers Inc	Burlington	VT	E	802 864-4566	17153
Stillwater Graphics Inc	Williamstown	VT	F	802 433-9898	17718
Stratford Publishing Services	Brattleboro	VT	E	802 254-6073	17100
Tuttle Law Print Inc	Rutland	VT	D	802 773-9171	17512
Villanti & Sons Printers Inc	Milton	VT	D	802 864-0723	17367

2796 Platemaking services

	CITY	ST	EMP	PHONE	ENTRY#
Baron Technology Inc	Milford	CT	F	203 452-0515	1800
Gateway Digital Inc	Norwalk	CT	F	203 853-4929	2503
Ghp Media Inc (PA)	West Haven	CT	D	203 479-7500	4107
Paul Dewitt	Danbury	CT	G	203 792-5610	795
Schmitt Realty Holdings Inc	Branford	CT	F	203 488-3252	275
Spm Management Inc	Shelton	CT	F	203 847-1112	3065
Urg Graphics Inc (PA)	Stafford Springs	CT	E	860 928-0835	3263
Belmont Printing Company	Belmont	MA	G	617 484-0833	6304
Chemi-Graphic Inc	Ludlow	MA	E	413 589-0151	9942
Csw Inc (PA)	Ludlow	MA	D	413 589-1311	9943
Desk Top Graphics Inc (HQ)	Peabody	MA	E	617 832-1927	11305
Excelsior Printing Company	North Adams	MA	D	413 663-3771	10807
Farganyd Inc	Canton	MA	C	781 575-1700	7790
Ghp Media Inc	North Adams	MA	D	413 663-3771	10808
ID Graphics Group Inc	South Easton	MA	E	508 238-8500	11945
J T Gardner Inc (PA)	Westborough	MA	E	800 540-4993	13112
Linmel Associates Inc	Marlborough	MA	F	508 481-6699	10180
Pure Imaging	Woburn	MA	G	781 537-6992	13642
Southern Brkshire Shppers Gide	Great Barrington	MA	F	413 528-0095	8978
Spectragraphic New England Inc	Boston	MA	E	617 737-3575	7049
Valley Etching Engrv Dsign Inc	Holyoke	MA	E	413 536-2256	9289
W Gillies Technologies LLC	Worcester	MA	E	508 852-2502	13827
Desk Top Graphics Inc	Portland	ME	F	207 828-0041	5208
Higgingbotham Management Corp	Portsmouth	NH	F	603 431-0142	15402
McClure Newspapers Inc	Williston	VT	C	802 863-3441	17740
Offset House Inc	Essex Junction	VT	C	802 878-4440	17242

28 CHEMICALS AND ALLIED PRODUCTS

2812 Alkalies and chlorine

	CITY	ST	EMP	PHONE	ENTRY#
Kuehne New Haven LLC	New Haven	CT	E	203 508-6703	2167
Driscolls Restaurant	Mansfield	MA	G	508 261-1574	10050
International Dioxide Inc	North Kingstown	RI	E	401 295-8800	16260

2813 Industrial gases

	CITY	ST	EMP	PHONE	ENTRY#
Airgas Usa LLC	Danbury	CT	C	203 792-1834	705
Aldlab Chemicals LLC	North Haven	CT	F	203 589-4934	2390
Hydrogen Highway LLC	North Branford	CT	G	203 871-1000	2368
Linde Gas & Equipment Inc	Danbury	CT	D	203 837-2162	774
Linde Gas & Equipment Inc (DH)	Danbury	CT	F	844 445-4633	775
Linde Inc (HQ)	Danbury	CT	B	203 837-2000	776
Linde Inc	Groton	CT	E	860 623-8211	1376
Messer LLC	Danbury	CT	E	908 464-8100	785
O2 Concepts LLC	Middlebury	CT	E	877 867-4008	1718
Airgas Usa LLC	Billerica	MA	E	978 439-1344	6398
American Industrial & Med Pdts (PA)	Auburn	MA	E	508 832-5785	6101
Electric Hydrogen Co	Natick	MA	F	617 546-5710	10480
Found Energy Co	Charlestown	MA	F	201 315-9955	7873
Hydro-Test Products Inc	Stow	MA	F	978 897-4647	12246
Hydrogen Energy California LLC	Concord	MA	F	978 287-9529	8120
Linde Gas & Equipment Inc	Palmer	MA	G	413 283-9906	11276
Messer LLC	Bellingham	MA	F	508 966-3148	6296
Messer LLC	Stoughton	MA	E	781 341-4575	12224
Neon Labs LLC	Boston	MA	G	847 867-4370	6907
Plz Corp	Fall River	MA	C	650 543-7600	8597
Shield Packaging Co Inc	Dudley	MA	E	508 949-0900	8323
Shield Realty California Inc (PA)	Canton	MA	E	909 628-4707	7829
Messer LLC	Kittery	ME	E	207 475-3102	4937
Hanna Instruments Inc (PA)	Woonsocket	RI	E	401 765-7500	16962
Linde Gas & Equipment Inc	Slatersville	RI	D	401 767-3450	16682
Messer LLC	Essex Junction	VT	E	802 878-6339	17240

2816 Inorganic pigments

	CITY	ST	EMP	PHONE	ENTRY#
Color Change Technology Inc	North Andover	MA	E	978 377-0050	10824
F & D Plastics Inc (PA)	Leominster	MA	E	978 668-5140	9662
Ecc Holdings Inc (HQ)	Providence	RI	E	401 331-9000	16511

2819 Industrial inorganic chemicals, nec

	CITY	ST	EMP	PHONE	ENTRY#
Advanced Pwr Systems Intl Inc	New Hartford	CT	G	860 921-0009	2097
Auterra Inc	Guilford	CT	G	518 382-9600	1385
Carbide Solutions LLC	Windsor	CT	G	860 515-8665	4264
Carbtrol Corporation	Stratford	CT	E	203 337-4340	3525
Chromatics Inc	Bethel	CT	D	203 743-6868	102

	CITY	ST	EMP	PHONE	ENTRY#
H Krevit and Company Inc	New Haven	CT	E	203 772-3350	2159
Joshua LLC (PA)	Guilford	CT	F	203 624-0080	1398
King Industries Inc (PA)	Norwalk	CT	C	203 866-5551	2523
Metamorphic Materials Inc	Winsted	CT	G	860 738-8638	4349
Miller-Stephenson Chemical Company Inc (PA)	Danbury	CT	E	800 442-3424	786
New Haven Chlor-Alkali LLC	New Haven	CT	D	203 772-3350	2178
RT Vanderbilt Holding Co Inc (PA)	Norwalk	CT	F	203 295-2141	2568
Solidification Pdts Intl Inc	Northford	CT	D	203 484-9494	2456
Solvay	Stamford	CT	E	203 321-2292	3464
Specialty Minerals Inc	Canaan	CT	F	860 824-5435	557
Tiger-Sul Products LLC	Shelton	CT	E	203 635-0190	3069
Total Specialty Chemicals Inc (PA)	New Canaan	CT	E	203 966-1525	2089
Tronox Incorporated (DH)	Stamford	CT	C	203 705-3800	3486
Vanderbilt Chemicals LLC	Bethel	CT	C	203 744-3900	139
Vanderbilt Chemicals LLC (HQ)	Norwalk	CT	C	203 295-2141	2589
A W Chesterton Company	Groveland	MA	B	781 438-7000	9013
Americanbio Inc	Canton	MA	E	508 655-4336	7768
Avient Colorants USA LLC (HQ)	Holden	MA	E	508 829-6321	9187
Cabot Corporation (PA)	Boston	MA	E	617 345-0100	6631
Cabot Corporation	Haverhill	MA	C	978 556-8400	9084
Cabot Holdings LLC	Boston	MA	G	617 345-0100	6632
Cabot Ii-Tn1w09 LLC	Boston	MA	F	617 723-7400	6633
Cabot Specialty Chemicals Inc (HQ)	Boston	MA	F	617 345-0100	6634
Captivate Bio LLC	Watertown	MA	G	617 607-4017	12867
CCL Industries Corporation (HQ)	Framingham	MA	D	508 872-4511	8749
CMC Materials Inc	Waltham	MA	F	781 530-3833	12633
Cmo Partners Inc	Billerica	MA	F	617 875-5449	6425
Cutting Edge Carbide Tech Inc	Athol	MA	G	888 210-9670	5977
Dow Chemical Company	Marlborough	MA	C	508 229-7676	10147
Eidp Inc	Boston	MA	E	617 482-9595	6708
Element Care	Methuen	MA	G	978 655-6195	10330
Fiberlock Technologies Inc	Andover	MA	F	978 623-9987	5882
Gcp Applied Technologies Inc	Cambridge	MA	E	617 876-1400	7578
Gws Tool Holdings LLC	Springfield	MA	E	800 523-8570	12098
Holland Company Inc	Adams	MA	E	413 743-1292	5773
Instrumentation Laboratory Co (DH)	Bedford	MA	A	781 861-0710	6233
Jordi Labs LLC	Mansfield	MA	E	508 719-8543	10061
Magellan Diagnostics Inc (HQ)	Chelmsford	MA	D	978 250-7000	7937
MD Stetson Company Inc	Mansfield	MA	E	781 986-6161	10066
Metalor USA Refining Corp (DH)	North Attleboro	MA	C	508 699-8800	10877
Nyacol Nano Technologies Inc	Ashland	MA	E	508 881-2220	5965
Omniglow LLC	West Springfield	MA	B	413 241-6010	13039
Qsa Global Inc (HQ)	Burlington	MA	D	781 272-2000	7416
Rohm Haas Electronic Mtls LLC (HQ)	Marlborough	MA	A	508 481-7950	10206
Saint-Gobain Ceramics Plas Inc	Northborough	MA	F	508 351-7754	11107
Saint-Gobain Ceramics Plas Inc	Worcester	MA	D	508 795-5000	13790
Saint-Gobain Ceramics Plas Inc	Worcester	MA	C	508 795-5000	13791
Solutia Inc	Indian Orchard	MA	C	734 676-4400	9474
Starmet Corporation (PA)	Concord	MA	E	978 369-5410	8134
Strem Chemicals Incorporated (HQ)	Newburyport	MA	D	978 499-1600	10718
Sud-Chemie Protech Inc	Needham Heights	MA	B	781 444-5188	10559
Synthomer LLC	Fitchburg	MA	E	978 342-5831	8678
The Sharp Tool Co Inc	Hudson	MA	E	978 568-9292	9418
Transene Company Inc (PA)	Danvers	MA	G	978 777-7860	8227
Trelleborg Offshore Boston Inc	Mansfield	MA	E	774 719-1400	10082
Trelleborg Offshore Boston Inc (HQ)	Randolph	MA	E	781 437-1171	11577
Twin Rivers Tech Holdings Inc	Quincy	MA	C	617 472-9200	11541
Twin Rivers Tech Mfg Corp	Quincy	MA	D	888 929-8780	11543
Twin Rivers Technologies Us Inc	Quincy	MA	E	617 472-9200	11544
Veolia N Amer Rgnrtion Svcs LL (DH)	Boston	MA	D	312 552-2800	7097
W R Grace & Co	Lexington	MA	E	617 876-1400	9793
Dalegip America Inc	Searsport	ME	E	207 323-1880	5452
Element All Stars	Lewiston	ME	E	207 576-6931	4958
Gac Chemical Corporation (PA)	Searsport	ME	D	207 548-2525	5453
General Alum New England Corp	Searsport	ME	D	207 548-2525	5454
Imerys Usa Inc	Skowhegan	ME	E	207 238-3567	5469
Specialty Minerals Inc	Jay	ME	E	207 897-4492	4916
Hampshire Chemical Corp (DH)	Nashua	NH	E	603 888-2320	15109
Pure Element	Derry	NH	G	603 235-4373	14207
Saint-Gobain Ceramics Plas Inc	Milford	NH	C	603 673-5831	15036
Z-Tech LLC	Bow	NH	E	603 228-1305	14016
Agilent Technologies Inc	North Kingstown	RI	D	800 338-1754	16229
Cal Chemical Corporation	Coventry	RI	E	401 821-0320	15808
Clariant Corporation	Coventry	RI	B	401 823-2000	15809
International Dioxcide Inc	North Kingstown	RI	E	401 295-8800	16260
Ne Finest LLC	Coventry	RI	F	800 215-6640	15817
Northern Products Inc	Woonsocket	RI	F		16969
Reade International Corp (PA)	East Providence	RI	E	401 433-7000	16041
Ultra Scientific Incorporated	North Kingstown	RI	E	800 338-1754	16290
Augmentus Group LLC	Burlington	VT	F		17119
Brunswick Square LLC	Burlington	VT	G	802 497-2575	17122
O M Y A Inc	Proctor	VT	E	802 499-8131	17458
Omya	Florence	VT	E	802 770-7537	17271
Omya Inc	Florence	VT	F	802 459-3311	17272
Omya Inc	Proctor	VT	E	802 459-3311	17459

2821 Plastics materials and resins

	CITY	ST	EMP	PHONE	ENTRY#
Allnex USA Inc	Wallingford	CT	D	203 269-4481	3769
Allread Products Co LLC	Terryville	CT	F	860 589-3566	3600
Arkadia Plastics Inc	New Britain	CT	E	860 612-0556	2001
Axel Plastics RES Labs Inc	Monroe	CT	E	718 672-8300	1905
Bakelite N Sumitomo Amer Inc (DH)	Manchester	CT	D	860 646-5500	1586
C Mather Company Inc	South Windsor	CT	G	860 528-5667	3124
Chessco Industries Inc (PA)	Westport	CT	E	203 255-2804	4160
Current Inc (PA)	East Haven	CT	D	203 469-1337	1039
Electric Cable Compounds Inc	Naugatuck	CT	D	203 723-2590	1957
Electrocal Inc	Manchester	CT	C	860 646-8153	1595
Engineered Polymers Inds Inc	Cheshire	CT	F	203 272-2233	590
Fimor North America Inc (HQ)	Cheshire	CT	E	203 272-3219	593
Forum Plastics LLC	Waterbury	CT	E	203 754-0777	3913
Henkel of America Inc (HQ)	Rocky Hill	CT	B	860 615-3395	2926
Henkel US Operations Corp (DH)	Rocky Hill	CT	B	860 571-5100	2927
Hexcel Corporation (PA)	Stamford	CT	E	203 969-0666	3374
Lanxess Solutions US Inc	Shelton	CT	A	203 573-2000	3027
Neu Spclty Engineered Mtls LLC	North Haven	CT	F	203 239-9629	2426
Oxford Industries Conn Inc	New Britain	CT	E	860 225-3700	2048
Oxford Performance Mtls Inc	South Windsor	CT	E	860 698-9300	3169
Oxpekk Performance Mtls Inc	South Windsor	CT	E	860 698-9300	3170
P I Liquidating Inc (PA)	Prospect	CT	E	203 758-6651	2838
Pastanch LLC	Naugatuck	CT	E	203 720-9478	1979
Plastics Color Corp Inc	Dayville	CT	G	800 922-9936	866
Polymer Resources Ltd (PA)	Farmington	CT	D	800 243-5176	1242
Presidium USA Inc	Darien	CT	E	203 803-2980	853
Ravago Americas LLC	Wilton	CT	D	203 855-6000	4245
Resinall Corp North Carolina (DH)	Stamford	CT	F	203 329-7100	3446
Roehm America LLC	Wallingford	CT	E	203 269-4481	3846
Rogers Corporation	Woodstock	CT	C	860 928-3622	4396
Seaview Plastic Recycling Inc	Bridgeport	CT	F	203 367-0070	370
Sjd Tech Inc	Wallingford	CT	D	203 269-9500	3849
Sonoco Prtective Solutions Inc	Putnam	CT	D	860 928-7795	2875
Spartech LLC	Stamford	CT	C	203 327-6010	3467
Stanchem Incorporated (HQ)	East Berlin	CT	E	860 828-0571	918
Summit Plastics LLC	Portland	CT	G	860 740-4482	2826
Thornton and Company Inc	Southington	CT	F	860 628-6771	3237
A Schulman Custom Compounding Ne Inc	Worcester	MA	C	508 756-0002	13695
Abcorp NA Inc	Boston	MA	B	617 325-9600	6503
Accurate Composites LLC	East Falmouth	MA	D	508 457-9097	8353
Accurate Plastics Inc	East Falmouth	MA	E	508 457-9097	8354
Acushnet Rubber Company Inc	New Bedford	MA	B	508 998-4000	10564
Allied Resin Technologies LLC	Leominster	MA	F	978 401-2267	9635
Altium Acqisition Holdings Inc	Boston	MA	A	617 516-2000	6539
Anchor-Seal Inc	Gloucester	MA	G	978 515-6004	8918
Argotec LLC	Greenfield	MA	B	413 772-2564	8982
Argotec LLC (HQ)	Greenfield	MA	C	413 772-2564	8983
Banzan Intl Group Corp	Acton	MA	F	978 263-3186	5739
Barrday Corporation	Millbury	MA	B	508 581-2100	10427
Bayer Corporation	Newton	MA	E	617 969-7690	10738
Bi-Qem Inc	Florence	MA	E	413 584-2472	8683
Blueshift Materials Inc	Spencer	MA	E	888 350-7586	12054
Cambridge Polymer Group Inc	Woburn	MA	E	617 629-4400	13539
CDF Corporation (PA)	Plymouth	MA	C	508 747-5858	11454
Chroma Color Corporation	Leominster	MA	E	978 537-3538	9652
Clinton BCI Inc	Clinton	MA	E	978 365-7335	8075
Cold Chain Technologies LLC (HQ)	Franklin	MA	D	508 429-1395	8826
Covestro LLC	Wilmington	MA	C	800 458-0014	13399
Dj Microlaminates Inc	Sudbury	MA	F	978 261-3188	12264
Dow Chemical Company	Marlborough	MA	C	508 229-7676	10147
DSM Neoresins Inc	Wilmington	MA	A	800 458-0014	13403
DSM Thermoplastics	Leominster	MA	G	978 537-6484	9659
Eastern Packaging Inc	Lawrence	MA	D	978 685-7723	9559
Enginred Syntactic Systems LLC	Attleboro	MA	G	508 226-3907	6013
Entec Polymers	Sutton	MA	F	508 865-2001	12280
Ernest Johnson	Marlborough	MA	G	508 259-6727	10148
Gare Incorporated	Haverhill	MA	E	978 373-9131	9096
Gelpac Poly Usa Inc (PA)	Haverhill	MA	E	978 372-3300	9097
George Patton Associates Inc	Fall River	MA	C	800 572-2194	8552
Gxt Green Inc	Cambridge	MA	F	978 735-4367	7597
Hapco Inc	Hanover	MA	E	781 826-8801	9034
Henkel Corporation	Canton	MA	E	781 717-1400	7796
Indusol Inc	Sutton	MA	E	508 865-9516	12282
Industrial Polymers & Chem Inc (PA)	Shrewsbury	MA	F	508 845-6112	11835
Ineos Melamines LLC	Springfield	MA	E	413 730-3811	12104
Isp Freetown Fine Chem Inc	Assonet	MA	D	508 672-0634	5974
L H C Inc (PA)	Lynn	MA	F	781 592-6444	9982

	CITY	ST	EMP	PHONE	ENTRY#
Lifoam Industries LLC	Peabody	MA	E	978 278-0008	11324
Plaskolite LLC	Sheffield	MA	E	800 628-5084	11798
Plaskolite LLC	Sheffield	MA	C	800 628-5084	11799
Plaskolite Massachusetts LLC	Sheffield	MA	C	413 229-8711	11800
Plastic Design Inc	North Chelmsford	MA	E	978 251-4830	10987
Port Plastics Inc	Chelmsford	MA	G	978 259-0002	7946
Primary Colors Inc	North Grafton	MA	E	508 839-3202	11025
Reinforced Structures For Elec	Worcester	MA	F	508 754-5316	13783
RES-Tech Corporation (HQ)	Hudson	MA	F	978 567-1000	9406
Resin Distribution Inc	Ayer	MA	F	978 772-1616	6192
Resin Technology LLC (DH)	Littleton	MA	F	978 448-6926	9835
Resource Colors LLC	Leominster	MA	F	978 537-3700	9702
Rig Grip Incorporated	Newton	MA	G	800 770-2666	10781
Royston Laboratories	Bridgewater	MA	G	412 828-1500	7237
S&E Specialty Polymers LLC	Lunenburg	MA	D	978 537-8261	9960
Sabic Innovative Plas US LLC	Pittsfield	MA	B	413 448-7110	11422
Sabic Innovative Plas US LLC	Tyngsboro	MA	E	978 772-5900	12465
Saint-Gobain Prfmce Plas Corp	Taunton	MA	C	508 823-7701	12366
Solutia Inc	Indian Orchard	MA	C	734 676-4400	9474
Solutia Inc	Springfield	MA	A	413 788-6911	12132
Space Age Accessories Inc	Foxboro	MA	E	508 543-3661	8725
Synthomer Inc	Fitchburg	MA	C	978 342-5831	8678
Tapecoat Company	Westwood	MA	E	781 332-0700	13322
Teknor Apex Elastomers Inc	Leominster	MA	D	978 466-5344	9709
Tuftane Extrusion Tech Inc	Fall River	MA	F	978 921-8200	8618
Unicore LLC	Palmer	MA	E	413 284-9995	11287
US Polymers Inc	Beverly	MA	G	978 921-8000	6391
Ware Rite Distributors Inc	East Bridgewater	MA	D	508 690-2145	8347
Zschimmer Schwarz Intrplymer I (DH)	Canton	MA	E	781 828-7120	7844
Bosal Foam and Fiber (PA)	Limerick	ME	E	207 793-2245	5000
Cyro Industry	Sanford	ME	F	207 324-6000	5393
G & G Products LLC	Kennebunk	ME	E	207 985-9100	4925
Neal Specialty Compounding LLC	Lewiston	ME	D	207 777-1122	4979
Roehm America LLC	Sanford	ME	E	207 324-6000	5412
Rynel Inc	Wiscasset	ME	D	207 882-0200	5700
Allstate Polyethylene Corp (PA)	Alexandria	NH	G	800 288-7659	13851
Avilite Inc	Merrimack	NH	G	603 626-4388	14974
Core Elastomers LLC	Portsmouth	NH	G	603 319-6912	15376
Desmarais Plastics LLC	Manchester	NH	D	603 669-8523	14841
Faber Industries LLC (HQ)	Salem	NH	F	603 681-0484	15522
Freudenberg-Nok General Partnr	Bristol	NH	B	603 744-0371	14034
Freudenberg-Nok General Partnr	Northfield	NH	C	603 286-1600	15265
Freudenberg-Nok General Partnr	Northfield	NH	D	603 286-1600	15266
Gates Tpu Inc	Salem	NH	E	603 890-1515	15531
Gelpac Poly Usa Inc	Salem	NH	E	603 685-8338	15532
Huntsman International LLC	Derry	NH	G	603 421-3500	14195
Keller Products Incorporated	Bow	NH	F	603 224-5502	14003
Metzger/Mcguire Inc	Bow	NH	F	603 224-6122	14005
MTI Polyexe Corporation	Brentwood	NH	F	603 778-1449	14023
Nylon Corporation America Inc	Manchester	NH	D	603 627-5150	14906
Nyltech North America	Manchester	NH	G	603 627-5150	14907
Omni Metals Company Inc	Somersworth	NH	E	603 692-6664	15619
Plan Tech Inc	Loudon	NH	E	603 783-4767	14798
Polyexe Corporation	Brentwood	NH	E	603 778-1143	14027
Resin Systems Corporation	Amherst	NH	D	603 673-1234	13886
Saint-Gobain Prfmce Plas Corp	Merrimack	NH	C	603 424-9000	15001
Scandia Plastics Inc	Plaistow	NH	E	603 382-6533	15350
Spaulding Composites Inc (PA)	Rochester	NH	D	603 332-0555	15494
Teknor Apex	Derry	NH	F	603 434-3056	14210
Textiles Coated Incorporated (PA)	Londonderry	NH	E	603 296-2221	14786
Textiles Coated Incorporated	Manchester	NH	C	603 296-2221	14943
Visual Polymer Tech LLC	Bedford	NH	G	603 488-5064	13953
Wembly Nycoa Holdings LLC	Manchester	NH	D	603 627-5150	14959
Amazing Mobile	Woonsocket	RI	G	401 597-0566	16947
Branch River Plastics Inc	Smithfield	RI	E	401 232-0270	16690
Development Associates Inc	North Kingstown	RI	F	401 884-1350	16244
Epoxytech Inc	Woonsocket	RI	E	401 726-4500	16958
G-Form LLC	North Smithfield	RI	E	401 769-0994	16323
HI Tech Profiles Inc	Ashaway	RI	E	401 377-2040	15741
Nar Industries LLC	Cranston	RI	E	401 941-3000	15897
Optical Polymers Lab Corp	Pawtucket	RI	F	401 722-0710	16398
Ralco Industries Inc (PA)	Woonsocket	RI	E	401 765-1000	16973
Rbc Industries Inc	Cranston	RI	D	401 941-3000	15906
Teknor Apex Company (PA)	Pawtucket	RI	A	401 725-8000	16420
Teknor Color Company LLC (HQ)	Pawtucket	RI	E		16422
Teknor Prfmce Elastomers Inc	Pawtucket	RI	E	401 725-8000	16423
Trico Specialty Films LLC	North Kingstown	RI	F	401 294-7022	16288
Txv Aerospace Composites LLC	Bristol	RI	F	425 785-0883	15785
QST Inc	Saint Albans	VT	E	802 524-7704	17529

2822 Synthetic rubber

	CITY	ST	EMP	PHONE	ENTRY#
Aardvark Polymers	Woodstock	CT	G	609 483-1013	4390
Chemtura USA Corporation	Middlebury	CT	A	203 573-2000	1714

	CITY	ST	EMP	PHONE	ENTRY#
Si Group Inc	Danbury	CT	C	203 702-6140	815
Stanchem Incorporated	East Berlin	CT	E	860 828-0571	917
Advanced Frp Systems Inc	East Weymouth	MA	G	508 927-6915	8423
Allcoat Technology Inc	Wilmington	MA	E	978 988-0880	13376
Heveatex Corporation	Fall River	MA	C	508 675-0181	8560
Labthink International Inc	Medford	MA	F	617 830-2190	10293
Cri-Sil LLC	Biddeford	ME	E	207 283-6422	4558
Southworth Intl Group Inc (PA)	Falmouth	ME	D	207 878-0700	4772
Contitech Thermopol LLC	Rochester	NH	E	603 692-6300	15471
Contitech Thermopol LLC	Somersworth	NH	E	603 692-6300	15614
Contitech Thermopol LLC (HQ)	Somersworth	NH	C	603 692-6300	15615
Ipotec LLC	Seabrook	NH	F	704 991-6978	15595
Sheergard Cmpsite Slutions Inc	Salem	NH	E	954 661-7372	15561
Conley Casting Supply Corp (PA)	Warwick	RI	F	401 461-4710	16797
Cool Polymers Inc	North Kingstown	RI	E	401 667-7830	16241
Rbc Industries Inc	Cranston	RI	D	401 941-3000	15906
QST Inc	Saint Albans	VT	E	802 524-7704	17529

2823 Cellulosic manmade fibers

	CITY	ST	EMP	PHONE	ENTRY#
Verbio North American Holdings	Stamford	CT	E	866 306-4777	3492
Global Materials Inc	Lowell	MA	E	978 322-1900	9880
Conform Automotive LLC	Auburn	ME	B	207 784-1118	4424
Formed Fiber Technologies Inc	Auburn	ME	A	207 784-1118	4433
Image 4 Concepts Inc	Manchester	NH	F	603 644-0077	14862

2824 Organic fibers, noncellulosic

	CITY	ST	EMP	PHONE	ENTRY#
Fairfield Processing Corp (PA)	Danbury	CT	C	203 744-2090	744
Proteus Industries Inc	Gloucester	MA	G	978 281-9545	8952
Solutia Inc	Indian Orchard	MA	C	734 676-4400	9474
Synergy Manufacturing LLC	Stoughton	MA	G	781 209-5538	12242
Texon Usa Inc	Russell	MA	E	413 862-3652	11695
Conform Automotive LLC	Auburn	ME	B	207 784-1118	4424
Formed Fiber Technologies Inc	Auburn	ME	A	207 784-1118	4433

2833 Medicinals and botanicals

	CITY	ST	EMP	PHONE	ENTRY#
American Distilling Inc (PA)	East Hampton	CT	D	860 267-4444	959
Biomed Health Inc	Glastonbury	CT	G	860 657-2258	1270
Candlewood Stars Inc	Danbury	CT	G	203 994-8826	720
Henkel of America Inc (HQ)	Rocky Hill	CT	B	860 615-3395	2926
Henkel US Operations Corp (DH)	Rocky Hill	CT	B	860 571-5100	2927
Mantrose-Haeuser Co Inc (HQ)	Westport	CT	E	203 454-1800	4182
Watson LLC (DH)	West Haven	CT	E	203 932-3000	4132
Asymchem Boston Corporation	Woburn	MA	G	781 896-3998	13517
BASF Bioresearch Corp	Worcester	MA	E	508 849-2500	13702
Cequr Corporation	Marlborough	MA	E	508 486-0010	10131
Curia Global Inc	Waltham	MA	F	781 672-4530	12646
Designing Health Inc	East Longmeadow	MA	F	661 257-1705	8373
Fulcrum Thrptics Scrities Corp	Cambridge	MA	E	617 651-8851	7576
GE Healthcare Inc (HQ)	Marlborough	MA	B	732 457-8667	10152
Herb Chambers Medford Inc	Medford	MA	F	617 739-6600	10288
Impact Nano LLC	Orange	MA	G	508 380-8423	11224
INSA Inc	Chicopee	MA	E	877 500-4672	8039
Ipsen Biopharmaceuticals Inc (HQ)	Cambridge	MA	C	973 903-4442	7617
Marimed Inc (PA)	Norwood	MA	E	781 277-0007	11193
Microbiotix Inc	Worcester	MA	E	508 757-2800	13759
Nitto Denko Avecia Inc (DH)	Milford	MA	C	508 532-2500	10408
Nova Biomedical Corporation	Billerica	MA	D	781 894-0800	6463
Nova Biomedical Corporation	Billerica	MA	D	781 647-3700	6464
Nova Biomedical Corporation (PA)	Waltham	MA	A	781 894-0800	12738
Perioq Inc	Leominster	MA	E	978 534-1249	9693
Tetraphase Pharmaceuticals Inc	Waltham	MA	D	617 715-3600	12795
Valo Health Inc (PA)	Boston	MA	E	617 237-6080	7096
Veranova LP	North Andover	MA	E	978 784-5000	10857
W R Grace & Co	Lexington	MA	E	617 876-1400	9793
Biodesign International	Saco	ME	E	207 283-6500	5363
Novel Beverage Co	Scarborough	ME	G	207 798-9610	5442
Seasmoke Extracts Inc	Auburn	ME	F	207 819-4114	4460
Ticked Off Inc	Dover	NH	G	603 742-0925	14253
C-End LLC	Portsmouth	RI	G	610 350-8674	16442
Saint Germain	Warwick	RI	G	401 738-2800	16857
Mylan Technologies Inc (HQ)	Saint Albans	VT	C	802 527-7792	17525
Troy Micro Five Inc	Saint Albans	VT	G	802 524-0076	17535

2834 Pharmaceutical preparations

	CITY	ST	EMP	PHONE	ENTRY#
Abbott Diagnostics	Southington	CT	G	860 463-0767	3200
Aeromics Inc	Branford	CT	G	216 772-1004	231
Alexion Pharma LLC (DH)	New Haven	CT	D	203 272-2596	2112
Aplicare Products LLC (HQ)	Meriden	CT	D	203 630-0500	1655
Aptuit (scientific Operations) LLC	Greenwich	CT	A	203 422-6600	1313
Arvinas Inc (PA)	New Haven	CT	B	203 535-1456	2119
Asepsis Inc	Waterbury	CT	F	203 573-2000	3887
Avara Pharmaceutical Svcs Inc (HQ)	Norwalk	CT	D	405 217-7670	2467
Avara US Holdings LLC (PA)	Norwalk	CT	E	203 655-1333	2468

SIC

	CITY	ST	EMP	PHONE	ENTRY#
Benefit Coatings Inc	Stratford	CT	F	203 572-0660	3519
Bioasis Biosciences Corp	Guilford	CT	G	203 533-7082	1387
Biohaven Pharmaceuticals Inc	New Haven	CT	D	203 404-0410	2127
Biohaven Phrm Holdg Co Ltd	New Haven	CT	F	203 691-6332	2128
Biohaven Phrm Holdg Co Ltd (HQ)	New Haven	CT	D	203 404-0410	2129
Biomed Health Inc	Glastonbury	CT	G	860 657-2258	1270
Bioxcel Therapeutics Inc	New Haven	CT	C	475 238-6837	2130
Boehringer Ingelheim Corp (DH)	Ridgefield	CT	A	203 798-9988	2886
Boehringer Ingelheim Data Dime	Ridgefield	CT	G	800 203-2916	2887
Boehringer Ingelheim USA Corp (DH)	Ridgefield	CT	E	203 798-9988	2888
Boehrnger Ingelheim Roxane Inc	Ridgefield	CT	E	800 243-0127	2889
Boehrnger Inglheim Phrmctcals	Ridgefield	CT	C	203 798-9988	2890
Boehrnger Inglheim Phrmctcals (DH)	Ridgefield	CT	A	203 798-9988	2891
Brands To Go Inc	Norwalk	CT	F		2476
Brookfeld Mdcl/Srgical Sup Inc	Brookfield	CT	F	203 775-0862	514
Cara Therapeutics Inc	Stamford	CT	D	203 406-3700	3302
Cardinal Health 414 LLC	East Hartford	CT	G	860 291-9135	978
Celldex Therapeutics Inc	New Haven	CT	F	203 483-3531	2136
Cogstate Sport Inc	New Haven	CT	F	203 773-5010	2137
Drug Farm Usa LLC	Guilford	CT	G	617 735-5205	1392
Evolveimmune Therapeutics Inc	Branford	CT	F	203 858-7389	254
Foster Delivery Science Inc (HQ)	Putnam	CT	F	860 541-5280	2857
Foster Delivery Science Inc	Putnam	CT	E	860 630-4515	2858
Frederick Purdue Company Inc (PA)	Stamford	CT	B	203 588-8000	3349
Hcrx Investments Holdco LP	Stamford	CT	G	203 487-8300	3369
Hcrx Master Gp LLC	Stamford	CT	F	203 487-8300	3370
Healthcare Royalty Inc (PA)	Stamford	CT	G	203 487-8300	3371
Humphreys Pharmacal Inc	East Hampton	CT	F	860 267-8710	962
Imbrium Therapeutics LP (DH)	Stamford	CT	E	888 827-0622	3380
Infirst Healthcare Inc	Westport	CT	F	203 222-1300	4176
Itc Group LLC	Orange	CT	F	203 260-5101	2670
Iterum Therapeutics Inc	Old Saybrook	CT	G	860 391-8349	2653
J&J Precision Inc	Thomaston	CT	D	860 283-8243	3622
Karos Pharmaceuticals Inc	New Haven	CT	F	203 535-0540	2165
Kasten Inc	Bridgeport	CT	F	702 860-2407	339
Knoa Pharma LLC (PA)	Stamford	CT	E	203 588-8000	3395
Kolltan Pharmaceuticals Inc (HQ)	New Haven	CT	E	203 773-3000	2166
Koster Keunen LLC (PA)	Watertown	CT	E	860 945-3333	4018
Life Chemicals Usa Inc	Woodbridge	CT	G	203 693-4563	4380
Loxo Oncology Inc (HQ)	Stamford	CT	E	203 653-3880	3405
Mannkind Corporation (PA)	Danbury	CT	D	818 661-5000	781
MD Solarsciences Corporation	Westport	CT	F	203 857-0095	4184
Meter Health Inc	Manchester	CT	G	833 638-3777	1617
Micro Source Discovery Systems	Gaylordsville	CT	G	860 350-8078	1265
New Leaf Pharmaceuticals LLC	Newtown	CT	F	203 270-4167	2343
Par Phrmceutical Companies Inc	Stratford	CT	D	203 290-6261	3563
Penfield Search Partners Ltd	Fairfield	CT	G	203 307-2600	1196
Perosphere Inc	Danbury	CT	F	203 885-1111	796
PF Laboratories Inc (DH)	Stamford	CT	F	973 256-3100	3430
Pfizer	Groton	CT	E	203 584-2793	1378
Pfizer Inc	Groton	CT	C	860 441-4100	1379
Pfizer Inc	New Haven	CT	F	203 401-0100	2184
Pgxhealthholding Inc (PA)	New Haven	CT	C	203 786-3400	2185
Pharmaceutical RES Assoc Inc	Stamford	CT	A	203 588-8000	3431
Pharmavite Corp	Simsbury	CT	E	860 651-1885	3095
PRA Holdings Inc	Stamford	CT	A	203 853-0123	3435
Purdue Pharma LP (HQ)	Stamford	CT	C	203 588-8000	3439
Purdue Pharma Manufacturing LP	Stamford	CT	F	252 265-1924	3440
Purdue Pharma Technologies Inc	Stamford	CT	A	203 588-8000	3441
PURDUE PRODUCTS LP	Stamford	CT	A	888 827-0624	3442
Quality Care Drg/Cntrbrook LLC	Centerbrook	CT	F	860 767-0206	563
Rallybio Corporation (PA)	New Haven	CT	F	203 859-3820	2190
Rhodes Pharmaceuticals LP	Stamford	CT	F	888 827-0616	3448
SDA Laboratories Inc	Greenwich	CT	F	203 861-0005	1350
Sheffield Pharmaceuticals LLC	Norwich	CT	F	860 442-4451	2616
Theracour Pharma Inc	West Haven	CT	G	203 937-6137	4129
Tower Laboratories Ltd	Clinton	CT	E	860 669-7078	652
Tower Laboratories Ltd (PA)	Centerbrook	CT	D	860 767-2127	564
Trevi Therapeutics Inc (PA)	New Haven	CT	F	203 304-2499	2213
Trirx Pharmaceutical Svcs LLC (PA)	Norwalk	CT	E	256 489-8867	2587
Unipharm Inc	Waterbury	CT	G	203 528-3230	3978
2seventy Bio Inc (PA)	Cambridge	MA	D	339 499-9300	7462
4th Dimension Bioprocess Inc	Gloucester	MA	G	978 979-4222	8916
AA Pharmaceuticals Inc	Woburn	MA	G	617 935-1241	13496
Abbott	Burlington	MA	G	978 387-5652	7330
Abbott Laboratories	Worcester	MA	F	508 849-2500	13696
Abfero Pharmaceuticals Inc (PA)	Boston	MA	G	781 266-7297	6504
Abpro Corporation	Woburn	MA	E	617 225-0808	13497
Acceleron Pharma Inc (HQ)	Boston	MA	D	617 649-9200	6508
Acceleron Pharma Inc	Cambridge	MA	C	617 576-2220	7465
Adicet Bio Inc (PA)	Boston	MA	G	857 315-5528	6516
Adnexus Therapeutics Inc	Waltham	MA	E	781 891-3745	12584
Adolor Corporation	Lexington	MA	B	781 860-8660	9720

	CITY	ST	EMP	PHONE	ENTRY#
Aerodesigns Inc	Cambridge	MA	E	617 491-6600	7468
Aerovate Therapeutics Inc (PA)	Boston	MA	G	858 443-2400	6520
Agios Pharmaceuticals Inc (PA)	Cambridge	MA	B	617 649-8600	7470
Aileron Therapeutics Inc (PA)	Boston	MA	G	617 995-0900	6522
Akebia Therapeutics Inc (PA)	Cambridge	MA	C	617 871-2098	7474
Akouos Inc (PA)	Boston	MA	E	857 410-1818	6528
Albireo Pharma Inc (DH)	Boston	MA	E	857 254-5555	6531
Alcami Carolinas Corporation	Pepperell	MA	G	910 619-3952	11380
Alcami Carolinas Corporation	Pepperell	MA	G	910 619-3952	11381
Alcami Carolinas Corporation	Pepperell	MA	F	910 619-3952	11382
Alcami Carolinas Corporation	Shirley	MA	G	910 619-3952	11813
Aldeyra Therapeutics Inc (PA)	Lexington	MA	F	781 761-4904	9723
Aleksia Therapeutics Inc	Watertown	MA	G	720 918-6610	12856
Alexion Pharmaceuticals Inc (HQ)	Boston	MA	A	475 230-2596	6532
Alkermes Inc	Cambridge	MA	C	617 441-3092	7475
Alkermes Inc (HQ)	Waltham	MA	A	781 609-6000	12589
Alkermes Cntrlled Therapeutics	Waltham	MA	B	877 706-0510	12590
Alnylam Pharmaceuticals Inc (PA)	Cambridge	MA	B	617 551-8200	7478
Alnylam Pharmaceuticals Inc	Cambridge	MA	E	617 551-8200	7479
Alnylam Pharmaceuticals Inc	Cambridge	MA	E	617 551-8200	7480
Alnylam US Inc (HQ)	Cambridge	MA	E	617 551-8200	7481
Alnylam US Inc	Norton	MA	D	617 551-8200	11122
Alopexx Pharmaceuticals LLC	Cambridge	MA	F	617 945-2510	7482
Alzheon Inc	Framingham	MA	E	508 861-7709	8740
Amgen Inc	Cambridge	MA	E	617 444-5000	7483
Amryt Pharmaceuticals Inc (DH)	Boston	MA	F	877 764-3131	6547
Amylyx Pharmaceuticals Inc (PA)	Cambridge	MA	C	617 682-0917	7486
Antolrx Inc	Cambridge	MA	G	617 902-0601	7487
Apellis Pharmaceuticals Inc (PA)	Waltham	MA	B	617 977-5700	12592
Aquinnah Pharmaceuticals Inc	Cambridge	MA	F	617 416-0530	7488
Aratana Therapeutics Inc	Boston	MA	G	617 425-9226	6554
Arbor Biotechnologies Inc	Cambridge	MA	E	857 301-6366	7489
Ardelyx Inc	Waltham	MA	D	510 745-1700	12595
Armstrong Pharmaceuticals Inc (HQ)	West Roxbury	MA	D	617 323-7404	13009
Army & Roche LLC	Boston	MA	G	617 936-0114	6558
Arqule Inc (HQ)	Burlington	MA	E	781 994-0300	7335
Arranta Bio Holdings LLC (DH)	Watertown	MA	G	785 760-3128	12859
Astellas Inst For Rgnrtive Mdc (HQ)	Westborough	MA	F	800 727-7003	13078
Astrea Bioseparations US Inc	Canton	MA	F	919 899-9087	7771
Astria Therapeutics Inc (PA)	Boston	MA	E	617 349-1971	6562
Atea Pharmaceuticals Inc (PA)	Boston	MA	E	857 284-8891	6571
Avedro Inc	Burlington	MA	C	781 768-3400	7337
Aveo Pharmaceuticals Inc (HQ)	Boston	MA	F	857 400-0101	6580
Avrobio Inc (PA)	Cambridge	MA	E	617 914-8420	7495
Azurity Pharmaceuticals Inc (HQ)	Wilmington	MA	F	800 461-7449	13385
Batavia Biosciences Inc	Woburn	MA	G	781 305-3921	13521
Baxalta US Inc	Cambridge	MA	B	312 656-8021	7498
Bedrock Brands LLC	Boston	MA	G	914 231-9550	6587
Beigene US Mfg Co Inc	Cambridge	MA	D	781 801-1800	7502
Beigene Usa Inc (HQ)	Cambridge	MA	E	781 801-1887	7503
Berg LLC (HQ)	Framingham	MA	E	617 588-0083	8743
Berkshire Sterile Mfg LLC	Lee	MA	E	413 243-0330	9611
Bfs Pharma Inc	Randolph	MA	F	781 767-2020	11551
Bial - Biotech Investments Inc	Cambridge	MA	F	508 332-9103	7505
Bicara Therapeutics Inc	Cambridge	MA	G	860 882-7478	7506
Bind Biosciences Inc	Cambridge	MA	F	617 679-9600	7507
Biocon Biologics Inc	Cambridge	MA	D	857 706-2596	7509
Biocytogen Boston Corp	Waltham	MA	D	781 587-3558	12606
Biodelivery Sciences Intl Inc (HQ)	Stoughton	MA	F	919 582-9050	12198
Biofrontera Inc (HQ)	Woburn	MA	F	781 245-1325	13524
Biogen Inc (PA)	Cambridge	MA	B	617 679-2000	7511
Biogen Inc	Cambridge	MA	D	617 914-8888	7512
Biophysics Pharma Inc	Peabody	MA	F	781 608-7738	11299
Bioverativ Inc (HQ)	Waltham	MA	D	781 663-4400	12607
Bioverativ Therapeutics Inc (DH)	Waltham	MA	E	781 663-4400	12608
Black Diamond Therapeutics Inc (PA)	Cambridge	MA	F	617 252-0848	7517
Bluefin Biomedicine Inc	Beverly	MA	E	925 524-3417	6334
Blueprint Medicines Corp (PA)	Cambridge	MA	A	617 374-7580	7518
Bms Pizza Inc	Tewksbury	MA	F	978 851-0540	12386
Boston Oncology LLC	Cambridge	MA	F	857 209-5052	7521
Bpg Bio Inc	Framingham	MA	F	617 588-0083	8748
Brammer Bio Holding Co LLC (HQ)	Cambridge	MA	E	386 418-8199	7523
Bright Horizons At Biogen Idec	Cambridge	MA	F	617 621-3383	7525
Bristol-Myers Squibb Company	Devens	MA	B	978 588-6001	8271
Bryan Oncor Inc	Somerville	MA	G	617 957-9858	11865
Bwt Pharma & Biotech Inc	Marlborough	MA	E	508 485-4291	10124
Cadent Therapeutics Inc	Cambridge	MA	F	617 949-5529	7526
Cambrex	Agawam	MA	E	413 786-1680	5783
Cambrex Bio Science	Hopkinton	MA	G	508 497-0700	9312
Carisma Therapeutics Inc	Cambridge	MA	F	617 444-8550	7532
Cartesian Therapeutics Inc (PA)	Watertown	MA	F	617 923-1400	12868
Catalent Massachusetts LLC	Chelsea	MA	F	617 660-4110	7976
Cedilla Therapeutics Inc	Cambridge	MA	E	617 581-9333	7533

Company	CITY	ST	EMP	PHONE	ENTRY#
Celgene Corporation	Amesbury	MA	F	857 225-2309	5832
Celldex Therapeutics Inc	Needham Heights	MA	F	781 433-0771	10534
Celyad Inc	Boston	MA	G	857 990-6900	6644
Central Admxture Phrm Svcs Inc	Woburn	MA	G	781 376-0032	13541
Centrexion Therapeutics Corp	Boston	MA	G	617 837-6911	6646
Cerevel Thrputics Holdings Inc (PA)	Cambridge	MA	F	844 304-2048	7536
Checkpoint Therapeutics Inc	Waltham	MA	E	781 652-4500	12624
Chiasma Inc	Waltham	MA	E	617 928-5300	12625
Chiesi Ventures Inc	Boston	MA	G	919 998-3330	6651
CinCor Pharma Inc	Waltham	MA	F	513 800-2585	12628
Citra Labs LLC	Braintree	MA	E	781 848-9386	7173
Civitas Therapeutics Inc	Chelsea	MA	E	617 884-3004	7978
Clade Therapeutics Inc	Boston	MA	E	617 546-7460	6659
Clementia Phrmcuticals USA Inc	Auburndale	MA	F	857 226-5588	6130
Cogent Biosciences Inc (PA)	Waltham	MA	F	617 945-5576	12634
Coley Pharmaceutical Group Inc	Wellesley	MA	D	781 431-9000	12939
Collegium Pharmaceutical Inc (PA)	Stoughton	MA	E	781 713-3699	12201
Colucid Pharmaceuticals Inc	Cambridge	MA	G	857 285-6495	7543
Concert Pharmaceuticals Inc (HQ)	Lexington	MA	E	781 860-0045	9731
Constlltion Phrmaceuticals Inc (DH)	Boston	MA	E	844 667-1992	6666
Corbus Pharmaceuticals Inc	Norwood	MA	G	617 963-0100	11169
Corium LLC	Boston	MA	C	855 253-2407	6672
Corvidia Therapeutics Inc	Waltham	MA	G	781 205-4755	12642
Courage Therapeutics Inc	Newton	MA	G	617 216-9921	10749
Cpec LLC	Lexington	MA	D	781 861-8444	9733
Cubist Pharmaceuticals LLC	Lexington	MA	D	781 860-8660	9735
Cue Biopharma Inc (PA)	Cambridge	MA	E	617 949-2680	7545
Curagen Corporation (HQ)	Needham Heights	MA	F	908 200-7500	10538
Curia Massachusetts Inc (DH)	Burlington	MA	E	781 270-7900	7358
Curirx Inc	Wilmington	MA	E	978 658-2962	13400
Curis Inc (PA)	Lexington	MA	E	617 503-6500	9736
Cyclerion Therapeutics Inc (PA)	Cambridge	MA	E	857 327-8778	7547
Cyteir Therapeutics Inc (PA)	Lexington	MA	E	857 285-4140	9737
Cytosol Laboratories Inc	Braintree	MA	E	781 848-9386	7178
Decibel Therapeutics Inc (HQ)	Boston	MA	E	617 370-8701	6686
Deciphera Pharmaceuticals LLC	Waltham	MA	B	781 209-6400	12648
Deciphera Pharmaceuticals Inc (PA)	Waltham	MA	C	781 209-6400	12649
Deepcure Inc	Boston	MA	G	617 417-2345	6687
Dicerna Pharmaceuticals Inc (HQ)	Lexington	MA	C	617 621-8097	9739
Disc Medicine Inc (PA)	Watertown	MA	F	617 674-9274	12871
Dlrc Incorporated	Cambridge	MA	G	617 999-3340	7552
DSM Nutritional Products LLC	Lexington	MA	C	781 259-7600	9741
Dusa Pharmaceuticals Inc (DH)	Billerica	MA	D	978 657-7500	6434
Dyne Therapeutics Inc (PA)	Waltham	MA	E	781 786-8230	12658
Eisai Inc	Cambridge	MA	F	978 837-4616	7556
Elan Pharma	Cambridge	MA	F	415 885-6780	7557
Elan Pharmaceuticals Inc	Cambridge	MA	A		7558
Elevatebio LLC (PA)	Cambridge	MA	E	413 297-7151	7559
Elevatebio Base Camp Inc	Waltham	MA	C	617 433-2600	12660
EMD Accnting Sltons Svcs Amer	Rockland	MA	C	781 982-9000	11642
EMD Serono Inc	Billerica	MA	F	781 982-9000	6439
EMD Serono Inc	Burlington	MA	F	978 715-1804	7368
EMD Serono Inc (DH)	Rockland	MA	A	781 982-9000	11643
EMD Serono Biotech Center Inc	Billerica	MA	E	978 294-1100	6440
EMD Serono Biotech Center Inc	Quincy	MA	E	978 294-1100	11515
EMD Serono Biotech Center Inc (HQ)	Rockland	MA	D	800 283-8088	11644
EMD Serono Holding Inc	Rockland	MA	E	781 982-9000	11645
EMD Serono RES & Dev Inst Inc	Billerica	MA	D	978 294-1100	6441
EMD Serono RES & Dev Inst Inc (HQ)	Rockland	MA	E	781 982-9000	11646
Emergent Biosolutions Inc	Canton	MA	F	781 302-3000	7788
Empiramed Inc	Maynard	MA	G	978 344-4300	10262
Enanta Pharmaceuticals Inc (PA)	Watertown	MA	D	617 607-0800	12872
Encyte Systems Inc	Braintree	MA	G	781 848-6772	7180
Ensem Therapeutics Inc	Waltham	MA	E	662 422-2488	12663
Entasis Thrputics Holdings Inc (HQ)	Waltham	MA	F	781 810-0120	12664
Entrada Therapeutics Inc (PA)	Boston	MA	D	857 520-9158	6717
Epirus Biopharmaceuticals Inc	Foxboro	MA	E	617 600-3497	8696
Epizyme Inc	Cambridge	MA	C	617 229-5872	7563
Epoxy Technology Inc (PA)	Billerica	MA	E	978 667-3805	6444
Eqrx Inc (HQ)	Cambridge	MA	E	617 315-2255	7564
Erytech Pharma Inc	Cambridge	MA	F	360 320-3325	7565
Euthymics Bioscience Inc	Cambridge	MA	F	617 758-0300	7567
Evopoint Biosciences Usa Inc	Concord	MA	G	646 750-2661	8117
Excelerarx Corp	Stoughton	MA	F	612 293-0378	12203
Exemplar Laboratories LLC	Fall River	MA	G	508 676-6726	8543
Exemplar Pharma LLC	Fall River	MA	F	508 676-6726	8544
Exo Therapeutics Inc	Cambridge	MA	F	860 908-6508	7568
FDA Group LLC	North Grafton	MA	E	413 330-7476	11023
Fergene Inc	Cambridge	MA	F	973 796-1600	7569
Flexion Thrptics Scrities Corp	Burlington	MA	C	781 305-7777	7374
Flo Chemical Corp	Ashburnham	MA	F	978 827-5101	5952
Fog Pharmaceuticals Inc	Cambridge	MA	D	617 945-9510	7571
Foghorn Therapeutics Inc (PA)	Cambridge	MA	E	617 586-3100	7572
Foldrx Pharmaceuticals Inc (HQ)	Cambridge	MA	F	617 252-5500	7573
Forma Therapeutics Inc (DH)	Watertown	MA	E	617 679-1970	12877
Fortress Biotech Inc	Waltham	MA	F	781 652-4500	12678
Fresenius Kabi Compounding LLC	Canton	MA	E	224 358-1150	7792
Fresenius Kabi Usa Inc	North Andover	MA	D	978 775-8050	10833
Fresenius Usa Inc (DH)	Waltham	MA	C	781 699-4191	12683
Fulcrum Therapeutics Inc (PA)	Cambridge	MA	E	617 651-8851	7575
Fusion Pharmaceuticals US Inc	Boston	MA	F	617 420-5698	6750
Generation Bio Co (PA)	Cambridge	MA	D	617 655-7500	7581
Genocea Biosciences Inc (PA)	Cambridge	MA	E	617 876-8191	7582
Genzyme Corporation	Allston	MA	E	617 252-7500	5821
Genzyme Corporation	Cambridge	MA	C	508 271-2919	7583
Genzyme Corporation	Cambridge	MA	B	617 494-8484	7584
Genzyme Corporation (DH)	Cambridge	MA	A	617 252-7500	7585
Genzyme Corporation	Cambridge	MA	D	617 252-7500	7586
Genzyme Corporation	Cambridge	MA	D	617 252-7999	7587
Genzyme Corporation	Cambridge	MA	D	617 252-7500	7588
Genzyme Corporation	Cambridge	MA	C	508 872-8400	7589
Genzyme Corporation	Framingham	MA	E	508 872-8400	8765
Genzyme Corporation	Framingham	MA	E	508 872-8400	8766
Genzyme Corporation	Framingham	MA	E	508 872-8400	8767
Genzyme Corporation	Framingham	MA	D	508 872-8400	8768
Genzyme Corporation	Framingham	MA	D	508 872-8400	8769
Genzyme Corporation	Framingham	MA	D	508 271-2642	8770
Genzyme Corporation	Framingham	MA	D	508 370-9690	8771
Genzyme Corporation	Framingham	MA	D	617 252-7500	8772
Genzyme Corporation	Framingham	MA	E	617 252-7500	8773
Genzyme Corporation	Framingham	MA	E	617 252-7500	8774
Genzyme Corporation	Northborough	MA	C	508 351-2699	11096
Genzyme Corporation	Waltham	MA	C	781 487-5728	12687
Genzyme Corporation	Westborough	MA	D	508 351-2600	13102
Genzyme Corporation	Westborough	MA	C	508 898-9001	13103
Genzyme Securities Corporation	Cambridge	MA	F	617 252-7500	7590
Getreskilled	Boston	MA	G	617 901-9268	6757
Ginger Acquisition Inc	Boston	MA	B	617 551-4000	6760
Global Lf Scnces Sltons USA LL	Marlborough	MA	A	800 526-3593	10153
Global Lf Scnces Sltons USA LL	Northampton	MA	C	413 586-7720	11065
Gloucester Pharmaceuticals Inc	Cambridge	MA	F	617 583-1300	7592
Gsk	Cambridge	MA	F	781 795-4165	7594
GTC Biotherapeutics Inc	Framingham	MA	E	508 370-5429	8776
Gurnet Holding Company	Cambridge	MA	C	508 588-4900	7595
Harbour Biomed Us Inc	Cambridge	MA	F	617 682-3679	7598
Homology Medicines Inc	Bedford	MA	C	781 301-7277	6229
Hopewell Therapeutics Inc	Woburn	MA	E	781 218-3318	13582
Houston Lonza Inc	Lexington	MA	F	201 316-9200	9750
I2o Therapeutics Inc	Cambridge	MA	G	303 596-0402	7608
Idenix Pharmaceuticals Inc (HQ)	Cambridge	MA	E	617 995-9800	7609
Ifm Therapeutics LLC	Boston	MA	E	857 327-9903	6805
Imabiotech Corp	Billerica	MA	F	978 362-1825	6451
Imbria Pharmaceuticals Inc	Boston	MA	G	617 941-3000	6808
Immuneering Corporation	Cambridge	MA	E	617 500-8080	7612
Immunmlecular Therapeutics Inc	Woburn	MA	G	617 356-8170	13584
Immunogen Inc (PA)	Waltham	MA	F	781 895-0600	12696
In Silico Biosciences Inc	Lexington	MA	F	781 861-1592	9751
Infinity Pharmaceuticals Inc (PA)	Cambridge	MA	F		7614
Inflammasome Therapeutics Inc	Newton	MA	F	617 331-1071	10762
Innoviva Spclty Thrpeutics Inc	Waltham	MA	F	800 651-3861	12701
Inotek Pharmaceuticals Corp	Lexington	MA	F	781 676-2100	9753
Integral Biosystems LLC	Bedford	MA	F	781 275-8059	6234
Invetx Inc	Natick	MA	F	802 233-3103	10483
Ipsen Biopharmaceuticals Inc (HQ)	Cambridge	MA	C	973 903-4442	7617
Ipsen Bioscience Inc	Cambridge	MA	E	617 679-8500	7618
Ironwood Pharmaceuticals Inc (PA)	Boston	MA	C	617 621-7722	6818
Iteos Therapeutics Inc (PA)	Watertown	MA	F	339 217-0161	12883
Jnj Global Enterprises LLC	Attleboro	MA	G	508 455-4945	6028
Johnson & Johnson	Woburn	MA	G	781 264-4804	13594
Juniper Pharmaceuticals Inc (DH)	Boston	MA	D	619 430-1500	6837
Kala Pharmaceuticals Inc (PA)	Arlington	MA	C	781 996-5252	5942
Kalvista Pharmaceuticals Inc (PA)	Cambridge	MA	E	857 999-0075	7621
Karuna Therapeutics Inc (PA)	Boston	MA	E	857 449-2244	6840
Karyopharm Therapeutics Inc (PA)	Newton	MA	C	617 658-0600	10766
Kaz Inc (HQ)	Marlborough	MA	G	508 490-7000	10174
Keros Therapeutics Inc (PA)	Lexington	MA	D	617 314-6297	9756
Keryx Biopharmaceuticals Inc (HQ)	Cambridge	MA	F	617 871-2098	7622
Kiniksa Pharmaceuticals Corp	Lexington	MA	C	781 431-9100	9757
Kiq Bio LLC	Cambridge	MA	D	617 945-5576	7623
Korro Bio Inc (PA)	Cambridge	MA	D	617 468-1999	7624
La Jolla Pharmaceutical Co (HQ)	Waltham	MA	E	617 715-3600	12708
Landmark Bio Pbllc	Watertown	MA	G	617 894-8629	12886
Lantheus Holdings Inc (PA)	North Billerica	MA	A	978 671-8001	10923
Lantheus Medical Imaging Inc (HQ)	North Billerica	MA	B	800 362-2668	10924
Lantheus MI Intermediate Inc	North Billerica	MA	A	978 671-8001	10925
Leaf Pharmaceuticals LLC	Woburn	MA	E	781 305-4192	13601

S I C

	CITY	ST	EMP	PHONE	ENTRY#
Leap Therapeutics Inc (PA)	Cambridge	MA	F	617 714-0360	7630
Lfb Usa Inc (DH)	Framingham	MA	E	508 370-5100	8785
Lfb Usa Inc	Spencer	MA	G	508 370-5100	12063
Logical Therapeutics Inc	Waltham	MA	F	781 290-0900	12711
Lonza Biologics Inc	Cambridge	MA	D	608 630-3758	7634
Lonza Biologics Inc	Lexington	MA	F	508 435-2331	9760
Luckwel Pharmaceuticals Inc	Cambridge	MA	G	617 430-5222	7635
Lutronic USA	Billerica	MA	F	888 588-7644	6459
Lykan Bioscience Holdings LLC	Hopkinton	MA	F	774 341-4200	9336
Lyndra Therapeutics Inc	Lexington	MA	D	857 201-5314	9761
Lyndra Therapeutics Inc (PA)	Watertown	MA	F	339 222-6519	12888
Lyne Laboratories Inc	Brockton	MA	D	508 583-8700	7292
Lyra Therapeutics Inc	Watertown	MA	E	617 393-4600	12889
Matrivax Research & Dev Corp	Boston	MA	G	617 385-7640	6880
MBL International Corporation (DH)	Woburn	MA	F	781 939-6964	13607
Medtherapy Biotechnology Inc	Quincy	MA	E	617 938-7082	11528
Merck Group	Bedford	MA	E	781 858-3284	6242
Merck Group	Danvers	MA	D	978 762-5280	8209
Merck Research Laboratories	Boston	MA	F	617 992-2000	6883
Merck Sharp & Dohme Corp	Boston	MA	F	617 992-2000	6884
Merrimack Pharmaceuticals Inc (PA)	Cambridge	MA	E	617 441-1000	7640
Mersana Therapeutics Inc (PA)	Cambridge	MA	D	617 498-0020	7641
Millennium Pharmaceuticals Inc	Cambridge	MA	C	617 679-7000	7645
Millennium Pharmaceuticals Inc (HQ)	Cambridge	MA	C	617 679-7000	7646
Millennium Pharmaceuticals Inc	Cambridge	MA	D	617 679-7000	7647
Millennium Pharmaceuticals Inc	Cambridge	MA	D	617 679-7000	7648
Millennium Pharmaceuticals Inc	Cambridge	MA	D	617 679-7000	7649
Millennium Pharmaceuticals Inc	Cambridge	MA	D	617 679-7000	7650
Millennium Pharmaceuticals Inc	Cambridge	MA	D	617 679-7000	7651
Millennium Pharmaceuticals Inc	Lexington	MA	D	617 679-7000	9763
Millennium Pharmaceuticals Inc	Winchester	MA	D	781 729-7435	13487
Minerva Nrscnces Scrities Corp	Waltham	MA	G	617 600-7373	12721
Mitsubshi Tnabe Phrma Amer Inc	Cambridge	MA	F	210 897-3473	7652
Modalis Therapeutics Inc	Waltham	MA	E	617 219-9808	12723
Moderna Inc (PA)	Cambridge	MA	B	617 714-6500	7653
Momenta Pharmaceuticals Inc (HQ)	Cambridge	MA	D	617 491-9700	7654
Montai Health Inc	Cambridge	MA	E	617 293-0578	7656
Morphic Holding Inc (PA)	Waltham	MA	E	781 996-0955	12725
Msm Protein Technologies Inc	Waltham	MA	G	781 373-2405	12726
Mural Oncology Inc	Waltham	MA	E	617 694-2481	12727
Navitor Pharmaceuticals Inc	Cambridge	MA	F	857 285-4300	7660
Nemucore Med Innovations Inc	Wellesley	MA	G	617 943-9983	12944
Neovii Biotech Na Inc	Boston	MA	E	781 966-3830	6908
Neuro Phage Phrmaceuticals Inc	Cambridge	MA	F	617 941-7004	7663
Neurobo Pharmaceuticals Inc (PA)	Cambridge	MA	F	617 864-2880	7664
Neurobo Therapeutics Inc	Boston	MA	F	617 313-7331	6911
New England Cmpunding Phrm Inc	Boston	MA	E	800 994-6322	6915
Nextpoint Therapeutics Inc	Cambridge	MA	G	917 208-0865	7666
Nimbus Lakshmi Inc	Boston	MA	F	857 999-2009	6922
Nitromed Inc	Lexington	MA	G	781 274-1248	9766
Nocion Therapeutics Inc	Waltham	MA	G	781 812-6176	12737
Novabiotics Inc	Boston	MA	D	866 259-4527	6926
Novartis Corporation	Cambridge	MA	E	617 225-0820	7667
Novartis Instttes For Bmdcal R (HQ)	Cambridge	MA	E	617 777-8276	7668
Novartis Mlclar Dagnostics LLC	Cambridge	MA	E	617 871-8441	7669
Novartis Vccnes Dagnostics Inc	Cambridge	MA	A	617 871-7000	7670
Novirio Pharmaceuticals Inc	Cambridge	MA	D	617 250-3100	7671
Novo Nordisk Inc	Lexington	MA	A	463 209-3849	9767
Nuvalent Inc (PA)	Cambridge	MA	E	857 357-7000	7672
Nypro Inc	Clinton	MA	C	978 368-6021	8088
Ocular Therapeutix Inc (PA)	Bedford	MA	E	781 357-4000	6250
Oncopeptides Inc	Boston	MA	C	866 596-6626	6933
Oncorus Inc (PA)	Andover	MA	E	857 334-9077	5904
Ono Pharma Usa Inc	Cambridge	MA	F	617 904-4500	7675
Organogenesis Holdings Inc (PA)	Canton	MA	F	781 575-0775	7814
Orgenesis Inc (PA)	Natick	MA	F	480 659-6404	10489
Orogen Therapeutics Inc	Woburn	MA	G	617 981-2156	13628
Overland Phrmaceuticals US Inc	Boston	MA	F	508 827-8686	6947
Oxeia Biopharmaceuticals Inc	Boston	MA	G	619 213-7697	6948
Padlock Therapeutics Inc	Cambridge	MA	F	978 381-9601	7680
Palleon Pharma Inc	Waltham	MA	F	857 285-5904	12746
Paratek Pharmaceuticals Inc (DH)	Boston	MA	G	617 807-6600	6954
Parexel International Corp	Billerica	MA	D	978 313-3900	6469
Pepgen Inc	Boston	MA	E	781 797-0979	6962
Pfizer Inc	Andover	MA	C	978 247-1000	5906
Pfizer Inc	Cambridge	MA	F	617 551-3000	7683
Pfizer Inc	Cambridge	MA	G	617 674-7436	7684
Pharmasol Corporation	South Easton	MA	C	508 238-0105	11948
Pharmctcal Strtgies Stffing LL	Stoneham	MA	F	781 835-2300	12185
Pharmion Corporation	Cambridge	MA	E	857 706-1311	7685
Phosphorex LLC	Hopkinton	MA	E	508 435-9100	9339
Pic Pharmaceutical Inc	Natick	MA	G	617 947-3883	10491
Plasma Biolife Services L P	Attleboro	MA	E	508 761-2902	6048
Pluromed Inc	Woburn	MA	E	781 932-0574	13638
Point3 Farma LLC	Northampton	MA	G	719 733-3900	11077
Polycarbon Industries Inc	Newburyport	MA	D	978 462-5555	10707
Pp Manufacturing Corporation	Framingham	MA	F	508 766-2700	8799
Praecis Pharmaceuticals Inc	Waltham	MA	A	781 795-4100	12751
Praxis Precision Medicines Inc (PA)	Boston	MA	E	617 300-8460	6974
Primatope Therapeutics Inc	Newton	MA	G	617 413-3020	10776
Prismic Pharmaceuticals Inc	Holden	MA	F	971 506-6415	9195
Progderm Inc	Boston	MA	F	617 419-1800	6982
Ptc Therapeutics Gt Inc	Cambridge	MA	E	781 799-9179	7691
Pulmatrix Inc (PA)	Bedford	MA	F	781 357-2333	6254
Pure Encapsulations LLC	Sudbury	MA	E	800 753-2277	12269
Puretech Health PLC	Boston	MA	D	617 482-2333	6985
Pyxis Oncology Inc (PA)	Boston	MA	E	617 221-9059	6987
Ra Pharmaceuticals Inc (DH)	Cambridge	MA	E	617 401-4060	7692
Radius Health Inc (PA)	Boston	MA	B	617 551-4000	6994
Rapid Micro Biosystems Inc (PA)	Lowell	MA	C	978 349-3200	9916
Rapport Therapeutics Inc	Boston	MA	E	512 636-1706	6998
Red Oak Sourcing LLC	Foxborough	MA	D	401 742-0701	8737
Regenacy Pharmaceuticals LLC	Waltham	MA	E	617 245-1306	12764
Regor Therapeutics Inc	Brighton	MA	F	617 407-4737	7244
Reistone Biopharma Inc	Boston	MA	F	978 429-5824	7004
Rentschler Biopharma Inc	Milford	MA	D	508 282-5800	10417
Revo Biologics Inc (DH)	Framingham	MA	F	508 620-9700	8802
Ribon Therapeutics Inc	Cambridge	MA	E	617 914-8700	7696
Ring Therapeutics Inc (PA)	Cambridge	MA	E	617 218-1549	7697
Roche Dgnostics Hematology Inc	Brighton	MA	D	508 329-2450	7245
Rodin Therapeutics Inc	Waltham	MA	G	857 201-2770	12773
Rubius Therapeutics	Foxboro	MA	F	401 349-0818	8717
Safecor Health LLC	Woburn	MA	G	781 933-8780	13658
Safecor Health LLC	Woburn	MA	E	781 933-8780	13659
Sage Therapeutics Inc (PA)	Cambridge	MA	A	617 299-8380	7700
Sana Biotechnology Inc (PA)	Cambridge	MA	G	202 790-0313	7701
Sanofi Pasteur Biologics LLC (HQ)	Cambridge	MA	E	617 866-4400	7703
Sanofi Pasteur Biologics LLC	Canton	MA	D	781 302-3000	7824
Sanofi US Services Inc	Cambridge	MA	C	617 562-4555	7704
Sanofi US Services Inc	Cambridge	MA	E	800 981-2491	7705
Sanofi US Services Inc	Framingham	MA	C	508 424-4485	8803
Sanova Bioscience Inc	Acton	MA	F	978 429-8079	5763
Santhera Pharmaceuticals usa	Burlington	MA	G	781 552-5145	7421
Sarepta Therapeutics	Burlington	MA	F	781 221-7805	7422
Sarepta Therapeutics Inc	Andover	MA	C	978 662-4800	5914
Sarepta Therapeutics Inc (PA)	Cambridge	MA	C	617 274-4000	7706
Scholar Rock Holding Corp (PA)	Cambridge	MA	F	857 259-3860	7708
Scidose LLC	Amherst	MA	F	866 956-4333	5864
Scpharmaceuticals Inc	Burlington	MA	E	617 517-0730	7425
Selvita Inc	Boston	MA	F	857 998-4075	7032
Semma Therapeutics Inc (HQ)	Cambridge	MA	E	857 529-6430	7709
Seres Therapeutics Inc (PA)	Cambridge	MA	D	617 945-9626	7710
Serono Inc	Rockland	MA	E	781 681-2137	11660
Servier US Inc (PA)	Boston	MA	F	610 506-8203	7034
Shire	Milford	MA	F	508 282-5731	10418
Shire Humn Gntic Therapies Inc (DH)	Lexington	MA	E	617 349-0200	9772
Shire Pharmaceuticals LLC	Cambridge	MA	A	617 588-8800	7712
Shire Pharmaceuticals LLC	Cambridge	MA	A	781 482-9245	7713
Shire Pharmaceuticals LLC (HQ)	Lexington	MA	C	617 349-0200	9773
Shire Pharmaceuticals LLC	Lexington	MA	E	617 349-0200	9774
Shire US Inc (HQ)	Lexington	MA	A	781 482-9222	9775
Sigilon Therapeutics Inc (HQ)	Cambridge	MA	D	617 336-7540	7714
Sirtex Medical US Holdings Inc	Woburn	MA	F	888 474-7839	13668
Sobi Inc (HQ)	Waltham	MA	F	781 786-7370	12781
Soleo Health Inc	Canton	MA	E	781 298-3427	7830
Spectrum Pharmaceuticals Inc (PA)	Boston	MA	E	617 586-3900	7051
Springleaf Therapeutics Inc	Boston	MA	F		7055
Sq Innovation Inc	Burlington	MA	G	617 500-0121	7433
Stallrgenes Greer Holdings Inc	Cambridge	MA	E	617 588-4900	7721
Stealth Biotherapeutics Inc (HQ)	Needham Heights	MA	F	617 600-6888	10558
Sumitomo Pharma America Inc (HQ)	Marlborough	MA	A	508 481-6700	10217
Supportive Therapeutics LLC	Cambridge	MA	G	860 625-9226	7726
Syndax Pharmaceuticals Inc (PA)	Waltham	MA	E	781 419-1400	12785
Syndax Securities Corporation	Waltham	MA	F	781 472-2985	12786
Syndexa Pharmaceuticals Corp	Watertown	MA	F	617 607-7283	12911
Syner-G Biopharma Group LLC (PA)	Framingham	MA	E	508 460-9700	8805
Synlogic Inc (PA)	Cambridge	MA	E	617 401-9975	7729
Synostics Inc	Weston	MA	G	781 248-5699	13290
Takeda	Belmont	MA	G	617 594-7199	6313
Takeda	Lexington	MA	D	781 266-5464	9780
Takeda Building 35 5	Cambridge	MA	E	617 444-4352	7730
Takeda Dev Ctr Americas Inc	Cambridge	MA	A	617 349-0200	7731
Takeda Manufacturing USA Inc	Lexington	MA	E	877 825-3327	9781
Takeda Pharmaceutical Co Ltd	Lexington	MA	D	877 872-3700	9782
Takeda Pharmaceuticals Inc	Cambridge	MA	E	617 679-7348	7732
Takeda Pharmaceuticals USA Inc	Cambridge	MA	F	781 733-5208	7733

Company	CITY	ST	EMP	PHONE	ENTRY#
Takeda Pharmaceuticals USA Inc	Lexington	MA	E	617 349-0200	9783
Takeda Pharmaceuticals USA Inc (HQ)	Lexington	MA	A	877 825-3327	9784
Takeda Pharmaceuticals USA Inc	North Reading	MA	G	781 482-1461	11046
Takeda Phrmaceuticals Amer Inc (DH)	Lexington	MA	D	224 554-6500	9785
Takeda Vaccines Inc	Cambridge	MA	E	970 672-4918	7734
Tango Therapeutics Inc (PA)	Boston	MA	F	857 302-4900	7069
Tarpon Biosystems Inc	Marlborough	MA	F	978 979-4222	10222
Tarveda Therapeutics Inc	Watertown	MA	E	617 923-4100	12912
Tesaro Inc (HQ)	Waltham	MA	D	339 970-0900	12793
Tesaro Securities Corporation	Waltham	MA	A	339 970-0900	12794
Tessera Therapeutics Inc	Somerville	MA	D	860 910-6030	11900
Tetraphase Pharmaceuticals Inc	Waltham	MA	D	617 715-3600	12795
Theseus Pharmaceuticals Inc (PA)	Cambridge	MA	F	857 400-9491	7740
Tiburio Therapeutics Inc	Cambridge	MA	G	617 231-6050	7741
Tolerx Inc	Cambridge	MA	E	617 354-8100	7742
Tonix Phrmceuticals Holdg Corp	New Bedford	MA	F	617 908-5040	10656
Torque Therapeutics Inc	Cambridge	MA	E	617 945-1082	7744
Trafa Pharmaceutical Inc	Chicopee	MA	F	866 998-7232	8063
Translate Bio Inc (HQ)	Lexington	MA	E	617 945-7361	9789
Transtulit LLC	West Springfield	MA	G	413 737-2600	13045
Tremeau Pharmaceuticals Inc	Concord	MA	F	617 485-0250	8137
Trine Pharmaceuticals Inc	Newton	MA	F	617 558-8789	10791
Ucb Inc	Cambridge	MA	E	844 599-2273	7746
Unicus Pharmaceuticals LLC (PA)	Taunton	MA	F	508 659-7002	12374
Uptite Company Inc	Haverhill	MA	G	978 377-0451	9138
Valo Health Inc (PA)	Boston	MA	E	617 237-6080	7096
Vaso Active Phrmaceuticals Inc	Beverly	MA	E	978 750-1991	6392
Vbi Vaccines Inc (PA)	Cambridge	MA	G	617 830-3031	7750
Vectura Incorporated	Southborough	MA	G	508 573-5700	12005
Veranova LP (HQ)	Devens	MA	C	484 581-0149	8288
Veranova LP	North Andover	MA	E	978 784-5000	10857
Verastem Inc (PA)	Needham	MA	G	781 292-4200	10528
Vertex Pharmaceuticals Del LLC	Boston	MA	F	617 341-6100	7100
Vertex Pharmaceuticals Inc (PA)	Boston	MA	A	617 341-6100	7101
Vertex Pharmaceuticals PR LLC	Boston	MA	E	617 341-6100	7102
Vertex Phrmaceuticals Dist Inc	Boston	MA	E	617 341-6100	7103
Verve Therapeutics Inc	Cambridge	MA	E	617 603-0070	7755
Verve Therapeutics Inc (PA)	Cambridge	MA	E	617 603-0070	7756
Viamet Phrmctcals Holdings LLC	Foxboro	MA	E	919 467-8539	8730
Vibalogics US Inc	Boxborough	MA	F	252 903-2213	7157
Vietaz Inc	Dorchester	MA	G	617 322-1933	8301
Vigil Neuroscience Inc (PA)	Watertown	MA	E	857 254-4445	12919
Visionaid Inc	Wareham	MA	E	508 295-3300	12849
Visterra Inc	Waltham	MA	E	617 498-1070	12814
Voyager Pharmaceutical Corp	Swampscott	MA	F	781 592-1945	12301
W F Young Incorporated (PA)	East Longmeadow	MA	E	800 628-9653	8402
Walden Biosciences Inc	Cambridge	MA	F	617 794-2733	7758
Werewolf Therapeutics Inc	Watertown	MA	E	617 952-0555	12920
West St Intrmdate Hldings Corp (PA)	Waltham	MA	D	781 434-5051	12817
Westwell Incorporated (DH)	Wellesley	MA	D	800 753-2277	12948
Wilex Inc	Cambridge	MA	F	617 492-3900	7760
Wilmington Partners LP	Wilmington	MA	C	978 658-6111	13476
Wyeth Pharmaceuticals LLC	Andover	MA	E	978 475-9214	5936
Xilio Therapeutics Inc	Waltham	MA	D	617 430-4680	12820
Zikani Therapeutics Inc	Watertown	MA	E	617 453-9091	12922
Znlabs LLC (HQ)	Woburn	MA	E	781 897-6966	13692
Biodesign International	Saco	ME	E	207 283-6500	5363
Clearh2o Inc	Westbrook	ME	E	207 221-0039	5621
Covetrus North America LLC (PA)	Portland	ME	C	888 280-2221	5202
Dermalogix Partners Inc	Scarborough	ME	F	207 883-4103	5431
Desert Harvest Inc	Ellsworth	ME	F	919 245-1853	4756
Idexx Laboratories Inc (PA)	Westbrook	ME	A	207 556-0300	5631
Lonza Bio Science Rockland Inc	Rockland	ME	E	207 594-3400	5337
Lonza Rockland Inc	Rockland	ME	D	207 594-3400	5338
M Drug LLC	Brewer	ME	G	207 973-9444	4618
Maine Biotechnology Svcs Inc	Portland	ME	F	207 797-5454	5239
Shearwater Allergy LLC	Yarmouth	ME	E	207 846-7676	5707
Tevelle Pharmaceuticals LLC	South Portland	ME	G	207 808-9771	5516
Alcami Carolinas Corporation	Amherst	NH	G	910 619-3952	13861
Bentley Pharmaceuticals Inc (HQ)	Exeter	NH	C	603 658-6100	14285
Cellgenix Inc	Portsmouth	NH	F	603 373-0408	15369
Critical Prcess Filtration Inc (PA)	Nashua	NH	E	603 595-0140	15085
Icad Inc (PA)	Nashua	NH	F	603 882-5200	15111
Ipura Consulting Group LLC	Hampton	NH	F	603 294-4002	14404
Lonza Biologics Inc	Portsmouth	NH	D	603 610-4696	15420
Lonza Biologics Inc	Portsmouth	NH	D	201 316-9200	15421
Lonza Biologics Inc (DH)	Portsmouth	NH	C	603 610-4500	15422
Lyophilization Svcs Neng Inc	Bedford	NH	D	603 626-5763	13942
Lyophilization Svcs Neng Inc	Bedford	NH	E	603 668-5763	13943
Lyophilization Svcs Neng Inc (HQ)	Manchester	NH	F	603 626-5763	14877
Msm Protein Technologies Inc	East Kingston	NH	F	617 504-9548	14272
Novo Nordisk US Bio Prod Inc	West Lebanon	NH	C	603 298-3169	15687
Tender Corporation (PA)	Littleton	NH	D	603 444-5464	14724
Tri-K Industries Inc	Derry	NH	E	973 298-8850	14211
Tri-K Industries Inc	Salem	NH	E	603 898-0811	15567
Trividia Mfg Solutions Inc (DH)	Lancaster	NH	C	603 788-2848	14680
Aidance Scientific Inc	Woonsocket	RI	D	401 432-7750	16946
Amgen Inc	West Greenwich	RI	D	401 392-1200	16882
Denison Pharmaceuticals LLC	Lincoln	RI	D	401 723-5500	16131
Denison Pharmaceuticals LLC (PA)	Lincoln	RI	C	401 723-5500	16132
Edesia Inc	North Kingstown	RI	D	401 272-5521	16247
Edesia Enterprises LLC	North Kingstown	RI	D	401 272-5521	16248
Immunex Rhode Island Corp	West Greenwich	RI	C	401 392-1200	16886
Luna Pharmaceuticals Inc	Providence	RI	G	401 383-0299	16556
Mmj Biopharma Cultivation Inc	Westerly	RI	F	800 586-7863	16936
Neurotech Pharmaceuticals Inc	Cumberland	RI	E	617 694-5520	15951
Noramco Coventry LLC	Coventry	RI	D	401 623-1174	15818
Ocean Biomedical Holdings Inc	Providence	RI	G	401 444-7375	16578
Onset Dermatologics LLC	Cumberland	RI	D	401 762-2000	15958
Phe Investments LLC	Johnston	RI	D	401 289-2900	16100
Purdue Pharma LP	Coventry	RI	F	203 588-8000	15819
Sea-Band International Inc	Newport	RI	G	401 841-5900	16222
Techtrak LLC	Coventry	RI	G	401 397-3983	15822
Tedor Pharma Inc	Cumberland	RI	E	401 658-5219	15967
Vertex Pharmaceuticals Inc	Providence	RI	F	857 529-6430	16639
Foodscience LLC (HQ)	Williston	VT	C	800 451-5190	17731
Mylan Technologies Inc	Saint Albans	VT	C	802 527-7792	17524
Mylan Technologies Inc (HQ)	Saint Albans	VT	C	802 527-7792	17525
New Chapter Inc (HQ)	Brattleboro	VT	C	800 543-7279	17096
PBM Nutritionals LLC (DH)	Milton	VT	C	802 527-0521	17363
Somalabs Inc	Milton	VT	F	802 355-3000	17364
Vermonts Original LLC	Lyndonville	VT	G	802 626-3610	17322

2835 Diagnostic substances

Company	CITY	ST	EMP	PHONE	ENTRY#
Ai Therapeutics Inc	Guilford	CT	F	203 458-7100	1383
Cardinal Health 414 LLC	East Hartford	CT	G	860 291-9135	978
Charles River Laboratories Inc	Storrs	CT	F	860 429-7261	3511
Abpro Corporation	Woburn	MA	E	617 225-0808	13497
Advandx Inc	Woburn	MA	E	866 376-0009	13500
Alere Inc (HQ)	Waltham	MA	A	781 647-3900	12587
Alere US Holdings LLC	Waltham	MA	F	781 647-3900	12588
Asimov Inc	Boston	MA	E	339 532-9982	6561
Associates of Cape Cod Inc (PA)	East Falmouth	MA	D	508 540-3444	8355
Axis-Shield Poc As	Norton	MA	F	508 285-4870	11123
Biokit U S A Inc	Bedford	MA	E	781 861-4064	6215
Bionostics Inc	Devens	MA	C	978 772-7070	8270
Bostonmolecules Inc	Waltham	MA	F	617 651-1016	12610
Cellanyx Diagnostics LLC	Beverly	MA	G	571 212-9991	6337
Cellay LLC	Cambridge	MA	E	617 995-1307	7535
Confer Health Inc	Charlestown	MA	G	617 433-8810	7866
Creatics LLC	Braintree	MA	F	781 843-2202	7175
Daktari Diagnostics Inc	Cambridge	MA	F	617 336-3299	7549
Esoterix Genetic Labs LLC (HQ)	Westborough	MA	E	508 389-6650	13101
Fresenius Usa Inc (DH)	Waltham	MA	C	781 699-4191	12683
Genzyme Corporation (DH)	Cambridge	MA	A	617 252-7500	7585
Glycozym Usa Inc	Beverly	MA	G	425 985-2556	6351
High Technology Inc	North Attleboro	MA	E	508 660-2221	10873
Instrumentation Laboratory Co (DH)	Bedford	MA	A	781 861-0710	6233
Intellia Therapeutics Inc (PA)	Cambridge	MA	C	857 285-6200	7616
Interleukin Genetics Inc	Waltham	MA	F	781 398-0700	12702
Inverness Medical - Biostar Inc	Waltham	MA	C	781 647-3900	12703
Lantheus Holdings Inc (PA)	North Billerica	MA	A	978 671-8001	10923
Medical Research Networx	Franklin	MA	E	508 530-4289	8850
Memed US Inc	Andover	MA	E	617 335-0349	5895
Nanobiosym Inc	Cambridge	MA	E	781 391-7979	7659
Petnet Solutions Inc	Woburn	MA	E	781 937-3600	13634
Piton Therapeutics Inc	Watertown	MA	F	857 327-7666	12900
Qsa Global Inc (HQ)	Burlington	MA	D	781 272-2000	7416
Quest Diagnostic Incorporated	Marlborough	MA	A	617 547-8900	10199
Quidel Corporation	Beverly	MA	F	866 800-5458	6377
Regenocell Therapeutics Inc	Natick	MA	E	508 651-1598	10495
Rootpath Genomics	Watertown	MA	F	857 209-1060	12906
T2 Biosystems Inc (PA)	Lexington	MA	D	781 761-4646	9779
Telome Inc	Waltham	MA	G	617 383-7565	12792
Third Wave Technologies Inc (HQ)	Marlborough	MA	F	608 273-8933	10224
Ultivue Inc (PA)	Cambridge	MA	E	617 945-2662	7747
Vital Biosciences Inc	Boston	MA	G	415 910-2994	7107
Werfen USA LLC	Bedford	MA	C	781 861-0710	6276
Alere Inc	Scarborough	ME	D	207 730-5714	5421
Bioprocessing Inc	Portland	ME	F	207 457-0025	5187
Covetrus North America LLC (PA)	Portland	ME	C	888 280-2221	5202
Idexx Distribution Inc	Westbrook	ME	D	207 556-0300	5630
Idexx Laboratories Inc (PA)	Westbrook	ME	A	207 556-0300	5631
Immucell Corporation	Portland	ME	E	207 878-2770	5226
Immucell Corporation (PA)	Portland	ME	E	207 878-2770	5227

	CITY	ST	EMP	PHONE	ENTRY#
Lgc Clinical Diagnostics Inc 4712	Cumberland Foreside	ME	D	207 892-1300	
Maine Biotechnology Svcs Inc	Portland	ME	F	207 797-5454	5239
Meridian Life Science Inc (HQ)	Saco	ME	G	207 283-6500	5373
Sun Diagnostics LLC	New Gloucester	ME	G	207 926-1125	5089

2836 Biological products, except diagnostic

	CITY	ST	EMP	PHONE	ENTRY#
Aqua Pulsar LLC	Norwalk	CT	G	772 320-9691	2463
Avian Vaccine Services LLC (PA)	Norwich	CT	D	860 889-1389	2602
Axiomx Inc	Branford	CT	E	203 208-1034	239
Bactana Corp	Farmington	CT	G	203 716-1230	1208
Biomx Inc	Branford	CT	C	203 408-3915	240
Coopersurgical Inc	Guilford	CT	G	203 453-1700	1390
Gilead Sciences Inc	Branford	CT	G	203 315-1222	261
Green Valley Packaging Inc	Danielson	CT	G	860 779-7970	839
Intensity Therapeutics Inc	Shelton	CT	F	203 221-7381	3023
Plasma Technology Incorporated	South Windsor	CT	E	860 282-0659	3173
Realhub Inc	Darien	CT	F	650 461-9210	854
Skin & Co North America LLC	West Haven	CT	G	888 444-9971	4126
3-D Matrix Inc (HQ)	Newton	MA	F	781 373-9020	10730
3dm Inc	Cambridge	MA	G	617 875-6204	7463
Acceleron Holding Ltd	Boston	MA	G	617 649-9200	6507
Acceleron Pharma Inc (HQ)	Boston	MA	D	617 649-9200	6508
ACS Division Biochemical Tech	Boston	MA	F	617 216-6144	6512
Affinivax Inc	Cambridge	MA	C	617 465-0865	7469
Agenus Inc (PA)	Lexington	MA	C	781 674-4400	9721
Allovir Inc (PA)	Waltham	MA	F	617 433-2605	12591
Ariad Pharmaceuticals Inc	Cambridge	MA	B		7490
Aura Biosciences Inc (PA)	Boston	MA	F	617 500-8864	6577
Axcella Health Inc (PA)	Cambridge	MA	G	857 320-2200	7496
Beam Therapeutics Inc (PA)	Cambridge	MA	C	857 327-8775	7500
Biobohemia Inc	Cambridge	MA	G	617 958-7900	7508
Biogen Inc (PA)	Cambridge	MA	B	617 679-2000	7511
Biogen MA Inc	Cambridge	MA	D	781 464-2000	7513
Biogen MA Inc (HQ)	Cambridge	MA	C	617 679-2000	7514
Biohelix Corporation	Beverly	MA	F	978 927-5056	6333
Biontech US Inc (HQ)	Cambridge	MA	E	617 337-4701	7515
Biose Industrie Inc	Woburn	MA	F	617 460-1842	13525
Black Diamond Therapeutics Inc (PA)	Cambridge	MA	F	617 252-0848	7517
Bluebird Bio Inc (PA)	Somerville	MA	A	339 499-9300	11864
C4 Therapeutics Inc (PA)	Watertown	MA	C	617 231-0700	12866
Captivate Bio LLC	Watertown	MA	G	617 607-4017	12867
Cellaria Biosciences LLC	Boxford	MA	G	617 981-4208	7158
Checkmate Pharmaceuticals Inc	Cambridge	MA	E	617 682-3625	7539
Circle Labs Bio Inc	Cambridge	MA	G	516 660-6045	7541
Codiak Biosciences Inc (PA)	Cambridge	MA	E	617 949-4100	7542
Compass Therapeutics Inc (PA)	Brighton	MA	G	617 500-8099	7239
Corium LLC	Boston	MA	C	855 253-2407	6672
Cullinan Oncology Inc (PA)	Cambridge	MA	F	617 410-4650	7546
Curia Global Inc	Burlington	MA	C	781 205-1691	7357
Diagnosys LLC (PA)	Lowell	MA	E	978 458-1600	9875
Dicerna Pharmaceuticals Inc (HQ)	Lexington	MA	C	617 621-8097	9739
Diversified Biotech Inc	Dedham	MA	F	781 326-6709	8242
Editas Medicine Inc (PA)	Cambridge	MA	C	617 401-9000	7555
Elevatebio LLC (PA)	Cambridge	MA	E	413 297-7151	7559
Finch Therapeutics Group Inc	Somerville	MA	C	617 229-6499	11873
Forma Thrapeutics Holdings Inc (HQ)	Watertown	MA	F	617 679-1970	12878
Fresenius Usa Inc (DH)	Waltham	MA	C	781 699-4191	12683
Genocea Biosciences Inc (PA)	Cambridge	MA	E	617 876-8191	7582
Genzyme Corporation (DH)	Cambridge	MA	A	617 252-7500	7585
Genzyme Corporation	Framingham	MA	E	617 252-7500	8773
Ginkgo Bioworks Inc (HQ)	Boston	MA	B	877 422-5362	6761
Ginkgo Bioworks Inc	Cambridge	MA	F	617 633-7972	7591
Ginkgo Bioworks Holdings Inc (PA)	Boston	MA	B	877 422-5362	6762
Greenlght Bscnces Holdings Pbc (PA)	Medford	MA	F	617 616-8188	10287
Hillevax Inc	Boston	MA	D	617 213-5054	6787
Hockey12com	Billerica	MA	G	781 910-2877	6450
Hooke Laboratories Inc	Lawrence	MA	D	617 475-5114	9569
ID Bimedical Corp Northborough	Northborough	MA	D	508 351-9333	11099
Ikena Oncology Inc (PA)	Boston	MA	E	857 273-8343	6806
Iteos Therapeutics Inc (PA)	Watertown	MA	F	339 217-0161	12883
Jounce Therapeutics Inc (PA)	Cambridge	MA	D	857 259-3840	7620
Joyn Bio LLC	Boston	MA	E	978 549-3723	6832
Kaleido Biosciences Inc (PA)	Lexington	MA	D	617 674-9000	9755
Kymera Therapeutics Inc (PA)	Watertown	MA	E	857 285-5300	12885
Lariat Biosciences Inc	Chelsea	MA	G	603 244-9657	7985
Launchworks LLC	Beverly	MA	E	978 338-3045	6361
Logicbio Therapeutics Inc	Lexington	MA	D	617 245-0399	9759
Massbiologics	Boston	MA	D	617 474-3000	6877
Moderna Inc (PA)	Cambridge	MA	B	617 714-6500	7653
Monte Rosa Therapeutics Inc (PA)	Boston	MA	D	617 949-2643	6895
Neumora Therapeutics Inc (PA)	Watertown	MA	D	857 760-0900	12896
Organogenesis Inc (HQ)	Canton	MA	C	781 575-0775	7815

	CITY	ST	EMP	PHONE	ENTRY#
Pillar Biosciences Inc	Natick	MA	D	781 856-5568	10492
Plasma Pen USA LLC	Woburn	MA	F	855 568-3776	13637
Project Plasma Holdings Corp	Milford	MA	C	508 244-6400	10415
Protagene Us Inc	Burlington	MA	F	857 829-3200	7414
Puretech Health LLC (HQ)	Boston	MA	D	617 482-2333	6984
Pyxis Oncology Inc (PA)	Boston	MA	E	617 221-9059	6987
Qiagen Beverly LLC	Beverly	MA	D	978 927-7027	6373
Relay Therapeutics Inc (PA)	Cambridge	MA	E	617 370-8837	7695
Repligen Corporation	Marlborough	MA	E	508 845-6400	10202
Repligen Corporation (PA)	Waltham	MA	C	781 250-0111	12765
Replimune Group Inc (PA)	Woburn	MA	F	781 222-9600	13649
Revbio Inc	Lowell	MA	F	617 460-6675	9918
Revo Biologics Inc	Spencer	MA	E	508 370-5451	12065
Safc Biosciences Inc	Burlington	MA	F	978 715-1700	7420
Scholar Rock Holding Corp (PA)	Cambridge	MA	F	857 259-3860	7708
Seqirus Inc	Waltham	MA	B	617 871-5734	12778
Sigma Research Biochemicals	Natick	MA	G	781 237-3828	10497
Solid Biosciences Inc (PA)	Charlestown	MA	E	617 337-4680	7883
Sqz Biotechnologies Company (PA)	Watertown	MA	E	617 758-8672	12909
Synageva Biopharma Corp	Lexington	MA	B	781 357-9900	9778
Tcr2 Therapeutics Inc (HQ)	Cambridge	MA	D	617 949-5200	7735
Tetragenetics Inc	Arlington	MA	F	617 500-7471	5949
Tscan Therapeutics Inc	Waltham	MA	D	857 399-9500	12807
Twentyfrst Cntury Bchmcals Inc	Marlborough	MA	E	508 303-8222	10225
Vbi Vaccines Inc (PA)	Cambridge	MA	G	617 830-3031	7750
Vericel Corporation (PA)	Cambridge	MA	B	617 588-5555	7752
Vor Biopharma Inc (PA)	Cambridge	MA	F	617 655-6580	7757
Voyager Therapeutics Inc (PA)	Lexington	MA	D	570 329-6851	9791
X4 Pharmaceuticals Inc (PA)	Boston	MA	D	857 529-8300	7135
Xcellerex Inc	Marlborough	MA	D	508 480-9235	10237
Zea Biosciences Corp	Walpole	MA	F	508 921-3280	12579
Hightech Extracts LLC	Biddeford	ME	F	207 590-3251	4569
Kennebec River Biosciences Inc	Richmond	ME	F	207 737-2637	5322
Lohmann Animal Health Intl Inc	Winslow	ME	C	207 873-3989	5683
Northeast Laboratory Svcs Inc (PA)	Winslow	ME	F	207 873-7711	5686
Standard Merger Sub LLC	Windham	ME	D	207 856-6151	5670
Avitide Inc	Lebanon	NH	E	603 965-2100	14683
Lyophilization Svcs Neng Inc	Bedford	NH	E	603 668-5763	13940
Lyophilization Svcs Neng Inc	Bedford	NH	E	603 626-9559	13941
Lyophilization Svcs Neng Inc	Bedford	NH	E	603 626-5763	13942
Lyophilization Svcs Neng Inc	Bedford	NH	E	603 626-5763	13943
Lyophilization Svcs Neng Inc (HQ)	Manchester	NH	F	603 626-5763	14877
Amgen Inc	West Greenwich	RI	D	401 392-1200	16882
Epivax Inc	Providence	RI	E	401 272-2123	16515
Population Media Center Inc	South Burlington	VT	E	802 985-8156	17595

2841 Soap and other detergents

	CITY	ST	EMP	PHONE	ENTRY#
Amodex Products Incorporated	Bridgeport	CT	E	203 335-1255	296
Beiersdorf North America Inc (DH)	Stamford	CT	F	203 563-5800	3292
Harvard Chemical LLC (HQ)	Bolton	CT	F	404 761-0657	220
Henkel Consumer Goods Inc (DH)	Stamford	CT	A	475 210-0230	3373
Pharmacal Research Labs Inc	Waterbury	CT	E	203 755-4908	3959
Simoniz USA Inc (PA)	Bolton	CT	D	860 646-0172	223
The Sun Products Corporation	Stamford	CT	E	203 254-6700	3480
Unilever Ascc AG	Shelton	CT	B	203 381-2482	3073
Unilever Home and Per Care NA	Trumbull	CT	C	203 502-0086	3736
Alpha Chemical Services Inc	Stoughton	MA	E	781 344-8688	12193
Blendco Systems LLC	Holyoke	MA	D	800 537-7797	9244
Car Gold Inc	Holyoke	MA	G	800 537-7797	9246
Christeyns Laundry Tech LLC	East Bridgewater	MA	F	617 203-2169	8337
Commonwealth Liquid Pdts LLC	Fall River	MA	F	508 676-9355	8530
Commonwlth Soap Toiletries Inc (PA)	Fall River	MA	E	508 676-9355	8531
Dynasol Industries Inc	Canton	MA	E	781 821-8888	7787
Ecolab Inc	Norwood	MA	F	781 688-2100	11171
MD Stetson Company Inc	Mansfield	MA	E	781 986-6161	10066
Spectrowax Corporation (PA)	Canton	MA	D	617 543-0400	7832
Synthetic Labs Inc	Dracut	MA	E	978 957-2919	8312
Greener Formulas LLC	North Walpole	NH	G	888 825-4460	15257
Sweet Grass Farm Inc	Greenland	NH	G	603 766-1651	14371
Ne Finest LLC	Coventry	RI	F	800 215-6640	15817
Original Brdford Soap Wrks Inc (DH)	West Warwick	RI	B	401 821-2141	16919
Rhode Island Chemical Corp	Providence	RI	F	401 274-3905	16602
Twincraft Inc (PA)	Winooski	VT	C	802 655-2200	17769
Vermont Country Soap Corp	Middlebury	VT	E	802 388-4302	17349
Whisper Hills	Quechee	VT	G	802 296-7627	17464

2842 Polishes and sanitation goods

	CITY	ST	EMP	PHONE	ENTRY#
Amodex Products Incorporated	Bridgeport	CT	E	203 335-1255	296
Armored Autogroup Parent Inc	Danbury	CT	C	203 205-2900	710
Charles K White	Hamden	CT	G	203 631-2540	1417
Citra-Solv LLC	Danbury	CT	G	203 778-0881	721
Edsan Chemical Company Inc	New Haven	CT	F	203 624-3123	2148
Extec Corp	Enfield	CT	F	860 741-3435	1133

	CITY	ST	EMP	PHONE	ENTRY#
Great Lakes Chemical Corp (DH)	Shelton	CT	E	203 573-2000	3010
Grill Daddy Brush Company	Old Greenwich	CT	E	888 840-7552	2633
Harvard Chemical LLC (HQ)	Bolton	CT	F	404 761-0657	220
Hubbard-Hall Inc (PA)	Waterbury	CT	D	203 756-5521	3919
Koster Keunen LLC (PA)	Watertown	CT	F	860 945-3333	4018
Lanxess Solutions US Inc	Shelton	CT	A	203 573-2000	3027
Macdermid Incorporated (HQ)	Waterbury	CT	C	203 575-5700	3933
NC Brands LP	Norwalk	CT	D	203 295-2300	2542
Nci Holdings Inc (PA)	Norwalk	CT	D	203 295-2300	2543
Shlomo Enterprises Inc (PA)	Enfield	CT	G	860 265-7995	1150
Simoniz USA Inc (PA)	Bolton	CT	D	860 646-0172	223
All-Way Service Corp	South Weymouth	MA	F	781 335-4533	11974
Alpha Chemical Services Inc	Stoughton	MA	E	781 344-8688	12193
Blendco Systems LLC	Holyoke	MA	D	800 537-7797	9244
Brady Enterprises Inc (PA)	East Weymouth	MA	F	781 340-4571	8427
Cape Cod Polish Company Inc	Dennis	MA	G	508 385-5099	8257
Car Gold Inc	Holyoke	MA	E	800 537-7797	9246
Chemco Corporation	Lawrence	MA	E	978 687-9000	9547
D J Bass Inc	New Bedford	MA	G	508 678-4499	10583
Detrapel Inc	Framingham	MA	F	617 514-7778	8757
Dynasol Industries Inc	Canton	MA	F	781 821-8888	7787
Hci Cleaning Products LLC	Westford	MA	F	508 864-5510	13241
Head 2 Toe LLC	Reading	MA	F	781 944-0286	11602
HI Tunes	Whately	MA	F	435 962-0405	13339
Hubbard-Hall Inc	Wilmington	MA	F	978 988-0077	13411
James Austin Company	Ludlow	MA	F	413 589-1600	9946
MD Stetson Company Inc	Mansfield	MA	E	781 986-6161	10066
Parker & Bailey Corp	Walpole	MA	F	508 660-0011	12572
Perma Incorporated	Bedford	MA	F	978 667-5161	6252
Perrco Inc	Woburn	MA	F	617 933-5300	13633
Porex Cleanroom Products Inc	Chicopee	MA	D	800 628-8606	8056
Rectorseal LLC	Fall River	MA	F	508 673-7561	8601
Rock-Tred 2 LLC	Andover	MA	E	888 762-5873	5912
Roger A Reed Inc	Reading	MA	F	781 944-4640	11607
Rule Industries LLC	Gloucester	MA	C	978 281-0440	8956
Safehands Distribution Ne LLC	Wilbraham	MA	F	413 244-1452	13363
Savin Products Company Inc	Randolph	MA	E	781 961-2743	11574
Shield Packaging Co Inc	Dudley	MA	E	508 949-0900	8323
Spectrowax Corporation (PA)	Canton	MA	D	617 543-0400	7832
Unimed-Midwest Inc	Woburn	MA	G	800 347-9023	13681
Union Specialties Inc	Newburyport	MA	E	978 465-1717	10724
Versum Materials Us LLC	Burlington	MA	E	978 715-1614	7444
Webco Chemical Corporation	Dudley	MA	D	508 943-2337	8327
Allens Environmental Svcs Inc	Presque Isle	ME	G	207 764-9336	5295
Controlled Envmt Eqp Corp	Westbrook	ME	F	207 854-9126	5622
F O Bailey Co Inc	Falmouth	ME	G	207 781-8001	4768
Coating Systems Inc	Nashua	NH	G	603 883-0553	15082
E-Cloth Inc	Dover	NH	E	603 765-9367	14227
Eco Knight Group LLC (PA)	Lebanon	NH	E	802 318-8760	14687
Hampshire Chemical Corp (DH)	Nashua	NH	E	603 888-2320	15109
Peg Kearsarge Co Inc	Bartlett	NH	G	603 374-2341	13918
Rochester Shoe Tree Co Inc (PA)	Ashland	NH	D	603 968-3301	13902
Service Experts LLC	Rochester	NH	F	603 332-6466	15493
Absorbent Specialty Pdts LLC	Pawtucket	RI	F	401 722-1177	16342
Del Nero Cleaners LLC	Newport	RI	G	508 679-0999	16208
Ne Finest LLC	Coventry	RI	F	800 215-6640	15817
Precision Plsg Ornamentals Inc	Pawtucket	RI	F	401 728-9994	16404
Brown Country Services LLC	West Dover	VT	G	802 464-5200	17689

2843 Surface active agents

	CITY	ST	EMP	PHONE	ENTRY#
Bethune Nonwovens Inc	East Windsor	CT	C	860 386-8001	1067
Henkel of America Inc (HQ)	Rocky Hill	CT	B	860 615-3395	2926
Henkel US Operations Corp (DH)	Rocky Hill	CT	B	860 571-5100	2927
Lanxess Solutions US Inc	Shelton	CT	A	203 573-2000	3027
New England Tooling Inc	Killingworth	CT	F	800 866-5105	1544
Solidification Pdts Intl Inc	Northford	CT	G	203 484-9494	2456
Unimetal Surface Finishing LLC (PA)	Thomaston	CT	F	860 283-0271	3640
Isp Freetown Fine Chem Inc	Assonet	MA	D	508 672-0634	5974
Union Specialties Inc	Newburyport	MA	E	978 465-1717	10724
Peg Kearsarge Co Inc	Bartlett	NH	G	603 374-2341	13918
CNc International Ltd Partnr	Woonsocket	RI	F	401 769-6100	16954
Ne Finest LLC	Coventry	RI	F	800 215-6640	15817

2844 Toilet preparations

	CITY	ST	EMP	PHONE	ENTRY#
American Distilling Inc (PA)	East Hampton	CT	D	860 267-4444	959
Amodex Products Incorporated	Bridgeport	CT	E	203 335-1255	296
Bedoukian Research Inc (PA)	Danbury	CT	E	203 830-4000	713
Beiersdorf Inc (DH)	Stamford	CT	G	203 563-5800	3291
Beiersdorf North America Inc (DH)	Stamford	CT	F	203 563-5800	3292
Bella Grace LLC	Fairfield	CT	E	929 533-2343	1177
Carrubba Incorporated	Monroe	CT	D	203 878-0605	1908
Conopco Inc	Clinton	CT	C	860 669-8601	640
Continental Fragrances Ltd	Stamford	CT	E	800 542-5903	3322

	CITY	ST	EMP	PHONE	ENTRY#
Crabtree & Evelyn Ltd (DH)	Woodstock	CT	C	800 272-2873	4393
Durol Laboratories LLC	New Haven	CT	F	866 611-9694	2146
Ecometics Inc	Norwalk	CT	E	203 853-7856	2495
Edgewell Per Care Brands LLC	Milford	CT	E	203 882-2300	1822
Edgewell Per Care Brands LLC (HQ)	Shelton	CT	B	203 944-5500	3002
Edgewell Personal Care Company (PA)	Shelton	CT	B	203 944-5500	3003
Ephemeral Solutions Inc	Milford	CT	E	203 312-7337	1826
Golden Sun Inc	Stamford	CT	E	800 575-7960	3356
Golden Sun Holdings Inc (HQ)	Stamford	CT	F	203 595-5228	3357
Henkel US Operations Corp	Darien	CT	A	203 655-8911	848
HRB Winddown Inc (HQ)	Stamford	CT	D	203 674-8080	3379
Jolen Cream Bleach Corp	Fairfield	CT	G	203 259-8779	1191
Milbar Labs Inc	East Haven	CT	F	203 467-1577	1046
Miyoshi America Inc (HQ)	Dayville	CT	D	860 779-3990	863
Parfums De Coeur Ltd (PA)	Stamford	CT	E	203 655-8807	3426
Playtex Products LLC (HQ)	Shelton	CT	D	203 944-5500	3050
Rjtb Initiatives Inc	Greenwich	CT	F	203 531-7216	1347
Russell Organics LLC	Wallingford	CT	G	203 285-6633	3847
Sheffield Pharmaceuticals LLC (PA)	New London	CT	C	860 442-4451	2233
Silgan Dspnsing Systems Thmsto	Thomaston	CT	B	860 283-2000	3630
Skin & Co North America LLC	West Haven	CT	G	888 444-9971	4126
T N Dickinson Company	East Hampton	CT	F	860 267-2279	966
Transom Symphony Opco LLC (PA)	Stamford	CT	D	203 503-7938	3485
Unilever Home and Per Care NA	Trumbull	CT	E	203 502-0086	3736
Unilever Hpc USA	Trumbull	CT	D	203 381-3311	3737
Unilever Trumbull RES Svcs Inc	Trumbull	CT	E	203 502-0086	3738
Wearspf LLC	East Haven	CT	G	203 466-4616	1056
Avava Inc (PA)	Waltham	MA	G	617 912-2680	12599
Beacon Wellness Brands Inc (PA)	Newton	MA	F	781 449-9500	10739
Candela Corporation	Wayland	MA	A	800 733-8550	12923
Catalystsmc Inc	Newton	MA	F	781 449-9500	10741
CCL Industries Corporation (HQ)	Framingham	MA	D	508 872-4511	8749
Commonwlth Soap Toiletries Inc (PA)	Fall River	MA	E	508 676-9355	8531
Conopco Inc	Foxboro	MA	F	508 543-6767	8693
Dentovations Inc	Boston	MA	G	617 737-1199	6691
European Cubicles LLC	Boston	MA	G	617 681-6700	6721
Gillette Company (HQ)	Boston	MA	A	617 463-3000	6758
Grooming Ventures - FL LLC (HQ)	Boston	MA	D	305 593-0667	6774
Iredale Cosmetics Inc (PA)	Great Barrington	MA	A	413 644-9900	8976
Novagenesis LLC	Sharon	MA	F	781 784-1149	11794
Pharmasol Corporation	South Easton	MA	C	508 238-0105	11948
Procter & Gamble Mfg Co	Andover	MA	F	978 749-5547	5908
Rare Beauty Brands Inc (PA)	Norwood	MA	F	888 243-0646	11205
Revela Inc	Woburn	MA	G	716 725-2657	13651
St Cyr Inc	Worcester	MA	F	508 752-2222	13805
Tropical Products Inc	Salem	MA	F	978 740-5665	11736
Brickell Brands LLC	South Portland	ME	D	877 598-0060	5492
Colgate - Palmolive Company	Sanford	ME	G	207 467-2224	5392
Evergreen Manufacturing Group LLC	Madawaska	ME	F	207 728-4900	5037
Hunter Dathan Hair Artistry	Portland	ME	G	207 774-8887	5224
Procter & Gamble Company	Auburn	ME	C	207 753-4000	4456
Toms of Maine Inc (HQ)	Kennebunk	ME	D	207 985-2944	4930
Cabot Hill Naturals LLC	Lancaster	NH	F	800 747-4372	14676
Chuckles Inc	Manchester	NH	E	603 669-4228	14828
Fizz Time	Salem	NH	F	603 870-0000	15527
Greener Formulas LLC	North Walpole	NH	G	888 825-4460	15257
Heleka Companies LLC (PA)	Chichester	NH	G	603 798-3674	14073
Heleka Companies LLC	Manchester	NH	F	303 856-5457	14858
Maybrook Inc	Derry	NH	F	603 898-0811	14202
Naturally Uncommon LLC	Atkinson	NH	G	603 458-2209	13905
Tri-K Industries Inc	Derry	NH	F	973 298-8850	14211
Trividia Mfg Solutions Inc (DH)	Lancaster	NH	C	603 788-2848	14680
WS Badger Company Inc	Gilsum	NH	D	603 357-2958	14344
WSbadger Company Inc	Gilsum	NH	D	603 357-2958	14345
Autumn Harp Inc	Bristol	VT	E	802 453-4807	17113
Autumn-Harp Inc	Essex Junction	VT	C	802 857-4600	17227
Lancaster Imageworks LLC	Williston	VT	F	802 399-2418	17738
Rozelle Inc	Westfield	VT	E	802 744-2270	17699
Tatas Natural Alchemy LLC	Whiting	VT	D	802 462-3958	17711
Tatas Natural Alchemy LLC (PA)	Whiting	VT	E	802 462-3814	17712

2851 Paints and allied products

	CITY	ST	EMP	PHONE	ENTRY#
A G C Incorporated	Meriden	CT	C	203 235-3361	1649
Albert Kemperle Inc	Hartford	CT	F	860 727-0933	1469
Albi Protective Coatings LLC	East Berlin	CT	F	860 828-0571	906
Brico LLC	Bloomfield	CT	G	860 242-7068	154
Chromalloy Component Svcs Inc	Windsor	CT	E	860 688-7798	4266
Colonial Coatings Inc	Milford	CT	E	203 783-9933	1811
Dur-A-Flex Inc (HQ)	East Hartford	CT	E	860 528-9838	989
Element 119 LLC	Thomaston	CT	F	860 358-0119	3619
Five Star Products Inc	Shelton	CT	E	203 336-7900	3006
Foam Systems LLC	Norwalk	CT	G	800 853-1577	2502
Fougera Pharmaceuticals Inc	Wallingford	CT	C	203 265-2086	3807

	CITY	ST	EMP	PHONE	ENTRY#
Fox Valley Paint Inc	Brookfield	CT	D	844 627-5255	520
Greenmaker Industries Conn LLC	West Hartford	CT	F	860 761-2830	4062
Handyscape LLC	Southington	CT	G	860 318-1067	3215
Jet Process Corporation	Wallingford	CT	G	203 985-6000	3823
M & D Coatings LLC	Stratford	CT	G	203 380-9466	3554
Mantrose-Haeuser Co Inc (HQ)	Westport	CT	E	203 454-1800	4182
Minteq International Inc	Canaan	CT	F	860 824-5435	556
Southern Diversified Pdts LLC	Bethel	CT	F	917 306-4138	134
Stanchem Incorporated (HQ)	East Berlin	CT	E	860 828-0571	918
A I C Inc (PA)	Georgetown	MA	D	978 352-4510	8904
A W Chesterton Company (PA)	Groveland	MA	E	781 438-7000	9012
Acton Research Corporation	Acton	MA	E	941 556-2601	5731
Altri Junk Removal Services	Revere	MA	E	781 629-2500	11616
Bemis Associates Inc (PA)	Shirley	MA	C	978 425-6761	11815
Breakthrough Coatings Inc	Buzzards Bay	MA	F	866 608-7625	7453
C L Hauthaway & Sons Corp	Lynn	MA	E	781 592-6444	9965
California Paint	Andover	MA	E	978 965-2122	5876
Camger Coatings Systems Inc	Norfolk	MA	E	508 528-5787	10797
Chase Speciality Coating	Westwood	MA	F	781 332-0700	13310
Coveris Advnced Ctngs Mtthews (DH)	West Springfield	MA	E	413 539-5547	13019
Covestro LLC	Wilmington	MA	C	800 458-0014	13399
Creative Material Tech Ltd	Palmer	MA	G	413 284-0000	11272
Dampney Company Inc	Everett	MA	E	617 389-2805	8485
DSM Neoresins Inc	Wilmington	MA	C	800 458-0014	13403
Durant Prfmce Coatings Inc	Revere	MA	F	781 289-1400	11618
Eastern Chem-Lac LLC (PA)	Chicopee	MA	E	413 592-4191	8029
Eastman Performance Films LLC	Holliston	MA	E	508 474-6002	9208
F & D Plastics Inc (PA)	Leominster	MA	F	978 668-5140	9662
Flo Chemical Corp	Ashburnham	MA	F	978 827-5101	5952
Franklin Paint Company Inc	Franklin	MA	E	800 486-0304	8838
Gare Incorporated	Haverhill	MA	E	978 373-9131	9096
Highland Labs Inc	Holliston	MA	G	508 429-2918	9215
ICP Construction Inc (HQ)	Andover	MA	C	978 623-9980	5887
Idp Holdings Inc (PA)	Boston	MA	G		6804
Innovative Chem Pdts Group LLC	Boston	MA	E	800 393-5250	6812
Katahdin Industries Inc (PA)	Hudson	MA	E	781 329-1420	9380
L & A Molding Corporation	Leominster	MA	D	978 537-3538	9675
L H C Inc (PA)	Lynn	MA	F	781 592-6444	9982
Mantrose-Haeuser Co Inc	Attleboro	MA	E	203 454-1800	6033
Michael Rogovsky	New Bedford	MA	F	508 487-3287	10622
NBD Nanotechnologies Inc	Lexington	MA	F	781 541-4192	9764
Norfolk Corporation	Marshfield	MA	F	781 319-0400	10242
Perma Incorporated	Bedford	MA	F	978 667-5161	6252
Perrco Inc	Woburn	MA	F	617 933-5300	13633
Recolor Paints LLC	Hanover	MA	F	833 732-6567	9040
Rock-Tred 2 LLC	Andover	MA	E	888 762-5873	5912
RPM Wood Finishes Group Inc	Westfield	MA	D	413 562-9655	13204
Rule Industries LLC	Gloucester	MA	C	978 281-0440	8956
Rustoleum Attleboro Plant	Attleboro	MA	G	508 222-3710	6060
Silverlining Holding Corp (PA)	Needham	MA	E	617 986-4600	10522
The Savogran Company	Norwood	MA	E	781 762-5400	11216
Tnemec East Inc	Wilmington	MA	E	978 988-9500	13467
Union Specialties Inc	Newburyport	MA	E	978 465-1717	10724
Waterlac Coating Inc	Lowell	MA	G	573 885-2506	9935
Chilton Paint Co Inc ME	Freeport	ME	G	207 865-4443	4800
Advanced Polymerics Inc	Salem	NH	D	603 328-8177	15502
Coating Systems Inc	Nashua	NH	D	603 883-0553	15082
Foundation Armor LLC	Amherst	NH	F	866 306-0246	13870
Hampshire Chemical Corp (DH)	Nashua	NH	E	603 888-2320	15109
Kretetek Industries LLC	Hudson	NH	F	603 402-3073	14518
Roymal Inc	Newport	NH	E	603 863-2410	15237
Beacon Rock Properties Inc	Providence	RI	D	401 421-3470	16482
Carroll Coatings Company Inc (PA)	Providence	RI	G	401 450-5500	16497
Development Associates Inc	North Kingstown	RI	F	401 884-1350	16244
Fri Resins Holding Company	Cranston	RI	F	401 946-5564	15863
Pg Imtech of Californ	East Providence	RI	G	401 521-2490	16038
Spectrum Coatings Labs Inc	Providence	RI	F	401 781-4847	16614
Teknor Color Company	Pawtucket	RI	E	401 725-8000	16421
C E Bradley Laboratories Inc (PA)	Brattleboro	VT	E	802 257-7971	17077

2865 Cyclic crudes and intermediates

	CITY	ST	EMP	PHONE	ENTRY#
Bioenergy International LLC	Quincy	MA	F	617 657-5200	11506
Breakthrough Coatings Inc	Buzzards Bay	MA	F	866 608-7625	7453
Chemgenes Corporation	Billerica	MA	E	978 694-4500	6422
EC Pigments USA Inc	Fall River	MA	C	508 676-3481	8539
Ferro Corporation	Williamstown	MA	E	413 743-3927	13366
Itk Chemicals Inc	Danvers	MA	F	978 531-2279	8194
Mra Laboratories Inc	Adams	MA	E	413 743-3927	5774
Walrus Enteprises LLC	Northampton	MA	E	413 387-4387	11085
Avient Colorants USA LLC	Lewiston	ME	B	207 784-0733	4951
Clariant Corporation	Coventry	RI	B	401 823-2000	15809
Ecc Holdings Inc (HQ)	Providence	RI	E	401 331-9000	16511
Teknor Color Company	Pawtucket	RI	E	401 725-8000	16421

2869 Industrial organic chemicals, nec

	CITY	ST	EMP	PHONE	ENTRY#
Accustandard Inc	New Haven	CT	D	203 786-5290	2111
Advanced Pwr Systems Intl Inc	New Hartford	CT	G	860 921-0009	2097
Arcadia Chem Preservative LLC	Shelton	CT	F	203 717-4750	2982
BASF Catalysts LLC	East Windsor	CT	D	860 623-9901	1066
Bedoukian Research Inc (PA)	Danbury	CT	E	203 830-4000	713
Brickenmore East LLC	East Windsor	CT	F	860 906-6116	1069
Carlson Fuel of Meriden Inc	Waterbury	CT	F	203 574-9396	3896
Carrubba Incorporated	Monroe	CT	D	203 878-0605	1908
Chemtura USA Corporation	Middlebury	CT	A	203 573-2000	1714
Dependable Energy Incorporated	Prospect	CT	G	203 758-5831	2833
Dymax Oligomers & Coatings	Torrington	CT	F	860 626-7006	3677
E&S Automotive Operations LLC	Bridgeport	CT	G	203 332-4555	318
Galaxy Fuel LLC	Milford	CT	G	203 878-8173	1829
Greenfield Global USA Inc (HQ)	Brookfield	CT	F	203 740-3471	524
Greenleaf Bfuels New Haven LLC	New Haven	CT	F	203 672-9028	2157
H Krevit and Company Inc	New Haven	CT	E	203 772-3350	2159
Hajan LLC	New Britain	CT	F	860 223-2005	2029
Hampford Research Inc (PA)	Stratford	CT	E	203 375-1137	3544
Henkel of America Inc (HQ)	Rocky Hill	CT	B	860 615-3395	2926
Husky Fuel LLC	Oxford	CT	G	203 783-0783	2698
Kolmar Americas Inc (HQ)	Bridgeport	CT	F	203 873-2051	341
Lanxess Solutions US Inc	Shelton	CT	A	203 573-2000	3027
Macdermid Brazil Inc	Waterbury	CT	C	203 575-5700	3938
Nalas Engineering Services	Norwich	CT	D	860 861-3691	2609
Olin Corporation	Wilton	CT	E	203 750-3100	4244
Pucks Putters & Fuel LLC	Milford	CT	E	203 877-5457	1872
RSA Corp	Danbury	CT	E	203 790-8100	807
RT Vanderbilt Holding Co Inc (PA)	Norwalk	CT	F	203 295-2141	2568
Si Group Inc	Danbury	CT	C	203 702-6140	815
Si Group USA Hldings Usha Corp (DH)	Danbury	CT	F	203 702-6140	816
Ultra Food and Fuel	New Britain	CT	G	860 223-2005	2073
Vanderbilt Chemicals LLC	Bethel	CT	C	203 744-3900	139
Vanderbilt Chemicals LLC (HQ)	Norwalk	CT	C	203 295-2141	2589
Veolia Es Tchncal Slutions LLC	Danbury	CT	F	203 748-9116	832
Victory Fuel LLC	Terryville	CT	G	860 585-0532	3614
Alaimo Fuel Corp	Boston	MA	G	617 436-3600	6529
Avient Colorants USA LLC (HQ)	Holden	MA	E	508 829-6321	9187
Belco Fuel Company Inc	Pembroke	MA	F	781 331-6521	11359
Borden & Remington Corp	Fall River	MA	E	508 675-0096	8528
Cambridge Isotope Labs Inc (DH)	Tewksbury	MA	D	978 749-8000	12389
Cannan Fuels	Mansfield	MA	E	508 339-3317	10040
Chasm Advanced Materials Inc (PA)	Canton	MA	G	781 821-0443	7778
Continuus Pharmaceuticals Inc	Woburn	MA	F	781 281-0115	13548
Dodge Company Inc (PA)	Billerica	MA	F	800 443-6343	6431
Electronic Fluorocarbons LLC (PA)	Hopkinton	MA	E	508 435-7700	9316
Epoxy Technology Inc (PA)	Billerica	MA	E	978 667-3805	6444
Fisher Scientific Intl LLC (HQ)	Waltham	MA	E	781 622-1000	12675
Fuel America	Brighton	MA	G	617 782-0999	7240
Fuel First Elm Inc	West Springfield	MA	E	413 732-5732	13027
Fuel Source Inc	Norwood	MA	G	781 469-8449	11173
Giner Life Sciences Inc	Auburndale	MA	F	781 529-0576	6135
Girouard Tool Corp	Leominster	MA	G	978 534-4147	9667
H I Five Renewables	Merrimac	MA	G	978 384-8032	10324
Homeland Fuels Company LLC	Canton	MA	F	781 737-1892	7797
Inversant Inc	Lynn	MA	F	617 423-0331	9978
Isp Freetown Fine Chem Inc	Assonet	MA	D	508 672-0634	5974
John G Shelley Co Inc	Woburn	MA	F	781 237-0900	13593
Joule Unlimited Technologies Inc	Foxboro	MA	D	781 533-9100	8703
Liquiglide Inc	Cambridge	MA	E	617 901-0700	7633
Liquiglide Inc	North Billerica	MA	G	617 833-8638	10927
Lisha & Nirali Fuel LLC	Middleton	MA	G	908 433-6504	10389
Manus Bio Inc (HQ)	Waltham	MA	E	617 299-8466	12713
MK Fuel Inc	Brimfield	MA	F	413 245-7507	7250
Myriant Lake Providence Inc	Woburn	MA	F	617 657-5200	13616
Northeast Chemicals Inc	Milford	MA	F	508 634-6900	10409
Nutrasweet Company	Waltham	MA	C	706 303-5600	12740
Onyx Environmental Svcs LLC (DH)	Boston	MA	E	617 849-6600	6936
Pttgc Innovation America Corp (HQ)	Woburn	MA	E	617 657-5234	13641
Rachad Fuel Inc	Burlington	MA	F	781 273-0292	7419
Rohm Haas Electronic Mtls LLC (HQ)	Marlborough	MA	A	508 481-7950	10206
S & E Fuels Inc	Taunton	MA	F	617 407-9977	12365
S & M Fuels Inc	Plymouth	MA	F	508 746-1495	11476
Safc Hitech Inc	Haverhill	MA	E	978 374-5200	9130
Strem Chemicals Incorporated (HQ)	Newburyport	MA	D	978 499-1600	10718
Swampscott Fuel Inc	Swampscott	MA	F	781 592-1065	12299
Szr Fuel LLC	Tyngsboro	MA	G	978 649-2409	12466
TK&k Services LLC	Beverly	MA	D	770 844-8710	6389
Twin Rivers Tech Ltd Partnr	Quincy	MA	C	617 472-9200	11542
Um Food Sciences	Amherst	MA	E	413 545-2276	5866
World Asset Management LLC	Boston	MA	F	617 889-7300	7131
World Energy Biox Biofuels LLC (PA)	Boston	MA	F	617 889-7300	7133

	CITY	ST	EMP	PHONE	ENTRY#
World Energy Rome LLC	Boston	MA	G	706 291-4829	7134
Yield10 Bioscience Inc (PA)	Woburn	MA	E	617 583-1700	13691
YSNC Fuel Inc	Brockton	MA	F	508 436-2716	7314
FMC Corporation	Rockland	ME	D	207 594-3200	5329
Harcros Chemicals Inc	Westbrook	ME	E	207 856-6756	5627
John Seavey Acadia Fuel	Trenton	ME	G	207 664-6050	5556
M A Haskell & Sons LLC	China	ME	G	207 993-2265	4696
Maine Bio-Fuel Inc	Portland	ME	F	207 878-3001	5238
Offshore Fuel	Gouldsboro	ME	G	207 963-7068	4840
Yoc	York	ME	G	207 363-9322	5720
Favorite Fuels LLC	Hampton Falls	NH	G	603 967-4889	14418
Hampshire Chemical Corp (DH)	Nashua	NH	E	603 888-2320	15109
Itaconix Corporation	Stratham	NH	E	603 775-4400	15636
Z-Tech LLC	Bow	NH	E	603 228-1305	14016
Agilent Technologies Inc	North Kingstown	RI	D	800 338-1754	16229
Aurora Fuel Company Inc	West Warwick	RI	E	401 345-5996	16904
Cal Chemical Corporation	Coventry	RI	E	401 821-0320	15808
Clariant Corporation	Coventry	RI	B	401 823-2000	15809
Epoxies Inc	Cranston	RI	F	401 946-5564	15857
Fri Resins Holding Company	Cranston	RI	F	401 946-5564	15863
Purevita Labs LLC	West Warwick	RI	F	401 258-8968	16921
Teknor Apex Company (PA)	Pawtucket	RI	A	401 725-8000	16420
Ultra Scientific Incorporated	North Kingstown	RI	E	800 338-1754	16290
Abba Fuels Inc	Underhill	VT	G	802 878-8095	17654
Accordant Energy LLC	Rutland	VT	G	802 772-7368	17488
Augmentus Group LLC	Burlington	VT	F		17119
Brosseau Fuels LLC	Morrisville	VT	G	802 888-9209	17380
C E Bradley Laboratories Inc (PA)	Brattleboro	VT	E	802 257-7971	17077

2873 Nitrogenous fertilizers

	CITY	ST	EMP	PHONE	ENTRY#
Ocean Crest Seafoods Inc (PA)	Gloucester	MA	E	978 281-0232	8949
Gac Chemical Corporation (PA)	Searsport	ME	D	207 548-2525	5453
Compost Plant L3c	Providence	RI	F	844 741-4653	16503

2875 Fertilizers, mixing only

	CITY	ST	EMP	PHONE	ENTRY#
Clinton Nursery Products Inc (PA)	Westbrook	CT	C	860 399-3000	4137
Grillo Services LLC	Milford	CT	E	203 877-5070	1831
Harrells LLC	New Milford	CT	F	863 680-2003	2247
New Milford Farms Inc	New Milford	CT	F	860 210-0250	2256
Scotts Company LLC	Lebanon	CT	E	860 642-7591	1550
Black Earth Compost LLC	Gloucester	MA	F	262 227-1067	8923
Bootstrap Compost Inc	Plainfield	MA	F	617 642-1979	11428
Conrad Fafard Inc	Agawam	MA	A	413 786-4343	5788
Diemand Egg Farm Inc	Millers Falls	MA	G	978 544-3806	10447
Divert Inc (PA)	Concord	MA	E	978 341-5430	8113
Fafard Inc	Agawam	MA	D	413 786-4343	5790
Massachusetts Natural Fert Inc	Westminster	MA	G	978 874-0744	13272
Ocean Crest Seafoods Inc (PA)	Gloucester	MA	E	978 281-0232	8949
Sun Gro Holdings Inc	Agawam	MA	E	413 786-4343	5809
Sun Gro Horticulture Dist Inc (HQ)	Agawam	MA	E	413 786-4343	5810
Sun Gro Horticulture Dist Inc	Agawam	MA	E	800 732-8667	5811
Sun Gro Horticulture Dist Inc	Agawam	MA	D	864 224-7989	5812

2879 Agricultural chemicals, nec

	CITY	ST	EMP	PHONE	ENTRY#
Bedoukian Research Inc (PA)	Danbury	CT	E	203 830-4000	713
Chemtura USA Corporation	Middlebury	CT	A	203 573-2000	1714
Clinton Nursery Products Inc (PA)	Westbrook	CT	C	860 399-3000	4137
Connecticut Tick Control LLC	Norwalk	CT	F	203 855-7849	2486
Mist Hill Property Maint LLC	Brookfield	CT	F	203 648-7434	530
Pic20 Group LLC	Norwalk	CT	F	203 957-3555	2558
TAC Acquisition Corp	Greenwich	CT	A	203 983-5276	1355
Waterbury Companies Inc	Waterbury	CT	C		3980
Cambridge Chemical Co Corp	Cambridge	MA	F	617 876-4484	7529
Rohm Haas Electronic Mtls LLC	Marlborough	MA	E	508 481-7950	10207
Shield Packaging Co Inc	Dudley	MA	E	508 949-0900	8323
Thermacell Repellents Inc	Bedford	MA	D	781 541-6900	6273
Northern Turf Prfessionals Inc	Brunswick	ME	F	207 522-8598	4652
Bio-Concept Laboratories Inc	Salem	NH	E	603 437-4990	15510
Pace Anlytical Lf Sciences LLC	Salem	NH	E	603 437-4990	15555
Rosalie Gendron LLC	Manchester	NH	G	603 836-3692	14922
Tender Corporation (PA)	Littleton	NH	D	603 444-5464	14724
Augmentus Group LLC	Burlington	VT	F		17119
Costa Enterprises Ltd Co	Waterville	VT	G	802 644-6782	17682

2891 Adhesives and sealants

	CITY	ST	EMP	PHONE	ENTRY#
Advanced Adhesive Systems Inc	Newington	CT	E	860 953-4100	2267
Apcm Manufacturing LLC	Plainfield	CT	G	860 564-7817	2731
Chessco Industries Inc (PA)	Westport	CT	E	203 255-2804	4160
Edison Coatings Inc	Plainville	CT	F	860 747-2220	2757
Five Star Products Inc	Shelton	CT	E	203 336-7900	3006
Grafted Coatings Inc	Stratford	CT	G	203 377-9979	3543
Henkel Loctite Corporation (DH)	Rocky Hill	CT	D	860 571-5100	2925
Henkel of America Inc (HQ)	Rocky Hill	CT	B	860 615-3395	2926

	CITY	ST	EMP	PHONE	ENTRY#
Henkel US Operations Corp (DH)	Rocky Hill	CT	B	860 571-5100	2927
Hexcel Corporation (PA)	Stamford	CT	E	203 969-0666	3374
Laticrete International Inc (PA)	Bethany	CT	B	203 393-0010	94
Metamorphic Materials Inc	Winsted	CT	G	860 738-8638	4349
Mica Corporation	Shelton	CT	E	203 922-8888	3031
Panacol-Usa Inc	Torrington	CT	F	860 738-7449	3691
Si Group Inc	Danbury	CT	C	203 702-6140	815
Stanchem Incorporated (HQ)	East Berlin	CT	E	860 828-0571	918
Vanderbilt Chemicals LLC	Bethel	CT	C	203 744-3900	139
Xg Industries LLC	Stratford	CT	F	475 282-4643	3586
3M Company	Rockland	MA	E	781 871-1400	11632
A W Chesterton Company (PA)	Groveland	MA	E	781 438-7000	9012
Acton Research Corporation	Acton	MA	E	941 556-2601	5731
Adhesive Applications Inc (PA)	Easthampton	MA	E	413 527-7120	8437
Allcoat Technology Inc	Wilmington	MA	E	978 988-0880	13376
American Adhesive Coatings LLC (PA)	Lawrence	MA	E	978 688-7400	9536
AP Plastics LLC	Peabody	MA	E	800 222-1117	11298
Bacon Industries Inc	Wrentham	MA	F	508 384-0780	13837
Bemis Associates Inc (PA)	Shirley	MA	F	978 425-6761	11815
Bostik Inc	Middleton	MA	C	978 777-0103	10382
C L Hauthaway & Sons Corp	Lynn	MA	E	781 592-6444	9965
Coating House Inc	East Longmeadow	MA	F	413 525-3100	8372
Coatings Adhesives Inks	Georgetown	MA	F	978 352-7273	8907
Creative Materials Inc	Ayer	MA	E	978 391-4700	6180
Delo Industrial Adhesives LLC	Sudbury	MA	E	978 254-5275	12263
Diemat Inc	Byfield	MA	F	978 499-0900	7457
Dorn Equipment Corp	Melrose	MA	F	781 662-9300	10316
Eastman Performance Films LLC	Holliston	MA	E	508 474-6002	9208
Emseal Joint Systems Ltd	Westborough	MA	E	508 836-0280	13100
Epoxy Technology Inc (PA)	Billerica	MA	E	978 667-3805	6444
Flexcon Company Inc (PA)	Spencer	MA	A	508 885-8200	12058
Functional Coatings LLC	Newburyport	MA	E	978 462-0796	10684
Granger Lynch Corp	Millbury	MA	C	508 756-6244	10435
Hapco Inc	Hanover	MA	E	781 826-8801	9034
Henkel Corporation	Canton	MA	C	781 737-1400	7796
Hero Coatings Inc	Newburyport	MA	G	978 462-0746	10688
Illinois Tool Works Inc	Danvers	MA	C	978 777-1100	8193
Indusol Inc	Sutton	MA	E	508 865-9516	12282
Innovative Chem Pdts Group LLC (PA)	Andover	MA	E	978 623-9980	5889
ITW Devcon Inc	Danvers	MA	F	978 777-1100	8195
ITW Performance Polymers	Danvers	MA	D	978 777-1100	8196
John G Shelley Co Inc	Woburn	MA	F	781 237-0900	13593
Key Polymer LLC	Lawrence	MA	F	978 683-9411	9573
Key Polymer Holdings LLC (PA)	Lawrence	MA	F	978 683-9411	9574
L H C Inc (PA)	Lynn	MA	E	781 592-6444	9982
Middlesex Research Mfg Co Inc	Hudson	MA	E	978 562-3697	9390
Mussel Bound LLC	Brewster	MA	G	774 212-5488	7215
Ngac LLC	Burlington	MA	E	781 258-0008	7400
North American Coating Sciences Inc	Lawrence	MA	G	978 691-5622	9590
Nova Sports Usa Inc	Milford	MA	E	508 473-6540	10410
Olympic Adhesives Inc (PA)	Norwood	MA	E	800 829-1871	11202
Parker-Hannifin Corporation	Woburn	MA	B	781 935-4850	13629
Perrco Inc	Woburn	MA	E	617 933-5300	13633
Rectorseal LLC	Fall River	MA	F	508 673-7561	8601
Resin Designs LLC (DH)	Woburn	MA	E	781 935-3133	13650
Saint-Gobain Abrasives Inc (HQ)	Worcester	MA	A	508 795-5000	13788
Saint-Gobain Corporation	Northborough	MA	A	508 351-7112	11108
Stahl (usa) Inc (DH)	Peabody	MA	E	978 968-1382	11344
Standard Rubber Products Inc	Hanover	MA	E	781 878-2626	9043
Surmet Corp (PA)	Burlington	MA	E	781 345-5721	7436
Transene Company Inc (PA)	Danvers	MA	E	978 777-7860	8227
Tyco Adhesives	Franklin	MA	G	508 918-1600	8873
Union Specialties Inc	Newburyport	MA	E	978 465-1717	10724
Enterprise Casting Corporation	Lewiston	ME	E	207 782-5511	4961
Gripwet Inc	South Portland	ME	E	207 239-0486	5504
Piping Specialties Inc	Portland	ME	F	207 878-3955	5256
Sheepscot Machine Works LLC	Newcastle	ME	G	207 563-2299	5096
Adhesive Engineering & Supply	Seabrook	NH	F	603 895-4028	15582
Adhesive Technologies Inc (PA)	Hampton	NH	E	603 926-1616	14396
Appli-Tec Inc	Salem	NH	E	603 685-0500	15508
Coating Systems Inc	Nashua	NH	G	603 883-0553	15082
Extreme Adhesives Inc	Raymond	NH	G	603 895-4028	15452
Hampshire Chemical Corp (DH)	Nashua	NH	E	603 888-2320	15109
Kretetek Industries Inc	Hudson	NH	F	855 573-8383	14517
Mereco Technologies Group Inc (HQ)	Londonderry	NH	E	401 822-9300	14769
Metachem Resins Corporation	Londonderry	NH	E		14770
Protavic America Inc	Londonderry	NH	G	603 623-8624	14780
Resin Technology Group LLC	Seabrook	NH	D	508 230-8070	15601
Royal Adhesives & Sealants LLC	Raymond	NH	G	860 788-3380	15457
Schul International Co LLC	Hudson	NH	F	603 889-6872	14544
Trellborg Pipe Sals Mlford Inc (DH)	Milford	NH	F	800 626-2180	15042
Worthen Industries Inc (HQ)	Nashua	NH	D	603 888-5443	15188
Worthen Industries Inc	Nashua	NH	E	603 886-0973	15189

Employee Codes: A=Over 500 employees, B=251-500
C=101-250, D=51-100, E=20-50, F=10-19, G=1-9

2024 Harris New England
Manufacturers Directory

885

S I C

	CITY	ST	EMP	PHONE	ENTRY#
Atom Adhesives LLC	Providence	RI	F	888 522-6742	16478
Epoxies Inc	Cranston	RI	F	401 946-5564	15857
Fri Resins Holding Company	Cranston	RI	F	401 946-5564	15863
Gurit (usa) Inc	Bristol	RI	D	401 396-5008	15767
Northern Products Inc	Woonsocket	RI	F		16969
Vesuvius America Inc **(DH)**	Providence	RI	E		16640
Mylan Technologies Inc **(HQ)**	Saint Albans	VT	C	802 527-7792	17525
Rutland Fire Clay Co **(PA)**	Rutland	VT	F	802 775-5519	17507

2892 Explosives

	CITY	ST	EMP	PHONE	ENTRY#
Austin Powder Company	Sterling	CT	E	860 564-5466	3499
Dyno Nobel Inc	Simsbury	CT	C	860 843-2000	3085
Independent Explosives Inc	Bloomfield	CT	G	860 243-0137	171
Maxam Initiation Systems LLC	Sterling	CT	E	860 556-4064	3502
Metal Finish Eqp & Sup Co Inc	Suffield	CT	E	860 668-1050	3593
Dj Semichem Inc	Nashua	NH	G	603 204-5101	15092

2893 Printing ink

	CITY	ST	EMP	PHONE	ENTRY#
Superior Printing Ink Co Inc	Hamden	CT	E	203 281-1921	1458
Superior Printing Ink Co Inc	North Haven	CT	G	203 777-9055	2438
A I C Inc **(PA)**	Georgetown	MA	E	978 352-4510	8904
Coatings Adhesives Inks	Georgetown	MA	F	978 352-7273	8907
Functional Inks Inc	West Springfield	MA	G	413 363-0770	13028
Gem Gravure Co Inc **(PA)**	Hanover	MA	D	781 878-0456	9032
Gotham Ink of New England Inc	Marlborough	MA	E	508 485-7911	10154
RPM Wood Finishes Group Inc	Westfield	MA	D	413 562-9655	13204
Superior Printing Ink Co Inc	Marlborough	MA	E	508 481-8250	10219
Three Dimensional Graphics Corp	Byfield	MA	E	978 774-8595	7460
Universal Color Corp Inc	Wilmington	MA	F	978 658-2300	13473
Winged Pegasus Consulting Inc	Andover	MA	E	978 667-0600	5935
Graphic Utilities Incorporated	Limestone	ME	E	207 370-9178	5004
Markem-Imaje Corporation **(HQ)**	Keene	NH	B	603 352-1130	14607
Wikoff Color Corporation	Hudson	NH	F	603 864-6456	14560

2895 Carbon black

	CITY	ST	EMP	PHONE	ENTRY#
Cabot Corporation	Billerica	MA	E	978 671-4000	6421
Cabot Corporation **(PA)**	Boston	MA	C	617 345-0100	6631
Cabot Corporation	Haverhill	MA	C	978 556-8400	9084

2899 Chemical preparations, nec

	CITY	ST	EMP	PHONE	ENTRY#
5n Plus Corp	Bridgeport	CT	F	608 846-1357	288
Advanced Pwr Systems Intl Inc	New Hartford	CT	G	860 921-0009	2097
Alent USA Holding Inc	Waterbury	CT	C	203 575-5727	3880
Armored Autogroup Parent Inc	Danbury	CT	C	203 205-2900	710
Bic Consumer Pdts Mfg Co Inc	Milford	CT	C	203 783-2000	1802
Bic Corporation **(HQ)**	Shelton	CT	A	203 783-2000	2985
Bic USA Inc **(DH)**	Shelton	CT	C	203 783-2000	2986
Brand-Nu Laboratories LLC **(PA)**	Meriden	CT	E	203 235-7989	1656
Caap Co Inc	Milford	CT	E	203 877-0375	1805
Carruba Incorporated	Milford	CT	D	203 878-0605	1809
Chemotex Prtctive Catings Corp **(PA)**	Durham	CT	F	860 349-0144	897
Chessco Industries Inc **(PA)**	Westport	CT	E	203 255-2804	4160
Command Chemical Corporation	Fairfield	CT	G	203 319-1857	1180
Crystal Rock Spring Water Co	Watertown	CT	B	860 945-0661	4007
Cytec Industries Inc	Stamford	CT	D	203 321-2200	3333
Dexsil Corporation	Hamden	CT	E	203 288-3509	1421
Engineered Coatings Inc	Litchfield	CT	G	860 567-5556	1557
Filmco Rust Protection LLC	Branford	CT	F	203 483-5017	256
Five Star Products Inc	Shelton	CT	E	203 336-7900	3006
Gotham Chemical Company Inc	Norwalk	CT	D	203 854-6644	2508
Great Lakes Chemical Corp **(DH)**	Shelton	CT	E	203 573-2000	3010
Harvard Chemical LLC **(HQ)**	Bolton	CT	F	404 761-0657	220
Henkel of America Inc **(HQ)**	Rocky Hill	CT	B	860 615-3395	2926
Henkel US Operations Corp **(DH)**	Rocky Hill	CT	B	860 571-5100	2927
Hubbard-Hall Inc **(PA)**	Waterbury	CT	D	203 756-5521	3919
Intersurface Dynamics Inc	Bethel	CT	F	203 778-9995	120
Inventec Prfmce Chem USA LLC	Deep River	CT	E	860 526-8300	878
King Industries Inc **(PA)**	Norwalk	CT	C	203 866-5551	2523
Kuehne New Haven LLC	New Haven	CT	E	203 508-6703	2167
Lanxess Corporation	Naugatuck	CT	E	203 714-8669	1970
Lanxess Solutions US Inc	Shelton	CT	A	203 573-2000	3027
Laticrete International Inc **(PA)**	Bethany	CT	B	203 393-0010	94
Lydall Inc **(HQ)**	Manchester	CT	E	860 646-1233	1614
Macdermid Incorporated **(HQ)**	Waterbury	CT	C	203 575-5700	3933
Macdermid Acumen Inc	Waterbury	CT	C	203 575-5700	3934
Macdermid AG Solutions Inc **(HQ)**	Waterbury	CT	F	203 575-5727	3935
Macdermid Anion Inc	Waterbury	CT	C	203 575-5700	3936
Macdermid Autotype Inc	Waterbury	CT	E	847 818-8262	3937
Macdermid Enthone Inc **(HQ)**	West Haven	CT	C	203 934-8611	4112
Macdermid Holdings LLC	Waterbury	CT	C	203 575-5700	3939
Macdermid Overseas Asia Ltd **(HQ)**	Waterbury	CT	E	203 575-5799	3940
Macdermid Prtg Sltons Acmen In	Waterbury	CT	C	203 575-5700	3941
Near Oak LLC	Stamford	CT	G	203 329-6500	3415

	CITY	ST	EMP	PHONE	ENTRY#
New England Tooling Inc	Killingworth	CT	F	800 866-5105	1544
Purification Technologies LLC **(DH)**	Chester	CT	F	860 526-7801	630
REM Chemicals Inc **(PA)**	Southington	CT	F	860 621-6755	3231
Smt International LLC	Deep River	CT	F	860 526-8803	883
Stanchem Incorporated **(HQ)**	East Berlin	CT	E	860 828-0571	918
A W Chesterton Company	Groveland	MA	B	781 438-7000	9013
Adaptive Surface Tech Inc	Hopkinton	MA	G	617 360-7080	9306
Aqua Laboratories Inc	Amesbury	MA	E	978 388-3989	5829
Aspen Aerogels Inc **(PA)**	Northborough	MA	C	508 691-1111	11088
Assayquant Technologies Inc	Marlborough	MA	E	774 278-3302	10113
Barclay Water Management Inc	Newton	MA	D	617 926-3400	10736
Blank Industries LLC	Hudson	MA	E	855 887-3123	9356
Bolger and OHearn Inc	Fall River	MA	E	508 676-1518	8527
Business and Prof Exch Inc	Beverly	MA	E	978 556-4100	6336
Cabot Corporation	Billerica	MA	E	978 671-4000	6421
Camco Manufacturing Inc	Leominster	MA	D	978 537-6777	9646
Clearwter Tech Cnslting Wtr Sv	Rockland	MA	F	781 871-5157	11640
Cold Chain Technologies LLC **(HQ)**	Franklin	MA	D	508 429-1395	8826
Creative Materials Inc	Ayer	MA	E	978 391-4700	6180
Cristy Corporation	Fitchburg	MA	E	978 343-4330	8650
Duraflow LLC	Tewksbury	MA	F	978 851-7439	12394
Ecpi Inc	Bolton	MA	F	774 823-6368	6496
Emco Services Inc	Fall River	MA	G	508 674-5504	8541
Gillette Company **(HQ)**	Boston	MA	A	617 463-3000	6758
Grate Products LLC	Westport	MA	E	800 649-6140	13296
Hiller Companies Inc	Peabody	MA	E	978 532-5730	11315
Holland Company Inc	Adams	MA	E	413 743-1292	5773
Hubbard-Hall Inc	Wilmington	MA	F	978 988-0077	13411
Katahdin Industries Inc **(PA)**	Hudson	MA	E	781 329-1420	9380
Kayaku Advanced Materials Inc	Newton	MA	E	617 965-5511	10767
Kayaku Advanced Materials Inc **(PA)**	Westborough	MA	E	617 965-5511	13113
King Fisher Co Inc	Lowell	MA	E	978 596-0214	9890
Lubrizol Global Management Inc	Wilmington	MA	C	978 642-5051	13427
MD Chemicals LLC	Mendon	MA	E	508 314-9664	10320
MD Stetson Company Inc	Mansfield	MA	E	781 986-6161	10066
Mexichem Spcalty Compounds Inc **(HQ)**	Leominster	MA	C	978 537-8071	9683
Morgan Advanced Ceramics Inc	New Bedford	MA	D	508 995-1725	10624
Osmo Labs Pbc	Cambridge	MA	F	508 439-4692	7679
Rectorseal LLC	Fall River	MA	F	508 673-7561	8601
Ro-59 Inc	Stoughton	MA	G	781 341-1222	12230
Rousselot Peabody Inc	Peabody	MA	F	978 573-3700	11339
Rule Industries LLC	Gloucester	MA	E	978 281-0440	8956
Salt & Pepper	Worcester	MA	F	508 755-1113	13793
Sigma-Aldrich Corporation	Burlington	MA	D	978 715-1804	7427
Thermo Fisher Scientific Inc	Beverly	MA	C	978 232-6000	6387
Tli Group Ltd	Carver	MA	F	508 866-9825	7858
Transene Company Inc **(PA)**	Danvers	MA	G	978 777-7860	8227
United States Biological Corp	Salem	MA	E	978 744-0345	11737
Walnut 65 Holdings Inc **(PA)**	Peabody	MA	E	978 532-4010	11352
Whittemore-Wright Company Inc	Charlestown	MA	F	617 242-1180	7884
Yankee Candle Company Inc **(DH)**	South Deerfield	MA	C	413 665-8306	11931
Yankee Holding Corp **(DH)**	South Deerfield	MA	D	413 665-8306	11933
Ycc Holdings LLC	South Deerfield	MA	A	413 665-8306	11934
Enterprise Casting Corporation	Lewiston	ME	E	207 782-5511	4961
FMC Corporation	Rockland	ME	D	207 594-3200	5329
Paine Products Inc	Auburn	ME	F	207 782-0931	4450
Salt and Pepper Me LLC	Wilton	ME	F	207 645-7035	5659
Albany International Corp **(PA)**	Rochester	NH	D	603 330-5850	15464
Atlas Pyrvsion Entrmt Group In **(PA)**	Jaffrey	NH	E	603 532-8324	14564
CIM Industries Inc	Peterborough	NH	D	603 924-9481	15313
Coating Systems Inc	Nashua	NH	G	603 883-0553	15082
Diversified Enterprises-ADT	Claremont	NH	G	603 543-0038	14088
Hampshire Chemical Corp **(DH)**	Nashua	NH	E	603 888-2320	15109
Onsite Drug Testing Neng	Concord	NH	G	603 226-3858	14150
Performance Chemicals LLC	Franklin	NH	F	603 228-1200	14322
Advanced Chemical Company	Warwick	RI	E	401 785-3434	16776
American Foam Technologies Inc	Newport	RI	F	304 497-3400	16200
Aspen Aerogels RI LLC	East Providence	RI	E	401 432-2612	16005
Bardon Industries Inc	East Greenwich	RI	F	401 884-1814	15973
Cranston Print Works Company **(PA)**	Cranston	RI	E	401 943-4800	15844
Dryvit Systems Inc	North Kingstown	RI	D	401 822-4100	16245
International Dioxcide Inc	North Kingstown	RI	E	401 295-8800	16260
New Brick Dryvit Systems	North Kingstown	RI	G	401 822-4100	16272
Technic Inc **(PA)**	Cranston	RI	C	401 781-6100	15919
Technic Inc	Pawtucket	RI	E	401 781-6100	16419
Town of Burrillville	Oakland	RI	G	401 568-6296	16335
Univar Solutions USA Inc	Providence	RI	E	518 762-3500	16633

29 PETROLEUM REFINING AND RELATED INDUSTRIES

2911 Petroleum refining

	CITY	ST	EMP	PHONE	ENTRY#
App Polonia LLC	Plainville	CT	G	860 747-3397	2747

	CITY	ST	EMP	PHONE	ENTRY#
Armored Autogroup Parent Inc	Danbury	CT	C	203 205-2900	710
CCI Corpus Christi LLC	Stamford	CT	F	203 564-8100	3304
Chessco Industries Inc (PA)	Westport	CT	E	203 255-2804	4160
CPI Operations LLC	Stamford	CT	F	210 249-9988	3323
Enviro-Fuels LLC	Suffield	CT	G	860 242-2325	3590
Koster Keunen Inc	Watertown	CT	D	860 945-3333	4017
Koster Keunen Mfg Inc	Watertown	CT	D	860 945-3333	4019
Lanxess Solutions US Inc	Shelton	CT	A	203 573-2000	3027
Mountain Creek Energy Inc	Manchester	CT	F	512 990-7886	1619
New Haven Chemicals LLC	New Haven	CT	E	475 241-1150	2177
Purification Technologies LLC (DH)	Chester	CT	F	860 526-7801	630
Si Group Inc	Danbury	CT	C	203 702-6140	815
Star Group LP (PA)	Stamford	CT	D	203 328-7310	3473
Stop N Go LLC	Hartford	CT	G	860 206-3950	1510
US Chemicals Inc	New Canaan	CT	G	203 655-8878	2093
Altair Paramount LLC	Boston	MA	G	617 889-7300	6538
Blue Rhino of Ne	Springfield	MA	G	413 781-3694	12079
Canadian Hills Wind LLC	Dedham	MA	G	617 977-2400	8237
Homeland Fuels Company LLC	Canton	MA	F	781 737-1892	7797
Isp Freetown Fine Chem Inc	Assonet	MA	F	508 672-0634	5974
Itk Chemicals Inc	Danvers	MA	F	978 531-2279	8194
Power Advocate Inc (HQ)	Boston	MA	D	857 453-5700	6971
Weymouth Gas LLC	Hanover	MA	F	781 826-4327	9048
Gaftek Inc	Bangor	ME	E	207 217-6515	4504
Maine Bio-Fuel Inc	Portland	ME	F	207 878-3001	5238
Baycorp Holdings Ltd (PA)	Portsmouth	NH	F	603 294-4850	15364
Prima America Corporation	Groveton	NH	F	603 631-5407	14379
Sail Energy LLC	Portsmouth	NH	C	844 301-7245	15434
White Mountain Biodiesel LLC	Littleton	NH	G	603 444-0335	14725
Glenn Inc	Warwick	RI	F	800 521-0065	16819
Burtco Inc	Westminster Station	VT	F	802 722-3358	17702
Proctor Gas Inc	Proctor	VT	E	802 459-3340	17460

2951 Asphalt paving mixtures and blocks

	CITY	ST	EMP	PHONE	ENTRY#
E B Asphalt & Landscaping LLC	Oakdale	CT	F	860 639-1921	2621
Firestone Building Pdts Co LLC	Bristol	CT	F	860 584-4516	447
O & G Industries Inc	Bridgeport	CT	B	203 366-4586	354
O & G Industries Inc	New Milford	CT	E	860 354-4438	2258
O & G Industries Inc	Southbury	CT	E	203 263-2195	3197
O & G Industries Inc (PA)	Torrington	CT	D	860 489-9261	3689
Tilcon Connecticut Inc (DH)	New Britain	CT	B	860 224-6010	2072
Tilcon Inc (DH)	Newington	CT	B	860 223-3651	2328
Wescon Corp of Conn	Pawcatuck	CT	G	860 599-2500	2728
Westchester Industries Inc	Greenwich	CT	F	203 661-0055	1360
A F Amorello & Sons Inc	Worcester	MA	E	508 791-8778	13694
Alton E Gleason Company Inc (PA)	Springfield	MA	F	413 732-8207	12073
Bond Construction Corporation	Spencer	MA	F	508 885-2480	12055
Brox Industries Inc (PA)	Dracut	MA	D	978 454-9105	8302
East Coast Pavers LLC	Tewksbury	MA	F	508 577-7832	12395
Fletcher Granite LLC (DH)	Westford	MA	G	978 692-1312	13238
Gem Asset Acquisition LLC	Worcester	MA	E	508 419-7710	13730
Granger Lynch Corp	Millbury	MA	C	508 756-6244	10435
Heffron Asphalt Corp (PA)	North Reading	MA	G	781 935-1455	11040
Holcim - Ner Inc (DH)	Saugus	MA	E	781 941-7200	11760
JH Lynch & Sons Inc	Millbury	MA	E	508 756-6244	10438
Jsl Asphalt Inc (PA)	Westfield	MA	F	413 568-8986	13177
Lane Construction Corporation	Northfield	MA	D	413 498-5586	11120
Lorusso Corp (PA)	Plainville	MA	E	508 668-6520	11437
Massachusetts Broken Stone Co (PA)	Berlin	MA	E	978 838-9999	6319
Massachusetts Broken Stone Co	Holden	MA	E	508 829-5353	9193
New England Grund Slutions LLC	Gloucester	MA	G	978 203-6277	8945
Norfolk Asphalt Paving Inc	Canton	MA	F	617 293-9775	7813
Ondrick Materials & Recycl LLC	Chicopee	MA	E	413 592-2566	8052
P A Landers Inc	Hanover	MA	F	508 747-1800	9039
Palmer Paving Corporation (PA)	Palmer	MA	E	413 283-8354	11281
Peckham Enterprises LLC	Montgomery	MA	G	413 862-3252	10459
PJ Keating Company	Dracut	MA	D	978 454-7878	8310
Rose Office Carl	East Sandwich	MA	G	508 833-8758	8405
Sbarzola Construction Corp	South Weymouth	MA	G	781 817-6485	11977
Sealmaster	Worcester	MA	G	508 926-8080	13796
T L Edwards Inc	Plymouth	MA	F	508 732-9148	11480
Ted Ondrick Company LLC (PA)	Chicopee	MA	F	413 592-2565	8062
Trew Corp	Deerfield	MA	G	413 773-9798	8256
Bruce A Manzer Inc	Farmington	ME	E	207 696-5881	4777
Dayton Sand & Gravel Inc	Dayton	ME	D	207 499-2306	4720
Eurovia Atlantic Coast LLC	Hermon	ME	E	703 230-0850	4881
F R Carroll Inc	Limerick	ME	E	207 793-8615	5001
Lane Construction Corporation	Bangor	ME	B	207 945-0850	4508
Lane Construction Corporation	Presque Isle	ME	E	207 764-4137	5301
Mattingly Products Company	North Anson	ME	E	207 635-2719	5107
Morin Brothers	Fort Kent	ME	G	207 834-5361	4790
Pike Industries Inc	Wells	ME	F	207 676-9973	5604

	CITY	ST	EMP	PHONE	ENTRY#
Shaw Brothers Construction Inc (PA)	Gorham	ME	C	207 839-2552	4835
Blaktop Inc (PA)	West Lebanon	NH	E	603 298-8885	15678
Pike Industries Inc (DH)	Belmont	NH	E	603 527-5100	13967
Pike Industries Inc	Gorham	NH	F	603 466-2772	14361
Pike Industries Inc	Portsmouth	NH	G	603 436-4332	15429
Cruz Construction Company Inc	Cumberland	RI	F	401 727-3770	15935
Hudson Liquid Asphalts Inc (PA)	Cranston	RI	D	401 274-2200	15874
JH Lynch & Sons Inc (PA)	Cumberland	RI	F	401 333-4300	15948
JH Lynch & Sons Inc	East Providence	RI	F	401 434-7100	16025
Narragansett Improvement Co (PA)	Providence	RI	F	401 331-0051	16571
Pavement Warehouse	Greenville	RI	G	401 233-3200	16062
Perry Paving	Warwick	RI	F	401 732-1730	16845
Watson Materials	East Greenwich	RI	G	401 885-0600	15997
Peckham Industries Inc	Shaftsbury	VT	F	802 442-4418	17552
Pike Industries Inc	Williston	VT	G	802 658-0453	17744

2952 Asphalt felts and coatings

	CITY	ST	EMP	PHONE	ENTRY#
Firestone Building Pdts Co LLC	Bristol	CT	F	860 584-4516	447
Owens Corning Sales LLC	East Hartford	CT	C	304 353-6945	1008
Omg Inc (PA)	Agawam	MA	B	413 789-0252	5803
Patriot Seal Coating	Worcester	MA	G	774 386-8531	13768
Sarnafil Services Inc	Canton	MA	C	781 828-5400	7825
Thomas J Cronin	Medfield	MA	G	508 510-2328	10277
Ta Property Maintenance LLC	Scarborough	ME	F	207 289-7158	5444
Andrade Sealcoating LLC	Gilmanton Iron Works	NH	F	603 435-3704	14340
Cameron Sealcoating LLC	Jefferson	NH	F	603 586-7945	14583
Cherubino Sealcoating LMC LLC	Salem	NH	G	781 272-1020	15514
Lsr Sealcoating	Concord	NH	G	603 715-4934	14141
Northern Elastomeric Inc	Brentwood	NH	D	603 778-8899	14025
Newmont Slate Co Inc (PA)	West Pawlet	VT	F	802 645-0203	17692
Quarry Slate Industries Inc	Poultney	VT	E	802 287-9701	17449
Vermont Structural Slate Co (PA)	Fair Haven	VT	E	802 265-4933	17252

2992 Lubricating oils and greases

	CITY	ST	EMP	PHONE	ENTRY#
Axel Plastics RES Labs Inc	Monroe	CT	E	718 672-8300	1905
Chessco Industries Inc (PA)	Westport	CT	E	203 255-2804	4160
Macdermid Incorporated (HQ)	Waterbury	CT	C	203 575-5700	3933
A W Chesterton Company (PA)	Groveland	MA	F	781 438-7000	9012
A W Chesterton Company	Groveland	MA	B	781 438-7000	9013
CCL Industries Corporation (HQ)	Framingham	MA	D	508 872-4511	8749
Change Logic	Gloucester	MA	F	617 274-8661	8928
Circuit Systems Inc (PA)	Westfield	MA	F	413 562-5019	13159
Homeland Fuels Company LLC	Canton	MA	F	781 737-1892	7797
Nye Lubricants Inc (HQ)	Fairhaven	MA	C	508 996-6721	8512
Perrco Inc	Woburn	MA	F	617 933-5300	13633
Ro-59 Inc	Stoughton	MA	G	781 341-1222	12230
S & K Unlimited LLC	Brownville	ME	F	207 965-6137	4638
Kluber Lubric North Amercia LP	Londonderry	NH	E	603 647-4104	14758
Kluber Lubrication North Ameri	Londonderry	NH	F	603 434-7704	14759
Vidarr Inc	Portsmouth	NH	G	877 636-8432	15448
Battenfeld of America Inc	West Warwick	RI	F	401 823-0700	16905

2999 Petroleum and coal products, nec

	CITY	ST	EMP	PHONE	ENTRY#
Koster Keunen LLC (PA)	Watertown	CT	E	860 945-3333	4018
Cnc International Inc	Woonsocket	RI	G	401 769-6100	16953

30 RUBBER AND MISCELLANEOUS PLASTIC PRODUCTS

3011 Tires and inner tubes

	CITY	ST	EMP	PHONE	ENTRY#
KCR Tire & Auto Inc	Ridgefield	CT	F	203 438-4042	2900
Toce Brothers Incorporated (PA)	Torrington	CT	E	860 496-2080	3700
BF Services Inc	Lexington	MA	F	781 862-9792	9728
Main Industrial Tires Ltd (PA)	Wakefield	MA	F	713 676-0251	12515
Maine Industrial Tire LLC	Wakefield	MA	C	781 914-3410	12516
Maine Rubber International	Wakefield	MA	B	877 648-1949	12517
Maxam Tire North America Inc (HQ)	Danvers	MA	F	844 629-2662	8203
New England Trck Tire Ctrs Inc (PA)	Sanford	ME	E	207 324-2262	5402

3021 Rubber and plastics footwear

	CITY	ST	EMP	PHONE	ENTRY#
Black Diamond Group Inc	Woburn	MA	F	781 939-7824	13527
Klone Lab LLC	Newburyport	MA	F	978 378-3434	10692
Macneill Engineering Co Inc	Westborough	MA	E	508 481-8830	13118
New Balance Athletics Inc	Lawrence	MA	B	978 685-8400	9586
32 North Corporation	Biddeford	ME	G	207 284-5010	4553
Homegrown For Good LLC	York	ME	F	857 540-6361	5713
New Balance Athletics Inc	Norridgewock	ME	E	207 634-3033	5103
New Balance Athletics Inc	Skowhegan	ME	F	207 474-2042	5474
Genfoot America Inc	Littleton	NH	D	603 575-5114	14719
Simply Footwear Utah LLC	Concord	NH	F	603 715-2259	14157

Employee Codes: A=Over 500 employees, B=251-500
C=101-250, D=51-100, E=20-50, F=10-19, G=1-9   2024 Harris New England
Manufacturers Directory   887

S I C

	CITY	ST	EMP	PHONE	ENTRY#
Norcross Safety Products LLC	Smithfield	RI	A	800 430-5490	16724
Codet-Newport Corporation (HQ)	Newport	VT	F	802 334-5811	17398
Genfoot America LLC	Milton	VT	F	802 893-4280	17358

3052 Rubber and plastics hose and beltings

	CITY	ST	EMP	PHONE	ENTRY#
Diversified Industrial Sup LLC	Charlestown	MA	F	800 244-3647	7868
Dresco Belting Co Inc	Hingham	MA	G	781 335-1350	9148
Greene Rubber Company Inc (PA)	Woburn	MA	D	781 937-9909	13577
Guardair Corporation	Chicopee	MA	E	413 594-4400	8035
Samar Co Inc	Stoughton	MA	E	781 297-7264	12233
Titeflex Commercial Inc	Springfield	MA	E	413 739-5631	12139
Titeflex Corporation (HQ)	Springfield	MA	B	413 739-5631	12140
Contitech Thermopol LLC	Rochester	NH	E	603 692-6300	15471
Contitech Thermopol LLC	Somersworth	NH	E	603 692-6300	15614
Contitech Thermopol LLC (HQ)	Somersworth	NH	C	603 692-6300	15615
Teknor Apex Company (PA)	Pawtucket	RI	A	401 725-8000	16420

3053 Gaskets; packing and sealing devices

	CITY	ST	EMP	PHONE	ENTRY#
A G C Incorporated	Meriden	CT	C	203 235-3361	1649
American Seal and Engrg Co Inc	Orange	CT	E	203 789-8819	2667
Ametek Inc	Wallingford	CT	E	203 265-6731	3770
Auburn Manufacturing Company	Middletown	CT	E	860 346-6677	1737
Beacon Group Inc (PA)	Newington	CT	E	860 594-5200	2275
Corru-Seals Inc	Wallingford	CT	F	203 265-9331	3795
Derby Cellular Products Inc	Shelton	CT	E	203 735-4661	2999
H-O Products Corporation	Winsted	CT	E	860 379-9875	4346
Parker-Hannifin Corporation	North Haven	CT	D	203 239-3341	2430
SKF USA Inc	Winsted	CT	E	860 379-8511	4356
Spirol International Corp (HQ)	Danielson	CT	C	860 774-8571	844
Standard Washer & Mat Inc	Manchester	CT	E	860 643-5125	1638
Vanguard Products Corporation	Danbury	CT	D	203 744-7265	831
A W Chesterton Company (PA)	Groveland	MA	D	781 438-7000	9012
A W Chesterton Company	Groveland	MA	B	781 438-7000	9013
Acushnet Rubber Company Inc	New Bedford	MA	B	508 998-4000	10564
Atlantic Rubber Company Inc	Littleton	MA	F	800 882-3666	9804
Boston Atlantic Corp	Worcester	MA	F	508 754-4076	13705
Coorstek Inc	Worcester	MA	B	774 317-2600	13710
D V Die Cutting Inc	Danvers	MA	E	978 777-0300	8177
Eastern Industrial Pdts Inc	Plymouth	MA	F	781 826-9511	11457
Emseal Joint Systems Ltd	Westborough	MA	E	508 836-0280	13100
Gasket Express Inc	Worcester	MA	G	508 754-4076	13727
Greene Rubber Company Inc (PA)	Woburn	MA	D	781 937-9909	13577
Hollingsworth & Vose Company (PA)	East Walpole	MA	C	508 850-2000	8418
I G Marston Company	Holbrook	MA	F	781 767-2894	9174
Interstate Gasket Company Inc	Sutton	MA	E	508 234-5500	12283
Interstate Specialty Pdts Inc	Sutton	MA	E	800 984-1811	12284
Northeast Equipment Inc	Fall River	MA	F	508 324-0083	8588
Parker-Hannifin Corporation	Woburn	MA	B	781 935-4850	13629
Parker-Hannifin Corporation	Woburn	MA	G	781 935-4850	13630
Parker-Hannifin Corporation	Woburn	MA	B	781 939-4278	13631
Saint-Gobain Prfmce Plas Corp	Worcester	MA	C	508 852-3072	13792
United Tool & Machine Corp	Lawrence	MA	E	978 686-4181	9608
Vellumoid Inc	Worcester	MA	E	508 853-2500	13821
Zd USA Holdings Inc	New Bedford	MA	B	508 998-4000	10662
Woodex Bearing Company Inc	Georgetown	ME	E	207 371-2210	4815
Felton Inc	Londonderry	NH	D	603 425-0200	14750
Ferrotec (usa) Corporation	Bedford	NH	E	603 472-6800	13930
Freudenberg-Nok General Partnr	Ashland	NH	D	603 968-7187	13900
Freudenberg-Nok General Partnr	Bristol	NH	C	603 934-7800	14035
Freudenberg-Nok General Partnr	Northfield	NH	C	603 286-1600	15265
Freudenberg-Nok General Partnr	Northfield	NH	E	603 286-1600	15266
Marco Group LLC (PA)	Seabrook	NH	E	603 468-3600	15596
New England Braiding Co Inc	Manchester	NH	F	603 669-1987	14897
Trellborg Pipe Sals Mlford Inc	Milford	NH	D	603 673-8680	15041
Trellborg Pipe Sals Mlford Inc (DH)	Milford	NH	F	800 626-2180	15042
Zhongding Laconia Inc	Laconia	NH	E	603 524-3367	14674
Jade Engineered Plastics Inc	Warren	RI	D	401 253-4440	16759
John Crane Sealol Inc (DH)	Warwick	RI	C	401 732-0715	16828
LK Goodwin Co Inc (PA)	West Greenwich	RI	E	401 781-5526	16888
Magnetic Seal LLC	Warren	RI	D	401 247-2800	16760
Flex-A-Seal Inc	Williston	VT	E	802 878-8307	17729
Flexaseal Engnred Sals Systems	Williston	VT	C	800 426-3594	17730

3061 Mechanical rubber goods

	CITY	ST	EMP	PHONE	ENTRY#
Acmt Inc	Manchester	CT	D	860 645-0592	1582
Airex Rubber Products Corporation	Portland	CT	E	860 342-0850	2816
Applied Rubber & Plastics Inc	Windsor	CT	F	860 987-9018	4261
Vanguard Products Corporation	Danbury	CT	D	203 744-7265	831
Acushnet Rubber Company Inc	New Bedford	MA	B	508 998-4000	10564
Biltrite Corporation (PA)	Brockton	MA	F	781 647-1700	7261
Device Technologies Inc	Southborough	MA	E	508 229-2000	11994
Greene Rubber Company Inc (PA)	Woburn	MA	D	781 937-9909	13577
Hutchinson Arospc & Indust Inc (DH)	Hopkinton	MA	B	508 417-7000	9330

	CITY	ST	EMP	PHONE	ENTRY#
Jefferson Rubber Works Inc	Worcester	MA	D	508 791-3600	13744
Pocasset Machine Corporation	Pocasset	MA	E	508 563-5572	11491
Saint-Gobain Prfmce Plas Corp	Worcester	MA	C	508 852-3072	13792
Freudenberg-Nok General Partnr	Northfield	NH	C	603 286-1600	15265
Z-Flex Realty Inc (DH)	Bedford	NH	E	603 669-5136	13957
Zhongding Laconia Inc	Laconia	NH	E	603 524-3367	14674
Etco Incorporated (PA)	Warwick	RI	D	401 467-2400	16815
Htp Meds LLC	Ashaway	RI	C	401 315-0654	15742
Moore Company	Westerly	RI	C	401 596-2816	16939
Garware Fulflex USA Inc	Brattleboro	VT	C	802 257-5256	17085

3069 Fabricated rubber products, nec

	CITY	ST	EMP	PHONE	ENTRY#
Acutek Adhesive Specialties	Windsor	CT	F	310 419-0190	4254
Airex Rubber Products Corporation	Portland	CT	E	860 342-0850	2816
American Roller Company LLC	Middlebury	CT	E	203 598-3100	1713
Auburn Manufacturing Company	Middletown	CT	E	860 346-6677	1737
Bite Tech Inc	Norwalk	CT	E	203 987-6898	2473
Cooper Crouse-Hinds LLC	Windsor	CT	D	860 683-4300	4268
Dodson Boatyard LLC	Stonington	CT	E	860 535-1507	3508
Edgewell Personal Care Company (PA)	Shelton	CT	E	203 944-5500	3003
Excelsior Inc	Cheshire	CT	F	203 491-2028	592
Gordon Rubber and Pkg Co Inc	Derby	CT	E	203 735-7441	889
Griswold LLC	Moosup	CT	E	845 986-2271	1930
H-O Products Corporation	Winsted	CT	E	860 379-9875	4346
IR Industries Inc	Bethel	CT	F	203 790-8273	121
Jonal Laboratories Inc	Meriden	CT	D	203 634-4444	1671
Kingfisher Marine Ltd	Clinton	CT	G	602 409-1460	646
Lord & Hodge Inc	Middletown	CT	F	860 632-7006	1760
Mayborn Usa Inc	Stamford	CT	F	781 269-7490	3409
Midsun Specialty Products Inc	Berlin	CT	E	860 378-0111	76
New England Foam Products LLC (PA)	Hartford	CT	E	860 524-0121	1496
Playtex Products LLC (HQ)	Shelton	CT	D	203 944-5500	3050
Reilly Foam Corp	Bloomfield	CT	F	860 243-8200	206
Standard Washer & Mat Inc	Manchester	CT	E	860 643-5125	1638
Talalay Global Inc (DH)	Shelton	CT	F	203 924-0700	3067
Universal Foam Products LLC	Bloomfield	CT	F	860 216-3015	215
Advent Medical Products Inc	Lincoln	MA	G	781 272-2813	9794
Alimed Inc	Dedham	MA	C	781 329-2900	8235
American Biltrite Inc (PA)	Wellesley	MA	B	781 237-6655	12935
American Retail Svc Inc	Randolph	MA	G	781 885-7369	11548
Au Milford LLC	Milford	MA	D	508 473-1870	10398
Avon Custom Mixing Svcs Inc	Holbrook	MA	F	781 767-0511	9169
Ballard Away Corporation	Lawrence	MA	C	978 689-2800	9542
Cataki International Inc	Wareham	MA	F	508 295-9630	12833
Cooper Crouse-Hinds LLC	Chelsea	MA	F	617 389-3707	7979
Cri-Tech Inc	Hanover	MA	E	781 826-5600	9028
Dorel Juvenile Group Inc	Foxboro	MA	C	800 544-1108	8694
Fabreeka International Inc (DH)	Stoughton	MA	G	781 341-3655	12206
Fabreeka Intl Holdings Inc (DH)	Stoughton	MA	E	781 341-3655	12207
Fastcast Consortium Inc	Worcester	MA	E	508 853-4500	13722
Gzsl Corp	North Attleboro	MA	E	508 695-0727	10872
Haartz Corporation (PA)	Acton	MA	B	978 264-2600	5751
Heveatex Corporation	Fall River	MA	C	508 675-0181	8560
Hytex Industries Inc	Randolph	MA	E	781 963-4400	11565
Jefferson Rubber Works Inc	Worcester	MA	D	508 791-3600	13744
John G Shelley Co Inc	Woburn	MA	F	781 237-0900	13593
JPS Elastomerics Corp	Easthampton	MA	C	413 779-1200	8448
New England Business Svc Inc (HQ)	Townsend	MA	D	978 448-6111	12441
Patten Machine Inc	Hudson	MA	F	978 562-9847	9399
Plymouth Rubber Company LLC	Canton	MA	F	781 828-0220	7820
Rubber Right Rollers Inc	Chelsea	MA	F	617 466-1447	7990
Rubber-Right Rollers Inc	Everett	MA	G	617 387-6060	8498
Saint-Gobain Prfmce Plas Corp	Worcester	MA	C	508 852-3072	13792
Sandbox Medical LLC	Pembroke	MA	E	781 826-6905	11377
Simons Stamps LLC	Turners Falls	MA	F	413 863-6800	12455
SRC Medical Inc	Hanover	MA	D	781 826-9100	9042
Standard Rubber Products Inc	Hanover	MA	E	781 878-2626	9043
Vibram Corporation (HQ)	Concord	MA	E	978 318-0000	8138
Vibram Corporation (DH)	North Brookfield	MA	C	508 867-6494	10964
Vystar Corporation	Worcester	MA	D	508 791-9114	13826
Watermillpreferred Partners LP	Waltham	MA	F	781 790-5045	12815
Bosal Foam and Fiber (PA)	Limerick	ME	E	207 793-2245	5000
Expanded Rubber Products Inc (PA)	Sanford	ME	F	207 324-8226	5395
Maine Industrial P & R Corp	Newcastle	ME	G	207 563-5532	5095
Off Center Harbor LLC	Brooklin	ME	G	401 487-2090	4634
Proknee Corp	Whitefield	ME	F	207 549-5018	5656
American Ppe Company LLC	Merrimack	NH	E	603 320-5123	14972
Diacom Corporation	Amherst	NH	D	603 880-1900	13866
Humphreys Industrial Pdts Inc	Rochester	NH	E	603 692-5005	15478
Hutchinson Sealing Systems Inc	Newfields	NH	C	603 772-3771	15205
Nora Systems Inc (DH)	Salem	NH	D	603 894-1021	15550
Nordson Medical (nh) Inc (HQ)	Salem	NH	C	603 327-0600	15551
Schaeferrolls Inc	Farmington	NH	E	603 335-1786	14311

	CITY	ST	EMP	PHONE	ENTRY#
Stowe Woodward LLC	Concord	NH	E	603 224-6300	14160
Tillotson Corporation (PA)	Nashua	NH	F	781 402-1731	15176
Worthen Industries Inc	Nashua	NH	E	978 365-6345	15190
Cara Incorporated	East Greenwich	RI	G	401 732-6535	15976
Cooley Incorporated (HQ)	Pawtucket	RI	C	401 724-9000	16357
Cooley Group Holdings Inc (PA)	Pawtucket	RI	C	401 724-0510	16358
Dewal Industries LLC	Narragansett	RI	C	401 789-9736	16189
Fuller Box Co Inc	Central Falls	RI	C	401 725-4300	15788
Givens Marine Survival Svc Co	Tiverton	RI	F	617 441-5400	16736
Gs Rubber Industries LLC	Coventry	RI	F	508 672-0742	15814
LK Goodwin Co Inc (PA)	West Greenwich	RI	F	401 781-5526	16888
Moore Company	Westerly	RI	E	401 596-2816	16939
Teknor Apex Company (PA)	Pawtucket	RI	A	401 725-8000	16420
TMC Rhode Island Company Inc	Westerly	RI	E	401 596-2816	16943
Garware Fulflex USA Inc	Brattleboro	VT	C	802 257-5256	17085

3081 Unsupported plastics film and sheet

	CITY	ST	EMP	PHONE	ENTRY#
American Polyfilm Inc (PA)	Branford	CT	G	203 483-9797	235
Apogee Corporation	Cromwell	CT	D	860 632-3550	686
Atlas Metallizing Inc	New Britain	CT	E	860 827-9777	2003
Berry Global Inc	East Hampton	CT	G	413 529-7602	960
Connecticut Clean Room Corp	Bristol	CT	E	860 589-0049	430
Engineering Services & Pdts Co (PA)	South Windsor	CT	D	860 528-1119	3144
Flagship Converters Inc	Danbury	CT	D	203 792-0034	746
Fortune Plastics Inc	Old Saybrook	CT	B	800 243-0306	2648
Orafol Americas Inc	Avon	CT	C	860 676-7100	35
Polymer Films Inc	West Haven	CT	E	203 932-3000	4119
Spartech LLC	Stamford	CT	C	203 327-6010	3467
Str Holdings Inc (PA)	Enfield	CT	F	860 272-4235	1154
Superior Plas Extrusion Co Inc	Cromwell	CT	E	860 234-1864	697
American Durafilm Co Inc	Holliston	MA	E	508 429-8000	9198
Applied Nnstrctred Sltions LLC	Billerica	MA	E	978 670-6959	6403
Argotec LLC	Greenfield	MA	B	413 772-2564	8982
Argotec LLC (HQ)	Greenfield	MA	C	413 772-2564	8983
Arlin Mfg Co Inc	Lowell	MA	F	978 454-9165	9854
Atlantic Poly Inc	Norwood	MA	E	781 769-4260	11163
Cabot Corporation (PA)	Boston	MA	C	617 345-0100	6631
Cabot Corporation	Haverhill	MA	C	978 556-8400	9084
CDF Corporation (PA)	Plymouth	MA	D	508 747-5858	11454
Charter Next Generation Inc	Turners Falls	MA	C	413 863-3171	12444
Cheer Pack North America LLC	West Bridgewater	MA	F	508 927-7800	12968
Coorstek Inc	Worcester	MA	B	774 317-2600	13710
Danafilms Corp	Westborough	MA	E	508 366-8884	13098
Dielectrics Inc	Chicopee	MA	C	413 594-8111	8024
Eastern Etching and Mfg Co	Chicopee	MA	E	413 594-6601	8030
Entegris Inc (PA)	Billerica	MA	A	978 436-6500	6443
Flexcon Company Inc (PA)	Spencer	MA	A	508 885-8200	12058
Gregory Manufacturing Inc	Holyoke	MA	D	413 536-5432	9257
Guardian Indus Pdts Inc Mass	Norfolk	MA	G	508 384-0060	10798
Hartwell Asscoiates	Cambridge	MA	G	617 686-7571	7599
Hudson Poly Bag Inc	Hudson	MA	F	978 562-7566	9374
Hytex Industries Inc	Randolph	MA	E	781 963-4400	11565
JP Plastics Inc	Bridgewater	MA	G	508 697-4202	7235
K2w LLC	Waltham	MA	G	617 818-2613	12706
Laddawn Inc (HQ)	Devens	MA	D	800 446-3639	8274
Micron Plastics Inc	Ayer	MA	G	978 772-6900	6186
New England Plastics Corp	New Bedford	MA	D	508 998-3111	10630
New England Plastics Corp (PA)	Woburn	MA	E	781 933-6004	13623
Packaging Products Corporation (PA)	New Bedford	MA	F	508 997-5150	10638
Polyvinyl Films Inc	Sutton	MA	D	508 865-3558	12290
Swm	Greenfield	MA	E	413 772-2564	9001
Tekni-Plex Inc	Ashland	MA	E	508 881-2440	5968
Tel Mnfacturing Engrg Amer Inc	Billerica	MA	E	978 436-2300	6487
Tri-Star Plastics Corp (PA)	Shrewsbury	MA	E	508 845-1111	11845
Walter Drake Incorporated (PA)	Holyoke	MA	G	413 536-5463	9290
Ward Process Inc	Holliston	MA	D	508 429-1165	9238
Zatec LLC	North Dighton	MA	E	508 880-3388	11006
Waterville Window Co Inc	Winslow	ME	E	207 873-0159	5689
Multi Technologies Industrial LLC	Brentwood	NH	E	603 778-1449	14024
SF Tools LLC	Newport	NH	F	603 863-7719	15238
Textiles Coated Incorporated (PA)	Londonderry	NH	E	603 296-2221	14786
Bruin Plastics Co Inc	Glendale	RI	E	800 556-7764	16054
Dewal Industries LLC	Narragansett	RI	C	401 789-9736	16189
Nelipak Corporation (PA)	Cranston	RI	E	401 946-2699	15899
Teknor Apex Company (PA)	Pawtucket	RI	A	401 725-8000	16420
Toray Plastics (america) Inc (DH)	North Kingstown	RI	A	401 294-4511	16287
Astenjohnson Inc	Williston	VT	D	802 658-2040	17722

3082 Unsupported plastics profile shapes

	CITY	ST	EMP	PHONE	ENTRY#
Cebal Americas (PA)	Norwalk	CT	A	203 845-6356	2480
Polymedex Discovery Group Inc (PA)	Putnam	CT	C	860 928-4102	2870
Web Industries Hartford Inc (HQ)	Dayville	CT	E	860 779-3197	870
Coorstek Inc	Worcester	MA	B	774 317-2600	13710

	CITY	ST	EMP	PHONE	ENTRY#
Fluorolite Plastics LLC	Hudson	MA	G	508 788-1200	9368
Kilder Corporation	North Billerica	MA	E	978 663-8800	10922
Saint-Gobain Abrasives Inc (HQ)	Worcester	MA	A	508 795-5000	13788
Samar Co Inc	Stoughton	MA	E	781 297-7264	12233
Tri-Star Plastics Corp (PA)	Shrewsbury	MA	E	508 845-1111	11845
Nordson Medical (nh) Inc (HQ)	Salem	NH	E	603 327-0600	15551
Teleflex Incorporated	Jaffrey	NH	D	603 532-7706	14580
Tfx Medical Incorporated	Jaffrey	NH	D	603 532-7706	14581

3083 Laminated plastics plate and sheet

	CITY	ST	EMP	PHONE	ENTRY#
Alcat Incorporated	Milford	CT	E	203 878-0648	1795
Beckson Manufacturing Inc (PA)	Bridgeport	CT	E	203 366-3644	301
CT Composites & Marine Svc LLC	South Windsor	CT	G	860 282-0100	3137
Current Inc (PA)	East Haven	CT	D	203 469-1337	1039
Diba Industries Inc (HQ)	Danbury	CT	E	203 744-0773	731
Futuramik Industries Inc	Hartford	CT	E	860 951-3121	1481
Hicks and Otis Prints Inc	Norwalk	CT	E	203 846-2087	2513
New Precision Technology LLC	Madison	CT	G	800 243-4565	1564
Panolam Industries Inc (HQ)	Shelton	CT	E	203 925-1556	3044
Pioneer Plastics Corporation (HQ)	Shelton	CT	E	203 925-1556	3047
Polymedex Discovery Group Inc (PA)	Putnam	CT	C	860 928-4102	2870
Quality Name Plate Inc	East Glastonbury	CT	D	860 633-9495	923
The E J Davis Company	North Haven	CT	E	203 239-5391	2439
3M Company	Chelmsford	MA	E	978 256-3911	7901
Atlas Fibre LLC	Westborough	MA	F	847 674-1234	13079
Bixby International Corp	Newburyport	MA	D	978 462-4100	10671
Custom Extrusion Inc (HQ)	Sheffield	MA	E	413 229-8748	11797
Fort Hill Sign Products Inc	Hopedale	MA	F	781 321-4320	9297
General Woodworking Inc (PA)	Lowell	MA	F	978 458-6625	9879
Geonautics Manufacturing Inc	Newburyport	MA	F	978 462-7161	10685
H Loeb Corporation	New Bedford	MA	E	508 996-3745	10597
High Speed Routing LLC	Haverhill	MA	F	603 527-8027	9103
Injectronics Corporation	Clinton	MA	D	978 365-1200	8078
MM Newman Corporation	Marblehead	MA	F	781 631-7100	10091
Neptco Incorporated (DH)	Westwood	MA	E	401 722-5500	13316
October Company Inc	Easthampton	MA	E	413 529-0718	8457
Samar Co Inc	Stoughton	MA	E	781 297-7264	12233
United Plastic Fabricating Inc (PA)	North Andover	MA	D	978 975-4520	10855
Advanced Building Products Inc	Sanford	ME	E	207 490-2306	5389
Pioneer Plastics Corporation	Auburn	ME	C	207 784-9111	4454
York Manufacturing Inc	Sanford	ME	F	207 324-1300	5418
American Marine Products Inc	Charlestown	NH	F	954 782-1400	14060
Global Laminates Inc	Portsmouth	NH	F	603 373-8323	15393
Kalwall Corporation (PA)	Manchester	NH	B	603 627-3861	14870
Nordson Medical (nh) Inc (HQ)	Salem	NH	C	603 327-0600	15551
Plasti-Clip Corporation	Milford	NH	F	603 672-1166	15034
Riley Mountain Products Inc	Antrim	NH	F	603 588-7234	13898
Scandia Plastics Inc	Plaistow	NH	E	603 382-6533	15350
Tech Resources Inc	Milford	NH	E	603 673-9000	15039
Teleflex Incorporated	Jaffrey	NH	D	603 532-7706	14580
Tfx Medical Incorporated	Jaffrey	NH	D	603 532-7706	14581
Nelipak Corporation (PA)	Cranston	RI	E	401 946-2699	15899
Tpi Inc	Warren	RI	E	401 247-4010	16769
Tpi Composites Inc	Warren	RI	F	401 247-4010	16770
Kaman Composites - Vermont Inc	Bennington	VT	C	802 442-9964	17046

3084 Plastics pipe

	CITY	ST	EMP	PHONE	ENTRY#
Advanced Drainage Systems Inc	Ludlow	MA	B	413 589-0515	9937
Applied Nnstrctred Sltions LLC	Billerica	MA	E	978 670-6959	6403
Asahi/America Inc	Lawrence	MA	G	800 343-3618	9539
Asahi/America Inc (HQ)	Lawrence	MA	E	781 321-5409	9540
Cabot Corporation (PA)	Boston	MA	C	617 345-0100	6631
Cabot Corporation	Haverhill	MA	C	978 556-8400	9084
Fiberspar Spoolable Pdts Inc (PA)	West Wareham	MA	E	508 291-1000	13064
Orion Enterprises Inc (HQ)	North Andover	MA	C	913 342-1653	10847
Plastics Unlimited of MA Inc	Worcester	MA	G	508 752-7842	13770

3085 Plastics bottles

	CITY	ST	EMP	PHONE	ENTRY#
Altium Packaging	Windsor	CT	F	860 683-8560	4258
Mayborn Usa Inc	Stamford	CT	F	781 269-7490	3409
Silgan Holdings Inc (PA)	Stamford	CT	C	203 975-7110	3459
Camco Manufacturing Inc	Leominster	MA	D	978 537-6777	9646
Weston Presidio MGT Co Inc (PA)	Boston	MA	E	617 988-2500	7118
Quality Containers of Neng	Yarmouth	ME	G	207 846-5420	5706
Carr Management Inc (PA)	Nashua	NH	F	603 888-1315	15077
Envases Usa Inc (HQ)	Amherst	NH	F	603 889-8311	13868
Foxx Life Sciences LLC (PA)	Salem	NH	F	603 890-3699	15528
Southeastern Container Inc	Hudson	NH	E	603 324-1204	14547
Plastic Technologies MD Inc	South Burlington	VT	G	802 658-6588	17592
Plastic Technologies NY LLC	South Burlington	VT	F	802 658-6588	17593
Plastic Technologies of Vermont Inc	South Burlington	VT	D	802 658-6588	17594

SIC

	CITY	ST	EMP	PHONE	ENTRY#

3086 Plastics foam products

	CITY	ST	EMP	PHONE	ENTRY#
Ansonia Plastics LLC	Ansonia	CT	D	203 736-5200	7
Claremont Sales Corporation	Durham	CT	E	860 349-4499	898
FC Meyer Packaging LLC **(HQ)**	Norwalk	CT	E	203 847-8500	2499
General Packaging Products Inc	Norwalk	CT	G	203 846-1340	2505
Gilman Corporation	Gilman	CT	E	860 887-7080	1266
H-O Products Corporation	Winsted	CT	E	860 379-9875	4346
Hhc LLC	Manchester	CT	E	860 456-0677	1602
HI-Tech Packaging Inc	Stratford	CT	E	203 378-2700	3547
Hopp Companies Inc **(PA)**	Southbury	CT	G	800 889-8425	3196
Hydrofera LLC	Manchester	CT	D	860 456-0677	1604
Madison Polymeric Engrg Inc	Branford	CT	E	203 488-4554	271
Merco Inc	Ellington	CT	E	860 871-1888	1110
New England Foam Products LLC **(PA)**	Hartford	CT	E	860 524-0121	1496
New England Industrial Sup LLC	Newington	CT	F	860 436-5959	2308
Plastic Forming Company Inc **(PA)**	Woodbridge	CT	E	203 397-1338	4382
Reilly Foam Corp	Bloomfield	CT	F	860 243-8200	206
Sealed Air Corporation	Danbury	CT	C	203 791-3597	814
Silgan Dspnsing Systems Cvit A	Thomaston	CT	B	860 274-6791	3629
Sonoco Prtective Solutions Inc	Putnam	CT	D	860 928-7795	2875
The Gilman Brothers Company	Gilman	CT	D	860 889-8444	1268
Universal Foam Products LLC	Bloomfield	CT	E	860 216-3015	215
Architects of Packaging Inc	Westfield	MA	G	413 568-3187	13148
Ashworth International Inc	Fall River	MA	F	508 674-4693	8522
Bbmc Inc	Hancock	MA	F	413 443-3333	9024
Concrete Block Insulg Systems	West Brookfield	MA	E	508 867-4241	12993
Danvers Industrial Packg Corp	Beverly	MA	E	978 777-0020	6344
Flexcon Industrial LLC **(HQ)**	Spencer	MA	D	210 798-1900	12059
Fuller Box Co Inc **(PA)**	North Attleboro	MA	D	508 695-2525	10871
Future Foam Inc	Mansfield	MA	F	508 339-0354	10052
Geonautics Manufacturing Inc	Newburyport	MA	E	978 462-7161	10685
Georgia-Pacific LLC	Leominster	MA	D	978 537-4701	9666
Hardigg Industries LLC **(HQ)**	South Deerfield	MA	E	413 665-2163	11924
Horn Corporation **(PA)**	Lancaster	MA	E	800 832-7020	9527
Imanova Packaging	Leominster	MA	F	978 537-8534	9670
Insulation Technology Inc	Bridgewater	MA	G	508 697-6926	7231
Jeffco Fibres Inc **(PA)**	Webster	MA	F	508 943-0440	12928
Lelanite Corporation **(PA)**	Webster	MA	E	508 987-2637	12929
Master Containers Inc	Andover	MA	D	800 881-6847	5892
Osaap America LLC	Chelmsford	MA	F	877 652-7227	7943
Packaging Products Corporation **(PA)**	New Bedford	MA	F	508 997-5150	10638
Polyfoam LLC	Northbridge	MA	C	508 234-6323	11117
Rogers Foam Automotive Corp	Somerville	MA	F	617 623-3010	11895
Rogers Foam Corporation **(PA)**	Somerville	MA	B	617 623-3010	11896
Sealed Air Corporation	Ayer	MA	E	508 521-5694	6193
Sealed Air Corporation	Holyoke	MA	C	413 534-0231	9280
Trelleborg Offshore Boston Inc **(HQ)**	Randolph	MA	F	781 437-1171	11577
Trexel Inc **(PA)**	Wilmington	MA	F	781 932-0202	13471
Ufp Technologies Inc	Haverhill	MA	F	978 352-2200	9136
Ufp Technologies Inc **(PA)**	Newburyport	MA	E	978 352-2200	10722
Waddington North America Inc	Chelmsford	MA	C	978 256-6551	7970
Ward Process Inc	Holliston	MA	D	508 429-1165	9238
Carlisle Construction Mtls LLC	Portland	ME	C	888 746-1114	5195
Deepwater Buoyancy Inc	Biddeford	ME	F	207 468-2565	4559
Der-Tex Corporation	Saco	ME	F	207 284-5931	5365
Enefco International Inc **(PA)**	Auburn	ME	E	207 514-7218	4428
Hunter Panels LLC	Portland	ME	C	888 746-1114	5225
Johns Manville Corporation	Saco	ME	E	207 283-8000	5370
Rynel Inc	Wiscasset	ME	D	207 882-0200	5700
Finally Free LLC	Manchester	NH	F	603 626-4388	14848
Index Packaging Inc	Milton	NH	C	603 350-0018	15046
Wayne Manufacturing Inds LLC	Brentwood	NH	F	978 416-0899	14032
Aqua Traction Marine LLC	North Kingstown	RI	F	320 237-2225	16232
Branch River Plastics Inc	Smithfield	RI	E	401 232-0270	16690
Eco Global Manufacturing LLC	Providence	RI	F	401 331-5129	16512
Lance Industries Inc **(PA)**	Lincoln	RI	D	401 365-6272	16144
MH Stallman Company Inc **(PA)**	Providence	RI	F	401 331-5129	16564
Tex Flock Inc	Woonsocket	RI	F	401 765-2340	16981
Vesuvius America Inc **(DH)**	Providence	RI	E		16640
Spring Fill	South Burlington	VT	F	802 846-5900	17599

3087 Custom compound purchased resins

	CITY	ST	EMP	PHONE	ENTRY#
Byk USA Inc	North Haven	CT	E	475 234-5317	2395
Foster Corporation **(HQ)**	Putnam	CT	E	860 928-4102	2855
Foster Corporation	Putnam	CT	E	860 377-7117	2856
Neu Spclty Engineered Mtls LLC	North Haven	CT	F	203 239-9629	2426
Pioneer Plastics Corporation **(HQ)**	Shelton	CT	E	203 925-1556	3047
Ercon Inc	Wareham	MA	E	508 291-1400	12835
Mexichem Spcalty Compounds Inc **(HQ)**	Leominster	MA	C	978 537-8071	9683
Shield Packaging Co Inc	Dudley	MA	F	508 949-0900	8323
Teknor Apex Company	Leominster	MA	E	978 534-1010	9708
Pioneer Plastics Corporation	Auburn	ME	C	207 784-9111	4454

	CITY	ST	EMP	PHONE	ENTRY#
New Hampshire Stamping Co Inc	Goffstown	NH	E	603 641-1234	14352
Elite Custom Compounding Inc	Warwick	RI	G	401 921-2136	16813
Teknor Apex Company **(PA)**	Pawtucket	RI	A	401 725-8000	16420

3088 Plastics plumbing fixtures

	CITY	ST	EMP	PHONE	ENTRY#
Keeney Holdings LLC	Farmington	CT	B	860 666-3342	1226
Leisure Zone Stores Inc	Putnam	CT	F	860 963-1181	2863
Neoperl Inc	Waterbury	CT	D	203 756-8891	3949
Syn-Mar Products Inc	Ellington	CT	F	860 872-8505	1117
Roma Marble Inc	Ludlow	MA	F	413 583-5017	9953
Sherle Wagner Intl LLC	Fall River	MA	F	212 758-3300	8606

3089 Plastics products, nec

	CITY	ST	EMP	PHONE	ENTRY#
24 Scitico LLC	Bethel	CT	G	203 791-9055	98
Aba-Pgt Inc **(PA)**	Manchester	CT	D	860 649-4591	1580
Able Coil and Electronics Co	Bolton	CT	E	860 646-5686	218
Advance Mold & Mfg Inc	Manchester	CT	C	860 432-5887	1583
Aero-Med Molding Technologies **(PA)**	Ansonia	CT	F	203 735-2331	5
All-Time Manufacturing Co Inc	Montville	CT	F	860 848-9258	1926
Altium Packaging	Windsor	CT	A	860 683-8560	4258
American Molded Products Inc	Bridgeport	CT	F	203 333-0183	295
American Plastic Products Inc	Waterbury	CT	C	203 596-2410	3883
Amplified Ink Co	Fairfield	CT	E	203 787-2184	1175
Apex Machine Tool Company Inc	Cheshire	CT	D	860 677-2884	571
Aptargroup Inc	Trumbull	CT	B	203 377-8100	3712
Architectural Supplements LLC	Waterbury	CT	F	203 591-5505	3886
Balfor Industries Inc	Oxford	CT	F	203 828-6473	2687
Berry Global Inc	East Hampton	CT	G	413 529-7602	960
Better Molded Products Inc **(PA)**	Bristol	CT	D	860 589-0066	415
Bidwell Industrial Group Inc	Middletown	CT	E	860 346-9283	1740
Bprex Halthcare Brookville Inc	Waterbury	CT	D	203 754-4141	3891
C Cowles & Company **(PA)**	North Haven	CT	D	203 865-3117	2396
Canevari Plastics Inc	Milford	CT	G	203 878-4319	1807
Carpin Manufacturing Inc	Waterbury	CT	C	203 574-2556	3897
CKS Packaging Inc	Naugatuck	CT	E	203 729-0716	1952
Coastline Environmental LLC	North Branford	CT	G	203 483-6898	2362
Coating Design Group Inc	Stratford	CT	E	203 878-3663	3528
Colts Plastics Company Inc	Dayville	CT	C	860 774-2277	861
Connecticut Plastics Inc	Wallingford	CT	E	203 265-3299	3793
Connecticut Tool Co Inc	Putnam	CT	E	860 928-0565	2850
Cowles Products Company Inc	North Haven	CT	C	203 865-3110	2405
Davis-Standard LLC **(HQ)**	Pawcatuck	CT	B	860 300-3928	2717
Dekarz Corporation	Seymour	CT	F	203 888-3102	2960
Delmar Products Inc	Berlin	CT	F	860 828-6501	64
Dfs In-Home Services	Danbury	CT	G	845 405-6464	730
Dymotek Corporation	Ellington	CT	E	860 875-2868	1104
Edco Industries Inc	Bridgeport	CT	F	203 333-8982	319
Enflo Corporation **(PA)**	Bristol	CT	E	860 589-0014	441
Ensinger Prcsion Cmponents Inc*(DH)**	Putnam	CT	D	860 928-7911	2854
Entegris Inc	Danbury	CT	C	800 766-2681	737
F F Screw Products Inc	Southington	CT	E	860 621-4567	3209
Farrel Corporation **(DH)**	Ansonia	CT	D	203 736-5500	14
Fimor North America Inc **(HQ)**	Cheshire	CT	E	203 272-3219	593
Fka Ppm Inc	Hartford	CT	E	781 871-4606	1480
Flagship Converters Inc	Danbury	CT	D	203 792-0034	746
Fluoropolymer Resources LLC **(PA)**	East Hartford	CT	G	860 423-7622	994
Form-All Plastics Corp	Meriden	CT	G	203 634-1137	1668
Fsm Plasticoid Mfg Inc	East Hartford	CT	F	860 623-1361	995
G & G Dissolution Corp	Glastonbury	CT	E	860 633-7099	1279
GP Industries	Taftville	CT	F	860 859-9938	3597
Hawk Integrated Plastics LLC	Columbia	CT	F	860 337-0310	670
Hexcel Corporation **(PA)**	Stamford	CT	E	203 969-0666	3374
HI Tech Profiles Inc	Pawcatuck	CT	G	401 377-2040	2722
Hosokawa Micron Intl Inc	Berlin	CT	E	860 828-0541	69
Hutzler Manufacturing Co Inc	Canaan	CT	E	860 824-5117	555
Idemia Identity & SEC USA LLC	Rocky Hill	CT	F	860 529-2559	2929
Idex Health & Science LLC	Bristol	CT	C	860 314-2880	456
Illinois Tool Works Inc	Lakeville	CT	E	860 435-2574	1546
Infiltrator Water Technologies LLC **(HQ)**	Old Saybrook	CT	D	860 577-7000	2651
Injectech Engineering LLC **(PA)**	New Hartford	CT	G	860 379-9781	2104
Inline Plastics Corp	Shelton	CT	B	800 826-5567	3021
Inline Plastics Corp **(PA)**	Shelton	CT	C	203 924-5933	3022
J&L Plastic Molding LLC	Wallingford	CT	G	203 265-6237	3821
James A Bean Corporation	Torrington	CT	F	860 489-1404	3685
Jarden LLC	Norwalk	CT	F	203 845-5300	2519
Kensco Inc **(PA)**	Ansonia	CT	G	203 734-8827	15
Kinamor Incorporated	Wallingford	CT	E	203 269-0380	3824
Lacey Manufacturing Co LLC	Bridgeport	CT	B	203 336-0121	343
Lawrence Holdings Inc	Wallingford	CT	F	203 949-1600	3826
Lehvoss North America LLC	Pawcatuck	CT	F	860 495-2046	2723
Lingol Corporation	Wallingford	CT	E	203 265-3608	3828
Lorex Plastics Co Inc	Norwalk	CT	F	203 286-0020	2529
Manchester Molding and Mfg Co	Manchester	CT	E	860 643-2141	1615

	CITY	ST	EMP	PHONE	ENTRY#		CITY	ST	EMP	PHONE	ENTRY#
Marlborough Plastics Inc	Marlborough	CT	G	860 295-9124	1644	Applied Plastic Technology Inc	Worcester	MA	E	508 752-5924	13700
Mbsw Inc	West Hartford	CT	E	860 243-0303	4071	Argos Corporation	Taunton	MA	F	508 828-5900	12318
Mdm Products LLC	Milford	CT	F	203 877-7070	1848	Art Plastics Mfg Corp	Leominster	MA	F	978 537-6640	9637
Mercury-Excelum Inc	East Windsor	CT	E	860 292-1800	1080	Asahi/America Inc (HQ)	Lawrence	MA	E	781 321-5409	9540
Merritt Extruder Corp	Hamden	CT	E	203 230-8100	1440	Atco Plastics Inc	Plainville	MA	F	508 695-3573	11429
Milfoam Corporation	Hamden	CT	F	203 248-8011	1442	Atlantic Auto & Trck Parts LLC	Rowley	MA	G	978 535-6777	11667
Mohawk Tool and Die Mfg Co Inc	Bridgeport	CT	F	203 367-2181	349	Axygen Bioscience Inc	Tewksbury	MA	F	978 442-2200	12385
MPS Plastics Incorporated	Marlborough	CT	F	860 295-1161	1645	Bacon Industries Inc	Wrentham	MA	F	508 384-0780	13837
Napco Plastics LLC	Terryville	CT	F	860 261-4819	3606	Beacon Engnred Sltons - MA LLC	Leominster	MA	F	978 466-9591	9640
Nevamar Company LLC (HQ)	Shelton	CT	B	203 925-1556	3037	Berry Global Inc	Easthampton	MA	E	812 424-2904	8439
New Christie Ventures LLC	Naugatuck	CT	E	203 720-9478	1977	Berry Global Inc	Franklin	MA	C	508 918-1714	8820
Orbit Design LLC	Meriden	CT	F	203 393-0171	1683	Berry Plastics Corp	Easthampton	MA	C	413 529-2183	8440
Owens Corning Sales LLC	East Hartford	CT	C	304 353-6945	1008	Big Rock Oyster Company Inc	Harwich	MA	G	774 408-7951	9067
Packaging and Crating Tech LLC	Watertown	CT	F	203 759-1799	4021	Billy Hill Tubs LLC	Sterling	MA	G	978 422-8800	12156
Panolam Industries Inc (HQ)	Shelton	CT	E	203 925-1556	3044	Biomedical Polymers Inc	Sterling	MA	D	978 632-2555	12157
Panolam Industries Intl Inc (PA)	Shelton	CT	E	203 925-1556	3045	Bixby International Corp	Newburyport	MA	D	978 462-4100	10671
Pastanch LLC	Naugatuck	CT	E	203 720-9478	1979	Black Diamond Mfg & Engrg Inc	Georgetown	MA	F	978 352-6716	8905
Plastic Assembly Systems LLC	Bethany	CT	F	203 393-0639	97	Brockton Plastics	Brockton	MA	G	508 587-2290	7264
Plastic Design Intl Inc (PA)	Middletown	CT	E	860 632-2001	1771	BSP Group Inc	Brockton	MA	D	508 587-1101	7265
Plastic Forming Company Inc (PA)	Woodbridge	CT	E	203 397-1338	4382	Budgetcard Inc	Attleboro Falls	MA	F	508 695-8762	6080
Plastic Molding Technology	Seymour	CT	G	203 881-1811	2966	C & C Lamination	Chicopee	MA	G	413 594-6910	8012
Plastics and Concepts Conn Inc	Glastonbury	CT	G	860 657-9655	1294	Cado Manufacturing Inc	Fitchburg	MA	F	978 343-2989	8646
Polymeric Converting LLC	Enfield	CT	E	860 623-1335	1142	Cado Products Inc	Fitchburg	MA	E	978 343-2989	8647
Precision Engineered Pdts LLC	Wallingford	CT	E	203 265-3299	3840	Cardinal Comb & Brush Mfg Corp	Leominster	MA	F	978 537-6330	9647
Precision Plastic Products Inc	Portland	CT	F	860 342-2233	2821	Castle Plastics Inc	Leominster	MA	G	978 534-6220	9648
Prospect Products Incorporated	Newington	CT	E	860 666-0323	2320	Cavallero Plastics Inc	Pittsfield	MA	D	413 443-0925	11395
Pta Corporation (PA)	Oxford	CT	D	203 888-0585	2709	CDF Corporation (PA)	Plymouth	MA	D	508 747-5858	11454
Rcd Chambers Inc	Brookfield	CT	F	203 775-4416	536	CE Baird Corporation (PA)	Leominster	MA	F	978 368-7250	9649
Rogers Manufacturing Company	Rockfall	CT	D	860 346-8648	2915	Chatham Plastic Ventures Inc	Brockton	MA	F	518 392-5761	7268
Savetime Corporation	Bridgeport	CT	F	203 382-2991	368	Cheer Pack North America LLC	West Bridgewater	MA	F	508 927-7800	12968
Scan Tool & Mold Inc	Trumbull	CT	E	203 459-4950	3731	Chesterfield Products Inc	Chesterfield	MA	F	413 296-0066	7997
Schaeffler Aerospace USA Corp (DH)	Danbury	CT	B	203 744-2211	809	Clean Products LLC	Fall River	MA	F	508 676-9355	8529
SD Goodspeed Inc	Deep River	CT	C	860 526-3200	881	Cmt Materials Inc	Attleboro	MA	F	508 226-3901	6005
Seitz LLC	Torrington	CT	C	860 489-0476	3695	Comeau Consulting Inc	Leominster	MA	F	978 466-5870	9653
Selectives LLC	Thomaston	CT	G	860 585-1956	3628	Comprehensive Identification Products Inc	Burlington	MA			C
Shoham Manufacturing Inc	East Windsor	CT	F	860 623-1361	1085	781 229-8780				7354	
Siemon Company (PA)	Watertown	CT	A	860 945-4200	4029	Cool Gear International LLC (DH)	Plymouth	MA	E	508 830-3440	11455
Siftex Equipment Company	South Windsor	CT	E	860 289-8779	3179	Cordmaster Engineering Co Inc	North Adams	MA	E	413 664-9371	10805
Silgan Dispensing	Torrington	CT	F	860 283-2025	3696	Countrywide National Services	Walpole	MA	G	508 346-3286	12558
Silgan Holdings Inc (PA)	Stamford	CT	C	203 975-7110	3459	Creative Extrusion & Tech Inc	Brockton	MA	E	508 587-2290	7271
Silgan Plastics LLC	Deep River	CT	C	860 526-6300	882	Custom Extrusion Inc (HQ)	Sheffield	MA	E	413 229-8748	11797
Somerset Plastics Company Inc	Middletown	CT	E	860 635-1601	1782	Dela Incorporated (PA)	Haverhill	MA	E	978 372-7783	9091
Sound View Plastics LLC	Deep River	CT	F	860 322-4139	884	Design Mark Industries Inc	New Bedford	MA	D	800 451-3275	10585
Southpack LLC	New Britain	CT	E	860 224-2242	2061	Di-MO Manufacturing Inc	Middleboro	MA	G	508 947-2200	10357
Spartech LLC	Stamford	CT	C	203 327-6010	3467	Diamond Windows Doors Mfg Inc	Boston	MA	E	617 282-1688	6693
Spartech Polycast Inc	Stamford	CT	C	203 327-6010	3468	Donahue Industries Inc	Shrewsbury	MA	E	508 845-6501	11830
Standard Washer & Mat Inc	Manchester	CT	E	860 643-5125	1638	Dorel Juvenile Group Inc	Foxboro	MA	C	800 544-1108	8694
Stelray Plastic Products Inc	Ansonia	CT	E	203 735-2331	20	Dupont Packaging Inc	Holyoke	MA	F	413 552-0048	9251
STI Incorporated	Old Saybrook	CT	E	860 577-7000	2663	E F Inc	Gardner	MA	F	978 630-3800	8885
Super Seal Company LLC	Stratford	CT	F	203 378-5015	3579	Eclipse Products Inc	Leominster	MA	F	978 343-8600	9661
Superior Plas Extrusion Co Inc (PA)	Putnam	CT	E	860 963-1976	2877	Elm Industries Inc	West Springfield	MA	E	413 734-7762	13023
Swpc Plastics LLC (DH)	Deep River	CT	C	860 526-9800	885	Entegris Inc (PA)	Billerica	MA	A	978 436-6500	6443
T & A Industries LLC	Bloomfield	CT	G	860 309-9211	212	Essemtec Usa LLC	Waltham	MA	F	856 218-1131	12666
Technical Industries Inc (PA)	Torrington	CT	B	860 489-2160	3698	F & D Plastics Inc (PA)	Leominster	MA	E	978 668-5140	9662
Technology Plastics LLC	Terryville	CT	F	860 583-1590	3611	F & M Tool & Plastics Inc	Leominster	MA	B	978 840-1897	9663
The Gilman Brothers Company	Gilman	CT	D	860 889-8444	1268	Fall River Tool & Die Co Inc	Fall River	MA	F	508 674-4621	8550
Trento Group LLC	East Hartford	CT	G	860 623-1361	1029	Fiberglass Building Pdts Inc	Halifax	MA	D	847 650-3045	9021
United Plastics Tech Inc	Madison	CT	F	860 224-1110	1575	Fibertec Inc	Bridgewater	MA	D	508 697-5100	7229
Upc LLC	Meriden	CT	F	877 466-1137	1711	Filtrona Extrusion of Massachusetts LLC	Athol	MA	C	978 249-5343	5979
Vanguard Plastics Corporation	Southington	CT	E	860 628-4736	3239	First Plastics Corp	Leominster	MA	F	978 537-0367	9664
Vision Technical Molding	Manchester	CT	G	860 783-5050	1640	Flagraphics Inc	Somerville	MA	E	617 776-7549	11874
Vision Technical Molding LLC	Manchester	CT	C	860 647-7787	1641	Fort Hill Sign Products Inc	Hopedale	MA	G	781 321-4320	9297
Watertown Plastics Inc	Watertown	CT	E	860 274-7535	4038	Fraen Corporation (PA)	Reading	MA	C	781 205-5300	11601
Wepco Plastics Inc	Middlefield	CT	E	860 349-3407	1731	Fusion Optix Inc	Woburn	MA	E	781 995-0805	13572
Westbrook Manufacturing LLC	Ivoryton	CT	F	860 767-2460	1534	G&F Medical Inc	Fiskdale	MA	E	978 560-2622	8638
175 Pioneer Drive LLC	Leominster	MA	B	978 840-1897	9629	G&F Precision Molding Inc	Danvers	MA	G	978 560-2622	8188
34 Tower Street Inc	Shirley	MA	E	978 425-2311	11812	G&F Precision Molding Inc (PA)	Fiskdale	MA	D	508 347-9132	8639
3dfortify Inc	Boston	MA	F	857 274-0483	6500	Globe Composite Solutions Ltd	Stoughton	MA	D	781 871-3700	12211
Aaron Industries Corp	Leominster	MA	E	978 534-6135	9630	Governor Supply Co	Lancaster	MA	G	978 870-6888	9526
Accellent Acquisition Corp	Wilmington	MA	A	978 570-6900	13370	Great Hill Industries Inc (PA)	Boston	MA	C	617 262-4314	6771
Accellent Holdings Corp	Wilmington	MA	A	978 570-6900	13371	Gregory Manufacturing Inc	Holyoke	MA	D	413 536-5432	9257
Accutech Packaging Inc	Foxboro	MA	D	508 543-3800	8689	Gregstrom Corporation	Woburn	MA	D	781 935-6600	13578
Accutech Packaging Inc	Mansfield	MA	F	508 543-3800	10035	Grove Products Inc	Leominster	MA	F	978 534-5188	9668
Advance Plastics Inc	Oxford	MA	G	508 987-7235	11248	Gzsl Corp	North Attleboro	MA	E	508 695-0727	10872
Advanced Prototypes & Molding	Leominster	MA	G	978 534-0584	9632	Hapco Inc	Hanover	MA	E	781 826-8801	9034
Air-Tite Holders Inc	North Adams	MA	F	413 664-2730	10802	Hardigg Industries LLC (HQ)	South Deerfield	MA	C	413 665-2163	11924
Alsco Industries Inc	Sturbridge	MA	D	508 347-1199	12248	Hartwell 131 Holdings Corp	Lexington	MA	E	781 328-3220	9746
Altium Packaging LLC	Franklin	MA	D	508 520-8800	8816	Hi-Tech Mold & Tool Inc	Pittsfield	MA	C	413 443-9184	11401
Altium Packaging LP	Marlborough	MA	E	508 485-2109	10107	Hillside Plastics Inc	Turners Falls	MA	C	413 863-2222	12448
Americad Technology Corp	Norwood	MA	E	781 551-8220	11159	Hytex Industries Inc	Randolph	MA	E	781 963-4400	11565
Anchor Plastics Inc	Dudley	MA	G	508 753-2169	8316	I G Marston Company	Holbrook	MA	F	781 767-2894	9174
Andrew Rolden PC	Ayer	MA	G	978 391-4655	6172	ID Graphics Group Inc	South Easton	MA	E	508 238-8500	11945
Apex Resource Technologies Inc	Pittsfield	MA	D	413 442-1414	11390	Illinois Tool Works Inc	Westminster	MA	C	978 874-0151	13271

SIC

	CITY	ST	EMP	PHONE	ENTRY#
Injected Solutions Inc	Lanesborough	MA	F	413 499-5800	9532
Injection Molding Entps LLC	Littleton	MA	F	978 339-4535	9820
Injectronics Corporation	Clinton	MA	D	978 365-1200	8078
Innovative Mold Solutions Inc	Leominster	MA	E	978 840-1503	9671
Innovative Tooling Company Inc	Lenox	MA	F	413 637-1031	9625
Integrity Mold Inc	Gardner	MA	F	978 669-0093	8891
Jam Plastics Inc	Leominster	MA	E	978 537-2570	9672
JMS Manufacturing Co Inc	Taunton	MA	G	508 675-1141	12345
K and C Plastics Inc	Leominster	MA	F	978 537-0605	9673
Knobby Krafters Inc	Attleboro	MA	F	508 222-7272	6029
Korolath of New England Inc	Hudson	MA	F	978 562-7366	9381
Krest Products Corp	Leominster	MA	E	978 537-1244	9674
Lacerta Group Inc	Mansfield	MA	G	508 339-3312	10063
Lacerta Group LLC (PA)	Mansfield	MA	C	508 339-3312	10064
Lakewood Industries Inc	Pittsfield	MA	F	413 499-3550	11404
Lamson and Goodnow LLC	Shelburne Falls	MA	F	413 625-0201	11806
Lansen Mold Co Inc	Hancock	MA	F	413 443-5328	9025
Lar Plastics LLC	Winchester	MA	B	617 860-2020	13485
LD Plastics Inc	Brockton	MA	E	508 584-7651	7289
Leaktite Corporation (DH)	Leominster	MA	E	978 537-8000	9676
Lee Plastics Inc	Sterling	MA	E	978 422-7611	12166
Little Kids Inc	Seekonk	MA	D	800 545-5437	11780
Lyman Conrad (PA)	South Hadley	MA	F	413 538-8200	11965
M & P Machine Company Inc	Stoughton	MA	F	781 344-5888	12218
Mac Lean-Fogg Company	Lexington	MA	D	781 328-3220	9762
Mack Prototype Inc	Gardner	MA	E	978 632-3700	8893
Macneill Engineering Co Inc	Westborough	MA	E	508 481-8830	13118
Magnus Molding Inc	Pittsfield	MA	E	413 443-1192	11408
Mair-Mac Machine Company Inc	Brockton	MA	F	508 895-9001	7294
Mar-Lee Companies Inc	Fitchburg	MA	G	978 343-9600	8661
Marland Mold Inc	Pittsfield	MA	E	413 443-4481	11409
Mauser Packg Solutions Holdg	Leominster	MA	F	978 728-5000	9682
Mayfield Plastics Inc	Holyoke	MA	E	508 865-8150	9267
Mayhew Basque Plastics LLC	Westminster	MA	F	978 537-5219	13273
Micron Products Inc	Fitchburg	MA	F	978 345-5000	8665
Midstatemolding LLC	Franklin	MA	F	508 520-0011	8852
Milacron Marketing Company LLC	Rowley	MA	C	978 238-7100	11679
Mill Valley Molding Inc	West Hatfield	MA	E	413 247-9313	13005
Millennium Plastics Inc	North Chelmsford	MA	F	978 372-4822	10984
Millham LLC	Sterling	MA	F	978 422-8621	12168
MJW Mass Inc	Winchester	MA	D	781 721-0332	13488
Modern Mold and Tool Inc (PA)	Pittsfield	MA	E	413 443-1192	11412
Molded Plastics Engrg Inc	Rowley	MA	G	978 948-7153	11680
Moldmaster Engineering Inc	Pittsfield	MA	E	413 442-5793	11413
National Vinyl LLC	Chicopee	MA	E	413 420-0548	8051
Netco Extruded Plastics Inc	Hudson	MA	E	978 562-3485	9395
Neu-Tool Design Inc	Wilmington	MA	E	978 658-5881	13437
Nevron Plastics Inc	Saugus	MA	F	781 233-1310	11763
New England Business Svc Inc (HQ)	Townsend	MA	D	978 448-6111	12441
New England Plastics Corp	New Bedford	MA	D	508 998-3111	10630
New England Plastics Corp (PA)	Woburn	MA	E	781 933-6004	13623
Newell Brands Inc	East Longmeadow MA		F	413 526-5150	8388
Northeast Plastics Inc	Wakefield	MA	F	781 245-5512	12523
Northern Products Inc	Leominster	MA	F	978 840-3383	9687
Northern Tool Mfg Co Inc	Springfield	MA	F	413 732-5549	12117
Ntp/Republic Clear Thru Corp	Holyoke	MA	F	413 493-6800	9272
Nypro Inc (HQ)	Clinton	MA	A	978 365-9721	8087
Nypro Inc	Devens	MA	B	978 784-2006	8283
Nypromold Inc (PA)	Clinton	MA	D	978 365-4547	8089
Ocean and Common Inc	Leominster	MA	E	978 537-4102	9689
Orbit Plastics Corp	Danvers	MA	E	978 465-5300	8214
Orion Enterprises Inc (HQ)	North Andover	MA	C	913 342-1653	10847
Pen Ro Mold and Tool Inc	Pittsfield	MA	E	413 499-0464	11416
Pep Industries LLC	Attleboro	MA	E	508 226-5600	6046
Pepperell Braiding Company Inc (PA)	Pepperell	MA	E	978 433-2133	11387
Pexco LLC	Athol	MA	C	978 249-5343	5982
Pilgrim Innovative Plas LLC	Plymouth	MA	F	508 732-0297	11472
Pioneer Packaging Inc (PA)	Chicopee	MA	D	413 378-6930	8054
Pittsfield Plastics Engrg LLC	Pittsfield	MA	D	413 442-0067	11419
Placon Corporation	West Springfield	MA	D	413 785-1553	13041
Plastic Assembly Corporation	Ayer	MA	F	978 772-4725	6191
Plastic Concepts Inc	North Billerica	MA	E	978 663-7996	10943
Plastic Distrs Fabricators Inc	Haverhill	MA	E	978 374-0300	9121
Plastic Molding Mfg Inc (PA)	Hudson	MA	E	978 567-1000	9400
Plastic Monofil Co Ltd	Medway	MA	F	732 629-7701	10311
Plastic Packaging Corporation	West Springfield	MA	C	413 785-1553	13042
Plastican Inc	Leominster	MA	A	978 728-5000	9696
Pobco Inc	Worcester	MA	F	508 791-6376	13771
Poly-Cel Inc	Acton	MA	F	508 229-8310	5761
Poly6 Technologies Inc	Burlington	MA	F	339 234-9300	7412
Polymer Corporation	Palmer	MA	E	413 267-5524	11282
Polymer Corporation (HQ)	Rockland	MA	D	781 871-4606	11656
Precision Engineered Pdts LLC (DH)	Attleboro	MA	G		6051
Pro Pel Plastech Inc (PA)	South Deerfield	MA	E	413 665-3379	11928
QEP Co Inc	Clinton	MA	G	978 368-8991	8090
Radical Plastics Inc	Marblehead	MA	G	781 631-7924	10093
Rainbow Visions Inc	Boston	MA	E	617 787-4084	6995
REc Manufacturing Corp	Hopedale	MA	E	508 634-7999	9301
Reeves Company Inc	Attleboro	MA	F	508 222-2877	6053
RES-Tech Corporation (HQ)	Hudson	MA	E	978 567-1000	9406
Restech Plastic Molding LLC (DH)	Hudson	MA	E	978 567-1000	9407
Rj Fountain Group Inc	Franklin	MA	F	508 429-9950	8859
Robert E Glidden	Hyannis	MA	G	508 775-6812	9447
Saint-Gobain Prfmce Plas Corp	East Taunton	MA	D	508 823-7701	8412
Saint-Gobain Prfmce Plas Corp	Worcester	MA	C	508 852-3072	13792
Seabury Splash Inc	Plymouth	MA	E	508 830-3440	11477
Sencorp Inc	Hyannis	MA	C	508 771-9400	9450
Shelpak Plastics Inc	Middleton	MA	G	781 844-2046	10393
Sinicon Plastics Inc	Dalton	MA	E	413 684-5290	8155
Slideways Inc	Worcester	MA	E	508 854-0799	13803
SMC Ltd	Devens	MA	D	978 422-6800	8287
Sonicron Systems Corporation	Westfield	MA	E	413 562-5218	13309
Sonolite Plastics Corporation	Gloucester	MA	F	978 281-0662	8959
Spectrum Plastics Group	Paxton	MA	G	203 736-5230	11291
Spirit Foodservice LLC	Andover	MA	C	978 964-1551	5925
SRC Medical Inc	Hanover	MA	D	781 826-9100	9042
Stergis Aluminum Products Corp	Attleboro	MA	E	508 455-0661	6065
Sterilite Corporation (PA)	Townsend	MA	C	978 597-1000	12442
Sterling Manufacturing Co Inc	Lancaster	MA	D	978 368-8733	9530
Streamline Plastics Co Inc	East Longmeadow MA		E	718 401-4000	8396
Stuart Allyn Co Inc	Pittsfield	MA	G	413 443-7306	11425
Super Brush LLC	Springfield	MA	D	413 543-1442	12136
Toner Plastics Inc	East Longmeadow MA		E	413 789-1300	8399
Trans Form Plastics Corp	Danvers	MA	E	978 777-1440	8226
Trexel Inc (PA)	Wilmington	MA	F	781 932-0202	13471
Tyca Corporation (PA)	Clinton	MA	E	978 612-0002	8093
United Comb & Novelty Corp (PA)	Leominster	MA	D	978 537-2096	9712
United Plastic Fabricating Inc (PA)	North Andover	MA	D	978 975-4520	10855
Universal Plastics Corporation (PA)	Holyoke	MA	E	413 592-4791	9286
Urthpact Innovations LLC	Leominster	MA	F	978 847-9747	9713
Vantec LLC	North Attleboro	MA	F	508 726-2830	10891
Vaupell Industrial Plas Inc	Agawam	MA	D	413 233-3801	5814
Viant Chicopee Inc	Chicopee	MA	C	413 612-2100	8068
W M Gulliksen Mfg Co Inc (PA)	South Weymouth	MA	F	617 323-5750	11979
Waddington North America Inc	Chelmsford	MA	C	978 256-6551	7970
Walter Drake Incorporated (PA)	Holyoke	MA	G	413 536-5463	9290
Watts Sea Tech Inc	North Andover	MA	E	978 688-1811	10860
Web Industries Inc (PA)	Marlborough	MA	G	508 898-2988	10234
Xponent Global Inc	Hudson	MA	E	978 562-3485	9426
Altium Packaging LLC	Portland	ME	E	207 772-7468	5177
Beacon Sales Acquisition Inc	Portland	ME	F	207 797-7950	5185
Conform Automotive LLC	Auburn	ME	B	207 784-1118	4424
Cpk Manufacturing LLC	Augusta	ME	F	207 622-6229	4470
Flotation Technologies LLC	Biddeford	ME	D	207 282-7749	4565
Formed Fiber Technologies Inc	Auburn	ME	A	207 784-1118	4433
G & G Products LLC	Kennebunk	ME	F	207 985-9100	4925
G Pro Industrial Services	Biddeford	ME	G	207 766-1671	4567
Genplex Inc	Skowhegan	ME	G	207 474-3500	5467
Jarden LLC	East Wilton	ME	F	207 645-2574	4741
K & R Holdings Inc	Portland	ME	C	207 797-7950	5230
Maine Container LLC	Poland	ME	E	603 888-1315	5161
Maine Manufacturing LLC	Sanford	ME	D	207 324-1754	5398
Maine Mold & Machine Inc	Hartford	ME	C	207 388-2732	4876
Mathews Brothers Company (PA)	Belfast	ME	C	207 338-3360	4535
Nursery Supplies Inc	Cornish	ME	G	207 625-9373	4706
Packgen Inc	Auburn	ME	E	207 784-4195	4449
Panolam Surface Systems	Auburn	ME	F	203 925-1556	4451
Paradigm Operating Company LLC	Portland	ME	C	877 994-6369	5255
Portland Plastic Pipe	South Portland	ME	G	207 774-0364	5512
R&V Industries Inc	Sanford	ME	E	207 324-5200	5408
Riverbend Fiberglass Inc	Dixfield	ME	G	207 562-7103	4727
Thermoformed Plastics Neng LLC	Biddeford	ME	F	207 286-1775	4591
Villeroy & Boch Usa Inc	Kittery	ME	F	207 439-6440	4940
Acw Plastic Products Inc	Concord	NH	F	603 227-9540	14112
Advantage Mold Inc	Londonderry	NH	G	603 647-6678	14728
Albany International Corp (PA)	Rochester	NH	D	603 330-5850	15464
Alex & Ryan Design LLC	Manchester	NH	F	603 518-8650	14808
Altium Packaging LLC	Londonderry	NH	D	603 624-6055	14731
Ambix Manufacturing Inc	Albany	NH	F	603 452-5247	13849
AP Extrusion Inc	Salem	NH	F	603 890-1086	15507
App-Jwb Inc	Concord	NH	E	603 227-9540	14113
Bayhead Products Corporation	Dover	NH	E	603 742-3000	14218
Bb Plastic Fabrication	Manchester	NH	G	603 622-9882	14818
Burbak Companies	Wilton	NH	D	603 654-2291	15703
Comstock Industries Inc	Meredith	NH	E	603 279-7045	14968
Dunn Industries Inc	Manchester	NH	E	603 666-4800	14845

	CITY	ST	EMP	PHONE	ENTRY#
Eptam Plastics Ltd (PA)	Northfield	NH	C	603 286-8009	15264
Faber Polivol LLC (DH)	Salem	NH	G	603 681-0484	15523
Fbn Plastics Inc	Salem	NH	G	603 894-4326	15524
Freudenberg-Nok Gnrl Prtnrshp	Londonderry	NH	F	603 628-7023	14752
Genfoot America Inc	Littleton	NH	D	603 575-5114	14719
GI Plastek LLC	Wolfeboro	NH	B	603 569-5100	15731
GI Plastek Ltd Partnership	Wolfeboro	NH	E	603 569-5100	15732
Granite State Plastics Inc	Hudson	NH	E	603 669-6715	14502
Hbn Shoe LLC	Salem	NH	G	603 622-0272	15536
Hcp Packaging Usa Inc	Hinsdale	NH	C	603 256-3141	14444
Hy-Ten Die & Development Corp	Milford	NH	E	603 673-1611	15029
Insulfab Plastics Inc	Franklin	NH	F	603 934-2770	14320
Janco Inc (PA)	Rollinsford	NH	D	603 742-0043	15495
Kalwall Corporation	Bow	NH	C	603 224-6881	14002
Kalwall Corporation (PA)	Manchester	NH	B	603 627-3861	14870
Keller Products Incorporated (PA)	Manchester	NH	E	603 627-7887	14871
Mills Industries Inc	Laconia	NH	E	603 528-4217	14659
Mrpc Northeast LLC	Hudson	NH	E	603 880-3616	14530
Newdtc LLC	Salem	NH	F	603 893-0992	15549
North American Plastics Ltd	Manchester	NH	E	603 644-1660	14902
Pbs Plastics Inc	Barrington	NH	F	603 868-1717	13915
Pelham Plastics Inc	Pelham	NH	D	603 886-7226	15293
Plan Tech Inc	Loudon	NH	E	603 783-4767	14798
Plastic Industries Inc (HQ)	Nashua	NH	D	603 888-1315	15149
Plastic Techniques Inc	Goffstown	NH	E	603 622-5570	14356
Plp Composite Technologies	Fitzwilliam	NH	E	603 585-9100	14315
Poly-Ject Inc	Amherst	NH	E	603 882-6570	13884
Precision Letter LLC	Manchester	NH	F	603 625-9625	14913
Precision Tool & Molding LLC	Derry	NH	F	603 437-6685	14206
Presby Plastics Inc	Whitefield	NH	E	603 837-3826	15700
Proto Labs Inc	Nashua	NH	C	763 479-2679	15152
Proto Part Inc	Hudson	NH	F	603 883-6531	14537
PSI Molded Plastics NH Inc	Wolfeboro	NH	D	603 569-5100	15735
Rehrig Pacific Company	Nottingham	NH	C	603 490-8722	15277
Summit Packaging Systems LLC (PA)	Manchester	NH	B	603 669-5410	14937
Talbot Hill Holdings Corp	Swanzey	NH	E	603 357-2523	15646
Tech Nh Inc (PA)	Merrimack	NH	D	603 424-4404	15007
W K Hillquist Inc	Hudson	NH	E	603 595-7790	14559
Welch Fluorocarbon Inc	Dover	NH	E	603 742-0164	14260
Worthen Industries Inc	Nashua	NH	E	978 365-6345	15190
Accurate Molded Products Inc	Warwick	RI	E	401 739-2400	16775
American Cord & Webbing Co Inc	Woonsocket	RI	E	401 762-5500	16948
Applied Plastics Tech Inc	Bristol	RI	E	401 253-0200	15753
Aspects Inc	Warren	RI	E	401 247-1854	16751
Blackstone Molding Inc	Woonsocket	RI	E	401 765-6700	16950
Bms Plastics Inc	Pawtucket	RI	F	401 465-3960	16351
Buick LLC	Hope Valley	RI	E	401 539-2432	16066
Cabinet Gallery Ltd (PA)	Woonsocket	RI	G	401 762-4300	16952
Cadence Mfg Inc	Cranston	RI	E	508 746-6082	15839
Capco Plastics Inc (PA)	Providence	RI	E	401 272-3833	16494
Case Hard	Little Compton	RI	G	401 635-8201	16159
Clear Carbon & Components Inc	Bristol	RI	E	401 254-5085	15758
Continental Plas & Packg Inc	Lincoln	RI	F	781 932-1115	16128
Custom Design Incorporated	North Kingstown	RI	E	401 294-0200	16243
Custom Molded Products Inc	North Providence	RI	G	401 464-9991	16298
Eagle Motors Inc	Harrisville	RI	F	401 568-2580	16065
Edward F Briggs Disposal Inc	East Greenwich	RI	G	401 294-6391	15984
Fielding Manufacturing Inc	Cranston	RI	D	401 461-0400	15860
G-Form LLC	North Smithfield	RI	E	401 769-0994	16323
HI Tech Profiles Inc	Ashaway	RI	E	401 377-2040	15741
International Packaging Corporation (PA)	Pawtucket	RI	A	401 724-1600	16376
Iselann - Moss Industries Inc	Cranston	RI	E	401 463-5950	15877
Island Mooring Supplies LLC	Prudence Island	RI	F	401 447-5387	16650
Jade Engineered Plastics Inc	Warren	RI	D	401 253-4440	16759
Jay Packaging Group Inc (DH)	Warwick	RI	D	401 244-1300	16827
K & C Industries Inc	Smithfield	RI	F	508 520-4600	16720
Liftbag Usa Inc	North Kingstown	RI	F	401 884-8801	16267
Mars 2000 Inc	Providence	RI	A	401 421-5275	16558
Mastercast Ltd	Pawtucket	RI	F	401 726-3100	16384
Matrix I LLC	East Providence	RI	F	401 434-3040	16030
Modern Plastics	Warwick	RI	F	401 732-0415	16839
Morris Transparent Box Co	East Providence	RI	F	401 438-6116	16032
Packaging Concepts Ltd	Rumford	RI	C	401 334-0344	16675
Parkinson Machinery & Manufacturing Corp	Woonsocket	RI	C	401 762-2100	16971
Parkinson Technologies Inc	Woonsocket	RI	D	401 762-2100	16972
Perry Blackburne Inc	North Providence	RI	F	401 231-7200	16307
Response Technologies LLC	Coventry	RI	E	401 585-5918	15820
Rihani Plastics Inc	Cranston	RI	F	401 942-7393	15907
Scarborough Faire Inc	Pawtucket	RI	E	401 724-4200	16416
Silgan Dspnsing Systems Sltrsv (DH)	Slatersville	RI	F	401 767-2400	16683
Subsalve USA LLC	North Kingstown	RI	F	401 884-8801	16282
Tri-Mack Plastics Mfg Corp	Bristol	RI	D	401 253-2140	15784

	CITY	ST	EMP	PHONE	ENTRY#
Worldwide Tooling LLC	Lincoln	RI	F	401 334-9806	16158
Altium Packaging LLC	South Burlington	VT	E	802 658-6588	17569
Arlington Industries Inc	Arlington	VT	E	802 375-6139	16985
Astenjohnson Inc	Williston	VT	D	802 658-2040	17722
Carris Financial Corp (PA)	Proctor	VT	F	802 773-9111	17456
Carris Reels Inc (HQ)	Proctor	VT	F	802 773-9111	17457
Dolliver Corporation	Williston	VT	G	802 879-0072	17728
K & E Plastics Inc	Bennington	VT	E	802 375-0011	17043
Kp Building Products Inc	Williston	VT	D	866 850-4447	17737
Mack Group Inc (PA)	Arlington	VT	B	802 375-2511	16988
Mack Molding Company Inc	Arlington	VT	C	802 375-0500	16989
Mack Molding Company Inc (HQ)	Arlington	VT	C	802 375-2511	16990
National Hanger Company Inc	North Bennington	VT	D	800 426-4377	17410
Nolato Gw Inc (HQ)	Bethel	VT	B	802 234-9941	17060
Nolato Gw Inc	South Royalton	VT	D	802 763-2194	17612
Precision Composites VT LLC	Lyndonville	VT	E	802 626-5900	17320
Progressive Plastics Inc	Williamstown	VT	E	802 433-1563	17717
Questech Corporation (PA)	Rutland	VT	E	802 773-1228	17505
T & M Enterprises Inc	Shaftsbury	VT	G	802 447-0601	17553
Teknor Apex Co	Saint Albans	VT	F	802 524-7704	17534

31 LEATHER AND LEATHER PRODUCTS

3111 Leather tanning and finishing

	CITY	ST	EMP	PHONE	ENTRY#
Hat Attack Inc (PA)	Stamford	CT	E	718 994-1000	3368
Alliance Leather Inc	Peabody	MA	F	978 531-6771	11295
Hawtan Leathers LLC	Newburyport	MA	C	978 465-3791	10687
Slattery Bros Inc	Westwood	MA	G	617 269-3025	13318
Gallery Leather Direct Inc	Trenton	ME	F	207 667-9474	5554
Gallery Leather Mfg Inc	Trenton	ME	G	207 667-9474	5555
Tasman Industries Inc	Hartland	ME	G	207 938-4491	4878
Tasman Leather Group LLC	Hartland	ME	C	207 553-3700	4879
Lotuff Leather	Providence	RI	G	888 763-2247	16555

3131 Footwear cut stock

	CITY	ST	EMP	PHONE	ENTRY#
Catskill Gran Countertops Inc	Newington	CT	F	860 667-1555	2279
Rm Dissolution Co LLC	Cheshire	CT	E	203 699-9125	615
Barbour Corporation (PA)	Brockton	MA	D	508 583-8200	7260
Counter Culture	Saugus	MA	G	781 439-9810	11755
Counteredge LLC	Waltham	MA	F	781 891-0050	12643
Furnished Quarters LLC	Cambridge	MA	F	212 367-9400	7577
Healthquarters Inc	Beverly	MA	F	978 922-4490	6354
Jones & Vining Incorporated (PA)	Brockton	MA	E	508 232-7470	7287
Leo F Maciver Co Inc	Brockton	MA	G	508 583-2501	7290
Macneill Engineering Co Inc	Westborough	MA	E	508 481-8830	13118
Montello Heel Mfg Inc	Brockton	MA	F	508 586-0603	7296
North American Chemical Co	Lawrence	MA	G	978 687-9500	9589
Sx Industries Inc (PA)	Stoughton	MA	F	781 828-7111	12241
Vibram Corporation (HQ)	Concord	MA	F	978 318-0000	8138
Enefco International Inc (PA)	Auburn	ME	E	207 514-7218	4428
Lunder Manufacturing Inc	Saco	ME	E	207 284-5961	5371

3143 Men's footwear, except athletic

	CITY	ST	EMP	PHONE	ENTRY#
Bh Shoe Holdings Inc (HQ)	Greenwich	CT	E	203 661-2424	1318
Fisher Footwear LLC	Greenwich	CT	F	203 302-2800	1330
HH Brown Shoe Company Inc (DH)	Greenwich	CT	F	203 661-2424	1334
Mbf Holdings LLC	Greenwich	CT	F	203 302-2812	1341
Mf-TFC LLC	Greenwich	CT	F	203 302-2820	1342
Allbirds Inc	Boston	MA	F	617 430-4500	6535
Allbirds Inc	Boston	MA	F	857 990-1373	6536
Allbirds Inc	Cambridge	MA	F	617 315-4210	7476
Allbirds Inc	Hingham	MA	F	781 208-6094	9140
Allbirds Inc	Wrentham	MA	F	774 847-1330	13836
C & J Clark America Inc (DH)	Waltham	MA	B	617 964-1222	12617
C & J Clark Latin America	Waltham	MA	F	617 243-4100	12618
HH Brown Shoe Company Inc	Andover	MA	F	978 933-4700	5886
Reebok International Ltd LLC (HQ)	Boston	MA	B	781 401-5000	7002
Saucony Inc (DH)	Waltham	MA	C	617 824-6000	12776
Falcon Performance Ftwr LLC	Auburn	ME	G	207 784-9186	4431
Footwear Specialties Inc	Biddeford	ME	G	207 284-5003	4566
L L Bean Inc	Brunswick	ME	F	207 725-0300	4647
New Balance Athletics Inc	Norridgewock	ME	E	207 634-3033	5103
Rancourt & Co Shoecrafters Inc	Lewiston	ME	F	855 999-3544	4989
Timberland LLC (HQ)	Stratham	NH	B	603 772-9500	15641

3144 Women's footwear, except athletic

	CITY	ST	EMP	PHONE	ENTRY#
Aj Casey LLC	Norwalk	CT	G	203 226-5961	2460
Dooney & Bourke Inc (HQ)	Norwalk	CT	E	203 853-7515	2492
Fisher Footwear LLC	Greenwich	CT	F	203 302-2800	1330
Fisher Sigerson Morrison LLC	Greenwich	CT	F	203 302-2800	1331
HH Brown Shoe Company Inc (DH)	Greenwich	CT	F	203 661-2424	1334
Mf-TFC LLC	Greenwich	CT	F	203 302-2820	1342

SIC

	CITY	ST	EMP	PHONE	ENTRY#
Cardinal Shoe Corporation	Lawrence	MA	F	978 686-9706	9546
HH Brown Shoe Company Inc	Andover	MA	F	978 933-4700	5886
Modern Shoe Company LLC	Hyde Park	MA	F	617 333-7470	9464
Reebok International Ltd LLC (HQ)	Boston	MA	B	781 401-5000	7002
Saucony Inc (DH)	Waltham	MA	C	617 824-6000	12776
Footwear Specialties Inc	Biddeford	ME	G	207 284-5003	4566
L L Bean Inc	Brunswick	ME	F	207 725-0300	4647
New Balance Athletics Inc	Norridgewock	ME	E	207 634-3033	5103
Colby Footwear Inc	Somersworth	NH	F	603 332-2283	15612
Timberland LLC (HQ)	Stratham	NH	B	603 772-9500	15641
White Mountain Intl LLC (PA)	Lisbon	NH	E	603 838-6694	14711

3149 Footwear, except rubber, nec

	CITY	ST	EMP	PHONE	ENTRY#
Acushnet Company (DH)	Fairhaven	MA	B	508 979-2000	8504
Barry Manufacturing Co Inc	Lynn	MA	E	781 598-1055	9962
New Balance Athletics Inc	Lawrence	MA	E	978 685-8400	9586
Reebok International Ltd LLC (HQ)	Boston	MA	B	781 401-5000	7002
Saucony Inc (DH)	Waltham	MA	C	617 824-6000	12776
Stride Rite Corporation (HQ)	Waltham	MA	B	617 824-6000	12783
Tommy Hilfiger Footwear Inc	Lexington	MA	E	617 824-6000	9788
Warrior Sports Inc (DH)	Boston	MA	C	800 968-7845	7113
Callaway Golf Ball Oprtons Inc	Richmond	ME	C	207 737-4324	5320
New Balance Athletics Inc	Norridgewock	ME	E	207 634-3033	5103
New Balance Athletics Inc	Skowhegan	ME	F	207 474-2042	5474

3161 Luggage

	CITY	ST	EMP	PHONE	ENTRY#
Calzone Ltd (PA)	Bridgeport	CT	E	203 367-5766	309
Case Concepts Intl LLC	Stamford	CT	E	203 883-8602	3303
Commercial Sewing Inc	Torrington	CT	C	860 482-5509	3675
Dooney & Bourke Inc (HQ)	Norwalk	CT	E	203 853-7515	2492
Fabrique Ltd (PA)	Branford	CT	G	203 481-2266	255
Manup LLC	Norwalk	CT	E	203 588-9861	2533
Smithfamily1938 LLC	Enfield	CT	G	424 341-8876	1153
Ats Cases Inc	Northborough	MA	G	508 393-9110	11089
Blw Holdings Inc (PA)	Fairhaven	MA	C	508 994-4000	8507
Brahmin Leather Works LLC	Fairhaven	MA	C	509 994-4000	8508
Currys Leather Shop Inc	Randolph	MA	G	781 963-0679	11554
Dance It Up Inc	North Grafton	MA	F	508 839-1648	11021
Hartmann Incorporated	Mansfield	MA	E	508 851-1400	10054
HI Operating LLC (DH)	Mansfield	MA	E	508 851-1400	10056
Byer Manufacturing Company	Bernard	ME	E	207 866-2171	4547
C B P Corp (PA)	Arundel	ME	F	207 985-9767	4409
L L Bean Inc	Brunswick	ME	F	207 725-0300	4647
Sea Bags Inc	Freeport	ME	F	207 939-3679	4803
Samsonite Company Stores LLC	Warren	RI	F	401 247-3301	16768
Van & Company Inc	Pawtucket	RI	F	401 722-9829	16428
Porta-Brace Inc	Bennington	VT	F	802 442-8171	17055

3171 Women's handbags and purses

	CITY	ST	EMP	PHONE	ENTRY#
Dooney & Bourke Inc (HQ)	Norwalk	CT	E	203 853-7515	2492
Blw Holdings Inc (PA)	Fairhaven	MA	C	508 994-4000	8507
Brahmin Leather Works LLC	Fairhaven	MA	C	509 994-4000	8508
W D C Holdings Inc	Attleboro	MA	E	508 699-4412	6073

3172 Personal leather goods, nec

	CITY	ST	EMP	PHONE	ENTRY#
Dooney & Bourke Inc (HQ)	Norwalk	CT	E	203 853-7515	2492
Mayan Corporation	Norwalk	CT	F	203 854-4711	2534
Alliance Leather Inc	Peabody	MA	F	978 531-6771	11295
Blw Holdings Inc (PA)	Fairhaven	MA	C	508 994-4000	8507
Brahmin Leather Works LLC	Fairhaven	MA	C	509 994-4000	8508
Charles Thomae & Son Inc	Attleboro	MA	F	508 222-0785	6001
Currys Leather Shop Inc	Randolph	MA	G	781 963-0679	11554
Fuller Box Co Inc (PA)	North Attleboro	MA	D	508 695-2525	10871
HI Operating LLC (DH)	Mansfield	MA	E	508 851-1400	10056
Miles Kedex Co Inc	Westminster	MA	E	978 874-1403	13274
Montello Heel Mfg Inc	Brockton	MA	E	508 586-0603	7296
Strong Group Inc (PA)	Gloucester	MA	D	978 281-3300	8960
Valkyrie Company Inc	Worcester	MA	F	508 756-3633	13818
Valkyrie Company Inc (PA)	Worcester	MA	D	508 756-3633	13819
Perfect Fit	Corinna	ME	F	207 278-3333	4703
Appalachian Stitching Co LLC (PA)	Littleton	NH	F	603 444-4422	14714
Jewel Case Corporation	Providence	RI	B	401 943-1400	16549
Numaco Packaging LLC	East Providence	RI	E	401 438-4952	16035
Perry Blackburne Inc	North Providence	RI	F	401 231-7200	16307

3199 Leather goods, nec

	CITY	ST	EMP	PHONE	ENTRY#
A X M S Inc	Woodbury	CT	G	203 263-5046	4384
Waterbury Leatherworks Co	Danbury	CT	G	203 755-7789	835
Currys Leather Shop Inc	Randolph	MA	G	781 963-0679	11554
Ebinger Brothers Lea Co Inc	Ipswich	MA	F	978 356-5701	9484
Safariland LLC	Dalton	MA	E	413 684-3104	8153
Strong Group Inc (PA)	Gloucester	MA	D	978 281-3300	8960
Westfield Whip Mfg Co	Westfield	MA	F	413 568-8244	13223

	CITY	ST	EMP	PHONE	ENTRY#
Perfect Fit	Corinna	ME	F	207 278-3333	4703
Safe-Approach Inc	Poland	ME	F	207 345-9900	5162
Jaeger Usa Inc	Rochester	NH	F	603 332-5816	15480
Mitch Rosen Extraordinary Gunl	Manchester	NH	F	603 647-2971	14891
Page Belting Company Inc	Boscawen	NH	E	603 796-2463	13992

32 STONE, CLAY, GLASS, AND CONCRETE PRODUCTS

3211 Flat glass

	CITY	ST	EMP	PHONE	ENTRY#
Insulpane Connecticut Inc	Hamden	CT	D	800 922-3248	1432
A B C Glass Co Inc	Springfield	MA	F	413 734-4524	12067
B & G Glass LLC	Pittsfield	MA	G	413 442-3113	11391
Contract Glass Service Inc	Billerica	MA	E	978 262-1323	6429
Custom Glass and Alum Co Inc	Tewksbury	MA	G	978 640-5800	12392
LTI Smart Glass Inc	Pittsfield	MA	D	413 637-5001	11407
Metro Glass & Metal LLC	Woburn	MA	E	781 281-0667	13612
Mygrant Glass Company Inc	Randolph	MA	F	781 767-3289	11569
Patriot Armred Systems Hldg LL	Lee	MA	F	413 637-1060	9617
Protective Armored Systems Inc	Lee	MA	F	413 637-1060	9618
Sharoc Realty Inc	South Easton	MA	D	508 238-0151	11953
Thermal Seal Insulating GL Inc	Uxbridge	MA	F	508 278-4243	12490
Glass Graphics Inc	Conway	NH	F	603 447-1900	14179
Guild Optical Associates Inc	Amherst	NH	F	603 889-6247	13872
New Erie Scientific LLC (DH)	Portsmouth	NH	E	603 430-6859	15425
Glass America Window Mfg Inc	Smithfield	RI	F	401 231-6000	16704

3221 Glass containers

	CITY	ST	EMP	PHONE	ENTRY#
Emhart Glass Manufacturing Inc (DH)	Windsor	CT	E	860 298-7340	4273
Saint-Gobain Corporation	Northborough	MA	A	508 351-7112	11108
Jarden LLC	East Wilton	ME	F	207 645-2574	4741
New Erie Scientific LLC (DH)	Portsmouth	NH	E	603 430-6859	15425

3229 Pressed and blown glass, nec

	CITY	ST	EMP	PHONE	ENTRY#
Bovano Industries Incorporated	Cheshire	CT	F	203 272-3208	576
Fiberoptics Technology Inc	Pomfret	CT	F	860 928-0443	2808
Flabeg Technical Glass US Corp	Naugatuck	CT	E	203 729-5227	1958
G Schoepferinc	Cheshire	CT	F	203 250-7794	594
Liberty Glass and Met Inds Inc	North Grosvenordale	CT	E	860 923-3623	2384
Norwix Inc	Norwich	CT	C	860 823-3090	2612
Nufern	East Granby	CT	D	860 408-5000	945
O E M Controls Inc (PA)	Shelton	CT	C	203 929-8431	3042
Owens Corning Sales LLC	East Hartford	CT	C	304 353-6945	1008
Pioneer Optics Company Inc	East Granby	CT	F	860 286-0071	948
Schaeffler Aerospace USA Corp	Winsted	CT	D	860 379-7558	4354
Stran Technologies LLC	Naugatuck	CT	G	203 720-6500	1988
Tero Design Holdings LLC	Norwalk	CT	G	203 899-9950	2580
Whalley Glass Company (PA)	Derby	CT	D	203 735-9388	895
A B C Glass Co Inc	Springfield	MA	F	413 734-4524	12067
Advance Coatings Co (PA)	Westminster	MA	F	978 874-5921	13268
Apogent Technologies Inc	Waltham	MA	A	781 622-1300	12594
Catalyst Acoustics Group Inc	Agawam	MA	C	413 789-1770	5785
Catalyst Acustics Holdings Inc (HQ)	Agawam	MA	D	413 789-1770	5786
Corning Incorporated	Tewksbury	MA	E	978 442-2200	12391
Diamond USA Inc (HQ)	North Billerica	MA	F	978 256-6544	10906
Eye Health Services Inc	Plymouth	MA	E	508 747-6425	11459
Eye Health Services Inc (PA)	Quincy	MA	E	617 472-5242	11517
Fused Fiberoptics LLC	Southbridge	MA	F	508 765-1652	12017
Hosokawa Alpine American Inc	Northborough	MA	F	508 655-1123	11097
Ipg Photonics Corporation (PA)	Marlborough	MA	B	508 373-1100	10169
Josh Smpson Cntemporary GL Inc	Shelburne Falls	MA	F	413 625-6145	11805
Mini-Systems Inc	Plainville	MA	E	508 695-2000	11439
Myriad Fiber Imaging Tech Inc	Dudley	MA	F	508 949-3000	8320
Omniglow LLC	West Springfield	MA	B	413 241-6010	13039
Optical Laboratory Inc	New Bedford	MA	E	508 997-9779	10637
Perx LLC	Pittsfield	MA	F	413 358-9020	11417
Pgc Acquisition LLC	Reading	MA	G	508 888-2344	11604
Schott North America Inc	Southbridge	MA	B	508 765-9744	12034
Sentinel Process Systems Inc	Southborough	MA	F	508 624-5577	12002
Simon Pearce US Inc	Boston	MA	G	617 450-8388	7039
Stiles & Hart Brick Company	Bridgewater	MA	E	508 697-6928	7238
T & T Machine Products Inc	Rockland	MA	F	781 878-3861	11662
Vaillancourt Folk Art Inc	Sutton	MA	E	508 476-3601	12294
Ward Process Inc	Holliston	MA	D	508 429-1165	9238
Corning Incorporated	Kennebunk	ME	D	207 985-3111	4924
McDonald Stain Glass Ltd	Boothbay Harbor	ME	F	207 633-4815	4603
Corning Incorporated	Keene	NH	F	603 357-7662	14594
Fiber Optic Hardware	Nashua	NH	F	603 325-4993	15101
Fibernext LLC	Concord	NH	E	603 226-2400	14130
M & M Glass Blowing Co Inc	Nashua	NH	G	603 598-8195	15129
New Erie Scientific LLC (DH)	Portsmouth	NH	E	603 430-6859	15425
Te Conctvity Phenix Optix Inc	Ashaway	RI	C	401 637-4600	15745

	CITY	ST	EMP	PHONE	ENTRY#
Thames Glass Inc	Newport	RI	F	401 846-0576	16226
Ao Glass LLC	Burlington	VT	E	802 735-5016	17118
Catamount Glassware Co Inc	Bennington	VT	E	802 442-5438	17038
Crest Studios	Townshend	VT	G	802 365-4200	17650
Little Rver Htglass Studio Inc	Stowe	VT	E	802 253-0889	17632
Simon Pearce (us) Inc	Quechee	VT	E	802 295-2711	17463
Simon Pearce US Inc	Windsor	VT	E	802 674-6280	17763

3231 Products of purchased glass

	CITY	ST	EMP	PHONE	ENTRY#
Baron Technology Inc	Milford	CT	F	203 452-0515	1800
Bovano Industries Incorporated	Cheshire	CT	F	203 272-3208	576
Capitol Glass Company Inc	West Hartford	CT	F	860 236-1936	4050
Compu-Data LLC	Newington	CT	D	800 666-0399	2282
Ecu & US International	East Hartford	CT	F	860 906-3390	991
Flabeg Technical Glass US Corp	Naugatuck	CT	E	203 729-5227	1958
Glass Industries America LLC	Wallingford	CT	G	203 269-6700	3810
High-Tech Conversions LLC	Enfield	CT	F	860 265-2633	1134
Naugatuck Glass LLC	Naugatuck	CT	E	203 729-5227	1975
U S Glass Distributors Inc	Enfield	CT	F	860 741-3658	1156
A B C Glass Co Inc	Springfield	MA	F	413 734-4524	12067
Acton Research Corporation	Acton	MA	E	941 556-2601	5731
Cambridge GL Fctry Condo LLC	Cambridge	MA	F	617 576-6701	7530
Canner Incorporated	West Groton	MA	F	978 448-3063	13001
Corning Incorporated	Tewksbury	MA	F	978 442-2200	12391
Diamond Windows Doors Mfg Inc	Boston	MA	E	617 282-1688	6693
Fibertec Inc	Bridgewater	MA	D	508 697-5100	7229
Idex Health & Science LLC	Middleboro	MA	C	774 213-0200	10362
LTI Smart Glass Inc	Pittsfield	MA	D	413 637-5001	11407
Mini-Systems Inc	Plainville	MA	E	508 695-2000	11439
Modern Mfg Inc Worcester	Rochdale	MA	F	508 791-7151	11628
Patriot Armored Systems LLC (PA)	Lenox Dale	MA	F	413 637-1060	9628
Pegasus Glassworks Inc	Sturbridge	MA	F	508 347-5656	12255
Prestige Cstm Mirror & GL Inc	Waltham	MA	F	781 647-0878	12752
Printguard Inc	Millbury	MA	F	508 890-8822	10441
Protective Armored Systems Inc	Lee	MA	F	413 637-1060	9618
Serpentino Stned Leaded GL Inc	Needham Heights	MA	G	781 449-2074	10556
Shelmar Inc	Wakefield	MA	F	781 245-1206	12535
SL 301b LLC	Cambridge	MA	G	888 315-9598	7718
Solutia Inc	Indian Orchard	MA	C	734 676-4400	9474
Stained Glass Resources Inc (PA)	Hampden	MA	E	413 566-5053	9023
Sundensity Inc (PA)	Boston	MA	F	617 642-1767	7065
McDonald Stain Glass Ltd	Boothbay Harbor	ME	G	207 633-4815	4603
Sigco LLC	Westbrook	ME	E	207 775-2676	5648
Sigco LLC (HQ)	Westbrook	ME	C	207 775-2676	5649
American Marine Products Inc	Charlestown	NH	F	954 782-1400	14060
Dan Dailey Inc	Kensington	NH	F	603 778-2303	14629
Glass Graphics Inc	Conway	NH	F	603 447-1900	14179
Hardric Laboratories Inc	Hudson	NH	E	978 251-1702	14506
Kheops International Inc (PA)	Stewartstown	NH	F	603 237-8188	15631
Klarmann Rulings Inc	Manchester	NH	F	603 424-2401	14872
New Erie Scientific LLC (DH)	Portsmouth	NH	E	603 430-6859	15425
Durastone Flexicore Inc	Smithfield	RI	F	401 231-4000	16696
Swarovski North America Ltd (DH)	Cranston	RI	A	401 463-6400	15915
Americas Grdening Resource Inc	Milton	VT	C	802 660-3500	17354

3241 Cement, hydraulic

	CITY	ST	EMP	PHONE	ENTRY#
Andrews Holdings Inc	Ayer	MA	E	978 772-4444	6173
Dragon Products Company LLC (DH)	Biddeford	ME	E	207 594-5555	4560
Dragon Products Company LLC	Thomaston	ME	E	207 594-5555	5544

3251 Brick and structural clay tile

	CITY	ST	EMP	PHONE	ENTRY#
K & G Corp	Manchester	CT	F	860 643-1133	1609
Redland Brick Inc	South Windsor	CT	E	860 528-1311	3177
Hi-Way Concrete Pdts Co Inc	Wareham	MA	E	508 295-0834	12837
Morgan Advanced Ceramics Inc	New Bedford	MA	D	508 995-1725	10624
Redi-Mix Services Incorporated	Taunton	MA	F	508 823-0771	12361
Stiles & Hart Brick Company	Bridgewater	MA	E	508 697-6928	7238
Rjf - Morin Brick LLC	Auburn	ME	D	207 784-9375	4459
Ventech Industries Inc	Eliot	ME	G	207 439-0069	4751
Morgan Advanced Ceramics Inc	Hudson	NH	E	603 598-9122	14529

3253 Ceramic wall and floor tile

	CITY	ST	EMP	PHONE	ENTRY#
Aspecta North America LLC	Norwalk	CT	G	855 400-7732	2466
Brass City Tile Designs LLC	Waterbury	CT	G	203 597-8764	3892
Hmtx Industries LLC (PA)	Norwalk	CT	G	203 299-3100	2515
Porcelanosa New York Inc	Riverside	CT	F	203 698-7618	2910
Quemere International LLC	Middletown	CT	G	914 934-8366	1775
Laminam USA Inc	Boston	MA	F	905 669-6679	6852
Ventech Industries Inc	Eliot	ME	G	207 439-0069	4751
Cabinets For Less LLC	Manchester	NH	G	603 935-7551	14825
Dal-Tile Corporation	Williston	VT	F	802 951-2030	17726

3255 Clay refractories

	CITY	ST	EMP	PHONE	ENTRY#
Redland Brick Inc	South Windsor	CT	E	860 528-1311	3177
Bay State Crucible Co	Taunton	MA	E	508 824-5121	12323
Bnz Materials Inc	North Billerica	MA	C	978 663-3401	10900
Lynn Products Co	Lynn	MA	F	781 593-2500	9986
Zampell Refractories Inc (PA)	Newburyport	MA	E	978 465-0055	10728
Zampell Refractories Inc	Auburn	ME	F	207 786-2400	4465
Conproco Corp (PA)	Somersworth	NH	F	603 743-5800	15613

3259 Structural clay products, nec

	CITY	ST	EMP	PHONE	ENTRY#
Eljen Corporation	East Hartford	CT	E	860 610-0426	992
North American Supaflu Systems	Scarborough	ME	F	207 883-1155	5441
Z-Flex (us) Inc	Bedford	NH	E	603 669-5136	13956
Rupe Slate Co Inc	Poultney	VT	G	802 287-9692	17450

3261 Vitreous plumbing fixtures

	CITY	ST	EMP	PHONE	ENTRY#
Syn-Mar Products Inc	Ellington	CT	F	860 872-8505	1117
Clivus Multrum Inc	Lawrence	MA	G	978 725-5591	9551
Kenney Manufacturing Company (PA)	Warwick	RI	B	401 739-2200	16831
Summer Infant Inc (HQ)	Woonsocket	RI	C	401 671-6550	16975

3263 Semivitreous table and kitchenware

	CITY	ST	EMP	PHONE	ENTRY#
Tero Design Holdings LLC	Norwalk	CT	G	203 899-9950	2580
Waddington North America Inc	Chelmsford	MA	C	978 256-6551	7970
Hope & Main	Warren	RI	G	401 245-7400	16758

3264 Porcelain electrical supplies

	CITY	ST	EMP	PHONE	ENTRY#
Coorstek Inc	East Granby	CT	C	860 653-8071	932
Newco Condenser Inc	Shelton	CT	F	475 582-4000	3039
Accumet Engineering Corp	Devens	MA	E	978 568-8311	8266
Coorstek Inc	Worcester	MA	B	774 317-2600	13710
Idex Health & Science LLC	Middleboro	MA	C	774 213-0200	10362
Ceramco Inc	Center Conway	NH	E	603 447-2090	14050
Coorstek Inc	Milford	NH	D	603 673-7560	15019
Superior Tchncal Ceramics Corp (HQ)	Saint Albans	VT	C	802 527-7726	17533

3269 Pottery products, nec

	CITY	ST	EMP	PHONE	ENTRY#
Mc Cann Bros Inc	Monroe	CT	F	203 335-8630	1916
Singer Company Inc	Waterford	CT	F	860 439-1234	3995
Bodycote lmt Inc (DH)	Andover	MA	D	978 470-0876	5873
Dpb Ceramics LLC	Boston	MA	G	617 259-1084	6701
Gare Incorporated	Haverhill	MA	E	978 373-9131	9096
Saint-Gobain Corporation	Northborough	MA	A	508 351-7112	11108
Sheffield Pottery Inc	Sheffield	MA	F	413 229-7700	11801
Vaillancourt Folk Art Inc	Sutton	MA	E	508 476-3601	12294
Georgetown Pottery	Georgetown	ME	G	207 371-2801	4814
Sheepscot River Pottery (PA)	Edgecomb	ME	F	207 882-9410	4748
Bennington Potters Inc (PA)	Bennington	VT	E	800 205-8033	17036
Beth Mueller Inc	Barre	VT	G	802 476-3582	16997
Simon Pearce (us) Inc (PA)	Windsor	VT	C	802 674-6280	17762

3271 Concrete block and brick

	CITY	ST	EMP	PHONE	ENTRY#
Connecticut Concrete Form Inc	Farmington	CT	F	860 674-1314	1213
Cromwell Concrete Products Incorporated	Cromwell	CT	E		690
Kobyluck Ready-Mix Inc	Waterford	CT	F	860 444-9604	3991
Laydon Industries LLC (PA)	New Haven	CT	E	203 562-7283	2169
Lda Construction LLC	East Haven	CT	F	203 469-3180	1044
Westbrook Con Block Co Inc	Westbrook	CT	E	860 399-6201	4146
Adolf Jandris & Sons Inc	Gardner	MA	E	978 632-0089	8878
Connecticut Valley Block Co Inc	West Springfield	MA	E		13018
Crystal Brook Ldscp Cnstr Inc	Springfield	MA	F	413 596-0055	12087
Hi-Way Concrete Pdts Co Inc	Wareham	MA	E	508 295-0834	12837
Ideal Concrete Block Co	Waltham	MA	E	781 894-3200	12694
Ideal Concrete Block Co (PA)	Westford	MA	E	978 692-3076	13242
Johns Building Supply Co Inc	Pittsfield	MA	F	413 442-7846	11403
Medway Block Co Inc	Medway	MA	E	508 533-6701	10307
Oldcastle Apg Northeast Inc	Holbrook	MA	D	781 506-9473	9183
P & M Brick & Block Inc	Watertown	MA	G	617 924-6020	12898
R Ducharme Inc	Chicopee	MA	G	413 534-4516	8057
Roberts Ldscp Design & Cnstr	Barnstable	MA	F	508 364-4878	6201
State Road Cement Block Co Inc	North Dartmouth	MA	G	508 993-9473	11002
Stiles & Hart Brick Company	Bridgewater	MA	E	508 697-6928	7238
Vynorius Prestress Inc	Salisbury	MA	F	978 462-7765	11746
Gagne & Son Con Blocks Inc	Auburn	ME	G	207 495-3313	4435
Gagne & Son Concrete Blocks Inc (PA)	Belgrade	ME	E	207 495-3313	4539
Rjf - Morin Brick LLC	Auburn	ME	D	207 784-9375	4459
Cs-Ma Inc	Newport	NH	F	603 863-1000	15227
Tilcon Arthur Whitcomb Inc (HQ)	North Swanzey	NH	F	603 352-0101	15256
Anchor Concrete	Cranston	RI	F	401 942-4800	15833

3272 Concrete products, nec

	CITY	ST	EMP	PHONE	ENTRY#
Arrow Concrete Products Inc (PA)	Granby	CT	E	860 653-5063	1305
Atlas Concrete Products Inc	New Britain	CT	F	860 224-2244	2002
Blakeslee Prestress Inc (PA)	Branford	CT	C	203 315-7090	241
Bonsal American Inc	Canaan	CT	F	860 824-7733	553
Connecticut Precast Corp	Monroe	CT	E	203 268-8688	1910
Coreslab Structures Conn Inc	Thomaston	CT	D	860 283-8281	3617
Cromwell Concrete Products Incorporated	Cromwell	CT			E
			690		
Custom Vault Corporation	New Fairfield	CT	G	203 746-0506	2094
Cv Custom Volt	Ridgefield	CT	G	203 431-7646	2895
Dalton Enterprises Inc (PA)	Cheshire	CT	D	203 272-3221	586
Dawn Enterprises LLC	Manchester	CT	G	860 646-8200	1591
Doric Vault Connecticut LLC	Branford	CT	G	203 494-0172	251
Eastern Precast Company Inc	Brookfield	CT	F	203 775-0230	519
Elm-Cap Industries Inc	West Hartford	CT	E	860 953-1060	4059
Essex Concrete Products Inc	Essex	CT	F	860 767-1768	1163
Forterra Pipe & Precast LLC	Wauregan	CT	F	860 564-9000	4040
Future Classics USA LLC (PA)	Roxbury	CT	F	860 838-4688	2944
Growspan LLC	South Windsor	CT	F	877 835-9996	3152
Jolley Precast Inc	Danielson	CT	C	860 774-9066	840
Lane Construction Corporation (DH)	Cheshire	CT	G	203 235-3351	603
Lane Industries Incorporated (DH)	Cheshire	CT	G	203 235-3351	604
M & M Precast Corp	Danbury	CT	F	203 743-5559	780
Mono-Crete Step Co Ct LLC	Bethel	CT	F	203 748-8419	129
Nicolock Paving Stones Ne LLC	North Haven	CT	F	203 234-2800	2428
Norwalk Wilbert Vault Go LLC	Oakville	CT	E	203 366-5678	2624
O & G Industries Inc	Stamford	CT	D	203 323-1111	3422
Oldcastle Infrastructure Inc	Avon	CT	F	860 673-3291	34
Pauls Marble Depot LLC	Stamford	CT	F	203 978-0669	3427
Platt Brothers & Company (PA)	Waterbury	CT	D	203 753-4194	3963
Quikrete Companies Inc	Wauregan	CT	F	860 564-3308	4041
Stone Image Custom Con LLC	Suffield	CT	F	860 668-2434	3595
Technometalpost Connecticut	Cheshire	CT	F	203 228-7094	618
United Concrete Products Inc	Yalesville	CT	C	203 269-3119	4399
Washington Concrete Pdts Inc	Plainville	CT	F	860 747-5242	2788
WJ Kettleworks LLC	Stratford	CT	G	203 377-5000	3585
Acme Precast Co Inc	West Falmouth	MA	F	508 548-9607	13000
Acme-Shorey Precast Co Inc	Carver	MA	G	508 548-9607	7852
Acme-Shorey Precast Co Inc (PA)	Harwich	MA	G	508 432-0530	9066
Acme-Shorey Precast Co Inc	South Yarmouth	MA	G	508 430-0956	11980
Bonsal American Inc	Oxford	MA	G	508 987-8188	11249
County Concrete Corp (PA)	Dalton	MA	F	413 499-3359	8149
DAngelo Burial Vaults	Franklin	MA	G	508 528-0385	8830
Diversitech Corporation	Taunton	MA	G	800 699-0453	12333
Dn Tanks Inc (PA)	Wakefield	MA	D	781 246-1133	12507
Dn Tanks LLC	Wakefield	MA	F	781 246-1133	12508
Fbne LLC	Boston	MA	F	617 571-6443	6733
Fireslate 2 Inc	East Wareham	MA	F	508 273-0047	8422
Flagg Palmer Precast Inc	Oxford	MA	F	508 987-3400	11253
Fletcher Granite LLC (DH)	Westford	MA	F	978 692-1312	13238
Forterra Pipe & Precast LLC	Ashland	MA	C	508 881-2000	5958
Hardy Doric Inc	Chelmsford	MA	G	978 250-1113	7930
J & R Pre-Cast Inc	Berkley	MA	F	508 822-3311	6316
Keating-Wilbert Vault Inc	Wilbraham	MA	F	413 543-1226	13361
L & L Concrete Products Inc	Oxford	MA	E	508 987-8175	11257
L J Gentile & Sons Inc	Norfolk	MA	G	508 384-5156	10800
Lamontagne Wilbert Burial Vlt	Sutton	MA	F	508 476-0040	12286
Lane Construction Corporation	Lee	MA	E	413 637-2511	9614
Lorusso Corp (PA)	Plainville	MA	E	508 668-6520	11437
Mackenzie Vault Inc	East Longmeadow	MA	F	413 525-8827	8385
Massachusetts Contr Sups Inc	Hudson	MA	G	978 413-2578	9389
Means Pre-Cast Co Inc	Braintree	MA	G	781 843-1909	7194
Nantucket Pavers Inc	Rehoboth	MA	F	508 336-5800	11611
National Con Tnks / Frguard JV	Concord	MA	F	978 505-5533	8127
Oldcastle Apg Northeast Inc	Holbrook	MA	D	781 506-9473	9183
Oldcastle Infrastructure Inc	Rehoboth	MA	E	508 336-7600	11613
Pavestone LLC	Middleboro	MA	D	508 947-6001	10373
Petricca Industries Inc (PA)	Pittsfield	MA	E	413 499-1441	11418
Pine-Tree Concrete Pdts Inc	Millville	MA	G	508 883-7072	10451
Portland Stone Ware Co Inc (PA)	Dracut	MA	E	978 459-7272	8311
Precast Specialties Corp	Abington	MA	E	781 878-7220	5727
Quintal Burial Vault Inc	Dighton	MA	F	508 669-5717	8294
Sbarzola Construction Corp	South Weymouth	MA	G	781 817-6485	11977
Scituate Concrete Pipe Corp	Scituate	MA	E	781 545-0564	11772
Scituate Concrete Products	Marshfield	MA	D	781 837-1747	10245
Scituate Concrete Products Cor	Marshfield	MA	E	617 837-1747	10246
Shea Concrete Products Inc (PA)	Amesbury	MA	E	978 658-2645	5851
Shea Concrete Products Inc	Amesbury	MA	E	978 388-1509	5852
Strafello Precast Inc	East Taunton	MA	E	774 501-2628	8413
Unistress Corp	Pittsfield	MA	B	413 499-1441	11426
Watertown Engineering Corp	Whitman	MA	E	781 857-2555	13351

	CITY	ST	EMP	PHONE	ENTRY#
Whitman Vault Inc	Whitman	MA	G	781 857-3031	13355
Wiggin Means Precast Co Inc	Pocasset	MA	G	508 564-6776	11493
Wiggin Precast Corp	Pocasset	MA	F	508 564-6776	11494
Williams Stone Co Inc	East Otis	MA	E	413 269-4544	8403
American Concrete Inds Inc (PA)	Auburn	ME	E	207 947-8334	4418
American Concrete Inds Inc	Bangor	ME	D	207 947-8334	4488
Aroostacast Inc	Presque Isle	ME	F	207 764-0077	5296
Elm Street Vault Inc	Biddeford	ME	F	207 284-4855	4563
FC Work & Sons Incorporated	Jackson	ME	F	207 722-3206	4912
Gagne & Son Con Blocks Inc	Auburn	ME	G	207 495-3313	4435
M G A Cast Stone Inc	Oxford	ME	E	207 926-5993	5147
Mattingly Products Company	North Anson	ME	E	207 635-2719	5107
Pepin Precast Inc	Sanford	ME	F	207 324-6125	5405
Richard Genest Inc	Sanford	ME	F	207 324-7215	5411
Sandelin Foundation Inc	Topsham	ME	F	207 725-7004	5552
Wilbert Swans Vault Co	Casco	ME	E	207 854-5324	4684
Alex Vault Co	Epping	NH	G	603 944-0132	14276
Andrew J Foss Co LLC	Farmington	NH	F	603 755-2515	14307
Bd Enterprises LLC	Claremont	NH	G	603 504-6231	14078
Concrete Systems Inc	Hudson	NH	D	603 886-5472	14491
Concrete Systems Inc	Londonderry	NH	F	603 432-1840	14736
Conproco Corp (PA)	Somersworth	NH	F	603 743-5800	15613
E-Z Crete LLC	Keene	NH	F	603 313-6462	14596
E-Z Crete LLC	Swanzey	NH	F	603 313-6462	15643
East Coast Concrete Pdts LLC	Amherst	NH	F	603 883-3042	13867
Hudson Quarry Corp	Hudson	NH	F	603 598-0142	14507
Michie Corporation	Henniker	NH	D	603 428-7426	14438
New England Vlts Monuments LLC	Berlin	NH	G	603 449-2165	13984
Newstress Inc	Epsom	NH	E	603 736-9000	14281
Northern Design Precast Inc	Loudon	NH	E	603 783-8989	14796
Quikrete Companies LLC	Brentwood	NH	E	603 778-2123	14028
Sabbow and Co Inc	Littleton	NH	F	603 444-6724	14722
Slate Corporation	Auburn	NH	F	603 234-5943	13912
Tfh Liquidation Company LLC	Dover	NH	G	603 742-4961	14252
Turn Key Lumber Inc	Fitzwilliam	NH	C	978 798-1370	14317
Ufp Londonderry LLC	Londonderry	NH	E	603 668-4113	14787
Wahsburn Vault Company Inc	Hinsdale	NH	F	603 256-6891	14445
William N Lamarre Con Pdts Inc	Greenville	NH	F	603 878-1340	14375
Anchor Concrete	Cranston	RI	F	401 942-4800	15833
Concrete Products Inc	Chepachet	RI	E	401 568-8874	15803
Durastone Corporation	Lincoln	RI	F	401 723-7100	16134
Durastone Flexicore Inc	Smithfield	RI	E	401 231-4000	16696
Forterra Pipe & Precast LLC	Peace Dale	RI	G	401 782-2600	16433
Preferred Precast Inc	Cumberland	RI	F	401 475-5560	15961
Caledonia Inc	Saint Johnsbury	VT	F	802 748-2319	17539
Camp Precast Concrete Products Inc	Milton	VT	E	802 893-2401	17355
Dailey Precast LLC (HQ)	Shaftsbury	VT	D	802 442-4418	17549
Joes Cstm Mfg Qlty Mmrals Inc	Barre	VT	G	800 787-4004	17011
Joseph P Carrara & Sons Inc	Middlebury	VT	D	802 388-6363	17344
Joseph P Carrara & Sons Inc (PA)	North Clarendon	VT	E	802 775-2301	17415
Londonderry Industrial Pk Inc	South Londonderry	VT	E	802 297-3760	17611
Washburn Vault Company Inc	Brattleboro	VT	E	802 254-9150	17107

3273 Ready-mixed concrete

	CITY	ST	EMP	PHONE	ENTRY#
A Aiudi & Sons LLC (PA)	Plainville	CT	G	860 747-5534	2742
Aiudi Concrete Inc	Westbrook	CT	G	860 399-9289	4136
B&R Sand and Gravel	Gales Ferry	CT	G	860 464-5099	1259
Barnes Concrete Co Inc	Putnam	CT	E	860 928-7242	2846
Builders Concrete East LLC	North Windham	CT	E	860 456-4111	2450
Century Acquisition	Canaan	CT	E	518 758-7229	554
Devine Brothers Incorporated	Norwalk	CT	E	203 866-4421	2490
Dp Concrete LLC	Farmington	CT	E	860 677-2626	1214
Enfield Transit Mix Inc	Enfield	CT	F	860 763-0864	1129
Essex Concrete Products Inc	Essex	CT	F	860 767-1768	1163
Federici Brands LLC (PA)	Wilton	CT	F	203 762-7667	4239
Five Star Products Inc	Shelton	CT	E	203 336-7900	3006
Iffland Lumber Company Inc	Torrington	CT	E	860 489-9218	3684
Miks Mix LLC	Milford	CT	G	203 521-7824	1851
Mohican Valley Concrete Corp	Fairfield	CT	E	203 254-7133	1194
O & G Industries Inc	Bridgeport	CT	B	203 366-4586	354
O & G Industries Inc	Danbury	CT	E	203 748-5694	791
O & G Industries Inc	Stamford	CT	D	203 977-1618	3421
O & G Industries Inc	Stamford	CT	D	203 323-1111	3422
Quikrete Companies Inc	Wauregan	CT	F	860 564-3308	4041
Sega Ready Mix Incorporated (PA)	New Milford	CT	F	860 354-3969	2260
Sega Ready Mix Incorporated	Waterbury	CT	G	203 465-1052	3968
Sterling Materials LLC	Branford	CT	G	203 315-6619	279
Suzio York Hill Companies	Meriden	CT	F	888 789-4626	1703
The L Suzio Asphalt Co Inc	Meriden	CT	E	203 237-8421	1705
The L Suzio Concrete Co Inc (PA)	Meriden	CT	E	203 237-8421	1706
Tilcon Connecticut Inc	East Granby	CT	E	860 844-7000	954
Tilcon Connecticut Inc (DH)	New Britain	CT	D	860 224-6010	2072
Tilcon Connecticut Inc	Portland	CT	G	860 342-1096	2827

	CITY	ST	EMP	PHONE	ENTRY#
Tilcon Inc **(DH)**	Newington	CT	B	860 223-3651	2328
Windham Materials LLC **(PA)**	Willimantic	CT	E	860 456-4111	4222
Windham Materials LLC	Willimantic	CT	D	860 456-3277	4223
York Hill Trap Rock Quarry Co	Meriden	CT	E	203 237-8421	1712
A Graziano Inc	Braintree	MA	E	781 843-7300	7166
Aggregate Industries	Swampscott	MA	F	781 596-4107	12297
Banas Sand and Gravel Co Inc	Ludlow	MA	E	413 583-8321	9941
Berkshire Concrete Corp **(HQ)**	Pittsfield	MA	E	413 443-4734	11392
Boro Sand & Stone Corp **(PA)**	North Attleboro	MA	E	508 699-2911	10869
Boston Sand & Gravel Company **(PA)**	Boston	MA	E	617 227-9000	6616
Boston Sand & Gravel Company	Charlestown	MA	C	617 242-5540	7863
Boston Sand & Gravel Company	Sandwich	MA	F	508 888-8002	11747
Boucher Con Foundation Sups	Middleboro	MA	G	508 947-4279	10351
Byrne Sand & Gravel Co Inc	Middleboro	MA	F	508 947-0724	10354
Cape Cod Ready Mix Inc	Orleans	MA	E	508 255-4600	11236
Chicopee Foundations Inc	Chicopee	MA	E	413 594-4700	8015
CP Dauphinais Inc	Sutton	MA	E	508 865-1755	12279
Crh Americas Inc	Leominster	MA	B	978 840-1176	9655
Cs-Ma LLC **(PA)**	Wilbraham	MA	E	413 733-6631	13356
Dauphinais & Son Inc	Wilbraham	MA	E	413 596-3964	13357
Dauphinais Concrete	Bellingham	MA	G	508 657-0941	6289
Dmjl Consulting LLC	Methuen	MA	F	978 989-0790	10327
E H Perkins Construction Inc	Sterling	MA	F	978 422-3388	12161
E H Perkins Construction Inc **(PA)**	Wayland	MA	E	978 562-3436	12925
Fall River Ready-Mix Con LLC	Fall River	MA	G	508 675-7540	8549
Falmouth Ready Mix Inc	East Falmouth	MA	F	508 548-6100	8359
Fuccillo Ready Mix Inc	East Falmouth	MA	F	508 540-2821	8360
Gloucester Transit Mix Inc	Gloucester	MA	G	978 283-9649	8938
GP Aggregate Corp	Gloucester	MA	F	978 283-5318	8940
Holcim - Ner Inc **(DH)**	Saugus	MA	E	781 941-7200	11760
J G Maclellan Con Co Inc	Amesbury	MA	F	978 458-1223	5839
J G Maclellan Con Co Inc **(PA)**	Lowell	MA	D	978 458-1223	9888
JG Maclellan	Wakefield	MA	G	781 245-7756	12514
L & S Industries Inc **(PA)**	New Bedford	MA	E	508 995-4654	10612
Lane Construction Corporation	Northfield	MA	D	413 498-5586	11120
Leo Concrete Service Inc	Chicopee	MA	F	413 536-3370	8045
McCabe Sand & Gravel Co Inc	Taunton	MA	E	508 823-0771	12349
Morse Ready Mix LLC	Plainville	MA	E	508 809-4644	11440
Morse Sand & Gravel Corp	Attleboro	MA	F	508 809-4644	6038
P A Landers Inc	Hanover	MA	F	508 747-1800	9039
Petricca Industries Inc **(PA)**	Pittsfield	MA	E	413 499-1441	11418
Preferred Concrete Corporation	East Freetown	MA	F	508 763-5500	8365
Ragged Hill Incorporated	East Templeton	MA	E	978 939-5712	8414
Redi-Mix LP	South Carver	MA	E	508 295-5111	11915
Redi-Mix Services Incorporated	Taunton	MA	F	508 823-0771	12361
Rosenfeld Concrete Corp **(HQ)**	Hopedale	MA	E	508 473-7200	9303
Rowley Ready Mix Inc	Rowley	MA	F	978 948-2544	11684
Southeastern Concrete Inc	Kingston	MA	F	617 227-9000	9511
Southeastern Concrete Inc	Weymouth	MA	F	781 848-9390	13335
Sterling Concrete Corp	North Oxford	MA	F	978 422-8282	11034
Torromeo Industries Inc **(PA)**	Methuen	MA	F	978 686-5634	10346
Varney Bros Sand & Gravel Inc	Bellingham	MA	F	508 966-1313	6302
Westfield Concrete Inc	Westfield	MA	G	413 562-4814	13218
Westfield Ready-Mix Inc	Chicopee	MA	F	413 594-4700	8070
Coleman Concrete	Bethel	ME	G	207 824-6300	4552
County Concrete & Cnstr Co	Columbia Falls	ME	E	207 483-4409	4698
Dayton Sand & Gravel Inc	Dayton	ME	D	207 499-2306	4720
Dragon Products Company LLC **(DH)**	Biddeford	ME	E	207 594-5555	4560
Dragon Products Company LLC	Portland	ME	E	207 879-2328	5212
Dragon Products Company LLC	Thomaston	ME	E	207 594-5555	5544
F R Carroll Inc	Limerick	ME	E	207 793-8615	5001
Ferraiolo Construction Inc	Rockland	ME	E	207 594-9840	5327
Haley Construction Inc	Farmington	ME	G	207 778-9990	4781
Lane Construction Corporation	Presque Isle	ME	E	207 764-4137	5301
Lees Concrete Inc	Bangor	ME	G	207 974-4936	4509
Mattingly Products Company	North Anson	ME	E	207 635-2719	5107
Owen J Folsom Inc	Old Town	ME	E	207 827-7625	5131
P & K Sand and Gravel Inc	Naples	ME	E	207 693-6765	5081
R A Cummings Inc	Auburn	ME	E	207 777-7100	4457
R Pepin & Sons Inc	Sanford	ME	E	207 324-6125	5407
State Sand & Gravel Co Inc	Belfast	ME	F	207 338-4070	4538
Alvin J Coleman & Son Inc **(PA)**	Albany	NH	F	603 447-5936	13847
Alvin J Coleman & Son Inc	Albany	NH	E	603 447-3056	13848
Boston Sand & Gravel Company	Rochester	NH	D	603 330-3999	15467
Carroll Concrete Co Inc	Newport	NH	F	603 863-1765	15226
Coleman Concrete Inc	Albany	NH	E	603 447-5936	13850
Crh Americas Inc	West Lebanon	NH	C	603 298-5959	15681
Crh Americas Materials Inc	Manchester	NH	G	603 669-2373	14839
Granite State Concrete Co Inc	Milford	NH	F	603 673-3327	15023
LE Weed & Son LLC **(PA)**	Newport	NH	G	603 863-1540	15230
Michie Corporation	Henniker	NH	D	603 428-7426	14438
N H Central Concrete Corp	Henniker	NH	F	603 428-7900	14439
Newport Concrete Block Co	Newport	NH	F	603 863-1540	15232
Newport Sand & Gravel Co Inc	Charlestown	NH	G	603 826-4444	14065
Newport Sand & Gravel Co Inc **(PA)**	Newport	NH	F	603 298-0199	15233
Newport Sand & Gravel Co Inc	West Lebanon	NH	F	603 298-8777	15686
Osborne Concrete	Northwood	NH	F	603 231-3604	15275
Persons Concrete	Belmont	NH	F	603 524-4434	13966
Redimix Companies Inc **(DH)**	Belmont	NH	E	603 524-4434	13969
Redimix Concrete	Belmont	NH	F	603 581-1805	13970
Seacoast Redimix Concrete LLC **(PA)**	Dover	NH	F	603 742-4441	14250
Tilcon Arthur Whitcomb Inc **(HQ)**	North Swanzey	NH	F	603 352-0101	15256
Torromeo Industries Inc	Kingston	NH	E	603 642-5564	14637
Consolidated Concrete Corp **(PA)**	East Providence	RI	G	401 438-4700	16009
Cumberland Quarry Corp	Cumberland	RI	F	401 658-4442	15937
Ferreira Concrete Forms Inc	East Providence	RI	F	401 639-0931	16019
Greenville Ready Mix	Smithfield	RI	G	401 231-3900	16706
Greenville Ready Mix Inc	Ashaway	RI	G	401 539-2333	15740
Heidelberg Materials Us Inc	Providence	RI	F	800 833-4157	16531
Heritage Concrete Corp	Exeter	RI	F	401 294-1524	16052
Material Concrete Corp	North Smithfield	RI	F	401 765-0204	16326
Mix Marketing Corp	Narragansett	RI	G	401 954-6121	16191
Pawtucket Hot Mix Asphalt Inc	Pawtucket	RI	E	401 722-4488	16400
Bourbeau Aggregate LLC	Saint Albans	VT	G	802 309-4699	17517
Carroll Concrete Co	Barre	VT	G	802 229-0191	16999
Dailey Precast LLC **(HQ)**	Shaftsbury	VT	D	802 442-4418	17549
Gray Rock Concrete	Milton	VT	F	802 379-5393	17359
Harrison Concrete Cnstr Inc	Fairfax	VT	E	802 849-6688	17259
Harrison Redi-Mix Corp	Fairfax	VT	E	802 849-6688	17260
Joseph P Carrara & Sons Inc	Middlebury	VT	D	802 388-6363	17344
Joseph P Carrara & Sons Inc **(PA)**	North Clarendon	VT	E	802 775-2301	17415
Matt Waite Excavation Inc	Pawlet	VT	F	802 325-3668	17441
Newport Sand & Gravel Co Inc	Newport	VT	F	802 334-2000	17403
Newport Sand & Gravel Co Inc	Swanton	VT	G	802 868-4119	17638
S D Ireland Con Cnstr Corp	Williston	VT	C	802 863-6222	17747

3274 Lime

Specialty Minerals Inc	Adams	MA	C	413 743-0591	5775
Dragon Products Company LLC **(DH)**	Biddeford	ME	E	207 594-5555	4560

3275 Gypsum products

County Concrete & Cnstr Co	Columbia Falls	ME	E	207 483-4409	4698
Georgia-Pacific LLC	Newington	NH	C	603 433-8000	15207
GP Gypsum Corp	Portsmouth	NH	G	603 433-8000	15394
USG Services Corporation	Pawtucket	RI	G	401 644-7098	16427

3281 Cut stone and stone products

Architectural Stone Group LLC	Bridgeport	CT	G	203 494-5451	298
Connecticut Solid Surface LLC	Canton	CT	E	860 410-9800	559
Connecticut Stone Supplies Inc **(PA)**	Milford	CT	D	203 882-1000	1814
Core Site Services LLC	New Haven	CT	G	475 227-9026	2140
Dan Beard Inc	Shelton	CT	E	203 924-4346	2996
Eastern Marble and Granite LLC	Milford	CT	F	203 882-8221	1820
Kenneth Lynch & Sons Inc	Oxford	CT	G	203 762-8363	2702
La Pietra Thinstone Veneer	Brookfield	CT	F	203 775-6162	528
Mildred Coppola **(PA)**	Stamford	CT	F	203 967-9300	3411
New England Stone Inc	Milford	CT	F	203 876-8606	1853
O & G Industries Inc	Beacon Falls	CT	F	203 729-4529	45
O & G Industries Inc	Stamford	CT	D	203 323-1111	3422
Paul H Gesswein & Company Inc	Old Saybrook	CT	G	860 388-0652	2660
Singer Company Inc	Waterford	CT	F	860 439-1234	3995
Skyline Quarry LLC	Stafford Springs	CT	F	860 875-3580	3259
Stone Workshop LLC	Bridgeport	CT	G	203 362-1144	376
270 University Avenue LLC	Westwood	MA	G	781 407-0836	13304
Aldrich Marble & Granite Co	Norwood	MA	G	781 762-6111	11158
All Granite & Marble Inc II	Charlton	MA	G	508 434-0611	7885
Atlantic MBL & Gran Group Inc	East Falmouth	MA	G	508 540-9770	8356
B R S Inc	Bridgewater	MA	E	508 697-5448	7221
Bates Bros Seam-Face Gran Co	East Weymouth	MA	F	781 337-1150	8426
Continental Stone MBL Gran Inc	Sterling	MA	E	978 422-8700	12159
Conterra LLC	Canton	MA	F	781 821-2100	7780
Crystal Gt Systems LLC	Salem	MA	F	978 745-0088	11708
Cumar Inc	Everett	MA	E	617 389-7818	8484
Discover Marble & Granite Inc **(PA)**	Millbury	MA	D	877 411-9900	10432
Divine Stoneworks LLC	Ashland	MA	F	774 221-6006	5956
E W Sykes General Contractors	Athol	MA	E	978 249-7655	5978
East Coast Marble & Gran Corp	Lynn	MA	F	781 760-0207	9970
Es Countertops LLC	West Springfield	MA	G	413 732-8128	13024
Fletcher Granite LLC **(DH)**	Westford	MA	G	978 692-1312	13238
Foxrock Granite LLC	Quincy	MA	F	617 249-8015	11520
G R Sands Monumental Works	Roslindale	MA	G	617 522-1001	11666
Galaxy Stone Inc	Amesbury	MA	G	617 461-2790	5835
Gerritystone Inc	Wilmington	MA	E	781 938-1820	13409
Hi-Way Concrete Pdts Co Inc	Wareham	MA	E	508 295-0834	12837
International Stone Inc	Woburn	MA	D	781 937-3300	13589
Ippolitos Stone Craft Inc	Seekonk	MA	F	508 336-9616	11778

Employee Codes: A=Over 500 employees, B=251-500
C=101-250, D=51-100, E=20-50, F=10-19, G=1-9
2024 Harris New England
Manufacturers Directory
897

	CITY	ST	EMP	PHONE	ENTRY#
Louis W Mian Incorporated **(PA)**	Boston	MA	F	617 241-7900	6863
Majestic Marble & Granite Inc	Canton	MA	G	781 830-1020	7807
Monarch Stone Inc	North Reading	MA	G	978 954-7021	11044
Nicholas Ieronimo	Middleboro	MA	G	508 947-5363	10369
Onyx Marble & Granite LLC	Framingham	MA	F	508 620-0775	8793
Quintal Burial Vault Inc	Dighton	MA	G	508 669-5717	8294
Ricciardi Marble & Granite Inc	Hyannis	MA	G	508 790-2734	9446
Santo C De Spirt Marble & Gran	Agawam	MA	G	413 786-7073	5806
Sherle Wagner Intl LLC	Fall River	MA	F	212 758-3300	8606
Steven Tedesco	Danvers	MA	G	978 777-4070	8222
Stone Decor Galleria Inc	Woburn	MA	F	781 937-9377	13673
Stone Design Marble & Gran Co	South Weymouth	MA	G	781 331-3000	11978
Stone Surfaces Inc	Woburn	MA	F	781 270-4600	13674
Stone Yard LLC	Littleton	MA	E	978 742-9800	9840
Vanity World Inc	Canton	MA	F	508 668-1800	7839
Williams Stone Co Inc	East Otis	MA	E	413 269-4544	8403
Dragon Products Company LLC **(DH)**	Biddeford	ME	G	207 594-5555	4560
Flagstone Inc	Mapleton	ME	G	207 227-5883	5045
Freshwater Stone & Brickwork	Orland	ME	E	207 469-6331	5132
Harpswell House Inc	Lisbon Falls	ME	G	207 353-2385	5021
Morningstar Marble & Gran Inc	Topsham	ME	F	207 725-7309	5551
Sheldon Slate Products Co Inc	Monson	ME	F	207 997-3615	5074
Arens Stoneworks Inc	Greenland	NH	G	603 436-8000	14367
Atlas Gran Countertop Flr Sup	Derry	NH	F	603 818-8899	14190
Barre Tile Inc	Lebanon	NH	F	802 476-0912	14684
Ripano Stoneworks Ltd	Nashua	NH	E	603 886-6655	15160
Rumford Stone Inc **(PA)**	Bow	NH	F	603 224-9876	14010
Swenson Granite Company LLC **(DH)**	Concord	NH	E	603 225-4322	14161
KB Surfaces LLC	North Smithfield	RI	F	401 727-6792	16324
Stone Systems New England LLC	North Smithfield	RI	E	401 766-3603	16333
Structural Stone LLC	North Kingstown	RI	F	401 667-4969	16281
Adams Granite Co Inc	Websterville	VT	D	802 476-5281	17683
Browns Quarried Slate Pdts Inc	Castleton	VT	F	802 468-2297	17171
Buttura & Sons Inc	Barre	VT	E	802 476-6646	16998
Camara Slate Products Inc	Fair Haven	VT	F	802 265-3200	17250
Gandin Brothers Inc	South Ryegate	VT	F	802 584-3521	17614
Gawet Marble & Granite Inc **(PA)**	Center Rutland	VT	G	802 773-8868	17174
Granite Importers Inc **(PA)**	Barre	VT	E	802 476-5812	17002
Granite Industries Vermont Inc	Barre	VT	D	800 451-3236	17003
Greenstone Slate Company Inc	Poultney	VT	F	802 287-4333	17448
Hillside Solid Surfaces	Barre	VT	F	802 479-2508	17005
International Stone Products **(PA)**	Barre	VT	D	802 476-6636	17009
J & G Hadeka Slate Flrg Inc	West Pawlet	VT	G	802 265-3351	17691
McCue Memorial Co Inc	Castleton	VT	E	802 468-5636	17173
Memorial Sandblast Inc	Barre	VT	E	802 476-7086	17013
Montpelier Granite Works Inc	Montpelier	VT	F	802 223-2581	17373
Newmont Slate Co Inc **(PA)**	West Pawlet	VT	E	802 645-0203	17692
Pepin Granite Company Inc	Barre	VT	F	802 476-6103	17015
Q-Seal LLC	Rutland	VT	G	802 773-1228	17504
Riverton Memorial Inc	Riverton	VT	F	802 485-3371	17483
Rock of Ages Corporation **(DH)**	Graniteville	VT	C	802 476-3115	17277
S W Granite Inc	Northfield	VT	G	713 933-0501	17434
Spruce Mountain Granites Inc	Barre	VT	F	802 476-7474	17016
Spruce Mtn Grntes Cstm Sndblas	Barre	VT	F	802 476-7474	17017
Swenson Granite Company LLC	Barre	VT	G	802 476-7021	17019
Troy Minerals Inc	Colchester	VT	E	802 878-5103	17205
Vermont Stone Art LLC	Barre	VT	E	802 238-1498	17023
Vermont Structural Slate Co **(PA)**	Fair Haven	VT	E	802 265-4933	17252
Vermont Unfding Green Slate In **(PA)**	Fair Haven	VT	F	802 265-3200	17253
Williams & Co Mining Inc	Perkinsville	VT	F	802 263-5404	17443

3291 Abrasive products

	CITY	ST	EMP	PHONE	ENTRY#
Ahlstrom Nonwovens LLC **(DH)**	Windsor Locks	CT	B	860 654-8300	4318
Avery Abrasives Inc	Trumbull	CT	E	203 372-3513	3713
Chessco Industries Inc **(PA)**	Westport	CT	E	203 255-2804	4160
Composition Materials Co Inc	Milford	CT	G	203 874-6500	1812
Extec Corp	Enfield	CT	F	860 741-3435	1133
Myllykoski North America	Norwalk	CT	E		2541
Pressure Blast Mfg Co Inc	South Windsor	CT	F	800 722-5278	3174
Syncote Chemical Company Inc	Newtown	CT	G	203 426-5526	2348
Triatic Inc	West Hartford	CT	F	860 236-2298	4085
United Abrasives Inc **(PA)**	North Windham	CT	B	860 456-7131	2451
Aspen Systems LLC **(PA)**	Marlborough	MA	E	508 281-5322	10112
Chas G Allen Realty LLC	Barre	MA	D	978 355-2911	6202
Darmann Abrasive Products Inc **(PA)**	Clinton	MA	D	978 365-4544	8076
Micro Abrasives Corporation	Westfield	MA	D	413 562-3641	13187
Mosher Company Inc	Chicopee	MA	F	413 598-8341	8050
Olsen & Silk Abrasives	Salem	MA	F	978 744-4720	11728
Prematech LLC	Worcester	MA	E	508 791-9549	13773
Rex Cut Products Incorporated	Fall River	MA	D	508 678-1985	8602
Saint-Gobain Abrasives Inc **(HQ)**	Worcester	MA	A	508 795-5000	13788
Textile Buff & Wheel Co Inc	Boston	MA	F	617 241-8100	7075
Vogel Capital Inc **(HQ)**	Marlborough	MA	E	508 481-5944	10232

	CITY	ST	EMP	PHONE	ENTRY#
Washington Mills Group Inc **(PA)**	North Grafton	MA	D	508 839-6511	11028
Washington Mills N Grafton Inc **(HQ)**	North Grafton	MA	D	508 839-6511	11029
Westfield Grinding Wheel Co	Westfield	MA	F	413 568-8634	13220
Best Machine Inc	Fremont	NH	G	603 895-4018	14326
Hones LLC	Hanover	NH	G	603 643-4223	14425
Johnson Abrasives Co Inc	Jaffrey	NH	E	603 532-4434	14569
Peg Kearsarge Co Inc	Bartlett	NH	G	603 374-2341	13918
RP Abrasives & Machine Inc	Rochester	NH	F	603 335-2132	15492
ACS Industries Inc **(PA)**	Lincoln	RI	E	401 769-4700	16116
Bates Abrasive Products Inc	Lincoln	RI	E	773 586-8700	16121
Bullard Abrasives Inc	Lincoln	RI	D	508 366-4300	16123
Joseph A Thomas Ltd	Bristol	RI	E	401 253-1330	15770
Marvel Abrasives Products LLC	Lincoln	RI	F	800 621-0673	16148
Meister Abrasives Usa Inc	North Kingstown	RI	F	401 294-4503	16271
Rhode Island Centerless Inc	Johnston	RI	F	401 942-0403	16104
Dessureau Machines Inc	Barre	VT	F	802 476-4561	17000
General Abrasives Inc	Sharon	VT	F	802 763-7264	17555

3292 Asbestos products

	CITY	ST	EMP	PHONE	ENTRY#
Bascom Environmental Co	Plymouth	MA	E	617 282-9500	11449

3295 Minerals, ground or treated

	CITY	ST	EMP	PHONE	ENTRY#
Micro-Mech Inc	Ipswich	MA	E	978 356-2966	9491
P J Albert Inc	Fitchburg	MA	D	978 345-7828	8671
The Schundler Company	Nahant	MA	E	732 287-2244	10460
Whittemore Company Inc	Lawrence	MA	E	978 681-8833	9609
Dicaperl Minerals	Thomaston	ME	G	207 594-8225	5543
FMC Corporation	Rockland	ME	D	207 594-3200	5329
Imerys	Searsport	ME	G	207 548-0900	5455
Pike Industries Inc **(DH)**	Belmont	NH	E	603 527-5100	13967
Isovolta Inc	North Clarendon	VT	F	802 775-5528	17414

3296 Mineral wool

	CITY	ST	EMP	PHONE	ENTRY#
Ecologic Energy Solutions LLC	Stamford	CT	D	203 889-0505	3342
Leek Building Products Inc	Norwalk	CT	E	203 853-3883	2527
Owens Corning Sales LLC	East Hartford	CT	C	304 353-6945	1008
The E J Davis Company	North Haven	CT	E	203 239-5391	2439
Bnz Materials Inc	North Billerica	MA	C	978 663-3401	10900
Eckel Industries Inc **(PA)**	Ayer	MA	E	978 772-0840	6181
Owens Corning Sales LLC	Canton	MA	G	800 438-7465	7816
Soundown Corporation **(PA)**	Salem	MA	E	978 745-7000	11732
Ward Process Inc	Holliston	MA	D	508 429-1165	9238
Johns Manville Corporation	Lewiston	ME	D	207 784-0123	4968
Duxbury Composite Products Inc	Fitzwilliam	NH	E	603 585-9100	14313
Owens Corning	Brentwood	NH	G	603 773-4246	14026
Vemployee	Portsmouth	RI	F	888 471-1982	16460

3297 Nonclay refractories

	CITY	ST	EMP	PHONE	ENTRY#
Joshua LLC **(PA)**	Guilford	CT	F	203 624-0080	1398
Specialty Minerals Inc	Canaan	CT	F	860 824-5435	557
Lvr Inc	Oxford	MA	G	508 987-2337	11260
Osram Sylvania Inc **(DH)**	Wilmington	MA	A	978 570-3000	13444
Saint-Gobain Abrasives Inc **(HQ)**	Worcester	MA	A	508 795-5000	13788
Saint-Gobain Ceramics Plas Inc	Northampton	MA	C	413 586-8167	11078
Zar Tech	Newburyport	MA	F	978 499-5122	10729
Infab Refractories Inc	Lewiston	ME	G	207 783-2075	4965
Newport Sand & Gravel Co Inc **(PA)**	Newport	NH	F	603 298-0199	15233

3299 Nonmetallic mineral products,

	CITY	ST	EMP	PHONE	ENTRY#
John Canning & Co Ltd	Cheshire	CT	E	203 272-9868	602
Luckey LLC	New Haven	CT	F	203 747-5270	2171
U S Stucco LLC	Newington	CT	G	860 667-1935	2330
International Crmic Engrg Corp **(PA)**	Worcester	MA	E	508 853-4700	13743
Nixon Company Incorporated	Indian Orchard	MA	F	413 543-3701	9472
Wee Forest Folk Inc	Carlisle	MA	G	978 369-0286	7851
Zink Imaging Inc	Billerica	MA	C	781 761-5400	6492
Ceramco Inc	Center Conway	NH	E	603 447-2090	14050
Cogebi Inc	Dover	NH	F	603 749-6896	14223
Lightblocks Inc	Merrimack	NH	E	603 889-1115	14989

33 PRIMARY METAL INDUSTRIES

3312 Blast furnaces and steel mills

	CITY	ST	EMP	PHONE	ENTRY#
American Standard Company	Southington	CT	E	860 628-9643	3203
Arnio Welding LLC	Central Village	CT	F	860 564-7696	565
ATI Flat Rlled Pdts Hldngs LLC	Waterbury	CT	F	203 756-7414	3888
Ball & Roller Bearing Co LLC	New Milford	CT	F	860 355-4161	2239
Boudreaus Welding Co Inc	Dayville	CT	F	860 774-2771	860
Ccr Products LLC	West Hartford	CT	E	860 953-0499	4052
CMI Specialty Products Inc	Bristol	CT	F	860 585-0409	429
Dufrane Nuclear Shielding Inc	Winsted	CT	F	860 379-2318	4340
Gerdau Ameristeel US Inc	Plainville	CT	G	860 351-9029	2762

	CITY	ST	EMP	PHONE	ENTRY#
J J Ryan Corporation	Plantsville	CT	C	860 628-0393	2793
Kanthal Corporation	Bethel	CT	E	203 744-1440	124
Kimchuk Incorporated (PA)	Danbury	CT	F	203 790-7800	766
Nucor Steel Connecticut Inc	Wallingford	CT	C	203 265-0615	3836
Plainville Special Tool LLC	Plainville	CT	F	860 747-2736	2777
Rain Commodities (usa) Inc	Stamford	CT	F	203 406-0535	3443
Rcd LLC	Shelton	CT	E	203 712-1900	3059
Redifoils LLC	Portland	CT	F	860 342-1500	2823
Rolltech Precision Metals	Portland	CT	G	412 246-8846	2824
Sal Steel Inc	New Britain	CT	F	860 826-2755	2058
Scp Management LLC	New Hartford	CT	E	860 738-2600	2108
Theis Precision Steel USA Inc (HQ)	Bristol	CT	C	860 589-5511	501
Tms International LLC	Greenwich	CT	F	203 629-8383	1356
Ulbrich Stainless Steels	Wallingford	CT	C	203 269-2507	3871
Ulbrich Stnless Steels Spcial M (PA)	North Haven	CT	D	203 239-4481	2442
Waterbury Rolling Mills Inc	Waterbury	CT	F	203 597-5000	3981
A A A Metals Company Inc	Hanson	MA	F	781 447-1220	9049
Ackles Steel and Iron Co Inc	Waltham	MA	F	781 893-6818	12581
Boston Elctrmetallurgical Corp (PA)	Woburn	MA	E	781 281-7657	13531
Concentric Fabrication LLC	Middleboro	MA	E	508 672-4098	10355
Dakota Systems Inc	Dracut	MA	D	978 275-0600	8303
Emerald Iron Works Inc	Tewksbury	MA	F	978 851-3028	12396
Ipswich Bay Glass Co Inc	Rowley	MA	C	978 948-6644	11677
Joy & Robert Cromwell	East Longmeadow	MA	G	413 224-1440	8382
Ludlow Tool Inc	Agawam	MA	F	413 786-6415	5800
Microgroup Inc	Medway	MA	C	508 533-4925	10308
Natale Co Safetycare LL	Wilmington	MA	E	781 933-7500	13436
Ne Stainless Steel Fab	Weymouth	MA	G	781 335-0121	13331
New England Stinless Distr LLC	Salisbury	MA	F	978 255-4830	11743
Nucor Hrris Rbar Northeast LLC	Westfield	MA	E	413 568-7803	13194
Rivinius & Sons Inc	Woburn	MA	E	781 933-5620	13653
Townsend Welding Co Inc	Wilmington	MA	E	978 657-5189	13468
Vortex Inc	Peabody	MA	D	978 535-8721	11351
Cmd Enterprises LLC	Dexter	ME	G	207 745-9985	4726
Millincket Fabrication Mch Inc (PA)	Millinocket	ME	F	207 723-9733	5067
Parshley Steel Fabricators Inc	North Berwick	ME	G	207 957-4040	5111
Avilite Inc	Merrimack	NH	G	603 626-4388	14974
Capitol Fire Protection Co Inc	Loudon	NH	E	603 783-4713	14794
Empire Sheetmetal Inc	Manchester	NH	E	603 622-4439	14847
Harding Metals Inc	Northwood	NH	E	603 942-5573	15273
Max Cohen & Sons Inc (HQ)	Concord	NH	E	603 224-3532	14144
New Hampshire Stamping Co Inc	Goffstown	NH	E	603 641-1234	14352
New Hmpshire Ball Bearings Inc	Laconia	NH	B	603 524-0004	14661
RSI Metal Fabrication LLC	East Kingston	NH	F	603 382-8367	14273
Shookus Special Tools Inc	Raymond	NH	F	603 895-1200	15458
Slinky Stainless Steel	Milford	NH	G	603 673-1104	15038
Stamping Technologies Inc	Laconia	NH	F	603 524-5958	14671
Talco Enterprises LLC	Nottingham	NH	F	603 765-8052	15278
ACS Industries Inc (PA)	Lincoln	RI	E	401 769-4700	16116
Capco Steel Erection Company	Providence	RI	F	401 383-9388	16495
Jebella LLC	Pawtucket	RI	G	401 475-1720	16378
Ldc Inc	East Providence	RI	F	401 861-4667	16029
LK Goodwin Co Inc (PA)	West Greenwich	RI	F	401 781-5526	16888
Philip Machine Company Inc	Pawtucket	RI	E	401 353-7383	16402
Maru Ltd DBA Greenleaf Metals	Starksboro	VT	G	802 985-5200	17626

3313 Electrometallurgical products

	CITY	ST	EMP	PHONE	ENTRY#
Alent USA Holding Inc	Waterbury	CT*	E	203 575-5727	3880
Desktop Metal Inc (PA)	Burlington	MA	C	978 224-1244	7361
Newton Materion Inc (HQ)	Newton	MA	C	617 630-5800	10772
Purecoat International LLC	Belmont	MA	E	561 844-0100	6309

3315 Steel wire and related products

	CITY	ST	EMP	PHONE	ENTRY#
Accel Intl Holdings Inc	Meriden	CT	E	203 237-2700	1650
Ametek Inc	Wallingford	CT	C	203 265-6731	3770
Bridgeport Insulated Wire Co (PA)	Bridgeport	CT	F	203 333-3191	304
Federal Prison Industries	Danbury	CT	E	203 743-6471	745
Hamden Metal Service Co Inc	Hamden	CT	F	203 281-1522	1427
International Pipe & Stl Corp	North Branford	CT	F	203 481-7102	2369
Kanthal Corporation	Bethel	CT	E	203 744-1440	124
Lee Spring Company LLC	Bristol	CT	F	860 584-0991	461
Lex Products LLC (PA)	Trumbull	CT	C	203 363-3738	3723
Loos & Co Inc (PA)	Pomfret	CT	B	860 928-7981	2809
Loos & Co Inc	Pomfret	CT	D	860 928-6681	2810
Nutmeg Wire	Baltic	CT	F	860 822-8616	38
Q-S Technologies Inc	Meriden	CT	E	203 237-2297	1687
Radcliff Wire Inc	Bristol	CT	E	312 876-1754	489
Rscc Wire & Cable LLC (DH)	East Granby	CT	B	860 653-8300	950
SA Candelora Enterprises Inc	North Branford	CT	F	203 484-2863	2374
Shuster-Mettler Corp	Plainville	CT	E	203 562-3178	2780
Specialty Cable Corp	Wallingford	CT	D	203 265-7126	3852
Stephens Pipe & Steel LLC	Manchester	CT	D	877 777-8721	1639
Tool Logistics II	Norwalk	CT	F	203 855-9754	2585

	CITY	ST	EMP	PHONE	ENTRY#
Tsmc Inc	Torrington	CT	A	860 283-8265	3703
Wiremold Company (DH)	West Hartford	CT	A	860 233-6251	4091
Wiretek Inc	Bloomfield	CT	F	860 242-9473	217
Accellent Acquisition Corp	Wilmington	MA	A	978 570-6900	13370
Accellent Holdings Corp	Wilmington	MA	A	978 570-6900	13371
Belden Inc	Leominster	MA	E	978 537-8911	9641
Bergeron Machine LLC	Westford	MA	E	978 577-6235	13225
Brookfield Wire Company Inc (HQ)	West Brookfield	MA	E	508 867-6474	12992
Cape Cod Fence Co (PA)	South Yarmouth	MA	F	508 398-6041	11982
Countrywide National Services	Walpole	MA	G	508 346-3286	12558
Fence Lines Inc	South Weymouth	MA	F	781 331-2121	11976
Flooring Pro Industries LLC	Auburn	MA	G	704 736-1004	6113
Frank L Reed Inc	Wilbraham	MA	E	413 596-3861	13359
General Wire Products Inc	Worcester	MA	E	508 752-8260	13731
Hampden Fence Supply Inc	Agawam	MA	F	413 786-4390	5792
Heat Trace Products LLC	Leominster	MA	E	978 534-2810	9669
James Cable LLC	Braintree	MA	E	781 356-8701	7189
James Monroe Wire & Cable Corp (PA)	South Lancaster	MA	D	978 368-0131	11971
Joe Miller Inc	Worcester	MA	E	508 753-8581	13745
Lanoco Specialty Wire Pdts Inc	Sutton	MA	E	508 865-1500	12287
Mersen USA Ep Corp (HQ)	Newburyport	MA	D	978 462-6662	10699
Moor Metals Inc (PA)	Holliston	MA	G	508 429-9446	9224
Perfection Fence Corp (PA)	Marshfield	MA	F	781 837-3600	10243
Precision Wire Shapes Inc	West Brookfield	MA	F	508 867-3859	12997
Profiles Incorporated	Palmer	MA	E	413 283-7790	11283
Quirk Wire Co Inc	West Brookfield	MA	E	508 867-3155	12998
S&S Industries Inc (PA)	Stoughton	MA	F	914 885-1500	12232
Sanderson-Macleod Incorporate	Palmer	MA	C	413 283-3481	11284
Temp-Flex LLC	South Grafton	MA	C	508 839-3120	11958
United Site Services Inc (PA)	Westborough	MA	F	508 594-2655	13141
Kelco Industries	Milbridge	ME	F	207 546-7562	5061
Acme Staple Company Inc	Franklin	NH	E	603 934-2320	14318
King Manufacturing Co Inc	Jaffrey	NH	F	603 532-6455	14570
ACS Industries Inc (PA)	Lincoln	RI	E	401 769-4700	16116
Dayton Superior Corporation	Warwick	RI	F	401 885-1934	16805
Sonco Worldwide Inc	Warwick	RI	F	401 406-3761	16863
Heb Manufacturing Company Inc	Chelsea	VT	E	802 685-4821	17178
Micro Wire Transm Systems Inc	Essex Junction	VT	F	802 876-7901	17241

3316 Cold finishing of steel shapes

	CITY	ST	EMP	PHONE	ENTRY#
Deringer-Ney Inc (PA)	Bloomfield	CT	C	860 242-2281	158
Eastern Co (PA)	Shelton	CT	E	203 729-2255	3001
Kanthal Corporation (DH)	Bethel	CT	D	203 744-1440	123
Kanthal Corporation	Bethel	CT	E	203 744-1440	124
North-East Fasteners Corp	Terryville	CT	E	860 589-3242	3607
Paradigm Manchester Inc	Manchester	CT	C	860 649-2888	1625
Shepard Steel Co Inc	Newington	CT	E	860 525-4446	2325
Telling Industries LLC	Windsor	CT	E	860 731-7975	4308
Ulbrich Stainless Steels	Wallingford	CT	C	203 269-2507	3871
Ulbrich Stnless Stels Spcial M (PA)	North Haven	CT	D	203 239-4481	2442
ATI Allegheny Ludlum Inc	New Bedford	MA	D	508 992-4067	10570
Fall River Mfg Co Inc	Fall River	MA	D	508 675-1125	8547
Frank L Reed Inc	Wilbraham	MA	E	413 596-3861	13359
Hub Technologies Inc	Middleboro	MA	E	508 947-3513	10361
Premier Roll & Tool Inc	North Attleboro	MA	E	508 695-2551	10885
Thompson Steel Company Inc	Canton	MA	C	781 828-8800	7834
New Amtrol Holdings Inc (DH)	West Warwick	RI	F	614 438-3210	16917

3317 Steel pipe and tubes

	CITY	ST	EMP	PHONE	ENTRY#
Gordon Corporation	Southington	CT	D	860 628-4775	3214
Nvi Weld Technology LLC	Waterbury	CT	G	203 707-0587	3953
3M Company	Chelmsford	MA	E	978 256-3911	7901
Accellent Acquisition Corp	Wilmington	MA	A	978 570-6900	13370
Accellent Holdings Corp	Wilmington	MA	A	978 570-6900	13371
Ke Tube Inc	Gardner	MA	E	978 630-1436	8892
Microgroup Inc	Medway	MA	C	508 533-4925	10308
New Can Holdings Inc (PA)	Holbrook	MA	E	781 767-1650	9182
Thermatron Engineering Inc	Methuen	MA	E	978 687-8844	10345
Wyman-Gordon Company (DH)	North Grafton	MA	B	508 839-8252	11030
Grover Gndrilling Holdings LLC (PA)	Oxford	ME	E	207 743-7051	5144
Unique Mechanical Services Inc	Bow	NH	G	603 856-0057	14013
Maxson Automatic Machinery Co (PA)	Westerly	RI	F	401 596-0162	16935
National Chmney Spply-Vrmont I	South Burlington	VT	D	802 861-2217	17586

3321 Gray and ductile iron foundries

	CITY	ST	EMP	PHONE	ENTRY#
Taylor & Fenn Company	Windsor	CT	D	860 219-9393	4307
Ej Usa Inc	Brockton	MA	F	508 586-3130	7275
G & W Foundry Corp	Millbury	MA	E	508 581-8719	10434
Henry Perkins Company	Bridgewater	MA	F	508 697-6978	7230
Kadant Inc (PA)	Westford	MA	E	978 776-2000	13244
Ulvac Technologies Inc (HQ)	Methuen	MA	E	978 686-7550	10347
Whitman Castings Inc (PA)	Whitman	MA	E	781 447-4417	13352
Millincket Fabrication Mch Inc (PA)	Millinocket	ME	E	207 723-9733	5067

SIC

	CITY	ST	EMP	PHONE	ENTRY#
Prr Enterprise Inc	Lewiston	ME	E	207 783-2991	4985
Nashua Foundries Inc	Nashua	NH	E	603 882-4811	15138
Cumberland Foundry Co Inc	Cumberland	RI	E	401 658-3300	15936
Fairmount Foundry Inc	Woonsocket	RI	E	401 769-1585	16959
Tyco Fire Products LP (DH)	Cranston	RI	C	215 362-0700	15924

3322 Malleable iron foundries

	CITY	ST	EMP	PHONE	ENTRY#
G & W Foundry Corp	Millbury	MA	E	508 581-8719	10434
Rodney Hunt-Fontaine Inc (HQ)	Orange	MA	E	978 544-2511	11232

3324 Steel investment foundries

	CITY	ST	EMP	PHONE	ENTRY#
Alphacoin LLC	Bethel	CT	G	475 256-4050	99
Doncasters Inc	Groton	CT	D	860 446-4803	1366
Doncasters US Hldings 2018 Inc	Groton	CT	F	860 449-1603	1368
Hexcel Corporation	South Windsor	CT	D	925 520-3232	3156
Howmet Corporation	Branford	CT	B	203 315-6150	265
Howmet Corporation	Branford	CT	A	203 481-3451	266
Integra-Cast Inc	New Britain	CT	D	860 225-7600	2032
Sturm Ruger & Company Inc (PA)	Southport	CT	B	203 259-7843	3247
A Young Casting	Attleboro	MA	F	508 222-8188	5987
Consoldted Precision Pdts Corp	Braintree	MA	E	781 848-3333	7174
Kervick Family Foundation Inc	Worcester	MA	E	508 853-4500	13748
Mascon Inc	Woburn	MA	E	781 938-5800	13605
Parts Tool and Die Inc	Agawam	MA	E	413 821-9718	5805
Tecomet Inc	Wilmington	MA	B	978 642-2400	13462
Wyman-Gordon Company (DH)	North Grafton	MA	B	508 839-8252	11030
New England Castings LLC	Standish	ME	E	207 642-3029	5528
Hitchiner Manufacturing Co Inc (PA)	Milford	NH	A	603 673-1100	15027
KW Thompson Tool Company Inc	Rochester	NH	D	603 330-8670	15483
PCC Structurals Groton	Franklin	NH	E	603 286-4301	14321
Sturm Ruger & Company Inc	Newport	NH	B	603 865-2424	15239
Sturm Ruger & Company Inc	Newport	NH	C	603 863-3300	15240
Xray Aerospace Corp	Claremont	NH	F	603 254-8051	14101

3325 Steel foundries, nec

	CITY	ST	EMP	PHONE	ENTRY#
Frank Roth Co Inc	Stratford	CT	D	203 377-2155	3539
Tenova Inc	Wallingford	CT	E	203 265-5684	3859
D W Clark Inc (PA)	East Bridgewater	MA	E	508 378-4014	8339
D W Clark Inc	Taunton	MA	G	508 378-4014	12330
Doncasters Inc	Springfield	MA	D	413 785-1801	12090
HMK Enterprises Inc (PA)	Lexington	MA	F	781 891-6660	9749
Trident Alloys Inc	Springfield	MA	E	413 737-1477	12142
Wollaston Alloys Inc	Braintree	MA	C	781 848-3333	7214
KW Thompson Tool Company Inc	Rochester	NH	D	603 330-8670	15483
Metal Casting Technology Inc	Milford	NH	E	603 673-9720	15033

3331 Primary copper

	CITY	ST	EMP	PHONE	ENTRY#
Ametek Inc	Wallingford	CT	C	203 265-6731	3770
Materion Technical Mtls Inc	Lincoln	RI	C	401 333-1700	16149

3334 Primary aluminum

	CITY	ST	EMP	PHONE	ENTRY#
All Steel LLC	Ellington	CT	G	860 871-6023	1099
Angelos Aluminum	East Haven	CT	E	203 469-3117	1035
Howmet Aerospace Inc	Winsted	CT	E	860 379-3314	4347
Wilson Partitions Inc	Stamford	CT	F	203 316-8033	3495
Gear/Tronics Inc	North Billerica	MA	E	781 933-1400	10914
Wakefield Engineering	Fall River	MA	G	603 417-8310	8624
Bill Lztte Archtctral GL Alum	Riverside	RI	E	401 383-9535	16652

3339 Primary nonferrous metals, nec

	CITY	ST	EMP	PHONE	ENTRY#
Alent USA Holding Inc	Waterbury	CT	E	203 575-5727	3880
Bal International Inc	Stamford	CT	E	203 359-6775	3290
Northeastern Metals Corp	Stamford	CT	G	203 348-8088	3419
Ulbrich Stainless Steels	Wallingford	CT	C	203 269-2507	3871
Aspen Systems LLC (PA)	Marlborough	MA	F	508 281-5322	10112
Cabot Corporation (PA)	Boston	MA	C	617 345-0100	6631
Cabot Corporation	Haverhill	MA	C	978 556-8400	9084
Glines & Rhodes Inc	Attleboro	MA	E	508 226-2000	6021
Global Advanced Metals USA Inc (PA)	Wellesley Hills	MA	F	781 996-7300	12951
HC Starck Tungsten LLC	Auburndale	MA	E	617 630-4843	6136
J T Inman Co Inc	Attleboro Falls	MA	E	508 226-0080	6088
Metalor Technologies USA Corp (DH)	North Attleboro	MA	E	508 699-8800	10876
Metalor USA Refining Corp (DH)	North Attleboro	MA	C	508 699-8800	10877
Newton Materion Inc (HQ)	Newton	MA	C	617 630-5800	10772
Spindle City Precious Metals	Somerset	MA	G	508 567-1597	11855
Junora Ltd	Biddeford	ME	F	207 284-4900	4573
Medalist Corp	Burnham	ME	E	615 620-8280	4660
Apogee Coins Precious Mtls LLC	Manchester	NH	G	603 391-6417	14813
Colt Refining Inc (PA)	Merrimack	NH	E	603 429-9966	14978
Harding Metals Inc	Northwood	NH	E	603 942-5573	15273
Advanced Chemical Company	Warwick	RI	E	401 785-3434	16776
Geib Refining Corporation	Warwick	RI	E	401 738-8560	16817
Materion Technical Mtls Inc	Lincoln	RI	C	401 333-1700	16149

3341 Secondary nonferrous metals

	CITY	ST	EMP	PHONE	ENTRY#
5n Plus Wisconsin Inc	Bridgeport	CT	F	203 384-0331	289
Alent USA Holding Inc	Waterbury	CT	E	203 575-5727	3880
Lajoie Auto Wrecking Co Inc	Norwalk	CT	E	203 870-0641	2525
MJ Metal Inc	Bridgeport	CT	E	203 334-3484	348
Paradigm Manchester Inc	Manchester	CT	C	860 649-2888	1625
Reliable Silver Corporation	Naugatuck	CT	F	203 574-7732	1984
Smm New England Corporation	New Haven	CT	E	203 777-7445	2201
Thyssenkrupp Materials NA Inc	Wallingford	CT	E	610 586-1800	3863
Ulbrich Stnless Stels Spcial M (PA)	North Haven	CT	D	203 239-4481	2442
Utitec Inc (HQ)	Watertown	CT	D	860 945-0605	4035
Willimantic Waste Paper Co Inc (HQ)	Willimantic	CT	C	860 423-4527	4221
Connell Limited Partnership (PA)	Boston	MA	E	617 737-2700	6665
George Apkin & Sons Inc	Adams	MA	F	413 664-4936	5772
Metalor Technologies USA Corp (DH)	North Attleboro	MA	E	508 699-8800	10876
Metalor USA Refining Corp (DH)	North Attleboro	MA	C	508 699-8800	10877
Special Metals Corporation	Worcester	MA	D	270 365-9551	13804
Wte Recycling Inc	Greenfield	MA	E	413 772-2200	9007
Maine Metal Recycling Inc	Auburn	ME	F	207 786-3531	4442
Colt Refining Inc (PA)	Merrimack	NH	E	603 429-9966	14978
Harding Metals Inc	Northwood	NH	E	603 942-5573	15273
Max Cohen & Sons Inc (HQ)	Concord	NH	E	603 224-3532	14144
N Kamenske & Co Inc	Nashua	NH	G	603 888-1007	15137
Sturm Ruger & Company Inc	Newport	NH	C	603 863-3300	15240
Gannon & Scott Inc (PA)	Cranston	RI	D	800 556-7296	15864
Glencore Recycling LLC	East Providence	RI	F	401 438-9220	16020
Kelley Metals Corp	East Providence	RI	F	401 434-8795	16028
Morgan Mill Metals LLC	Johnston	RI	F	401 270-9944	16097
Noble Metals Services Inc	Cranston	RI	F	866 695-4806	15901
Pease & Curren Incorporated	Warwick	RI	E	401 738-6449	16844
Xstrata Recycling Inc	East Providence	RI	F	401 438-9220	16049
Earth Waste Systems Inc (PA)	Rutland	VT	E	802 775-7722	17494

3351 Copper rolling and drawing

	CITY	ST	EMP	PHONE	ENTRY#
Waterbury Rolling Mills Inc	Waterbury	CT	D	203 597-5000	3981
Aimtek Inc (PA)	Auburn	MA	E	508 832-5035	6099
Data Guide Cable Corporation	Gardner	MA	D	978 632-0900	8883
Ems Engnred Mtls Solutions LLC (DH)	Attleboro	MA	C	508 342-2100	6012
Frank L Reed Inc	Wilbraham	MA	E	413 596-3861	13359
McIntire Brass Works Inc	Lincoln	MA	G	617 547-1819	9797
Pep Industries LLC	Attleboro	MA	F	508 226-5600	6046
Precision Engineered Pdts LLC (DH)	Attleboro	MA	G		6051
Sanderson-Macleod Incorporate	Palmer	MA	C	413 283-3481	11284
Thermatron Engineering Inc	Methuen	MA	E	978 687-8844	10345
Advanced Building Products Inc	Sanford	ME	F	207 490-2306	5389
York Manufacturing Inc	Sanford	ME	F	207 324-1300	5418
Aetna Insulated Wire LLC	Milford	NH	C	757 460-3381	15011
House of Stainless Inc	Cranston	RI	E	800 556-3470	15873
J L Anthony & Company	Providence	RI	G	401 467-9700	16547
Millard Wire Company (PA)	Warwick	RI	E	401 737-9330	16838

3353 Aluminum sheet, plate, and foil

	CITY	ST	EMP	PHONE	ENTRY#
Clarke International Bus Inc	Middletown	CT	E	860 632-1149	1743
CMI Specialty Products Inc	Bristol	CT	F	860 585-0409	429
Ram Welding Co Inc	Naugatuck	CT	E	203 720-0535	1983
Republic Foil Inc	Danbury	CT	D	203 743-2731	805
Boyd Biomedical Inc (PA)	Lee	MA	E	413 243-2000	9612
Innovative Designs & Disp Inc	Hatfield	MA	F	413 586-9854	9072
GA Rel Manufacturing Company	Providence	RI	F	401 331-5455	16524
J L Anthony & Company	Providence	RI	G	401 467-9700	16547

3354 Aluminum extruded products

	CITY	ST	EMP	PHONE	ENTRY#
Narragansett Screw Co	Winsted	CT	F	860 379-4059	4351
Porcelen Limited Connecticut LLC (PA)	Hamden	CT	D	203 248-6346	1449
Porcelen Ltd Connecticut LLC	Hamden	CT	E	203 248-6346	1450
Republic Foil Inc	Danbury	CT	D	203 743-2731	805
The Petit Tool Co	Thomaston	CT	E	860 283-9626	3636
Unique Extrusions Incorporated	Cromwell	CT	E	860 632-1314	698
Atrenne Cmpt Solutions LLC	Brockton	MA	D	508 588-6110	7258
Atrenne Cmpt Solutions LLC (DH)	Brockton	MA	B	508 588-6110	7259
Erd Metal Inc	Westfield	MA	E	508 232-3684	13165
Maki Building Centers Inc (HQ)	Gardner	MA	E	978 343-7422	8894
Mestek Inc (PA)	Westfield	MA	E	470 898-4533	13186
Silver City Aluminum Corp	Taunton	MA	D	508 824-8631	12367
Wakefeld Thermal Solutions Inc (HQ)	Nashua	NH	C	603 635-2800	15185
Hall Inc	Bristol	RI	D	401 253-4858	15768

3355 Aluminum rolling and drawing, nec

	CITY	ST	EMP	PHONE	ENTRY#
Acme Monaco Corporation (PA)	New Britain	CT	C	860 224-1349	1995
Alpha-Core Inc	Shelton	CT	E	203 954-0050	2980
Erickson Metals Corporation (PA)	Cheshire	CT	G	203 272-2918	591
Republic Foil Inc	Danbury	CT	D	203 743-2731	805

	CITY	ST	EMP	PHONE	ENTRY#
IBC Corporation	South Easton	MA	D	508 238-7941	11944
Joseph Freedman Co Inc	Springfield	MA	E	413 781-4444	12107
Joseph Freedman Co Inc (PA)	Springfield	MA	D	888 677-7818	12108
Replica Works Inc	Orange	MA	E	978 544-7000	11231

3356 Nonferrous rolling and drawing, nec

	CITY	ST	EMP	PHONE	ENTRY#
Aerospace Metals Inc	Hartford	CT	A	860 522-3123	1468
Alent USA Holding Inc	Waterbury	CT	E	203 575-5727	3880
Alpha Assembly Solutions Inc	Waterbury	CT	E	203 575-5696	3881
Doncasters Inc	Groton	CT	D	860 446-4803	1366
Doncasters Inc (PA)	Groton	CT	D	860 449-1603	1367
Platt Brothers & Company (PA)	Waterbury	CT	D	203 753-4194	3963
Tico Titanium Inc (PA)	Wallingford	CT	E	248 446-0400	3864
Titanium Electric LLC	Norwalk	CT	G	203 810-4050	2582
Titanium Metals Corporation	East Windsor	CT	C	860 627-7051	1088
Torrey S Crane Company	Plantsville	CT	E	860 628-4778	2799
Ulbrich Stainless Steels	Wallingford	CT	C	203 269-2507	3871
Ulbrich Stnless Stels Spcial M (PA)	North Haven	CT	D	203 239-4481	2442
United Sttes Sign Fbrction Cor	Trumbull	CT	F	203 601-1000	3739
Waterbury Rolling Mills Inc	Waterbury	CT	D	203 597-5000	3981
6k Energy LLC	North Andover	MA	F	978 258-1645	10815
Ascend Elements Inc (PA)	Westborough	MA	G	508 936-7701	13077
Comtran Cable LLC	Attleboro	MA	C	800 842-7809	6007
EF Leach & Company	Attleboro	MA	C	508 643-3309	6011
Newton Materion Inc (HQ)	Newton	MA	C	617 630-5800	10772
President Titanium Co Inc	Hanson	MA	E	781 294-0000	9055
Replica Works Inc	Orange	MA	E	978 544-7000	11231
Special Metals Corporation	Worcester	MA	D	270 365-9551	13804
Sx Industries Inc (PA)	Stoughton	MA	F	781 828-7111	12241
Elmet Technologies Inc	Lewiston	ME	C	207 784-3591	4959
Elmet Technologies LLC (PA)	Lewiston	ME	C	207 333-6100	4960
Jarden LLC	East Wilton	ME	F	207 645-2574	4741
Dgf Indstrial Innvtons Group L	Gilford	NH	F	603 528-6591	14335
Microspec Corporation	Peterborough	NH	E	603 924-4300	15319
1st Casting Company	Johnston	RI	F	401 272-0750	16071
Aim Products LLC (HQ)	Cranston	RI	E	401 463-5605	15825
American Iron & Metal USA Inc (HQ)	Cranston	RI	F	401 463-5605	15831
Callico Metals Inc	North Kingstown	RI	G	401 398-8238	16236
Cimini & Associates Inc	Westerly	RI	E	401 348-0388	16929
J L Anthony & Company	Providence	RI	G	401 467-9700	16547
Nickel Corporaxion	Providence	RI	G	401 351-6555	16575

3357 Nonferrous wiredrawing and insulating

	CITY	ST	EMP	PHONE	ENTRY#
A J R Inc	Bridgeport	CT	F	203 384-0400	290
Algonquin Industries Inc (HQ)	Guilford	CT	D	203 453-4348	1384
Alpha-Core Inc	Shelton	CT	E	203 954-0050	2980
Altek Electronics Inc	Torrington	CT	C	860 482-7626	3669
Autac Incorporated (PA)	Branford	CT	D	203 481-3444	238
Bellevue Private Equity Inc	Naugatuck	CT	G	781 893-6721	1949
Bridgeport Insulated Wire Co (PA)	Bridgeport	CT	F	203 333-3191	304
Bridgeport Insulated Wire Co	Stratford	CT	G	203 375-9579	3523
Bridgeport Magnetics Group Inc	Shelton	CT	E	203 954-0050	2988
Cable Technology Inc	Willington	CT	E	860 429-7889	4224
Fiberqa LLC	Old Lyme	CT	E	860 254-7275	2641
Hamden Metal Service Co Inc	Hamden	CT	F	203 281-1522	1427
Insulated Wire Inc	Bethel	CT	E	203 791-1999	119
Kanthal Corporation (DH)	Bethel	CT	D	203 744-1440	123
Kanthal Corporation	Bethel	CT	E	203 744-1440	124
King Network Services Inc	Plainville	CT	F	860 479-8029	2766
Loos & Co Inc (PA)	Pomfret	CT	B	860 928-7981	2809
Lucent Specialty Fiber Tech	Avon	CT	G	320 258-3035	30
Luvata Waterbury Inc (HQ)	Waterbury	CT	D	203 753-5215	3931
Multi-Cable Corp	Bristol	CT	F	860 589-9035	473
Norfield Data Products Inc	Norwalk	CT	F	203 849-0292	2546
Ofs Fitel LLC	Avon	CT	B	860 678-0371	33
Omerin Usa Inc	Meriden	CT	E	475 343-3450	1682
Ortronics Inc (DH)	New London	CT	D	860 445-3900	2232
Ortronics Inc	West Hartford	CT	F	877 295-3472	4076
Platt Brothers & Company (PA)	Waterbury	CT	D	203 753-4194	3963
Prysmian Cbles Systems USA LLC	Willimantic	CT	C	860 456-8000	4220
Radcliff Wire Inc	Bristol	CT	E	312 876-7574	489
REA Magnet Wire Company Inc	Guilford	CT	D	203 738-6100	1404
Rscc Wire & Cable LLC	East Granby	CT	D	860 653-8300	949
Rscc Wire & Cable LLC (DH)	East Granby	CT	B	860 653-8300	950
Siemon Company (PA)	Watertown	CT	A	860 945-4200	4029
Specialty Cable Corp	Wallingford	CT	D	203 265-7126	3852
Tek Wire and Cable Corp	Stamford	CT	E	914 663-2100	3479
Times Fiber Communications Inc (HQ)	Wallingford	CT	D	800 677-2288	3865
Times Microwave Systems Inc (HQ)	Wallingford	CT	B	203 949-8400	3866
Volpe Cable Corporation	Branford	CT	C	203 623-1818	284
Winchester Interconnect CM Corporation	Dayville	CT	C	860 774-4812	871
Wiretek Inc	Bloomfield	CT	F	860 242-9473	217
AFL Telecommunications LLC	North Grafton	MA	F	508 890-7100	11018

	CITY	ST	EMP	PHONE	ENTRY#
American Cable Assemblies Inc (PA)	Palmer	MA	F	413 283-2515	11270
American Insulated Wire Corporation (HQ) 508 964-1200 10037	Mansfield	MA		MA	E
Anomet Products Inc	Shrewsbury	MA	E	508 842-0174	11827
Belden Inc	Leominster	MA	E	978 537-8911	9641
Belden Inc	Worcester	MA	G	508 754-4858	13703
Brookfield Wire Company Inc (HQ)	West Brookfield	MA	E	508 867-6474	12992
Caton Connector Corp	Kingston	MA	E	781 585-4315	9505
Champlain Cable Leeds Corporation	Leeds	MA	E	413 584-3853	9620
Cubit Wire & Cable Co Inc	Holyoke	MA	E	413 539-9892	9249
Data Guide Cable Corporation	Gardner	MA	D	978 632-0900	8883
Denardo Wire and Cable Co Inc	Fitchburg	MA	E	978 343-6412	8652
Dielectric Sciences Inc	Chelmsford	MA	E	978 250-1507	7923
Draka Cableteq Usa Inc	Boston	MA	B	888 520-1200	6702
East Cast McRwave Sls Dist LLC	Woburn	MA	E	781 279-0900	13562
Eis Wire & Cable Inc	South Hadley	MA	D	413 536-0152	11961
Electronic Assemblies Mfg Inc	Methuen	MA	E	978 374-6840	10329
Gavitt Wire and Cable Co Inc	West Brookfield	MA	D	508 867-6476	12994
General Wire Products Inc	Worcester	MA	E	508 752-8260	13731
IBC Corporation	South Easton	MA	D	508 238-7941	11944
James Monroe Wire & Cable Corp (PA)	South Lancaster	MA	D	978 368-0131	11971
Judd Wire Inc (DH)	Turners Falls	MA	B	800 545-5833	12450
L-Com Inc (DH)	North Andover	MA	D	978 682-6936	10842
Madison Cable Corporation	Worcester	MA	D	800 522-6752	13755
Manage Inc	Springfield	MA	E	413 593-9128	12112
Mercury Wire Products Inc	Spencer	MA	C	508 885-6363	12064
Milford Manufacturing Svcs LLC	Hopedale	MA	E	508 478-8544	9299
Mohawk Chicago Distribution	Leominster	MA	F	781 334-4976	9684
Mor-Wire & Cable Inc	Lowell	MA	F	978 453-1782	9909
Motorola Mobility LLC	Lowell	MA	E	978 614-2900	9910
Ofs Brightwave LLC	Sturbridge	MA	E	508 347-2261	12252
Ofs Fitel LLC	Sturbridge	MA	B	508 347-2261	12253
Prysmian Group Spclty Cbles LL	Taunton	MA	C	508 822-0246	12357
Prysmian Group Spclty Cbles LL (DH)	Taunton	MA	C	774 501-7600	12358
Prysmian Group Spclty Cbles LL	Taunton	MA	C	508 822-5444	12359
Quabbin Wire & Cable Co Inc (PA)	Ware	MA	D	413 967-6281	12827
Quirk Wire Co Inc	West Brookfield	MA	E	508 867-3155	12998
Saint-Gobain Prfmce Plas Corp	Worcester	MA	C	508 852-3072	13792
Segue Manufacturing Svcs LLC	North Billerica	MA	D	978 970-1200	10952
Senko Advanced Components Inc (HQ)	Hudson	MA	E	508 481-9999	9412
Supercon Incorporated	Shrewsbury	MA	E	508 842-0174	11843
Taurus Technologies Corp	South Grafton	MA	F	508 234-6372	11957
Tech-Etch Inc	Fall River	MA	E	508 675-5757	8614
Temp-Flex LLC	South Grafton	MA	C	508 839-3120	11958
Tricab (usa) Inc	Worcester	MA	E	508 421-4680	13813
V-Tron Electronics Corp	Attleboro	MA	D	508 761-9100	6072
Verrillon Inc	North Grafton	MA	D	508 890-7100	11027
Eldur Corporation	Bangor	ME	E	207 942-6592	4499
Transparent Audio Inc	Saco	ME	E	207 284-1100	5380
Aetna Insulated Wire LLC	Milford	NH	C	757 460-3381	15011
AFL Telecommunications LLC	Belmont	NH	E	603 528-7780	13958
Amphenol Corporation	Nashua	NH	B	603 879-3000	15061
Amphenol Printed Circuits Inc (HQ)	Nashua	NH	D	603 324-4500	15062
Belden Inc	Keene	NH	G	603 359-7355	14590
Burton Wire & Cable LLC	Hooksett	NH	F	603 624-2427	14463
Cable Assemblies Inc	Amherst	NH	F	603 889-4090	13863
Elektrisola Incorporated (PA)	Boscawen	NH	C	603 796-2114	13989
Enterasys Networks Inc (HQ)	Salem	NH	D	603 952-5000	15521
Marmon Aerospace & Defense LLC (DH)	Manchester	NH	F	603 622-3500	14880
Marmon Utility LLC	Amherst	NH	C	603 673-2040	13878
Marmon Utility LLC (DH)	Milford	NH	C	603 673-2040	15032
Microspec Corporation	Peterborough	NH	E	603 924-4300	15319
Proterial Cable America Inc	Manchester	NH	C	603 669-4347	14917
Prysmian Cbles Systems USA LLC	Manchester	NH	D	603 668-1620	14918
Retcomp Inc	New Boston	NH	F	603 487-5010	15194
Rscc Wire & Cable LLC	Manchester	NH	D	603 622-3500	14923
Stonewall Cable Inc	Rumney	NH	D	603 536-1601	15498
Subcom Cable Systems LLC	Newington	NH	B	603 436-6100	15214
Teledyne Instruments Inc	Portsmouth	NH	C	603 474-5571	15442
Electro Standards Lab Inc	Cranston	RI	D	401 946-1164	15853
Okonite Company Inc	Cumberland	RI	E	401 333-3500	15947
Prysmian Cbles Systems USA LLC	Lincoln	RI	C	401 333-4848	16151
Champlain Cable Corporation (PA)	Colchester	VT	C	802 654-4200	17187
Phoenix Wire Inc	South Hero	VT	G	802 372-4561	17609
Super-Temp Wire & Cable Inc	South Burlington	VT	E	802 655-4211	17603

3363 Aluminum die-castings

	CITY	ST	EMP	PHONE	ENTRY#
Arrow Diversified Tooling Inc	Ellington	CT	E	860 872-9072	1101
Custom Metal Crafters Inc	Newington	CT	E	860 953-4210	2283
Texas Die Casting LLC	Norwalk	CT	C	903 845-2224	2581
Diecast Connections Co Inc	Plymouth	MA	E	413 592-8444	11456
Kennedy Die Castings Inc	Worcester	MA	C	508 791-5594	13747
Kingston Aluminum Foundry Inc	Kingston	MA	G	781 585-6631	9509

SIC

	CITY	ST	EMP	PHONE	ENTRY#
Mystic Valley Foundry Inc	Lincoln	MA	G	617 547-1819	9798
Pace Industries LLC	North Billerica	MA	C	978 667-8400	10941
Connectcut Prcsion Cstings Inc	Claremont	NH	G	603 542-3373	14085
Diamond Casting and Mch Co LLC	Hollis	NH	E	603 465-2263	14450
Hebert Manufacturing Company (PA)	Laconia	NH	F	603 524-2065	14653
Wyman-Gordon Company	Franklin	NH	F	603 934-6630	14325
Miniature Casting Corporation	Cranston	RI	F	401 463-5090	15896

3364 Nonferrous die-castings except aluminum

	CITY	ST	EMP	PHONE	ENTRY#
Custom Metal Crafters Inc	Newington	CT	E	860 953-4210	2283
Integra-Cast Inc	New Britain	CT	D	860 225-7600	2032
Narragansett Screw Co	Winsted	CT	F	860 379-4059	4351
Advanced Metal Concepts Inc	North Attleboro	MA	F	508 695-6400	10864
Fall River Tool & Die Co Inc	Fall River	MA	F	508 674-4621	8550
Industrial Foundry Corporation	Uxbridge	MA	G	508 278-5523	12481
Kennedy Die Castings Inc	Worcester	MA	C	508 791-5594	13747
Kingston Aluminum Foundry Inc	Kingston	MA	E	781 585-6631	9509
Pace Industries LLC	North Billerica	MA	C	978 667-8400	10941
Diamond Casting and Mch Co LLC	Hollis	NH	E	603 465-2263	14450
Hebert Manufacturing Company (PA)	Laconia	NH	F	603 524-2065	14653
Watts Regulator Co	Franklin	NH	A	603 934-5110	14323
Fielding Manufacturing Inc	Cranston	RI	D	401 461-0400	15860
Fielding Mfg - Zinc Dcsting In	Cranston	RI	D	401 461-0400	15861
Ridco Casting Co	Pawtucket	RI	F	401 724-0400	16412
New England Precision Inc	Randolph	VT	D	800 293-4112	17471

3365 Aluminum foundries

	CITY	ST	EMP	PHONE	ENTRY#
Dwyer Aluminum Mast Co Inc	North Branford	CT	F	203 484-0419	2366
Integra-Cast Inc	New Britain	CT	D	860 225-7600	2032
JET Corporation	Bridgeport	CT	F	203 334-3317	334
Oberdorfer LLC	Hartford	CT	C		1498
Pcx Aerosystems LLC	Newington	CT	E	860 666-2471	2317
Arcam Cad To Metal Inc	Woburn	MA	E	781 281-1718	13513
Black Bay Ventures Vi LLC	Palmer	MA	F	413 283-2976	11271
Consoldted Precision Pdts Corp	Braintree	MA	F	781 848-3333	7174
Industrial Bmdcal Sensors Corp	Waltham	MA	F	781 891-4201	12698
Industrial Foundry Corporation	Uxbridge	MA	G	508 278-5523	12481
Kingston Aluminum Foundry Inc	Kingston	MA	E	781 585-6631	9509
Marlborough Foundry Inc	Marlborough	MA	E	508 485-2848	10182
Mystic Valley Foundry Inc	Lincoln	MA	G	617 547-1819	9798
Nanoal LLC (HQ)	Ashland	MA	G	774 777-3369	5963
Pace Industries LLC	North Billerica	MA	C	978 667-8400	10941
Parts Tool and Die Inc	Agawam	MA	E	413 821-9718	5805
Tecomet Inc	Wilmington	MA	B	978 642-2400	13462
Westfield Gage Co Inc	Southwick	MA	F	413 569-9444	12050
Bronze Craft Corporation	Nashua	NH	D	603 883-7747	15074
Diamond Casting and Mch Co LLC	Hollis	NH	E	603 465-2263	14450
Nu-Cast Inc	Londonderry	NH	E	603 432-1600	14777
Patriot Foundry & Castings LLC	Pelham	NH	F	603 934-3919	15292
Hall Inc	Bristol	RI	F	401 253-4858	15768
Jade Manufacturing Company LLC	Warwick	RI	E	401 737-2400	16826
Michael Healy Designs Inc	Manville	RI	G	401 597-5900	16165

3366 Copper foundries

	CITY	ST	EMP	PHONE	ENTRY#
American Sleeve Bearing LLC	Stafford Springs	CT	E	860 684-8060	3253
Spirol International Corp (HQ)	Danielson	CT	C	860 774-8571	844
Alloy Castings Co Inc	East Bridgewater	MA	E	508 378-2541	8334
D W Clark Inc (PA)	East Bridgewater	MA	E	508 378-4014	8339
D W Clark Inc	Taunton	MA	G	508 378-4014	12330
Komtek Forge LLC	Worcester	MA	E	508 853-4500	13750
Mystic Valley Foundry Inc	Lincoln	MA	G	617 547-1819	9798
Palmer Foundry Inc	Palmer	MA	D	413 283-2976	11280
Western Bronze Inc	West Springfield	MA	F	413 737-1319	13053
Bronze Craft Corporation	Nashua	NH	D	603 883-7747	15074
Hebert Foundry & Machine Inc	Laconia	NH	E	603 524-2065	14652
KW Thompson Tool Company Inc	Rochester	NH	D	603 330-8670	15483
New Hmpshire Ball Bearings Inc	Laconia	NH	B	603 524-0004	14661
UNI-Cast LLC	Londonderry	NH	C	603 625-5761	14788
Friends Foundry Inc	Woonsocket	RI	F	401 769-0160	16961
Michael Healy Designs Inc	Manville	RI	G	401 597-5900	16165
Paul King Foundry Inc	Johnston	RI	G	401 231-3120	16099
Truex Incorporated	Pawtucket	RI	F	401 722-5023	16426
New England Precision Inc	Randolph	VT	D	800 293-4112	17471

3369 Nonferrous foundries, nec

	CITY	ST	EMP	PHONE	ENTRY#
Consoldted Inds Acqsition Corp	Cheshire	CT	D	203 272-5371	582
Custom Metal Crafters Inc	Newington	CT	E	860 953-4210	2283
Doncasters Inc	Groton	CT	D	860 446-4803	1366
PCC Structurals Groton (DH)	Groton	CT	C	860 405-3700	1377
Sycast Inc	Hartford	CT	F	860 308-2122	1512
The Commercial Foundry Company	New Britain	CT	E	860 224-1794	2071
Tighitco Inc	Berlin	CT	C	860 828-0298	87
Yankee Casting Co Inc	Enfield	CT	D	860 749-6171	1161

	CITY	ST	EMP	PHONE	ENTRY#
Accent On Industrial Metal Inc	Springfield	MA	F	413 785-1654	12069
Advanced Metal Concepts Inc	North Attleboro	MA	E	508 695-6400	10864
Castechnologies Inc	Attleboro	MA	F	508 222-2915	6000
D W Clark Inc (PA)	East Bridgewater	MA	E	508 378-4014	8339
D W Clark Inc	Taunton	MA	G	508 378-4014	12330
Kennedy Die Castings Inc	Worcester	MA	C	508 791-5594	13747
Kervick Family Foundation Inc	Worcester	MA	E	508 853-4500	13748
Mack Prototype Inc	Gardner	MA	E	978 632-3700	8893
MPingo Multi Casting	Springfield	MA	E	413 241-2500	12115
Pace Industries LLC	North Billerica	MA	C	978 667-8400	10941
Parts Tool and Die Inc	Agawam	MA	E	413 821-9718	5805
Tecomet Inc	Wilmington	MA	B	978 642-2400	13462
Trident Alloys Inc	Springfield	MA	E	413 737-1477	12142
Whitman Castings Inc (PA)	Whitman	MA	E	781 447-4417	13352
Wollaston Alloys Inc	Braintree	MA	E	781 848-3333	7214
Hawk Motors Inc	York	ME	G	207 363-4716	5712
Al CU Met Inc	Londonderry	NH	E	603 432-6220	14729
Diamond Casting and Mch Co LLC	Hollis	NH	E	603 465-2263	14450
Graphicast Inc	Jaffrey	NH	E	603 532-4481	14568
PCC Structurals Groton	Northfield	NH	C	603 286-4301	15267
Component Technologies Corpora	Bristol	RI	G	401 965-2699	15759
Fielding Manufacturing Inc	Cranston	RI	D	401 461-0400	15860
New England Union Co In	West Warwick	RI	E	401 821-0000	16918
Optical Polymers Lab Corp	Pawtucket	RI	F	401 722-0710	16398
Osram Sylvania Inc	Central Falls	RI	C	401 723-1378	15794
Providence Casting Inc	North Providence	RI	G	401 231-0860	16308
Ridco Casting Co	Pawtucket	RI	F	401 724-0400	16412

3398 Metal heat treating

	CITY	ST	EMP	PHONE	ENTRY#
A G C Incorporated	Meriden	CT	C	203 235-3361	1649
A-1 Heat Treating Inc	Ansonia	CT	F	914 220-2179	4
Accurate Brazing Corporation	Manchester	CT	F	860 432-1840	1581
American Heat Treating Inc	Monroe	CT	E	203 268-1750	1904
Amk Welding Inc	South Windsor	CT	E	860 289-5634	3113
Aqua Blasting Corp	Bloomfield	CT	E	860 242-8855	146
Bodycote Thermal Proc Inc	Berlin	CT	E	860 225-7691	52
Bodycote Thermal Proc Inc	Berlin	CT	D	508 754-1724	53
Bodycote Thermal Proc Inc	South Windsor	CT	E	860 282-1371	3121
Eastern Metal Treating Inc	Enfield	CT	F	860 763-4311	1128
Hydro Honing Laboratories Inc (PA)	East Hartford	CT	E	860 289-4328	999
Johnstone Company Inc	North Haven	CT	E	203 239-5834	2419
Metal Improvement Company LLC	East Windsor	CT	E	860 523-9901	1081
Metal Improvement Company LLC	Middletown	CT	E	860 635-9994	1762
Metal Improvement Company LLC	New Britain	CT	E	860 224-9148	2042
Metal Improvement Company LLC	Windsor	CT	E	860 688-6201	4291
Metallurgical Processing	West Hartford	CT	G	860 916-5015	4073
Metallurgical Processing Incorporated	New Britain	CT	D	860 224-2648	2044
Nelson Heat Treating Co Inc	Waterbury	CT	F	203 754-0670	3948
O & W Heat Treat Inc	South Windsor	CT	E	860 528-9239	3168
P&G Metal Components Corp	Bloomfield	CT	F	860 243-2220	199
Paradigm Manchester Inc	Manchester	CT	C	860 649-2888	1625
Peening Technologies Eqp LLC	East Hartford	CT	E	860 289-4328	1010
Sousa Corp	Newington	CT	E	860 523-9090	2326
Specialty Steel Treating Inc	East Granby	CT	E	860 653-0061	953
Walter A Beach Inc	East Hartford	CT	G	860 282-7440	1033
Bodycote Imt Inc (DH)	Andover	MA	D	978 470-0876	5873
Bodycote Thermal Proc Inc	Ipswich	MA	E	978 356-3818	9478
Engelhard Surface Tech	Wilmington	MA	G	978 658-0032	13406
Fireball Heat Treating Co Inc	Attleboro	MA	F	508 222-2617	6017
Hardline Heat Treating Inc	Southbridge	MA	E	508 764-6669	12018
Hy Temp Inc	Attleboro	MA	F	508 222-6626	6024
Industrial Heat Treating Inc	North Quincy	MA	E	617 328-1010	11036
Materials Development Corp	Andover	MA	D	781 391-0400	5893
Metal Improvement Company LLC	Wakefield	MA	F	781 246-3848	12519
Metal Improvement Company LLC	Wilmington	MA	D	978 658-0032	13430
Metal Processing Co Inc	Tyngsboro	MA	G	978 649-1289	12461
Norking Company Inc	Attleboro	MA	E	508 222-3100	6043
Northeast Metals Tech LLC	Rowley	MA	E	978 948-2633	11682
S M Engineering Co Inc	North Attleboro	MA	F	508 699-4484	10886
Thermo Electron F S C Inc	Waltham	MA	C	781 622-1000	12798
United-County Industries Corp	Millbury	MA	E	508 865-5885	10444
Enterprise Casting Corporation	Lewiston	ME	E	207 782-5511	4961
Accurate Brazing Corporation (HQ)	Goffstown	NH	E	603 945-3750	14346
Bodycote Thermal Proc Inc	Laconia	NH	E	603 524-7886	14647
Brazecom Industries LLC	Weare	NH	E	603 529-2080	15670
Mushield Company Inc	Londonderry	NH	D	603 666-4433	14776
Smiths Tblar Systms-Lconia Inc	Laconia	NH	C	603 524-2064	14670
Tsi Group Inc (DH)	Hampton	NH	E	603 964-0296	14416
Turbocam Energy Solutions LLC	Dover	NH	E	603 905-0200	14255
Windy Ridge Corporation	Tamworth	NH	G	603 323-2323	15650
Induplate Inc (PA)	North Providence	RI	D	401 231-5770	16303
Metallurgical Solutions Inc	Providence	RI	F	401 941-2100	16563
S & P Heat Treating Inc	Warwick	RI	F	401 737-9272	16856

	CITY	ST	EMP	PHONE	ENTRY#
Spectrum Thermal Proc LLC	Cranston	RI	F	401 808-6249	15912
Bodycote Surface Tech Inc	Rutland	VT	E	802 773-4278	17490
Trow & Holden Co Inc	Barre	VT	E	802 476-7221	17022

3399 Primary metal products

	CITY	ST	EMP	PHONE	ENTRY#
Abbott Ball Company	West Hartford	CT	D	860 236-5901	4046
Alinabal Inc **(HQ)**	Milford	CT	C	203 877-3241	1796
Alinabal Holdings Corporation **(PA)**	Milford	CT	B	203 877-3241	1797
Allied Sinterings Incorporated	Danbury	CT	F	203 743-7502	706
Allread Products Co LLC	Terryville	CT	F	860 589-3566	3600
Ametek Inc	Wallingford	CT	C	203 265-6731	3770
Ccr Products LLC	West Hartford	CT	E	860 953-0499	4052
Conn Engineering Assoc Corp	Sandy Hook	CT	F	203 426-4733	2948
Hartford Technologies Inc	Rocky Hill	CT	E	860 571-3602	2924
Lincoln Thompson	Bristol	CT	F	860 516-0472	462
Norwalk Powdered Metals Inc	Stratford	CT	D	203 338-8000	3560
Schaeffler Aerospace USA Corp **(DH)**	Danbury	CT	B	203 744-2211	809
Schaeffler Aerospace USA Corp	Winsted	CT	D	860 379-7558	4354
Sterling Sintered Technologies Inc	Winsted	CT	D	860 379-2753	4357
Trd Specialties Inc	Pine Meadow	CT	G	860 738-4505	2729
Cable Harness Resources Inc	Leicester	MA	F	508 892-9495	9622
Capstan Industries Inc	Wrentham	MA	C	508 384-3100	13839
Cryogenic Institute Neng Inc	Worcester	MA	F	508 459-7447	13712
Integratech Solutions Corp	Hudson	MA	D	978 567-1000	9376
Sem-Tec Inc	Worcester	MA	E	508 798-8551	13797
Starmet Corporation **(PA)**	Concord	MA	F	978 369-5410	8134
US Packaging Specialties	Fall River	MA	F	508 674-3636	8621
Eastern Metals Inc	Londonderry	NH	E	603 818-8639	14745
Powdered Metal Technology Corp	Nashua	NH	F	617 642-4135	15150
J Arakelian Inc	Johnston	RI	F	401 943-7366	16090
MCM Technologies Inc	Providence	RI	D	401 785-9204	16561
Stanley Fastening Systems LP **(HQ)**	East Greenwich	RI	C	401 884-2500	15993
Tracy Glover Objects & Ltg Inc	Pawtucket	RI	G	401 724-1100	16425
Ultra Fine Specialty Pdts LLC	Woonsocket	RI	F	401 488-4987	16982

34 FABRICATED METAL PRODUCTS

3411 Metal cans

	CITY	ST	EMP	PHONE	ENTRY#
CCL Label Inc	Shelton	CT	F	203 926-1253	2990
Silgan Closures Intl Holdg Co	Stamford	CT	F	203 975-7110	3457
Silgan Containers Corporation	Stamford	CT	A	203 975-7110	3458
Silgan Holdings Inc **(PA)**	Stamford	CT	C	203 975-7110	3459
Silgan White Cap Corporation	Stamford	CT	G	630 515-8383	3460
CCL Industries Corporation **(HQ)**	Framingham	MA	D	508 872-4511	8749
CCL Label Inc **(HQ)**	Framingham	MA	D	508 872-4511	8750
Leaktite Corporation **(DH)**	Leominster	MA	E	978 537-8000	9676
Tin Can Alley	Provincetown	MA	G	508 487-1648	11499
Can-One (usa) Inc	Nashua	NH	F	860 299-4608	15075

3412 Metal barrels, drums, and pails

	CITY	ST	EMP	PHONE	ENTRY#
Architectural Supplements LLC	Waterbury	CT	F	203 591-5505	3886
Champlin-Packrite Inc	Manchester	CT	E	860 559-6373	1589
Connecticut Container Corp **(PA)**	North Haven	CT	C	203 248-2161	2399
Mobile Mini Inc	Suffield	CT	G	860 668-1888	3594
Cold Chain Technologies LLC **(HQ)**	Franklin	MA	D	508 429-1395	8826
Hardigg Industries LLC **(HQ)**	South Deerfield	MA	C	413 665-2163	11924
Mass Engineering & Tank Inc	Middleboro	MA	F	508 947-8669	10366
Roche Bros Barrel Drum Co Inc	Lowell	MA	F	978 454-9135	9920
Roche Manufacturing Inc	Lowell	MA	F	978 454-9135	9921
Index Packaging Inc	Milton	NH	C	603 350-0018	15046
Modern Metal Solutions LLC	Hudson	NH	F	603 402-3022	14528
Rand-Whitney Container LLC	Pawtucket	RI	D	401 729-7900	16411

3421 Cutlery

	CITY	ST	EMP	PHONE	ENTRY#
Acme United Corporation **(PA)**	Shelton	CT	D	203 254-6060	2978
Bic Corporation **(HQ)**	Shelton	CT	A	203 783-2000	2985
Bic USA Inc **(DH)**	Shelton	CT	C	203 783-2000	2986
Edgewell Per Care Brands LLC **(HQ)**	Shelton	CT	B	203 944-5500	3002
Edgewell Personal Care Company	Milford	CT	D	203 882-2308	1823
Edgewell Personal Care Company **(PA)**	Shelton	CT	E	203 944-5500	3003
Energizer Holdings	Shelton	CT	E	314 985-2000	3004
Dexter-Russell Inc	Southbridge	MA	C	508 765-0201	12014
Donahue Industries Inc	Shrewsbury	MA	E	508 845-6501	11830
Georgia-Pacific LLC	Leominster	MA	D	978 537-4701	9666
Gillette Company **(HQ)**	Boston	MA	A	617 463-3000	6758
Gillette De Mexico Inc	Boston	MA	E	617 421-7000	6759
Grooming Ventures - FL LLC **(HQ)**	Boston	MA	D	305 590-0667	6774
Hyde Group Inc **(PA)**	Southbridge	MA	D	800 872-4933	12020
Lamson and Goodnow LLC	Shelburne Falls	MA	F	413 625-0201	11806
Lamson and Goodnow Mfg Co	Shelburne Falls	MA	E	413 625-6311	11807
Longcap Lamson Products LLC	Westfield	MA	F	413 642-8135	13179
Mandes Inc	Stoughton	MA	G	781 344-6915	12220

	CITY	ST	EMP	PHONE	ENTRY#
Silver Greenfield Inc	Greenfield	MA	C	413 774-2774	8999
York-Cmbrland Assn For Hndcppe **(PA)**	Portland	ME	E	207 879-1140	5292
Zootility Co	Portland	ME	F	207 536-0639	5293
Colonial Cutlery Intl Inc	North Kingstown	RI	E	401 737-0024	16238
Perry Blackburne Inc	North Providence	RI	F	401 231-7200	16307
Edgewell Per Care Brands LLC	Saint Albans	VT	F	802 524-2151	17521
Germani Inc	South Burlington	VT	G	802 862-3653	17579

3423 Hand and edge tools, nec

	CITY	ST	EMP	PHONE	ENTRY#
Atlantic Woodcraft Inc	Enfield	CT	F	860 749-4887	1121
Ben Hughes Communication Products Co		Chester		CT	E
860 526-4337	623				
Bessette Holdings Inc	East Hartford	CT	E	860 289-6000	975
Cambridge Specialty Co Inc	Berlin	CT	D	860 828-3579	57
Chapman Manufacturing Company	Durham	CT	F	860 349-9228	896
Crrc LLC	Cromwell	CT	D	860 635-2200	691
Crrc LLC **(PA)**	South Windsor	CT	F	877 684-6464	3136
E & S Gage Inc	Tolland	CT	F	860 872-5917	3658
Easco Hand Tools Inc	Simsbury	CT	A	860 843-7351	3086
Esico Triton LLC	Chester	CT	E	860 526-9535	629
Fletcher-Terry Company LLC **(PA)**	East Berlin	CT	D	860 828-3400	911
Hart Tool & Engineering	Oxford	CT	G	203 264-9776	2696
Integrity Mfg LLC	Farmington	CT	F	860 678-1599	1223
Irwin Industrial Tool Company	New Britain	CT	E	860 438-3460	2035
J J Ryan Corporation	Plantsville	CT	C	860 628-0393	2793
Jesco Iron Crafts Inc	Oxford	CT	F	201 488-4545	2701
Kell-Strom Tool Co Inc **(PA)**	Wethersfield	CT	F	860 529-6851	4209
Kell-Strom Tool Intl Inc	Wethersfield	CT	F	860 529-6851	4210
Lewmar Inc **(DH)**	Guilford	CT	E	203 458-6200	1399
Online River LLC	Westport	CT	F	203 801-5900	4191
Power-Dyne LLC	Middletown	CT	E	860 346-9283	1772
Skillcraft Machine Tool Co	South Windsor	CT	F	860 953-1246	3180
Stanley Black & Decker Inc **(PA)**	New Britain	CT	C	860 225-5111	2065
Stanley Black & Decker Inc	New Britain	CT	C	860 225-5111	2067
Tiger Enterprises Inc	Plantsville	CT	E	860 621-9155	2798
Trumpf Inc	Farmington	CT	C	860 255-6000	1254
Trumpf Inc **(DH)**	Farmington	CT	C	860 255-6000	1255
Trumpf Inc	Plainville	CT	G	860 255-6000	2786
Ullman Devices Corporation	Ridgefield	CT	D	203 438-6577	2908
Unger Enterprises LLC **(PA)**	Bridgeport	CT	C	203 366-4884	381
Uniprise International Inc	Terryville	CT	E	860 589-7262	3613
Wadsworth Falls Mfg Co	Rockfall	CT	F	860 346-3644	2916
Amos Grt-Grt-Granddaughter Inc	Leominster	MA	E	413 773-5471	9636
Apco Mossberg Co	Attleboro	MA	G	508 222-0340	5993
D & S Manufacturing Company Incorporated		Auburn		MA	F
508 799-7812	6111				
Dexter-Russell Inc	Southbridge	MA	C	508 765-0201	12014
Feteria Tool & Findings	Attleboro	MA	G	508 222-7788	6014
Fine Edge Tool Company Inc	Attleboro	MA	G	508 222-7511	6016
Great Neck Saw Mfrs Inc	Millbury	MA	D	508 865-4482	10436
Hot Tools Incorporated	Marblehead	MA	F	781 639-1000	10088
Hyde Group Inc **(PA)**	Southbridge	MA	D	800 872-4933	12020
Hyde Tools	Southbridge	MA	F	508 764-4344	12021
Lamson and Goodnow LLC	Shelburne Falls	MA	F	413 625-0201	11806
Lamson and Goodnow Mfg Co	Shelburne Falls	MA	E	413 625-6311	11807
Lowell Corporation	West Boylston	MA	E	508 835-2900	12964
LS Starrett Company **(PA)**	Athol	MA	A	978 249-3551	5981
Ludlow Tool	Ludlow	MA	G	413 786-6360	9950
Mayhew Steel Products Inc **(PA)**	Turners Falls	MA	F	413 625-6351	12452
MM Newman Corporation	Marblehead	MA	F	781 631-7100	10091
Peterson and Nash Inc	Norwell	MA	G	781 826-9085	11145
Replica Works Inc	Orange	MA	E	978 544-7000	11231
Riverdale Mills Corporation	Northbridge	MA	C	508 234-8715	11118
Safe-T-Cut Inc	Monson	MA	F	413 267-9984	10456
Seekonk Manufacturing Co Inc	Seekonk	MA	E	508 761-8284	11785
Silpro LLC **(PA)**	Ayer	MA	E	978 772-4444	6196
Silver Greenfield Inc	Greenfield	MA	C	413 774-2774	8999
Simonds Saw LLC	Leominster	MA	E	800 343-1616	9703
Skew Products Incorporated	West Bridgewater	MA	F	508 580-5800	12980
Stan Rubinstein Associates Inc	Walpole	MA	F	508 668-6044	12576
Wrentham Tool Group LLC	Bellingham	MA	F	508 966-2332	6303
Advanced Indus Solutions Inc **(PA)**	Augusta	ME	F	207 623-9599	4466
Garland Manufacturing Co	Saco	ME	E	207 283-3693	5367
Grs Group Inc	Portland	ME	F	207 775-6139	5220
Lie-Nielsen Toolworks Inc	Warren	ME	D	800 327-2520	5584
Peavey Manufacturing Company	Eddington	ME	E	207 843-7861	4746
Xuron Corp	Saco	ME	E	207 283-1401	5382
Axe Play LLC	Hudson	NH	G	603 809-9081	14485
Trellborg Pipe Sals Mlford Inc **(DH)**	Milford	NH	F	800 626-2180	15042
Central Tools Inc **(PA)**	Cranston	RI	E	401 467-8211	15841
Joseph A Thomas Ltd	Bristol	RI	E	401 253-1330	15770
Materion Technical Mtls Inc	Lincoln	RI	C	401 333-1700	16149
Americas Grdening Resource Inc **(PA)**	Burlington	VT	C	802 660-3500	17117

	CITY	ST	EMP	PHONE	ENTRY#
Americas Grdening Resource Inc	Milton	VT	C	802 660-3500	17354
Ames Companies Inc	Wallingford	VT	E	802 446-2601	17670
Edlund Company LLC	Burlington	VT	D	802 862-9661	17133
Gardenmats	Worcester	VT	G	802 498-3314	17781
Innovtive Grdening Slutions Inc	Burlington	VT	C	888 560-1037	17139

3425 Saw blades and handsaws

	CITY	ST	EMP	PHONE	ENTRY#
Blackstone Industries LLC	Bethel	CT	D	203 792-8622	101
Disston Company	Chicopee	MA	E	800 272-4436	8025
LS Starrett Company (PA)	Athol	MA	A	978 249-3551	5981
Lie-Nielsen Toolworks Inc	Warren	ME	D	800 327-2520	5584
Sands Business Eqp & Sups LLC	York	ME	F	207 351-3334	5716
Malco Saw Co Inc	Cranston	RI	G	401 942-7380	15891
Thurston Manufacturing Company	Smithfield	RI	E	401 232-9100	16732
T S S Inc	Waterbury	VT	E	802 244-8101	17678

3429 Hardware, nec

	CITY	ST	EMP	PHONE	ENTRY#
Air-Lock Incorporated	Milford	CT	E	203 878-4691	1794
Assa Inc	New Haven	CT	F	800 235-7482	2120
Assa Abloy ACC Door Cntrls Gro	Berlin	CT	C	865 986-7511	50
Assa Abloy ACC Door Cntrls Gro	New Haven	CT	D	901 365-2160	2121
Assa Abloy Access Egress Hdwr	Berlin	CT	B	860 225-7411	51
Assa Abloy Inc (HQ)	New Haven	CT	B	203 562-2151	2122
Beckson Manufacturing Inc (PA)	Bridgeport	CT	C	203 366-3644	301
Bourdon Forge Co Inc	Middletown	CT	C	860 632-2740	1741
Brookfield Industries Inc	Thomaston	CT	E	860 283-6211	3615
C Sherman Johnson Company Inc	East Haddam	CT	F	860 873-8697	955
Colonial Bronze Company	Torrington	CT	D	860 489-9233	3674
Corbin Russwin	New Haven	CT	C	860 225-7411	2139
Cornell-Carr Co Inc	Monroe	CT	E	203 261-2529	1911
Crrc LLC	Cromwell	CT	D	860 635-2200	691
Crrc LLC (PA)	South Windsor	CT	D	877 684-6464	3136
Dwyer Aluminum Mast Co Inc	North Branford	CT	F	203 484-0419	2366
Eastern Co (PA)	Shelton	CT	E	203 729-2255	3001
Fsb Inc	Berlin	CT	F	203 404-4700	67
GK Mechanical Systems LLC	Brookfield	CT	G	203 775-4970	521
Hartford Aircraft Products Inc	Bloomfield	CT	E	860 242-8228	168
Hdb Inc	Thomaston	CT	F	860 379-9901	3621
Heckmann Building Products Inc	Norwalk	CT	E	708 865-2403	2511
Hicks and Otis Prints Inc	Norwalk	CT	E	203 846-2087	2513
Incjet	Norwich	CT	F	860 823-1427	2607
James Ippolito & Co Conn Inc	Bridgeport	CT	E	203 366-3840	333
James L Howard and Company Inc	Bloomfield	CT	E	860 242-3581	176
Kell-Strom Tool Co Inc (PA)	Wethersfield	CT	F	860 529-6851	4209
Kell-Strom Tool Intl Inc	Wethersfield	CT	F	860 529-6851	4210
Lab Security Systems Corp	Bristol	CT	F	860 589-6037	460
Lassy Tools Inc	Plainville	CT	G	860 747-2748	2768
Lewmar Inc (DH)	Guilford	CT	E	203 458-6200	1399
Loctec Corporation	Newtown	CT	G	203 364-1000	2340
Meadow Manufacturing Inc	Bristol	CT	F	860 357-3785	467
Outland Engineering Inc	Milford	CT	F	800 797-3709	1861
Paneloc Corporation	Farmington	CT	E	860 677-6711	1238
Paradigm Manchester Inc	Manchester	CT	F	860 649-2888	1625
Perry Technology Corporation	New Hartford	CT	D	860 738-2525	2107
Roller Bearing Co Amer Inc	Middlebury	CT	F	203 758-8272	1720
Sargent Manufacturing Company	New Haven	CT	A	203 562-2147	2194
Stanley Black & Decker Inc	New Britain	CT	C	860 225-5111	2063
Stanley Black & Decker Inc	New Britain	CT	G	860 225-5111	2064
Stanley Black & Decker Inc (PA)	New Britain	CT	C	860 225-5111	2065
Stanley Black & Decker Inc	New Britain	CT	F	860 827-5025	2066
Stanley Black & Decker Inc	New Britain	CT	C	860 225-5111	2067
Stanley Black Dcker Asia Hldng (HQ)	New Britain	CT	F	860 225-5111	2068
Stanley Industrial & Auto LLC	New Britain	CT	C	800 800-8005	2070
Tiger Enterprises Inc	Plantsville	CT	C	860 621-9155	2798
Unger Industrial LLC	Bridgeport	CT	G	203 336-3344	382
Vector Engineering Inc	Mystic	CT	F	860 572-0422	1944
Westfalia Inc	Bristol	CT	E	860 314-2920	505
Zephyr Lock LLC	Newtown	CT	F	866 937-4971	2355
Acorn Manufacturing Co Inc	Mansfield	MA	E	508 339-4500	10036
Afc Cable Systems Inc	New Bedford	MA	B	508 998-1131	10566
Anderson Component Corporation	Malden	MA	F	781 324-0350	10001
Architctral Fireplaces of Neng	Auburn	MA	F	508 757-0622	6104
Atlantic RES Mktg Systems Inc	West Bridgewater	MA	F	508 584-7816	12966
Atrenne Cmpt Solutions LLC (DH)	Brockton	MA	B	508 588-6110	7259
Autonomous Marine Systems Inc	Somerville	MA	G	703 348-4778	11862
Boston Gar Flrg & Cabinets LLC	Hanover	MA	F	339 788-9580	9026
Craft Inc	Attleboro	MA	E	508 761-7917	6008
De-Ice Technologies Inc	Somerville	MA	F	857 829-7651	11868
Delaware Valley Corp	Tewksbury	MA	F	978 459-6932	12393
Device Technologies Inc	Southborough	MA	E	508 229-2000	11994
Dorel Juvenile Group Inc	Foxboro	MA	C	800 544-1108	8694
Everett Aluminum Inc	Everett	MA	F	617 389-3839	8488
Gardner Screw Corporation	Gardner	MA	F	978 632-0850	8887

	CITY	ST	EMP	PHONE	ENTRY#
H&H Propeller and Shaft Inc	Salem	MA	F	800 325-0117	11720
Hostar Mar Trnspt Systems Inc	Wareham	MA	F	508 295-2900	12838
Hudson Lock LLC (PA)	Hudson	MA	D	978 562-3481	9373
Inner-Tite Corp	Holden	MA	D	508 829-6361	9191
Jibo Inc	Boston	MA	D	617 542-5426	6825
Ketcham Supply Co Inc	New Bedford	MA	E	508 997-4787	10609
Ketcham Traps	New Bedford	MA	G	508 997-4787	10610
Max Cuff LLC	Pittsfield	MA	G	413 553-3511	11410
McStowe Engrg & Met Pdts Inc	East Bridgewater	MA	F	508 378-7400	8343
Mooring Systems Incorporated	Cataumet	MA	G	508 776-0254	7859
New England Door Closer Inc	West Springfield	MA	E	413 733-7889	13037
Newera Services Corporation (PA)	New Bedford	MA	E	508 995-9711	10631
Qc Industries Inc (PA)	Mansfield	MA	D	781 344-1000	10073
Renovators Supply Inc	Erving	MA	E	413 423-3300	8471
Rolls-Royce Marine North Amer (DH)	Walpole	MA	C	508 668-9610	12574
Roses Oil Service Inc (PA)	Gloucester	MA	E	877 283-3334	8955
Schaefer Marine Inc	New Bedford	MA	E	508 995-9511	10648
Schlage Lock Company LLC	Canton	MA	G	781 828-6655	7826
Taunton Stove Company Inc	North Dighton	MA	E	508 823-0786	11004
Tph Inc	Taunton	MA	E	401 431-1791	12372
Vectrix LLC	New Bedford	MA	G	508 717-6510	10658
W J Roberts Co Inc	Saugus	MA	E	781 233-8176	11767
Watts Sea Tech Inc	North Andover	MA	E	978 688-1811	10860
Worcester Tool & Stamping Co	Rochdale	MA	E	508 892-8194	11630
Xcerra Corporation (HQ)	Norwood	MA	C	781 461-1000	11220
Morse Hardware & Lumber LLC	Wells	ME	F	207 646-5700	5603
Sands Business Eqp & Sups LLC	York	ME	F	207 351-3334	5716
Accutech Marine Propeller Inc	Dover	NH	G	603 617-3626	14213
Bronze Craft Corporation	Nashua	NH	D	603 883-7747	15074
Cascaded Purchase Holdings Inc (PA)	Claremont	NH	D	603 448-1090	14083
Coyote Mountain Farm Inc	Ossipee	NH	G	603 662-2164	15282
American Cord & Webbing Co Inc	Woonsocket	RI	E	401 762-5500	16948
Beacon Rock Properties Inc	Providence	RI	D	401 421-3470	16482
Drapery House Inc	North Providence	RI	E	401 724-3400	16300
Fulford Manufacturing Company (PA)	Riverside	RI	F	401 431-2000	16655
Groov-Pin Corporation (PA)	Smithfield	RI	D	770 251-5054	16707
Hindley Manufacturing Co Inc	Cumberland	RI	D	401 722-2550	15943
J&E Home Products LLC	Lincoln	RI	E	401 464-8677	16142
New England Boatworks Inc	Portsmouth	RI	D	401 683-4000	16449
Ronstan International Inc	Portsmouth	RI	F	401 293-0539	16456
Siren Marine Inc	Newport	RI	F	401 619-4774	16224
Tracey Gear Inc	Pawtucket	RI	F	401 725-3920	16424
Grate Ideas of America LLC	Colchester	VT	G	844 292-6044	17193
Repiper US Inc	Woodstock	VT	G	802 230-5703	17777

3431 Metal sanitary ware

	CITY	ST	EMP	PHONE	ENTRY#
Kensco Inc (PA)	Ansonia	CT	G	203 734-8827	15
Acushnet International Inc (DH)	Fairhaven	MA	C	508 979-2000	8506
Kohler Sgnture Str By Sup Neng	Burlington	MA	F	781 365-0168	7388
Shelmar Inc	Wakefield	MA	F	781 245-1206	12535
Sherle Wagner Intl LLC	Fall River	MA	F	212 758-3300	8606
Rk Parisi Enterprises Inc	Keene	NH	F	844 438-7674	14616
Palmer Industries Inc	North Providence	RI	F	800 398-9676	16306

3432 Plumbing fixture fittings and trim

	CITY	ST	EMP	PHONE	ENTRY#
2023 Holdings LLC (PA)	Newington	CT	C	603 239-6371	2263
Bead Industries Inc (PA)	Milford	CT	E	203 301-0270	1801
Burt Process Equipment Inc (PA)	Hamden	CT	E	203 287-1985	1415
Colonial Bronze Company	Torrington	CT	D	860 489-9233	3674
F W Webb Company	New Haven	CT	F	203 865-6124	2151
Fitzgerald and Wood Inc	Branford	CT	G	203 488-2553	257
Granite Group Wholesalers LLC	Colchester	CT	G	860 537-7600	659
Macristy Industries Inc (PA)	Newington	CT	F	860 225-4637	2305
McGuire Manufacturing Co Inc	Cheshire	CT	E	203 699-1801	606
Neoperl Inc	Waterbury	CT	D	203 756-8891	3949
F W Webb Company	Needham	MA	F	781 247-0300	10510
Ferguson Enterprises LLC	Chicopee	MA	F	413 593-1219	8032
Idex Health & Science LLC	Middleboro	MA	F	774 213-0200	10362
Orion Enterprises Inc (HQ)	North Andover	MA	C	913 342-1653	10847
Renovators Supply Inc	Erving	MA	E	413 423-3300	8471
Sherle Wagner Intl LLC	Fall River	MA	F	212 758-3300	8606
Symmons Industries Inc	Avon	MA	D	508 857-2352	6163
Symmons Industries Inc (PA)	Braintree	MA	C	800 796-6667	7207
Viola Associates Inc	Hyannis	MA	F	508 771-3457	9455
F W Webb Company	Windham	ME	F	207 892-5302	5661
2023 Holdings LLC	Winchester	NH	D	603 239-6371	15713
Fulford Manufacturing Company (PA)	Riverside	RI	F	401 431-2000	16655
Quick Fitting Inc	East Providence	RI	D	401 734-9500	16040

3433 Heating equipment, except electric

	CITY	ST	EMP	PHONE	ENTRY#
Aquacomfort Solutions LLC	Wallingford	CT	G	203 265-0100	3774
Cowles Operating Company	North Haven	CT	C	203 680-9401	2404
Hamworthy Peabody Combustn Inc (DH)	Shelton	CT	E	203 922-1199	3012

	CITY	ST	EMP	PHONE	ENTRY#
Jad LLC	South Windsor	CT	E	860 289-1551	3158
John Zink Company LLC	Shelton	CT	E	203 925-0380	3025
Macristy Industries Inc (PA)	Newington	CT	F	860 225-4637	2305
Manufacturing PDT Systems Inc	Windsor	CT	F	877 689-1860	4288
McIntire Company (HQ)	Bristol	CT	F	860 585-8559	465
Omega Engineering Inc (DH)	Norwalk	CT	C	203 359-1660	2549
Preferred Utilities Mfg Corp (HQ)	Danbury	CT	D	203 743-6741	799
Proliance International Inc	New Haven	CT	E	203 401-6450	2188
Pumc Holding Corporation (PA)	Danbury	CT	F	203 743-6741	802
Babcock Power Inc (PA)	Danvers	MA	G	978 646-3300	8166
Babcock Power Renewables LLC (HQ)	Danvers	MA	G	978 646-3300	8167
Cox Engineering Company (PA)	Canton	MA	C	781 302-3300	7781
Ganado Storage LLC	Andover	MA	D	617 605-4322	5884
H B Smith Company Inc	Westfield	MA	F	413 568-3148	13170
J & J Heating & AC Inc	Dracut	MA	F	978 454-8197	8306
Lake Industries Inc	Stoneham	MA	D	781 438-8814	12180
Marios Oil Corp	Everett	MA	G	617 202-8259	8493
Mestek Inc	Westfield	MA	E	413 568-9571	13185
Metromatic Manufacturing Company Inc	Byfield	MA	F	781 396-5300	7458
Rasa Incorporated	Shrewsbury	MA	F	508 425-3261	11840
Rdp Manufacturing Inc	East Longmeadow	MA	D	413 525-7700	8392
Riley Power Inc	Marlborough	MA	B	508 852-7100	10204
Runtal North America Inc	Haverhill	MA	F	800 526-2621	9128
Spire Solar Inc (HQ)	Bedford	MA	G	781 275-6000	6271
Sundrum Solar Inc	Northborough	MA	G	508 740-6256	11110
Thermal Circuits Inc	Salem	MA	C	978 745-1162	11734
Tunstall Corporation (PA)	Chicopee	MA	E	413 594-8695	8064
GS Inc	Rockland	ME	G	207 593-7730	5332
Jotul North America Inc	Gorham	ME	D	207 797-5912	4823
Maine Stove & Chimney LLC	Sanford	ME	F	207 324-4440	5399
Onix Corporation	Caribou	ME	F	866 290-5362	4678
Bradford White Corp	Rochester	NH	G	603 332-0116	15468
Efficiency Plus	Center Ossipee	NH	G	603 539-8125	14057
Osram Sylvania Inc	Exeter	NH	B	603 772-4331	14299
R Filion Manufacturing Inc	Newport	NH	F	603 865-1893	15236
Woodstock Soapstone Co Inc	West Lebanon	NH	F	800 866-4344	15692
Nasons Ug Inc (PA)	Middletown	RI	G	401 847-2497	16180
Taco Inc (PA)	Cranston	RI	B	401 942-8000	15917
Bullrock Solar LLC	South Burlington	VT	F	802 985-1460	17575
L & G Fabricators Inc	Bennington	VT	F	802 447-0965	17047

3441 Fabricated structural metal

	CITY	ST	EMP	PHONE	ENTRY#
Accutron Inc (PA)	Windsor	CT	D	860 683-8300	4253
Action Steel LLC	Colchester	CT	E	860 537-9499	653
Alken Industries Inc	Newington	CT	E	631 467-2000	2269
All Panel Systems LLC	Branford	CT	D	203 208-3142	234
All Phase Steel Works LLC	New Haven	CT	F	203 375-8881	2113
Alloy Welding & Mfg Co Inc	Bristol	CT	F	860 582-3638	394
Anco Engineering Inc	Shelton	CT	D	203 925-9235	2981
Ansonia Stl Fabrication Co Inc	Beacon Falls	CT	E	203 888-4509	39
Applied Laser Solutions Inc	Danbury	CT	G	203 739-0179	709
Atlantic Eqp Installers Inc	Wallingford	CT	F	203 284-0402	3777
Atlantic Fabricating Co Inc	South Windsor	CT	F	860 291-9882	3117
Atlas Metal Works LLC	South Windsor	CT	F	860 282-1030	3118
Berlin Steel Construction Co (PA)	Kensington	CT	E	860 828-3531	1538
Boudreaus Welding Co Inc	Dayville	CT	F	860 774-2771	860
Capital Steel LLC	Berlin	CT	E	860 828-9353	58
Capin Manufacturing Inc	Waterbury	CT	D	203 574-2556	3897
Central Construction Inds LLC	Putnam	CT	E	860 963-8902	2848
Clearspan Fabr Strctres Intl I	Glastonbury	CT	E	866 643-1010	1274
Coastal Steel Corporation	Waterford	CT	F	860 443-4073	3986
Collins & Jewell Company Inc	Bozrah	CT	D	860 887-8813	227
Connecticut Iron Works Inc	Greenwich	CT	G	203 869-0657	1327
Contractors Steel Supply Inc	North Haven	CT	F	203 782-1221	2400
Di-Cor Industries Inc	Bristol	CT	E	860 585-5583	436
Division 5 LLC	Stafford Springs	CT	F	860 752-4127	3254
Eagle Manufacturing Co Inc	Colchester	CT	E	860 537-3759	656
East Windsor Metal Fabg Inc	South Windsor	CT	F	860 528-7107	3139
Engineered Building Pdts Inc	Bloomfield	CT	E	860 243-1110	161
ES Metal Fabrications Inc	Terryville	CT	F	860 585-6067	3602
Feman Steel LLC	Bloomfield	CT	F	860 982-6393	164
Focus Fabrication LLC	Woodstock	CT	G	860 604-8018	4394
Fox Steel Products LLC	Orange	CT	F	203 799-2356	2669
General Wldg & Fabrication Inc	Watertown	CT	E	860 274-9668	4014
George H Olson Steel Company	Stratford	CT	F	203 375-5656	3541
Gulf Manufacturing Inc	Rocky Hill	CT	E	860 529-8601	2923
HRF Fastener Systems Inc	Bristol	CT	D	860 589-0750	455
J Steele Services LLC	Mystic	CT	G	860 415-9720	1938
Jozef Custom Ironworks Inc	Bridgeport	CT	E	203 384-6363	337
Jwc Steel Co LLC	Hartford	CT	E	860 296-5517	1489
Kinamor Incorporated	Wallingford	CT	E	203 269-0380	3824
LH Gault & Son Incorporated	Westport	CT	D	203 227-5181	4180

	CITY	ST	EMP	PHONE	ENTRY#
Logan Steel Inc (PA)	Meriden	CT	E	203 235-0811	1672
Magna Steel Sales Inc	Beacon Falls	CT	F	203 888-0300	42
Mayarc Industries Inc	Ellington	CT	G	860 871-1872	1109
Mobile Mini Inc	Suffield	CT	G	860 668-1888	3594
Pcx Aerostructures LLC	Newington	CT	E	860 666-2471	2316
Pds Engineering & Construction	Bloomfield	CT	E	860 242-8586	201
Platt & Labonia Company LLC	Waterbury	CT	E	800 505-9099	3962
Post Road Iron Works Inc	Greenwich	CT	E	203 869-6322	1343
Qsr Steel Corporation LLC	Hartford	CT	E	860 548-0248	1502
Ram Welding Co Inc	Naugatuck	CT	E	203 720-0535	1983
Romco Contractors Inc	Bloomfield	CT	F	860 243-8872	208
Rwt Corporation	Madison	CT	E	203 245-2731	1568
Shepard Steel Co Inc (PA)	Hartford	CT	D	860 525-4446	1507
Shepard Steel Co Inc	Newington	CT	E	860 525-4446	2325
Sound Construction & Engrg Co	Bloomfield	CT	F	860 242-2109	210
Stamford Iron & Stl Works Inc	Stamford	CT	E	203 324-6751	3470
State Welding & Fabg Inc	Clinton	CT	G	203 294-4071	650
Steeltech Building Pdts Inc	South Windsor	CT	D	860 290-8930	3184
Stratford Steel LLC	Stratford	CT	E	203 612-7350	3576
Stratford Stl Fabrication LLC	Stratford	CT	E	203 612-7350	3577
Strocchia Iron Works	Bridgeport	CT	F	203 296-4600	377
Tico Titanium Inc (PA)	Wallingford	CT	E	248 446-0400	3864
Tinsley GROup-Ps&w (HQ)	Milford	CT	F	919 742-5832	1896
Total Fab LLC	East Haven	CT	F	475 238-8176	1055
United Steel Inc	East Hartford	CT	C	860 289-2323	1032
Varnum Enterprises LLC	Bethel	CT	F	203 743-4443	140
Vernier Metal Fabricating Inc	Seymour	CT	D	203 881-3133	2975
Welding Works Inc	Madison	CT	E	203 245-2731	1576
2I Inc	Hudson	MA	F	978 567-8867	9350
3-D Welding Inc	Attleboro	MA	F	508 222-2500	5986
A G Industries Inc	North Attleboro	MA	F	508 695-4219	10863
Accufab Ironworks Inc	Goshen	MA	F	413 268-7133	8966
All Steel Fabricating Inc	North Grafton	MA	E	508 839-4471	11019
Astro Welding & Fabg Inc	Boxborough	MA	F	978 429-8666	7148
Auciello Iron Works Inc	Hudson	MA	E	978 568-8382	9355
Bay Steel Co Inc	Bridgewater	MA	F	508 697-7083	7222
Bellingham Metal Works LLC	Franklin	MA	G	617 519-5958	8819
Berkshire Bridge & Iron Co Inc	Dalton	MA	E	413 684-3182	8148
Blue Atlantic Fabricators LLC	Boston	MA	F	617 874-8503	6598
Boston Steel Fabricators Inc	Holbrook	MA	G	781 767-1540	9170
Bradford Steel Co Inc	East Freetown	MA	F	508 763-5921	8363
Brayton Wilson Cole Corp	Hingham	MA	G	781 803-6624	9144
Butler Metal Fabricators Inc	Indian Orchard	MA	E	413 306-5762	9470
Cape Cod Iron Corp	Wareham	MA	F	508 322-9985	12831
Cape House Realty Inc	Attleboro Falls	MA	E	508 695-6800	6081
Capone Iron Corporation	Rowley	MA	F	978 948-8000	11670
Carl Fisher Co Inc	Springfield	MA	E	413 736-3661	12082
Diamond Iron Works Inc	Lawrence	MA	F	978 794-4640	9557
Dublin Steel Corporation	Palmer	MA	E	413 289-1218	11273
E T Duval & Sons Inc	Leominster	MA	G	978 537-7596	9660
Eastern Metal Industries Inc	Saugus	MA	F	781 231-5220	11757
Emseal Joint Systems Ltd	Westborough	MA	E	508 836-0280	13100
Ernest Johnson	Marlborough	MA	G	508 259-6727	10148
Fitchburg Welding Co Inc	Westminster	MA	E	978 874-2911	13270
Flametech Steels Inc	Lawrence	MA	F	978 686-9518	9562
G&E Steel Fabricators Inc	Salem	MA	F	978 741-0391	11717
General Steel Products Co Inc	Lexington	MA	E	617 387-5400	9745
Gill Metal Fab Inc	Brockton	MA	E	508 580-4445	7281
Harris Rebar	Canton	MA	F	781 575-8999	7794
Hunter Industries Inc	Attleboro Falls	MA	F	508 695-6800	6087
Industrial Metal Pdts Co Inc	Sharon	MA	D	781 762-3330	11793
Industrial Stl Boiler Svcs Inc	Chicopee	MA	E	413 532-7788	8038
Ironman Inc	Mansfield	MA	G	989 386-8975	10060
James F Stearns Co LLP	Pembroke	MA	F	781 829-0095	11371
Kent Fabrications Inc	Pembroke	MA	G	339 244-4533	11373
L & J Enterprises Inc	Malden	MA	G	781 233-1966	10018
Leblanc Enterprises Inc	Lawrence	MA	E	978 682-5112	9578
Mbs Fabrication Inc (PA)	Southbridge	MA	G	508 765-0900	12029
Metfab Engineering Inc	Attleboro Falls	MA	E	508 695-1007	6091
Mid-State Welding Inc	Southbridge	MA	F	508 987-9410	12031
Mill City Iron Fabricators	Dracut	MA	F	978 957-6833	8309
MIW Corp	Fall River	MA	E	508 672-4029	8585
Moseley Corporation	Franklin	MA	E	508 520-4004	8853
MPS Products Corp	Rowley	MA	F	978 817-2144	11681
National Coating Corporation	Rockland	MA	G	781 878-2781	11653
Nevron Plastics Inc	Saugus	MA	F	781 233-1310	11763
New England Bridge Pdts Inc	Lynn	MA	G	781 592-2444	9987
North Shore Steel Co Inc (PA)	Lynn	MA	E	781 598-1645	9988
Nucor Hrris Rbar Northeast LLC	South Deerfield	MA	D	413 665-2381	11925
Nucor Hrris Rbar Northeast LLC	Westfield	MA	E	413 568-7803	13194
O W Landergren Inc	Pittsfield	MA	E	413 442-5632	11415
Package Steel Systems Inc	Sutton	MA	E	508 865-5871	12289
Payne Engrg Fabrication Co Inc	Canton	MA	E	781 828-9046	7817

	CITY	ST	EMP	PHONE	ENTRY#
Precision Metal Works Inc	North Billerica	MA	E	978 667-0180	10944
Quinn Bros of Essex Inc	Essex	MA	E	978 768-6929	8479
R I Baker Co Inc (PA)	Clarksburg	MA	E	413 663-3791	8073
Ranor Inc	Westminster	MA	D	978 874-0591	13276
Rens Welding & Fabricating	Taunton	MA	F	508 828-1702	12362
Republic Iron Works Inc	Chicopee	MA	G	413 594-8819	8058
Rodney Hunt-Fontaine Inc (HQ)	Orange	MA	E	978 544-2511	11232
Sajawi Corporation	Littleton	MA	E	978 486-9050	9837
Scannell Boiler Works	Lowell	MA	F	978 454-5629	9923
Schrimpf Wldg Fabrication Inc	Woburn	MA	G	339 298-2311	13661
Shawmut Metal Products Inc	Swansea	MA	E	508 379-0803	12311
Smj Metal Company Inc	Northampton	MA	E	413 586-3535	11081
Southstern Mtal Fbricators Inc	Rockland	MA	E	781 878-1505	11661
Spector Metal Products Co Inc	Holbrook	MA	E	781 767-5600	9185
Standex International Corp	North Billerica	MA	D	978 667-2771	10959
Starkweather Engineering Inc	Tewksbury	MA	F	978 858-3700	12419
Steel Connections Inc	Franklin	MA	F	508 958-5129	8865
Steel-Fab Inc	Fitchburg	MA	E	978 345-1112	8676
Steel-Fab Engineering & Sales	Fitchburg	MA	G	978 345-0035	8677
Stoughton Steel Company Inc	Hanover	MA	E	781 826-6496	9044
Superior Rail and Ir Works Inc	East Bridgewater	MA	E	508 378-4025	8345
Techprecision Corporation (PA)	Westminster	MA	F	978 874-0591	13280
Topper & Griggs Group LLC	Agawam	MA	E	860 747-5737	5813
Townsend Welding Co Inc	Wilmington	MA	E	978 657-5189	13468
Tuckerman Steel Fabricators Inc	Boston	MA	D	617 569-8373	7087
Ty-Wood Corporation	Holliston	MA	E	508 429-4011	9235
V & G Iron Works Inc	Tewksbury	MA	F	978 851-9191	12424
Vertex Fab & Design LLC	Middleboro	MA	E	508 947-3513	10379
Village Forge Inc	Boston	MA	F	617 361-2591	7104
Web Industries Inc (PA)	Marlborough	MA	G	508 898-2988	10234
Westwood Systems Inc	Canton	MA	F	781 821-1117	7840
Worcester County Welding Inc	Rochdale	MA	G	508 892-4884	11629
Advanced Rsrces Cnstr Entps In	Kingfield	ME	E	207 265-2646	4932
Bachmann Industries Inc	New Gloucester	ME	E	207 440-2888	5083
Bangor Steel Service Inc	Bangor	ME	F	207 947-2773	4494
Casco Bay Steel Structures Inc	South Portland	ME	F	207 780-6722	5494
Cianbro Fbrcation Coating Corp	Pittsfield	ME	C	207 487-3311	5158
Cives Corporation	Augusta	ME	C	207 622-6141	4469
Clark Metal Fabrication Inc	Turner	ME	E	207 330-6322	5561
Design Fab Inc	Auburn	ME	F	207 786-2446	4426
Douglas Brothers Georgia Inc	Portland	ME	F	800 341-0926	5210
Global Metal Fabrication LLC	Turner	ME	E	207 753-0001	5562
Glover Company Inc	Rockport	ME	F	207 236-8644	5349
Howies Wldg & Fabrication Inc	Jay	ME	G	207 645-2581	4913
J F Hutchinson Co	New Gloucester	ME	F	207 926-3676	5085
James A McBrady Inc	Scarborough	ME	E	207 883-4176	5435
Knowlton Machine Company	Gorham	ME	E	207 854-8471	4824
L M C Light Iron Inc	Limerick	ME	F	207 793-9957	5002
Lane Conveyors & Drives Inc	Brewer	ME	F	207 989-4560	4616
Magco Inc	Wells	ME	D	207 324-8060	5600
Malings Welding Svc Inc	Kennebunk	ME	G	207 985-9769	4926
McCann Fabrication	New Gloucester	ME	E	207 926-4118	5087
Megquier & Jones Inc	Topsham	ME	E	207 799-8555	5550
New England Stl Fbricators Inc	Alfred	ME	F	207 324-1846	4403
Nif Inc	Newport	ME	E	207 368-4344	5097
North E Wldg & Fabrication Inc	Auburn	ME	E	207 786-2446	4448
Prescott Metal (PA)	Biddeford	ME	E	207 283-0115	4584
Ramsays Welding & Machine Inc	Lincoln	ME	F	207 794-8839	5012
Rbw Inc	Windham	ME	F	207 786-2446	5668
Robert Mitchell Co Inc (DH)	Portland	ME	F	207 797-6771	5266
Senior Operations LLC	Lewiston	ME	E	207 784-2338	4992
Steel-Pro Inc	Rockland	ME	E	207 596-0061	5342
Tigpro Inc	Portland	ME	G	207 878-1190	5282
Tis Brewer LLC	Brewer	ME	E	207 989-4560	4621
Tri State Steel Inc	Auburn	ME	G	207 784-9371	4461
Velux America LLC	Wells	ME	D	207 216-4500	5607
Wahlcometroflex Inc	Lewiston	ME	B	207 784-2338	4995
Ace Welding Co Inc	Merrimack	NH	E	603 424-9936	14971
Alpine Machine Co Inc	Berlin	NH	E	603 752-1441	13979
American Steel Fabricators Inc	Peterborough	NH	E	603 547-6311	15311
Apollo Steel LLC	Jaffrey	NH	F	603 532-1156	14563
Atlas Prcision Met Fabricators	Dover	NH	F	603 742-1226	14217
Canam Bridges US Inc	Claremont	NH	E	603 542-5202	14081
Charles Leonard Steel Svcs LLC	Concord	NH	F	603 225-0211	14121
Charles Smith Steel LLC	Boscawen	NH	G	603 753-9844	13988
Cross Machine Inc	Berlin	NH	F	603 752-6111	13981
East Coast Metal Works Co Inc	Kingston	NH	G	603 642-9600	14634
Fronek Anchor Darling Entp	Laconia	NH	F	603 528-1931	14651
Fwm Inc	Hudson	NH	F	603 578-3366	14497
Gilchrist Metal Fabg Co Inc	Hudson	NH	F	603 889-2600	14499
Gilchrist Metal Fabg Co Inc (PA)	Hudson	NH	E	603 889-2600	14500
Granite State Plasma Cutting	Portsmouth	NH	E	603 536-4415	15395
Mill City Iron	Manchester	NH	G	603 622-0042	14888
Netc Liquidating Corporation	Center Tuftonboro	NH	E	603 569-3100	14059
New Hampshire Stl Erectors LLC	Goffstown	NH	E	603 668-3464	14353
New Hmpshire Stl Fbrcators LLC	Goffstown	NH	E	603 668-3464	14354
NH Steel Fabricators	Amherst	NH	B	603 213-6357	13882
Novel Iron Works Inc	Greenland	NH	C	603 436-7950	14369
Nsa Industries LLC	Groveton	NH	D	802 748-5007	14377
Nucor Hrris Rbar Northeast LLC	Canaan	NH	D	603 632-5222	14047
Pipe Shields Inc	Laconia	NH	G	603 528-1931	14663
Quality Fabricators LLC	Barrington	NH	G	603 905-9012	13916
Redline Welding Inc	Hampstead	NH	F	603 489-2266	14391
S L Chasse Welding & Fabg Inc	Hudson	NH	D	603 886-3436	14543
Smiths Tblar Systms-Lconia Inc	Laconia	NH	C	603 524-2064	14670
Soucy Industries Inc (PA)	Pelham	NH	E	603 883-4500	15297
Superior Steel Fabricators Inc	Brookline	NH	F	603 673-7509	14041
Tri-State Iron Works Inc	Concord	NH	E	603 228-0020	14165
Valley Welding & Fabg Inc	Hollis	NH	E	603 465-3266	14460
Viking Wldg & Fabrication LLC	Kensington	NH	G	603 394-7887	14631
Winchester Precision Tech Ltd	Winchester	NH	F	603 239-6326	15718
Amaral Custom Fabrications Inc	Rumford	RI	F	401 396-5663	16661
American Welding Company Inc	West Greenwich	RI	E	401 397-9155	16881
Blount Boats Inc	Warren	RI	D	401 245-8300	16754
Capco Steel LLC	Providence	RI	D	401 861-1220	16496
Custom Iron Works Inc	Coventry	RI	E	401 826-3310	15812
Dominion Rebar Company	Pawtucket	RI	E	401 724-9200	16365
Engineering Wldg & Fabg Co Inc	North Kingstown	RI	G	401 884-1484	16252
Farber Industrial Fabricating	Pawtucket	RI	G	401 725-2492	16368
Getchell & Son Inc	Smithfield	RI	F	401 231-3850	16703
LK Goodwin Co Inc (PA)	West Greenwich	RI	F	401 781-5526	16888
Luthers Repair Shop Inc	Bristol	RI	F	401 253-5550	15773
Ne Steel Fabricators LLC	Cranston	RI	F	401 785-1234	15898
Regal Components Inc	East Providence	RI	F	727 299-0800	16042
Browns Certified Welding Inc	Bristol	VT	F	802 453-3351	17115
Custom Mtal Fabricators VT LLC	Hyde Park	VT	G	802 888-0033	17299
K V Sbardella Slate Inc	Fair Haven	VT	G	802 265-9955	17251
L & G Fabricators Inc	Bennington	VT	F	802 447-0965	17047
Milton Vermont Sheet Metal Inc	Milton	VT	D	802 893-1581	17362
Nops Metal Works	Middlebury	VT	F	802 382-9300	17347
PG Adams Inc	South Burlington	VT	E	802 862-8664	17590
S & A Trombley Corporation	Morrisville	VT	E	802 888-2394	17388
Stairs Unlimited Inc	Richford	VT	G	802 848-7030	17476
Thomann Steel LLC	Vergennes	VT	G	802 462-3066	17662
Vermont Indexable Tooling Inc	Fairfax	VT	G	802 752-2002	17264

3442 Metal doors, sash, and trim

	CITY	ST	EMP	PHONE	ENTRY#
Advanced Window Systems LLC	Cromwell	CT	F	800 841-6544	684
All-Time Manufacturing Co Inc	Montville	CT	F	860 848-9258	1926
Arcadia Architectural Pdts Inc	Stamford	CT	E	203 316-8000	3285
Bilco Holding Company	New Haven	CT	E	203 507-2751	2126
Capitol Glass Company Inc	West Hartford	CT	F	860 236-1936	4050
Ckh Industries Inc	Wethersfield	CT	D	860 563-2999	4203
Cooper Group LLC	Pawcatuck	CT	F	860 599-2481	2716
Cornell-Carr Co Inc	Monroe	CT	E	203 261-2529	1911
Girardin Moulding Inc	Windsor Locks	CT	F	860 623-4486	4326
Gordon Corporation	Southington	CT	D	860 628-4775	3214
Legere Group Ltd	Avon	CT	D	860 674-0392	29
Liberty Glass and Met Inds Inc	North Grosvenordale	CT	E	860 923-3623	2384
Mercury-Excelum Inc	East Windsor	CT	E	860 292-1800	1080
Odorox Iaq Inc	Stamford	CT	G	203 541-5577	3423
Post Road Iron Works Inc	Greenwich	CT	E	203 869-6322	1343
Stent Metal Corp	Hamden	CT	G	203 287-9007	1457
Stonington Services LLC	Gales Ferry	CT	E	860 464-1991	1261
The Bilco Company (DH)	West Haven	CT	C	203 934-6363	4128
Aluminum Products Cape Cod Inc (PA)	Dennis Port	MA	E	508 398-8546	8259
Architctral Glzing Systems Inc	Avon	MA	E	508 588-4845	6142
Architectural Openings Inc	Somerville	MA	E	617 776-9223	11861
Brunswick Enclosure Company	North Billerica	MA	F	978 670-1124	10902
Centco Architectural Mtls Inc	East Bridgewater	MA	E	508 456-1888	8336
Coastal Industries Inc	Haverhill	MA	E	978 373-1543	9087
Diamond Windows Doors Mfg Inc	Boston	MA	E	617 282-1688	6693
ER Lewin Inc	Wrentham	MA	E	508 384-0363	13841
Everett Aluminum Inc	Everett	MA	F	617 389-3839	8488
Far Industries Inc	Assonet	MA	F	508 644-3122	5973
Harvey Industries LLC	Springfield	MA	E	413 731-7700	12099
Harvey Industries LLC (PA)	Waltham	MA	C	800 598-5400	12691
Harvey Industries LLC	Woburn	MA	F	781 935-7990	13581
Island Pond Industries Inc	Agawam	MA	G	413 732-6625	5796
Jeld-Wen Inc	Avon	MA	F	541 528-1931	6152
Modern Mfg Inc Worcester	Rochdale	MA	E	508 791-7151	11628
Nashoba Security Inc	Littleton	MA	F	978 486-8615	9827
National Store Fronts Co Inc	Avon	MA	F	508 584-8880	6154
Philipp Manufacturing Company	Easthampton	MA	E	413 527-4444	8459
Portal Inc	Avon	MA	E	800 966-3030	6157

	CITY	ST	EMP	PHONE	ENTRY#
Precision Door & Window Inc (PA)	Stoughton	MA	F	781 344-6900	12228
Shelmar Inc	Wakefield	MA	F	781 245-1206	12535
Stergis Aluminum Products Corp	Attleboro	MA	E	508 455-0661	6065
Ultimate Windows Inc	Lawrence	MA	G	978 687-9444	9605
Watertown Engineering Corp	Whitman	MA	F	781 857-2555	13351
West Side Metal Door Corp	Ludlow	MA	F	413 589-0945	9956
Harvey Industries Inc	Augusta	ME	F	207 629-3737	4472
Overhead Door Co Bangor Inc	Hermon	ME	F	207 848-7200	4888
Win-Pressor LLC	Unity	ME	G	207 948-4800	5568
R G Tombs Door Company Inc	Hooksett	NH	E	603 624-5040	14471
Central FLS Plate & Win GL Co	Central Falls	RI	F	401 722-1267	15787
Columbus Door Company	Warwick	RI	D	401 781-7792	16796
Jsg Holdings Inc	Warwick	RI	E	401 738-3800	16829
Lockheed Archtctral Sltons Inc	Pascoag	RI	C	401 568-3061	16339
E I J Inc	Tunbridge	VT	F	802 889-3432	17653

3443 Fabricated plate work (boiler shop)

	CITY	ST	EMP	PHONE	ENTRY#
Angel Fuel LLC	Waterbury	CT	G	203 597-8759	3885
Apcompower Inc (PA)	Windsor	CT	E	860 688-1911	4260
C Cowles & Company (PA)	North Haven	CT	D	203 865-3117	2396
Certuss America LP	Windsor	CT	G	440 454-6172	4265
Connectcut Boiler Repr Mfg Inc	West Hartford	CT	E	860 953-9117	4054
Hayes Services LLC	East Lyme	CT	E	860 739-2273	1059
HI Stone & Son Inc	Southbury	CT	E	203 264-8656	3195
JFd Tube & Coil Products Inc	Hamden	CT	E	203 288-6941	1435
Johnstone Company Inc	North Haven	CT	E	203 239-5834	2419
L & L Mechanical LLC	Goshen	CT	F	860 491-4007	1303
Mastercraft Tool and Mch Co	Southington	CT	F	860 628-5551	3220
MB Aerospace East Granby Limited Partnership 860 653-5041	East Granby	CT			C 942
Mitchell-Bate Company	Waterbury	CT	E	203 233-0862	3946
Modine LLC	Killingworth	CT	F	860 452-4194	1543
Mp Systems Inc	East Granby	CT	F	860 687-3460	944
Porobond Products LLC	Hamden	CT	F	203 288-7477	1451
SMR Metal Technology LLC	South Windsor	CT	G	860 291-8259	3181
Thermaxx LLC (HQ)	West Haven	CT	G	203 672-1021	4130
United Steel Inc	East Hartford	CT	C	860 289-2323	1032
Vitta Corporation	Bethel	CT	E	203 790-8155	141
Vulcan Industries Inc	Windsor	CT	C	860 683-2005	4313
Walz & Krenzer Inc	Oxford	CT	G	203 267-5712	2714
Wanho Manufacturing LLC	Cheshire	CT	E	203 759-3744	621
Westbrook Manufacturing LLC	Ivoryton	CT	F	860 767-2460	1534
Whitcraft LLC (PA)	Eastford	CT	C	860 974-0786	1093
Whitcraft Scrborough/Tempe LLC (HQ)	Eastford	CT	E	860 974-0786	1094
Alfa Laval Inc	Newburyport	MA	D	978 465-5777	10666
All Metal Fabricators Inc	Acton	MA	F	978 263-3904	5733
All Steel Fabricating Inc	North Grafton	MA	E	508 839-4471	11019
Alloy Fabricators Neng Inc	Randolph	MA	F	781 986-6400	11547
Alvin Johnson	East Longmeadow	MA	G	413 525-6334	8368
Atlantic Industrial Models LLC	Essex	MA	E	978 768-7686	8473
Babcock Power Capital Corp (HQ)	Danvers	MA	E	978 646-3300	8165
Babcock Power Inc (PA)	Danvers	MA	E	978 646-3300	8166
Babcock Power Renewables LLC (HQ)	Danvers	MA	E	978 646-3300	8167
Bath Systems Massachusetts Inc	West Bridgewater	MA	G	508 521-2700	12967
BE Peterson Inc	Avon	MA	D	508 436-7900	6144
Boston Steel & Mfg Co	Haverhill	MA	F	781 324-3000	9080
Boyd Corporation (woburn) Inc (DH)	Woburn	MA	C	781 933-7300	13534
Braden Manufacturing LLC	Auburn	MA	D	508 797-8000	6108
Cape Cod Cupola Co Inc	North Dartmouth	MA	F	508 994-2119	10990
Connell Limited Partnership (PA)	Boston	MA	F	617 737-2700	6665
Consolidated Machine Corporation	Billerica	MA	E	617 782-6072	6428
Cotter Corporation	Danvers	MA	E	978 774-6777	8175
Credit Card Supplies Corp	Marlborough	MA	F	508 485-4230	10139
Fiba Tech	Littleton	MA	F	978 486-0586	9814
Fiba Technologies Inc (PA)	Littleton	MA	B	508 887-7100	9815
Fisher Contracting Corporation	Worcester	MA	G	508 421-6989	13723
Flexcon Industries Inc	Randolph	MA	F	781 986-2424	11557
Framingham Welding & Engineering Corporation	Framingham	MA			E 8763
Frank I Rounds Company (PA)	Randolph	MA	E	401 333-5014	11559
Garbage Gone Inc	Barnstable	MA	G	508 737-4995	6200
Geo Knight & Co Inc	Brockton	MA	E	508 588-0186	7280
Gill Metal Fab Inc	Brockton	MA	E	508 580-4445	7281
Green Brothers Fabricating (PA)	Taunton	MA	E	508 880-3608	12339
Gregory Engineering Corp	Marlborough	MA	F	508 481-0480	10156
H & H Engineering Company Inc	Methuen	MA	F	978 682-0567	10333
Heat Fab Inc	Turners Falls	MA	F	413 863-2242	12447
Helfrich Bros Boiler Works Inc	Lawrence	MA	E	978 975-2464	9566
Helfrich Construction Svcs LLC	Lawrence	MA	E	978 683-7244	9567
Herb Chambers Brookline Inc	Brookline	MA	D	617 278-3920	7318
Industrial Stl Boiler Svcs Inc	Chicopee	MA	E	413 532-7788	8038
J F White Contracting Co	Stoughton	MA	C	781 436-8497	12216
Larson Tool & Stamping Company	Attleboro	MA	D	508 222-0897	6031

	CITY	ST	EMP	PHONE	ENTRY#
Lytron Fs Inc	Woburn	MA	F	781 933-7300	13604
Mair-Mac Machine Company Inc	Brockton	MA	F	508 895-9001	7294
Mascon Inc	Woburn	MA	E	781 938-5800	13605
Mass Engineering & Tank Inc	Middleboro	MA	F	508 947-8669	10366
Mass Tank Inspection Svcs LLC	Middleboro	MA	E	508 923-3445	10367
Mass Tank Sales Corp	Middleboro	MA	E	508 947-8826	10368
Merrimac Industrial Sales Inc (PA)	Haverhill	MA	E	978 372-6006	9115
Mersen USA Ep Corp (HQ)	Newburyport	MA	D	978 462-6662	10699
Momentum Mfg Group LLC (HQ)	Georgetown	MA	E	978 659-6960	8910
Mooring Systems Incorporated	Cataumet	MA	G	508 776-0254	7859
Riley Power Inc	Marlborough	MA	B	508 852-7100	10204
Russell James Engineering Works Inc	Boston	MA	E	617 265-2240	7018
Scannell Boiler Works	Lowell	MA	F	978 454-5629	9923
Sharon Vacuum Co Inc	Brockton	MA	F	508 588-2323	7304
Steel-Fab Inc	Fitchburg	MA	E	978 345-1113	8676
Surmet Corp (PA)	Burlington	MA	E	781 345-5721	7436
Therma-Flow Inc	Watertown	MA	E	617 924-3877	12913
Thermatron Engineering Inc	Methuen	MA	E	978 687-8844	10345
Triangle Engineering Inc	Hanover	MA	F	781 878-1500	9046
United Metal Fabracators Inc	Worcester	MA	E	508 754-1800	13815
Vent-Rite Valve Corp (PA)	Randolph	MA	F	781 986-2000	11578
XI Technology Systems Inc	Rockland	MA	E	781 982-1220	11665
Bear Pond Dumpster LLC	Turner	ME	G	207 224-0337	5560
Knowlton Machine Company	Gorham	ME	F	207 854-8471	4824
Millincket Fabrication Mch Inc (PA)	Millinocket	ME	E	207 723-9733	5067
Onix Corporation	Caribou	ME	F	866 290-5362	4678
Steel-Pro Inc	Rockland	ME	E	207 596-0061	5342
Westmor Industries LLC	Brewer	ME	F	207 989-0100	4624
Boston Environmental LLC	Portsmouth	NH	E	603 334-1000	15366
Chart Inc	Salem	NH	D	603 382-6551	15513
Controlair LLC	Amherst	NH	E	603 886-9400	13865
Core Assemblies Inc	Gilford	NH	F	603 293-0270	14334
Gilchrist Metal Fabg Co Inc (PA)	Hudson	NH	E	603 889-2600	14500
Hyde Specialty Products LLC	Merrimack	NH	F	603 883-7400	14984
Ingersoll-Rand Energy Systems Corporation 603 430-7000	Portsmouth	NH			D 15408
Laars Heating Systems Company	Rochester	NH	C	603 335-6300	15484
Recycling Mechanical Neng LLC	Allenstown	NH	F	603 268-8028	13855
Skaff Cryogenics Inc	Brentwood	NH	F	603 775-0350	14029
Tsi Group Inc (DH)	Hampton	NH	E	603 964-0296	14416
Valley Welding & Fabg Inc	Hollis	NH	E	603 465-3266	14460
Amtrol Holdings Inc	West Warwick	RI	A	401 884-6300	16899
Amtrol Inc (DH)	West Warwick	RI	B	401 884-6300	16900
Amtrol Intl Investments Inc (DH)	West Warwick	RI	F	401 884-6300	16901
Ariston Usa LLC (HQ)	Providence	RI	E	508 763-8071	16474
Fiberglass Fabricators Inc	Smithfield	RI	E	401 231-3552	16700
Modine Manufacturing Company	West Kingston	RI	D	401 792-1231	16894
Seifert Systems Inc	North Kingstown	RI	F	401 294-6960	16279
Stackbin Corporation	Lincoln	RI	F	401 333-1600	16155
Taco Inc (PA)	Cranston	RI	B	401 942-8000	15917
West Warwick Welding Inc	West Warwick	RI	F	401 822-8200	16926
Burtco Inc	Westminster Station	VT	F	802 722-3358	17702

3444 Sheet metalwork

	CITY	ST	EMP	PHONE	ENTRY#
A B & F Sheet Metal	Cheshire	CT	G	203 272-9340	566
A B & F Sheet Metal Pdts Inc	Cheshire	CT	G	203 272-9340	567
A G C Incorporated	Meriden	CT	C	203 235-3361	1649
A Plus Exterior LLC	Milford	CT	F	203 516-1729	1792
Advanced Sheetmetal Assoc LLC	Middlefield	CT	E	860 349-1644	1723
Advantage Sheet Metal Mfg LLC	Naugatuck	CT	E	203 720-0929	1946
Aerocor Inc	East Windsor	CT	F	860 281-9274	1064
American Marketing Intl LLC	Clinton	CT	E	860 669-4100	635
Anco Engineering Inc	Shelton	CT	D	203 925-9235	2981
Ansonia Stl Fabrication Co Inc	Beacon Falls	CT	E	203 888-4509	39
Atlantic Vent & Eqp Co Inc	Cromwell	CT	E	860 635-1300	687
Atlas Industrial Services LLC	Branford	CT	E	203 315-4538	237
Buckley Associates Inc	Stratford	CT	G	203 380-2405	3524
Bull Metal Products Inc	Middletown	CT	E	860 346-9691	1742
Carlson Sheet Metal LLC	New Milford	CT	G	860 354-4660	2240
CBS Contractors Inc	Ansonia	CT	F	203 734-8015	10
Chapco Inc (PA)	Chester	CT	E	860 526-9535	625
Coastal Exteriors LLC	Wallingford	CT	F	203 626-5396	3790
Complete Sheet Metal LLC	Berlin	CT	G	860 310-5447	61
Custom & Precision Pdts Inc	Hamden	CT	F	203 281-0818	1419
Denlar Fire Protection LLC	Chester	CT	G	860 526-9846	626
Ductco LLC	Bloomfield	CT	E	860 243-0350	160
Dufrane Nuclear Shielding Inc	Winsted	CT	F	860 379-2318	4340
Dyco Industries Inc	South Windsor	CT	F	860 289-4957	3138
East Coast Sheet Metal LLC	Litchfield	CT	F	860 283-1126	1556
East Windsor Metal Fabg Inc	South Windsor	CT	F	860 528-7107	3139
Engineered Building Pdts Inc	Bloomfield	CT	E	860 243-1110	161
Erickson Metals Corporation (PA)	Cheshire	CT	G	203 272-2918	591

Company	CITY	ST	EMP	PHONE	ENTRY#
Farrell Prcsion Mtalcraft Corp	New Milford	CT	E	860 355-2651	2243
General Dynamics Info Tech Inc	Pawcatuck	CT	D	860 441-2400	2720
General Sheet Metal Works Inc	Bridgeport	CT	F	203 333-6111	324
Hdb Inc	Thomaston	CT	F	860 379-9901	3621
Highway Safety LLC (HQ)	Glastonbury	CT	D	860 633-9445	1286
Hispanic Enterprises Inc	Bridgeport	CT	E	203 588-9334	329
I2s LLC	Wallingford	CT	C	203 265-5684	3816
Illinois Tool Works Inc	Naugatuck	CT	F	203 720-1676	1964
Jared Manufacturing Co Inc	Norwalk	CT	F	203 846-1732	2520
Jesco Iron Crafts Inc	Oxford	CT	F	201 488-4545	2701
Jgs Properties LLC	Milford	CT	E	203 378-7508	1840
Jhs Restoration Inc	South Windsor	CT	F	860 757-3870	3159
Lee Manufacturing Inc	Wallingford	CT	D	203 284-0466	3827
Leek Building Products Inc	Norwalk	CT	E	203 853-3883	2527
Link Mechanical Services Inc	New Britain	CT	E	860 826-5880	2038
Lostocco Refuse Service LLC	Danbury	CT	E	203 748-9296	779
Lyons Slitting Inc	Waterbury	CT	F	203 755-4564	3932
M & J Sheet Metal LLC	Winsted	CT	G	860 379-2907	4348
M & O Corporation	Bridgeport	CT	E	203 367-4292	345
M & W Sheet Metal LLC	North Franklin	CT	E	860 642-7748	2382
M Cubed Technologies Inc (HQ)	Newtown	CT	E	203 304-2940	2341
Manufacturers Service Co Inc	Woodbridge	CT	G	203 389-9595	4381
MB Aerospace East Granby Limited Partnership 860 653-5041	East Granby	CT	942		C
McMullin Manufacturing Corp	Brookfield	CT	E	203 740-3360	529
Midget Louver Company Inc	Milford	CT	G	203 783-1444	1850
Milford Fabricating Co Inc	Milford	CT	D	203 878-2476	1852
Mrnd LLC	Enfield	CT	E	860 749-0256	1138
Paradigm Manchester Inc	Manchester	CT	G	860 646-4048	1624
Paradigm Manchester Inc	Manchester	CT	C	860 649-2888	1625
Progressive Sheetmetal LLC	South Windsor	CT	E	860 436-9884	3176
Quality Sheet Metal Inc	Naugatuck	CT	E	203 729-2244	1982
R & D Precision Inc	Meriden	CT	F	203 284-3396	1689
R & D Precision Inc	Wallingford	CT	F	203 284-3396	3844
R W E Inc	Putnam	CT	E	860 974-1101	2871
R-D Mfg Inc	East Lyme	CT	F	860 739-3986	1062
Ram Welding Co Inc	Naugatuck	CT	E	203 720-0535	1983
Seconn Automation Solutions	Waterford	CT	E	860 442-4325	3993
Seconn Fabrication LLC	Waterford	CT	D	860 443-0000	3994
Shoreline Metal Services LLC	East Haven	CT	G	203 466-7372	1050
Snow Goose 2019 Inc	Meriden	CT	E	203 237-3444	1700
Sound Manufacturing Inc	Old Saybrook	CT	D	860 388-4466	2662
Stauffer Sheet Metal LLC	Windsor	CT	E	860 623-0518	4304
Strategic Value Partners LLC (PA)	Greenwich	CT	D	203 618-3500	1354
Target Custom Manufacturing Co	Haddam	CT	G	860 388-5848	1410
Tech-Air Incorporated	Uncasville	CT	E	860 848-1287	3744
The Bilco Company (DH)	West Haven	CT	C	203 934-6363	4128
The Petit Tool Co	Thomaston	CT	E	203 283-9626	3636
Trumpf Photonics Inc	Farmington	CT	F	860 255-6000	1256
U-Sealusa LLC	Newington	CT	F	860 667-0911	2331
United Steel Inc	East Hartford	CT	C	860 289-2323	1032
United Sttes Sign Fbrction Cor	Trumbull	CT	F	203 601-1000	3739
Valley Tool and Mfg LLC	Milford	CT	E	203 878-2476	1897
Vernier Metal Fabricating Inc	Seymour	CT	D	203 881-3133	2975
Vulcan Industries Inc	Windsor	CT	C	860 683-2005	4313
Whitcraft LLC (PA)	Eastford	CT	C	860 974-0786	1093
Whitcraft Scrborough/Tempe LLC (HQ)	Eastford	CT	C	860 974-0786	1094
White Welding Company	Waterbury	CT	G	203 753-1197	3984
Yost Manufacturing & Sup Inc	Waterford	CT	F	800 872-9678	4000
A & D Metal Inc	Westfield	MA	F	413 485-7505	13145
A G Miller Company Inc	Springfield	MA	E	413 732-9297	12068
Aaron Morin	West Hatfield	MA	G	413 247-0550	13003
Absolute Sheet Metal	Billerica	MA	F	978 667-0236	6395
Advanced Air Systems Inc	Abington	MA	F	781 878-5733	5721
Aero Manufacturing Corp	Beverly	MA	D	978 720-1000	6323
Aero-Space Fabricators Inc	Waltham	MA	G	781 899-4535	12586
Afc Cable Systems Inc	New Bedford	MA	B	508 998-1131	10566
Algonquin Industries Inc (PA)	Bellingham	MA	E	508 966-4600	6283
All Metal Fabricators Inc	Acton	MA	F	978 263-3904	5733
Allstate Hood & Duct Inc	Westfield	MA	F	413 568-4663	13147
Aluminum Products Cape Cod Inc (PA)	Dennis Port	MA	F	508 398-8546	8259
Amaral Custom Fabrications Inc	Seekonk	MA	E	508 336-6681	11774
American Sheet Metal LLC	Salisbury	MA	E	978 578-8360	11738
Apahouser Inc	Marlborough	MA	E	508 786-0309	10110
Arcam Cad To Metal Inc	Woburn	MA	F	781 281-1718	13513
Atlantic Air Products Mfg LLC	Quincy	MA	F	603 410-3900	11504
Auciello Iron Works Inc	Hudson	MA	E	978 568-8382	9355
AW Airflo Industries Inc	Newburyport	MA	F	978 465-6260	10668
B & J Sheet Metal Inc	Hyde Park	MA	F	617 590-2295	9456
Bedard Sheet Metal Company Inc	Westfield	MA	G	413 572-3774	13151
Bomco Inc	Gloucester	MA	C	978 283-9000	8924
Braden Manufacturing LLC	Auburn	MA	D	508 797-8000	6108
Brideau Shtmtl Fabrication Inc	Leominster	MA	E	978 537-3372	9643
Brouillette Hvac & Shtmtl Inc	East Taunton	MA	G	508 822-4800	8406
Buckley Associates Inc (PA)	Hanover	MA	D	781 878-5000	9027
C S H Industries Inc	Plymouth	MA	E	508 747-1990	11452
Cambridgeport	Randolph	MA	E	781 302-3347	11553
Cambridgeport Air Systems Inc	Georgetown	MA	C	978 465-8481	8906
Carbone Sheet Metal Corp	Chelsea	MA	E	617 884-0237	7975
Carl Fisher Co Inc	Springfield	MA	E	413 736-3661	12082
Century-Tywood J3 Corp	Holliston	MA	F	508 429-4011	9204
Ceric Fabrication Co Inc	Ayer	MA	F	978 772-9034	6178
Churchill Corporation	Melrose	MA	E	781 665-4700	10315
Columbia ASC Inc	Lawrence	MA	F	978 683-2205	9554
Computron Metal Products Inc	Whitman	MA	E	781 447-2265	13348
Connell Limited Partnership (PA)	Boston	MA	F	617 737-2700	6665
Cox Engineering Company (PA)	Canton	MA	C	781 302-3300	7781
Crocker Architectural Shtmtl	North Oxford	MA	E	508 987-9900	11031
CTR Enterprises Inc	Haverhill	MA	G	978 794-2093	9089
D J Fabricators Inc	Ipswich	MA	F	978 356-0228	9482
Dg Service Company Inc	Mattapoisett	MA	F	508 758-7906	10257
Dimark Incorporated	Whitman	MA	E	781 447-7990	13349
Dosco Sheet Metal and Mfg Inc	Millbury	MA	G	508 865-9998	10433
Draper Elevator Cab Co Inc	Holbrook	MA	F	781 961-3146	9171
Draper Metal Fabrication Inc	Holbrook	MA	F	781 961-3146	9172
Duc-Pac Corporation	Springfield	MA	E	413 525-3302	12091
E T Duval & Sons Inc	Leominster	MA	G	978 537-7596	9660
Eckel Industries Inc (PA)	Ayer	MA	F	978 772-0840	6181
Electrnic Shtmtal Crftsmen Inc	Stoughton	MA	E	781 341-3260	12202
Essex Engineering Inc	Lynn	MA	F	781 595-2114	9972
Everett Aluminum Inc	Everett	MA	F	617 389-3839	8488
Expansion Opportunities Inc	Northborough	MA	E	508 393-8200	11095
Fabco Mfg Inc	Hudson	MA	E	978 568-8519	9366
Fabtron Corporation	Waltham	MA	E	781 891-4430	12674
Far Industries Inc	Assonet	MA	F	508 644-3122	5973
First Quality Metal Pdts Corp	Plympton	MA	G	781 585-5820	11484
Francer Industries Inc	Carver	MA	E		7854
Franklin Sheet Metal Works Inc	Franklin	MA	G	508 528-3600	8839
Frs Company Inc	Medford	MA	F	781 322-6252	10285
Gas Path Solutions LLC	Hubbardston	MA	F	978 229-5460	9348
Gill Metal Fab Inc	Brockton	MA	E	508 580-4445	7281
Green Brothers Fabricating (PA)	Taunton	MA	F	508 880-3608	12339
Gtr Manufacturing LLC	Brockton	MA	D	508 588-3240	7282
Harrington Air Systems LLC	Watertown	MA	F	781 341-1999	12880
Heat Fab Inc	Turners Falls	MA	F	413 863-2242	12447
Helfrich Bros Boiler Works Inc	Lawrence	MA	E	978 975-2464	9566
Herfco Inc	Shirley	MA	E	978 772-4758	11816
Hi-Tech Metals Inc	Bellingham	MA	D	508 966-0332	6291
Horizon Sheet Metal Inc	Springfield	MA	D	413 734-6966	12102
Howard Products Incorporated	Worcester	MA	F	508 757-2440	13738
Ideal Sheet Metal Corp	Worcester	MA	F	508 799-2781	13739
Ideas Inc	Lowell	MA	G	978 453-6864	9886
Improved Consumer Products Inc	North Attleboro	MA	F	508 695-6841	10875
Industrial Metal Pdts Co Inc	Sharon	MA	D	781 762-3330	11793
Integrated Dynamic Metals Corp	Marlborough	MA	E	508 624-7271	10165
J & J Heating & AC Inc	Dracut	MA	E	978 454-8197	8306
Jay Salem Inc	Middleton	MA	G	978 774-4999	10387
Jgpg Inc	Waltham	MA	F	781 891-9640	12705
Kennedy Sheet Metal Inc	East Weymouth	MA	F	781 331-7764	8431
Kleeberg Sheet Metal Inc	Ludlow	MA	D	413 589-1854	9947
Lamb & Ritchie Company Inc	Saugus	MA	E	781 941-2700	11762
Le Bel Inc	Abington	MA	D	781 878-7279	5725
Lehi Sheet Metal Corporation	Westborough	MA	E	508 366-8550	13116
Lyman Conrad (PA)	South Hadley	MA	F	413 538-8200	11965
Lyman Sheet Metal Co Inc	Southampton	MA	G	413 527-0848	11988
Manufacturing Tech Group Inc	Westfield	MA	D	413 562-4337	13181
Marblehead Engineering	Essex	MA	F	978 432-1386	8477
McGarvin Engineering Inc	Lowell	MA	F	978 454-2741	9904
Mestek Inc	Westfield	MA	E	413 568-9571	13185
Metal Men	Chicopee	MA	F	413 533-0513	8048
Metal Tronics Inc	Georgetown	MA	E	978 659-6960	8909
Metalcrafters Inc	Methuen	MA	E	978 683-7097	10338
MLS Sheet Metal LLC	Bedford	MA	F	781 275-2265	6243
Momentum Mfg Group LLC (HQ)	Georgetown	MA	D	978 659-6960	8910
Moseley Corporation	Franklin	MA	E	508 520-4004	8853
New England Fab Mtls Inc	Leominster	MA	E	978 466-7823	9685
New England Metalform Inc	Plainville	MA	E	508 695-9340	11441
New England Sheets LLC (PA)	Devens	MA	E	978 487-2500	8281
New-Com Metal Pdts Group LLC	Randolph	MA	E	781 767-7520	11570
Northeastern Metals LLC	Greenfield	MA	F	800 506-7090	8997
Norwood Sheet Metal Corp	Norwood	MA	F	781 762-0720	11201
Noyes Sheet Metal	Milford	MA	F	508 482-9302	10411
Omg Inc (DH)	Agawam	MA	B	413 789-0252	5803
Ornamental Ironworks Inc	Fall River	MA	F	508 678-0687	8592
P G L Industries Inc	Swansea	MA	F	508 679-8845	12309
P M S Manufactured Pdts Inc	Gloucester	MA	E	978 281-2600	8950

	CITY	ST	EMP	PHONE	ENTRY#
Parker-Hannifin Corporation	Woburn	MA	B	781 935-4850	13629
Payne Engrg Fabrication Co Inc	Canton	MA	E	781 828-9046	7817
Phoenix Sheet Metal	South Dartmouth	MA	G	508 994-4046	11919
Precise Industries Inc	Lowell	MA	E	978 453-8490	9915
Precision Engineering LLC	Uxbridge	MA	E	508 278-5700	12488
Precision Metal Works Inc	North Billerica	MA	E	978 667-0180	10944
Quality Air Metals Inc	Holbrook	MA	E	781 986-9967	9184
R F Sheet Metal and Mech Inc	Hyannis	MA	G	508 367-0533	9445
R I Baker Co Inc (PA)	Clarksburg	MA	E	413 663-3791	8073
R R Leduc Corp	Holyoke	MA	E	413 536-4329	9275
Rgm Metals Inc	Hudson	MA	G	978 562-9773	9408
Ricks Sheet Metal Inc	Fall River	MA	F	774 488-9576	8603
Riverside Shtmtl & Contg Inc	Medford	MA	F	781 396-0070	10296
Roar Industries Inc	Hopedale	MA	F	508 429-5952	9302
Roberts Welding Inc	Brookfield	MA	E	508 867-7640	7315
Roland Gatchell	Georgetown	MA	G	978 352-6132	8912
S and S Concrete Forms Cnstr	Swansea	MA	G	508 379-0191	12310
Salem Metal Inc	Middleton	MA	E	978 774-2100	10392
Sme Ltd	Dedham	MA	G	617 842-4682	8251
Southbridge Shtmtl Works Inc	Sturbridge	MA	E	508 347-7800	12258
Standex International Corp	North Billerica	MA	D	978 667-2771	10959
Sx Industries Inc (PA)	Stoughton	MA	F	781 828-7111	12241
Tamer Industries Inc	Somerset	MA	D	508 677-0900	11856
Taunton Stove Company Inc	North Dighton	MA	E	508 823-0786	11004
Tech Fab Inc	South Hadley	MA	E	413 532-9022	11967
Tech-Etch Inc	Fall River	MA	E	508 675-5757	8614
Techncal Metal Fabricators Inc	Mendon	MA	F	508 473-2223	10322
Techni-Products Inc	East Longmeadow	MA	E	413 525-6321	8398
Tecomet Inc (HQ)	Wilmington	MA	C	978 642-2400	13463
Teltron Engineering Inc	Foxboro	MA	F	508 543-6600	8727
Thermo-Craft Engineering Corp	Lynn	MA	E	781 599-4023	9992
Thl-Nortek Investors LLC (PA)	Boston	MA	D	617 227-1050	7077
Todrin Industries Inc	Lakeville	MA	F	508 946-3600	9522
Townsend Welding Co Inc	Wilmington	MA	E	978 657-5189	13468
Ty-Wood Corporation	Holliston	MA	G	508 429-4011	9235
United Hvac Co Inc	Rockland	MA	E	781 871-1060	11663
United Metal Fabracators Inc	Worcester	MA	F	508 754-1800	13815
US Sheetmetal Inc	West Bridgewater	MA	G	508 427-0500	12987
Vortex Inc	Peabody	MA	D	978 535-8721	11351
Vulcan Industries Inc	Hudson	MA	E	978 562-0003	9425
Waynes Sheet Metal Inc	Rehoboth	MA	G	508 431-8057	11615
Weiss Sheet Metal Inc	Avon	MA	E	508 583-8300	6167
Welch Welding and Trck Eqp Inc	North Chelmsford	MA	F	978 251-8726	10989
Weld Rite	Jamaica Plain	MA	G	617 524-9747	9504
Welding Craftsmen Co Inc	South Easton	MA	F	508 230-7878	11956
Wrobel Engineering Co Inc	Avon	MA	D	508 586-8338	6169
XYZ Sheet Metal Inc	Abington	MA	F	781 878-1419	5729
Architectural Skylight Co Inc	Waterboro	ME	F	207 247-6747	5589
Collins Sheet Metal Inc	Berwick	ME	F	207 384-4428	4549
Down East Shtmtl & Certif Wldg	Brewer	ME	G	207 989-3443	4611
DSM Metal Fabrication Inc	Biddeford	ME	E	207 282-6740	4561
Eagle Industries Inc	Hollis Center	ME	E	207 929-3700	4893
Ekto Manufacturing Corp	Sanford	ME	E	207 324-4427	5394
Fastco Fabrication Inc	Lincoln	ME	E	207 794-3030	5007
Futureguard Building Pdts Inc (PA)	Auburn	ME	E	800 858-5818	4434
Gagne & Son Con Blocks Inc	Auburn	ME	E	207 495-3313	4435
Hahnel Bros Co (PA)	Lewiston	ME	C	207 784-6477	4963
Kinetics Group Inc	Scarborough	ME	F	207 541-4712	5436
Knowlton Machine Company	Gorham	ME	E	207 854-8471	4824
MC Faulkner & Sons Inc	Gorham	ME	F	207 929-4545	4826
N E Tech-Air Inc	Scarborough	ME	C	207 347-7577	5439
North E Wldg & Fabrication Inc	Auburn	ME	E	207 786-2446	4448
Prescott Metal (PA)	Biddeford	ME	E	207 283-0115	4584
Ridlons Metal Shop	Casco	ME	G	207 655-7997	4683
Tri Star Sheet Metal Company	Turner	ME	F	207 225-2043	5563
Advance Concrete Form Inc	Manchester	NH	G	603 669-4496	14805
Approved Sheet Metal LLC	Hudson	NH	E	603 883-1510	14484
Charles P Blouin Inc (PA)	Seabrook	NH	C	603 474-3400	15586
David Streeter	Charlestown	NH	G	603 542-6045	14061
Ddg Fabrication LLC	Nashua	NH	G	603 883-9292	15088
Dgf Indstrial Innvtons Group L	Gilford	NH	F	603 528-6591	14335
Donovan Equipment Company Inc	Londonderry	NH	D	603 669-2250	14743
East Coast Metal Works Co Inc	Kingston	NH	G	603 642-9600	14634
Empire Sheetmetal Inc	Manchester	NH	E	603 622-4439	14847
Evs New Hampshire Inc	Keene	NH	D	603 352-3000	14598
Excell Solutions Inc	Nashua	NH	G	978 663-6100	15097
Garvin Industries Incorporated	Auburn	NH	G	603 647-5410	13908
Gilchrist Metal Fabg Co Inc (PA)	Hudson	NH	E	603 889-2600	14500
H&H Custom Metal Fabg Inc	Plaistow	NH	G	603 382-2818	15347
Hi-Tech Fabricators Inc	Milford	NH	F	603 672-3766	15025
Inofab LLC	Pittsfield	NH	F	603 435-5082	15333
Keebowil Inc (PA)	Keene	NH	E	603 352-4232	14605
Ken-Mar LLC	Salem	NH	E	603 898-1268	15539
LAD Welding & Fabrication	Hooksett	NH	F	603 228-6617	14466
M&H Liquidating Company LLC	Amherst	NH	D	603 889-8320	13876
Macy Industries Inc	Hooksett	NH	E	603 623-5568	14468
Martin Intl Enclosures LLC	Seabrook	NH	E	603 474-2626	15597
Metal Works Inc	Londonderry	NH	D	603 669-6180	14771
MJ Murphy and Sons Inc	Dover	NH	E	603 767-4200	14236
Nashua Fabrication Co Inc	Hudson	NH	E	603 889-2181	14531
Northeastern Sheet Metal Inc	Goffstown	NH	D	603 497-4166	14355
Novia Corporation	Salem	NH	E	603 898-8600	15552
Omni Metals Company Inc	Somersworth	NH	E	603 692-6664	15619
Palmer and Sicard Inc	Exeter	NH	D	603 778-1841	14300
Profile Metal Forming Inc (HQ)	Newmarket	NH	E	603 659-8323	15222
Progressive Manufacturing Inc	West Lebanon	NH	E	603 298-5778	15688
Prototek Dgtal Mfg Concord LLC (PA)	Contoocook	NH	D	603 746-2001	14173
Prototek Intrmdate Hldings Inc	Contoocook	NH	F	800 403-9777	14174
Ran/All Metal Technology Inc	Hooksett	NH	G	603 668-1907	14472
Rapid Group	Nashua	NH	F	603 821-7300	15155
Rapid Manufacturing Group LLC	Nashua	NH	F	603 686-8980	15156
Rockingham Sheet Metal Inc	Pelham	NH	G	603 886-1799	15296
S&H Precision Mfg Co Inc (PA)	Newmarket	NH	E	603 659-8323	15223
Sebabo South Inc	Nashua	NH	F	603 881-8720	15165
South Main Manchester Housing	Manchester	NH	G	603 626-3034	14935
Sparton Technology Corp	Hudson	NH	D	603 880-3692	14548
Spiral Air Manufacturing LLC	Derry	NH	G	603 624-6647	14208
Superior Sheet Metal LLC	Hudson	NH	E	866 468-3828	14549
Sylro Sales Corporation	Pelham	NH	E	603 595-4556	15298
Sylvester Sheet Metal LLC	Manchester	NH	E	603 624-4586	14938
Technical Machine Components	Hudson	NH	F	603 880-0444	14550
Tecta America Corp	Keene	NH	D	603 352-4232	14627
Total Air Supply LLC	Nashua	NH	E	603 889-0100	15177
Tsi Group Inc (DH)	Hampton	NH	E	603 964-0296	14416
Valley Welding & Fabg Inc	Hollis	NH	F	603 465-3266	14460
Will-Mor Manufacturing LLC	Seabrook	NH	D	603 474-8971	15606
All-State Fabricators Limited Partnership	Cranston	RI	D	401 785-3900	15827
Century Sheet Metal Inc	Riverside	RI	G	401 433-1380	16653
Cosco LLC	Woonsocket	RI	G	401 765-0009	16955
EMI Industries LLC	Cranston	RI	D	401 785-3900	15855
Engineering Wldg & Fabg Co Inc	North Kingstown	RI	G	401 884-1484	16252
Ferguson Perforating Company (DH)	Providence	RI	D	401 941-8876	16518
Frank J Newman & Son Inc	North Scituate	RI	G	401 231-0550	16315
Frank Lombardo and Sons Inc	Providence	RI	F	401 461-4547	16521
GA Rel Manufacturing Company	Providence	RI	F	401 331-5455	16524
H V Holland Inc	Jamestown	RI	F	401 423-0614	16069
J & R Senior Sheet Metal Inc	Westerly	RI	G	401 322-1509	16933
Lightship Group LLC (PA)	North Kingstown	RI	E	401 294-3341	16268
Metalworks Corporation	Tiverton	RI	F	401 624-4400	16737
Morris & Broms LLC	Johnston	RI	F	401 781-3134	16098
Nasons Ug Inc (PA)	Middletown	RI	F	401 847-2497	16180
Renaisance Cornice	Johnston	RI	G	401 275-6500	16103
Renaissance Sheet Metal L	North Kingstown	RI	G	401 294-3703	16278
Stackbin Corporation	Lincoln	RI	E	401 333-1600	16155
Wards Manufacturing LLC	Warren	RI	G	404 441-0453	16671
Fab-Tech Inc	Colchester	VT	E	802 655-8800	17190
Gloucester Associates Inc	Barre	VT	E	802 479-1088	17001
Hutchins Roofing Company Inc	Barre	VT	F	802 476-5591	17007
Ke Usa Inc	Middlebury	VT	E	802 388-7309	17345
Keebowil Inc	Rutland	VT	F	802 775-3572	17502
Kimtek Corporation	Orleans	VT	G	802 754-9000	17438
McGill Airflow LLC	Bennington	VT	G	802 442-1900	17051
McKernon Group Inc	Brandon	VT	D	802 247-8500	17068
Milton Vermont Sheet Metal Inc	Milton	VT	F	802 893-1581	17362
Momentum Mfg Group - N LLC (PA)	Saint Johnsbury	VT	C	802 748-5007	17545
Nevtec Inc	Newport	VT	F	802 334-7800	17401
New England Supply Inc (PA)	Williston	VT	D	802 858-4577	17742
Northeastern Htg Vent AC Corp	Williston	VT	F	802 865-8008	17743
Real Vermont Roofing Slate	West Pawlet	VT	G	802 884-8091	17693
Sheet Metal Design	Essex Junction	VT	G	802 288-9700	17246
Vhv Company (PA)	Winooski	VT	C	802 655-8805	17771

3446 Architectural metalwork

	CITY	ST	EMP	PHONE	ENTRY#
Artistic Iron Works LLC	Norwalk	CT	G	203 838-9200	2464
Boudreaus Welding Co Inc	Dayville	CT	F	860 774-2771	860
Clarke International Bus Inc	Middletown	CT	E	860 632-1149	1743
Connecticut Iron Works Inc	Greenwich	CT	G	203 869-0657	1327
Dyco Industries Inc	South Windsor	CT	E	860 289-4957	3138
East Windsor Metal Fabg Inc	South Windsor	CT	E	860 528-7107	3139
Eastern Metal Works Inc	Milford	CT	E	203 878-6995	1821
Edi Landscape LLC	Hartford	CT	F	860 216-6871	1477
Engineered Building Pdts Inc	Bloomfield	CT	E	860 243-1110	161
Euro Tech Metal Creations Inc	Danbury	CT	G	914 325-1760	742
Feman Steel LLC	Bloomfield	CT	F	860 982-6393	164
Garden Iron LLC	Westbrook	CT	G	860 767-9917	4138
Ida International Inc	Derby	CT	E	203 736-9249	890

SIC

	CITY	ST	EMP	PHONE	ENTRY#
International Pipe & Stl Corp	North Branford	CT	F	203 481-7102	2369
Kammetal Inc (PA)	Naugatuck	CT	F	718 722-9991	1969
Kenneth Lynch & Sons Inc	Oxford	CT	G	203 762-8363	2702
Leed - Himmel Industries Inc	Hamden	CT	D	203 288-8484	1436
Leek Building Products Inc	Norwalk	CT	E	203 853-3883	2527
Loyal Fence Company LLC	Rockfall	CT	G	203 530-7046	2914
Lpg Metal Crafts LLC	Plainville	CT	G	860 982-3573	2770
Luckey LLC	New Haven	CT	F	203 747-5270	2171
Mono-Crete Step Co Ct LLC	Bethel	CT	F	203 748-8419	129
Musano Inc	Wolcott	CT	E	203 879-4651	4369
Naugatuck Stair Company Inc	Naugatuck	CT	F	203 729-7134	1976
Patwil LLC	Bristol	CT	G	860 589-9085	480
Quality Stairs Inc	Bridgeport	CT	F	203 367-8390	364
Shepard Steel Co Inc (PA)	Hartford	CT	D	860 525-4446	1507
Shepard Steel Co Inc	Newington	CT	E	860 525-4446	2325
Southington Metal Fabg Co	Southington	CT	F	860 621-0149	3233
Stately Stair Co Inc	Naugatuck	CT	F	203 575-1966	1987
T Woodward Stair Building LLC	North Branford	CT	G	860 664-0515	2376
The Bilco Company (DH)	West Haven	CT	C	203 934-6363	4128
United Steel Inc	East Hartford	CT	C	860 289-2323	1032
Washington Concrete Pdts Inc	Plainville	CT	F	860 747-5242	2788
Wrought Iron Works LLC	West Hartford	CT	E	860 523-4457	4093
AP Iron Design Inc	Everett	MA	G	617 389-0001	8482
Boston Retail Products Inc (PA)	Tewksbury	MA	D	781 395-7417	12387
Boston Steel Fabricators Inc	Holbrook	MA	G	781 767-1540	9170
Brayton Wilson Cole Corp	Hingham	MA	G	781 803-6624	9144
Cape Cod Fence Co (PA)	South Yarmouth	MA	F	508 398-6041	11982
Cassidy Bros Forge Inc	Rowley	MA	E	978 948-7303	11671
Clayton LLC DBA Blbird Grphic	Woburn	MA	E	617 250-8500	13542
Concentric Fabrication LLC	Somerset	MA	G	774 955-5692	11851
Concentric Fabrication LLC	Middleboro	MA	E	508 672-4098	10355
DC Scaffold Inc	West Bridgewater	MA	G	508 580-5100	12971
Deangelis Iron Work Inc (PA)	South Easton	MA	E	508 238-4310	11941
Eckel Industries Inc (PA)	Ayer	MA	F	978 772-0840	6181
Flagraphics Inc	Somerville	MA	F	617 776-7549	11874
Green Brothers Fabricating (PA)	Taunton	MA	E	508 880-3608	12339
Kamrowski Refinishing Co Inc	Framingham	MA	F	508 877-0367	8783
M Cohen and Sons	Mashpee	MA	G	774 228-2193	10253
Make Archtectural Metalworking	West Wareham	MA	F	508 273-7603	13067
Mezzanine Safeti-Gates Inc	Essex	MA	G	978 768-3000	8478
Nucor Grating	Milford	MA	F	724 934-5320	10412
Ornamental Ironworks Inc	Fall River	MA	F	508 678-0687	8592
Pbd Productions LLC	Hopedale	MA	F	508 482-9300	9300
Perfection Fence Corp (PA)	Marshfield	MA	F	781 837-3600	10243
Period Lighting Fixtures Inc	Clarksburg	MA	F	413 664-7141	8072
Quinn Bros of Essex Inc	Essex	MA	F	978 768-6929	8479
Rens Welding & Fabricating	Taunton	MA	F	508 828-1702	12362
Rolls-Royce Marine North Amer (DH)	Walpole	MA	C	508 668-9610	12574
Ryan Iron Works Inc	Raynham	MA	E	508 821-2058	11596
Somerville Orna Ir Works Inc	Somerville	MA	G	617 666-8872	11898
Southeast Railing Co Inc	Cantoh	MA	F	781 828-7088	7831
Southern Mtal Fbricators Inc	Rockland	MA	E	781 878-1505	11661
Sunsetter Products Ltd Partnr	Malden	MA	D	781 321-9600	10029
Superior Rail and Ir Works Inc	East Bridgewater	MA	E	508 378-4025	8345
Village Forge Inc	Boston	MA	F	617 361-2591	7104
Watertown Ironworks Inc	Woburn	MA	E	781 491-0229	13687
Welch Welding and Trck Eqp Inc	North Chelmsford	MA	F	978 251-8726	10989
Weld Rite	Jamaica Plain	MA	G	617 524-9747	9504
Anchor Corporation	Kennebunk	ME	F	207 985-6018	4920
Cives Corporation	Augusta	ME	C	207 622-6141	4469
Clark Metal Fabrication Inc	Turner	ME	G	207 330-6322	5561
Mainely Gates & Handrails	Benton	ME	G	207 314-1083	4546
Mainely Handrails LLC	Fairfield	ME	F	207 314-1083	4764
Sigco Inc	Westbrook	ME	E	207 775-2676	5648
Sigco LLC (HQ)	Westbrook	ME	C	207 775-2676	5649
Asca Inc (PA)	Portsmouth	NH	E	603 433-6700	15361
Environmental Interiors Inc	Nashua	NH	E	603 889-9290	15095
Mf Blouin Mdsg Solution	Dover	NH	G	800 394-1632	14234
Mfb Holdings LLC	Dover	NH	E	603 742-0104	14235
New Hampshire Stl Erectors LLC	Goffstown	NH	E	603 668-3464	14353
Plp Composite Technologies	Fitzwilliam	NH	E	603 585-9100	14315
S L Chasse Welding & Fabg Inc	Hudson	NH	D	603 886-3436	14543
Soucy Industries Inc (PA)	Pelham	NH	E	603 883-4500	15297
Superior Steel Fabricators Inc	Brookline	NH	F	603 673-7509	14041
Upnovr Inc	Pelham	NH	E	603 625-8639	15299
Vanguard Manufacturing Inc	New Ipswich	NH	D	603 878-2083	15200
379 Charles RI Inc	North Providence	RI	F	401 521-1101	16293
Custom Iron Works Inc	Coventry	RI	E	401 826-3310	15812
Ne Steel Fabricators LLC	Cranston	RI	E	401 785-1234	15898
Burtco Inc	Westminster Station	VT	F	802 722-3358	17702
Hubbardton Forge LLC	Castleton	VT	C	802 468-3090	17172
S & A Trombley Corporation	Morrisville	VT	E	802 888-2394	17388

	CITY	ST	EMP	PHONE	ENTRY#
Springfield Fence Company Inc	North Springfield	VT	F	802 886-2221	17424

3448 Prefabricated metal buildings

	CITY	ST	EMP	PHONE	ENTRY#
Cover-It Inc	West Haven	CT	C	203 931-4747	4100
Eb Carports & Metal Structures	Newington	CT	F	860 263-3797	2287
Engineered Building Pdts Inc	Bloomfield	CT	E	860 243-1110	161
Fabbrica LLC (PA)	Windsor	CT	C	860 253-4136	4275
Illinois Tool Works Inc	Waterbury	CT	C	203 574-2119	3920
Mdm Products LLC	Milford	CT	F	203 877-7070	1848
Mobile Mini Inc	Suffield	CT	G	860 668-1888	3594
Morin Corporation (DH)	Bristol	CT	D	860 584-0900	472
Rwt Corporation	Madison	CT	D	203 245-2731	1568
Star Steel Structures Inc	Somers	CT	G	860 763-5681	3100
Steel Modular Inc	Essex	CT	F	310 227-3714	1172
Walpole Outdoors LLC	Ridgefield	CT	E	508 668-2800	2909
Welding Works Inc	Madison	CT	E	203 245-2731	1576
Brady-Built Inc	Auburn	MA	G	508 798-2600	6109
Freight Farms Inc	Boston	MA	E	877 687-4326	6748
Gordon Industries Inc (PA)	Randolph	MA	E	857 401-8398	11561
Green Brothers Fabricating (PA)	Taunton	MA	E	508 880-3608	12339
Jf2 LLC	Holliston	MA	C	508 429-1022	9218
Longhorn Steel Inc	Peabody	MA	G	978 265-3646	11325
Marzilli Machine Co	Fall River	MA	E	508 567-4145	8574
Mobile Mini Inc	West Bridgewater	MA	F	508 427-5395	12975
Morton Buildings Inc	Westfield	MA	F	413 562-7028	13191
New England Foundation Co Inc (PA)	Hyde Park	MA	D	617 361-9750	9465
Package Industries Inc	Sutton	MA	E	508 865-5871	12288
Space Building Corp	Lakeville	MA	E	508 947-7277	9521
The Cricket System Inc	Newburyport	MA	G	617 905-1420	10719
Walpole Outdoors LLC	East Falmouth	MA	E	508 540-0300	8362
Walpole Outdoors LLC	Wilmington	MA	E	978 658-3373	13475
Ekto Manufacturing Corp	Sanford	ME	E	207 324-4427	5394
Great Northern Docks Inc (PA)	Naples	ME	G	207 693-3770	5080
Rubb Inc	Sanford	ME	D	207 324-2877	5413
Sheridan Corporation (HQ)	Fairfield	ME	E	207 453-9311	4765
Walpole Outdoors LLC	Chester	ME	E	207 794-2248	4694
Concrete Systems Inc	Hudson	NH	D	603 886-5672	14491
Concrete Systems Inc	Londonderry	NH	F	603 432-1840	14736
Dyer S Docking Systems Corp	West Nottingham	NH	F	603 942-5122	15693
Inofab LLC	Pittsfield	NH	F	603 435-5082	15333
Rimol Greenhouse Systems Inc	Hooksett	NH	F	603 629-9004	14474
Ufp Shelf 1 LLC	Wilton	NH	F	603 824-9690	15711

3449 Miscellaneous metalwork

	CITY	ST	EMP	PHONE	ENTRY#
Aerospace Alloys Inc	Bloomfield	CT	D	860 882-0019	144
Boudreaus Welding Co Inc	Dayville	CT	F	860 774-2771	860
C & S Engineering Inc	Meriden	CT	F	203 235-5727	1657
Clarke International Bus Inc	Middletown	CT	E	860 632-1149	1743
Conntech Products Corporation	Cheshire	CT	E	203 272-2261	581
Eastern Metal Works Inc	Milford	CT	E	203 878-6995	1821
Engineered Building Pdts Inc	Bloomfield	CT	E	860 243-1110	161
Nucor Hrris Rbar Northeast LLC	South Windsor	CT	D	860 282-1860	3166
Nucor Steel Connecticut Inc	Wallingford	CT	C	203 265-0615	3836
Quality Engineering Svcs Inc	Wallingford	CT	E	203 269-5054	3843
Simpson Strong-Tie Company Inc	Enfield	CT	D	860 741-8923	1152
The Carby Corporation	Watertown	CT	E	860 274-6741	4032
Artisan Industries Inc	Stoughton	MA	D	781 893-6800	12195
Building Envelope Systems LLC	Plainville	MA	D	508 381-0429	11430
Cdp Manufacturing LLC	Brockton	MA	F	508 588-6400	7267
Marblehead Engineering	Essex	MA	F	978 432-1386	8477
Mill City Iron Fabricators	Dracut	MA	F	978 957-6833	8309
Nucor Hrris Rbar Northeast LLC	Westfield	MA	E	413 568-7803	13194
Rebars & Mesh Inc	Haverhill	MA	E	978 374-2244	9126
Schrimpf Wldg Fabrication Inc	Woburn	MA	G	339 298-2311	13661
Megquier & Jones Inc	Topsham	ME	E	207 799-8555	5550
Ingenven Flrplymer Sltions LLC	Hampton	NH	F	603 601-0877	14403
Nucor Hrris Rbar Northeast LLC	Canaan	NH	E	603 632-5222	14047
Audette Group LLC	Providence	RI	F	401 667-5884	16479
Dominion Rebar Company	Pawtucket	RI	E	401 724-9200	16365
Ne Steel Fabricators LLC	Cranston	RI	E	401 785-1234	15898
Nucor Hrris Rbar Northeast LLC	Pawtucket	RI	E	401 724-9200	16396
Rusco Steel Company	Warwick	RI	D	401 732-0548	16855

3451 Screw machine products

	CITY	ST	EMP	PHONE	ENTRY#
Atp Industries LLC (PA)	Plainville	CT	F	860 479-5007	2748
B&T Screw Machine Co Inc	Bristol	CT	F	860 314-4410	402
Bar Work Manufacturing Co Inc	Waterbury	CT	E	203 753-4103	3889
C & A Machine Co Inc	Newington	CT	E	860 667-0605	2278
Cadcom Inc	Milford	CT	F	203 877-0640	1806
Cole S Crew Machine Products	North Haven	CT	E	203 723-1418	2398
Creed 20 LLC	New Britain	CT	G	860 826-4004	2016
Creed Assets Inc	New Britain	CT	B	860 225-7884	2017
Curtis Products LLC	Bristol	CT	F	203 754-4155	433

	CITY	ST	EMP	PHONE	ENTRY#
Dacruz Manufacturing Inc	Bristol	CT	E	860 584-5315	434
Day Machine Systems Inc	New Britain	CT	F	860 229-3440	2020
Devon Precision Industries Inc	Wolcott	CT	D	203 879-1437	4363
Duda and Goodwin Incorporated	Woodbury	CT	F	203 263-4353	4387
Durco Manufacturing Co Inc	Waterbury	CT	G	203 575-0446	3908
Electro-Tech Inc	Cheshire	CT	E	203 271-1976	589
F F Screw Products Inc	Southington	CT	E	860 621-4567	3209
Forestville Machine Company	Plainville	CT	F	860 747-6000	2760
G M T Manufacturing Co Inc	Plantsville	CT	G	860 628-6757	2792
Garmac Screw Machines Inc	Naugatuck	CT	F	203 723-6911	1960
GK Automatics Incorporated	Thomaston	CT	F	860 283-5878	3620
Horst Engineering & Manufacturing Co **(PA)** 860 289-8209	East Hartford CT 997				D
J J Ryan Corporation	Plantsville	CT	C	860 628-0393	2793
James Wright Precision Pdts	Putnam	CT	E	860 928-7756	2862
Jay Sons Screw Mch Pdts Inc	Milldale	CT	E	860 621-0141	1901
Kamatics Corporation **(DH)**	Bloomfield	CT	E	860 243-9704	184
Leipold Inc	Windsor	CT	E	860 298-9791	4286
Mailly Mfg Co Inc	Wolcott	CT	G	203 879-1445	4367
Manufacturers Associates Inc	West Haven	CT	E	203 931-4344	4113
Marvel Screw Machine Pdts Inc	Waterbury	CT	E	203 756-7058	3943
Matthew Warren Inc	Seymour	CT	G	203 888-2133	2964
Microbest Inc	Waterbury	CT	C	203 597-0355	3944
Multi-Metal Manufacturing Inc	Naugatuck	CT	C	203 723-8887	1974
OEM Sources LLC	Milford	CT	G	203 283-5415	1857
Olson Brothers Company	Plainville	CT	F	860 747-6844	2775
P-A-R Precision Inc	Wolcott	CT	F	860 491-4181	4372
Palladin Precision Pdts Inc	Waterbury	CT	F	203 574-0246	3958
Petron Automation Inc	Watertown	CT	F	860 274-9091	4024
Precision Methods Incorporated	Wolcott	CT	F	203 879-1449	4373
Prime Engneered Components Inc	Watertown	CT	D	860 274-6773	4025
Prime Engnred Cmpnnts - Brstol	Bristol	CT	F	860 584-5964	484
Pro-Manufactured Products Inc	Plainfield	CT	G	860 564-2197	2737
Quality Automatics Inc **(PA)**	Oakville	CT	F	860 945-4795	2625
Rgd Technologies Corp	Bristol	CT	F	860 589-0756	492
Royal Screw Machine Pdts Co	Bristol	CT	F	860 845-8920	495
Selectcom Manufacturing Co Inc	Wolcott	CT	F	203 879-9900	4376
Sga Components Group LLC	Prospect	CT	G	203 758-3702	2842
Sheldon Precision LLC	Prospect	CT	E	203 758-4441	2843
Sperry Automatics Co Inc	Naugatuck	CT	F	203 729-4589	1986
Sun Corp	Morris	CT	G	860 567-0817	1934
Supreme-Lake Mfg Inc	Plantsville	CT	D	860 621-8911	2797
T & A Screw Products Inc	Waterbury	CT	F	203 756-2770	3972
T & J Screw Machine Pdts LLC	Oakville	CT	F	860 417-3801	2627
Thomastn-Mdtown Screw Mch Pdts	Thomaston	CT	F	860 283-9796	3637
Thomaston Industries Inc	Thomaston	CT	F	860 283-4358	3638
Tomz Corporation	Berlin	CT	C	860 829-0670	88
Tremco Swiss Inc	Waterbury	CT	F	203 573-8584	3975
Tri-Star Industries Inc	Seymour	CT	E	860 828-7570	2973
Triem Industries LLC	Terryville	CT	E	203 888-1212	3612
Vigue Holding Company Inc	Plainville	CT	E	860 747-6000	2787
Ville Swiss Automatics Inc	Waterbury	CT	F	203 756-2825	3979
Waterbury Screw Mch Pdts Co	Waterbury	CT	F	203 756-8084	3982
Alpha Grainger Mfg Inc	Franklin	MA	C	508 520-4005	8815
Atc Screw Machine Inc	Haverhill	MA	F	781 939-0725	9075
Automatic Machine Pdts Sls Co	Taunton	MA	F	508 822-4226	12320
Berkmatics Inc	North Adams	MA	F	413 664-6152	10803
Boston Centerless Inc	Avon	MA	E	508 587-3500	6145
Burlington Machine Inc	Wilmington	MA	F	978 284-6525	13396
C F G Corporation	Saugus	MA	F	781 233-6110	11754
Condon Mfg Co Inc	Springfield	MA	F	413 543-1250	12085
Device Technologies Inc	Southborough	MA	E	508 229-2000	11994
E F Inc	Gardner	MA	F	978 630-3800	8885
FC Phillips Inc	Stoughton	MA	F	781 344-9400	12208
Fraen Corporation **(PA)**	Reading	MA	C	781 205-5300	11601
Geonautics Manufacturing Inc	Newburyport	MA	F	978 462-7161	10685
Louis C Morin Co Inc	North Billerica	MA	E	978 670-1222	10928
Lutco Bearings Inc	Worcester	MA	D	508 756-6296	13754
Marver Med Inc	Stoughton	MA	F	781 341-9372	12221
Mgb Us Inc	Franklin	MA	F	774 415-0060	8851
North Easton Machine Co Inc	North Easton	MA	F	508 238-6219	11011
Plymtron Industries Inc	Plymouth	MA	F	508 746-1126	11473
Rosellis Machine & Mfg Co	Westfield	MA	F	413 562-4317	13203
San-Tron Inc **(PA)**	Ipswich	MA	D	978 356-1585	9496
Specialized Turning Inc	Peabody	MA	F	978 977-0444	11342
Swissturn/Usa Inc	Oxford	MA	D	508 987-6211	11264
Weber Realty Trust	Auburn	MA	F	508 756-4290	6127
Yankee Hill Machine Co Inc	Easthampton	MA	D	413 584-1400	8464
Arundel Holdings Inc	Arundel	ME	D	207 985-8555	4408
Elmet Technologies Inc	Lewiston	ME	C	207 784-3591	4959
Barco Manufacturing Inc	Tilton	NH	E	603 286-3324	15652
D & E Screw Machine Pdts Inc	Colebrook	NH	F	508 658-7344	14104
Intelitek Inc	Derry	NH	E	800 221-2763	14196
JT Manufacturing Corporation	Pelham	NH	E	603 821-5720	15291
Liberty Research Co Inc **(PA)**	Rochester	NH	E	603 332-2730	15486
New Hampshire Machine Pdts Inc	Exeter	NH	G	603 772-4404	14297
Omni Components Corp **(HQ)**	Hudson	NH	C	603 882-4467	14533
Parker & Harper Companies Inc **(PA)**	Raymond	NH	D	603 895-4761	15455
W H Bagshaw Co Inc	Nashua	NH	E	603 883-7758	15184
Blackhawk Machine Products Inc	Smithfield	RI	E	401 232-7563	16689
Esmond Manufacturing Co Inc	Cranston	RI	G	401 942-9103	15858
Greystone Incorporated	Lincoln	RI	F	401 333-0444	16139
Greystone of Lincoln Inc **(PA)**	Lincoln	RI	C	401 333-0444	16140
Groov-Pin Corporation **(PA)**	Smithfield	RI	D	770 251-5054	16707
M F Engineering Company Inc	Bristol	RI	F	401 253-6163	15774
Machinex Company Inc	Smithfield	RI	G	401 231-3230	16723
Moody Machine Products Inc	Providence	RI	G	401 941-5130	16569
Precision Trned Cmponents Corp	Smithfield	RI	D	401 232-3377	16726
Quality Screw Machine Pdts Inc	Smithfield	RI	F	401 231-8900	16727
Rhode Island Precision Co	Providence	RI	F	401 421-6661	16604
Swissline Precision LLC	Cumberland	RI	E	216 362-3814	15964
Wellington Manufacturing Inc	Providence	RI	F	401 461-2248	16645
West Warwick Screw Pdts Co Inc	West Warwick	RI	G	401 821-4729	16925
Lebanon Screw Products Inc	Windsor	VT	F	802 674-6347	17759

3452 Bolts, nuts, rivets, and washers

	CITY	ST	EMP	PHONE	ENTRY#
Aerotech Fasteners Inc	Putnam	CT	F	860 928-6300	2845
Ametek Inc	Wallingford	CT	C	203 265-6731	3770
Atp Industries LLC **(PA)**	Plainville	CT	F	860 479-5007	2748
Bead Industries Inc **(PA)**	Milford	CT	E	203 301-0270	1801
Cast Global Manufacturing Corp	Oxford	CT	F	203 828-6147	2688
Click Bond Inc	Watertown	CT	E	860 274-5435	4005
Contorq Components LLC	New Britain	CT	F	860 225-3366	2015
Crescent Mnfacturing Operating	Burlington	CT	E	860 673-2591	547
Deringer-Ney Inc **(PA)**	Bloomfield	CT	C	860 242-2281	158
Eastern Co **(PA)**	Shelton	CT	E	203 729-2255	3001
Edson Manufacturing Inc	Wolcott	CT	F	203 879-1441	4364
Holo-Krome USA	Wallingford	CT	E	800 879-6205	3815
Horst Engineering & Manufacturing Co **(PA)** 860 289-8209	East Hartford CT 997				D
Howard Engineering LLC	Naugatuck	CT	E	203 729-5213	1963
L & M Manufacturing Co Inc	New Hartford	CT	E	860 379-2751	2105
Lab Security Systems Corp	Bristol	CT	E	860 589-6037	460
Matthew Warren Inc	Seymour	CT	G	203 888-2133	2964
McMellon Bros Incorporated	Stratford	CT	E	203 375-5685	3555
Metalform Acquisition LLC **(PA)**	New Britain	CT	F	860 224-2630	2043
Metallics Inc	Bristol	CT	E	860 589-4186	468
Microbest Inc	Waterbury	CT	C	203 597-0355	3944
Narragansett Screw Co	Winsted	CT	F	860 379-4059	4351
North-East Fasteners Corp	Terryville	CT	E	860 589-3242	3607
Nucap US Inc **(DH)**	Wolcott	CT	F	203 879-1423	4371
Plastic Met Components Co Inc	Milford	CT	F	203 877-2723	1866
Spirol International Corp **(HQ)**	Danielson	CT	C	860 774-8571	844
Spirol Intl Holdg Corp **(PA)**	Danielson	CT	C	860 774-8571	845
Stanley Black & Decker Inc **(PA)**	New Britain	CT	C	860 225-5111	2065
Tico Titanium Inc **(PA)**	Wallingford	CT	E	248 446-0400	3864
Universal Thread Grinding Co	Fairfield	CT	F	203 336-1849	1204
2is Inc	Walpole	MA	E	508 850-7520	12545
A1 Screw Machine Products Inc	Chicopee	MA	F	413 594-8939	8004
Alcoa Global Fasteners Inc	Stoughton	MA	C	412 553-4545	12192
American Bolt & Nut Co Inc	Chelsea	MA	G	617 884-3331	7974
Antenna Associates Inc	Brockton	MA	E	508 583-3241	7257
Astron Inc **(PA)**	Pepperell	MA	E	978 433-9500	11383
Crystal Engineering Co Inc **(PA)**	Newburyport	MA	E	978 465-7007	10677
Donahue Industries Inc	Shrewsbury	MA	E	508 845-6501	11830
Fall River Mfg Co Inc	Fall River	MA	D	508 675-1125	8547
Gardner Screw Corporation	Gardner	MA	F	978 632-0850	8887
Omg Inc **(DH)**	Agawam	MA	B	413 789-0252	5803
Q Pin2s Billiards	West Springfield	MA	G	413 285-7971	13043
Reed & Prince Mfg Corp	Leominster	MA	F	978 466-6903	9700
Reeves Company Inc	Attleboro	MA	F	508 222-2877	6053
Robbins Manufacturing Co Inc	Fall River	MA	E	508 675-2555	8605
Standard Lock Washer & Mfg Co	Worcester	MA	F	508 757-4508	13807
Stanlok Corporation	Worcester	MA	F	508 757-4508	13808
Tiberio Manufacturing Corp	Holliston	MA	D	508 429-4011	9232
Tph Inc	Taunton	MA	E	401 431-1791	12372
Haydon Kerk Mtion Slutions Inc	Milford	NH	D	603 213-6290	15024
Allesco Industries Inc **(PA)**	Cranston	RI	F	401 943-0680	15828
Alloy Fasteners Inc **(HQ)**	Cranston	RI	F	401 943-0639	15830
Bobby Pins	Cranston	RI	G	401 461-3400	15837
Eastern Screw Company	Cranston	RI	C	401 943-0680	15852
Groov-Pin Corporation **(PA)**	Smithfield	RI	D	770 251-5054	16707
Hindley Manufacturing Co Inc	Cumberland	RI	D	401 722-2550	15943
Research Engineering & Mfg Inc	Middletown	RI	F	401 841-8880	16184
Applied Bolting Tech Pdts LLC	Bellows Falls	VT	E	802 460-3100	17028

SIC

Employee Codes: A=Over 500 employees, B=251-500   2024 Harris New England
C=101-250, D=51-100, E=20-50, F=10-19, G=1-9   Manufacturers Directory

911

	CITY	ST	EMP	PHONE	ENTRY#

3462 Iron and steel forgings

	CITY	ST	EMP	PHONE	ENTRY#
Bourdon Forge Co Inc	Middletown	CT	C	860 632-2740	1741
Bristol Instrument Gears Inc	Bristol	CT	F	860 583-1395	420
Consoldted Inds Acqsition Corp	Cheshire	CT	D	203 272-5371	582
East Shore Wire Rope	East Haven	CT	G	203 469-5204	1040
J J Ryan Corporation	Plantsville	CT	C	860 628-0393	2793
OEM Sources LLC	Milford	CT	D	203 283-5415	1857
Paradigm Manchester Inc	Manchester	CT	C	860 649-2888	1625
Perry Technology Corporation	New Hartford	CT	D	860 738-2525	2107
Roller Bearing Co Amer Inc	Middlebury	CT	F	203 758-8272	1720
Secondaries Inc	Wolcott	CT	C	203 879-4633	4375
United Gear and Machine Co Inc	Suffield	CT	F	860 623-6618	3596
2is Inc	Walpole	MA	E	508 850-7520	12545
Acorn Manufacturing Co Inc	Mansfield	MA	E	508 339-4500	10036
Boulevard Machine & Gear Inc	Westfield	MA	E	413 788-6466	13154
Diamond Hrseshoe Dev Group LLC	Quincy	MA	G	617 755-6100	11510
Doncasters Inc	Springfield	MA	D	413 785-1801	12090
Engineered Pressure Systems Inc	Haverhill	MA	E	978 469-8280	9094
Horseshoe Sunday LLC	Haverhill	MA	G	978 476-9766	9104
Insco Corporation	Groton	MA	E	978 448-6368	9010
Kervick Family Foundation Inc	Worcester	MA	E	508 853-4500	13748
Paradigm Prcision Holdings LLC	Malden	MA	E	781 321-0480	10022
Schrader Electronics Inc	Attleboro	MA	B	615 384-0089	6061
Schrimpf Wldg Fabrication Inc	Woburn	MA	G	339 298-2311	13661
St Pierre Manufacturing Corp	Worcester	MA	E	508 853-8010	13806
Suncor Stainless Inc	Plymouth	MA	D	508 732-9191	11479
US Tsubaki Automotive LLC (DH)	Chicopee	MA	C	413 593-1100	8067
Wyman-Gordon Company	Millbury	MA	B	800 343-6070	10446
Wyman-Gordon Company (DH)	North Grafton	MA	B	508 839-8252	11030
Wyman-Gordon Company	Worcester	MA	D	508 839-8253	13835
ME Industries	Biddeford	ME	G	207 286-2030	4579
Tem Inc	Buxton	ME	E	207 929-8700	4665
Horseshoe Pond Place Commnty	Concord	NH	E	603 224-8390	14137
J C B Leasing Inc	Weare	NH	F	603 529-7974	15671
New Hampshire Forge Inc	Keene	NH	E	603 357-5692	14613
Blue Horseshoe LLC	Bristol	RI	G	401 253-0037	15755
Greystone of Lincoln Inc (PA)	Lincoln	RI	F	401 333-0444	16140
Perry Blackburne Inc	North Providence	RI	F	401 231-7200	16307
Wiesner Manufacturing Company	Warwick	RI	F	401 421-2406	16879

3463 Nonferrous forgings

	CITY	ST	EMP	PHONE	ENTRY#
Consolidated Industries Inc	Cheshire	CT	D	203 272-5371	583
Charles A Richardson Inc	Mansfield	MA	F	508 339-8600	10041
Kervick Family Foundation Inc	Worcester	MA	E	508 853-4500	13748
Wyman-Gordon Company (DH)	North Grafton	MA	B	508 839-8252	11030
Wyman-Gordon Company	Worcester	MA	D	508 839-8253	13835
Tem Inc	Buxton	ME	E	207 929-8700	4665
Granite Forge LLC	Hudson	NH	F	603 589-9480	14501
Smiths Tblar Systms-Lconia Inc	Laconia	NH	C	603 524-2064	14670

3465 Automotive stampings

	CITY	ST	EMP	PHONE	ENTRY#
3M Company	Meriden	CT	F	203 237-5541	1647
C Cowles & Company (PA)	North Haven	CT	D	203 865-3117	2396
Energy Release LLC	Hudson	MA	G	978 466-9700	9363
Illinois Tool Works Inc	Westminster	MA	C	978 874-0151	13271

3466 Crowns and closures

	CITY	ST	EMP	PHONE	ENTRY#
Assa Abloy ACC Door Cntrls Gro	New Haven	CT	C	901 365-2160	2121
Eyelet Design Inc	Waterbury	CT	D	203 754-4141	3911
Orca Inc	New Britain	CT	E	860 223-4180	2047
American Cord & Webbing Co Inc	Woonsocket	RI	E	401 762-5500	16948

3469 Metal stampings, nec

	CITY	ST	EMP	PHONE	ENTRY#
A & D Components Inc	Bristol	CT	G	860 582-9541	389
Acme Monaco Corporation (PA)	New Britain	CT	C	860 224-1349	1995
Addamo Manufacturing Inc	Newington	CT	G	860 667-2601	2266
Alinabal Inc (HQ)	Milford	CT	C	203 877-3241	1796
Alinabal Holdings Corporation (PA)	Milford	CT	B	203 877-3241	1797
American Standard Company	Southington	CT	E	860 628-9643	3203
Arcade Technology LLC	Bridgeport	CT	D	203 366-3871	297
Arrow Manufacturing Company	Bristol	CT	E		397
Atlantic Precision Spring Inc	Bristol	CT	E	860 583-1864	399
Atlas Stamping & Mfg Corp	Newington	CT	E	860 757-3233	2273
Avna Inc (PA)	New Britain	CT	C	860 225-8707	2004
Barlow Metal Stamping Inc	Bristol	CT	E	860 583-1387	403
Barnes Group Inc	Bristol	CT	D	860 582-9581	404
Barnes Group Inc (PA)	Bristol	CT	C	860 583-7070	406
Barnes Group Inc	Farmington	CT	G	860 298-7740	1209
Ben-Art Manufacturing Co Inc	Prospect	CT	G	203 758-4435	2829
Berkley Associates Inc	Waterbury	CT	D	203 757-9221	3890
Bessette Holdings Inc	East Hartford	CT	E	860 289-6000	975
Beta Shim Co	Shelton	CT	E	203 926-1150	2983

	CITY	ST	EMP	PHONE	ENTRY#
Blase Manufacturing Company (PA)	Stratford	CT	E	203 375-5646	3520
Bml Tool & Mfg Corp	Monroe	CT	D	203 880-9485	1907
Bracone Metal Spinning Inc	Southington	CT	E	860 628-5927	3204
Bridgeport TI & Stamping Corp	Bridgeport	CT	E	203 336-2501	305
Bristol Tool & Die Company	Bristol	CT	F	860 582-2577	423
Carpin Manufacturing Inc	Waterbury	CT	D	203 574-2556	3897
Century Spring Mfg Co Inc	Bristol	CT	E	860 582-3344	425
Cheshire Manufacturing Co Inc	Cheshire	CT	G	203 272-3586	580
Cly-Del Manufacturing Company	Waterbury	CT	C	203 574-2100	3898
Companion Industries Inc	Southington	CT	D	860 628-0504	3207
Component Engineers Inc	Wallingford	CT	D	203 269-0557	3791
Connectcut Spring Stmping Corp	Farmington	CT	B	860 677-1341	1212
Consulting Engrg Dev Svcs Inc	Oxford	CT	D	203 828-6528	2691
Cowles Stamping Inc	North Haven	CT	E	203 865-3117	2406
Demsey Manufacturing Inc	Watertown	CT	E	860 274-6209	4008
Deringer-Ney Inc (PA)	Bloomfield	CT	C	860 242-2281	158
Durham Manufacturing Company (PA)	Durham	CT	D	860 349-3427	899
E & E Tool & Mfg Co Inc	Winsted	CT	F	860 738-8577	4342
Empire Industries Inc	Manchester	CT	E	860 647-1431	1596
Excel Spring & Stamping LLC	Bristol	CT	G	860 585-1495	444
Eyelet Design Inc	Waterbury	CT	D	203 754-4141	3911
Eyelet Tech LLC	Wolcott	CT	E	203 879-5306	4365
Eyelet Toolmakers Inc	Watertown	CT	E	860 274-5423	4012
Forrest Machine Inc	Berlin	CT	D	860 563-1796	66
Four Star Manufacturing Co	Bristol	CT	E	860 583-1614	448
Fourslide Spring Stamping Inc	Bristol	CT	E	860 583-1688	449
G L C Inc	Watertown	CT	F	860 945-6166	4013
Gem Manufacturing LLC	Waterbury	CT	D	203 574-1466	3914
Gemco Manufacturing Co Inc	Southington	CT	E	860 628-5529	3211
Globe Tool & Met Stampg Co Inc	Southington	CT	E	860 621-6807	3213
Government Surplus Sales Inc	Hartford	CT	G	860 247-7787	1484
H&T Waterbury Inc	Waterbury	CT	C	203 574-2240	3916
Hexcel Corporation (PA)	Stamford	CT	E	203 969-0666	3374
HMC Enterprises Inc	New Hartford	CT	E	860 379-8506	2101
Hob Industries Inc	Cheshire	CT	E	203 879-3028	599
Hobson and Motzer Incorporated (PA)	Durham	CT	C	860 349-1756	901
Howard Engineering LLC	Naugatuck	CT	E	203 729-5213	1963
Hylie Products Incorporated	Cheshire	CT	E	203 439-8786	600
Illinois Tool Works Inc	Naugatuck	CT	F	203 720-1676	1964
Illinois Tool Works Inc	Waterbury	CT	C	203 574-2119	3920
Insulpane Connecticut Inc	Hamden	CT	D	800 922-3248	1432
ITW Highland Manufacturing Inc	Waterbury	CT	D	203 574-3200	3923
J&J Precision Inc	Thomaston	CT	D	860 283-8243	3622
Joma Incorporated	Waterbury	CT	E	203 759-0848	3926
Lawrence Holdings Inc	Wallingford	CT	F	203 949-1600	3826
Marion Manufacturing Company	Cheshire	CT	E	203 272-5376	605
Mastercraft Tool and Mch Co	Southington	CT	F	860 628-5551	3220
Maurer Metalcraft Inc	Orange	CT	G	203 799-8800	2676
McM Stamping Corporation	Danbury	CT	E	203 792-3080	783
McMullin Manufacturing Corp	Brookfield	CT	E	203 740-3360	529
Meriden Manufacturing Inc	Meriden	CT	D	203 237-7481	1675
Metalform Acquisition LLC (PA)	New Britain	CT	F	860 224-2630	2043
Metallon Inc	Thomaston	CT	E	860 283-8265	3624
MJM Marga LLC	Naugatuck	CT	G	203 729-0600	1973
Mohawk Manufacturing Company	Middletown	CT	F	860 632-2345	1766
National Die Company	Wolcott	CT	G	203 879-1408	4370
National Spring & Stamping Inc	Thomaston	CT	F	860 283-0203	3625
New Hartford Industrial Pk Inc	New Hartford	CT	F	860 379-8506	2106
Nucap US Inc (DH)	Wolcott	CT	E	203 879-1423	4371
OEM Sources LLC	Milford	CT	G	203 283-5415	1857
Oscar Jobs	Bristol	CT	G	860 583-7834	477
Owen Tool and Mfg Co Inc	Southington	CT	G	860 628-6540	3227
P&G Metal Components Corp	Bloomfield	CT	F	860 243-2220	199
Pa-Ted Spring Company LLC	Bristol	CT	E	860 582-6368	479
Paradigm Prcision Holdings LLC	Manchester	CT	E	860 649-2888	1626
Platt Brothers & Company (PA)	Waterbury	CT	D	203 753-4194	3963
Pr-MX Holdings Company LLC (HQ)	Shelton	CT	D	203 925-0012	3051
Precision Resource Inc (PA)	Shelton	CT	C	203 925-0012	3053
Preferred Tool & Die Inc (PA)	Shelton	CT	E	203 925-8525	3054
Pressure Blast Mfg Co Inc	South Windsor	CT	F	800 722-5278	3174
Prospect Machine Products Inc	Prospect	CT	F	203 758-4448	2840
Record Products America Inc	Hamden	CT	F	203 248-6371	1453
Richards Metal Products Inc	Wolcott	CT	F	203 879-2555	4374
Rowley Spring & Stamping Corp	Bristol	CT	C	860 582-8175	494
SA Manchester LLC	Manchester	CT	D	860 533-7500	1634
Satellite Aerospace Inc	Manchester	CT	E	860 643-2771	1635
Schaeffler Aerospace USA Corp (DH)	Danbury	CT	B	203 744-2211	809
Siemon Company (PA)	Watertown	CT	A	860 945-4200	4029
Solla Eyelet Products Inc	Watertown	CT	E	860 274-5729	4030
Southington Tool & Mfg Corp	Plantsville	CT	E	860 276-0021	2796
Spirol International Corp (HQ)	Danielson	CT	C	860 774-8571	844
Spirol Intl Holdg Corp (PA)	Danielson	CT	C	860 774-8571	845
Stevens Company Incorporated	Thomaston	CT	D	860 283-8201	3631

Company	CITY	ST	EMP	PHONE	ENTRY#
Stewart Efi LLC	Thomaston	CT	F	860 283-2523	3632
Stewart Efi LLC (PA)	Thomaston	CT	C	860 283-8213	3633
Stewart Efi Connecticut LLC	Thomaston	CT	C	860 283-8213	3634
Taco Fasteners Inc	Plainville	CT	F	860 747-5597	2782
Target Custom Manufacturing Co	Haddam	CT	G	860 388-5848	1410
The Lyons Tool & Die Company	Meriden	CT	E	203 238-2689	1707
The Romatic Manufacturing Company	Southbury	CT	C	203 264-8203	3199
Tiger Enterprises Inc	Plantsville	CT	E	860 621-9155	2798
Touche Manufacturing Company	Glastonbury	CT	F	860 254-5080	1299
Tru-Precision Corporation	Farmington	CT	G	860 269-6230	1252
Truelove & Maclean Inc	Watertown	CT	C	860 274-9600	4034
Tyger Tool Inc	Stratford	CT	F	203 375-4344	3581
Utitec Inc (HQ)	Watertown	CT	D	860 945-0605	4035
Utitec Holdings Inc	Watertown	CT	D	860 945-0601	4036
Valley Tool & Manufacturing Inc	Orange	CT	D	203 799-8800	2683
Wces Inc	Waterbury	CT	F	203 573-1325	3983
Weimann Brothers Mfg Co	Derby	CT	F	203 735-3311	894
West Shore Metals LLC	Enfield	CT	G	860 749-8013	1158
34 Tower Street Inc	Shirley	MA	F	978 425-2311	11812
A Luongo & Sons Incorporated	Bridgewater	MA	G	508 226-0788	7218
Aero Manufacturing Corp	Beverly	MA	D	978 720-1000	6323
Ainslie Corporation	Walpole	MA	G	781 848-0850	12548
Astron Inc (PA)	Pepperell	MA	E	978 433-9500	11383
Atrenne Cmpt Solutions LLC (DH)	Brockton	MA	B	508 588-6110	7259
Automatic Specialties Inc	Marlborough	MA	E	508 481-2370	10114
Barber Elc Enclosures Mfg Inc	North Attleboro	MA	F	508 699-4872	10867
Berkshire Mnufactured Pdts Inc	Newburyport	MA	C	978 462-8161	10670
Bnz Materials Inc	North Billerica	MA	C	978 663-3401	10900
Brainin-Advance Industries LLC (HQ)	Attleboro	MA	C	508 226-1200	5998
Carlstrom Pressed Metal Co Inc	Westborough	MA	E	508 366-4472	13086
Century-Tywood J3 Corp	Holliston	MA	F	508 429-4011	9204
Charles A Richardson Inc	Mansfield	MA	F	508 339-8600	10041
Cobra Precision Machining Corp	Petersham	MA	G	603 434-8424	11388
Collt Mfg Inc	Millis	MA	E	508 376-2525	10449
Craft Inc	Attleboro	MA	E	508 761-7917	6008
Crystal Engineering Co Inc (PA)	Newburyport	MA	E	978 465-7007	10677
Cunningham Machine Co Inc	Chelmsford	MA	G	978 256-7541	7921
Dakin Road Investments Inc	Littleton	MA	F	978 443-4020	9809
Deltran Inc	Attleboro Falls	MA	F	508 699-7506	6083
Elite Metal Fabricators Inc	Ludlow	MA	G	413 547-2588	9944
Enjet Aero Malden LLC	Malden	MA	D	781 321-0366	10013
Excel Tool & Die Co Inc	Quincy	MA	G	617 472-0473	11516
Far Industries Inc	Assonet	MA	F	508 644-3122	5973
Fine Edge Tool Company Inc	Attleboro	MA	G	508 222-7511	6016
Fraen Corporation (PA)	Reading	MA	C	781 205-5300	11601
Fraen Corporation	Woburn	MA	D	781 937-8825	13570
Gardner Screw Corporation	Gardner	MA	F	978 632-0850	8887
Green Brothers Fabricating (PA)	Taunton	MA	E	508 880-3608	12339
Hi-Tech Inc	Attleboro	MA	F	401 454-4086	6023
International Metal Pdts Inc	Chicopee	MA	E	413 532-2411	8040
Interplex Etch Logic LLC	Attleboro	MA	E	508 399-6810	6025
Killeen Machine and TI Co Inc	Auburn	MA	D	508 754-1714	6118
Larson Tool & Stamping Company	Attleboro	MA	D	508 222-0897	6031
Lee Tool Co Inc	Ludlow	MA	F	413 583-8750	9948
Martran Corp	Attleboro Falls	MA	F	508 699-7506	6089
Matrix Metal Products Inc	Attleboro	MA	F	508 226-2374	6035
New Can Company Inc (HQ)	Holbrook	MA	E	330 928-1191	9181
New England Metalform Inc	Plainville	MA	E	508 695-9340	11441
Norking Company Inc	Attleboro	MA	E	508 222-3100	6043
Norpin Mfg Co Inc	Wilbraham	MA	F	413 599-1628	13362
O W Landergren Inc	Pittsfield	MA	E	413 442-5632	11415
P M S Manufactured Pdts Inc	Gloucester	MA	E	978 281-2600	8950
Paramount Tool LLC	Fall River	MA	E	508 672-0844	8594
Pep Industries LLC	Attleboro	MA	F	508 226-5600	6046
Peter Forg Manufacturing Co	Somerville	MA	F	617 625-0337	11888
Pocasset Machine Corporation	Pocasset	MA	F	508 563-5572	11491
Precision Engineered Pdts LLC (DH)	Attleboro	MA	G		6051
Replica Works Inc	Orange	MA	E	978 544-7000	11231
Samtan Engineering Corp	Malden	MA	E	781 322-7880	10026
Shawmut Engineering Company	Wrentham	MA	F	508 850-9500	13845
Skg Associates Inc	Dedham	MA	G	781 878-7250	8250
Sp Machine Inc	Hudson	MA	E	978 562-2019	9414
Springfield Spring Corporation (PA)	East Longmeadow	MA	E	413 525-6837	8395
Standex International Corp	North Billerica	MA	D	978 667-2711	10959
Tech Fab Inc	South Hadley	MA	E	413 532-9022	11967
Tech-Etch Inc	Fall River	MA	E	508 675-5757	8614
Tech-Etch Inc (PA)	Plymouth	MA	B	508 747-0300	11481
Techncal Hrdfcing McHining Inc	Attleboro	MA	F	508 223-2900	6069
The Wakefield Corporation	Wakefield	MA	E	781 587-1925	12539
Thomas Smith Company Inc	Worcester	MA	E	508 792-5000	13812
Tiberio Manufacturing Corp	Holliston	MA	D	508 429-4011	9232
Timco Corporation	Stoughton	MA	E	781 821-1041	12243
True Machine Co Inc	Swansea	MA	G	508 379-0329	12314
Uneco Manufacturing Inc	Chicopee	MA	E	413 594-2700	8066
United Tool & Machine Corp (PA)	Lawrence	MA	E	978 658-5500	9607
United Tool & Machine Corp	Lawrence	MA	E	978 686-4181	9608
Universal Tool Co Inc	Springfield	MA	E	413 732-4807	12145
Valentine Tool & Stamping Inc	Norton	MA	F	508 285-6911	11137
Westwood Mills Corp	Hingham	MA	F	781 335-4466	9165
Whitman Tool & Die Company Inc	Whitman	MA	E	781 447-0421	13354
Worcester Manufacturing Inc	Worcester	MA	E	508 756-0301	13830
Worcester Tool & Stamping Co	Rochdale	MA	E	508 892-8194	11630
Numberall Stamp & Tool Co	Sangerville	ME	F	207 876-3541	5420
Alan T Seeler Inc	New Hampton	NH	F	603 744-3736	15195
Ameriforge Group Inc	Newport	NH	E	603 863-1270	15225
Costello/April Design Inc	Dover	NH	E	603 749-6755	14224
J Tool Inc	Belmont	NH	E	603 524-5813	13962
Laird Technologies Inc	Manchester	NH	E	603 627-7877	14875
Mushield Company Inc	Londonderry	NH	E	603 666-6433	14776
New England Industries Inc	Lebanon	NH	E	603 448-5330	14696
New Hampshire Stamping Co Inc	Goffstown	NH	E	603 641-1234	14352
Rk Parisi Enterprises Inc	Keene	NH	F	844 438-7674	14616
Samson Manufacturing Corp	Keene	NH	E	603 355-3903	14617
Stamping Technologies Inc	Laconia	NH	F	603 524-5958	14671
Sunset Tool Inc	Keene	NH	E	603 355-2246	14623
Technical Tool & Design LLC	Northfield	NH	C	603 286-1600	15269
Wilton Pressed Metals	Newport	NH	E	603 863-1488	15241
Amt Acquisition Inc	Warren	RI	E	401 247-1680	16749
Angelo Di Maria Inc	Providence	RI	E	401 274-0100	16472
Aro-Sac Inc	North Providence	RI	E	401 231-6655	16297
Artic Tool & Engrg Co LLC	Greenville	RI	E	401 785-2210	16055
Atamian Manufacturing Corp	Providence	RI	E	401 944-9614	16477
C Sjoberg & Son Inc	Cranston	RI	F	401 461-8220	15838
Crest Manufacturing Company	Lincoln	RI	F	401 333-1350	16129
Crystal Stamping LLC	Pawtucket	RI	F	401 724-5880	16361
Csc Inc	Pawtucket	RI	F	401 724-5880	16362
Demaich Industries Inc	Johnston	RI	F	401 944-3576	16080
Eastern Manufacturing Company	North Providence	RI	F	401 231-8330	16301
Etco Incorporated (PA)	Warwick	RI	D	401 467-2400	16815
Evans Findings Company Inc	East Providence	RI	E	401 434-5600	16018
Everett J Prescott Inc	Lincoln	RI	G	401 333-8588	16135
Ferguson Perforating Company (DH)	Providence	RI	D	401 941-8876	16518
Fulford Manufacturing Company (PA)	Riverside	RI	F	401 431-2000	16655
Interplex Industries Inc (DH)	Rumford	RI	F	401 434-6543	16672
Ira Green Inc (PA)	Providence	RI	C	800 663-7487	16543
Lorac Company Inc	Providence	RI	E	401 781-3330	16554
Morris & Broms LLC	Johnston	RI	F	401 781-3134	16098
Norcross Safety Products LLC	Smithfield	RI	A	800 430-5490	16724
Philip Machine Company Inc	Pawtucket	RI	E	401 353-7383	16402
Providence Mint Inc	Providence	RI	E	401 272-7760	16592
Quality Stamping	Providence	RI	G	401 272-7760	16598
Salvadore Tool & Findings Inc (PA)	Providence	RI	F	401 331-6000	16609
Schroff Inc (HQ)	Warwick	RI	B	763 204-7700	16859
Tercat Tool and Die Co II Inc	Providence	RI	E	401 421-3371	16620
Truex Incorporated	Pawtucket	RI	D	401 722-5023	16426
United States Associates LLC	Providence	RI	E	401 272-7760	16632
Ann Clark Ltd	Rutland	VT	E	802 773-7886	17489
Cold Hollow Precision Inc	Enosburg Falls	VT	G	802 933-5542	17221
Heb Manufacturing Company Inc	Chelsea	VT	E	802 685-4821	17178
New England Precision Inc	Randolph	VT	D	800 293-4112	17471
Shelburne Corporation (PA)	Shelburne	VT	F	802 985-3321	17561

3471 Plating and polishing

Company	CITY	ST	EMP	PHONE	ENTRY#
A-1 Chrome and Polishing Corp	Newington	CT	F	860 666-4593	2265
Accurate Burring Co LLC	Plainville	CT	F	860 747-8640	2745
Allied Metal Finishing LLC	South Windsor	CT	G	860 290-8865	3111
Alpha Plating and Finishing Co	Plainville	CT	E	860 747-5002	2746
Aluminum Finishing Company Inc	Bridgeport	CT	E	203 366-5871	293
American Electro Products Inc	Waterbury	CT	C	203 756-7051	3882
Anodic Incorporated	Stevenson	CT	F	203 268-9966	3506
Aqua Blasting Corp	Bloomfield	CT	F	860 242-8855	146
B & P Plating Equipment LLC	Bristol	CT	F	860 589-5799	401
Baron & Young Co Inc	Bristol	CT	G	860 589-3235	407
Bass Plating Company	Bloomfield	CT	E	860 243-2557	149
Berkley Associates Inc	Waterbury	CT	D	203 757-9221	3890
Broad Peak Manufacturing LLC	Wallingford	CT	E	203 678-4664	3784
C & S Engineering Inc	Meriden	CT	F	203 235-5727	1657
Chromalloy Component Svcs Inc	Shelton	CT	D	203 924-1666	2992
Colonial Coatings Inc	Milford	CT	E	203 783-9933	1811
Component Technologies Inc (PA)	Newington	CT	E	860 667-1065	2281
Conn Anodizing Finshg Co Inc	Bridgeport	CT	E	203 367-1765	312
CRC Chrome Corporation	Meriden	CT	E	203 630-1008	1662
Custom Chrome Plating	Wallingford	CT	G	203 265-5667	3798
Ddm Metal Finishing Company	Tolland	CT	G	860 872-4683	3657
Deburr Co	Plantsville	CT	F	860 621-6634	2790
Deburring House Inc	East Berlin	CT	E	860 828-0889	909

S I C

	CITY	ST	EMP	PHONE	ENTRY#
Deburring Laboratories Inc	New Britain	CT	F	860 829-6300	2022
E & J Parts Cleaning Inc	Waterbury	CT	F	203 757-1716	3909
Etherington Brothers Inc	Bristol	CT	G	860 585-5624	442
Giering Metal Finishing Incorporated	Hamden	CT	E	203 248-5583	1426
Gybenorth Industries LLC	Milford	CT	F	203 876-9876	1832
Halco Inc	Waterbury	CT	D	203 575-9450	3917
Har-Conn Chrome Company **(PA)**	West Hartford	CT	D	860 236-6801	4063
Hi-Tech Polishing Inc	Newington	CT	F	860 665-1399	2300
Hubbard-Hall Inc **(PA)**	Waterbury	CT	D	203 756-5521	3919
Jarvis Precision Polishing	Bristol	CT	F	860 589-5822	458
Light Metals Coloring Co Inc	Southington	CT	D	860 621-0145	3219
Linde Inc **(HQ)**	Danbury	CT	B	203 837-2000	776
Logan Steel Inc **(PA)**	Meriden	CT	E	203 235-0811	1672
Marsam Metal Finishing Co	New Britain	CT	E	860 826-5489	2039
Mirabello Holdings LLC	Bristol	CT	E	860 582-9517	470
Mirror Polishing & Pltg Co Inc	Waterbury	CT	E	203 574-5400	3945
National Chromium Company Inc	Putnam	CT	E	860 928-7965	2865
P&G Metal Components Corp	Bloomfield	CT	F	860 243-2220	199
Plainville Plating Company Inc	Plainville	CT	D	860 747-1624	2776
Plasma Technology Incorporated	South Windsor	CT	E	860 282-0659	3173
Porcelen Limited Connecticut LLC **(PA)**	Hamden	CT	D	203 248-6346	1449
Precision Finishing Svcs Inc	Windsor	CT	E	860 882-1073	4295
Preventative Maintenance Corp	Poquonock	CT	F	860 683-1180	2815
Quality Rolling Deburring Inc	Thomaston	CT	E	860 283-0271	3626
Rayco Inc	New Britain	CT	F	860 357-4693	2056
Rayco Metal Finishing Inc	Middletown	CT	F	860 347-7434	1776
Reliable Pltg & Polsg Co Inc	Bridgeport	CT	E	203 366-5261	365
Scott Metal Finishing LLC	Bristol	CT	F	860 589-3778	496
Seaboard Metal Finishing Co	New Britain	CT	F	203 933-1603	2060
Seidel LLC	Waterbury	CT	D	203 757-7349	3969
Sousa Corp	Newington	CT	E	860 523-9090	2326
Spec Plating Inc	Bridgeport	CT	F	203 366-3638	374
Summit Corporation of America	Thomaston	CT	D	860 283-4391	3635
Superior Plating Company	Southport	CT	D	203 255-1501	3248
Superior Technology Corp **(PA)**	Southport	CT	C	203 255-1501	3249
Technical Metal Finishing Inc	Wallingford	CT	E	203 284-7825	3857
The Romatic Manufacturing Company	Southbury	CT	C	203 264-8203	3199
Unimetal Surface Finishing LLC	Naugatuck	CT	E	203 729-8244	1991
Uprising LLC	Torrington	CT	F	860 960-3781	3705
Whyco Finishing Tech LLC	Thomaston	CT	E	860 283-5826	3645
Absolute Metal Finishing Inc	Norwood	MA	E	781 551-8235	11153
Accumet Engineering Corp	Devens	MA	E	978 568-8311	8266
Accurate Metal Finishing LLC	Randolph	MA	E	781 963-7300	11546
Ace Metal Finishing Inc	Lawrence	MA	E	978 683-2082	9534
Acton Metal Processing Corp	Waltham	MA	F	781 893-5890	12582
Alternate Finishing Inc	Hudson	MA	G	978 567-9205	9353
Anomet Products Inc	Shrewsbury	MA	E	508 842-0174	11827
Aotco Holdings LLC **(PA)**	Billerica	MA	F	978 667-8298	6401
Aotco Metal Finishing LLC	Billerica	MA	D	978 667-8298	6402
Arborway Metal Finishing Inc	Rockland	MA	E	781 982-0137	11635
Automated Finishing Co Inc	Attleboro	MA	E	508 222-6262	5996
B & J Manufacturing Corp	Taunton	MA	D	508 822-1990	12322
Bay State Plating Inc	Holyoke	MA	G	413 533-6927	9243
Berkshire Mnufactured Pdts Inc	Newburyport	MA	C	978 462-8161	10670
Bradford Finshg Powdr Coat Inc	Haverhill	MA	G	978 469-9965	9081
Central Metal Finishing Inc	North Andover	MA	D	978 291-0500	10823
CIL Electroplating Inc **(PA)**	Lawrence	MA	D	978 683-2082	9548
CIL Electroplating Inc	Lawrence	MA	D	978 683-2082	9549
CIL Inc	Lawrence	MA	D	978 685-8300	9550
Coating Systems Inc	Lowell	MA	D	978 937-3712	9868
Cryogenic Institute Neng Inc	Worcester	MA	F	508 459-7447	13712
D & S Plating Co Inc	Holyoke	MA	F	413 533-7771	9250
Dav-Tech Plating Inc	Marlborough	MA	E	508 485-8472	10143
Electropolishing Systems Inc	Plymouth	MA	E	508 830-1717	11458
F M Callahan and Son Inc	Malden	MA	D	781 324-5101	10014
Five Star Plating LLC	Lawrence	MA	E	978 655-4081	9561
Fountain Plating Company LLC	West Springfield	MA	D	413 781-4651	13025
General Metal Finishing LLC	Attleboro	MA	D	508 222-9683	6020
Glasseal Products Inc	New Bedford	MA	E	732 370-9100	10595
H Larosee and Sons Inc	Blackstone	MA	F	978 562-9417	6494
H O Wire Co Inc	West Boylston	MA	F	508 243-7177	12963
Hubbard-Hall Inc	Wilmington	MA	F	978 988-0077	13411
Indepenent Plating Co	Worcester	MA	F	508 756-0301	13740
Katahdin Industries Inc **(PA)**	Hudson	MA	E	781 329-1420	9380
Light Metal Platers LLC	Waltham	MA	E	781 899-8855	12709
Lone Star Holdings Inc **(HQ)**	Chelsea	MA	E	781 935-2224	7986
Luster-On Products Inc	Springfield	MA	F	413 739-2541	12111
Mueller Corporation	East Bridgewater	MA	C	508 456-4500	8344
New England Elctrpolishing Inc	Fall River	MA	E	508 672-6616	8587
New Method Plating Co Inc	Worcester	MA	E	508 754-2671	13766
Nu Chrome Corp	Seekonk	MA	F	508 557-1418	11782
Ouellette Industries Inc	Attleboro Falls	MA	G	508 695-0964	6093
Paul McNamara	Bridgewater	MA	F	508 245-5654	7236
Pep Industries LLC	Attleboro	MA	F	508 226-5600	6046
Plating For Electronics LLC	Waltham	MA	D	781 893-2368	12750
Plating Technology Inc	New Bedford	MA	E	508 996-4006	10640
Poly-Metal Finishing Inc	Springfield	MA	D	413 781-4535	12122
Poly-Plating Inc	Chicopee	MA	E	413 593-5477	8055
Precision Engineered Pdts LLC **(DH)**	Attleboro	MA	G		6051
Purecoat North LLC	Belmont	MA	D	617 489-2750	6310
Qc Industries Inc **(PA)**	Mansfield	MA	D	781 344-1000	10073
R L Barry Inc	Attleboro	MA	F	508 226-3350	6052
Reliable Electro Plating Inc	Chartley	MA	G	508 222-0620	7896
River St Metal Finishing Inc	Braintree	MA	F	781 843-9351	7200
Sdpd Holdings Inc	Waltham	MA	E	781 893-2368	12777
Specialized Plating Inc	Haverhill	MA	E	978 373-8030	9131
Spencer Metal Finishing Inc **(HQ)**	Brookfield	MA	E	508 885-6477	7316
Sweet Metal Finishing Inc	Attleboro	MA	F	508 226-4359	6068
T & T Anodizing Inc	Lowell	MA	F	978 454-9631	9926
T & T Anodizing Incorporated	Lowell	MA	F	978 454-9631	9927
T D F Metal Finishing Co Inc	Danvers	MA	E	978 223-4292	8223
Tdf Metal Finishing Co Inc	Danvers	MA	F	978 223-4292	8224
Transene Company Inc **(PA)**	Danvers	MA	G	978 777-7860	8227
Valentine Plating Company Inc	West Springfield	MA	E	413 732-0009	13050
Valley Plating Inc	Springfield	MA	D	413 788-7375	12147
Westfield Electroplating Co **(PA)**	Westfield	MA	C	413 568-3716	13219
Whitman Company Inc	Whitman	MA	E	781 447-2422	13353
Worcester Manufacturing Inc	Worcester	MA	E	508 756-0301	13830
Jarden LLC	East Wilton	ME	F	207 645-2574	4741
Mbw Tractor Sales LLC	Berwick	ME	F	207 384-2001	4551
Silvex Incorporated	Westbrook	ME	D	207 761-0392	5650
Southern Maine Industries Corp	Windham	ME	F	207 856-7391	5669
Turbine Specialists LLC	Brewer	ME	F	207 947-9327	4622
Aerodynamics LLC	Seabrook	NH	E	603 474-2547	15583
Dyna Roll Inc	Seabrook	NH	F	603 474-2547	15590
Finishield Corp	Londonderry	NH	F	603 641-2164	14751
Jmd Industries Inc	Hudson	NH	E	603 882-3198	14513
Medina Plating Corp	Londonderry	NH	E	330 725-4155	14766
Peg Kearsarge Co Inc	Bartlett	NH	G	603 374-2341	13918
Pure Source LLC	Durham	NH	F	626 442-6784	14267
Snf Finishing LLC	Keene	NH	G	603 355-3903	14622
A & F Plating Co Inc	Providence	RI	F	401 861-3597	16462
A & H Duffy Polsg & Finshg Co	Providence	RI	E	401 785-9203	16463
Accent Plating Company Inc	Pawtucket	RI	F	401 722-6306	16343
American Ring Co Inc	Cranston	RI	F	401 467-4480	15832
American Ring Co Inc **(PA)**	East Providence	RI	F	401 438-9060	16003
Anton Enterprises Inc	Cranston	RI	F	401 781-3120	15834
Chemart Company **(PA)**	Lincoln	RI	D	401 333-9200	16126
Dura-Kote Technology Ltd	Johnston	RI	F	401 331-6460	16082
Electrolizing Inc	Providence	RI	E	401 861-5900	16513
G Tanury Plating Co Inc	North Providence	RI	D	401 232-2330	16302
Ideal Plating & Polsg Co Inc	Providence	RI	F	401 455-1700	16537
Induplate Inc **(PA)**	North Providence	RI	D	401 231-5770	16303
International Chromium Pltg Co	Providence	RI	G	401 421-0205	16540
Interplex Engineered Pdts Inc	Rumford	RI	D	401 434-6543	16670
Interplex Engineered Pdts Inc	Rumford	RI	C	508 399-6810	16671
Interplex Industries Inc **(DH)**	Rumford	RI	F	401 434-6543	16672
Jrb Associates Inc	Cranston	RI	E	401 351-8693	15881
Monarch Metal Finishing Co Inc	Providence	RI	E	401 785-3200	16568
New Annex Plating Inc	North Providence	RI	E	401 349-0911	16305
Nu-Lustre Finishing Corp	Providence	RI	E	401 521-7800	16576
Precision Plsg Ornamentals Inc	Pawtucket	RI	F	401 728-9994	16404
Providence Metallizing Co Inc **(PA)**	Pawtucket	RI	D	401 722-5300	16406
Reed Allison Group Inc	Providence	RI	D	617 846-1237	16599
Tanury Industries Inc	Lincoln	RI	C	800 428-6213	16156
Unique Plating Co	Johnston	RI	G	401 943-7366	16109
Universal Plating Co Inc	Providence	RI	G	401 861-3530	16634
Westwell Industries Inc	Providence	RI	F	401 467-2992	16646
Finish Solutions LLC	Saint Albans	VT	G	802 540-0326	17522

3479 Metal coating and allied services

	CITY	ST	EMP	PHONE	ENTRY#
Advanced Graphics Incorporated	Stratford	CT	E	203 378-0471	3515
American Roller Company LLC	Middlebury	CT	E	203 598-3100	1713
Ann S Davis	Lebanon	CT	F	860 642-7228	1548
Baron & Young Co Inc	Bristol	CT	G	860 589-3235	407
Biomerics LLC	Monroe	CT	D	203 268-7238	1906
Cametoid Technologies Inc	South Windsor	CT	E	860 646-4667	3125
Central Conn Coatings Inc	East Hartford	CT	G	860 528-8281	980
Colonial Coatings Inc	Milford	CT	E	203 783-9933	1811
Conard Corporation	Glastonbury	CT	E	860 659-0591	1275
Connecticut Plasma Tech LLC	South Windsor	CT	F	860 289-5500	3132
Donwell Company	Manchester	CT	E	860 649-5374	1593
Electrostatic Coating Technologies Corp	South Windsor	CT	F	860 610-9097	3142
Farrell Prcsion Mtalcraft Corp	New Milford	CT	E	860 355-2651	2243
Giering Metal Finishing Incorporated	Hamden	CT	E	203 248-5583	1426
Gybenorth Industries LLC	Milford	CT	F	203 876-9876	1832

	CITY	ST	EMP	PHONE	ENTRY#
Halco Inc	Waterbury	CT	D	203 575-9450	3917
Highway Safety LLC **(HQ)**	Glastonbury	CT	D	860 633-9445	1286
Identification Products Corp	Bridgeport	CT	F	203 334-5969	331
Identification Products Corp **(PA)**	Shelton	CT	E	203 334-5969	3019
Imperial Metal Finishing Inc	Stratford	CT	G	203 377-1229	3549
ITW Hlographic Specialty Films	Bloomfield	CT	G	860 243-0343	174
Jet Process Corporation	Wallingford	CT	G	203 985-6000	3823
K & G Corp	Manchester	CT	F	860 643-1133	1609
Linde Advanced Mtl Tech Inc	Danbury	CT	C	203 837-2000	773
Linde Advanced Mtl Tech Inc	Manchester	CT	C	860 646-0700	1612
Linde Inc **(HQ)**	Danbury	CT	B	203 837-2000	776
Line-X of Hartford	Hartford	CT	G	860 216-6180	1490
Marjan Inc	Waterbury	CT	E	203 573-1742	3942
Materion Lrge Area Catings LLC **(DH)**	Windsor	CT	D	216 486-4200	4289
Metallizing Svc Holdings LLC **(PA)**	West Hartford	CT	D	860 953-1144	4072
Metamorphic Materials Inc	Winsted	CT	G	860 738-8638	4349
Mitchell-Bate Company	Waterbury	CT	E	203 233-0862	3946
Niem Holdings Inc	Watertown	CT	E	203 267-1510	4020
Northeast Laser Engraving Inc	Monroe	CT	E	203 268-7238	1918
Paint & Powder Works LLC	New Britain	CT	F	860 225-2019	2049
Pauway Corp	Wallingford	CT	F	203 265-3939	3837
Plas-TEC Coatings Inc	South Windsor	CT	F	860 289-6029	3172
Plasma Coatings Inc	Middlebury	CT	F	203 598-3100	1719
Plasma Coatings Inc	Waterbury	CT	G	203 598-3100	3961
Plastonics Inc	Hartford	CT	E	860 249-5455	1499
Prestige Industrial Finshg Co	Shelton	CT	E	203 924-7720	3056
Pti Industries Inc **(HQ)**	Enfield	CT	E	800 318-8438	1143
Rtg Coatings	Manchester	CT	G	860 643-1133	1633
Summit Corporation of America	Thomaston	CT	D	860 283-4391	3635
Suraci Corp	New Haven	CT	E	203 624-1345	2204
Vitek Research Corporation	Naugatuck	CT	F	203 735-1813	1992
Willington Nameplate Inc	Stafford Springs	CT	D	860 684-4281	3264
Actnano Inc **(PA)**	Cambridge	MA	F	857 333-8631	7467
American Durafilm Co Inc	Holliston	MA	E	508 429-8000	9198
Amex Inc	Boston	MA	E	617 569-5630	6545
Anjen Finishing	Marlborough	MA	F	508 251-1532	10109
Applied Graphics Inc	Amesbury	MA	E	978 241-5300	5828
Applied Plastics Co Inc	Norwood	MA	E	781 762-1881	11161
Applied Plastics LLC	Norwood	MA	E	781 762-1881	11162
Ariston Engraving & Mch Co Inc	Woburn	MA	G	781 935-2328	13515
Automated Finishing Co Inc	Attleboro	MA	G	508 222-6262	5996
Bagge Inc	Holliston	MA	G	508 429-8080	9202
Bay State Surface Technologies	Auburn	MA	F	508 832-5035	6107
Bells Powder Coating Inc	Attleboro Falls	MA	F	508 643-2222	6079
Bemis Associates Inc **(PA)**	Shirley	MA	E	978 425-6761	11815
Berkshire Custom Coating Inc	Pittsfield	MA	F	413 442-3757	11393
Boyd Coatings Research Co Inc	Hudson	MA	D	978 562-7561	9358
Central Coating Tech Inc	West Boylston	MA	D	508 835-6225	12956
Chase Corp Inc	Westwood	MA	F	781 332-0700	13308
Chase Corporation	Oxford	MA	F	508 731-2710	11250
Chase Corporation **(HQ)**	Westwood	MA	F	781 332-0700	13309
Chemi-Graphic Inc	Ludlow	MA	E	413 589-0151	9942
CIL Inc	Lawrence	MA	D	978 685-8300	9550
Coating Application Tech	Woburn	MA	F	781 491-0699	13543
Collt Mfg Inc	Millis	MA	E	508 376-2525	10449
Covestro LLC	Wilmington	MA	C	800 458-0014	13399
Custom Coatings	Hyannis	MA	G	508 771-8830	9433
Diamond Custom Coatings Inc	Westfield	MA	G	413 562-2734	13161
DSM Neoresins Inc	Wilmington	MA	C	800 458-0014	13403
Duncan Galvanizing Corporation	Everett	MA	D	617 389-8440	8487
E V Yeuell Inc	Woburn	MA	E	781 933-2984	13560
East Coast Plastics Inc	Framingham	MA	G	508 429-8080	8760
Eastern Etching and Mfg Co	Chicopee	MA	E	413 594-6601	8030
Elenel Industries Inc **(PA)**	Milford	MA	E	508 478-2025	10401
Feeleys Company Inc	Quincy	MA	G	617 773-1711	11518
Fort Hill Sign Products Inc	Hopedale	MA	G	781 321-4320	9297
Foundry Specialty Coatings LLC	Tewksbury	MA	F	978 518-9990	12400
G T R Finishing Corporation	Brockton	MA	E	508 588-3240	7279
Gvd Corporation **(PA)**	Cambridge	MA	F	617 661-0060	7596
Hayden Corporation	West Springfield	MA	E	413 734-4981	13029
Indepenent Plating Co	Worcester	MA	D	508 756-0301	13740
Industrial Etching Inc	East Longmeadow	MA	F	413 525-4110	8380
Innovative Coatings Inc	Medway	MA	F	508 533-6101	10306
Jet-Tech Incorporated	Lynn	MA	F	781 599-8685	9979
Jr Chemical Coatings LLC	Harwich	MA	E	508 896-3383	9068
Light Metal Platers LLC	Waltham	MA	E	781 899-8855	12709
Manning Way Cpitl Partners LLC	Bellingham	MA	E	508 966-4800	6293
Medical Cmpnent Spcialists Inc **(PA)**	Bellingham	MA	E	508 966-0992	6295
N2 Biomedical LLC	Bedford	MA	E	781 275-6001	6244
NBD Nanotechnologies Inc	Lexington	MA	F	781 541-4192	9764
New England Etching Co Inc	Holyoke	MA	E	413 532-9482	9269
North East Indus Coatings Inc	Ipswich	MA	G	978 356-1200	9492
Pace Industries LLC	North Billerica	MA	C	978 667-8400	10941
Paratronix Inc	Westborough	MA	F	508 222-8979	13129
Patriot Coating Inc	Hudson	MA	G	978 567-9006	9398
Pg Technologies Inc	Westfield	MA	G	413 562-1354	13198
Poly-Metal Finishing Inc	Springfield	MA	D	413 781-4535	12122
Powder Pro Powder Coating Inc	New Bedford	MA	G	508 991-5999	10642
Precision Coating Co Inc	Hudson	MA	E	978 562-7561	9403
Precision Coating Co Inc **(HQ)**	Hudson	MA	E	781 329-1420	9404
Rapid Coatings Inc	Haverhill	MA	G	339 227-6490	9125
Reeves Company Inc	Attleboro	MA	F	508 222-2877	6053
Richard Gaudreau Engraving	Eastham	MA	G	508 240-2940	8435
RPM Wood Finishes Group Inc	Westfield	MA	D	413 562-9655	13204
Specialty Restoration Inc	Clinton	MA	G	978 365-1700	8091
Spencer Industrial Painting	Spencer	MA	F	508 885-5406	12066
Spencer Metal Finishing Inc **(HQ)**	Brookfield	MA	E	508 885-6477	7316
Spray Maine Inc	Newburyport	MA	F	207 384-2273	10717
Stainless Steel Coatings Inc	Lancaster	MA	F	978 365-9828	9529
Stickamayka Packaging Inc	Andover	MA	F	978 474-1930	5926
Tech-Etch Inc **(PA)**	Plymouth	MA	B	508 747-0300	11481
Titus Engrv & Stonesetting Inc	Plainville	MA	F	508 695-6842	11443
Ultrasonic Systems Inc	Haverhill	MA	E	978 521-0095	9137
V&S Taunton Galvanizing LLC	Taunton	MA	E	508 828-9499	12375
Vw Quality Coating	Norton	MA	G	617 963-6503	11138
Westfield Electroplating Co **(PA)**	Westfield	MA	C	413 568-3716	13219
Westside Finishing Co Inc	Holyoke	MA	E	413 533-4909	9291
Worcester Manufacturing Inc	Worcester	MA	E	508 756-0301	13830
Xtalic Corporation	Marlborough	MA	E	508 485-9730	10238
Cianbro Fbrcation Coating Corp	Pittsfield	ME	C	207 487-3311	5158
Futureguard Building Pdts Inc **(PA)**	Auburn	ME	F	800 858-5818	4434
Jarden LLC	East Wilton	ME	F	207 645-2574	4741
Linde Advanced Mtl Tech Inc	Biddeford	ME	D	207 282-3787	4575
New England Powder Coating	Lebanon	ME	F	207 432-6679	4945
Northeast Coating Tech Inc	Kennebunk	ME	E	207 985-3232	4927
Performance Products Painting	Auburn	ME	E	207 783-4222	4453
Superior Wldg Fabrication Inc	Ellsworth	ME	F	207 664-2121	4760
Advanced Polymerics Inc	Salem	NH	F	603 328-8177	15502
Allweather Coatings LLC	Claremont	NH	G	603 504-4474	14074
Brapsards Powder Coating LLC	Franklin	NH	G	603 630-4014	14319
Ionbond LLC	Portsmouth	NH	F	603 610-4460	15411
Omni Metals Company Inc	Somersworth	NH	E	603 692-6664	15619
Parker-Hannifin Corporation	Hudson	NH	C	603 880-4807	14534
Pf Pro Fnshg Silkscreening Inc	Hampstead	NH	G	603 329-8344	14389
Rapid Finishing LLC	Nashua	NH	E	603 889-4234	15154
Rapid Finishing North	Londonderry	NH	G	603 641-2164	14781
Specialty Coating Systems	Amherst	NH	F	603 883-3339	13891
American Trophy and Supply Inc	East Providence	RI	G	401 438-3060	16004
Best Engineered Surfc Tech LLC	Rumford	RI	F	401 724-2230	16662
Chemart Company	Lincoln	RI	E	401 333-9200	16125
Chemart Company **(PA)**	Lincoln	RI	D	401 333-9200	16126
Development Associates Inc	North Kingstown	RI	F	401 884-1350	16244
Difruscia Industries Inc	Cranston	RI	F	401 943-9900	15850
Duralectra-Chn LLC	Woonsocket	RI	D	401 597-5000	16957
GA Rel Manufacturing Company	Providence	RI	F	401 331-5455	16524
Industrial & Commercial Finshg	Johnston	RI	G	401 942-4680	16089
International Etching Inc	Providence	RI	F	401 781-6800	16541
J Arakelian Inc	Johnston	RI	F	401 943-7366	16090
Me-92 Operations Inc	Providence	RI	E	401 831-9200	16562
Providence Metallizing Co Inc **(PA)**	Pawtucket	RI	D	401 722-5300	16406
Quality Spraying Tech Inc	Providence	RI	D	401 861-2413	16597
Technodic Inc	Providence	RI	E	401 467-6660	16618
Wehr Industries Inc	Warwick	RI	E	401 732-6565	16878
G S P Coatings Inc	Brattleboro	VT	E	802 257-5858	17083
Gds Manufacturing Company	Williston	VT	G	802 862-7610	17732
Ideal Powder Coating Inc	Brandon	VT	G	802 345-7532	17067
Vermont Ware Inc	St George	VT	G	802 482-4426	17624

3482 Small arms ammunition

	CITY	ST	EMP	PHONE	ENTRY#
General Dynamics Ordnance	Avon	CT	F	860 404-0162	25
Illinois Tool Works Inc	Waterbury	CT	C	203 574-2119	3920
Smith & Wesson Brands Inc **(PA)**	Springfield	MA	A	800 331-0852	12129
Starmet Corporation **(PA)**	Concord	MA	E	978 369-5410	8134
Bzgunz LLC	Gilmanton	NH	G	603 491-8019	14339
Green Mountain Risk MGT LLC	Dover	NH	F	802 683-8586	14229
Green Mtn Rifle Barrel Co Inc	Conway	NH	F	603 447-1095	14180

3483 Ammunition, except for small arms, nec

	CITY	ST	EMP	PHONE	ENTRY#
Geneve Corporation **(HQ)**	Stamford	CT	E	203 358-8000	3355
Starmet Corporation **(PA)**	Concord	MA	E	978 369-5410	8134
Textron Systems Corporation	Wilmington	MA	E	978 657-5111	13465
Textron Systems Corporation **(DH)**	Wilmington	MA	E	978 657-5111	13466
Tech Resources Inc	Milford	NH	E	603 673-9000	15039

3484 Small arms

	CITY	ST	EMP	PHONE	ENTRY#
Black Phoenix Customs LLC	Bristol	CT	G	860 681-3162	416

	CITY	ST	EMP	PHONE	ENTRY#
Colt Defense LLC (HQ)	West Hartford	CT	B	860 232-4489	4053
Connecticut Shotgun Manufacturing Co	New Britain	CT	D	860 225-6581	2012
Continental Machine TI Co Inc	New Britain	CT	D	860 223-2896	2014
Deburring House Inc	East Berlin	CT	E	860 828-0889	909
Mike Sadlak	Coventry	CT	G	860 742-0227	680
New Colt Holding Corp	West Hartford	CT	C	860 236-6311	4074
New Designz Realty LLC	Cheshire	CT	G	860 384-1809	608
O F Mossberg & Sons Inc (HQ)	North Haven	CT	C	203 230-5300	2429
Standard Mfg Co LLC	New Britain	CT	F	860 225-3401	2062
Sturm Ruger & Company Inc	Southport	CT	B	203 256-3895	3246
Sturm Ruger & Company Inc (PA)	Southport	CT	B	203 259-7843	3247
Caliber Company (PA)	Westfield	MA	F	413 642-4260	13156
International Security Assista	Woburn	MA	F	617 590-7942	13588
Mascon Inc	Woburn	MA	E	781 938-5800	13605
Remsport Mfg LLC	Ludlow	MA	F	413 589-1911	9952
Saeilo USA Inc	Worcester	MA	E	508 795-3919	13787
Savage Arms Inc (DH)	Westfield	MA	C	413 642-4135	13206
Savage Sports Corporation (HQ)	Westfield	MA	F	413 568-7001	13208
Thompson/Center Arms Co Inc (HQ)	Springfield	MA	D	800 331-0852	12138
Windham Weaponry Inc	Windham	ME	G	207 893-2223	5676
Alex & Ryan Design LLC	Manchester	NH	F	603 518-8650	14808
Green Mtn Rifle Barrel Co Inc	Conway	NH	F	603 447-1095	14180
Q LLC	Dover	NH	G	603 294-0047	14246
Sig Sauer Inc	Exeter	NH	C	603 610-3000	14301
Sig Sauer Inc	Exeter	NH	B	603 772-2302	14302
Sig Sauer Inc (DH)	Newington	NH	C	603 610-3000	15210
Sturm Ruger & Company Inc	Newport	NH	B	603 865-2424	15239
Sturm Ruger & Company Inc	Newport	NH	C	603 863-3300	15240
Tandem Kross LLC	Weare	NH	G	603 369-7060	15673
Century International Arms Inc	Fairfax	VT	D	802 527-1252	17257
Foster Industries Inc	Wolcott	VT	F	802 472-6147	17774
General Dynamics Corp	Burlington	VT	F	703 876-3631	17137
Z M Weapons High Performance	Richmond	VT	G	802 777-8964	17482

3489 Ordnance and accessories, nec

	CITY	ST	EMP	PHONE	ENTRY#
Kaman Aerospace Corporation	Middletown	CT	C	860 632-1000	1755
Entwistle Company LLC (PA)	Hudson	MA	D	508 481-4000	9364
Pathiakis Nickolas	Rangeley	ME	G	207 864-3474	5313
Joseph A Cura	Nashua	NH	G	508 254-4624	15119
Sig Sauer US Holding LP	Newington	NH	F	603 610-3000	15211
McLaughlin Research Corp	Middletown	RI	C	401 849-4010	16179

3491 Industrial valves

	CITY	ST	EMP	PHONE	ENTRY#
Belimo Technology (usa) Inc	Danbury	CT	D	203 791-9915	717
BNL Industries Inc	Vernon	CT	E	860 870-6222	3751
Contemporary Products LLC	Middletown	CT	F	860 346-9283	1744
Conval Inc	Enfield	CT	D	860 749-0761	1126
Curtiss-Wright Corporation	East Windsor	CT	G	864 486-9311	1070
Fisher Controls Intl LLC	North Stonington	CT	F	860 599-1140	2449
Kip Inc	Farmington	CT	C	860 677-0272	1227
Motion Industries Inc	Bloomfield	CT	A	860 687-5000	195
Parker-Hannifin Corporation	New Britain	CT	C	860 827-2300	2050
Peter Paul Electronics Co Inc	New Britain	CT	C	860 229-4884	2051
Arichell Technologies Inc	Newton	MA	D	617 796-9001	10734
Asahi/America Inc (HQ)	Lawrence	MA	E	781 321-5409	9540
Circor Energy LLC	Burlington	MA	F	781 270-1200	7349
Circor German Holdings LLC (DH)	Burlington	MA	D	781 270-1200	7350
Circor International Inc (HQ)	Burlington	MA	E	781 270-1200	7351
Cobra Precision Machining Corp	Petersham	MA	G	603 434-8424	11388
Conant Controls Inc	Woburn	MA	E	781 395-2240	13544
Condon Mfg Co Inc	Springfield	MA	E	413 543-1250	12085
Crosby Valve & Gage Intl Inc	Mansfield	MA	E	508 384-3121	10048
Diebolt & Company	East Longmeadow	MA	G	860 434-2222	8374
Emerson Atmtn Sltons Fnal Ctrl	Mansfield	MA	D	508 594-4411	10051
Gordon Martin	Newbury	MA		351 201-6065	10665
Millennium Power Services Inc (PA)	Westfield	MA	E	413 562-5332	13189
Mks Instruments Inc	Andover	MA	E	978 645-5500	5898
Mks Instruments Inc (PA)	Andover	MA	B	978 645-5500	5899
Mks Msc Inc	Wilmington	MA	D	978 284-4000	13434
Rodney Hunt-Fontaine Inc (HQ)	Orange	MA	E	978 544-2511	11232
Valves and Controls Us Inc	Ipswich	MA	D	978 744-5690	9499
Vent-Rite Valve Corp (PA)	Randolph	MA	F	781 986-2000	11578
Watts Regulator Co	North Andover	MA	A	978 688-1811	10858
Watts Regulator Co (HQ)	North Andover	MA	C	978 689-6000	10859
Watts Water Technologies Inc (PA)	North Andover	MA	C	978 688-1811	10861
Allagash International Inc	Portland	ME	G	207 781-8831	5176
Broen-Lab Inc	Bedford	NH	F	603 310-5089	13920
Controlair LLC	Amherst	NH	E	603 886-9400	13865
Quality Controls Inc	Northfield	NH	E	603 286-3321	15268
Ruggles-Klingemann Mfg Co	Seabrook	NH	G	603 474-8500	15603
Watts Regulator Co	Franklin	NH	A	603 934-5110	14323
Watts Water Technologies Inc	Franklin	NH	E	603 934-1369	14324
Velan Valve Corp (DH)	Williston	VT	D	802 863-2561	17751

3492 Fluid power valves and hose fittings

	CITY	ST	EMP	PHONE	ENTRY#
Atp Industries LLC (PA)	Plainville	CT	F	860 479-5007	2748
Crane Aerospace Inc (DH)	Stamford	CT	C	203 363-7300	3325
Crane Controls Inc (DH)	Stamford	CT	C	203 363-7300	3327
Crane Intl Holdings Inc (HQ)	Stamford	CT	C	203 363-7300	3328
Crane Merger Co LLC	Stamford	CT	F	203 363-7300	3329
Crane Overseas LLC (HQ)	Stamford	CT	E	203 363-7300	3330
Enfield Technologies LLC	Trumbull	CT	F	203 375-3100	3719
Faxon Engineering Company Inc (PA)	Bloomfield	CT	F	860 286-4266	163
Fluid Dynamics LLC	Manchester	CT	F	860 791-6325	1598
Norgren LLC	Farmington	CT	C	860 677-0272	1232
Parker-Hannifin Corporation	New Britain	CT	C	860 827-2300	2050
Redco Corporation (HQ)	Stamford	CT	D	203 363-7300	3445
Circor Inc	Burlington	MA	E	781 270-1200	7348
Conant Controls Inc	Woburn	MA	E	781 395-2240	13544
Controls For Automation Inc	Taunton	MA	E	508 802-6005	12328
Crane Nxt Co (PA)	Waltham	MA	C	610 430-2510	12644
Guardair Corporation	Chicopee	MA	E	413 594-4400	8035
Hope Inc	Needham	MA	E	781 455-1145	10512
McGill Hose & Coupling Inc (PA)	East Longmeadow	MA	E	413 525-3977	8387
Microgroup Inc	Medway	MA	C	508 533-4925	10308
Navtec Rigging Solutions Inc	Groton	MA	E		9011
Portland Valve LLC (DH)	Warren	MA	E	704 289-6511	12852
Tapcoenpro Tracker LLC	Burlington	MA	E	781 270-1200	7437
Windward Power Systems Inc	Fairhaven	MA	G	774 992-0059	8515
PRC Acquisition Company Inc	Gorham	ME	F	207 854-3702	4832
Parker-Hannifin Corporation	Hollis	NH	C	603 595-1500	14456
Quality Controls Inc	Northfield	NH	E	603 286-3321	15288
Eaton Corporation	Rumford	RI	E	401 473-2214	16666
John Crane Sealol Inc (DH)	Warwick	RI	C	401 732-0715	16828

3493 Steel springs, except wire

	CITY	ST	EMP	PHONE	ENTRY#
Acme Monaco Corporation (PA)	New Britain	CT	C	860 224-1349	1995
Arrow Manufacturing Company	Bristol	CT	E		397
Atlantic Precision Spring Inc	Bristol	CT	E	860 583-1864	399
Century Spring Mfg Co Inc	Bristol	CT	E	860 582-3344	425
Connectcut Spring Stmping Corp	Farmington	CT	B	860 677-1341	1212
Excel Spring & Stamping LLC	Bristol	CT	G	860 585-1495	444
Fourslide Spring Stamping Inc	Bristol	CT	E	860 583-1688	449
HMC Enterprises Inc	New Hartford	CT	E	860 379-8506	2101
Lee Spring Company LLC	Bristol	CT	F	860 584-0991	461
Matthew Warren Inc	Southington	CT	D	860 621-7358	3221
Newcomb Spring Corp	Southington	CT	D	860 621-0111	3224
Old Dmfg Inc	Farmington	CT	E	860 677-8561	1234
Oscar Jobs	Bristol	CT	G	860 583-7834	477
Pa-Ted Spring Company LLC	Bristol	CT	E	860 582-6368	479
Rowley Spring & Stamping Corp	Bristol	CT	C	860 582-8175	494
Spring Computerized Inds LLC	Harwinton	CT	G	860 605-9206	1523
Spring Tollman Company Incorporated (PA) 860 583-1326	Bristol	CT	D		497
Leggett & Platt Incorporated	Oxford	MA	D	508 987-8706	11258
Solid Earth Technologies Inc	Amherst	NH	G	603 882-5319	13890
D & W Tool & Findings Inc	Pawtucket	RI	F	401 727-3030	16363

3494 Valves and pipe fittings, nec

	CITY	ST	EMP	PHONE	ENTRY#
Carten Controls Inc	Cheshire	CT	E	203 699-2100	577
Enfield Technologies LLC	Trumbull	CT	F	203 375-3100	3719
Fisher Controls Intl LLC	North Stonington	CT	F	860 599-1140	2449
Houston-Weber Systems Inc	Branford	CT	G	203 481-0115	264
Hydrolevel Company	North Haven	CT	F	203 776-0473	2414
Idex Health & Science LLC	Bristol	CT	C	860 314-2880	456
Ppi Gas Distribution Inc	Naugatuck	CT	G		1981
Redco Corporation (HQ)	Stamford	CT	D	203 363-7300	3445
Automatic Machine Pdts Sls Co	Taunton	MA	E	508 822-4226	12320
Axenics Inc	Tyngsboro	MA	F	978 774-9393	12456
C M S Landscaping Corporation	Holyoke	MA	F	413 533-3300	9245
Carpenter & Paterson Inc	Woburn	MA	E	781 935-7036	13540
Colfax Fluid Handling	Warren	MA	G	413 436-7711	12850
Conant Controls Inc	Woburn	MA	E	781 395-2240	13544
Crane Nxt Co (PA)	Waltham	MA	C	610 430-2510	12644
F W Webb Company	Stoughton	MA	E	781 341-1100	12205
Ferguson Enterprises LLC	Chicopee	MA	G	413 593-1219	8032
Improved Consumer Products Inc	North Attleboro	MA	F	508 695-6841	10875
Ltp Corporation (DH)	Northborough	MA	D	508 393-7660	11101
Microgroup Inc	Medway	MA	C	508 533-4925	10308
Mks Instruments Inc	Andover	MA	E	978 645-5500	5898
Mks Instruments Inc (PA)	Andover	MA	B	978 645-5500	5899
Mks Msc Inc	Wilmington	MA	D	978 284-4000	13434
Portland Valve LLC (DH)	Warren	MA	E	704 289-6511	12852
Reggies Oil Company Inc	Quincy	MA	F	617 471-2095	11536
Rodney Hunt-Fontaine Inc (HQ)	Orange	MA	E	978 544-2511	11232
Scully Signal Company (PA)	Wilmington	MA	D	617 692-8600	13452

	CITY	ST	EMP	PHONE	ENTRY#
Sem-Tec Inc	Worcester	MA	E	508 798-8551	13797
Sloan Valve Company	Andover	MA	C	617 796-9001	5922
Swiss Precision Products Inc (DH)	North Oxford	MA	E	508 987-8003	11035
Symmons Industries Inc (PA)	Braintree	MA	C	800 796-6667	7207
Watts Regulator Co (HQ)	North Andover	MA	C	978 689-6000	10859
Watts Water Technologies Inc (PA)	North Andover	MA	C	978 688-1811	10861
Flue Gas Solutions Inc	Auburn	ME	G	207 893-1510	4432
Alan T Seeler Inc	New Hampton	NH	F	603 744-3736	15195
Controlair LLC	Amherst	NH	F	603 886-9400	13865
Fronek Anchor Darling Entp	Laconia	NH	F	603 528-1931	14651
Mem-Co Fittings Inc	Hampstead	NH	G	603 329-9633	14386
Parker & Harper Companies Inc (PA)	Raymond	NH	D	603 895-4761	15455
Quality Controls Inc	Northfield	NH	G	603 286-3321	15268
Everett J Prescott Inc	Lincoln	RI	G	401 333-8588	16135
Guill Tool & Engrg Co Inc	West Warwick	RI	D	401 822-8186	16908
Leonard Valve Company LLC	Cranston	RI	E	800 222-1208	15884
Tyco Fire Products LP (DH)	Cranston	RI	C	215 362-0700	15924

3495 Wire springs

	CITY	ST	EMP	PHONE	ENTRY#
Atlantic Precision Spring Inc	Bristol	CT	E	860 583-1864	399
Barnes Group Inc	Bristol	CT	D	860 582-9581	404
Barnes Group Inc (PA)	Bristol	CT	C	860 583-7070	406
Barnes Group Inc	Farmington	CT	G	860 298-7740	1209
Century Spring Mfg Co Inc	Bristol	CT	E	860 582-3344	425
Chestnut United Corporation	Bristol	CT	D	860 584-0594	426
Connectcut Spring Stmping Corp	Farmington	CT	B	860 677-1341	1212
Dcp Spring Acquisition Co Inc	Bristol	CT	E	860 589-3231	435
Engineering Specialties Inc	North Branford	CT	E	203 488-2266	2367
Excel Spring & Stamping LLC	Bristol	CT	G	860 585-1495	444
Fourslide Spring Stamping Inc	Bristol	CT	E	860 583-1688	449
Gemco Manufacturing Co Inc	Southington	CT	E	860 628-5529	3211
Hardware Products Company LP	Bristol	CT	E	617 884-9410	452
Lee Spring Company LLC	Bristol	CT	F	860 584-0991	461
Matthew Warren Inc	Southington	CT	D	860 621-7358	3221
National Spring & Stamping Inc	Thomaston	CT	F	860 283-0203	3625
Newcomb Spring Corp	Southington	CT	D	860 621-0111	3224
Newcomb Springs Connecticut	Southington	CT	E	860 621-0111	3225
Old Dmfg Inc	Farmington	CT	E	860 677-8561	1234
Oscar Jobs	Bristol	CT	G	860 583-7834	477
Plymouth Spring Company Inc	Bristol	CT	D	860 584-0594	482
Rd Ventures Inc	Plainville	CT	F	860 747-2709	2779
Rowley Spring & Stamping Corp	Bristol	CT	C	860 582-8175	494
Southington Tool & Mfg Corp	Plantsville	CT	E	860 276-0021	2796
Spring Computerized Inds LLC	Harwinton	CT	G	860 605-9206	1523
Spring Tollman Company Incorporated (PA)	Bristol	CT			D
860 583-1326	497				
Springfield Spring Corporation	Bristol	CT	F	860 584-6560	498
Thomas Spring Co Conn Inc	Milford	CT	G	203 874-7030	1895
Device Technologies Inc	Southborough	MA	E	508 229-2000	11994
Leggett & Platt Incorporated	Oxford	MA	D	508 987-8706	11258
Spring Manufacturing Corp	Tewksbury	MA	F	978 658-7396	12417
Springfield Spring Corporation (PA)	East Longmeadow MA		E	413 525-6837	8395
D & W Tool & Findings Inc	Pawtucket	RI	F	401 727-3030	16363

3496 Miscellaneous fabricated wire products

	CITY	ST	EMP	PHONE	ENTRY#
Acme Monaco Corporation (PA)	New Britain	CT	C	860 224-1349	1995
Acme Wire Products Co Inc	Mystic	CT	E	860 572-0511	1935
Amtec Corporation	Plainfield	CT	E	860 230-0006	2730
Armored Shield Technologies	Redding	CT	F	714 848-5796	2881
Arrow Manufacturing Company	Bristol	CT	E		397
Bes-Cut Inc	Bristol	CT	G	860 582-8660	414
Bridgeport Insulated Wire Co (PA)	Bridgeport	CT	F	203 333-3191	304
Bridgeport Insulated Wire Co	Stratford	CT	G	203 375-9579	3523
C O Jelliff Corporation (PA)	Southport	CT	E	203 259-1615	3244
Cco Llc	Rocky Hill	CT	F	860 757-3434	2917
East Shore Wire Rope Rgging Su	North Haven	CT	F	203 469-5204	2407
ERA Wire Inc	West Haven	CT	D	203 933-0480	4106
Excel Spring & Stamping LLC	Bristol	CT	G	860 585-1495	444
Gemco Manufacturing Co Inc	Southington	CT	E	860 628-5529	3211
Habasit Abt Inc	Middletown	CT	C	860 632-2211	1749
Habasit America Inc	Middletown	CT	C	860 632-2211	1750
Harding Company Inc (HQ)	Putnam	CT	G	860 778-7070	2859
Harding Company Inc	Putnam	CT	F	860 928-0475	2860
International Pipe & Stl Corp	North Branford	CT	F	203 481-7102	2369
Luvata Waterbury Inc	Branford	CT	E	203 488-5956	269
Meyer Wire & Cable Company LLC	Hamden	CT	E	203 281-0817	1441
Netsource Inc (PA)	Manchester	CT	E	860 649-6000	1620
New England Cage & Fence Corp	North Haven	CT	F	860 688-8148	2427
Northeastern Shaped Wire Inc	Southington	CT	E	860 621-8991	3226
Novo Precision LLC	Bristol	CT	E	860 583-0517	476
Nucor Steel Connecticut Inc	Wallingford	CT	C	203 265-0615	3836
Pa-Ted Spring Company LLC	Bristol	CT	E	860 582-6368	479
Protopac Inc	Watertown	CT	G	860 274-6796	4027

	CITY	ST	EMP	PHONE	ENTRY#
Prysmian Cbles Systems USA LLC	Willimantic	CT	C	860 456-8000	4220
Radcliff Wire Inc	Bristol	CT	E	312 876-1754	489
Redco Audio Inc	Monroe	CT	F	203 502-7600	1920
Rowley Spring & Stamping Corp	Bristol	CT	C	860 582-8175	494
Siri Manufacturing Co Inc	Danielson	CT	E	860 236-5901	842
Siri Wire Co	Danielson	CT	G	860 774-0607	843
Specialty Wire & Cord Sets Inc	Hamden	CT	F	203 498-2932	1456
Spring Tollman Company Incorporated (PA)	Bristol	CT			D
860 583-1326	497				
Tiger Enterprises Inc	Plantsville	CT	E	860 621-9155	2798
Ultimate Wireforms Inc	Bristol	CT	D	860 582-9111	504
Wiremold Company (DH)	West Hartford	CT	A	860 233-6251	4091
Alvin Johnson	East Longmeadow MA		F	413 525-6334	8368
Atlee Delaware Incorporated	Melrose	MA	F	978 681-1003	10313
Automatic Specialties Inc	Marlborough	MA	E	508 481-2370	10114
Bay State Wire & Cable Co Inc	Lowell	MA	E	978 454-2444	9861
Cape Cod Fence Co (PA)	South Yarmouth	MA	F	508 398-6041	11982
Citiworks Corp	Attleboro	MA	F	508 761-7400	6004
Comprehensive Identification Products Inc	Burlington	MA			C
781 229-8780	7354				
Custom Convyrs Fabrication Inc	North Oxford	MA	F	508 922-0283	11032
Dolan-Jenner Industries Inc	Boxborough	MA	E	978 263-1400	7151
Eastern Sling & Supply	Avon	MA	F	617 464-4422	6150
Ekiton Corporation	Boston	MA	G	617 464-4422	6709
Electro-Prep Inc	Wareham	MA	E	508 291-2880	12834
Frank L Reed Inc	Wilbraham	MA	E	413 596-3861	13359
Garlan Chain Co Inc	Attleboro Falls	MA	E	508 399-7288	6085
General Wire Products Inc	Worcester	MA	E	508 752-8260	13731
Horizon Fence Company Inc	Spencer	MA	F	774 289-9254	12061
I & I Sling Inc	Norwood	MA	E	781 575-0600	11178
Icarus Corporation	Auburn	MA	F	508 832-3481	6114
Innovive LLC	Billerica	MA	E	617 500-1691	6452
International Metal Pdts Inc	Chicopee	MA	E	413 532-2411	8040
Joe Miller Inc	Worcester	MA	E	508 753-8581	13745
Ketcham Supply Co Inc	New Bedford	MA	E	508 997-4787	10609
Lanoco Specialty Wire Pdts Inc	Sutton	MA	E	508 865-1500	12287
Markwell Manufacturing Co Inc	Norwood	MA	G	781 769-6610	11194
Merchants Metals LLC	Chicopee	MA	D	413 562-9981	8047
Micro Wire Products Inc	Holbrook	MA	D	508 584-0200	9180
Neptco Incorporated (DH)	Westwood	MA	E	401 722-5500	13316
New England Wire Products Inc (PA)	Leominster	MA	D	800 254-9473	9686
New England Wirecloth Co LLC	Fitchburg	MA	G	978 343-4998	8669
O/K Machinery Corporation	Marlborough	MA	E	508 303-8286	10188
Profiles Incorporated	Palmer	MA	E	413 283-7790	11283
Quirk Wire Co Inc	West Brookfield	MA	E	508 867-3155	12998
Reliable Fnce C/Wstern Div Inc	Ashland	MA	F	508 877-1200	5966
Riverdale Mills Corporation	Northbridge	MA	C	508 234-8715	11118
S&S Industries Inc (PA)	Stoughton	MA	C	914 885-1500	12232
Saint-Gobain Prfmce Plas Corp	Worcester	MA	C	508 852-3072	13792
St Pierre Manufacturing Corp	Worcester	MA	D	508 853-8010	13806
US Tsubaki Automotive LLC (DH)	Chicopee	MA	C	413 593-1100	8067
Viamed Corp	South Easton	MA	F	508 238-0220	11955
W D C Holdings Inc	Attleboro	MA	E	508 699-4412	6073
Whitney & Son Inc	Fitchburg	MA	E	978 343-6353	8682
Wirefab Inc	Worcester	MA	E	508 754-5359	13829
Worcester Manufacturing Inc	Worcester	MA	E	508 756-0301	13830
Anchor Corporation	Kennebunk	ME	F	207 985-6018	4920
Downeast Fishing Gear	Trenton	ME	E	207 667-3131	5553
Ftc Inc (PA)	Friendship	ME	E	207 354-2545	4806
Kardex Remstar LLC (HQ)	Westbrook	ME	E	207 854-1861	5633
Kelco Industries	Milbridge	ME	E	207 546-7562	5061
New England Wire Products Inc	Kingfield	ME	E	207 265-2176	4934
Tire Chains Requiredcom	Oakland	ME	G	207 465-7276	5121
Albany International Corp (PA)	Rochester	NH	D	603 330-5850	15464
Amphenol Corporation	Nashua	NH	B	603 879-3000	15061
Continental Cable LLC	Hinsdale	NH	D	800 229-5131	14443
Elektrisola Incorporated (PA)	Boscawen	NH	C	603 796-2114	13989
Felton Inc	Londonderry	NH	D	603 425-0200	14750
Guidewire Technologies Inc	Salem	NH	F	603 894-4399	15534
New England Wire Tech Corp (HQ)	Lisbon	NH	B	603 838-6624	14710
Plasti-Clip Corporation	Milford	NH	F	603 672-1166	15034
Prysmian Cbles Systems USA LLC	Manchester	NH	D	603 668-1620	14918
Wire Belt Company of America (PA)	Bedford	NH	D	603 644-2500	13955
ACS Industries Inc (PA)	Lincoln	RI	D	401 769-4700	16116
Alloy Holdings LLC	Providence	RI	D	401 353-7500	16467
Ametek Scp Inc (HQ)	Westerly	RI	D	401 596-6658	16927
Ammega US Inc	Warwick	RI	G	401 732-8131	16778
Electro Standards Lab Inc	Cranston	RI	D	401 946-1164	15853
Ferguson Perforating Company (DH)	Providence	RI	D	401 941-8876	16518
Fortune Rope & Metal Co Inc (PA)	Bristol	RI	E	800 416-6595	15765
Hindley Manufacturing Co Inc	Cumberland	RI	D	401 722-2550	15943
Perry Blackburne Inc	North Providence	RI	F	401 231-7200	16307
Quality Chain & Cable LLC	East Providence	RI	G	401 575-8323	16039

	CITY	ST	EMP	PHONE	ENTRY#
Royal Diversified Products	Warren	RI	E	401 245-6900	16767
Sh Consulting Co	Warwick	RI	F	508 695-6611	16862
Signature Cable Mfg Tech Inc	Cranston	RI	E	401 383-1008	15910
Weissenfels Usa Inc	Portsmouth	RI	F	401 683-2900	16461
Astenjohnson Inc	Williston	VT	D	802 658-2040	17722
One-Pull Sltons Wire Cable LLC	Randolph	VT	D	833 663-7855	17472
Vermont Wireform Inc	Chelsea	VT	F	802 889-3200	17179
Westwood Fences Inc	Irasburg	VT	F	802 754-8486	17303

3497 Metal foil and leaf

	CITY	ST	EMP	PHONE	ENTRY#
Cthru Metals Inc	North Branford	CT	F	203 884-1017	2364
Dexmet Corporation	Wallingford	CT	D	203 294-4440	3800
Foilmark Inc	Bloomfield	CT	F	860 243-0343	165
Republic Foil Inc	Danbury	CT	D	203 743-2731	805
Foilmark Inc (HQ)	Newburyport	MA	D	978 225-8200	10683
Hazen Paper Company (PA)	Holyoke	MA	C	413 538-8204	9259
Global Laminates Inc	Portsmouth	NH	F	603 373-8323	15393

3498 Fabricated pipe and fittings

	CITY	ST	EMP	PHONE	ENTRY#
Diba Industries Inc (HQ)	Danbury	CT	E	203 744-0773	731
EA Patten Co LLC	Manchester	CT	D	860 649-2851	1594
Howden Roots LLC	Windsor	CT	D	860 688-8361	4281
JFd Tube & Coil Products Inc	Hamden	CT	E	203 288-6941	1435
Leggett Platt Arspc Mddltown L	Middletown	CT	F	860 635-8811	1759
Macristy Industries Inc (PA)	Newington	CT	F	860 225-4637	2305
Pegasus Manufacturing Inc	Middletown	CT	E	860 635-8811	1769
Plastics and Concepts Conn Inc	Glastonbury	CT	G	860 657-9655	1294
Spencer Turbine Company (DH)	Windsor	CT	E	860 688-8361	4301
Vas Integrated LLC	Berlin	CT	G	860 748-4058	90
Bergen Pipe Supports Inc (HQ)	Woburn	MA	E	781 935-9550	13522
Fiberspar Linepipe LLC	New Bedford	MA	C	281 854-2636	10590
Improved Consumer Products Inc	North Attleboro	MA	F	508 695-6841	10875
L & R Manufacturing Co Inc	Worcester	MA	F	508 853-0562	13751
Microgroup Inc	Medway	MA	C	508 533-4925	10308
New England Stinless Distr LLC	Salisbury	MA	F	978 255-4830	11743
Piping Systems Inc	Assonet	MA	E	508 644-2221	5976
Platinum Fire Prtction Svcs LL (PA)	Marlborough	MA	E	508 481-8242	10196
Starmet Corporation (PA)	Concord	MA	E	978 369-5410	8134
Teshima International Corp	Cambridge	MA	G	617 830-1886	7739
Triangle Engineering Inc	Hanover	MA	F	781 878-1500	9046
Victaulic Company	Mansfield	MA	G	508 406-3220	10083
Worcester Manufacturing Inc	Worcester	MA	E	508 756-0301	13830
Wardwell Piping Inc	Windham	ME	F	207 892-0034	5674
ASC Engineered Solutions LLC	Portsmouth	NH	F	708 534-1414	15360
Long Island Pipe Supply NH Inc	Salem	NH	G	603 685-3200	15543
Micro Bends Corp	Peterborough	NH	E	603 924-0022	15318
New England Small Tube Corp	Litchfield	NH	D	603 429-1600	14713
Smiths Tblar Systms-Lconia Inc	Laconia	NH	C	603 524-2064	14670
Trellborg Pipe Sals Mlford Inc (DH)	Milford	NH	F	800 626-2180	15042
ASC Engineered Solutions LLC	North Kingstown	RI	C	401 886-3000	16233
ATW Companies Inc (PA)	Warwick	RI	D	401 244-1002	16785
Maley Laser Processing Inc	Warwick	RI	F	303 552-8941	16834
New England Union Co Inc	West Warwick	RI	E	401 821-0800	16918
Osram Sylvania Inc	Central Falls	RI	C	401 723-1378	15794
Prcess Critical Systems Group	Colchester	VT	F	802 448-5860	17200
Raymond Gadues Inc	Swanton	VT	E	802 868-2033	17641

3499 Fabricated metal products, nec

	CITY	ST	EMP	PHONE	ENTRY#
Airpot Corporation	Norwalk	CT	E	800 848-7681	2459
Alvarez Industries LLC	Orange	CT	D	203 799-2356	2666
Aptargroup Inc	Trumbull	CT	B	203 377-8100	3712
Beta Shim Co	Shelton	CT	E	203 926-1150	2983
Concord Industries Inc	Norwalk	CT	E	203 750-6060	2485
Cvc II Inc (DH)	Bethel	CT	D	203 401-4205	105
Dcg-Pmi Inc	Bethel	CT	E	203 743-5525	106
Farmington Engineering Inc	North Haven	CT	G	800 428-7584	2412
Farmington Mtal Fbrication LLC	Bristol	CT	G	860 402-5148	446
Feman Steel LLC	Bloomfield	CT	F	860 982-6393	164
General Wldg & Fabrication Inc	Watertown	CT	E	860 274-9668	4014
Greco Industries Inc	Bethel	CT	G	203 798-7804	117
H G Steinmetz Mch Works Inc	Stamford	CT	E	203 794-1880	3360
K-Tech International Inc	Torrington	CT	E	860 489-9399	3687
M & B Enterprise LLC	Derby	CT	F	888 983-2670	891
Nvi Weld Technology LLC	Waterbury	CT	G	203 707-0587	3953
Oxford General Industries Inc	Prospect	CT	F	203 758-4467	2837
Performance Connection Systems	Meriden	CT	G	203 868-5517	1684
Spirol International Corp (HQ)	Danielson	CT	C	860 774-8571	844
Spirol Intl Holdg Corp (PA)	Danielson	CT	F	860 774-8571	845
Tek-Motive Inc	Branford	CT	F	203 468-2224	281
Torqmaster Inc	Stamford	CT	E	203 326-5945	3484
Waterbury Companies Inc	Waterbury	CT	C		3980
Yarde Metals Inc (HQ)	Southington	CT	B	860 406-6061	3241
Alliance Sheet Metal Inc	Avon	MA	G	508 587-0314	6141

	CITY	ST	EMP	PHONE	ENTRY#
Alloy Fabricators Neng Inc	Randolph	MA	F	781 986-6400	11547
B & J Manufacturing Corp	Taunton	MA	D	508 822-1990	12322
Bete Fog Nozzle Inc (PA)	Greenfield	MA	C	413 772-0846	8985
Boston America Corp	Woburn	MA	C	781 933-3535	13529
Capstan Atlantic	Wrentham	MA	C	508 384-3100	13838
Century-Tywood J3 Corp	Holliston	MA	F	508 429-4011	9204
Conference Medal & Trophy Co	Buzzards Bay	MA	F	508 563-3600	7454
Draper Elevator Cab Co Inc	Holbrook	MA	F	781 961-3146	9171
Hampden Fence Supply Inc	Agawam	MA	F	413 786-4390	5792
Industrial Transfer & Stor Inc	Southbridge	MA	E	508 765-9178	12022
Jaco Inc	Franklin	MA	C	508 553-1000	8844
Lynn Ladder Scaffolding Co Inc (HQ)	Lynn	MA	D	781 598-6010	9985
Malden Intl Designs Inc	Middleboro	MA	E	508 946-2270	10365
Martin Benjamin Corporation	Dedham	MA	E	781 326-8311	8246
Metal Tech Industries Inc	Bourne	MA	G	508 566-8132	7140
Mooring Systems Incorporated	Cataumet	MA	G	508 776-0254	7859
Noyes Sheet Metal	Milford	MA	F	508 482-9302	10411
Nsd Metal Fabrication Inc	Merrimac	MA	G	978 346-0045	10326
October Company Inc (PA)	Easthampton	MA	D	413 527-9380	8456
October Company Inc	Easthampton	MA	E	413 529-0718	8457
Payne Engrg Fabrication Co Inc	Canton	MA	E	781 828-9046	7817
Production Basics Inc	Billerica	MA	E	617 926-8100	6473
Spoontiques Inc	Stoughton	MA	D	781 344-9530	12238
St Pierre Manufacturing Corp	Worcester	MA	E	508 853-8010	13806
Thureon Inc	Hopkinton	MA	F	774 249-8110	9346
Veloxint Corporation	Framingham	MA	F	774 777-3369	8806
VH Blackinton & Co Inc	Attleboro Falls	MA	C	508 699-4436	6096
Visi-Flash Rentals Eastern	West Bridgewater	MA	E	508 583-9100	12988
William McCaskie Inc	Westport	MA	G	508 636-8845	13301
Barrette Outdoor Living Inc	Biddeford	ME	E	800 866-8101	4556
Brooks Inc (PA)	Thomaston	ME	E	207 354-8763	5542
Cynthia Carroll Pallian	Wells	ME	G	207 646-1600	5599
Elmet Technologies LLC (PA)	Lewiston	ME	C	207 333-6100	4960
Minuteman Metal LLC	Wilton	ME	G	207 217-8908	5658
Rodco Enterprises	Lewiston	ME	F	207 786-2931	4990
Saunders Mfg Co Inc (PA)	Readfield	ME	E	207 685-9860	5318
Harmony Metal Products North Inc	Portsmouth	NH	E	603 536-6012	15399
Spraying Systems Co	Bedford	NH	F	603 471-0505	13950
Spraying Systems Co	Merrimack	NH	E	603 517-1854	15006
Summit Packaging Systems LLC (PA)	Manchester	NH	B	603 669-5410	14937
American Trophy and Supply Inc	East Providence	RI	G	401 438-3060	16004
Artvac Corporation	Lincoln	RI	E	401 333-6120	16120
Aspects Inc	Warren	RI	E	401 247-1854	16751
Capco Steel Erection Company	Providence	RI	F	401 383-9388	16495
Case Future Corp	Johnston	RI	E	401 944-0402	16078
Cathedral Art Metal Co Inc	Providence	RI	E	401 273-7200	16498
Fulford Manufacturing Company (PA)	Riverside	RI	F	401 431-2000	16655
International Packaging Corporation (PA)	Pawtucket	RI	A	401 724-1600	16376
Jewel Case Corporation	Providence	RI	B	401 943-1400	16549
Josef Creations Inc (PA)	Chepachet	RI	E	401 421-4198	15805
Kenney Manufacturing Company (PA)	Warwick	RI	B	401 739-2200	16831
Weingeroff Enterprises Inc	Cranston	RI	C	401 467-2200	15929
Whetstone Workshop LLC	East Providence	RI	G	401 368-7410	16048
World Trophies Company Inc	Providence	RI	F	401 272-5846	16649
Carris Financial Corp (PA)	Proctor	VT	F	802 773-9111	17456
Carris Reels Inc (HQ)	Proctor	VT	E	802 773-9111	17457
S & A Trombley Corporation	Morrisville	VT	E	802 888-2394	17388

35 INDUSTRIAL AND COMMERCIAL MACHINERY AND COMPUTER EQUIPMENT

3511 Turbines and turbine generator sets

	CITY	ST	EMP	PHONE	ENTRY#
Advanced Turbine Services LLC	Wallingford	CT	G	203 269-7977	3767
Asea Brown Boveri Inc	Norwalk	CT	A	203 750-2200	2465
Becon Incorporated (PA)	Bloomfield	CT	E	860 243-1428	151
Blastech Overhaul & Repr Corp	Bloomfield	CT	E	860 243-8811	152
Doncasters Inc (PA)	Groton	CT	D	860 449-1603	1367
GE Engine Svcs UNC Holdg I Inc	New Haven	CT	F	518 380-0767	2153
General Electric Company	Norwalk	CT	A	203 797-0840	2504
General Electric Company	Stamford	CT	F	866 419-4096	3354
Interntnl Turbine Systems Inc	Bloomfield	CT	F	860 761-0358	173
Mitsubishi Power Aero LLC (HQ)	Glastonbury	CT	C	860 368-5900	1290
Precision Combustion Inc	North Haven	CT	E	203 287-3700	2432
R&D Dynamics Corporation	Bloomfield	CT	D	860 726-1204	205
Wood Group Pratt & Whitney	Windsor Locks	CT	G	860 687-1686	4337
Camar Corp	Northborough	MA	F	508 845-9263	11093
Concepts Nrec LLC	Chelmsford	MA	F	781 935-9050	7920
Ethosenergy Tc Inc (DH)	Chicopee	MA	C	802 257-2721	8031
GE Energy Parts Intl LLC	Boston	MA	E	617 443-3000	6752
GE Vernova International LLC (HQ)	Cambridge	MA	C	617 443-3000	7580
General Electric Company (PA)	Boston	MA	A	617 443-3000	6754

	CITY	ST	EMP	PHONE	ENTRY#
Jet Industries Inc	Agawam	MA	E	413 786-2010	5798
Knm Holdings LLC	Marlborough	MA	G	508 229-1400	10177
LKM Industries Inc	Woburn	MA	D	781 935-9210	13602
New Bedford Ocean Cluster Inc	New Bedford	MA	F	508 474-8902	10627
Riley Power Inc	Marlborough	MA	B	508 852-7100	10204
Shaft Current Solutions Inc	Florence	MA	G	413 267-0590	8686
Trireme Manufacturing Co Inc	Topsfield	MA	E	978 887-2132	12440
General Electric Company	Bangor	ME	A	207 941-2500	4505
Machining Innovations Inc	Oakland	ME	G	207 465-2500	5120
Peregrine Turbine Tech LLC	Wiscasset	ME	F	207 687-8333	5699
Pika Energy Inc	Westbrook	ME	F	207 887-9105	5641
PJ Schwalbenberg & Assoc Inc	Cushing	ME	G	207 354-0700	4714
Energy Resources Group Inc (PA)	Farmington	NH	E	603 335-2535	14309
Flex Leasing Power & Svc LLC	Portsmouth	NH	E	603 430-7000	15384
Flexenergy Inc	Portsmouth	NH	D	603 430-7000	15385
Flexenergy Energy Systems Inc	Portsmouth	NH	E	877 477-6937	15386
Flexenergy Green Solutions Inc (PA)	Portsmouth	NH	E	603 430-7000	15387
Flexenergy Holdings LLC	Portsmouth	NH	D	603 430-7000	15388
Flexenergy Power Solutions LLC	Portsmouth	NH	D	603 430-7000	15389
Ingersoll-Rand Energy Systems Corporation 603 430-7000	Portsmouth	NH	D		15408
Concepts Nrec LLC (PA) 17707	White River Junction	VT	D	802 296-2321	
Village Industrial Power Inc	Bradford	VT	F	802 522-8584	17065

3519 Internal combustion engines, nec

	CITY	ST	EMP	PHONE	ENTRY#
Bell Power Systems LLC	Essex	CT	D	860 767-7502	1162
CAM Group LLC	Manchester	CT	F	860 646-2378	1587
Cummins - Allison Corp	Cheshire	CT	G	203 794-9200	585
Cummins Enviro Tech Inc	Old Lyme	CT	G	860 388-6377	2638
Cummins Inc	Rocky Hill	CT	F	860 529-7474	2920
Jacobs Vehicle Systems Inc	Bloomfield	CT	B	860 243-5222	175
Kco Numet Inc	Orange	CT	E	203 375-4995	2671
Liquidpiston Inc	Bloomfield	CT	E	860 838-2677	190
Smith Hill of Delaware Inc	Essex	CT	E	860 767-7502	1171
Andy Collazzo	Danvers	MA	G	978 539-8962	8162
Cummins Inc	Springfield	MA	G	413 737-2659	12088
Cummins Northeast LLC (HQ)	Braintree	MA	E	781 801-1700	7176
Governors America Corporation	Agawam	MA	C	413 233-1888	5791
Growth I M33 L P	Boston	MA	E	617 877-0046	6776
JH Westerbeke Corp	Taunton	MA	E	508 823-7677	12344
Js Sale Corp	Worcester	MA	E	508 753-2979	13746
Salem Preferred Partners LLC (PA)	Boston	MA	C	540 389-3922	7021
Thermo Power Corporation	Waltham	MA	A	781 622-1400	12802
Westerbeke Corporation	Avon	MA	E	508 823-7677	6168
Westerbeke Corporation (PA)	Taunton	MA	E	508 977-4273	12377
Melton Sales and Service Inc	Hallowell	ME	G	207 623-8895	4860
Vitaminsea LLC	Buxton	ME	G	207 671-0955	4666
Davis Village Solutions LLC	New Ipswich	NH	F	603 878-3662	15197

3523 Farm machinery and equipment

	CITY	ST	EMP	PHONE	ENTRY#
Double H Acres LLC	Broad Brook	CT	G	860 250-3311	508
Engineering Services & Pdts Co (PA)	South Windsor	CT	D	860 528-1119	3144
Salsco Inc	Cheshire	CT	D	203 271-1682	616
Stephens Pipe & Steel LLC	Manchester	CT	G	877 777-8721	1639
American Robotics Inc	Marlborough	MA	E	617 942-2101	10108
I B A Inc (PA)	Sutton	MA	E	508 865-6911	12281
Innovasea Systems Inc (PA)	Boston	MA	E	207 322-3219	6811
Oesco Inc	Conway	MA	E	413 369-4335	8143
Ondas Holdings Inc	Marlborough	MA	E	617 862-2101	10191
Allagash Timberlands LP	St John Plt	ME	G	207 834-6348	5524
Central Maine Dairy Eqp Inc	Skowhegan	ME	G	207 453-6727	5465
Harold Haines Inc	Presque Isle	ME	F	207 762-1411	5300
Northeast Structures Barns LLC	Porter	ME	G	207 512-0503	5167
Clark Summit Alpacas LLC	Deering	NH	G	603 464-2588	14187
SPI LLC	North Woodstock	NH	E	603 745-3911	15262
Country Home Products Inc	Charlotte	VT	E	802 771-7202	17175

3524 Lawn and garden equipment

	CITY	ST	EMP	PHONE	ENTRY#
Salsco Inc	Cheshire	CT	D	203 271-1682	616
Woodland Power Products Inc	West Haven	CT	F	888 531-7253	4133
Armatron International Inc (PA)	Medford	MA	D	781 321-2300	10280
Aubin Equipment and Automotive	East Dennis	MA	G	508 385-3237	8348
Essex County Coop Farming Assn	Topsfield	MA	F	978 887-2300	12433
Lps Enterprises Inc	East Freetown	MA	E	508 763-3830	8364
R I Baker Co Inc (PA)	Clarksburg	MA	E	413 663-3791	8073
Douglas Dynamics LLC	Rockland	ME	F	207 701-4200	5325
Machining Innovations Inc	Oakland	ME	G	207 465-2500	5120
North Country Tractor Inc	Dover	NH	F	603 742-5488	14241
Country Home Products Inc	Charlotte	VT	E	802 771-7202	17175
Vermont Ware Inc	St George	VT	G	802 482-4426	17624

3531 Construction machinery

	CITY	ST	EMP	PHONE	ENTRY#
Capewell Aerial Systems LLC (PA)	South Windsor	CT	D	860 610-0700	3126
Conair LLC	Torrington	CT	D	800 492-7464	3676
CT Crane and Hoist Service LLC	Plymouth	CT	G	860 283-4320	2806
DR Charles Envmtl Cnstr LLC	Monroe	CT	G	203 445-0412	1913
Ezflow Limited Partnership (DH)	Old Saybrook	CT	E	860 577-7064	2647
H Barber & Sons Inc	Naugatuck	CT	E	203 729-9000	1962
Indeco North America Inc	Milford	CT	E	203 713-1030	1838
Interstate Elec Svcs Corp	Windsor	CT	E	860 243-5644	4284
LH Gault & Son Incorporated	Westport	CT	D	203 227-5181	4180
Maretron LLP	Plainville	CT	F	602 861-1707	2771
Megadoor USA Inc	Meriden	CT	C	203 238-2700	1673
Naiad Dynamics Us Inc (HQ)	Shelton	CT	E	203 929-6355	3033
Naiad Maritime Group Inc (PA)	Shelton	CT	E	203 944-1932	3034
Numa Tool Company (PA)	Thompson	CT	D	860 923-9551	3652
Promein Steel LLC	Berlin	CT	F	860 828-1944	81
Salsco Inc	Cheshire	CT	D	203 271-1682	616
Show Motion Inc	Milford	CT	E	203 866-1866	1884
Terex Advance Mixer Inc	Westport	CT	E	203 222-7170	4198
Terex Corporation (PA)	Norwalk	CT	F	203 222-7170	2578
Terex Usa LLC (HQ)	Norwalk	CT	B	203 222-7170	2579
Tinsley GROup-Ps&w (HQ)	Milford	CT	E	919 742-5832	1896
Town of Ledyard	Gales Ferry	CT	F	860 464-9060	1262
Washington Terex Inc	Westport	CT	F	203 222-7170	4200
West Shore LLC	East Hampton	CT	G	860 267-1764	967
Altec Inc	Shrewsbury	MA	D	508 752-0660	11826
Altec Inc	Natick	MA	F	508 545-8200	10468
American Crane and Hoist Corp	Boston	MA	C	617 482-8383	6540
Amos Grt-Grt-Granddaughter Inc	Leominster	MA	G	413 773-5471	9636
Atlantic Broom Service Inc	East Bridgewater	MA	E	774 226-1300	8335
Bonsal American Inc	Oxford	MA	G	508 987-8188	11249
Costello Dismantling Co Inc (PA)	West Wareham	MA	E	508 291-2324	13058
Ecpi Inc	Bolton	MA	F	774 823-6368	6496
Ghm Industries Inc (PA)	Charlton	MA	F	508 248-3941	7888
Hercules Slr (us) Inc	New Bedford	MA	G	508 992-9519	10600
Hercules Slr (us) Inc (PA)	New Bedford	MA	E	508 993-0010	10601
Industrial Stl Boiler Svcs Inc	Chicopee	MA	E	413 532-7788	8038
Lewicki & Sons Excavating Inc	Plainville	MA	G	508 695-0122	11436
Louie and Teds Blacktop Inc	Swansea	MA	F	508 678-4948	12306
Omg Inc	Agawam	MA	G	413 786-0516	5802
Omg Inc (DH)	Agawam	MA	B	413 789-0252	5803
Roadsafe Traffic Systems	Stoughton	MA	G	781 436-5006	12231
Rockland Equipment Company LLC	Rockland	MA	F	781 871-4400	11659
Rt Engineering Corporation	Franklin	MA	E	800 343-1182	8861
Shemin Nurseries Inc	Lexington	MA	E	781 861-1111	9771
Ship Street Capital LLC	New Bedford	MA	E	508 995-9711	10650
Stoughton Steel Company Inc	Hanover	MA	E	781 826-6496	9044
Vulcan Company Inc (PA)	Hingham	MA	D	781 337-5970	9163
County Concrete & Cnstr Co	Columbia Falls	ME	E	207 483-4409	4698
Douglas Dynamics LLC	Rockland	ME	F	207 701-4200	5325
Howard P Fairfield LLC (DH)	Skowhegan	ME	F	207 474-9836	5468
North E Wldg & Fabrication Inc	Auburn	ME	F	207 786-2446	4448
Somatex Inc	Detroit	ME	E	207 487-6141	4725
A & G Crane LLC	Hooksett	NH	G	603 668-5844	14462
Admix Inc	Londonderry	NH	G	603 627-2340	14727
Advanced Concrete Tech Inc	Greenland	NH	G	603 431-5661	14365
Continental Biomass Industries	Newton	NH	F	603 382-0556	15242
Davis Village Solutions LLC	New Ipswich	NH	F	603 878-3662	15197
J C B Leasing Inc	Weare	NH	F	603 529-7974	15671
Ragnartech Inc	Fremont	NH	F	603 244-7575	14331
Ray-Tech Infrared Corporation	Charlestown	NH	F	603 826-3030	14068
Rwc Landscape Services MGT	Concord	NH	E	603 279-1411	14154
Terex Usa LLC	Newton	NH	D	603 382-0556	15245
Trellborg Pipe Sals Mlford Inc (DH)	Milford	NH	F	800 626-2180	15042
American Equipment & Fabg Corp	East Providence	RI	F	401 438-2626	16002
Colebrook Intrlcking Pvers Wll	Little Compton	RI	F	401 835-6934	16160
Dig Rite Company Inc	Johnston	RI	F	401 862-5895	16081
Hudson Terminal Corp	Cranston	RI	G	401 941-0500	15875
Hudson Terminal Corp (PA)	Providence	RI	F	401 274-2200	16535
Interstate Elec Svcs Corp	East Providence	RI	E	401 369-7890	16024
Vibco Inc (PA)	Wyoming	RI	D	401 539-2392	16983
Built Rite Manufacturing Inc	Ludlow	VT	F	802 228-7293	17314
Champlain Construction Co Inc	Middlebury	VT	F	802 388-2652	17341

3532 Mining machinery

	CITY	ST	EMP	PHONE	ENTRY#
Bove Brothers LLC	Oakdale	CT	E	860 443-9200	2620
Numa Tool Company (PA)	Thompson	CT	D	860 923-9551	3652
Eldred Wheeler Company	Hanover	MA	G	781 924-5067	9030
Haymart LLC	Patten	ME	G	207 528-2058	5153
Northeast Pellets LLC	Ashland	ME	F	207 435-6230	4412
Buckeye Blasting Corporation	Epsom	NH	G	603 736-4681	14279
Intertech Process Technology	Atkinson	NH	G	603 893-9566	13904

S I C

	CITY	ST	EMP	PHONE	ENTRY#
Joseph A Thomas Ltd	Bristol	RI	E	401 253-1330	15770

3533 Oil and gas field machinery

	CITY	ST	EMP	PHONE	ENTRY#
Cameron International Corp	Glastonbury	CT	F	860 633-0277	1273
General Electric Company	Norwalk	CT	A	203 797-0840	2504
General Electric Company	Stamford	CT	F	866 419-4096	3354
Numa Tool Company (PA)	Thompson	CT	D	860 923-9551	3652
Oil Purification Systems Inc	Waterbury	CT	F	203 346-1800	3955
Slickbar Products Corp	Seymour	CT	E	203 888-7700	2969
Solidification Pdts Intl Inc	Northford	CT	E	203 484-9494	2455
GE Vernova International LLC (HQ)	Cambridge	MA	C	617 443-3000	7580
General Electric Company (PA)	Boston	MA	A	617 443-3000	6754
Kyle Equipment Co Inc	Sterling	MA	F	978 422-8448	12165
Deepwater Buoyancy Inc	Biddeford	ME	F	207 468-2565	4559
Shannon Drilling	Machias	ME	G	207 255-6149	5034

3534 Elevators and moving stairways

	CITY	ST	EMP	PHONE	ENTRY#
Ascend Elevator Inc	Bloomfield	CT	D	215 703-0358	148
Bay State Elevator Company Inc	Bloomfield	CT	F	860 243-9030	150
K-Tech International Inc	Torrington	CT	E	860 489-9399	3687
Otis Elevator Company	Bloomfield	CT	B	860 242-3632	198
Otis Elevator Company (HQ)	Farmington	CT	C	860 674-3000	1235
Otis Elevator Intl Inc	Farmington	CT	C	860 676-6000	1236
Otis Worldwide Corporation (PA)	Farmington	CT	A	860 674-3000	1237
Bay State Elevator Company Inc (HQ)	Agawam	MA	E	413 786-7000	5779
Gillespie Corporation	Ware	MA	E	413 967-4980	12825
Hamilton Elevator Interiors	Saugus	MA	F	781 233-9540	11759
Interstate Elevator Corp	Woburn	MA	G	603 560-3377	13590
Keystone Elev Svc Mdrnztion LL	Weymouth	MA	G	781 340-3860	13328
Otis Elevator Company	Auburn	MA	F	401 232-7282	6122
Stairway Manufacturers Assoc	Fall River	MA	G	508 646-1313	8608

3535 Conveyors and conveying equipment

	CITY	ST	EMP	PHONE	ENTRY#
Affordable Conveyor Svcs LLC	Southington	CT	F	860 582-1800	3202
Alvest (usa) Inc (DH)	Windsor	CT	F	860 602-3400	4259
ID Mail Systems Inc	New Britain	CT	F	860 344-3333	2031
Industrial Magnetics Inc	Windsor	CT	D	508 853-3232	4283
International Robotics Inc	Stamford	CT	F	914 630-1060	3385
Mk North America Inc	Bloomfield	CT	E	860 769-5500	194
Production Equipment Company	Meriden	CT	E	800 758-5697	1685
Roller Bearing Co Amer Inc	Middlebury	CT	F	203 758-8272	1720
Walker Magnetics Group Inc	Windsor	CT	D	508 853-3232	4314
AMA Engnring - Smrtmove Cnvyor	Westport	MA	F	508 636-7740	13292
Amazon Robotics LLC (HQ)	North Reading	MA	C	781 221-4640	11037
Anaconda Usa Inc	Natick	MA	F	800 285-5721	10470
Ascend Robotics LLC	Cambridge	MA	F	978 451-0170	7491
Barrett Technology Inc	Cambridge	MA	F	617 252-9000	7497
Belt Technologies Inc (PA)	Agawam	MA	E	413 786-9922	5780
Chelsea Industries Inc	Newton	MA	A	617 232-6060	10745
Dg Marshall Associates Inc	Charlton	MA	E	508 943-2394	7887
Fabreeka International Inc (DH)	Stoughton	MA	G	781 341-3655	12206
Fabreeka Intl Holdings Inc (DH)	Stoughton	MA	F	781 341-3655	12207
Kleenline LLC	Newburyport	MA	F	978 463-0827	10691
Magnemotion Inc	Devens	MA	D	978 757-9100	8277
Omtec Corp	Marlborough	MA	F	508 481-3322	10190
TEC Engineering Corp	Oxford	MA	F	508 987-0231	11266
Modula Inc (DH)	Lewiston	ME	D	207 440-5100	4976
Plastic Techniques Inc	Goffstown	NH	E	603 622-5570	14356
Action Conveyor Tech Inc	Smithfield	RI	F	401 722-2300	16685
Hall Inc	Bristol	RI	D	401 253-4858	15768
Niko Us LLC	Portsmouth	RI	G	401 683-7525	16451

3536 Hoists, cranes, and monorails

	CITY	ST	EMP	PHONE	ENTRY#
Genie Lease Management LLC	Westport	CT	G	203 222-7170	4169
New England Lift Systems LLC	Newington	CT	G	860 372-4040	2309
Production Equipment Company	Meriden	CT	E	800 758-5697	1685
Terex Corporation (PA)	Norwalk	CT	F	203 222-7170	2578
American Crane and Hoist Corp	Boston	MA	C	617 482-8383	6540
Capco Crane & Hoist Inc	Rowley	MA	F	978 948-2998	11668
Capco Crane & Hoist Parts Inc	Rowley	MA	G	978 948-2998	11669
Gillespie Corporation	Ware	MA	E	413 967-4980	12825
Konecranes Inc	Chelmsford	MA	F	978 256-5525	7935
Leon Eg Company Inc	Boston	MA	E	617 482-8383	6856
Lincoln Precision Machining Co	North Grafton	MA	E	508 839-2175	11024
Nai Cranes LLC	Woburn	MA	D	781 897-4100	13617
New England Crane Inc	Tyngsboro	MA	E	207 782-7353	12462
St Pierre Manufacturing Corp	Worcester	MA	E	508 853-8010	13806
Somatex Inc	Detroit	ME	E	207 487-6141	4725
Thermopol Inc	Somersworth	NH	G	603 692-6300	15626

3537 Industrial trucks and tractors

	CITY	ST	EMP	PHONE	ENTRY#
Doleco Usa Inc	Meriden	CT	G	203 440-1940	1663
Dri-Air Industries Inc	East Windsor	CT	E	860 627-5110	1071

	CITY	ST	EMP	PHONE	ENTRY#
Innovativ Hoisting LLC	Willington	CT	F	860 969-4477	4225
New Haven Companies Inc	East Haven	CT	F	203 469-6421	1048
Northside Minis LLC	Old Saybrook	CT	G	860 388-6871	2656
Terex Corporation (PA)	Norwalk	CT	F	203 222-7170	2578
Ada Fabricators Inc	Wilmington	MA	F	978 262-9900	13372
Brownell Boat Stands Inc	Mattapoisett	MA	F	508 758-3671	10255
Craufurd Manufacturing LLC	Belchertown	MA	F	413 323-4628	6279
Crown Equipment Corporation	Woburn	MA	D	781 933-3366	13551
Daves Truck Repair Inc	Springfield	MA	E	413 734-8898	12089
Entwistle Company LLC (PA)	Hudson	MA	D	508 481-4000	9364
Greenwood Emrgncy Vehicles LLC (HQ)	Attleboro Falls	MA	D	508 695-7138	6086
Hostar Mar Trnspt Systems Inc	Wareham	MA	F	508 295-2900	12838
Ite LLC	Brockton	MA	G	508 313-5600	7286
KS Baxter Logistics Co Inc	Boston	MA	F	607 203-5921	6848
Martel Welding & Sons Inc	Tewksbury	MA	F	978 458-0661	12406
Masart Inc	Watertown	MA	F	781 786-8774	12892
Maybury Associates Inc	East Longmeadow	MA	D	413 525-4216	8386
MEI Rigging & Crating LLC	Salisbury	MA	F	978 685-7700	11742
Steele Canvas Basket Corp	Chelsea	MA	E	800 541-8929	7994
Tally Transportation LLC	Randolph	MA	E	781 510-2411	11576
WB Engineering Inc	Foxboro	MA	E	508 952-4000	8731
Brown Construction Inc	Houlton	ME	F	207 532-0910	4898
Crown Equipment Corporation	Scarborough	ME	E	207 773-4049	5429
KSd ATL Trnspt Systems Inc	Westbrook	ME	D	207 591-4150	5634
North Country Tractor Inc	Sanford	ME	F	207 324-5646	5403
Southworth Intl Group Inc (PA)	Falmouth	ME	D	207 878-0700	4772
Southworth Products Corp (HQ)	Falmouth	ME	F	207 878-0700	4773
WB Engineering Inc (HQ)	Falmouth	ME	E	207 878-0700	4775
Davis Village Solutions LLC	New Ipswich	NH	F	603 878-3662	15197
Hawkes Motorsports LLC	Goffstown	NH	G	603 660-9864	14349

3541 Machine tools, metal cutting type

	CITY	ST	EMP	PHONE	ENTRY#
Atp Industries LLC (PA)	Plainville	CT	F	860 479-5007	2748
Branson Ultrasonics Corp (DH)	Brookfield	CT	B	203 796-0400	512
C V Tool Company Inc (PA)	Southington	CT	E	978 353-7901	3206
Cnc Engineering Inc	Enfield	CT	E	860 749-1780	1124
Coastal Industrial Distrs Inc	Berlin	CT	F	207 286-3319	59
Connecticut Tool & Cutter Co	Bristol	CT	F	860 314-1740	431
Deburring Laboratories Inc	New Britain	CT	F	860 829-6300	2022
Extec Corp	Enfield	CT	F	860 741-3435	1133
Fletcher-Terry Company LLC (PA)	East Berlin	CT	D	860 828-3400	911
Gary Tool Company	Stratford	CT	G	203 377-3077	3540
Gmn Usa LLC	Bristol	CT	F	800 686-1679	451
Hanwha Aerospace USA LLC (DH)	Cheshire	CT	C	203 806-2090	597
Hanwha Aerospace USA LLC	East Windsor	CT	D	860 789-2511	1075
Iamaw	Hebron	CT	G	860 228-0049	1528
J & L Mfg Watertown Inc	Waterbury	CT	E	203 591-9124	3924
JL Lucas Machinery Co Inc	Waterbury	CT	F	203 597-1300	3925
L C M Tool Co	Waterbury	CT	G	203 757-1575	3930
Laser Tool Co Inc	Thomaston	CT	F	860 283-8284	3623
Machine Builders Neng LLC	Milford	CT	F	203 922-9446	1847
Marena Industries Inc	East Hartford	CT	F	860 528-9701	1004
Microbest Inc	Waterbury	CT	C	203 597-0355	3944
Moon Cutter Co Inc	Hamden	CT	E	203 288-9249	1444
Moore Tool Company Inc (HQ)	Bridgeport	CT	F	203 366-3224	350
National Screw Manufacturing	East Haven	CT	F	203 469-7109	1047
New England Cnc Inc	Hamden	CT	D	203 288-8241	1446
New England Die Co Inc	Waterbury	CT	F	203 574-5140	3950
New England Machine Tools Inc	Bristol	CT	G	860 583-4001	475
New England Plasma Dev Corp	Putnam	CT	F	860 928-6561	2866
New England Tooling Inc	Killingworth	CT	F	800 866-5105	1544
Nowak Products Inc	Newington	CT	G	860 666-9685	2311
P-A-R Precision Inc	Wolcott	CT	F	860 491-4181	4372
Pmt Group Inc (PA)	Bridgeport	CT	C	203 367-8675	359
Producto Corporation (HQ)	Bridgeport	CT	E	203 366-3224	363
Ramdy Corporation	Oakville	CT	E	860 274-3716	2626
Ready Tool Company	West Hartford	CT	E	860 524-7811	4079
Sadlak Industries LLC	Coventry	CT	E	860 742-0227	681
Service Network Inc	Farmington	CT	D	860 679-7432	1247
Shuster-Mettler Corp	Plainville	CT	E	203 562-3178	2780
Sonitek Corporation	Milford	CT	E	203 878-9321	1886
Sperry Automatics Co Inc	Naugatuck	CT	E	203 729-4589	1986
Stanley Engnered Fastening LLC (HQ)	Danbury	CT	F	800 783-6427	821
Syzygy Global Technology LLC	Darien	CT	G	203 818-2166	856
Tetco Inc	Plainville	CT	F	860 747-1280	2783
The Viking Tool Company	Shelton	CT	E	203 929-1457	3068
Turbine Controls Inc (PA)	Bloomfield	CT	D	860 242-0448	214
U S Tool Grinding Inc	Danbury	CT	F	203 797-5036	829
United Tool & Die Company (PA)	West Hartford	CT	C	860 246-6531	4088
US Avionics Inc / Superabr	South Windsor	CT	G	860 528-1114	3188
Watertown Jig Bore Service Inc	Watertown	CT	E	860 274-5898	4037
Acp Waterjet Inc	Littleton	MA	F	800 951-5127	9799
American Holt Corporation (PA)	Norwood	MA	F	781 440-9993	11160

	CITY	ST	EMP	PHONE	ENTRY#
American Spcialty Grinding Inc (HQ)	Chicopee	MA	E	413 593-5412	8007
Amherst Machine Co	Amherst	MA	F	413 549-4551	5858
Boston Centerless Inc (PA)	Woburn	MA	D	781 994-5000	13530
Central MA Waterjet Inc	Millbury	MA	G	508 769-4308	10429
Component Sources Intl Inc	Westborough	MA	F	508 986-2300	13092
Compumachine Inc	Danvers	MA	F	978 777-8440	8173
Desktop Metal Operating Inc (HQ)	Burlington	MA	C	978 224-1244	7362
Donahue Industries Inc	Shrewsbury	MA	E	508 845-6501	11830
Dumont Company LLC	Greenfield	MA	F	413 773-3675	8990
Duval Precision Grinding Inc	Chicopee	MA	E	413 593-3060	8028
E T Duval & Sons Inc	Leominster	MA	G	978 537-7596	9660
Grob Inc	Weston	MA	G	617 817-3123	13285
Hendrick Manufacturing Corp (PA)	Salem	MA	F	781 631-4400	11723
Intech Inc	Acton	MA	E	978 263-2210	5756
JT Machine Inc	East Douglas	MA	E	508 476-1508	8351
Kinefac Corporation	Worcester	MA	D	508 754-6901	13749
Mainline Tool & Grind Inc	Westfield	MA	G	413 626-9601	13180
Merit Machine Mfg Inc	Fitchburg	MA	F	978 342-7677	8664
Mrse Inc	West Brookfield	MA	F	508 867-5083	12996
Nova Analytics Corporation	Beverly	MA	E	781 897-1208	6368
Peterson and Nash Inc	Norwell	MA	G	781 826-9085	11145
Phoenix Inc	Seekonk	MA	E	508 399-7100	11783
Production Tool & Grinding	Athol	MA	F	978 544-8206	5983
Professional TI Grinding Inc (PA)	South Easton	MA	E	508 230-3535	11951
Pys Enterprises Inc	Springfield	MA	F	413 732-7470	12123
Simonds Industries Intl	Fitchburg	MA	F	978 424-0100	8674
Toolmex Indus Solutions Inc (PA)	Northborough	MA	D	508 653-8897	11114
True Machine Co Inc	Swansea	MA	G	508 379-0329	12314
Uva Lidkoping Inc	Milford	MA	G	508 634-4301	10422
Fabco Inc	Winthrop	ME	E	207 377-6909	5692
OBrien Consolidated Inds	Lewiston	ME	E	207 783-8543	4981
Sands Business Eqp & Sups LLC	York	ME	F	207 351-3334	5716
Valmet Inc	Winthrop	ME	D	207 377-6909	5696
Airmar Technology Corp (PA)	Milford	NH	B	603 673-9570	15013
Ametek Precitech Inc (HQ)	Keene	NH	D	603 357-2510	14588
Centricut Inc	West Lebanon	NH	G	603 298-7849	15679
Centricut Manufacturing LLC	West Lebanon	NH	F	603 298-6191	15680
Cnc North Inc	Claremont	NH	G	603 542-3361	14084
Datron Dynamics Inc	Milford	NH	E	603 215-5850	15020
Express Assemblyproducts LLC	Nashua	NH	F	603 424-5590	15098
Fremont Machine & Tool Co Inc	Fremont	NH	E	603 895-9445	14327
Hypertherm Inc (PA)	Hanover	NH	A	603 643-3441	14426
Hypertherm Inc	Hanover	NH	F	716 434-3755	14427
Jarvis Company Inc (PA)	Rochester	NH	D	603 332-9000	15481
Thermacut Inc	Claremont	NH	D	603 543-0585	14098
Thermal Dynamics Corporation (DH)	West Lebanon	NH	B	603 298-5711	15690
Trellborg Pipe Sals Mlford Inc (DH)	Milford	NH	F	800 626-2180	15042
Williams & Hussey Mch Co Inc	Amherst	NH	F	603 732-0219	13895
Aargo Environmental Inc	North Kingstown	RI	G	401 267-0077	16228
Jfl Enterprises Inc	Smithfield	RI	E	401 231-1020	16718
Malco Saw Co Inc	Cranston	RI	G	401 942-7380	15891
Piatek Machine Company Inc	Pawtucket	RI	F	401 728-9930	16403
Supfina Machine Co Inc	North Kingstown	RI	E	401 294-6600	16283
Fellows Corporation	Windsor	VT	E	802 674-6500	17758
Neil H Daniels Inc	Ascutney	VT	F	802 674-6323	16993
Yankee Corporation	Fairfax	VT	D	802 527-0177	17265

3542 Machine tools, metal forming type

	CITY	ST	EMP	PHONE	ENTRY#
American Actuator Corporation	Redding	CT	G	203 324-6334	2880
Arna Machine Company	Bristol	CT	F	860 583-0628	396
Arrow Diversified Tooling Inc	Ellington	CT	E	860 872-9072	1101
Avna Inc (PA)	New Britain	CT	C	860 225-8707	2004
Cole S Crew Machine Products	North Haven	CT	E	203 723-1418	2398
Deringer-Ney Inc (PA)	Bloomfield	CT	C	860 242-2281	158
Eyelet Tech LLC	Wolcott	CT	E	203 879-5306	4365
Fenn LLC	East Berlin	CT	E	860 259-6600	910
Grant Manufacturing and Mch Co	Bridgeport	CT	F	203 366-4557	326
Joining Tech Automtn Inc	East Granby	CT	F	203 784-1967	936
Joshua LLC (PA)	Guilford	CT	F	203 624-0080	1398
L M Gill Welding and Mfr LLC (PA)	Manchester	CT	D	860 647-9931	1610
Lou-Jan Tool & Die Inc	Bristol	CT	F	203 272-3536	463
Merritt Extruder Corp	Hamden	CT	E	203 230-8100	1440
OEM Sources LLC	Milford	CT	G	203 283-5415	1857
Oxford General Industries Inc	Prospect	CT	F	203 758-4467	2837
Raymon Tool LLC	Hamden	CT	F	203 248-2199	1452
Sandviks Inc (PA)	Danbury	CT	G	866 984-0188	808
Sirois Tool Company Inc (PA)	Berlin	CT	E	860 828-5327	85
St Liquidation Corporation	Southington	CT	F	860 628-9090	3234
Trumpf Inc	Farmington	CT	E	860 255-6000	1253
Trumpf Inc	Farmington	CT	E	860 255-6000	1254
Trumpf Inc (DH)	Farmington	CT	E	860 255-6000	1255
Trumpf Inc	Plainville	CT	G	860 255-6000	2786
Ab-Wey Machine & Die Co Inc	Pembroke	MA	F	781 294-8031	11356

	CITY	ST	EMP	PHONE	ENTRY#
Alcoa Global Fasteners Inc	Stoughton	MA	C	412 553-4545	12192
Altra Industrial Motion Corp (HQ)	Braintree	MA	C	781 917-0600	7167
American Flwform Machining LLC (HQ)	Billerica	MA	E	978 667-0202	6399
Automatic Press Inc	Franklin	MA	G	508 528-2000	8818
Compumachine Inc	Danvers	MA	F	978 777-8440	8173
Form Roll Die Corp (PA)	Worcester	MA	E	508 755-2010	13725
Form Roll Die Corp	Worcester	MA	F	508 755-5302	13726
Kinefac Corporation	Worcester	MA	D	508 754-6901	13749
Mestek Inc (PA)	Westfield	MA	C	470 898-4533	13186
PCC Specialty Products Inc	Auburn	MA	C	503 417-4800	6123
Sonolite Plastics Corporation	Gloucester	MA	F	978 281-0662	8959
Thermoplastics Engineering Corp	Leominster	MA	F		9710
Thomson Service Corp	Franklin	MA	F	508 528-2000	8872
Valentine Tool & Stamping Inc	Norton	MA	F	508 285-6911	11137
Warner Electric	Braintree	MA	D	781 917-0600	7212
Westfield Tool & Die Co Inc	Westfield	MA	E	413 562-2393	13222
Whitman Castings Inc (PA)	Whitman	MA	E	781 447-4417	13352
Greenerd Press & Mch Co LLC (PA)	Nashua	NH	F	603 889-4101	15108
Linde Advanced Mtl Tech Inc	Concord	NH	D	603 224-9585	14140
Nbr Diamond Tool Corp	South Hampton	NH	G	603 394-2113	15629
Tafa Incorporated (DH)	Concord	NH	E	603 224-9585	14162
Durant Tool Company Inc	North Kingstown	RI	E	401 781-7800	16246
Gasbarre Products Inc	Cranston	RI	F	401 467-5200	15865
Joraco Inc	Smithfield	RI	E	401 232-1710	16719
Laser Fare Inc (PA)	Smithfield	RI	E	401 231-4400	16721
Parkinson Machinery & Manufacturing Corp	Woonsocket	RI		401 762-2100	C 16971
Vermont Machine Tool Corp	Springfield	VT	F	802 885-5161	17622
Whitney Blake Company (PA)	Bellows Falls	VT	D	800 323-0479	17033

3543 Industrial patterns

	CITY	ST	EMP	PHONE	ENTRY#
Arrow Diversified Tooling Inc	Ellington	CT	E	860 872-9072	1101
Roehr Tool Corp	Sterling	MA	E	978 562-4488	12169
S Ralph Cross and Sons Inc	Holyoke	MA	E	508 865-8512	9279
Clear Carbon & Components Inc	Bristol	RI	E	401 254-5085	15758
Goodwin-Bradley Pattern Co Inc	Providence	RI	F	401 461-5220	16525

3544 Special dies, tools, jigs, and fixtures

	CITY	ST	EMP	PHONE	ENTRY#
A & H Tool Works LLC	Harwinton	CT	G	860 302-9284	1518
Aba-Pgt Inc (PA)	Manchester	CT	D	860 649-4591	1580
Accurate Tool & Die Inc	Stamford	CT	E	203 967-1200	3270
Acson Tool Company	Bridgeport	CT	F	203 334-8050	292
Advance Mold & Mfg Inc	Manchester	CT	C	860 432-5887	1583
Airex Rubber Products Corporation	Portland	CT	E	860 342-0850	2816
Alinabal Inc (HQ)	Milford	CT	C	203 877-3241	1796
All Five Tool Co Inc	Berlin	CT	F	860 583-1693	48
American Kuhne Inc	North Stonington	CT	E	401 326-6200	2446
American Molded Products Inc	Bridgeport	CT	F	203 333-0183	295
Apex Machine Tool Company Inc	Cheshire	CT	D	860 677-2884	571
Arcade Technology LLC	Bridgeport	CT	D	203 366-3871	297
Arrow Diversified Tooling Inc	Ellington	CT	E	860 872-9072	1101
Atlas Stamping & Mfg Corp	Newington	CT	E	860 757-3233	2273
B & D Machine Inc	Tolland	CT	E	860 871-9226	3655
B & P Plating Equipment LLC	Bristol	CT	F	860 589-5799	401
Bessette Holdings Inc	East Hartford	CT	E	860 289-6000	975
Better Molded Products Inc (PA)	Bristol	CT	D	860 589-0066	415
Bml Tool & Mfg Corp	Monroe	CT	D	203 880-9485	1907
Bremser Technologies Inc	Stratford	CT	F	203 378-8486	3521
Bridgeport TI & Stamping Corp	Bridgeport	CT	E	203 336-2501	305
Bristol Tool & Die Company	Bristol	CT	F	860 582-2577	423
C V Tool Company Inc (PA)	Southington	CT	F	978 353-7901	3206
Cambridge Specialty Co Inc	Berlin	CT	D	860 828-3579	57
Candlewood Tool and Mch Sp Inc	Gaylordsville	CT	F	860 355-1892	1263
Century Tool Co Inc	Thompson	CT	F	860 923-9523	3648
Charles J Angelo Mfg Group LLC	Manchester	CT	F	860 646-2378	1590
Connecticut Tool Co Inc	Putnam	CT	E	860 928-0565	2850
D & B Tool Co LLC	Milford	CT	G	203 878-6026	1815
Delta Tool Co Inc	Thompson	CT	G	860 923-2012	3649
E & E Tool & Mfg Co Inc	Winsted	CT	F	860 738-8577	4342
E and S Gage Inc	Tolland	CT	F	860 872-5917	3659
Edco Engineering Inc	Newington	CT	D	860 667-8292	2289
Fad Tool Company LLC	Bristol	CT	F	860 582-7890	445
Ferron Mold and Tool LLC	Dayville	CT	G	860 774-5555	862
Fka Ppm Inc	Hartford	CT	E	781 871-4606	1480
Foilmark Inc	Bloomfield	CT	G	860 243-0343	165
G & G Dissolution Corp	Glastonbury	CT	E	860 633-7099	1279
G L C Inc	Watertown	CT	F	860 945-6166	4013
G P Tool Co Inc	Danbury	CT	E	203 744-0310	749
Gary Tool Company	Stratford	CT	G	203 377-3077	3540
Globe Tool & Met Stampg Co Inc	Southington	CT	E	860 621-6807	3213
Gordon Rubber and Pkg Co Inc	Derby	CT	E	203 735-7441	889
Hamden Packaging Inc	Hamden	CT	E	203 288-0200	1428
Heise Industries Inc	East Berlin	CT	D	860 828-6538	912

	CITY	ST	EMP	PHONE	ENTRY#		CITY	ST	EMP	PHONE	ENTRY#
Herman Schmidt Precision Workh	South Windsor	CT	G	860 289-3347	3154	De Mari Pasta Dies USA Inc	Dracut	MA	G	978 454-4099	8304
Highland Manufacturing Inc	Manchester	CT	E	860 646-5142	1603	Diecutting Tooling Svcs Inc **(PA)**	Chicopee	MA	G	413 331-3500	8023
Hobson and Motzer Incorporated **(PA)**	Durham	CT	C	860 349-1756	901	Fall River Tool & Die Co Inc	Fall River	MA	F	508 674-4621	8550
Ivanhoe Tool & Die Company Inc	Thompson	CT	E	860 923-9541	3650	Foilmark Inc **(HQ)**	Newburyport	MA	D	978 225-8200	10683
J & L Mfg Watertown Inc	Waterbury	CT	E	203 591-9124	3924	Fort Hill Sign Products Inc	Hopedale	MA	G	781 321-4320	9297
J & L Tool Company Inc	Wallingford	CT	E	203 265-6237	3820	G&F Precision Molding Inc	Danvers	MA	G	978 560-2622	8188
Jovek Tool and Die	Bristol	CT	G	860 261-5020	459	G&F Precision Molding Inc **(PA)**	Fiskdale	MA	D	508 347-9132	8639
Kovacs Machine and Tool Co	Wallingford	CT	F	203 269-4949	3825	Gare Incorporated	Haverhill	MA	E	978 373-9131	9096
Larosa Manufacturing LLC	Plainville	CT	G	860 819-7066	2767	Geonautics Manufacturing Inc	Newburyport	MA	E	978 462-7161	10685
Lassy Tools Inc	Plainville	CT	G	860 747-2748	2768	Hapco Inc	Hanover	MA	E	781 826-8801	9034
Lawrence Holdings Inc	Wallingford	CT	F	203 949-1600	3826	Hoppe Technologies Inc	Chicopee	MA	D	413 592-9213	8036
Lou-Jan Tool & Die Inc	Bristol	CT	F	203 272-3536	463	Ideal Industries Inc	Sterling	MA	G	978 422-3600	12163
Manchester Molding and Mfg Co	Manchester	CT	E	860 643-2141	1615	Innovative Tooling Company Inc	Lenox	MA	F	413 637-1031	9625
Mastercraft Tool and Mch Co	Southington	CT	E	860 628-5551	3220	Interstate Design Company Inc	Agawam	MA	E	413 786-7730	5794
Matthew Porio	Westport	CT	F	203 227-3695	4183	Interstate Mfg Co Inc	Agawam	MA	G	413 789-8674	5795
Mohawk Tool and Die Mfg Co Inc	Bridgeport	CT	F	203 367-2181	349	J-K Tool Co Inc	Agawam	MA	E	413 789-0613	5797
Moldvision LLC	Thompson	CT	G	860 315-1025	3651	Lakewood Industries Inc	Pittsfield	MA	F	413 499-3550	11404
Moore Tool Company Inc **(HQ)**	Bridgeport	CT	E	203 366-3224	350	Lansen Mold Co Inc	Hancock	MA	F	413 443-5328	9025
Newhart Products Inc	Milford	CT	E	203 878-3546	1854	M & H Engineering Co Inc	Danvers	MA	E	978 777-1222	8200
Noujaim Tool Co Inc	Waterbury	CT	E	203 753-4441	3952	Mack Prototype Inc	Gardner	MA	E	978 632-3700	8893
Oxford General Industries Inc	Prospect	CT	F	203 758-4467	2837	Magnus Molding Inc	Pittsfield	MA	E	413 443-1192	11408
P&G Metal Components Corp	Bloomfield	CT	F	860 243-2220	199	Mar-Lee Companies Inc **(HQ)**	Fitchburg	MA	D	978 343-9600	8662
Paragon Tool Company Inc	Manchester	CT	G	860 647-9935	1627	Mayhew Basque Plastics LLC	Westminster	MA	F	978 537-5219	13273
Plainville Machine & TI Co Inc	Bristol	CT	E	860 589-5595	481	Millennium Die Group Inc	Three Rivers	MA	E	413 283-3500	12430
Plastic Design Intl Inc **(PA)**	Middletown	CT	E	860 632-2001	1771	Modern Mold and Tool Inc **(PA)**	Pittsfield	MA	E	413 443-1192	11412
Pmt Group Inc **(PA)**	Bridgeport	CT	C	203 367-8675	359	Moldmaster Engineering Inc	Pittsfield	MA	E	413 442-5793	11413
Precision Punch + Tooling Corp **(PA)**	Berlin	CT	D	860 229-9902	79	Mtd Micro Molding Inc	Charlton	MA	E	508 248-0111	7893
Preferred Tool & Die Inc **(PA)**	Shelton	CT	E	203 925-8525	3054	Neu-Tool Design Inc	Wilmington	MA	E	978 658-5881	13437
Producto Corporation **(HQ)**	Bridgeport	CT	F	203 366-3224	363	New England Die Cutting Inc	Methuen	MA	E	978 374-0789	10340
Quality Engineering Svcs Inc	Wallingford	CT	E	203 269-5054	3843	Northeast Plastics Inc	Wakefield	MA	E	781 245-5512	12523
Quality Wire Edm Inc	Bristol	CT	G	860 583-9867	487	Ocean and Common Inc	Leominster	MA	E	978 537-4102	9689
R&R Tool & Die LLC	East Windsor	CT	G	860 627-9197	1083	Orchard Tool & Die Inc	Indian Orchard	MA	G	413 433-1233	9473
Ramar-Hall Inc	Middlefield	CT	E	860 349-1081	1728	Packaging Devices Inc **(PA)**	Teaticket	MA	F	508 548-0224	12379
Reno Machine Company Inc	Newington	CT	D	860 666-5641	2321	Pearl Die-Cutting & Finshg LLC	Woburn	MA	F	781 721-9000	13632
Reynolds Carbide Die Co Inc	Thomaston	CT	E	860 283-8246	3627	Pen Ro Mold and Tool Inc	Pittsfield	MA	E	413 499-0464	11416
Richards Machine Tool Co Inc	Newington	CT	F	860 436-2938	2322	Pilgrim Tool & Die Co Inc	Worcester	MA	G	508 753-0190	13769
Rintec Corporation	Waterbury	CT	F	860 274-3697	3966	Pittsfield Plastics Engrg LLC	Pittsfield	MA	D	413 442-0067	11419
Roto-Die Company Inc	East Windsor	CT	E	860 292-7030	1084	Premier Roll & Tool Inc	North Attleboro	MA	E	508 695-2551	10885
Royal Machine and Tool Corp	Berlin	CT	F	860 828-6555	83	S Ralph Cross and Sons Inc	Holyoke	MA	E	978 865-8112	9279
SA Manchester LLC	Manchester	CT	D	860 533-7500	1634	Samtan Engineering Corp	Malden	MA	E	781 322-7880	10026
Sandur Tool Co	Waterbury	CT	G	203 753-0004	3967	Sancliff Inc	Worcester	MA	E	508 795-0747	13794
Scan Tool & Mold Inc	Trumbull	CT	E	203 459-4950	3731	Skg Associates Inc	Dedham	MA	G	781 878-7250	8250
Sirois Tool Company Inc **(PA)**	Berlin	CT	E	860 828-5327	85	Sonicron Systems Corporation	Westfield	MA	F	413 562-5218	13209
Skico Manufacturing Co LLC	Hamden	CT	G	203 230-1305	1455	Southbridge Tool & Mfg Inc	Dudley	MA	E	508 764-6819	8324
Skillcraft Machine Tool Co	South Windsor	CT	F	860 953-1246	3180	Srd Holdings Inc	North Attleboro	MA	E	508 695-5656	10888
Somerset Plastics Company Inc	Middletown	CT	E	860 635-1601	1782	Star Base Technologies Inc	Pittsfield	MA	E	413 499-4005	11424
Straton Industries Inc	Stratford	CT	D	203 375-4488	3578	Stuart Allyn Co Inc	Pittsfield	MA	G	413 443-7306	11425
Taco Fasteners Inc	Plainville	CT	F	860 747-5597	2782	Superior Die & Stamping Inc	Attleboro	MA	E	774 203-3674	6067
The Lyons Tool & Die Company	Meriden	CT	E	203 238-2689	1707	Synventive Molding Solutions Inc **(HQ)**	Peabody	MA	C	978 750-8065	11345
Total Concept Tool Inc	Branford	CT	E	203 483-1130	283	Tech Ridge Inc	Chelmsford	MA	E	978 256-5741	7963
Watertown Jig Bore Service Inc	Watertown	CT	E	860 274-5898	4037	Thomson Service Corp	Franklin	MA	F	508 528-2000	8872
Watertown Plastics Inc	Watertown	CT	E	860 274-7535	4038	Ultraclad Corporation	Newburyport	MA	G	978 358-7945	10723
Weimann Brothers Mfg Co	Derby	CT	F	203 735-3311	894	Uneco Manufacturing Inc	Chicopee	MA	E	413 594-2700	8066
Wepco Plastics Inc	Middlefield	CT	E	860 349-3407	1731	United Tool & Machine Corp **(PA)**	Lawrence	MA	E	978 658-5500	9607
West-Conn Tool and Die Inc	Shelton	CT	E	203 538-5081	3077	V&M Tool & Die Inc	Leominster	MA	E	978 534-8814	9715
Westminster Tool Inc	Plainfield	CT	E	860 564-6966	2741	Vogform Tool & Die Co Inc	West Springfield	MA	F	413 737-6947	13051
Winthrop Tool LLC	Essex	CT	G	860 526-9079	1173	W M Gulliksen Mfg Co Inc **(PA)**	South Weymouth	MA	F	617 323-5750	11979
A & M Tool & Die Company Inc	Southbridge	MA	E	508 764-3241	12008	Westfield Tool & Die Co Inc	Westfield	MA	E	413 562-2393	13222
A Luongo & Sons Incorporated	Bridgewater	MA	G	508 226-0788	7218	Whip City Tool & Die Corp	Southwick	MA	E	413 569-5528	12053
Abco Tool & Die Inc	Hyannis	MA	E	508 771-3225	9428	Whitman Tool & Die Company Inc	Whitman	MA	E	781 447-0421	13354
Accutech Packaging Inc	Foxboro	MA	D	508 543-3800	8689	Kennebec Technologies	Augusta	ME	D	207 626-0188	4474
Adt/Diversity Inc	Attleboro	MA	G	508 222-9601	5991	Maine Mold & Machine Inc	Hartford	ME	G	207 388-2732	4876
Advanced Prototypes & Molding	Leominster	MA	G	978 534-0584	9632	OBrien Consolidated Inds	Lewiston	ME	E	207 783-8543	4981
Alsco Industries Inc	Sturbridge	MA	D	508 347-1199	12248	Aluminum Castings Inc	Wilton	NH	G	603 654-9695	15701
Amherst Machine Co	Amherst	MA	E	413 549-4551	5858	Atlantic Microtool	Salem	NH	G	603 898-3212	15509
Anderson Power Products Inc **(HQ)**	Sterling	MA	D	978 422-3600	12154	Berube Tool & Die Inc	Plaistow	NH	G	603 382-2224	15337
Ar-Ro Engineering Company Inc	Uxbridge	MA	F	401 766-6669	12477	Bocra Industries Inc	Seabrook	NH	E	603 474-3598	15585
Atco Plastics Inc	Plainville	MA	F	508 695-3573	11429	Comstock Industries Inc	Meredith	NH	E	603 279-7045	14968
Banner Mold & Die Co Inc	Leominster	MA	E	978 534-6558	9638	Contour Fine Tooling Inc	Keene	NH	G	603 876-4908	14593
Baril Corporation	Haverhill	MA	E	978 373-7910	9076	Freudenberg-Nok General Partnr	Ashland	NH	D	603 968-7187	13900
Barnard Die Inc	Wakefield	MA	F	781 246-9117	12500	Hy-Ten Tool & Development Corp	Milford	NH	E	603 673-1611	15029
Berkshire Mnufactured Pdts Inc	Newburyport	MA	C	978 462-8161	10670	Live Free or Die Alliance	Hampton	NH	F	210 232-8779	14406
Bermer Tool & Die Inc	Southbridge	MA	E	508 764-2521	12011	Mrpc Northeast LLC	Hudson	NH	E	603 880-3616	14530
Boniface Tool & Die Inc	Dudley	MA	E	508 764-3248	8317	New England Industries Inc	Lebanon	NH	E	603 448-5330	14696
Brolan Tool Inc	Leominster	MA	E	978 537-0290	9644	North East Cutting Die Corp	Dover	NH	E	603 436-8952	14242
Cavallero Plastics Inc	Pittsfield	MA	D	413 443-0925	11395	Precision Depaneling Mchs LLC	Fremont	NH	F	540 248-1381	14329
CE Baird Corporation	Lancaster	MA	F	978 365-3867	9525	Rays Tool & Die Co Inc	Somersworth	NH	G	603 692-5978	15623
CE Baird Corporation	Leominster	MA	F	978 751-8432	9650	Stamping Technologies Inc	Laconia	NH	E	603 524-5958	14671
Columbia ASC Inc	Lawrence	MA	F	978 683-2205	9554	Sunset Tool Inc	Keene	NH	E	603 355-2246	14623
Connell Limited Partnership **(PA)**	Boston	MA	F	617 737-2700	6665	Talbot Hill Holdings Corp	Swanzey	NH	E	603 357-2523	15646
Costa Precision Mfg Corp **(PA)**	Chicopee	MA	E	603 542-5229	8021	Technical Tool & Design LLC	Northfield	NH	C	603 286-1600	15269
Csw Inc **(PA)**	Ludlow	MA	D	413 589-1311	9943	Temco Tool Company Inc	Manchester	NH	E	603 622-6989	14941
D V Die Cutting Inc	Danvers	MA	E	978 777-0300	8177	Whelen Engineering Co	Charlestown	NH	A	860 526-9504	14069

Company	CITY	ST	EMP	PHONE	ENTRY#
Clear Carbon & Components Inc	Bristol	RI	E	401 254-5085	15758
Conley Casting Supply Corp (PA)	Warwick	RI	F	401 461-4710	16797
Fielding Manufacturing Inc	Cranston	RI	D	401 461-0400	15860
Formex Inc	East Greenwich	RI	F	401 885-9800	15986
GA Rel Manufacturing Company	Providence	RI	F	401 331-5455	16524
Goodwin-Bradley Pattern Co Inc	Providence	RI	F	401 461-5220	16525
Guill Tool & Engrg Co Inc	West Warwick	RI	D	401 822-8186	16908
Henry A Evers Corp	Cranston	RI	F	401 781-4767	15872
Ldc Inc	East Providence	RI	F	401 861-4667	16029
Matrix I LLC	East Providence	RI	D	401 434-3040	16030
Mono Die Cutting Co Inc	Riverside	RI	F	401 434-1274	16658
Newport Tool & Die Inc	Middletown	RI	F	401 847-6711	16181
Rol-Flo Engineering Inc	Westerly	RI	F	401 596-0060	16942
Royal Diversified Products	Warren	RI	E	401 245-6900	16767
Stearns Tool Company	Providence	RI	G	401 351-4765	16616
Tri-Bro Tool Co Inc	Cranston	RI	E	401 781-6323	15921
Nolato Gw Inc (HQ)	Bethel	VT	B	802 234-9941	17060
North Hartland Tool Corp (PA)	North Hartland	VT	D	802 295-3196	17420
Preci-Manufacturing Inc	Winooski	VT	F	802 655-2414	17768
Raymond Gadues Inc	Swanton	VT	E	802 868-2033	17641
Richard Mrchssult DBA Bngtson	Canaan	VT	G	802 266-9666	17169
Vermont Mold & Tool Corp	Barnet	VT	G	802 633-2300	16995
Vmt LLC	Groton	VT	E	802 592-3146	17279
Yankee Medical Inc (DH)	Burlington	VT	F	802 863-4591	17164

3545 Machine tool accessories

Company	CITY	ST	EMP	PHONE	ENTRY#
Accu-Rite Tool & Mfg Co	Tolland	CT	F	860 688-4844	3654
Alden Corporation	Wolcott	CT	D	203 879-8830	4361
Alden Tool Company Inc	Berlin	CT	E	860 828-3556	47
All Five Tool Co Inc	Berlin	CT	E	860 583-1693	48
American Grippers Inc	Trumbull	CT	F	203 459-8345	3710
Apex Machine Tool Company Inc	Cheshire	CT	D	860 677-2884	571
Arna Machine Company	Bristol	CT	F	860 583-0628	396
Center Broach & Machine Co	Meriden	CT	G	203 235-6329	1659
Century Tool and Design Inc	Milldale	CT	F	860 621-6748	1900
Danjon Manufacturing Corp	Cheshire	CT	E	203 272-7258	587
Drill Masters-Eldorado Tool Inc	Milford	CT	F	203 878-1711	1819
E and S Gage Inc	Tolland	CT	F	860 872-5917	3659
Eastern Broach Inc	Plainville	CT	F	860 828-4800	2755
Edmunds Manufacturing Company (PA)	Farmington	CT	D	860 677-2813	1218
Edrive Actuators Inc	Newington	CT	G	860 953-0588	2290
Enjet Aero Newington Inc	Newington	CT	D	860 953-0686	2291
Ewald Instruments Corp	Lakeville	CT	F	860 491-9042	1545
Fletcher-Terry Company LLC (PA)	East Berlin	CT	D	860 828-3400	911
Floyd Manufacturing Co Inc	Cromwell	CT	F	860 829-1920	692
Goldenrod Corporation	Beacon Falls	CT	E	203 723-4400	40
Guhring Inc	Bloomfield	CT	E	860 216-5948	167
H & B Tool & Eng Co Inc	South Windsor	CT	F	860 528-9341	3153
Hermann Schmidt Company Inc	South Windsor	CT	F	860 289-3347	3155
Highland Manufacturing Inc	Manchester	CT	E	860 646-5142	1603
Industrial Magnetics Inc	Windsor	CT	D	508 853-3232	4283
Iswiss Corporation	Manchester	CT	G	860 327-4200	1606
Jetct Inc	Southington	CT	E	860 621-5381	3217
Jjioc Inc	Southington	CT	E	860 628-4655	3218
Johnson Gage Company	Bloomfield	CT	E	860 242-5541	177
Kinetic Tool Co Inc	East Windsor	CT	F	860 627-5882	1078
Leeco Inc	Avon	CT	G	860 404-8876	28
LLC Dow Gage	Berlin	CT	G	860 828-5327	74
Lord & Hodge Inc	Middletown	CT	F	860 632-7006	1760
Marena Industries Inc	East Hartford	CT	F	860 528-9701	1004
Meyer Gage Co Inc	South Windsor	CT	F	860 528-6526	3163
Micro Insert Incorporated	Milldale	CT	G	860 621-5789	1902
Miracle Instruments Co	Lebanon	CT	F	860 642-7745	1549
Moon Cutter Co Inc	Hamden	CT	E	203 288-9249	1444
Moore Tool Company Inc (HQ)	Bridgeport	CT	E	203 366-3224	350
New England Tooling Inc	Killingworth	CT	F	800 866-5105	1544
O S Walker Company Inc (HQ)	Windsor	CT	E	508 853-3232	4292
Paradigm Prcision Holdings LLC	East Berlin	CT	D	860 829-3663	915
Perry Technology Corporation	New Hartford	CT	D	860 738-2525	2107
Pmt Group Inc (PA)	Bridgeport	CT	C	203 367-8675	359
Powerhold Inc	Middlefield	CT	F	860 349-1044	1727
Preferred Tool & Die Inc	Shelton	CT	E	203 925-8525	3055
Preferred Utilities Mfg Corp (HQ)	Danbury	CT	D	203 743-6741	799
Producto Corporation (HQ)	Bridgeport	CT	D	203 366-3224	363
Q Alpha Inc	Colchester	CT	E	860 357-7340	664
R&R Tool & Die LLC	East Windsor	CT	G	860 627-9197	1083
Ringfeder Pwr Transm USA Corp (HQ)	Bolton	CT	F	201 666-3320	222
Royal Machine and Tool Corp	Berlin	CT	E	860 828-6555	83
Seals-It Inc	Ellington	CT	G	860 979-0060	1114
Sirois Tool Company Inc (PA)	Berlin	CT	E	860 828-5327	85
Sjm Properties Inc	Ellington	CT	G	860 979-0060	1115
Skico Manufacturing Co LLC	Hamden	CT	G	203 230-1305	1455
Somma Tool Company	Waterbury	CT	E	203 753-2114	3970

Company	CITY	ST	EMP	PHONE	ENTRY#
Southwick & Meister Inc	Meriden	CT	C	203 237-0000	1701
Space Electronics LLC	Berlin	CT	E	860 829-0001	86
Swanson Tool Manufacturing Inc	West Hartford	CT	E	860 953-1641	4084
The Lyons Tool & Die Company	Meriden	CT	E	203 238-2689	1707
The Viking Tool Company	Shelton	CT	E	203 929-1457	3068
Thought Out Co LLC	Monroe	CT	G	203 987-5452	1925
Walker Magnetics Group Inc	Windsor	CT	D	508 853-3232	4314
Zero Check LLC	Thomaston	CT	G	860 283-5629	3647
Ade Technologies Inc (HQ)	Westwood	MA	D	781 467-3500	13305
Allegion Access Tech LLC	South Easton	MA	E	508 230-2350	11936
American Saw & Mfg Company Inc	East Longmeadow	MA	C	413 525-3961	8369
Ar-Ro Engineering Company Inc	Uxbridge	MA	F	401 766-6669	12477
Arborjet Inc	Woburn	MA	F	781 935-9070	13512
Automec Inc	Waltham	MA	E	781 893-3403	12598
B & E Group LLC	Southwick	MA	E	413 569-5585	12041
Ben Franklin Design Mfg Co Inc	Agawam	MA	F	413 786-4220	5781
Berkshire Precision Tool LLC	Pittsfield	MA	D	413 499-3875	11394
Boston Centerless Inc (PA)	Woburn	MA	D	781 994-5000	13530
Cobra Precision Machining Corp	Petersham	MA	G	603 434-8424	11388
Columbia ASC Inc	Lawrence	MA	E	978 683-2205	9554
Coorstek Inc	Worcester	MA	B	774 317-2600	13710
Cutting Edge Carbide Tech Inc	Athol	MA	G	888 210-9670	5977
D & R Products Co Inc	Hudson	MA	E	978 562-4137	9361
Dff Corp	Agawam	MA	C	413 786-8880	5789
Dienes Corporation	Spencer	MA	E	508 885-6301	12057
Dmt Export Inc	Marlborough	MA	F	508 481-5944	10144
Double E Company LLC (PA)	West Bridgewater	MA	C	508 588-8099	12972
Dynisco Instruments LLC (HQ)	Franklin	MA	C	508 541-9400	8831
Emuge Corp	West Boylston	MA	E	508 595-3600	12962
Esco Technologies Inc	Holliston	MA	E	508 429-4441	9209
Form Roll Die Corp (PA)	Worcester	MA	E	508 755-2010	13725
G & D Tool Co Inc	Salem	MA	F	978 745-0020	11716
Great Neck Saw Mfrs Inc	Millbury	MA	D	508 865-4482	10436
Hassay Savage Broach Co Inc	Turners Falls	MA	F	413 863-9052	12446
Hoppe Technologies Inc	Chicopee	MA	D	413 592-9213	8036
Hutchinson Arospc & Indust Inc	Hopkinton	MA	C	508 417-7000	9328
Industrial Cutting Tools Inc	Westfield	MA	G	413 562-2996	13171
Joma Diamond Tool LLC	East Longmeadow	MA	E	413 525-0760	8381
Kennametal Inc	Greenfield	MA	D	802 626-3331	8994
L Hardy Company Inc (PA)	Worcester	MA	E	508 757-3480	13752
Lapointe Hudson Broach Co Inc	Hudson	MA	E	978 562-7943	9383
Lee Tool Co Inc	Ludlow	MA	F	413 583-8750	9948
LS Starrett Company	Athol	MA	G	978 249-3551	5980
LS Starrett Company (PA)	Athol	MA	A	978 249-3551	5981
Martran Corp	Attleboro Falls	MA	F	508 699-7506	6089
Michael Brisebois	Easthampton	MA	F	413 527-9590	8450
Microcut Inc	Plymouth	MA	G	781 582-8090	11466
Mk Services Corp	Middleton	MA	E	978 777-2196	10390
New England Carbide Inc	Topsfield	MA	E	978 887-0313	12437
Nortek Inc	West Springfield	MA	E	413 781-4777	13038
Pilot Precision Products LLC	South Deerfield	MA	E	413 350-5200	11927
Poly-Tech Diamond Co Inc	North Attleboro	MA	F	508 695-5561	10882
Proto XYZ Inc	New Bedford	MA	F	508 525-6363	10644
Quabbin Inc	Orange	MA	F	978 544-3872	11230
Reed Machinery Inc (PA)	Worcester	MA	F	508 595-9090	13782
Richards Micro-Tool LLC	Plymouth	MA	F	508 746-6900	11474
Safe-T-Cut Inc	Monson	MA	F	413 267-9984	10456
Saint-Gobain Abrasives Inc (HQ)	Worcester	MA	A	508 795-5000	13788
Simonds Saw LLC (PA)	Leominster	MA	G	800 343-1616	9704
Standex International Corp	Wakefield	MA	D	978 538-0808	12537
Symmetry Med New Bedford Inc	New Bedford	MA	F	781 447-6661	10654
Tektron Inc	Topsfield	MA	F	978 887-0091	12439
Thomas Machine Works Inc	Newburyport	MA	G	978 462-7182	10720
Tool Technology Inc	Middleton	MA	F	978 777-5006	10396
Toolmex Indus Solutions Inc (PA)	Northborough	MA	D	508 653-8897	11114
Vogel Capital Inc (HQ)	Marlborough	MA	E	508 481-5944	10232
Vulcan Company Inc (PA)	Hingham	MA	D	781 337-5970	9163
Waverly Tool Rental & Sales Co	Framingham	MA	F	508 872-8866	8811
Wells Tool Company	Greenfield	MA	F	413 773-3465	9005
Contour360 Corp	Cornish	ME	E	207 625-4000	4704
Core Cutter LLC	Farmingdale	ME	F	207 588-7519	4776
Enercon (HQ)	Gray	ME	D	207 657-7000	4841
Maine Scale LLC	Auburn	ME	F	207 777-9500	4443
Mid State Machine Products (PA)	Winslow	ME	C	207 873-6136	5685
Peavey Manufacturing Company	Eddington	ME	E	207 843-7861	4746
Sands Business Eqp & Sups LLC	York	ME	F	207 351-3334	5716
Xuron Corp	Saco	ME	E	207 283-1401	5382
Abrasives & Tools NH Inc	Pembroke	NH	E	603 224-5376	15301
Abtech Inc	Fitzwilliam	NH	E	603 585-7106	14312
Ametek Precitech Inc (HQ)	Keene	NH	D	603 357-2510	14588
Axard LLC	Grantham	NH	F	603 306-7679	14362
Bocra Industries Inc	Seabrook	NH	E	603 474-3598	15585
Chadwick & Trefethen Inc	Portsmouth	NH	F	603 436-2568	15370

	CITY	ST	EMP	PHONE	ENTRY#
Contour Fine Tooling Inc	Keene	NH	G	603 876-4908	14593
Cutting Tool Technologies Inc	Wilton	NH	E	603 654-2550	15704
Datron Dynamics Inc	Milford	NH	E	603 215-5850	15020
Jarvis Cutting Tools Inc	Rochester	NH	D	603 332-9000	15482
Onvio LLC **(PA)**	Salem	NH	F	603 685-0404	15553
R & J Tool Inc **(PA)**	Laconia	NH	G	603 366-4925	14664
Will-Mor Manufacturing LLC	Seabrook	NH	D	603 474-8971	15606
Central Tools Inc **(PA)**	Cranston	RI	E	401 467-8211	15841
Comtorgage Corporation	North Smithfield	RI	F	401 765-0900	16321
Durant Tool Company Inc	North Kingstown	RI	E	401 781-7800	16246
Fielding Mfg - Zinc Dcsting In	Cranston	RI	D	401 461-0400	15861
Hexagon Mfg Intelligence Inc **(DH)**	North Kingstown	RI	D	401 886-2000	16255
Mouldcam Inc	Bristol	RI	G	401 396-5522	15775
Numaco Packaging LLC	East Providence	RI	F	401 438-4952	16035
Rol-Flo Engineering Inc	Westerly	RI	F	401 596-0060	16942
Thurston Manufacturing Company	Smithfield	RI	E	401 232-9100	16732
W L Fuller Inc	Warwick	RI	E	401 467-2900	16876
Wei Inc **(PA)**	Cranston	RI	E	401 781-3904	15928
Kollmorgen Corporation	Brattleboro	VT	E	802 258-3020	17092
Lovejoy Tool Company Inc	Springfield	VT	E	802 885-2194	17620
Preci-Manufacturing Inc	Winooski	VT	D	802 655-2414	17768
Sterling Gun Drills Inc	North Bennington	VT	E	802 442-3525	17412
Tivoly Inc	Derby Line	VT	C	802 873-3106	17213
Trow & Holden Co Inc	Barre	VT	E	802 476-7221	17022
Vermont Precision Tools Inc **(PA)**	Swanton	VT	C	802 868-4246	17645
Vermont Thread Gage LLC	Swanton	VT	F	802 868-4246	17646
Yankee Corporation	Fairfax	VT	D	802 527-0177	17265

3546 Power-driven handtools

	CITY	ST	EMP	PHONE	ENTRY#
Air Tool Sales & Svc Co Inc **(PA)**	Unionville	CT	G	860 673-2714	3746
Alden Corporation	Wolcott	CT	D	203 879-8830	4361
Apex Machine Tool Company Inc	Cheshire	CT	D	860 677-2884	571
Black & Decker (us) Inc	New Britain	CT	G	860 225-5111	2008
Blackstone Industries LLC	Bethel	CT	D	203 792-8622	101
Frasal Tool Co Inc	Newington	CT	F	860 666-3524	2295
HRF Fastener Systems Inc	Bristol	CT	F	860 589-0750	455
Ridge View Associates Inc	Milford	CT	D	203 878-8560	1878
Stanley Black & Decker Inc **(PA)**	New Britain	CT	E	860 225-5111	2065
Stanley Black & Decker Inc	New Britain	CT	C	860 225-5111	2067
Stanley Black & Decker Inc	Southington	CT	F	860 460-9122	3235
Stihl Incorporated	Oxford	CT	E	203 929-8488	2712
Trumpf Inc	Farmington	CT	E	860 255-6000	1254
Trumpf Inc **(DH)**	Farmington	CT	E	860 255-6000	1255
Trumpf Inc	Plainville	CT	G	860 255-6000	2786
Aube Precision Tool Co Inc	Ludlow	MA	G	413 589-9048	9939
Black & Decker (us) Inc	Westwood	MA	F	781 329-3407	13306
Guardair Corporation	Chicopee	MA	E	413 594-4400	8035
Stanley Black & Decker	Boston	MA	G	781 460-4511	7059
Vulcan Company Inc **(PA)**	Hingham	MA	D	781 337-5970	9163
Gary Raymond	Caribou	ME	G	207 498-2549	4675
Reggies Sales & Service	Auburn	ME	G	207 783-0558	4458
Sands Business Eqp & Sups LLC	York	ME	F	207 351-3334	5716
Adhesive Technologies Inc **(PA)**	Hampton	NH	G	603 926-1616	14396
Pneutek Inc	Hudson	NH	F	603 883-1660	14535
Malco Saw Co Inc	Cranston	RI	G	401 942-7380	15891
Textron Inc	Providence	RI	A	401 421-2800	16623
Champlain Valley Equipment Inc	Saint Albans	VT	G	802 524-6782	17518
Leos Small Engines Inc	Morrisville	VT	F	802 888-7247	17384

3547 Rolling mill machinery

	CITY	ST	EMP	PHONE	ENTRY#
Adam Z Golas **(PA)**	New Britain	CT	G	860 224-7178	1996
Compass Group Management LLC **(PA)**	Westport	CT	F	203 221-1703	4162
Ulbrich Stainless Steels	Wallingford	CT	C	203 269-2507	3871
Idex Mpt Inc **(HQ)**	Westwood	MA	D	630 530-3333	13312
JP Plastics Inc	Foxboro	MA	E	508 203-2420	8704
Kinefac Corporation	Worcester	MA	D	508 754-6901	13749
N Ferrara Inc	Somerset	MA	F	508 679-2440	11853
Pfe Rolls Inc	Chicopee	MA	F	978 544-7803	8053
Winchester Precision Tech Ltd	Winchester	NH	F	603 239-6326	15718
Millard Wire Company	Warwick	RI	F	401 737-9330	16837
Millard Wire Company **(PA)**	Warwick	RI	E	401 737-9330	16838

3548 Welding apparatus

	CITY	ST	EMP	PHONE	ENTRY#
Air-Vac Engineering Co Inc **(PA)**	Seymour	CT	E	203 888-9900	2955
Branson Ultrasonics Corp **(DH)**	Brookfield	CT	B	203 796-0400	512
Cadi Co Inc **(PA)**	Naugatuck	CT	F	203 729-1111	1951
Jt Automation LLC	East Granby	CT	F	860 784-1967	938
Linde Advanced Mtl Tech Inc	Manchester	CT	C	860 646-0700	1612
Magnatech LLC	East Granby	CT	D	860 653-2573	939
Sonics & Materials Inc **(PA)**	Newtown	CT	D	203 270-4600	2347
Sonitek Corporation	Milford	CT	E	203 878-9321	1886
AGM Industries Inc	Brockton	MA	E	508 587-3900	7254
Hydro-Test Products Inc	Stow	MA	F	978 897-4647	12246

	CITY	ST	EMP	PHONE	ENTRY#
Kamweld Industries Inc	Norwood	MA	G	617 558-7500	11185
Kamweld Technologies Inc	Norwood	MA	F	781 762-6922	11186
Mitchell Machine Incorporated **(PA)**	Springfield	MA	F	413 739-9693	12114
Power Systems Integrity Inc	Northborough	MA	F	508 393-1655	11106
Precision Electronics Corp	Marshfield	MA	F	781 834-6677	10244
Stan Rubinstein Associates Inc	Walpole	MA	F	508 668-6044	12576
Triad Inc	Plainville	MA	G	508 695-2247	11444
Weld Engineering Co Inc	Shrewsbury	MA	F	508 842-2224	11848
Bortech Corporation	Keene	NH	F	603 358-4030	14591
Centruct Manufacturing LLC	West Lebanon	NH	F	603 298-6191	15680
Contract Fusion Inc	East Providence	RI	E	401 438-1298	16010
Nordson Efd LLC **(DH)**	East Providence	RI	C	401 431-7000	16034
Vesuvius America Inc **(DH)**	Providence	RI	E		16640
YS Enterprises Inc	East Ryegate	VT	G	802 238-0902	17219

3549 Metalworking machinery, nec

	CITY	ST	EMP	PHONE	ENTRY#
Adamczyk Enterprises Inc	Enfield	CT	G	860 745-9830	1120
Alpha-Core Inc	Shelton	CT	E	203 954-0050	2980
Fletcher-Terry Company LLC **(PA)**	East Berlin	CT	D	860 828-3400	911
Foilmark Inc	Bloomfield	CT	G	860 243-0343	165
J & P Manufacturing LLC	Plainville	CT	F	860 919-8287	2765
Jovil Universal LLC	Danbury	CT	F	203 792-6700	763
L M Gill Welding and Mfr LLC **(PA)**	Manchester	CT	D	860 647-9931	1610
Merritt Extruder Corp	Hamden	CT	E	203 230-8100	1440
Nni Liquidation Corp	Shelton	CT	F	203 929-2221	3040
P/A Industries Inc **(PA)**	Bloomfield	CT	E	860 243-8306	200
Rotad Inc	Stamford	CT	F	203 708-8900	3453
Shuster-Mettler Corp	Plainville	CT	E	203 562-3178	2780
Te Connectivity Corporation	Stafford Springs	CT	E	860 684-8000	3260
True Position Mfg LLC	South Windsor	CT	G	860 291-2987	3186
Tyger Tool Inc	Stratford	CT	F	203 375-4344	3581
Automec Inc	Waltham	MA	E	781 893-3403	12598
Broomfield Laboratories Inc **(PA)**	Bolton	MA	F	978 779-6600	6495
Entwistle Company LLC **(PA)**	Hudson	MA	D	508 481-4000	9364
Entwistle Trust	Hudson	MA	C	508 481-4000	9365
Foilmark Inc **(HQ)**	Newburyport	MA	D	978 225-8200	10683
Gear/Tronics Industries Inc	North Billerica	MA	D	781 933-1400	10915
Gorman Machine Corp	Middleboro	MA	E	508 923-9462	10359
Kamrowski Metal Refinishing	Boston	MA	G	508 877-0367	6839
Ktron Incorporated	Marlborough	MA	E	508 229-0919	10178
Lawrence Sigler	Princeton	MA	G	510 782-6737	11495
Mestek Inc	Westfield	MA	E	413 568-9571	13185
Mestek Inc **(PA)**	Westfield	MA	E	470 898-4533	13186
Micro Electronics Inc	Seekonk	MA	F	508 761-9161	11781
Milara Inc	Milford	MA	D	508 533-5322	10404
Shanklin Research Corporation	Ayer	MA	G	978 772-2090	6195
Soft Robotics Inc	Bedford	MA	D	617 391-0612	6269
Symbotic LLC **(HQ)**	Wilmington	MA	C	978 284-2800	13460
Teledyne Instruments Inc	North Falmouth	MA	E	508 563-1000	11017
Hill-Loma Inc	Gorham	ME	E	207 854-9791	4822
Granite State Manufacturing	Manchester	NH	F	800 464-7646	14855
Precision Depaneling Mchs LLC	Fremont	NH	F	540 248-1381	14329
Standex International Corp **(PA)**	Salem	NH	E	603 893-9701	15563
Applitek Technologies Corp	Providence	RI	G	401 467-0007	16473
Cove Metal Company Inc **(PA)**	Pawtucket	RI	F	401 724-3500	16359
Custom Centric Machining LLC	Bristol	RI	G	401 952-1804	15761
Durant Tool Company Inc	North Kingstown	RI	E	401 781-7800	16246
Gasbarre Products Inc	Cranston	RI	F	401 467-5200	15865
Huestis Machine Corporation	Bristol	RI	E	401 253-5500	15769
Providence Wire Creations Inc	Providence	RI	F	401 490-3227	16594
Wardwell Braiding Machine Company **(PA)**	Central Falls	RI	E		
401 724-8800	15801				
Abacus Automation Inc	Bennington	VT	E	802 442-3662	17035

3552 Textile machinery

	CITY	ST	EMP	PHONE	ENTRY#
Image Star LLC	Middletown	CT	G	888 632-5515	1753
Reynolds Carbide Die Co Inc	Thomaston	CT	E	860 283-8246	3627
Sonic Corp	Stratford	CT	F	203 375-0063	3575
Systematic Automation Inc	Farmington	CT	E	310 218-3361	1249
Accellent Acquisition Corp	Wilmington	MA	A	978 570-6900	13370
Accellent Holdings Corp	Wilmington	MA	A	978 570-6900	13371
Holyoke Machine Company	Holyoke	MA	E	413 534-5612	9261
Lamb Knitting Machine Corp	Chicopee	MA	G	413 592-2501	8044
Lloyd & Bouvier Inc	Clinton	MA	E	978 365-5700	8082
Micrex Corporation	Walpole	MA	F	508 660-1900	12569
Maine Stitching Spc LLC	Skowhegan	ME	F	207 812-5207	5472
Orion Ropeworks LLC	Winslow	ME	D	207 877-2224	5688
Ametek Precitech Inc **(HQ)**	Keene	NH	D	603 357-2510	14588
Harrisville Designs Inc **(PA)**	Harrisville	NH	G	603 827-3333	14432
Cove Metal Company Inc **(PA)**	Pawtucket	RI	F	401 724-3500	16359
Greystone Incorporated	Lincoln	RI	F	401 333-0444	16139
James L Gallagher Inc	Little Compton	RI	F	508 758-3102	16161

	CITY	ST	EMP	PHONE	ENTRY#
Parkinson Machinery & Manufacturing Corp	Woonsocket	RI			C
401 762-2100	16971				
Reed Gowdey Company	Central Falls	RI	G	401 723-6114	15795
Richmond Graphic Products Inc	Providence	RI	F	401 233-2700	16605
Standard Mill Machinery Corp	West Warwick	RI	G	401 822-7871	16923
Stolberger Incorporated	Central Falls	RI	E	401 724-8800	15797
Texcel Inc	Cumberland	RI	F	401 727-2113	15968
Wardwell Braiding Machine Company (PA)	Central Falls	RI			E
401 724-8800	15801				

3553 Woodworking machinery

	CITY	ST	EMP	PHONE	ENTRY#
United Abrasives Inc (PA)	North Windham	CT	B	860 456-7131	2451
Woodcrafters LLP	Thomaston	CT	G	860 355-1022	3646
Heyes Forest Products Inc	Orange	MA	G	978 544-8801	11223
Lawrence Sigler	Princeton	MA	F	510 782-6737	11495
Simonds International LLC (HQ)	Fitchburg	MA	B	978 424-0100	8675
Downeast Machine & Engrg Inc (PA)	Mechanic Falls	ME	F	207 345-8111	5050
Machinery Service Co Inc	Wiscasset	ME	G	207 882-6788	5698
HMC Corporation (PA)	Hopkinton	NH	E	603 746-3399	14477
Williams & Hussey Mch Co Inc	Amherst	NH	F	603 732-0219	13895

3554 Paper industries machinery

	CITY	ST	EMP	PHONE	ENTRY#
Andritz Shw Inc	Torrington	CT	E	860 496-8888	3670
Bar-Plate Manufacturing Co	Hamden	CT	F	203 397-0033	1413
Dcg-Apvh Acquisition Co LLC	Newington	CT	E	636 488-3200	2286
Goldenrod Corporation	Beacon Falls	CT	E	203 723-4400	40
Sonic Corp	Stratford	CT	F	203 375-0063	3575
Zatorski Coating Co Inc	East Hampton	CT	F	860 267-9889	968
Andritz Inc	Springfield	MA	C	413 733-6603	12075
Butler Automatic Inc (PA)	Middleboro	MA	D	508 923-0544	10353
First Mate Prtg Converting Inc (HQ)	Gardner	MA	D	978 630-1028	8886
Functional Coatings LLC	Newburyport	MA	D	978 462-0796	10684
Holyoke Machine Company	Holyoke	MA	E	413 534-5612	9261
Kadant Inc	Auburn	MA	C	508 791-8171	6115
Kadant Inc	Auburn	MA	C	508 791-8171	6116
Kadant Inc (PA)	Westford	MA	C	978 776-2000	13244
Magnat-Fairview Inc	Chicopee	MA	D	413 593-5742	8046
Micrex Corporation	Walpole	MA	F	508 660-1900	12569
Mitchell Machine Incorporated (PA)	Springfield	MA	F	413 739-9693	12114
Mm-Apvh Acquisition Co LLC (HQ)	Westminster	MA	F	978 516-7050	13275
Montague Industries Inc	Turners Falls	MA	F	413 863-4301	12453
Snyder Machine Co Inc	Ipswich	MA	F	978 356-4488	9497
Thomas M Leonard Inc	West Bridgewater	MA	G		12984
Thomson Service Corp	Franklin	MA	F	508 528-2000	8872
Valmet Inc	Lenox	MA	C	413 637-2424	9627
Webco Engineering Inc	Southborough	MA	F	508 303-0500	12006
C P Technologies Inc (PA)	Saco	ME	F	207 286-1167	5364
Johnston Dandy Company (PA)	Lincoln	ME	E	207 794-6571	5009
Southworth Intl Group Inc (PA)	Falmouth	ME	D	207 878-0700	4772
Valmet Inc	Biddeford	ME	C	207 282-1521	4593
Bfmc LLC	Berlin	NH	E	603 752-4550	13980
Dahle North America Inc	Peterborough	NH	F	603 924-0003	15314
GL&v USA Inc	Nashua	NH	B	603 882-2711	15105
Valmet Inc	Nashua	NH	C	603 882-2711	15181
Maxson Automatic Machinery Co (PA)	Westerly	RI	E	401 596-0162	16935
Stearns Tool Company	Providence	RI	G	401 351-4765	16616
Ashe America Inc	Brattleboro	VT	E	802 254-0200	17073

3555 Printing trades machinery

	CITY	ST	EMP	PHONE	ENTRY#
Arico Engineering Inc	North Franklin	CT	G	860 642-7040	2381
Dymo Corporation	Norwalk	CT	D		2494
I Q Technology LLC	Enfield	CT	E	860 749-7255	1135
Image Star LLC	Middletown	CT	G	888 632-5515	1753
Santec Corporation	Milford	CT	F	203 878-1379	1882
Systematic Automation Inc	Farmington	CT	E	310 218-3361	1249
Trimech Solutions LLC	Deep River	CT	F	860 526-5869	886
Verico Technology LLC (HQ)	Enfield	CT	F	860 871-1200	1157
2l Inc	Hudson	MA	F	978 567-8867	9350
Armstrong Machine Co Inc	Beverly	MA	F	978 232-9466	6326
Art Swiss Corporation	New Bedford	MA	G	508 999-3281	10569
Aurora Imaging Technology Inc	Wellesley	MA	D	617 522-6900	12937
Autoroll Print Technologies LLC	Middleton	MA	F	978 777-2160	10380
Blade Tech Systems Inc	Plymouth	MA	G	508 830-9506	11451
Butler Automatic Inc (PA)	Middleboro	MA	D	508 923-0544	10353
Ecrm Incorporated (PA)	North Andover	MA	E	978 581-0207	10830
Flex-O-Graphic Prtg Plate Inc	Worcester	MA	E	508 752-8100	13724
Gem Gravure Co Inc (PA)	Hanover	MA	D	781 878-0456	9032
Honorcraft LLC	Stoughton	MA	F	781 341-0410	12214
Hosokawa Micron Intl Inc	Northborough	MA	E	508 655-1123	11098
Inscribe Inc	Woburn	MA	E	781 933-3331	13586
Integrted Web Fnshg Systems In	Avon	MA	E	508 580-5809	6151
Jet Graphics LLC	Avon	MA	G	508 580-5809	6153
Jnj Industries Inc	Franklin	MA	E	508 553-0529	8846

	CITY	ST	EMP	PHONE	ENTRY#
Milara Inc	Milford	MA	D	508 533-5322	10404
Nes Worldwide Inc	Westfield	MA	E	413 562-8000	13192
Photop Aegis Inc	Woburn	MA	G	781 904-4000	13636
Signature Engrv Systems Inc	Holyoke	MA	E	413 533-7500	9281
Teca-Print USA Corp	Winchester	MA	F	781 369-1084	13492
Tecnau Inc (DH)	North Andover	MA	E	978 608-0500	10851
Thomas M Leonard Inc	West Bridgewater	MA	G		12984
Tooling Research Inc (PA)	Walpole	MA	F	508 668-1950	12578
W Gillies Technologies LLC	Worcester	MA	E	508 852-2502	13827
W Oliver Tripp Company (PA)	Weymouth	MA	E	781 848-1230	13338
Westcon Mfg Inc	Brunswick	ME	E	207 725-5537	4657
Cc1 Inc	Portsmouth	NH	E	603 319-2000	15368
Electronics For Imaging Inc	West Lebanon	NH	B	603 279-6800	15683
Gp2 Technologies Inc	Bow	NH	G	603 226-0336	13998
Manroland Goss Web Systems AMR (DH)	Exeter	NH			B
603 750-6600	14294				
Manroland Web Systems Inc	Exeter	NH	F	630 920-5850	14295
Prodways	Merrimack	NH	G	763 568-7966	14999
Vidarr Inc	Portsmouth	NH	G	877 636-8432	15448
A2b Tracking Solutions Inc	Portsmouth	RI	E	401 683-5215	16434
Dasko Identification Products	Warren	RI	F	401 435-6500	16757
Fine Line Graphics Inc (PA)	Smithfield	RI	E	401 349-3300	16701
R & D Technologies Inc	North Kingstown	RI	E	401 885-6400	16276

3556 Food products machinery

	CITY	ST	EMP	PHONE	ENTRY#
A & I Concentrate LLC	Shelton	CT	E	203 447-1938	2977
Capricorn Investors III LP (PA)	Greenwich	CT	F	203 861-6600	1326
Conair LLC	Torrington	CT	D	800 492-7464	3676
EMI Inc	Clinton	CT	G	860 669-1199	643
Jarvis Products Corporation (HQ)	Middletown	CT	F	860 347-7271	1754
Pro Scientific Inc	Oxford	CT	F	203 267-4600	2708
Sonic Corp	Stratford	CT	F	203 375-0063	3575
Taylor Coml Foodservice Inc	Farmington	CT	A	336 245-6400	1250
Treif USA Inc	Shelton	CT	F	203 929-9930	3072
Watercure Farm LLC	Pomfret Center	CT	G	860 208-4083	2814
Alfa Laval Inc	Newburyport	MA	D	978 465-5777	10666
Baker Parts Inc	Westport	MA	G	508 878-5436	13293
C H Babb Co Inc	Raynham	MA	G	508 977-0600	11582
Consolidated Machine Corporation	Billerica	MA	E	617 782-6072	6428
Electrolyzer Corp	West Newbury	MA	G	978 363-5349	13008
Glenpharmer Distillery LLC	Franklin	MA	E	508 654-6577	8841
Grandten Distilling LLC	Boston	MA	G	617 269-0497	6770
Jbt Aerotech Corp	Boston	MA	E	857 574-3170	6821
Jimsan Enterprises Inc	West Bridgewater	MA	G	508 587-3666	12973
Maxant Industries Inc	Devens	MA	F	978 772-0576	8279
Oesco Inc	Conway	MA	E	413 369-4335	8143
Reiser Creations	Easthampton	MA	G	508 259-5794	8460
Sharp Services Inc	Saugus	MA	G	781 854-3334	11766
Somerset Industries Inc	Lowell	MA	F	978 667-3355	9924
South Shore Packing Inc	Brockton	MA	E	508 941-0458	7307
Wilevco Inc	Billerica	MA	F	978 667-0400	6491
Acana Northeast Inc	Pembroke	NH	G	800 922-2629	15302
Admix Inc	Londonderry	NH	E	603 627-2340	14727
Burlodge USA Inc	Litchfield	NH	E	336 776-1010	14712
Cooking Solutions Group Inc (HQ)	Salem	NH	F	603 893-9701	15516
Distillery Network Inc	Manchester	NH	G	603 997-6786	14842
Heat and Control Inc	Pembroke	NH	E	603 225-5190	15303
Mastermatic Inc	Pembroke	NH	G	603 225-5190	15304
Superior Ice Cream Eqp LLC	Bow	NH	F	603 225-4207	14011
Univex Corporation	Salem	NH	D	603 893-6191	15569
Charcuterie Artisans	Mapleville	RI	F	401 426-9499	16166
Cooking Solutions Group Inc	Essex Junction	VT	C	864 963-3471	17231
Edlund Company LLC	Burlington	VT	D	802 862-9661	17133
Mfi Corp	Burlington	VT	D	802 658-6600	17145
Vermont Evaporator Company LLC (PA)	Montpelier	VT	G	802 522-8499	17376

3559 Special industry machinery, nec

	CITY	ST	EMP	PHONE	ENTRY#
Asml Us LLC	Wilton	CT	A	203 761-4000	4231
Bausch Advanced Tech Inc (PA)	Clinton	CT	C	860 669-7380	637
Berkshire Photonics LLC	Torrington	CT	G	860 868-0412	3671
Davis-Standard Holdings Inc (PA)	Pawcatuck	CT	B	860 599-1010	2718
Day Machine Systems Inc	New Britain	CT	F	860 229-3440	2020
Devivo Industries Inc	Waterbury	CT	E	203 270-1552	3906
Edward Segal Inc	Thomaston	CT	E	860 283-5821	3618
Emhart Glass Inc (DH)	Windsor	CT	D	860 298-7340	4272
Environmental Systems Products Inc	East Granby	CT	C	860 653-0081	933
Farrel Corporation (DH)	Ansonia	CT	D	203 736-5500	14
Gerber Technology LLC (HQ)	Tolland	CT	B	800 321-2448	3662
Industrial Magnetics Inc	Windsor	CT	F	508 853-3232	4283
Intact Solutions LLC	New Milford	CT	G	860 350-1900	2248
Interlab Incorporated	Danbury	CT	E	203 794-0209	759
James A Bean Corporation	Torrington	CT	F	860 489-1404	3685
Jet Process Corporation	Wallingford	CT	G	203 985-6000	3823

SIC

	CITY	ST	EMP	PHONE	ENTRY#
Johnstone Company Inc	North Haven	CT	E	203 239-5834	2419
Lyman Products Corporation (PA)	Middletown	CT	D	860 632-2020	1761
Lynch Corp	Greenwich	CT	F	203 452-3007	1340
Media One LLC	Hamden	CT	E	203 745-5825	1439
Merritt Extruder Corp	Hamden	CT	E	203 230-8100	1440
Mikro Industrial Finishing Co	Vernon	CT	G	860 875-6357	3754
Modern Metal Finishing LLC	Oxford	CT	E	203 267-1510	2704
Omega Engineering Inc	Norwalk	CT	D	714 540-4914	2548
Pmp Corporation	Avon	CT	D	860 677-9656	36
Prospect Products Incorporated	Newington	CT	E	860 666-0323	2320
Puritan Industries Inc	Collinsville	CT	G	860 693-0791	668
PYC Deborring LLC F/K/A C &	Berlin	CT	G	860 828-6806	82
Smokeloudz LLC (PA)	Meriden	CT	E	203 909-3556	1699
Startech Environmental Corp (PA)	Wilton	CT	F	203 762-2499	4248
Tkh Security LLC (PA)	Cheshire	CT	D	203 220-6544	619
Unipharm Inc	Waterbury	CT	E	203 528-3230	3978
Walker Magnetics Group Inc	Windsor	CT	D	508 853-3232	4314
Windham Automated Machines Inc	South Windham	CT	E	860 208-5297	3105
Wittmann Usa Inc (DH)	Torrington	CT	D	860 496-9603	3708
A B Engineering & Co	Oxford	MA	G	508 987-0318	11247
American & Schoen Machinery Co	Beverly	MA	E	978 524-0168	6324
American Recycled Mtls Inc	Holliston	MA	G	508 429-1455	9199
Applied Materials Inc	Gloucester	MA	F	978 282-2000	8919
Artisan Industries Inc	Stoughton	MA	E	781 893-6800	12195
Axcelis Technologies Inc (PA)	Beverly	MA	A	978 787-4000	6330
Azenta Inc (PA)	Burlington	MA	A	978 262-2400	7339
Azenta Inc	Chelmsford	MA	B	978 262-2795	7914
Bay State Plating Inc	Holyoke	MA	F	413 533-6927	9243
Biopharm Engneered Systems LLC	Lawrence	MA	E	978 691-2737	9543
Bisco Environmental Inc	Danvers	MA	F	508 738-5100	8169
Carpe Diem Technologies Inc	Franklin	MA	E	508 541-2055	8822
Celeros Inc	Newton	MA	E	248 478-2800	10742
Chemical Systems Services Inc	Attleboro	MA	F	508 431-9995	6003
Chucks Auto Body Towing	Chicopee	MA	G	413 459-4636	8017
Cotter Brothers Corporation	Danvers	MA	E	978 777-5001	8174
Csi Mfg Inc	Westborough	MA	E	508 986-2300	13096
DCI Automation Inc	West Boylston	MA	D	508 752-3071	12960
Degreasing Devices Co	Southbridge	MA	G	508 765-0045	12013
Gloucester Engineering Co Inc (DH)	Gloucester	MA	F	978 281-1800	8935
Gloucester Engineering Co Inc	Gloucester	MA	E	978 515-7008	8936
Gradiant Osmotics Inc	Woburn	MA	G	781 819-5034	13576
Hardigg Industries LLC (HQ)	South Deerfield	MA	C	413 665-2163	11924
Healthstar Inc	Braintree	MA	F	781 428-3696	7187
Highland Labs Inc	Holliston	MA	G	508 429-2918	9215
Hosokawa Micron Intl Inc	Northborough	MA	E	508 655-1123	11098
Innovent Technologies LLC	Peabody	MA	E	978 538-0808	11318
J P Ruthier Sons Recycl Corp (PA)	Littleton	MA	E	978 772-4251	9821
Jgp Enterprises Inc	Lawrence	MA	E	978 691-2737	9572
Lacerta Group Inc	Mansfield	MA	D	508 339-3312	10063
Lacerta Group LLC (PA)	Mansfield	MA	C	508 339-3312	10064
Lambient Technologies LLC	Cambridge	MA	G	857 242-3963	7627
Maxant Industries Inc	Devens	MA	F	978 772-0576	8279
Mediatek USA Inc	Woburn	MA	D	781 503-8000	13609
Merrow Manufacturing LLC (PA)	Fall River	MA	B	508 689-4095	8578
Microfluidics Intl Corp	Westwood	MA	E	617 969-5452	13315
Millers Petroleum Systems Inc	Pittsfield	MA	G	413 499-2314	11411
Mitchell Machine Incorporated (PA)	Springfield	MA	F	413 739-9693	12114
New England Alpaca Fibr Pool I	Fall River	MA	G	508 659-6731	8586
Nypro Inc (HQ)	Clinton	MA	A	978 365-9721	8087
O K Engineering Inc	Hudson	MA	E	978 562-1010	9397
Oasys Water Inc	Foxboro	MA	E	617 963-0450	8711
Optikos Corporation	Wakefield	MA	D	617 354-7557	12525
Overlook Industries Inc	Easthampton	MA	E	413 527-4344	8458
Purecoat International LLC	Belmont	MA	E	561 844-0100	6309
Ranger Automation Systems Inc	Millbury	MA	E	508 842-6500	10442
Reifenhauser Incorporated	Danvers	MA	G	847 669-9972	8218
Reliable	Winchendon	MA	G	978 230-2689	13481
Rethink Robotics Inc	Boston	MA	F	617 500-2487	7008
Rocheleau Tool and Die Co Inc	Fitchburg	MA	D	978 345-1723	8673
Rt Engineering Corporation	Franklin	MA	E	800 343-1182	8861
Safety-Kleen Systems Inc (HQ)	Norwell	MA	B	800 669-5740	11146
Saint-Gobain Abrasives Inc (HQ)	Worcester	MA	A	508 795-5000	13788
Sancliff Inc	Worcester	MA	E	508 795-0747	13794
Sonicron Systems Corporation	Westfield	MA	F	413 562-5218	13209
Sturtevant Inc (PA)	Hanover	MA	E	781 829-6501	9045
Synventive Molding Solutions Inc (HQ)	Peabody	MA	C	978 750-8065	11345
TEC Engineering Corp	Oxford	MA	F	508 987-0231	11266
Tecomet Inc	Woburn	MA	A	781 762-6400	13675
Thermoplastics Company Inc	Worcester	MA	E	508 754-4668	13811
Universal Pharma Tech LLC	North Andover	MA	G	978 975-7216	10856
Uspack Inc	Leominster	MA	E	978 466-9700	9714
Uspack Inc	Hudson	MA	E	978 562-8522	9423
Vacuum Barrier Corporation	Woburn	MA	E	781 933-3570	13682
Varian Semicdtr Eqp Assoc Inc	Newburyport	MA	E	978 463-1500	10725
Waste Mgmt Inc	Springfield	MA	F	413 747-9294	12149
Welton Technology LLC	Leominster	MA	G	978 425-0160	9716
Whitney & Son Inc	Fitchburg	MA	E	978 343-6353	8682
Whoop Inc (PA)	Boston	MA	B	617 670-1074	7122
Witricity Corporation (PA)	Watertown	MA	F	617 926-2700	12921
Arcast Inc	Oxford	ME	G	207 539-9638	5140
Lanco Assembly Systems Inc (PA)	Westbrook	ME	D	207 773-2060	5635
Mid-Cape Restoration Inc	Hollis Center	ME	F	207 929-4759	4894
Pamco Machine Company Inc	Lewiston	ME	F	207 783-1763	4982
Admix Inc	Londonderry	NH	E	603 627-2340	14727
CET Technology LLC	Windham	NH	F	603 894-6100	15724
Ishigaki USA Ltd	Portsmouth	NH	F	603 433-3334	15412
Jenesco Inc	Lyndeborough	NH	F	603 673-4830	14800
Land and Sea Inc	Concord	NH	D	603 226-3966	14139
MTS Associates Londonderry LLC	Londonderry	NH	E	603 425-2562	14775
Mushield Company Inc	Londonderry	NH	E	603 666-4433	14776
Pica Mfg Solutions Inc (PA)	Derry	NH	E	603 845-3258	14204
Premier Recycling Eqp Inc	Seabrook	NH	F	855 223-5859	15600
Province Kiln Dried Firewood	Belmont	NH	G	603 524-4447	13968
Puritan Electronics Inc	Manchester	NH	E	800 343-8649	14919
White Mountain Imaging	Concord	NH	E	603 228-2630	14166
White Mountain Imaging (PA)	Webster	NH	E	603 648-2124	15675
Conley Casting Supply Corp (PA)	Warwick	RI	F	401 461-4710	16797
Environmental Ctrl Systems Inc	East Providence	RI	F	401 437-8612	16016
Fueling Services LLC	Johnston	RI	F	401 764-0711	16087
Greco Bros Inc	Providence	RI	E	401 421-9306	16529
High Purity New England Inc (PA)	Smithfield	RI	F	401 349-4477	16710
High Purity New England Inc	Smithfield	RI	D	401 349-4477	16711
Impreglon Inc	Woonsocket	RI	F	401 766-3353	16965
Technic Inc (PA)	Cranston	RI	C	401 781-6100	15919
US Extruders Inc	Westerly	RI	F	401 584-4710	16945
Yushin America Inc (HQ)	Cranston	RI	D	401 463-1800	15930
Advanced Illumination Inc	Rochester	VT	F	802 767-3830	17484
Hazelett Strip-Casting Corp (HQ)	Colchester	VT	C	802 863-6376	17195
Simon Pearce (us) Inc	Quechee	VT	E	802 295-2711	17463
Triex LLC	Barre	VT	G	802 505-6772	17021
Trow & Holden Co Inc	Barre	VT	E	802 476-7221	17022

3561 Pumps and pumping equipment

	CITY	ST	EMP	PHONE	ENTRY#
2600 Albany Avenue LLC	Torrington	CT	G	336 632-0005	3665
A V I International Inc	Torrington	CT	G	860 482-8345	3666
Beckson Manufacturing Inc (PA)	Bridgeport	CT	E	203 366-3644	301
Connecticut Basement Systems Inc	Seymour	CT	C	203 881-5090	2959
Draught Technologies LLC	Farmington	CT	G	860 840-7555	1215
Foleys Pump Service Inc	Danbury	CT	E	203 792-2236	747
Hamworthy Peabody Combustn Inc (DH)	Shelton	CT	E	203 922-1199	3012
Hisco Pump Incorporated (PA)	Bloomfield	CT	F	860 243-2705	170
Idex Health & Science LLC	Wallingford	CT	E	203 774-4422	3817
Industrial Flow Sltons Oper LL	New Haven	CT	E	860 399-5937	2163
ITT Goulds Pumps Inc (HQ)	Stamford	CT	E	315 568-2811	3387
ITT Water & Wastewater USA Inc (HQ)	Shelton	CT	D	262 548-8181	3024
Marsars Wtr Rescue Systems Inc	Beacon Falls	CT	G	203 924-7315	43
McVac Environmental Svcs Inc	New Haven	CT	E	203 497-1960	2173
Megadoor USA Inc	Meriden	CT	C	203 238-2700	1673
MSC Filtration Tech Inc	Enfield	CT	F	860 745-7475	1139
Omega Engineering Inc	Norwalk	CT	D	714 540-4914	2548
Preferred Utilities Mfg Corp (HQ)	Danbury	CT	D	203 743-6741	799
Proflow Inc	North Haven	CT	E	203 230-4700	2433
Pump Technology Incorporated	Ansonia	CT	E	203 736-8890	18
Sfc Koenig LLC	North Haven	CT	D	203 245-1100	2436
Sonic Corp	Stratford	CT	F	203 375-0063	3575
Stancor LP	Monroe	CT	E	203 268-7513	1922
Sulzer Pump Solutions US Inc (PA)	Wallingford	CT	E	203 238-2700	3856
Trane Technologies Company LLC	Rocky Hill	CT	F	860 616-6600	2939
Trane Technologies Company LLC	Torrington	CT	G	860 626-2085	3702
Xylem Water Solutions USA Inc	Shelton	CT	D	203 450-3715	3080
A W Chesterton Company	Groveland	MA	B	781 438-7000	9013
Azenta Inc	Chelmsford	MA	B	978 262-2795	7914
BEE International Inc	South Easton	MA	E	508 238-5558	11937
Flow Control LLC	Beverly	MA	E	978 281-0440	6348
Flowserve US Inc	Lawrence	MA	C	978 682-5248	9563
Harvard Apparatus Inc	Holliston	MA	D	508 893-8999	9213
Hayes Pump Inc (PA)	Concord	MA	E	978 369-8800	8119
Iwaki America Incorporated (HQ)	Holliston	MA	E	508 429-1440	9216
Iwaki Pumps Inc (DH)	Holliston	MA	E	508 429-1440	9217
Lawrence Pumps Inc	Lawrence	MA	C	978 682-5248	9577
Lewa/Nikkiso America Inc (DH)	Holliston	MA	E	508 429-7403	9220
Mass Vac Inc	North Billerica	MA	E	978 667-2393	10932
Monalex Manufacturing Inc	East Douglas	MA	G	508 476-1200	8352
Newera Services Corporation (PA)	New Bedford	MA	E	508 995-9711	10631
Northeast Equipment Inc	Fall River	MA	F	508 324-0083	8588
Rule Industries LLC	Gloucester	MA	C	978 281-0440	8956

	CITY	ST	EMP	PHONE	ENTRY#
Tark Inc	Billerica	MA	F	978 663-8074	6486
The Tyler Co Inc	Hudson	MA	E	978 568-3400	9419
Trane Technologies Company LLC	Northborough	MA	D	781 961-2063	11115
Trane Technologies Company LLC	Shrewsbury	MA	E	508 842-5769	11844
Warren Pumps LLC	Warren	MA	E	413 436-7711	12853
Xylem Water Solutions USA Inc	Woburn	MA	F	781 935-6515	13690
Bison Pumps	Houlton	ME	F	207 532-2600	4897
Cascon Inc	Yarmouth	ME	F	207 846-6202	5702
Stevens Electric Pump Service	Monmouth	ME	G	207 933-2143	5073
Brailsford & Company Inc	Antrim	NH	F	603 588-2880	13896
Pfeiffer Vacuum Inc (DH)	Nashua	NH	E	317 328-8492	15147
Universal Envmtl Tech Inc	Nashua	NH	G	603 883-9312	15180
Williamson Electrical Co Inc	Epping	NH	D	617 884-9200	14277
Aquamotion Inc	Warwick	RI	E	401 785-3000	16783
Boydco Inc (PA)	East Providence	RI	F	401 438-6900	16007
Bsm Pump Corp	North Kingstown	RI	F	401 471-6350	16235
Mesco Corporation	Portsmouth	RI	G	401 683-2677	16447
Taco Inc (PA)	Cranston	RI	B	401 942-8000	15917
Taco International Ltd	Cranston	RI	F	401 942-8000	15918
Apex Sealing Inc	Fairfax	VT	F	802 524-7100	17254
Hayward Tyler Inc (DH)	Colchester	VT	E	802 655-4444	17194
Ivek Corp (PA)	North Springfield	VT	C	802 886-2238	17422
PBL Incorporated	Colchester	VT	F	802 893-0111	17199
Whale Water Systems Inc	Manchester	VT	F	802 367-1091	17325

3562 Ball and roller bearings

	CITY	ST	EMP	PHONE	ENTRY#
Abek LLC	Bristol	CT	F	860 314-3905	390
Ball & Roller Bearing Co LLC	New Milford	CT	F	860 355-4161	2239
Buswell Manufacturing Company	Bridgeport	CT	F	203 334-6069	307
C & S Engineering Inc	Meriden	CT	E	203 235-5727	1657
Del-Tron Precision Inc	Bethel	CT	E	203 778-2727	107
Gwilliam Company Inc	New Milford	CT	F	860 354-2884	2246
Hartford Technologies Inc	Rocky Hill	CT	E	860 571-3602	2924
K A F Manufacturing Co Inc	Stamford	CT	E	203 324-3012	3394
Kamatics Corporation (DH)	Bloomfield	CT	E	860 243-9704	184
Kamatics Corporation	Bloomfield	CT	C	860 243-7230	185
Nn Inc	Wallingford	CT	F	203 793-7132	3835
Nordex Incorporated	Brookfield	CT	E	203 775-4877	532
Rbc Aircraft Products Inc	Torrington	CT	D	860 626-7800	3692
Rbc Bearings Incorporated (PA)	Oxford	CT	C	203 267-7001	2710
Schaeffler Aerospace USA Corp (DH)	Danbury	CT	B	203 744-2211	809
Schaeffler Aerospace USA Corp	Winsted	CT	D	860 379-7558	4354
Schaeffler Holding LLC (DH)	Danbury	CT	B	203 790-5474	810
SKF Specialty Balls	Winsted	CT	F	860 379-8511	4355
SKF USA Inc	Winsted	CT	E	860 379-8511	4356
Wind Corporation	Newtown	CT	E	800 946-3267	2354
Nn Inc	North Attleboro	MA	E	508 695-7700	10880
Vulcan Industries Inc	East Longmeadow	MA	G	413 525-8846	8401
Mpb Corporation (HQ)	Keene	NH	D	603 352-0310	14611
Mpb Corporation	Lebanon	NH	A	603 448-3000	14694
Mpb Corporation	Lebanon	NH	A	603 448-3000	14695
New Hmpshire Ball Bearings Inc	Laconia	NH	B	603 524-0004	14661
New Hmpshire Ball Bearings Inc	Peterborough	NH	E	818 407-9300	15320

3563 Air and gas compressors

	CITY	ST	EMP	PHONE	ENTRY#
Afcon Products Inc	Bethany	CT	F	203 393-9301	91
Nordson Efd LLC	Norwich	CT	D	860 889-3383	2610
Norwalk Compreseer Company	Stratford	CT	E	203 386-1234	3559
P&G Metal Components Corp	Bloomfield	CT	F	860 243-2220	199
Stead-Fast Custom Linings LLC	East Haven	CT	F	203 466-8000	1052
Stylair LLC	Plainville	CT	E	860 747-4588	2781
Anver Corporation	Hudson	MA	D	978 568-0221	9354
Artisan Industries Inc	Stoughton	MA	D	781 893-6800	12195
Atlas Copco Compressors LLC	Ludlow	MA	G	413 589-7439	9938
Atlas Copco Compressors LLC	West Springfield	MA	F	413 493-7290	13015
Atlas Copco Compressors LLC	Westfield	MA	G	518 765-3344	13149
Azenta Inc (PA)	Burlington	MA	A	978 262-2400	7339
Azenta Inc	Chelmsford	MA	B	978 262-2795	7914
Brooks Automation Us LLC	Chelmsford	MA	C	978 262-4613	7916
Craftech Upton	Upton	MA	F	508 529-4505	12472
Edwards Vacuum LLC	Chelmsford	MA	F	978 262-2400	7924
Guardair Corporation	Chicopee	MA	E	413 594-4400	8035
Mass Vac Inc	North Billerica	MA	E	978 667-2393	10932
Millibar Inc	Hudson	MA	F	508 488-9870	9391
Ruwac Inc	Holyoke	MA	F	413 532-4030	9278
V Power Equipment LLC	Wareham	MA	F	508 273-7596	12847
Vacuum Technology Assoc Inc	Hingham	MA	D	781 740-8600	9161
General Electric Company	Bangor	ME	A	207 941-2500	4505
Linde Advanced Mtl Tech Inc	Concord	NH	D	603 224-9585	14140
Nexvac Inc (PA)	Sandown	NH	F	603 887-0015	15580
Tafa Incorporated (DH)	Concord	NH	E	603 224-9585	14162
Aargo Environmental Inc	Exeter	RI	G	401 678-6444	16050

3564 Blowers and fans

	CITY	ST	EMP	PHONE	ENTRY#
Atlantic Vent & Eqp Co Inc	Cromwell	CT	E	860 635-1300	687
Clean Air Group Inc (PA)	Fairfield	CT	G	203 335-3700	1179
EBM-Papst Inc (DH)	Farmington	CT	B	860 674-1515	1217
Environmental Monitor Svc Inc	Meriden	CT	G	203 935-0102	1667
Environmental Systems Products Inc	East Granby	CT	C	860 653-0081	933
Guardian Envmtl Tech Inc	New Milford	CT	F	860 350-2200	2245
Howden Roots LLC	Windsor	CT	D	860 688-8361	4281
Kennedy Gustafson and Cole Inc	Berlin	CT	E	860 828-2594	72
Liberty Industries Inc	East Berlin	CT	E	860 828-6361	913
Lydall Inc (HQ)	Manchester	CT	E	860 646-1233	1614
McIntire Company (HQ)	Bristol	CT	F	860 585-8559	465
Mechanical Engnered Systems LLC	New Canaan	CT	G	203 400-4658	2083
Nq Industries Inc	Hamden	CT	F	860 258-3466	1448
Planet Biopharmaceuticals Inc	Ridgefield	CT	F	800 255-3749	2904
Planet Technologies Inc	Ridgefield	CT	D	800 255-3749	2905
Spencer Turbine Company (DH)	Windsor	CT	E	860 688-8361	4301
Stylair LLC	Plainville	CT	E	860 747-4588	2781
Treadwell Corporation	Thomaston	CT	E	860 283-7600	3639
7ac Technologies Inc	Beverly	MA	F	781 574-1348	6322
APA LLC	Canton	MA	F	781 986-5900	7769
B G Wickberg Company Inc	East Weymouth	MA	E	781 335-7800	8425
Bmac Inc	Ayer	MA	E	978 772-3310	6175
Gremarco Industries Inc	West Brookfield	MA	F	508 867-5244	12995
Headwaters Inc	Marblehead	MA	F	781 715-6404	10087
Heat Fab Inc	Turners Falls	MA	F	413 863-2242	12447
Hendrick Manufacturing Corp (PA)	Salem	MA	F	781 631-4400	11723
Impolit Envmtl Ctrl Corp	Beverly	MA	E	978 927-4304	6356
Jarvis Welding & Mfg Co	Turners Falls	MA	F	413 863-9541	12449
Kovalus Spration Solutions LLC (PA)	Wilmington	MA	C	978 694-7000	13421
Kse Inc	Sunderland	MA	F	413 549-5506	12274
Manchester Corporation	Harvard	MA	E	978 772-2900	9065
Metalmark Innovations Pbc	Cambridge	MA	G	617 714-4026	7642
Metromatic Manufacturing Company Inc	Byfield	MA	F	781 396-5300	7458
Munters Corporation (DH)	Amesbury	MA	C	978 241-1100	5845
Pall Northborough (DH)	Northborough	MA	E	978 263-9888	11105
Parker-Hannifin Corporation	Haverhill	MA	C	978 858-0505	9120
Riley Power Inc	Marlborough	MA	B	508 852-7100	10204
Spruce Environmental Tech Inc	Haverhill	MA	E	978 521-0901	9134
Vacuum Technology Inc	Gloucester	MA	G	510 333-6562	8962
Weld Engineering Co Inc	Shrewsbury	MA	E	508 842-2224	11848
Zwitterco Inc	Woburn	MA	E	301 442-5662	13693
Air Control Industries Inc	Windsor	ME	E	207 445-2518	5677
N E Tech-Air Inc	Scarborough	ME	C	207 347-7577	5439
Parker-Hannifin Corporation	Kittery	ME	D	207 439-9511	4938
Airex Corporation	Hudson	NH	E	603 821-3065	14481
Brailsford & Company Inc	Antrim	NH	F	603 588-2880	13896
Electrocraft New Hampshire Inc (DH)	Dover	NH	E	603 742-3330	14228
Pollution Research & Dev Corp (PA)	Newport	NH	G	603 863-7553	15234
Ocean State Air LLC	Pawtucket	RI	G	401 722-2447	16397

3565 Packaging machinery

	CITY	ST	EMP	PHONE	ENTRY#
B & B Equipment LLC	Portland	CT	G	860 342-5773	2817
Bausch Advanced Tech Inc (PA)	Clinton	CT	C	860 669-7380	637
Dymo Corporation	Norwalk	CT	D		2494
Hasler Inc	Milford	CT	B	203 301-3400	1833
Millwood Inc	North Haven	CT	D	203 248-7902	2425
OEM Sources LLC	Milford	CT	G	203 283-5415	1857
Packard Inc	Prospect	CT	E	203 758-6219	2839
PDC International Corp	Norwalk	CT	D	203 853-1516	2552
Staban Engineering Corp	Wallingford	CT	F	203 294-1997	3854
Standard Knapp Inc	Portland	CT	D	860 342-1100	2825
A & M Tool & Die Company Inc	Southbridge	MA	E	508 764-3241	12008
Accutech Packaging Inc	Foxboro	MA	D	508 543-3800	8689
Butler Automatic Inc (PA)	Middleboro	MA	E	508 923-0544	10353
Chesterfield Products Inc	Chesterfield	MA	E	413 296-0066	7997
Dtm Massman LLC	Hingham	MA	E	781 749-1866	9149
Econocorp Inc	Randolph	MA	E	781 986-7500	11555
Energy Sciences Inc	Wilmington	MA	E	978 694-9000	13405
Hydration Labs Inc (PA)	Charlestown	MA	E	617 315-4715	7876
Illinois Tool Works Inc	Hopkinton	MA	E	508 520-0083	9331
Lock Inspection Systems Inc	Leominster	MA	E	978 343-3716	9679
Maruho Htsujyo Innovations Inc (PA)	Norwell	MA	E	617 653-1617	11143
Mrsi Systems LLC	Tewksbury	MA	E	978 667-9449	12411
Nova Packaging Systems Inc	Leominster	MA	D	978 537-8534	9688
O/K Machinery Corporation	Marlborough	MA	E	508 303-8286	10188
Pac Machinery Group	Stoneham	MA	G	214 724-8523	12184
Package Machinery Company Inc	Holyoke	MA	G	413 315-3801	9274
Packaging Devices Inc (PA)	Teaticket	MA	F	508 548-0224	12379
Sencorp Inc	Hyannis	MA	C	508 771-9400	9450
Shanklin Corporation (HQ)	Ayer	MA	C	978 487-2204	6194
Speedline Technologies Inc	Franklin	MA	B	508 541-4867	8864

SIC

	CITY	ST	EMP	PHONE	ENTRY#
Sperry Product Innovation Inc	Bedford	MA	F	781 271-1400	6270
Tooling Research Inc (PA)	Walpole	MA	F	508 668-1950	12578
Eami Inc	Biddeford	ME	F	207 283-3001	4562
Oizero9 Inc	Sanford	ME	E	207 324-3582	5404
Wrabacon Inc	Oakland	ME	F	207 465-2068	5122
Zajac LLC	Saco	ME	E	207 286-9100	5384
Computype Inc	Concord	NH	G	603 225-5500	14122
Folder-Glr Techl Svs Grp LLC	Pelham	NH	G	603 635-7400	15288
George Gordon Associates Inc	Merrimack	NH	F	603 424-5204	14981
Labels Inc	Hampton	NH	F	603 929-3088	14405
Njm Packaging LLC (DH)	Lebanon	NH	F	603 448-0300	14697
Nestech Machine Systems Inc	Hinesburg	VT	G	802 482-4575	17296

3566 Speed changers, drives, and gears

	CITY	ST	EMP	PHONE	ENTRY#
Advanced Torque Products LLC	Newington	CT	G	860 828-1523	2268
Carlyle Johnson Machine Co LLC (DH)	Bolton	CT	F	860 643-1531	219
Control Concepts Inc (PA)	Brooklyn	CT	F	860 928-6551	545
JET Corporation	Bridgeport	CT	F	203 334-3317	334
Nordex Incorporated	Brookfield	CT	E	203 775-4877	532
Roller Bearing Co Amer Inc	Middlebury	CT	F	203 758-8272	1720
Bendon Gear and Machine Inc	Rockland	MA	F	781 878-8100	11636
Commercial Gear Sprocket Inc	East Walpole	MA	E	508 668-1073	8417
Control Resources Inc	Littleton	MA	E	978 486-4160	9806
Custom Machine & Tool Co Inc	Hanover	MA	E	781 924-1003	9029
Gear/Tronics Industries Inc	North Billerica	MA	D	781 933-1400	10915
Gefran Inc (DH)	North Andover	MA	E	781 729-5249	10836
Harmonic Drive LLC (HQ)	Beverly	MA	D	978 532-1800	6353
Hersey Clutch Company LLC	Orleans	MA	F	508 255-2533	11239
Insco Corporation	Groton	MA	E	978 448-6368	9010
Ksew	Southbridge	MA	G	774 230-4995	12026
Lampin Corporation (PA)	Uxbridge	MA	F	508 278-2422	12484
Lenze Americas Corporation (DH)	Uxbridge	MA	E	508 278-9100	12485
Maxon Precision Motors Inc (HQ)	Taunton	MA	E	508 677-0520	12348
Newera Services Corporation (PA)	New Bedford	MA	E	508 995-9711	10631
Std Precision Gear & Instr Inc	West Bridgewater	MA	E	508 580-0035	12982
Allard Nazarian Group Inc (PA)	Manchester	NH	C	603 668-1900	14810
Electrocraft New Hampshire Inc (DH)	Dover	NH	E	603 742-3330	14228
Onvio Servo LLC	Salem	NH	C	603 685-0404	15554

3567 Industrial furnaces and ovens

	CITY	ST	EMP	PHONE	ENTRY#
Birk Manufacturing Inc	East Lyme	CT	D	800 531-2070	1058
Cober Inc	Stratford	CT	E	203 855-8755	3529
Dri-Air Industries Inc	East Windsor	CT	F	860 627-5110	1071
Duralite Incorporated	Riverton	CT	F	860 379-3113	2912
Etter Engineering Company Incorporated	Bristol	CT	E	860 584-8842	443
Furnace Source LLC	Terryville	CT	F	860 582-4201	3603
Hamworthy Peabody Combustn Inc (DH)	Shelton	CT	E	203 922-1199	3012
Hearth Kitchen Products Inc	Stamford	CT	G	203 325-8800	3372
Industrial Heater Corp	Cheshire	CT	D	203 250-0500	601
Jad LLC	South Windsor	CT	E	860 289-1551	3158
Kanthal Corporation	Bethel	CT	E	203 744-1440	124
Manufacturers Coml Fin LLC	West Hartford	CT	E	860 242-6287	4070
Preferred Utilities Mfg Corp (HQ)	Danbury	CT	D	203 743-6741	799
Sshc Inc	Westbrook	CT	F	860 399-5434	4143
Warmup Inc	Danbury	CT	F		834
Allen Morgan	Bridgewater	MA	G	714 538-7492	7219
Avs Incorporated	Ayer	MA	D	978 772-0710	6174
Bruce Technologies Inc	North Billerica	MA	F	978 670-5501	10901
Calorique LLC	West Wareham	MA	F	508 291-2000	13057
Dalton Electric Heating Co Inc	Ipswich	MA	F	978 356-9844	9483
Dcaf of Massachusetts Inc	West Wareham	MA	F	508 291-2000	13060
Duc-Pac Corporation	Springfield	MA	E	413 525-3302	12091
East Coast Induction Inc	Brockton	MA	F	508 587-2800	7274
H B Smith Company Inc	Westfield	MA	E	413 568-3148	13170
Mestek Inc	Westfield	MA	E	413 568-9571	13183
Radio Frequency Company Inc	Millis	MA	E	508 376-9555	10450
Runtal North America Inc	Haverhill	MA	E	800 526-2621	9128
S M Engineering Co Inc	North Attleboro	MA	F	508 699-4484	10886
Tevtech LLC	North Billerica	MA	F	978 667-4557	10962
The Sentry Company	Foxboro	MA	G	508 543-5391	8728
Arcast Inc	Oxford	ME	F	207 539-9638	5141
N E Tech-Air Inc	Scarborough	ME	E	207 347-7577	5439
Onix Corporation	Caribou	ME	F	866 290-5362	4678
Vulcan Electric Company (PA)	Porter	ME	D	207 625-3231	5171
Centorr/Vacuum Industries LLC (PA)	Nashua	NH	E	603 595-7233	15078
Ebner Furnaces Inc	Londonderry	NH	G	603 552-3806	14746
Hollis Line Machine Co Inc	Milford	NH	E	603 673-1166	15028
Materials Research Frncs Inc	Allenstown	NH	E	603 485-2394	13853
Mellen Company Inc (DH)	Concord	NH	E	603 228-2929	14145
OXY-Gon Industries Inc	Epsom	NH	E	603 736-8422	14283
Gasbarre Products Inc	Cranston	RI	F	401 467-5200	15865
Rmb Ltd	Warren	RI	E	401 245-3700	16766
Sargeant & Wilbur Inc	Pawtucket	RI	F	401 726-0013	16415

	CITY	ST	EMP	PHONE	ENTRY#
Purmo Group USA Inc	Williston	VT	F	802 654-7500	17746
Rettig USA Inc	Colchester	VT	G	802 654-7500	17201

3568 Power transmission equipment, nec

	CITY	ST	EMP	PHONE	ENTRY#
Altra Industrial Motion Corp	New Hartford	CT	E	860 379-1673	2098
American Collars Couplings Inc	Winsted	CT	F	860 379-7043	4338
American Sleeve Bearing LLC	Stafford Springs	CT	E	860 684-8060	3253
Bead Industries Inc (PA)	Milford	CT	E	203 301-0270	1801
Carlyle Johnson Machine Co LLC (DH)	Bolton	CT	F	860 643-1531	219
Cmhanb LLC	Hartford	CT	G	860 241-0112	1474
Del-Tron Precision Inc	Bethel	CT	E	203 778-2727	107
F-K Bearings Inc	Southington	CT	F	860 621-4567	3210
Gwilliam Company Inc	New Milford	CT	F	860 354-2884	2246
Helander Products Inc	Clinton	CT	F	860 669-7953	644
Industrial Tecto	Oxford	CT	F	310 537-3750	2699
Inertia Dynamics LLC	New Hartford	CT	C	860 379-1252	2102
Magnetic Technologies Ltd	Putnam	CT	F	508 987-3303	2864
Nordex Incorporated	Brookfield	CT	E	203 775-4877	532
Perry Technology Corporation	New Hartford	CT	D	860 738-2525	2107
Rolease Acmeda Inc (HQ)	Stamford	CT	D	203 964-1573	3451
Roller Bearing Co Amer Inc	Middlebury	CT	F	203 758-8272	1720
Altra Industrial Motion Corp (HQ)	Braintree	MA	C	781 917-0600	7167
Altra Power Transmission Inc	Braintree	MA	B	781 917-0600	7168
Ameridrives International LLC	Quincy	MA	E	617 689-6237	11502
Antenna Associates Inc	Brockton	MA	E	508 583-3241	7257
Bauer Gear Motor LLC	Braintree	MA	E	732 469-8770	7169
Belt Technologies Inc (PA)	Agawam	MA	E	413 786-9922	5780
C F G Corporation	Saugus	MA	F	781 233-6110	11754
Custom Machine & Tool Co Inc	Hanover	MA	E	781 924-1003	9029
Double E Company LLC (PA)	West Bridgewater	MA	C	508 588-8099	12972
Emseal Joint Systems Ltd	Westborough	MA	E	508 836-0280	13100
Fabreeka International Inc (DH)	Stoughton	MA	G	781 341-3655	12206
Fabreeka Intl Holdings Inc (DH)	Stoughton	MA	E	781 341-3655	12207
Hersey Clutch Company LLC	Orleans	MA	F	508 255-2533	11239
Kevlin Corporation	Methuen	MA	C	978 689-8331	10336
Lampin Corporation (PA)	Uxbridge	MA	F	508 278-2422	12484
Lm/Tarbell Inc	East Longmeadow	MA	F	413 525-4166	8383
Lovejoy LLC	Ludlow	MA	F	413 737-0281	9949
Mass-Flex Research Inc	Medford	MA	G	781 391-3640	10295
Renbrandt Inc	Gloucester	MA	F	617 445-8910	8954
Ruland Manufacturing Co Inc	Marlborough	MA	E	508 485-1000	10208
Stafford Manufacturing Corp (PA)	Wilmington	MA	E	978 657-8000	13458
Tb Woods Corporation	Braintree	MA	E	781 917-0600	7209
US Tsubaki Automotive LLC (DH)	Chicopee	MA	C	413 593-1100	8067
US Tsubaki Power Transm LLC	Holyoke	MA	C	413 536-1576	9288
Valley Enterprises Inc	Springfield	MA	F	413 737-0281	12146
Warner Electric	Braintree	MA	D	781 917-0600	7212
Wgi Inc	Southwick	MA	C	413 569-9444	12051
Montalvo Corporation	Gorham	ME	E	207 856-2501	4827
Woodex Bearing Company Inc	Georgetown	ME	E	207 371-2210	4815
Accutech Marine Propeller Inc	Dover	NH	G	603 617-3626	14213
Ametek Precitech Inc (HQ)	Keene	NH	D	603 357-2510	14588
Ferrotec (usa) Corporation	Bedford	NH	E	603 472-6800	13930
Mpb Corporation	Lebanon	NH	A	603 448-3000	14695
Nhi Mechanical Motion LLC	Claremont	NH	F	603 448-1090	14095
Nim-Cor Inc	Nashua	NH	F	603 889-2153	15142
Tracey Gear Inc	Pawtucket	RI	E	401 725-3920	16424
Whittet-Higgins Company	Central Falls	RI	E	401 728-0700	15802

3569 General industrial machinery,

	CITY	ST	EMP	PHONE	ENTRY#
3M Purification Inc (HQ)	Meriden	CT	B	203 237-5541	1648
Act Robots Inc	Bristol	CT	G	860 314-1557	392
Alstom Power Co	Windsor	CT	E	860 688-1911	4257
Applied Porous Tech Inc	Tariffville	CT	F	860 408-9793	3598
Arthur G Russell Company Inc	Bristol	CT	D	860 583-4109	398
Automation Inc	West Hartford	CT	E	860 236-5991	4048
Cable Management LLC	Meriden	CT	E	860 670-1890	1658
D&D Fltrtion Cons Sppliers Inc	Kensington	CT	E	860 829-3690	1539
Environmantal Systems Cor	Hartford	CT	E	860 953-5167	1479
Gyre9 LLC	Southbury	CT	E	203 702-4010	3194
Hamilton Standard Space	Windsor Locks	CT	E	860 654-6000	4329
Linde Inc (HQ)	Danbury	CT	B	203 837-2000	776
Mott Corporation (PA)	Farmington	CT	D	860 864-5017	1230
MSC Filtration Tech Inc	Enfield	CT	E	860 745-7475	1139
Naiad Dynamics Us Inc (HQ)	Shelton	CT	E	203 929-6355	3033
On Site Gas Systems Inc	Newington	CT	E	860 667-8888	2313
Packard Inc	Prospect	CT	E	203 758-6219	2839
Pallflex Products Company	Putnam	CT	E	860 928-7761	2869
Proton Energy Systems Inc	Wallingford	CT	E	203 678-2000	3841
Qsonica LLC	Newtown	CT	G	203 426-0101	2344
Rondo America Incorporated	Naugatuck	CT	C	203 723-5831	1985
Sonics & Materials Inc (PA)	Newtown	CT	D	203 270-4600	2347
Terex Corporation (PA)	Norwalk	CT	F	203 222-7170	2578

	CITY	ST	EMP	PHONE	ENTRY#
The Gas Equipment Engineering Corporation	Milford	CT			F
	1894				
Tinny Corporation	Middletown	CT	E	860 854-6121	1786
Triad Concepts Inc	Westbrook	CT	G	860 399-4045	4145
Angstrom Advanced Inc	Stoughton	MA	D	781 519-4765	12194
Armstrong Machine Co Inc	Beverly	MA	F	978 232-9466	6326
Avenger Inc	Gloucester	MA	F	978 356-7311	8920
Azelis Americas LLC	Sterling	MA	D	212 915-8178	12155
Babcock Power Inc (PA)	Danvers	MA	G	978 646-3300	8166
Balyo Inc (HQ)	Woburn	MA	G	781 281-7957	13519
Barrett Technology LLC	Newton	MA	E	617 252-9000	10737
Barrett Technology Inc	Newtonville	MA	E	617 252-9000	10796
Berkshire Grey Inc (PA)	Bedford	MA	E	833 848-9900	6214
Corindus Inc (HQ)	Auburndale	MA	E	508 653-3335	6131
Dresser Msnlan Ctrl Vlves Avon (DH)	Avon	MA	D	508 586-4600	6149
East Coast Filter Inc	Wrentham	MA	G	716 649-2326	13840
Encore Fire Protection	Needham	MA	F	617 903-3191	10509
Evoqua Water Technologies LLC	Tewksbury	MA	E	978 863-4600	12397
Filter-Kleen Manufacturing Co	Westford	MA	F	978 692-5137	13237
Flexhead Industries Inc	Holliston	MA	E	508 893-9596	9210
Flexhead Industries Massachusetts Business Trust	Holliston		MA		F
508 893-9596	9211				
Hostar Mar Trnspt Systems Inc	Wareham	MA	F	508 295-2900	12838
Hydro-Test Products Inc	Stow	MA	F	978 897-4647	12246
Illinois Tool Works Inc	Hopkinton	MA	E	508 520-0083	9331
Ipsumm Inc (PA)	Amesbury	MA	E	603 570-4050	5838
Irobot Corporation (PA)	Bedford	MA	B	781 430-3000	6235
Isp Freetown Fine Chem Inc	Assonet	MA	D	508 672-0634	5974
King Fisher Co Inc	Lowell	MA	E	978 596-0214	9890
Kovalus Spration Solutions LLC (PA)	Wilmington	MA	C	978 694-7000	13421
Locus Robotics Corp (PA)	Wilmington	MA	F	844 562-8700	13426
Ltp Corporation (DH)	Northborough	MA	D	508 393-7660	11101
McIntire Brass Works Inc	Lincoln	MA	G	617 547-1819	9797
Mestek Inc	Westfield	MA	D	413 564-5530	13184
Methods 3d Inc	Sudbury	MA	G	978 443-5388	12268
Munters Corporation (DH)	Amesbury	MA	C	978 241-1100	5845
Nery Corporation	New Bedford	MA	G	508 990-9800	10626
New England Gen-Connect LLC	Hingham	MA	F	617 571-6884	9155
Pall Corporation	Framingham	MA	G	508 259-5107	8797
Pall Corporation	Westborough	MA	B	508 871-5380	13127
Parker-Hannifin Corporation	Haverhill	MA	C	978 858-0505	9120
Persimmon Technologies Corp	Wakefield	MA	F	781 587-0677	12527
Polytech Fltration Systems Inc	Hudson	MA	F	978 562-7700	9402
Precision Feeding Systems Inc	East Longmeadow	MA	G	413 525-9200	8389
Riley Power Inc	Marlborough	MA	B	508 852-7100	10204
Russell James Engineering Works Inc	Boston	MA	E	617 265-2240	7018
Rypos Inc (PA)	Franklin	MA	E	508 429-4552	8862
Siemens Hlthcare Dgnostics Inc	Andover	MA	F	212 258-4000	5919
Soft Robotics Inc	Bedford	MA	D	617 391-0612	6269
Speedline Technologies Inc	Franklin	MA	B	508 541-4867	8864
St Equipment & Technology LLC	Needham	MA	E	781 972-2319	10524
Teledyne Flir Unmnned Grund Sy (DH)	Chelmsford	MA	D	978 769-9333	7964
Town of Westminster	Westminster	MA	F	978 874-2313	13281
Tyco Fire Products LP	Avon	MA	G	508 583-8447	6165
US Nortek Inc	Worcester	MA	F	774 314-4006	13817
Comnav Engineering Inc	Portland	ME	E	207 221-8524	5201
Lapoint Industries Inc (PA)	Auburn	ME	D	207 777-3100	4439
Micronics Engnred Fltrtion Gro	Winthrop	ME	F	207 377-2626	5693
Micronics Engnred Fltrtion Gro	Winthrop	ME	F	207 377-2626	5694
National Filter Media Corp	Winthrop	ME	C	207 327-2626	5695
Oizero9 Inc	Sanford	ME	E	207 324-3582	5404
SKF	Charlotte	ME	F	207 454-8078	4686
United Fbrcnts Strainrite Corp (HQ)	Auburn	ME	D	207 376-1600	4463
Wrabacon Inc	Oakland	ME	F	207 465-2068	5122
Devprotek Inc	Hollis	NH	G	603 577-5557	14449
James W McClellan & Associates Inc	Bedford	NH	E	603 644-1247	13935
JP Sercel Associates Inc	Manchester	NH	E	603 595-7048	14869
M & A Advnced Design Cnstr Inc (PA)	Hampstead	NH	F	603 329-9515	14385
Mikrolar Inc	Hampton	NH	F	603 617-2508	14408
ACS Industries Inc (PA)	Lincoln	RI	E	401 769-4700	16116
Bioprocessh2o LLC	Portsmouth	RI	E	401 683-5400	16438
Tyco Fire Products LP	Cranston	RI	E	401 781-8220	15923
Tyco Fire Products LP (DH)	Cranston	RI	C	215 362-0700	15924
4smartpro LLC	Saint Johnsbury	VT	F	802 745-8797	17537
Kalow Technologies LLC	Rutland	VT	D	802 775-4633	17501

3571 Electronic computers

	CITY	ST	EMP	PHONE	ENTRY#
Black Rock Tech Group LLC	Bridgeport	CT	F	203 916-7200	302
Cyberresearch Inc	Branford	CT	E	203 643-5000	247
Cyclone Microsystems Inc	Hamden	CT	E	203 786-5536	1420
Fairfix CT Inc	Fairfield	CT	F	203 516-4137	1185
Frontier Vision Tech Inc	Rocky Hill	CT	E	860 953-0240	2922
General Digital Corporation	East Hartford	CT	D	860 282-2900	996

	CITY	ST	EMP	PHONE	ENTRY#
Glacier Computer LLC	New Milford	CT	F	603 882-1560	2244
Hoffman Engineering LLC (DH)	Stamford	CT	D	203 425-8900	3378
Interactive Marketing Corp	North Haven	CT	G	203 248-5324	2416
Kimchuk Incorporated	Danbury	CT	C	203 798-0799	765
Mohegan Digital Services LLC	Uncasville	CT	G	888 226-7711	3741
Abaco Systems Technology Corp	Wilmington	MA	D	256 382-8115	13369
Acbel (usa) Polytech Inc	Hopkinton	MA	G	508 625-1768	9305
Acumentrics Rups LLC	Walpole	MA	E	617 932-7877	12546
Advanced Electronic Design Inc	Attleboro Falls	MA	E	508 699-0249	6078
Biscom Inc	Westford	MA	D	978 250-1800	13226
Bull Data Systems Inc	Chelmsford	MA	A	978 294-6000	7919
Comark LLC (HQ)	Milford	MA	E	508 359-8161	10399
Dell Technologies Inc	Concord	MA	D	781 259-2552	8112
E E S Companies Inc	Framingham	MA	F	508 653-6911	8758
Foundation Devices Inc	Boston	MA	F	617 283-8306	6746
General Dynamics Mission	Dedham	MA	B	781 410-9635	8244
General Dynamics Mission	Taunton	MA	A	508 880-4000	12337
Hiper Global Us LLC (PA)	North Andover	MA	D	978 486-0300	10838
Hp Inc	Littleton	MA	D	800 222-5547	9816
HP Inc	Littleton	MA	E	650 857-1501	9817
Industrial Bmdcal Sensors Corp	Waltham	MA	F	781 891-4201	12698
International Parallel Mchs	New Bedford	MA	G	508 990-2977	10604
Keimos 1988 US Inc (PA)	Norwood	MA	F	508 921-4590	11187
Kinetic Systems Inc	Boston	MA	F	617 522-8700	6842
Mack Technologies Inc (HQ)	Westford	MA	C	978 392-5500	13247
Manufacturers Services Limited	Concord	MA	E	617 330-7682	8124
Mediavue Systems LLC	Hingham	MA	F	781 926-0676	9154
Mercury Commercial Electronics Inc	Chelmsford	MA	C	978 967-1364	7938
Microway Inc	Plymouth	MA	F	508 746-7341	11467
Oracle America Inc	Bedford	MA	E	781 328-4770	6251
Oracle America Inc	Burlington	MA	E	281 710-2881	7405
Oracle Corporation	Burlington	MA	D	678 815-6637	7406
Power Systems Integrity Inc	Northborough	MA	G	508 393-1655	11106
Sie Computing Solutions Inc	Brockton	MA	D	508 588-6110	7305
Source Code LLC (PA)	Norwood	MA	E	781 688-2248	11209
Source Code Midco LLC (PA)	Norwood	MA	E	781 255-2022	11210
Sybase Inc	Watertown	MA	G	617 673-1200	12910
Tag Global Systems LLC	Pembroke	MA	G	800 630-4708	11378
Thinkflood Inc	Needham	MA	F	617 299-2000	10526
Advanced Programs Inc	Salem	NH	F	603 685-6748	15503
Alacron Inc	Nashua	NH	F	603 891-2750	15056
Celestica New England Inc	Newington	NH	B	603 334-3450	15206
Dutile Glines & Higgins Inc	Manchester	NH	F	603 622-0452	14846
Lexington Data Incorporated	Rindge	NH	G	603 899-5673	15460
Monarch International Inc	Amherst	NH	F	603 883-3390	13881
Wagz Inc (PA)	Portsmouth	NH	F	603 570-6015	15449
Jerrys At Misquamicut Inc	Westerly	RI	E	401 596-3155	16934
Onlogic Inc	South Burlington	VT	C	802 861-2300	17587

3572 Computer storage devices

	CITY	ST	EMP	PHONE	ENTRY#
BEI Holdings Inc	Wallingford	CT	F	203 741-9300	3780
J R Merritt Controls Inc (PA)	Stratford	CT	E	203 381-0100	3551
Kaman Aerospace Corporation	Middletown	CT	C	860 632-1000	1755
Mini LLC	Naugatuck	CT	G	203 464-5495	1972
Pexagon Technology Inc	Guilford	CT	E	203 458-3364	1402
Quantum Bpower Southington LLC	Southington	CT	F	860 201-0621	3230
Quantum Circuits Inc	New Haven	CT	E	203 872-4723	2189
Acbel (usa) Polytech Inc	Hopkinton	MA	G	508 625-1768	9305
ARA Dell EMC MA Rsa Bedfo	Bedford	MA	F	508 431-4084	6210
Cambex Corporation (PA)	Westborough	MA	F	508 983-1200	13085
EMC Corporation	Franklin	MA	E	800 275-8777	8834
EMC Corporation	Franklin	MA	D	508 435-1000	8835
EMC Corporation	Franklin	MA	D	866 438-3622	8836
EMC Corporation	Hopkinton	MA	F	508 435-0369	9317
EMC Corporation	Hopkinton	MA	D	800 445-2588	9318
EMC Corporation	Hopkinton	MA	E	508 346-2900	9319
EMC Corporation	Hopkinton	MA	D	508 435-2581	9320
EMC Corporation	Hopkinton	MA	D	508 249-5883	9321
EMC Corporation (HQ)	Hopkinton	MA	B	508 435-1000	9322
EMC Corporation	Milford	MA	E	508 634-2774	10402
EMC Corporation	Newton	MA	D	617 618-3400	10755
EMC Global Holdings Company	Hopkinton	MA	D	508 544-2852	9323
EMC International Holdings Inc	Hopkinton	MA	A	508 435-1000	9324
Emc1 Continental Ave LLC	Boston	MA	G	617 875-2687	6713
Infinidat Inc	Waltham	MA	F	781 907-7585	12699
Iwave Software LLC	Hopkinton	MA	E		9333
Manufacturers Services Limited	Concord	MA	E	617 330-7682	8124
Nanoramic Laboratories	Wakefield	MA	F	857 403-6031	12521
Raid Inc	Lawrence	MA	D	978 683-6444	9595
Seagate Technology LLC	Shrewsbury	MA	F	508 770-3111	11841
Sencorpwhite Inc (HQ)	Hyannis	MA	C	508 771-9400	9451
Sepaton Inc	Marlborough	MA	D	508 490-7900	10210
Silk Technologies Inc	Needham Heights	MA	D	877 982-2555	10557

SIC

Company	CITY	ST	EMP	PHONE	ENTRY#
Springboard Technology Corporation	Springfield	MA	D		12133
Sudbury Systems Inc	Bedford	MA	E	800 876-8888	6272
Unicom Engineering Inc (HQ)	Canton	MA	E	781 332-1000	7836
Vagrants Inc	Somerville	MA	F	857 400-8870	11909
Vce Company LLC	Marlborough	MA	A	831 247-1660	10228
Winchester Systems Inc (PA)	Littleton	MA	E	781 265-0200	9845
Cybernorth LLC	South Portland	ME	G	207 331-3310	5496
Centilla Corporation	Windham	NH	F	603 658-3801	15723
Memtec Corporation	Amherst	NH	F	603 893-8080	13880
Visit WEI	Salem	NH	F	603 893-0900	15570
It Synergy Group LLC	Warwick	RI	F	866 767-4874	16824

3575 Computer terminals

Company	CITY	ST	EMP	PHONE	ENTRY#
General Digital Corporation	East Hartford	CT	D	860 282-2900	996
Omega Engineering Inc (DH)	Norwalk	CT	C	203 359-1660	2549
Precision Electronic Assembly	Monroe	CT	F	203 452-1839	1919
Tech II Business Services Inc	Rocky Hill	CT	F	518 587-1565	2936
Actuality Systems Inc	Arlington	MA	G	617 325-9230	5938
Cortron Inc	Lowell	MA	E	978 975-5445	9871
Csi Keyboards Inc	Peabody	MA	E	978 532-8181	11304
EPC Space LLC	Andover	MA	F	978 208-1334	5881
Igt Global Solutions Corp	Braintree	MA	G	781 849-5642	7188
Leidos Inc	Tewksbury	MA	G	781 221-7627	12402
Rampage Systems Inc	Waltham	MA	E	781 891-1001	12758
Ferrite Microwave Tech LLC	Nashua	NH	E	603 881-5234	15100
Igt Global Solutions Corp	West Greenwich	RI	E	401 392-7025	16885
Igt Global Solutions Corporation (HQ)	Providence	RI	D	401 392-7077	16538
Vesuvius America Inc (DH)	Providence	RI	E		16640

3577 Computer peripheral equipment, nec

Company	CITY	ST	EMP	PHONE	ENTRY#
Alinabal Holdings Corporation (PA)	Milford	CT	B	203 877-3241	1797
Braxton Manufacturing Co Inc	Watertown	CT	C	860 274-6781	4003
Computer Express LLC	Berlin	CT	F	860 829-1310	62
Contek International Corp	New Canaan	CT	F	203 972-7330	2078
Control Module Inc (PA)	Enfield	CT	F	860 745-2433	1125
Dark Field Technologies Inc	Shelton	CT	F	203 298-0731	2997
Data Technology Inc	Tolland	CT	A	860 871-8082	3656
Dictaphone Corporation (DH)	Stratford	CT	F	203 381-7000	3533
Dymo Corporation	Norwalk	CT	D		2494
Eloque LLC	Norwalk	CT	F	203 849-5567	2497
Flo-Tech LLC (PA)	New Haven	CT	D	860 613-3333	2152
Fremco LLC	Stamford	CT	F	203 857-0522	3351
Frontier Vision Tech Inc	Rocky Hill	CT	E	860 953-0240	2922
General Digital Corporation	East Hartford	CT	D	860 282-2900	996
Gerber Scientific LLC (PA)	Tolland	CT	C	860 871-8082	3661
LTI Portfolio Management Corp	Wilton	CT	F	203 563-1100	4243
Macdermid Incorporated (HQ)	Waterbury	CT	C	203 575-5700	3933
Magnetec Corporation	Wallingford	CT	D	203 949-9933	3829
Marco International Inc	Ridgefield	CT	D	203 894-8000	2902
Measurement Systems Inc	Wallingford	CT	E	203 949-3500	3831
Morse Watchmans Inc	Oxford	CT	E	203 264-4949	2705
O E M Controls Inc (PA)	Shelton	CT	C	203 929-8431	3042
OEM Design Services LLC	East Haven	CT	E	203 467-5993	1049
Omega Engineering Inc (DH)	Norwalk	CT	C	203 359-1660	2549
Online River LLC	Westport	CT	F	203 801-5900	4191
Ortronics Inc (DH)	New London	CT	D	860 445-3900	2232
Ortronics Inc	West Hartford	CT	F	877 295-3472	4076
Ortronics Legrand	Ivoryton	CT	G	860 767-3515	1531
Recycle 4 Vets LLC	Westport	CT	G	203 222-7300	4194
Resavue Inc	Orange	CT	F	203 878-0944	2682
Scan-Optics LLC	Manchester	CT	D	860 645-7878	1636
Spectrum Virtual LLC	Cheshire	CT	G	203 303-7540	617
Syferlock Technology Corp	Waterbury	CT	G	203 292-5441	3971
Symbol Technologies LLC	Stamford	CT	E	203 359-5677	3476
Team Logic It	Vernon	CT		320 760-9084	3757
Therap Techne LLC	Torrington	CT	G	203 596-7553	3699
Ventus Technologies LLC	Norwalk	CT	F	203 642-2800	2591
Verico Technology LLC (HQ)	Enfield	CT	F	860 871-1200	1157
Xerox Corporation (HQ)	Norwalk	CT	B	203 849-5216	2598
Xerox Holdings Inc	Norwalk	CT	A	203 968-3000	2599
Xerox Holdings Corporation (PA)	Norwalk	CT	B	203 849-5216	2600
Yellowfin Holdings Inc	Ellington	CT	G	866 341-0979	1119
3M Touch Systems Inc	Norwood	MA	E	781 386-2770	11152
3M Touch Systems Inc	Westborough	MA	D	508 871-1840	13075
Adaptive Optics Associates Inc (DH)	Devens	MA	D	978 757-9600	8269
Aereo Inc	Hopedale	MA	F	617 861-8287	9293
Bmf Precision Inc	Maynard	MA	E	978 637-2050	10261
Bull Data Systems Inc	Chelmsford	MA	A	978 294-6000	7919
Camiant Inc (PA)	Marlborough	MA	F	508 486-9996	10126
Cgi Information Systems & Management Consultants Inc	Andover	MA	A	978 946-3000	5878
Cisco Systems Inc	Boxborough	MA	F	978 936-0000	7149
Corero Network Security Inc	Marlborough	MA	E	978 212-1500	10136
Cortron Inc	Lowell	MA	E	978 975-5445	9871
Csi Keyboards Inc	Peabody	MA	E	978 532-8181	11304
Csp Inc (PA)	Lowell	MA	E	978 954-5038	9872
Data Translation Inc (PA)	Norton	MA	E	508 481-3700	11126
Dowslake Microsystems Corp	North Andover	MA	G	978 691-5700	10826
EMC Corporation (HQ)	Hopkinton	MA	B	508 435-1000	9322
EMC International Holdings Inc	Hopkinton	MA	A	508 435-1000	9324
Equipe Communications Corp	Acton	MA	C	978 635-1999	5747
Evolv Tech Holdings Inc (PA)	Waltham	MA	G	781 374-8100	12669
Evolv Technologies Inc (HQ)	Waltham	MA	D	781 374-8100	12670
Fujifilm Rcrding Media USA Inc (DH)	Bedford	MA	D	781 271-4400	6228
Garrettcom Inc	North Andover	MA	E	978 688-8807	10835
Humanscale Corporation	Boston	MA	D	617 338-0077	6800
Intel Massachusetts Inc	Hudson	MA	A	978 553-4000	9377
INTEL Network Systems Inc (HQ)	Hudson	MA	C	978 553-4000	9378
International Parallel Mchs	New Bedford	MA	G	508 990-2977	10604
Inteset Technologies LLC	Hanover	MA	G	781 826-1560	9035
Juniper Networks Inc	Shrewsbury	MA	F	508 523-0427	11836
Kamel Peripherals Inc (PA)	Hopkinton	MA	E	508 435-7771	9334
Kemp Technologies Inc	Rochdale	MA	G	631 418-8407	11627
Kentron Technologies Inc	Wilmington	MA	G	978 988-9100	13419
L-Com Inc (DH)	North Andover	MA	D	978 682-6936	10842
M8trix Tech LLC	Canton	MA	E	617 925-7030	7806
Mack Technologies Inc (HQ)	Westford	MA	C	978 392-5500	13247
Madison Cable Corporation	Worcester	MA	D	800 522-6752	13755
Manufacturers Services Limited	Concord	MA	E	617 330-7682	8124
Markforged Holding Corporation (PA)	Watertown	MA	E	866 496-1805	12891
Mazu Networks LLC	Cambridge	MA	E	617 354-9292	7639
Metroblity Optical Systems Inc	North Billerica	MA	F	781 255-5300	10935
Microway Inc	Plymouth	MA	E	508 746-7341	11467
Milford Manufacturing Svcs LLC	Hopedale	MA	E	508 478-8544	9299
Mimoco Inc	Needham Heights	MA	F	617 783-1100	10552
N3k Informatik Inc	Boston	MA	F	617 289-9282	6901
Netscout Systems Inc (PA)	Westford	MA	E	978 614-4000	13253
Netsilicon Inc (HQ)	Waltham	MA	D	781 647-1234	12736
Network Equipment Tech Inc (DH)	Westford	MA	E	510 713-7300	13254
New England Keyboard Inc	Fitchburg	MA	E	978 345-8332	8668
New England Technology Group	Cambridge	MA	F	617 864-5551	7665
Newcastle Systems Inc	Amesbury	MA	E	781 935-3450	5848
Parallel Systems Corp	Georgetown	MA	E	978 352-7100	8911
Pison Technology Inc	Boston	MA	G	540 394-0998	6966
Power Systems Integrity Inc	Northborough	MA	G	508 393-1655	11106
Primary Pdc Inc (PA)	Waltham	MA	G	781 386-2000	12753
Project Resources Inc	Wareham	MA	F	508 295-7444	12842
Psjl Corporation	Billerica	MA	E	978 313-2500	6474
Rampage Systems Inc	Waltham	MA	E	781 891-1001	12758
Rapiscan Systems Inc	Billerica	MA	F	978 933-4375	6475
Retro-Fit Technologies Inc	Taunton	MA	E	508 478-2222	12363
Rsa Security LLC (PA)	Bedford	MA	A	800 995-5095	6268
Samsara	Northampton	MA	G	413 570-4130	11079
Sick Inc	Stoughton	MA	D	781 302-2500	12235
Sky Computers Inc	Chelmsford	MA	F	978 250-2420	7958
Smart Modular Technologies Inc	Tewksbury	MA	D	978 221-3513	12416
Sycamore Networks Inc	Chelmsford	MA	C	978 250-2900	7962
Voxel8 Inc	Somerville	MA	F	916 396-3714	11912
Williams Lea Boston	Boston	MA	E	617 371-2300	7125
Winchester Systems Inc (PA)	Littleton	MA	E	781 265-0200	9845
Wind River Systems Inc	Canton	MA	D	781 364-2200	7841
Wright Line LLC (HQ)	Worcester	MA	B	508 852-4300	13834
Allen Datagraph Systems Inc	Salem	NH	E	603 216-6344	15504
Allied Telesis Inc	Portsmouth	NH	D	603 334-6058	15358
Bantry Components Inc	Manchester	NH	E	603 668-3210	14817
Corportion For Lser Optics Res (PA)	Londonderry	NH	E	603 430-2023	14738
CTS Corporation	Londonderry	NH	D	603 421-2546	14740
Dutile Glines & Higgins Inc	Manchester	NH	F	603 622-0452	14846
Dzs Inc	Portsmouth	NH	F	510 777-7000	15380
Enterasys Networks Inc (HQ)	Salem	NH	D	603 952-5000	15521
Extech Instruments Corporation	Nashua	NH	D	877 439-8324	15099
Fujifilm Dimatix Inc	Lebanon	NH	D	603 443-5300	14689
H32 Design and Development LLC (PA)	Concord	NH	G	603 865-1000	14135
Lantos Technologies Inc	Derry	NH	E	781 443-7633	14198
Memtec Corporation	Amherst	NH	F	603 893-8080	13880
Minim Inc (PA)	Manchester	NH	E	833 966-4646	14889
Riverbed Technology Inc	Nashua	NH	G	603 402-5200	15161
Seamark International LLC	Nashua	NH	E	603 546-0100	15164
Solidscape Inc	Merrimack	NH	E	603 424-0590	15003
Tech Resources Inc	Milford	NH	E	603 673-9000	15039
Xor Media Inc	Greenville	NH	F	603 878-6400	14376
Astronova Inc (PA)	West Warwick	RI	C	401 828-4000	16902
Astronova Inc	West Warwick	RI	C	401 828-4000	16903
Electro Standards Lab Inc	Cranston	RI	D	401 946-1164	15853
Florlink Inc	Newport	RI	F	617 221-2200	16210
Vishay Efi Inc	Warwick	RI	E	401 738-9150	16873

	CITY	ST	EMP	PHONE	ENTRY#		CITY	ST	EMP	PHONE	ENTRY#
Alken Inc	Colchester	VT	E	802 655-3159	17185	7ac Technologies Inc	Beverly	MA	F	781 574-1348	6322
Image Tek Mfg Inc	Springfield	VT	E	802 885-6208	17618	Aipco Inc	Taunton	MA	E	508 823-7003	12316
Mack Group Inc (PA)	Arlington	VT	B	802 375-2511	16988	Air-Mart Heating & Cooling LLC	Lowell	MA	G	603 821-1416	9852
Mack Molding Company Inc (HQ)	Arlington	VT	C	802 375-2511	16990	Airxchange Inc	Rockland	MA	D	781 871-4816	11633
Ovr Tech LLC	Burlington	VT	G	802 391-4172	17149	Alpha Instruments Inc	Acton	MA	F	978 264-2966	5735
Preci-Manufacturing Inc	Winooski	VT	D	802 655-2414	17768	Aspen Systems LLC (PA)	Marlborough	MA	F	508 281-5322	10112
						Backer Hotwatt Inc	Danvers	MA	E	978 777-0070	8168

3578 Calculating and accounting equipment

	CITY	ST	EMP	PHONE	ENTRY#		CITY	ST	EMP	PHONE	ENTRY#
Blackwold Inc	Chester	CT	D	860 526-0800	624	Boyd Corporation (woburn) Inc (DH)	Woburn	MA	C	781 933-7300	13534
Hopp Companies Inc (PA)	Southbury	CT	G	800 889-8425	3196	Cambridgeport Air Systems Inc	Georgetown	MA	C	978 465-8481	8906
Marinero Express 809 East	Stamford	CT	F	203 487-0636	3408	Controlled Envmt Systems LLC (PA)	Mansfield	MA	E	508 339-4237	10042
Danversbank	South Hamilton	MA	G	978 468-2243	11969	Cox Engineering Company (PA)	Canton	MA	C	781 302-3300	7781
Diebold Nixdorf Incorporated	North Dartmouth	MA	D	508 984-5936	10994	Duc-Pac Corporation	Springfield	MA	E	413 525-3302	12091
Diebold Nixdorf Incorporated	Swansea	MA	D	508 646-4378	12304	Economy Plumbing & Htg Sup Co	Mattapan	MA	E	617 433-1200	10254
Atlantic Precision Services	Gorham	ME	G	207 329-1043	4816	Harris Envmtl Systems Inc	Andover	MA	D	978 470-8600	5885
Securecash Advantage	Portland	ME	G	207 797-4838	5269	Heat-Flo Inc	Uxbridge	MA	G	508 278-2400	12480
Crane Payment Solutions Inc (DH)	Bedford	NH	D	603 685-6999	13923	Hkd Turbo	Natick	MA	F	508 878-3798	10482
Diebold Nixdorf Incorporated	Hudson	NH	G	603 577-9519	14493	J & J Heating & AC Inc	Dracut	MA	F	978 454-8197	8306
Diebold Nixdorf Incorporated	Warwick	RI	G	401 823-8665	16806	Lake Industries Inc	Stoneham	MA	D	781 438-8814	12180
Diebold Nixdorf Incorporated	Woonsocket	RI	G	401 766-3606	16956	Lenox Special Needs	Lenox	MA	G	413 637-5571	9626
Displays By Garo Inc	Lincoln	RI	F	401 305-3511	16133	Merrimac Industrial Sales Inc (PA)	Haverhill	MA	F	978 372-6006	9114
Plastics Plus Inc	Cumberland	RI	E	401 727-1447	15960	Mestek Inc	Westfield	MA	D	413 564-5530	13184
						Mestek Inc (PA)	Westfield	MA	E	470 898-4533	13186

3579 Office machines, nec

	CITY	ST	EMP	PHONE	ENTRY#		CITY	ST	EMP	PHONE	ENTRY#
Accu-Time Systems Inc (DH)	Windsor	CT	E	860 870-5000	4252	Metromatic Manufacturing Company Inc	Byfield	MA	F	781 396-5300	7458
Acme United Corporation (PA)	Shelton	CT	D	203 254-6060	2978	Munters Corporation	Amesbury	MA	F	978 388-2666	5844
Agissar Corporation	Stratford	CT	E	203 375-8662	3516	Munters Corporation (DH)	Amesbury	MA	C	978 241-1100	5845
Bell and Howell LLC	Deep River	CT	E	860 526-9561	873	Munters Corporation	Amesbury	MA	E	978 241-1100	5846
Bidwell Industrial Group Inc	Middletown	CT	E	860 346-9283	1740	Munters USA Inc	Amesbury	MA	A	978 241-1100	5847
Dictaphone Corporation (DH)	Stratford	CT	C	203 381-7000	3533	Process Cooling Systems Inc	Leominster	MA	F	978 537-1996	9697
Dmt Solutions Global Corp (HQ)	Danbury	CT	D	833 874-0552	733	Renewable Energy Systems LLC	Scituate	MA	F	781 545-3320	11769
Energy Saving Pdts & Sls Corp	Burlington	CT	E	860 675-6443	549	Rubix Composites Inc	Woburn	MA	G	781 856-0342	13657
Gbr Systems Corporation	Deep River	CT	E	860 526-9561	877	Snow Economics Inc	Natick	MA	G	508 655-3232	10498
ID Mail Systems Inc	New Britain	CT	F	860 344-3333	2031	Suburban Service Corp Norwood	Westwood	MA	F	781 769-1515	13320
Its New England Inc	Wallingford	CT	F	203 265-8100	3819	Tecogen Inc (PA)	Waltham	MA	E	781 466-6402	12790
Pitney Bowes Inc	Shelton	CT	G	203 356-5000	3048	Tecomet Inc	Woburn	MA	A	781 782-6400	13675
Pitney Bowes Inc	Shelton	CT	E	203 922-4000	3049	Thermal Circuits Inc	Salem	MA	C	978 745-1162	11734
Pitney Bowes Inc (PA)	Stamford	CT	A	203 356-5000	3433	Thermo Power Corporation	Waltham	MA	A	781 622-1400	12802
Pitney Bowes RE Fing Corp	Stamford	CT	C	203 356-5000	3434	Thl-Nortek Investors LLC (PA)	Boston	MA	D	617 227-1050	7077
Pyramid Time Systems LLC	Meriden	CT	E	203 238-0550	1686	Thomas H Lee Equity Fund V LP	Boston	MA	E	617 227-1050	7078
Quadient Inc (DH)	Milford	CT	C	203 301-3400	1874	Trane Comercial Systems	Springfield	MA	F	413 271-3001	12141
Quadient Finance Usa Inc (DH)	Milford	CT	E	203 301-3400	1875	Trane Inc	Wilmington	MA	D	978 737-3900	13470
Stanley Fastening Systems LP	New Britain	CT	E	860 225-5111	2069	Watka Corporation	Lakeville	MA	F	508 946-5555	9523
Xerox Corporation (HQ)	Norwalk	CT	B	203 849-5216	2598	Beer Saver USA	Kennebunk	ME	F	207 299-2826	4922
Xerox Holdings Inc	Norwalk	CT	A	203 968-3000	2599	Fisher Engineering	Rockland	ME	C	207 701-4200	5328
Xerox Holdings Corporation (PA)	Norwalk	CT	B	203 849-5216	2600	Flexware Control Tech LLC	Bangor	ME	G	207 262-9682	4501
C P Bourg Inc (PA)	New Bedford	MA	E	508 998-2171	10577	Maine Market Refrigeration LLC (PA)	Fayette	ME	E	207 685-3504	4783
Markwell Manufacturing Co Inc	Norwood	MA	G	781 769-6610	11194	N E Tech-Air Inc	Scarborough	ME	C	207 347-7577	5439
Str Grinnell GP Holding LLC	Westminster	MA	F	978 731-2500	13279	Nyle International Corp (PA)	Bangor	ME	C	207 989-4335	4512
Sudbury Systems Inc	Bedford	MA	E	800 876-8888	6272	Nyle Systems LLC	Bangor	ME	E	207 989-4335	4513
Acme Staple Company Inc	Franklin	NH	F	603 934-2320	14318	Pool Environments Inc	Gorham	ME	F	207 839-8225	4831
Stanley Fastening Systems LP (HQ)	East Greenwich	RI	C	401 884-2500	15993	Trane US Inc	Westbrook	ME	F	844 807-2282	5652
						Ventech Industries Inc	Eliot	ME	G	207 439-0069	4751
						Aavid Laboratories Inc	Laconia	NH	C	603 528-3400	14639

3581 Automatic vending machines

	CITY	ST	EMP	PHONE	ENTRY#		CITY	ST	EMP	PHONE	ENTRY#
Blackwold Inc	Chester	CT	D	860 526-0800	624	Filtrine Manufacturing Co Inc	Keene	NH	D	603 352-5500	14599
Eastern Co	Chester	CT	D	860 526-0800	628	Hussmann Corporation	Salem	NH	E	603 893-7770	15538
Century Food Service Inc	Acushnet	MA	F	508 995-3221	5770	Jmd Duct Fabrication LLC	Weare	NH	G	603 235-9314	15672
DMC Inc	Somerville	MA	G	617 758-8517	11869	Precision Temperature Control	Jaffrey	NH	G	603 471-9023	15672
Next Generation Vending LLC	Stoughton	MA	A	781 828-2345	12226	Standex International Corp (PA)	Salem	NH	E	603 893-9701	15563
SOS Group Inc	Boston	MA	G	978 496-7947	7047	Tracs Industrial Coolers	Ossipee	NH	G	603 707-2241	15284
						Amtrol Holdings Inc	West Warwick	RI	A	401 884-6300	16899

3582 Commercial laundry equipment

	CITY	ST	EMP	PHONE	ENTRY#		CITY	ST	EMP	PHONE	ENTRY#
Rema Dri-Vac Corp	Norwalk	CT	F	203 847-2464	2566	Amtrol Inc (DH)	West Warwick	RI	B	401 884-6300	16900
American Dryer Corporation	Fall River	MA	C	508 678-9000	8519	Amtrol Intl Investments Inc (DH)	West Warwick	RI	F	401 884-6300	16901
Baystate Business Ventures LLC	Taunton	MA	F	508 828-9274	12324	Bsg Handcraft	Providence	RI	F	508 636-5154	16492
Gordon Brothers Intl LLC (HQ)	Boston	MA	D	888 424-1903	6767	Davidon Industries Inc	Warwick	RI	F	401 737-8380	16803
Two Go Drycleaning Inc	South Burlington	VT	E	802 658-9469	17606	John Hazen Whote Corporation	Cranston	RI	F	401 942-8000	15879
						Nasons Ug Inc (PA)	Middletown	RI	F	401 847-2497	16180

3585 Refrigeration and heating equipment

	CITY	ST	EMP	PHONE	ENTRY#		CITY	ST	EMP	PHONE	ENTRY#
116 Lenox Eo LLC	Stamford	CT	G	973 854-1999	3265	Trane US Inc	Riverside	RI	E	617 908-6710	16660
261 Pascone Place LLC	Newington	CT	G	860 666-7845	2264	Standex International Corp	Essex Junction	VT	F	864 963-3471	17247
Alvest (usa) Inc (DH)	Windsor	CT	E	860 602-3400	4259	Trane Company	Williston	VT	G	802 864-3816	17750
Demartino Fixture Co Inc	Windsor	CT	F	203 628-4899	4270						
Hartford Compressors Inc	West Hartford	CT	E		4064						

3586 Measuring and dispensing pumps

	CITY	ST	EMP	PHONE	ENTRY#		CITY	ST	EMP	PHONE	ENTRY#
Latin American Holding Inc (HQ)	Farmington	CT	F	860 674-3000	1228	Proflow Inc	North Haven	CT	E	203 230-4700	2433
Mechancal Engnered Systems LLC	New Canaan	CT	G	203 400-4658	2083	Fishman Corporation	Hopkinton	MA	E	508 435-2115	9325
Pfm Holding Co	Fairfield	CT	B	203 335-3300	1197	Lewa-Nikkiso America Inc (DH)	Holliston	MA	E	508 429-7403	9220
Rtx Corporation	East Hartford	CT	F	860 565-7622	1021	Liquid Metronics Incorporated	Acton	MA	E	978 263-9800	5757
Rtx Corporation	Middletown	CT	C	860 704-7133	1779	Sensing Systems Corporation	Dartmouth	MA	F	508 992-0872	8231
Trane Inc	New Haven	CT	F	860 437-6208	2211	Nordson Efd LLC (HQ)	East Providence	RI	C	401 431-7000	16034
Trane US Inc	Farmington	CT	F	860 470-3901	1251						

3589 Service industry machinery, nec

	CITY	ST	EMP	PHONE	ENTRY#		CITY	ST	EMP	PHONE	ENTRY#
Ultra Flow Dispense LLC	Windsor	CT	F	866 827-2534	4311	3M Purification Inc (HQ)	Meriden	CT	B	203 237-5541	1648
York International Corporation	Danbury	CT	F	203 730-8100	838	Aqualogic Inc	North Haven	CT	E	203 248-8959	2393
						Atlas Filtri North America LLC	Wallingford	CT	F	203 284-0080	3778
						Crystal Rock Holdings Inc	Watertown	CT	B	860 945-0661	4006
						Devivo Industries Inc	Waterbury	CT	E	203 270-1552	3906

	CITY	ST	EMP	PHONE	ENTRY#
Ds Services of America Inc	Watertown	CT	B	860 945-0661	4009
Evoqua Water Technologies LLC	South Windsor	CT	D	860 528-6512	3146
Goodway Technologies Corporation (PA)	Stamford	CT	D	203 359-4708	3358
Gotham Technologies Inc	Norwalk	CT	F	800 468-4261	2509
Guardian Envmtl Tech Inc	New Milford	CT	F	860 350-2200	2245
H Krevit and Company Inc	New Haven	CT	E	203 772-3350	2159
Howden Roots LLC	Windsor	CT	D	860 688-8361	4281
Hydro Service & Supplies Inc	Middletown	CT	G	203 265-3995	1751
Kx Technologies LLC (DH)	West Haven	CT	E	203 799-9000	4111
Megadoor USA Inc	Meriden	CT	C	203 238-2700	1673
New Milford Commission	New Milford	CT	G	860 354-3758	2255
Redco Corporation (HQ)	Stamford	CT	D	203 363-7300	3445
Rhema 320 LLC (PA)	New Haven	CT		475 434-8581	2191
Smithfamily1938 LLC	Enfield	CT	G	424 341-8876	1153
Spencer Turbine Company (DH)	Windsor	CT	E	860 688-8361	4301
Stormtech LLC	Rocky Hill	CT	E	860 529-8188	2935
Town of Montville	Uncasville	CT	D	860 848-3830	3745
Town of Vernon	Vernon	CT	D	860 870-3545	3758
Uncle Sams Contractors LLC (PA)	East Hartford	CT	F	833 487-2776	1031
All-Way Service Corp	South Weymouth	MA	F	781 335-4533	11974
American Water Systems LLC	Canton	MA	F	781 830-9722	7767
Atlas Water Systems Inc	Waltham	MA	D	781 373-4700	12597
Auto-Chlor System NY Cy Inc	Foxboro	MA	C	508 543-6767	8691
Barletta Fschbach Green Line D	Canton	MA	F	781 737-1705	7773
Battle Grounds Coffee Co LLC	Haverhill	MA	F	978 891-5860	9077
Bluedrop LLC	South Easton	MA	E	877 662-7873	11938
Continental Metal Pdts Co Inc	Woburn	MA	F	781 935-4400	13546
Crane Mdsg Systems Inc	Dedham	MA	G	781 501-5800	8240
Crane Nxt Co (PA)	Waltham	MA	C	610 430-2510	12644
Crosstek Membrane Tech LLC	Billerica	MA	F	978 761-9601	6430
Den Mar Corporation	North Dartmouth	MA	F	508 999-3295	10993
Diamond Water Systems Inc	Chicopee	MA	E	413 536-8186	8022
Duraflow LLC	Tewksbury	MA	F	978 851-7439	12394
Essex Silverline Corporation (PA)	Dracut	MA	F	978 957-2116	8305
Evoqua Water Technologies LLC	Tewksbury	MA	E	978 863-4600	12397
Evoqua Water Technologies LLC	Tewksbury	MA	D	908 851-4250	12398
Evoqua Water Technologies LLC	Tewksbury	MA	C	978 934-9349	12399
Filtered Air Systems Inc	Woburn	MA	F	781 491-0508	13565
H2o Care Inc	Middleton	MA	F	978 777-8330	10384
Heartland Water Technology Inc	Hudson	MA	F	603 490-9203	9372
Hydrotech Services Inc	North Attleboro	MA	F	508 699-5977	10874
I Robot Corp - Closed	Burlington	MA	F	781 345-0200	7377
JDM Company Inc	North Chelmsford	MA	G	978 251-1121	10979
Keller Products Inc	North Chelmsford	MA	F	978 264-1911	10980
Kerfoot Technologies Inc	Falmouth	MA	F	508 539-3002	8634
KLA Systems Inc	Assonet	MA	G	508 644-5555	5975
L T Technologies	East Bridgewater	MA	G	508 456-0315	8342
Metro Group Inc	Wilmington	MA	F	781 932-9911	13431
Motion Technology Inc	Hudson	MA	G	508 460-9800	9392
Nanostone Water Inc	Waltham	MA	C	781 209-6900	12732
North Amrcn Fltration Mass Inc	Walpole	MA	F	508 660-9016	12570
Remediation Lockwood Tech	Leominster	MA	E	404 666-5857	9701
Safve Inc	Scituate	MA	F	781 545-3546	11770
Sarid Inc	Lexington	MA	G	781 315-1105	9769
Security Engineered McHy Inc (PA)	Westborough	MA	E	508 366-1488	13133
Spilldam Environmental Inc	Brockton	MA	F	508 583-7850	7309
Thermo Wave Technologies LLC	Peabody	MA	F	800 733-9615	11347
Town of Westborough	Westborough	MA	E	508 366-7615	13140
Tryxus Investment & Trdg Inc	Weston	MA	F	800 981-6616	13291
Uvtech Systems Inc	Carlisle	MA	G	978 440-7282	7849
Veralto Corporation	Waltham	MA	G	781 755-3655	12810
Voltea Inc	Worcester	MA	F	510 861-3719	13825
Whipps Inc	Athol	MA	D	978 249-7924	5984
Alan S Bolster	Brewer	ME	F	207 989-5143	4608
Hil Technology Inc (DH)	Portland	ME	F	207 756-6200	5222
Micronetixx Technologies LLC	Lewiston	ME	G	207 786-2000	4975
Williams Partners Ltd	East Boothbay	ME	G	207 633-3111	4738
Aquatic Solutions LLC	Hampton	NH	G	888 704-7665	14398
City of Manchester	Manchester	NH	F	603 624-6482	14829
Filtrine Manufacturing Co Inc	Keene	NH	D	603 352-5500	14599
Global Filtration Systems	Wolfeboro	NH	G	603 651-8777	15733
GS Blodgett Corporation	Bow	NH	D	603 225-5688	14000
Pentair Rsdntial Fltration LLC	Dover	NH	B	603 749-1610	14244
Pitco Frialator Inc (HQ)	Bow	NH	D	603 225-6684	15306
Pitco Frialator Inc	Pembroke	NH	D	603 225-6684	15307
PSI Water Systems LLC (PA)	Hooksett	NH	F	603 624-5110	14470
Sponge-Jet Inc (PA)	Newington	NH	G	603 610-7950	15212
Utrafryer Systems Inc	Bow	NH	C	603 225-6684	14012
Benson Neptune Inc (DH)	Warwick	RI	D	401 821-7140	16790
Service Tech Inc (PA)	North Providence	RI	G	401 353-3664	16310
Westfall Manufacturing Co	Bristol	RI	F	401 253-3799	15786
Bering Technology Inc	Waitsfield	VT	G	408 364-6500	17663
GS Blodgett LLC (HQ)	Essex Junction	VT	C	802 860-3700	17236

	CITY	ST	EMP	PHONE	ENTRY#
GS Blodgett Corporation	Essex Junction	VT	D	802 860-3700	17237

3592 Carburetors, pistons, rings, valves

	CITY	ST	EMP	PHONE	ENTRY#
Air Valves LLC	Bethlehem	CT	G	203 266-7175	142
Carten Controls Inc	Cheshire	CT	E	203 699-2100	577
Nutek Aerospace Corp	New Milford	CT	G	860 355-3169	2257
Schwing Bioset Technologies	Danbury	CT	C	203 744-2100	813
Conant Controls Inc	Woburn	MA	E	781 395-2240	13544
Heart Valve Society	Beverly	MA	F	212 561-9879	6355
Tooling Research Inc	Walpole	MA	F	508 668-5583	12577
Valmet Flow Control Inc	Shrewsbury	MA	C	508 852-0200	11846
Valmet Flow Control Inc (HQ)	Shrewsbury	MA	C	508 852-0200	11847
Maine Valve Rebuilders	Gorham	ME	G	207 856-6735	4825
Butler Valve & Fittings	Portsmouth	RI	G	401 849-3833	16441

3593 Fluid power cylinders and actuators

	CITY	ST	EMP	PHONE	ENTRY#
Airpot Corporation	Norwalk	CT	E	800 848-7681	2459
Parker & Harper Companies Inc (PA)	Raymond	NH	D	603 895-4761	15455
Quality Controls Inc	Northfield	NH	E	603 286-3321	15268
Watts Regulator Co	Franklin	NH	A	603 934-5110	14323

3594 Fluid power pumps and motors

	CITY	ST	EMP	PHONE	ENTRY#
Hamilton Sundstrand Corp (HQ)	Windsor Locks	CT	A	619 714-9442	4330
ITT Inc (PA)	Stamford	CT	C	914 641-2000	3388
Redco Corporation (HQ)	Stamford	CT	D	203 363-7300	3445
Reidville Hydraulics & Mfg Inc	Torrington	CT	E	860 496-1133	3694
Sfc Koenig LLC	North Haven	CT	E	203 245-1100	2436
Crane Nxt Co (PA)	Waltham	MA	C	610 430-2510	12644
Hostar Mar Trnspt Systems Inc	Wareham	MA	F	508 295-2900	12838
Kerfoot Technologies Inc	Falmouth	MA	F	508 539-3002	8634
Marine Hydraulics Inc	New Bedford	MA	F	508 990-2866	10619
Navtec Rigging Solutions Inc	Groton	MA	E		9011
Newera Services Corporation (PA)	New Bedford	MA	E	508 995-9711	10631
Apex Sealing Inc	Fairfax	VT	G	802 524-7100	17254

3596 Scales and balances, except laboratory

	CITY	ST	EMP	PHONE	ENTRY#
Compuweigh Corporation (PA)	Woodbury	CT	F	203 262-9400	4386
Hasler Inc	Milford	CT	B	203 301-3400	1833
The A H Emery Company (PA)	Seymour	CT	E	203 881-9333	2970
Commercial Scale Balance Inc	Agawam	MA	F	413 789-9990	5787
Highland Labs Inc	Holliston	MA	G	508 429-2918	9215
Hyer Industries Inc	Pembroke	MA	G	781 826-8101	11370
M & M Scale Company Inc	Danvers	MA	F	781 321-2737	8202
New Bedford Scale Co Inc	New Bedford	MA	G	508 997-6730	10628
Setra Systems Inc	Boxboro	MA	F	978 263-1400	7145
Public Scales	Lewiston	ME	F	207 784-9466	4986
Edlund Company LLC	Burlington	VT	D	802 862-9661	17133
Tridyne Process Systems Inc	South Burlington	VT	G	802 863-6873	17605

3599 Industrial machinery, nec

	CITY	ST	EMP	PHONE	ENTRY#
300 Wood Avenue LLC	Stratford	CT	G	763 479-6605	3514
A D Grinding	Plainville	CT	F	860 747-6630	2743
A Hardiman Machine Co Inc	East Windsor	CT	F	860 623-8133	1063
Able Machine Tool	Cheshire	CT	G	203 272-5459	568
Abstract Tool Inc	Deep River	CT	F	860 526-4635	872
Accupaulo Holding Corporation (PA)	Bristol	CT	E	860 666-5621	391
Accurate Tool & Die Inc	Stamford	CT	E	203 967-1200	3270
Accutrol LLC	Danbury	CT	E	203 445-9991	703
Accuturn Manufacturing Co LLC	South Windsor	CT	F	860 289-6355	3106
Acucut Inc	Southington	CT	E	860 793-7012	3201
Addamo Manufacturing Inc	Newington	CT	G	860 667-2601	2266
Advance Development & Mfg Corp	Guilford	CT	F	203 453-4325	1382
Aerospace Techniques Inc	Middletown	CT	F	860 347-1200	1733
Aeroswiss LLC	Meriden	CT	F	203 634-4545	1652
Agreda & Son Inc	South Windsor	CT	D	860 289-2520	3109
AIW-Alton Inc	Windsor Locks	CT	G		4323
Allied Machining Co Inc	Newington	CT	G	860 665-1228	2271
Allyn Tool Company	Ellington	CT	G	860 979-0041	1100
Altek Electronics Inc	Torrington	CT	C	860 482-7626	3669
American Precision Mfg LLC	Ansonia	CT	F	203 734-1800	6
American Tool & Mfg Corp	Newington	CT	F	860 666-2255	2272
Anmor Machining Company LLC	New Britain	CT	F	860 224-7774	2000
Arcade Technology LLC	Bridgeport	CT	D	203 366-3871	297
Arcor Systems LLC	Suffield	CT	G	860 370-9780	3588
Arna Machine Company	Bristol	CT	F	860 583-0628	396
ASap Mch Sp Fabrication Inc	Plainfield	CT	G	860 564-4114	2733
Atlas Precision Mfg LLC	South Windsor	CT	E	860 290-9114	3119
B & A Company Inc	Milford	CT	E	203 876-7527	1798
B & F Machine Co Inc (PA)	New Britain	CT	C	860 225-6349	2006
Balding Precision Inc	Milford	CT	G	203 878-9135	1799
Barnes Technical Products LLC	New Haven	CT	G	203 931-8852	2123
Bay State Machine Inc	Plainfield	CT	G	860 230-0054	2735
Bmi Cad Services Inc	Simsbury	CT	F	860 658-0808	3083

	CITY	ST	EMP	PHONE	ENTRY#		CITY	ST	EMP	PHONE	ENTRY#
Bracone Metal Spinning Inc	Southington	CT	E	860 628-5927	3204	Jeff Mfg Inc	Torrington	CT	F	860 482-1387	3686
Bristol Tool & Die Company	Bristol	CT	F	860 582-2577	423	Jensen Machine Company	Newington	CT	G	860 666-5438	2301
British Precision Inc	Glastonbury	CT	F	860 633-3343	1272	Jeskey LLC	North Haven	CT	E	203 772-6675	2418
Budney Overhaul & Repair Ltd	Berlin	CT	C	860 828-0585	56	Joval Machine Co Inc	Yalesville	CT	E	203 284-0082	4398
Burke Precision Machine Co Inc	East Granby	CT	G	860 408-1394	926	JV Precision Machine Co	Seymour	CT	E	203 888-0748	2962
Buswell Manufacturing Company	Bridgeport	CT	F	203 334-6069	307	K & E Auto Machine L L C	Naugatuck	CT	F	203 723-7189	1968
C & A Machine Co Inc	Newington	CT	E	860 667-0605	2278	K4 Machining LLC	Waterbury	CT	F	203 437-8764	3927
C V Tool Company Inc (PA)	Southington	CT	E	978 353-7901	3206	Kania Darius	Newington	CT	G	860 667-4400	2302
Candlewood Tool and Mch Sp Inc	Gaylordsville	CT	F	860 355-1892	1263	Karas Engineering Company Inc	New Milford	CT	G	860 355-3153	2249
Carolina Precision Technologie	Putnam	CT	F	860 315-9017	2847	Kell-Strom Tool Co Inc (PA)	Wethersfield	CT	F	860 529-6851	4209
Central Conn Sls & Mfg Inc	Newington	CT	G	860 667-1411	2280	Kell-Strom Tool Intl Inc	Wethersfield	CT	F	860 529-6851	4210
Chapco Inc (PA)	Chester	CT	F	860 526-9535	625	Kksp Precision Machining LLC	Watertown	CT	D	860 274-6773	4016
Con-Tec Inc	Naugatuck	CT	F	203 723-8942	1953	Kovacs Machine and Tool Co	Wallingford	CT	F	203 269-4949	3825
Concentric Tool & Mfg Co Inc	Waterbury	CT	F	203 756-9145	3901	Loric Tool Inc	North Grosvenordale	CT	F	860 928-0171	
Connectcut Mch Toling Cast Inc	Milford	CT	F	203 874-8300	1813						2385
Connecticut Coining Inc	Bethel	CT	D	203 743-3861	103	Lynn Welding Co Inc	Newington	CT	D	860 667-4400	2304
Connecticut Department Trnsp	Portland	CT	G	860 342-5996	2818	M Cubed Technologies Inc	Monroe	CT	E	203 452-2333	1915
Consulting Engrg Dev Svcs Inc	Oxford	CT	D	203 828-6528	2691	M Cubed Technologies Inc (HQ)	Newtown	CT	E	203 304-2940	2341
Continental Machine TI Co Inc	New Britain	CT	D	860 223-2896	2014	M T D Corporation	Trumbull	CT	E	203 261-3721	3724
Continuity Engine Inc	Ridgefield	CT	F	866 631-5556	2893	Macton Oxford LLC	Oxford	CT	E	203 267-1500	2703
Controlled Fluidics LLC	Wallingford	CT	F	603 673-4323	3794	Manchester TI & Design ADP LLC	North Haven	CT	G	860 296-6541	2422
Coronet Machinery Corp	Bethel	CT	E	203 744-8009	104	Marenna Amusements LLC	Orange	CT	F	203 623-4386	2675
CPI Manufacturing LLC	Berlin	CT	F		63	Max-Tek LLC	Prospect	CT	F	860 372-4900	2836
CT Hone Inc	Plainville	CT	G	860 747-3884	2752	Mega Precision LLC	Newington	CT	E	203 887-5718	2306
Darly Custom Technology Inc	Windsor	CT	F	860 298-7966	4269	Megowen LLC	East Hartford	CT	F	860 528-9701	1005
Dawid Manufacturing Inc	Ansonia	CT	G	203 734-1800	12	Metalpro Inc	Old Saybrook	CT	E	860 388-1811	2655
Dell Acquisition LLC	Plainville	CT	F	860 677-8545	2753	Micro Precision LLC	South Windham	CT	F	860 423-4575	3103
Delta-Ray Industries Inc	Bridgeport	CT	F	203 367-6910	316	Microbest Inc	Waterbury	CT	C	203 597-0355	3944
Demusz Mfg Co Inc	East Hartford	CT	E	860 528-9845	985	Mikco Manufacturing Inc	Wallingford	CT	F	203 269-2250	3833
Dependable Repair Inc	North Branford	CT	F	203 481-9706	2365	Mill Manufacturing Inc	Bridgeport	CT	G	203 367-9572	347
Dickson Product Dev Inc	Norwalk	CT	G	203 846-2128	2491	Naiad Dynamics Us Inc (HQ)	Shelton	CT	E	203 929-6355	3033
Drt Aerospace LLC	East Hartford	CT	F	937 298-7391	986	Necst Inc	Southington	CT	F	860 628-2515	3223
Dso Manufacturing Company Inc	New Britain	CT	E	860 224-2641	2023	New Designz Inc	Wallingford	CT	F	203 439-7784	3834
Dufrane Nuclear Shielding Inc	Winsted	CT	F	860 379-2318	4340	New England Cnc Inc	Hamden	CT	F	203 288-8241	1446
Durol Co	Hamden	CT	F	203 288-3383	1422	New England Tool Corporation (PA)	Manchester	CT	F	860 783-5555	1621
E O Manufacturing Company Inc	West Haven	CT	E	203 932-5981	4105	New Horizon Machine Co Inc	Stamford	CT	G	203 316-9355	3416
E-B Manufacturing Company Inc	Middletown	CT	E	860 632-8563	1745	Northwest Conn Mfg Co Inc	Winsted	CT	G	860 379-1553	4352
EA Patten Co LLC	Manchester	CT	D	860 649-2851	1594	Noujaim Tool Co Inc	Waterbury	CT	E	203 753-4441	3952
East Branch Engrg & Mfg Inc	New Milford	CT	F	860 355-9661	2242	Nova Machining LLC	Unionville	CT	G	860 675-8131	3750
East Coast Metal Hose Inc	Naugatuck	CT	G	203 723-7459	1956	Nvi Weld Technology LLC	Waterbury	CT	G	203 707-0587	3953
Eastern Broach & Machine LLC	Farmington	CT	G	860 678-7490	1216	Oakville Quality Products LLC	Waterbury	CT	F	203 757-5525	3954
Eclas Realty Corporation	Plainville	CT	E	860 747-5773	2756	Par Manufacturing Inc	Farmington	CT	G	860 677-1797	1239
El Mar Inc	West Hartford	CT	G	860 729-7232	4058	Paramount Machine Company Inc	Manchester	CT	D	860 643-5549	1628
Elks Manufacturing Corporation	Meriden	CT	F	203 235-2528	1666	Parason Machine Inc	Deep River	CT	F	860 526-3565	880
Emp Co Inc (PA)	Bristol	CT	G	860 589-3233	440	Phoenix Manufacturing Inc	Enfield	CT	D	860 745-2080	1141
Engineered Inserts Systems Inc (PA)	Milford	CT	F	203 301-3334	1824	Pinto Manufacturing LLC	Glastonbury	CT	G	860 659-9543	1293
Engineering Specialties Inc	North Branford	CT	E	203 488-2266	2367	Polar Corporation	Farmington	CT	F	862 225-6000	1241
Esteem Manufacturing Corp	South Windsor	CT	E	860 282-9964	3145	Precision Aerospace Inc	Milford	CT	E	203 888-3022	1868
Excello Tool Engrg & Mfg Co	Milford	CT	E	203 878-4073	1827	Precision Grinding Company	New Britain	CT	F	860 229-9652	2055
Expermental Prototype Pdts Inc	South Windsor	CT	F	860 289-4948	3147	Precision Metal Products Inc	Milford	CT	C	203 877-4258	1869
Expressway Lube Centers	Danbury	CT	F	203 744-2511	743	Precision Punch + Tooling Corp	Berlin	CT	G	860 225-4159	80
F W Manufacturing & Engrg Co	South Windsor	CT	F	860 291-8580	3148	Pro Tool and Design Inc	Newington	CT	F	860 828-4667	2318
Fairchild Industries Inc	Winsted	CT	F	860 379-2725	4345	Projects Inc	Glastonbury	CT	C	860 633-4615	1295
Famp Inc	Colebrook	CT	E	860 379-2725	666	Quality Machine Inc	New Milford	CT	G	860 354-6794	2259
Focus Technologies Inc	Berlin	CT	F	860 829-8998	65	Quality Wire Edm Inc	Bristol	CT	G	860 583-9867	487
Forrati Manufacturing & TI LLC	Plantsville	CT	G	860 426-1105	2791	Quest Machining & Mfg LLC	East Hartford	CT	F	860 290-1145	1018
Frank Roth Co Inc	Stratford	CT	D	203 377-2155	3539	Quick Machining Services LLC	Meriden	CT	G	203 634-8822	1688
Frasal Tool Co Inc	Newington	CT	F	860 666-3524	2295	Quick Turn Machine Company Inc	Windsor Locks	CT	F	860 623-2569	4332
G L C Inc	Watertown	CT	F	860 945-6166	4013	R & I Manufacturing Co	Terryville	CT	F	860 589-5864	3608
Gen-El-Mec Associates LLC	Oxford	CT	E	203 828-6566	2694	Ralph Industries Inc	Bristol	CT	F	860 666-5621	490
General Machine Company Inc	Southington	CT	F	860 426-9295	3212	Rand Machine & Fabrication Co	Cheshire	CT	F	203 272-1352	613
Genovese Manufacturing Co	Terryville	CT	F	860 582-9944	3604	Rand Sheaves & Pulleys LLC	Cheshire	CT	G	203 272-1352	614
Grace Machine Company LLC	Berlin	CT	F	860 828-8789	68	Raym-Co Inc	Farmington	CT	F	860 678-8292	1243
Gregor Technologies LLC	Torrington	CT	E	860 482-2569	3683	Reed and Stefanow Mch TI Co	Bristol	CT	E	860 583-7834	491
Gulf Manufacturing Inc	Rocky Hill	CT	E	860 529-8601	2923	Reidville Hydraulics & Mfg Inc	Torrington	CT	F	860 496-1133	3694
Gypsum Systems LLC	Burlington	CT	G	860 470-3916	550	Remarc LLC	Granby	CT	G	860 844-8939	1308
H & B Tool & Eng Co Inc	South Windsor	CT	F	860 528-9341	3153	Renchel Tool LLC	Putnam	CT	F	860 315-9017	2873
H G Steinmetz Mch Works Inc	Stamford	CT	E	203 794-1880	3360	Reno Machine Company Inc	Newington	CT	D	860 666-5641	2321
Harwest Holdings One Inc	South Windham	CT	E	860 423-8334	3102	Richards Machine Tool Co Inc	Newington	CT	F	860 436-2938	2322
Hfo Chicago LLC	Windsor	CT	G	860 285-0709	4280	RK Manufacturing Corp Conn	Danbury	CT	D	203 797-8700	806
Hfw Inc	Norwalk	CT	G	203 854-9584	2512	Ross Mfg & Design LLC	Milford	CT	F	203 878-0187	1881
Houston-Weber Systems Inc	Branford	CT	G	203 481-0115	264	RWK Tool Inc	Cromwell	CT	F	860 635-0116	696
HW Machine LLC	Berlin	CT	G	860 828-7679	70	Salform Inc	New Britain	CT	F	860 559-6359	2059
Hygrade Precision Tech LLC	Plainville	CT	F	860 747-5773	2764	Satellite Tool & Mch Co Inc	South Windsor	CT	F	860 290-8558	3178
Integra-Cast Inc	New Britain	CT	D	860 225-7600	2032	Secondaries Inc	Wolcott	CT	G	203 879-4633	4375
Integral Technologies Inc (DH)	Enfield	CT	G	860 741-2281	1136	Senior Operations LLC	Enfield	CT	E	860 741-2546	1148
Interface Devices Incorporated	Milford	CT	G	203 878-4648	1839	Seymour - Sheridan Incorporated	Monroe	CT	D	203 261-4009	1921
Irex Machining Inc	Tolland	CT	F	860 870-1885	3663	Silver City Manufacturing LLC	Meriden	CT	F	203 238-0027	1698
J & L Machine Co Inc (PA)	Manchester	CT	E	860 649-3539	1607	Simsbury Precision Pdts Inc	Simsbury	CT	G	860 658-6909	3097
J & L Mfg Watertown Inc	Waterbury	CT	E	203 591-9124	3924	Simson Corporation	Wallingford	CT	F	203 265-9882	3848
Jan Manufacturing Co	Wolcott	CT	G	203 879-0580	4366	Sirois Tool Company Inc (PA)	Berlin	CT	E	860 828-5327	85
Jared Manufacturing Co Inc	Norwalk	CT	E	203 846-1732	2520	Skico Manufacturing Co LLC	Hamden	CT	G	203 230-1305	1455
Jbsbt LLC	Durham	CT	F	860 349-0631	902	Soldream Spcial Process - Wldg	Tolland	CT	G	860 858-5247	3664

	CITY	ST	EMP	PHONE	ENTRY#		CITY	ST	EMP	PHONE	ENTRY#
Spargo Machine Products Inc	Terryville	CT	F	860 583-3925	3609	Atlantic Industrial Model	Essex	MA	G	978 768-4568	8472
Specialty Components Inc	Wallingford	CT	G	203 284-9112	3853	Aube Precision Tool Co Inc	Ludlow	MA	G	413 589-9048	9939
Spectrum Machine & Design LLC	Windsor Locks	CT	E	860 386-6490	4334	Automatic Machine Products Co	Taunton	MA	E	508 822-4226	12321
SS Fabrications Inc	Eastford	CT	G	860 974-1910	1092	Axis Cnc Incorporated	Ware	MA	F	413 967-6803	12824
Ssi Manufacturing Tech Corp	Bristol	CT	E	860 589-8004	499	Axis Technologies Inc	Lowell	MA	E	978 275-9908	9858
Standard Bellows Co (PA)	Windsor Locks	CT	E	860 623-2307	4335	B & R Machine Inc	Ludlow	MA	E	413 589-0246	9940
Sterling Engineering Corp	Pleasant Valley	CT	C	860 379-3366	2804	B S E International Corp	Concord	MA	G	781 863-5270	8104
Sterling Prcsion Machining Inc	Sterling	CT	F	860 564-4043	3504	B-C-D Metal Products Inc	Malden	MA	F	781 397-9922	10004
Stevens Manufacturing Co Inc	Milford	CT	E	203 878-2328	1890	Ball Slides Inc	Millis	MA	G	508 359-4348	10448
Straton Industries Inc	Stratford	CT	D	203 375-4488	3578	Banacek Invstgtons Srch Recove	Sharon	MA	G	781 784-1400	11792
Summit Screw Machine Corp	Milford	CT	G	203 693-2727	1891	Bartley Machine & Mfg Co Inc	Amesbury	MA	E		5831
Sunnycor Incorporated	Terryville	CT	F	860 582-9667	3610	Bees Manufacturing LLC	Needham	MA	F	781 400-1280	10506
T & J Manufacturing LLP	Middletown	CT	E	860 632-8655	1785	Bendon Gear and Machine Inc	Rockland	MA	E	781 878-8100	11636
T M I Liquidating Inc	East Berlin	CT	E	860 828-0344	919	Berkshire Mnufactured Pdts Inc	Newburyport	MA	C	978 462-8161	10670
TET Mfg Co Inc	Middlefield	CT	E	860 349-1004	1729	Berner Precision Products LLC	Southbridge	MA	E	508 764-2521	12010
TG Industries Inc	Meriden	CT	E	203 235-3239	1704	Bigwood Corporation	Mashpee	MA	E	508 477-2220	10249
Thavenet Machine Company Inc	Pawcatuck	CT	G	860 599-4495	2726	Boniface Tool & Die Inc	Dudley	MA	E	508 764-3248	8317
Thermatool Corp (HQ)	East Haven	CT	D	203 468-4100	1053	Borg Design Inc	Hudson	MA	F	978 562-1559	9357
Timna Manufacturing Inc	Wallingford	CT	G	203 265-4656	3868	Boston Centerless Inc	Avon	MA	E	508 587-3500	6145
To Wind Down LLC	Newtown	CT	D	203 426-3030	2353	Boulevard Machine & Gear Inc	Westfield	MA	E	413 788-6466	13154
Tool Logistics II	Norwalk	CT	D	203 855-9754	2585	Boynton Machine Company Inc	Waltham	MA	F	781 899-9900	12611
Toolmax Designing Tooling Inc	Ashford	CT	F	860 477-0373	22	Brennan Machine Co Inc	Hanson	MA	E	781 293-3997	9050
Top Flight Machine Tool LLC	Plainville	CT	G	860 747-4726	2784	Brodeur Machine Company Inc	New Bedford	MA	E	508 995-2662	10574
Total Concept Tool Inc	Branford	CT	E	203 483-1130	283	Brook Pond Machining Inc	Westfield	MA	G	413 562-7411	13155
TP Cycle & Engineering Inc	Danbury	CT	E	203 744-4960	826	Brookline Machine Company Inc (PA)	Waltham	MA	E	617 782-4018	12612
Tri-Mar Manufacturing Company	Southington	CT	E	860 628-4791	3238	Brooks Precision Machining Inc	Chelmsford	MA	F	978 256-7477	7918
Triumph Manufacturing Co Inc	Middletown	CT	F	860 635-8811	1787	Bruce Diamond Corporation	Attleboro	MA	E	508 222-3755	5999
Tropax Precision Manufacturing	Danbury	CT	F	203 794-0733	827	Burr Industries Inc	Danvers	MA	G	978 774-2527	8172
Twin Mfg Co DBA Twin Mro	South Windsor	CT	D	860 289-6041	3187	C & C Fabricating Inc	Ipswich	MA	F	978 356-9980	9479
Unas Grinding Corporation	East Hartford	CT	E	860 289-1538	1030	C & C Machine Inc	Tyngsboro	MA	F	978 649-0285	12459
Uniprise International Inc	Terryville	CT	F	860 589-7262	3613	C & C Metals Engineering Inc	West Boylston	MA	F	508 835-9011	12955
United Gear and Machine Co Inc	Suffield	CT	F	860 623-6618	3596	C & G Machine Tool Co Inc	Granby	MA	F	413 467-9556	8970
W & W Machine Co Inc	Milford	CT	F		1899	C V Tool Company Inc	Fitchburg	MA	F	978 353-7901	8645
Wallingford Industries Inc	Branford	CT	F	203 481-0359	285	C-R Machine Co Inc (PA)	Billerica	MA	D	978 663-3989	6420
Warner Precision Machining & F	Hamden	CT	E	203 281-3660	1463	Cape Cod Cupola Co Inc	North Dartmouth	MA	F	508 994-2119	10990
Wdss Corporation	Norwalk	CT	F	203 854-5930	2594	Capeway Welding Inc	Plymouth	MA	F	508 747-6666	11453
Weld-All Inc	Southington	CT	G	860 621-3156	3240	Capstan Atlantic	Walpole	MA	E	508 660-6001	12554
Wendell Enterprises Inc	Farmington	CT	C	860 846-0800	1258	Catapult Sports LLC	Boston	MA	E	312 762-5332	6643
Wendon Company Inc	Easton	CT	F		1098	Cbm Industries Inc	Taunton	MA	E	508 821-4555	12326
Wentworth Manufacturing LLC	South Windham	CT	D	860 423-4575	3104	Chas G Allen Realty LLC	Barre	MA	D	978 355-2911	6202
Westbrook Manufacturing LLC	Ivoryton	CT	F	860 767-2460	1534	City Machine Corporation	Holyoke	MA	G	413 538-9766	9247
Westminster Tool Inc	Sterling	CT	E	860 317-1039	3505	Clarkworks Machine	Westford	MA	G	978 692-2556	13230
Westport Precision LLC	Stratford	CT	D	203 378-2175	3583	Clematis Machine & Fix Co Inc	Waltham	MA	E	781 894-0777	12631
Wilde Manufacturing LLC	North Haven	CT	G	203 693-3939	2444	CNE Machine Inc	Walpole	MA	G	508 668-4110	12556
Winthrop Tool Inc	Essex	CT	G	860 526-9079	1173	Colcord Machine Co Inc	Hopedale	MA	E	508 634-8840	9295
Wood Grinding Unlimited	Bridgeport	CT	F	203 333-9047	385	Collins Manufacturing Inc	Essex	MA	F	978 768-2553	8474
325 Silver Street Inc	Agawam	MA	E	413 789-1800	5776	Continental Feed Screw Inc	Gardner	MA	F	978 630-1300	8882
A & A Industries Inc	Peabody	MA	E	978 977-9660	11292	Contract Engineering Inc	Beverly	MA	F	978 921-0501	6342
A & G Centerless Grinding Inc	Woburn	MA	F	781 281-0007	13494	Costa Precision Mfg Corp (PA)	Chicopee	MA	E	603 542-5229	8021
A1 Screw Machine Products Inc	Chicopee	MA	F	413 594-8939	8004	Cotter Machine Co Inc (PA)	West Wareham	MA	E	508 291-7400	13059
Ab-Wey Machine & Die Co Inc	Pembroke	MA	F	781 294-8031	11356	Cunningham Engineering Inc	Danvers	MA	E	978 774-4169	8176
Accudynamics LLC	Lakeville	MA	E	508 946-4545	9515	Cunningham Machine Co Inc	Chelmsford	MA	F	978 256-7641	7921
Accumet Engineering Inc	Devens	MA	E	978 692-6180	8265	Custom Arospc Components LLC	Woburn	MA	D	781 935-4940	13552
Accurounds Inc	Avon	MA	D	508 587-3500	6140	Custom Machine LLC	Woburn	MA	F	781 935-4940	13554
Accutech Machine Inc	Danvers	MA	F	978 922-7271	8160	D & D Precision Machine Co Inc	Middleboro	MA	E	508 946-8010	10356
Ace Precision Inc	Agawam	MA	F	413 789-7536	5777	D and D Manufacturing LLC	Ipswich	MA	E		9481
Advance Machine & Tool Inc	Pittsfield	MA	F	413 499-4900	11389	D S Greene Co Inc	Wakefield	MA	F	781 245-2644	12506
Advance Mfgco Inc	Westfield	MA	C	413 568-2411	13146	Dale Engineering & Son Inc	Bedford	MA	F	781 541-6055	6221
Advanced Engineering Corp	Danvers	MA	F	978 777-7147	8161	Dalton Manufacturing Co Inc	Amesbury	MA	F	978 388-2227	5833
Advanced Precision Engineering Incorporated 978 356-7303	Ipswich 9477	MA	E	MA	E	Dalton Manufacturing Group Inc	Amesbury	MA	F	978 388-2227	5834
						David Gilbert	Framingham	MA	G	508 879-1507	8755
Afc Cable Systems Inc	New Bedford	MA	B	508 998-1131	10566	David Packard Company Inc	Oxford	MA	G	508 987-2998	11252
Ainslie Corporation	Walpole	MA	G	781 848-0850	12548	Debco Machine Inc	Natick	MA	G	508 655-4469	10476
Aj Precision Inc	Southwick	MA	G	413 998-3291	12040	Decker Machine Works Inc	Greenfield	MA	E	413 628-3300	8989
Algonquin Industries Inc	Hopedale	MA	G	508 634-3733	9294	Denault Inc	North Adams	MA	G	413 664-6771	10806
Allied Machined Products Corp	Auburn	MA	D	508 756-4290	6100	Dimark Precision Machining Inc	Pembroke	MA	F	781 447-7990	11362
Alpine Precision LLC	North Billerica	MA	G	978 600-0035	10896	Ding Fann Enterprises LLC	Malden	MA	F	781 322-7121	10009
Alpine Precision LLC	North Billerica	MA	F	978 667-6333	10897	Diversified Metals Inc	Monson	MA	D	413 267-5101	10455
Alvin Johnson	East Longmeadow	MA	G	413 525-6334	8368	DL Tech Machine Inc	North Billerica	MA	G	978 439-0500	10908
Amarello S Machining	Plymouth	MA	G	508 746-8010	11446	Dps Packaging LLC	Holden	MA	G	508 459-8917	9188
American Screw and Barrels Inc	Gardner	MA	F	978 630-1300	8879	Eastern Machine & Design Corp	Hanson	MA	F	781 293-6391	9051
AMS Precision Machining Inc	Brockton	MA	G	508 588-2283	7256	Eastern Mass Machined Pdts Inc	Salisbury	MA	F	978 462-9301	11741
Andys Machine Inc	Middleboro	MA	E	508 947-1192	10350	Eastern Tool Corporation	Stoneham	MA	F	781 395-1472	12176
Antron Engrg & Mch Co Inc	Bellingham	MA	D	508 966-2803	6285	Easthampton Machine & Tool Inc	Easthampton	MA	G	413 527-8770	8444
Anver Corporation	Hudson	MA	D	978 568-0221	9354	Easthampton Precision Mfg	Easthampton	MA	G	413 527-1650	8445
Applied Precision Technology	Attleboro	MA	F	508 226-8700	5994	Element Precision LLC	Southbridge	MA	F	774 318-1777	12015
Arbo Machine Co Inc	Rockland	MA	G	781 871-3449	11634	Ely Tool Inc	Springfield	MA	E	413 732-2347	12093
Arch Med & Arospc Woburn LLC	Woburn	MA	D	781 933-1760	13514	Emco Tool & Gauge Corporation	Ludlow	MA	E	413 385-0200	9945
Arland Tool & Mfg Inc (PA)	Sturbridge	MA	D	508 347-3368	12249	Enos Engineering LLC	Acton	MA	G	978 654-6522	5745
Arland Tool & Mfg Inc	West Brookfield	MA	F	508 867-3085	12991	Entwistle Company LLC (PA)	Hudson	MA	D	508 481-4000	9364
Arlowe Corporation	Littleton	MA	F	978 486-9050	9802	Essex Bay Engineering Inc	Ipswich	MA	E	978 412-9600	9486
Arwood Machine Corporation	Newburyport	MA	D	978 463-3777	10667	Essex Engineering Inc	Lynn	MA	E	781 595-2114	9972
Assabet Machine Corp	Boxborough	MA	E	978 263-2900	7147	Evans Industries LLC	Topsfield	MA	C	978 887-8561	12434

Company	CITY	ST	EMP	PHONE	ENTRY#
Evans Machine Co Inc	Brockton	MA	E	508 584-8085	7277
Eyesaver International Inc	Hanover	MA	D	781 829-0808	9031
F H Peterson Machine Corp	Stoughton	MA	D	781 341-4930	12204
Fairview Machine Company Inc	Topsfield	MA	F	978 887-2141	12435
Ferro-Ceramic Grinding Inc	Wilmington	MA	E	781 245-1833	13407
Filtec Precision Ceramics Corp	Westford	MA	G	978 204-2288	13236
Fitz Machine Inc	Wakefield	MA	F	781 245-5966	12510
Form Centerless Grinding Inc	Franklin	MA	F	508 520-0900	8837
Form Roll Die Corp	Worcester	MA	F	508 755-5302	13726
Fraen Machining Corporation (PA)	Woburn	MA	D	781 205-5400	13571
Framingham Welding & Engineering Corporation	Framingham	MA		E	8763
Galaxie Labs Inc	Burlington	MA	G	781 272-3750	7375
Gaskin Manufacturing Corp	Plainville	MA	F	508 695-8949	11433
General Machine Inc	Holyoke	MA	G	413 533-5744	9256
General Products & Gear Corp	Rowley	MA	F	978 948-8146	11674
Gill Metal Fab Inc	Brockton	MA	E	508 580-4445	7281
Grassetti Sales Associates Inc	Springfield	MA	G	413 737-2283	12097
Graycer Screw Products Co Inc	Bellingham	MA	E	508 966-1810	6290
H & S Tool and Engineering Inc	Fall River	MA	E	508 672-6509	8559
H & T Specialty Co Inc	Waltham	MA	E	781 893-3866	12689
H H Arnold Co Inc	Rockland	MA	E	781 878-0346	11648
Hannah Engineering Inc	Danvers	MA	E	978 777-5892	8189
Harvard Products Inc	Harvard	MA	F	978 772-0309	9063
Helical Solutions LLC	Rowley	MA	E	207 854-5581	11676
Higgins Location LLC	Acton	MA	E	978 266-1200	5752
High Tech Machinists Inc	Chelmsford	MA	E	978 256-1600	7932
Hillside Engineering Inc	Danvers	MA	G	978 762-6640	8190
Holyoke Machine Company	Holyoke	MA	E	413 534-5612	9261
Honematic Machine Corporation	Boylston	MA	E	508 869-2131	7162
Howestemco Inc	Taunton	MA	D		12341
HT Machine Co Inc	Webster	MA	F	508 949-1105	12926
IBC Advanced Alloys Inc-Belac	Wilmington	MA	E	978 284-8900	13412
Ideal Instrument Inc	Canton	MA	F	781 828-0881	7799
Industrial Precision Inc	Westfield	MA	E	413 562-5161	13172
Innovative Tooling Company Inc	Lenox	MA	F	413 637-1031	9625
Intech Inc	Acton	MA	E	978 263-2210	5756
Intellicut Inc	Middleton	MA	F	617 417-5236	10386
Invincible Metal Corp	Marshfield	MA	F	781 536-4589	10239
Ital-Tech Engineering Co Inc	Groveland	MA	F	978 373-6773	9014
Ital-Tech Machined Pdts LLC	Groveland	MA	F	978 373-6773	9015
J & L Welding & Machine Co	Gloucester	MA	E	978 283-3388	8942
J W Machining Inc	Hudson	MA	F	978 562-5611	9379
J&E Precision TI Holdings LLC (PA)	Southampton	MA	E	413 527-8778	11986
J&E Precision Tool LLC	Southampton	MA	D	413 527-8778	11987
J&J Machine Company Inc	Marlborough	MA	F	508 481-8166	10170
James F Mullen Co Inc	Merrimac	MA	D	978 346-0045	10325
Jet Machined Products LLC	East Bridgewater	MA	F	508 378-3200	8341
Jeto Engineering Inc	Essex	MA	F	978 768-6472	8475
JG Machine Co Inc	Wilmington	MA	F	978 447-5279	13418
Jmc Asset Holdings Inc	Hanson	MA	G	781 447-9264	9052
John Covey	Peabody	MA	F	978 535-4681	11321
Joma LLC	Haverhill	MA	G	978 374-0034	9106
JT Machine Inc	East Douglas	MA	E	508 476-1508	8351
K & M Engineering Inc	Marlborough	MA	F	978 235-7923	10173
K-F Liquidation Inc	Franklin	MA	G	508 528-2000	8847
Kad Machine Inc	Chicopee	MA	G	413 538-8684	8042
Kc Precision Machining LLC	Ipswich	MA	E	978 356-8900	9487
Keystone Precision & Engrg Inc	Pepperell	MA	E	978 433-8484	11385
Kind Grind Incorporated	Amherst	MA	F	413 367-2478	5861
Kingston Manufacturing Co Inc	Kingston	MA	G	781 585-4476	9510
Kms Machine Works Inc	Taunton	MA	F	508 822-3151	12346
Knight Machine & Tool Co Inc	South Hadley	MA	F	413 532-2507	11964
Kodiak Machining Co Inc	Ipswich	MA	F	978 356-9876	9488
L & M Machine Inc	Everett	MA	F	617 294-0378	8489
L K M Industries Woburn	Woburn	MA	G	781 935-9210	13598
Lake Manufacturing Co Inc	Newburyport	MA	F	978 465-1617	10694
Lampin Corporation (PA)	Uxbridge	MA	F	508 278-2422	12484
Lanford Manufacturing Corp	Lawrence	MA	F	978 557-0240	9575
Laser Process Mfg Inc	Peabody	MA	F	978 531-6003	11323
Lavallee Machinery Inc	Southbridge	MA	G	508 764-2896	12027
Lavelle Machine & Tool Co Inc	Westford	MA	E	978 692-8825	13245
Lawrence Sigler	Princeton	MA	G	510 782-6737	11495
Legacy Machine & Mfg LLC	Amesbury	MA	G	978 388-0956	5841
Lentros Engineering Inc	Ashland	MA	E	508 881-1160	5961
Lincoln Tool & Machine Corp	Hudson	MA	E	508 485-2940	9385
Line Bore Industries Inc	Oxford	MA	F	508 987-6509	11259
Little Enterprises LLC (DH)	Ipswich	MA	D	978 356-7422	9489
M & H Engineering Co Inc	Danvers	MA	F	978 777-1222	8200
M & P Machine Company Inc	Stoughton	MA	E	781 344-5888	12218
MA Industrial Fall River LLC	Fall River	MA	G	508 672-5217	8571
MA Mfg LLC	Fitchburg	MA	E	978 400-9991	8660
Macdiarmid LLC	Newburyport	MA	F	978 465-3546	10696
Macdiarmid Machine Corp	Newburyport	MA	F	978 465-3546	10697
Mach Machine Inc	Hudson	MA	F	978 274-5700	9387
Machine Incorporated	Stoughton	MA	E	781 297-3700	12219
Machine Technology Inc	Beverly	MA	E	978 927-1900	6363
Machining For Electronics Inc	Hudson	MA	G	978 562-7554	9388
Mackenzie Machine & Design Inc	Pembroke	MA	F	339 933-8157	11374
Magnat-Fairview Inc	Chicopee	MA	D	413 593-5742	8046
Mair-Mac Machine Company Inc	Brockton	MA	F	508 895-9001	7294
Maplewood Machine Co Inc	Fall River	MA	F	508 673-6710	8573
Markforged Inc (HQ)	Waltham	MA	C	866 496-1805	12715
Marox Corporation	Holyoke	MA	F	413 536-1300	9266
Marver Med Inc	Stoughton	MA	F	781 341-9372	12221
Mass Machine Inc	Walpole	MA	F	781 467-3550	12566
Massachusetts Mch Works Inc	Walpole	MA	F	781 467-3550	12567
MB Machining Inc	Westborough	MA	F	508 251-8663	13119
Med Tech Machine Company Inc	Rockland	MA	F	781 878-2250	11650
Menton Machine Co Inc	Hanson	MA	G	781 293-8394	9054
Meridian Industrial Group LLC	Holyoke	MA	E	413 538-9880	9268
Merit Machine Mfg Inc	Fitchburg	MA	F	978 342-7677	8664
Merrimac Tool Company Inc (PA)	Amesbury	MA	G	978 388-7159	5843
Mfg Mach Corp	Fall River	MA	F	774 294-4285	8580
Mica-Tron Products Corp	Holbrook	MA	F	781 767-2163	9179
Microwave Cmpnnts Spclists Inc	North Billerica	MA	F	978 667-1215	10937
Midas Technology Inc	Woburn	MA	F	781 938-0069	13613
Mikes Precision Machine Inc	North Billerica	MA	F	978 667-9793	10938
Millrite Machine Inc	Westfield	MA	E	413 562-9212	13390
Monks Manufacturing Co Inc	Wilmington	MA	F	978 657-8282	13435
Montague Industries Inc	Turners Falls	MA	F	413 863-4301	12453
Morrison Berkshire Inc	North Adams	MA	E	413 663-6501	10812
MRM Seller Entity LLC	Hudson	MA	F	978 568-1330	9393
Myriad Engineering Co Inc	North Oxford	MA	F	508 731-6416	11033
Nadco International Inc	Marion	MA	G	781 767-1797	10098
Nash Mfg & Grinding Svcs Inc	Springfield	MA	F	413 301-5416	12116
Nationwide Die Cutng Svcs LLC	Uxbridge	MA	G	617 306-6886	12487
Nevada Heat Treating LLC	Clinton	MA	E	978 365-4999	8085
Noremac Manufacturing Corp	Westborough	MA	E	508 366-8822	13124
Norgaard Machine Inc	Feeding Hills	MA	G	413 789-1291	8636
North American Tool & Mch Corp	Charlton	MA	F	508 248-9862	7894
Northampton Machine Co Inc	Easthampton	MA	E	413 529-2530	8455
Northeast Industrial Tech Inc	Lawrence	MA	F	617 360-7220	9591
Northeast Manufacturing Co Inc	Stoneham	MA	E	781 438-3022	12183
Nuforj LLC	Springfield	MA	F	413 530-0349	12119
Numeric Inc	Westfield	MA	F	413 732-6544	13195
O W Landergren Inc	Pittsfield	MA	F	413 442-5632	11415
O-D Tool & Cutter Inc	Mansfield	MA	E	508 339-7507	10071
Oliver Welding & Fabg Inc	Ipswich	MA	G	978 356-4488	9493
Olympic Engineering Service	Haverhill	MA	G	978 373-2789	9119
Olympic Systems Corporation	Winchester	MA	E	781 721-2740	13489
Optimum Parts Company	Agawam	MA	G	413 273-1865	5804
Ortiz Tool LLC	Springfield	MA	G	413 733-1206	12120
Paragon Mfg Inc	Westfield	MA	F	413 562-7202	13196
Paramount Tool LLC	Fall River	MA	E	508 672-0844	8594
Parkway Manufacturing Co Inc	West Bridgewater	MA	G	508 559-6686	12976
Patten Machine Inc	Hudson	MA	F	978 562-9847	9399
Payne Engrg Fabrication Co Inc	Canton	MA	E	781 828-9046	7817
Peerless Precision Inc	Westfield	MA	E	413 562-2359	13197
Pegasus Inc	Holliston	MA	E	508 429-2461	9227
Pferd Inc	Leominster	MA	E	978 840-6420	9694
Phillips Precision Inc	Boylston	MA	E	508 869-3344	7164
Phillips Precision Inc	Boylston	MA	E	508 869-0373	7165
Photofabrication Engrg Inc (HQ)	Milford	MA	E	508 478-2025	10414
Pierce Machine Co Inc (PA)	Dalton	MA	F	413 684-0056	8152
Pioneer Valley Machine LLC	Westfield	MA	G	413 204-0358	13200
Plus One Corporation	Peabody	MA	F	978 532-3700	11334
Pocasset Machine Corporation	Pocasset	MA	E	508 563-5572	11491
Ponn Machine Cutting Co	Woburn	MA	F	781 937-3373	13639
Poplar Hill Machine Inc	Conway	MA	F	413 369-4252	8144
Portance Corp	Fitchburg	MA	F	978 400-9991	8672
Portland Valve LLC (DH)	Warren	MA	E	704 289-6511	12852
Prattnella Machine & TI Co Inc	Peabody	MA	D	978 538-5229	11335
Precision Machinists Co Inc	Franklin	MA	F	508 528-2325	8857
Precision Technologies Inc	Tyngsboro	MA	F	978 649-8715	12464
Prematechnoligies LLC	Worcester	MA	E	508 791-9549	13774
Premco Inc	Hingham	MA	D	781 749-0333	9157
Proteus Manufacturing Company Inc	Beverly	MA	E	781 939-0919	6372
Proto XYZ Inc	New Bedford	MA	G	508 525-6363	10644
Psjl Corporation	Billerica	MA	C	978 313-2500	6474
Pv Engineering & Mfg Inc	Salisbury	MA	E	978 465-1221	11744
QCI Inc	Seekonk	MA	F	508 399-8983	11784
Quabbin Inc	Orange	MA	F	978 544-3872	11230
Queen Screw & Mfg Inc	Waltham	MA	D	781 894-8110	12756
Quick Manufacturing Co	Danvers	MA	G	978 750-4202	8215
R & S Redco Inc	Weymouth	MA	G	781 792-1717	13334

	CITY	ST	EMP	PHONE	ENTRY#
R B Machine Co Inc	Wareham	MA	G	508 830-0567	12843
R I Baker Co Inc (PA)	Clarksburg	MA	E	413 663-3791	8073
R L Barry Inc	Attleboro	MA	F	508 226-3350	6052
R M Precision Machine Corp	Tewksbury	MA	F	978 640-2900	12413
Ramco Machine LLC	Rowley	MA	F	978 948-3778	11683
Ranor Inc	Westminster	MA	D	978 874-0591	13276
Ree Machine Works Inc	North Billerica	MA	G	978 663-9105	10950
Regional Industries Inc	Danvers	MA	G	978 750-8787	8217
Riverside Engineering Co Inc	Peabody	MA	G	978 531-1556	11337
Robert J Moran Inc	Littleton	MA	G	978 486-4718	9836
Roberts Machine Shop Inc	Beverly	MA	G	978 927-6111	6379
Rock Valley Tool LLC	Easthampton	MA	E	413 527-2350	8461
Rogers General Machining Inc	Chicopee	MA	F	413 532-4673	8059
Rolls-Royce Marine North Amer (DH)	Walpole	MA	C	508 668-9610	12574
Roses Oil Service Inc (PA)	Gloucester	MA	E	877 283-3334	8955
Ryszard A Kokosinski	Dudley	MA	E	508 943-2700	8321
S & F Machine Co Inc	Haverhill	MA	F	978 374-1552	9129
S & S Machine and Welding Inc	Savoy	MA	G	413 743-5714	11768
S&H Engineering Inc	Chelmsford	MA	F	978 256-7231	7953
Saeilo Inc	Worcester	MA	E	508 799-9809	13786
Saliga Machine Co Inc	Hudson	MA	E	978 562-7959	9409
Samtan Engineering Corp	Malden	MA	E	781 322-7880	10026
Segue LLC	Marion	MA	G	970 274-9801	10100
Semco Machine Corp	Plainville	MA	E	508 384-8303	11442
Senior Operations LLC	Sharon	MA	C	781 784-1400	11795
Sharp Manufacturing Inc	West Bridgewater	MA	G	508 583-4080	12978
Sigler Machine Co	Sterling	MA	F	978 422-7868	12170
Simfer Precision Machine Co	Billerica	MA	E	978 667-1138	6482
Simpsons Inc of Lawrence	Lawrence	MA	F	978 683-2417	9597
Sisson Engineering Corp	Orange	MA	E	413 498-2840	11234
Snyder Machine Co Inc	Ipswich	MA	F	978 356-4488	9497
South Shore Manufacturing Inc	Hanson	MA	F	781 447-9264	9056
Sp Machine Inc	Hudson	MA	E	978 562-2019	9414
Specialty Manufacturing Inc	Amesbury	MA	F	978 388-1601	5853
Spring Hill Machine Co Inc	Haverhill	MA	F	978 374-4461	9133
Standex International Corp	North Billerica	MA	D	978 667-2771	10959
Standley Bros Machine Co Inc	Beverly	MA	E	978 927-0278	6385
Sterling Precision Inc	Clinton	MA	E	978 365-4999	8092
Stoneridge Design Inc	Littleton	MA	F	978 486-9626	9841
Swiss Concept Inc	Waltham	MA	G	781 894-1281	12784
Swiss Precision Products Inc (DH)	North Oxford	MA	E	508 987-8003	11035
T & D Specialties Inc	Oxford	MA	E	508 987-8344	11265
T G G Inc	Middleton	MA	E	978 777-5010	10395
Tattersall Machining Inc	Upton	MA	G	508 529-2300	12474
Taunton Stove Company Inc	North Dighton	MA	E	508 823-0786	11004
Tebaldi Enterprises Inc	Holyoke	MA	F	413 532-3261	9283
Tech Ridge Inc	Chelmsford	MA	E	978 256-5741	7963
Techncal Hrdfcing McHining Inc	Attleboro	MA	F	508 222-2900	6069
Techni-Products Inc	East Longmeadow	MA	E	413 525-6321	8398
Techprecision Corporation (PA)	Westminster	MA	F	978 874-0591	13280
Tecomet Inc	Woburn	MA	A	781 782-6400	13675
Tektron Inc	Topsfield	MA	F	978 887-0091	12439
Thermo-Craft Engineering Corp	Lynn	MA	E	781 599-4023	9992
Thomas M Leonard Inc	West Bridgewater	MA	G		12984
Titeflex Commercial Inc	Springfield	MA	E	413 739-5631	12139
Titeflex Corporation (HQ)	Springfield	MA	B	413 739-5631	12140
Tmh Machining & Welding Corp	West Bridgewater	MA	G	508 580-6899	12985
TOC Finishing Corp	Somerville	MA	E	617 623-3310	11902
Tog Manufacturing Company Inc	North Adams	MA	F	949 888-7700	10813
Tova Industries Inc	Southwick	MA	F	413 569-5688	12048
Tri-Star Plastics Corp (PA)	Shrewsbury	MA	E	508 845-1111	11845
Trivak Incorporated	Lowell	MA	E	978 453-7123	9929
True Precision Inc	West Springfield	MA	E	413 788-4226	13046
True Precision Industries Inc	West Springfield	MA	F	413 788-4226	13047
Truex Machine Co Inc	Hanover	MA	G	781 826-6875	9047
Tucker Engineering Inc	Peabody	MA	E	978 532-5900	11350
Twin City Machining Inc	Westminster	MA	G	978 874-1940	13282
Unimacts Manufacturing Mx LLC	Lexington	MA	F	410 415-6070	9790
Union Machine Company Lynn Inc (PA)	Groveland	MA	E	978 521-5100	9016
United GL To Met Sealing Inc	Lawrence	MA	F	978 327-5880	9606
United Machining Inc	Sutton	MA	G	508 865-3035	12293
United Metal Fabracators Inc	Worcester	MA	F	508 754-1800	13815
United Tool & Machine Corp (PA)	Lawrence	MA	E	978 658-5500	9607
Universal Mch & Design Corp	Fitchburg	MA	G	978 343-4688	8679
Van - Wal Machine Inc	Bellingham	MA	E	508 966-0733	6301
Van Pelt Precision Inc	Westfield	MA	F	413 527-1204	13215
Vangy Tool Company Inc	Worcester	MA	G	508 754-2669	13820
Vat Inc	Woburn	MA	E	781 537-5402	13684
Vibration & Shock Tech LLC	Beverly	MA	E	781 281-0721	6393
Villa Machine Associates Inc	Dedham	MA	F	781 326-5969	8255
Vinyl Technologies Inc	Fitchburg	MA	E	978 342-9800	8680
Vita Needle Company	Needham	MA	E	781 444-1780	10529
Volo Aero Mro Inc	East Longmeadow	MA	G	413 525-7211	8400
W J Roberts Co Inc	Saugus	MA	E	781 233-8176	11767
Wear-Rite Corp	Oxford	MA	F	508 987-0361	11268
Whalley Precision Inc	Southwick	MA	F	413 569-1400	12052
Woodman Precision Engrg Inc	Peabody	MA	F	978 538-9544	11355
WS Anderson Associates Inc	Auburn	MA	E	508 832-5550	6129
Wyz Machine Co Inc	Agawam	MA	F	413 786-6816	5816
Xtreme Tub Grinding Svcs Inc	North Dighton	MA	G	508 386-6015	11005
Albion Manufacturing	Winslow	ME	F	207 873-5633	5679
Alexanders Welding & Mch Inc	Greenfield Twp	ME	F	207 827-3300	4849
Align Precision - Arundel LLC	Arundel	ME	C	207 985-8555	4407
Arundel Holdings Inc	Arundel	ME	D	207 985-8555	4408
B & B Precise Products Inc	Benton	ME	E	207 453-8118	4544
Brackett Machine Inc	Westbrook	ME	E	207 854-9789	5618
Brady Enterprises Inc	Portland	ME	G	207 653-9990	5191
Cole Gunsmithing Inc	South Harpswell	ME	G	207 833-5027	5486
Custom Milling & Machining Inc	Waterboro	ME	G	207 776-8137	5590
D & G Machine Products Inc	Westbrook	ME	D	207 854-1500	5624
D and GM Achine Products	Gorham	ME	E	207 854-1500	4817
Dearborn Bortec LLC	Fryeburg	ME	F	207 935-2502	4808
Dewitt Mch & Fabrication Inc	Medford	ME	E	207 732-3530	5054
Elmet Technologies LLC (PA)	Lewiston	ME	C	207 333-6100	4960
Grover Gundrilling LLC	Oxford	ME	E	207 743-7051	5145
Howard Tool Company	Hermon	ME	E	207 942-1203	4884
Hunting Dearborn Inc	Fryeburg	ME	C	207 935-2171	4809
J & M Machining Inc	Skowhegan	ME	F	207 474-7300	5470
J B J Machine Company	North Berwick	ME	E	207 676-3380	5110
Kennebec Technologies	Augusta	ME	D	207 626-0188	4474
Kenniston Machine & Engrg	Rockland	ME	G	207 594-7810	5336
Knowlton Machine Company	Gorham	ME	E	207 854-8471	4824
Knox Machine Company	Warren	ME	D	207 273-2296	5582
Kw Products LLC	Canton	ME	G	207 357-3798	4671
Lane Conveyors & Drives Inc	Brewer	ME	D	207 989-4560	4616
Lank Machining Co LLC	Arundel	ME	G	207 286-9549	4410
Liberty Machine Inc	Gray	ME	G	207 376-6224	4842
Limerick Machine Company Inc	Limerick	ME	E	207 793-2288	5003
Little Enterprises LLC	Whitefield	ME	F	207 549-7232	5655
M & M Machine Inc	Presque Isle	ME	F	207 764-4199	5303
Machinery Service Co Inc	Wiscasset	ME	G	207 882-6788	5698
Machining Innovations Inc	Oakland	ME	G	207 465-2500	5120
Maine Machine Products Company (PA)	South Paris	ME	C	207 743-6344	5489
Maine Parts & Machine Inc	Portland	ME	E	207 797-0024	5242
Maine Tool & Machine LLC	Lisbon Falls	ME	F	207 576-4319	5022
Masters Machine Company	Bristol	ME	C	207 529-5191	4631
McAllister Machine Inc	Biddeford	ME	E	207 282-8655	4578
McKenney Machine & Tool Co	Corinna	ME	F	207 278-7091	4701
Melton Sales and Service Inc	Hallowell	ME	E	207 623-8895	4860
Metal Specialties Inc	Auburn	ME	E	207 786-4268	4444
Mid State Machine Products (PA)	Winslow	ME	C	207 873-6136	5685
Millincket Fabrication Mch Inc (PA)	Millinocket	ME	E	207 723-9733	5067
Montalvo Corporation	Gorham	ME	E	207 856-2501	4827
Mountain Machine Works	Auburn	ME	E	207 783-6680	4446
Nikel Precision Group LLC	Saco	ME	D	207 282-6080	5375
North Country Wind Bells Inc	Round Pond	ME	E	207 677-2224	5353
Northeast Doran Inc	Skowhegan	ME	G	207 474-2000	5475
OBrien Consolidated Inds	Lewiston	ME	F	207 783-8543	4981
Odat Machine Inc	Gorham	ME	E	207 854-2455	4828
Oizero9 Inc	Sanford	ME	E	207 324-3582	5404
Patten Tool and Engrg Inc	Kittery	ME	F	207 439-1555	4939
Precision Screw Mch Pdts Inc	Biddeford	ME	E	207 283-0121	4583
Ramsays Welding & Machine Inc	Lincoln	ME	F	207 794-8839	5012
Sabattus Machine Works Inc	Sabattus	ME	G	207 375-6222	5362
Soleras Advanced Coatings Ltd (PA)	Biddeford	ME	E	207 282-5699	4588
Technical Sales & Svc of Neng	Greene	ME	F	207 946-5506	4848
Tis Brewer LLC	Brewer	ME	E	207 989-4560	4621
Titan Machine Products Inc	Westbrook	ME	D	207 775-0011	5651
TK Machining Inc	Waterboro	ME	F	207 247-3114	5592
Tri-State Packing Supply	Scarborough	ME	E	207 883-5218	5446
Tube Hollows International	Windham	ME	E	844 721-8823	5673
W S Bessett Inc	Sanford	ME	E	207 324-9232	5417
Yankee Machine Inc	Casco	ME	E	207 627-4277	4685
Abtech Inc	Fitzwilliam	NH	E	603 585-7106	14312
Ace Machine Inc	East Hampstead	NH	E	603 329-6716	14269
Adax Machine Co Inc	Hudson	NH	E	603 598-6777	14479
Advanced Cnc Machine Inc	Manchester	NH	E	603 625-6631	14806
Advanced Fabricating McHy Inc	Kingston	NH	F	603 642-4906	14632
Aero Precision East LLC	Somersworth	NH	D	603 750-7100	15609
Aka Tool Inc	Laconia	NH	E	603 524-1868	14644
Allard Nazarian Group Inc (PA)	Manchester	NH	C	603 668-1900	14810
Alpine Machine Co Inc	Berlin	NH	E	603 752-1441	13979
Aluminum Castings Inc	Wilton	NH	G	603 654-9695	15701
Ameriforge Group Inc	Newport	NH	E	603 863-1270	15225
AMG-Awetis Mfg Group Corp	Gilford	NH	F	603 286-1645	14333
Artemas Industries Inc	Farmington	NH	G	603 755-9777	14308

Company	CITY	ST	EMP	PHONE	ENTRY#
Barco Manufacturing Inc	Tilton	NH	E	603 286-3324	15652
Baron Machine Company Inc	Laconia	NH	D	603 524-6800	14645
Beaumac Company Inc	Epsom	NH	E	603 736-9321	14278
Best Machine Inc	Fremont	NH	E	603 895-4018	14326
Bfmc LLC	Berlin	NH	E	603 752-4550	13980
Brians Machine Shop LLC	Concord	NH	G	603 224-4333	14117
Burbak Companies	Wilton	NH	D	603 654-2291	15703
C & M Machine Products Inc	Hudson	NH	D	603 594-8100	14489
CAM Tech	Plaistow	NH	E	603 382-2900	15338
Cariman 44 LLC	Nashua	NH	G	603 889-5160	15076
Carr Tool Co LLC	Londonderry	NH	F	603 669-0177	14734
Chamberlain Machine LLC	Walpole	NH	F	603 756-2560	15660
Comstock Industries Inc	Meredith	NH	E	603 279-7045	14968
Controlled Fluidics LLC (PA)	Milford	NH	F	603 673-4323	15018
Core Assemblies Inc	Gilford	NH	F	603 293-0270	14334
Cph Program & Machine Tool Des	Loudon	NH	F	603 716-3849	14795
Cz Machine Inc	East Hampstead	NH	G	603 382-4259	14270
Davis Village Solutions LLC	New Ipswich	NH	F	603 878-3662	15197
Dgf Indstrial Innvtons Group L	Gilford	NH	F	603 528-6591	14335
Diamond Casting and Mch Co LLC	Hollis	NH	E	603 465-2263	14450
Dmr Industries Inc	Rochester	NH	G	603 335-0325	15474
Dra Precision Machine	Brentwood	NH	F	603 734-2139	14020
Elpakco Inc	Ashland	NH	G	603 968-9950	13899
Emm Precision Inc	Center Conway	NH	F	603 356-8892	14051
Feature Products Ltd	Bedford	NH	G	603 669-0800	13928
Fuller Machine Co Inc	Alstead	NH	F	603 835-6559	13857
Fwm Inc	Hudson	NH	E	603 578-3366	14497
G & A Machine Inc	Salem	NH	E	603 894-6965	15530
GKN Aerospace New England Inc	Charlestown	NH	D	603 542-5135	14063
Green Mountain Metals of VT	Claremont	NH	F	603 542-0005	14090
GS Precision LLC-Keene Div	Keene	NH	D	603 355-1166	14602
Gti Spindle Technology Inc (DH)	Manchester	NH	E	603 669-5993	14857
H & S Machine Company Inc	Plaistow	NH	F	978 686-2321	15346
Hagan Design and Machine Inc	Newmarket	NH	G	603 292-1101	15220
Hawk Quality Products Inc	Derry	NH	E	603 432-3319	14194
Hicks Enterprises Inc	Walpole	NH	E	603 756-3671	15662
High Speed Technologies Inc	Bow	NH	E	603 483-0333	14001
Highland Tool Co Inc	Nashua	NH	F	603 882-6907	15110
Hillsgrove Machine Inc	Alton	NH	F	603 776-5090	13859
Hitchiner LLC	Milford	NH	G	603 672-9630	15026
HM Machine LLC	Dover	NH	G	603 617-3450	14231
HMC Solutions LLC	Peterborough	NH	G	501 255-0498	15316
Howard Precision Inc	Gilford	NH	F	603 293-8012	14337
HPM NH LLC	Seabrook	NH	F	603 474-1879	15593
Industrial Cnc LLC	Hollis	NH	E	603 320-3484	14452
Innovative Machine & Sup Inc	Winchester	NH	F	603 239-8082	15714
Intec Automation Inc	Rochester	NH	E	603 833-9329	15479
J Tool Inc	Belmont	NH	F	603 524-5813	13962
Jarvis Auto Machine LLC	Claremont	NH	F	603 504-6144	14091
Joa Tools LLC	Goffstown	NH	G	850 529-3567	14350
JR Poirier Tool & Machine Co	Amherst	NH	F	603 882-9279	13875
Js Machine	Hampstead	NH	G	603 329-3790	14383
Karl Gschwind Machineworks LLC	Derry	NH	E	603 434-4211	14197
Lake Machine Co Inc	Claremont	NH	F	603 542-8884	14092
Latva Machine LLC	Newport	NH	G	603 863-5155	15229
Lennartz Enterprises LLC	Nashua	NH	F	978 663-6100	15126
Lighthouse Manufacturing LLC	Portsmouth	NH	E	978 532-5999	15417
Linear & Metric Co	Londonderry	NH	E	603 432-1700	14764
Machine Craft Company Inc	Concord	NH	F	603 225-0958	14142
Machined Integrations LLC	Merrimack	NH	G	603 420-8871	14991
Maclean Precision Mch Co Inc	Madison	NH	E	603 367-9011	14803
Magnum Machine Inc	Raymond	NH	F	603 895-0545	15453
Micro-Tech Prod Mch Co Inc	Londonderry	NH	G	603 434-1743	14773
Micromatics Machine Co Inc	Hollis	NH	F	603 889-2115	14454
Mikros Technologies LLC	Claremont	NH	E	603 690-2020	14094
Mitee-Bite Products LLC	Center Ossipee	NH	F	603 539-4538	14058
Monadnock Grinding LLC	Fitzwilliam	NH	G	603 585-7275	14314
Netc Liquidating Corporation	Center Tuftonboro	NH	E	603 569-3100	14059
New England Innovations Corp	Dover	NH	F	603 742-6247	14240
NH Rapid Machining LLC	Nashua	NH	G	603 821-5200	15141
North East Cutting Die Corp	Dover	NH	F	603 436-8952	14242
Northern Fbrction Slutions LLC	Tamworth	NH	G	603 539-4333	15647
Omni Components Corp (HQ)	Hudson	NH	C	603 882-4467	14533
Palmer Machine Company Inc	Conway	NH	F	603 447-2069	14181
Peterboro Tool Company Inc	Peterborough	NH	E	603 924-3034	15325
Photomachining Inc	Pelham	NH	F	603 882-9944	15294
Pj Diversified Machining Inc	Merrimack	NH	G	603 459-8655	14998
Plastech Machining Fabrication	Bow	NH	F	603 228-7601	14009
Priority Machine LLC	Concord	NH	F	603 677-2507	14152
Profile Precision Machine	Somersworth	NH	G	603 692-4116	15622
Quality Machine Inc	Plaistow	NH	G	603 382-2334	15349
R & K Machine	Laconia	NH	F	603 528-0221	14665
R D S Machine Inc (PA)	Newport	NH	G	603 863-4131	15235
R S Machine Inc	Hudson	NH	G	603 880-3177	14538
Robinson Precision Tool Corp	Hudson	NH	F	603 889-1625	14542
Rowe Machine Co	Hampton	NH	F	603 926-0029	14411
S & S Machine LLC	Amherst	NH	F	603 204-5542	13889
Seacoast Machine Company LLC	Newmarket	NH	F	603 659-3404	15224
Skytrans Mfg LLC	Contoocook	NH	F	802 230-7783	14175
Sparton Technology Corp	Hudson	NH	D	603 880-3692	14548
Stone Machine Co Inc	Chester	NH	F	603 887-4287	14071
Sunset Tool Inc	Keene	NH	E	603 355-2246	14623
Technical Machine Components	Hudson	NH	F	603 880-0444	14550
Tee Enterprises	Conway	NH	F	603 447-5662	14182
Teleflex Incorporated	Jaffrey	NH	D	603 532-7706	14580
Tfx Medical Incorporated	Jaffrey	NH	D	603 532-7706	14581
Tilton - Nrthfeld Rcrtion Cnci	Northfield	NH	G	603 286-8653	15270
TNT Precision LLC	Hudson	NH	G	603 595-6813	14556
Tru Form Precision Mfg LLC	Plaistow	NH	F	603 974-2552	15353
Tsi Group Inc (DH)	Hampton	NH	E	603 964-0296	14416
Turbocam Inc (PA)	Barrington	NH	C	603 905-0200	13917
Unistar Corporation	Tamworth	NH	G	603 323-9327	15649
United Mch & TI Design Co Inc	Fremont	NH	F	603 642-3601	14332
Vck Best Machining LLC	Nashua	NH	F	603 880-8858	15183
Wdw Machine Inc	Hampstead	NH	G	603 329-9604	14394
White Mountain Wood Grinding	Contoocook	NH	G	603 455-6931	14176
Winchester Precision Tech Ltd	Winchester	NH	F	603 239-6326	15718
Agar Machining & Welding Inc	Pawtucket	RI	F	401 724-2260	16344
American Tool Company	Lincoln	RI	E	401 333-0111	16118
Artic Tool & Engrg Co LLC	Greenville	RI	F	401 785-2210	16055
Austrian Machine Corp	Cranston	RI	F	401 946-4090	15835
Automated Industrial Mch Inc	Smithfield	RI	F	401 232-1710	16688
Axis Machining Inc	Woonsocket	RI	G	401 766-9911	16949
Bpm LLC	Warwick	RI	F	401 615-0700	16792
Brada Manufacturing Inc	Warwick	RI	E	401 739-3774	16793
Chase Machine Co Inc	West Warwick	RI	E	401 821-8879	16907
Chewbarka Inc	Johnston	RI	F	404 464-9911	16079
Colonial Machine & Tool Co Inc	Coventry	RI	E	401 826-1883	15810
Contract Fusion Inc	East Providence	RI	E	401 438-1298	16010
D & B Machining Inc	Cumberland	RI	F	401 726-2347	15938
D Simpson Inc	Smithfield	RI	E	401 232-3638	16693
Dean Machine Incorporated	Cranston	RI	E	401 919-5100	15847
Demaich Industries Inc	Johnston	RI	F	401 944-3576	16080
Droitcour Company	Warwick	RI	D	401 737-4646	16809
E & M Enterprises Ltd	Johnston	RI	E	401 274-7405	16083
Ersa Inc	Westerly	RI	E	401 348-4000	16930
Formex Inc	East Greenwich	RI	F	401 885-9800	15986
Fred Ricci Tool Co Inc	Johnston	RI	F	401 464-9911	16086
Guill Tool & Engrg Co Inc	West Warwick	RI	D	401 822-8186	16908
Guill Tool and Engrg Co Inc	West Warwick	RI	F	401 828-7600	16909
Hawkins Machine Company Inc	Coventry	RI	E	401 828-1424	15815
HB Precision Products Inc	Greenville	RI	F	401 767-4340	16059
Huestis Machine Corporation	Bristol	RI	E	401 253-5500	15769
Jade Manufacturing Company Inc	Warwick	RI	E	401 737-2400	16825
Jade Manufacturing Company LLC	Warwick	RI	F	401 737-2400	16826
John Crane Sealol Inc (DH)	Warwick	RI	C	401 732-0715	16828
Joraco Inc	Smithfield	RI	E	401 232-1710	16719
Laser Fare Inc (PA)	Smithfield	RI	E	401 231-4400	16721
Lavigne Manufacturing Inc	Cranston	RI	C	401 490-4627	15883
Little Rhody Machine Repr Inc	Coventry	RI	F	401 828-1919	15816
Machinex Company Inc	Smithfield	RI	G	401 231-3230	16723
Mtr Machining Inc	North Smithfield	RI	F	401 766-0200	16327
Nagel Machine Co Inc	West Warwick	RI	F	401 827-8962	16912
Newport Tool & Die Inc	Middletown	RI	F	401 847-6711	16181
Niantic Seal Inc	Lincoln	RI	E	401 334-6870	16150
Page McLellan Inc	West Greenwich	RI	G	401 397-2799	16890
Parmatech 3d Inc	Warwick	RI	E	401 739-0740	16843
Piatek Machine Company Inc	Pawtucket	RI	F	401 728-9930	16403
Porter Machine Inc	West Greenwich	RI	E	401 397-8889	16891
Precision Products	North Smithfield	RI	G	401 766-0200	16331
R & R Machine Industries Inc	North Smithfield	RI	F	401 766-2505	16332
Rhode Island Engine Co Inc	Narragansett	RI	E	401 789-1021	16195
Rosco Manufacturing LLC	Central Falls	RI	E	401 228-0120	15796
Rounds Service Station Inc	North Scituate	RI	F	401 934-9877	16316
Sandberg Enterprises Inc (PA)	Mapleville	RI	F	401 568-1602	16168
Sandberg Enterprises Inc	Pascoag	RI	E	401 568-1602	16341
Sandstorm Crbide Pdts Corp Inc	Warwick	RI	F	401 739-5220	16858
Swissline Precision Mfg Inc	Cumberland	RI	D	401 333-8888	15965
Swissline Products Inc	Cumberland	RI	D	401 333-8888	15966
T Tech Machine Inc	Warwick	RI	F	401 732-3590	16867
Thomas Engineering	Coventry	RI	G	401 822-1235	15823
Abacus Automation Inc	Bennington	VT	F	802 442-3662	17035
Advanced Machine and TI Co Inc	Milton	VT	F	802 893-6322	17353
Ascutney Metal Products Inc	Windsor	VT	F	802 674-6721	17757
CAM Dvlpment McRo Cmpnents Inc	Hydeville	VT	F	802 265-3240	17301
Carter Machine Inc	Marshfield	VT	G	802 426-3501	17333

SIC

	CITY	ST	EMP	PHONE	ENTRY#
Cave Manufacturing Inc	Brattleboro	VT	E	802 257-9253	17079
Dessureau Machines Inc	Barre	VT	F	802 476-4561	17000
G S Precision Inc **(PA)**	Brattleboro	VT	B	802 257-5200	17084
Gloucester Associates Inc	Barre	VT	E	802 479-1088	17001
Jenne Machine LLC	Lyndonville	VT	F	802 626-1106	17318
Kad Models & Prototypes Inc	East Randolph	VT	F	510 229-8764	17218
Lauzon Machine and Engrg Inc	Bennington	VT	E	802 442-3116	17048
Metal-Flex Welded Bellows Inc	Newport	VT	E	802 334-5550	17400
Milton Vermont Sheet Metal Inc	Milton	VT	D	802 893-1581	17362
North Country Engineering Inc	Derby	VT	E	802 766-5396	17212
North East Precision Inc	Saint Johnsbury	VT	D	802 748-1440	17546
Pre-Tech Plastics Inc **(PA)**	Williston	VT	E	802 879-9441	17745
Precision Cutter Grinding Inc	Hartland	VT	G	802 436-2039	17287
S & A Trombley Corporation	Morrisville	VT	E	802 888-2394	17388
Sathorn Corporation	Williston	VT	E	802 860-2121	17748
Stephens Precision Inc	Bradford	VT	F	802 222-9600	17064
Sterling Technologies Inc	Morrisville	VT	G	802 888-4753	17389
Sterling Technologies Inc	Morrisville	VT	F	802 363-6883	17390
Vermont Aerospace Inds LLC	Saint Johnsbury	VT	D	802 828-6705	17547
Vermont Aerospace Manufacturing Inc	Lyndonville	VT	E	802 748-8705	17321
Vermont Engine Service Inc	Williston	VT	G	802 863-2326	17752
Vermont Indexable Tooling Inc	Fairfax	VT	G	802 752-2002	17264
W & Mb Inc	Brattleboro	VT	F	802 257-1935	17105

36 ELECTRONIC & OTHER ELECTRICAL EQUIPMENT & COMPONENTS

3612 Transformers, except electric

	CITY	ST	EMP	PHONE	ENTRY#
ABB Enterprise Software Inc	Stamford	CT	F	203 329-8771	3268
ABB Inc	Danbury	CT	C	203 790-8588	701
ABB Inc	Windsor	CT	C	860 285-0183	4251
Able Coil and Electronics Co	Bolton	CT	E	860 646-5686	218
Alpha-Core Inc	Shelton	CT	E	203 954-0050	2980
Altus II LLC	Stamford	CT	G	203 698-0090	3279
Asea Brown Boveri Inc	Norwalk	CT	A	203 750-2200	2465
Bicron Electronics LLC **(HQ)**	Torrington	CT	D	860 482-2524	3672
Bridgeport Magnetics Group Inc	Shelton	CT	E	203 954-0050	2988
Carling Technologies Inc **(HQ)**	Plainville	CT	C	860 793-9281	2750
Linden Vft LLC	Stamford	CT	E	203 357-4740	3401
Neeltran Inc	New Milford	CT	C	860 350-5964	2254
Tortran Inc	Shelton	CT	F	203 538-5062	3070
Transformer Technology Inc	Durham	CT	F	860 349-1061	905
Unipower LLC	Brookfield	CT	F	203 740-8555	540
Universal Voltronics Corp	Brookfield	CT	D	203 740-8555	541
Atrex Energy Inc **(PA)**	Walpole	MA	E	781 461-8251	12551
BP Fly Corporation **(PA)**	Tyngsboro	MA	F	978 649-9114	12457
Cgit Westboro Inc	Westborough	MA	E	508 836-4000	13087
Ethosenergy Tc Inc **(DH)**	Chicopee	MA	C	802 257-2721	8031
GEC Durham Industries Inc **(PA)**	New Bedford	MA	E	508 995-2636	10594
International Coil Inc	South Easton	MA	G	508 580-8515	11946
Magnetika/East Ltd Partnership	Marlborough	MA	F	508 485-7555	10181
McElroy Electronics Corp	Shirley	MA	F	978 425-4055	11820
MCI Transformer Corporation	Orange	MA	F	978 544-8272	11226
Micheal John	Brookline	MA	E	857 239-0277	7320
Phoenix Electric Corp	Canton	MA	E	781 821-0200	7819
Precision Electronics Corp	Marshfield	MA	F	781 834-6677	10244
Pwb	Hopkinton	MA	F	508 497-3930	9342
Schneider Electric Usa Inc **(DH)**	Boston	MA	A	978 975-9600	7026
Schneider Electric Usa Inc	Foxboro	MA	E	508 549-3385	8724
Total Recoil Magnetics Inc	Holliston	MA	F	508 429-9600	9234
Trans Mag Corp	Carlisle	MA	G	978 458-1487	7847
Parker-Hannifin Corporation	Kittery	ME	D	207 439-9511	4938
Trans Utility Inc	Baileyville	ME	G	207 454-1162	4485
Airex LLC	Laconia	NH	E	603 841-2040	14643
Century Magnetics Holdings Inc	Northfield	NH	F	603 934-4931	15263
Controlair LLC	Amherst	NH	F	603 886-9400	13865
Laconia Magnetics Inc	Laconia	NH	F	603 528-2766	14655
Russound/Fmp Inc	Portsmouth	NH	C	603 659-5170	15433
Semper Fi Power Supply Inc	Manchester	NH	G	603 656-9729	14927
SPI LLC	North Woodstock	NH	E	603 745-3911	15262
Standex Elctrnic Magnetics Inc	Concord	NH	D	800 805-8991	14158
Vishay Hirel Systems LLC	Dover	NH	D	603 742-4375	14257
Wall Industries Inc	Exeter	NH	E	603 778-2300	14305
Voltserver Inc **(PA)**	East Greenwich	RI	F	401 885-8658	15996
Dynapower Company LLC **(DH)**	South Burlington	VT	D	802 860-7200	17577
Omni Measurement Systems Inc	Colchester	VT	E	802 497-2253	17198

3613 Switchgear and switchboard apparatus

	CITY	ST	EMP	PHONE	ENTRY#
ABB Enterprise Software Inc	Plainville	CT	A	860 747-7111	2744
ABB Finance (usa) Inc	Norwalk	CT	E	919 856-2360	2458
Accutron Inc **(PA)**	Windsor	CT	D	860 683-8300	4253

	CITY	ST	EMP	PHONE	ENTRY#
Allied Controls Inc	Stamford	CT	F	860 628-8443	3277
Asea Brown Boveri Inc	Norwalk	CT	A	203 750-2200	2465
Bass Products LLC	Bristol	CT	G	860 585-7923	408
Capitol Electronics Inc	Wilton	CT	F	203 744-3300	4235
Carling Technologies Inc **(HQ)**	Plainville	CT	C	860 793-9281	2750
Control Concepts Inc **(PA)**	Brooklyn	CT	F	860 928-6551	545
Faria Beede Instruments Inc	North Stonington	CT	C	860 848-9271	2448
GE Grid Solutions LLC	Windsor	CT	G	425 250-2695	4278
Gems Sensors Inc **(HQ)**	Plainville	CT	B	860 747-3000	2761
General Electro Components	Glastonbury	CT	G	860 659-3573	1280
Hubbell Incorporated Delaware **(HQ)**	Shelton	CT	B	475 882-4000	3018
Industrial Cnnctons Sltons LLC	Bloomfield	CT	E	678 216-5817	172
Lex Products LLC **(PA)**	Trumbull	CT	C	203 363-3738	3723
Madison Company **(PA)**	Branford	CT	E	203 488-4477	270
MH Rhodes Cramer LLC	South Windsor	CT	G	860 291-8402	3164
Mil-Con Inc	Naugatuck	CT	F	630 595-2366	1971
Newco Condenser Inc	Shelton	CT	F	475 882-4000	3039
Omega Engineering Inc	Norwalk	CT	D	714 540-4914	2548
Precision Graphics Inc	East Berlin	CT	F	860 828-6561	916
Quality Name Plate Inc	East Glastonbury	CT	D	860 633-9495	923
Schulz Electric Company	New Haven	CT	C	203 562-5811	2195
Siemon Company **(PA)**	Watertown	CT	A	860 945-4200	4029
The Plainville Electrical Products Co	Bristol	CT	E	860 583-1144	500
C & K Components LLC **(HQ)**	Waltham	MA	D	617 969-3700	12619
Cgit Westboro Inc	Westborough	MA	E	508 836-4000	13087
Cole Hersee Company **(HQ)**	Boston	MA	D	617 268-2100	6662
Columbia Electrical Contrs Inc	Westborough	MA	C	508 366-8297	13091
Control 7 Inc	Bridgewater	MA	E	508 697-3197	7228
Cordmaster Engineering Co Inc	North Adams	MA	E	413 664-9371	10805
Eastprint Inc	North Andover	MA	D	978 975-5255	10829
Eaton Corporation	Franklin	MA	E	508 520-2444	8833
Echolab Inc	North Billerica	MA	E		10910
Electro Switch Corp	Weymouth	MA	C	781 607-3306	13324
Electro Switch Corp	Weymouth	MA	E	781 335-1195	13325
Emx Controls Inc	East Douglas	MA	E	508 876-9700	8350
Huber+suhner Polatis Inc **(DH)**	Bedford	MA	E	781 275-5080	6231
Infra-Red Bldg & Pwr Svc Inc **(PA)**	Holbrook	MA	F	781 767-0888	9175
Koovera International	Beverly	MA	E	978 867-0867	6359
McStowe Engrg & Met Pdts Inc	East Bridgewater	MA	F	508 378-7400	8343
Mersen USA Ev LLC	Newburyport	MA	F	978 518-7648	10700
Mettler-Toledo Thornton Inc **(DH)**	Billerica	MA	D	978 262-0210	6460
Microtek Inc	Chicopee	MA	C	413 593-1025	8049
Pancon Corporation **(PA)**	East Taunton	MA	C	781 297-6000	8410
Pickering Interfaces Inc	Chelmsford	MA	E	781 897-1710	7945
Power Systems Integrity Inc	Northborough	MA	G	508 393-1655	11106
Project Resources Inc	Wareham	MA	F	508 295-7444	12842
Russelectric Inc	Hingham	MA	B	781 749-6000	9158
Schneider Electric Usa Inc **(DH)**	Boston	MA	A	978 975-9600	7026
Schneider Electric Usa Inc	Foxboro	MA	E	508 549-3385	8724
Siemens Industry Inc	Hingham	MA	B	781 749-6000	9159
Stellant PST Corp	Topsfield	MA	F	978 887-5754	12438
Suns International LLC	Chelmsford	MA	B	978 349-2329	7960
Teknikor Automtn & Contrls Inc	Fall River	MA	F	508 679-9474	8615
Tektron Inc	Topsfield	MA	F	978 887-0091	12439
Texas Instruments Incorporated	Attleboro	MA	E	508 236-3800	6070
Vicor Corporation **(PA)**	Andover	MA	F	978 470-2900	5933
Whitmor Company Inc **(PA)**	Revere	MA	F	781 284-8000	11625
General Electric Company	Auburn	ME	C	207 786-5100	4436
Huber Engineered Woods LLC	Easton	ME	D	207 488-6700	4742
Siemens Industry Inc	Falmouth	ME	D	207 878-3367	4771
Triangle Design Group LLC	Biddeford	ME	F	207 776-3177	4592
Bittware Inc **(DH)**	Concord	NH	E	603 226-0404	14115
Electrcal Installations LLC Ei	Moultonborough	NH	E	603 253-4525	15053
Fanaras Elc & Indus Contrls	Kensington	NH	G	603 772-3425	14630
Hoyt Elec Instr Works Inc	Concord	NH	E	603 753-6321	14138
Vidarr Inc	Portsmouth	NH	G	877 636-8432	15448
Kearney-National Inc	North Kingstown	RI	C	401 943-2686	16264
SE Mass Devlopment LLC	East Providence	RI	F	401 434-3329	16043
Wei Inc	Cranston	RI	F	401 781-3904	15927
Wei Inc **(PA)**	Cranston	RI	E	401 781-3904	15928
Dynapower Company LLC **(DH)**	South Burlington	VT	D	802 860-7200	17577

3621 Motors and generators

	CITY	ST	EMP	PHONE	ENTRY#
A-1 Machining Co LLC	New Britain	CT	D	860 223-6420	1994
Ac/Dc Industrial Electric LLC	Bozrah	CT	G	860 886-2232	225
Afcon Products Inc	Bethany	CT	F	203 393-9301	91
Coils Plus Inc	Wolcott	CT	E	203 879-0755	4362
Cramer Company	South Windsor	CT	F	860 291-8402	3135
Crrc LLC **(PA)**	South Windsor	CT	D	877 684-6464	3136
Cubico Palmetto Holdings LLC	Stamford	CT	E	646 513-4981	3331
D & M Group LLC	Putnam	CT	F	860 928-5010	2852
Elinco International Jpc Inc **(PA)**	Fairfield	CT	G	203 334-7537	1183
Engineered Electric Company	Bridgeport	CT	B	203 366-5211	320

	CITY	ST	EMP	PHONE	ENTRY#
Fuelcell Energy Inc	Torrington	CT	E	860 496-1111	3682
GE Steam Power Inc (HQ)	Windsor	CT	A	866 257-8664	4279
Generators On Demand LLC	Old Lyme	CT	F	860 662-4090	2642
Hamilton Sundstrand Corp (HQ)	Windsor Locks	CT	A	619 714-9442	4330
Japanese Products Corporation	Fairfield	CT	F	203 334-7537	1190
Kanthal Corporation	Bethel	CT	E	203 744-1440	124
Ktcr Holding	Westport	CT	G	203 227-4115	4179
Novanta Motion USA Inc (HQ)	Marlborough	CT	D	860 295-6102	1646
Polaris Management Inc	Easton	CT	G	203 261-6399	1097
Rowley Spring & Stamping Corp	Bristol	CT	C	860 582-8175	494
Schulz Electric Company	New Haven	CT	C	203 562-5811	2195
Tritex Corporation	Waterbury	CT	C	203 756-7441	3977
TT Trade Group LLC (PA)	Bethel	CT	F	800 354-4502	137
Ward Leonard CT LLC (DH)	Thomaston	CT	D	860 283-5801	3641
Ward Leonard CT LLC	Thomaston	CT	E	860 283-2894	3642
Ward Leonard Operating LLC (DH)	Thomaston	CT	E	860 283-5801	3643
Ward Lonard Houma Holdings LLC	Thomaston	CT	D	860 283-5801	3644
ACS Group Inc	Everett	MA	E	617 381-0822	8481
American Superconductor Corp (PA)	Ayer	MA	D	978 842-3000	6171
Ametek Inc	Wilmington	MA	A	978 988-4101	13377
Ametek Arizona Instrument LLC	Middleboro	MA	C	508 946-6200	10349
Andrus Power Solutions Inc	Lee	MA	F	413 243-0043	9610
Atlantic Pwr US GP Hldings Inc	Dedham	MA	G	617 977-2400	8236
Aurora Wind Project LLC	Andover	MA	F	978 409-9712	5871
BP Logue & Co	Chelmsford	MA	F	978 251-4433	7915
Comprehensive Power Inc	Marlborough	MA	E	508 460-0010	10134
Dkd Solutions Inc	Worcester	MA	G	508 762-9114	13717
Dzi	Easthampton	MA	F	413 527-4500	8443
Electro Switch Corp	Weymouth	MA	C	781 607-3306	13324
Emergncy Pwr Gnrators Neng LLC	Chelmsford	MA	G	978 455-0461	7925
Enbw North America Inc	Boston	MA	F	857 753-4623	6714
Horlick Company Inc	Randolph	MA	G	781 963-0090	11564
Hy9 Corporation	Foxboro	MA	G	508 698-1040	8699
L3 Technologies Inc	Northampton	MA	A	413 586-2330	11069
Maxon Precision Motors Inc (HQ)	Taunton	MA	E	508 677-0520	12348
New England Gen-Connect LLC	Hingham	MA	G	617 571-6884	9155
Nidec America Corporation (HQ)	Braintree	MA	E	781 848-4970	7196
Northern Lights Inc	Methuen	MA	G	978 258-7412	10342
Peak Scientific Inc (DH)	North Billerica	MA	E	978 234-4679	10942
Power Equipment Co Inc (PA)	Attleboro	MA	E	508 226-3410	6050
Precision Electronics Corp	Marshfield	MA	F	781 834-6471	10244
Sparkcharge Inc	Somerville	MA	E	866 906-2330	11899
Superpedestrian Inc (PA)	Cambridge	MA	C	877 678-7518	7725
Viking Industrial Products	Marlborough	MA	E	508 481-4600	10231
Weld Power Generator Inc	Millbury	MA	F	800 288-6016	10445
Bear Swamp Power Company LLC	Millinocket	ME	F	207 723-4341	5064
Powr Pt Generator Pwr Systems	Saco	ME	F	207 864-2787	5377
Raven Technology LLC	Brunswick	ME	F	207 729-7904	4654
Ashland Electric Products Inc	Rochester	NH	E	603 335-1100	15466
Data Electronic Devices Inc	Salem	NH	C	603 893-2047	15517
Dmi Technology Corp (PA)	Dover	NH	F	603 742-3330	14226
Electrocraft (HQ)	Stratham	NH	E	855 697-7966	15634
Electrocraft New Hampshire Inc (DH)	Dover	NH	E	603 742-3330	14228
Electrocraft New Hampshire Inc	Stratham	NH	E	740 441-6208	15635
Ion Physics Corp	Fremont	NH	G	603 895-5100	14328
Megatrnics US Ultimate Hldco LL (PA)	Salem	NH	E	888 706-0230	15544
Sumake North America LLC	Amherst	NH	F	603 402-2924	13892
Teledyne Instruments Inc	Portsmouth	NH	C	603 474-5571	15442
Wall Industries Inc	Exeter	NH	E	603 778-2300	14305
Green Development LLC	Cranston	RI	D	401 295-4998	15870
Kearney-National Inc	North Kingstown	RI	C	401 943-2686	16264
Wei Inc (PA)	Cranston	RI	E	401 781-3904	15928
Apex Sealing Inc	Fairfax	VT	F	802 524-7100	17254
Dynapower Company LLC (DH)	South Burlington	VT	D	802 860-7200	17577
Hayward Tyler Inc (DH)	Colchester	VT	E	802 655-4444	17194

3624 Carbon and graphite products

	CITY	ST	EMP	PHONE	ENTRY#
Carbon Products Inc	Somersville	CT	G	860 749-0614	3101
Hexcel Corporation (PA)	Stamford	CT	E	203 969-0666	3374
Joshua LLC (PA)	Guilford	CT	F	203 624-0080	1398
Minteq International Inc	Canaan	CT	F	860 824-5435	556
Morgan A M T	Durham	CT	F	860 349-4444	903
Applied Nnstrctred Sltions LLC	Billerica	MA	E	978 670-6959	6403
Geonautics Manufacturing Inc	Newburyport	MA	E	978 462-7161	10685
Hyperion Catalysis Intl Inc (PA)	Cambridge	MA	D	617 354-9678	7607
N12 Technologies Inc	Foxboro	MA	G	857 259-6622	8709
Via Separations Inc	Watertown	MA	D	781 354-7945	12918
Clear Carbon & Components Inc	Bristol	RI	E	401 254-5085	15758
Composite Energy Tech Inc	Bristol	RI	E	401 253-2670	15760
Hall Inc	Bristol	RI	D	401 253-4858	15768
TEAM INC	Woonsocket	RI	E	401 762-1500	16980

3625 Relays and industrial controls

	CITY	ST	EMP	PHONE	ENTRY#
ABB Inc	Danbury	CT	E	203 798-6210	702
Advanced Micro Controls Inc	Terryville	CT	E	860 585-1254	3599
Alinabal Inc (HQ)	Milford	CT	C	203 877-3241	1796
Allied Controls Inc	Stamford	CT	F	860 628-8443	3277
Altek Company	Torrington	CT	C	860 482-7626	3668
Altek Electronics Inc	Torrington	CT	C	860 482-7626	3669
Asea Brown Boveri Inc	Norwalk	CT	A	203 750-2200	2465
Ashcroft (DH)	Stratford	CT	B	203 378-8281	3517
Baumer Ltd (DH)	Bristol	CT	F	860 621-2121	410
Belimo Aircontrols (usa) Inc (HQ)	Danbury	CT	C	800 543-9038	715
Carlyle Johnson Machine Co LLC (DH)	Bolton	CT	F	860 643-1531	219
Cet Inc	Milford	CT	G	203 882-8057	1810
Clarktron Products Inc	Fairfield	CT	G	203 333-6517	1178
Computer Components Inc	East Granby	CT	E	860 653-9909	931
Conntrol International Inc	Putnam	CT	F	860 928-0567	2851
Control Concepts Inc (PA)	Brooklyn	CT	F	860 928-6551	545
Conveyco Technologies Inc (PA)	Bristol	CT	E	860 589-8215	432
Crrc LLC (PA)	South Windsor	CT	D	877 684-6464	3136
Delta Elevator Service Corp (DH)	Canton	CT	E	860 676-6152	560
Devar Inc	Bridgeport	CT	E	203 368-6751	317
Digatron Power Electronics Inc	Shelton	CT	E	203 446-8000	3000
Dufrane Technologies LLC	Winsted	CT	F	860 379-2318	4341
Dynamic Bldg Enrgy Sltions LLC (PA)	North Stonington	CT	F	860 599-1872	2447
Ewald Instruments Corp	Lakeville	CT	F	860 491-9042	1545
Gems Sensors Inc (HQ)	Plainville	CT	B	860 747-3000	2761
General Electric Company	Bridgeport	CT	D	203 396-7200	323
General Electro Components	Glastonbury	CT	G	860 659-3573	1280
Gordon Products Incorporated	Brookfield	CT	E	203 775-4501	523
Hamilton Sundstrand Corp (HQ)	Windsor Locks	CT	A	619 714-9442	4330
Idevices LLC	Avon	CT	D	860 352-5252	27
Inertia Dynamics LLC	New Hartford	CT	C	860 379-1252	2102
ITT Inc (PA)	Stamford	CT	A	914 641-2000	3388
J R Merritt Controls Inc (PA)	Stratford	CT	E	203 381-0100	3551
Kimchuk Incorporated (PA)	Danbury	CT	F	203 790-7800	766
Linemaster Switch Corporation	Woodstock	CT	C	860 630-4920	4395
Magnetic Technologies Ltd	Putnam	CT	E	508 987-3303	2864
Measurement Systems Inc	Wallingford	CT	E	203 949-3500	3831
Minarik Corporation	Bloomfield	CT	C	860 687-5000	192
Naiad Dynamics Us Inc (HQ)	Shelton	CT	E	203 929-6355	3033
New England Lift Systems LLC	Newington	CT	G	860 372-4040	2309
New England Machine Tools Inc	Bristol	CT	G	860 583-4001	475
New Haven Companies Inc	East Haven	CT	F	203 469-6421	1048
North American Elev Svcs Co (DH)	Farmington	CT	E	860 676-6000	1233
O E M Controls Inc (PA)	Shelton	CT	C	203 929-8431	3042
P-Q Controls Inc (PA)	Bristol	CT	E	860 583-6994	478
P/A Industries Inc (PA)	Bloomfield	CT	E	860 243-8306	200
Park Distributories Inc	Bridgeport	CT	G	203 366-7200	355
Park Distributories Inc	Bridgeport	CT	G	203 366-7200	356
Park Distributories Inc (PA)	Bridgeport	CT	G	203 579-2140	357
Quality Name Plate Inc	East Glastonbury	CT	D	860 633-9495	923
T & T Automation Inc	Windsor	CT	F	860 683-8788	4306
Thomas Products Ltd	Southington	CT	F	860 621-9101	3236
Ward Leonard CT LLC (DH)	Thomaston	CT	D	860 283-5801	3641
Airloc Corporation	Franklin	MA	G	508 528-0022	8814
Altra Industrial Motion Corp (HQ)	Braintree	MA	C	781 917-0600	7167
Applied Dynamics Corporation (PA)	Greenfield	MA	E	413 774-7268	8981
Asahi/America Inc (HQ)	Lawrence	MA	F	781 321-5409	9540
Ben Franklin Design Mfg Co Inc	Agawam	MA	F	413 786-4220	5781
Complete Energy Services Corp	Raynham	MA	F	833 237-2677	11584
Control Resources Inc	Littleton	MA	F	978 486-4160	9806
Control Technology Corporation (PA)	Hopkinton	MA	E	508 435-9596	9313
Cordmaster Engineering Co Inc	North Adams	MA	F	413 664-9371	10805
Dolan-Jenner Industries Inc	Boxborough	MA	E	978 263-1400	7151
Dynisco Instruments LLC (HQ)	Franklin	MA	E	508 541-9400	8831
Electro Switch Corp	Weymouth	MA	C	781 607-3306	13324
Electro Switch Corp	Weymouth	MA	F	781 335-1195	13325
Emx Controls Inc	East Douglas	MA	E	508 876-9700	8350
EPC Corporation	Middleboro	MA	E	508 923-9503	10358
Fil-Tech Inc	Boston	MA	G	617 227-1133	6735
Fluigent Inc	North Chelmsford	MA	F	978 934-5283	10976
Gefran Inc (DH)	North Andover	MA	E	781 729-5249	10836
General Dynmics Def Systems In	Pittsfield	MA	C	413 494-1110	11397
High Voltage Engineering Corp	Wakefield	MA	E	781 224-1001	12511
Horlick Company Inc	Randolph	MA	G	781 963-0090	11564
Ideal Electric Co Inc	Peabody	MA	E	781 284-2525	11317
International Parallel Mchs	New Bedford	MA	E	508 990-2977	10604
Invetech Inc	Boxborough	MA	E	508 475-3400	7152
Iwaki America Incorporated (HQ)	Holliston	MA	E	508 429-1440	9216
Kenneth Crosby Co Inc	Hopkinton	MA	F	508 497-0048	9335
Kidde-Fenwal Inc (HQ)	Ashland	MA	A	508 881-2000	5960
Koso America Inc	West Bridgewater	MA	D	774 517-5300	12974

SIC

	CITY	ST	EMP	PHONE	ENTRY#
L3 Technologies Inc	Northampton	MA	A	413 586-2330	11069
Ltp Corporation (DH)	Northborough	MA	D	508 393-7660	11101
Lynx System Developers Inc	Haverhill	MA	E	978 556-9780	9111
Manufctring Resource Group Inc	Norwood	MA	C	781 440-9700	11192
Massa Products Corporation	Hingham	MA	D	781 749-3120	9152
Maxon Precision Motors Inc (HQ)	Taunton	MA	E	508 677-0520	12348
Motion Industries Inc	Danvers	MA	E	978 774-7100	8210
Murata Power Solutions Inc (DH)	Westborough	MA	C	508 339-3000	13122
Omni Control Technology Inc	Whitinsville	MA	E	508 234-9121	13343
Panametrics LLC (DH)	Billerica	MA	A	978 437-1000	6468
Performance Motion Devices Inc	Boxborough	MA	E	978 266-1210	7153
Radar Technology Inc	Newburyport	MA	E		10711
Rexa Inc	West Bridgewater	MA	D	508 584-1199	12977
RLB Industries Inc	Attleboro	MA	D	508 226-3350	6057
Rockwell Automation Inc	Chelmsford	MA	D	978 441-9500	7952
Rockwell Automation Inc	Marlboro	MA	F	508 357-8400	10205
Schneider Electric Usa Inc (DH)	Boston	MA	A	978 975-9600	7026
Schneider Electric Usa Inc	Foxboro	MA	E	508 549-3385	8724
Scully Signal Company (PA)	Wilmington	MA	D	617 692-8600	13452
Sensata Technologies Ind Inc (DH)	Attleboro	MA	A	508 236-3800	6063
Setra Systems Inc	Boxboro	MA	F	978 263-1400	7145
Sick Inc	Stoughton	MA	D	781 302-2500	12235
Sick Auto Ident Inc (DH)	Stoughton	MA	D	781 302-2500	12236
SMC Corporation of America	Danvers	MA	F	978 767-2328	8220
Suns International LLC	Chelmsford	MA	B	978 349-2329	7960
Teknikor Automtn & Contrls Inc	Fall River	MA	F	508 679-9474	8615
Tektron Inc	Topsfield	MA	F	978 887-0091	12439
Texas Instruments Incorporated	Attleboro	MA	E	508 236-3800	6070
Todd Clark and Associates Inc	Danvers	MA	E	978 774-7100	8225
Viking Industrial Products	Marlborough	MA	E	508 481-4600	10231
Wabash Technologies Inc (DH)	Attleboro	MA	D	260 355-4100	6075
Waja Associates Inc	Franklin	MA	E	508 543-6050	8874
Warner Electric	Braintree	MA	D	781 917-0600	7212
Caron Engineering Inc	Wells	ME	E	207 646-6071	5598
Electrnic Mobility Contrls LLC	Augusta	ME	F	207 512-8009	4471
Elscott Manufacturing LLC (PA)	Gouldsboro	ME	E	207 422-6747	4839
F W Webb Company	Winslow	ME	E	207 873-7741	5682
Illinois Tool Works Inc	Mechanic Falls	ME	E	207 998-5140	5051
James Eaton	Standish	ME	F	207 522-3944	5527
ME Title	Bangor	ME	G	207 942-1988	4510
Montalvo Corporation	Gorham	ME	E	207 856-2501	4827
Richmond Contract Mfg	Bowdoinham	ME	E	207 737-4385	4606
Southworth Intl Group Inc (PA)	Falmouth	ME	D	207 878-0700	4772
Anaren Ceramics Inc	Salem	NH	D	603 898-2883	15505
Antrim Controls & Systems	Bennington	NH	G	603 588-6297	13974
Dmi Technology Corp (PA)	Dover	NH	F	603 742-3330	14226
Dover Flexo Electronics Inc	Rochester	NH	E	603 332-6150	15475
Electrocraft Inc (HQ)	Stratham	NH	E	855 697-7966	15634
Electrocraft New Hampshire Inc (DH)	Dover	NH	E	603 742-3330	14228
Elmo Motion Control Inc	Nashua	NH	F	603 821-9979	15094
Hampshire Controls Corp	Dover	NH	F	603 749-9424	14230
Ie Chemical Systems Inc	Nashua	NH	F	603 888-4777	15112
Spartronics Plaistow Inc	Plaistow	NH	E	603 382-3840	15352
Coto Technology	Warwick	RI	G	401 943-2686	16799
Coto Technology Inc	North Kingstown	RI	B	401 943-2686	16242
Eagle Industries Inc	Ashaway	RI	E	401 596-8111	15739
Kearflex Engineering Company	Warwick	RI	F	401 781-4900	16830
Kearney-National Inc	North Kingstown	RI	C	401 943-2686	16264
Lv Controls Incorporated	Cranston	RI	G	401 228-3937	15889
Raytheon Company	Portsmouth	RI	D	401 847-8000	16454
Regent Controls Inc	Greenville	RI	F	203 732-6200	16063
Walco Electric Company	Providence	RI	D	401 467-6500	16642
Wei Inc	Cranston	RI	F	401 781-3904	15927
Wei Inc (PA)	Cranston	RI	F	401 781-3904	15928
Cooper Lighting Inc	Essex Junction	VT	E	800 767-3674	17232
Dynapower Company LLC (DH)	South Burlington	VT	D	802 860-7200	17577
Westinghouse Electric Co LLC	Brattleboro	VT	E	802 254-9353	17108

3629 Electrical industrial apparatus

	CITY	ST	EMP	PHONE	ENTRY#
90 River Street LLC	New Haven	CT	G	203 772-4700	2109
Advanced Sonics LLC	Oxford	CT	G	203 266-4440	2684
B S T Systems Inc	Plainfield	CT	D	860 564-4078	2734
Control Module Inc (PA)	Enfield	CT	D	860 745-2433	1125
Digatron Power Electronics Inc	Shelton	CT	E	203 446-8000	3000
Harby Power Solutions LLC	Wallingford	CT	G	203 265-0012	3811
Interacter Inc	Wallingford	CT	F	203 949-0199	3818
Pressure Blast Mfg Co Inc	South Windsor	CT	F	800 722-5278	3174
Proliance International Inc	New Haven	CT	E	203 401-6450	2188
3M Company	Chelmsford	MA	E	978 256-3911	7901
Aerovox Incorporated	New Bedford	MA	A	508 994-9661	10565
Asco Power Technologies LP	Marlborough	MA	D	508 624-0466	10111
Assurance Technology Corp (PA)	Carlisle	MA	D	978 369-8848	7845
Assurance Technology Corp	Chelmsford	MA	D	978 250-8060	7912

	CITY	ST	EMP	PHONE	ENTRY#
Atrex Energy Inc (PA)	Walpole	MA	E	781 461-8251	12551
Ballard Unmanned Systems Inc	Southborough	MA	F	508 687-4970	11990
Bel Power Inc	Westborough	MA	D	508 870-9775	13082
Desco Industries Inc	Canton	MA	E	781 821-8370	7784
Gutor Electronic Americas LLC	Foxboro	MA	D	713 397-3798	8698
Lavo USA LLC	Winchester	MA	E	781 600-4123	13486
Murata Power Solutions Inc (DH)	Westborough	MA	C	508 339-3000	13122
Phoenix Electric Corp	Canton	MA	E	781 821-0200	7819
Schneider Electric It Corp (DH)	Foxboro	MA	A	508 543-8750	8723
Solectria Renewables LLC	Lawrence	MA	C	978 683-9700	9599
Sun Catalytix Corporation	Cambridge	MA	E	617 374-3797	7722
Superconductivity Inc (HQ)	Ayer	MA	D	608 831-5773	6197
Tasi Holdings Inc (PA)	Marlborough	MA	F	513 202-5182	10223
Thermo Fisher Scientific Inc (PA)	Waltham	MA	C	781 622-1000	12800
Wafer LLC	Beverly	MA	F	978 304-3821	6394
Illinois Tool Works Inc	Mechanic Falls	ME	E	207 998-5140	5051
Kyocera AVX Cmpnnts Bddford Co	Biddeford	ME	C	207 282-5111	4574
Aak Power Supply Corporation	Plaistow	NH	F	603 382-2222	15335
Desco Industries Inc	Rochester	NH	G	603 332-0717	15473
El-Op US Inc	Merrimack	NH	C	603 889-2500	14980
KMC Systems Inc	Merrimack	NH	D	866 742-0442	14987
Kollsman Inc (DH)	Merrimack	NH	A	603 889-2500	14988
Milpower Source Inc	Belmont	NH	C	603 267-8865	13963
Stentech Inc (PA)	Derry	NH	D	603 505-4470	14209
Thomas Instruments Inc	Spofford	NH	G	603 363-4500	15630
Vicor Corporation	Manchester	NH	E	603 623-3222	14953
International Technologies Inc	Warwick	RI	F	401 467-6907	16823
Veterans Assembled Elec LLC (PA)	North Kingstown	RI	G	401 228-6165	16291

3631 Household cooking equipment

	CITY	ST	EMP	PHONE	ENTRY#
Conair LLC (HQ)	Stamford	CT	B	203 351-9000	3320
Kenyon International Inc	Clinton	CT	E	860 664-4906	645
South Windsor Golf Course LLC	South Windsor	CT	D	860 648-4653	3182
General Electric Company (PA)	Boston	MA	A	617 443-3000	6754
Ray Murray Inc	Lee	MA	D	413 243-2164	9619
Taunton Stove Company Inc	North Dighton	MA	E	508 823-0786	11004
M & S Enterprises Inc	Brewer	ME	G	207 989-0077	4617
Cooking Solutions Group Inc (HQ)	Salem	NH	F	603 893-9701	15516
Cooking Solutions Group Inc	Essex Junction	VT	C	864 963-3471	17231
GS Blodgett LLC (HQ)	Essex Junction	VT	C	802 860-3700	17236

3632 Household refrigerators and freezers

	CITY	ST	EMP	PHONE	ENTRY#
Coldsnap Corp	Billerica	MA	E	617 733-9935	6426
General Electric Company (PA)	Boston	MA	A	617 443-3000	6754
Raytheon Sutheast Asia Systems (DH)	Waltham	MA	E	978 470-5000	12762

3634 Electric housewares and fans

	CITY	ST	EMP	PHONE	ENTRY#
Bkmfg Corp	Winsted	CT	E	860 738-2200	4339
Black & Decker (us) Inc	New Britain	CT	E	860 225-5111	2008
Conair LLC (HQ)	Stamford	CT	B	203 351-9000	3320
Conair LLC	Stamford	CT	F	203 348-6684	3321
Conair LLC	Torrington	CT	D	800 492-7464	3676
Crrc LLC	Cromwell	CT	D	860 635-2200	691
Jarden LLC	Norwalk	CT	E	203 845-5300	2519
Mayborn Usa Inc	Stamford	CT	F	781 269-7490	3409
McIntire Company (HQ)	Bristol	CT	F	860 585-8559	465
Puraclenz LLC	New Canaan	CT	G	561 213-1411	2085
Aeris Health Inc	Bedford	MA	F	917 685-6504	6206
Convectronics Inc	Haverhill	MA	E	978 374-7714	9088
De-Ice Technologies Inc	Somerville	MA	F	857 829-7651	11868
Ecovent Corp	Charlestown	MA	F	620 983-6863	7869
Gillette Company (HQ)	Boston	MA	A	617 463-3000	6758
Headwaters Inc	Marblehead	MA	G	781 715-6404	10087
Kaz Usa Inc	Marlborough	MA	D	508 490-7000	10175
Mestek Inc (PA)	Westfield	MA	E	470 898-4533	13186
QCI Inc	Seekonk	MA	F	508 399-8983	11784
REST LLC	North Reading	MA	F	781 788-8113	11045
Revolution Cooking LLC	Woburn	MA	F	301 710-0590	13652
Springfield Wire Inc	Ludlow	MA	A	413 385-0115	9954
Spruce Environmental Tech Inc	Haverhill	MA	D	978 521-0901	9134
Thl-Nortek Investors LLC (PA)	Boston	MA	D	617 227-1050	7077
Vaughn Thermal Corporation	Salisbury	MA	E	978 462-6683	11745
Mills & Co Inc	Windham	ME	G	207 893-1115	5665
Eichenauer Inc	Newport	NH	E	603 863-1454	15228
Infinite Creative Entps Inc (PA)	Seabrook	NH	E	603 347-6006	15594
Bedjet LLC	Newport	RI	F	401 404-5250	16205

3635 Household vacuum cleaners

	CITY	ST	EMP	PHONE	ENTRY#
Headwaters Inc	Marblehead	MA	G	781 715-6404	10087
Irobot Corporation (PA)	Bedford	MA	B	781 430-3000	6235
Static Solutions Inc (PA)	Hudson	MA	F	978 310-7251	9415
Vacuum Engineering Inc	West Springfield	MA	G	413 734-4400	13049

3639 Household appliances, nec

Company	CITY	ST	EMP	PHONE	ENTRY#
Clarke Distribution Corp	Norwalk	CT	G	203 838-9385	2482
Conair LLC (HQ)	Stamford	CT	B	203 351-9000	3320
Eemax Inc	Waterbury	CT	D	203 267-7890	3910
The Electric Heater Company	Stratford	CT	D	800 647-3165	3580
Euro-Pro Holdco LLC	Needham Heights	MA	E	617 243-0235	10543
Merrow Superior LLC	Fall River	MA	G	212 691-3400	8579
Sharkninja Inc	Needham	MA	A	617 243-0235	10520
Sharkninja Operating LLC (PA)	Needham	MA	E	617 243-0235	10521
Therma-Flow Inc	Watertown	MA	E	617 924-3877	12913
Vaughn Thermal Corporation	Salisbury	MA	E	978 462-6683	11745
W S Bessett Inc	Sanford	ME	E	207 324-9232	5417
Vermont Culinary Islands LLC	Brattleboro	VT	F	802 387-8591	17103

3641 Electric lamps

Company	CITY	ST	EMP	PHONE	ENTRY#
Electro-Lite Corporation	Bethel	CT	F	203 743-4059	114
Lcd Lighting Inc	Orange	CT	C	203 799-7877	2674
Revolution Lighting Tech Inc (PA)	Stamford	CT	E	877 578-2536	3447
Whelen Engineering Company Inc (PA)	Chester	CT	B	860 526-9504	634
Analytik Jena US LLC (DH)	Tewksbury	MA	D	909 946-3197	12384
Dolan-Jenner Industries Inc	Boxborough	MA	E	978 263-1400	7151
International Light Tech Inc	Peabody	MA	E	978 818-6180	11319
Lucidity Lights Inc (PA)	Charlestown	MA	E	781 995-2405	7878
Neenas Lighting	Cambridge	MA	G	617 864-5757	7661
Osram Sylvania Inc (DH)	Wilmington	MA	A	978 570-3000	13444
Partylite Inc (HQ)	Plymouth	MA	D	203 661-1926	11471
Philips Holding USA Inc (HQ)	Cambridge	MA	A	978 687-1501	7686
Luminescent Systems Inc	Lebanon	NH	C	603 643-7766	14693
Osram Sylvania Inc	Exeter	NH	B	603 772-4331	14299
Osram Sylvania Inc	Hillsborough	NH	B	978 750-3900	14441
Osram Sylvania Inc	Hillsborough	NH	B	603 464-7235	14442
Brownlie Lamar Design Group	Warren	RI	G	401 714-9371	16756
Osram Sylvania Inc	Central Falls	RI	C	401 723-1378	15794
First Light Technologies Inc	Poultney	VT	D	802 287-4195	17447

3643 Current-carrying wiring devices

Company	CITY	ST	EMP	PHONE	ENTRY#
ABB Enterprise Software Inc	Plainville	CT	A	860 747-7111	2744
Allied Controls Inc	Stamford	CT	F	860 628-8443	3277
Amphenol Corporation	Stamford	CT	D	203 327-7300	3281
Amphenol Corporation (PA)	Wallingford	CT	D	203 265-8900	3771
Bead Industries Inc (PA)	Milford	CT	E	203 301-0270	1801
Carling Technologies Inc (HQ)	Plainville	CT	C	860 793-9281	2750
Deringer-Ney Inc (PA)	Bloomfield	CT	C	860 242-2281	158
Deringer-Ney Inc	Bloomfield	CT	C	860 242-2281	159
East Coast Lightning Eqp Inc	Winsted	CT	E	860 379-9072	4343
Ek-Ris Cable Company Inc	New Britain	CT	E	860 223-4327	2025
Electric Motion Company Inc (DH)	Winsted	CT	C	860 379-8515	4344
Faria Beede Instruments Inc	North Stonington	CT	C	860 848-9271	2448
Gold Line Connector Inc (PA)	Redding	CT	E	203 938-2588	2882
Gordon Products Incorporated	Brookfield	CT	E	203 775-4501	523
Hubbell Incorporated	Newtown	CT	D	203 426-2555	2338
Hubbell Power Systems Inc	Cromwell	CT	D	860 635-2200	694
Legrand Holding Inc (DH)	West Hartford	CT	E	860 233-6251	4067
Lex Products LLC (PA)	Trumbull	CT	C	203 363-3738	3723
Luvata Waterbury Inc (HQ)	Waterbury	CT	D	203 753-5215	3931
Old Cambridge Products Corp	Bloomfield	CT	F	860 243-1761	197
On Line Building Systems LLC	Danbury	CT	G	203 798-1194	792
Phoenix Assets Holdings Ltd	Norwalk	CT	E	800 323-9562	2557
Siemon Company (PA)	Watertown	CT	A	860 945-4200	4029
Spectrum Associates Inc	Milford	CT	F	203 878-4618	1889
Thomas Products Ltd	Southington	CT	F	860 621-9101	3236
Times Wire and Cable Company (HQ)	Wallingford	CT	D	203 949-8400	3867
Willconn Connections Inc	North Branford	CT	E	203 481-8080	2379
Winchster Interconnect Rf Corp (DH)	Norwalk	CT	D	978 532-0775	2596
Wiremold Company (DH)	West Hartford	CT	A	860 233-6251	4091
World Cord Sets Inc	Enfield	CT	G	203 763-2100	1160
Anderson Airmotive Inc	Fall River	MA	F	508 646-0950	8521
Anderson Power Products Inc (HQ)	Sterling	MA	D	978 422-3600	12154
Anomet Products Inc	Shrewsbury	MA	E	508 842-0174	11827
Artisan Industries Inc	Stoughton	MA	D	781 893-6800	12195
Atlee Delaware Incorporated	Melrose	MA	F	978 681-1003	10313
Baystate Lghtning Prtction Inc	Bridgewater	MA	G	508 697-7727	7223
Brainin-Advance Industries LLC (HQ)	Attleboro	MA	C	508 226-1200	5998
C & K Components LLC (HQ)	Waltham	MA	E	617 969-3700	12619
Caton Connector Corp	Kingston	MA	E	781 585-4315	9505
Checon LLC	Attleboro	MA	F	508 838-2060	6002
Cole Hersee Company (HQ)	Boston	MA	E	617 268-2100	6662
Component Sources Intl Inc	Westborough	MA	F	508 986-2300	13092
Cordmaster Engineering Co Inc	North Adams	MA	E	413 664-9371	10805
Csi Keyboards Inc	Peabody	MA	E	978 532-8181	11304
Data Guide Cable Corporation	Gardner	MA	D	978 632-0900	8883
Dielectric Sciences Inc	Chelmsford	MA	E	978 250-1507	7923
Dorn Equipment Corp	Melrose	MA	F	781 662-9300	10316
Electro Switch Corp	Weymouth	MA	C	781 607-3306	13324
Electro-Term Inc	Springfield	MA	D	413 734-6469	12092
Equipe Communications Corp	Acton	MA	C	978 635-1999	5747
First Electronics Corporation (DH)	Dorchester	MA	E	617 288-2430	8299
General Wire Products Inc	Worcester	MA	E	508 752-8260	13731
Glasseal Products Inc	New Bedford	MA	E	732 370-9100	10595
Ideal Industries Inc	Sterling	MA	G	978 422-3600	12163
Intersense Incorporated	Billerica	MA	E	781 541-6330	6455
ITW Ark-Les Corporation (HQ)	Stoughton	MA	E	781 297-6000	12215
Kidde-Fenwal Inc (HQ)	Ashland	MA	A	508 881-2000	5960
Madison Cable Corporation	Worcester	MA	D	800 522-6752	13755
Mestek Inc	Westfield	MA	F	413 568-9571	13183
Mini-Systems Inc	Plainville	MA	E	508 695-2000	11439
Opalala Inc	Fall River	MA	F	508 646-0950	8591
Osram Sylvania Inc (DH)	Wilmington	MA	A	978 570-3000	13444
Paneltek Inc	Attleboro Falls	MA	F	920 906-9457	6094
Paneltek LLC	Attleboro Falls	MA	F	920 906-9457	6095
Pep Industries LLC	Attleboro	MA	F	508 226-5600	6046
Phoenix Electric Corp	Canton	MA	E	781 821-0200	7819
Portwest Corporation (PA)	North Attleboro	MA	C	508 809-5112	10884
Precision Engineered Pdts LLC (DH)	Attleboro	MA	G		6051
Quabbin Wire & Cable Co Inc (PA)	Ware	MA	D	413 967-6281	12827
San Franciso Market	Lynn	MA	E	781 780-3731	9990
San-Tron Inc (PA)	Ipswich	MA	D	978 356-1585	9496
Schneider Electric Usa Inc (DH)	Boston	MA	A	978 975-9600	7026
Schneider Electric Usa Inc	Foxboro	MA	E	508 549-3385	8724
Segue Manufacturing Svcs LLC	North Billerica	MA	D	978 970-1200	10952
T & T Machine Products Inc	Rockland	MA	F	781 878-3861	11662
Te Connectivity Corporation	Northborough	MA	F	717 592-4299	11111
Teradyne Inc	Boston	MA	G	978 370-2700	7074
Teradyne Inc (PA)	North Reading	MA	A	978 370-2700	11048
Teradyne Inc	Woburn	MA	F	978 370-2700	13677
Texas Instruments Incorporated	Attleboro	MA	E	508 236-3800	6070
Tru Technologies Inc	Peabody	MA	F	978 532-0775	11349
W J Roberts Co Inc	Saugus	MA	E	781 233-8176	11767
General Electric Company	Auburn	ME	C	207 786-5100	4436
Amphenol Corporation	Nashua	NH	B	603 879-3000	15061
Burndy Americas Inc (HQ)	Manchester	NH	D	603 647-5000	14822
Burndy Americas Intl Holdg LLC	Manchester	NH	A	603 647-5000	14823
Burndy LLC (DH)	Manchester	NH	B	603 647-5000	14824
Fci Electrical-Brundy Products	Littleton	NH	D	603 444-6781	14718
Hubbell Incorporated	Londonderry	NH	E	800 346-4175	14756
Hubbell Incorporated	Manchester	NH	F	603 647-5000	14860
Inside Track Cabling Inc	Hudson	NH	E	603 886-8013	14509
Jr Hinds Const Serv	Tilton	NH	G	603 496-2344	15654
O Brien D G Inc	Seabrook	NH	G	603 474-5571	15599
Osram Sylvania Inc	Exeter	NH	B	603 772-4331	14299
Parker & Harper Companies Inc (PA)	Raymond	NH	D	603 895-4761	15455
Q A Technology Company Inc	Hampton	NH	D	603 926-1193	14409
Spire Technology Solutions LLC	Nashua	NH	F	603 594-0005	15173
Teledyne Instruments Inc	Portsmouth	NH	C	603 474-5571	15442
Ametek Scp Inc (HQ)	Westerly	RI	D	401 596-6658	16927
Precision Trned Cmponents Corp	Smithfield	RI	D	401 232-3377	16726
Quick Fitting Inc	East Providence	RI	D	401 734-9500	16040
Thermoswitch International Ltd	Providence	RI	F	401 467-7550	16626
Tower Manufacturing Corp	Providence	RI	D	401 467-7550	16629
Cooper Lighting Inc	Essex Junction	VT	E	800 767-3674	17232
Whitney Blake Company (PA)	Bellows Falls	VT	D	800 323-0479	17033

3644 Noncurrent-carrying wiring devices

Company	CITY	ST	EMP	PHONE	ENTRY#
Arcade Technology LLC	Bridgeport	CT	D	203 366-3871	297
Bridgeport Fittings LLC	Stratford	CT	C	203 377-5944	3522
Hubbell Incorporated Delaware (HQ)	Shelton	CT	E	475 882-4000	3018
Wiremold Company	Rocky Hill	CT	D	860 233-6251	2942
Wiremold Company (DH)	West Hartford	CT	A	860 233-6251	4091
Wiremold Company	West Hartford	CT	E	860 263-3115	4092
Chase Corp Inc	Westwood	MA	D	781 332-0700	13308
Chase Corporation	Oxford	MA	G	508 731-2710	11250
Chase Corporation (HQ)	Westwood	MA	G	781 332-0700	13309
H Loeb Corporation	New Bedford	MA	E	508 996-3745	10597
ITW Ark-Les Corporation (HQ)	Stoughton	MA	E	781 297-6000	12215
Matkim Industries Inc	Oxford	MA	E	508 987-3599	11262
McStowe Engrg & Met Pdts Inc	East Bridgewater	MA	F	508 378-7400	8343
Reinforced Structures For Elec	Worcester	MA	F	508 754-5316	13783
Signal Communications Corp	Woburn	MA	E	781 933-0998	13666
Speedboard Usa Inc	Rowley	MA	G	978 884-3900	11685
Transene Company Inc (PA)	Danvers	MA	G	978 777-7860	8227
Baker Company Inc (PA)	Sanford	ME	E	207 324-8773	5390
Continental Cable LLC	Hinsdale	NH	D	800 229-5131	14443
Intellihome of Vermont L L C	Wilmington	VT	F	802 464-2499	17754
Isovolta Inc	North Clarendon	VT	E	802 775-5528	17414
Superior Tchncal Ceramics Corp (HQ)	Saint Albans	VT	C	802 527-7726	17533

SIC

Employee Codes: A=Over 500 employees,
C=101-250, D=51-100, E=20-50, F=10-19, G=1-9
   B=251-500

2024 Harris New England
Manufacturers Directory

941

	CITY	ST	EMP	PHONE	ENTRY#
Weidmann Electrical Technology Inc **(DH)**	Saint Johnsbury	VT	B	802 748-8106	17548

3645 Residential lighting fixtures

	CITY	ST	EMP	PHONE	ENTRY#
E-Lite Technologies Inc	Trumbull	CT	E	203 371-2070	3718
Gs Thermal Solutions Inc	Danbury	CT	G	475 289-4625	755
Seesmart Inc	Stamford	CT	E	203 504-1111	3454
Atlantic Lighting Inc	Fall River	MA	E	508 678-5411	8523
Blanche P Field LLC	Boston	MA	F	617 423-0715	6596
Chapman Manufacturing Company Inc **(PA)**	Avon			MA	E
508 588-3200	6147				
Color Kinetics	Burlington	MA	D	617 423-9999	7353
Period Lighting Fixtures Inc	Clarksburg	MA	F	413 664-7141	8072
Renovators Supply Inc	Erving	MA	E	413 423-3300	8471
Telefluent Communications Inc	Northborough	MA	F	508 919-0902	11112
Brownlie Lamar Design Group	Warren	RI	G	401 714-9371	16756
Icon International Inc	North Kingstown	RI	D	401 295-2533	16259
Lexington Lighting Group LLC	Rumford	RI	E	860 564-4512	16674
Mastro Lighting Mfg Co Inc **(PA)**	Providence	RI	G	401 467-7700	16559
SCW Corporation	Warwick	RI	E	401 808-6849	16860
Authentic Designs Inc	West Rupert	VT	F	802 394-7715	17694
Hubbardton Forge LLC	Castleton	VT	C	802 468-3090	17172
Light Logic Inc	Hyde Park	VT	E	802 888-7984	17300

3646 Commercial lighting fixtures

	CITY	ST	EMP	PHONE	ENTRY#
C Cowles & Company **(PA)**	North Haven	CT	D	203 865-3117	2396
Lcd Lighting Inc	Orange	CT	C	203 799-7877	2674
Nutron Manufacturing Inc	Norwich	CT	E	860 887-4550	2613
Pathway Lighting Products Inc	Old Saybrook	CT	D	860 388-6881	2659
Pegasus Capital Advisors LP **(PA)**	Stamford	CT	F	203 869-4400	3429
Seesmart Inc	Stamford	CT	E	203 504-1111	3454
Sylvan R Shemitz Designs LLC **(PA)**	West Haven	CT	D	203 931-4455	4127
The L C Doane Company	Ivoryton	CT	D	860 767-8295	1533
Tri-State Led Inc	Greenwich	CT	F	203 813-3791	1357
Whelen Engineering Company Inc	Chester	CT	E	860 526-9504	633
Whelen Engineering Company Inc **(PA)**	Chester	CT	B	860 526-9504	634
Arch Lighting Group Inc	Taunton	MA	E		12317
Asd Lighting Corp	Canton	MA	E	781 739-3977	7770
Atlantic Lighting Inc	Fall River	MA	E	508 678-5411	8523
Dion Signs and Service Inc	New Bedford	MA	F	401 724-4459	10586
International Light Tech Inc	Peabody	MA	E	978 818-6180	11319
Jlc-Tech LLC	Pembroke	MA	F	781 826-8162	11372
Litecontrol Corporation	Plympton	MA	C	781 294-0100	11485
Lumenpulse Lighting Corp	Boston	MA	E	617 307-5700	6865
Micro-Lite Inc	Three Rivers	MA	F	413 289-1313	12429
Norwell Mfg Co Inc	East Taunton	MA	E	508 822-2831	8409
O C White Company	Thorndike	MA	E	413 289-1751	12427
Osram Sylvania Inc **(DH)**	Wilmington	MA	A	978 570-3000	13444
Philips Colorkinetics	Burlington	MA	G	323 251-4758	7411
Renovators Supply Inc	Erving	MA	E	413 423-3300	8471
Rpt Holdings LLC	Middleton	MA	F	877 997-3674	10391
Signify North America Corp	Boston	MA	C	617 423-9999	7036
Signify North America Corp	Burlington	MA	B	508 679-8131	7428
Spectrum Lighting Inc	Fall River	MA	E	508 678-2303	8607
Affinity Led Light LLC	Dover	NH	F	978 378-5338	14214
Lw Holding Lc	Hollis	NH	E	913 851-3000	14453
National Energy & Light LLC	Nashua	NH	E	603 821-9954	15139
Plastic Techniques Inc	Goffstown	NH	E	603 622-5570	14356
Signify North America Corp	Manchester	NH	D	603 645-6061	14929
Central Tools Inc **(PA)**	Cranston	RI	E	401 467-8211	15841
Icon International Inc	North Kingstown	RI	D	401 295-2533	16259
Lexington Lighting Group LLC	Rumford	RI	E	860 564-4512	16674
Lumetta Inc	Warwick	RI	E	401 691-3994	16833
Mastro Lighting Mfg Co Inc **(PA)**	Providence	RI	G	401 467-7700	16559
Orion Ret Svcs & Fixturing Inc	Smithfield	RI	E	401 334-5000	16725
PMC Lighting Inc	Warwick	RI	E	401 738-7266	16846
Renova Lighting Systems Inc	Warwick	RI	E	800 635-6682	16848
SCW Corporation	Warwick	RI	E	401 808-6849	16860
Authentic Designs Inc	West Rupert	VT	F	802 394-7715	17694
Cooper Lighting Inc	Essex Junction	VT	E	800 767-3674	17232

3647 Vehicular lighting equipment

	CITY	ST	EMP	PHONE	ENTRY#
Cornell-Carr Co Inc	Monroe	CT	E	203 261-2529	1911
Ecu & US International	East Hartford	CT	F	860 906-3390	991
Hoffman Engineering LLC **(DH)**	Stamford	CT	D	203 425-8900	3378
Ridge View Associates Inc	Milford	CT	D	203 878-8560	1878
The L C Doane Company	Ivoryton	CT	D	860 767-8295	1533
Whelen Engineering Company Inc **(PA)**	Chester	CT	B	860 526-9504	634
Osram Sylvania Inc **(DH)**	Wilmington	MA	A	978 570-3000	13444
B/E Aerospace Inc	Hampton	NH	F	603 926-5700	14399

3648 Lighting equipment, nec

	CITY	ST	EMP	PHONE	ENTRY#
Blp Technologies Inc	Wallingford	CT	E	203 678-4224	3781
Cooper Crouse-Hinds LLC	Windsor	CT	D	860 683-4300	4268

	CITY	ST	EMP	PHONE	ENTRY#
Eaton Electric Holdings LLC	Windsor	CT	F	860 683-4300	4271
Electrix LLC	New Haven	CT	D	203 776-5577	2149
Fidelux Lighting LLC **(PA)**	Middletown	CT	F	203 774-5653	1746
ME Products LLC	New Britain	CT	E	860 832-8960	2041
Pathway Lighting Products Inc	Old Saybrook	CT	D	860 388-6881	2659
Pegasus Capital Advisors LP **(PA)**	Stamford	CT	F	203 869-4400	3429
Pennsylvania Globe Gaslight Co	North Branford	CT	E	203 484-7749	2371
Point Lighting Corporation	Bloomfield	CT	E	860 243-0600	202
Reflex Ltg Group of CT LLC	Wethersfield	CT	G	860 666-1548	4214
Rsl Fiber Systems LLC	East Hartford	CT	F	860 282-4930	1019
Sensor Switch Inc **(DH)**	New Haven	CT	E	203 265-2842	2198
Solais Lighting Inc	Stamford	CT	F	203 683-6222	3463
Sorenson Lighted Controls Inc **(PA)**	West Hartford	CT	D	860 527-3092	4081
Sylvan R Shemitz Designs LLC	New Haven	CT	D	203 776-5577	2205
Whelen Engineering Company Inc **(PA)**	Chester	CT	B	860 526-9504	634
Acton Research Corporation	Acton	MA	G	941 556-2601	5731
Ainslie Corporation	Walpole	MA	G	781 848-0850	12548
Brite-Strike Technologies Inc	Duxbury	MA	G	781 585-3525	8329
Color Kinetics	Burlington	MA	D	617 423-9999	7353
Creative Mktg Concepts Corp	Boxford	MA	G	800 272-8267	7159
Current Lighting Solutions LLC	Boston	MA	F	713 521-6500	6678
Current Ltg Employeeco LLC	Boston	MA	A	216 266-2906	6679
Cyalume Technologies Inc **(HQ)**	West Springfield	MA	F	888 858-7881	13020
Dolan-Jenner Industries Inc	Boxborough	MA	E	978 263-1400	7151
Dorel Juvenile Group Inc	Foxboro	MA	C	800 544-1108	8694
Excelitas Tech Holdg Corp	Waltham	MA	A	781 522-5914	12671
Excelitas Tech Holdings Corp **(PA)**	Waltham	MA	F	781 522-5900	12672
Excelitas Technologies Corp **(DH)**	Waltham	MA	E	855 382-2677	12673
Lansea Systtems Inc	Quincy	MA	G	617 877-9773	11526
Lighting By Hammerworks **(PA)**	Worcester	MA	E	508 755-3434	13753
Micro-Lite Inc	Three Rivers	MA	F	413 289-1313	12429
Nedap Inc	Burlington	MA	F	844 876-3327	7396
Needham Electric Supply LLC **(DH)**	Canton	MA	D	781 828-9494	7811
Optoglo Inc	Leominster	MA	E	978 235-0201	9690
Pelican Products Inc	South Deerfield	MA	E	413 665-2163	11926
Period Lighting Fixtures Inc	Clarksburg	MA	F	413 664-7141	8072
Spotlight LLC	Danvers	MA	F	978 762-8352	8221
Sunrise Technologies LLC	Raynham	MA	F	508 884-9732	11598
Tmlp Ernest Mello	Taunton	MA	G	508 823-4849	12371
Xenon Corporation **(PA)**	Wilmington	MA	E	978 661-9033	13477
ARC Electronics Inc	Hampstead	NH	F	603 458-2089	14380
Luminescent Systems Inc	Lebanon	NH	C	603 643-7766	14693
Visible Light Inc	Hampton	NH	G	603 926-6049	14417
Emissive Energy Corp	North Kingstown	RI	D	401 294-2030	16251
Cooper Lighting Inc	Essex Junction	VT	E	800 767-3674	17232
Uv III Systems Inc	Alburg	VT	F	508 883-4881	16984

3651 Household audio and video equipment

	CITY	ST	EMP	PHONE	ENTRY#
C Speaker Corp	Stamford	CT	C		3299
D&C Global Enterprise LLC	Bridgeport	CT	G	810 553-2360	313
Harman Bcker Auto Systems Mfg	Stamford	CT	G	203 328-3501	3362
Harman Consumer Inc	Stamford	CT	E	203 328-3500	3363
Harman International Inds Inc	Stamford	CT	E	203 328-3500	3364
Harman International Inds Inc **(HQ)**	Stamford	CT	A	203 328-3500	3365
Harman KG Holding LLC **(DH)**	Stamford	CT	D	203 328-3500	3366
Insight Plus Technology LLC	Bristol	CT	G	860 930-4763	457
Interspace Industries LLC	Brookfield	CT	E	520 745-5009	526
Ki Inc	Orange	CT	D	203 641-5492	2672
Krell Industries LLC	Orange	CT	F	203 298-4000	2673
Microphase Corporation	Shelton	CT	E	203 866-8000	3032
PMC Technologies LLC	Weston	CT	G	203 222-0000	4151
Redco Audio Inc	Monroe	CT	F	203 502-7600	1920
Telefunken Usa LLC	South Windsor	CT	F	860 882-5919	3185
Visionpoint LLC	Newington	CT	E	860 436-9673	2333
Whelen Engineering Company Inc **(PA)**	Chester	CT	B	860 526-9504	634
Access Advance LLC	Boston	MA	F	617 367-4802	6510
Aerial Acoustics Corporation	Lawrence	MA	F	978 988-1600	9535
Andover Audio LLC	North Andover	MA	F	978 775-3670	10818
Artel Video Systems Corp	Westford	MA	E	978 263-5775	13224
Bose Corporation **(PA)**	Framingham	MA	A	508 879-7330	8745
Bose Corporation	Framingham	MA	F	508 766-1265	8746
Bose Corporation	Framingham	MA	E	508 879-7330	8747
Bose Corporation	Stow	MA	E	508 766-7330	12244
Boston Acoustics Inc **(DH)**	Wakefield	MA	D	978 538-5000	12503
Bowers and Wilkins Group	North Reading	MA	E	978 357-0428	11038
Brown Innovations Inc **(PA)**	Boston	MA	G	773 477-7500	6625
Cambridge Soundworks Inc	Westwood	MA	E	781 329-2777	13307
Cco Holdings LLC	Harvard	MA	C	978 615-1032	9060
Cco Holdings LLC	Longmeadow	MA	C	413 754-0616	9849
Cco Holdings LLC	North Grafton	MA	C	774 293-4026	11020
Cco Holdings LLC	Upton	MA	C	774 462-6577	12470
Courtsmart Digital Systems Inc	North Chelmsford	MA	E	978 251-3300	10973
Fargo Ta LLC	Boston	MA	E	617 345-0066	6731

	CITY	ST	EMP	PHONE	ENTRY#
Fishman Transducers Inc	Andover	MA	D	978 988-9199	5883
Genelec Inc	Natick	MA	F	508 652-0900	10481
Headwaters Inc	Marblehead	MA	G	781 715-6404	10087
Industrial Video & Ctrl Co LLC	Newton	MA	E	617 467-3059	10761
Inter-Ego Systems Inc (PA)	Hatfield	MA	F	516 576-9052	9073
Loud Audio LLC	Whitinsville	MA	C	508 234-6158	13341
Metalpro USA Inc	Plymouth	MA	G	508 942-9746	11465
Mini-Systems Inc (PA)	North Attleboro	MA	D	508 695-1420	10878
Outlaw Audio LLC	Norton	MA	F	508 286-4110	11131
Philips	North Andover	MA	F	978 258-7110	10848
Pine and Baker Mfg Inc	Tewksbury	MA	F	978 851-1215	12412
Rf Venue Inc	Walpole	MA	G	800 795-0817	12573
Runco Capital Corporation	Newburyport	MA	E	978 462-0320	10716
Savant Systems Inc (PA)	Hyannis	MA	E	508 683-2500	9449
Technomad Associates LLC	South Deerfield	MA	F	413 665-6704	11929
Thomson Video Networks Americas LLC	Southwick	MA	E	413 998-1200	12046
Venmill Industries Inc	Oxford	MA	F	508 363-0410	11267
Views Record Label LLC	Springfield	MA	F	413 204-0930	12148
Viking Industrial Products	Marlborough	MA	E	508 481-4600	10231
Volicon Inc	Burlington	MA	E	781 221-7400	7447
Yamaha Unfied Cmmnications Inc	Sudbury	MA	E	978 610-4040	12272
Transparent Audio Inc	Saco	ME	E	207 284-1100	5380
Cc1 Inc	Portsmouth	NH	E	603 319-2000	15368
Russound/Fmp Inc	Portsmouth	NH	C	603 659-5170	15433
Tradeport USA LLC	Dover	NH	F	603 692-2900	14254
Vx1 Corporation	Dover	NH	F	603 742-2888	14258
Cambridge Signal Tech Inc	Providence	RI	F	401 490-5682	16493
Constant Technologies Inc	North Kingstown	RI	E	800 518-7369	16240
Ion Audio LLC (HQ)	Cumberland	RI	F	401 658-3743	15947
Cco Holdings LLC	Montpelier	VT	C	802 778-0497	17371
Westinghouse Electric Co LLC	Brattleboro	VT	E	802 254-9353	17108

3652 Prerecorded records and tapes

	CITY	ST	EMP	PHONE	ENTRY#
Bff Holdings Inc (HQ)	Old Saybrook	CT	C	860 510-0100	2645
Covalent Networks Inc	Boston	MA	F	781 296-7952	6673
Image Software Services Inc	Shirley	MA	G	978 425-3600	11817
Intent Solutions Group (PA)	Norwell	MA	G	617 909-4714	11142
Qwiklabs Inc	Carlisle	MA	F	978 760-0732	7846
Teranode Inc	Dedham	MA	F	781 493-6900	8252
Barefoot Technologies Corp	Henniker	NH	F	603 428-6255	14433
Porter Music Box Co Inc	Randolph	VT	G	802 728-9694	17473

3661 Telephone and telegraph apparatus

	CITY	ST	EMP	PHONE	ENTRY#
Action-Dctgraph Tlecomuncation	Meriden	CT	G	203 238-2322	1651
Ahead Communications Systems	Naugatuck	CT	E	203 720-0227	1947
Amphenol Corporation (PA)	Wallingford	CT	D	203 265-8900	3771
Canoga Perkins Corporation	Seymour	CT	G	203 888-7914	2956
Dac Systems Inc	Shelton	CT	F	203 924-7000	2995
Freedom Technologies LLC	Glastonbury	CT	F	860 633-0452	1278
General Datacomm Inds Inc (PA)	Naugatuck	CT	F	203 729-0271	1961
IPC Systems Inc	Fairfield	CT	E	860 271-4100	1189
IPC Systems Inc	Old Saybrook	CT	F	860 952-9575	2652
K-Tech International Inc	Torrington	CT	E	860 489-9399	3687
Mercury Cabling Systems LLC	Stratford	CT	F	203 378-9008	3556
Microphase Corporation	Shelton	CT	E	203 866-8000	3032
Nutmeg Utility Products Inc (PA)	Cheshire	CT	E	203 250-8802	609
Opticonx Inc	Putnam	CT	E	888 748-6855	2868
Pitney Bowes Inc (PA)	Stamford	CT	A	203 356-5000	3433
Radio Frequency Systems Inc (DH)	Meriden	CT	E	203 630-3311	1690
Sigmavoip Llc	Westport	CT	G	203 541-5450	4196
Tango Modem LLC	Madison	CT	G	203 421-2245	1572
Total Communications Inc (PA)	East Hartford	CT	D	860 282-9999	1028
Adtran Networks North Amer Inc	Chelmsford	MA	F	978 674-6800	7902
Artel Video Systems Corp	Westford	MA	E	978 263-5775	13224
Avaya LLC	Billerica	MA	F	908 953-6000	6407
Biscom Inc	Westford	MA	D	978 250-1800	13226
Cantata Technology Inc (DH)	Needham Heights	MA	C	781 449-4100	10533
Century-Tywood J3 Corp	Holliston	MA	F	508 429-4011	9204
Crown Cstle Fibr Holdings Corp (HQ)	Boxborough	MA	F	978 264-6001	7150
Digital 128 First Avenue LLC	Needham	MA	E	781 726-7736	10508
Em4 Inc (DH)	Bedford	MA	F	781 275-7501	6223
Equipe Communications Corp	Acton	MA	C	978 635-1999	5747
General Dynmics Mssion Systems	Taunton	MA	F	508 880-4000	12338
Global Connector Tech Ltd	Lawrence	MA	F	978 208-1618	9565
Gn Audio USA Inc (DH)	Lowell	MA	B	800 826-4656	9881
Grandstream Networks Inc (PA)	Boston	MA	F	617 566-9300	6769
Interntonal Micro Photonix Inc	North Andover	MA	G	978 685-3800	10840
Manufacturers Services Limited	Concord	MA	E	617 330-7682	8124
Mayflower Communications Inc	Bedford	MA	E	781 359-9500	6239
MB Westfield Inc	Westfield	MA	C	413 568-8676	13182
Mrv Communications Americas Inc	Chelmsford	MA	C	978 674-6800	7940
Nokia of America Corporation	Westford	MA	D	978 952-1616	13256
Opus Telecom Inc	Framingham	MA	F	508 875-4444	8794

	CITY	ST	EMP	PHONE	ENTRY#
Photonex Corporation	Maynard	MA	F	978 723-2200	10264
Sandy Bay Machine Inc	Gloucester	MA	C	978 546-1331	8957
Sanwa Technologies Inc	Westborough	MA	E	508 616-9500	13132
Seaborn Networks Holdings LLC (PA)	Beverly	MA	F	978 471-3171	6382
Shintron Co Inc	Cambridge	MA	F	617 491-8701	7711
Siemens Energy Inc	Westford	MA	E	978 577-6413	13262
Signal Communications Corp	Woburn	MA	E	781 933-0998	13666
Spectrsite Bradcast Towers Inc	Boston	MA	F	888 348-3667	7050
Xphotonics LLC	Littleton	MA	G	978 952-2568	9846
SPX Corporation	Raymond	ME	E	207 655-8525	5316
Amphenol Corporation	Nashua	NH	B	603 879-3000	15061
At Comm Corp	Manchester	NH	F	603 624-4424	14815
Deborah Frost	Bedford	NH	F	603 882-3100	13924
Dialogic (us) Inc	Salem	NH	E	603 890-7240	15518
Exacom Inc	Concord	NH	E	603 228-0706	14129
H&L Instruments LLC	North Hampton	NH	F	603 964-1818	15251
Minim Inc (PA)	Manchester	NH	E	833 966-4646	14889
Northeast Innovations Inc	Pembroke	NH	F	603 226-4000	15306
Ripley Odm LLC	Belmont	NH	F	603 524-8350	13971
Subcom LLC	Newington	NH	D	603 319-5041	15213
Aldotech Corporation	Warwick	RI	E	401 467-6100	16777
Eartec Company Inc	Narragansett	RI	F	401 789-8700	16190
Electro Standards Lab Inc	Cranston	RI	D	401 946-1164	15853
Global Photonix LLC	East Greenwich	RI	G	401 474-8158	15987
Okonite Company Inc	Cumberland	RI	E	401 333-3500	15957
Ramtel Corporation	Johnston	RI	F	401 231-3340	16102
Telecom Installation Svcs Inc	Middletown	RI	E	401 258-2095	16185

3663 Radio and t.v. communications equipment

	CITY	ST	EMP	PHONE	ENTRY#
Arris Technology Inc	Wallingford	CT	E	678 473-8493	3776
Ashcroft Inc (DH)	Stratford	CT	B	203 378-8281	3517
Commscope Technologies LLC	Prospect	CT	F	203 699-4100	2831
Comsat Inc	Southbury	CT	F	203 264-4091	3192
Connecticut Radio Inc	Rocky Hill	CT	G	860 563-4867	2919
Cuescript Inc	Stratford	CT	G	203 763-4030	3532
Ericsson	New Haven	CT	E	203 776-0631	2150
Frontier Vision Tech Inc	Rocky Hill	CT	E	860 953-0240	2922
Gold Line Connector Inc (PA)	Redding	CT	E	203 938-2588	2882
Latino Multiservice LLC	New Haven	CT	G	203 691-9715	2168
Links Point Inc	Norwalk	CT	E	203 853-4600	2528
Media Links Inc	Windsor	CT	F	860 206-9163	4290
Microphase Corporation	Shelton	CT	E	203 866-8000	3032
Microtech Inc	Cheshire	CT	D	203 272-3234	607
Northastern Communications Inc	Stratford	CT	F	203 381-9008	3558
Radio Frequency Systems Inc (DH)	Meriden	CT	E	203 630-3311	1690
Retcomm Inc	Guilford	CT	F	203 453-2389	1405
Stamford Mdia Ctr Prdctons LLC	Stamford	CT	G	203 905-4000	3471
Symbol Technologies LLC	Stamford	CT	G	203 359-5677	3476
Video Messengercom Corp	Stratford	CT	G	203 358-8842	3582
Wpcs International- Hartford Inc (HQ)	Windsor	CT	E		4315
Accelerated Media Tech Inc	Auburn	MA	E	508 459-0300	6097
Adaptive Networks Inc	Needham	MA	E	781 444-4170	10504
Aerial Wireless Services LLC	Bellingham	MA	D	508 657-1213	6282
Ainslie Corporation	Walpole	MA	G	781 848-0850	12548
Antenna Research Assoc Inc	Pembroke	MA	E	781 829-4740	11357
Arris Technology Inc	Lowell	MA	F	978 614-2900	9855
Artel Video Systems Corp	Westford	MA	E	978 263-5775	13224
Asco Power Technologies LP	Marlborough	MA	D	508 624-0466	10111
Assurance Technology Corp	Chelmsford	MA	D	978 250-8060	7912
Atc Ponderosa B-I LLC	Boston	MA	F	617 375-7500	6563
Atc Ponderosa B-II LLC	Boston	MA	F	617 375-7500	6564
Atc Ponderosa H-I LLC	Boston	MA	F	617 375-7500	6565
Atc Ponderosa H-II LLC	Boston	MA	F	617 375-7500	6566
Atc Ponderosa K LLC	Boston	MA	G	617 375-7500	6567
Atc Ponderosa K Ohio LLC	Boston	MA	F	617 375-7500	6568
Atc Sequoia LLC	Boston	MA	F	617 375-7500	6569
Atc Tower Services LLC	Boston	MA	F	617 375-7500	6570
Atlantic Microwave Corporation	Lowell	MA	C		9856
Axiom Microdevices Inc	Woburn	MA	E	781 376-3000	13518
Benu Networks Inc	Burlington	MA	D	978 223-4700	7340
Burk Technology Inc	Littleton	MA	F	978 486-0086	9805
Casa Systems Inc (PA)	Andover	MA	B	978 688-6706	5877
Catalog Technologies Inc	Boston	MA	F	617 768-7222	6641
Cco Holdings LLC	Harvard	MA	C	978 615-1032	9060
Cco Holdings LLC	Longmeadow	MA	C	413 754-0616	9849
Cco Holdings LLC	North Grafton	MA	C	774 293-4026	11020
Cco Holdings LLC	Upton	MA	C	774 462-6577	12470
Comcast Sportsnet Neng LLC	Needham Heights	MA	D	617 630-5000	10537
Communications & Pwr Inds LLC	Beverly	MA	B	978 922-6000	6340
Comrex Corporation	Devens	MA	F	978 784-1776	8272
Copley Controls Corporation (DH)	Canton	MA	B	781 828-8090	7779
Courtsmart Digital Systems Inc	North Chelmsford	MA	E	978 251-3300	10973
Cowbell Technologies Inc	Hudson	MA	F	508 733-1778	9360

	CITY	ST	EMP	PHONE	ENTRY#
Cowbell Technologies Inc (PA)	Westborough	MA	G	508 733-1778	13094
CPI Essco Inc	Ayer	MA	C	978 568-5100	6179
CPI Radant Tech Div Inc (DH)	Stow	MA	D	978 562-3866	12245
David Clark Company Inc (PA)	Worcester	MA	C	508 756-6216	13713
Fat Hen LLC	Somerville	MA	E	617 764-1412	11871
Global Tower Holdings LLC	Boston	MA	F	617 375-7500	6764
Hitachi Kokusai Electric Comark LLC	Southwick	MA	D	413 998-1100	12043
Hxi LLC	Harvard	MA	B	978 772-7774	9064
Legacy Broadcast Inc	North Billerica	MA	F	978 330-9300	10926
Leidos SEC Dtction Automtn Inc	Haverhill	MA	F	781 939-3800	9108
Leidos SEC Dtction Automtn Inc	Tewksbury	MA	F	781 939-3800	12404
Linx Consulting LLC	Webster	MA	E	508 461-6333	12930
Loud Audio LLC	Whitinsville	MA	C	508 234-6158	13341
Macom Technology Solutions Inc	Lowell	MA	E	978 656-2500	9899
Macom Technology Solutions Inc (HQ)	Lowell	MA	B	978 656-2500	9900
Manage Inc	Springfield	MA	E	413 593-9128	12112
Manufacturers Services Limited	Concord	MA	E	617 330-7682	8124
Megapulse Incorporated	Bedford	MA	E	781 538-5299	6241
Microwave Engineering Corp	North Andover	MA	D	978 685-2776	10844
Millitech Inc	Northampton	MA	D	413 582-9620	11073
Motion Industries Inc	Danvers	MA	E	978 774-7100	8210
Newedge Signal Solutions LLC (PA)	Ayer	MA	G	978 425-5400	6188
Novelsat Inc	Newton	MA	E	617 658-1419	10773
Ondas Holdings Inc (PA)	Waltham	MA	F	888 350-9994	12744
Panametrics LLC (DH)	Billerica	MA	A	978 437-1000	6468
Qd Vision Inc	Foxboro	MA	D	781 652-7500	8715
Radio Waves Inc	North Billerica	MA	E	978 459-8800	10946
Raytheon Company (HQ)	Waltham	MA	B	781 522-3000	12759
Raytheon Korean Support Co (DH)	Waltham	MA	E	339 645-6111	12761
Raytheon Sutheast Asia Systems (DH)	Waltham	MA	E	978 470-5000	12762
Royalty Brdcstg Svcs & Trnsp	Springfield	MA	F	413 777-7868	12127
Ruckus Wireless Inc	Lowell	MA	C	978 614-2900	9922
Ruckus Wireless Inc	Westborough	MA	C	508 870-1184	13131
Seachange International Inc (PA)	Boston	MA	D	978 897-0100	7029
Smiths Interconnect Inc	Northampton	MA	D	413 582-9620	11080
Starent Networks LLC (HQ)	Tewksbury	MA	F	978 851-1100	12418
Stellant PST Corp	Topsfield	MA	F	978 887-5754	12438
Sunu Inc	Cambridge	MA	F	617 980-9807	7723
Syntonic Microwave LLC	Andover	MA	G	408 866-5900	5929
Talamas Company Inc	Waltham	MA	F	617 928-3437	12788
Technical Communications Corp (PA)	Concord	MA	E	978 287-5100	8135
Todd Clark and Associates Inc	Danvers	MA	E	978 774-7100	8225
Trackcam LLC	Rehoboth	MA	G	508 556-1955	11614
Unisite LLC	Boston	MA	E	781 926-7135	7091
Viasat Inc	Marlborough	MA	E	508 229-6500	10230
Victor Microwave Inc	Wakefield	MA	E	781 245-4472	12541
Zeevee Inc (PA)	Littleton	MA	E	978 467-1395	9847
Howell Laboratories Inc (PA)	Bridgton	ME	E	207 647-3327	4629
Maine Radio	Scarborough	ME	F	207 883-2929	5438
Mwave Industries LLC	Windham	ME	E	207 892-0011	5666
Nautel Maine Inc	Bangor	ME	C	207 947-8200	4511
P-Cube Inc	South Portland	ME	F	207 318-3349	5511
Pearpoint Inc	Raymond	ME	C	760 343-7350	5314
SPX Corporation	Raymond	ME	C	207 655-8100	5317
Aerosat Avionics LLC	Amherst	NH	D	603 943-8680	13860
Airlinx Communications Inc	New Ipswich	NH	F	603 878-1926	15196
Audio Accessories Inc	Marlow	NH	E	603 446-3335	14966
Cellular Specialties Inc	Manchester	NH	D	603 626-6677	14826
Cobham Exeter Inc	Exeter	NH	E	714 841-4976	14288
Communction Cmpnent Flters Inc (PA)	Seabrook	NH	G	603 294-4685	15588
Data Radio Management Co Inc	Merrimack	NH	G	603 598-1222	14979
Edge Velocity Corporation	Salem	NH	G	603 912-5618	15519
Haigh-Farr Inc	Bedford	NH	D	603 644-6170	13932
Hro Inc	Salem	NH	G	603 898-3750	15537
Laird Technologies Inc	Manchester	NH	E	603 627-7877	14875
Nhrc LLC	Pembroke	NH	F	603 485-2248	15305
Raytheon Company	Merrimack	NH	G	978 313-0201	15000
Research In Motion Rf Inc (HQ)	Nashua	NH	E	603 598-8880	15158
Applied Radar Inc	North Kingstown	RI	E	401 295-0062	16231
Blackhawk Machine Products Inc	Smithfield	RI	E	401 232-7563	16689
Kvh Industries Inc	Middletown	RI	C	401 847-3327	16176
Kvh Industries Inc (PA)	Middletown	RI	C	401 847-3327	16177
L3 Technologies Inc	Ashaway	RI	E	401 377-2300	15744
Porta Phone Co Inc	Narragansett	RI	E	401 789-8700	16194
Cco Holdings LLC	Montpelier	VT	C	802 778-0497	17371
Lcs Controls Inc	Rochester	VT	E	802 767-3128	17486
Secure Pnt Inc	Shelburne	VT	G	201 401-4207	17560

3669 Communications equipment, nec

	CITY	ST	EMP	PHONE	ENTRY#
Allstate Fire Systems LLC	Middletown	CT	E	860 246-7711	1734
Applied Physical Sciences Corp (HQ)	Groton	CT	D	860 448-3253	1364
Carrier Fire SEC Americas Corp	Farmington	CT	E	941 739-4200	1211
Essential Trading Systems Corp	Colchester	CT	F	860 295-8100	657

	CITY	ST	EMP	PHONE	ENTRY#
Fire-Lite Alarms Inc	Northford	CT	B	203 484-7161	2452
Magik Eye Inc	Stamford	CT	G	917 676-7436	3407
Nutmeg Utility Products Inc (PA)	Cheshire	CT	E	203 250-8802	609
Onsite Services Inc	Clinton	CT	F	860 669-3988	648
Preusser Research Group Inc (PA)	Trumbull	CT	F	203 459-8700	3729
Protection Industries Corp (PA)	Stratford	CT	E	203 375-9393	3569
Rtx Corporation	Farmington	CT	B	954 485-6501	1244
Trans-Tek Inc	Ellington	CT	E	860 872-8351	1118
Visionpoint LLC	Newington	CT	E	860 436-9673	2333
Xtralis Inc	Northford	CT	E	800 229-4434	2457
Accelenet By Itc A Div Viasat	Quincy	MA	G	617 773-3369	11500
Alarmsafe Inc	Chelmsford	MA	E	978 658-6717	7903
Altiostar Networks Inc (PA)	Lexington	MA	D	855 709-0701	9724
Convergent Networks Inc	Boston	MA	F	978 262-0231	6667
Coredge Networks Inc	Boston	MA	F	617 267-5205	6671
Courtsmart Digital Systems Inc	North Chelmsford	MA	E	978 251-3300	10973
Fall Prevention Alarms Inc	Southbridge	MA	G	508 765-5050	12016
General Dynmics Mssion Systems	Needham Heights	MA	D	954 846-3000	10549
General Dynmics Mssion Systems	Pittsfield	MA	A	413 494-1110	11398
Housing Devices Inc	Medford	MA	F	781 395-5200	10289
I F Engineering Corp	Dudley	MA	E	860 935-0280	8319
Image Stream Medical Inc	Littleton	MA	D	978 486-8494	9818
Keltron Corporation (HQ)	Waltham	MA	F	781 894-8710	12707
Kidde-Fenwal Inc (HQ)	Ashland	MA	A	508 881-2000	5960
King Fisher Co Inc	Lowell	MA	E	978 596-0214	9890
Lifeline Systems Company (HQ)	Framingham	MA	A	855 600-6127	8787
Octoscope Inc	Littleton	MA	E	978 486-3130	9829
Philips Hlthcare Infrmtics Inc	Marlborough	MA	F	508 988-1000	10195
Protectowire Co Inc	Pembroke	MA	E	781 826-3878	11376
Segue Manufacturing Svcs LLC	North Billerica	MA	D	978 970-1200	10952
Shufro Security Company Inc	Newton	MA	G	617 244-3355	10784
Signal Communications Corp	Woburn	MA	E	781 933-0998	13666
Simplex Time Recorder LLC (DH)	Westminster	MA	C		13278
Space Age Electronics Inc (PA)	Sterling	MA	E		12171
Space Age Electronics Inc	Templeton	MA	E	978 652-5421	12382
Suns International LLC	Chelmsford	MA	B	978 349-2329	7960
Talamas Company Inc	Waltham	MA	F	617 928-3437	12788
Tidal Communications LLC	North Andover	MA	F	978 687-0900	10852
Visonic Inc (HQ)	Westford	MA	E	860 243-0833	13267
Vivox Inc	Framingham	MA	E	508 650-3571	8808
Coastal Traffic	York	ME	E	207 351-8673	5711
Frazier Signal Tech LLC (PA)	Veazie	ME	G	207 991-0543	5571
Sierra Peaks Corporation	Camden	ME	E	207 236-3301	4668
Wentworth Technology Inc	Saco	ME	G	207 571-9744	5381
Astronics Aerosat Corporation	Manchester	NH	D	603 879-0205	14814
Fireye Inc (DH)	Derry	NH	C	603 432-4100	14193
Nextmove Technologies LLC	Hollis	NH	G	603 654-1280	14455
Nestor Inc (PA)	Providence	RI	E	401 274-5345	16574
Nestor Traffic Systems Inc (PA)	Pawtucket	RI	E	401 714-7781	16391
Royal Group Inc (PA)	Rutland	VT	E	802 773-3313	17506
Worksafe Traffic Ctrl Inds Inc (PA)	Barre	VT	G	802 223-8948	17025

3671 Electron tubes

	CITY	ST	EMP	PHONE	ENTRY#
Connecticut Coining Inc	Bethel	CT	D	203 743-3861	103
Whelen Engineering Company Inc (PA)	Chester	CT	B	860 526-9504	634
Adaptas Solutions LLC (PA)	Palmer	MA	E	413 284-9975	11269
Fil-Tech Inc	Boston	MA	G	617 227-1133	6735
Motion Industries Inc	Danvers	MA	E	978 774-7100	8210
Photonis Scientific Inc (DH)	Sturbridge	MA	F	508 347-4000	12257
Todd Clark and Associates Inc	Danvers	MA	E	978 774-7100	8225
Osram Sylvania Inc	Exeter	NH	B	603 772-4331	14299
Narragansett Imaging Usa LLC	North Smithfield	RI	E	401 762-3800	16328

3672 Printed circuit boards

	CITY	ST	EMP	PHONE	ENTRY#
AB Electronics LLC	Brookfield	CT	E	203 740-2793	509
Accutron Inc (PA)	Windsor	CT	D	860 683-8300	4253
Altek Electronics Inc	Torrington	CT	C	860 482-7626	3669
American Backplane Inc	Morris	CT	E	860 567-2360	1932
Apct-Wallingford Inc	Wallingford	CT	E	203 269-3311	3773
Argo Transdata Corp	Clinton	CT	E	860 669-2233	636
Carlton Industries Corp	Hamden	CT	E	203 288-5605	1416
Cyclone Microsystems Inc	Hamden	CT	E	203 786-5536	1420
Eastern Co	Clinton	CT	C	860 669-2233	642
Electronic Spc Conn Inc	Hamden	CT	E	203 288-1707	1423
Limat Graphics Inc	Danbury	CT	E	203 798-9711	772
Microboard Processing Inc	Seymour	CT	C	203 881-4300	2965
Midstate Electronics Co	Wallingford	CT	F	203 265-9900	3832
Norfield Data Products Inc	Norwalk	CT	F	203 849-0292	2546
Northeast Circuit Tech LLC	Glastonbury	CT	G	860 633-1967	1291
Precise Circuit Company Inc	Shelton	CT	D	203 924-2512	3052
Silicon Integration Inc	Milford	CT	E	203 876-2844	1885
Tallinn Fulfillment Limited	Milford	CT	E	203 878-2155	1893
Te Connectivity Corporation	Stafford Springs	CT	E	860 684-8000	3260

	CITY	ST	EMP	PHONE	ENTRY#
Technical Manufacturing Corp	Durham	CT	E	860 349-1735	904
Tek Industries Inc	Vernon Rockville	CT	E	860 870-0001	3763
Ttm Printed Circuit Group Inc	Stafford Springs	CT	C	860 684-8000	3261
Ttm Technologies Inc	Stafford	CT	B	860 684-5881	3251
Ttm Technologies Inc	Stafford Springs	CT	D	860 684-8000	3262
Accusemble Electronics Inc (PA)	North Billerica	MA	G	508 254-4538	10893
Adcotron Ems Inc	Boston	MA	C	617 598-3000	6514
Azores Corp	Wilmington	MA	F	978 253-6200	13384
Bitflow Inc	Woburn	MA	F	781 932-2900	13526
Boardtech Solutions Inc	North Attleboro	MA	G	508 643-3684	10868
Case Assembly Solutions Inc	South Easton	MA	E	508 238-5665	11939
Chase Corporation	Oxford	MA	G	508 731-2710	11250
Chase Corporation (HQ)	Westwood	MA	G	781 332-0700	13309
Circuit Technology Center Inc	Haverhill	MA	E	978 374-5000	9086
Coghlin Companies Inc (PA)	Westborough	MA	C	508 753-2354	13089
Creation Technologies Inc (PA)	Boston	MA	E	877 734-7456	6675
Creation Technologies Intl Inc (PA)	Boston	MA	E	877 734-7456	6676
Dilla St Corp	Milford	MA	G	508 478-3419	10400
Distron Corporation	Attleboro Falls	MA	C	508 695-8786	6084
East West Boston LLC	Boston	MA	D	617 598-3000	6706
Epec LLC (PA)	New Bedford	MA	D	508 995-5171	10589
Essemtec Usa LLC	Waltham	MA	F	856 218-1131	12666
Ftg Circuits Haverhill Inc	Haverhill	MA	E	978 373-9190	9095
Integratech Solutions Corp	Hudson	MA	D	978 567-1000	9376
J & J Technologies Inc	Wareham	MA	D	508 291-3803	12839
Jabil Inc	Clinton	MA	E	978 365-9721	8079
Jnj Industries Inc	Franklin	MA	E	508 553-0529	8846
Kalt Incorporated (PA)	Lowell	MA	E	978 805-5001	9889
Liberty Engineering Inc	Newton	MA	E	617 965-6644	10768
Ltpc Holdings Inc	Waltham	MA	E	781 893-6672	12712
M C Test Service Inc	North Billerica	MA	C	781 218-7550	10929
Mc Assembly International LLC	North Billerica	MA	B	978 215-9501	10933
Measurement Computing Corp (DH)	Norton	MA	E	508 946-5100	11128
Mercury Systems Inc (PA)	Andover	MA	B	978 256-1300	5896
Mfg Electronics Inc	North Billerica	MA	G	978 671-5490	10936
Micro-Precision Tech Inc (PA)	Lawrence	MA	F	978 688-1299	9580
Micron Corporation	Norwood	MA	E	781 769-5771	11196
Milford Manufacturing Svcs LLC	Hopedale	MA	E	508 478-8544	9299
Mini-Systems Inc (PA)	North Attleboro	MA	D	508 695-1420	10878
Murata Power Solutions Inc (DH)	Westborough	MA	C	508 339-3000	13122
Nano Dimension USA Inc	Waltham	MA	E	650 209-2866	12729
Neo Tech	Westborough	MA	G	508 329-6270	13123
New Age Technologies Inc	Attleboro	MA	E	508 226-6090	6041
Oncore Manufacturing LLC	Westborough	MA	D	978 737-3640	13125
Parlex	Methuen	MA	F	978 946-2500	10343
Photo Tool Engineering Inc	Lowell	MA	F	978 805-5000	9913
Prodrive Technologies Inc	Canton	MA	G	617 475-1617	7822
Proxy Manufacturing Inc	Methuen	MA	E	978 687-3138	10344
Remtec Incorporated (PA)	Norwood	MA	E	781 762-9191	11207
RLB Industries Inc	Attleboro	MA	D	508 226-3350	6057
Specialized Coating Svcs LLC	North Billerica	MA	E	978 362-0346	10957
Sunburst Elctrnic Mfg Sltons I (PA)	West Bridgewater	MA	D	508 580-1881	12983
Tech-Etch Inc (PA)	Plymouth	MA	B	508 747-0300	11481
Technical Services Inc	Raynham	MA	F	781 389-8342	11599
Technology Design Mfg Svcs LLC	Springfield	MA	E	413 730-4444	12137
Techtrade Inc	Needham	MA	F	781 724-7878	10525
Whitman Products Company Inc	North Andover	MA	E	978 975-0502	10862
Worthington Assembly Inc	South Deerfield	MA	F	413 397-8265	11930
Alternative Manufacturing Inc	Winthrop	ME	D	207 377-9377	5690
David Saunders Inc	South Portland	ME	E	207 228-1888	5497
Elscott Manufacturing LLC (PA)	Gouldsboro	ME	E	207 422-6747	4839
Enercon	Auburn	ME	E	207 657-7001	4429
Enercon (HQ)	Gray	ME	E	207 657-7000	4841
Marja Corporation	Sanford	ME	F	207 324-2994	5400
A Ttm Technologies Company	Salem	NH	G	603 870-4580	15501
Aci - Pcb Inc	Laconia	NH	G	603 528-7711	14642
Agility Mfg Inc	Dover	NH	E	603 742-7339	14215
Amphenol Corporation	Nashua	NH	B	603 879-3000	15060
Amphenol Printed Circuits Inc (HQ)	Nashua	NH	D	603 324-4500	15062
Anaren Ceramics Inc	Salem	NH	D	603 898-2883	15505
Azego Technology Svcs US Inc	Portsmouth	NH	E	603 610-0030	15363
Benchmark Electronics Inc	Nashua	NH	B	603 879-7000	15070
Circuit Connect Inc	Nashua	NH	E	603 880-7447	15080
Circuit Technology LLC	Merrimack	NH	D	603 424-2200	14977
Cirtronics Corporation	Milford	NH	C	603 249-9190	15016
Colonial Electronic Mfrs Inc	Nashua	NH	E	603 881-8244	15083
Core Assemblies Inc	Gilford	NH	F	603 293-0270	14334
Data Electronic Devices Inc	Salem	NH	C	603 893-2047	15517
Electronics Aid Inc	Marlborough	NH	G	603 876-4161	14964
Equipment Technologies Inc	Windham	NH	F	603 548-0875	15725
Gorilla Circuits Inc	Nashua	NH	F	603 864-0283	15106
Greensource Fabrication LLC (PA)	Charlestown	NH	D	603 283-9880	14064
Hadco Corporation (HQ)	Salem	NH	B	603 421-3400	15535

	CITY	ST	EMP	PHONE	ENTRY#
Insulectro	Londonderry	NH	E	603 629-4403	14757
Intelligent Mfg Solutons LLC	Manchester	NH	E	603 296-1160	14864
Intervala LLC	Hudson	NH	D	603 595-1987	14512
Manufacturing Services Group	Manchester	NH	F	603 883-1022	14878
Mass Design Inc (PA)	Nashua	NH	D	603 886-6460	15130
Megatronics US Ultimate Hldco LL (PA)	Salem	NH	E	888 706-0230	15544
Mercury Systems Inc	Hudson	NH	A	603 883-2900	14527
Merrimack Micro LLC	Merrimack	NH	G	603 809-4183	14992
Miraco Inc	Manchester	NH	E	603 665-9449	14890
Ncab Group Usa Inc (DH)	Hampstead	NH	E	603 329-4551	14388
Pica Mfg Solutions Inc (PA)	Derry	NH	E	603 845-3258	14204
Precision Placement Mchs Inc (PA)	Fremont	NH	F	603 895-5112	14330
Princeton Technology Corp	Hudson	NH	D	603 595-1987	14536
Retcomp Inc	New Boston	NH	F	603 487-5010	15194
Sanmina Corporation	Manchester	NH	C	603 621-1800	14924
Seica	Salem	NH	F	978 376-7254	15560
Singulrity Elctrnic Systems In	Portsmouth	NH	G	603 430-6000	15437
Sonic Manufacturing Co Inc	Hudson	NH	E	603 882-1020	14546
Sparton Beckwood LLC	Plaistow	NH	D	603 382-3840	15351
Stellar Manufacturing Inc	Salem	NH	E	978 241-9537	15564
Two In One Manufacturing Inc	Nashua	NH	E	603 595-8212	15179
Varitron Technologies USA Inc	Hudson	NH	E	603 577-8855	14557
Willis & Pham LLC	Salem	NH	G	603 893-6029	15572
Aldotech Corporation	Warwick	RI	E	401 467-6100	16777
Vr Industries Inc	Warwick	RI	E	401 732-6800	16875
Image Tek Mfg Inc	Springfield	VT	E	802 885-6208	17618
Purchasing Inventory Cons Inc	Windsor	VT	F	802 674-2620	17761
Vemas Corporation	Poultney	VT	E	802 287-4100	17454
Vermont Circuits Inc	Brattleboro	VT	D	802 257-4571	17102

3674 Semiconductors and related devices

	CITY	ST	EMP	PHONE	ENTRY#
AG Semiconductor Services LLC	Stamford	CT	E	203 322-5300	3274
Carten-Fujikin Incorporated	Cheshire	CT	F	203 699-2134	578
Clear Edge Power International Service LLC 860 727-2200	South Windsor	CT	C		3128
Code Red Electronics LLC	North Branford	CT	G		2363
Coherent Inc	East Granby	CT	E	860 408-5066	928
Comet Technologies USA Inc (DH)	Shelton	CT	E	203 447-3200	2993
Compugraphics USA Inc (HQ)	Waterbury	CT	D	510 249-2600	3900
Delcom Products Inc	Danbury	CT	G	914 934-5170	729
Edal Industries Inc	East Haven	CT	E	203 467-2591	1041
Emosyn America Inc	Danbury	CT	E	203 794-1100	735
Entegris Prof Solutions Inc (HQ)	Danbury	CT	C	203 794-1100	738
Fuelcell Energy Inc (PA)	Danbury	CT	C	203 825-6000	748
Fuelcell Energy Inc	Torrington	CT	E	860 496-1111	3682
Gordon Products Incorporated	Brookfield	CT	E	203 775-4501	523
Hi-Rel Group LLC	Essex	CT	G	860 767-9031	1166
Hi-Rel Products LLC	Essex	CT	E	860 767-9031	1167
Hipotronics Inc (HQ)	Shelton	CT	E	845 279-3644	3013
Hoffman Engineering LLC (DH)	Stamford	CT	D	203 425-8900	3378
Hyaxiom Inc (HQ)	East Hartford	CT	E	860 727-2200	998
LLC Dow Gage	Berlin	CT	G	860 828-5327	75
Luvata Waterbury Inc (HQ)	Waterbury	CT	D	203 753-5215	3931
Marco International Inc	Ridgefield	CT	D	203 894-8000	2902
Merrick Services	North Grosvenordale	CT	F	508 802-3751	2386
Microphase Corporation	Shelton	CT	E	203 866-8000	3032
Newco Condenser Inc	Shelton	CT	F	475 882-4000	3039
Photronics Inc (PA)	Brookfield	CT	B	203 775-9000	533
Photronics Texas Inc	Brookfield	CT	E	203 546-3039	534
Photronics Texas I LLC	Brookfield	CT	G	203 775-9000	535
Radeco Inc	Plainfield	CT	G	860 823-1220	2738
Revolution Lighting Tech Inc (PA)	Stamford	CT	E	877 578-2536	3447
Servers Storage Networking LLC	Norwalk	CT	G	203 433-0808	2570
Specialty Coating Systems Inc	Milford	CT	E	203 283-0087	1887
Strain Measurement Devices Inc	Wallingford	CT	E	203 294-5800	3855
Transwitch Corporation	Shelton	CT	C	203 929-8810	3071
Vishay Americas Inc (HQ)	Shelton	CT	B	203 452-5648	3076
ABB Enterprise Software Inc	Boston	MA	E	617 574-1130	6502
Acacia Communications Inc (HQ)	Maynard	MA	C	978 938-4896	10259
Accuprobe Corporation	Salem	MA	F	978 745-7878	11699
Ace Residential Solar LLC	North Andover	MA	E	800 223-1462	10816
Aceinna Inc	Tewksbury	MA	E	978 965-3200	12383
Advanced Micro Devices Inc	Boxborough	MA	D	978 795-2500	7146
Advanced Microsensors Corp	Shrewsbury	MA	D	508 770-6600	11825
Aetruim Incorporated	Billerica	MA	E	651 773-4200	6397
Allegro Microsystems LLC	Marlborough	MA	C	508 853-5000	10106
American Superconductor Corp (PA)	Ayer	MA	D	978 842-3000	6171
American Superconductor Corp	Westminster	MA	E	978 842-3000	13269
Ametek Inc	New Bedford	MA	D	508 998-4335	10568
Amkor Technology Inc	Stoneham	MA	G	781 438-7800	12174
Analog Devices Inc (PA)	Wilmington	MA	A	781 935-5565	13379
Analog Devices Federal LLC (HQ)	Chelmsford	MA	B	978 250-3373	7906

S I C

	CITY	ST	EMP	PHONE	ENTRY#		CITY	ST	EMP	PHONE	ENTRY#
Analog Devices Intl Inc (HQ)	Wilmington	MA	E	800 262-5643	13380	Micro-Precision Tech Inc (PA)	Lawrence	MA	F	978 688-1299	9580
Anokiwave Inc	Billerica	MA	D	781 820-1049	6400	Microsemi Corp- Massachusetts	Lawrence	MA	B	978 620-2600	9581
Apple Mill Holding Company Inc	Pembroke	MA	F	781 826-9706	11358	Microsemi Corp- Massachusetts	Lowell	MA	C	978 442-5600	9906
Applehill Systems Inc	Lynnfield	MA	G	781 334-7009	9994	Microsemi Corp-Colorado	Lawrence	MA	D	480 941-6300	9582
Applied Materials Inc	Gloucester	MA	F	978 282-2000	8919	Microsemi Corporation	Beverly	MA	G	978 232-0040	6365
Ardeo Systems Inc	Haverhill	MA	G	978 373-4680	9074	Microsemi Corporation	Lawrence	MA	D	781 665-1071	9583
Arm Inc	Waltham	MA	B	978 264-7300	12596	Microsemi Corporation	Lowell	MA	E	978 442-5637	9907
Arradiance LLC	Littleton	MA	F	508 202-0593	9803	Microsemi Corporation	Tewksbury	MA	F	978 232-3793	12410
Ase (us)inc	Woburn	MA	F	781 305-5900	13516	Microsemi Nes Inc	Lawrence	MA	E	978 794-1666	9584
Asmpt Nexx Inc	Billerica	MA	E	978 436-4600	6406	Microtronic Inc	Edgartown	MA	E	508 627-8951	8467
Astex Plasmaquest Inc	Wilmington	MA	G	781 937-6272	13382	Mini-Systems Inc (PA)	North Attleboro	MA	D	508 695-1420	10878
Athinia Technologies LLC	Cambridge	MA	F	781 491-4189	7494	Mini-Systems Inc	Plainville	MA	E	508 695-2000	11439
Atlas Devices LLC	Chelmsford	MA	F	617 415-1657	7913	Murata Power Solutions Inc (DH)	Westborough	MA	C	508 339-3000	13122
Atomera Incorporated	Wellesley Hills	MA	G	617 219-0600	12950	Nantero Inc	Woburn	MA	E	781 932-5338	13618
Aware Inc (PA)	Bedford	MA	E	781 276-4000	6213	Nissin Ion Equipment Usa Inc	North Billerica	MA	F	978 362-2590	10940
Axcel Photonics Inc	Marlborough	MA	E	508 481-9200	10115	North East Silicon Tech Inc	New Bedford	MA	D	508 999-2001	10634
Bae Systems Info Elctrnic Syst	Lexington	MA	C	603 885-4321	9726	Optomistic Products Inc	Leominster	MA	F	207 865-9181	9691
Black Earth Technologies Inc	Dighton	MA	G	508 397-1335	8292	Orbotech Inc (DH)	Billerica	MA	D	978 667-6037	6466
Borgwarner Massachusetts Inc (HQ)	Northborough	MA	E	508 281-5500	11092	Ox3 Corporation	Devens	MA	F	978 772-1222	8284
Broadcom Corporation	Andover	MA	C	978 719-1300	5874	Panametrics LLC (DH)	Billerica	MA	A	978 437-1000	6468
Brooks Automation Us LLC (DH)	Chelmsford	MA	D	978 262-2400	7917	Performance Motion Devices Inc	Boxborough	MA	E	978 266-1210	7153
Bruce Technologies Inc	North Billerica	MA	F	978 670-5501	10901	Philips Advanced Metrology Sys	Billerica	MA	F	508 647-8400	6470
Business and Prof Exch Inc	Beverly	MA	E	978 556-4100	6336	Philips Holding USA Inc (HQ)	Cambridge	MA	A	978 687-1501	7686
Ceramic Process Systems	Taunton	MA	G	508 222-0614	12327	Piconics Inc	Tyngsboro	MA	F	978 649-7501	12463
Cicor Americas Inc	Cambridge	MA	F	617 576-2005	7540	Precision Sensing Devices Inc	Medfield	MA	G	508 359-2833	10274
CMC Materials Inc (HQ)	Billerica	MA	D	978 436-6500	6424	Qbit Semiconductor Ltd	Littleton	MA	G	351 205-0005	9834
Comdel Inc	Gloucester	MA	F	978 282-0620	8930	Qorvo Inc	Chelmsford	MA	E	978 770-2158	7947
Control Resources Inc	Littleton	MA	F	978 486-4160	9806	Qorvo Us Inc	Chelmsford	MA	E	978 467-4290	7948
CPS Technologies Corp	Norton	MA	C	508 222-0614	11124	Qualcomm Technologies Inc	Boston	MA	E	617 447-9846	6988
Crystal Gt Systems LLC	Salem	MA	F	978 745-0088	11708	Qualcomm Technologies Inc	Burlington	MA	F	781 791-6000	7418
Cubicpv Inc (PA)	Bedford	MA	F	800 570-1120	6218	R F Integration Inc (PA)	North Billerica	MA	G	978 654-6770	10945
Design Centers Com	Worcester	MA	F	800 570-1120	13716	Radio Act Corporation	Brookline	MA	G	617 731-6542	7326
Digital Lumens Incorporated	Boston	MA	C		6696	Raytheon Sutheast Asia Systems (DH)	Waltham	MA	E	978 470-5000	12762
Distron Corporation	Attleboro Falls	MA	C	508 695-8786	6084	Reinforced Structures For Elec	Worcester	MA	F	508 754-5316	13783
Dolan-Jenner Industries Inc	Boxborough	MA	E	978 263-1400	7151	Remote Sensing Solutions Inc	Buzzards Bay	MA	F	508 362-9400	7456
Dover Microsystems Inc	Waltham	MA	G	781 577-0300	12655	Renesas Electronics Amer Inc	Westford	MA	E	978 577-6340	13259
Drs Development LLC	Rochester	MA	G	774 271-0533	11631	Rochester Electronics LLC	Newburyport	MA	F	978 462-1248	10714
Druck LLC (HQ)	Billerica	MA	C	978 437-1000	6432	Rochester Electronics LLC (PA)	Newburyport	MA	C	978 462-9332	10715
Eastwind Communications Inc	Hyannis	MA	F	508 862-8600	9435	Sand 9 Inc	Cambridge	MA	G	617 358-0957	7702
Electronic Products Inds Inc	Newburyport	MA	E	978 462-8101	10681	Semigear Inc	Wakefield	MA	E	781 213-3066	12534
Elpakco Inc (PA)	Westford	MA	F	978 392-0400	13235	Seminex Corporation	Danvers	MA	F	978 326-7700	8219
Entegris Inc (PA)	Billerica	MA	A	978 436-6500	6443	Sensera Inc	Woburn	MA	F	978 606-2600	13663
Epi II Inc	Newburyport	MA	D	978 462-1514	10682	Sheaumann Laser Inc	Billerica	MA	E	508 970-0600	6481
Eta Devices Inc	Cambridge	MA	F	617 577-8300	7566	Sick Inc	Stoughton	MA	D	781 302-2500	12235
Excelitas Technologies Corp (DH)	Waltham	MA	B	855 382-2677	12673	Sige Semiconductor Inc (HQ)	Andover	MA	E	978 327-6920	5920
Flir Systems-Boston Inc (DH)	North Billerica	MA	B	978 901-8000	10911	Signet Products Corporation	North Attleboro	MA	G	650 592-3575	10887
Forward Photonics LLC	Woburn	MA	F	978 224-5488	13569	Silex Microsystems Inc	Boston	MA	F	617 834-7197	7038
Gigantum Inc	Foxboro	MA	G	301 960-8012	8697	Silicon Transistor Corporation	Chelmsford	MA	F	978 256-3321	7957
Global Silicon Tech Inc	New Bedford	MA	F	508 999-2001	10596	Sionyx LLC (PA)	Beverly	MA	F	978 922-0684	6384
Googleplex Technologies LLC	Hudson	MA	G	978 897-0880	9370	Skyworks Solutions Inc	Andover	MA	F	978 327-6850	5921
Gridedge Networks Inc	Acton	MA	F	978 569-2000	5749	Skyworks Solutions Inc	Woburn	MA	D	781 935-5150	13669
HCC Aegis Inc (DH)	New Bedford	MA	C	508 998-3141	10599	Soitec Usa Inc (HQ)	Gloucester	MA	G	978 531-2222	8958
Hittite Microwave LLC (HQ)	Chelmsford	MA	D	978 250-3343	7933	Solar Five LLC	Lexington	MA	F	781 301-7233	9776
Huber + Shner Platis Photonics	Bedford	MA	F	781 275-5080	6230	Solect Energy Development LLC (PA)	Hopkinton	MA	G	508 598-3511	9344
Ii-VI Photonics (us) Inc (HQ)	Woburn	MA	D	781 938-1222	13583	Spectris Inc (HQ)	Westborough	MA	E	508 768-6400	13137
Immedia Semiconductor Inc	North Reading	MA	F	978 296-4950	11041	Spectrum Microwave Inc	Marlborough	MA	D	508 485-0336	10212
Infineon Tech Americas Corp	Andover	MA	F	978 851-1298	5888	Spire Corporation (PA)	Billerica	MA	D	978 584-3958	6484
Innovion Corporation	Wilmington	MA	F	978 267-4064	13415	Spire Solar LLC	Newton	MA	E	617 332-4040	10787
Integris Inc	Billerica	MA	G	978 294-2633	6454	Springboard Technology Corporation	Springfield	MA	D		12133
Interface Engineering Corp	Randolph	MA	F	781 986-2600	11566	Sst Components Inc (PA)	Lawrence	MA	D	978 670-7300	9601
Ipg Photonics Corporation (PA)	Marlborough	MA	B	508 373-1100	10169	Starlink North America Inc	Woburn	MA	G	877 823-1566	13672
Iqe Kc LLC	Taunton	MA	D	508 824-6696	12343	Stellar Industries Corp	Millbury	MA	E	508 865-1668	10443
Isilon Systems LLC	Hopkinton	MA	E	206 315-7500	9332	Stmicroelectronics Inc	Burlington	MA	G	781 861-2650	7435
Iwaki Pumps Inc (DH)	Holliston	MA	E	508 429-1440	9217	Tego Inc	Waltham	MA	F	781 547-5680	12791
Ixys Intgrted Circuits Div LLC (DH)	Beverly	MA	D	978 524-6700	6357	Tel Mnfacturing Engrg Amer Inc	Billerica	MA	E	978 436-2300	6487
Kcb Solutions LLC	Shirley	MA	F	978 425-0400	11819	Teradyne Inc	Boston	MA	G	978 370-2700	7074
Kopin Corporation	Taunton	MA	E	508 824-6696	12347	Teradyne Inc (PA)	North Reading	MA	A	978 370-2700	11048
Kopin Corporation (PA)	Westborough	MA	E	508 870-5959	13114	Texas Instruments Incorporated	Attleboro	MA	E	508 236-3800	6070
L T X International Inc	Norwood	MA	D	781 461-1000	11189	That Corporation (PA)	Milford	MA	E	508 478-9200	10420
Lightmatter Inc	Boston	MA	D	857 244-0460	6859	Tier 7 Communications	Shirley	MA	G	978 425-9543	11823
Linear Singapore Holding LLC	Norwood	MA	F	781 329-4700	11190	Transene Company Inc (PA)	Danvers	MA	E	978 777-7860	8227
Linear Technology LLC	North Chelmsford	MA	G	978 656-4750	10981	Trebia Networks Inc	Acton	MA	E	978 264-3700	5766
Macom Metelics LLC	Lowell	MA	C	978 656-2500	9897	Ulvac Technologies Inc (HQ)	Methuen	MA	E	978 686-7550	10347
Macom Tech Sltons Holdings Inc (PA)	Lowell	MA	C	978 656-2500	9898	Union Miniere	Boston	MA	E	617 960-5900	7090
Macom Technology Solutions Inc (HQ)	Lowell	MA	B	978 656-2500	9900	University Wafer Inc	Boston	MA	E	617 331-7747	7095
Magellan Distribution Corp	Boston	MA	F	617 399-7900	6868	Upstart Power Inc	Southborough	MA	E	614 877-8278	12003
Massachusetts Bay Tech Inc	Stoughton	MA	F	781 344-8809	12222	Vacuum Plus Manufacturing Inc	Chelmsford	MA	F	978 441-3100	7968
Maxim Integrated Products Inc	North Chelmsford	MA	F	978 934-7600	10983	Varian Semicdtr Eqp Assoc Inc	Andover	MA	G	978 282-2807	5932
MB Westfield Inc	Westfield	MA	F	413 568-8676	13182	Varian Semicdtr Eqp Assoc Inc (HQ)	Gloucester	MA	C	978 282-2000	8963
Mediatek USA Inc	Woburn	MA	C	781 503-8000	13609	Vsea Inc	Gloucester	MA	E	978 282-2000	8964
Metalenz Inc	Weston	MA	E	844 770-1300	13287	Xosoft Inc	Framingham	MA	E	800 225-5224	8812
Metelics Corp	Lowell	MA	E	408 737-8197	9905	Xp Power LLC	Gloucester	MA	D	978 282-0620	8965
Micro Magnetics Inc	Fall River	MA	F	508 672-4489	8581	Yankee Electrical Mfg Co	Wilbraham	MA	G	413 596-8256	13364

	CITY	ST	EMP	PHONE	ENTRY#
Asml Us LLC	Westbrook	ME	G	207 541-5000	5615
Delkin Inc	Cumberland Center	ME	G	207 370-0703	4708
Fairchild Energy LLC	South Portland	ME	E	207 775-8100	5499
Fairchild Semiconductor Corp	South Portland	ME	C	801 562-7000	5500
Fairchild Semiconductor Corp	South Portland	ME	C	207 775-8100	5501
Fairchild Semiconductor Corp (DH)	South Portland	ME	B	207 775-8100	5502
Nanoscale Components Inc	Portland	ME	F	207 671-7028	5248
Vulcan Flex Circuit Corp	Porter	ME	D	603 883-1500	5172
Allegro Microsystems Inc (HQ)	Manchester	NH	B	603 626-2300	14811
Allegro Microsystems LLC (HQ)	Manchester	NH	B	603 626-2300	14812
Analog Devices Inc	Nashua	NH	G	603 883-2430	15063
Bantry Components Inc	Manchester	NH	E	603 668-3210	14817
Bluglass Inc	Nashua	NH	F	617 869-5150	15072
Corfin Industries Inc	Manchester	NH	D	603 893-9900	14837
Cxe Equipment Services LLC	Seabrook	NH	G	603 437-2477	15589
Cyclones Arena	Hudson	NH	F	603 880-4424	14492
Dutile Glines & Higgins Inc	Manchester	NH	F	603 622-0452	14846
Eigenlight Corporation	Newmarket	NH	E	603 692-9800	15219
Gosolar NH LLC	Barrington	NH	G	603 948-1189	13914
Gpd Optoelectronics Corp	Salem	NH	E	603 894-6865	15533
Gt Advanced Technologies Inc (DH)	Hudson	NH	D	603 883-5200	14503
Gt Advanced Technologies Ltd	Hudson	NH	G	603 883-5200	14504
Gt Equipment Holdings Inc	Merrimack	NH	F	603 883-5200	14983
Gtat Corporation (DH)	Hudson	NH	D	603 883-5200	14505
Ibmnh Inc (PA)	Manchester	NH	G	603 644-2326	14861
Jenesco Inc	Lyndeborough	NH	F	603 673-4830	14800
Laird Connectivity LLC	Manchester	NH	C	603 627-7877	14874
Macom Tech Sltons Holdings Inc	Londonderry	NH	D	603 641-3800	14765
Masimo Semiconductor Inc	Hudson	NH	E	603 595-8900	14525
Melexis Inc	Nashua	NH	E	603 223-2362	15133
Micro-Metrics Inc	Londonderry	NH	D	603 641-3800	14772
Micro-Precision Tech Inc	Salem	NH	E	603 893-7600	15545
Microfab Inc	Manchester	NH	F	603 621-9522	14885
Microsembly LLC	Merrimack	NH	E	603 718-8445	14993
Microsemi Corporation	Manchester	NH	F	978 232-3793	14886
Micross Components LLC	Manchester	NH	C	603 893-9900	14887
NORTH PENN TECHNOLOGY INC	Manchester	NH	E	603 893-9900	14903
Paragon Electronic Systems	Manchester	NH	F	603 645-7630	14910
Premier Semiconductor Svcs LLC (DH)	Manchester	NH	D	267 954-0130	14914
Qmagiq LLC	Nashua	NH	F	603 821-3092	15153
Saint-Gobain Glass Corporation	Milford	NH	E	603 673-7560	15037
Semi-General Inc	Londonderry	NH	D	603 641-3800	14783
Semikron Inc (HQ)	Hudson	NH	E	603 883-8102	14545
Sparton Beckwood LLC	Plaistow	NH	D	603 382-3840	15351
Stockeryale Inc	Salem	NH	G	603 893-8778	15565
Texas Instruments Incorporated	Manchester	NH	G	603 222-8500	14942
Two In One Manufacturing Inc	Nashua	NH	E	603 595-8212	15179
Ultrasource Inc	Hollis	NH	D	603 881-7799	14459
Unitrode Corporation (HQ)	Manchester	NH	B	603 222-8500	14948
Vishay Dale Electronics LLC	Hollis	NH	D	603 881-7799	14461
Xilinx Inc	Nashua	NH	F	603 891-1096	15191
Ampleon USA Inc	Smithfield	RI	E	401 830-5420	16687
ATW Companies Inc (PA)	Warwick	RI	D	401 244-1002	16785
Cherry Semiconductor Corp	East Greenwich	RI	F	401 885-3600	15977
Enow Inc	Warwick	RI	F	401 732-7080	16814
Infineon Tech Americas Corp	Warwick	RI	G	401 773-7501	16822
Integrated Device Technology	Smithfield	RI	G	401 719-1686	16716
Interplex Industries Inc (DH)	Rumford	RI	F	401 434-6543	16672
Narragansett Imaging Usa LLC	North Smithfield	RI	E	401 762-3800	16328
Numark International Inc	Cumberland	RI	F	954 761-7550	15956
Reed Semiconductor Corp (PA)	Warwick	RI	F	401 886-0857	16847
Veterans Assembled Elec LLC (PA)	North Kingstown	RI	G	401 228-6165	16291
Vishay Efi Inc	Warwick	RI	E	401 738-9150	16873
Wei Inc (PA)	Cranston	RI	E	401 781-3904	15928
4382412 Canada Inc	Randolph	VT	F	802 225-5911	17465
Allearth Renewables Inc	Williston	VT	F	802 872-9600	17721
Globalfoundries US 2 LLC	Essex Junction	VT	A	408 462-4452	17234
Leddynamics Inc	Randolph	VT	D	802 728-4533	17470
Marvell Gvrnment Solutions LLC	Burlington	VT	E	845 245-8066	17143
Nehp Inc	Williston	VT	D	802 652-1444	17741

3675 Electronic capacitors

	CITY	ST	EMP	PHONE	ENTRY#
Code Red Electronics LLC	North Branford	CT	G		2363
Hipotronics Inc (HQ)	Shelton	CT	C	845 279-3644	3013
Newco Condenser Inc	Shelton	CT	F	475 882-4000	3039
Aerovox Incorporated	New Bedford	MA	A	508 994-9661	10565
Cornell-Dubilier Elec Inc	New Bedford	MA	A	508 996-8561	10580
Magellan Distribution Corp	Boston	MA	F	617 399-7900	6868
Rf Aero LLC	New Bedford	MA	E	508 910-3500	10646
Steinerfilm Inc	Williamstown	MA	C	413 458-9525	13368
Tdl Inc	Canton	MA	E	781 828-3366	7833
Kyocera AVX Cmpnnts Bddford Co	Biddeford	ME	C	207 282-5111	4574

	CITY	ST	EMP	PHONE	ENTRY#
Standex International Corp (PA)	Salem	NH	E	603 893-9701	15563
Evans Capacitor Company LLC	East Providence	RI	E	401 435-3555	16017
Vishay Efi Inc	Warwick	RI	E	401 738-9150	16873

3676 Electronic resistors

	CITY	ST	EMP	PHONE	ENTRY#
Able Coil and Electronics Co	Bolton	CT	E	860 646-5686	218
Code Red Electronics LLC	North Branford	CT	G		2363
Prime Technology LLC	North Branford	CT	E	203 481-5721	2373
Vishay Americas Inc (HQ)	Shelton	CT	B	203 452-5648	3076
Magellan Distribution Corp	Boston	MA	F	617 399-7900	6868
Mini-Systems Inc	Attleboro	MA	E	508 695-0203	6037
Mini-Systems Inc (PA)	North Attleboro	MA	D	508 695-1420	10878
Mini-Systems Inc	Plainville	MA	E	508 695-2000	11439
Phoenix Electric Corp	Canton	MA	E	781 821-0200	7819
Sensata Technologies Ind Inc (DH)	Attleboro	MA	E	508 236-3800	6063
Wabash Technologies Inc (DH)	Attleboro	MA	D	260 355-4100	6075
Bantry Components Inc	Manchester	NH	E	603 668-3210	14817
Two In One Manufacturing Inc	Nashua	NH	E	603 595-8212	15179
Cx Thin Films LLC	Cranston	RI	F	401 461-5500	15846
Vishay Efi Inc	Warwick	RI	E	401 738-9150	16873

3677 Electronic coils and transformers

	CITY	ST	EMP	PHONE	ENTRY#
3M Purification Inc	Stafford Springs	CT	B	860 684-8628	3252
Able Coil and Electronics Co	Bolton	CT	E	860 646-5686	218
Bicron Electronics LLC (HQ)	Torrington	CT	D	860 482-2524	3672
Cable Technology Inc	Willington	CT	E	860 429-7889	4224
Classic Coil Company Inc	Bristol	CT	D	860 583-7600	427
Coils Plus Inc	Wolcott	CT	E	203 879-0755	4362
Future Manufacturing Inc	Bristol	CT	F	860 584-0685	450
Henkel Loctite Corporation (DH)	Rocky Hill	CT	D	860 571-5100	2925
Hipotronics Inc (HQ)	Shelton	CT	C	845 279-3644	3013
Microphase Corporation	Shelton	CT	E	203 866-8000	3032
Microtech Inc	Cheshire	CT	D	203 272-3234	607
Neeltran Inc	New Milford	CT	C	860 350-5964	2254
Qtran Inc (PA)	Milford	CT	E	203 367-8777	1873
Quality Coils Incorporated (PA)	Bristol	CT	C	860 584-0927	485
Tortran Inc	Shelton	CT	F	203 538-5062	3070
Ainslie Corporation	Walpole	MA	G	781 848-0850	12548
American Sub Assmbly Prdcers I	Dudley	MA	E	508 949-2320	8315
Atrex Energy Inc (PA)	Walpole	MA	E	781 461-8251	12551
ATW Electronics Inc	Charlestown	MA	F	617 304-3579	7861
Degreasing Devices Co	Southbridge	MA	G	508 765-0045	12013
Excelitas Technologies Corp	Salem	MA	C	800 775-6786	11714
Magellan Distribution Corp	Boston	MA	F	617 399-7900	6868
MCI Transformer Corporation	Orange	MA	F	978 544-8272	11226
Microwave Engineering Corp	North Andover	MA	D	978 685-2776	10844
Modular Air Filtration Systems	Raynham	MA	E	508 823-4900	11594
Precision Electronics Corp	Marshfield	MA	F	781 834-6677	10244
Schneider Electric It Corp (DH)	Foxboro	MA	A	508 543-8750	8723
Transcon Technologies Inc	Westfield	MA	E	413 562-7684	13212
Porvair Filtration Group Inc	Caribou	ME	F	207 493-3027	4679
Design Consultants Associates	Hampstead	NH	F	603 329-4541	14382
Gowanda Rcd LLC	Manchester	NH	C	716 532-2234	14853
Jmk Inc	Amherst	NH	F	603 886-4100	13874
Laconia Magnetics Inc	Laconia	NH	F	603 528-2766	14655
Ladesco Inc	Manchester	NH	C	603 623-3772	14873
Rme Filters Inc	Amherst	NH	F	603 595-4573	13887
Technicoil LLC	Ossipee	NH	F	603 569-3100	15283
Vishay Hirel Systems LLC	Dover	NH	D	603 742-4375	14257
Wire Winders Inc	Milford	NH	G	603 673-1763	15044
Bioholdings Ltd	Portsmouth	RI	F	401 683-5400	16437
Crest Manufacturing Company	Lincoln	RI	E	401 333-1350	16129
Gets LLC	Lincoln	RI	D	401 314-5550	16138
Kearney-National Inc	North Kingstown	RI	C	401 943-2686	16264
Dynapower Company LLC (DH)	South Burlington	VT	D	802 860-7200	17577
Vishay Intertechnology Inc	Bennington	VT	F	802 440-8571	17057

3678 Electronic connectors

	CITY	ST	EMP	PHONE	ENTRY#
Amphenol Corporation	Danbury	CT	C	203 743-9272	707
Amphenol Corporation	Hamden	CT	D	203 287-2272	1412
Amphenol Corporation (PA)	Wallingford	CT	D	203 265-8900	3771
Amphenol International Ltd (HQ)	Wallingford	CT	C	203 265-8900	3772
Bead Industries Inc (PA)	Milford	CT	E	203 301-0270	1801
Electro-Tech Inc	Cheshire	CT	E	203 271-1976	589
Fct Electronics LP	Torrington	CT	D	860 482-2800	3678
Fct Electronics Management Inc	Torrington	CT	F	860 482-2800	3679
Hubbell Incorporated (PA)	Shelton	CT	A	475 882-4000	3017
Microtech Inc	Cheshire	CT	D	203 272-3234	607
Palco Connector Inc	Naugatuck	CT	E	203 729-9090	1978
Phoenix Company of Chicago Inc (PA)	Naugatuck	CT	D	630 595-2300	1980
RC Connectors LLC	Weatogue	CT	G	860 413-2196	4042
Telect Mfg LLC	Wallingford	CT	F	877 858-3855	3858
Teledyne Bolt Inc	Norwalk	CT	C	203 853-0700	2577

	CITY	ST	EMP	PHONE	ENTRY#
Times Microwave Systems Inc (HQ)	Wallingford	CT	B	203 949-8400	3866
Winchester Interconnect Corp (DH)	Norwalk	CT	E	203 741-5400	2595
Winchster Interconnect Rf Corp (DH)	Norwalk	CT	D	978 532-0775	2596
Amphenol Alden Products Co (HQ)	Brockton	MA	C	508 427-7000	7255
Anderson Power Products Inc (HQ)	Sterling	MA	D	978 422-3600	12154
Atlee Delaware Incorporated	Melrose	MA	F	978 681-1003	10313
C & K Components LLC (HQ)	Waltham	MA	D	617 969-3700	12619
Component Sources Intl Inc	Westborough	MA	F	508 986-2300	13092
Cristek Interconnects LLC	North Billerica	MA	G	978 735-2161	10903
Delta Electronics Mfg Corp	Beverly	MA	C	978 927-1060	6345
Electro-Term Inc	Springfield	MA	D	413 734-6469	12092
Elpakco Inc (PA)	Westford	MA	F	978 392-0400	13235
Glasseal Products Inc	New Bedford	MA	E	732 370-9100	10595
Global Interconnect Inc (PA)	Pocasset	MA	D	508 563-6306	11487
Hypertronics Corporation	Hudson	MA	C	978 568-0451	9375
Ideal Industries Inc	Sterling	MA	D	978 422-3600	12163
Infinite Electronics Intl Inc	North Andover	MA	E	800 341-5266	10839
L-Com Inc (DH)	North Andover	MA	D	978 682-6936	10842
Magellan Distribution Corp	Boston	MA	F	617 399-7900	6868
Microwave Engineering Corp	North Andover	MA	D	978 685-2776	10844
Nabson Inc	Taunton	MA	G	617 323-1101	12350
Paricon Technologies Corp	Taunton	MA	F	508 823-0876	12354
Reinforced Structures For Elec	Worcester	MA	F	508 754-5316	13783
San-Tron Inc (PA)	Ipswich	MA	D	978 356-1585	9496
Te Connectivity Corporation	Northborough	MA	F	717 592-4299	11111
Te Connectivity Corporation	Norwood	MA	F	781 278-5200	11213
Te Connectivity Corporation	Norwood	MA	F	781 278-5273	11214
Texas Instruments Incorporated	Attleboro	MA	E	508 236-3800	6070
Trego Inc	Wareham	MA	G	508 291-3816	12846
Tru Technologies Inc	Peabody	MA	F	978 532-0775	11349
Winchester Interconnect Corp	Peabody	MA	D	978 532-0775	11353
Winchester Interconnect Corp	Peabody	MA	D	978 532-0775	11354
Xybol Interlynks Inc	Ipswich	MA	F	978 356-0750	9500
Set Connectors Inc	Norway	ME	G	207 527-2876	5118
Amphenol Corporation	Nashua	NH	D	603 879-3000	15061
Amphenol Printed Circuits Inc (HQ)	Nashua	NH	D	603 324-4500	15062
Electronics Aid Inc	Marlborough	NH	G	603 876-4161	14964
Hubbell Incorporated	Manchester	NH	F	603 647-5000	14860
Incon Inc	Hudson	NH	B	603 595-0550	14508
Ksaria Corporation	Hudson	NH	C	866 457-2742	14519
Q A Technology Company Inc	Hampton	NH	D	603 926-1193	14409
Special Hermetic Products Inc	Wilton	NH	E	603 654-2002	15710
Teledyne Instruments Inc	Portsmouth	NH	C	603 474-5571	15442
Wavelink LLC	Manchester	NH	F	603 606-7489	14958
Xma Corporation	Manchester	NH	D	603 222-2256	14961
Advanced Interconnections Corp	West Warwick	RI	D	401 823-5200	16898
Ametek Scp Inc (HQ)	Westerly	RI	D	401 596-6658	16927
Precision Trned Cmponents Corp	Smithfield	RI	D	401 232-3377	16726
Teka Interconnection Systems Inc	Rumford	RI	D	401 785-4110	16677

3679 Electronic components, nec

	CITY	ST	EMP	PHONE	ENTRY#
AB Electronics LLC	Brookfield	CT	E	203 740-2793	509
Able Coil and Electronics Co	Bolton	CT	E	860 646-5686	218
Alpha-Core Inc	Shelton	CT	E	203 954-0050	2980
Arccos Golf LLC (PA)	Stamford	CT	E	844 692-7226	3286
Ashcroft Inc (DH)	Stratford	CT	B	203 378-8281	3517
Bead Industries Inc (PA)	Milford	CT	E	203 301-0270	1801
Bicron Electronics LLC (HQ)	Torrington	CT	D	860 482-2524	3672
Bloomy Controls Inc (PA)	South Windsor	CT	E	860 298-9925	3120
Bridgeport Magnetics Group Inc	Shelton	CT	E	203 954-0050	2988
Data Signal Corporation	Milford	CT	E	203 882-5393	1816
Doltronics LLC	Branford	CT	E	203 488-8766	250
Dsaencore LLC	Brookfield	CT	D	203 740-4200	518
Ebl Products Inc	East Hartford	CT	F	860 290-3737	990
Edal Industries Inc	East Haven	CT	E	203 467-2591	1041
Electro-Tech Inc	Cheshire	CT	E	203 271-1976	589
ESI Electronic Products Corp	Prospect	CT	E	203 758-4401	2834
General Electro Components	Glastonbury	CT	G	860 659-3573	1280
Goodrich Corporation	Danbury	CT	B	505 345-9031	750
Hermetic Solutions Group Inc (HQ)	Essex	CT	F	215 645-9420	1165
Hipotronics Inc (HQ)	Shelton	CT	C	845 279-3644	3013
Imperial Elctrnic Assembly Inc	Brookfield	CT	D	203 740-8425	525
Insys Micro Inc	Norwalk	CT	G	917 566-5045	2518
K B C Electronics Inc	Milford	CT	F	203 298-9654	1842
Linemaster Switch Corporation	Plainfield	CT	G	860 564-7713	2736
Lq Mechatronics Inc	Branford	CT	E	203 433-4430	268
Marmon Indus Enrgy Infrstrctur	East Granby	CT	E	860 653-8300	940
Microsemi Corporation	Simsbury	CT	D	860 651-0211	3093
Microtech Inc	Cheshire	CT	D	203 272-3234	607
Mil-Con Inc	Naugatuck	CT	F	630 595-2366	1971
Neeltran Inc	New Milford	CT	C	860 350-5964	2254
Northeast Electronics Corp	Milford	CT	D	203 878-3511	1855
Osda Inc	Milford	CT	G	203 878-2155	1860

	CITY	ST	EMP	PHONE	ENTRY#
Park Distributories Inc	Bridgeport	CT	G	203 366-7200	356
Precision Electronic Assembly	Monroe	CT	F	203 452-1839	1919
Prime Technology LLC	North Branford	CT	E	203 481-5721	2373
Protronix Inc	Wallingford	CT	F	203 269-5858	3842
Qtran Inc (PA)	Milford	CT	E	203 367-8777	1873
Rel-Tech Electronics Inc	Milford	CT	D	203 877-8770	1876
Robert Warren LLC (PA)	Westport	CT	E	203 247-3347	4195
Rogers Corporation	Rogers	CT	C	860 774-9605	2943
Siemon Company (PA)	Watertown	CT	A	860 945-4200	4029
Sysdyne Technologies LLC	Stamford	CT	F	203 327-3649	3477
Technical Manufacturing Corp	Durham	CT	E	860 349-1735	904
Times Microwave Systems Inc (HQ)	Wallingford	CT	B	203 949-8400	3866
Topex Inc	Danbury	CT	F	203 748-5918	825
Tornik Inc	Rocky Hill	CT	C	860 282-6081	2937
Tornik LLC	Rocky Hill	CT	F	860 282-6081	2938
Transformer Technology Inc	Durham	CT	F	860 349-1061	905
Tri TEC Electronics Inc	Waterbury	CT	G	203 573-8491	3976
Tritex Corporation	Waterbury	CT	C	203 756-7441	3977
Validus DC Systems LLC	Brookfield	CT	G	203 448-3600	542
Accellent Acquisition Corp	Wilmington	MA	A	978 570-6900	13370
Accellent Holdings Corp	Wilmington	MA	A	978 570-6900	13371
Adcotron Ems Inc	Boston	MA	C	617 598-3000	6514
Advent Technologies Inc (PA)	Boston	MA	F	617 655-6000	6519
Ainslie Corporation	Walpole	MA	G	781 848-0850	12548
American Sub Assmbly Prdcers I	Dudley	MA	E	508 949-2320	8315
Aquila Technology Corp	Burlington	MA	F	781 993-9004	7334
Aved Electronics LLC	North Billerica	MA	D	978 453-6393	10898
Bae Systems Info Elctrnic Syst	Lexington	MA	C	603 885-4321	9726
Bowers and Wilkins Group	North Reading	MA	E	978 357-0428	11038
C & K Components LLC (HQ)	Waltham	MA	D	617 969-3700	12619
Caes Mission Systems LLC	Woburn	MA	C	781 729-9450	13538
Cape Light Compact	Barnstable	MA	F	508 375-6703	6199
Case Assembly Solutions Inc	South Easton	MA	E	508 238-5665	11939
Cbm Industries Inc	Taunton	MA	E	508 821-4555	12326
Ceramic To Metal Seals Inc	Melrose	MA	F	781 665-5002	10314
Cirtec Medical Corp	Lowell	MA	C	978 703-6822	9867
Coactive Technologies LLC	Newton	MA	C	617 969-3700	10747
Comprehensive Power Inc	Marlborough	MA	E	508 460-0010	10134
Cooper Crouse-Hinds LLC	Chelsea	MA	E	617 889-3700	7979
Copley Controls Corporation (DH)	Canton	MA	B	781 828-8090	7779
Corning Incorporated	Tewksbury	MA	E	978 442-2200	12391
Courtsmart Digital Systems Inc	North Chelmsford	MA	E	978 251-3300	10973
Creation Technologies Intl Inc (PA)	Boston	MA	E	877 734-7456	6676
Crystal Gt Systems LLC	Salem	MA	F	978 745-0088	11708
Csr Technology Inc	Burlington	MA	E	781 791-6000	7356
Datacon Inc	Chelmsford	MA	E	781 273-5800	7922
Delta Electronics Mfg Corp	Beverly	MA	C	978 927-1060	6345
Desco Electronics Inc	Plainville	MA	E	508 643-1950	11431
Design Mark Industries Inc	New Bedford	MA	D	800 451-3275	10585
Diamond Antenna Microwave Corp	Littleton	MA	D	978 486-0039	9811
DI Technology LLC	Haverhill	MA	E	978 374-6451	9092
Dss Circuits Inc	Worcester	MA	D	508 852-8061	13719
East West Boston LLC	Boston	MA	D	617 598-3000	6706
Electronic Assemblies Mfg Inc	Methuen	MA	E	978 374-6840	10329
Embr Labs Inc	Charlestown	MA	F	413 218-0629	7871
Excelitas Technologies Corp	Salem	MA	A	800 775-6786	11714
Excelitas Technologies Corp (DH)	Waltham	MA	E	855 382-2677	12673
First Electronics Corporation	Braintree	MA	D	617 704-4248	7183
First Electronics Corporation	Chelsea	MA	E	617 288-2430	7981
First Electronics Corporation (DH)	Dorchester	MA	E	617 288-2430	8299
Flintec Inc	Hudson	MA	E	978 562-4548	9367
Fourstar Connections Inc	Hudson	MA	D	978 568-9800	9369
Fraen Corporation (PA)	Reading	MA	E	781 205-5300	11601
General Manufacturing Corp	North Billerica	MA	D	978 667-5514	10917
Glasseal Products Inc	New Bedford	MA	E	732 370-9100	10595
Global Interconnect Inc (PA)	Pocasset	MA	D	508 563-6306	11487
Gutz LLC	Lowell	MA	G	978 805-5001	9883
H & T Specialty Co Inc	Waltham	MA	E	781 893-3866	12689
Harvard Scientific Corporation	Cambridge	MA	F	617 876-5033	7604
Hdm Systems Corporation	Brighton	MA	F	617 562-4054	7242
Heilind Electronics Inc (PA)	Wilmington	MA	D	978 657-4870	13410
High Voltage Engineering Corp	Wakefield	MA	E	781 224-1001	12511
Hottinger Bruel & Kjaer Inc (DH)	Marlborough	MA	D	508 485-7480	10164
Hxi LLC	Harvard	MA	F	978 772-7774	9064
Intellisense Software Corp	Lynnfield	MA	F	781 933-8098	9997
Interface Engineering Corp	Randolph	MA	F	781 986-2600	11566
Jem Electronics Inc	Franklin	MA	C	508 520-3105	8845
Kaiser Systems Inc	Salem	MA	D	978 224-4135	11725
Kevlin Corporation	Methuen	MA	C	978 689-8331	10336
Keystone Precision Inc	Pepperell	MA	G	978 433-8484	11386
Kopin Targeting Corporation	Westborough	MA	D	508 870-5959	13115
Leidos Inc	Tewksbury	MA	G	781 221-7627	12402
Macom Technology Solutions Inc	Lowell	MA	E	978 656-2500	9899

	CITY	ST	EMP	PHONE	ENTRY#
Macom Technology Solutions Inc **(HQ)**	Lowell	MA	B	978 656-2500	9900
Manage Inc	Springfield	MA	E	413 593-9128	12112
Massa Products Corporation	Hingham	MA	D	781 749-3120	9152
Massmicroelectronics LLC	Canton	MA	F	781 828-6110	7808
Metal Processing Co Inc	Tyngsboro	MA	G	978 649-1289	12461
Metalogic Industries LLC	Southbridge	MA	F	508 461-6787	12030
Microtek Inc	Chicopee	MA	C	413 593-1025	8049
Microwave Cmpnents Systems Inc	Westborough	MA	F	508 466-8400	13121
Microwave Development Labs Inc	Needham Heights	MA	D	781 292-6600	10551
Microwave Engineering Corp	North Andover	MA	D	978 685-2776	10844
Midas Technology Inc	Woburn	MA	F	781 938-0069	13613
Millitech Inc	Northampton	MA	D	413 582-9620	11073
Mornsun America LLC	Milford	MA	G	978 293-3923	10406
Mti-Milliren Technologies Inc	Newburyport	MA	E	978 465-6064	10703
Murata Power Solutions Inc **(DH)**	Westborough	MA	C	508 339-3000	13122
Nanosemi Inc	Waltham	MA	E	781 472-2832	12731
Noeveon Inc	Wilmington	MA	G	978 642-5004	13439
Nypro Healthcare Baja Inc **(DH)**	Clinton	MA	D	619 498-9250	8086
O R M Inc	Northborough	MA	F	508 393-7054	11104
Orion Industries Incorporated	Ayer	MA	E	978 772-0020	6190
Paricon Technologies Corp	Taunton	MA	F	508 823-0876	12354
Parisi Associates LLC	Chelmsford	MA	F	978 667-8700	7944
PCA LLC	Andover	MA	F	978 494-0550	5905
Photonis Scientific Inc **(DH)**	Sturbridge	MA	F	508 347-4000	12257
Pickering Interfaces Inc	Chelmsford	MA	G	781 897-1710	7945
Polyonics Corporation	Newburyport	MA	F	978 462-3600	10708
Quartzite Processing Inc	Malden	MA	F	781 322-3611	10024
REA Associates Inc	North Billerica	MA	G	209 521-2727	10949
Sensata Technologies Inc **(HQ)**	Attleboro	MA	A	508 236-3800	6062
Sensata Technologies Mass Inc **(DH)**	Attleboro	MA	A	508 236-3800	6064
Sie Computing Solutions Inc	Brockton	MA	D	508 588-6110	7305
Sinclair Manufacturing Co LLC	Norton	MA	D	508 222-7440	11135
Skyworks Solutions Inc	Woburn	MA	D	781 935-5150	13669
Smiths Interconnect Inc	Northampton	MA	B	413 582-9620	11080
Smiths Intrcnnect Americas Inc	Hudson	MA	C	978 568-0451	9413
Socomec Inc **(DH)**	Watertown	MA	F	617 245-0447	12908
Spectrum Microwave Inc	Marlborough	MA	D	508 485-0336	10212
Spectrum Microwave Inc	Marlborough	MA	C	508 251-6400	10213
Spectrum Microwave Inc	Marlborough	MA	G	603 459-1600	10214
Star Engineering Inc	North Attleboro	MA	E	508 316-1492	10889
Sunburst Elctrnic Mfg Sltons I **(PA)**	West Bridgewater	MA	D	508 580-1881	12983
Synqor Inc **(PA)**	Boxborough	MA	C	978 849-0600	7155
Synqor Holdings LLC	Boxborough	MA	F	978 849-0600	7156
Texas Instruments Incorporated	Attleboro	MA	E	508 236-3800	6070
That Corporation	Milford	MA	E	508 478-9200	10420
Thorndike Corporation	East Bridgewater	MA	F	508 378-9797	8346
Tmd Technologies LLC	Beverly	MA	C	978 922-6000	6390
Tru Technologies Inc	Peabody	MA	F	978 532-0775	11349
Ulvac Technologies Inc **(HQ)**	Methuen	MA	E	978 686-7550	10347
Utz Technologies Inc **(PA)**	Lowell	MA	E	973 339-1100	9933
V-Tron Electronics Corp	Attleboro	MA	D	508 761-9100	6072
Vicor Corporation **(PA)**	Andover	MA	A	978 470-2900	5933
Victor Microwave Inc	Wakefield	MA	E	781 245-4472	12541
Wasik Associates Inc	Dracut	MA	F	978 454-9787	8314
Artel Inc	Westbrook	ME	E	207 854-0860	5614
603 Manufacturing LLC	Hudson	NH	D	603 578-9876	14478
Aavid Corporation	Laconia	NH	A	603 528-3400	14638
Advanced Design & Mfg Inc	Portsmouth	NH	E	603 430-7573	15357
Amphenol Printed Circuits Inc **(HQ)**	Nashua	NH	D	603 324-4500	15062
Anaren Ceramics Inc	Salem	NH	D	603 898-2883	15505
Asia Direct LLC	Plaistow	NH	F	603 382-9485	15336
Bae Systems Info Elctrnic Syst	Hudson	NH	A	603 885-4321	14486
Bae Systems Info Elctrnic Syst	Merrimack	NH	B	603 885-4321	14975
Boyd Laconia LLC **(DH)**	Laconia	NH	B	603 528-3400	14649
Data Electronic Devices Inc	Salem	NH	C	603 893-2047	15517
Electronics Aid Inc	Marlborough	NH	G	603 876-4161	14964
Frontier Design Group LLC	Lebanon	NH	E	603 448-6283	14688
Gill Design Inc	Windham	NH	G	603 890-1237	15727
Great Bay Manufacturing LLC	Rochester	NH	F	603 948-1212	15477
Ica Northeast Inc	Exeter	NH	E	603 773-2386	14293
Impact Science & Technology Inc	Nashua	NH	C	603 459-2200	15113
Intervala LLC	Hudson	NH	D	603 595-1987	14512
Janco Electronics Inc	Rollinsford	NH	D	603 742-1581	15496
Jenesco Inc	Lyndeborough	NH	F	603 673-4830	14800
K E I Incorporated	Nashua	NH	F	978 656-2575	15120
Ksaria Corporation	Hudson	NH	C	866 457-2742	14519
Lnx Corporation	Hudson	NH	D	603 898-6800	14524
Maynesboro Industries Inc	Berlin	NH	F	603 752-3366	13982
Megatrnics US Ultmate Hldco LL **(PA)**	Salem	NH	E	888 706-0230	15544
Meggitt (new Hampshire) Inc	Londonderry	NH	C	603 669-0940	14767
Miltronics Mfg Svcs Inc	Keene	NH	F	603 352-3333	14609
Miraco Inc	Manchester	NH	E	603 665-9449	14890
Monzite Corporation **(HQ)**	Nashua	NH	G	617 429-7050	15136
New Model Inc	Belmont	NH	E	603 267-8225	13964
Pgc Wire & Cable LLC	Derry	NH	F	603 821-7300	14203
Princeton Technology Corp	Hudson	NH	D	603 595-1987	14536
Remcon/North Corporation	Meredith	NH	D	603 279-7091	14969
Rf Logic LLC	Hudson	NH	E	603 578-9876	14541
RH Laboratories Inc	Nashua	NH	E	603 459-5900	15159
Rotary Vacuum Products Inc	Salem	NH	G	603 890-6001	15558
Scott Electronics Inc **(PA)**	Salem	NH	D	603 893-2845	15559
Sonesys LLC	Merrimack	NH	F	603 423-9000	15004
Special Hermetic Products Inc	Wilton	NH	E	603 654-2002	15710
Stellar Manufacturing Inc	Salem	NH	E	978 241-9537	15564
Technical Research and Manufacturing Inc	Bedford	NH		D	
603 627-6000					13951
Vectronics Microwave Corp **(PA)**	Hudson	NH	E	973 244-1040	14558
Versatile Subcontracting LLC	Northfield	NH	G	603 286-8081	15271
Vette Thermal Solutions LLC **(HQ)**	Pelham	NH	F	603 635-2800	15300
Xp Power LLC	Salem	NH	F	603 894-4420	15574
Andon Electronics Corporation	Lincoln	RI	E	401 333-0388	16119
Cooliance Inc **(PA)**	Warwick	RI	F	401 921-6500	16798
Federal Electronics Inc	Cranston	RI	D	401 944-6200	15859
Fpp Holdings LLC	Cranston	RI	F	401 684-1443	15862
IDS Highway Safety Inc	Cumberland	RI	D	401 425-2205	15945
Igus Bearings Inc **(PA)**	Rumford	RI	C	800 521-2747	16669
International Mfg Svcs Inc	Portsmouth	RI	E	401 683-9700	16445
Kearney-National Inc	North Kingstown	RI	C	401 943-2686	16264
L L Rowe Company	Ashaway	RI	E	781 729-7860	15743
Narragansett Imaging Usa LLC	North Smithfield	RI	E	401 762-3800	16328
Precision Trned Cmponents Corp	Smithfield	RI	D	401 232-3377	16726
Raytheon Company	Portsmouth	RI	D	401 847-8000	16454
Ritronics Inc	Warwick	RI	F	401 732-8175	16852
Staffall Inc	Cranston	RI	E	401 461-5554	15913
Vesuvius America Inc **(DH)**	Providence	RI	E		16640
Veterans Assembled Elec LLC **(PA)**	North Kingstown	RI	G	401 228-6165	16291
Vishay Efi Inc	Warwick	RI	E	401 738-9150	16873
Aviatron Inc	South Burlington	VT	E	802 865-9318	17570
Dynapower Company LLC **(DH)**	South Burlington	VT	D	802 860-7200	17577
Image Tek Mfg Inc	Springfield	VT	E	802 885-6208	17618
Necsel Intllctual Property Inc	Vergennes	VT	E	802 877-6432	17658
Prom Software Inc	South Burlington	VT	F	802 862-7500	17597
Vemas Corporation	Poultney	VT	E	802 287-4100	17454
Village of Orleans	Orleans	VT	G	802 754-8584	17440

3691 Storage batteries

	CITY	ST	EMP	PHONE	ENTRY#
Alcad Inc	North Haven	CT	E	203 985-2500	2389
B S T Systems Inc	Plainfield	CT	D	860 564-4078	2734
Duracell Company	Bethel	CT	E	203 796-4000	110
Duracell International Inc	Bethel	CT	A	203 796-4000	111
Duracell Manufacturing LLC	Bethel	CT	C	203 796-4000	112
Duracell US Holding LLC **(HQ)**	Bethel	CT	E	203 796-4000	113
Evercel Inc	Stamford	CT	C	781 741-8800	3346
Hbl America Inc **(HQ)**	Manchester	CT	G	860 257-9800	1601
Johnson Controls Inc	Meriden	CT	F	678 297-4040	1670
Nofet LLC	New Haven	CT	E	203 848-9064	2180
Saft America Inc	North Haven	CT	E	203 234-8333	2435
24m Technologies Inc **(PA)**	Cambridge	MA	E	617 553-1012	7461
A123 Systems Inc	Watertown	MA	E	617 972-3400	12854
A123 Systems LLC	Hopkinton	MA	D	508 497-7200	9304
A123 Systems LLC	Waltham	MA	C	617 778-5700	12580
Atlantic Battery Company Inc	Watertown	MA	F	617 924-2868	12860
Avanti Battery Company	Watertown	MA	F	617 209-9434	12861
B456 Systems Inc	Waltham	MA	A	617 778-5100	12600
Battery Resourcers LLC	Westborough	MA	F	206 948-6325	13081
Factorial Inc **(PA)**	Woburn	MA	E	617 315-9733	13563
Fastcap Systems Corporation **(PA)**	Wakefield	MA	F	857 403-6031	12509
Integer Holdings Corporation	Canton	MA	C	781 830-5800	7801
Interstate All Battery Center	South Yarmouth	MA	F	508 394-9400	11984
Lg Energy Solution Vertech Inc **(DH)**	Westborough	MA	E	508 497-7319	13117
Nyobolt Inc	Bedford	MA	G	978 884-2220	6249
Solidenergy Systems LLC	Woburn	MA	D	617 972-3412	13670
Technical Power Systems Inc	Middleboro	MA	E	630 719-1471	10378
Titan Advnced Enrgy Sltons Inc	Salem	MA	F	561 654-5558	11735
Tracer Technologies Inc	Somerville	MA	E	617 776-6410	11904
Xilectric Inc	Fall River	MA	G	781 247-4567	8627
Sustainx Inc	Exeter	NH	F	603 601-7800	14303
Eaglepicher Technologies LLC	East Greenwich	RI	F	401 471-6580	15981
Ener-Tek International Inc	East Greenwich	RI	E	401 471-6580	15985
Yardney Technical Products Inc	East Greenwich	RI	C	401 471-6580	15998
Edgewell Per Care Brands LLC	Bennington	VT	E	802 442-5551	17039

3692 Primary batteries, dry and wet

	CITY	ST	EMP	PHONE	ENTRY#
B S T Systems Inc	Plainfield	CT	D	860 564-4078	2734
Videndum Prod Solutions Inc **(HQ)**	Shelton	CT	E	203 929-1100	3075
Electrochem Solutions Inc	Raynham	MA	C	781 575-0800	11589

SIC

	CITY	ST	EMP	PHONE	ENTRY#
Integer Holdings Corporation	Canton	MA	C	781 830-5800	7801
Largo Clean Energy Corp (HQ)	Wilmington	MA	E	978 566-8220	13425
Ener-Tek International Inc	East Greenwich	RI	E	401 471-6580	15985

3694 Engine electrical equipment

	CITY	ST	EMP	PHONE	ENTRY#
Simmonds Precision Pdts Inc	Danbury	CT	F	203 797-5000	818
Teledyne Bolt Inc	Norwalk	CT	C	203 853-0700	2577
Bay State Wire & Cable Co Inc	Lowell	MA	E	978 454-2444	9861
BBA Remanufacturing Inc	Taunton	MA	E	508 822-4490	12325
Liquidsky Technologies Inc	Chestnut Hill	MA	F	857 389-9893	8000
Magna Elec Roadscape Auto LLC (HQ)	Lowell	MA	G	978 656-2500	9901
Magna Electronics LLC	Lowell	MA	C	978 674-6500	9902
Pellion Technologies Inc	Arlington	MA	E		5944
Tanyx Measurements Inc	Billerica	MA	G	978 671-0183	6485
Veoneer Roadscape Auto Inc	Lowell	MA	G	978 656-2500	9934
Gauss Corporation	Scarborough	ME	F	207 883-4121	5432
Launchpad Electric Solutions	Kittery	ME	F	603 828-2919	4936
Electrocraft New Hampshire Inc (DH)	Dover	NH	F	603 742-3330	14228
Hubbell Incorporated	Manchester	NH	F	603 647-5000	14860
Ricks Mtorsport Electrics Inc	Hampstead	NH	E	603 329-9901	14392
Antaya Inc	Warwick	RI	E	401 941-7050	16780
Antaya Technologies Corp	Warwick	RI	C	401 921-3197	16781
Simmonds Precision Products (DH)	Vergennes	VT	A	802 877-4000	17661

3695 Magnetic and optical recording media

	CITY	ST	EMP	PHONE	ENTRY#
20/20 Software Inc	Stamford	CT	G	203 316-5500	3266
Cogz Systems LLC	Woodbury	CT	F	203 263-7882	4385
Dataquest Korea Inc	Stamford	CT	F	239 561-4862	3334
Dictaphone Corporation (DH)	Stratford	CT	C	203 381-7000	3533
Adaptive Optics Associates Inc (DH)	Devens	MA	D	978 757-9600	8269
Intellisense Software Corp	Lynnfield	MA	F	781 933-8098	9997
Omniview Sports Inc	Boston	MA	E	781 583-3534	6929
Primary Pdc Inc (PA)	Waltham	MA	G	781 386-2000	12753
Portfolio Software Inc	Richmond	VT	F	802 434-4000	17481

3699 Electrical equipment and supplies, nec

	CITY	ST	EMP	PHONE	ENTRY#
Alent Inc	Waterbury	CT	D	203 575-5980	3879
Alent USA Holding Inc	Waterbury	CT	E	203 575-5727	3880
Arcor Laser Services LLC	Suffield	CT	E	860 370-9780	3587
Arthur J Hurley Company	East Hartford	CT	G	860 257-5505	972
Assa Abloy Inc (HQ)	New Haven	CT	B	203 562-2151	2122
Bevin Bros Manufacturing Co	East Hampton	CT	E	860 267-4431	961
Branson Ultrasonics Corp (DH)	Brookfield	CT	B	203 796-0400	512
Brookfield Industries Inc	Thomaston	CT	E	860 283-6211	3615
Cadence Ct Inc	Suffield	CT	D	860 370-9780	3589
Circuit Breaker Sales Ne LLC	Seymour	CT	E	203 888-7500	2958
Coherent Corp	Bloomfield	CT	C	860 243-9557	156
Coherent-Deos LLC	Bloomfield	CT	D	860 243-9557	157
Command Corporation	East Granby	CT	E	800 851-6012	930
E-J Electric T & D LLC	Wallingford	CT	D	203 626-9625	3803
Eastern Electric Cnstr Co	Harwinton	CT	G	860 485-1100	1519
Eastside Electric Inc	Harwinton	CT	F	860 485-0700	1520
Ebtec Corporation	East Windsor	CT	E	860 789-2462	1072
Electro Mech Specialists LLC	Bozrah	CT	G	860 887-2613	228
Fuelcell Energy Inc	Torrington	CT	E	860 496-1111	3682
Hamar Laser Instruments Inc	Danbury	CT	E	203 730-4600	756
Hubbell Incorporated (PA)	Shelton	CT	A	475 882-4000	3017
Hubbell Incorporated Delaware (HQ)	Shelton	CT	B	475 882-4000	3018
Insight Plus Technology LLC	Bristol	CT	G	860 930-4763	457
Integral Technologies Inc (DH)	Enfield	CT	G	860 741-2281	1136
Isupportws Inc	Stamford	CT	E	203 569-7600	3386
Jared Manufacturing Co Inc	Norwalk	CT	E	203 846-1732	2520
Luvata Waterbury Inc (HQ)	Waterbury	CT	D	203 753-5215	3931
Magnatech LLC	East Granby	CT	D	860 653-2573	939
Miracle Instruments Co	Lebanon	CT	G	860 642-7745	1549
Morse Watchmans Inc	Oxford	CT	F	203 264-4949	2705
Nabco Entrances Inc	Bridgeport	CT	F	262 679-0045	351
Newco Condenser Inc	Shelton	CT	E	475 882-4000	3039
Ptr - Precision Technologies Inc (DH)	Enfield	CT	E	860 741-2281	1144
Razberi Technologies Inc	Danbury	CT	E	469 828-3380	804
Rtx Corporation	Farmington	CT	B	954 485-6501	1244
Snow Goose 2019 Inc	Meriden	CT	F	203 237-3444	1700
Stanley Black & Decker Inc	Farmington	CT	F	860 677-2861	1248
Stanley Black & Decker Inc	New Britain	CT	F	860 225-5111	2063
Stanley Black & Decker Inc (PA)	New Britain	CT	C	860 225-5111	2065
Total Register Inc	New Milford	CT	F	860 210-0465	2262
Trine Access Technology Inc	Bethel	CT	F	203 730-1756	136
Ultra Clean Equipment Inc	Madison	CT	G	860 669-1354	1574
Varnum Enterprises LLC	Bethel	CT	E	203 743-4443	140
World Cord Sets Inc	Enfield	CT	G	860 763-2100	1160
Abisee Inc	Acton	MA	E	978 637-2900	5730
AES Corporation	Peabody	MA	D	978 535-7310	11293
AES International Corporation	Peabody	MA	F	978 535-7310	11294

	CITY	ST	EMP	PHONE	ENTRY#
All Security Co Inc	New Bedford	MA	E	508 993-4271	10567
Arcam Cad To Metal Inc	Woburn	MA	E	781 281-1718	13513
Armatron International Inc (PA)	Medford	MA	D	781 321-2300	10280
Asco Power Technologies LP	Marlborough	MA	D	508 624-0466	10111
Azz Inc	Medway	MA	E	774 854-0700	10302
Branson Ultrasonics Corp	Acton	MA	G	978 262-9040	5741
Byrna Technologies Inc (PA)	Andover	MA	C	978 868-5011	5875
Clearswift Corporation	Waltham	MA	B	781 839-7321	12630
Compu-Gard Inc	Swansea	MA	E	508 679-8845	12303
Concord Electric Supply Ltd	Hyannis	MA	A	774 552-2185	9432
Concord Electric Supply Ltd	Nantucket	MA	A	774 325-5142	10461
Convergent - Photonics LLC (DH)	Chicopee	MA	E	413 598-5200	8020
Cooper Crouse-Hinds LLC	Chelsea	MA	E	617 889-3700	7980
Cordmaster Engineering Co Inc	North Adams	MA	E	413 664-9371	10805
Cortron Inc	Lowell	MA	E	978 975-5445	9871
Degreasing Devices Co	Southbridge	MA	G	508 765-0045	12013
Diamond-Roltran LLC	Littleton	MA	F	978 486-0039	9812
Distribution & Control Product	Malden	MA	G	781 324-0070	10010
Dogwatch Inc (PA)	Natick	MA	G	508 650-0600	10478
Dorel Juvenile Group Inc	Foxboro	MA	C	800 544-1108	8694
Electri-Cord Manufacturing Co	Westborough	MA	G	508 836-3510	13099
Electronic Components Inc	Framingham	MA	G	508 881-8399	8762
Exatel Visual Systems Inc	Burlington	MA	G	781 221-7400	7372
Excel Dryer Inc	East Longmeadow	MA	E	413 525-4531	8375
Excel Technology Inc (HQ)	Bedford	MA	D	781 266-5700	6226
Giner Elx Sub LLC	Auburndale	MA	F	781 392-0300	6134
Green Brothers Fabricating (PA)	Taunton	MA	E	508 880-3608	12339
Grove Labs Inc	Somerville	MA	F	703 608-8178	11878
Headwaters Inc	Marblehead	MA	G	781 715-6404	10087
Hutchinson Arospc & Indust Inc	Hopkinton	MA	D	508 417-7000	9329
Inner-Tite Corp	Holden	MA	D	508 829-6361	9191
Interntnal Br-Tech Sltions Inc (PA)	Springfield	MA	G	413 739-2271	12106
Ipg Photonics Corporation	Marlborough	MA	F	508 373-1100	10167
Ipg Photonics Corporation	Marlborough	MA	E	508 506-2812	10168
Ipg Photonics Corporation (PA)	Marlborough	MA	B	508 373-1100	10169
Ipg Photonics Corporation	Oxford	MA	F	508 506-2585	11255
Lightspeed Mfg Co LLC	Haverhill	MA	F	978 521-7676	9109
Litron LLC	Agawam	MA	D		5799
Lumeway Products Inc	Holden	MA	G	508 829-2112	9192
Lumina Power Inc	Haverhill	MA	E	978 241-8260	9110
M & S Electrical Contrs LLC	Brockton	MA	E	781 389-4465	7293
Magiq Technologies Inc (PA)	Somerville	MA	E	617 661-8300	11884
Markarian Electric LLC	Watertown	MA	G	617 393-9700	12890
Matec Instrument Companies Inc (PA)	Northborough	MA	E	508 393-0155	11102
Mc10 Inc	Tewksbury	MA	E	617 234-4448	12408
McLane Research Labs Inc (PA)	East Falmouth	MA	G	508 495-4000	8361
Mettlr-Tledo Prcess Anlytics I	Billerica	MA	D	781 301-8800	6461
Multi-Concept Inc	Mansfield	MA	F	508 366-7676	10067
Nextek LLC	North Billerica	MA	E	978 486-0582	10939
Nhv America Inc	Methuen	MA	E	978 682-4900	10341
Nkt Photonics Inc (DH)	Boston	MA	F	503 444-8404	6923
Novanta Corporation (HQ)	Bedford	MA	C	781 266-5700	6245
Novanta Inc (PA)	Bedford	MA	C	781 266-5700	6246
Oatsystems Inc	Waltham	MA	D	781 907-6100	12741
Optowares Incorporated	Woburn	MA	E	781 427-7106	13627
Panametrics LLC (DH)	Billerica	MA	A	978 437-1000	6468
Photonwares Corporation (PA)	Woburn	MA	D	781 935-1200	13635
Polar Controls Inc	Shirley	MA	G	978 425-2233	11822
Polytec Inc	Hudson	MA	E	508 417-1040	9401
Product Resources LLC	Newburyport	MA	E	978 524-8500	10709
Rofin-Baasel Inc (HQ)	Devens	MA	E	978 635-9100	8286
Sancliff Inc	Worcester	MA	E	508 795-0747	13794
Schneider Automation Inc	Andover	MA	E	978 975-9600	5915
Socomec Inc (DH)	Watertown	MA	F	617 245-0447	12908
Sonosystems N Schunk Amer Corp (DH)	Wilmington	MA	E	978 658-9400	13454
Static Clean International Inc	North Billerica	MA	F	781 229-7799	10960
Steel Root Inc	Salem	MA	E	978 312-7668	11733
Stellar Industries Corp	Millbury	MA	E	508 865-1668	10443
Sunrise Technologies Inc	Raynham	MA	F	508 821-1597	11597
Sysnova LLC	Mansfield	MA	G	508 309-9264	10077
Tel Mnfacturing Engrg Amer Inc	Billerica	MA	E	978 436-2300	6487
Teledyne Instruments Inc	North Falmouth	MA	C	508 548-2077	11016
Teradiode Inc	Wilmington	MA	D	978 988-1040	13464
Thermal Circuits Inc	Salem	MA	C	978 745-1162	11734
Videoiq Inc	Somerville	MA	C	781 222-3069	11911
W J Roberts Co Inc	Saugus	MA	E	781 233-8176	11767
Whyte Electric LLC	Braintree	MA	G	781 348-6239	7213
Wire Techniques Ltd	Amesbury	MA	E	978 372-1300	5855
Wrapsol LLC	Canton	MA	E		7843
Zorean Inc	Chelmsford	MA	E	978 250-9144	7973
Chandler Security Systems Inc	Lewiston	ME	G	207 576-3418	4954
Design Architectural Heating	Lewiston	ME	F	207 784-0309	4955
Eami Inc	Biddeford	ME	F	207 283-3001	4562

	CITY	ST	EMP	PHONE	ENTRY#
Electrotech Inc	Rockland	ME	F	207 596-0556	5326
Enercon (HQ)	Gray	ME	D	207 657-7000	4841
Waughs Mountainview Elec	Mexico	ME	F	207 545-2421	5059
Brailsford & Company Inc	Antrim	NH	F	603 588-2880	13896
Corportion For Lser Optics Res (PA)	Londonderry	NH	G	603 430-2023	14738
Electronics Aid Inc	Marlborough	NH	G	603 876-4161	14964
Enertgetic Baltic MI	Enfield	NH	G	603 252-0804	14274
Hardric Laboratories Inc	Hudson	NH	E	978 251-1702	14506
Ipg Photonics Corporation	Nashua	NH	F	603 518-3200	15116
JP Sercel Associates Inc	Manchester	NH	E	603 595-7048	14869
Laser Advantage LLC	Nashua	NH	F	603 886-9464	15125
Laser Light Engines Inc	Salem	NH	F	603 952-4550	15542
Laser Projection Technologies Inc	Londonderry	NH	E	603 421-0209	14762
Lenric Corp	Nashua	NH	E	603 886-6772	15127
Namtek Corp	Bedford	NH	F	603 262-1630	13945
Omega Six Security LLC	Bedford	NH	F	888 866-9954	13946
Orion Entrance Control Inc	Laconia	NH	E	603 527-4187	14662
Prime Power Inc	Hampstead	NH	F	603 329-4675	14390
Spartronics Plaistow Inc	Plaistow	NH	F	603 382-3840	15352
Spinnaker Contract Mfg Inc	Tilton	NH	D	603 286-4366	15657
Tech Resources Inc	Milford	NH	E	603 673-9000	15039
Teledyne Instruments Inc	Portsmouth	NH	C	603 474-5571	15442
Thermal Arc Inc	West Lebanon	NH	D	800 462-2782	15689
Wilcox Industries Corp (PA)	Newington	NH	D	603 431-1331	15216
Wilcox Industries Corp	Newington	NH	E	603 431-1331	15217
Clariant Corporation	Coventry	RI	B	401 823-2000	15809
Endiprev Usa LLC	Providence	RI	D	401 519-3600	16514
Kenney Manufacturing Company (PA)	Warwick	RI	B	401 739-2200	16831
Laser Fare Inc (PA)	Smithfield	RI	E	401 231-4400	16721
Laservall North America LLC	Pawtucket	RI	G	401 724-0076	16382
Lfi Inc (PA)	Smithfield	RI	E	401 231-4400	16722
Maley Laser Processing Inc	Warwick	RI	F	303 952-8941	16834
Newport Electric Corporation	Portsmouth	RI	F	401 293-0527	16450
Nordson Efd LLC (HQ)	East Providence	RI	C	401 431-7000	16034
Ritec Inc	Warwick	RI	F	401 738-3660	16851
Vesuvius America Inc (DH)	Providence	RI	E		16640
Champlain Door Company Inc	Milton	VT	F	802 524-7595	17356
Limoge & Sons Garage Doors Inc	Williston	VT	F	802 878-4338	17739
Omni Measurement Systems Inc	Colchester	VT	E	802 497-2253	17198
Westinghouse Electric Co LLC	Brattleboro	VT	E	802 254-9353	17108

37 TRANSPORTATION EQUIPMENT

3711 Motor vehicles and car bodies

	CITY	ST	EMP	PHONE	ENTRY#
Henry Furtera	New Haven	CT	G	762 200-7318	2160
Meriden Fire Marshals Office	Meriden	CT	F	203 630-4010	1674
Mhq Inc	Middletown	CT	F	888 242-1118	1763
Old Gate Automotive LLC	Milford	CT	G	203 878-7688	1858
Oshkosh Corporation	East Granby	CT	F	860 653-5548	946
Universal Body and Eqp Co LLC	Oakville	CT	F	860 274-7541	2628
Allegiance Fire & Rescue LLC	Walpole	MA	F	800 225-4808	12550
Bayonet Ocean Vehicles Inc	Plymouth	MA	F	802 434-6033	11450
Cabot Coach Builders Inc (PA)	Haverhill	MA	E	978 374-4530	9083
CPI Essco Inc	Ayer	MA	C	978 568-5100	6179
Greenwood Emrgncy Vehicles LLC (HQ)	Attleboro Falls	MA	D	508 695-7138	6086
Lawton Truck Equipment Inc	Topsfield	MA	F	978 887-0005	12436
Lenco Industries Inc	Pittsfield	MA	D	413 443-7359	11406
Mhq Inc (PA)	Marlborough	MA	D	508 573-2600	10184
Prfrred Lancaster Partners LLC	Boston	MA	F	717 299-0782	6980
Textron Systems Corporation	Wilmington	MA	E	978 657-5111	13465
Wgi Inc	Southwick	MA	C	413 569-9444	12051
Douglas Dynamics LLC	Rockland	ME	F	207 701-4200	5325
Epping Volunteer Fire District	Columbia Falls	ME	G	207 483-2036	4699
Messer Truck Equipment (PA)	Westbrook	ME	E	207 854-9751	5638
Sugarloaf Ambulance and Rescue 4680	Carrabassett Valley	ME	F	207 235-2222	
Costello/April Design Inc	Dover	NH	E	603 749-6755	14224
Larry Dingee	Cornish	NH	G	603 542-9682	14183
Patsys Bus Sales and Service	Concord	NH	F	603 226-2222	14151
Swnh Fire Mutual Aid Radio	Keene	NH	G	603 352-8635	14625
Valley Transportation Inc (PA)	Bradford	NH	G	603 938-2271	14018
Dejana Trck Utility Eqp Co LLC	Smithfield	RI	D	401 231-9797	16695
North Atlantic Dist Inc	North Kingstown	RI	B	401 667-7000	16274
Lance Smith Inc	Milton	VT	D	802 655-3354	17361
Town of Hartford 17710	White River Junction	VT	E	802 295-9425	

3713 Truck and bus bodies

	CITY	ST	EMP	PHONE	ENTRY#
Rj 15 Inc	Bristol	CT	F	860 585-0111	493
Robert-Kenneth Andrade LLC	West Haven	CT	G	203 937-8697	4121
Universal Body and Eqp Co LLC	Oakville	CT	F	860 274-7541	2628
Bart Truck Equipment LLC	West Springfield	MA	G	413 737-2766	13017

	CITY	ST	EMP	PHONE	ENTRY#
Boston Trailer Manufacturing	Walpole	MA	F	508 668-2242	12553
Bostonian Body Inc	Everett	MA	F	617 944-0985	8483
Commonwlth Vntr Fnding Group I (PA)	Waltham	MA	G	781 684-0095	12636
Consolidated Truck & Eqp Inc	Seekonk	MA	G	508 252-3330	11775
Curtis Industries LLC (PA)	West Boylston	MA	F	508 853-2200	12958
Dattco Sales & Service	Saugus	MA	E	860 229-4878	11756
DC Bates Equipment Co Inc	Hopedale	MA	E	508 473-0041	9296
James A Kiley Company	Somerville	MA	E	617 776-0344	11882
L W Tank Repair Incorporated	Uxbridge	MA	E	508 234-6000	12483
Middlesex Truck & Auto Body	Boston	MA	E	617 442-3000	6887
Moroney Bodyworks Inc	Worcester	MA	F	508 792-2878	13762
New England Wheels Inc (PA)	Billerica	MA	E	978 663-9724	6462
Tom Berkowitz Trucking Inc (PA)	Whitinsville	MA	E	508 234-2920	13346
Hcb Holdings Inc (PA)	South Portland	ME	E	207 767-2136	5505
Messer Truck Equipment (PA)	Westbrook	ME	E	207 854-9751	5638
Shyft Group Inc	Waterville	ME	C	207 692-7178	5596
Vld Inc	Bangor	ME	G	207 947-6148	4519
Custom Truck One Source LP	Hooksett	NH	E	574 370-2740	14464
Donovan Equipment Company Inc	Londonderry	NH	D	603 669-2250	14743
Gpi Nh-T Inc	Manchester	NH	D	603 624-1800	14854
Larry Dingee	Cornish	NH	G	603 542-9682	14183
Nashua Fabrication Co Inc	Hudson	NH	E	603 889-2181	14531
Vanguard Manufacturing Inc	New Ipswich	NH	D	603 878-2083	15200
Dejana Trck Utility Eqp Co LLC	Smithfield	RI	D	401 231-9797	16695
Utility Systems Inc	Johnston	RI	E	401 351-6681	16110
Iroquois Manufacturing Company	Hinesburg	VT	E	802 482-2155	17295

3714 Motor vehicle parts and accessories

	CITY	ST	EMP	PHONE	ENTRY#
Aerospace Techniques Inc	Middletown	CT	D	860 347-1200	1733
Airpot Corporation	Norwalk	CT	E	800 848-7681	2459
Alinabal Inc (HQ)	Milford	CT	C	203 877-3241	1796
Alinabal Holdings Corporation (PA)	Milford	CT	B	203 877-3241	1797
Beacon Group Inc (PA)	Newington	CT	E	860 594-5200	2275
Callaway Cars Inc	Old Lyme	CT	F	860 434-9002	2636
Callaway Companies Inc (PA)	Old Lyme	CT	F	860 434-9002	2637
Cambridge Specialty Co Inc	Berlin	CT	D	860 828-3579	57
Cheshire Manufacturing Co Inc	Cheshire	CT	G	203 272-3586	580
Competition Engineering Inc	Guilford	CT	D	203 453-5200	1389
Continental Machine TI Co Inc	New Britain	CT	D	860 223-2896	2014
CT Driveshaft Service LLC	East Hartford	CT	G	860 289-6459	984
Danbury A LLC	Danbury	CT	E	203 744-5202	724
Defeo Manufacturing Inc	Brookfield	CT	E	203 775-0254	517
Energizer Auto Sales Inc	Danbury	CT	E	203 205-2900	736
Express Lube & Tire LLC	Windsor	CT	G	860 690-3066	4274
Expressway Lube Centers	Danbury	CT	F	203 744-2511	743
Genuine Parts Company	Windsor Locks	CT	G	860 623-4479	4325
Inertia Dynamics Inc	New Hartford	CT	E	860 379-1252	2103
International Auto Entps Inc	New Britain	CT	F	860 223-7979	2033
International Auto Entps Inc (PA)	New Britain	CT	F	860 224-0253	2034
Jobin Machine Inc	West Hartford	CT	E	860 953-1631	4065
Johnson Controls Inc	Meriden	CT	F	678 297-4040	1670
Kongsberg Acttion Systems II L (PA)	Suffield	CT	D	860 668-1285	3592
Lac Landscaping LLC	Milford	CT	E	203 807-1067	1843
Lee Company (PA)	Westbrook	CT	A	860 399-6281	4140
Lewmar (DH)	Guilford	CT	E	203 458-6200	1399
Littlejohn Partners IV LP	Greenwich	CT	A	203 552-3500	1338
Lydall Inc (HQ)	Manchester	CT	E	860 646-1233	1614
Moroso Performance Pdts Inc (PA)	Guilford	CT	C	203 453-6571	1401
Nickson Industries Inc	Plainville	CT	E	860 747-1671	2774
Nucap US Inc (DH)	Wolcott	CT	E	203 879-1423	4371
Park Avenue Securities	Farmington	CT	E	860 677-2600	1240
Phillips Fuel Systems Inc	Stratford	CT	F	203 908-3323	3567
Platt-Labonia of N Haven Inc	North Haven	CT	D	203 239-5681	2431
Pratt & Whitney Eng Svcs Inc	Middletown	CT	B	860 344-4000	1773
Proliance International Inc	Windsor	CT	G	860 688-7644	4297
Tek-Motive Inc	Branford	CT	F	203 468-2224	281
Thule Inc (DH)	Seymour	CT	C	203 881-9600	2971
Thule Holding Inc (DH)	Seymour	CT	C	203 881-9600	2972
Tru-Hitch Inc	Pleasant Valley	CT	F	860 379-7772	2805
Turbine Technologies Inc (PA)	Farmington	CT	D	860 678-1642	1257
Unitec	Danbury	CT	G	203 778-0400	830
Vulcan Industries Inc	Windsor	CT	C	860 683-2005	4313
Westfalia Inc	Bristol	CT	E	860 314-2920	505
AAm Inc	Weston	MA	F	781 330-9857	13284
Aptiv Services Us LLC	Boston	MA	D	781 864-9230	6553
Armatron International Inc (PA)	Medford	MA	F	781 321-2300	10280
Blendco Systems LLC	Holyoke	MA	D	800 537-7797	9244
Borgwarner Inc	Northborough	MA	E	508 281-5500	11091
Borgwarner Massachusetts Inc (HQ)	Northborough	MA	E	508 281-5500	11092
Boston Steel & Mfg Co	Haverhill	MA	E	781 324-3000	9080
Car Gold Inc	Holyoke	MA	E	800 537-7797	9246
Clearmotion Inc (PA)	Billerica	MA	G	617 313-0822	6423
Currex LLC	Newton	MA	G	206 883-0209	10751

	CITY	ST	EMP	PHONE	ENTRY#
Curtis Industries LLC **(PA)**	West Boylston	MA	F	508 853-2200	12958
Daves Truck Repair Inc	Springfield	MA	E	413 734-8898	12089
Davico Inc	New Bedford	MA	F	508 998-1150	10584
Dynex/Rivett Inc	Ashland	MA	G	508 881-5110	5957
Fabreeka International Inc **(DH)**	Stoughton	MA	G	781 341-3655	12206
Fabreeka Intl Holdings Inc **(DH)**	Stoughton	MA	G	781 341-3655	12207
Factory Five Racing Inc	Wareham	MA	E	508 291-3443	12836
General Electric Company	Lynn	MA	A	781 594-2218	9975
Geoorbital Inc	Somerville	MA	F	617 651-1102	11877
Gtb Innovative Solutions Inc	Westfield	MA	F	413 733-0146	13168
H&H Propeller Shop Inc **(PA)**	Salem	MA	E	978 744-3806	11721
Haufe Group	Stoneham	MA	G	781 376-3737	12179
Helvetia LLC	Holden	MA	F	508 829-7607	9190
Hi-Tech Inc	Attleboro	MA	F	401 454-4086	6023
High Voltage Engineering Corp	Wakefield	MA	E	781 224-1001	12511
Hutchinson Arospc & Indust Inc **(DH)**	Hopkinton	MA	B	508 417-7000	9330
Insco Corporation	Groton	MA	F	978 448-6368	9010
Joseph Palmer Inc	Woburn	MA	F	781 376-0130	13595
Kirby Corporation	Springfield	MA	G	413 363-0005	12110
Lfr Chassis Inc	Shrewsbury	MA	F	508 425-3117	11837
Magmotor Technologies Inc	Worcester	MA	F	508 835-4305	13756
Newera Services Corporation **(PA)**	New Bedford	MA	E	508 995-9711	10631
North Shore Laboratories Corp	Peabody	MA	F	978 531-5954	11327
OMV	Attleboro	MA	G	508 243-6236	6045
Ryca Inc	Tewksbury	MA	F	978 851-3265	12415
Shaft Current Solutions Inc	Florence	MA	G	413 267-0590	8686
Textron Systems Corporation	Wilmington	MA	E	978 657-5111	13405
Trucbrush Corporation	South Easton	MA	F	877 783-0237	11954
V Power Equipment LLC	Wareham	MA	F	508 273-7596	12847
Xl Hybrids Inc **(HQ)**	Brighton	MA	E	617 718-0329	7247
Xxpress Auto Repair Shop LLC	Hyde Park	MA	F	800 591-2068	9468
Yokohama Tws North America Inc	Wakefield	MA	G	781 914-3410	12544
ZF Active Safety & Elec US LLC	Westminster	MA	D	978 874-0151	13283
ZF Chassis Components LLC	Boston	MA	F	859 334-3834	7139
Angstrom Fiber Auburn LLC	Auburn	ME	G	734 756-1164	4420
Coastal Metal Fab	Topsham	ME	E	207 729-5101	5547
Crescent Industries Company	Auburn	ME	G	207 777-3500	4425
Electrnic Mobility Contrls LLC	Augusta	ME	F	207 512-8009	4471
Marketing Worldwide Corp **(PA)**	Rockland	ME	G	631 444-8090	5339
Ms Ambrogio North America LLC	Auburn	ME	E	832 834-3641	4447
Nichols Portland LLC **(PA)**	Portland	ME	B	207 774-6121	5251
Somic America Inc	Brewer	ME	D	207 989-1759	4619
Allard Nazarian Group Inc	Manchester	NH	F	603 314-0017	14809
Down To Fab LLC	Canaan	NH	G	603 728-8299	14045
Eco Touch Inc	Somersworth	NH	C	603 319-1762	15616
Freudenberg-Nok General Partnr	Northfield	NH	C	603 286-1600	15265
Freudenberg-Nok General Partnr	Northfield	NH	D	603 286-1600	15266
General Electric Company	Hooksett	NH	A	603 666-8300	14465
Granite Shore Power LLC	Bow	NH	C	603 634-2299	13999
Jenesco Inc	Lyndeborough	NH	F	603 673-4830	14800
Kautex Inc	Dover	NH	B	603 743-2431	14232
Larry Dingee	Cornish	NH	G	603 542-9682	14183
Moveras LLC	Salem	NH	F	877 866-8372	15546
Osram Sylvania Inc	Hillsborough	NH	B	603 464-7235	14442
Sanner	Nashua	NH	G	603 577-9087	15163
Vibracoustic Usa Inc	Londonderry	NH	F	603 413-7262	14790
Kennedy Incorporated	North Kingstown	RI	F	401 295-7800	16265
M & T Manufacturing	Wakefield	RI	G	401 789-0472	16742
Rhode Island Wiring Svc Inc	West Kingston	RI	G	401 789-1955	16896
Vensys Energy Inc	Warwick	RI	F	401 295-0006	16870
General Electric Company	Rutland	VT	A	802 775-9842	17497
JBM Sherman Carmel Inc	Bennington	VT	E	802 442-5115	17042
NSK Steering Systems Amer Inc	Bennington	VT	B	802 442-5448	17054
Sonnax Industries Inc	Bellows Falls	VT	G	802 463-0240	17031
Sonnax Transmission Company **(DH)**	Bellows Falls	VT	D	802 463-9722	17032
T M Services Inc	Rutland	VT	F	802 775-2948	17511

3715 Truck trailers

Boston Trailer Manufacturing	Walpole	MA	F	508 668-2242	12553
Daves Truck Repair Inc	Springfield	MA	E	413 734-8898	12089
Jason Trucks Inc	Medford	MA	F	781 396-8300	10292
Lins Propane Trucks Corp	Dighton	MA	F	508 669-6665	8293
Martel Welding & Sons Inc	Tewksbury	MA	F	978 458-0661	12406
Motor Service Inc	Shrewsbury	MA	F	508 832-6291	11839
U-Haul Co Mass & Ohio Inc **(DH)**	Somerville	MA	E	617 625-2789	11908
Alcom LLC **(PA)**	Winslow	ME	F	207 861-9800	5680
Innovative Specialties LLC	Pittsfield	ME	F	207 948-1500	5160
On The Road Inc	Warren	ME	F	207 273-3780	5585
Pelletier Manufacturing Inc	Millinocket	ME	F	207 723-6500	5068
Reed Truck Services Inc	Claremont	NH	F	603 542-5032	14097

3716 Motor homes

National Van Sales Inc	Attleboro	MA	F	508 222-2272	6040

3721 Aircraft

	CITY	ST	EMP	PHONE	ENTRY#
Aircastle Advisor LLC	Stamford	CT	D	203 504-1020	3276
Amco Precision Tools Inc **(PA)**	Berlin	CT	E	860 828-5640	49
Aquiline Drones Corporation	Hartford	CT	E	973 980-6596	1471
B & F Design Incorporated	New Britain	CT	E	860 357-4317	2005
Cs Group - Usa Inc	East Hartford	CT	E	860 944-0041	983
Cyient Defense Services Inc	New Britain	CT	E	860 357-4317	2019
Embraer Executive Jet Svcs LLC	Windsor Locks	CT	G	860 804-4600	4324
GKN Aerospace Newington LLC	Newington	CT	F	860 830-5810	2296
Gulfstream Aerospace Corp	East Granby	CT	F	912 965-3000	935
Hanwha Aerospace USA LLC	Glastonbury	CT	D	860 633-9474	1284
Hartford Jet Center LLC	Hartford	CT	F	860 548-9334	1487
Kaman Aerospace Corporation **(DH)**	Bloomfield	CT	A	860 242-4461	179
Kaman Aerospace Corporation	Bloomfield	CT	E	860 242-4461	180
Kaman Aerospace Corporation	Bloomfield	CT	G	860 242-4461	181
Kaman Aerospace Group Inc **(HQ)**	Bloomfield	CT	F	860 243-7100	182
Kaman Corporation **(PA)**	Bloomfield	CT	D	860 243-7100	183
Learjet Inc	Windsor Locks	CT	C	860 627-9491	4331
MB Aerospace	East Granby	CT	E	860 653-0569	941
New England Airfoil Pdts Inc	Farmington	CT	F	860 677-1376	1231
Schweizer Aircraft Corp	Stratford	CT	B	203 386-4356	3570
Sikorsky Aircraft Corporation	Bridgeport	CT	D	203 384-7532	372
Sikorsky Aircraft Corporation	Shelton	CT	F	203 386-7861	3062
Sikorsky Aircraft Corporation	Shelton	CT	E	203 386-4000	3063
Sikorsky Aircraft Corporation **(HQ)**	Stratford	CT	A	203 386-4000	3571
Sikorsky Export Corporation	Stratford	CT	D	203 386-4000	3574
Straton Industries Inc	Stratford	CT	D	203 375-4488	3578
Aerovironment Inc	Burlington	MA	E	805 520-8350	7333
American Robotics Inc	Marlborough	MA	E	617 862-2101	10108
Ascent Aerosystems Inc	Wilmington	MA	E	330 554-6334	13381
Bombardier Services Corp	Boston	MA	C	617 464-0323	6600
Echelon Industries Corporation	Westfield	MA	E	413 562-6659	13163
General Dynamics Aviation Svcs	Westfield	MA	D	413 562-5860	13166
Greensight Inc	Charlestown	MA	E	617 633-4919	7875
Gulfstream Aerospace Corp	Westfield	MA	C	413 562-5866	13169
Liquiglide Inc	Cambridge	MA	E	617 901-0700	7633
Lockheed Martin Corporation	Andover	MA	E	407 356-2374	5891
Lockheed Mrtin Advnced Enrgy S	Waltham	MA	G	972 603-7611	12710
Northeast Seat Company Inc	Palmer	MA	G	413 283-6236	11278
Ondas Holdings Inc	Marlborough	MA	E	617 862-2101	10191
Raytheon Sutheast Asia Systems **(DH)**	Waltham	MA	E	978 470-5000	12762
Spike Aerospace Inc	Boston	MA	F	617 338-1400	7052
Terrafugia Inc	Woburn	MA	F	781 491-0812	13678
Thermo Fisher Scientific Inc	Franklin	MA	C	713 272-0404	8869
Transcend Air Corporation	Carlisle	MA	G	781 883-4818	7848
Lockheed Martin	Wayne	ME	F	603 966-6031	5597
Sonic Blue Aerospace Inc	Portland	ME	G	207 776-2471	5275
CHI Aerospace	Portsmouth	NH	F	603 380-9951	15372
John E Boeing Company Inc	Nashua	NH	F	603 897-8000	15118
Marmon Aerospace & Defense LLC	Manchester	NH	G	603 622-3500	14879
Uav - America Inc	Nottingham	NH	G	603 389-6364	15279
Bell Helicopter Miami Inc	Providence	RI	G	401 421-2800	16485
Bell Textron Rhode Island Inc	Providence	RI	E	401 421-2800	16486
Textron Aviation RI Inc	Providence	RI	F	401 421-2800	16621
Textron Fluid and Power Inc	Providence	RI	F	401 588-3400	16622
Textron Inc **(PA)**	Providence	RI	A	401 421-2800	16623
Textron Inc	Warwick	RI	F	401 457-2310	16868
Beta Technologies Inc	South Burlington	VT	E	802 281-3623	17572
BF Goodrich Aerspce Aircrft In	Vergennes	VT	G	802 877-2911	17656
Lockheed Martin Corporation	South Burlington	VT	F	802 503-8699	17584

3724 Aircraft engines and engine parts

A-1 Machining Co LLC	New Britain	CT	D	860 223-6420	1994
Accupaulo Holding Corporation **(PA)**	Bristol	CT	E	860 666-5621	391
Acmt Inc	Manchester	CT	E	860 645-0592	1582
Aerospace Techniques Inc	Middletown	CT	D	860 347-1200	1733
AGC Acquisition LLC	Meriden	CT	C	203 639-7125	1653
Agreda Industries LLC	South Windsor	CT	E	860 436-5551	3110
Air Transport Intl Inc	Windsor Locks	CT	G	937 287-8455	4322
Alloy Specialties LLC	Manchester	CT	E	860 646-4587	1585
American Design & Mfg Inc	South Windsor	CT	E	860 282-2719	3112
ATI Ladish Machining Inc **(DH)**	East Hartford	CT	E	860 688-3688	973
ATI Ladish Machining Inc	East Hartford	CT	E	860 688-3688	974
ATI Ladish Machining Inc	South Windsor	CT	D	860 688-3688	3116
Barnes Group Inc	Bristol	CT	C	513 759-3503	405
Barnes Group Inc **(PA)**	Bristol	CT	C	860 583-7070	406
Beacon Group Inc **(PA)**	Newington	CT	E	860 594-5200	2275
Budney Industries Inc	Berlin	CT	C	860 828-1950	55
Cambridge Specialty Co Inc	Berlin	CT	D	860 828-3579	57
CBS Manufacturing Company	East Granby	CT	E	860 653-8100	927
Chromalloy Component Svcs Inc	Windsor	CT	E	860 688-7798	4266
Chromalloy Gas Turbine LLC	Windsor	CT	D	860 688-7798	4267

	CITY	ST	EMP	PHONE	ENTRY#
Columbia Manufacturing Inc	Columbia	CT	D	860 228-2259	669
Deburring House Inc	East Berlin	CT	E	860 828-0889	909
Drt Aerospace LLC	Meriden	CT	E	203 781-8020	1664
Electro-Methods Inc	South Windsor	CT	B	860 289-8661	3140
Electro-Methods Inc (PA)	South Windsor	CT	C	860 289-8661	3141
Engine Alliance LLC	Glastonbury	CT	B	860 565-2239	1277
Enjet Aero Bloomfield LLC	Bloomfield	CT	C	860 242-2211	162
Enjet Aero Manchester LLC	Manchester	CT	F	913 717-7396	1597
First Equity Group Inc (PA)	Westport	CT	F	203 291-7700	4168
General Electric Company	Stamford	CT	F	866 419-4096	3354
GKN Aerospace Newington LLC (DH)	Newington	CT	C	860 667-8502	2297
GKN Arspace Svcs Strctures LLC	Cromwell	CT	C	860 613-0236	693
GKN Arspace Svcs Strctures LLC	Wallingford	CT	B	203 303-1408	3809
Global Trbine Cmpnent Tech LLC	South Windsor	CT	E	860 528-4722	3151
Hanwha Aerospace USA LLC (DH)	Cheshire	CT	C	203 806-2090	597
Hanwha Aerospace USA LLC	East Windsor	CT	E	860 789-2500	1074
Hanwha Aerospace USA LLC	East Windsor	CT	D	860 789-2511	1075
Hanwha Aerospace USA LLC	Farmington	CT	D	860 677-2603	1221
Honeywell International Inc	Northford	CT	E	203 484-7161	2453
Honeywell International Inc	Northford	CT	B	203 484-7161	2454
Horst Engineering & Manufacturing Co (PA) 860 289-8209	East Hartford	CT	D		997
Hsb Aircraft Components LLC	New Britain	CT	F	860 505-7349	2030
I & J Machine Tool Company	Milford	CT	F	203 877-5376	1836
Iae International Aero Engs AG	East Hartford	CT	C	860 565-1773	1000
International Aero Engines LLC	East Hartford	CT	F	860 565-5515	1002
Kaman Aerospace Corporation	Bloomfield	CT	G	860 242-4461	181
Kaman Aerospace Group Inc (HQ)	Bloomfield	CT	F	860 243-7100	182
Kamatics Corporation (DH)	Bloomfield	CT	E	860 243-9704	184
Leading Edge Aero LLC	Bethel	CT	D	203 797-1200	125
Lewis Machine LLC	East Hartford	CT	E	860 289-3468	1003
Lighthouse International LLC	South Windsor	CT	F	860 528-4722	3161
MB Aerospace East Granby Limited Partnership 860 653-5041	East Granby	CT	C		942
MB Aerspace Acp Hldngs III Cor (PA)	East Granby	CT	E	586 772-2500	943
Meadow Manufacturing Inc	Bristol	CT	F	860 357-3785	467
Micro Farmington Sub LLC	New Britain	CT	D	860 677-2646	2045
Msj Investments Inc	Stafford Springs	CT	F	860 684-9956	3257
New England Airfoil Pdts Inc	Farmington	CT	E	860 677-1376	1231
Numet Machining Techniques LLC	Orange	CT	E	203 375-4995	2679
Palmer Manufacturing Co LLC	East Berlin	CT	F	860 828-0344	914
Pcx Aerosystems-Manchester LLC	Manchester	CT	C	860 649-0000	1630
Pdq Inc (PA)	Rocky Hill	CT	E	860 529-9051	2932
Point Machine Company	Berlin	CT	G	860 828-6901	78
Polar Corp	New Britain	CT	G	860 225-6000	2053
Polar Corporation	New Britain	CT	E	860 223-7891	2054
Pratt & Whitney Cenco Inc	East Hartford	CT	F	860 565-4321	1013
Pratt & Whitney Company Inc	East Hartford	CT	A	860 565-4321	1014
Pratt & Whitney Eng Svcs Inc	Cheshire	CT	B	203 250-4000	611
Pratt & Whitney Eng Svcs Inc	East Hartford	CT	E	860 565-4321	1015
Pratt & Whitney Eng Svcs Inc	East Hartford	CT	E	860 610-7478	1016
Pratt & Whitney Eng Svcs Inc	Middletown	CT	B	860 344-4000	1773
Pratt & Whitney Engine Lsg LLC	Hartford	CT	D	860 565-4321	1500
Pratt & Whitney Services Inc	East Hartford	CT	D	860 565-5489	1017
Precision Speed Mfg LLC	Middletown	CT	E	860 635-8811	1774
Purdy Corporation	Manchester	CT	C	860 649-0000	1631
Rockville Technology LLC	Vernon	CT	E	860 871-6883	3756
Rtx Corporation	East Hartford	CT	A	860 610-7000	1020
Rtx Corporation	Farmington	CT	C	860 678-4500	1245
Rtx Corporation	Windsor Locks	CT	D	860 654-7519	4333
SA Manchester LLC	Manchester	CT	D	860 533-7500	1634
Saar Corporation	Farmington	CT	F	860 674-9440	1246
Scap Motors Inc	Fairfield	CT	F	203 384-0005	1200
Sikorsky Aircraft Corporation	Stratford	CT	E	203 386-4000	3572
Simmonds Precision Pdts Inc	Danbury	CT	F	203 797-5000	818
Soto Holdings Inc	New Haven	CT	E	203 781-8020	2202
Specialty Tool Company USA LLC	Milford	CT	E	203 874-2009	1888
Triumph Eng Ctrl Systems LLC (HQ)	West Hartford	CT	D	860 236-0651	4087
Tru-Precision Corporation	Farmington	CT	G	860 269-6230	1252
Turbine Components Inc	Oxford	CT	E	858 678-8568	2713
Turbine Kinetics Inc	Glastonbury	CT	F	860 633-8520	1300
Turbine Technologies Inc (PA)	Farmington	CT	D	860 678-1642	1257
United Gear and Machine Co Inc	Suffield	CT	F	860 623-6618	3596
United Tool & Die Company (PA)	West Hartford	CT	C	860 246-6531	4088
Whitney Pratt	Willington	CT	G	860 565-6431	4227
Winslow Automatics Inc	New Britain	CT	D	860 225-6321	2075
325 Silver Street Inc	Agawam	MA	E	413 789-1800	5776
Actronics Incorporated	Waltham	MA	F	781 890-7030	12583
Aero Turbine Components Inc	Worcester	MA	F	508 755-2121	13698
Aerobond Composites LLC	Springfield	MA	E	413 734-2224	12071
Ametek Arospc Pwr Holdings Inc (HQ)	Wilmington	MA	D	978 988-4771	13378
De-Ice Technologies Inc	Somerville	MA	F	857 829-7651	11868
Fountain Plating Company LLC	West Springfield	MA	D	413 781-4651	13025
General Electric Company (PA)	Boston	MA	A	617 443-3000	6754
General Electric Company	Lynn	MA	A	781 594-0100	9974
General Electric Company	Lynn	MA	A	781 594-2218	9975
Goodrich Corporation	Westford	MA	A	978 303-6700	13239
Honeywell International Inc	Canton	MA	G	781 298-2700	7798
Honeywell International Inc	Southborough	MA	A	508 490-7100	11997
Hutchinson Arospc & Indust Inc (DH)	Hopkinton	MA	B	508 417-7000	9330
Jet Industries Inc	Agawam	MA	E	413 786-2010	5798
LKM Industries Inc	Woburn	MA	F	781 935-9210	13602
Magellan Aerospace Usa Inc (DH)	Haverhill	MA	F	978 774-6000	9112
Magellan Arospc Haverhill Inc	Haverhill	MA	C	978 774-6000	9113
Materials Development Corp	Andover	MA	D	781 391-0400	5893
MB Westfield Inc	Westfield	MA	C	413 568-8676	13182
Palmer Manufacturing Co Llc (DH)	Malden	MA	C	781 321-0480	10021
Palmer Manufacturing Co LLC	Peabody	MA	F	781 321-0480	11330
Paradigm Prcision Holdings LLC	Peabody	MA	C	978 278-7100	11331
Parker-Hannifin Corporation	Devens	MA	C	978 784-1200	8285
Si-Rel Inc	Chelmsford	MA	G	978 455-8737	7956
Tell Tool Inc	Westfield	MA	D	413 568-1671	13210
Tell Tool Acquisition Inc (DH)	Westfield	MA	E	413 568-1671	13211
Traincroft Inc (PA)	Medford	MA	E	781 393-6943	10299
Union Machine Company Lynn Inc (PA)	Groveland	MA	E	978 521-5100	9016
Wgi Inc	Southwick	MA	C	413 569-9444	12051
Pratt & Whitney Eng Svcs Inc	North Berwick	ME	B	207 676-4100	5112
Tem Inc	Buxton	ME	E	207 929-8700	4665
General Electric Company	Hooksett	NH	A	603 666-8300	14465
GKN Aerospace New England Inc	Charlestown	NH	D	603 542-5135	14063
Ingersoll-Rand Energy Systems Corporation 603 430-7000	Portsmouth	NH	D		15408
Pratt & Whitney	Londonderry	NH	F	800 742-5877	14779
Avco Corporation (DH)	Providence	RI	C	401 421-2800	16480
Honeywell International Inc	Smithfield	RI	F	401 757-2560	16712
Textron Inc (PA)	Providence	RI	A	401 421-2800	16623
Textron Lycoming Corp (HQ)	Providence	RI	A	401 421-2800	16624
General Electric Company	Rutland	VT	A	802 775-9842	17497
Honeywell International Inc	Williston	VT	G	877 841-2840	17735
Pratt & Whitney Eng Svcs Inc	South Burlington	VT	E	802 658-2208	17596
Simmonds Precision Products (DH)	Vergennes	VT	A	802 877-4000	17661
Superior Tchncal Ceramics Corp (HQ)	Saint Albans	VT	C	802 527-7726	17533

3728 Aircraft parts and equipment, nec

	CITY	ST	EMP	PHONE	ENTRY#
A G C Incorporated	Meriden	CT	C	203 235-3361	1649
A-1 Machining Co LLC	New Britain	CT	D	860 223-6420	1994
AAR Government Services Inc	Windsor	CT	F	860 298-0144	4250
Acmt Inc	Manchester	CT	D	860 645-0592	1582
Admill Machine Co LLC	New Britain	CT	C	860 356-0330	1998
Aero Gear Incorporated	Windsor	CT	C	860 688-0888	4255
Aero Tube Technologies LLC	South Windsor	CT	E	860 289-2520	3107
Aerocision LLC	Chester	CT	D	860 526-9700	622
Aerocomposites Inc	Kensington	CT	F	860 829-6809	1537
Aerospace Techniques Inc	Middletown	CT	D	860 347-1200	1733
Agreda Industries LLC	South Windsor	CT	E	860 436-5551	3110
Air-Lock Incorporated	Milford	CT	E	203 878-4691	1794
Airborne Industries Inc	Branford	CT	F	203 315-0200	232
Alinabal Inc (HQ)	Milford	CT	C	203 877-3241	1796
Alken Industries Inc	Newington	CT	E	631 467-2000	2269
Arrow Diversified Tooling Inc	Ellington	CT	E	860 872-9072	1101
Athens Industries Inc	Plantsville	CT	G	860 621-8957	2789
B/E Aerospace Inc	Farmington	CT	D	410 266-2048	1207
B&N Aerospace Inc	Newington	CT	E	860 665-0134	2274
Barnes Group Inc	Windsor	CT	A	860 298-7740	4262
Beacon Industries Inc	Newington	CT	C	860 594-5200	2276
Brandstrom Instruments Inc	Ridgefield	CT	E	203 544-9341	2892
Budney Aerospace Inc	Berlin	CT	D	860 828-0585	54
C V Tool Company Inc (PA)	Southington	CT	E	978 353-7901	3206
Cambridge Specialty Co Inc	Berlin	CT	D	860 828-3579	57
Carey Manufacturing Co Inc	Cromwell	CT	F	860 829-1803	689
CBS Manufacturing Company	East Granby	CT	E	860 653-8100	927
Connecticut Tool & Mfg Co LLC	Plainville	CT	D	860 846-0800	2751
Continental Machine TI Co Inc	New Britain	CT	D	860 223-2896	2014
Crane Manufacturing Co Inc (DH)	Stamford	CT	C	203 363-7300	3325
Doncasters Inc (PA)	Groton	CT	D	860 449-1603	1367
Electro-Methods Inc (PA)	South Windsor	CT	C	860 289-8661	3141
Enjet Aero Bloomfield LLC	Bloomfield	CT	C	860 242-2211	162
Enjet Aero New Britain LLC	New Britain	CT	C	860 356-0330	2026
Flight Support Inc	North Haven	CT	E	203 562-1415	2413
Forrest Machine Inc	Berlin	CT	D	860 563-1796	66
Gelder Aerospace LLC	Shelton	CT	G	203 283-9524	3008
GKN Aerospace Newington LLC (DH)	Newington	CT	C	860 667-8502	2297
Global Trbine Cmpnent Tech LLC	South Windsor	CT	E	860 528-4722	3151
Glyne Manufacturing Co Inc	Stratford	CT	F	203 375-9524	3542
Goodrich Corporation	Danbury	CT	C	704 423-7000	751
Goodrich Corporation	Danbury	CT	B	203 797-5000	752

	CITY	ST	EMP	PHONE	ENTRY#
H & B Tool & Eng Co Inc	South Windsor	CT	E	860 528-9341	3153
Hamilton Standard Space	Windsor Locks	CT	E	860 654-6000	4329
Hamilton Sundstrand Corp **(HQ)**	Windsor Locks	CT	A	619 714-9442	4330
Hanwha Aerospace USA LLC	Glastonbury	CT	D	860 633-9474	1284
Hanwha Aerospace USA LLC	Newington	CT	D	860 667-2134	2298
Hanwha Aerospace USA LLC	Newington	CT	D	860 667-2134	2299
Helicopter Support Inc **(DH)**	Trumbull	CT	B	203 416-4000	3721
Hexcel Corporation **(PA)**	Stamford	CT	E	203 969-0666	3374
Hexcel Pottsville Corporation	Stamford	CT	E	203 969-0666	3375
Horst Engineering & Manufacturing Co **(PA)**	East Hartford	CT			D
860 289-8209	997				
I & J Machine Tool Company	Milford	CT	F	203 877-5376	1836
Ithaco Space Systems Inc	Danbury	CT	E	607 272-7640	760
Jarvis Airfoil Inc	Portland	CT	D	860 342-5000	2820
Jobin Machine Inc	West Hartford	CT	E	860 953-1631	4065
Kaman Acquisition Usa Inc **(HQ)**	Bloomfield	CT	F	860 243-7100	178
Kaman Aerospace Corporation **(DH)**	Bloomfield	CT	A	860 242-4461	179
Kaman Aerospace Corporation	Bloomfield	CT	E	860 242-4461	180
Kaman Aerospace Corporation	Bloomfield	CT	G	860 242-4461	181
Kaman Aerospace Group Inc **(HQ)**	Bloomfield	CT	A	860 243-7100	182
Kaman Corporation **(PA)**	Bloomfield	CT	D	860 243-7100	183
Kamatics Corporation **(DH)**	Bloomfield	CT	E	860 243-9704	184
L M Gill Welding and Mfr LLC	Manchester	CT	D	860 647-9931	1611
Leading Edge Aero LLC	Bethel	CT	E	203 797-1200	125
Leading Edge Concepts Inc	Bethel	CT	G	203 797-1200	126
Lee Company **(PA)**	Westbrook	CT	A	860 399-6281	4140
Liftwing LLC	Shelton	CT	F	203 913-2308	3028
LM Gill Welding & Mfg LLC	Manchester	CT	E	860 647-9931	1613
MB Aerospace East Granby Limited Partnership	East Granby	CT			C
860 653-5041	942				
McMellon Bros Incorporated	Stratford	CT	E	203 375-5685	3555
Metallon Inc	Thomaston	CT	E	860 283-8265	3624
MTM Corporation	Andover	CT	G	860 742-9600	2
Naiad Dynamics Us Inc **(HQ)**	Shelton	CT	E	203 929-6355	3033
Nanni Manufacturing Co Inc	Winsted	CT	E		4350
Nelson Tool & Machine Co Inc	Bristol	CT	G	860 589-8004	474
Overhaul Support Services LLC **(PA)**	East Granby	CT	D	860 264-2101	947
Paradigm Manchester Inc **(DH)**	Manchester	CT	B	772 287-7770	1623
Paragon Tool Company Inc	Manchester	CT	G	860 647-9935	1627
Pas Technologies Inc	Manchester	CT	D	860 649-2727	1629
Pcx Aerostructures LLC **(PA)**	Newington	CT	C	860 666-2471	2315
Pcx Aerosystems-Manchester LLC	Manchester	CT	C	860 649-0000	1630
Perry Technology Corporation	New Hartford	CT	D	860 738-2525	2107
Polamer Precision Inc	New Britain	CT	C	860 259-6200	2052
Polar Corporation	New Britain	CT	E	860 223-7891	2054
Pratt & Whitney Eng Svcs Inc	Middletown	CT	B	860 344-4000	1773
Precision Metals and Plastics	Winsted	CT	G	860 238-4320	4353
Precision Speed Mfg LLC	Middletown	CT	E	860 635-8811	1774
Purdy Corporation	Manchester	CT	C	860 649-0000	1631
Ramar-Hall Inc	Middlefield	CT	E	860 349-1081	1728
Rbc Bearings Incorporated **(PA)**	Oxford	CT	C	203 267-7001	2710
Redco Corporation **(HQ)**	Stamford	CT	D	203 363-7300	3445
Richard Manufacturing Co Inc	Milford	CT	E	203 874-3617	1877
Rotair Aerospace Corporation	Bridgeport	CT	E	203 576-6545	367
Rotating Composite Tech LLC	Kensington	CT	G	860 829-6809	1540
Saf Industries LLC **(HQ)**	Meriden	CT	E	203 729-4900	1696
Sargent Controls and Aerospace	Oxford	CT	G	520 744-1000	2711
Schweizer Aircraft Corp	Stratford	CT	B	203 386-4356	3570
Senior Operations LLC	Enfield	CT	D	860 741-2546	1147
Simmonds Precision Pdts Inc	Danbury	CT	F	203 797-5000	818
Straton Industries Inc	Stratford	CT	E	203 375-4488	3578
Tachwa Enterprises Inc	Hamden	CT	G	203 691-5772	1459
Thompson Aerospace LLC	Bristol	CT	F	860 516-0472	502
TLD America Corporation **(DH)**	Windsor	CT	F	860 602-3400	4309
Toolmax Designing Tooling Inc	Ashford	CT	F	860 477-0373	22
Triumph Acttion Systems - Conn **(HQ)**	Windsor	CT	D	860 687-5412	4310
Triumph Eng Ctrl Systems LLC	West Hartford	CT	B	860 597-7173	4086
Triumph Eng Ctrl Systems LLC **(HQ)**	West Hartford	CT	D	860 236-0651	4087
Triumph Group Inc	Bloomfield	CT	G	860 726-9378	213
United Avionics Inc	Seymour	CT	E	203 723-1404	2974
Valley Tool and Mfg LLC **(HQ)**	Milford	CT	E	203 799-8800	1898
W and G Machine Company Inc	Hamden	CT	F	203 288-3871	1462
Whitcraft LLC **(PA)**	Eastford	CT	C	860 974-0786	1093
Whitcraft Scrborough/Tempe LLC **(HQ)**	Eastford	CT	E	860 974-0786	1094
Whitcraft South Windsor LLC	South Windsor	CT	B	860 436-5551	3191
2is Inc	Walpole	MA	E	508 850-7520	12545
325 Silver Street Inc	Agawam	MA	E	413 789-1800	5776
Actronics Incorporated	Waltham	MA	F	781 890-7030	12583
Aerobond Composites LLC	Springfield	MA	E	413 734-2224	12071
Anderson Airmotive Inc	Fall River	MA	F	508 646-0950	8521
B & E Tool Company Inc	Southwick	MA	D	413 569-5585	12042
Blue Tactical LLC	Westfield	MA	F	413 315-6344	13153
Boniface Tool & Die Inc	Dudley	MA	E	508 764-3248	8317
Collins Aerospace	Westford	MA	E	978 303-6700	13231
Crane Nxt Co **(PA)**	Waltham	MA	C	610 430-2510	12644
De-Ice Technologies Inc	Somerville	MA	F	857 829-7651	11868
Fgc Plasma Solutions Inc	Middleton	MA	E	617 999-9078	10383
GE Aviation Systems LLC	Lynn	MA	E	513 552-3272	9973
Goodrich Corporation	Peabody	MA	E	978 532-2350	11311
Goodrich Corporation	Westford	MA	A	978 303-6700	13239
Goodrich Corporation	Westford	MA	E	978 303-6700	13240
Jet Industries Inc	Agawam	MA	E	413 786-2010	5798
Ltp Corporation **(DH)**	Northborough	MA	D	508 393-7660	11101
Opalala Inc	Fall River	MA	F	508 646-0950	8591
Parker-Hannifin Corporation	Devens	MA	C	978 784-1200	8285
Parts Tool and Die Inc	Agawam	MA	E	413 821-9718	5805
Pcx Aerostructures LLC	Boylston	MA	D	508 869-2131	7163
Raytheon Company	Marlborough	MA	A	508 490-1000	10201
Rockwell Collins	Peabody	MA	F	978 532-2350	11338
Rodney Hunt-Fontaine Inc **(HQ)**	Orange	MA	E	978 544-2511	11232
Roscid Technologies Inc	Woburn	MA	G	781 933-4007	13656
Union Machine Company Lynn Inc **(PA)**	Groveland	MA	E	978 521-5100	9016
Whitcraft Scrborough/Tempe LLC	Newburyport	MA	C	763 780-0060	10727
Wyman-Gordon Company **(DH)**	North Grafton	MA	B	508 839-8252	11030
Clamar Floats Inc	Brunswick	ME	G	603 828-5373	4644
Elmet Technologies LLC **(PA)**	Lewiston	ME	C	207 333-6160	4960
General Dynamics Ots Cal Inc	Saco	ME	C	207 283-3611	5368
B/E Aerospace Inc	Hampton	NH	F	603 926-5700	14399
Bae Systems Info Elctrnic Syst	Merrimack	NH	B	603 885-4321	14975
Brazonics Inc **(DH)**	Hampton	NH	C	603 758-6237	14400
Continental Cable LLC	Hinsdale	NH	D	800 229-5131	14443
Exothermics Inc	Amherst	NH	F	603 821-5660	13869
General Electric Company	Hooksett	NH	A	603 666-8300	14465
Hardric Laboratories Inc	Hudson	NH	E	978 251-1702	14506
Integrated Deicing Svcs LLC **(DH)**	Manchester	NH	B	603 647-1717	14863
Lakes Region Tubular Pdts Inc	Laconia	NH	E	603 528-2838	14657
Lanair Research & Dev Inc	Portsmouth	NH	G	603 433-6134	15415
Matrix Aerospace Corp	Claremont	NH	D	603 542-0191	14093
Meggitt (new Hampshire) Inc	Londonderry	NH	C	603 669-0940	14767
Screw-Matic Corporation	Laconia	NH	E	603 468-1610	14668
Sierra Nevada Corporation	Bedford	NH	E	775 331-0222	13949
Avco Corporation **(DH)**	Providence	RI	C	401 421-2800	16480
Bell Helicopter Korea Inc	Providence	RI	E	401 421-2800	16484
Clear Carbon & Components Inc	Bristol	RI	E	401 254-5085	15758
Magnetic Seal LLC	Warren	RI	D	401 247-2800	16760
Textron Inc **(PA)**	Providence	RI	A	401 421-2800	16623
Textron Lycoming Corp **(HQ)**	Providence	RI	E	401 421-2800	16624
Collins Aerospace	Vergennes	VT	D	802 877-4000	17657
General Dynamics Ots Cal Inc	Williston	VT	B	802 662-7000	17733
Liquid Measurement Systems Inc	Fairfax	VT	E	802 528-8100	17261
Preci-Manufacturing Inc	Winooski	VT	D	802 655-2414	17768
Sathorn Corporation	Williston	VT	E	802 860-2121	17748
Simmonds Precision Pdts Inc	Vergennes	VT	F	802 877-2911	17660
Simmonds Precision Products **(DH)**	Vergennes	VT	A	802 877-4000	17661
Vermont Aerospace Manufacturing Inc	Lyndonville	VT	C	802 748-8705	17321

3731 Shipbuilding and repairing

	CITY	ST	EMP	PHONE	ENTRY#
Electric Boat Corporation	Groton	CT	D	860 433-0503	1369
Electric Boat Corporation **(HQ)**	Groton	CT	B	860 433-3000	1370
Electric Boat Corporation	Groton	CT	A	860 433-3000	1371
Electric Boat Corporation	New London	CT	A	860 433-3000	2227
General Dynamics Corporation	Groton	CT	A	860 433-3000	1372
Globenix Inc	Norwalk	CT	G	203 740-7070	2506
Hornblower Shipyard LLC	Bridgeport	CT	E	203 572-0378	330
LM Gill Welding & Mfg LLC	Manchester	CT	E	860 647-9931	1613
Naiad Dynamics Us Inc **(HQ)**	Shelton	CT	E	203 929-6355	3033
Naiad Maritime Group Inc **(PA)**	Shelton	CT	E	203 944-1932	3034
Thames Shipyard & Repair Co	New London	CT	D	860 442-5349	2234
Boston Ship Repair LLC	Boston	MA	C	617 330-5045	6617
Dive Technologies Inc	Quincy	MA	G	339 236-4599	11511
F L Tripp & Sons Inc	Westport Point	MA	F	508 636-4058	13303
Hydroid LLC	Pocasset	MA	D	508 563-6565	11488
L W Tank Repair Incorporated	Uxbridge	MA	E	508 234-6000	12483
L3 Oceanserver Inc **(DH)**	Fall River	MA	E	508 678-0550	8567
Navtec Rigging Solutions Inc	Groton	MA	E		9011
The Duclos Corporation	Somerset	MA	D	508 676-8596	11857
Bath Iron Works Corporation **(HQ)**	Bath	ME	A	207 443-3311	4525
Bath Iron Works Corporation	Brunswick	ME	E	207 442-1266	4641
Rockland Marine Corporation	Rockland	ME	E	207 594-7860	5341
Virginia Project Inc	Bath	ME	F	207 443-4242	4531
Washburn & Doughty Assoc Inc	East Boothbay	ME	D	207 633-6517	4737
Yankee Marina Inc	Yarmouth	ME	E	207 846-9120	5710
Ksaria Service Corporation	Hudson	NH	E	978 933-0000	14520
United States Dept of Navy	Portsmouth	NH	C	207 438-2714	15446
Aramid Rigging Inc	Portsmouth	RI	G	401 683-6966	16436
Blount Boats Inc	Warren	RI	D	401 245-8300	16754

	CITY	ST	EMP	PHONE	ENTRY#
Electric Boat Corporation	North Kingstown	RI	A	401 268-2410	16250
Fast Forward Composites Inc	Bristol	RI	F	207 350-1773	15764
Iyrs School Tech & Trades	Newport	RI	E	401 846-2587	16212
J Goodison Company **(PA)**	North Kingstown	RI	E	401 667-5938	16261
Promet Marine Service Corp	Providence	RI	E	401 467-3730	16588
Relentless Inc	North Kingstown	RI	F	401 295-2585	16277
Senesco Marine LLC	North Kingstown	RI	B	401 295-0373	16280
Armach Robotics Inc	Richmond	VT	F	802 434-6080	17478
Lake Champlain Trnsp Co	Burlington	VT	D	802 660-3495	17141

3732 Boatbuilding and repairing

	CITY	ST	EMP	PHONE	ENTRY#
B I L Inc	Groton	CT	F	860 446-8058	1365
Casavant Corporation	Burlington	CT	G	860 605-5937	546
Chester Boatworks	Deep River	CT	G	860 526-2227	874
Dodson Boatyard LLC	Stonington	CT	F	860 535-1507	3508
Gregs Outboard Service LLC	Old Saybrook	CT	G	860 339-5139	2649
Seaport Marine Inc	Mystic	CT	G	860 536-9651	1942
Vespoli Usa Inc	New Haven	CT	E	203 773-0311	2215
Allen Harbor Marine Svc Inc	Harwich Port	MA	G	508 432-0353	9070
Bctz Ltd	Lexington	MA	G	781 863-0405	9727
Beetle Inc	Wareham	MA	G	508 295-8585	12829
Best Marine and Outdoors Inc	Boston	MA	G	617 644-7711	6590
Boston Boatworks LLC	Charlestown	MA	E	617 561-9111	7862
Cape Cod Shipbuilding Co	Wareham	MA	F	508 295-3550	12832
Concordia Co Inc	South Dartmouth	MA	E	508 999-1381	11916
Crosby Yacht Yard Inc	Osterville	MA	E	508 428-6900	11245
CW Hood Yachts Inc	Marblehead	MA	G	781 631-0192	10086
Falmouth Mar Yachting Ctr Inc	Falmouth	MA	F	508 548-4600	8631
Hannah Boden Corp	New Bedford	MA	F	508 992-3334	10598
Hawthorne Cove Marina Inc	Salem	MA	G	978 740-9890	11722
Heritage Wharf Company LLC	Dartmouth	MA	G	508 990-1011	8230
Inriver Tank & Boat Inc	Concord	MA	G	978 287-9534	8121
Karls Boat Shop Inc	Harwich	MA	G	508 432-4488	9069
Marine Usa Inc	Worcester	MA	E	508 791-7116	13757
Marshall Marine Corporation	South Dartmouth	MA	F	508 994-0414	11917
Montreal Fishing Corp	New Bedford	MA	G	508 993-0275	10623
Nauset Marine Inc **(PA)**	Orleans	MA	F	508 255-0777	11240
Northern Light Mar Group Inc	Manchester	MA	E	978 526-7911	10033
P B Y A Inc	South Orleans	MA	F	508 255-0994	11973
Ribcraft Usa LLC	Marblehead	MA	E	781 639-9065	10094
Sperry Sails Inc	Marion	MA	G	508 748-2581	10101
The Duclos Corporation	Somerset	MA	D	508 676-8596	11857
Alley Road LLC	Boothbay Harbor	ME	F	207 633-3171	4600
Belmont Boatworks LLC	Belmont	ME	F	207 342-2885	4542
Brooklin Boat Yard Inc **(PA)**	Brooklin	ME	E	207 359-2236	4632
Crossfox Inc	Brooklin	ME	F	207 664-2900	4633
Dana Robes Boat Builders	Round Pond	ME	G	207 529-2433	5352
Dark Harbor Boatyard Corp	Islesboro	ME	F	207 734-2246	4908
Ebw Windup	Edgecomb	ME	G	207 882-5038	4747
Ellis Boat Co Inc	Southwest Harbor	ME	F	207 244-9221	5518
F V Tigger	South Harpswell	ME	G	207 721-0875	5487
Flowers Boat Works Inc	Walpole	ME	G	207 563-7404	5581
French Webb & Co Inc	Belfast	ME	F	207 338-6706	4533
General Marine Inc	Biddeford	ME	G	207 284-7517	4568
Gowen Inc	Portland	ME	F	207 773-1761	5219
Greene Marine Inc	Yarmouth	ME	G	207 846-3184	5705
H & H Marine Inc	Steuben	ME	F	207 546-7477	5532
Hodgdon Shipbuilding LLC	Damariscotta	ME	D	207 563-7033	4715
Hodgdon Yachts Inc **(PA)**	East Boothbay	ME	D	207 737-2802	4736
J O Brown & Son Inc	North Haven	ME	F	207 867-4621	5114
James H Rich Boatyard	Bernard	ME	G	207 244-3208	4548
Johansons Boatworks	Rockland	ME	F	207 596-7060	5335
John M Williams Company	Mount Desert	ME	F	207 244-7854	5077
Johnson Otdoors Watercraft Inc **(HQ)**	Old Town	ME	E	207 827-5513	5126
Lyman Morse Boatbuilding Inc	Camden	ME	D	207 236-4378	4667
Lyman Morse Boatbuilding Inc	Thomaston	ME	F	207 354-6904	5545
Lyman Morse Boatbuilding Inc **(PA)**	Thomaston	ME	C	207 354-6904	5546
Maine Cat	Lincolnville	ME	F	207 529-6500	5015
Mastercraft Inc	Skowhegan	ME	F	207 431-2056	5473
My Ease Inc **(PA)**	Bass Harbor	ME	D	207 667-6235	4524
My Ease Inc	Trenton	ME	F	207 667-8237	5557
North End Composites LLC	Rockland	ME	E	207 594-8427	5340
Padebco Custom Boats	Round Pond	ME	G	207 529-5106	5354
Portland Company	Portland	ME	E	207 774-1067	5257
Puffin Boats LLC	Hampden	ME	F	207 907-4385	4866
Sabra Corporation	Raymond	ME	C	207 655-3831	5315
Sabre Yachts Inc	South Casco	ME	C	207 655-3831	5484
Seaway Boats Inc	Oxford	ME	F	207 539-8116	5150
Shipyard In Boothbay Hbr LLC	Boothbay Harbor	ME	E	207 633-3171	4604
SW Boatworks	Lamoine	ME	F	207 667-7427	4944
Talaria Company LLC	Southwest Harbor	ME	E	207 244-5572	5519
Talaria Company LLC	Trenton	ME	D	207 667-1891	5558
Washburn & Doughty Assoc Inc	East Boothbay	ME	D	207 633-6517	4737

	CITY	ST	EMP	PHONE	ENTRY#
Wesmac Custom Boats Inc	Surry	ME	F	207 667-4822	5540
American Marine Products Inc	Charlestown	NH	F	954 782-1400	14060
Chisletts Boating & Design LLC	Dover	NH	G	603 755-6815	14222
Eastern Boats Inc	Milton	NH	E	603 652-9213	15045
Juliet Marine Systems Inc	Portsmouth	NH	F	603 319-8412	15413
Liberty Cycle LLC	Deering	NH	G	603 620-1851	14188
New England Boat & Motor Inc	Laconia	NH	G	603 527-9435	14660
Pompanette LLC **(PA)**	Charlestown	NH	D	717 569-2300	14067
Special Projects Group LLC	Gilford	NH	G	603 391-9700	14338
Viking Wldg & Fabrication LLC	Kensington	NH	G	603 394-7887	14631
Alden Yachts Corporation	Bristol	RI	E	401 683-4200	15752
Anchorage Inc	Warren	RI	F	401 245-3300	16750
Berthon Usa Inc	Newport	RI	F	401 846-8404	16206
Blount Boats Inc	Warren	RI	D	401 245-8300	16754
C & C Fibrgls Components Inc	Bristol	RI	F	401 254-4342	15757
Clean Away Inc	East Greenwich	RI	F	860 985-6743	15979
Cove Haven Corp	Barrington	RI	F	401 246-1600	15747
Dur A Flex Motor Sports	Warwick	RI	G	401 739-0202	16811
Element Industries Inc	Bristol	RI	F	401 253-8802	15762
Eric Goetz Custom Sailboats	Bristol	RI	E	401 253-2670	15763
Fairhaven Marine Corporation	Riverside	RI	F	401 433-3010	16654
Fulcrum Speedworks LLC	Rumford	RI	F	401 524-3953	16667
Gecko Marine Inc	Bristol	RI	F	401 237-6117	15766
Gunboat	Newport	RI	F	401 619-1055	16211
Hall Inc	Bristol	RI	D	401 253-4858	15768
Hunt Yachts LLC	Portsmouth	RI	F	401 324-4201	16444
Iyrs School Tech & Trades	Newport	RI	E	401 846-2587	16212
Lenmarine Inc **(PA)**	Bristol	RI	E	401 253-2200	15772
Mc Millen Yachts	Portsmouth	RI	F	401 682-2610	16446
Morris Yachts LLC	Portsmouth	RI	G	207 667-2499	15780
Naiad Inflatables Newport Inc	Newport	RI	F		16218
New England Boatworks Inc	Portsmouth	RI	D	401 683-4000	16449
Oldport Marine Services Inc	Newport	RI	F	401 847-9109	16220
Resolute Racing LLC	Bristol	RI	F	401 253-7384	15775
Rhode Northsales Island Inc	Portsmouth	RI	F	401 683-7997	16455
Seamless North America	Bristol	RI	G	401 714-2925	15780
Shannon Boat Company Inc	Bristol	RI	E	401 253-2441	15781
Sparkman & Stephens LLC **(PA)**	Newport	RI	F	401 847-5449	16225
Squirrel Works LLC	Portsmouth	RI	E	401 247-3000	16457
Talaria Company LLC **(PA)**	Portsmouth	RI	F	401 683-7100	16458
Talaria Company LLC	Portsmouth	RI	D	401 683-7280	16459
Darlings Boatworks Inc	Charlotte	VT	G	802 425-2004	17176

3743 Railroad equipment

	CITY	ST	EMP	PHONE	ENTRY#
James L Howard and Company Inc	Bloomfield	CT	E	860 242-3581	176
Transit Systems Inc	Plainville	CT	G	860 747-3669	2785
Winchester Industries Inc	Winsted	CT	G	860 379-5336	4359
Winslow Automatics Inc	New Britain	CT	D	860 225-6321	2075
Crrc MA Corporation	Springfield	MA	C	617 415-7190	12086
Motive Power	Boston	MA	C	857 350-3765	6897
RI Controls LLC	Woburn	MA	D	781 932-3349	13654
Okonite Company Inc	Cumberland	RI	E	401 333-3500	15957

3751 Motorcycles, bicycles, and parts

	CITY	ST	EMP	PHONE	ENTRY#
Cycling Sports Group Inc **(HQ)**	Wilton	CT	D	203 845-8300	4238
Frank Roth Co Inc	Stratford	CT	D	203 377-2155	3539
Kobuta Choppers LLC	North Haven	CT	G	203 234-6047	2421
Madd Gear LLC	Stamford	CT	F	410 800-4423	3406
Independent Fabrication Inc	Somerville	MA	F	617 666-3609	11881
Montague Corporation	Cambridge	MA	F	617 491-7200	7655
Mustang Motorcycle Pdts LLC	Three Rivers	MA	D	413 283-6236	12431
Mystic Valley Wheel Works Inc **(PA)**	Belmont	MA	E	617 489-3577	6308
New Vectrix LLC	Boston	MA	E	858 674-6099	6919
Parlee Composites Inc	Beverly	MA	F	978 998-4880	6371
Superpedestrian Inc **(PA)**	Cambridge	MA	C	877 678-7518	7725
Choppers of New England	Nashua	NH	G	603 809-4391	15079
Moto Tassinari LLC	West Lebanon	NH	F	603 298-6646	15684
Motorway Engineering Inc	Manchester	NH	F	603 668-6315	14893

3761 Guided missiles and space vehicles

	CITY	ST	EMP	PHONE	ENTRY#
Kaman Corporation **(PA)**	Bloomfield	CT	D	860 243-7100	183
Assurance Technology Corp **(PA)**	Carlisle	MA	D	978 369-8848	7845
Raytheon Company **(HQ)**	Waltham	MA	B	781 522-3000	12759
Raytheon Korean Support Co **(DH)**	Waltham	MA	E	339 645-6111	12761
Raytheon Lgstics Spport Trning **(DH)**	Bedford	MA	F	310 647-9438	6256
Blushift Aerospace Inc	Brunswick	ME	F	207 619-1703	4642
Valt Enterprizes Inc	Presque Isle	ME	F	207 560-5188	5311
Raytheon Company	Merrimack	NH	G	978 313-0201	15000
Rogue Space Systems Corp	Laconia	NH	F	603 460-5069	14666

3764 Space propulsion units and parts

	CITY	ST	EMP	PHONE	ENTRY#
United Gear and Machine Co Inc	Suffield	CT	F	860 623-6618	3596
Ae Red Holdings LLC **(PA)**	Marlborough	MA	F	561 372-7820	10105

	CITY	ST	EMP	PHONE	ENTRY#
Busek Co Inc	Natick	MA	E	508 655-5565	10471
Wormtown Atomic Propulsion	Waltham	MA	F	781 487-7777	12819
Blushift Aerospace Inc	Brunswick	ME	F	207 619-1703	4642
Exothermics Inc	Amherst	NH	F	603 821-5660	13869
Mentis Sciences Inc	Warner	NH	E	603 624-9197	15666

3769 Space vehicle equipment, nec

	CITY	ST	EMP	PHONE	ENTRY#
Accupaulo Holding Corporation (PA)	Bristol	CT	E	860 666-5621	391
Braxton Manufacturing Co Inc	Watertown	CT	C	860 274-6781	4003
Hanwha Aerospace USA LLC (DH)	Cheshire	CT	C	203 806-2090	597
Hanwha Aerospace USA LLC	East Windsor	CT	D	860 789-2511	1075
Kaman Aerospace Group Inc (HQ)	Bloomfield	CT	F	860 243-7100	182
Meriden Manufacturing Inc	Meriden	CT	D	203 237-7481	1675
Ramar-Hall Inc	Middlefield	CT	E	860 349-1081	1728
SA Manchester LLC	Manchester	CT	D	860 533-7500	1634
Sterling Engineering Corp	Pleasant Valley	CT	C	860 379-3366	2804
United Tool & Die Company (PA)	West Hartford	CT	E	860 246-6531	4088
325 Silver Street Inc	Agawam	MA	E	413 789-1800	5776
Busek Co Inc	Natick	MA	E	508 655-5565	10471
Entwistle Company LLC (PA)	Hudson	MA	D	508 481-4000	9364
Geonautics Manufacturing Inc	Newburyport	MA	E	978 462-7161	10685
Industrial Precision Inc	Westfield	MA	E	413 562-5161	13172
Raytheon International Inc (PA)	Waltham	MA	F	781 522-3000	12760
Technology Service Corporation	Plymouth	MA	E	508 275-5113	11482
Technology Service Corporation	Plymouth	MA	D	508 275-5113	11483
Tell Tool Inc	Westfield	MA	D	413 568-1671	13210
Tell Tool Acquisition Inc (DH)	Westfield	MA	E	413 568-1671	13211
Wgi Inc	Southwick	MA	C	413 569-9444	12051
Elmet Technologies LLC (PA)	Lewiston	ME	C	207 333-6100	4960
Fiber Materials Inc (DH)	Biddeford	ME	C	207 282-5911	4564
Intermat	Biddeford	ME	E	207 283-1156	4572
Mentis Sciences Inc	Warner	NH	E	603 624-9197	15666
Swissline Products Inc	Cumberland	RI	D	401 333-8888	15966
Superior Tchncal Ceramics Corp (HQ)	Saint Albans	VT	C	802 527-7726	17533

3792 Travel trailers and campers

	CITY	ST	EMP	PHONE	ENTRY#
3333 LLC	Manchester	CT	G	860 643-1384	1579
Thule Holding Inc (DH)	Seymour	CT	E	203 881-9600	2972
Boston Trailer Manufacturing	Walpole	MA	F	508 668-2242	12553
Yankee Custom Inc (PA)	Tewksbury	MA	F	978 851-9024	12426
Perseus Partners LLC	Warren	ME	F	207 273-3780	5586
Port-Lite LLC	Alna	ME	G	678 575-9065	4405
American Keder Inc (PA)	Rindge	NH	G	603 899-3233	15459
New Hmpshire Cntry Campers LLC	Epsom	NH	G	802 223-6417	14280

3795 Tanks and tank components

	CITY	ST	EMP	PHONE	ENTRY#
New England Airfoil Pdts Inc	Farmington	CT	E	860 677-1376	1231
General Dynmics Def Systems In	Pittsfield	MA	C	413 494-1110	11397
L W Tank Repair Incorporated	Uxbridge	MA	E	508 234-6000	12483
Natgun Corporation	Wakefield	MA	F	781 224-5180	12522
New England Stinless Distr LLC	Salisbury	MA	F	978 255-4830	11743
Arundel Holdings Inc	Arundel	ME	D	207 985-8555	4408
Howe & Howe Technologies Inc	Waterboro	ME	F	207 247-2777	5591

3799 Transportation equipment, nec

	CITY	ST	EMP	PHONE	ENTRY#
Danbury Powersports Inc	Danbury	CT	F	203 791-1310	726
Littlejohn Partners IV LP	Greenwich	CT	A	203 552-3500	1338
New Haven Chemicals LLC	New Haven	CT	F	475 241-1150	2177
Beals & Sons Inc	Northborough	MA	G	508 393-1833	11090
Hostar Mar Trnspt Systems Inc	Wareham	MA	F	508 295-2900	12838
Moseley Corporation	Franklin	MA	F	508 520-4004	8853
Places To Go LLC	New Bedford	MA	G	774 202-7756	10639
Steele Canvas Basket Corp	Chelsea	MA	E	800 541-8929	7994
Wright Trailers Inc	Seekonk	MA	F	508 336-8530	11790
Eimskip USA Inc	Portland	ME	F	207 221-5268	5214
Southern Maine Atv Club	North Berwick	ME	G	207 676-1152	5113
Davis Village Solutions LLC	New Ipswich	NH	F	603 878-3662	15197
Rokon International Inc	Rochester	NH	F	603 335-3200	15491
Eagle Motors Inc	Harrisville	RI	F	401 568-2580	16065
Textron Inc (PA)	Providence	RI	A	401 421-2800	16623

38 MEASURING, PHOTOGRAPHIC, MEDICAL, & OPTICAL GOODS, & CLOCKS

3812 Search and navigation equipment

	CITY	ST	EMP	PHONE	ENTRY#
Ais Global Holdings LLC	Cheshire	CT	E	203 250-3500	570
Alpha Q Inc (PA)	Colchester	CT	D	860 537-4681	654
Atlantic Inertial Systems Inc (DH)	Cheshire	CT	B	203 250-3500	572
Atlantic Inertial Systems Inc	Cheshire	CT	C	203 250-3500	573
Beacon Group Inc (PA)	Newington	CT	E	860 594-5200	2275
Brandstrom Instruments Inc	Ridgefield	CT	E	203 544-9341	2892

	CITY	ST	EMP	PHONE	ENTRY#
Chromalloy Component Svcs Inc	Windsor	CT	E	860 688-7798	4266
Connecticut Analytical Corp	Bethany	CT	F	203 393-9666	92
Crane Company (PA)	Stamford	CT	D	203 363-7300	3326
Drs Naval Power Systems Inc	Bethel	CT	B	203 366-5211	108
Drs Naval Power Systems Inc	Danbury	CT	B	203 798-3000	734
Electro-Methods Inc (PA)	South Windsor	CT	C	860 289-8661	3141
Ensign-Bickford Arospc Def Co (HQ)	Simsbury	CT	D	860 843-2289	3089
Ensign-Bickford Company (HQ)	Simsbury	CT	F	860 843-2001	3090
Gems Sensors Inc (HQ)	Plainville	CT	B	860 747-3000	2761
Hanwha Aerospace USA LLC	Glastonbury	CT	D	860 633-9474	1284
Hartford Aircraft Products Inc	Bloomfield	CT	E	860 242-8228	168
ITT Inc (PA)	Stamford	CT	C	914 641-2000	3388
Kaman Corporation	Middletown	CT	E	860 632-1000	1756
Kaman Precision Products Inc	Middletown	CT	C	860 632-1000	1757
Lee Company (PA)	Westbrook	CT	A	860 399-6281	4140
Lewis Machine LLC	East Hartford	CT	E	860 289-3468	1003
Meriden Manufacturing Inc	Meriden	CT	D	203 237-7481	1675
Msj Investments Inc	Stafford Springs	CT	F	860 684-9956	3257
Mtu Aero Engines N Amer Inc	Rocky Hill	CT	C	860 258-9700	2931
Northrop Grumman Corporation	East Hartford	CT	E	860 282-4461	1007
Polar Corporation	New Britain	CT	E	860 223-7891	2054
Saf Industries LLC (HQ)	Meriden	CT	E	203 729-4900	1696
Sensor Switch Inc (DH)	New Haven	CT	E	203 265-2842	2198
Sikorsky Aircraft Corporation	Stratford	CT	E	203 380-3142	3573
Sikorsky Aircraft Corporation	Trumbull	CT	G	203 386-7794	3733
Sperian Prtction Instrmnttion	Middletown	CT	D	860 344-1079	1783
Thayermahan Inc (PA)	Groton	CT	E	860 785-9994	1381
Triumph Eng Ctrl Systems LLC (HQ)	West Hartford	CT	D	860 236-0651	4087
UTC Corporation	Newington	CT	F	860 665-1770	2332
3deo Inc	Norwood	MA	G	781 999-3447	11151
Accusonic Technologies (DH)	New Bedford	MA	E	508 495-6600	10560
Adcole LLC (PA)	Marlborough	MA	C	508 485-9100	10103
Advanced Device Technology	Andover	MA	G	603 894-1402	5867
American Robotics Inc	Marlborough	MA	E	617 862-2101	10108
Ametek Inc	Wilmington	MA	D	978 988-4101	13377
Ametek Arospc Pwr Holdings Inc (HQ)	Wilmington	MA	D	978 988-4771	13378
Analogic Corporation (HQ)	Peabody	MA	A	978 326-4000	11296
Atk Space Systems LLC	Hopkinton	MA	D	508 497-9457	9308
Autonodyne LLC (PA)	Boston	MA	E	321 751-8402	6579
Avwatch Inc	Plymouth	MA	F	508 274-7937	11448
Ba-Insight Inc	Boston	MA	G	339 368-7234	6581
Bascom-Turner Instruments Inc	Norwood	MA	D	781 769-9660	11164
Cobham Defense Electronic Systems Corporation 978 779-7000	Lowell	MA			A 9869
Cobham Electronic Systems Inc	Lowell	MA	A	978 442-4700	9870
CPI Radant Tech Div Inc (DH)	Stow	MA	D	978 562-3866	12245
De-Ice Technologies Inc	Somerville	MA	F	857 829-7651	11868
Defensecom Inc	Boston	MA	G	203 912-8679	6688
Drs Naval Power Systems Inc	Fitchburg	MA	C	978 343-9719	8653
E S Ritchie & Sons Inc	Pembroke	MA	E	781 826-5131	11364
Edgeone LLC	West Wareham	MA	G	508 291-0057	13061
Edgeone LLC	West Wareham	MA	G	508 291-0960	13062
Entwistle Company LLC (PA)	Hudson	MA	D	508 481-4000	9364
Evolv Tech Holdings Inc (PA)	Waltham	MA	G	781 374-8100	12669
Evolv Technologies Inc (HQ)	Waltham	MA	D	781 374-8100	12670
Falmouth Scientific Inc (PA)	Pocasset	MA	F	508 564-7640	11486
Flir Systems-Boston Inc (DH)	North Billerica	MA	B	978 901-8000	10911
General Dynamics Def Systems In	Pittsfield	MA	C	413 494-1110	11397
General Dynmics Mssion Systems	Pittsfield	MA	A	413 494-1110	11398
General Dynmics Mssion Systems	Quincy	MA	D	617 715-7000	11522
Glasseal Products Inc	New Bedford	MA	E	732 370-9100	10595
Hxi LLC	Harvard	MA	F	978 772-7774	9064
Idss Holdings Inc	Boxboro	MA	D	978 237-0236	7144
Implant Sciences Corp	Wilmington	MA	E	978 752-1700	13413
J W Fishers Mfg Inc	East Taunton	MA	F	508 822-7330	8407
L3 Technologies Inc	Northampton	MA	A	413 586-2330	11069
Leidos SEC Dtction Automtn Inc	Tewksbury	MA	F	571 526-6000	12403
Lockheed Martin Corporation	Bedford	MA	A	781 863-5235	6237
Lockheed Martin Corporation	Chelmsford	MA	E	978 256-4113	7936
Mascon Inc	Woburn	MA	E	781 938-5800	13605
Massa Products Corporation	Hingham	MA	D	781 749-3120	9152
Megapulse Incorporated	Bedford	MA	E	781 538-5299	6241
Mettler-Toledo Thornton Inc (DH)	Billerica	MA	D	978 262-0210	6460
Mikel Inc (PA)	Fall River	MA	G	401 846-0052	8582
MSI Transducers Corp	Littleton	MA	F	978 486-0404	9826
Navionics Inc	Wareham	MA	E	508 291-6000	12841
Northrop Grumman Systems Corp	Hopkinton	MA	F	508 589-6291	9337
Ondas Holdings Inc	Marlborough	MA	E	617 862-2101	10191
Parts Tool and Die Inc	Agawam	MA	E	413 821-9718	5805
Perspecta Svcs & Solutions Inc (DH)	Waltham	MA	G	781 684-4000	12747
Photonis Scientific Inc (DH)	Sturbridge	MA	F	508 347-4000	12257
Princton Gamma-Tech Instrs Inc	Franklin	MA	E	609 924-7310	8858
Prosensing Inc	Amherst	MA	F	413 549-4402	5863

	CITY	ST	EMP	PHONE	ENTRY#
Qualtre Inc (HQ)	Sudbury	MA	E	508 658-8360	12270
Quincy Electronics Co Inc	Quincy	MA	G	617 471-7700	11534
Radar Technology Inc	Newburyport	MA	E		10711
Raytheon Company	Andover	MA	C	978 470-5000	5909
Raytheon Company	Marlborough	MA	B	978 440-1000	10200
Raytheon Company	Marlborough	MA	E	508 490-1000	10201
Raytheon Company (HQ)	Waltham	MA	B	781 522-3000	12759
Raytheon Company	Woburn	MA	C	781 933-1863	13647
Raytheon Company	Woburn	MA	C	339 645-6000	13648
Raytheon International Inc (PA)	Waltham	MA	F	781 522-3000	12760
Raytheon Italy Liaison Company	Andover	MA	D	978 684-5300	5910
Raytheon Korean Support Co (DH)	Waltham	MA	E	339 645-6111	12761
Raytheon Sutheast Asia Systems (DH)	Waltham	MA	E	978 470-5000	12762
Raytheon Systems Support Co (DH)	Tewksbury	MA	E	978 851-2134	12414
Remote Sensing Solutions Inc	Buzzards Bay	MA	F	508 362-9400	7456
Rigaku Analytical Devices Inc	Wilmington	MA	E	855 785-1064	13449
Rule Industries LLC	Gloucester	MA	C	978 281-0440	8956
Secure Point Technologies Inc	Boston	MA	D	978 752-1700	7031
Sensar Marine Us Inc	Lexington	MA	F	800 910-2150	9770
Spectrum Microwave Inc	Marlborough	MA	C	508 251-6400	10213
Spike Aerospace Inc	Boston	MA	F	617 338-1400	7052
Ssg Optronics	Wilmington	MA	G	978 694-9991	13457
Symetrica Inc	Westford	MA	E	508 718-5610	13265
Teledyne Benthos Inc	North Falmouth	MA	C	508 563-1000	11013
Teledyne Instruments Inc	North Falmouth	MA	C	508 563-1000	11014
Tmd Technologies LLC	Beverly	MA	C	978 922-6000	6390
Tru Technologies Inc	Peabody	MA	F	978 532-0775	11349
Ultra Elec Ocean Systems Inc (DH)	Braintree	MA	D	781 848-3400	7211
Ursa Navigation Solutions Inc	North Billerica	MA	E	781 538-5299	10963
Vacuum Barrier Corporation	Woburn	MA	E	781 933-3570	13682
Where Inc	Boston	MA	F	617 502-3100	7121
Xchange Imc LLC	Maynard	MA	F	978 298-2100	10267
Xiphos Partners Inc	Dartmouth	MA	G	508 991-1014	8233
American Rhnmetall Systems LLC	Biddeford	ME	E	207 571-5850	4554
Arundel Holdings Inc	Arundel	ME	D	207 985-8555	4408
General Dynamics Ots Cal Inc	Saco	ME	C	207 283-3611	5368
Hunting Dearborn Inc	Fryeburg	ME	C	207 935-2171	4809
Lander Group LLC	Greenville	ME	F	207 974-3104	4850
Lockheed Martin Corporation	Bath	ME	G	207 442-3125	4529
Northrop Grmmn Spce & Mssn Sys	Bath	ME	C	207 442-5097	4530
Ropeless Systems Inc	Biddeford	ME	G	207 468-8545	4586
Aero Defense International LLC	Manchester	NH	G	603 644-0305	14807
Alex & Ryan Design LLC	Manchester	NH	F	603 518-8650	14808
Allard Nazarian Group Inc	Manchester	NH	F	603 314-0017	14809
Allard Nazarian Group Inc (PA)	Manchester	NH	C	603 668-1900	14810
American Ir Solutions LLC	Hudson	NH	G	662 626-2477	14483
ARC Technology Solutions LLC	Nashua	NH	D	603 883-3027	15064
Bae Systems Elctronic Solution	Nashua	NH	D	603 885-3653	15066
Bae Systems Info Elctrnic Syst	Hudson	NH	A	603 885-4321	14486
Bae Systems Info Elctrnic Syst	Merrimack	NH	A	603 885-4321	14976
Bae Systems Info Elctrnic Syst	Nashua	NH	A	603 885-4321	15067
Bae Systems Info Elctrnic Syst (DH)	Nashua	NH	A	603 885-4321	15068
CHI Aerospace	Portsmouth	NH	F	603 380-9951	15372
Cobham	Exeter	NH	D	603 418-9786	14287
Cobham Def Electronic Systems	Manchester	NH	G	603 518-2716	14832
Contintential Microwave	Exeter	NH	F	603 775-5200	14289
Critical Cmmnctons Cntrls Inst	Exeter	NH	F		14290
Cubic Corporation	Concord	NH	F	603 369-5504	14127
El-Op US Inc	Merrimack	NH	C	603 889-2500	14980
Fireye Inc (DH)	Derry	NH	C	603 432-4100	14193
Flir Maritime Us Inc	Hudson	NH	E	603 324-7900	14496
Frontgrade Technologies Inc	Exeter	NH	B	603 775-5200	14292
Gentex Corporation	Manchester	NH	C	603 657-1200	14851
Klein Marine Systems Inc	Salem	NH	D	603 893-6131	15540
KMC Systems Inc	Merrimack	NH	D	866 742-0442	14987
Kollsman Inc (DH)	Merrimack	NH	A	603 889-2500	14988
Lockheed Martin Corporation	Merrimack	NH	F	603 885-5295	14990
Lockheed Martin Corporation	Nashua	NH	D	603 885-4321	15128
Meggitt (new Hampshire) Inc	Londonderry	NH	C	603 669-0940	14767
Memtec Corporation	Amherst	NH	F	603 893-8080	13880
Mevatec Corp	Nashua	NH	E	603 885-4321	15134
Northrop Grumman Systems Corp	Hudson	NH	G	603 886-4270	14532
Raytheon Company	Merrimack	NH	G	978 313-0201	15000
Raytheon Company	Pelham	NH	F	603 635-6800	15295
Research In Motion Rf Inc (HQ)	Nashua	NH	G	603 598-8880	15158
Resurrection Defense LLC	Winchester	NH	G	603 313-1040	15716
Sealite Usa LLC	Tilton	NH	F	603 737-1310	15656
Sierra Nevada Corporation	Bedford	NH	E	775 331-0222	13949
Signalquest LLC	Lebanon	NH	E	603 448-6266	14698
Skeyetrac LLC	Salem	NH	F	603 898-8000	15562
Tomtom North America Inc	Lebanon	NH	D	978 405-1677	14700
Tomtom North America Inc	Lebanon	NH	A	603 643-0330	14701
Exail Defense Systems Inc	Lincoln	RI	E	401 475-4400	16136

	CITY	ST	EMP	PHONE	ENTRY#
Kearflex Engineering Company	Warwick	RI	F	401 781-4900	16830
Kvh Industries Inc (PA)	Middletown	RI	C	401 847-3327	16177
Northrop Grumman Systems Corp	Middletown	RI	B	401 849-6270	16183
Raytheon Company	Portsmouth	RI	D	401 847-8000	16454
Syqwest Inc	Cranston	RI	E	401 432-7129	15916
Wei Inc (PA)	Cranston	RI	E	401 781-3904	15928
BF Goodrich Aerspce Aircrft In	Vergennes	VT	G	802 877-2911	17656
General Dynamics Ots Cal Inc	Williston	VT	B	802 662-7000	17733
Liquid Measurement Systems Inc	Fairfax	VT	E	802 528-8100	17261

3821 Laboratory apparatus and furniture

	CITY	ST	EMP	PHONE	ENTRY#
Arecna Holdings Inc	Branford	CT	F	203 819-2322	236
Ebs Acquisition Inc	Niantic	CT	F	860 653-0411	2356
Environics Inc	Tolland	CT	F	860 872-1111	3660
Eppendorf Inc (DH)	Enfield	CT	G	860 253-3400	1130
Eppendorf Holding Inc (DH)	Enfield	CT	E	860 253-3417	1131
Extec Corp	Enfield	CT	F	860 741-3435	1133
Idex Health & Science LLC	Bristol	CT	C	860 314-2880	456
Kent Scientific Corporation	Torrington	CT	F	860 626-1172	3688
Mayborn Usa Inc	Stamford	CT	F	781 269-7490	3409
Novamont North America Inc	Shelton	CT	F	203 744-8801	3041
Origio Midatlantic Devices Inc	Trumbull	CT	D	856 762-2000	3727
Tomtec Inc	Hamden	CT	D	203 281-6790	1460
Aja International Inc	Hingham	MA	F	781 545-7365	9139
Apogent Technologies Inc	Waltham	MA	A	781 622-1300	12594
Blacktrace Inc	Norwell	MA	G	617 848-1211	11140
Bluecatbio MA Inc	Concord	MA	G	978 405-2533	8106
Bmac Inc	Ayer	MA	F	978 772-3310	6175
Bnz Materials Inc	North Billerica	MA	C	978 663-3401	10900
Consolidated Machine Corporation	Billerica	MA	E	617 782-6072	6428
Corning Incorporated	Tewksbury	MA	E	978 442-2200	12391
Digilab Inc	Hopkinton	MA	D	508 305-2410	9315
Erbi Biosystems Inc	Stoneham	MA	G	617 297-7422	12177
Excelerarx Corp	Stoughton	MA	F	612 293-0378	12203
Fisher Scientific Intl LLC (HQ)	Waltham	MA	C	781 622-1000	12675
GE Health Care	Northampton	MA	E	413 586-7720	11064
Hamilton Storage Tech Inc	Franklin	MA	G	508 544-7000	8842
Idex Health & Science LLC	Middleboro	MA	C	774 213-0200	10362
Inert Corporation	Amesbury	MA	E	978 462-4415	5837
Infors USA Inc	Weymouth	MA	F	781 335-3108	13326
Inphotonics Inc	Norwood	MA	F	781 440-0202	11181
Jeio Tech Inc	Billerica	MA	E	781 376-0700	6457
Kinetic Systems Inc	Boston	MA	E	617 522-8700	6842
Lab Frnture Instlltons Sls Inc	Middleton	MA	F	978 646-0600	10388
Labcentral Inc (PA)	Cambridge	MA	E	617 863-3650	7626
Labminds Inc	Somerville	MA	E	844 956-8327	11883
Matrix Technologies	Tewksbury	MA	G	603 521-0547	12407
Micro-Lite Inc	Three Rivers	MA	F	413 289-1313	12429
Microfluidics Intl Corp	Westwood	MA	E	617 969-5452	13315
Nexcelom Bioscience LLC (HQ)	Lawrence	MA	E	978 327-5340	9588
Openclinica LLC	Needham Heights	MA	E	617 621-8585	10554
Pall Northborough (DH)	Northborough	MA	D	978 263-9888	11105
Parallel Systems Corp	Georgetown	MA	E	978 352-7100	8911
Pinpoint Laser Systems Inc	Peabody	MA	E	978 532-8001	11333
Setra Systems Inc	Boxboro	MA	F	978 263-1400	7145
Spectris (HQ)	Westborough	MA	E	508 768-6400	13137
Thermo Fisher Scientific Inc	Beverly	MA	A	978 232-6000	6387
Thermo Fisher Scientific Inc	Franklin	MA	C	713 272-0404	8869
Thomas Scientific LLC	Thorndike	MA	D	413 406-6588	12428
Vacuum Technology Inc	Gloucester	MA	G	510 333-6562	8962
Wright Line LLC (HQ)	Worcester	MA	F	508 852-4300	13834
Baker Company Inc (PA)	Sanford	ME	C	207 324-8773	5390
Emerson Apparatus Company	Gorham	ME	F	207 856-0055	4818
Kimball Physics Inc	Wilton	NH	F	603 878-1616	15705
Materials Research Frncs Inc	Allenstown	NH	F	603 485-2394	13853
Matrix Technologies LLC	Hudson	NH	A	603 595-0505	14526
New Erie Scientific LLC (DH)	Portsmouth	NH	E	603 430-6859	15425
Rochester USA	Rochester	NH	F	603 332-0717	15490
Analytical Services Company	Narragansett	RI	G	401 792-3537	16186
Surplus Solutions LLC	Woonsocket	RI	F	401 526-0055	16978
Pre-Tech Plastics Inc (PA)	Williston	VT	E	802 879-9441	17745
Raj Communications Ltd	Essex Junction	VT	E	802 658-4961	17243

3822 Environmental controls

	CITY	ST	EMP	PHONE	ENTRY#
Automated Logic Corporation	Wallingford	CT	E	203 284-0100	3779
Belimo Aircontrols (usa) Inc (HQ)	Danbury	CT	C	800 543-9038	715
Belimo Automation AG	Danbury	CT	E	203 749-3319	716
Center For Discovery	Southport	CT	E	203 955-1381	3245
Emme Controls LLC	Bristol	CT	G	503 793-3792	437
Emme E2ms LLC	Bristol	CT	F	860 845-8810	438
Emme E2ms LLC	Bristol	CT	F	860 845-8810	439
Environmental Systems Corp	West Hartford	CT	C	860 953-8800	4060
Food Atmtn - Svc Tchniques LLC (PA)	Stratford	CT	E	203 377-4414	3537

SIC

Company	CITY	ST	EMP	PHONE	ENTRY#
Hamilton Standard Space	Windsor Locks	CT	E	860 654-6000	4329
Hamilton Sundstrand Corp (HQ)	Windsor Locks	CT	A	619 714-9442	4330
Innovative Fusion Inc	Naugatuck	CT	E	203 729-3873	1965
J & B Service Company LLC	Bethel	CT	G	203 743-9357	122
Johnson Controls Inc	Meriden	CT	F	678 297-4040	1670
Lightstat Inc	Pleasant Valley	CT	E	860 738-4111	2802
Nats USA Incorporated	Middletown	CT	F	860 398-0035	1767
Omega Engineering Inc	Norwalk	CT	D	714 540-4914	2548
Process Automtn Solutions Inc (HQ)	Danbury	CT	E	203 207-9917	801
Rich Plastic Products Inc	Meriden	CT	G	203 235-4241	1694
Tek-Air Systems Inc	Monroe	CT	E	203 791-1400	1923
The Electric Heater Company	Stratford	CT	D	800 647-3165	3580
7ac Technologies Inc	Beverly	MA	F	781 574-1348	6322
Automated Logic Corporation	Chicopee	MA	F	413 547-6595	8008
Burnell Controls Inc	Danvers	MA	E	978 646-9992	8171
Control Resources Inc	Littleton	MA	E	978 486-4160	9806
Division 15 Hvac Inc	Pembroke	MA	F	781 285-3115	11363
Ene Systems Inc (PA)	Canton	MA	D	781 828-6770	7789
Johnson Controls Inc	Lynnfield	MA	E	781 246-5500	9998
Johnson Controls Inc	Wrentham	MA	E	508 384-0018	13843
Kidde-Fenwal Inc (HQ)	Ashland	MA	A	508 881-2000	5960
Lee Electric Inc	Danvers	MA	C	978 777-0070	8198
Massachusetts Clean Energy Ctr	Boston	MA	E	617 315-9355	6873
Mestek Inc	Westfield	MA	F	413 568-9571	13185
Mettlr-Tledo Prcess Anlytics I	Billerica	MA	D	781 301-8800	6461
Molecular Health Inc	Boston	MA	D	832 482-3898	6894
Motion Industries Inc	Danvers	MA	E	978 774-7100	8210
Munters Corporation (DH)	Amesbury	MA	C	978 241-1100	5845
Mv3 LLC	Buzzards Bay	MA	G	617 658-4420	7455
Nanmac Corp	Milford	MA	E	508 872-4811	10407
New England Water Heater Co	Framingham	MA	F	781 647-7004	8792
On-Sight Insight	Boston	MA	G	617 502-5985	6931
Product Resources LLC	Newburyport	MA	E	978 524-8500	10709
Sensitech Inc (DH)	Beverly	MA	D	978 927-7033	6383
Sigma Systems Corp	Mansfield	MA	E	781 688-2354	10076
Static Solutions Inc (PA)	Hudson	MA	F	978 310-7251	9415
Sud-Chemie Protech Inc	Needham Heights	MA	B	781 444-5188	10559
Todd Clark and Associates Inc	Danvers	MA	E	978 774-7100	8225
Parker-Hannifin Corporation	Kittery	ME	D	207 439-9511	4938
Rexx Company Inc	Cumberland Center	ME	F	207 200-9000	4710
Senior Operations LLC	Lewiston	ME	E	207 784-2338	4992
Wahlcometroflex Inc	Lewiston	ME	B	207 784-2338	4995
Ene Systems of Nh Inc	Bow	NH	G	603 856-0330	13996
Hampshire Controls Corp	Dover	NH	F	603 749-9424	14230
Hansa Consult North Amer LLC (PA)	Portsmouth	NH	F	603 422-8833	15398
Hurricane Farm LLC	West Swanzey	NH	E	603 352-0053	15695
Meggitt (new Hampshire) Inc	Londonderry	NH	C	603 669-0940	14767
RMA Manufacturing LLC	West Swanzey	NH	E	603 352-0053	15697
Amtrol Holdings Inc	West Warwick	RI	A	401 884-6300	16899
Avtech Software Inc (PA)	Warren	RI	F	401 628-1600	16752
Energy MGT & Ctrl Svcs Inc	Cranston	RI	F	401 946-1440	15856
Goldline Controls (DH)	North Kingstown	RI	D	401 583-1100	16253
Taco Inc (PA)	Cranston	RI	B	401 942-8000	15917
Thermoswitch International Ltd	Providence	RI	F	401 467-7550	16626

3823 Process control instruments

Company	CITY	ST	EMP	PHONE	ENTRY#
Ai-Tek Instruments LLC	Cheshire	CT	E	203 271-6927	569
Ametek Inc	Wallingford	CT	C	203 265-6731	3770
Appleton Grp LLC	East Granby	CT	F	860 653-1603	925
Ashcroft Inc (DH)	Stratford	CT	B	203 378-8281	3517
Bristol Inc (HQ)	Watertown	CT	B	860 945-2200	4004
Buck Scientific Inc	Norwalk	CT	E	203 853-9444	2477
C F D Engineering Company	Waterbury	CT	F	203 754-2807	3895
Cidra Chemical Management Inc (HQ)	Wallingford	CT	D	203 265-0035	3786
Cidra Corporate Services Inc (HQ)	Wallingford	CT	D	203 265-0035	3787
Cidra Corporation	Wallingford	CT	D	203 265-0035	3788
Cidra Minerals Processing Inc	Wallingford	CT	D	203 265-0035	3789
Clinton Instrument Company	Clinton	CT	E	860 669-7548	638
Cyberresearch Inc	Branford	CT	E	203 643-5000	247
Danaher Tool Group	Wallingford	CT	F	203 284-7000	3799
Devar Inc	Bridgeport	CT	E	203 368-6751	317
Diba Industries Inc (HQ)	Danbury	CT	E	203 744-0773	731
Ecochlor Inc	North Haven	CT	D	978 298-1463	2408
Environics Inc	Tolland	CT	F	860 872-1111	3660
Faria Beede Instruments Inc	North Stonington	CT	C	860 848-9271	2448
Food Atmtn - Svc Tchniques LLC (PA)	Stratford	CT	E	203 377-4414	3537
Frank Smith	Naugatuck	CT	E	203 729-6434	1959
GE Steam Power Inc (HQ)	Windsor	CT	A	866 257-8664	4279
Gordon Engineering Corporation	Brookfield	CT	G	203 775-4501	522
H & B Tool & Eng Co Inc	South Windsor	CT	E	860 528-9341	3153
Hamilton Sundstrand Corp (HQ)	Windsor Locks	CT	A	619 714-9442	4330
Haydon Kerk Mtion Slutions Inc (HQ)	Waterbury	CT	D	203 756-7441	3918

Company	CITY	ST	EMP	PHONE	ENTRY#
He Technologies Inc	Milford	CT	G	203 878-6892	1835
Idex Health & Science LLC	Bristol	CT	C	860 314-2880	456
ITT Inc (PA)	Stamford	CT	C	914 641-2000	3388
Jad LLC	South Windsor	CT	E	860 289-1551	3158
Johnson Gage Company	Bloomfield	CT	E	860 242-5541	177
Kahn Instruments Incorporated	Wethersfield	CT	G	860 529-8643	4208
Kaman Aerospace Corporation	Middletown	CT	C	860 632-1000	1755
Kem Liquidating Company Inc	Glastonbury	CT	E	860 430-5100	1287
Laticrete Supercap LLC	Bethany	CT	G	203 393-4558	95
Lee Company	Westbrook	CT	E	860 399-6281	4139
Lee Company (PA)	Westbrook	CT	A	860 399-6281	4140
Lee Company HC	Westbrook	CT	E	860 399-6281	4141
Lq Mechatronics Inc	Branford	CT	G	203 433-4430	268
Madison Company (PA)	Branford	CT	E	203 488-4477	270
Minteq International Inc	Canaan	CT	F	860 824-5435	556
Moeller Instrument Company Inc	Ivoryton	CT	F	800 243-9310	1530
Norwalk Indus Components LLC	Manchester	CT	G	860 645-5340	1622
Omega Engineering Inc (DH)	Norwalk	CT	C	203 359-1660	2549
Omega Engineering Inc	Stamford	CT	C	203 359-7922	3424
Orange Research Inc	Milford	CT	D	203 877-5657	1859
PMC Engineering LLC	Danbury	CT	E	203 792-8686	798
Prime Technology LLC	North Branford	CT	E	203 481-5721	2373
Proflow Inc	North Haven	CT	E	203 230-4700	2433
Projects Inc	Glastonbury	CT	C	860 633-4615	1295
Seymour - Sheridan Incorporated	Monroe	CT	D	203 261-4009	1921
Sperian Prtction Instrmnttion	Middletown	CT	D	860 344-1079	1783
Tek-Air Systems Inc	Monroe	CT	E	203 791-1400	1923
Underground Systems Inc (PA)	Bethel	CT	E	203 792-3444	138
Veeder-Root Company (HQ)	Weatogue	CT	D	860 651-2700	4043
Vertiv Corporation	Wallingford	CT	F	203 294-6020	3874
Whitman Controls LLC	Bristol	CT	F	800 233-4401	506
Accusonic Technologies (DH)	New Bedford	MA	F	508 495-6600	10560
Adcole LLC (PA)	Marlborough	MA	C	508 485-9100	10103
Advanced Thermal Solutions Inc (PA)	Norwood	MA	F	781 769-2800	11157
AGFA Healthcare Corporation	Canton	MA	D	978 284-7900	7766
Ametek Arizona Instrument LLC	Middleboro	MA	C	508 946-6200	10349
Applied Analytics Inc	Chelmsford	MA	E	978 294-8214	7907
Arichell Technologies Inc	Newton	MA	D	617 796-9001	10734
Arklay S Richards Co Inc	Newton	MA	F	617 527-4385	10735
Assembly Guidance Systems Inc	Chelmsford	MA	F	978 244-1166	7911
Auburn International Inc	Beverly	MA	G	978 777-2460	6328
Auburn Systems LLC	Beverly	MA	G	978 777-2460	6329
Azenta Inc (PA)	Burlington	MA	A	978 262-2400	7339
Bae Systems Info Elctrnic Syst	Lexington	MA	C	603 885-4321	9726
Bedrock Automtn Platforms Inc	Wilmington	MA	E	781 821-0280	13390
Big Belly Solar LLC (PA)	Needham Heights	MA	E	888 820-0300	10530
Central Tools Inc	Framingham	MA	G	781 893-0095	8752
Cimetrics Inc	Malden	MA	D	617 350-7550	10007
Cognex Corporation (PA)	Natick	MA	B	508 650-3000	10472
Cognex Europe Inc (HQ)	Natick	MA	A	855 426-4639	10473
Cognex International Inc (HQ)	Natick	MA	G	508 650-3000	10475
Controlled Envmt Systems LLC (PA)	Mansfield	MA	E	508 339-4237	10042
Cybertools	Harvard	MA	G	800 894-9206	9061
Data Industrial Corporation	Mattapoisett	MA	E	508 758-6390	10256
Dias Infrared Corp	West Boylston	MA	F	845 987-8152	12961
Dolan-Jenner Industries Inc	Boxborough	MA	E	978 263-1400	7151
Druck LLC (HQ)	Billerica	MA	E	978 437-1000	6432
Dynisco Instruments LLC (HQ)	Franklin	MA	C	508 541-9400	8831
Dynisco Parent Inc	Billerica	MA	B	978 667-5301	6436
E Gs Gauging Incorporated	Wilmington	MA	E	978 262-3100	13404
Edgetech Instruments Inc	Hudson	MA	F	508 263-5900	9362
Electro Switch Corp	Weymouth	MA	F	781 335-1195	13325
Emerson Prcess MGT Pwr Wtr Slt	Lawrence	MA	E	978 689-2800	9560
Entegris Inc	Billerica	MA	E	978 436-6500	6442
Evoqua Water Technologies LLC	Tewksbury	MA	E	978 863-4600	12397
Flir Systems-Boston Inc (DH)	North Billerica	MA	B	978 901-8000	10911
Gefran Isi Inc	North Andover	MA	E	781 729-0842	10837
Got Interface	Peabody	MA	F	781 547-5700	11312
Hamilton Storage Tech Inc (DH)	Franklin	MA	E	508 544-7000	8843
Honeywell Data Instruments Inc	Acton	MA	E	978 264-9550	5754
Impolit Envmtl Ctrl Corp	Beverly	MA	E	978 927-4304	6356
Industrial Bmdcal Sensors Corp	Waltham	MA	F	781 891-4201	12698
International Parallel Mchs	New Bedford	MA	G	508 990-2977	10604
Invetech Inc	Boxborough	MA	E	508 475-3400	7152
Iwaki America Incorporated (HQ)	Holliston	MA	E	508 429-1440	9216
Jowa Usa Inc	Littleton	MA	E	978 486-9800	9822
Kadant Fibergen Inc (HQ)	Bedford	MA	F	781 275-3600	6236
Kidde-Fenwal Inc (HQ)	Ashland	MA	A	508 881-2000	5960
Krohne Inc (DH)	Beverly	MA	C	978 535-6060	6360
Lewa Process Technologies Inc	Devens	MA	D	978 487-1100	8275
Liquid Metronics Incorporated	Acton	MA	E	978 263-9800	5757
Liquid Solids Control Inc (PA)	Upton	MA	E	508 529-3377	12473
LS Starrett Company (PA)	Athol	MA	A	978 249-3551	5981

	CITY	ST	EMP	PHONE	ENTRY#
Lynn Products Co	Lynn	MA	F	781 593-2500	9986
M & K Industries Inc	Leominster	MA	E	978 514-9850	9680
Magmotor Technologies Inc	Worcester	MA	F	508 835-4305	13756
Mathworks Inc	Natick	MA	A	508 647-7000	10485
Mathworks Inc (PA)	Natick	MA	A	508 647-7000	10486
Mettler-Toledo Thornton Inc (DH)	Billerica	MA	D	978 262-0210	6460
Mks Instruments Inc	Andover	MA	E	978 645-5500	5898
Mks Instruments Inc (PA)	Andover	MA	B	978 645-5500	5899
Mks Instruments Inc	Haverhill	MA	F	978 284-4015	9117
Mks Instruments Inc	Lawrence	MA	F	978 975-2350	9585
Mks Instruments Inc	Methuen	MA	E	978 682-3512	10339
Mks Instruments Inc	Wilmington	MA	C	978 284-4000	13433
Mks Msc Inc	Wilmington	MA	C	978 284-4000	13434
Motion Industries Inc	Danvers	MA	E	978 774-7100	8210
National Resource MGT Inc (PA)	Canton	MA	E	781 828-8877	7809
Netzsch Instruments N Amer LLC (DH)	Burlington	MA	E	781 272-5353	7398
Onset Computer Corporation	Bourne	MA	C	508 759-9500	7141
Orbotech Inc (DH)	Billerica	MA	D	978 667-6037	6466
Panametrics LLC (DH)	Billerica	MA	A	978 437-1000	6468
Patriot Worldwide Inc	Milford	MA	F	800 786-4669	10413
Performance Motion Devices Inc	Boxborough	MA	E	978 266-1210	7153
Phoenix Electric Corp	Canton	MA	E	781 821-0200	7819
Pid Analyzers LLC	Sandwich	MA	F	774 413-5281	11752
Precision Digital Corporation	Hopkinton	MA	E	508 655-7300	9340
Pressure Signal Inc	Rockland	MA	E	781 871-5629	11657
Rigaku Analytical Devices Inc	Wilmington	MA	E	855 785-1064	13449
Roscid Technologies Inc	Woburn	MA	F	781 933-4007	13656
Rosemount Inc	Mansfield	MA	G	508 261-2928	10075
Schneder Elc Systems Argntina	Foxboro	MA	C	508 543-8750	8718
Schneider Elc Systems USA Inc	Foxboro	MA	F	508 543-8750	8719
Schneider Elc Systems USA Inc	Foxboro	MA	A	508 543-8750	8720
Schneider Elc Systems USA Inc (DH)	Foxboro	MA	E	508 543-8750	8721
Schneider Electric Foxboro	Foxboro	MA	B	508 543-8750	8722
Schneider Electric Usa Inc (DH)	Boston	MA	A	978 975-9600	7026
Schneider Electric Usa Inc	Foxboro	MA	A	508 549-3385	8724
Scully Signal Company (PA)	Wilmington	MA	D	617 692-8600	13452
Semilab USA LLC	Billerica	MA	E	508 647-8400	6479
Sensitech Inc (DH)	Beverly	MA	D	978 927-7033	6383
Sensortech Systems Inc	Westborough	MA	F	805 981-3735	13134
Set Americas Inc	Easthampton	MA	G	413 203-6130	8462
Setra Systems Inc	Boxboro	MA	F	978 263-1400	7145
Shawmut Advertising Inc (PA)	Peabody	MA	E	978 762-7500	11340
Sick Inc	Stoughton	MA	D	781 302-2500	12235
Spectro Scientific Inc (HQ)	Chelmsford	MA	D	978 486-0123	7959
Tasi Holdings Inc (PA)	Marlborough	MA	F	513 202-5182	10223
Tecomet Inc	Woburn	MA	A	781 782-6400	13675
Teknikor Automtn & Contrls Inc	Fall River	MA	F	508 679-9474	8615
Teledyne Instruments Inc	North Falmouth	MA	E	508 563-1000	11015
Temp-Pro Incorporated	Northampton	MA	E	413 584-3165	11082
Temptronic Corporation (HQ)	Mansfield	MA	E	781 688-2300	10079
Thermo Egs Gauging LLC	Chelmsford	MA	C	978 663-2300	7965
Thermo Envmtl Instrs LLC (HQ)	Franklin	MA	C	508 520-0430	8868
Thermo Fisher Scientific Inc (PA)	Waltham	MA	C	781 622-1000	12800
Thermo Process Instruments LP	Franklin	MA	C	508 553-6913	8870
Thermonics Inc	Mansfield	MA	F	408 542-5900	10080
Todd Clark and Associates Inc	Danvers	MA	E	978 774-7100	8225
United Electric Controls Company (PA)	Watertown	MA	C	617 926-1000	12917
Water Analytics Inc	Andover	MA	F	978 749-9949	5934
Williamson Corporation	Concord	MA	E	978 369-9607	8141
Wintriss Controls Group LLC	Acton	MA	E	978 268-2700	5768
Ymc America Inc	Devens	MA	E	978 487-1130	8290
David Saunders Inc	South Portland	ME	E	207 228-1888	5497
F W Webb Company	Winslow	ME	E	207 873-7741	5682
Montalvo Corporation	Gorham	ME	E	207 856-2501	4827
Bantry Components Inc	Manchester	NH	E	603 668-3210	14817
Degree Controls Inc (PA)	Nashua	NH	E	603 672-8900	15089
Dover Flexo Electronics Inc	Rochester	NH	E	603 332-6150	15475
Dutile Glines & Higgins Inc	Manchester	NH	F	603 622-0452	14846
Extech Instruments Corporation	Nashua	NH	D	877 439-8324	15099
Jewell Instruments LLC (PA)	Manchester	NH	C	603 669-5121	14868
Madgetech Inc (PA)	Warner	NH	F	603 456-2011	15665
Meggitt (new Hampshire) Inc	Londonderry	NH	C	603 669-0940	14767
Memtec Corporation	Amherst	NH	F	603 893-8080	13880
Monarch International Inc	Amherst	NH	E	603 883-3390	13881
Parker-Hannifin Corporation	Hollis	NH	C	603 595-1500	14456
Pneucleus Technologies LLC	Hollis	NH	G	603 465-7346	14457
Teledyne Instruments Inc	Hampton	NH	G	603 474-5571	14415
Tomtom North America Inc	Lebanon	NH	A	603 643-0330	14701
Tvc Inc	Portsmouth	NH	F	603 431-5251	15445
Valde Systems Inc	Brookline	NH	G	603 577-1728	14042
Wilcom Inc	Belmont	NH	E	603 524-2622	13973
Z Thunderline Inc	Hampstead	NH	E	603 329-4050	14395
Astonish Results LP	Warwick	RI	F	401 921-6220	16784
Celestial Monitoring Corp (HQ)	Narragansett	RI	E	401 782-1045	16187
Cool Polymers Inc	North Kingstown	RI	E	401 667-7830	16241
Crest Manufacturing Company	Lincoln	RI	E	401 333-1350	16129
E H Benz Co Inc	Providence	RI	G	401 331-5650	16510
Hanna Instruments Inc (PA)	Woonsocket	RI	E	401 765-7500	16962
Hexagon Mfg Intelligence Inc (DH)	North Kingstown	RI	D	401 886-2000	16255
Primary Flow Signal Inc (PA)	Cranston	RI	D	401 461-6366	15905
Instrumart LLC (HQ)	South Burlington	VT	E	802 863-0085	17580
NRG Systems Inc	Hinesburg	VT	E	802 482-2255	17297
Step Ahead Innovations Inc	South Burlington	VT	F	802 233-0211	17600
Vermont Precision Tools Inc (PA)	Swanton	VT	C	802 868-4246	17645

3824 Fluid meters and counting devices

	CITY	ST	EMP	PHONE	ENTRY#
Alinabal Holdings Corporation (PA)	Milford	CT	B	203 877-3241	1797
Bidwell Industrial Group Inc	Middletown	CT	E	860 346-9283	1740
Denominator Company Inc	Waterbury	CT	F	203 263-3210	3905
Faria Beede Instruments Inc	North Stonington	CT	C	860 848-9271	2448
Gems Sensors Inc (HQ)	Plainville	CT	B	860 747-3000	2761
Habco Industries LLC	Glastonbury	CT	E	860 682-6800	1283
Kem Liquidating Company Inc	Glastonbury	CT	E	860 430-5100	1287
Kongsberg Dgtal Simulation Inc	Groton	CT	F	860 405-2300	1375
Lq Mechatronics Inc	Branford	CT	G	203 433-4430	268
Veeder-Root Company (HQ)	Weatogue	CT	D	860 651-2700	4043
Acentech Incorporated (PA)	Cambridge	MA	E	617 499-8000	7466
Ametek Arizona Instrument LLC	Middleboro	MA	C	508 946-6200	10349
Block Mems LLC	Southborough	MA	F	508 251-3100	11992
Data Industrial Corporation	Mattapoisett	MA	E	508 758-6390	10256
Dff Corp	Agawam	MA	C	413 786-8880	5789
Druck LLC (HQ)	Billerica	MA	B	978 437-1000	6432
High Voltage Engineering Corp	Wakefield	MA	E	781 224-1001	12511
Schleifring North America LLC	Chelmsford	MA	E	978 677-2500	7954
Setra Systems Inc	Boxboro	MA	F	978 263-1400	7145
Small Water Systems Svcs LLC	Littleton	MA	E	978 486-1008	9838
Cei Flowmaster Products LLC	Hudson	NH	G	603 880-0094	14490
Monarch International Inc	Amherst	NH	E	603 883-3390	13881

3825 Instruments to measure electricity

	CITY	ST	EMP	PHONE	ENTRY#
Altek Electronics Inc	Torrington	CT	C	860 482-7626	3669
ARS Products Inc	Plainfield	CT	E	860 564-0208	2732
Bloomy Controls Inc (PA)	South Windsor	CT	E	860 298-9925	3120
Clinton Instrument Company	Clinton	CT	E	860 669-7548	638
Dictaphone Corporation (DH)	Stratford	CT	C	203 381-7000	3533
Digatron Power Electronics Inc	Shelton	CT	E	203 446-8000	3000
Eneon US LLC (HQ)	Fairfield	CT	F	312 724-6886	1184
Faria Beede Instruments Inc	North Stonington	CT	C	860 848-9271	2448
Forte Rts Inc	Ledyard	CT	G	860 464-5221	1551
Gold Line Connector Inc (PA)	Redding	CT	E	203 938-2588	2882
Habco Industries LLC	Glastonbury	CT	E	860 682-6800	1283
Hipotronics Inc (HQ)	Shelton	CT	C	845 279-3644	3013
Hoffman Engineering LLC (DH)	Stamford	CT	D	203 425-8900	3378
International Contact Tech Inc	Oxford	CT	E	203 264-5757	2700
Kem Liquidating Company Inc	Glastonbury	CT	E	860 430-5100	1287
Microtools Inc	Simsbury	CT	G	860 651-6170	3094
Nutmeg Utility Products Inc (PA)	Cheshire	CT	E	203 250-8802	609
Omega Engineering Inc	Norwalk	CT	D	714 540-4914	2548
Prime Technology LLC	North Branford	CT	E	203 481-5721	2373
Space Electronics LLC	Berlin	CT	E	860 829-0001	86
Tektronix	Danbury	CT	E	203 730-2730	824
Think Energy LLC	Southport	CT	D	917 202-3574	3250
Trans-Tek Inc	Ellington	CT	E	860 872-8351	1118
Wentworth Laboratories Inc (PA)	Brookfield	CT	C	203 775-0448	544
Accelrf Corporation	Devens	MA	E	978 391-4009	8264
Acentech Incorporated (PA)	Cambridge	MA	E	617 499-8000	7466
Advanced Mechanical Tech Inc (PA)	Watertown	MA	E	617 923-4174	12855
Aetruim Incorporated	Billerica	MA	E	651 773-4200	6397
Agilent Technologies Inc	Andover	MA	E	978 794-3664	5868
Agilent Technologies Inc	Chicopee	MA	E	413 593-2900	8005
Agilent Technologies Inc	Lexington	MA	C	781 861-7200	9722
Ametek Inc	Wilmington	MA	E	978 988-4101	13377
Ametek Arizona Instrument LLC	Middleboro	MA	C	508 946-6200	10349
Analog Devices Intl Inc (HQ)	Wilmington	MA	A	800 262-5643	13380
Analogic Corporation (HQ)	Peabody	MA	A	978 326-4000	11296
Analogic Corporation	Peabody	MA	A	978 977-3000	11297
ARC Technologies LLC (HQ)	Amesbury	MA	D	978 388-2993	5830
Axiam Inc (PA)	Gloucester	MA	G	978 281-3550	8921
Bascom-Turner Instruments Inc	Norwood	MA	D	781 769-9660	11164
Bose Corporation	Framingham	MA	F	508 766-1265	8746
Brewer Electric & Utilities In	South Yarmouth	MA	G	508 771-2040	11981
Business and Prof Exch Inc	Beverly	MA	E	978 556-4100	6336
Cami Research Inc	Acton	MA	F	978 266-2655	5742
Central Tools Inc	Framingham	MA	G	781 893-0095	8752
Connected Auto Systems Neng In	South Easton	MA	E	508 238-5855	11940
Copley Global Services LLC	Waltham	MA	G	617 970-9617	12641

S I C

	CITY	ST	EMP	PHONE	ENTRY#
CTS Valpey Corporation (HQ)	Hopkinton	MA	D	508 435-6831	9314
Day-Ahead Instrumentation LLC	Littleton	MA	G	978 952-2444	9810
Doble Engineering Company (HQ)	Marlborough	MA	F	617 926-4900	10145
Durridge Company Inc (PA)	Billerica	MA	F	978 667-9556	6433
Dynisco Instruments LLC (HQ)	Franklin	MA	G	508 541-9400	8831
Electro-Fix Inc	Plainville	MA	E	508 695-0228	11432
Engement Company Inc	Topsfield	MA	G	603 537-2088	12432
Etec Inc	West Roxbury	MA	G	617 477-4308	13010
Exinda Inc	Boston	MA	G	617 973-6477	6724
Fishman Transducers Inc	Andover	MA	D	978 988-9199	5883
Flintec Inc	Hudson	MA	E	978 562-4548	9367
Group Four Transducers Inc (PA)	East Longmeadow	MA	G	413 525-2705	8378
H & W Test Products Inc	Seekonk	MA	F	508 336-3200	11776
Hampden Engineering Corp	East Longmeadow	MA	D	413 525-3981	8379
Hid Global Corporation	Newton	MA	E	617 581-6200	10759
High Voltage Engineering Corp	Wakefield	MA	E	781 224-1001	12511
Hivec Holdings Inc	Wakefield	MA	E	781 224-1001	12512
Honeywell Data Instruments Inc	Acton	MA	E	978 264-9550	5754
Iet Labs Inc	West Roxbury	MA	F	617 969-0804	13011
Ilab Solutions LLC	Boston	MA	E	617 297-2805	6807
Ineoquest Technologies Inc (HQ)	Westwood	MA	E	508 339-2497	13313
Inspectrology LLC	Wilmington	MA	E	978 212-3100	13416
Kidde-Fenwal Inc (HQ)	Ashland	MA	A	508 881-2000	5960
Krohn-Hite Corporation	Brockton	MA	E	508 580-1660	7288
L T X International Inc	Norwood	MA	D	781 461-1000	11189
Lynn Products Co	Lynn	MA	F	781 593-2500	9986
Magellan Diagnostics Inc (HQ)	Chelmsford	MA	D	978 250-7000	7937
Matec Instrument Companies Inc (PA)	Northborough	MA	E	508 393-0155	11102
Mercury Commercial Electronics Inc	Chelmsford	MA	C	978 967-1364	7938
Microsemi Frequency Time Corp	Beverly	MA	E	978 232-0040	6366
Middlesex General Inds Inc	Newburyport	MA	E	781 935-8870	10702
Mini-Systems Inc	Plainville	MA	E	508 695-2000	11439
Mks Instruments Inc	Lawrence	MA	F	978 975-2350	9585
Mti-Milliren Technologies Inc	Newburyport	MA	E	978 465-6064	10703
Murata Power Solutions Inc (DH)	Westborough	MA	C	508 339-3000	13122
Novotechnik US Inc	Southborough	MA	G	508 485-2244	12000
Pharmatron Inc	Westborough	MA	F	603 645-6766	13130
Power Systems Integrity Inc	Northborough	MA	G	508 393-1655	11106
Powerhydrant LLC (PA)	Boston	MA	G	617 686-9632	6972
Programmed Test Sources Inc	Littleton	MA	F	978 486-3008	9833
Quadtech Inc	Marlborough	MA	D	978 461-2100	10198
Rika Denshi America Inc	Attleboro	MA	E	508 226-2080	6056
Rotek Instrument Corp	Waltham	MA	E	781 899-4611	12774
Scully Signal Company (PA)	Wilmington	MA	D	617 692-8600	13452
Spirent Communications Inc	Littleton	MA	G	774 463-0281	9839
Tech180 Corp	Easthampton	MA	F	413 203-6123	8463
Teradar Inc	Cambridge	MA	E	508 433-0269	7737
Teradyne Inc	Boston	MA	G	978 370-2700	7074
Teradyne Inc	North Reading	MA	E	978 370-2700	11047
Teradyne Inc (PA)	North Reading	MA	A	978 370-2700	11048
Teradyne Inc	North Reading	MA	F	978 370-2700	11049
Teradyne Inc	Woburn	MA	F	978 370-2700	13677
Transcat Inc	Andover	MA	F	888 975-5061	5930
Tts Mexican Holding Company	Wakefield	MA	G	781 224-1001	12540
Vaunix Technology Corporation	Newburyport	MA	F	978 662-7839	10726
Victor Microwave Inc	Wakefield	MA	E	781 245-4472	12541
Xcerra Corporation (HQ)	Norwood	MA	C	781 461-1000	11220
Xilectric Inc	Fall River	MA	G	781 247-4567	8627
Zurich Instruments Usa Inc	Waltham	MA	F	949 682-5172	12823
Micronetixx Technologies LLC	Lewiston	ME	G	207 786-2000	4975
Aclara Technologies LLC	Somersworth	NH	D	603 749-8376	15608
Airmar Technology Corp	Milford	NH	F	603 673-9570	15012
Airmar Technology Corp (PA)	Milford	NH	B	603 673-9570	15013
Amphenol Corporation	Nashua	NH	B	603 879-3000	15061
ARC Technology Solutions LLC	Nashua	NH	D	603 883-3027	15064
Bantry Components Inc	Manchester	NH	E	603 668-3210	14817
Dover Flexo Electronics Inc	Rochester	NH	E	603 332-6150	15475
Eagle Test Systems Inc	Bedford	NH	B	603 624-5757	13926
Eastern Time Designs Inc	Candia	NH	F	603 483-5876	14048
Electrocraft New Hampshire Inc (DH)	Dover	NH	E	603 742-3330	14228
Everett Charles Tech LLC	Nashua	NH	E	603 882-2621	15096
Extech Instruments Corporation	Nashua	NH	D	877 439-8324	15099
Hoyt Elec Instr Works Inc	Concord	NH	E	603 753-6321	14138
Innovative Test Solutions LLC	Nashua	NH	G	603 288-0280	15115
Ion Physics Corp	Fremont	NH	E	603 895-5100	14328
Keysight Technologies Inc	Nashua	NH	G	800 829-4444	15123
Leusin Microwave LLC	Hampstead	NH	F	603 329-7270	14384
Martel Electronics Corp	Derry	NH	E	603 434-6033	14201
Monarch International Inc	Amherst	NH	E	603 883-3390	13881
Physical Measurement Tech Inc	Marlborough	NH	G	603 876-9990	14965
Q A Technology Company Inc	Hampton	NH	D	603 926-1193	14409
Tech Resources Inc	Milford	NH	E	603 673-9000	15039
Ultrasystems Electronics Inc	Amherst	NH	F	603 578-0444	13893

	CITY	ST	EMP	PHONE	ENTRY#
Wilcom Inc	Belmont	NH	E	603 524-2622	13973
Agilent Technologies Inc	North Kingstown	RI	D	800 338-1754	16229
Aurora Performance Pdts LLC	Jamestown	RI	G	401 398-2959	16068
Central Tools Inc (PA)	Cranston	RI	F	401 467-8211	15841
Hanna Instruments Inc	Cumberland	RI	F	401 335-3677	15941
Hanna Instruments Inc (PA)	Woonsocket	RI	E	401 765-7500	16962
Hanna Instruments US Inc	Smithfield	RI	E	401 765-7500	16708
Interplex Industries Inc (DH)	Rumford	RI	F	401 434-6543	16672
Biotek Instruments Inc	Winooski	VT	G	802 655-4040	17766
Draker Laboratories Inc	Burlington	VT	D	802 922-1162	17131
Omni Measurement Systems Inc	Colchester	VT	E	802 497-2253	17198
Vermont Mold & Tool Corp	Barnet	VT	F	802 633-2300	16995

3826 Analytical instruments

	CITY	ST	EMP	PHONE	ENTRY#
Albrayco Technologies Inc	Cromwell	CT	G	860 635-3369	685
Applied Biosystems LLC	Norwalk	CT	F	781 271-0045	2462
Buck Scientific Inc	Norwalk	CT	E	203 853-9444	2477
Cam2 Technologies LLC	Danbury	CT	F	203 628-4833	719
Carestream Hlth Mlclar Imging	New Haven	CT	F	888 777-0072	2134
Connecticut Analytical Corp	Bethany	CT	F	203 393-9666	92
Crane Company (PA)	Stamford	CT	D	203 363-7300	3326
Dexsil Corporation	Hamden	CT	E	203 288-3509	1421
Diasys Corp	Waterbury	CT	F	302 636-5400	3907
Energy Beam Sciences Inc	Niantic	CT	F	860 653-0411	2357
Hamilton Sndstrand Space Syste	Windsor Locks	CT	E	860 654-6000	4328
Hoffman Engineering LLC (DH)	Stamford	CT	D	203 425-8900	3378
Idex Health & Science LLC	Bristol	CT	C	860 314-2880	456
Ihs Herold Inc (DH)	Norwalk	CT	D	203 857-0215	2516
K A F Manufacturing Co Inc	Stamford	CT	E	203 324-3012	3394
MLS Acq Inc	East Windsor	CT	E	860 386-6878	1082
Nats USA Incorporated	Middletown	CT	F	860 398-0035	1767
Omega Engineering Inc (DH)	Norwalk	CT	C	203 359-1660	2549
Perkinelmer US LLC (PA)	Shelton	CT	D	203 925-4600	3046
Precipio Inc (PA)	New Haven	CT	F	203 787-7888	2187
Prospect Products Incorporated	Newington	CT	E	860 666-0323	2320
Real-Time Analyzers Inc	Middletown	CT	G	860 635-9800	1777
Revvity Inc	Shelton	CT	G	203 925-4600	3060
Revvity Health Sciences Inc	Shelton	CT	F	203 925-4600	3061
Spectral LLC	Putnam	CT	F	860 928-7726	2876
Spectro Analytical Instrs Inc	Danbury	CT	F	203 778-8837	820
Tomtec Inc	Hamden	CT	D	203 281-6790	1460
AB Sciex Sales LP	Framingham	MA	E	508 383-7700	8739
Acton Research Corporation	Acton	MA	E	941 556-2601	5731
Advanced Instruments LLC (DH)	Norwood	MA	E	781 320-9000	11156
Advanced Thermal Solutions Inc (PA)	Norwood	MA	E	781 769-2800	11157
Agilone Inc (HQ)	Boston	MA	E	877 769-3047	6521
American Ult Cryogenics Inc (PA)	Woburn	MA	E	781 491-0888	13507
American Ult Cryogenics LLC	Woburn	MA	E	781 491-0999	13508
Analytik Jena US LLC (DH)	Tewksbury	MA	D	909 946-3197	12384
Andor Technology Inc	Concord	MA	E	978 405-1116	8098
Andor Technology Ltd (DH)	Concord	MA	F	860 290-9211	8099
Antec (usa) LLC	Boston	MA	G	888 572-0012	6549
Apogent Holding Company (HQ)	Waltham	MA	F	781 622-1300	12593
Applied Biosystems LLC	Bedford	MA	F	781 271-0045	6209
Applied Biosystems LLC	Framingham	MA	F	508 877-1307	8741
Autogen Inc	Holliston	MA	E	508 429-5965	9200
Block Engineering LLC	Southborough	MA	E	508 480-9643	11991
Bmac Inc	Ayer	MA	E	978 772-3310	6175
Boston Piezo-Optics Inc	Bellingham	MA	F	508 966-4988	6287
Brammer Bio Ma LLC (HQ)	Cambridge	MA	B	877 765-7676	7524
Bruker Biospin Corporation (HQ)	Billerica	MA	C	978 667-9580	6412
Bruker Biospin Mri Inc	Billerica	MA	F	978 667-9580	6413
Bruker Corporation (PA)	Billerica	MA	A	978 663-3660	6414
Bruker Corporation	Billerica	MA	C	978 663-3660	6415
Bruker Detection Corporation	Billerica	MA	B	978 663-3660	6416
Bruker Enrgy Supercon Tech Inc (HQ)	Billerica	MA	D	978 901-7550	6417
Bruker Scientific LLC	Billerica	MA	A	978 667-9580	6418
Bruker Scientific LLC (HQ)	Billerica	MA	A	978 439-9899	6419
Business and Prof Exch Inc	Beverly	MA	E	978 556-4100	6336
Caliper Life Sciences Inc (DH)	Hopkinton	MA	C	203 954-9442	9310
Carl Zeiss Nts LLC (DH)	Peabody	MA	D	978 826-1500	11301
Cohesive Technologies Inc (HQ)	Franklin	MA	E	508 528-7989	8824
Copious Imaging LLC	Lexington	MA	E	781 918-6554	9732
Corindus Inc (HQ)	Auburndale	MA	E	508 653-3335	6131
Corning Incorporated	Tewksbury	MA	E	978 442-2200	12391
Covaris Inc	Woburn	MA	E	781 932-3959	13549
Day Zero Diagnostics Inc	Watertown	MA	E	857 770-1125	12870
Doble Engineering Company (HQ)	Marlborough	MA	F	617 926-4900	10145
DOE & Inglls Msschstts Oprting	Peabody	MA	E	781 391-0090	11307
Dpp Inc	Sudbury	MA	G	978 443-9995	12265
Duke River Engineering Co	Newton	MA	G	617 965-7255	10753
E Fjeld Co Inc	North Billerica	MA	G	978 667-1416	10909
Edgeone LLC (PA)	West Wareham	MA	F	508 291-0057	13063

Company	CITY	ST	EMP	PHONE	ENTRY#
EMD Millipore Corporation	Bedford	MA	C	781 533-6000	6224
EMD Millipore Corporation	Bedford	MA	C	781 533-6000	6225
EMD Millipore Corporation	Billerica	MA	B	978 715-4321	6438
EMD Millipore Corporation	Danvers	MA	F	978 762-5100	8185
EMD Millipore Corporation	Quincy	MA	F	800 637-7872	11514
EMD Millipore Corporation	Taunton	MA	D	781 533-5754	12334
EMD Millipore Corporation	Waltham	MA	E	781 533-5858	12661
Endeavor Robotic Holdings Inc (DH)	Chelmsford	MA	F	978 769-9333	7927
Evident Scientific Inc (PA)	Waltham	MA	A	781 419-3900	12668
Evoqua Water Technologies LLC	Tewksbury	MA	E	978 863-4600	12397
Exergen Corporation	Watertown	MA	D	617 923-9900	12873
Exeter Analytical Inc	North Chelmsford	MA	F	978 251-1411	10975
Eye Pint Phrmctcals Scrties Co	Watertown	MA	F	617 926-5000	12874
Eyepoint Pharmaceuticals Inc (PA)	Watertown	MA	D	617 926-5000	12875
Fiberlock Technologies Inc	Andover	MA	F	978 623-9987	5882
Fisher Scientific Intl LLC	Billerica	MA	F	978 670-7460	6447
Fluid Management Systems Inc	Billerica	MA	E	617 393-2396	6448
Fswh Intl Holdings LLC (HQ)	Waltham	MA	E	781 622-1000	12685
Genomic Solutions Inc	Holliston	MA	F	734 975-4800	9212
High Voltage Engineering Corp	Wakefield	MA	E	781 224-1001	12511
Honle Uv America Inc	Marlborough	MA	G	508 229-7774	10163
Illinois Tool Works Inc	Norwood	MA	B	781 828-2500	11179
Imaging W Varex Holdings Inc	Waltham	MA	E	781 663-6900	12695
Innov-X Systems Inc	Waltham	MA	C	781 938-5005	12700
Intelcoat Tech Dgtal Imging HI	West Springfield	MA	E	413 536-7800	13030
International Light Tech Inc	Peabody	MA	E	978 818-6180	11319
Ionsense Inc	Billerica	MA	F	781 231-1739	6456
Izon Science US Limited	Medford	MA	G	617 945-5936	10290
Izon Science US LLC	Medford	MA	F	617 945-5936	10291
Jentek Sensors Inc	Marlborough	MA	F	781 642-9666	10171
Jeol Usa Inc (HQ)	Peabody	MA	C	978 535-5900	11320
Kramer Scientific LLC	Amesbury	MA	G	978 388-7159	5840
Krohn-Hite Corporation	Brockton	MA	F	508 580-1660	7288
Labthink International Inc	Medford	MA	F	617 830-2190	10293
Lase Innovation Inc	Woburn	MA	G	617 599-0003	13600
Leica Biosystems	Danvers	MA	D	978 471-0625	8199
Life Technologies Corporation	Framingham	MA	E	508 383-7700	8786
Listen Inc	Boston	MA	E	617 556-4104	6860
M-R Resources Inc	Fitchburg	MA	F	978 345-9010	8659
Magellan Biosciences Inc (HQ)	North Billerica	MA	F	978 856-2345	10930
Magellan Diagnostics Inc (HQ)	Chelmsford	MA	D	978 250-7000	7937
Magellan Diagnostics Inc	North Billerica	MA	E	978 856-2345	10931
Malvern Panalytical Inc	Northampton	MA	E	413 586-7720	11070
Matec Instrument Companies Inc (PA)	Northborough	MA	E	508 393-0155	11102
Medica Corporation (PA)	Bedford	MA	C	781 275-4892	6240
Memed US Inc	Andover	MA	E	617 335-0349	5895
Microcal LLC	Northampton	MA	F	413 586-7720	11072
Midac Corporation	Westfield	MA	F	413 642-5595	13188
Minuteman Laboratories Inc	Chelmsford	MA	F	978 263-2632	7939
Mj Research Inc (HQ)	Waltham	MA	C	510 724-7000	12722
Mtoz Biolabs Inc	Cambridge	MA	E	617 401-8103	7657
New Objective Inc	Littleton	MA	F	781 933-9560	9828
Nova Biomedical Corporation (PA)	Waltham	MA	A	781 894-0800	12738
Nova Metrix LLC	Woburn	MA	F	781 897-1200	13625
Omniprobe Inc	Concord	MA	E		8129
On-Site Analysis Inc (DH)	Chelmsford	MA	G	561 775-5756	7942
Optra Inc	Wilmington	MA	F	978 887-6600	13443
Organomation Associates Inc	Berlin	MA	F	978 838-7300	6320
Particles Plus Inc	Stoughton	MA	F	781 341-6898	12227
Philips North America LLC	Natick	MA	D	508 647-1130	10490
Photonis Scientific Inc (DH)	Sturbridge	MA	F	508 347-4000	12257
Physical Sciences Inc (PA)	Andover	MA	D	978 689-0003	5907
Pion Inc	Billerica	MA	F	978 528-2020	6472
Pp Systems International Inc	Amesbury	MA	G	978 834-0505	5849
Precision Systems Inc	Natick	MA	E	508 655-7010	10494
Proveris Scientific Corp (PA)	Hudson	MA	E	508 460-8822	9405
Pvd Products Inc	Wilmington	MA	F	978 694-9455	13448
Rapid Micro Biosystems Inc (PA)	Lowell	MA	C	978 349-3200	9916
Resonance Research Inc	Billerica	MA	E	978 671-0811	6476
Revvity Inc	Billerica	MA	E	978 439-5511	6477
Revvity Inc	Boston	MA	F	617 596-9909	7009
Revvity Inc	Hopkinton	MA	F	508 435-9500	9343
Revvity Inc (PA)	Waltham	MA	C	781 663-6900	12767
Revvity Health Sciences Inc (DH)	Waltham	MA	D	781 663-6900	12768
Rigaku Analytical Devices Inc	Wilmington	MA	E	855 785-1064	13449
Roscid Technologies Inc	Woburn	MA	G	781 933-4007	13656
Sage Science Inc	Beverly	MA	F	617 922-1832	6380
Schoeffel International Corp	Chelmsford	MA	E	978 256-4512	7955
Sciaps Inc (PA)	Woburn	MA	E	339 222-2585	13662
Scientific Instrument Facility	Boston	MA	F	617 353-5056	7027
Semilab USA LLC	North Billerica	MA	F	508 647-8400	10953
Semtech Solutions Inc	North Billerica	MA	E	978 663-9822	10954
Sensitech Inc (DH)	Beverly	MA	D	978 927-7033	6383

Company	CITY	ST	EMP	PHONE	ENTRY#
Sensortech Systems Inc	Westborough	MA	F	805 981-3735	13134
Sick Inc	Stoughton	MA	D	781 302-2500	12235
Skyray Instrument Inc	Stoughton	MA	F	617 202-3879	12237
Spectra Analysis Inc (PA)	Marlborough	MA	G	508 281-6232	10211
Spectral Evolution Inc	Haverhill	MA	G	978 687-1833	9132
Spectris Inc (HQ)	Westborough	MA	E	508 768-6400	13137
Spectro Analytical Instruments Inc (HQ)	Wilmington	MA	E	201 642-3000	13456
Teledyne Flir LLC	North Billerica	MA	C	978 901-8000	10961
Thermedetec Inc	Waltham	MA	F	508 520-0430	12797
Thermo Eberline LLC (HQ)	Franklin	MA	F	508 553-1582	8867
Thermo Envmtl Instrs LLC (HQ)	Franklin	MA	C	508 520-0430	8868
Thermo Fisher	Somerville	MA	F	781 325-8726	11901
Thermo Fisher Fincl Svcs Inc	Waltham	MA	D	781 622-1000	12799
Thermo Fisher Scientific Inc	Chelmsford	MA	E	978 250-7000	7966
Thermo Fisher Scientific Inc	Franklin	MA	C	713 272-0404	8869
Thermo Fisher Scientific Inc	Tewksbury	MA	D	781 622-1000	12422
Thermo Fisher Scientific Inc (PA)	Waltham	MA	C	781 622-1000	12800
Thermo Ice Inc (HQ)	Milford	MA	D		10421
Thermo Orion Inc (HQ)	Chelmsford	MA	E	800 225-1480	7967
Thermo Scntfic Prtble Anlytcal (HQ)	Tewksbury	MA	C	978 657-5555	12423
Thoratec LLC	Burlington	MA	C	781 272-0139	7440
Thrive Bioscience Inc	Beverly	MA	G	978 720-8048	6388
Umass Mem Mri Imaging Ctr LLC	Worcester	MA	F	508 756-7300	13814
Union Biometrica Inc (PA)	Holliston	MA	F	508 893-3115	9236
Unity Scientific LLC	Westborough	MA	E	203 740-2999	13142
Vacuum Process Technology LLC	Cambridge	MA	E	508 732-7200	7749
Vacuum Technology Inc	Gloucester	MA	G	510 333-6562	8962
Viken Detection Corporation	Burlington	MA	E	617 467-5526	7445
Waters Associates Inc	Milford	MA	A	508 634-4500	10423
Waters Corporation (PA)	Milford	MA	A	508 478-2000	10424
Waters Technologies Corp	Franklin	MA	E	508 482-4807	8875
Waters Technologies Corp (HQ)	Milford	MA	A	508 478-2000	10425
Waters Technologies Corp	Taunton	MA	F	508 482-5223	12376
Waveguide Corporation	Waltham	MA	G	617 892-9700	12816
Williamson Corporation	Concord	MA	F	978 369-9607	8141
Witec Instruments Corp	Concord	MA	F	865 690-5550	8142
Xenogen Corporation (DH)	Hopkinton	MA	D	508 435-9500	9347
American Healthcare	Scarborough	ME	F	888 567-7733	5423
Artel Inc	Westbrook	ME	E	207 854-0860	5614
Envirologix Inc (PA)	Portland	ME	E	207 797-0300	5215
Fhc Inc (PA)	Bowdoin	ME	D	207 666-8190	4605
Idexx Distribution Inc	Westbrook	ME	D	207 556-0300	5630
Idexx Operations Inc (HQ)	Westbrook	ME	E	207 556-4388	5632
Wjb Associates Inc	Mount Vernon	ME	G	207 293-2457	5078
Yokogawa Fluid Imging Tech Inc	Scarborough	ME	E	207 289-3200	5448
Allen Datagraph Systems Inc	Salem	NH	E	603 216-6344	15504
Brailsford & Company Inc	Antrim	NH	F	603 588-2880	13896
Diversified Enterprises-ADT	Claremont	NH	G	603 543-0038	14088
EMD Millipore Corporation	Jaffrey	NH	B	603 532-8711	14567
Environmental Test Pdts Inc (PA)	Hollis	NH	Gj	603 924-5010	14451
Integra Biosciences Corp	Hudson	NH	F	603 578-5800	14510
Integra Biosciences Corp	Hudson	NH	F	603 578-5800	14511
Integra Biosciences Corp	Merrimack	NH	G	603 578-5800	14985
Kentek Corporation (PA)	Boscawen	NH	E	603 223-4900	13990
Labsphere Inc	North Sutton	NH	C	603 927-4266	15254
M Braun Inc	Stratham	NH	D	603 773-9333	15638
Metavac LLC	Portsmouth	NH	F	631 207-2344	15423
Microelectrodes Inc	Bedford	NH	G	603 668-0692	13944
Optical Filter Corporation	Keene	NH	A	603 357-7662	14614
Owl Separation Systems LLC	Newington	NH	D	603 559-9297	15209
Poly-Vac Inc	Manchester	NH	C	603 647-7822	14912
Teledyne Flir LLC	Hudson	NH	E	603 324-7783	14551
Teledyne Flir Coml Systems Inc	Hudson	NH	C	603 324-7824	14552
Teledyne Instrs Leeman Labs	Hudson	NH	D	603 521-3299	14553
Teledyne Instruments Inc	Hudson	NH	D	603 886-8400	14554
Teledyne Tekmar Company Inc	Hudson	NH	D	603 886-8400	14555
Thermo Fisher Scientific Inc (HQ)	Portsmouth	NH	E	603 431-8410	15443
Thermo Neslab LLC	Newington	NH	G	603 436-9444	15215
Valmet Inc	Nashua	NH	C	603 882-2711	15181
Wilbur Technical Services LLC	Mont Vernon	NH	G	603 880-7100	15050
Agilent Technologies Inc	North Kingstown	RI	D	800 338-1754	16229
Dewetron Inc	East Greenwich	RI	E	401 284-3750	15980
G&G Technologies Inc	Coventry	RI	F	401 295-4000	15813
Hanna Instruments Inc (PA)	Woonsocket	RI	E	401 765-7500	16962
Thermo Fisher Scientific Inc	North Kingstown	RI	A	401 294-1234	16286
Ultra Scientific Incorporated	North Kingstown	RI	E	800 338-1754	16290
Agilent Technologies Inc	Winooski	VT	F	802 861-8597	17765
Biotek Instruments Inc (HQ)	Winooski	VT	C	802 655-4040	17767
Med Associates Inc (PA)	Fairfax	VT	D	802 527-2343	17262
Raj Communications Ltd	Essex Junction	VT	E	802 658-4961	17243

3827 Optical instruments and lenses

Company	CITY	ST	EMP	PHONE	ENTRY#
4 D Technology Corporation	East Hampton	CT	E	860 365-0420	957

	CITY	ST	EMP	PHONE	ENTRY#
Adaptive Optics Associates Inc	East Hartford	CT	F	860 282-4401	969
Aperture Optical Sciences Inc (PA)	Meriden	CT	E	860 316-2589	1654
Coating Design Group Inc	Stratford	CT	E	203 878-3663	3528
Coburn Technologies Inc (DH)	South Windsor	CT	E	860 648-6600	3129
Coburn Technologies Intl Inc (DH)	South Windsor	CT	E	860 648-6600	3130
Conoptics Inc	Danbury	CT	F	203 743-3349	722
Crystal Fairfield Tech LLC	New Milford	CT	G	860 354-2111	2241
CT Fiberoptics	Somers	CT	F	860 763-4341	3098
Data Technology Inc	Tolland	CT	A	860 871-8082	3656
Eschenbach Optik America Inc (PA)	Danbury	CT	F	203 702-1600	739
Fiberoptics Technology Inc (PA)	Pomfret	CT	C	860 928-0443	2807
Flabeg Technical Glass US Corp	Naugatuck	CT	E	203 729-5227	1958
Flemming Tinker Incorporated	Durham	CT	F	860 316-2589	900
Gerber Coburn Optical Inc (DH)	South Windsor	CT	C	800 843-1479	3150
Lenscrafters	Milford	CT	G	203 878-8511	1845
Nntechnology Moore Systems LLC	Bridgeport	CT	D	203 366-3224	352
Orafol Americas Inc	Avon	CT	C	860 676-7100	35
Retina Systems Inc	Seymour	CT	E	203 881-1311	2968
Scope Technology Incorporated	Plainfield	CT	F	860 963-1141	2739
Tower Optical Company Inc	Norwalk	CT	C	203 866-4535	2586
United Technologies Optical Systems Inc	Windsor Locks	CT	C	860 654-6000	4336
Zygo Corporation (HQ)	Middlefield	CT	G	860 347-8506	1732
Acton Research Corporation	Acton	MA	E	941 556-2601	5731
Adaptive Optics Associates Inc	Devens	MA	F	978 391-0000	8267
Adaptive Optics Associates Inc	Devens	MA	F	978 757-9600	8268
Adaptive Optics Associates Inc (DH)	Devens	MA	D	978 757-9600	8269
AMF Optical Solutions LLC	Woburn	MA	F	781 933-6125	13509
Amplitude Laser Inc	Cambridge	MA	F	857 285-5952	7485
Angstrom Advanced Inc	Stoughton	MA	D	781 519-4765	12194
Applied Science Group Inc	Billerica	MA	E	781 275-4000	6404
Atlantic RES Mktg Systems Inc	West Bridgewater	MA	F	508 584-7816	12966
Atlantic Vision Inc	Shrewsbury	MA	G	508 845-8401	11828
Axsun Technologies Inc	Billerica	MA	D	978 262-0049	6408
Bae Systems Info Elctrnic Syst	Lexington	MA	C	603 885-4321	9726
Bern Optics Inc	Westfield	MA	F	413 568-6800	13152
Boston Piezo-Optics Inc	Bellingham	MA	F	508 966-4988	6287
Cambrdge RES Instrmntation Inc	Hopkinton	MA	E	781 935-9099	9311
Carl Zeiss Vision Inc	Marlborough	MA	G	800 327-9735	10130
Dynasil Corporation America (PA)	Concord	MA	E	617 668-6855	8116
Eidolon Corporation	Natick	MA	G	781 400-0586	10479
Enos Engineering LLC	Acton	MA	G	978 654-6522	5745
Eo Vista LLC	Acton	MA	F	978 635-8080	5746
Excel Technology Inc (HQ)	Bedford	MA	D	781 266-5700	6226
Excelitas Technologies Corp	Billerica	MA	D	978 262-0049	6446
Excelitas Technologies Corp (DH)	Waltham	MA	E	855 382-2677	12673
Eye Health Services Inc	Plymouth	MA	E	508 747-6425	11459
Eye Health Services Inc (PA)	Quincy	MA	E	617 472-5242	11517
Genscope Inc	East Longmeadow	MA	F	413 526-0802	8377
Headwall Photonics Inc	Bolton	MA	D	978 353-4100	6497
Hilsinger Company Parent LLC (PA)	Mansfield	MA	E	508 699-4406	10055
Holographix LLC	Marlborough	MA	F	978 562-4474	10162
I-Optics Corp	Burlington	MA	G	508 366-1600	7378
Incom Inc	Charlton	MA	C	508 909-2200	7889
Innovations In Optics Inc	Woburn	MA	F	781 933-4477	13585
Instrument Technology Inc	Westfield	MA	E	413 562-3512	13173
J P Mfg Inc	Southbridge	MA	G	508 764-2538	12023
Kinetic Systems Inc	Boston	MA	E	617 522-8700	6842
L3 Technologies Inc	Northampton	MA	A	413 586-2330	11069
L3 Technologies Inc	Wilmington	MA	C	978 694-9991	13422
Materion Prcsion Optics Thin F (DH)	Westford	MA	F	978 692-7513	13249
McAllister Optical Inc	Woburn	MA	E	781 938-0456	13608
Newport Corporation	Franklin	MA	D	508 553-5035	8855
Novotech Inc	Acton	MA	F	978 929-9458	5760
Opco Laboratory Inc	Fitchburg	MA	E	978 345-2522	8670
Ophir Optics LLC	Wilmington	MA	D	978 657-6410	13441
Opticraft Inc	Woburn	MA	F	781 938-0456	13626
Optikos Corporation	Wakefield	MA	D	617 354-7557	12525
Optimum Technologies Inc	Southbridge	MA	F	508 765-8100	12032
Opto-Line International Inc	Wilmington	MA	F	978 658-7255	13442
Optometrics Corporation (HQ)	Littleton	MA	E	978 772-1700	9830
Optos Inc	Marlborough	MA	D	508 787-1400	10192
Optra Inc	Wilmington	MA	F	978 887-6600	13443
Orpro Vision LLC	Billerica	MA	G	617 676-1101	6467
Pioneer Precision Optics Inc	Florence	MA	F	413 341-3992	8685
Plymouth Grating Lab Inc	Carver	MA	F	508 465-2274	7857
Polychromix	Wilmington	MA	F	978 284-6000	13447
Precision Optics Corp Inc (PA)	Gardner	MA	D	978 630-1800	8898
Primary Pdc Inc (PA)	Waltham	MA	G	781 386-2000	12753
Prior Scientific Inc (HQ)	Rockland	MA	F	781 878-8442	11658
Rubil Associates Inc	Billerica	MA	F	978 670-7192	6478
S I Howard Glass Company Inc	Worcester	MA	E	508 753-8146	13785
Scientific Solutions Inc	North Chelmsford	MA	F	978 251-4554	10988
Spectro Scientific Inc (HQ)	Chelmsford	MA	D	978 486-0123	7959
Sycamore Networks Inc	Chelmsford	MA	C	978 250-2900	7962
Tel Mnfacturing Engrg Amer Inc	Billerica	MA	E	978 436-2300	6487
Thermo Vision Corp (HQ)	Franklin	MA	E	508 520-0083	8871
Thin Film Imaging Technologies	Greenfield	MA	F	413 774-6692	9002
Transom Scopes Inc	Westfield	MA	E	413 562-3606	13213
United Lens Company Inc	Southbridge	MA	C	508 765-5421	12037
Vacuum Process Technology LLC	Cambridge	MA	E	508 732-7200	7749
Zibra Corporation	Westport	MA	F	508 636-6606	13302
Lh Liquidation LLC	Windham	ME	E	207 893-8233	5664
Ametek Precitech Inc (HQ)	Keene	NH	D	603 357-2510	14588
Andover Corporation	Salem	NH	E	603 893-6888	15506
Bae Systems Oasys LLC	Hudson	NH	D	603 232-8221	14487
Bond Optics LLC	Lebanon	NH	F	603 448-2300	14685
Clear Align LLC	Nashua	NH	F	603 889-2116	15081
Contour Fine Tooling Inc	Keene	NH	G	603 876-4908	14593
G5 Infrared LLC	Hudson	NH	G	603 304-5722	14498
General Dynmics Mssion Systems	Nashua	NH	F	603 864-6300	15103
Gooch & Housego (keene) LLC	Keene	NH	E	603 358-5577	14601
Guidewire Technologies Inc	Salem	NH	F	603 894-4399	15534
Guild Optical Associates Inc	Amherst	NH	F	603 889-6247	13872
Hardric Laboratories Inc	Hudson	NH	E	978 251-1702	14506
Janos Technology Inc	Keene	NH	F	603 757-0070	14603
Janos Technology LLC (DH)	Keene	NH	D	603 757-0070	14604
Km Holding Inc	Hudson	NH	D	603 566-2704	14516
L3 Technologies Inc	Londonderry	NH	A	603 626-4800	14760
Moore Nntechnology Systems LLC (DH)	Swanzey	NH	F	603 352-3030	15645
National Aperture Inc	Salem	NH	F	603 893-7393	15547
Optical Filter Corporation	Keene	NH	A	603 357-7662	14614
Optical Solutions Inc	Charlestown	NH	G	603 826-4411	14066
Optics 1 Inc (DH)	Bedford	NH	F	603 296-0469	13947
Puritan Electronics Inc	Manchester	NH	E	800 343-8649	14919
Space Optics Research Labs LLC	Merrimack	NH	F	978 250-8640	15005
Wilcox Industries Corp (PA)	Newington	NH	D	603 431-1331	15216
Wilcox Industries Corp	Newington	NH	E	603 431-1331	15217
Adolf Meller Company (PA)	Providence	RI	E	800 821-0180	16465
Knight Optical (usa) LLC	North Kingstown	RI	G	401 521-7000	16266
Nippon American Limited	East Greenwich	RI	F	401 885-7353	15992
Pyramid Case Co Inc	Providence	RI	D	401 273-0643	16595
89 North Inc	Williston	VT	F	802 881-0302	17719
Chroma Technology Corp	Bellows Falls	VT	C	802 428-2500	17029
Diffraction Ltd	Waitsfield	VT	G	802 496-6640	17666
J & L Metrology Inc	Springfield	VT	G	802 885-8291	17619
Omega Optical Holdings LLC (PA)	Brattleboro	VT	F	802 251-7300	17098
Vermont Precision Machine Svcs	Springfield	VT	G	802 885-8291	17623

3829 Measuring and controlling devices, nec

	CITY	ST	EMP	PHONE	ENTRY#
AKO Inc	Windsor	CT	E	860 298-9765	4256
American Design & Mfg Inc	South Windsor	CT	E	860 282-2719	3112
Bauer Inc	Bristol	CT	D	860 583-9100	409
Clinton Instrument Company	Clinton	CT	D	860 669-7548	638
Cooper-Atkins Corporation (HQ)	Middlefield	CT	C	860 349-3473	1724
Data Technology Inc	Tolland	CT	A	860 871-8082	3656
Edmunds Manufacturing Company (PA)	Farmington	CT	D	860 677-2813	1218
Electro-Methods Inc (PA)	South Windsor	CT	C	860 289-8661	3141
Fischer Technology Inc (DH)	Windsor	CT	E	860 683-0781	4276
Gold Line Connector Inc (PA)	Redding	CT	E	203 938-2884	2882
Graywolf Sensing Solutions LLC (PA)	Shelton	CT	G	203 402-0477	3009
Habco Industries LLC	Glastonbury	CT	E	860 682-6800	1283
Harcosemco LLC	Branford	CT	C	203 483-3700	263
Hayward Turnstiles Inc	Milford	CT	E	203 647-9144	1834
Hipotronics Inc (HQ)	Shelton	CT	C	845 279-3644	3013
Hitachi Aloka Medical Ltd	Wallingford	CT	F	203 269-5088	3813
Hitachi Aloka Medical Amer Inc	Wallingford	CT	D	800 872-5652	3814
Image Insight Inc	East Hartford	CT	G	888 667-9244	1001
Jurman Metrics Inc	Monroe	CT	F	203 261-9388	1914
Kahn Industries Inc	East Hampton	CT	E	860 529-8643	963
Kem Liquidating Company Inc	Glastonbury	CT	G	860 430-5100	1287
Leica Geosystems Inc	Danbury	CT	F	203 744-8362	768
Lex Products LLC (PA)	Trumbull	CT	C	203 363-3738	3723
Miracle Instruments Co	Lebanon	CT	F	860 642-7745	1549
Mirion Tech Canberra Inc (DH)	Meriden	CT	D	203 238-2351	1677
Omega Engineering Inc	Norwalk	CT	D	714 540-4914	2548
Online River LLC	Westport	CT	F	203 801-5900	4191
Perey Turnstiles Inc	Bridgeport	CT	E	203 333-9400	358
Power-Dyne LLC	Middletown	CT	E	860 346-9283	1772
Pratt Whtney Msrment Systems I	Bloomfield	CT	E	860 286-8181	203
Precision Sensors Inc	Milford	CT	E	203 877-2795	1870
Preferred Utilities Mfg Corp (HQ)	Danbury	CT	D	203 743-6741	799
Projects Inc	Glastonbury	CT	C	860 633-4615	1295
Semco Instruments Inc	Branford	CT	E	661 362-6117	276
Semco Instruments Inc (DH)	Branford	CT	C	203 483-3700	277
Simmonds Precision Pdts Inc	Danbury	CT	F	203 797-5000	818
Soldream Inc	Vernon Rockville	CT	E	860 871-6883	3762

	CITY	ST	EMP	PHONE	ENTRY#
Sperian Prtction Instrmnttion	Middletown	CT	D	860 344-1079	1783
Star Equity Holdings Inc (PA)	Old Greenwich	CT	D	203 489-9500	2635
Technisonic Research Inc	Fairfield	CT	G	203 368-3600	1201
Tek-Air Systems Inc	Monroe	CT	E	203 791-1400	1923
Teledyne Bolt Inc	Norwalk	CT	C	203 853-0700	2577
Trans-Tek Inc	Ellington	CT	E	860 872-8351	1118
Unholtz-Dickie Corporation	Wallingford	CT	E	203 265-3929	3872
Weigh & Test Systems Inc	Riverside	CT	F	203 698-9681	2911
Abbess Instrs & Systems Inc	Holliston	MA	F	508 429-0002	9197
Accusonic Technologies (DH)	New Bedford	MA	F	508 495-6600	10560
Adaptive Wreless Solutions LLC	Hudson	MA	E	978 875-6000	9351
Ade Technologies Inc (HQ)	Westwood	MA	D	781 467-3500	13305
Admet Inc	Norwood	MA	G	781 769-0850	11155
Advanced Mechanical Tech Inc (PA)	Watertown	MA	E	617 923-4174	12855
Advanced Thermal Solutions Inc (PA)	Norwood	MA	E	781 769-2800	11157
Aja International Inc	Hingham	MA	E	781 545-7365	9139
Allm USA Inc	Cambridge	MA	F	857 209-5065	7477
Ametek Inc	Wilmington	MA	D	978 988-4101	13377
Anderson Power Products Inc (HQ)	Sterling	MA	D	978 422-3600	12154
Artemis Capital Partners LLC (PA)	Boston	MA	G	857 327-5606	6559
Associated Envmtl Systems Inc (PA)	Acton	MA	C	978 772-0022	5738
Auburn Filtersense LLC	Beverly	MA	E	978 777-2460	6327
Axcelis Technologies Inc (PA)	Beverly	MA	A	978 787-4000	6330
Barbour Stockwell Inc	Woburn	MA	E	781 933-5200	13520
Barrett Technology LLC	Newton	MA	E	617 252-9000	10737
Business and Prof Exch Inc	Beverly	MA	E	978 556-4100	6336
C2sense Inc	Watertown	MA	E	617 651-3991	12865
Capacitec Inc (PA)	Ayer	MA	F	978 772-6033	6176
Control Resources Inc	Littleton	MA	E	978 486-4160	9806
Convectronics Inc	Haverhill	MA	E	978 374-7714	9088
CTS Valpey Corporation (HQ)	Hopkinton	MA	D	508 435-6831	9314
Doble Engineering Company (HQ)	Marlborough	MA	F	617 926-4900	10145
Druck LLC (HQ)	Billerica	MA	C	978 437-1000	6432
Dynisco Instruments LLC	Billerica	MA	E	978 215-3401	6435
Dynisco Instruments LLC (HQ)	Franklin	MA	C	508 541-9400	8831
Dynisco LLC (HQ)	Franklin	MA	D	508 541-3195	8832
Dynisco Parent Inc	Billerica	MA	B	978 667-5301	6436
Electro Switch Corp	Weymouth	MA	F	781 335-1195	13325
Electro-Fix Inc	Plainville	MA	E	508 695-0228	11432
Evident Scientific Inc (PA)	Waltham	MA	A	781 419-3900	12668
Fabreeka Intl Holdings Inc (DH)	Stoughton	MA	E	781 341-3655	12207
Fitbit Inc	Boston	MA	D	857 277-0594	6738
Forte Technology Inc	South Easton	MA	F	508 297-2363	11943
Galvanic Applied Scnces USA In	North Billerica	MA	F	978 848-2701	10913
Gefran Isi Inc	North Andover	MA	F	781 729-0842	10837
GTC Falcon Inc	Plymouth	MA	F	508 746-0200	11462
Hamilton Thorne Inc (PA)	Beverly	MA	E	978 921-2050	6352
Hefring Inc	Gloucester	MA	F	617 938-9544	8941
Hitec Products Inc	Pepperell	MA	F	978 772-6963	11384
Human Systems Integration Inc	East Walpole	MA	F	508 660-2500	8419
Ide Acquisition Corp	Westwood	MA	G	781 326-5700	13311
Ideal Industries Inc	Sterling	MA	G	978 422-3600	12163
Illinois Tool Works Inc	Norwood	MA	B	781 828-2500	11179
Industrial Physics PDT Intgrit	Devens	MA	F	978 772-0970	8273
Instron Japan Company Ltd	Norwood	MA	B	781 828-2500	11184
Integrated Dynamics Engrg Inc (HQ)	Mansfield	MA	F	781 300-6561	10059
International Light Tech Inc	Peabody	MA	E	978 818-6180	11319
Johnson Controls Inc	Wrentham	MA	E	508 384-0018	13843
Kerfoot Technologies Inc	Falmouth	MA	F	508 539-3002	8634
Kinetic Systems Inc	Boston	MA	E	617 522-8700	6842
Krohn-Hite Corporation	Brockton	MA	F	508 580-1660	7288
M-R Resources Inc	Fitchburg	MA	E	978 345-9010	8659
Matec Instrument Companies Inc (PA)	Northborough	MA	E	508 393-0155	11102
Materials Systems Inc	Littleton	MA	G	978 486-0404	9824
Maximum Inc	New Bedford	MA	G	508 995-2200	10621
Microsense LLC (HQ)	Lowell	MA	E	978 843-7670	9908
Mistras Group Inc	Auburn	MA	D	508 832-5500	6121
Mks Instruments Inc	Lawrence	MA	F	978 975-2350	9585
Nanmac Corp	Milford	MA	E	508 872-4811	10407
New England Phtoconductor Corp	Norton	MA	E	508 285-5561	11130
Nortekusa Inc	Boston	MA	G	617 206-5755	6924
Novanta Inc	Bedford	MA	D	781 266-5200	6247
Novanta Inc	Bedford	MA	C	781 266-5700	6248
Onto Innovation Inc (PA)	Wilmington	MA	C	978 253-6200	13440
Optra Inc	Wilmington	MA	F	978 887-6600	13443
Oxford Instrs Msrement Systems	Concord	MA	E	978 369-9933	8130
Oxford Instruments America Inc (HQ)	Concord	MA	E	978 369-9933	8131
Photonis Scientific Inc (DH)	Sturbridge	MA	F	508 347-4000	12257
Physical Sciences Inc (PA)	Andover	MA	D	978 689-0003	5907
Pinpoint Laser Systems Inc	Peabody	MA	F	978 532-8001	11333
Princton Gamma-Tech Instrs Inc	Franklin	MA	E	609 924-7310	8858
Prior Scientific Inc (HQ)	Rockland	MA	F	781 878-8442	11658
Quadtech Inc	Marlborough	MA	D	978 461-2100	10198
Quality Engineering Assoc Inc	Chelmsford	MA	G	978 528-2034	7949
Radiation Monitoring Dvcs Inc (HQ)	Watertown	MA	E	617 668-6800	12902
Rmd Instruments Corp	Watertown	MA	F	617 668-6900	12905
Rotek Instrument Corp	Waltham	MA	E	781 899-4611	12774
Rudolph Technologies Inc (HQ)	Wilmington	MA	D	978 253-6200	13450
Schenck USA Corp	Hudson	MA	E	978 562-6017	9410
Schneeberger Inc (DH)	Woburn	MA	G	781 271-0140	13660
Schoeffel International Corp	Chelmsford	MA	F	978 256-4512	7955
Second Wind Systems Inc	Newton	MA	F	617 581-6090	10782
Second Wind Systems Inc	Newton	MA	F	617 467-1500	10783
Secure Point Technologies Inc	Boston	MA	D	978 752-1700	7031
Semiconsoft Inc	Southborough	MA	F	617 388-6832	12001
Sensortech Systems Inc	Westborough	MA	F	805 981-3735	13134
Setra Systems Inc	Boxboro	MA	F	978 263-1400	7145
Sick Inc	Stoughton	MA	D	781 302-2500	12235
Silverside Detectors Inc	Waltham	MA	G	617 684-5925	12779
Spectris Inc (HQ)	Westborough	MA	E	508 768-6400	13137
Spectro Scientific Inc (HQ)	Chelmsford	MA	D	978 486-0123	7959
Spire Metering Technology LLC	Marlborough	MA	F	978 263-7100	10215
Square Robot Inc	Marlborough	MA	E	617 274-8389	10216
Sundance Wind Project LLC	Andover	MA	D	978 409-9712	5928
Technical Manufacturing Corp (HQ)	Peabody	MA	D	978 532-6330	11346
Tekscan Inc	Norwood	MA	D	617 464-4500	11215
Teledyne Lecroy Inc	Marion	MA	E	508 748-0103	10102
Test Devices Inc	Hudson	MA	E	978 562-6017	9417
Testing Machines Inc	Swansea	MA	D	302 613-5600	12313
Thermalogic Corporation	Hudson	MA	E	800 343-4492	9420
Thermo Envmtl Instrs LLC (HQ)	Franklin	MA	C	508 520-0430	8868
Thermo Instrument Systems Inc	Waltham	MA	F	781 622-1000	12801
Thermo Process Instruments LP	Franklin	MA	C	508 553-6913	8870
Toolmex Indus Solutions Inc (PA)	Northborough	MA	D	508 653-8897	11114
Trans Metrics Inc (HQ)	Watertown	MA	E	617 926-1000	12916
Triangle Engineering Inc	Hanover	MA	F	781 878-1500	9046
United Innovations Inc	Holyoke	MA	F	413 533-7500	9285
Vaisala Inc	Newton	MA	E	617 467-1500	10792
Vaisala Inc	Woburn	MA	G	508 574-1163	13683
Veralto Enterprise LLC (PA)	Waltham	MA	A	603 860-7300	12811
Waters Corporation (PA)	Milford	MA	A	508 478-2000	10424
Waters Technologies Corp (HQ)	Milford	MA	A	508 478-2000	10425
Whoop Inc (PA)	Boston	MA	B	617 670-1074	7122
Wildlife Acoustics Inc	Maynard	MA	E	978 369-5225	10266
Xchange Imc LLC	Maynard	MA	F	978 298-2100	10267
Franklin Grid Solutions LLC (HQ)	Saco	ME	E	207 571-1123	5366
Ibcontrols	Windham	ME	E	207 893-0080	5662
Idexx Distribution Inc	Westbrook	ME	D	207 556-0300	5630
Illinois Tool Works Inc	Mechanic Falls	ME	E	207 998-5140	5051
Sensor Research and Dev Corp	Orono	ME	G	207 866-0100	5137
Airmar Technology Corp (PA)	Milford	NH	B	603 673-9570	15013
Allard Nazarian Group Inc (PA)	Manchester	NH	C	603 668-1900	14810
ARC Technology Solutions LLC	Nashua	NH	D	603 883-3027	15064
Automated Video Insptn Dvcs	Portsmouth	NH	F	603 559-9700	15362
Cc1 Inc	Portsmouth	NH	E	603 319-2000	15368
Chauvin Arnoux Inc (PA)	Dover	NH	F	603 749-6434	14221
Enertrac Inc	Portsmouth	NH	F	603 821-0003	15382
Geokon Inc	Lebanon	NH	D	603 448-1562	14690
Geophysical Survey Systems Inc (DH)	Nashua	NH	D	603 893-1109	15104
Guidewire Technologies Inc	Salem	NH	E	603 894-4399	15534
Hampshire Controls Corp	Dover	NH	F	603 749-9424	14230
Kimball Physics Inc	Wilton	NH	E	603 878-1616	15705
Meggitt (new Hampshire) Inc	Londonderry	NH	C	603 669-0940	14767
Meggitt (orange County) Inc	Londonderry	NH	D	603 657-2603	14768
Microvision Inc (PA)	Seabrook	NH	F	603 474-5566	15598
Motorway Engineering Inc	Manchester	NH	F	603 668-6315	14893
National Aperture Inc	Salem	NH	F	603 893-7393	15547
Nexus Technology Inc	Nashua	NH	F	877 595-8116	15140
Oz Holding Corp	Merrimack	NH	F	603 546-0090	14996
Proteq Solutions LLC	Nashua	NH	F	603 888-6630	15151
RDF Corporation	Hudson	NH	D	603 882-5195	14539
Secure Care Products LLC	Concord	NH	D	603 223-0745	14156
Thomas Instruments Inc	Spofford	NH	G	603 363-4500	15630
Topcon Positioning Systems Inc	Concord	NH	G	800 421-0125	14164
United Sensor Corporation	Amherst	NH	F	603 672-0909	13894
Vibrac LLC (PA)	Manchester	NH	G	603 882-6777	14952
American Ecotech LLC	Warren	RI	F	877 247-0403	16748
Aspects Inc	Warren	RI	E	401 247-1854	16751
Astronova Inc (PA)	West Warwick	RI	C	401 828-4000	16902
Crest Manufacturing Company	Lincoln	RI	E	401 333-1350	16129
Kearflex Engineering Company	Warwick	RI	F	401 781-4900	16830
Raytheon Company	Portsmouth	RI	D	401 847-8000	16454
Textron Inc (PA)	Providence	RI	A	401 421-2800	16623
Verichem Laboratories Inc	Providence	RI	G	401 461-0180	16638
Alken Inc	Colchester	VT	E	802 655-3159	17185
Applied Research Assoc Inc	Randolph	VT	E	802 728-4588	17467

	CITY	ST	EMP	PHONE	ENTRY#
Bowles Corporation	North Ferrisburgh	VT	F	802 425-3447	17419
NRG Systems Inc	Hinesburg	VT	C	802 482-2255	17297
Senix Corporation	Hinesburg	VT	F	802 489-7300	17298
Simmonds Precision Products (DH)	Vergennes	VT	A	802 877-4000	17661

3841 Surgical and medical instruments

	CITY	ST	EMP	PHONE	ENTRY#
3M Company	Wallingford	CT	F	203 949-1630	3766
Abbott Associates Inc	Milford	CT	C	203 878-2370	1793
Abyrx Inc	Stamford	CT	C	855 475-9175	3269
Acme Monaco Corporation (PA)	New Britain	CT	C	860 224-1349	1995
Aegea Medical Inc	Trumbull	CT	E	650 701-1125	3709
Aerospace Techniques Inc	Middletown	CT	D	860 347-1200	1733
Apiject Systems Corp (PA)	Stamford	CT	E	203 461-7121	3284
Aplicare Products LLC (HQ)	Meriden	CT	D	203 630-0500	1655
Bartron Medical Imaging LLC	New Haven	CT	G	203 498-2184	2124
Becton Dickinson and Company	Canaan	CT	D	860 824-5487	552
Beekley Medical	Bristol	CT	E	860 583-4700	412
Bio-Med Devices Inc	Guilford	CT	D	203 458-0202	1386
Biosig Technologies Inc (PA)	Westport	CT	E	203 409-5444	4158
Blairden Precision Instruments Inc	Trumbull	CT	G	203 799-2000	3714
Boston Endo-Surgical Tech LLC	Bridgeport	CT	B	203 336-6479	303
Carwild Corporation (PA)	New London	CT	E	860 442-4914	2224
Cas Medical Systems Inc	Branford	CT	E	203 488-6056	242
Catachem Inc	Oxford	CT	G	203 262-0330	2689
CD Management LLC	Bristol	CT	F	203 269-0090	424
Cirtec Medical Corp	Enfield	CT	C	860 814-3973	1123
Clinical Dynamics Conn LLC	Bristol	CT	G	203 269-0090	428
Connecticut Hypodermics Inc	Wallingford	CT	D	203 265-4881	3792
Convexity Scientific Inc	New Haven	CT	G	844 359-7632	2138
Coopersurgical Inc (DH)	Trumbull	CT	C	203 601-5200	3716
Covidien Holding Inc	North Haven	CT	C	203 492-5000	2401
Covidien LP	New Haven	CT	C	781 839-1722	2141
Covidien LP	North Haven	CT	B	203 492-6332	2402
Covidien LP	North Haven	CT	A	203 492-5000	2403
Creo Medical Inc	Danbury	CT	F	860 670-6054	723
Cygnus Medical LLC	Branford	CT	G	800 990-7489	248
Dcg-Pmi Inc	Bethel	CT	E	203 743-5525	106
Epicurean Feast Medtron O	North Haven	CT	C	203 492-5000	2410
Eppendorf Manufacturing Corp	Enfield	CT	C	860 253-3400	1132
Frank Roth Co Inc	Stratford	CT	D	203 377-2155	3539
Furnace Source LLC	Terryville	CT	F	860 582-4201	3603
Hamilton Sndstrand Space Syste	Windsor Locks	CT	E	860 654-6000	4328
Hitachi Aloka Medical Ltd	Wallingford	CT	F	203 269-5088	3813
Hitachi Aloka Medical Amer Inc	Wallingford	CT	D	800 872-5652	3814
Hobbs Medical Inc	Stafford Springs	CT	E	860 684-5875	3256
Hologic Inc	Danbury	CT	C	203 790-1188	757
Hyperfine Operations Inc	Guilford	CT	E	866 796-6767	1396
Iodine Holdings Inc	Meriden	CT	C	203 630-0500	1669
K B C Electronics Inc	Milford	CT	F	203 298-9654	1842
Kinetic Concepts Inc	Newington	CT	F	860 594-1043	2303
Lacey Manufacturing Co LLC	Bridgeport	CT	B	203 336-0121	343
Lambda Investors LLC	Greenwich	CT	F	203 862-7000	1337
Lee Company (PA)	Westbrook	CT	A	860 399-6281	4140
Lensesonly LLC	Bloomfield	CT	F	860 769-2020	187
Lorad Corporation	Danbury	CT	C	203 790-5544	778
Lumendi LLC	Westport	CT	G	203 528-0316	4181
Madison Medical LLC	Madison	CT	E	203 245-0306	1563
Marel Corporation	West Haven	CT	G	203 934-8187	4114
Medtronic Inc	North Haven	CT	C	203 492-5764	2424
Memry Corporation (HQ)	Bethel	CT	B	203 739-1100	128
Microspecialities Inc	Middletown	CT	F	203 874-1832	1764
Microspecialties Inc	Milford	CT	G	203 874-1832	1849
Minimally Invasive Surgeon	Hartford	CT	G	860 241-0870	1493
Monopol Corporation	Bristol	CT	F	860 583-3852	471
Newmark Medical Components Inc	Waterbury	CT	F	203 753-1158	3951
Nordex Incorporated	Brookfield	CT	E	203 775-4877	532
Oerlikon AM Medical Inc	Shelton	CT	D	203 712-1030	3043
Opticare Health Systems Inc (DH)	Waterbury	CT	C	203 574-2020	3957
Oxford Science Inc	Oxford	CT	F	203 881-3115	2707
Perosphere Technologies Inc	Danbury	CT	G	475 218-4600	797
Precision Engineered Pdts LLC	Bridgeport	CT	G	203 336-6479	361
Promisim Inc	Greenwich	CT	E	203 554-2707	1344
Putnam Plastics Corporation	Dayville	CT	C	860 774-1559	867
Rapid Usa Inc	Stamford	CT	F	203 461-7121	3444
Rom Technologies Inc	Brookfield	CT	A	888 374-0855	537
Saar Corporation	Farmington	CT	F	860 674-9440	1246
SEI II Inc	Milford	CT	F	203 877-8488	1883
Sequel Special Products LLC	Wolcott	CT	D	203 759-1020	4377
Sleep Management Solutions LLC (DH)	Hartford	CT	F	888 497-5337	1508
Smiths Medical	East Granby	CT	G	860 413-3230	952
Smiths Medical Asd Inc	Southington	CT	E	860 621-9111	3232
Southington Tool & Mfg Corp	Plantsville	CT	E	860 276-0021	2796
Spine Wave Inc	Shelton	CT	D	203 944-9494	3064
Stryker Corporation	East Hartford	CT	F	860 528-1111	1024
Supernova Diagnostics Inc	New Canaan	CT	G	301 792-4345	2088
Surgiquest Inc	Milford	CT	D	203 799-2400	1892
Tarry Medical Products Inc	Danbury	CT	F	203 791-9001	823
Team Technologies Inc	Watertown	CT	G	860 945-9125	4031
Teleflex Incorporated	Coventry	CT	E	860 742-8821	683
Ultimate Wireforms Inc	Bristol	CT	D	860 582-9111	504
United Ophthalmics LLC	Middletown	CT	F	203 500-3332	1788
Utitec Inc (HQ)	Watertown	CT	D	860 945-0605	4035
Utitec Holdings Inc	Watertown	CT	D	860 945-0601	4036
Valleylab	Stamford	CT	E	203 461-9075	3490
Vilex LLC	Granby	CT	E	860 413-9875	1309
Vivax Medical Corporation	Naugatuck	CT	F	203 729-0514	1993
Wallach Surgical Devices Inc (PA)	Trumbull	CT	E	203 799-2000	3740
West-Conn Tool and Die Inc	Shelton	CT	E	203 538-5081	3077
Winslow Automatics Inc	New Britain	CT	D	860 225-6321	2075
3eo Health Inc	Beverly	MA	E	508 308-4805	6321
Abiomed R&D Inc (DH)	Danvers	MA	F	978 646-1400	8159
Accellent Acquisition Corp	Wilmington	MA	A	978 570-6900	13370
Accellent Holdings Corp	Wilmington	MA	A	978 570-6900	13371
Accellent LLC	Brimfield	MA	F	413 245-7144	7248
Activ Surgical Inc	Boston	MA	D	202 688-5648	6513
Advansource Biomaterials Corporation	Wilmington	MA	F	978 657-0075	13374
Akili Inc (PA)	Boston	MA	E	617 313-8853	6527
Allen Medical Systems Inc (DH)	Acton	MA	F	978 263-7727	5734
American Optics Limited	Wellesley Hills	MA	F	905 631-5377	12949
American Surgical Company LLC	Salem	MA	E	781 592-7200	11701
Amide Technologies Inc	Cambridge	MA	F	508 245-6839	7484
Amplitude Vascular Systems Inc	Boston	MA	F	754 755-1530	6546
Andover Healthcare Inc	Salisbury	MA	B	978 465-0044	11739
Anika Therapeutics Inc (PA)	Bedford	MA	C	781 457-9000	6207
Applied Tissue Tech LLC	Hingham	MA	G	781 366-3848	9141
Arrow International LLC	Chelmsford	MA	D	978 250-5100	7908
Arrow Interventional Inc	Chelmsford	MA	D	919 314-4948	7909
Arteriocyte Med Systems Inc	Hopkinton	MA	C	508 395-5998	9307
Arthrosurface Incorporated	Franklin	MA	D	508 520-3003	8817
Atc Technologies Inc	Wilmington	MA	E	781 939-0725	13383
Atrium Innovations	Sudbury	MA	E	978 579-2346	12260
Aurora Imaging Technology Inc (PA)	Danvers	MA	E	877 975-7530	8164
Avedro Inc (HQ)	Burlington	MA	C	781 768-3400	7337
Axiomed LLC	Malden	MA	F	978 232-3990	10002
Axya Medical Inc	Beverly	MA	F	978 232-9997	6331
Beaver Group LLC	Waltham	MA	G	781 647-5775	12603
Beaver-Visitec Intl Inc	Waltham	MA	F	781 906-8080	12604
Belmont Instrument LLC (PA)	Billerica	MA	E	978 663-0212	6409
Bfly Operations Inc	Burlington	MA	G	781 557-4800	7341
Bio Sphere Medical Inc	Rockland	MA	E	208 844-5008	11637
Biodevek Inc	Allston	MA	G	617 768-8246	5819
Boston Scientific Corporation	Marlborough	MA	B	508 382-0200	10118
Boston Scientific Corporation (PA)	Marlborough	MA	A	508 683-4000	10119
Boston Scientific Corporation	Quincy	MA	B	617 689-6000	11507
Boston Scientific Corporation	Watertown	MA	F	617 972-4000	12863
Boston Scientific Funding LLC	Marlborough	MA	G	508 683-4000	10120
Boston Scientific Intl Corp	Marlborough	MA	F	508 683-4000	10121
Brimfield Precision LLC	Brimfield	MA	C	413 245-7144	7249
Btl Industries Inc	Marlborough	MA	C	866 285-1656	10122
Bvi Medical Inc (PA)	Waltham	MA	E	866 906-8080	12615
Cambridge Heart Inc (PA)	Foxborough	MA	F	978 654-7600	8734
Cambridge Interventional LLC	Burlington	MA	F	978 793-2674	7342
Cardiofocus Inc	Marlborough	MA	D	508 658-7200	10129
Cerenovus Inc	Raynham	MA	D	908 704-4024	11583
Cheetah Medical Inc (PA)	Newton	MA	D	617 964-0613	10744
Chmc Otlrynglgic Fundation Inc (PA)	Boston	MA	F	617 355-8290	6654
Claret Medical Inc	Marlborough	MA	F	707 528-9300	10132
Clinical Instruments Intl	Burlington	MA	F	781 221-2266	7352
Codman & Shurtleff Inc	Bridgewater	MA	D	508 880-8100	7227
Cognex Germany Inc	Natick	MA	D	508 650-3000	10474
Cold Chain Technologies LLC	Franklin	MA	F	508 429-1395	8825
Cold Chain Technologies LLC (HQ)	Franklin	MA	D	508 429-1395	8826
Concert Medical LLC	Attleboro Falls	MA	E	781 261-7400	6082
Confluent Surgical Inc	Waltham	MA	D	781 839-1700	12638
Conformis Inc (HQ)	Billerica	MA	D	781 345-9001	6427
Conmed Corporation	Westborough	MA	F	508 366-3668	13093
Corindus Vascular Robotics Inc (PA)	Auburndale	MA	E	508 653-3335	6132
Covidien France Holdings Inc	Mansfield	MA	D	508 261-8000	10043
Covidien LP	Mansfield	MA	F	508 261-8000	10044
Covidien LP	Mansfield	MA	B	508 261-8000	10045
Covidien LP (HQ)	Mansfield	MA	C	763 514-4000	10046
Covidien LP	Woburn	MA	D	800 962-9888	13550
Covidien Sales LLC	Mansfield	MA	E	508 261-8000	10047
Cytonome/St LLC	Bedford	MA	F	617 330-5030	6220
Dale Medical Products Inc (PA)	Franklin	MA	D	800 343-3980	8829
David Clark Company Inc (PA)	Worcester	MA	C	508 756-6216	13713

	CITY	ST	EMP	PHONE	ENTRY#
Dentsply Ih Inc (HQ)	Waltham	MA	C	781 890-6800	12650
Depuy Mitek LLC	Raynham	MA	B	508 880-8100	11586
Depuy Synthes Products Inc (DH)	Raynham	MA	F	508 880-8100	11588
Diagnosys LLC (PA)	Lowell	MA	E	978 458-1600	9875
Diamond Diagnostics Inc (PA)	Holliston	MA	D	508 429-0450	9206
Digilab Genomic Solutions Inc	Holliston	MA	F	508 893-3130	9207
Digital Cognition Tech Inc	Waltham	MA	E	617 433-1777	12653
Direx Systems Corp	Canton	MA	G	339 502-6013	7785
Domain Surgical Inc	Lexington	MA	E	801 924-4950	9740
Draeger Medical Systems Inc	Andover	MA	B	800 437-2437	5880
Eagle Vision Inc	Dennis	MA	G	508 385-2283	8258
Earlysense Inc	Woburn	MA	F	781 373-3228	13561
Endodynamix Inc	Salem	MA	F	978 740-0400	11713
Eos Imaging Inc	Cambridge	MA	F	678 564-5400	7562
Erika of Texas Inc	Waltham	MA	A	956 783-4689	12665
Escalon Digital Solutions Inc	Stoneham	MA	F	610 688-6830	12178
Etex Corporation	Braintree	MA	E	617 577-7270	7182
Everest Halthcare Holdings Inc (DH)	Waltham	MA	G	781 699-9000	12667
Eyepoint Pharmaceuticals Inc (PA)	Watertown	MA	D	617 926-5000	12875
Fci Ophthalmics Inc	Pembroke	MA	F	781 826-9060	11365
Femtonics Usa Inc	Beverly	MA	E	361 210-3349	6347
Five Star Manufacturing Inc	New Bedford	MA	D	508 998-1404	10592
Five Star Surgical Inc	New Bedford	MA	D	508 998-1404	10593
Flodesign Sonics Inc	Wilbraham	MA	E	413 596-5900	13358
Fms New York Services LLC (DH)	Waltham	MA	F	781 699-9000	12677
Fresenius Med Care Hldings Inc (DH)	Waltham	MA	A	781 699-9000	12679
Fresenius Med Care Rnal Thrpie	Waltham	MA	F	781 699-9000	12680
Fresenius Med Care Vntures LLC (DH)	Waltham	MA	F	781 699-9000	12681
Fresenius Med Svcs Group LLC	Waltham	MA	F	781 699-9000	12682
Fresenius Usa Inc (DH)	Waltham	MA	C	781 699-4191	12683
Fresenius USA Marketing Inc (DH)	Waltham	MA	F	781 699-9000	12684
Functional Assessment Tech Inc	North Billerica	MA	F	978 663-2800	10912
Gcb Medical LLC	Duxbury	MA	F	617 699-6715	8331
Gregory Manufacturing Inc	Holyoke	MA	D	413 536-5432	9257
Guidant Corporation	Marlborough	MA	D	508 683-4000	10157
Gyrus Acmi LLC (DH)	Westborough	MA	C	508 804-2600	13104
Haemonetics Asia Incorporated (HQ)	Braintree	MA	F	781 848-7100	7186
Haemonetics Corporation (PA)	Boston	MA	A	781 848-7100	6780
Hallowell Engrg & Mfg Corp	Pittsfield	MA	G	413 445-4263	11400
Hamilton Thorne Inc (PA)	Beverly	MA	E	978 921-2050	6352
Harvard Apparatus Inc	Holliston	MA	D	508 893-8999	9213
Harvard Apprtus Rgnrtive Tech (PA)	Holliston	MA	D	774 233-7300	9214
Heartware International Inc (DH)	Framingham	MA	E	508 739-0950	8777
Hemanext Inc	Lexington	MA	F	240 301-7474	9747
Hemedex Inc	Waltham	MA	F	617 577-1759	12692
Highland Labs Inc	Holliston	MA	G	508 429-2918	9215
Hightech Amercn Indus Labs Inc	Lexington	MA	F	781 862-9884	9748
Hologic Inc (PA)	Marlborough	MA	A	508 263-2900	10159
Hologic Inc	Methuen	MA	C	508 263-2900	10334
Horsepower Technologies Inc	Lowell	MA	E	844 514-6773	9884
Hydrocision Inc	North Billerica	MA	E	978 474-9300	10918
Image Stream Medical Inc	Littleton	MA	D	978 486-8494	9818
Inspiremd Inc (PA)	Boston	MA	E	857 305-2410	6813
Instrumentation Laboratory Co (DH)	Bedford	MA	A	781 861-0710	6233
Insulet Corporation (PA)	Acton	MA	B	978 600-7000	5755
Insulet MA Securities Corp	Billerica	MA	D	978 600-7000	6453
Intech Inc	Acton	MA	E	978 263-2210	5756
Integra Lfscnces Holdings Corp	Burlington	MA	G	800 466-6814	7380
Integra Lifesciences	Boston	MA	F	617 268-1616	6815
Integra Lifesciences Prod Corp	Mansfield	MA	F	781 971-5682	10058
Intelon Optics Inc	Woburn	MA	F	310 804-9392	13587
Intralign Holdings LLC	Foxboro	MA	G	602 773-8506	8702
Inverness Medical - Biostar Inc	Waltham	MA	C	781 647-3900	12703
Jarvis Surgical Inc	Westfield	MA	E	413 562-6659	13174
Jlp Machine and Welding LLC	Kingston	MA	G	781 585-1744	9508
Johnson Johnson Healthcar	Bridgewater	MA	E	508 828-6194	7234
Karl Storz Endovision Inc	Charlton	MA	A	508 248-9011	7890
Karl Storz Endscpy-America Inc	Auburn	MA	C	508 248-9011	6117
Kinaset Therapeutics Inc (PA)	Medfield	MA	G	508 858-5810	10271
Kirwan Surgical Products LLC	Marshfield	MA	D	781 834-9500	10240
KS Manufacturing Inc	Allston	MA	G	508 427-5727	5822
Kyra Medical Inc	Northborough	MA	G	888 611-5972	11100
Lab Medical Manufacturing Inc	Billerica	MA	D	978 663-2475	6458
Lake Region Manufacturing Inc (HQ)	Wilmington	MA	A	952 361-2515	13423
Lake Region Medical Inc (HQ)	Wilmington	MA	E	978 570-6900	13424
Lantheus Medical Imaging Inc (HQ)	North Billerica	MA	B	800 362-2668	10924
Lantheus MI Intermediate Inc	North Billerica	MA	A	978 671-8001	10925
LDR Care Inc	Concord	MA	G	978 786-5110	8122
Lemaitre Vascular Inc (PA)	Burlington	MA	E	781 221-2266	7389
Lightlab Imaging Inc	Westford	MA	B	978 577-3400	13246
Logan Instruments Inc	Braintree	MA	F	617 394-0601	7193
Lymol Medical Corp (PA)	Woburn	MA	G	781 935-0004	13603
M & W Industries Inc	Mansfield	MA	F	508 406-2100	10065

	CITY	ST	EMP	PHONE	ENTRY#
Majestic Medical Inc	Raynham	MA	F	508 824-1944	11590
Maruho Htsujyo Innovations Inc (PA)	Norwell	MA	E	617 653-1617	11143
Mauna Kea Technologies Inc	Allston	MA	G	617 216-4263	5823
Mds Nxstage Corporation (DH)	Waltham	MA	E	866 697-8243	12718
Medcon Biolab Technologies Inc	Grafton	MA	G	508 839-4203	8968
Medical Device Bus Svcs Inc	Raynham	MA	F	508 880-8100	11591
Medical-Technical Gases Inc	North Billerica	MA	E	781 395-1946	10934
Medicametrix LLC	Woburn	MA	G	617 488-9233	13610
Medline Industries LP	Uxbridge	MA	E	847 949-5500	12486
Medrobotics Corporation	Raynham	MA	E	508 692-6460	11592
Medsource Tech Holdings LLC (DH)	Wilmington	MA	F	978 570-6900	13428
Medsource Technologies LLC (DH)	Wilmington	MA	F	978 570-6900	13429
Medtrnic Intrvntnal Vsclar Inc	Danvers	MA	A	978 777-0042	8206
Medtronic Inc	Danvers	MA	F	978 777-0042	8207
Medtronic Inc	Danvers	MA	F	978 739-3080	8208
Merit Medical Systems Inc (HQ)	Rockland	MA	F	781 681-7900	11651
Microline Surgical Inc (HQ)	Beverly	MA	C	978 922-9810	6364
Micron Products Inc	Fitchburg	MA	E	978 345-5000	8665
Microport Navibot Intl LLC	Foxborough	MA	F	774 215-5471	8735
Mitsubishi Chemical Amer Inc	Wilmington	MA	F	978 657-0075	13432
Mobius Imaging LLC	Shirley	MA	D	978 796-5068	11821
Morgan Scientific Inc (PA)	Haverhill	MA	F	978 521-4440	9118
N P Medical Inc	Clinton	MA	E	978 365-9721	8084
Nanodx Inc	Southborough	MA	E	508 599-2400	11998
Nanoentek Inc	Waltham	MA	G	781 472-2559	12730
Navilyst Medical Inc	Marlborough	MA	D	508 658-7990	10186
Needletech Products Inc	North Attleboro	MA	C	508 431-4000	10879
Nellcor Puritan Bennett LLC (DH)	Mansfield	MA	B	508 261-8000	10069
Neurologica Corp	Danvers	MA	D	978 564-8500	8211
Neurometrix Inc (PA)	Woburn	MA	G	781 890-9989	13621
Neurotherm Inc	Wilmington	MA	E	888 655-3500	13438
New View Surgical Inc	Boston	MA	F	774 284-2283	6920
Nn Inc	Mansfield	MA	E	508 406-2100	10070
Nvision Medical Corporation	Marlborough	MA	F	408 655-3577	10187
Nypro Healthcare Baja Inc (DH)	Clinton	MA	D	619 498-9250	8086
Nypro Inc (HQ)	Clinton	MA	A	978 365-9721	8087
Obp Surgical Corporation	Lawrence	MA	F	978 291-6853	9593
Optim LLC	Sturbridge	MA	E	508 347-5100	12254
Oxford Immunotec USA Inc	Marlborough	MA	D	833 682-6933	10193
Palomar Medical Tech LLC (DH)	Burlington	MA	C	781 993-2330	7409
Paradigm Biodevices Inc	Rockland	MA	G	781 982-9950	11655
Pep Industries LLC	Attleboro	MA	F	508 226-5600	6046
Photo Diagnostic Systems Inc	Boxborough	MA	E	978 266-0420	7154
Precision Engineered Pdts LLC (DH)	Attleboro	MA	G		6051
Precision Systems Inc	Natick	MA	E	508 655-7010	10494
Pressure Biosciences Inc (PA)	South Easton	MA	F	508 230-1828	11950
Primo Medical Group Inc (PA)	Stoughton	MA	C	781 297-5700	12229
Primrose Medical Inc	East Walpole	MA	F	508 660-8688	8421
Professnal Cntract Strlztion I	Taunton	MA	F	508 822-5524	12356
QCI Inc	Seekonk	MA	F	508 399-8983	11784
Radius Medical Tech Inc	Stow	MA	F	978 263-4466	12247
Ranfac Corp	Avon	MA	D	508 588-4400	6159
Rebiscan Inc	Boston	MA	F	857 600-0982	6999
Renalguard Solutions Inc (HQ)	Milford	MA	F	508 541-8800	10416
Repjtm LLC	Mansfield	MA	E	508 406-2100	10074
Respironics Novametrix LLC	Andover	MA	A	724 882-4120	5911
Rest Ensured Medical Inc	Norwood	MA	G	603 225-2860	11208
Rhealth Corporation	Bedford	MA	E	617 913-7630	6267
Rph Enterprises Inc	Franklin	MA	D	508 238-3351	8860
Sapphiros Ai Bio LLC	Boston	MA	E	617 297-7993	7023
Schuerch Corporation	Abington	MA	E	781 982-7000	5728
Scion Medical Techologies LLC	Newton Upper Falls	MA	G	617 455-5186	10795
Sekisui Diagnostics LLC (DH)	Burlington	MA	D	781 652-7800	7426
Smith & Nephew Inc	Andover	MA	E	978 749-1000	5923
Smith & Nephew Endoscopy Inc	Andover	MA	C	978 749-1000	5924
Sonivie Inc	Boston	MA	E	857 415-4814	7046
Spectra Medical Devices LLC	Wilmington	MA	B	978 657-0889	13455
Spinefrontier Inc	Malden	MA	E	978 232-3990	10028
SRS Medical Systems Inc (PA)	North Billerica	MA	E	978 663-2800	10958
Starmet Corporation (PA)	Concord	MA	KS	978 369-5410	8134
Statspin Inc	Westwood	MA	E	781 551-0100	13319
Steris Corporation	Northborough	MA	D	508 393-9323	11109
Stryker Corporation	Hopkinton	MA	F	508 416-5200	9345
Surgical Specialties Corp (HQ)	Westwood	MA	C	781 751-1000	13321
Surgical Tables Incorporated	Middleton	MA	F	978 777-4031	10394
Swiss Precision Products Inc (DH)	North Oxford	MA	E	508 987-8003	11035
Symmetry Med New Bedford Inc	New Bedford	MA	F	781 447-6661	10654
Symmetry Medical Inc	New Bedford	MA	C	508 998-1104	10655
T & T Machine Products Inc	Rockland	MA	F	781 878-3861	11662
T2 Biosystems Inc (PA)	Lexington	MA	D	781 761-4646	9779
T2 Biosystems Inc	Wilmington	MA	E	978 447-1069	13461
Target Therapeutics Inc (HQ)	Marlborough	MA	B	508 683-4000	10221

	CITY	ST	EMP	PHONE	ENTRY#
Tecomet Inc	Wilmington	MA	B	978 642-2400	13462
Tecomet Inc (HQ)	Wilmington	MA	C	978 642-2400	13463
Tecostar Holdings Inc (PA)	Woburn	MA	C	978 642-2400	13676
Tegra Medical LLC (HQ)	Franklin	MA	C	508 541-4200	8866
Tei Biosciences Inc (DH)	Boston	MA	D	617 268-1616	7072
Teleflex Incorporated	Mansfield	MA	E	508 964-6021	10078
Tenacity Medical Inc	Lexington	MA	G	617 299-8001	9786
Tepha Inc (HQ)	Lexington	MA	D	781 357-1700	9787
Teratech Corporation	Burlington	MA	E	781 270-4143	7438
Thermo Fisher Scientific Inc	Beverly	MA	C	978 232-6000	6387
Toxikon Corporation	Bedford	MA	D	978 942-5554	6274
Tsi Liquidation Inc	Hudson	MA	E	978 567-9033	9421
Ufp Technologies Inc	Chicopee	MA	E	800 372-3172	8065
Valeritas Inc	Marlborough	MA	E	908 927-9920	10227
Varian Medical Systems Inc	Ashland	MA	G	650 493-4000	5969
Vasca (PA)	Tewksbury	MA	E	978 640-0431	12425
Verax Biomedical Incorporated	Marlborough	MA	F	866 948-3729	10229
Viamed Corp	South Easton	MA	F	508 238-0220	11955
Viant AS&o Holdings LLC	Wilmington	MA	C	866 899-1392	13474
Visionquest Holdings LLC	Littleton	MA	F	978 776-9518	9843
Vita Needle Company	Needham	MA	E	781 444-1780	10529
Warner Instruments	Holliston	MA	G	203 776-0664	9239
Weavr Health Corp	Billerica	MA	E	617 430-6920	6489
Wotton Enterprises Inc	Sturbridge	MA	F	855 383-7678	12259
Xact Robotics Inc	Hingham	MA	G	781 252-9143	9166
Xenotherapeutics LLC	Boston	MA	G	617 750-1907	7136
Zyno Medical LLC	Natick	MA	F	508 650-2008	10501
Biotronik Inc	Brewer	ME	D	207 944-5515	4610
Idexx Distribution Inc	Westbrook	ME	D	207 556-0300	5630
Medical Resources Inc	Brunswick	ME	E	207 721-1110	4650
Standard Merger Sub LLC	Windham	ME	D	207 856-6151	5670
Accellent Endoscopy Inc	Laconia	NH	E	603 528-1211	14641
Atrium Medical Corporation (HQ)	Merrimack	NH	B	973 709-7654	14973
Cambridge Heart Inc	Windham	NH	F	978 654-7600	15721
Design Standards Corp	Charlestown	NH	D	603 826-7744	14062
Dutch Ophthalmic Usa Inc	Exeter	NH	F	603 778-6929	14291
Extrusion Alternatives Inc	Portsmouth	NH	E	603 430-9600	15383
Eye Exam 2000	Bedford	NH	G	603 836-5353	13927
Getinge Group Logis Ameri LLC	Merrimack	NH	A	603 880-1433	14982
Icad Inc (PA)	Nashua	NH	F	603 882-5200	15111
Imagene Technology Inc	Lebanon	NH	F	603 448-9940	14981
KMC Systems Inc	Merrimack	NH	D	866 742-0442	14987
Laborie Medical Technologies Corp (HQ)	Portsmouth	NH	F	802 857-1300	15414
Lake Region Medical Inc	Laconia	NH	E	603 528-1211	14656
Maxilon Laboratories Inc	Amherst	NH	G	603 594-9300	13879
Mdi East Inc	Jaffrey	NH	E	603 532-5656	14574
Merrimack Manufacturing LLC	Manchester	NH	E	603 206-0200	14883
Multi-Med Inc	Keene	NH	F	603 357-8733	14612
Nciea	Dover	NH	G	603 749-0733	14237
New England Small Tube Corp	Litchfield	NH	D	603 429-1600	14713
Nextphase Medical Devices LLC (PA)	Rochester	NH	E	201 968-9400	15487
Nextphase Medical Devices LLC	Rochester	NH	D	603 332-8900	15488
Prepco Inc	Colebrook	NH	G	603 237-4080	14108
Prometheus Group of NH Ltd	Dover	NH	F	800 442-2325	14245
Seacoast Technologies Inc	Portsmouth	NH	G	603 766-9800	15436
Sequel Med Tech LLC (PA)	Manchester	NH	G	212 883-1007	14928
Sims Portex Inc	Keene	NH	G	603 352-3812	14619
Smiths Medical Asd Inc	Keene	NH	F	603 352-3812	14620
Smiths Medical Asd Inc	Keene	NH	D	603 352-3812	14621
Teleflex Incorporated	Jaffrey	NH	D	603 532-7706	14580
Tfx Medical Incorporated	Jaffrey	NH	D	603 532-7706	14581
Ticked Off Inc	Dover	NH	G	603 742-0925	14253
Vapotherm Inc (PA)	Exeter	NH	E	603 658-0011	14304
Vascular Technology Inc	Nashua	NH	G	603 594-9700	15182
Viant Medical LLC	Laconia	NH	D	603 528-1211	14673
Vygon Corporation	Dover	NH	C	603 743-5988	14259
Alcor Scientific LLC	Smithfield	RI	D	401 737-3774	16686
American Access Care RI LLC	Providence	RI	F	401 277-9729	16469
Astronova Inc	West Warwick	RI	C	401 828-4000	16903
Biomedical Structures LLC	Warwick	RI	F	401 223-0990	16791
Bnr Supplies	Cranston	RI	G	401 461-9132	15836
C R Bard Inc	Warwick	RI	E	401 825-8300	16794
Cadence Science Inc	Cranston	RI	C	401 942-1031	15840
Contech Medical Inc	Providence	RI	D	401 351-4890	16504
Davol Inc (DH)	Warwick	RI	E	401 825-8300	16804
Huestis Machine Corporation	Bristol	RI	E	401 253-5500	15769
Luv2bu Inc	Cranston	RI	G	401 612-9585	15888
Nu-Lustre Finishing Corp	Providence	RI	E	401 521-7800	16576
RJ Mansour Inc	Providence	RI	F	401 521-7800	16606
Unetixs Vascular Inc	Warwick	RI	E	401 583-0089	16869
Ascension Technology Corp	Shelburne	VT	E	802 893-6657	17556
Biotek Instruments Inc (HQ)	Winooski	VT	C	802 655-4040	17767
PBL Incorporated	Colchester	VT	F	802 893-0111	17199
Preci-Manufacturing Inc	Winooski	VT	D	802 655-2414	17768
Raj Communications Ltd	Essex Junction	VT	E	802 658-4961	17243
Stellar Lasers LLC	Worcester	VT	G	802 299-5411	17782

3842 Surgical appliances and supplies

	CITY	ST	EMP	PHONE	ENTRY#
Acme United Corporation (PA)	Shelton	CT	D	203 254-6060	2978
Becton Dickinson and Company	Canaan	CT	D	860 824-5487	552
Beiersdorf North America Inc (DH)	Stamford	CT	F	203 563-5800	3292
Bio Med Packaging Systems Inc	Norwalk	CT	F	203 846-1923	2472
Cardiopulmonary Corp	Milford	CT	E	203 877-1999	1808
Carwild Corporation (PA)	New London	CT	E	860 442-4914	2224
Cellu Tissue Corporation	East Hartford	CT	A	860 289-7496	979
Contemporary Products LLC	Middletown	CT	F	860 346-9283	1744
Coopersurgical Inc	Trumbull	CT	G	203 601-5200	3715
Coopersurgical Inc (DH)	Trumbull	CT	C	203 601-5200	3716
Danbury Ortho	Danbury	CT	G	203 797-1500	725
Ethicon Inc	Southington	CT	B	860 621-9111	3208
First Aid Bandage Co Inc	New London	CT	E	860 443-8499	2228
Gordon Engineering Corporation	Brookfield	CT	G	203 775-4501	522
Hamilton Standard Space	Windsor Locks	CT	E	860 654-6000	4329
Hermell Products Inc	Bloomfield	CT	E	860 242-6550	169
K B C Electronics Inc	Milford	CT	F	203 298-9654	1842
K W Griffen Company	Norwalk	CT	F	203 846-1923	2521
Kelyniam Global Inc	Collinsville	CT	G	800 280-8192	667
Linde Inc	Danbury	CT	E	800 772-9247	777
McIntire Company (HQ)	Bristol	CT	F	860 585-8559	465
McNeil Healthcare Inc	West Haven	CT	A	203 934-8187	4115
Playtex Products LLC (HQ)	Shelton	CT	D	203 944-5500	3050
Schaeffler Aerospace USA Corp (DH)	Danbury	CT	B	203 744-2211	809
Seongyun Corporation	West Haven	CT	F	203 668-6803	4125
Stride Inc	Middlebury	CT	F	203 758-8307	1721
Unisoft Medical Corporation	Torrington	CT	F	860 482-6848	3704
United Seating & Mobility LLC	Rocky Hill	CT	D	806 761-0700	2940
A-T Surgical Mfg Co Inc	Holyoke	MA	G	413 532-4551	9240
Adhesive Tapes Intl Inc	Easthampton	MA	G	203 792-8279	8438
Aearo Technologies LLC	Auburn	MA	B	317 692-6645	6098
Amatech Corporation (DH)	Acton	MA	E	978 263-5401	5736
Amatech Corporation	Acton	MA	E	978 263-5401	5737
Americal Sergical Company	Salem	MA	G	781 592-7200	11700
American Surgical Company LLC	Salem	MA	E	781 592-7200	11701
Angel Guard Products Inc	Worcester	MA	G	508 791-1073	13699
Arcam Cad To Metal Inc	Woburn	MA	E	781 281-1718	13513
Arrow Interventional Inc	Chelmsford	MA	D	919 433-4948	7909
At Surgical Company	Holyoke	MA	F	888 233-4069	9241
Axya Medical Inc	Beverly	MA	F	978 232-9997	6331
Bay State Elevator Company Inc (HQ)	Agawam	MA	E	413 786-7000	5779
Bionx Medical Technologies Inc	Cambridge	MA	D		7516
Blauer Manufacturing Co Inc (PA)	Boston	MA	E	800 225-6715	6597
Bonesupport Inc	Needham Heights	MA	E	781 772-1756	10531
Boston Medical Products Inc	Shrewsbury	MA	E	508 898-9300	11829
Brimfield Precision LLC	Brimfield	MA	C	413 245-7144	7249
Brownmed Inc (PA)	Boston	MA	F	857 317-3354	6626
Cardiotech International Inc	Wilmington	MA	F	978 657-0075	13397
Cause For Change LLC	Sudbury	MA	E	617 571-6990	12262
Chamberlain Group LLC	Great Barrington	MA	E	413 528-7744	8975
Cohen Slvstri Rogoff Hammer PC	Boston	MA	E	617 426-6011	6661
Consolidated Machine Corporation	Billerica	MA	E	617 782-6072	6428
Consumer Hearing Cons Inc	Walpole	MA	G	866 658-8800	12557
Continental Metal Pdts Co Inc	Woburn	MA	F	781 935-4400	13546
Cornell Orthotics Prosthetics (PA)	Beverly	MA	G	978 922-2866	6343
Covidien LP (HQ)	Mansfield	MA	C	763 514-4000	10046
David Clark Company Inc (PA)	Worcester	MA	C	508 756-6216	13713
Depuy Spine LLC (HQ)	Raynham	MA	B	508 880-8100	11587
Eddies Wheels Inc	Shelburne Falls	MA	F	413 625-0033	11804
Emotionrx Inc	Cambridge	MA	F	617 500-5976	7561
Fleming Industries Inc	Chicopee	MA	E	413 593-3300	8033
Fosta-Tek Optics Inc (PA)	Leominster	MA	D	978 534-6511	9665
Fresenius Usa Inc (DH)	Waltham	MA	C	781 699-4191	12683
Freudenberg Medical LLC	Beverly	MA	C	978 281-2023	6349
Gentex Corporation	Boston	MA	F	617 670-3547	6755
Genzyme Corporation (DH)	Cambridge	MA	A	617 252-7500	7585
Genzyme Corporation	Framingham	MA	E	617 252-7500	8773
Gta-Nht Inc (HQ)	Rockland	MA	C	781 331-5900	11647
Gzsl Corp	North Attleboro	MA	E	508 695-0727	10872
Handy Pad Supply Inc	Paxton	MA	E	978 791-2289	11289
Honeywell Data Instruments Inc	Acton	MA	E	978 264-9550	5754
Hood E Benson Laboratories	Pembroke	MA	F	781 826-7573	11367
Louis M Gerson Co Inc	Middleboro	MA	F	508 947-4000	10363
Louis M Gerson Co Inc (PA)	Middleboro	MA	D	508 947-4000	10364
Lovepop Inc (PA)	Boston	MA	G	888 687-9589	6864
Marine Polymer Tech Inc (PA)	Tewksbury	MA	E	781 270-3200	12405
Medical Device Bus Svcs Inc	Norton	MA	D	508 828-2726	11129
Medical Products Mfg LLC	West Wareham	MA	F	508 291-1830	13069

	CITY	ST	EMP	PHONE	ENTRY#
Medsource Technologies LLC (DH)	Wilmington	MA	F	978 570-6900	13429
Medtronic Inc	Danvers	MA	F	978 777-0042	8207
Medtronic Inc	Danvers	MA	E	978 739-3080	8208
Myomo Inc (PA)	Boston	MA	D	617 996-9058	6900
Numotion	Taunton	MA	G	401 681-2153	12353
Ocean Orthopedic Services Inc (PA)	Hopkinton	MA	F	401 725-5240	9338
Oi Sellers Fund LLC	Wakefield	MA	G	781 587-3242	12524
Omni Life Science Inc (DH)	Raynham	MA	E	508 824-2444	11595
Ops-Core Inc	Boston	MA	F	617 670-3547	6940
Palomar Medical Products LLC	Burlington	MA	E	781 993-2300	7408
Progderm Inc	Boston	MA	F	617 419-1800	6982
Ranfac Corp	Avon	MA	D	508 588-4400	6159
Rewalk Robotics Inc (HQ)	Marlborough	MA	G	508 251-1154	10203
Rogerson Orthopedic Appls Inc	Boston	MA	F	617 268-1135	7011
Rph Enterprises Inc	Franklin	MA	D	508 238-3351	8860
Rrk Walker Inc	Mendon	MA	G	508 541-8100	10321
Safariland LLC	Dalton	MA	E	413 684-3104	8153
Salk Company Inc	Allston	MA	F	617 782-4030	5825
Sals Clothing & Fabric Restor	Everett	MA	F	617 387-6726	8499
Spinal Technology LLC (PA)	West Yarmouth	MA	E	508 775-0990	13073
St Jude Medical LLC	Westford	MA	G	978 577-3400	13264
Surgical Specialties Corp (HQ)	Westwood	MA	C	781 751-1000	13321
Tesco Associates Incorporated (PA)	Tyngsboro	MA	F	978 649-5527	12467
Tillotson Rubber Co Inc	Seekonk	MA	B	781 402-1731	11789
Touch Bionics	Mansfield	MA	F	774 719-2199	10081
Visionaid Inc	Wareham	MA	E	508 295-3300	12849
W D C Holdings Inc	Attleboro	MA	F	508 699-4412	6073
Babac Inc	Winslow	ME	F	207 872-0889	5681
Globe Footwear LLC (HQ)	Auburn	ME	D	207 784-9186	4437
Maine Artfl Limb Orthotics Co	Portland	ME	F	207 773-4963	5236
Maine Orthtic Prsthtic Rhab Sv	Portland	ME	F	207 773-8818	5241
Pine Tree Orthopedic Lab Inc	Livermore Falls	ME	F	207 897-5558	5025
Puritan Medical Pdts Co I LP	Guilford	ME	B	207 876-3311	4856
Puritan Medical Pdts Co LLC (PA)	Guilford	ME	B	207 876-3311	4857
Qsa Optical Co Inc	Lewiston	ME	E	207 783-8523	4988
Tena Group LLC	Windham	ME	G	207 893-2920	5671
Wheelchair	Lewiston	ME	F	207 782-8400	4996
Allied Orthotic Inc	Londonderry	NH	G	603 434-7722	14730
Atrium Medical Corporation (HQ)	Merrimack	NH	B	973 709-7654	14973
Cg Holdings LLC (PA)	Manchester	NH	E	603 623-3344	14827
Fireye Inc (DH)	Derry	NH	C	603 432-4100	14193
Galvion Ltd (HQ)	Portsmouth	NH	F	514 739-4444	15392
Globe Manufacturing Co LLC (DH)	Pittsfield	NH	B	603 435-8323	15332
Healthco International LLC	Colebrook	NH	G	603 255-3771	14106
Labonville Inc	Gorham	NH	G	603 752-4400	14360
New England Brace Co Inc (PA)	Concord	NH	F	508 588-6060	14148
Next Step Bnics Prsthetics Inc (PA)	Manchester	NH	F	603 668-3831	14901
Poly-Vac Inc	Manchester	NH	C	603 647-7822	14912
Seabrook Medical LLC	Seabrook	NH	C	603 474-1919	15605
The Great N Woods Assoc/ Blind	Colebrook	NH	G	603 490-9877	14109
AF Group Inc	Lincoln	RI	C	401 757-3910	16117
Ashaway Line & Twine Mfg Co	Ashaway	RI	D	401 377-2221	15738
Atlantic Footcare Inc	North Smithfield	RI	D	401 568-4918	16318
Cintas Corporation No 2	Pawtucket	RI	G	401 723-7300	16354
Honeywell Safety Pdts USA Inc	Smithfield	RI	D	401 757-2249	16713
Honeywell Safety Pdts USA Inc	Smithfield	RI	E	401 757-2106	16714
Johnson & Johnson	Cumberland	RI	F	401 762-6751	15949
New England Orthopedics Inc (PA)	Warwick	RI	G	401 739-9838	16841
Norcross Safety Products LLC	Smithfield	RI	A	800 430-5490	16724
North Safety Products LLC	Cranston	RI	A	401 943-4400	15902
Power Chair Recyclers Neng LLC	North Kingstown	RI	G	401 294-4111	16275
Simply Safer Products LLC	Providence	RI	F	401 474-4957	16611
Sperian Protection Usa Inc (DH)	Smithfield	RI	E	401 232-1200	16731
Summer Infant Inc (HQ)	Woonsocket	RI	C	401 671-6550	16975
Aadco Medical Inc	Randolph	VT	D	802 728-3400	17466
Biomedic Appliances Inc	Essex Junction	VT	G	802 878-0930	17228
Yankee Medical Inc (DH)	Burlington	VT	F	802 863-4591	17164

3843 Dental equipment and supplies

	CITY	ST	EMP	PHONE	ENTRY#
Acme Monaco Corporation (PA)	New Britain	CT	C	860 224-1349	1995
Aero-Med LLC	South Windsor	CT	F	860 659-2270	3108
Centrix Inc	Shelton	CT	D	203 929-5582	2991
DRM Research Laboratories Inc	Branford	CT	F	203 488-5555	252
Essel Dental	East Windsor	CT	G	860 254-6955	1073
J Palmero Sales Company Inc	Stratford	CT	F	203 377-6424	3550
Jensen Industries Inc (PA)	North Haven	CT	D	203 285-1402	2417
Kerr Corporation	Danbury	CT	D	203 748-0030	764
Palmero Healthcare LLC	Stratford	CT	F	203 377-6424	3562
Proxysoft Worldwide Inc	Bethel	CT	G	203 730-0084	133
Scott Woodford	Madison	CT	G	203 245-4266	1569
Surfctcom Inc	Naugatuck	CT	E	203 720-9209	1989
Ultimate Companies Inc (PA)	Bristol	CT	G	860 582-9111	503
Ultimate Wireforms Inc	Bristol	CT	D	860 582-9111	504

	CITY	ST	EMP	PHONE	ENTRY#
Winslow Automatics Inc	New Britain	CT	D	860 225-6321	2075
3d Diagnostix Inc	Allston	MA	F	617 820-5279	5817
Apogent Technologies Inc	Waltham	MA	A	781 622-1300	12594
Benco Dental	Hopkinton	MA	E	508 435-3000	9309
Bicon LLC (PA)	Boston	MA	D	617 524-4443	6593
Cataki International Inc	Wareham	MA	F	508 295-9630	12833
Convergent Dental Inc (PA)	Waltham	MA	E	508 500-5656	12640
Dentovations Inc	Boston	MA	F	617 737-1199	6690
Dillon Laboratories Inc	Abington	MA	G	781 871-2333	5723
Enamel Pure Inc	Worcester	MA	F	508 335-4824	13720
Ergonomic Products Inc	Fall River	MA	F	508 636-2263	8542
Keystone Dental Inc (PA)	Burlington	MA	D	781 328-3300	7386
New England Orthdontic Lab Inc	Andover	MA	E	800 922-6365	5900
Pulpdent Corporation	Watertown	MA	D	617 926-6666	12901
Sterngold Dental LLC	Attleboro	MA	E	508 226-5660	6066
Straumann Usa LLC	Andover	MA	C	978 747-2500	5927
Triseptagon LLC	Springfield	MA	F	413 732-2131	12144
National Dentex LLC	Manchester	NH	C	561 537-8301	14895

3844 X-ray apparatus and tubes

	CITY	ST	EMP	PHONE	ENTRY#
Associated X-Ray Corp (PA)	East Haven	CT	F	203 466-2446	1036
Bidwell Industrial Group Inc	Middletown	CT	E	860 346-9283	1740
Biowave Innovations LLC	Wilton	CT	C	203 982-8157	4232
Hologic Inc	Danbury	CT	F	203 790-1188	757
Kub Technologies Inc	Stratford	CT	E	203 364-8544	3553
Lorad Corporation	Danbury	CT	C	203 790-5544	778
Parker Medical Inc	Danbury	CT	D	860 350-4304	794
Precision X-Ray Inc	Madison	CT	F	203 484-2011	1567
Precision X-Ray Inc	North Branford	CT	F	203 484-2011	2372
Topex Inc	Danbury	CT	F	203 748-5918	825
Yxlon	Shelton	CT	G	234 284-7862	3081
Biolucent LLC	Marlborough	MA	F	508 263-2900	10116
Bruker Corporation (PA)	Billerica	MA	A	978 663-3660	6414
Finch Therapeutics Inc	Somerville	MA	D	617 229-6499	11872
Hologic Inc	Marlborough	MA	A	508 263-2900	10158
Hologic Inc (PA)	Marlborough	MA	A	508 263-2900	10159
Hologic Inc	Methuen	MA	E	508 263-2900	10334
Panalytical Inc	Westborough	MA	D	508 647-1100	13128
Princton Gamma-Tech Instrs Inc	Franklin	MA	F	609 924-7310	8858
Qsa Global Inc (HQ)	Burlington	MA	D	781 272-2000	7416
Scholz Frank X Ray Corp	Brockton	MA	F		7303
VJ Electronix Inc	Chelmsford	MA	F	631 589-8800	7969
Xenocs Inc	Holyoke	MA	F	413 587-4000	9292
Hologic Inc	Londonderry	NH	E	508 263-2900	14755
Telcor	Hancock	NH	G	603 525-4769	14420
Huestis Machine Corporation	Bristol	RI	F	401 253-5500	15769
Aadco Medical Inc	Randolph	VT	D	802 728-3400	17466

3845 Electromedical equipment

	CITY	ST	EMP	PHONE	ENTRY#
Acute Care Gases of Ct LLC	Wolcott	CT	F	855 399-1224	4360
Amco Precision Tools Inc (PA)	Berlin	CT	E	860 828-5640	49
American Dream Unlimited LLC	Andover	CT	G	860 742-5055	1
Atlantic Inertial Systems Inc	Cheshire	CT	C	203 250-3500	573
Bartron Medical Imaging LLC	New Haven	CT	G	203 498-2184	2124
Bio-Med Devices Inc	Guilford	CT	D	203 458-0202	1386
Cardiac Pacemakers Inc	East Hartford	CT	A	651 582-3201	977
Coherent Corp	Bloomfield	CT	C	860 243-9557	156
Coopersurgical Inc (DH)	Trumbull	CT	C	203 601-5200	3716
Defibtech LLC (HQ)	Guilford	CT	D	866 333-4248	1391
Digirad Health LLC	Old Greenwich	CT	B	800 947-6134	2632
Focus Medical LLC	Bethel	CT	C	203 730-8885	116
General Electric Company	Norwalk	CT	A	203 797-0840	2504
General Electric Company	Stamford	CT	F	866 419-4096	3354
Hobbs Medical Inc	Stafford Springs	CT	E	860 684-5875	3256
Hyperfine Inc (PA)	Guilford	CT	C	203 458-7100	1395
Industrial Magnetics Inc	Windsor	CT	D	508 853-3232	4283
Innovatorslink Corporation	Groton	CT	G	860 446-8058	1374
Integrated Medical Systems Inc	Gales Ferry	CT	F	860 949-2929	1260
Ivy Biomedical Systems Inc	Branford	CT	E	203 481-4183	267
Jeffrey Gold	Hamden	CT	G	203 281-5737	1434
Mobile Sense Technologies Inc	Darien	CT	F	203 914-5375	852
Philips Ultrasound Inc	Waterbury	CT	F	203 753-5215	3960
Pioneer Optics Company Inc	East Granby	CT	F	860 286-0071	948
Ram Technologies LLC	Guilford	CT	F	203 453-3916	1403
Sorbus Inc	Branford	CT	F	203 481-2810	278
Star Equity Holdings Inc (PA)	Old Greenwich	CT	D	203 489-9500	2635
Textspeak Corporation	Westport	CT	F	203 803-1069	4199
Tomtec Inc	Hamden	CT	F	203 281-6790	1460
Walker Magnetics Group Inc	Windsor	CT	G	508 853-3232	4314
Abiomed Inc (HQ)	Danvers	MA	B	978 646-1400	8157
Abiomed Cardiovascular Inc	Danvers	MA	D	978 777-5410	8158
Adeza Biomedical Corp	Marlborough	MA	F	508 263-8390	10104
AGFA Healthcare Corporation	Canton	MA	D	978 284-7900	7766

SIC

	CITY	ST	EMP	PHONE	ENTRY#
American Optics Limited	Wellesley Hills	MA	F	905 631-5377	12949
Arrhythmia Research Technology	Fitchburg	MA	F	978 602-1436	8642
Arteriocyte Med Systems Inc	Hopkinton	MA	C	508 395-5998	9307
Aurora Healthcare US Corp	Danvers	MA	F	978 204-5240	8163
Axiomed Spine Corporation (PA)	Malden	MA	F	978 232-3990	10003
Axya Medical Inc	Beverly	MA	F	978 232-9997	6331
Belmont Instrument LLC (PA)	Billerica	MA	E	978 663-0212	6409
Beta Bionics Inc	Concord	MA	E	855 745-3800	8105
Biolucent LLC	Marlborough	MA	F	508 263-2900	10116
Bioview (usa) Inc	Billerica	MA	G	978 670-4741	6410
Cambridge Heart Inc (PA)	Foxborough	MA	F	978 654-7600	8734
Candela Corporation (DH)	Marlborough	MA	C	508 358-7400	10127
Candela Medical Inc	Marlborough	MA	A	508 358-7400	10128
Cardiofocus Inc	Marlborough	MA	E	508 658-7200	10129
Cardiovascular Instrument Corp	Wakefield	MA	F	781 245-7799	12504
Clozex Medical Inc	West Bridgewater	MA	G	781 237-1673	12969
Cosman Medical LLC	Marlborough	MA	D	781 272-6561	10137
Covidien LP (HQ)	Mansfield	MA	C	763 514-4000	10046
Csa Medical Inc	Lexington	MA	D	443 921-8053	9734
Cyduct Diagnostics Inc	Boston	MA	E	617 360-9700	6682
Cynosure LLC (HQ)	Westford	MA	B	978 256-4200	13233
Cytyc Corporation	Marlborough	MA	E	508 303-4746	10140
Cytyc Corporation (HQ)	Marlborough	MA	B	508 263-2900	10141
Cytyc Surgical Products LLC (HQ)	Marlborough	MA	E	508 263-2900	10142
Delsys Inc	Natick	MA	F	508 545-8200	10477
Dermal Photonics Corporation	Danvers	MA	F	781 451-1717	8180
Diagnosys LLC (PA)	Lowell	MA	F	978 458-1600	9875
Docbox Inc	Waltham	MA	F	978 987-2569	12654
Eldersafe Technologies Inc	Harvard	MA	E	617 852-3018	9062
Electrosonics Medical Inc	Boston	MA	G	216 357-3310	6711
En-Pro Management Inc	Chelmsford	MA	F	866 352-5433	7926
Excelitas Tech Holdg Corp	Waltham	MA	A	781 522-5914	12671
GE Medcal Systems Info Tech In	Boston	MA	B	617 424-6800	6753
General Electric Company (PA)	Boston	MA	A	617 443-3000	6754
Gentuity LLC	Sudbury	MA	E	978 202-4108	12267
Haemonetics Asia Incorporated (HQ)	Braintree	MA	F	781 848-7100	7186
Haemonetics Corporation (PA)	Boston	MA	A	781 848-7100	6780
Henke Sass Wolf America Inc	Dudley	MA	D	508 671-9300	8318
Hologic Inc (PA)	Marlborough	MA	A	508 263-2900	10159
Hologic Inc	Methuen	MA	E	508 263-2900	10334
Hologic Foreign Sales Corp	Marlborough	MA	A	781 999-7300	10160
Hologic Sales and Service LLC	Marlborough	MA	B	508 263-2900	10161
Imactis Inc	Cambridge	MA	G	617 576-2005	7611
Image Diagnostics Inc	Fitchburg	MA	E	978 829-0009	8657
Infobionic Inc	Chelmsford	MA	E	978 674-8304	7934
Infraredx Inc	Bedford	MA	D	781 221-0053	6232
Innovheart US Inc	Newton	MA	F	858 349-8652	10763
Integer Holdings Corporation	Canton	MA	C	781 830-5800	7801
Interlace Medical Inc	Marlborough	MA	E	800 442-9892	10166
L3 Technologies Inc	Northampton	MA	A	413 586-2330	11069
Lake Region Manufacturing Inc (HQ)	Wilmington	MA	A	952 361-2515	13423
Lantos Technologies Inc	Foxboro	MA	G	781 443-7633	8706
M-R Resources Inc	Fitchburg	MA	E	978 345-9010	8659
Medical Products Mfg LLC	West Wareham	MA	F	508 291-1830	13069
Medtronic Inc	Danvers	MA	F	978 777-0042	8207
Medtronic Inc	Danvers	MA	F	978 739-3080	8208
Mettlr-Tledo Prcess Anlytics I	Billerica	MA	D	781 301-8800	6461
Mevion Medical Systems Inc (PA)	Littleton	MA	C	978 486-1006	9825
Micro-Leads Inc	Somerville	MA	F	617 580-3030	11886
Micron Solutions Inc (PA)	Fitchburg	MA	E	978 345-5000	8666
Mindsciences Inc	Worcester	MA	G	516 658-2985	13760
Myriad Fiber Imaging Tech Inc	Dudley	MA	F	508 949-3000	8320
Nellcor Puritan Bennett LLC (DH)	Mansfield	MA	B	508 261-8000	10069
Neutron Therapeutics LLC	Danvers	MA	E	978 777-0846	8212
Novanta Inc (PA)	Bedford	MA	C	781 266-5700	6246
Nxstage Medical Inc (DH)	Lawrence	MA	D	978 687-4700	9592
Palomar Medical Products LLC	Burlington	MA	E	781 993-2300	7408
Palomar Medical Tech LLC (DH)	Burlington	MA	C	781 993-2330	7409
Pendar Technologies LLC (PA)	Cambridge	MA	F	617 588-2128	7682
Precision Optics Corp Inc (PA)	Gardner	MA	D	978 630-1800	8898
Proven Process Med Dvcs Inc	Mansfield	MA	D	508 261-0800	10072
Pyramid Technical Cons Inc	Waltham	MA	F	781 402-1700	12755
Quanttus Inc	Newton	MA	G	617 401-2648	10778
Radiation Monitoring Dvcs Inc (HQ)	Watertown	MA	E	617 668-6800	12902
Respiratory Motion Inc	Watertown	MA	E	508 954-2706	12904
Respironics Novametrix LLC	Andover	MA	A	724 882-4120	5911
Revvity Inc (PA)	Waltham	MA	C	781 663-6900	12767
Smith & Nephew Endoscopy Inc	Andover	MA	C	978 749-1000	5924
Steward Pet Imaging LLC	Fall River	MA	E	508 259-8919	8609
Suros Surgical Systems Inc	Marlborough	MA	D	508 263-2900	10220
Tenacity Medical Inc	Lexington	MA	G	617 299-8001	9786
Thermo Envmtl Instrs LLC (HQ)	Franklin	MA	C	508 520-0430	8868
Thermo Fisher Scientific Inc (PA)	Waltham	MA	C	781 622-1000	12800
Third Pole Inc (PA)	Waltham	MA	F	908 310-0596	12803
Thoratec LLC	Burlington	MA	C	781 272-0139	7439
Thoratec LLC	Burlington	MA	C	781 272-0139	7440
Transmedics Inc (PA)	Andover	MA	C	978 552-0443	5931
Tsi Liquidation Inc	Hudson	MA	E	978 567-9033	9421
US Biochips Corp	Waban	MA	G	617 504-5502	12497
Vasca Inc (PA)	Tewksbury	MA	E	978 640-0431	12425
Viking Systems Inc	Westborough	MA	E	508 366-3668	13143
Vita Needle Company	Needham	MA	E	781 444-1780	10529
Zoll Medical Corporation	Burlington	MA	C	781 229-0020	7451
Zoll Medical Corporation	Chelmsford	MA	E	978 421-9132	7971
Zoll Medical Corporation (HQ)	Chelmsford	MA	A	978 421-9655	7972
Artel Inc	Westbrook	ME	E	207 854-0860	5614
David Saunders Inc	South Portland	ME	E	207 228-1888	5497
Electrnic Mobility Contrls LLC	Augusta	ME	F	207 512-8009	4471
Fhc Inc (PA)	Bowdoin	ME	D	207 666-8190	4605
Hawkin Dynamics LLC	Westbrook	ME	F	207 405-9142	5628
Lh Liquidation LLC	Windham	ME	E	207 893-8233	5664
Medrhythms Inc	Portland	ME	E	207 447-2177	5244
Vuetek Scientific LLC	Gray	ME	G	207 657-6565	4844
Cytyc Corporation	Londonderry	NH	E	603 668-7688	14741
Mbraun	Stratham	NH	D	603 773-9333	15639
Memtec Corporation	Amherst	NH	F	603 893-8080	13880
Monarch International Inc	Amherst	NH	E	603 883-3390	13881
Sleepnet Corp	Hampton	NH	E	603 758-6600	14412
Criticare Technologies Inc	Warwick	RI	E	401 667-3837	16800
Hanna Instruments Inc (PA)	Woonsocket	RI	E	401 765-7500	16962
Zoll Medical Corporation	Pawtucket	RI	B	401 729-1400	16432
Zoll Medical Corporation	Rumford	RI	D	401 729-1400	16681
Raj Communications Ltd	Essex Junction	VT	E	802 658-4961	17243

3851 Ophthalmic goods

	CITY	ST	EMP	PHONE	ENTRY#
Coburn Technologies Inc (DH)	South Windsor	CT	E	860 648-6600	3129
Encore Optics	South Windsor	CT	G	860 282-0082	3143
Gerber Coburn Optical Inc (DH)	South Windsor	CT	E	800 843-1479	3150
Gerber Scientific LLC (PA)	Tolland	CT	C	860 871-8082	3661
Hoya Corporation	South Windsor	CT	E	860 289-5379	3157
Lensesonly LLC	Bloomfield	CT	F	860 769-2020	187
Aearo Technologies LLC	Auburn	MA	B	317 692-6645	6098
Bausch & Lomb Incorporated	Wilmington	MA	C	978 658-6111	13388
Bcpe Seminole Holdings LP (PA)	Boston	MA	F	617 516-2000	6585
Beaver-Visitec Intl Inc	Waltham	MA	F	781 906-8080	12604
Bomas Machine Specialties Inc	Woburn	MA	F	617 628-3831	13528
Chicopee Vision Center Inc	Springfield	MA	G	413 796-7570	12083
Claris Vision LLC	North Dartmouth	MA	E	508 994-1400	10991
Eye Health Services Inc	Plymouth	MA	E	508 747-6425	11459
Eye Health Services Inc (PA)	Quincy	MA	E	617 472-5242	11517
Fosta-Tek Optics Inc (PA)	Leominster	MA	D	978 534-6511	9665
Hilsinger Company Parent LLC (PA)	Mansfield	MA	E	508 699-4406	10055
Optical Laboratory Inc	New Bedford	MA	E	508 997-9779	10637
Paramount Corp	North Dartmouth	MA	D	508 999-4442	11000
Perx LLC	Pittsfield	MA	F	413 358-9020	11417
Randolph Engineering Inc	Randolph	MA	E	781 961-6070	11573
Thea Pharma Inc	Waltham	MA	D	781 832-3667	12796
Vision Dynamics LLC	Worcester	MA	G	203 271-1944	13824
Visionaid Inc	Wareham	MA	E	508 295-3300	12849
Wilmington Partners LP	Wilmington	MA	C	978 658-6111	13476
McLeod Optical Company Inc	Augusta	ME	G	207 623-3841	4478
Qsa Optical Co Inc	Lewiston	ME	E	207 783-8523	4988
General Dynmics Mssion Systems	Nashua	NH	F	603 864-6300	15103
New Hampshire Optical Co Inc (PA)	Allenstown	NH	E	603 268-0741	13854
Optical Filter Corporation	Keene	NH	A	603 357-7662	14614
Vibez Sunglasses LLC	Hooksett	NH	G	603 818-2207	14476
Accu Rx Inc	Johnston	RI	E	401 454-2920	16072
Costa Inc	Providence	RI	E	401 333-1200	16506
Fgx International Holdings Ltd (HQ)	Smithfield	RI	B	401 231-3800	16698
Fgx International Inc	Smithfield	RI	A	401 231-3800	16699
Honeywell Safety Pdts USA Inc	Smithfield	RI	E	401 757-2106	16714
Jones Safety Equipment Company	East Providence	RI	G	401 434-4010	16026
McLeod Optical Company Inc (PA)	Warwick	RI	E	401 467-3000	16836
Sperian Eye & Face Protection Inc	Smithfield	RI	C	401 232-1200	16730
Sperian Protection Usa Inc (DH)	Smithfield	RI	E	401 232-1200	16731
Uvex Safety Manufacturing Ltd	Smithfield	RI	F	401 232-1200	16733
Galvion Ballistics Ltd	Essex Junction	VT	D	802 334-2774	17233
Prolens Inc	North Troy	VT	G	802 988-1018	17430
Revision Military Ltd (PA)	Essex Junction	VT	E	802 879-7002	17245

3861 Photographic equipment and supplies

	CITY	ST	EMP	PHONE	ENTRY#
Base-Line II Inc (PA)	Danbury	CT	E	203 826-7031	712
Bidwell Industrial Group Inc	Middletown	CT	E	860 346-9283	1740
Bpi Reprographics	Norwalk	CT	F	203 866-5600	2475
Cag Imaging LLC	Norwich	CT	G	860 887-0836	2603
Cine Magnetics Inc (HQ)	Stamford	CT	D	914 273-7600	3312

	CITY	ST	EMP	PHONE	ENTRY#
Freedom Grafix LLC	Fairfield	CT	G	815 900-6189	1186
Fujifilm Elctrnic Mtls USA Inc	Stamford	CT	E	203 363-3360	3352
Kenyon Laboratories LLC	Higganum	CT	G	860 345-2097	1529
Midstate Arc Inc	Meriden	CT	D	203 238-9001	1676
Oce-USA Holding Inc	Trumbull	CT	A	773 714-8500	3726
Recycle 4 Vets LLC	Westport	CT	G	203 222-7300	4194
Rosco Laboratories Inc (HQ)	Stamford	CT	E	203 708-8900	3452
Sixmil Holdings Inc (PA)	Stamford	CT	D	203 708-8900	3462
Verico Technology LLC (HQ)	Enfield	CT	E	860 871-1200	1157
Videndum Prod Solutions Inc (HQ)	Shelton	CT	E	203 929-1100	3075
Xerox Corporation (HQ)	Norwalk	CT	B	203 849-5216	2598
Xerox Holdings Inc	Norwalk	CT	A	203 968-3000	2599
Xerox Holdings Corporation (PA)	Norwalk	CT	B	203 849-5216	2600
Adaptive Optics Associates Inc (DH)	Devens	MA	D	978 757-9600	8269
Advance Reproductions Corp	North Andover	MA	D	978 685-2911	10817
AGFA Corporation	Wilmington	MA	B	978 658-5600	13375
Apogee Imaging Systems Inc	Concord	MA	F		8100
Avid Technology Inc (PA)	Burlington	MA	A	978 640-3000	7338
Boston Light & Sound Inc (PA)	Malden	MA	F	617 787-3131	10005
Broadcast Pix Inc	Tyngsboro	MA	E	978 600-1100	12458
Comprehensive Identification Products Inc 781 229-8780	Burlington	MA	C		7354
Etchomatic Inc	Lowell	MA	F	978 656-0011	9877
Fujifilm Hlthcare Amricas Corp (DH)	Lexington	MA	C	203 324-2000	9743
Georgia-Pacific LLC	Leominster	MA	D	978 537-4701	9666
Glidecam Industries Inc (PA)	Pembroke	MA	F	508 577-6261	11366
Greensight Inc	Charlestown	MA	E	617 633-4919	7875
Intelligent Network Sales LLC	Walpole	MA	F	508 446-3646	12562
Ix Cameras Inc	Woburn	MA	F	617 225-0080	13592
Kasalis Inc	Burlington	MA	E	781 273-6400	7383
Primary Pdc Inc (PA)	Waltham	MA	G	781 386-2000	12753
Process Solutions Inc	East Longmeadow	MA	G	413 525-5870	8390
Progress Enterprises LLC	Westfield	MA	E	413 562-2736	13201
R & B Splicer Systems Inc	Avon	MA	G	508 580-3500	6158
Solutek Corporation	Boston	MA	E	617 445-5335	7044
Spinnakervideo Inc	Boston	MA	F	617 591-2200	7054
Valentine Tool & Stamping Inc	Norton	MA	F	508 285-6911	11137
Dewal Industries LLC	Narragansett	RI	C	401 789-9736	16189
Hutchison Company Inc	North Kingstown	RI	F	401 294-3503	16258

3873 Watches, clocks, watchcases, and parts

	CITY	ST	EMP	PHONE	ENTRY#
Accu-Time Systems Inc (DH)	Windsor	CT	E	860 870-5000	4252
Morristown Star Struck LLC	Bethel	CT	E	203 778-4925	130
Pyramid Time Systems LLC	Meriden	CT	E	203 238-0550	1686
Timex Group Usa Inc (HQ)	Middlebury	CT	C	203 346-5000	1722
West Hartford Lock Co LLC	West Hartford	CT	F	860 236-0671	4089
Centerline Machine Company Inc	Beverly	MA	F	978 524-8842	6338
Chelsea Clock LLC	Chelsea	MA	E	617 884-0250	7977
Electric Time Company Inc	Medfield	MA	E	508 359-4396	10270
Fraen Corporation (PA)	Reading	MA	C	781 205-5300	11601
Lampin Corporation (PA)	Uxbridge	MA	F	508 278-2422	12484

39 MISCELLANEOUS MANUFACTURING INDUSTRIES

3911 Jewelry, precious metal

	CITY	ST	EMP	PHONE	ENTRY#
Amy Kahn Russell LLC (PA)	Ridgefield	CT	F	203 438-2133	2885
Brannkey Inc	Old Saybrook	CT	E	860 510-0501	2646
Dt Holdings Incorporated	Stamford	CT	F	203 602-6969	3339
Elm City Mfg Jewelers Inc	Hamden	CT	D	203 248-2195	1425
Jewelry Designs Inc	Danbury	CT	E	203 797-0389	761
Joseph Hannoush Family Inc	Farmington	CT	F	860 561-4651	1225
Karavas Fashions Ltd	Norwalk	CT	F	203 866-4000	2522
AB Group Inc	Attleboro	MA	G	508 222-1404	5989
Adina Inc (PA)	Norwood	MA	E	781 762-4477	11154
Artinian Garabet Corporation	Concord	MA	F	978 371-7110	8102
Ashworth Assoc Mfg Whl Jwelers	North Attleboro	MA	F	508 695-1900	10866
B & L Manufacturing Inc	Bellingham	MA	G	508 966-3066	6286
Barmakian Brothers Ltd Partnr	Boston	MA	E	617 227-3724	6583
Charles Thomae & Son Inc	Attleboro	MA	F	508 222-0785	6001
Chris Ploof Designs Inc	Leominster	MA	G	978 728-4905	9651
Dance It Up Inc	North Grafton	MA	F	508 839-1648	11021
Dilon Company Inc	Attleboro	MA	G	508 223-3400	6009
E A Dion Inc	Attleboro	MA	F	800 445-1007	6010
EF Leach & Company	Attleboro	MA	C	508 643-3309	6011
Findings Incorporated	Attleboro	MA	D	508 222-7449	6015
G Austin Young Inc	Attleboro	MA	G	508 222-4700	6019
Goldman-Kolber Inc	Norwood	MA	F	781 769-6362	11175
J T Inman Co Inc	Attleboro Falls	MA	E	508 226-0080	6088
Jewelry Solutions LLC	Canton	MA	G	781 821-6100	7803
M S Company	Attleboro	MA	G	508 222-1700	6032
Marathon Co	Attleboro	MA	C	508 222-5544	6034
McVan Inc	Attleboro	MA	F	508 431-2400	6036
Melanie Casey LLC	Andover	MA	E	781 640-8910	5894
Mr Idea Inc	Attleboro	MA	E	508 222-0155	6039
Natalia Marketing Corp	Waltham	MA	E	781 693-4900	12733
Newpro Designs Inc	Norwood	MA	E	781 762-4477	11200
North Attleboro Jewelry Co Inc	Attleboro	MA	E	508 222-4660	6044
Ozcan Jewelers Inc	Boston	MA	F	617 338-6844	6949
Richline Group Inc	Attleboro	MA	F	774 203-1199	6055
Robbins Company	Attleboro	MA	C	508 222-2900	6058
Silva Jewelers of Osterville	Osterville	MA	F	508 428-2872	11246
Sweet Metal Finishing Inc	Attleboro	MA	F	508 226-4359	6068
Touch Inc	Waltham	MA	F	781 894-8133	12805
W E Richards Co Inc	Attleboro	MA	G	508 226-1036	6074
William J Hirten Co LLC	Attleboro	MA	F	401 334-5370	6076
Zero Porosity Casting Inc	Waltham	MA	F	617 391-0008	12821
A Silver Lining Inc	Boothbay Harbor	ME	G	207 633-4103	4599
Brown Goldsmiths & Co Inc	Freeport	ME	F	207 865-4126	4799
Daunis	Portland	ME	F	207 773-6011	5205
Bellman Jewelers Inc	Manchester	NH	G	603 625-4653	14819
M J Harrington & Co Inc (PA)	Newport	NH	F	603 863-1662	15231
Nazarian Jewelers NH Inc (PA)	Salem	NH	F	603 893-1600	15548
Newsshop of Portsmouth LLC	Newington	NH	G	603 431-5665	15208
Sawyers Jewelry Inc	Laconia	NH	F	603 527-1000	14667
Accessories Assoc Inc	Smithfield	RI	G	401 231-3800	16684
Aetna Manufacturing Company	Providence	RI	F	401 751-3260	16466
Alviti Link - All Inc	Johnston	RI	G	401 861-6656	16074
Anatone Jewelry Co Inc	North Providence	RI	G	401 728-0490	16294
Arden Jewelry Mfg Co	Johnston	RI	E	401 274-9800	16076
Armbrust International Ltd	Providence	RI	C	401 781-3300	16475
Atamian Manufacturing Corp	Providence	RI	E	401 944-9614	16477
Bazar Group Inc (PA)	East Providence	RI	E	401 434-2595	16006
Bliss Manufacturing Co Inc	Pawtucket	RI	F	401 729-1690	16350
Carla Corp	East Providence	RI	C	401 438-7070	16008
Chronomatic Inc	East Greenwich	RI	E	401 884-6361	15978
CJ International Inc	Providence	RI	E	401 944-4700	16499
Discovery Mint Inc	Pawtucket	RI	E	401 722-6530	16364
Erm LLC	Johnston	RI	G	401 934-2544	16084
Esposito Jewelry Inc	Providence	RI	F	401 943-1900	16516
FAF Inc (PA)	Greenville	RI	D	401 949-3000	16058
Fashion Accents LLC (PA)	Providence	RI	F	401 331-6626	16517
Fiesta Jewelry Corporation	Pawtucket	RI	E	212 564-6847	16369
First Card Co Inc	Johnston	RI	F	401 434-6140	16685
Gem-Craft Inc	Cranston	RI	G	401 854-1200	15867
Grant Foster Group L P	Smithfield	RI	F	401 231-4077	16705
Herff Jones LLC	Warwick	RI	F	401 331-1240	16820
Hogan & Bolas	Providence	RI	G	401 349-2988	16532
Imperial-Deltah Inc	East Providence	RI	D	401 434-2597	16023
J Arakelian Inc	Johnston	RI	F	401 943-7366	16090
J Cal Inc	Providence	RI	D	401 941-7700	16545
J Cal Inc (PA)	Providence	RI	F	401 941-7700	16546
J H Breakell & Company Inc	Newport	RI	F	401 849-3522	16213
Jcc Residual Ltd	Woonsocket	RI	F	508 699-4401	16966
Jji International Inc	Cranston	RI	E	401 780-8668	15878
Kennedy Incorporated	North Kingstown	RI	F	401 295-7800	16265
Kerissa Creations Inc	Greenville	RI	F	401 949-5100	16061
Klitzner Industries Inc	Lincoln	RI	E	800 621-0161	16143
Lees Manufacturing Co Inc	Providence	RI	F	401 275-2383	16552
LImage Inc	Johnston	RI	E	401 369-7141	16093
Luca + Danni Inc	Cranston	RI	E	401 275-5337	15887
Mag Jewelry Co Inc	Cranston	RI	G	401 942-1840	15890
Marketplace Inc Corporate	East Greenwich	RI	F	401 336-3000	15990
Martins Soldering	Johnston	RI	G	401 521-2280	16095
Narragasett Jewelry Inc	Providence	RI	E	401 944-2200	16572
National Chain Company (PA)	Warwick	RI	D	401 732-3634	16840
Racecar Jewelry Co Inc	Pawtucket	RI	G	401 475-5701	16409
Reed Allison Group Inc	Providence	RI	D	617 846-1237	16599
Rolyn Inc (PA)	Cranston	RI	E	401 944-0844	15908
Stylecraft Inc	Cranston	RI	D	401 463-9944	15914
Sunshine Minting Inc	North Providence	RI	F	401 265-8383	16311
T Sardelli and Sons Inc	Providence	RI	G	401 429-2144	16617
Tahoe Jewelry Inc	East Providence	RI	F	401 435-4114	16045
Tme Co Inc	Providence	RI	F	860 354-0686	16628
Two Hands Inc	Providence	RI	F	401 785-2727	16631
Uncas International LLC (PA)	West Warwick	RI	D	401 231-0266	16924
US Emblem LLC	East Greenwich	RI	F	401 487-4327	15995
Village Goldsmith	Warwick	RI	F	401 944-8404	16872
Wehr Industries Inc	Warwick	RI	E	401 732-6565	16878
Whiting & Davis LLC	Pawtucket	RI	F	508 699-4412	16431
Wiesner Manufacturing Company	Warwick	RI	F	401 421-2406	16879
Bixler University	Burlington	VT	F	888 361-4558	17120
PBL Incorporated	Colchester	VT	F	802 893-0111	17199

3914 Silverware and plated ware

	CITY	ST	EMP	PHONE	ENTRY#
Boardman Silversmiths Inc	Wallingford	CT	F	203 265-9978	3782

	CITY	ST	EMP	PHONE	ENTRY#
Oldani Brothers LLC **(PA)**	Meriden	CT	G	203 630-6565	1681
Tero Design Holdings LLC	Norwalk	CT	G	203 899-9950	2580
Woodbury Pewterers Inc	Woodbury	CT	E	203 263-2668	4389
Alviti Creations Inc	Attleboro	MA	G	508 222-4030	5992
Conference Medal & Trophy Co	Buzzards Bay	MA	F	508 563-3600	7454
Dipwell Company Inc	Northampton	MA	G	413 587-4673	11059
Hilliard Precision Products LLC	Bellingham	MA	E	508 541-9100	6292
J T Inman Co Inc	Attleboro Falls	MA	E	508 226-0080	6088
Silver Greenfield Inc	Greenfield	MA	E	413 774-2774	8999
Syratech Acquisition Corp **(HQ)**	Medford	MA	C	781 539-0100	10298
J H Breakell & Company Inc	Newport	RI	F	401 849-3522	16213
Village Goldsmith	Warwick	RI	F	401 944-8404	16872

3915 Jewelers' materials and lapidary work

	CITY	ST	EMP	PHONE	ENTRY#
Carat Systems Inc	Stoneham	MA	E	781 560-8082	12175
Cold River Mining Inc	Turners Falls	MA	E	413 863-5445	12445
EF Leach & Company	Attleboro	MA	C	508 643-3309	6011
FE Knight Inc **(PA)**	Chestnut Hill	MA	G	508 520-1666	7999
Guyot Brothers Company Inc	Attleboro	MA	E	508 222-2000	6022
Idex Health & Science LLC	Middleboro	MA	C	774 213-0200	10362
Joseph P Stachura Company Inc	Uxbridge	MA	E	508 278-6525	12482
M S Company	Attleboro	MA	D	508 222-1700	6032
Richard H Bird & Co Inc	Waltham	MA	E	781 894-0160	12770
Ronald Pratt Company Inc	Attleboro	MA	E	508 222-9601	6059
Alex and Ani LLC **(HQ)**	East Greenwich	RI	E	401 633-1486	15972
Angelo Di Maria Inc	Providence	RI	E	401 274-0100	16472
APAC Tool Inc	North Providence	RI	F	401 724-6090	16295
Aro-Sac Inc	North Providence	RI	E	401 231-6655	16297
Contract Fusion Inc	East Providence	RI	E	401 438-1298	16010
Crystal Hord Corporation	Pawtucket	RI	F	401 723-2989	16360
Discovery Mint Inc	Pawtucket	RI	F	401 722-6530	16364
Eagle Tool Inc	Warwick	RI	E	401 421-5105	16812
Evans Findings Company Inc	East Providence	RI	E	401 434-5600	16018
Fulford Manufacturing Company **(PA)**	Riverside	RI	F	401 431-2000	16655
Kefi Development Inc	East Providence	RI	E	401 272-6513	16027
Lorac Company Inc	Providence	RI	E	401 781-3330	16554
Robert Baxter Associates Inc	Warwick	RI	F	401 739-8222	16853
Roland and Whytock Company Inc	Providence	RI	E	401 781-1234	16607
Rolyn Inc **(PA)**	Cranston	RI	E	401 944-0844	15908
Salvadore Tool & Findings Inc **(PA)**	Providence	RI	F	401 331-6000	16609
Tercat Tool and Die Co II Inc	Providence	RI	E	401 421-3371	16620
Tiffany & Co	Cumberland	RI	C	212 755-8000	15970
Tri-Bro Tool Co Inc	Cranston	RI	E	401 781-6323	15921
Venturi Inc	Warwick	RI	G	401 781-2647	16871
Village Goldsmith	Warwick	RI	F	401 944-8404	16872
W R Cobb Company	East Providence	RI	C	401 438-7000	16047

3931 Musical instruments

	CITY	ST	EMP	PHONE	ENTRY#
Austin Organs Incorporated	Hartford	CT	F	860 522-8293	1472
Harps Unlimited Intl LLC	Burlington	CT	G	860 675-0227	551
Rokr Distribution Us Inc	Bloomfield	CT	B	860 509-8888	207
Andover Organ Company Inc	Lawrence	MA	F	978 686-9600	9537
Avedis Zildjian Co **(PA)**	Norwell	MA	C	781 871-2200	11139
Brannen Brothers-Flutemakers	Woburn	MA	E	781 935-9522	13535
Burgett Brothers Incorporated	Haverhill	MA	E	978 374-8888	9082
C B Fisk Inc	Gloucester	MA	E	978 283-1909	8926
Carl Swanson Harp Rentals Inc **(PA)**	Boston	MA	G	617 569-6642	6639
FA Finale Inc	Boston	MA	E	617 226-7888	6728
Fishman Transducers Inc	Andover	MA	D	978 988-9199	5883
Main Street Blanchard LLC	Reading	MA	G	781 944-4000	11603
SE Shires Inc	Holliston	MA	E	508 634-6805	9228
Vater Percussion Inc	Holbrook	MA	E	781 767-1877	9186
Verne Q Powell Flutes Inc	Maynard	MA	D	978 461-6111	10265
Pantheon Guitars LLC	Lewiston	ME	F	207 755-0003	4983
Alesis LP	Cumberland	RI	C	401 658-4032	15931
Clear Carbon & Components Inc	Bristol	RI	E	401 254-5085	15758
Island Woods Performance Inc	Smithfield	RI	G	401 349-4644	16717

3942 Dolls and stuffed toys

	CITY	ST	EMP	PHONE	ENTRY#
Nancy Sales Co Inc	Chelsea	MA	D	617 884-1700	7987
Oyo Sportstoys Inc	Brookline	MA	D	978 264-2000	7323
Woobo Inc	Cambridge	MA	F	630 639-6326	7762
Chrisha Creations Ltd	Smithfield	RI	F		16691
Hasbro Inc **(PA)**	Pawtucket	RI	A	401 431-8697	16373
Sproutel Inc	Providence	RI	G	914 806-6514	16615
Hibernation Holding Co Inc **(PA)**	Shelburne	VT	C	802 985-3001	17558
R John Wright Dolls Inc	Bennington	VT	F	802 447-7072	17056
Vermont Teddy Bear Co Inc **(HQ)**	Shelburne	VT	C	802 985-3001	17563

3944 Games, toys, and children's vehicles

	CITY	ST	EMP	PHONE	ENTRY#
A Piece of Pzzle Bhvral Intrvn	West Hartford	CT	F	860 250-8054	4045
Essex Wood Products Inc	Colchester	CT	F	860 537-3451	658
Immucor Trnsplant Dgnstics Inc **(DH)**	Stamford	CT	D	203 328-9500	3381

	CITY	ST	EMP	PHONE	ENTRY#
Infinity Stone Inc	Waterbury	CT	F	203 575-9484	3922
Lego Systems Inc **(DH)**	Enfield	CT	A	860 698-9367	1137
Milton & Goose LLC	Stamford	CT	G	203 539-1073	3412
Roto-Die Company Inc	East Windsor	CT	G	860 292-7030	1084
S & S Worldwide Inc	Colchester	CT	B	860 537-3451	665
Tegu	Norwalk	CT	D	877 834-8869	2576
US Games Systems Inc	Stamford	CT	E	800 544-2637	3488
Walts Tropper Factory LLC	North Branford	CT	G	203 871-9254	2378
Air Canada	Boston	MA	G	617 567-7157	6523
Burnham Associates Inc	Salem	MA	F	978 745-1788	11706
Cartamundi East Longmeadow LLC	East Longmeadow	MA	B	413 526-2000	8371
Ceaco Inc	Canton	MA	E	617 926-8080	7777
Charles Thomae & Son Inc	Attleboro	MA	F	508 222-0785	6001
Digi-Block Inc	Cambridge	MA	E	617 926-9300	7550
Dorel Juvenile Group Inc	Foxboro	MA	C	508 216-1800	8695
Flying Kites	Wellesley	MA	F	401 575-0009	12941
Gold Water Technology Inc	Walpole	MA	G	781 551-3590	12559
Greenbrier Games LLP	Marlborough	MA	G	978 618-8442	10155
Hitpoint Inc **(PA)**	Greenfield	MA	E	413 992-6663	8993
Koplow Games Inc	Boston	MA	F	617 482-4011	6846
Leap Year Publishing LLC	Newburyport	MA	F	978 688-9900	10695
Little Kids Inc	Seekonk	MA	G	800 545-5437	11780
Merida Meridian Inc	Boston	MA	E	617 464-5400	6885
Monahan Products LLC **(PA)**	Rockland	MA	D	844 823-3132	11652
Neuromotion Inc	Boston	MA	F	415 676-9326	6912
Norade Inc **(DH)**	Holyoke	MA	F	413 533-7159	9271
Oyo Sportstoys Inc	Brookline	MA	D	978 264-2000	7323
Paul K Guillow Inc	Wakefield	MA	E	781 245-5255	12526
Piecing Puzzle	Carver	MA	G	508 450-0323	7856
Piecing Puzzle Inc	Middleboro	MA	F	508 465-0417	10374
Piecing Puzzle Inc	Lakeville	MA	G	508 465-0417	9520
Puzzle Pieces LLC	Quincy	MA	E	617 481-2304	11533
Weston Presidio MGT Co Inc **(PA)**	Boston	MA	E	617 988-2500	7118
Winning Moves Inc	Danvers	MA	F	978 777-7464	8229
Zen Art & Design Inc	Hadley	MA	G	800 215-6010	9019
Atlantic Standard Molding Inc	Portland	ME	F	207 797-0727	5179
Bluejacket Inc	Searsport	ME	F	207 548-9970	5451
Downeast Concepts Inc	Yarmouth	ME	F	207 846-3726	5703
Elms Puzzles Inc	Harrison	ME	F	207 583-6262	4875
Elves & Angels Inc	Hodgdon	ME	G	207 456-7575	4891
Delta Education LLC	Nashua	NH	B	800 258-1302	15090
Puzzle House	Jaffrey	NH	F	603 532-4442	14577
Sempco Inc	Nashua	NH	F	603 889-1830	15166
Two In One Manufacturing Inc	Nashua	NH	E	603 595-8212	15179
Hasbro Inc	Pawtucket	RI	E	401 726-2090	16371
Hasbro Inc	Pawtucket	RI	D	401 431-8412	16372
Hasbro Inc **(PA)**	Pawtucket	RI	A	401 431-8697	16373
Hasbro Inc	Providence	RI	E	401 431-2090	16530
Hasbro International Inc **(HQ)**	Pawtucket	RI	A	401 431-8697	16374
Sproutel Inc	Providence	RI	G	914 806-6514	16615
Maple Landmark Inc	Middlebury	VT	E	802 388-0627	17346
Real Good Toys Inc	Montpelier	VT	F	802 479-2217	17734
Stave Puzzles Incorporated	Wilder	VT	F	802 295-5200	17715
Vermont Christmas Company	Milton	VT	G	802 893-1670	17366

3949 Sporting and athletic goods, nec

	CITY	ST	EMP	PHONE	ENTRY#
Ammunition Stor Components LLC	New Britain	CT	G	860 225-3548	1999
Aqua Massage International Inc	Mystic	CT	F	860 536-3735	1936
Bob Vess Building LLC	Cromwell	CT	G	860 729-2536	688
Ei-Rec LLC	Stafford Springs	CT	F	860 851-9014	3255
Force3 Pro Gear LLC	Stratford	CT	F	315 367-2331	3538
Gilman Corporation	Gilman	CT	E	860 887-7080	1266
Golf Galaxy Inc	Norwalk	CT	F	203 855-0500	2507
Homeland Fundraising	East Windsor	CT	G	860 386-6698	1076
Jaypro Sports LLC	Waterford	CT	E	860 447-3001	3990
Marty Gilman Incorporated	Bozrah	CT	G	860 889-7334	229
Marty Gilman Incorporated **(PA)**	Gilman	CT	G	860 889-7334	1267
Mike Sadlak	Coventry	CT	G	860 742-0227	680
Probatter Sports LLC	Milford	CT	G	203 874-2500	1871
Protek Ski Racing Inc	Southington	CT	G	860 628-9643	3229
Rampage LLC	Trumbull	CT	G	203 521-1645	3730
Recreational Equipment Inc	West Hartford	CT	F	860 313-0128	4080
Sadlak Industries LLC	Coventry	CT	E	860 742-0227	681
Samsara Fitness LLC	Chester	CT	G	860 895-8533	632
Stache Co LLC	South Windsor	CT	G	860 719-1727	3183
TI Partners LLC	Norwalk	CT	G	203 956-6181	2583
Unified Sports Incorporated **(PA)**	Waterford	CT	E	860 447-3001	3998
Wiffle Ball Incorporated	Shelton	CT	F	203 924-4643	3079
Wild Card Golf LLC	Hartford	CT	G	860 296-1661	1517
Acushnet Company	Acushnet	MA	F	508 979-2000	5769
Acushnet Company	Brockton	MA	F	508 979-2309	7252
Acushnet Company **(DH)**	Fairhaven	MA	B	508 979-2000	8504
Acushnet Company	New Bedford	MA	F	508 979-2156	10561

Company	CITY	ST	EMP	PHONE	ENTRY#
Acushnet Company	New Bedford	MA	F	508 979-2000	10562
Acushnet Company	New Bedford	MA	E	508 979-2000	10563
Acushnet Holdings Corp (HQ)	Fairhaven	MA	E	800 225-8500	8505
Boomerangs	Cambridge	MA	G	617 758-6128	7519
Callaway Golf Company	Chicopee	MA	E	413 536-1200	8013
Cherry Hill Construction Corp	Pembroke	MA	G	781 826-6886	11360
Cns Outdoor Technologies LLC	Greenfield	MA	E	413 475-3840	8986
Cookes Skate Supply Inc	Wilmington	MA	G	978 657-7586	13398
Creative Playthings Ltd (PA)	Framingham	MA	F	508 620-0900	8753
Cuesport Inc	Southfield	MA	G	413 229-6626	12039
Cybex International Inc	Medway	MA	C	508 533-4167	10304
Dark Monk LLC	Salem	MA	G	978 766-5315	11709
Dart World Inc	Lynn	MA	E	781 581-6035	9966
East Basin Sports Inc (PA)	Newton	MA	E	781 492-2747	10754
Fitness Em LLC	Uxbridge	MA	E		12479
Fitnow Inc	Boston	MA	E	617 699-5585	6739
Great Neck Saw Mfrs Inc	Millbury	MA	D	508 865-4482	10436
Hogy Lure Company LLC	Falmouth	MA	G	617 699-5157	8633
Hollrock Engineering Inc	Hadley	MA	E	413 586-2256	9018
Hudson Poly Bag Inc	Hudson	MA	F	978 562-7566	9374
Hydro-Test Products Inc	Stow	MA	F	978 897-4647	12246
Imperial Pools Inc	Taunton	MA	F	508 339-3830	12342
Inov-8 Inc	Westborough	MA	E	508 251-4904	13109
Insignia Athletics LLC	Worcester	MA	G	508 756-3633	13742
Life+gear Inc	Wellesley Hills	MA	F	858 755-2099	12952
Macneill Engineering Co Inc	Westborough	MA	E	508 481-8830	13118
Mylec Inc (PA)	Winchendon	MA	D	978 297-0089	13480
New England Spt Ventures LLC	Boston	MA	F	617 267-9440	6916
Nokona USA Baseball	Ashland	MA	G	508 309-3527	5964
Omniview Sports Inc	Boston	MA	G	781 583-3534	6929
Outdoor Outfitters Inc	Orleans	MA	E	508 255-0455	11241
Promounds Inc (PA)	Randolph	MA	E	508 580-6171	11572
Savage Range Systems Inc	Westfield	MA	G	413 568-7001	13207
Sickday Inc	Wellfleet	MA	G	508 214-4158	12953
Surfari Inc	Gloucester	MA	G	978 283-7873	8961
Swimex Inc	Fall River	MA	E	508 646-1600	8613
Thomas & Thomas Rodmakers	Greenfield	MA	F	413 475-3840	9003
Tom Waters Golf Shop	Manchester	MA	G	978 526-7311	10034
Warrior Sports Inc (DH)	Boston	MA	C	800 968-7845	7113
Xenith	Lowell	MA	E	978 328-5297	9936
Xthera Corporation	Franklin	MA	G	508 528-3100	8877
Bigelow Mountain Partners LLC	Freeport	ME	F	207 865-9208	4798
Cedarworks of Maine Inc	Rockland	ME	E	207 596-0771	5324
E Skip Grindle & Sons	Ellsworth	ME	F	207 460-0334	4758
Eastern ME Shooting Sups Inc	Milo	ME	F	207 943-8808	5069
Extreme Dim Wildlife Calls LLC	Hampden	ME	G	207 862-2825	4863
Faulkner Corporation	Brewer	ME	G	207 989-3792	4612
Hyperlite Mountain Gear Inc	Biddeford	ME	F	800 464-9208	4570
Johnson Outdoors Inc	Old Town	ME	F	603 518-1634	5127
Pride Manufacturing Co LLC (PA)	Burnham	ME	C	207 487-3322	4661
Sports Fields Inc	Monmouth	ME	F	207 933-3547	5072
Thomas Hall	Scarborough	ME	F	207 956-0020	5445
Advanced Fitnes Components LLC	Hudson	NH	G	603 595-1967	14480
Bauer Hockey LLC	Exeter	NH	A	603 430-2111	14284
Mikel Surfboards LLC	Hampton	NH	G	603 767-7662	14407
Old Bh Inc	Exeter	NH	B	603 430-2111	14298
Pat Trap Inc	Henniker	NH	G	603 428-3396	14440
Ragged Mountain Equipment Inc	Intervale	NH	E	603 356-3042	14561
Richardson Mfg Co Inc	Silver Lake	NH	G	603 367-9018	15607
Santa Cruz Gunlocks LLC	Webster	NH	G	603 746-7740	15674
Simbex LLC	Lebanon	NH	E	603 448-2367	14699
Sunapee Difference LLC	Newbury	NH	D	603 763-3500	15204
Ashaway Line & Twine Mfg Co	Ashaway	RI	D	401 377-2221	15738
Firecracker Sports LLC	Cumberland	RI	F	401 595-0233	15939
Great American Recrtl Eqp	Cranston	RI	F	401 463-5587	15869
Hayward Industries Inc	North Kingstown	RI	C	401 583-1150	16254
Kane Motor Car Co Inc	North Kingstown	RI	G	401 294-4634	16263
Matthew W Robinson	Riverside	RI	G	401 480-3975	16657
Mearthane Products LLC (PA)	Cranston	RI	E	401 946-4400	15893
Mighty Well Inc	Newport	RI	G	617 804-1233	16217
Parsonskellogg LLC	East Providence	RI	D	866 602-8398	16037
Planet Eclipse LLC	Warren	RI	G	401 247-9061	16763
Sports Systems Custom Bags	Woonsocket	RI	D	401 767-3770	16974
Waterrower Inc	Warren	RI	D	800 852-2210	16772
Waterrower International LLC	Warren	RI	G	800 852-2210	16773
Burton Corporation (PA)	Burlington	VT	A	800 881-3138	17123
Concept2 Inc (PA)	Morrisville	VT	F	802 888-7971	17381
Gordini USA Inc (PA)	Essex Junction	VT	D	802 879-5211	17235
Gw Ski Inc	West Dover	VT	F	802 464-3464	17690
Manufacturing Solutions Inc	Morrisville	VT	E	802 888-3289	17386
Orvis Company Inc	Manchester	VT	E	802 362-3750	17324
Red Corp	Burlington	VT	E	802 862-4500	17155
Snowshoe Pond Mple Sgrwrks LLC	Enosburg Falls	VT	G	802 777-9676	17224
The Orvis Company Inc (PA)	Sunderland	VT	B	802 362-3622	17635
Whistlekick LLC	Montpelier	VT	F	802 225-6676	17379

3951 Pens and mechanical pencils

Company	CITY	ST	EMP	PHONE	ENTRY#
Bic Consumer Pdts Mfg Co Inc	Milford	CT	C	203 783-2000	1802
Bic Consumer Pdts Mfg Co Inc (DH)	Shelton	CT	D	203 783-2000	2984
Bic Corporation (HQ)	Shelton	CT	A	203 783-2000	2985
Bic USA Inc (DH)	Shelton	CT	C	203 783-2000	2986
Mega Sound and Light LLC	Danbury	CT	G	203 743-4200	784
EF Leach & Company	Attleboro	MA	C	508 643-3309	6011
Gillette Company (HQ)	Boston	MA	A	617 463-3000	6758
Goodkind Pen Company Inc	Rockland	ME	E	207 594-6207	5331
AT Cross Company LLC (HQ)	Providence	RI	E	401 333-1200	16476
Becker Manufacturing Company	Newport	RI	G	401 821-1450	16204
Costa Inc	Providence	RI	E	401 333-1200	16506
Sheaffer Pen Corporation	Lincoln	RI	A	319 372-7444	16154

3952 Lead pencils and art goods

Company	CITY	ST	EMP	PHONE	ENTRY#
Bic Corporation (HQ)	Shelton	CT	A	203 783-2000	2985
Color Craft Ltd	East Granby	CT	F	800 509-6563	929
Chartpak Inc (HQ)	Leeds	MA	D	413 584-5446	9621
Jen Mfg Inc	Millbury	MA	E	508 753-1076	10437
Pucker Gallery Inc	Somerville	MA	F	617 261-1817	11891
Scratch Art Company Inc (PA)	Avon	MA	F	508 583-8085	6161
Sprout USA LLC	Boston	MA	G	617 650-1958	7056
Goodkind Pen Company Inc	Rockland	ME	E	207 594-6207	5331
Hunter Dathan Hair Artistry	Portland	ME	G	207 774-8887	5224
Dahle North America Inc	Peterborough	NH	E	603 924-0003	15314
Sheaffer Pen Corporation	Lincoln	RI	A	319 372-7444	16154
Wood & Wood Inc	Waitsfield	VT	G	802 496-3000	17669

3953 Marking devices

Company	CITY	ST	EMP	PHONE	ENTRY#
A D Perkins Company	New Haven	CT	G	203 777-3456	2110
Acme Sign Co (PA)	Stamford	CT	F	324 224-2263	3272
American Sign Inc	New Haven	CT	F	203 624-2991	2115
Biomerics LLC	Monroe	CT	D	203 268-7238	1906
Liftline Capital LLC	Old Saybrook	CT	F	860 395-0150	2654
Mallace Industries Corp	Clinton	CT	E	860 669-9001	647
Mbsw Inc	West Hartford	CT	E	860 243-0303	4071
Northeast Laser Engraving Inc	Monroe	CT	E	203 268-7238	1918
Schwerdtle Stamp Company	Bridgeport	CT	E	203 330-2750	369
United Sttes Sign Fbrction Cor	Trumbull	CT	F	203 601-1000	3739
Van Deusen & Levitt Assoc Inc	Weston	CT	G	203 445-6244	4154
AA White Company	Uxbridge	MA	G	508 779-0821	12476
Kalt Incorporated (PA)	Lowell	MA	F	978 805-5001	9889
Lincoln Press Co Inc	Fall River	MA	F	508 673-3241	8569
Logan Stamp Works Inc	Boston	MA	G	617 569-2121	6861
Making Your Mark Inc	Quincy	MA	G	617 479-0999	11527
New England Expert Tech Corp	Greenfield	MA	E	413 773-8200	8995
Opsec Security Inc	Boston	MA	D	617 226-3000	6941
Owl Stamp Company Inc	Lowell	MA	G	978 452-4541	9912
Rofin-Baasel Inc (HQ)	Devens	MA	E	978 635-9100	8286
Titus & Bean Graphics Inc	Kingston	MA	F	781 585-1355	9513
Top Half Inc	Tyngsboro	MA	F	978 454-5440	12468
Visimark Inc (PA)	Worcester	MA	E	866 344-7721	13823
Armstrong Family Inds Inc	Hermon	ME	E	207 848-7300	4880
Davis-Joncas Enterprises Inc	Scarborough	ME	E	207 883-6200	5430
Granite State Stamps Inc	Manchester	NH	F	603 669-9322	14856

3955 Carbon paper and inked ribbons

Company	CITY	ST	EMP	PHONE	ENTRY#
Envirmntal Office Sltions Inc (PA)	East Hartford	CT	E	860 291-1900	993
Avcarb LLC	Lowell	MA	D	978 452-8961	9857
Electronics For Imaging Inc	Londonderry	NH	B	603 285-9800	14747
Electronics For Imaging Inc (HQ)	Londonderry	NH	E	650 357-3500	14748

3961 Costume jewelry

Company	CITY	ST	EMP	PHONE	ENTRY#
Buisson Jewelers Inc	Greenwich	CT	G	203 869-8895	1324
Dt Holdings Incorporated	Stamford	CT	F	203 602-6969	3339
Mystic Knotwork LLC	Mystic	CT	G	860 889-3793	1939
AB Group Inc	Attleboro	MA	G	508 222-1404	5989
Adina Inc (PA)	Norwood	MA	G	781 762-4477	11154
American Biltrite Inc (PA)	Wellesley	MA	G	781 237-6655	12935
Ashworth Assoc Mfg Whl Jwelers	North Attleboro	MA	F	508 695-1900	10866
Charles Thomae & Son Inc	Attleboro	MA	F	508 222-0785	6001
ESP Solutions Inc	Taunton	MA	F	508 285-0017	12335
Garlan Chain Co Inc	Attleboro Falls	MA	G	508 399-7288	6085
J & K Sales Co Inc	Rehoboth	MA	G	508 252-6235	11610
Natalia Marketing Corp	Waltham	MA	F	781 693-4900	12733
Newpro Designs Inc	Norwood	MA	E	781 762-4477	11200
North Attleboro Jewelry Co Inc	Attleboro	MA	G	508 222-4660	6044
Plastic Craft Novelty Co Inc	Attleboro	MA	F	508 222-1486	6049
Sweet Metal Finishing Inc	Attleboro	MA	F	508 226-4359	6068
AG & G Inc (PA)	Johnston	RI	E	401 946-4330	16073

SIC

Employee Codes: A=Over 500 employees, B=251-500
C=101-250, D=51-100, E=20-50, F=10-19, G=1-9   2024 Harris New England
Manufacturers Directory   971

	CITY	ST	EMP	PHONE	ENTRY#
American Ring Co Inc (PA)	East Providence	RI	F	401 438-9060	16003
Barrington Manufacturing Inc	Warren	RI	G	401 245-1737	16753
Bazar Group Inc (PA)	East Providence	RI	E	401 434-2595	16006
Bliss Manufacturing Co Inc	Pawtucket	RI	E	401 729-1690	16350
Chronomatic Inc	East Greenwich	RI	E	401 884-6361	15978
CJ International Inc	Providence	RI	E	401 944-4700	16499
Decor Craft Inc	Providence	RI	E	401 621-2324	16507
Dina Inc	Cranston	RI	G	401 942-9633	15851
Esposito Jewelry Inc	Providence	RI	F	401 943-1900	16516
Fulford Manufacturing Company (PA)	Riverside	RI	F	401 431-2000	16655
Gennaro Inc	Cranston	RI	F	401 632-4100	15868
J Arakelian Inc	Johnston	RI	F	401 943-7366	16090
J Cal Inc (PA)	Providence	RI	D	401 941-7700	16546
Jcc Residual Ltd	Woonsocket	RI	F	508 699-4401	16966
Josef Creations Inc (PA)	Chepachet	RI	E	401 421-4198	15805
Kefi Development Inc	East Providence	RI	E	401 272-6513	16027
Kennedy Incorporated	North Kingstown	RI	F	401 295-7800	16265
Klitzner Industries Inc	Lincoln	RI	E	800 621-0161	16143
Luca + Danni Inc	Cranston	RI	E	401 275-5337	15887
Mag Jewelry Co Inc	Cranston	RI	E	401 942-1840	15890
Michael Healy Designs Inc	Manville	RI	G	401 597-5900	16165
Modern Manufacturing Inc	Johnston	RI	F	401 944-9230	16096
Perry Blackburne Inc	North Providence	RI	F	401 231-7200	16307
R & D Manufacturing Co Inc	Pawtucket	RI	F	401 305-7662	16408
Reed Allison Group Inc	Providence	RI	D	617 846-1237	16599
Rgt Inc	Providence	RI	D	401 431-5016	16601
Rolyn Inc (PA)	Cranston	RI	E	401 944-0844	15908
Salvadore Tool & Findings Inc (PA)	Providence	RI	F	401 331-6000	16609
Snow & Stars Corporation	Providence	RI	F	401 421-4134	16613
Stylecraft Inc	Cranston	RI	D	401 463-9944	15914
Swarovski North America Ltd (DH)	Cranston	RI	A	401 463-6400	15915
Training Thru Placement Inc	North Providence	RI	E	401 353-0220	16312
Ubio Inc	Johnston	RI	G	401 541-9172	16108
Venturi Inc	Warwick	RI	G	401 781-2647	16871
Wehr Industries Inc	Warwick	RI	F	401 732-6565	16878
Weingeroff Enterprises Inc	Cranston	RI	C	401 467-2200	15929
Winkler Group Ltd (PA)	Rumford	RI	C	401 272-2885	16680
Mainstream Inc (PA)	Bennington	VT	F	802 442-8859	17050

3965 Fasteners, buttons, needles, and pins

	CITY	ST	EMP	PHONE	ENTRY#
Braxton Manufacturing Co Inc	Watertown	CT	C	860 274-6781	4003
Eyelet Tech LLC	Wolcott	CT	E	203 879-5306	4365
Illinois Tool Works Inc	Naugatuck	CT	F	203 720-1676	1964
ITW Powertrain Fastening	Naugatuck	CT	E	203 720-1676	1967
J&J Precision Inc	Thomaston	CT	D	860 283-8243	3622
Lord & Hodge Inc	Middletown	CT	F	860 632-7006	1760
Manchester TI & Design ADP LLC	North Haven	CT	G	860 296-6541	2422
Metalform Acquisition LLC (PA)	New Britain	CT	F	860 224-2630	2043
Midwest Motor Supply Co	Newtown	CT	E	800 233-1294	2342
Nucap US Inc (DH)	Wolcott	CT	E	203 879-1423	4371
OGS TECHNOLOGIES LLC	Cheshire	CT	E	203 271-9055	610
Paneloc Corporation	Farmington	CT	E	860 677-6711	1238
Platt Brothers & Company (PA)	Waterbury	CT	D	203 753-4194	3963
Rings Wire Inc (PA)	Milford	CT	E	203 874-6719	1879
Rome Fastener Corporation	Milford	CT	E	203 874-6719	1880
Stevens Company Incorporated	Thomaston	CT	D	860 283-8201	3631
US Button Corporation	Putnam	CT	C	860 928-2707	2878
Buckleguycom LLC	Newburyport	MA	G	978 213-9989	10673
Charles Thomae & Son Inc	Attleboro	MA	F	508 222-7085	6001
Great Northern Industries Inc (PA)	Boston	MA	C	617 262-4314	6771
Icarus Corporation	Auburn	MA	F	508 832-3481	6114
Nixon Company Incorporated	Indian Orchard	MA	F	413 543-3701	9472
Reed & Prince Mfg Corp	Leominster	MA	F	978 466-6903	9700
Reeves Company Inc	Attleboro	MA	F	508 222-2877	6053
Warwick Fasteners	West Bridgewater	MA	G	401 739-9200	12989
Velcro USA Inc (DH)	Manchester	NH	A	800 225-0180	14951
W H Bagshaw Co Inc	Nashua	NH	E	603 883-7758	15184
J Arakelian Inc	Johnston	RI	F	401 943-7366	16090
Precision Plsg Ornamentals Inc	Pawtucket	RI	F	401 728-9994	16404

3991 Brooms and brushes

	CITY	ST	EMP	PHONE	ENTRY#
Liftline Capital LLC	Old Saybrook	CT	F	860 395-0150	2654
Loos & Co Inc	Pomfret	CT	D	860 928-6681	2810
Angel Guard Products Inc	Worcester	MA	G	508 791-1073	13699
Atlantic Broom Service Inc	East Bridgewater	MA	F	774 226-1300	8335
Butler Home Products LLC (HQ)	Hudson	MA	F	508 597-8000	9359
Cardinal Comb & Brush Mfg Corp	Leominster	MA	E	978 537-6330	9647
Jaz Brush USA Inc	New Bedford	MA	G	774 992-7996	10605
Jen Mfg Inc	Millbury	MA	F	508 753-1076	10437
Sanderson-Macleod Incorporate	Palmer	MA	C	413 283-3481	11284
Howard P Fairfield LLC (DH)	Skowhegan	ME	E	207 474-9836	5468
American Brush Company Inc	Claremont	NH	F	603 542-9951	14075
Felton Inc	Londonderry	NH	D	603 425-0200	14750

	CITY	ST	EMP	PHONE	ENTRY#
ACS Industries Inc (PA)	Lincoln	RI	E	401 769-4700	16116
Northeast Ldscpg Tree Svcs Inc	Westerly	RI	F	860 405-5274	16941
Tucel Industries Inc	Forest Dale	VT	F	802 247-6824	17274

3993 Signs and advertising specialties

	CITY	ST	EMP	PHONE	ENTRY#
A D Perkins Company	New Haven	CT	G	203 777-3456	2110
ABC Sign Corporation	Bridgeport	CT	E	203 513-8110	291
Acme Sign Co (PA)	Stamford	CT	F	203 324-2263	3272
Adams Ahern Sign Solutions	West Hartford	CT	G	860 523-8835	4047
Adamsahern Sign Solutions Inc	Hartford	CT	F	860 523-8835	1467
American Sign Inc	New Haven	CT	F	203 624-2991	2115
Applied Advertising Inc	Danbury	CT	F	860 640-0800	708
Arnco Sign Company	Wallingford	CT	D	203 238-1224	3775
Arteffects Incorporated	Bloomfield	CT	E	860 242-0031	147
Asi Sign Systems Inc	East Berlin	CT	G	860 828-3331	907
Camaro Signs Inc (PA)	Jewett City	CT	G	860 886-1553	1535
Classic Graphics Corp	Stamford	CT	G	203 323-6635	3315
Concord Industries Inc	Norwalk	CT	E	203 750-6060	2485
Connecticut Container Corp (PA)	North Haven	CT	C	203 248-2161	2399
Connecticut Sign Service LLC	Deep River	CT	G	860 767-7446	875
Copy Cats Inc	New London	CT	F	860 442-8424	2225
Creative Dimensions Inc	Cheshire	CT	E	203 250-6500	584
CT Sign Service LLC	Deep River	CT	G	860 322-3954	876
Displaycraft Inc	Plainville	CT	E	860 747-9110	2754
Farmington Displays Inc	Farmington	CT	E	860 677-2497	1219
Fg Signs LLC	Stratford	CT	G	203 612-4447	3536
Gerber Scientific LLC (PA)	Tolland	CT	C	860 871-8082	3661
Horizons Unlimited Inc	Willimantic	CT	F	860 423-1931	4219
Hot Tops LLC	Shelton	CT	F	203 926-2067	3016
Identification Products Corp (PA)	Shelton	CT	E	203 334-5969	3019
John Oldham Studios Inc	Wethersfield	CT	E	860 529-3331	4207
Jornik Manufacturing Corp	Stamford	CT	F	203 969-0500	3393
Lamar Advertising Company	Windsor	CT	G	860 246-6546	4285
Lauretano Sign Group Inc	Terryville	CT	E	860 582-0233	3605
Lewtan Industries Corporation	West Hartford	CT	E	860 278-9800	4068
McIntire Company (HQ)	Bristol	CT	F	860 585-8559	465
Michael Zoppa	South Windsor	CT	G	860 289-5881	3165
National Sign Corporation (PA)	Berlin	CT	F	860 829-9060	77
OGS TECHNOLOGIES LLC	Cheshire	CT	E	203 271-9055	610
PRC Synergy Corp	Bridgeport	CT	B	203 331-9100	360
Precision Graphics Inc	East Berlin	CT	E	860 828-6561	916
Priority One Inc	Danbury	CT	G	203 244-7093	800
Project Graphics Inc	Woodbury	CT	E	802 488-8789	4388
Revolution Lighting Tech Inc (PA)	Stamford	CT	F	877 578-2536	3447
Rokap Inc	East Hampton	CT	E	203 265-6895	965
Shiner Signs Inc	Meriden	CT	E	203 634-4331	1697
Sign Factory	Enfield	CT	F	860 763-1085	1151
Sign Fast	Bridgeport	CT	G	203 549-8500	371
Sign Pro Inc	Plantsville	CT	F	860 229-1812	2795
Signs On Demand Usa LLC	Middletown	CT	G	860 346-1720	1780
Signs Plus Inc (PA)	East Granby	CT	G	860 653-0547	951
Skyline Exhibits Graphics Inc	Middletown	CT	F	860 635-2400	1781
Sonalysts Inc	Waterford	CT	B	860 442-4355	3997
Spencer Norb	West Hartford	CT	F	860 231-8079	4082
The Gilman Brothers Company	Gilman	CT	D	860 889-8444	1268
United Sttes Sign Fbrction Cor	Trumbull	CT	F	203 601-1000	3739
Wad Inc	East Berlin	CT	F	860 828-3331	920
Whaling City Graphics LLC	Waterford	CT	F	860 437-7446	3999
Wingsite Displays Inc	Wethersfield	CT	E	860 257-3300	4215
Yankee Plak Co Inc	Bridgeport	CT	F	203 333-3168	387
Accurate Graphics Inc	Lynn	MA	G	781 593-1630	9961
Ace Signs Inc	Springfield	MA	F	413 739-3814	12070
Ad-A-Day Company Inc	Taunton	MA	E	508 824-8676	12315
Advanced Signing LLC	Medway	MA	E	508 533-9000	10301
Aerial Skyvertising Inc	Brockton	MA	G	508 586-4076	7253
Agnoli Sign Company Inc	Springfield	MA	E	413 732-5111	12072
All American Signs Inc	Plymouth	MA	F	508 830-0505	11445
Apifia Inc	Boston	MA	E	585 506-2787	6550
Apple Mill Holding Company Inc	Pembroke	MA	F	781 826-9706	11358
Atlantic Broom Service Inc	East Bridgewater	MA	F	774 226-1300	8335
Back Bay Sign LLC	Wilmington	MA	F	781 475-1001	13386
Baker Sign Works Inc	Fall River	MA	F	508 674-6600	8524
Batten Bros Inc	Wakefield	MA	F	781 245-4800	12501
Boston Sign Company Inc	Boston	MA	G	617 338-2114	6618
Business Signs LLC	Woburn	MA	G	781 808-3153	13537
C & D Signs Inc	Tewksbury	MA	E	978 851-2424	12388
Cadwell Products Company Inc	Holliston	MA	F	508 429-3100	9203
Casey & Hayes Inc	Hingham	MA	C	617 269-5900	9146
Clayton LLC DBA Blbird Grphic	Woburn	MA	E	617 250-8500	13542
Design Communications Ltd (PA)	Avon	MA	D	617 542-9620	6148
Dg International Holdings Corp	Needham Heights	MA	F	781 577-2016	10541
Dinn Bros Inc (PA)	West Springfield	MA	D	413 750-3466	13022
E A Dion Inc	Attleboro	MA	C	800 445-1007	6010

	CITY	ST	EMP	PHONE	ENTRY#
E V Yeuell Inc	Woburn	MA	E	781 933-2984	13560
Eastern Etching and Mfg Co	Chicopee	MA	E	413 594-6601	8030
Eratech Inc	Ashfield	MA	F	413 628-3219	5954
Expansion Opportunities Inc	Northborough	MA	E	508 393-8200	11095
Far Reach Graphics Inc	Needham Heights	MA	G	781 444-4889	10545
Fastsigns	Needham Heights	MA	G	781 444-4889	10546
Fastsigns of Attleboro	Rehoboth	MA	F	508 699-6699	11608
Fnsj Inc	Quincy	MA	F	617 302-2882	11519
General Display Inc	Medway	MA	F	508 533-6676	10305
George Patton Associates Inc	Fall River	MA	C	800 572-2194	8552
Gloucester Graphics Inc (PA)	Gloucester	MA	G	978 281-4500	8937
Grand Image Inc	Hudson	MA	E	888 973-2622	9371
Graphic Impact Signs Inc	Pittsfield	MA	E	413 499-0382	11399
Hamilton Sign & Design Inc	Worcester	MA	G	508 459-9731	13736
Higgins Location LLC	Acton	MA	F	978 266-1200	5752
Honorcraft LLC	Stoughton	MA	F	781 341-0410	12214
ID Graphics Group Inc	South Easton	MA	E	508 238-8500	11945
Image Signs	New Bedford	MA	G	774 328-8059	10603
Innovative Media Group Inc	Weymouth	MA	F	781 335-8773	13327
Insignia Incorporated	Haverhill	MA	E	978 372-3721	9105
Insignia Incorporated	Norwood	MA	E	781 278-0150	11182
John J Cahill Displays Inc	East Weymouth	MA	G	617 737-3232	8430
Keating Communication Group	Canton	MA	F	781 828-9030	7804
Lane Printing Co Inc	Holbrook	MA	F	781 767-4450	9178
Ldr Inc	Salem	MA	E	978 825-0020	11726
Massachstts Sign Instlltion Co	Worcester	MA	F	508 793-0956	13758
Mediavue Systems Inc	Hingham	MA	E	781 926-0676	9153
Mystic Scenic Studios Inc	Norwood	MA	D	781 440-0914	11198
National Sign Corp	Attleboro Falls	MA	E	508 809-4638	6092
New England Flag & Banner	Watertown	MA	F	617 782-1892	12897
New England Sign Group Inc	Worcester	MA	G	508 779-0821	13764
New England Wire Products Inc (PA)	Leominster	MA	D	800 254-9473	9686
New England Wooden Ware Corp (PA)	Gardner	MA	E	978 632-3600	8896
Newman Enterprises Inc	Southborough	MA	G	508 875-7446	11999
Oldsignsnstuffcom Inc	Gardner	MA	F	978 407-6718	8897
Owl Stamp Company Inc	Lowell	MA	G	978 452-4541	9912
Pg Technologies Inc	Westfield	MA	G	413 562-1354	13198
Poyant Signs Inc (PA)	New Bedford	MA	E	800 544-0961	10643
Quick Clean Car Wash Systems I (PA)	Wakefield	MA	F	781 245-6809	12531
Quick Print Ltd Inc	Chelmsford	MA	G	978 256-1822	7950
Raders Engraving Inc	Boston	MA	F	617 227-2921	6993
Ready 2 Run Graphics Signs Inc	Worcester	MA	F	508 459-9977	13781
Reeves Company Inc	Attleboro	MA	F	508 222-2877	6053
Roadsafe Traffic Systems Inc	Avon	MA	D	508 580-6700	6160
Rustic Marlin Designs LLC	Hanover	MA	E	508 376-1004	9041
Serrato Signs LLC	Worcester	MA	G	508 756-7004	13799
Sign Art Inc	Malden	MA	F	781 322-3785	10027
Sign By Tommorrow	Norton	MA	G	508 222-1900	11134
Sign Company	Dennis Port	MA	F	508 760-5400	8262
Sign Design Inc	Brockton	MA	D	508 580-0094	7306
Sign Solutions Unlimited	Woburn	MA	G	781 537-6156	13665
Sign Techniques Inc	Chicopee	MA	F	413 594-8240	8061
Signarama	Worcester	MA	G	508 459-9731	13801
Signs By J Inc	Boston	MA	G	617 825-9855	7037
Signs To Go Inc	Woburn	MA	F	781 808-3153	13667
Signworks Group Inc	Watertown	MA	F	617 924-0292	12907
Silver Screen Design Inc	Greenfield	MA	F	413 773-1692	9000
Space Age Accessories Inc	Foxboro	MA	E	508 543-3661	8725
Speedy Sign-A-Rama USA	Braintree	MA	G	781 849-1161	7203
Steel Art Company Inc	Norwood	MA	D	617 566-4079	11211
Stickamayka Packaging Inc	Andover	MA	E	978 474-1930	5926
Strong Group Inc (PA)	Gloucester	MA	D	978 281-3300	8960
Sunshine Sign Company Inc	North Grafton	MA	C	508 839-5588	11026
Titus & Bean Graphics Inc	Kingston	MA	F	781 585-1355	9513
Wood Art Incorporated	Cherry Valley	MA	G	508 892-8058	7995
Affordable Exhibit Displays	Auburn	ME	F	207 782-6175	4417
American Nameplate	Brewer	ME	G	207 848-7187	4609
Bailey Sign Inc	Westbrook	ME	E	207 774-2843	5617
Bangor Neon	Bangor	ME	F	207 947-2766	4492
Burr Signs	Westbrook	ME	G	207 396-6111	5619
Central Equipment Company	Stillwater	ME	F	207 827-6193	5533
Davis-Joncas Enterprises Inc	Scarborough	ME	E	207 883-6200	5430
Geiger Bros (PA)	Lewiston	ME	B	207 755-2000	4962
Glidden Signs Inc	Scarborough	ME	F	207 396-6111	5433
H4 Holdings LLC	Saco	ME	G	207 494-8085	5369
Neokraft Signs Inc	Lewiston	ME	E	207 782-9654	4980
Print-Mail of Maine Inc	Portland	ME	F	207 878-8000	5262
Sign Concepts LLC	Portland	ME	F	207 699-2920	5271
Sign Design Inc	Portland	ME	F	207 856-2600	5272
Sign Services Inc	Stetson	ME	F	207 296-2400	5531
T R Sign Design Inc	Portland	ME	F	207 856-2600	5279
Transformit (PA)	Gorham	ME	E	207 856-9911	4837

	CITY	ST	EMP	PHONE	ENTRY#
Winter People Inc	Cumberland Center	ME	E	207 865-6636	4711
American Flgging Trffic Ctrl I	Hudson	NH	D	603 890-1154	14482
Bigraphics Inc	Nashua	NH	G	603 594-8686	15071
Classic Signs Inc	Amherst	NH	F	603 883-0384	13864
Corportion For Lser Optics Res (PA)	Londonderry	NH	F	603 430-2023	14738
Db Signs LLC	Concord	NH	G	603 225-4081	14128
Fast Signs of Plaistow	Plaistow	NH	F	603 894-7446	15343
Fastrax Signs Inc	Brentwood	NH	G	603 775-7500	14021
Granite State Stamps Inc	Manchester	NH	F	603 669-9322	14856
Ink Outside Box Incorporated	Pelham	NH	G	603 635-2292	15290
J H Dunning Corporation	North Walpole	NH	E	603 445-5591	15258
Jackson Signsmith	Jackson	NH	F	603 383-8900	14562
Jutras Signs Inc	Bedford	NH	F	603 622-2344	13936
Kevin L Woolbert	North Walpole	NH	G	603 445-5222	15259
Maineline Graphics LLC	Antrim	NH	F	603 588-3177	13897
Plw Inc	Greenland	NH	F	603 889-4126	14370
Powerplay Management LLC	Portsmouth	NH	E	603 436-3030	15431
Precision Letter LLC	Manchester	NH	F	603 625-9625	14913
Snap Site Studios LLC	Manchester	NH	G	603 782-3395	14931
Sousa Signs LLC	Manchester	NH	F	603 622-5067	14934
Spectrum Monthly LLC	Manchester	NH	C	603 627-0042	14936
Synergy Signworks LLC	Manchester	NH	F	603 440-3519	14939
Abar Color Labs Neng Inc	Lincoln	RI	F	401 351-8644	16114
Accent Display Corp	Lincoln	RI	E	401 461-8787	16115
Anchors Aweigh Together LLC	Warwick	RI	G	401 738-8055	16779
Dasko Identification Products	Warren	RI	F	401 435-6500	16757
Dexter Enterprises Corp	East Providence	RI	G	401 434-2300	16013
Dexter Sign Co	East Providence	RI	F	401 434-1100	16014
Gepp LLC	Warwick	RI	F	401 808-8004	16818
Hub-Federal Inc	Providence	RI	G	401 421-3400	16534
Hutchison Company Inc	North Kingstown	RI	F	401 294-3503	16258
Josef Creations Inc (PA)	Chepachet	RI	E	401 421-4198	15805
LSI Industries Inc	Woonsocket	RI	G	401 766-7446	16968
Mandeville Signs Inc	Lincoln	RI	G	401 334-9100	16146
Mastercast Ltd	Pawtucket	RI	F	401 726-3100	16384
National Marker Company	North Smithfield	RI	D	401 762-9700	16329
Nmc Solar LLC	North Smithfield	RI	D	401 762-9700	16330
Orion Ret Svcs & Fixturing Inc	Smithfield	RI	D	401 334-5000	16725
Progressive Displays Inc	Warren	RI	F	401 245-2909	16764
Rose Displays	Pawtucket	RI	F	978 219-8120	16413
RTC Holdings Inc	Pawtucket	RI	F	401 728-6980	16414
Scope Display & Box Co Inc (PA)	Cranston	RI	E	401 942-7150	15909
SES America Inc	Warwick	RI	F	401 232-3370	16861
Spirit Recognition Inc (PA)	Pawtucket	RI	F	401 722-6400	16417
The Elliott Sales Group Inc	Providence	RI	D	401 944-0002	16625
Fastsigns - 490101	South Burlington	VT	G	802 238-1247	17578
Twin State Signs Inc	Essex Junction	VT	G	802 872-8949	17248
Wood & Wood Inc	Waitsfield	VT	G	802 496-3000	17669
Yellow Sign Commercial Inc	South Burlington	VT	G	802 324-8500	17608

3996 Hard surface floor coverings, nec

	CITY	ST	EMP	PHONE	ENTRY#
Industrial Floor Covering Inc	North Billerica	MA	G	978 362-8655	10921
Natco Products Corporation (PA)	West Warwick	RI	B	401 828-0300	16916

3999 Manufacturing industries, nec

	CITY	ST	EMP	PHONE	ENTRY#
Acme United Corporation (PA)	Shelton	CT	D	203 254-6060	2978
Advanced Specialist LLC	Watertown	CT	G	860 945-9125	4001
Aero-Precision Mfg LLC	Wallingford	CT	G	203 675-7625	3768
American Hydrogen Northeast	Bridgeport	CT	G	203 449-4614	294
Amerpet LLC	Stamford	CT	G	475 619-9512	3280
Andher Mfg LLC	East Hartford	CT	G	860 874-8816	970
Ann S Davis	Lebanon	CT	F	860 642-7228	1548
Arrow Lock Manufacturing Co	New Haven	CT	G	203 603-5959	2118
Bic Corporation (HQ)	Shelton	CT	A	203 783-2000	2985
Bic USA Inc (DH)	Shelton	CT	C	203 783-2000	2986
Bnl Manufacturing LLC	Vernon Rockville	CT	G	860 870-6222	3760
Boom LLC	New Canaan	CT	E	212 317-2005	2076
Cardinal Shehan Center Inc	Bridgeport	CT	E	203 336-4468	310
Carlin Mfg Kitchens To Go	Mystic	CT	G	413 519-2822	1937
CCI Cyrus River Terminal LLC	Stamford	CT	G	203 761-8000	3305
Cici Bevin Gordon	Marlborough	CT	G	860 365-5731	1642
CJ First Candle	New Canaan	CT	G	203 966-1300	2077
Components For Mfg LLC	Noank	CT	G	860 572-1671	2359
Conair LLC (HQ)	Stamford	CT	B	203 351-9000	3320
Concentric Tool and Mfg Co	Naugatuck	CT	G	203 756-9145	1954
Connecticut Metal Industries	Ansonia	CT	G	203 736-0790	11
Crystal Journey Candles LLC	Branford	CT	E	203 433-4735	245
Customized Foods Mfg LLC	Waterbury	CT	G	203 759-1645	3902
CV Industries Corporation	Oxford	CT	E	203 828-6566	2692
Ddk Industries LLC	Shelton	CT	G	203 641-4218	2998
Delcon Industries	Trumbull	CT	G	203 371-5711	3717
Delta-Source LLC	West Hartford	CT	F	860 461-1600	4056

Company	CITY	ST	EMP	PHONE	ENTRY#
Diversified Manufacturing LLC	Ansonia	CT	F	203 734-0379	13
DRM Research Laboratories Inc	Branford	CT	F	203 488-5555	252
East Coast Precision Mfg	Chester	CT	F	860 322-4624	627
Elite Group Manufacturing LLC	Portland	CT	G	860 788-6413	2819
Ellis Manufacturing LLC	Plainville	CT	G	865 518-0531	2758
Ensign Bickford Industries	Simsbury	CT	F	203 843-2126	3087
Fire Prevention Services	Trumbull	CT	F	203 866-6357	3720
Firestable Insulation Co	Essex	CT	G	860 767-8773	1164
Formatron Ltd	Farmington	CT	F	860 676-0227	1220
Global Scenic Services Inc	Bridgeport	CT	E	203 334-2130	325
Hpi Manufacturing Inc	Hamden	CT	F	203 777-5395	1431
Idelle Management Company	Danbury	CT	E		758
Incord Ltd	Oakdale	CT	E	860 537-1414	2622
Ironhorse Industries LLC	Harwinton	CT	G	203 598-8720	1521
Jenray Products Inc	Brookfield	CT	E	914 375-5596	527
Jera Industries LLC	Stamford	CT	G	203 428-6588	3391
K and R Precision Grinding	New Britain	CT	F	860 505-8030	2036
Katy Industries Inc	Middlebury	CT	G	314 656-4321	1715
LDM Manufacturing Inc	Plainville	CT	G	860 410-9804	2769
Leisure Learning Products Inc	Stamford	CT	F	203 325-2800	3397
Lesco	Stamford	CT	F	203 353-0061	3398
Line Sets Inc	Ansonia	CT	G	203 732-6700	16
Mafcote Industries	Norwalk	CT	F	601 776-9006	2531
Marmon Engnered Wire Cable LLC	Hartford	CT	F	860 653-8300	1491
Mk Millwork LLC	Morris	CT	F	860 567-0173	1933
Modelvision Inc	New Milford	CT	G	860 355-3884	2253
Nac Industries Inc	Oxford	CT	F	845 214-0659	2706
Northeast Wood Products LLC	Uncasville	CT	F	860 862-6350	3742
O & G Industries Inc	Beacon Falls	CT	E	203 881-5192	44
O & G Industries Inc	Harwinton	CT	F	860 485-6600	1522
O Berk Company Neng LLC	West Haven	CT	F	203 932-8000	4117
Ouidad Products LLC	Danbury	CT	G		793
Outdoor Industries LLC	Madison	CT	F	203 350-2275	1565
Picture This Hartford Inc	East Hartford	CT	G	860 528-1409	1011
Pleasant Valley Fence Co Inc	Pleasant Valley	CT	G	860 379-0088	2803
Polster Industries LLC	Fairfield	CT	G	203 521-8517	1198
Precision Express Mfg LLC	Bristol	CT	F	860 584-2627	483
Precision Fire Fabrication LLC	Plantsville	CT	F	203 706-0749	2794
Qds LLC	Shelton	CT	F	203 338-9668	3057
Quality Bead Craft Inc	Bloomfield	CT	G	860 242-2167	204
RC Industries Inc	Wilton	CT	F	203 423-9419	4246
Regional Industries LLC	Clinton	CT	F	860 227-3627	649
Rockwood Manufacturing Co	New Haven	CT	F	800 582-2424	2192
Rome Fastener Corporation	Milford	CT	E	203 874-6719	1880
Sadlak Manufacturing LLC	Coventry	CT	F	860 742-0227	682
Show Motion Inc	Milford	CT	E	203 866-1866	1884
Solidification Pdts Intl Inc	Northford	CT	G	203 484-9494	2456
Solon Manufacturing	North Haven	CT	F	203 230-5300	2437
Spv Industries LLC	West Hartford	CT	G	860 953-5928	4083
Thermospas Hot Tub Products	Wallingford	CT	E	203 303-0005	3861
Thomas S Klise Co	Mystic	CT	G	860 536-4200	1943
Thomaston Industries Inc	Thomaston	CT	F	860 283-4358	3638
UST LLC	Stamford	CT	A	203 817-3000	3489
Vr Industries LLC	Torrington	CT	F	860 618-2772	3706
West-Conn Tool and Die Inc	Shelton	CT	E	203 538-5081	3077
Whiff LLC	Fairfield	CT	F	917 420-0397	1206
10beauty Inc	Burlington	MA	E	215 356-8680	7329
99degrees Custom Inc	Lawrence	MA	E	978 655-3362	9533
Act Manufacturing Securities C	Foxboro	MA	G	508 481-5246	8690
Advanced CAM Manufacturing LLC	Hudson	MA	F	978 562-2825	9352
Alpha Tech Pet Inc	Littleton	MA	G	978 486-3690	9800
Altium Packaging LP	Marlborough	MA	E	508 485-2109	10107
Anthony Industries Inc	Woburn	MA	G	781 305-3750	13511
Atlantic Industrial Models LLC	Essex	MA	F	978 768-7686	8473
Audiospectrum Inc	Randolph	MA	E	781 767-1331	11549
Axial Industries	Wakefield	MA	G	781 224-0421	12499
Batch Inc	New Braintree	MA	F	203 948-9212	10663
Blanche P Field LLC	Boston	MA	F	617 423-0715	6596
Byblos Industries Corporation	Norwood	MA	G	781 727-4764	11167
Callenstitch LLC	Concord	MA	F	978 369-9080	8107
Cartamundi East Longmeadow LLC	East Longmeadow	MA	B	413 526-2000	8371
Cassjack Industries Inc	Westfield	MA	G	413 786-1800	13157
Century-Tywood J3 Corp	Holliston	MA	F	508 429-4011	9204
CIM Industries Inc	Bridgewater	MA	E	800 543-3458	7226
CJS Workshop LLC	Groton	MA	F	323 445-5012	9008
Cory Manufacturing Inc	West Bridgewater	MA	F	508 680-2111	12970
Couture Brands LLC	Marlborough	MA	G	512 626-7544	10138
Createk-Stone Inc	Southbridge	MA	G	888 786-6389	12012
Crosby Whistle Stop	Charlestown	MA	G	617 974-7410	7867
Cultivate Licensing LLC	Leicester	MA	F	508 859-8130	9623
Currys Leather Shop Inc	Randolph	MA	G	781 963-0679	11554
Custom Group Ctr For Mfg Tech	Woburn	MA	G	781 935-4940	13553
Custom Learning Designs Inc	Belmont	MA	D	617 489-1702	6305
Dalton Manufacturing Group Inc	Amesbury	MA	F	978 388-2227	5834
David W Wallace	Shelburne Falls	MA	G	413 625-6523	11803
Diamondhead Usa Inc	West Springfield	MA	F	413 537-4806	13021
Don-Jo Mfg Inc	Sterling	MA	E	978 422-3377	12160
Erica Wilson Inc (PA)	Nantucket	MA	F	212 348-6196	10463
Fire Defenses New England LLC	Danvers	MA	F	978 304-1506	8186
Graphite Insulg Systems Inc	Gardner	MA	F	978 630-8988	8890
Greenfield Industries Inc	Greenfield	MA	G	413 772-3200	8992
Gzsl Corp	North Attleboro	MA	F	508 695-0727	10872
Hedge Hog Industries Corp	Springfield	MA	F	413 363-2528	12100
High Purity Natural Pdts LLC	Southbridge	MA	G	508 864-6072	12019
Highland Labs Inc	Holliston	MA	G	508 429-2918	9215
HMh Religious Mfg Inc	Plainville	MA	G	508 699-9464	11434
Houghton Mifflin Harcourt Co (HQ)	Boston	MA	D	617 351-5000	6796
Hydro-Test Products Inc	Stow	MA	F	978 897-4647	12246
International Light Tech Inc	Peabody	MA	E	978 818-6180	11319
Inverness Corporation (DH)	Attleboro	MA	G	774 203-1130	6026
Ivey Industries	Holyoke	MA	G	413 736-6464	9263
Jab Industries Inc	Attleboro	MA	F	401 447-9668	6027
Jameco Industries Inc	North Andover	MA	F	978 688-1811	10841
JP Saw Mfg Inc	Fall River	MA	G	508 567-0469	8563
Laurence Cndle Mfg Ch Sups Inc (PA)	Millbury	MA	E	508 865-6061	10439
Lavoie Industries LLC	Fall River	MA	G	508 542-1062	8568
Liberty Compassion Inc	Clinton	MA	E	978 213-8757	8081
Lighthouse Distributors Inc	Marshfield	MA	G	781 319-9828	10241
Ls Industries Inc	Lynnfield	MA	F	781 844-8115	9999
LS Starrett Company (PA)	Athol	MA	A	978 249-3551	5981
Makers Tool and Mfg Co LLC	Oxford	MA	F	774 633-0658	11261
Manomet Manufacturing Inc	New Bedford	MA	G	508 997-1795	10617
Maple Leaf Industries	Lakeville	MA	G	508 728-9581	9517
Market Forge Industries Inc	Everett	MA	G	617 387-4100	8494
Mbm Building Systems Ltd	Boston	MA	F	617 478-3466	6881
McNeilly Ems Educators Inc	Danvers	MA	E	978 278-3008	8204
MCR Labs LLC	Framingham	MA	D	508 872-6666	8789
MCS Industries Inc	Natick	MA	F	508 651-3755	10487
Megatech Corporation	Tewksbury	MA	F	978 937-9600	12409
Milani Industries Incorporated	Stoughton	MA	G	781 344-3377	12225
Mooneytunco Inc	Weymouth	MA	G	781 331-4445	13330
Mountain Base Mfg LLC	Easthampton	MA	G	413 527-9590	8451
Mystic Scenic Studios Inc	Norwood	MA	D	781 440-0914	11198
Navitar Industries LLC	Woburn	MA	G	781 933-6125	13619
Neenas Lighting	Cambridge	MA	G	617 864-5757	7661
Nixoh Company Incorporated	Indian Orchard	MA	F	413 543-3701	9472
Olimpia Industries Inc	Bellingham	MA	F	508 966-3392	6299
P Wiles Inc (PA)	Orleans	MA	F	508 385-4321	11242
Partlite Inc (HQ)	Plymouth	MA	D	203 661-1926	11471
Partylite Worldwide LLC (DH)	Norwell	MA	C	888 999-5706	11144
Patriot Custom Mfg Inc	Southbridge	MA	F	508 764-7342	12033
Perkins School For Blind	Watertown	MA	A	617 924-3434	12899
Pha Industries Incorporated	Orange	MA	F	978 544-8770	11229
Pilgrim Candle Company Inc (PA)	Westfield	MA	E	413 562-2635	13199
Prysm Inc	Marlborough	MA	F	978 405-3091	10197
Reeves Company Inc	Attleboro	MA	F	508 222-2877	6053
Rgb Industries Inc	Holyoke	MA	G	413 536-3100	9277
Rockland Industries Inc	Braintree	MA	F	781 849-7918	7201
Rv Manufacturing Inc	Middleboro	MA	F	508 488-6612	10377
Sencorpwhite Holdings LLC	Hyannis	MA	F	508 771-9400	9452
Sheffield Pottery Inc	Sheffield	MA	E	413 229-7700	11801
Sira Naturals Inc	Milford	MA	G	508 422-0145	10419
Sjogren Industries Inc	Worcester	MA	F	508 987-3206	13802
Skin Catering Inc	Springfield	MA	F	413 349-8199	12128
Smtc Manufacturing	North Billerica	MA	F	508 207-6355	10956
Solchroma Technologies Inc	Billerica	MA	F	401 829-0024	6483
Std Manufacturing Inc	Stoughton	MA	F	781 828-4400	12239
Std Med Inc	West Bridgewater	MA	G	781 828-4400	12981
Stilisti	Boston	MA	A	617 262-2234	7062
Stran & Company Inc (PA)	Quincy	MA	F	617 822-6950	11540
Sunstar Spa Covers Inc	New Bedford	MA	F	508 993-5830	10653
Syratech Acquisition Corp (HQ)	Medford	MA	C	781 539-0100	10298
Technical Power Systems Inc	Middleboro	MA	G	630 719-1471	10378
Tml Manufacturing Inc	Foxboro	MA	G	508 264-0494	8729
Turning Leaf Ctrs Nrthmpton LL	Northampton	MA	G	413 204-4749	11083
Weather Guard Industries LLC	Northampton	MA	F	954 703-0563	11086
Wendi C Smith	Yarmouth Port	MA	F	508 362-4595	13846
Whiffletree Cntry Str Gift Sp	Billerica	MA	F	978 663-6346	6490
Yankee Candle Company Inc (DH)	South Deerfield	MA	C	413 665-8306	11931
Yankee Candle Company Inc	Whately	MA	G	413 665-8306	13340
Yankee Candle Investments LLC (DH)	South Deerfield	MA	G	413 665-8306	11932
Yankee Holding Corp (DH)	South Deerfield	MA	D	413 665-8306	11933
Ycc Holdings LLC	South Deerfield	MA	A	413 665-8306	11934
York Athletics Mfg Inc	Boston	MA	F	617 777-3125	7138
Zycal Bioceuticals Mfg LLC	Shrewsbury	MA	E	888 779-9225	11850
Alexanders Welding & Mch Inc	Greenfield Twp	ME	F	207 827-3300	4849

	CITY	ST	EMP	PHONE	ENTRY#
Auburn Asphalt LLC	Auburn	ME	F	207 894-5040	4421
Barringer Industries LLC	Scarborough	ME	F	207 730-7125	5424
Cellblock Fcs LLC	Standish	ME	E	800 440-4119	5526
Danica Design	Rockport	ME	F	207 236-3060	5347
Gardner Chpmlls Mllinocket LLC	Chester	ME	F	207 794-2223	4693
Hanscom Construction Inc	Marshfield	ME	F	207 255-8067	5046
Hope Association (PA)	Rumford	ME	E	207 364-4561	5356
Lie-Nielsen Toolworks Inc	Warren	ME	D	800 327-2520	5584
LLC Park Hill	Westbrook	ME	G	207 239-7741	5636
Lockwood Mfg Inc	Presque Isle	ME	G	207 764-4196	5302
Lux Box Company Inc	Portland	ME	G	301 832-0622	5235
Maine Pet Supply	Wells	ME	G	207 360-0005	5601
McSwain Manufacturing Inc	Winslow	ME	G	513 619-1222	5684
Moore-Clark USA Inc	Westbrook	ME	F	207 591-7077	5639
New Portland Publishing Inc	Falmouth	ME	G	207 536-5210	4770
Northeast Patients Group	South Portland	ME	E	855 848-6740	5509
Phocam Manufacturing LLC	Gorham	ME	F	207 854-8471	4830
Pieceworks Inc	Montville	ME	G	207 589-3451	5075
Planet Ventures Inc (PA)	Westbrook	ME	F	207 761-1515	5642
Stonewall Kitchen LLC	Wells	ME	D	207 251-4800	5606
TSS-Maine LLC	Waldoboro	ME	E	207 832-6344	5579
Two Rivers Pet Products Inc	Turner	ME	E	207 225-3965	5565
Village Candle Inc	Wells	ME	D	207 251-4800	5608
Whitney Originals	Whitneyville	ME	D	207 255-5857	5657
Alene Candles LLC (PA)	Milford	NH	C	603 673-5050	15014
Allard Nazarian Group Inc (PA)	Nashua	NH	D	603 320-8755	15057
and Fauna LLC	Holderness	NH	G	603 968-7490	14446
Axard LLC	Grantham	NH	F	603 306-7679	14362
Bryant Group Inc	Contoocook	NH	F	603 746-1166	14167
Cbms LLC	Hampton	NH	G	508 776-2647	14401
Clearly Balanced Days LLC	Belmont	NH	G	833 223-4040	13960
D D Bean & Sons Co (PA)	Jaffrey	NH	C	603 532-8311	14565
Enviromart Industries Inc	Plaistow	NH	F	603 378-0154	15341
Garaventa U S A Inc	Manchester	NH	F	603 669-6553	14850
GKN Aerospace New England Inc	Charlestown	NH	D	603 542-5135	14063
Hampshire Fire Protection LLC (PA)	Londonderry	NH	D	603 432-8221	14753
Hampshire Hives LLC	Gilsum	NH	G	603 313-0186	14342
Happy House Amusement Inc	Goffstown	NH	F	603 497-4151	14348
Hardwater Industries LLC	Gilford	NH	G	603 867-9240	14336
Houghton Mifflin Harcourt Co	Portsmouth	NH	C	630 467-7000	15406
Imed Mfg	Atkinson	NH	G	603 489-5184	13903
Ingu LLC	Portsmouth	NH	F	603 770-5969	15409
Kevin S Boghigian	Nashua	NH	G	603 883-0236	15122
Key Industries	New Ipswich	NH	F	603 369-9634	15198
Keyspin Manufacturing LLC	Merrimack	NH	G	603 420-8508	14986
Lamarre Industries LLC	Nashua	NH	G	603 889-0165	15124
Lupine Inc	Center Conway	NH	D	603 356-7371	14055
Marklin Candle Design LLC	Contoocook	NH	F	603 746-2211	14171
Marques Guitars LLC	Manchester	NH	G	603 321-4833	14881
Natural Playgrounds Shop LLC	Concord	NH	F	888 290-8405	14147
New Hampshire Novelty LLC (PA)	Winchester	NH	G	413 325-7648	15715
Pleasant View Gardens Inc (PA)	Loudon	NH	D	603 435-8361	14799
Polytite Manufacturing Corp	Derry	NH	G	603 952-9327	14205
Ragnar Inc	Newton	NH	D	603 382-0556	15244
Ricor Usa Inc	Salem	NH	F	603 718-8903	15557
Ride-Away Inc (HQ)	Londonderry	NH	E	603 437-4444	14782
Siglab Industries LLC	Merrimack	NH	G	603 860-2931	15002
Valid Mfg Inc	Londonderry	NH	F	603 880-0948	14789
Voda Industries LLC	Mont Vernon	NH	G	908 531-8156	15049
Aro Industrial Finishing LLC	North Providence	RI	G	401 349-4848	16296
Barrette Fabrication LLC	Coventry	RI	F	401 996-6691	15807
Barrette Fabrication LLC (PA)	Warwick	RI	G	401 822-0860	16787
Cas America LLC	North Smithfield	RI	F	401 884-8556	16320
Custom Built Window Mfg LLC	Warwick	RI	E	401 738-3800	16801
GA Rel Manufacturing Company	Providence	RI	F	401 331-5455	16524
Graco Awards Manufacturing Inc	Providence	RI	F	281 255-2161	16527
Hodges Badge Company Inc (PA)	Portsmouth	RI	D	401 682-2000	16443
Hope Valley Industries Inc	North Kingstown	RI	G	401 667-7780	16257
International Insignia Corp	Providence	RI	D	401 784-0000	16542
Ira Green Inc (PA)	Providence	RI	C	800 663-7487	16543
Lance Industries	North Providence	RI	G	401 654-5394	16304
Mel-Co-Ed Inc	Pawtucket	RI	E	401 724-2160	16386
Michael Healy Designs Inc	Manville	RI	G	401 597-5900	16165
MP Manufacturing Inc	West Greenwich	RI	G	203 915-2235	16889
Numaco Packaging LLC	East Providence	RI	F	401 438-4952	16035
Officers Equipment Company	Providence	RI	F	703 221-1912	16580
Rgt Inc	Providence	RI	D	401 431-5016	16601
RJ Mansour Inc	Providence	RI	F	401 521-7800	16606
Scope Display & Box Co Inc (PA)	Cranston	RI	E	401 942-7150	15909
Screencraft Tileworks LLC	Lincoln	RI	G	401 427-2816	16153
Thank-U Company Inc	North Kingstown	RI	G	401 739-3100	16285
Up Country Inc	East Providence	RI	E	401 431-2940	16046
Village Goldsmith	Warwick	RI	F	401 944-8404	16872

	CITY	ST	EMP	PHONE	ENTRY#
Vision Industries Corp	Johnston	RI	G	401 764-0916	16111
Advanced Animations	Stockbridge	VT	E	802 746-8974	17628
Ask-Inttag LLC	Essex Junction	VT	E	802 288-7210	17226
Aunt Sadies Inc	Lunenburg	VT	F	802 892-5267	17316
Cbd Events LLC	South Burlington	VT	G	802 310-8810	17576
Champlain Industries Inc	Burlington	VT	F	802 651-0708	17125
Dock Doctors LLC	Ferrisburgh	VT	E	802 877-6756	17268
Green Mountain Cbd Inc	Hardwick	VT	G	802 595-3258	17283
Hyzer Industries	Montpelier	VT	G	802 223-8277	17372
Leo D Bernstein & Sons Inc	Shaftsbury	VT	D	802 442-8029	17550
Leo D Bernstein and Sons Inc	Shaftsbury	VT	E	212 337-9578	17551
McNeills Manufacturing	Brattleboro	VT	G	802 246-1171	17095
Miti Manufacturing Co Inc	Saint Johnsbury	VT	F	802 424-1671	17544
Porter Music Box Co Inc	Randolph	VT	G	802 728-9694	17473
Select Design Ltd	Burlington	VT	D	802 864-9075	17158
Vermont Center Wreaths Inc	Newport Center	VT	G	802 334-6432	17408
Vermont Juvenile Furn Mfg Inc	West Rutland	VT	F	802 438-2231	17697
Way Out Wax Inc	Montgomery Center	VT	F	802 730-8069	17369
Yankee Medical Inc (DH)	Burlington	VT	F	802 863-4591	17164

41 LOCAL & SUBURBAN TRANSIT & INTERURBAN HIGHWAY TRANSPORTATION

4119 Local passenger transportation, nec

	CITY	ST	EMP	PHONE	ENTRY#
Sugarloaf Ambulance and Rescue	Carrabassett Valley	ME	F	207 235-2222	4680
Skytrans Mfg LLC	Contoocook	NH	F	802 230-7783	14175

4151 School buses

	CITY	ST	EMP	PHONE	ENTRY#
Valley Transportation Inc (PA)	Bradford	NH	G	603 938-2271	14018

42 MOTOR FREIGHT TRANSPORTATION

4212 Local trucking, without storage

	CITY	ST	EMP	PHONE	ENTRY#
HI Stone & Son Inc	Southbury	CT	E	203 264-8656	3195
Royalty Consulting LLC	Rocky Hill	CT	F	800 474-5157	2934
Thomas Keegan & Sons Inc	Wallingford	CT	F	203 239-9248	3862
Tradebe Treatment and Recycling Northeast LLC (DH)	Meriden	CT	D	203 238-8102	1710
All-Way Service Corp	South Weymouth	MA	F	781 335-4533	11974
Big Foot Moving & Storage Inc	Acton	MA	E	781 488-3090	5740
Capital Industries Corporation	East Weymouth	MA	F	781 337-9807	8428
Everson Distributing Co Inc	Worcester	MA	E	413 533-9261	13721
Garbage Gone Inc	Barnstable	MA	G	508 737-4995	6200
J P Ruthier Sons Recycl Corp (PA)	Littleton	MA	E	978 772-4251	9821
Mainstream Global Inc	Lawrence	MA	E	978 682-6767	9579
Safety-Kleen Systems Inc (HQ)	Norwell	MA	B	800 669-5740	11146
Earl W Gerrish & Sons	Brownville	ME	F	207 965-2171	4637
M B Eastman Logging Inc	Parsonsfield	ME	G	207 625-8020	5151
R C McLucas Trucking Inc	Porter	ME	G	207 625-8915	5168
Roland H Tyler Logging Inc	Dixfield	ME	G	207 562-7282	4728
Thompson Trucking Inc	Lincoln	ME	F	207 794-6101	5014
Tracy J Morrison	Harmony	ME	G	207 683-2371	4874
Coating Systems Inc	Nashua	NH	G	603 883-0553	15082
Hinesburg Sand & Gravel Co Inc	Hinesburg	VT	E	802 482-2335	17294
P and L Trucking	Chester	VT	G	802 875-2819	17182
Sheehan & Sons Lumber	Perkinsville	VT	G	802 263-5545	17442

4213 Trucking, except local

	CITY	ST	EMP	PHONE	ENTRY#
Grillo Services LLC	Milford	CT	E	203 877-5070	1831
Laydon Industries LLC (PA)	New Haven	CT	E	203 562-7283	2169
Casey & Hayes Inc	Hingham	MA	C	617 269-5900	9146
Horn International Packg Inc (HQ)	Lancaster	MA	E	978 667-8797	9528
Ser Logistics Inc	Worcester	MA	F	508 757-3397	13798
On The Road Inc	Warren	ME	E	207 273-3780	5585
Padebco Custom Boats	Round Pond	ME	G	207 529-5106	5354
McLaughlin Oil Corp (PA)	Nashua	NH	E	603 882-5500	15132
Roy and Laurel Amey Inc	Pittsburg	NH	G	603 538-7767	15329
New England Boatworks Inc	Portsmouth	RI	D	401 683-4000	16449

4214 Local trucking with storage

	CITY	ST	EMP	PHONE	ENTRY#
All-Way Service Corp	South Weymouth	MA	F	781 335-4533	11974
Big Foot Moving & Storage Inc	Acton	MA	E	781 488-3090	5740
Casey & Hayes Inc	Hingham	MA	C	617 269-5900	9146
McLaughlin Oil Corp (PA)	Nashua	NH	E	603 882-5500	15132

4215 Courier services, except by air

	CITY	ST	EMP	PHONE	ENTRY#
Better Lists Incorporated	Stamford	CT	E	203 324-4171	3294

Employee Codes: A=Over 500 employees, B=251-500
C=101-250, D=51-100, E=20-50, F=10-19, G=1-9

2024 Harris New England
Manufacturers Directory

SIC

	CITY	ST	EMP	PHONE	ENTRY#

4222 Refrigerated warehousing and storage

	CITY	ST	EMP	PHONE	ENTRY#
Natural Country Farms Inc	Ellington	CT	C	860 872-8346	1112
Merrill Blueberry Farms Inc	Hancock	ME	F	207 667-2541	4872

4225 General warehousing and storage

	CITY	ST	EMP	PHONE	ENTRY#
Dayleen Intimates Inc	Brookfield	CT	F	914 969-5900	516
L P Macadams Company Inc	Bridgeport	CT	D	203 366-3647	342
Big Foot Moving & Storage Inc	Acton	MA	E	781 488-3090	5740
Cardinal Shoe Corporation	Lawrence	MA	F	978 686-9706	9546
Horn International Packg Inc (HQ)	Lancaster	MA	E	978 667-8797	9528
Pucker Gallery Inc	Somerville	MA	F	617 261-1817	11891
Veoneer Roadscape Auto Inc	Lowell	MA	G	978 656-2500	9934
Coca-Cola Btlg Sthstern Neng I	Rutland	VT	F	802 773-2768	17492

4226 Special warehousing and storage, nec

	CITY	ST	EMP	PHONE	ENTRY#
CD Solutions Inc	Branford	CT	G	203 481-5895	243
Macristy Industries Inc (PA)	Newington	CT	F	860 225-4637	2305
Concordia Co Inc	South Dartmouth	MA	E	508 999-1381	11916
Holcim - Ner Inc (DH)	Saugus	MA	E	781 941-7200	11760
Pepsi-Cola Metro Btlg Co Inc	Sagamore Beach	MA	E	508 833-5600	11697
Quintal Burial Vault Inc	Dighton	MA	F	508 669-5717	8294
State-Line Graphics Inc	Everett	MA	E	617 389-1200	8501
Sterilite Corporation (PA)	Townsend	MA	C	978 597-1000	12442

4231 Trucking terminal facilities

	CITY	ST	EMP	PHONE	ENTRY#
New Haven Chemicals LLC	New Haven	CT	E	475 241-1150	2177

44 WATER TRANSPORTATION

4424 Deep sea domestic transportation of freight

	CITY	ST	EMP	PHONE	ENTRY#
Eagle Ship Management LLC (HQ)	Stamford	CT	C	203 276-8100	3340

4489 Water passenger transportation

	CITY	ST	EMP	PHONE	ENTRY#
Oldport Marine Services Inc	Newport	RI	F	401 847-9109	16220

4491 Marine cargo handling

	CITY	ST	EMP	PHONE	ENTRY#
Falmouth Mar Yachting Ctr Inc	Falmouth	MA	F	508 548-4600	8631
Dock Doctors LLC	Ferrisburgh	VT	E	802 877-6756	17268

4492 Towing and tugboat service

	CITY	ST	EMP	PHONE	ENTRY#
Cape Cod Shipbuilding Co	Wareham	MA	E	508 295-3550	12832

4493 Marinas

	CITY	ST	EMP	PHONE	ENTRY#
Dodson Boatyard LLC	Stonington	CT	E	860 535-1507	3508
Allen Harbor Marine Svc Inc	Harwich Port	MA	E	508 432-0353	9070
Cape Cod Shipbuilding Co	Wareham	MA	E	508 295-3550	12832
Crosby Yacht Yard Inc	Osterville	MA	E	508 428-6900	11245
F L Tripp & Sons Inc	Westport Point	MA	F	508 636-4058	13303
Falmouth Mar Yachting Ctr Inc	Falmouth	MA	F	508 548-4600	8631
Hawthorne Cove Marina Inc	Salem	MA	G	978 740-9890	11722
Marshall Marine Corporation	South Dartmouth	MA	F	508 994-0414	11917
Northern Light Mar Group Inc	Manchester	MA	E	978 526-7911	10033
P B Y A Inc	South Orleans	MA	G	508 255-0994	11973
Roses Oil Service Inc (PA)	Gloucester	MA	E	877 283-3334	8955
Brooklin Boat Yard Inc (PA)	Brooklin	ME	E	207 359-2236	4632
Dark Harbor Boatyard Corp	Islesboro	ME	F	207 734-2246	4908
Ellis Boat Co Inc	Southwest Harbor	ME	F	207 244-9221	5518
Gowen Inc	Portland	ME	F	207 773-1761	5219
J O Brown & Son Inc	North Haven	ME	G	207 867-4621	5114
James H Rich Boatyard	Bernard	ME	G	207 244-3208	4548
John M Williams Company	Mount Desert	ME	F	207 244-7854	5077
Shipyard In Boothbay Hbr LLC	Boothbay Harbor	ME	E	207 633-3171	4604
Yankee Marina Inc	Yarmouth	ME	E	207 846-9120	5710
Alden Yachts Corporation	Bristol	RI	E	401 683-4200	15752
Cove Haven Corp	Barrington	RI	F	401 246-1600	15747
Lenmarine Inc (PA)	Bristol	RI	E	401 253-2200	15772
New England Boatworks Inc	Portsmouth	RI	D	401 683-4000	16449

4499 Water transportation services, nec

	CITY	ST	EMP	PHONE	ENTRY#
Northern Light Mar Group Inc	Manchester	MA	E	978 526-7911	10033
Alden Yachts Corporation	Bristol	RI	E	401 683-4200	15752

45 TRANSPORTATION BY AIR

4581 Airports, flying fields, and services

	CITY	ST	EMP	PHONE	ENTRY#
Aerospace Techniques Inc	Middletown	CT	D	860 347-1200	1733
Helicopter Support Inc (DH)	Trumbull	CT	B	203 416-4000	3721
Sikorsky Aircraft Corporation (HQ)	Stratford	CT	A	203 386-4000	3571
Turbine Controls Inc (PA)	Bloomfield	CT	D	860 242-0448	214
Integrated Deicing Svcs LLC (DH)	Manchester	NH	B	603 647-1717	14863

	CITY	ST	EMP	PHONE	ENTRY#
4smartpro LLC	Saint Johnsbury	VT	F	802 745-8797	17537

47 TRANSPORTATION SERVICES

4724 Travel agencies

	CITY	ST	EMP	PHONE	ENTRY#
Smarter Travel Media LLC	Boston	MA	C	617 886-5555	7041
Hideaways International Inc	Portsmouth	NH	F	603 430-4433	15401

4731 Freight transportation arrangement

	CITY	ST	EMP	PHONE	ENTRY#
ITT Industries Holdings Inc (DH)	Stamford	CT	G	914 641-2000	3389
Evergreen Manufacturing Group LLC	Madawaska	ME	E	207 728-4900	5037
Vidarr Inc	Portsmouth	NH	G	877 636-8432	15448
Vermont Heritage Distrs Inc	Newport	VT	G	802 334-6503	17407

4783 Packing and crating

	CITY	ST	EMP	PHONE	ENTRY#
Park City Packaging Inc (PA)	Stratford	CT	E	203 378-7384	3564
Abbott-Action Inc	Canton	MA	E	781 702-5710	7765
Big Foot Moving & Storage Inc	Acton	MA	E	781 488-3090	5740
Horn Corporation (PA)	Lancaster	MA	E	800 832-7020	9527
Eimskip USA Inc	Portland	ME	F	207 221-5268	5214
P2k Printing LLC	North Conway	NH	G	603 356-2010	15249
Contech Medical Inc	Providence	RI	D	401 351-4890	16504

4789 Transportation services, nec

	CITY	ST	EMP	PHONE	ENTRY#
Cw Solutions LLC	New Britain	CT	D	860 229-7700	2018
Ethosenergy Tc Inc (DH)	Chicopee	MA	C	802 257-2721	8031
Everson Distributing Co Inc	Worcester	MA	E	413 533-9261	13721
Tally Transportation LLC	Randolph	MA	E	781 510-2411	11576

48 COMMUNICATIONS

4812 Radiotelephone communication

	CITY	ST	EMP	PHONE	ENTRY#
Ahead Communications Systems	Naugatuck	CT	E	203 720-0227	1947
Southern Neng Telecom Corp (HQ)	New Haven	CT	B	203 771-5200	2203
Wpcs International- Hartford Inc (HQ)	Windsor	CT	E		4315
BJs Wholesale Club Inc	Franklin	MA	D	508 553-9889	8821
Verizon New York Inc	Winchester	MA	F	781 721-5957	13493
Maine Radio	Scarborough	ME	F	207 883-2929	5438
Verizon Communications Inc	Bedford	NH	E	603 472-2090	13952

4813 Telephone communication, except radio

	CITY	ST	EMP	PHONE	ENTRY#
20/20 Software Inc	Stamford	CT	G	203 316-5500	3266
Ahead Communications Systems	Naugatuck	CT	E	203 720-0227	1947
Blc Holdings LLC (PA)	Norwalk	CT	E	203 229-1007	2474
Cst Incorporated	Wallingford	CT	F	203 949-9900	3796
Mercury Cabling Systems LLC	Stratford	CT	E	203 378-9008	3556
Mirion Tech Canberra Inc (DH)	Meriden	CT	D	203 238-2351	1677
Sigmavoip Llc	Westport	CT	G	203 541-5450	4196
Southern Neng Telecom Corp (HQ)	New Haven	CT	B	203 771-5200	2203
Atc Sequoia LLC	Boston	MA	E	617 375-7500	6569
Atc Tower Services LLC	Boston	MA	E	617 375-7500	6570
Benu Networks Inc	Burlington	MA	D	978 223-4700	7340
Brightcove Inc (PA)	Boston	MA	B	888 882-1880	6623
Evotext Inc	Billerica	MA	F	781 272-1830	6445
Family Education Network Inc	Boston	MA	E	617 671-3435	6730
Grandstream Networks Inc (PA)	Boston	MA	F	617 566-9300	6769
Gridedge Networks Inc	Acton	MA	F	978 569-2000	5749
Swymed Incorporated	Lexington	MA	F	855 799-6366	9777
Vaunix Technology Corporation	Newburyport	MA	F	978 662-7839	10726
Verizon New York Inc	Winchester	MA	F	781 721-5957	13493
Dataxoom Corp (PA)	Manchester	NH	F	510 474-0044	14840

4822 Telegraph and other communications

	CITY	ST	EMP	PHONE	ENTRY#
Southern Neng Telecom Corp (HQ)	New Haven	CT	B	203 771-5200	2203
Northeast Publishing Company	Dover Foxcroft	ME	G	207 564-8355	4730

4832 Radio broadcasting stations

	CITY	ST	EMP	PHONE	ENTRY#
Christian Science Pubg Soc (PA)	Boston	MA	B	617 450-2000	6655
Off The Dial Media LLC	Cambridge	MA	F	617 929-3424	7673
Omniview Sports Inc	Boston	MA	G	781 583-3534	6929
GS Inc	Rockland	ME	G	207 593-7730	5332

4833 Television broadcasting stations

	CITY	ST	EMP	PHONE	ENTRY#
Christian Science Pubg Soc (PA)	Boston	MA	B	617 450-2000	6655
Diversified Communications (HQ)	Portland	ME	E	207 842-5500	5209

4841 Cable and other pay television services

	CITY	ST	EMP	PHONE	ENTRY#
Hubbell Power Systems Inc	Cromwell	CT	D	860 635-2200	694
Cco Holdings LLC	Harvard	MA	E	978 615-1032	9060
Cco Holdings LLC	Longmeadow	MA	C	413 754-0616	9849
Cco Holdings LLC	North Grafton	MA	C	774 293-4026	11020

	CITY	ST	EMP	PHONE	ENTRY#
Cco Holdings LLC	Upton	MA	C	774 462-6577	12470
Comcast Sportsnet Neng LLC	Needham Heights	MA	D	617 630-5000	10537
Cco Holdings LLC	Montpelier	VT	C	802 778-0497	17371

4899 Communication services, nec

	CITY	ST	EMP	PHONE	ENTRY#
Textspeak Corporation	Westport	CT	F	203 803-1069	4199
Aquila Technology Corp	Burlington	MA	E	781 993-9004	7334
Cisco Systems Inc	Boxborough	MA	F	978 936-0000	7149
Millitech Inc	Northampton	MA	D	413 582-9620	11073
Smiths Interconnect Inc	Northampton	MA	D	413 582-9620	11080

49 ELECTRIC, GAS AND SANITARY SERVICES

4911 Electric services

	CITY	ST	EMP	PHONE	ENTRY#
Direct Energy Inc (HQ)	Stamford	CT	E	800 260-0300	3338
GE Steam Power Inc (HQ)	Windsor	CT	A	866 257-8664	4279
Right of Way Solutions LLC	Salem	CT	G	860 917-0608	2945
Ace Residential Solar LLC	North Andover	MA	F	800 223-1462	10816
Atlantic Pwr US GP Hldings Inc	Dedham	MA	G	617 977-2400	8236
Intercntnental Enrgy Group LLC	Hingham	MA	G	781 749-9800	9151
National Grid USA Svc Co Inc (DH)	Waltham	MA	G	800 260-0054	12734
Sundensity Inc (PA)	Boston	MA	F	617 642-1767	7065
Tecomet Inc	Woburn	MA	A	781 782-6400	13675
Maine & Maritimes Corporation (PA)	Presque Isle	ME	F	207 760-2499	5304
Granite Shore Power LLC	Bow	NH	C	603 634-2299	13999
Green Development LLC	Cranston	RI	D	401 295-4998	15870
National Grid USA Svc Co Inc	Providence	RI	A	401 784-7224	16573
Simon Pearce (us) Inc (PA)	Windsor	VT	C	802 674-6280	17762

4931 Electric and other services combined

	CITY	ST	EMP	PHONE	ENTRY#
GE Steam Power Inc (HQ)	Windsor	CT	A	866 257-8664	4279
Ace Residential Solar LLC	North Andover	MA	F	800 223-1462	10816

4941 Water supply

	CITY	ST	EMP	PHONE	ENTRY#
Evoqua Water Technologies LLC	Tewksbury	MA	E	978 863-4600	12397

4953 Refuse systems

	CITY	ST	EMP	PHONE	ENTRY#
City Carting Inc	Stamford	CT	D	888 413-3344	3313
G & G Beverage Distributors	Yalesville	CT	E	203 949-6220	4397
Grillo Services LLC	Milford	CT	E	203 877-5070	1831
HI Stone & Son Inc	Southbury	CT	E	203 264-8656	3195
Lostocco Refuse Service LLC	Danbury	CT	E	203 748-9296	779
MJ Metal Inc	Bridgeport	CT	E	203 334-3484	348
Seaview Plastic Recycling Inc	Bridgeport	CT	F	203 367-0070	370
Tradebe Treatment and Recycling Northeast LLC (DH) 203 238-8102	Meriden 1710	CT			D
Veolia Es Tchncal Slutions LLC	Danbury	CT	F	203 748-9116	832
All-Way Service Corp	South Weymouth	MA	F	781 335-4533	11974
American Recycled Mtls Inc	Holliston	MA	G	508 429-1455	9199
Blacksmith Shop Farms Inc	East Falmouth	MA	G	508 548-7714	8357
Copley Global Services LLC	Waltham	MA	F	617 970-9617	12641
Divert Inc (PA)	Concord	MA	E	978 341-5430	8113
Garbage Gone Inc	Barnstable	MA	G	508 737-4995	6200
Northstar Pulp & Paper Co Inc	Springfield	MA	D	413 263-6000	12118
Ondrick Materials & Recycl LLC	Chicopee	MA	E	413 592-2566	8052
Onyx Environmental Svcs LLC (DH)	Boston	MA	E	617 849-6600	6936
Safety-Kleen Systems Inc (HQ)	Norwell	MA	B	800 669-5740	11146
Ted Ondrick Company LLC (PA)	Chicopee	MA	E	413 592-2565	8062
Wte Recycling Inc	Greenfield	MA	E	413 772-2200	9007
Zwitterco Inc	Woburn	MA	E	301 442-5662	13693
Coating Systems Inc	Nashua	NH	G	603 883-0553	15082
Harding Metals Inc	Northwood	NH	E	603 942-5573	15273
Max Cohen & Sons Inc (HQ)	Concord	NH	E	603 224-3532	14144
Compost Plant L3c	Providence	RI	F	844 741-4653	16503
P M Recycling	Woonsocket	RI	F	401 765-0330	16970
Earth Waste Systems Inc (PA)	Rutland	VT	E	802 775-7722	17494

4959 Sanitary services, nec

	CITY	ST	EMP	PHONE	ENTRY#
Hayes Services LLC	East Lyme	CT	E	860 739-2273	1059
Innovative Environmental LLC	Colchester	CT	F	860 871-7582	660
McVac Environmental Svcs Inc	New Haven	CT	E	203 497-1960	2173
Cotton Tree Service Inc	Northampton	MA	F	413 584-9104	11057
Spilldam Environmental Inc	Brockton	MA	F	508 583-7850	7309
Copp Excavating Inc	Durham	ME	E	207 926-4988	4732
E Skip Grindle & Sons	Ellsworth	ME	F	207 460-0334	4758
P & K Sand and Gravel Inc	Naples	ME	F	207 693-6765	5081
Garland Lumber Company Inc	Center Conway	NH	E	603 356-5636	14053
Djs Tree Service & Log Inc	Colchester	VT	F	802 655-0264	17189

4961 Steam and air-conditioning supply

	CITY	ST	EMP	PHONE	ENTRY#
P&G Metal Components Corp	Bloomfield	CT	F	860 243-2220	199

50 WHOLESALE TRADE - DURABLE GOODS

5012 Automobiles and other motor vehicles

	CITY	ST	EMP	PHONE	ENTRY#
MH Rhodes Cramer LLC	South Windsor	CT	G	860 291-8402	3164
New Haven Companies Inc	East Haven	CT	F	203 469-6421	1048
B&B Micro Manufacturing Inc	Adams	MA	E	413 281-9431	5771
Bostonian Body Inc	Everett	MA	F	617 944-0985	8483
Greenwood Emrgncy Vehicles LLC (HQ)	Attleboro Falls	MA	E	508 695-7138	6086
Tel Mnfacturing Engrg Amer Inc	Billerica	MA	E	978 436-2300	6487
Hcb Holdings Inc (PA)	South Portland	ME	F	207 767-2136	5505
Innovative Specialties LLC	Pittsfield	ME	F	207 948-1500	5160
Vld Inc	Bangor	ME	G	207 947-6148	4519
Donovan Equipment Company Inc	Londonderry	NH	D	603 669-2250	14743

5013 Motor vehicle supplies and new parts

	CITY	ST	EMP	PHONE	ENTRY#
Genuine Parts Company	Windsor Locks	CT	G	860 623-4479	4325
Tek-Motive Inc	Branford	CT	F	203 468-2224	281
WH Rose Inc	Columbia	CT	E	860 228-8258	671
Blendco Systems LLC	Holyoke	MA	D	800 537-7797	9244
Car Gold Inc	Holyoke	MA	D	800 537-7797	9246
Connected Auto Systems Neng In	South Easton	MA	E	508 238-5855	11940
Consolidated Truck & Eqp Inc	Seekonk	MA	G	508 252-3330	11775
Factory Five Racing Inc	Wareham	MA	E	508 291-3443	12836
Moroney Bodyworks Inc	Worcester	MA	F	508 792-2878	13762
National Van Sales Inc	Attleboro	MA	F	508 222-2272	6040
Simpsons of Lawrence	Lawrence	MA	F	978 683-2417	9597
Vld Inc	Bangor	ME	G	207 947-6148	4519
Donovan Equipment Company Inc	Londonderry	NH	D	603 669-2250	14743
Freudenberg-Nok General Partnr	Northfield	NH	D	603 286-1600	15266
Ride-Away Inc (HQ)	Londonderry	NH	E	603 437-4444	14782
Beacon Rock Properties Inc	Providence	RI	D	401 421-3470	16482
Dejana Trck Utility Eqp Co LLC	Smithfield	RI	D	401 231-9797	16695
Scarborough Faire Inc	Pawtucket	RI	E	401 724-4200	16416

5014 Tires and tubes

	CITY	ST	EMP	PHONE	ENTRY#
Bergson Tire Co Inc	Ellington	CT	F	860 872-7729	1102
Derby Tire Company	Branford	CT	F	203 481-8473	249
Firestone Building Pdts Co LLC	Bristol	CT	F	860 584-4516	447
Reliable Auto Tire Company Inc	Hartford	CT	G	860 247-7977	1504
Toce Brothers Incorporated (PA)	Torrington	CT	E	860 496-2080	3700
Aronson Tire Company Inc	Auburn	MA	F	508 832-3244	6105
City Tire Co Inc	Pittsfield	MA	G	413 445-5578	11396
City Tire Co Inc (PA)	Springfield	MA	E	413 737-1419	12084
Holyoke Tire & Auto Svc Inc	Springfield	MA	G	413 733-2141	12101
K & W Tire Company Inc	Ayer	MA	F	978 772-5700	6184
Rolands Tire Service Inc (PA)	Fairhaven	MA	E	508 997-4501	8514
Central Tire Co Inc (PA)	Sanford	ME	E	207 324-4250	5391
Lag Inc (PA)	Topsham	ME	E	207 729-1676	5548
Maine Commercial Tire Inc (PA)	Hermon	ME	E	207 848-5540	4885
Maine Commercial Tire Inc	Waterville	ME	F	207 622-3200	5595
Maine Tire & Appliance Co (PA)	Falmouth	ME	F	207 781-3136	4769
New England Trck Tire Ctrs Inc (PA)	Sanford	ME	E	207 324-2262	5402
Belknap Tire Co Holdings Inc	Laconia	NH	F	603 524-4517	14646
Mountain Tire Corp	Berlin	NH	F	603 752-8473	13983
Northeast Tire Service Inc	Belmont	NH	G	603 524-7973	13965
Ocean State Tire Co Inc	Cranston	RI	E	401 946-0880	15903
Petes Tire Barns Inc	Providence	RI	G	401 521-2240	16583

5015 Motor vehicle parts, used

	CITY	ST	EMP	PHONE	ENTRY#
Consolidated Truck & Eqp Inc	Seekonk	MA	G	508 252-3330	11775

5021 Furniture

	CITY	ST	EMP	PHONE	ENTRY#
Baldwin Lawn Furniture LLC	Middletown	CT	F	860 347-1306	1738
Di-Cor Industries Inc	Bristol	CT	E	860 585-5583	436
Donghia Inc	Milford	CT	C	800 366-4442	1818
Focal Metals	Bethel	CT	C	203 743-4443	115
Thule Inc (DH)	Seymour	CT	C	203 881-9600	2971
CAM Office Services Inc (PA)	Marlborough	MA	F	781 932-9868	10125
Chapman Manufacturing Company Inc (PA) 508 588-3200	Avon 6147	MA			E
Drive-O-Rama Inc	Dennis Port	MA	G	508 394-0028	8260
Jordans Furniture Inc (HQ)	East Taunton	MA	A	508 828-4000	8408
Marthas Vineyard Furn Co LLC	Vineyard Haven	MA	G	508 687-9555	12491
Restmore Inc	Brockton	MA	D	508 559-9944	7302
Jackson Caldwell	Oxford	ME	G	207 539-2325	5146
York-Cmbrland Assn For Hndcppe (PA)	Portland	ME	E	207 879-1140	5292
Cw Keller & Associates LLC	Plaistow	NH	D	603 382-2028	15339
Gabriel Business Group Co Ltd	Brookline	NH	F	877 401-5544	14039
Installed Building Pdts LLC	Auburn	NH	B	603 645-1604	13909
Mkind Inc	Manchester	NH	G	603 493-6882	14892
Classic Dsgns By Mtthew Brak I	Saint Johnsbury	VT	E	802 748-6062	17541

Employee Codes: A=Over 500 employees, B=251-500
C=101-250, D=51-100, E=20-50, F=10-19, G=1-9   2024 Harris New England
Manufacturers Directory   977

5023 Homefurnishings

	CITY	ST	EMP	PHONE	ENTRY#
Glass Industries America LLC	Wallingford	CT	G	203 269-6700	3810
Mc Cann Bros Inc	Monroe	CT	F	203 335-8630	1916
Porcelen Limited Connecticut LLC (PA)	Hamden	CT	D	203 248-6346	1449
Tero Design Holdings LLC	Norwalk	CT	G	203 899-9950	2580
Viking Kitchen Cabinets LLC (PA)	New Britain	CT	E	860 223-7101	2074
Whalley Glass Company (PA)	Derby	CT	D	203 735-9388	895
Architctral Fireplaces of Neng	Auburn	MA	F	508 757-0622	6104
Blanche P Field LLC	Boston	MA	F	617 423-0715	6596
Matter Surfaces Inc (PA)	Stoughton	MA	F	800 628-7462	12223
Merida Meridian Inc	Boston	MA	E	617 464-5400	6885
Mr Idea Inc	Attleboro	MA	E	508 222-0155	6039
Neenas Lighting	Cambridge	MA	G	617 864-5757	7661
Partylite Inc (HQ)	Plymouth	MA	D	203 661-1926	11471
Petermans Boards and Bowls Inc	Gill	MA	G	413 863-2116	8915
Pgc Acquisition LLC	Reading	MA	G	508 888-2344	11604
Sherle Wagner Intl LLC	Fall River	MA	F	212 758-3300	8606
Sheepscot River Pottery (PA)	Edgecomb	ME	E	207 882-9410	4748
Cabinets For Less LLC	Manchester	NH	G	603 935-7551	14825
Dci Inc (PA)	Lisbon	NH	D	800 552-8286	14708
J & R Langley Co Inc	Manchester	NH	E	603 622-9653	14866
International Textile Mfg Inc	Cumberland	RI	G		15946
KAY DEE DESIGNS INC (PA)	Hope Valley	RI	E	401 539-2400	16067
Natco Products Corporation (PA)	West Warwick	RI	B	401 828-0300	16916
Stupell Industries Inc	Johnston	RI	E	401 831-5640	16107
Swarovski North America Ltd (DH)	Cranston	RI	A	401 463-6400	15915
Anichini Inc	Tunbridge	VT	E	802 889-9430	17651
Bennington Potters Inc (PA)	Bennington	VT	E	800 205-8033	17036
Gordons Window Decor Inc (PA)	Williston	VT	F	802 655-7777	17734

5031 Lumber, plywood, and millwork

	CITY	ST	EMP	PHONE	ENTRY#
Advanced Window Systems LLC	Cromwell	CT	F	800 841-6544	684
Bridgwell Rsurces Holdings LLC (HQ)	Greenwich	CT	E	203 622-9138	1322
Devine Brothers Incorporated	Norwalk	CT	E	203 866-4421	2490
Hardwood Lumber Manufacturing	Scotland	CT	B	860 423-2447	2953
Hull Forest Products Inc	Pomfret Center	CT	E	860 974-0127	2812
Professional Trades Netwrk LLC	Watertown	CT	G	860 567-0173	4026
Redco Corporation (HQ)	Stamford	CT	D	203 363-7300	3445
S J Pappas Inc	Meriden	CT	G	203 237-7701	1695
Stanley Black & Decker Inc	Farmington	CT	F	860 677-2861	1248
Steeltech Building Pdts Inc	South Windsor	CT	D	860 290-8930	3184
Stelray Plastic Products Inc	Ansonia	CT	E	203 735-2331	20
Viking Kitchen Cabinets LLC (PA)	New Britain	CT	E	860 223-7101	2074
West Hartford Lock Co LLC	West Hartford	CT	F	860 236-0671	4089
Willco Sales & Service Inc (PA)	Stratford	CT	F	203 366-3895	3584
Advanced Bldg Components LLC	Middleboro	MA	F	508 733-4889	10348
Architectural Timber Mllwk Inc	Hadley	MA	F	413 586-3045	9017
Brockway-Smith Company	West Hatfield	MA	C	413 247-9674	13004
Coastal-N-Counters Inc	Mashpee	MA	F	508 539-3500	10251
Crane Nxt Co (PA)	Waltham	MA	C	610 430-2510	12644
Creative Material Tech Ltd	Palmer	MA	G	413 284-0000	11272
F M Callahan and Son Inc	Malden	MA	D	781 324-5101	10014
Fiberglass Building Pdts Inc	Halifax	MA	F	847 650-3045	9021
Great Northern Dunnage LLC	Fitchburg	MA	E	978 343-2300	8656
Harvey Industries LLC	Springfield	MA	F	413 731-7700	12099
Harvey Industries LLC (PA)	Waltham	MA	C	800 598-5400	12691
Holt and Bugbee Company (PA)	Tewksbury	MA	C	978 851-7201	12401
Joe Miller Inc	Worcester	MA	F	508 753-8581	13745
Keiver Willard-Lumber Corp	Newburyport	MA	D	978 462-7193	10690
Maki Corp (PA)	Gardner	MA	E	978 343-7422	8895
Metalcraft Door Co Inc	Woburn	MA	E	781 933-2861	13611
New England Shrlines Companies	Hanover	MA	F	781 826-0140	9037
North Atlantic Corp	Somerset	MA	C	508 235-4830	11854
Perfection Fence Corp (PA)	Marshfield	MA	F	781 837-3600	10243
Precision Door & Window Inc (PA)	Stoughton	MA	F	781 344-6900	12228
Specialty Wholesale Sup Corp	Gardner	MA	E	978 632-1472	8901
Bagala Window Works	Westbrook	ME	G	207 887-9231	5616
Bear Paw Lumber Corp (PA)	Fryeburg	ME	F	207 935-3052	4807
Hammond Lumber Company (PA)	Belgrade	ME	C	207 495-3303	4540
Harvey Industries Inc	Augusta	ME	F	207 629-3737	4472
Hillside Lumber Company Inc	Westbrook	ME	E	207 839-2575	5629
K & D Millworks Inc	Windham	ME	E	207 892-5188	5663
Kelly Lumber Sales Inc	Old Town	ME	E	207 435-4950	5128
Oxford Timber Inc	Oxford	ME	F	207 539-9656	5148
Paradigm Operating Company LLC	Portland	ME	C	877 994-6369	5255
Parent Lumber Company Inc	Mechanic Falls	ME	G	207 998-2322	5053
Pre-Hung Doors Inc	Auburn	ME	F	207 783-3881	4455
R E Lowell Lumber Co Inc	Buckfield	ME	E	207 336-2901	4658
S W Collins	Lincoln	ME	E	207 794-6113	5013
T and P Lumber Inc (PA)	Orrington	ME	E	207 825-3317	5139
David D Douglas Inc	Londonderry	NH	G	603 437-1151	14742
FC Hammond & Son Co Inc	Canaan	NH	F	603 523-4353	14046
Fernald Lumber Inc	Nottingham	NH	F	603 679-2997	15276
Forest Northland Products Inc (PA)	Kingston	NH	E	603 642-3665	14635
Granite State Ktchens Dstrs In	Bedford	NH	E	603 472-4080	13931
Harvey Industries LLC	Londonderry	NH	E	603 216-8300	14754
Hhp Inc (PA)	Henniker	NH	E	603 428-3298	14436
Millwork Masters Ltd (PA)	Keene	NH	F	603 358-3038	14608
R P Williams & Sons Inc	Bristol	NH	F	603 744-5446	14037
Tommila Brothers Inc	Fitzwilliam	NH	F	603 242-7774	14316
Arnold Lumber Co (PA)	West Kingston	RI	D	401 783-2266	16893
Cas America LLC	North Smithfield	RI	F	401 884-8556	16320
Columbus Door Company	Warwick	RI	D	401 781-7792	16796
A Johnson Co	Bristol	VT	D	802 453-4884	17112
Britton Lumber Company Inc (PA)	Fairlee	VT	F	802 333-4388	17267
H Hirschmann Ltd	West Rutland	VT	F	802 438-4447	17695
Jack Tarmy Lumber Co Inc	Brattleboro	VT	F	802 257-0427	17089
Manchester Lumber Inc	Johnson	VT	F	802 635-2315	17309
Mill River Lumber Ltd	North Clarendon	VT	D	802 775-0032	17417
N W P Inc	Pownal	VT	G	802 442-4749	17455

5032 Brick, stone, and related material

	CITY	ST	EMP	PHONE	ENTRY#
Adelman Sand & Gravel Inc	Bozrah	CT	F	860 889-3394	226
Brass City Tile Designs LLC	Waterbury	CT	G	203 597-8764	3892
Connecticut Stone Supplies Inc (PA)	Milford	CT	D	203 882-1000	1814
Dan Beard Inc	Shelton	CT	E	203 924-4346	2996
Desiato Sand & Gravel Corp	Storrs Mansfield	CT	E	860 429-6479	3512
Devine Brothers Incorporated	Norwalk	CT	E	203 866-4421	2490
Lane Construction Corporation (DH)	Cheshire	CT	C	203 235-3351	603
Lane Industries Incorporated (DH)	Cheshire	CT	G	203 235-3351	604
LH Gault & Son Incorporated	Westport	CT	D	203 227-5181	4180
Midwood Quarry and Cnstr Inc (PA)	East Hartford	CT	F	860 289-1414	1006
Mildred Coppola Inc	Stamford	CT	F	203 967-9300	3411
Monroe Recycl & Aggregates LLC	Monroe	CT	G	203 644-7748	1917
New England Stone Inc	Milford	CT	F	203 876-8606	1853
O & G Industries Inc	Southbury	CT	E	203 263-2195	3197
O & G Industries Inc (PA)	Torrington	CT	D	860 489-9261	3689
Pauls Marble Depot LLC	Stamford	CT	F	203 978-0669	3427
Porcelanosa New York Inc	Riverside	CT	F	203 698-7618	2910
Quikrete Companies Inc	Wauregan	CT	F	860 564-3308	4041
Rawson Development Inc	Putnam	CT	F	860 928-4536	2872
Skyline Quarry LLC	Stafford Springs	CT	F	860 875-3580	3259
Suzio York Hill Companies	Meriden	CT	F	888 789-4626	1703
Tilcon Connecticut Inc	East Granby	CT	E	860 844-7000	954
Tilcon Connecticut Inc (DH)	New Britain	CT	D	860 224-6010	2072
Tilcon Inc (DH)	Newington	CT	B	860 223-3651	2328
Washington Concrete Pdts Inc	Plainville	CT	F	860 747-5242	2788
Windham Materials LLC (PA)	Willimantic	CT	E	860 456-4111	4222
A Graziano Inc	Braintree	MA	E	781 843-7300	7166
Aldrich Marble & Granite Co	Norwood	MA	G	781 762-6111	11158
B R S Inc	Bridgewater	MA	E	508 697-5448	7221
Boro Sand & Stone Corp (PA)	North Attleboro	MA	E	508 699-2911	10869
Cape Cod Aggregates Corp (PA)	Hyannis	MA	E	508 775-3716	9429
Connecticut Valley Block Co Inc	West Springfield	MA	E		13018
Cumar Inc	Everett	MA	F	617 389-7818	8484
Dauphinais & Son Inc	Wilbraham	MA	E	413 596-3964	13357
Dauphinais Concrete	Bellingham	MA	G	508 657-0941	6289
E H Perkins Construction Inc	Sterling	MA	F	978 422-3388	12161
E H Perkins Construction Inc (PA)	Wayland	MA	F	978 562-3436	12925
George D Judd & Sons LLC	Goshen	MA	G	413 268-7590	8967
Heffron Asphalt Corp (PA)	North Reading	MA	G	781 935-1455	11040
Holcim - Ner Inc (DH)	Saugus	MA	F	781 941-7200	11760
Ideal Concrete Block Co	Waltham	MA	E	781 894-3200	12694
Ideal Concrete Block Co (PA)	Westford	MA	F	978 692-3076	13242
International Stone Inc	Woburn	MA	D	781 937-3300	13589
J G Maclellan Con Co Inc	Amesbury	MA	E	978 458-1223	5839
JH Lynch & Sons Inc	Millbury	MA	E	508 756-6244	10438
Lane Construction Corporation	Lee	MA	E	413 637-2511	9614
Louis W Mian Incorporated (PA)	Boston	MA	F	617 241-7900	6863
McCabe Sand & Gravel Co Inc	Taunton	MA	E	508 823-0771	12349
Nicholas Ieronimo	Middleboro	MA	G	508 947-5363	10369
PJ Keating Company	Dracut	MA	D	978 454-7878	8310
Portland Stone Ware Co Inc (PA)	Dracut	MA	F	978 459-7272	8311
Rangeway Supply LLC	North Billerica	MA	G	978 667-8500	10947
S Lane John & Son Incorporated	Oxford	MA	F	508 987-3959	11263
Specialty Minerals Inc	Adams	MA	C	413 743-0591	5775
State Road Cement Block Co Inc	North Dartmouth	MA	E	508 993-9473	11002
Stone Decor Galleria Inc	Woburn	MA	F	781 937-9377	13673
Stone Design Marble & Gran Co	South Weymouth	MA	G	781 331-3000	11978
Stone Yard LLC	Littleton	MA	F	978 742-9800	9840
T L Edwards Inc	Plymouth	MA	F	508 732-9148	11480
Torromeo Industries Inc (PA)	Methuen	MA	F	978 686-5634	10346
WJ Graves Cnstr Co Inc (PA)	East Templeton	MA	F	978 939-5568	8416
Morningstar Marble & Gran Co	Topsham	ME	F	207 725-7309	5551
Pike Industries Inc	Wells	ME	F	207 676-9973	5604

	CITY	ST	EMP	PHONE	ENTRY#
R Pepin & Sons Inc	Sanford	ME	E	207 324-6125	5407
Rjf - Morin Brick LLC	Auburn	ME	D	207 784-9375	4459
Alvin J Coleman & Son Inc (PA)	Albany	NH	F	603 447-5936	13847
Benevento Aggregates LLC	Loudon	NH	F	603 783-4723	14793
Cs-Ma Inc	Newport	NH	F	603 863-1000	15227
Tilcon Arthur Whitcomb Inc (HQ)	North Swanzey	NH	F	603 352-0101	15256
Torromeo Industries Inc	Kingston	NH	E	603 642-5564	14637
Dailey Precast LLC (HQ)	Shaftsbury	VT	D	802 442-4418	17549
Dal-Tile Corporation	Williston	VT	E	802 951-2030	17726
Hinesburg Sand & Gravel Co Inc	Hinesburg	VT	E	802 482-2335	17294
McCue Memorial Co	Castleton	VT	F	802 468-5636	17173
Shelburne Limestone Corp (PA)	Colchester	VT	F	802 878-2656	17203
Shelburne Limestone Corp	Swanton	VT	E	802 868-3357	17642
Vermont Quarries Corp	Rutland	VT	E	802 775-1065	17514
Washburn Vault Company Inc	Brattleboro	VT	G	802 254-9150	17107

5033 Roofing, siding, and insulation

	CITY	ST	EMP	PHONE	ENTRY#
Dfs In-Home Services	Danbury	CT	G	845 405-6464	730
Mercury-Excelum Inc	East Windsor	CT	E	860 292-1800	1080
The Petit Tool Co	Thomaston	CT	E	860 283-9626	3636
Aspen Aerogels Inc (PA)	Northborough	MA	C	508 691-1111	11088
Harvey Industries LLC	Springfield	MA	E	413 731-7700	12099
Harvey Industries LLC (PA)	Waltham	MA	C	800 598-5400	12691
Harvey Industries LLC	Woburn	MA	F	781 935-7990	13581
Beacon Sales Acquisition Inc	Portland	ME	F	207 797-7950	5185
Harvey Industries Inc	Augusta	ME	F	207 629-3737	4472
K & R Holdings Inc	Portland	ME	C	207 797-7950	5230
Britton Lumber Company Inc (PA)	Fairlee	VT	E	802 333-4388	17267
Kp Building Products Inc	Williston	VT	D	866 850-4447	17737

5039 Construction materials, nec

	CITY	ST	EMP	PHONE	ENTRY#
Bridgwell Rsurces Holdings LLC (HQ)	Greenwich	CT	E	203 622-9138	1322
Heckmann Building Products Inc	Norwalk	CT	E	708 865-2403	2511
Laydon Industries LLC (PA)	New Haven	CT	E	203 562-7283	2169
Liberty Glass and Met Inds Inc	North Grosvenordale	CT	E	860 923-3623	2384
New England Cage & Fence Corp	North Haven	CT	F	860 688-8148	2427
TAC Acquisition Corp	Greenwich	CT	A	203 983-5276	1355
U S Glass Distributors Inc	Enfield	CT	E	860 741-3658	1156
Architectural Timber Mllwk Inc	Hadley	MA	F	413 586-3045	9017
Boston Area Door Company	Bridgewater	MA	G	508 857-4722	7224
Joe Miller Inc	Worcester	MA	F	508 753-8581	13745
Massachusetts Contr Sups Inc	Hudson	MA	G	978 413-2578	9389
Mygrant Glass Company Inc	Randolph	MA	F	781 767-3289	11569
Schrimpf Wldg Fabrication Inc	Woburn	MA	G	339 298-2311	13661
Anchor Corporation	Kennebunk	ME	F	207 985-6018	4920
Elm Street Vault Inc	Biddeford	ME	G	207 284-4855	4563
Gagne & Son Con Blocks Inc	Auburn	ME	G	207 495-3313	4435
North American Supaflu Systems	Scarborough	ME	F	207 883-1155	5441
Nucor Hrris Rbar Northeast LLC	Canaan	NH	D	603 632-5222	14047
Sonco Worldwide Inc	Warwick	RI	F	401 406-3761	16863
Springfield Fence Company Inc	North Springfield	VT	F	802 886-2221	17424

5043 Photographic equipment and supplies

	CITY	ST	EMP	PHONE	ENTRY#
Fujifilm Elctrnic Mtls USA Inc	Stamford	CT	E	203 363-3360	3352
Boston Light & Sound Inc (PA)	Malden	MA	F	617 787-3131	10005
Comprehensive Identification Products Inc	Burlington	MA			C
781 229-8780	7354				
Fujifilm Hlthcare Amricas Corp (DH)	Lexington	MA	C	203 324-2000	9743

5044 Office equipment

	CITY	ST	EMP	PHONE	ENTRY#
Agissar Corporation	Stratford	CT	E	203 375-8662	3516
Cvc II Inc (DH)	Bethel	CT	D	203 401-4205	105
Hasler Inc	Milford	CT	B	203 301-3400	1833
Oce-USA Holding Inc	Trumbull	CT	A	773 714-8500	3726
C P Bourg Inc (PA)	New Bedford	MA	E	508 998-2171	10577
CAM Office Services Inc (PA)	Marlborough	MA	F	781 932-9868	10125
Hosokawa Micron Intl Inc	Northborough	MA	G	508 655-1123	11098
MBI Graphics & Printing Corp	Southbridge	MA	F	508 765-0658	12028
Sands Business Eqp & Sups LLC	York	ME	F	207 351-3304	5716
Dahle North America Inc	Peterborough	NH	F	603 924-0003	15314
Relyco Sales Inc (PA)	Dover	NH	E	603 742-0999	14248

5045 Computers, peripherals, and software

	CITY	ST	EMP	PHONE	ENTRY#
3M Company	Wallingford	CT	F	203 949-1630	3766
Cyberresearch Inc	Branford	CT	E	203 643-5000	247
Envirnmntal Office Sltions Inc (PA)	East Hartford	CT	F	860 291-1900	993
Flo-Tech LLC (PA)	New Haven	CT	D	860 613-3333	2152
Frontier Vision Tech Inc	Rocky Hill	CT	G	860 953-0240	2922
Marco International Inc	Ridgefield	CT	D	203 894-8000	2902
Online River LLC	Westport	CT	F	203 801-5900	4191
Radio Frequency Systems Inc (DH)	Meriden	CT	E	203 630-3311	1690
Syferlock Technology Corp	Waterbury	CT	G	203 292-5441	3971

	CITY	ST	EMP	PHONE	ENTRY#
American Well Corporation (PA)	Boston	MA	B	617 204-3500	6543
Beacon Application Svcs Corp (PA)	Framingham	MA	E	508 663-4433	8742
Bynder LLC	Boston	MA	C	857 310-5434	6630
Canvas Gfx Inc	Boston	MA	E	833 721-0829	6637
Cisco Systems Inc	Boxborough	MA	F	978 936-0000	7149
Compart North America Inc	Andover	MA	F	877 237-2725	5879
Copley Global Services LLC	Waltham	MA	G	617 970-9617	12641
Datarobot Inc (PA)	Boston	MA	D	617 765-4500	6684
Double-Take Software Inc (DH)	Burlington	MA	F	949 253-6500	7365
Dynatrace LLC (HQ)	Waltham	MA	C	781 530-1000	12657
Electro-Prep Inc	Wareham	MA	F	508 291-2880	12834
Evotext Inc	Billerica	MA	F	781 272-1830	6445
Fev Tutor Inc	Woburn	MA	D	781 376-6925	13564
Free Software Foundation Inc	Boston	MA	F	617 542-5942	6747
Full Circle Technologies Inc	Boston	MA	E	617 722-0100	6749
Inteset Technologies LLC	Hanover	MA	F	781 826-1560	9035
Ivory Onyx	Boston	MA	G	617 454-4980	6820
Medical Manager Pcn Inc	Walpole	MA	F	508 850-3500	12568
Mimoco Inc	Needham Heights	MA	F	617 783-1100	10552
Modus Media Inc	Waltham	MA	F	781 663-5000	12724
Morgan Scientific Inc (PA)	Haverhill	MA	F	978 521-4440	9118
Netsilicon Inc (HQ)	Waltham	MA	D	781 647-1234	12736
New England Business Svc Inc (HQ)	Townsend	MA	B	978 448-6111	12441
Philips Holding USA Inc (HQ)	Cambridge	MA	A	978 687-1501	7686
Retro-Fit Technologies Inc	Taunton	MA	E	508 478-2222	12363
RSD America Inc	Waltham	MA	F	201 996-1000	12775
Source Code LLC (PA)	Norwood	MA	E	781 688-2248	11209
Source Code Midco LLC (PA)	Norwood	MA	E	781 255-2022	11210
Visible Systems Corporation (PA)	Boston	MA	G	617 902-0767	7106
Westrex International Inc	Boston	MA	F	617 254-1200	7119
Wordstock Inc	Bedford	MA	F	781 646-7700	6277
Centilla Corporation	Windham	NH	F	603 658-3881	15723
Enterasys Networks Inc (HQ)	Salem	NH	D	603 952-5000	15521
H32 Design and Development LLC (PA)	Concord	NH	G	603 865-1000	14135
Maynesboro Industries Inc	Berlin	NH	F	603 752-3366	13982
A2b Tracking Solutions Inc	Portsmouth	RI	E	401 683-5215	16434
Radley Corporation	Lincoln	RI	E	616 554-9060	16152
Onlogic Inc	South Burlington	VT	E	802 861-2300	17587
Rectrac LLC	Essex Junction	VT	D	802 879-6993	17244

5046 Commercial equipment, nec

	CITY	ST	EMP	PHONE	ENTRY#
American Marketing Intl LLC	Clinton	CT	E	860 669-4100	635
Ardent Inc (PA)	East Hartford	CT	F	860 528-6000	971
Capricorn Investors III LP (PA)	Greenwich	CT	F	203 861-6600	1326
Cummins - Allison Corp	Cheshire	CT	F	203 794-9200	585
Saccuzzo Company Inc	Newington	CT	G	860 665-1101	2323
Steeltech Building Pdts Inc	South Windsor	CT	D	860 290-8930	3184
Treif USA Inc	Shelton	CT	F	203 929-9930	3072
Battle Grounds Coffee Co LLC	Haverhill	MA	F	978 891-5860	9077
Fitness Em LLC	Uxbridge	MA	F		12479
Halmark Systems LLC	Stoughton	MA	E	781 630-0123	12212
Markwell Manufacturing Co Inc	Norwood	MA	G	781 769-6610	11194
Mike Sheas Cffhouse Trdtnals In	Fairhaven	MA	F	508 807-5754	8509
Jsi Store Fixtures Inc (HQ)	Milo	ME	C	207 943-5203	5070
Public Scales	Lewiston	ME	F	207 784-9466	4986
Heat and Control Inc	Pembroke	NH	F	603 225-5190	15303
LK Goodwin Co Inc (PA)	West Greenwich	RI	F	401 781-5526	16888
Walco Electric Company	Providence	RI	D	401 467-6500	16642
Ann Clark Ltd	Rutland	VT	E	802 773-7886	17489
Leo D Bernstein & Sons Inc	Shaftsbury	VT	D	802 442-8029	17550

5047 Medical and hospital equipment

	CITY	ST	EMP	PHONE	ENTRY#
Associated X-Ray Corp (PA)	East Haven	CT	F	203 466-2446	1036
Boston Endo-Surgical Tech LLC	Bridgeport	CT	B	203 336-6479	303
Brit Systems LLC	Wallingford	CT	F	214 630-0636	3783
Contemporary Products LLC	Middletown	CT	F	860 346-9283	1744
Coopersurgical Inc	Trumbull	CT	G	203 601-5200	3715
Coopersurgical Inc (DH)	Trumbull	CT	C	203 601-5200	3716
Hitachi Aloka Medical Ltd	Wallingford	CT	F	203 269-5088	3813
Hitachi Aloka Medical Amer Inc	Wallingford	CT	D	800 872-5652	3814
Lenscrafters	Milford	CT	G	203 878-8511	1845
Marel Corporation	West Haven	CT	G	203 934-8187	4114
O Berk Company Neng LLC	West Haven	CT	F	203 932-8000	4117
Origio Midatlantic Devices Inc	Trumbull	CT	D	856 762-2000	3727
Precision Engineered Pdts LLC	Bridgeport	CT	G	203 336-6479	361
Realhub Inc	Darien	CT	F	650 461-9210	854
Tarry Medical Products Inc	Danbury	CT	F	203 791-9001	823
Z-Medica LLC	Wallingford	CT	D	203 294-0000	3876
Alimed Inc	Dedham	MA	C	781 329-2900	8235
Amatech Corporation	Acton	MA	D	978 263-5401	5737
American Industrial & Med Pdts (PA)	Auburn	MA	F	508 832-5785	6101
American Optics Limited	Wellesley Hills	MA	F	905 631-5377	12949
Biokit U S A Inc	Bedford	MA	G	781 861-4064	6215

SIC

	CITY	ST	EMP	PHONE	ENTRY#
Boston Medical Products Inc	Shrewsbury	MA	E	508 898-9300	11829
Brownmed Inc (PA)	Boston	MA	E	857 317-3354	6626
Carl Zeiss Nts LLC (DH)	Peabody	MA	D	978 826-1500	11301
Cellanyx Diagnostics LLC	Beverly	MA	G	571 212-9991	6337
Dale Medical Products Inc (PA)	Franklin	MA	E	800 343-3980	8829
Dentovations Inc	Boston	MA	G	617 737-1199	6691
Diamond Diagnostics Inc (PA)	Holliston	MA	D	508 429-0450	9206
Dlrc Incorporated	Cambridge	MA	E	617 999-3340	7552
FDA Group LLC	North Grafton	MA	E	413 330-7476	11023
Fujifilm Hlthcare Amricas Corp (DH)	Lexington	MA	C	203 324-2000	9743
Gyrus Acmi LLC (DH)	Westborough	MA	C	508 804-2600	13104
High Technology Inc	North Attleboro	MA	E	508 660-2221	10873
Image Diagnostics Inc	Fitchburg	MA	F	978 829-0009	8657
Image Stream Medical Inc	Littleton	MA	D	978 486-8494	9818
Inert Corporation	Amesbury	MA	E	978 462-4415	5837
Interlace Medical Inc	Marlborough	MA	E	800 442-9892	10166
Izon Science US LLC	Medford	MA	F	617 945-5936	10291
Kaz Inc (HQ)	Marlborough	MA	D	508 490-7000	10174
Lemaitre Vascular Inc (PA)	Burlington	MA	E	781 221-2266	7389
M-R Resources Inc	Fitchburg	MA	F	978 345-9010	8659
Mascon Inc	Woburn	MA	E	781 938-5800	13605
Novartis Mlclar Dagnostics LLC	Cambridge	MA	E	617 871-8441	7669
Perx LLC	Pittsfield	MA	F	413 358-9020	11417
Philips Holding USA Inc (HQ)	Cambridge	MA	A	978 687-1501	7686
Straumann Usa LLC	Andover	MA	C	978 747-2500	5927
Tenacity Medical Inc	Lexington	MA	G	617 299-8001	9786
Third Pole Inc (PA)	Waltham	MA	F	908 310-0596	12803
Wotton Enterprises Inc	Sturbridge	MA	F	855 383-7678	12259
Baker Company Inc (PA)	Sanford	ME	C	207 324-8773	5390
Maine Orthtic Prsthtic Rhab Sv	Portland	ME	F	207 773-8818	5241
Nyle International Corp (PA)	Bangor	ME	F	207 989-4335	4512
LDI Solutions LLC	Rochester	NH	E	603 436-0077	15485
Vygon Corporation	Dover	NH	C	603 743-5988	14259
White Mountain Imaging	Concord	NH	E	603 228-2631	14166
White Mountain Imaging (PA)	Webster	NH	F	603 648-2124	15675
Surplus Solutions LLC	Woonsocket	RI	F	401 526-0055	16978
Aadco Medical Inc	Randolph	VT	D	802 728-3400	17466
Yankee Medical Inc (DH)	Burlington	VT	F	802 863-4591	17164

5048 Ophthalmic goods

	CITY	ST	EMP	PHONE	ENTRY#
Avedro Inc (HQ)	Burlington	MA	E	781 768-3400	7337
Perx LLC	Pittsfield	MA	F	413 358-9020	11417
McLeod Optical Company Inc	Augusta	ME	G	207 623-3841	4478
New Hampshire Optical Co Inc (PA)	Allenstown	NH	E	603 268-0741	13854
McLeod Optical Company Inc (PA)	Warwick	RI	E	401 467-3000	16836

5049 Professional equipment, nec

	CITY	ST	EMP	PHONE	ENTRY#
Coburn Technologies Intl Inc (DH)	South Windsor	CT	F	860 648-6600	3130
Electro-Lite Corporation	Bethel	CT	F	203 743-4059	114
Globenix Inc	Norwalk	CT	G	203 740-7070	2506
Hoya Corporation	South Windsor	CT	E	860 289-5379	3157
Joseph Merritt & Company Inc	Danbury	CT	G	203 743-6734	762
S & S Worldwide Inc	Colchester	CT	B	860 537-3451	665
Technical Reproductions Inc	Norwalk	CT	F	203 849-9100	2575
Tower Optical Company Inc	Norwalk	CT	G	203 866-4535	2586
A W McMullen Co Inc	Brockton	MA	F	508 583-2072	7251
AMF Optical Solutions LLC	Woburn	MA	F	781 933-6125	13509
Atlantic Vision Inc	Shrewsbury	MA	G	508 845-8401	11828
Boston Piezo-Optics Inc	Bellingham	MA	F	508 966-4988	6287
Bruker Scientific LLC	Billerica	MA	A	978 667-9580	6418
Bruker Scientific LLC (HQ)	Billerica	MA	A	978 439-9899	6419
Cyduct Diagnostics Inc	Boston	MA	G	617 360-9700	6682
Edgeone LLC	West Wareham	MA	G	508 291-0960	13062
Fisher Scientific Intl LLC (HQ)	Waltham	MA	C	781 622-1000	12675
Harvard Apparatus Inc	Holliston	MA	D	508 893-8999	9213
High Technology Inc	North Attleboro	MA	E	508 660-2221	10873
Izon Science US LLC	Medford	MA	F	617 945-5936	10291
Jeio Tech Inc	Billerica	MA	G	781 376-0700	6457
Kayaku Advanced Materials Inc (PA)	Westborough	MA	E	617 965-5511	13113
Kse Inc	Sunderland	MA	F	413 549-5506	12274
M-R Resources Inc	Fitchburg	MA	F	978 345-9010	8659
McVan Inc	Attleboro	MA	F	508 431-2400	6036
Organomation Associates Inc	Berlin	MA	F	978 838-7300	6320
Oxford Instruments America Inc (HQ)	Concord	MA	E	978 369-9933	8131
Pion Inc	Billerica	MA	F	978 528-2020	6472
Princton Gamma-Tech Instrs Inc	Franklin	MA	E	609 924-7310	8858
Sage Science Inc	Beverly	MA	F	617 922-1832	6380
Tech180 Corp	Easthampton	MA	F	413 203-6123	8463
William J Hirten Co LLC	Attleboro	MA	F	401 334-5370	6076
Witec Instruments Corp	Concord	MA	F	865 690-5550	8142
Contour360 Corp	Cornish	ME	F	207 625-4400	4704
Qsa Optical Co Inc	Lewiston	ME	E	207 783-8523	4988
Axard LLC	Grantham	NH	F	603 306-7679	14362

	CITY	ST	EMP	PHONE	ENTRY#
Contour Fine Tooling Inc	Keene	NH	G	603 876-4908	14593
Optical Solutions Inc	Charlestown	NH	G	603 826-4411	14066
Analytical Services Company	Narragansett	RI	G	401 792-3537	16186
Raj Communications Ltd	Essex Junction	VT	E	802 658-4961	17243

5051 Metals service centers and offices

	CITY	ST	EMP	PHONE	ENTRY#
Aerospace Alloys Inc	Bloomfield	CT	D	860 882-0019	144
Alloy Specialties LLC	Manchester	CT	E	860 646-4587	1585
American Metals Coal Intl Inc (HQ)	Greenwich	CT	F	203 625-9200	1311
ATI Flat Rlled Pdts Hldngs LLC	Waterbury	CT	F	203 756-7414	3888
Contractors Steel Supply Inc	North Haven	CT	F	203 782-1221	2400
East Shore Wire Rope Rgging Su	North Haven	CT	F	203 469-5204	2407
Eastern Metal Works Inc	Milford	CT	E	203 878-6995	1821
Erickson Metals Corporation (PA)	Cheshire	CT	G	203 272-2918	591
Fox Steel Products LLC	Orange	CT	F	203 799-2356	2669
I2s LLC	Wallingford	CT	C	203 265-5684	3816
International Pipe & Stl Corp	North Branford	CT	F	203 481-7102	2369
Logan Steel Inc (PA)	Meriden	CT	E	203 235-0811	1672
Loos & Co Inc (PA)	Pomfret	CT	B	860 928-7981	2809
M Cubed Technologies Inc (HQ)	Newtown	CT	E	203 304-2940	2341
Magna Steel Sales Inc	Beacon Falls	CT	F	203 888-0300	42
Newhart Products Inc	Milford	CT	E	203 878-3546	1854
Scott Metal Finishing LLC	Bristol	CT	F	860 589-3778	496
Smm New England Corporation	New Haven	CT	E	203 777-7445	2201
St Liquidation Corporation	Southington	CT	F	860 628-9090	3234
Stephens Pipe & Steel LLC	Manchester	CT	D	877 777-8721	1639
Thyssenkrupp Materials NA Inc	Wallingford	CT	F	610 586-1800	3863
Tico Titanium Inc (PA)	Wallingford	CT	E	248 446-0400	3864
Titanium Metals Corporation	East Windsor	CT	C	860 627-7051	1088
Tsmc Inc	Torrington	CT	A	860 283-8265	3703
Ulbrich Stnless Stels Spcial M (PA)	North Haven	CT	D	203 239-4481	2442
Yarde Metals Inc (HQ)	Southington	CT	B	860 406-6061	3241
A A A Metals Company Inc	Hanson	MA	F	781 447-1220	9049
Baxter Inc	West Yarmouth	MA	F	508 775-0375	13072
Bradford Steel Co Inc	East Freetown	MA	F	508 763-5921	8363
Diversified Metals Inc	Monson	MA	D	413 267-5101	10455
Erd Metal Inc	Westfield	MA	F	508 232-3684	13165
Innovative Designs & Disp Inc	Hatfield	MA	F	413 586-9854	9072
Mersen USA Ep Corp (HQ)	Newburyport	MA	D	978 462-6662	10699
Microgroup Inc	Medway	MA	C	508 533-4925	10308
Moor Metals Inc (PA)	Holliston	MA	G	508 429-9446	9224
Portland Stone Ware Co Inc (PA)	Dracut	MA	E	978 459-7272	8311
President Titanium Co Inc	Hanson	MA	F	781 294-0000	9055
Rebars & Mesh Inc	Haverhill	MA	E	978 374-2244	9126
Special Metals Corporation	Worcester	MA	F	270 365-9551	13804
Thompson Steel Company Inc	Canton	MA	C	781 828-8800	7834
Vita Needle Company	Needham	MA	E	781 444-1780	10529
Wakefield Engineering	Fall River	MA	G	603 417-8310	8624
Bangor Steel Service Inc	Bangor	ME	F	207 947-2773	4494
Ftc Inc (PA)	Friendship	ME	E	207 354-2545	4806
Canam Bridges US Inc	Claremont	NH	E	603 542-5202	14081
Capitol Fire Protection Co Inc	Loudon	NH	E	603 783-4713	14794
KW Thompson Tool Company Inc	Rochester	NH	D	603 330-8670	15483
Micro Bends Corp	Peterborough	NH	G	603 924-0022	15318
New England Small Tube Corp	Litchfield	NH	D	603 429-1600	14713
Nucor Hrris Rbar Northeast LLC	Canaan	NH	D	603 632-5222	14047
Windy Ridge Corporation	Tamworth	NH	G	603 323-2323	15650
Aim Products LLC (HQ)	Cranston	RI	E	401 463-5605	15825
Reade International Corp (PA)	East Providence	RI	F	401 433-7000	16041
Raymond Gadues Inc	Swanton	VT	E	802 868-2033	17641
Whitney Blake Company (PA)	Bellows Falls	VT	D	800 323-0479	17033

5052 Coal and other minerals and ores

	CITY	ST	EMP	PHONE	ENTRY#
American Metals Coal Intl Inc (HQ)	Greenwich	CT	F	203 625-9200	1311
H J Baker & Bro Inc	Westport	CT	B	203 682-9200	4171
HJ Baker & Bro LLC (PA)	Shelton	CT	E	203 682-9200	3014

5063 Electrical apparatus and equipment

	CITY	ST	EMP	PHONE	ENTRY#
Ac/DC Industrial Electric LLC	Bozrah	CT	G	860 886-2232	225
Asea Brown Boveri Inc	Norwalk	CT	A	203 750-2200	2465
Autac Incorporated (PA)	Branford	CT	G	203 481-3444	238
B & J Electric Motor Repair Co Inc	Ansonia	CT	F	203 734-1695	8
Carlyle Johnson Machine Co LLC (DH)	Bolton	CT	F	860 643-1531	219
Circuit Breaker Sales Ne LLC	Seymour	CT	D	203 888-7500	2958
Electric Enterprise Inc	Stratford	CT	D	203 378-7311	3534
Elinco International Jpc Inc (PA)	Fairfield	CT	G	203 334-7537	1183
Hartford Fire Equipment	Plainville	CT	F	860 747-2757	2763
Hubbell Power Systems Inc	Cromwell	CT	D	860 635-2200	694
Industrial Drives Contrls Inc (PA)	Waterbury	CT	F	203 753-5103	3921
Japanese Products Corporation	Fairfield	CT	F	203 334-7537	1190
Joining Technologies Inc	East Granby	CT	D	860 653-0111	937
Marmon Engnered Wire Cable LLC	Hartford	CT	F	860 653-8300	1491
Mil-Con Inc	Naugatuck	CT	F	630 595-2366	1971

	CITY	ST	EMP	PHONE	ENTRY#
On Line Building Systems LLC	Danbury	CT	G	203 798-1194	792
Palmers Elc Mtrs & Pumps Inc	Norwalk	CT	G	203 348-7378	2551
Pathway Lighting Products Inc	Old Saybrook	CT	D	860 388-6881	2659
Pennsylvania Globe Gaslight Co	North Branford	CT	E	203 484-7749	2371
Phoenix Company of Chicago Inc **(PA)**	Naugatuck	CT	D	630 595-2300	1980
Piela Electric Inc	Preston	CT	F	860 889-8476	2828
Point Lighting Corporation	Bloomfield	CT	E	860 243-0600	202
Precision Devices Inc **(PA)**	Wallingford	CT	F	203 265-9308	3839
Protection Industries Corp **(PA)**	Stratford	CT	E	203 375-9393	3569
Rel-Tech Electronics Inc	Milford	CT	D	203 877-8770	1876
Reliable Electric Motor Inc	Hartford	CT	F	860 522-2257	1505
SEC Electrical Inc	New Haven	CT	F	203 562-5811	2196
Specialty Cable Corp	Wallingford	CT	D	203 265-7126	3852
Stanley Black & Decker Inc	New Britain	CT	F	860 827-5025	2066
Times Wire and Cable Company **(HQ)**	Wallingford	CT	D	203 949-8400	3867
Traver Electric Motor Co Inc	Waterbury	CT	E	203 753-5103	3974
TT Trade Group LLC **(PA)**	Bethel	CT	F	800 354-4502	137
Underground Systems Inc **(PA)**	Bethel	CT	E	203 792-3444	138
A123 Systems LLC	Waltham	MA	C	617 778-5700	12580
Anchor Electric LLC	Agawam	MA	G	413 786-6788	5778
Applied Dynamics Corporation **(PA)**	Greenfield	MA	E	413 774-7268	8981
Bay State Wire & Cable Co Inc	Lowell	MA	E	978 454-2444	9861
Citiworks Corp	Attleboro	MA	F	508 761-7400	6004
Complete Energy Services Corp	Raynham	MA	F	833 237-2677	11584
Concord Electric Supply Ltd	Hyannis	MA	A	774 552-2185	9432
Concord Electric Supply Ltd	Nantucket	MA	A	774 325-5142	10461
Copley Global Services LLC	Waltham	MA	G	617 970-9617	12641
Cummins Northeast LLC **(HQ)**	Braintree	MA	E	781 801-1700	7176
Current Lighting Solutions LLC	Boston	MA	F	713 521-6500	6678
Current Ltg Employeeco LLC	Boston	MA	A	216 266-2906	6679
Electrochem Solutions Inc	Raynham	MA	C	781 575-0800	11589
Electronic Assemblies Mfg Inc	Methuen	MA	E	978 374-6840	10329
Fluorolite Plastics LLC	Hudson	MA	G	508 788-1200	9368
Heilind Electronics Inc **(PA)**	Wilmington	MA	D	978 657-4870	13410
Hiller Companies Inc	Peabody	MA	E	978 532-5730	11315
Infra-Red Bldg & Pwr Svc Inc **(PA)**	Holbrook	MA	F	781 767-0888	9175
Interstate All Battery Center	South Yarmouth	MA	F	508 394-9400	11984
James Monroe Wire & Cable Corp **(PA)**	South Lancaster	MA	D	978 368-0131	11971
Lighting By Hammerworks **(PA)**	Worcester	MA	E	508 755-3434	13753
Lloyd & Bouvier Inc	Clinton	MA	E	978 365-5700	8082
Lucidity Lights Inc **(PA)**	Charlestown	MA	E	781 995-2405	7878
Merrimac Industrial Sales Inc **(PA)**	Haverhill	MA	E	978 372-6006	9114
Micro-Lite Inc	Three Rivers	MA	F	413 289-1313	12429
Multi-Concept Inc	Mansfield	MA	F	508 366-7676	10067
Needham Electric Supply LLC **(DH)**	Canton	MA	D	781 828-9494	7811
New England Elc Mtr Svc Corp	Chelsea	MA	E	617 884-9200	7988
Newton Distributing Co Inc	Natick	MA	F	617 969-4002	10488
Period Lighting Fixtures Inc	Clarksburg	MA	F	413 664-7141	8072
Phoenix Electric Corp	Canton	MA	E	781 821-0200	7819
Polytec Inc	Hudson	MA	G	508 417-1040	9401
Ralco Electric Inc	Westport	MA	D	508 679-3363	13299
Rt Engineering Corporation	Franklin	MA	E	800 343-1182	8861
Schneider Electric Usa Inc **(DH)**	Boston	MA	A	978 975-9600	7026
Schneider Electric Usa Inc	Foxboro	MA	E	508 549-3385	8724
Soitec Usa Inc **(HQ)**	Gloucester	MA	G	978 531-2222	8958
Toolmex Indus Solutions Inc **(PA)**	Northborough	MA	D	508 653-8897	11114
AC Electric Corp **(PA)**	Auburn	ME	E	207 784-7341	4416
Enercon	Auburn	ME	E	207 657-7001	4429
Enercon **(HQ)**	Gray	ME	D	207 657-7000	4841
Gowen Inc	Portland	ME	F	207 773-1761	5219
Burndy Americas Inc **(HQ)**	Manchester	NH	D	603 647-5000	14822
Burndy Americas Intl Holdg LLC	Manchester	NH	A	603 647-5000	14823
Burndy LLC **(DH)**	Manchester	NH	B	603 647-5000	14824
Chase Electric Motors LLC	Bedford	NH	G	603 669-2565	13921
Hubbell Incorporated	Londonderry	NH	E	800 346-4175	14756
Leo Algers NH Elc Mtrs Inc	Laconia	NH	G	603 524-3729	14658
Miraco Inc	Manchester	NH	E	603 665-9449	14890
National Energy & Light LLC	Nashua	NH	E	603 821-9954	15139
Rk Parisi Enterprises Inc	Keene	NH	F	844 438-7674	14616
Williamson Electrical Co Inc	Epping	NH	D	617 884-9200	14277
Eaton Corporation	Rumford	RI	E	401 473-2214	16666
Igus Bearings Inc **(HQ)**	Rumford	RI	C	800 521-2747	16669
Jet Electric Motor Co Inc	Pawtucket	RI	E	401 725-9050	16379
SES America Inc	Warwick	RI	F	401 232-3370	16861
Walco Electric Company	Providence	RI	D	401 467-6500	16642
Hubbardton Forge LLC	Castleton	VT	C	802 468-3090	17172
Royal Group Inc **(PA)**	Rutland	VT	E	802 773-3313	17506

5064 Electrical appliances, television and radio

	CITY	ST	EMP	PHONE	ENTRY#
Conair LLC	Torrington	CT	D	800 492-7464	3676
Aerial Acoustics Corporation	Lawrence	MA	F	978 988-1600	9535
Creative Mktg Concepts Corp	Boxford	MA	G	800 272-8267	7159
Economy Plumbing & Htg Sup Co	Mattapan	MA	E	617 433-1200	10254
Philips Holding USA Inc **(HQ)**	Cambridge	MA	A	978 687-1501	7686
Tom Berkowitz Trucking Inc **(PA)**	Whitinsville	MA	E	508 234-2920	13346
Stonewall Kitchen LLC **(PA)**	York	ME	C	207 351-2713	5717

5065 Electronic parts and equipment, nec

	CITY	ST	EMP	PHONE	ENTRY#
Carrier Fire SEC Americas Corp	Farmington	CT	E	941 739-4200	1211
Connecticut Radio Inc	Rocky Hill	CT	G	860 563-4867	2919
Fct Electronics LP	Torrington	CT	D	860 482-2800	3678
Fiberoptics Technology Inc **(PA)**	Pomfret	CT	C	860 928-0443	2807
Globenix Inc	Norwalk	CT	G	203 740-7070	2506
Marco International Inc	Ridgefield	CT	D	203 894-8000	2902
Midstate Electronics Co	Wallingford	CT	F	203 265-9900	3832
Mil-Con Inc	Naugatuck	CT	F	630 595-2366	1971
Park Distributories Inc	Bridgeport	CT	G	203 366-7200	355
Park Distributories Inc **(PA)**	Bridgeport	CT	G	203 579-2140	357
Phoenix Company of Chicago Inc **(PA)**	Naugatuck	CT	D	630 595-2300	1980
Radio Frequency Systems Inc **(DH)**	Meriden	CT	E	203 630-3311	1690
Razberi Technologies Inc	Danbury	CT	E	469 828-3380	804
Servers Storage Networking LLC	Norwalk	CT	G	203 433-0808	2570
Southern Neng Telecom Corp **(HQ)**	New Haven	CT	B	203 771-5200	2203
Tech II Business Services Inc	Rocky Hill	CT	E	518 587-1565	2936
Total Communications Inc **(PA)**	East Hartford	CT	D	860 282-9999	1028
Wanho Manufacturing LLC	Cheshire	CT	E	203 759-3744	621
Altiostar Networks Inc **(PA)**	Lexington	MA	D	855 709-0701	9724
Anderson Power Products Inc **(HQ)**	Sterling	MA	D	978 422-3600	12154
Assocted Electro-Mechanics Inc	Springfield	MA	D	413 781-4276	12076
Bruce Technologies Inc	North Billerica	MA	F	978 670-5501	10901
Cbm Industries Inc	Taunton	MA	E	508 821-4555	12326
Cornell-Dubilier Elec Inc	New Bedford	MA	E	508 996-8561	10580
Electrochem Solutions Inc	Raynham	MA	C	781 575-0800	11589
Electronic Assemblies Mfg Inc	Methuen	MA	E	978 374-6840	10329
Elpakco Inc **(PA)**	Westford	MA	F	978 392-0400	13235
Etchomatic Inc	Lowell	MA	F	978 656-0011	9877
Heilind Electronics Inc **(PA)**	Wilmington	MA	D	978 657-4870	13410
Ideal Industries Inc	Sterling	MA	G	978 422-3600	12163
Jem Electronics Inc	Franklin	MA	C	508 520-3105	8845
Magellan Distribution Corp	Boston	MA	F	617 399-7900	6868
Mainstream Global Inc	Lawrence	MA	E	978 682-6767	9579
MCI Transformer Corporation	Orange	MA	F	978 544-8272	11226
Nabson Inc	Taunton	MA	G	617 323-1101	12350
Orbotech Inc **(DH)**	Billerica	MA	D	978 667-6037	6466
Psjl Corporation	Billerica	MA	C	978 313-2500	6474
Rf Aero LLC	New Bedford	MA	E	508 910-3500	10646
Rochester Electronics LLC **(PA)**	Newburyport	MA	C	978 462-9332	10715
Semigear Inc	Wakefield	MA	E	781 213-3066	12534
Socomec Inc **(DH)**	Watertown	MA	F	617 245-0447	12908
Static Clean International Inc	North Billerica	MA	F	781 229-7799	10960
Stmicroelectronics Inc	Burlington	MA	G	781 861-2650	7435
Tdl Inc	Canton	MA	E	781 828-3366	7833
Varian Semicdtr Eqp Assoc Inc **(HQ)**	Gloucester	MA	C	978 282-2000	8963
Asml Us LLC	Westbrook	ME	G	207 541-5000	5615
Comnav Engineering Inc	Portland	ME	E	207 221-8524	5201
Critical Cmmnctons Cntrls Inst	Exeter	NH	F		14290
CTS Corporation	Londonderry	NH	D	603 421-2546	14740
Ferrite Microwave Tech LLC	Nashua	NH	E	603 881-5234	15100
Gowanda Rcd LLC	Manchester	NH	C	716 532-2234	14853
Insulectro	Londonderry	NH	E	603 629-4403	14757
Intelligent Mfg Solutons LLC	Manchester	NH	E	603 296-1160	14864
Klein Marine Systems Inc	Salem	NH	D	603 893-6131	15540
Prime Power Inc	Hampstead	NH	F	603 329-4675	14390
Rme Filters Inc	Amherst	NH	F	603 595-4573	13887
Xma Corporation	Manchester	NH	D	603 222-2256	14961
Advanced Interconnections Corp	West Warwick	RI	D	401 823-5200	16898
Andon Electronics Corporation	Lincoln	RI	E	401 333-0388	16119
Signature Cable Mfg Tech Inc	Cranston	RI	E	401 383-1008	15910
Galvion Ballistics Ltd	Essex Junction	VT	D	802 334-2774	17233
Marvell Gvrnment Solutions LLC	Burlington	VT	E	845 245-8066	17143

5072 Hardware

	CITY	ST	EMP	PHONE	ENTRY#
Air Tool Sales & Svc Co Inc **(PA)**	Unionville	CT	G	860 673-2714	3746
Bloomfield Wood & Melamine Inc	Bloomfield	CT	F	860 243-3226	153
Carey Manufacturing Co Inc	Cromwell	CT	F	860 829-1803	689
East Coast Lightning Eqp Inc	Winsted	CT	E	860 379-9072	4343
East Shore Wire Rope Rgging Su	North Haven	CT	F	203 469-5204	2407
Kell-Strom Tool Intl Inc	Wethersfield	CT	F	860 529-6851	4210
Loctec Corporation	Newtown	CT	G	203 364-1000	2340
Plastic Met Components Co Inc	Milford	CT	F	203 877-2723	1866
Steeltech Building Pdts Inc	South Windsor	CT	D	860 290-8930	3184
Viking Kitchen Cabinets LLC **(PA)**	New Britain	CT	E	860 223-7101	2074
Wind Corporation	Newtown	CT	E	800 946-3267	2354
Apco Mossberg Co	Attleboro	MA	G	508 222-0340	5993
Coating House Inc	East Longmeadow	MA	F	413 525-3100	8372
Disston Company	Chicopee	MA	E	800 272-4436	8025

SIC

	CITY	ST	EMP	PHONE	ENTRY#
F W Webb Company	Needham	MA	F	781 247-0300	10510
Gardner Screw Corporation	Gardner	MA	F	978 632-0850	8887
Hudson Lock LLC (PA)	Hudson	MA	D	978 562-3481	9373
Markwell Manufacturing Co Inc	Norwood	MA	G	781 769-6610	11194
Express Assemblyproducts LLC	Nashua	NH	F	603 424-5590	15098
Allesco Industries Inc (PA)	Cranston	RI	E	401 943-0680	15828
Alloy Fasteners Inc (HQ)	Cranston	RI	E	401 943-0639	15830
Columbus Door Company	Warwick	RI	D	401 781-7792	16796
Eastern Screw Company	Cranston	RI	C	401 943-0680	15852
Gardenmats	Worcester	VT	G	802 498-3314	17781

5074 Plumbing and hydronic heating supplies

	CITY	ST	EMP	PHONE	ENTRY#
2023 Holdings LLC (PA)	Newington	CT	C	603 239-6371	2263
5n Plus Corp	Bridgeport	CT	F	608 846-1357	288
F W Webb Company	New Haven	CT	F	203 865-6124	2151
Granite Group Wholesalers LLC	Colchester	CT	G	860 537-7600	659
John Zink Company LLC	Shelton	CT	E	203 925-0380	3025
Jolley Precast Inc	Danielson	CT	E	860 774-9066	840
Keeney Holdings LLC	Farmington	CT	B	860 666-3342	1226
Kensco Inc (PA)	Ansonia	CT	E	203 734-8827	15
Neoperl Inc	Waterbury	CT	D	203 756-8891	3949
Tinny Corporation	Middletown	CT	E	860 854-6121	1786
Aluminum Products Cape Cod Inc (PA)	Dennis Port	MA	F	508 398-8546	8259
Atlas Water Systems Inc	Waltham	MA	F	781 373-4700	12597
Economy Plumbing & Htg Sup Co	Mattapan	MA	E	617 433-1200	10254
F W Webb Company	Needham	MA	F	781 247-0300	10510
F W Webb Company	Stoughton	MA	F	781 341-1100	12205
Ferguson Enterprises LLC	Chicopee	MA	G	413 593-1219	8032
Francer Industries Inc	Carver	MA	E		7854
Frank I Rounds Company (PA)	Randolph	MA	E	401 333-5014	11559
H2o Care Inc	Middleton	MA	F	978 777-8330	10384
Metromatic Manufacturing Company Inc	Byfield	MA	F	781 396-5300	7458
Newton Distributing Co Inc	Natick	MA	F	617 969-4002	10488
Orion Enterprises Inc (HQ)	North Andover	MA	C	913 342-1653	10847
R I Baker Co Inc (PA)	Clarksburg	MA	E	413 663-3791	8073
Spire Solar Inc (HQ)	Bedford	MA	G	781 275-6000	6271
Symmons Industries Inc	Avon	MA	D	508 857-2352	6163
F W Webb Company	Windham	ME	F	207 892-5302	5661
F W Webb Company	Winslow	ME	F	207 873-7741	5682
M & S Enterprises Inc	Brewer	ME	G	207 989-0077	4617

5075 Warm air heating and air conditioning

	CITY	ST	EMP	PHONE	ENTRY#
Belimo Aircontrols (usa) Inc (HQ)	Danbury	CT	C	800 543-9038	715
Buckley Associates Inc	Stratford	CT	G	203 380-2405	3524
Outland Engineering Inc	Milford	CT	F	800 797-3709	1861
Buckley Associates Inc (PA)	Hanover	MA	D	781 878-5000	9027
Merrimac Industrial Sales Inc (PA)	Haverhill	MA	E	978 372-6006	9114
Mestek Inc	Westfield	MA	F	413 568-9571	13183
Metromatic Manufacturing Company Inc	Byfield	MA	F	781 396-5300	7458
Ray Murray Inc (PA)	Lee	MA	F	413 243-2164	9619
Cogebi Inc	Dover	NH	F	603 749-6896	14223
Total Air Supply LLC	Nashua	NH	E	603 889-0100	15177
Energy MGT & Ctrl Svcs Inc	Cranston	RI	F	401 946-1440	15856

5078 Refrigeration equipment and supplies

	CITY	ST	EMP	PHONE	ENTRY#
Mp Systems Inc	East Granby	CT	F	860 687-3460	944
Bluedrop LLC	South Easton	MA	F	877 662-7873	11938
Mv3 LLC	Buzzards Bay	MA	G	617 658-4420	7455
Bev-Tech Inc	Eliot	ME	F	207 439-8061	4749
Flexware Control Tech LLC	Bangor	ME	G	207 262-9682	4501
United Fbrcnts Strainrite Corp (HQ)	Auburn	ME	F	207 376-1600	4463
Hussmann Corporation	Salem	NH	E	603 893-7770	15538

5082 Construction and mining machinery

	CITY	ST	EMP	PHONE	ENTRY#
Bell Power Systems LLC	Essex	CT	D	860 767-7502	1162
Merrick Services	North Grosvenordale	CT	F	508 802-3751	2386
Numa Tool Company (PA)	Thompson	CT	D	860 923-9551	3652
Astro Welding & Fabg Inc	Boxborough	MA	F	978 429-8666	7148
Ideal Concrete Block Co	Waltham	MA	E	781 894-3200	12694
Knm Holdings LLC	Marlborough	MA	G	508 229-1400	10177
Lyn-Lad Group Ltd (PA)	Lynn	MA	F	781 598-6010	9984
Lynn Ladder Scaffolding Co Inc (HQ)	Lynn	MA	D	781 598-6010	9985
Waverly Tool Rental & Sales Co	Framingham	MA	F	508 872-8866	8811
FC Work & Sons Incorporated	Jackson	ME	F	207 722-3206	4912
North Country Tractor Inc	Sanford	ME	F	207 324-5646	5403
Hudson Quarry Corp	Hudson	NH	F	603 598-0142	14507
Labonville Inc (PA)	Gorham	NH	F	603 752-4400	14360
North Country Tractor Inc	Dover	NH	F	603 742-5488	14241
Ray-Tech Infrared Corporation	Charlestown	NH	F	603 826-3030	14068
Vanguard Manufacturing Inc	New Ipswich	NH	D	603 878-2083	15200
Windy Ridge Corporation	Tamworth	NH	F	603 323-2323	15650
American Equipment & Fabg Corp	East Providence	RI	F	401 438-2626	16002

	CITY	ST	EMP	PHONE	ENTRY#
Dig Rite Company Inc	Johnston	RI	F	401 862-5895	16081
Rhode Island Engine Co Inc	Narragansett	RI	E	401 789-1021	16195

5083 Farm and garden machinery

	CITY	ST	EMP	PHONE	ENTRY#
Engineering Services & Pdts Co (PA)	South Windsor	CT	D	860 528-1119	3144
Mist Hill Property Maint LLC	Brookfield	CT	F	203 648-7434	530
Stihl Incorporated	Oxford	CT	E	203 929-8488	2712
Blacksmith Shop Farms Inc	East Falmouth	MA	G	508 548-7714	8357
I B A Inc (PA)	Sutton	MA	E	508 865-6911	12281
Nedap Inc	Burlington	MA	F	844 876-3327	7396
Oesco Inc	Conway	MA	E	413 369-4335	8143
Lyle Guptill	East Machias	ME	F	207 255-4130	4740
Bascom Maple Farms Inc (PA)	Alstead	NH	D	603 835-2230	13856
Champlain Valley Equipment Inc	Saint Albans	VT	G	802 524-6782	17518

5084 Industrial machinery and equipment

	CITY	ST	EMP	PHONE	ENTRY#
Advanced Pwr Systems Intl Inc	New Hartford	CT	G	860 921-0009	2097
Air Tool Sales & Svc Co Inc (PA)	Unionville	CT	G	860 673-2714	3746
Airgas Usa LLC	Danbury	CT	C	203 792-1834	705
Arthur G Russell Company Inc	Bristol	CT	D	860 583-4109	398
Baumer Ltd (DH)	Bristol	CT	F	860 621-2121	410
Bloomy Controls Inc (PA)	South Windsor	CT	E	860 298-9925	3120
Bremser Technologies Inc	Stratford	CT	F	203 378-8486	3521
Conveyco Technologies Inc (PA)	Bristol	CT	E	860 589-8215	432
CT Crane and Hoist Service LLC	Plymouth	CT	G	860 283-4320	2806
Cummins Inc	Rocky Hill	CT	F	860 529-7474	2920
Del-Tron Precision Inc	Bethel	CT	E	203 778-2727	107
Devar Inc	Bridgeport	CT	E	203 368-6751	317
EBM-Papst Inc (DH)	Farmington	CT	B	860 674-1515	1217
Etter Engineering Company Incorporated	Bristol	CT	E	860 584-8842	443
F & W Rentals Inc	Orange	CT	F	203 795-0591	2668
Faxon Engineering Company Inc (PA)	Bloomfield	CT	F	860 236-4266	163
Fortis Solutions Group LLC	Ellington	CT	E	860 872-6311	1107
Frc Founders Corporation (PA)	Stamford	CT	F	203 661-6601	3348
Gems Sensors Inc (HQ)	Plainville	CT	B	860 747-3000	2761
Goldenrod Corporation	Beacon Falls	CT	E	203 723-4400	40
Hamar Laser Instruments Inc	Danbury	CT	E	203 730-4600	756
Hauser Eqp & Wldg Svcs Inc	Stratford	CT	F	203 377-7072	3545
Helander Products Inc	Clinton	CT	F	860 669-7953	644
Hisco Pump Incorporated (PA)	Bloomfield	CT	F	860 243-2705	170
Howden Roots LLC	Windsor	CT	D	860 688-8361	4281
Industrial Flow Sltons Oper LL	New Haven	CT	F	860 399-5937	2163
Interface Devices Incorporated	Milford	CT	G	203 878-4648	1839
ITT Goulds Pumps Inc (HQ)	Stamford	CT	E	315 568-2811	3387
Jad LLC	South Windsor	CT	E	860 289-1551	3158
JL Lucas Machinery Co Inc	Waterbury	CT	E	203 597-1300	3925
Jovil Universal LLC	Danbury	CT	F	203 792-6700	763
Kahn Instruments Incorporated	Wethersfield	CT	G	860 529-8643	4208
L M Gill Welding and Mfr LLC (PA)	Manchester	CT	D	860 647-9931	1610
Leppert/Nutmeg Inc	Bloomfield	CT	E	860 243-1737	188
Linde Gas & Equipment Inc (DH)	Danbury	CT	F	844 445-4633	775
Metal Finish Eqp & Sup Co Inc	Suffield	CT	E	860 668-1050	3593
Mikro Industrial Finishing Co	Vernon	CT	G	860 875-6357	3754
Millwood Inc	North Haven	CT	D	203 248-7902	2425
MSC Filtration Tech Inc	Enfield	CT	F	860 745-7475	1139
Northeastern Metals Corp	Stamford	CT	G	203 348-8088	3419
Novo Precision LLC	Bristol	CT	E	860 583-0517	476
Otis Elevator Company	Bloomfield	CT	B	860 242-3632	198
Proflow Inc	North Haven	CT	E	203 230-4700	2433
Pump Technology Incorporated	Ansonia	CT	E	203 736-8890	18
Realhub Inc	Darien	CT	F	650 461-9210	854
Record Products America Inc	Hamden	CT	F	203 248-6371	1453
Rema Dri-Vac Corp	Norwalk	CT	F	203 847-2464	2566
Ringfeder Pwr Transm USA Corp (HQ)	Bolton	CT	E	201 666-3320	222
Royal Machine and Tool Corp	Berlin	CT	E	860 828-6555	83
Seitz LLC	Torrington	CT	C	860 489-0476	3695
Shuster-Mettler Corp	Plainville	CT	E	203 562-3178	2780
Spectrum Associates Inc	Milford	CT	F	203 878-4618	1889
Spencer Turbine Company (DH)	Windsor	CT	E	860 688-8361	4301
Stancor LP	Monroe	CT	E	203 268-7513	1922
Sulzer Pump Solutions US Inc (PA)	Wallingford	CT	E	203 238-2700	3856
Swanson Tool Manufacturing Inc	West Hartford	CT	E	860 953-1641	4084
Tenova Inc	Wallingford	CT	E	203 265-5684	3859
Thavenet Machine Company Inc	Pawcatuck	CT	G	860 599-4495	2726
The Viking Tool Company	Shelton	CT	E	203 929-1457	3068
Willco Sales & Service Inc (PA)	Stratford	CT	F	203 366-3895	3584
Wittman Usa Inc (DH)	Torrington	CT	D	860 496-9603	3708
Acme-Shorey Precast Co Inc (PA)	Harwich	MA	F	508 432-0530	9066
American Industrial & Med Pdts (PA)	Auburn	MA	F	508 832-5785	6101
Anver Corporation	Hudson	MA	D	978 568-0221	9354
Ashmont Welding Company Inc	Bridgewater	MA	F	508 279-1977	7220
Assocted Electro-Mechanics Inc	Springfield	MA	D	413 781-4276	12076
Auburn Systems LLC	Beverly	MA	G	978 777-2460	6329

	CITY	ST	EMP	PHONE	ENTRY#
Autoroll Print Technologies LLC	Middleton	MA	E	978 777-2160	10380
Baker Parts Inc	Westport	MA	G	508 878-5436	13293
BEE International Inc	South Easton	MA	E	508 238-5558	11937
Carpe Diem Technologies Inc	Franklin	MA	F	508 541-2055	8822
Compumachine Inc	Danvers	MA	E	978 777-8440	8173
Controls For Automation Inc	Taunton	MA	E	508 802-6005	12328
Cummins Northeast LLC (HQ)	Braintree	MA	E	781 801-1700	7176
Degreasing Devices Co	Southbridge	MA	G	508 765-0045	12013
Dienes Corporation	Spencer	MA	E	508 885-6301	12057
Dynisco Instruments LLC (HQ)	Franklin	MA	C	508 541-9400	8831
Emuge Corp	West Boylston	MA	E	508 595-3600	12962
Emx Controls Inc	East Douglas	MA	E	508 876-9700	8350
Frank I Rounds Company (PA)	Randolph	MA	E	401 333-5014	11559
Gorman Machine Corp	Middleboro	MA	E	508 923-9462	10359
Harvard Products Inc	Harvard	MA	F	978 772-0309	9063
Hayes Pump Inc (PA)	Concord	MA	F	978 369-8800	8119
Hope Inc	Needham	MA	E	781 455-1145	10512
Industrial Packaging Sup Inc	Worcester	MA	F	978 514-9960	13741
Industrial Packaging Supply Inc (PA)	Webster	MA	F	508 499-1600	12927
Innovasea Systems Inc (PA)	Boston	MA	E	207 322-3219	6811
Iwaki America Incorporated (HQ)	Holliston	MA	E	508 429-1440	9216
Jeio Tech Inc	Billerica	MA	G	781 376-0700	6457
JP Plastics Inc	Foxboro	MA	G	508 203-2420	8704
Js Sale Corp	Worcester	MA	F	508 753-2979	13746
Kadant Inc	Auburn	MA	C	508 791-8171	6116
Kamweld Industries Inc	Norwood	MA	G	617 558-7500	11185
Labthink International Inc	Medford	MA	E	617 830-2190	10293
Lewa-Nikkiso America Inc (DH)	Holliston	MA	E	508 429-7403	9220
Liquid Solids Control Inc (PA)	Upton	MA	E	508 529-3377	12473
Ltp Corporation (DH)	Northborough	MA	D	508 393-7660	11101
Luster-On Products Inc	Springfield	MA	F	413 739-2541	12111
Marine Hydraulics Inc	New Bedford	MA	F	508 990-2866	10619
Mascon Inc	Woburn	MA	E	781 938-5800	13605
Mass Vac Inc	North Billerica	MA	E	978 667-2393	10932
Maybury Associates Inc	East Longmeadow	MA	D	413 525-4216	8386
Merrimac Industrial Sales Inc (PA)	Haverhill	MA	E	978 372-6006	9114
Merrimac Industrial Sales Inc (PA)	Haverhill	MA	E	978 372-6006	9115
Mettler-Toledo Thornton Inc (DH)	Billerica	MA	D	978 262-0210	6460
Mezzanine Safeti-Gates Inc	Essex	MA	G	978 768-3000	8478
N Ferrara Inc	Somerset	MA	F	508 679-2440	11853
Nidec America Corporation (HQ)	Braintree	MA	F	781 848-0970	7196
Omtec Corp	Marlborough	MA	F	508 481-3322	10190
Otis Elevator Company	Auburn	MA	F	401 232-7282	6122
Pacific Packaging Products Inc (PA)	Wilmington	MA	C	978 657-9100	13445
Panametrics LLC (DH)	Billerica	MA	A	978 437-1000	6468
Polytech Fltration Systems Inc	Hudson	MA	F	978 562-7700	9402
Ray Murray Inc (PA)	Lee	MA	D	413 243-2164	9619
Sanger Equipment Corporation	Conway	MA	F	413 625-8304	8145
Spectro Scientific Inc (HQ)	Chelmsford	MA	D	978 486-0123	7959
St Pierre Manufacturing Corp	Worcester	MA	E	508 853-8010	13806
Stan Rubinstein Associates Inc	Walpole	MA	F	508 668-6044	12576
TEC Engineering Corp	Oxford	MA	F	508 987-0231	11266
Testing Machines Inc	Swansea	MA	D	302 613-5600	12313
The Tyler Co Inc	Hudson	MA	E	978 568-3400	9419
Thermoplastics Company Inc	Worcester	MA	E	508 754-4668	13811
Thomson Service Corp	Franklin	MA	F	508 528-2000	8872
Toolmex Indus Solutions Inc (PA)	Northborough	MA	D	508 653-8897	11114
Trans Metrics Inc (HQ)	Watertown	MA	F	617 926-1000	12916
Ulvac Technologies Inc (HQ)	Methuen	MA	E	978 686-7550	10347
Weld Engineering Co Inc	Shrewsbury	MA	E	508 842-2224	11848
Whitmor Company Inc (PA)	Revere	MA	F	781 284-8000	11625
Whitney & Son Inc	Fitchburg	MA	E	978 343-6353	8682
Bev-Tech Inc	Eliot	ME	F	207 439-8061	4749
Cascon Inc	Yarmouth	ME	F	207 846-6202	5702
Downeast Machine & Engrg Inc (PA)	Mechanic Falls	ME	F	207 345-8111	5050
Enterprise Casting Corporation	Lewiston	ME	E	207 782-5511	4961
Faulkner Corporation	Brewer	ME	F	207 989-3792	4612
Gac Chemical Corporation (PA)	Searsport	ME	D	207 548-2525	5453
Gary Raymond	Caribou	ME	G	207 498-2549	4675
Kardex Remstar LLC (HQ)	Westbrook	ME	E	207 854-1861	5633
Melton Sales and Service Inc	Hallowell	ME	G	207 623-8895	4860
Oizero9 Inc	Sanford	ME	E	207 324-3582	5404
Pamco Machine Company Inc	Lewiston	ME	F	207 783-1763	4982
PRC Acquisition Company Inc	Gorham	ME	F	207 854-3702	4832
Somatex Inc	Detroit	ME	F	207 487-6141	4725
Southworth Products Corp (HQ)	Falmouth	ME	E	207 878-0700	4773
Barre Tile Inc	Lebanon	NH	F	802 476-0912	14684
Centilla Corporation	Windham	NH	F	603 658-3881	15723
Controlair LLC	Amherst	NH	F	603 886-9400	13865
Federal Spice Corp (PA)	North Conway	NH	E	603 356-6381	15248
HMC Corporation (PA)	Hopkinton	NH	E	603 746-3399	14477
Hyde Specialty Products LLC	Merrimack	NH	F	603 883-7400	14984
Jarvis Company Inc (PA)	Rochester	NH	D	603 332-9000	15481

	CITY	ST	EMP	PHONE	ENTRY#
Labonville Inc (PA)	Gorham	NH	E	603 752-4030	14360
Martel Electronics Corp	Derry	NH	E	603 434-6033	14201
Moore Nntechnology Systems LLC (DH)	Swanzey	NH	F	603 352-3030	15645
Premier Recycling Eqp Inc	Seabrook	NH	F	855 223-5859	15600
Sponge-Jet Inc (PA)	Newington	NH	G	603 610-7950	15212
Technical Tool & Design LLC	Northfield	NH	C	603 286-1600	15269
Thermal Dynamics Corporation (DH)	West Lebanon	NH	B	603 298-5711	15690
Williamson Electrical Co Inc	Epping	NH	D	617 884-9200	14277
Ariston Usa LLC (HQ)	Providence	RI	E	508 763-8071	16474
Atlantic Automation Group LLC	Bristol	RI	E	401 424-1840	15754
Contract Fusion Inc	East Providence	RI	E	401 438-1298	16010
Glencore Recycling LLC	East Providence	RI	F	401 438-9220	16020
Linde Gas & Equipment Inc	Slatersville	RI	F	401 767-3450	16682
LK Goodwin Co Inc (PA)	West Greenwich	RI	F	401 781-5526	16888
Primary Flow Signal Inc (PA)	Cranston	RI	F	401 461-6366	15905
Rbc Industries Inc	Cranston	RI	D	401 941-3000	15906
Vogue Industries Ltd Partnr	Central Falls	RI	F	401 722-0900	15800
Walco Electric Company	Providence	RI	D	401 467-6500	16642
Yushin America Inc (HQ)	Cranston	RI	D	401 463-1800	15930
Apex Sealing Inc	Fairfax	VT	F	802 524-7100	17254
Ashe America Inc	Brattleboro	VT	E	802 254-0200	17073
Fellows Corporation	Windsor	VT	E	802 674-6500	17758
Galvion Ballistics Ltd	Essex Junction	VT	D	802 334-2774	17233
Leos Small Engines Inc	Morrisville	VT	F	802 888-7247	17384
Triex LLC	Barre	VT	G	802 505-6772	17021
Vermont Machine Tool Corp	Springfield	VT	F	802 885-5161	17622
Worksafe Traffic Ctrl Inds Inc (PA)	Barre	VT	G	802 223-8948	17025

5085 Industrial supplies

	CITY	ST	EMP	PHONE	ENTRY#
Airgas Usa LLC	Danbury	CT	C	203 792-1834	705
Altra Industrial Motion Corp	New Hartford	CT	E	860 379-1673	2098
Applied Rubber & Plastics Inc	Windsor	CT	F	860 987-9018	4261
Automation Inc	West Hartford	CT	E	860 236-5991	4048
B I L Inc	Groton	CT	F	860 446-8058	1365
Ball & Roller Bearing Co LLC	New Milford	CT	F	860 355-4161	2239
Burt Process Equipment Inc (PA)	Hamden	CT	F	203 287-1985	1415
Carlyle Johnson Machine Co LLC (DH)	Bolton	CT	F	860 643-1531	219
Composition Materials Co Inc	Milford	CT	G	203 874-6500	1812
F-K Bearings Inc	Southington	CT	F	860 621-4567	3210
Faxon Engineering Company Inc (PA)	Bloomfield	CT	F	860 236-4266	163
Fluid Dynamics LLC	Manchester	CT	F	860 791-6325	1598
Gordon Rubber and Pkg Co Inc	Derby	CT	E	203 735-7441	889
Kaman Aerospace Corporation	Bloomfield	CT	E	860 242-4461	180
Kaman Corporation (PA)	Bloomfield	CT	D	860 243-7100	183
Kell-Strom Tool Intl Inc	Wethersfield	CT	F	860 529-6851	4210
Lee Spring Company LLC	Bristol	CT	F	860 584-0991	461
Motion Industries Inc	Bloomfield	CT	A	860 687-5000	195
MSC Filtration Tech Inc	Enfield	CT	F	860 745-7475	1139
Nucor Hrris Rbar Northeast LLC	South Windsor	CT	D	860 282-1860	3166
O Berk Company Neng LLC	West Haven	CT	F	203 932-8000	4117
Pa-Ted Spring Company LLC	Bristol	CT	E	860 582-6368	479
Plastic Met Components Co Inc	Milford	CT	F	203 877-2723	1866
Protek Ski Racing LLC	Southington	CT	G	860 628-9643	3229
Rbc Aircraft Products Inc	Torrington	CT	D	860 626-7800	3692
Rbc Bearings Incorporated (PA)	Oxford	CT	C	203 267-7001	2710
Seals-It Inc	Ellington	CT	G	860 979-0060	1114
Spectrum Associates Inc	Milford	CT	F	203 878-4618	1889
Sperry Automatics Co Inc	Naugatuck	CT	E	203 729-4589	1986
Spirol International Corp (HQ)	Danielson	CT	C	860 774-8571	844
Stanley Black & Decker Inc	New Britain	CT	C	860 225-5111	2067
Tinny Corporation	Middletown	CT	E	860 854-6121	1786
Wadsworth Falls Mfg Co	Rockfall	CT	F	860 346-3644	2916
Afc Cable Systems Inc	New Bedford	MA	B	508 998-1131	10566
Airgas Usa LLC	Billerica	MA	E	978 439-1344	6398
Altra Industrial Motion Corp (HQ)	Braintree	MA	C	781 917-0600	7167
Altra Power Transmission Inc	Braintree	MA	B	781 917-0600	7168
American Holt Corporation (PA)	Norwood	MA	F	781 440-9993	11160
Ar-Ro Engineering Company Inc	Uxbridge	MA	F	401 766-6669	12477
Autoroll Print Technologies LLC	Middleton	MA	E	978 777-2160	10380
Bascom-Turner Instruments Inc	Norwood	MA	D	781 769-9660	11164
Boston Atlantic Corp	Worcester	MA	F	508 754-4076	13705
C F G Corporation	Saugus	MA	E	781 233-6110	11754
Cbm Industries Inc	Taunton	MA	E	508 821-4555	12326
Circor LLC	Burlington	MA	E	781 270-1200	7348
Creative Imprints Inc	Norton	MA	E	508 285-7650	11125
Crosby Valve & Gage Intl Inc	Mansfield	MA	E	508 384-3121	10048
Esco Technologies Inc	Holliston	MA	E	508 429-4441	9209
Essex Silverline Corporation (PA)	Dracut	MA	F	978 957-2116	8305
Fabreeka International Inc (DH)	Stoughton	MA	G	781 341-3655	12206
Fabreeka Intl Holdings Inc (DH)	Stoughton	MA	F	781 341-3655	12207
Gardner Screw Corporation	Gardner	MA	F	978 632-0850	8887
Greene Rubber Company Inc (PA)	Woburn	MA	D	781 937-9909	13577
Hope Inc	Needham	MA	E	781 455-1145	10512

	CITY	ST	EMP	PHONE	ENTRY#
Horn International Packg Inc (HQ)	Lancaster	MA	E	978 667-8797	9528
John G Shelley Co Inc	Woburn	MA	F	781 237-0900	13593
Joma Diamond Tool LLC	East Longmeadow	MA	F	413 525-0760	8381
Kinefac Corporation	Worcester	MA	D	508 754-6901	13749
Leggett & Platt Incorporated	Oxford	MA	D	508 987-8706	11258
Lm/Tarbell Inc	East Longmeadow	MA	F	413 525-4166	8383
Ltp Corporation (DH)	Northborough	MA	D	508 393-7660	11101
Markwell Manufacturing Co Inc	Norwood	MA	G	781 769-6610	11194
McGill Hose & Coupling Inc (PA)	East Longmeadow	MA	F	413 525-3977	8387
Motion Industries Inc	Danvers	MA	E	978 774-7100	8210
Mrse Inc	West Brookfield	MA	F	508 867-5083	12996
Ray Murray Inc (PA)	Lee	MA	D	413 243-2164	9619
Reed & Prince Mfg Corp	Leominster	MA	F	978 466-6903	9700
Safe-T-Cut Inc	Monson	MA	F	413 267-9984	10456
Safety-Kleen Systems Inc (HQ)	Norwell	MA	B	800 669-5740	11146
Sentinel Process Systems Inc	Southborough	MA	F	508 624-5577	12002
Standard Lock Washer & Mfg Co	Worcester	MA	E	508 757-4508	13807
Ulvac Technologies Inc (HQ)	Methuen	MA	E	978 686-7550	10347
Warner Electric	Braintree	MA	D	781 917-0600	7212
AC Electric Corp	Bangor	ME	F	207 945-9487	4487
Advanced Indus Solutions Inc	Waldoboro	ME	F	207 832-0569	5573
C P Technologies Inc (PA)	Saco	ME	F	207 286-1167	5364
Deepwater Buoyancy Inc	Biddeford	ME	F	207 468-2565	4559
Lane Conveyors & Drives Inc	Brewer	ME	D	207 989-4560	4616
Lapoint Industries Inc (PA)	Auburn	ME	D	207 777-3100	4439
Pieceworks Inc	Montville	ME	G	207 589-3451	5075
PRC Acquisition Company Inc	Gorham	ME	F	207 854-3702	4832
Quality Containers of Neng	Yarmouth	ME	E	207 846-5420	5706
Tis Brewer LLC	Brewer	ME	E	207 989-4560	4621
Tri-State Packing Supply	Scarborough	ME	F	207 883-5218	5446
Abrasives & Tools NH Inc	Pembroke	NH	E	603 224-5376	15301
Cogebi Inc	Dover	NH	E	603 749-6896	14223
Marco Group LLC (PA)	Seabrook	NH	E	603 468-3600	15596
Monadnock Paper Mills Inc (HQ)	Bennington	NH	D	603 588-3311	13977
New Hmpshire Ball Bearings Inc	Peterborough	NH	E	818 407-9300	15320
Z-Flex Realty Inc (DH)	Bedford	NH	F	603 669-5136	13957
Bullard Abrasives Inc	Lincoln	RI	D	508 366-4300	16123
Igus Bearings Inc (HQ)	Rumford	RI	C	800 521-2747	16669
Meister Abrasives Usa Inc	North Kingstown	RI	E	401 294-4503	16271
Niantic Seal Inc	Lincoln	RI	F	401 334-6870	16150
Tyco Fire Products LP (DH)	Cranston	RI	C	215 362-0700	15924
W L Fuller Inc	Warwick	RI	F	401 467-2900	16876
Apex Sealing Inc	Fairfax	VT	F	802 524-7100	17254
Flex-A-Seal Inc	Williston	VT	E	802 878-8307	17729
Velan Valve Corp (DH)	Williston	VT	D	802 863-2561	17751

5087 Service establishment equipment

	CITY	ST	EMP	PHONE	ENTRY#
American Marketing Intl LLC	Clinton	CT	E	860 669-4100	635
Cummins - Allison Corp	Cheshire	CT	G	203 794-9200	585
Edsan Chemical Company Inc	New Haven	CT	F	203 624-3123	2148
New England Industrial Sup LLC	Newington	CT	F	860 436-5959	2308
Baystate Business Ventures LLC	Taunton	MA	F	508 828-9274	12324
Blendco Systems LLC	Holyoke	MA	D	800 537-7797	9244
Car Gold Inc	Holyoke	MA	F	800 537-7797	9246
Dodge Company Inc (PA)	Billerica	MA	F	800 443-6343	6431
ERC Acquisition Inc	Lynn	MA	E	781 593-4000	9971
Greenwood Emrgncy Vehicles LLC (HQ)	Attleboro Falls	MA	D	508 695-7138	6086
Keating-Wilbert Vault Inc	Wilbraham	MA	F	413 543-1226	13361
Quintal Burial Vault Inc	Dighton	MA	F	508 669-5717	8294
Safehands Distribution Ne LLC	Wilbraham	MA	F	413 244-1452	13363
Vibram Corporation (DH)	North Brookfield	MA	C	508 867-6494	10964
E-Cloth Inc	Dover	NH	F	603 765-9367	14227
Royal Group Inc (PA)	Rutland	VT	E	802 773-3313	17506

5088 Transportation equipment and supplies

	CITY	ST	EMP	PHONE	ENTRY#
Acmt Inc	Manchester	CT	D	860 645-0592	1582
B I L Inc	Groton	CT	F	860 446-8058	1365
Columbia Manufacturing Inc	Columbia	CT	G	860 228-2259	669
Dawid Manufacturing Inc	Ansonia	CT	D	203 734-1800	12
Defender Industries Inc	Waterford	CT	C	860 701-3400	3989
Helicopter Support Inc (DH)	Trumbull	CT	B	203 416-4000	3721
TLD America Corporation (DH)	Windsor	CT	E	860 602-3400	4309
Hercules Slr (us) Inc	New Bedford	MA	G	508 992-9519	10600
Hercules Slr (us) Inc (PA)	New Bedford	MA	F	508 993-0010	10601
New England Expert Tech Corp	Greenfield	MA	E	413 773-8200	8995
QCI Inc	Seekonk	MA	F	508 399-8983	11784
Quincy Electronics Co Inc	Quincy	MA	G	617 471-7700	11534
Textron Systems Corporation (DH)	Wilmington	MA	E	978 657-5111	13466
Watts Sea Tech Inc	North Andover	MA	E	978 688-1811	10860
John M Williams Company	Mount Desert	ME	F	207 244-7854	5077
Puffin Boats LLC	Hampden	ME	G	207 907-4385	4866
Exail Defense Systems Inc	Lincoln	RI	E	401 475-4400	16136
Ronstan International Inc	Portsmouth	RI	F	401 293-0539	16456

	CITY	ST	EMP	PHONE	ENTRY#
Dock Doctors LLC	Ferrisburgh	VT	E	802 877-6756	17268

5091 Sporting and recreation goods

	CITY	ST	EMP	PHONE	ENTRY#
Bic Corporation (HQ)	Shelton	CT	A	203 783-2000	2985
Golf Galaxy LLC	Norwalk	CT	F	203 855-0500	2507
Jaypro Sports LLC	Waterford	CT	E	860 447-3001	3990
Shelterlogic Corp (HQ)	Watertown	CT	E	860 945-6442	4028
Slogic Holding Corp (PA)	New Canaan	CT	F	203 966-2800	2086
Wild Card Golf LLC	Hartford	CT	G	860 296-1661	1517
CMI Restructuring Inc	Westfield	MA	D	413 562-3664	13160
Creative Playthings Ltd (PA)	Framingham	MA	F	508 620-0900	8753
Fitness Em LLC	Uxbridge	MA	E		12479
Full Circle Padding Inc	Norton	MA	F	508 285-2500	11127
Hollrock Engineering Inc	Hadley	MA	E	413 586-2256	9018
Inov-8 Inc	Westborough	MA	E	508 251-4643	13109
Jarvis Welding & Mfg Co	Turners Falls	MA	G	413 863-9541	12449
Montague Corporation	Cambridge	MA	F	617 491-7200	7655
Outdoor Outfitters Inc	Orleans	MA	E	508 255-0455	11241
Paramount Industries Inc	Medway	MA	F	508 533-8480	10310
Schlage Lock Company LLC	Canton	MA	G	781 828-6655	7826
Thomas & Thomas Rodmakers	Greenfield	MA	F	413 475-3840	9003
Downeast Fishing Gear	Trenton	ME	E	207 667-3131	5553
Hyperlite Mountain Gear Inc	Biddeford	ME	D	800 464-9208	4570
Lyle Guptill	East Machias	ME	F	207 255-4130	4740
Collins Sports Center LLC	Rochester	NH	G	603 335-1417	15470
Happy House Amusement Inc	Goffstown	NH	F	603 497-4151	14348
Labonville Inc (PA)	Gorham	NH	F	603 752-4030	14360
Planet Eclipse LLC	Warren	RI	G	401 247-9061	16763
Trawlworks Inc	Narragansett	RI	F	401 789-3964	16198
Century International Arms Inc	Fairfax	VT	D	802 527-1252	17257
Dock Doctors LLC	Ferrisburgh	VT	E	802 877-6756	17268
Gw Ski Inc	West Dover	VT	F	802 464-3464	17690
Keiths II Sports Ltd	Pittsford	VT	F	802 483-6050	17444

5092 Toys and hobby goods and supplies

	CITY	ST	EMP	PHONE	ENTRY#
Lego Systems Inc (DH)	Enfield	CT	A	860 698-9367	1137
Leisure Learning Products Inc	Stamford	CT	F	203 325-2800	3397
Nicks Enterprises Inc (PA)	Hamden	CT	F	203 287-9990	1447
US Games Systems Inc	Stamford	CT	F	800 544-2637	3488
Beacon Wellness Brands Inc (PA)	Newton	MA	F	781 449-9500	10739
Catalystsmc Inc	Newton	MA	F	781 449-9500	10741
Digi-Block Inc	Cambridge	MA	E	617 926-9300	7550
Erica Wilson Inc (PA)	Nantucket	MA	F	212 348-6196	10463
Nancy Sales Co Inc	Chelsea	MA	D	617 884-1700	7987
Bluejacket Inc	Searsport	ME	F	207 548-9970	5451
Downeast Concepts Inc	Yarmouth	ME	E	207 846-3726	5703
Elves & Angels Inc	Hodgdon	ME	G	207 456-7575	4891

5093 Scrap and waste materials

	CITY	ST	EMP	PHONE	ENTRY#
Lajoie Auto Wrecking Co Inc	Norwalk	CT	E	203 870-0641	2525
MJ Metal Inc	Bridgeport	CT	E	203 334-3484	348
Willimantic Waste Paper Co Inc (HQ)	Willimantic	CT	C	860 423-4527	4221
American Paper Recycling Corp (PA)	Mansfield	MA	A	800 422-3220	10038
Costello Dismantling Co Inc (PA)	West Wareham	MA	F	508 291-2324	13058
George Apkin & Sons Inc	Adams	MA	F	413 664-4936	5772
Spector Textile Products Inc (PA)	Lawrence	MA	F	978 688-3501	9600
United Paper Stock Co Inc	Worcester	MA	E	401 724-5700	13816
Wte Recycling Inc	Greenfield	MA	E	413 772-2200	9007
Casella Recycling LLC (HQ)	Scarborough	ME	E	207 883-4600	5427
Maine Metal Recycling Inc	Auburn	ME	F	207 786-3531	4442
Colt Refining Inc (PA)	Merrimack	NH	E	603 429-9966	14978
Harding Metals Inc	Northwood	NH	E	603 942-5573	15273
Max Cohen & Sons Inc (HQ)	Concord	NH	E	603 224-3532	14144
Hyman Brickle & Son Inc (PA)	Woonsocket	RI	F	401 769-0189	16964
Earth Waste Systems Inc (PA)	Rutland	VT	E	802 775-7722	17494

5094 Jewelry and precious stones

	CITY	ST	EMP	PHONE	ENTRY#
Barker Advg Specialty Co Inc (PA)	Cheshire	CT	D	203 272-2222	575
Elm City Mfg Jewelers Inc	Hamden	CT	F	203 248-2195	1425
Northeastern Metals Corp	Stamford	CT	G	203 348-8088	3419
American Biltrite Inc (PA)	Wellesley	MA	G	781 237-6655	12935
Artinian Garabet Corporation	Concord	MA	F	978 371-7110	8102
Findings Incorporated	Attleboro	MA	D	508 222-7449	6015
Joseph P Stachura Company Inc	Uxbridge	MA	G	508 278-6525	12482
Natalia Marketing Corp	Waltham	MA	F	781 693-4900	12733
Ozcan Jewelers Inc	Boston	MA	F	617 338-6844	6949
Paramount Industries Inc	Medway	MA	F	508 533-8480	10310
A Silver Lining Inc	Boothbay Harbor	ME	G	207 633-4103	4599
Glass Graphics Inc	Conway	NH	F	603 447-1900	14179
Alloy Holdings LLC	Providence	RI	D	401 353-7500	16467
Bazar Group Inc (PA)	East Providence	RI	E	401 434-2595	16006
Cimini & Associates Inc	Westerly	RI	E	401 348-0388	16929
Imperial-Deltah Inc	East Providence	RI	D	401 434-2597	16023

	CITY	ST	EMP	PHONE	ENTRY#
Ldc Inc	East Providence	RI	F	401 861-4667	16029
R & D Manufacturing Co Inc	Pawtucket	RI	E	401 305-7662	16408
Snow & Stars Corporation	Providence	RI	F	401 421-4134	16613
Uncas International LLC (PA)	West Warwick	RI	D	401 231-0266	16924

5099 Durable goods, nec

	CITY	ST	EMP	PHONE	ENTRY#
Acme Sign Co (PA)	Stamford	CT	F	203 324-2263	3272
Barile Printers LLC	New Britain	CT	F	860 224-0127	2007
Consumer Product Distrs LLC	Stratford	CT	G	203 378-2193	3531
Ecu & US International	East Hartford	CT	F	860 906-3390	991
Eylward Timber Co	Wallingford	CT	G	203 265-4276	3806
New England Industrial Sup LLC	Newington	CT	F	860 436-5959	2308
Online River LLC	Westport	CT	F	203 801-5900	4191
Rokr Distribution Us Inc	Bloomfield	CT	B	860 509-8888	207
Vision Designs LLC	Brookfield	CT	F	203 778-9898	543
47 Brand LLC	Boston	MA	D	617 437-1384	6501
Audiospectrum Inc	Randolph	MA	E	781 767-1331	11549
Blauer Manufacturing Co Inc (PA)	Boston	MA	E	800 225-6715	6597
Boston Light & Sound Inc (PA)	Malden	MA	F	617 787-3131	10005
FA Finale Inc	Boston	MA	E	617 226-7888	6728
Forced Exposure Inc	Arlington	MA	E	781 321-0320	5940
G R Sands Monumental Works	Roslindale	MA	G	617 522-1001	11666
Lar Plastics LLC	Winchester	MA	B	617 860-2020	13485
Life+gear Inc	Wellesley Hills	MA	F	858 755-2099	12952
Lighthouse Distributors Inc	Marshfield	MA	G	781 319-9828	10241
Nancy Sales Co Inc	Chelsea	MA	D	617 884-1700	7987
Simons Stamps Inc	Turners Falls	MA	E	413 863-6800	12455
Spector Textile Products Inc (PA)	Lawrence	MA	E	978 688-3501	9600
Verne Q Powell Flutes Inc	Maynard	MA	D	978 461-6111	10265
Visi-Flash Rentals Eastern	West Bridgewater	MA	E	508 583-9100	12988
West End Firewood Inc	Whitinsville	MA	G	508 234-4747	13347
Pantheon Guitars LLC	Lewiston	ME	F	207 755-0003	4983
Glass Graphics Inc	Conway	NH	F	603 447-1900	14179
Middleton Building Supply (PA)	Middleton	NH	C	603 473-2210	15008
Ossipee Mountain Land Co LLC	Tamworth	NH	G	603 323-7677	15648
Fgx International Holdings Ltd (HQ)	Smithfield	RI	B	401 231-3800	16698
Fgx International Inc (DH)	Smithfield	RI	A	401 231-3800	16699
Metro Inc (PA)	Cranston	RI	E	401 461-2200	15894
Century International Arms Inc	Fairfax	VT	D	802 527-1252	17257
McCue Memorial Co Inc	Castleton	VT	E	802 468-5636	17173

51 WHOLESALE TRADE - NONDURABLE GOODS

5111 Printing and writing paper

	CITY	ST	EMP	PHONE	ENTRY#
Mega Sound and Light LLC	Danbury	CT	G	203 743-4200	784
Wallingford Prtg Bus Forms Inc	Branford	CT	F	203 481-1911	286
Medical Manager Pcn Inc	Walpole	MA	F	508 850-3500	12568
Judd Paper Company	Rumford	RI	F	413 534-5661	16673

5112 Stationery and office supplies

	CITY	ST	EMP	PHONE	ENTRY#
Adkins Printing Company	New Britain	CT	F	800 228-9745	1997
Compu-Data LLC	Newington	CT	D	800 666-0399	2282
Envirnmntal Office Sltions Inc (PA)	East Hartford	CT	E	860 291-1900	993
Executive Greetings (HQ)	New Hartford	CT	B	860 379-9911	2100
Massachusetts Envelope Co Inc	Hartford	CT	F	860 727-9100	1492
Mega Sound and Light LLC	Danbury	CT	G	203 743-4200	784
Olympia Sales Inc	Enfield	CT	D	860 749-0751	1140
Recycle 4 Vets LLC	Westport	CT	G	203 222-7300	4194
Ames Safety Envelope Company (DH)	Somerville	MA	F	617 684-1000	11860
Brady Business Forms Inc	Lowell	MA	G	978 458-2585	9865
CAM Office Services Inc (PA)	Marlborough	MA	F	781 932-9868	10125
Continuprint Inc	Woburn	MA	F	781 933-1800	13547
Da Rosas	Oak Bluffs	MA	E	508 693-0110	11221
Expressive Design Group Inc	Holyoke	MA	E	413 315-6296	9255
Ils Business Services Inc	Agawam	MA	G	413 789-4555	5793
Lovepop Inc (PA)	Boston	MA	G	888 687-9589	6864
Massachusetts Envelope Co Inc (PA)	Woburn	MA	F	617 623-8000	13606
Medical Manager Pcn Inc	Walpole	MA	F	508 850-3500	12568
State-Line Graphics Inc	Everett	MA	F	617 389-1200	8501
Sterling Business Products Inc	Stoneham	MA	F	781 481-1234	12186
W G Fry Corp	Florence	MA	E	413 747-2551	8687
Gallery Leather Mfg Inc	Trenton	ME	E	207 667-9474	5555
Wise Business Forms Inc	Portland	ME	C	207 774-6560	5290
Fiberkraft Inc	Salem	NH	E	603 621-0090	15525
Kelley Solutions Inc	Rye	NH	G	603 431-3881	15499
Papergraphics Print & Copy Inc	Merrimack	NH	F	603 880-1835	14997
Relyco Sales Inc (PA)	Dover	NH	E	603 742-0999	14248
Savron Graphics Inc (PA)	Jaffrey	NH	G	603 532-7726	14579
AT Cross Company LLC (HQ)	Providence	RI	D	401 333-1200	16476
Costa Inc	Providence	RI	E	401 333-1200	16506
Fred F Waltz Co Inc	Cumberland	RI	F	401 769-4900	15940
Sheaffer Pen Corporation	Lincoln	RI	A	319 372-7444	16154

	CITY	ST	EMP	PHONE	ENTRY#
First Step Print Shop LLC	Burlington	VT	G	802 899-2708	17135

5113 Industrial and personal service paper

	CITY	ST	EMP	PHONE	ENTRY#
Fortis Solutions Group LLC	Ellington	CT	E	860 872-6311	1107
Hudson Paper Company (PA)	Stratford	CT	E	203 378-8759	3548
IR Industries Inc	Bethel	CT	F	203 790-8273	121
Penmar Industries Inc	Stratford	CT	F	203 853-4868	3565
Boyd Biomedical Inc (PA)	Lee	MA	E	413 243-2000	9612
Diamond Water Systems Inc	Chicopee	MA	E	413 536-8186	8022
Expressive Design Group Inc	Holyoke	MA	E	413 315-6296	9255
Horn Corporation (PA)	Lancaster	MA	E	800 832-7020	9527
LCI Paper Company	Hudson	MA	F	508 281-5088	9384
McLaughlin Paper Co Inc (PA)	West Springfield	MA	F	413 732-7485	13033
Pacific Packaging Products Inc (PA)	Wilmington	MA	C	978 657-9100	13445
United Paper Stock Co Inc	Worcester	MA	E	401 524-5700	13816
Visionstep Consulting Inc	Fitchburg	MA	F	978 422-1447	8681
Vidarr Inc	Portsmouth	NH	G	877 636-8432	15448
Admiral Packaging Inc	Providence	RI	D	401 274-5588	16464
Judd Paper Company	Rumford	RI	F	413 534-5661	16673
Wcm LLC	Providence	RI	F	401 273-0444	16644
Bees Wrap LLC	Middlebury	VT	E	802 643-2132	17338
K&H Group Inc	Bennington	VT	C	802 442-5455	17045

5122 Drugs, proprietaries, and sundries

	CITY	ST	EMP	PHONE	ENTRY#
Beiersdorf North America Inc (DH)	Stamford	CT	F	203 563-5800	3292
Boom LLC	New Canaan	CT	E	212 317-2005	2076
Crabtree & Evelyn Ltd (DH)	Woodstock	CT	C	800 272-2933	4393
First Aid Bandage Co Inc	New London	CT	E	860 443-8499	2228
Frederick Purdue Company Inc (PA)	Stamford	CT	B	203 588-8000	3349
Knoa Pharma LLC (PA)	Stamford	CT	E	203 588-8000	3395
Mantrose-Haeuser Co Inc (HQ)	Westport	CT	E	203 454-1800	4182
Pharmaceutical RES Assoc Inc	Stamford	CT	A	203 588-8000	3431
PRA Holdings Inc	Stamford	CT	A	203 853-0123	3435
Purdue Pharma LP (HQ)	Stamford	CT	C	203 588-8000	3439
Sheffield Pharmaceuticals LLC (PA)	New London	CT	E	860 442-4451	2233
T N Dickinson Company	East Hampton	CT	F	860 267-2279	966
Amylyx Pharmaceuticals Inc (PA)	Cambridge	MA	C	617 682-0917	7486
Batavia Biosciences Inc	Woburn	MA	G	781 305-3921	13521
Bedrock Brands LLC	Boston	MA	G	914 231-9550	6587
Beigene Usa Inc (HQ)	Cambridge	MA	E	781 801-1887	7503
Central Admxture Phrm Svcs Inc	Woburn	MA	G	781 376-0032	13541
Corvidia Therapeutics Inc	Waltham	MA	G	781 205-4755	12642
Covidien LP (HQ)	Mansfield	MA	C	763 514-4000	10046
Encyte Systems Inc	Braintree	MA	G	781 848-6772	7180
GE Healthcare Inc (HQ)	Marlborough	MA	B	732 457-8667	10152
Genzyme Corporation (DH)	Cambridge	MA	A	617 252-7500	7585
Genzyme Corporation	Framingham	MA	E	617 252-7500	8773
Grooming Ventures - FL LLC (HQ)	Boston	MA	D	305 593-0667	6774
Iredale Cosmetics (PA)	Great Barrington	MA	D	413 644-9900	8976
MBL International Corporation (DH)	Woburn	MA	F	781 939-6964	13607
Progderm Inc	Boston	MA	F	617 419-1800	6982
Pure Encapsulations LLC	Sudbury	MA	E	800 753-2277	12269
Rare Beauty Brands Inc (PA)	Norwood	MA	F	888 243-0646	11205
Revela Inc	Woburn	MA	G	716 725-2657	13651
Sanofi Pasteur Biologics LLC	Canton	MA	D	781 302-3000	7824
Sobi Inc	Waltham	MA	F	781 786-7370	12781
Triseptagon LLC	Springfield	MA	F	413 732-2131	12144
Westwell Incorporated (DH)	Wellesley	MA	D	800 753-2277	12948
Brickell Brands LLC	South Portland	ME	D	877 598-0060	5492
Desert Harvest Inc	Ellsworth	ME	F	919 245-1853	4756
Downeast Concepts Inc	Yarmouth	ME	F	207 846-3726	5703
Meridian Life Science Inc (HQ)	Saco	ME	G	207 283-6500	5373
Boston Ntrceutical Science LLC	Providence	RI	F	617 848-4560	16488
G&G Technologies Inc	Coventry	RI	F	401 295-4000	15813
Sea-Band International Inc	Newport	RI	G	401 841-5900	16222
Surplus Solutions LLC	Woonsocket	RI	F	401 526-0055	16978
Foodscience LLC (HQ)	Williston	VT	C	800 451-5190	17731
Seventh Generation Inc (DH)	Burlington	VT	C	802 658-3773	17159

5131 Piece goods and notions

	CITY	ST	EMP	PHONE	ENTRY#
Donghia Inc	Milford	CT	C	800 366-4442	1818
Fortis Solutions Group LLC	Ellington	CT	E	860 872-6311	1107
Harding Company Inc	Putnam	CT	F	860 928-0475	2860
Patricia Spratt For Home LLC	Old Lyme	CT	F	860 434-9291	2644
Soapstone Media Inc	Ellington	CT	F	860 749-0455	1116
Thomas W Raftery Inc	Hartford	CT	F	860 278-9870	1514
Accent Banner LLC	Medford	MA	F	781 391-7300	10278
Emtex Inc	Peabody	MA	F	978 907-4500	11309
Microfibres Inc	Foxboro	MA	F	401 725-4883	8708
Precision Coating Co Inc (HQ)	Hudson	MA	E	781 329-1420	9404
Time-Out Sports Inc	Whitman	MA	F	781 447-6670	13350
Bosal Foam and Fiber (PA)	Limerick	ME	E	207 793-2245	5000
Fiber Materials Inc (DH)	Biddeford	ME	C	207 282-5911	4564

	CITY	ST	EMP	PHONE	ENTRY#
Custom Banner & Graphics LLC	Rochester	NH	G	603 332-2067	15472
American Cord & Webbing Co Inc	Woonsocket	RI	E	401 762-5500	16948

5136 Men's and boy's clothing

	CITY	ST	EMP	PHONE	ENTRY#
Del Arbour LLC	Milford	CT	F	203 882-8501	1817
Gima LLC	Hartford	CT	F	860 296-4441	1483
Nicks Enterprises Inc (PA)	Hamden	CT	F	203 287-9990	1447
Accurate Services Inc	Fall River	MA	E	508 674-5773	8518
Advanced Print Technology Inc	Fitchburg	MA	G	978 342-0093	8640
Austins Sportswear Inc	West Yarmouth	MA	F	508 775-0554	13071
Birch Outfitters LLC	Salem	MA	F	978 498-4631	11703
Corporate Casuals LLC	Concord	MA	F	978 369-5935	8110
Piesco Sporting Goods Inc	North Easton	MA	F	508 238-5599	11012
Sickday Inc	Wellfleet	MA	F	508 214-4158	12953
Soft-As-A-grape Inc (PA)	Wareham	MA	E	508 295-9900	12844
Top Half Inc	Tyngsboro	MA	F	978 454-5440	12468
Highland Belts & Fine Lea Gds	Brewer	ME	F	207 989-2597	4614
Rodco Enterprises	Lewiston	ME	F	207 786-2931	4990
Woodland Studios Inc	Ellsworth	ME	F	207 667-3286	4761
Business Shirtmasters	Chichester	NH	F	603 798-3787	14072
G-Form LLC (HQ)	Providence	RI	E	401 250-5555	16523
New York Accessory Group Inc	Bristol	RI	D	401 245-6096	15776
Squadlocker Inc	Warwick	RI	D	888 885-6253	16864
Cabot Hosiery Mills Inc (PA)	Northfield	VT	F	802 485-6066	17432
Outfitters Inc Corporate	Saint Albans	VT	G	802 527-0204	17528
Vermont Flannel Co (PA)	East Barre	VT	F	802 476-5226	17215

5137 Women's and children's clothing

	CITY	ST	EMP	PHONE	ENTRY#
Del Arbour LLC	Milford	CT	F	203 882-8501	1817
Accurate Services Inc	Fall River	MA	E	508 674-5773	8518
Action Apparel Inc	Stoneham	MA	G	781 435-2342	12173
Advanced Print Technology Inc	Fitchburg	MA	G	978 342-0093	8640
Austins Sportswear Inc	West Yarmouth	MA	F	508 775-0554	13071
Birch Outfitters LLC	Salem	MA	F	978 498-4631	11703
Broder Bros Co	Middleboro	MA	C	508 923-4800	10352
Cause For Change LLC	Sudbury	MA	E	617 571-6990	12262
Image Factory	Pocasset	MA	G	508 295-3876	11489
Mahi Gold Inc	Chatham	MA	F	508 348-5487	7898
Piesco Sporting Goods Inc	North Easton	MA	F	508 238-5599	11012
Shop Therapy Imports	Provincetown	MA	G	508 487-8970	11497
Soft-As-A-grape Inc (PA)	Wareham	MA	E	508 295-9900	12844
Imeldas Fabrics & Designs	New Sharon	ME	G	207 778-0665	5090
New York Accessory Group Inc	Bristol	RI	D	401 245-6096	15776
Officers Equipment Company	Providence	RI	F	703 221-1912	16580
Samsonite Company Stores LLC	Warren	RI	F	401 247-3301	16768
Squadlocker Inc	Warwick	RI	D	888 885-6253	16864
Cabot Hosiery Mills Inc (PA)	Northfield	VT	D	802 485-6066	17432
Cornell Online LLC	Burlington	VT	E	802 448-3281	17128
Nomad Communications Inc 17709	White River Junction	VT	F	802 649-1995	
Outfitters Inc Corporate	Saint Albans	VT	G	802 527-0204	17528
Vermont Flannel Co (PA)	East Barre	VT	F	802 476-5226	17215

5139 Footwear

	CITY	ST	EMP	PHONE	ENTRY#
Black Diamond Group Inc	Woburn	MA	F	781 939-7824	13527
C & J Clark America Inc (DH)	Waltham	MA	B	617 964-1222	12617
C & J Clark Latin America	Waltham	MA	A	617 243-4100	12618
Modern Shoe Company LLC	Hyde Park	MA	F	617 333-7470	9464
Stride Rite Corporation (HQ)	Waltham	MA	B	617 824-6000	12783
Hbn Shoe LLC	Salem	NH	G	603 622-0272	15536
White Mountain Intl LLC (PA)	Lisbon	NH	F	603 838-6694	14711
Forsake Inc	Stowe	VT	G	585 576-6358	17631

5141 Groceries, general line

	CITY	ST	EMP	PHONE	ENTRY#
Norpaco Inc	Middletown	CT	D	860 632-2299	1768
Albano Sales Inc	North Billerica	MA	F	978 667-9100	10895
Cambridge Packing Co Inc	Boston	MA	D	617 464-6000	6635
Colony Foods Inc	Lawrence	MA	E	978 794-1500	9553
Dahlicious Holdings LLC	Leominster	MA	F	978 401-2103	9656
Pvk Inc	Lynn	MA	F	781 595-7771	9989
Wohrles Foods Inc (PA)	Pittsfield	MA	E	413 442-1518	11427
B Del Toro & Sons Inc	Providence	RI	F	401 421-5820	16481
Portion Meat Associates Inc	Providence	RI	F	401 421-2438	16585
Supreme Dairy Farms	Woonsocket	RI	F	401 739-8180	16977
Back Roads Food Co LLC	Brattleboro	VT	F	802 579-1135	17074

5142 Packaged frozen goods

	CITY	ST	EMP	PHONE	ENTRY#
Cambridge Packing Co Inc	Boston	MA	D	617 464-6000	6635
F W Bryce Inc (DH)	Gloucester	MA	E	978 283-7080	8934
Willow Tree Poultry Farm Inc	Attleboro	MA	D	508 222-2479	6077
Wohrles Foods Inc (PA)	Pittsfield	MA	E	413 442-1518	11427
Getchell Bros Inc	Sanford	ME	F	207 490-0809	5397

5143 Dairy products, except dried or canned

	CITY	ST	EMP	PHONE	ENTRY#
Guida-Seibert Dairy Company (HQ)	New Britain	CT	C	800 832-8929	2028
Mozzicato Fmly Investments LLC	Wethersfield	CT	F	860 296-0426	4212
Ndr Liuzzi Inc	Hamden	CT	E	203 287-8477	1445
295 Tremont Inc	Attleboro	MA	D	508 222-2884	5985
Albano Sales Inc	North Billerica	MA	F	978 667-9100	10895
Brighams Inc (HQ)	Arlington	MA	F	800 242-2423	5939
Colony Foods Inc	Lawrence	MA	E	978 794-1500	9553
Freeze Operations Holding Corp (PA)	Wilbraham	MA	A	413 543-2445	13360
Hershey Creamery Company	Seekonk	MA	F	508 399-8560	11777
Casco Bay Butter Company Inc	Westbrook	ME	G	207 712-9148	5620
Getchell Bros Inc (PA)	Brewer	ME	E	800 949-4423	4613
Getchell Bros Inc	Sanford	ME	F	207 490-0809	5397
Oakhurst Dairy (HQ)	Portland	ME	C	207 772-7468	5253
Shains	Sanford	ME	D	207 324-1449	5415
Annblles Ntral Ice Cream Ygur	Portsmouth	NH	G	603 436-3400	15359
Sunrise Foods Incorporated	Brentwood	NH	F	603 772-4420	14031
Cabot Creamery Cooperative Inc	Waitsfield	VT	B	888 792-2268	17664
H P Hood-Booth Brothers Dairy	Barre	VT	F	802 476-6605	17004
Monument Farms Inc	Weybridge	VT	E	802 545-2119	17703
Vermonts Orginal Ice Cream Inc	Arlington	VT	G	802 375-1133	16992

5144 Poultry and poultry products

	CITY	ST	EMP	PHONE	ENTRY#
Carls Boned Chicken Inc	New Haven	CT	E	203 777-9048	2135
Moark LLC (HQ)	North Franklin	CT	E	951 332-3300	2383
Radlo Foods LLC (PA)	Watertown	MA	G	617 926-7070	12903
Samuel Holmes Incorporated	Everett	MA	F	617 269-5740	8500
Somerville Live Poultry Co Inc	Boston	MA	G	617 547-9191	7045

5145 Confectionery

	CITY	ST	EMP	PHONE	ENTRY#
Thompson Brands LLC	Meriden	CT	D	203 235-2541	1708
Everson Distributing Co Inc	Worcester	MA	E	413 533-9261	13721
Frito-Lay North America Inc	Wilmington	MA	F	978 657-8344	13408
Stage Stop Candy Ltd Inc	Dennis Port	MA	G	508 394-1791	8263
Grandy Organics LLC (PA)	Hiram	ME	E	207 935-7415	4890
Wilburs ME Choclat Confections	Freeport	ME	E	207 865-4071	4805
Fredericks Pastries (PA)	Amherst	NH	F	603 882-7725	13871
Granite State Candy Shoppe LLC (PA)	Concord	NH	F	603 225-2591	14131
Tom and Sallys Handmade Choco	Westerly	RI	F	800 289-8783	16944
Tradest1	East Greenwich	RI	G	401 884-4949	15994
Quirion Luc (PA)	Newport	VT	G	802 673-8386	17406

5146 Fish and seafoods

	CITY	ST	EMP	PHONE	ENTRY#
Cambridge Packing Co Inc	Boston	MA	D	617 464-6000	6635
Hannah Boden Corp	New Bedford	MA	F	508 992-3334	10598
Jordan Bros Seafood Co Inc	Boston	MA	F	508 583-9797	6831
National Fish and Seafood Inc	Gloucester	MA	B	978 282-7880	8944
North Coast Sea-Foods Corp (PA)	Boston	MA	C	617 345-4400	6925
Northern Wind LLC (HQ)	New Bedford	MA	D	508 997-0727	10635
Ocean Crest Seafoods Inc (PA)	Gloucester	MA	E	978 281-0232	8949
Sea Star Seafood Corp	Marlborough	MA	E		10209
Southeast Shellfish Inc	Wareham	MA	F	508 273-0323	12845
Wohrles Foods Inc (PA)	Pittsfield	MA	E	413 442-1518	11427
Bristol Seafood LLC (HQ)	Portland	ME	F	207 761-4251	5192
Bristol Seafood Holdings Inc (PA)	Portland	ME	D	207 761-4251	5193
Browne Trading Co	Portland	ME	E	207 766-2402	5194
Carver Shellfish Inc	Beals	ME	E	207 497-2261	4532
Inland Fresh Sfood Corp Amer I	South Portland	ME	F	207 546-7591	5506
Isf Trading Inc	Portland	ME	C	207 879-1575	5228
Looks Gourmet Food Co Inc (HQ)	Machias	ME	F	207 259-3341	5031
North Atlantic Inc	Portland	ME	G	207 774-6025	5252
High Liner Foods USA Inc	Portsmouth	NH	F	603 818-5555	15403
Tri-State Seafoods Inc	Somersworth	NH	F	603 692-7201	15627
American Mussel Harvesters Inc	North Kingstown	RI	E	401 294-8999	16230
Endeavor Seafood LLC	Newport	RI	E	401 841-8637	16209
Ngc Inc (PA)	Narragansett	RI	D	401 789-2200	16192
South Pier Fish Company Inc	Narragansett	RI	F	401 783-6611	16196
Tase-Rite Co Inc	Wakefield	RI	F	401 783-7300	16746

5147 Meats and meat products

	CITY	ST	EMP	PHONE	ENTRY#
App Polonia LLC	Plainville	CT	G	860 747-3397	2747
Baretta Provision Inc	East Berlin	CT	F	860 828-0802	908
Jbs Aves Ltda	Stamford	CT	F	203 357-5920	3390
Manchester Packing Company Inc	Manchester	CT	D	860 646-5000	1616
Cambridge Packing Co Inc	Boston	MA	D	617 464-6000	6635
Chicopee Provision Company Inc	Chicopee	MA	E	413 594-4765	8016
Colony Foods Inc	Lawrence	MA	E	978 794-1500	9553
DOro Foods Inc	Malden	MA	E	781 324-1310	10011
Home Market Foods Inc	Norwood	MA	B	781 948-1500	11176
Kelly Corned Beef Co Chicago	Norwood	MA	F	773 588-2882	11188
Lisbon Sausage Co Inc	New Bedford	MA	F	508 993-7645	10613
New England Box Beef Company	Taunton	MA	E	781 320-3232	12352

	CITY	ST	EMP	PHONE	ENTRY#
Wohrles Foods Inc (PA)	Pittsfield	MA	E	413 442-1518	11427
Native Maine Operations Inc	Westbrook	ME	E	207 856-1100	5640
Bp Inc	Providence	RI	E	401 274-7900	16490
Lincoln Packing Co	Cranston	RI	C	401 943-0878	15885
Quality Beef Co Inc	Providence	RI	F	401 421-5668	16596
Tase-Rite Co Inc	Wakefield	RI	F	401 783-7300	16746
Vermont Packinghouse LLC	North Springfield	VT	F	802 886-8688	17426

5148 Fresh fruits and vegetables

	CITY	ST	EMP	PHONE	ENTRY#
Gracies Kitchens Inc	New Haven	CT	F	203 773-0795	2156
Garden Fresh Salad Co Inc	Chelsea	MA	E	617 889-1580	7982
Native Maine Operations Inc	Westbrook	ME	E	207 856-1100	5640
Spear Farms Inc	Nobleboro	ME	E	207 832-4488	5101
B Del Toro & Sons Inc	Providence	RI	F	401 421-5820	16481
Taylor Farms New England Inc	North Kingstown	RI	E	877 323-7374	16284

5149 Groceries and related products, nec

	CITY	ST	EMP	PHONE	ENTRY#
Apicellas Bakery Inc	New Haven	CT	E	203 865-6204	2116
Blue Buffalo Company Ltd (DH)	Wilton	CT	D	203 762-9751	4233
Cofco Americas Resources Corp (HQ)	Stamford	CT	F	203 658-2820	3316
Crabtree & Evelyn Ltd (DH)	Woodstock	CT	C	800 272-2873	4393
Crystal Rock Spring Water Co	Watertown	CT	B	860 945-0661	4007
D & M Packing LLC	Waterbury	CT	E	203 591-8986	3903
G & G Beverage Distributors	Yalesville	CT	E	203 949-6220	4397
Gracies Kitchens Inc	New Haven	CT	F	203 773-0795	2156
Guida-Seibert Dairy Company (HQ)	New Britain	CT	C	800 832-8929	2028
Herbasway Laboratories LLC	Wallingford	CT	F	203 269-6991	3812
Jmf Group LLC	East Windsor	CT	D	860 627-7003	1077
Mozzicato Pastry & Bake Sp Inc	Hartford	CT	E	860 296-0426	1495
Old Lyme Gourmet Company	Deep River	CT	E	860 434-7347	879
Omar Coffee Company	Newington	CT	E	860 667-8889	2312
Pasta Vita Inc	Old Saybrook	CT	G	860 395-1452	2658
Saccuzzo Company Inc	Newington	CT	G	860 665-1101	2323
Superior Bakery Inc	North Grosvenordale	CT	E	860 923-9555	2387
Battle Grounds Coffee Co LLC	Haverhill	MA	F	978 891-5860	9077
Boston Chipyard The Inc	Boston	MA	E	617 742-9537	6607
Boyajian Inc	Canton	MA	F	781 828-9966	7774
Buzzards Bay Brewing Inc	Westport	MA	G	508 636-2288	13294
Cape Cod Ginger LLC	Wareham	MA	G	508 295-2795	12830
Chmuras Bakery Inc (PA)	Indian Orchard	MA	F	413 543-2521	9471
Coca-Cola Bevs Northeast Inc	Sandwich	MA	E	508 888-0001	11749
Coca-Cola Refreshments USA Inc	Greenfield	MA	F	413 772-2617	8988
Comfort Foods Inc	North Andover	MA	F	978 557-0009	10825
Dunajski Dairy Inc	Peabody	MA	F	978 531-1457	11308
East Baking Company Inc	Holyoke	MA	C	413 536-2300	9252
Easton Springs Corporation	South Easton	MA	F	508 238-2741	11942
George Howell Coffee Co LLC	Acton	MA	F	978 635-9033	5748
Healthy Truth LLC	Walpole	MA	E	774 256-5800	12560
James C Cannell Coffees Inc	West Wareham	MA	F	508 295-7009	13066
Jedwards International Inc (PA)	Braintree	MA	E	617 340-9461	7191
La Patisserie Inc	Revere	MA	F	781 729-9441	11621
Lqc Inc	Norwood	MA	G	617 586-5139	11191
Mange LLC	Somerville	MA	G	917 880-2104	11885
Mike Sheas Cffhuse Trdtnals In	Fairhaven	MA	F	508 807-5754	8509
New England Partnership Inc	Norwood	MA	C	800 225-3537	11199
North Star Distributors Inc (PA)	Vineyard Haven	MA	E	508 693-2000	12494
Olivenation LLC (PA)	Avon	MA	F	781 351-1499	6156
Pasta Bene Inc	Brockton	MA	F	508 583-1515	7300
Polar Corp (PA)	Worcester	MA	A	508 753-6383	13772
Pvk Inc	Lynn	MA	F	781 595-7771	9989
Rohtstein Corp (PA)	Woburn	MA	D	781 935-8300	13655
Tatte Holdings LLC	Boston	MA	C	617 577-1111	7070
Vitasoy USA Inc	Woburn	MA	C	781 430-8988	13686
Maine Coast Sea Vegetables Inc	Hancock	ME	E	207 412-0094	4871
Native Maine Operations Inc	Westbrook	ME	E	207 856-1100	5640
Northeast Merchandising Corp	Skowhegan	ME	E	207 474-3321	5476
R & N Inc	Unity	ME	G	207 948-2613	5567
Stonewall Kitchen LLC (PA)	York	ME	C	207 351-2713	5717
Bascom Maple Farms Inc (PA)	Alstead	NH	D	603 835-2230	13856
Coca-Cola Bevs Northeast Inc	Londonderry	NH	E	603 437-3530	14735
Craft Beer Guild LLC	Portsmouth	NH	E	603 319-8508	15377
Dutch Gold Honey Inc	Littleton	NH	F	603 444-6246	14717
Fredericks Pastries (PA)	Amherst	NH	F	603 882-7725	13871
Granite State Candy Shoppe LLC (PA)	Concord	NH	F	603 225-2591	14131
Lindt & Sprungli (usa) Inc (HQ)	Stratham	NH	C	603 778-8100	15637
Monadnock Mountain Spring Water Inc	Wilton	NH	D	603 654-2728	15706
Coca-Cola Refreshments USA Inc	Providence	RI	E	401 331-1981	16501
Edesia Industries LLC	North Kingstown	RI	D	401 272-5521	16249
Excellent Coffee Co Inc (PA)	Pawtucket	RI	C	401 724-6393	16367
Henry Gonsalves Co	Smithfield	RI	E	401 231-6700	16709
Mills Coffee Roasting Co	Providence	RI	G	401 781-7860	16565
Ann Clark Ltd	Rutland	VT	E	802 773-7886	17489

	CITY	ST	EMP	PHONE	ENTRY#
BB&c Wholesale LLC (PA)	Bristol	VT	F	802 453-7708	17114
Birnn Chocolates Vermont Inc	South Burlington	VT	F	802 860-1047	17573
Cold Hollow Cider Mill Inc	Waterbury Center	VT	E	802 244-8771	17680
Commonwealth Dairy LLC	Guilford	VT	D	802 251-2300	17280
Fudge Factory Inc	Manchester Center	VT	F	888 669-7425	17328
Highland Sugarworks Inc	Websterville	VT	E	802 479-1747	17684
Klingers Bread Company	South Burlington	VT	E	802 860-6322	17582
Runamok Maple LLC	Fairfax	VT	E	802 849-7943	17263
Sogle Property LLC	Cambridge	VT	E	802 849-7943	17168

5153 Grain and field beans

	CITY	ST	EMP	PHONE	ENTRY#
Bridgwell Rsurces Holdings LLC (HQ)	Greenwich	CT	E	203 622-9138	1322
Central Conn Cooperative Farme	South Windsor	CT	F	860 649-4523	3127
Cofco Americas Resources Corp (HQ)	Stamford	CT	F	203 658-2820	3316
Louis Dreyfus Holdg Co US LLC (HQ)	Wilton	CT	B	203 761-2000	4242
New England Tortilla Inc	Boston	MA	E	617 889-6462	6917
TruRoots LLC (PA)	Needham	MA	E	800 288-3637	10527
Feed Commodities Intl Inc (HQ)	Middlebury	VT	E	800 639-3191	17343
Poulin Grain Inc	Swanton	VT	E	802 868-3323	17640
Poulin Grain Inc (PA)	Newport	VT	D	802 334-6731	17404

5159 Farm-product raw materials, nec

	CITY	ST	EMP	PHONE	ENTRY#
CSC Sugar LLC	Westport	CT	E	203 846-5610	4163
Nuway Tobacco Company	South Windsor	CT	D	860 289-6414	3167

5162 Plastics materials and basic shapes

	CITY	ST	EMP	PHONE	ENTRY#
Delmar Products Inc	Berlin	CT	F	860 828-6501	64
Edco Industries Inc	Bridgeport	CT	F	203 333-8982	319
Extec Corp	Enfield	CT	F	860 741-3435	1133
Neu Spclty Engineered Mtls LLC	North Haven	CT	F	203 239-9629	2426
Nevamar Company LLC (HQ)	Shelton	CT	B	203 925-1556	3037
Orafol Americas Inc	Avon	CT	C	860 676-7100	35
Thornton and Company Inc	Southington	CT	F	860 628-6771	3237
Web Industries Hartford Inc (HQ)	Dayville	CT	E	860 779-3197	870
Atlantic Poly Inc	Norwood	MA	F	781 769-4260	11163
Covestro LLC	Wilmington	MA	C	800 458-0014	13399
DSM Neoresins Inc	Wilmington	MA	C	800 458-0014	13403
Eastman Performance Films LLC	Holliston	MA	E	508 474-6002	9208
Fluorolite Plastics LLC	Hudson	MA	F	508 788-1200	9368
Kilder Corporation	North Billerica	MA	E	978 663-8800	10922
Millennium Plastics Inc	North Chelmsford	MA	F	978 372-4822	10984
Pacific Packaging Products Inc (PA)	Wilmington	MA	C	978 657-9100	13445
Plastic Concepts Inc	North Billerica	MA	E	978 663-7996	10943
Plastic Design Inc	North Chelmsford	MA	E	978 251-4830	10987
Plastics Unlimited of MA Inc	Worcester	MA	D	508 752-7842	13770
Polymer Corporation (HQ)	Rockland	MA	D	781 871-4606	11656
Tri-Star Plastics Corp (PA)	Shrewsbury	MA	E	508 845-1111	11845
Web Industries Inc (PA)	Marlborough	MA	G	508 898-2988	10234
Morris Transparent Box Co	East Providence	RI	F	401 438-6116	16032
Seventh Generation Inc (DH)	Burlington	VT	C	802 658-3773	17159

5169 Chemicals and allied products, nec

	CITY	ST	EMP	PHONE	ENTRY#
Airgas Usa LLC	Danbury	CT	C	203 792-1834	705
Arcadia Chem Preservative LLC	Shelton	CT	F	203 717-4750	2982
Auburn Manufacturing Company	Middletown	CT	E	860 346-6677	1737
Connecticut Analytical Corp	Bethany	CT	F	203 393-9666	92
Engineered Fibers Tech LLC	Shelton	CT	F	203 922-1810	3005
Greenfield Global USA Inc (HQ)	Brookfield	CT	F	203 740-3471	524
Hubbard-Hall Inc (PA)	Waterbury	CT	D	203 756-5521	3919
Kolmar Americas Inc (HQ)	Bridgeport	CT	F	203 873-2051	341
Lanxess Corporation	Naugatuck	CT	E	203 714-8669	1970
Miyoshi America Inc (HQ)	Dayville	CT	D	860 779-3990	863
Near Oak LLC	Stamford	CT	G	203 329-6500	3415
New England Tooling Inc	Killingworth	CT	E	800 866-5105	1544
RT Vanderbilt Holding Co Inc (PA)	Norwalk	CT	F	203 295-2141	2568
Seaview Plastic Recycling Inc	Bridgeport	CT	F	203 367-0070	370
Shlomo Enterprises Inc (PA)	Enfield	CT	G	860 265-7995	1150
Total Specialty Chemicals Inc (PA)	New Canaan	CT	E	203 966-1525	2089
US Chemicals Inc	New Canaan	CT	G	203 655-8878	2093
Vanderbilt Chemicals LLC (HQ)	Norwalk	CT	E	203 295-2141	2589
A W Chesterton Company (PA)	Groveland	MA	E	781 438-7000	9012
Airgas Usa LLC	Billerica	MA	F	978 439-1344	6398
B&C Cryotech Services Inc	Sutton	MA	G	508 277-5440	12277
Blank Industries LLC	Hudson	MA	E	855 887-3123	9356
Borden & Remington Corp	Fall River	MA	E	508 675-0096	8528
Cryogenic Institute Neng Inc	Worcester	MA	F	508 459-7447	13712
Fisher Scientific Intl LLC (HQ)	Waltham	MA	C	781 622-1000	12675
Guardian Indus Pdts Inc Mass	Norfolk	MA	G	508 384-0060	10798
Hubbard-Hall Inc	Wilmington	MA	F	978 988-0077	13411
Lubrizol Global Management Inc	Wilmington	MA	C	978 642-5051	13427
MD Stetson Company Inc	Mansfield	MA	E	781 986-6161	10066
Parker & Bailey Corp	Walpole	MA	F	508 660-0011	12572
Redi-Mix Services Incorporated	Taunton	MA	F	508 823-0771	12361

S
I
C

	CITY	ST	EMP	PHONE	ENTRY#
Safc Hitech Inc	Haverhill	MA	E	978 374-5200	9130
Savin Products Company Inc	Randolph	MA	E	781 961-2743	11574
Shield Packaging Co Inc	Dudley	MA	E	508 949-0900	8323
The Savogran Company	Norwood	MA	E	781 762-5400	11216
Avient Colorants USA LLC	Lewiston	ME	B	207 784-0733	4951
Gac Chemical Corporation (PA)	Searsport	ME	D	207 548-2525	5453
Harcros Chemicals Inc	Westbrook	ME	G	207 856-6756	5627
Allstate Polyethylene Corp (PA)	Alexandria	NH	G	800 288-7659	13851
Appli-Tec Inc	Salem	NH	E	603 685-0500	15508
Gates Tpu Inc	Salem	NH	E	603 890-1515	15531
Agilent Technologies Inc	North Kingstown	RI	D	800 338-1754	16229
Electrolizing Inc	Providence	RI	E	401 861-5900	16513
Simply Safer Products LLC	Providence	RI	F	401 474-4957	16611
Ultra Scientific Incorporated	North Kingstown	RI	E	800 338-1754	16290
Univar Solutions USA Inc	Providence	RI	E	518 762-3500	16633
QST Inc	Saint Albans	VT	E	802 524-7704	17529
Seventh Generation Inc (DH)	Burlington	VT	C	802 658-3773	17159

5172 Petroleum products, nec

	CITY	ST	EMP	PHONE	ENTRY#
Anz Petroleum Inc	New Milford	CT	F	860 261-4798	2238
Eagle Ship Management LLC (HQ)	Stamford	CT	C	203 276-8100	3340
Equinor US Holdings Inc (DH)	Stamford	CT	C	203 978-6900	3345
Arclight Enrgy Prtners Fund VI (PA)	Boston	MA	E	617 531-6300	6557
Cumberland Farms Inc (DH)	Westborough	MA	B	800 225-9702	13097
Ray Murray Inc (PA)	Lee	MA	D	413 243-2164	9619
Roses Oil Service Inc (PA)	Gloucester	MA	E	877 283-3334	8955
Safety-Kleen Systems Inc (HQ)	Norwell	MA	B	800 669-5740	11146
Highlands Fuel Delivery LLC (HQ)	Portsmouth	NH	D	603 559-8700	15404

5181 Beer and ale

	CITY	ST	EMP	PHONE	ENTRY#
A & I Concentrate LLC	Shelton	CT	E	203 447-1938	2977
G & G Beverage Distributors	Yalesville	CT	E	203 949-6220	4397
Harpoon Distributing Co Inc	Boston	MA	F	617 574-9551	6781
Murder Hill LLC (PA)	Whitinsville	MA	G	774 757-4411	13342
Capitol Distributors Inc	Bow	NH	F	603 223-2086	13995
Finestkind Brewing LLC	Hampton	NH	D	603 436-4026	14402
Smuttynose Brewing Company Inc	Hampton	NH	D	603 436-4026	14413
Martignetti Companies RI	Central Falls	RI	C	401 722-8008	15792
Fiddlehead Brewing Company LLC	Shelburne	VT	F	802 489-5090	17557

5182 Wine and distilled beverages

	CITY	ST	EMP	PHONE	ENTRY#
Truro Vineyards Cape Cod LLC	North Truro	MA	F	508 487-6200	11051
Viva Beverages Inc	Boston	MA	F	617 712-3488	7108
All Night Long Inc	Newport	RI	F	860 306-3189	16199
Johnson Brothers RI Inc	North Kingstown	RI	F	401 583-0050	16262
Martignetti Companies RI	Central Falls	RI	C	401 722-8008	15792
Sakonnet Vineyards LP	Little Compton	RI	F	401 635-8486	16162
Caledonia Spirits Inc	Montpelier	VT	E	802 472-8000	17370

5191 Farm supplies

	CITY	ST	EMP	PHONE	ENTRY#
Central Conn Cooperative Farme	South Windsor	CT	E	860 649-4523	3127
Clinton Nursery Products Inc (PA)	Westbrook	CT	C	860 399-3000	4137
Grillo Services LLC	Milford	CT	E	203 877-5070	1831
H J Baker & Bro Inc	Westport	CT	B	203 682-9200	4171
HJ Baker & Bro LLC (PA)	Shelton	CT	B	203 682-9200	3014
Pic20 Group LLC	Norwalk	CT	F	203 957-3555	2558
Waterbury Companies Inc	Waterbury	CT	C		3980
Conrad Fafard Inc	Agawam	MA	A	413 786-4343	5788
I B A Inc (PA)	Sutton	MA	E	508 865-6911	12281
Sun Gro Holdings Inc	Agawam	MA	E	413 786-4343	5809
Sports Fields Inc	Monmouth	ME	F	207 933-3547	5072
Rimol Greenhouse Systems Inc	Hooksett	NH	F	603 629-9004	14474
Americas Grdening Resource Inc (PA)	Burlington	VT	C	802 660-3500	17117
Americas Grdening Resource Inc	Milton	VT	C	802 660-3500	17354
Cargill Incorporated	Swanton	VT	A	802 868-3232	17636
Mill River Lumber Ltd	North Clarendon	VT	D	802 775-0032	17417
Shelburne Limestone Corp (PA)	Colchester	VT	F	802 878-2656	17203

5192 Books, periodicals, and newspapers

	CITY	ST	EMP	PHONE	ENTRY#
Scholastic Inc (DH)	Danbury	CT	D	212 343-6100	811
Scholastic Library Pubg Inc (HQ)	Danbury	CT	A	203 797-3500	812
Cheng & Tsui Co Inc	Boston	MA	F	617 988-2400	6649
Courier Companies Inc (PA)	North Chelmsford	MA	F	978 251-6000	10969
Horizon House Publications Inc (PA)	Norwood	MA	D	781 769-9750	11177
Quarto Pubg Group USA Inc	Beverly	MA	F	425 827-7120	6375
Redwheel/Weiser LLC (PA)	Newburyport	MA	G	978 465-0504	10712
Robert Bentley Inc	Cambridge	MA	F	617 547-4170	7698
Storey Publishing LLC (DH)	Clarksburg	MA	E	413 346-2100	8074
Sundance Newbridge Publishing	Marlborough	MA	F	508 303-3920	10218
Westborough Books Inc (PA)	Westborough	MA	E	508 366-4292	13144

5193 Flowers and florists supplies

	CITY	ST	EMP	PHONE	ENTRY#
Clinton Nursery Products Inc (PA)	Westbrook	CT	C	860 399-3000	4137

	CITY	ST	EMP	PHONE	ENTRY#
Mc Cann Bros Inc	Monroe	CT	F	203 335-8630	1916
Shemin Nurseries Inc	Lexington	MA	E	781 861-1111	9771

5194 Tobacco and tobacco products

	CITY	ST	EMP	PHONE	ENTRY#
Consumer Product Distrs LLC	Stratford	CT	G	203 378-2193	3531
Foundation Cigar Company LLC	Ellington	CT	G	203 738-9377	1108
Hay Island Holding Corporation (PA)	Darien	CT	C	203 656-8000	847
Smokey Mountain Chew Inc	Darien	CT	C	203 304-9200	855

5198 Paints, varnishes, and supplies

	CITY	ST	EMP	PHONE	ENTRY#
Color Craft Ltd	East Granby	CT	F	800 509-6563	929
Donghia Inc	Milford	CT	C	800 366-4442	1818
Grafted Coatings Inc	Stratford	CT	F	203 377-9979	3543
Advanced Frp Systems Inc	East Weymouth	MA	G	508 927-6915	8423
Detrapel Inc	Framingham	MA	F	617 514-7778	8757
Maki Corp (PA)	Gardner	MA	E	978 343-7422	8895
Merida Meridian Inc	Boston	MA	E	617 464-5400	6885
Chilton Paint Co Inc ME	Freeport	ME	G	207 865-4443	4800

5199 Nondurable goods, nec

	CITY	ST	EMP	PHONE	ENTRY#
Color Craft Ltd	East Granby	CT	F	800 509-6563	929
Concord Industries Inc	Norwalk	CT	E	203 750-6060	2485
Executive Greetings Inc (HQ)	New Hartford	CT	B	860 379-9911	2100
Greenwich Workshop Inc (PA)	Seymour	CT	E	203 881-3336	2961
Hudson Paper Company (PA)	Stratford	CT	E	203 378-8759	3548
McWeeney Marketing Group Inc	Orange	CT	G	203 891-8100	2677
Nicks Enterprises Inc (PA)	Hamden	CT	F	203 287-9990	1447
Park City Packaging Inc (PA)	Stratford	CT	F	203 378-7384	3564
Penmar Industries Inc	Stratford	CT	F	203 853-4868	3565
Professional Mktg Svcs Inc	Stratford	CT	F	203 610-6222	3568
S & S Worldwide Inc	Colchester	CT	B	860 537-3451	665
Smokeloudz LLC (PA)	Meriden	CT	G	203 909-3556	1699
Technical Reproductions Inc	Norwalk	CT	F	203 849-9100	2575
Ad-A-Day Company Inc	Taunton	MA	E	508 824-8676	12315
Alpha Tech Pet Inc	Littleton	MA	G	978 486-3690	9800
Canson Inc	South Hadley	MA	D	413 538-9250	11959
Cause For Change LLC	Sudbury	MA	E	617 571-6990	12262
Danvers Industrial Packg Corp	Beverly	MA	E	978 777-0020	6344
Dawson Forte Holdings LLC (PA)	Canton	MA	E	508 651-7910	7782
Gloucester Graphics Inc (PA)	Gloucester	MA	G	978 281-4500	8937
Hawtan Leathers LLC	Newburyport	MA	C	978 465-3791	10687
Horn International Packg Inc (HQ)	Lancaster	MA	E	978 667-8797	9528
Hyde Group Inc (PA)	Southbridge	MA	D	800 872-4933	12020
J W I N Promotional Corp	Westport	MA	G	508 636-1993	13297
Jeffco Fibres Inc (PA)	Webster	MA	C	508 943-0440	12928
Ketcham Traps	New Bedford	MA	G	508 997-4787	10610
Louis A Green Corp	North Adams	MA	F	781 535-6199	10810
Mooneytunco Inc	Weymouth	MA	G	781 331-4445	13330
Nancy Sales Co Inc	Chelsea	MA	E	617 884-1700	7987
National Reprographics Inc	Boston	MA	F	857 383-3700	6904
North Atlantic PCF Seafood LLC	Danvers	MA	F	401 969-3886	8213
Pacific Packaging Products Inc (PA)	Wilmington	MA	C	978 657-9100	13445
Packaging Products Corporation	New Bedford	MA	F	508 997-5150	10638
Packaging Specialties Inc	Newburyport	MA	D	978 462-1300	10706
Partylite Inc (HQ)	Plymouth	MA	D	203 661-1926	11471
Pgc Acquisition LLC	Reading	MA	E	508 888-2344	11604
Prolamina Corporation (DH)	Westfield	MA	A	413 562-2315	13202
Sealed Air Corporation	Holyoke	MA	C	413 534-0231	9280
Shawmut Advertising Inc (PA)	Peabody	MA	E	978 762-7500	11340
Smartpak Equine LLC (DH)	Plymouth	MA	D	774 773-1100	11478
Strong Group Inc (PA)	Gloucester	MA	D	978 281-3300	8960
Superior Printing Company Inc	Medford	MA	F	781 391-9090	10297
Time-Out Sports Inc	Whitman	MA	F	781 447-6670	13350
W Oliver Tripp Company (PA)	Weymouth	MA	E	781 848-1230	13338
Walker-Clay Inc	Hanson	MA	F	781 294-1100	9057
Ambrose G McCarthy Jr	Skowhegan	ME	G	207 474-8837	5462
Bosal Foam and Fiber (PA)	Limerick	ME	E	207 793-2245	5000
Downeast Concepts Inc	Yarmouth	ME	E	207 846-3726	5703
Geiger Bros (PA)	Lewiston	ME	B	207 755-2000	4962
Harpswell House Inc	Lisbon Falls	ME	G	207 353-2385	5021
Kelco Industries	Milbridge	ME	E	207 546-7562	5061
Lux Box Company Inc	Portland	ME	G	301 832-0622	5235
Maine Potato Growers Inc	Caribou	ME	F	207 764-3131	4676
Quince & Company Inc	Saco	ME	F	207 210-6630	5378
Ship-Pac Corp	Portland	ME	F	207 797-7444	5270
Tasman Industries Inc	Hartland	ME	F	207 938-4491	4878
U S Felt Company Inc	Sanford	ME	E	207 324-0063	5416
American Keder Inc (PA)	Rindge	NH	G	603 899-3233	15459
E Print Inc	Hudson	NH	G	603 594-0009	14495
Glass Graphics Inc	Conway	NH	F	603 447-1900	14179
Harrisville Designs Inc (PA)	Harrisville	NH	G	603 827-3333	14432
Powerplay Management LLC	Portsmouth	NH	E	603 436-3030	15431
Taggart Ice Inc	Nashua	NH	F	603 888-4630	15174

	CITY	ST	EMP	PHONE	ENTRY#
Continental Plas & Packg Inc	Lincoln	RI	F	781 932-1115	16128
Eco Global Manufacturing LLC	Providence	RI	E	401 331-5129	16512
Ira Green Inc (PA)	Providence	RI	C	800 663-7487	16543
Pet Food Experts Inc (PA)	Pawtucket	RI	C	401 721-5593	16401
Providence Yarn Company Inc	Pawtucket	RI	G	401 722-5600	16407
Ann Clark Ltd	Rutland	VT	E	802 773-7886	17489

52 BUILDING MATERIALS, HARDWARE, GARDEN SUPPLIES & MOBILE HOMES

5211 Lumber and other building materials

	CITY	ST	EMP	PHONE	ENTRY#
Bernhard Thmas Bldg Systems LL	Southport	CT	F	203 925-0414	3243
Bonito Manufacturing Inc	North Haven	CT	D	203 234-8786	2394
Chapman Lumber Inc	Thomaston	CT	E	860 283-6213	3616
Conway Hardwood Products LLC	Gaylordsville	CT	E	860 355-4030	1264
Desiato Sand & Gravel Corp	Storrs Mansfield	CT	E	860 429-6479	3512
Devine Brothers Incorporated	Norwalk	CT	E	203 866-4421	2490
Focal Metals	Bethel	CT	G	203 743-4443	115
Harris Enterprise Corp	Manchester	CT	E	860 649-4663	1600
Iffland Lumber Company Inc	Torrington	CT	E	860 489-9218	3684
Kensco Inc (PA)	Ansonia	CT	G	203 734-8827	15
La Pietra Thinstone Veneer	Brookfield	CT	F	203 775-6162	528
Leek Building Products Inc	Norwalk	CT	E	203 853-3883	2527
LH Gault & Son Incorporated	Westport	CT	D	203 227-5181	4180
Martin Cabinet Inc (PA)	Plainville	CT	E	860 747-5769	2772
Midwood Quarry and Cnstr Inc (PA)	East Hartford	CT	F	860 289-1414	1006
O & G Industries Inc	Stamford	CT	D	203 323-1111	3422
Rawson Development Inc	Putnam	CT	F	860 928-4536	2872
Royal Woodcraft Inc	Ansonia	CT	F	203 847-3461	19
Viking Kitchen Cabinets LLC (PA)	New Britain	CT	E	860 223-7101	2074
Walpole Outdoors LLC	Ridgefield	CT	E	508 668-2800	2909
Windham Materials LLC (PA)	Willimantic	CT	E	860 456-4111	4222
Aluminum Products Cape Cod Inc (PA)	Dennis Port	MA	F	508 398-8546	8259
Amherst Woodworking & Supply Inc	Northampton	MA	E	413 584-3003	11052
Baxter Sand & Gravel Inc	Chicopee	MA	E	413 536-3370	8009
Berkshire Concrete Corp (HQ)	Pittsfield	MA	E	413 443-4734	11392
Bond Construction Corporation	Spencer	MA	F	508 885-2480	12055
Boston Area Door Company	Bridgewater	MA	G	508 857-4722	7224
Brightman Corporation	Assonet	MA	F	508 644-2620	5972
Cape Cod Fence Co (PA)	South Yarmouth	MA	F	508 398-6041	11982
Cape Cod Lumber Co Inc	Abington	MA	C	781 878-0715	5722
Coastal-N-Counters Inc	Mashpee	MA	F	508 539-3500	10251
Complete Energy Services Corp	Raynham	MA	F	833 237-2677	11584
Creative Material Tech Ltd	Palmer	MA	G	413 284-0000	11272
Dauphinais & Son Inc	Wilbraham	MA	F	413 596-3964	13357
Dauphinais Concrete	Bellingham	MA	G	508 657-0941	6289
Dedham Cabinet Shop Inc	Canton	MA	F	781 326-4090	7783
Delano Saw Mill Inc	North Dartmouth	MA	G	508 994-8752	10992
Delta Sand and Gravel Inc	Sunderland	MA	F	413 665-4051	12273
Diemand Egg Farm Inc	Millers Falls	MA	G	978 544-3806	10447
Everett Aluminum Inc	Everett	MA	F	617 389-3839	8488
J B Sash & Door Company Inc	Chelsea	MA	E	617 884-8940	7983
Jamesbrook Enterprises Inc	Shirley	MA	F	978 425-6166	11818
JH Lynch & Sons Inc	Millbury	MA	E	508 756-6244	10438
Joe Miller Inc	Worcester	MA	F	508 753-8581	13745
Johns Building Supply Co Inc	Pittsfield	MA	F	413 442-7846	11403
Louis W Mian Incorporated (PA)	Boston	MA	E	617 241-7900	6863
Maki Building Centers Inc (HQ)	Gardner	MA	E	978 343-7422	8894
Medway Block Co Inc	Medway	MA	E	508 533-6701	10307
Morse Sand & Gravel Corp	Attleboro	MA	F	508 809-4644	6038
P & M Brick & Block Inc	Watertown	MA	G	617 924-6020	12898
P A Landers Inc	Hanover	MA	F	508 747-1800	9039
Perfection Fence Corp (PA)	Marshfield	MA	F	781 837-3600	10243
Precision Door & Window Inc (PA)	Stoughton	MA	F	781 344-6900	12228
Rangeway Supply LLC	North Billerica	MA	G	978 667-8500	10947
RD Contractors Inc	North Billerica	MA	E	978 667-6545	10948
Rebars & Mesh Inc	Haverhill	MA	F	978 374-2244	9126
Reliable Fnce C/Wstern Div Inc	Ashland	MA	F	508 877-1200	5966
Rowley Ready Mix Inc	Rowley	MA	F	978 948-2544	11684
Shea Concrete Products Inc	Amesbury	MA	E	978 388-1509	5852
Shelmar Inc	Wakefield	MA	F	781 245-1206	12535
Southeastern Millwork Co Inc	Bourne	MA	F	508 888-6038	7142
Ultimate Windows Inc	Lawrence	MA	G	978 687-9444	9605
Walpole Outdoors LLC	East Falmouth	MA	E	508 540-0300	8362
American Concrete Inds Inc	Bangor	ME	D	207 947-8334	4488
Anchor Corporation	Kennebunk	ME	F	207 985-6018	4920
Bangor Millwork & Supply Inc (PA)	Bangor	ME	F	207 947-6019	4491
Deweys Lumber LLC	Liberty	ME	G	207 589-4126	4998
Ernest R Palmer Lumber Co Inc	Sangerville	ME	F	207 876-2725	5419
Gagne & Son Con Blocks Inc	Auburn	ME	G	207 495-3313	4435
Gagne & Son Concrete Blocks Inc (PA)	Belgrade	ME	E	207 495-3313	4539

	CITY	ST	EMP	PHONE	ENTRY#
Hanscom Construction Inc	Marshfield	ME	F	207 255-8067	5046
Hillside Lumber Company Inc	Westbrook	ME	E	207 839-2575	5629
Maschino & Sons Lumber Co Inc	New Gloucester	ME	F	207 926-4288	5086
Morse Hardware & Lumber LLC	Wells	ME	F	207 646-5700	5603
N C Hunt Inc	Damariscotta	ME	E	207 563-8503	4716
New England Building Materials LLC	Sanford	ME	B	207 324-3350	5401
Parent Lumber Company Inc	Mechanic Falls	ME	G	207 998-2322	5053
Phinney Lumber Co	Gorham	ME	E	207 839-3336	4829
Pre-Hung Doors Inc	Auburn	ME	F	207 783-3881	4455
R E Lowell Lumber Co Inc	Buckfield	ME	E	207 336-2901	4658
Rjf - Morin Brick LLC	Auburn	ME	D	207 784-9375	4459
State Sand & Gravel Co Inc	Belfast	ME	F	207 338-4070	4538
Sunny Side Land Holdings LLC	Presque Isle	ME	F	207 768-1020	5310
T and P Lumber Inc (PA)	Orrington	ME	F	207 825-3317	5139
Walpole Outdoors LLC	Chester	ME	E	207 794-2248	4694
Wilbert Swans Vault Co	Casco	ME	E	207 854-5324	4684
Alvin J Coleman & Son Inc (PA)	Albany	NH	F	603 447-5936	13847
Barre Tile Inc	Lebanon	NH	F	802 476-0912	14684
Boulia-Gorrell Lumber Co LLC	Laconia	NH	F	603 524-1300	14648
Cabinets For Less LLC	Manchester	NH	G	603 935-7551	14825
Chasco Inc	Portsmouth	NH	F	603 436-2141	15371
Cs-Ma Inc	Newport	NH	F	603 863-1000	15227
DH Hardwick & Sons Inc	Bennington	NH	F	603 588-6618	13975
Fernald Lumber Inc	Nottingham	NH	F	603 679-2997	15276
Goss Lumber Co Inc	Henniker	NH	G	603 428-3363	14434
Granite State Ktchns Dstrs In	Bedford	NH	E	603 472-4080	13931
Granite State Log Homes Inc (PA)	Campton	NH	F	603 536-4949	14044
Hudson Quarry Corp	Hudson	NH	F	603 598-0142	14507
Middleton Building Supply (PA)	Middleton	NH	C	603 473-2210	15008
Millwork Masters Ltd (PA)	Keene	NH	F	603 358-3038	14608
Northern Design Precast Inc	Loudon	NH	F	603 783-8989	14796
Nucor Hrris Rbar Northeast LLC	Canaan	NH	D	603 632-5222	14047
R P Williams & Sons Inc	Bristol	NH	F	603 744-5446	14037
Seacoast Redimix Concrete LLC (PA)	Dover	NH	F	603 742-4441	14250
Tommila Brothers Inc	Fitzwilliam	NH	F	603 242-7774	14316
Triumph Interiors LLC	Rindge	NH	F	603 899-5184	15461
Turn Key Lumber Inc	Fitzwilliam	NH	C	978 798-1370	14317
White Mountain Lumber Co Inc	Berlin	NH	E	603 752-1000	13987
Wilkins Lumber Co Inc	Milford	NH	F	603 673-2545	15043
Windy Ridge Corporation	Tamworth	NH	G	603 323-2323	15650
Arnold Lumber Co	Coventry	RI	F	401 792-0979	15806
Arnold Lumber Co (PA)	West Kingston	RI	D	401 783-2266	16893
Cabinet Gallery Ltd (PA)	Woonsocket	RI	G	401 762-4300	16952
Concrete Products Inc	Chepachet	RI	F	401 568-8874	15803
Cooley Group Holdings Inc (PA)	Pawtucket	RI	C	401 724-0510	16358
Tsco Inc	North Kingstown	RI	F	401 295-0669	16289
A Johnson Co	Bristol	VT	D	802 453-4884	17112
Allearth Renewables Inc	Williston	VT	E	802 872-9600	17721
Champlain Door Company Inc	Milton	VT	F	802 524-7595	17356
City Feed and Lumber Co Inc (PA)	Saint Albans	VT	E	802 524-2136	17519
Dailey Precast LLC (HQ)	Shaftsbury	VT	D	802 442-4418	17549
H Hirschmann Ltd	West Rutland	VT	F	802 438-4447	17695
Limoge & Sons Garage Doors Inc	Williston	VT	F	802 878-4338	17739
M Piette & Sons Lumber Inc	Irasburg	VT	F	802 754-8876	17302
McCue Memorial Co Inc	Castleton	VT	F	802 468-5636	17173
Mill River Lumber Ltd	North Clarendon	VT	D	802 775-0032	17417
RK Miles Inc (PA)	Manchester Center	VT	C	802 362-1952	17330
Springfield Fence Company Inc	North Springfield	VT	F	802 886-2221	17424

5231 Paint, glass, and wallpaper stores

	CITY	ST	EMP	PHONE	ENTRY#
Capitol Glass Company Inc	West Hartford	CT	F	860 236-1936	4050
Chapman Lumber Inc	Thomaston	CT	E	860 283-6213	3616
Color Craft Ltd	East Granby	CT	F	800 509-6563	929
Ethan Allen Retail Inc (HQ)	Danbury	CT	B	203 743-8000	741
A B C Glass Co Inc	Springfield	MA	F	413 734-4524	12067
Detrapel Inc	Framingham	MA	F	617 514-7778	8757
Durant Prfmce Coatings Inc	Revere	MA	F	781 289-1400	11618
Irvings Home Center Inc	Brockton	MA	G	508 583-4421	7285
Maki Building Centers Inc (HQ)	Gardner	MA	E	978 343-7422	8894
Maki Corp (PA)	Gardner	MA	E	978 343-7422	8895
National Lumber Company	Newton	MA	E	617 244-8020	10770
National Lumber Company LLC (HQ)	Mansfield	MA	C	508 339-8020	10068
Hammond Lumber Company (PA)	Belgrade	ME	C	207 495-3303	4540
Morse Hardware & Lumber LLC	Wells	ME	F	207 646-5700	5603
S W Collins	Lincoln	ME	F	207 794-6113	5013
Central FLS Plate & Win GL Co	Central Falls	RI	F	401 722-1267	15787
RK Miles Inc (PA)	Manchester Center	VT	C	802 362-1952	17330

5251 Hardware stores

	CITY	ST	EMP	PHONE	ENTRY#
Chapman Manufacturing Company	Durham	CT	F	860 349-9228	896
F W Webb Company	New Haven	CT	F	203 865-6124	2151
Plastic Met Components Co Inc	Milford	CT	F	203 877-2723	1866
Proflow Inc	North Haven	CT	E	203 230-4700	2433

SIC

	CITY	ST	EMP	PHONE	ENTRY#
Sulzer Pump Solutions US Inc **(PA)**	Wallingford	CT	E	203 238-2700	3856
Swanson Tool Manufacturing Inc	West Hartford	CT	E	860 953-1641	4084
Essex County Coop Farming Assn	Topsfield	MA	F	978 887-2300	12433
F W Webb Company	Needham	MA	F	781 247-0300	10510
Irvings Home Center Inc	Brockton	MA	G	508 583-4421	7285
Lyn-Lad Group Ltd **(PA)**	Lynn	MA	E	781 598-6010	9984
Maki Building Centers Inc **(HQ)**	Gardner	MA	E	978 343-7422	8894
Maki Corp **(PA)**	Gardner	MA	E	978 343-7422	8895
National Lumber Company	Newton	MA	E	617 244-8020	10770
National Lumber Company LLC **(HQ)**	Mansfield	MA	C	508 339-8020	10068
Renovators Supply Inc	Erving	MA	E	413 423-3300	8471
Safe-T-Cut Inc	Monson	MA	F	413 267-9984	10456
F W Webb Company	Windham	ME	F	207 892-5302	5661
Gary Raymond	Caribou	ME	G	207 498-2549	4675
Hammond Lumber Company **(PA)**	Belgrade	ME	C	207 495-3303	4540
Kelco Industries	Milbridge	ME	F	207 546-7562	5061
Lyle Guptill	East Machias	ME	F	207 255-4130	4740
N C Hunt Inc **(PA)**	Jefferson	ME	E	207 549-0922	4918
R E Lowell Lumber Co Inc	Buckfield	ME	F	207 336-2901	4658
S W Collins	Lincoln	ME	E	207 794-6113	5013
Gilberte Interiors LLC **(PA)**	Hanover	NH	F	603 643-3727	14423
White Mountain Lumber Co Inc	Berlin	NH	E	603 752-1000	13987
379 Charles RI Inc	North Providence	RI	F	401 521-1101	16293

5261 Retail nurseries and garden stores

	CITY	ST	EMP	PHONE	ENTRY#
American Standard Company	Southington	CT	E	860 628-9643	3203
DR Charles Envmtl Cnstr LLC	Monroe	CT	G	203 445-0412	1913
Grillo Services LLC	Milford	CT	E	203 877-5070	1831
Midwood Quarry and Cnstr Inc **(PA)**	East Hartford	CT	F	860 289-1414	1006
W H Preuss Sons Incorporated	Bolton	CT	G	860 643-9492	224
Blacksmith Shop Farms Inc	East Falmouth	MA	F	508 548-7714	8357
Nicholas Ieronimo	Middleboro	MA	G	508 947-5363	10369
P Wiles Inc **(PA)**	Orleans	MA	F	508 385-4321	11242
Burger-Roy Inc	Madison	ME	E	207 696-3978	5041
Gary Raymond	Caribou	ME	G	207 498-2549	4675
Reggies Sales & Service	Auburn	ME	G	207 783-0558	4458
Hudson Quarry Corp	Hudson	NH	F	603 598-0142	14507
Americas Grdening Resource Inc **(PA)**	Burlington	VT	C	802 660-3500	17117
Americas Grdening Resource Inc	Milton	VT	C	802 660-3500	17354
Champlain Valley Equipment Inc	Saint Albans	VT	G	802 524-6782	17518
Innovtive Grdning Slutions Inc	Burlington	VT	C	888 560-1037	17139
Leos Small Engines Inc	Morrisville	VT	F	802 888-7247	17384
Mill River Lumber Ltd	North Clarendon	VT	D	802 775-0032	17417

53 GENERAL MERCHANDISE STORES

5311 Department stores

	CITY	ST	EMP	PHONE	ENTRY#
Gordon Brothers Intl LLC **(HQ)**	Boston	MA	D	888 424-1903	6767

5399 Miscellaneous general merchandise

	CITY	ST	EMP	PHONE	ENTRY#
BJs Wholesale Club Inc	Franklin	MA	D	508 553-9889	8821

54 FOOD STORES

5411 Grocery stores

	CITY	ST	EMP	PHONE	ENTRY#
Cco Llc	Rocky Hill	CT	F	860 757-3434	2917
Wizards Nuts Holdings LLC **(PA)**	Greenwich	CT	D	708 483-1315	1362
Atkins Fruit Bowl Inc	Amherst	MA	C	413 253-9528	5859
Big Y Foods Inc	Longmeadow	MA	D	413 567-6231	9848
Boston Food Cooperative **(PA)**	Cambridge	MA	C	617 661-1580	7520
Cumberland Farms Inc **(DH)**	Westborough	MA	B	800 225-9702	13097
Lacascias Bakery Inc	Medford	MA	F	781 395-8612	10294
North Star Distributors Inc **(PA)**	Vineyard Haven	MA	E	508 693-2000	12494
Old Creamery Grocery Store	Cummington	MA	G	413 634-5560	8147
Roche Bros Supermarkets LLC	Norton	MA	C	508 285-3600	11133
Um Food Sciences	Amherst	MA	E	413 545-2276	5866
Wohrles Foods Inc **(PA)**	Pittsfield	MA	E	413 442-1518	11427
Natural Selection Inc	Brunswick	ME	F	207 725-6287	4651
Market Basket Produce Inc	Concord	NH	D	603 224-5479	14143
Eastern Food Industries Inc	East Greenwich	RI	C	401 884-8798	15983
Pearl Street Beverage Inc	Burlington	VT	F	802 658-1574	17150

5421 Meat and fish markets

	CITY	ST	EMP	PHONE	ENTRY#
Manchester Packing Company Inc	Manchester	CT	D	860 646-5000	1616
Martin Rosols Inc	New Britain	CT	E	860 223-2707	2040
Newington Meat Center	Newington	CT	G	860 666-3431	2310
Chair City Meats Inc	Gardner	MA	G	978 630-1050	8881
Ice Cream Machine Co	Cumberland	RI	F	401 333-5053	15944
Tase-Rite Co Inc	Wakefield	RI	F	401 783-7300	16746

5431 Fruit and vegetable markets

	CITY	ST	EMP	PHONE	ENTRY#
Lyman Farm Incorporated **(PA)**	Middlefield	CT	C	860 349-1793	1725
Atkins Fruit Bowl Inc	Amherst	MA	C	413 253-9528	5859
Nashoba Valley Spirits Limited	Bolton	MA	E	978 779-5521	6498
Training Thru Placement Inc	North Providence	RI	F	401 353-0220	16312

5441 Candy, nut, and confectionery stores

	CITY	ST	EMP	PHONE	ENTRY#
Bridgewater Chocolate LLC	Brookfield	CT	G	203 775-2286	513
Fascias Chocolates Inc	Waterbury	CT	F	203 753-0515	3912
Munsons Candy Kitchen Inc **(PA)**	Bolton	CT	F	860 649-4332	221
Thompson Brands LLC	Meriden	CT	D	203 235-2541	1708
Thompson Candy Company	Meriden	CT	D	203 235-2541	1709
Arthur Mapes Inc	Chelmsford	MA	F	978 256-4061	7910
Bb Walpole Liquidation NH Inc	Cambridge	MA	G	617 491-4340	7499
Ben & Bills Chocolate Emporium	Falmouth	MA	F	508 548-7878	8628
Ben & Blls Chclat Emporium Inc **(PA)**	Northampton	MA	F	413 584-5695	11053
C&J Dreams Inc **(PA)**	North Easton	MA	E	508 238-6231	11008
Dorothy Coxs Candies Inc	Fall River	MA	E	774 678-0654	8534
Fastachi Ltd	Watertown	MA	F	617 924-8787	12876
Fedele and Carter Inc	Dennis Port	MA	F	508 394-1791	8261
Furlongs Cttage Cndies Ice Cre	Norwood	MA	F	781 762-4124	11174
Hebert Confections LLC	Shrewsbury	MA	F		11833
Hebert Retail LLC	Shrewsbury	MA	D	508 845-8051	11834
Nichols Candies Inc	Gloucester	MA	F	978 283-9850	8946
Russos Inc	Saugus	MA	G	781 233-1737	11765
Seven Sweets Inc	Marblehead	MA	F	781 631-0303	10095
Stage Stop Candy Ltd Inc	Dennis Port	MA	G	508 394-1791	8263
Harbor Candy Shop Inc	Ogunquit	ME	F	207 646-8078	5123
Len Libbys Inc	Scarborough	ME	F	207 883-4897	5437
Wilburs ME Choclat Confections	Freeport	ME	F	207 865-4071	4805
Fredericks Pastries **(PA)**	Amherst	NH	F	603 882-7725	13871
Granite State Candy Shoppe LLC **(PA)**	Concord	NH	F	603 225-2591	14131
Lindt & Sprungli (usa) Inc **(HQ)**	Stratham	NH	C	603 778-8100	15637
Van Otis Chocolates LLC **(PA)**	Manchester	NH	G	603 627-1611	14949
Anchor Toffee LLC	Newport	RI	E	401 619-1044	16201
Hauser Foods Inc	Westerly	RI	F	401 596-8866	16932
Lady Ann Candies Inc	Warwick	RI	F	401 738-4321	16832
Sweenors Chocolates Inc **(PA)**	Wakefield	RI	E	401 783-4433	16745
Tom and Sallys Handmade Choco	Westerly	RI	F	800 289-8783	16944
Tradest1	East Greenwich	RI	G	401 884-4949	15994
Champlain Chocolate Company **(PA)**	Burlington	VT	D	800 465-5909	17124
Champlain Chocolate Company	Williston	VT	D	802 864-1808	17725
Fudge Factory Inc	Manchester Center	VT	F	888 669-7425	17328
Nu Chocolat LLC	Burlington	VT	F	802 735-7770	17147
Quirion Luc **(PA)**	Newport	VT	G	802 673-8386	17406

5451 Dairy products stores

	CITY	ST	EMP	PHONE	ENTRY#
Cold Stone Creamery	Clinton	CT	G	860 669-7025	639
295 Tremont Inc	Attleboro	MA	D	508 222-2884	5985
C&J Dreams Inc **(PA)**	North Easton	MA	E	508 238-6231	11008
Meletharb Inc	Wakefield	MA	G	781 245-4946	12518
Peaceful Meadows Ice Cream Inc **(PA)**	Carver	MA	F	781 447-3700	7855
Russos Inc	Saugus	MA	G	781 233-1737	11765
White Mountain Creamery Inc	Chestnut Hill	MA	F	617 527-8790	8003
Whittier Farms Inc	Sutton	MA	G	508 865-1096	12295
Franks Bake Shop Inc	Bangor	ME	G	207 947-4594	4502
Shains	Sanford	ME	D	207 324-1449	5415
Walpole Creamery Ltd	Walpole	NH	G	603 445-5700	15664
Newport Creamery LLC	Cranston	RI	F	401 946-4000	15900
Wrights Dairy Farm Inc	North Smithfield	RI	E	401 767-3014	16334
Cabot Creamery Cooperative Inc	Waitsfield	VT	B	888 792-2268	17664
Monument Farms Inc	Weybridge	VT	E	802 545-2119	17703

5461 Retail bakeries

	CITY	ST	EMP	PHONE	ENTRY#
Amoun Pita & Distribution LLC	South Windsor	CT	F	866 239-9990	3114
Apicellas Bakery Inc	New Haven	CT	E	203 865-6204	2116
Capricorn Investors II LP	Greenwich	CT	E	203 861-6600	1325
DAndrea Corporation **(PA)**	West Haven	CT	G	203 932-6000	4101
Lupis Incorporated	New Haven	CT	F	203 562-9491	2172
Milite Bakery	Wolcott	CT	G	203 753-9451	4368
Modern Pastry Shop Inc	Hartford	CT	G	860 296-7628	1494
Mozzicato Pastry & Bake Sp Inc	Hartford	CT	F	860 296-0426	1495
Oasis Coffee Corp	Norwalk	CT	G	203 847-0554	2547
Realejo Donuts Inc	Portland	CT	F	860 342-5120	2822
Whole Donut	Enfield	CT	F	860 745-3041	1159
Abp Corporation **(PA)**	Boston	MA	E	617 423-0629	6505
Bagel Works Inc	Amherst	MA	F	413 835-0561	5860
Boston Chipyard The Inc	Boston	MA	E	617 742-9537	6607
Chmuras Bakery Inc **(PA)**	Indian Orchard	MA	F	413 543-2521	9471
Concord Teacakes Etcetera Inc	Concord	MA	F	978 369-7644	8109
D D J	Oxford	MA	F	508 987-0417	11251
Depot Donuts Inc	North Easton	MA	F	508 230-2888	11009

	CITY	ST	EMP	PHONE	ENTRY#
Driscolls Restaurant	Mansfield	MA	G	508 261-1574	10050
Dunkin Donuts of Methuen	Methuen	MA	G	978 681-8123	10328
G H Bent Company	Milton	MA	D	617 322-9287	10452
Ginsco Inc (PA)	Fall River	MA	F	508 677-4767	8554
Hamilton Orchards	New Salem	MA	F	978 544-6867	10664
Harbar LLC	Canton	MA	C	781 828-0848	7793
Hole In One	Eastham	MA	F	508 255-5359	8384
Iggys Bread Ltd (PA)	Cambridge	MA	D	617 491-7600	7610
Kookla Inc	Southbridge	MA	F	508 765-0442	12025
Kookla Inc (PA)	Sturbridge	MA	E	508 347-2623	12251
Korner Bagel Partnership	Seekonk	MA	G	508 336-5204	11779
La Patisserie Inc	Revere	MA	F	781 729-9441	11621
Lacascias Bakery Inc	Medford	MA	F	781 395-8612	10294
Lori Donuts Inc	East Longmeadow	MA	E	413 526-9944	8384
Meadowbrook Orchards Inc	Sterling	MA	F	978 365-7617	12167
Rob Roy Foods Inc	Worcester	MA	G	508 755-8393	13784
Spinelli Ravioli Mfg Co Inc	Boston	MA	E	617 567-1992	7053
Stone House Farm Inc	West Boxford	MA	G	978 352-2323	12954
Superior Baking Co Inc	Brockton	MA	F	508 586-6601	7310
Tripoli Bakery Inc	Lawrence	MA	F	978 682-7754	9604
Cape Whpie Mnes Grmet Whpie Pl	South Portland	ME	F	207 799-9207	5493
Donut Hole Inc	Buxton	ME	F	207 929-5060	4662
Dunkin Donuts (PA)	Auburn	ME	F	207 783-0408	4427
Franks Bake Shop Inc	Bangor	ME	G	207 947-4594	4502
Holy Donut Inc (PA)	Portland	ME	E	207 761-7775	5223
Italian Bakery Products Co	Lewiston	ME	F	207 782-8312	4967
Lepage Bakeries Inc	Auburn	ME	A	207 783-9161	4440
Lepage Bakeries Park St LLC	Auburn	ME	F	207 783-9161	4441
Lepage Bakeries Park St LLC (HQ)	Lewiston	ME	E	207 783-9161	4971
Natural Selection Inc	Brunswick	ME	E	207 725-6287	4651
Tonys Donut Shop	Portland	ME	G	207 772-2727	5285
A & M Donuts Inc	Plymouth	NH	E	603 536-7622	15354
ANM Donuts Inc	Tilton	NH	E	603 286-2770	15651
Crosby Bakery Inc	Nashua	NH	F	603 882-1851	15086
Fredericks Pastries (PA)	Amherst	NH	F	603 882-7725	13871
Loxsmith Bagel Corporation	Dover	NH	F	603 362-9060	14233
Manco LLC	Allenstown	NH	G	603 485-5327	13852
Bristol Bagel Works Ltd	Bristol	RI	F	401 254-1390	15756
Dunkin Donuts	Warwick	RI	F	401 822-2434	16810
Eastern Food Industries Inc	East Greenwich	RI	G	401 884-8798	15983
Tienda Y Panaderia El Quiche	Providence	RI	F	401 521-5154	16627
Wrights Dairy Farm Inc	North Smithfield	RI	E	401 767-3014	16334
Fudge Factory Inc	Manchester Center	VT	F	888 669-7425	17328
Klingers Bread Company	South Burlington	VT	E	802 860-6322	17582
Queen Dog LLC	Burlington	VT	F	802 660-2733	17154

5499 Miscellaneous food stores

	CITY	ST	EMP	PHONE	ENTRY#
Crystal Rock Spring Water Co	Watertown	CT	B	860 945-0661	4007
First Chance Inc	Middletown	CT	F	860 346-3663	1747
Grotto Always Inc	Waterbury	CT	F	203 754-0295	3915
Harvest Hill Holdings LLC (PA)	Stamford	CT	F	203 914-1620	3367
Masas Usa Inc	East Haven	CT	E	305 603-8868	1045
Miami Bay Beverage Company LLC	Guilford	CT	F	203 453-0090	1400
Boyajian Inc	Canton	MA	F	781 828-9966	7774
David W Wallace	Shelburne Falls	MA	G	413 625-6523	11803
Designing Health Inc	East Longmeadow	MA	F	661 257-1705	8373
North Star Distributors Inc (PA)	Vineyard Haven	MA	E	508 693-2000	12494
Olivenation LLC (PA)	Avon	MA	F	781 351-1499	6156
Perioq Inc	Leominster	MA	G	978 534-1249	9693
Somerville Live Poultry Co Inc	Boston	MA	G	617 547-9191	7045
Willow Tree Poultry Farm Inc	Attleboro	MA	D	508 222-2479	6077
Ambrose G McCarthy Jr	Skowhegan	ME	G	207 474-8837	5462
Auburn Spring Water Company (PA)	Auburn	ME	G	207 782-1521	4422
Modernist Pantry LLC	Eliot	ME	G	207 200-3817	4750
Vera Roasting Company	Portsmouth	NH	G	603 969-7970	15447
Bolt Coffee Company LLC	Providence	RI	E	401 533-6506	16487
Coffee Exchange Ltd	Providence	RI	F	401 273-1198	16502
Daves Coffee LLC (PA)	Narragansett	RI	F	800 483-4436	16188
Bread & Chocolate Inc	Wells River	VT	G	802 429-2920	17686
Cold Hollow Cider Mill Inc	Waterbury Center	VT	E	802 244-8771	17680
Keurig Green Mountain Inc (DH)	Waterbury	VT	D	877 879-2326	17675
Rea Inc	Saint Albans	VT	F	802 527-7437	17530
Speeder & Earls Inc	Burlington	VT	F	802 660-3996	17160

55 AUTOMOTIVE DEALERS AND GASOLINE SERVICE STATIONS

5511 New and used car dealers

	CITY	ST	EMP	PHONE	ENTRY#
Danbury A LLC	Danbury	CT	E	203 744-5202	724
Scap Motors Inc	Fairfield	CT	C	203 384-0005	1200
Steven Pelletier	Fort Kent	ME	F	207 834-3191	4794

	CITY	ST	EMP	PHONE	ENTRY#
Gpi Nh-T Inc	Manchester	NH	D	603 624-1800	14854
Ride-Away Inc (HQ)	Londonderry	NH	E	603 437-4444	14782

5521 Used car dealers

	CITY	ST	EMP	PHONE	ENTRY#
Landes Enterprises LLC	Attleboro	MA	G	508 761-7800	6030
Eagle Motors Inc	Harrisville	RI	F	401 568-2580	16065

5531 Auto and home supply stores

	CITY	ST	EMP	PHONE	ENTRY#
Bridgestone Ret Operations LLC	Bristol	CT	G	860 584-2727	417
Bridgestone Ret Operations LLC	Hamden	CT	G	203 288-1634	1414
Bridgestone Ret Operations LLC	Milford	CT	G	203 878-6859	1803
Bridgestone Ret Operations LLC	New Britain	CT	F	860 229-0348	2009
Bridgestone Ret Operations LLC	New Haven	CT	G	203 787-1208	2132
Bridgestone Ret Operations LLC	Newington	CT	G	860 594-0594	2277
Bridgestone Ret Operations LLC	Southington	CT	G	860 628-9621	3205
Bridgestone Ret Operations LLC	Waterbury	CT	F	203 754-6119	3893
Bridgestone Ret Operations LLC	West Haven	CT	F	203 933-7750	4095
Derby Tire Company	Branford	CT	F	203 481-8473	249
Firestone Building Pdts Co LLC	Bristol	CT	F	860 584-4516	447
Genuine Parts Company	Windsor Locks	CT	F	860 623-4479	4325
International Auto Entps Inc (PA)	New Britain	CT	F	860 224-0253	2034
Line-X of Hartford	Hartford	CT	G	860 216-6180	1490
Line-X of New England LLC	New Milford	CT	G	860 355-6997	2252
Reliable Auto Tire Company Inc	Hartford	CT	G	860 247-7977	1504
Star Tires Plus Wheels LLC	Hartford	CT	F	860 296-9799	1509
Stead-Fast Custom Linings LLC	East Haven	CT	F	203 466-8000	1052
Tire Country of Enfield Inc	Enfield	CT	G	860 763-0846	1155
Toce Brothers Incorporated (PA)	Torrington	CT	F	860 496-2080	3700
American Tire Svc & Sls Inc	Springfield	MA	G	413 739-5369	12074
Aronson Tire Company Inc	Auburn	MA	E	508 832-3244	6105
Atlantic Auto & Trck Parts LLC	Rowley	MA	F	978 535-6777	11667
Bodyshop World By Wagner Inc	Worcester	MA	F	508 853-0300	13704
Bridgestone Ret Operations LLC	Auburn	MA	G	508 832-9671	6110
Bridgestone Ret Operations LLC	Boston	MA	G	617 327-1100	6622
Bridgestone Ret Operations LLC	Braintree	MA	F	781 843-2870	7172
Bridgestone Ret Operations LLC	Brockton	MA	G	508 588-8866	7262
Bridgestone Ret Operations LLC	Hingham	MA	G	781 749-6454	9145
Bridgestone Ret Operations LLC	Northampton	MA	G	413 586-1584	11054
Bridgestone Ret Operations LLC	Quincy	MA	G	617 479-3208	11508
Bridgestone Ret Operations LLC	Springfield	MA	F	413 543-1312	12080
Bridgestone Ret Operations LLC	Watertown	MA	F	617 924-3989	12864
Bridgestone Ret Operations LLC	Wilmington	MA	F	978 658-5660	13394
City Tire Co Inc	Chicopee	MA	E	413 534-2946	8018
City Tire Co Inc	Pittsfield	MA	G	413 445-5578	11396
City Tire Co Inc (PA)	Springfield	MA	E	413 737-1419	12084
Consolidated Truck & Eqp Inc	Seekonk	MA	F	508 252-3330	11775
Goodyear Tire & Rubber Company	Lynn	MA	F	781 598-4500	9976
Holyoke Tire & Auto Svc Inc	Springfield	MA	G	413 733-2141	12101
Interstate All Battery Center	South Yarmouth	MA	F	508 394-9400	11984
K & W Tire Company Inc	Ayer	MA	F	978 772-5700	6184
Lawton Truck Equipment Inc	Topsfield	MA	F	978 887-0005	12436
Lynn Ladder Scaffolding Co Inc (HQ)	Lynn	MA	D	781 598-6010	9985
Middlesex Truck & Auto Body	Boston	MA	F	617 442-3000	6887
Petes Tire Barns Inc (PA)	Orange	MA	D	978 544-8811	11228
Rolands Tire Service Inc (PA)	Fairhaven	MA	E	508 997-4501	8514
Sullivan Investment Co Inc (PA)	Norwell	MA	E	781 982-1550	11147
Sullivan Tire Co Inc	North Attleboro	MA	E	508 695-9920	10890
Tebaldi Enterprises Inc	Holyoke	MA	F	413 532-3261	9283
Yankee Custom Inc (PA)	Tewksbury	MA	F	978 851-9024	12426
Baude Inc	Houlton	ME	F	207 532-6571	4896
Central Tire Co Inc (PA)	Sanford	ME	F	207 324-4250	5391
Coastal Metal Fab	Topsham	ME	E	207 729-5101	5547
Hanscom Construction Inc	Marshfield	ME	F	207 255-8067	5046
Lag Inc (PA)	Topsham	ME	E	207 729-1676	5548
Lees Tire	Topsham	ME	E	207 729-1676	5549
Maine Tire & Appliance Co	Augusta	ME	G	207 623-1171	4477
Maine Tire & Appliance Co (PA)	Falmouth	ME	F	207 781-3136	4769
McQuade Tidd Industries	Houlton	ME	F	207 532-6571	4902
Tki Inc	Skowhegan	ME	G	207 474-5322	5479
Belknap Tire Co Holdings Inc	Laconia	NH	F	603 524-4517	14646
Bridgestone Ret Operations LLC	Manchester	NH	F	603 668-1123	14821
DC Tire Service Inc	Milford	NH	G	603 673-9211	15021
Freedom Tire Inc (PA)	Plaistow	NH	F	603 382-7223	15344
Mountain Tire Corp	Berlin	NH	F	603 752-8473	13983
Northeast Tire Service Inc	Belmont	NH	F	603 524-7973	13965
Reed Truck Services Inc	Claremont	NH	F	603 542-5032	14097
Bec Corp	Pawtucket	RI	G	401 725-3535	16347
Bridgestone Ret Operations LLC	North Smithfield	RI	F	401 766-0233	16319
Bridgestone Ret Operations LLC	Providence	RI	F	401 521-6622	16491
Petes Tire Barns Inc	Providence	RI	G	401 521-2240	16583
Scarborough Faire Inc	Pawtucket	RI	E	401 724-4200	16416
Lance Smith Inc	Milton	VT	D	802 655-3354	17361
Vianor Inc (HQ)	Colchester	VT	E	802 864-7108	17207

SIC

	CITY	ST	EMP	PHONE	ENTRY#
5541 Gasoline service stations					
Cumberland Farms Inc (DH)	Westborough	MA	B	800 225-9702	13097
Old Creamery Grocery Store	Cummington	MA	G	413 634-5560	8147
Quick Clean Car Wash Systems I (PA)	Wakefield	MA	F	781 245-6809	12531
Dark Harbor Boatyard Corp	Islesboro	ME	F	207 734-2246	4908
Highlands Fuel Delivery LLC (HQ)	Portsmouth	NH	D	603 559-8700	15404
Rounds Service Station Inc	North Scituate	RI	F	401 934-9877	16316
Hemmings Motor News Inc	Bennington	VT	A	802 442-3101	17040
5551 Boat dealers					
Defender Industries Inc	Waterford	CT	C	860 701-3400	3989
Dodson Boatyard LLC	Stonington	CT	E	860 535-1507	3508
Seaport Marine Inc	Mystic	CT	G	860 536-9651	1942
Vespoli Usa Inc	New Haven	CT	F	203 773-0311	2215
Allen Harbor Marine Svc Inc	Harwich Port	MA	E	508 432-0353	9070
Crosby Yacht Yard Inc	Osterville	MA	E	508 428-6900	11245
F L Tripp & Sons Inc	Westport Point	MA	F	508 636-4058	13303
Falmouth Mar Yachting Ctr Inc	Falmouth	MA	F	508 548-4600	8631
Hercules Slr (us) Inc	New Bedford	MA	G	508 992-9519	10600
Hercules Slr (us) Inc (PA)	New Bedford	MA	F	508 993-0010	10601
Karls Boat Shop Inc	Harwich	MA	G	508 432-4488	9069
Marine Usa Inc	Worcester	MA	E	508 791-7116	13757
Nauset Marine Inc (PA)	Orleans	MA	E	508 255-0777	11240
P B Y A Inc	South Orleans	MA	G	508 255-0994	11973
Ribcraft Usa LLC	Marblehead	MA	F	781 639-9065	10094
Roses Oil Service Inc (PA)	Gloucester	MA	E	877 283-3334	8955
Windward Power Systems Inc	Fairhaven	MA	G	774 992-0059	8515
Dark Harbor Boatyard Corp	Islesboro	ME	F	207 734-2246	4908
Gowen Inc	Portland	ME	F	207 773-1761	5219
Howell Laboratories Inc (PA)	Bridgton	ME	E	207 647-3327	4629
J O Brown & Son Inc	North Haven	ME	G	207 867-4621	5114
John M Williams Company	Mount Desert	ME	F	207 244-7854	5077
Navigator Publishing LLC	Portland	ME	E	207 822-4350	5249
Accutech Marine Propeller Inc	Dover	NH	G	603 617-3626	14213
Eastern Boats Inc	Milton	NH	E	603 652-9213	15045
Aramid Rigging Inc	Portsmouth	RI	F	401 683-6966	16436
Berthon Usa Inc	Newport	RI	F	401 846-8404	16206
Cove Haven Corp	Barrington	RI	F	401 246-1600	15747
Gecko Marine Inc	Bristol	RI	F	401 237-6117	15766
Iyrs School Tech & Trades	Newport	RI	E	401 846-2587	16212
Lightship Group LLC (PA)	North Kingstown	RI	E	401 294-3341	16268
Oldport Marine Services Inc	Newport	RI	F	401 847-9109	16220
Quantum Newport	Portsmouth	RI	G	401 849-7700	16452
5561 Recreational vehicle dealers					
Gary Raymond	Caribou	ME	G	207 498-2549	4675
Lyle Guptill	East Machias	ME	F	207 255-4130	4740
5571 Motorcycle dealers					
Danbury Powersports Inc	Danbury	CT	F	203 791-1310	726
Government Surplus Sales Inc	Hartford	CT	G	860 247-7787	1484
Gary Raymond	Caribou	ME	G	207 498-2549	4675
Moto Tassinari LLC	West Lebanon	NH	F	603 298-6646	15684
Rowe Machine Co	Hampton	NH	F	603 926-0029	14411
5599 Automotive dealers, nec					
Sikorsky Aircraft Corporation (HQ)	Stratford	CT	A	203 386-4000	3571
Innovative Specialties LLC	Pittsfield	ME	F	207 948-1500	5160
On The Road Inc	Warren	ME	E	207 273-3780	5585
North Atlantic Dist Inc	North Kingstown	RI	B	401 667-7000	16274

56 APPAREL AND ACCESSORY STORES

	CITY	ST	EMP	PHONE	ENTRY#
5611 Men's and boys' clothing stores					
Arocam Inc	Taunton	MA	F	508 822-1220	12319
Dawson Forte Holdings LLC (PA)	Canton	MA	E	508 651-7910	7782
Sickday Inc	Wellfleet	MA	F	508 214-4158	12953
Top Half Inc	Tyngsboro	MA	F	978 454-5440	12468
Chuck Roast Equipment Inc (PA)	Conway	NH	F	603 447-5492	14178
Spirit Recognition Inc (PA)	Pawtucket	RI	F	401 722-6400	16417
Nomad Communications Inc 17709	White River Junction	VT	F	802 649-1995	
5621 Women's clothing stores					
Arocam Inc	Taunton	MA	F	508 822-1220	12319
Dawson Forte Holdings LLC (PA)	Canton	MA	E	508 651-7910	7782
Lane Printing Co Inc	Holbrook	MA	F	781 767-4450	9178
Sickday Inc	Wellfleet	MA	F	508 214-4158	12953
B Peachee Inc	Biddeford	ME	G	207 602-6262	4555
Chuck Roast Equipment Inc (PA)	Conway	NH	F	603 447-5492	14178
Spirit Recognition Inc (PA)	Pawtucket	RI	F	401 722-6400	16417

	CITY	ST	EMP	PHONE	ENTRY#
Mainstream Inc (PA)	Bennington	VT	F	802 442-8859	17050
Nomad Communications Inc 17709	White River Junction	VT	F	802 649-1995	
5632 Women's accessory and specialty stores					
Bondi Band LLC	Simsbury	CT	F	207 576-4191	3084
Dance It Up Inc	North Grafton	MA	F	508 839-1648	11021
Dawson Forte Holdings LLC (PA)	Canton	MA	E	508 651-7910	7782
Sea Bags LLC (PA)	Portland	ME	F	207 780-0744	5268
Nomad Communications Inc 17709	White River Junction	VT	F	802 649-1995	
5641 Children's and infants' wear stores					
Classic Prep Childrenswear Inc	Norwalk	CT	G	203 286-6204	2483
Chuck Roast Equipment Inc (PA)	Conway	NH	F	603 447-5492	14178
Ragged Mountain Equipment Inc	Intervale	NH	E	603 356-3042	14561
Thanksben10 LLC	Milford	NH	F	603 206-5116	15040
5651 Family clothing stores					
Fyc Apparel Group LLC (PA)	Branford	CT	D	203 481-2420	260
Chillybear Inc (PA)	Needham	MA	F	781 455-6321	10507
Good Clothing Company Inc	Fall River	MA	F	508 419-6152	8556
Image Factory	Pocasset	MA	G	508 295-3876	11489
Santacroce Graphics Inc	Charlton	MA	F	802 447-0020	7895
Synergy Sportswear Inc (PA)	Keene	NH	G	603 352-8681	14626
Thanksben10 LLC	Milford	NH	F	603 206-5116	15040
Wool Advisor LLC	Johnson	VT	F	802 635-2271	17312
5661 Shoe stores					
Arocam Inc	Taunton	MA	F	508 822-1220	12319
C & J Clark America Inc (DH)	Waltham	MA	B	617 964-1222	12617
C & J Clark Latin America	Waltham	MA	E	617 243-4100	12618
Reebok International Ltd LLC (HQ)	Boston	MA	B	781 401-5000	7002
Santacroce Graphics Inc	Charlton	MA	F	802 447-0020	7895
Stride Rite Corporation (HQ)	Waltham	MA	B	617 824-6000	12783
Vibram Corporation (HQ)	Concord	MA	E	978 318-0000	8138
Wear-Guard Corporation	Norwell	MA	A	781 871-4100	11150
Pine Tree Orthopedic Lab Inc	Livermore Falls	ME	F	207 897-5558	5025
5699 Miscellaneous apparel and accessories					
Air Tool Sales & Svc Co Inc (PA)	Unionville	CT	G	860 673-2714	3746
Al-Lynn Sales LLC	Shelton	CT	G	203 922-7840	2979
Lenscrafters	Milford	CT	G	203 878-8511	1845
Birch Outfitters LLC	Salem	MA	F	978 498-4631	11703
Chillybear Inc (PA)	Needham	MA	F	781 455-6321	10507
Guertins Graphics Inc	Worcester	MA	F	508 754-0200	13735
Maverick Work Wear Inc	North Reading	MA	E	860 944-3776	11043
Omniview Sports Inc	Boston	MA	G	781 583-3534	6929
Rainbow Visions Inc	Boston	MA	G	617 787-4084	6995
Soft-As-A-grape Inc (PA)	Wareham	MA	E	508 295-9900	12844
Wear-Guard Corporation	Norwell	MA	A	781 871-4100	11150
Allen Uniforms Inc	South Portland	ME	G	207 775-7364	5491
Winter People Inc 4711	Cumberland Center	ME	E	207 865-6636	
Blue Dolphin Screenprint Inc	Somersworth	NH	E	603 692-2500	15611
Chuck Roast Equipment Inc (PA)	Conway	NH	F	603 447-5492	14178
Firecracker Sports LLC	Cumberland	RI	G	401 595-0233	15939
Merchbro Inc	Pawtucket	RI	F	866 428-0095	16387
Teespring Inc	Providence	RI	E	855 833-7774	16619
Vermont Teddy Bear Co Inc (HQ)	Shelburne	VT	C	802 985-3001	17563

57 HOME FURNITURE, FURNISHINGS AND EQUIPMENT STORES

	CITY	ST	EMP	PHONE	ENTRY#
5712 Furniture stores					
Cerrito Furniture Inds Inc	Branford	CT	F	203 481-2580	244
Deane Inc	Stamford	CT	E	203 327-7008	3335
Domino Media Group Inc	Westport	CT	F	877 223-7844	4165
Ethan Allen Interiors Inc (PA)	Danbury	CT	C	203 743-8000	740
Ethan Allen Retail Inc (HQ)	Danbury	CT	B	203 743-8000	741
Ian Ingersoll Cabinetmaker	West Cornwall	CT	F	860 672-6334	4044
Lovesac Company (PA)	Stamford	CT	D	888 636-1223	3404
Pemac Construction	Oakdale	CT	F	860 437-0007	2623
Porta Door Co	Seymour	CT	E	203 888-6191	2967
S J Pappas Inc	Meriden	CT	G	203 237-7701	1695
W B Mason Co Inc	East Windsor	CT	D	888 926-2766	1089
W B Mason Co Inc	Norwalk	CT	E	888 926-2766	2593
W B Mason Co Inc	Norwich	CT	C	888 926-2766	2619
Walpole Outdoors LLC	Ridgefield	CT	E	508 668-2800	2909
Acton Woodworks Inc	Acton	MA	G	978 263-0222	5732
Affordable Intr Systems Inc (HQ)	Leominster	MA	D	978 562-7500	9633

	CITY	ST	EMP	PHONE	ENTRY#
Albert E Cadrette	West Townsend	MA	F	978 597-2312	13056
Atlantic Furniture Inc	South Deerfield	MA	E	413 665-4700	11920
CAM Office Services Inc (PA)	Marlborough	MA	F	781 932-9868	10125
Conklin Office Services Inc (PA)	Holyoke	MA	E	413 315-4924	9248
Drive-O-Rama Inc (PA)	Hyannis	MA	G	508 771-8100	9434
Drive-O-Rama Inc	Dennis Port	MA	G	508 394-0028	8260
Ecin Industries Inc	Fall River	MA	E	508 675-6920	8540
Grace Lee Designs Shilling	Cambridge	MA	G	617 661-7090	7593
HMK Enterprises Inc (PA)	Lexington	MA	F	781 891-6660	9749
Jay Salem Inc	Middleton	MA	G	978 774-4999	10387
Jobart Inc (PA)	Methuen	MA	F	978 689-4414	10335
Jordans Furniture Inc (HQ)	East Taunton	MA	A	508 828-4000	8408
Marthas Vineyard Furn Co LLC	Vineyard Haven	MA	G	508 687-9555	12491
Officeworks Inc (PA)	Burlington	MA	F	781 270-9000	7403
Twin Cy Upholstering Mat Inc	Braintree	MA	F	781 843-1780	7210
US Bedding Inc	Fall River	MA	F	508 678-6988	8620
W B Mason Co Inc	Framingham	MA	D	888 926-2766	8809
W B Mason Co Inc	Greenfield	MA	E	888 926-2766	9004
Walpole Outdoors LLC	East Falmouth	MA	E	508 540-0300	8362
Walpole Outdoors LLC	Wilmington	MA	E	978 658-3373	13475
Chilton Paint Co Inc ME	Freeport	ME	G	207 865-4443	4800
Maine Bunk Beds LLC	Buxton	ME	F	207 929-4499	4663
Portland Mattress Makers (PA)	Biddeford	ME	E	207 282-9583	4582
W B Mason Co Inc	Augusta	ME	E	888 926-2766	4481
W B Mason Co Inc	Bangor	ME	E	888 926-2766	4520
W B Mason Co Inc	Portland	ME	E	888 926-2766	5288
Walpole Outdoors LLC	Chester	ME	E	207 794-2248	4694
Aubin Woodworking Inc	Bow	NH	F	603 224-5512	13993
Chamberlain Companies Inc	Salem	NH	E	603 893-2606	15512
Cw Keller & Associates LLC	Plaistow	NH	D	603 382-2028	15339
Design Brand Partners Inc	Bedford	NH	G	603 232-3490	13925
Gilberte Interiors LLC (PA)	Hanover	NH	F	603 643-3727	14423
W B Mason Co Inc	Manchester	NH	D	888 926-2766	14957
Arnold Lumber Co	Coventry	RI	E	401 792-0979	15806
Cole Cabinet Co Inc	Cranston	RI	F	401 467-4343	15842
W B Mason Co Inc	Cranston	RI	D	888 926-2766	15926
Community Apostolic Order Inc (PA)	Island Pond	VT	F	802 723-4452	17304
W B Mason Co Inc	Brattleboro	VT	E	888 926-2766	17106
W B Mason Co Inc	South Burlington	VT	E	888 926-2766	17607
Wcw Inc (PA)	Manchester Center	VT	D	802 362-8053	17332

5713 Floor covering stores

	CITY	ST	EMP	PHONE	ENTRY#
Agw Clssic Hardwood Floors LLC	Westbrook	CT	G	203 640-3106	4135
Elizabeth Eakins Inc	Norwalk	CT	E	203 831-9347	2496
Ethan Allen Retail Inc (HQ)	Danbury	CT	B	203 743-8000	741
Mildred Coppola (PA)	Stamford	CT	F	203 967-9300	3411
Aldrich Marble & Granite Co	Norwood	MA	G	781 762-6111	11158
Cape Cod Braided Rug Co Inc	Marstons Mills	MA	F	508 432-3133	10247
Irvings Home Center Inc	Brockton	MA	G	508 583-4421	7285
TMI Industries Inc	Palmer	MA	E	413 283-9021	11285
Proknee Corp	Whitefield	ME	E	207 549-5018	5656
Robin Industries Inc	Bristol	RI	E	401 253-8350	15779

5714 Drapery and upholstery stores

	CITY	ST	EMP	PHONE	ENTRY#
Irvings Home Center Inc	Brockton	MA	G	508 583-4421	7285
New England Worldwide Export	Quincy	MA	G	617 472-0251	11529
Reliable Fabrics Inc	Everett	MA	F	617 387-5321	8497
Custom Canvas & Upholstery LLC	Bridgton	ME	F	207 241-8518	4627
Maine Stitching Spc LLC	Skowhegan	ME	F	207 812-5207	5472
Gilberte Interiors LLC (PA)	Hanover	NH	F	603 643-3727	14423
Drapery House Inc	North Providence	RI	E	401 724-3400	16300
Marion Mfg Co	Lincoln	RI	E	401 331-4343	16147

5719 Miscellaneous homefurnishings

	CITY	ST	EMP	PHONE	ENTRY#
Acme Sign Co (PA)	Stamford	CT	F	203 324-2263	3272
Arrow Win Shade Mfg of Mrden I	Wethersfield	CT	G	860 563-4035	4202
Ethan Allen Retail Inc (HQ)	Danbury	CT	B	203 743-8000	741
Hearth Kitchen Products Inc	Stamford	CT	F	203 325-8800	3372
Kensington GL & Frmng Co Inc	Berlin	CT	F	860 828-9428	73
Mirror Polishing & Pltg Co Inc	Waterbury	CT	E	203 574-5400	3945
Picture This Hartford Inc	East Hartford	CT	G	860 528-1409	1011
Porcelen Limited Connecticut LLC (PA)	Hamden	CT	D	203 248-6346	1449
Tero Design Holdings LLC	Norwalk	CT	G	203 899-9950	2580
A B C Glass Co Inc	Springfield	MA	F	413 734-4524	12067
Architctral Fireplaces of Neng	Auburn	MA	F	508 757-0622	6104
Chilsons Shops Inc	Easthampton	MA	E	413 529-8062	8441
Irvings Home Center Inc	Brockton	MA	G	508 583-4421	7285
Lighthouse Distributors Inc	Marshfield	MA	G	781 319-9828	10241
Lighting By Hammerworks (PA)	Worcester	MA	G	508 755-3434	13753
Petermans Boards and Bowls Inc	Gill	MA	G	413 863-2116	8915
Pgc Acquisition LLC	Reading	MA	G	508 888-2344	11604
Plastican Inc	Leominster	MA	A	978 728-5000	9696
Ray Murray Inc (PA)	Lee	MA	D	413 243-2164	9619

	CITY	ST	EMP	PHONE	ENTRY#
Reliable Fabrics Inc	Everett	MA	F	617 387-5321	8497
Sheffield Pottery Inc	Sheffield	MA	E	413 229-7700	11801
Bangor Steel Service Inc	Bangor	ME	E	207 947-2773	4494
Enefco International Inc (PA)	Auburn	ME	E	207 514-7218	4428
Georgetown Pottery	Georgetown	ME	G	207 371-2801	4814
Sheepscot River Pottery (PA)	Edgecomb	ME	F	207 882-9410	4748
Gilberte Interiors LLC (PA)	Hanover	NH	F	603 643-3727	14423
Installed Building Pdts LLC	Auburn	NH	B	603 645-1604	13909
J & R Langley Co Inc	Manchester	NH	E	603 622-9653	14866
Scarlet Aspen LLC	Portsmouth	NH	F	603 509-3990	15435
Central FLS Plate & Win GL Co	Central Falls	RI	F	401 722-1267	15787
J K Adams Company Inc	Dorset	VT	E	802 362-2303	17214
Simon Pearce (us) Inc (PA)	Windsor	VT	C	802 674-6280	17762

5722 Household appliance stores

	CITY	ST	EMP	PHONE	ENTRY#
Clarke Distribution Corp	Norwalk	CT	G	203 838-9385	2482
W H Preuss Sons Incorporated	Bolton	CT	G	860 643-9492	224
Nidec America Corporation (HQ)	Braintree	MA	E	781 848-0970	7196
W S Bessett Inc	Sanford	ME	E	207 324-9232	5417
Proctor Gas Inc	Proctor	VT	E	802 459-3340	17460
Trane Company	Williston	VT	G	802 864-3816	17750

5731 Radio, television, and electronic stores

	CITY	ST	EMP	PHONE	ENTRY#
Alpha-Core Inc	Shelton	CT	E	203 954-0050	2980
Idevices LLC	Avon	CT	D	860 352-5252	27
Krystal Inc LLC	Granby	CT	G	860 844-1267	1307
All Security Co Inc	New Bedford	MA	E	508 993-4271	10567
Bose Corporation (PA)	Framingham	MA	A	508 879-7330	8745
Bose Corporation	Stow	MA	E	508 766-7330	12244
Cowbell Technologies Inc	Hudson	MA	F	508 733-1778	9360
Cowbell Technologies Inc (PA)	Westborough	MA	G	508 733-1778	13094
Fargo Ta LLC	Boston	MA	E	617 345-0066	6731
Omniview Sports Inc	Boston	MA	G	781 583-3534	6929
Trackcam LLC	Rehoboth	MA	G	508 556-1955	11614
Hro Inc	Salem	NH	E	603 898-3750	15537
Russound/Fmp Inc	Portsmouth	NH	C	603 659-5170	15433
Tradeport USA LLC	Dover	NH	F	603 692-2900	14254

5734 Computer and software stores

	CITY	ST	EMP	PHONE	ENTRY#
Glacier Computer LLC	New Milford	CT	F	603 882-1560	2244
Cimcon Software LLC (PA)	Westford	MA	D	978 464-9180	13229
Covalent Networks Inc	Boston	MA	F	781 296-7952	6673
E E S Companies Inc	Framingham	MA	F	508 653-6911	8758
Free Software Foundation Inc	Boston	MA	F	617 542-5942	6747
Mimoco Inc	Needham Heights	MA	F	617 783-1100	10552
Omniview Sports Inc	Boston	MA	G	781 583-3534	6929
Retro-Fit Technologies Inc	Taunton	MA	E	508 478-2222	12363
Valora Technologies Inc	Carlisle	MA	F	781 229-2265	7850
Hawkin Dynamics LLC	Westbrook	ME	F	207 405-9142	5628
Electronics For Imaging Inc	West Lebanon	NH	B	603 279-6800	15683
Infor (us) LLC	Nashua	NH	E	678 319-8000	15114
Tomtom North America Inc	Lebanon	NH	D	978 405-1677	14700
Quantifacts Inc	Riverside	RI	G	401 421-8300	16659
Portfolio Software Inc	Richmond	VT	F	802 434-4000	17481

58 EATING AND DRINKING PLACES

5812 Eating places

	CITY	ST	EMP	PHONE	ENTRY#
Bagelman III Inc	Danbury	CT	F	203 792-0030	711
Big Dipper Ice Cream Fctry Inc	Prospect	CT	F	203 758-3200	2830
Capricorn Investors III LP (PA)	Greenwich	CT	F	203 861-6600	1326
Cold Stone Creamery	Clinton	CT	G	860 669-7025	639
Creole Jos LLC	Glastonbury	CT	F	203 893-2875	1276
Daybrake Donuts Inc	Bridgeport	CT	G	203 368-4962	314
Grotto Always Inc	Waterbury	CT	F	203 754-0295	3915
If Not Now When Inc	Groton	CT	G	860 445-5276	1373
J Foster Ice Cream	Simsbury	CT	D	860 651-1499	3092
Krystal Inc LLC	Granby	CT	G	860 844-1267	1307
Michaels Dairy Inc	New London	CT	E	860 443-7617	2230
Olive Oil Factory LLC	Waterbury	CT	E	203 437-8286	3956
Provisionaire & Co LLC	Westport	CT	E	646 681-8600	4193
Sharpe Hill Vineyard Inc	Pomfret	CT	F	860 974-3549	2811
Smoothie King	Waterford	CT	F	860 574-9382	3996
Whole Donut	Enfield	CT	F	860 745-3041	1159
Yosi Kosher Catering LLC	Windsor	CT	F	860 688-6677	4316
295 Tremont Inc	Attleboro	MA	D	508 222-2884	5985
Abp Corporation (PA)	Boston	MA	C	617 423-0629	6505
Amherst Brewing Co Inc	Amherst	MA	F	413 253-4400	5856
Bakery To Go Inc	Boston	MA	G	617 482-1015	6582
Barrel House Z LLC	Hingham	MA	E	617 480-2880	9142
Battle Grounds Coffee Co LLC	Haverhill	MA	F	978 891-5860	9077
Bay Colony Associates (PA)	Boston	MA	G	617 287-9100	6584

SIC

	CITY	ST	EMP	PHONE	ENTRY#
Brighams Inc (HQ)	Arlington	MA	F	800 242-2423	5939
Cambridge Brewing Co Inc	Cambridge	MA	E	617 494-1994	7528
Cold Harbor Brewing Co LLC	Westborough	MA	E	508 768-5232	13090
Dairy Queen	West Boylston	MA	F	508 853-2700	12959
Diemand Egg Farm Inc	Millers Falls	MA	F	978 544-3806	10447
Foxees Co Inc	Falmouth	MA	E	508 548-8485	8632
Freeze Operations Holding Corp (PA)	Wilbraham	MA	A	413 543-2445	13360
Furlongs Cttage Cndies Ice Cre	Norwood	MA	F	781 762-4124	11174
G H Bent Company	Milton	MA	D	617 322-9287	10452
Ginsco Inc (PA)	Fall River	MA	F	508 677-4767	8554
Goldacre Realty Inc	Spencer	MA	F	508 885-2748	12060
Highlands Lunchette	Fall River	MA	G	508 674-6206	8561
Hole In One	Eastham	MA	F	508 255-5359	8434
Honey Dew Rehoboth	Rehoboth	MA	F	508 431-2784	11609
John Harvards Brewhouse Llc	Braintree	MA	B	508 875-2337	7192
Julesan Inc	Boston	MA	E	617 437-6860	6835
Kookla Inc (PA)	Sturbridge	MA	F	508 347-2623	12251
Korner Bagel Partnership	Seekonk	MA	G	508 336-5204	11779
La Patisserie Inc	Revere	MA	F	781 729-9441	11621
Metzys Taqueria LLC	Newburyport	MA	F	978 992-1451	10701
Mike Sheas Cffhuse Trdtnals In	Fairhaven	MA	F	508 807-5754	8509
Neovii Biotech Na Inc	Boston	MA	E	781 966-3830	6908
North Star Distributors Inc (PA)	Vineyard Haven	MA	E	508 693-2000	12494
Paramount South Boston	Boston	MA	E	617 269-9999	6953
PDKD Enterprises Inc	Saugus	MA	E	781 233-8499	11764
Peaceful Meadows Ice Cream Inc (PA)	Carver	MA	F	781 447-3700	7855
Phillips Candy House Inc	Boston	MA	E	617 282-2090	6965
Piantedosi Baking Co Inc (PA)	Malden	MA	C	781 321-3400	10023
Plan B Burger LLC	Springfield	MA	F	413 285-8296	12121
Queen Associates Inc	Woburn	MA	D	781 389-8494	13644
Reasons To Be Cheerful	Concord	MA	F	978 610-6248	8132
Rescor Inc (PA)	Boston	MA	F	617 723-3635	7006
Richardsons Ice Cream	Reading	MA	G	781 944-9121	11606
Rob Roy Foods Inc	Worcester	MA	G	508 755-8933	13784
Salt & Pepper	Worcester	MA	F	508 755-1113	13793
Sarro Cohasset Incorporated	Hull	MA	D	781 383-1704	9427
Shaans Panini & Roast Beef LLC	North Billerica	MA	F	617 230-3166	10955
Slesar Bros Brewing Co Inc	Boston	MA	F	978 745-2337	7040
Spinelli Ravioli Mfg Co Inc	Boston	MA	E	617 567-1992	7053
Sunday River Brewing Co Inc	Boston	MA	G	207 824-4253	7064
Tatte Holdings LLC	Boston	MA	C	617 577-1111	7070
Tessis Pizza & Roast Beef	Tewksbury	MA	F	978 851-8700	12421
True North Ale Company LLC	Ipswich	MA	F	978 312-6473	9498
Westborough Books Inc (PA)	Westborough	MA	E	508 366-4292	13144
White Mountain Creamery Inc	Chestnut Hill	MA	F	617 527-8790	8003
Ashleigh Inc (PA)	Kennebunk	ME	E	207 967-4311	4921
Brays Brewing Company	Naples	ME	E	207 693-6806	5079
Coffee By Design Inc (PA)	Portland	ME	G	207 879-2233	5200
Flame Grilling Products Inc	Waldoboro	ME	E	800 724-5510	5576
Franks Bake Shop Inc	Bangor	ME	G	207 947-4594	4502
Gelato Fiasco Inc	Portland	ME	G	207 607-4002	5218
Kjpl Restaurants Inc	Greene	ME	F	207 577-1728	4846
Natural Selection Inc	Brunswick	ME	F	207 725-6287	4651
Orono House of Pizza	Orono	ME	F	207 866-5505	5135
Round Top Ice Cream Inc	Damariscotta	ME	F	207 563-5307	4717
Sams Italian Foods Inc (PA)	Lewiston	ME	F	207 782-9145	4991
Shains	Sanford	ME	D	207 324-1449	5415
Slab LLC	Portland	ME	E	207 245-3088	5273
Wpf Liquidating Co Inc (PA)	York	ME	D	207 363-0612	5719
7th Settlement Brewery LLC	Dover	NH	F	603 534-5292	14212
Annables Ntral Ice Cream Ygur	Portsmouth	NH	G	603 436-3400	15359
Debra Rivest Ltd	Keene	NH	E	603 355-3335	14595
Federal Spice Corp (PA)	North Conway	NH	E	603 356-6381	15248
Grist For Mill LLC	Bristol	NH	F	603 744-0405	14036
Loxsmith Bagel Corporation	Dover	NH	F	603 362-9060	14233
Nuttin Ordinary LLC	Peterborough	NH	F	603 567-7916	15322
Parkers Maple Barn Corn Crib	Mason	NH	A	603 878-2308	14967
Pro Dough Inc	Manchester	NH	G	603 623-6844	14916
Smoothie Bus LLC	Manchester	NH	F	603 303-7353	14930
Waterwheel Breakfast Gift Hse	Jefferson	NH	G	603 586-4313	14587
Coffee Exchange Ltd	Providence	RI	F	401 273-1198	16502
Ben & Jerrys Homemade Inc (HQ)	South Burlington	VT	E	802 846-1500	17571
Bennington Potters Inc (PA)	Bennington	VT	E	800 205-8033	17036
Community Apostolic Order Inc (PA)	Island Pond	VT	F	802 723-4452	17304
DC Enterprizes Inc	Hinesburg	VT	F	802 865-4480	17290
Dosa Kitchen LLC	Brattleboro	VT	G	802 246-7592	17082
Fudge Factory Inc	Manchester Center	VT	F	888 669-7425	17328
Klingers Bread Company	South Burlington	VT	E	802 860-6322	17582
Lost Nation Brewing LLC	Morrisville	VT	F	802 851-8041	17385
McHolbe-Noonan Corporation	Burlington	VT	G	802 865-0500	17144
Nourish Llc	Saint Albans	VT	G	802 782-0012	17526
Simon Pearce (us) Inc	Quechee	VT	E	802 295-2711	17463
Simon Pearce (us) Inc (PA)	Windsor	VT	C	802 674-6280	17762

	CITY	ST	EMP	PHONE	ENTRY#
Speeder & Earls Inc	Burlington	VT	F	802 660-3996	17160
Whetstone Stn Rest Brewry LLC (PA)	Brattleboro	VT	E	802 490-2354	17109
Woodbelly Pizza LLC (PA)	Cabot	VT	G	802 552-3476	17166

5813 Drinking places

	CITY	ST	EMP	PHONE	ENTRY#
Beerd Brewing Co LLC (PA)	Stonington	CT	E	860 857-1014	3507
Swagnificent Ent LLC	Bridgeport	CT	G	203 449-0124	378
Thimble Island Brewing Company	Branford	CT	E	203 208-2827	282
Amherst Brewing Co Inc	Amherst	MA	E	413 253-4400	5856
Bad Martha Farmers Brewery LLC	Edgartown	MA	F	978 335-9879	8465
Berkshire Brewing Company Inc (PA)	South Deerfield	MA	F	413 665-6600	11921
City Winery Boston LLC	Boston	MA	E	617 933-8047	6658
Four Phantoms Brewing Co LLC	Greenfield	MA	G	931 247-0315	8991
Murder Hill LLC (PA)	Whitinsville	MA	G	774 757-4411	13342
Penny Pinchers Brewing Co LLC	Millbury	MA	F	774 696-7885	10440
Phillips Candy House Inc	Boston	MA	E	617 282-2090	6965
Sarro Cohasset Incorporated	Hull	MA	D	781 383-1704	9427
Sunday River Brewing Co Inc	Boston	MA	G	207 824-4253	7064
Turtle Swamp Brewing LLC	Boston	MA	F	617 314-2952	7089
Untold Brewing LLC (PA)	Scituate	MA	F	781 378-0559	11773
Wormtown Brewery LLC	Foxborough	MA	F	774 215-5403	8738
Wormtown Brewery LLC	Worcester	MA	F	774 239-1555	13833
Ashleigh Inc (PA)	Kennebunk	ME	E	207 967-4311	4921
Brays Brewing Company	Naples	ME	E	207 693-6806	5079
Nonesuch River Brewing LLC	Scarborough	ME	F	207 219-8948	5440
Rising Tide Brewing Co LLC	Portland	ME	F	207 370-2337	5265
Saco River Brewing LLC	Fryeburg	ME	F	207 256-3028	4810
Cisco Brewers Portsmouth LLC	Portsmouth	NH	E	603 380-7575	15373
Debra Rivest Ltd	Keene	NH	E	603 355-3335	14595
Hobbs Tavern & Brewing Co LLC	West Ossipee	NH	G	603 539-2000	15694
Apponaug Brewing Company	Warwick	RI	E	401 681-4321	16782
Foam Brewers LLC	Burlington	VT	F	802 399-2511	17136
Lost Nation Brewing LLC	Morrisville	VT	F	802 851-8041	17385
McHolbe-Noonan Corporation	Burlington	VT	G	802 865-0500	17144

59 MISCELLANEOUS RETAIL

5912 Drug stores and proprietary stores

	CITY	ST	EMP	PHONE	ENTRY#
Big Y Foods Inc	Longmeadow	MA	D	413 567-6231	9848
Soleo Health Inc	Canton	MA	E	781 298-3427	7830
Walgreen Co	North Attleboro	MA	F	781 244-9431	10892

5921 Liquor stores

	CITY	ST	EMP	PHONE	ENTRY#
Brockton Beer Company LLC	Brockton	MA	G	508 521-9711	7263
Gt Spirits Inc	Boston	MA	E	617 276-5209	6777
Mass Bay Brewing Company Inc (PA)	Boston	MA	C	617 574-9551	6870
Old Creamery Grocery Store	Cummington	MA	G	413 634-5560	8147
Sunday River Brewing Co Inc	Boston	MA	G	207 824-4253	7064
Tremont Street Lq Group Inc (PA)	Boston	MA	F	617 262-0379	7085
True North Ale Company LLC	Ipswich	MA	F	978 312-6473	9498
Truro Vineyards Cape Cod LLC	North Truro	MA	F	508 487-6200	11051
Finestkind Brewing LLC	Hampton	NH	D	603 436-4026	14402
Smuttynose Brewing Company Inc	Hampton	NH	D	603 436-4026	14413
Sakonnet Vineyards LP	Little Compton	RI	F	401 635-8486	16162
Mbbc Vermont LLC	Windsor	VT	F	802 674-5491	17760
Pearl Street Beverage Inc	Burlington	VT	F	802 658-1574	17150
Rea Inc	Saint Albans	VT	F	802 527-7437	17530

5932 Used merchandise stores

	CITY	ST	EMP	PHONE	ENTRY#
E Skip Grindle & Sons	Ellsworth	ME	F	207 460-0334	4758
F O Bailey Co Inc	Falmouth	ME	G	207 781-8001	4768
Maine Antique Digest Inc	Waldoboro	ME	F	207 832-7534	5578

5941 Sporting goods and bicycle shops

	CITY	ST	EMP	PHONE	ENTRY#
Connecticut Shotgun Manufacturing Co	New Britain	CT	D	860 225-6581	2012
Del Arbour LLC	Milford	CT	F	203 882-8501	1817
Golf Galaxy LLC	Norwalk	CT	F	203 855-0500	2507
Liberty Industries Inc	East Berlin	CT	E	860 828-6361	913
Lyman Farm Incorporated (PA)	Middlefield	CT	C	860 349-1793	1725
Manup LLC	Norwalk	CT	F	203 588-9861	2533
Probatter Sports LLC	Milford	CT	G	203 874-2500	1871
TI Partners LLC	Norwalk	CT	G	203 956-6181	2583
April Twenty One Corporation	Billerica	MA	F	978 667-6424	6405
Arocam Inc	Taunton	MA	E	508 822-1220	12319
Cookes Skate Supply Inc	Wilmington	MA	G	978 657-7586	13398
Creative Playthings Ltd (PA)	Framingham	MA	F	508 620-0900	8753
Full Circle Padding Inc	Norton	MA	E	508 285-2500	11127
Mystic Valley Wheel Works Inc (PA)	Belmont	MA	F	617 489-3577	6308
Nova Sports Usa Inc	Milford	MA	F	508 473-6540	10410
Rosellis Machine & Mfg Co	Westfield	MA	F	413 562-4317	13203
Thomas & Thomas Rodmakers	Greenfield	MA	F	413 475-3840	9003
Downeast Fishing Gear	Trenton	ME	E	207 667-3131	5553

	CITY	ST	EMP	PHONE	ENTRY#
Hyperlite Mountain Gear Inc	Biddeford	ME	D	800 464-9208	4570
Portland Dry Goods Inc	Portland	ME	G	207 699-5575	5258
T J Ryan LLC	Brewer	ME	F	207 989-7183	4620
Alex & Ryan Design LLC	Manchester	NH	F	603 518-8650	14808
Collins Sports Center LLC	Rochester	NH	G	603 335-1417	15470
Ragged Mountain Equipment Inc	Intervale	NH	E	603 356-3042	14561
Matthew W Robinson	Riverside	RI	G	401 480-3975	16657
Trawlworks Inc	Narragansett	RI	F	401 789-3964	16198
Keiths II Sports Ltd	Pittsford	VT	F	802 483-6050	17444
Orvis Company Inc	Manchester	VT	E	802 362-3750	17324
The Orvis Company Inc **(PA)**	Sunderland	VT	B	802 362-3622	17635

5942 Book stores

	CITY	ST	EMP	PHONE	ENTRY#
Westborough Books Inc **(PA)**	Westborough	MA	E	508 366-4292	13144
Sellers Publishing Inc	South Portland	ME	D	207 772-6833	5514
Fred F Waltz Co Inc	Cumberland	RI	G	401 769-4900	15940

5943 Stationery stores

	CITY	ST	EMP	PHONE	ENTRY#
Adkins Printing Company	New Britain	CT	F	800 228-9745	1997
Hartford Business Supply Inc	Hartford	CT	E	860 233-2138	1485
W B Mason Co Inc	East Windsor	CT	D	888 926-2766	1089
W B Mason Co Inc	Norwalk	CT	E	888 926-2766	2593
W B Mason Co Inc	Norwich	CT	C	888 926-2766	2619
Brooks Interiors Group Inc	Wilmington	MA	E	978 988-1300	13395
Celebrations	Falmouth	MA	F	508 457-0530	8629
Da Rosas	Oak Bluffs	MA	E	508 693-0110	11221
Neenah Technical Materials Inc **(DH)**	Dalton	MA	F	678 518-3343	8151
W B Mason Co Inc	Framingham	MA	D	888 926-2766	8809
W B Mason Co Inc	Greenfield	MA	E	888 926-2766	9004
W B Mason Co Inc	Augusta	ME	E	888 926-2766	4481
W B Mason Co Inc	Bangor	ME	E	888 926-2766	4520
W B Mason Co Inc	Portland	ME	E	888 926-2766	5288
B & E Enterprises Inc	Peterborough	NH	G	603 924-7203	15312
W B Mason Co Inc	Manchester	NH	D	888 926-2766	14957
AT Cross Company LLC **(HQ)**	Providence	RI	D	401 333-1200	16476
W B Mason Co Inc	Cranston	RI	D	888 926-2766	15926
Portfolio Software Inc	Richmond	VT	F	802 434-4000	17481
W B Mason Co Inc	Brattleboro	VT	E	888 926-2766	17106
W B Mason Co Inc	South Burlington	VT	E	888 926-2766	17607

5944 Jewelry stores

	CITY	ST	EMP	PHONE	ENTRY#
Buisson Jewelers Inc	Greenwich	CT	G	203 869-8895	1324
Dt Holdings Incorporated	Stamford	CT	F	203 602-6969	3339
Elm City Mfg Jewelers Inc	Hamden	CT	F	203 248-2195	1425
Jewelry Designs Inc	Danbury	CT	F	203 797-0389	761
Joseph Hannoush Family Inc	Farmington	CT	F	860 561-4651	1225
Artinian Garabet Corporation	Concord	MA	F	978 371-7110	8102
Barmakian Brothers Ltd Partnr	Boston	MA	E	617 227-3724	6583
Charles Thomae & Son Inc	Attleboro	MA	F	508 222-0785	6001
Findings Incorporated	Attleboro	MA	D	508 222-7449	6015
G Austin Young Inc	Attleboro	MA	G	508 222-4700	6019
Mahi Gold Inc	Chatham	MA	F	508 348-5487	7898
Plastic Craft Novelty Co Inc	Attleboro	MA	F	508 222-1486	6049
Silva Jewelers of Osterville	Osterville	MA	G	508 428-2872	11246
A Silver Lining Inc	Boothbay Harbor	ME	G	207 633-4103	4599
Brown Goldsmiths & Co Inc	Freeport	ME	F	207 865-4126	4799
Daunis	Portland	ME	F	207 773-6011	5205
Bellman Jewelers Inc	Manchester	NH	G	603 625-4653	14819
M J Harrington & Co Inc **(PA)**	Newport	NH	F	603 863-1662	15231
Nazarian Jewelers NH Inc **(PA)**	Salem	NH	F	603 893-1600	15548
Sawyers Jewelry Inc	Laconia	NH	F	603 527-1000	14667
APAC Tool Inc	North Providence	RI	F	401 724-6090	16295
Dina Inc	Cranston	RI	G	401 942-9633	15851
J Cal Inc **(PA)**	Providence	RI	D	401 941-7700	16546
Ldc Inc	East Providence	RI	F	401 861-4667	16029
Racecar Jewelry Co	Pawtucket	RI	G	401 475-5701	16409
Robert Baxter Associates Inc	Warwick	RI	F	401 739-8222	16853

5945 Hobby, toy, and game shops

	CITY	ST	EMP	PHONE	ENTRY#
American Girl Brands LLC	Natick	MA	E	508 810-3461	10469
Digi-Block Inc	Cambridge	MA	E	617 926-9300	7550
Bluejacket Inc	Searsport	ME	F	207 548-9970	5451
Elves & Angels Inc	Hodgdon	ME	G	207 456-7575	4891
Sheepscot River Pottery **(PA)**	Edgecomb	ME	F	207 882-9410	4748
R John Wright Dolls Inc	Bennington	VT	F	802 447-7072	17056

5946 Camera and photographic supply stores

	CITY	ST	EMP	PHONE	ENTRY#
Ix Cameras Inc	Woburn	MA	F	617 225-0080	13592

5947 Gift, novelty, and souvenir shop

	CITY	ST	EMP	PHONE	ENTRY#
Bovano Industries Incorporated	Cheshire	CT	F	203 272-3208	576
Crystal Journey Candles LLC	Branford	CT	F	203 433-4735	245
Hudson Paper Company **(PA)**	Stratford	CT	E	203 378-8759	3548
Munsons Candy Kitchen Inc **(PA)**	Bolton	CT	E	860 649-4332	221
Mystic Seaport Museum Inc	Mystic	CT	B	860 572-0711	1940
Nicks Enterprises Inc **(PA)**	Hamden	CT	F	203 287-9990	1447
47 Brand LLC	Boston	MA	D	617 437-1384	6501
Albert E Cadrette	West Townsend	MA	F	978 597-2312	13056
Celebrations	Falmouth	MA	F	508 457-0530	8629
Dance It Up Inc	North Grafton	MA	F	508 839-1648	11021
David W Wallace	Shelburne Falls	MA	G	413 625-6523	11803
Drive-O-Rama Inc **(PA)**	Hyannis	MA	G	508 771-8100	9434
Green Mountain Choclat Co Inc **(PA)**	Hopedale	MA	G	508 473-9060	9298
Laurence Cndle Mfg Ch Sups Inc **(PA)**	Millbury	MA	E	508 865-6061	10439
Omniglow LLC	West Springfield	MA	B	413 241-6010	13039
Pilgrim Candle Company Inc **(PA)**	Westfield	MA	F	413 562-2635	13199
Vaillancourt Folk Art Inc	Sutton	MA	E	508 476-3601	12294
Whiffletree Cntry Str Gift Sp	Billerica	MA	G	978 663-6346	6490
Harbor Candy Shop Inc	Ogunquit	ME	F	207 646-8078	5123
Renaissance Greeting Cards Inc	Sanford	ME	E	207 324-4153	5409
B & E Enterprises Inc	Peterborough	NH	G	603 924-7203	15312
Kellerhaus Inc	Laconia	NH	F	603 366-4466	14654
Parkers Maple Barn Corn Crib	Mason	NH	A	603 878-2308	14967
Sawyers Jewelry Inc	Laconia	NH	F	603 527-1000	14667
Waterwheel Breakfast Gift Hse	Jefferson	NH	G	603 586-4313	14587
E Frances Paper Inc	Middletown	RI	F	857 250-0036	16173
Cold Hollow Cider Mill Inc	Waterbury Center	VT	F	802 244-8771	17680
Harringtons In Vermont Inc **(PA)**	Richmond	VT	F	802 434-7535	17479
Hemmings Motor News Inc	Bennington	VT	A	802 442-3101	17040
Lake Champlain Trnsp Co	Burlington	VT	D	802 660-3495	17141
Little Rver Htglass Studio Inc	Stowe	VT	F	802 253-0889	17632
Vermont Nut Free Choclat Inc	Colchester	VT	F	802 372-4654	17206
Windham Foundation Inc **(PA)**	Grafton	VT	F	802 843-2211	17275

5948 Luggage and leather goods stores

	CITY	ST	EMP	PHONE	ENTRY#
Sea Bags Inc	Freeport	ME	F	207 939-3679	4803

5949 Sewing, needlework, and piece goods

	CITY	ST	EMP	PHONE	ENTRY#
R & M Associates Inc	Glastonbury	CT	F	860 633-0721	1296
Dial Fabrics Co Inc	Taunton	MA	E	508 822-5333	12332
E W Winship Ltd Inc	Nantucket	MA	G	508 228-1908	10462
Erica Wilson Inc **(PA)**	Nantucket	MA	F	212 348-6196	10463
Hardwick Knitted Fabric Inc	Warren	MA	G	413 436-7704	12851
Northeast Knitting Mills Inc **(PA)**	Fall River	MA	E	508 678-7553	8589
Optimum Sportswear Inc	Lawrence	MA	F	978 689-2290	9594
P Straker Ltd	South Dartmouth	MA	G	508 996-4804	11918
Harrisville Designs Inc **(PA)**	Harrisville	NH	G	603 827-3333	14432
Ragged Mountain Equipment Inc	Intervale	NH	E	603 356-3042	14561
Say It In Stitches Inc	Concord	NH	G	603 224-6470	14155
North East Knitting Inc	Pawtucket	RI	C	401 727-0500	16395
Providence Yarn Company Inc	Pawtucket	RI	F	401 722-5600	16407
Green Mountain Spinnery Inc	East Dummerston	VT	G	802 387-4528	17216
Keiths II Sports Inc	Pittsford	VT	F	802 483-6050	17444
Simon Pearce (us) Inc **(PA)**	Windsor	VT	C	802 674-6280	17762

5961 Catalog and mail-order houses

	CITY	ST	EMP	PHONE	ENTRY#
Cogz Systems LLC	Woodbury	CT	F	203 263-7882	4385
Color Craft Ltd	East Granby	CT	F	800 509-6563	929
Defender Industries Inc	Waterford	CT	C	860 701-3400	3989
Del Arbour LLC	Milford	CT	F	203 882-8501	1817
Envirmntal Office Sltions Inc **(PA)**	East Hartford	CT	E	860 291-1900	993
Geneve Corporation **(HQ)**	Stamford	CT	E	203 358-8000	3355
Kent Scientific Corporation	Torrington	CT	F	860 626-1172	3688
Olympia Sales Inc	Enfield	CT	D	860 749-0751	1140
Scholastic Library Pubg Inc **(HQ)**	Danbury	CT	A	203 797-3500	812
Atlantic RES Mktg Systems Inc	West Bridgewater	MA	F	508 584-7816	12966
Audiospectrum Inc	Randolph	MA	F	781 767-1331	11549
Birch Outfitters LLC	Salem	MA	F	978 498-4631	11703
David W Wallace	Shelburne Falls	MA	G	413 625-6523	11803
Designing Health Inc	East Longmeadow	MA	F	661 257-1705	8373
Erica Wilson Inc **(PA)**	Nantucket	MA	F	212 348-6196	10463
Flag Fables Inc	Springfield	MA	E	413 747-0525	12095
Forced Exposure Inc	Arlington	MA	E	781 321-0320	5940
Leo F Maciver Co Inc	Brockton	MA	G	508 583-2501	7290
Lighting By Hammerworks **(PA)**	Worcester	MA	F	508 755-3434	13753
Partylite Worldwide LLC **(DH)**	Norwell	MA	C	888 999-5706	11144
Period Lighting Fixtures Inc	Clarksburg	MA	F	413 664-7141	8072
Renovators Supply Inc	Erving	MA	E	413 423-3300	8471
Southworth Company	Agawam	MA	C	413 789-1200	5807
Storey Publishing LLC **(DH)**	Clarksburg	MA	E	413 346-2100	8074
Wear-Guard Corporation	Norwell	MA	A	781 871-4100	11150
Desert Harvest Inc	Ellsworth	ME	F	919 245-1853	4756
Island Approaches	Sunset	ME	F	207 348-2459	5539
Kelco Industries	Milbridge	ME	E	207 546-7562	5061
Bascom Maple Farms Inc **(PA)**	Alstead	NH	D	603 835-2230	13856
Butcher Block Inc	Claremont	NH	E	800 258-4304	14080

SIC

	CITY	ST	EMP	PHONE	ENTRY#
Granite State Candy Shoppe LLC **(PA)**	Concord	NH	F	603 225-2591	14131
Mountain Corporation **(HQ)**	Keene	NH	E	603 355-2272	14610
Rk Parisi Enterprises Inc	Keene	NH	F	844 438-7674	14616
Tandem Kross LLC	Weare	NH	G	603 369-7060	15673
Black Dog Corporation	Portsmouth	RI	E	401 683-5858	16439
G-Form LLC **(HQ)**	Providence	RI	E	401 250-5555	16523
J H Breakell & Company Inc	Newport	RI	F	401 849-3522	16213
Lady Ann Candies Inc	Warwick	RI	F	401 738-4321	16832
Merchbro Inc	Pawtucket	RI	F	866 428-0095	16387
Americas Grdening Resource Inc **(PA)**	Burlington	VT	C	802 660-3500	17117
Americas Grdening Resource Inc	Milton	VT	C	802 660-3500	17354
Beau Ties of Vermont LLC	Middlebury	VT	E	802 388-0108	17337
Classic Dsgns By Mtthew Brak I	Saint Johnsbury	VT	F	802 748-6062	17541
Cold Hollow Cider Mill Inc	Waterbury Center	VT	E	802 244-8771	17680
Country Home Products Inc	Charlotte	VT	E	802 771-7202	17175
Hemmings Motor News Inc	Bennington	VT	A	802 442-3101	17040
Hibernation Holding Co Inc **(PA)**	Shelburne	VT	F	802 985-3001	17558
Orvis Company Inc	Manchester	VT	E	802 362-3750	17324
Speeder & Earls Inc	Burlington	VT	F	802 660-3996	17160
Sugarbush Farm Inc	Woodstock	VT	F	802 457-1757	17778
The Orvis Company Inc **(PA)**	Sunderland	VT	B	802 362-3622	17635
Vermont Christmas Company	Milton	VT	G	802 893-1670	17366
Vermont Teddy Bear Co Inc **(HQ)**	Shelburne	VT	C	802 985-3001	17563

5962 Merchandising machine operators

	CITY	ST	EMP	PHONE	ENTRY#
Coca-Cola Bottling Company of Southeastern New England Inc **(DH)**	Waterford 860 443-2816	CT	F		3987
Thomson Service Corp	Franklin	MA	F	508 528-2000	8872

5963 Direct selling establishments

	CITY	ST	EMP	PHONE	ENTRY#
Bluetriton Brands Inc	Stamford	CT	F	203 531-4100	3295
Bluetriton Brands Inc **(HQ)**	Stamford	CT	B	888 747-7437	3296
Scholastic Library Pubg Inc **(HQ)**	Danbury	CT	A	203 797-3500	812
Taunton Inc	Newtown	CT	A	203 426-8171	2349
Bcg Connect LLC	Wilmington	MA	F	978 528-7999	13389
Bluecatbio MA Inc	Concord	MA	G	978 405-2533	8106
Craft Beer Guild Distrg VT LLC **(PA)**	Kingston	MA	E	781 585-5165	9507
Easton Springs Corporation	South Easton	MA	F	508 238-2741	11942
Gatehouse Media LLC	Worcester	MA	F	508 829-5981	13728
Scarlet Aspen LLC	Portsmouth	NH	F	603 509-3990	15435
Walpole Creamery Ltd	Walpole	NH	G	603 445-5700	15664
Sogle Property LLC	Cambridge	VT	E	802 849-7943	17168

5983 Fuel oil dealers

	CITY	ST	EMP	PHONE	ENTRY#
Devine Brothers Incorporated	Norwalk	CT	E	203 866-4421	2490
Falmouth Mar Yachting Ctr Inc	Falmouth	MA	F	508 548-4600	8631
R J McDonald Inc	Barre	MA	F	978 355-6649	6203
Reggies Oil Company Inc	Quincy	MA	F	617 471-2095	11536
Mike Murphy & Sons Inc	Kingston	NH	F	603 362-4879	14636
Sail Energy LLC	Portsmouth	NH	C	844 301-7245	15434

5984 Liquefied petroleum gas dealers

	CITY	ST	EMP	PHONE	ENTRY#
Proctor Gas Inc	Proctor	VT	E	802 459-3340	17460

5989 Fuel dealers, nec

	CITY	ST	EMP	PHONE	ENTRY#
West End Firewood Inc	Whitinsville	MA	G	508 234-4747	13347

5992 Florists

	CITY	ST	EMP	PHONE	ENTRY#
Roche Bros Supermarkets LLC	Norton	MA	C	508 285-3600	11133
Wendi C Smith	Yarmouth Port	MA	F	508 362-4595	13846

5993 Tobacco stores and stands

	CITY	ST	EMP	PHONE	ENTRY#
Foundation Cigar Company LLC	Ellington	CT	G	203 738-9377	1108
Cultivate Licensing LLC	Leicester	MA	F	508 859-8130	9623

5995 Optical goods stores

	CITY	ST	EMP	PHONE	ENTRY#
Opticare Health Systems Inc **(DH)**	Waterbury	CT	C	203 574-2020	3957
BJs Wholesale Club Inc	Franklin	MA	D	508 553-9889	8821
Eye Health Services Inc	Plymouth	MA	E	508 747-6425	11459
Eye Health Services Inc **(PA)**	Quincy	MA	E	617 472-5242	11517
Perx LLC	Pittsfield	MA	F	413 358-9020	11417
Eye Exam 2000	Bedford	NH	G	603 836-5353	13927

5999 Miscellaneous retail stores, nec

	CITY	ST	EMP	PHONE	ENTRY#
Acme Sign Co **(PA)**	Stamford	CT	F	203 324-2263	3272
Barile Printers LLC	New Britain	CT	F	860 224-0127	2007
BEI Holdings Inc	Wallingford	CT	F	203 741-9300	3780
Bella Grace LLC	Fairfield	CT	E	929 533-2343	1177
Carey Manufacturing Co Inc	Cromwell	CT	F	860 829-1803	689
Ecu & US International	East Hartford	CT	F	860 906-3390	991
Flagman of America LLC	Avon	CT	G	860 678-0275	24
Foam Systems LLC	Norwalk	CT	G	800 853-1577	2502
Granite Group Wholesalers LLC	Colchester	CT	G	860 537-7600	659

	CITY	ST	EMP	PHONE	ENTRY#
Greenwich Workshop Inc **(PA)**	Seymour	CT	E	203 881-3336	2961
Keeney Holdings LLC	Farmington	CT	B	860 666-3342	1226
Kensco Inc **(PA)**	Ansonia	CT	G	203 734-8827	15
Kent Scientific Corporation	Torrington	CT	F	860 626-1172	3688
Linde Gas & Equipment Inc **(DH)**	Danbury	CT	F	844 445-4633	775
Mhq Inc	Middletown	CT	E	888 242-1118	1763
Northastern Communications Inc	Stratford	CT	F	203 381-9008	3558
Palmers Elc Mtrs & Pumps Inc	Norwalk	CT	G	203 348-7378	2551
Pic20 Group LLC	Norwalk	CT	F	203 957-3555	2558
Smithfamily1938 LLC	Enfield	CT	G	424 341-8876	1153
Soapstone Media Inc	Ellington	CT	F	860 749-0455	1116
Technical Reproductions Inc	Norwalk	CT	F	203 849-9100	2575
Washington Concrete Pdts Inc	Plainville	CT	F	860 747-5242	2788
West Hartford Lock Co LLC	West Hartford	CT	F	860 236-0671	4089
Accent Banner LLC	Medford	MA	F	781 391-7300	10278
American Water Systems LLC	Canton	MA	F	781 830-9722	7767
Atlas Water Systems Inc	Waltham	MA	D	781 373-4700	12597
Automatic Press Inc	Franklin	MA	G	508 528-2000	8818
Bluedrop LLC	South Easton	MA	F	877 662-7873	11938
Boston Business Printing Inc	Boston	MA	F	617 482-7955	6606
Chartpak Inc **(HQ)**	Leeds	MA	D	413 584-5446	9621
Clean Run Productions LLC	South Hadley	MA	F	413 532-1389	11960
Cultivate Licensing LLC	Leicester	MA	F	508 859-8130	9623
Cumar Inc	Everett	MA	E	617 389-7818	8484
Dartmouth Awning Co Inc	Westport	MA	G	508 636-6838	13295
Dinn Bros Inc **(PA)**	West Springfield	MA	D	413 750-3466	13022
East Cast McRwave Sls Dist LLC	Woburn	MA	E	781 279-0900	13562
Eastern Ice Company Inc	Fall River	MA	F	508 672-1800	8538
Essex County Coop Farming Assn	Topsfield	MA	F	978 887-2300	12433
First Electric Motor Svc Inc	Woburn	MA	F	781 491-1100	13567
Flag Fables Inc	Springfield	MA	E	413 747-0525	12095
GPA Global US Holding Inc	Mansfield	MA	F	800 334-1113	10053
Grooming Ventures - FL LLC **(HQ)**	Boston	MA	D	305 593-0667	6774
H2o Care Inc	Middleton	MA	F	978 777-8330	10384
Inert Corporation	Amesbury	MA	E	978 462-4415	5837
Jay Salem Inc	Middleton	MA	G	978 774-4999	10387
Kink Pieces of A Dream LLC	Framingham	MA	F	508 748-5417	8784
Laurence Cndle Mfg Ch Sups Inc **(PA)**	Millbury	MA	E	508 865-6061	10439
Leominster Ice Company Inc	Leominster	MA	G	978 537-5322	9678
Limelight Productions Inc	Lee	MA	G	413 243-4950	9616
Mhq Inc **(PA)**	Marlborough	MA	D	508 573-2600	10184
Motorola Mobility LLC	Lowell	MA	E	978 614-2900	9910
National Reprographics Inc	Boston	MA	F	857 383-3700	6904
Oesco Inc	Conway	MA	E	413 369-4335	8143
Pilgrim Candle Company Inc **(PA)**	Westfield	MA	E	413 562-2635	13199
Ralco Electric Inc	Westport	MA	D	508 679-3363	13299
Reliance Electric Svc Co Inc	Holyoke	MA	G	413 533-3557	9276
Santo C De Spirt Marble & Gran	Agawam	MA	G	413 786-7073	5806
Simons Stamps Inc	Turners Falls	MA	F	413 863-6800	12455
Smartpak Equine LLC **(DH)**	Plymouth	MA	D	774 773-1100	11478
Talamas Company Inc	Waltham	MA	F	617 928-3437	12788
Tech180 Corp	Easthampton	MA	F	413 203-6123	8463
Universal Color Corp Inc	Wilmington	MA	F	978 658-2300	13473
Walgreen Co	North Attleboro	MA	F	781 244-9431	10892
Yankee Candle Company Inc **(DH)**	South Deerfield	MA	C	413 665-8306	11931
Yankee Candle Investments LLC **(DH)**	South Deerfield	MA	F	413 665-8306	11932
Ycc Holdings LLC	South Deerfield	MA	A	413 665-8306	11934
Alan S Bolster	Brewer	ME	F	207 989-5143	4608
Brickell Brands LLC	South Portland	ME	D	877 598-0060	5492
Custom Canvas & Upholstery LLC	Bridgton	ME	F	207 241-8518	4627
D R Designs Inc	Manchester	ME	G	207 622-3303	5044
Enefco International Inc **(PA)**	Auburn	ME	E	207 514-7218	4428
Getchell Bros Inc	Sanford	ME	F	207 490-0809	5397
Maine Artfl Limb Orthotics Co	Portland	ME	F	207 773-4963	5236
Motor Power Inc	Lewiston	ME	G	207 782-0616	4977
Reggies Sales & Service	Auburn	ME	G	207 783-0558	4458
Two Rivers Pet Products Inc	Turner	ME	E	207 225-3965	5565
Aquatic Solutions LLC	Hampton	NH	G	888 704-7665	14398
Chase Electric Motors LLC	Bedford	NH	G	603 669-2565	13921
Image Awnings Incorporated	Wolfeboro	NH	G	603 569-6680	15734
R Filion Manufacturing Inc	Newport	NH	F	603 865-1893	15236
Ripano Stoneworks Ltd	Nashua	NH	E	603 886-6655	15160
Accessories Assoc Inc	Smithfield	RI	G	401 231-3800	16684
Arnold Art Inc **(PA)**	Newport	RI	F	401 847-2273	16203
Fiberglass Fabricators Inc	Smithfield	RI	E	401 231-3552	16700
Fred F Waltz Co Inc	Cumberland	RI	G	401 769-4900	15940
Grant Foster Group L P	Smithfield	RI	F	401 231-4077	16705
Hodges Badge Company Inc **(PA)**	Portsmouth	RI	D	401 682-2000	16443
Ion Audio LLC **(HQ)**	Cumberland	RI	F	401 658-3743	15947
Linde Gas & Equipment Inc	Slatersville	RI	D	401 767-3450	16682
Numaco Packaging LLC	East Providence	RI	F	401 438-4952	16035
Rhode Island Textile Company **(PA)**	Cumberland	RI	C	401 722-3700	15963
Sperian Protection Usa Inc **(DH)**	Smithfield	RI	E	401 232-1200	16731

	CITY	ST	EMP	PHONE	ENTRY#
Telecom Installation Svcs Inc	Middletown	RI	E	401 258-2095	16185
Thank-U Company Inc	North Kingstown	RI	G	401 739-3100	16285
Applejack Art Partners Inc	Manchester Center	VT	E	802 362-3662	17326
Biomedic Appliances Inc	Essex Junction	VT	G	802 878-0930	17228
Champlain Valley Equipment Inc	Saint Albans	VT	G	802 524-6782	17518
Gawet Marble & Granite Inc (PA)	Center Rutland	VT	G	802 773-8868	17174
Ke Usa Inc	Williston	VT	E	802 864-3009	17736
McCue Memorial Co Inc	Castleton	VT	E	802 468-5636	17173
Royal Group Inc (PA)	Rutland	VT	E	802 773-3313	17506
Swenson Granite Company LLC	Barre	VT	G	802 476-7021	17019
Yankee Medical Inc (DH)	Burlington	VT	F	802 863-4591	17164
Zephyr Designs Ltd	Brattleboro	VT	G	802 254-2788	17110

60 DEPOSITORY INSTITUTIONS

6061 Federal credit unions

	CITY	ST	EMP	PHONE	ENTRY#
Mpb Corporation (HQ)	Keene	NH	C	603 352-0310	14611

6099 Functions related to depository banking

	CITY	ST	EMP	PHONE	ENTRY#
Creative Success Alliance Corp	Rockland	MA	E	781 878-7114	11641

61 NONDEPOSITORY CREDIT INSTITUTIONS

6141 Personal credit institutions

	CITY	ST	EMP	PHONE	ENTRY#
Cross Country Motor Club Inc (HQ)	Medford	MA	A	781 393-9300	10283

6153 Short-term business credit

	CITY	ST	EMP	PHONE	ENTRY#
Capricorn Investors III LP (PA)	Greenwich	CT	F	203 861-6600	1326
General Electric Company	Norwalk	CT	A	203 797-0840	2504

6159 Miscellaneous business credit

	CITY	ST	EMP	PHONE	ENTRY#
Southern Neng Telecom Corp (HQ)	New Haven	CT	B	203 771-5200	2203

62 SECURITY & COMMODITY BROKERS, DEALERS, EXCHANGES & SERVICES

6211 Security brokers and dealers

	CITY	ST	EMP	PHONE	ENTRY#
Isupportws Inc	Stamford	CT	F	203 569-7600	3386
Stamford Capital Group Inc (PA)	Stamford	CT	F	800 977-7837	3469
Debt Exchange Inc	Boston	MA	D	617 531-3400	6685
Monadnock Associates Inc (PA)	Watertown	MA	F	617 924-7032	12894
New Generation Research Inc	Boston	MA	F	617 573-9550	6918

6221 Commodity contracts brokers, dealers

	CITY	ST	EMP	PHONE	ENTRY#
Boehringer Ingelheim Corp (DH)	Ridgefield	CT	A	203 798-9988	2886
Cofco Americas Resources Corp (HQ)	Stamford	CT	F	203 658-2820	3316
Louis Dreyfus Holdg Co US LLC (HQ)	Wilton	CT	B	203 761-2000	4242

6282 Investment advice

	CITY	ST	EMP	PHONE	ENTRY#
Asset International Inc	Greenwich	CT	E	203 629-5014	1314
Compass Group Management LLC (PA)	Westport	CT	F	203 221-1703	4162
Eagle Investment Systems LLC	West Hartford	CT	F	860 561-4602	4057
Geneve Corporation (HQ)	Stamford	CT	E	203 358-8000	3355
Ihs Herold Inc (DH)	Norwalk	CT	D	203 857-0215	2516
Wexford Capital LP (PA)	Greenwich	CT	G	203 862-7000	1361
Debt Exchange Inc	Boston	MA	D	617 531-3400	6685
Eagle Investment Systems LLC (HQ)	Wellesley	MA	E	781 943-2200	12940
Partners Capital Inv Group LLP	Boston	MA	F	617 292-2570	6955

63 INSURANCE CARRIERS

6321 Accident and health insurance

	CITY	ST	EMP	PHONE	ENTRY#
Blc Holdings LLC (PA)	Norwalk	CT	E	203 229-1007	2474

6324 Hospital and medical service plans

	CITY	ST	EMP	PHONE	ENTRY#
Essel Dental	East Windsor	CT	G	860 254-6955	1073

6331 Fire, marine, and casualty insurance

	CITY	ST	EMP	PHONE	ENTRY#
Cross Country Motor Club Inc (HQ)	Medford	MA	A	781 393-9300	10283

6351 Surety insurance

	CITY	ST	EMP	PHONE	ENTRY#
Tryxus Investment & Trdg Inc	Weston	MA	F	800 981-6616	13291

64 INSURANCE AGENTS, BROKERS AND SERVICE

6411 Insurance agents, brokers, and service

	CITY	ST	EMP	PHONE	ENTRY#
Boston Software Corp	Needham Heights	MA	F	781 449-8585	10532
Fev Tutor Inc	Woburn	MA	D	781 376-6925	13564
HMK Enterprises Inc (PA)	Lexington	MA	F	781 891-6660	9749
Joseph G Pulitano Insur Agcy	Newton	MA	F	617 783-2622	10765

65 REAL ESTATE

6512 Nonresidential building operators

	CITY	ST	EMP	PHONE	ENTRY#
American Metals Coal Intl Inc (HQ)	Greenwich	CT	F	203 625-9200	1311
Fletcher-Terry Company LLC (PA)	East Berlin	CT	D	860 828-3400	911
Louis Dreyfus Holdg Co US LLC (HQ)	Wilton	CT	B	203 761-2000	4242
Macristy Industries Inc (PA)	Newington	CT	F	860 225-4637	2305
Jewish Advocate Pubg Corp	Boston	MA	F	617 523-6232	6823
Sx Industries Inc (PA)	Stoughton	MA	F	781 828-7111	12241
Weber Realty Trust	Auburn	MA	F	508 756-4290	6127
Bosal Foam and Fiber (PA)	Limerick	ME	F	207 793-2245	5000
North Country Engineering Inc	Derby	VT	E	802 766-5396	17212

6513 Apartment building operators

	CITY	ST	EMP	PHONE	ENTRY#
CP Dauphinais Inc	Sutton	MA	E	508 865-1755	12279
Sawmill Park	Southwick	MA	G	413 569-3393	12045

6514 Dwelling operators, except apartments

	CITY	ST	EMP	PHONE	ENTRY#
Peaceful Meadows Ice Cream Inc (PA)	Carver	MA	F	781 447-3700	7855
Ambrose G McCarthy Jr	Skowhegan	ME	G	207 474-8837	5462

6519 Real property lessors, nec

	CITY	ST	EMP	PHONE	ENTRY#
Greystone Incorporated	Lincoln	RI	F	401 333-0444	16139

6531 Real estate agents and managers

	CITY	ST	EMP	PHONE	ENTRY#
Icon Capital Management LLC	Greenwich	CT	G	203 542-7792	1335
Louis Dreyfus Holdg Co US LLC (HQ)	Wilton	CT	B	203 761-2000	4242
Royalty Consulting LLC	Rocky Hill	CT	F	800 474-5157	2934
Bruno Diduca	Waltham	MA	G	781 894-5300	12613
Chas G Allen Realty LLC	Barre	MA	F	978 355-2911	6202
Coldwell Banker	Tewksbury	MA	F	978 851-3731	12390
East Coast Publications Inc (PA)	Norwell	MA	F	781 878-4540	11141
Gordon Brothers Intl LLC (HQ)	Boston	MA	D	888 424-1903	6767
Just Publications Inc	Brookline	MA	G	617 739-5878	7319
Massachusetts Assn Realtors (PA)	Foxboro	MA	F	781 890-3700	8707
Nery Corporation	New Bedford	MA	G	508 990-9800	10626
Platinum Investments Ltd	Brookline	MA	F	617 731-2447	7325
Rowe Contracting Co	Melrose	MA	G	781 620-0052	10319
Southern Brkshire Shppers Gide	Great Barrington	MA	F	413 528-0095	8978
Weber Realty Trust	Auburn	MA	F	508 756-4290	6127
Woodmeister Master Bldrs Inc (PA)	Holden	MA	C	774 345-1000	9196
Ambrose G McCarthy Jr	Skowhegan	ME	G	207 474-8837	5462
Leland Boggs II	Warren	ME	G	207 273-2610	5583
Finally Free LLC	Manchester	NH	F	603 626-4388	14848
Granite Commercial RE LLC	Nashua	NH	F	603 669-2770	15107
Cersosimo Industries Inc (PA)	Brattleboro	VT	D	802 254-4500	17080

6552 Subdividers and developers, nec

	CITY	ST	EMP	PHONE	ENTRY#
Richard Riggio and Sons Inc	Ivoryton	CT	F	860 767-0812	1532
The Bilco Company (DH)	West Haven	CT	C	203 934-6363	4128
Emery Development Ltd	Springfield	MA	G	413 782-1990	12094
Fox Homes Inc	Lee	MA	F	413 243-1950	9613
Wells Development L L C	Arlington	MA	G	781 727-5560	5950
Wesco Building & Design Inc	Stoneham	MA	G	781 279-0490	12188
Wescor Ltd (PA)	Stoneham	MA	G	781 279-0490	12189
Narragansett Improvement Co (PA)	Providence	RI	D	401 331-0051	16571

67 HOLDING AND OTHER INVESTMENT OFFICES

6712 Bank holding companies

	CITY	ST	EMP	PHONE	ENTRY#
Diversified Communications (HQ)	Portland	ME	E	207 842-5500	5209

6719 Holding companies, nec

	CITY	ST	EMP	PHONE	ENTRY#
Avara US Holdings LLC (PA)	Norwalk	CT	E	203 655-1333	2468
Kco Numet Inc	Orange	CT	E	203 375-4995	2671
Legrand Holding Inc (DH)	West Hartford	CT	E	860 233-6251	4067
Longview Holding Corporation (HQ)	Greenwich	CT	G	203 869-6734	1339
Naiad Maritime Group Inc (PA)	Shelton	CT	E	203 944-1932	3034
Polymedex Discovery Group Inc (PA)	Putnam	CT	C	860 928-4102	2870
Video Messengercom Corp	Stratford	CT	G	203 358-8842	3582
Wizards Nuts Holding LLC (PA)	Greenwich	CT	D	708 483-1315	1362
Altium Acqisition Holdings Inc	Boston	MA	A	617 516-2000	6539
Connell Limited Partnership (PA)	Boston	MA	F	617 737-2700	6665
Dawson Forte Holdings LLC (PA)	Canton	MA	E	508 651-7910	7782
Euro-Pro Holdco LLC	Needham Heights	MA	D	617 243-0235	10543
Ginger Acquisition Inc	Boston	MA	B	617 551-4000	6760
Gurnet Holding Company	Cambridge	MA	C	617 588-4900	7595

SIC

	CITY	ST	EMP	PHONE	ENTRY#
Kettle Cuisine Holdings LLC	Lynn	MA	C	617 409-1100	9981
Source Code Midco LLC (PA)	Norwood	MA	E	781 255-2022	11210
Kullson Engineered Tech Inc	Lewiston	ME	E	207 576-9808	4969
Ibmnh Inc (PA)	Manchester	NH	G	603 644-2326	14861
Cooley Group Holdings Inc (PA)	Pawtucket	RI	E	401 724-0510	16358
Mack Group Inc (PA)	Arlington	VT	B	802 375-2511	16988

6722 Management investment, open-ended

	CITY	ST	EMP	PHONE	ENTRY#
Blue Bell Mattress Company LLC (HQ)	East Windsor	CT	E	860 292-6372	1068
Arclight Enrgy Prtners Fund VI (PA)	Boston	MA	E	617 531-6300	6557
Eagle Investment Systems LLC (HQ)	Wellesley	MA	E	781 943-2200	12940
Platinum Investments Ltd	Brookline	MA	F	617 731-2447	7325

6726 Investment offices, nec

	CITY	ST	EMP	PHONE	ENTRY#
L & L Capital Partners LLC	Wilton	CT	F	203 834-6222	4241
Longworth Venture Partners LP (PA)	Norfolk	MA	G	781 663-3600	10801

6732 Trusts: educational, religious, etc.

	CITY	ST	EMP	PHONE	ENTRY#
Labcentral Inc (PA)	Cambridge	MA	E	617 863-3650	7626

6733 Trusts, nec

	CITY	ST	EMP	PHONE	ENTRY#
Strategic Value Partners LLC (PA)	Greenwich	CT	D	203 618-3500	1354
West Bridgewater Fd Pantry Inc	West Bridgewater	MA	G	339 987-1684	12990

6794 Patent owners and lessors

	CITY	ST	EMP	PHONE	ENTRY#
Capricorn Investors II LP	Greenwich	CT	E	203 861-6600	1325
Capricorn Investors III LP (PA)	Greenwich	CT	F	203 861-6600	1326
The Bilco Company (DH)	West Haven	CT	E	203 934-6363	4128
Biogen MA Inc	Cambridge	MA	D	781 464-2000	7513
Brighams Inc (HQ)	Arlington	MA	F	800 242-2423	5939
Gordon Industries Inc (PA)	Randolph	MA	E	857 401-8398	11561
Qualcomm Technologies Inc	Burlington	MA	F	781 791-6000	7418
Revo Biologics Inc (DH)	Framingham	MA	F	508 620-9700	8802
Revo Biologics Inc	Spencer	MA	E	508 370-5451	12065
White Mountain Creamery Inc	Chestnut Hill	MA	F	617 527-8790	8003
Applejack Art Partners Inc	Manchester Center	VT	E	802 362-3662	17326
Ben & Jerrys Homemade Inc (HQ)	South Burlington	VT	C	802 846-1500	17571

6798 Real estate investment trusts

	CITY	ST	EMP	PHONE	ENTRY#
Smithfamily1938 LLC	Enfield	CT	G	424 341-8876	1153

6799 Investors, nec

	CITY	ST	EMP	PHONE	ENTRY#
Atlantic Street Capitl MGT LLC (PA)	Stamford	CT	E	203 428-3158	3289
Cobra Green LLC	Norwalk	CT	A	203 354-5000	2484
Abry Partners V L P	Boston	MA	A	617 859-2959	6506
Bcpe Seminole Holdings LP (PA)	Boston	MA	F	617 516-2000	6585
BV Investment Partners LP (PA)	Boston	MA	E	617 224-0057	6629
Gemini Investors V LP (PA)	Wellesley	MA	E	781 237-7001	12942
Platinum Investments Ltd	Brookline	MA	F	617 731-2447	7325
Tryxus Investment & Trdg Inc	Weston	MA	F	800 981-6616	13291
Weston Presidio MGT Co Inc (PA)	Boston	MA	E	617 988-2500	7118

70 HOTELS, ROOMING HOUSES, CAMPS, AND OTHER LODGING PLACES

7011 Hotels and motels

	CITY	ST	EMP	PHONE	ENTRY#
Bay Colony Associates (PA)	Boston	MA	G	617 287-9100	6584
Sarro Cohasset Incorporated	Hull	MA	D	781 383-1704	9427
Northeast Structures Barns LLC	Porter	ME	G	207 512-0503	5167
Federal Spice Corp (PA)	North Conway	NH	F	603 356-6381	15248
Jordan Associates	Pittsburg	NH	F	603 246-8998	15328
Sunapee Difference LLC	Newbury	NH	D	603 763-3500	15204
Windham Foundation Inc (PA)	Grafton	VT	F	802 843-2211	17275

72 PERSONAL SERVICES

7211 Power laundries, family and commercial

	CITY	ST	EMP	PHONE	ENTRY#
Dependable Cleaners Inc (PA)	Quincy	MA	F	617 770-9232	11509

7213 Linen supply

	CITY	ST	EMP	PHONE	ENTRY#
A&P Coat Apron & Linen Sup LLC	Hartford	CT	D	914 840-3200	1466

7216 Drycleaning plants, except rugs

	CITY	ST	EMP	PHONE	ENTRY#
Dependable Cleaners Inc (PA)	Quincy	MA	F	617 770-9232	11509

7217 Carpet and upholstery cleaning

	CITY	ST	EMP	PHONE	ENTRY#
Craftech Upton	Upton	MA	F	508 529-4505	12472

7218 Industrial launderers

	CITY	ST	EMP	PHONE	ENTRY#
A&P Coat Apron & Linen Sup LLC	Hartford	CT	D	914 840-3200	1466

	CITY	ST	EMP	PHONE	ENTRY#
Unifirst Corporation (PA)	Wilmington	MA	B	978 658-8888	13472
Controlled Envmt Eqp Corp	Westbrook	ME	F	207 854-9126	5622
Sperian Protection Usa Inc (DH)	Smithfield	RI	E	401 232-1200	16731

7221 Photographic studios, portrait

	CITY	ST	EMP	PHONE	ENTRY#
Cine Magnetics Inc (HQ)	Stamford	CT	D	914 273-7600	3312
Lestat Production 81 Corp	Bedford	NH	E	866 557-4478	13939

7231 Beauty shops

	CITY	ST	EMP	PHONE	ENTRY#
Skin Catering Inc	Springfield	MA	F	413 349-8199	12128
St Cyr Inc	Worcester	MA	F	508 752-2222	13805
Stilisti	Boston	MA	G	617 262-2234	7062
Hunter Dathan Hair Artistry	Portland	ME	G	207 774-8887	5224

7261 Funeral service and crematories

	CITY	ST	EMP	PHONE	ENTRY#
Tfh Liquidation Company LLC	Dover	NH	G	603 742-4961	14252

7291 Tax return preparation services

	CITY	ST	EMP	PHONE	ENTRY#
Nationwide Tax & Business Svcs	New Bedford	MA	E	774 473-8444	10625

7299 Miscellaneous personal services

	CITY	ST	EMP	PHONE	ENTRY#
Cst Incorporated	Wallingford	CT	F	203 949-9900	3796
Eagle Investment Systems LLC	West Hartford	CT	F	860 561-4602	4057
Ephemeral Solutions Inc	Milford	CT	E	203 312-7337	1826
Surfctcom Inc	Naugatuck	CT	E	203 720-9209	1989
T-Shirts Etc Inc	Glastonbury	CT	G	860 657-3551	1298
This Old House Ventures LLC	Stamford	CT	E	475 209-8665	3481
Urban Exposition LLC (DH)	Shelton	CT	E	203 242-8717	3074
Lyman Conrad (PA)	South Hadley	MA	F	413 538-8200	11965
Opendatasoft LLC	Cambridge	MA	D	781 952-0515	7676
Toledo Woodworking Inc	Holliston	MA	G	508 280-3354	9233

73 BUSINESS SERVICES

7311 Advertising agencies

	CITY	ST	EMP	PHONE	ENTRY#
Applied Advertising Inc	Danbury	CT	F	860 640-0800	708
Directory Assistants Inc	Avon	CT	F	860 633-0122	23
Adlife Advertising & Graphics	Walpole	MA	F	508 668-4109	12547
Allison Advertising Inc	Boston	MA	F	617 368-6800	6537
Carnegie Communications LLC	Westford	MA	E	978 692-5092	13227
Carnegie Dartlet LLC (PA)	Westford	MA	D	978 692-5092	13228
Monster Tech	Weston	MA	F	978 897-0832	13288
RMS Media Group Inc	Newburyport	MA	E	978 623-8020	10713
Toth Inc (PA)	Concord	MA	E	617 577-6400	8136
Vocero Hispano Newspaper Inc	Southbridge	MA	F	866 846-6397	12038
Northeast Publishing Company	Caribou	ME	G	207 496-3251	4677
Hideaways International Inc	Portsmouth	NH	F	603 430-4433	15401
Uvp Liquidation Inc	North Haverhill	NH	D	603 787-7000	15253
Scarborough Faire Inc	Pawtucket	RI	E	401 724-4200	16416

7312 Outdoor advertising services

	CITY	ST	EMP	PHONE	ENTRY#
Lamar Advertising Company	Windsor	CT	G	860 246-6546	4285
All American Signs Inc	Plymouth	MA	F	508 830-0505	11445
Lane Printing Co Inc	Holbrook	MA	F	781 767-4450	9178
Davis-Joncas Enterprises Inc	Scarborough	ME	E	207 883-6200	5430

7313 Radio, television, publisher representatives

	CITY	ST	EMP	PHONE	ENTRY#
Comcast Sportsnet Neng LLC	Needham Heights	MA	D	617 630-5000	10537
Dixie Media LLC	Danvers	MA	E	508 739-1999	8183
Eagle-Tribune Publishing Co	Haverhill	MA	F	978 374-0321	9093
Local Media Group Inc	New Bedford	MA	C	508 997-7411	10614
Lowell Sun Publishing Company	Ayer	MA	F	978 433-6685	6185
Newhomesale LLC	Franklin	MA	F	508 541-8900	8854
Portuguese Times Inc	New Bedford	MA	G	508 997-3118	10641
Vocero Hispano Newspaper Inc	Southbridge	MA	F	866 846-6397	12038
Northeast Publishing Company	Dover Foxcroft	ME	G	207 564-8355	4730
North Eastern Publishing Co	Bennington	VT	D	802 447-7567	17053

7319 Advertising, nec

	CITY	ST	EMP	PHONE	ENTRY#
Applied Advertising Inc	Danbury	CT	F	860 640-0800	708
Chief Executive Group LLC (PA)	Stamford	CT	E	785 832-0303	3310
National Publishing Co Inc	Westport	CT	E	203 221-2300	4188
Resavue Inc	Orange	CT	F	203 878-0944	2682
Valley Container Inc	Bridgeport	CT	E	203 368-6546	383
Aerial Skyvertising Inc	Brockton	MA	G	508 586-4076	7253
Carnegie Communications LLC	Westford	MA	E	978 692-5092	13227
Carnegie Dartlet LLC (PA)	Westford	MA	D	978 692-5092	13228
Liberty Publishing Inc	Beverly	MA	F	978 777-8200	6362
Vocero Hispano Newspaper Inc	Southbridge	MA	F	866 846-6397	12038
Parsonskellogg LLC	East Providence	RI	D	866 602-8398	16037
Nomad Communications Inc	White River Junction	VT	F	802 649-1995	17709

	CITY	ST	EMP	PHONE	ENTRY#
Verizon	Swanton	VT	G	802 879-4954	17644

7331 Direct mail advertising services

	CITY	ST	EMP	PHONE	ENTRY#
Action Letter Inc (PA)	Stamford	CT	E	203 323-2466	3273
Automated Mailing Services LLC	Cheshire	CT	G	203 439-2763	574
Better Lists Incorporated	Stamford	CT	E	203 324-4171	3294
Brescias Printing Services Inc	East Hartford	CT	G	860 528-4254	976
Fairfield Marketing Group Inc (PA)	Easton	CT	F	203 261-0884	1095
Joseph Merritt & Company Inc (PA)	Hartford	CT	E	860 296-2500	1488
L P Macadams Company Inc	Bridgeport	CT	D	203 366-3647	342
Life Study Fllwship Foundation	Darien	CT	G	203 655-1436	851
Oddo Print Shop Inc	Torrington	CT	G	860 489-6585	3690
Technique Printers Inc	Clinton	CT	G	860 669-2516	651
Transmonde USa Inc	North Branford	CT	D	203 484-1528	2377
ABS Printing Inc	Swansea	MA	G	401 826-0870	12302
Boston Business Printing Inc	Boston	MA	F	617 482-7955	6606
Carnegie Communications LLC	Westford	MA	E	978 692-5092	13227
Carnegie Dartlet LLC (PA)	Westford	MA	D	978 692-5092	13228
Clark Mailing Service Inc	Worcester	MA	E	508 752-1953	13708
Communication Ink Inc	Peabody	MA	E	978 977-4595	11302
Harte Hanks Inc (PA)	Chelmsford	MA	E	512 434-1100	7931
Ils Business Services Inc	Agawam	MA	G	413 789-4555	5793
Massachusetts Envelope Co Inc (PA)	Woburn	MA	E	617 623-8000	13606
Newhomesale LLC	Franklin	MA	F	508 541-8900	8854
Owl Stamp Company Inc	Lowell	MA	G	978 452-4541	9912
Quad/Graphics Inc	East Longmeadow	MA	D	413 525-8552	8391
Red Mill Graphics Incorporated	Chelmsford	MA	F	978 251-4081	7951
Rivkind Associates Inc (PA)	South Easton	MA	F	781 269-2415	11952
Shawmut Advertising Inc (PA)	Peabody	MA	E	978 762-7500	11340
Tom Snyder Productions Inc (HQ)	Watertown	MA	D	617 600-2145	12915
Winter & Company Inc	Quincy	MA	F	617 773-7605	11545
Bangor Ltr Sp & Color Copy Ctr	Bangor	ME	G	207 945-9311	4490
Print-Mail of Maine Inc	Portland	ME	F	207 878-8000	5262
Turner Publishing Inc	Turner	ME	F	207 225-2076	5564
Echo Communications Inc	New London	NH	E	603 526-6006	15203
Puritan Press Inc (PA)	Hollis	NH	E	603 889-4500	14458
Spectrum Monthly LLC	Manchester	NH	C	603 627-0042	14936
Johnson & Wales University	Providence	RI	G	401 598-1824	16550
L Brown and Sons Printing Inc	Barre	VT	E	802 476-3164	17012
Offset House Inc	Essex Junction	VT	C	802 878-4440	17242
Paw Prints Press Inc	South Burlington	VT	F	802 865-2872	17589
Villanti & Sons Printers Inc	Milton	VT	D	802 864-0723	17367

7334 Photocopying and duplicating services

	CITY	ST	EMP	PHONE	ENTRY#
Action Letter Inc (PA)	Stamford	CT	E	203 323-2466	3273
Alliance Graphics Inc	Newington	CT	F	860 666-7992	2270
Baker Graphics Corporation	Westport	CT	F	203 226-6928	4157
Bpi Reprographics	Norwalk	CT	F	203 866-5600	2475
Brescias Printing Services Inc	East Hartford	CT	G	860 528-4254	976
Copy Cats Inc	New London	CT	G	860 442-8424	2225
Custom Printing & Copy Inc (PA)	Enfield	CT	F	860 290-6890	1127
Derosa Printing Company Inc	Manchester	CT	F	860 646-1698	1592
Hedges & Hedges Ltd	Wethersfield	CT	G	860 257-3170	4205
Oddo Print Shop Inc	Torrington	CT	G	860 489-6585	3690
Tech-Repro Inc	Stamford	CT	F	203 348-8884	3478
Technical Reproductions Inc	Norwalk	CT	F	203 849-9100	2575
Andrew T Johnson Company Inc (PA)	Boston	MA	F	617 742-1610	6548
Apex Press Inc	Westborough	MA	F	508 366-1110	13076
Boston Business Printing Inc	Boston	MA	F	617 482-7955	6606
Copy Cop The Digital Printing Company LLC	Boston	MA	E		
617 267-8899	6669				
Fars Inc	Northampton	MA	E	413 586-1332	11061
Fasprint Inc (PA)	Brockton	MA	F	508 588-9961	7278
Flashprint Graphics Inc	Cambridge	MA	G	617 492-7767	7570
Gorilla Graphics Inc (PA)	Malden	MA	F	617 623-2838	10016
Hercules Press	Boston	MA	G	617 323-1950	6786
John K Dietrich & Assoc Inc	Watertown	MA	G	617 868-4140	12884
John Karl Dietrich & Assoc	Cambridge	MA	G	617 868-4140	7619
Marcus Company Inc	Holyoke	MA	E	413 534-3303	9265
Milk Street Press Inc	Boston	MA	F	617 742-7900	6888
Northast Dcment Cnsrvtion Ctr	Andover	MA	F	978 470-1010	5901
R & H Communications Inc (PA)	Waltham	MA	F	781 893-6221	12757
Shafiis Inc (PA)	East Longmeadow	MA	E	413 224-2100	8394
Smudge Ink Incorporated	Charlestown	MA	G	617 242-8228	7882
Thomas & Thomas Inc	Lowell	MA	F	978 453-7444	9928
Tri Star Printing & Graphics	Somerville	MA	G	617 666-4480	11905
We Print Today LLC	Kingston	MA	F	781 585-6021	9514
Weston Corporation	Hingham	MA	F	781 749-0936	9164
Central Street Corporation	Bangor	ME	F	207 947-8049	4495
Coastal Business Center Inc	Wiscasset	ME	G	207 882-7197	5697
Copy Center (PA)	Winthrop	ME	F	207 623-1452	5691
Curry Printing & Copy Center	Portland	ME	F	207 772-5897	5203
First Choice Printing Inc	Lisbon Falls	ME	G	207 353-8006	5020

	CITY	ST	EMP	PHONE	ENTRY#
Gossamer Press	Benton	ME	G	207 827-9881	4545
Northeast Publishing Company	Dover Foxcroft	ME	G	207 564-8355	4730
Print Bangor	Bangor	ME	G	207 947-8049	4515
Alpha Grphics Prntshop of Ftur	Nashua	NH	F	603 595-1444	15058
Baker Graphics Inc	Manchester	NH	G	603 625-5427	14816
Boles Enterprises Inc	Manchester	NH	G	603 622-4282	14820
Fedex Office & Print Svcs Inc	Bedford	NH	F	603 644-2679	13929
Jalbert Printing LLC	Amherst	NH	G	603 623-4677	13873
New England Duplicator Inc	Manchester	NH	G	603 623-6847	14898
P2k Printing LLC	North Conway	NH	G	603 356-2010	15249
Papergraphics Print & Copy Inc	Merrimack	NH	F	603 880-1835	14997
Ram Printing Incorporated (PA)	East Hampstead	NH	E	603 382-7045	14271
RB Graphics Inc	Hooksett	NH	G	603 624-4025	14473
Southport Management Group LLC	Portsmouth	NH	G	603 433-4664	15438
Digital Press Printers LLC	Williston	VT	G	802 863-5579	17727
First Step Print Shop LLC	Burlington	VT	G	802 899-2708	17135

7335 Commercial photography

	CITY	ST	EMP	PHONE	ENTRY#
Cag Imaging LLC	Norwich	CT	G	860 887-0836	2603
James W Sewall Company	Bangor	ME	G	207 817-5410	4506
James W Sewall Company (PA)	Old Town	ME	E	207 827-4456	5125

7336 Commercial art and graphic design

	CITY	ST	EMP	PHONE	ENTRY#
A To A Studio Solutions Ltd	Stamford	CT	F	203 388-9050	3267
Arteffects Incorporated	Bloomfield	CT	E	860 242-0031	147
Barker Advg Specialty Co Inc (PA)	Cheshire	CT	D	203 272-2222	575
Franklin Impressions Inc	Norwich	CT	F	860 887-1661	2605
Gerber Scientific LLC (PA)	Tolland	CT	C	860 871-8082	3661
HJ Hoffman Company	Norwalk	CT	G	203 853-7740	2514
Hot Tops LLC	Shelton	CT	F	203 926-2067	3016
Image Processing	Guilford	CT	G	203 488-3252	1397
Lettering Inc of New York (PA)	Stamford	CT	E	203 329-7759	3400
Michael Zoppa	South Windsor	CT	G	860 289-5881	3165
P C I Group	Stamford	CT	F	203 327-0410	3425
Pj Specialties	Willington	CT	G	860 429-7626	4226
Play-It Productions Inc	Colchester	CT	F	212 695-6530	663
Project Graphics Inc	Woodbury	CT	E	802 488-8789	4388
Schwerdtle Stamp Company	Bridgeport	CT	E	203 330-2750	369
Spm Management Inc	Shelton	CT	F	203 847-1112	3065
TSS & A Inc	Prospect	CT	F	203 758-6303	2844
Xtreme Designs LLC	East Haven	CT	G	203 773-9303	1057
Allison Advertising Inc	Boston	MA	F	617 368-6800	6537
Argosy Publishing Inc (PA)	Newton	MA	D	617 527-9999	10733
Bay State Apparel Inc	Leominster	MA	G	978 534-5810	9639
Chesterfield Products Inc	Chesterfield	MA	E	413 296-0066	7997
Clayton LLC DBA Blbird Grphic	Woburn	MA	F	617 250-8500	13542
Creamer Associates Inc	Cambridge	MA	G	617 374-6000	7544
Creative Publishing Corp Amer (PA)	Peabody	MA	G	978 532-5880	11303
Desk Top Graphics Inc (HQ)	Peabody	MA	F	617 832-1927	11305
Digital Graphics Inc	North Billerica	MA	G	781 270-3670	10907
Elite Envelope & Graphics Inc	Randolph	MA	F	781 961-1800	11556
ESP Solutions Inc	Taunton	MA	F	508 285-0017	12335
Gloucester Graphics Inc (PA)	Gloucester	MA	F	978 281-4500	8937
Icl Imaging Corp	Framingham	MA	E	508 872-3280	8778
J L Enterprises Inc	Canton	MA	G	781 821-6300	7802
Lane Printing Co Inc	Holbrook	MA	F	781 767-4450	9178
Light Metal Platers LLC	Waltham	MA	F	781 899-8855	12709
M & P Machine Company Inc	Stoughton	MA	E	781 344-5888	12218
Pg Technologies Inc	Westfield	MA	G	413 562-1354	13198
Quarto Pubg Group USA Inc	Beverly	MA	E	425 827-7120	6375
Rainbow Graphics Inc	Springfield	MA	F	413 733-3376	12124
Silver Screen Design Inc	Greenfield	MA	F	413 773-1692	9000
Spray Maine Inc	Newburyport	MA	F	207 384-2273	10717
St Associates Inc	Wakefield	MA	E		12536
Stephen Gould Corporation	Tewksbury	MA	F	978 851-2500	12420
Top Half Inc	Tyngsboro	MA	F	978 454-5440	12468
Toth Inc (PA)	Concord	MA	F	617 577-6400	8136
Universal Screening Studio Inc	Everett	MA	G	617 387-1832	8502
Valley Etching Engrv Dsign Inc	Holyoke	MA	G	413 536-2256	9289
Weston Corporation	Hingham	MA	E	781 749-0936	9164
Winter & Company Inc	Quincy	MA	F	617 773-7605	11545
BBH Apparel	Boothbay Harbor	ME	F	207 633-0601	4601
DVE Manufacturing Inc	Lewiston	ME	G	207 783-9895	4957
S & K Unlimited LLC	Brownville	ME	F	207 965-6137	4638
Winter People Inc	Cumberland Center	ME	E	207 865-6636	
4711					
E Print Inc	Hudson	NH	G	603 594-0009	14495
Franklin Exeter Inc	Portsmouth	NH	F	603 836-8590	15391
Insty-Prints of Bedford Inc	Bedford	NH	G	603 622-3821	13934
Lestat Production 81 Corp	Bedford	NH	E	866 557-4478	13939
Maineline Graphics LLC	Antrim	NH	G	603 588-3177	13897
P2k Printing LLC	North Conway	NH	G	603 356-2010	15249
Pf Pro Fnshg Silkscreening Inc	Hampstead	NH	G	603 329-8344	14389

SIC

	CITY	ST	EMP	PHONE	ENTRY#
Rapid Finishing LLC	Nashua	NH	E	603 889-4234	15154
Savvy Workshop	Manchester	NH	G	603 792-0080	14926
Tk Sports and Associates Inc	Enfield	NH	G	603 442-6770	14275
Fine Line Graphics Inc (PA)	Smithfield	RI	E	401 349-3300	16701
S G Inc	Pascoag	RI	E	401 568-1110	16340
Garlic Press Inc	Colchester	VT	F	802 864-0670	17192
Oatmeal Studios Inc	Rochester	VT	F	802 967-8014	17487
Stillwater Graphics Inc	Williamstown	VT	F	802 433-9898	17718

7338 Secretarial and court reporting

	CITY	ST	EMP	PHONE	ENTRY#
Nsight Inc	Andover	MA	E	781 273-6300	5902

7342 Disinfecting and pest control services

	CITY	ST	EMP	PHONE	ENTRY#
Connecticut Tick Control LLC	Norwalk	CT	F	203 855-7849	2486
Pfm Holding Co	Fairfield	CT	B	203 335-3300	1197
Cambridge Chemical Co Corp	Cambridge	MA	F	617 876-4484	7529

7349 Building maintenance services, nec

	CITY	ST	EMP	PHONE	ENTRY#
Cw Solutions LLC	New Britain	CT	D	860 229-7700	2018
E & J Parts Cleaning Inc	Waterbury	CT	F	203 757-1716	3909
Front Line Apparel Group LLC	Hebron	CT	F	860 859-3524	1527
Hartford Fire Equipment	Plainville	CT	F	860 747-2757	2763
Innovative Environmental LLC	Colchester	CT	F	860 871-7582	660
New England Industrial Sup LLC	Newington	CT	F	860 436-5959	2308
Pfm Holding Co	Fairfield	CT	B	203 335-3300	1197
Lps Enterprises Inc	East Freetown	MA	E	508 763-3830	8364
Maine Turnpike Authority	Cumberland Center	ME	D	207 829-4531	
4709					
4smartpro LLC	Saint Johnsbury	VT	F	802 745-8797	17537

7352 Medical equipment rental

	CITY	ST	EMP	PHONE	ENTRY#
Vivax Medical Corporation	Naugatuck	CT	F	203 729-0514	1993
Tenacity Medical Inc	Lexington	MA	G	617 299-8001	9786

7353 Heavy construction equipment rental

	CITY	ST	EMP	PHONE	ENTRY#
Baxter Inc	West Yarmouth	MA	F	508 775-0375	13072
Central Equipment Company	Stillwater	ME	F	207 827-6193	5533
Granite Shore Power LLC	Bow	NH	C	603 634-2299	13999
American Equipment & Fabg Corp	East Providence	RI	F	401 438-2626	16002
Acer Holdings Starksboro Inc	Starksboro	VT	F	802 453-4438	17625

7359 Equipment rental and leasing, nec

	CITY	ST	EMP	PHONE	ENTRY#
3333 LLC	Manchester	CT	G	860 643-1384	1579
Aircastle Advisor LLC	Stamford	CT	D	203 504-1020	3276
Mobile Mini Inc	Suffield	CT	G	860 668-1888	3594
Pastanch LLC	Naugatuck	CT	E	203 720-9478	1979
Pitney Bowes Inc (PA)	Stamford	CT	A	203 356-5000	3433
Quadient Inc (DH)	Milford	CT	C	203 301-3400	1874
The Bilco Company (DH)	West Haven	CT	C	203 934-6363	4128
Thomas Keegan & Sons Inc	Wallingford	CT	F	203 239-9248	3862
Audiospectrum Inc	Randolph	MA	E	781 767-1331	11549
B R T Inc	Worcester	MA	E	508 791-2383	13701
Bluedrop LLC	South Easton	MA	F	877 662-7873	11938
Boston Gar Flrg & Cabinets LLC	Hanover	MA	F	339 788-9580	9026
Boston Light & Sound Inc (PA)	Malden	MA	F	617 787-3131	10005
Doble Engineering Company (HQ)	Marlborough	MA	F	617 926-4900	10145
Easton Springs Corporation	South Easton	MA	F	508 238-2741	11942
Limelight Productions Inc	Lee	MA	G	413 243-4950	9616
Lyn-Lad Group Ltd (PA)	Lynn	MA	E	781 598-6010	9984
Lynn Ladder Scaffolding Co Inc (HQ)	Lynn	MA	D	781 598-6010	9985
Maki Corp (PA)	Gardner	MA	E	978 343-7422	8895
MEI Rigging & Crating LLC	Salisbury	MA	F	978 685-7700	11742
Reading Diagnostic Center	Reading	MA	F	781 942-9876	11605
Tent Connection Inc	Northbridge	MA	G	508 234-8746	11119
United Site Services Inc (PA)	Westborough	MA	C	508 594-2655	13141
Visi-Flash Rentals Eastern	West Bridgewater	MA	E	508 583-9100	12988
Waverly Tool Rental & Sales Co	Framingham	MA	F	508 872-8866	8811
Whitney & Son Inc	Fitchburg	MA	F	978 343-6353	8682
Wilevco Inc	Billerica	MA	E	978 667-0400	6491
Grs Group Inc	Portland	ME	F	207 775-6139	5220
Leavitt & Parris Inc	Portland	ME	F	207 797-0100	5233
Maine Bay Canvas Inc	Portland	ME	F	207 878-8888	5237
Sonco Worldwide Inc	Warwick	RI	F	401 406-3761	16863

7361 Employment agencies

	CITY	ST	EMP	PHONE	ENTRY#
ABB Enterprise Software Inc	Plainville	CT	A	860 747-7111	2744
Opportunity Works Inc (PA)	Newburyport	MA	E	978 462-6144	10705
Traincroft Inc (PA)	Medford	MA	E	781 393-6943	10299
Voltea Inc	Worcester	MA	F	510 861-3719	13825

7363 Help supply services

	CITY	ST	EMP	PHONE	ENTRY#
New England Industrial Sup LLC	Newington	CT	F	860 436-5959	2308
Honeywell DMC Services LLC	Danvers	MA	B	978 774-3007	8192

	CITY	ST	EMP	PHONE	ENTRY#
Nsight Inc	Andover	MA	E	781 273-6300	5902
Traincroft Inc (PA)	Medford	MA	E	781 393-6943	10299

7371 Custom computer programming services

	CITY	ST	EMP	PHONE	ENTRY#
Active Internet Tech LLC (PA)	Glastonbury	CT	C	800 592-2469	1269
Arecna Holdings Inc	Branford	CT	F	203 819-2322	236
Cnc Engineering Inc	Enfield	CT	E	860 749-1780	1124
Compuweigh Corporation (PA)	Woodbury	CT	F	203 262-9400	4386
Gerber Technology LLC (HQ)	Tolland	CT	B	800 321-2448	3662
Gss Infotech Ct Inc	Glastonbury	CT	C	860 709-0933	1282
Isupportws Inc	Stamford	CT	F	203 569-7600	3386
Kimchuk Incorporated (PA)	Danbury	CT	F	203 790-7800	766
Microtools Inc	Simsbury	CT	G	860 651-6170	3094
Otis Elevator Company (HQ)	Farmington	CT	C	860 674-3000	1235
Peerless Systems Corporation (DH)	Stamford	CT	G	203 350-0040	3428
Powerphone Inc	Madison	CT	E	203 245-8911	1566
R4 Technologies Inc (PA)	Ridgefield	CT	E	203 461-7100	2906
Scholastic Library Pubg Inc (HQ)	Danbury	CT	A	203 797-3500	812
SS&c Technologies Inc (HQ)	Windsor	CT	C	800 234-0556	4302
Vertafore Inc	Windsor	CT	E	860 602-6000	4312
Vinegar Syndrome LLC	Bridgeport	CT	G	475 731-1778	384
Visionpoint LLC	Newington	CT	E	860 436-9673	2333
21st Century Software Tech Inc	Boston	MA	D	610 341-9017	6499
2is Inc	Walpole	MA	E	508 850-7520	12545
Able Software Corp (PA)	Lexington	MA	G	781 862-2804	9719
American Business Systems Inc	Chelmsford	MA	F	978 250-0335	7905
Apama Inc	Bedford	MA	F	781 280-4000	6208
Apiphani Inc	Boston	MA	E	800 215-0811	6551
Apogee Imaging Systems Inc	Concord	MA	F		8100
Aquila Technology Corp	Burlington	MA	E	781 993-9004	7334
Aries Systems Corporation	North Andover	MA	E	978 975-7570	10820
Aspen Technology Inc (HQ)	Bedford	MA	D	781 221-6400	6211
Aspentech Corporation (DH)	Bedford	MA	C	781 221-6400	6212
Belle Artfl Intelligence Corp	Cambridge	MA	F	650 291-9410	7504
Bellhawk Systems Corporation	Millbury	MA	G	508 865-8070	10428
Biobright LLC (HQ)	Boston	MA	G	617 444-9007	6595
Bitflow Inc	Woburn	MA	F	781 932-2900	13526
Bridgeline Digital Inc (PA)	Woburn	MA	F	781 376-5555	13536
Bvsn LLC	Waltham	MA	F	781 290-0710	12616
Bynder LLC	Boston	MA	C	857 310-5434	6630
Cami Research Inc	Acton	MA	F	978 266-2655	5742
Cantata Technology Inc (DH)	Needham Heights	MA	C	781 449-4100	10533
Canvas Gfx Inc	Boston	MA	E	833 721-0829	6637
Catapult Sports Inc (HQ)	Boston	MA	E	978 447-5220	6642
Centerity Systems Inc	Newton	MA	F	339 225-7007	10743
Channelwave Software Inc (DH)	Cambridge	MA	F	617 621-1700	7538
Cimcon Software LLC (PA)	Westford	MA	D	978 464-9180	13229
Circle Labs Bio Inc	Cambridge	MA	G	516 660-6045	7541
Claricode Inc	Dedham	MA	F	781 449-2450	8238
CLC Bio LLC	Beverly	MA	F	617 945-0178	6339
Connected Auto Systems Neng In	South Easton	MA	E	508 238-5855	11940
Cosmic Software Inc	North Chelmsford	MA	F	978 667-2556	10967
Creativestar Solution Inc	Waltham	MA	F	617 326-5308	12645
CST of America LLC	Framingham	MA	E	508 665-4400	8754
Datarobot Inc (PA)	Boston	MA	D	617 765-4500	6684
Demandware LLC (HQ)	Burlington	MA	D	888 553-9216	7360
Diacritech Inc	Boston	MA	F	617 236-7500	6692
Dinner Daily LLC	Westford	MA	F	978 392-5887	13234
Double-Take Software Inc (DH)	Burlington	MA	C	949 253-6500	7365
EMC Corporation (HQ)	Hopkinton	MA	B	508 435-1000	9322
Expertek Systems Inc	Marlborough	MA	E	508 624-0006	10149
Forefield Inc	Marlborough	MA	E	508 630-1100	10150
Full Circle Technologies Inc	Boston	MA	E	617 722-0100	6749
Grove Labs Inc	Somerville	MA	F	703 608-8178	11878
Hirezon Corporation	Westborough	MA	F	508 836-3800	13105
Hottinger Bruel & Kjaer Inc (DH)	Marlborough	MA	D	508 485-7480	10164
Human Resource Dev Press (PA)	Belchertown	MA	E	413 253-3488	6280
Iconics Inc (HQ)	Foxboro	MA	E		8700
Iet Solutions LLC (DH)	Canton	MA	E	818 838-0606	7800
Infinidat Inc	Waltham	MA	D	781 907-7585	12699
Inscribe Inc	Woburn	MA	E	781 933-3331	13586
Intuvision Inc	Woburn	MA	G	781 497-1015	13591
Ivory Onyx	Boston	MA	F	617 454-4980	6820
Kemp Technologies Inc	Rochdale	MA	E	631 418-8407	11627
King Fisher Co Inc	Lowell	MA	F	978 596-0214	9890
Kognito Solutions LLC	Burlington	MA	E	212 675-2651	7387
Leanix Inc (DH)	Watertown	MA	F	781 321-6500	12887
Leidos Inc	Tewksbury	MA	F	781 221-7627	12402
Mathworks Inc	Natick	MA	A	508 647-7000	10485
Mathworks Inc (PA)	Natick	MA	A	508 647-7000	10486
Meta Software Corporation (PA)	Burlington	MA	F	781 238-0293	7393
Metalmark Innovations Pbc	Cambridge	MA	G	617 714-4026	7642
Microsemi Frequency Time Corp	Beverly	MA	E	978 232-0040	6366

	CITY	ST	EMP	PHONE	ENTRY#
Modus Media Inc	Waltham	MA	E	781 663-5000	12724
Monotype Imaging Holdings Inc (DH)	Woburn	MA	D	781 970-6000	13614
Monotype Imaging Inc (DH)	Woburn	MA	D	781 970-6000	13615
MTI Systems Inc	West Springfield	MA	F	413 733-1972	13035
Nara Logics Inc	Boston	MA	F	617 945-2049	6902
Neuromotion Inc	Boston	MA	F	415 676-9326	6912
Ntt Data Intl Svcs Inc (DH)	Boston	MA	B	800 745-3263	6927
On Technology Corp (PA)	Waltham	MA	D	781 487-3300	12743
Para Research Inc	Gloucester	MA	G	978 282-1100	8951
Pegasystems Inc (PA)	Cambridge	MA	A	617 374-9600	7681
Phase Forward	Waltham	MA	E	781 626-1256	12748
Picis Clinical Solutions Inc (DH)	Wakefield	MA	C	336 397-5336	12528
Pmweb Inc	Wakefield	MA	D	617 207-7080	12529
Progress Software Corporation (PA)	Burlington	MA	C	781 280-4000	7413
Ptc Inc (PA)	Boston	MA	A	781 370-5000	6983
Rampage Systems Inc	Waltham	MA	E	781 891-1001	12758
Raytheon Company	Marlborough	MA	E	508 490-1000	10201
Research Applctons Fncl Trckin	Boston	MA	E	800 939-7238	7007
Revvity Signals Software Inc (DH)	Waltham	MA	E	781 663-6900	12769
Rocket Software Systems Inc	Waltham	MA	E	248 833-9000	12772
Rockstar New England Inc	Andover	MA	E	978 409-6272	5913
Sdl Xyenterprise LLC (PA)	Wakefield	MA	E	781 756-4400	12533
Seachange International Inc (PA)	Boston	MA	D	978 897-0100	7029
Sepaton Inc	Marlborough	MA	D	508 490-7900	10210
Silverthread Inc	Cambridge	MA	G	800 674-9366	7715
Solusoft Inc	North Andover	MA	E	978 375-6021	10849
Speechworks International	Burlington	MA	E	781 565-5000	7432
Squareworks Consulting LLC	Boston	MA	E	800 779-6285	7057
Stmicroelectronics Inc	Burlington	MA	G	781 861-2650	7435
Superpedestrian Inc (PA)	Cambridge	MA	E	877 678-7518	7725
Svh Software Inc	Chelmsford	MA	G	978 566-1812	7961
Syberworks Inc	Arlington	MA	E	781 891-1999	5948
Tom Snyder Productions Inc (HQ)	Watertown	MA	D	617 600-2145	12915
Tomorrow Companies Inc	Boston	MA	F	800 735-7075	7080
Ukg Kronos Systems LLC (DH)	Lowell	MA	B	978 250-9800	9931
VMS Software Inc	Boston	MA	D	425 766-1692	7110
Voxel8 Inc	Somerville	MA	F	916 396-3714	11912
Waters Corporation (PA)	Milford	MA	A	508 478-2000	10424
Window Book Inc	Cambridge	MA	D	617 395-4500	7761
Xiphos Partners Inc	Dartmouth	MA	G	508 991-1014	8233
Zlink Inc	Maynard	MA	D	978 309-3628	10268
Covetrus North America LLC (PA)	Portland	ME	G	888 280-2221	5202
Cybernorth LLC	South Portland	ME	G	207 331-3310	5496
Garmin International Inc	Yarmouth	ME	F	800 561-5105	5704
Hawkin Dynamics LLC	Westbrook	ME	F	207 405-9142	5628
Team Augmented Reality Inc	Nobleboro	ME	G	207 350-0460	5102
Tyler Technologies Inc	Bangor	ME	F	207 947-4494	4517
CNi Corp	Milford	NH	G	603 249-5075	15017
Dataxoom Corp (PA)	Manchester	NH	F	510 474-0044	14840
Impact Science & Technology Inc	Nashua	NH	C	603 459-2200	15113
Kbace Technologies Inc (HQ)	Nashua	NH	D	603 821-7000	15121
Loftware Holdings Inc (PA)	Portsmouth	NH	F	603 766-3630	15419
Loxsmith Bagel Corporation	Dover	NH	F	603 362-9060	14233
Mmis Inc	Portsmouth	NH	D	603 929-5078	15424
North Tecom LLC	Manchester	NH	F	603 851-5165	14904
Premier Semiconductor Svcs LLC (DH)	Manchester	NH	D	267 954-0130	14914
Profitkey International Inc	Salem	NH	E	603 898-9800	15556
Softech Inc (HQ)	Nashua	NH	E	513 942-7100	15170
Tomtom North America Inc	Lebanon	NH	A	603 643-0330	14701
A2b Tracking Solutions Inc	Portsmouth	RI	E	401 683-5215	16434
Avtech Software Inc (PA)	Warren	RI	F	401 628-1600	16752
Hexagon Mfg Intllgnce- Mtrlogy	North Kingstown	RI	D	401 886-2000	16256
McLaughlin Research Corp	Middletown	RI	C	401 849-4010	16179
MTI Film LLC (HQ)	Providence	RI	G	401 831-1315	16570
Purevita Labs LLC	West Warwick	RI	F	401 258-8968	16921
Radley Corporation	Lincoln	RI	E	616 554-9060	16152
Sproutel Inc	Providence	RI	F	914 806-6514	16615
Datamann Inc	Wilder	VT	E	802 295-6600	17714
Ivy Computer Inc	Waterbury Center	VT	F	802 244-7880	17681
Natworks Inc	Northfield	VT	F	802 485-6818	17433
Prom Software Inc	South Burlington	VT	F	802 862-7500	17597
Rectrac LLC	Essex Junction	VT	D	802 879-6993	17244
Wellsky Humn Social Svcs Corp	Essex Junction	VT	D	802 316-3000	17249

7372 Prepackaged software

	CITY	ST	EMP	PHONE	ENTRY#
3 Story Software LLC	New Milford	CT	G	860 799-6366	2236
360alumni LLC	Ridgefield	CT	F	203 253-5860	2884
5381 Partners LLC	Fairfield	CT	E	203 255-7985	1174
Active Internet Tech LLC (PA)	Glastonbury	CT	C	860 592-2469	1269
Advanced Decisions Inc	Orange	CT	G	203 402-0603	2665
Akademos LLC	Norwalk	CT	D	203 866-0190	2461
API Wizard LLC	Stamford	CT	E	800 691-8714	3283
Ataccama Corp US	Stamford	CT	E	203 564-1488	3287

	CITY	ST	EMP	PHONE	ENTRY#
Atconsulting LLC	Stamford	CT	G	203 987-5355	3288
Automatech Inc	Unionville	CT	F	860 673-5940	3747
Becaid LLC	New Haven	CT	G	203 915-6914	2125
Beqom North America Inc	Southport	CT	E	888 995-3028	3242
Blc Holdings LLC (PA)	Norwalk	CT	E	203 229-1007	2474
Blue Sky Studios Inc	Greenwich	CT	C	203 992-6000	1319
Brit Systems LLC	Wallingford	CT	F	214 630-0636	3783
CD Solutions Inc	Branford	CT	G	203 481-5895	243
Channel Sources LLC	Brookfield	CT	E	203 775-6464	515
Cobra Green LLC	Norwalk	CT	A	203 354-5000	2484
Computer Prgrm & Systems Inc (PA)	Stamford	CT	G	203 324-9203	3319
Continuity Engine Inc	Ridgefield	CT	F	866 631-5556	2893
Continuum	Norwich	CT	G	860 383-2562	2604
Coss Systems Inc (not Inc)	Old Greenwich	CT	G	732 447-7724	2631
Cratedigger Inc	New Canaan	CT	G	203 594-1488	2081
Criterion Inc	Norwalk	CT	D	203 703-9000	2488
Cst Incorporated	Wallingford	CT	F	203 949-9900	3796
Cya Technologies Inc	Shelton	CT	F	203 513-3111	2994
Datto Holding Corp (DH)	Norwalk	CT	D	888 995-1431	2489
Device42 Inc	West Haven	CT	F	203 409-7242	4103
Eagle Investment Systems LLC	West Hartford	CT	F	860 561-4602	4057
Earnix Inc	Westport	CT	F	203 557-8077	4166
Ebrevia Inc	Stamford	CT	F	203 870-3000	3341
Edge2web Inc	Southbury	CT	G	203 770-2588	3193
Enginuity Plm LLC (DH)	Milford	CT	F	203 218-7225	1825
Explain Everything Sales Inc	Ridgefield	CT	G	646 825-8552	2897
Flexiinternational Sftwr Inc (PA)	Shelton	CT	E	203 925-3040	3007
Flitsai Inc	Ellington	CT	F	203 586-8201	1106
Freethink Technologies Inc	Branford	CT	F	860 237-5800	258
Frevvo Inc	Branford	CT	F	203 208-3117	259
Frevvo LLC	Wallingford	CT	G	203 208-3117	3808
Gerber Scientific LLC (PA)	Tolland	CT	C	860 871-8082	3661
Graybark Enterprises LLC	Fairfield	CT	G	203 255-4503	1187
Grey Wall Software LLC	New Haven	CT	F	203 782-5944	2158
Gss Infotech Ct Inc	Glastonbury	CT	C	860 709-0933	1282
Halo Technology Holdings Inc	Stamford	CT	C	203 422-2950	3361
Harpoon Acquisition Corp	Glastonbury	CT	E	860 815-5736	1285
Healthper Inc	Hamden	CT	E	203 506-0957	1429
Hexplora LLC	Rocky Hill	CT	D	860 760-7601	2928
Hypack Inc (HQ)	Middletown	CT	F	860 635-1500	1752
Intellgent Clearing Netwrk Inc	North Haven	CT	G	203 972-0861	2415
Intellinet Corporation	Farmington	CT	G	860 677-4427	1224
Kol LLC	Woodbridge	CT	F	203 393-2924	4379
Lablite LLC	New Milford	CT	F	860 355-8817	2251
Leap Pond LLC	Milford	CT	G	203 361-9200	1844
Lessonbee Inc	Stamford	CT	G	646 582-2040	3399
Lifetoken Software Inc	Cos Cob	CT	G	203 515-9686	678
Litigation Analytics Inc (PA)	Ridgefield	CT	G	203 431-0300	2901
Locallive Networks Inc	Stamford	CT	F	877 355-6225	3402
Mobile Global Esports Inc	Westport	CT	F	475 666-8401	4186
Navtech Systems Inc	Old Greenwich	CT	G	203 661-7800	2634
Nexvue Information Systems Inc	Stamford	CT	E	203 327-0800	3418
Norfield Data Products Inc	Norwalk	CT	F	203 849-0292	2546
Objectif Lune Inc	Milford	CT	G	203 878-7206	1856
Peerless Systems Corporation (DH)	Stamford	CT	G	203 350-0040	3428
Phesi Inc	East Lyme	CT	G	800 679-0068	1061
Pitney Bowes Inc (PA)	Stamford	CT	A	203 356-5000	3433
Primatics Financial LLC (HQ)	Windsor	CT	E	703 342-0040	4296
Protegrity Usa Inc (PA)	Stamford	CT	E	203 326-7200	3438
Qualedi Inc	Shelton	CT	G	203 538-5320	3058
R4 Technologies Inc (PA)	Ridgefield	CT	E	203 461-7100	2906
Regenerative Medicine LLC (PA)	Greenwich	CT	G	203 969-4877	1346
Rite-Solutions Inc (PA)	Pawcatuck	CT	F	401 847-3399	2725
Sagemaker Inc	Fairfield	CT	D	203 368-4888	1199
Securities Software & Consulti	Windsor	CT	E	860 298-4500	4299
Shibumicom Inc	Norwalk	CT	F	855 744-2864	2571
Shippinginsight	Weston	CT	G	203 260-0480	4153
Sigmund Software LLC	Danbury	CT	F	800 448-6975	817
Smartpay Solutions LLC	New Haven	CT	E	860 986-7659	2200
Solve Advisors Inc (PA)	Stamford	CT	F	646 699-5041	3465
SS&c Technologies Inc (HQ)	Windsor	CT	A	800 234-0556	4302
SS&c Technologies Holdings Inc (PA)	Windsor	CT	A	860 298-4500	4303
Stamford Risk Analytics LLC	Stamford	CT	F	203 559-0883	3472
Swing By Swing Golf Inc	Hartford	CT	E	804 869-6983	1511
Technolutions Inc	New Haven	CT	D	203 404-4835	2206
Telenity Inc	Monroe	CT	B	203 445-2000	1924
Tethereducation Inc	New Haven	CT	E	203 691-0131	2207
Thebeamer LLC	East Hartford	CT	F	860 212-5071	1027
TMC Liquidating Corp	Wallingford	CT	D	800 344-5901	3869
Torino Systems LLC	Madison	CT	G	203 871-1118	1573
Uniworld Bus Publications Inc	Darien	CT	G	201 384-4900	857
Valen Technologies Inc	Hartford	CT	E	720 570-3333	1515
Venan Entertainment Inc	Middletown	CT	G	860 704-6330	1789

	CITY	ST	EMP	PHONE	ENTRY#		CITY	ST	EMP	PHONE	ENTRY#
Veoci Inc	New Haven	CT	D	203 782-5944	2214	Blubox Security Inc	Andover	MA	E	508 414-3517	5872
Vertafore Inc	Windsor	CT	E	860 602-6000	4312	Blue Cow Software LLC	Wakefield	MA	F	781 245-2583	12502
Voice Glance LLC	Mystic	CT	F	800 260-3025	1945	Blueconic Inc	Boston	MA	E	888 440-2583	6599
Webilent Technology Inc	South Windsor	CT	E	860 254-6169	3190	Bluesnap Inc (PA)	Waltham	MA	E	781 790-5013	12609
Wipl-D (usa) LLC	West Hartford	CT	E	860 570-0678	4090	Boston Software Corp	Needham Heights	MA	F	781 449-8585	10532
128 Technology Inc (PA)	Lowell	MA	C	781 203-8400	9850	Botify Corporation	Cambridge	MA	G	617 576-2005	7522
21st Century Software Tech Inc	Boston	MA	D	610 341-9017	6499	Boxcar Media LLC	North Adams	MA	F	413 663-3384	10804
3rd Millennium Inc	Cambridge	MA	F	781 890-4440	7464	BR Holdings Inc (PA)	Gloucester	MA	C	978 281-3723	8925
4tell Solutions LP	Foxboro	MA	G	207 828-7900	8688	Bridgeline Digital Inc (PA)	Woburn	MA	E	781 376-5555	13536
AB Ovo North America Inc	Somerville	MA	G	617 718-0765	11859	Brightcove Inc (PA)	Boston	MA	B	888 882-1880	6623
Able Software Corp (PA)	Lexington	MA	G	781 862-2804	9719	Buildium LLC	Boston	MA	G	888 414-1988	6627
Accelevents Inc	Boston	MA	D	857 254-8035	6509	Bullhorn Inc (PA)	Boston	MA	D	617 478-9100	6628
Accodale Technolgy Inc	Franklin	MA	F	508 520-1400	8813	Business Forecast Systems Inc	Waltham	MA	F	617 484-5050	12614
Accufund Inc	Needham	MA	G	781 433-0233	10502	Business Systems Incorporated	Marlborough	MA	G	508 624-4600	10123
Acktify Inc	Melrose	MA	E	781 462-3942	10312	Bvsn LLC	Waltham	MA	F	781 290-0710	12616
Aclara Software Inc	Wellesley	MA	D	781 283-9160	12933	Bynder LLC	Boston	MA	C	857 310-5434	6630
Acme Packet Inc	Bedford	MA	A	781 328-4400	6205	Caliper Corporation	Newton	MA	E	617 527-4700	10740
Acquia Inc (PA)	Boston	MA	A	888 922-7842	6511	Cambridge Semantics Inc (PA)	Boston	MA	D	617 245-0517	6636
Acronis Inc	Burlington	MA	E	781 782-9100	7331	Canvas Gfx Inc	Boston	MA	C	833 721-0829	6637
Actifio Federal Inc	Needham	MA	F	781 795-9182	10503	Carbon Black LLC (DH)	Waltham	MA	B	617 393-7400	12620
Actuality Systems Inc	Arlington	MA	G	617 325-9230	5938	Care International Exch Inc	Waltham	MA	D	781 642-5900	12621
Adobe Inc	Newton	MA	D	617 467-6760	10731	Carrier Eq LLC	Boston	MA	D	617 841-7207	6640
Adobe Inc	Waltham	MA	A	408 536-6000	12585	Casenet LLC (HQ)	Bedford	MA	E	781 357-2700	6217
Advance Systems Inc	Newton	MA	F	888 238-8704	10732	Cazena Inc	Waltham	MA	E	781 897-6380	12622
Advanced Entp Systems Corp	Boston	MA	E	508 431-7607	6517	Centage Corporation	Framingham	MA	D	800 366-5111	8751
Advantage Data Inc (HQ)	Boston	MA	F	212 227-8870	6518	Centerity Systems Inc	Newton	MA	F	339 225-7007	10743
Agrify Corporation (PA)	North Billerica	MA	E	617 896-5243	10894	Centive Inc	Lowell	MA	F	866 469-2285	9866
Airworks Solutions Inc	Boston	MA	E	857 990-1060	6524	Centra Software Inc (DH)	Lexington	MA	D	781 861-7000	9729
Aislebuyer Lllc	Boston	MA	F	617 606-7062	6525	Cerence Inc (PA)	Burlington	MA	D	857 362-7300	7343
Aiven Inc	Boston	MA	E	860 908-6924	6526	Cerence Operating Company (HQ)	Burlington	MA	E	857 362-7300	7344
Akamai Technologies Inc	Cambridge	MA	G	203 969-5161	7471	Cerner Corporation	Waltham	MA	E	781 434-2200	12623
Akamai Technologies Inc	Cambridge	MA	E	415 994-2299	7472	Certeon Inc	Burlington	MA	F	781 425-5099	7345
Akamai Technologies Inc (PA)	Cambridge	MA	B	617 444-3000	7473	Channelwave Software Inc (DH)	Cambridge	MA	E	617 621-1700	7538
Alfresco Software Inc (DH)	Wellesley	MA	D	888 317-3395	12934	Check Point Software Tech Inc	Acton	MA	D	978 635-0300	5743
Algorithmia Inc	Boston	MA	G	415 741-1491	6533	Chef Software Inc (HQ)	Burlington	MA	C	206 508-4799	7346
Alignable Inc	Boston	MA	F	978 376-5852	6534	Cheshire Software Inc	Newton	MA	F	617 527-4000	10746
Alivia Analytics LLC	Woburn	MA	E	617 227-5111	13504	Cimcon Software LLC (PA)	Westford	MA	D	978 464-9180	13229
Alivia Capital LLC (PA)	Woburn	MA	G	781 569-5212	13505	City Pblcations Greater Boston	Wayland	MA	G	617 549-7622	12924
Alm Works Inc	Chelmsford	MA	E	617 600-4369	7904	Claricode Inc	Dedham	MA	E	781 449-2450	8238
Almusnet Inc	Woburn	MA	E	781 933-1846	13506	CLC Bio LLC	Beverly	MA	F	617 945-0178	6339
American Business Systems Inc	Chelmsford	MA	E	978 250-0335	7905	Codiscope LLC	Boston	MA	F	617 804-5428	6660
American Robotics Inc	Marlborough	MA	E	617 862-2101	10108	Coherent Path Inc	Waltham	MA	E	508 612-4557	12635
American Well Corporation (PA)	Boston	MA	B	617 204-3500	6543	Compart North America Inc	Andover	MA	E	877 237-2725	5879
Analytix Bus Solutions LLC (PA)	Woburn	MA	G	781 503-9000	13510	Complete Technology Resources	Marlborough	MA	F	508 909-5961	10133
Apama Inc	Bedford	MA	F	781 280-4000	6208	Computer Corporation America (HQ)	Waltham	MA	D	781 577-4402	12637
Apifia Inc	Boston	MA	E	585 506-2787	6550	Computer Software Associates	Boston	MA	F	808 891-0099	6664
Apiphani Inc	Boston	MA	E	800 215-0811	6551	Constant Contact Inc (DH)	Waltham	MA	B	781 472-8100	12639
Apriori Technologies Inc (PA)	Concord	MA	D	978 371-2006	8101	Core Sdi Inc (PA)	Boston	MA	G	617 695-1109	6670
Apryse Corp	Boston	MA	E	617 982-2646	6552	Corporate Rmbursement Svcs Inc	Newton	MA	D	888 312-0788	10748
Aries Systems Corporation	North Andover	MA	E	978 975-7570	10820	Cosmic Software Inc	North Chelmsford	MA	F	978 667-2556	10967
Arinsights LLC	Needham	MA	E	508 233-3494	10505	Creativestar Solution Inc	Waltham	MA	F	617 326-5308	12645
Aspen Technology Inc (HQ)	Bedford	MA	D	781 221-6400	6211	Crio Inc	Boston	MA	E	617 302-9845	6677
Aspentech Corporation (DH)	Bedford	MA	A	781 221-6400	6212	Cross Country Motor Club Inc (HQ)	Medford	MA	A	781 393-9300	10283
Aternity Inc	Cambridge	MA	C	508 475-0414	7492	Csp Inc (PA)	Lowell	MA	E	978 954-5038	9872
Aternity LLC (DH)	Cambridge	MA	E	617 250-5309	7493	CST of America LLC	Framingham	MA	E	508 665-4400	8754
Athenahealth Inc (PA)	Boston	MA	B	617 402-1000	6572	Cura Software Solutions Co	Bedford	MA	F	781 325-7158	6219
Atiim Inc	Boston	MA	F	800 735-4071	6573	Customergauge USA LLC	Burlington	MA	G	844 211-3932	7359
Atlantis Technology Corp	Concord	MA	G	978 341-0999	8103	Cyberark Software Inc (HQ)	Newton	MA	C	617 965-1544	10752
Atlas Devices LLC	Chelmsford	MA	F	617 415-1657	7913	Cyberbit Inc	Boston	MA	E	415 960-5750	6680
Atlassian Pty Ltd	Boston	MA	G	401 864-1481	6575	Cybereason Government Inc	Boston	MA	F	978 618-6992	6681
Atrex Energy Inc (PA)	Walpole	MA	E	781 461-8251	12551	Cybergrx Inc	Concord	MA	C	877 929-2374	8111
Attivio Inc	Boston	MA	D	857 226-5040	6576	Cyglass Inc	Littleton	MA	D	978 665-0280	9808
Attunity Inc (DH)	Burlington	MA	E	781 730-4070	7336	Daedalus Software Inc	Cambridge	MA	F	617 851-5157	7548
Auctionmethod LLC	Shelburne Falls	MA	F	413 489-1389	11802	Dashboard Advantage LLC	Boston	MA	G	949 232-7409	7693
Autodesk Inc	Boston	MA	E	857 233-4149	6578	Data Plus Incorporated	North Chelmsford	MA	F	978 888-6300	10974
Automatech Inc (PA)	Plymouth	MA	G	508 830-0088	11447	Data Translation Inc (PA)	Norton	MA	E	508 481-3700	11126
Avid Technology Inc (PA)	Burlington	MA	A	978 640-3000	7338	Datanational Corporation	Pembroke	MA	E	781 826-3400	11361
Aware Inc (PA)	Bedford	MA	E	781 276-4000	6213	Datarobot Inc (PA)	Boston	MA	D	617 765-4500	6684
Backlight Parent Corporation (PA)	Lexington	MA	F	617 665-8844	9725	Datawatch Corporation (HQ)	Bedford	MA	D	978 441-2200	6222
Bamboo Rose LLC (PA)	Gloucester	MA	C	978 281-3723	8922	Debt Exchange Inc	Boston	MA	D	617 531-3400	6685
Bare Bones Software Inc	North Chelmsford	MA	F	978 251-0500	10965	Deerwalk Inc	Lexington	MA	C	781 325-1775	9738
Battery Ventures Vi LP	Waltham	MA	F	781 577-1000	12601	Definitive Healthcare Corp (PA)	Framingham	MA	A	508 720-4224	8756
Beacon Application Svcs Corp (PA)	Framingham	MA	E	508 663-4433	8742	Delve Labs Inc	Boston	MA	F	617 820-9798	6689
Beacon Biosignals Inc	Boston	MA	D	401 225-5782	6586	Demandware LLC (HQ)	Burlington	MA	D	888 553-9216	7360
Bearer Inc	Cambridge	MA	F	657 297-5335	7501	Demarey Insurance Software	Hampden	MA	G	413 531-3991	9022
Belarc Inc	Maynard	MA	E	978 461-1100	10260	Dg3 Group America Inc	Woburn	MA	G	617 241-5600	13557
Belle Artfl Intelligence Corp	Cambridge	MA	F	650 291-9410	7504	Digital Immunity LLC	Burlington	MA	G	508 630-0321	7363
Bellhawk Systems Corporation	Millbury	MA	G	508 865-8070	10428	Dimensional Insight Inc (PA)	Burlington	MA	E	781 229-9111	7364
Bi-Sam	Boston	MA	F	617 933-4400	6592	Double-Take Software Inc (DH)	Burlington	MA	C	949 253-6500	7365
Bigtime Software Inc	Boston	MA	E	781 859-5308	6594	Doubleyard Inc (PA)	Boston	MA	F	857 314-1400	6699
Bigtincan Mobile Pty Ltd	Waltham	MA	G	617 981-7557	12605	Drizly LLC (HQ)	Boston	MA	E	774 234-1033	6703
Biobright LLC (HQ)	Boston	MA	G	617 444-9007	6595	Dropgenie Inc	Cambridge	MA	G	617 901-7422	7553
Biscom Inc	Westford	MA	D	978 250-1800	13226	Duck Creek Technologies Inc (HQ)	Boston	MA	F	949 214-1000	6704

	CITY	ST	EMP	PHONE	ENTRY#
Duck Creek Technologies LLC (DH)	Boston	MA	E	833 798-7789	6705
Dynamicops Inc	Burlington	MA	E	781 221-2136	7366
Dynatrace Inc (PA)	Waltham	MA	C	781 530-1000	12656
Dynatrace LLC (HQ)	Waltham	MA	C	781 530-1000	12657
Eagle Investment Systems LLC (HQ)	Wellesley	MA	E	781 943-2200	12940
Ebsnet Inc	Groton	MA	G	978 448-9000	9009
Eclypses Inc	Boston	MA	E	719 323-6680	6707
Econiq	Burlington	MA	G	781 588-2223	7367
Edgil Associates Inc	Danvers	MA	F	978 262-9799	8184
Ekran System Inc	Needham Heights	MA	E	424 242-8838	10542
Elcom International Inc (PA)	Braintree	MA	F	781 501-4000	7179
Electra Vehicles Inc (PA)	Boston	MA	F	617 313-7842	6710
Elerts Corporation	South Weymouth	MA	F	781 803-6362	11975
EMC Corporation (HQ)	Hopkinton	MA	B	508 435-1000	9322
EMC Corporation	Newton	MA	D	617 618-3400	10755
Endowmentsolutions LLC	Auburn	MA	G	617 308-7231	6112
Endurance Intl Group-West Inc	Burlington	MA	C	781 852-3200	7369
Endure Dgtal Intrmdate Hldngs	Burlington	MA	A	781 852-3200	7370
Engagesmart Inc (PA)	Braintree	MA	F	781 848-3733	7181
Engene Usa Inc	Waltham	MA	F	857 246-8765	12662
Enterprise Gvrnnce Systems Cor (PA)	Boston	MA	G	888 655-4125	6715
Enterprise Gvrnnce Systems Cor	Boston	MA	E	888 655-4125	6716
Epicenter	Westfield	MA	D	413 568-1360	13164
Erecruit Holdings LLC	Boston	MA	D	617 535-3720	6718
Eskill Corporation	Boston	MA	F	978 649-8010	6719
Esm Software LLC	Lincoln	MA	F	781 541-4462	9795
Esm Software Group Inc	Lincoln	MA	F	781 541-4465	9796
Evergage Inc	Somerville	MA	D	888 310-0589	11870
Evotext Inc	Billerica	MA	F	781 272-1830	6445
Exa Corporation (DH)	Burlington	MA	E	781 564-0200	7371
Exari Group Inc	Boston	MA	E	617 938-3777	6722
Exari Systems Inc	Boston	MA	D	617 938-3777	6723
Excelergy Corp (PA)	Lexington	MA	E	781 274-0420	9742
Exony Inc	Boston	MA	F	617 854-7486	6725
Expertek Systems Inc	Marlborough	MA	E	508 624-0006	10149
Extreme Protocol Solutions Inc	Uxbridge	MA	G	508 278-3600	12478
Eze Castle Software Inc (DH)	Boston	MA	C	617 316-1000	6726
Eze Castle Software LLC (DH)	Boston	MA	G	617 316-1000	6727
Fablevision Learning LLC	Dedham	MA	F	781 320-3225	8243
Fairmarkit Inc (PA)	Boston	MA	D	774 364-4446	6729
Fev Tutor Inc	Woburn	MA	D	781 376-6925	13564
Finastra USA Corporation	Burlington	MA	D	781 203-9200	7373
Fis Systems International LLC	Boston	MA	G	617 728-7722	6737
Flimp Media	Hopkinton	MA	D	508 435-5220	9326
Flux Cyber Inc	Boston	MA	G	617 440-4655	6741
Focused Impressions Tech LLC	Boston	MA	E	857 453-6771	6742
Forefield Inc	Marlborough	MA	E	508 630-1100	10150
Formation Inc	Boston	MA	F	650 257-2277	6744
Free Software Foundation Inc	Boston	MA	F	617 542-5942	6747
Frendzi Inc	Newton	MA	F	617 899-0234	10756
Full Circle Technologies Inc	Boston	MA	E	617 722-0100	6749
Gain Life Inc	Boston	MA	F	888 412-6041	6751
Galaxy Software Inc	Quincy	MA	G	617 773-7790	11521
GE Digital LLC (HQ)	Cambridge	MA	E	925 242-6200	7579
Geisel Software Inc	Worcester	MA	F	508 853-5310	13729
Geometric Informatics Inc	Somerville	MA	G	617 440-1078	11876
Ginger Software Inc	Newton	MA	F	617 755-0160	10757
Goodrich Corporation	Westford	MA	A	978 303-6700	13239
GoTo Group Inc (PA)	Boston	MA	A		6768
Gotuit Media Corp	Woburn	MA	F	801 592-5575	13575
Graphisoft North America Inc	Waltham	MA	E	617 485-4219	12688
Grip Security Inc	Boston	MA	E	757 439-5650	6773
Gty Technology Holdings Inc (PA)	Boston	MA	F	702 945-2898	6778
Guardicore Inc	Boston	MA	F	781 789-8904	6779
Gurukrupa I LLC	Middleboro	MA	F	508 947-1080	10360
Harte Hanks Inc (PA)	Chelmsford	MA	E	512 434-1100	7931
Haystack ID	Boston	MA	F	617 422-0075	6785
Healthedge Software Inc (HQ)	Burlington	MA	D	781 285-1300	7376
HealthFleet Inc	Needham Heights	MA	D	203 810-5400	10550
Heraldapi Inc	Somerville	MA	F	781 799-1165	11879
Hirezon Corporation	Westborough	MA	F	508 836-3800	13105
Homeportfolio Inc	Newton	MA	E	617 559-1197	10760
Honeywell DMC Services LLC	Danvers	MA	B	978 774-3007	8192
Horizon International Inc	Belmont	MA	F	617 489-6666	6306
Hoylu Inc	Pembroke	MA	F	877 554-6958	11369
Hubengage Inc	Cambridge	MA	E	877 704-6662	7605
Hubspot Inc (PA)	Cambridge	MA	A	888 482-7768	7606
Human Care Systems Inc (HQ)	Boston	MA	F	617 720-7838	6799
Human Care Systems Inc	Lynnfield	MA	E	781 587-0414	9996
Human Care Systems Inc	Weston	MA	E	781 609-2194	13286
Hycu Inc (DH)	Boston	MA	C	617 681-9100	6801
Iconics Inc (HQ)	Foxboro	MA	E		8700
Id123 Inc	Waltham	MA	G	617 936-0210	12693
Iet Solutions LLC (DH)	Canton	MA	E	818 838-0606	7800
Ifs Enterprises LLC	North Billerica	MA	F	781 369-9500	10920
Image Source Inc	North Chelmsford	MA	F		10977
Imbellus Inc	Waban	MA	G	203 710-4667	12496
IMD Soft Inc (DH)	Dedham	MA	E	781 449-5567	8245
Imprivata Inc (HQ)	Waltham	MA	B	781 674-2700	12697
Inbalance Inc	Lexington	MA	G	339 223-6636	9752
Industrial Defender Inc	Foxboro	MA	D	617 675-4206	8701
Infinite Forest Inc (PA)	Cambridge	MA	F	617 299-1382	7613
Infinite Iq Inc	Wellesley	MA	F	781 710-8696	12943
Inflight Corporation	Easthampton	MA	F	800 853-7505	8447
Infogix Inc (HQ)	Burlington	MA	C	630 505-1800	7379
Infogix Inc	Westborough	MA	E	508 366-1400	13107
Infor Inc	Littleton	MA	F	678 319-8000	9819
Ingenico Inc	Boston	MA	E	888 589-5885	6809
Innoneo Health Tech Inc (PA)	Boston	MA	D	617 336-3202	6810
Inscribe Inc	Woburn	MA	E	781 933-3331	13586
Insightfulvr	Lowell	MA	G	978 429-7874	9887
Intellgent Cmpression Tech Inc	Quincy	MA	E	617 773-3369	11523
Intelligent Bus Entrmt Inc	Watertown	MA	G	617 519-4172	12882
Intelycare Inc	Quincy	MA	C	617 971-8344	11524
Intempo Software Inc (PA)	Springfield	MA	F	800 950-2221	12105
Intent Ai LLC	Bridgewater	MA	G	415 871-0605	7232
Intuvision Inc	Woburn	MA	G	781 497-1015	13591
Iperia Inc	Waltham	MA	G	781 839-3800	12704
Isubscribed Inc	Burlington	MA	E	617 750-4975	7381
Itrica Corp	Boston	MA	G	617 340-7777	6819
Ivory Onyx	Boston	MA	F	617 454-4980	6820
Jenzabar Inc (PA)	Boston	MA	D	617 492-9099	6822
Jrni Inc	Boston	MA	E	857 305-6477	6833
Jumptap Inc	Boston	MA	E	617 301-4550	6836
Juniper Networks Inc	Westford	MA	B	978 589-5800	13243
Juriba Limited	Boston	MA	E	617 356-8681	6838
Kenexa Brassring Inc	Littleton	MA	C	781 530-5000	9823
Kenexa Compensation Inc (DH)	Needham	MA	E	877 971-9171	10516
Kimble Applications Inc	Boston	MA	E	617 651-5600	6841
Kintent Inc	Arlington	MA	F	512 294-4201	5943
Kitewheel LLC	Boston	MA	E	617 447-2138	6843
Kliks Inc	Boston	MA	F	617 230-0544	6844
Knowledge Ai Inc (PA)	Boston	MA	D	415 321-9059	6845
Kognito Solutions LLC	Burlington	MA	E	212 675-2651	7387
Kronos International MGT LLC (DH)	Lowell	MA	F	978 250-9800	9892
Kronos Securities Corporation	Lowell	MA	F	978 250-9800	9893
Kronos Solutions Inc (DH)	Lowell	MA	E	978 805-9971	9894
Kronos Tech Systems Ltd Partnr	Lowell	MA	F	978 250-9800	9895
Ksplice Inc	Cambridge	MA	G	765 577-5423	7625
Kubotek Usa Inc	Marlborough	MA	E	508 229-2020	10179
Kyruus Inc	Boston	MA	C	617 419-2060	6849
Lakeside Software LLC (PA)	Boston	MA	E	248 686-1700	6851
Leading Market Tech Inc	Boston	MA	E	617 494-4747	6854
Leanix Inc (DH)	Watertown	MA	F	781 321-6500	12887
Learning Pool Inc (PA)	Boston	MA	F	857 284-1420	6855
Lexia Learning Systems LLC	Concord	MA	E	800 435-3942	8123
Libring Technologies Inc	Cambridge	MA	F	617 553-1015	7632
Life Image Inc	Newton	MA	C	617 244-8411	10769
Lifecloud Inc	Amesbury	MA	G	978 621-9572	5842
Loadspring Solutions Inc (PA)	Burlington	MA	F	978 685-9715	7390
Logicmanager Inc	Boston	MA	E	617 530-1200	6862
Longworth Venture Partners LP (PA)	Norfolk	MA	G	781 663-3600	10801
Luzy Technologies LLC	Boston	MA	E	514 577-2295	6866
Machinemetrics Inc	Easthampton	MA	E	413 341-5747	8449
Magma	Gloucester	MA	G	978 381-3494	8943
Magnitude Software Inc	Burlington	MA	E	781 202-3200	7391
Mam Software Inc	Westford	MA	E	978 392-0941	13248
Massachsetts Brewers Guild Inc	Framingham	MA	F	508 405-9115	8788
Material Impact Inc	Boston	MA	E	617 917-4123	6879
Materialise Dental Inc	Waltham	MA	F	443 557-0121	12717
Mathsoft Corporate Holdings (HQ)	Charlestown	MA	D	617 444-8000	7879
Measurement Computing Corp (DH)	Norton	MA	E	508 946-5100	11128
Meddata Group LLC	Danvers	MA	F	978 887-0039	8205
Medical Information Tech Inc (PA)	Westwood	MA	A	781 821-3000	13314
Mega Na Inc	Raynham	MA	E	781 784-7684	11593
Memento Inc	Burlington	MA	E	781 221-3030	7392
Mendix Inc	Boston	MA	C	857 263-8200	6882
Mercury Systems Inc (PA)	Andover	MA	A	978 256-1300	5896
Merlinone Inc (PA)	Braintree	MA	F	617 328-6645	7195
Meta Software Corporation (PA)	Burlington	MA	F	781 238-0293	7393
Metalogix Software Corp	Waltham	MA	G	202 609-9100	12719
Microcad Trning Consulting Inc (PA)	Watertown	MA	F	617 923-0500	12893
Micros Systems Inc	Westborough	MA	G	508 655-7500	13120
Microsoft Corporation	Cambridge	MA	E	781 398-4600	7643
Microsoft Corporation	Cambridge	MA	E	857 453-6000	7644
Microsol	Boston	MA	G	857 263-7249	6886

	CITY	ST	EMP	PHONE	ENTRY#		CITY	ST	EMP	PHONE	ENTRY#
Mindedge Inc	Waltham	MA	D	781 250-1805	12720	Power Object Inc	Newton	MA	G	617 630-5701	10775
Mixfit Inc	Boston	MA	G	617 902-8082	6889	Preservica Inc	Boston	MA	E	617 294-6676	6975
Mobile Messaging Solutions	Boston	MA	F	857 202-3132	6891	Proficient Software Corp	Newton	MA	G	617 964-3457	10777
Mobile Software Inc	Boston	MA	F	617 719-8660	6892	Profitect Inc **(HQ)**	Dedham	MA	F	781 290-0009	8247
Moca Systems Inc **(PA)**	Boston	MA	E	617 581-6622	6893	Progress Software Corporation **(PA)**	Burlington	MA	C	781 280-4000	7413
Mocana Corporation	Marlborough	MA	G	508 251-5086	10185	Prophet Corp	Auburn	MA	F	774 253-0909	6124
Monadnock Associates Inc **(PA)**	Watertown	MA	F	617 924-7032	12894	Ptc Inc **(PA)**	Boston	MA	A	781 370-5000	6983
Monotonyai Inc	Watertown	MA	F	202 607-8193	12895	Ptc Inc	Waltham	MA	G	617 792-7622	12754
Monotype Imaging Holdings Inc **(DH)**	Woburn	MA	D	781 970-6000	13614	Pulse Network Inc	Norwood	MA	F	781 688-8000	11203
Monotype Imaging Inc **(DH)**	Woburn	MA	D	781 970-6000	13615	Quadramed Quantim Corporation	Burlington	MA	F	781 565-5000	7417
Morgan Scientific Inc **(PA)**	Haverhill	MA	F	978 521-4440	9118	Qualcomm Technologies Inc	Burlington	MA	F	781 791-6000	7418
Morphisec Inc	Boston	MA	E	617 826-1212	6896	Quality Solutions Inc **(DH)**	Newburyport	MA	E	978 465-7755	10710
MTI Systems Inc	West Springfield	MA	F	413 733-1972	13035	Quantum Simulation Tech Inc	Boston	MA	F	847 626-5535	6990
Mtp Software LLC	Needham	MA	G	508 353-6221	10517	Queues Enforth Development Inc	Woburn	MA	F	781 870-1100	13646
Myperfectgig Inc	Maynard	MA	E	978 461-6700	10263	Quickbase Inc **(PA)**	Boston	MA	B	855 725-2293	6991
N-Able Inc **(PA)**	Wakefield	MA	E	781 328-6490	12520	Radar Wind Up Corporation **(HQ)**	Cambridge	MA	F	917 488-6050	7693
N-Able Technologies Inc	Burlington	MA	A	855 679-0817	7395	Radiant Sage Ventures LLC	Belmont	MA	E	855 723-7243	6311
Nara Logics Inc	Boston	MA	F	617 945-2049	6902	Rapid7 Inc **(PA)**	Boston	MA	B	617 247-1717	6996
Native Instruments Usa Inc **(PA)**	Boston	MA	D	617 577-7799	6905	Rapid7 LLC **(HQ)**	Boston	MA	G	617 247-1717	6997
Neolane Inc	Newton	MA	D	617 467-6760	10771	Real Relational Solutions LLC	Arlington	MA	G	781 646-7326	5945
Netbrain Technologies Inc **(PA)**	Burlington	MA	C	781 221-7199	7397	Red Frames Inc	Boston	MA	E	617 477-8740	7000
Netcracker Technology Corp **(HQ)**	Waltham	MA	C	781 419-3300	12735	Red Hat Inc	Westford	MA	F	978 392-1000	13258
Netsuite	Boston	MA	E	877 638-7848	6910	Red Point Positioning Corp **(PA)**	Newton	MA	F	339 222-0261	10779
Newfold Dgtal Hldngs Group Inc **(HQ)**	Burlington	MA	C	781 852-3200	7399	Redi2 Technologies Inc **(HQ)**	Boston	MA	E	617 910-3282	7001
Nexthink Inc	Boston	MA	E	617 861-8257	6921	Redstone Aggregator LP	Bedford	MA	E	781 515-5000	6257
NH Learning Solutions Corp	Woburn	MA	D	781 224-1113	13624	Redstone Buyer LLC	Bedford	MA	E	781 515-5000	6258
Novell Inc	Waltham	MA	F	781 464-8000	12739	Redstone GP Holdco 1 LLC	Bedford	MA	E	781 515-5000	6259
Ntt Data Inc	Rockland	MA	E	877 532-6312	11654	Redstone GP Holdco 2 LLC	Bedford	MA	E	781 515-5000	6260
Ntt Data Intl Svcs Inc **(DH)**	Boston	MA	B	800 745-3263	6927	Redstone Holdco 1 LP	Bedford	MA	E	781 515-5000	6261
Nuance Communications Inc **(HQ)**	Burlington	MA	A	781 565-5000	7401	Redstone Holdco 2 LP	Bedford	MA	E	781 515-5000	6262
Nuance Hlthcare Dgnstics Slton	Burlington	MA	A	404 575-4222	7402	Redstone Intrmdate Archer Hldc	Bedford	MA	E	781 515-5000	6263
Object First (us) Inc	Beverly	MA	E	844 569-0653	6370	Redstone Intrmdate Fri Hldco L	Bedford	MA	F	781 515-5000	6264
Octo Telematics North Amer LLC	Auburndale	MA	G	617 916-1080	6138	Redstone Intrmdate Scrid Hldco	Bedford	MA	E	781 515-5000	6265
Off The Dial Media LLC	Cambridge	MA	F	617 929-3424	7673	Redstone Parent LP	Bedford	MA	E	781 515-5000	6266
Omnify Software Inc	Andover	MA	G	508 527-1956	5903	Reify Health Inc **(PA)**	Boston	MA	C	617 861-8261	7003
On Technology Corp **(PA)**	Waltham	MA	D	781 487-3300	12743	Research Applctons Fncl Trckin	Boston	MA	E	800 939-7238	7007
Onapsis Inc **(PA)**	Boston	MA	F	617 603-9932	6932	Research Cmpt Consulting Svcs **(PA)**	Canton	MA	E	781 821-1221	7823
Ondas Holdings Inc	Marlborough	MA	E	617 862-2101	10191	Revulytics Inc **(DH)**	Waltham	MA	F	781 398-3400	12766
Ondas Holdings Inc **(PA)**	Waltham	MA	F	888 350-9994	12744	Revvity Signals Software Inc **(DH)**	Waltham	MA	D	781 663-6900	12769
One Hippo	Boston	MA	G	857 233-4886	6934	Rivermeadow Software Inc	Westford	MA	F	617 448-4990	13260
Onepin Inc	Westborough	MA	E	508 475-1000	13126	Rocket Software Inc **(PA)**	Waltham	MA	C	781 577-4323	12771
Oneview Commerce Inc	Hingham	MA	D	617 279-0549	9156	Rocket Software Systems Inc	Waltham	MA	F	248 833-9000	12772
Online Marketing Solutions Inc	Lowell	MA	E	978 937-2363	9911	Rockstar New England Inc	Andover	MA	E	978 409-6272	5913
Onshape Inc	Boston	MA	F	844 667-4273	6935	Rogue Amoeba Software Inc	Boston	MA	G	609 213-4380	7012
Openair Inc	Boston	MA	E	617 351-0232	6937	Rsa Security LLC **(PA)**	Bedford	MA	A	800 995-5095	6268
Openbridge Inc	Boston	MA	G	857 234-1008	6938	Rsa Security LLC	Lexington	MA	F	781 515-6258	9768
Opendatasoft LLC	Cambridge	MA	D	781 952-0515	7676	RSD America Inc	Waltham	MA	F	201 996-1000	12775
Opportunityspace Inc	Boston	MA	E	857 366-1666	6939	Sage Learning Inc	Boston	MA	F	778 951-9312	7020
Optikos Corporation	Wakefield	MA	D	617 354-7557	12525	Salesforcecom Inc	Boston	MA	F	857 415-3510	7022
Optirtc Inc	Boston	MA	F	844 678-4782	6942	Saylent Technologies Inc	Franklin	MA	E	508 570-2161	8863
Oracle America Inc	Burlington	MA	D	650 506-7000	7404	SBE Vision Inc	Wakefield	MA	F	612 237-0128	12532
Oracle Corporation	Burlington	MA	G	650 506-7000	7407	Scan Soft Inc	Burlington	MA	D	781 565-5000	7423
Oracle Corporation	Cambridge	MA	F	617 497-7713	7677	Scheduling Systems Inc	Framingham	MA	G	508 620-0390	8804
Oracle Corporation	Waltham	MA	E	781 314-8001	12745	Schneider Electric It Corp **(DH)**	Foxboro	MA	A	508 543-8750	8723
Oracle Otc Subsidiary LLC	Cambridge	MA	A	617 386-1000	7678	School Family Media LLC	Wrentham	MA	E	508 384-0394	13844
Oracle Systems Corporation	Boston	MA	F	617 247-7900	6943	Sdl Xyenterprise LLC **(PA)**	Wakefield	MA	E	781 756-4400	12533
Outcomes4me Inc	Boston	MA	E	617 812-1010	6945	Sea Street Technologies Inc	Canton	MA	E	617 600-5150	7827
Outsystems Inc **(PA)**	Boston	MA	D	617 837-6840	6946	Seavus Group	Andover	MA	E	978 623-7221	5916
Overtone Studio Inc	Framingham	MA	G	774 290-2900	8795	Seavus Usa Inc	Acton	MA	F	888 573-2887	5765
Owncloud Inc	Foxboro	MA	D	617 515-3664	8712	Seceon Inc	Westford	MA	F	978 923-0040	13261
Ozone Technologies Inc	Boston	MA	G	617 955-4188	6950	Secure Code Warrior Inc	Boston	MA	E	617 901-3005	7030
Pactolus Cmmnctions Sftwr Corp	Marlborough	MA	F	508 616-0900	10194	Semrush Holdings Inc **(PA)**	Boston	MA	B	800 815-9959	7033
Padakshep	Brookline	MA	G	801 652-5589	7324	Sidechannel Inc	Worcester	MA	F	508 925-0114	13800
Panalgo LLC	Boston	MA	F	781 290-0808	6951	Silverthread Inc	Cambridge	MA	G	800 674-9366	7715
Para Research Inc	Gloucester	MA	G	978 282-1100	8951	Similarweb Inc	Burlington	MA	F	800 540-1086	7429
Parametric Holdings Inc **(HQ)**	Needham Heights	MA	E	781 370-5000	10555	Simsoft Corp	Westborough	MA	E	508 366-5451	13136
Parametric Technology Corp	Boston	MA	D	781 370-5000	6952	Sinauer Associates Inc	Sunderland	MA	E	413 549-4300	12275
Partners Capital Inv Group LLP	Boston	MA	F	617 292-2570	6955	Skelmir LLC	Arlington	MA	F	617 625-1551	5947
Pathai Inc **(PA)**	Boston	MA	E	617 543-5250	6956	Small Plnet Communications Inc	Lawrence	MA	G	978 794-2201	9598
Peak Technologies LLC	Littleton	MA	E	978 393-5900	9832	Smart Software Inc	Belmont	MA	E	617 489-2743	6312
Peergrade Inc	Boston	MA	G	857 302-4023	6961	Smartco Services LLC	Taunton	MA	E	508 880-0816	12368
Pegasystems Inc **(PA)**	Cambridge	MA	A	617 374-9600	7681	Snowbound Software Corporation	Needham	MA	D	617 607-2000	10523
Percussion Software Inc	Burlington	MA	F	781 438-9900	7410	Soapstone Networks Inc	Burlington	MA	D	617 719-3897	7430
Pet Pocketbook Inc	Boston	MA	G	857 246-9884	6964	Sofnet Technology Inc	Newton	MA	F	857 272-2568	10785
Phase Forward	Waltham	MA	F	781 626-1256	12748	Soft10 Inc	Boston	MA	G	857 263-7375	7043
Picis Clinical Solutions Inc **(DH)**	Wakefield	MA	C	336 397-5336	12528	Softinway Inc	Burlington	MA	F	781 328-4310	7431
Plannuh Inc	Newton	MA	E	617 965-7393	10774	Software Experts Inc	Westford	MA	G	978 692-5343	13263
Planon Corporation	Braintree	MA	F	781 356-0999	7198	Solusoft Inc	North Andover	MA	F	978 375-6021	10849
Plataine Inc	Waltham	MA	D	336 905-0900	12749	Spaceclaim Corporation	Concord	MA	D	978 482-2100	8133
Platformq Education Inc	Needham	MA	E	617 938-6000	10519	Spatter Inc	Newton	MA	G	617 510-0498	10786
Plumriver LLC	Wellesley	MA	F	781 431-7477	12945	Speechworks International	Burlington	MA	E	781 565-5000	7432
Pmweb Inc	Wakefield	MA	D	617 207-7080	12529	Spotbus Inc	Westborough	MA	G	774 262-4052	13138
Pointillist Inc	Boston	MA	E	617 752-2214	6967	Sqdm Inc	Woburn	MA	F	888 993-9674	13671

	CITY	ST	EMP	PHONE	ENTRY#		CITY	ST	EMP	PHONE	ENTRY#
Squareworks Consulting LLC	Boston	MA	E	800 779-6285	7057	Winshuttle LLC (HQ)	Burlington	MA	D	425 368-2708	7449
SS&c Technologies Inc	Burlington	MA	F	781 654-6498	7434	Wordstock Inc	Bedford	MA	F	781 646-7700	6277
Starent Networks LLC (HQ)	Tewksbury	MA	E	978 851-1100	12418	Wordstream Inc	Boston	MA	F	617 963-0555	7130
Starfish Storage Corporation	Waltham	MA	G	781 250-3000	12782	Wyebot Inc	Marlborough	MA	E	508 481-2603	10236
Statisys Inc	Boston	MA	G	617 804-1284	7060	Yieldx Inc	Boston	MA	E	646 328-9803	7137
Stellar Menus Inc	Provincetown	MA	G	617 882-2800	11498	Zappix Inc	Burlington	MA	E	781 214-8124	7450
Stone Tablet LLC	Newton	MA	F	781 380-8800	10788	Zlink Inc	Maynard	MA	D	978 309-3628	10268
Stratgic Corp Asssment System	Medfield	MA	G	508 359-1966	10276	Zoll Medical Corporation (HQ)	Chelmsford	MA	A	978 421-9655	7972
Streetscan Inc	Wakefield	MA	E	617 399-8236	12538	Zoran Corporation	Burlington	MA	E	408 523-6500	7452
Stuart Karon	Newton	MA	F	802 649-1911	10789	Zylotech	Cambridge	MA	G	845 802-3188	7764
Supplyscape Corporation	Foxboro	MA	D	781 503-7426	8726	Abacus Labs Inc	Portland	ME	E	917 426-6642	5174
Survey Software Services	Braintree	MA	F	781 849-8118	7206	Anodyne Health Partners Inc (HQ)	Falmouth	ME	E	207 347-7400	4767
Suse LLC	Cambridge	MA	D	617 613-2000	7727	Cassiopae Us Inc	Vinalhaven	ME	E	435 647-9940	5572
Sustainable Minds LLC	Cambridge	MA	F	617 401-2269	7728	Certify Inc (PA)	Portland	ME	E	207 773-6100	5197
Svh Software Inc	Chelmsford	MA	E	978 566-1812	7961	Change Hlthcare Phrm Sltons In	Augusta	ME	D	207 622-7153	4468
Swymed Incorporated	Lexington	MA	F	855 799-6366	9777	Coursestorm Inc	Orono	ME	F	207 866-0328	5134
Syberworks Inc	Arlington	MA	E	781 891-1999	5948	Highbyte Inc	Portland	ME	F	844 328-2677	5221
Synopsys Inc	Westborough	MA	G	508 870-6500	13139	Kinotek Inc	Portland	ME	F	207 805-1919	5232
Sysaid Technologies Inc	Newton	MA	E	800 686-7047	10790	Maine & Maritimes Corporation (PA)	Presque Isle	ME	F	207 760-2499	5304
Tactai Inc	Waltham	MA	F	617 391-7915	12787	Mathemtics Problem Solving LLC	South Portland	ME	F	207 772-2846	5508
Tagup Inc	Boston	MA	E	513 262-0159	7067	Nearpeer Inc	Portland	ME	E	207 615-0414	5250
Tausight Inc	Boston	MA	E	339 364-1246	7071	Rockstep Solutions Inc (PA)	Portland	ME	F	844 800-7625	5267
Teletypesetting Company Inc	Boston	MA	F	617 542-6220	7073	Salty Cultivation LLC	Sanford	ME	F	207 752-7549	5414
Televeh Inc	Auburndale	MA	F	857 400-1938	6139	Syllaworks LLC	Brunswick	ME	F	617 564-3727	4656
Terrapin	Cambridge	MA	G	508 487-8181	7738	Team Augmented Reality Inc	Nobleboro	ME	G	207 350-0460	5102
Timelinx Software Inc	North Andover	MA	F	978 296-4090	10853	Tyler Technologies Inc	Bangor	ME	F	207 947-4494	4517
Timelinx Software LLC	North Andover	MA	G	978 662-1171	10854	Tyler Technologies Inc	Portland	ME	F	207 879-7243	5287
Toast Inc (PA)	Boston	MA	A	617 297-1005	7079	Tyler Technologies Inc	Yarmouth	ME	C	207 781-2260	5708
Tom Snyder Productions Inc (HQ)	Watertown	MA	D	617 600-2145	12915	Workgroup Tech Partners Inc (PA)	Westbrook	ME	E	207 856-5312	5653
Tomorrow Companies Inc	Boston	MA	F	800 735-7075	7080	Actio Software Corporation	Portsmouth	NH	D	603 433-2300	15356
Toolsgroup Inc	Boston	MA	E	617 263-0080	7081	Acuant Inc	Manchester	NH	F	603 641-8443	14804
Tor Project Inc	Somerville	MA	F	206 512-5312	11903	Akken Inc	Nashua	NH	D	866 590-6695	15054
Touch Ahead Software LLC	Boston	MA	F	866 960-9301	7082	Akumina Inc (PA)	Nashua	NH	E	603 318-8269	15055
Town of Billerica	Billerica	MA	F	978 671-0954	6488	Altscale Cloud Services Inc	Nashua	NH	E	603 558-5814	15059
Tr3 Solutions Inc	Stoneham	MA	F	781 481-0642	12187	Atlantic Turnkey Cons Corp	Amherst	NH	D	603 673-9447	13862
Tracelink Inc (PA)	Wilmington	MA	C	781 914-4900	13469	Autovirt Inc	Nashua	NH	G	603 546-2900	15065
Transparency-One Inc	Boston	MA	E	617 645-2176	7084	Bid2win Software LLC	Portsmouth	NH	C	800 336-3808	15365
Trilog Group Inc	Woburn	MA	F	781 937-9963	13679	Bottomline Technologies Inc (PA)	Portsmouth	NH	A	603 436-0700	15367
Tripcraft LLC	Waltham	MA	F	781 588-9100	12806	Cassiopae US Inc	Salem	NH	G	603 685-3223	15511
Triple Seat Software LLC	Acton	MA	F	978 635-0615	5767	Chyme	Salem	NH	G	603 893-7683	15515
Tripleshot LLC	Boston	MA	G	646 812-7548	7086	Cloud Software Group Inc	Manchester	NH	A	603 622-5109	14831
Tufin Software North Amer Inc	Boston	MA	F	877 270-7711	7088	CNi Corp	Milford	NH	G	603 249-5075	15017
Tulip Interfaces Inc (PA)	Somerville	MA	C	833 468-8547	11907	Conest Software Systems Inc	Londonderry	NH	E	603 437-9353	14737
Typesafe Inc	Cambridge	MA	G	617 622-2200	7745	Connexient LLC	Manchester	NH	F	603 669-1300	14834
Ukg Inc (HQ)	Lowell	MA	C	978 947-2855	9930	Crawford Sftwr Consulting Inc	Londonderry	NH	G	603 537-9630	14739
Ukg Kronos Systems LLC (DH)	Lowell	MA	B	978 250-9800	9931	Datanomix Inc	Nashua	NH	E	843 885-4639	15087
Unica Corporation	Cambridge	MA	A	781 839-8000	7748	Dataxoom Corp (PA)	Manchester	NH	F	510 474-0044	14840
Unicom Engineering Inc (HQ)	Canton	MA	F	781 332-1000	7836	DCI Training Inc	West Lebanon	NH	G	603 643-6066	15682
Unit4 Business Software Inc (PA)	Burlington	MA	F	877 704-5974	7441	Denali Software Inc	Nashua	NH	F	603 566-0991	15091
Uptodate Inc (DH)	Waltham	MA	D	781 392-2000	12808	Dino Software	Sandown	NH	F	603 612-0418	15579
Valiantys America Inc	Dedham	MA	F	781 375-2494	8253	Entelligence Computer Svcs LLC	Salem	NH	G	603 893-4800	15520
Validated Cloud Inc (PA)	Waltham	MA	F	617 849-8650	12809	Eversolve LLC	Windham	NH	E	603 870-9739	15726
Valora Technologies Inc	Carlisle	MA	F	781 229-2265	7850	Fis Systems International LLC	Salem	NH	F	603 898-6185	15526
Vantage Reporting Inc	Dedham	MA	E	212 750-2256	8254	Glh Systems	Dunbarton	NH	G	603 774-6374	14264
Varstreet Inc	Burlington	MA	F	781 262-0610	7442	Hopto Inc (PA)	Concord	NH	G	408 688-2674	14136
Vblearning LLC	Newton	MA	E	781 527-9999	10793	Ibis LLC	Bedford	NH	E	603 471-0951	13933
Vector Software USA Corp	Cambridge	MA	F	305 332-1703	7751	Infor (us) LLC	Nashua	NH	B	678 319-8000	15114
Veeam Software	Westford	MA	C	978 660-3276	13266	Innovairre Studios Inc	Milford	NH	E	603 579-1600	15030
Veeam Software Corporation	Swampscott	MA	A	781 592-0752	12300	Internet Systems Cnsortium Inc (PA)	Newmarket	NH	F	650 423-1300	15221
Veradigm Inc	Burlington	MA	F	800 720-7351	7443	Kana Software Inc	Bedford	NH	C	650 614-8300	13937
Verity LLC (PA)	Boston	MA	D	617 482-2634	7098	Kbace Technologies Inc (HQ)	Nashua	NH	D	603 821-7000	15121
Vermilion Software	Boston	MA	G	617 279-0799	7099	Kentico Software LLC	Bedford	NH	E	866 328-8998	13938
Vertica Systems LLC	Cambridge	MA	E	617 386-4400	7754	Koncert LLC	Salem	NH	C	800 955-5040	15541
Via Science Inc (PA)	Somerville	MA	F	857 600-2171	11910	Loftware Holdings Inc (PA)	Portsmouth	NH	F	603 766-3630	15419
Virtual Software Systems Inc	Waltham	MA	G	781 424-4899	12812	Loyalty Builders Inc (PA)	North Hampton	NH	F	603 610-8800	15252
Visible Measures Corp (PA)	Boston	MA	E	617 482-0222	7105	Mmis Inc	Portsmouth	NH	D	603 929-5078	15424
Visible Systems Corporation (PA)	Boston	MA	E	617 902-0767	7106	Namtek Corp	Bedford	NH	E	603 262-1630	13945
Vision Gvernment Solutions Inc	Hudson	MA	C	800 628-1013	9424	Narrative 1 Software LLC	Plymouth	NH	F	603 968-2233	15355
Vivantio Inc	Boston	MA	E	617 982-0390	7109	Nitrosecurity Inc (DH)	Portsmouth	NH	F	603 766-8160	15426
VMS Software Inc	Boston	MA	D	425 766-1692	7110	North Tecom LLC	Manchester	NH	F	603 851-5165	14904
Vmturbo Inc	Burlington	MA	F	914 584-5263	7446	Ntp Software of Ca Inc (PA)	Nashua	NH	G	603 641-6937	15143
Voatz Inc	Boston	MA	G	617 395-8091	7111	Omada Technologies LLC	Portsmouth	NH	F	603 610-8282	15428
Vulncheck Inc	Lexington	MA	F	781 879-6863	9792	Oracle Corporation	Manchester	NH	E	603 668-4998	14908
Wanderlust Group Inc	Cambridge	MA	F	617 784-3696	7759	Oracle Systems Corporation	Nashua	NH	E	603 897-3000	15146
Warrior Trading Inc	Great Barrington	MA	E	413 591-1100	8980	Pickup Patrol LLC	Mont Vernon	NH	G	877 394-7774	15048
Waters Corporation (PA)	Milford	MA	A	508 478-2000	10424	Premier Packaging LLC	Hooksett	NH	G	603 485-7465	14469
Wealth2kcom Inc	Boston	MA	F	781 989-5200	7115	Professnal Sftwr For Nrses Inc	Amherst	NH	D	800 889-7627	13885
Wellcoin Inc	Newton	MA	G	617 512-8617	10794	Profitkey International Inc	Salem	NH	E	603 898-9800	15556
Wespire Inc	Boston	MA	E	617 531-8970	7117	Redblack Software LLC (HQ)	Bedford	NH	F	603 232-9404	13948
Wiiisdom Usa Inc	Boston	MA	F	617 319-3563	7123	Regdox Solutions Inc	Nashua	NH	D	603 589-4830	15157
William-Sever Inc	Worcester	MA	F	617 651-2483	13828	Retrieve LLC	Manchester	NH	E	603 413-0022	14920
Windesco Inc	Boston	MA	G	617 480-9379	7128	Sdv Software Inc	Hampstead	NH	G	603 329-8164	14393
Window Book Inc	Cambridge	MA	D	617 395-4500	7761	Skillsoft (US) LLC (DH)	Nashua	NH	C	603 324-3000	15167

SIC

Company	CITY	ST	EMP	PHONE	ENTRY#
Skillsoft Corp	Nashua	NH	F	603 889-8834	15168
Skillsoft Ltd	Nashua	NH	C	603 324-3000	15169
Softech Inc **(HQ)**	Nashua	NH	E	513 942-7100	15170
Software Outside Inc	Peterborough	NH	G	603 820-1994	15327
Spantech Software Inc	Nashua	NH	F	603 589-4044	15171
Spectrum Controls Inc	Hampton	NH	G	603 686-4442	14414
Sports Visio Inc	Dunbarton	NH	F	603 774-1339	14265
Strolid Inc	Salem	NH	F	978 655-8550	15566
Syam Software Incorporated	Londonderry	NH	F	603 598-9575	14785
Synap Inc	Dover	NH	G	888 572-1150	14251
Team Eda Inc	Manchester	NH	G	603 656-5200	14940
Techfourfive LLC	Nashua	NH	G	603 438-5760	15175
Weather Source LLC	Salem	NH	F	844 813-2617	15571
White Star Software LLC	Nashua	NH	G	603 897-0396	15187
Agitar Technologies Inc	Cranston	RI	G	401 572-3150	15824
Agk Soft	Tiverton	RI	G	401 466-4213	16734
Andera Inc	Providence	RI	D	401 621-7900	16471
Avtech Software Inc **(PA)**	Warren	RI	F	401 628-1600	16752
Backflip Studios LLC	Pawtucket	RI	E	720 475-1970	16346
Boothroyd Dewhurst Inc	East Greenwich	RI	F	401 783-5840	15975
Bottomline Technologies	Cumberland	RI	F	401 954-2200	15933
Dealership Software LLC	Lincoln	RI	F	401 305-3740	16130
Hello Tomorrow LLC	Pawtucket	RI	G	401 727-0070	16375
Hexagon Mfg Intllgnce- Mtrlogy	North Kingstown	RI	D	401 886-2000	16256
Igt Global Solutions Corp	West Greenwich	RI	E	401 392-7025	16885
Igt Global Solutions Corporation **(HQ)**	Providence	RI	D	401 392-7077	16538
Leidos Inc	Middletown	RI	E	401 849-8900	16178
MTI Film LLC **(HQ)**	Providence	RI	F	401 831-1315	16570
Quantifacts Inc	Riverside	RI	G	401 421-8300	16659
Radley Corporation	Lincoln	RI	E	616 554-9060	16512
Raybern Utility Solutions LLC	Portsmouth	RI	D	303 775-5041	16453
Rxvantage Inc	Providence	RI	E	866 464-2157	16608
Simpatico Software Systems Inc	Barrington	RI	F	401 246-1358	15750
Voicescript Technologies	Warwick	RI	E	401 524-2246	16874
Agilent Technologies Inc	Winooski	VT	F	802 861-8597	17765
Concepts Eti Inc 17706	White River Junction	VT	D	802 296-2321	
Concepts Nrec LLC **(PA)** 17707	White River Junction	VT	D	802 296-2321	
Core Value Software	Norwich	VT	F	802 473-3147	17437
Datamann Inc	Wilder	VT	E	802 295-6600	17714
Faraday Inc	Burlington	VT	E	802 658-2034	17134
Isystems LLC **(HQ)**	South Burlington	VT	F	802 655-8347	17581
Ivy Computer Inc	Waterbury Center	VT	F	802 244-7880	17681
Mach 7 Technologies Inc	South Burlington	VT	D	802 861-7745	17585
Natworks Inc	Northfield	VT	F	802 485-6818	17433
Notabli Inc	Burlington	VT	F	802 448-0810	17146
Ohmd Inc	Burlington	VT	E	802 578-6369	17148
Piematrix Inc	Burlington	VT	F	802 318-4891	17151
Preava Inc	Essex	VT	G	202 935-1566	17225
Rectrac LLC	Essex Junction	VT	D	802 879-6993	17244
Ringmaster Software Corp	Burlington	VT	F	802 383-1050	17157
Systems & Software Inc	Colchester	VT	E	802 655-4400	17204
Topaz Legal Inc	Burlington	VT	E	802 540-2504	17162
Visible Electrophysiology LLC	Colchester	VT	F	802 847-4539	17208
Wellsky Humn Social Svcs Corp	Essex Junction	VT	D	802 316-3000	17249
Workwise LLC	Waterbury	VT	F	802 881-8178	17679

7373 Computer integrated systems design

Company	CITY	ST	EMP	PHONE	ENTRY#
Bpi Reprographics	Norwalk	CT	F	203 866-5600	2475
Crane Company **(PA)**	Stamford	CT	D	203 363-7300	3326
Cst Incorporated	Wallingford	CT	F	203 949-9900	3796
Cyberresearch Inc	Branford	CT	E	203 643-5000	247
Enginuity Plm LLC **(DH)**	Milford	CT	F	203 218-7225	1825
Environmental Systems Corp	West Hartford	CT	C	860 953-8800	4060
Frontier Vision Tech Inc	Rocky Hill	CT	E	860 953-0240	2922
General Dynamics Info Tech Inc	Pawcatuck	CT	D	860 441-2400	2720
Harpoon Acquisition Corp	Glastonbury	CT	E	860 815-5736	1285
Insys Micro Inc	Norwalk	CT	G	917 566-5045	2518
Interactive Marketing Corp	North Haven	CT	G	203 248-5324	2416
Kimchuk Incorporated **(PA)**	Danbury	CT	F	203 790-7800	766
Norfield Data Products Inc	Norwalk	CT	F	203 849-0292	2546
Process Automtn Solutions Inc **(HQ)**	Danbury	CT	E	203 207-9917	801
Rite-Solutions Inc **(PA)**	Pawcatuck	CT	F	401 847-3399	2725
Sonalysts Inc **(PA)**	Waterford	CT	B	860 442-4355	3997
Tek Industries Inc	Vernon Rockville	CT	F	860 870-0001	3763
Vertafore Inc	Windsor	CT	E	860 602-6000	4312
Visionpoint LLC	Newington	CT	E	860 436-9673	2333
Amazon Robotics LLC **(HQ)**	North Reading	MA	C	781 221-4640	11037
Analytix Bus Solutions LLC **(PA)**	Woburn	MA	G	781 503-9000	13510
Belle Artfl Intelligence Corp	Cambridge	MA	F	650 291-9410	7504
Bellhawk Systems Corporation	Millbury	MA	G	508 865-8070	10428
Canvas Gfx Inc	Boston	MA	E	833 721-0829	6637

Company	CITY	ST	EMP	PHONE	ENTRY#
Cgi Information Systems & Management Consultants Inc 978 946-3000 5878	Andover	MA			A
Csp Inc **(PA)**	Lowell	MA	E	978 954-5038	9872
DCI Automation Inc	West Boylston	MA	D	508 752-3071	12960
Diacritech Inc	Boston	MA	F	617 236-7500	6692
Double-Take Software Inc **(DH)**	Burlington	MA	C	949 253-6500	7365
E E S Companies Inc	Framingham	MA	F	508 653-6911	8758
Eclypses Inc	Boston	MA	E	719 323-6680	6707
EMC Corporation	Milford	MA	E	508 634-2774	10402
Engement Company Inc	Topsfield	MA	G	603 537-2088	12432
Exa Corporation **(DH)**	Burlington	MA	E	781 564-0200	7371
Infinite Iq Inc	Wellesley	MA	F	781 710-8696	12943
INTEL Network Systems Inc **(HQ)**	Hudson	MA	C	978 553-4000	9378
Juniper Networks Inc	Westford	MA	B	978 589-5800	13243
Kubotek Usa Inc	Marlborough	MA	E	508 229-2020	10179
L T X International Inc	Norwood	MA	D	781 461-1000	11189
Mediavue Systems Inc	Hingham	MA	E	781 926-0676	9153
Milford Manufacturing Svcs LLC	Hopedale	MA	E	508 478-8544	9299
Netscout Systems Inc **(PA)**	Westford	MA	E	978 614-4000	13253
On Technology Corp **(PA)**	Waltham	MA	D	781 487-3300	12743
Paneltek LLC	Attleboro Falls	MA	F	920 906-9457	6095
Ptc Inc **(PA)**	Boston	MA	A	781 370-5000	6983
Revvity Signals Software Inc **(DH)**	Waltham	MA	D	781 663-6900	12769
Rsa Security LLC **(PA)**	Bedford	MA	A	800 995-5095	6268
Sencorpwhite Inc **(HQ)**	Hyannis	MA	C	508 771-9400	9451
Soapstone Networks Inc	Burlington	MA	D	617 719-3897	7430
Speechworks International	Burlington	MA	E	781 565-5000	7432
Superpedestrian Inc **(PA)**	Cambridge	MA	C	877 678-7518	7725
Syberworks Inc	Arlington	MA	E	781 891-1999	5948
Tactai Inc	Waltham	MA	F	617 391-7915	12787
Timelinx Software LLC	North Andover	MA	G	978 662-1171	10854
Ukg Kronos Systems LLC **(DH)**	Lowell	MA	B	978 250-9800	9931
Valiantys America Inc	Dedham	MA	F	781 375-2494	8253
Verizon New York Inc	Winchester	MA	F	781 721-5957	13493
Window Book Inc	Cambridge	MA	D	617 395-4500	7761
Caron Engineering Inc	Wells	ME	E	207 646-6071	5598
Ibcontrols	Windham	ME	E	207 893-0080	5662
Workgroup Tech Partners Inc **(PA)**	Westbrook	ME	E	207 856-5312	5653
Entelligence Computer Svcs LLC	Salem	NH	G	603 893-4800	15520
Enterasys Networks Inc **(HQ)**	Salem	NH	D	603 952-5000	15521
Namtek Corp	Bedford	NH	E	603 262-1630	13945
Omada Technologies LLC	Portsmouth	NH	F	603 610-8282	15428
Profitkey International Inc	Salem	NH	E	603 898-9800	15556
Softech Inc **(HQ)**	Nashua	NH	E	513 942-7100	15170
Electro Standards Lab Inc	Cranston	RI	D	401 946-1164	15853
It Synergy Group LLC	Warwick	RI	F	866 767-4874	16824
Jerrys At Misquamicut Inc	Westerly	RI	E	401 596-3155	16934
Leidos Inc	Middletown	RI	E	401 849-8900	16178
Nestor Inc **(PA)**	Providence	RI	E	401 274-5345	16574
Northrop Grumman Systems Corp	Middletown	RI	B	401 849-6270	16183
Ivy Computer Inc	Waterbury Center	VT	F	802 244-7880	17681

7374 Data processing and preparation

Company	CITY	ST	EMP	PHONE	ENTRY#
A To A Studio Solutions Ltd	Stamford	CT	F	203 388-9050	3267
Aquiline Drones Corporation	Hartford	CT	E	973 980-6596	1471
Better Lists Incorporated	Stamford	CT	E	203 324-4171	3294
Hexplora LLC	Rocky Hill	CT	D	860 760-7601	2928
Joseph Merritt & Company Inc **(PA)**	Hartford	CT	E	860 296-2500	1488
Shibumicom Inc	Norwalk	CT	F	855 744-2864	2571
Spectrum Virtual LLC	Cheshire	CT	G	203 303-7540	617
Xerox Corporation **(HQ)**	Norwalk	CT	B	203 849-5216	2598
Xerox Holdings Inc	Norwalk	CT	A	203 968-3000	2599
Xerox Holdings Corporation **(PA)**	Norwalk	CT	B	203 849-5216	2600
Akamai Technologies Inc **(PA)**	Cambridge	MA	B	617 444-3000	7473
Cgi Information Systems & Management Consultants Inc 978 946-3000 5878	Andover	MA			A
Corporate Rmbursement Svcs Inc	Newton	MA	D	888 312-0788	10748
Creamer Associates Inc	Cambridge	MA	G	617 374-6000	7544
Debt Exchange Inc	Boston	MA	D	617 531-3400	6685
Desk Top Graphics Inc **(HQ)**	Peabody	MA	E	617 832-1927	11305
Diacritech Inc	Boston	MA	F	617 236-7500	6692
Gty Technology Holdings Inc **(PA)**	Boston	MA	F	702 945-2898	6778
Homeportfolio Inc	Newton	MA	E	617 559-1197	10760
Logicmanager Inc	Boston	MA	E	617 530-1200	6862
Material Impact Inc	Boston	MA	F	617 917-4123	6879
Research Cmpt Consulting Svcs **(PA)**	Canton	MA	G	781 821-1221	7823
School Family Media LLC	Wrentham	MA	E	508 384-0394	13844
Scully Signal Company **(PA)**	Wilmington	MA	D	617 692-8600	13452
Tactai Inc	Waltham	MA	F	617 391-7915	12787
Toast Inc **(PA)**	Boston	MA	A	617 297-1005	7079
Zlink Inc	Maynard	MA	D	978 309-3628	10268
Edge Media Group	Bangor	ME	F	207 942-2901	4498
S & K Unlimited LLC	Brownville	ME	F	207 965-6137	4638

	CITY	ST	EMP	PHONE	ENTRY#
Ipura Consulting Group LLC	Hampton	NH	F	603 294-4002	14404
Oracle Systems Corporation	Nashua	NH	E	603 897-3000	15146
Snap Site Studios LLC	Manchester	NH	G	603 782-3395	14931
Weather Source LLC	Salem	NH	F	844 813-2617	15571
Igt Global Solutions Corporation (HQ)	Providence	RI	D	401 392-7077	16538
Northrop Grumman Systems Corp	Middletown	RI	B	401 849-6270	16183
Datamann Inc	Wilder	VT	E	802 295-6600	17714

7375 Information retrieval services

	CITY	ST	EMP	PHONE	ENTRY#
Cst Incorporated	Wallingford	CT	F	203 949-9900	3796
Windhover Information Inc (DH)	Norwalk	CT	E	203 838-4401	2597
Aquila Technology Corp	Burlington	MA	F	781 993-9004	7334
Debt Exchange Inc	Boston	MA	D	617 531-3400	6685
Ebsco Publishing Inc (DH)	Ipswich	MA	A	978 356-6500	9485
Homeportfolio Inc	Newton	MA	E	617 559-1197	10760
Kyruus Inc	Boston	MA	C	617 419-2060	6849
Research Cmpt Consulting Svcs (PA)	Canton	MA	G	781 821-1221	7823
Bald Hill Reach Inc	Ellsworth	ME	D	207 667-2576	4754
Tower Publishing (PA)	Standish	ME	F	207 642-5400	5529
Winter People Inc	Cumberland Center	ME	E	207 865-6636	4711
Actio Software Corporation	Portsmouth	NH	D	603 433-2300	15356
Weather Source LLC	Salem	NH	F	844 813-2617	15571
Caledonian Record Pubg Co Inc (PA)	Saint Johnsbury	VT	D	802 748-8121	17540

7376 Computer facilities management

	CITY	ST	EMP	PHONE	ENTRY#
Environmental Systems Corp	West Hartford	CT	C	860 953-8800	4060
Research Cmpt Consulting Svcs (PA)	Canton	MA	G	781 821-1221	7823
It Synergy Group LLC	Warwick	RI	F	866 767-4874	16824

7378 Computer maintenance and repair

	CITY	ST	EMP	PHONE	ENTRY#
Frontier Vision Tech Inc	Rocky Hill	CT	E	860 953-0240	2922
Xerox Corporation (HQ)	Norwalk	CT	B	203 849-5216	2598
Xerox Holdings Inc	Norwalk	CT	A	203 968-3000	2599
Xerox Holdings Corporation (PA)	Norwalk	CT	B	203 849-5216	2600
Bull Data Systems Inc	Chelmsford	MA	A	978 294-6000	7919
Complete Technology Resources	Marlborough	MA	F	508 909-5961	10133
Deerwalk Inc (HQ)	Lexington	MA	C	781 325-1775	9738
Retro-Fit Technologies Inc	Taunton	MA	F	508 478-2222	12363
Sdl Xyenterprise LLC (PA)	Wakefield	MA	E	781 756-4400	12533
Valora Technologies Inc	Carlisle	MA	F	781 229-2265	7850
Xxpress Auto Repair Shop LLC	Hyde Park	MA	F	800 591-2068	9468
Tyler Technologies Inc	Bangor	ME	F	207 947-4494	4517
Techfourfive LLC	Nashua	NH	G	603 438-5760	15175
Igt Global Solutions Corporation (HQ)	Providence	RI	D	401 392-7077	16538

7379 Computer related services, nec

	CITY	ST	EMP	PHONE	ENTRY#
Advanced Decisions Inc	Orange	CT	G	203 402-0603	2665
Advanced Sonics LLC	Oxford	CT	G	203 266-4440	2684
Cst Incorporated	Wallingford	CT	F	203 949-9900	3796
Environmental Systems Corp	West Hartford	CT	C	860 953-8800	4060
Fremco LLC	Stamford	CT	F	203 857-0522	3351
General Dynamics Info Tech Inc	Pawcatuck	CT	D	860 441-2400	2720
Gss Infotech Ct Inc	Glastonbury	CT	C	860 709-0933	1282
Isupportws Inc	Stamford	CT	F	203 569-7600	3386
Norfield Data Products Inc	Norwalk	CT	F	203 849-0292	2546
Process Automtn Solutions Inc (HQ)	Danbury	CT	E	203 207-9917	801
21st Century Software Tech Inc	Boston	MA	D	610 341-9017	6499
Apiphani Inc	Boston	MA	E	800 215-0811	6551
Automatech Inc (PA)	Plymouth	MA	F	508 830-0088	11447
Belle Artfl Intelligence Corp	Cambridge	MA	F	650 291-9410	7504
Datarobot Inc (PA)	Boston	MA	D	617 765-4500	6684
Expertek Systems Inc	Marlborough	MA	E	508 624-0006	10149
GoTo Group Inc (PA)	Boston	MA	A		6768
Intelligent Bus Entrmt Inc	Watertown	MA	F	617 519-4172	12882
Ivory Onyx	Boston	MA	F	617 454-4980	6820
Kenexa Brassring Inc	Littleton	MA	C	781 530-5000	9823
M8trix Tech LLC	Canton	MA	F	617 925-7030	7806
Mobile Software Inc	Boston	MA	G	617 719-8660	6892
Modus Media Inc	Waltham	MA	E	781 663-5000	12724
National Reprographics Inc	Boston	MA	F	857 383-3700	6904
Octo Telematics North Amer LLC	Auburndale	MA	G	617 916-1080	6138
Oneview Commerce Inc	Hingham	MA	D	617 279-0549	9156
Opportunityspace Inc	Boston	MA	E	857 366-1666	6939
Pathai Inc (PA)	Boston	MA	E	617 543-5250	6956
Pegasystems Inc (PA)	Cambridge	MA	A	617 374-9600	7681
Research Cmpt Consulting Svcs (PA)	Canton	MA	G	781 821-1221	7823
RSD America Inc	Waltham	MA	F	201 996-1000	12775
Squareworks Consulting LLC	Boston	MA	E	800 779-6285	7057
Tactai Inc	Waltham	MA	F	617 391-7915	12787
Westrex International Inc	Boston	MA	F	617 254-1200	7119
Cybernorth LLC	South Portland	ME	G	207 331-3310	5496
North Tecom LLC	Manchester	NH	F	603 851-5165	14904

	CITY	ST	EMP	PHONE	ENTRY#
Profitkey International Inc	Salem	NH	E	603 898-9800	15556
Spantech Software Inc	Nashua	NH	F	603 589-4044	15171
It Synergy Group LLC	Warwick	RI	F	866 767-4874	16824
Leidos Inc	Middletown	RI	E	401 849-8900	16178
Ovr Tech LLC	Burlington	VT	G	802 391-4172	17149
Purchasing Inventory Cons Inc	Windsor	VT	F	802 674-2620	17761

7381 Detective and armored car services

	CITY	ST	EMP	PHONE	ENTRY#
International Security Assista	Woburn	MA	C	617 590-7942	13588

7382 Security systems services

	CITY	ST	EMP	PHONE	ENTRY#
BEI Holdings Inc	Wallingford	CT	F	203 741-9300	3780
Environmental Systems Corp	West Hartford	CT	C	860 953-8800	4060
Insight Plus Technology LLC	Bristol	CT	G	860 930-4763	457
Isupportws Inc	Stamford	CT	F	203 569-7600	3386
Manup LLC	Norwalk	CT	G	203 588-9861	2533
Mercury Cabling Systems LLC	Stratford	CT	E	203 378-9008	3556
AES Corporation	Peabody	MA	D	978 535-7310	11293
AES International Corporation	Peabody	MA	F	978 535-7310	11294
Cisco Systems Inc	Boxborough	MA	F	978 936-0000	7149
Idss Holdings Inc	Boxboro	MA	D	978 237-0236	7144
Imprivata Inc (HQ)	Waltham	MA	B	781 674-2700	12697
Nashoba Security Inc	Littleton	MA	F	978 486-8615	9827
Simplex Time Recorder LLC (DH)	Westminster	MA	C		13278
Videoiq Inc	Somerville	MA	E	781 222-3069	11911
Orion Entrance Control Inc	Laconia	NH	E	603 527-4187	14662
It Synergy Group LLC	Warwick	RI	F	866 767-4874	16824
General Dynamics Ots Cal Inc	Williston	VT	B	802 662-7000	17733

7383 News syndicates

	CITY	ST	EMP	PHONE	ENTRY#
Provincetown Banner Inc	Provincetown	MA	F	508 487-7400	11496

7384 Photofinish laboratories

	CITY	ST	EMP	PHONE	ENTRY#
Cine Magnetics Inc (HQ)	Stamford	CT	D	914 273-7600	3312
Queen Graphics Printworks Inc	West Haven	CT	F	203 464-7337	4120
Yankee Plak Co Inc	Bridgeport	CT	F	203 333-3168	387
Icl Imaging Corp	Framingham	MA	E	508 872-3280	8778
Market Basket Produce Inc	Concord	NH	D	603 224-5479	14143
Abar Color Labs Neng Inc	Lincoln	RI	F	401 351-8644	16114

7389 Business services, nec

	CITY	ST	EMP	PHONE	ENTRY#
20/20 Software Inc	Stamford	CT	G	203 316-5500	3266
A D Perkins Company	New Haven	CT	G	203 777-3456	2110
Acme Wire Products Co Inc	Mystic	CT	E	860 572-0511	1935
Aerospace Alloys Inc	Bloomfield	CT	D	860 882-0019	144
American Sign Inc	New Haven	CT	F	203 624-2991	2115
Ann S Davis	Lebanon	CT	F	860 642-7228	1548
API Wizard LLC	Stamford	CT	E	800 691-8714	3283
Arnco Sign Company	Wallingford	CT	E	203 238-1224	3775
B & F Design Incorporated	New Britain	CT	F	860 357-4317	2005
Barker Advg Specialty Co Inc (PA)	Cheshire	CT	D	203 272-2222	575
Biomerics LLC	Monroe	CT	E	203 268-7238	1906
Century Tool and Design Inc	Milldale	CT	F	860 621-6748	1900
Chapin Packaging LLC	Darien	CT	G	203 202-2747	846
Cyient Defense Services Inc	New Britain	CT	E	860 357-4317	2019
D&D Fltrtion Cons Sppliers Inc	Kensington	CT	F	860 829-3690	1539
DS Sewing Inc	New Haven	CT	F	203 773-1344	2145
Dufrane Nuclear Shielding Inc	Winsted	CT	F	860 379-2318	4340
Environmental Monitor Svc Inc	Meriden	CT	G	203 935-0102	1667
Federal Business Products Inc	Torrington	CT	E	860 482-6231	3680
First Equity Group Inc (PA)	Westport	CT	F	203 291-7700	4168
Flagship Converters Inc	Danbury	CT	D	203 792-0034	746
Flitsai Inc	Ellington	CT	F	203 586-8201	1106
Gyre9 LLC	Southbury	CT	E	203 702-4010	3194
Hornblower Shipyard LLC	Bridgeport	CT	E	203 572-0378	330
Indigo Coast Inc	Kent	CT	G	860 592-0088	1541
John Oldham Studios Inc	Wethersfield	CT	E	860 529-3331	4207
Joseph Merritt & Company Inc (PA)	Hartford	CT	E	860 296-2500	1488
Karen Callan Designs Inc	Greenwich	CT	E	203 762-9914	1336
Kimchuk Incorporated (PA)	Danbury	CT	F	203 790-7800	766
Kirchoff Wohlberg Inc	Madison	CT	F	212 644-2020	1562
Lifetoken Software Inc	Cos Cob	CT	G	203 515-9686	678
Lmt Communications Inc	Newtown	CT	E	203 426-4568	2339
Lyons Slitting Inc	Waterbury	CT	F	203 755-4564	3932
Mdf Systems Inc	Bristol	CT	D	860 584-4750	466
N C T Inc	Colchester	CT	F	860 666-8424	662
New England Tooling Inc	Killingworth	CT	F	800 866-5105	1544
New Haven Chemicals LLC	New Haven	CT	E	475 241-1150	2177
Nofet LLC	New Haven	CT	F	203 848-9064	2180
Northeast Laser Engraving Inc	Monroe	CT	E	203 268-7238	1918
Olive Oil Factory LLC	Waterbury	CT	E	203 437-8286	3956
Olympia Sales Inc	Enfield	CT	D	860 749-0751	1140
On Line Building Systems LLC	Danbury	CT	G	203 798-1194	792

Name	CITY	ST	EMP	PHONE	ENTRY#
Perosphere Inc	Danbury	CT	F	203 885-1111	796
Pta Corporation (PA)	Oxford	CT	D	203 888-0585	2709
Regenerative Medicine LLC (PA)	Greenwich	CT	G	203 969-4877	1346
Rhema 320 LLC (PA)	New Haven	CT	G	475 434-8581	2191
Rokap Inc	East Hampton	CT	G	203 265-6895	965
Show Management Associates LLC	Norwalk	CT	G	203 939-9901	2572
Skin & Co North America LLC	West Haven	CT	G	888 444-9971	4126
Skull Kingdom Entrmt LLC	Ledyard	CT	G	262 804-8193	1553
Society Plastics Engineers Inc (PA)	Danbury	CT	E	203 740-5422	819
Technical Reproductions Inc	Norwalk	CT	F	203 849-9100	2575
Tethereducation Inc	New Haven	CT	E	203 691-0131	2207
Uniworld Bus Publications Inc	Darien	CT	G	201 384-4900	857
UPS Authorized Retailer	Fairfield	CT	F	203 256-9991	1205
Urban Exposition LLC (DH)	Shelton	CT	E	203 242-8717	3074
Wingsite Displays Inc	Wethersfield	CT	E	860 257-3300	4215
Yolanda Dubose Records and	West Haven	CT	F	203 823-6699	4134
943 Enteretainment Corp	Somerville	MA	F	617 608-6943	11858
Accumet Engineering Corp	Devens	MA	E	978 568-8311	8266
Actifio Federal LLC	Needham	MA	F	781 795-9182	10503
Acumentrics Rups LLC	Walpole	MA	F	617 932-7877	12546
Aetruim Incorporated	Billerica	MA	E	651 773-4200	6397
Airworks Solutions Inc	Boston	MA	E	857 990-1060	6524
Americas Test Kitchen Limited Partnership	Boston		MA		C
617 232-1000	6544				
Andritz Inc	Springfield	MA	C	413 733-6603	12075
Architects of Packaging Inc	Westfield	MA	G	413 568-3187	13148
Associated Mktg Systems Inc	Holbrook	MA	E	781 767-9001	9168
Atlas Devices LLC	Chelmsford	MA	F	617 415-1657	7913
Audiospectrum Inc	Randolph	MA	E	781 767-1331	11549
Bcg Connect LLC	Wilmington	MA	E	978 528-7999	13389
Bew Corp	Randolph	MA	F	781 963-0315	11550
Bloom & Company Inc	Framingham	MA	F	617 923-1526	8744
Bluedrop LLC	South Easton	MA	F	877 662-7873	11938
Booktalk Event	Lowell	MA	E	952 836-5617	9863
Boston Sports Journal LLC	Medway	MA	G	617 306-0166	10303
Bradford Finshg Powdr Coat Inc	Haverhill	MA	G	978 469-9965	9081
Business and Prof Exch Inc	Beverly	MA	E	978 556-4100	6336
Carriage Hse Developments LLC	Winchester	MA	F	339 221-4253	13483
Chillybear Inc (PA)	Needham	MA	F	781 455-6321	10507
Chris Ploof Designs Inc	Leominster	MA	G	978 728-4905	9651
CJS Workshop LLC	Groton	MA	E	323 445-5012	9008
Corporate Casuals LLC	Concord	MA	F	978 369-5935	8110
Dinner Daily LLC	Westford	MA	F	978 392-5887	13234
Dion Signs and Service Inc	New Bedford	MA	F	401 724-4459	10586
Drizly LLC (HQ)	Boston	MA	E	774 234-1033	6703
Duval Precision Grinding Inc	Chicopee	MA	F	413 593-3060	8028
East Basin Sports Inc (PA)	Newton	MA	E	781 492-2747	10754
Edge Embossing Inc	Charlestown	MA	G	617 850-2868	7870
Edgewater Marine Inds LLC	New Bedford	MA	F	508 992-6555	10588
Etec Inc	West Roxbury	MA	F	617 477-4308	13010
Feteria Tool & Findings	Attleboro	MA	G	508 222-7788	6014
Fire Defenses New England LLC	Danvers	MA	F	978 304-1655	8186
First Sail Group Inc	South Yarmouth	MA	G	425 409-2783	11983
Focused Impressions Tech LLC	Boston	MA	E	857 453-6771	6742
Frendzi Inc	Newton	MA	F	617 899-0234	10756
Gem Group Inc (PA)	Lawrence	MA	B	978 691-2000	9564
George Patton Associates Inc	Fall River	MA	C	800 572-2194	8552
Greenbrier Games LLP	Marlborough	MA	G	978 618-8442	10155
Grey Barn Farm Enterprises LLC	Chilmark	MA	G	508 645-4854	8071
Heat-Flo Inc	Uxbridge	MA	G	508 278-2400	12480
Horizon House Publications Inc (PA)	Norwood	MA	D	781 769-9750	11177
Horn Corporation (PA)	Lancaster	MA	E	800 832-7020	9527
Idex Health & Science LLC	Middleboro	MA	C	774 213-0200	10362
Industrial Packaging Sup Inc	Worcester	MA	F	978 514-9960	13741
Industrial Packaging Supply Inc (PA)	Webster	MA	F	508 499-1600	12927
Infinite Iq Inc	Wellesley	MA	F	781 710-8696	12943
Innovative Publishing Company	Edgartown	MA	F	267 266-8876	8466
Insco Corporation	Groton	MA	F	978 448-6368	9010
Insignia Incorporated	Haverhill	MA	E	978 372-3721	9105
Insignia Incorporated	Norwood	MA	E	781 278-0150	11182
Institute For Applied Ntwrk SE	Boston	MA	E	617 399-8100	6814
Institute For Fgn Plicy Analis (PA)	Cambridge	MA	E	617 492-2116	7615
Intelon Optics Inc	Woburn	MA	F	310 804-9392	13587
International Data Group Inc (HQ)	Needham	MA	F	508 875-5000	10514
J L Enterprises Inc	Canton	MA	G	781 821-6300	7802
Jamesbrook Enterprises Inc	Shirley	MA	G	978 425-6166	11818
John McGillicuddy Inc	Milton	MA	F	617 388-6324	10453
JP Progressive Comm Group LLC	New Bedford	MA	F	800 477-4681	10607
Kink Pieces of A Dream LLC	Framingham	MA	F	508 748-5417	8784
Klone Lab LLC	Newburyport	MA	F	978 378-3434	10692
Leblanc Enterprises Inc	Lawrence	MA	E	978 682-5112	9578
Lifecloud Inc	Amesbury	MA	G	978 621-9572	5842
M P Brewing Company	Fall River	MA	F	508 944-8531	8570
Marthas Vineyard Furn Co LLC	Vineyard Haven	MA	G	508 687-9555	12491
Massachsetts Brewers Guild Inc	Framingham	MA	F	508 405-9115	8788
Mbm Building Systems Ltd	Boston	MA	F	617 478-3466	6881
Merida Meridian Inc	Boston	MA	F	617 464-5400	6885
Microwave Development Labs Inc	Needham Heights	MA	D	781 292-6600	10551
Modus Media Inc	Waltham	MA	E	781 663-5000	12724
Monalex Manufacturing Inc	East Douglas	MA	G	508 476-1200	8352
Mystic Scenic Studios Inc	Norwood	MA	D	781 440-0914	11198
Nationwide Tax & Business Svcs	New Bedford	MA	F	774 473-8444	10625
Nery Corporation	New Bedford	MA	G	508 990-9800	10626
North Atlantic PCF Seafood LLC	Danvers	MA	F	401 969-3886	8213
North Shore Laboratories Corp	Peabody	MA	F	978 531-5954	11327
Nvision Medical Corporation	Marlborough	MA	G	408 655-3577	10187
Nypro Inc (HQ)	Clinton	MA	A	978 365-9721	8087
Owl Stamp Company Inc	Lowell	MA	G	978 452-4541	9912
Ozone Technologies Inc	Boston	MA	G	617 955-4188	6950
Perioq Inc	Leominster	MA	G	978 534-1249	9693
Plastilam Inc	Salem	MA	E	978 745-5563	11730
Queen Associates Inc	Woburn	MA	D	781 389-8494	13644
Radar Wind Up Corporation (HQ)	Cambridge	MA	F	917 488-6050	7693
Raders Engraving Inc	Boston	MA	G	617 227-2921	6993
Rand-Whitney Packaging Corp	Worcester	MA	D	508 929-3400	13780
Red Point Positioning Corp (PA)	Newton	MA	F	339 222-0261	10779
Roadsafe Traffic Systems Inc	Avon	MA	D	508 580-6700	6160
Safecor Health LLC	Woburn	MA	G	781 933-8780	13658
Safety-Kleen Systems Inc (HQ)	Norwell	MA	B	800 669-5740	11146
Safve Inc	Scituate	MA	G	781 545-3546	11770
Sampco Inc (PA)	Pittsfield	MA	C	413 442-4043	11423
Sara Campbell Ltd (PA)	Boston	MA	G	617 423-3134	7025
Scidose LLC	Amherst	MA	F	866 956-4333	5864
Security Engineered McHy Inc (PA)	Westborough	MA	E	508 366-1488	13133
Ser Logistics Inc	Worcester	MA	F	508 757-3397	13798
Serrato Signs LLC	Worcester	MA	G	508 756-7004	13799
Silva Jewelers of Osterville	Osterville	MA	F	508 428-2872	11246
Sst Components Inc (PA)	Lawrence	MA	E	978 670-7300	9601
Stellar Menus Inc	Provincetown	MA	G	617 882-2800	11498
Stone Tablet LLC	Newton	MA	F	781 380-8800	10788
Streetscan Inc	Wakefield	MA	E	617 399-8236	12538
Tanyx Measurements Inc	Billerica	MA	G	978 671-0183	6485
TCI America Inc	Seekonk	MA	F	508 336-6633	11786
Telco Communications Inc	Seekonk	MA	F	508 336-6633	11788
Terrapin	Cambridge	MA	G	508 487-8181	7738
Three Twins Productions Inc	Watertown	MA	G	617 926-0377	12914
TMI Industries Inc	Palmer	MA	E	413 283-9021	11285
Trackcam LLC	Rehoboth	MA	G	508 556-1955	11614
Tri Textiles Corporation (PA)	Fall River	MA	G	631 420-0011	8617
True Machine Co Inc	Swansea	MA	G	508 379-0329	12314
United Paper Stock Co Inc	Worcester	MA	E	401 724-5700	13816
US Packaging Specialties	Fall River	MA	F	508 674-3636	8621
Veloxint Corporation	Framingham	MA	F	774 777-3369	8806
Vision Gvernment Solutions Inc	Hudson	MA	C	800 628-1013	9424
Webco Chemical Corporation	Dudley	MA	D	508 943-2337	8327
Witricity Corporation (PA)	Watertown	MA	F	617 926-2700	12921
Advanced Indus Solutions Inc (PA)	Augusta	ME	F	207 623-9599	4466
Ambrose G McCarthy Jr	Skowhegan	ME	F	207 474-8837	5462
B & B Precise Products Inc	Benton	ME	F	207 453-8118	4544
Bangor Neon	Bangor	ME	F	207 947-2766	4492
Barrett Made (PA)	Portland	ME	E	207 650-6500	5184
BBH Apparel	Boothbay Harbor	ME	F	207 633-0601	4601
Contour360 Corp	Cornish	ME	F	207 625-4000	4704
Coursestorm Inc	Orono	ME	F	207 866-0328	5134
D E Enterprise Inc	Rockport	ME	E	207 594-9544	5346
Diversified Communications (HQ)	Portland	ME	F	207 842-5500	5209
Enefco International Inc (PA)	Auburn	ME	F	207 514-7218	4428
Erin Flett	Gorham	ME	G	207 887-9253	4819
Evergreen Manufacturing Group LLC	Madawaska	ME	E	207 728-4900	5037
F O Bailey Co Inc	Falmouth	ME	F	207 781-8001	4768
Fiber Materials Inc (DH)	Biddeford	ME	C	207 282-5911	4564
J & M Machining Inc	Skowhegan	ME	F	207 474-7300	5470
Kbs Builders Inc	South Paris	ME	C	207 739-2400	5488
Knickerbocker Group Inc	Boothbay	ME	D	207 541-9333	4598
Nikel Precision Group LLC	Saco	ME	F	207 282-6080	5375
Packgen Inc	Auburn	ME	E	207 784-4195	4449
Print Bangor	Bangor	ME	G	207 947-8049	4515
Rockstep Solutions Inc (PA)	Portland	ME	F	844 800-7625	5267
Somatex Inc	Detroit	ME	G	207 487-6141	4725
Ta Property Maintenance LLC	Scarborough	ME	F	207 289-7158	5444
Transformnt (PA)	Gorham	ME	E	207 856-9911	4837
Tranztape LLC	Appleton	ME	G	207 785-2467	4406
Valt Enterprizes Inc	Presque Isle	ME	F	207 560-5188	5311
A & R Sawyer Co Inc	Windham	NH	G	603 893-5752	15719
A B Excavating Inc	Lancaster	NH	E	603 788-5110	14675
Alex & Ryan Design LLC	Manchester	NH	F	603 518-8650	14808

	CITY	ST	EMP	PHONE	ENTRY#
American Flgging Trffic Ctrl I	Hudson	NH	D	603 890-1154	14482
AP Dley Cstm Laminating Corp	Windham	NH	E	603 437-6666	15720
Bellman Jewelers Inc	Manchester	NH	G	603 625-4653	14819
Blue Dolphin Screenprint Inc	Somersworth	NH	E	603 692-2500	15611
Cdc Enterprises Llc	Windham	NH	G	603 437-3090	15722
Eco Knight Group LLC **(PA)**	Lebanon	NH	G	802 318-8760	14687
Gilberte Interiors LLC **(PA)**	Hanover	NH	F	603 643-3727	14423
Glass Graphics Inc	Conway	NH	F	603 447-1900	14179
Hammar & Sons Inc	Pelham	NH	F	603 635-2292	15289
Helmers Publishing Inc	Dublin	NH	E	603 563-1631	14261
Hopkinton For Land Claring Inc	Henniker	NH	E	603 428-8400	14437
Image 4 Concepts Inc	Manchester	NH	F	603 644-0077	14862
Ingersoll-Rand Energy Systems Corporation	Portsmouth	NH			D
603 430-7000	15408				
Innovairre Studios Inc	Milford	NH	E	603 579-1600	15030
J-Pac LLC **(HQ)**	Somersworth	NH	D	603 692-9955	15617
Lestat Production 81 Corp	Bedford	NH	E	866 557-4478	13939
Miraco Inc	Manchester	NH	E	603 665-9449	14890
National Embroidery Corp	Manchester	NH	F	603 647-1995	14896
Nazarian Jewelers NH Inc **(PA)**	Salem	NH	F	603 893-1600	15548
New Model Inc	Belmont	NH	E	603 267-8225	13964
Prime Power Inc	Hampstead	NH	F	603 329-4675	14390
Resin Technology Group LLC	Seabrook	NH	D	508 230-8070	15601
Sousa Signs LLC	Manchester	NH	G	603 622-5067	14934
Sports Visio Inc	Dunbarton	NH	F	603 774-1339	14265
Starkey Welding Crane Service	Brentwood	NH	G	603 679-2553	14030
Synap Inc	Dover	NH	G	888 572-1150	14251
Tolles Communications Corp	Manchester	NH	F	603 627-9500	14945
Vidarr Inc	Portsmouth	NH	G	877 636-8432	15448
Wagz Inc **(PA)**	Portsmouth	NH	F	603 570-6015	15449
Alden Yachts Corporation	Bristol	RI	E	401 683-4200	15752
Cabinet Gallery Ltd **(PA)**	Woonsocket	RI	G	401 762-4300	16952
Classsick Custom LLC	Pawtucket	RI	F	401 475-7288	16355
Constant Technologies Inc	North Kingstown	RI	E	800 518-7369	16240
Contech Medical Inc	Providence	RI	D	401 351-4890	16504
Dexter Enterprises Corp	East Providence	RI	G	401 434-2300	16013
Dexter Sign Co	East Providence	RI	F	401 434-1100	16014
Drapery House Inc	North Providence	RI	G	401 724-3400	16300
Florlink Inc	Newport	RI	F	617 221-2200	16210
Hilco Athletic & Graphics Inc	West Warwick	RI	F	401 822-1775	16910
IDS Highway Safety Inc	Cumberland	RI	D	401 425-2205	15945
Johnson & Wales University	Providence	RI	E	401 598-1824	16550
Matlet Group LLC	Pawtucket	RI	B	401 834-3007	16385
Modern Industries Inc	Providence	RI	E	401 331-8000	16566
Parsonskellogg LLC	East Providence	RI	D	866 602-8398	16037
Sonco Worldwide Inc	Warwick	RI	F	401 406-3761	16863
Sparkman & Stephens LLC **(PA)**	Newport	RI	F	401 847-5449	16225
Tsco Inc	North Kingstown	RI	F	401 295-0669	16289
DC Enterprizes Inc	Hinesburg	VT	F	802 865-4480	17290
Leo D Bernstein & Sons Inc	Shaftsbury	VT	D	802 442-8029	17550
McKernon Group Inc	Brandon	VT	D	802 247-8500	17068
Precision Cutter Grinding Inc	Hartland	VT	G	802 436-2039	17287
RK Miles Inc **(PA)**	Manchester Center	VT	C	802 362-1952	17330
Select Design Ltd	Burlington	VT	D	802 864-9075	17158
Sogle Property LLC	Cambridge	VT	F	802 849-7943	17168
Twin State Signs Inc	Essex Junction	VT	G	802 872-8949	17248
Twincraft Inc **(PA)**	Winooski	VT	C	802 655-2200	17769

75 AUTOMOTIVE REPAIR, SERVICES AND PARKING

7513 Truck rental and leasing, without drivers

	CITY	ST	EMP	PHONE	ENTRY#
Standard Welding Company Inc	East Hartford	CT	G	860 528-9628	1022
U-Haul Co Mass & Ohio Inc **(DH)**	Somerville	MA	E	617 625-2789	11908
Baude Inc	Houlton	ME	F	207 532-6571	4896

7514 Passenger car rental

	CITY	ST	EMP	PHONE	ENTRY#
Big Foot Moving & Storage Inc	Acton	MA	E	781 488-3090	5740

7532 Top and body repair and paint shops

	CITY	ST	EMP	PHONE	ENTRY#
Rokap Inc	East Hampton	CT	G	203 265-6895	965
Bodyshop World By Wagner Inc	Worcester	MA	F	508 853-0300	13704
Fastsigns	Needham Heights	MA	G	781 444-4889	10546
Lynn Ladder Scaffolding Co Inc **(HQ)**	Lynn	MA	D	781 598-6010	9985
Martel Welding & Sons Inc	Tewksbury	MA	F	978 458-0661	12406
Middlesex Truck & Auto Body	Boston	MA	E	617 442-3000	6887
National Van Sales Inc	Attleboro	MA	F	508 222-2272	6040
Marketing Worldwide Corp **(PA)**	Rockland	ME	G	631 444-8090	5339
Mbw Tractor Sales LLC	Berwick	ME	F	207 384-2001	4551
Bri-Weld Industries LLC	Auburn	NH	F	603 622-9480	13906
Larry Dingee	Cornish	NH	G	603 542-9682	14183
Ride-Away Inc **(HQ)**	Londonderry	NH	E	603 437-4444	14782
Special Projects Group LLC	Gilford	NH	G	603 391-9700	14338

	CITY	ST	EMP	PHONE	ENTRY#
Kane Motor Car Co Inc	North Kingstown	RI	G	401 294-4634	16263
Giroux Body Shop Inc	Hinesburg	VT	F	802 482-2162	17291
Iroquois Manufacturing Company	Hinesburg	VT	E	802 482-2155	17295

7533 Auto exhaust system repair shops

	CITY	ST	EMP	PHONE	ENTRY#
Monro Inc	Swanzey	NH	G	603 352-7822	15644
T M Services Inc	Rutland	VT	E	802 775-2948	17511

7534 Tire retreading and repair shops

	CITY	ST	EMP	PHONE	ENTRY#
Bergson Tire Co Inc	Ellington	CT	F	860 872-7729	1102
Bridgestone Ret Operations LLC	Bristol	CT	G	860 584-2727	417
Bridgestone Ret Operations LLC	Hamden	CT	G	203 288-1634	1414
Bridgestone Ret Operations LLC	Milford	CT	G	203 878-6859	1803
Bridgestone Ret Operations LLC	New Britain	CT	F	860 229-0348	2009
Bridgestone Ret Operations LLC	New Haven	CT	G	203 787-1208	2132
Bridgestone Ret Operations LLC	Newington	CT	G	860 594-0594	2277
Bridgestone Ret Operations LLC	Southington	CT	G	860 628-9621	3205
Bridgestone Ret Operations LLC	Waterbury	CT	F	203 754-6119	3893
Bridgestone Ret Operations LLC	West Haven	CT	G	203 933-7750	4095
Derby Tire Company	Branford	CT	F	203 481-8473	249
Firestone Building Pdts Co LLC	Bristol	CT	G	860 584-4516	447
Oasis Truck Tire Service LLC **(PA)**	Old Saybrook	CT	G	860 296-8749	2657
Reliable Auto Tire Company Inc	Hartford	CT	G	860 247-7977	1504
Star Tires Plus Wheels LLC	Hartford	CT	F	860 296-9799	1509
Tire Country of Enfield Inc	Enfield	CT	G	860 763-0846	1155
American Tire Svc & Sls Inc	Springfield	MA	G	413 739-5369	12074
Aronson Tire Company Inc	Auburn	MA	E	508 832-3244	6105
Autocraft Collision Inc	Reading	MA	G	781 670-9001	11600
BJs Wholesale Club Inc	Franklin	MA	D	508 553-9889	8821
Bodyshop World By Wagner Inc	Worcester	MA	F	508 853-0300	13704
Bridgestone Ret Operations LLC	Auburn	MA	G	508 832-9671	6110
Bridgestone Ret Operations LLC	Boston	MA	G	617 327-1100	6622
Bridgestone Ret Operations LLC	Braintree	MA	G	781 843-2870	7172
Bridgestone Ret Operations LLC	Brockton	MA	G	508 588-8866	7262
Bridgestone Ret Operations LLC	Hingham	MA	G	781 749-6454	9145
Bridgestone Ret Operations LLC	Northampton	MA	G	413 586-1584	11054
Bridgestone Ret Operations LLC	Quincy	MA	G	617 479-3208	11508
Bridgestone Ret Operations LLC	Springfield	MA	F	413 543-1312	12080
Bridgestone Ret Operations LLC	Watertown	MA	F	617 924-3989	12864
Bridgestone Ret Operations LLC	Wilmington	MA	G	978 658-5660	13394
City Tire Co Inc	Chicopee	MA	E	413 534-2946	8018
City Tire Co Inc	Pittsfield	MA	E	413 445-5578	11396
City Tire Co Inc **(PA)**	Springfield	MA	E	413 737-1419	12084
Goodyear Tire & Rubber Company	Lynn	MA	F	781 598-4500	9976
Holyoke Tire & Auto Svc Inc	Springfield	MA	G	413 733-2141	12101
K & W Tire Company Inc	Ayer	MA	F	978 772-5700	6184
Petes Tire Barns Inc **(PA)**	Orange	MA	D	978 544-8811	11228
Rolands Tire Service Inc **(PA)**	Fairhaven	MA	E	508 997-4501	8514
Sullivan Investment Co Inc **(PA)**	Norwell	MA	F	781 982-1550	11147
Sullivan Tire Co Inc	North Attleboro	MA	G	508 695-9920	10890
Tire & Auto Service Centers	Brockton	MA	G	508 559-6802	7312
Baude Inc	Houlton	ME	F	207 532-6571	4896
Central Tire Co Inc **(PA)**	Sanford	ME	G	207 324-4250	5391
Lag Inc **(PA)**	Topsham	ME	G	207 729-1676	5548
Lees Tire	Topsham	ME	E	207 729-1676	5549
Maine Commercial Tire Inc **(PA)**	Hermon	ME	E	207 848-5540	4885
Maine Commercial Tire Inc	Waterville	ME	F	207 622-3200	5595
Maine Tire & Appliance Co	Augusta	ME	G	207 623-1171	4477
Maine Tire & Appliance Co **(PA)**	Falmouth	ME	F	207 781-3136	4769
McQuade Tidd Industries	Houlton	ME	F	207 532-6571	4902
New England Trck Tire Ctrs Inc **(PA)**	Sanford	ME	E	207 324-2262	5402
Steven Pelletier	Fort Kent	ME	F	207 834-3191	4794
Tki Inc	Skowhegan	ME	G	207 474-5322	5479
Belknap Tire Co Holdings Inc	Laconia	NH	F	603 524-4517	14646
Bridgestone Ret Operations LLC	Manchester	NH	G	603 668-1123	14821
DC Tire Service Inc	Milford	NH	G	603 673-9211	15021
Freedom Tire Inc **(PA)**	Plaistow	NH	F	603 382-7223	15344
Monro Inc	Swanzey	NH	G	603 352-7822	15644
Mountain Tire Corp	Berlin	NH	F	603 752-8473	13983
Northeast Tire Service Inc	Belmont	NH	G	603 524-7973	13965
Bec Corp	Pawtucket	RI	G	401 725-3535	16347
Bridgestone Ret Operations LLC	North Smithfield	RI	F	401 766-0233	16319
Bridgestone Ret Operations LLC	Providence	RI	F	401 521-6622	16491
Ocean State Tire Co Inc	Cranston	RI	E	401 946-0880	15903
Petes Tire Barns Inc	Providence	RI	F	401 521-2240	16583
Sullivan Tire Co Inc	Warwick	RI	F	401 737-5251	16866
John Penfield Ltd	Brattleboro	VT	G	802 254-5411	17090
Vianor Inc **(HQ)**	Colchester	VT	E	802 864-7108	17207
Vianor Inc	Montpelier	VT	F	802 223-1747	17378
Vianor Inc	Morrisville	VT	E	802 888-7961	17392

7536 Automotive glass replacement shops

	CITY	ST	EMP	PHONE	ENTRY#
Capitol Glass Company Inc	West Hartford	CT	F	860 236-1936	4050

SIC

	CITY	ST	EMP	PHONE	ENTRY#

7537 Automotive transmission repair shops

	CITY	ST	EMP	PHONE	ENTRY#
Bridgestone Ret Operations LLC	West Haven	CT	G	203 933-7750	4095

7538 General automotive repair shops

	CITY	ST	EMP	PHONE	ENTRY#
Bridgestone Ret Operations LLC	West Haven	CT	G	203 933-7750	4095
Danbury A LLC	Danbury	CT	E	203 744-5202	724
Tire Country of Enfield Inc	Enfield	CT	G	860 763-0846	1155
Boston Trailer Manufacturing	Walpole	MA	F	508 668-2242	12553
Daves Truck Repair Inc	Springfield	MA	E	413 734-8898	12089
Holyoke Tire & Auto Svc Inc	Springfield	MA	E	413 733-2141	12101
Motor Service Inc	Shrewsbury	MA	F	508 832-6291	11839
Sullivan Tire Co Inc	North Attleboro	MA	G	508 695-9920	10890
U-Haul Co Mass & Ohio Inc (DH)	Somerville	MA	E	617 625-2789	11908
Central Tire Co Inc (PA)	Sanford	ME	F	207 324-4250	5391
Hanscom Construction Inc	Marshfield	ME	F	207 255-8067	5046
Hcb Holdings Inc (PA)	South Portland	ME	E	207 767-2136	5505
J O Brown & Son Inc	North Haven	ME	G	207 867-4621	5114
Lees Tire	Topsham	ME	F	207 729-1676	5549
Melton Sales and Service Inc	Hallowell	ME	G	207 623-8895	4860
Steven Pelletier	Fort Kent	ME	F	207 834-3191	4794
Weymouths Garage Inc	Milford	ME	G	207 827-2069	5063
Belknap Tire Co Holdings Inc	Laconia	NH	F	603 524-4517	14646
Donovan Equipment Company Inc	Londonderry	NH	D	603 669-2250	14743
Northeast Tire Service Inc	Belmont	NH	G	603 524-7993	13965
Ralph L Osgood Inc	Claremont	NH	F	603 543-1703	14096
Reed Truck Services Inc	Claremont	NH	F	603 542-5032	14097
Eagle Motors Inc	Harrisville	RI	F	401 568-2580	16065
Kane Motor Car Co Inc	North Kingstown	RI	G	401 294-4634	16263
Rounds Service Station Inc	North Scituate	RI	F	401 934-9877	16316
Sullivan Tire Co Inc	Warwick	RI	G	401 737-5251	16866

7539 Automotive repair shops, nec

	CITY	ST	EMP	PHONE	ENTRY#
Advanced Torque Products LLC	Newington	CT	G	860 828-1523	2268
Bridgestone Ret Operations LLC	Southington	CT	G	860 628-9621	3205
Seals-It Inc	Ellington	CT	G	860 979-0060	1114
WH Rose Inc	Columbia	CT	E	860 228-8258	671
Boston Trailer Manufacturing	Walpole	MA	F	508 668-2242	12553
Centerline Machine Company Inc	Beverly	MA	F	978 524-8842	6338
Dattco Sales & Service	Saugus	MA	G	860 229-4878	11756
Daves Truck Repair Inc	Springfield	MA	E	413 734-8898	12089
Joseph Palmer Inc	Woburn	MA	F	781 376-0130	13595
Tire & Auto Service Centers	Brockton	MA	G	508 559-6802	7312
U-Haul Co Mass & Ohio Inc (DH)	Somerville	MA	E	617 625-2789	11908
Wright Trailers Inc	Seekonk	MA	F	508 336-8530	11790
Maine & Maritimes Corporation (PA)	Presque Isle	ME	F	207 760-2499	5304
Hagan Design and Machine Inc	Newmarket	NH	F	603 292-1101	15220
Monro Inc	Swanzey	NH	G	603 352-7822	15644
Lance Smith Inc	Milton	VT	D	802 655-3354	17361
T M Services Inc	Rutland	VT	E	802 775-2948	17511
Vermont Engine Service Inc	Williston	VT	G	802 863-2326	17752

7542 Carwashes

	CITY	ST	EMP	PHONE	ENTRY#
Quick Clean Car Wash Systems I (PA)	Wakefield	MA	F	781 245-6809	12531

7549 Automotive services, nec

	CITY	ST	EMP	PHONE	ENTRY#
Environmental Systems Products Inc	East Granby	CT	C	860 653-0081	933
Standard Welding Company Inc	East Hartford	CT	G	860 528-9628	1022
Tire Country of Enfield Inc	Enfield	CT	G	860 763-0846	1155
Cross Country Motor Club Inc (HQ)	Medford	MA	A	781 393-9300	10283
Daves Truck Repair Inc	Springfield	MA	E	413 734-8898	12089
Jiffy Lube	Mashpee	MA	G	508 539-8888	10252
Xxpress Auto Repair Shop LLC	Hyde Park	MA	F	800 591-2068	9468
Melton Sales and Service Inc	Hallowell	ME	G	207 623-8895	4860
Monro Inc	Swanzey	NH	G	603 352-7822	15644
East Greenwich Oil Co Inc	East Greenwich	RI	G	401 884-2454	15982
North Atlantic Dist Inc	North Kingstown	RI	F	401 667-7000	16274
T M Services Inc	Rutland	VT	E	802 775-2948	17511

76 MISCELLANEOUS REPAIR SERVICES

7622 Radio and television repair

	CITY	ST	EMP	PHONE	ENTRY#
Retcomm Inc	Guilford	CT	F	203 453-2389	1405

7623 Refrigeration service and repair

	CITY	ST	EMP	PHONE	ENTRY#
Jason Trucks Inc	Medford	MA	F	781 396-8300	10292
Tecogen Inc (PA)	Waltham	MA	F	781 466-6402	12790
Watka Corporation	Lakeville	MA	F	508 946-5555	9523
Hussmann Corporation	Salem	NH	E	603 893-7770	15538

7629 Electrical repair shops

	CITY	ST	EMP	PHONE	ENTRY#
Afcon Products Inc	Bethany	CT	F	203 393-9301	91

	CITY	ST	EMP	PHONE	ENTRY#
Agissar Corporation	Stratford	CT	E	203 375-8662	3516
Air Tool Sales & Svc Co Inc (PA)	Unionville	CT	G	860 673-2714	3746
Conair LLC	Torrington	CT	D	800 492-7464	3676
Electro-Methods Inc (PA)	South Windsor	CT	C	860 289-8661	3141
Hyaxiom Inc (HQ)	East Hartford	CT	E	860 727-2200	998
Leppert/Nutmeg Inc	Bloomfield	CT	E	860 243-1737	188
Microboard Processing Inc	Seymour	CT	C	203 881-4300	2965
N C T Inc	Colchester	CT	F	860 666-8424	662
On Line Building Systems LLC	Danbury	CT	G	203 798-1194	792
Quadient Inc (DH)	Milford	CT	C	203 301-3400	1874
Tech II Business Services Inc	Rocky Hill	CT	E	518 587-1565	2936
TLD America Corporation (DH)	Windsor	CT	F	860 602-3400	4309
Total Communications Inc (PA)	East Hartford	CT	D	860 282-9999	1028
W H Preuss Sons Incorporated	Bolton	CT	G	860 643-9492	224
Xerox Corporation (HQ)	Norwalk	CT	B	203 849-5216	2598
Xerox Holdings Inc	Norwalk	CT	A	203 968-3000	2599
Xerox Holdings Corporation (PA)	Norwalk	CT	B	203 849-5216	2600
Applied Dynamics Corporation (PA)	Greenfield	MA	E	413 774-7268	8981
Blanche P Field LLC	Boston	MA	F	617 423-0715	6596
BP Logue & Co	Chelmsford	MA	F	978 251-4433	7915
Cowbell Technologies Inc	Hudson	MA	F	508 733-1778	9360
Cowbell Technologies Inc (PA)	Westborough	MA	G	508 733-1778	13094
Genelec Inc	Natick	MA	F	508 652-0900	10481
L T X International Inc	Norwood	MA	D	781 461-1000	11189
RI Controls LLC	Woburn	MA	D	781 932-3349	13654
Sandy Bay Machine Inc	Gloucester	MA	C	978 546-1331	8957
Thomson Service Corp	Franklin	MA	F	508 528-2000	8872
Wasik Associates Inc	Dracut	MA	F	978 454-9787	8314
AC Electric Corp (PA)	Auburn	ME	E	207 784-7341	4416
Chase Electric Motors LLC	Bedford	NH	G	603 669-2565	13921
Dover Flexo Electronics Inc	Rochester	NH	F	603 332-6150	15475
Singularity Elctrnic Systems In	Portsmouth	NH	G	603 430-6000	15437
Ersa Inc	Westerly	RI	E	401 348-4000	16930
Schroff Inc (HQ)	Warwick	RI	B	763 204-7700	16859
Walco Electric Company	Providence	RI	D	401 467-6500	16642

7631 Watch, clock, and jewelry repair

	CITY	ST	EMP	PHONE	ENTRY#
Joseph Hannoush Family Inc	Farmington	CT	F	860 561-4651	1225
Ozcan Jewelers Inc	Boston	MA	F	617 338-6844	6949
Silva Jewelers of Osterville	Osterville	MA	G	508 428-2872	11246
Brown Goldsmiths & Co Inc	Freeport	ME	F	207 865-4126	4799
Sawyers Jewelry Inc	Laconia	NH	F	603 527-1000	14667
Village Goldsmith	Warwick	RI	F	401 944-8404	16872

7641 Reupholstery and furniture repair

	CITY	ST	EMP	PHONE	ENTRY#
Bonito Manufacturing Inc	North Haven	CT	D	203 234-8786	2394
General Seating Solutions LLC	South Windsor	CT	F	860 242-3307	3149
Joshua Friedman & Co LLC	New London	CT	F	860 439-1637	2229
Canner Incorporated	West Groton	MA	F	978 448-3063	13001
Columbia ASC Inc	Lawrence	MA	F	978 683-2205	9554
Conklin Office Services Inc (PA)	Holyoke	MA	E	413 315-4924	9248
Copley Furniture Company Inc	Boston	MA	G	617 566-1000	6668
Crimson Upholstery Company Inc	Newton	MA	F	617 332-0758	10750
Furniture Concepts	Malden	MA	G	781 324-8668	10015
McLaughlin Upholstering Co Inc	Everett	MA	F	617 389-0761	8495
F O Bailey Co Inc	Falmouth	ME	G	207 781-8001	4768
Mavrikis Uphlstring Furn Dsign	Nashua	NH	G	603 883-6868	15131

7692 Welding repair

	CITY	ST	EMP	PHONE	ENTRY#
24/7 LLC	Branford	CT	G	203 410-5151	230
Acceleron Inc	East Granby	CT	E	860 651-9333	924
Accurate Welding Services LLC	Windsor Locks	CT	F	860 623-9500	4317
Amk Welding Inc	South Windsor	CT	F	860 289-5634	3113
Ansonia Stl Fabrication Co Inc	Beacon Falls	CT	E	203 888-4509	39
Arp Welding LLC	Oxford	CT	F	203 344-7528	2686
B & F Machine Co Inc (PA)	New Britain	CT	C	860 225-6349	2006
C V Tool Company Inc (PA)	Southington	CT	F	978 353-7901	3206
Carlucci Wldg Fabrication Inc	Norwalk	CT	F	203 588-0746	2479
Cheshire Manufacturing Co Inc	Cheshire	CT	G	203 272-3586	580
Connecticut Machine & Welding	Stratford	CT	G	203 502-2605	3530
Dasco Welded Products Inc	Waterbury	CT	F	203 754-9353	3904
DBF Industries Inc	New Britain	CT	F	860 827-8283	2021
Dyco Industries Inc	South Windsor	CT	E	860 289-4957	3138
East Windsor Metal Fabg Inc	South Windsor	CT	F	860 528-7107	3139
Ebtec Corporation	East Windsor	CT	D	860 789-2462	1072
EZ Welding LLC	New Britain	CT	F	860 707-3100	2027
F & W Rentals Inc	Orange	CT	F	203 795-0591	2668
Fabtron Incorporated	Plainville	CT	G	860 410-1801	2759
Farrell Prcsion Mtalcraft Corp	New Milford	CT	F	860 355-2651	2243
H G Steinmetz Mch Works Inc	Stamford	CT	E	203 794-1880	3360
Hauser Eqp & Wldg Svcs Inc	Stratford	CT	F	203 377-7072	3545
Hurley Mtal Fbrication Mfg LLC	Windsor	CT	F	860 688-8844	4282
Innovative Fusion Inc	Naugatuck	CT	E	203 729-3873	1965

Company	CITY	ST	EMP	PHONE	ENTRY#
J & L Mfg Watertown Inc	Waterbury	CT	E	203 591-9124	3924
Jeff Mfg Inc	Torrington	CT	F	860 482-1387	3686
Joining Technologies LLC	East Granby	CT	D	860 653-0111	937
Kell-Strom Tool Intl Inc	Wethersfield	CT	F	860 529-6851	4210
Kti Inc (HQ)	East Windsor	CT	G	860 623-2511	1079
L M Gill Welding and Mfr LLC	Manchester	CT	D	860 647-9931	1611
Line-X of New England LLC	New Milford	CT	G	860 355-6997	2252
LM Gill Welding & Mfg LLC	Manchester	CT	F	860 647-9931	1613
Lostocco Refuse Service LLC	Danbury	CT	E	203 748-9296	779
Lynn Welding Co Inc	Newington	CT	D	860 667-4400	2304
N C T Inc	Colchester	CT	F	860 666-8424	662
National Welding LLC	Middlefield	CT	G	860 818-1240	1726
Parama Corporation	Bethel	CT	G	203 790-8155	131
Paul Welding Company Inc	Newington	CT	F	860 229-9945	2314
Quality Welding LLC	Bristol	CT	G	860 585-1121	486
Ram Welding Co Inc	Naugatuck	CT	E	203 720-0535	1983
Reno Machine Company Inc	Newington	CT	D	860 666-5641	2321
Salsco Inc	Cheshire	CT	D	203 271-1682	616
SS Fabrications Inc	Eastford	CT	G	860 974-1910	1092
Standard Welding Company Inc	East Hartford	CT	G	860 528-9628	1022
State Welding & Fabg Inc	Clinton	CT	G	203 294-4071	650
Sterzingers Welding LLC	Danbury	CT	G	203 685-1575	822
Sua Prformance Fabrication LLC	East Hartford	CT	F	860 904-6068	1025
Tinsley GROup-Ps&w Inc (HQ)	Milford	CT	E	919 742-5832	1896
Total Fab LLC	East Haven	CT	F	475 238-8176	1055
United Steel Inc	East Hartford	CT	C	860 289-2323	1032
Weld-All Inc	Southington	CT	F	860 621-3156	3240
WH Rose Inc	Columbia	CT	E	860 228-8258	671
White Welding Company	Waterbury	CT	G	203 753-1197	3984
Advanced Welding & Design Inc	Woburn	MA	F	781 938-7644	13499
Aero Brazing Corporation	Woburn	MA	F	781 933-7511	13502
Aero Manufacturing Corp	Beverly	MA	D	978 720-1000	6323
Alvin Johnson	East Longmeadow	MA	G	413 525-6334	8368
Ashmont Welding Company Inc	Bridgewater	MA	F	508 279-1977	7220
Assocted Electro-Mechanics Inc	Springfield	MA	D	413 781-4276	12076
Astro Welding & Fabg Inc	Boxborough	MA	F	978 429-8666	7148
B&C Cryotech Services Inc	Sutton	MA	G	508 277-5440	12277
Baxter Inc	West Yarmouth	MA	F	508 775-0375	13072
Blue Fleet Welding Service	New Bedford	MA	G	508 997-5513	10572
Boston Welding & Design Inc	Woburn	MA	F	781 932-0035	13532
Bostonia Welding Supply Inc	Boston	MA	G	617 268-1025	6621
Capeway Welding Inc	Plymouth	MA	F	508 747-6666	11453
City Welding & Fabrication Inc	Worcester	MA	E	508 853-6000	13707
Composite Company Inc	Sherborn	MA	G	508 651-1681	11810
David Gilbert	Framingham	MA	G	508 879-1507	8755
Dockside Repairs Inc	New Bedford	MA	E	508 993-6730	10587
East Cast Wldg Fabrication LLC	Newburyport	MA	E	978 465-2338	10680
Feeneys Fence Inc	Hyde Park	MA	F	617 364-1407	9460
Fitchburg Welding Co Inc	Westminster	MA	E	978 874-2911	13270
Framingham Welding & Engineering Corporation	Framingham	MA			E
					8763
Gem Welding	North Billerica	MA	F	978 362-3873	10916
Gill Metal Fab Inc	Brockton	MA	E	508 580-4445	7281
Horacios Inc	New Bedford	MA	F	508 985-9940	10602
International Beam Wldg Corp	West Springfield	MA	F	413 781-4368	13031
J & L Welding & Machine Co	Gloucester	MA	E	978 283-3388	8942
Jacquier Welding LLC	Ashley Falls	MA	G	413 248-1204	5971
Kielb Welding Enterprises Inc	Springfield	MA	F	413 734-4544	12109
Lima Fredy	Everett	MA	F	781 599-3055	8491
Marblehead Engineering	Essex	MA	F	978 432-1386	8477
Martel Welding & Sons Inc	Tewksbury	MA	F	978 458-0661	12406
Morrell Metalsmiths Ltd	Colrain	MA	G	413 624-1200	8096
New England Welding Inc	Avon	MA	F	508 580-2024	6155
Noremac Manufacturing Corp	Westborough	MA	E	508 366-8822	13124
Northeast Stainless Inc	North Andover	MA	G	781 589-9000	10846
O W Landergren Inc	Pittsfield	MA	E	413 442-5632	11415
Oliver Welding & Fabg Inc	Ipswich	MA	G	978 356-4488	9493
Patricia Barrett	Leominster	MA	F	978 537-0458	9692
Podgurski Wldg & Hvy Eqp Repr	Canton	MA	E	781 830-9901	7821
Precision Metal Works Inc	North Billerica	MA	E	978 667-0180	10944
Rae Js	Shelburne Falls	MA	F	413 625-9228	11808
Rens Welding & Fabricating	Taunton	MA	F	508 828-1702	12362
Roar Industries Inc	Hopedale	MA	F	508 429-5952	9302
Schrimpf Wldg Fabrication Inc	Woburn	MA	G	339 298-2311	13661
Shaw Welding Company Inc	Billerica	MA	F	978 667-0197	6480
Standex International Corp	North Billerica	MA	D	978 667-2771	10959
Thermo-Craft Engineering Corp	Lynn	MA	E	781 599-4023	9992
Todd & Weld LLP	Sharon	MA	F	781 784-1026	11796
Townsend Welding Co Inc	Wilmington	MA	E	978 657-5189	13468
Triad Inc	Plainville	MA	G	508 695-2247	11444
Trivak Incorporated	Lowell	MA	E	978 453-7123	9929
Union Machine Company Lynn Inc (PA)	Groveland	MA	E	978 521-5100	9016
Villa Machine Associates Inc	Dedham	MA	F	781 326-5969	8255
Welch Welding and Trck Eqp Inc	North Chelmsford	MA	F	978 251-8726	10989
Weld Rite	Jamaica Plain	MA	G	617 524-9747	9504
Welding Craftsmen Co Inc	South Easton	MA	F	508 230-7878	11956
With Weld	Boston	MA	F	800 288-6016	7129
Worcester County Welding Inc	Rochdale	MA	G	508 892-4884	11629
Crosbys Welding LLC	Bangor	ME	F	207 974-7815	4497
Davis Brothers Inc	Chester	ME	F	207 794-1001	4691
Down East Shtmtl & Certif Wldg	Brewer	ME	F	207 989-3443	4611
Howies Wldg & Fabrication Inc	Jay	ME	E	207 645-2581	4913
Linde Advanced Mtl Tech Inc	Biddeford	ME	D	207 282-3787	4575
North E Wldg & Fabrication Inc	Auburn	ME	E	207 786-2446	4448
Ramsays Welding & Machine Inc	Lincoln	ME	F	207 794-8839	5012
Weymouths Garage Inc	Milford	ME	E	207 827-2069	5063
Ace Welding Co Inc	Merrimack	NH	E	603 424-9936	14971
Anderson Welding LLC	Dover	NH	F	603 996-6225	14216
ARC Maintenance Machining	Londonderry	NH	G	603 626-8046	14732
Baron Machine Company Inc	Laconia	NH	D	603 524-6800	14645
Bay State Industrial Weldin	Hudson	NH	E	603 881-7663	14488
Bocra Industries Inc	Seabrook	NH	E	603 474-3598	15585
Bri-Weld Industries LLC	Auburn	NH	F	603 622-9480	13906
East Coast Metal Works Co Inc	Kingston	NH	G	603 642-9600	14634
Hollis Line Machine Co Inc	Milford	NH	F	603 673-1166	15028
Ken-Mar LLC	Salem	NH	E	603 898-1268	15539
Merrimack County Customs	Bradford	NH	F	603 938-5855	14017
Multi-Weld Services Inc	Contoocook	NH	F	603 746-4604	14172
Radenhausen & ONeill Inc	Jaffrey	NH	F	603 532-4879	14578
Ralph L Osgood Inc	Claremont	NH	F	603 543-1703	14096
Recycling Mechanical Neng LLC	Allenstown	NH	F	603 268-8028	13855
S L Chasse Welding & Fabg Inc	Hudson	NH	D	603 886-3436	14543
Shawn Dudek	Laconia	NH	G	603 387-1859	14669
Smiths Tblar Systms-Lconia Inc	Laconia	NH	C	603 524-2064	14670
Starkey Welding Crane Service	Brentwood	NH	F	603 679-2553	14030
Stone Machine Co Inc	Chester	NH	F	603 887-4287	14071
Valley Welding & Fabg Inc	Hollis	NH	E	603 465-3266	14460
Weidner Services LLC	Jaffrey	NH	E	603 532-4833	14582
Will-Mor Manufacturing LLC	Seabrook	NH	D	603 474-8971	15606
A D&D Wldg & Boiler Works Inc	Warwick	RI	F	401 732-5222	16774
Artic Tool & Engrg Co LLC	Greenville	RI	F	401 785-2210	16055
Formex Inc	East Greenwich	RI	F	401 885-9800	15986
Guill Tool & Engrg Co Inc	West Warwick	RI	D	401 822-8186	16908
H B Welding Inc	Johnston	RI	E	401 727-0323	16088
Laser Fare Inc (PA)	Smithfield	RI	F	401 231-4400	16721
Luthers Repair Shop Inc	Bristol	RI	F	401 253-5550	15773
Southern New England Wldg LLC	Coventry	RI	G	401 822-0596	15821
West Warwick Welding Inc	West Warwick	RI	F	401 822-8200	16926
Bellavance Welding LLC	Wolcott	VT	F	802 793-9327	17773
Browns Certified Welding Inc	Bristol	VT	F	802 453-3351	17115
Cave Manufacturing Inc	Brattleboro	VT	F	802 257-9253	17079
Giroux Body Shop Inc	Hinesburg	VT	F	802 482-2162	17291
Gloucester Associates Inc	Barre	VT	F	802 479-1088	17001
Milton Vermont Sheet Metal Inc	Milton	VT	D	802 893-1581	17362
Mulholland Wldg & Fabrication	Chester	VT	F	802 875-5500	17181
North Country Engineering Inc	Derby	VT	F	802 766-5396	17212
PG Adams Inc	South Burlington	VT	E	802 862-8664	17590
Pre-Tech Plastics Inc (PA)	Williston	VT	E	802 879-9441	17745

7694 Armature rewinding shops

Company	CITY	ST	EMP	PHONE	ENTRY#
B & J Electric Motor Repair Co Inc	Ansonia	CT	F	203 734-1695	8
Electric Enterprise Inc	Stratford	CT	F	203 378-7311	3534
Industrial Drives Contrls Inc (PA)	Waterbury	CT	F	203 753-5103	3921
Jan Manufacturing Co	Wolcott	CT	G	203 879-0580	4366
Leppert/Nutmeg Inc	Bloomfield	CT	E	860 243-1737	188
Nepv LLC	Niantic	CT	F	860 739-2200	2358
Palmers Elc Mtrs & Pumps Inc	Norwalk	CT	F	203 348-7378	2551
Piela Electric Inc	Preston	CT	G	860 889-8476	2828
Precision Devices Inc (PA)	Wallingford	CT	F	203 265-9308	3839
Reliable Electric Motor Inc	Hartford	CT	F	860 522-2257	1505
Schulz Electric Company	New Haven	CT	C	203 562-5811	2195
SEC Electrical Inc	New Haven	CT	F	203 562-5811	2196
Traver Electric Motor Co Inc	Waterbury	CT	E	203 753-5103	3974
Ward Leonard Operating LLC (DH)	Thomaston	CT	F	860 283-5801	3643
Ward Lonard Houma Holdings LLC	Thomaston	CT	D	860 283-5801	3644
Anchor Electric LLC	Agawam	MA	G	413 786-6788	5778
Applied Dynamics Corporation (PA)	Greenfield	MA	E	413 774-7268	8981
First Electric Motor Svc Inc	Woburn	MA	F	781 491-1100	13567
General Electric Company	Medford	MA	G	781 396-9600	10286
Landes Enterprises LLC	Attleboro	MA	G	508 761-7800	6030
Maxon Precision Motors Inc (HQ)	Taunton	MA	F	508 677-0520	12348
New England Elc Mtr Svc Corp	Chelsea	MA	F	617 884-9200	7988
Potomac Electric Corp	Boston	MA	E	617 364-0400	6970
Ralco Electric Inc	Westport	MA	D	508 679-3363	13299
Reliance Electric Svc Co Inc	Holyoke	MA	G	413 533-3557	9276
Stearns Perry & Smith Company	Quincy	MA	G	617 423-4775	11539

	CITY	ST	EMP	PHONE	ENTRY#
AC Electric Corp **(PA)**	Auburn	ME	E	207 784-7341	4416
AC Electric Corp	Bangor	ME	F	207 945-9487	4487
Maine Industrial Repair Service Inc	Augusta	ME	E	207 623-7500	4476
Motor Power Inc	Lewiston	ME	G	207 782-0616	4977
Prime Electric Motors	Gorham	ME	F	207 591-7800	4833
Timken Motor & Crane Svcs LLC	Portland	ME	F	207 699-2501	5284
Chase Electric Motors LLC	Bedford	NH	G	603 669-2565	13921
Leo Algers NH Elc Mtrs Inc	Laconia	NH	G	603 524-3729	14658
Rays Electric & Gen Contg Inc	Berlin	NH	F	603 752-1370	13985
Atlantic Automation Group LLC	Bristol	RI	E	401 424-1840	15754
Delta-Electro Power LLC	Cranston	RI	E	401 944-8350	15848
Jet Electric Motor Co Inc	Pawtucket	RI	F	401 725-9050	16379
Pioneer Motors and Drives Inc	South Burlington	VT	F	802 651-0114	17591

7699 Repair services, nec

	CITY	ST	EMP	PHONE	ENTRY#
A V I International Inc	Torrington	CT	G	860 482-8345	3666
Afcon Products Inc	Bethany	CT	F	203 393-9301	91
Air Tool Sales & Svc Co Inc **(PA)**	Unionville	CT	G	860 673-2714	3746
American Marketing Intl LLC	Clinton	CT	E	860 669-4100	635
Amk Welding Inc	South Windsor	CT	E	860 289-5634	3113
Ampd Air Quality Servics LLC	Hamden	CT	G	203 387-1709	1411
Aqua Blasting Corp	Bloomfield	CT	F	860 242-8855	146
Arico Engineering Inc	North Franklin	CT	G	860 642-7040	2381
Church Hill Classics Ltd	Monroe	CT	D	800 477-9005	1909
Cnc Engineering Inc	Enfield	CT	F	860 749-1780	1124
Coastline Environmental LLC	North Branford	CT	G	203 483-6898	2362
Coburn Technologies Intl Inc **(DH)**	South Windsor	CT	F	860 648-6600	3130
Connectcut Boiler Repr Mfg Inc	West Hartford	CT	G	860 953-9117	4054
Dependable Repair Inc	North Branford	CT	F	203 481-9706	2365
Dodson Boatyard LLC	Stonington	CT	E	860 535-1507	3508
Doncasters Inc **(PA)**	Groton	CT	D	860 449-1603	1367
Eastern Broach Inc	Plainville	CT	F	860 828-4800	2755
Environmental Monitor Svc Inc	Meriden	CT	G	203 935-0102	1667
Ewald Instruments Corp	Lakeville	CT	F	860 491-9042	1545
Faxon Engineering Company Inc **(PA)**	Bloomfield	CT	F	860 236-4266	163
H G Steinmetz Mch Works Inc	Stamford	CT	E	203 794-1880	3360
Hauser Eqp & Wldg Svcs Inc	Stratford	CT	F	203 377-7072	3545
Hisco Pump Incorporated **(PA)**	Bloomfield	CT	F	860 243-2705	170
Hydro Service & Supplies Inc	Middletown	CT	G	203 265-3995	1751
Machine Builders Neng LLC	Milford	CT	F	203 922-9446	1847
Nepv LLC	Niantic	CT	F	860 739-2200	2358
North American Elev Svcs Co **(DH)**	Farmington	CT	E	860 676-6000	1233
OEM Design Services LLC	East Haven	CT	G	203 467-5993	1049
Otis Elevator Company **(HQ)**	Farmington	CT	C	860 674-3000	1235
Otis Worldwide Corporation **(PA)**	Farmington	CT	A	860 674-3000	1237
Parker Septic LLC	Somers	CT	G	860 749-8220	3099
Picture This Hartford Inc	East Hartford	CT	G	860 528-1409	1011
Power-Dyne LLC	Middletown	CT	E	860 346-9283	1772
Projects Inc	Glastonbury	CT	C	860 633-4615	1295
Quick Machining Services LLC	Meriden	CT	G	203 634-8822	1688
Rokap Inc	East Hampton	CT	G	203 265-6895	965
Skico Manufacturing Co LLC	Hamden	CT	G	203 230-1305	1455
Stanley Black & Decker Inc	Farmington	CT	F	860 677-2861	1248
W H Preuss Sons Incorporated	Bolton	CT	G	860 643-9492	224
West Hartford Lock Co LLC	West Hartford	CT	F	860 236-0671	4089
Acme Precast Co Inc	West Falmouth	MA	F	508 548-9607	13000
Aj Precision Inc	Southwick	MA	E	413 998-3291	12040
All Security Co Inc	New Bedford	MA	E	508 993-4271	10567
American Water Systems LLC	Canton	MA	F	781 830-9722	7767
Andover Organ Company Inc	Lawrence	MA	E	978 686-9600	9537
Azenta Inc **(PA)**	Burlington	MA	A	978 262-2400	7339
B G Wickberg Company Inc	East Weymouth	MA	G	781 335-7800	8425
Bay State Elevator Company Inc **(HQ)**	Agawam	MA	G	413 786-7000	5779
Bellingham Metal Works LLC	Franklin	MA	E	617 519-5958	8819
Boston Document Systems Inc **(PA)**	Marlborough	MA	E	800 616-8576	10117
Carl Swanson Harp Rentals Inc **(PA)**	Boston	MA	G	617 569-6642	6639
Chas G Allen Realty LLC	Barre	MA	D	978 355-2911	6202
Commercial Scale Balance Inc	Agawam	MA	E	413 789-9990	5787
Concordia Co Inc	South Dartmouth	MA	E	508 999-1381	11916
Cryogenic Institute Neng Inc	Worcester	MA	F	508 459-7447	13712
Cyduct Diagnostics Inc	Boston	MA	G	617 360-9700	6682
Falmouth Mar Yachting Ctr Inc	Falmouth	MA	F	508 548-4600	8631
Henke Sass Wolf America Inc	Dudley	MA	D	508 671-9300	8318
High Technology Inc	North Attleboro	MA	E	508 660-2221	10873
Industrial Stl Boiler Svcs Inc	Chicopee	MA	E	413 532-7788	8038
Inert Corporation	Amesbury	MA	E	978 462-4415	5837
Iwaki Pumps Inc **(DH)**	Holliston	MA	E	508 429-1440	9217
JDM Company Inc	North Chelmsford	MA	G	978 251-1121	10979
Keystone Elev Svc Mdrnztion LL	Weymouth	MA	G	781 340-3860	13328
Liquid Solids Control Inc **(PA)**	Upton	MA	F	508 529-3377	12473
M & M Scale Company Inc	Danvers	MA	F	781 321-2737	8202
Mainstream Global Inc	Lawrence	MA	E	978 682-6767	9579
Majestic Medical Inc	Raynham	MA	F	508 824-1944	11590

	CITY	ST	EMP	PHONE	ENTRY#
Marine Usa Inc	Worcester	MA	E	508 791-7116	13757
Marzilli Machine Co	Fall River	MA	E	508 567-4145	8574
Mass Tank Inspection Svcs LLC	Middleboro	MA	E	508 923-3445	10367
Mass Vac Inc	North Billerica	MA	E	978 667-2393	10932
Mystic Valley Wheel Works Inc **(PA)**	Belmont	MA	E	617 489-3577	6308
Nashoba Security Inc	Littleton	MA	F	978 486-8615	9827
New Bedford Scale Co Inc	New Bedford	MA	G	508 997-6730	10628
Newera Services Corporation **(PA)**	New Bedford	MA	E	508 995-9711	10631
Optical Laboratory Inc	New Bedford	MA	E	508 997-9779	10637
P B Y A Inc	South Orleans	MA	G	508 255-0994	11973
Quincy Electronics Co Inc	Quincy	MA	G	617 471-7700	11534
T & D Specialties Inc	Oxford	MA	E	508 987-8344	11265
The Sharp Tool Co Inc	Hudson	MA	E	978 568-9292	9418
Thermo Egs Gauging LLC	Chelmsford	MA	C	978 663-2300	7965
Thermoplastics Company Inc	Worcester	MA	E	508 754-4668	13811
Ulvac Technologies Inc **(HQ)**	Methuen	MA	E	978 686-7550	10347
Webco Engineering Inc	Southborough	MA	F	508 303-0500	12006
C P Technologies Inc **(PA)**	Saco	ME	F	207 286-1167	5364
Cole Gunsmithing Inc	South Harpswell	ME	G	207 833-5027	5486
Knowlton Machine Company	Gorham	ME	E	207 854-8471	4824
Leavitt & Parris Inc	Portland	ME	F	207 797-0100	5233
Machinery Service Co Inc	Wiscasset	ME	G	207 882-6788	5698
Maine Industrial Repair Service Inc	Augusta	ME	E	207 623-7500	4476
Reggies Sales & Service	Auburn	ME	E	207 783-0558	4458
Timken Motor & Crane Svcs LLC	Portland	ME	F	207 699-2501	5284
Accutech Marine Propeller Inc	Dover	NH	G	603 617-3626	14213
Contour Fine Tooling Inc	Keene	NH	E	603 876-4908	14593
David Streeter	Charlestown	NH	G	603 542-6045	14061
Dgf Indstrial Innvtons Group L	Gilford	NH	F	603 528-6591	14335
Gti Spindle Technology Inc **(DH)**	Manchester	NH	E	603 669-5993	14857
Heat and Control Inc	Pembroke	NH	E	603 225-5190	15303
M & A Advnced Design Cnstr Inc **(PA)**	Hampstead	NH	F	603 329-9515	14385
Macy Industries Inc	Hooksett	NH	E	603 623-5568	14468
Manroland Goss Web Systems AMR **(DH)**	Exeter	NH			B
603 750-6600	14294				
Nexvac Inc **(PA)**	Sandown	NH	F	603 887-0015	15580
Slate Corporation	Auburn	NH	F	603 234-5943	13912
379 Charles RI Inc	North Providence	RI	F	401 521-1101	16293
A D& D Wldg & Boiler Works Inc	Warwick	RI	F	401 732-5222	16774
E H Benz Co Inc	Providence	RI	G	401 331-5650	16510
Exail Defense Systems Inc	Lincoln	RI	E	401 475-4400	16136
J Goodison Company **(PA)**	North Kingstown	RI	E	401 667-5938	16261
Michael Healy Designs Inc	Manville	RI	G	401 597-5900	16165
Rhode Island Engine Co Inc	Narragansett	RI	E	401 789-1021	16195
4smartpro LLC	Saint Johnsbury	VT	F	802 745-8797	17537
Apex Sealing Inc	Fairfax	VT	E	802 524-7100	17254
Hayward Tyler Inc **(DH)**	Colchester	VT	E	802 655-4444	17194
Limoge & Sons Garage Doors Inc	Williston	VT	F	802 878-4338	17739
T S S Inc	Waterbury	VT	E	802 244-8101	17678

78 MOTION PICTURES

7812 Motion picture and video production

	CITY	ST	EMP	PHONE	ENTRY#
Bff Holdings Inc **(HQ)**	Old Saybrook	CT	C	860 510-0100	2645
Blue Sky Studios Inc	Greenwich	CT	C	203 992-6000	1319
Play-It Productions Inc	Colchester	CT	F	212 695-6530	663
Taunton Inc	Newtown	CT	A	203 426-8171	2349
The Taunton Press Inc **(PA)**	Newtown	CT	C	203 426-8171	2352
Venan Entertainment Inc	Middletown	CT	G	860 704-6330	1789
World Wrestling Entrmt LLC **(DH)**	Stamford	CT	C	203 352-8600	3497
Channing Bete Company Inc **(PA)**	South Deerfield	MA	C	413 665-7611	11922
Human Resource Dev Press **(PA)**	Belchertown	MA	E	413 253-3488	6280
Sinauer Associates Inc	Sunderland	MA	E	413 549-4300	12275

7819 Services allied to motion pictures

	CITY	ST	EMP	PHONE	ENTRY#
Cine Magnetics Inc **(HQ)**	Stamford	CT	D	914 273-7600	3312
Play-It Productions Inc	Colchester	CT	F	212 695-6530	663
Boston Light & Sound Inc **(PA)**	Malden	MA	F	617 787-3131	10005
Community of Jesus Inc **(PA)**	Orleans	MA	E	508 255-1094	11237
MTI Film LLC **(HQ)**	Providence	RI	G	401 831-1315	16570

7822 Motion picture and tape distribution

	CITY	ST	EMP	PHONE	ENTRY#
Seachange International Inc **(PA)**	Boston	MA	D	978 897-0100	7029
Wooden Kiwi Productions LLC	Waltham	MA	G	781 209-2623	12818

7841 Video tape rental

	CITY	ST	EMP	PHONE	ENTRY#
Cataki International Inc	Wareham	MA	F	508 295-9630	12833

79 AMUSEMENT AND RECREATION SERVICES

	CITY	ST	EMP	PHONE	ENTRY#

7911 Dance studios, schools, and halls

	CITY	ST	EMP	PHONE	ENTRY#
Dance It Up Inc	North Grafton	MA	F	508 839-1648	11021

7922 Theatrical producers and services

	CITY	ST	EMP	PHONE	ENTRY#
Stamford Mdia Ctr Prdctons LLC	Stamford	CT	G	203 905-4000	3471
Americas Test Kitchen Limited Partnership	Boston	MA			C
617 232-1000	6544				
Wooden Kiwi Productions LLC	Waltham	MA	G	781 209-2623	12818

7929 Entertainers and entertainment groups

	CITY	ST	EMP	PHONE	ENTRY#
Bondi Band LLC	Simsbury	CT	F	207 576-4191	3084
World Wrestling Entrmt LLC (DH)	Stamford	CT	C	203 352-8600	3497
Yolanda Dubose Records and	West Haven	CT	F	203 823-6699	4134
CJS Workshop LLC	Groton	MA	E	323 445-5012	9008
Grist For Mill LLC	Bristol	NH	F	603 744-0405	14036

7933 Bowling centers

	CITY	ST	EMP	PHONE	ENTRY#
Bay Colony Associates (PA)	Boston	MA	G	617 287-9100	6584

7941 Sports clubs, managers, and promoters

	CITY	ST	EMP	PHONE	ENTRY#
Video Messengercom Corp	Stratford	CT	G	203 358-8842	3582
Cape Cod Life LLC	Mashpee	MA	F	508 419-7381	10250
Nokona USA Baseball	Ashland	MA	G	508 309-3527	5964
Rhee Gold Company Inc	Norton	MA	F	508 285-6650	11132
Terika Smith Ministries Corp	Lawrence	MA	E	978 233-0576	9603
T J Ryan LLC	Brewer	ME	F	207 989-7183	4620
Firecracker Sports LLC	Cumberland	RI	G	401 595-0233	15939

7992 Public golf courses

	CITY	ST	EMP	PHONE	ENTRY#
Lyman Farm Incorporated (PA)	Middlefield	CT	C	860 349-1793	1725

7993 Coin-operated amusement devices

	CITY	ST	EMP	PHONE	ENTRY#
Happy House Amusement Inc	Goffstown	NH	F	603 497-4151	14348

7997 Membership sports and recreation clubs

	CITY	ST	EMP	PHONE	ENTRY#
South Windsor Golf Course LLC	South Windsor	CT	D	860 648-4653	3182
Northeast Outdoors Inc	Paxton	MA	G	508 752-8762	11290
Southern Maine Atv Club	North Berwick	ME	G	207 676-1152	5113

7999 Amusement and recreation, nec

	CITY	ST	EMP	PHONE	ENTRY#
Lyman Farm Incorporated (PA)	Middlefield	CT	C	860 349-1793	1725
Drive-O-Rama Inc (PA)	Hyannis	MA	G	508 771-8100	9434
Harvard Debate Incorporated	Cambridge	MA	G	617 876-5003	7600
Hollrock Engineering Inc	Hadley	MA	E	413 586-2256	9018
Terika Smith Ministries Corp	Lawrence	MA	E	978 233-0576	9603
Rich Associates Incorporated	Kennebunk	ME	G	207 985-5999	4929
Axe Play LLC	Hudson	NH	G	603 809-9081	14485
Cg Roxane LLC	Moultonborough	NH	F	603 476-8844	15051
Sig Sauer Inc (DH)	Newington	NH	C	603 610-3000	15210
Firecracker Sports LLC	Cumberland	RI	G	401 595-0233	15939
Igt Global Solutions Corporation (HQ)	Providence	RI	D	401 392-7077	16538
Matthew W Robinson	Riverside	RI	G	401 480-3975	16657
Oldport Marine Services Inc	Newport	RI	F	401 847-9109	16220

80 HEALTH SERVICES

8011 Offices and clinics of medical doctors

	CITY	ST	EMP	PHONE	ENTRY#
Childrens Medical Group (PA)	Bloomfield	CT	E	860 242-8330	155
Jeffrey Gold	Hamden	CT	G	203 281-5737	1434
Yale New Haven Hlth Svcs Corp	New Haven	CT	A	203 688-2100	2217
Cosman Medical LLC	Marlborough	MA	D	781 272-6561	10137
Eye Health Services Inc	Plymouth	MA	E	508 747-6425	11459
Eye Health Services Inc (PA)	Quincy	MA	E	617 472-5242	11517
Innoneo Health Tech Inc (PA)	Boston	MA	D	617 336-3202	6810
Ranfac Corp	Avon	MA	D	508 588-4400	6159
Springfield Eye Associates	Springfield	MA	E	413 739-7367	12134
Umass Mem Mri Imaging Ctr LLC	Worcester	MA	F	508 756-7300	13814
Uptodate Inc (DH)	Waltham	MA	D	781 392-2000	12808
Shearwater Allergy LLC	Yarmouth	ME	G	207 846-7676	5707
Cg Holdings LLC (PA)	Manchester	NH	E	603 623-3344	14827

8021 Offices and clinics of dentists

	CITY	ST	EMP	PHONE	ENTRY#
Essel Dental	East Windsor	CT	G	860 254-6955	1073
Ultimate Wireforms Inc	Bristol	CT	D	860 582-9111	504
Cohen Slvstri Rogoff Hammer PC	Boston	MA	E	617 426-6011	6661
Perioq Inc	Leominster	MA	G	978 534-1249	9693

8041 Offices and clinics of chiropractors

	CITY	ST	EMP	PHONE	ENTRY#
Sorbus Inc	Branford	CT	F	203 481-2810	278

8042 Offices and clinics of optometrists

	CITY	ST	EMP	PHONE	ENTRY#
Opticare Health Systems Inc (DH)	Waterbury	CT	C	203 574-2020	3957
Eye Health Services Inc	Plymouth	MA	E	508 747-6425	11459
Eye Health Services Inc (PA)	Quincy	MA	E	617 472-5242	11517
Vision Dynamics LLC	Worcester	MA	G	203 271-1944	13824

8049 Offices of health practitioner

	CITY	ST	EMP	PHONE	ENTRY#
Lenscrafters	Milford	CT	G	203 878-8511	1845
Maine Orthtic Prsthtic Rhab Sv	Portland	ME	F	207 773-8818	5241

8062 General medical and surgical hospitals

	CITY	ST	EMP	PHONE	ENTRY#
Bcpe Seminole Holdings LP (PA)	Boston	MA	F	617 516-2000	6585
Cistercian Abbey Spencer Inc	Spencer	MA	E	508 885-8700	12056

8071 Medical laboratories

	CITY	ST	EMP	PHONE	ENTRY#
Acuren Inspection Inc (HQ)	Danbury	CT	A	203 702-8740	704
Immucor Trnsplant Dgnstics Inc (DH)	Stamford	CT	D	203 328-9500	3381
Alere Inc (HQ)	Waltham	MA	A	781 647-3900	12587
Day Zero Diagnostics Inc	Watertown	MA	F	857 770-1125	12870
Esoterix Genetic Labs LLC (HQ)	Westborough	MA	E	508 389-6650	13101
Genzyme Corporation (DH)	Cambridge	MA	A	617 252-7500	7585
Genzyme Corporation	Framingham	MA	E	617 252-7500	8773
Genzyme Corporation	Framingham	MA	E	617 252-7500	8774
Kalvista Pharmaceuticals Inc (PA)	Cambridge	MA	E	857 999-0075	7621
Labthink International Inc	Medford	MA	F	617 830-2190	10293
Magellan Diagnostics Inc (HQ)	Chelmsford	MA	D	978 250-7000	7937
Magellan Diagnostics Inc	North Billerica	MA	E	978 856-2345	10931
Massbiologics	Boston	MA	C	617 474-3000	6877
Quest Diagnostic Incorporated	Marlborough	MA	A	617 547-8900	10199
Reading Diagnostic Center	Reading	MA	F	781 942-9876	11605
Vigil Neuroscience Inc (PA)	Watertown	MA	E	857 254-4445	12919
Kennebec River Biosciences Inc	Richmond	ME	F	207 737-2637	5322

8072 Dental laboratories

	CITY	ST	EMP	PHONE	ENTRY#
Dillon Laboratories Inc	Abington	MA	G	781 871-2333	5723
New England Orthdontic Lab Inc	Andover	MA	E	800 922-6365	5900
National Dentex LLC	Manchester	NH	C	561 537-8301	14895

8082 Home health care services

	CITY	ST	EMP	PHONE	ENTRY#
Fev Tutor Inc	Woburn	MA	D	781 376-6925	13564
Kaz Inc (HQ)	Marlborough	MA	D	508 490-7000	10174

8092 Kidney dialysis centers

	CITY	ST	EMP	PHONE	ENTRY#
Fresenius Med Care Hldings Inc (DH)	Waltham	MA	A	781 699-9000	12679
Fresenius Med Svcs Group LLC	Waltham	MA	F	781 699-9000	12682

8099 Health and allied services, nec

	CITY	ST	EMP	PHONE	ENTRY#
C S M S-I P A	North Haven	CT	G	203 562-7228	2397
Innoneo Health Tech Inc (PA)	Boston	MA	D	617 336-3202	6810
Outcomes4me Inc	Boston	MA	E	617 812-1010	6945
Siemens Hlthcare Dgnostics Inc	Andover	MA	F	212 258-4000	5919
Simulconsult Inc	Chestnut Hill	MA	G	617 566-5383	8001

81 LEGAL SERVICES

8111 Legal services

	CITY	ST	EMP	PHONE	ENTRY#
Massachstts Cntning Lgal Edcat	Boston	MA	E	617 482-2205	6871

82 EDUCATIONAL SERVICES

8211 Elementary and secondary schools

	CITY	ST	EMP	PHONE	ENTRY#
Crane Data LLC	Westborough	MA	F	508 439-4419	13095
NH Learning Solutions Corp	Woburn	MA	D	781 224-1113	13624
Perkins School For Blind	Watertown	MA	A	617 924-3434	12899

8221 Colleges and universities

	CITY	ST	EMP	PHONE	ENTRY#
Wesleyan University	Middletown	CT	G	860 685-2980	1790
Yale University	New Haven	CT	E	203 764-4333	2218
Yale University (PA)	New Haven	CT	E	203 432-2550	2219
Yale University	New Haven	CT	E	203 737-1244	2220
Yale University	New Haven	CT	G	203 432-2880	2221
Cengage Learning Inc	Boston	MA	F	518 348-2300	6645
Massachusetts Institute Tech	Cambridge	MA	C	617 253-5646	7637
Massachusetts Institute Tech	Cambridge	MA	G	617 253-7183	7638
President and Fellows of Harvard College (PA)	Cambridge	MA			A
617 496-4873	7688				
President Fllows Hrvard Cllege	Boston	MA	E	617 495-5581	6976
Technology Review Inc	Cambridge	MA	E	617 475-8000	7736
Trustees of Boston College	Chestnut Hill	MA	F	617 552-2844	8002
Trustees of Tufts College	Medford	MA	G	617 628-5000	10300

SIC

	CITY	ST	EMP	PHONE	ENTRY#
Trustees of Tufts College (PA)	Somerville	MA	B	617 628-5000	11906
University of Maine System	Orono	ME	F	207 581-2843	5138
Southern New Hampshire Univ	Manchester	NH	G	603 629-4631	14963
Trustees of Dartmouth College	Hanover	NH	G	603 646-2256	14431
Trustees of Dartmouth College	Lebanon	NH	E	603 448-1533	14702

8222 Junior colleges

Mathworks Inc	Natick	MA	A	508 647-7000	10485
Mathworks Inc (PA)	Natick	MA	A	508 647-7000	10486

8243 Data processing schools

Learntoprogramtv Incorporated	Bridgeport	CT	F	860 840-7090	344
Compart North America Inc	Andover	MA	E	877 237-2725	5879
Datarobot Inc (PA)	Boston	MA	D	617 765-4500	6684
Microcad Trning Consulting Inc (PA)	Watertown	MA	F	617 923-0500	12893
Secure Code Warrior Inc	Boston	MA	E	617 901-3005	7030
Sunrise Group USA LLC	Shrewsbury	MA	E	508 873-1519	11842

8249 Vocational schools, nec

Cortina Learning Intl Inc (PA)	Wilton	CT	F	800 245-2145	4237
Cengage Learning Inc	Boston	MA	F	518 348-2300	6645
North Shore Press Inc	Melrose	MA	G	781 662-6757	10317
Varian Semicdtr Eqp Assoc Inc	Newburyport	MA	E	978 463-1500	10725
Kbace Technologies Inc (HQ)	Nashua	NH	D	603 821-7000	15121

8299 Schools and educational services

Aquiline Drones Corporation	Hartford	CT	E	973 980-6596	1471
Overseas Ministries Study Ctr	New Haven	CT	E	203 624-6672	2182
Esm Software LLC	Lincoln	MA	F	781 541-4462	9795
Esm Software Group Inc	Lincoln	MA	F	781 541-4465	9796
Harvard Debate Incorporated	Cambridge	MA	G	617 876-5003	7600
Massachstts Cntning Lgal Edcat	Boston	MA	E	617 482-2205	6871
Syberworks Inc	Arlington	MA	E	781 891-1999	5948
Terika Smith Ministries Corp	Lawrence	MA	E	978 233-0576	9603
Um Food Sciences	Amherst	MA	E	413 545-2276	5866
Mathemtics Problem Solving LLC	South Portland	ME	D	207 772-2846	5508
DCI Training Inc	West Lebanon	NH	G	603 643-6066	15682
Nippon American Limited	East Greenwich	RI	F	401 885-7353	15992
Shelburne Farms	Shelburne	VT	D	802 985-8498	17562

83 SOCIAL SERVICES

8322 Individual and family services

Midstate Arc Inc	Meriden	CT	D	203 238-9001	1676
Saint Vincent De Paul Place	Norwich	CT	G	860 889-7374	2615
Opportunity Works Inc (PA)	Newburyport	MA	E	978 462-6144	10705
Phase Forward	Waltham	MA	E	781 626-1256	12748
Hope Association (PA)	Rumford	ME	E	207 364-4561	5356
York-Cmbrland Assn For Hndcppe (PA)	Portland	ME	E	207 879-1140	5292
Kevin Emery	Farmington	NH	G	603 433-5784	14310
Epivax Inc	Providence	RI	E	401 272-2123	16515

8331 Job training and related services

Powerphone Inc	Madison	CT	E	203 245-8911	1566
Asian American Civic Assn Inc (PA)	Boston	MA	E	617 426-9492	6560
Cengage Learning Inc	Boston	MA	F	518 348-2300	6645
Hcpro Inc (HQ)	Middleton	MA	E	781 639-1872	10385
International Security Assista	Woburn	MA	C	617 590-7942	13588
Opportunity Works Inc (PA)	Newburyport	MA	E	978 462-6144	10705
Goodwill Industries Nthrn Neng (PA)	Gorham	ME	D	207 774-6323	4820
Training Thru Placement Inc	North Providence	RI	F	401 353-0220	16312

8399 Social services, nec

Stratcomm Inc	Natick	MA	C	508 907-7000	10499
Shelburne Farms	Shelburne	VT	D	802 985-8498	17562

84 MUSEUMS, ART GALLERIES AND BOTANICAL AND ZOOLOGICAL GARDENS

8412 Museums and art galleries

Greenwich Workshop Inc (PA)	Seymour	CT	E	203 881-3336	2961
Mystic Seaport Museum Inc	Mystic	CT	B	860 572-0711	1940
Blazing Editions	East Greenwich	RI	G	401 885-4329	15974

86 MEMBERSHIP ORGANIZATIONS

8611 Business associations

Chief Executive Group LLC (PA)	Stamford	CT	E	785 832-0303	3310
Limra International Inc (PA)	Windsor	CT	E	860 688-3358	4287

	CITY	ST	EMP	PHONE	ENTRY#
National Shting Spt Fndtion In	Shelton	CT	D	203 426-1320	3036
Decas Cranberry Products Inc (PA)	Carver	MA	E	508 866-8506	7853
Massachusetts Assn Realtors (PA)	Foxboro	MA	F	781 890-3700	8707
Tree Care Industry Assn Inc	Manchester	NH	E	603 314-5380	14946
Rhode Island Assn Realtors Inc (PA)	Warwick	RI	G	401 785-3650	16849

8621 Professional organizations

C S M S-I P A	North Haven	CT	G	203 562-7228	2397
Financial Accnting Foundation (PA)	Norwalk	CT	C	203 847-0700	2500
Society Plastics Engineers Inc (PA)	Danbury	CT	E	203 740-5422	819
Wire Association Intl Inc (PA)	Madison	CT	F	203 453-2777	1577
American Mteorological Soc Inc (PA)	Boston	MA	D	617 227-2425	6541
American Soc Law Mdcine Ethics	Boston	MA	E	617 262-4990	6542
Archaeological Institute Amer	Boston	MA	F	617 353-9361	6555
Massachusetts Medical Society	Boston	MA	E	617 734-9800	6874
Massachusetts Medical Society	Waltham	MA	E	781 434-7950	12716
American Mathematical Society Inc (PA)	Providence	RI	C	401 455-4000	16470

8641 Civic and social associations

Asian American Civic Assn Inc (PA)	Boston	MA	E	617 426-9492	6560
School Family Media LLC	Wrentham	MA	E	508 384-0394	13844
Island Institute	Rockland	ME	E	207 594-9209	5334

8661 Religious organizations

A Guideposts Church Corp (PA)	Danbury	CT	C	203 749-0203	699
NRG Connecticut LLC	Hartford	CT	F	860 231-2424	1497
Cistercian Abbey Spencer Inc	Spencer	MA	E	508 885-8700	12056
Community of Jesus Inc (PA)	Orleans	MA	E	508 255-1094	11237
First Ch of Chrst Scntist In B (PA)	Boston	MA	E	617 450-2000	6736
Society of St John The Evang	Cambridge	MA	E	617 876-3037	7719
Terika Smith Ministries Corp	Lawrence	MA	E	978 233-0576	9603
Unitarian Universalist Assn (PA)	Boston	MA	C	617 742-2100	7092
T J Ryan LLC	Brewer	ME	F	207 989-7183	4620
Community Apostolic Order Inc (PA)	Island Pond	VT	F	802 723-4452	17304

8699 Membership organizations, nec

Massachsetts Brewers Guild Inc	Framingham	MA	F	508 405-9115	8788
Massachstts Soc For Prvntion C (PA)	Boston	MA	C	617 522-7282	6872
Padakshep	Brookline	MA	E	801 652-5589	7324
Hanover Review Inc	Hanover	NH	G	603 643-4370	14424
Hideaways International Inc	Portsmouth	NH	F	603 430-4433	15401
Hinesburg Record Inc	Hinesburg	VT	F	802 482-2350	17293

87 ENGINEERING, ACCOUNTING, RESEARCH, AND MANAGEMENT SERVICES

8711 Engineering services

AB Electronics LLC	Brookfield	CT	E	203 740-2793	509
Act Robots Inc	Bristol	CT	G	860 314-1557	392
Alstom Power Co	Windsor	CT	E	860 688-1911	4257
Apcompower Inc (PA)	Windsor	CT	E	860 688-1911	4260
Apex Machine Tool Company Inc	Cheshire	CT	D	860 677-2884	571
Applied Physical Sciences Corp (HQ)	Groton	CT	D	860 448-3253	1364
Asea Brown Boveri Inc	Norwalk	CT	A	203 750-2200	2465
Atp Industries LLC (PA)	Plainville	CT	F	860 479-5007	2748
B & F Design Incorporated	New Britain	CT	F	860 357-4317	2005
Connecticut Analytical Corp	Bethany	CT	F	203 393-9666	92
Cs Group - Usa Inc	East Hartford	CT	E	860 944-0041	983
Cummins Enviro Tech Inc	Old Lyme	CT	G	860 388-6377	2638
Cyient Defense Services Inc	New Britain	CT	E	860 357-4317	2019
Dark Field Technologies Inc	Shelton	CT	F	203 298-0731	2997
Delcom Products Inc	Danbury	CT	G	914 934-5170	729
Dufrane Nuclear Shielding Inc	Winsted	CT	F	860 379-2318	4340
Electric Boat Corporation (HQ)	Groton	CT	B	860 433-3000	1370
Electric Boat Corporation	Groton	CT	A	860 433-3000	1371
Engineered Fibers Tech LLC	Shelton	CT	F	203 922-1810	3005
Engineering Specialties Inc	North Branford	CT	E	203 488-2266	2367
ESI Electronic Products Corp	Prospect	CT	E	203 758-4401	2834
GE Steam Power Inc (HQ)	Windsor	CT	A	866 257-8664	4279
General Digital Corporation	East Hartford	CT	D	860 282-2900	996
General Dynamics Info Tech Inc	Pawcatuck	CT	D	860 441-2400	2720
Goldenrod Corporation	Beacon Falls	CT	E	203 723-4400	40
Goodrich Corporation	Danbury	CT	B	505 345-9031	750
Henkel Loctite Corporation (DH)	Rocky Hill	CT	D	860 571-5100	2925
John Zink Company LLC	Shelton	CT	E	203 925-0380	3025
Johnson Gage Company	Bloomfield	CT	E	860 242-5541	177
Jonal Laboratories Inc	Meriden	CT	D	203 634-4444	1671
Kem Liquidating Company Inc	Glastonbury	CT	E	860 430-5100	1287
Mike Sadlak	Coventry	CT	G	860 742-0227	680
New England Machine Tools Inc	Bristol	CT	E	860 583-4001	475
Preferred Utilities Mfg Corp (HQ)	Danbury	CT	D	203 743-6741	799

	CITY	ST	EMP	PHONE	ENTRY#		CITY	ST	EMP	PHONE	ENTRY#
Prospect Machine Products Inc	Prospect	CT	F	203 758-4448	2840	Xp Power LLC	Gloucester	MA	D	978 282-0620	8965
Pta Corporation **(PA)**	Oxford	CT	D	203 888-0585	2709	Bachmann Industries Inc	New Gloucester	ME	E	207 440-2888	5083
Pumc Holding Corporation **(PA)**	Danbury	CT	F	203 743-6741	802	Bath Iron Works Corporation **(HQ)**	Bath	ME	A	207 443-3311	4525
Quality Engineering Svcs Inc	Wallingford	CT	E	203 269-5054	3843	C P Technologies Inc **(PA)**	Saco	ME	F	207 286-1167	5364
R&D Dynamics Corporation	Bloomfield	CT	D	860 726-1204	205	Cascades Auburn Fiber Inc	Auburn	ME	E	207 753-5300	4423
Rite-Solutions Inc **(PA)**	Pawcatuck	CT	F	401 847-3399	2725	Comnav Engineering Inc	Portland	ME	E	207 221-8524	5201
Seals-It Inc	Ellington	CT	G	860 979-0060	1114	Enercon **(HQ)**	Gray	ME	D	207 657-7000	4841
SEI II Inc	Milford	CT	F	203 877-8488	1883	Intermat	Biddeford	ME	E	207 283-1156	4572
Silicon Integration Inc	Milford	CT	E	203 876-2844	1885	James W Sewall Company	Bangor	ME	G	207 817-5410	4506
Sonalysts Inc **(PA)**	Waterford	CT	B	860 442-4355	3997	James W Sewall Company **(PA)**	Old Town	ME	E	207 827-4456	5125
Stanley Engnered Fastening LLC **(HQ)**	Danbury	CT	F	800 783-6427	821	Knowlton Machine Company	Gorham	ME	E	207 854-8471	4824
Systematic Automation Inc	Farmington	CT	E	310 218-3361	1249	Modula Inc **(DH)**	Lewiston	ME	D	207 440-5100	4976
Tek Industries Inc	Vernon Rockville	CT	E	860 870-0001	3763	Nichols Portland LLC **(PA)**	Portland	ME	B	207 774-6121	5251
Tenova Inc	Wallingford	CT	E	203 265-5684	3859	Oizero9 Inc	Sanford	ME	E	207 324-3582	5404
Tornik Inc	Rocky Hill	CT	C	860 282-6081	2937	Patten Tool and Engrg Inc	Kittery	ME	F	207 439-1555	4939
TP Cycle & Engineering Inc	Danbury	CT	E	203 744-4960	826	S & K Unlimited LLC	Brownville	ME	F	207 965-6137	4638
Vector Engineering Inc	Mystic	CT	F	860 572-0422	1944	Senior Operations LLC	Lewiston	ME	E	207 784-2338	4992
Veolia Es Tchncal Slutions LLC	Danbury	CT	F	203 748-9116	832	Wahlcometroflex Inc	Lewiston	ME	B	207 784-2338	4995
Vertafore Inc	Windsor	CT	E	860 602-6000	4312	Zajac LLC	Saco	ME	E	207 286-9100	5384
2is Inc	Walpole	MA	E	508 850-7520	12545	ARC Technology Solutions LLC	Nashua	NH	D	603 883-3027	15064
Ae Red Holdings LLC **(PA)**	Marlborough	MA	F	561 372-7820	10105	Astronics Aerosat Corporation	Manchester	NH	E	603 879-0205	14814
Andritz Inc	Springfield	MA	C	413 733-6603	12075	Bay State Industrial Weldin	Hudson	NH	E	603 881-7663	14488
Assurance Technology Corp **(PA)**	Carlisle	MA	F	978 369-8848	7845	Chart Inc	Salem	NH	D	603 382-6551	15513
Atomera Incorporated	Wellesley Hills	MA	G	617 219-0600	12950	Design Consultants Associates	Hampstead	NH	F	603 329-4541	14382
B & E Group LLC	Southwick	MA	E	413 569-5585	12041	Fronek Anchor Darling Entp	Laconia	NH	F	603 528-1931	14651
Bluecatbio MA Inc	Concord	MA	G	978 405-2533	8106	Gill Design Inc	Windham	NH	G	603 890-1237	15727
Brown Innovations Inc **(PA)**	Boston	MA	G	773 477-7500	6625	Haigh-Farr Inc	Bedford	NH	D	603 644-6170	13932
Chemical Systems Services Inc	Attleboro	MA	F	508 431-9995	6003	Newdtc LLC	Salem	NH	F	603 893-0992	15549
Comdel Inc	Gloucester	MA	F	978 282-0620	8930	Premier Recycling Eqp Inc	Seabrook	NH	F	855 223-5859	15600
Concepts Nrec LLC	Chelmsford	MA	F	781 935-9050	7920	Simbex LLC	Lebanon	NH	E	603 448-2367	14699
Costello Dismantling Co Inc **(PA)**	West Wareham	MA	E	508 291-2324	13058	Tech Nh Inc **(PA)**	Merrimack	NH	D	603 424-4404	15007
Dale Engineering & Son Inc	Bedford	MA	F	781 541-6055	6221	Two In One Manufacturing Inc	Nashua	NH	E	603 595-8212	15179
Distron Corporation	Attleboro Falls	MA	C	508 695-8786	6084	Universal Envmtl Tech Inc	Nashua	NH	G	603 883-9312	15180
Division 15 Hvac Inc	Pembroke	MA	E	781 285-3115	11363	Applied Radar Inc	North Kingstown	RI	E	401 295-0062	16231
Eclypses Inc	Boston	MA	E	719 323-6680	6707	Cambridge Signal Tech Inc	Providence	RI	F	401 490-5682	16493
GE Vernova International LLC **(HQ)**	Cambridge	MA	C	617 443-3000	7580	Celestial Monitoring Corp **(HQ)**	Narragansett	RI	E	401 782-1045	16187
Gillespie Corporation	Ware	MA	E	413 967-4980	12825	Eagle Industries Inc	Ashaway	RI	E	401 596-8111	15739
Graphite Insulg Systems Inc	Gardner	MA	F	978 630-8988	8890	Electric Boat Corporation	North Kingstown	RI	A	401 268-2410	16250
Greensight Inc	Charlestown	MA	E	617 633-4919	7875	Ersa Inc	Westerly	RI	E	401 348-4000	16930
Hardigg Industries LLC **(HQ)**	South Deerfield	MA	C	413 665-2163	11924	Hall Inc	Bristol	RI	D	401 253-4858	15768
Hosokawa Micron Intl Inc	Northborough	MA	E	508 655-1123	11098	Leidos Inc	Middletown	RI	H	401 849-8900	16178
Improved Consumer Products Inc	North Attleboro	MA	F	508 695-6841	10875	McLaughlin Research Corp	Middletown	RI	C	401 849-4010	16179
Interstate Design Company Inc	Agawam	MA	E	413 786-7730	5794	Metallurgical Solutions Inc	Providence	RI	E	401 941-2100	16563
Ipsumm Inc **(PA)**	Amesbury	MA	E	603 570-4050	5838	Palmer Industries Inc	North Providence	RI	F	800 398-9676	16306
J & J Heating & AC Inc	Dracut	MA	F	978 454-8197	8306	Sproutel Inc	Providence	RI	G	914 806-6514	16615
Lewa Process Technologies Inc	Devens	MA	D	978 487-1100	8275	Veterans Assembled Elec LLC **(PA)**	North Kingstown	RI	F	401 228-6165	16291
Louie and Teds Blacktop Inc	Swansea	MA	F	508 678-4948	12306	Applied Bolting Tech Pdts LLC	Bellows Falls	VT	E	802 460-3100	17028
Luster-On Products Inc	Springfield	MA	F	413 739-2541	12111	Applied Research Assoc Inc	Randolph	VT	E	802 728-4588	17467
Makers Tool and Mfg Co LLC	Oxford	MA	F	774 633-0658	11261	Cersosimo Industries Inc **(PA)**	Brattleboro	VT	D	802 254-4500	17080
Manchester Corporation	Harvard	MA	F	978 772-2900	9065	Westinghouse Electric Co LLC	Brattleboro	VT	E	802 254-9353	17108
Marblehead Engineering	Essex	MA	F	978 432-1386	8477						
Medsource Tech Holdings LLC **(DH)**	Wilmington	MA	F	978 570-6900	13428	**8712 Architectural services**					
Motorola Mobility LLC	Lowell	MA	E	978 614-2900	9910	Coreslab Structures Conn Inc	Thomaston	CT	D	860 283-8281	3617
National Resource MGT Inc **(PA)**	Canton	MA	E	781 828-8877	7809	Architctral Fireplaces of Neng	Auburn	MA	F	508 757-0622	6104
Nn Inc	Mansfield	MA	E	508 406-2100	10070	Boston Sign Company Inc	Boston	MA	G	617 338-2114	6618
Nypro Inc **(HQ)**	Clinton	MA	A	978 365-9721	8087	Faverco Inc	Boston	MA	G	617 247-1440	6732
Oncore Manufacturing LLC	Westborough	MA	D	978 737-3640	13125	Moca Systems Inc **(PA)**	Boston	MA	E	617 581-6622	6893
Onyx Environmental Svcs LLC **(DH)**	Boston	MA	E	617 849-6600	6936	South Mountain Company Inc	West Tisbury	MA	E	508 693-4850	13055
Optikos Corporation	Wakefield	MA	D	617 354-7557	12525	Zlink Inc	Maynard	MA	D	978 309-3628	10268
Optimum Technologies Inc	Southbridge	MA	F	508 765-8100	12032	Barrett Made **(PA)**	Portland	ME	E	207 650-6500	5184
Physical Sciences Inc **(PA)**	Andover	MA	D	978 689-0003	5907	Northern Design Precast Inc	Loudon	NH	E	603 783-8989	14796
Product Resources LLC	Newburyport	MA	E	978 524-8500	10709	Universal Envmtl Tech Inc	Nashua	NH	G	603 883-9312	15180
Proto XYZ Inc	New Bedford	MA	G	508 525-6363	10644	Herrick & White Ltd	Cumberland	RI	D	401 658-0440	15942
Pyramid Technical Cons Inc	Waltham	MA	F	781 402-1700	12755	William H Moore Inc	Waitsfield	VT	G	802 496-3595	17668
Quality Engineering Assoc Inc	Chelmsford	MA	G	978 528-2034	7949						
R & S Redco Inc	Weymouth	MA	G	781 792-1717	13334	**8713 Surveying services**					
Repjtm LLC	Mansfield	MA	E	508 406-2100	10074	Airworks Solutions Inc	Boston	MA	E	857 990-1060	6524
Roscid Technologies Inc	Woburn	MA	G	781 933-4007	13656	Greensight Inc	Charlestown	MA	E	617 633-4919	7875
Rt Engineering Corporation	Franklin	MA	E	800 343-1182	8861	Zink Imaging Inc	Billerica	MA	E	781 761-5400	6492
Schneder Elc Systems Argntina	Foxboro	MA	C	508 543-8750	8718						
Schneider Elc Systems USA Inc	Foxboro	MA	F	508 543-8750	8719	**8721 Accounting, auditing, and bookkeeping**					
Schneider Elc Systems USA Inc	Foxboro	MA	F	508 543-8750	8720	Cobra Green LLC	Norwalk	CT	A	203 354-5000	2484
Schneider Elc Systems USA Inc **(DH)**	Foxboro	MA	E	508 543-8750	8721	Eagle Investment Systems LLC	West Hartford	CT	F	860 561-4602	4057
Softinway Inc	Burlington	MA	F	781 328-4310	7431	Analytix Bus Solutions LLC **(PA)**	Woburn	MA	G	781 503-9000	13510
Star Engineering Inc	North Attleboro	MA	F	508 316-1492	10889	Eagle Investment Systems LLC **(HQ)**	Wellesley	MA	E	781 943-2200	12940
Surmet Corp **(PA)**	Burlington	MA	E	781 345-5721	7436	Nationwide Tax & Business Svcs	New Bedford	MA	F	774 473-8444	10625
The Duclos Corporation	Somerset	MA	D	508 676-8596	11857	Numeric Inc	Westfield	MA	F	413 732-6544	13195
TK&k Services LLC	Beverly	MA	D	770 844-8710	6389	Verizon New York Inc	Winchester	MA	F	781 721-5957	13493
Todd Clark and Associates Inc	Danvers	MA	E	978 774-7100	8225	Waja Associates Inc	Franklin	MA	E	508 543-6050	8874
Triangle Engineering Inc	Hanover	MA	F	781 878-1500	9046	Anodyne Health Partners Inc **(HQ)**	Falmouth	ME	E	207 347-7400	4767
US Nortek Inc	Worcester	MA	F	774 314-4006	13817	Outer Limits Publishing LLC	Killington	VT	F	802 422-2399	17313
Vacuum Process Technology LLC	Cambridge	MA	E	508 732-7200	7749						
Woods Hole Group Inc **(DH)**	Bourne	MA	E	301 925-4411	7143						

S
I
C

8731 Commercial physical research

Company	CITY	ST	EMP	PHONE	ENTRY#
Accustandard Inc	New Haven	CT	D	203 786-5290	2111
Arvinas Inc (PA)	New Haven	CT	B	203 535-1456	2119
Cara Therapeutics Inc	Stamford	CT	D	203 406-3700	3302
Charles River Laboratories Inc	Storrs	CT	F	860 429-7261	3511
Clear Edge Power International Service LLC	South Windsor	CT			C
860 727-2200					3128
Connecticut Analytical Corp	Bethany	CT	F	203 393-9666	92
Cytec Industries Inc	Stamford	CT	D	203 321-2200	3333
Doltronics LLC	Branford	CT	E	203 488-8766	250
DRM Research Laboratories Inc	Branford	CT	E	203 488-5555	252
Frc Founders Corporation (PA)	Stamford	CT	E	203 661-6601	3348
Hampford Research Inc (PA)	Stratford	CT	E	203 375-1137	3544
Henkel Loctite Corporation (DH)	Rocky Hill	CT	D	860 571-5100	2925
Herbasway Laboratories LLC	Wallingford	CT	F	203 269-6991	3812
Imbrium Therapeutics LP (DH)	Stamford	CT	E	888 827-0622	3380
Integral Technologies Inc (DH)	Enfield	CT	G	860 741-2281	1136
Jet Process Corporation	Wallingford	CT	E	203 985-6000	3823
Lambda Investors LLC	Greenwich	CT	F	203 862-7000	1337
Pfizer Inc	Groton	CT	C	860 441-4100	1379
Pratt & Whitney Eng Svcs Inc	East Hartford	CT	E	860 610-7478	1016
Precipio Inc (PA)	New Haven	CT	E	203 787-7888	2187
Precision Combustion Inc	North Haven	CT	E	203 287-3700	2432
Thayermahan Inc (PA)	Groton	CT	E	860 785-9994	1381
Ventus Technologies LLC	Norwalk	CT	F	203 642-2800	2591
2is Inc	Walpole	MA	E	508 850-7520	12545
Adaptive Optics Associates Inc (DH)	Devens	MA	D	978 757-9600	8269
Adicet Bio Inc (PA)	Boston	MA	G	857 315-5528	6516
Advent Technologies Inc (PA)	Boston	MA	F	617 655-6000	6519
Agenus Inc (PA)	Lexington	MA	C	781 674-4400	9721
Agios Pharmaceuticals Inc (PA)	Cambridge	MA	B	617 649-8600	7470
Aileron Therapeutics Inc (PA)	Boston	MA	G	617 995-0900	6522
Alcami Carolinas Corporation	Pepperell	MA	G	910 619-3952	11380
Alcami Carolinas Corporation	Pepperell	MA	G	910 619-3952	11381
Alcami Carolinas Corporation	Pepperell	MA	F	910 619-3952	11382
Alcami Carolinas Corporation	Shirley	MA	G	910 619-3952	11813
Alkermes Inc (HQ)	Waltham	MA	E	781 609-6000	12589
Alnylam Pharmaceuticals Inc (PA)	Cambridge	MA	B	617 551-8200	7478
Amylyx Pharmaceuticals Inc (PA)	Cambridge	MA	C	617 682-0917	7486
Ardelyx Inc	Waltham	MA	A	510 745-1700	12595
Ariad Pharmaceuticals Inc	Cambridge	MA	B		7490
Arichell Technologies Inc	Newton	MA	D	617 796-9001	10734
Arqule Inc (HQ)	Burlington	MA	E	781 994-0300	7335
Atea Pharmaceuticals Inc (PA)	Boston	MA	C	857 284-8891	6571
Aura Biosciences Inc (PA)	Boston	MA	F	617 500-8864	6577
Axcella Health Inc (PA)	Cambridge	MA	G	857 320-2200	7496
Barrett Technology LLC	Newton	MA	E	617 252-9000	10737
BASF Bioresearch Corp	Worcester	MA	E	508 849-2500	13702
Beigene Usa Inc (HQ)	Cambridge	MA	E	781 801-1887	7503
Biogen Inc (PA)	Cambridge	MA	B	617 679-2000	7511
Biogen MA Inc (HQ)	Cambridge	MA	C	617 679-2000	7514
Biontech US Inc (HQ)	Cambridge	MA	E	617 337-4701	7515
Bluebird Bio Inc (PA)	Somerville	MA	A	339 499-9300	11864
Bostonmolecules Inc	Waltham	MA	F	617 651-1016	12610
Brammer Bio Holding Co LLC (HQ)	Cambridge	MA	E	386 418-8199	7523
Brammer Bio Ma LLC (HQ)	Cambridge	MA	B	877 765-7676	7524
C4 Therapeutics Inc (PA)	Watertown	MA	E	617 231-0700	12866
Cambrdge RES Instrmntation Inc	Hopkinton	MA	E	781 935-9099	9311
Cambridge Polymer Group Inc	Woburn	MA	E	617 629-4400	13539
Carpe Diem Technologies Inc	Franklin	MA	F	508 541-2055	8822
Checkmate Pharmaceuticals Inc	Cambridge	MA	F	617 682-3625	7539
Chemgenes Corporation	Billerica	MA	E	978 694-4500	6422
Cogent Biosciences Inc (PA)	Waltham	MA	F	617 945-5576	12634
Concepts Nrec LLC	Chelmsford	MA	F	781 935-9050	7920
Corium LLC	Boston	MA	C	855 253-2407	6672
CPI Radant Tech Div Inc (DH)	Stow	MA	D	978 562-3866	12245
Creative Materials Inc	Ayer	MA	E	978 391-4700	6180
Crystal Gt Systems LLC	Salem	MA	F	978 745-0088	11708
Curia Global Inc	Burlington	MA	G	781 205-1691	7357
Dicerna Pharmaceuticals Inc (HQ)	Lexington	MA	C	617 621-8097	9739
Disc Medicine Inc (PA)	Watertown	MA	F	617 674-9274	12871
Dynasil Corporation America (PA)	Concord	MA	F	617 668-6855	8116
Eclypses Inc	Boston	MA	E	719 323-6680	6707
Elevatebio LLC (PA)	Cambridge	MA	E	413 297-7151	7559
Elevatebio Base Camp Inc	Waltham	MA	C	617 433-2600	12660
Empiramed Inc	Maynard	MA	G	978 344-4300	10262
Enanta Pharmaceuticals Inc (PA)	Watertown	MA	D	617 607-0800	12872
Epizyme Inc	Cambridge	MA	C	617 229-5872	7563
Ercon Inc	Wareham	MA	E	508 291-1400	12835
Esoterix Genetic Labs LLC (HQ)	Westborough	MA	E	508 389-6650	13101
Ferro Corporation	Williamstown	MA	F	413 743-3927	13366
Flintec Inc	Hudson	MA	E	978 562-4548	9367
Folia Materials Inc	Bedford	MA	G	315 559-2135	6227
Gentex Corporation	Boston	MA	F	617 670-3547	6755
Ginger Acquisition Inc	Boston	MA	B	617 551-4000	6760
Gurnet Holding Company	Cambridge	MA	C	617 588-4900	7595
Homology Medicines Inc	Bedford	MA	C	781 301-7277	6229
Hood E Benson Laboratories	Pembroke	MA	F	781 826-7573	11367
ID Bimedical Corp Northborough	Northborough	MA	D	508 351-9333	11099
Imbria Pharmaceuticals Inc	Boston	MA	G	617 941-3000	6808
Immuneering Corporation	Cambridge	MA	E	617 500-8080	7612
Immunlecular Therapeutics Inc	Woburn	MA	G	617 356-8170	13584
Infinity Pharmaceuticals Inc (PA)	Cambridge	MA	F		7614
Instrumentation Laboratory Co (DH)	Bedford	MA	A	781 861-0710	6233
Integral Biosystems LLC	Bedford	MA	F	781 275-8059	6234
Intellia Therapeutics Inc (PA)	Cambridge	MA	C	857 285-6200	7616
Interleukin Genetics Inc	Waltham	MA	F	781 398-0700	12702
International Parallel Mchs	New Bedford	MA	G	508 990-2977	10604
Intuvision Inc	Woburn	MA	G	781 497-1015	13591
Inverness Medical - Biostar Inc	Waltham	MA	C	781 647-3900	12703
Ironwood Pharmaceuticals Inc	Boston	MA	C	617 621-7722	6818
Joule Unlimited Technologies Inc	Foxboro	MA	D	781 533-9100	8703
Jounce Therapeutics Inc (PA)	Cambridge	MA	D	857 259-3840	7620
Kaleido Biosciences Inc (PA)	Lexington	MA	D	617 674-9000	9755
La Jolla Pharmaceutical Co (HQ)	Waltham	MA	E	617 715-3600	12708
Landmark Bio Pbllc	Watertown	MA	G	617 894-8629	12886
Leidos Inc	Tewksbury	MA	G	781 221-7627	12402
Lyne Laboratories Inc	Brockton	MA	D	508 583-8700	7292
Manus Bio Inc (HQ)	Waltham	MA	E	617 299-8466	12713
McLane Research Labs Inc (PA)	East Falmouth	MA	G	508 495-4000	8361
Medtherapy Biotechnology Inc	Quincy	MA	E	617 938-7082	11528
Mersana Therapeutics Inc (PA)	Cambridge	MA	D	617 498-0020	7641
Micro Magnetics Inc	Fall River	MA	E	508 672-4489	8581
Microbiotix Inc	Worcester	MA	E	508 757-2800	13759
Millennium Pharmaceuticals Inc	Cambridge	MA	C	617 679-7000	7647
Mra Laboratories Inc	Adams	MA	F	413 743-3927	5774
Mural Oncology Inc	Waltham	MA	A	617 694-2481	12727
New Balance Athletics Inc	Lawrence	MA	B	978 685-8400	9586
Novirio Pharmaceuticals Inc	Cambridge	MA	D	617 250-3100	7671
Optra Inc	Wilmington	MA	F	978 887-6600	13443
Peak Technologies LLC	Littleton	MA	E	978 393-5900	9832
Pellion Technologies Inc	Arlington	MA	E		5944
Pepgen Inc	Boston	MA	E	781 797-0979	6962
Perspecta Svcs & Solutions Inc (DH)	Waltham	MA	G	781 684-4000	12747
Physical Sciences Inc (PA)	Andover	MA	D	978 689-0003	5907
Pion Inc	Billerica	MA	F	978 528-2020	6472
Praxis Precision Medicines Inc (PA)	Boston	MA	E	617 300-8460	6974
Radius Health Inc (PA)	Boston	MA	B	617 551-4000	6994
Red Point Positioning Corp (PA)	Newton	MA	F	339 222-0261	10779
Remote Sensing Solutions Inc	Buzzards Bay	MA	E	508 362-9400	7416
Revela Inc	Woburn	MA	G	716 725-2657	13651
Sanofi Pasteur Biologics LLC (HQ)	Cambridge	MA	C	617 866-4400	7703
Sarepta Therapeutics Inc	Andover	MA	C	978 662-4800	5914
Scientific Solutions Inc	North Chelmsford	MA	F	978 251-4554	10988
Sensera Inc	Woburn	MA	F	978 606-2600	13663
Sigma Research Biochemicals	Natick	MA	G	781 237-3828	10497
Soft Robotics Inc	Bedford	MA	D	617 391-0612	6269
Solid Biosciences Inc (PA)	Charlestown	MA	E	617 337-4680	7883
Spire Solar Inc (HQ)	Bedford	MA	G	781 275-6000	6271
Synlogic Inc (PA)	Cambridge	MA	E	617 401-9975	7729
T2 Biosystems Inc	Wilmington	MA	E	978 447-1069	13461
Tango Therapeutics Inc (PA)	Boston	MA	F	857 302-4900	7069
Tepha Inc (HQ)	Lexington	MA	D	781 357-1700	9787
Thermo Power Corporation	Waltham	MA	A	781 622-1400	12802
Theseus Pharmaceuticals Inc (PA)	Cambridge	MA	F	857 400-9491	7740
Torque Therapeutics Inc	Cambridge	MA	E	617 945-1082	7744
Tracer Technologies Inc	Somerville	MA	E	617 776-6410	11904
Ultraclad Corporation	Newburyport	MA	G	978 358-7945	10723
Universal Pharma Tech LLC	North Andover	MA	G	978 975-7216	10856
Vaso Active Phrmaceuticals Inc	Beverly	MA	G	978 750-1991	6392
Veranova LP (HQ)	Devens	MA	C	484 581-0149	8288
Veranova LP	North Andover	MA	E	978 784-5000	10857
Vertex Pharmaceuticals Inc (PA)	Boston	MA	A	617 341-6100	7101
Videoiq Inc	Somerville	MA	E	781 222-3069	11911
Vigil Neuroscience Inc (PA)	Watertown	MA	E	857 254-4445	12919
Voltea Inc	Worcester	MA	F	510 861-3719	13825
Voyager Therapeutics Inc (PA)	Lexington	MA	D	570 329-6851	9791
Werewolf Therapeutics Inc	Watertown	MA	E	617 952-0555	12920
Xilectric Inc	Fall River	MA	G	781 247-4567	8627
Biodesign International	Saco	ME	E	207 283-6500	5363
David Saunders Inc	South Portland	ME	E	207 228-1888	5497
Lgc Clinical Diagnostics Inc	Cumberland Foreside	ME	D	207 892-1300	
4712					
Maine Orthtic Prsthtic Rhab Sv	Portland	ME	F	207 773-8818	5241
Wjb Associates Inc	Mount Vernon	ME	G	207 293-2457	5078

	CITY	ST	EMP	PHONE	ENTRY#
Alcami Carolinas Corporation	Amherst	NH	G	910 619-3952	13861
At Comm Corp	Manchester	NH	F	603 624-4424	14815
Bae Systems Info Elctrnic Syst	Hudson	NH	A	603 885-4321	14486
Bio-Concept Laboratories Inc	Salem	NH	E	603 437-4990	15510
Corportion For Lser Optics Res **(PA)**	Londonderry	NH	G	603 430-2023	14738
Exothermics Inc	Amherst	NH	F	603 821-5660	13869
Ingersoll-Rand Energy Systems Corporation	Portsmouth	NH			D
603 430-7000		15408			
Ion Physics Corp	Fremont	NH	G	603 895-5100	14328
Ipura Consulting Group LLC	Hampton	NH	F	603 294-4002	14404
Mentis Sciences Inc	Warner	NH	E	603 624-9197	15666
Metal Casting Technology Inc	Milford	NH	E	603 673-9720	15033
Mikros Technologies LLC	Claremont	NH	E	603 690-2020	14094
Oracle Systems Corporation	Nashua	NH	E	603 897-3000	15146
Pace Anlytical Lf Sciences LLC	Salem	NH	E	603 437-4990	15555
Simbex LLC	Lebanon	NH	E	603 448-2367	14699
Amgen Inc	West Greenwich	RI	D	401 392-1200	16882
Analytical Services Company	Narragansett	RI	G	401 792-3537	16186
Bioprocessh2o LLC	Portsmouth	RI	E	401 683-5400	16438
Electro Standards Lab Inc	Cranston	RI	D	401 946-1164	15853
Epivax Inc	Providence	RI	E	401 272-2123	16515
Leidos Inc	Middletown	RI	E	401 849-8900	16178
McLaughlin Research Corp	Middletown	RI	C	401 849-4010	16179
Ultra Scientific Incorporated	North Kingstown	RI	E	800 338-1754	16290
Vertex Pharmaceuticals Inc	Providence	RI	F	857 529-6430	16639
Xstrata Recycling Inc	East Providence	RI	E	401 438-9220	16049
Applied Research Assoc Inc	Randolph	VT	E	802 728-4588	17467
Diffraction Ltd	Waitsfield	VT	G	802 496-6640	17666
Triex LLC	Barre	VT	G	802 505-6772	17021

8732 Commercial nonphysical research

	CITY	ST	EMP	PHONE	ENTRY#
Callaway Companies Inc **(PA)**	Old Lyme	CT	F	860 434-9002	2637
Freethink Technologies Inc	Branford	CT	F	860 237-5800	258
Litigation Analytics Inc **(PA)**	Ridgefield	CT	G	203 431-0300	2901
Madison Medical LLC	Madison	CT	E	203 245-0306	1563
Sonalysts Inc **(PA)**	Waterford	CT	B	860 442-4355	3997
Vitek Research Corporation	Naugatuck	CT	F	203 735-1813	1992
Angel Guard Products Inc	Worcester	MA	G	508 791-1073	13699
Barrett Technology Inc	Newtonville	MA	E	617 252-9000	10796
Continuus Pharmaceuticals Inc	Woburn	MA	F	781 281-0115	13548
Education Development Ctr Inc **(PA)**	Waltham	MA	A	617 969-7100	12659
Euro International Ltd	Boston	MA	F	617 670-2265	6720
Idg Corporate Services Group	Framingham	MA	G	508 875-5000	8781
International Data Group Inc **(HQ)**	Needham	MA	F	508 875-5000	10514
Lightlab Imaging Inc	Westford	MA	B	978 577-3400	13246
Power Advocate Inc **(HQ)**	Boston	MA	D	857 453-5700	6971
President and Fellows of Harvard College **(PA)**	Cambridge	MA			A
617 496-4873		7688			
President Fllows Hrvard Cllege	Boston	MA	C	617 495-5581	6976
T & D Specialties Inc	Oxford	MA	E	508 987-8344	11265
Howe & Howe Technologies Inc	Waterboro	ME	F	207 247-2777	5591
Tower Publishing **(PA)**	Standish	ME	F	207 642-5400	5529
Population Media Center Inc	South Burlington	VT	E	802 985-8156	17595

8733 Noncommercial research organizations

	CITY	ST	EMP	PHONE	ENTRY#
Alexion Pharma LLC **(DH)**	New Haven	CT	D	203 272-2596	2112
Advanced Mechanical Tech Inc **(PA)**	Watertown	MA	E	617 923-4174	12855
Cambrdge RES Instrmntation Inc	Hopkinton	MA	E	781 935-9099	9311
Confluent Surgical Inc	Waltham	MA	D	781 839-1700	12638
In Silico Biosciences Inc	Lexington	MA	F	781 861-1592	9751
Institute For Fgn Plicy Analis **(PA)**	Cambridge	MA	E	617 492-2116	7615
Inverness Medical - Biostar Inc	Waltham	MA	C	781 647-3900	12703
Lfb Usa Inc **(DH)**	Framingham	MA	E	508 370-5100	8785
Logan Instruments Inc	Braintree	MA	F	617 394-0601	7193
Medical Research Networx	Franklin	MA	E	508 530-4289	8850
Silverthread Inc	Cambridge	MA	G	800 674-9366	7715
Valo Health Inc **(PA)**	Boston	MA	F	617 237-6080	7096
Sensor Research and Dev Corp	Orono	ME	G	207 866-0100	5137
Haigh-Farr Inc	Bedford	NH	D	603 644-6170	13932

8734 Testing laboratories

	CITY	ST	EMP	PHONE	ENTRY#
AKO Inc	Windsor	CT	E	860 298-9765	4256
Cogstate Sport Inc	New Haven	CT	F	203 773-5010	2137
Enginuity Plm LLC **(DH)**	Milford	CT	F	203 218-7225	1825
Hoffman Engineering LLC **(DH)**	Stamford	CT	D	203 425-8900	3378
Nats USA Incorporated	Middletown	CT	F	860 398-0035	1767
Precipio Inc **(PA)**	New Haven	CT	F	203 787-7888	2187
Pti Industries Inc **(HQ)**	Enfield	CT	E	800 318-8438	1143
Sousa Corp	Newington	CT	E	860 523-9090	2326
Alcami Carolinas Corporation	Pepperell	MA	G	910 619-3952	11380
Alcami Carolinas Corporation	Pepperell	MA	G	910 619-3952	11381
Alcami Carolinas Corporation	Pepperell	MA	F	910 619-3952	11382
Alcami Carolinas Corporation	Shirley	MA	G	910 619-3952	11813

	CITY	ST	EMP	PHONE	ENTRY#
Aspen Systems LLC **(PA)**	Marlborough	MA	F	508 281-5322	10112
Barbour Stockwell Inc	Woburn	MA	E	781 933-5200	13520
Bmac Inc	Ayer	MA	E	978 772-3310	6175
Cambridge Polymer Group Inc	Woburn	MA	E	617 629-4400	13539
Cryogenic Institute Neng Inc	Worcester	MA	F	508 459-7447	13712
Hardigg Industries LLC **(HQ)**	South Deerfield	MA	E	413 665-2163	11924
Jordi Labs LLC	Mansfield	MA	E	508 719-8543	10061
Kse Inc	Sunderland	MA	F	413 549-5506	12274
Netzsch Instruments N Amer LLC **(DH)**	Burlington	MA	E	781 272-5353	7398
Parker-Hannifin Corporation	Woburn	MA	B	781 939-4278	13631
Schenck USA Corp	Hudson	MA	E	978 562-6017	9410
Test Devices Inc	Hudson	MA	E	978 562-6017	9417
Covetrus North America LLC **(PA)**	Portland	ME	F	888 280-2221	5202
Kennebec River Biosciences Inc	Richmond	ME	F	207 737-2637	5322
Northeast Laboratory Svcs Inc **(PA)**	Winslow	ME	D	207 873-7711	5686
Wjb Associates Inc	Mount Vernon	ME	G	207 293-2457	5078
Alcami Carolinas Corporation	Amherst	NH	G	910 619-3952	13861
Klarmann Rulings Inc	Manchester	NH	F	603 424-2401	14872
Smiths Tblar Systms-Lconia Inc	Laconia	NH	C	603 524-2064	14470
American Iron & Metal USA Inc **(HQ)**	Cranston	RI	F	401 463-5605	15831
Verichem Laboratories Inc	Providence	RI	G	401 461-0180	16638

8741 Management services

	CITY	ST	EMP	PHONE	ENTRY#
Brennan Realty LLC **(PA)**	Shelton	CT	C	203 929-6314	2987
Cogstate Sport Inc	New Haven	CT	F	203 773-5010	2137
Conair LLC	Torrington	CT	D	800 492-7464	3676
Dt Holdings Incorporated	Stamford	CT	F	203 602-6969	3339
Frc Founders Corporation **(PA)**	Stamford	CT	F	203 661-6601	3348
General Dynamics Ordnance	Avon	CT	F	860 404-0162	25
Hasler Inc	Milford	CT	B	203 301-3400	1833
Sleep Management Solutions LLC **(DH)**	Hartford	CT	F	888 497-5337	1508
SS&c Technologies Inc **(HQ)**	Windsor	CT	C	800 234-0556	4302
Urban Exposition LLC **(DH)**	Shelton	CT	E	203 242-8717	3074
Wexford Capital LP **(PA)**	Greenwich	CT	G	203 862-7000	1361
Yale New Haven Hlth Svcs Corp	New Haven	CT	A	203 688-2100	2217
Automatic Press Inc	Franklin	MA	G	508 528-2000	8818
Biokit U S A Inc	Bedford	MA	E	781 861-4064	6215
Cross Country Motor Club Inc **(HQ)**	Medford	MA	A	781 393-9300	10283
John McGillicuddy Inc	Milton	MA	F	617 388-6324	10453
Linx Consulting LLC	Webster	MA	F	508 461-6333	12930
Logicmanager Inc	Boston	MA	E	617 530-1200	6862
Massachusetts Envelope Co Inc **(PA)**	Woburn	MA	F	617 623-8000	13606
Schneder Elc Systems Argntina	Foxboro	MA	C	508 543-8750	8718
Schneider Elc Systems USA Inc	Foxboro	MA	F	508 543-8750	8719
Schneider Elc Systems USA Inc **(DH)**	Foxboro	MA	F	508 543-8750	8721
Coca-Cola Bevs Northeast Inc	Belmont	NH	B	603 267-8834	13961
Gabriel Business Group Co Ltd	Brookline	NH	F	877 401-5544	14039
Beacon Rock Properties Inc	Providence	RI	D	401 421-3470	16482
Douglas Wine & Spirits Inc	North Providence	RI	F	401 353-6400	16299
Ener-Tek International Inc	East Greenwich	RI	E	401 471-6580	15985

8742 Management consulting services

	CITY	ST	EMP	PHONE	ENTRY#
Chief Executive Group LLC **(PA)**	Stamford	CT	E	785 832-0303	3310
Chief Executive Group LP **(PA)**	Stamford	CT	G	203 930-2700	3311
Computer Prgrm & Systems Inc **(PA)**	Stamford	CT	G	203 324-9203	3319
D&D Fltrtion Cons Sppliers Inc	Kensington	CT	F	860 829-9350	1539
Enginuity Plm LLC **(DH)**	Milford	CT	F	203 218-7225	1825
Fairfield Marketing Group Inc **(PA)**	Easton	CT	F	203 261-0884	1095
Forecast International Inc	Sandy Hook	CT	E	203 426-0800	2951
Gss Infotech Ct Inc	Glastonbury	CT	C	860 709-0933	1282
Ihs Herold Inc **(DH)**	Norwalk	CT	D	203 857-0215	2516
Merrill Anderson Company Inc	Stratford	CT	E	203 377-4996	3557
O & W Heat Treat Inc	South Windsor	CT	E	860 528-9239	3168
Phocuswright Inc **(HQ)**	Sherman	CT	F	860 350-4084	3082
Powerphone Inc	Madison	CT	E	203 245-8911	1566
PRA Holdings Inc	Stamford	CT	A	203 853-0123	3435
R4 Technologies Inc **(PA)**	Ridgefield	CT	E	203 461-7100	2906
Reac Ready LLC	Wethersfield	CT	G	860 550-5049	4213
Relocation Information Svc Inc	Norwalk	CT	F	203 855-1234	2564
Rothstein Associates Inc	Brookfield	CT	G	203 740-7400	538
Sfc Koenig LLC	North Haven	CT	E	203 245-1100	2436
Stonington Services LLC	Gales Ferry	CT	E	860 464-1991	1261
4tell Solutions LP	Foxboro	MA	E	207 828-7900	8688
Acentech Incorporated **(PA)**	Cambridge	MA	E	617 499-8000	7466
Alere Inc **(HQ)**	Waltham	MA	A	781 647-3900	12587
Alpha Tech Pet Inc	Littleton	MA	E	978 486-3690	9800
Apiphani Inc	Boston	MA	E	800 215-0811	6551
Atlantic Inc	Boston	MA	F	617 720-3700	6574
Beacon Application Svcs Corp **(PA)**	Framingham	MA	F	508 663-4433	8742
Berkshire Grey Inc **(PA)**	Bedford	MA	E	833 848-9900	6214
Caliper Corporation	Newton	MA	E	617 527-4700	10740
Cape Cod Life LLC	Mashpee	MA	F	508 419-7381	10250
Cerulli Associates Inc **(PA)**	Boston	MA	E	617 437-0084	6647

	CITY	ST	EMP	PHONE	ENTRY#
Citiworks Corp	Attleboro	MA	F	508 761-7400	6004
City Pblcations Greater Boston	Wayland	MA	G	617 549-7622	12924
Clearwter Tech Cnslting Wtr Sv	Rockland	MA	F	781 871-5157	11640
Copley Global Services LLC	Waltham	MA	G	617 970-9617	12641
Debt Exchange Inc	Boston	MA	D	617 531-3400	6685
Dixie Media LLC	Danvers	MA	E	508 739-1999	8183
Esm Software LLC	Lincoln	MA	F	781 541-4462	9795
Esm Software Group Inc	Lincoln	MA	F	781 541-4465	9796
First Sail Group Inc	South Yarmouth	MA	G	425 409-2783	11983
Graphic Arts Institute of Neng	Southborough	MA	F	508 804-4100	11995
Hcpro Inc **(HQ)**	Middleton	MA	E	781 639-1872	10385
Infogix Inc **(HQ)**	Burlington	MA	C	630 505-1800	7379
Innoneo Health Tech Inc **(PA)**	Boston	MA	D	617 336-3202	6810
Innovative Chem Pdts Group LLC **(PA)**	Andover	MA	E	978 623-9980	5889
Innovative Publishing Company	Edgartown	MA	F	267 266-8876	8466
International Security Assista	Woburn	MA	G	617 590-7942	13588
Intralign Holdings LLC	Foxboro	MA	G	602 773-8506	8702
Joseph G Pulitano Insur Agcy	Newton	MA	F	617 783-2622	10765
Kognito Solutions LLC	Burlington	MA	E	212 675-2651	7387
Material Impact Inc	Boston	MA	F	617 917-4123	6879
MSP Digital Marketing Mass Inc **(HQ)**	Hudson	MA	E	978 567-6000	9394
Network World Inc	Needham Heights	MA	E	800 622-1108	10553
Nsd Seafood Inc **(PA)**	Gloucester	MA	C	978 282-7880	8947
Oliveri & Associates Inc	Plymouth	MA	F	781 320-9090	11470
Physical Sciences Inc **(PA)**	Andover	MA	D	978 689-0003	5907
Product Resources LLC	Newburyport	MA	E	978 524-8500	10709
Sbarzola Construction Corp	South Weymouth	MA	G	781 817-6485	11977
Square Robot Inc	Marlborough	MA	G	617 274-8389	10216
St Associates Inc	Wakefield	MA	E		12536
Stratcomm Inc	Natick	MA	C	508 907-7000	10499
Vdc Research Group Inc **(PA)**	Southborough	MA	E	508 653-9000	12004
Vocero Hispano Newspaper Inc	Southbridge	MA	F	866 846-6397	12038
Xiphos Partners Inc	Dartmouth	MA	G	508 991-1014	8233
Barrett Made **(PA)**	Portland	ME	F	207 650-6500	5184
Change Hlthcare Phrm Sltons In	Augusta	ME	D	207 622-7153	4468
S & K Unlimited LLC	Brownville	ME	F	207 965-6137	4638
Sunny Side Land Holdings LLC	Presque Isle	ME	F	207 768-1020	5310
Thomas Hall	Scarborough	ME	F	207 956-0020	5445
Actio Software Corporation	Portsmouth	NH	D	603 433-2300	15356
Atlantic Turnkey Cons Corp	Amherst	NH	F	603 673-9447	13862
Granite Commercial RE LLC	Nashua	NH	F	603 669-2770	15107
Image 4 Concepts Inc	Manchester	NH	F	603 644-0077	14862
Ingersoll-Rand Energy Systems Corporation	Portsmouth	NH			D
603 430-7000	15408				
Ipura Consulting Group LLC	Hampton	NH	F	603 294-4002	14404
Kbace Technologies Inc **(HQ)**	Nashua	NH	D	603 821-7000	15121
Mmis Inc	Portsmouth	NH	D	603 929-5078	15424
Powerplay Management LLC	Portsmouth	NH	E	603 436-3030	15431
R & J Tool Inc **(PA)**	Laconia	NH	G	603 366-4925	14664
Scribliotech Inc	Orange	NH	G	603 306-9000	15280
Universal Envmtl Tech Inc	Nashua	NH	G	603 883-9312	15180
Durastone Corporation	Lincoln	RI	F	401 723-7100	16134
Eagle Industries Inc	Ashaway	RI	G	401 596-8111	15739
Endeavor Seafood LLC	Newport	RI	G	401 841-8637	16209
G&G Technologies Inc	Coventry	RI	F	401 295-4000	15813
Raybern Utility Solutions LLC	Portsmouth	RI	G	303 775-5041	16453
Trimed Media Group Inc	Providence	RI	F	401 919-5165	16630
DC Enterprizes Inc	Hinesburg	VT	F	802 865-4480	17290
Select Design Ltd	Burlington	VT	D	802 864-9075	17158
Triex LLC	Barre	VT	F	802 505-6772	17021
YS Enterprises Inc	East Ryegate	VT	G	802 238-0902	17219

8743 Public relations services

	CITY	ST	EMP	PHONE	ENTRY#
Fairfield Marketing Group Inc **(PA)**	Easton	CT	F	203 261-0884	1095
Sales Solutions Inc	Scituate	MA	G	781 588-2703	11771
Zajac LLC	Saco	ME	E	207 286-9100	5384
Innovairre Studios Inc	Milford	NH	E	603 579-1600	15030
Country Home Products Inc	Charlotte	VT	E	802 771-7202	17175

8744 Facilities support services

	CITY	ST	EMP	PHONE	ENTRY#
DR Charles Envmtl Cnstr LLC	Monroe	CT	G	203 445-0412	1913
Johnson Controls Inc	Meriden	CT	F	678 297-4040	1670
Pitney Bowes Inc **(PA)**	Stamford	CT	A	203 356-5000	3433
Bostonian Clg Restoration Inc	Braintree	MA	F	781 356-3303	7170
Milk Street Press Inc	Boston	MA	F	617 742-7900	6888
Remediation Lockwood Tech	Leominster	MA	E	404 666-5857	9701
Universal Envmtl Tech Inc	Nashua	NH	G	603 883-9312	15180

8748 Business consulting, nec

	CITY	ST	EMP	PHONE	ENTRY#
Childrens Health Market Inc	Wilton	CT	G	203 762-2938	4236
Cobra Green LLC	Norwalk	CT	A	203 354-5000	2484
D&D Fltrtion Cons Sppliers Inc	Kensington	CT	F	860 829-3690	1539
Draught Technologies LLC	Farmington	CT	G	860 840-7555	1215

	CITY	ST	EMP	PHONE	ENTRY#
Dufrane Nuclear Shielding Inc	Winsted	CT	F	860 379-2318	4340
Dynamic Bldg Enrgy Sltions LLC **(PA)**	North Stonington	CT	F	860 599-1872	2447
Informa Tech Holdings LLC	Darien	CT	F	203 662-6501	849
Joseph Merritt & Company Inc **(PA)**	Hartford	CT	E	860 296-2500	1488
Mercury Cabling Systems LLC	Stratford	CT	E	203 378-9008	3556
Penfield Search Partners Ltd	Fairfield	CT	G	203 307-2600	1196
Powerphone Inc	Madison	CT	E	203 245-8911	1566
Preusser Research Group Inc **(PA)**	Trumbull	CT	F	203 459-8700	3729
R4 Technologies Inc **(PA)**	Ridgefield	CT	E	203 461-7100	2906
Royalty Consulting LLC	Rocky Hill	CT	F	800 474-5157	2934
Sonalysts Inc **(PA)**	Waterford	CT	B	860 442-4355	3997
Advanced Electronic Design Inc	Attleboro Falls	MA	E	508 699-0249	6078
Agrify Corporation **(PA)**	North Billerica	MA	E	617 896-5243	10894
Applied Science Group Inc	Billerica	MA	E	781 275-4000	6404
Aqua Laboratories Inc	Amesbury	MA	E	978 388-3989	5829
Assurance Technology Corp **(PA)**	Carlisle	MA	D	978 369-8848	7845
Cisco Systems Inc	Boxborough	MA	E	978 936-0000	7149
Complete Energy Services Corp	Raynham	MA	G	833 237-2677	11584
D L Maher Co	North Reading	MA	F	781 933-3210	11039
Edgeone LLC **(PA)**	West Wareham	MA	F	508 291-0057	13063
Elcom International Inc **(PA)**	Braintree	MA	F	781 501-4000	7179
Ercon Inc	Wareham	MA	E	508 291-1400	12835
Evotext Inc	Billerica	MA	F	781 272-1830	6445
Foundtion For Dmcracy In Ukrin	Cambridge	MA	G	617 496-8816	7574
Honeywell DMC Services LLC	Danvers	MA	B	978 774-3007	8192
Horizon House Publications Inc **(PA)**	Norwood	MA	D	781 769-9750	11177
Innovasea Systems Inc **(PA)**	Boston	MA	E	207 322-3219	6811
Interleukin Genetics Inc	Waltham	MA	F	781 398-0700	12702
Kerfoot Technologies Inc	Falmouth	MA	F	508 539-3002	8634
Labthink International Inc	Medford	MA	F	617 830-2190	10293
Moseley Corporation	Franklin	MA	F	508 520-4004	8853
National Resource MGT Inc **(PA)**	Canton	MA	E	781 828-8877	7809
Nsight Inc	Andover	MA	E	781 273-6300	5902
Rt Engineering Corporation	Franklin	MA	B	800 343-1182	8861
Silverthread Inc	Cambridge	MA	G	800 674-9366	7715
Sofnet Technology Inc	Newton	MA	F	857 272-2568	10785
Solectria Renewables LLC	Lawrence	MA	C	978 683-9700	9599
Syberworks Inc	Arlington	MA	F	781 891-1999	5948
Tupelo Press Inc	North Adams	MA	F	413 664-9611	10814
Visible Systems Corporation **(PA)**	Boston	MA	E	617 902-0767	7106
Cybernorth LLC	South Portland	ME	E	207 331-3310	5496
James W Sewall Company	Bangor	ME	E	207 817-5410	4506
James W Sewall Company **(PA)**	Old Town	ME	E	207 827-4456	5125
Kennebec River Biosciences Inc	Richmond	ME	F	207 737-2637	5322
Actio Software Corporation	Portsmouth	NH	D	603 433-2300	15356
Data Radio Management Co Inc	Merrimack	NH	G	603 598-1222	14979
DCI Training Inc	West Lebanon	NH	G	603 643-6066	15682
Entelligence Computer Svcs LLC	Salem	NH	G	603 893-4800	15520
Impact Science & Technology Inc	Nashua	NH	C	603 459-2200	15113
Ipura Consulting Group LLC	Hampton	NH	F	603 294-4002	14404
Lenric Corp	Nashua	NH	E	603 886-6772	15127
Northrop Grumman Systems Corp	Hudson	NH	E	603 886-4270	14532
Universal Envmtl Tech Inc	Nashua	NH	G	603 883-9312	15180
Hope & Main	Warren	RI	G	401 245-7400	16758
Nestor Traffic Systems Inc **(PA)**	Pawtucket	RI	E	401 714-7781	16391

89 SERVICES, NOT ELSEWHERE CLASSIFIED

8999 Services, nec

	CITY	ST	EMP	PHONE	ENTRY#
Coastline Environmental LLC	North Branford	CT	G	203 483-6898	2362
Computer Prgrm & Systems Inc **(PA)**	Stamford	CT	G	203 324-9203	3319
Connecticut Forest Pk Assn Inc	Rockfall	CT	F	860 346-2372	2913
John Canning & Co Ltd	Cheshire	CT	E	203 272-9868	602
Acacia Communications Inc **(HQ)**	Maynard	MA	C	978 938-4896	10259
Celebrations	Falmouth	MA	F	508 457-0530	8629
Chasm Advanced Materials Inc **(PA)**	Canton	MA	G	781 821-0443	7778
Hager Geoscience Inc	Woburn	MA	G	781 935-8111	13579
Kink Pieces of A Dream LLC	Framingham	MA	F	508 748-5417	8784
Michael Rogovsky	New Bedford	MA	F	508 487-3287	10622
Tomorrow Companies Inc	Boston	MA	G	800 735-7075	7080
Tr3 Solutions Inc	Stoneham	MA	F	781 481-0642	12187
Traincroft Inc **(PA)**	Medford	MA	E	781 393-6943	10299
United States Biological Corp	Salem	MA	F	978 744-0345	11737
Scribliotech Inc	Orange	NH	G	603 306-9000	15280
Buildinggreen Inc	Brattleboro	VT	E	802 257-7300	17076

91 EXECUTIVE, LEGISLATIVE & GENERAL GOVERNMENT, EXCEPT FINANCE

	CITY	ST	EMP	PHONE	ENTRY#
9199 General government, nec					
City of Boston	Boston	MA	C	617 635-3700	6657
Town of Westborough	Westborough	MA	E	508 366-7615	13140

92 JUSTICE, PUBLIC ORDER AND SAFETY

9223 Correctional institutions

	CITY	ST	EMP	PHONE	ENTRY#
Federal Prison Industries	Danbury	CT	E	203 743-6471	745

95 ADMINISTRATION OF ENVIRONMENTAL QUALITY AND HOUSING PROGRAMS

9511 Air, water, and solid waste management

	CITY	ST	EMP	PHONE	ENTRY#
Town of Billerica	Billerica	MA	F	978 671-0954	6488
City of Manchester	Manchester	NH	F	603 624-6482	14829

96 ADMINISTRATION OF ECONOMIC PROGRAMS

9621 Regulation, administration of transportation

	CITY	ST	EMP	PHONE	ENTRY#
Connecticut Department Trnsp	Portland	CT	G	860 342-5996	2818

97 NATIONAL SECURITY AND INTERNATIONAL AFFAIRS

9711 National security

	CITY	ST	EMP	PHONE	ENTRY#
United States Dept of Navy	Portsmouth	NH	C	207 438-2714	15446

SIC

National Gadget Mfg Co..216 999-7777
  853 Industrial Rd Cleveland, OH (44198) **(G-301801)** — *Geographic Section entry number where full company information appears*

National Glass Co 480 Lewis Lexington, KY (40505) **(G-20615)**........606 477-9000

National Group Mfg 920 247-4000
  1234 W Waldo Ave Green Bay, WI (54301) **(G-36751)**

Address, city & ZIP → National Gypsum Wall..773 490-8888 — *Business phone*
  65 S Rio Dr Chicago, IL (6060) **(G-18901)**

See footnotes for symbols and codes identification.
- Companies listed alphabetically.
- Complete physical or mailing address.

(Parent Is Oerlikon Usa Holding Inc, Trafford, Pa.), Shelton *Also Called: Oerlikon AM Medical Inc* **(G-3043)**

0 Mohawk LLC..203 622-7180
  97 Valley Rd Cos Cob (06807) **(G-673)**

101.7 FM, Providence *Also Called: Boston Phoenix Inc* **(G-16489)**

10beauty Inc..215 356-8680
  10 Ray Ave Burlington (01803) **(G-7329)**

116 Lenox Eo LLC......................................973 854-1999
  707 Summer St Fl 5 Stamford (06901) **(G-3265)**

128 Technology Inc **(PA)**............................**781 203-8400**
  10 Technology Dr Lowell (01851) **(G-9850)**

136 Express Printing Inc..............................401 253-0136
  380 Metacom Ave Bristol (02809) **(G-15751)**

136 Express Prtg & Copy Ctr, Bristol *Also Called: 136 Express Printing Inc* **(G-15751)**

16 Acres Optical, Springfield *Also Called: Chicopee Vision Center Inc* **(G-12083)**

16sur20 Management LLC...............................413 637-5061
  30 Kemble St Lenox (01240) **(G-9624)**

175 Pioneer Drive LLC................................978 840-1897
  175 Pioneer Dr Leominster (01453) **(G-9629)**

18th Century Woodworks...............................401 829-8760
  272 James Trl West Kingston (02892) **(G-16892)**

1st Casting Company..................................401 272-0750
  64 Dyerville Ave Johnston (02919) **(G-16071)**

2 Dogs Treats LLC....................................617 286-4844
  171 Neponset Ave Dorchester (02122) **(G-8295)**

20/20 Software Inc...................................203 316-5500
  2001 W Main St Ste 270 Stamford (06902) **(G-3266)**

2023 Holdings LLC **(PA)**............................**603 239-6371**
  1170 Main St Newington (06111) **(G-2263)**

2023 Holdings LLC....................................603 239-6371
  75 Plumb Pak Dr Winchester (03470) **(G-15713)**

21st, Marlborough *Also Called: Twentyfrst Cntury Bchmcals Inc* **(G-10225)**

21st Century Fox America Inc.........................203 563-6600
  20 Westport Rd Wilton (06897) **(G-4228)**

21st Century Software, Boston *Also Called: 21st Century Software Tech Inc* **(G-6499)**

21st Century Software Tech Inc.......................610 341-9017
  6 Liberty Sq Boston (02109) **(G-6499)**

24 Scitico LLC.......................................203 791-9055
  15 Whitney Rd Bethel (06801) **(G-98)**

24/7 LLC...203 410-5151
  107 Short Beach Rd Branford (06405) **(G-230)**

24m Technologies Inc **(PA)**.........................**617 553-1012**
  130 Brookline St Ste 200 Cambridge (02139) **(G-7461)**

2600 Albany Avenue LLC...............................336 632-0005
  1688 E Main St Torrington (06790) **(G-3665)**

261 Pascone Place LLC................................860 666-7845
  261 Pascone Pl Newington (06111) **(G-2264)**

270 University Avenue LLC............................781 407-0836
  270 University Ave Westwood (02090) **(G-13304)**

290 Industrial Stitching Inc........................978 355-0271
  49 Main St South Barre (01074) **(G-11914)**

295 Tremont Inc......................................508 222-2884
  711 Park St Attleboro (02703) **(G-5985)**

2is Inc..508 850-7520
  75 West St Walpole (02081) **(G-12545)**

2I Inc...978 567-8867
  4 Kane Industrial Dr Hudson (01749) **(G-9350)**

2seventy Bio Inc **(PA)**.............................**339 499-9300**
  60 Binney St Cambridge (02142) **(G-7462)**

3 Story Software LLC.................................860 799-6366
  63 Bridge St New Milford (06776) **(G-2236)**

3-D Matrix Inc **(HQ)**...............................**781 373-9020**
  1234 Chestnut St Ste 2 Newton (02464) **(G-10730)**

3-D Welding Inc......................................508 222-2500
  5 Howard Ireland Dr Attleboro (02703) **(G-5986)**

300 Wood Avenue LLC..................................763 479-6605
  45 Plane Tree Rd Stratford (06614) **(G-3514)**

32 North Corporation.................................207 284-5010
  16 Pomerleau St Biddeford (04005) **(G-4553)**

320 Ink LLC..207 835-0038
  2 Karen Dr Westbrook (04092) **(G-5613)**

325 Silver Street Inc...............................413 789-1800
  325 Silver St Agawam (01001) **(G-5776)**

3333 LLC...860 643-1384
  42 Hilliard St Manchester (06042) **(G-1579)**

34 Tower Street Inc..................................978 425-2311
  76 Walker Rd Shirley (01464) **(G-11812)**

360alumni LLC..203 253-5860
  85 Ethan Allen Hwy Ridgefield (06877) **(G-2884)**

379 Charles RI Inc...................................401 521-1101
  862 Charles St Unit 1 North Providence (02904) **(G-16293)**

3d Diagnostix Inc....................................617 820-5279
  24 Denby Rd Allston (02134) **(G-5817)**

3d Logging Co Inc....................................603 915-3020
  302 Howard St Berlin (03570) **(G-13978)**

3d-Matrix, Cambridge *Also Called: 3dm Inc* **(G-7463)**

3ddx, Allston *Also Called: 3d Diagnostix Inc* **(G-5817)**

3deo Inc...781 999-3447
  106 Access Rd Ste 6 Norwood (02062) **(G-11151)**

3dfortify Inc..857 274-0483
  75 Hood Park Dr Fl 1 Boston (02129) **(G-6500)**

3dm Inc..617 875-6204
  245 1st St Cambridge (02142) **(G-7463)**

3eo Health Inc.......................................508 308-4805
  48 Dunham Rd Ste 4350 Beverly (01915) **(G-6321)**

3M, Meriden *Also Called: 3M Company* **(G-1647)**

3M, Stafford Springs *Also Called: 3M Purification Inc* **(G-3252)**

3M, Wallingford *Also Called: 3M Company* **(G-3766)**

3M, Chelmsford *Also Called: 3M Company* **(G-7901)**

3M, Rockland *Also Called: 3M Company* **(G-11632)**

3M, Tilton *Also Called: Innovative Paper Tech LLC* **(G-15653)**

3M Company... 203 237-5541
   400 Research Pkwy Meriden (06450) *(G-1647)*

3M Company... 203 949-1630
   100 Barnes Rd Wallingford (06492) *(G-3766)*

3M Company... 978 256-3911
   279 Billerica Rd Chelmsford (01824) *(G-7901)*

3M Company... 781 871-1400
   30 Commerce Rd Rockland (02370) *(G-11632)*

3M Purification Inc (HQ)...203 237-5541
   400 Research Pkwy Meriden (06450) *(G-1648)*

3M Purification Inc.. 860 684-8628
   32 River Rd Stafford Springs (06076) *(G-3252)*

3M Touch Systems Inc... 781 386-2770
   1 Upland Rd Norwood (02062) *(G-11152)*

3M Touch Systems Inc... 508 871-1840
   115 Flanders Rd Westborough (01581) *(G-13075)*

3rd Millennium Inc... 781 890-4440
   125 Cambridgepark Dr Ste 301 Cambridge (02140) *(G-7464)*

4 D Technology Corporation... 860 365-0420
   91 Daniel St East Hampton (06424) *(G-957)*

4 D TECHNOLOGY CORPORATION, East Hampton *Also Called: 4 D Technology Corporation*
(G-957)

42 Design Fab Studio Inc.. 413 203-4948
   34 Front St Indian Orchard (01151) *(G-9469)*

4382412 Canada Inc.. 802 225-5911
   44 Hull St Ste D Randolph (05060) *(G-17465)*

47 Brand LLC.. 617 437-1384
   19 Jersey St Boston (02215) *(G-6501)*

4smartpro LLC.. 802 745-8797
   599 Farmer Dr Saint Johnsbury (05819) *(G-17537)*

4tell Solutions LP... 207 828-7900
   124 Washington St Ste 101 Foxboro (02035) *(G-8688)*

4th Dimension Bioprocess Inc... 978 979-4222
   27 Rowley Shr Gloucester (01930) *(G-8916)*

5381 Partners LLC... 203 255-7985
   5381 Congress St Fairfield (06824) *(G-1174)*

59 Beecher Street LLC.. 631 734-6200
   59 Beecher St Southbridge (01550) *(G-12007)*

5n Plus, Bridgeport *Also Called: 5n Plus Wisconsin Inc (G-289)*

5n Plus Corp.. 608 846-1357
   380 Horace St Bridgeport (06610) *(G-288)*

5n Plus Wisconsin Inc.. 203 384-0331
   380a Horace St Bridgeport (06610) *(G-289)*

603 Brewery, Londonderry *Also Called: 603 Brewery LLC (G-14726)*

603 Brewery LLC.. 603 630-7745
   12 Liberty Dr Unit 7 Londonderry (03053) *(G-14726)*

603 Manufacturing LLC... 603 578-9876
   21 Park Ave Hudson (03051) *(G-14478)*

6k Energy LLC.. 978 258-1645
   25 Commerce Way Ste 6 North Andover (01845) *(G-10815)*

7 South Sandwich Company LLC...................................... 802 388-3354
   1396 Route 7 S Ste 4 Middlebury (05753) *(G-17334)*

73-75 Magazine Street LLC... 617 787-1913
   1125 Commonwealth Ave Allston (02134) *(G-5818)*

77 Mattatuck Heights LLC... 203 597-9338
   77 Mattatuck Heights Rd Waterbury (06705) *(G-3878)*

7ac Technologies Inc.. 781 574-1348
   100 Cummings Ctr Ste 265g Beverly (01915) *(G-6322)*

7th Settlement Brewery LLC.. 603 534-5292
   47 Washington St Dover (03820) *(G-14212)*

802 Print LLC... 802 598-0967
   61 Main St Vergennes (05491) *(G-17655)*

88 Acres Foods Inc.. 617 208-8651
   196 Quincy St Ste 5 Dorchester (02121) *(G-8296)*

89 North, Williston *Also Called: 89 North Inc (G-17719)*

89 North Inc.. 802 881-0302
   20 Winter Sport Ln Ste 135 Williston (05495) *(G-17719)*

90 River Street LLC.. 203 772-4700
   90 River St New Haven (06513) *(G-2109)*

943 Enteretainment Corp.. 617 608-6943
   21 Cypress St Somerville (02143) *(G-11858)*

99degrees Custom Inc... 978 655-3362
   360 Merrimack St Ste 132 Lawrence (01843) *(G-9533)*

A & A Industries Inc... 978 977-9660
   320 Jubilee Dr Peabody (01960) *(G-11292)*

A & A Wheeler Mfg Inc.. 603 659-4446
   300 Calef Hwy Lee (03861) *(G-14704)*

A & B Electronics Co, Berlin *Also Called: Maynesboro Industries Inc (G-13982)*

A & D Components Inc... 860 582-9541
   33 Stafford Ave Ste 2 Bristol (06010) *(G-389)*

A & D Metal Inc... 413 485-7505
   555 Southampton Rd Westfield (01085) *(G-13145)*

A & F Plating Co Inc... 401 861-3597
   45 River Ave Providence (02908) *(G-16462)*

A & G Centerless Grinding Inc.. 781 281-0007
   15 Linscott Rd Woburn (01801) *(G-13494)*

A & G Crane LLC.. 603 668-5844
   7 Craneway Hooksett (03106) *(G-14462)*

A & H Composition and Prtg Inc....................................... 401 438-1200
   5 Almeida Ave East Providence (02914) *(G-15999)*

A & H Duffy Polsg & Finshg Co.. 401 785-9203
   175 Dupont Dr Providence (02907) *(G-16463)*

A & H Mfg. Co., Johnston *Also Called: Amring Worldwide Inc (G-16075)*

A & H Tool Works LLC... 860 302-9284
   101 Rocky Rd E Harwinton (06791) *(G-1518)*

A & I Concentrate LLC... 203 447-1938
   2 Corporate Dr Ste 136 Shelton (06484) *(G-2977)*

A & M Donuts Inc... 603 536-7622
   384 Tenney Mountain Hwy Plymouth (03264) *(G-15354)*

A & M Tool & Die Company Inc... 508 764-3241
   64 Mill St Ste 1 Southbridge (01550) *(G-12008)*

A & R Sawyer Co Inc.. 603 893-5752
   67 Rockingham Rd Windham (03087) *(G-15719)*

A A A Metals Company Inc... 781 447-1220
   68 Industrial Blvd Ste 9 Hanson (02341) *(G-9049)*

A A S, Newington *Also Called: Advanced Adhesive Systems Inc (G-2267)*

A Aiudi & Sons LLC (PA)...860 747-5534
   190 Camp St Plainville (06062) *(G-2742)*

A B & F Sheet Metal.. 203 272-9340
   327 Sandbank Rd Cheshire (06410) *(G-566)*

A B & F Sheet Metal Pdts Inc... 203 272-9340
   327 Sandbank Rd Ste C3 Cheshire (06410) *(G-567)*

A B A Tool & Die Div, Manchester *Also Called: Aba-Pgt Inc (G-1580)*

A B B Power Transmission, Norwalk *Also Called: Asea Brown Boveri Inc (G-2465)*

A B C Glass & Mirror Works, Springfield *Also Called: A B C Glass Co Inc (G-12067)*

A B C Glass Co Inc... 413 734-4524
   722 Liberty St Springfield (01104) *(G-12067)*

A B C Printing & Mailing, East Haven *Also Called: ABC Printing Inc (G-1034)*

A B E Enterprises LLC... 781 271-0000
   4 Preston Ct Ste 200 Bedford (01730) *(G-6204)*

A B Engineering & Co.. 508 987-0318
   3 Old Cudworth Rd Oxford (01540) *(G-11247)*

A B Excavating Inc.. 603 788-5110
   653 Main St Lancaster (03584) *(G-14675)*

A B Group, Attleboro *Also Called: W E Richards Co Inc (G-6074)*

A B Munroe Dairy Inc (PA)..401 438-4450
   151 N Brow St East Providence (02914) *(G-16000)*

A Bismark Company... 508 675-2002
   5 Probber Ln Ste 1 Fall River (02720) *(G-8516)*

A C S, Stoughton *Also Called: Alpha Chemical Services Inc (G-12193)*

A C T, Greenland *Also Called: Advanced Concrete Tech Inc (G-14365)*

A C W, Woonsocket *Also Called: American Cord & Webbing Co Inc (G-16948)*

A D Grinding... 860 747-6630
   54 Lewis St Plainville (06062) *(G-2743)*

A D M, Portsmouth *Also Called: Advanced Design & Mfg Inc (G-15357)*

A D Perkins Company.. 203 777-3456
   43 Elm St New Haven (06510) *(G-2110)*

A D& D Wldg & Boiler Works Inc....................................... 401 732-5222
   33 Bleachery Ct Warwick (02886) *(G-16774)*

A Drop of Joy LLC... 802 598-6419
   166 Boyer Cir Williston (05495) *(G-17720)*

A E Staley Manufacturing Co.................... 207 532-9523
  48 Morningstar Rd Houlton (04730) *(G-4895)*

A F Amorello & Sons Inc.......................... 508 791-8778
  115 Sw Cutoff Ste 1 Worcester (01604) *(G-13694)*

A G C, Meriden *Also Called: A G C Incorporated (G-1649)*

A G C Incorporated................................ 203 235-3361
  106 Evansville Ave Meriden (06451) *(G-1649)*

A G I Automation, Trumbull *Also Called: American Grippers Inc (G-3710)*

A G Industries Inc................................ 508 695-4219
  75 Chestnut St North Attleboro (02760) *(G-10863)*

A G Miller Company Inc........................... 413 732-9297
  53 Batavia St Springfield (01109) *(G-12068)*

A Graziano Inc................................... 781 843-7300
  71 Adams St Braintree (02184) *(G-7166)*

A Group Inc...................................... 781 756-3163
  76 Holton St Woburn (01801) *(G-13495)*

A Guideposts Church Corp **(PA)**.............. **203 749-0203**
  100 Reserve Rd Ste E200 Danbury (06810) *(G-699)*

A Hardiman Machine Co Inc....................... 860 623-8133
  94 Newberry Rd East Windsor (06088) *(G-1063)*

A I C Inc **(PA)**............................. **978 352-4510**
  7 Martel Way Georgetown (01833) *(G-8904)*

A I S, Leominster *Also Called: Affordable Intr Systems Inc (G-9633)*

A I S, Leominster *Also Called: Ais Group Holdings LLC (G-9634)*

A J R Inc.. 203 384-0400
  67 Poland St Ste 4 Bridgeport (06605) *(G-290)*

A Johnson Co..................................... 802 453-4884
  106 Andrew Johnson Dr Bristol (05443) *(G-17112)*

A L Ellis Inc.................................... 508 672-4799
  113 Griffin St Ste 1 Fall River (02724) *(G-8517)*

A Luongo & Sons Incorporated.................... 508 226-0788
  160 Fireworks Cir Bridgewater (02324) *(G-7218)*

A Lyons & Company Inc........................... 978 526-4244
  40 Beach St Ste 105 Manchester (01944) *(G-10032)*

A M C Design and Manufacturing, Cranston *Also Called: Austrian Machine Corp (G-15835)*

A M C I, Greenwich *Also Called: American Metals Coal Intl Inc (G-1311)*

A M I, Mystic *Also Called: Aqua Massage International Inc (G-1936)*

A M I, Winthrop *Also Called: Alternative Manufacturing Inc (G-5690)*

A M T, Milton *Also Called: Advanced Machine and TI Co Inc (G-17353)*

A P C M G E, Foxboro *Also Called: Schneider Electric It Corp (G-8723)*

A P M, Leominster *Also Called: Advanced Prototypes & Molding (G-9632)*

A P M Sterngold, Attleboro *Also Called: Sterngold Dental LLC (G-6066)*

A Piece of Pzzle Bhvral Intrvn.................. 860 250-8054
  1100 New Britain Ave Ste 105 West Hartford (06110) *(G-4045)*

A Plus Exterior, Milford *Also Called: A Plus Exterior LLC (G-1792)*

A Plus Exterior LLC.............................. 203 516-1729
  215 Bridgeport Ave Milford (06460) *(G-1792)*

A S C Scientific, Narragansett *Also Called: Analytical Services Company (G-16186)*

A Schulman Custom Compounding Ne Inc............ 508 756-0002
  53 Millbrook St Ste 2 Worcester (01606) *(G-13695)*

A Silver Lining Inc............................. 207 633-4103
  17 Townsend Ave Boothbay Harbor (04538) *(G-4599)*

A T S, Windsor *Also Called: Accu-Time Systems Inc (G-4252)*

A To A Studio Solutions Ltd..................... 203 388-9050
  47 Euclid Ave Stamford (06902) *(G-3267)*

A To Z Foods Inc................................ 781 413-0221
  797 Massachusetts Ave Arlington (02476) *(G-5937)*

A Ttm Technologies Company...................... 603 870-4580
  27 Northwestern Dr Salem (03079) *(G-15501)*

A V I International Inc.......................... 860 482-8345
  3240 Winsted Rd Torrington (06790) *(G-3666)*

A V X, Biddeford *Also Called: Kyocera AVX Cmpnnts Bddford Co (G-4574)*

A View of Vermont LLC........................... 802 748-0880
  1632 Memorial Dr Saint Johnsbury (05819) *(G-17538)*

A W Chaffee...................................... 207 426-8588
  163 Hinckley Rd Clinton (04927) *(G-4697)*

A W Chesterton Company **(PA)**................ **781 438-7000**
  860 Salem St Groveland (01834) *(G-9012)*

A W Chesterton Company.......................... 781 438-7000
  860 Salem St Groveland (01834) *(G-9013)*

A W McMullen Co Inc............................. 508 583-2072
  12 Field St Brockton (02301) *(G-7251)*

A X M S Inc..................................... 203 263-5046
  27 Woodside Cir Woodbury (06798) *(G-4384)*

A Young Casting................................. 508 222-8188
  35 County St Attleboro (02703) *(G-5987)*

A-1 Chrome and Polishing Corp................... 860 666-4593
  125 Stamm Rd Newington (06111) *(G-2265)*

A-1 Heat Treating Inc........................... 914 220-2179
  22 Maple St Ansonia (06401) *(G-4)*

A-1 Machining Co LLC............................ 860 223-6420
  235 John Downey Dr New Britain (06051) *(G-1994)*

A-1 Machining Co., New Britain *Also Called: A-1 Machining Co LLC (G-1994)*

A-1 Stairs & Rails Llc.......................... 203 792-7367
  2 Mill Plain Rd Danbury (06811) *(G-700)*

A-1 Stairs By Wesconn Stairs, Danbury *Also Called: Wesconn Stairs Inc (G-836)*

A-T Surgical Mfg Co Inc......................... 413 532-4551
  115 Clemente St Holyoke (01040) *(G-9240)*

A.C., Beals *Also Called: Carver Shellfish Inc (G-4532)*

A.M.I. Contract Foodservice, Clinton *Also Called: American Marketing Intl LLC (G-635)*

A&G Vineyard Inc................................ 508 226-4483
  1 North Ave Attleboro (02703) *(G-5988)*

A&M Design, North Providence *Also Called: Aro-Sac Inc (G-16297)*

A&P Coat Apron & Linen Sup LLC.................. 914 840-3200
  420 Ledyard St Hartford (06114) *(G-1466)*

A&S Innersprings Usa LLC........................ 860 298-0401
  4 Market Cir Windsor (06095) *(G-4249)*

A1 Beyond Video Services, Boston *Also Called: Spinnakervideo Inc (G-7054)*

A1 Pallets Inc.................................. 978 838-2720
  163 River Rd W Berlin (01503) *(G-6318)*

A1 Screw Machine Products Inc................... 413 594-8939
  717 Fuller Rd Chicopee (01020) *(G-8004)*

A123 Systems Inc................................ 617 972-3400
  1 Kingsbury Ave Watertown (02472) *(G-12854)*

A123 Systems LLC................................ 508 497-7200
  10 Avenue E Hopkinton (01748) *(G-9304)*

A123 Systems LLC................................ 617 778-5700
  200 West St Waltham (02451) *(G-12580)*

A2b Tracking Solutions Inc...................... 401 683-5215
  207 Highpoint Ave Ste 7 Portsmouth (02871) *(G-16434)*

AA Pharmaceuticals Inc.......................... 617 935-1241
  470 Wildwood Ave Ste 3 Woburn (01801) *(G-13496)*

Aa Thrifty Sign & Awning, Warwick *Also Called: Anchors Aweigh Together LLC (G-16779)*

AA White Company............................... 508 779-0821
  867 Quaker Hwy Unit A Uxbridge (01569) *(G-12476)*

Aacc, Lawrence *Also Called: American Adhesive Coatings LLC (G-9536)*

Aadco Medical Inc............................... 802 728-3400
  2279 Vt Route 66 Randolph (05060) *(G-17466)*

Aak Power Supply Corporation.................... 603 382-2222
  73 Newton Rd Ste 103 Pmb 2 Plaistow (03865) *(G-15335)*

Aalberts Surface Technologies, Woonsocket *Also Called: Impreglon Inc (G-16965)*

AAm Inc.. 781 330-9857
  839 Boston Post Rd Weston (02493) *(G-13284)*

AAR Defense Systems Logistics, Windsor *Also Called: AAR Government Services Inc (G-4250)*

AAR Government Services Inc..................... 860 298-0144
  754 Rainbow Rd Ste C Windsor (06095) *(G-4250)*

Aardvark Polymers............................... 609 483-1013
  73 Underwood Rd Ste 13 Woodstock (06281) *(G-4390)*

Aargo Environmental Inc......................... 401 678-6444
  35 Beechwood Hill Trl Exeter (02822) *(G-16050)*

Aargo Environmental Inc......................... 401 267-0077
  376 Dry Bridge Rd Ste A2 North Kingstown (02852) *(G-16228)*

Aaron, Leominster *Also Called: Aaron Industries Corp (G-9630)*

Aaron Industries Corp........................... 978 534-6135
  20 Mohawk Dr Ste 1 Leominster (01453) *(G-9630)*

Aaron Morin.................................... 413 247-0550
  140 West St West Hatfield (01088) *(G-13003)*

Aavid Corporation.............................. 603 528-3400
  1 Aavid Cir Laconia (03246) *(G-14638)*

Aavid Laboratories Inc......................... 603 528-3400
  1 Aavid Cir Laconia (03246) *(G-14639)*

A L P H A B E T I C

Aavid Thermal Div Boyd Corp, Laconia *Also Called: Aavid Laboratories Inc (G-14639)*

AB Electronics LLC... 203 740-2793
　61 Commerce Dr Brookfield (06804) *(G-509)*

AB Engineering & Company, Oxford *Also Called: A B Engineering & Co (G-11247)*

AB Group Inc.. 508 222-1404
　40 John Williams St Attleboro (02703) *(G-5989)*

AB Ovo North America Inc....................................... 617 718-0765
　285 Washington St Ste 101 Somerville (02143) *(G-11859)*

AB Sciex, Framingham *Also Called: AB Sciex Sales LP (G-8739)*

AB Sciex Sales LP.. 508 383-7700
　500 Old Connecticut Path Bldg B Framingham (01701) *(G-8739)*

Ab-Wey Machine & Die Co Inc................................... 781 294-8031
　51 School St Pembroke (02359) *(G-11356)*

AB&f Sheet Metal Products, Cheshire *Also Called: A B & F Sheet Metal (G-566)*

Aba-Pgt Inc **(PA)**... **860 649-4591**
　10 Gear Dr Manchester (06042) *(G-1580)*

Abaco Systems Technology Corp................................. 256 382-8115
　50 Fordham Rd Wilmington (01887) *(G-13369)*

Abacus Automation Inc... 802 442-3662
　264 Shields Dr Bennington (05201) *(G-17035)*

Abacus Labs Inc... 917 426-6642
　320 Cumberland Ave Portland (04101) *(G-5174)*

Abar Color Labs Neng Inc...................................... 401 351-8644
　9 Powder Hill Rd Lincoln (02865) *(G-16114)*

Abas Accessories, Worcester *Also Called: Valkyrie Company Inc (G-13819)*

ABB Enterprise Software Inc.................................... 860 747-7111
　41 Woodford Ave Plainville (06062) *(G-2744)*

ABB Enterprise Software Inc.................................... 203 329-8771
　900 Long Ridge Rd Stamford (06902) *(G-3268)*

ABB Enterprise Software Inc.................................... 617 574-1130
　2 Oliver St Boston (02109) *(G-6502)*

ABB ENTERPRISE SOFTWARE INC., Stamford *Also Called: ABB Enterprise Software Inc (G-3268)*

ABB ENTERPRISE SOFTWARE INC., Boston *Also Called: ABB Enterprise Software Inc (G-6502)*

ABB Finance (usa) Inc... 919 856-2360
　501 Merritt 7 Norwalk (06851) *(G-2458)*

ABB Inc... 203 790-8588
　24 Commerce Dr Danbury (06810) *(G-701)*

ABB Inc... 203 798-6210
　152 Deer Hill Ave Ste 304 Danbury (06810) *(G-702)*

ABB Inc... 860 285-0183
　5 Waterside Xing Ste 204a Windsor (06095) *(G-4251)*

Abba Fuels Inc.. 802 878-8095
　1018 Vt Route 15 Underhill (05489) *(G-17654)*

Abbess Instrs & Systems Inc................................... 508 429-0002
　75 October Hill Rd Holliston (01746) *(G-9197)*

Abbess Instruments, Holliston *Also Called: Abbess Instrs & Systems Inc (G-9197)*

Abbott.. 978 387-5652
　168 Middlesex Tpke Burlington (01803) *(G-7330)*

Abbott Associates Inc... 203 878-2370
　261a Pepes Farm Rd Milford (06460) *(G-1793)*

Abbott Ball Company... 860 236-5901
　19 Railroad Pl West Hartford (06110) *(G-4046)*

Abbott Diagnostics.. 860 463-0767
　178 Old Cider Mill Rd Southington (06489) *(G-3200)*

Abbott Laboratories... 508 849-2500
　100 Research Dr Worcester (01605) *(G-13696)*

Abbott Manufacturing, West Hartford *Also Called: Lewtan Industries Corporation (G-4068)*

Abbott-Action Inc **(PA)**.................................... **401 722-2100**
　3 Venus Way Attleboro (02703) *(G-5990)*

Abbott-Action Inc... 781 702-5710
　10 Campanelli Cir Canton (02021) *(G-7765)*

ABC Imaging, Boston *Also Called: Washington ABC Imaging Inc (G-7114)*

ABC Printing Inc.. 203 468-1245
　875 Foxon Rd East Haven (06513) *(G-1034)*

ABC Sign Corporation.. 203 513-8110
　125 Front St Bridgeport (06606) *(G-291)*

Abco Tool & Die Inc... 508 771-3225
　11 Thornton Dr Hyannis (02601) *(G-9428)*

Abcorp NA Inc... 617 325-9600
　225 Rivermoor St Boston (02132) *(G-6503)*

Abcrosby & Company Inc.. 978 827-6064
　20 S Maple Ave Ashburnham (01430) *(G-5951)*

Abek LLC.. 860 314-3905
　492 Birch St Bristol (06010) *(G-390)*

Abfero Pharmaceuticals Inc **(PA)**........................... **781 266-7297**
　867 Boylston St Fl 5 Boston (02116) *(G-6504)*

Abiomed, Danvers *Also Called: Abiomed Inc (G-8157)*

Abiomed Inc **(HQ)**.. **978 646-1400**
　22 Cherry Hill Dr Danvers (01923) *(G-8157)*

Abiomed Cardiovascular Inc.................................... 978 777-5410
　22 Cherry Hill Dr Danvers (01923) *(G-8158)*

Abiomed R&D Inc **(DH)**...................................... **978 646-1400**
　22 Cherry Hill Dr Danvers (01923) *(G-8159)*

Abisee Inc.. 978 637-2900
　30 Sudbury Rd Ste 1b Acton (01720) *(G-5730)*

Able Coil and Electronics Co.................................. 860 646-5686
　25 Howard Rd Bolton (06043) *(G-218)*

Able Machine Tool... 203 272-5459
　110 Hitchcock Ct Cheshire (06410) *(G-568)*

Able Software Corp **(PA)**................................... **781 862-2804**
　5 Appletree Ln Lexington (02420) *(G-9719)*

Abp Corporation **(PA)**...................................... **617 423-0629**
　19 Fid Kennedy Ave Boston (02210) *(G-6505)*

Abpro, Woburn *Also Called: Abpro Corporation (G-13497)*

Abpro Corporation... 617 225-0808
　68 Cummings Park Woburn (01801) *(G-13497)*

Abrasives & Tools NH Inc...................................... 603 224-5376
　49 Sheep Davis Rd Pembroke (03275) *(G-15301)*

Abry Partners V L P... 617 859-2959
　111 Huntington Ave Fl 30 Boston (02199) *(G-6506)*

ABS, Chelmsford *Also Called: American Business Systems Inc (G-7905)*

ABS Printing Inc.. 401 826-0870
　837 Pearse Rd Swansea (02777) *(G-12302)*

ABS Pumps, Meriden *Also Called: Megadoor USA Inc (G-1673)*

Absolute Marble & Granite, Canton *Also Called: Vanity World Inc (G-7839)*

Absolute Metal Finishing Inc.................................. 781 551-8235
　90 Morse St Norwood (02062) *(G-11153)*

Absolute Sheet Metal.. 978 667-0236
　559 Boston Rd Billerica (01821) *(G-6395)*

Absorbent Specialty Pdts LLC.................................. 401 722-1177
　30 Hamlet St Pawtucket (02861) *(G-16342)*

Abstract Tool Inc... 860 526-4635
　500 Main St Ste 15 Deep River (06417) *(G-872)*

Abtech Inc.. 603 585-7106
　126 Rte 12 N Fitzwilliam (03447) *(G-14312)*

Abyrx Inc... 855 475-9175
　700 Fairfield Ave Ste 1 Stamford (06902) *(G-3269)*

AC, Auburn *Also Called: AC Electric Corp (G-4416)*

AC Electric, Bangor *Also Called: AC Electric Corp (G-4487)*

AC Electric Corp **(PA)**..................................... **207 784-7341**
　120 Merrow Rd Auburn (04210) *(G-4416)*

AC Electric Corp.. 207 945-9487
　40 Target Cir Bangor (04401) *(G-4487)*

Ac/DC Industrial Electric LLC................................. 860 886-2232
　16b Stockhouse Rd Bozrah (06334) *(G-225)*

Acacia, Maynard *Also Called: Acacia Communications Inc (G-10259)*

Acacia Communications Inc **(HQ)**............................ **978 938-4896**
　3 Mill And Main Pl Ste 400 Maynard (01754) *(G-10259)*

Acadia Leather, Hartland *Also Called: Tasman Leather Group LLC (G-4879)*

Acana Northeast Inc... 800 922-2629
　360 Commerce Way Unit 3 Pembroke (03275) *(G-15302)*

Acara Holdings LLC.. 603 434-3175
　14 Lexington Dr Ste 2 Laconia (03246) *(G-14640)*

Acbel (usa) Polytech Inc...................................... 508 625-1768
　227 South St Hopkinton (01748) *(G-9305)*

ACC, East Falmouth *Also Called: Associates of Cape Cod Inc (G-8355)*

Accel International, Meriden *Also Called: Accel Intl Holdings Inc (G-1650)*

Accel Intl Holdings Inc....................................... 203 237-2700
　508 N Colony St Meriden (06450) *(G-1650)*

Accelenet By Itc A Div Viasat................................. 617 773-3369
　1250 Hancock St Ste 701n Quincy (02169) *(G-11500)*

Accelerated Media Tech Inc.. 508 459-0300
  19 Technology Dr Auburn (01501) *(G-6097)*

Accelerating Biologics, Burlington *Also Called: Protagene Us Inc (G-7414)*

Acceleron, Boston *Also Called: Acceleron Pharma Inc (G-6508)*

Acceleron Inc... 860 651-9333
  21 Lordship Rd Ste 1 East Granby (06026) *(G-924)*

Acceleron Holding Ltd... 617 649-9200
  33 Avenue Louis Pasteur Boston (02115) *(G-6507)*

Acceleron Pharma Inc **(HQ)**.................................... **617 649-9200**
  33 Avenue Louis Pasteur Boston (02115) *(G-6508)*

Acceleron Pharma Inc... 617 576-2220
  149 Sidney St Cambridge (02139) *(G-7465)*

Accelevents Inc.. 857 254-8035
  10 Post Office Sq Ste 800 Boston (02109) *(G-6509)*

Accellent Acquisition Corp.. 978 570-6900
  100 Fordham Rd Bldg C Wilmington (01887) *(G-13370)*

Accellent Endoscopy Inc.. 603 528-1211
  45 Lexington Dr Laconia (03246) *(G-14641)*

Accellent Holdings Corp.. 978 570-6900
  100 Fordham Rd Wilmington (01887) *(G-13371)*

Accellent Laconia, Laconia *Also Called: Lake Region Medical Inc (G-14656)*

Accellent LLC... 413 245-7144
  68 Mill Ln Brimfield (01010) *(G-7248)*

Accelrf Corporation... 978 391-4009
  94 Jackson Rd Devens (01434) *(G-8264)*

Accent Banner LLC.. 781 391-7300
  17 Locust St Medford (02155) *(G-10278)*

Accent Display, Lincoln *Also Called: Accent Display Corp (G-16115)*

Accent Display Corp.. 401 461-8787
  11 Dario Dr Lincoln (02865) *(G-16115)*

Accent On Industrial Metal Inc................................... 413 785-1654
  179 Page Blvd Springfield (01104) *(G-12069)*

Accent Plating Company Inc....................................... 401 722-6306
  25 Esten Ave Unit 5 Pawtucket (02860) *(G-16343)*

Access Advance LLC.. 617 367-4802
  100 Cambridge St Ste 21400 Boston (02114) *(G-6510)*

Accessories Assoc Inc... 401 231-3800
  500 Washington Hwy Smithfield (02917) *(G-16684)*

Accodale Technolgy Inc... 508 520-1400
  124 Grove St Franklin (02038) *(G-8813)*

Accordant Energy LLC... 802 772-7368
  225 S Main St Ste 2 Rutland (05701) *(G-17488)*

Accu Rx Inc... 401 454-2920
  100 Federal Way Johnston (02919) *(G-16072)*

Accu-Machining Corporation, Providence *Also Called: Roland and Whytock Company Inc
(G-16607)*

Accu-Rite Tool & Mfg Co.. 860 688-4844
  23 Industrial Park Rd W Ste A Tolland (06084) *(G-3654)*

Accu-Time Systems Inc **(DH)**................................. **860 870-5000**
  20 International Dr Windsor (06095) *(G-4252)*

Accucon Incorporated... 978 840-0337
  12 Mount Pleasant Ave Ste 100 Leominster (01453) *(G-9631)*

Accudynamics LLC.. 508 946-4545
  240 Kenneth Welch Dr Lakeville (02347) *(G-9515)*

Accufab Ironworks Inc.. 413 268-7133
  82 S Main St Goshen (01032) *(G-8966)*

Accufund Inc... 781 433-0233
  400 Hillside Ave Ste 5 Needham (02494) *(G-10502)*

Accumet Engineering Inc.. 978 692-6180
  41 Lake George St Devens (01434) *(G-8265)*

Accumet Engineering Corp... 978 568-8311
  41 Lake George St Devens (01434) *(G-8266)*

Accupaulo Holding Corporation **(PA)**...................... **860 666-5621**
  33 Stafford Ave Ste 5 Bristol (06010) *(G-391)*

Accuprobe, Salem *Also Called: Accuprobe Corporation (G-11699)*

Accuprobe Corporation.. 978 745-7878
  35 Congress St Ste 201 Salem (01970) *(G-11699)*

Accura Printing... 802 476-4429
  80 East Rd Barre (05641) *(G-16996)*

Accurate Brazing Corporation..................................... 860 432-1840
  4 Progress Dr Manchester (06042) *(G-1581)*

Accurate Brazing Corporation **(HQ)**........................ **603 945-3750**
  36 Cote Ave Ste 5 Goffstown (03045) *(G-14346)*

Accurate Burring Co LLC.. 860 747-8640
  161 Woodford Ave Ste 19 Plainville (06062) *(G-2745)*

Accurate Composites LLC.. 508 457-9097
  33 Technology Park Dr East Falmouth (02536) *(G-8353)*

Accurate Graphics Inc... 781 593-1630
  26 Alley St Lynn (01902) *(G-9961)*

Accurate Metal Finishing LLC................................... 781 963-7300
  414 South St Randolph (02368) *(G-11546)*

Accurate Molded Products Inc.................................... 401 739-2400
  459 Warwick Industrial Dr Warwick (02886) *(G-16775)*

Accurate Plastics, East Falmouth *Also Called: Accurate Composites LLC (G-8353)*

Accurate Plastics Inc.. 508 457-9097
  33 Technology Park Dr East Falmouth (02536) *(G-8354)*

Accurate Services, Fall River *Also Called: Accurate Services Inc (G-8518)*

Accurate Services Inc.. 508 674-5773
  951 Broadway Ste 4 Fall River (02724) *(G-8518)*

Accurate Threaded Products, Bristol *Also Called: Accupaulo Holding Corporation (G-391)*

Accurate Threaded Products Co, Bristol *Also Called: Ralph Industries Inc (G-490)*

Accurate Tool & Die Inc.. 203 967-1200
  16 Leon Pl Stamford (06902) *(G-3270)*

Accurate Welding Services LLC................................. 860 623-9500
  7 Industrial Rd Windsor Locks (06096) *(G-4317)*

Accurounds, Avon *Also Called: Boston Centerless Inc (G-6145)*

Accurounds Inc... 508 587-3500
  15 Doherty Ave Avon (02322) *(G-6140)*

Accusemble Electronics Inc **(PA)**.......................... **508 254-4538**
  5 Esquire Rd North Billerica (01862) *(G-10893)*

Accusonic Technologies **(DH)**................................ **508 495-6600**
  259 Samuel Barnet Blvd Unit 1 New Bedford (02745) *(G-10560)*

Accustandard Inc.. 203 786-5290
  125 Market St New Haven (06513) *(G-2111)*

Accutech, Foxboro *Also Called: Accutech Packaging Inc (G-8689)*

Accutech Machine Inc.. 978 922-7271
  370 Andover St Danvers (01923) *(G-8160)*

Accutech Marine Propeller Inc.................................... 603 617-3626
  24 Crosby Rd Ste 6 Dover (03820) *(G-14213)*

Accutech Packaging Inc... 508 543-3800
  157 Green St Foxboro (02035) *(G-8689)*

Accutech Packaging Inc... 508 543-3800
  71 Hampden Rd Mansfield (02048) *(G-10035)*

Accutrol LLC.. 203 445-9991
  21 Commerce Dr Danbury (06810) *(G-703)*

Accutron Inc **(PA)**.. **860 683-8300**
  149 Addison Rd Windsor (06095) *(G-4253)*

Accutronics, Chelmsford *Also Called: Zorean Inc (G-7973)*

Accuturn Manufacturing Co LLC.................................. 860 289-6355
  100 Commerce Way South Windsor (06074) *(G-3106)*

Ace Castings, Colchester *Also Called: PBL Incorporated (G-17199)*

Ace Energy LLC... 860 623-3308
  152 Broad Brook Rd Broad Brook (06016) *(G-507)*

Ace Hardware, Thomaston *Also Called: Chapman Lumber Inc (G-3616)*

Ace Hardware, Brockton *Also Called: Irvings Home Center Inc (G-7285)*

Ace Hardware, Berlin *Also Called: White Mountain Lumber Co Inc (G-13987)*

Ace Machine Inc.. 603 329-6716
  563 Rte 111 East Hampstead (03826) *(G-14269)*

Ace Metal Finishing, Lawrence *Also Called: Ace Metal Finishing Inc (G-9534)*

Ace Metal Finishing, Lawrence *Also Called: CIL Electroplating Inc (G-9548)*

Ace Metal Finishing Inc... 978 683-2082
  125 Glenn St Lawrence (01843) *(G-9534)*

Ace Precision Inc... 413 789-7536
  1123 Suffield St Agawam (01001) *(G-5777)*

Ace Residential Solar LLC.. 800 223-1462
  16 High St North Andover (01845) *(G-10816)*

Ace Signs Inc... 413 739-3814
  477 Cottage St Springfield (01104) *(G-12070)*

Ace Solar, North Andover *Also Called: Ace Residential Solar LLC (G-10816)*

Ace Torwel, Bellingham *Also Called: Hilliard Precision Products LLC (G-6292)*

Ace Welding Co Inc.. 603 424-9936
  715a Daniel Webster Hwy Merrimack (03054) *(G-14971)*

A
L
P
H
A
B
E
T
I
C

Ace-Lon Corporation................................ 781 322-7121
   960 Eastern Ave Malden (02148) *(G-10000)*

Aceinna Inc.. 978 965-3200
   3 Highwood Dr Ste 101w Tewksbury (01876) *(G-12383)*

Acentech Incorporated **(PA)**...................... **617 499-8000**
   33 Moulton St Cambridge (02138) *(G-7466)*

Acer Holdings Starksboro Inc........................ 802 453-4438
   22 Varney Hill Rd Starksboro (05487) *(G-17625)*

Aci - Pcb Inc.. 603 528-7711
   254 Court St Ste A Laconia (03246) *(G-14642)*

Aci Industries Converting Ltd....................... 740 368-4166
   1266 E Main St Ste 700r Stamford (06902) *(G-3271)*

Acitronics, Branford *Also Called: Schmitt Realty Holdings Inc* **(G-275)**

Ackles Steel and Iron Co Inc........................ 781 893-6818
   12 Sun St Waltham (02453) *(G-12581)*

Acktify Inc.. 781 462-3942
   142 Franklin St Melrose (02176) *(G-10312)*

Aclara Software Inc.................................. 781 283-9160
   16 Laurel Ave Ste 100 Wellesley (02481) *(G-12933)*

Aclara Technologies LLC............................. 603 749-8376
   130 Main St Somersworth (03878) *(G-15608)*

Acme Apparel, Gloucester *Also Called: Acme Merchandise and AP Inc* **(G-8917)**

Acme Bookbinding, Billerica *Also Called: Acme Bookbinding Company Inc* **(G-6396)**

Acme Bookbinding Company, Billerica *Also Called: Hf Group LLC* **(G-6449)**

Acme Bookbinding Company Inc....................... 617 242-1100
   27 Woodcliff Dr Billerica (01821) *(G-6396)*

Acme Merchandise and AP Inc........................ 978 282-4800
   46 Blackburn Ctr Ste 47 Gloucester (01930) *(G-8917)*

Acme Monaco Corporation **(PA)**.................... **860 224-1349**
   75 Winchell Rd New Britain (06052) *(G-1995)*

Acme Packet Inc..................................... 781 328-4400
   100 Crosby Dr Bedford (01730) *(G-6205)*

Acme Precast Co Inc................................. 508 548-9607
   509 Thomas B Landers Rd West Falmouth (02574) *(G-13000)*

Acme Printing, Canton *Also Called: Universal Wilde Inc* **(G-7838)**

Acme Sign Co **(PA)**................................ **203 324-2263**
   12 Research Dr Stamford (06906) *(G-3272)*

Acme Staple Company Inc............................ 603 934-2320
   87 Hill Rd Franklin (03235) *(G-14318)*

Acme United Corporation **(PA)**.................... **203 254-6060**
   1 Waterview Dr Ste 200 Shelton (06484) *(G-2978)*

Acme Wire Products Co Inc........................... 860 572-0511
   7 Broadway Avenue Ext Mystic (06355) *(G-1935)*

Acme-Shorey Precast Co Inc......................... 508 548-9607
   334 Tremont St Carver (02330) *(G-7852)*

Acme-Shorey Precast Co Inc **(PA)**................ **508 432-0530**
   36 Great Western Rd Harwich (02645) *(G-9066)*

Acme-Shorey Precast Co Inc......................... 508 430-0956
   351 Whites Path South Yarmouth (02664) *(G-11980)*

Acmt Inc.. 860 645-0592
   369 Progress Dr Manchester (06042) *(G-1582)*

Acorda Therapeutics, Chelsea *Also Called: Civitas Therapeutics Inc* **(G-7978)**

Acorn Manufacturing Co Inc.......................... 508 339-4500
   457 School St Mansfield (02048) *(G-10036)*

Acp Waterjet Inc.................................... 800 951-5127
   170 Ayer Rd Littleton (01460) *(G-9799)*

Acquia Inc **(PA)**................................. **888 922-7842**
   53 State St Ste 1101 Boston (02109) *(G-6511)*

Acra-Cut, Acton *Also Called: Intech Inc* **(G-5756)**

Acro-Matic Plastics, Leominster *Also Called: Ocean and Common Inc* **(G-9689)**

Acronis Inc... 781 782-9100
   1 Van De Graaff Dr Ste 301 Burlington (01803) *(G-7331)*

ACS, Bedford *Also Called: Deborah Frost* **(G-13924)**

ACS Division Biochemical Tech....................... 617 216-6144
   42 Chauncy St Ste 10a Boston (02111) *(G-6512)*

ACS Group Inc....................................... 617 381-0822
   27 Carter St Everett (02149) *(G-8481)*

ACS Industries, Lincoln *Also Called: ACS Industries Inc* **(G-16116)**

ACS Industries Inc **(PA)**........................ **401 769-4700**
   1 New England Way Unit 1 Lincoln (02865) *(G-16116)*

Acson Tool Company................................. 203 334-8050
   62 Carroll Ave Bridgeport (06607) *(G-292)*

Act Manufacturing Securities C..................... 508 481-5246
   124 Washington St Ste 101 Foxboro (02035) *(G-8690)*

Act Robots Inc...................................... 860 314-1557
   95 Wooster Ct Bristol (06010) *(G-392)*

Acti, Waltham *Also Called: Alkermes Cntrlled Therapeutics* **(G-12590)**

Actifio Federal Inc................................. 781 795-9182
   105 Cabot St Ste 301e Needham (02494) *(G-10503)*

Actio, Portsmouth *Also Called: Actio Software Corporation* **(G-15356)**

Actio Software Corporation.......................... 603 433-2300
   1 Nh Ave Ste 207 Portsmouth (03801) *(G-15356)*

Action Apparel Inc.................................. 781 435-2342
   100a Maple St Stoneham (02180) *(G-12173)*

Action Container, Attleboro *Also Called: Abbott-Action Inc* **(G-5990)**

Action Conveyor Tech Inc............................ 401 722-2300
   90 Douglas Pike Smithfield (02917) *(G-16685)*

Action Letter Inc **(PA)**.......................... **203 323-2466**
   11 Elm Ct Stamford (06902) *(G-3273)*

Action Screen Printing.............................. 207 795-7786
   41 Chestnut St Ste 5 Lewiston (04240) *(G-4949)*

Action Steel LLC.................................... 860 537-9499
   34 Oconnell Road Ext Colchester (06415) *(G-653)*

Action Systems Company Div, Meriden *Also Called: Action-Dctgraph Tlecomuncation* **(G-1651)**

Action Unlimited Newspaper, Concord *Also Called: Doncar Inc* **(G-8115)**

Action-Dctgraph Tlecomuncation...................... 203 238-2326
   55 Colony St Meriden (06451) *(G-1651)*

Activ Surgical Inc.................................. 202 688-5648
   30 Thomson Pl Boston (02210) *(G-6513)*

Active Internet Tech LLC **(PA)**................... **800 592-2469**
   655 Winding Brook Dr Ste 10 Glastonbury (06033) *(G-1269)*

Actnano, Cambridge *Also Called: Actnano Inc* **(G-7467)**

Actnano Inc **(PA)**................................ **857 333-8631**
   85 Bolton St Ste 105 Cambridge (02140) *(G-7467)*

Acton Metal Processing Corp......................... 781 893-5890
   41 Athletic Field Rd Waltham (02451) *(G-12582)*

Acton Research Corporation.......................... 941 556-2601
   15 Discovery Way Acton (01720) *(G-5731)*

Acton Woodworks.................................... 978 263-0222
   2 School St Acton (01720) *(G-5732)*

Actronics Incorporated.............................. 781 890-7030
   166 Bear Hill Rd Waltham (02451) *(G-12583)*

Actuality Systems Inc............................... 617 325-9230
   1337 Massachusetts Ave Arlington (02476) *(G-5938)*

Actuarial Bookstore, Greenland *Also Called: Archimedia Advantage Inc* **(G-14366)**

Actuaries Division, Stamford *Also Called: Computer Prgrm & Systems Inc* **(G-3319)**

Acuant Inc.. 603 641-8443
   200 Perimeter Rd Manchester (03103) *(G-14804)*

Acucut Inc.. 860 793-7012
   200 Town Line Rd Southington (06489) *(G-3201)*

Acumentrics Rups LLC................................ 617 932-7877
   10 Walpole Park S Walpole (02081) *(G-12546)*

Acuren Inspection Inc **(HQ)**...................... **203 702-8740**
   30 Main St Ste 402 Danbury (06810) *(G-704)*

Acuren Inspection Inc............................... 203 869-6734
   43 Arch St Greenwich (06830) *(G-1310)*

Acushnet, Fairhaven *Also Called: Acushnet Holdings Corp* **(G-8505)**

Acushnet Company................................... 508 979-2000
   4 Slocum St Acushnet (02743) *(G-5769)*

Acushnet Company................................... 508 979-2309
   144 Field St Brockton (02302) *(G-7252)*

Acushnet Company **(DH)**........................... **508 979-2000**
   333 Bridge St Fairhaven (02719) *(G-8504)*

Acushnet Company................................... 508 979-2156
   256 Samuel Barnet Blvd New Bedford (02745) *(G-10561)*

Acushnet Company................................... 508 979-2000
   215 Duchaine Blvd New Bedford (02745) *(G-10562)*

Acushnet Company................................... 508 979-2000
   700 Belleville Ave New Bedford (02745) *(G-10563)*

Acushnet Holdings Corp **(HQ)**..................... **800 225-8500**
   333 Bridge St Fairhaven (02719) *(G-8505)*

Acushnet International Inc **(DH)** 508 979-2000
333 Bridge St Fairhaven (02719) **(G-8506)**

Acushnet Rubber Company Inc 508 998-4000
744 Belleville Ave New Bedford (02745) **(G-10564)**

Acute Care Gases of Ct LLC 855 399-1224
23 Nutmeg Valley Rd Wolcott (06716) **(G-4360)**

Acutek, Windsor *Also Called: Acutek Adhesive Specialties* **(G-4254)**

Acutek Adhesive Specialties 310 419-0190
111 Great Pond Dr Windsor (06095) **(G-4254)**

Acw Plastic Products Inc 603 227-9540
38 Henniker St Concord (03301) **(G-14112)**

Ad-A-Day Company Inc 508 824-8676
245 W Water St Taunton (02780) **(G-12315)**

Ad-Tech, Hampton *Also Called: Adhesive Technologies Inc* **(G-14396)**

Ada Fabricators Inc 978 262-9900
323 Andover St Ste 3 Wilmington (01887) **(G-13372)**

Adam Z Golas **(PA)** 860 224-7178
99 John Downey Dr New Britain (06051) **(G-1996)**

Adamczyk Enterprises Inc 860 745-9830
3 Palomba Dr Enfield (06082) **(G-1120)**

Adams Ahern Sign Solutions 860 523-8835
120 Vanderbilt Ave West Hartford (06110) **(G-4047)**

Adams Granite Co Inc 802 476-5281
58 Pitman Rd Websterville (05678) **(G-17683)**

Adamsahern Sign Solutions Inc 860 523-8835
30 Arbor St Hartford (06106) **(G-1467)**

Adaptas Solutions LLC **(PA)** 413 284-9975
9 2nd St Palmer (01069) **(G-11269)**

Adaptive Networks Inc 781 444-4170
123 Highland Ave Needham (02494) **(G-10504)**

Adaptive Optics Associates Inc 860 282-4401
121 Prestige Park Cir East Hartford (06108) **(G-969)**

Adaptive Optics Associates Inc 978 391-0000
53 Jackson Rd Devens (01434) **(G-8267)**

Adaptive Optics Associates Inc 978 757-9600
115 Jackson Rd Devens (01434) **(G-8268)**

Adaptive Optics Associates Inc **(DH)** 978 757-9600
115 Jackson Rd Devens (01434) **(G-8269)**

Adaptive Surface Tech Inc 617 360-7080
106 South St # 2 Hopkinton (01748) **(G-9306)**

Adaptive Wreless Solutions LLC 978 875-6000
577 Main St Ste 300 Hudson (01749) **(G-9351)**

Adax Machine Co Inc 603 598-6777
5 Flagstone Dr Hudson (03051) **(G-14479)**

Adcole LLC **(PA)** 508 485-9100
669 Forest St Marlborough (01752) **(G-10103)**

Adcotron Ems Inc 617 598-3000
12 Channel St Marine Industrial Park Boston (02210) **(G-6514)**

Addamo Manufacturing Inc 860 667-2601
360 Stamm Rd Newington (06111) **(G-2266)**

Adden Furniture Inc 978 454-7848
444 Washington St Ste 206 Woburn (01801) **(G-13498)**

Addison Independent, Middlebury *Also Called: Addison Press Inc* **(G-17335)**

Addison Press Inc 802 388-4944
58 Maple St Middlebury (05753) **(G-17335)**

Addison-Wesley 617 848-6300
501 Boylston St Ste 900 Boston (02116) **(G-6515)**

Addivant, Danbury *Also Called: Si Group USA Hldings Usha Corp* **(G-816)**

Ade Technologies Inc **(HQ)** 781 467-3500
80 Wilson Way Westwood (02090) **(G-13305)**

Adelman Sand & Gravel Inc 860 889-3394
34 Bozrah St Bozrah (06334) **(G-226)**

Adeza Biomedical Corp 508 263-8390
250 Campus Dr Marlborough (01752) **(G-10104)**

Adhesive Applications Inc **(PA)** 413 527-7120
41 Oneil St Easthampton (01027) **(G-8437)**

Adhesive Engineering & Supply 603 895-4028
15 Batchelder Rd Seabrook (03874) **(G-15582)**

Adhesive Tapes Intl Inc 203 792-8279
41 Oneil St Easthampton (01027) **(G-8438)**

Adhesive Technologies Inc **(PA)** 603 926-1616
3 Merrill Industrial Dr Hampton (03842) **(G-14396)**

Adhesives Prepregs, Plainfield *Also Called: Apcm Manufacturing LLC* **(G-2731)**

ADI, Wilmington *Also Called: Analog Devices Inc* **(G-13379)**

Adicet Bio Inc **(PA)** 857 315-5528
500 Boylston St Ste 1300 Boston (02116) **(G-6516)**

Adina Inc **(PA)** 781 762-4477
90 Kerry Pl Ste 5 Norwood (02062) **(G-11154)**

Adirondack Beverages Corp 800 734-9800
1001 Southbridge St Worcester (01610) **(G-13697)**

Adjective Art & Framing Inc 617 281-4661
471 Page St Ste 5 Stoughton (02072) **(G-12190)**

Adkins, New Britain *Also Called: Adkins Printing Company* **(G-1997)**

Adkins Printing Company 800 228-9745
40 South St Ste 2 New Britain (06051) **(G-1997)**

Adlife, Walpole *Also Called: Adlife Advertising & Graphics* **(G-12547)**

Adlife Advertising & Graphics 508 668-4109
470 High Plain St Walpole (02081) **(G-12547)**

ADM Group LLC 860 354-3208
18 Round Table Rd New Milford (06776) **(G-2237)**

Admet Inc 781 769-0850
51 Morgan Dr Norwood (02062) **(G-11155)**

Admill Machine Co LLC 860 356-0330
150 John Downey Dr New Britain (06051) **(G-1998)**

Administrative Professionals, Portland *Also Called: Journal Publishing Company* **(G-5229)**

Admiral Packaging Inc 401 274-5588
10 Admiral St Providence (02908) **(G-16464)**

Admiral Packaging Co., Providence *Also Called: Admiral Packaging Inc* **(G-16464)**

Admix Inc 603 627-2340
144 Harvey Rd Londonderry (03053) **(G-14727)**

Adnexus Therapeutics Inc 781 891-3745
100 Beaver St Waltham (02453) **(G-12584)**

Adobe Inc 617 467-6760
275 Washington St Ste 305 Newton (02458) **(G-10731)**

Adobe Inc 408 536-6000
1075 Main St Waltham (02451) **(G-12585)**

Adolf Jandris & Sons Inc 978 632-0089
202 High St Gardner (01440) **(G-8878)**

Adolf Meller Company **(PA)** 800 821-0180
120 Corliss St Providence (02904) **(G-16465)**

Adolor Corporation 781 860-8660
65 Hayden Ave Lexington (02421) **(G-9720)**

ADP Rivet, North Haven *Also Called: Manchester TI & Design ADP LLC* **(G-2422)**

Adt/Diversity Inc 508 222-9601
50 Perry Ave Attleboro (02703) **(G-5991)**

Adtran Networks North Amer Inc 978 674-6800
300 Apollo Dr Chelmsford (01824) **(G-7902)**

Advance Coatings Co **(PA)** 978 874-5921
42 Depot Rd Westminster (01473) **(G-13268)**

Advance Concrete Form Inc 603 669-4496
241 Pepsi Rd Manchester (03109) **(G-14805)**

Advance Development & Mfg Corp 203 453-4325
325 Soundview Rd Guilford (06437) **(G-1382)**

Advance Form & Supply, Manchester *Also Called: Advance Concrete Form Inc* **(G-14805)**

Advance Machine & Tool Inc 413 499-4900
50 Greenway St Pittsfield (01201) **(G-11389)**

Advance Mfgco Inc 413 568-2411
8 Turnpike Industrial Rd Westfield (01085) **(G-13146)**

Advance Mold & Mfg Inc 860 432-5887
71 Utopia Rd Manchester (06042) **(G-1583)**

Advance Plastics Inc 508 987-7235
27 Industrial Park Rd E Oxford (01540) **(G-11248)**

Advance Reproductions Corp 978 685-2911
100 Flagship Dr North Andover (01845) **(G-10817)**

Advance Systems, Newton *Also Called: Advance Systems Inc* **(G-10732)**

Advance Systems Inc 888 238-8704
79a Chapel St Newton (02458) **(G-10732)**

Advance Welding, Springfield *Also Called: Kielb Welding Enterprises Inc* **(G-12109)**

Advanced Adhesive Systems Inc 860 953-4100
681 N Mountain Rd Newington (06111) **(G-2267)**

Advanced Air Systems Inc 781 878-5733
43 Highland Rd Ste J Abington (02351) **(G-5721)**

Advanced Animations.. 802 746-8974
   534 Vt Route 107 Stockbridge (05772) *(G-17628)*

Advanced Bldg Components LLC................................ 508 733-4889
   321 W Grove St Middleboro (02346) *(G-10348)*

Advanced Building Products Inc................................. 207 490-2306
   95 Cyro Dr Sanford (04073) *(G-5389)*

Advanced CAM Manufacturing LLC............................. 978 562-2825
   526 Main St Hudson (01749) *(G-9352)*

Advanced Chemical Company.................................... 401 785-3434
   105 Bellows St 131 Warwick (02888) *(G-16776)*

Advanced Cnc Machine Inc....................................... 603 625-6631
   722 E Indus Pk Dr Unit 15 Manchester (03109) *(G-14806)*

Advanced Concrete Tech Inc..................................... 603 431-5661
   300 Portsmouth Ave Greenland (03840) *(G-14365)*

Advanced Control Systems Div, East Haven *Also Called: Associated X-Ray Corp* *(G-1036)*

Advanced Custom Cabinets Inc.................................. 603 772-6211
   13 Prescott Rd Brentwood (03833) *(G-14019)*

Advanced Decisions Inc.. 203 402-0603
   350 Woodland Ln Orange (06477) *(G-2665)*

Advanced Design & Mfg Inc...................................... 603 430-7573
   350 Heritage Ave Portsmouth (03801) *(G-15357)*

Advanced Design Construction, Hampstead *Also Called: M & A Advnced Design Cnstr Inc* *(G-14385)*

Advanced Development Cente, New Bedford *Also Called: Tonix Phrmceuticals Holdg Corp* *(G-10656)*

Advanced Device Technology...................................... 603 894-1402
   6 Yardley Rd Andover (01810) *(G-5867)*

Advanced Drainage Systems Inc................................ 413 589-0515
   58 Wyoming St Ludlow (01056) *(G-9937)*

Advanced Electronic Design Inc................................. 508 699-0249
   344 John L Dietsch Blvd Attleboro Falls (02763) *(G-6078)*

Advanced Embroidery, Hyannis *Also Called: Threadhead Inc* *(G-9453)*

Advanced Engineering Corp....................................... 978 777-7147
   45 Prince St Danvers (01923) *(G-8161)*

Advanced Entp Systems Corp.................................... 508 431-7607
   179 Lincoln St Boston (02111) *(G-6517)*

Advanced Exhibits, Stockbridge *Also Called: Advanced Animations* *(G-17628)*

Advanced Fabricating McHy Inc.................................. 603 642-4906
   65 Route 125 Kingston (03848) *(G-14632)*

Advanced Fitnes Components LLC.............................. 603 595-1967
   17 Hampshire Dr Ste 18 Hudson (03051) *(G-14480)*

Advanced Frp Systems Inc.. 508 927-6915
   20 Mathewson Dr East Weymouth (02189) *(G-8423)*

Advanced Graphics Incorporated................................ 203 378-0471
   55 Old South Ave Stratford (06615) *(G-3515)*

Advanced Illumination Inc.. 802 767-3830
   440 State Garage Rd Rochester (05767) *(G-17484)*

Advanced Imaging Inc.. 978 658-7776
   234 Ballardvale St Wilmington (01887) *(G-13373)*

Advanced Indus Solutions Inc **(PA)**.......................... **207 623-9599**
   36 Anthony Ave Augusta (04330) *(G-4466)*

Advanced Indus Solutions Inc.................................... 207 832-0569
   151 One Pie Rd Waldoboro (04572) *(G-5573)*

Advanced Instruments LLC **(DH)**............................ **781 320-9000**
   2 Technology Way Norwood (02062) *(G-11156)*

Advanced Interconnections Corp................................ 401 823-5200
   5 Energy Way West Warwick (02893) *(G-16898)*

Advanced Kiosks, Concord *Also Called: H32 Design and Development LLC* *(G-14135)*

Advanced Machine and TI Co Inc............................... 802 893-6322
   63 Gonyeau Rd Ste B Milton (05468) *(G-17353)*

Advanced Mechanical Tech Inc **(PA)**........................ **617 923-4174**
   176 Waltham St Watertown (02472) *(G-12855)*

Advanced Media Corporation...................................... 800 844-0599
   159 Thomas Burgin Pkwy Quincy (02169) *(G-11501)*

Advanced Metal Concepts Inc................................... 508 695-6400
   385 John L Dietsch Blvd North Attleboro (02763) *(G-10864)*

Advanced Micro Controls Inc.................................... 860 585-1254
   20 Gear Dr Terryville (06786) *(G-3599)*

Advanced Micro Devices Inc..................................... 978 795-2500
   90 Central St Boxborough (01719) *(G-7146)*

Advanced Microsensors Corp..................................... 508 770-6600
   333 South St Bldg 2 Shrewsbury (01545) *(G-11825)*

Advanced Mixing Technologies, Londonderry *Also Called: Admix Inc* *(G-14727)*

Advanced Polymerics Inc... 603 328-8177
   32 Hampshire Rd Salem (03079) *(G-15502)*

Advanced Precision Engineering Incorporated............... 978 356-7303
   16 Mitchell Rd Ipswich (01938) *(G-9477)*

Advanced Print Solutions Inc.................................... 508 655-8434
   45 Bishop Rd Sharon (02067) *(G-11791)*

Advanced Print Tech LLC.. 401 434-8802
   18 Laura St East Providence (02914) *(G-16001)*

Advanced Print Technology Inc.................................. 978 342-0093
   76 Laurel St Fitchburg (01420) *(G-8640)*

Advanced Printing Services Inc.................................. 860 583-1906
   135 Cross St Bristol (06010) *(G-393)*

Advanced Products Operation, North Haven *Also Called: Parker-Hannifin Corporation* *(G-2430)*

Advanced Programs Inc... 603 685-6748
   21 Northwestern Dr Salem (03079) *(G-15503)*

Advanced Prototypes & Molding................................. 978 534-0584
   21 Howe St Leominster (01453) *(G-9632)*

Advanced Pwr Systems Intl Inc.................................. 860 921-0009
   18 Hemlock Dr New Hartford (06057) *(G-2097)*

Advanced Recycling, Concord *Also Called: Max Cohen & Sons Inc* *(G-14144)*

Advanced Resources Marketing, Newton *Also Called: Joseph G Pulitano Insur Agcy* *(G-10765)*

Advanced Rsrces Cnstr Entps In................................ 207 265-2646
   27 Commercial Rd Kingfield (04947) *(G-4932)*

Advanced Safety Systems, Peabody *Also Called: Hiller Companies Inc* *(G-11315)*

Advanced Sheetmetal Assoc LLC............................... 860 349-1644
   52 Industrial Park Access Rd Middlefield (06455) *(G-1723)*

Advanced Signing LLC... 508 533-9000
   4 Industrial Park Rd Medway (02053) *(G-10301)*

Advanced Sonic Proc Systems, Oxford *Also Called: Advanced Sonics LLC* *(G-2684)*

Advanced Sonics LLC.. 203 266-4440
   324 Christian St Oxford (06478) *(G-2684)*

Advanced Specialist LLC.. 860 945-9125
   162 Commercial St Watertown (06795) *(G-4001)*

Advanced Specialty Metals, Nashua *Also Called: Powdered Metal Technology Corp* *(G-15150)*

Advanced Thermal Solutions Inc **(PA)**...................... **781 769-2800**
   89 Access Rd Ste 27 Norwood (02062) *(G-11157)*

Advanced Tooling Design, Derry *Also Called: Stentech Inc* *(G-14209)*

Advanced Torque Products LLC.................................. 860 828-1523
   56 Budney Rd Newington (06111) *(G-2268)*

Advanced Turbine Services LLC................................. 203 269-7977
   856 N Main Street Ext Wallingford (06492) *(G-3767)*

Advanced Vacuum Systems, Ayer *Also Called: Avs Incorporated* *(G-6174)*

Advanced Visibility LLC.. 603 660-6033
   983 John Fitch Hwy Fitchburg (01420) *(G-8641)*

Advanced Welding & Design Inc................................. 781 938-7644
   6 Draper St Woburn (01801) *(G-13499)*

Advanced Window Systems LLC................................ 800 841-6544
   14 Alcap Rdg Ste 4 Cromwell (06416) *(G-684)*

Advanced Woodworking Tech LLC.............................. 978 937-1400
   258 W Manchester St Lowell (01852) *(G-9851)*

Advancepierre Foods Inc... 207 541-2800
   54 Saint John St Portland (04102) *(G-5175)*

Advandx Inc... 866 376-0009
   400 Tradecenter Ste 6990 Woburn (01801) *(G-13500)*

Advansource Biomaterials Corporation........................ 978 657-0075
   229 Andover St Wilmington (01887) *(G-13374)*

Advanstar Communications Inc.................................. 339 298-4200
   70 Blanchard Rd Ste 301 Burlington (01803) *(G-7332)*

Advantage Data Inc **(HQ)**....................................... **212 227-8870**
   1 Federal St Fl 25 Boston (02110) *(G-6518)*

Advantage Mold Inc... 603 647-6678
   576 Mammoth Rd Ste 23 Londonderry (03053) *(G-14728)*

Advantage Plastic Products, Concord *Also Called: Acw Plastic Products Inc* *(G-14112)*

Advantage Sheet Metal Mfg LLC................................ 203 720-0929
   51 Elm St Naugatuck (06770) *(G-1946)*

Advent Medical Products Inc..................................... 781 272-2813
   55 Beaver Pond Rd Lincoln (01773) *(G-9794)*

Advent Technologies Inc **(PA)**................................ **617 655-6000**
   500 Rutherford Ave Ste 101 Boston (02129) *(G-6519)*

2024 Harris New England
Manufacturers Directory

(G-0000) Company's Geographic Section entry number

Adventure Ready Brands, Littleton *Also Called: Tender Corporation* **(G-14724)**

Advisor...203 239-4121
  83 State St North Haven (06473) **(G-2388)**

Advisor Perspectives Inc..781 376-0050
  10 State St 2nd Fl Woburn (01801) **(G-13501)**

Ae Red Holdings LLC **(PA)**...................................**561 372-7820**
  669 Forest St Marlborough (01752) **(G-10105)**

AE&f, East Providence *Also Called: American Equipment & Fabg Corp* **(G-16002)**

Aearo Technologies, Auburn *Also Called: Aearo Technologies LLC* **(G-6098)**

Aearo Technologies LLC...317 692-6645
  48 Sword St Ste 101 Auburn (01501) **(G-6098)**

Aegea Medical Inc..650 701-1125
  50 Corporate Dr Trumbull (06611) **(G-3709)**

Aegis Container, Milford *Also Called: Aegis Holdings LLC* **(G-15010)**

Aegis Holdings LLC..603 673-8900
  Riverway W Milford (03055) **(G-15010)**

Aegis Semiconductor Security, Woburn *Also Called: Ii-VI Photonics (us) Inc* **(G-13583)**

Aem, Springfield *Also Called: Assocted Electro-Mechanics Inc* **(G-12076)**

Aemc Instruments, Dover *Also Called: Chauvin Arnoux Inc* **(G-14221)**

Aereo Inc...617 861-8287
  2 Rosenfeld Dr Ste F Hopedale (01747) **(G-9293)**

Aerex Manufacturing, South Windsor *Also Called: ATI Ladish Machining Inc* **(G-3116)**

Aerial Acoustics Corporation.......................................978 988-1600
  15 Union St Lawrence (01840) **(G-9535)**

Aerial Skyvertising Inc...508 586-4076
  55 Boyle Rd Brockton (02302) **(G-7253)**

Aerial Wireless Services LLC.......................................508 657-1213
  125 Depot St Bellingham (02019) **(G-6282)**

Aeris Health Inc..917 685-6504
  8 Crosby Dr Bedford (01730) **(G-6206)**

Aero Brazing Corporation...781 933-7511
  223 New Boston St Woburn (01801) **(G-13502)**

Aero Defense International LLC....................................603 644-0305
  400 Bedford St Ste 136 Manchester (03101) **(G-14807)**

Aero Gear Incorporated...860 688-0888
  1050 Day Hill Rd Windsor (06095) **(G-4255)**

Aero Manufacturing Corp..978 720-1000
  100 Sam Fonzo Dr Ste 1 Beverly (01915) **(G-6323)**

Aero Precision East LLC...603 750-7100
  10 Willand Dr Somersworth (03878) **(G-15609)**

Aero Tube Technologies LLC.......................................860 289-2520
  425 Sullivan Ave South Windsor (06074) **(G-3107)**

Aero Turbine Components Inc......................................508 755-2121
  993 Millbury St Worcester (01607) **(G-13698)**

Aero-Med LLC..860 659-2270
  571 Nutmeg Rd N South Windsor (06074) **(G-3108)**

Aero-Med Molding Technologies **(PA)**........................**203 735-2331**
  50 Westfield Ave Ansonia (06401) **(G-5)**

Aero-Precision Mfg LLC...203 675-7625
  71 S Turnpike Rd Wallingford (06492) **(G-3768)**

Aero-Space Fabricators Inc...781 899-4535
  116 Harvard St Waltham (02453) **(G-12586)**

Aerobond Composites LLC..413 734-2224
  1 Allen St Ste 201 Springfield (01108) **(G-12071)**

Aerocision LLC...860 526-9700
  12a Inspiration Ln Chester (06412) **(G-622)**

Aerocomposites Inc...860 829-6809
  49 Cambridge Hts Kensington (06037) **(G-1537)**

Aerocor Inc..860 281-9274
  59 Newberry Rd East Windsor (06088) **(G-1064)**

Aerodesigns Inc..617 491-6600
  161 1st St Ste 3 Cambridge (02142) **(G-7468)**

Aerodynamics LLC..603 474-2547
  142 Batchelder Rd Seabrook (03874) **(G-15583)**

Aerodynamics Metal Finishing, Seabrook *Also Called: Aerodynamics LLC* **(G-15583)**

Aeroflex Metelics, Londonderry *Also Called: Micro-Metrics Inc* **(G-14772)**

Aeromics Inc..216 772-1004
  11000 Cedar Ave Ste 270 Branford (06405) **(G-231)**

Aerontics Systems Arspc Strctr, Hopkinton *Also Called: Northrop Grumman Systems Corp* **(G-9337)**

Aerosat, Amherst *Also Called: Aerosat Avionics LLC* **(G-13860)**

Aerosat Avionics LLC...603 943-8680
  60 State Route 101a Amherst (03031) **(G-13860)**

Aerospace, Berlin *Also Called: Amco Precision Tools Inc* **(G-49)**

Aerospace Alloys Inc..860 882-0019
  11 Britton Dr Bloomfield (06002) **(G-144)**

Aerospace Manufacturing, Manchester *Also Called: Acmt Inc* **(G-1582)**

Aerospace Metals Inc...860 522-3123
  239 W Service Rd Hartford (06120) **(G-1468)**

Aerospace Semiconductor, Lawrence *Also Called: Micro-Precision Tech Inc* **(G-9580)**

Aerospace Techniques, Middletown *Also Called: Aerospace Techniques Inc* **(G-1733)**

Aerospace Techniques Inc...860 347-1200
  1100 Country Club Rd Middletown (06457) **(G-1733)**

Aeroswiss, Meriden *Also Called: Aeroswiss LLC* **(G-1652)**

Aeroswiss LLC..203 634-4545
  20 Powers Dr Meriden (06451) **(G-1652)**

Aerotech Fasteners Inc...860 928-6300
  1 Ridge Rd Putnam (06260) **(G-2845)**

Aerovate Therapeutics Inc **(PA)**.............................**858 443-2400**
  200 Berkeley St Ste 18 Boston (02116) **(G-6520)**

Aerovironment Inc...805 520-8350
  141 S Bedford St Ste 250 Burlington (01803) **(G-7333)**

Aerovox, New Bedford *Also Called: Aerovox Incorporated* **(G-10565)**

Aerovox Incorporated...508 994-9661
  167 John Vertente Blvd New Bedford (02745) **(G-10565)**

Aerus, Brewer *Also Called: Alan S Bolster* **(G-4608)**

AES Corporation..978 535-7310
  285 Newbury St Ste 1 Peabody (01960) **(G-11293)**

AES International Corporation......................................978 535-7310
  285 Newbury St Ste 1 Peabody (01960) **(G-11294)**

Aesthetic Blacksmithing, Bridgeport *Also Called: Jozef Custom Ironworks Inc* **(G-337)**

Aetna Insulated Wire LLC..757 460-3381
  53 Old Wilton Rd Milford (03055) **(G-15011)**

Aetna Jewelery Mfg, Providence *Also Called: Aetna Manufacturing Company* **(G-16466)**

Aetna Manufacturing Company.....................................401 751-3260
  720 Harris Ave Providence (02909) **(G-16466)**

Aetruim Incorporated...651 773-4200
  4 Federal St Billerica (01821) **(G-6397)**

AF Group Inc..401 757-3910
  24 Albion Rd Ste 210 Lincoln (02865) **(G-16117)**

Afc Cable Systems Inc..508 998-1131
  960 Flaherty Dr New Bedford (02745) **(G-10566)**

Afcon Products Inc..203 393-9301
  35 Sargent Dr Bethany (06524) **(G-91)**

Affinity, Clinton *Also Called: Liberty Compassion Inc* **(G-8081)**

Affinity Led Light LLC..978 378-5338
  1 Washington St Ste 5121 Dover (03820) **(G-14214)**

Affinity Led Lighting, Dover *Also Called: Affinity Led Light LLC* **(G-14214)**

Affinivax Inc...617 465-0865
  301 Binney St Ste 302 Cambridge (02142) **(G-7469)**

Affordable Conveyor Svcs LLC......................................860 582-1800
  72 Industrial Dr Southington (06489) **(G-3202)**

Affordable Exhibit Displays...207 782-6175
  142 Turner St Auburn (04210) **(G-4417)**

Affordable Intr Systems Inc **(HQ)**............................**978 562-7500**
  25 Tucker Dr Leominster (01453) **(G-9633)**

AFL, Belmont *Also Called: AFL Telecommunications LLC* **(G-13958)**

AFL Telecommunications LLC..508 890-7100
  15 Centennial Dr North Grafton (01536) **(G-11018)**

AFL Telecommunications LLC..603 528-7780
  16 Eastgate Park Dr Belmont (03220) **(G-13958)**

AG & G Inc **(PA)**...**401 946-4330**
  21 Mill St Johnston (02919) **(G-16073)**

AG Semiconductor Services LLC...................................203 322-5300
  1111 Summer St Fl 4 Stamford (06905) **(G-3274)**

AG Structures LLC...603 648-2987
  96 Old Turnpike Rd Salisbury (03268) **(G-15575)**

Against Grn Gourmet Foods LLC....................................802 258-3838
  22 Browne Ct Unit 119 Brattleboro (05301) **(G-17072)**

Agar Machining & Welding Inc......................................401 724-2260
  270 York Ave Pawtucket (02860) **(G-16344)**

AGC Acquisition LLC.. 203 639-7125
  106 Evansville Ave Meriden (06451) *(G-1653)*

Agenus, Lexington *Also Called: Agenus Inc (G-9721)*

Agenus Inc **(PA)**.. **781 674-4400**
  3 Forbes Rd Lexington (02421) *(G-9721)*

AGFA Corporation.. 978 658-5600
  200 Ballardvale St Wilmington (01887) *(G-13375)*

AGFA Finance Group, Wilmington *Also Called: AGFA Corporation (G-13375)*

AGFA Healthcare Corporation................................ 978 284-7900
  150 Royall St Ste 107 Canton (02021) *(G-7766)*

Aggregate Industries.. 781 596-4107
  30 Danvers Rd Swampscott (01907) *(G-12297)*

Aggregate Products, Shelton *Also Called: Brennan Realty LLC (G-2987)*

Agi-Shorewood, Stamford *Also Called: Agi-Shorewood Group Us LLC (G-3275)*

Agi-Shorewood Group Us LLC................................ 203 324-4839
  300 Atlantic St Ste 206 Stamford (06901) *(G-3275)*

Agi-Shorewood U.S., Greenwich *Also Called: Atlas Agi Holdings LLC (G-1315)*

Agile Magnetics, Concord *Also Called: Standex Elctrnic Magnetics Inc (G-14158)*

Agilent Technologies Inc...................................... 978 794-3664
  40 Shattuck Rd Ste 201 Andover (01810) *(G-5868)*

Agilent Technologies Inc...................................... 413 593-2900
  300 Griffith Rd Chicopee (01022) *(G-8005)*

Agilent Technologies Inc...................................... 781 861-7200
  121 Hartwell Ave Lexington (02421) *(G-9722)*

Agilent Technologies Inc...................................... 800 338-1754
  250 Smith St North Kingstown (02852) *(G-16229)*

Agilent Technologies Inc...................................... 802 861-8597
  100 Tigan St Winooski (05404) *(G-17765)*

Agility Mfg Inc.. 603 742-7339
  279 Locust St Dover (03820) *(G-14215)*

Agilone Inc **(HQ)**.. **877 769-3047**
  53 State St 10th Fl Boston (02109) *(G-6521)*

Agios, Cambridge *Also Called: Agios Pharmaceuticals Inc (G-7470)*

Agios Pharmaceuticals Inc **(PA)**.......................... **617 649-8600**
  88 Sidney St Cambridge (02139) *(G-7470)*

Agissar Corporation.. 203 375-8662
  526 Benton St Stratford (06615) *(G-3516)*

Agitar Technologies Inc.. 401 572-3150
  41 Sharpe Dr Cranston (02920) *(G-15824)*

Agk Soft.. 401 466-4213
  1420 Main Rd Tiverton (02878) *(G-16734)*

AGM Industries Inc.. 508 587-3900
  16 Jonathan Dr Brockton (02301) *(G-7254)*

Agnoli Sign Company Inc...................................... 413 732-5111
  722 Worthington St Springfield (01105) *(G-12072)*

Agreda & Son Inc.. 860 289-2520
  425 Sullivan Ave Ste 5 South Windsor (06074) *(G-3109)*

Agreda Industries LLC.. 860 436-5551
  425 Sullivan Ave Ste 6 South Windsor (06074) *(G-3110)*

Agri-Mark Inc **(PA)**.. **978 552-5500**
  40 Shattuck Rd Ste 301 Andover (01810) *(G-5869)*

Agrify, North Billerica *Also Called: Agrify Corporation (G-10894)*

Agrify Corporation **(PA)**...................................... **617 896-5243**
  76 Treble Cove Rd Ste 3 North Billerica (01862) *(G-10894)*

Agriphar Crop Solutions, Waterbury *Also Called: Macdermid AG Solutions Inc (G-3935)*

Agw Clssic Hardwood Floors LLC.......................... 203 640-3106
  1871 Boston Post Rd Westbrook (06498) *(G-4135)*

Agway, Madison *Also Called: Burger-Roy Inc (G-5041)*

Agway, Orleans *Also Called: P Wiles Inc (G-11242)*

Ahead Communications Systems............................ 203 720-0227
  6 Rubber Ave Naugatuck (06770) *(G-1947)*

Ahlstrom Nonwovens LLC **(DH)**.......................... **860 654-8300**
  2 Elm St Windsor Locks (06096) *(G-4318)*

Ahlstrom USA Inc **(DH)**...................................... **860 654-8300**
  2 Elm St Windsor Locks (06096) *(G-4319)*

Ahlstrom-Munksjo Nonwovens LLC........................ 860 654-8300
  11 Canal Bank Rd Windsor Locks (06096) *(G-4320)*

Ahlstrom-Munksjo Nonwovens LLC, Windsor Locks *Also Called: Ahlstrom Nonwovens LLC (G-4318)*

AHLSTROM-MUNKSJO NONWOVENS LLC, Windsor Locks *Also Called: Ahlstrom-Munksjo Nonwovens LLC (G-4320)*

Ahlstrom-Munksjo Paper Inc.................................. 860 654-8300
  2 Elm St Windsor Locks (06096) *(G-4321)*

Ahlstrom-Munksjo USA Inc., Windsor Locks *Also Called: Ahlstrom USA Inc (G-4319)*

Ai, Boston *Also Called: Activ Surgical Inc (G-6513)*

Ai Therapeutics Inc.. 203 458-7100
  530 Old Whitfield St Guilford (06437) *(G-1383)*

Ai-Tek, Cheshire *Also Called: Ai-Tek Instruments LLC (G-569)*

Ai-Tek Instruments LLC.. 203 271-6927
  152 Knotter Dr Cheshire (06410) *(G-569)*

Aidance Scientific Inc.. 401 432-7750
  184 Burnside Ave Woonsocket (02895) *(G-16946)*

Aidance Skncare Tpcal Slutions, Woonsocket *Also Called: Aidance Scientific Inc (G-16946)*

Aileron Therapeutics, Boston *Also Called: Aileron Therapeutics Inc (G-6522)*

Aileron Therapeutics Inc **(PA)**............................ **617 995-0900**
  285 Summer St Ste 101 Boston (02210) *(G-6522)*

Aim Joraco, Smithfield *Also Called: Automated Industrial Mch Inc (G-16688)*

Aim Products, Auburn *Also Called: American Industrial & Med Pdts (G-6101)*

Aim Products LLC **(HQ)**...................................... **401 463-5605**
  25 Kenney Dr Cranston (02920) *(G-15825)*

Aim Solder, Cranston *Also Called: Aim Products LLC (G-15825)*

Aimco, Auburn *Also Called: Aimtek Inc (G-6099)*

Aimtek Inc **(PA)**.. **508 832-5035**
  201 Washington St Auburn (01501) *(G-6099)*

Ainslie Corporation.. 781 848-0850
  88 Peach St Walpole (02081) *(G-12548)*

Aipco Inc.. 508 823-7003
  75 John Hancock Rd Taunton (02780) *(G-12316)*

Air Age Inc.. 203 431-9000
  88 Danbury Rd Ste 2b Wilton (06897) *(G-4229)*

Air Canada.. 617 567-7157
  200 Terminal B Ste 5 Boston (02128) *(G-6523)*

Air Control Industries Inc...................................... 207 445-2518
  76 Augusta Rockland Rd Windsor (04363) *(G-5677)*

Air Graphics, Quincy *Also Called: Applied Image Rprographics Inc (G-11503)*

Air Graphics, Watertown *Also Called: Applied Image Rprgrphics of Wt (G-12858)*

Air Handling Systems, Woodbridge *Also Called: Manufacturers Service Co Inc (G-4381)*

Air Tool Sales & Svc Co Inc **(PA)**........................ **860 673-2714**
  1 Burnham Ave Unionville (06085) *(G-3746)*

Air Transport Intl Inc.. 937 287-8455
  100 Cargo Rd Windsor Locks (06096) *(G-4322)*

Air Treatment Division, Amesbury *Also Called: Munters Corporation (G-5845)*

Air Valves LLC.. 203 266-7175
  78 Thomson Rd Bethlehem (06751) *(G-142)*

Air-Lock Incorporated.. 203 878-4691
  108 Gulf St Milford (06460) *(G-1794)*

Air-Mart Heating & Cooling LLC............................ 603 821-1416
  225 Stedman St Ste 13 Lowell (01851) *(G-9852)*

Air-Tite Holders Inc.. 413 664-2730
  1560 Curran Hwy North Adams (01247) *(G-10802)*

Air-Vac Engineering Co Inc **(PA)**........................ **203 888-9900**
  30 Progress Ave Ste 2 Seymour (06483) *(G-2955)*

Airborne Industries Inc.. 203 315-0200
  6 Sycamore Way Ste 2 Branford (06405) *(G-232)*

Aircastle, Stamford *Also Called: Aircastle Advisor LLC (G-3276)*

Aircastle Advisor LLC.. 203 504-1020
  201 Tresser Blvd Ste 400 Stamford (06901) *(G-3276)*

Aircraft, Plainville *Also Called: Top Flight Machine Tool LLC (G-2784)*

Airex LLC.. 603 841-2040
  98 Paugus Park Rd Laconia (03246) *(G-14643)*

Airex Corporation.. 603 821-3065
  17 Executive Dr Hudson (03051) *(G-14481)*

Airex Rubber Products Corporation........................ 860 342-0850
  100 Indian Hill Ave Portland (06480) *(G-2816)*

Airfox, Boston *Also Called: Carrier Eq LLC (G-6640)*

Airgas Usa LLC.. 203 792-1834
  50 Mill Plain Rd Danbury (06811) *(G-705)*

Airgas Usa LLC.. 978 439-1344
  1 Plank St Billerica (01821) *(G-6398)*

Airlinx Communications Inc.................................. 603 878-1926
  111 Old Country Rd New Ipswich (03071) *(G-15196)*

Airloc Corporation.. 508 528-0022
   42 Hayward St Franklin (02038) *(G-8814)*

Airloc Products Division, Franklin *Also Called: Clark-Cutler-Mcdermott Company (G-8823)*

Airmar Technology Corp.. 603 673-9570
   40 Meadowbrook Dr Milford (03055) *(G-15012)*

Airmar Technology Corp **(PA)**.................................. **603 673-9570**
   35 Meadowbrook Dr Milford (03055) *(G-15013)*

Airpot Corporation.. 800 848-7681
   35 Lois St Norwalk (06851) *(G-2459)*

Airs, Hudson *Also Called: American Ir Solutions LLC (G-14483)*

Airtight Ink, Richmond *Also Called: Z M Weapons High Performance (G-17482)*

Airworks Solutions Inc... 857 990-1060
   226 Causeway St Ste 1 Boston (02114) *(G-6524)*

Airxchange Inc.. 781 871-4816
   85 Longwater Dr Rockland (02370) *(G-11633)*

Ais Global Holdings LLC... 203 250-3500
   250 Knotter Dr Cheshire (06410) *(G-570)*

Ais Group Holdings LLC.. 978 562-7500
   25 Tucker Dr Leominster (01453) *(G-9634)*

Aislebuyer Lllc... 617 606-7062
   321 Summer St Fl 8 Boston (02210) *(G-6525)*

Aiudi Concrete Inc... 860 399-9289
   129 Norris Ave Westbrook (06498) *(G-4136)*

Aiven Inc.. 860 908-6924
   1 Lincoln St Boston (02111) *(G-6526)*

AIW-Alton Inc
   545 Spring St Unit E Windsor Locks (06096) *(G-4323)*

Aj Casey LLC... 203 226-5961
   597 Westport Ave Unit C363 Norwalk (06851) *(G-2460)*

Aj Nonwovens - Hampton LLC...................................... 603 929-6000
   11 Merrill Industrial Dr Hampton (03842) *(G-14397)*

Aj Precision Inc.. 413 998-3291
   13 Industrial Rd Southwick (01077) *(G-12040)*

Aja International Inc... 781 545-7365
   72 Sharp St Ste B Hingham (02043) *(G-9139)*

Ajinomoto Cambrooke Inc **(DH)**................................ **508 782-2300**
   4 Copeland Dr Ayer (01432) *(G-6170)*

AKa McHlngelo Strbuilder LLC..................................... 508 238-9054
   31 Randall St North Easton (02356) *(G-11007)*

Aka Tool Inc.. 603 524-1868
   477 Province Rd Ste 1 Laconia (03246) *(G-14644)*

Akademos LLC.. 203 866-0190
   200 Connecticut Ave Ste 2b Norwalk (06854) *(G-2461)*

Akamai Technologies Inc... 203 969-5161
   1 Hampshire St Ste 6 Cambridge (02139) *(G-7471)*

Akamai Technologies Inc... 415 994-2299
   8 Cambridge Ctr Cambridge (02142) *(G-7472)*

Akamai Technologies Inc **(PA)**................................. **617 444-3000**
   145 Broadway Cambridge (02142) *(G-7473)*

Akebia Therapeutics Inc **(PA)**................................. **617 871-2098**
   245 1st St Ste 1400 Cambridge (02142) *(G-7474)*

Akili Inc **(PA)**.. **617 313-8853**
   125 Broad St Fl 5 Boston (02110) *(G-6527)*

Akken Inc... 866 590-6695
   98 Spit Brook Rd Ste 402 Nashua (03062) *(G-15054)*

AKO Inc... 860 298-9765
   50 Baker Hollow Rd Windsor (06095) *(G-4256)*

Akouos, Boston *Also Called: Akouos Inc (G-6528)*

Akouos Inc **(PA)**.. **857 410-1818**
   645 Summer St Ste 200 Boston (02210) *(G-6528)*

Akumina Inc **(PA)**... **603 318-8269**
   30 Temple St Ste 301 Nashua (03060) *(G-15055)*

Al CU Met Inc.. 603 432-6220
   3 Planeview Dr Londonderry (03053) *(G-14729)*

Al-Lynn Sales, Shelton *Also Called: Al-Lynn Sales LLC (G-2979)*

Al-Lynn Sales LLC.. 203 922-7840
   25 Brook St Ste 102 Shelton (06484) *(G-2979)*

Al's Beverage Company, East Windsor *Also Called: Jmf Group LLC (G-1077)*

Alacron Inc... 603 891-2750
   71 Spit Brook Rd Ste 200 Nashua (03060) *(G-15056)*

Aladdin Manufacturing Corp.. 508 660-8913
   15 Walpole Park S Walpole (02081) *(G-12549)*

Alaimo Fuel Corp... 617 436-3600
   165 Norfolk St Boston (02124) *(G-6529)*

Alan S Bolster... 207 989-5143
   413 Wilson St Brewer (04412) *(G-4608)*

Alan T Seeler Inc... 603 744-3736
   87 New Hampshire Rte 132n New Hampton (03256) *(G-15195)*

Alaris USA, Windham *Also Called: Mwave Industries LLC (G-5666)*

Alarmsafe Inc... 978 658-6717
   6 Omni Way Chelmsford (01824) *(G-7903)*

Alaskan Captain ME Lobster CLB, Rockland *Also Called: US Oceans LLC (G-5344)*

Albano Sales Inc.. 978 667-9100
   101 Billerica Ave Ste 5-203 North Billerica (01862) *(G-10895)*

Albany Engineered Composites, Rochester *Also Called: Albany Engnered Composites Inc (G-15463)*

Albany Engnered Composites Inc................................... 603 330-5851
   216 Airport Dr Rochester (03867) *(G-15462)*

Albany Engnered Composites Inc **(HQ)**.......................... **603 330-5800**
   216 Airport Dr Rochester (03867) *(G-15463)*

Albany International Corp **(PA)**................................. **603 330-5850**
   216 Airport Dr Rochester (03867) *(G-15464)*

Albea, Thomaston *Also Called: Silgan Dspnsing Systems Thmsto (G-3630)*

Albea Metal Americas, Thomaston *Also Called: Silgan Dspnsing Systems Cvit A (G-3629)*

Albert Basse Associates Inc.. 781 344-3555
   175 Campanelli Pkwy Stoughton (02072) *(G-12191)*

Albert E Cadrette.. 978 597-2312
   419a Main St West Townsend (01474) *(G-13056)*

Albert K Stokes, Hudson *Also Called: Stokes Woodworking Co Inc (G-9416)*

Albert Kemperle Inc.. 860 727-0933
   141 Locust St Hartford (06114) *(G-1469)*

Alberto Vasallo Jr.. 617 522-5060
   175 Wlliam F Mcclllan Hwy Boston (02128) *(G-6530)*

Albi Protective Coatings LLC....................................... 860 828-0571
   401 Berlin St East Berlin (06023) *(G-906)*

Albion Manufacturing.. 207 873-5633
   133 Halifax St Winslow (04901) *(G-5679)*

Albireo Pharma Inc **(DH)**....................................... **857 254-5555**
   53 State St Fl 19 Boston (02109) *(G-6531)*

Albrayco Technologies Inc.. 860 635-3369
   38 River Rd Cromwell (06416) *(G-685)*

Albright Silicone, Leominster *Also Called: Comeau Consulting Inc (G-9653)*

Alcad Inc... 203 985-2500
   3 Powdered Metal Rd North Haven (06473) *(G-2389)*

Alcad Standby Batteries, North Haven *Also Called: Alcad Inc (G-2389)*

Alcami Carolinas Corporation....................................... 910 619-3952
   27 Lomar Park Pepperell (01463) *(G-11380)*

Alcami Carolinas Corporation....................................... 910 619-3952
   10 Lomar Park Ste 4 Pepperell (01463) *(G-11381)*

Alcami Carolinas Corporation....................................... 910 619-3952
   20 Mill St Pepperell (01463) *(G-11382)*

Alcami Carolinas Corporation....................................... 910 619-3952
   3 Patterson Rd Shirley (01464) *(G-11813)*

Alcami Carolinas Corporation....................................... 910 619-3952
   2 Howe Dr Amherst (03031) *(G-13861)*

Alcan Packaging, Norwalk *Also Called: Cebal Americas (G-2480)*

Alcat Incorporated.. 203 878-0648
   116 W Main St Milford (06460) *(G-1795)*

Alchemist Stowe, The, Stowe *Also Called: Alchemy Brewing Stowe LLC (G-17629)*

Alchemy Brewing Stowe LLC.. 802 882-8165
   100 Cottage Club Rd Stowe (05672) *(G-17629)*

Alcoa, Stoughton *Also Called: Alcoa Global Fasteners Inc (G-12192)*

Alcoa Global Fasteners Inc.. 412 553-4545
   44 Campanelli Pkwy Stoughton (02072) *(G-12192)*

Alcom LLC **(PA)**... **207 861-9800**
   6 Millennium Dr Winslow (04901) *(G-5680)*

Alcor Scientific LLC.. 401 737-3774
   20 Thurber Blvd Smithfield (02917) *(G-16686)*

Alden Corporation.. 203 879-8830
   1 Hillside Dr Wolcott (06716) *(G-4361)*

Alden Tool Company Inc.. 860 828-3556
   199 New Park Dr Berlin (06037) *(G-47)*

A L P H A B E T I C

Alden Yachts Brokerage, Bristol *Also Called: Alden Yachts Corporation* (G-15752)

Alden Yachts Corporation.................................... 401 683-4200
  99 Poppasquash Rd Unit I Bristol (02809) *(G-15752)*

Alden-Hauk Inc.. 781 281-0154
  215 Salem St Ste G Woburn (01801) *(G-13503)*

Aldeyra Therapeutics, Lexington *Also Called: Aldeyra Therapeutics Inc* (G-9723)

Aldeyra Therapeutics Inc **(PA)**.......................... **781 761-4904**
  131 Hartwell Ave Ste 320 Lexington (02421) *(G-9723)*

Aldlab Chemicals LLC....................................... 203 589-4934
  410 Sackett Point Rd North Haven (06473) *(G-2390)*

Aldo, Warwick *Also Called: Aldotech Corporation* (G-16777)

Aldotech Corporation....................................... 401 467-6100
  71 Norwood Ave Warwick (02888) *(G-16777)*

Aldrich Marble & Granite Co................................ 781 762-6111
  83 Morse St Ste 3 Norwood (02062) *(G-11158)*

Aldrich Stone, Norwood *Also Called: Aldrich Marble & Granite Co* (G-11158)

Aleias Gluten Free Foods LLC.............................. 203 488-5556
  4 Pin Oak Dr Branford (06405) *(G-233)*

Aleksia Therapeutics Inc................................... 720 918-6610
  65 Grove St Ste 102 Watertown (02472) *(G-12856)*

Alene Candles, Milford *Also Called: Alene Candles LLC* (G-15014)

Alene Candles LLC **(PA)**................................. **603 673-5050**
  51 Scarborough Ln Milford (03055) *(G-15014)*

Alent Inc.. 203 575-5980
  245 Freight St Waterbury (06702) *(G-3879)*

Alent USA Holding Inc...................................... 203 575-5727
  245 Freight St Waterbury (06702) *(G-3880)*

Alere Inc.. 207 730-5714
  10 Southgate Rd Scarborough (04074) *(G-5421)*

Alere Inc **(HQ)**... **781 647-3900**
  51 Sawyer Rd Ste 200 Waltham (02453) *(G-12587)*

Alere US Holdings LLC...................................... 781 647-3900
  51 Sawyer Rd Ste 200 Waltham (02453) *(G-12588)*

Alert Solutions Inc.. 401 427-2100
  201 Hillside Rd Ste 2 Cranston (02920) *(G-15826)*

Alesis LP.. 401 658-4032
  200 Scenic View Dr Ste 201 Cumberland (02864) *(G-15931)*

Alex & Ryan Design LLC.................................... 603 518-8650
  630 Harvard St # 2 Manchester (03103) *(G-14808)*

Alex and Ani, East Greenwich *Also Called: Alex and Ani LLC* (G-15972)

Alex and Ani LLC **(HQ)**................................. **401 633-1486**
  10 Briggs Dr East Greenwich (02818) *(G-15972)*

Alex Vault Co... 603 944-0132
  25 Molly Way Epping (03042) *(G-14276)*

Alexanders Mech Solutions, Greenfield Twp *Also Called: Alexanders Welding & Mch Inc* (G-4849)

Alexanders Welding & Mch Inc.............................. 207 827-3300
  1462 Greenfield Rd Greenfield Twp (04418) *(G-4849)*

Alexion, Boston *Also Called: Alexion Pharmaceuticals Inc* (G-6532)

Alexion Pharma LLC **(DH)**............................... **203 272-2596**
  100 College St New Haven (06510) *(G-2112)*

Alexion Pharmaceuticals Inc **(HQ)**...................... **475 230-2596**
  121 Seaport Blvd Boston (02210) *(G-6532)*

Alexion Rare Dsase By Astrznec, New Haven *Also Called: Alexion Pharma LLC* (G-2112)

Alfa Laval Inc.. 978 465-5777
  111 Parker St Newburyport (01950) *(G-10666)*

Alfa Laval Thermal-Food Ctr, Newburyport *Also Called: Alfa Laval Inc* (G-10666)

Alfred's Upholstrey and Co., Alfred *Also Called: Alfreds Uphlstring Cstm Fbrcti* (G-4402)

Alfreds Uphlstring Cstm Fbrcti............................ 207 536-5565
  181 Waterboro Rd Alfred (04002) *(G-4402)*

Alfresco Software Inc **(DH)**............................ **888 317-3395**
  100 Worcester St Ste 203 Wellesley (02481) *(G-12934)*

Algonquin Industries Inc **(HQ)**........................ **203 453-4348**
  129 Soundview Rd Guilford (06437) *(G-1384)*

Algonquin Industries Inc **(PA)**........................ **508 966-4600**
  139 Farm St Bellingham (02019) *(G-6283)*

Algonquin Industries Inc................................. 508 634-3733
  2 Business Way Hopedale (01747) *(G-9294)*

Algorithmia, Boston *Also Called: Algorithmia Inc* (G-6533)

Algorithmia Inc.. 415 741-1491
  225 Franklin St Boston (02110) *(G-6533)*

Align Precision - Arundel LLC............................. 207 985-8555
  20 Technology Dr Arundel (04046) *(G-4407)*

Alignable Inc... 978 376-5852
  205 Portland St Ste 500 Boston (02114) *(G-6534)*

Aligned Vision, Chelmsford *Also Called: Assembly Guidance Systems Inc* (G-7911)

Alimed Inc.. 781 329-2900
  297 High St Dedham (02026) *(G-8235)*

Alinabal Inc **(HQ)**..................................... **203 877-3241**
  28 Woodmont Rd Milford (06460) *(G-1796)*

Alinabal Holdings Corporation **(PA)**.................... **203 877-3241**
  28 Woodmont Rd Milford (06460) *(G-1797)*

Alivia Analytics LLC...................................... 617 227-5111
  400 Tradecenter Ste 5900 Woburn (01801) *(G-13504)*

Alivia Capital LLC **(PA)**............................... **781 569-5212**
  400 Tradecenter Ste 5900 Woburn (01801) *(G-13505)*

Alivia Technology, Woburn *Also Called: Alivia Capital LLC* (G-13505)

Alkegen, Manchester *Also Called: Lydall Inc* (G-1614)

Alken Inc... 802 655-3159
  40 Hercules Dr Colchester (05446) *(G-17185)*

Alken Industries Inc...................................... 631 467-2000
  300 Fenn Rd Newington (06111) *(G-2269)*

Alkermes Inc.. 617 441-3092
  30 Rindge Ave Apt 2 Cambridge (02140) *(G-7475)*

Alkermes Inc **(HQ)**..................................... **781 609-6000**
  900 Winter St Waltham (02451) *(G-12589)*

Alkermes Cntrlled Therapeutics........................... 877 706-0510
  852 Winter St Waltham (02451) *(G-12590)*

All American Signs Inc.................................... 508 830-0505
  15 Roberts Rd Ste G Plymouth (02360) *(G-11445)*

All American Signs Plus, Plymouth *Also Called: All American Signs Inc* (G-11445)

All Five Tool Co Inc...................................... 860 583-1693
  169 White Oak Dr Berlin (06037) *(G-48)*

All Granite & Marble Inc II............................... 508 434-0611
  379 Worcester Rd Charlton (01507) *(G-7885)*

All Metal Fabricators Inc................................. 978 263-3904
  82 Hayward Rd Acton (01720) *(G-5733)*

All Night Long Inc.. 860 306-3189
  52 Berkeley Ave Newport (02840) *(G-16199)*

All Panel Systems LLC.................................... 203 208-3142
  9 Baldwin Dr Unit 1 Branford (06405) *(G-234)*

All Phase Steel Works LLC................................ 203 375-8881
  57 Trumbull St New Haven (06510) *(G-2113)*

All Security Co Inc....................................... 508 993-4271
  771 Kempton St New Bedford (02740) *(G-10567)*

All Steel LLC... 860 871-6023
  240 Crystal Lake Rd Ellington (06029) *(G-1099)*

All Steel Fabricating Inc................................. 508 839-4471
  84 Creeper Hill Rd North Grafton (01536) *(G-11019)*

All Tube Div, Medway *Also Called: Microgroup Inc* (G-10308)

All-City Screen Printing Inc.............................. 781 665-0000
  983 Main St Wakefield (01880) *(G-12498)*

All-State Fabricators, Cranston *Also Called: EMI Industries LLC* (G-15855)

All-State Fabricators Limited Partnership................. 401 785-3900
  1485 Elmwood Ave Cranston (02910) *(G-15827)*

All-Time Manufacturing Co Inc............................ 860 848-9258
  Bridge St Montville (06353) *(G-1926)*

All-Way Service Corp...................................... 781 335-4533
  1182 Main St South Weymouth (02190) *(G-11974)*

Allagash International, Portland *Also Called: Allagash International Inc* (G-5176)

Allagash International Inc................................. 207 781-8831
  70 Ingersol Dr Portland (04103) *(G-5176)*

Allagash Timberlands LP................................... 207 834-6348
  1798 St John Road St J St John Plt (04743) *(G-5524)*

Allard Nazarian Group Inc................................. 603 314-0017
  111 Joliette St Ste 9 Manchester (03102) *(G-14809)*

Allard Nazarian Group Inc **(PA)**....................... **603 668-1900**
  124 Joliette St Manchester (03102) *(G-14810)*

Allard Nazarian Group Inc **(PA)**....................... **603 320-8755**
  140 Burke St Nashua (03060) *(G-15057)*

Allbirds Inc.. 617 430-4500
  205 Newbury St Boston (02116) *(G-6535)*

(G-0000) Company's Geographic Section entry number

Allbirds Inc.. 800 Boylston St Boston (02199) *(G-6536)*	857 990-1373
Allbirds Inc.. 29 Brattle St Cambridge (02138) *(G-7476)*	617 315-4210
Allbirds Inc.. 94 Derby St Hingham (02043) *(G-9140)*	781 208-6094
Allbirds Inc.. 1 Premium Outlet Blvd Ste 475 Wrentham (02093) *(G-13836)*	774 847-1330
Allcoat Technology Inc.. 100 Eames St Wilmington (01887) *(G-13376)*	978 988-0880
Allearth Renewables, Williston *Also Called: Allearth Renewables Inc (G-17721)*	
Allearth Renewables Inc...................................... 94 Harvest Ln Williston (05495) *(G-17721)*	802 872-9600
Allegiance Fire & Rescue LLC............................... 2181 Providence Hwy Walpole (02081) *(G-12550)*	800 225-4808
Allegion Access Tech LLC.................................... 24 Black Brook Rd South Easton (02375) *(G-11936)*	508 230-2350
Allegra Print & Imaging, Boston *Also Called: Milk Street Press Inc (G-6888)*	
Allegra Print & Imaging, Brockton *Also Called: Fasprint Inc (G-7278)*	
Allegra Print & Imaging No 196, Kingston *Also Called: Key Graphics Inc (G-16113)*	
Allegra Print and Imaging, Waltham *Also Called: R & H Communications Inc (G-12757)*	
Allegro, Manchester *Also Called: Allegro Microsystems Inc (G-14811)*	
Allegro Microsystems Inc **(HQ)**.......................... 955 Perimeter Rd Manchester (03103) *(G-14811)*	**603 626-2300**
Allegro Microsystems LLC.................................... 100 Crowley Dr Marlborough (01752) *(G-10106)*	508 853-5000
Allegro Microsystems LLC **(HQ)**......................... 955 Perimeter Rd Manchester (03103) *(G-14812)*	**603 626-2300**
Allen Datagraph Systems Inc............................... 45a Northwestern Dr Salem (03079) *(G-15504)*	603 216-6344
Allen Harbor Marine Svc Inc................................. 335 Lower County Rd Harwich Port (02646) *(G-9070)*	508 432-0353
Allen Manufacturing.. 41 Canal St Lewiston (04240) *(G-4950)*	207 333-3385
Allen Medical Systems Inc **(DH)**......................... 100 Discovery Way Ste 100 Acton (01720) *(G-5734)*	**978 263-7727**
Allen Morgan.. 32 Scotland Blvd Bridgewater (02324) *(G-7219)*	714 538-7492
Allen Science With Impact, Scarborough *Also Called: Allen Screen Printing (G-5422)*	
Allen Screen Printing... 25 Washington Ave Scarborough (04074) *(G-5422)*	207 510-6800
Allen Screen Printing, Brunswick *Also Called: Identity Group Holdings Corp (G-4646)*	
Allen Uniform Sales, South Portland *Also Called: Allen Uniforms Inc (G-5491)*	
Allen Uniforms Inc... 385 Main St Rear 3 South Portland (04106) *(G-5491)*	207 775-7364
Allen Woodworking LLC.. 200 Center St Bellingham (02019) *(G-6284)*	617 306-6479
Allen's Drain Cleaning Service, Presque Isle *Also Called: Allens Environmental Svcs Inc (G-5295)*	
Allens Blueberry Freezer Inc **(HQ)**.................... 244 Main St Ellsworth (04605) *(G-4753)*	**207 667-5561**
Allens Environmental Svcs Inc.............................. 75 Davis St Presque Isle (04769) *(G-5295)*	207 764-9336
Allesco Industries Inc **(PA)**............................... 15 Amflex Dr Cranston (02921) *(G-15828)*	**401 943-0680**
Alley Road LLC.. 120 Commercial St Boothbay Harbor (04538) *(G-4600)*	207 633-3171
Alliance Carpet Cushion Co **(HQ)**...................... 180 Church St Torrington (06790) *(G-3667)*	**860 489-4273**
Alliance Energy LLC.. Merritt Parkway New Haven (06535) *(G-2114)*	203 933-2511
Alliance Graphics Inc... 16 Progress Cir Newington (06111) *(G-2270)*	860 666-7992
Alliance Leather Inc.. 58 Pulaski St Ste 2 Peabody (01960) *(G-11295)*	978 531-6771
Alliance Paper Company Inc................................. 33 India St Pawtucket (02860) *(G-16345)*	401 722-0295
Alliance Press, The, Brunswick *Also Called: Alliance Printers LLC (G-4639)*	
Alliance Printers LLC... 3 Business Pkwy Ste 1 Brunswick (04011) *(G-4639)*	207 504-8200
Alliance Sheet Metal Inc...................................... 21 Ledin Dr Avon (02322) *(G-6141)*	508 587-0314
Allied Controls Inc.. 25 Forest St Apt 14a Stamford (06901) *(G-3277)*	860 628-8443
Allied Engineering, Newington *Also Called: Allied Machining Co Inc (G-2271)*	
Allied Group LLC **(PA)**...................................... 25 Amflex Dr Cranston (02921) *(G-15829)*	**401 946-6100**
Allied Group, The, Cranston *Also Called: Allied Group LLC (G-15829)*	
Allied Machined Products Corp............................. 4 Westec Dr Auburn (01501) *(G-6100)*	508 756-4290
Allied Machining Co Inc....................................... 50 Progress Cir Ste 3 Newington (06111) *(G-2271)*	860 665-1228
Allied Metal Finishing LLC.................................... 379 Chapel Rd South Windsor (06074) *(G-3111)*	860 290-8865
Allied Metel Products, Auburn *Also Called: Weber Realty Trust (G-6127)*	
Allied Orthotic Inc.. 3 Commercial Ln Ste E Londonderry (03053) *(G-14730)*	603 434-7722
Allied Printing Services Inc **(PA)**....................... 1 Allied Way Manchester (06042) *(G-1584)*	**860 643-1101**
Allied Resin Technologies LLC.............................. 25 Litchfield St Leominster (01453) *(G-9635)*	978 401-2267
Allied Sinterings Incorporated.............................. 29 Briar Ridge Rd Danbury (06810) *(G-706)*	203 743-7502
Allied Telesis, Portsmouth *Also Called: Allied Telesis Inc (G-15358)*	
Allied Telesis Inc.. 15 Rye St Portsmouth (03801) *(G-15358)*	603 334-6058
Allison Advertising Inc... 123 South St Ste 7 Boston (02111) *(G-6537)*	617 368-6800
Allison Associates, Boston *Also Called: Allison Advertising Inc (G-6537)*	
Allison Taylor, Branford *Also Called: Fyc Apparel Group LLC (G-260)*	
Allm USA Inc... 125 Cambridgepark Dr Cambridge (02140) *(G-7477)*	857 209-5065
Allnex USA Inc.. 528 S Cherry St Wallingford (06492) *(G-3769)*	203 269-4481
Allovir, Waltham *Also Called: Allovir Inc (G-12591)*	
Allovir Inc **(PA)**.. 1100 Winter St Waltham (02451) *(G-12591)*	**617 433-2605**
Alloy Castings Co Inc.. 151 W Union St East Bridgewater (02333) *(G-8334)*	508 378-2541
Alloy Fabricators Neng Inc................................... 39 York Ave Randolph (02368) *(G-11547)*	781 986-6400
Alloy Fasteners Inc **(HQ)**................................. 15 Amflex Dr Cranston (02921) *(G-15830)*	**401 943-0639**
Alloy Holdings LLC.. 160 Niantic Ave Providence (02907) *(G-16467)*	401 353-7500
Alloy Specialties LLC... 110 Batson Dr Manchester (06042) *(G-1585)*	860 646-4587
Alloy Welding & Mfg Co Inc.................................. 233 Riverside Ave Bristol (06010) *(G-394)*	860 582-3638
Allread Products Co LLC...................................... 22 S Main St Terryville (06786) *(G-3600)*	860 589-3566
Allstate Fire Equipment, Danvers *Also Called: Fire Defenses New England LLC (G-8186)*	
Allstate Fire Systems LLC.................................... 35 Phil Mack Dr Middletown (06457) *(G-1734)*	860 246-7711
Allstate Hood & Duct Inc..................................... 88 Notre Dame St Westfield (01085) *(G-13147)*	413 568-4663
Allstate Polyethylene Corp **(PA)**....................... 236 Ragged Mountain Hwy Alexandria (03222) *(G-13851)*	**800 288-7659**
Alltec Laser Technology.. 50 Optical Dr Southbridge (01550) *(G-12009)*	508 765-6666
Allweather Coatings LLC...................................... 29 Old Newport Rd Claremont (03743) *(G-14074)*	603 504-4474
Allyn Tool Company... 164 Maple St Ellington (06029) *(G-1100)*	860 979-0041
Allyndale Corporation.. 40 Allyndale Rd East Canaan (06024) *(G-921)*	860 824-7959
Alm Works Inc... 12 Biltmore Ave Chelmsford (01824) *(G-7904)*	617 600-4369
Almont Company Inc... 293 Libbey Industrial Pkwy Ste 500 East Weymouth (02189) *(G-8424)*	617 269-8244
Almusnet Inc... 400 Tradecenter Ste 4900 Woburn (01801) *(G-13506)*	781 933-1846

ALPHABETIC

Alnylam, Cambridge *Also Called: Alnylam Pharmaceuticals Inc (G-7478)*

Alnylam Alewife Mfg Fcilty, Cambridge *Also Called: Alnylam Pharmaceuticals Inc (G-7479)*

Alnylam Pharmaceuticals Inc **(PA)**.. **617 551-8200**
675 W Kendall St Cambridge (02142) *(G-7478)*

Alnylam Pharmaceuticals Inc.. 617 551-8200
665 Concord Ave Cambridge (02138) *(G-7479)*

Alnylam Pharmaceuticals Inc.. 617 551-8200
300 3rd St Cambridge (02142) *(G-7480)*

Alnylam US Inc **(HQ)**... **617 551-8200**
675 W Kendall St Cambridge (02142) *(G-7481)*

Alnylam US Inc.. 617 551-8200
20 Commerce Way Norton (02766) *(G-11122)*

Alopexx, Cambridge *Also Called: Alopexx Pharmaceuticals LLC (G-7482)*

Alopexx Pharmaceuticals LLC.. 617 945-2510
50 Buckingham St Cambridge (02138) *(G-7482)*

Alpha Advanced Materials, Waterbury *Also Called: Alpha Assembly Solutions Inc (G-3881)*

Alpha Assembly Solutions Inc.. 203 575-5696
245 Freight St Waterbury (06702) *(G-3881)*

Alpha Chemical Services Inc... 781 344-8688
46 Morton St Stoughton (02072) *(G-12193)*

Alpha Grainger Mfg Inc.. 508 520-4005
20 Discovery Way Franklin (02038) *(G-8815)*

Alpha Grphics Prntshop of Ftur.. 603 595-1444
97 Main St Ste 1 Nashua (03060) *(G-15058)*

Alpha Instruments Inc... 978 264-2966
468 Great Rd Ste 3 Acton (01720) *(G-5735)*

Alpha Plating and Finishing Co... 860 747-5002
169 W Main St Plainville (06062) *(G-2746)*

Alpha Press, Waltham *Also Called: Bruno Diduca (G-12613)*

Alpha Q Inc **(PA)**.. **860 537-4681**
87 Upton Rd Colchester (06415) *(G-654)*

Alpha Tech Pet Inc.. 978 486-3690
25 Porter Rd Ste 210 Littleton (01460) *(G-9800)*

Alpha-Core Inc... 203 954-0050
6 Waterview Dr Shelton (06484) *(G-2980)*

Alphacoin LLC.. 475 256-4050
10 Trowbridge Dr Bethel (06801) *(G-99)*

Alphagary, Leominster *Also Called: Mexichem Spcalty Compounds Inc (G-9683)*

AlphaGraphics.. 203 847-8884
16 Dyke Ln Stamford (06902) *(G-3278)*

AlphaGraphics.. 508 380-8344
192 Sudbury Rd Concord (01742) *(G-8097)*

AlphaGraphics.. 617 924-4091
376 Arsenal St Watertown (02472) *(G-12857)*

AlphaGraphics.. 401 648-0078
28 Wolcott St Providence (02908) *(G-16468)*

AlphaGraphics, Greenwich *Also Called: Turnstone Inc (G-1358)*

AlphaGraphics, Oxford *Also Called: Digitaldruker Inc (G-2693)*

AlphaGraphics, Stamford *Also Called: AlphaGraphics (G-3278)*

AlphaGraphics, Attleboro *Also Called: Rhode Island Mktg & Prtg Inc (G-6054)*

AlphaGraphics, Boston *Also Called: Boston Print Specialists LLC (G-6613)*

AlphaGraphics, Concord *Also Called: AlphaGraphics (G-8097)*

AlphaGraphics, Framingham *Also Called: Elbonais Incorporated (G-8761)*

AlphaGraphics, Watertown *Also Called: AlphaGraphics (G-12857)*

AlphaGraphics, Worcester *Also Called: Documents On Demand Inc (G-13718)*

AlphaGraphics, Worcester *Also Called: Massachstts Sign Instlltion Co (G-13758)*

AlphaGraphics, Nashua *Also Called: Alpha Grphics Prntshop of Ftur (G-15058)*

Alpine Machine Co Inc... 603 752-1441
355 Goebel St Berlin (03570) *(G-13979)*

Alpine Precision LLC.. 978 600-0035
152 Rangeway Rd North Billerica (01862) *(G-10896)*

Alpine Precision LLC.. 978 667-6333
23 Sullivan Rd North Billerica (01862) *(G-10897)*

Alpinist Magazine, Jeffersonville *Also Called: Height Land Publications Ltd (G-17306)*

Alps Sportswear Mfg Co Inc... 978 685-5159
5 Commonwealth Rd Ste 1a Natick (01760) *(G-10467)*

Als Beverage Company Inc... 860 627-7003
13 Revay Rd East Windsor (06088) *(G-1065)*

Alsco Industries Inc... 508 347-1199
174 Charlton Rd Sturbridge (01566) *(G-12248)*

Alstom Power Co... 860 688-1911
175 Addison Rd Windsor (06095) *(G-4257)*

Alstom Power Co, Windsor *Also Called: GE Steam Power Inc (G-4279)*

Altair Paramount LLC... 617 889-7300
225 Franklin St Ste 2330 Boston (02110) *(G-6538)*

Altamira Lighting, Warren *Also Called: Brownlie Lamar Design Group (G-16756)*

Altana, North Haven *Also Called: Byk USA Inc (G-2395)*

Altec Inc.. 508 752-0660
10 Fortune Blvd Shrewsbury (01545) *(G-11826)*

Altec Inc.. 508 545-8200
23 Strathmore Rd Ste 2 Natick (01760) *(G-10468)*

Altek Company... 860 482-7626
89 Commercial Blvd Ste 1 Torrington (06790) *(G-3668)*

Altek Electronics Inc.. 860 482-7626
89 Commercial Blvd Torrington (06790) *(G-3669)*

Alternate Finishing Inc... 978 567-9205
15 Kane Industrial Dr Hudson (01749) *(G-9353)*

Alternative Energy Retailer, Oxford *Also Called: Zackin Publications Inc (G-2715)*

Alternative Manufacturing Inc.. 207 377-9377
30 Summer St Ste B Winthrop (04364) *(G-5690)*

Altiostar Networks Inc **(PA)**.. **855 709-0701**
1 Cranberry Hl Ste 203 Lexington (02421) *(G-9724)*

Altium Acqisition Holdings Inc.. 617 516-2000
200 Clarendon St Boston (02116) *(G-6539)*

Altium Packaging... 860 683-8560
4 Market Cir Windsor (06095) *(G-4258)*

Altium Packaging LLC... 207 772-7468
364 Forest Ave Portland (04101) *(G-5177)*

Altium Packaging LLC... 508 520-8800
1253 W Central St Franklin (02038) *(G-8816)*

Altium Packaging LLC... 603 624-6055
27 Industrial Dr Londonderry (03053) *(G-14731)*

Altium Packaging LLC... 802 658-6588
8 Harbor View Rd South Burlington (05403) *(G-17569)*

Altium Packaging LP.. 508 485-2109
1 Dangelo Dr Marlborough (01752) *(G-10107)*

Alton E Gleason Company Inc **(PA)**.. **413 732-8207**
658 Berkshire Ave Springfield (01109) *(G-12073)*

Altra, Braintree *Also Called: Altra Industrial Motion Corp (G-7167)*

Altra Industrial Motion Corp.. 860 379-1673
31 Industrial Park Rd New Hartford (06057) *(G-2098)*

Altra Industrial Motion Corp **(HQ)**... **781 917-0600**
300 Granite St Ste 201 Braintree (02184) *(G-7167)*

Altra Power Transmission Inc... 781 917-0600
300 Granite St Ste 201 Braintree (02184) *(G-7168)*

Altri Junk Removal Services... 781 629-2500
40a Waite St Revere (02151) *(G-11616)*

Altscale Cloud Services Inc.. 800 558-5814
23 Middle Dunstable Rd Nashua (03062) *(G-15059)*

Altus II LLC... 203 698-0090
2200 Atlantic St Fl 6 Stamford (06902) *(G-3279)*

Alumasign, Brockton *Also Called: Sign Design Inc (G-7306)*

Aluminum Castings Inc... 603 654-9695
4 Hampshire Hills Ln Wilton (03086) *(G-15701)*

Aluminum Finishing Company Inc... 203 366-5871
1575 Railroad Ave Bridgeport (06605) *(G-293)*

Aluminum Products Cape Cod Inc **(PA)**...................................... **508 398-8546**
476 Main St Dennis Port (02639) *(G-8259)*

Alvarez Industries LLC... 203 799-2356
312 Boston Post Rd Orange (06477) *(G-2666)*

Alvest (usa) Inc **(DH)**.. **860 602-3400**
812 Bloomfield Ave Windsor (06095) *(G-4259)*

Alvin J Coleman, Bethel *Also Called: Coleman Concrete (G-4552)*

Alvin J Coleman & Son Inc **(PA)**.. **603 447-5936**
9 Nh Route 113 Albany (03818) *(G-13847)*

Alvin J Coleman & Son Inc... 603 447-3056
9 Nh Route 113 Albany (03818) *(G-13848)*

Alvin Johnson... 413 525-6334
26 Maple Ct East Longmeadow (01028) *(G-8368)*

Alviti Creations, Attleboro *Also Called: Alviti Creations Inc (G-5992)*

Alviti Creations Inc.. 508 222-4030
67 Mechanic St Unit 4 Attleboro (02703) *(G-5992)*

Alviti Link - All Inc.. 401 861-6656
  165 Dyerville Ave Unit 1 Johnston (02919) *(G-16074)*

Always On Time Signs & Design, Barre *Also Called: Worksafe Traffic Ctrl Inds Inc (G-17025)*

Alzheon, Framingham *Also Called: Alzheon Inc (G-8740)*

Alzheon Inc.. 508 861-7709
  111 Speen St Ste 306 Framingham (01701) *(G-8740)*

AM, South Windsor *Also Called: American Design & Mfg Inc (G-3112)*

AM Lithography Corporation.................................... 413 737-9412
  694 Center St Ste 2 Chicopee (01013) *(G-8006)*

AMA Engnring - Smrtmove Cnvyor........................... 508 636-7740
  683 American Legion Hwy Westport (02790) *(G-13292)*

Amaral Custom Fabrications Inc............................... 508 336-6681
  40 Mead St Seekonk (02771) *(G-11774)*

Amaral Custom Fabrications Inc............................... 401 396-5663
  310 Bourne Ave Ste 5 Rumford (02916) *(G-16661)*

Amaral's, New Bedford *Also Called: Lisbon Sausage Co Inc (G-10613)*

Amarello S Machining.. 508 746-8010
  8 Meadow Park Rd Plymouth (02360) *(G-11446)*

Amatech Corporation **(DH)**................................... **978 263-5401**
  100 Discovery Way Acton (01720) *(G-5736)*

Amatech Corporation... 978 263-5401
  531 Main St Acton (01720) *(G-5737)*

Amatech International, Acton *Also Called: Amatech Corporation (G-5736)*

Amatom Electronic Hardware, Cromwell *Also Called: Carey Manufacturing Co Inc (G-689)*

Amazing Mobile.. 401 597-0566
  1096 Social St Woonsocket (02895) *(G-16947)*

Amazon Robotics LLC **(HQ)**.................................. **781 221-4640**
  300 Riverpark Dr North Reading (01864) *(G-11037)*

Ambassador Woodworks Inc................................... 916 858-1092
  44 Sproul Rd Walpole (04573) *(G-5580)*

Amber Style Inc.. 401 405-0089
  3335 Mendon Rd Cumberland (02864) *(G-15932)*

Amber Synthetics, Stamford *Also Called: Near Oak LLC (G-3415)*

Ambit Creative Group, Concord *Also Called: Dmr Print Inc (G-8114)*

Ambix Manufacturing Inc....................................... 603 452-5247
  1369 Nh Route 16 Albany (03818) *(G-13849)*

Ambrose G McCarthy Jr... 207 474-8837
  228 North Ave Skowhegan (04976) *(G-5462)*

AMC, Newburyport *Also Called: Arwood Machine Corporation (G-10667)*

Amci, Terryville *Also Called: Advanced Micro Controls Inc (G-3599)*

Amco Precision Tools Inc **(PA)**.............................. **860 828-5640**
  921 Farmington Ave Berlin (06037) *(G-49)*

Amcraft, Pawtucket *Also Called: Mastercast Ltd (G-16384)*

Amerbelle Textiles LLC
  104 E Main St Vernon Rockville (06066) *(G-3759)*

America Extract Corporation.................................... 860 267-4444
  31 E High St East Hampton (06424) *(G-958)*

America's Test Kitchen, Boston *Also Called: Americas Test Kitchen Limited Partnership (G-6544)*

Americad Technology Corp..................................... 781 551-8220
  700 Pleasant St Norwood (02062) *(G-11159)*

Americal Sergical Company.................................... 781 592-7200
  45 Congress St Salem (01970) *(G-11700)*

American & Schoen Machinery Co............................ 978 524-0168
  100 Cummings Ctr Ste 140a Beverly (01915) *(G-6324)*

American Access Care RI LLC................................. 401 277-9729
  100 Highland Ave Providence (02906) *(G-16469)*

American Accessories Co., East Providence *Also Called: American Ring Co Inc (G-16003)*

American Acoustical Products, Holliston *Also Called: Ward Process Inc (G-9238)*

American Actuator Corporation................................ 203 324-6334
  292 Newtown Tpke Redding (06896) *(G-2880)*

American Adhesive Coatings LLC **(PA)**.................... **978 688-7400**
  12 Osgood St Lawrence (01843) *(G-9536)*

American Backplane Inc... 860 567-2360
  355 Bantam Lake Rd Morris (06763) *(G-1932)*

American Bacon Boston Felt Inc.............................. 603 332-7000
  31 Front St Rochester (03868) *(G-15465)*

American Biltrite Inc **(PA)**.................................... **781 237-6655**
  57 River St Ste 302 Wellesley (02481) *(G-12935)*

American Bolt & Nut Co Inc.................................... 617 884-3331
  124 Carter St # 38 Chelsea (02150) *(G-7974)*

American Brush Company Inc.................................. 603 542-9951
  112 Industrial Blvd Claremont (03743) *(G-14075)*

American Building Systems Inc............................... 860 589-0215
  200 Terryville Ave Ste 1 Bristol (06010) *(G-395)*

American Business Systems Inc.............................. 978 250-0335
  315 Littleton Rd Unit 1 Chelmsford (01824) *(G-7905)*

American Cable Assemblies Inc **(PA)**..................... **413 283-2515**
  21 Wilbraham St Unit A12 Palmer (01069) *(G-11270)*

American Canvas & Aluminum, South Hadley *Also Called: Lyman Conrad (G-11965)*

American Canvas Co, Boston *Also Called: Harry Miller Co LLC (G-6783)*

American Coated Products, Clinton *Also Called: Mallace Industries Corp (G-647)*

American Collars Couplings Inc............................... 860 379-7043
  88 Hubbard St Winsted (06098) *(G-4338)*

American College & Schl Press, Rockport *Also Called: Down East Enterprise Inc (G-5348)*

American Colorized Coins, Pawtucket *Also Called: RTC Holdings Inc (G-16414)*

American Concrete Inds Inc **(PA)**........................... **207 947-8334**
  982 Minot Ave Auburn (04210) *(G-4418)*

American Concrete Inds Inc.................................... 207 947-8334
  1717 Stillwater Ave Bangor (04401) *(G-4488)*

American Cookie Cutter, Rutland *Also Called: Ann Clark Ltd (G-17489)*

American Cord & Webbing Co Inc............................ 401 762-5500
  88 Century Dr Ste 1 Woonsocket (02895) *(G-16948)*

American Crane and Hoist Corp.............................. 617 482-8383
  1234 Washington St Boston (02118) *(G-6540)*

American Design & Mfg Inc.................................... 860 282-2719
  145 Commerce Way South Windsor (06074) *(G-3112)*

American Devices, Darien *Also Called: Realhub Inc (G-854)*

American Disposables Inc....................................... 413 967-6201
  2705 Greenwich Rd Hardwick (01082) *(G-9059)*

American Distilling Inc **(PA)**................................. **860 267-4444**
  31 E High St East Hampton (06424) *(G-959)*

American Dream Unlimited LLC............................... 860 742-5055
  212 Gilead Rd Andover (06232) *(G-1)*

American Dry Ice Corporation, Palmer *Also Called: Mass Dry Ice Corporation (G-11277)*

American Dry Stripping, Milford *Also Called: Gybenorth Industries LLC (G-1832)*

American Dryer Corporation.................................... 508 678-9000
  88 Currant Rd Fall River (02720) *(G-8519)*

American Durafilm Co Inc....................................... 508 429-8000
  55 Boynton Rd Holliston (01746) *(G-9198)*

American Ecotech LLC... 877 247-0403
  426 Metacom Ave Warren (02885) *(G-16748)*

American Electro Products, Waterbury *Also Called: American Electro Products Inc (G-3882)*

American Electro Products Inc................................. 203 756-7051
  1358 Thomaston Ave Waterbury (06704) *(G-3882)*

American Equipment & Fabg Corp........................... 401 438-2626
  100 Water St East Providence (02914) *(G-16002)*

American Flgging Trffic Ctrl I.................................. 603 890-1154
  4 Rebel Rd Hudson (03051) *(G-14482)*

American Fltbread - Brlngton H, Burlington *Also Called: Third Place Inc (G-17161)*

American Flwform Machining LLC **(HQ)**................... **978 667-0202**
  12 Suburban Park Dr Billerica (01821) *(G-6399)*

American Foam Technologies Inc............................. 304 497-3000
  221 3rd St Ste 101 Newport (02840) *(G-16200)*

American Folding Table Mfg, Northbridge *Also Called: Tent Connection Inc (G-11119)*

American Foods LLC.. 978 682-1855
  33 Bridge St Pelham (03076) *(G-15286)*

American Girl Brands LLC...................................... 508 810-3461
  1245 Worcester St Ste 109 Natick (01760) *(G-10469)*

American Grippers Inc... 203 459-8345
  171 Spring Hill Rd Trumbull (06611) *(G-3710)*

American Healthcare.. 888 567-7733
  6 Lincoln Ave Scarborough (04074) *(G-5423)*

American Heat Treating Inc..................................... 203 268-1750
  16 Commerce Dr Monroe (06468) *(G-1904)*

American Holt Corporation **(PA)**............................ **781 440-9993**
  203 Carnegie Row Norwood (02062) *(G-11160)*

American Hydrogen Northeast................................. 203 449-4614
  520 Savoy St Bridgeport (06606) *(G-294)*

American Industrial & Med Pdts **(PA)**..................... **508 832-5785**
  201 Washington St Auburn (01501) *(G-6101)*

ALPHABETIC

American Insulated Panel Co, Taunton *Also Called: Aipco Inc (G-12316)*

American Insulated Wire Corporation **(HQ)** **508 964-1200**
   260 Forbes Blvd Mansfield (02048) *(G-10037)*

American Ir Solutions LLC 662 626-2477
   1 Wall St Hudson (03051) *(G-14483)*

American Iron & Metal, Cranston *Also Called: American Iron & Metal USA Inc (G-15831)*

American Iron & Metal USA Inc **(HQ)** **401 463-5605**
   25 Kenney Dr Cranston (02920) *(G-15831)*

American Keder Inc **(PA)** **603 899-3233**
   22 Perkins Rd Rindge (03461) *(G-15459)*

American Kuhne Inc 401 326-6200
   75 Frontage Rd North Stonington (06359) *(G-2446)*

American Library Association 860 347-6933
   575 Main St Ste 300 Middletown (06457) *(G-1735)*

American Marine Products Inc 954 782-1400
   73 Southwest St Charlestown (03603) *(G-14060)*

American Marketing Intl LLC 860 669-4100
   20 Knollwood Dr Clinton (06413) *(G-635)*

American Mathematical Society Inc **(PA)** **401 455-4000**
   201 Charles St Providence (02904) *(G-16470)*

American Metals Coal Intl Inc **(HQ)** **203 625-9200**
   475 Steamboat Rd 2nd Fl Greenwich (06830) *(G-1311)*

American Molded Products Inc. 203 333-0183
   130 Front St Bridgeport (06606) *(G-295)*

American Mteorological Soc Inc **(PA)** **617 227-2425**
   45 Beacon St Boston (02108) *(G-6541)*

American Mussel Harvesters Inc. 401 294-8999
   165 Tidal Dr North Kingstown (02852) *(G-16230)*

American Nameplate 207 848-7187
   103 Center St Brewer (04412) *(G-4609)*

American Natural Soda Ash Corp **(PA)** **203 226-9056**
   15 Riverside Ave Ste 2 Westport (06880) *(G-4156)*

American Optics Limited 905 631-5377
   34 Washington St Ste 230 Wellesley Hills (02481) *(G-12949)*

American Paper Recycling Corp **(PA)** **800 422-3220**
   87 Central St Bldg 1 Mansfield (02048) *(G-10038)*

American Plastic Products Inc. 203 596-2410
   2114 Thomaston Ave Waterbury (06704) *(G-3883)*

American Plating, Cranston *Also Called: American Ring Co Inc (G-15832)*

American Players, Fall River *Also Called: American Power Source Inc (G-8520)*

American Police Beat, Cambridge *Also Called: On The Beat Inc (G-7674)*

American Polyfilm Inc **(PA)** **203 483-9797**
   15 Baldwin Dr Branford (06405) *(G-235)*

American Power Source Inc **(PA)** **508 672-8847**
   15 Shaw St Fall River (02724) *(G-8520)*

American Ppe Company LLC 603 320-5123
   21 Continental Blvd Merrimack (03054) *(G-14972)*

American Precision Mfg LLC 203 734-1800
   26 Beaver St Ste 1 Ansonia (06401) *(G-6)*

American Prefab, Bloomfield *Also Called: American Prefab Wood Pdts Co (G-145)*

American Prefab Wood Pdts Co. 860 242-5468
   1217 Blue Hills Ave Bloomfield (06002) *(G-145)*

American Printing, Rumford *Also Called: Branch Graphics Inc (G-16663)*

American Prtg & Envelope Inc. 508 832-6100
   211 Southbridge St Auburn (01501) *(G-6102)*

American Pulley Cover, South Windsor *Also Called: Siftex Equipment Company (G-3179)*

American Recycled Mtls Inc. 508 429-1455
   157 Lowland St 165 Holliston (01746) *(G-9199)*

American Reprographics, Norwalk *Also Called: Bpi Reprographics (G-2475)*

American Retail Svc Inc 781 885-7369
   39 Teed Dr Randolph (02368) *(G-11548)*

American Rhnmetall Systems LLC. 207 571-5850
   15 Morin St Ste B Biddeford (04005) *(G-4554)*

American Ring Co Inc. 401 467-4480
   41 Wheatland Ave Cranston (02910) *(G-15832)*

American Ring Co Inc **(PA)** **401 438-9060**
   19 Grosvenor Ave East Providence (02914) *(G-16003)*

American Robotics Inc. 617 862-2101
   53 Brigham St Unit 4 Marlborough (01752) *(G-10108)*

American Robotics Inc, Marlborough *Also Called: Ondas Holdings Inc (G-10191)*

American Roller Company LLC 203 598-3100
   84 Turnpike Dr Middlebury (06762) *(G-1713)*

American Saw & Mfg Company Inc. 413 525-3961
   301 Chestnut St East Longmeadow (01028) *(G-8369)*

American Screw and Barrels Inc. 978 630-1300
   60 Linus Allain Ave Gardner (01440) *(G-8879)*

American Seal and Engrg Co Inc. 203 789-8819
   295 Indian River Rd Orange (06477) *(G-2667)*

American Sheet Metal LLC. 978 578-8360
   4 Fanaras Dr Salisbury (01952) *(G-11738)*

American Sign, New Haven *Also Called: American Sign Inc (G-2115)*

American Sign Inc. 203 624-2991
   614 Ferry St New Haven (06513) *(G-2115)*

American Sleeve Bearing, Stafford Springs *Also Called: American Sleeve Bearing LLC (G-3253)*

American Sleeve Bearing LLC. 860 684-8060
   1 Spring St Stafford Springs (06076) *(G-3253)*

American Soc Law Mdcine Ethics 617 262-4990
   765 Commonwealth Ave Ste 1634 Boston (02215) *(G-6542)*

American Spcialty Grinding Inc **(HQ)** **413 593-5412**
   904 Sheridan St Chicopee (01022) *(G-8007)*

American Standard Company 860 628-9643
   85 Ladyslipper Ln Southington (06489) *(G-3203)*

American Steel Fabricators Inc. 603 547-6311
   590 Hancock Rd Peterborough (03458) *(G-15311)*

American Sub Assmbly Prdcers I. 508 949-2320
   137 Schofield Ave Dudley (01571) *(G-8315)*

American Superconductor Corp **(PA)** **978 842-3000**
   114 E Main St Ayer (01432) *(G-6171)*

American Superconductor Corp. 978 842-3000
   95 Aubuchon Dr Westminster (01473) *(G-13269)*

American Surgical Company LLC. 781 592-7200
   45 Congress St Ste 153 Salem (01970) *(G-11701)*

American Tire Svc & Sls Inc. 413 739-5369
   160 Tapley St Springfield (01104) *(G-12074)*

American Tool & Mfg Corp. 860 666-2255
   125 Rockwell Rd Newington (06111) *(G-2272)*

American Tool Company. 401 333-0111
   623 George Washington Hwy Lincoln (02865) *(G-16118)*

American Trophy and Supply Inc. 401 438-3060
   110 Russell Ave East Providence (02914) *(G-16004)*

American Ult Cryogenics Inc **(PA)** **781 491-0888**
   30 Briarwood Rd Woburn (01801) *(G-13507)*

American Ult Cryogenics LLC. 781 491-0999
   30 Briarwood Rd Woburn (01801) *(G-13508)*

American Water Systems LLC. 781 830-9722
   9 Pequot Way Canton (02021) *(G-7767)*

American Welding Company Inc. 401 397-9155
   689 Hopkins Hill Rd West Greenwich (02817) *(G-16881)*

American Well Corporation **(PA)** **617 204-3500**
   75 State St Fl 26 Boston (02109) *(G-6543)*

American Wood Products. 203 248-4433
   301 State St North Haven (06473) *(G-2391)*

American-Republican Inc **(PA)** **203 574-3636**
   389 Meadow St Waterbury (06702) *(G-3884)*

Americanbio Inc. 508 655-4336
   20 Dan Rd Canton (02021) *(G-7768)*

Americas Grdening Resource Inc **(PA)** **802 660-3500**
   128 Intervale Rd Burlington (05401) *(G-17117)*

Americas Grdening Resource Inc. 802 660-3500
   947 Route 7 S Milton (05468) *(G-17354)*

Americas Test Kitchen Limited Partnership. 617 232-1000
   21 Drydock Ave Ste 210 Boston (02210) *(G-6544)*

Ameridrives International LLC. 617 689-6237
   14 Hayward St Quincy (02171) *(G-11502)*

Amerifix LLC. 203 931-7290
   278 Washington Ave West Haven (06516) *(G-4094)*

Ameriforge Group Inc. 603 863-1270
   452 Sunapee St Newport (03773) *(G-15225)*

Ameripharma, Waterbury *Also Called: Unipharm Inc (G-3978)*

Amerpet LLC. 475 619-9512
   48 Union St Ste 2d Stamford (06906) *(G-3280)*

Ames Color File Div, Somerville *Also Called: Ames Safety Envelope Company (G-11860)*

Ames Companies Inc... 802 446-2601
82 Creek Rd Wallingford (05773) *(G-17670)*

Ames Construction, Sebec *Also Called: SDR Logging Inc (G-5457)*

Ames Safety Envelope Company **(DH)**.. **617 684-1000**
12 Tyler St Somerville (02143) *(G-11860)*

Ames Textile Corporation.. 978 934-8850
710 Chelmsford St Lowell (01851) *(G-9853)*

Amesbury Community Televi... 978 388-5900
5 Highland St Amesbury (01913) *(G-5827)*

Ametek Inc... 203 265-6731
21 Toelles Rd Wallingford (06492) *(G-3770)*

Ametek Inc... 508 998-4335
50 Welby Rd New Bedford (02745) *(G-10568)*

Ametek Inc... 978 988-4101
50 Fordham Rd Wilmington (01887) *(G-13377)*

Ametek Aegis, New Bedford *Also Called: HCC Aegis Inc (G-10599)*

Ametek Aerospace & Defense, New Bedford *Also Called: Ametek Inc (G-10568)*

Ametek Arizona Instrument LLC.. 508 946-6200
11 Commerce Blvd Middleboro (02346) *(G-10349)*

Ametek Arospc Pwr Holdings Inc **(HQ)**....................................... **978 988-4771**
50 Fordham Rd Wilmington (01887) *(G-13378)*

Ametek Brookfield, Middleboro *Also Called: Ametek Arizona Instrument LLC (G-10349)*

Ametek Precitech Inc **(HQ)**... **603 357-2510**
44 Black Brook Rd Keene (03431) *(G-14588)*

Ametek Scp Inc **(HQ)**... **401 596-6658**
52 Airport Rd Westerly (02891) *(G-16927)*

Ametek Sea Connect Products, Westerly *Also Called: Ametek Scp Inc (G-16927)*

Ametek Specialty Metal Pdts, Wallingford *Also Called: Ametek Inc (G-3770)*

Amex Inc... 617 569-5630
256 Marginal St Ste 3 Boston (02128) *(G-6545)*

AMF Optical Solutions LLC.. 781 933-6125
30 Nashua St Ste 3 Woburn (01801) *(G-13509)*

AMF Technologies, Rockland *Also Called: Arborway Metal Finishing Inc (G-11635)*

AMG-Awetis Mfg Group Corp... 603 286-1645
18 Colonial Dr Gilford (03249) *(G-14333)*

Amgen, Cambridge *Also Called: Amgen Inc (G-7483)*

Amgen Inc.. 617 444-5000
360 Binney St Cambridge (02142) *(G-7483)*

Amgen Inc.. 401 392-1200
40 Technology Way West Greenwich (02817) *(G-16882)*

Amgraph.. 860 822-2000
190 Inland Rd Lisbon (06351) *(G-1554)*

Amgraph Packaging Inc **(PA)**... **860 822-2000**
90 Paper Mill Rd Baltic (06330) *(G-37)*

Amherst Brewing Co Inc.. 413 253-4400
36 N Pleasant St Amherst (01002) *(G-5856)*

Amherst College Public Affairs.. 413 542-2321
306 Converse Hall Amherst (01002) *(G-5857)*

Amherst Label Inc.. 603 673-7849
15 Westchester Dr Milford (03055) *(G-15015)*

Amherst Machine Co.. 413 549-4551
16 Cowls Rd Amherst (01002) *(G-5858)*

Amherst Tire, Springfield *Also Called: City Tire Co Inc (G-12084)*

Amherst Woodworking & Supply Inc... 413 584-3003
30 Industrial Dr Northampton (01060) *(G-11052)*

AMI, Middleboro *Also Called: Andys Machine Inc (G-10350)*

Amide Technologies Inc.. 508 245-6839
750 Main St Ste 328 Cambridge (02139) *(G-7484)*

Amk Technical Services, South Windsor *Also Called: Amk Welding Inc (G-3113)*

Amk Welding Inc.. 860 289-5634
283 Sullivan Ave South Windsor (06074) *(G-3113)*

Amkor Technology Inc.. 781 438-7800
105 Central St Ste 2300 Stoneham (02180) *(G-12174)*

Ammega US Inc.. 401 732-8131
46 Warwick Industrial Dr Warwick (02886) *(G-16778)*

Ammunition Stor Components LLC... 860 225-3548
206 Newington Ave New Britain (06051) *(G-1999)*

Amodex Products Incorporated.. 203 335-1255
1354 State St Bridgeport (06605) *(G-296)*

Amos Grt-Grt-Granddaughter Inc.. 413 773-5471
554 Willard St Leominster (01453) *(G-9636)*

Amoun Bakery & Distribution, South Windsor *Also Called: Amoun Pita & Distribution LLC (G-3114)*

Amoun Pita & Distribution LLC.. 866 239-9990
361 Pleasant Valley Rd South Windsor (06074) *(G-3114)*

AMP, Warwick *Also Called: Accurate Molded Products Inc (G-16775)*

Ampac Holdings LLC.. 603 542-0411
130 Sullivan St Claremont (03743) *(G-14076)*

Ampd Air Quality Servics LLC.. 203 387-1709
51 Greenes Ridge Rd Hamden (06514) *(G-1411)*

Amped-Up Electric Rides, Springfield *Also Called: Kirby Corporation (G-12110)*

AMPHENOL, Wallingford *Also Called: Amphenol Corporation (G-3771)*

Amphenol, Wallingford *Also Called: Times Wire and Cable Company (G-3867)*

Amphenol Alden, Brockton *Also Called: Amphenol Alden Products Co (G-7255)*

Amphenol Alden Products Co **(HQ)**.. **508 427-7000**
117 N Main St Brockton (02301) *(G-7255)*

Amphenol Corporation.. 203 743-9272
4 Old Newtown Rd Danbury (06810) *(G-707)*

Amphenol Corporation.. 203 287-2272
720 Sherman Ave Hamden (06514) *(G-1412)*

Amphenol Corporation.. 203 327-7300
316 Courtland Ave Ste 100 Stamford (06906) *(G-3281)*

Amphenol Corporation **(PA)**.. **203 265-8900**
358 Hall Ave Wallingford (06492) *(G-3771)*

Amphenol Corporation.. 603 879-3000
91 Northeastern Blvd Nashua (03062) *(G-15060)*

Amphenol Corporation.. 603 879-3000
200 Innovative Way Ste 201 Nashua (03062) *(G-15061)*

Amphenol International Ltd **(HQ)**... **203 265-8900**
358 Hall Ave Wallingford (06492) *(G-3772)*

Amphenol Nexus Technologies, Stamford *Also Called: Amphenol Corporation (G-3281)*

Amphenol Printed Circuits, Nashua *Also Called: Amphenol Corporation (G-15060)*

Amphenol Printed Circuits Inc **(HQ)**... **603 324-4500**
91 Northeastern Blvd Nashua (03062) *(G-15062)*

Amphenol Rf, Danbury *Also Called: Amphenol Corporation (G-707)*

Ampleon, Smithfield *Also Called: Ampleon USA Inc (G-16687)*

Ampleon USA Inc.. 401 830-5420
310 Washington Hwy Ste 500 Smithfield (02917) *(G-16687)*

Amplified Ink Co.. 203 787-2184
188 Farmstead Hill Rd Fairfield (06824) *(G-1175)*

Amplitude Laser Inc.. 857 285-5952
185 Alewife Brook Pkwy Cambridge (02138) *(G-7485)*

Amplitude Vascular Systems Inc... 754 755-1530
451 D St Ste 802 Boston (02210) *(G-6546)*

Amramp, Randolph *Also Called: Gordon Industries Inc (G-11561)*

Amri, Waltham *Also Called: Curia Global Inc (G-12646)*

Amri Global, Burlington *Also Called: Curia Massachusetts Inc (G-7358)*

Amring Worldwide Inc.. 401 943-5040
1 Carding Ln Johnston (02919) *(G-16075)*

Amryt Pharmaceuticals Inc **(DH)**... **877 764-3131**
160 Federal St Fl 21 Boston (02110) *(G-6547)*

AMS, Boston *Also Called: American Mteorological Soc Inc (G-6541)*

AMS Precision Machining Inc.. 508 588-2283
959 W Chestnut St Ste 1 Brockton (02301) *(G-7256)*

Amsc, Ayer *Also Called: American Superconductor Corp (G-6171)*

Amstep Products, Bristol *Also Called: Patwil LLC (G-480)*

Amt Acquisition Inc.. 401 247-1680
5 Greenlawn Ave Warren (02885) *(G-16749)*

Amtec Corporation... 860 230-0006
30 Center Pkwy Plainfield (06374) *(G-2730)*

Amtech Solder, Deep River *Also Called: Smt International LLC (G-883)*

Amti, Watertown *Also Called: Advanced Mechanical Tech Inc (G-12855)*

Amtrol, West Warwick *Also Called: Amtrol Holdings Inc (G-16899)*

Amtrol Holdings Inc.. 401 884-6300
1400 Division Rd West Warwick (02893) *(G-16899)*

Amtrol Inc **(DH)**.. **401 884-6300**
1400 Division Rd West Warwick (02893) *(G-16900)*

Amtrol Intl Investments Inc **(DH)**... **401 884-6300**
1400 Division Rd West Warwick (02893) *(G-16901)*

A L P H A B E T I C

Amwell, Boston *Also Called: American Well Corporation* *(G-6543)*

Amy Kahn Russell LLC **(PA)**.. 203 438-2133
225 S Salem Rd Ridgefield (06877) *(G-2885)*

Amylyx, Cambridge *Also Called: Amylyx Pharmaceuticals Inc* *(G-7486)*

Amylyx Pharmaceuticals Inc **(PA)**................................... 617 682-0917
43 Thorndike St Ste 12 Cambridge (02141) *(G-7486)*

Anaconda Usa Inc... 800 285-5721
154 E Central St Natick (01760) *(G-10470)*

Analog Devices Inc **(PA)**.. 781 935-5565
1 Analog Way Wilmington (01887) *(G-13379)*

Analog Devices Inc.. 603 883-2430
20 Cotton Rd Ste 101 Nashua (03063) *(G-15063)*

Analog Devices Federal LLC **(HQ)**................................. 978 250-3373
20 Alpha Rd Chelmsford (01824) *(G-7906)*

Analog Devices Intl Inc **(HQ)**.. 800 262-5643
1 Analog Way Wilmington (01887) *(G-13380)*

Analogic, Peabody *Also Called: Analogic Corporation* *(G-11296)*

Analogic Corporation **(HQ)**.. 978 326-4000
8 Centennial Dr Peabody (01960) *(G-11296)*

Analogic Corporation.. 978 977-3000
8 Centennial Dr Peabody (01960) *(G-11297)*

Analytical Instruments, Medford *Also Called: Izon Science US Limited* *(G-10290)*

Analytical Services Company... 401 792-3537
10 Dean Knauss Dr Narragansett (02882) *(G-16186)*

Analytik Jena US LLC **(DH)**... 909 946-3197
3 Highwood Dr Ste 103e Tewksbury (01876) *(G-12384)*

Analytix Bus Solutions LLC **(PA)**................................. 781 503-9000
800 W Cummings Park Ste 2000 Woburn (01801) *(G-13510)*

Analytix Solutions, Woburn *Also Called: Analytix Bus Solutions LLC* *(G-13510)*

Anaren Ceramics Inc.. 603 898-2883
27 Northwestern Dr Salem (03079) *(G-15505)*

Anatone Jewelry Co Inc... 401 728-0490
10 Mark Dr North Providence (02904) *(G-16294)*

Anchor Concrete... 401 942-4800
30 Budlong Rd Cranston (02920) *(G-15833)*

Anchor Corporation.. 207 985-6018
2 Bragdon Ln 1 Kennebunk (04043) *(G-4920)*

Anchor Electric LLC... 413 786-6788
687 Silver St Agawam (01001) *(G-5778)*

Anchor Fence, Kennebunk *Also Called: Anchor Corporation* *(G-4920)*

Anchor Plastics Inc.. 508 753-2169
26 Knollwood Rd Dudley (01571) *(G-8316)*

Anchor Toffee LLC... 401 619-1044
8 Bowens Wharf Newport (02840) *(G-16201)*

Anchor-Seal Inc... 978 515-6004
54 Great Republic Dr Gloucester (01930) *(G-8918)*

Anchorage Inc.. 401 245-3300
57 Miller St Warren (02885) *(G-16750)*

Anchorage Inc-Dyer Boats, Warren *Also Called: Anchorage Inc* *(G-16750)*

Anchors and Thread LLC.. 401 248-8645
300 Highpoint Ave Portsmouth (02871) *(G-16435)*

Anchors Aweigh Together LLC... 401 738-8055
221 Jefferson Blvd Warwick (02888) *(G-16779)*

Anco, Shelton *Also Called: Anco Engineering Inc* *(G-2981)*

Anco Engineering Inc... 203 925-9235
217 Long Hill Cross Rd Shelton (06484) *(G-2981)*

Anco Tool & Manufacturing, Watertown *Also Called: G L C Inc* *(G-4013)*

and Fauna LLC... 603 968-7490
949 Us Route 3 Holderness (03245) *(G-14446)*

Andaluna Enterprises Inc... 617 335-3204
159 Indian Hill St West Newbury (01985) *(G-13006)*

Andera Inc... 401 621-7900
15 Park Row W Ste 200 Providence (02903) *(G-16471)*

Anderson Airmotive Inc.. 508 646-0950
994 Jefferson St Ste 10 Fall River (02721) *(G-8521)*

Anderson Airmotive Products Co, Fall River *Also Called: Anderson Airmotive Inc* *(G-8521)*

Anderson Component Corporation....................................... 781 324-0350
61 Clinton St Malden (02148) *(G-10001)*

Anderson Grnwood Crsby Vlve Ga, Mansfield *Also Called: Crosby Valve & Gage Intl Inc* *(G-10048)*

Anderson Power Products Inc **(HQ)**.............................. 978 422-3600
13 Pratts Junction Rd Sterling (01564) *(G-12154)*

Anderson Stair & Railing.. 203 288-0117
348 Sackett Point Rd North Haven (06473) *(G-2392)*

Anderson Welding LLC... 603 996-6225
3 Dean Dr Dover (03820) *(G-14216)*

Andher Mfg LLC... 860 874-8816
24 Emely St East Hartford (06108) *(G-970)*

Andon Electronics Corporation... 401 333-0388
4 Court Dr Lincoln (02865) *(G-16119)*

Andor Technology Inc... 978 405-1116
300 Baker Ave Ste 150 Concord (01742) *(G-8098)*

Andor Technology Ltd **(DH)**.. 860 290-9211
300 Baker Ave Ste 150 Concord (01742) *(G-8099)*

Andover Audio LLC.. 978 775-3670
15 High St North Andover (01845) *(G-10818)*

Andover Corporation.. 603 893-6888
4 Commercial Dr Salem (03079) *(G-15506)*

Andover Healthcare Inc.. 978 465-0044
9 Fanaras Dr Salisbury (01952) *(G-11739)*

Andover Organ Company Inc.. 978 686-9600
560 Broadway Lawrence (01841) *(G-9537)*

Andover Printing Inc.. 978 475-4945
79 N Main St Andover (01810) *(G-5870)*

Andover Publishing Company... 978 475-7000
100 Turnpike St North Andover (01845) *(G-10819)*

Andover Townsman, North Andover *Also Called: Eagle-Tribune Publishing Co* *(G-10828)*

Andover Townsmen, North Andover *Also Called: Andover Publishing Company* *(G-10819)*

Andrade Sealcoating LLC... 603 435-3704
215 Middle Rte Gilmanton Iron Works (03837) *(G-14340)*

Andre Furniture Industries LLC.. 860 528-8826
55 Sandra Dr South Windsor (06074) *(G-3115)*

Andrew Irish Logging... 207 562-8839
1264 Auburn Rd Peru (04290) *(G-5155)*

Andrew J Foss Co LLC... 603 755-2515
100 Cocheco Rd Farmington (03835) *(G-14307)*

Andrew Pearce Bowls LLC... 802 356-4632
59 Us Route 4 Taftsville (05073) *(G-17647)*

Andrew Rolden PC... 978 391-4655
39 Main St Ayer (01432) *(G-6172)*

Andrew T Johnson Company Inc **(PA)**.......................... 617 742-1610
15 Tremont Pl Boston (02108) *(G-6548)*

Andrews Holdings Inc... 978 772-4444
2 New England Way Ayer (01432) *(G-6173)*

Andritz Inc... 413 733-6603
40 Progress Ave Springfield (01104) *(G-12075)*

Andritz Shw Inc.. 860 496-8888
90 Commercial Blvd Torrington (06790) *(G-3670)*

Andrus Power Solutions Inc... 413 243-0043
690 Pleasant St Lee (01238) *(G-9610)*

Andy Collazzo.. 978 539-8962
15 Mill St Danvers (01923) *(G-8162)*

Andys Machine Inc... 508 947-1192
23 Abbey Ln Middleboro (02346) *(G-10350)*

Angel Fuel LLC.. 203 597-8759
56 Knoll St Waterbury (06705) *(G-3885)*

Angel Guard Products Inc.. 508 791-1073
120 Goddard Memorial Dr Worcester (01603) *(G-13699)*

Angelo Di Maria Inc... 401 274-0100
395 Admiral St Providence (02908) *(G-16472)*

Angelos Aluminum... 203 469-3117
55 Thompson St Apt 14g East Haven (06513) *(G-1035)*

Angelrox, Biddeford *Also Called: B Peachee Inc* *(G-4555)*

Angiotech, Westwood *Also Called: Surgical Specialties Corp* *(G-13321)*

Angostura International Ltd... 207 786-3200
176 First Flight Dr Auburn (04210) *(G-4419)*

Angstrom Advanced Inc... 781 519-4765
95 Mill St Stoughton (02072) *(G-12194)*

Angstrom Fiber Auburn.. 734 756-1164
125 Allied Rd Auburn (04210) *(G-4420)*

Anichini Inc... 802 889-9430
4 Larkin Rd Tunbridge (05077) *(G-17651)*

Anichini Linea Casa, Tunbridge *Also Called: Anichini Inc (G-17651)*

Anika, Bedford *Also Called: Anika Therapeutics Inc (G-6207)*

Anika Therapeutics Inc **(PA)**.. **781 457-9000**
  32 Wiggins Ave Bedford (01730) *(G-6207)*

ANIMAL MAGAZINE, Boston *Also Called: Massachstts Soc For Prvntion C (G-6872)*

Anjen Finishing.. 508 251-1532
  432 Northboro Road Central Marlborough (01752) *(G-10109)*

ANM Donuts Inc.. 603 286-2770
  65 Laconia Rd Tilton (03276) *(G-15651)*

Anmor Machining Company LLC... 860 224-7774
  20 Hudson Pl New Britain (06051) *(G-2000)*

Ann Clark Ltd... 802 773-7886
  453 Quality Ln Rutland (05701) *(G-17489)*

Ann S Davis... 860 642-7228
  754 Exeter Rd Lebanon (06249) *(G-1548)*

Annablles Ntral Ice Cream Ygur... 603 436-3400
  49 Ceres St Portsmouth (03801) *(G-15359)*

Anne At Home, Lincoln *Also Called: J&E Home Products LLC (G-16142)*

Anne Queen Woodworking... 203 720-1781
  74 Great Hill Rd Naugatuck (06770) *(G-1948)*

Annex Plating, North Providence *Also Called: New Annex Plating Inc (G-16305)*

Annies Gluten Free Bakery.. 978 425-5385
  2 Shaker Rd Ste C205a Shirley (01464) *(G-11814)*

Anodic Incorporated.. 203 268-9966
  1480 Monroe Tpke Stevenson (06491) *(G-3506)*

Anodyne Health Partners Inc **(HQ)**... **207 347-7400**
  400 Us Route 1 Ste 1 Falmouth (04105) *(G-4767)*

Anokiwave Inc.. 781 820-1049
  296 Concord Rd Ste 300 Billerica (01821) *(G-6400)*

Anomet Products Inc.. 508 842-0174
  830 Boston Tpke Shrewsbury (01545) *(G-11827)*

Anothercreationbymichele.. 203 322-4277
  1351 Riverbank Rd Stamford (06903) *(G-3282)*

Anpesil Distribution Services LLC
  1 Spectacle Pond Rd Littleton (01460) *(G-9801)*

Ansac, Westport *Also Called: American Natural Soda Ash Corp (G-4156)*

Ansel Label and Packaging Corp.. 203 452-0311
  204 Spring Hill Rd Ste 3 Trumbull (06611) *(G-3711)*

Ansonia Plastics LLC... 203 736-5200
  401 Birmingham Blvd Ansonia (06401) *(G-7)*

Ansonia Stl Fabrication Co Inc... 203 888-4509
  164 Pines Bridge Rd Beacon Falls (06403) *(G-39)*

Antaya Inc... 401 941-7050
  333 Strawberry Field Rd Ste 3 Warwick (02886) *(G-16780)*

Antaya Technologies Inc... 401 921-3197
  333 Strawberry Field Rd Warwick (02886) *(G-16781)*

Antec (usa) LLC... 888 572-0012
  1 Boston Pl Fl 26 Boston (02108) *(G-6549)*

Antec Scientific USA, Boston *Also Called: Antec (usa) LLC (G-6549)*

Antenna Associates Inc... 508 583-3241
  21 Burke Dr Brockton (02301) *(G-7257)*

Antenna Research Assoc Inc... 781 829-4740
  28 Riverside Dr Ste 2 Pembroke (02359) *(G-11357)*

Anthony Industries Inc.. 781 305-3750
  5r Green St Woburn (01801) *(G-13511)*

Anthony Manufacturing Co Inc.. 781 396-1400
  410 Riverside Ave Medford (02155) *(G-10279)*

Antiqueweb.com, Middlefield *Also Called: Times Publishing LLC (G-1730)*

Antoinette Leonard Associates, Woodstock *Also Called: Longhill Partners Inc (G-17776)*

Antolrx Inc.. 617 902-0601
  1 Kendall Sq Bldg 1400 Cambridge (02139) *(G-7487)*

Anton Enterprises Inc... 401 781-3120
  430 Wellington Ave Cranston (02910) *(G-15834)*

Antrim Controls & Systems.. 603 588-6297
  76 N Bennington Rd Bennington (03442) *(G-13974)*

Antron Engrg & Mch Co Inc... 508 966-2803
  170 Mechanic St Bellingham (02019) *(G-6285)*

Anver, Hudson *Also Called: Anver Corporation (G-9354)*

Anver Corporation... 978 568-0221
  36 Parmenter Rd Hudson (01749) *(G-9354)*

Anvil CT LLP.. 860 619-0589
  324 Christian St Oxford (06478) *(G-2685)*

Anz Petroleum Inc.. 860 261-4798
  291 Danbury Rd Unit 2a New Milford (06776) *(G-2238)*

Ao Glass LLC.. 802 735-5016
  29 Ledge Rd Burlington (05401) *(G-17118)*

Aoa Xinetics, East Hartford *Also Called: Adaptive Optics Associates Inc (G-969)*

Aoa Xinetics, Devens *Also Called: Adaptive Optics Associates Inc (G-8267)*

Aoa Xinetics, Devens *Also Called: Adaptive Optics Associates Inc (G-8268)*

Aoa Xinetics, Devens *Also Called: Adaptive Optics Associates Inc (G-8269)*

Aotco Holdings LLC **(PA)**.. **978 667-8298**
  11 Suburban Park Dr Billerica (01821) *(G-6401)*

Aotco Metal Finishing LLC.. 978 667-8298
  11 Suburban Park Dr Billerica (01821) *(G-6402)*

AP Disposition LLC... 860 889-1344
  387 N Main St Norwich (06360) *(G-2601)*

AP Dley Cstm Laminating Corp... 603 437-6666
  6 Ledge Rd Windham (03087) *(G-15720)*

AP Extrusion Inc... 603 890-1086
  10 Manor Pkwy Ste E Salem (03079) *(G-15507)*

AP Iron Design Inc.. 617 389-0001
  40 Crescent St Everett (02149) *(G-8482)*

AP Plastics LLC.. 800 222-1117
  103 Foster St Peabody (01960) *(G-11298)*

APA LLC... 781 986-5900
  4 Campanelli Cir Canton (02021) *(G-7769)*

APAC Tool Inc.. 401 724-6090
  49 Hurdis St North Providence (02904) *(G-16295)*

Apahouser Inc.. 508 786-0309
  40 Hayes Memorial Dr Marlborough (01752) *(G-10110)*

Apama Inc... 781 280-4000
  14 Oak Park Dr Bedford (01730) *(G-6208)*

APC Paper Company Inc **(DH)**.. **603 542-0411**
  130 Sullivan St Claremont (03743) *(G-14077)*

APC Paper Group, Claremont *Also Called: APC Paper Company Inc (G-14077)*

APC Phno, Nashua *Also Called: Amphenol Printed Circuits Inc (G-15062)*

Apcm Manufacturing LLC.. 860 564-7817
  1366 Norwich Rd Plainfield (06374) *(G-2731)*

Apco Mossberg Co.. 508 222-0340
  104 County St Attleboro (02703) *(G-5993)*

Apcompower Inc **(PA)**.. **860 688-1911**
  200 Great Pond Dr Windsor (06095) *(G-4260)*

Apct-Wallingford Inc... 203 269-3311
  340 Quinnipiac St Unit 25 Wallingford (06492) *(G-3773)*

Apellis, Waltham *Also Called: Apellis Pharmaceuticals Inc (G-12592)*

Apellis Pharmaceuticals Inc **(PA)**.. **617 977-5700**
  100 5th Ave Fl 3 Waltham (02451) *(G-12592)*

Aperture Optical Sciences Inc **(PA)**.. **860 316-2589**
  170 Pond View Dr Meriden (06450) *(G-1654)*

Apex Machine Tool Company Inc... 860 677-2884
  500 Knotter Dr Cheshire (06410) *(G-571)*

Apex Plastics, Nashua *Also Called: Spire Technology Solutions LLC (G-15173)*

Apex Press Inc... 508 366-1110
  122 Turnpike Rd Westborough (01581) *(G-13076)*

Apex Resource Technologies Inc.. 413 442-1414
  17 Downing Three Park Bldg 1 Pittsfield (01201) *(G-11390)*

Apex Sealing Inc... 802 524-7100
  164 Yankee Park Rd Fairfax (05454) *(G-17254)*

API, Branford *Also Called: American Polyfilm Inc (G-235)*

API Holdings Inc **(PA)**... **603 668-2648**
  19 Stoney Brook Dr Wilton (03086) *(G-15702)*

API Technologies, Marlborough *Also Called: Spectrum Microwave Inc (G-10212)*

API Wizard LLC.. 800 691-8714
  1127 High Ridge Rd Ste 238 Stamford (06905) *(G-3283)*

Apicellas Bakery Inc.. 203 865-6204
  365 Grand Ave New Haven (06513) *(G-2116)*

Apifia Inc.. 585 506-2787
  200 State St. Marketplace Center N Bld, 3rd Fl Boston (02109) *(G-6550)*

Apiject Systems Corp **(PA)**.. **203 461-7121**
  2 High Ridge Park Fl 1 Stamford (06905) *(G-3284)*

A L P H A B E T I C

Apiphani, Boston *Also Called: Apiphani Inc (G-6551)*

Apiphani Inc..800 215-0811
53 State St Fl 5 Boston (02109) *(G-6551)*

APJ Test Consulting, Nashua *Also Called: Everett Charles Tech LLC (G-15096)*

Aplicare Products LLC **(HQ)**..**203 630-0500**
550 Research Pkwy Meriden (06450) *(G-1655)*

Apogee Coins Precious Mtls LLC...................................603 391-6417
Manchester (03108) *(G-14813)*

Apogee Corporation...860 632-3550
154 West St Ste C Cromwell (06416) *(G-686)*

Apogee Imaging Systems Inc
300 Baker Ave Ste 150 Concord (01742) *(G-8100)*

Apogee Precision Parts, Warwick *Also Called: National Chain Company (G-16840)*

Apogent Holding Company **(HQ)**....................................**781 622-1300**
81 Wyman St Waltham (02451) *(G-12593)*

Apogent Technologies Inc...781 622-1300
81 Wyman St Waltham (02451) *(G-12594)*

Apollo Steel LLC...603 532-1156
35 Maria Dr Jaffrey (03452) *(G-14563)*

App Gap, Middlebury *Also Called: Xagd Inc (G-17351)*

App Polonia LLC...860 747-3397
95 Metacomet Rd Plainville (06062) *(G-2747)*

App Polonia Trading, Plainville *Also Called: App Polonia LLC (G-2747)*

App-Jwb Inc..603 227-9540
38 Henniker St Concord (03301) *(G-14113)*

Appalachian Stitching Co LLC **(PA)**...............................**603 444-4422**
90 Badger St Littleton (03561) *(G-14714)*

Appalchian Engineered Flrg Inc.....................................802 988-1073
105 Industrial Park Dr North Troy (05859) *(G-17428)*

Apparel Marketing Associates, Burlington *Also Called: Select Design Ltd (G-17158)*

Appels Prtg & Mailing Bur Inc.......................................860 522-8189
307 Homestead Ave Hartford (06112) *(G-1470)*

Apperian, Boston *Also Called: Red Frames Inc (G-7000)*

Apple Mill Holding Company Inc.....................................781 826-9706
720 Washington St Pembroke (02359) *(G-11358)*

Applehill Systems Inc..781 334-7009
130 Summer St Lynnfield (01940) *(G-9994)*

Applejack Art Partners Inc..802 362-3662
450 Applejack Rd Manchester Center (05255) *(G-17326)*

Appleton Grp LLC...860 653-1603
2 Connecticut South Dr East Granby (06026) *(G-925)*

Appli-Tec Inc..603 685-0500
7 Industrial Way Ste 1 Salem (03079) *(G-15508)*

Applicator Sales & Service, Portland *Also Called: Beacon Sales Acquisition Inc (G-5185)*

Applied Advertising Inc..860 640-0800
71 Newtown Rd Ste 5 Danbury (06810) *(G-708)*

Applied Analytics Inc...978 294-8214
21 Alpha Rd Chelmsford (01824) *(G-7907)*

Applied Biosystems LLC..781 271-0045
301 Merritt 7 Ste 23 Norwalk (06851) *(G-2462)*

Applied Biosystems LLC..781 271-0045
2 Preston Ct Bedford (01730) *(G-6209)*

Applied Biosystems LLC..508 877-1307
1455 Concord St Ste 8 Framingham (01701) *(G-8741)*

Applied Bolting Tech Pdts LLC.......................................802 460-3100
1413 Rockingham Rd Bellows Falls (05101) *(G-17028)*

Applied Bosystems Part Lf Tech, Bedford *Also Called: Applied Biosystems LLC (G-6209)*

Applied Dynamics Corporation **(PA)**..............................**413 774-7268**
38 Butternut St Greenfield (01301) *(G-8981)*

Applied Graphics Inc...978 241-5300
61 S Hunt Rd Amesbury (01913) *(G-5828)*

Applied Image Rprgrphics of Wt.....................................617 924-6060
63 Pleasant St Ste 1 Watertown (02472) *(G-12858)*

Applied Image Rprographics Inc **(PA)**............................**617 471-3373**
82 Sagamore St Quincy (02171) *(G-11503)*

Applied Language Technologies, Burlington *Also Called: Speechworks International (G-7432)*

Applied Laser Solutions Inc...203 739-0179
28 Commerce Dr Danbury (06810) *(G-709)*

Applied Machine Technology, Warren *Also Called: Amt Acquisition Inc (G-16749)*

Applied Materials Inc...978 282-2000
35 Dory Rd Gloucester (01930) *(G-8919)*

Applied Materials Varian, Gloucester *Also Called: Varian Semicdtr Eqp Assoc Inc (G-8963)*

Applied Mtls Vrian Smicdtr Eqp, Andover *Also Called: Varian Semicdtr Eqp Assoc Inc (G-5932)*

Applied Mtls Vrian Smicdtr Eqp, Newburyport *Also Called: Varian Semicdtr Eqp Assoc Inc (G-10725)*

Applied Nnstrctred Sltions LLC......................................978 670-6959
157 Concord Rd Billerica (01821) *(G-6403)*

Applied Physical Sciences Corp **(HQ)**............................**860 448-3253**
475 Bridge St Ste 100 Groton (06340) *(G-1364)*

Applied Plastic Technology Inc.......................................508 752-5924
169 Fremont St Worcester (01603) *(G-13700)*

Applied Plastics, Norwood *Also Called: Applied Plastics Co Inc (G-11161)*

Applied Plastics Co Inc...781 762-1881
25 Endicott St Norwood (02062) *(G-11161)*

Applied Plastics LLC..781 762-1881
25 Endicott St Norwood (02062) *(G-11162)*

Applied Plastics Tech Inc..401 253-0200
45 Broadcommon Rd Bristol (02809) *(G-15753)*

Applied Porous Tech Inc...860 408-9793
2 Tunxis Rd Ste 103 Tariffville (06081) *(G-3598)*

Applied Precision Technology...508 226-8700
81 West St Attleboro (02703) *(G-5994)*

Applied Radar Inc..401 295-0062
315 Commerce Park Rd Unit P2 North Kingstown (02852) *(G-16231)*

Applied Research Assoc Inc..802 728-4538
250 Beanville Rd Randolph (05060) *(G-17467)*

Applied Rubber & Plastics Inc..860 987-9018
100 Skitchewaug St Windsor (06095) *(G-4261)*

Applied Science Group Inc..781 275-4000
900 Middlesex Tpke Bldg 5 Billerica (01821) *(G-6404)*

Applied Science Laboratories, Billerica *Also Called: Applied Science Group Inc (G-6404)*

Applied Tissue Tech LLC..781 366-3848
99 Derby St Ste 200 Hingham (02043) *(G-9141)*

Applitek Technologies Corp...401 467-0007
160 Georgia Ave Providence (02905) *(G-16473)*

Appolo Vineyards LLC..603 421-6052
49 Lawrence Rd Derry (03038) *(G-14189)*

Apponaug Brewing Company...401 681-4321
334 Knight St Ste 11101 Warwick (02886) *(G-16782)*

Approved Sheet Metal LLC...603 883-1510
7 Security Dr Hudson (03051) *(G-14484)*

Apricot Home LLC..203 552-1791
15 Sheffield Way Greenwich (06831) *(G-1312)*

April Cornell, Burlington *Also Called: Cornell Online LLC (G-17128)*

April Twenty One Corporation..978 667-8472
749 Boston Rd Billerica (01821) *(G-6405)*

Apriori Technologies Inc **(PA)**.....................................**978 371-2006**
300 Baker Ave Ste 370 Concord (01742) *(G-8101)*

Apryse Corp..617 982-2646
530 Harrison Ave Ste 2 Boston (02118) *(G-6552)*

APS, Lee *Also Called: Andrus Power Solutions Inc (G-9610)*

APT, Fitchburg *Also Called: Advanced Print Technology Inc (G-8640)*

Aptargroup Inc...203 377-8100
60 Commerce Dr # 1 Trumbull (06611) *(G-3712)*

Aptiv Services Us LLC...781 864-9230
100 Northern Ave Boston (02210) *(G-6553)*

Aptuit (scientific Operations) LLC...................................203 422-6600
2 Greenwich Office Park Greenwich (06831) *(G-1313)*

Aqua Blasting Corp..860 242-8855
2 Northwood Dr Bloomfield (06002) *(G-146)*

Aqua Laboratories Inc..978 388-3989
8 Industrial Way Amesbury (01913) *(G-5829)*

Aqua Massage International Inc.......................................860 536-3735
800 Flanders Rd Unit 1-3 Mystic (06355) *(G-1936)*

Aqua Pulsar LLC..772 320-9591
95b Rowayton Ave Ste 1 Norwalk (06853) *(G-2463)*

Aqua Traction Marine LLC..320 237-2225
376 Dry Bridge Rd Ste F1 North Kingstown (02852) *(G-16232)*

Aqua Vitea Kombucha, Middlebury *Also Called: Aqua Vitea LLC (G-17336)*

Aqua Vitea LLC..802 453-8590
153 Pond Ln Middlebury (05753) *(G-17336)*

Aquacomfort Solutions LLC...203 265-0100
8 Fairfield Blvd Ste 115 Wallingford (06492) *(G-3774)*

Aqualogic Inc.. 203 248-8959
  30 Devine St North Haven (06473) *(G-2393)*

Aquamesh, Northbridge *Also Called: Riverdale Mills Corporation (G-11118)*

Aquamotion Inc... 401 785-3000
  88 Jefferson Blvd Ste C Warwick (02888) *(G-16783)*

Aquas Group, East Providence *Also Called: Environmental Ctrl Systems Inc (G-16016)*

Aquatic Solutions LLC....................................... 888 704-7665
  45 Lafayette Rd Hampton (03842) *(G-14398)*

Aquidneck Awning, Bristol *Also Called: Kinder Industries Inc (G-15771)*

Aquila Technology, Burlington *Also Called: Aquila Technology Corp (G-7334)*

Aquila Technology Corp...................................... 781 993-9004
  20 Burlington Mall Rd Ste 230 Burlington (01803) *(G-7334)*

Aquiline Drones Corporation................................ 973 980-6596
  750 Main St Ph Hartford (06103) *(G-1471)*

Aquinnah Pharmaceuticals Inc............................. 617 416-0530
  700 Main St Cambridge (02139) *(G-7488)*

AR Walton Construction, Presque Isle *Also Called: Sunny Side Land Holdings LLC (G-5310)*

Ar-Ro Engineering Company Inc........................... 401 766-6669
  406 Pond St Uxbridge (01569) *(G-12477)*

ARA Dell EMC MA Rsa Bedfo............................... 508 431-4084
  174 Middlesex Tpke Bedford (01730) *(G-6210)*

Aramid Rigging Inc... 401 683-6966
  14 Regatta Way Ste 3 Portsmouth (02871) *(G-16436)*

Aratana Therapeutics Inc.................................... 617 425-9226
  200 Clarendon St 54th Fl Boston (02116) *(G-6554)*

Arbo Machine Co Inc... 781 871-3449
  45 Union St Rockland (02370) *(G-11634)*

Arbor Biotechnologies Inc................................... 857 301-6366
  20 Acorn Park Dr Ste 500 Cambridge (02140) *(G-7489)*

Arborjet Inc.. 781 935-9070
  99 Blueberry Hill Rd Woburn (01801) *(G-13512)*

Arborway Metal Finishing Inc............................... 781 982-0137
  401 Vfw Dr Rockland (02370) *(G-11635)*

ARC Electronics Inc.. 603 458-2089
  16 Peaslee Ct Hampstead (03841) *(G-14380)*

ARC Enterprises, Kingfield *Also Called: Advanced Rsrces Cnstr Entps In (G-4932)*

ARC Maintenance Machining................................ 603 626-8046
  14 Tinker Ave Unit 2 Londonderry (03053) *(G-14732)*

ARC Technologies LLC **(HQ)**............................... **978 388-2993**
  37 S Hunt Rd Amesbury (01913) *(G-5830)*

ARC Technology Solutions LLC............................. 603 883-3027
  165 Ledge St Ste 4 Nashua (03060) *(G-15064)*

Arcade Industries Inc.. 508 832-6300
  205 Southbridge St Auburn (01501) *(G-6103)*

Arcade Metal Stampings, Bridgeport *Also Called: Arcade Technology LLC (G-297)*

Arcade Snacks & Dried Fruits, Auburn *Also Called: Arcade Industries Inc (G-6103)*

Arcade Technology LLC...................................... 203 366-3871
  38 Union Ave Bridgeport (06607) *(G-297)*

Arcadia, Stamford *Also Called: Wilson Partitions Inc (G-3495)*

Arcadia Architectural Pdts Inc.............................. 203 316-8000
  110 Viaduct Rd Stamford (06907) *(G-3285)*

Arcadia Chem Preservative LLC........................... 203 717-4750
  100 Beard Sawmill Rd Ste 348 Shelton (06484) *(G-2982)*

Arcam Cad To Metal Inc..................................... 781 281-1718
  6 Gill St Woburn (01801) *(G-13513)*

Arcast Inc.. 207 539-9638
  264 Main St Oxford (04270) *(G-5140)*

Arcast Inc.. 207 539-9638
  5 Park Rd Oxford (04270) *(G-5141)*

Arcat Inc... 203 929-9444
  173 Sherman St Fairfield (06824) *(G-1176)*

Arccos Golf LLC **(PA)**...................................... **844 692-7226**
  700 Canal St Ste 19 Stamford (06902) *(G-3286)*

Arch Lighting Group Inc
  30 Sherwood Dr Taunton (02780) *(G-12317)*

Arch Med & Arospc Woburn LLC........................... 781 933-1760
  166 New Boston St Woburn (01801) *(G-13514)*

Arch Parent Inc... 860 336-4856
  82 Storrs Rd Willimantic (06226) *(G-4216)*

Arch Parent Inc... 207 492-5414
  25 Emond Rd Connor Twp (04736) *(G-4700)*

Arch Parent Inc... 413 504-1433
  1129 Riverdale St West Springfield (01089) *(G-13013)*

Arch Parent Inc... 401 388-9802
  13 Airport Rd Westerly (02891) *(G-16928)*

Archaeological Institute Amer............................... 617 353-9361
  44 Beacon St Boston (02108) *(G-6555)*

Archangel Woodworks Inc................................... 603 347-5345
  3 New Boston Rd Kingston (03848) *(G-14633)*

Archer Roose Inc... 646 283-4152
  6 Liberty Sq Boston (02109) *(G-6556)*

Archer Roose Wine, Boston *Also Called: Archer Roose Inc (G-6556)*

Archerdx Inc... 978 232-3570
  123 Brimbal Ave Beverly (01915) *(G-6325)*

Archimedia Advantage Inc................................... 603 430-1252
  69 Greenland (03840) *(G-14366)*

Architctral Fireplaces of Neng.............................. 508 757-0622
  4 Washington St Auburn (01501) *(G-6104)*

Architctral Glzing Systems Inc.............................. 508 588-4845
  40 Murphy Dr Avon (02322) *(G-6142)*

Architects of Packaging Inc................................. 413 568-3187
  11 Mainline Dr Westfield (01085) *(G-13148)*

Architectural Building Svcs, Cumberland *Also Called: Herrick & White Ltd (G-15942)*

Architectural Components Inc............................... 413 367-9441
  26 N Leverett Rd Montague (01351) *(G-10458)*

Architectural Elements, Boston *Also Called: Boston Sign Company Inc (G-6618)*

Architectural Interiors Group, Providence *Also Called: Modern Industries Inc (G-16566)*

Architectural Kitchens Inc.................................. 781 239-9750
  310b Washington St Wellesley (02481) *(G-12936)*

Architectural Openings Inc.................................. 617 776-9223
  16 Garfield Ave Somerville (02145) *(G-11861)*

Architectural Skylight Co Inc................................ 207 247-6747
  661 Main St Waterboro (04087) *(G-5589)*

Architectural Stone Group LLC............................. 203 494-5451
  9 Island Brook Ave Bridgeport (06606) *(G-298)*

Architectural Supplements LLC............................. 203 591-5505
  567 S Leonard St Bldg 1b Waterbury (06708) *(G-3886)*

Architectural Timber Mllwk Inc............................. 413 586-3045
  49 Mount Warner Rd Hadley (01035) *(G-9017)*

Arclight Enrgy Prtners Fund VI **(PA)**..................... **617 531-6300**
  200 Clarendon St 55th Fl Boston (02116) *(G-6557)*

Arclin, East Longmeadow *Also Called: Arclin Surfaces - E Longmeadow (G-8370)*

Arclin Surfaces - E Longmeadow.......................... 678 781-5341
  82 Deer Park Dr East Longmeadow (01028) *(G-8370)*

Arcor Laser Services LLC.................................... 860 370-9780
  4 Kenny Roberts Memorial Dr Suffield (06078) *(G-3587)*

Arcor Systems LLC... 860 370-9780
  4 Kenny Roberts Memorial Dr Suffield (06078) *(G-3588)*

Arctic Pack, New Bedford *Also Called: Packaging Products Corporation (G-10638)*

Ardelyx, Waltham *Also Called: Ardelyx Inc (G-12595)*

Ardelyx Inc.. 510 745-1700
  400 5th Ave Ste 210 Waltham (02451) *(G-12595)*

Arden Jewelry Mfg Co.. 401 274-9800
  10 Industrial Ln Johnston (02919) *(G-16076)*

Ardent Inc **(PA)**... **860 528-6000**
  95 Leggett St East Hartford (06108) *(G-971)*

Ardent Displays & Packaging, East Hartford *Also Called: Ardent Inc (G-971)*

Ardeo Systems Inc... 978 373-4680
  17 Parkridge Rd Ste 2 Haverhill (01835) *(G-9074)*

Arecna Holdings Inc.. 203 819-2322
  15 Commercial St Branford (06405) *(G-236)*

Arens Stoneworks Inc.. 603 436-8000
  434 Portsmouth Ave Greenland (03840) *(G-14367)*

Arentzen Ohlander Glass, Burlington *Also Called: Ao Glass LLC (G-17118)*

Arey's Pond Boat Yard, South Orleans *Also Called: P B Y A Inc (G-11973)*

Arga Controls, Weymouth *Also Called: Electro Switch Corp (G-13325)*

Arga Prsnlzed Dcment Solutions............................ 203 401-3650
  25 James St New Haven (06513) *(G-2117)*

Argo Ems, Clinton *Also Called: Eastern Co (G-642)*

Argo Transdata Corp... 860 669-2233
  1 Heritage Park Rd Clinton (06413) *(G-636)*

A L P H A B E T I C

Argos Corporation..508 828-5900
 84 Independence Dr Taunton (02780) *(G-12318)*

Argosy, Newton *Also Called: Argosy Publishing Inc (G-10733)*

Argosy Publishing Inc **(PA)**.........................**617 527-9999**
 109 Oak St Ste 102 Newton (02464) *(G-10733)*

Argotec, Greenfield *Also Called: Argotec LLC (G-8983)*

Argotec LLC..413 772-2564
 53 Silvio O Conte Dr Greenfield (01301) *(G-8982)*

Argotec LLC **(HQ)**...**413 772-2564**
 53 Silvio O Conte Dr Greenfield (01301) *(G-8983)*

Argotec, LLC, Greenfield *Also Called: Argotec LLC (G-8982)*

Argus Analyzers, Jamestown *Also Called: Aurora Performance Pdts LLC (G-16068)*

Argyle Associates Inc...603 226-4300
 30 Terrill Park Dr Concord (03301) *(G-14114)*

Ariad Pharmaceuticals Inc
 40 Landsdowne St Cambridge (02139) *(G-7490)*

Arichell Technologies Inc.....................................617 796-9001
 55 Border St Newton (02465) *(G-10734)*

Arico Engineering Inc..860 642-7040
 841 Route 32 Ste 19 North Franklin (06254) *(G-2381)*

Aries Systems Corporation...................................978 975-7570
 50 High St Ste 21 North Andover (01845) *(G-10820)*

Arinsights LLC..508 233-3494
 163 Highland Ave # 1038 Needham (02494) *(G-10505)*

Arista Industries Inc **(PA)**..............................**203 761-1009**
 187 Danbury Rd Ste 3a Wilton (06897) *(G-4230)*

Aristocrat Metal Box Company, Warren *Also Called: Pusterla Us Inc (G-16765)*

Aristocrat Products Inc...626 287-4110
 17 Taft St Upton (01568) *(G-12469)*

Ariston Engraving & Mch Co Inc...........................781 935-2328
 56 Dragon Ct Woburn (01801) *(G-13515)*

Ariston Usa LLC **(HQ)**.....................................**508 763-8071**
 225 Dyer St Fl 1 Providence (02903) *(G-16474)*

Arizona Polymer Flooring, Andover *Also Called: ICP Construction Inc (G-5887)*

Arkadia Plastics Inc...860 612-0556
 315 John Downey Dr New Britain (06051) *(G-2001)*

Arklay S Richards Co Inc.....................................617 527-4385
 72 Winchester St Newton (02461) *(G-10735)*

Arkwear Inc...401 846-9903
 337 Thames St Unit 1 Newport (02840) *(G-16202)*

Arkwright Advanced Coating Inc **(HQ)**...........**401 821-1000**
 538 Main St Fiskeville (02823) *(G-16053)*

Arland Tool, Sturbridge *Also Called: Arland Tool & Mfg Inc (G-12249)*

Arland Tool & Mfg Inc **(PA)**...........................**508 347-3368**
 421 Main St Sturbridge (01566) *(G-12249)*

Arland Tool & Mfg Inc..508 867-3085
 45 Freight House Rd West Brookfield (01585) *(G-12991)*

Arlin Mfg Co Inc...978 454-9165
 239 Industrial Ave E Lowell (01852) *(G-9854)*

Arlington Industries Inc..802 375-6139
 2617 Vt Route 7a Arlington (05250) *(G-16985)*

Arlington Sample Book Co Inc **(PA)**..............**603 763-9082**
 100 Fernwood Point Rd Sunapee (03782) *(G-15642)*

Arlowe Corporation..978 486-9050
 24 Porter Rd Littleton (01460) *(G-9802)*

Arm Inc..978 264-7300
 100 5th Ave Fl 5 Waltham (02451) *(G-12596)*

Armach Robotics Inc..802 434-6080
 10 E Main St Richmond (05477) *(G-17478)*

Armatron International Inc **(PA)**.....................**781 321-2300**
 17 Locust St Medford (02155) *(G-10280)*

Armbrust International Ltd.....................................401 781-3300
 735 Allens Ave Providence (02905) *(G-16475)*

Armenian Mirror-Spectator, Watertown *Also Called: Baikar Association Inc (G-12862)*

Armetta LLC..860 788-2369
 90 Industrial Park Rd Middletown (06457) *(G-1736)*

Armin Innovative Products Inc...............................508 822-4629
 1424 Somerset Ave Dighton (02715) *(G-8291)*

Armor Roll, Jamaica Plain *Also Called: Weld Rite (G-9504)*

Armored Autogroup Parent Inc..............................203 205-2900
 44 Old Ridgebury Rd Ste 300 Danbury (06810) *(G-710)*

Armored Shield Technologies...............................714 848-5796
 3655 W Mcfadden Ave Redding (06896) *(G-2881)*

Arms, West Bridgewater *Also Called: Atlantic RES Mktg Systems Inc (G-12966)*

Armstrong Family Inds Inc....................................207 848-7300
 1 Printers Dr Hermon (04401) *(G-4880)*

Armstrong Machine Co Inc...................................978 232-9466
 117 Elliott St Ste 3 Beverly (01915) *(G-6326)*

Armstrong Pharmaceuticals Inc **(HQ)**............**617 323-7404**
 423 Lagrange St West Roxbury (02132) *(G-13009)*

Army & Roche LLC..617 936-0114
 1 Beacon St Fl 23 Boston (02108) *(G-6558)*

Arna Machine Company...860 583-0628
 95 Wooster Ct Bristol (06010) *(G-396)*

Arnco Sign Company..203 238-1224
 1133 S Broad St Wallingford (06492) *(G-3775)*

Arnio Welding LLC..860 564-7696
 12 Water St Central Village (06332) *(G-565)*

Arnold Art Inc **(PA)**..**401 847-2273**
 210 Thames St Newport (02840) *(G-16203)*

Arnold Art Store & The Gallery, Newport *Also Called: Arnold Art Inc (G-16203)*

Arnold Lumber Co...401 792-0979
 11 Industrial Dr Coventry (02816) *(G-15806)*

Arnold Lumber Co **(PA)**...................................**401 783-2266**
 251 Fairgrounds Rd West Kingston (02892) *(G-16893)*

Aro Industrial Finishing LLC.................................401 349-4848
 1 Warren Ave North Providence (02911) *(G-16296)*

Aro-Sac Inc..401 231-6655
 1 Warren Ave North Providence (02911) *(G-16297)*

Arocam Inc..508 822-1220
 605 Myles Standish Blvd Taunton (02780) *(G-12319)*

Aroma Therapy International, Boston *Also Called: Euro International Ltd (G-6720)*

Aronson Tire Company Inc.....................................508 832-3244
 510 Washington St Auburn (01501) *(G-6105)*

Aroostacast Inc..207 764-0077
 217 Parsons Rd Presque Isle (04769) *(G-5296)*

Aroostook Republic and News, Caribou *Also Called: Northeast Publishing Company (G-4677)*

Aroostook Republican, Presque Isle *Also Called: Northeast Publishing Company (G-5307)*

Aroostook Shredding, Presque Isle *Also Called: Aroostook Trusses Inc (G-5297)*

Aroostook Trusses Inc..207 768-5817
 655 Missile St Presque Isle (04769) *(G-5297)*

Aroostook Woodsmiths...207 728-7100
 149 Main St Saint Agatha (04772) *(G-5385)*

Arp Welding LLC...203 344-7528
 6 Fox Hollow Rd Oxford (06478) *(G-2686)*

Arqule, Burlington *Also Called: Arqule Inc (G-7335)*

Arqule Inc **(HQ)**..**781 994-0300**
 1 Wall St Ste 603 Burlington (01803) *(G-7335)*

Arradiance LLC...508 202-0593
 11a Beaver Brook Rd Littleton (01460) *(G-9803)*

Arranta Bio, Watertown *Also Called: Arranta Bio Holdings LLC (G-12859)*

Arranta Bio Holdings LLC **(DH)**......................**785 760-3128**
 650 Pleasant St Watertown (02472) *(G-12859)*

Arrhythmia Research Technology............................978 602-1436
 25 Sawyer Passway Fitchburg (01420) *(G-8642)*

Arris International, Westborough *Also Called: Ruckus Wireless Inc (G-13131)*

Arris Technology Inc..678 473-8493
 15 Sterling Dr Wallingford (06492) *(G-3776)*

Arris Technology Inc..978 614-2900
 900 Chelmsford St Lowell (01851) *(G-9855)*

Arrow Concrete Products Inc **(PA)**..................**860 653-5063**
 560 Salmon Brook St Granby (06035) *(G-1305)*

Arrow Diversified Tooling Inc.................................860 872-9072
 17 Pinney St Ellington (06029) *(G-1101)*

Arrow International LLC...978 250-5100
 16 Elizabeth Dr Chelmsford (01824) *(G-7908)*

Arrow Interventional Inc..919 433-4948
 16 Elizabeth Dr Chelmsford (01824) *(G-7909)*

Arrow Lock Manufacturing Co.................................203 603-5959
 110 Sargent Dr New Haven (06511) *(G-2118)*

Arrow Manufacturing Company
 16 Jeannette St Bristol (06010) *(G-397)*

Arrow Shed LLC..	800 560-8383
150 Callender Rd Watertown (06795) *(G-4002)*	
Arrow Thompson Metals, Canton *Also Called: Thompson Steel Company Inc (G-7834)*	
Arrow Win Shade Mfg of Mrden I................................	860 563-4035
47 Oxford St Wethersfield (06109) *(G-4202)*	
Arrowhead Athletics, Andover *Also Called: Shawsheen Rubber Co Inc (G-5918)*	
ARS Products Inc...	860 564-0208
43 Lathrop Road Ext Plainfield (06374) *(G-2732)*	
Art Licensing Intl Inc...	802 362-3662
6366 Vt Route 7a Arlington (05250) *(G-16986)*	
Art Plastics Mfg Corp..	978 537-6640
75 Water St Leominster (01453) *(G-9637)*	
Art Swiss Corporation...	508 999-3281
1357 E Rodney French Blvd New Bedford (02744) *(G-10569)*	
Artco Offset Inc...	781 830-7900
15 Darin Dr Augusta (04330) *(G-4467)*	
Artcraft, Hudson *Also Called: United Stretch Design Corp (G-9422)*	
Artcraft Co Inc...	508 695-4042
200 John L Dietsch Blvd North Attleboro (02763) *(G-10865)*	
Arteffects Incorporated...	860 242-0031
27 Britton Dr Bloomfield (06002) *(G-147)*	
Artek, Antrim *Also Called: Riley Mountain Products Inc (G-13898)*	
Artel Inc..	207 854-0860
25 Bradley Dr Westbrook (04092) *(G-5614)*	
Artel Video Systems Corp..	978 263-5775
5b Lyberty Way Westford (01886) *(G-13224)*	
Artemas Industries Inc..	603 755-9777
20 Sarah Greenfield Way Farmington (03835) *(G-14308)*	
Artemis Capital Partners LLC **(PA)**..............................	**857 327-5606**
160 Federal St 23rd Boston (02110) *(G-6559)*	
Arteriocyte Med Systems Inc...	508 395-5998
45 South St Ste 3c Hopkinton (01748) *(G-9307)*	
Artforms **(PA)**...	**800 828-8518**
128 Maine St Brunswick (04011) *(G-4640)*	
Artfx Signs, Bloomfield *Also Called: Arteffects Incorporated (G-147)*	
Arthrosurface Incorporated..	508 520-3003
28 Forge Pkwy Franklin (02038) *(G-8817)*	
Arthur G Lombardi Seltzer, Derby *Also Called: Castle Seltzer Inc (G-888)*	
Arthur G Russell Company Inc......................................	860 583-4109
750 Clark Ave Bristol (06010) *(G-398)*	
Arthur J Hurley Company..	860 257-5505
60 Meadow St East Hartford (06108) *(G-972)*	
Arthur Mapes Inc..	978 256-4061
292 Chelmsford St Chelmsford (01824) *(G-7910)*	
Arthur Whitcomb, West Lebanon *Also Called: Crh Americas Inc (G-15681)*	
Artic Tool & Engrg Co LLC..	401 785-2210
29 Lark Industrial Pkwy Greenville (02828) *(G-16055)*	
Artinian Garabet Corporation..	978 371-7110
39 Main St Concord (01742) *(G-8102)*	
Artisan Chef Manufacturing LLC **(HQ)**.......................	**978 691-6100**
117 Water St Lawrence (01841) *(G-9538)*	
Artisan Industries Inc...	781 893-6800
44 Campanelli Pkwy Stoughton (02072) *(G-12195)*	
Artisan Surfaces Inc...	802 885-8677
200 Clinton St Springfield (05156) *(G-17616)*	
Artistic Iron Works LLC..	203 838-9200
11 Reynolds St Norwalk (06855) *(G-2464)*	
Arts International Wholesale...	508 822-7181
104 Forge River Pkwy Raynham (02767) *(G-11581)*	
Arturo Milite and Spinella Bky, Wolcott *Also Called: Milite Bakery (G-4368)*	
Artvac Corporation..	401 333-6120
17 New England Way Lincoln (02865) *(G-16120)*	
Arundel Holdings Inc..	207 985-8555
20 Technology Dr Arundel (04046) *(G-4408)*	
Arvinas Inc **(PA)**..	**203 535-1456**
395 Winchester Ave New Haven (06511) *(G-2119)*	
Arwood Machine Corporation...	978 463-3777
95 Parker St Ste 4 Newburyport (01950) *(G-10667)*	
AS Hudak Lumber..	802 527-9802
24 Beverly Ct Saint Albans (05478) *(G-17515)*	
Asahi/America Inc...	800 343-3618
655 Andover St Lawrence (01843) *(G-9539)*	

Asahi/America Inc **(HQ)**..	**781 321-5409**
655 Andover St Lawrence (01843) *(G-9540)*	
ASAP, Dudley *Also Called: American Sub Assmbly Prdcers I (G-8315)*	
ASap Mch Sp Fabrication Inc..	860 564-4114
89 Mill Brook Rd Plainfield (06374) *(G-2733)*	
ASC Engineered Solutions LLC.....................................	708 534-1414
75 Portsmouth Blvd Ste 210 Portsmouth (03801) *(G-15360)*	
ASC Engineered Solutions LLC.....................................	401 886-3000
160 Frenchtown Rd North Kingstown (02852) *(G-16233)*	
Asca Inc **(PA)**...	**603 433-6700**
112 Corporate Dr Ste 1 Portsmouth (03801) *(G-15361)*	
Ascend Elements Inc **(PA)**..	**508 936-7701**
133 Flanders Rd Westborough (01581) *(G-13077)*	
Ascend Elevator Inc..	215 703-0358
212 W Newberry Rd Bloomfield (06002) *(G-148)*	
Ascend Robotics LLC..	978 451-0170
245 1st St Ste 18 Cambridge (02142) *(G-7491)*	
Ascension, Shelburne *Also Called: Ascension Technology Corp (G-17556)*	
Ascension Technology Corp...	802 893-6657
120 Graham Way Ste 130 Shelburne (05482) *(G-17556)*	
Ascent Aerosystems Inc..	330 554-6334
100 Research Dr Ste 3 Wilmington (01887) *(G-13381)*	
Asco Power Technologies LP...	508 624-0466
2 Maple St Marlborough (01752) *(G-10111)*	
Ascutney Metal Products Inc...	802 674-6721
2637 Us Route 5 N Windsor (05089) *(G-17757)*	
Asd Lighting Corp...	781 739-3977
120 Shawmut Rd Canton (02021) *(G-7770)*	
Ase (us)inc...	781 305-5900
400 Tradecenter Ste 4950 Woburn (01801) *(G-13516)*	
Asea Brown Boveri Inc...	203 750-2200
501 Merritt 7 Norwalk (06851) *(G-2465)*	
Asepsis Inc...	203 573-2000
199 Benson Rd Waterbury (06749) *(G-3887)*	
Ashaway Line & Twine Mfg Co......................................	401 377-2221
24 Laurel St Ashaway (02804) *(G-15738)*	
Ashcroft Inc **(DH)**..	**203 378-8281**
250 E Main St Stratford (06614) *(G-3517)*	
Ashe America Inc...	802 254-0200
23 Marlboro Rd Brattleboro (05301) *(G-17073)*	
Ashe Converting Equipment, Brattleboro *Also Called: Ashe America Inc (G-17073)*	
Ashland Cabinet Corporation...	508 303-8100
150 Cordaville Rd Ste 100 Southborough (01772) *(G-11989)*	
Ashland Electric Products Inc..	603 335-1100
10 Indl Way Rochester (03867) *(G-15466)*	
Ashleigh Inc **(PA)**...	**207 967-4311**
8 Western Ave Ste 6 Kennebunk (04043) *(G-4921)*	
Ashley & Harmon Logging Inc.......................................	207 259-2043
230 Chases Mill Rd East Machias (04630) *(G-4739)*	
Ashmont Welding Company Inc.....................................	508 279-1977
10 Cranmore Dr Bridgewater (02324) *(G-7220)*	
Ashworth Assoc Mfg Whl Jwelers................................	508 695-1900
41 Richards Ave North Attleboro (02760) *(G-10866)*	
Ashworth Awards, North Attleboro *Also Called: Ashworth Assoc Mfg Whl Jwelers (G-10866)*	
Ashworth International Inc..	508 674-4693
222 Milliken Blvd Ste 7 Fall River (02721) *(G-8522)*	
Asi Modulex, East Berlin *Also Called: Wad Inc (G-920)*	
Asi Sign Systems Inc..	860 828-3331
100 Clark Dr East Berlin (06023) *(G-907)*	
Asia Direct LLC...	603 382-9485
91 Main St Ste 14 Plaistow (03865) *(G-15336)*	
Asian American Civic Assn Inc **(PA)**...........................	**617 426-9492**
87 Tyler St Ste 5f Boston (02111) *(G-6560)*	
Asimov Inc...	339 532-9982
201 Brookline Ave Boston (02215) *(G-6561)*	
Ask Services, North Kingstown *Also Called: Lightship Group LLC (G-16268)*	
Ask-Inttag LLC..	802 288-7210
1000 River St Bldg 966 Essex Junction (05452) *(G-17226)*	
Asml Us LLC...	203 761-4000
77 Danbury Rd Wilton (06897) *(G-4231)*	
Asml Us LLC...	207 541-5000
590 County Rd Westbrook (04092) *(G-5615)*	

A
L
P
H
A
B
E
T
I
C

Asmpt Nexx Inc.. 978 436-4600
  900 Middlesex Tpke Bldg 6 Billerica (01821) *(G-6406)*

Asp Fibermark Holdings LLC................................. 413 736-4554
  70 Front St West Springfield (01089) *(G-13014)*

Aspecta North America LLC................................... 855 400-7732
  15 Oakwood Ave Norwalk (06850) *(G-2466)*

Aspects, Warren *Also Called: Aspects Inc (G-16751)*

Aspects Inc... 401 247-1854
  245 Child St Warren (02885) *(G-16751)*

Aspen Aerogels, Northborough *Also Called: Aspen Aerogels Inc (G-11088)*

Aspen Aerogels Inc **(PA)**................................... **508 691-1111**
  30 Forbes Rd Bldg B Northborough (01532) *(G-11088)*

Aspen Aerogels RI LLC... 401 432-2612
  3 Dexter Rd East Providence (02914) *(G-16005)*

Aspen Systems LLC **(PA)**.................................. **508 281-5322**
  24 Saint Martin Dr Ste 3 Marlborough (01752) *(G-10112)*

Aspen Technology Inc **(HQ)**............................... **781 221-6400**
  20 Crosby Dr Bedford (01730) *(G-6211)*

Aspenone, Bedford *Also Called: Aspentech Corporation (G-6212)*

Aspentech Corporation **(DH)**.............................. **781 221-6400**
  20 Crosby Dr Bedford (01730) *(G-6212)*

Assa, New Haven *Also Called: Assa Abloy Inc (G-2122)*

Assa Inc... 800 235-7482
  110 Sargent Dr New Haven (06511) *(G-2120)*

Assa Abloy ACC Door Cntrls Gro........................ 865 986-7511
  225 Episcopal Rd Berlin (06037) *(G-50)*

Assa Abloy ACC Door Cntrls Gro........................ 901 365-2160
  110 Sargent Dr New Haven (06511) *(G-2121)*

Assa Abloy Access Egress Hdwr.......................... 860 225-7411
  225 Episcopal Rd Berlin (06037) *(G-51)*

Assa Abloy Inc **(HQ)**.. **203 562-2151**
  110 Sargent Dr New Haven (06511) *(G-2122)*

Assa Abloy USA, New Haven *Also Called: Sargent Manufacturing Company (G-2194)*

Assa High Security Locks, New Haven *Also Called: Assa Inc (G-2120)*

Assabet Machine Corp.. 978 263-2900
  1145 Massachusetts Ave Boxborough (01719) *(G-7147)*

Assayquant Technologies Inc................................ 774 278-3302
  260 Cedar Hill St Marlborough (01752) *(G-10113)*

Assembly Guidance Systems Inc.......................... 978 244-1166
  27 Industrial Ave Unit 4 Chelmsford (01824) *(G-7911)*

Assembly Test Division, North Reading *Also Called: Teradyne Inc (G-11047)*

Asset International Inc.. 203 629-5014
  125 Greenwich Ave Ste 3 Greenwich (06830) *(G-1314)*

Associated Envmtl Systems, Acton *Also Called: Associated Envmtl Systems Inc (G-5738)*

Associated Envmtl Systems Inc **(PA)**................ **978 772-0022**
  8 Post Office Sq Acton (01720) *(G-5738)*

Associated Mktg Systems Inc.............................. 781 767-9001
  2 Kleen Way Holbrook (02343) *(G-9168)*

Associated X-Ray Corp **(PA)**............................ **203 466-2446**
  246 Dodge Ave East Haven (06512) *(G-1036)*

Associates of Cape Cod Inc **(PA)**.................... **508 540-3444**
  124 Bernard E Saint Jean East Falmouth (02536) *(G-8355)*

Assocted Electro-Mechanics Inc........................... 413 781-4276
  185 Rowland St Springfield (01107) *(G-12076)*

Assoction For Grvstone Studies............................ 413 772-0836
  278 Main St Ste 209 Greenfield (01301) *(G-8984)*

Assurance Technology Corp **(PA)**..................... **978 369-8848**
  84 South St Carlisle (01741) *(G-7845)*

Assurance Technology Corp.................................. 978 250-8060
  303 Littleton Rd Chelmsford (01824) *(G-7912)*

Assuretec Systems, Manchester *Also Called: Acuant Inc (G-14804)*

AST, Hopkinton *Also Called: Adaptive Surface Tech Inc (G-9306)*

Astellas Inst For Rgnrtive Mdc **(HQ)**................ **800 727-7003**
  9 Technology Dr Westborough (01581) *(G-13078)*

Astenjohnson Inc.. 413 733-6603
  40 Progress Ave Springfield (01104) *(G-12077)*

Astenjohnson Inc.. 802 658-2040
  192 Industrial Ave Williston (05495) *(G-17722)*

Astex Plasmaquest Inc... 781 937-6272
  90 Industrial Way Wilmington (01887) *(G-13382)*

Astonish Results LP... 401 921-6220
  300 Metro Center Blvd Warwick (02886) *(G-16784)*

Astrea Bioseparations, Canton *Also Called: Astrea Bioseparations US Inc (G-7771)*

Astrea Bioseparations US Inc............................... 919 899-9087
  960 Turnpike St Canton (02021) *(G-7771)*

Astrella Ink... 508 865-5028
  50 Howe Ave Ste 2 Millbury (01527) *(G-10426)*

Astria Therapeutics Inc **(PA)**........................... **617 349-1971**
  75 State St Ste 1400 Boston (02109) *(G-6562)*

Astro Welding, Boxborough *Also Called: Astro Welding & Fabg Inc (G-7148)*

Astro Welding & Fabg Inc.................................... 978 429-8666
  200 Codman Hill Rd Boxborough (01719) *(G-7148)*

Astron Inc **(PA)**... **978 433-9500**
  21 Lomar Park Pepperell (01463) *(G-11383)*

Astronics Aerosat Corporation.............................. 603 879-0205
  220 Hackett Hill Rd Manchester (03102) *(G-14814)*

Astronova, West Warwick *Also Called: Astronova Inc (G-16902)*

Astronova Inc **(PA)**... **401 828-4000**
  600 E Greenwich Ave West Warwick (02893) *(G-16902)*

Astronova Inc... 401 828-4000
  600 E Greenwich Ave West Warwick (02893) *(G-16903)*

Asymchem, Woburn *Also Called: Asymchem Boston Corporation (G-13517)*

Asymchem Boston Corporation.............................. 781 896-3998
  10 Gill St Ste J Woburn (01801) *(G-13517)*

At Comm Corp.. 603 624-4424
  150 Dow St Ste 404 Manchester (03101) *(G-14815)*

AT Cross Company LLC **(HQ)**........................... **401 333-1200**
  295 Promenade St Providence (02908) *(G-16476)*

At Surgical Company.. 888 233-4069
  115 Clemente St Holyoke (01040) *(G-9241)*

AT&T, New Haven *Also Called: Southern Neng Telecom Corp (G-2203)*

Ata Piping, Windham *Also Called: Wardwell Piping Inc (G-5674)*

Ataccama Corp US... 203 564-1488
  263 Tresser Blvd Fl 9 Stamford (06901) *(G-3287)*

Atamian Manufacturing Corp................................. 401 944-9614
  910 Plainfield St Providence (02909) *(G-16477)*

Atc Ponderosa B-I LLC... 617 375-7500
  116 Huntington Ave Boston (02116) *(G-6563)*

Atc Ponderosa B-II LLC.. 617 375-7500
  116 Huntington Ave Boston (02116) *(G-6564)*

Atc Ponderosa H-I LLC... 617 375-7500
  116 Huntington Ave Boston (02116) *(G-6565)*

Atc Ponderosa H-II LLC.. 617 375-7500
  116 Huntington Ave Boston (02116) *(G-6566)*

Atc Ponderosa K LLC... 617 375-7500
  116 Huntington Ave Boston (02116) *(G-6567)*

Atc Ponderosa K Ohio LLC................................... 617 375-7500
  116 Huntington Ave Boston (02116) *(G-6568)*

Atc Screw Machine Inc... 781 939-0725
  419 River St Haverhill (01832) *(G-9075)*

Atc Sequoia LLC.. 617 375-7500
  116 Huntington Ave Boston (02116) *(G-6569)*

Atc Technologies Inc.. 781 939-0725
  30b Upton Dr Wilmington (01887) *(G-13383)*

Atc Tower Services LLC.. 617 375-7500
  116 Huntington Ave Ste 1100 Boston (02116) *(G-6570)*

Atco Lanair, Portsmouth *Also Called: Lanair Research & Dev Inc (G-15415)*

Atco Plastics Inc.. 508 695-3573
  31 W Bacon St Plainville (02762) *(G-11429)*

Atconsulting LLC.. 203 987-5355
  151 Cascade Rd Stamford (06903) *(G-3288)*

ATEA PHARMACEUTICALS, Boston *Also Called: Atea Pharmaceuticals Inc (G-6571)*

Atea Pharmaceuticals Inc **(PA)**......................... **857 284-8891**
  225 Franklin St Ste 2100 Boston (02110) *(G-6571)*

Aternity Inc... 508 475-0414
  125 Cambridgepark Dr Ste 402 Cambridge (02140) *(G-7492)*

Aternity LLC **(DH)**.. **617 250-5309**
  125 Cambridgepark Dr Cambridge (02140) *(G-7493)*

Atg, Cambridge *Also Called: Oracle Otc Subsidiary LLC (G-7678)*

Athenahealth Inc **(PA)**...................................... **617 402-1000**
  80 Guest St Boston (02135) *(G-6572)*

Athens Industries Inc.. 860 621-8957
220 West St Plantsville (06479) *(G-2789)*

Athinia Technologies LLC.. 781 491-4189
245 1st St Ste 18 Cambridge (02142) *(G-7494)*

Athletic Emblem Lettering Inc....................................... 413 733-8151
189 Taylor St Springfield (01105) *(G-12078)*

ATI Allegheny Ludlum Inc.. 508 992-4067
1357 E Rodney French Blvd New Bedford (02744) *(G-10570)*

ATI Flat Rlled Pdts Hldngs LLC...................................... 203 756-7414
271 Railroad Hill St Waterbury (06708) *(G-3888)*

ATI Flat Rolled Products, Waterbury *Also Called: ATI Flat Rlled Pdts Hldngs LLC (G-3888)*

ATI Flat Rolled Products, New Bedford *Also Called: ATI Allegheny Ludlum Inc (G-10570)*

ATI Forged Products, East Hartford *Also Called: ATI Ladish Machining Inc (G-973)*

ATI Ladish Machiring Inc **(DH)**.................................... **860 688-3688**
311 Prestige Park Rd East Hartford (06108) *(G-973)*

ATI Ladish Machining Inc... 860 688-3688
311 Prestige Park Rd East Hartford (06108) *(G-974)*

ATI Ladish Machining Inc... 860 688-3688
34 S Satellite Rd South Windsor (06074) *(G-3116)*

Atiim Inc.. 800 735-4071
399 Boylston St Fl 6 Boston (02116) *(G-6573)*

Atk Space Systems LLC.. 508 497-9457
65 South St Ste 105 Hopkinton (01748) *(G-9308)*

Atkins Farm Country Market, Amherst *Also Called: Atkins Fruit Bowl Inc (G-5859)*

Atkins Fruit Bowl Inc... 413 253-9528
1150 West St Amherst (01002) *(G-5859)*

Atlantic Acm.. 617 720-3700
31 State St Ste 2 Boston (02109) *(G-6574)*

Atlantic Air Products Mfg LLC.. 603 410-3900
1266 Furnace Brook Pkwy Ste 300 Quincy (02169) *(G-11504)*

Atlantic Auto & Trck Parts LLC...................................... 978 535-6777
26 Hammond St Rowley (01969) *(G-11667)*

Atlantic Automation Group LLC..................................... 401 424-1840
19 Broadcommon Rd Bristol (02809) *(G-15754)*

Atlantic Battery Company Inc....................................... 617 924-2868
309 Main St Rear Watertown (02472) *(G-12860)*

Atlantic Bookbinders Inc.. 978 365-4524
87 Flagg St South Lancaster (01561) *(G-11970)*

Atlantic Broom Service Inc... 774 226-1300
600 N Bedford St Ste 300 East Bridgewater (02333) *(G-8335)*

Atlantic Cotton Company, Portland *Also Called: Atlantic Sportswear Inc (G-5178)*

Atlantic Eqp Installers Inc.. 203 284-0402
55 N Plains Industrial Rd Wallingford (06492) *(G-3777)*

Atlantic Fabricating Co Inc.. 860 291-9882
71 Edwin Rd South Windsor (06074) *(G-3117)*

Atlantic Fish & Seafcod, Gloucester *Also Called: Nsd Seafood Inc (G-8947)*

Atlantic Footcare, North Smithfield *Also Called: Atlantic Footcare Inc (G-16318)*

Atlantic Footcare Inc.. 401 568-4918
229 Quaker Hwy North Smithfield (02896) *(G-16318)*

Atlantic Furniture Inc.. 413 665-4700
5 Industrial Dr W South Deerfield (01373) *(G-11920)*

Atlantic Highway Sign Company, East Bridgewater *Also Called: Atlantic Broom Service Inc (G-8335)*

Atlantic Industrial Model.. 978 768-4568
197 Western Ave Essex (01929) *(G-8472)*

Atlantic Industrial Models LLC....................................... 978 768-7686
7 Essex Park Rd Essex (01929) *(G-8473)*

Atlantic Inertial Systems, Cheshire *Also Called: Ais Global Holdings LLC (G-570)*

Atlantic Inertial Systems Inc **(DH)**............................... **203 250-3500**
250 Knotter Dr Cheshire (06410) *(G-572)*

Atlantic Inertial Systems Inc.. 203 250-3500
250 Knotter Dr Cheshire (06410) *(G-573)*

Atlantic Laboratories Inc... 207 832-5376
41 Cross St Waldoboro (04572) *(G-5574)*

Atlantic Lighting Inc... 508 678-5411
231 Commerce Dr Fall River (02720) *(G-8523)*

Atlantic MBL & Gran Group Inc...................................... 508 540-9770
59 Technology Park Dr East Falmouth (02536) *(G-8356)*

Atlantic Microtool.. 603 898-3212
91 Stiles Rd Ste 207 Salem (03079) *(G-15509)*

Atlantic Microwave Corporation
1001 Pawtucket Blvd Lowell (01854) *(G-9856)*

Atlantic Millwork, North Haven *Also Called: Elm City Manufacturing LLC (G-2409)*

Atlantic Poly Inc... 781 769-4260
86 Morse St Norwood (02062) *(G-11163)*

Atlantic Precision Services... 207 329-1043
397 Ossipee Trl Gorham (04038) *(G-4816)*

Atlantic Precision Spring Inc... 860 583-1864
125 Ronzo Rd Bristol (06010) *(G-399)*

Atlantic Printing Co Inc.. 781 449-2700
5 Causeway Ln Medfield (02052) *(G-10269)*

Atlantic Pwr US GP Hldings Inc...................................... 617 977-2400
3 Allied Dr Ste 155 Dedham (02026) *(G-8236)*

Atlantic RES Mktg Systems LLC...................................... 508 584-7816
230 W Center St West Bridgewater (02379) *(G-12966)*

Atlantic Rubber Company Inc.. 800 882-3666
37 Ayer Rd Ste 6 Littleton (01460) *(G-9804)*

Atlantic Sea Farms, Biddeford *Also Called: Ocean Approved Inc (G-4580)*

Atlantic Sportswear Inc... 207 797-5028
36 Waldron Way Portland (04103) *(G-5178)*

Atlantic Standard Molding Inc....................................... 207 797-0727
380 Warren Ave Apt 2 Portland (04103) *(G-5179)*

Atlantic Street Capitl MGT LLC **(PA)**............................. **203 428-3158**
281 Tresser Blvd Fl 6 Stamford (06901) *(G-3289)*

Atlantic Turnkey Cons Corp.. 603 673-9447
54 Ponemah Rd Amherst (03031) *(G-13862)*

Atlantic Vent & Eqp Co Inc... 860 635-1300
125 Sebethe Dr Cromwell (06416) *(G-687)*

Atlantic Vision Inc... 508 845-8401
810 Boston Tpke Ste 2 Shrewsbury (01545) *(G-11828)*

Atlantic Woodcraft Inc.. 860 749-4887
199 Moody Rd Enfield (06082) *(G-1121)*

Atlantic-Acm, Boston *Also Called: Atlantic Acm (G-6574)*

Atlantis Technology Corp.. 978 341-0999
1620 Sudbury Rd Ste 1 Concord (01742) *(G-8103)*

Atlas Advanced Pyrotechnics, Jaffrey *Also Called: Atlas Pyrvsion Entrmt Group In (G-14564)*

Atlas Agi Holdings LLC... 203 622-9138
100 Northfield St Greenwich (06830) *(G-1315)*

Atlas Barrell & Pallet Inc... 401 568-2900
50 Old Mill St Harrisville (02830) *(G-16064)*

Atlas Box and Crating Co Inc **(PA)**.............................. **508 865-1155**
223 Worcester Providence Tpke Sutton (01590) *(G-12276)*

Atlas Concrete Products Inc... 860 224-2244
65 Burritt St New Britain (06053) *(G-2002)*

Atlas Copco, Ludlow *Also Called: Atlas Copco Compressors LLC (G-9938)*

Atlas Copco Compressors LLC.. 413 589-7439
151 Carmelinas Cir Ludlow (01056) *(G-9938)*

Atlas Copco Compressors LLC.. 413 493-7290
92 Interstate Dr West Springfield (01089) *(G-13015)*

Atlas Copco Compressors LLC.. 518 765-3344
94 N Elm St Fl 4 Westfield (01085) *(G-13149)*

Atlas Devices, Chelmsford *Also Called: Atlas Devices LLC (G-7913)*

Atlas Devices LLC... 617 415-1657
21 Alpha Rd Ste B Chelmsford (01824) *(G-7913)*

Atlas Distributing Inc.. 508 791-6221
44 Southbridge St Auburn (01501) *(G-6106)*

Atlas Fibre LLC... 847 674-1234
116 Flanders Rd Ste 3000 Westborough (01581) *(G-13079)*

Atlas Filtri North America LLC.. 203 284-0080
1068 N Farms Rd Ste 3 Wallingford (06492) *(G-3778)*

Atlas Global Solutions, Sutton *Also Called: Atlas Box and Crating Co Inc (G-12276)*

Atlas Gran Countertop Flr Sup....................................... 603 818-8899
4 Windham Depot Rd Derry (03038) *(G-14190)*

Atlas Industrial Services LLC.. 203 315-4538
30 Ne Industrial Rd Branford (06405) *(G-237)*

Atlas Metal Works, South Windsor *Also Called: Atlas Metal Works LLC (G-3118)*

Atlas Metal Works LLC.. 860 282-1030
48 Commerce Way South Windsor (06074) *(G-3118)*

Atlas Metallizing Inc... 860 827-9777
5 East St New Britain (06051) *(G-2003)*

Atlas Pallet, Harrisville *Also Called: Atlas Barrell & Pallet Inc (G-16064)*

Atlas Prcision Met Fabricators....................................... 603 742-1226
49 Industrial Park Dover (03820) *(G-14217)*

Atlas Precision Manufacturing, South Windsor *Also Called: Atlas Precision Mfg LLC* **(G-3119)**

Atlas Precision Mfg LLC.. 860 290-9114
   508 Burnham St South Windsor (06074) *(G-3119)*

Atlas Pyrvsion Entrmt Group In **(PA)**.............................. **603 532-8324**
   136 Old Sharon Rd Jaffrey (03452) *(G-14564)*

Atlas Stamping & Mfg Corp... 860 757-3233
   729 N Mountain Rd Newington (06111) *(G-2273)*

Atlas Water Systems Inc... 781 373-4700
   301 2nd Ave Waltham (02451) *(G-12597)*

Atlassian Pty Ltd.. 401 864-1481
   239 Causeway St Ste 300 Boston (02114) *(G-6575)*

Atlee Delaware Incorporated... 978 681-1003
   9 Clinton Rd Melrose (02176) *(G-10313)*

Atmi, Inc., Danbury *Also Called: Entegris Prof Solutions Inc* **(G-738)**

Atmosair, Fairfield *Also Called: Clean Air Group Inc* **(G-1179)**

Atnh, Pembroke *Also Called: Abrasives & Tools NH Inc* **(G-15301)**

Atom Adhesives LLC.. 888 522-6742
   1 Acorn St Providence (02903) *(G-16478)*

Atomera Incorporated.. 617 219-0600
   20 Walnut St Ste 8 Wellesley Hills (02481) *(G-12950)*

Atomic Cafe Inc **(PA)**... **978 910-0489**
   45 Mason St Ste 1 Salem (01970) *(G-11702)*

Atp Industries LLC **(PA)**.. **860 479-5007**
   75 Northwest Dr Plainville (06062) *(G-2748)*

Atrenne Cmpt Solutions LLC... 508 588-6110
   11 Burke Dr Brockton (02301) *(G-7258)*

Atrenne Cmpt Solutions LLC **(DH)**..................................... **508 588-6110**
   10 Mupac Dr Brockton (02301) *(G-7259)*

Atrex Energy Inc **(PA)**... **781 461-8251**
   19 Walpole Park S Walpole (02081) *(G-12551)*

Atrium Innovations... 978 579-2346
   33 Union Ave Sudbury (01776) *(G-12260)*

Atrium Medical, Merrimack *Also Called: Atrium Medical Corporation* **(G-14973)**

Atrium Medical Corporation **(HQ)**.................................... **973 709-7654**
   40 Continental Blvd Merrimack (03054) *(G-14973)*

Ats, Wallingford *Also Called: Advanced Turbine Services LLC* **(G-3767)**

Ats Cases Inc... 508 393-9110
   172 Otis St Ste 4 Northborough (01532) *(G-11089)*

Ats Manufacturing,, Holyoke *Also Called: At Surgical Company* **(G-9241)**

Ats Precision, New Hampton *Also Called: Alan T Seeler Inc* **(G-15195)**

Attivio Inc... 857 226-5040
   100 Summer St Ste 3100 Boston (02110) *(G-6576)*

Attleboro Sand & Gravel Corp.. 508 222-2870
   125 Tiffany St Attleboro (02703) *(G-5995)*

Attleboro's Jewelry Makers, Attleboro *Also Called: G Austin Young Inc* **(G-6019)**

Attunity Inc **(DH)**... **781 730-4070**
   70 Blanchard Rd Burlington (01803) *(G-7336)*

ATW Companies Inc **(PA)**.. **401 244-1002**
   125 Metro Center Blvd Ste 3001 Warwick (02886) *(G-16785)*

ATW Electronics Inc.. 617 304-3579
   24 Spice St Ste 2 Charlestown (02129) *(G-7861)*

Au Bon Pain, Boston *Also Called: Abp Corporation* **(G-6505)**

Au Milford LLC... 508 473-1870
   213 Central St Milford (01757) *(G-10398)*

Aube Precision Tool Co Inc... 413 589-9048
   54 Moody St Ludlow (01056) *(G-9939)*

Aubin Equipment and Automotive...................................... 508 385-3237
   372 Hokum Rock Rd East Dennis (02641) *(G-8348)*

Aubin Woodworking Inc... 603 224-5512
   359 River Rd Ste 15 Bow (03304) *(G-13993)*

Auburn, Middletown *Also Called: Auburn Manufacturing Company* **(G-1737)**

Auburn Asphalt LLC.. 207 894-5040
   3189 Hotel Rd Auburn (04210) *(G-4421)*

Auburn Concrete, Auburn *Also Called: R A Cummings Inc* **(G-4457)**

Auburn Filtersense LLC... 978 777-2460
   800 Cummings Ctr Ste 355w Beverly (01915) *(G-6327)*

Auburn International Inc.. 978 777-2460
   800 Cummings Ctr Ste 355w Beverly (01915) *(G-6328)*

Auburn Manufacturing Company.. 860 346-6677
   29 Stack St Middletown (06457) *(G-1737)*

Auburn Manufacturing Inc... 207 345-8271
   5125 Walker Rd Mechanic Falls (04256) *(G-5048)*

Auburn Manufacturing Inc **(PA)**... **207 345-8271**
   34 Walker Rd Mechanic Falls (04256) *(G-5049)*

Auburn Spring Water Company **(PA)**.................................. **207 782-1521**
   24 Brickyard Cir Auburn (04210) *(G-4422)*

Auburn Systems LLC... 978 777-2460
   800 Cummings Ctr Ste 355w Beverly (01915) *(G-6329)*

Auciello Iron Works Inc... 978 568-8382
   560 Main St Hudson (01749) *(G-9355)*

Auctionmethod LLC.. 413 489-1389
   30 Williams St Shelburne Falls (01370) *(G-11802)*

Audette Group LLC... 401 667-5884
   144 Westminster St Ste 302 Providence (02903) *(G-16479)*

Audi Danbury, Danbury *Also Called: Danbury A LLC* **(G-724)**

Audia Woodworking.. 603 817-1309
   161 Portsmouth Ave Stratham (03885) *(G-15633)*

Audio Accessories Inc... 603 446-3335
   25 Mill St Marlow (03456) *(G-14966)*

Audio Line, Marlow *Also Called: Audio Accessories Inc* **(G-14966)**

Audio Spectrum, Randolph *Also Called: Audiospectrum Inc* **(G-11549)**

Audiospectrum Inc... 781 767-1331
   50 Mazzeo Dr Randolph (02368) *(G-11549)*

Augmentus Group LLC
   57 Loomis St # 3 Burlington (05401) *(G-17119)*

Augmentus Ltd Co, Burlington *Also Called: Augmentus Group LLC* **(G-17119)**

Aunt Sadies Inc... 802 892-5267
   108 S Lunenburg Rd Lunenburg (05906) *(G-17316)*

AURA, Boston *Also Called: Aura Biosciences Inc* **(G-6577)**

Aura Biosciences Inc **(PA)**... **617 500-8864**
   80 Guest St Fl 5 Boston (02135) *(G-6577)*

Aurora Fuel Company Inc... 401 345-5996
   191 Pulaski St West Warwick (02893) *(G-16904)*

Aurora Healthcare US Corp.. 978 204-5240
   8 Electronics Ave Ste 1 Danvers (01923) *(G-8163)*

Aurora Imaging Technology Inc **(PA)**.................................. **877 975-7530**
   8 Electronics Ave Ste 1 Danvers (01923) *(G-8164)*

Aurora Imaging Technology Inc.. 617 522-6900
   165 Worcester St Wellesley (02481) *(G-12937)*

Aurora Performance Pdts LLC.. 401 398-2959
   56 Green Ln Jamestown (02835) *(G-16068)*

Aurora Plastics, Lunenburg *Also Called: S&E Specialty Polymers LLC* **(G-9960)**

Aurora Wind Project LLC.. 978 409-9712
   100 Brickstone Sq Ste 300 Andover (01810) *(G-5871)*

Austin Electronics, Chester *Also Called: Whelen Engineering Company Inc* **(G-633)**

Austin Organs Incorporated... 860 522-8293
   156 Woodland St Hartford (06105) *(G-1472)*

Austin Powder Company... 860 564-5466
   332 Ekonk Hill Rd Sterling (06377) *(G-3499)*

Austin Screenprint, West Yarmouth *Also Called: Austins Sportswear Inc* **(G-13071)**

Austins Sportswear Inc.. 508 775-0554
   223 Mid Tech Dr West Yarmouth (02673) *(G-13071)*

Austrian Machine Corp... 401 946-4090
   25 Stamp Farm Rd Cranston (02921) *(G-15835)*

Autac Incorporated **(PA)**... **203 481-3444**
   25 Thompson Rd Branford (06405) *(G-238)*

Auterra Inc.. 518 382-9600
   333 White Birch Dr Guilford (06437) *(G-1385)*

Authentic Designs Inc... 802 394-7715
   154 Mill Rd West Rupert (05776) *(G-17694)*

Author Reputation Press LLC... 800 220-7660
   45 Dan Rd Canton (02021) *(G-7772)*

Auto Chlor Systems Co, Foxboro *Also Called: Conopco Inc* **(G-8693)**

Auto Hunter Magazine, Saugus *Also Called: Hunter Associates Inc* **(G-11761)**

Auto-Chlor System NY Cy Inc.. 508 543-6767
   140 Washington St Ste 1 Foxboro (02035) *(G-8691)*

Autocraft Collision Inc.. 781 670-9001
   943 Main St Reading (01867) *(G-11600)*

Autocrat Coffee, Lincoln *Also Called: Finlay EXT Ingredients USA Inc* **(G-16137)**

Autodesk Inc.. 857 233-4149
   23 Drydock Ave Ste 610e Boston (02210) *(G-6578)*

Autodesk Reseller, Watertown *Also Called: Microcad Trning Consulting Inc* ***(G-12893)***

Autogen Inc. 508 429-5965
84 October Hill Rd Ste 5 Holliston (01746) ***(G-9200)***

Automatech Inc. 860 673-5940
21 Westview Ter Unionville (06085) ***(G-3747)***

Automatech Inc **(PA)** **508 830-0088**
138 Industrial Park Rd Plymouth (02360) ***(G-11447)***

Automated Finishing Co Inc. 508 222-6262
90 County St Attleboro (02703) ***(G-5996)***

Automated Industrial Mch Inc. 401 232-1710
347 Farnum Pike Smithfield (02917) ***(G-16688)***

Automated Logic Corporation 203 284-0100
23 Village Ln Wallingford (06492) ***(G-3779)***

Automated Logic Corporation 413 547-6595
260 Griffith Rd Chicopee (01022) ***(G-8008)***

Automated Mailing Services LLC 203 439-2763
1687 Reinhard Rd Cheshire (06410) ***(G-574)***

Automated Video Insptn Dvcs 603 559-9700
222 International Dr Ste 195 Portsmouth (03801) ***(G-15362)***

Automatic Machine Pdts Sls Co. 508 822-4226
400 Constitution Dr Taunton (02780) ***(G-12320)***

Automatic Machine Products Co. 508 822-4226
400 Constitution Dr Taunton (02780) ***(G-12321)***

Automatic Press Inc. 508 528-2000
842 Union St Ste 1 Franklin (02038) ***(G-8818)***

Automatic Rolls of New England, Dayville *Also Called: Northeast Foods Inc* ***(G-864)***

Automatic Specialties Inc. 508 481-2370
422 Northboro Road Central Marlborough (01752) ***(G-10114)***

Automating Information, Cambridge *Also Called: Window Book Inc* ***(G-7761)***

Automation Inc. 860 236-5991
707 Oakwood Ave West Hartford (06110) ***(G-4048)***

Automec Inc. 781 893-3403
82 Calvary St Waltham (02453) ***(G-12598)***

Automotive & Miniature Ltg, Hillsborough *Also Called: Osram Sylvania Inc* ***(G-14442)***

Autonodyne LLC **(PA)** **321 751-8402**
320 Congress St Fl 1 Boston (02210) ***(G-6579)***

Autonomous Marine Systems Inc. 703 348-4778
28 Dane St Somerville (02143) ***(G-11862)***

Autoroll Machine, Middleton *Also Called: Autoroll Print Technologies LLC* ***(G-10380)***

Autoroll Print Technologies LLC 978 777-2160
11 River St Middleton (01949) ***(G-10380)***

Autovirt Inc. 603 546-2900
12 Murphy Dr Nashua (03062) ***(G-15065)***

Autumn Harp Inc. 802 453-4807
61 Pine St Bristol (05443) ***(G-17113)***

Autumn-Harp Inc. 802 857-4600
26 Thompson Dr Essex Junction (05452) ***(G-17227)***

Ava Anderson, Johnston *Also Called: Phe Investments LLC* ***(G-16100)***

Avanti Battery Company 617 209-9434
149 Grove St Watertown (02472) ***(G-12861)***

Avara Pharmaceutical Svcs Inc **(HQ)** **405 217-7670**
401 Merritt 7 Norwalk (06851) ***(G-2467)***

Avara US Holdings LLC **(PA)** **203 655-1333**
101 Merritt 7 Norwalk (06851) ***(G-2468)***

Avava Inc **(PA)** **617 912-2680**
275 Second Ave Ste 3 Waltham (02451) ***(G-12599)***

Avaya, Billerica *Also Called: Avaya LLC* ***(G-6407)***

Avaya LLC 908 953-6000
600 Technology Park Dr Ste 1 Billerica (01821) ***(G-6407)***

Avcarb LLC 978 452-8961
2 Indl Ave Lowell (01851) ***(G-9857)***

Avcarb Material Solutions, Lowell *Also Called: Avcarb LLC* ***(G-9857)***

Avco Corporation **(DH)** **401 421-2800**
40 Westminster St Providence (02903) ***(G-16480)***

Aved Electronics LLC 978 453-6393
95 Billerica Ave North Billerica (01862) ***(G-10898)***

Avedis Zildjian Co **(PA)** **781 871-2200**
22 Longwater Dr Norwell (02061) ***(G-11139)***

Avedro Inc **(HQ)** **781 768-3400**
30 North Ave Ste 1 Burlington (01803) ***(G-7337)***

Avenger Inc. 978 356-7311
129 Thatcher Rd Gloucester (01930) ***(G-8920)***

Avenger Filter Force, Gloucester *Also Called: Avenger Inc* ***(G-8920)***

Avenir, Johnston *Also Called: LImage Inc* ***(G-16093)***

Aveo Oncology, Boston *Also Called: Aveo Pharmaceuticals Inc* ***(G-6580)***

Aveo Pharmaceuticals Inc **(HQ)** **857 400-0101**
1 Marina Park Dr Fl 12 Boston (02210) ***(G-6580)***

Averill House Vineyard LLC 603 371-2296
21 Averill Rd Brookline (03033) ***(G-14038)***

Avery Abrasives Inc. 203 372-3513
2225 Reservoir Ave Ste 1 Trumbull (06611) ***(G-3713)***

Avery Dennison Corporation 978 353-2100
224 Industrial Rd Fitchburg (01420) ***(G-8643)***

Avery Dennison Corporation 603 217-4144
7 Fruite St Unit 7 # G Belmont (03220) ***(G-13959)***

Avery Dennison Fastener Div, Fitchburg *Also Called: Avery Dennison Corporation* ***(G-8643)***

Avery Dnnson Dgtal Ink Sltions, Belmont *Also Called: Avery Dennison Corporation* ***(G-13959)***

Avery Products Corporation 508 893-1000
89 Cross St Holliston (01746) ***(G-9201)***

Avian Vaccine Services LLC **(PA)** **860 889-1389**
1 Wisconsin Ave Norwich (06360) ***(G-2602)***

Aviatron Inc. 802 865-9318
25 Customs Dr South Burlington (05403) ***(G-17570)***

Avid, Portsmouth *Also Called: Automated Video Insptn Dvcs* ***(G-15362)***

Avid Technology Inc **(PA)** **978 640-3000**
75 Blue Sky Dr Burlington (01803) ***(G-7338)***

Avient Colorants USA LLC 207 784-0733
17 Foss Rd Lewiston (04240) ***(G-4951)***

Avient Colorants USA LLC **(HQ)** **508 829-6321**
85 Industrial Dr Holden (01520) ***(G-9187)***

Avila Textiles Inc. 508 828-5882
620 Spring St North Dighton (02764) ***(G-11003)***

Avilite LLC 603 626-4388
59 Daniel Webster Hwy Ste 100 Merrimack (03054) ***(G-14974)***

Avitide Inc. 603 965-2100
16 Cavendish Ct Ste 151 Lebanon (03766) ***(G-14683)***

Avlite Systems, Tilton *Also Called: Sealite Usa LLC* ***(G-15656)***

Avna Inc **(PA)** **860 225-8707**
200 Ellis St New Britain (06051) ***(G-2004)***

Avo Cedar Fences, Stoughton *Also Called: Avo Fence & Supply Inc* ***(G-12196)***

Avo Fence & Supply Inc **(PA)** **781 341-2963**
50 Washington St Stoughton (02072) ***(G-12196)***

Avocus Publishing Inc. 603 357-0236
4 White Brook Rd Gilsum (03448) ***(G-14341)***

Avon Cstm EMB & Screenprinting 781 341-4663
4 Brentwood Ave Avon (02322) ***(G-6143)***

Avon Custom EMB & Screen Prtg, Avon *Also Called: Avon Cstm EMB & Screenprinting* ***(G-6143)***

Avon Custom Mixing Svcs Inc. 781 767-0511
55 High St Holbrook (02343) ***(G-9169)***

Avon Food Company LLC 781 341-4981
30 James Massey Ln Stoughton (02072) ***(G-12197)***

Avrio Health L.P., Stamford *Also Called: PURDUE PRODUCTS LP* ***(G-3442)***

Avrobio Inc **(PA)** **617 914-8420**
1 Kendall Sq Ste B2001 Cambridge (02139) ***(G-7495)***

Avs Incorporated 978 772-0710
60 Fitchburg Rd Ayer (01432) ***(G-6174)***

Avs Bio, Norwich *Also Called: Avian Vaccine Services LLC* ***(G-2602)***

Avson Brewing LLC 781 727-5789
89 Baldwin St West Springfield (01089) ***(G-13016)***

Avtech Software Inc **(PA)** **401 628-1600**
16 Cutler St Warren (02885) ***(G-16752)***

Avwatch Inc. 508 274-7937
246 S Meadow Rd Ste 55 Plymouth (02360) ***(G-11448)***

AW Airflo Industries Inc. 978 465-6260
52 Parker St Newburyport (01950) ***(G-10668)***

Aware, Bedford *Also Called: Aware Inc* ***(G-6213)***

Aware Inc **(PA)** **781 276-4000**
40 Middlesex Tpke Bedford (01730) ***(G-6213)***

Awning Systems, Hyannis *Also Called: Robert E Glidden* ***(G-9447)***

Axard, Grantham *Also Called: Axard LLC* ***(G-14362)***

Axard LLC 603 306-7679
742 Route 114 Grantham (03753) ***(G-14362)***

ALPHABETIC

Axcel Photonics Inc...	508 481-9200
45 Bartlett St Marlborough (01752) *(G-10115)*	
Axcelis, Beverly *Also Called: Axcelis Technologies Inc (G-6330)*	
Axcelis Technologies Inc (PA).......................................	**978 787-4000**
108 Cherry Hill Dr Beverly (01915) *(G-6330)*	
Axcella, Cambridge *Also Called: Axcella Health Inc (G-7496)*	
Axcella Health Inc (PA)..	**857 320-2200**
840 Memorial Dr Ste 3 Cambridge (02139) *(G-7496)*	
Axe Play LLC...	603 809-9081
142 Lowell Rd Unit 19 Hudson (03051) *(G-14485)*	
Axel Plastics RES Labs Inc...	718 672-8300
50 Cambridge Dr Monroe (06468) *(G-1905)*	
Axenics Inc..	978 774-9393
200 Business Park Dr # 30 Tyngsboro (01879) *(G-12456)*	
Axewraps, Portland *Also Called: Sign Concepts LLC (G-5271)*	
Axial Industries..	781 224-0421
27 Water St Ste 111 Wakefield (01880) *(G-12499)*	
Axiam Inc (PA)..	**978 281-3550**
90 Blackburn Ctr Gloucester (01930) *(G-8921)*	
Axiom Microdevices Inc...	781 376-3000
20 Sylvan Rd Woburn (01801) *(G-13518)*	
Axiomatics, Wilmington *Also Called: Trexel Inc (G-13471)*	
Axiomed LLC...	978 232-3990
350 Main St 2nd Fl Malden (02148) *(G-10002)*	
Axiomed Spine Corporation (PA)...................................	**978 232-3990**
350 Main St Malden (02148) *(G-10003)*	
Axiomx Inc..	203 208-1034
688 E Main St Branford (06405) *(G-239)*	
Axis Cnc Incorporated..	413 967-6803
39 Gould Rd Ware (01082) *(G-12824)*	
Axis Machining Inc..	401 766-9911
549 River St Woonsocket (02895) *(G-16949)*	
Axis New England, Danvers *Also Called: Motion Industries Inc (G-8210)*	
Axis New England, Danvers *Also Called: Todd Clark and Associates Inc (G-8225)*	
Axis Technologies Inc..	978 275-9908
39 Wilbur St Ste 2 Lowell (01851) *(G-9858)*	
Axis-Shield Poc As..	508 285-4870
15 Commerce Way Ste E Norton (02766) *(G-11123)*	
Axsun Technologies Inc..	978 262-0049
1 Fortune Dr Billerica (01821) *(G-6408)*	
Axya Medical Inc..	978 232-9997
100 Cummings Ctr Ste 444c Beverly (01915) *(G-6331)*	
Axygen Bioscience Inc...	978 442-2200
836 North St Bldg 300 Tewksbury (01876) *(G-12385)*	
Azego Technology Svcs US Inc..	603 610-0030
300 Heritage Ave Unit 1 Portsmouth (03801) *(G-15363)*	
Azelis Americas LLC..	212 915-8178
100 Leominster Rd Sterling (01564) *(G-12155)*	
Azenta Inc (PA)...	**978 262-2400**
200 Summit Dr Ste 600 Burlington (01803) *(G-7339)*	
Azenta Inc..	978 262-2795
12 Elizabeth Dr Chelmsford (01824) *(G-7914)*	
Azores Corp..	978 253-6200
16 Jonspin Rd Wilmington (01887) *(G-13384)*	
Azurity Pharmaceuticals Inc (HQ).................................	**800 461-7449**
841 Woburn St Wilmington (01887) *(G-13385)*	
Azz Inc...	774 854-0700
51 Alder St Medway (02053) *(G-10302)*	
B & A Company Inc...	203 876-7527
160 Wampus Ln Milford (06460) *(G-1798)*	
B & B Equipment LLC...	860 342-5773
80 Main St Ste D Portland (06480) *(G-2817)*	
B & B Precise Products Inc..	207 453-8118
25 Neck Rd Benton (04901) *(G-4544)*	
B & D Machine Inc..	860 871-9226
30 Industrial Park Rd E Tolland (06084) *(G-3655)*	
B & D Pallet Co, Westfield *Also Called: B & D Pllet Bldg Indus Sup Inc (G-13150)*	
B & D Pllet Bldg Indus Sup Inc..	413 568-9624
997 Western Ave Westfield (01085) *(G-13150)*	
B & E Enterprises Inc...	603 924-7203
40 Main St Peterborough (03458) *(G-15312)*	

B & E Group LLC..	413 569-5585
10 Hudson Dr Southwick (01077) *(G-12041)*	
B & E Juices Inc...	203 333-1802
550 Knowlton St Bridgeport (06608) *(G-299)*	
B & E Tool Company Inc..	413 569-5585
10 Hudson Dr Southwick (01077) *(G-12042)*	
B & F Design Incorporated...	860 357-4317
120 Production Ct New Britain (06051) *(G-2005)*	
B & F Machine Co Inc (PA)..	**860 225-6349**
370 John Downey Dr New Britain (06051) *(G-2006)*	
B & G Cabinet..	978 465-6455
253 Low St Ste 8 Newburyport (01950) *(G-10669)*	
B & G Glass LLC...	413 442-3113
35 1st St Pittsfield (01201) *(G-11391)*	
B & J Electric Motor Repair Co Inc....................................	203 734-1695
30 Maple St Ansonia (06401) *(G-8)*	
B & J Manufacturing Corp..	508 822-1990
55 Constitution Dr Taunton (02780) *(G-12322)*	
B & J Sheet Metal Inc..	617 590-2295
232 Turtle Pond Pkwy Hyde Park (02136) *(G-9456)*	
B & L Finishing Shop Inc...	860 583-1164
400 Middle St Ste 6 Bristol (06010) *(G-400)*	
B & L Manufacturing Inc..	508 966-3066
8 William Way Bellingham (02019) *(G-6286)*	
B & M Printing, Cumberland *Also Called: WEB Printing Inc (G-15971)*	
B & P Plating Equipment LLC...	860 589-5799
74 Broderick Rd Bristol (06010) *(G-401)*	
B & R Machine Inc..	413 589-0246
305a Moody St Ste A Ludlow (01056) *(G-9940)*	
B & W Press Inc...	978 352-6100
17 Meadowsweet Rd West Newbury (01985) *(G-13007)*	
B B & S Treated Lumber Neng, North Kingstown *Also Called: BB&s Acquisition Corp (G-16234)*	
B C T, Naugatuck *Also Called: Business Cards Tomorrow Inc (G-1950)*	
B Copy, Westbrook *Also Called: Cybercopy Inc (G-5623)*	
B Del Toro & Sons Inc..	401 421-5820
393 Harris Ave Providence (02909) *(G-16481)*	
B G Wickberg Company Inc..	781 335-7800
30 Woodrock Rd East Weymouth (02189) *(G-8425)*	
B I L Inc..	860 446-8058
973 North Rd Groton (06340) *(G-1365)*	
B L R, Old Saybrook *Also Called: Bff Holdings Inc (G-2645)*	
B L Tees, Chicopee *Also Called: Bltees Inc (G-8011)*	
B Peachee Inc..	207 602-6262
40 Main St Ste 13-109 Biddeford (04005) *(G-4555)*	
B R S Inc...	508 697-5448
1453 Plymouth St Bridgewater (02324) *(G-7221)*	
B R T Inc...	508 791-2383
240 Salisbury St Worcester (01609) *(G-13701)*	
B S E International Corp..	781 863-5270
79 Macone Farm Ln Concord (01742) *(G-8104)*	
B S T Systems Inc...	860 564-4078
78 Plainfield Pike Plainfield (06374) *(G-2734)*	
B T Building Systems, Southport *Also Called: Bernhard Thmas Bldg Systems LL (G-3243)*	
B-C-D Metal Products Inc..	781 397-9922
205 Maplewood St Malden (02148) *(G-10004)*	
B-Fresh Inc..	401 349-0001
37 Lark Industrial Pkwy Unit A Greenville (02828) *(G-16056)*	
B/E Aerospace Inc..	410 266-2048
9 Farm Springs Rd Farmington (06032) *(G-1207)*	
B/E Aerospace Inc..	603 926-5700
94 Tide Mill Rd Hampton (03842) *(G-14399)*	
B&B Micro Manufacturing Inc...	413 281-9431
201 Howland Ave Adams (01220) *(G-5771)*	
B&C Cryotech Services Inc..	508 277-5440
12 John Rd Sutton (01590) *(G-12277)*	
B&C Kitchen and Bath, Enfield *Also Called: Atlantic Woodcraft Inc (G-1121)*	
B&E Precision Arcft Components, Southwick *Also Called: B & E Tool Company Inc (G-12042)*	
B&G Foods Inc..	207 772-8341
1 Beanpot Cir Portland (04103) *(G-5180)*	
B&N Aerospace Inc...	860 665-0134
44 Rockwell Rd Newington (06111) *(G-2274)*	

(G-0000) Company's Geographic Section entry number

B&R Sand and Gravel... 860 464-5099
   1358 Baldwin Hill Rd Gales Ferry (06335) *(G-1259)*

B&T Pallet Recycling Inc... 207 784-9048
   13 Fireslate Pl Lewiston (04240) *(G-4952)*

B&T Screw Machine Co Inc.. 860 314-4410
   571 Broad St Bristol (06010) *(G-402)*

B2w, Portsmouth *Also Called: Bid2win Software LLC (G-15365)*

B456 Systems Inc... 617 778-5700
   200 West St Waltham (02451) *(G-12600)*

Ba-Insight Inc... 339 368-7234
   401 Congress St Ste 1850 Boston (02210) *(G-6581)*

Babac Inc.. 207 872-0889
   166 China Rd Winslow (04901) *(G-5681)*

Babbco, Raynham *Also Called: C H Babb Co Inc (G-11582)*

Babcock Power Capital Corp **(HQ)**.......................... **978 646-3300**
   222 Rosewood Dr Fl 3 Danvers (01923) *(G-8165)*

Babcock Power Inc **(PA)**... **978 646-3300**
   222 Rosewood Dr Fl 3 Danvers (01923) *(G-8166)*

Babcock Power Renewables LLC **(HQ)**.................... **978 646-3300**
   222 Rosewood Dr Fl 3 Danvers (01923) *(G-8167)*

Bachmann Industries Inc.. 207 440-2888
   60 Pineland Dr Ste 230 New Gloucester (04260) *(G-5083)*

Back Bay Sign LLC... 781 475-1001
   65i Industrial Way Wilmington (01887) *(G-13386)*

Back Cove Yachts, Rockland *Also Called: North End Composites LLC (G-5340)*

Back Roads Food Co LLC... 802 579-1135
   74 Cotton Mill Hl Unit A110 Brattleboro (05301) *(G-17074)*

Back Roads Granola, Brattleboro *Also Called: Back Roads Food Co LLC (G-17074)*

Backbay Roasters... 844 532-6269
   10 Jewel Dr Wilmington (01887) *(G-13387)*

Backer Hotwatt Inc... 978 777-0070
   16a Electronics Ave Danvers (01923) *(G-8168)*

Backflip Studios LLC.. 720 475-1970
   1027 Newport Ave Pawtucket (02861) *(G-16346)*

Backlight Parent Corporation **(PA)**.......................... **617 665-8844**
   450 Bedford St Lexington (02420) *(G-9725)*

Bacon Industries Inc.. 508 384-0780
   65 Warren Dr Wrentham (02093) *(G-13837)*

Bacou-Dalloz Eye & Face Protec, Smithfield *Also Called: Honeywell Safety Pdts USA Inc (G-16714)*

Bactana Animal Health, Farmington *Also Called: Bactana Corp (G-1208)*

Bactana Corp.. 203 716-1230
   400 Farmington Ave Farmington (06032) *(G-1208)*

Bad Dog Tools, Bristol *Also Called: Joseph A Thomas Ltd (G-15770)*

Bad Martha Farmers Brewery LLC.............................. 978 335-9879
   270 Upper Main St Edgartown (02539) *(G-8465)*

Badger, Gilsum *Also Called: WS Badger Company Inc (G-14344)*

Badges of America, Pawtucket *Also Called: Racecar Jewelry Co (G-16409)*

Bae Systems Elctronic Solution................................. 603 885-3653
   65 Spit Brook Rd Nashua (03060) *(G-15066)*

Bae Systems Info Elctrnic Syst................................. 603 885-4321
   2 Forbes Rd Lexington (02421) *(G-9726)*

Bae Systems Info Elctrnic Syst................................. 603 885-4321
   65 River Rd Hudson (03051) *(G-14486)*

Bae Systems Info Elctrnic Syst................................. 603 885-4321
   144 Daniel Webster Hwy # 24 Merrimack (03054) *(G-14975)*

Bae Systems Info Elctrnic Syst................................. 603 885-4321
   130 Daniel Webster Hwy Bldg 15 Merrimack (03054) *(G-14976)*

Bae Systems Info Elctrnic Syst................................. 603 885-4321
   95 Canal St Nashua (03064) *(G-15067)*

Bae Systems Info Elctrnic Syst **(DH)**...................... **603 885-4321**
   65 Spit Brook Rd Nashua (03060) *(G-15068)*

BAE SYSTEMS INFORMATION AND ELECTRONIC SYSTEMS INTEGRATION INC., Lexington *Also Called: Bae Systems Info Elctrnic Syst (G-9726)*

BAE SYSTEMS INFORMATION AND ELECTRONIC SYSTEMS INTEGRATION INC., Hudson *Also Called: Bae Systems Info Elctrnic Syst (G-14486)*

BAE SYSTEMS INFORMATION AND ELECTRONIC SYSTEMS INTEGRATION INC., Merrimack *Also Called: Bae Systems Info Elctrnic Syst (G-14975)*

BAE Systems Information And Electronic Systems Integration Inc., Merrimack *Also Called: Bae Systems Info Elctrnic Syst (G-14976)*

BAE SYSTEMS INFORMATION AND ELECTRONIC SYSTEMS INTEGRATION INC., Nashua *Also Called: Bae Systems Info Elctrnic Syst (G-15067)*

Bae Systems Oasys LLC.. 603 232-8221
   65 River Rd Hudson (03051) *(G-14487)*

Baffoni's Wholesale & Retail, Johnston *Also Called: Baffonis Poultry Farm Inc (G-16077)*

Baffonis Poultry Farm Inc.. 401 231-6315
   324 Greenville Ave Johnston (02919) *(G-16077)*

Bafs Inc **(PA)**... **207 942-5226**
   61 Florida Ave Ste 101 Bangor (04401) *(G-4489)*

Bag Balm, Lyndonville *Also Called: Vermonts Original LLC (G-17322)*

Bagala Window Works.. 207 887-9231
   677 Main St Westbrook (04092) *(G-5616)*

Bagdon Advertising Inc... 508 366-5500
   32 South St Westborough (01581) *(G-13080)*

Bagel Alley Baker, Nashua *Also Called: Bagel Alley of NH Inc (G-15069)*

Bagel Alley of NH Inc... 603 882-9343
   1 Eldridge St Nashua (03060) *(G-15069)*

Bagel Boy LLC... 978 682-8646
   485 S Union St Lawrence (01843) *(G-9541)*

Bagel Works Inc... 413 835-0561
   48 N Pleasant St Amherst (01002) *(G-5860)*

Bagelman III Inc... 203 792-0030
   40 1/2 Padanaram Rd Danbury (06811) *(G-711)*

Bagge Inc... 508 429-8080
   150 Kuniholm Dr Ste 4 Holliston (01746) *(G-9202)*

Bags and Things, Enfield *Also Called: Tk Sports and Associates Inc (G-14275)*

Baikar Association Inc **(PA)**..................................... **617 924-4420**
   755 Mount Auburn St Watertown (02472) *(G-12862)*

Bailey Sign Inc... 207 774-2843
   9 Thomas Dr Westbrook (04092) *(G-5617)*

Bake-N-Joy Foods, North Andover *Also Called: Frozen Batters Inc (G-10834)*

Bake-N-Joy Foods Inc **(PA)**..................................... **978 683-1414**
   351 Willow St North Andover (01845) *(G-10821)*

Bakelite N Sumitomo Amer Inc **(DH)**....................... **860 646-5500**
   24 Mill St Manchester (06042) *(G-1586)*

Baker Commodities Inc.. 978 454-8811
   134 Billerica Ave North Billerica (01862) *(G-10899)*

Baker Commodities Inc.. 401 821-3003
   4 Riverdale Ct Warwick (02886) *(G-16786)*

Baker Commodities Inc.. 802 658-0721
   354 Avenue B Williston (05495) *(G-17723)*

Baker Company Inc **(PA)**.. **207 324-8773**
   175 Gate House Rd Sanford (04073) *(G-5390)*

Baker Company, The, Sanford *Also Called: Baker Company Inc (G-5390)*

Baker Graphics Corporation....................................... 203 226-6928
   1753 Post Rd E Westport (06880) *(G-4157)*

Baker Graphics Inc.. 603 625-5427
   143 Middle St Ste 1 Manchester (03101) *(G-14816)*

Baker Grphics Reproduction Ctr, Westport *Also Called: Baker Graphics Corporation (G-4157)*

Baker Hughes Holdings LLC....................................... 508 668-0400
   1600 Providence Hwy Ste 4 Walpole (02081) *(G-12552)*

Baker Parts Inc.. 508 878-5436
   407 Cornell Rd Westport (02790) *(G-13293)*

Baker Sign Works Inc... 508 674-6600
   75 Ferry St Ste 5 Fall River (02721) *(G-8524)*

Baker's Dozen Bakery, Colchester *Also Called: Bakers Dozen Inc (G-17186)*

Bakers Dozen Inc... 802 879-4001
   70 Roosevelt Hwy Ste 2 Colchester (05446) *(G-17186)*

Bakery To Go Inc.. 617 482-1015
   314 Shawmut Ave Boston (02118) *(G-6582)*

Bal International Inc.. 203 359-6775
   281 Tresser Blvd Fl 12 Stamford (06901) *(G-3290)*

Bald Hill Reach Inc.. 207 667-2576
   1 Printing House Sq Ellsworth (04605) *(G-4754)*

Balding Precision Inc... 203 878-9135
   61 Woodmont Rd Milford (06460) *(G-1799)*

Baldwin Cooke, New Hartford *Also Called: Executive Greetings Inc (G-2100)*

Baldwin Lawn Furniture LLC....................................... 860 347-1306
   440 Middlefield St Ste 1 Middletown (06457) *(G-1738)*

Balfor Industries Inc.. 203 828-6473
   327 Riggs St Oxford (06478) *(G-2687)*

Ball & Roller Bearing, New Milford *Also Called: Ball & Roller Bearing Co LLC (G-2239)*

ALPHABETIC

Ball & Roller Bearing Co LLC........................ 860 355-4161
  46 Old State Rd Ste 4 New Milford (06776) *(G-2239)*

Ball Slides Inc... 508 359-4348
  42 Union St Millis (02054) *(G-10448)*

Ballard Away Corporation.............................. 978 689-2800
  12 Ballard Way Lawrence (01843) *(G-9542)*

Ballard Material Products Inc......................... 978 452-8961
  2 Industrial Ave Lowell (01851) *(G-9859)*

Ballard Unmanned Systems Inc...................... 508 687-4970
  153 Northboro Rd Ste 1 Southborough (01772) *(G-11990)*

Ballhaus Bev Co LLC..................................... 828 302-5837
  101 Mystic Ave Medford (02155) *(G-10281)*

Balyo Inc **(HQ)**... **781 281-7957**
  78b Olympia Ave Woburn (01801) *(G-13519)*

Bam Lab LLC.. 603 973-9388
  186 Blackwater Rd Somersworth (03878) *(G-15610)*

Bamboo Rose, Gloucester *Also Called: BR Holdings Inc* *(G-8925)*

Bamboo Rose LLC **(PA)**................................ **978 281-3723**
  17 Rogers St Gloucester (01930) *(G-8922)*

Bamboo Rose Software, Gloucester *Also Called: Bamboo Rose LLC* *(G-8922)*

Banacek Invstgtons Srch Recove.................... 781 784-1400
  1075 Providence Hwy Sharon (02067) *(G-11792)*

Banas Sand and Gravel Co Inc....................... 413 583-8321
  246 Fuller St Ludlow (01056) *(G-9941)*

Bangor Daily News, Bangor *Also Called: Bangor Publishing Company* *(G-4493)*

Bangor Daily News Hancock Bur, Ellsworth *Also Called: Bangor Publishing Company* *(G-4755)*

Bangor Ltr Sp & Color Copy Ctr..................... 207 945-9311
  99 Washington St Bangor (04401) *(G-4490)*

Bangor Millwork & Supply Inc **(PA)**............... **207 947-6019**
  355 Target Cir Bangor (04401) *(G-4491)*

Bangor Millwork & Supply Inc........................ 207 878-8548
  460 Riverside St Portland (04103) *(G-5181)*

Bangor Neon... 207 947-2766
  1567 Hammond St Bangor (04401) *(G-4492)*

Bangor Publishing Company **(PA)**................. **207 990-8000**
  1 Merchants Plz Bangor (04401) *(G-4493)*

Bangor Publishing Company............................ 207 667-9393
  98 Main St Ste B Ellsworth (04605) *(G-4755)*

Bangor Steel Service Inc................................ 207 947-2773
  123 Dowd Rd Bangor (04401) *(G-4494)*

Bangor Wholesale Laminates, Bangor *Also Called: Bangor Millwork & Supply Inc* *(G-4491)*

Bangs Island Mussels, Portland *Also Called: Wild Ocean Aquaculture LLC* *(G-5289)*

Banks Publications LLC.................................. 617 996-2283
  519 Somerville Ave Somerville (02143) *(G-11863)*

Banner Glass Shelmar, Wakefield *Also Called: Shelmar Inc* *(G-12535)*

Banner Mold & Die Co Inc.............................. 978 534-6558
  251 Florence St Leominster (01453) *(G-9638)*

Bannish Lumber Inc....................................... 413 354-2279
  632 Route 20 Chester (01011) *(G-7996)*

Bantry Components Inc.................................. 603 668-3210
  160 Bouchard St Manchester (03103) *(G-14817)*

Banzan International Group, Acton *Also Called: Banzan Intl Group Corp* *(G-5739)*

Banzan Intl Group Corp.................................. 978 263-3186
  15 Craig Rd Acton (01720) *(G-5739)*

Bar Co American, North Haven *Also Called: American Wood Products* *(G-2391)*

Bar Harbor Foods, Machias *Also Called: Looks Gourmet Food Co Inc* *(G-5031)*

Bar Work Manufacturing Co Inc....................... 203 753-4103
  1198 Highland Ave Waterbury (06708) *(G-3889)*

Bar-Plate Manufacturing Co............................ 203 397-0033
  1180 Sherman Ave Hamden (06514) *(G-1413)*

Barber Elc Enclosures Mfg Inc........................ 508 699-4872
  30 Chestnut St North Attleboro (02760) *(G-10867)*

Barber Foods LLC... 207 772-1934
  70 Saint John St Portland (04102) *(G-5182)*

Barber Foods LLC **(DH)**............................... **207 482-5500**
  56 Milliken St Portland (04103) *(G-5183)*

Barbour Corporation **(PA)**............................. **508 583-8200**
  1001 N Montello St Brockton (02301) *(G-7260)*

Barbour Plastics, Brockton *Also Called: Barbour Corporation* *(G-7260)*

Barbour Stockwell Inc.................................... 781 933-5200
  45 6th Rd Woburn (01801) *(G-13520)*

Barcia LLC.. 203 367-1010
  50 Hurd Ave Bridgeport (06604) *(G-300)*

Barclay Furniture Associates.......................... 413 536-8084
  532 Main St Ste 6 Holyoke (01040) *(G-9242)*

Barclay Water Management Inc....................... 617 926-3400
  55 Chapel St Ste 400 Newton (02458) *(G-10736)*

Barco Engineering Co, Tilton *Also Called: Barco Manufacturing Inc* *(G-15652)*

Barco Manufacturing Inc................................ 603 286-3324
  505 W Main St Tilton (03276) *(G-15652)*

Bardell Office Sty & Sups, East Haven *Also Called: Bardell Printing Corp* *(G-1037)*

Bardell Printing Corp..................................... 203 469-2441
  42 Michael St East Haven (06513) *(G-1037)*

Bardon Industries Inc.................................... 401 884-1814
  3377 S County Trl Unit 6 East Greenwich (02818) *(G-15973)*

Bardons Technology, East Greenwich *Also Called: Bardon Industries Inc* *(G-15973)*

Bare Bones Software Inc................................ 978 251-0500
  73 Princeton St Ste 206 North Chelmsford (01863) *(G-10965)*

Barefoot Technologies Corp............................ 603 428-6255
  41 Liberty Hill Rd Henniker (03242) *(G-14433)*

Baretta Provision Inc..................................... 860 828-0802
  172 Commerce St East Berlin (06023) *(G-908)*

Bargain News Free Clssfied Adv...................... 203 377-3000
  720 Barnum Avenue Cutoff Ofc Stratford (06614) *(G-3518)*

Bariatrix Nutrition Corp.................................. 802 527-2500
  308 Industrial Park Rd Fairfax (05454) *(G-17255)*

Baril Corporation.. 978 373-7910
  50 Ward Hill Ave Haverhill (01835) *(G-9076)*

Barile Printers LLC.. 860 224-0127
  43 Viets St New Britain (06053) *(G-2007)*

Barker Advg Specialty Co Inc **(PA)**............... **203 272-2222**
  27 Realty Dr Cheshire (06410) *(G-575)*

Barker Screen Printers, Meriden *Also Called: Multiprints Inc* *(G-1678)*

Barker Specialty Co, Cheshire *Also Called: Barker Advg Specialty Co Inc* *(G-575)*

Barletta Fschbach Green Line D....................... 781 737-1705
  40 Shawmut Rd Ste 200 Canton (02021) *(G-7773)*

Barlow Architectural Mllwk LLC....................... 603 329-6026
  30 Gigante Dr Hampstead (03841) *(G-14381)*

Barlow Metal Stamping Inc............................. 860 583-1387
  2 Barlow St Bristol (06010) *(G-403)*

Barmakian Brothers Ltd Partnr........................ 617 227-3724
  333 Washington St Ste 720 Boston (02108) *(G-6583)*

Barn Door Screen Printers.............................. 603 447-5369
  56 Pleasant St Conway (03818) *(G-14177)*

Barnard Die Inc... 781 246-3117
  431 Water St Frnt Wakefield (01880) *(G-12500)*

Barnard Water Jet Cutting, Wakefield *Also Called: Barnard Die Inc* *(G-12500)*

Barnes, Bristol *Also Called: Barnes Group Inc* *(G-406)*

Barnes Aerospace, Windsor *Also Called: Barnes Group Inc* *(G-4262)*

Barnes Aerospace W Chester Div, Bristol *Also Called: Barnes Group Inc* *(G-405)*

Barnes Concrete Co Inc.................................. 860 928-7242
  873 Providence Pike Putnam (06260) *(G-2846)*

Barnes Group Inc.. 860 582-9581
  18 Main St Bristol (06010) *(G-404)*

Barnes Group Inc.. 513 759-3503
  123 Main St Bristol (06010) *(G-405)*

Barnes Group Inc **(PA)**................................ **860 583-7070**
  123 Main St Bristol (06010) *(G-406)*

Barnes Group Inc.. 860 298-7740
  80 Scott Swamp Rd Farmington (06032) *(G-1209)*

Barnes Group Inc.. 860 298-7740
  169 Kennedy Rd Windsor (06095) *(G-4262)*

Barnes Technical Products LLC........................ 203 931-8852
  15 High St New Haven (06510) *(G-2123)*

Barney Rabin Company Inc............................. 781 639-0593
  2 Foss Ter Marblehead (01945) *(G-10084)*

Baron & Young Co Inc.................................... 860 589-3235
  400 Middle St Ste 13 Bristol (06010) *(G-407)*

Baron Machine Company Inc........................... 603 524-6800
  40 Primrose Dr S Laconia (03246) *(G-14645)*

Baron Technology Inc.................................... 203 452-0515
  86 Raton Rd Milford (06461) *(G-1800)*

(G-0000) Company's Geographic Section entry number

Barrday Advanced Mtl Solutions, Millbury *Also Called: Barrday Corporation* **(G-10427)**

Barrday Corporation.. 508 581-2100
86 Providence St Bldg 3 Millbury (01527) **(G-10427)**

Barre Tile Inc.. 802 476-0912
187 Mechanic St Lebanon (03766) **(G-14684)**

Barrel House, Hingham *Also Called: Barrel House Z LLC* **(G-9142)**

Barrel House Z LLC.. 617 480-2880
14 Union St Hingham (02043) **(G-9142)**

Barrett Made **(PA)**... **207 650-6500**
65 Hanover St Portland (04101) **(G-5184)**

Barrett Technology Inc... 617 252-9000
139 Main St Cambridge (02142) **(G-7497)**

Barrett Technology LLC.. 617 252-9000
320 Nevada St Rear Newton (02460) **(G-10737)**

Barrett Technology Inc... 617 252-9000
320 Nevada St Newtonville (02460) **(G-10796)**

Barrette Fabrication LLC... 401 996-6691
46 Capwell Ave Coventry (02816) **(G-15807)**

Barrette Fabrication LLC **(PA)**.............................. **401 822-0860**
1077 Toll Gate Rd Warwick (02886) **(G-16787)**

Barrette Outdoor Living Inc....................................... 800 866-8101
8 Morin St Biddeford (04005) **(G-4556)**

Barringer Industries LLC.. 207 730-7125
2 Washington Ave Scarborough (04074) **(G-5424)**

Barrington Enterprises LLC....................................... 401 943-8300
334 Knight St Ste S1a Warwick (02886) **(G-16788)**

Barrington Manufacturing Inc.................................... 401 245-1737
8 Rockland Rd Warren (02885) **(G-16753)**

Barrington Printing, East Greenwich *Also Called: Meridian Printing Inc* **(G-15991)**

Barrington Printing, Warwick *Also Called: Barrington Enterprises LLC* **(G-16788)**

Barry Callebaut USA LLC... 802 524-9711
400 Industrial Park Rd Saint Albans (05478) **(G-17516)**

Barry Controls, Hopkinton *Also Called: Hutchinson Arospc & Indust Inc* **(G-9328)**

Barry Manufacturing Co Inc....................................... 781 598-1055
15 Bubier St Lynn (01901) **(G-9962)**

Barry T Chouinard Inc **(HQ)**.................................. **802 485-8600**
127 N Main St Northfield (05663) **(G-17431)**

Bart Truck Equipment LLC... 413 737-2766
358 River St West Springfield (01089) **(G-13017)**

Bartley Machine & Mfg Co Inc
35 Water St Amesbury (01913) **(G-5831)**

Barton, Seabrook *Also Called: Barton Corporation Salisbury* **(G-15584)**

Barton Corporation Salisbury..................................... 603 760-2669
34 Folly Mill Rd Ste 4 Seabrook (03874) **(G-15584)**

Bartron Medical Imaging LLC...................................... 203 498-2184
91 Shelton Ave New Haven (06511) **(G-2124)**

Basco Leather Goods, Worcester *Also Called: Valkyrie Company Inc* **(G-13818)**

Bascom Environmental Co.. 617 282-9500
7 Pleasant Harbour Rd Plymouth (02360) **(G-11449)**

Bascom Maple Farms Inc **(PA)**............................... **603 835-2230**
56 Sugar House Rd Alstead (03602) **(G-13856)**

Bascom-Turner Instruments Inc.................................. 781 769-9660
111 Downey St Norwood (02062) **(G-11164)**

Base Line, Danbury *Also Called: Base-Line II Inc* **(G-712)**

Base-Line II Inc **(PA)**... **203 826-7031**
30 Main St Ste 406 Danbury (06810) **(G-712)**

BASF Bioresearch Corp... 508 849-2500
100 Research Dr Worcester (01605) **(G-13702)**

BASF Catalysts LLC.. 860 623-9901
12 Thompson Rd East Windsor (06088) **(G-1066)**

Bass Plating Company.. 860 243-2557
82 Old Windsor Rd Bloomfield (06002) **(G-149)**

Bass Products LLC... 860 585-7923
435 Lake Ave Bristol (06010) **(G-408)**

Bass Ready Rooter, New Bedford *Also Called: D J Bass Inc* **(G-10583)**

Bassett & Cassidy... 978 452-9595
1527 Middlesex St Apt 1 Lowell (01851) **(G-9860)**

Bassette Printers LLC... 413 781-7140
326 Barton Ave Belchertown (01007) **(G-6278)**

Bast Road Collection, West Rupert *Also Called: Authentic Designs Inc* **(G-17694)**

Batavia Biosciences Inc.. 781 305-3921
300 Tradecenter Ste 6650 Woburn (01801) **(G-13521)**

Batch Inc.. 203 948-9212
80 Slein Rd New Braintree (01531) **(G-10663)**

Bates & Klinke, Taunton *Also Called: B & J Manufacturing Corp* **(G-12322)**

Bates Abrasive Products Inc...................................... 773 586-8700
6 Carol Dr Lincoln (02865) **(G-16121)**

Bates Bros Seam-Face Gran Co................................... 781 337-1150
611 Pleasant St East Weymouth (02189) **(G-8426)**

Bath Iron Works Corporation **(HQ)**......................... **207 443-3311**
700 Washington St Bath (04530) **(G-4525)**

Bath Iron Works Corporation...................................... 207 442-1266
Mallet Park Brunswick (04011) **(G-4641)**

Bath Systems Massachusetts Inc................................ 508 521-2700
25 Turnpike St West Bridgewater (02379) **(G-12967)**

Batten Bros Inc.. 781 245-4800
893 Main St Wakefield (01880) **(G-12501)**

Batten Sign, Wakefield *Also Called: Batten Bros Inc* **(G-12501)**

Battenfeld of America Inc.. 401 823-0700
31 James P Murphy Ind Hwy West Warwick (02893) **(G-16905)**

Battenkill Communications LLP.................................... 802 362-3981
5515 Main St Manchester Center (05255) **(G-17327)**

Battery Graphics, Burlington *Also Called: Queen City Printers Inc* **(G-17153)**

Battery Resourcers, Westborough *Also Called: Battery Resourcers LLC* **(G-13081)**

Battery Resourcers LLC... 206 948-6325
133 Flanders Rd Westborough (01581) **(G-13081)**

Battery Ventures Vi LP... 781 577-1000
930 Winter St Ste 2500 Waltham (02451) **(G-12601)**

Battle Grounds Coffee Co LLC..................................... 978 891-5860
39 Washington St Haverhill (01832) **(G-9077)**

Battle Grounds Coffee Company, Haverhill *Also Called: Battle Grounds Coffee Co LLC* **(G-9077)**

Baude Inc.. 207 532-6571
76 Smyrna St Houlton (04730) **(G-4896)**

Bauer Inc.. 860 583-9100
175 Century Dr Bristol (06010) **(G-409)**

Bauer Gear Motor LLC.. 732 469-8770
300 Granite St Ste 201 Braintree (02184) **(G-7169)**

Bauer Hockey LLC... 603 430-2111
100 Domain Dr Exeter (03833) **(G-14284)**

Baumer Electric, Bristol *Also Called: Baumer Ltd* **(G-410)**

Baumer Ltd **(DH)**.. **860 621-2121**
5 Century Dr Bristol (06010) **(G-410)**

Bausch & Lomb Incorporated..................................... 978 658-6111
100 Research Dr Ste 2 Wilmington (01887) **(G-13388)**

Bausch Advanced Tech Inc **(PA)**............................ **860 669-7380**
115 Nod Rd Clinton (06413) **(G-637)**

Baxalta US Inc.. 312 656-8021
650 E Kendall St Cambridge (02142) **(G-7498)**

Baxter Crane & Rigging, West Yarmouth *Also Called: Baxter Inc* **(G-13072)**

Baxter Inc... 508 775-0375
10 Bayview St West Yarmouth (02673) **(G-13072)**

Baxter Sand & Gravel Inc.. 413 536-3370
652 Prospect St Chicopee (01020) **(G-8009)**

Bay Colony Associates **(PA)**.................................. **617 287-9100**
818 William T Morrissey Blvd Boston (02122) **(G-6584)**

Bay State Apparel Inc... 978 534-5810
44 Mead St Leominster (01453) **(G-9639)**

Bay State Apparrel, Leominster *Also Called: Bay State Apparel Inc* **(G-9639)**

Bay State Crucible Co... 508 824-5121
740 W Water St Taunton (02780) **(G-12323)**

Bay State Elevator Company Inc.................................. 860 243-9030
105 W Dudley Town Rd Ste H Bloomfield (06002) **(G-150)**

Bay State Elevator Company Inc **(HQ)**..................... **413 786-7000**
275 Silver St Agawam (01001) **(G-5779)**

Bay State Envelope Inc **(PA)**................................. **508 337-8900**
440 Chauncy St Mansfield (02048) **(G-10039)**

Bay State Industrial Weldin.. 603 881-7663
10 Flagstone Dr Hudson (03051) **(G-14488)**

Bay State Machine Inc.. 860 230-0054
21 Center Pkwy Plainfield (06374) **(G-2735)**

Bay State Milling Co, Quincy *Also Called: Bay State Milling Company* **(G-11505)**

ALPHABETIC

Bay State Milling Company **(PA)**.................... 617 328-4400
   100 Congress St Quincy (02169) *(G-11505)*

Bay State Pallet Co Inc.................... 978 374-4840
   125 Ward Hill Ave Haverhill (01835) *(G-9078)*

Bay State Plating Inc.................... 413 533-6927
   18 N Bridge St Holyoke (01040) *(G-9243)*

Bay State Surface Technologies.................... 508 832-5035
   201 Washington St Auburn (01501) *(G-6107)*

Bay State Wire & Cable Co Inc.................... 978 454-2444
   645 Lawrence St Ste 3 Lowell (01852) *(G-9861)*

Bay Steel Co Inc.................... 508 697-7083
   81 Bridge St Bridgewater (02324) *(G-7222)*

Bayard Inc **(DH)**.................... **860 437-3012**
   1 Montauk Ave Ste 3 New London (06320) *(G-2222)*

Baycorp Holdings Ltd **(PA)**.................... **603 294-4850**
   953 Islington St Ste 22 Portsmouth (03801) *(G-15364)*

Bayer Corporation.................... 617 969-7690
   45 Industrial Pl Newton (02461) *(G-10738)*

Bayhead Products Corporation.................... 603 742-3000
   173 Crosby Rd Dover (03820) *(G-14218)*

Baynets Safety Systems, Colchester *Also Called: International Cordage East Ltd (G-661)*

Bayonet Ocean Vehicles Inc.................... 802 434-6033
   10 Cordage Park Cir Ste 243 Plymouth (02360) *(G-11450)*

Bayside Print Services, Portland *Also Called: Davic Inc (G-5206)*

Baystate Business Ventures LLC.................... 508 828-9274
   705 Myles Standish Blvd Ste 3 Taunton (02780) *(G-12324)*

Baystate Lghtning Prtction Inc.................... 508 697-7727
   55 Three Rivers Dr Bridgewater (02324) *(G-7223)*

Baystate Machine Co., Easthampton *Also Called: Northampton Machine Co Inc (G-8455)*

Bazar Group Inc **(PA)**.................... **401 434-2595**
   795 Waterman Ave East Providence (02914) *(G-16006)*

Bazzano, J Cedar Products, Pleasant Valley *Also Called: Pleasant Valley Fence Co Inc (G-2803)*

Bb Plastic Fabrication.................... 603 622-9882
   726 East Industrial Park Dr Unit 5 Manchester (03109) *(G-14818)*

Bb Walpole Liquidation NH Inc.................... 617 491-4340
   52d Brattle St Cambridge (02138) *(G-7499)*

BB&c Wholesale LLC **(PA)**.................... **802 453-7708**
   61 Pine St Bristol (05443) *(G-17114)*

BB&s Acquisition Corp.................... 401 295-3200
   61 Bonneau Rd North Kingstown (02852) *(G-16234)*

BBA Remanufacturing Inc.................... 508 822-4490
   300 Myles Standish Blvd Ste 8 Taunton (02780) *(G-12325)*

BBC Printing and Products Inc.................... 781 647-4646
   21 Hill Rd Waltham (02451) *(G-12602)*

BBH Apparel.................... 207 633-0601
   45 Commercial St Boothbay Harbor (04538) *(G-4601)*

Bbi Solutions, Portland *Also Called: Maine Biotechnology Svcs Inc (G-5239)*

Bbmc Inc.................... 413 443-3333
   1 N Main St Hancock (01237) *(G-9024)*

Bcg Connect LLC.................... 978 528-7999
   1 Jewel Dr Wilmington (01887) *(G-13389)*

Bcpe Seminole Holdings LP **(PA)**.................... **617 516-2000**
   200 Clarendon St Boston (02116) *(G-6585)*

Bctz Ltd.................... 781 863-0405
   401 Lowell St Lexington (02420) *(G-9727)*

Bd Enterprises LLC.................... 603 504-6231
   111 Twistback Rd Claremont (03743) *(G-14078)*

BDS, Marlborough *Also Called: Boston Document Systems Inc (G-10117)*

BE Peterson Inc.................... 508 436-7900
   40 Murphy Dr Ste 2 Avon (02322) *(G-6144)*

Be Youneeq LLC.................... 603 244-3933
   62 Langford Rd Raymond (03077) *(G-15451)*

Beacon Application Svcs Corp **(PA)**.................... **508 663-4433**
   40 Speen St Ste 104 Framingham (01701) *(G-8742)*

Beacon Biosignals Inc.................... 401 225-5782
   80 Revere St Apt 10 Boston (02114) *(G-6586)*

Beacon Communications Inc.................... 401 732-3100
   1944 Warwick Ave Warwick (02889) *(G-16789)*

Beacon Design Company, Lincoln *Also Called: Chemart Company (G-16126)*

Beacon Engnred Sltons - MA LLC.................... 978 466-9591
   32 Jungle Rd Leominster (01453) *(G-9640)*

Beacon Group Inc **(PA)**.................... **860 594-5200**
   549 Cedar St Newington (06111) *(G-2275)*

BEACON HILL TIMES,THE, Revere *Also Called: Independent Newspaper Group (G-11620)*

Beacon Industries Inc.................... 860 594-5200
   549 Cedar St Newington (06111) *(G-2276)*

Beacon Power, Tyngsboro *Also Called: BP Fly Corporation (G-12457)*

BEACON PRESS, Boston *Also Called: Unitarian Universalist Assn (G-7092)*

Beacon Press Inc.................... 207 282-1535
   457 Alfred St Biddeford (04005) *(G-4557)*

Beacon Rock Properties Inc.................... 401 421-3470
   125 Whipple St Ste 3 Providence (02908) *(G-16482)*

Beacon Sales Acquisition Inc.................... 207 797-7950
   400 Warren Ave Portland (04103) *(G-5185)*

Beacon Wellness Brands, Newton *Also Called: Catalystsmc Inc (G-10741)*

Beacon Wellness Brands Inc **(PA)**.................... **781 449-9500**
   85 Wells Ave Ste 106 Newton (02459) *(G-10739)*

Bead Electronics, Milford *Also Called: Bead Industries Inc (G-1801)*

Bead Industries Inc **(PA)**.................... **203 301-0270**
   11 Cascade Blvd Milford (06460) *(G-1801)*

Beadery Craft Products, The, Hope Valley *Also Called: Buick LLC (G-16066)*

Beal Manufacturing Inc.................... 704 824-9961
   2 Shelton Rd Swampscott (01907) *(G-12298)*

Beals & Sons Inc.................... 508 393-1833
   440 Green St Northborough (01532) *(G-11090)*

Beam Therapeutics, Cambridge *Also Called: Beam Therapeutics Inc (G-7500)*

Beam Therapeutics Inc **(PA)**.................... **857 327-8775**
   238 Main St Cambridge (02142) *(G-7500)*

Beantown Bedding LLC.................... 781 608-9915
   137 Main St Hingham (02043) *(G-9143)*

Bear Dog Enterprises, Middlebury *Also Called: Champlain Construction Co Inc (G-17341)*

Bear Island Paper Company LLC.................... 203 661-3344
   80 Field Point Rd Ste 3 Greenwich (06830) *(G-1316)*

Bear Paw Lumber Corp **(PA)**.................... **207 935-3052**
   103 Main St Fryeburg (04037) *(G-4807)*

Bear Pond Dumpster LLC.................... 207 224-0337
   250 Bear Pond Rd Turner (04282) *(G-5560)*

Bear Swamp Power Company LLC.................... 207 723-4341
   1024 Central St Millinocket (04462) *(G-5064)*

Bearer Inc.................... 657 297-5335
   185 Alewife Brook Pkwy Cambridge (02138) *(G-7501)*

Beau Tech, Portland *Also Called: Grs Group Inc (G-5220)*

Beau Ties Limited of Vermont, Middlebury *Also Called: Btl Holdings LLC (G-17339)*

Beau Ties of Vermont LLC.................... 802 388-0108
   69 Industrial Ave Middlebury (05753) *(G-17337)*

Beaumac Company Inc.................... 603 736-9321
   382 Suncook Valley Hwy Epsom (03234) *(G-14278)*

Beautiful Day.................... 617 733-9289
   66 Benefit St Fl 1 Providence (02904) *(G-16483)*

Beauty Quest Group, Stamford *Also Called: Transom Symphony Opco LLC (G-3485)*

Beaver Dam Partners Inc.................... 508 717-9799
   125 Cromesett Rd Wareham (02571) *(G-12828)*

Beaver Group LLC.................... 781 647-5775
   411 Waverley Oaks Rd Waltham (02452) *(G-12603)*

Beaver-Visitec Intl Inc.................... 781 906-8080
   500 Totten Pond Rd 10 City Pt Waltham (02451) *(G-12604)*

Bec Corp.................... 401 725-3535
   588 Brdwy Pawtucket (02860) *(G-16347)*

Becaid LLC.................... 203 915-6914
   5 Science Park New Haven (06511) *(G-2125)*

Becker Manufacturing Company.................... 401 821-1450
   18 Annandale Rd Newport (02840) *(G-16204)*

BECker&mayer, Beverly *Also Called: Quarto Pubg Group USA Inc (G-6375)*

Beckson Manufacturing Inc **(PA)**.................... **203 366-3644**
   165 Holland Ave Bridgeport (06605) *(G-301)*

Becon Incorporated **(PA)**.................... **860 243-1428**
   522 Cottage Grove Rd Bldg H Bloomfield (06002) *(G-151)*

Becton Dickinson and Company.................... 860 824-5487
   Rt 7 & Grace Way Canaan (06018) *(G-552)*

Bed Works, The, Bangor *Also Called: Waterworks (G-4521)*

Bedard Sheet Metal Company Inc.................... 413 572-3774
   123 Medieros Way Ste 2 Westfield (01085) *(G-13151)*

Bedjet LLC..401 404-5250
  17 Connell Hwy Newport (02840) *(G-16205)*

Bedoukian Research Inc **(PA)**.......................**203 830-4000**
  6 Commerce Dr Danbury (06810) *(G-713)*

Bedrock Automation, Wilmington *Also Called: Bedrock Automtn Platforms Inc (G-13390)*

Bedrock Automtn Platforms Inc........................781 821-0280
  1 Analog Way Wilmington (01887) *(G-13390)*

Bedrock Brands LLC..914 231-9550
  20 Custom House St # 920 Boston (02110) *(G-6587)*

Bee Fiberglass, Taunton *Also Called: JMS Manufacturing Co Inc (G-12345)*

BEE International Inc..508 238-5558
  46 Eastman St Ste 5 South Easton (02375) *(G-11937)*

Beekley Corporation **(PA)**.............................**860 583-4700**
  1 Prestige Ln Bristol (06010) *(G-411)*

Beekley Medical...860 583-4700
  1 Prestige Ln Bristol (06010) *(G-412)*

Beer Saver USA...207 299-2826
  16 Sylvan Cir Kennebunk (04043) *(G-4922)*

Beerd Brewing Co LLC **(PA)**..........................**860 857-1014**
  22 Bayview Ave Stonington (06378) *(G-3507)*

Bees Manufacturing LLC..................................781 400-1280
  40 Wildwood Dr Needham (02492) *(G-10506)*

Bees Wrap LLC..802 643-2132
  383 Exchange St Middlebury (05753) *(G-17338)*

Beetle Inc...508 295-8585
  3 Thacher Ln Wareham (02571) *(G-12829)*

Beeze Tees LLC...603 357-1400
  117 Main St Keene (03431) *(G-14589)*

Begell House Inc...203 456-6161
  50 North St Danbury (06810) *(G-714)*

Begum Brands Corporation..............................617 269-8400
  60 Old Colony Ave Boston (02127) *(G-6588)*

BEI Holdings Inc...203 741-9300
  6 Capital Dr Wallingford (06492) *(G-3780)*

Beiersdorf Inc **(DH)**.....................................**203 563-5800**
  301 Tresser Blvd Ste 1500 Stamford (06901) *(G-3291)*

Beiersdorf North America Inc **(DH)**................**203 563-5800**
  301 Tresser Blvd Ste 1500 Stamford (06901) *(G-3292)*

Beigene US Mfg Co Inc....................................781 801-1800
  55 Cambrdge Pkwy Ste 700w Cambridge (02142) *(G-7502)*

Beigene Usa Inc **(HQ)**..................................**781 801-1887**
  55 Cambridge Pkwy Ste 700w Cambridge (02142) *(G-7503)*

Bel Power Inc..508 870-9775
  2400 Computer Dr Westborough (01581) *(G-13082)*

Belarc Inc...978 461-1100
  2 Mill And Main Pl Ste 520 Maynard (01754) *(G-10260)*

Belco Fuel Company Inc..................................781 331-6521
  38 Mountain Ash Ln Pembroke (02359) *(G-11359)*

Belden Inc..978 537-8911
  128 Tolman Ave Leominster (01453) *(G-9641)*

Belden Inc..508 754-4858
  324 Clark St Worcester (01606) *(G-13703)*

Belden Inc..603 359-7355
  20 Forest St Keene (03431) *(G-14590)*

Beldotti Bakeries LLC......................................203 348-9029
  605 Newfield Ave Stamford (06905) *(G-3293)*

Belimo Air Controls USA, Danbury *Also Called: Belimo Aircontrols (usa) Inc (G-715)*

Belimo Aircontrols (usa) Inc **(HQ)**................**800 543-9038**
  33 Turner Rd Danbury (06810) *(G-715)*

Belimo Automation AG.....................................203 749-3319
  33 Turner Rd Danbury (06810) *(G-716)*

Belimo Technology (usa) Inc............................203 791-9915
  33 Turner Rd Danbury (06810) *(G-717)*

Belknap Tire Co Holdings Inc...........................603 524-4517
  670 Union Ave Laconia (03246) *(G-14646)*

Bell and Howell LLC..860 526-9561
  6 Winter Ave Deep River (06417) *(G-873)*

Bell Atlantic Yellow Pages, Williston *Also Called: Supermedia LLC (G-17749)*

Bell Helicopter Korea Inc.................................401 421-2800
  40 Westminster St Providence (02903) *(G-16484)*

Bell Helicopter Miami Inc.................................401 421-2800
  40 Westminster St Providence (02903) *(G-16485)*

Bell Helicopter RI Inc, Providence *Also Called: Bell Textron Rhode Island Inc (G-16486)*

Bell Label Co., Lewiston *Also Called: Bell Manufacturing Co (G-4953)*

Bell Manufacturing Co.....................................207 784-2961
  777 Main St Lewiston (04240) *(G-4953)*

Bell Power Systems LLC..................................860 767-7502
  34 Plains Rd Essex (06426) *(G-1162)*

Bell Textron Rhode Island Inc..........................401 421-2800
  40 Westminster St Providence (02903) *(G-16486)*

Bell's Foods, East Weymouth *Also Called: Brady Enterprises Inc (G-8427)*

Bella Cabinets Inc...401 722-0038
  296 Beverage Hill Ave Pawtucket (02861) *(G-16348)*

Bella Grace LLC..929 533-2343
  857 Post Rd Fairfield (06824) *(G-1177)*

Bellamy-Robie, Boston *Also Called: American Crane and Hoist Corp (G-6540)*

Bellaonline...508 865-9593
  80 Lincoln Rd Sutton (01590) *(G-12278)*

Bellavance Welding LLC...................................802 793-9327
  5471 Vt Rte 15 Wolcott (05680) *(G-17773)*

Belle Artfl Intelligence Corp.............................650 291-9410
  245 1st St Ste 18 Cambridge (02142) *(G-7504)*

Bellecraft Woodworking Co Inc........................978 297-2672
  540 River St Winchendon (01475) *(G-13478)*

Belleflower Brewing Co LLC.............................617 365-9536
  66 Cove St Portland (04101) *(G-5186)*

Bellevue Private Equity Inc..............................781 893-6721
  39 Great Hill Rd Naugatuck (06770) *(G-1949)*

Bellhawk Systems Corporation........................508 865-8070
  2 Jacques Pkwy Millbury (01527) *(G-10428)*

Bellingham Metal Works, Franklin *Also Called: Bellingham Metal Works LLC (G-8819)*

Bellingham Metal Works LLC............................617 519-5958
  101 Jefferson Rd Franklin (02038) *(G-8819)*

Bellman Jewelers Inc.......................................603 625-4653
  1650 Elm St Ste 102 Manchester (03101) *(G-14819)*

Bells Powder Coating Inc.................................508 643-2222
  500 John L Dietsch Blvd Attleboro Falls (02763) *(G-6079)*

Belmont Boatworks LLC...................................207 342-2885
  163 Augusta Rd Belmont (04952) *(G-4542)*

Belmont Corporation..860 589-5700
  60 Crystal Pond Pl Bristol (06010) *(G-413)*

Belmont Instrument LLC **(PA)**.......................**978 663-0212**
  780 Boston Rd Ste 3 Billerica (01821) *(G-6409)*

Belmont Medical Technologies, Billerica *Also Called: Belmont Instrument LLC (G-6409)*

Belmont Printing Company...............................617 484-0833
  46 Brighton St Belmont (02478) *(G-6304)*

Belmont Wheel Works, Belmont *Also Called: Mystic Valley Wheel Works Inc (G-6308)*

Belt Technologies Inc **(PA)**..........................**413 786-9922**
  11 Bowles Rd Agawam (01001) *(G-5780)*

Belvoir Media Group, Norwalk *Also Called: Belvoir Publications Inc (G-2470)*

Belvoir Media Group LLC.................................203 857-3100
  535 Connecticut Ave Ste 100 Norwalk (06854) *(G-2469)*

Belvoir Publications Inc **(PA)**........................**203 857-3100**
  800 Connecticut Ave Ste 4w02 Norwalk (06854) *(G-2470)*

Bemis, Shirley *Also Called: Bemis Associates Inc (G-11815)*

Bemis Associates Inc **(PA)**...........................**978 425-6761**
  1 Bemis Way Shirley (01464) *(G-11815)*

BEN & BILL'S CHOCOLATE EMPORIUM, Falmouth *Also Called: Ben & Bills Chocolate Emporium (G-8628)*

Ben & Bills Chocolate Emporium......................508 548-7878
  209 Main St Falmouth (02540) *(G-8628)*

Ben & Blls Chclat Emporium Inc **(PA)**............**413 584-5695**
  143 Main St Northampton (01060) *(G-11053)*

Ben & Jerry's Ice Cream, South Burlington *Also Called: Ben & Jerrys Homemade Inc (G-17571)*

Ben & Jerrys Homemade Inc **(HQ)**................**802 846-1500**
  530 Community Dr Ste 1 South Burlington (05403) *(G-17571)*

Ben Franklin Design Mfg Co Inc.......................413 786-4220
  938 Suffield St Agawam (01001) *(G-5781)*

Ben Franklin Manufacturing, Agawam *Also Called: Ben Franklin Design Mfg Co Inc (G-5781)*

Ben Franklin Print Co Inc.................................978 624-7341
  177 N Main St Ste 611 Middleton (01949) *(G-10381)*

Ben Hughes Communication Products Co.........860 526-4337
  207 Middlesex Ave Chester (06412) *(G-623)*

Ben Savage Logging Inc................................ 207 735-6699
  30 North Rd Sebec (04481) *(G-5456)*

Ben-Art Manufacturing Co Inc...................... 203 758-4435
  109 Waterbury Rd Prospect (06712) *(G-2829)*

Benchmark Carbide, Springfield *Also Called: Gws Tool Holdings LLC (G-12098)*

Benchmark Electronics Inc............................ 603 879-7000
  100 Innovative Way Nashua (03062) *(G-15070)*

Benco Dental.. 508 435-3000
  63 South St Hopkinton (01748) *(G-9309)*

Bender Management Inc............................... 203 847-3865
  235 Westport Ave Norwalk (06851) *(G-2471)*

Bender Showrooms, Norwalk *Also Called: Bender Management Inc (G-2471)*

Bendon Gear and Machine Inc...................... 781 878-8100
  100 Weymouth St Ste A1 Rockland (02370) *(G-11636)*

Benefit Coatings Inc.................................... 203 572-0660
  550 Long Beach Blvd Stratford (06615) *(G-3519)*

Benevento Aggregates LLC........................... 603 783-4723
  528 Route 106 N Loudon (03307) *(G-14793)*

Benevento Asphalt, Wilmington *Also Called: Benevento Asphalt Corp (G-13391)*

Benevento Asphalt, Wilmington *Also Called: Benevento Sand & Stone Corp (G-13392)*

Benevento Asphalt Corp............................... 978 658-5300
  900 Salem St Wilmington (01887) *(G-13391)*

Benevento Sand & Stone Corp...................... 978 658-4762
  200 Salem St Wilmington (01887) *(G-13392)*

Benifit Port, Norwalk *Also Called: Blc Holdings LLC (G-2474)*

Benjamin D Knapp....................................... 603 660-8172
  108 Perkins Pond Rd Weare (03281) *(G-15668)*

Benjamin K Lepesqueur................................ 802 933-5500
  799 Pudvah Hill Rd Enosburg Falls (05450) *(G-17220)*

Benjamin Moore Authorized Ret, Belgrade *Also Called: Hammond Lumber Company (G-4540)*

Benjamin Moore Authorized Ret, Wells *Also Called: Morse Hardware & Lumber LLC (G-5603)*

Benjamin Moore Authorized Ret, Manchester Center *Also Called: RK Miles Inc (G-17330)*

Bennettisville Printing, Hebron *Also Called: Bennettsville Holdings LLC (G-1525)*

Bennettsville Holdings LLC............................ 860 444-9400
  33 Pendleton Dr # A Hebron (06248) *(G-1525)*

Bennington Banner, Bennington *Also Called: North Eastern Publishing Co (G-17053)*

Bennington Potters Inc **(PA)**.................... **800 205-8033**
  324 County St Bennington (05201) *(G-17036)*

Bennington Shriff GLC Slar LLC..................... 802 233-3370
  811 Us Route 7 S Bennington (05201) *(G-17037)*

Bennington Sports & Graphic, Charlton *Also Called: Santacroce Graphics Inc (G-7895)*

Benson Neptune Inc **(DH)**........................ **401 821-7140**
  334 Knight St Unit 3100 Warwick (02886) *(G-16790)*

Benson Woodhomes, Walpole *Also Called: Benson Woodworking Company Inc (G-15659)*

Benson Woodworking Company Inc................ 603 756-3600
  6 Blackjack Xing Walpole (03608) *(G-15659)*

Bent Water Brewing Co................................ 781 780-9948
  180 Commercial St Lynn (01905) *(G-9963)*

Bent's Cookie Factory, Milton *Also Called: G H Bent Company (G-10452)*

Bentley Pharmaceuticals Inc **(HQ)**........... **603 658-6100**
  2 Holland Way Exeter (03833) *(G-14285)*

Bentley Publishers, Cambridge *Also Called: Robert Bentley Inc (G-7698)*

Benu Networks Inc...................................... 978 223-4700
  154 Middlesex Tpke Ste 2 Burlington (01803) *(G-7340)*

Benz, Edwin H Co, Providence *Also Called: E H Benz Co Inc (G-16510)*

Beqom North America Inc............................. 888 995-3028
  132 Old Post Rd Southport (06890) *(G-3242)*

Bera Company, Rochester *Also Called: Inner Traditions International (G-17485)*

Berg, Framingham *Also Called: Berg LLC (G-8743)*

Berg LLC **(HQ)**....................................... **617 588-0083**
  500 Old Connecticut Path Ste 3 Framingham (01701) *(G-8743)*

Bergan Architectural Wdwkg Inc................... 860 346-0869
  55 N Main St Middletown (06457) *(G-1739)*

Bergen Pipe Supports Inc **(HQ)**................ **781 935-9550**
  225 Merrimac St Woburn (01801) *(G-13522)*

Berger & Company Recycling Inc................... 401 723-7240
  126 Front St Pawtucket (02860) *(G-16349)*

Bergeron Machine LLC................................. 978 577-6235
  65 Powers Rd Westford (01886) *(G-13225)*

Bergson Tire Co Inc..................................... 860 872-7729
  40 West Rd Ellington (06029) *(G-1102)*

Bering Technology Inc.................................. 408 364-6500
  5086 Main St Waitsfield (05673) *(G-17663)*

Berkley Associates Inc................................. 203 757-9221
  2712 S Main St Waterbury (06706) *(G-3890)*

Berkmatics Inc... 413 664-6152
  59 Demond Ave North Adams (01247) *(G-10803)*

Berkshire, Great Barrington *Also Called: Berkshire Corporation (G-8973)*

Berkshire Brewing Company Inc **(PA)**........ **413 665-6600**
  12 Railroad St South Deerfield (01373) *(G-11921)*

Berkshire Bridge & Iron Co Inc..................... 413 684-3182
  140 E Housatonic St Dalton (01226) *(G-8148)*

Berkshire Concrete Corp **(HQ)**................. **413 443-4734**
  550 Cheshire Rd Pittsfield (01201) *(G-11392)*

Berkshire Corporation **(HQ)**..................... **413 528-2602**
  21 River St Great Barrington (01230) *(G-8973)*

Berkshire Custom Coating Inc....................... 413 442-3757
  50 Downing Industrial Park Pittsfield (01201) *(G-11393)*

Berkshire Grey Inc **(PA)**.......................... **833 848-9900**
  140 South Rd Bedford (01730) *(G-6214)*

Berkshire Mnufactured Pdts Inc.................... 978 462-8161
  116 Parker St Newburyport (01950) *(G-10670)*

Berkshire Photonics LLC............................... 860 868-0412
  89 Commercial Blvd Ste 4 Torrington (06790) *(G-3671)*

Berkshire Plate Glass, Pittsfield *Also Called: B & G Glass LLC (G-11391)*

Berkshire Precision Tool LLC......................... 413 499-3875
  9 Betnr Industrial Dr Pittsfield (01201) *(G-11394)*

Berkshire Publishing Group LLC.................... 413 528-0206
  122 Castle St Great Barrington (01230) *(G-8974)*

Berkshire Reference Works, Great Barrington *Also Called: Berkshire Publishing Group LLC (G-8974)*

Berkshire Sterile Mfg LLC............................. 413 243-0330
  480 Pleasant St Lee (01238) *(G-9611)*

Berlin Foundary & Achine Co, Berlin *Also Called: Bfmc LLC (G-13980)*

Berlin Operations, East Berlin *Also Called: Paradigm Prcision Holdings LLC (G-915)*

Berlin Steel, Kensington *Also Called: Berlin Steel Construction Co (G-1538)*

Berlin Steel Construction Co **(PA)**............. **860 828-3531**
  76 Depot Rd Kensington (06037) *(G-1538)*

Berlyn Reporter, Meredith *Also Called: Salmon Press LLC (G-14970)*

Bermer Precision Products LLC...................... 508 764-2521
  94 Ashland Ave Southbridge (01550) *(G-12010)*

Bermer Tool & Die Inc................................. 508 764-2521
  81 Ashland Ave Southbridge (01550) *(G-12011)*

Bern Optics Inc... 413 568-6800
  579 Southampton Rd Westfield (01085) *(G-13152)*

Bernardinos Bakery Inc **(PA)**.................... **413 592-1944**
  105 Exchange St Chicopee (01013) *(G-8010)*

Bernardo Manufacturing, Rumford *Also Called: Winkler Group Ltd (G-16680)*

Bernhard Thmas Bldg Systems LL.................. 203 925-0414
  281 Pequot Ave Southport (06890) *(G-3243)*

Bernstein Display, Shaftsbury *Also Called: Leo D Bernstein & Sons Inc (G-17550)*

Berq Rng Holdings Usa LLC **(PA)**.............. **412 656-8863**
  591 W Putnam Ave Greenwich (06830) *(G-1317)*

Berq US Operations, Greenwich *Also Called: Berq Rng Holdings Usa LLC (G-1317)*

Berry Global Inc.. 413 529-7602
  44 Oneill Ln East Hampton (06424) *(G-960)*

Berry Global Inc.. 812 424-2904
  44 Oneil St Easthampton (01027) *(G-8439)*

Berry Global Inc.. 508 918-1714
  25 Forge Pkwy Franklin (02038) *(G-8820)*

Berry Plastics, Franklin *Also Called: Berry Global Inc (G-8820)*

Berry Plastics Corp...................................... 413 529-2183
  122 Pleasant St Easthampton (01027) *(G-8440)*

Berry Twist... 857 362-7455
  200 Faneuil Hall Market Pl Boston (02109) *(G-6589)*

Berstein Display, Shaftsbury *Also Called: Leo D Bernstein and Sons Inc (G-17551)*

Bertek Systems, Milton *Also Called: Industrial Marking Systems Corp (G-17360)*

Berthon Usa Inc.. 401 846-8404
  40 Mary St Newport (02840) *(G-16206)*

Berube Tool & Die Inc.. 603 382-2224
    34 Main St Plaistow (03865) *(G-15337)*

Bes-Cut Inc... 860 582-8660
    400 Middle St Bristol (06010) *(G-414)*

Bess Home Fashions Inc.. 401 828-0300
    155 Brookside Ave West Warwick (02893) *(G-16906)*

Bessette Holdings Inc.. 860 289-6000
    95 Leggett St East Hartford (06108) *(G-975)*

Best Embroidery... 857 258-0333
    231 Park Ave Revere (02151) *(G-11617)*

Best Engineered Surfc Tech LLC.................................... 401 724-2230
    10 New Rd Rumford (02916) *(G-16662)*

Best Felts Liquidation Corp.. 207 596-0566
    17 Dexter St Thomaston (04861) *(G-5541)*

Best Home Fashions, West Warwick *Also Called: Natco Home Fashions Inc (G-16915)*

Best Machine Inc.. 603 895-4018
    79 Beede Hill Rd Fremont (03044) *(G-14326)*

Best Marine and Outdoors Inc.. 617 644-7711
    100 Cambridge St Boston (02114) *(G-6590)*

Beta Bionics, Concord *Also Called: Beta Bionics Inc (G-8105)*

Beta Bionics Inc.. 855 745-3800
    300 Baker Ave Ste 301 Concord (01742) *(G-8105)*

Beta Shim Co... 203 926-1150
    11 Progress Dr Shelton (06484) *(G-2983)*

Beta Technologies Inc.. 802 281-3623
    1150 Airport Dr Ste 101 South Burlington (05403) *(G-17572)*

Bete Fog Nozzle Inc **(PA)**.. **413 772-0846**
    50 Greenfield St Greenfield (01301) *(G-8985)*

Beth Mueller Inc.. 802 476-3582
    13 Pleasant St Barre (05641) *(G-16997)*

Beth Mueller Design, Barre *Also Called: Beth Mueller Inc (G-16997)*

Bethel Citizen, Albany Twp *Also Called: Citizen Printers Incorporated (G-4400)*

Bethel Division, Bethel *Also Called: Vanderbilt Chemicals LLC (G-139)*

Bethel Mail Service... 203 730-1399
    211 Greenwood Ave Ste 2 Bethel (06801) *(G-100)*

Bethel Mail Service Center, Bethel *Also Called: Bethel Mail Service (G-100)*

Bethune Nonwovens Inc.. 860 386-8001
    1 Hartfield Blvd Ste 101 East Windsor (06088) *(G-1067)*

Better Lists Incorporated.. 203 324-4171
    64 Sunnyside Ave Stamford (06902) *(G-3294)*

Better Molded Products Inc **(PA)**................................. **860 589-0066**
    95 Valley St Ste 2 Bristol (06010) *(G-415)*

Better Stones & Garden, East Hartford *Also Called: Midwood Quarry and Cnstr Inc (G-1006)*

Betterhalf.ai, Cambridge *Also Called: Infinite Forest Inc (G-7613)*

Betty Reez Whoopiez... 207 865-1735
    67 Carter Rd Freeport (04032) *(G-4797)*

Bev-Tech Inc.. 207 439-8061
    56 Julie Ln Eliot (03903) *(G-4749)*

Beverage Mart, Saint Albans *Also Called: Rea Inc (G-17530)*

Beverly Citizen.. 978 927-2777
    48 Dunham Rd Beverly (01915) *(G-6332)*

Beverly Feldman, Norwalk *Also Called: Aj Casey LLC (G-2460)*

Bevi, Charlestown *Also Called: Hydration Labs Inc (G-7876)*

Bevin Bells, East Hampton *Also Called: Bevin Bros Manufacturing Co (G-961)*

Bevin Bros Manufacturing Co... 860 267-4431
    17 Watrous St East Hampton (06424) *(G-961)*

Bevovations LLC... 978 227-5469
    320 Industrial Rd Leominster (01453) *(G-9642)*

Bew Corp.. 781 963-0315
    280 Pond St Randolph (02368) *(G-11550)*

Beyond Shaker LLC... 617 461-6608
    124a Cummings Park Woburn (01801) *(G-13523)*

BF Goodrich Aerspce Aircrft In.. 802 877-2911
    100 Panton Rd Vergennes (05491) *(G-17656)*

BF Services Inc... 781 862-9792
    35 Bedford St Ste 15 Lexington (02420) *(G-9728)*

Bff Holdings Inc **(HQ)**... **860 510-0100**
    141 Mill Rock Rd E Old Saybrook (06475) *(G-2645)*

BFI Print Communications Inc **(PA)**............................... **781 447-1199**
    255 State St Fl 7 Boston (02109) *(G-6591)*

Bfly Operations Inc... 781 557-4800
    1600 District Ave Burlington (01803) *(G-7341)*

Bfmc LLC.. 603 752-4550
    489 Goebel St Berlin (03570) *(G-13980)*

Bfs Pharma Inc... 781 767-2020
    78 Pacella Park Dr 80 Randolph (02368) *(G-11551)*

Bh Media Inc **(HQ)**... **617 426-3000**
    491 Dutton St Ste 1 Lowell (01854) *(G-9862)*

Bh Shoe Holdings Inc **(HQ)**....................................... **203 661-2424**
    124 W Putnam Ave Ste 1 Greenwich (06830) *(G-1318)*

Bhs-Torin, Manchester *Also Called: L M Gill Welding and Mfr LLC (G-1610)*

Bi-Qem Inc.. 413 584-2472
    238 Nonotuck St Florence (01062) *(G-8683)*

Bi-Sam.. 617 933-4400
    53 State St Ste 1203 Boston (02109) *(G-6592)*

Bial - Biotech Investments Inc.. 508 332-9103
    19 Blackstone St Fl 2 Cambridge (02139) *(G-7505)*

Bibo International LLC.. 774 232-4248
    34 Morton Ave # 2 Newport (02840) *(G-16207)*

Bic Consumer Pdts Mfg Co Inc....................................... 203 783-2000
    565 Bic Dr Milford (06461) *(G-1802)*

Bic Consumer Pdts Mfg Co Inc **(DH)**............................. **203 783-2000**
    1 Bic Way Ste 1 Shelton (06484) *(G-2984)*

Bic Corporation **(HQ)**.. **203 783-2000**
    1 Bic Way Ste 1 Shelton (06484) *(G-2985)*

Bic Graphic USA, Shelton *Also Called: Bic Corporation (G-2985)*

Bic USA Inc **(DH)**.. **203 783-2000**
    1 Bic Way Ste 1 Shelton (06484) *(G-2986)*

Bicara Therapeutics Inc.. 860 882-7478
    245 Main St Cambridge (02142) *(G-7506)*

Bicon LLC **(PA)**.. **617 524-4443**
    501 Arborway Boston (02130) *(G-6593)*

Bicon Dental Implants, Boston *Also Called: Bicon LLC (G-6593)*

Bicron Electronics LLC **(HQ)**...................................... **860 482-2524**
    427 Goshen Rd Torrington (06790) *(G-3672)*

Bid2win Software LLC.. 800 336-3808
    99 Bow St Ste 500 Portsmouth (03801) *(G-15365)*

Biddeford Saco Courier, Biddeford *Also Called: Mainely Newspapers Inc (G-4577)*

Bidwell Industrial Group Inc... 860 346-9283
    2055 S Main St Middletown (06457) *(G-1740)*

Big Belly Solar LLC **(PA)**... **888 820-0300**
    150 A St Ste 103 Needham Heights (02494) *(G-10530)*

Big Bill, Newport *Also Called: Codet-Newport Corporation (G-17398)*

Big Dipper, Prospect *Also Called: Big Dipper Ice Cream Fctry Inc (G-2830)*

Big Dipper Ice Cream Fctry Inc....................................... 203 758-3200
    91 Waterbury Rd Prospect (06712) *(G-2830)*

Big Foot Moving & Storage Inc.. 781 488-3090
    5 Craig Rd Acton (01720) *(G-5740)*

Big Foote Crushing LLC.. 603 345-0695
    1225 River Rd Weare (03281) *(G-15669)*

Big G Seafood Inc.. 508 994-5113
    48 Antonio Costa Ave New Bedford (02740) *(G-10571)*

Big Rock Oyster Company Inc.. 774 408-7951
    501 Depot St Harwich (02645) *(G-9067)*

Big Y Foods Inc.. 413 567-6231
    802 Williams St Longmeadow (01106) *(G-9848)*

Big Y Pharmacy, Longmeadow *Also Called: Big Y Foods Inc (G-9848)*

Bigelow Mountain Partners LLC....................................... 207 865-9208
    208 Us Route 1 Freeport (04032) *(G-4798)*

Bigraphics Inc.. 603 594-8686
    472 Amherst St Unit 18 Nashua (03063) *(G-15071)*

Bigrep America Inc... 781 281-0569
    50-E Concord St Ste 100 Wilmington (01887) *(G-13393)*

Bigtime Software Inc... 781 859-5308
    98 N Washington St Ste 410 Boston (02114) *(G-6594)*

Bigtincan Mobile Pty Ltd... 617 981-7557
    260 Charles St Ste 101 Waltham (02453) *(G-12605)*

Bigwood Corporation.. 508 477-2220
    57 Industrial Dr Mashpee (02649) *(G-10249)*

Bilco Holding Company.. 203 507-2751
    370 James St Ste 201 New Haven (06513) *(G-2126)*

A L P H A B E T I C

Bill Lztte Archtctral GL Alum.................... 401 383-9535
  400 Wampanoag Trl Riverside (02915) *(G-16652)*

Billerica Minute-Man, Concord *Also Called: Gatehouse Media Mass I Inc (G-8118)*

Billy Hill Tubs LLC.................... 978 422-8800
  47 Chocksett Rd Sterling (01564) *(G-12156)*

Billy's Bakery, Fairfield *Also Called: Katona Bakery LLC (G-1193)*

Biltrite Corporation **(PA)**.................... **781 647-1700**
  1350 Belmont St Brockton (02301) *(G-7261)*

Bind Biosciences Inc.................... 617 679-9600
  325 Vassar St Cambridge (02139) *(G-7507)*

Bio Med Packaging Systems Inc.................... 203 846-1923
  100 Pearl St Norwalk (06850) *(G-2472)*

Bio Pharmaceutical, Boston *Also Called: Puretech Health LLC (G-6984)*

Bio Sphere Medical Inc.................... 208 844-5008
  1050 Hingham St Fl 1 Rockland (02370) *(G-11637)*

Bio-Concept Laboratories Inc.................... 603 437-4990
  13 Industrial Way Salem (03079) *(G-15510)*

Bio-Detek, Pawtucket *Also Called: Zoll Medical Corporation (G-16432)*

Bio-Med Devices Inc.................... 203 458-0202
  61 Soundview Rd Guilford (06437) *(G-1386)*

Bio-Mold Division, Wilmington *Also Called: Neu-Tool Design Inc (G-13437)*

Bio-Oregon, Westbrook *Also Called: Moore-Clark USA Inc (G-5639)*

Bioasis Biosciences Corp.................... 203 533-7082
  14 Water St Ste A Guilford (06437) *(G-1387)*

Biobohemia Inc.................... 617 958-7900
  1 Broadway Ste 14 Cambridge (02142) *(G-7508)*

Biobright, Boston *Also Called: Biobright LLC (G-6595)*

Biobright LLC **(HQ)**.................... **617 444-9007**
  85 Merrimac St Ste 200 Boston (02114) *(G-6595)*

Biocon Biologics Inc.................... 857 706-2596
  245 Main St Fl 2 Cambridge (02142) *(G-7509)*

Biocytogen Boston Corp.................... 781 587-3558
  300 3rd Ave Fl 6 Waltham (02451) *(G-12606)*

Biodata Inc.................... 512 593-5521
  625 Massachusetts Ave Ste 1 Cambridge (02139) *(G-7510)*

Biodelivery Sciences Intl Inc **(HQ)**.................... **919 582-9050**
  100 Technology Center Dr Ste 300 Stoughton (02072) *(G-12198)*

Biodesign International.................... 207 283-6500
  60 Industrial Park Rd Saco (04072) *(G-5363)*

Biodevek Inc.................... 617 768-8246
  127 Western Ave Allston (02134) *(G-5819)*

Bioenergy International LLC.................... 617 657-5200
  3 Batterymarch Park Ste 301 Quincy (02169) *(G-11506)*

Biofrontera, Woburn *Also Called: Biofrontera Inc (G-13524)*

Biofrontera Inc **(HQ)**.................... **781 245-1325**
  120 Presidential Way Ste 330 Woburn (01801) *(G-13524)*

Biogen, Cambridge *Also Called: Biogen Inc (G-7511)*

Biogen Inc **(PA)**.................... **617 679-2000**
  225 Binney St Cambridge (02142) *(G-7511)*

Biogen Inc.................... 617 914-8888
  6 Cambridge Ctr Cambridge (02142) *(G-7512)*

Biogen MA Inc.................... 781 464-2000
  225 Binney St Cambridge (02142) *(G-7513)*

Biogen MA Inc **(HQ)**.................... **617 679-2000**
  225 Binney St Cambridge (02142) *(G-7514)*

Biohaven Labs, New Haven *Also Called: Biohaven Phrm Holdg Co Ltd (G-2128)*

Biohaven Pharmaceuticals, New Haven *Also Called: Biohaven Phrm Holdg Co Ltd (G-2129)*

Biohaven Pharmaceuticals Inc.................... 203 404-0410
  215 Church St New Haven (06510) *(G-2127)*

Biohaven Phrm Holdg Co Ltd.................... 203 691-6332
  25 Science Park Ste 2d New Haven (06511) *(G-2128)*

Biohaven Phrm Holdg Co Ltd **(HQ)**.................... **203 404-0410**
  215 Church St New Haven (06510) *(G-2129)*

Biohelix Corporation.................... 978 927-5056
  500 Cummings Ctr Ste 5550 Beverly (01915) *(G-6333)*

Bioholdings Ltd.................... 401 683-5400
  45 Highpoint Ave Ste 3 Portsmouth (02871) *(G-16437)*

Biokit U S A Inc.................... 781 861-4064
  180 Hartwell Rd Bedford (01730) *(G-6215)*

Biologics Production, Winslow *Also Called: Lohmann Animal Health Intl Inc (G-5683)*

Biolucent LLC.................... 508 263-2900
  250 Campus Dr Marlborough (01752) *(G-10116)*

Biom, Cambridge *Also Called: Bionx Medical Technologies Inc (G-7516)*

Biomed Health Inc.................... 860 657-2258
  70 Oakwood Dr Ste 8 Glastonbury (06033) *(G-1270)*

Biomed Packing Systems, Norwalk *Also Called: K W Griffen Company (G-2521)*

Biomedic Appliances Inc.................... 802 878-0930
  8a Ewing Pl Essex Junction (05452) *(G-17228)*

Biomedical Polymers Inc.................... 978 632-2555
  16 Chocksett Rd Sterling (01564) *(G-12157)*

Biomedical Structures LLC.................... 401 223-0990
  60 Commerce Dr Warwick (02886) *(G-16791)*

Biomerics LLC.................... 203 268-7238
  246 Main St Ste C Monroe (06468) *(G-1906)*

Biomx Inc.................... 203 408-3915
  36 E Industrial Rd Ste 1 Branford (06405) *(G-240)*

Bionostics Inc.................... 978 772-7070
  7 Jackson Rd Devens (01434) *(G-8270)*

Biontech US Inc **(HQ)**.................... **617 337-4701**
  40 Erie St Ste 110 Cambridge (02139) *(G-7515)*

Bionx Medical Technologies Inc
  27 Moulton St Cambridge (02138) *(G-7516)*

Biopharm Engineered Systems, Lawrence *Also Called: Jgp Enterprises Inc (G-9572)*

Biopharm Engneered Systems LLC.................... 978 691-2737
  421 Merrimack St # 1 Lawrence (01843) *(G-9543)*

Biophysics Pharma Inc.................... 781 608-7738
  9 Centennial Dr Unit 102 Peabody (01960) *(G-11299)*

Bioprocessh2o LLC.................... 401 683-5400
  45 Highpoint Ave Ste 3 Portsmouth (02871) *(G-16438)*

Bioprocessing Inc.................... 207 457-0025
  1045 Riverside St Portland (04103) *(G-5187)*

Bioraft, Boston *Also Called: Research Applctons Fncl Trckin (G-7007)*

Biose Industrie Inc.................... 617 460-1842
  12 Gill St Ste 5700 Woburn (01801) *(G-13525)*

Biosig Technologies, Westport *Also Called: Biosig Technologies Inc (G-4158)*

Biosig Technologies Inc **(PA)**.................... **203 409-5444**
  55 Greens Farms Rd Ste 1 Westport (06880) *(G-4158)*

Biosolutions, Meriden *Also Called: Brand-Nu Laboratories LLC (G-1656)*

BIOSTAGE, Holliston *Also Called: Harvard Apprtus Rgnrtive Tech (G-9214)*

Biotech, Cambridge *Also Called: Arbor Biotechnologies Inc (G-7489)*

Biotek, Winooski *Also Called: Biotek Instruments Inc (G-17767)*

Biotek Instruments Inc.................... 802 655-4040
  15 Tigan St Winooski (05404) *(G-17766)*

Biotek Instruments Inc **(HQ)**.................... **802 655-4040**
  100 Tigan St Winooski (05404) *(G-17767)*

Biotronik Inc.................... 207 944-5515
  3 Clover Ln Brewer (04412) *(G-4610)*

Bioverativ Inc **(HQ)**.................... **781 663-4400**
  225 2nd Ave Waltham (02451) *(G-12607)*

Bioverativ Therapeutics Inc **(DH)**.................... **781 663-4400**
  225 2nd Ave Waltham (02451) *(G-12608)*

Bioview (usa) Inc.................... 978 670-4741
  44 Manning Rd Ste 104 Billerica (01821) *(G-6410)*

Biowave Innovations LLC.................... 203 982-8157
  274 Ridgefield Rd Wilton (06897) *(G-4232)*

Bioxcel Therapeutics Inc.................... 475 238-6837
  555 Long Wharf Dr Fl 12 New Haven (06511) *(G-2130)*

Birch Outfitters LLC.................... 978 498-4631
  27 Congress St Ste 210 Salem (01970) *(G-11703)*

Birch Stream Farms, Bangor *Also Called: Bafs Inc (G-4489)*

Birchcraft Studios, Abington *Also Called: New England Art Publishers Inc (G-5726)*

Bird Precision, Waltham *Also Called: Richard H Bird & Co Inc (G-12770)*

Birk Manufacturing Inc.................... 800 531-2070
  14 Capitol Dr East Lyme (06333) *(G-1058)*

Birkhauser, Boston *Also Called: Walter De Gruyter Inc (G-7112)*

Birnn Chocolates Vermont Inc.................... 802 860-1047
  102 Kimball Ave Ste 4 South Burlington (05403) *(G-17573)*

Bisco Environmental Inc.................... 508 738-5100
  55 Ferncroft Rd Ste 110 Danvers (01923) *(G-8169)*

Biscom Inc.................... 978 250-1800
  10 Technology Park Dr Ste 102 Westford (01886) *(G-13226)*

Bishop Audio, Newburyport *Also Called: Runco Capital Corporation (G-10716)*

Bison Pumps... 207 532-2600
   98 Bangor St Houlton (04730) *(G-4897)*

Biszko Contracting Corp..................................... 508 679-0518
   20 Development St Fall River (02721) *(G-8525)*

Bite Ne Live Bait, Newport *Also Called: Arkwear Inc (G-16202)*

Bite Tech Inc... 203 987-6898
   20 Glover Ave Ste 1 Norwalk (06850) *(G-2473)*

Bitflow Inc... 781 932-2900
   400 W Cummings Park Ste 5050 Woburn (01801) *(G-13526)*

Bittersweet Herb Farm, Shelburne Falls *Also Called: David W Wallace (G-11803)*

Bittware Inc **(DH)**... **603 226-0404**
   45 S Main St Fl 2 Concord (03301) *(G-14115)*

Bittware Fpga Cmpt Systems, Concord *Also Called: Bittware Inc (G-14115)*

Bixby & Co LLC... 207 691-1778
   1 Sea Street Pl Rockland (04841) *(G-5323)*

Bixby Chocolate, Rockland *Also Called: Bixby & Co LLC (G-5323)*

Bixby International Corp...................................... 978 462-4100
   1 Preble Rd Newburyport (01950) *(G-10671)*

Bixler University.. 888 361-4558
   227 Main St Burlington (05401) *(G-17120)*

Bixler's, Burlington *Also Called: Bixler University (G-17120)*

BJ's Brewhouse, Pawtucket *Also Called: Isle Brewers Guild LLC (G-16377)*

BJ's Wholesale Club, Franklin *Also Called: BJs Wholesale Club Inc (G-8821)*

Bji Enterprises, Westport *Also Called: Dartmouth Awning Co Inc (G-13295)*

BJs Wholesale Club Inc...................................... 508 553-9889
   100 Corporate Dr Franklin (02038) *(G-8821)*

Bki Worldwide, Salem *Also Called: Cooking Solutions Group Inc (G-15516)*

Bki Worldwide, Essex Junction *Also Called: Cooking Solutions Group Inc (G-17231)*

Bki Worldwide, Essex Junction *Also Called: Standex International Corp (G-17247)*

Bkmfg Corp.. 860 738-2200
   200 International Way Winsted (06098) *(G-4339)*

BL&s, Malden *Also Called: Boston Light & Sound Inc (G-10005)*

Black & Decker (us) Inc...................................... 860 225-5111
   700 Stanley Dr New Britain (06053) *(G-2008)*

Black & Decker (us) Inc...................................... 781 329-3407
   377 University Ave Westwood (02090) *(G-13306)*

Black Bay Ventures Vi LLC.................................. 413 283-2976
   22 Mount Dumplin Rd Palmer (01069) *(G-11271)*

Black Bear Granite, Wilmington *Also Called: Gerritystone Inc (G-13409)*

Black Cove Cabinetry... 207 883-8901
   137 Pleasant Hill Rd Scarborough (04074) *(G-5425)*

Black Diamond Group Inc.................................... 781 939-7824
   400 Tradecenter Ste 2990 Woburn (01801) *(G-13527)*

Black Diamond Mfg & Engrg Inc.......................... 978 352-6716
   8 Searle St Georgetown (01833) *(G-8905)*

Black Diamond Therapeutics, Cambridge *Also Called: Black Diamond Therapeutics Inc (G-7517)*

Black Diamond Therapeutics Inc **(PA)**................ **617 252-0848**
   1 Main St Ste 1040 Cambridge (02142) *(G-7517)*

Black Dog Corporation.. 401 683-5858
   1 Maritime Dr Ste 3 Portsmouth (02871) *(G-16439)*

Black Earth Compost LLC................................... 262 227-1067
   2 Hillside Rd Gloucester (01930) *(G-8923)*

Black Earth Technologies Inc............................... 508 397-1335
   2575 County St Dighton (02715) *(G-8292)*

Black Infusions.. 617 212-1046
   396 Washington St Ste 264 Wellesley (02481) *(G-12938)*

Black Phoenix Customs LLC................................ 860 681-3162
   43 Elm St Bristol (06010) *(G-416)*

Black Pond Brews.. 860 207-5295
   1001 Hartford Pike Dayville (06241) *(G-858)*

Black Rock Tech Group LLC................................ 203 916-7200
   211 State St Ste 203 Bridgeport (06604) *(G-302)*

Blackhawk Machine Products Inc.......................... 401 232-7563
   6 Industrial Dr Smithfield (02917) *(G-16689)*

Blacksmith Shop Farms Inc................................. 508 548-7714
   716 Blacksmith Shop Rd East Falmouth (02536) *(G-8357)*

Blackstone Industries LLC.................................. 203 792-8622
   16 Stony Hill Rd Bethel (06801) *(G-101)*

Blackstone Molding Inc...................................... 401 765-6700
   100 Founders Dr Woonsocket (02895) *(G-16950)*

Blackstone Supply, Providence *Also Called: Beacon Rock Properties Inc (G-16482)*

Blacktrace Inc.. 617 848-1211
   156 Norwell Ave Norwell (02061) *(G-11140)*

Blackwold Inc... 860 526-0800
   212 Middlesex Ave Chester (06412) *(G-624)*

Blade Tech Systems Inc...................................... 508 830-9506
   100 Armstrong Rd Ste 103 Plymouth (02360) *(G-11451)*

Blairden Precision Instruments Inc........................ 203 799-2000
   95 Corporate Dr Trumbull (06611) *(G-3714)*

Blakeslee Prestress Inc **(PA)**.......................... **203 315-7090**
   Rt 139 At Mc Dermott Rd Branford (06405) *(G-241)*

Blaktop Inc **(PA)**.. **603 298-8885**
   73 Elm St W West Lebanon (03784) *(G-15678)*

Blanchard Awnings, Wakefield *Also Called: William Blanchard Co Inc (G-12543)*

Blanche P Field LLC.. 617 423-0715
   22 Elkins St Ste 2 Boston (02127) *(G-6596)*

Blank Industries LLC... 855 887-3123
   17 Brent Dr Hudson (01749) *(G-9356)*

Blase Manufacturing Company **(PA)**................. **203 375-5646**
   60 Watson Blvd Stratford (06615) *(G-3520)*

Blase Tool & Manufacturing Co, Stratford *Also Called: Blase Manufacturing Company (G-3520)*

Blastech Overhaul & Repr Corp............................ 860 243-8811
   86 W Dudley Town Rd Bloomfield (06002) *(G-152)*

Blauer, Boston *Also Called: Blauer Manufacturing Co Inc (G-6597)*

Blauer Manufacturing Co Inc **(PA)**................... **800 225-6715**
   20 Aberdeen St Boston (02215) *(G-6597)*

Blazing Editions.. 401 885-4329
   42 Ladd St Ste 12 East Greenwich (02818) *(G-15974)*

Blazing Editions, East Greenwich *Also Called: Blazing Editions (G-15974)*

Blc Holdings LLC **(PA)**................................... **203 229-1007**
   20 Glover Ave Norwalk (06850) *(G-2474)*

Blendco Systems LLC.. 800 537-7797
   630 Beaulieu St Holyoke (01040) *(G-9244)*

Blethen Maine Newspapers, Augusta *Also Called: Seattle Times Company (G-4480)*

Blethen Maine Newspapers Inc............................ 207 791-6650
   390 Congress St Portland (04101) *(G-5188)*

Blind Pig Tavern.. 207 592-0776
   266 Water St Gardiner (04345) *(G-4812)*

Blind Tiger LLP.. 603 498-7005
   3 Wright Ln Exeter (03833) *(G-14286)*

Blink, North Reading *Also Called: Immedia Semiconductor Inc (G-11041)*

Blinky Products, Ayer *Also Called: Plastic Assembly Corporation (G-6191)*

Bliss Manufacturing Co Inc................................. 401 729-1690
   50 Bacon St Pawtucket (02860) *(G-16350)*

Block Engineering LLC...................................... 508 480-9643
   132 Turnpike Rd Ste 110 Southborough (01772) *(G-11991)*

Block Mems LLC.. 508 251-3100
   132 Turnpike Rd Ste 110 Southborough (01772) *(G-11992)*

Blodgett Oven Company, The, Essex Junction *Also Called: GS Blodgett LLC (G-17236)*

Bloom & Company Inc.. 617 923-1526
   220 Baldwin Ave Framingham (01701) *(G-8744)*

Bloomfield Wood & Melamine Inc.......................... 860 243-3226
   1 Griffin Rd S Bloomfield (06002) *(G-153)*

Bloomy Controls Inc **(PA)**.............................. **860 298-9925**
   68 Nutmeg Rd S South Windsor (06074) *(G-3120)*

Bloomy Energy Systems, South Windsor *Also Called: Bloomy Controls Inc (G-3120)*

Blouin Display, Dover *Also Called: Mfb Holdings LLC (G-14235)*

Blount Boats Inc... 401 245-8300
   461 Water St Warren (02885) *(G-16754)*

Blount Fine Foods, Fall River *Also Called: Blount Fine Foods Corp (G-8526)*

Blount Fine Foods Corp **(PA)**.......................... **774 888-1300**
   630 Currant Rd Fall River (02720) *(G-8526)*

Blp Technologies Inc... 203 678-4224
   2a Research Pkwy Wallingford (06492) *(G-3781)*

Bltees Inc... 413 594-7547
   165 Front St Ste 3 Chicopee (01013) *(G-8011)*

Blubox Security Inc... 508 414-3517
   1 Tech Dr Ste 110 Andover (01810) *(G-5872)*

Blue Atlantic Fabricators LLC.............................. 617 874-8503
   256 Marginal St Ste 2 Boston (02128) *(G-6598)*

A L P H A B E T I C

Blue Barn LLC.. 207 536-8002
  15 Washington Ave Unit 9 Scarborough (04074) *(G-5426)*

Blue Barn Inc... 617 894-6987
  708 Whitney St Gardner (01440) *(G-8880)*

Blue Bell Mattress Company LLC **(HQ)**.................. **860 292-6372**
  24 Thompson Rd East Windsor (06088) *(G-1068)*

Blue Buffalo Company Ltd **(DH)**.......................... **203 762-9751**
  11 River Rd Ste 200 Wilton (06897) *(G-4233)*

Blue Buffalo Pet Products Inc **(HQ)**.................... **203 762-9751**
  11 River Rd Ste 103 Wilton (06897) *(G-4234)*

Blue Cow Software LLC.. 781 245-2583
  19 Garden Ln Wakefield (01880) *(G-12502)*

Blue Dolphin Screenprint Inc................................ 603 692-2500
  22 Canal St Unit 425 Somersworth (03878) *(G-15611)*

Blue Fleet Welding Service.................................... 508 997-5513
  102 Wamsutta St New Bedford (02740) *(G-10572)*

Blue Hill Transformer, Holliston *Also Called: Total Recoil Magnetics Inc (G-9234)*

Blue Horseshoe LLC.. 401 253-0037
  114 Aaron Ave Bristol (02809) *(G-15755)*

Blue Lobster Wine Company.................................. 207 671-1154
  219 Anderson St Ste 2 Portland (04101) *(G-5189)*

Blue Moon Foods Inc.. 802 295-1165
  568 N Main St Ste 1 White River Junction (05001) *(G-17704)*

Blue Moon Sorbet, White River Junction *Also Called: Blue Moon Foods Inc (G-17704)*

Blue Ox Malthouse LLC.. 207 649-0018
  41 Capital Ave Lisbon Falls (04252) *(G-5019)*

Blue Rhino of Ne.. 413 781-3694
  1709 Page Blvd Springfield (01104) *(G-12079)*

Blue Sky Inc... 207 772-0073
  987 Riverside St Portland (04103) *(G-5190)*

Blue Sky Studios Inc.. 203 992-6000
  1 American Ln Ste 301 Greenwich (06831) *(G-1319)*

Blue Sky/Vifx, Greenwich *Also Called: Blue Sky Studios Inc (G-1319)*

Blue Tactical LLC.. 413 315-6344
  109 Apremont Way Westfield (01085) *(G-13153)*

Blue Triton Brands, Stamford *Also Called: Bluetriton Brands Inc (G-3295)*

Bluebird, Somerville *Also Called: Bluebird Bio Inc (G-11864)*

BLUEBIRD BIO, Cambridge *Also Called: 2seventy Bio Inc (G-7462)*

Bluebird Bio Inc **(PA)**.. **339 499-9300**
  455 Grand Union Blvd Somerville (02145) *(G-11864)*

Bluebird Graphic Solutions, Woburn *Also Called: Clayton LLC DBA Blbird Grphic (G-13542)*

Bluecatbio, Concord *Also Called: Bluecatbio MA Inc (G-8106)*

Bluecatbio MA Inc.. 978 405-2533
  58 Elsinore St Concord (01742) *(G-8106)*

Blueconic Inc... 888 440-2583
  179 Lincoln St Ste 501 Boston (02111) *(G-6599)*

Bluecrest, Danbury *Also Called: Dmt Solutions Global Corp (G-733)*

Bluedge, Boston *Also Called: National Reprographics Inc (G-6904)*

Bluedrop LLC... 877 662-7873
  24 Norfolk Ave Ste A South Easton (02375) *(G-11938)*

Bluefin Biomedicine Inc.. 925 524-3417
  32 Tozer Rd Beverly (01915) *(G-6334)*

Bluejacket Inc.. 207 548-9970
  160 E Main St Searsport (04974) *(G-5451)*

Blueprint Medicines Corp **(PA)**.......................... **617 374-7580**
  45 Sidney St Cambridge (02139) *(G-7518)*

Blueshift, Spencer *Also Called: Blueshift Materials Inc (G-12054)*

Blueshift Materials Inc.. 888 350-7586
  5 S Spencer Rd Spencer (01562) *(G-12054)*

Bluesnap Inc **(PA)**.. **781 790-5013**
  800 South St Ste 640 Waltham (02453) *(G-12609)*

Bluet, Scarborough *Also Called: Blue Barn LLC (G-5426)*

Bluetriton Brands Inc.. 203 531-4100
  900 Long Ridge Rd Stamford (06902) *(G-3295)*

Bluetriton Brands Inc **(HQ)**.............................. **888 747-7437**
  900 Long Ridge Rd Bldg 2 Stamford (06902) *(G-3296)*

Bluetriton Brands Inc.. 207 998-4315
  109 Poland Spring Dr Poland Spring (04274) *(G-5163)*

Bluglass Inc.. 617 869-5150
  77 Northeastern Blvd Ste 103 Nashua (03062) *(G-15072)*

Blushift Aerospace Inc.. 207 619-1703
  2 Pegasus St Ste 2 Brunswick (04011) *(G-4642)*

Blw Holdings Inc **(PA)**...................................... **508 994-4000**
  77 Alden Rd Fairhaven (02719) *(G-8507)*

Bmac Inc... 978 772-3310
  31 Willow Rd Ayer (01432) *(G-6175)*

Bmd, Guilford *Also Called: Bio-Med Devices Inc (G-1386)*

Bmf Precision Inc.. 978 637-2050
  8 Mill And Main Pl Ste 310 Maynard (01754) *(G-10261)*

Bmi, Warren *Also Called: Barrington Manufacturing Inc (G-16753)*

Bmi Cad Services Inc.. 860 658-0808
  8a Herman Dr Simsbury (06070) *(G-3083)*

Bml Tool & Mfg Corp.. 203 880-9485
  67 Enterprise Dr Monroe (06468) *(G-1907)*

Bmp Medical, Sterling *Also Called: Biomedical Polymers Inc (G-12157)*

Bms Pizza Inc.. 978 851-0540
  1475 Main St Tewksbury (01876) *(G-12386)*

Bms Plastics Inc... 401 465-3960
  535 Prospect St Pawtucket (02860) *(G-16351)*

Bn Logging, Cranston *Also Called: Green Development LLC (G-15870)*

BNL Industries Inc... 860 870-6222
  30 Industrial Park Rd Vernon (06066) *(G-3751)*

Bnl Manufacturing LLC.. 860 870-6222
  30 Industrial Park Rd Vernon Rockville (06066) *(G-3760)*

Bnr Supplies.. 401 461-9132
  18 Gallup Ave Cranston (02910) *(G-15836)*

Bnz Materials Inc... 978 663-3401
  400 Iron Horse Park North Billerica (01862) *(G-10900)*

Boardman Silversmiths Inc.................................... 203 265-9978
  22 N Plains Industrial Rd Ste 6c Wallingford (06492) *(G-3782)*

Boardtech Solutions Inc.. 508 643-3684
  322 E Washington St Unit 2 North Attleboro (02760) *(G-10868)*

Bob Bean Company Inc... 603 818-4390
  44 Nashua Rd Unit 2 Londonderry (03053) *(G-14733)*

Bob The Baker, Brookfield *Also Called: Bob The Baker LLC (G-510)*

Bob The Baker LLC... 203 775-1032
  594 Federal Rd Brookfield (06804) *(G-510)*

Bob Vess Building LLC.. 860 729-2536
  605 Main St Cromwell (06416) *(G-688)*

Bobby Pins.. 401 461-3400
  2208 Broad St Cranston (02905) *(G-15837)*

Bobguide Publishing... 207 827-3782
  478 Beechwood Ave Old Town (04468) *(G-5124)*

Bobken Automatics, Waterbury *Also Called: Oakville Quality Products LLC (G-3954)*

Boc Gases, Bellingham *Also Called: Messer LLC (G-6296)*

Boc Gases, Stoughton *Also Called: Messer LLC (G-12224)*

Bocra Industries Inc... 603 474-3598
  140 Batchelder Rd Seabrook (03874) *(G-15585)*

Body Mind & Spirit Magazine, Providence *Also Called: Island Publishing Company (G-16544)*

Body Rags, Pelham *Also Called: C K Productions Inc (G-15287)*

Bodycote Andover, Andover *Also Called: Bodycote Imt Inc (G-5873)*

Bodycote Imt Inc **(DH)**...................................... **978 470-0876**
  155 River St Andover (01810) *(G-5873)*

Bodycote Surface Tech Inc.................................... 802 773-4278
  112 Quality Ln Rutland (05701) *(G-17490)*

Bodycote Thermal Proc Inc................................... 860 225-7691
  675 Christian Ln Berlin (06037) *(G-52)*

Bodycote Thermal Proc Inc................................... 508 754-1724
  675 Christian Ln Berlin (06037) *(G-53)*

Bodycote Thermal Proc Inc................................... 860 282-1371
  45 Connecticut Ave South Windsor (06074) *(G-3121)*

Bodycote Thermal Proc Inc................................... 978 356-3818
  11 Old Right Rd Ste C Ipswich (01938) *(G-9478)*

Bodycote Thermal Proc Inc................................... 603 524-7886
  187 Water St Laconia (03246) *(G-14647)*

Bodyshop World By Wagner Inc............................. 508 853-0300
  700 Plantation St Worcester (01605) *(G-13704)*

Boehringer Ingelheim, Ridgefield *Also Called: Boehringer Ingelheim USA Corp (G-2888)*

Boehringer Ingelheim, Ridgefield *Also Called: Boehrnger Inglheim Phrmctcals (G-2891)*

Boehringer Ingelheim Corp **(DH)**........................ **203 798-9988**
  900 Ridgebury Rd Ridgefield (06877) *(G-2886)*

(G-0000) Company's Geographic Section entry number

Boehringer Ingelheim Data Dime.................................... 800 203-2916
   900 Ridgebury Rd Ridgefield (06877) *(G-2887)*

Boehringer Ingelheim USA Corp (DH)........................ 203 798-9988
   900 Ridgebury Rd Ridgefield (06877) *(G-2888)*

Boehrnger Ingelheim Roxane Inc..................................... 800 243-0127
   900 Ridgebury Rd Ridgefield (06877) *(G-2889)*

Boehrnger Inglheim Phrmctcals.. 203 798-9988
   39 Briar Ridge Rd Ridgefield (06877) *(G-2890)*

Boehrnger Inglheim Phrmctcals (DH)......................... 203 798-9988
   900 Ridgebury Rd Ridgefield (06877) *(G-2891)*

Boggs Mobile Homes, Warren *Also Called: Leland Boggs II (G-5583)*

Bogner of America Inc (PA)... 802 451-4417
   128 Lakeside Ave Ste 302 Burlington (05401) *(G-17121)*

Bogner's, Manchester *Also Called: Manchester Packing Company Inc (G-1616)*

Bold Maker LLC.. 978 891-5920
   45 Wingate St Haverhill (01832) *(G-9079)*

Bold Wood Interiors LLC... 203 907-4077
   138 Haven St New Haven (06513) *(G-2131)*

Boles Enterprises Inc... 603 622-4282
   143 Middle St Ste 1 Manchester (03101) *(G-14820)*

Bolger and OHearn Inc.. 508 676-1518
   47 Slade St Fall River (02724) *(G-8527)*

Bollore Inc.. 860 774-2930
   60 Louisa Viens Dr Dayville (06241) *(G-859)*

Bolt Coffee Company LLC... 401 533-6506
   96 Calverley St Providence (02908) *(G-16487)*

Bolton Aerospace, Manchester *Also Called: Pas Technologies Inc (G-1629)*

Boltprintingcom.. 203 885-0571
   20 Old Grays Bridge Rd Brookfield (06804) *(G-511)*

Bomas Machine Specialties Inc...................................... 617 628-3831
   6 Jefferson Ave Woburn (01801) *(G-13528)*

Bomb Cosmetics, Salem *Also Called: Fizz Time (G-15527)*

Bombardier, Windsor Locks *Also Called: Learjet Inc (G-4331)*

Bombardier Mass Transit, Boston *Also Called: Bombardier Services Corp (G-6600)*

Bombardier Services Corp.. 617 464-0323
   2 Frontage Rd Boston (02118) *(G-6600)*

Bomco Inc... 978 283-9000
   125 Gloucester Ave Gloucester (01930) *(G-8924)*

Bond Construction Corporation....................................... 508 885-2480
   98 N Spencer Rd Spencer (01562) *(G-12055)*

Bond Optics LLC.. 603 448-2300
   76 Etna Rd Lebanon (03766) *(G-14685)*

Bond Painting Company Inc... 212 944-0070
   27 Meadowbank Rd Old Greenwich (06870) *(G-2630)*

Bond Sand Gravel & Asphalt, Spencer *Also Called: Bond Construction Corporation (G-12055)*

Bonded Abrasives, Worcester *Also Called: Saint-Gobain Abrasives Inc (G-13788)*

Bondi Band LLC... 207 576-4191
   24 Metacom Dr Simsbury (06070) *(G-3084)*

Bonesupport, Needham Heights *Also Called: Bonesupport Inc (G-10531)*

Bonesupport Inc... 781 772-1756
   117 4th Ave Needham Heights (02494) *(G-10531)*

Boniface Tool & Die Inc... 508 764-3248
   181 Southbridge Rd Dudley (01571) *(G-8317)*

Bonito Manufacturing Inc.. 203 234-8786
   445 Washington Ave North Haven (06473) *(G-2394)*

Bonollos, Providence *Also Called: Bp Inc (G-16490)*

Bonsal American Inc.. 860 824-7733
   43 Clayton Rd Canaan (06018) *(G-553)*

Bonsal American Inc.. 508 987-8188
   Old Webster Rd Oxford (01540) *(G-11249)*

Book-Mart Press Inc.. 978 251-6000
   15 Wellman Ave North Chelmsford (01863) *(G-10966)*

Books On Disk, Boston *Also Called: Teletypesetting Company Inc (G-7073)*

Booktalk, Lowell *Also Called: Booktalk Event (G-9863)*

Booktalk Event... 952 836-6275
   125 Charant Rd Lowell (01854) *(G-9863)*

Booktriblifecom LLC... 203 226-0199
   155 Post Rd E Westport (06880) *(G-4159)*

Boom Creative Development, New Canaan *Also Called: Boom LLC (G-2076)*

Boom LLC... 212 317-2005
   11 Forest St Ste 3 New Canaan (06840) *(G-2076)*

Boomerangs.. 617 758-6128
   563 Massachusetts Ave Cambridge (02139) *(G-7519)*

Boot Strap Press, Northampton *Also Called: Council On Intl Pub Affirs Inc (G-11058)*

Boothbay Harbor Shipyard, Boothbay Harbor *Also Called: Shipyard In Boothbay Hbr LLC (G-4604)*

Boothbay Home Builders, Boothbay *Also Called: Knickerbocker Group Inc (G-4598)*

Boothroyd Dewhurst Inc.. 401 783-5840
   4474 Post Rd East Greenwich (02818) *(G-15975)*

Bootstrap Compost Inc... 617 642-1979
   470 W Main St Plainfield (01070) *(G-11428)*

Bopkg Inc (HQ).. 978 343-3067
   251 Authority Dr Fitchburg (01420) *(G-8644)*

Borden, Fall River *Also Called: Borden & Remington Corp (G-8528)*

Borden & Remington Corp... 508 675-0096
   63 Water St Ste 1 Fall River (02721) *(G-8528)*

Borealis Press Inc.. 800 669-6845
   35 Tenney Hl Blue Hill (04614) *(G-4595)*

Borg Design Inc.. 978 562-1559
   19 Brent Dr Hudson (01749) *(G-9357)*

Borgwarner Inc... 508 281-5500
   100 Otis St Ste 1 Northborough (01532) *(G-11091)*

Borgwarner Massachusetts Inc (HQ)......................... 508 281-5500
   100 Otis St Northborough (01532) *(G-11092)*

Boro Sand & Stone Corp (PA)................................... 508 699-2911
   192 Plain St North Attleboro (02760) *(G-10869)*

Bortech Corporation... 603 358-4030
   66 Victoria St Keene (03431) *(G-14591)*

Bosal Foam and Fiber (PA).. 207 793-2245
   171 Washington St Limerick (04048) *(G-5000)*

Bosal Foam Products, Limerick *Also Called: Bosal Foam and Fiber (G-5000)*

Bose Corporate Center, Framingham *Also Called: Bose Corporation (G-8745)*

Bose Corporation (PA)... 508 879-7330
   100 The Mountain Rd Framingham (01701) *(G-8745)*

Bose Corporation... 508 766-1265
   145 Pennsylvania Ave Framingham (01701) *(G-8746)*

Bose Corporation... 508 879-7330
   1 New York Ave Framingham (01701) *(G-8747)*

Bose Corporation... 508 766-7330
   688 Great Rd Stow (01775) *(G-12244)*

Bostik Inc... 978 777-0103
   211 Boston St Middleton (01949) *(G-10382)*

Boston Academic Publishing... 617 851-8655
   175 Portland St Fl 2 Boston (02114) *(G-6601)*

Boston Acoustics Inc (DH)... 978 538-5000
   301 Edgewater Pl Ste 100 Wakefield (01880) *(G-12503)*

Boston America Corp.. 781 933-3535
   55 6th Rd Ste 8 Woburn (01801) *(G-13529)*

Boston Area Door Company.. 508 857-4722
   75 1st St Unit 3 Bridgewater (02324) *(G-7224)*

Boston Area Door Company, Bridgewater *Also Called: Boston Area Door Company (G-7224)*

Boston Atlantic Corp.. 508 754-4076
   7 Harris Ct Worcester (01610) *(G-13705)*

Boston Atlantic Gasket and Rbr, Worcester *Also Called: Boston Atlantic Corp (G-13705)*

Boston Bagel Inc.. 617 364-6900
   101 Sprague St Ste 3 Hyde Park (02136) *(G-9457)*

Boston Beer, Boston *Also Called: Boston Beer Company Inc (G-6603)*

Boston Beer Company Inc.. 617 368-5080
   30 Germania St Ste 1 Boston (02130) *(G-6602)*

Boston Beer Company Inc (PA)................................. 617 368-5000
   1 Design Center Pl Ste 850 Boston (02210) *(G-6603)*

Boston Beer Corporation (DH)................................... 617 368-5000
   1 Design Center Pl Ste 850 Boston (02210) *(G-6604)*

Boston Billows Inc.. 603 598-1200
   55 Lake St Nashua (03060) *(G-15073)*

Boston Boatworks, Charlestown *Also Called: Boston Boatworks LLC (G-7862)*

Boston Boatworks LLC... 617 561-9111
   333 Terminal St Charlestown (02129) *(G-7862)*

Boston Brands of Maine, Lewiston *Also Called: Mr Boston Brands LLC (G-4978)*

Boston Brisket Company Inc... 617 442-8814
   323 Dodge St Beverly (01915) *(G-6335)*

A L P H A B E T I C

Boston Business Journal Inc................................. 617 330-1000
   70 Franklin St Ste 800 Boston (02110) *(G-6605)*

Boston Business Printing Inc............................... 617 482-7955
   115 Broad St Boston (02110) *(G-6606)*

Boston Centerless Inc.. 508 587-3500
   15 Doherty Ave Avon (02322) *(G-6145)*

Boston Centerless Inc **(PA)**.............................. **781 994-5000**
   11 Presidential Way Woburn (01801) *(G-13530)*

Boston Chipyard, Boston *Also Called: Boston Chipyard The Inc (G-6607)*

Boston Chipyard The Inc.................................... 617 742-9537
   257 Faneuil Hall Market Pl Boston (02109) *(G-6607)*

Boston Coffee Exchange, Providence *Also Called: Coffee Exchange Ltd (G-16502)*

Boston Design Guide Inc.................................... 978 443-9886
   277 Concord Rd Sudbury (01776) *(G-12261)*

Boston Document Systems Inc **(PA)**................... **800 616-8576**
   417 South St Ste 9 Marlborough (01752) *(G-10117)*

Boston Elctrmetallurgical Corp **(PA)**.................. **781 281-7657**
   6c Gill St Woburn (01801) *(G-13531)*

Boston Endo-Surgical Tech, Bridgeport *Also Called: Precision Engineered Pdts LLC (G-361)*

Boston Endo-Surgical Tech LLC........................... 203 336-6479
   1146 Barnum Ave Bridgeport (06610) *(G-303)*

Boston Environmental LLC................................... 603 334-1000
   600 State St Ste 7 Portsmouth (03801) *(G-15366)*

Boston Fabrications.. 781 762-9185
   39 Franklin R Mckay Rd Attleboro (02703) *(G-5997)*

Boston Food Cooperative **(PA)**.......................... **617 661-1580**
   580 Massachusetts Ave Cambridge (02139) *(G-7520)*

Boston Gar Flrg & Cabinets LLC........................... 339 788-9580
   145 Webster St Ste 2 Hanover (02339) *(G-9026)*

Boston Globe, Boston *Also Called: Ne Media Group Inc (G-6906)*

Boston Globe LLC... 617 929-2684
   53 State St Lbby 2& Boston (02109) *(G-6608)*

Boston Globe Mdia Partners LLC.......................... 617 929-2000
   1 Exchange Pl Ste 201 Boston (02109) *(G-6609)*

Boston Globe, The, Boston *Also Called: Boston Globe Mdia Partners LLC (G-6609)*

Boston Hatian Reporter, Boston *Also Called: Boston Neighborhood News Inc (G-6611)*

Boston Herald, Lowell *Also Called: Bh Media Inc (G-9862)*

Boston Irish Reporter.. 617 436-1222
   150 Mount Vernon St Ste 120 Dorchester (02125) *(G-8297)*

Boston Iron Works, Everett *Also Called: Lima Fredy (G-8491)*

Boston Korean... 617 254-4654
   161 Harvard Ave Ste 13 Allston (02134) *(G-5820)*

Boston Legion LLC... 508 718-8912
   6 Liberty Sq Boston (02109) *(G-6610)*

Boston Light & Sound Inc **(PA)**......................... **617 787-3131**
   420 Pearl St Malden (02148) *(G-10005)*

Boston Logan Intl Arprt, Boston *Also Called: Massachusetts Port Authority (G-6875)*

Boston Materials Inc.. 617 306-2396
   8 Federal St # A Billerica (01821) *(G-6411)*

Boston Medical Products Inc.............................. 508 898-9300
   70 Chestnut St Shrewsbury (01545) *(G-11829)*

Boston Metal, Woburn *Also Called: Boston Elctrmetallurgical Corp (G-13531)*

Boston Micro Fabrication, Maynard *Also Called: Bmf Precision Inc (G-10261)*

Boston Neighborhood News Inc.......................... 617 436-1222
   150 Mount Vernon St Ste 120 Boston (02125) *(G-6611)*

Boston Ntrceutical Science LLC.......................... 617 848-4560
   1 Turks Head Pl Providence (02903) *(G-16488)*

Boston Oncology LLC....................................... 857 209-5052
   245 1st St Ste 1800 Cambridge (02142) *(G-7521)*

Boston Paper Board Corp.................................. 617 666-1154
   40 Roland St Boston (02129) *(G-6612)*

Boston Phoenix Inc **(PA)**................................. **617 536-5390**
   1 Chestnut St Ste 1 Providence (02903) *(G-16489)*

Boston Piezo-Optics Inc.................................... 508 966-4988
   38b Maple St Bellingham (02019) *(G-6287)*

Boston Print Specialists LLC.............................. 617 742-9585
   12 Channel St Ste 804 Boston (02210) *(G-6613)*

Boston Retail, Tewksbury *Also Called: Boston Retail Products Inc (G-12387)*

Boston Retail Products Inc **(PA)**....................... **781 395-7417**
   3 Highwood Dr Ste 100w Tewksbury (01876) *(G-12387)*

Boston Salads, Boston *Also Called: Boston Salads and Provs Inc (G-6615)*

Boston Salads and Provs Inc.............................. 617 541-9054
   26 Chesterton St Boston (02119) *(G-6614)*

Boston Salads and Provs Inc **(PA)**..................... **617 307-6340**
   225 Southampton St Boston (02118) *(G-6615)*

Boston Sand & Gravel Company **(PA)**.................. **617 227-9000**
   100 N Washington St 2nd Fl Boston (02114) *(G-6616)*

Boston Sand & Gravel Company........................... 617 242-5540
   40 Bunker Hill Industrial Park Charlestown (02129) *(G-7863)*

Boston Sand & Gravel Company........................... 508 888-8002
   181 Kiahs Way Sandwich (02563) *(G-11747)*

Boston Sand & Gravel Company........................... 603 330-3999
   69 N Coast Rd Rochester (03868) *(G-15467)*

Boston Sand and Gravel, Kingston *Also Called: Southeastem Concrete Inc (G-9511)*

Boston Scientific, Marlborough *Also Called: Boston Scientific Corporation (G-10119)*

BOSTON SCIENTIFIC, Marlborough *Also Called: Boston Scientific Funding LLC (G-10120)*

Boston Scientific Corporation............................. 508 382-0200
   100 Boston Scientific Way Marlborough (01752) *(G-10118)*

Boston Scientific Corporation **(PA)**.................... **508 683-4000**
   300 Boston Scientific Way Marlborough (01752) *(G-10119)*

Boston Scientific Corporation............................. 617 689-6000
   500 Commander Shea Blvd Quincy (02171) *(G-11507)*

Boston Scientific Corporation............................. 617 972-4000
   480 Pleasant St Watertown (02472) *(G-12863)*

Boston Scientific Funding LLC............................ 508 683-4000
   300 Boston Scientific Way Marlborough (01752) *(G-10120)*

Boston Scientific Intl Corp................................. 508 683-4000
   300 Boston Scientific Way Marlborough (01752) *(G-10121)*

Boston Ship Repair LLC.................................... 617 330-5045
   32a Drydock Ave Boston (02210) *(G-6617)*

Boston Sign Company Inc.................................. 617 338-2114
   40 Plympton St Ste 1 Boston (02118) *(G-6618)*

Boston Ski Tennis, Newton *Also Called: East Basin Sports Inc (G-10754)*

Boston Smoked Fish Company LLC....................... 617 819-5476
   20 Fish Pier St W Boston (02210) *(G-6619)*

Boston Software Corp....................................... 781 449-8585
   189 Reservoir St Needham Heights (02494) *(G-10532)*

Boston Sports Journal LLC................................. 617 306-0166
   4 Daniels Rd Medway (02053) *(G-10303)*

Boston Steel & Mfg Co...................................... 781 324-3000
   89 Newark St Haverhill (01832) *(G-9080)*

Boston Steel Fabricators Inc.............................. 781 767-1540
   610 South St Holbrook (02343) *(G-9170)*

Boston Stone and Cabinet.................................. 781 352-3623
   165 Lenox St Norwood (02062) *(G-11165)*

Boston Trailer Manufacturing.............................. 508 668-2242
   1 Production Rd Walpole (02081) *(G-12553)*

Boston Welding & Design Inc.............................. 781 932-0035
   7 Micro Dr Woburn (01801) *(G-13532)*

BOSTON'S CHILDREN HOSPTIAL, Boston *Also Called: Chmc Otlrynglgic Fundation Inc (G-6654)*

Bostoncom LLC.. 617 929-8593
   320 Congress St Fl 2 Boston (02210) *(G-6620)*

Bostoncounters LLC.. 781 281-1622
   78h Olympia Ave Woburn (01801) *(G-13533)*

Bostonia Welding Supply Inc.............................. 617 268-1025
   61 Dorchester Ave Boston (02127) *(G-6621)*

Bostonian, Waltham *Also Called: C & J Clark America Inc (G-12617)*

Bostonian Body Inc.. 617 944-0985
   151 Bow St Everett (02149) *(G-8483)*

Bostonian Clg Restoration Inc............................ 781 356-3303
   26 Quincy Ave Braintree (02184) *(G-7170)*

Bostonmolecules Inc.. 617 651-1016
   204 2nd Ave Ste 1 Waltham (02451) *(G-12610)*

Bostonsportsjournal.com, Medway *Also Called: Boston Sports Journal LLC (G-10303)*

Bosworth Printing Co Inc................................... 781 341-2992
   28 Tosca Dr Stoughton (02072) *(G-12199)*

Botify Corporation... 617 576-2005
   185 Alewife Brook Pkwy Ste 210 Cambridge (02138) *(G-7522)*

Bottle King Redemption Center........................... 207 563-1520
   116 Mills Rd Newcastle (04553) *(G-5092)*

Botto's Bakery, Westbrook *Also Called: Mathews Bakery Inc (G-5637)*

Bottomline Technologies.. 401 954-2200
  36 Ridgeland Drive Cumberland (02864) *(G-15933)*

Bottomline Technologies Inc **(PA)**   **603 436-0700**
  325 Corporate Dr Portsmouth (03801) *(G-15367)*

Boucher Con Foundation Sups.. 508 947-4279
  80 Cambridge St Middleboro (02346) *(G-10351)*

Bouckaert Indus Textiles Inc.. 401 769-5474
  235 Singleton St Woonsocket (02895) *(G-16951)*

Boudreaus Welding Co Inc... 860 774-2771
  1029 N Main St Dayville (06241) *(G-860)*

Bouffard Metal Goods, Waterbury *Also Called: H&T Waterbury Inc (G-3916)*

Boulevard Machine & Gear Inc... 413 788-6466
  326 Lockhouse Rd Westfield (01085) *(G-13154)*

Boulia-Gorrell Lumber Co LLC.. 603 524-1300
  176 Fair St Laconia (03246) *(G-14648)*

Bouncepad North America Inc... 617 804-0110
  50 Terminal St Unit 710 Charlestown (02129) *(G-7864)*

Bouncyband LLC... 860 916-9978
  148 Eastern Blvd Ste 308 Glastonbury (06033) *(G-1271)*

Boundary Co.. 207 668-4193
  25 Talpey Rd Moose River (04945) *(G-5076)*

Bourbeau Aggregate LLC... 802 309-4699
  1881 Sheldon Rd Saint Albans (05478) *(G-17517)*

Bourdon Forge Co Inc... 860 632-2740
  99 Tuttle Rd Middletown (06457) *(G-1741)*

Bourdons Institutional Sls Inc... 603 542-8709
  85 Plains Rd Claremont (03743) *(G-14079)*

Bourg Collaters System, New Bedford *Also Called: C P Bourg Inc (G-10577)*

Bourgeois Guitars, Lewiston *Also Called: Pantheon Guitars LLC (G-4983)*

Boutin/Mcquiston Inc **(PA)**   **802 863-8038**
  365 Dorset St South Burlington (05403) *(G-17574)*

Bouyea-Fassetts, Rutland *Also Called: Unilever Bestfoods North Amer (G-17513)*

Bovano Industries Incorporated.. 203 272-3208
  830 S Main St Ofc A Cheshire (06410) *(G-576)*

Bovano of Cheshire, Cheshire *Also Called: Bovano Industries Incorporated (G-576)*

Bove Brothers LLC... 860 443-9200
  18 Sachatello Industrial Dr Oakdale (06370) *(G-2620)*

Bovie Screen Process Prtg Inc... 603 224-0651
  4 Northeast Ave Bow (03304) *(G-13994)*

Bowers and Wilkins Group.. 978 357-0428
  54 Concord St North Reading (01864) *(G-11038)*

Bowles Corporation.. 802 425-3447
  445 Longpoint Rd North Ferrisburgh (05473) *(G-17419)*

Boxcar Media LLC.. 413 663-3384
  102 Main St North Adams (01247) *(G-10804)*

Boxerbrand, East Weymouth *Also Called: Almont Company Inc (G-8424)*

Boyajian Inc... 781 828-9966
  144 Will Dr Canton (02021) *(G-7774)*

Boyce Highland, Concord *Also Called: Boyce Highlands Furn Co Inc (G-14116)*

Boyce Highlands Furn Co Inc.. 603 753-1042
  14 Whitney Rd Concord (03301) *(G-14116)*

Boyd Biomedical Inc **(PA)**   **413 243-2000**
  501 Pleasant St Lee (01238) *(G-9612)*

Boyd Coatings, Hudson *Also Called: Precision Coating Co Inc (G-9403)*

Boyd Coatings Research Co Inc... 978 562-7561
  51 Parmenter Rd Hudson (01749) *(G-9358)*

Boyd Corporation (woburn) Inc **(DH)**   **781 933-7300**
  55 Dragon Ct Woburn (01801) *(G-13534)*

Boyd Laconia LLC **(DH)**   **603 528-3400**
  1 Aavid Cir Laconia (03246) *(G-14649)*

Boydco Inc **(PA)**   **401 438-6900**
  101 Commercial Way East Providence (02914) *(G-16007)*

Boynton Machine Company Inc.. 781 899-9900
  101 Clematis Ave Ste 6 Waltham (02453) *(G-12611)*

Bp Inc... 401 274-7900
  55 Clarkson St Providence (02908) *(G-16490)*

BP Custom Woodworking... 401 787-8750
  500 Mendon Rd Cumberland (02864) *(G-15934)*

BP Fly Corporation **(PA)**   **978 649-9114**
  65 Middlesex Rd Tyngsboro (01879) *(G-12457)*

BP Logging... 207 398-4457
  562 Main St Saint Francis (04774) *(G-5387)*

BP Logue & Co.. 978 251-4433
  10 Jean Ave Ste 16 Chelmsford (01824) *(G-7915)*

Bpg Bio Inc **(PA)**   **617 588-0083**
  500 Old Connecticut Path Framingham (01701) *(G-8748)*

Bpi, Westport *Also Called: Baker Parts Inc (G-13293)*

Bpi Reprographics.. 203 866-5600
  87 Taylor Ave Norwalk (06854) *(G-2475)*

Bpm LLC.. 401 615-0700
  33 College Hill Rd Ste 15b Warwick (02886) *(G-16792)*

Bprex Halthcare Brookville Inc.. 203 754-4141
  574 E Main St Waterbury (06702) *(G-3891)*

Bps Division, Bristol *Also Called: Freudenberg-Nok General Partnr (G-14035)*

BR Holdings Inc **(PA)**   **978 281-3723**
  17 Rogers St Ste 2 Gloucester (01930) *(G-8925)*

Brackett Machine Inc.. 207 854-9789
  355 Saco St Westbrook (04092) *(G-5618)*

Bracone Metal Spinning Inc.. 860 628-5927
  39 Depaolo Dr Southington (06489) *(G-3204)*

Brada Manufacturing Inc.. 401 739-3774
  46 Warwick Industrial Dr Warwick (02886) *(G-16793)*

Bradbury Barrel Co, Bridgewater *Also Called: E G W Bradbury Enterprises Inc (G-4625)*

Bradbury Enterprises, Rumford *Also Called: Clinton G Bradbury Inc (G-5355)*

Braden Manufacturing LLC... 508 797-8000
  17 Saint Mark St Auburn (01501) *(G-6108)*

Bradford & Bigelow Inc... 978 904-3112
  3 Perkins Way Newburyport (01950) *(G-10672)*

Bradford & Bigelow Realty LLC... 978 777-1200
  1 Industrial Dr Danvers (01923) *(G-8170)*

Bradford Coatings Inc... 978 459-4100
  75 Rogers St Lowell (01852) *(G-9864)*

Bradford Finshg Powdr Coat Inc.. 978 469-9965
  2 S Grove St Haverhill (01835) *(G-9081)*

Bradford Industries, Lowell *Also Called: Bradford Coatings Inc (G-9864)*

Bradford Machine, Brattleboro *Also Called: Cave Manufacturing Inc (G-17079)*

Bradford Price Book, Littleton *Also Called: Harrison Publishing House Inc (G-14720)*

Bradford Soap Works, West Warwick *Also Called: Original Brdford Soap Wrks Inc (G-16919)*

Bradford Steel Co Inc... 508 763-5921
  46 Braley Rd East Freetown (02717) *(G-8363)*

Bradford White Corp.. 603 332-0116
  20 Industrial Way Rochester (03867) *(G-15468)*

Brady Business Forms Inc.. 978 458-2585
  171 Lincoln St Ste 1 Lowell (01852) *(G-9865)*

Brady Enterprises Inc... 207 653-9990
  80 Exchange St Ste 30 Portland (04101) *(G-5191)*

Brady Enterprises Inc **(PA)**   **781 340-4571**
  167 Moore Rd East Weymouth (02189) *(G-8427)*

Brady-Built Inc.. 508 798-2600
  160 Southbridge St Auburn (01501) *(G-6109)*

Brady-Built Sunrooms, Auburn *Also Called: Brady-Built Inc (G-6109)*

Brady-Built Sunrooms, Auburn *Also Called: Marvic Inc (G-6119)*

Brahmin Leather Works, Fairhaven *Also Called: Blw Holdings Inc (G-8507)*

Brahmin Leather Works LLC.. 509 994-4000
  77 Alden Rd Fairhaven (02719) *(G-8508)*

Brailsford & Company Inc.. 603 588-2880
  15 Elm Ave Antrim (03440) *(G-13896)*

Brainin-Advance Industries LLC **(HQ)**   **508 226-1200**
  48 Frank Mossberg Dr Attleboro (02703) *(G-5998)*

Braintree Printing Inc... 781 848-5300
  230 Wood Rd Braintree (02184) *(G-7171)*

Brammer Bio Holding Co LLC **(HQ)**   **386 418-8199**
  250 Binney St Cambridge (02142) *(G-7523)*

Brammer Bio Ma LLC **(HQ)**   **877 765-7676**
  250 Binney St Cambridge (02142) *(G-7524)*

Branch Graphics Inc... 401 861-1830
  260 Narragansett Park Dr Rumford (02916) *(G-16663)*

Branch River Plastics Inc... 401 232-0270
  15 Thurber Blvd Smithfield (02917) *(G-16690)*

Brand & Oppenheimer Co Inc... 781 271-0000
  4 Preston Ct Ste 200 Bedford (01730) *(G-6216)*

A L P H A B E T I C

Brand & Oppenheimer Co Inc **(PA)**............................ **401 293-5500**
   208 Clock Tower Sq Portsmouth (02871) **(G-16440)**

Brand Services, Gales Ferry *Also Called: Stonington Services LLC* **(G-1261)**

Brand-Nu Laboratories LLC **(PA)**............................ **203 235-7989**
   377 Research Pkwy Ste 2 Meriden (06450) **(G-1656)**

Brands To Go Inc
   65 East Ave Norwalk (06851) **(G-2476)**

Brandstrom Instruments Inc.............................. 203 544-9341
   85 Ethan Allen Hwy Ridgefield (06877) **(G-2892)**

Brannen Brothers-Flutemakers.......................... 781 935-9522
   58 Dragon Ct Woburn (01801) **(G-13535)**

Brannen Flutes, Woburn *Also Called: Brannen Brothers-Flutemakers* **(G-13535)**

Brannkey Inc... 860 510-0501
   137 Mill Rock Rd E Old Saybrook (06475) **(G-2646)**

Branson Ultrasonics Corp **(DH)**............................ **203 796-0400**
   120 Park Ridge Rd Brookfield (06804) **(G-512)**

Branson Ultrasonics Corp................................. 978 262-9040
   58 Skyline Dr Acton (01720) **(G-5741)**

Brant Industries Inc **(PA)**............................ **203 661-3344**
   80 Field Point Rd Fl 3 Greenwich (06830) **(G-1320)**

Brant Paper Inc.. 203 661-3344
   80 Field Point Rd Ste 3 Greenwich (06830) **(G-1321)**

Brapsards Powder Coating LLC........................ 603 630-4014
   52 Thompson Park Franklin (03235) **(G-14319)**

Brass City Tile Designs LLC............................. 203 597-8764
   29 S Commons Rd Ste 3 Waterbury (06704) **(G-3892)**

Brattleboro Kiln Dry & Milling........................... 802 254-4528
   1103 Vernon St Brattleboro (05301) **(G-17075)**

Brattleboro Reformer, Brattleboro *Also Called: New England Newspapers Inc* **(G-17097)**

Brattleboro Tire, Brattleboro *Also Called: John Penfield Ltd* **(G-17090)**

Bravo LLC... 860 896-1899
   1084 Hartford Tpke Vernon (06066) **(G-3752)**

Braxton Manufacturing Co Inc.......................... 860 274-6781
   858 Echo Lake Rd Watertown (06795) **(G-4003)**

Bray's Brew Pub & Eatery, Naples *Also Called: Brays Brewing Company* **(G-5079)**

Brays Brewing Company................................... 207 693-6806
   678 Roosevelt Trl Naples (04055) **(G-5079)**

Brayton Wilson Cole Corp................................ 781 803-6624
   70 Sharp St Hingham (02043) **(G-9144)**

Brazecom Industries LLC................................. 603 529-2080
   45 B And B Ln Weare (03281) **(G-15670)**

Brazonics Inc **(DH)**............................ **603 758-6237**
   94 Tide Mill Rd Hampton (03842) **(G-14400)**

Bread & Chocolate Inc.................................... 802 429-2920
   1538 Industrial Park Wells River (05081) **(G-17686)**

Breakthrough Coatings, Buzzards Bay *Also Called: Breakthrough Coatings Inc* **(G-7453)**

Breakthrough Coatings Inc............................... 866 608-7625
   169 Clay Pond Rd Ste 1 Buzzards Bay (02532) **(G-7453)**

Breakwater Foods LLC.................................... 617 335-6475
   82 Sanderson Ave Lynn (01902) **(G-9964)**

Brede, Hingham *Also Called: Casey & Hayes Inc* **(G-9146)**

Breeze Publications Inc................................... 401 334-9555
   6 Blackstone Valley Pl Ste 204 Lincoln (02865) **(G-16122)**

Breezy Hill, Oxford *Also Called: Jackson Caldwell* **(G-5146)**

Breezy Hill Lumber Co..................................... 603 496-8870
   78 Province Rd Barnstead (03218) **(G-13913)**

Bremser Technologies Inc................................ 203 378-8486
   305 Sniffens Ln Stratford (06615) **(G-3521)**

Brennan Machine Co Inc.................................. 781 293-3997
   820 Monponsett St Hanson (02341) **(G-9050)**

Brennan Realty LLC **(PA)**............................ **203 929-6314**
   70 Platt Rd Shelton (06484) **(G-2987)**

Brescias Printing Services Inc.......................... 860 528-4254
   66 Connecticut Blvd East Hartford (06108) **(G-976)**

Bresna Hand Ice, Gloucester *Also Called: Cape Pond Ice Company* **(G-8927)**

Brew Your Own, Manchester Center *Also Called: Battenkill Communications LLP* **(G-17327)**

Brewer Electric & Utilities In............................. 508 771-2040
   110 Old Town House Rd South Yarmouth (02664) **(G-11981)**

Brewer's Cove Haven Marina, Barrington *Also Called: Cove Haven Corp* **(G-15747)**

Brewery Legitimus LLC.................................... 860 810-8894
   283 Main St New Hartford (06057) **(G-2099)**

Brewster Home Fashions, Randolph *Also Called: Brewster Wallpaper LLC* **(G-11552)**

Brewster Wallpaper LLC................................... 800 366-1700
   67 Pacella Park Dr Randolph (02368) **(G-11552)**

Bri-Weld Industries LLC................................... 603 622-9480
   55 Gold Ledge Ave Auburn (03032) **(G-13906)**

Brians Machine Shop LLC................................ 603 224-4333
   27 Industrial Park Dr Ste 1 Concord (03301) **(G-14117)**

Briar Hill, Poultney *Also Called: Quarry Slate Industries Inc* **(G-17449)**

Briarwood Printing Company Inc....................... 860 747-6805
   301 Farmington Ave Plainville (06062) **(G-2749)**

Brickell Brands LLC.. 877 598-0060
   167 Rumery St South Portland (04106) **(G-5492)**

Brickell Men's Products, South Portland *Also Called: Brickell Brands LLC* **(G-5492)**

Brickenmore East LLC.................................... 860 906-6116
   9 Thompson Rd East Windsor (06088) **(G-1069)**

Brickmill Marketing Services, Milford *Also Called: Innovairre Studios Inc* **(G-15030)**

Brico LLC... 860 242-7068
   6c Northwood Dr Bloomfield (06002) **(G-154)**

Brideau Shtmtl Fabrication Inc.......................... 978 537-3372
   29 Phillips St Leominster (01453) **(G-9643)**

Bridge & Byron Inc... 603 225-5221
   45 S State St Concord (03301) **(G-14118)**

Bridge Building Images, Milton *Also Called: Vermont Christmas Company* **(G-17366)**

Bridge Byron Printers, Concord *Also Called: Bridge & Byron Inc* **(G-14118)**

BRIDGELINE DIGITAL, Woburn *Also Called: Bridgeline Digital Inc* **(G-13536)**

Bridgeline Digital Inc **(PA)**............................ **781 376-5555**
   100 Sylvan Rd Ste G700 Woburn (01801) **(G-13536)**

Bridgemedica, Mansfield *Also Called: Nn Inc* **(G-10070)**

Bridgemedica, LLC, Mansfield *Also Called: Repjtm LLC* **(G-10074)**

Bridgeport, Stratford *Also Called: Bridgeport Fittings LLC* **(G-3522)**

Bridgeport Fittings LLC.................................... 203 377-5944
   705 Lordship Blvd Stratford (06615) **(G-3522)**

Bridgeport Insulated Wire Co **(PA)**............................ **203 333-3191**
   51 Brookfield Ave Bridgeport (06610) **(G-304)**

Bridgeport Insulated Wire Co............................ 203 375-9579
   514 Surf Ave Stratford (06615) **(G-3523)**

Bridgeport Magnetics, Shelton *Also Called: Tortran Inc* **(G-3070)**

Bridgeport Magnetics Group, Shelton *Also Called: Bridgeport Magnetics Group Inc* **(G-2988)**

Bridgeport Magnetics Group Inc........................ 203 954-0050
   6 Waterview Dr Shelton (06484) **(G-2988)**

Bridgeport Nat Bindery Inc............................... 413 789-1981
   662 Silver St Agawam (01001) **(G-5782)**

Bridgeport TI & Stamping Corp......................... 203 336-2501
   35 Burr Ct Bridgeport (06605) **(G-305)**

Bridgestone Ret Operations LLC....................... 860 584-2727
   700 Farmington Ave Bristol (06010) **(G-417)**

Bridgestone Ret Operations LLC....................... 203 288-1634
   2300 Dixwell Ave Ste A Hamden (06514) **(G-1414)**

Bridgestone Ret Operations LLC....................... 203 878-6859
   1063 Boston Post Rd Milford (06460) **(G-1803)**

Bridgestone Ret Operations LLC....................... 860 229-0348
   55 Chestnut St New Britain (06051) **(G-2009)**

Bridgestone Ret Operations LLC....................... 203 787-1208
   680 Chapel St New Haven (06510) **(G-2132)**

Bridgestone Ret Operations LLC....................... 860 594-0594
   2897 Berlin Tpke Newington (06111) **(G-2277)**

Bridgestone Ret Operations LLC....................... 860 628-9621
   288 Queen St Southington (06489) **(G-3205)**

Bridgestone Ret Operations LLC....................... 203 754-6119
   809 Wolcott St Waterbury (06705) **(G-3893)**

Bridgestone Ret Operations LLC....................... 203 933-7750
   525 Saw Mill Rd West Haven (06516) **(G-4095)**

Bridgestone Ret Operations LLC....................... 508 832-9671
   450 Southbridge St Auburn (01501) **(G-6110)**

Bridgestone Ret Operations LLC....................... 617 327-1100
   1528a Vfw Pkwy Boston (02132) **(G-6622)**

Bridgestone Ret Operations LLC....................... 781 843-2870
   535 Granite St Braintree (02184) **(G-7172)**

Bridgestone Ret Operations LLC....................... 508 588-8866
   126 Warren Ave Brockton (02301) **(G-7262)**

Bridgestone Ret Operations LLC............................. 781 749-6454
  22 Whiting St Hingham (02043) *(G-9145)*

Bridgestone Ret Operations LLC............................. 413 586-1584
  327 King St Northampton (01060) *(G-11054)*

Bridgestone Ret Operations LLC............................. 617 479-3208
  2 School St Quincy (02169) *(G-11508)*

Bridgestone Ret Operations LLC............................. 413 543-1312
  1666 Boston Rd Springfield (01129) *(G-12080)*

Bridgestone Ret Operations LLC............................. 617 924-3989
  40 Arsenal St Watertown (02472) *(G-12864)*

Bridgestone Ret Operations LLC............................. 978 658-5660
  496 Main St Wilmington (01887) *(G-13394)*

Bridgestone Ret Operations LLC............................. 603 668-1123
  300 Elm St Manchester (03101) *(G-14821)*

Bridgestone Ret Operations LLC............................. 401 766-0233
  22 Dowling Village Blvd North Smithfield (02896) *(G-16319)*

Bridgestone Ret Operations LLC............................. 401 521-6622
  987 N Main St Providence (02904) *(G-16491)*

Bridgewater Chocolate LLC.................................... 203 775-2286
  559 Federal Rd Brookfield (06804) *(G-513)*

Bridgewater Prtg Copy Ctr LLC............................... 508 697-5227
  100 Broad St Bridgewater (02324) *(G-7225)*

Bridgewater Raynham Sand Stone, Bridgewater *Also Called: B R S Inc (G-7221)*

Bridgton News Corporation..................................... 207 647-2851
  118 Main St Bridgton (04009) *(G-4626)*

Bridgton News The, Bridgton *Also Called: Bridgton News Corporation (G-4626)*

Bridgwell Rsources Holdings LLC **(HQ)**.............. **203 622-9138**
  1 Sound Shore Dr Ste 302 Greenwich (06830) *(G-1322)*

Brigade Qm Prince George Co, Providence *Also Called: Ira Green Inc (G-16543)*

Briggs Lumber Products.. 978 630-4207
  336 E County Rd Rutland (01543) *(G-11696)*

Brigham's, Arlington *Also Called: Brighams Inc (G-5939)*

Brighams Inc **(HQ)**... **800 242-2423**
  30 Mill St Arlington (02476) *(G-5939)*

Bright Horizons At Biogen Idec............................. 617 621-3383
  105 Broadway Cambridge (02142) *(G-7525)*

Brightcove, Boston *Also Called: Brightcove Inc (G-6623)*

Brightcove Inc **(PA)**... **888 882-1880**
  281 Summer St Boston (02210) *(G-6623)*

Brightman Corporation... 508 644-2620
  181 S Main St Assonet (02702) *(G-5972)*

Brightman Lumber Co, Assonet *Also Called: Brightman Corporation (G-5972)*

Brill Academic Publishers, Boston *Also Called: Brill Usa Inc (G-6624)*

Brill Usa Inc.. 617 263-2323
  10 Liberty Sq Boston (02109) *(G-6624)*

Brimfield Flemarket.com, Sturbridge *Also Called: Journal of Antq & Collectibles (G-12250)*

Brimfield Precision LLC.. 413 245-7144
  68 Mill Ln Brimfield (01010) *(G-7249)*

Brio Promotions, Rockland *Also Called: Trems Inc (G-5343)*

Brisco Graphics LLC
  21 Commerce Park North Bedford (03110) *(G-13919)*

Bristal Cushion & ACC LLC.................................... 401 247-4499
  6 Commercial Way Warren (02885) *(G-16755)*

Bristol Inc **(HQ)**... **860 945-2200**
  1100 Buckingham St Watertown (06795) *(G-4004)*

Bristol Adult Resource Ctr Inc............................... 860 583-8721
  97 Peck Ln Bristol (06010) *(G-418)*

Bristol Bagel Works Ltd... 401 254-1390
  420 Hope St Bristol (02809) *(G-15756)*

Bristol Bakery & Cafe, Bristol *Also Called: BB&c Wholesale LLC (G-17114)*

Bristol Bay LLC... 978 744-4272
  70 Washington St Ste 310 Salem (01970) *(G-11704)*

Bristol Hospitality LLC... 860 589-7766
  42 Century Dr Bristol (06010) *(G-419)*

Bristol Instrument Gears Inc.................................. 860 583-1395
  164 Central St Ste 1 Bristol (06010) *(G-420)*

Bristol Marine, Bristol *Also Called: Lenmarine Inc (G-15772)*

Bristol Press... 860 845-8686
  188 Main St Bristol (06010) *(G-421)*

Bristol Press... 860 584-0501
  188 Main St Torrington (06790) *(G-3673)*

Bristol Rtary Schlrship Fund I................................ 860 314-1871
  123 Farmington Ave Ste 111 Bristol (06010) *(G-422)*

Bristol Seafood LLC **(HQ)**.............................. **207 761-4251**
  5 Portland Fish Pier Portland (04101) *(G-5192)*

Bristol Seafood Holdings Inc **(PA)**.................. **207 761-4251**
  5 Portland Fish Pier Portland (04101) *(G-5193)*

Bristol Tool & Die Company.................................... 860 582-2577
  550 Broad St Ste 13 Bristol (06010) *(G-423)*

Bristol-Myers Squibb, Devens *Also Called: Bristol-Myers Squibb Company (G-8271)*

Bristol-Myers Squibb Company.............................. 978 588-6001
  38 Jackson Rd Devens (01434) *(G-8271)*

Brit Systems LLC.. 214 630-0636
  135 N Plains Industrial Rd Wallingford (06492) *(G-3783)*

Brite Strike Tctcal Illmntion, Duxbury *Also Called: Brite-Strike Technologies Inc (G-8329)*

Brite-Strike Technologies Inc................................ 781 585-3525
  1145 Franklin St Duxbury (02332) *(G-8329)*

British Motor Heritage, Pawtucket *Also Called: Scarborough Faire Inc (G-16416)*

British Precision Inc.. 860 633-3343
  20 Sequin Dr Glastonbury (06033) *(G-1272)*

British Transco Capital Inc.................................... 781 907-3646
  25 Research Dr Westborough (01581) *(G-13083)*

Brito Ice LLC.. 978 744-7727
  17 Canal St Salem (01970) *(G-11705)*

Brittany Global Tech Corp...................................... 508 999-3281
  1357 E Rodney French Blvd New Bedford (02744) *(G-10573)*

Britton Lumber Company Inc **(PA)**.................. **802 333-4388**
  7 Ely Rd Fairlee (05045) *(G-17267)*

Broad Peak, Wallingford *Also Called: Broad Peak Manufacturing LLC (G-3784)*

Broad Peak Manufacturing LLC.............................. 203 678-4664
  10 Beaumont Rd Ste 1 Wallingford (06492) *(G-3784)*

Broadcast Pix Inc.. 978 600-1100
  141 Middlesex Rd Ste 1 Tyngsboro (01879) *(G-12458)*

Broadcastmed LLC **(PA)**................................ **860 953-2900**
  195 Farmington Ave Farmington (06032) *(G-1210)*

Broadcom Corporation... 978 719-1300
  200 Brickstone Sq Ste 401 Andover (01810) *(G-5874)*

Broadrdge Cstmer Cmmnctons E L **(PA)**........ **860 290-7000**
  125 Ellington Rd South Windsor (06074) *(G-3122)*

Broadvision Waltham, Waltham *Also Called: Bvsn LLC (G-12616)*

Broadway Tire and Auto Service, Pawtucket *Also Called: Bec Corp (G-16347)*

Brockton Beer Company LLC.................................. 508 521-9711
  121 Main St Brockton (02301) *(G-7263)*

Brockton Plastics... 508 587-2290
  230 Elliot St Brockton (02302) *(G-7264)*

Brockway-Smith Company...................................... 413 247-9674
  125 Chestnut St West Hatfield (01088) *(G-13004)*

Broden Millworks LLC.. 401 846-0271
  185 Oliphant Ln Middletown (02842) *(G-16170)*

Broder Bros Co... 508 923-4800
  154 Campanelli Dr Middleboro (02346) *(G-10352)*

Brodeur Machine Company Inc............................... 508 995-2662
  62 Wood St New Bedford (02745) *(G-10574)*

Brody Printing Company Inc.................................. 203 384-9313
  265 Central Ave Bridgeport (06607) *(G-306)*

Broen-Lab Inc... 603 310-5089
  15 Constitution Dr Ste 122 Bedford (03110) *(G-13920)*

Broil King, Winsted *Also Called: Bkmfg Corp (G-4339)*

Brolan Tool Inc... 978 537-0290
  25 Jytek Rd Leominster (01453) *(G-9644)*

Bromar.. 207 474-3784
  17 Parlin St Skowhegan (04976) *(G-5463)*

Bronze Craft Corporation....................................... 603 883-7747
  37 Will St Nashua (03060) *(G-15074)*

Brook & Whittle Limited **(PA)**......................... **203 483-5602**
  20 Carter Dr Guilford (06437) *(G-1388)*

Brook & Whittle Limited... 203 483-5602
  260 Branford Rd North Branford (06471) *(G-2361)*

Brook Pond Machining Inc..................................... 413 562-7411
  170 Lockhouse Rd Ste 5 Westfield (01085) *(G-13155)*

Brooke Taylor Farm LLC **(PA)**........................ **860 974-1263**
  848 Route 171 Woodstock (06281) *(G-4391)*

Brookfeld Mdcl/Srgical Sup Inc.................................... 203 775-0862
  60 Old New Milford Rd Ste 1b Brookfield (06804) *(G-514)*

Brookfield Industries Inc.. 860 283-6211
  99 W Hillside Ave Thomaston (06787) *(G-3615)*

Brookfield Phrm Compounding, Brookfield Also Called: Brookfield Mdcl/Srgical Sup Inc *(G-514)*

Brookfield Wire Company Inc **(HQ)**.......................... **508 867-6474**
  231 E Main St West Brookfield (01585) *(G-12992)*

Brooklin Boat Yard Inc **(PA)**................................... **207 359-2236**
  44 Center Harbor Rd Ste 44 Brooklin (04616) *(G-4632)*

Brookline Machine Company Inc **(PA)**...................... **617 782-4018**
  184 Riverview Ave Ste A Waltham (02453) *(G-12612)*

Brooks Inc **(PA)**.. **207 354-8763**
  211 Beechwood St Thomaston (04861) *(G-5542)*

Brooks Automation Us LLC....................................... 978 262-4613
  12 Elizabeth Dr Chelmsford (01824) *(G-7916)*

Brooks Automation Us LLC **(DH)**............................ **978 262-2400**
  15 Elizabeth Dr Chelmsford (01824) *(G-7917)*

Brooks Interiors Group Inc....................................... 978 988-1300
  5 Waltham St Ste 3 Wilmington (01887) *(G-13395)*

Brooks Precision Machining Inc................................. 978 256-7477
  4 Kidder Rd Chelmsford (01824) *(G-7918)*

Brooks Trap Mill, Thomaston Also Called: Brooks Inc *(G-5542)*

Brookside Flvors Ingrdents LLC **(HQ)**...................... **203 595-4520**
  201 Tresser Blvd Ste 320 Stamford (06901) *(G-3297)*

Brookwood Finishing, Kenyon Also Called: Kenyon Industries Inc *(G-16112)*

Brookwood Laminating Inc.. 860 774-5001
  275 Putnam Rd Wauregan (06387) *(G-4039)*

Brookwood Roll Goods Group, Wauregan Also Called: Brookwood Laminating Inc *(G-4039)*

Broomfield Laboratories Inc **(PA)**.......................... **978 779-6600**
  164 Still River Rd Bolton (01740) *(G-6495)*

Brosseau Fuels LLC... 802 888-9209
  2148 Cadys Falls Rd Morrisville (05661) *(G-17380)*

Brothers Artisanal Inc.. 508 938-9161
  32 William St Unit 1 New Bedford (02740) *(G-10575)*

Brouillette Hvac & Shtmtl Inc.................................... 508 822-4800
  13 Stevens St East Taunton (02718) *(G-8406)*

Brouillette Woodworking Co Inc................................. 401 499-4867
  48 Barrington Ave Barrington (02806) *(G-15746)*

Brown & Sharpe Pumps, North Kingstown Also Called: Bsm Pump Corp *(G-16235)*

Brown Construction Inc... 207 532-0910
  68 Bangor St Houlton (04730) *(G-4898)*

Brown Country Services LLC..................................... 802 464-5200
  131 Vt Route 100 West Dover (05356) *(G-17689)*

Brown Goldsmiths & Co Inc...................................... 207 865-4126
  11 Mechanic St Freeport (04032) *(G-4799)*

Brown Innovations Inc **(PA)**................................... **773 477-7500**
  369 Congress St Fl 4 Boston (02210) *(G-6625)*

Brown Med, Boston Also Called: Brownmed Inc *(G-6626)*

Brown Publishing Network Inc **(PA)**........................ **781 547-7600**
  10 City Sq Ste 3 Charlestown (02129) *(G-7865)*

Brown Shop, North Haven Also Called: J O Brown & Son Inc *(G-5114)*

Browne Trading Co... 207 766-2402
  260 Commercial St Portland (04101) *(G-5194)*

Brownell & Company Inc **(PA)**................................ **860 873-8625**
  423 E Haddam Moodus Rd Moodus (06469) *(G-1929)*

Brownell Boat Stands Inc... 508 758-3671
  5 Boat Rock Rd Mattapoisett (02739) *(G-10255)*

Brownell Boatstands, Mattapoisett Also Called: Brownell Boat Stands Inc *(G-10255)*

Brownlie Lamar Design Group.................................... 401 714-9371
  79 Joyce St Warren (02885) *(G-16756)*

Brownmed Inc **(PA)**... **857 317-3354**
  101 Federal St Fl 29 Boston (02110) *(G-6626)*

Browns Certified Welding Inc.................................... 802 453-3351
  275 S 116 Rd Bristol (05443) *(G-17115)*

Browns Quarried Slate Pdts Inc................................. 802 468-2297
  2504 S Street Ext Castleton (05735) *(G-17171)*

Browns River Bindery Inc... 802 878-3335
  1 Allen Martin Dr Essex Junction (05452) *(G-17229)*

Browns Rver Rec Prsrvtion Svcs, Essex Junction Also Called: Browns River Bindery Inc *(G-17229)*

Brox, Dracut Also Called: Brox Industries Inc *(G-8302)*

Brox Industries Inc **(PA)**...................................... **978 454-9105**
  1471 Methuen St Dracut (01826) *(G-8302)*

Bruce A Manzer Inc... 207 696-5881
  189 Main St Farmington (04938) *(G-4777)*

Bruce Diamond Corporation...................................... 508 222-3755
  1231 County St Attleboro (02703) *(G-5999)*

Bruce Technologies Inc... 978 670-5501
  23 Esquire Rd North Billerica (01862) *(G-10901)*

Bruin Plastics Co Inc.. 800 556-7764
  61 Joslin Rd Glendale (02826) *(G-16054)*

Bruker, Billerica Also Called: Bruker Corporation *(G-6414)*

Bruker Biospin Corporation **(HQ)**........................... **978 667-9580**
  15 Fortune Dr Billerica (01821) *(G-6412)*

Bruker Biospin Mri Inc.. 978 667-9580
  15 Fortune Dr Billerica (01821) *(G-6413)*

Bruker Corporation **(PA)**...................................... **978 663-3660**
  40 Manning Rd Billerica (01821) *(G-6414)*

Bruker Corporation... 978 663-3660
  40 Manning Rd Billerica (01821) *(G-6415)*

Bruker Detection Corporation.................................... 978 663-3660
  40 Manning Rd Billerica (01821) *(G-6416)*

Bruker Enrgy Supercon Tech Inc **(HQ)**.................... **978 901-7550**
  15 Fortune Dr Billerica (01821) *(G-6417)*

Bruker Scientific LLC.. 978 667-9580
  40 Manning Rd Billerica (01821) *(G-6418)*

Bruker Scientific LLC **(HQ)**................................... **978 439-9899**
  40 Manning Rd Billerica (01821) *(G-6419)*

Brumberg Publications Inc....................................... 617 734-1979
  124 Harvard St Ste 9 Brookline (02446) *(G-7317)*

Brunarhans Inc.. 860 928-0887
  263 Woodstock Rd Woodstock (06281) *(G-4392)*

Bruno Diduca... 781 894-5300
  57 Harvard St Waltham (02453) *(G-12613)*

Brunswick Enclosure Company.................................. 978 670-1124
  25 Sullivan Rd Ste 6 North Billerica (01862) *(G-10902)*

Brunswick Publishing LLC.. 802 747-6121
  77 Grove St Ste 102 Rutland (05701) *(G-17491)*

Brunswick Publishing LLC.. 207 729-3311
  3 Business Pkwy Brunswick (04011) *(G-4643)*

Brunswick Square LLC... 802 497-2575
  208 Flynn Ave Burlington (05401) *(G-17122)*

Brunt Workwear, North Reading Also Called: Maverick Work Wear Inc *(G-11043)*

Brunwick Biomedical Tech, West Wareham Also Called: Medical Products Mfg LLC *(G-13069)*

Bryan, Woburn Also Called: Lymol Medical Corp *(G-13603)*

Bryan Oncor Inc... 617 957-9858
  141 Powder House Blvd Somerville (02144) *(G-11865)*

Bryant Group Inc... 603 746-1166
  28 Riverside Dr Contoocook (03229) *(G-14167)*

Bryant Manufacturing Assoc, Ayer Also Called: Bmac Inc *(G-6175)*

Bsg, Providence Also Called: Bsg Handcraft *(G-16492)*

Bsg Handcraft.. 508 636-5154
  250 Niantic Ave Providence (02907) *(G-16492)*

Bsiw, Hudson Also Called: Bay State Industrial Weldin *(G-14488)*

Bsm Pump Corp... 401 471-6350
  180 Frenchtown Rd North Kingstown (02852) *(G-16235)*

BSP Group Inc.. 508 587-1101
  135 Oak Hill Way Brockton (02301) *(G-7265)*

Btl Aesthetics, Marlborough Also Called: Btl Industries Inc *(G-10122)*

Btl Holdings LLC.. 917 596-3660
  69 Industrial Ave Middlebury (05753) *(G-17339)*

Btl Industries Inc... 866 285-1656
  362 Elm St Ste 5 Marlborough (01752) *(G-10122)*

Buck Brothers, Millbury Also Called: Great Neck Saw Mfrs Inc *(G-10436)*

Buck Scientific Inc... 203 853-9444
  58 Fort Point St Norwalk (06855) *(G-2477)*

Buck's Ice Cream, Milford Also Called: Bucks Spumoni Company Inc *(G-1804)*

Buckeye Blasting Corporation.................................... 603 736-4681
  48 Old Town Road Ext Epsom (03234) *(G-14279)*

Buckleguy, Newburyport Also Called: Buckleguycom LLC *(G-10673)*

Buckleguycom LLC... 978 213-9989
  15 Graf Rd Newburyport (01950) *(G-10673)*

Buckley Air Products, Hanover *Also Called: Buckley Associates Inc (G-9027)*

Buckley Associates Inc... 203 380-2405
  350 Long Beach Blvd Stratford (06615) *(G-3524)*

Buckley Associates Inc **(PA)**... **781 878-5000**
  385 King St Hanover (02339) *(G-9027)*

Bucks Spumoni Company Inc... 203 874-2007
  229 Pepes Farm Rd Milford (06460) *(G-1804)*

Budd Foods, Manchester *Also Called: Msn Corporation (G-14894)*

BUDGET BLINDS, Portsmouth *Also Called: Scarlet Aspen LLC (G-15435)*

Budgetcard Inc... 508 695-8762
  171 Commonwealth Ave Attleboro Falls (02763) *(G-6080)*

Budney Aerospace Inc.. 860 828-0585
  131 New Park Dr Berlin (06037) *(G-54)*

Budney Industries Inc... 860 828-1950
  40 New Park Dr Berlin (06037) *(G-55)*

Budney Overhaul & Repair Ltd... 860 828-0585
  131 New Park Dr Berlin (06037) *(G-56)*

Buffalo Gulf Cast Trminals LLC... 203 930-3802
  100 W Putnam Ave Greenwich (06830) *(G-1323)*

Buick LLC... 401 539-2432
  106 Canonchet Rd Hope Valley (02832) *(G-16066)*

Builders Concrete East LLC.. 860 456-4111
  79 Boston Post Rd North Windham (06256) *(G-2450)*

Builders Insulation NH, Auburn *Also Called: Installed Building Pdts LLC (G-13909)*

Building Blocks, Newton *Also Called: Homeportfolio Inc (G-10760)*

Building Envelope Systems LLC.. 508 381-0429
  20 High St Plainville (02762) *(G-11430)*

Buildinggreen Inc.. 802 257-7300
  122 Birge St Ste 30 Brattleboro (05301) *(G-17076)*

Buildium LLC... 888 414-1988
  3 Center Plz Ste 400 Boston (02108) *(G-6627)*

Built Rite Manufacturing Inc.. 802 228-7293
  750 E Hill Rd Ludlow (05149) *(G-17314)*

Buisson Jewelers Inc.. 203 869-8895
  200 Railroad Ave Ste 201 Greenwich (06830) *(G-1324)*

Buitoni Food Company **(PA)**... **475 210-0128**
  1 High Ridge Park Ste 201 Stamford (06905) *(G-3298)*

Bull Data Systems Inc.. 978 294-6000
  285 Billerica Rd Ste 200 Chelmsford (01824) *(G-7919)*

Bull Display, Middletown *Also Called: Bull Metal Products Inc (G-1742)*

Bull Metal Products Inc.. 860 346-9691
  191 Saybrook Rd Middletown (06457) *(G-1742)*

Bullard Abrasives Inc... 508 366-4300
  6 Carol Dr Lincoln (02865) *(G-16123)*

Bulletin Newspapers Inc **(PA)**.. **617 361-8400**
  695 Truman Hwy Ste 99 Hyde Park (02136) *(G-9458)*

Bulletin Newspapers Inc.. 617 361-8400
  661 Washington St Ste 202 Norwood (02062) *(G-11166)*

Bullhorn Inc **(PA)**... **617 478-9100**
  100 Summer St Ste 1700 Boston (02110) *(G-6628)*

Bullock Cove Marine, Riverside *Also Called: Fairhaven Marine Corporation (G-16654)*

Bullrock Solar LLC.. 802 985-1460
  228 Aviation Ave Ste 200 South Burlington (05403) *(G-17575)*

Bumwraps Inc **(PA)**... **802 326-4080**
  578 Vt Route 242 Montgomery Center (05471) *(G-17368)*

Buon Appetito From Italy LLC.. 860 437-3668
  15 Shaw St New London (06320) *(G-2223)*

Burbak Companies.. 603 654-2291
  361 Forest Rd Wilton (03086) *(G-15703)*

Burbak Plastic, Wilton *Also Called: Burbak Companies (G-15703)*

Burell Bros Inc.. 860 455-9681
  Rr 97 Hampton (06247) *(G-1464)*

Burger-Roy Inc... 207 696-3978
  66 Main St Madison (04950) *(G-5041)*

Burgett Brothers Incorporated.. 978 374-8888
  35 Duncan St Haverhill (01830) *(G-9082)*

Burk Technology Inc... 978 486-0086
  7 Beaver Brook Rd Littleton (01460) *(G-9805)*

Burke Aerospace, Farmington *Also Called: Turbine Technologies Inc (G-1257)*

Burke Precision Machine Co Inc.. 860 408-1394
  7 Hatchett Hill Rd East Granby (06026) *(G-926)*

Burlington Coat Factory, Danbury *Also Called: Burlington Coat Fctry Whse Cor (G-718)*

Burlington Coat Fctry Whse Cor... 203 748-8583
  1 Padanaram Rd Ste 25 Danbury (06811) *(G-718)*

Burlington Free Press, Williston *Also Called: McClure Newspapers Inc (G-17740)*

Burlington Machine Inc... 978 284-6525
  340b Fordham Rd Wilmington (01887) *(G-13396)*

Burlodge USA Inc.. 336 776-1010
  24 Pearson St Litchfield (03052) *(G-14712)*

Burndy Americas Inc **(HQ)**.. **603 647-5000**
  47 East Industrial Park Dr Manchester (03109) *(G-14822)*

Burndy Americas Intl Holdg LLC.. 603 647-5000
  47 East Industrial Park Dr Manchester (03109) *(G-14823)*

Burndy LLC **(DH)**... **603 647-5000**
  47 East Industrial Park Dr Manchester (03109) *(G-14824)*

Burnell Controls Inc... 978 646-9992
  153 Andover St Ste 202 Danvers (01923) *(G-8171)*

Burnham & Morrill, Portland *Also Called: B&G Foods Inc (G-5180)*

Burnham Associates Inc... 978 745-1788
  14 Franklin St Salem (01970) *(G-11706)*

Burr Industries Inc... 978 774-2527
  495 Newbury St Danvers (01923) *(G-8172)*

Burr Signs.. 207 396-6111
  2 Karen Dr Stop 4 Westbrook (04092) *(G-5619)*

Burr Signs, Scarborough *Also Called: Glidden Signs Inc (G-5433)*

Burrillville Waste Water, Oakland *Also Called: Town of Burrillville (G-16335)*

Burt Process Equipment Inc **(PA)**.................................... **203 287-1985**
  100 Overlook Dr Hamden (06514) *(G-1415)*

Burtco Inc.. 802 722-3358
  185 Rte 123 Westminster Station (05159) *(G-17702)*

Burton Corporation **(PA)**.. **800 881-3138**
  180 Queen City Park Rd Burlington (05401) *(G-17123)*

Burton Wire & Cable LLC.. 603 624-2427
  4 Brookside West Hooksett (03106) *(G-14463)*

Busek Co Inc... 508 655-5565
  11 Tech Cir Natick (01760) *(G-10471)*

Business and Prof Exch Inc.. 978 556-4100
  100 Cummings Ctr Ste 344c Beverly (01915) *(G-6336)*

Business Card Express, Laconia *Also Called: Acara Holdings LLC (G-14640)*

Business Cards Tomorrow Inc... 203 723-5858
  69 Raytkwich Rd Naugatuck (06770) *(G-1950)*

Business Electronics, Wallingford *Also Called: BEI Holdings Inc (G-3780)*

Business Financial Pubg LLC.. 802 865-9886
  380 Hurricane Ln Ste 202 Williston (05495) *(G-17724)*

Business Forecast Systems Inc.. 617 484-5050
  465 Waverley Oaks Rd Waltham (02452) *(G-12614)*

Business Journals Inc... 203 853-6015
  50 Day St Norwalk (06854) *(G-2478)*

Business New Haven, New Haven *Also Called: Second Wind Media Limited (G-2197)*

Business Resources Inc.. 508 433-4600
  8 Lyman St Ste 200 Westborough (01581) *(G-13084)*

Business Shirtmasters... 603 798-3787
  349 Dover Rd Chichester (03258) *(G-14072)*

Business Signs LLC... 781 808-3153
  155a New Boston St Woburn (01801) *(G-13537)*

Business Systems Incorporated.. 508 624-4600
  208 Cedar Hill St Marlborough (01752) *(G-10123)*

Business West... 413 781-8600
  1441 Main St Ste 604 Springfield (01103) *(G-12081)*

Business West On Line, Springfield *Also Called: Business West (G-12081)*

Buswell Manufacturing Company... 203 334-6069
  229 Merriam St Bridgeport (06604) *(G-307)*

Butcher & Pantry LLC... 315 396-6464
  871 Route 44 Brownsville (05037) *(G-17116)*

Butcher Block Inc... 800 258-4304
  19 Syd Clarke Dr Claremont (03743) *(G-14080)*

Butler & Macmaster Engines, Hallowell *Also Called: Melton Sales and Service Inc (G-4860)*

Butler Architectural Wdwkg Inc... 508 985-9980
  200 Theodore Rice Blvd New Bedford (02745) *(G-10576)*

Butler Automatic Inc **(PA)**.. **508 923-0544**
  41 Leona Dr Middleboro (02346) *(G-10353)*

A
L
P
H
A
B
E
T
I
C

Butler Home Products LLC **(HQ)**..................... **508 597-8000**
  2 Cabot Rd Ste 1 Hudson (01749) *(G-9359)*

Butler Metal Fabricators Inc............................ 413 306-5762
  91 Pinevale St Indian Orchard (01151) *(G-9470)*

Butler Valve & Fittings.................................. 401 849-3833
  81 Black Point Ln Portsmouth (02871) *(G-16441)*

Butternut Mountain Farm, Johnson *Also Called: Vermont Maple Sugar Co Inc (G-17310)*

Butternut Mountain Farm, Johnson *Also Called: Vermont Maple Sugar Co Inc (G-17311)*

Butternut Mountain Farm, Morrisville *Also Called: Vermont Maple Sugar Co Inc (G-17391)*

Buttura & Sons Inc...................................... 802 476-6646
  109 Boynton St Barre (05641) *(G-16998)*

Buttura Gherardi Gran Artisans, Barre *Also Called: Buttura & Sons Inc (G-16998)*

Buyers Digest, Fairfax *Also Called: Gannett River States Pubg Corp (G-17258)*

Buyers Digest Press Inc................................. 802 893-4214
  57 Yankee Park Rd Fairfax (05454) *(G-17256)*

Buzzards Bay Brewing Inc.............................. 508 636-2288
  98 Horseneck Rd Westport (02790) *(G-13294)*

BV Investment Partners LP **(PA)**.................. **617 224-0057**
  125 High St Ste 1711 Boston (02110) *(G-6629)*

Bvi Medical Inc **(PA)**................................ **866 906-8080**
  500 Totten Pond Rd Fl 5 Waltham (02451) *(G-12615)*

Bvsn LLC.. 781 290-0710
  255 Bear Hill Rd Ste 3 Waltham (02451) *(G-12616)*

Bwi of MA LLC... 978 534-4065
  248 Industrial Rd Leominster (01453) *(G-9645)*

Bwt Pharma & Biotech Inc............................. 508 485-4291
  417 South St Ste 5 Marlborough (01752) *(G-10124)*

Byblos Industries Corporation......................... 781 727-4764
  1220 Washington St Norwood (02062) *(G-11167)*

Byer Manufacturing Company.......................... 207 866-2171
  41 Gunlow Pond Rd Bernard (04612) *(G-4547)*

Byer of Maine, Bernard *Also Called: Byer Manufacturing Company (G-4547)*

Byk USA Inc.. 475 234-5317
  33 Stiles Ln North Haven (06473) *(G-2395)*

Bynder LLC... 857 310-5434
  321 Summer St Fl 1 Boston (02210) *(G-6630)*

Byrna Technologies Inc **(PA)**...................... **978 868-5011**
  100 Burtt Rd Ste 115 Andover (01810) *(G-5875)*

Byrne Group Inc... 203 573-0100
  156 Grand St Waterbury (06702) *(G-3894)*

Byrne Sand & Gravel Co Inc.......................... 508 947-0724
  210 Wood St Middleboro (02346) *(G-10354)*

Byrne Woodworking Inc................................. 203 953-3205
  170 Herbert St Bridgeport (06604) *(G-308)*

Bzgunz LLC.. 603 491-8019
  22 Stockwell Hill Rd Gilmanton (03237) *(G-14339)*

C & A Machine Co Inc.................................. 860 667-0605
  49 Progress Cir Newington (06111) *(G-2278)*

C & C Fabricating Inc................................... 978 356-9980
  24 Hayward St Ste A Ipswich (01938) *(G-9479)*

C & C Fibrgls Components Inc......................... 401 254-4342
  75 Ballou Blvd Bristol (02809) *(G-15757)*

C & C Lamination... 413 594-6910
  34 Pajak St Chicopee (01013) *(G-8012)*

C & C Logging.. 860 683-0071
  416 Pigeon Hill Rd Windsor (06095) *(G-4263)*

C & C Machine... 978 649-0285
  78 Progress Ave Tyngsboro (01879) *(G-12459)*

C & C Metals Engineering Inc......................... 508 835-9011
  104 Hartwell St West Boylston (01583) *(G-12955)*

C & D, Deblois *Also Called: Jasper Wyman & Son (G-4721)*

C & D Signs Inc.. 978 851-2424
  170 Lorum St Tewksbury (01876) *(G-12388)*

C & G Machine Tool Co Inc............................ 413 467-9556
  180 W State St Granby (01033) *(G-8970)*

C & J Clark America Inc **(DH)**..................... **617 964-1222**
  60 Tower Rd Waltham (02451) *(G-12617)*

C & J Clark Latin America.............................. 617 243-4100
  201 Jones Rd Ste 1 Waltham (02451) *(G-12618)*

C & J Jewelry, Providence *Also Called: Narragasett Jewelry Inc (G-16572)*

C & K Components LLC **(HQ)**...................... **617 969-3700**
  465 Waverley Oaks Rd Ste 400 Waltham (02452) *(G-12619)*

C & M, Dayville *Also Called: Winchester Interconnect CM Corporation (G-871)*

C & M Machine Products Inc.......................... 603 594-8100
  25 Flagstone Dr Hudson (03051) *(G-14489)*

C & S Engineering Inc.................................. 203 235-5727
  956 Old Colony Rd Meriden (06451) *(G-1657)*

C & S Packing Co., Providence *Also Called: Capco Plastics Inc (G-16494)*

C & T Print Finishing Inc............................... 860 282-0616
  67 Commerce Way South Windsor (06074) *(G-3123)*

C A Construction Inc.................................... 207 422-3493
  41 Tucker Mountain Rd Gouldsboro (04607) *(G-4838)*

C B Fisk Inc.. 978 283-1909
  21 Kondelin Rd Gloucester (01930) *(G-8926)*

C B P Corp **(PA)**..................................... **207 985-9767**
  39 Limerick Rd Unit 2 Arundel (04046) *(G-4409)*

C C F, Seabrook *Also Called: Communction Cmpnent Filters Inc (G-15588)*

C Cowles & Company **(PA)**........................ **203 865-3117**
  126 Bailey Rd North Haven (06473) *(G-2396)*

C Cramer & Co Inc...................................... 603 742-3838
  20 Venture Dr Dover (03820) *(G-14219)*

C E Bradley Laboratories Inc **(PA)**............... **802 257-7971**
  56 Bennett Dr Brattleboro (05301) *(G-17077)*

C E D, Oxford *Also Called: Consulting Engrg Dev Svcs Inc (G-2691)*

C E I, Wallingford *Also Called: Component Engineers Inc (G-3791)*

C E Maple LLC... 802 387-5944
  663 Bemis Hill Rd Westminster (05158) *(G-17700)*

C F D Engineering Company........................... 203 754-2807
  105 Avenue Of Industry Waterbury (06705) *(G-3895)*

C F G Corporation....................................... 781 233-6110
  181 Central St Saugus (01906) *(G-11754)*

C H Babb Co Inc... 508 977-0600
  445 Paramount Dr Raynham (02767) *(G-11582)*

C H P Marketing Services, Charlotte *Also Called: Country Home Products Inc (G-17175)*

C I Medical, Norton *Also Called: Creative Imprints Inc (G-11125)*

C J Cranam Inc.. 207 739-1016
  15 Madison Ave Oxford (04270) *(G-5142)*

C J Fox Company, Providence *Also Called: Cjf Group Ltd (G-16500)*

C K Productions Inc..................................... 603 893-5069
  60a Pulpit Rock Rd Pelham (03076) *(G-15287)*

C L Hauthaway & Sons Corp.......................... 781 592-6444
  638 Summer St Lynn (01905) *(G-9965)*

C L O V, Winooski *Also Called: Whiteside Holdings Inc (G-17772)*

C M S Landscaping Corporation...................... 413 533-3300
  175 Suffolk St Holyoke (01040) *(G-9245)*

C Mather Company Inc.................................. 860 528-5667
  339 Chapel Rd South Windsor (06074) *(G-3124)*

C O Jelliff Corporation **(PA)**....................... **203 259-1615**
  354 Pequot Ave Ste 300 Southport (06890) *(G-3244)*

C P Bourg Inc **(PA)**.................................. **508 998-2171**
  50 Samuel Barnet Blvd New Bedford (02745) *(G-10577)*

C P Dauphinais Landscape, Sutton *Also Called: CP Dauphinais Inc (G-12279)*

C P Technologies Inc **(PA)**......................... **207 286-1167**
  64 Industrial Park Rd Saco (04072) *(G-5364)*

C P Tek, Saco *Also Called: C P Technologies Inc (G-5364)*

C P W, Cranston *Also Called: Cranston Print Works Company (G-15844)*

C Q P Bakery... 978 557-5626
  19 Blanchard St Lawrence (01843) *(G-9544)*

C R Bard Inc... 401 825-8300
  100 Crossings Blvd Warwick (02886) *(G-16794)*

C R I, Hopkinton *Also Called: Cambrdge RES Instrmntation Inc (G-9311)*

C R S, Newton *Also Called: Corporate Rmbursement Svcs Inc (G-10748)*

C S H Industries Inc.................................... 508 747-1990
  15 Appollo 11 Rd Plymouth (02360) *(G-11452)*

C S M S-I P A.. 203 562-7228
  127 Washington Ave Ste 3 North Haven (06473) *(G-2397)*

C Sherman Johnson Company Inc.................... 860 873-8697
  1 Matthews Dr East Haddam (06423) *(G-955)*

C Sjoberg & Son Inc.................................... 401 461-8220
  415 Station St Cranston (02910) *(G-15838)*

C Speaker Corp
  46 Southfield Ave Ste 300 Stamford (06902) *(G-3299)*

C T C, Hopkinton *Also Called: Control Technology Corporation (G-9313)*

C T P, Fitchburg *Also Called: Crocker Technical Papers Inc (G-8651)*

C V Tool Company Inc **(PA)**................................... 978 353-7901
44 Robert Porter Rd Southington (06489) *(G-3206)*

C V Tool Company Inc................................... 978 353-7901
12 Baltic Ln Ste 1 Fitchburg (01420) *(G-8645)*

C W Timber, Colebrook *Also Called: W Craig Washburn (G-14110)*

C Z Machine Shop, East Hampstead *Also Called: Cz Machine Inc (G-14270)*

C-End LLC................................... 610 350-8674
409 Vanderbilt Ln Portsmouth (02871) *(G-16442)*

C-R Machine Co Inc **(PA)**................................... 978 663-3989
13 Alexander Rd Ste 10 Billerica (01821) *(G-6420)*

C. S. Williams Lacquer Company, Providence *Also Called: Spectrum Coatings Labs Inc (G-16614)*

C/A Design, Dover *Also Called: Costello/April Design Inc (G-14224)*

C&C Ventures, Chicopee *Also Called: Eastern Chem-Lac LLC (G-8029)*

C&J Dreams Inc **(PA)**................................... 508 238-6231
316 Main St North Easton (02356) *(G-11008)*

C&K Switches, Waltham *Also Called: C & K Components LLC (G-12619)*

C&M Precision Tech, Hudson *Also Called: C & M Machine Products Inc (G-14489)*

C2sense Inc................................... 617 651-3991
480 Arsenal Way # 110 Watertown (02472) *(G-12865)*

C4 Therapeutics Inc **(PA)**................................... 617 231-0700
490 Arsenal Way Ste 200 Watertown (02472) *(G-12866)*

C7, Bridgewater *Also Called: Control 7 Inc (G-7228)*

C8 Sciences, New Haven *Also Called: Becaid LLC (G-2125)*

CA J&L Enterprises Inc................................... 781 963-6666
225 Bodwell St Avon (02322) *(G-6146)*

Caap Co Inc................................... 203 877-0375
152 Pepes Farm Rd Milford (06460) *(G-1805)*

Cabby Chic, Woonsocket *Also Called: Cabinet Gallery Ltd (G-16952)*

Cabinet Depot Outlet Inc................................... 508 485-7777
3 Atwood Rd Southborough (01772) *(G-11993)*

Cabinet Gallery Ltd **(PA)**................................... 401 762-4300
245 Privilege St Woonsocket (02895) *(G-16952)*

Cabinet Harward Specialti................................... 860 231-1192
50 Chelton Ave West Hartford (06110) *(G-4049)*

Cabinets For Less LLC................................... 603 935-7551
679 Mast Rd Manchester (03102) *(G-14825)*

Cabinets To Go LLC................................... 800 222-4638
10 Technology Dr Wallingford (06492) *(G-3785)*

Cable Assemblies Inc................................... 603 889-4090
13 Columbia Dr Unit 17 Amherst (03031) *(G-13863)*

Cable Harness Resources Inc................................... 508 892-9495
3 Brickyard Rd Leicester (01524) *(G-9622)*

Cable Management LLC................................... 860 670-1890
290 Pratt St Ste 1108 Meriden (06450) *(G-1658)*

Cable Manufacturing Business, Redding *Also Called: Armored Shield Technologies (G-2881)*

Cable Prep, Chester *Also Called: Ben Hughes Communication Products Co (G-623)*

Cable Technology Inc................................... 860 429-7889
73 River Rd Willington (06279) *(G-4224)*

Cabletron, Salem *Also Called: Enterasys Networks Inc (G-15521)*

Cableworks, Putnam *Also Called: Harding Company Inc (G-2860)*

Cabot, Billerica *Also Called: Cabot Corporation (G-6421)*

CABOT, Boston *Also Called: Cabot Corporation (G-6631)*

Cabot, Boston *Also Called: Cabot li-Tn1w09 LLC (G-6633)*

Cabot, Haverhill *Also Called: Cabot Corporation (G-9084)*

Cabot Coach Builders Inc **(PA)**................................... 978 374-4530
99 Newark St Haverhill (01832) *(G-9083)*

Cabot Corporation................................... 978 671-4000
157 Concord Rd Billerica (01821) *(G-6421)*

Cabot Corporation **(PA)**................................... 617 345-0100
2 Seaport Ln Ste 1300 Boston (02210) *(G-6631)*

Cabot Corporation................................... 978 556-8400
50 Rogers Rd Ste 1 Haverhill (01835) *(G-9084)*

Cabot Creamery, Andover *Also Called: Agri-Mark Inc (G-5869)*

Cabot Creamery, Waitsfield *Also Called: Cabot Creamery Cooperative Inc (G-17664)*

Cabot Creamery Cooperative Inc................................... 888 792-2268
193 Home Farm Way Waitsfield (05673) *(G-17664)*

Cabot Heritage Corporation................................... 978 745-5532
176 North St Salem (01970) *(G-11707)*

Cabot Hill Naturals LLC................................... 800 747-4372
62 Bridge St Lancaster (03584) *(G-14676)*

Cabot Holdings LLC................................... 617 345-0100
2 Seaport Ln Ste 1300 Boston (02210) *(G-6632)*

Cabot Hosiery Mills Inc **(PA)**................................... 802 485-6066
364 Whetstone Dr Northfield (05663) *(G-17432)*

Cabot li-Tn1w09 LLC................................... 617 723-7400
1 Beacon St Ste 1700 Boston (02108) *(G-6633)*

Cabot Market Letter, Salem *Also Called: Cabot Heritage Corporation (G-11707)*

Cabot Specialty Chemicals Inc **(HQ)**................................... 617 345-0100
2 Seaport Ln Ste 1300 Boston (02210) *(G-6634)*

Cadcom Inc................................... 203 877-0640
110 Raton Rd Milford (06461) *(G-1806)*

Cadence Aerospace, Westfield *Also Called: Tell Tool Inc (G-13210)*

Cadence Ct Inc................................... 860 370-9780
4 Kenny Roberts Memorial Dr Suffield (06078) *(G-3589)*

Cadence Mfg Inc................................... 508 746-6082
2080 Plainfield Pike Cranston (02921) *(G-15839)*

Cadence Science Inc................................... 401 942-1031
2080 Plainfield Pike Cranston (02921) *(G-15840)*

Cadent Therapeutics Inc................................... 617 949-5529
250 Massachusetts Ave Cambridge (02139) *(G-7526)*

Cadi Co Inc **(PA)**................................... 203 729-1111
60 Rado Dr Naugatuck (06770) *(G-1951)*

Cadi Company, Naugatuck *Also Called: Cadi Co Inc (G-1951)*

Cadmus................................... 203 595-3000
200 Stamford Pl Fl 2 Stamford (06902) *(G-3300)*

Cado Manufacturing Inc................................... 978 343-2989
1 Princeton Rd Ste 2 Fitchburg (01420) *(G-8646)*

Cado Products Inc................................... 978 343-2989
1 Princeton Rd Ste 2 Fitchburg (01420) *(G-8647)*

Cadwell Company, Holliston *Also Called: Cadwell Products Company Inc (G-9203)*

Cadwell Products Company Inc................................... 508 429-3100
3 Kuniholm Dr Holliston (01746) *(G-9203)*

Caes Mission Systems LLC................................... 781 729-9450
10 Sonar Dr Woburn (01801) *(G-13538)*

Cag Imaging LLC................................... 860 887-0836
387 N Main St Norwich (06360) *(G-2603)*

Cai Inks, Georgetown *Also Called: A I C Inc (G-8904)*

Cal Chemical Corporation................................... 401 821-0320
592 Arnold Rd Coventry (02816) *(G-15808)*

Calabro Cheese Corporation................................... 203 469-1311
580 Coe Ave East Haven (06512) *(G-1038)*

Calco, Saint Johnsbury *Also Called: Caledonia Inc (G-17539)*

Caledonia Inc **(PA)**................................... 802 748-2319
2878 Vt Route 18 Saint Johnsbury (05819) *(G-17539)*

Caledonia Spirits, Montpelier *Also Called: Caledonia Spirits Inc (G-17370)*

Caledonia Spirits Inc................................... 802 472-8000
116 Gin Ln Montpelier (05602) *(G-17370)*

Caledonian Record Pubg Co Inc................................... 603 444-7141
263 Main St Littleton (03561) *(G-14715)*

Caledonian Record Pubg Co Inc **(PA)**................................... 802 748-8121
190 Federal St Saint Johnsbury (05819) *(G-17540)*

Caledonian-Record, Saint Johnsbury *Also Called: Caledonian Record Pubg Co Inc (G-17540)*

Calendar Press Inc................................... 508 531-1860
18 Rainbow Cir Peabody (01960) *(G-11300)*

Caliber Company **(PA)**................................... 413 642-4260
100 Springdale Rd Westfield (01085) *(G-13156)*

California Brazing, Clinton *Also Called: Nevada Heat Treating LLC (G-8085)*

California Paint................................... 978 965-2122
150 Dascomb Rd Andover (01810) *(G-5876)*

Caliper Corporation................................... 617 527-4700
1172 Beacon St Ste 302 Newton (02461) *(G-10740)*

Caliper Life Sciences Inc **(DH)**................................... 203 954-9442
68 Elm St Hopkinton (01748) *(G-9310)*

Caliper Woodworking Corp................................... 781 322-9760
49 Clinton St Malden (02148) *(G-10006)*

Calise & Sons Bakery Inc **(PA)**................................... 401 334-3444
2 Quality Dr Lincoln (02865) *(G-16124)*

ALPHABETIC

Calise Bakery, Lincoln *Also Called: Calise & Sons Bakery Inc* **(G-16124)**

Calkins Rock Products Inc.................................... 802 626-5755
   34 Calkins Dr Lyndonville (05851) **(G-17317)**

Calkins Sand & Gravel, Lyndonville *Also Called: Calkins Rock Products Inc* **(G-17317)**

Calkins Sand & Gravel Inc................................... 802 334-8418
   3258 Vt Route 14 N Newport (05855) **(G-17397)**

Callahan, Robert, Tilton *Also Called: Nes Embroidery Inc* **(G-15655)**

Callaway Cars Inc... 860 434-9002
   3 High St Old Lyme (06371) **(G-2636)**

Callaway Companies Inc **(PA)**........................... **860 434-9002**
   3 High St Old Lyme (06371) **(G-2637)**

Callaway Golf Ball Oprtons Inc............................ 207 737-4324
   County Rd Richmond (04357) **(G-5320)**

Callaway Golf Company.. 413 536-1200
   425 Meadow St Chicopee (01013) **(G-8013)**

CALLAWAY GOLF COMPANY, Chicopee *Also Called: Callaway Golf Company* **(G-8013)**

Callenstitch LLC... 978 369-9080
   52 Domino Dr Concord (01742) **(G-8107)**

Callico Metals Inc.. 401 398-8238
   512 Old Baptist Rd North Kingstown (02852) **(G-16236)**

Calling All Cargo LLC.. 603 740-1900
   69 Venture Dr Unit 4 Dover (03820) **(G-14220)**

Calling All Cargo Moving Co, Dover *Also Called: Calling All Cargo LLC* **(G-14220)**

Calorique, West Wareham *Also Called: Dcaf of Massachusetts Inc* **(G-13060)**

Calorique LLC.. 508 291-2000
   2380 Cranberry Hwy Ste 6 West Wareham (02576) **(G-13057)**

Calverley Club, Providence *Also Called: Bolt Coffee Company LLC* **(G-16487)**

Calzone Ltd **(PA)**... **203 367-5766**
   225 Black Rock Ave Bridgeport (06605) **(G-309)**

Calzone Case Company, Bridgeport *Also Called: Calzone Ltd* **(G-309)**

CAM Dvlpment McRo Cmpnents Inc..................... 802 265-3240
   84 Blissville Rd Hydeville (05750) **(G-17301)**

CAM Group LLC... 860 646-2378
   130 Chapel Rd Manchester (06042) **(G-1587)**

CAM Logging, Skowhegan *Also Called: Ambrose G McCarthy Jr* **(G-5462)**

CAM Office Services Inc **(PA)**.......................... **781 932-9868**
   41 Brigham St Unit 2 Marlborough (01752) **(G-10125)**

CAM Tech.. 603 382-2900
   129 Newton Rd Plaistow (03865) **(G-15338)**

Cam2 Technologies LLC....................................... 203 628-4833
   41 Eagle Rd Danbury (06810) **(G-719)**

Camar Corp... 508 845-9263
   55 Church St Northborough (01532) **(G-11093)**

Camara Slate Products Inc................................... 802 265-3200
   963 S Main St Fair Haven (05743) **(G-17250)**

Camaro Signs Inc **(PA)**................................... **860 886-1553**
   268 Edmond Rd Jewett City (06351) **(G-1535)**

Cambex Corporation **(PA)**................................ **508 983-1200**
   115 Flanders Rd Westborough (01581) **(G-13085)**

Cambrdge RES Instrmntation Inc.......................... 781 935-9099
   68 Elm St Hopkinton (01748) **(G-9311)**

Cambrex... 413 786-1680
   104 Gold St Agawam (01001) **(G-5783)**

Cambrex Bio Science.. 508 497-0700
   97 South St Hopkinton (01748) **(G-9312)**

Cambridge Brands Mfg Inc.................................. 617 491-2500
   810 Main St Cambridge (02139) **(G-7527)**

Cambridge Brewing Co Inc................................... 617 494-1994
   1 Kendall Sq Ste B1102 Cambridge (02139) **(G-7528)**

Cambridge Brickhouse Inc.................................... 978 725-8001
   60 Island St Ste 2 Lawrence (01840) **(G-9545)**

Cambridge Chemical Co Corp.............................. 617 876-4484
   58 Dudley St Cambridge (02140) **(G-7529)**

Cambridge Chemical Company, Cambridge *Also Called: Cambridge Chemical Co Corp* **(G-7529)**

Cambridge GL Fctry Condo LLC........................... 617 576-6701
   169 Monsignor Obrien Hwy Cambridge (02141) **(G-7530)**

Cambridge Heart, Windham *Also Called: Cambridge Heart Inc* **(G-15721)**

Cambridge Heart Inc **(PA)**............................... **978 654-7600**
   124 Washington St Foxborough (02035) **(G-8734)**

Cambridge Heart Inc... 978 654-7600
   7 Searles Rd Windham (03087) **(G-15721)**

Cambridge Interventional LLC.............................. 978 793-2674
   78 Cambridge St Burlington (01803) **(G-7342)**

Cambridge Isotope Labs, Tewksbury *Also Called: Cambridge Isotope Labs Inc* **(G-12389)**

Cambridge Isotope Labs Inc **(DH)**.................... **978 749-8000**
   3 Highwood Dr Tewksbury (01876) **(G-12389)**

Cambridge Offsett Printing, Fall River *Also Called: Potters Printing Inc* **(G-8598)**

Cambridge Packing Co Inc................................... 617 464-6000
   4143 Food Mart Rd Boston (02118) **(G-6635)**

Cambridge Polymer Group Inc............................. 617 629-4400
   100 Sylvan Rd Ste 200 Woburn (01801) **(G-13539)**

Cambridge Repro Graphics, Malden *Also Called: Gorilla Graphics Inc* **(G-10016)**

Cambridge Semantics Inc **(PA)**........................ **617 245-0517**
   1 Beacon St Ste 3400 Boston (02108) **(G-6636)**

Cambridge Signal Tech Inc.................................. 401 490-5682
   60 Eddy St Ste 3 Providence (02903) **(G-16493)**

Cambridge Soundworks Inc................................. 781 329-2777
   26 Dartmouth St Westwood (02090) **(G-13307)**

Cambridge Specialty Co Inc................................. 860 828-3579
   588 Four Rod Rd Berlin (06037) **(G-57)**

Cambridgeeditors... 617 876-2855
   293 Sidney St Cambridge (02139) **(G-7531)**

Cambridgeport... 781 302-3347
   21 Pacella Park Dr Randolph (02368) **(G-11553)**

Cambridgeport Air Systems Inc............................ 978 465-8481
   4 Carleton Dr Georgetown (01833) **(G-8906)**

Cambrooke Foods, Ayer *Also Called: Ajinomoto Cambrooke Inc* **(G-6170)**

Camco Display & Screen Prtg, Providence *Also Called: Cathedral Art Metal Co Inc* **(G-16498)**

Camco Manufacturing Inc.................................... 978 537-6777
   165 Pioneer Dr Leominster (01453) **(G-9646)**

CAMCO MANUFACTURING, INC., Leominster *Also Called: Camco Manufacturing Inc* **(G-9646)**

Camden Designs, Wells *Also Called: Village Candle Inc* **(G-5608)**

Camelot Enterprises Inc....................................... 781 341-9100
   213 Turnpike St Ste 1 Stoughton (02072) **(G-12200)**

Cameron International Corp.................................. 860 633-0277
   256 Oakwood Dr Ste 1 Glastonbury (06033) **(G-1273)**

Cameron Sealcoating LLC.................................... 603 586-7945
   115 Couture Rd Jefferson (03583) **(G-14583)**

Cametoid Technologies Inc.................................. 860 646-4667
   45 S Satellite Rd Unit D South Windsor (06074) **(G-3125)**

Camger Coatings Systems Inc.............................. 508 528-5787
   364 Main St Norfolk (02056) **(G-10797)**

Cami Research Inc... 978 266-2655
   42 Nagog Park Ste 115 Acton (01720) **(G-5742)**

Camiant Inc **(PA)**... **508 486-9996**
   200 Nickerson Rd Ste 200 Marlborough (01752) **(G-10126)**

Camio Custom Cabinetry Inc................................ 781 562-1573
   130 Jackson St Ste 2 Canton (02021) **(G-7775)**

Camio Kitchens, East Weymouth *Also Called: Industrial Woodworking Co Inc* **(G-8429)**

Camp Precast Concrete Products Inc..................... 802 893-2401
   78 Precast Rd Milton (05468) **(G-17355)**

Campbell Enterprises Corp................................... 401 753-7778
   1 Campbell St Pawtucket (02860) **(G-16352)**

Campus Crystal, Conway *Also Called: Glass Graphics Inc* **(G-14179)**

Can-One (usa) Inc... 860 299-4608
   141 Burke St Nashua (03060) **(G-15075)**

Canaan Division, Canaan *Also Called: Nucor Hrris Rbar Northeast LLC* **(G-14047)**

Canadian Hills Wind LLC..................................... 617 977-2400
   3 Allied Dr Ste 155 Dedham (02026) **(G-8237)**

Canam Bridges US Inc... 603 542-5202
   386 River Rd Claremont (03743) **(G-14081)**

Canberra Industries, Meriden *Also Called: Mirion Tech Canberra Inc* **(G-1677)**

Candela Corporation **(DH)**................................ **508 358-7400**
   251 Locke Dr Marlborough (01752) **(G-10127)**

Candela Corporation.. 800 733-8550
   530 Boston Post Rd Wayland (01778) **(G-12923)**

Candela Medical Inc.. 508 358-7400
   251 Locke Dr Marlborough (01752) **(G-10128)**

Candle Cabin, The, Montgomery Center *Also Called: Way Out Wax Inc* **(G-17369)**

Candlewick Press Inc... 617 661-3330
   99 Dover St Ste 3 Somerville (02144) **(G-11866)**

Candlewood Stars Inc.. 203 994-8826
60 Newtown Rd Ste 32 Danbury (06810) *(G-720)*

Candlewood Tool and Mch Sp Inc............................. 860 355-1892
24 Martha Ln Gaylordsville (06755) *(G-1263)*

Canevari Plastics Inc... 203 878-4319
10 Furniture Row Milford (06460) *(G-1807)*

Canidae LLC.. 475 208-1789
1 Dock St Ste 502 Stamford (06902) *(G-3301)*

Canidae Pet Foods, Stamford *Also Called: Canidae LLC (G-3301)*

Cannan Fuels.. 508 339-3317
157 Pratt St Mansfield (02048) *(G-10040)*

Cannelli Printing Co Inc... 203 932-1719
39 Wood St West Haven (06516) *(G-4096)*

Canner Incorporated.. 978 448-3063
1 Cannery Row West Groton (01472) *(G-13001)*

Cannondale Sports Group, Wilton *Also Called: Cycling Sports Group Inc (G-4238)*

Canoga Perkins Corporation..................................... 203 888-7914
100 Bank St Seymour (06483) *(G-2956)*

Canopy Timber Alternatives Inc................................. 802 388-1548
30 Grist Mill Rd Middlebury (05753) *(G-17340)*

Canson Inc... 413 538-9250
21 Industrial Dr South Hadley (01075) *(G-11959)*

Cantata Technology Inc **(DH)**................................ **781 449-4100**
15 Crawford St Ste 201 Needham Heights (02494) *(G-10533)*

Canton Citizen Inc.. 781 821-4418
866 Washington St Canton (02021) *(G-7776)*

Canvas Gfx Inc... 833 721-0829
192 South St Ste 250 Boston (02111) *(G-6637)*

Canvasworks Inc... 207 985-2419
8 Bragdon Ln Kennebunk (04043) *(G-4923)*

Capacitec Inc **(PA)**.. **978 772-6033**
87 Fitchburg Rd Ayer (01432) *(G-6176)*

Capco Crane & Hoist Inc... 978 948-2998
58 Forest Ridge Dr Rowley (01969) *(G-11668)*

Capco Crane & Hoist Parts Inc................................. 978 948-2998
58 Forest Ridge Dr Rowley (01969) *(G-11669)*

Capco Plastics Inc **(PA)**....................................... **401 272-3833**
297 Dexter St Providence (02907) *(G-16494)*

Capco Steel Erection Company................................. 401 383-9388
33 Acorn St Unit 2 Providence (02903) *(G-16495)*

Capco Steel LLC.. 401 861-1220
25 Acorn St Ste 1 Providence (02903) *(G-16496)*

Cape Cod, Hyannis *Also Called: Cape Cod Potato Chip Company Inc (G-9430)*

Cape Cod Aggregates Corp **(PA)**............................ **508 775-3716**
1550 Phinneys Ln Hyannis (02601) *(G-9429)*

Cape Cod Braided Rug Co Inc.................................. 508 432-3133
75 Olde Homestead Dr Marstons Mills (02648) *(G-10247)*

Cape Cod Chronicle, Chatham *Also Called: Hyora Publications Inc (G-7897)*

Cape Cod Cupola Co Inc... 508 994-2119
78 State Rd North Dartmouth (02747) *(G-10990)*

Cape Cod Fence Co **(PA)**....................................... **508 398-6041**
1093 Route 28 South Yarmouth (02664) *(G-11982)*

Cape Cod Ginger LLC.. 508 295-2795
8 Kendrick Rd Wareham (02571) *(G-12830)*

Cape Cod Ice.. 401 438-4555
1 Noyes Ave Bldg C Rumford (02916) *(G-16664)*

Cape Cod Iron Corp... 508 322-9985
2707 Cranberry Hwy Wareham (02571) *(G-12831)*

Cape Cod Life LLC.. 508 419-7381
13 Steeple St Ste 204 Mashpee (02649) *(G-10250)*

Cape Cod Life Publications, Mashpee *Also Called: Cape Cod Life LLC (G-10250)*

Cape Cod Lumber Co Inc... 781 878-0715
225 Groveland St Abington (02351) *(G-5722)*

Cape Cod Metal Polsg Cloths, Dennis *Also Called: Cape Cod Polish Company Inc (G-8257)*

Cape Cod Polish Company Inc.................................. 508 385-5099
348 Hokum Rock Rd Dennis (02638) *(G-8257)*

Cape Cod Potato Chip Company Inc......................... 888 881-2447
100 Breeds Hill Rd Hyannis (02601) *(G-9430)*

Cape Cod Ready Mix Inc.. 508 255-4600
300 Route 6 A Orleans (02653) *(G-11236)*

Cape Cod Shipbuilding Co.. 508 295-3550
7 Narrows Rd Wareham (02571) *(G-12832)*

Cape Cod Textile, Sandwich *Also Called: Gonco Inc (G-11750)*

Cape Cod Winery Inc.. 508 457-5592
4 Oxbow Rd Teaticket (02536) *(G-12378)*

Cape House Realty Inc... 508 695-6800
266 John L Dietsch Blvd Attleboro Falls (02763) *(G-6081)*

Cape Light Compact.. 508 375-6703
3195 Main St Barnstable (02630) *(G-6199)*

Cape Pond Ice Company **(PA)**................................ **978 283-0174**
104 Commercial St Gloucester (01930) *(G-8927)*

Cape Shore, Yarmouth *Also Called: Downeast Concepts Inc (G-5703)*

Cape Whpie Mnes Grmet Whpie Pl............................ 207 799-9207
185 Cottage Rd South Portland (04106) *(G-5493)*

Capeway Printing & Copy Center............................... 781 878-1600
71 Reservoir Park Dr Rockland (02370) *(G-11638)*

Capeway Welding Inc... 508 747-6666
9 Appollo 11 Rd Plymouth (02360) *(G-11453)*

Capeway Yarns Inc.. 401 624-1311
209 Horizon Dr Tiverton (02878) *(G-16735)*

Capewell, South Windsor *Also Called: Crrc LLC (G-3136)*

Capewell Aerial Systems LLC **(PA)**........................ **860 610-0700**
105 Nutmeg Rd S South Windsor (06074) *(G-3126)*

Capital Cities Communications.................................. 203 784-8800
8 Elm St New Haven (06510) *(G-2133)*

Capital Growth Advertising, Williamstown *Also Called: Fidelity Ind Advser Newsletter (G-13367)*

Capital Industries Corporation................................... 781 337-9807
200 Libbey Industrial Pkwy East Weymouth (02189) *(G-8428)*

Capital Offset Co Inc... 603 225-3308
95 Runnells Bridge Rd Hollis (03049) *(G-14448)*

Capital Steel LLC... 860 828-9353
190 New Park Dr Berlin (06037) *(G-58)*

Capitol Distributors Inc.. 603 223-2086
510 Hall St Bow (03304) *(G-13995)*

Capitol Distributors Inc.. 603 224-3348
114 Hall St Concord (03301) *(G-14119)*

Capitol Electronics Inc... 203 744-3300
18 Keelers Ridge Rd Wilton (06897) *(G-4235)*

Capitol Fire Protection Co Inc................................... 603 783-4713
141 N Village Rd Loudon (03307) *(G-14794)*

Capitol Glass Company Inc....................................... 860 236-1936
75 Grassmere Ave West Hartford (06110) *(G-4050)*

Capitol Printing Co Inc... 860 522-1547
52 Pratt St Hartford (06103) *(G-1473)*

Capitol Screen Prtg & Embro..................................... 603 234-7000
276 N State St Concord (03301) *(G-14120)*

Capone Iron Corporation.. 978 948-8000
20 Turcotte Memorial Dr Rowley (01969) *(G-11670)*

Capricorn Investors II LP... 203 861-6600
30 E Elm St Greenwich (06830) *(G-1325)*

Capricorn Investors III LP **(PA)**.............................. **203 861-6600**
30 E Elm St Greenwich (06830) *(G-1326)*

Capstan Inc.. 508 384-3100
263 Georgetown Rd Weston (06883) *(G-4147)*

Capstan Atlantic.. 508 660-6001
24 Walpole Park S Walpole (02081) *(G-12554)*

Capstan Atlantic.. 508 384-3100
10 Cushing Dr Wrentham (02093) *(G-13838)*

Capstan Industries Inc... 508 384-3100
10 Cushing Dr Wrentham (02093) *(G-13839)*

Captivate Bio LLC.. 617 607-4017
142 Galen St Fl 2 Watertown (02472) *(G-12867)*

Captivating Kitchens.. 860 236-6500
555 New Park Ave West Hartford (06110) *(G-4051)*

Car Gold Inc.. 800 537-7797
630 Beaulieu St Holyoke (01040) *(G-9246)*

Cara, Stamford *Also Called: Cara Therapeutics Inc (G-3302)*

Cara Incorporated.. 401 732-6535
620 Main St Apt 12 East Greenwich (02818) *(G-15976)*

Cara Therapeutics Inc... 203 406-3700
400 Atlantic St Ste 500 Stamford (06901) *(G-3302)*

Carando Foods, Springfield *Also Called: Smithfield Foods Inc (G-12131)*

Carando Gourmet Foods Corp **(PA)**........................ **413 737-0183**
175 Main St Agawam (01001) *(G-5784)*

ALPHABETIC

Carando Gourmet Frozen Foods, Agawam *Also Called: Carando Gourmet Foods Corp (G-5784)*

Carat Systems Inc... 781 560-8082
17 Manison St Stoneham (02180) *(G-12175)*

Caraustar Industries Inc... 413 593-9700
70 Better Way Chicopee (01022) *(G-8014)*

Caraustar Industries Inc... 978 665-2632
100 Newark Ave Fitchburg (01420) *(G-8648)*

Carbide Solutions LLC... 860 515-8665
800 Marshall Phelps Rd Windsor (06095) *(G-4264)*

Carbon Black LLC **(DH)**.. **617 393-7400**
1100 Winter St Ste 4900 Waltham (02451) *(G-12620)*

Carbon Felt Inc... 603 542-0202
98 Plains Rd Claremont (03743) *(G-14082)*

Carbon Products Inc... 860 749-0614
40 Scitico Rd Somersville (06072) *(G-3101)*

Carboncraft, Barre *Also Called: Srg Inc (G-17018)*

Carbone Metal Fabricator, Chelsea *Also Called: Carbone Sheet Metal Corp (G-7975)*

Carbone Sheet Metal Corp... 617 884-0237
240 Marginal St Chelsea (02150) *(G-7975)*

Carbtrol Corporation... 203 337-4340
200 Benton St Stratford (06615) *(G-3525)*

Carby, Watertown *Also Called: The Carby Corporation (G-4032)*

Cardiac Pacemakers Inc... 651 582-3201
East Hartford (06128) *(G-977)*

Cardinal Comb & Brush Mfg Corp............................... 978 537-6330
106 Carter St Ste 3 Leominster (01453) *(G-9647)*

Cardinal Comb Mfg, Leominster *Also Called: Cardinal Comb & Brush Mfg Corp (G-9647)*

Cardinal Health 414, East Hartford *Also Called: Cardinal Health 414 LLC (G-978)*

Cardinal Health 414 LLC... 860 291-9135
131 Hartland St Ste 8 East Hartford (06108) *(G-978)*

Cardinal Shehan Center Inc....................................... 203 336-4468
1494 Main St Bridgeport (06604) *(G-310)*

Cardinal Shoe Corporation... 978 686-9706
468 N Canal St Ste 3 Lawrence (01840) *(G-9546)*

Cardiofocus, Marlborough *Also Called: Cardiofocus Inc (G-10129)*

Cardiofocus Inc.. 508 658-7200
500 Nickerson Rd Ste 500200 Marlborough (01752) *(G-10129)*

Cardiopulmonary Corp... 203 877-1999
200 Cascade Blvd Ste B Milford (06460) *(G-1808)*

Cardiotech International Inc....................................... 978 657-0075
229 Andover St Wilmington (01887) *(G-13397)*

Cardiovascular Instrument Corp.................................. 781 245-7799
102 Foundry St Wakefield (01880) *(G-12504)*

Care International Exch Inc.. 781 642-5900
77 4th Ave Ste 5 Waltham (02451) *(G-12621)*

Career Press Inc **(PA)**.. **201 848-0310**
65 Parker St Ste 7 Newburyport (01950) *(G-10674)*

Carefree Building Co Inc **(PA)**................................ **860 267-7600**
48 Westchester Rd Colchester (06415) *(G-655)*

Carestream Hlth Mlclar Imging................................... 888 777-2072
4 Science Park New Haven (06511) *(G-2134)*

Carestream Molecular Imaging, New Haven *Also Called: Carestream Hlth Mlclar Imging (G-2134)*

Carey Manufacturing Co Inc....................................... 860 829-1803
5 Pasco Hill Rd Unit B Cromwell (06416) *(G-689)*

Cargill, Swanton *Also Called: Cargill Incorporated (G-17636)*

Cargill Incorporated.. 802 868-3232
149 Jonergin Dr Swanton (05488) *(G-17636)*

Caribe Cmmnctions Pblctions Inc................................ 617 522-5060
175 William F Mcclellan Hwy Ste 1 Boston (02128) *(G-6638)*

Caribe Communications, Boston *Also Called: Alberto Vasallo Jr (G-6530)*

Cariman 44 LLC... 603 889-5160
2 Knights Bridge Dr Nashua (03063) *(G-15076)*

Caring Pharmacy 2, Dorchester *Also Called: Vietaz Inc (G-8301)*

Carisma Therapeutics Inc.. 617 444-8550
245 1st St Ste 1800 Cambridge (02142) *(G-7532)*

Carl Associates, North Hartland *Also Called: North Hartland Tool Corp (G-17420)*

Carl Fisher Co Inc.. 413 736-3661
42 Wilcox St Springfield (01105) *(G-12082)*

Carl Swanson Harp Rentals Inc **(PA)**....................... **617 569-6642**
137 Webster St Boston (02128) *(G-6639)*

Carl Zeiss Nts LLC **(DH)**.. **978 826-1500**
1 Corporate Pl Ste 3 Peabody (01960) *(G-11301)*

Carl Zeiss Vision Inc.. 800 327-9735
257 Simarano Dr Ste 107 Marlborough (01752) *(G-10130)*

Carla Corp... 401 438-7070
33 Sutton Ave East Providence (02914) *(G-16008)*

Carla's Pasta, South Windsor *Also Called: CP Foods LLC (G-3134)*

Carlat Publishing LLC... 978 499-0583
2 Prince Pl Newburyport (01950) *(G-10675)*

Carlin Combustion Tech Inc, North Haven *Also Called: Cowles Operating Company (G-2404)*

Carlin Mfg Kitchens To Go... 413 519-2822
31 Masons Island Rd Mystic (06355) *(G-1937)*

Carling Technologies Inc **(HQ)**............................... **860 793-9281**
60 Johnson Ave Plainville (06062) *(G-2750)*

Carlisle Construction Mtls LLC.................................... 888 746-1114
15 Franklin St Portland (04101) *(G-5195)*

Carls Boned Chicken Inc... 203 777-9048
208 Food Terminal Plz New Haven (06511) *(G-2135)*

Carlson Fuel of Meriden Inc....................................... 203 574-9396
532 S Leonard St Waterbury (06708) *(G-3896)*

Carlson Sheet Metal LLC... 860 354-4660
24 Bostwick Pl New Milford (06776) *(G-2240)*

Carlstrom Pressed Metal Co Inc................................. 508 366-4472
65 Fisher St Westborough (01581) *(G-13086)*

Carlton Industries Corp... 203 288-5605
33 Rossotto Dr Hamden (06514) *(G-1416)*

Carlton Newton Corporation LLC................................. 802 579-1413
55 Marlboro Rd Ste 7 Brattleboro (05301) *(G-17078)*

Carlucci Wldg Fabrication Inc..................................... 203 588-0746
205 Wilson Ave Norwalk (06854) *(G-2479)*

Carlyle Johnson Machine Co LLC **(DH)**..................... **860 643-1531**
291 Boston Tpke Bolton (06043) *(G-219)*

Carnegie Communications LLC.................................... 978 692-5092
210 Littleton Rd Ste 100 Westford (01886) *(G-13227)*

Carnegie Dartlet LLC **(PA)**..................................... **978 692-5092**
210 Littleton Rd Ste 100 Westford (01886) *(G-13228)*

Carolina Binding & Textile, Bedford *Also Called: A B E Enterprises LLC (G-6204)*

Carolina Precision Technologie.................................... 860 315-9017
51 Ridge Rd Putnam (06260) *(G-2847)*

Carols Canvas Company Inc....................................... 781 871-8288
273 Weymouth St Rockland (02370) *(G-11639)*

Caron Engineering Inc.. 207 646-6071
116 Willie Hill Rd Wells (04090) *(G-5598)*

Carousel Cabinets.. 978 846-8763
489 Neck Rd Lancaster (01523) *(G-9524)*

Carpe Diem Technologies Inc..................................... 508 541-2055
34 Saxon St Franklin (02038) *(G-8822)*

Carpenter & Paterson Inc.. 781 935-7036
225 Merrimac St Woburn (01801) *(G-13540)*

Carpin, Waterbury *Also Called: Carpin Manufacturing Inc (G-3897)*

Carpin Manufacturing Inc.. 203 574-2556
411 Austin Rd Waterbury (06705) *(G-3897)*

Carr Management Inc **(PA)**..................................... **603 888-1315**
1 Tara Blvd Ste 303 Nashua (03062) *(G-15077)*

Carr Tool Co LLC... 603 669-0177
19 Tinker Ave Unit 2 Londonderry (03053) *(G-14734)*

Carr-Dee Corp... 781 391-4500
37 Linden St Medford (02155) *(G-10282)*

Carrara, North Clarendon *Also Called: Joseph P Carrara & Sons Inc (G-17415)*

Carriage Hse Developments LLC.................................. 339 221-4253
253 Swanton St Winchester (01890) *(G-13483)*

Carriage Towne News.. 603 642-4499
100 Turnpike St North Andover (01845) *(G-10822)*

Carrier Chipping Inc.. 207 858-4277
100 Carrier Ln Skowhegan (04976) *(G-5464)*

Carrier Commercial Rfrgn, Farmington *Also Called: Rtx Corporation (G-1245)*

Carrier Eq LLC.. 617 841-7207
186 Lincoln St Fl 3 Boston (02111) *(G-6640)*

Carrier Fire SEC Americas Corp.................................. 941 739-4200
30 Batterson Park Rd Ste 100 Farmington (06032) *(G-1211)*

Carris Community of Companies, Proctor *Also Called: Carris Financial Corp (G-17456)*

Carris Financial Corp **(PA)**......................................802 773-9111
  49 Main St Proctor (05765) *(G-17456)*

Carris Plastics, Proctor *Also Called: Carris Reels Inc (G-17457)*

Carris Reels Connecticut Inc.................................860 749-8308
  11 Randolph St Enfield (06082) *(G-1122)*

Carris Reels Inc **(HQ)**...802 773-9111
  49 Main St Proctor (05765) *(G-17457)*

Carris Reels of CT, Enfield *Also Called: Carris Reels Connecticut Inc (G-1122)*

Carroll Coatings Company Inc **(PA)**......................401 450-5500
  150 Ernest St Providence (02905) *(G-16497)*

Carroll Concrete, Newport *Also Called: Newport Sand & Gravel Co Inc (G-15233)*

Carroll Concrete Co...802 229-0191
  379 Granger Rd Barre (05641) *(G-16999)*

Carroll Concrete Co, Charlestown *Also Called: Newport Sand & Gravel Co Inc (G-14065)*

Carroll Concrete Co, West Lebanon *Also Called: Newport Sand & Gravel Co Inc (G-15686)*

Carroll Concrete Co, Newport *Also Called: Newport Sand & Gravel Co Inc (G-17403)*

Carroll Concrete Co Inc..603 863-1765
  8 Reeds Mill Rd Newport (03773) *(G-15226)*

Carrubba Incorporated..203 878-0605
  70 Research Dr Milford (06460) *(G-1809)*

Carrubba Incorporated..203 878-0605
  500 Pepper St Monroe (06468) *(G-1908)*

Cartamundi East Longmeadow LLC.........................413 526-2000
  443 Shaker Rd East Longmeadow (01028) *(G-8371)*

Carten Controls Inc..203 699-2100
  604 W Johnson Ave Cheshire (06410) *(G-577)*

Carten-Fujikin Incorporated.....................................203 699-2134
  604 W Johnson Ave Cheshire (06410) *(G-578)*

Carter Machine Inc..802 426-3501
  360 Pattys Xing Marshfield (05658) *(G-17333)*

Cartesian Therapeutics Inc **(PA)**...........................617 923-1400
  65 Grove St Watertown (02472) *(G-12868)*

Carts Vermont, Saint Johnsbury *Also Called: Momentum Mfg Group - N LLC (G-17545)*

Carver Shellfish Inc..207 497-2261
  125 Black Duck Cove Rd Beals (04611) *(G-4532)*

Carvers' Guild, West Groton *Also Called: Canner Incorporated (G-13001)*

Carwild Corporation **(PA)**.....................................860 442-4914
  3 State Pier Rd New London (06320) *(G-2224)*

Cas America, North Smithfield *Also Called: Cas America LLC (G-16320)*

Cas America LLC..401 884-8556
  20 Providence Pike North Smithfield (02896) *(G-16320)*

Cas Medical Systems Inc..203 488-6056
  44 E Industrial Rd Branford (06405) *(G-242)*

Cas of New England, South Easton *Also Called: Connected Auto Systems Neng In (G-11940)*

Casa Systems, Andover *Also Called: Casa Systems Inc (G-5877)*

Casa Systems Inc **(PA)**...978 688-6706
  100 River Rd Andover (01810) *(G-5877)*

Casavant Corporation..860 605-5937
  5 Cricket Ln Burlington (06013) *(G-546)*

Cascaded Purchase Holdings Inc **(PA)**.................603 448-1090
  35 Connecticut River Bend Rd Claremont (03743) *(G-14083)*

Cascades Auburn Fiber Inc......................................207 753-5300
  586 Lewiston Junction Rd Auburn (04210) *(G-4423)*

Cascades Holding US Inc...718 340-2136
  1 Edmund Rd Newtown (06470) *(G-2336)*

Casco Bay Butter Company Inc...............................207 712-9148
  25 Thomas Dr Westbrook (04092) *(G-5620)*

Casco Bay Creamery, Westbrook *Also Called: Casco Bay Butter Company Inc (G-5620)*

Casco Bay Sbstnce Abuse Rsrces...........................207 773-7993
  205 Ocean Ave Portland (04103) *(G-5196)*

Casco Bay Steel Structures Inc................................207 780-6722
  1 Wallace Ave South Portland (04106) *(G-5494)*

Cascon Inc..207 846-6202
  65 Forest Falls Dr Yarmouth (04096) *(G-5702)*

Cascon Pump, Yarmouth *Also Called: Cascon Inc (G-5702)*

Case Assembly Solutions Inc...................................508 238-5665
  19 Norfolk Ave Ste B South Easton (02375) *(G-11939)*

Case Concepts Intl LLC...203 883-8602
  112 Prospect St Unit A Stamford (06901) *(G-3303)*

Case Future Corp...401 944-0402
  27 Mill St Johnston (02919) *(G-16078)*

Case Hard...401 635-8201
  56 Indian Rd Little Compton (02837) *(G-16159)*

Casella Recycling LLC **(HQ)**.................................207 883-4600
  13 Gibson Rd Scarborough (04074) *(G-5427)*

Casenet LLC **(HQ)**..781 357-2700
  34 Crosby Dr Ste 100 Bedford (01730) *(G-6217)*

Casey & Hayes Inc..617 269-5900
  100 Industrial Park Rd Hingham (02043) *(G-9146)*

Casinelli Design, Cranston *Also Called: Gennaro Inc (G-15868)*

Casmed, Branford *Also Called: Cas Medical Systems Inc (G-242)*

Caspari Inc **(PA)**...203 888-1100
  99 Cogwheel Ln Seymour (06483) *(G-2957)*

Cassidy Bros Forge Inc...978 948-7303
  282 Newburyport Tpke Rowley (01969) *(G-11671)*

Cassiopae Us Inc..435 647-9940
  183 Roberts Cemetery Rd Vinalhaven (04863) *(G-5572)*

Cassiopae US Inc..603 685-3223
  224 Main St Ste 3a Salem (03079) *(G-15511)*

Cassjack Industries Inc...413 786-1800
  174 Main St Westfield (01085) *(G-13157)*

Cast Global Manufacturing Corp...............................203 828-6147
  66 Prokop Rd Oxford (06478) *(G-2688)*

Castaldo Proudcts, Chestnut Hill *Also Called: FE Knight Inc (G-7999)*

Castechnologies Inc...508 222-2915
  40 Townsend Rd Attleboro (02703) *(G-6000)*

Castle Beverages Inc..203 732-0883
  105 Myrtle Ave Ansonia (06401) *(G-9)*

Castle Gate Invstmnts Ltd Lblt..................................617 596-1126
  36 Carl Rd Walpole (02081) *(G-12555)*

Castle Island Brewing Co LLC...................................781 951-2029
  31 Astor Ave Norwood (02062) *(G-11168)*

Castle Plastics Inc..978 534-6220
  11 Francis St Leominster (01453) *(G-9648)*

Castle Seltzer Inc...203 736-6887
  245 Francis St Derby (06418) *(G-888)*

Catachem Inc...203 262-0330
  353 Christian St Ste 2 Oxford (06478) *(G-2689)*

Cataki International Inc...508 295-9630
  14 Kendrick Rd Ste 5 Wareham (02571) *(G-12833)*

Catalent Massachusetts LLC....................................617 660-4110
  190 Everett Ave Chelsea (02150) *(G-7976)*

Catalog Technologies Inc...617 768-7222
  529 Main St Ste 127 Boston (02129) *(G-6641)*

Catalyst Acoustics Group Inc...................................413 789-1770
  50 Almgren Dr S Agawam (01001) *(G-5785)*

Catalyst Acustics Holdings Inc **(HQ)**.....................413 789-1770
  50 Almgren Dr S Agawam (01001) *(G-5786)*

Catalystsmc Inc...781 449-9500
  85 Wells Ave Ste 106 Newton (02459) *(G-10741)*

Catamount Color, Essex Junction *Also Called: Offset House Inc (G-17242)*

Catamount Glassware Co Inc...................................802 442-5438
  309 County St Bennington (05201) *(G-17038)*

Catamount North Cabinetry LLC...............................802 264-9009
  15 Corporate Dr Essex Junction (05452) *(G-17230)*

Catania Oils, Ayer *Also Called: Catania-Spagna Corporation (G-6177)*

Catania-Spagna Corporation....................................978 772-7900
  90 Nemco Way Ayer (01432) *(G-6177)*

Catanzaro Food Products Inc...................................401 255-1700
  203 Concord St Unit 457 Pawtucket (02860) *(G-16353)*

Catapult Sports Inc **(HQ)**.....................................978 447-5220
  10 Post Office Square Fl 9 Boston (02109) *(G-6642)*

Catapult Sports LLC...312 762-5332
  10 Post Office Sq Ste 900s Boston (02109) *(G-6643)*

Catelli Brothers Family Foods, Sutton *Also Called: J&G (2021) Inc (G-12285)*

Cathedral Art Metal Co Inc......................................401 273-7200
  25 Manton Ave Providence (02909) *(G-16498)*

Cathedral Ledge Distillery Inc...................................612 386-4829
  3340 White Mountain Hwy North Conway (03860) *(G-15246)*

Caton, Kingston *Also Called: Caton Connector Corp (G-9505)*

Caton Connector Corp...781 585-4315
  26 Wapping Rd Ste 1 Kingston (02364) *(G-9505)*

Catskill Gran Countertops Inc.. 860 667-1555
  156 Pane Rd Ste A Newington (06111) *(G-2279)*

Cause For Change LLC.. 617 571-6990
  359 Boston Post Rd Ste 2 Sudbury (01776) *(G-12262)*

Cavallero Plastics Inc... 413 443-0925
  1250 North St Pittsfield (01201) *(G-11395)*

Cavanagh, Greenville *Also Called: Cavanagh Company (G-16057)*

Cavanagh Company... 401 949-4000
  610 Putnam Pike Greenville (02828) *(G-16057)*

Cave Manufacturing Inc.. 802 257-9253
  22 Browne Ct Unit 104 Brattleboro (05301) *(G-17079)*

Cave Moose Farm, Cambridge *Also Called: Sogle Property LLC (G-17168)*

Cazena Inc.. 781 897-6380
  1601 Trapelo Rd Ste 205 Waltham (02451) *(G-12622)*

CB Ventures LLC... 603 434-3175
  14 Lexington Dr Ste 2 Laconia (03246) *(G-14650)*

Cbd Events LLC.. 802 310-8810
  35 Hummingbird Ln South Burlington (05403) *(G-17576)*

CBI, Newton *Also Called: Ragnar Inc (G-15244)*

Cbis, West Brookfield *Also Called: Concrete Block Insulg Systems (G-12993)*

Cbm Industries Inc.. 508 821-4555
  470 Constitution Dr Taunton (02780) *(G-12326)*

Cbms LLC... 508 776-2647
  6 Fieldstone Cir Hampton (03842) *(G-14401)*

Cbr, West Hartford *Also Called: Connectcut Boiler Repr Mfg Inc (G-4054)*

CBS Contractors, Ansonia *Also Called: CBS Contractors Inc (G-10)*

CBS Contractors Inc.. 203 734-8015
  1 Riverside Dr Ste D Ansonia (06401) *(G-10)*

CBS Manufacturing Company... 860 653-8100
  35 Kripes Rd East Granby (06026) *(G-927)*

Cc1 Inc... 603 319-2000
  170 West Rd Ste 7 Portsmouth (03801) *(G-15368)*

CCC Acquisition Holdings, Inc., Boston *Also Called: Altium Acqisition Holdings Inc (G-6539)*

CCI, Putnam *Also Called: Central Construction Inds LLC (G-2848)*

CCI Corpus Christi LLC.. 203 564-8100
  2200 Atlantic St Ste 800 Stamford (06902) *(G-3304)*

CCI Cyrus River Terminal LLC.. 203 761-8000
  2200 Atlantic St Ste 800 Stamford (06902) *(G-3305)*

CCI Robinsons Bend LLC... 203 564-8571
  2200 Atlantic St Ste 800 Stamford (06902) *(G-3306)*

CCL Design, Framingham *Also Called: CCL Label Inc (G-8750)*

CCL Industries Corporation.. 203 926-1253
  15 Controls Dr Shelton (06484) *(G-2989)*

CCL Industries Corporation **(HQ)**.................................. **508 872-4511**
  161 Worcester Rd Ste 403 Framingham (01701) *(G-8749)*

CCL Label, Framingham *Also Called: CCL Industries Corporation (G-8749)*

CCL Label Inc... 203 926-1253
  15 Controls Dr Shelton (06484) *(G-2990)*

CCL Label Inc **(HQ)**... **508 872-4511**
  161 Worcester Rd Ste 403 Framingham (01701) *(G-8750)*

Ccmc, Medford *Also Called: Cross Country Motor Club Inc (G-10283)*

Cco Llc.. 860 757-3434
  2138 Silas Deane Hwy Ste 101 Rocky Hill (06067) *(G-2917)*

Cco Holdings LLC... 978 615-1032
  289 Ayer Rd Harvard (01451) *(G-9060)*

Cco Holdings LLC... 413 754-0616
  400 Longmeadow St Longmeadow (01106) *(G-9849)*

Cco Holdings LLC... 774 293-4026
  100 Worcester St North Grafton (01536) *(G-11020)*

Cco Holdings LLC... 774 462-6577
  9 Walker Dr Upton (01568) *(G-12470)*

Cco Holdings LLC... 802 778-0497
  89 Main St Montpelier (05602) *(G-17371)*

Ccr Products LLC.. 860 953-0499
  175 South St West Hartford (06110) *(G-4052)*

CD Aero, LLC, New Bedford *Also Called: Rf Aero LLC (G-10646)*

CD Management LLC... 203 269-0090
  225 N Main St Bristol (06010) *(G-424)*

CD Solutions Inc... 203 481-5895
  420 E Main St Ste 16 Branford (06405) *(G-243)*

Cdc Enterprises Llc... 603 437-3090
  3 Lexington Rd Unit 1a Windham (03087) *(G-15722)*

CDF Corporation **(PA)**... **508 747-5858**
  77 Industrial Park Rd Plymouth (02360) *(G-11454)*

Cdi LLC A Valley Forge Co... 508 587-7000
  637 N Montello St Brockton (02301) *(G-7266)*

Cdp Manufacturing LLC... 508 588-6400
  15 Jonathan Dr Ste 6 Brockton (02301) *(G-7267)*

CE Baird Corporation... 978 365-3867
  851 Sterling Rd Lancaster (01523) *(G-9525)*

CE Baird Corporation **(PA)**... **978 368-7250**
  32 Jungle Rd Leominster (01453) *(G-9649)*

CE Baird Corporation... 978 751-8432
  11 Jytek Rd Leominster (01453) *(G-9650)*

Ceaco Inc... 617 926-8080
  250 Royall St Canton (02021) *(G-7777)*

Cebal Americas **(PA)**... **203 845-6356**
  101 Merritt 7 Ste 2 Norwalk (06851) *(G-2480)*

Cedar Crest Cabinetry, Manchester *Also Called: Revolution Furnishings LLC (G-14921)*

Cedarworks of Maine Inc.. 207 596-0771
  12 Merrill Dr Rockland (04841) *(G-5324)*

Cedarworks of Maine Inc **(PA)**...................................... **207 596-1010**
  799 Commercial St Rockport (04856) *(G-5345)*

Cedarworks Playsets, Rockland *Also Called: Cedarworks of Maine Inc (G-5324)*

Cedarworks Playsets, Rockport *Also Called: Cedarworks of Maine Inc (G-5345)*

Cedilla Therapeutics Inc.. 617 581-9333
  245 1st St Ste 300 Cambridge (02142) *(G-7533)*

Cei Flowmaster Products LLC... 603 880-0094
  18 Park Ave Hudson (03051) *(G-14490)*

Celebrations.. 508 457-0530
  210 Main St Falmouth (02540) *(G-8629)*

Celera Motion, Bedford *Also Called: Novanta Inc (G-6247)*

Celeros Inc... 248 478-2800
  1188 Centre St Ste 1 Newton (02459) *(G-10742)*

Celeros Separations, Newton *Also Called: Celeros Inc (G-10742)*

Celestial Monitoring Corp **(HQ)**.................................... **401 782-1045**
  24 Celestial Dr Ste B Narragansett (02882) *(G-16187)*

Celestica New England Inc... 603 334-3450
  72 Pease Blvd Newington (03801) *(G-15206)*

Celgene Corporation.. 857 225-2309
  100 Macy St Unit F174 Amesbury (01913) *(G-5832)*

Cell Nique.. 888 417-9343
  12 Old Stage Coach Rd Weston (06883) *(G-4148)*

Cell Press Inc... 617 397-2800
  50 Hampshire St Cambridge (02139) *(G-7534)*

Cellanyx Diagnostics LLC.. 571 212-9991
  100 Cummings Ctr Ste 451d Beverly (01915) *(G-6337)*

Cellaria Biosciences LLC... 617 981-4208
  26 Bennett Rd Boxford (01921) *(G-7158)*

Cellars.. 207 288-3907
  854 State Highway 3 Bar Harbor (04609) *(G-4522)*

Cellay LLC... 617 995-1307
  100 Inman St Ste 207 Cambridge (02139) *(G-7535)*

Cellblock Fcs LLC... 800 440-4119
  234 Northeast Rd Ste 5 Standish (04084) *(G-5526)*

Celldex Therapeutics Inc... 203 483-3531
  300 George St Ste 503 New Haven (06511) *(G-2136)*

Celldex Therapeutics Inc... 781 433-0771
  119 4th Ave Needham Heights (02494) *(G-10534)*

Cellgenix Inc.. 603 373-0408
  1 Nh Ave Ste 125 Portsmouth (03801) *(G-15369)*

Cellu Tissue Corporation.. 860 289-7496
  2 Forbes St East Hartford (06108) *(G-979)*

Cellular Specialties Inc.. 603 626-6677
  670 North Commercial St Ste 202 Manchester (03101) *(G-14826)*

Celyad Inc.. 857 990-6900
  2 Seaport Ln Boston (02210) *(G-6644)*

Cemcolift Elevator Systems, Bloomfield *Also Called: Ascend Elevator Inc (G-148)*

Cengage Learning Inc.. 518 348-2300
  200 Pier 4 Blvd Ste 200 Boston (02210) *(G-6645)*

Centage Corporation.. 800 366-5111
  330 Cochituate Rd Unit 807 Framingham (01701) *(G-8751)*

Centco Architectural Mtls Inc.. 508 456-1888
523 Spring St East Bridgewater (02333) *(G-8336)*

Center Broach & Machine Co... 203 235-6329
525 N Colony St Meriden (06450) *(G-1659)*

Center For Discovery... 203 955-1381
1320 Mill Hill Rd Southport (06890) *(G-3245)*

Center For Work and Family, Chestnut Hill *Also Called: Trustees of Boston College (G-8002)*

Center Point Inc.. 207 568-3717
600 Brooks Rd Knox (04986) *(G-4943)*

Center Point Publishing, Knox *Also Called: Center Point Inc (G-4943)*

Centerity Systems Inc... 339 225-7007
154 Wells Ave Ste 4 Newton (02459) *(G-10743)*

Centerline Machine Company Inc.. 978 524-8842
60 Park St Beverly (01915) *(G-6338)*

Centilla Corporation.. 603 658-3881
11 Bedros St Windham (03087) *(G-15723)*

Centive Inc.. 866 469-2285
900 Chelmsford St Lowell (01851) *(G-9866)*

Centorr/Vacuum Industries LLC **(PA)**.............................. **603 595-7233**
55 Northeastern Blvd Unit 2 Nashua (03062) *(G-15078)*

Centra Software Inc **(DH)**.. **781 861-7000**
430 Bedford St Ste 220 Lexington (02420) *(G-9729)*

Central Admxture Phrm Svcs Inc... 781 376-0032
55 6th Rd Woburn (01801) *(G-13541)*

Central Coating, West Boylston *Also Called: Central Coating Tech Inc (G-12956)*

Central Coating Tech Inc... 508 835-6225
165 Shrewsbury St West Boylston (01583) *(G-12956)*

Central Conn Cmmunications LLC... 860 225-4601
1 Court St Fl 4 New Britain (06051) *(G-2010)*

Central Conn Coatings Inc... 860 528-8281
52 Village St East Hartford (06108) *(G-980)*

Central Conn Cooperative Farme... 860 649-4523
1050 Sullivan Ave Ste A3 South Windsor (06074) *(G-3127)*

Central Conn Sls & Mfg Inc... 860 667-1411
37 Stanwell Rd Newington (06111) *(G-2280)*

Central Construction Inds LLC.. 860 963-8902
30 Harris St Putnam (06260) *(G-2848)*

Central Equipment Company.. 207 827-6193
45 Dempsey-Greaves Ln Stillwater (04489) *(G-5533)*

Central Falls Glass Co, Central Falls *Also Called: Central FLS Plate & Win GL Co (G-15787)*

Central FLS Plate & Win GL Co... 401 722-1267
481 Broad St Central Falls (02863) *(G-15787)*

Central MA Waterjet Inc.. 508 769-4308
32 Grafton St Millbury (01527) *(G-10429)*

Central Maine Dairy Eqp Inc.. 207 453-6727
793 Skowhegan Rd Skowhegan (04976) *(G-5465)*

Central Maine Morning Sentinel... 207 873-3341
31 Front St Waterville (04901) *(G-5593)*

Central Metal Finishing Inc.. 978 291-0500
80 Flagship Dr North Andover (01845) *(G-10823)*

Central Pallet & Box Co LLC... 860 224-4416
271 John Downey Dr New Britain (06051) *(G-2011)*

Central Street Corporation... 207 947-8049
80 Central St Bangor (04401) *(G-4495)*

Central Tire Co Inc **(PA)**.. **207 324-4250**
1307 Main St Sanford (04073) *(G-5391)*

Central Tools Inc... 781 893-0095
1644 Concord St Framingham (01701) *(G-8752)*

Central Tools Inc **(PA)**... **401 467-8211**
456 Wellington Ave Cranston (02910) *(G-15841)*

Centrexion Therapeutics Corp.. 617 837-6911
200 State St Ste 6 Boston (02109) *(G-6646)*

Centricut Inc... 603 298-7849
2 Technology Dr West Lebanon (03784) *(G-15679)*

Centricut Manufacturing LLC.. 603 298-6191
16 Airpark Rd West Lebanon (03784) *(G-15680)*

Centrix, Shelton *Also Called: Centrix Inc (G-2991)*

Centrix Inc.. 203 929-5582
770 River Rd Shelton (06484) *(G-2991)*

Centurian Mechanical Seals, Rumford *Also Called: Eaton Corporation (G-16666)*

Century Acquisition... 518 758-7229
49 Clayton Rd Canaan (06018) *(G-554)*

Century Box, Methuen *Also Called: Gooby Industries Corp (G-10332)*

Century Food Service Inc.. 508 995-3221
107 S Main St Acushnet (02743) *(G-5770)*

Century International Arms Inc... 802 527-1252
236 Bryce Blvd Fairfax (05454) *(G-17257)*

Century Magnetics Holdings Inc... 603 934-4931
27 Sargent St Northfield (03276) *(G-15263)*

Century Products, New Canaan *Also Called: Contek International Corp (G-2078)*

Century Sheet Metal Inc.. 401 433-1380
19 Maple Ave Riverside (02915) *(G-16653)*

Century Spring Mfg Co Inc.. 860 582-3344
100 Wooster Ct Bristol (06010) *(G-425)*

Century Tool and Design Inc.. 860 621-6748
260 Canal St Milldale (06467) *(G-1900)*

Century Tool Co Inc... 860 923-9523
753 Thompson Rd Thompson (06277) *(G-3648)*

Century Warehouse Office, Fairfax *Also Called: Century International Arms Inc (G-17257)*

Century Woodworking Inc.. 860 379-7538
40 River Rd Pleasant Valley (06063) *(G-2800)*

Century-Tywood, Holliston *Also Called: Century-Tywood J3 Corp (G-9204)*

Century-Tywood J3 Corp.. 508 429-4011
79 Lowland St Holliston (01746) *(G-9204)*

Cenveo... 203 595-3109
63 Hawks Cir Westfield (01085) *(G-13158)*

Cenveo Corporation.. 303 790-8023
200 Stamford Pl Fl 2 Stamford (06902) *(G-3307)*

Cenveo Enterprises Inc **(PA)**....................................... **203 595-3000**
200 Stamford Pl 2nd Fl Stamford (06902) *(G-3308)*

Cenveo Worldwide Limited **(DH)**.................................. **203 595-3000**
200 Stamford Pl Stamford (06902) *(G-3309)*

Cequr, Marlborough *Also Called: Cequr Corporation (G-10131)*

Cequr Corporation.. 508 486-0010
734 Forest St Ste 100 Marlborough (01752) *(G-10131)*

Ceramco Inc.. 603 447-2090
1467 E Main St Center Conway (03813) *(G-14050)*

Ceramic Process Systems.. 508 222-0614
111 Worcester St Taunton (02780) *(G-12327)*

Ceramic To Metal Seals Inc... 781 665-5002
78 Stone Pl Ste 4 Melrose (02176) *(G-10314)*

Cerbone Bakery, Stamford *Also Called: Beldotti Bakeries LLC (G-3293)*

Cerence, Burlington *Also Called: Cerence Inc (G-7343)*

Cerence Inc **(PA)**.. **857 362-7300**
1 Burlington Woods Dr Ste 301a Burlington (01803) *(G-7343)*

Cerence Operating Company **(HQ)**............................... **857 362-7300**
1 Burlington Woods Dr Ste 301a Burlington (01803) *(G-7344)*

Cerenovus, Raynham *Also Called: Depuy Synthes Products Inc (G-11588)*

Cerenovus Inc... 908 704-4024
325 Paramount Dr Raynham (02767) *(G-11583)*

Cerenovus, Inc, Raynham *Also Called: Cerenovus Inc (G-11583)*

Cerevel Thrputics Holdings Inc **(PA)**............................. **844 304-2048**
222 Jacobs St Unit 200 Cambridge (02141) *(G-7536)*

Ceric Fab Systems, Ayer *Also Called: Ceric Fabrication Co Inc (G-6178)*

Ceric Fabrication Co Inc.. 978 772-9034
70 Nemco Way Ayer (01432) *(G-6178)*

Cerner Corporation... 781 434-2200
51 Sawyer Rd Ste 600 Waltham (02453) *(G-12623)*

Cerner DHT, Waltham *Also Called: Cerner Corporation (G-12623)*

Cerrito Furniture Inds Inc.. 203 481-2580
7 Venice St Branford (06405) *(G-244)*

Cerritos Upholstery Concepts, Branford *Also Called: Cerrito Furniture Inds Inc (G-244)*

Cersosimo Industries Inc **(PA)**..................................... **802 254-4500**
439 West River Road Route 30 Brattleboro (05301) *(G-17080)*

Cersosimo Lumber Company Inc **(PA)**........................... **802 254-4508**
1103 Vernon St Brattleboro (05301) *(G-17081)*

Certeon Inc... 781 425-5099
5 Wall St Fl 5 Burlington (01803) *(G-7345)*

Certify Inc **(PA)**.. **207 773-6100**
320 Cumberland Ave Portland (04101) *(G-5197)*

Certuss America LP... 440 454-6172
800 Marshall Phelps Rd Windsor (06095) *(G-4265)*

ALPHABETIC

Cerulli Associates Inc **(PA)**.................... 617 437-0084
  699 Boylston St Ste 1100 Boston (02116) *(G-6647)*

Cervena Barva Press LLC.................... 617 764-2229
  294 Highland Ave Apt 2 Somerville (02144) *(G-11867)*

Cesyl Mills Inc.................... 508 865-6129
  95 W Main St Millbury (01527) *(G-10430)*

CET, Milford *Also Called: Cet Inc (G-1810)*

Cet Inc.................... 203 882-8057
  270 Rowe Ave Ste D Milford (06461) *(G-1810)*

CET Technology LLC.................... 603 894-6100
  27 Roulston Rd A Windham (03087) *(G-15724)*

CFI Millwork Inc.................... 860 643-7580
  41 Chapel St Manchester (06042) *(G-1588)*

CFPA, Rockfall *Also Called: Connecticut Forest Pk Assn Inc (G-2913)*

Cg Holdings LLC **(PA)**.................... 603 623-3344
  669 East Industrial Park Dr Manchester (03109) *(G-14827)*

Cg Roxane LLC.................... 603 476-8844
  455 Ossipee Park Rd Moultonborough (03254) *(G-15051)*

Cgi, Andover *Also Called: Cgi Information Systems & Management Consultants Inc (G-5878)*

Cgi Information Systems & Management Consultants Inc.................... 978 946-3000
  600 Federal St Andover (01810) *(G-5878)*

Cgit Westboro Inc.................... 508 836-4000
  30 Oak St Westborough (01581) *(G-13087)*

Chadwick & Trefethen Inc.................... 603 436-2568
  50 Borthwick Ave Portsmouth (03801) *(G-15370)*

Chadwick Yarn Co., West Greenwich *Also Called: Conneaut Industries Inc (G-16883)*

Chair City Meats Inc.................... 978 630-1050
  766 W Broadway Gardner (01440) *(G-8881)*

Chamberlain Companies Inc.................... 603 893-2606
  14 Delaware Dr Salem (03079) *(G-15512)*

Chamberlain Group, Great Barrington *Also Called: Chamberlain Group LLC (G-8975)*

Chamberlain Group LLC.................... 413 528-7744
  934 Main St Great Barrington (01230) *(G-8975)*

Chamberlain Machine LLC.................... 603 756-2560
  17 Huntington Ln Walpole (03608) *(G-15660)*

Champion Enterprises Inc.................... 860 429-3537
  19 Greenfield Ln Storrs (06268) *(G-3510)*

Champion Polymers Recycling, Old Saybrook *Also Called: Infiltrator Water Technologies LLC (G-2651)*

Champlain Cable, Colchester *Also Called: Champlain Cable Corporation (G-17187)*

Champlain Cable Corporation **(PA)**.................... 802 654-4200
  175 Hercules Dr Colchester (05446) *(G-17187)*

Champlain Cable Leeds Corporation.................... 413 584-3853
  118 River Rd Leeds (01053) *(G-9620)*

Champlain Chocolate Company **(PA)**.................... 800 465-5909
  750 Pine St Burlington (05401) *(G-17124)*

Champlain Chocolate Company.................... 802 864-1808
  290 Boyer Cir Williston (05495) *(G-17725)*

Champlain Construction Co Inc.................... 802 388-2652
  1050 Route 7 S Middlebury (05753) *(G-17341)*

Champlain Door Company Inc.................... 802 524-7595
  4182 Highbridge Rd Milton (05468) *(G-17356)*

Champlain Industries Inc.................... 802 651-0708
  17 Oak St Burlington (05401) *(G-17125)*

Champlain Software, Gloucester *Also Called: Para Research Inc (G-8951)*

Champlain Valley Equipment Inc.................... 802 524-6782
  7 Franklin Park W Saint Albans (05478) *(G-17518)*

Champlin-Packrite LLC.................... 860 559-6373
  151 Batson Dr Manchester (06042) *(G-1589)*

Chand LLC.................... 310 483-5769
  99 Circuit St Roxbury (02119) *(G-11688)*

Chandler Security Systems Inc.................... 207 576-3418
  1260 Lisbon St Lewiston (04240) *(G-4954)*

Chang Shing Tofu Inc.................... 617 868-8878
  37 Rogers St Cambridge (02142) *(G-7537)*

Change Hlthcare Phrm Sltons In.................... 207 622-7153
  45 Commerce Dr Ste 5 Augusta (04330) *(G-4468)*

Change Logic.................... 617 274-8661
  30 Trask St Gloucester (01930) *(G-8928)*

Channel Fish Co Inc.................... 617 569-3200
  370 E Eagle St Boston (02128) *(G-6648)*

Channel Sources LLC.................... 203 775-6464
  246 Federal Rd Ste A12-1 Brookfield (06804) *(G-515)*

Channel Sources Company, Brookfield *Also Called: Channel Sources LLC (G-515)*

Channelwave Software Inc **(DH)**.................... 617 621-1700
  1 Kendall Sq Bldg 200 Cambridge (02139) *(G-7538)*

Channing Bete Company Inc **(PA)**.................... 413 665-7611
  1 Community Pl South Deerfield (01373) *(G-11922)*

Channing-Bete, South Deerfield *Also Called: Channing Bete Company Inc (G-11922)*

Chante, Cranston *Also Called: Rolyn Inc (G-15908)*

Chapco Inc **(PA)**.................... 860 526-9535
  10 Denlar Dr Chester (06412) *(G-625)*

Chapin Packaging LLC.................... 203 202-2747
  1078 Post Rd Ste 1 Darien (06820) *(G-846)*

Chapin Printing Group, Darien *Also Called: Chapin Packaging LLC (G-846)*

Chapman Lumber Inc.................... 860 283-6213
  224 Watertown Rd Thomaston (06787) *(G-3616)*

Chapman Manufacturing Company.................... 860 349-9228
  471 New Haven Rd Durham (06422) *(G-896)*

Chapman Manufacturing Company Inc **(PA)**.................... 508 588-3200
  481 W Main St Avon (02322) *(G-6147)*

Charbert Inc.................... 401 364-7751
  830 Boylston St Ste 209 Chestnut Hill (02467) *(G-7998)*

Charbert Fabrics, Chestnut Hill *Also Called: Charbert Inc (G-7998)*

Charcuterie Artisans.................... 401 426-9499
  1000 Danielle Dr Mapleville (02839) *(G-16166)*

Charles A Richardson Inc.................... 508 339-8600
  330 Otis St Mansfield (02048) *(G-10041)*

Charles E Tuttle Co Inc **(DH)**.................... 802 773-8930
  364 Innovation Dr North Clarendon (05759) *(G-17413)*

Charles J Angelo Mfg Group LLC.................... 860 646-2378
  130 Chapel Rd Manchester (06042) *(G-1590)*

Charles K White.................... 203 631-2540
  2259 State St Hamden (06517) *(G-1417)*

Charles Leonard Steel Svcs LLC.................... 603 225-0211
  183 Pembroke Rd Concord (03301) *(G-14121)*

Charles P Blouin Inc **(PA)**.................... 603 474-3400
  203 New Zealand Rd Seabrook (03874) *(G-15586)*

Charles River Door Works.................... 617 828-3946
  3 Austin St Blackstone (01504) *(G-6493)*

Charles River Laboratories Inc.................... 860 429-7261
  67 Baxter Rd Storrs (06268) *(G-3511)*

Charles Rosenberg, Burlington *Also Called: Cherrybrook Kitchen LLC (G-7347)*

Charles Shcklton Mrnda Thmas L.................... 802 672-5175
  102 Mill Rd Bridgewater (05034) *(G-17111)*

Charles Smith Steel Inc.................... 603 753-9844
  115 N Main St Boscawen (03303) *(G-13988)*

Charles Thomae & Son Inc.................... 508 222-0785
  15 Maynard St Attleboro (02703) *(G-6001)*

Charlesbridge Publishing Inc **(PA)**.................... 617 926-0329
  9 Galen St Ste 220 Watertown (02472) *(G-12869)*

Chart Dist & Stor Group, Salem *Also Called: Chart Inc (G-15513)*

Chart Inc.................... 603 382-6551
  68 Stiles Rd Ste B Salem (03079) *(G-15513)*

Charter Next Generation Inc.................... 413 863-3171
  18 Industrial Blvd Turners Falls (01376) *(G-12444)*

Chartpak Inc **(HQ)**.................... 413 584-5446
  1 River Rd Leeds (01053) *(G-9621)*

Chas G Allen Realty LLC.................... 978 355-2911
  25 Williamsville Rd Barre (01005) *(G-6202)*

Chasco Inc.................... 603 436-2141
  15 Banfield Rd Unit 6 Portsmouth (03801) *(G-15371)*

Chase, Westwood *Also Called: Chase Corporation (G-13309)*

Chase Corp Inc.................... 781 332-0700
  375 University Ave Westwood (02090) *(G-13308)*

Chase Corporation.................... 508 731-2710
  24 Dana Rd Oxford (01540) *(G-11250)*

Chase Corporation **(HQ)**.................... 781 332-0700
  375 University Ave Westwood (02090) *(G-13309)*

Chase Electric Motors LLC.................... 603 669-2565
  10 Iron Horse Dr Bedford (03110) *(G-13921)*

Chase Graphics Inc.................... 860 315-9006
  124 School St Putnam (06260) *(G-2849)*

Chase Machine & Engineering, West Warwick *Also Called: Chase Machine Co Inc (G-16907)*

Chase Machine Co Inc.. 401 821-8879
  324 Washington St West Warwick (02893) *(G-16907)*

Chase Media Group... 914 962-3871
  31 Pecks Ln Ste 3 Newtown (06470) *(G-2337)*

Chase Press, Newtown *Also Called: Shop Smart Central Inc (G-2346)*

Chase Speciality Coating.. 781 332-0700
  375 University Ave Westwood (02090) *(G-13310)*

Chasm Advanced Materials Inc **(PA)**..................... **781 821-0443**
  480 Neponset St Ste 6 Canton (02021) *(G-7778)*

Chatco, Brockton *Also Called: Chatham Plastic Ventures Inc (G-7268)*

Chatham Plastic Ventures Inc....................................... 518 392-5761
  1200 W Chestnut St Brockton (02301) *(G-7268)*

Chaucer Accessories Inc... 978 373-1566
  143 Essex St Ste 3 Haverhill (01832) *(G-9085)*

Chaucer Leather, Haverhill *Also Called: Chaucer Accessories Inc (G-9085)*

Chauvin Arnoux Inc **(PA)**.. **603 749-6434**
  15 Faraday Dr Dover (03820) *(G-14221)*

Check Point Software Tech Inc...................................... 978 635-0300
  179 Great Rd Ste 111a Acton (01720) *(G-5743)*

Checkerboard Ltd... 508 835-2475
  216 W Boylston St West Boylston (01583) *(G-12957)*

Checkmate, Cambridge *Also Called: Checkmate Pharmaceuticals Inc (G-7539)*

Checkmate Pharmaceuticals Inc.................................... 617 682-3625
  245 Main St Fl 2 Cambridge (02142) *(G-7539)*

Checkpoint Therapeutics Inc... 781 652-4500
  95 Sawyer Rd Ste 110 Waltham (02453) *(G-12624)*

Checksforlesscom.. 800 245-5775
  200 Riverside Industrial Pkwy Portland (04103) *(G-5198)*

Checon, North Attleboro *Also Called: Portwest Corporation (G-10884)*

Checon LLC.. 508 838-2060
  527 Pleasant St Bldg 11 Attleboro (02703) *(G-6002)*

Cheer Pack North America, West Bridgewater *Also Called: Cheer Pack North America LLC (G-12968)*

Cheer Pack North America LLC..................................... 508 927-7800
  1 United Dr West Bridgewater (02379) *(G-12968)*

Cheetah Medical Inc **(PA)**...................................... **617 964-0613**
  1320 Centre St Ste 400 Newton (02459) *(G-10744)*

Chef Software Inc **(HQ)**... **206 508-4799**
  15 Wayside Rd Ste 400 Burlington (01803) *(G-7346)*

Chef-A-Roni, East Greenwich *Also Called: Eastern Food Industries Inc (G-15983)*

Chefs Equipment Emporium, Windsor *Also Called: Demartino Fixture Co Inc (G-4270)*

Chelsea Clock LLC... 617 884-0250
  101 2nd St Chelsea (02150) *(G-7977)*

Chelsea Green Publishing Co.. 802 295-6300
  85 N Main St Ste 120 White River Junction (05001) *(G-17705)*

Chelsea Industries Inc.. 617 232-6060
  46a Glen Ave Newton (02459) *(G-10745)*

Chelsea Record, Revere *Also Called: Independant Newspaper Group (G-11619)*

Chemart Company.. 401 333-9200
  11 New England Way Lincoln (02865) *(G-16125)*

Chemart Company **(PA)**.. **401 333-9200**
  15 New England Way Lincoln (02865) *(G-16126)*

Chemco Corporation... 978 687-9000
  46 Stafford St Lawrence (01841) *(G-9547)*

Chemetal Division, Easthampton *Also Called: October Company Inc (G-8456)*

Chemetal Division, Easthampton *Also Called: October Company Inc (G-8457)*

Chemgenes, Billerica *Also Called: Chemgenes Corporation (G-6422)*

Chemgenes Corporation.. 978 694-4500
  900 Middlesex Tpke Bldg 2 Billerica (01821) *(G-6422)*

Chemi-Graphic Inc... 413 589-0151
  340 State St Ludlow (01056) *(G-9942)*

Chemical & Metallurgical Div, Exeter *Also Called: Osram Sylvania Inc (G-14299)*

Chemical Consolidated Division, Nashua *Also Called: Coating Systems Inc (G-15082)*

Chemical Systems Services Inc...................................... 508 431-9995
  12 Field Rd Attleboro (02703) *(G-6003)*

Chemotex Prtctive Catings Corp **(PA)**.................... **860 349-0144**
  15 Commerce Cir Durham (06422) *(G-897)*

Chemtura, Middlebury *Also Called: Chemtura USA Corporation (G-1714)*

Chemtura USA, Shelton *Also Called: Lanxess Solutions US Inc (G-3027)*

Chemtura USA Corporation.. 203 573-2000
  199 Benson Rd Middlebury (06762) *(G-1714)*

Cheng & Tsui Co Inc.. 617 988-2400
  25 West St Boston (02111) *(G-6649)*

Chep.. 207 883-0244
  7 Washington Ave Scarborough (04074) *(G-5428)*

Cherise Cpl LLC.. 203 238-3482
  57 S Broad St Meriden (06450) *(G-1660)*

Cherry Hill Construction Corp....................................... 781 826-6886
  722 Washington St Pembroke (02359) *(G-11360)*

Cherry Hill Pool & Spa, Pembroke *Also Called: Cherry Hill Construction Corp (G-11360)*

Cherry Point Products Inc... 207 546-0930
  54 Wyman Rd Milbridge (04658) *(G-5060)*

Cherry Semiconductor Corp.. 401 885-3600
  2000 S County Trl East Greenwich (02818) *(G-15977)*

Cherrybrook Kitchen LLC.. 781 272-0400
  20 Mall Rd Ste 410 Burlington (01803) *(G-7347)*

Cherryfield Foods Inc **(DH)**.................................... **207 546-7573**
  320 Ridge Rd Cherryfield (04622) *(G-4688)*

Cherubino Sealcoating LMC LLC.................................... 781 272-1020
  103 Cluff Crossing Rd Apt M1 Salem (03079) *(G-15514)*

Chesapeake Sciences - Ashaway, Ashaway *Also Called: L3 Technologies Inc (G-15744)*

Cheshire Cml LLC.. 203 238-3482
  21 Diana Ct Cheshire (06410) *(G-579)*

Cheshire Division, Cheshire *Also Called: Atlantic Inertial Systems Inc (G-573)*

Cheshire Herald, Wallingford *Also Called: True Publishing Company (G-3870)*

Cheshire Manufacturing Co Inc..................................... 203 272-3586
  312 E Johnson Ave Ste 1 Cheshire (06410) *(G-580)*

Cheshire Software Inc.. 617 527-4000
  1170 Walnut St Newton (02461) *(G-10746)*

Chessco Industries Inc **(PA)**.................................. **203 255-2804**
  1330 Post Rd E Ste 2 Westport (06880) *(G-4160)*

Chester Boatworks.. 860 526-2227
  444 Main St Deep River (06417) *(G-874)*

Chesterfield Custom, Chesterfield *Also Called: Chesterfield Products Inc (G-7997)*

Chesterfield Products Inc.. 413 296-0066
  11 Bofat Hill Rd Chesterfield (01012) *(G-7997)*

Chesterton, Groveland *Also Called: A W Chesterton Company (G-9012)*

Chestnut United Corporation... 860 584-0594
  281 Lake Ave Bristol (06010) *(G-426)*

Chew LLC... 617 945-1868
  1255 Boylston St Ste 3 Boston (02215) *(G-6650)*

Chew Publishing Inc.. 401 808-0648
  190 E Main Rd Ste 3 Middletown (02842) *(G-16171)*

Chewbarka Inc.. 404 464-9911
  165 Dyerville Ave Unit 2 Johnston (02919) *(G-16079)*

Chewbarka's Tags, Johnston *Also Called: Fred Ricci Tool Co Inc (G-16086)*

CHI Aerospace... 603 380-9951
  44 Durham St Portsmouth (03801) *(G-15372)*

Chiasma Inc.. 617 928-5300
  460 Totten Pond Rd Ste 530 Waltham (02451) *(G-12625)*

Chick Embroidery... 603 332-5487
  556 Portland St Rochester (03867) *(G-15469)*

Chick Trucking Inc... 603 659-3566
  Route 152 Newmarket (03857) *(G-15218)*

Chicken Soup For Soul LLC... 203 861-4000
  132 E Putnam Ave Ste 20 Cos Cob (06807) *(G-674)*

Chicken Soup For Soul Prdctons **(PA)**.................... **855 398-0443**
  132 E Putnam Ave Ste 20 Cos Cob (06807) *(G-675)*

Chicopee Foundations Inc... 413 594-4700
  158 New Lombard Rd Chicopee (01020) *(G-8015)*

Chicopee Provision Company Inc................................... 413 594-4765
  19 Sitarz Ave Chicopee (01013) *(G-8016)*

Chicopee Vision Center Inc... 413 796-7570
  1907 Wilbraham Rd Springfield (01129) *(G-12083)*

Chief Executive Group, Stamford *Also Called: Chief Executive Group LLC (G-3310)*

Chief Executive Group LLC **(PA)**............................ **785 832-0303**
  9 W Broad St Ste 430 Stamford (06902) *(G-3310)*

Chief Executive Group LP **(PA)**.............................. **203 930-2700**
  9 W Broad St Ste 430 Stamford (06902) *(G-3311)*

Chief Executive Magazine, Stamford *Also Called: Chief Executive Group LP (G-3311)*

**A
L
P
H
A
B
E
T
I
C**

Chief Logging & Cnstr Inc... 802 584-3868
   2494 Stone Rd South Ryegate (05069) *(G-17613)*

Chiesi Ventures Inc... 919 998-3330
   10 Post Office Sq Ste 1305 Boston (02109) *(G-6651)*

Childrens Health Market Inc..................................... 203 762-2938
   27 Cannon Rd Ste 1b Wilton (06897) *(G-4236)*

Childrens Medical Group **(PA)**................................ **860 242-8330**
   6 Northwestern Dr Ste 101 Bloomfield (06002) *(G-155)*

Chillybars Tddy Dog Bntown Brn, Needham *Also Called: Chillybear Inc* *(G-10507)*

Chillybear Inc **(PA)**... **781 455-6321**
   6 Brook Rd Needham (02494) *(G-10507)*

Chilmark Archtctural Wdwkg LLC............................ 508 856-9200
   705 Plantation St Worcester (01605) *(G-13706)*

Chilsons Shops Inc.. 413 529-8062
   8 Industrial Pkwy Easthampton (01027) *(G-8441)*

Chilton Furniture and Paint, Freeport *Also Called: Chilton Paint Co Inc ME* *(G-4800)*

Chilton Paint Co Inc ME... 207 865-4443
   184 Lower Main St Freeport (04032) *(G-4800)*

Chinamerica Fd Manufacture Inc............................. 617 426-1818
   133 Newmarket Sq Boston (02118) *(G-6652)*

Chinese Spaghetti Factory Inc................................ 617 445-7714
   83 Newmarket Sq Boston (02118) *(G-6653)*

Chinetco... 207 873-3351
   242 College Ave Waterville (04901) *(G-5594)*

Chipping & Logging... 207 625-4056
   37 Cross Rd Porter (04068) *(G-5165)*

Chisletts Boating & Design LLC.............................. 603 755-6815
   35 Industrial Park Dover (03820) *(G-14222)*

Chmc Otlrynglgic Fundation Inc **(PA)**.................... **617 355-8290**
   300 Longwood Ave Rm 273 Boston (02115) *(G-6654)*

Chmuras Bakery Inc **(PA)**.................................. **413 543-2521**
   12 Pulaski St Ste 14 Indian Orchard (01151) *(G-9471)*

Chocolate Delicacies, East Greenwich *Also Called: Tradest1* *(G-15994)*

Chocorua Valley Lumber Company........................... 508 883-6878
   1210 Pulaski Blvd Bellingham (02019) *(G-6288)*

Choice Graphics Inc... 978 948-2789
   140 Central St Ste 4 Rowley (01969) *(G-11672)*

Choice Magazine, Middletown *Also Called: American Library Association* *(G-1735)*

Chomerics Division, Hudson *Also Called: Parker-Hannifin Corporation* *(G-14534)*

Chopmist Hill Woodworks Ltd................................. 401 374-3143
   1586 Chopmist Hill Rd North Scituate (02857) *(G-16314)*

Chopper One Inc.. 207 444-5476
   215 Old Main St Eagle Lake (04739) *(G-4734)*

Choppers of New England....................................... 603 809-4391
   50 Bridge St Nashua (03060) *(G-15079)*

Chris Cross LLC.. 203 386-8426
   294 Benton St Stratford (06615) *(G-3526)*

Chris Ploof Designs Inc... 978 728-4905
   57 Nashua St Leominster (01453) *(G-9651)*

Chrisha Creations Ltd
   7 Industrial Dr S Smithfield (02917) *(G-16691)*

Christeyns Laundry Tech LLC................................. 617 203-2169
   100 Laurel St Ste 120 East Bridgewater (02333) *(G-8337)*

Christian Science Monitor, Boston *Also Called: Christian Science Pubg Soc* *(G-6655)*

Christian Science Pubg Soc **(PA)**........................ **617 450-2000**
   210 Massachusetts Ave Boston (02115) *(G-6655)*

Christopher Peacock Home LLC.............................. 203 388-4022
   9 Bettswood Rd Norwalk (06851) *(G-2481)*

Christopher-Gordon Publishing.............................. 781 762-5577
   3 Bailey St Foxboro (02035) *(G-8692)*

Christopoulos Designs Inc..................................... 203 576-1110
   195 Dewey St Bridgeport (06605) *(G-311)*

Chroma Color Corporation..................................... 978 537-3538
   50 Francis St Leominster (01453) *(G-9652)*

Chroma Technology Corp.. 802 428-2500
   10 Imtec Ln Bellows Falls (05101) *(G-17029)*

Chromalloy Component Svcs Inc............................. 203 924-1666
   415 Howe Ave Shelton (06484) *(G-2992)*

Chromalloy Component Svcs Inc............................. 860 688-7798
   601 Marshall Phelps Rd Windsor (06095) *(G-4266)*

Chromalloy Connecticut, Windsor *Also Called: Chromalloy Gas Turbine LLC* *(G-4267)*

Chromalloy Gas Turbine LLC.................................. 860 688-7798
   601 Marshall Phelps Rd Windsor (06095) *(G-4267)*

Chromatics Inc.. 203 743-6868
   19 Francis J Clarke Cir Bethel (06801) *(G-102)*

Chronicle Inc.. 802 525-3531
   133 Water Barton (05822) *(G-17027)*

Chronicle Printing Company................................... 860 423-8466
   1 Chronicle Rd Willimantic (06226) *(G-4217)*

Chronicle, The, Willimantic *Also Called: Chronicle Printing Company* *(G-4217)*

Chronicle, The, Barton *Also Called: Chronicle Inc* *(G-17027)*

Chronoflex, Wilmington *Also Called: Advansource Biomaterials Corporation* *(G-13374)*

Chronomatic Inc... 401 884-6361
   1503 S County Trl East Greenwich (02818) *(G-15978)*

Chuck Roast Equipment Inc **(PA)**....................... **603 447-5492**
   90 Odell Hill Rd Conway (03818) *(G-14178)*

Chuck Rose Inc... 603 746-2311
   100 Chase Farm Rd Contoocook (03229) *(G-14168)*

Chuckles Inc... 603 669-4228
   11925 S Willow St Manchester (03103) *(G-14828)*

Chucks Auto Body Towing...................................... 413 459-4636
   78 West St Chicopee (01013) *(G-8017)*

Church Hill Classics Ltd.. 800 477-9005
   594 Pepper St Monroe (06468) *(G-1909)*

Churchill Corporation... 781 665-4700
   344 Franklin St Melrose (02176) *(G-10315)*

Chyme... 603 893-7683
   50 Northwestern Dr Ste 11 Salem (03079) *(G-15515)*

CIA Ink, Fall River *Also Called: Corporate Image Apparel Inc* *(G-8532)*

Cianbro Fbrcation Coating Corp.............................. 207 487-3311
   335 Hunnewell Ave Pittsfield (04967) *(G-5158)*

Cici Bevin Gordon.. 860 365-5731
   9 Austin Dr Marlborough (06447) *(G-1642)*

Cico, Norwalk *Also Called: Twenty-Five Commerce Inc* *(G-2588)*

Cicor Americas Inc.. 617 576-2005
   185 Alewife Brook Pkwy Ste 410 Cambridge (02138) *(G-7540)*

Cid Performance Tool, Berlin *Also Called: Coastal Industrial Distrs Inc* *(G-59)*

Cidermillrunsterlingcom.. 978 422-8675
   15 Waushacum Ave Sterling (01564) *(G-12158)*

Cidra Chemical Management Inc **(HQ)**................. **203 265-0035**
   50 Barnes Park Rd N Ste 103 Wallingford (06492) *(G-3786)*

Cidra Corporate Services Inc **(HQ)**..................... **203 265-0035**
   50 Barnes Park Rd N Wallingford (06492) *(G-3787)*

Cidra Corporation.. 203 265-0035
   50 Barnes Park Rd N Ste 103 Wallingford (06492) *(G-3788)*

Cidra Minerals Processing Inc................................ 203 265-0035
   50 Barnes Park Rd N Wallingford (06492) *(G-3789)*

CIL Electroplating Inc **(PA)**................................ **978 683-2082**
   125 Glenn St Lawrence (01843) *(G-9548)*

CIL Electroplating Inc... 978 683-2082
   9 Mill St Lawrence (01840) *(G-9549)*

CIL Inc.. 978 685-8300
   400 Canal St Lawrence (01840) *(G-9550)*

CIM Industries Inc... 800 543-3458
   26 Summer St Bridgewater (02325) *(G-7226)*

CIM Industries Inc... 603 924-9481
   23 Elm St Ste 2 Peterborough (03458) *(G-15313)*

Cimcon Software, Westford *Also Called: Cimcon Software LLC* *(G-13229)*

Cimcon Software LLC **(PA)**................................ **978 464-9180**
   234 Littleton Rd Ste 2h Westford (01886) *(G-13229)*

Cimetrics Inc.. 617 350-7550
   376 Washington St Ste 104 Malden (02148) *(G-10007)*

Cimini & Associates Inc.. 401 348-0388
   46 Airport Rd Westerly (02891) *(G-16929)*

Cimpress, Waltham *Also Called: Cimpress USA Incorporated* *(G-12627)*

Cimpress USA Incorporated................................... 866 207-4955
   275 Wyman St Waltham (02451) *(G-12626)*

Cimpress USA Incorporated **(DH)**....................... **781 652-6300**
   170 Data Dr Waltham (02451) *(G-12627)*

Cinco Medical, Wakefield *Also Called: Cardiovascular Instrument Corp* *(G-12504)*

CinCor Pharma Inc... 513 800-2585
   230 3rd Ave Ste 6 Waltham (02451) *(G-12628)*

Cindy's Kitchen, Brockton *Also Called: Custom Blends Inc* **(G-7272)**

Cine Magnetics Inc **(HQ)**... **914 273-7600**
   9 W Broad St Ste 730 Stamford (06902) **(G-3312)**

Cintas, Pawtucket *Also Called: Cintas Corporation No 2* **(G-16354)**

Cintas Corporation No 2.. 401 723-7300
   700 Narragansett Park Dr Pawtucket (02861) **(G-16354)**

Cira, New Haven *Also Called: Yale University* **(G-2218)**

Circle Labs Bio Inc.. 516 660-6045
   400 Technology Sq Ste 602 Cambridge (02139) **(G-7541)**

Circle Wire, Pepperell *Also Called: Astron Inc* **(G-11383)**

Circor, Burlington *Also Called: Circor International Inc* **(G-7351)**

Circor LLC.. 781 270-1200
   30 Corporate Dr Ste 200 Burlington (01803) **(G-7348)**

Circor Energy LLC.. 781 270-1200
   30 Corporate Dr Ste 200 Burlington (01803) **(G-7349)**

Circor German Holdings LLC **(DH)**.................................. **781 270-1200**
   30 Corporate Dr Ste 200 Burlington (01803) **(G-7350)**

Circor International, Burlington *Also Called: Circor LLC* **(G-7348)**

Circor International **(HQ)**.. **781 270-1200**
   30 Corporate Dr Ste 200 Burlington (01803) **(G-7351)**

Circuit Breaker Sales Ne LLC... 203 888-7500
   79 Main St Seymour (06483) **(G-2958)**

Circuit Breaker Sales Ne Inc., Seymour *Also Called: Circuit Breaker Sales Ne LLC* **(G-2958)**

Circuit Connect Inc... 603 880-7447
   4 State St Nashua (03063) **(G-15080)**

Circuit Systems Inc **(PA)**... **413 562-5019**
   54 Mainline Dr Ste B Westfield (01085) **(G-13159)**

Circuit Technology Center Inc... 978 374-5000
   22 Parkridge Rd Haverhill (01835) **(G-9086)**

Circuit Technology LLC... 603 424-2200
   6a Continental Blvd Merrimack (03054) **(G-14977)**

Circuitmedic, Haverhill *Also Called: Circuit Technology Center Inc* **(G-9086)**

Cirtec Medical Corp... 860 814-3973
   99 Print Shop Rd Enfield (06082) **(G-1123)**

Cirtec Medical Corp... 978 703-6822
   1001 Pawtucket Blvd Lowell (01854) **(G-9867)**

Cirtech, Merrimack *Also Called: Circuit Technology LLC* **(G-14977)**

Cirtronics Corporation... 603 249-9190
   528 Route 13 S Ste 130 Milford (03055) **(G-15016)**

Cisco Brewers Portsmouth, Portsmouth *Also Called: Cisco Brewers Portsmouth LLC* **(G-15373)**

Cisco Brewers Portsmouth LLC... 603 380-7575
   35 Corporate Dr Portsmouth (03801) **(G-15373)**

Cisco Brwers Dstlrs Vntners Sp... 508 325-5929
   85 Northern Ave Boston (02210) **(G-6656)**

Cisco Systems Inc... 978 936-0000
   500 Beaver Brook Rd R Boxborough (01719) **(G-7149)**

Cistercian Abbey Spencer Inc... 508 885-8700
   167 N Spencer Rd Spencer (01562) **(G-12056)**

Citius Printing & Graphics LLC.. 781 547-5550
   20 Clematis Ave Waltham (02453) **(G-12629)**

Citiworks Corp.. 508 761-7400
   20 Rutledge Dr Attleboro (02703) **(G-6004)**

Citiworks RI, Attleboro *Also Called: Citiworks Corp* **(G-6004)**

Citizen Cider LLC... 802 288-0576
   180 Flynn Ave Burlington (05401) **(G-17126)**

Citizen Cider LLC **(PA)**... **802 448-3278**
   316 Pine St Ste 114 Burlington (05401) **(G-17127)**

Citizen Printers Incorporated.. 207 824-2444
   19 Crooked River Cswy Albany Twp (04217) **(G-4400)**

Citra Labs LLC... 781 848-9386
   55 Messina Dr Ste 4 Braintree (02184) **(G-7173)**

Citra-Solv LLC.. 203 778-0881
   98 Mill Plain Rd Ste 4c Danbury (06811) **(G-721)**

City Boy Logs LLC.. 802 496-4372
   612 Mansfield Rd Waitsfield (05673) **(G-17665)**

City Carting, Stamford *Also Called: City Carting Inc* **(G-3313)**

City Carting Inc... 888 413-3344
   8 Viaduct Rd Stamford (06907) **(G-3313)**

City Feed and Lumber Co Inc **(PA)**................................. **802 524-2136**
   44 Lower Newton St Saint Albans (05478) **(G-17519)**

City Fresh Foods, Roxbury *Also Called: City Fresh Foods Inc* **(G-11689)**

City Fresh Foods, Roxbury *Also Called: City Fresh Foods Inc* **(G-11690)**

City Fresh Foods Inc... 617 606-7123
   77 Shirley St Roxbury (02119) **(G-11689)**

City Fresh Foods Inc... 617 606-7123
   69 Shirley St Roxbury (02119) **(G-11690)**

City Machine Corporation... 413 538-9766
   155 N Canal St Holyoke (01040) **(G-9247)**

City of Boston.. 617 635-3700
   174 North St Boston (02109) **(G-6657)**

City of Manchester... 603 624-6482
   1581 Lake Shore Rd Manchester (03109) **(G-14829)**

City Pblcations Greater Boston... 617 549-7622
   18 Lake Shore Dr Wayland (01778) **(G-12924)**

City Tire Co Inc.. 413 534-2946
   1385 Memorial Dr Chicopee (01020) **(G-8018)**

City Tire Co Inc.. 413 445-5578
   560 Hubbard Ave Pittsfield (01201) **(G-11396)**

City Tire Co Inc **(PA)**.. **413 737-1419**
   25 Avocado St Springfield (01104) **(G-12084)**

City Welding & Fabrication Inc.. 508 853-6000
   10 Ararat St Ste 1 Worcester (01606) **(G-13707)**

City Winery Boston LLC.. 617 933-8047
   80 Beverly St Boston (02114) **(G-6658)**

Cives Corporation.. 207 622-6141
   103 Lipman Rd Augusta (04330) **(G-4469)**

Cives Steel, Augusta *Also Called: Cives Corporation* **(G-4469)**

Civitas Therapeutics Inc... 617 884-3004
   190 Everett Ave Chelsea (02150) **(G-7978)**

CJ First Candle.. 203 966-1300
   21 Locust Ave Ste 2b New Canaan (06840) **(G-2077)**

CJ International Inc... 401 944-4700
   150 Niantic Ave Providence (02907) **(G-16499)**

Cjf Group Ltd... 401 421-2000
   40 Brenton Ave Providence (02906) **(G-16500)**

Cjmco, Bolton *Also Called: Carlyle Johnson Machine Co LLC* **(G-219)**

CJS Millwork Inc.. 203 708-0080
   425 Fairfield Ave Ste 12 Stamford (06902) **(G-3314)**

CJS Workshop LLC.. 323 445-5012
   31 Adams Ave Groton (01450) **(G-9008)**

Ckg Limited... 781 893-2514
   39 Revere St Gloucester (01930) **(G-8929)**

Ckh Industries Inc.. 860 563-2999
   365 Silas Deane Hwy Ste 1 Wethersfield (06109) **(G-4203)**

CKS Packaging Inc... 203 729-0716
   10 Great Hill Rd Naugatuck (06770) **(G-1952)**

Clade Therapeutics Inc... 617 546-7460
   201 Brookline Ave Ste 1002 Boston (02215) **(G-6659)**

Clamar Floats Inc.. 603 828-5373
   74 Orion St Brunswick (04011) **(G-4644)**

Clandestine Kitchen LLC.. 415 516-0378
   3 Birch Cir Hingham (02043) **(G-9147)**

Claremont Sales Corporation... 860 349-4499
   35 Winsome Rd Durham (06422) **(G-898)**

Claret Medical Inc.. 707 528-9300
   300 Boston Scientific Way Marlborough (01752) **(G-10132)**

Clariant Corporation... 401 823-2000
   500 Washington St Coventry (02816) **(G-15809)**

Claricode Inc... 781 449-2450
   980 Washington St Ste 330 Dedham (02026) **(G-8238)**

Clarion Ux, Shelton *Also Called: Urban Exposition LLC* **(G-3074)**

Clarios LLC.. 603 222-2400
   477 Congress St 6th Fl Portland (04101) **(G-5199)**

Clarios LLC.. 603 222-2400
   915 Holt Ave Unit 7 Manchester (03109) **(G-14830)**

Clarios LLC.. 401 235-6700
   6 Blackstone Valley Pl Ste 202 Lincoln (02865) **(G-16127)**

Claris Vision LLC... 508 994-1400
   51 State Rd North Dartmouth (02747) **(G-10991)**

Clarity Output Solutions LLC.. 800 414-1624
   860 Honeyspot Rd Stratford (06615) **(G-3527)**

A
L
P
H
A
B
E
T
I
C

Clark Hammerbeam Corporation............................ 781 461-1946
  886 Washington St Dedham (02026) *(G-8239)*

Clark Mailing Service Inc.................................... 508 752-1953
  41 Jackson St Worcester (01608) *(G-13708)*

Clark Metal Fabrication Inc................................... 207 330-6322
  1463 Auburn Rd Turner (04282) *(G-5561)*

Clark Solutions, Hudson *Also Called: The Tyler Co Inc (G-9419)*

Clark Summit Alpacas LLC.................................. 603 464-2588
  168 Wolf Hill Rd Deering (03244) *(G-14187)*

Clark-Cutler-Mcdermott Company............................ 508 528-1200
  5 Fisher St Franklin (02038) *(G-8823)*

Clarke Distribution Corp.................................... 203 838-9385
  64 S Main St Norwalk (06854) *(G-2482)*

Clarke International Bus Inc................................. 860 632-1149
  7232 Town Pl Middletown (06457) *(G-1743)*

Clarkie Industries.. 508 404-0202
  182 Grant St North Attleboro (02760) *(G-10870)*

Clarktron Products Inc...................................... 203 333-6517
  1525 Kings Hwy Ste 7 Fairfield (06824) *(G-1178)*

Clarkworks Machine... 978 692-2556
  496 Groton Rd Ste 5 Westford (01886) *(G-13230)*

Clarus, Westford *Also Called: Carnegie Dartlet LLC (G-13228)*

Classic Coil Company Inc................................... 860 583-7600
  205 Century Dr Bristol (06010) *(G-427)*

Classic Copy & Printing, Cambridge *Also Called: John Karl Dietrich & Assoc (G-7619)*

Classic Dsgns By Mtthew Brak I............................ 802 748-6062
  84 Central St Ste 104 Saint Johnsbury (05819) *(G-17541)*

Classic Envelope Inc....................................... 508 731-6747
  120 Gilboa St Unit 1 East Douglas (01516) *(G-8349)*

Classic Graphics Corp...................................... 203 323-6635
  652 Glenbrook Rd Ste 3-308 Stamford (06906) *(G-3315)*

Classic Kitchen Design Inc................................. 508 775-3075
  127 Airport Rd Hyannis (02601) *(G-9431)*

Classic Kitchens & Interiors, Hyannis *Also Called: Classic Kitchen Design Inc (G-9431)*

Classic Label Inc.. 203 389-3535
  10 Research Dr Woodbridge (06525) *(G-4378)*

Classic Prep Childrenswear Inc............................. 203 286-6204
  161 Rowayton Ave Norwalk (06853) *(G-2483)*

Classic Signs Inc.. 603 883-0384
  13 Columbia Dr Unit 16 Amherst (03031) *(G-13864)*

Classic Tractor Services LLC............................... 781 585-2050
  8b Grove St Kingston (02364) *(G-9506)*

Classsick Custom LLC...................................... 401 475-7288
  5 Carpenter St Ste 101 Pawtucket (02860) *(G-16355)*

Clay Furniture, Manchester *Also Called: CFI Millwork Inc (G-1588)*

Clayton LLC DBA Blbird Grphic.............................. 617 250-8500
  17 Everberg Rd Ste E Woburn (01801) *(G-13542)*

CLC Bio LLC... 617 945-0178
  100 Cummings Ctr Ste 407j Beverly (01915) *(G-6339)*

Clean Air Group Inc **(PA)**.............................. **203 335-3700**
  418 Meadow St Ste 204 Fairfield (06824) *(G-1179)*

Clean Away Inc... 860 985-6743
  154 Peirce St East Greenwich (02818) *(G-15979)*

Clean Products LLC... 508 676-9355
  537 Quequechan St Fall River (02721) *(G-8529)*

Clean Run Productions LLC.................................. 413 532-1389
  17 Industrial Dr South Hadley (01075) *(G-11960)*

Clean Water Ventures Inc................................... 858 437-3294
  81 Ocean State Dr North Kingstown (02852) *(G-16237)*

Cleaner Home Living, Hudson *Also Called: Butler Home Products LLC (G-9359)*

Clear Align LLC.. 603 889-2116
  24 Simon St Nashua (03060) *(G-15081)*

Clear Carbon & Components Inc.............................. 401 254-5085
  108 Tupelo St Bristol (02809) *(G-15758)*

Clear Edge Power International Service LLC.................. 860 727-2200
  195 Governors Hwy South Windsor (06074) *(G-3128)*

Clear Water Plasma, Norwalk *Also Called: Aqua Pulsar LLC (G-2463)*

Clearh2o Inc.. 207 221-0039
  85 Bradley Dr Westbrook (04092) *(G-5621)*

Clearly Balanced Days LLC................................. 833 223-4040
  7 Fruite St Unit C Belmont (03220) *(G-13960)*

Clearmotion, Billerica *Also Called: Clearmotion Inc (G-6423)*

Clearmotion Inc **(PA)**.................................. **617 313-0822**
  805 Middlesex Tpke Billerica (01821) *(G-6423)*

Clearspan, Glastonbury *Also Called: Clearspan Fabr Strctres Intl I (G-1274)*

Clearspan, South Windsor *Also Called: Engineering Services & Pdts Co (G-3144)*

Clearspan Fabr Strctres Intl I.............................. 866 643-1010
  703 Hebron Ave Ste 3 Glastonbury (06033) *(G-1274)*

Clearswift Corporation...................................... 781 839-7321
  1050 Winter St Ste 1000 Waltham (02451) *(G-12630)*

Clearwter Tech Cnslting Wtr Sv............................. 781 871-5157
  83 E Water St Rockland (02370) *(G-11640)*

Cleary Millwork Company Inc................................ 800 486-7600
  2049 Silas Deane Hwy Ste 1 Rocky Hill (06067) *(G-2918)*

Cleco Manufacturing, Hudson *Also Called: Concrete Systems Inc (G-14491)*

Clematis Machine & Fix Co Inc.............................. 781 894-0777
  42 Clematis Ave Waltham (02453) *(G-12631)*

Clementia Phrmcuticals USA Inc............................ 857 226-5588
  275 Grove St Ste 2400 Auburndale (02466) *(G-6130)*

Clever Green Cabinets LLC.................................. 508 963-6776
  738 Main St Waltham (02451) *(G-12632)*

Click Bond Inc... 860 274-5435
  18 Park Rd Watertown (06795) *(G-4005)*

Cliggott Publishing, Darien *Also Called: Informa Tech Holdings LLC (G-849)*

Clinical Dynamics, Bristol *Also Called: CD Management LLC (G-424)*

Clinical Dynamics Conn LLC................................ 203 269-0090
  225 N Main St Bristol (06010) *(G-428)*

Clinical Instruments Intl................................... 781 221-2266
  63 2nd Ave Burlington (01803) *(G-7352)*

Clinton BCI Inc.. 978 365-7335
  179 Woodlawn St Clinton (01510) *(G-8075)*

Clinton G Bradbury Inc..................................... 207 562-8014
  1180 Route 2 Ste 5 Rumford (04276) *(G-5355)*

Clinton Instrument Company................................. 860 669-7548
  295 E Main St Clinton (06413) *(G-638)*

Clinton Instrument Company, Clinton *Also Called: Clinton Instrument Company (G-638)*

Clinton Nursery Products Inc **(PA)**..................... **860 399-3000**
  517 Pond Meadow Rd Westbrook (06498) *(G-4137)*

Clinton Nypro, Clinton *Also Called: Nypro Inc (G-8087)*

Clivus Multrum Inc... 978 725-5591
  15 Union St Ste 412 Lawrence (01840) *(G-9551)*

Close To Home, Glastonbury *Also Called: R & M Associates Inc (G-1296)*

Closets By Design, Shirley *Also Called: Jamesbrook Enterprises Inc (G-11818)*

Closettec, North Smithfield *Also Called: KB Surfaces LLC (G-16324)*

Cloud Peak Energy Inc **(PA)**........................... **307 687-6000**
  606 Post Rd E # 624 Westport (06880) *(G-4161)*

Cloud Software Group Inc................................... 603 622-5109
  150 Dow St Manchester (03101) *(G-14831)*

Clown Shoes Beer, Boston *Also Called: Harpoon Distributing Co Inc (G-6781)*

Clozex Medical Inc... 781 237-1673
  375 West St West Bridgewater (02379) *(G-12969)*

Clss, Concord *Also Called: Charles Leonard Steel Svcs LLC (G-14121)*

Cly-Del Manufacturing Company.............................. 203 574-2100
  151 Sharon Rd Waterbury (06705) *(G-3898)*

Clyde Bergemann Bachmann, New Gloucester *Also Called: Bachmann Industries Inc (G-5083)*

CM Almy & Son Inc... 207 487-3232
  133 Ruth St Pittsfield (04967) *(G-5159)*

CMC Materials Inc **(HQ)**............................... **978 436-6500**
  129 Concord Rd Billerica (01821) *(G-6424)*

CMC Materials Inc... 781 530-3833
  1050 Winter St Waltham (02451) *(G-12633)*

Cmd, Dexter *Also Called: Cmd Enterprises LLC (G-4726)*

Cmd Enterprises LLC....................................... 207 745-9985
  363 Garland Rd Dexter (04930) *(G-4726)*

Cmd Logging.. 603 986-5055
  520 N Barnstead Rd Center Barnstead (03225) *(G-14049)*

Cme, North Adams *Also Called: Cordmaster Engineering Co Inc (G-10805)*

Cmhanb LLC... 860 241-0112
  1 Financial Plz Fl 16 Hartford (06103) *(G-1474)*

CMI, Enfield *Also Called: Control Module Inc (G-1125)*

CMI, Ayer *Also Called: Creative Materials Inc (G-6180)*

CMI Media Management, Stamford *Also Called: Cine Magnetics Inc (G-3312)*

CMI Restructuring Inc.. 413 562-3664
1 Cycle St Westfield (01085) *(G-13160)*

CMI Specialty Products Inc.. 860 585-0409
105 Redstone Hill Rd Bristol (06010) *(G-429)*

Cmo Partners Inc.. 617 875-5449
8 Cook St 10 Billerica (01821) *(G-6425)*

Cmp, Woburn *Also Called: Continental Metal Pdts Co Inc (G-13546)*

Cmt Materials Inc.. 508 226-3901
107 Frank Mossberg Dr Attleboro (02703) *(G-6005)*

CN Custom Cabinets Inc.. 978 300-5531
599 Canal St Lawrence (01840) *(G-9552)*

Cnc Engineering Inc... 860 749-1780
19 Bacon Rd Enfield (06082) *(G-1124)*

Cnc International Inc... 401 769-6100
20 Privilege St Woonsocket (02895) *(G-16953)*

CNc International Ltd Partnr.. 401 769-6100
20 Privilege St Woonsocket (02895) *(G-16954)*

Cnc North Inc.. 603 542-3361
16 Industrial Blvd Claremont (03743) *(G-14084)*

CNE Machine Inc... 508 668-4110
2000 Main St Ste 4 Walpole (02081) *(G-12556)*

CNi Corp.. 603 249-5075
468 Route 13 S Milford (03055) *(G-15017)*

Cns Outdoor Technologies LLC...................................... 413 475-3840
627 Barton Rd Greenfield (01301) *(G-8986)*

Co Op Creamery.. 802 524-6581
140 Federal St Saint Albans (05478) *(G-17520)*

Coactive Technologies LLC... 617 969-3700
15 Riverdale Ave Ste 1 Newton (02458) *(G-10747)*

Coast To Cast Ff E Instlltons.. 603 433-0164
2 Spring Hill Rd Greenland (03840) *(G-14368)*

Coastal Blueberry Service Inc **(PA)**............................... **207 667-9750**
Rural Rte 4 Thorsen Rd Hancock (04640) *(G-4868)*

Coastal Business Center Inc.. 207 882-7197
62 Old Ferry Rd Wiscasset (04578) *(G-5697)*

Coastal Exteriors, Wallingford *Also Called: Coastal Exteriors LLC (G-3790)*

Coastal Exteriors LLC... 203 626-5396
10 Winding Brook Ln Wallingford (06492) *(G-3790)*

Coastal Industrial Distrs Inc.. 207 286-3319
56 Willow Brook Dr Berlin (06037) *(G-59)*

Coastal Industries Inc.. 978 373-1543
77 Newark St Haverhill (01832) *(G-9087)*

Coastal McHnery Eqpment Apprse, New Bedford *Also Called: Nery Corporation (G-10626)*

Coastal Metal Fab.. 207 729-5101
120 Old Lisbon Rd Topsham (04086) *(G-5547)*

Coastal Printing, Newburyport *Also Called: Harborside Printing Co Inc (G-10686)*

Coastal Speedpro, Portsmouth *Also Called: Franklin Exeter Inc (G-15391)*

Coastal Steel Corporation... 860 443-4073
10 Mallard Ln Waterford (06385) *(G-3986)*

Coastal Style LLC.. 603 328-2000
259 Grant Ave Portsmouth (03801) *(G-15374)*

Coastal Traffic... 207 351-8673
26 Brickyard Ct Ste 1 York (03909) *(G-5711)*

Coastal Woodworking Inc.. 207 563-1072
16 Sand Hill Dr Nobleboro (04555) *(G-5100)*

Coastal Woodworks & Display, Nobleboro *Also Called: Coastal Woodworking Inc (G-5100)*

Coastal-N-Counters Inc... 508 539-3500
92 Industrial Dr Mashpee (02649) *(G-10251)*

Coastline Environmental LLC... 203 483-6898
12 Ridgetop Ln North Branford (06471) *(G-2362)*

Coaters Inc... 508 996-5700
305 Nash Rd Unit 1 New Bedford (02746) *(G-10578)*

Coating Application Tech... 781 491-0699
219 New Boston St Woburn (01801) *(G-13543)*

Coating Design Group Inc... 203 878-3663
430 Sniffens Ln Stratford (06615) *(G-3528)*

Coating House Inc... 413 525-3100
15 Benton Dr Ste 14 East Longmeadow (01028) *(G-8372)*

Coating Systems Inc.. 978 937-3712
90 Phoenix Ave Lowell (01852) *(G-9868)*

Coating Systems Inc.. 603 883-0553
55 Crown St Nashua (03060) *(G-15082)*

Coatings Adhesives Inks.. 978 352-7273
7 Martel Way Georgetown (01833) *(G-8907)*

Cobb/Ballou Findings, East Providence *Also Called: W R Cobb Company (G-16047)*

Cober Inc.. 203 855-8755
30 Moffitt St Stratford (06615) *(G-3529)*

Cobham... 603 418-9786
32 Industrial Dr Exeter (03833) *(G-14287)*

Cobham Antenna Systems, Exeter *Also Called: Cobham (G-14287)*

Cobham Def Electronic Systems....................................... 603 518-2716
336 Abby Rd Manchester (03103) *(G-14832)*

Cobham Defense Electronic Systems Corporation.............. 978 779-7000
1001 Pawtucket Blvd Lowell (01854) *(G-9869)*

Cobham Defense Electronics, Lowell *Also Called: Cobham Electronic Systems Inc (G-9870)*

Cobham Electronic Systems Inc.. 978 442-4700
1001 Pawtucket Blvd Lowell (01854) *(G-9870)*

Cobham Exeter Inc... 714 841-4976
11 Continental Dr Exeter (03833) *(G-14288)*

Cobham Metelics, Londonderry *Also Called: Macom Tech Sltons Holdings Inc (G-14765)*

Cobham Sensor Systems, Methuen *Also Called: Kevlin Corporation (G-10336)*

Cobra Green LLC.. 203 354-5000
50 N Water St Norwalk (06854) *(G-2484)*

Cobra Precision Machining Corp...................................... 603 434-8424
57 Birch Dr Petersham (01366) *(G-11388)*

Coburn Technologies Inc **(DH)**.................................... **860 648-6600**
83 Gerber Rd W South Windsor (06074) *(G-3129)*

Coburn Technologies Intl Inc **(DH)**............................... **860 648-6600**
55 Gerber Rd E South Windsor (06074) *(G-3130)*

Coca Cola Btlg Co of Cape Cod.. 508 888-0001
370 Route 130 Sandwich (02563) *(G-11748)*

Coca-Cola, South Windsor *Also Called: Coca-Cola Bevs Northeast Inc (G-3131)*

Coca-Cola, Waterford *Also Called: Coca-Cola Bottling Company of Southeastern New England Inc (G-3987)*

Coca-Cola, Farmington *Also Called: Farmington Coca Cola Btlg Dstr (G-4779)*

Coca-Cola, Presque Isle *Also Called: Coca-Cola Bevs Northeast Inc (G-5298)*

Coca-Cola, South Portland *Also Called: Coca-Cola Bevs Northeast Inc (G-5495)*

Coca-Cola, South Portland *Also Called: Maine Beverage Association (G-5507)*

Coca-Cola, Needham Heights *Also Called: Coca-Cola Bevs Northeast Inc (G-10535)*

Coca-Cola, Needham Heights *Also Called: Coca-Cola Btlg Sthstern Neng I (G-10536)*

Coca-Cola, Northampton *Also Called: Coca-Cola Btlg Sthstern Neng I (G-11055)*

Coca-Cola, Northampton *Also Called: Coca-Cola Refreshments USA Inc (G-11056)*

Coca-Cola, Sandwich *Also Called: Coca Cola Btlg Co of Cape Cod (G-11748)*

Coca-Cola, Sandwich *Also Called: Coca-Cola Bevs Northeast Inc (G-11749)*

Coca-Cola, Westborough *Also Called: Coca-Cola Btlg Sthstern Neng I (G-13088)*

Coca-Cola, Bedford *Also Called: Coca-Cola Beverages Northeast Inc (G-13922)*

Coca-Cola, Belmont *Also Called: Coca-Cola Bevs Northeast Inc (G-13961)*

Coca-Cola, Londonderry *Also Called: Coca-Cola Bevs Northeast Inc (G-14735)*

Coca-Cola, Manchester *Also Called: Coca-Cola Bevs Northeast Inc (G-14833)*

Coca-Cola, Seabrook *Also Called: Coca-Cola Bevs Northeast Inc (G-15587)*

Coca-Cola, Providence *Also Called: Coca-Cola Refreshments USA Inc (G-16501)*

Coca-Cola Beverages Northeast Inc **(HQ)**...................... **603 627-7871**
1 Executive Park Dr Ste 330 Bedford (03110) *(G-13922)*

Coca-Cola Bevs Northeast Inc.. 860 895-5100
451 Main St East Hartford (06118) *(G-981)*

Coca-Cola Bevs Northeast Inc.. 800 241-2653
359 Ellington Rd South Windsor (06074) *(G-3131)*

Coca-Cola Bevs Northeast Inc.. 207 764-4481
991 Skyway St Presque Isle (04769) *(G-5298)*

Coca-Cola Bevs Northeast Inc.. 207 773-5505
316 Western Ave South Portland (04106) *(G-5495)*

Coca-Cola Bevs Northeast Inc.. 978 459-9378
9 B St Needham Heights (02494) *(G-10535)*

Coca-Cola Bevs Northeast Inc.. 508 888-0001
370 Route 130 Sandwich (02563) *(G-11749)*

Coca-Cola Bevs Northeast Inc.. 603 267-8834
495 Depot St Belmont (03220) *(G-13961)*

Coca-Cola Bevs Northeast Inc.. 603 437-3530
7 Symmes Dr Londonderry (03053) *(G-14735)*

Coca-Cola Bevs Northeast Inc.................................. 603 623-6033
  99 Eddy Rd Manchester (03102) *(G-14833)*

Coca-Cola Bevs Northeast Inc.................................. 603 926-0404
  118 Stard Rd Seabrook (03874) *(G-15587)*

Coca-Cola Bottling Company of Southeastern New England Inc **(DH)**.............. **860 443-2816**
  150 Waterford Parkway S Waterford (06385) *(G-3987)*

Coca-Cola Btlg Sthstern Neng I.................................. 860 569-0037
  471 Main St # 471 East Hartford (06118) *(G-982)*

Coca-Cola Btlg Sthstern Neng I.................................. 413 448-8296
  180 Silvio O Conte Dr Greenfield (01301) *(G-8987)*

Coca-Cola Btlg Sthstern Neng I.................................. 781 449-4300
  9 B St Needham Heights (02494) *(G-10536)*

Coca-Cola Btlg Sthstern Neng I.................................. 413 586-8450
  45 Industrial Dr Northampton (01060) *(G-11055)*

Coca-Cola Btlg Sthstern Neng I.................................. 508 836-5200
  2 Sassacus Dr Westborough (01581) *(G-13088)*

Coca-Cola Btlg Sthstern Neng I.................................. 802 773-2768
  30 Quality Ln Rutland (05701) *(G-17492)*

Coca-Cola Refreshments USA Inc.................................. 413 772-2617
  180 Silvio O Conte Dr Greenfield (01301) *(G-8988)*

Coca-Cola Refreshments USA Inc.................................. 413 586-8450
  45 Industrial Dr Northampton (01060) *(G-11056)*

Coca-Cola Refreshments USA Inc.................................. 401 331-1981
  95 Pleasant Valley Pkwy Providence (02908) *(G-16501)*

Coccomo Brothers Drilling LLC.................................. 860 828-1632
  1897 Berlin Tpke Berlin (06037) *(G-60)*

Code Red Electronics LLC
  999 Foxon Rd Ste 30 North Branford (06471) *(G-2363)*

Codet-Newport Corporation **(HQ)**.................................. **802 334-5811**
  294 Crawford Rd Newport (05855) *(G-17398)*

Codiak Biosciences Inc **(PA)**.................................. **617 949-4100**
  35 Cambridgepark Dr Ste 500 Cambridge (02140) *(G-7542)*

Codiscope LLC.................................. 617 804-5428
  20 Park Plz Ste 1400 Boston (02116) *(G-6660)*

Codman & Shurtleff Inc.................................. 508 880-8100
  50 Scotland Park Dr Bridgewater (02324) *(G-7227)*

CODMAN & SHURTLEFF INC, Bridgewater *Also Called: Codman & Shurtleff Inc (G-7227)*

Cofco Americas Resources Corp **(HQ)**.................................. **203 658-2820**
  107 Elm St Fl 11 Stamford (06902) *(G-3316)*

Cofco-Gri Cof Cot Grins Sug Di, Stamford *Also Called: Cofco Americas Resources Corp (G-3316)*

Coffee By Design Inc **(PA)**.................................. **207 879-2233**
  1 Diamond St Portland (04101) *(G-5200)*

Coffee Enterprises, Hinesburg *Also Called: DC Enterprizes Inc (G-17290)*

Coffee Exchange Ltd.................................. 401 273-1198
  207 Wickenden St Providence (02903) *(G-16502)*

Cofmic Computers, Norwalk *Also Called: Norfield Data Products Inc (G-2546)*

Cogebi Inc.................................. 603 749-6896
  14 Faraday Dr Dover (03820) *(G-14223)*

COGENT BIOSCIENCES, Waltham *Also Called: Cogent Biosciences Inc (G-12634)*

Cogent Biosciences Inc **(PA)**.................................. **617 945-5576**
  275 Wyman St Fl 3 Waltham (02451) *(G-12634)*

Coghlin Companies Inc **(PA)**.................................. **508 753-2354**
  27 Otis St Westborough (01581) *(G-13089)*

Cognex, Natick *Also Called: Cognex Corporation (G-10472)*

Cognex, Natick *Also Called: Cognex Europe Inc (G-10473)*

Cognex, Natick *Also Called: Cognex Germany Inc (G-10474)*

Cognex, Natick *Also Called: Cognex International Inc (G-10475)*

Cognex Corporation **(PA)**.................................. **508 650-3000**
  1 Vision Dr Natick (01760) *(G-10472)*

Cognex Europe Inc **(HQ)**.................................. **855 426-4639**
  1 Vision Dr Natick (01760) *(G-10473)*

Cognex Germany Inc.................................. 508 650-3000
  1 Vision Dr Natick (01760) *(G-10474)*

Cognex International Inc **(HQ)**.................................. **508 650-3000**
  1 Vision Dr Natick (01760) *(G-10475)*

Cogstate Sport Inc.................................. 203 773-5010
  195 Church St Fl 10 New Haven (06510) *(G-2137)*

Cogz Systems LLC.................................. 203 263-7882
  58 Steeple View Ln Woodbury (06798) *(G-4385)*

Cohasa Publishing Inc.................................. 802 222-5281
  Rte 5 Bradford (05033) *(G-17061)*

Cohasset Redemption Inc.................................. 781 383-3100
  166 King St Cohasset (02025) *(G-8094)*

Cohen Slvstri Rogoff Hammer PC.................................. 617 426-6011
  3 Post Office Sq Ste 900 Boston (02109) *(G-6661)*

Coherent Inc.................................. 860 408-5066
  7 Airport Park Rd East Granby (06026) *(G-928)*

Coherent Bloomfield, Bloomfield *Also Called: Coherent Corp (G-156)*

Coherent Corp.................................. 860 243-9557
  1280 Blue Hills Ave Ste A Bloomfield (06002) *(G-156)*

Coherent Path Inc.................................. 508 612-4557
  183 Crescent St Waltham (02453) *(G-12635)*

Coherent-Deos LLC.................................. 860 243-9557
  1280 Blue Hills Ave Bloomfield (06002) *(G-157)*

Cohesion, Andover *Also Called: Nsight Inc (G-5902)*

Cohesive Biotechnologies, Franklin *Also Called: Cohesive Technologies Inc (G-8824)*

Cohesive Technologies Inc **(HQ)**.................................. **508 528-7989**
  101 Constitution Blvd Ste G Franklin (02038) *(G-8824)*

Coils Plus Inc.................................. 203 879-0755
  30 Town Line Rd Wolcott (06716) *(G-4362)*

Colby Footwear Inc.................................. 603 332-2283
  364 Route 108 Somersworth (03878) *(G-15612)*

Colcord Machine Co Inc.................................. 508 634-8840
  2 Rosenfeld Dr Ste G Hopedale (01747) *(G-9295)*

Cold Chain Technologies LLC.................................. 508 429-1395
  135 Constitution Blvd Franklin (02038) *(G-8825)*

Cold Chain Technologies LLC **(HQ)**.................................. **508 429-1395**
  135 Constitution Blvd Franklin (02038) *(G-8826)*

Cold Harbor Brewing Co LLC.................................. 508 768-5232
  66 Otis St Westborough (01581) *(G-13090)*

Cold Hollow Cider Mill Inc.................................. 802 244-8771
  3600 Waterbury-Stowe Rd Waterbury Center (05677) *(G-17680)*

Cold Hollow Precision Inc.................................. 802 933-5542
  154 Butternut Hollow Rd Enosburg Falls (05450) *(G-17221)*

Cold River Mining Inc.................................. 413 863-5445
  17 Masonic Ave Turners Falls (01376) *(G-12445)*

Cold Springs Spirits LLC.................................. 802 496-6973
  156 Cold Springs Farm Rd Warren (05674) *(G-17671)*

Cold Stone Creamery.................................. 860 669-7025
  7 Glenwood Rd Unit F Clinton (06413) *(G-639)*

Coldsnap Corp.................................. 617 733-9935
  6 Enterprise Rd Billerica (01821) *(G-6426)*

Coldwell Banker.................................. 978 851-3731
  1201 Main St Unit 1 Tewksbury (01876) *(G-12390)*

Cole Cabinet Co Inc.................................. 401 467-4343
  530 Wellington Ave Cranston (02910) *(G-15842)*

Cole Gunsmithing Inc.................................. 207 833-5027
  21 Bog Hollow Rd South Harpswell (04079) *(G-5486)*

Cole Hersee Company **(HQ)**.................................. **617 268-2100**
  20 Old Colony Ave Boston (02127) *(G-6662)*

Cole S Crew Machine Products.................................. 203 723-1418
  69 Dodge Ave North Haven (06473) *(G-2398)*

Colebrook Intrlcking Pvers Wll.................................. 401 835-6934
  114 Colebrook Rd Little Compton (02837) *(G-16160)*

Coleman Concrete.................................. 207 824-6300
  Nwbethel Rd Bethel (04217) *(G-4552)*

Coleman Concrete Inc.................................. 603 447-5936
  9 Nh Route 113 Albany (03818) *(G-13850)*

Coleman Concrete Division, Albany *Also Called: Alvin J Coleman & Son Inc (G-13848)*

Coley Pharmaceutical Group Inc.................................. 781 431-9000
  93 Worcester St Ste 101 Wellesley (02481) *(G-12939)*

Colfax Fluid Handling.................................. 413 436-7711
  82 Bridge St Warren (01083) *(G-12850)*

Colgate - Palmolive Company.................................. 207 467-2224
  27 Community Dr Sanford (04073) *(G-5392)*

Colins Aerospace, Farmington *Also Called: B/E Aerospace Inc (G-1207)*

Collabric.................................. 207 945-5095
  1017 School St Veazie (04401) *(G-5570)*

Collegium Pharmaceutical, Stoughton *Also Called: Collegium Pharmaceutical Inc (G-12201)*

Collegium Pharmaceutical Inc **(PA)**.................................. **781 713-3699**
  100 Technology Center Dr Ste 300 Stoughton (02072) *(G-12201)*

Collins, Rochester *Also Called: Collins Sports Center LLC (G-15470)*

(G-0000) Company's Geographic Section entry number

Collins & Jewell Company Inc.................................... 860 887-8813
  5 Rachel Dr Bozrah (06334) *(G-227)*

Collins Aerospace.. 978 303-6700
  7 Technology Park Dr Westford (01886) *(G-13231)*

Collins Aerospace.. 802 877-4000
  100 Panton Rd Vergennes (05491) *(G-17657)*

Collins Aerospace, Danbury *Also Called: Goodrich Corporation (G-751)*

Collins Aerospace, Windsor Locks *Also Called: Hamilton Sundstrand Corp (G-4330)*

Collins Aerospace, Peabody *Also Called: Rockwell Collins Inc (G-11338)*

Collins Manufacturing Inc... 978 768-2553
  239 Western Ave Essex (01929) *(G-8474)*

Collins Sheet Metal Inc... 207 384-4428
  510 Portland St Berwick (03901) *(G-4549)*

Collins Sports Center LLC... 603 335-1417
  663 Columbus Ave Rochester (03867) *(G-15470)*

Collt Mfg Inc... 508 376-2525
  1375 Main St Millis (02054) *(G-10449)*

Colonial Bronze Company.. 860 489-9233
  511 Winsted Rd Torrington (06790) *(G-3674)*

Colonial Coatings Inc... 203 783-9933
  66 Erna Ave Milford (06461) *(G-1811)*

Colonial Corrugated Pdts Inc..................................... 203 597-1707
  118 Railroad Hill St Waterbury (06708) *(G-3899)*

Colonial Cutlery Intl Inc... 401 737-0024
  606 Ten Rod Rd North Kingstown (02852) *(G-16238)*

Colonial Electronic Mfrs Inc....................................... 603 881-8244
  1 Chestnut St Ste 203 Nashua (03060) *(G-15083)*

Colonial Instant Printing, Warwick *Also Called: Romano Investments Inc (G-16854)*

Colonial Knife Company, North Kingstown *Also Called: Colonial Cutlery Intl Inc (G-16238)*

Colonial Lithograph Inc... 508 222-1832
  129 Bank St Ste 5 Attleboro (02703) *(G-6006)*

Colonial Machine & Tool Co Inc.................................. 401 826-1883
  5 Salvas Ave Coventry (02816) *(G-15810)*

Colonial Mills, Rumford *Also Called: Colonial Mills Inc (G-16665)*

Colonial Mills Inc... 401 724-6279
  77 Pawtucket Ave Rumford (02916) *(G-16665)*

Colonial Oil, Providence *Also Called: Sanoil LLC (G-16610)*

Colonial Printing Inc (PA)....................................... 401 691-3400
  333 Strawberry Field Rd Ste 11 Warwick (02886) *(G-16795)*

Colonial Times Publishing.. 781 274-9997
  805 Massachusetts Ave Lexington (02420) *(G-9730)*

Colonial Wood Products Inc....................................... 203 932-9003
  250 Callegari Dr West Haven (06516) *(G-4097)*

Colonial Woodworking Inc.. 203 866-5844
  841 Cove Rd Stamford (06902) *(G-3317)*

Coloniel Printing, Manchester *Also Called: Boles Enterprises Inc (G-14820)*

Colony Foods Inc... 978 794-1500
  439 Haverhill St Lawrence (01841) *(G-9553)*

Color, Londonderry *Also Called: Corportion For Lser Optics Res (G-14738)*

Color Change Technology Inc..................................... 978 377-0050
  30 Masschstts Ave Ste 306 North Andover (01845) *(G-10824)*

Color Craft Ltd.. 800 509-6563
  14 Airport Park Rd East Granby (06026) *(G-929)*

Color Kinetics.. 617 423-9999
  1 Van De Graaff Dr Burlington (01803) *(G-7353)*

Color Resource Concentrates, Leominster *Also Called: Resource Colors LLC (G-9702)*

Color-Tex International Inc... 617 269-8020
  28 Damrell St Boston (02127) *(G-6663)*

Colorgraphix LLC... 203 264-5212
  91 Willenbrock Rd Ste B5 Oxford (06478) *(G-2690)*

Colrain Sand and Gravel Inc...................................... 413 624-5118
  465 Jacksonville Rd Colrain (01340) *(G-8095)*

Colt Defense Holding, West Hartford *Also Called: Colt Defense LLC (G-4053)*

Colt Defense LLC (HQ).. 860 232-4489
  547 New Park Ave West Hartford (06110) *(G-4053)*

Colt Heel Div Montello Heel, Brockton *Also Called: Montello Heel Mfg Inc (G-7296)*

Colt Refining Inc (PA)... 603 429-9966
  12a Star Dr Merrimack (03054) *(G-14978)*

Colts Plastics Company Inc....................................... 860 774-2277
  969 N Main St Dayville (06241) *(G-861)*

Colucid Pharmaceuticals Inc...................................... 857 285-6495
  222 3rd St Ste 1320 Cambridge (02142) *(G-7543)*

Columbia, Westfield *Also Called: CMI Restructuring Inc (G-13160)*

Columbia ASC Inc.. 978 683-2205
  165 S Broadway Ste167 Lawrence (01843) *(G-9554)*

Columbia Electrical Contrs Inc................................... 508 366-8297
  27 Otis St Ste 300 Westborough (01581) *(G-13091)*

Columbia Forest Products Inc..................................... 207 760-3800
  395 Missile St Presque Isle (04769) *(G-5299)*

Columbia Forest Products Inc..................................... 802 334-6711
  115 Columbia Way Newport (05855) *(G-17399)*

Columbia Manufacturing Inc....................................... 860 228-2259
  165 Route 66 E Columbia (06237) *(G-669)*

Columbia Sand & Gravel Inc...................................... 603 237-5729
  Rr 3 Colebrook (03576) *(G-14103)*

Columbia Tech, Westborough *Also Called: Coghlin Companies Inc (G-13089)*

Columbia Tech, Westborough *Also Called: Columbia Electrical Contrs Inc (G-13091)*

Columbus Door Company.. 401 781-7792
  1884 Elmwood Ave Warwick (02888) *(G-16796)*

Comark LLC (HQ).. 508 359-8161
  440 Fortune Blvd Milford (01757) *(G-10399)*

Comark Communications, Southwick *Also Called: Hitachi Kokusai Electric Comark LLC (G-12043)*

Comcast Sportsnet Neng LLC..................................... 617 630-5000
  189 B St Needham Heights (02494) *(G-10537)*

Comdec Incorporated... 978 462-3399
  25 Hale St Newburyport (01950) *(G-10676)*

Comdel Inc.. 978 282-0620
  11 Kondelin Rd Gloucester (01930) *(G-8930)*

Comdel Rf Power Systems, Gloucester *Also Called: Comdel Inc (G-8930)*

Comeau Consulting Inc... 978 466-5870
  30 Patriots Cir Leominster (01453) *(G-9653)*

Comet Technologies USA Inc (DH)............................. 203 447-3200
  100 Trap Falls Road Ext Shelton (06484) *(G-2993)*

Comfort Colors Dyehouse, Northfield *Also Called: Barry T Chouinard Inc (G-17431)*

Comfort Foods Inc... 978 557-0009
  25 Commerce Way Ste 5 North Andover (01845) *(G-10825)*

Comicana Inc... 203 968-0748
  61 Studio Rd Stamford (06903) *(G-3318)*

Command Chemical Corporation.................................. 203 319-1857
  2490 Black Rock Tpke # 359 Fairfield (06825) *(G-1180)*

Command Corporation... 800 851-6012
  4 Creamery Brk East Granby (06026) *(G-930)*

Commercial Gear Sprocket Inc.................................... 508 668-1073
  618 Washington St East Walpole (02032) *(G-8417)*

Commercial Paving, Gorham *Also Called: Shaw Brothers Construction Inc (G-4835)*

Commercial Scale Balance Inc..................................... 413 789-9990
  36 Russo Cir Agawam (01001) *(G-5787)*

Commercial Sewing Inc.. 860 482-5509
  65 Grant St Torrington (06790) *(G-3675)*

Common Crossing Inc... 508 822-8225
  11 N Main St Berkley (02779) *(G-6314)*

Commonwealth Dairy LLC.. 802 251-2300
  66 Pauls Rd Guilford (05301) *(G-17280)*

Commonwealth Liquid Pdts LLC.................................. 508 676-9355
  537 Quequechan St Fall River (02721) *(G-8530)*

Commonwealth Packaging Corp................................... 413 593-1482
  1146 Sheridan St Chicopee (01022) *(G-8019)*

Commonwlth Soap Toiletries Inc (PA)....................... 508 676-9355
  537 Quequechan St Fall River (02721) *(G-8531)*

Commonwlth Vntr Fnding Group I (PA)....................... 781 684-0095
  391 Totten Pond Rd Ste 402 Waltham (02451) *(G-12636)*

Comms At Mill River... 203 287-0082
  75 Washington Ave Hamden (06518) *(G-1418)*

Commscope Technologies LLC.................................... 203 699-4100
  33 Union City Rd Ste 2 Prospect (06712) *(G-2831)*

Commtank Cares Inc.. 781 224-1021
  84 New Salem St Wakefield (01880) *(G-12505)*

Communction Cmpnent Flters Inc (PA)...................... 603 294-4685
  145 Batchelder Rd Seabrook (03874) *(G-15588)*

Communication Ink Inc.. 978 977-4595
  140 Summit St Peabody (01960) *(G-11302)*

A
L
P
H
A
B
E
T
I
C

Communications & Pwr Inds LLC...................... 978 922-6000
  150 Sohier Rd Beverly (01915) *(G-6340)*

Community Advocate, Westborough *Also Called: Bagdon Advertising Inc (G-13080)*

Community Apostolic Order Inc **(PA)**................... **802 723-4452**
  Cross St & Main St Island Pond (05846) *(G-17304)*

Community Newspaper, Beverly *Also Called: Gatehouse Media Mass I Inc (G-6350)*

Community Newspaper Inc.......................... 781 639-4800
  122 Washington St Marblehead (01945) *(G-10085)*

Community of Jesus Inc **(PA)**........................ **508 255-1094**
  5 Bay View Dr Orleans (02653) *(G-11237)*

Community Shellfish Co LLC........................ 207 529-2700
  656 Waldoboro Rd Bremen (04551) *(G-4607)*

Community Shopper, Worcester *Also Called: Worcester Telegram Gazette Inc (G-13831)*

Comnav Engineering Inc............................ 207 221-8524
  430 Riverside St Portland (04103) *(G-5201)*

Companion Industries Inc.......................... 860 628-0504
  891 W Queen St Southington (06489) *(G-3207)*

Companystuffcom Inc.............................. 978 282-1525
  45 S Main St Ipswich (01938) *(G-9480)*

Compart North America Inc......................... 877 237-2725
  6 Wild Rose Dr Andover (01810) *(G-5879)*

Compass Group Management LLC **(PA)**.............. **203 221-1703**
  301 Riverside Ave Westport (06880) *(G-4162)*

Compass Therapeutics Inc **(PA)**.................... **617 500-8099**
  80 Guest St Brighton (02135) *(G-7239)*

Competition Engineering Inc........................ 203 453-5200
  80 Carter Dr Guilford (06437) *(G-1389)*

Complete Energy Services Corp..................... 833 237-2677
  407 South St E Ste A2 Raynham (02767) *(G-11584)*

Complete Sheet Metal LLC.......................... 860 310-5447
  500 Four Rod Rd Ste 122 Berlin (06037) *(G-61)*

Complete Technology Resources.................... 508 909-5961
  2 Mount Royal Ave Ste 350 Marlborough (01752) *(G-10133)*

Completely Custom LLC............................ 401 667-0059
  376 Dry Bridge Rd Ste D1 North Kingstown (02852) *(G-16239)*

Compliance Week, Boston *Also Called: Wilmington Compliance Week Inc (G-7127)*

Component Engineers Inc........................... 203 269-0557
  108 N Plains Industrial Rd Wallingford (06492) *(G-3791)*

Component Sources Intl Inc......................... 508 986-2300
  121 Flanders Rd Westborough (01581) *(G-13092)*

Component Technologies Corpora.................... 401 965-2699
  14 Griswold Ave Bristol (02809) *(G-15759)*

Component Technologies Inc **(PA)**.................. **860 667-1065**
  68 Holmes Rd Newington (06111) *(G-2281)*

Components Division, Bristol *Also Called: Freudenberg-Nok General Partnr (G-14034)*

Components For Mfg LLC............................ 860 572-1671
  26 High St Noank (06340) *(G-2359)*

Composite Company Inc............................ 508 651-1681
  19 Kendall Ave Sherborn (01770) *(G-11810)*

Composite Energy Tech Inc......................... 401 253-2670
  52 Ballou Blvd Bristol (02809) *(G-15760)*

Composition Materials Co Inc....................... 203 874-6500
  249 Pepes Farm Rd Milford (06460) *(G-1812)*

Compost Plant L3c................................. 844 741-4653
  190 Swan St Providence (02905) *(G-16503)*

Compounding Solutions, Lewiston *Also Called: Neal Specialty Compounding LLC (G-4979)*

Comprehensive Identification Products Inc........... 781 229-8780
  209 Middlesex Tpke Burlington (01803) *(G-7354)*

Comprehensive Land Tech Inc....................... 207 445-3151
  665 Rte 3 South China (04358) *(G-5485)*

Comprehensive Power Inc........................... 508 460-0010
  420 Northboro Rd Marlborough (01752) *(G-10134)*

Compu-Data LLC.................................. 800 666-0399
  597 N Mountain Rd Newington (06111) *(G-2282)*

Compu-Gard Inc.................................. 508 679-8845
  1432 Gar Hwy Swansea (02777) *(G-12303)*

Compugraphics, Waterbury *Also Called: Compugraphics USA Inc (G-3900)*

Compugraphics USA Inc **(HQ)**...................... **510 249-2600**
  245 Freight St Waterbury (06702) *(G-3900)*

Compumachine, Danvers *Also Called: Compumachine Inc (G-8173)*

Compumachine Inc................................ 978 777-8440
  6 Electronics Ave Danvers (01923) *(G-8173)*

Computer Components Inc.......................... 860 653-9909
  18 Kripes Rd East Granby (06026) *(G-931)*

Computer Connection, Wilder *Also Called: Datamann Inc (G-17714)*

Computer Corporation America **(HQ)**............... **781 577-4402**
  77 4th Ave Ste 100 Waltham (02451) *(G-12637)*

Computer Express LLC.............................. 860 829-1310
  365 New Britain Rd Ste D Berlin (06037) *(G-62)*

Computer Imprntble Lbel System.................... 877 512-8763
  1500 District Ave Burlington (01803) *(G-7355)*

Computer Network Integrators, Milford *Also Called: CNi Corp (G-15017)*

Computer Prgrm & Systems Inc **(PA)**............... **203 324-9203**
  1011 High Ridge Rd Ste 208 Stamford (06905) *(G-3319)*

Computer Simulation Technology, Framingham *Also Called: CST of America LLC (G-8754)*

Computer Software Associates...................... 808 891-0099
  31 Saint James Ave Ste 1100 Boston (02116) *(G-6664)*

Computer Store Northern VT, Fairfax *Also Called: Med Associates Inc (G-17262)*

Computing and Media Center, New Haven *Also Called: Yale University (G-2220)*

Computron Metal Products Inc...................... 781 447-2265
  66 Pond St Whitman (02382) *(G-13348)*

Computype Inc................................... 603 225-5500
  38 Locke Rd Ste 4 Concord (03301) *(G-14122)*

Compuweigh Corporation **(PA)**..................... **203 262-9400**
  50 Middle Quarter Rd Woodbury (06798) *(G-4386)*

Comrex Corporation............................... 978 784-1776
  19 Pine Rd Devens (01434) *(G-8272)*

Comsat Inc....................................... 203 264-4091
  2120 River Rd Southbury (06488) *(G-3192)*

Comsat Inc., Southbury *Also Called: Comsat Inc (G-3192)*

Comstock Industries Inc........................... 603 279-7045
  Foundry Ave Meredith (03253) *(G-14968)*

Comtorgage Corporation........................... 401 765-0900
  58 Industrial Dr North Smithfield (02896) *(G-16321)*

Comtran Cable LLC................................ 800 842-7809
  330 Turner St Attleboro (02703) *(G-6007)*

Con-Tec Inc...................................... 203 723-8942
  41 Raytkwich Rd Naugatuck (06770) *(G-1953)*

Conair LLC **(HQ)**................................ **203 351-9000**
  1 Cummings Point Rd Stamford (06902) *(G-3320)*

Conair LLC....................................... 203 348-6684
  1 Cummings Point Rd Stamford (06902) *(G-3321)*

Conair LLC....................................... 800 492-7464
  314 Ella Grasso Ave Torrington (06790) *(G-3676)*

Conant Controls Inc............................... 781 395-2240
  215 Salem St Ste K Woburn (01801) *(G-13544)*

Conard Corporation............................... 860 659-0591
  101 Commerce St Glastonbury (06033) *(G-1275)* ·

Concentric Fabrication LLC......................... 774 955-5692
  179 Riverside Ave Somerset (02725) *(G-11851)*

Concentric Fabrication LLC......................... 508 672-4098
  7 Coombs St Middleboro (02346) *(G-10355)*

Concentric Tool & Mfg Co Inc....................... 203 756-9145
  133 S Leonard St Waterbury (06708) *(G-3901)*

Concentric Tool and Mfg Co......................... 203 756-9145
  550 Spring St Naugatuck (06770) *(G-1954)*

Concept Displays, Rumford *Also Called: Packaging Concepts Ltd (G-16675)*

Concept Manufacturing Company, Waltham *Also Called: Swiss Concept Inc (G-12784)*

Concept2 Inc **(PA)**............................... **802 888-7971**
  105 Industrial Park Dr Morrisville (05661) *(G-17381)*

Concepts Eti Inc.................................. 802 296-2321
  217 Billings Farm Rd White River Junction (05001) *(G-17706)*

Concepts Nrec, White River Junction *Also Called: Concepts Eti Inc (G-17706)*

Concepts Nrec LLC................................ 781 935-9050
  285 Billerica Rd Ste 102 Chelmsford (01824) *(G-7920)*

Concepts Nrec LLC **(PA)**.......................... **802 296-2321**
  217 Billings Farm Rd White River Junction (05001) *(G-17707)*

Concert, Lexington *Also Called: Concert Pharmaceuticals Inc (G-9731)*

Concert Medical LLC............................... 781 261-7400
  452 John L Dietsch Blvd Attleboro Falls (02763) *(G-6082)*

Concert Pharmaceuticals Inc **(HQ)**................ **781 860-0045**
  65 Hayden Ave Ste 3000n Lexington (02421) *(G-9731)*

Conco Wood Working Inc.... 203 934-9665
755 1st Ave West Haven (06516) *(G-4098)*

Concord Awning & Canvas, Bow *Also Called: Yarra Design & Fabrication LLC (G-14014)*

Concord Distributing, Norwalk *Also Called: Concord Industries Inc (G-2485)*

Concord Electric Supply, Hyannis *Also Called: Concord Electric Supply Ltd (G-9432)*

Concord Electric Supply, Nantucket *Also Called: Concord Electric Supply Ltd (G-10461)*

Concord Electric Supply Ltd.... 774 552-2185
1336 Phinneys Ln Hyannis (02601) *(G-9432)*

Concord Electric Supply Ltd.... 774 325-5142
5 Teasdale Cir Nantucket (02554) *(G-10461)*

Concord Foods LLC **(PA)**.... **508 580-1700**
10 Minuteman Way Brockton (02301) *(G-7269)*

Concord Industries Inc.... 203 750-6060
19 Willard Rd Norwalk (06851) *(G-2485)*

Concord Litho Group LLC **(PA)**.... **603 224-1202**
92 Old Turnpike Rd Concord (03301) *(G-14123)*

Concord Medical Products, Lincoln *Also Called: Advent Medical Products Inc (G-9794)*

Concord Monitor.... 603 224-5301
60 Manor Rd Concord (03303) *(G-14124)*

Concord Photo Engraving Co Inc.... 603 225-3681
12 Commercial St Concord (03301) *(G-14125)*

Concord Teacakes Etcetera Inc **(PA)**.... **978 369-2409**
30 Domino Dr Ste 1 Concord (01742) *(G-8108)*

Concord Teacakes Etcetera Inc.... 978 369-7644
59 Commonwealth Ave Concord (01742) *(G-8109)*

Concordia Co Inc.... 508 999-1381
300 Gulf Rd South Dartmouth (02748) *(G-11916)*

Concordia Fibers, Coventry *Also Called: Concordia Manufacturing LLC (G-15811)*

Concordia Manufacturing LLC.... 401 828-1100
4 Laurel Ave Coventry (02816) *(G-15811)*

Concordian LLC.... 603 225-5660
462 Josiah Bartlett Rd Concord (03301) *(G-14126)*

Concrete Block Insulg Systems.... 508 867-4241
25 Freight House Rd West Brookfield (01585) *(G-12993)*

Concrete Products Inc.... 401 568-8874
36 Terry Ln Chepachet (02814) *(G-15803)*

Concrete Systems Inc.... 603 886-5472
14 Park Ave Hudson (03051) *(G-14491)*

Concrete Systems Inc.... 603 432-1840
15 Independence Dr Londonderry (03053) *(G-14736)*

Condon Mfg Co Inc.... 413 543-1250
310 Verge St Springfield (01129) *(G-12085)*

Conductrf, Methuen *Also Called: Electronic Assemblies Mfg Inc (G-10329)*

Conest Software Systems Inc.... 603 437-9353
136a Harvey Rd Ste 102 Londonderry (03053) *(G-14737)*

Confer Health Inc.... 617 433-8810
56 Roland St Ste 208 Charlestown (02129) *(G-7866)*

Conference Medal & Trophy Co.... 508 563-3600
530 Macarthur Blvd Buzzards Bay (02532) *(G-7454)*

Confidential Copy, Cranston *Also Called: Crosstown Press Inc (G-15845)*

Confluent Maine, Windham *Also Called: Tube Hollows International (G-5673)*

Confluent Surgical Inc.... 781 839-1700
101 1st Ave Ste 4 Waltham (02451) *(G-12638)*

Conform Automotive, Auburn *Also Called: Conform Automotive LLC (G-4424)*

Conform Automotive, Auburn *Also Called: Formed Fiber Technologies Inc (G-4433)*

Conform Automotive LLC.... 207 784-1118
125 Allied Rd Auburn (04210) *(G-4424)*

Conformis, Billerica *Also Called: Conformis Inc (G-6427)*

Conformis Inc **(HQ)**.... **781 345-9001**
600 Technology Park Dr Ste 3 Billerica (01821) *(G-6427)*

Conklin Office Furniture, Holyoke *Also Called: Conklin Office Services Inc (G-9248)*

Conklin Office Services Inc **(PA)**.... **413 315-4924**
75 Appleton St Holyoke (01040) *(G-9248)*

Conley Casting Supply Corp **(PA)**.... **401 461-4710**
124 Maple St Warwick (02888) *(G-16797)*

Conmed Corporation.... 508 366-3668
134 Flanders Rd Westborough (01581) *(G-13093)*

Conn Anodizing Finshg Co Inc.... 203 367-1765
128 Logan St Bridgeport (06607) *(G-312)*

Conn Engineering Assoc Corp.... 203 426-4733
27 Philo Curtis Rd Sandy Hook (06482) *(G-2948)*

Conn Shed Company, Colchester *Also Called: Carefree Building Co Inc (G-655)*

Conneaut Industries Inc.... 401 392-1110
89 Hopkins Hill Rd West Greenwich (02817) *(G-16883)*

Connectcut Boiler Repr Mfg Inc.... 860 953-9117
694 Oakwood Ave West Hartford (06110) *(G-4054)*

Connectcut Hspnic Yellow Pages.... 860 560-8713
2074 Park St Ste 2 Hartford (06106) *(G-1475)*

Connectcut Mch Toling Cast Inc.... 203 874-8300
93 Research Dr Milford (06460) *(G-1813)*

Connectcut Prcsion Cstings Inc.... 603 542-3373
20 Wentworth Pl Claremont (03743) *(G-14085)*

Connectcut Rver Vly Yllow Pges.... 603 727-4700
103 Hanover St Ste 9 Lebanon (03766) *(G-14686)*

Connectcut Spring Stmping Corp.... 860 677-1341
48 Spring Ln Farmington (06032) *(G-1212)*

Connected Auto Systems Neng In.... 508 238-5855
87 Eastman St South Easton (02375) *(G-11940)*

Connected Office Tech LLC.... 603 380-7333
933 Us Highway 1 Byp Portsmouth (03801) *(G-15375)*

Connecticut Analytical Corp.... 203 393-9666
696 Amity Rd Ste 13 Bethany (06524) *(G-92)*

Connecticut Basement Systems Inc.... 203 881-5090
60 Silvermine Rd Seymour (06483) *(G-2959)*

Connecticut Carpentry, Meriden *Also Called: Connecticut Carpentry LLC (G-1661)*

Connecticut Carpentry LLC.... 203 639-8585
290 Pratt St Ofc Meriden (06450) *(G-1661)*

Connecticut Clean Room Corp.... 860 589-0049
32 Valley St Ste 2 Bristol (06010) *(G-430)*

Connecticut Coining, Bethel *Also Called: Connecticut Coining Inc (G-103)*

Connecticut Coining Inc.... 203 743-3861
10 Trowbridge Dr Bethel (06801) *(G-103)*

Connecticut Concrete Form Inc.... 860 674-1314
168 Brickyard Rd Farmington (06032) *(G-1213)*

Connecticut Container Corp **(PA)**.... **203 248-2161**
455 Sackett Point Rd North Haven (06473) *(G-2399)*

Connecticut Cue Parts, Wolcott *Also Called: Jan Manufacturing Co (G-4366)*

Connecticut Department Trnsp.... 860 342-5996
263 Freestone Ave Portland (06480) *(G-2818)*

Connecticut Die Cutting Svc, East Hartford *Also Called: Bessette Holdings Inc (G-975)*

Connecticut Forest Pk Assn Inc.... 860 346-2372
16 Meriden Rd Rockfall (06481) *(G-2913)*

Connecticut Galvanizing, Glastonbury *Also Called: Highway Safety LLC (G-1286)*

Connecticut Hypodermics Inc.... 203 265-4881
519 Main St Wallingford (06492) *(G-3792)*

Connecticut Iron Works Inc.... 203 869-0657
59 Davenport Ave Greenwich (06830) *(G-1327)*

Connecticut Machine & Welding.... 203 502-2605
425 Harding Ave Stratford (06615) *(G-3530)*

Connecticut Metal Industries.... 203 736-0790
1 Riverside Dr Ste G Ansonia (06401) *(G-11)*

Connecticut Millwork Inc.... 860 875-2860
80 Spring St Vernon (06066) *(G-3753)*

Connecticut Parent Magazine.... 203 483-1700
311 Bartlett Dr Madison (06443) *(G-1561)*

Connecticut Plasma Tech LLC.... 860 289-5500
273 Chapel Rd South Windsor (06074) *(G-3132)*

Connecticut Plastics Inc.... 203 265-3299
1264 Old Colony Rd Wallingford (06492) *(G-3793)*

Connecticut Post, Norwalk *Also Called: Medianews Group Inc (G-2535)*

Connecticut Precast Corp.... 203 268-8688
555 Fan Hill Rd Monroe (06468) *(G-1910)*

Connecticut Radio Inc.... 860 563-4867
1208 Cromwell Ave Ste C Rocky Hill (06067) *(G-2919)*

Connecticut Refining Co, New Haven *Also Called: Alliance Energy LLC (G-2114)*

Connecticut Shotgun Manufacturing Co.... 860 225-6581
100 Burritt St New Britain (06053) *(G-2012)*

Connecticut Sign Service LLC.... 860 767-7446
500 Industrial Park Rd Deep River (06417) *(G-875)*

Connecticut Solid, Canton *Also Called: Connecticut Solid Surface LLC (G-559)*

Connecticut Solid Surface LLC.... 860 410-9800
85 Washburn Rd Canton (06019) *(G-559)*

Connecticut Spring & Stamping, Farmington *Also Called: Connectcut Spring Stmping Corp* *(G-1212)*

Connecticut Stone, Milford *Also Called: Connecticut Stone Supplies Inc* *(G-1814)*

Connecticut Stone Supplies Inc **(PA)**..................... **203 882-1000**
  138 Woodmont Rd Milford (06460) *(G-1814)*

Connecticut Tick Control, Norwalk *Also Called: Connecticut Tick Control LLC* *(G-2486)*

Connecticut Tick Control LLC....................... 203 855-7849
  15 Chapel St Norwalk (06850) *(G-2486)*

Connecticut Tool & Cutter Co....................... 860 314-1740
  280 Redstone Hill Rd Ste 1 Bristol (06010) *(G-431)*

Connecticut Tool & Mfg Co LLC....................... 860 846-0800
  35 Corp Ave Plainville (06062) *(G-2751)*

Connecticut Tool Co Inc....................... 860 928-0565
  6 Highland Dr Putnam (06260) *(G-2850)*

Connecticut Valley Bindery....................... 860 229-7637
  1 Hartford Sq Ste 1w New Britain (06052) *(G-2013)*

Connecticut Valley Block Co Inc
  55 Circuit Ave West Springfield (01089) *(G-13018)*

Connell Communications Inc....................... 603 924-7271
  155 Washington St Keene (03431) *(G-14592)*

Connell Limited Partnership **(PA)**..................... **617 737-2700**
  1 International Pl 31th Fl Boston (02110) *(G-6665)*

Connexient LLC....................... 603 669-1300
  33 S Coml St Ste 302 Manchester (03101) *(G-14834)*

Connolly Printing LLC....................... 781 932-8885
  17b Gill St Woburn (01801) *(G-13545)*

Connor Homes LLC....................... 802 382-9082
  1741 Route 7 S Middlebury (05753) *(G-17342)*

Connors Design Ltd....................... 508 481-1930
  257 Simarano Dr Ste 105 Marlborough (01752) *(G-10135)*

Connors Footwear, Lisbon *Also Called: White Mountain Intl LLC* *(G-14711)*

Conntech Products Corporation....................... 203 272-2261
  30 Grandview Ct Cheshire (06410) *(G-581)*

Conntrol International Inc....................... 860 928-0567
  135 Park Rd Putnam (06260) *(G-2851)*

Conopco Inc....................... 860 669-8601
  1 John St Clinton (06413) *(G-640)*

Conopco Inc....................... 508 543-6767
  140 Washington St Ste 1 Foxboro (02035) *(G-8693)*

Conoptics Inc....................... 203 743-3349
  19 Eagle Rd Danbury (06810) *(G-722)*

Conproco, Somersworth *Also Called: Conproco Corp* *(G-15613)*

Conproco Corp **(PA)**..................... **603 743-5800**
  388 High St Somersworth (03878) *(G-15613)*

Conquest Business Media Inc....................... 978 299-1200
  152 Conant St Ste 3 Beverly (01915) *(G-6341)*

Conrad Fafard Inc....................... 413 786-4343
  770 Silver St Agawam (01001) *(G-5788)*

Conrad-Jarvis Inc....................... 401 722-8700
  217 Conant St Pawtucket (02860) *(G-16356)*

Conservation Systems, Bridgton *Also Called: Howell Laboratories Inc* *(G-4629)*

Consolidated Sterilizer Systems, Billerica *Also Called: Consolidated Machine Corporation* *(G-6428)*

Consoldted Inds Acqsition Corp....................... 203 272-5371
  677 Mixville Rd Cheshire (06410) *(G-582)*

Consoldted Precision Pdts Corp....................... 781 848-3333
  205 Wood Rd Braintree (02184) *(G-7174)*

Consolidated Coating Company, Bellingham *Also Called: Manning Way Cpitl Partners LLC* *(G-6293)*

Consolidated Concrete Corp **(PA)**..................... **401 438-4700**
  835 Taunton Ave Unit 1 East Providence (02914) *(G-16009)*

Consolidated Fabricators, Auburn *Also Called: Braden Manufacturing LLC* *(G-6108)*

Consolidated Industries, Cheshire *Also Called: Consoldted Inds Acqsition Corp* *(G-582)*

Consolidated Industries Inc....................... 203 272-5371
  677 Mixville Rd Cheshire (06410) *(G-583)*

Consolidated Machine Corporation....................... 617 782-6072
  3 Enterprise Rd 3c Billerica (01821) *(G-6428)*

Consolidated Thread Mills, Fall River *Also Called: Dhm Thread Corporation* *(G-8533)*

Consolidated Truck & Eqp Inc....................... 508 252-3330
  1727 Fall River Ave Seekonk (02771) *(G-11775)*

Constant Contact Inc **(DH)**..................... **781 472-8100**
  1601 Trapelo Rd Ste 329 Waltham (02451) *(G-12639)*

Constant Tech, North Kingstown *Also Called: Constant Technologies Inc* *(G-16240)*

Constant Technologies Inc....................... 800 518-7369
  125 Steamboat Ave Ste 2 North Kingstown (02852) *(G-16240)*

Constlltion Phrmaceuticals Inc **(DH)**..................... **844 667-1992**
  470 Atlantic Ave Ste 1401 Boston (02210) *(G-6666)*

Constrction Smmary New Hmpshr/....................... 603 627-8856
  734 Chestnut St Manchester (03104) *(G-14835)*

Construction, Meriden *Also Called: Northeast Companies Inc* *(G-1680)*

Construction, Brookline *Also Called: Gabriel Business Group Co Ltd* *(G-14039)*

Construction Aggregates, Henniker *Also Called: Michie Corporation* *(G-14438)*

Construction Service, Wilbraham *Also Called: Cs-Ma LLC* *(G-13356)*

Construction Service Division, Wilbraham *Also Called: Dauphinais & Son Inc* *(G-13357)*

Construction Source MGT LLC....................... 508 484-5100
  33 Commercial St Raynham (02767) *(G-11585)*

Consulting Engrg Dev Svcs Inc....................... 203 828-6528
  3 Fox Hollow Rd Oxford (06478) *(G-2691)*

Consumer Hearing Cons Inc....................... 866 658-8800
  869 Main St Ste 7 Walpole (02081) *(G-12557)*

Consumer Product Distrs LLC....................... 203 378-2193
  1075 Honeyspot Rd Stratford (06615) *(G-3531)*

Contech Medical, Providence *Also Called: Contech Medical Inc* *(G-16504)*

Contech Medical Inc....................... 401 351-4890
  99 Hartford Ave Providence (02909) *(G-16504)*

Contek International Corp....................... 203 972-7330
  93 Cherry St New Canaan (06840) *(G-2078)*

Contempo Card Co Inc **(PA)**..................... **401 272-4210**
  69 Tingley St Providence (02903) *(G-16505)*

Contemporary Products LLC....................... 860 346-9283
  2055 S Main St Middletown (06457) *(G-1744)*

Continental Biomass Industries....................... 603 382-0556
  22 Whittier St Newton (03858) *(G-15242)*

Continental Cable LLC....................... 800 229-5131
  253 Monument Rd Hinsdale (03451) *(G-14443)*

Continental Consolidated Inds, Worcester *Also Called: Continental Woodcraft Inc* *(G-13709)*

Continental Consumer Products, Stamford *Also Called: Continental Fragrances Ltd* *(G-3322)*

Continental Feed Screw Inc....................... 978 630-1300
  60 Linus Allain Ave Gardner (01440) *(G-8882)*

Continental Fragrances Ltd....................... 800 542-5903
  333 Ludlow St Ste 2 Stamford (06902) *(G-3322)*

Continental Machine TI Co Inc....................... 860 223-2896
  533 John Downey Dr New Britain (06051) *(G-2014)*

Continental Metal Pdts Co Inc....................... 781 935-4400
  35 Olympia Ave Woburn (01801) *(G-13546)*

Continental Plas & Packg Inc....................... 781 932-1115
  21 Powder Hill Rd Lincoln (02865) *(G-16128)*

Continental Plastics, Lincoln *Also Called: Continental Plas & Packg Inc* *(G-16128)*

Continental Stone, Sterling *Also Called: Continental Stone MBL Gran Inc* *(G-12159)*

Continental Stone MBL Gran Inc....................... 978 422-8700
  287 Leominster Rd Sterling (01564) *(G-12159)*

Continental Woodcraft Inc **(PA)**..................... **508 581-9560**
  7 Coppage Dr Worcester (01603) *(G-13709)*

Contintential Microwave....................... 603 775-5200
  32 Industrial Dr Exeter (03833) *(G-14289)*

Continuity Engine Inc....................... 866 631-5556
  426 Main St # 2 Ridgefield (06877) *(G-2893)*

Continuprint Inc....................... 781 933-1800
  247 Salem St Woburn (01801) *(G-13547)*

Continuum....................... 860 383-2562
  34 Thomas Ave Norwich (06360) *(G-2604)*

Continuum, Cambridge *Also Called: Amplitude Laser Inc* *(G-7485)*

Continuus Pharmaceuticals Inc....................... 781 281-0115
  25r Olympia Ave Woburn (01801) *(G-13548)*

Contitech Thermopol LLC....................... 603 692-6300
  35 Industrial Way Ste 204 Rochester (03867) *(G-15471)*

Contitech Thermopol LLC....................... 603 692-6300
  10 Interstate Dr Somersworth (03878) *(G-15614)*

Contitech Thermopol LLC **(HQ)**..................... **603 692-6300**
  9 Interstate Dr Somersworth (03878) *(G-15615)*

Contorq Components LLC....................... 860 225-3366
  433 John Downey Dr New Britain (06051) *(G-2015)*

Contour Fine Tooling Inc... 603 876-4908
   310 Marlboro St Ste 121 Keene (03431) *(G-14593)*

Contour360 Corp.. 207 625-4000
   5 Industrial Way Cornish (04020) *(G-4704)*

Contract Decor Intl Inc.. 508 587-7000
   637 N Montello St Brockton (02301) *(G-7270)*

Contract Engineering Inc.. 978 921-0501
   128 Park St Ste B5 Beverly (01915) *(G-6342)*

Contract Fusion Inc... 401 438-1298
   99 Massasoit Ave East Providence (02914) *(G-16010)*

Contract Glass Service Inc.. 978 262-1323
   44 Dunham Rd Billerica (01821) *(G-6429)*

Contract Support Group, Belmont *Also Called: New Model Inc (G-13964)*

Contractors Steel Supply Inc...................................... 203 782-1221
   111 Quinnipiac Ave North Haven (06473) *(G-2400)*

Contrak Drapery Manufacturing, North Providence *Also Called: Drapery House Inc (G-16300)*

Control 7 Inc... 508 697-3197
   55 Scotland Blvd Bridgewater (02324) *(G-7228)*

Control Concepts Inc **(PA)**.................................... **860 928-6551**
   19 S Main St Brooklyn (06234) *(G-545)*

Control Module Inc **(PA)**...................................... **860 745-2433**
   89 Phoenix Ave Enfield (06082) *(G-1125)*

Control Resources Inc... 978 486-4160
   11 Beaver Brook Rd Littleton (01460) *(G-9806)*

Control Technology Corporation **(PA)**......................... **508 435-9596**
   25 South St Hopkinton (01748) *(G-9313)*

Controlair LLC.. 603 886-9400
   8 Columbia Dr Amherst (03031) *(G-13865)*

Controlled Envmt Eqp Corp.. 207 854-9126
   55 Bradley Dr Westbrook (04092) *(G-5622)*

Controlled Envmt Systems LLC **(PA)**........................... **508 339-4237**
   137 High St Mansfield (02048) *(G-10042)*

Controlled Fluidics LLC... 603 673-4323
   1262 Old Colony Rd Wallingford (06492) *(G-3794)*

Controlled Fluidics LLC... 603 673-4323
   18 Hollow Oak Ln Milford (03055) *(G-15018)*

Controls For Automation Inc....................................... 508 802-6005
   25 Constitution Dr Taunton (02780) *(G-12328)*

Conval Inc... 860 749-0761
   96 Phoenix Ave Enfield (06082) *(G-1126)*

Convanta Holliston... 508 429-9750
   115 Washington St Holliston (01746) *(G-9205)*

Convectronics Inc.. 978 374-7714
   111 Neck Rd Haverhill (01835) *(G-9088)*

Convergent - Photonics LLC **(DH)**............................. **413 598-5200**
   711 E Main St Chicopee (01020) *(G-8020)*

Convergent Dental Inc **(PA)**.................................. **508 500-5656**
   100 5th Ave Fl 1 Waltham (02451) *(G-12640)*

Convergent Networks Inc.. 978 262-0231
   500 Boylston St Fl 4 Boston (02116) *(G-6667)*

Conversion Marketing, Ridgefield *Also Called: R4 Technologies Inc (G-2906)*

Convexity Scientific Inc.. 844 359-7632
   85 Willow St Lbby New Haven (06511) *(G-2138)*

Conveyco Technologies Inc **(PA)**.............................. **860 589-8215**
   47 Commerce Dr Bristol (06010) *(G-432)*

Conveyor Installation, Smithfield *Also Called: Action Conveyor Tech Inc (G-16685)*

Conway Daily Sun, North Conway *Also Called: Country News Club Inc (G-15247)*

Conway Hardwood Products, Gaylordsville *Also Called: Conway Hardwood Products LLC (G-1264)*

Conway Hardwood Products LLC..................................... 860 355-4030
   37 Gaylord Rd Gaylordsville (06755) *(G-1264)*

Cook Company, Upton *Also Called: Cook Forest Products Inc (G-12471)*

Cook Forest Products Inc.. 508 634-3300
   252 Milford St Upton (01568) *(G-12471)*

Cooked Perfect, Norwood *Also Called: Home Market Foods Inc (G-11176)*

Cookes Skate Supply Inc.. 978 657-7586
   446 Main St Wilmington (01887) *(G-13398)*

Cooking Solutions Group Inc **(HQ)**........................... **603 893-9701**
   23 Keewaydin Dr Ste 205 Salem (03079) *(G-15516)*

Cooking Solutions Group Inc...................................... 864 963-3471
   42 Allen Martin Dr Essex Junction (05452) *(G-17231)*

Cool Air Creations Inc... 401 830-5780
   10 Business Park Dr Smithfield (02917) *(G-16692)*

Cool Gear International LLC **(DH)**............................ **508 830-3440**
   36 Cordage Park Cir Plymouth (02360) *(G-11455)*

Cool Polymers Inc.. 401 667-7830
   51 Circuit Dr North Kingstown (02852) *(G-16241)*

Cool Tropics, Bedford *Also Called: Tropical Paradise Inc (G-6275)*

Coolback, Portsmouth *Also Called: Global Laminates Inc (G-15393)*

Cooley Incorporated.. 401 721-6374
   5 Slater Rd Cranston (02920) *(G-15843)*

Cooley Incorporated **(HQ)**................................... **401 724-9000**
   350 Esten Ave Pawtucket (02860) *(G-16357)*

Cooley Ashalt Paving, Belmont *Also Called: Pike Industries Inc (G-13967)*

Cooley Building Products, Pawtucket *Also Called: Cooley Incorporated (G-16357)*

Cooley Group Holdings Inc **(PA)**............................. **401 724-0510**
   350 Esten Ave Pawtucket (02860) *(G-16358)*

Cooley/Group, Pawtucket *Also Called: Cooley Group Holdings Inc (G-16358)*

Cooliance Inc **(PA)**... **401 921-6500**
   60 Alhambra Rd Ste 1 Warwick (02886) *(G-16798)*

Coombs Family Farms, Alstead *Also Called: Bascom Maple Farms Inc (G-13856)*

Cooper Controls, Essex Junction *Also Called: Cooper Lighting Inc (G-17232)*

Cooper Crouse-Hinds LLC.. 860 683-4300
   1200 Kennedy Rd Windsor (06095) *(G-4268)*

Cooper Crouse-Hinds LLC.. 617 889-3700
   222 Williams St Chelsea (02150) *(G-7979)*

Cooper Crouse-Hinds LLC.. 617 889-3700
   222 Williams St Chelsea (02150) *(G-7980)*

Cooper Group LLC... 860 599-2481
   25 White Rock Bridge Rd Pawcatuck (06379) *(G-2716)*

Cooper Lighting Inc.. 800 767-3674
   16 Perkins Dr Essex Junction (05452) *(G-17232)*

Cooper Products, Inc., Laconia *Also Called: Zhongding Laconia Inc (G-14674)*

Cooper Surgical, Trumbull *Also Called: Blairden Precision Instruments Inc (G-3714)*

Cooper-Atkins Corporation **(HQ)**............................. **860 349-3473**
   33 Reeds Gap Rd Middlefield (06455) *(G-1724)*

Coopersurgical Inc... 203 453-1700
   393 Soundview Rd Guilford (06437) *(G-1390)*

Coopersurgical Inc... 203 601-5200
   120 Corporate Dr Trumbull (06611) *(G-3715)*

Coopersurgical Inc **(DH)**.................................... **203 601-5200**
   75 Corporate Dr Trumbull (06611) *(G-3716)*

Coorstek Inc... 860 653-8071
   10 Airport Park Rd East Granby (06026) *(G-932)*

Coorstek Inc... 774 317-2600
   5 Norton Dr Worcester (01606) *(G-13710)*

Coorstek Inc... 603 673-7560
   47 Powers St Milford (03055) *(G-15019)*

Coorstek East Granby, East Granby *Also Called: Coorstek Inc (G-932)*

Coorstek Milford, Milford *Also Called: Coorstek Inc (G-15019)*

Coorstek Worcester, Worcester *Also Called: Coorstek Inc (G-13710)*

Copar Industries, Middletown *Also Called: Armetta LLC (G-1736)*

Copenhgen Offshore Prtners Inc................................... 508 717-8964
   700 Pleasant St New Bedford (02740) *(G-10579)*

Copies Now, Wethersfield *Also Called: Hedges & Hedges Ltd (G-4205)*

Copies Plus Info Booth, Manchester *Also Called: Southern New Hampshire Univ (G-14963)*

Copious Imaging LLC.. 781 918-6554
   83 Hartwell Ave Lexington (02421) *(G-9732)*

Copley Apholstery Company, Boston *Also Called: Copley Furniture Company Inc (G-6668)*

Copley Controls Corporation **(DH)**........................... **781 828-8090**
   20 Dan Rd Canton (02021) *(G-7779)*

Copley Furniture Company Inc..................................... 617 566-1000
   120 Landseer St Boston (02132) *(G-6668)*

Copley Global, Waltham *Also Called: Copley Global Services LLC (G-12641)*

Copley Global Services LLC....................................... 617 970-9617
   303 Wyman St Ste 300 Waltham (02451) *(G-12641)*

Copp Excavating Inc.. 207 926-4988
   190 Pinkham Brook Rd Durham (04222) *(G-4732)*

Copper Beech Millwork, Northampton *Also Called: Amherst Woodworking & Supply Inc (G-11052)*

A L P H A B E T I C

Copper Lease, Stewartstown *Also Called: Kheops International Inc* **(G-15631)**

Coppola Marble, Stamford *Also Called: Mildred Coppola* **(G-3411)**

Copy Art, Stamford *Also Called: Classic Graphics Corp* **(G-3315)**

Copy Cats Inc.. 860 442-8424
458 Williams St Ste 1 New London (06320) **(G-2225)**

Copy Center **(PA)**.. **207 623-1452**
1921 Us Route 202 Winthrop (04364) **(G-5691)**

Copy Center Plus The, Winthrop *Also Called: Copy Center* **(G-5691)**

Copy Cop The Digital Printing Company LLC....................... 617 267-8899
12 Channel St Boston (02210) **(G-6669)**

Copy Express LLC... 603 625-4960
923 Elm St Manchester (03101) **(G-14836)**

Copy Masters Inc... 508 824-7187
106 Oak St Ste 2 Taunton (02780) **(G-12329)**

Copy Shop, The, Wiscasset *Also Called: Coastal Business Center Inc* **(G-5697)**

Copy World, East Providence *Also Called: A & H Composition and Prtg Inc* **(G-15999)**

Copy World Inc.. 401 438-1200
5 Almeida Ave East Providence (02914) **(G-16011)**

Copy-All, Providence *Also Called: Providence Label & Tag Co* **(G-16591)**

Copycop, Boston *Also Called: Copy Cop The Digital Printing Company LLC* **(G-6669)**

Copyworld II, East Providence *Also Called: Signature Printing Inc* **(G-16044)**

Corbin Russwin... 860 225-7411
110 Sargent Dr New Haven (06511) **(G-2139)**

Corbin Russwin Arch Hdwr, Berlin *Also Called: Assa Abloy Access Egress Hdwr* **(G-51)**

Corbus Pharmaceuticals, Norwood *Also Called: Corbus Pharmaceuticals Inc* **(G-11169)**

Corbus Pharmaceuticals Inc... 617 963-0100
500 River Ridge Dr Ste 2 Norwood (02062) **(G-11169)**

Cordmaster Engineering Co Inc.. 413 664-9371
1544 Curran Hwy North Adams (01247) **(G-10805)**

Core Assemblies Inc.. 603 293-0270
21 Meadowbrook Ln Unit 4 Gilford (03249) **(G-14334)**

Core Concepts Inc.. 508 528-0070
305 Union St Ste 7 Franklin (02038) **(G-8827)**

Core Cutter LLC... 207 588-7519
362 Maine Ave Farmingdale (04344) **(G-4776)**

Core Elastomers LLC... 603 319-6912
170 West Rd Portsmouth (03801) **(G-15376)**

Core Sdi Inc **(PA)**.. **617 695-1109**
41 Farnsworth St Fl 6 Boston (02210) **(G-6670)**

Core Security Technologies, Boston *Also Called: Core Sdi Inc* **(G-6670)**

Core Site Services LLC.. 475 227-9026
470 James St Ste 7 New Haven (06513) **(G-2140)**

Core Value Software.. 802 473-3147
316 Main St Norwich (05055) **(G-17437)**

Coredge Networks Inc.. 617 267-5205
50 Commonwealth Ave # 504 Boston (02116) **(G-6671)**

Corenco, Warwick *Also Called: Baker Commodities Inc* **(G-16786)**

Corenco Div, North Billerica *Also Called: Baker Commodities Inc* **(G-10899)**

Corero Network Security Inc... 978 212-1500
293 Boston Post Rd W Ste 310 Marlborough (01752) **(G-10136)**

Coreslab Structures Conn Inc... 860 283-8281
1023 Waterbury Rd Thomaston (06787) **(G-3617)**

Corfin Industries, Manchester *Also Called: Micross Components LLC* **(G-14887)**

Corfin Industries Inc.. 603 893-9900
1050 Perimeter Rd Manchester (03103) **(G-14837)**

Corindus Inc **(HQ)**.. **508 653-3335**
275 Grove St Ste 1110 Auburndale (02466) **(G-6131)**

Corindus Vascular Robotics Inc **(PA)**.............................. **508 653-3335**
275 Grove St Ste 1100 Auburndale (02466) **(G-6132)**

Corium, Boston *Also Called: Corium LLC* **(G-6672)**

Corium LLC.. 855 253-2407
11 Farnsworth St Fl 4 Boston (02210) **(G-6672)**

Cork Technologies, Lawrence *Also Called: North American Chemical Co* **(G-9589)**

Cork Technologies LLC.. 978 687-9500
29 S Canal St Ste 204 Lawrence (01843) **(G-9555)**

Cornell Online LLC.. 802 448-3281
131 Battery St Burlington (05401) **(G-17128)**

Cornell Orthotics Prosthetics **(PA)**.............................. **978 922-2866**
100 Cummings Ctr Ste 207h Beverly (01915) **(G-6343)**

Cornell-Carr Co Inc.. 203 261-2529
626 Main St Monroe (06468) **(G-1911)**

Cornell-Dubilier Elec Inc.. 508 996-8561
1661 E Rodney French Blvd New Bedford (02744) **(G-10580)**

Corning, Kennebunk *Also Called: Corning Incorporated* **(G-4924)**

Corning, Tewksbury *Also Called: Corning Incorporated* **(G-12391)**

Corning Incorporated... 207 985-3111
2 Alfred Rd Kennebunk (04043) **(G-4924)**

Corning Incorporated... 978 442-2200
836 North St Ste 3401 Tewksbury (01876) **(G-12391)**

Corning Incorporated... 603 357-7662
69 Island St Ste T Keene (03431) **(G-14594)**

Corning Netoptix, Keene *Also Called: Optical Filter Corporation* **(G-14614)**

Coronet Machinery Corp... 203 744-8009
8 Trowbridge Dr Bethel (06801) **(G-104)**

Corporate, Windsor *Also Called: ABB Inc* **(G-4251)**

Corporate Casuals LLC.. 978 369-5935
52 Domino Dr Concord (01742) **(G-8110)**

Corporate Image Apparel Inc.. 508 676-3099
596 Airport Rd Fall River (02720) **(G-8532)**

Corporate Outfitters, Saint Albans *Also Called: Outfitters Inc Corporate* **(G-17528)**

Corporate Press... 781 769-6656
89 Access Rd Ste 17 Norwood (02062) **(G-11170)**

Corporate Rmbursement Svcs Inc....................................... 888 312-0788
233 Needham St Ste 540 Newton (02464) **(G-10748)**

Corporation, Lexington *Also Called: Sarid Inc* **(G-9769)**

Corporation, Gtat, Salem *Also Called: Crystal Gt Systems LLC* **(G-11708)**

Corportion For Lser Optics Res **(PA)**............................ **603 430-2023**
95 Mammoth Rd Londonderry (03053) **(G-14738)**

Corru-Seals Inc... 203 265-9331
24 Capital Dr Wallingford (06492) **(G-3795)**

Corrugated Packaging Inc.. 978 342-6076
215 Cleghorn Fitchburg (01420) **(G-8649)**

Corrugated Stitcher Service.. 508 823-2844
88 Jerome St Berkley (02779) **(G-6315)**

Cortelyou Inc.. 203 847-2000
129 Glover Ave Norwalk (06850) **(G-2487)**

Cortina Famous Schools, Wilton *Also Called: Cortina Learning Intl Inc* **(G-4237)**

Cortina Learning Intl Inc **(PA)**...................................... **800 245-2145**
33 Catalpa Rd Wilton (06897) **(G-4237)**

Cortron Inc... 978 975-5445
59 Technology Dr Lowell (01851) **(G-9871)**

Corvidia, Waltham *Also Called: Corvidia Therapeutics Inc* **(G-12642)**

Corvidia Therapeutics Inc... 781 205-4755
35 Gatehouse Dr Waltham (02451) **(G-12642)**

Cory Manufacturing Inc.. 508 680-2111
343 Manley St West Bridgewater (02379) **(G-12970)**

Cosco LLC... 401 765-0009
707 Park East Dr Woonsocket (02895) **(G-16955)**

Cosman Medical LLC... 781 272-6561
300 Boston Scientific Way Marlborough (01752) **(G-10137)**

Cosmic Software Inc.. 978 667-2556
55 Middlesex St Unit 215 North Chelmsford (01863) **(G-10967)**

Cosmo, Byfield *Also Called: Starensier Inc* **(G-7459)**

Cosmos Food Products Inc... 800 942-6766
200 Callegari Dr West Haven (06516) **(G-4099)**

Coss Systems Inc (not Inc).. 732 447-7724
26 Arcadia Rd Old Greenwich (06870) **(G-2631)**

Costa Enterprises Ltd Co... 802 644-6782
2953 Vt Route 109 Waterville (05492) **(G-17682)**

Costa Inc... 401 333-1200
295 Promenade St # 1 Providence (02908) **(G-16506)**

Costa Packaging LLC.. 860 282-2535
70 Bidwell Rd South Windsor (06074) **(G-3133)**

Costa Precision Mfg Corp **(PA)**..................................... **603 542-5229**
475 Lombard Rd Chicopee (01020) **(G-8021)**

Costantino's Venda Ravioli, Providence *Also Called: Venda Ravioli Inc* **(G-16636)**

Costantino's Venda Ravioli, Providence *Also Called: Venda Ravioli Inc* **(G-16637)**

Costello Dismantling Co Inc **(PA)**................................. **508 291-2324**
15 Cranberry Hwy Unit 1 West Wareham (02576) **(G-13058)**

Costello/April Design Inc... 603 749-6755
  180 Crosby Rd Dover (03820) *(G-14224)*

Coto Technology.. 401 943-2686
  171 Service Ave Ste 330 Warwick (02886) *(G-16799)*

Coto Technology, North Kingstown *Also Called: Kearney-National Inc (G-16264)*

Coto Technology Inc.. 401 943-2686
  66 Whitecap Dr North Kingstown (02852) *(G-16242)*

Coto Technology USA, North Kingstown *Also Called: Coto Technology Inc (G-16242)*

Cotswold Furniture Makers, Hinesburg *Also Called: Greenrange Furniture Company (G-17292)*

Cottages & Grdns Publications, Norwalk *Also Called: Dulce Domum LLC (G-2493)*

Cotter Brothers Corporation.. 978 777-5001
  8 Southside Rd Danvers (01923) *(G-8174)*

Cotter Corporation.. 978 774-6777
  8 Southside Rd Danvers (01923) *(G-8175)*

Cotter Machine Co Inc **(PA)**....................................... **508 291-7400**
  7 Little Brook Rd West Wareham (02576) *(G-13059)*

Cotton Tree Service Inc... 413 584-9104
  248 Hatfield St Northampton (01060) *(G-11057)*

Coulter Press, Worcester *Also Called: Worcester Tlegram Gazette Corp (G-13832)*

Council On Intl Pub Affirs Inc **(PA)**............................ **212 972-9878**
  3 Mont View Ave Northampton (01060) *(G-11058)*

Counter Culture... 781 439-9810
  60 Main St Saugus (01906) *(G-11755)*

Counter Pro Inc.. 603 647-2444
  210 Lincoln St Manchester (03103) *(G-14838)*

Counteredge LLC.. 781 891-0050
  108 Clematis Ave Unit 2 Waltham (02453) *(G-12643)*

Counterra LLC.. 781 821-2100
  399 Neponset St Ste 202 Canton (02021) *(G-7780)*

Counters, Newington *Also Called: Catskill Gran Countertops Inc (G-2279)*

Country Carpenters Inc.. 860 228-2276
  326 Gilead St Hebron (06248) *(G-1526)*

Country Courier, Turner *Also Called: Turner Publishing Inc (G-5564)*

Country Courier, Barre *Also Called: Ta Update Inc (G-17020)*

Country Home Products Inc.. 802 771-7202
  823 Ferry Rd Charlotte (05445) *(G-17175)*

Country Kitchen, Auburn *Also Called: Lepage Bakeries Inc (G-4440)*

Country Kitchen, Lewiston *Also Called: Lepage Bakeries Park St LLC (G-4972)*

Country Kitchen, Hudson *Also Called: Lepage Bakeries Park St LLC (G-14521)*

Country Log Homes, Goshen *Also Called: Country Log Homes Inc (G-1302)*

Country Log Homes Inc... 413 229-8084
  27 Rockwall Ct Goshen (06756) *(G-1302)*

Country News Club Inc... 603 356-2999
  64 Seavey St North Conway (03860) *(G-15247)*

Country Press, New London *Also Called: Echo Communications Inc (G-15203)*

Country Press Inc... 508 947-4485
  1 Commercial Dr Lakeville (02347) *(G-9516)*

Country Pure Foods, Ellington *Also Called: Natural Country Farms Inc (G-1112)*

Country Pure Foods Inc.. 330 753-2293
  58 West Rd Ellington (06029) *(G-1103)*

Countryside Woodcraft LLP.. 413 862-3276
  665 Huntington Rd Russell (01071) *(G-11694)*

Countrywide National Services....................................... 508 346-3286
  220 Norfolk St Walpole (02081) *(G-12558)*

County Concrete & Cnstr Co... 207 483-4409
  125 Pit Rd Columbia Falls (04623) *(G-4698)*

County Concrete Corp **(PA)**....................................... **413 499-3359**
  290 Hubbard Ave Dalton (01226) *(G-8149)*

County Courier Inc.. 802 933-4375
  342 Main St Enosburg Falls (05450) *(G-17222)*

County Heat Treat, Millbury *Also Called: United-County Industries Corp (G-10444)*

County Qwik Print Inc... 207 492-0360
  56 Sweden St Caribou (04736) *(G-4674)*

Courage Therapeutics Inc... 617 216-9921
  64 Homer St Newton (02459) *(G-10749)*

Courier Communications LLC **(DH)**........................... **978 251-6000**
  15 Wellman Ave North Chelmsford (01863) *(G-10968)*

Courier Companies Inc **(PA)**..................................... **978 251-6000**
  15 Wellman Ave North Chelmsford (01863) *(G-10969)*

Courier Corporation.. 978 251-6000
  15 Wellman Ave North Chelmsford (01863) *(G-10970)*

Courier Epic, North Chelmsford *Also Called: Courier New Media Inc (G-10972)*

Courier Fulfillment Services, Westford *Also Called: Courier Westford Inc (G-13232)*

Courier Intl Holdings LLC... 978 251-6000
  15 Wellman Ave North Chelmsford (01863) *(G-10971)*

Courier New Media Inc **(PA)**..................................... **978 251-3945**
  15 Wellman Ave North Chelmsford (01863) *(G-10972)*

Courier Westford Inc.. 978 251-6482
  22 Town Farm Rd Westford (01886) *(G-13232)*

Coursestorm Inc... 207 866-0328
  148 Main St Orono (04473) *(G-5134)*

Courtsmart Digital Systems Inc...................................... 978 251-3300
  51 Middlesex St Unit 128 North Chelmsford (01863) *(G-10973)*

Cousineau Wood Products ME LLC................................ 207 635-4445
  3 Valley Rd North Anson (04958) *(G-5104)*

Couture Brands LLC... 512 626-7544
  19 Brigham St Unit 9c Marlborough (01752) *(G-10138)*

Covalent Networks Inc.. 781 296-7952
  24 Hanson St Boston (02118) *(G-6673)*

Covaris Inc... 781 932-3959
  14 Gill St Unit H Woburn (01801) *(G-13549)*

Cove Haven Corp.. 401 246-1600
  101 Narragansett Ave Unit 2 Barrington (02806) *(G-15747)*

Cove Metal Company Inc **(PA)**.................................. **401 724-3500**
  160 Grenville St Pawtucket (02860) *(G-16359)*

Cove Press, Stamford *Also Called: US Games Systems Inc (G-3488)*

Cove Shoe Company Division, Greenwich *Also Called: HH Brown Shoe Company Inc (G-1334)*

Cove Textile Machinery Co, Pawtucket *Also Called: Cove Metal Company Inc (G-16359)*

Cover-It Inc.. 203 931-4747
  17 Wood St West Haven (06516) *(G-4100)*

Coveris Advnced Ctngs Mtthews **(DH)**....................... **413 539-5547**
  69 William Frank Dr West Springfield (01089) *(G-13019)*

Covestro LLC.. 800 458-0014
  730 Main St Wilmington (01887) *(G-13399)*

Covetrus, Portland *Also Called: Covetrus North America LLC (G-5202)*

Covetrus North America LLC **(PA)**............................ **888 280-2221**
  12 Mountfort St Portland (04101) *(G-5202)*

Covey Engineering, Peabody *Also Called: John Covey (G-11321)*

Covia Finance Company LLC... 203 966-8880
  258 Elm St New Canaan (06840) *(G-2079)*

Covia Specialty Minerals Inc... 203 966-8880
  258 Elm St New Canaan (06840) *(G-2080)*

Covidien, Mansfield *Also Called: Covidien LLC (G-10044)*

Covidien, Mansfield *Also Called: Covidien LP (G-10046)*

Covidien, Mansfield *Also Called: Nellcor Puritan Bennett LLC (G-10069)*

Covidien France Holdings Inc... 508 261-8000
  15 Hampshire St Mansfield (02048) *(G-10043)*

Covidien Holding Inc.. 203 492-5000
  195 Mcdermott Rd North Haven (06473) *(G-2401)*

Covidien LLC.. 508 261-8000
  777 West St Mansfield (02048) *(G-10044)*

Covidien LP.. 781 839-1722
  555 Long Wharf Dr Fl 4 New Haven (06511) *(G-2141)*

Covidien LP.. 203 492-6332
  195 Mcdermott Rd North Haven (06473) *(G-2402)*

Covidien LP.. 203 492-5000
  60 Middletown Ave North Haven (06473) *(G-2403)*

Covidien LP.. 508 261-8000
  777 West St Mansfield (02048) *(G-10045)*

Covidien LP **(HQ)**.. **763 514-4000**
  15 Hampshire St Mansfield (02048) *(G-10046)*

Covidien LP.. 800 962-9888
  12 Gill St Ste 3500 Woburn (01801) *(G-13550)*

Covidien Sales LLC.. 508 261-8000
  15 Hampshire St Mansfield (02048) *(G-10047)*

Cowbell Technologies Inc... 508 733-1778
  59 Apsley St Unit 11d Hudson (01749) *(G-9360)*

Cowbell Technologies Inc **(PA)**................................. **508 733-1778**
  150 E Main St Unit 960 Westborough (01581) *(G-13094)*

Cowles Operating Company... 203 680-9401
  126 Bailey Rd North Haven (06473) *(G-2404)*

Cowles Products Company Inc........................ 203 865-3110
  126 Bailey Rd North Haven (06473) *(G-2405)*

Cowles Stamping Inc.................................... 203 865-3117
  126 Bailey Rd North Haven (06473) *(G-2406)*

Cox Engineering Company **(PA)**.................. **781 302-3300**
  35 Industrial Dr Canton (02021) *(G-7781)*

Coyote Mountain Farm Inc........................... 603 662-2164
  93 Duncan Lake Rd Ossipee (03864) *(G-15282)*

CP Dauphinais Inc..................................... 508 865-1755
  203 Worcester Providence Tpke Sutton (01590) *(G-12279)*

CP Foods LLC... 860 436-4042
  50 Talbot Ln South Windsor (06074) *(G-3134)*

Cpec LLC... 781 861-8444
  99 Hayden Ave Lexington (02421) *(G-9733)*

Cph Program & Machine Tool Des................. 603 716-3849
  26 Shaker Brook Park Loudon (03307) *(G-14795)*

CPI, Marlborough *Also Called: Comprehensive Power Inc* *(G-10134)*

CPI Essco Inc... 978 568-5100
  90 Nemco Way Ayer (01432) *(G-6179)*

CPI Manufacturing LLC
  128 Old Brickyard Ln Berlin (06037) *(G-63)*

CPI Operations LLC................................... 210 249-9988
  750 Wshngton Blvd Ste 600 Stamford (06901) *(G-3323)*

CPI Radant Tech Div Inc **(DH)**................... **978 562-3866**
  255 Hudson Rd Stow (01775) *(G-12245)*

Cpk Manufacturing LLC.............................. 207 622-6229
  681 Riverside Dr Augusta (04330) *(G-4470)*

Cpo Science, Nashua *Also Called: Delta Education LLC* *(G-15090)*

Cpp-Boston, Braintree *Also Called: Wollaston Alloys Inc* *(G-7214)*

CPS Technologies Corp............................... 508 222-0614
  111 S Worcester St Norton (02766) *(G-11124)*

Crabtree & Evelyn Ltd **(DH)**..................... **800 272-2873**
  102 Peake Brook Rd Woodstock (06281) *(G-4393)*

Craft Inc... 508 761-7917
  1929 County St Attleboro (02703) *(G-6008)*

Craft Beer Guild Distrg VT LLC **(PA)**.......... **781 585-5165**
  35 Elder Ave Kingston (02364) *(G-9507)*

Craft Beer Guild LLC.................................. 603 319-8508
  4 Cutts St Unit 4 Portsmouth (03801) *(G-15377)*

Craft Beer Guild of Vermont, Kingston *Also Called: Craft Beer Guild Distrg VT LLC* *(G-9507)*

Craft Brew Alliance Inc............................... 603 430-8600
  35 Corporate Dr Portsmouth (03801) *(G-15378)*

Craft Corrugated Box Inc............................ 508 998-2115
  4674 Acushnet Ave New Bedford (02745) *(G-10581)*

Craftech Upton... 508 529-4505
  1 Walker Dr Upton (01568) *(G-12472)*

Craftline, North Haven *Also Called: Platt-Labonia of N Haven Inc* *(G-2431)*

Crafts Technology, Attleboro *Also Called: Craft Inc* *(G-6008)*

Craftsmen Printing Group Inc....................... 203 327-2817
  104 Lincoln Ave Stamford (06902) *(G-3324)*

Cramaro Tarpaulin Systems Inc.................... 508 393-3062
  51 Sw Cutoff Northborough (01532) *(G-11094)*

Cramer Company.. 860 291-8402
  105 Nutmeg Rd S South Windsor (06074) *(G-3135)*

Cramer Fabrics, Inc., Dover *Also Called: C Cramer & Co Inc* *(G-14219)*

Crane, Stamford *Also Called: Crane Intl Holdings Inc* *(G-3328)*

Crane, Stamford *Also Called: Redco Corporation* *(G-3445)*

Crane & Co Inc **(HQ)**............................. **617 648-3799**
  30 South St Dalton (01226) *(G-8150)*

Crane Aerospace Inc **(DH)**....................... **203 363-7300**
  100 Stamford Pl Stamford (06902) *(G-3325)*

Crane Company **(PA)**.............................. **203 363-7300**
  100 Stamford Pl Ste 300 Stamford (06902) *(G-3326)*

Crane Composition Inc............................... 774 338-5183
  23 Ploughed Neck Rd East Sandwich (02537) *(G-8404)*

Crane Controls Inc **(DH)**......................... **203 363-7300**
  100 Stamford Pl Stamford (06902) *(G-3327)*

Crane Currency, Dalton *Also Called: Crane & Co Inc* *(G-8150)*

Crane Currency, Nashua *Also Called: Crane Security Tech Inc* *(G-15084)*

Crane Currency Us LLC.............................. 617 648-3710
  1 Beacon St Boston (02108) *(G-6674)*

Crane Data LLC.. 508 439-4419
  110 Turnpike Rd Ste 213 Westborough (01581) *(G-13095)*

Crane Intl Holdings Inc **(HQ)**................... **203 363-7300**
  100 Stamford Pl Stamford (06902) *(G-3328)*

Crane Mdsg Systems Inc............................. 781 501-5800
  990 Washington St Ste 205 Dedham (02026) *(G-8240)*

Crane Merger Co LLC................................. 203 363-7300
  100 Stamford Pl Stamford (06902) *(G-3329)*

Crane Nxt Co **(PA)**................................. **610 430-2510**
  950 Winter St Fl 4 Waltham (02451) *(G-12644)*

Crane Overseas LLC **(HQ)**....................... **203 363-7300**
  100 Stamford Pl Stamford (06902) *(G-3330)*

Crane Payment Solutions Inc **(DH)**............ **603 685-6999**
  1 Bedford Farms Dr Ste 103 Bedford (03110) *(G-13923)*

Crane Pro Services, Chelmsford *Also Called: Konecranes Inc* *(G-7935)*

Crane Security Tech Inc.............................. 603 881-1860
  1 Cellu Dr Nashua (03063) *(G-15084)*

Cranston Print Works Company **(PA)**.......... **401 943-4800**
  1381 Cranston St Cranston (02920) *(G-15844)*

Cranston Print Works Company.................... 401 397-2442
  25 Hopkins Hill Rd West Greenwich (02817) *(G-16884)*

Cranston Trucking, West Greenwich *Also Called: Cranston Print Works Company* *(G-16884)*

Cratedigger Inc.. 203 594-1488
  53 Turtle Back Rd New Canaan (06840) *(G-2081)*

Crauford Mfg, Belchertown *Also Called: Craufurd Manufacturing LLC* *(G-6279)*

Craufurd Manufacturing LLC....................... 413 323-4628
  401 Mill Valley Rd Belchertown (01007) *(G-6279)*

Crawford Sftwr Consulting Inc..................... 603 537-9630
  1e Commons Dr Unit 26 Londonderry (03053) *(G-14739)*

CRC Chrome Corporation............................ 203 630-1008
  169 Pratt St # R Meriden (06450) *(G-1662)*

Creamer Associates Inc.............................. 617 374-6000
  501 Cambridge St Ste 101 Cambridge (02141) *(G-7544)*

Createk, Southbridge *Also Called: Createk-Stone Inc* *(G-12012)*

Createk-Stone Inc..................................... 888 786-6389
  833 Main St Ste 2 Southbridge (01550) *(G-12012)*

Createx Colors, East Granby *Also Called: Color Craft Ltd* *(G-929)*

Creatics LLC.. 781 843-2202
  60 Columbian St Braintree (02184) *(G-7175)*

Creation Technologies Inc **(PA)**................. **877 734-7456**
  1 Beacon St Fl 23 Boston (02108) *(G-6675)*

Creation Technologies Intl Inc **(PA)**........... **877 734-7456**
  1 Beacon St Boston (02108) *(G-6676)*

Creative Apparel, Belmont *Also Called: Creative Apparel Assoc LLC* *(G-4543)*

Creative Apparel Assoc LLC........................ 207 342-2814
  318 Augusta Rd Belmont (04952) *(G-4543)*

Creative Communications, New London *Also Called: Bayard Inc* *(G-2222)*

Creative Companies, The, Bangor *Also Called: Creative Digital Imaging* *(G-4496)*

Creative Digital Imaging............................. 207 973-0500
  24 Dowd Rd Bangor (04401) *(G-4496)*

Creative Dimensions Inc............................. 203 250-6500
  345 Mccausland Ct Ste 2 Cheshire (06410) *(G-584)*

Creative Extrusion & Tech Inc...................... 508 587-2290
  230 Elliot St Brockton (02302) *(G-7271)*

Creative Imprints Inc................................. 508 285-7650
  15 Commerce Way Ste A Norton (02766) *(G-11125)*

Creative Marketing Services........................ 802 775-9500
  27 Wales St Rutland (05701) *(G-17493)*

Creative Material Tech Ltd........................... 413 284-0000
  21 Wilbraham St Unit B11 Palmer (01069) *(G-11272)*

Creative Materials Inc................................ 978 391-4700
  12 Willow Rd Ayer (01432) *(G-6180)*

Creative Media Applications......................... 203 226-0544
  22 Old Orchard Dr Weston (06883) *(G-4149)*

Creative Mktg Concepts Corp....................... 800 272-8267
  167 Killam Hill Rd Boxford (01921) *(G-7159)*

Creative Packaging Inc **(PA)**..................... **508 756-7275**
  175 James St Worcester (01603) *(G-13711)*

Creative Playthings Ltd **(PA)**..................... **508 620-0900**
  33 Loring Dr Framingham (01702) *(G-8753)*

Creative Print Products Inc.......................... 978 534-2030
  243 Whitney St Leominster (01453) *(G-9654)*

2024 Harris New England
Manufacturers Directory

(G-0000) Company's Geographic Section entry number

Creative Publishing Corp Amer **(PA)**.................... **978 532-5880**
  2 1st Ave Ste 103 Peabody (01960) *(G-11303)*

Creative Success Alliance Corp.......................... 781 878-7114
  100 Weymouth St Ste D2 Rockland (02370) *(G-11641)*

Creativestar Solution Inc................................. 617 326-5308
  1601 Trapelo Rd Ste 260 Waltham (02451) *(G-12645)*

Credit Card Supplies Corp................................. 508 485-4230
  105 Bartlett St Marlborough (01752) *(G-10139)*

Creed 20 LLC.. 860 826-4004
  1 Pucci Park New Britain (06051) *(G-2016)*

Creed Assets Inc.. 860 225-7884
  1 Pucci Park New Britain (06051) *(G-2017)*

Creed Monarch, New Britain *Also Called: Creed 20 LLC (G-2016)*

Creed Monarch, New Britain *Also Called: Creed Assets Inc (G-2017)*

Creo Medical Inc.. 860 670-6054
  100 Reserve Rd Ste B400 Danbury (06810) *(G-723)*

Creole Jos LLC.. 203 893-2875
  2389 Main St Ste 100 Glastonbury (06033) *(G-1276)*

Crescent Industries Company.............................. 207 777-3500
  191 Washington St S Auburn (04210) *(G-4425)*

Crescent Lumber & Building Sup, Orrington *Also Called: T and P Lumber Inc (G-5139)*

Crescent Mnfacturing Operating........................... 860 673-2591
  700 George Washington Tpke Burlington (06013) *(G-547)*

Crest Manufacturing Company.............................. 401 333-1350
  5 Hood Dr Lincoln (02865) *(G-16129)*

Crest Studios... 802 365-4200
  1096 Vt Route 30 Townshend (05353) *(G-17650)*

Crestline, Lewiston *Also Called: Geiger Bros (G-4962)*

Crh Americas Inc.. 978 840-1176
  14 Monument Sq Ste 302 Leominster (01453) *(G-9655)*

Crh Americas Inc.. 603 298-5959
  35 Glen Rd West Lebanon (03784) *(G-15681)*

Crh Americas Materials Inc................................ 603 669-2373
  1 Sundial Ave Ste 310 Manchester (03103) *(G-14839)*

Cri-Sil LLC... 207 283-6422
  359 Hill St Biddeford (04005) *(G-4558)*

Cri-Sil Silicone Technologies, Biddeford *Also Called: Cri-Sil LLC (G-4558)*

Cri-Tech Inc.. 781 826-5600
  85 Winter St Hanover (02339) *(G-9028)*

Cricket Press Inc... 860 521-9279
  236 Park Rd West Hartford (06119) *(G-4055)*

Cricket Radio LLC... 802 825-8368
  260 Battery St Burlington (05401) *(G-17129)*

Crimson Upholstery Company Inc............................ 617 332-0758
  175 North St Rear Newton (02460) *(G-10750)*

Crimzon Rose, West Warwick *Also Called: Uncas International LLC (G-16924)*

Crio Inc.. 617 302-9845
  177 Huntington Ave Ste 1703 Pmb 32876 Boston (02115) *(G-6677)*

Cristek Interconnects LLC................................. 978 735-2161
  95 Billerica Ave North Billerica (01862) *(G-10903)*

Cristy Corporation.. 978 343-4330
  260 Authority Dr Fitchburg (01420) *(G-8650)*

Criterion Inc... 203 703-9000
  301 Merritt 7 Norwalk (06851) *(G-2488)*

Critical Cmmnctons Cntrls Inst
  8 Commerce Way Exeter (03833) *(G-14290)*

Critical Prcess Filtration Inc **(PA)**.................... **603 595-0140**
  1 Chestnut St Ste 221 Nashua (03060) *(G-15085)*

Critical Scrn Printg & EMB................................ 860 443-4327
  82 Boston Post Rd Waterford (06385) *(G-3988)*

Criticare Technologies Inc................................ 401 667-3837
  333 Strawberry Field Rd Ste 11 Warwick (02886) *(G-16800)*

Crocetti Oakdale Pkg Co Inc **(PA)**...................... **508 587-0035**
  378 Pleasant St East Bridgewater (02333) *(G-8338)*

Crocker Architectural Shtmtl.............................. 508 987-9900
  129 Southbridge Rd North Oxford (01537) *(G-11031)*

Crocker Technical Papers Inc.............................. 978 345-7771
  431 Westminster St Fitchburg (01420) *(G-8651)*

Cromwell Concrete Products Incorporated
  667 Main St Cromwell (06416) *(G-690)*

Cronin Cabinets - Marine LLP.............................. 508 248-7026
  164 Sturbridge Rd Ste 20 Charlton (01507) *(G-7886)*

Crosby Bakery Inc... 603 882-1851
  51 E Pearl St Nashua (03060) *(G-15086)*

Crosby Valve & Gage Intl Inc.............................. 508 384-3121
  55 Cabot Blvd Mansfield (02048) *(G-10048)*

Crosby Whistle Stop....................................... 617 974-7410
  24 Roland St Charlestown (02129) *(G-7867)*

Crosby Yacht Yard Inc..................................... 508 428-6900
  72 Crosby Cir Ste 1 Osterville (02655) *(G-11245)*

Crosbys Welding LLC....................................... 207 974-7815
  99 Farm Rd Bangor (04401) *(G-4497)*

Cross Country Motor Club Inc **(HQ)**..................... **781 393-9300**
  1 Cabot Rd Medford (02155) *(G-10283)*

Cross Machine Inc... 603 752-6111
  167 Glen Ave Berlin (03570) *(G-13981)*

Crossfox Inc.. 207 664-2900
  Flye Point Rd Brooklin (04616) *(G-4633)*

Crosstek Membrane Tech LLC................................ 978 761-9601
  900 Technology Park Dr Ste 101 Billerica (01821) *(G-6430)*

Crosstown Press Inc....................................... 401 941-4061
  829 Park Ave Cranston (02910) *(G-15845)*

Crown Cstle Fibr Holdings Corp **(HQ)**................... **978 264-6001**
  80 Central St Ste 240 Boxborough (01719) *(G-7150)*

Crown Equipment Corporation............................... 207 773-4049
  165 Innovation Way Scarborough (04074) *(G-5429)*

Crown Equipment Corporation............................... 781 933-3366
  2 Presidential Way Woburn (01801) *(G-13551)*

Crown Lift Trucks, Scarborough *Also Called: Crown Equipment Corporation (G-5429)*

Crown Lift Trucks, Woburn *Also Called: Crown Equipment Corporation (G-13551)*

Crown Point Cabinetry Corp................................ 603 542-1273
  462 River Rd Claremont (03743) *(G-14086)*

Crown Point Excavation LLC................................ 802 291-4817
  890 Chester Rd Springfield (05156) *(G-17617)*

Crown Point Realty Corp Inc............................... 603 543-1208
  153 Charlestown Rd Claremont (03743) *(G-14087)*

Crrc LLC.. 860 635-2200
  46 Nooks Hill Rd Cromwell (06416) *(G-691)*

Crrc LLC **(PA)**... **877 684-6464**
  105 Nutmeg Rd S South Windsor (06074) *(G-3136)*

Crrc MA Corporation....................................... 617 415-7190
  655 Page Blvd Springfield (01104) *(G-12086)*

Cruz Construction Company Inc............................. 401 727-3770
  23 Maple St Ste 6 Cumberland (02864) *(G-15935)*

Crymed Technologies, Lexington *Also Called: Csa Medical Inc (G-9734)*

Cryogas International, Lexington *Also Called: Gasworld Publishing LLC (G-9744)*

Cryogenic Institute Neng Inc.............................. 508 459-7447
  78 Chilmark St Worcester (01604) *(G-13712)*

Crystal Brook Decorative Con, Springfield *Also Called: Crystal Brook Ldscp Cnstr Inc (G-12087)*

Crystal Brook Ldscp Cnstr Inc............................. 413 596-0055
  52 Hardy St Springfield (01129) *(G-12087)*

Crystal Engineering Co Inc **(PA)**....................... **978 465-7007**
  2 Stanley Tucker Dr Newburyport (01950) *(G-10677)*

Crystal Fairfield Tech LLC................................ 860 354-2111
  8 S End Plz New Milford (06776) *(G-2241)*

Crystal Gt Systems LLC.................................... 978 745-0088
  35 Congress St Salem (01970) *(G-11708)*

Crystal Hord Corporation.................................. 401 723-2989
  33 York Ave Ste 45 Pawtucket (02860) *(G-16360)*

Crystal Ice Co Inc.. 508 997-7522
  178 Front St New Bedford (02740) *(G-10582)*

Crystal Journey Candles LLC............................... 203 433-4735
  69 N Branford Rd Branford (06405) *(G-245)*

Crystal Rock Holdings Inc................................. 860 945-0661
  1050 Buckingham St Watertown (06795) *(G-4006)*

Crystal Rock Spring Water Co.............................. 860 945-0661
  1050 Buckingham St Watertown (06795) *(G-4007)*

Crystal Rock Water & Coffee Co, Watertown *Also Called: Crystal Rock Spring Water Co (G-4007)*

Crystal Stamping LLC...................................... 401 724-5880
  51 Charlton Ave Pawtucket (02860) *(G-16361)*

Cs Group - Usa Inc.. 860 944-0041
  222 Pitkin St Ste 123 East Hartford (06108) *(G-983)*

A
L
P
H
A
B
E
T
I
C

Cs-Ma Inc.. 603 863-1000
  8 Reeds Mill Rd Newport (03773) *(G-15227)*

Cs-Ma LLC **(PA)**.. **413 733-6631**
  2420 Boston Rd Wilbraham (01095) *(G-13356)*

Csa Medical Inc... 443 921-8053
  131 Hartwell Ave Ste 100 Lexington (02421) *(G-9734)*

Csc Inc... 401 724-5880
  51 Charlton Ave Pawtucket (02860) *(G-16362)*

CSC El Paso, Westport *Also Called: CSC Sugar LLC (G-4163)*

CSC Sugar LLC **(PA)**.. 203 846-5610
  33 Riverside Ave Ste 101 Westport (06880) *(G-4163)*

Csi, Harwinton *Also Called: Spring Computerized Inds LLC (G-1523)*

Csi Keyboards Inc... 978 532-8181
  56 Pulaski St Unit 1 Peabody (01960) *(G-11304)*

Csi Mfg Inc.. 508 986-2300
  121 Flanders Rd Westborough (01581) *(G-13096)*

Csourceauto, Raynham *Also Called: Construction Source MGT LLC (G-11585)*

Csp Inc **(PA)**... **978 954-5038**
  175 Cabot St Ste 210 Lowell (01854) *(G-9872)*

CSPI, Lowell *Also Called: Csp Inc (G-9872)*

Csr Technology Inc.. 781 791-6000
  1 Wall St Burlington (01803) *(G-7356)*

CST, Fall River *Also Called: Commonwlth Soap Toiletries Inc (G-8531)*

Cst Incorporated... 203 949-9900
  65 N Plains Industrial Rd Ste 3 Wallingford (06492) *(G-3796)*

CST of America LLC... 508 665-4400
  492 Old Connecticut Path Ste 500 Framingham (01701) *(G-8754)*

Csw Inc **(PA)**.. **413 589-1311**
  45 Tyburski Rd Ludlow (01056) *(G-9943)*

CT Acquisitions LLC.. 888 441-0537
  1 Grand St Wallingford (06492) *(G-3797)*

CT Composites & Marine Svc LLC...................................... 860 282-0100
  620 Sullivan Ave South Windsor (06074) *(G-3137)*

CT Crane and Hoist Service LLC.. 860 283-4320
  19 Burr Rd Plymouth (06782) *(G-2806)*

CT Driveshaft Service LLC.. 860 289-6459
  77 Cherry St East Hartford (06108) *(G-984)*

CT Fiberoptics Inc.. 860 763-4341
  64 Field Rd Ste 5a Somers (06071) *(G-3098)*

CT Hone Inc... 860 747-3884
  9 Grace Ave Plainville (06062) *(G-2752)*

CT Precast, Monroe *Also Called: Connecticut Precast Corp (G-1910)*

CT Sign Service LLC.. 860 322-3954
  500 Industrial Park Rd Deep River (06417) *(G-876)*

Cthru Metals Inc.. 203 884-1017
  14 Commerce Dr North Branford (06471) *(G-2364)*

CTI, Newington *Also Called: Component Technologies Inc (G-2281)*

CTR Enterprises Inc.. 978 794-2093
  60 Railroad St Ste 1 Haverhill (01835) *(G-9089)*

CTS Corporation... 603 421-2546
  34 Londonderry Rd Unit A1 Londonderry (03053) *(G-14740)*

CTS Interconnect Systems, Londonderry *Also Called: CTS Corporation (G-14740)*

CTS Valpey Corporation **(HQ)**... **508 435-6831**
  75 South St Hopkinton (01748) *(G-9314)*

Cubic Corporation... 603 369-5504
  54 Regional Dr Concord (03301) *(G-14127)*

Cubico Palmetto Holdings LLC.. 646 513-4981
  208 Harbor Dr Stamford (06902) *(G-3331)*

Cubicpv Inc **(PA)**... **781 861-1611**
  6-8 Preston Ct Bedford (01730) *(G-6218)*

Cubist Pharmaceuticals LLC... 781 860-8660
  65 Hayden Ave Lexington (02421) *(G-9735)*

Cubit Wire & Cable Co Inc... 413 539-9892
  164 Race St Ste 100 Holyoke (01040) *(G-9249)*

Cue Biopharma Inc **(PA)**... **617 949-2680**
  21 Erie St Ste 1 Cambridge (02139) *(G-7545)*

Cuescript Inc... 203 763-4030
  555 Lordship Blvd Unit G Stratford (06615) *(G-3532)*

Cuesport Inc.. 413 229-6626
  1415 Canaan Southfield Rd Southfield (01259) *(G-12039)*

Cullinan Oncology Inc **(PA)**... **617 410-4650**
  1 Main St Ste 1350 Cambridge (02142) *(G-7546)*

Culpepper's Bakery & Cafe, Worcester *Also Called: Rob Roy Foods Inc (G-13784)*

Cultivate, Leicester *Also Called: Cultivate Licensing LLC (G-9623)*

Cultivate Licensing LLC.. 508 859-8130
  1794 Main St Leicester (01524) *(G-9623)*

Culture Fresh Foods Inc... 203 632-8433
  162 Spring St Naugatuck (06770) *(G-1955)*

Culver Company LLC.. 978 463-1700
  104 Bridge Rd Salisbury (01952) *(G-11740)*

Cumar Inc... 617 389-7818
  69 Norman St Ste 4 Everett (02149) *(G-8484)*

Cumar Marble and Granite, Everett *Also Called: Cumar Inc (G-8484)*

Cumberland Farms Inc **(DH)**.. **800 225-9702**
  165 Flanders Rd Westborough (01581) *(G-13097)*

Cumberland Foundry Co Inc.. 401 658-3300
  310 W Wrentham Rd Cumberland (02864) *(G-15936)*

Cumberland Quarry Corp.. 401 658-4442
  6 Manville Hill Rd Cumberland (02864) *(G-15937)*

Cummings Printing Company, Hooksett *Also Called: Lew A Cummings Co Inc (G-14467)*

Cummins, Old Lyme *Also Called: Cummins Enviro Tech Inc (G-2638)*

Cummins, Braintree *Also Called: Cummins Northeast LLC (G-7176)*

Cummins - Allison Corp.. 203 794-9200
  125 Commerce Ct Ste 6 Cheshire (06410) *(G-585)*

Cummins Allison, Cheshire *Also Called: Cummins - Allison Corp (G-585)*

Cummins Enviro Tech Inc... 860 388-6377
  29 Mile Creek Rd Old Lyme (06371) *(G-2638)*

Cummins Inc.. 860 529-7474
  914 Cromwell Ave Rocky Hill (06067) *(G-2920)*

Cummins Inc.. 413 737-2659
  177 Rocus St Ste 1 Springfield (01104) *(G-12088)*

Cummins Northeast LLC **(HQ)**.. **781 801-1700**
  30 Braintree Hill Park Ste 101 Braintree (02184) *(G-7176)*

Cunningham Engineering Inc... 978 774-4169
  9 Electronics Ave Danvers (01923) *(G-8176)*

Cunningham Machine Co Inc... 978 256-7541
  35 Hunt Rd Chelmsford (01824) *(G-7921)*

Cura Software Solutions Co... 781 325-7158
  34 Crosby Dr Bedford (01730) *(G-6219)*

Curagen Corporation **(HQ)**.. **908 200-7500**
  119 4th Ave Needham Heights (02494) *(G-10538)*

Curia Global Inc... 781 205-1691
  20 Blanchard Rd Burlington (01803) *(G-7357)*

Curia Global Inc... 781 672-4530
  201 Jones Rd Ste 300 Waltham (02451) *(G-12646)*

Curia Massachusetts Inc **(DH)**....................................... **781 270-7900**
  99 S Bedford St Burlington (01803) *(G-7358)*

Curirx Inc... 978 658-2962
  205 Lowell St # 1c Wilmington (01887) *(G-13400)*

CURIS, Lexington *Also Called: Curis Inc (G-9736)*

Curis Inc **(PA)**.. **617 503-6500**
  128 Spring St Ste 510 Lexington (02421) *(G-9736)*

Current Composites, East Haven *Also Called: Current Inc (G-1039)*

Current Inc **(PA)**... **203 469-1337**
  30 Tyler Street Ext East Haven (06512) *(G-1039)*

Current Lighting Solutions LLC.. 713 521-6500
  745 Atlantic Ave Boston (02111) *(G-6678)*

Current Ltg Employeeco LLC... 216 266-2906
  745 Atlantic Ave Boston (02111) *(G-6679)*

Currex America, Newton *Also Called: Currex LLC (G-10751)*

Currex LLC.. 206 883-0209
  539 Commonwealth Ave Newton (02459) *(G-10751)*

Curriculum Associates, Littleton *Also Called: Curriculum Associates LLC (G-9807)*

Curriculum Associates LLC... 978 313-1276
  1 Distribution Center Cir Ste 200 Littleton (01460) *(G-9807)*

Curriculum Associates LLC **(PA)**..................................... **978 667-8000**
  153 Rangeway Rd North Billerica (01862) *(G-10904)*

Curry Copy and Printing Center, Manchester *Also Called: Baker Graphics Inc (G-14816)*

Curry Printing, Westborough *Also Called: J T Gardner Inc (G-13112)*

Curry Printing & Copy Center.. 207 772-5897
  10 City Ctr Portland (04101) *(G-5203)*

Curry's Leather Products, Randolph *Also Called: Currys Leather Shop Inc (G-11554)*

Currys Leather Shop Inc.. 781 963-0679
314 High St Randolph (02368) *(G-11554)*

Curtis Corporation A Del Corp.................................. 203 426-5861
44 Berkshire Rd Sandy Hook (06482) *(G-2949)*

Curtis Industries LLC **(PA)**.................................... **508 853-2200**
70 Hartwell St West Boylston (01583) *(G-12958)*

Curtis Packaging Corporation.................................. 203 426-5861
44 Berkshire Rd Sandy Hook (06482) *(G-2950)*

Curtis Products LLC.. 203 754-4155
70 Halcyon Dr Bristol (06010) *(G-433)*

Curtis Tractor Cab, West Boylston *Also Called: Curtis Industries LLC (G-12958)*

Curtiss Woodworking, Prospect *Also Called: Curtiss Woodworking Inc (G-2832)*

Curtiss Woodworking Inc.. 203 527-9305
123 Union City Road, Route 68 Prospect (06712) *(G-2832)*

Curtiss Wright Surface Tech, Wakefield *Also Called: Metal Improvement Company LLC (G-12519)*

Curtiss-Wright Corporation...................................... 864 486-9311
12 Thompson Rd East Windsor (06088) *(G-1070)*

Curtiss-Wright Surface Tech, Wilmington *Also Called: Metal Improvement Company LLC (G-13430)*

Curved Glass Distributors, Derby *Also Called: Whalley Glass Company (G-895)*

Custom & Miller Box Company.................................. 401 431-9007
25 Almeida Ave East Providence (02914) *(G-16012)*

Custom & Precision Pdts Inc.................................... 203 281-0818
2893 State St Rear Hamden (06517) *(G-1419)*

Custom Arospc Components LLC.............................. 781 935-4940
30 Nashua St Ste 3 Woburn (01801) *(G-13552)*

Custom Banner & Graphics LLC............................... 603 332-2067
184 Milton Rd Rochester (03868) *(G-15472)*

Custom Blends Inc.. 508 583-2995
40 Industrial Blvd Brockton (02301) *(G-7272)*

Custom Built Window Mfg LLC................................. 401 738-3800
80 Meadow St Warwick (02886) *(G-16801)*

Custom Canvas & Upholstery LLC............................ 207 241-8518
721 Portland Rd Bridgton (04009) *(G-4627)*

Custom Centric Machining, Bristol *Also Called: Custom Centric Machining LLC (G-15761)*

Custom Centric Machining LLC................................. 401 952-1804
500 Wood St Ste 21 Bristol (02809) *(G-15761)*

Custom Cft Ktchens By Rzio Bro.............................. 203 268-0271
8 Maple Dr Monroe (06468) *(G-1912)*

Custom Chrome Plating... 203 265-5667
400 S Orchard St Wallingford (06492) *(G-3798)*

Custom Coatings.. 508 771-8830
104 Enterprise Rd Hyannis (02601) *(G-9433)*

Custom Coatings Inc... 401 766-1500
22 Steel St North Smithfield (02896) *(G-16322)*

Custom Convyrs Fabrication Inc............................... 508 922-0283
140 Southbridge Rd North Oxford (01537) *(G-11032)*

Custom Cordage LLC, Waldoboro *Also Called: Advanced Indus Solutions Inc (G-5573)*

Custom Cordage, LLC, Augusta *Also Called: Advanced Indus Solutions Inc (G-4466)*

Custom Covers LLC... 860 669-4169
20 Riverside Dr Clinton (06413) *(G-641)*

Custom Design Incorporated.................................... 401 294-0200
370 Commerce Park Rd North Kingstown (02852) *(G-16243)*

Custom Design Woodworks LLC............................... 860 434-0515
10 Maywood Dr Old Lyme (06371) *(G-2639)*

Custom Extrusion Inc **(HQ)**.................................. **413 229-8748**
34 Home Road Sheffield (01257) *(G-11797)*

Custom Furniture & Design, Litchfield *Also Called: Custom Furniture & Design LLC (G-1555)*

Custom Furniture & Design LLC............................... 860 567-3519
601 Bantam Rd Litchfield (06759) *(G-1555)*

Custom Glass and Alum Co Inc............................... 978 640-5800
120 Lumber Ln Unit 4 Tewksbury (01876) *(G-12392)*

Custom Group Ctr For Mfg Tech.............................. 781 935-4940
30 Nashua St Woburn (01801) *(G-13553)*

Custom Iron Works Inc.. 401 826-3310
1600 Flat River Rd Coventry (02816) *(G-15812)*

Custom Ktchens By Chmpagne Inc........................... 508 528-7919
170 Grove St Franklin (02038) *(G-8828)*

Custom Learning Designs Inc.................................. 617 489-1702
375 Concord Ave Ste 101 Belmont (02478) *(G-6305)*

Custom Log Homes... 603 786-9082
10 Coursey Ln Rumney (03266) *(G-15497)*

Custom Machine & Tool Co Inc................................ 781 924-1003
301 Winter St Ste 2 Hanover (02339) *(G-9029)*

Custom Machine LLC.. 781 935-4940
30 Nashua St Ste 2 Woburn (01801) *(G-13554)*

Custom Metal Crafters Inc...................................... 860 953-4210
815 N Mountain Rd Newington (06111) *(G-2283)*

Custom Metal Crafters CMC, Newington *Also Called: Custom Metal Crafters Inc (G-2283)*

Custom Milling & Machining Inc............................... 207 776-8137
1087 Main St Waterboro (04087) *(G-5590)*

Custom Molded Products Inc.................................... 401 464-9991
24 Thelma St North Providence (02904) *(G-16298)*

Custom Mtal Fabricators VT LLC.............................. 802 888-0033
327 Ferry St Hyde Park (05655) *(G-17299)*

Custom Office Furn Boston Inc................................ 781 933-9970
10 Atlantic Ave Ste 3 Woburn (01801) *(G-13555)*

Custom Printing & Copy Inc **(PA)**.......................... **860 290-6890**
16 Debra St Enfield (06082) *(G-1127)*

Custom Publishing, Brewster *Also Called: The Pohly Company (G-7217)*

Custom Seasonings Inc... 978 762-6300
12 Heritage Way Gloucester (01930) *(G-8931)*

Custom Tees Plus.. 203 752-1071
365 Whalley Ave New Haven (06511) *(G-2142)*

Custom Truck One Source LP.................................. 574 370-2740
6 Sutton Cir Hooksett (03106) *(G-14464)*

Custom TS n More LLC... 203 438-1592
135 Ethan Allen Hwy Ridgefield (06877) *(G-2894)*

Custom Vault Corporation.. 203 746-0506
6 Jeremy Dr New Fairfield (06812) *(G-2094)*

Customer Fulfillment Center, Quincy *Also Called: Boston Scientific Corporation (G-11507)*

Customergauge USA LLC.. 844 211-3932
3 Burlington Woods Dr Ste 302 Burlington (01803) *(G-7359)*

Customic Adjustable Bedz, Natick *Also Called: Ppj LLC (G-10493)*

Customink LLC... 781 205-4035
30 Forbes Rd Ste H Braintree (02184) *(G-7177)*

Customized Foods Mfg LLC..................................... 203 759-1645
8 S Commons Rd Waterbury (06704) *(G-3902)*

Customvault Convergint, Bethel *Also Called: Cvc II Inc (G-105)*

Cutter & Locke Inc **(PA)**...................................... **802 889-3500**
234 Monarch Hill Rd Tunbridge (05077) *(G-17652)*

Cutting Edge Carbide Tech Inc................................ 888 210-9670
438 Wallingford Ave Athol (01331) *(G-5977)*

Cutting Edge Technologies, Plymouth *Also Called: Richards Micro-Tool LLC (G-11474)*

Cutting Edge Texstyles, Bedford *Also Called: Brand & Oppenheimer Co Inc (G-6216)*

Cutting Tool Technologies Inc.................................. 603 654-2550
327 Forest Rd Wilton (03086) *(G-15704)*

Cv Custom Volt.. 203 431-7646
162 Danbury Rd Ridgefield (06877) *(G-2895)*

CV Industries Corporation.. 203 828-6566
2 Fox Hollow Rd Oxford (06478) *(G-2692)*

Cvc II Inc **(DH)**.. **203 401-4205**
4 Research Dr Bethel (06801) *(G-105)*

CW Hood Yachts Inc... 781 631-0192
3 Beacon St Ste 4 Marblehead (01945) *(G-10086)*

Cw Keller & Associates LLC..................................... 603 382-2028
9 Hale Spring Rd Plaistow (03865) *(G-15339)*

Cw Solutions LLC... 860 229-7700
200 Myrtle St New Britain (06053) *(G-2018)*

Cwindows, Portland *Also Called: Paradigm Operating Company LLC (G-5255)*

Cwl Enterprises Inc **(HQ)**.................................... **303 790-8023**
200 Stamford Pl 2nd Fl Stamford (06902) *(G-3332)*

Cx Thin Films LLC.. 401 461-5500
1515 Elmwood Ave Cranston (02910) *(G-15846)*

Cxe Equipment Services, Seabrook *Also Called: Cxe Equipment Services LLC (G-15589)*

Cxe Equipment Services LLC................................... 603 437-2477
33 Beckman Lndg Seabrook (03874) *(G-15589)*

Cxo Media, Needham Heights *Also Called: Cxo Media Inc (G-10539)*

Cxo Media Inc **(DH)**... **508 766-5696**
140 Kendrick St # B Needham Heights (02494) *(G-10539)*

Cya Technologies Inc.. 203 513-3111
   3 Enterprise Dr Ste 408 Shelton (06484) *(G-2994)*

Cyalume, West Springfield *Also Called: Cyalume Technologies Inc (G-13020)*

Cyalume Technologies Inc **(HQ)**.................................. **888 858-7881**
   96 Windsor St West Springfield (01089) *(G-13020)*

Cyber Global Risk Exchange, Concord *Also Called: Cybergrx Inc (G-8111)*

Cyberark Software Inc **(HQ)**.. **617 965-1544**
   60 Wells Ave Ste 103 Newton (02459) *(G-10752)*

Cyberbit Inc.. 415 960-5750
   71 Commercial St Ste 26 Boston (02109) *(G-6680)*

Cyberchrome Inc.. 203 488-9594
   19 Business Park Dr Ste B Branford (06405) *(G-246)*

Cybercopy Inc.. 207 775-2679
   55 Bradley Dr Ste A Westbrook (04092) *(G-5623)*

Cybereason Government Inc.. 978 618-6992
   200 Berkeley St Boston (02116) *(G-6681)*

Cybergrx Inc... 877 929-2374
   33 Bradford St Concord (01742) *(G-8111)*

Cybernorth LLC.. 207 331-3310
   15 Cottage Rd Unit 2433 South Portland (04116) *(G-5496)*

Cyberresearch Inc.. 203 643-5000
   29 Business Park Dr Ste D Branford (06405) *(G-247)*

Cybertools.. 800 894-9206
   249 Ayer Rd Ste 302 Harvard (01451) *(G-9061)*

Cybex International Inc... 508 533-4167
   51 Alder St Medway (02053) *(G-10304)*

Cyclerion, Cambridge *Also Called: Cyclerion Therapeutics Inc (G-7547)*

Cyclerion Therapeutics Inc **(PA)**................................. **857 327-8778**
   245 1st St Ste 18 Cambridge (02142) *(G-7547)*

Cycling Sports Group Inc **(HQ)**................................... **203 845-8300**
   1 Cannondale Way Wilton (06897) *(G-4238)*

Cyclone Microsystems Inc.. 203 786-5536
   25 Marne St Hamden (06514) *(G-1420)*

Cyclone Rake, West Haven *Also Called: Woodland Power Products Inc (G-4133)*

Cyclones Arena.. 603 880-4424
   20 Constitution Dr Hudson (03051) *(G-14492)*

Cyduct Diagnostics Inc... 617 360-9700
   65 Sprague St Boston (02136) *(G-6682)*

Cyglass, Littleton *Also Called: Cyglass Inc (G-9808)*

Cyglass Inc... 978 665-0280
   305 Foster St Ste 200 Littleton (01460) *(G-9808)*

Cygnus Inc... 603 431-8989
   95 Brewery Ln Unit 16 Portsmouth (03801) *(G-15379)*

Cygnus Medical LLC.. 800 990-7489
   965 W Main St Ste 2 Branford (06405) *(G-248)*

Cyient Defense Services Inc... 860 357-4317
   120 Production Ct New Britain (06051) *(G-2019)*

Cynosure LLC **(HQ)**.. **978 256-4200**
   5 Carlisle Rd Westford (01886) *(G-13233)*

Cynthia Carroll Pallian... 207 646-1600
   2049 Post Rd Wells (04090) *(G-5599)*

Cypress Woodworks LLC.. 802 338-0538
   150 Stuart Ln Waterbury (05676) *(G-17673)*

Cyr Lumber Inc... 802 893-4448
   215 Poor Farm Rd Milton (05468) *(G-17357)*

Cyr Woodworking Inc... 860 232-1991
   139 Summit St Newington (06111) *(G-2284)*

Cyro Industry... 207 324-6000
   1796 Main St Sanford (04073) *(G-5393)*

Cytec Industries Inc.. 203 321-2200
   1937 W Main St Ste 1 Stamford (06902) *(G-3333)*

Cyteir Therapeutics Inc **(PA)**..................................... **857 285-4140**
   128 Spring St Bldg A Lexington (02421) *(G-9737)*

Cytonome/St LLC... 617 330-5030
   9 Oak Park Dr Bedford (01730) *(G-6220)*

Cytosol Laboratories Inc... 781 848-9386
   55 Messina Dr Braintree (02184) *(G-7178)*

Cytyc Corporation.. 508 303-4746
   445 Simarano Dr Marlborough (01752) *(G-10140)*

Cytyc Corporation **(HQ)**.. **508 263-2900**
   250 Campus Dr Marlborough (01752) *(G-10141)*

Cytyc Corporation... 603 668-7688
   2 E Perimeter Rd Londonderry (03053) *(G-14741)*

Cytyc Surgical Products LLC **(HQ)**.............................. **508 263-2900**
   250 Campus Dr Marlborough (01752) *(G-10142)*

Cz Machine Inc... 603 382-4259
   110 Hunt Rd East Hampstead (03826) *(G-14270)*

D & B Machining Inc... 401 726-2347
   53 John St Cumberland (02864) *(G-15938)*

D & B Tool Co LLC... 203 878-6026
   83 Erna Ave Milford (06461) *(G-1815)*

D & D Filtration, Kensington *Also Called: D&D Fltrtion Cons Sppliers Inc (G-1539)*

D & D Precision Machine Co Inc..................................... 508 946-8010
   395 Plymouth St Middleboro (02346) *(G-10356)*

D & E Screw Machine Pdts Inc.. 508 658-7344
   34 Bill Bromage Dr Colebrook (03576) *(G-14104)*

D & G, Westbrook *Also Called: D & G Machine Products Inc (G-5624)*

D & G Machine Products Inc.. 207 854-1500
   50 Eisenhower Dr Westbrook (04092) *(G-5624)*

D & L Associates Inc.. 781 400-5068
   679 Highland Ave Rear Needham Heights (02494) *(G-10540)*

D & M Group LLC... 860 928-5010
   18 Maple St Putnam (06260) *(G-2852)*

D & M Packing LLC... 203 591-8986
   407 Brookside Rd Ste 1 Waterbury (06708) *(G-3903)*

D & R Products Co Inc.. 978 562-4137
   455 River Rd Hudson (01749) *(G-9361)*

D & S Manufacturing, Southwick *Also Called: Tova Industries Inc (G-12048)*

D & S Manufacturing Company Incorporated................... 508 799-7812
   14 Sword St Ste 4 Auburn (01501) *(G-6111)*

D & S Plating Co Inc.. 413 533-7771
   102 Cabot St Ste 6 Holyoke (01040) *(G-9250)*

D & W Tool & Findings Inc.. 401 727-3030
   601 Mineral Spring Ave Pawtucket (02860) *(G-16363)*

D and D Manufacturing LLC
   49 Mitchell Rd Ipswich (01938) *(G-9481)*

D and GM Achine Products... 207 854-1500
   20 Hutcherson Dr Gorham (04038) *(G-4817)*

D B S Industries Inc.. 978 373-4748
   144 Hilldale Ave Haverhill (01832) *(G-9090)*

D B Welding, Leominster *Also Called: Patricia Barrett (G-9692)*

D C M Services, Framingham *Also Called: David Gilbert (G-8755)*

D D Bean & Sons Co **(PA)**... **603 532-8311**
   207 Peterborough St Jaffrey (03452) *(G-14565)*

D D J.. 508 987-0417
   17 Sutton Ave Oxford (01540) *(G-11251)*

D E Enterprise Inc.. 207 594-9544
   680 Commercial St Rockport (04856) *(G-5346)*

D F E, Rochester *Also Called: Dover Flexo Electronics Inc (G-15475)*

D F Richard Inc... 603 742-2020
   124 Broadway Dover (03820) *(G-14225)*

D G C, Gardner *Also Called: Data Guide Cable Corporation (G-8883)*

D J Bass Inc.. 508 678-4499
   84 Bates St New Bedford (02745) *(G-10583)*

D J Fabricators Inc... 978 356-0228
   94 Turnpike Rd Ipswich (01938) *(G-9482)*

D L Maher Co.. 781 933-3210
   71 Concord St North Reading (01864) *(G-11039)*

D M I, Woburn *Also Called: Duplication Management Inc (G-13559)*

D R Designs Inc... 207 622-3303
   980 Western Ave Manchester (04351) *(G-5044)*

D R Dimes & Co Ltd.. 603 942-8050
   49 Dimes Rd Northwood (03261) *(G-15272)*

D R Logging Inc.. 207 316-6434
   11 Pinette Ln Fort Kent (04743) *(G-4786)*

D S G, Lowell *Also Called: D S Graphics Inc (G-9873)*

D S Graphics Inc **(PA)**... **978 970-1359**
   120 Stedman St Lowell (01851) *(G-9873)*

D S Greene Co Inc.. 781 245-2644
   431 Water St Wakefield (01880) *(G-12506)*

D Simpson Inc.. 401 232-3638
   13 Industrial Dr Smithfield (02917) *(G-16693)*

(G-0000) Company's Geographic Section entry number

D V Die Cutting Inc		978 777-0300
45 Prince St Danvers (01923) *(G-8177)*		
D W Clark Inc **(PA)**		**508 378-4014**
692 N Bedford St East Bridgewater (02333) *(G-8339)*		
D W Clark Inc		508 378-4014
36 Allison Ave Taunton (02780) *(G-12330)*		
D. F. Richard Energy, Dover *Also Called: D F Richard Inc (G-14225)*		
D.M.I. Manufacturing, North Kingstown *Also Called: Durant Tool Company Inc (G-16246)*		
D.R. Charles Envmtl Excav, Monroe *Also Called: DR Charles Envmtl Cnstr LLC (G-1913)*		
D'Andrea USA, Berlin *Also Called: Delmar Products Inc (G-64)*		
D&C Global Enterprise LLC		810 553-2360
290 East Ave Bridgeport (06610) *(G-313)*		
D&D Fltrtion Cons Sppliers Inc		860 829-3690
612 Four Rod Rd Kensington (06037) *(G-1539)*		
D&R Marine Upholstery & Canvas		860 989-9646
369 Old Main St Rocky Hill (06067) *(G-2921)*		
D&S Engineered Products, Attleboro *Also Called: Bruce Diamond Corporation (G-5999)*		
Da Capo Publishing Inc		802 864-5684
255 S Champlain St Ste 5 Burlington (05401) *(G-17130)*		
Da Rosas		508 693-0110
46 Circuit Ave Oak Bluffs (02557) *(G-11221)*		
Daaquam Lumber Maine Inc **(HQ)**		**207 435-6401**
1203 Aroostook Scenic Hwy Masardis (04732) *(G-5047)*		
Dac Systems Inc		203 924-7000
2 Corporate Dr Ste 949 Shelton (06484) *(G-2995)*		
Dacruz Manufacturing Inc		860 584-5315
100 Broderick Rd Bristol (06010) *(G-434)*		
Dadanco - Mestek, Westfield *Also Called: Mestek Inc (G-13186)*		
Daedalon, Waldoboro *Also Called: TSS-Maine LLC (G-5579)*		
Daedalus Software Inc		617 851-5157
215 First St Ste 7 Cambridge (02142) *(G-7548)*		
Dagle Electrical Cnstr Corp		800 379-1459
68 Industrial Way Wilmington (01887) *(G-13401)*		
Dahle North America Inc		603 924-0003
49 Vose Farm Rd Suite 100 Peterborough (03458) *(G-15314)*		
Dahlicious, Leominster *Also Called: Dahlicious Holdings LLC (G-9656)*		
Dahlicious Holdings LLC		978 401-2103
320 Hamilton St Ste 3 Leominster (01453) *(G-9656)*		
Dahlicious LLC		505 200-0396
320 Hamilton St Ste 3 Leominster (01453) *(G-9657)*		
Dailey Precast LLC **(HQ)**		**802 442-4418**
295 Airport Rd Shaftsbury (05262) *(G-17549)*		
Dailey-Mc Neil, Kensington *Also Called: Dan Dailey Inc (G-14629)*		
Daily Gardener		802 223-7851
2930 Dugar Brook Rd Calais (05648) *(G-17167)*		
Daily Hampshire Gazette		413 527-4000
72 Main St Easthampton (01027) *(G-8442)*		
Daily News-Mercury, Malden *Also Called: Eastern Mddlsex Press Pblctons (G-10012)*		
Daily Times Chronicle, Woburn *Also Called: Wobum Daily Times Inc (G-13689)*		
Daily Woburn Times Inc		978 658-2346
1 Arrow Drive Wilmington (01887) *(G-13402)*		
Dairy Queen		508 853-2700
328 W Boylston St West Boylston (01583) *(G-12959)*		
Dairy Queen, Spencer *Also Called: Goldacre Realty Inc (G-12060)*		
Dairy Queen, West Boylston *Also Called: Dairy Queen (G-12959)*		
Dakin Road Investments Inc		978 443-4020
162 Ayer Rd Littleton (01460) *(G-9809)*		
Dakota Life Sciences, Bridgeport *Also Called: Kasten Inc (G-339)*		
Dakota Systems Inc		978 275-0600
1057 Bdwy Rd Rte 113 Dracut (01826) *(G-8303)*		
Daktari Diagnostics Inc		617 336-3299
85 Bolton St Ste 229 Cambridge (02140) *(G-7549)*		
Dal-Tile Corporation		802 951-2030
44 Miller Ln Ste 20 Williston (05495) *(G-17726)*		
DAL-TILE CORPORATION, Williston *Also Called: Dal-Tile Corporation (G-17726)*		
Dale E Crawford		603 473-2738
2453 Lovell Lake Rd Sanbornville (03872) *(G-15578)*		
Dale E Percy Inc		802 253-8503
269 Weeks Hill Rd Stowe (05672) *(G-17630)*		
Dale Engineering & Son Inc		781 541-6055
3 Alfred Cir Bedford (01730) *(G-6221)*		

Dale Medical Products Inc **(PA)**		**800 343-3980**
40 Kenwood Cir Ste 7 Franklin (02038) *(G-8829)*		
Dale Rand Printing Inc		207 773-8198
508 Riverside St Ste A Portland (04103) *(G-5204)*		
Dalegip America Inc		207 323-1880
34 Kidder Point Rd Searsport (04974) *(G-5452)*		
Dalton Electric Heating Co Inc		978 356-9844
28 Hayward St Ipswich (01938) *(G-9483)*		
Dalton Enterprises Inc **(PA)**		**203 272-3221**
131 Willow St Cheshire (06410) *(G-586)*		
Dalton Manufacturing Co Inc		978 388-2227
6 Clark St Amesbury (01913) *(G-5833)*		
Dalton Manufacturing Group Inc		978 388-2227
6 Clark St Amesbury (01913) *(G-5834)*		
Dama Jewelry, East Providence *Also Called: Kefi Development Inc (G-16027)*		
Dampney Company Inc		617 389-2805
85 Paris St Everett (02149) *(G-8485)*		
Dan Beard Inc		203 924-4346
64 Hawthorne Ave Shelton (06484) *(G-2996)*		
Dan Dailey Inc		603 778-2303
2 North Rd Kensington (03833) *(G-14629)*		
Dana Robes Boat Builders		207 529-2433
75 Southern Point Rd Round Pond (04564) *(G-5352)*		
Danafilms Corp		508 366-8884
5 Otis St Westborough (01581) *(G-13098)*		
Danaher Tool Group		203 284-7000
61 Barnes Industrial Park N Wallingford (06492) *(G-3799)*		
Danaher Tool Group, Simsbury *Also Called: Easco Hand Tools Inc (G-3086)*		
Danbury A LLC		203 744-5202
25 Sugar Hollow Rd Danbury (06810) *(G-724)*		
Danbury Ortho		203 797-1500
2 Riverview Dr Danbury (06810) *(G-725)*		
Danbury Powersports Inc		203 791-1310
41 Lake Avenue Ext Danbury (06811) *(G-726)*		
Danbury Sheet Metal, Bethel *Also Called: Varnum Enterprises LLC (G-140)*		
Danbury Square Box Company		203 744-4611
1a Broad St Danbury (06810) *(G-727)*		
Dance It Up Inc		508 839-1648
36 N Main St North Grafton (01536) *(G-11021)*		
DAndrea Corporation **(PA)**		**203 932-6000**
985 Boston Post Rd West Haven (06516) *(G-4101)*		
Danecraft, Providence *Also Called: J Cal Inc (G-16546)*		
DAngelo Burial Vaults		508 528-0385
30 Raymond St Franklin (02038) *(G-8830)*		
Danica Candle Works, Rockport *Also Called: Danica Design (G-5347)*		
Danica Design		207 236-3060
569 West St Rockport (04856) *(G-5347)*		
Daniel F Crapa		203 746-5706
17 Calverton Dr New Fairfield (06812) *(G-2095)*		
Daniele, Mapleville *Also Called: Daniele International LLC (G-16167)*		
Daniele Inc		401 568-6228
105 Davis Dr Pascoag (02859) *(G-16336)*		
Daniele International Inc		401 568-6228
105 Davis Dr Pascoag (02859) *(G-16337)*		
Daniele International Inc		401 568-6228
180 Davis Dr Pascoag (02859) *(G-16338)*		
Daniele International LLC **(PA)**		**401 371-2000**
1000 Charcuterie Dr Mapleville (02839) *(G-16167)*		
Daniele International, Inc., Pascoag *Also Called: Daniele International Inc (G-16337)*		
DANIELE INTERNATIONAL, INC., Pascoag *Also Called: Daniele International Inc (G-16338)*		
Daniels Construction, Ascutney *Also Called: Neil H Daniels Inc (G-16993)*		
Danjon Manufacturing Corp		203 272-7258
1075 S Main St Cheshire (06410) *(G-587)*		
Danly IEM, Boston *Also Called: Connell Limited Partnership (G-6665)*		
Danver, Wallingford *Also Called: CT Acquisitions LLC (G-3797)*		
Danvers Herald		978 774-0505
152 Sylvan St Danvers (01923) *(G-8178)*		
Danvers Industrial Packg Corp		978 777-0020
39 Tozer Rd Beverly (01915) *(G-6344)*		
Danversbank		978 468-2243
25 Railroad Ave South Hamilton (01982) *(G-11969)*		

Dark Field Technologies Inc.................... 203 298-0731
  5 Research Dr Shelton (06484) *(G-2997)*

Dark Harbor Boatyard Corp.................... 207 734-2246
  700 Acre Is Islesboro (04848) *(G-4908)*

Dark Monk LLC.................... 978 766-5315
  21 Conant St Salem (01970) *(G-11709)*

Darlings Boatworks Inc.................... 802 425-2004
  821 Ferry Rd Charlotte (05445) *(G-17176)*

Darlington Fabrics, Westerly *Also Called: Moore Company (G-16938)*

Darly Custom Technology Inc.................... 860 298-7966
  276 Addison Rd Windsor (06095) *(G-4269)*

Darmann Abrasive Products Inc **(PA)**.................... **978 365-4544**
  100 Sterling St Clinton (01510) *(G-8076)*

Darn Tough Vermont, Northfield *Also Called: Cabot Hosiery Mills Inc (G-17432)*

Darrell C McGuire & Sons Inc.................... 207 532-0511
  1157 Hodgdon Corner Rd Houlton (04730) *(G-4899)*

Dart World Inc.................... 781 581-6035
  140 Linwood St Ste 1 Lynn (01905) *(G-9966)*

Dartmouth Inc.................... 603 646-2600
  6175 Robinson Hall Hanover (03755) *(G-14421)*

Dartmouth Alumni Magazine, Hanover *Also Called: Trustees of Dartmouth College (G-14431)*

Dartmouth Awning Co Inc.................... 508 636-6838
  45 Beeden Rd Westport (02790) *(G-13295)*

Dartmouth Journal Services Inc.................... 802 244-1457
  5 Pilgrim Park Rd Ste 5 Waterbury (05676) *(G-17674)*

Dartmouth Printing Company **(DH)**.................... **603 643-2220**
  69 Lyme Rd Hanover (03755) *(G-14422)*

Dartmouth Review, Hanover *Also Called: Hanover Review Inc (G-14424)*

DARTMOUTH, THE, Hanover *Also Called: Dartmouth Inc (G-14421)*

Darwin A Lewis Inc.................... 802 457-4521
  243 Densmore Hill Rd Hartland (05048) *(G-17286)*

Dasco Welded Products Inc.................... 203 754-9353
  2038 Thomaston Ave Waterbury (06704) *(G-3904)*

Dashboard Advantage LLC.................... 949 232-7409
  207 Webster St Boston (02128) *(G-6683)*

Dasko Identification Products.................... 401 435-6500
  1 New Industrial Way Ste 2 Warren (02885) *(G-16757)*

Dasko Label, Warren *Also Called: Dasko Identification Products (G-16757)*

Data Associates, Waltham *Also Called: Data Associates Business Trust (G-12647)*

Data Associates Business Trust
  280 Bear Hill Rd Waltham (02451) *(G-12647)*

Data Binding Inc.................... 401 738-7901
  10 New England Way Warwick (02886) *(G-16802)*

Data Electronic Devices Inc.................... 603 893-2047
  32 Northwestern Dr Salem (03079) *(G-15517)*

Data Guide Cable Corporation.................... 978 632-0900
  232 Sherman St Gardner (01440) *(G-8883)*

Data Industrial Corporation.................... 508 758-6390
  6 County Rd Ste 6 Mattapoisett (02739) *(G-10256)*

Data Management Incorporated.................... 860 677-8586
  537 New Britain Ave Unionville (06085) *(G-3748)*

Data Plus Incorporated.................... 978 888-6300
  55 Middlesex St Unit 219 North Chelmsford (01863) *(G-10974)*

Data Print Inc.................... 781 935-3350
  18 Cranes Ct Woburn (01801) *(G-13556)*

Data Radio Management Co Inc.................... 603 598-1222
  30 Daniel Webster Hwy Ste 9 Merrimack (03054) *(G-14979)*

Data Signal Corporation.................... 203 882-5393
  16 Higgins Dr Milford (06460) *(G-1816)*

Data Technology Inc.................... 860 871-8082
  24 Industrial Park Rd W Tolland (06084) *(G-3656)*

Data Translation Inc **(PA)**.................... **508 481-3700**
  10 Commerce Way Ste E # F Norton (02766) *(G-11126)*

Data-Graphics Inc.................... 860 667-0435
  240 Hartford Ave Newington (06111) *(G-2285)*

Datacon Inc.................... 781 273-5800
  10 Elizabeth Dr Unit 8 Chelmsford (01824) *(G-7922)*

Dataed, Salem *Also Called: Data Electronic Devices Inc (G-15517)*

Datamann Inc.................... 802 295-6600
  1994 Hartford Ave Wilder (05088) *(G-17714)*

Datanational Corporation.................... 781 826-3400
  100 Schoosett St Ste 2a Pembroke (02359) *(G-11361)*

Datanomix Inc.................... 843 885-4639
  71 Spit Brook Rd # 210 Nashua (03060) *(G-15087)*

Dataquest Korea Inc.................... 239 561-4862
  56 Top Gallant Rd Stamford (06902) *(G-3334)*

Datarobot Inc **(PA)**.................... **617 765-4500**
  225 Franklin St Fl 13 Boston (02110) *(G-6684)*

Datasite Global Corporation.................... 617 389-7900
  40 Commercial St Everett (02149) *(G-8486)*

Datawatch Corporation **(HQ)**.................... **978 441-2200**
  4 Crosby Dr Bedford (01730) *(G-6222)*

Dataxoom Corp **(PA)**.................... **510 474-0044**
  25 Sundial Ave Ste 316 Manchester (03103) *(G-14840)*

Datron Dynamics Inc.................... 603 215-5850
  115 Emerson Rd Milford (03055) *(G-15020)*

Dattco Sales & Service.................... 860 229-4878
  121 Ballard St Saugus (01906) *(G-11756)*

Datto, Norwalk *Also Called: Datto Holding Corp (G-2489)*

Datto Holding Corp **(DH)**.................... **888 995-1431**
  101 Merritt 7 Norwalk (06851) *(G-2489)*

Daunis.................... 207 773-6011
  616 Congress St Ste 2 Portland (04101) *(G-5205)*

Daunis Fine Jewelry, Portland *Also Called: Daunis (G-5205)*

Dauphinais & Son Inc.................... 413 596-3964
  2420 Boston Rd Wilbraham (01095) *(G-13357)*

Dauphinais Concrete.................... 508 657-0941
  79 Hartford Ave Bellingham (02019) *(G-6289)*

Dav-Tech Plating Inc.................... 508 485-8472
  40 Cedar Hill St Marlborough (01752) *(G-10143)*

Daves Coffee LLC **(PA)**.................... **800 483-4436**
  35 Walts Way Narragansett (02882) *(G-16188)*

Daves Fresh Mrktplace MGT Inc.................... 401 830-5650
  371 Putnam Pike Ste 590 Smithfield (02917) *(G-16694)*

Daves Truck Repair Inc.................... 413 734-8898
  1023 Page Blvd Springfield (01104) *(G-12089)*

Davic Inc.................... 207 774-0093
  417 Congress St Portland (04101) *(G-5206)*

Davico Inc.................... 508 998-1150
  95 Brook St New Bedford (02746) *(G-10584)*

Davico Manufacturing, New Bedford *Also Called: Davico Inc (G-10584)*

David Bird LLC.................... 207 832-0569
  151 One Pie Rd Waldoboro (04572) *(G-5575)*

David Clark, Worcester *Also Called: David Clark Company Inc (G-13713)*

David Clark Company Inc **(PA)**.................... **508 756-6216**
  360 Franklin St Worcester (01604) *(G-13713)*

David D Douglas Inc.................... 603 437-1151
  23 Londonderry Rd Unit 19 Londonderry (03053) *(G-14742)*

David Gilbert.................... 508 879-1507
  10 Olympic St Framingham (01701) *(G-8755)*

David Lefort.................... 781 826-9033
  13 Arrowhead Path Halifax (02338) *(G-9020)*

David Packard Company Inc.................... 508 987-2998
  15 Industrial Park Rd E Oxford (01540) *(G-11252)*

David R Burl.................... 603 235-2661
  56 N Mast St Goffstown (03045) *(G-14347)*

David R Godine Publisher Inc.................... 603 532-4100
  426 Nutting Rd Jaffrey (03452) *(G-14566)*

David Rich Co, Wellesley *Also Called: Watson Printing Co Inc (G-12947)*

David Saunders Inc.................... 207 228-1888
  192 Gannett Dr South Portland (04106) *(G-5497)*

David Streeter.................... 603 542-6045
  853 River Rd Charlestown (03603) *(G-14061)*

David W Wallace.................... 413 625-6523
  635 Mohawk Trl Shelburne Falls (01370) *(G-11803)*

Davidon Alloys, Warwick *Also Called: Davidon Industries Inc (G-16803)*

Davidon Industries Inc.................... 401 737-8380
  87 Dewey Ave Warwick (02886) *(G-16803)*

Davies Family Selections Inc.................... 508 317-6024
  255 Hill And Plain Rd East Falmouth (02536) *(G-8358)*

Davinci Laboratories, Williston *Also Called: Foodscience LLC (G-17731)*

Davis Art Images, Worcester *Also Called: Davis Publications Inc (G-13715)*

Davis Brothers Inc.................... 207 794-1001
  86 Access Rd Chester (04457) *(G-4691)*

Davis Corp Worcester Inc **(PA)**.. **508 754-7201**	
44 Portland St Worcester (01608) *(G-13714)*	
Davis Forestry Products Inc.. 207 448-2625	
Danforth (04424) *(G-4718)*	
Davis Publications, Worcester *Also Called: Davis Corp Worcester Inc (G-13714)*	
Davis Publications Inc.. 508 754-7201	
50 Portland St Fl 3 Worcester (01608) *(G-13715)*	
Davis Tree & Logging LLC... 203 938-2153	
57 North St Ste 209 Danbury (06810) *(G-728)*	
Davis Village Solutions LLC... 603 878-3662	
167 Davis Village Rd New Ipswich (03071) *(G-15197)*	
Davis Zac Fine Woodworking... 207 926-4710	
321 Gloucester Hill Rd New Gloucester (04260) *(G-5084)*	
Davis-Joncas Enterprises Inc... 207 883-6200	
7 Lincoln Ave Scarborough (04074) *(G-5430)*	
Davis-Standard LLC **(HQ)**.. **860 300-3928**	
1 Extrusion Dr Pawcatuck (06379) *(G-2717)*	
Davis-Standard Holdings Inc **(PA)**.................................. **860 599-1010**	
1 Extrusion Dr Pawcatuck (06379) *(G-2718)*	
Davol Inc **(DH)**.. **401 825-8300**	
100 Crossings Blvd Warwick (02886) *(G-16804)*	
Davol/Taunton Printing Inc.. 508 824-4305	
330 Winthrop St Ste 3 Taunton (02780) *(G-12331)*	
Dawid Manufacturing Inc... 203 734-1800	
26 Beaver St Ansonia (06401) *(G-12)*	
Dawn Enterprises LLC... 860 646-8200	
275 Progress Dr Ste B Manchester (06042) *(G-1591)*	
Dawson Forte Holdings LLC **(PA)**................................... **508 651-7910**	
40 Shawmut Rd Canton (02021) *(G-7782)*	
Day Lumber Company, Chicopee *Also Called: KG Pallet LLC (G-8043)*	
Day Machine Systems Inc.. 860 229-3440	
221 South St Bldg F2 New Britain (06051) *(G-2020)*	
Day Publishing Company **(HQ)**....................................... **860 701-4200**	
47 Eugene Oneill Dr New London (06320) *(G-2226)*	
Day Zero Diagnostics Inc... 857 770-1125	
85 Walnut St Ste 320 Watertown (02472) *(G-12870)*	
Day-Ahead Instrumentation LLC....................................... 978 952-2444	
410 Great Rd Ste B6 Littleton (01460) *(G-9810)*	
Day-O-Lite Fluorescent Fixs, Warwick *Also Called: SCW Corporation (G-16860)*	
Day, The, New London *Also Called: Day Publishing Company (G-2226)*	
Daybrake Donuts Inc... 203 368-4962	
941 Madison Ave Bridgeport (06606) *(G-314)*	
Dayken Pallet, Leeds *Also Called: Gerrity Company Incorporated (G-4948)*	
Dayleen Intimates Inc... 914 969-5900	
57 Commerce Dr Brookfield (06804) *(G-516)*	
Dayon Mfg., Inc., Farmington *Also Called: Old Dmfg Inc (G-1234)*	
Dayton Sand & Gravel Inc.. 207 499-2306	
928 Goodwins Mills Rd Dayton (04005) *(G-4720)*	
Dayton Superior Corporation.. 401 885-1934	
3970 Post Rd Warwick (02886) *(G-16805)*	
Db Signs LLC... 603 225-4081	
249 Sheep Davis Rd Ste 4 Concord (03301) *(G-14128)*	
DB&f Industries, New Britain *Also Called: DBF Industries Inc (G-2021)*	
DBF Industries Inc.. 860 827-8283	
145 Edgewood Ave New Britain (06051) *(G-2021)*	
Dbi, Chester *Also Called: Davis Brothers Inc (G-4691)*	
DC Bates Equipment Co Inc... 508 473-0041	
10 Airport Rd Hopedale (01747) *(G-9296)*	
DC Enterprizes Inc.. 802 865-4480	
110 Riggs Rd # B Hinesburg (05461) *(G-17290)*	
DC Scaffold Inc.. 508 580-5100	
400 West St Ste 2 West Bridgewater (02379) *(G-12971)*	
DC Tire Service Inc... 603 673-9211	
6 Prospect St Milford (03055) *(G-15021)*	
DCA Business Media LLC... 203 227-1699	
256 Post Rd E Ste 206 Westport (06880) *(G-4164)*	
Dcaf of Massachusetts Inc... 508 291-2000	
2380 Cranberry Hwy West Wareham (02576) *(G-13060)*	
Dcci, New Haven *Also Called: Dow Cover Company Incorporated (G-2144)*	
Dcg Precision Manufacturing, Bethel *Also Called: Dcg-Pmi Inc (G-106)*	

Dcg-Apvh Acquisition Co LLC.. 636 488-3200	
53 Rockwell Rd Newington (06111) *(G-2286)*	
Dcg-Pmi Inc.. 203 743-5525	
9 Trowbridge Dr Bethel (06801) *(G-106)*	
DCI, Providence *Also Called: Decor Craft Inc (G-16507)*	
Dci Inc **(PA)**.. **800 552-8286**	
265 S Main St Lisbon (03585) *(G-14708)*	
DCI Automation Inc.. 508 752-3071	
70 Hartwell St West Boylston (01583) *(G-12960)*	
DCI Furniture, Lisbon *Also Called: Dci Inc (G-14708)*	
DCI Training Inc.. 603 643-6066	
1 Oak Ridge Rd Ste 8a West Lebanon (03784) *(G-15682)*	
Dciamerica, West Lebanon *Also Called: DCI Training Inc (G-15682)*	
Dcp Spring Acquisition Co Inc.. 860 589-3231	
95 Valley St Bristol (06010) *(G-435)*	
Ddg Fabrication LLC... 603 883-9292	
29 Crown St Nashua (03060) *(G-15088)*	
Ddk Industries LLC... 203 641-4218	
70 Center St Shelton (06484) *(G-2998)*	
Ddm Metal Finishing Company... 860 872-4683	
25 Industrial Park Rd W Tolland (06084) *(G-3657)*	
De Mari Pasta Dies USA Inc.. 978 454-4099	
48 Chuck Dr Dracut (01826) *(G-8304)*	
De-Ice Technologies Inc.. 857 829-7651	
444 Somerville Ave Ste 2 Somerville (02143) *(G-11868)*	
Deacon Giles Inc... 781 883-8256	
75 Canal St Salem (01970) *(G-11710)*	
Dealership Software, Lincoln *Also Called: Dealership Software LLC (G-16130)*	
Dealership Software LLC... 401 305-3740	
85 Industrial Cir Ste 201 Lincoln (02865) *(G-16130)*	
Dean Machine Incorporated... 401 919-5100	
25 Sharpe Dr Unit 1 Cranston (02920) *(G-15847)*	
Deane Inc.. 203 327-7008	
1267 E Main St Stamford (06902) *(G-3335)*	
Deangelis Iron Work Inc **(PA)**....................................... **508 238-4310**	
46 Eastman St South Easton (02375) *(G-11941)*	
Dearborn Bortec, Fryeburg *Also Called: Dearborn Bortec LLC (G-4808)*	
Dearborn Bortec LLC.. 207 935-2502	
12 Budrich Dr Fryeburg (04037) *(G-4808)*	
Dearnley Brothers Inc... 508 865-2267	
190 W Main St Millbury (01527) *(G-10431)*	
Debco Machine Inc... 508 655-4469	
85 North Ave Natick (01760) *(G-10476)*	
Deborah Frost.. 603 882-3100	
20 Commerce Park North Ste 106 Bedford (03110) *(G-13924)*	
Debra Rivest Ltd.. 603 355-3335	
222 West St Unit 46 Keene (03431) *(G-14595)*	
Debt Exchange Inc.. 617 531-3400	
225 Franklin St Fl 26 Boston (02110) *(G-6685)*	
Debtx, Boston *Also Called: Debt Exchange Inc (G-6685)*	
Deburr Co.. 860 621-6634	
201 Atwater St Plantsville (06479) *(G-2790)*	
Deburring House Inc... 860 828-0889	
230 Berlin St East Berlin (06023) *(G-909)*	
Deburring Laboratories Inc.. 860 829-6300	
206 Newington Ave New Britain (06051) *(G-2022)*	
Decas Cranberry Products Inc **(PA)**............................... **508 866-8506**	
4 Old Forge Way Ste 1 Carver (02330) *(G-7853)*	
Decibel Therapeutics Inc **(HQ)**..................................... **617 370-8701**	
1325 Boylston St Ste 500 Boston (02215) *(G-6686)*	
DECIPHERA, Waltham *Also Called: Deciphera Pharmaceuticals Inc (G-12649)*	
Deciphera Pharmaceuticals LLC....................................... 781 209-6400	
200 Smith St Waltham (02451) *(G-12648)*	
Deciphera Pharmaceuticals Inc **(PA)**............................. **781 209-6400**	
200 Smith St Waltham (02451) *(G-12649)*	
Decker Machine Works Inc.. 413 628-3300	
201 Munson St Greenfield (01301) *(G-8989)*	
Deco Manufacturing, East Hartford *Also Called: Megowen LLC (G-1005)*	
Decor Craft Inc.. 401 621-2324	
24 Arnold St Providence (02906) *(G-16507)*	
Decorator Services Inc.. 203 384-8144	
25 Wells St Ste 1 Bridgeport (06604) *(G-315)*	

A
L
P
H
A
B
E
T
I
C

Dedham Cabinet Shop Inc.................................... 781 326-4090
  550 Turnpike St Canton (02021) *(G-7783)*

Dedham Recycled Gravel Co Inc............................ 781 329-1044
  1039 East St Dedham (02026) *(G-8241)*

Deep Blue Sea Trading, Boston *Also Called: Iqbal Shaheen (G-6817)*

Deep River Snacks, Deep River *Also Called: Old Lyme Gourmet Company (G-879)*

Deepcure Inc.. 617 417-2345
  100 City Hall Plz Boston (02108) *(G-6687)*

Deepwater, Biddeford *Also Called: Deepwater Buoyancy Inc (G-4559)*

Deepwater Buoyancy Inc..................................... 207 468-2565
  394 Hill St Biddeford (04005) *(G-4559)*

Deer Creek Fabrics Inc.. 203 964-0922
  11b Riverbend Dr S Stamford (06907) *(G-3336)*

Deerfield Machine & Tool Co, North Adams *Also Called: Denault Inc (G-10806)*

Deerfield Valley News, Wilmington *Also Called: Vermont Media Corp (G-17756)*

Deerwalk Inc (HQ).. **781 325-1775**
  430 Bedford St Ste 175 Lexington (02420) *(G-9738)*

Defender Industries Inc...................................... 860 701-3400
  42 Great Neck Rd Waterford (06385) *(G-3989)*

Defender Warehouse Outlet Str, Waterford *Also Called: Defender Industries Inc (G-3989)*

Defensecom Inc... 203 912-8679
  17 Claremont Park Boston (02118) *(G-6688)*

Defeo Manufacturing Inc...................................... 203 775-0254
  115 Commerce Dr Brookfield (06804) *(G-517)*

Defiance Graphics Corp...................................... 978 948-2789
  140 Central St Rowley (01969) *(G-11673)*

Defibtech LLC (HQ).. **866 333-4248**
  741 Boston Post Rd Ste 201 Guilford (06437) *(G-1391)*

Definitive Brewing Company LLC............................ 207 446-4746
  35 Industrial Way Portland (04103) *(G-5207)*

Definitive Healthcare Corp (PA).......................... **508 720-4224**
  492 Old Connecticut Path Ste 401 Framingham (01701) *(G-8756)*

Degreasing Devices Co.. 508 765-0045
  105 Dresser St Southbridge (01550) *(G-12013)*

Degree C, Nashua *Also Called: Degree Controls Inc (G-15089)*

Degree Controls Inc (PA).................................. **603 672-8900**
  300 Innovative Way Ste 222 Nashua (03062) *(G-15089)*

Deitsch Plastic Company Inc................................. 203 934-6601
  14 Farwell St West Haven (06516) *(G-4102)*

Dejana Trck Utility Eqp Co LLC.............................. 401 231-9797
  9 Business Park Dr Smithfield (02917) *(G-16695)*

Dejana Truck & Utility Eqp, Smithfield *Also Called: Dejana Trck Utility Eqp Co LLC (G-16695)*

Dekarz Corporation.. 203 888-3102
  31 Silvermine Rd Seymour (06483) *(G-2960)*

Dekarz Engineering, Seymour *Also Called: Dekarz Corporation (G-2960)*

Del Arbour LLC... 203 882-8501
  152 Old Gate Ln Milford (06460) *(G-1817)*

Del Nero Cleaners LLC.. 508 679-0999
  11 Farewell St Newport (02840) *(G-16208)*

Del-Tron Precision Inc.. 203 778-2727
  5 Trowbridge Dr Ste 1 Bethel (06801) *(G-107)*

Dela Incorporated (PA).................................... **978 372-7783**
  175 Ward Hill Ave Ste 1 Haverhill (01835) *(G-9091)*

Dela Lamimnation Solutions, Haverhill *Also Called: Dela Incorporated (G-9091)*

Delaite Trucking, Chester *Also Called: Delaite Trucking Inc (G-4692)*

Delaite Trucking Inc... 207 794-6844
  45 Gray Rd Chester (04457) *(G-4692)*

Delano Saw Mill Inc.. 508 994-8752
  157 Cross Rd North Dartmouth (02747) *(G-10992)*

Delaware Dimatix, Lebanon *Also Called: Fujifilm Dimatix Inc (G-14689)*

Delaware Valley Corp (PA)................................ **978 688-6995**
  500 Broadway Lawrence (01841) *(G-9556)*

Delaware Valley Corp.. 978 459-6932
  600 Woburn St Tewksbury (01876) *(G-12393)*

Delcom Products Inc... 914 934-5170
  45 Backus Ave Danbury (06810) *(G-729)*

Delcon Industries.. 203 371-5711
  31 Frenchtown Rd Trumbull (06611) *(G-3717)*

Delkin Inc.. 207 370-0703
  286 Harris Rd Cumberland Center (04021) *(G-4708)*

Dell Acquisition LLC... 860 677-8545
  35 Corporate Ave Plainville (06062) *(G-2753)*

Dell EMC, Hopkinton *Also Called: EMC Corporation (G-9322)*

Dell Manufacturing, Plainville *Also Called: Dell Acquisition LLC (G-2753)*

Dell Technologies Inc... 781 259-2552
  777 Virginia Rd Concord (01742) *(G-8112)*

Dell'amore Pasta Sauce, Colchester *Also Called: Dellamore Enterprises Inc (G-17188)*

Dellamore Enterprises Inc.................................... 802 655-6264
  948 Hercules Dr Ste 1 Colchester (05446) *(G-17188)*

Delmar Products Inc... 860 828-6501
  400 Christian Ln Berlin (06037) *(G-64)*

Delo Industrial Adhesives, Sudbury *Also Called: Delo Industrial Adhesives LLC (G-12263)*

Delo Industrial Adhesives LLC.............................. 978 254-5275
  144 North Rd Ste 2650 Sudbury (01776) *(G-12263)*

Delsys Inc.. 508 545-8200
  23 Strathmore Rd Ste 1 Natick (01760) *(G-10477)*

Delta Education LLC... 800 258-1302
  80 Northwest Blvd Nashua (03063) *(G-15090)*

Delta Electronics Mfg Corp................................... 978 927-1060
  416 Cabot St Beverly (01915) *(G-6345)*

Delta Elevator Service, Farmington *Also Called: North American Elev Svcs Co (G-1233)*

Delta Elevator Service Corp (DH)........................ **860 676-6152**
  1 Farm Springs Rd Canton (06019) *(G-560)*

Delta Mechanical Seals, Fall River *Also Called: Northeast Equipment Inc (G-8588)*

Delta Sand and Gravel Inc.................................... 413 665-4051
  562 Amherst Rd Sunderland (01375) *(G-12273)*

Delta Tool Co Inc.. 860 923-2012
  Rr 193 Thompson (06277) *(G-3649)*

Delta-Electro Power LLC...................................... 401 944-8350
  215 Niantic Ave Cranston (02907) *(G-15848)*

Delta-Ray Industries Inc...................................... 203 367-6910
  805 Housatonic Ave Bridgeport (06604) *(G-316)*

Delta-Source LLC.. 860 461-1600
  138 Beacon Hill Dr West Hartford (06117) *(G-4056)*

Deltran Inc... 508 699-7506
  65 John L Dietsch Blvd Ste A Attleboro Falls (02763) *(G-6083)*

Delve Labs Inc... 617 820-9798
  31 Saint James Ave Boston (02116) *(G-6689)*

Demaich Industries Inc.. 401 944-3576
  70 Mill St Johnston (02919) *(G-16080)*

Demakes Enterprises Inc...................................... 978 739-1506
  18 Electronics Ave Danvers (01923) *(G-8179)*

Demakes Enterprises Inc (PA)............................ **781 417-1100**
  37 Waterhill St Lynn (01905) *(G-9967)*

Demakes Enterprises Inc...................................... 781 586-0212
  34 Riley Way Lynn (01905) *(G-9968)*

Demandware LLC (HQ)...................................... **888 553-9216**
  5 Wall St Fl 2 Burlington (01803) *(G-7360)*

Demarey Insurance Software.................................. 413 531-3991
  10 Chestnut Hill Rd Hampden (01036) *(G-9022)*

Demartino Fixture Co Inc...................................... 203 628-4899
  360 Bloomfield Ave Ste 301 Windsor (06095) *(G-4270)*

Deme, Mechanic Falls *Also Called: Downeast Machine & Engrg Inc (G-5050)*

Demsey Manufacturing Co Inc................................ 860 274-6209
  78 New Wood Rd Watertown (06795) *(G-4008)*

Demusz Mfg Co Inc.. 860 528-9845
  303 Burnham St East Hartford (06108) *(G-985)*

Den Mar Corporation.. 508 999-3295
  1005 Reed Rd North Dartmouth (02747) *(G-10993)*

Denali Software Inc.. 603 566-0991
  154 Broad St Ste 1535 Nashua (03063) *(G-15091)*

Denardo Wire and Cable Co Inc.............................. 978 343-6412
  149 Industrial Rd Fitchburg (01420) *(G-8652)*

Denault Inc... 413 664-6771
  79 Walden St North Adams (01247) *(G-10806)*

Denison Pharmaceuticals LLC................................ 401 723-5500
  100 Higginson Ave Lincoln (02865) *(G-16131)*

Denison Pharmaceuticals LLC (PA)...................... **401 723-5500**
  1 Powder Hill Rd Lincoln (02865) *(G-16132)*

Denlar Fire Protection LLC.................................... 860 526-9846
  20 Denlar Dr Chester (06412) *(G-626)*

Dennecrepe Corporation.................................... 978 630-8669
  70 Fredette St Gardner (01440) *(G-8884)*

Denominator Company Inc................................. 203 263-3210
  20 S Commons Rd Waterbury (06704) *(G-3905)*

Dent Herb Company, Lancaster *Also Called: Cabot Hill Naturals LLC (G-14676)*

Dentovations Inc.. 617 737-1199
  1 Beacon St Boston (02108) *(G-6690)*

Dentovations Inc.. 617 737-1199
  1 Beacon St Fl 15 Boston (02108) *(G-6691)*

Dentovations Company, Boston *Also Called: Dentovations Inc (G-6691)*

Dentsply Ih Inc **(HQ)**...................................... **781 890-6800**
  590 Lincoln St Waltham (02451) *(G-12650)*

Dependable Cleaners Inc **(PA)**...................... **617 770-9232**
  320 Quincy Ave Quincy (02169) *(G-11509)*

Dependable Energy Incorporated....................... 203 758-5831
  9 Gramar Ave Prospect (06712) *(G-2833)*

Dependable Fuel, Prospect *Also Called: Dependable Energy Incorporated (G-2833)*

Dependable Hydraulics, North Branford *Also Called: Dependable Repair Inc (G-2365)*

Dependable Launderers & Clrs, Quincy *Also Called: Dependable Cleaners Inc (G-11509)*

Dependable Repair Inc... 203 481-9706
  2110 Foxon Rd North Branford (06471) *(G-2365)*

Depot Donuts Inc... 508 230-2888
  700 Depot St North Easton (02356) *(G-11009)*

Depuy Mitek LLC... 508 880-8100
  325 Paramount Dr Raynham (02767) *(G-11586)*

Depuy Spine LLC **(HQ)**.................................. **508 880-8100**
  325 Paramount Dr Raynham (02767) *(G-11587)*

Depuy Synthes Products Inc **(DH)**................. **508 880-8100**
  325 Paramount Dr Raynham (02767) *(G-11588)*

Der-Tex Corporation.. 207 284-5931
  1 Lehner Rd Saco (04072) *(G-5365)*

Derby Cellular Products Inc................................. 203 735-4661
  680 Bridgeport Ave Ste 3 Shelton (06484) *(G-2999)*

Derby Tire Company... 203 481-8473
  34 N Main St Branford (06405) *(G-249)*

Deringer-Ney Inc **(PA)**.................................. **860 242-2281**
  353 Woodland Ave Bloomfield (06002) *(G-158)*

Deringer-Ney Inc... 860 242-2281
  2 Douglas St Bloomfield (06002) *(G-159)*

Dermal Photonics Corporation............................ 781 451-1717
  153 Andover St Ste 111 Danvers (01923) *(G-8180)*

Dermalogix Partners Inc...................................... 207 883-4103
  672 Us Route 1 Scarborough (04074) *(G-5431)*

Derosa Printing Company Inc.............................. 860 646-1698
  485 Middle Tpke E Manchester (06040) *(G-1592)*

Derry News, Derry *Also Called: Eagle-Tribune Publishing Co (G-14192)*

Des Printing, Barrington *Also Called: Rlcp Inc (G-15749)*

Descal Inc.. 781 736-9400
  1275 Main St Ste 1 Waltham (02451) *(G-12651)*

Deschamps Printing, Salem *Also Called: Deschamps Printing Co Inc (G-11711)*

Deschamps Printing Co Inc.................................. 978 744-2152
  3 Dodge St Salem (01970) *(G-11711)*

Deschenes & Cooper Architectur......................... 860 599-2481
  25 White Rock Bridge Rd Pawcatuck (06379) *(G-2719)*

Desco Electronics Inc.. 508 643-1950
  36 Bacon Sq Plainville (02762) *(G-11431)*

Desco Industries Inc.. 781 821-8370
  1 Colgate Way Canton (02021) *(G-7784)*

Desco Industries Inc.. 603 332-0717
  73 Allen St Rochester (03867) *(G-15473)*

Desert Harvest Inc... 919 245-1853
  192 Main St Ellsworth (04605) *(G-4756)*

Desiato Sand & Gravel Corp................................ 860 429-6479
  999 Stafford Rd Storrs Mansfield (06268) *(G-3512)*

Design Architectural Heating............................... 207 784-0309
  141 Howe St Lewiston (04240) *(G-4955)*

Design Brand Partners Inc................................... 603 232-3490
  2 Bedford Farms Dr Ste 108 Bedford (03110) *(G-13925)*

Design Centers Com.. 800 570-1120
  725 Southbridge St Worcester (01610) *(G-13716)*

Design Communications Ltd **(PA)**................. **617 542-9620**
  85 Bodwell St Ste 1 Avon (02322) *(G-6148)*

Design Consultants Associates........................... 603 329-4541
  1 Owens Ct Hampstead (03841) *(G-14382)*

Design Contempo.. 603 838-6544
  265 S Main St Lisbon (03585) *(G-14709)*

Design Fab, Windham *Also Called: Rbw Inc (G-5668)*

Design Fab Inc... 207 786-2446
  928 Minot Ave Auburn (04210) *(G-4426)*

Design Fabricators Inc... 401 944-5294
  72 Stamp Farm Rd Cranston (02921) *(G-15849)*

Design Label Manufacturing Inc.......................... 860 739-6266
  12 Nottingham Dr Old Lyme (06371) *(G-2640)*

Design Mark Industries, New Bedford *Also Called: Design Mark Industries Inc (G-10585)*

Design Mark Industries Inc.................................. 800 451-3275
  22 Logan St Unit 1 New Bedford (02740) *(G-10585)*

Design Research Optics, East Greenwich *Also Called: Nippon American Limited (G-15992)*

Design Standards Corp... 603 826-7744
  957 Claremont Rd Charlestown (03603) *(G-14062)*

Designing Health Inc.. 661 257-1705
  302 Benton Dr East Longmeadow (01028) *(G-8373)*

Desk Top Graphics Inc... 207 828-0041
  477 Congress St Portland (04101) *(G-5208)*

Desk Top Graphics Inc **(HQ)**....................... **617 832-1927**
  1 1st Ave Peabody (01960) *(G-11305)*

Desk Top Solutions Inc.. 781 890-7500
  70 Industrial Ave E Lowell (01852) *(G-9874)*

Desktop Engineering Magazine, Dublin *Also Called: Helmers Publishing Inc (G-14261)*

Desktop Metal Inc **(PA)**................................ **978 224-1244**
  63 3rd Ave Burlington (01803) *(G-7361)*

Desktop Metal Operating Inc **(HQ)**.............. **978 224-1244**
  63 3rd Ave Burlington (01803) *(G-7362)*

Desmarais Plastics LLC.. 603 669-8523
  1 Bouchard St Manchester (03103) *(G-14841)*

Dessureau Machines Inc...................................... 802 476-4561
  53 Granite St Barre (05641) *(G-17000)*

Detail Millwork Inc... 781 893-2250
  160 Riverview Ave Waltham (02453) *(G-12652)*

Detotec North America Inc................................... 860 564-1012
  401 Snake Meadow Hill Rd Sterling (06377) *(G-3500)*

Detrapel Inc... 617 514-7778
  92 Blandin Ave Ste H Framingham (01702) *(G-8757)*

Devar Inc... 203 368-6751
  706 Bostwick Ave Bridgeport (06605) *(G-317)*

Development Associates Inc................................. 401 884-1350
  300 Old Baptist Rd North Kingstown (02852) *(G-16244)*

Development Resources, Westborough *Also Called: Business Resources Inc (G-13084)*

Device Technologies Inc....................................... 508 229-2000
  155 Northboro Rd Ste 8 Southborough (01772) *(G-11994)*

Device42 Inc... 203 409-7242
  600 Saw Mill Rd West Haven (06516) *(G-4103)*

Devincentis Press Inc.. 781 605-3796
  988 Eastern Ave Malden (02148) *(G-10008)*

Devine Brothers Incorporated............................. 203 866-4421
  38 Commerce St Norwalk (06850) *(G-2490)*

Devivo Industries Inc... 203 270-1552
  211 Brookside Rd Waterbury (06708) *(G-3906)*

Devon Precision Industries Inc............................ 203 879-1437
  251 Munson Rd Wolcott (06716) *(G-4363)*

Devon Precision Industries., Wolcott *Also Called: Devon Precision Industries Inc (G-4363)*

Devon's Place, Mansfield *Also Called: Driscolls Restaurant (G-10050)*

Devprotek Inc.. 603 577-5557
  4 Clinton Dr Hollis (03049) *(G-14449)*

Dewal Industries LLC... 401 789-9736
  15 Ray Trainor Dr Narragansett (02882) *(G-16189)*

Dewetron Inc... 401 284-3750
  2850 S County Trl Unit 1 East Greenwich (02818) *(G-15980)*

Deweys Lumber LLC.. 207 589-4126
  140 Kager Mountain Rd Liberty (04949) *(G-4998)*

Dewitt Mch & Fabrication Inc............................... 207 732-3530
  1152 Medford Center Rd Medford (04463) *(G-5054)*

Dewolfe New England RE, Tewksbury *Also Called: Coldwell Banker (G-12390)*

Dexmet Corporation.. 203 294-4440
  22 Barnes Industrial Rd S Wallingford (06492) *(G-3800)*

A
L
P
H
A
B
E
T
I
C

Dexsil Corporation.............................203 288-3509
  1 Hamden Park Dr Hamden (06517) *(G-1421)*

Dexter, Southbridge *Also Called: Dexter-Russell Inc (G-12014)*

Dexter Co The, East Providence *Also Called: Dexter Enterprises Corp (G-16013)*

Dexter Crane Service, East Providence *Also Called: Dexter Sign Co (G-16014)*

Dexter Enterprises Corp.......................401 434-2300
  70 Waterman Ave East Providence (02914) *(G-16013)*

Dexter Sign Co.................................401 434-1100
  70 Waterman Ave East Providence (02914) *(G-16014)*

Dexter-Russell Inc............................508 765-0201
  44 River St Southbridge (01550) *(G-12014)*

Dff Corp......................................413 786-8880
  59 Gen Creighton W Abrams Dr Agawam (01001) *(G-5789)*

DFI Tactical Coatings Group, Cranston *Also Called: Difruscia Industries Inc (G-15850)*

Dfs In-Home Services..........................845 405-6464
  15 Great Pasture Rd Danbury (06810) *(G-730)*

Dg International Holdings Corp.................781 577-2016
  75 2nd Ave Ste 720 Needham Heights (02494) *(G-10541)*

Dg Marshall Associates Inc....................508 943-2394
  6 H Putnam Rd Charlton (01507) *(G-7887)*

Dg Precision Manufacturing, Woodbury *Also Called: Duda and Goodwin Incorporated (G-4387)*

Dg Service Company Inc........................508 758-7906
  23c County Rd Mattapoisett (02739) *(G-10257)*

Dg3 Digital Pubg Solutions, Woburn *Also Called: Dg3 Group America Inc (G-13557)*

Dg3 Group America Inc.........................617 241-5600
  500 W Cummings Park Ste 4500 Woburn (01801) *(G-13557)*

Dgf Indstrial Invvations Group, Gilford *Also Called: Dgf Indstrial Innvtons Group L (G-14335)*

Dgf Indstrial Innvtons Group L................603 528-6591
  25 Waterford Pl Gilford (03249) *(G-14335)*

Dgi Communications LLC **(PA)**................**781 285-6972**
  101 Billerica Ave Bldg 6-1 North Billerica (01862) *(G-10905)*

Dgi Invisuals, North Billerica *Also Called: Dgi Communications LLC (G-10905)*

DH Hardwick & Sons Inc........................603 588-6618
  301 Francestown Rd Bennington (03442) *(G-13975)*

Dhm Thread Corporation........................508 672-0032
  192 Anawan St Ste 301 Fall River (02721) *(G-8533)*

Di MO Tool, Middleboro *Also Called: Di-MO Manufacturing Inc (G-10357)*

Di-Cor Industries Inc.........................860 585-5583
  139 Center St Bristol (06010) *(G-436)*

Di-MO Manufacturing Inc.......................508 947-2200
  35 Harding St Middleboro (02346) *(G-10357)*

Diacom Corporation............................603 880-1900
  5 Howe Dr Amherst (03031) *(G-13866)*

Diacritech, Boston *Also Called: Diacritech Inc (G-6692)*

Diacritech Inc................................617 236-7500
  1 S Market St Ste 4 Boston (02109) *(G-6692)*

Diageo Investment Corporation.................203 229-2100
  200 Elm St Ste 200 Stamford (06902) *(G-3337)*

Diageo Loyal Spirits Corp.....................401 284-4006
  1425 Kingstown Rd Wakefield (02879) *(G-16740)*

Diageo North America Inc......................802 362-4700
  3567 Main St Manchester (05254) *(G-17323)*

Diagnosys LLC **(PA)**........................**978 458-1600**
  55 Technology Dr Ste 1 Lowell (01851) *(G-9875)*

Dial Fabrics Co Inc...........................508 822-5333
  20 Cushman St Taunton (02780) *(G-12332)*

Dialogic, Needham Heights *Also Called: Cantata Technology Inc (G-10533)*

Dialogic (us) Inc.............................603 890-7240
  18 Keewaydin Dr Salem (03079) *(G-15518)*

Diamond Antenna Microwave Corp................978 486-0039
  59 Porter Rd Littleton (01460) *(G-9811)*

Diamond Casting and Mch Co LLC................603 465-2263
  95 Proctor Hill Rd Hollis (03049) *(G-14450)*

Diamond Custom Coatings Inc...................413 562-2734
  3 Progress Ave Westfield (01085) *(G-13161)*

Diamond Deans Dollhouse Co, Montpelier *Also Called: Real Good Toys Inc (G-17374)*

Diamond Diagnostics -USA, Holliston *Also Called: Diamond Diagnostics Inc (G-9206)*

Diamond Diagnostics Inc **(PA)**..............**508 429-0450**
  333 Fiske St Holliston (01746) *(G-9206)*

Diamond Hrseshoe Dev Group LLC................617 755-6100
  1266 Furnace Brook Pkwy Ste 300 Quincy (02169) *(G-11510)*

Diamond Iron Works Inc........................978 794-4640
  109 Blanchard St Lawrence (01843) *(G-9557)*

Diamond Machining Technology, Marlborough *Also Called: Vogel Capital Inc (G-10232)*

Diamond Systems, Lewiston *Also Called: Modula Inc (G-4976)*

Diamond USA Inc **(HQ)**......................**978 256-6544**
  85 Rangeway Rd Ste 3 North Billerica (01862) *(G-10906)*

Diamond Water Systems Inc.....................413 536-8186
  863 Montgomery St Chicopee (01013) *(G-8022)*

Diamond Windows, Boston *Also Called: Diamond Windows Doors Mfg Inc (G-6693)*

Diamond Windows Doors Mfg Inc.................617 282-1688
  99 E Cottage St Boston (02125) *(G-6693)*

Diamond-Roltran LLC...........................978 486-0039
  59 Porter Rd Ste 2 Littleton (01460) *(G-9812)*

Diamondhead Usa Inc...........................413 537-4806
  622 Union St West Springfield (01089) *(G-13021)*

Diane L Ivey..................................617 763-9736
  1203 River St Hyde Park (02136) *(G-9459)*

Diannes Fine Desserts Inc **(PA)**...........**800 435-2253**
  4 Graf Rd Newburyport (01950) *(G-10678)*

Diannes Fine Desserts Inc.....................978 463-3881
  1 Perry Way Newburyport (01950) *(G-10679)*

Dias Infrared Corp............................845 987-8152
  75 Sterling St West Boylston (01583) *(G-12961)*

Diasys Corp...................................302 636-5400
  21 W Main St Waterbury (06702) *(G-3907)*

Diba Industries Inc **(HQ)**.................**203 744-0773**
  4 Precision Rd Danbury (06810) *(G-731)*

Dicaperl Minerals.............................207 594-8225
  94 Buttermilk Ln Thomaston (04861) *(G-5543)*

Dicerna, Lexington *Also Called: Dicerna Pharmaceuticals Inc (G-9739)*

Dicerna Pharmaceuticals Inc **(HQ)**.........**617 621-8097**
  75 Hayden Ave Lexington (02421) *(G-9739)*

Dickinson's Cosmetics, East Hampton *Also Called: T N Dickinson Company (G-966)*

Dickson Product Dev Inc.......................203 846-2128
  14 Perry Ave Norwalk (06850) *(G-2491)*

Dicon, North Branford *Also Called: Willconn Connections Inc (G-2379)*

Dicronite Dry Lube, Westfield *Also Called: Circuit Systems Inc (G-13159)*

Dictaphone Corporation **(DH)**..............**203 381-7000**
  3191 Broadbridge Ave Stratford (06614) *(G-3533)*

Diebold Nixdorf Incorporated..................508 984-5936
  506 State Rd North Dartmouth (02747) *(G-10994)*

Diebold Nixdorf Incorporated..................508 646-4378
  400 Swansea Mall Dr Swansea (02777) *(G-12304)*

Diebold Nixdorf Incorporated..................603 577-9519
  7 Walmart Blvd Hudson (03051) *(G-14493)*

Diebold Nixdorf Incorporated..................401 823-8665
  25 Pace Blvd Warwick (02886) *(G-16806)*

Diebold Nixdorf Incorporated..................401 766-3606
  1919 Diamond Hill Rd Woonsocket (02895) *(G-16956)*

Diebolt & Company.............................860 434-2222
  341 Shaker Rd East Longmeadow (01028) *(G-8374)*

Diecast Connections Co Inc....................413 592-8444
  10 Cordage Park Cir Ste 222 Plymouth (02360) *(G-11456)*

Diecutting Tooling Svcs Inc **(PA)**.........**413 331-3500**
  680 Meadow St Chicopee (01013) *(G-8023)*

Dielectric Sciences Inc.......................978 250-1507
  88 Turnpike Rd Chelmsford (01824) *(G-7923)*

Dielectrics Inc...............................413 594-8111
  300 Burnett Rd Chicopee (01020) *(G-8024)*

Diemand Egg Farm Inc..........................978 544-3806
  126 Mormon Hollow Rd Millers Falls (01349) *(G-10447)*

Diemand Farm, Millers Falls *Also Called: Diemand Egg Farm Inc (G-10447)*

Diemat Inc....................................978 499-0900
  19 Central St Ste 9 Byfield (01922) *(G-7457)*

Dienes Corporation............................508 885-6301
  27 W Main St Spencer (01562) *(G-12057)*

Dietzgen Corporation..........................813 849-4334
  351 Morgan Ln West Haven (06516) *(G-4104)*

Diffraction Ltd...............................802 496-6640
  193 Home Farm Way 2 Waitsfield (05673) *(G-17666)*

Difruscia Industries Inc......................401 943-9900
  1425 Cranston St Cranston (02920) *(G-15850)*

Dig Publishing LLC.. 617 426-8942
  242 E Berkeley St Ste 2 Boston (02118) *(G-6694)*

Dig Rite Company Inc... 401 862-5895
  572 Central Ave Johnston (02919) *(G-16081)*

Digatron Power Electronics Inc................................. 203 446-8000
  240 Long Hill Cross Rd Shelton (06484) *(G-3000)*

Digboston.. 617 426-8942
  242 E Berkeley St Boston (02118) *(G-6695)*

Digi-Block Inc... 617 926-9300
  122 Brattle St Cambridge (02138) *(G-7550)*

Digilab, Holliston *Also Called: Digilab Genomic Solutions Inc (G-9207)*

Digilab Inc.. 508 305-2410
  35 Parkwood Dr Hopkinton (01748) *(G-9315)*

Digilab Genomic Solutions Inc.................................. 508 893-3130
  84 October Hill Rd Ste 7 Holliston (01746) *(G-9207)*

Digipress Inc (PA)... 617 832-1927
  1 1st Ave Ste 1 Peabody (01960) *(G-11306)*

Digirad Health LLC.. 800 947-6134
  53 Forest Ave Old Greenwich (06870) *(G-2632)*

Digital 128 First Avenue LLC................................... 781 726-7736
  128 1st Ave Needham (02494) *(G-10508)*

Digital Cognition Tech Inc.. 617 433-1777
  210 Bear Hill Rd Ste 301 Waltham (02451) *(G-12653)*

Digital Graphics Inc... 781 270-3670
  101 Billerica Ave Bldg 6 North Billerica (01862) *(G-10907)*

Digital Immunity, Burlington *Also Called: Digital Immunity LLC (G-7363)*

Digital Immunity LLC.. 508 630-0321
  60 Mall Rd Ste 309 Burlington (01803) *(G-7363)*

Digital Lumens Incorporated
  374 Congress St Ste 601 Boston (02210) *(G-6696)*

Digital On Demand LLC.. 978 224-7900
  44 Garden St Ste 3 Danvers (01923) *(G-8181)*

Digital Press Printers LLC.. 802 863-5579
  128 Commerce St Williston (05495) *(G-17727)*

Digital Printing Concepts Inc................................... 401 751-4953
  225 Freeman Pkwy Providence (02906) *(G-16508)*

Digital Products, Waltham *Also Called: Netsilicon Inc (G-12736)*

Digital Stream Energy Inc.. 310 488-2743
  160 Federal St Fl 18 Boston (02110) *(G-6697)*

Digitaldruker Inc.. 203 888-6001
  11 Old Farm Rd Oxford (06478) *(G-2693)*

Dilla St Corp... 508 478-3419
  130 Cedar St Milford (01757) *(G-10400)*

Dillon Dental Laboratories, Abington *Also Called: Dillon Laboratories Inc (G-5723)*

Dillon Laboratories Inc.. 781 871-2333
  4 Thicket St Abington (02351) *(G-5723)*

Dilon Company Inc.. 508 223-3400
  65 Newcomb St Attleboro (02703) *(G-6009)*

Diluigis Inc.. 978 750-9900
  41 Popes Ln Danvers (01923) *(G-8182)*

Dimark Incorporated.. 781 447-7990
  205 Commercial St Whitman (02382) *(G-13349)*

Dimark Precision Machining Inc............................... 781 447-7990
  745 Washington St Pembroke (02359) *(G-11362)*

Dimension Lumber.. 207 897-9973
  85 Jug Hill Rd Peru (04290) *(G-5156)*

Dimension-Polyant Inc.. 860 928-8314
  78 Highland Dr Putnam (06260) *(G-2853)*

Dimensional Insight Inc (PA)................................ 781 229-9111
  60 Mall Rd Ste 210 Burlington (01803) *(G-7364)*

Dimitria Delights Inc.. 508 839-1638
  81 Creeper Hill Rd North Grafton (01536) *(G-11022)*

Dina Inc... 401 942-9633
  357 Dyer Ave Cranston (02920) *(G-15851)*

Ding Fann Enterprises LLC...................................... 781 322-7121
  960 Eastern Ave Malden (02148) *(G-10009)*

Dingee Machine Co, Cornish *Also Called: Larry Dingee (G-14183)*

Dingley Press Inc.. 207 782-1529
  40 Westminster St Lewiston (04240) *(G-4956)*

Dinn Bros Inc (PA)... 413 750-3466
  221 Interstate Dr West Springfield (01089) *(G-13022)*

Dinn Bros Trophies & Plaques, West Springfield *Also Called: Dinn Bros Inc (G-13022)*

Dinner Daily LLC... 978 392-5887
  26 Colonial Dr Westford (01886) *(G-13234)*

Dinning Out -Main Coast, Wolfeboro Falls *Also Called: Panoramic Publishing Group LLC (G-15736)*

Dino Software.. 603 612-0418
  10 Loggers Ln Sandown (03873) *(G-15579)*

Dion Label Printing Inc.. 413 568-3713
  539 North Rd Westfield (01085) *(G-13162)*

Dion Signs and Service Inc..................................... 401 724-4459
  125 Samuel Barnet Blvd New Bedford (02745) *(G-10586)*

Dionex, Chelmsford *Also Called: Magellan Diagnostics Inc (G-7937)*

Diplomaframe.com, Monroe *Also Called: Church Hill Classics Ltd (G-1909)*

Diprizio Pines Sales, Middleton *Also Called: Middleton Building Supply (G-15008)*

Dipwell Company Inc... 413 587-4673
  82 Industrial Dr Unit 3 Northampton (01060) *(G-11059)*

Direct Display Publishing Co.................................... 207 443-4800
  765 High St Ste 5 Bath (04530) *(G-4526)*

Direct Energy Inc (HQ)... 800 260-0300
  263 Tresser Blvd Fl 8 Stamford (06901) *(G-3338)*

Directional Technologies Inc.................................... 203 294-9200
  89 N Main St Wallingford (06492) *(G-3801)*

Directions To Maine Dovetail.................................... 207 829-2759
  36 Rochester St Westbrook (04092) *(G-5625)*

Directory Assistants Inc.. 860 633-0122
  34 Valley View Dr Avon (06001) *(G-23)*

Direx Systems Corp... 339 502-6013
  956 Turnpike St Canton (02021) *(G-7785)*

Dirigo Stitching Inc.. 207 474-8421
  40 Dane Ave Skowhegan (04976) *(G-5466)*

Disc Medicine Inc (PA)... 617 674-9274
  321 Arsenal St Ste 101 Watertown (02472) *(G-12871)*

Discount Labels Montgomery Co, Stamford *Also Called: Cenveo Worldwide Limited (G-3309)*

Discover Marble & Granite Inc (PA)...................... 877 411-9900
  1 Latti Farm Rd Millbury (01527) *(G-10432)*

Discovery Mint Inc.. 401 722-6530
  151 Exchange St Pawtucket (02860) *(G-16364)*

Dispatch News... 978 458-7100
  491 Dutton St Lowell (01854) *(G-9876)*

Dispatch Plant, Chicopee *Also Called: Chicopee Foundations Inc (G-8015)*

Displaycraft Inc... 860 747-9110
  335 S Washington St Plainville (06062) *(G-2754)*

Displays By Garo Inc... 401 305-3511
  2 Carol Dr Lincoln (02865) *(G-16133)*

Displays For Less, Warren *Also Called: Progressive Displays Inc (G-16764)*

Displays2go, Fall River *Also Called: George Patton Associates Inc (G-8552)*

Dissertation Editor LLC.. 857 600-2241
  1 Mifflin Pl Ste 400 Cambridge (02138) *(G-7551)*

Disston Company... 800 272-4436
  45 Plainfield St Chicopee (01013) *(G-8025)*

Distillery Network Inc... 603 997-6786
  21 W Auburn St Ste 30 Manchester (03101) *(G-14842)*

Distribution & Control Product................................. 781 324-0070
  730 Eastern Ave Malden (02148) *(G-10010)*

Distron Corporation... 508 695-8786
  87 John L Dietsch Sq Attleboro Falls (02763) *(G-6084)*

Ditusa Corporation.. 978 335-5259
  19 Shepherd St Gloucester (01930) *(G-8932)*

Div of Bttnfeld Glcester Engrg, Newport *Also Called: SF Tools LLC (G-15238)*

Dive Technologies Inc.. 339 236-4599
  258 Willard St Quincy (02169) *(G-11511)*

Diversified Biotech Inc.. 781 326-6709
  65 Commerce Way Dedham (02026) *(G-8242)*

Diversified Bus Communications, Portland *Also Called: Diversified Communications (G-5209)*

Diversified Business Systems, Haverhill *Also Called: D B S Industries Inc (G-9090)*

Diversified Communications (HQ).......................... 207 842-5500
  121 Free St Portland (04101) *(G-5209)*

Diversified Enterprises, Claremont *Also Called: Diversified Enterprises-ADT (G-14088)*

Diversified Enterprises-ADT..................................... 603 543-0038
  101 Mulberry St Ste 2n Claremont (03743) *(G-14088)*

A
L
P
H
A
B
E
T
I
C

Diversified Industrial Sup LLC.................................... 800 244-3647
  100 Terminal St Charlestown (02129) *(G-7868)*

Diversified Manufacturing LLC................................... 203 734-0379
  1 Riverside Dr Ste H Ansonia (06401) *(G-13)*

Diversified Metals LLC... 413 267-5101
  49 Main St Monson (01057) *(G-10455)*

Diversified Precast, Claremont *Also Called: Bd Enterprises LLC (G-14078)*

Diversified Prtg Solutions Inc.................................... 203 826-7198
  128 E Liberty St Danbury (06810) *(G-732)*

Diversitech Corporation... 800 699-0453
  391 W Water St Taunton (02780) *(G-12333)*

Divert Inc **(PA)**... **978 341-5430**
  23 Bradford St Ste 3 Concord (01742) *(G-8113)*

Divine Stoneworks LLC.. 774 221-6006
  60 Pleasant St Ashland (01721) *(G-5956)*

Division 15 Hvac Inc.. 781 285-3115
  300 Oak St Ste 930 Pembroke (02359) *(G-11363)*

Division 5 LLC.. 860 752-4127
  99 Cooper Ln Stafford Springs (06076) *(G-3254)*

Dixie Chopper of Vermont, Williston *Also Called: Vermont Engine Service Inc (G-17752)*

Dixie Consumer Products LLC................................... 978 537-4701
  149 Hamilton St Leominster (01453) *(G-9658)*

Dixie Media LLC... 508 739-1999
  199 Rosewood Dr Ste 230 Danvers (01923) *(G-8183)*

Dixon Bros Millwork Inc.. 781 261-9962
  200 Wales St Abington (02351) *(G-5724)*

Dj Instruments, Franklin *Also Called: Dynisco Instruments LLC (G-8831)*

Dj Instruments, Franklin *Also Called: Dynisco LLC (G-8832)*

Dj Microlaminates Inc... 978 261-3188
  490 Boston Post Rd Sudbury (01776) *(G-12264)*

Dj Printing Inc... 207 773-0439
  800 Main St Ste 1 South Portland (04106) *(G-5498)*

Dj Semichem Inc.. 603 204-5101
  28 Charron Ave Nashua (03063) *(G-15092)*

Dj's Tree Service and Ldscpg, Colchester *Also Called: Djs Tree Service & Log Inc (G-17189)*

Djs Tree Service & Log Inc....................................... 802 655-0264
  65 Colchester Point Rd Colchester (05446) *(G-17189)*

Dkd Solutions Inc.. 508 762-9114
  77 E Worcester St Worcester (01604) *(G-13717)*

DL Tech Machine Inc... 978 439-0500
  144b Rangeway Rd North Billerica (01862) *(G-10908)*

Dl Technology, Haverhill *Also Called: Dl Technology LLC (G-9092)*

Dl Technology LLC.. 978 374-6451
  216 River St Haverhill (01832) *(G-9092)*

Dlrc Incorporated.. 617 999-3340
  1 Broadway Cambridge (02142) *(G-7552)*

Dlz Architectural Mill Work....................................... 860 883-7562
  510 Ledyard St Hartford (06114) *(G-1476)*

DManelly Ex Multiservices LLC.................................. 401 490-2900
  918 Atwells Ave Providence (02909) *(G-16509)*

DMC Inc.. 617 758-8517
  20 Holland St Ste 408 Somerville (02144) *(G-11869)*

DMC Steel, Providence *Also Called: Capco Steel Erection Company (G-16495)*

Dmi Technology, Dover *Also Called: Dmi Technology Corp (G-14226)*

Dmi Technology Corp **(PA)**.................................... **603 742-3330**
  1 Progress Dr Dover (03820) *(G-14226)*

Dmjl Consulting LLC.. 978 989-0790
  145 Milk St Methuen (01844) *(G-10327)*

Dmr Industries Inc... 603 335-0325
  181 Milton Rd Rochester (03868) *(G-15474)*

Dmr Print Inc **(PA)**.. **617 876-3688**
  13 Dover St Concord (01742) *(G-8114)*

DMS Machining & Fabrication, Barre *Also Called: Gloucester Associates Inc (G-17001)*

Dmt Export Inc... 508 481-5944
  85 Hayes Memorial Dr Marlborough (01752) *(G-10144)*

Dmt Solutions Global Corp **(HQ)**.......................... **833 874-0552**
  37 Executive Dr Danbury (06810) *(G-733)*

Dn Tanks, Wakefield *Also Called: Dn Tanks Inc (G-12507)*

Dn Tanks Inc **(PA)**... **781 246-1133**
  11 Teal Rd Wakefield (01880) *(G-12507)*

Dn Tanks LLC... 781 246-1133
  11 Teal Rd Wakefield (01880) *(G-12508)*

Dn Tanks of Wyoming, Wakefield *Also Called: Dn Tanks LLC (G-12508)*

Do It Best, Lincoln *Also Called: S W Collins (G-5013)*

Do It Best, Mansfield *Also Called: National Lumber Company LLC (G-10068)*

Doble Engineering Company **(HQ)**......................... **617 926-4900**
  123 Felton St Marlborough (01752) *(G-10145)*

Docbox Inc... 978 987-2569
  77 Rumford Ave Ste 4 Waltham (02453) *(G-12654)*

Dock Doctors LLC.. 802 877-6756
  19 Little Otter Ln Ferrisburgh (05456) *(G-17268)*

Dock Doctors, The, Ferrisburgh *Also Called: Dock Doctors LLC (G-17268)*

Docking Systems, West Nottingham *Also Called: Dyer S Docking Systems Corp (G-15693)*

Dockside Repairs Inc... 508 993-6730
  14 Hervey Tichon Ave New Bedford (02740) *(G-10587)*

Doctors Designs, Milton *Also Called: Somalabs Inc (G-17364)*

Documents On Demand Inc.. 508 793-0956
  184 Main St Worcester (01608) *(G-13718)*

Docuprint & Imaging Inc... 203 776-6000
  27 Whitney Ave New Haven (06510) *(G-2143)*

Docuprintnow, New Haven *Also Called: Docuprint & Imaging Inc (G-2143)*

Docuserve Inc... 508 786-5820
  72 Cedar Hill St Ste B Marlborough (01752) *(G-10146)*

Dodge Company Inc **(PA)**..................................... **800 443-6343**
  9 Progress Rd Billerica (01821) *(G-6431)*

Dodson Boatyard LLC.. 860 535-1507
  194 Water St Stonington (06378) *(G-3508)*

DOE & Inglls Msschstts Oprting................................ 781 391-0090
  300 Jubilee Dr # 400 Peabody (01960) *(G-11307)*

Dogwatch Inc **(PA)**... **508 650-0600**
  10 Michigan Dr Natick (01760) *(G-10478)*

Doire Distilling LLC... 603 765-4353
  1 E Broadway Derry (03038) *(G-14191)*

Dolan-Jenner Industries Inc...................................... 978 263-1400
  159 Swanson Rd Boxborough (01719) *(G-7151)*

Doleco Usa Inc.. 203 440-1940
  290 Pratt St Meriden (06450) *(G-1663)*

Dolliver Corporation.. 802 879-0072
  209 Blair Park Rd Williston (05495) *(G-17728)*

Doltronics LLC... 203 488-8766
  65-4 N Branford Rd Branford (06405) *(G-250)*

Dom's Sausage Co, Malden *Also Called: DOro Foods Inc (G-10011)*

Domain Surgical Inc.. 801 924-4950
  4 Maguire Rd # 2 Lexington (02421) *(G-9740)*

Dome Enterprises Trust **(PA)**................................ **401 738-7900**
  10 New England Way Warwick (02886) *(G-16807)*

Dome Publishing Company Inc **(HQ)**...................... **401 738-7900**
  10 New England Way Warwick (02886) *(G-16808)*

Domestic Kitchens Inc... 203 368-1651
  515 Commerce Dr Fairfield (06825) *(G-1181)*

Dominion Rebar Company... 401 724-9200
  30 Lockbridge St Pawtucket (02860) *(G-16365)*

Dominique Intimate Apparel, Brookfield *Also Called: Dayleen Intimates Inc (G-516)*

Domino Media Group Inc... 877 223-7844
  16 Taylor Pl Westport (06880) *(G-4165)*

Domino.com, Westport *Also Called: Domino Media Group Inc (G-4165)*

Domtar Paper Company LLC...................................... 207 427-6400
  144 Main St Bajleyville (04694) *(G-4482)*

Don-Jo Mfg Inc.. 978 422-3377
  70 Pratts Junction Rd Sterling (01564) *(G-12160)*

Donahue Industries Inc.. 508 845-6501
  5 Industrial Dr Shrewsbury (01545) *(G-11830)*

Doncar Inc... 978 371-2442
  100 Domino Dr 1 Concord (01742) *(G-8115)*

Doncasters Inc... 860 446-4803
  835 Poquonnock Rd Groton (06340) *(G-1366)*

Doncasters Inc **(PA)**... **860 449-1603**
  835 Poquonnock Rd Groton (06340) *(G-1367)*

Doncasters Inc... 413 785-1801
  160 Cottage St Springfield (01104) *(G-12090)*

(G-0000) Company's Geographic Section entry number

Doncasters Precision Castings-, Groton *Also Called: Doncasters Inc* **(G-1366)**

DONCASTERS STORMS FORGE, Groton *Also Called: Doncasters Inc* **(G-1367)**

Doncasters US Hldings 2018 Inc.................................... 860 449-1603
835 Poquonnock Rd Groton (06340) **(G-1368)**

Donelan Fmly Wine Cellars LLC.................................... 707 591-0782
34 Circle Dr E Ridgefield (06877) **(G-2896)**

Donghia Furniture and Textiles, Milford *Also Called: Donghia Inc* **(G-1818)**

Donghia Inc... 800 366-4442
500 Bic Dr Ste 200 Milford (06461) **(G-1818)**

Donham Crafts, Naugatuck *Also Called: Unimetal Surface Finishing LLC* **(G-1991)**

Donovan Equipment Company Inc.................................. 603 669-2250
6 Enterprise Dr Londonderry (03053) **(G-14743)**

Donovan Marine-Atlantic, Biddeford *Also Called: ME Industries* **(G-4579)**

Donut Hole, Buxton *Also Called: Donut Hole Inc* **(G-4662)**

Donut Hole Inc... 207 929-5060
4 Pierce Dr Buxton (04093) **(G-4662)**

Donwell, Manchester *Also Called: Donwell Company* **(G-1593)**

Donwell Company.. 860 649-5374
130 Sheldon Rd Manchester (06042) **(G-1593)**

Dooney & Bourke Inc **(HQ)**.................................... **203 853-7515**
1 Regent St Norwalk (06855) **(G-2492)**

Dooney Woodworks LLC **(PA)**................................. **203 340-9770**
105 River Rd Cos Cob (06807) **(G-676)**

Dooney Woodworks LLC.. 203 869-5457
55 Conyers Farm Dr Greenwich (06831) **(G-1328)**

Doosan, East Hartford *Also Called: Hyaxiom Inc* **(G-998)**

Dorchester Beer Holdings LLC..................................... 617 869-7092
1250 Massachusetts Ave Boston (02125) **(G-6698)**

Dorchester Reporter, Dorchester *Also Called: Boston Irish Reporter* **(G-8297)**

Dorel Design & Development Ctr, Foxboro *Also Called: Dorel Juvenile Group Inc* **(G-8695)**

Dorel Juvenile Group Inc... 800 544-1108
25 Forbes Blvd Unit 4 Foxboro (02035) **(G-8694)**

Dorel Juvenile Group Inc... 508 216-1800
25 Forbes Blvd Unit 4 Foxboro (02035) **(G-8695)**

Doric Vault Connecticut LLC....................................... 203 494-0172
23 Thistle Meadow Ln Branford (06405) **(G-251)**

Dorman Logging LLC.. 603 437-4403
506 Mammoth Rd Londonderry (03053) **(G-14744)**

Dorn Equipment Corp... 781 662-9300
27 Upham St Melrose (02176) **(G-10316)**

DOro Foods Inc.. 781 324-1310
10 Riverside Park Malden (02148) **(G-10011)**

Dorothy Cox Chocolates, Fall River *Also Called: Dorothy Coxs Candies Inc* **(G-8534)**

Dorothy Coxs Candies Inc.. 774 678-0654
100 Griffin St Fall River (02724) **(G-8534)**

Dosa Kitchen, Brattleboro *Also Called: Dosa Kitchen LLC* **(G-17082)**

Dosa Kitchen LLC.. 802 246-7592
209 Austine Dr Brattleboro (05301) **(G-17082)**

Dosco Sheet Metal and Mfg Inc................................... 508 865-9998
6 Grafton St Millbury (01527) **(G-10433)**

Double E Company LLC **(PA)**.................................. **508 588-8099**
319 Manley St West Bridgewater (02379) **(G-12972)**

Double H Acres LLC... 860 250-3311
47 Broad Brook Rd Broad Brook (06016) **(G-508)**

Double-Take, Burlington *Also Called: Double-Take Software Inc* **(G-7365)**

Double-Take Software Inc **(DH)**............................... **949 253-6500**
1700 District Ave Ste 300 Burlington (01803) **(G-7365)**

Doubleyard Inc **(PA)**... **857 314-1400**
201 Washington St Ste 3630 Boston (02108) **(G-6699)**

Dough Connection Corp... 877 693-6844
32a Holton St Woburn (01801) **(G-13558)**

Doughvinci Inc... 603 494-8769
Manchester (03108) **(G-14843)**

Douglas Bros Div, Portland *Also Called: Robert Mitchell Co Inc* **(G-5266)**

Douglas Brothers Georgia Inc...................................... 800 341-0926
423 Riverside Industrial Pkwy Portland (04103) **(G-5210)**

Douglas Dynamics LLC.. 207 701-4200
50 Gordon Dr Rockland (04841) **(G-5325)**

Douglas Wine & Spirits Inc... 401 353-6400
1661 Mineral Spring Ave North Providence (02904) **(G-16299)**

Dover Flexo Electronics Inc... 603 332-6150
307 Pickering Rd Rochester (03867) **(G-15475)**

Dover Microsystems Inc... 781 577-0300
203 Crescent St Ste 108 Waltham (02453) **(G-12655)**

Dover Motion, Boxborough *Also Called: Invetech Inc* **(G-7152)**

Dow Chemical, Marlborough *Also Called: Dow Chemical Company* **(G-10147)**

Dow Chemical Company... 508 229-7676
455 Forest St Marlborough (01752) **(G-10147)**

Dow Cover Company Incorporated................................. 203 469-5394
373 Lexington Ave New Haven (06513) **(G-2144)**

Dow Jones, Chicopee *Also Called: Dow Jones & Company Inc* **(G-8026)**

Dow Jones, Chicopee *Also Called: Dow Jones & Company Inc* **(G-8027)**

Dow Jones & Company Inc.. 212 416-3858
84 2nd Ave Chicopee (01020) **(G-8026)**

Dow Jones & Company Inc.. 413 598-4000
200 Burnett Rd Chicopee (01020) **(G-8027)**

Down East Enterprise Inc... 207 594-9544
680 Commercial St Rockport (04856) **(G-5348)**

Down East Shtmtl & Certif Wldg.................................... 207 989-3443
19 Sparks Ave Brewer (04412) **(G-4611)**

Down To Fab LLC.. 603 728-8299
453 Us Route 4 Canaan (03741) **(G-14045)**

Downeast Cider House, Mansfield *Also Called: Downeast Cider House LLC* **(G-10049)**

Downeast Cider House LLC **(PA)**.............................. **857 301-8881**
256 Marginal St Ste 2 Boston (02128) **(G-6700)**

Downeast Cider House LLC... 650 279-2417
31 Plymouth St Ste 2 Mansfield (02048) **(G-10049)**

Downeast Coffee Roasters, Pawtucket *Also Called: Excellent Coffee Co Inc* **(G-16367)**

Downeast Concepts Inc... 207 846-3726
86 Downeast Dr Yarmouth (04096) **(G-5703)**

Downeast Fishing Gear.. 207 667-3131
12 Bar Harbor Rd Trenton (04605) **(G-5553)**

Downeast Graphics & Prtg Inc...................................... 207 667-5582
477 Washington Junction Rd Ellsworth (04605) **(G-4757)**

Downeast Machine & Engrg Inc **(PA)**......................... **207 345-8111**
26 Maple St Mechanic Falls (04256) **(G-5050)**

Downeast Manufacturing, Gouldsboro *Also Called: Elscott Manufacturing LLC* **(G-4839)**

Downeaster, The, Topsham *Also Called: Coastal Metal Fab* **(G-5547)**

Dowslake Microsystems Corp....................................... 978 691-5700
21 High St Ste 306 North Andover (01845) **(G-10826)**

Doyle Sailmakers Inc **(PA)**.................................... **978 740-5950**
96 Swampscott Rd Ste 8 Salem (01970) **(G-11712)**

Doyle Sails Newport Partnr... 401 849-9400
23 Johnny Cake Hill Rd Middletown (02842) **(G-16172)**

Dp Concrete LLC... 860 677-2626
164 Brickyard Rd Farmington (06032) **(G-1214)**

Dp Foods L L C.. 203 271-6212
152 Knotter Dr Cheshire (06410) **(G-588)**

Dpb Ceramics LLC... 617 259-1084
800 Boylston St Ste 200 Boston (02199) **(G-6701)**

Dpp Inc.. 978 443-9995
385 Boston Post Rd Sudbury (01776) **(G-12265)**

Dps Packaging LLC.. 508 459-8917
1010 Main St Ste 1 Holden (01520) **(G-9188)**

Dr Biron Incorporated **(PA)**................................... **603 622-5222**
20 East Industrial Park Dr Unit 2 Manchester (03109) **(G-14844)**

DR Charles Envmtl Cnstr LLC....................................... 203 445-0412
189 Monroe Tpke Monroe (06468) **(G-1913)**

Dr Pepper, Portland *Also Called: Dr Pepper Bottling Co Portland* **(G-5211)**

Dr Pepper Bottling Co Portland.................................... 207 773-4258
250 Canco Rd Portland (04103) **(G-5211)**

Dra Precision Machine.. 603 734-2139
424 Commercial Pl Unit 13 Calef Hwy 125 Brentwood (03833) **(G-14020)**

Dra-Cor Industries Inc.. 508 580-3770
65 N Main St Brockton (02301) **(G-7273)**

Draeger Medical Systems Inc....................................... 800 437-2437
6 Tech Dr Andover (01810) **(G-5880)**

Dragon Products Company LLC **(DH)**.......................... **207 594-5555**
2 Main St Ste 18-221 Biddeford (04005) **(G-4560)**

Dragon Products Company LLC..................................... 207 879-2328
960 Ocean Ave Portland (04103) **(G-5212)**

Dragon Products Company LLC.................... 207 594-5555
   107 New County Rd Thomaston (04861) *(G-5544)*

Draka, Boston *Also Called: Draka Cableteq Usa Inc (G-6702)*

Draka Cableteq, Taunton *Also Called: Prysmian Group Spclty Cbles LL (G-12359)*

Draka Cableteq Usa Inc.................... 888 520-1200
   Boston (02101) *(G-6702)*

Draker Laboratories Inc.................... 802 922-1162
   431 Pine St Ste 114 Burlington (05401) *(G-17131)*

Draper Elevator Cab Co Inc.................... 781 961-3146
   260 Centre St Holbrook (02343) *(G-9171)*

Draper Knitting Company Inc.................... 781 828-0029
   28 Draper Ln Canton (02021) *(G-7786)*

Draper Metal Fabrication Inc.................... 781 961-3146
   260 Centre St Unit A Holbrook (02343) *(G-9172)*

Draperies Intrors Grenwich LLC.................... 203 489-3010
   238 E Putnam Ave Cos Cob (06807) *(G-677)*

Drapery House Inc.................... 401 724-3400
   1307 Mineral Spring Ave North Providence (02904) *(G-16300)*

Draught Technologies LLC.................... 860 840-7555
   592 New Britain Ave Farmington (06032) *(G-1215)*

Dresco Belting Co Inc.................... 781 335-1350
   24 French St Hingham (02043) *(G-9148)*

Dresser Measurement Control, Avon *Also Called: Dresser Msnlan Ctrl Vlves Avon (G-6149)*

Dresser Msnlan Ctrl Vlves Avon **(DH)**.................... **508 586-4600**
   85 Bodwell St Avon (02322) *(G-6149)*

Drew's All Natural, Chester *Also Called: Drews LLC (G-17180)*

Drews LLC **(HQ)**.................... **802 875-1184**
   926 Vt Route 103 S Chester (05143) *(G-17180)*

Dri-Air Industries, East Windsor *Also Called: Dri-Air Industries Inc (G-1071)*

Dri-Air Industries Inc.................... 860 627-5110
   16 Thompson Rd East Windsor (06088) *(G-1071)*

Driggin Sandra DBA Extra Extra.................... 617 773-6996
   21 Mayor Thomas J Mcgrath Hwy Ste 405 Quincy (02169) *(G-11512)*

Drill Masters-Eldorado Tool Inc.................... 203 878-1711
   336 Boston Post Rd Milford (06460) *(G-1819)*

Drill-Out, Wolcott *Also Called: Alden Corporation (G-4361)*

Drillmasters of Vermont, North Bennington *Also Called: Sterling Gun Drills Inc (G-17412)*

Drink Maple Inc.................... 978 610-6408
   144 North Rd Ste 1050 Sudbury (01776) *(G-12266)*

Driscolls Restaurant.................... 508 261-1574
   535 S Main St Mansfield (02048) *(G-10050)*

Drive-O-Rama Inc **(PA)**.................... **508 771-8100**
   270 Communication Way Unit 6 Hyannis (02601) *(G-9434)*

Drive-O-Rama Inc.................... 508 394-0028
   Drive-O-Rama Inc Dennis Port (02639) *(G-8260)*

Driving Impressions, East Providence *Also Called: Parsonskellogg LLC (G-16037)*

Drizly LLC **(HQ)**.................... **774 234-1033**
   334 Boylston St Ste 301 Boston (02116) *(G-6703)*

DRM Research Laboratories Inc.................... 203 488-5555
   8 Juniper Point Rd Branford (06405) *(G-252)*

Droitcour Company.................... 401 737-4646
   28 Graystone St Warwick (02886) *(G-16809)*

Drop, Essex Junction *Also Called: Gordini USA Inc (G-17235)*

Dropgenie Inc.................... 617 901-7422
   750 Main St Cambridge (02139) *(G-7553)*

Drs Development LLC.................... 774 271-0533
   10 Marion Rd Rochester (02770) *(G-11631)*

Drs Fermont, Bridgeport *Also Called: Engineered Electric Company (G-320)*

Drs Naval Power Systems Inc.................... 203 366-5211
   11 Durant Ave Bethel (06801) *(G-108)*

Drs Naval Power Systems Inc.................... 203 798-3000
   21 South St Danbury (06810) *(G-734)*

Drs Naval Power Systems Inc.................... 978 343-9719
   166 Boulder Dr Ste 201 Fitchburg (01420) *(G-8653)*

Drt Aerospace LLC.................... 937 298-7391
   221 Burnham St East Hartford (06108) *(G-986)*

Drt Aerospace LLC.................... 203 781-8020
   620 Research Pkwy Meriden (06450) *(G-1664)*

Druck LLC **(HQ)**.................... **978 437-1000**
   1100 Technology Park Dr Ste 300 Billerica (01821) *(G-6432)*

Drug Farm Usa LLC.................... 617 735-5205
   88 Greenbrier Dr Guilford (06437) *(G-1392)*

Dryvit, North Kingstown *Also Called: Dryvit Systems Inc (G-16245)*

Dryvit Systems Inc **(DH)**.................... **401 822-4100**
   200 Frenchtown Rd North Kingstown (02852) *(G-16245)*

Ds Huntington Co LLC.................... 603 784-5136
   9 Vose Farm Rd Peterborough (03458) *(G-15315)*

Ds Services of America Inc.................... 860 945-0661
   1050 Buckingham St Watertown (06795) *(G-4009)*

DS Sewing Inc.................... 203 773-1344
   260 Wolcott St New Haven (06513) *(G-2145)*

Dsaencore LLC.................... 203 740-4200
   50 Pocono Rd Brookfield (06804) *(G-518)*

DSM Coating Resins, Wilmington *Also Called: DSM Neoresins Inc (G-13403)*

DSM Metal Fabrication Inc.................... 207 282-6740
   129 Precourt St Biddeford (04005) *(G-4561)*

DSM Neoresins Inc.................... 800 458-0014
   730 Main St Wilmington (01887) *(G-13403)*

DSM Nutritional Products LLC.................... 781 259-7600
   60 Westview St Lexington (02421) *(G-9741)*

DSM Thermoplastics.................... 978 537-6484
   29 Fuller St Leominster (01453) *(G-9659)*

Dso Manufacturing Company Inc.................... 860 224-2641
   390 John Downey Dr New Britain (06051) *(G-2023)*

Dss Circuits Inc.................... 508 852-8061
   29 Oriental St Worcester (01605) *(G-13719)*

Dt Holdings Incorporated.................... 203 602-6969
   72 Camp Ave Stamford (06907) *(G-3339)*

Dti, Southborough *Also Called: Device Technologies Inc (G-11994)*

Dtm Massman LLC.................... 781 749-1866
   150 Recreation Park Dr Ste 5 Hingham (02043) *(G-9149)*

Dtm Packaging & Custom Automtn, Hingham *Also Called: Dtm Massman LLC (G-9149)*

Dublin Steel Corporation.................... 413 289-1218
   95 2nd St Palmer (01069) *(G-11273)*

Duc-Pac Corporation.................... 413 525-3302
   1125 Page Blvd Springfield (01104) *(G-12091)*

Duck Creek, Boston *Also Called: Duck Creek Technologies Inc (G-6704)*

Duck Creek Technologies Inc **(HQ)**.................... **949 214-1000**
   22 Boston Wharf Rd Fl 10 Boston (02210) *(G-6704)*

Duck Creek Technologies LLC **(DH)**.................... **833 798-7789**
   22 Boston Wharf Rd Fl 10 Boston (02210) *(G-6705)*

Ducktrap River of Maine, LLC, Belfast *Also Called: Mowi Ducktrap LLC (G-4537)*

Ductco LLC.................... 860 243-0350
   13 Britton Dr Bloomfield (06002) *(G-160)*

Duda and Goodwin Incorporated.................... 203 263-4353
   90 Washington Rd Woodbury (06798) *(G-4387)*

Dufrane Nuclear Shielding Inc.................... 860 379-2318
   150 Price Rd Winsted (06098) *(G-4340)*

Dufrane Technologies LLC.................... 860 379-2318
   150 Price Rd Winsted (06098) *(G-4341)*

Duhamel Family Farm LLC.................... 802 868-4954
   107 Franklin Rd Highgate Center (05459) *(G-17288)*

Duke River Engineering, Newton *Also Called: Duke River Engineering Co (G-10753)*

Duke River Engineering Co.................... 617 965-7255
   30 Ossipee Rd Newton (02464) *(G-10753)*

Dulce Domum LLC.................... 203 227-1400
   40 Richards Ave Ste 4 Norwalk (06854) *(G-2493)*

Dumont Company LLC.................... 413 773-3675
   289 Wells St Greenfield (01301) *(G-8990)*

Dunajski Dairy Inc.................... 978 531-1457
   22 Buxton Ln Peabody (01960) *(G-11308)*

Duncan Galvanizing Corporation.................... 617 389-8440
   69 Norman St Ste 2 Everett (02149) *(G-8487)*

Dune Denim LLC.................... 203 241-5409
   6 Meadow Ln Bethel (06801) *(G-109)*

Dunkin Donuts **(PA)**.................... **207 783-0408**
   360 Center St Auburn (04210) *(G-4427)*

Dunkin Donuts.................... 401 822-2434
   341 Providence St Warwick (02886) *(G-16810)*

Dunkin Donuts of Methuen.................... 978 681-8123
   464 Lowell St Methuen (01844) *(G-10328)*

(G-0000) Company's Geographic Section entry number

Dunkin' Donuts, Portland *Also Called: Realejo Donuts Inc (G-2822)*

Dunkin' Donuts, West Haven *Also Called: DAndrea Corporation (G-4101)*

Dunkin' Donuts, East Longmeadow *Also Called: Lori Donuts Inc (G-8384)*

Dunkin' Donuts, Methuen *Also Called: Dunkin Donuts of Methuen (G-10328)*

Dunkin' Donuts, North Easton *Also Called: Depot Donuts Inc (G-11009)*

Dunkin' Donuts, Oxford *Also Called: D D J (G-11251)*

Dunkin' Donuts, Southbridge *Also Called: Kookla Inc (G-12025)*

Dunkin' Donuts, Sturbridge *Also Called: Kookla Inc (G-12251)*

Dunkin' Donuts, Allenstown *Also Called: Manco LLC (G-13852)*

Dunkin' Donuts, Plymouth *Also Called: A & M Donuts Inc (G-15354)*

Dunkin' Donuts, Tilton *Also Called: ANM Donuts Inc (G-15651)*

Dunkin' Donuts, Warwick *Also Called: Dunkin Donuts (G-16810)*

Dunn & Co Inc... 978 368-8505
  75 Green St Ste 1 Clinton (01510) *(G-8077)*

Dunn Industries Inc... 603 666-4800
  123 Abby Rd Manchester (03103) *(G-14845)*

Dunn Paper Holdings Inc.. 860 289-7496
  2 Forbes St East Hartford (06108) *(G-987)*

Dunn Paper LLC.. 860 466-4141
  2 Forbes St East Hartford (06108) *(G-988)*

Duplication Management Inc...................................... 781 935-7224
  215 Salem St Ste B Woburn (01801) *(G-13559)*

Dupont, Boston *Also Called: Eidp Inc (G-6708)*

Dupont Electronics & Imaging, Marlborough *Also Called: Rohm Haas Electronic Mtls LLC (G-10207)*

Dupont Packaging Inc.. 413 552-0048
  68b Winter St # 4 Holyoke (01040) *(G-9251)*

Dupont Water Technologies, North Kingstown *Also Called: International Dioxcide Inc (G-16260)*

Dur A Flex Motor Sports... 401 739-0202
  875 W Shore Rd Warwick (02889) *(G-16811)*

Dur-A-Flex Inc **(HQ)**.. **860 528-9838**
  95 Goodwin St East Hartford (06108) *(G-989)*

Dura-Kote Technology Ltd... 401 331-6460
  2 Industrial Ln Johnston (02919) *(G-16082)*

Durable Technologies, Worcester *Also Called: Visimark Inc (G-13823)*

Duracell Company... 203 796-4000
  Berkshire Corporate Bldg Bethel (06801) *(G-110)*

Duracell International Inc.. 203 796-4000
  14 Research Dr Bethel (06801) *(G-111)*

Duracell Manufacturing LLC...................................... 203 796-4000
  14 Research Dr Bethel (06801) *(G-112)*

Duracell US Holding LLC **(HQ)**................................ **203 796-4000**
  14 Research Dr Bethel (06801) *(G-113)*

Duraflow LLC... 978 851-7439
  120 Lumber Ln Unit 15 Tewksbury (01876) *(G-12394)*

Duralectra-Chn LLC... 401 597-5000
  1 Shorr Ct Woonsocket (02895) *(G-16957)*

Duralite Incorporated... 860 379-3113
  15 School St Riverton (06065) *(G-2912)*

Duramag, Waterville *Also Called: Shyft Group Inc (G-5596)*

Durant Performance Coatings, Revere *Also Called: Durant Prfmce Coatings Inc (G-11618)*

Durant Prfmce Coatings Inc...................................... 781 289-1400
  112 Railroad Ave Revere (02151) *(G-11618)*

Durant Tool Company Inc... 401 781-7800
  200 Circuit Dr North Kingstown (02852) *(G-16246)*

Durastone Corporation... 401 723-7100
  150 Higginson Ave Lincoln (02865) *(G-16134)*

Durastone Flexicore Inc... 401 231-4000
  550 Washington Hwy Smithfield (02917) *(G-16696)*

Durco Manufacturing Co Inc..................................... 203 575-0446
  493 S Leonard St Waterbury (06708) *(G-3908)*

Durgin and Crowell Lbr Co Inc.................................. 603 763-2860
  231 Fisher Corner Rd New London (03257) *(G-15202)*

Durham Manufacturing Company **(PA)**...................... **860 349-3427**
  201 Main St Durham (06422) *(G-899)*

Durkee-Mower Inc.. 781 593-8007
  2 Empire St Corner Columbia St Lynn (01902) *(G-9969)*

Duro Hilex Poly LLC... 203 639-7070
  850 Murdock Ave Meriden (06450) *(G-1665)*

Duro Textiles LLC... 508 675-0102
  110 Chace St Fall River (02724) *(G-8535)*

Duro Textiles LLC... 508 679-0076
  206 Globe Mills Ave Fall River (02724) *(G-8536)*

Duro-Fiber Co Inc.. 603 881-4200
  11 Park Ave Hudson (03051) *(G-14494)*

Durol Co... 203 288-3383
  2580 State St Hamden (06517) *(G-1422)*

Durol Cosmetic Laboratories, New Haven *Also Called: Durol Laboratories LLC (G-2146)*

Durol Laboratories LLC... 866 611-9694
  116 Welton St New Haven (06511) *(G-2146)*

Durridge Company Inc **(PA)**................................... **978 667-9556**
  900 Technology Park Dr Billerica (01821) *(G-6433)*

Dusa Pharmaceuticals Inc **(DH)**............................. **978 657-7500**
  29 Dunham Rd Billerica (01821) *(G-6434)*

Dutch Gold Honey Inc... 603 444-6246
  46 N Littleton Rd Littleton (03561) *(G-14716)*

Dutch Gold Honey Inc... 603 444-6246
  46 N Littleton Rd Littleton (03561) *(G-14717)*

Dutch Maid Bakery Inc.. 617 265-5417
  50 Park St Ste 2 Dorchester (02122) *(G-8298)*

Dutch Ophthalmic Usa Inc.. 603 778-6929
  10 Continental Dr Bldg 1 Exeter (03833) *(G-14291)*

Dutile Glines & Higgins Inc...................................... 603 622-0452
  850 Perimeter Rd Manchester (03103) *(G-14846)*

Duva Distributors Inc... 508 841-8182
  479 Hartford Tpke Shrewsbury (01545) *(G-11831)*

Duval Precision Grinding Inc..................................... 413 593-3060
  940 Sheridan St Chicopee (01022) *(G-8028)*

Duxbury Clipper Inc... 781 934-2811
  11 S Station St Duxbury (02332) *(G-8330)*

Duxbury Composite Products Inc................................ 603 585-9100
  57 Creamery Rd Fitzwilliam (03447) *(G-14313)*

DVE Manufacturing Inc.. 207 783-9895
  550 Lisbon St Lewiston (04240) *(G-4957)*

Dwyer Aluminum Mast Co Inc................................... 203 484-0419
  2 Commerce Dr Ste 1 North Branford (06471) *(G-2366)*

Dycem Corporation **(DH)**...................................... **401 738-4420**
  33 Appian Way Smithfield (02917) *(G-16697)*

Dyco Industries Inc.. 860 289-4957
  229 S Satellite Rd South Windsor (06074) *(G-3138)*

Dyer S Docking Systems Corp.................................... 603 942-5122
  404 Stage Rd West Nottingham (03291) *(G-15693)*

Dykrex Wire Die Machinery Div, Worcester *Also Called: Sancliff Inc (G-13794)*

Dymax Oligomers & Coatings.................................... 860 626-7006
  318 Industrial Ln Torrington (06790) *(G-3677)*

Dymo Corporation..
  383 Main Ave Ste 4 Norwalk (06851) *(G-2494)*

Dymotek Corporation... 860 875-2868
  7 Main St Ellington (06029) *(G-1104)*

Dyna Roll Inc.. 603 474-2547
  146 Batchelder Rd Seabrook (03874) *(G-15590)*

Dynamic Bldg Enrgy Sltions LLC **(PA)**.................... **860 599-1872**
  183 Providence New London Tpke Ste W3 North Stonington (06359) *(G-2447)*

Dynamic Coating Solutions, Palmer *Also Called: Creative Material Tech Ltd (G-11272)*

Dynamic Gunver Technologies, Manchester *Also Called: Paradigm Manchester Inc (G-1625)*

Dynamicops Inc.. 781 221-2136
  1 Wall St Ste 201 Burlington (01803) *(G-7366)*

Dynapower Company LLC **(DH)**.............................. **802 860-7200**
  85 Meadowland Dr South Burlington (05403) *(G-17577)*

Dynasil, Concord *Also Called: Dynasil Corporation America (G-8116)*

Dynasil Corporation America **(PA)**.......................... **617 668-6855**
  200 Baker Ave Ste 301 Concord (01742) *(G-8116)*

Dynasol Industries Inc... 781 821-8888
  330 Pine St Canton (02021) *(G-7787)*

Dynatrace, Waltham *Also Called: Dynatrace Inc (G-12656)*

Dynatrace Inc **(PA)**... **781 530-1000**
  1601 Trapelo Rd Ste 116 Waltham (02451) *(G-12656)*

Dynatrace LLC **(HQ)**.. **781 530-1000**
  1601 Trapelo Rd Ste 116 Waltham (02451) *(G-12657)*

Dynavac, Hingham *Also Called: Vacuum Technology Assoc Inc (G-9161)*

ALPHABETIC

Dyne Therapeutics, Waltham *Also Called: Dyne Therapeutics Inc (G-12658)*

Dyne Therapeutics Inc (PA)..**781 786-8230**
  1560 Trapelo Rd Waltham (02451) *(G-12658)*

Dynex/Rivett Inc..508 881-5110
  54 Nickerson Rd Ashland (01721) *(G-5957)*

Dynisco Instruments LLC..978 215-3401
  37 Manning Rd Ste 2 Billerica (01821) *(G-6435)*

Dynisco Instruments LLC (HQ)......................................**508 541-9400**
  38 Forge Pkwy Franklin (02038) *(G-8831)*

Dynisco LLC (HQ)..**508 541-3195**
  38 Forge Pkwy Franklin (02038) *(G-8832)*

Dynisco Parent Inc...978 667-5301
  37 Manning Rd Ste 2 Billerica (01821) *(G-6436)*

Dyno Nobel Inc..860 843-2000
  660 Hopmeadow St Simsbury (06070) *(G-3085)*

Dzi..413 527-4500
  150 Pleasant St Ste 320 Easthampton (01027) *(G-8443)*

Dzs Inc...510 777-7000
  112 Corporate Dr Ste 1 Portsmouth (03801) *(G-15380)*

E & A Enterprises Inc...203 250-8050
  10 Capital Dr # A Wallingford (06492) *(G-3802)*

E & E Tool & Mfg Co Inc..860 738-8577
  100 International Way Winsted (06098) *(G-4342)*

E & J Parts Cleaning Inc..203 757-1716
  1669 Thomaston Ave Waterbury (06704) *(G-3909)*

E & M Enterprises Ltd...401 274-7405
  16 Sunnyside Ave Johnston (02919) *(G-16083)*

E & S Gage Inc..860 872-5917
  38 Gerber Dr Tolland (06084) *(G-3658)*

E & S Gauge Company, Tolland *Also Called: E and S Gage Inc (G-3659)*

E A Dion Inc..800 445-1007
  33 Franklin R Mckay Rd Attleboro (02703) *(G-6010)*

E A M, Biddeford *Also Called: Eami Inc (G-4562)*

E and S Gage Inc...860 872-5917
  38 Gerber Dr Tolland (06084) *(G-3659)*

E B Asphalt & Landscaping LLC...860 639-1921
  1650 Old Colchester Rd Unit 1 Oakdale (06370) *(G-2621)*

E B Buffing, Bristol *Also Called: Etherington Brothers Inc (G-442)*

E C I, Westfield *Also Called: Transcon Technologies Inc (G-13212)*

E C S, Fall River *Also Called: Teknikor Automtn & Contrls Inc (G-8615)*

E Cook Associates Inc..860 283-9849
  15 Mountain View Rd Watertown (06795) *(G-4010)*

E D A X International Division, Natick *Also Called: Philips North America LLC (G-10490)*

E D C, Waltham *Also Called: Education Development Ctr Inc (G-12659)*

E E S Companies Inc...508 653-6911
  841 Worcester Rd Ste 503 Framingham (01701) *(G-8758)*

E F D, East Providence *Also Called: Nordson Efd LLC (G-16034)*

E F Inc..978 630-3800
  88 Suffolk Ln Gardner (01440) *(G-8885)*

E F Shea Neng Con Pdts I, Amesbury *Also Called: Shea Concrete Products Inc (G-5852)*

E Fjeld Co Inc..978 667-1416
  152 Rangeway Rd North Billerica (01862) *(G-10909)*

E Frances Paper Inc...857 250-0036
  114 W Main Rd # 2 Middletown (02842) *(G-16173)*

E G W Bradbury Enterprises Inc...207 429-8141
  100 Main St Bridgewater (04735) *(G-4625)*

E Gs Gauging Incorporated...978 262-3100
  200 Research Dr Wilmington (01887) *(G-13404)*

E H Benz Co Inc...401 331-5650
  73 Maplehurst Ave Providence (02908) *(G-16510)*

E H Perkins Construction Inc...978 422-3388
  194 Worcester Rd Sterling (01564) *(G-12161)*

E H Perkins Construction Inc (PA)................................**978 562-3436**
  560 Main St Wayland (01778) *(G-12925)*

E H Publishing Inc (PA)..**508 663-1500**
  111 Speen St Ste 200 Framingham (01701) *(G-8759)*

E I J Inc...802 889-3432
  467 Vt Route 110 Tunbridge (05077) *(G-17653)*

E I Printing Co...207 797-4838
  200 Riverside Industrial Pkwy Portland (04103) *(G-5213)*

E Ink Corporation...617 499-6000
  1000 Technology Park Dr Billerica (01821) *(G-6437)*

E J Carrier Inc...207 668-4457
  Rte 201 Jackman (04945) *(G-4909)*

E O Manufacturing Company Inc...203 932-5981
  474 Frontage Rd West Haven (06516) *(G-4105)*

E O S, East Hartford *Also Called: Envirnmntal Office Sltions Inc (G-993)*

E P S I, Haverhill *Also Called: Engineered Pressure Systems Inc (G-9094)*

E P X Group, Portland *Also Called: Wise Business Forms Inc (G-5290)*

E Print Inc..603 594-0009
  10 Rebel Rd Hudson (03051) *(G-14495)*

E R Hinman & Sons Inc..860 673-9170
  77 Milford St Burlington (06013) *(G-548)*

E R Hitchcock Company...860 229-2024
  191 John Downey Dr New Britain (06051) *(G-2024)*

E S I, Hanover *Also Called: Eyesaver International Inc (G-9031)*

E S Ritchie & Sons Inc...781 826-5131
  243 Oak St Pembroke (02359) *(G-11364)*

E Skip Grindle & Sons...207 460-0334
  485 North St Ellsworth (04605) *(G-4758)*

E T Duval & Sons Inc...978 537-7596
  386 Main St Leominster (01453) *(G-9660)*

E T I, Cheshire *Also Called: Electro-Tech Inc (G-589)*

E T M Manufacturing Company, Littleton *Also Called: Arlowe Corporation (G-9802)*

E T Wright, Norwell *Also Called: Wear-Guard Corporation (G-11150)*

E V Yeuell Inc...781 933-2984
  17 Gill St Woburn (01801) *(G-13560)*

E W Sykes, Athol *Also Called: E W Sykes General Contractors (G-5978)*

E W Sykes General Contractors..978 249-7655
  5567 S Athol Rd Athol (01331) *(G-5978)*

E W Winship Ltd Inc...508 228-1908
  51 Main St Nantucket (02554) *(G-10462)*

E-B Manufacturing Company Inc...860 632-8563
  825 Middle St Middletown (06457) *(G-1745)*

E-Cloth Inc...603 765-9367
  131 Broadway Dover (03820) *(G-14227)*

E-I-E-I-o Incorporated..508 324-9311
  502 Bedford St Fall River (02720) *(G-8537)*

E-J Electric T & D LLC..203 626-9625
  53 N Plains Industrial Rd Wallingford (06492) *(G-3803)*

E-Lite Technologies Inc...203 371-2070
  2285 Reservoir Ave Trumbull (06611) *(G-3718)*

E-Skylight.com, Waterboro *Also Called: Architectural Skylight Co Inc (G-5589)*

E-Z Audit, Stamford *Also Called: Atconsulting LLC (G-3288)*

E-Z Crete LLC..603 313-6462
  502 Winchester St Keene (03431) *(G-14596)*

E-Z Crete LLC..603 313-6462
  126 Monadnock Hwy Swanzey (03446) *(G-15643)*

E. Hartford Production, East Hartford *Also Called: Coca-Cola Bevs Northeast Inc (G-981)*

E.F. Cook Company, Lincoln *Also Called: Johnston Dandy Company (G-5009)*

E&S Automotive Operations LLC...203 332-4555
  425 Boston Ave Bridgeport (06610) *(G-318)*

EA Patten Co LLC...860 649-2851
  303 Wetherell St Manchester (06040) *(G-1594)*

Eagle Div, Warwick *Also Called: John Crane Sealol Inc (G-16828)*

Eagle Electric, Ashaway *Also Called: Eagle Industries Inc (G-15739)*

Eagle Industries Inc...207 929-3700
  118 Hollis Rd Hollis Center (04042) *(G-4893)*

Eagle Industries Inc...401 596-8111
  23 Gray Ln Ashaway (02804) *(G-15739)*

Eagle Investment Systems LLC...860 561-4602
  65 Lasalle Rd Ste 305 West Hartford (06107) *(G-4057)*

Eagle Investment Systems LLC (HQ).............................**781 943-2200**
  45 William St Wellesley (02481) *(G-12940)*

Eagle Manufacturing Co Inc..860 537-3759
  13 Homonick Rd Colchester (06415) *(G-656)*

Eagle Motors Inc...401 568-2580
  172 Chapel St Harrisville (02830) *(G-16065)*

Eagle Motors Victory, Harrisville *Also Called: Eagle Motors Inc (G-16065)*

Eagle Publications..603 543-3100
  45 Crescent St Claremont (03743) *(G-14089)*

(G-0000) Company's Geographic Section entry number

Eagle Ship Management LLC **(HQ)**..................**203 276-8100**
300 Stamford Pl Stamford (06902) *(G-3340)*

Eagle Test Systems Inc.................................603 624-5757
2 Commerce Dr Ste 102 Bedford (03110) *(G-13926)*

Eagle Times, Claremont *Also Called: Eagle Publications Inc (G-14089)*

Eagle Tool Inc...401 421-5105
101 Venturi Ave Warwick (02888) *(G-16812)*

Eagle Tribune, The, North Andover *Also Called: Eagle-Tribune Publishing Co (G-10827)*

Eagle Vision Inc.......................................508 385-2283
1017 Main St Dennis (02638) *(G-8258)*

Eagle Woodworking Inc.................................978 681-6194
678 Andover St Ste 1 Lawrence (01843) *(G-9558)*

Eagle-Tribune Publishing Co..........................978 282-0077
36 Whittemore St Gloucester (01930) *(G-8933)*

Eagle-Tribune Publishing Co..........................978 374-0321
181 Merrimack St Haverhill (01830) *(G-9093)*

Eagle-Tribune Publishing Co..........................978 946-2000
100 Turnpike St North Andover (01845) *(G-10827)*

Eagle-Tribune Publishing Co **(DH)**..................**978 946-2000**
100 Turnpike St North Andover (01845) *(G-10828)*

Eagle-Tribune Publishing Co..........................603 437-7000
46 W Broadway Derry (03038) *(G-14192)*

Eaglepicher Technologies LLC.........................401 471-6580
2000 S County Trl East Greenwich (02818) *(G-15981)*

Eaglepicher Yardney Division, East Greenwich *Also Called: Eaglepicher Technologies LLC*
(G-15981)

Eami Inc..207 283-3001
19 Pomerleau St Biddeford (04005) *(G-4562)*

Earl W Gerrish & Sons................................207 965-2171
2 Charlottes Rd Brownville (04414) *(G-4637)*

Early Advantage LLC..................................203 259-6480
426 Mine Hill Rd Fairfield (06824) *(G-1182)*

Earlysense Inc.......................................781 373-3228
800 W Cummings Park Ste 6400 Woburn (01801) *(G-13561)*

Earnix Inc...203 557-8077
191 Post Rd W Westport (06880) *(G-4166)*

Eartec Company Inc...................................401 789-8700
145 Dean Knauss Dr Narragansett (02882) *(G-16190)*

Earth Eagle Brewings LLC.............................603 817-2773
175 High St Apt 6 Portsmouth (03801) *(G-15381)*

Earth Waste Systems Inc **(PA)**......................**802 775-7722**
49 Wales St Rutland (05701) *(G-17494)*

Earthlink..508 735-1508
4 Saint James Cir Acton (01720) *(G-5744)*

Easco Hand Tools Inc.................................860 843-7351
125 Powder Forest Dr Simsbury (06070) *(G-3086)*

East Baking Company Inc..............................413 536-2300
104 Whiting Farms Rd Holyoke (01040) *(G-9252)*

East Basin Sports Inc **(PA)**........................**781 492-2747**
153 Needham St Newton (02464) *(G-10754)*

East Bay Newspapers, Bristol *Also Called: Phoenix-Times Publishing Co (G-15777)*

East Branch Engrg & Mfg Inc..........................860 355-9661
57 S End Plz New Milford (06776) *(G-2242)*

East Cast McRwave Sls Dist LLC.......................781 279-0900
470 Wildwood Ave Ste 4 Woburn (01801) *(G-13562)*

East Cast Wldg Fabrication LLC.......................978 465-2338
104 Parker St Newburyport (01950) *(G-10680)*

East Coast Concrete Pdts LLC.........................603 883-3042
5 Northern Blvd Ste 15 Amherst (03031) *(G-13867)*

East Coast Filter Inc................................716 649-2326
560 Washington St Ste 3 Wrentham (02093) *(G-13840)*

East Coast Induction Inc.............................508 587-2800
506 N Warren Ave Brockton (02301) *(G-7274)*

East Coast Interiors Inc.............................508 995-4200
4 Ledgewood Blvd North Dartmouth (02747) *(G-10995)*

East Coast Lightning Eqp Inc.........................860 379-9072
24 Lanson Dr Winsted (06098) *(G-4343)*

East Coast Marble & Gran Corp........................781 760-0207
142 Lynnfield St Lynn (01904) *(G-9970)*

East Coast Metal Hose Inc............................203 723-7459
41 Raytkwich Rd Naugatuck (06770) *(G-1956)*

East Coast Metal Works Co Inc........................603 642-9600
21 Route 125 Unit 2 Kingston (03848) *(G-14634)*

East Coast Pavers LLC................................508 577-7832
1777 Main St Tewksbury (01876) *(G-12395)*

East Coast Perfection Coating, Holliston *Also Called: Bagge Inc (G-9202)*

East Coast Plastic, Framingham *Also Called: East Coast Plastics Inc (G-8760)*

East Coast Plastics Inc..............................508 429-8080
763 Waverley St Ste 3 Framingham (01702) *(G-8760)*

East Coast Precision Mfg.............................860 322-4624
221 Middlesex Ave Chester (06412) *(G-627)*

East Coast Printing Inc..............................781 331-5635
2 Keith Way Ste 5 Hingham (02043) *(G-9150)*

East Coast Publications Inc **(PA)**..................**781 878-4540**
17 Accord Park Dr Ste 207 Norwell (02061) *(G-11141)*

East Coast Roof Specialties, Winsted *Also Called: East Coast Lightning Eqp Inc (G-4343)*

East Coast Sheet Metal LLC...........................860 283-1126
141 Woodruff St Litchfield (06759) *(G-1556)*

East Greenwich Oil Co Inc............................401 884-2454
390 Main St East Greenwich (02818) *(G-15982)*

East Hartford Operations, East Hartford *Also Called: ATI Ladish Machining Inc (G-974)*

East Meets West, Boston *Also Called: Bakery To Go Inc (G-6582)*

East Passage Yachting Center, Portsmouth *Also Called: New England Boatworks Inc (G-16449)*

East Providence Mohawks.............................401 829-1411
78 Vine St East Providence (02914) *(G-16015)*

East Rock Brewing Company LLC **(PA)**................**203 530-3484**
285 Nicoll St New Haven (06511) *(G-2147)*

East Shore Wire Rope................................203 469-5204
5 Old Bradley St East Haven (06512) *(G-1040)*

East Shore Wire Rope Rgging Su......................203 469-5204
78 Rebeschi Dr North Haven (06473) *(G-2407)*

East Tronix, Billerica *Also Called: Tanyx Measurements Inc (G-6485)*

East West Boston LLC................................617 598-3000
12 Channel St Ste 301 Boston (02210) *(G-6706)*

East Windsor Metal Fabg Inc.........................860 528-7107
91 Glendale Rd South Windsor (06074) *(G-3139)*

Eastern Awning Systems Inc..........................860 274-9218
843 Echo Lake Rd Watertown (06795) *(G-4011)*

Eastern Boats, Milton *Also Called: Eastern Boats Inc (G-15045)*

Eastern Boats Inc...................................603 652-9213
31 Industrial Way Milton (03851) *(G-15045)*

Eastern Broach & Machine LLC........................860 678-7490
24 Skyline Dr Farmington (06032) *(G-1216)*

Eastern Broach Inc..................................860 828-4800
10 Sparks St Plainville (06062) *(G-2755)*

Eastern Chem-Lac LLC **(PA)**........................**413 592-4191**
33 Haynes Cir Chicopee (01020) *(G-8029)*

Eastern Co..860 526-0800
212 Middlesex Ave Chester (06412) *(G-628)*

Eastern Co..860 669-2233
1 Heritage Park Rd Clinton (06413) *(G-642)*

Eastern Co **(PA)**..................................**203 729-2255**
3 Enterprise Dr Ste 408 Shelton (06484) *(G-3001)*

Eastern Design Inc..................................401 765-0558
70 New River Rd Manville (02838) *(G-16163)*

Eastern Electric Cnstr Co...........................860 485-1100
75 North Rd Harwinton (06791) *(G-1519)*

Eastern Etching, Chicopee *Also Called: Eastern Etching and Mfg Co (G-8030)*

Eastern Etching and Mfg Co..........................413 594-6601
35 Lower Grape St Chicopee (01013) *(G-8030)*

Eastern Food Industries Inc.........................401 884-8798
2832 S County Trl East Greenwich (02818) *(G-15983)*

Eastern Ice Company Inc.............................508 672-1800
281 Commerce Dr Fall River (02720) *(G-8538)*

Eastern Industrial Pdts Inc.........................781 826-9511
3 Collins Ave Plymouth (02360) *(G-11457)*

Eastern Laundry Systems, Taunton *Also Called: Baystate Business Ventures LLC (G-12324)*

Eastern Machine & Design Corp.......................781 293-6391
1062 Main St Hanson (02341) *(G-9051)*

Eastern Maine Industries, Milo *Also Called: Eastern ME Shooting Sups Inc (G-5069)*

Eastern Manufacturing Company.......................401 231-8330
9 Humbert St North Providence (02911) *(G-16301)*

A L P H A B E T I C

Eastern Marble and Granite LLC.............. 203 882-8221
  201 Buckingham Ave Milford (06460) *(G-1820)*

Eastern Mass Machined Pdts Inc.............. 978 462-9301
  164 Elm St Salisbury (01952) *(G-11741)*

Eastern Mddlsex Press Pblctons **(PA)**.......... **781 321-8000**
  277 Commercial St Malden (02148) *(G-10012)*

Eastern ME Shooting Sups Inc.............. 207 943-8808
  71 Main St Milo (04463) *(G-5069)*

Eastern Metal Industries Inc.............. 781 231-5220
  910 Broadway Rear Saugus (01906) *(G-11757)*

Eastern Metal Treating Inc.............. 860 763-4311
  28 Bacon Rd Enfield (06082) *(G-1128)*

Eastern Metal Works Inc.............. 203 878-6995
  333 Woodmont Rd Milford (06460) *(G-1821)*

Eastern Metals Inc.............. 603 818-8639
  4 Old Nashua Rd Londonderry (03053) *(G-14745)*

Eastern Packaging Inc.............. 978 685-7723
  283 Lowell St Lawrence (01840) *(G-9559)*

Eastern Plastics, Bristol *Also Called: Idex Health & Science LLC (G-456)*

Eastern Precast Company Inc.............. 203 775-0230
  1 Commerce Dr Brookfield (06804) *(G-519)*

Eastern Screw Company.............. 401 943-0680
  15 Amflex Dr Cranston (02921) *(G-15852)*

Eastern Sling & Supply.............. 617 464-4422
  230 Bodwell St Avon (02322) *(G-6150)*

Eastern Sling & Supply, Boston *Also Called: Ekiton Corporation (G-6709)*

Eastern Time Designs Inc.............. 603 483-5876
  143 Raymond Rd Candia (03034) *(G-14048)*

Eastern Tool Corporation.............. 781 395-1472
  105 High St Stoneham (02180) *(G-12176)*

Eastern Woodworks Llc.............. 978 352-2005
  132 Tenney St Georgetown (01833) *(G-8908)*

Easthampton Machine & Tool Inc.............. 413 527-8770
  72 Parsons St Easthampton (01027) *(G-8444)*

Easthampton Precision Mfg.............. 413 527-1650
  16 Arthur St Easthampton (01027) *(G-8445)*

Eastman Performance Films LLC.............. 508 474-6002
  35 Jeffrey Ave Holliston (01746) *(G-9208)*

Easton Springs Corporation.............. 508 238-2741
  719 Washington St South Easton (02375) *(G-11942)*

Eastprint Inc.............. 978 975-5255
  350 Willow St North Andover (01845) *(G-10829)*

Eastside Electric Inc.............. 860 485-0700
  178 Birge Park Rd Harwinton (06791) *(G-1520)*

Eastview Associates Inc.............. 802 773-4040
  162 N Main St Ste 8 Rutland (05701) *(G-17495)*

Eastwind Communications Inc.............. 508 862-8600
  75 Perseverance Way Hyannis (02601) *(G-9435)*

Eastwood Printing Inc.............. 860 529-6673
  501 Middletown Ave Wethersfield (06109) *(G-4204)*

Eastwoods Arms LLC.............. 203 615-3476
  37 Orcutt Dr Guilford (06437) *(G-1393)*

Eating Well Inc.............. 802 425-5700
  50 Lakeside Ave Burlington (05401) *(G-17132)*

Eatingwell Media Group, Burlington *Also Called: Eating Well Inc (G-17132)*

Eaton Corporation.............. 508 520-2444
  165 Grove St Ste 10 Franklin (02038) *(G-8833)*

Eaton Corporation.............. 401 473-2214
  10 New Rd Rumford (02916) *(G-16666)*

Eaton Electric Holdings LLC.............. 860 683-4300
  1200 Kennedy Rd Windsor (06095) *(G-4271)*

Eaton Wright Line, Worcester *Also Called: Wright Line LLC (G-13834)*

Eb Carports & Metal Structures.............. 860 263-3797
  357 Alumni Rd Newington (06111) *(G-2287)*

Eba, East Longmeadow *Also Called: Alvin Johnson (G-8368)*

EBA&d, Simsbury *Also Called: Ensign-Bickford Arospc Def Co (G-3089)*

Ebinger Brothers Lea Co Inc.............. 978 356-5701
  44 Mitchell Rd Ste 1 Ipswich (01938) *(G-9484)*

Ebiz Tech LLC.............. 603 233-8481
  134 Haines St Unit 2 Nashua (03060) *(G-15093)*

Ebl Products Inc.............. 860 290-3737
  22 Prestige Park Cir East Hartford (06108) *(G-990)*

EBM-Papst Inc **(DH)**.............. **860 674-1515**
  100 Hyde Rd Farmington (06032) *(G-1217)*

Ebner Furnaces.............. 603 552-3806
  51 Harvey Rd Unit C Londonderry (03053) *(G-14746)*

Ebrevia Inc.............. 203 870-3000
  6 Landmark Sq Ste B Stamford (06901) *(G-3341)*

Ebs Acquisition Inc.............. 860 653-0411
  2 Oak St Niantic (06357) *(G-2356)*

Ebsco Publishing Inc **(DH)**.............. **978 356-6500**
  10 Estes St Ipswich (01938) *(G-9485)*

Ebscohost, Ipswich *Also Called: Ebsco Publishing Inc (G-9485)*

Ebsnet Inc.............. 978 448-9000
  274e Main St Groton (01450) *(G-9009)*

Ebtec Corporation.............. 860 789-2462
  68 Prospect Hill Rd East Windsor (06088) *(G-1072)*

Ebw Windup.............. 207 882-5038
  957 Boothbay Rd Edgecomb (04556) *(G-4747)*

Ebws LLC.............. 802 765-4180
  61 Rockbottom Rd Strafford (05072) *(G-17634)*

EC Pigments USA Inc.............. 508 676-3481
  749 Quequechan St Fall River (02721) *(G-8539)*

Ecc Holdings Inc **(HQ)**.............. **401 331-9000**
  35 Livingston St Providence (02904) *(G-16511)*

Echelon Industries Corporation.............. 413 562-6659
  53 Airport Rd Westfield (01085) *(G-13163)*

Echo Communications Inc.............. 603 526-6006
  59 Pleasant St New London (03257) *(G-15203)*

Echo Industries, Orange *Also Called: Replica Works Inc (G-11231)*

Echolab Inc
  267 Boston Rd Ste 11 North Billerica (01862) *(G-10910)*

Ecin Industries Inc.............. 508 675-6920
  1 Ace St Unit 2 Fall River (02720) *(G-8540)*

Eckel Industries Inc **(PA)**.............. **978 772-0840**
  100 Groton Shirley Rd Ayer (01432) *(G-6181)*

Eckoustic Division, Ayer *Also Called: Eckel Industries Inc (G-6181)*

Eclas Realty Corporation.............. 860 747-5773
  329 Cooke St Plainville (06062) *(G-2756)*

Eclipse Products Inc.............. 978 343-8600
  60 Commonwealth Cir Leominster (01453) *(G-9661)*

Eclypses Inc.............. 719 323-6680
  33 Broad St Ste 1100 Boston (02109) *(G-6707)*

Eco Division, Somerville *Also Called: Tracer Technologies Inc (G-11904)*

Eco Global Manufacturing LLC.............. 401 331-5129
  292 Charles St Providence (02904) *(G-16512)*

Eco Knight Group LLC **(PA)**.............. **802 318-8760**
  68 Mountain View Dr Lebanon (03766) *(G-14687)*

Eco Millwork LLC.............. 860 266-5744
  697 Cedar St Newington (06111) *(G-2288)*

Eco Touch, Somersworth *Also Called: Eco Touch Inc (G-15616)*

Eco Touch Inc.............. 603 319-1762
  22 Canal St Unit 125 Somersworth (03878) *(G-15616)*

Ecochlor Inc.............. 978 298-1463
  285 State St Ste 8 North Haven (06473) *(G-2408)*

Ecocor LLC.............. 207 342-2085
  22 Main St N Searsmont (04973) *(G-5449)*

Ecolab, Norwood *Also Called: Ecolab Inc (G-11171)*

Ecolab Inc.............. 781 688-2100
  1 Edgewater Dr Ste 210 Norwood (02062) *(G-11171)*

Ecologic Energy Solutions LLC.............. 203 889-0505
  48 Union St Ste 14 Stamford (06906) *(G-3342)*

Ecological Fibers Inc **(PA)**.............. **978 537-0003**
  40 Pioneer Dr Lunenburg (01462) *(G-9958)*

Ecological Fibers Inc.............. 401 725-9700
  730 York Ave Pawtucket (02861) *(G-16366)*

Ecometics Inc.............. 203 853-7856
  19 Concord St Norwalk (06854) *(G-2495)*

Econiq.............. 781 588-2223
  101 Cambridge St Ste 385 Burlington (01803) *(G-7367)*

Econocorp Inc.............. 781 986-7500
  72 Pacella Park Dr Randolph (02368) *(G-11555)*

Economy Energy LLC.............. 203 227-5181
  11 Ferry Ln W Westport (06880) *(G-4167)*

Economy Plumbing, Mattapan *Also Called: Economy Plumbing & Htg Sup Co* **(G-10254)**

Economy Plumbing & Htg Sup Co........................... 617 433-1200
875 Morton St Mattapan (02126) **(G-10254)**

Economy Printing, Danbury *Also Called: Paul Dewitt* **(G-795)**

Economy Spring, Southington *Also Called: Matthew Warren Inc* **(G-3221)**

Ecovent, Charlestown *Also Called: Ecovent Corp* **(G-7869)**

Ecovent Corp... 620 983-6863
24 Cambridge St Ste 6 Charlestown (02129) **(G-7869)**

Ecpi Inc.. 774 823-6368
83 Wilder Rd Bolton (01740) **(G-6496)**

Ecrm Imaging Systems, North Andover *Also Called: Ecrm Incorporated* **(G-10830)**

Ecrm Incorporated **(PA)**............................... **978 581-0207**
25 Commerce Way Ste 6 North Andover (01845) **(G-10830)**

Ect, South Windsor *Also Called: Electrostatic Coating Technologies Corp* **(G-3142)**

Ecu & US International.................................. 860 906-3390
43 Franklin St East Hartford (06108) **(G-991)**

Edac Machinery, Farmington *Also Called: Service Network Inc* **(G-1247)**

Edac ND, Glastonbury *Also Called: Hanwha Aerospace USA LLC* **(G-1284)**

Edal Industries Inc...................................... 203 467-2591
51 Commerce St East Haven (06512) **(G-1041)**

Edaron, Inc., Holyoke *Also Called: Norade Inc* **(G-9271)**

Edco Engineering Inc.................................... 860 667-8292
100 Rockwell Rd Newington (06111) **(G-2289)**

Edco Industries, Bridgeport *Also Called: Edco Industries Inc* **(G-319)**

Edco Industries Inc..................................... 203 333-8982
203 Dekalb Ave Bridgeport (06607) **(G-319)**

Eddies Wheels Inc...................................... 413 625-0033
140 State St Shelburne Falls (01370) **(G-11804)**

Edesia Inc **(PA)**..................................... **401 272-5521**
550 Romano Vineyard Way North Kingstown (02852) **(G-16247)**

Edesia Enterprises LLC................................. 401 272-5521
550 Romano Vineyard Way North Kingstown (02852) **(G-16248)**

Edesia Industries LLC.................................. 401 272-5521
550 Romano Vineyard Way North Kingstown (02852) **(G-16249)**

Edge Embossing Inc.................................... 617 850-2868
56 Roland St Ste 211 Charlestown (02129) **(G-7870)**

Edge Media Group...................................... 207 942-2901
1 Cumberland Pl Ste 204 Bangor (04401) **(G-4498)**

Edge Velocity Corporation.............................. 603 912-5618
68 Stiles Rd Ste G Salem (03079) **(G-15519)**

Edge2web Inc.. 203 770-2588
800 Main St S Southbury (06488) **(G-3193)**

Edgeone LLC... 508 291-0057
4 Little Brook Rd West Wareham (02576) **(G-13061)**

Edgeone LLC... 508 291-0960
4 Little Brook Rd West Wareham (02576) **(G-13062)**

Edgeone LLC **(PA)**.................................. **508 291-0057**
4 Little Brook Rd West Wareham (02576) **(G-13063)**

Edgetech, West Wareham *Also Called: Edgeone LLC* **(G-13063)**

Edgetech Instruments Inc.............................. 508 263-5900
399 River Rd Hudson (01749) **(G-9362)**

Edgewater Marine Inds LLC............................ 508 992-6555
90 Hatch St Unit 1 New Bedford (02745) **(G-10588)**

EDGEWELL, Shelton *Also Called: Edgewell Personal Care Company* **(G-3003)**

Edgewell Per Care Brands LLC......................... 203 882-2300
10 Leighton Rd Milford (06460) **(G-1822)**

Edgewell Per Care Brands LLC **(HQ)**................. **203 944-5500**
6 Research Dr Shelton (06484) **(G-3002)**

Edgewell Per Care Brands LLC......................... 802 442-5551
401 Gage St Bennington (05201) **(G-17039)**

Edgewell Per Care Brands LLC......................... 802 524-2151
75 Swanton Rd Saint Albans (05478) **(G-17521)**

Edgewell Personal Care Company....................... 203 882-2308
10 Leighton Rd Milford (06460) **(G-1823)**

Edgewell Personal Care Company **(PA)**.............. **203 944-5500**
6 Research Dr Ste 400 Shelton (06484) **(G-3003)**

Edgil Associates Inc.................................... 978 262-9799
222 Rosewood Dr Unit 210 Danvers (01923) **(G-8184)**

Edi Landscape LLC.................................... 860 216-6871
32 Belmont St Hartford (06106) **(G-1477)**

Edigene Inc... 617 682-5731
700 Main St Cambridge (02139) **(G-7554)**

Edison Coatings Inc................................... 860 747-2220
3 Northwest Dr Plainville (06062) **(G-2757)**

Edison Press, Sanford *Also Called: RH Rosenfield Co* **(G-5410)**

Editas, Cambridge *Also Called: Editas Medicine Inc* **(G-7555)**

Editas Medicine Inc **(PA)**.......................... **617 401-9000**
11 Hurley St Cambridge (02141) **(G-7555)**

Editorial Ofc Indtrl Lser Solt, Sturbridge *Also Called: Penwell* **(G-12256)**

Edlund Company LLC.................................. 802 862-9661
319 Queen City Park Rd Burlington (05401) **(G-17133)**

Edmond Roy & Sons Inc............................... 877 425-8491
101 Main Street Jackman (04945) **(G-4910)**

Edmunds Gages, Farmington *Also Called: Edmunds Manufacturing Company* **(G-1218)**

Edmunds Manufacturing Company **(PA)**.............. **860 677-2813**
45 Spring Ln Farmington (06032) **(G-1218)**

Edrive Actuators Inc.................................. 860 953-0588
385 Stamm Rd Newington (06111) **(G-2290)**

Edsan Chemical Company Inc........................... 203 624-3123
150 Whittier Rd New Haven (06515) **(G-2148)**

Edson Manufacturing Inc.............................. 203 879-1411
10 Venus Dr Wolcott (06716) **(G-4364)**

Edson Marine, New Bedford *Also Called: Ship Street Capital LLC* **(G-10650)**

Edson Pump Div, New Bedford *Also Called: Newera Services Corporation* **(G-10631)**

Education Development Ctr Inc **(PA)**................. **617 969-7100**
300 5th Ave 2010 Waltham (02451) **(G-12659)**

Educational Instrument, Nashua *Also Called: Sempco Inc* **(G-15166)**

Educators Publishing Service, Cambridge *Also Called: Ssi Liquidating Inc* **(G-7720)**

Edward Elgar Publishing Inc........................... 413 584-5551
9 Dewey Ct Northampton (01060) **(G-11060)**

Edward F Briggs Disposal Inc.......................... 401 294-6391
Carrs Pond Rd East Greenwich (02818) **(G-15984)**

Edward Group Inc..................................... 802 775-1029
194 Seward Rd Rutland (05701) **(G-17496)**

Edward Segal Inc..................................... 860 283-5821
360 Reynolds Bridge Rd Thomaston (06787) **(G-3618)**

Edwards Detection & Alarm, Farmington *Also Called: Carrier Fire SEC Americas Corp* **(G-1211)**

Edwards Home Furnishings, Lisbon Falls *Also Called: Miller Industries Inc* **(G-5023)**

Edwards Vacuum LLC.................................. 978 262-2400
15 Elizabeth Dr Chelmsford (01824) **(G-7924)**

Eemax, Inc.. 203 267-7890
400 Captain Neville Dr Waterbury (06705) **(G-3910)**

EF Leach & Company.................................. 508 643-3309
8 N Main St Ste 500 Attleboro (02703) **(G-6011)**

Efficiency Plus....................................... 603 539-8125
49 Leavitt Rd Center Ossipee (03814) **(G-14057)**

Efficient Air Systems, Gorham *Also Called: Pool Environments Inc* **(G-4831)**

Efi Inkjet Solutions, Londonderry *Also Called: Electronics For Imaging Inc* **(G-14747)**

Egan Church Supply, Millbury *Also Called: Laurence Cndle Mfg Ch Sups Inc* **(G-10439)**

Egan, Strling Nrm Kllion Ltol, Pawcatuck *Also Called: Davis-Standard Holdings Inc* **(G-2718)**

Eggrock Inc... 978 952-8800
265 Foster St Littleton (01460) **(G-9813)**

Eglean Inc.. 617 229-5863
1266 Furnace Brook Pkwy Quincy (02169) **(G-11513)**

Eglean.com, Quincy *Also Called: Eglean Inc* **(G-11513)**

Egs Elctrcal Group Nlson Heat, East Granby *Also Called: Appleton Grp LLC* **(G-925)**

Ehs Publishing....................................... 203 216-5800
10 Newmarket Rd Durham (03824) **(G-14266)**

Ehv-Weidmann Industries, Saint Johnsbury *Also Called: Weidmann Electrical Technology Inc* **(G-17548)**

Ei-Rec LLC... 860 851-9014
17 Middle River Dr Stafford Springs (06076) **(G-3255)**

Eichenauer Inc....................................... 603 863-1454
292 Sunapee St Newport (03773) **(G-15228)**

Eidolon Corporation.................................. 781 400-0586
3 Erie Dr Natick (01760) **(G-10479)**

Eidp Inc... 617 482-9595
123 E Dedham St Boston (02118) **(G-6708)**

Eigenlight Corporation................................ 603 692-9200
13 Water St Apt B Newmarket (03857) **(G-15219)**

A
L
P
H
A
B
E
T
I
C

Eimskip USA Inc.. 207 221-5268
   468 Commercial St Portland (04101) *(G-5214)*

Eis, Milford *Also Called: Engineered Inserts Systems Inc (G-1824)*

Eis Wire & Cable Inc.. 413 536-0152
   775 New Ludlow Rd South Hadley (01075) *(G-11961)*

Eisai Inc.. 978 837-4616
   35 Cambridgepark Dr Ste 200 Cambridge (02140) *(G-7556)*

EJ Jaxtimer Builder Inc....................................... 508 778-4911
   48 Rosary Ln Hyannis (02601) *(G-9436)*

Ej Usa Inc... 508 586-3130
   1125 Pearl St Brockton (02301) *(G-7275)*

Ek-Ris Cable, New Britain *Also Called: Ek-Ris Cable Company Inc (G-2025)*

Ek-Ris Cable Company Inc................................... 860 223-4327
   503 Burritt St Apt 7 New Britain (06053) *(G-2025)*

Ekiton Corporation... 617 464-4422
   17 Power House St R Boston (02127) *(G-6709)*

Ekran System Inc.. 424 242-8838
   60 Kendrick St Ste 201 Needham Heights (02494) *(G-10542)*

Ekto Manufacturing Corp..................................... 207 324-4427
   83 Eagle Dr Sanford (04073) *(G-5394)*

El Mar Inc... 860 729-7232
   38 Cody St # 2 West Hartford (06110) *(G-4058)*

El Mundo Newspapers, Boston *Also Called: Caribe Cmmnctons Pblctions Inc (G-6638)*

El Paso Prod Oil Gas Texas LP.............................. 860 293-1990
   490 Capitol Ave Hartford (06106) *(G-1478)*

El-Op US Inc... 603 889-2500
   220 Daniel Webster Hwy Merrimack (03054) *(G-14980)*

Elan, Cambridge *Also Called: Elan Pharmaceuticals Inc (G-7558)*

Elan Pharma.. 415 885-6780
   300 Technology Sq Ste 3 Cambridge (02139) *(G-7557)*

Elan Pharmaceuticals Inc
   300 Technology Sq Ste 1 Cambridge (02139) *(G-7558)*

Elan Publishing Company Inc................................ 603 253-6002
   72 Whittier Hwy Unit 3 Moultonborough (03254) *(G-15052)*

Elbonais Incorporated... 508 626-2318
   1451 Concord St Ste 1 Framingham (01701) *(G-8761)*

Elcom, Braintree *Also Called: Elcom International Inc (G-7179)*

Elcom International Inc **(PA)**.............................. **781 501-4000**
   50 Braintree Hill Park Ste 309 Braintree (02184) *(G-7179)*

Eldersafe Technologies Inc.................................. 617 852-3018
   127 Poor Farm Rd Harvard (01451) *(G-9062)*

Eldred Wheeler Company..................................... 781 924-5067
   199 Winter St Ste 3 Hanover (02339) *(G-9030)*

Eldur AG, Bangor *Also Called: Eldur Corporation (G-4499)*

Eldur Corporation.. 207 942-6592
   448 Griffin Rd Bangor (04401) *(G-4499)*

Electra, Boston *Also Called: Electra Vehicles Inc (G-6710)*

Electra Vehicles Inc **(PA)**................................ **617 313-7842**
   110 K St Ste 330 Boston (02127) *(G-6710)*

Electrcal Installations LLC Ei................................ 603 253-4525
   397 Whittier Hwy Moultonborough (03254) *(G-15053)*

Electri-Cord Manufacturing Co............................... 508 836-3510
   133 Flanders Rd Westborough (01581) *(G-13099)*

Electric Boat Corporation.................................... 860 433-0503
   210 Mitchell St Groton (06340) *(G-1369)*

Electric Boat Corporation **(HQ)**.......................... **860 433-3000**
   75 Eastern Point Rd Groton (06340) *(G-1370)*

Electric Boat Corporation.................................... 860 433-3000
   75 Eastern Point Rd Groton (06340) *(G-1371)*

Electric Boat Corporation.................................... 860 433-3000
   50 Pequot Ave New London (06320) *(G-2227)*

Electric Boat Corporation.................................... 401 268-2410
   165 Dillabur Ave North Kingstown (02852) *(G-16250)*

Electric Boat Fairwater Div, Groton *Also Called: Electric Boat Corporation (G-1371)*

Electric Cable Compounds Inc.............................. 203 723-2590
   108 Rado Dr Naugatuck (06770) *(G-1957)*

Electric Catalytic Pdts Group, Tewksbury *Also Called: Evoqua Water Technologies LLC (G-12398)*

Electric Enterprise Inc....................................... 203 378-7311
   1410 Stratford Ave Stratford (06615) *(G-3534)*

Electric Hydrogen Co... 617 546-5710
   1 Strathmore Rd Natick (01760) *(G-10480)*

Electric Motion Company Inc **(DH)**...................... **860 379-8515**
   110 Groppo Dr Winsted (06098) *(G-4344)*

Electric Time Company Inc.................................. 508 359-4396
   97 West St Medfield (02052) *(G-10270)*

Electrix LLC.. 203 776-5577
   45 Spring St New Haven (06519) *(G-2149)*

Electrnic Mobility Contrls LLC............................... 207 512-8009
   26 Gabriel Dr Augusta (04330) *(G-4471)*

Electrnic Shtmtal Crftsmen Inc.............................. 781 341-3260
   120 Central St Stoughton (02072) *(G-12202)*

Electrnic Vsion Access Sltns/V, Westerly *Also Called: Jerrys At Misquamicut Inc (G-16934)*

Electro Mech Specialists LLC............................... 860 887-2613
   6 Commerce Park Rd Bozrah (06334) *(G-228)*

Electro Standards Lab Inc................................... 401 946-1164
   36 Western Industrial Dr Cranston (02921) *(G-15853)*

Electro Standards Laboratories, Cranston *Also Called: Electro Standards Lab Inc (G-15853)*

Electro Switch Corp... 781 607-3306
   180 King Ave Weymouth (02188) *(G-13324)*

Electro Switch Corp... 781 335-1195
   180 King Ave Weymouth (02188) *(G-13325)*

Electro-Fix Inc... 508 695-0228
   300 South St Plainville (02762) *(G-11432)*

Electro-Flex Heat, West Hartford *Also Called: Manufacturers Coml Fin LLC (G-4070)*

Electro-Lite Corporation...................................... 203 743-4059
   6 Trowbridge Dr Bethel (06801) *(G-114)*

Electro-Methods Inc... 860 289-8661
   525 Nutmeg Rd N South Windsor (06074) *(G-3140)*

Electro-Methods Inc **(PA)**................................ **860 289-8661**
   330 Governors Hwy South Windsor (06074) *(G-3141)*

Electro-Prep Inc... 508 291-2880
   8 Kendrick Rd Ste 1 Wareham (02571) *(G-12834)*

Electro-Tech Inc... 203 271-1976
   408 Sandbank Rd Cheshire (06410) *(G-589)*

Electro-Term Inc.. 413 734-6469
   50 Warehouse St Springfield (01118) *(G-12092)*

Electro-Term/Hollingsworth, Springfield *Also Called: Electro-Term Inc (G-12092)*

Electrocal Inc.. 860 646-8153
   375 New State Rd Manchester (06042) *(G-1595)*

Electrochem Solutions Inc................................... 781 575-0800
   670 Paramount Dr Raynham (02767) *(G-11589)*

Electrocraft Inc **(HQ)**.................................... **855 697-7966**
   2 Marin Way Ste 3 Stratham (03885) *(G-15634)*

Electrocraft New Hampshire Inc **(DH)**.................. **603 742-3330**
   1 Progress Dr Dover (03820) *(G-14228)*

Electrocraft New Hampshire Inc............................ 740 441-6208
   2 Marin Way Ste 3 Stratham (03885) *(G-15635)*

Electrodyne Systems, Scarborough *Also Called: Gauss Corporation (G-5432)*

Electrolizing Inc... 401 861-5900
   20 Houghton St Providence (02904) *(G-16513)*

Electrolyzer Corp.. 978 363-5349
   22 Bachelor St West Newbury (01985) *(G-13008)*

Electronic Assemblies Mfg Inc.............................. 978 374-6840
   126 Merrimack St Methuen (01844) *(G-10329)*

Electronic Assembly Service, Sanford *Also Called: Marja Corporation (G-5400)*

Electronic Components Inc................................... 508 881-8399
   39 Loring Dr Framingham (01702) *(G-8762)*

Electronic Finishing Company, Bridgeport *Also Called: Park Distributories Inc (G-356)*

Electronic Fluorocarbons LLC **(PA)**...................... **508 435-7700**
   239 South St Hopkinton (01748) *(G-9316)*

Electronic House, Framingham *Also Called: E H Publishing Inc (G-8759)*

Electronic Imaging Mtls Inc.................................. 603 357-1459
   20 Forge St Keene (03431) *(G-14597)*

Electronic Products, Newburyport *Also Called: Electronic Products Inds Inc (G-10681)*

Electronic Products Inds Inc................................. 978 462-8101
   85 Parker St Newburyport (01950) *(G-10681)*

Electronic Spc Conn Inc...................................... 203 288-1707
   19 Hamden Park Dr Hamden (06517) *(G-1423)*

Electronic Surface Coatings, Lincoln *Also Called: Tanury Industries Inc (G-16156)*

Electronic Test Energy Co, West Roxbury *Also Called: Etec Inc (G-13010)*

Electronics Aid Inc.. 603 876-4161
   32 Roxbury Rd Marlborough (03455) *(G-14964)*

Electronics For Imaging Inc.. 603 285-9800
  12 Innovatiion Way Londonderry (03053) *(G-14747)*

Electronics For Imaging Inc **(HQ)**.............................. **650 357-3500**
  12 Innovatiion Way Londonderry (03053) *(G-14748)*

Electronics For Imaging Inc.. 603 279-6800
  79 E Wilder Rd Ste 1 West Lebanon (03784) *(G-15683)*

Electropolishing Systems Inc.. 508 830-1717
  24 Aldrin Rd Plymouth (02360) *(G-11458)*

Electrosonics Medical Inc.. 216 357-3310
  2 Oliver St Ste 616 Boston (02109) *(G-6711)*

Electrostatic Coating Technologies Corp........................... 860 610-9097
  1265 John Fitch Blvd Ste 12 South Windsor (06074) *(G-3142)*

Electrotech Inc.. 207 596-0556
  344 Park St Rockland (04841) *(G-5326)*

Elektrisola Incorporated **(PA)**.. **603 796-2114**
  126 High St Boscawen (03303) *(G-13989)*

Element 119, Thomaston *Also Called: Element 119 LLC (G-3619)*

Element 119 LLC... 860 358-0119
  296 Reynolds Bridge Rd Thomaston (06787) *(G-3619)*

Element All Stars.. 207 576-6931
  746 Main St Lewiston (04240) *(G-4958)*

Element Care... 978 655-6195
  209 Lawrence St Methuen (01844) *(G-10330)*

Element Industries Inc.. 401 253-8802
  48 Ballou Blvd Bristol (02809) *(G-15762)*

Element Precision LLC... 774 318-1777
  10 Cabot St Southbridge (01550) *(G-12015)*

Element Real Estate, Burlington *Also Called: Brunswick Square LLC (G-17122)*

Elenel Industries Inc **(PA)**.. **508 478-2025**
  500 Fortune Blvd Milford (01757) *(G-10401)*

Elerts Corporation... 781 803-6362
  1132 Main St Ste 300 South Weymouth (02190) *(G-11975)*

Elevatebio LLC **(PA)**.. **413 297-7151**
  139 Main St Ste 500 Cambridge (02142) *(G-7559)*

Elevatebio Base Camp, Cambridge *Also Called: Elevatebio LLC (G-7559)*

Elevatebio Base Camp Inc.. 617 433-2600
  200 Smith St Ste 301 Waltham (02451) *(G-12660)*

Elie Baking Corporation.. 508 584-4890
  204 N Montello St Brockton (02301) *(G-7276)*

Elinco International Jpc Inc **(PA)**.................................... **203 334-7537**
  1525 Kings Hwy Fairfield (06824) *(G-1183)*

Elite Custom Compounding Inc... 401 921-2136
  303 Kilvert St Warwick (02886) *(G-16813)*

Elite Envelope, Randolph *Also Called: Elite Envelope & Graphics Inc (G-11556)*

Elite Envelope & Graphics Inc.. 781 961-1800
  280 Pond St Randolph (02368) *(G-11556)*

Elite Group Manufacturing LLC... 860 788-6413
  173 E Cotton Hill Rd Portland (06480) *(G-2819)*

Elite Metal Fabricators Inc... 413 547-2588
  100 State St Bldg 203 Ludlow (01056) *(G-9944)*

Elizabeth Eakins Inc... 203 831-9347
  5 Taft St Norwalk (06854) *(G-2496)*

Eljen Corporation.. 860 610-0426
  125 Mckee St East Hartford (06108) *(G-992)*

Elkins & Co Inc... 207 633-0109
  103 Industrial Park Rd Boothbay (04537) *(G-4597)*

Elks Manufacturing Corporation... 203 235-2528
  290 Pratt St Ste 15 Meriden (06450) *(G-1666)*

Ellen McLaughlin.. 207 746-3398
  Rte 157 Medway (04460) *(G-5055)*

Ellington Printery Inc.. 860 875-3310
  25 West Rd Ste B Ellington (06029) *(G-1105)*

Elliott Group, Providence *Also Called: The Elliott Sales Group Inc (G-16625)*

Ellis Boat Co Inc... 207 244-9221
  265 Seawall Rd Southwest Harbor (04679) *(G-5518)*

Ellis Manufacturing LLC.. 865 518-0531
  161 Woodford Ave Plainville (06062) *(G-2758)*

Elloit Wright Workroom Inc... 617 542-3605
  535 Albany St Ste 18 Boston (02118) *(G-6712)*

Elm City Cheese Company Inc.. 203 865-5768
  2240 State St Hamden (06517) *(G-1424)*

Elm City Management, Hamden *Also Called: Elm City Mfg Jewelers Inc (G-1425)*

Elm City Manufacturing LLC... 203 248-1969
  370 Sackett Point Rd North Haven (06473) *(G-2409)*

Elm City Mfg Jewelers Inc.. 203 248-2195
  29 Marne St Hamden (06514) *(G-1425)*

Elm Industries Inc... 413 734-7762
  380 Union St Ste 67 West Springfield (01089) *(G-13023)*

Elm Press Incorporated... 860 583-3600
  16 Tremco Dr Terryville (06786) *(G-3601)*

Elm Street Vault Inc.. 207 284-4855
  38 Landry St Biddeford (04005) *(G-4563)*

Elm-Cap Industries Inc.. 860 953-1060
  111 South St West Hartford (06110) *(G-4059)*

Elmet Technologies, Lewiston *Also Called: Elmet Technologies LLC (G-4960)*

Elmet Technologies Inc... 207 784-3591
  1560 Lisbon St Lewiston (04240) *(G-4959)*

Elmet Technologies LLC **(PA)**.. **207 333-6100**
  1560 Lisbon St Lewiston (04240) *(G-4960)*

Elmo Motion Control Inc.. 603 821-9979
  42 Technology Way Nashua (03060) *(G-15094)*

Elms Puzzles Inc... 207 583-6262
  Hobbs Hill Ln Harrison (04040) *(G-4875)*

Elmwood Countertop Inc... 401 785-1677
  50 Webb St Cranston (02920) *(G-15854)*

Elmwood Manufacturing Inc, Cranston *Also Called: Fielding Mfg - Zinc Dcsting In (G-15861)*

Eloque LLC.. 203 849-5567
  201 Merritt 7 Norwalk (06851) *(G-2497)*

Elpakco Inc **(PA)**.. **978 392-0400**
  2 Carl Thompson Rd Westford (01886) *(G-13235)*

Elpakco Inc.. 603 968-9950
  Main St Ashland (03217) *(G-13899)*

Elscott Manufacturing LLC **(PA)**.................................. **207 422-6747**
  38 Route 1 Gouldsboro (04607) *(G-4839)*

Elsevier Inc... 781 663-5200
  50 Hampshire St 5th Fl Cambridge (02139) *(G-7560)*

Elves & Angels Inc.. 207 456-7575
  506 White Settlement Rd Hodgdon (04730) *(G-4891)*

Ely Tool Inc... 413 732-2347
  455 Cottage St Springfield (01104) *(G-12093)*

Em4 Inc **(DH)**... **781 275-7501**
  7 Oak Park Dr Bedford (01730) *(G-6223)*

Embassy Creations, Providence *Also Called: Pyramid Case Co Inc (G-16595)*

Embr Labs Inc... 413 218-0629
  24 Roland St Ste 1 Charlestown (02129) *(G-7871)*

Embraer Executive Jet Svcs LLC.. 860 804-4600
  41 Perimeter Rd Windsor Locks (06096) *(G-4324)*

Embraer Executive Jets, Windsor Locks *Also Called: Embraer Executive Jet Svcs LLC (G-4324)*

Embroidery Place... 508 842-5311
  10 Broushane Cir Shrewsbury (01545) *(G-11832)*

EMC, Augusta *Also Called: Electrnic Mobility Contrls LLC (G-4471)*

EMC Corporation... 800 275-8777
  55 Constitution Blvd Franklin (02038) *(G-8834)*

EMC Corporation... 508 435-1000
  50 Constitution Blvd Franklin (02038) *(G-8835)*

EMC Corporation... 866 438-3622
  111 Constitution Blvd Franklin (02038) *(G-8836)*

EMC Corporation... 508 435-0369
  117 South St Hopkinton (01748) *(G-9317)*

EMC Corporation... 800 445-2588
  80 South St Hopkinton (01748) *(G-9318)*

EMC Corporation... 508 346-2900
  171 South St Hopkinton (01748) *(G-9319)*

EMC Corporation... 508 435-2581
  45 South St Hopkinton (01748) *(G-9320)*

EMC Corporation... 508 249-5883
  228 South St Mailstop Hopkinton (01748) *(G-9321)*

EMC Corporation **(HQ)**... **508 435-1000**
  176 South St Hopkinton (01748) *(G-9322)*

EMC Corporation... 508 634-2774
  5 Technology Dr Milford (01757) *(G-10402)*

EMC Corporation... 617 618-3400
  95 Wells Ave Ste 160 Newton (02459) *(G-10755)*

ALPHABETIC

EMC Global Holdings Company..................... 508 544-2852
  176 South St Hopkinton (01748) *(G-9323)*

EMC International Holdings Inc..................... 508 435-1000
  176 South St Hopkinton (01748) *(G-9324)*

EMC Services, Cranston *Also Called: Energy MGT & Ctrl Svcs Inc (G-15856)*

Emc1 Continental Ave LLC......................... 617 875-2687
  529 Columbus Ave Apt 18 Boston (02118) *(G-6713)*

Emc2, Hopkinton *Also Called: EMC International Holdings Inc (G-9324)*

Emco Services Inc................................. 508 674-5504
  37 Slade St Fall River (02724) *(G-8541)*

Emco Tool & Gauge Corporation.................... 413 385-0206
  100 State St Bldg 206 Ludlow (01056) *(G-9945)*

EMD Accnting Sltons Svcs Amer.................... 781 982-9000
  1 Technology Pl Rockland (02370) *(G-11642)*

EMD Millipore Corporation......................... 781 533-6000
  80 Ashby Rd Bedford (01730) *(G-6224)*

EMD Millipore Corporation......................... 781 533-6000
  75 Wiggins Ave Bedford (01730) *(G-6225)*

EMD Millipore Corporation......................... 978 715-4321
  290 Concord Rd # 2 Billerica (01821) *(G-6438)*

EMD Millipore Corporation......................... 978 762-5100
  17 Cherry Hill Dr Danvers (01923) *(G-8185)*

EMD Millipore Corporation......................... 800 637-7872
  4 Batterymarch Park Ste 200 Quincy (02169) *(G-11514)*

EMD Millipore Corporation......................... 781 533-5754
  530 John Hancock Rd Taunton (02780) *(G-12334)*

EMD Millipore Corporation......................... 781 533-5858
  300 2nd Ave Waltham (02451) *(G-12661)*

EMD Millipore Corporation......................... 603 532-8711
  11 Prescott Rd Jaffrey (03452) *(G-14567)*

EMD Pharmaceuticals, Burlington *Also Called: EMD Serono Inc (G-7368)*

EMD Pharmaceuticals, Rockland *Also Called: EMD Serono Inc (G-11643)*

EMD Serono Inc.................................... 781 982-9000
  290 Concord Rd Billerica (01821) *(G-6439)*

EMD Serono Inc.................................... 978 715-1804
  400 Summit Dr Fl 4 Burlington (01803) *(G-7368)*

EMD Serono Inc **(DH)**............................ **781 982-9000**
  1 Technology Pl Rockland (02370) *(G-11643)*

EMD Serono Biotech Center Inc.................... 978 294-1100
  45a Middlesex Tpke Billerica (01821) *(G-6440)*

EMD Serono Biotech Center Inc.................... 978 294-1100
  4 Batterymarch Park Ste 2 Quincy (02169) *(G-11515)*

EMD Serono Biotech Center Inc **(HQ)**........... **800 283-8088**
  1 Technology Pl Rockland (02370) *(G-11644)*

EMD Serono Holding Inc........................... 781 982-9000
  1 Technology Pl Rockland (02370) *(G-11645)*

EMD Serono RES & Dev Inst Inc................... 978 294-1100
  45 Middlesex Tpke Billerica (01821) *(G-6441)*

EMD Serono RES & Dev Inst Inc **(HQ)**........... **781 982-9000**
  1 Technology Pl Rockland (02370) *(G-11646)*

EMD Serono Research Inst Inc, Rockland *Also Called: EMD Serono RES & Dev Inst Inc (G-11646)*

EMD Srdi, Billerica *Also Called: EMD Serono RES & Dev Inst Inc (G-6441)*

Emerald Ems, Salem *Also Called: Megatrnics US Ultimate Hldco LL (G-15544)*

Emerald Iron Works Inc........................... 978 851-3028
  662 Clark Rd Ste 1 Tewksbury (01876) *(G-12396)*

Emergent Biosolutions Inc......................... 781 302-3000
  50 Shawmut Rd Canton (02021) *(G-7788)*

Emergncy Pwr Gnrators Neng LLC.................. 978 455-0461
  4 Etta Rd Chelmsford (01824) *(G-7925)*

Emerson Apparatus Company....................... 207 856-0055
  59 Sanford Dr Unit 12 Gorham (04038) *(G-4818)*

Emerson Atmtn Sltons Fnal Ctrl.................... 508 594-4411
  55 Cabot Blvd Mansfield (02048) *(G-10051)*

Emerson Prcess MGT Pwr Wtr Slt.................. 978 689-2800
  12 Ballard Way Lawrence (01843) *(G-9560)*

Emerson Rmote Automtn Solution, Watertown *Also Called: Bristol Inc (G-4004)*

Emerson Textiles, Peabody *Also Called: Emtex Inc (G-11309)*

Emery Development Ltd............................. 413 782-1990
  179 Cooley St Springfield (01128) *(G-12094)*

Emery Winslow Scale Co, Seymour *Also Called: The A H Emery Company (G-2970)*

Emhart Glass Inc **(DH)**......................... **860 298-7340**
  123 Great Pond Dr Windsor (06095) *(G-4272)*

Emhart Glass Manufacturing Inc **(DH)**........... **860 298-7340**
  123 Great Pond Dr Windsor (06095) *(G-4273)*

EMI Inc... 860 669-1199
  4 Heritage Park Rd Clinton (06413) *(G-643)*

EMI Industries LLC................................ 401 785-3900
  1485 Elmwood Ave Cranston (02910) *(G-15855)*

Emissive Energy Corp.............................. 401 294-2030
  135 Circuit Dr North Kingstown (02852) *(G-16251)*

Emm Precision Inc................................ 603 356-8892
  619 E Conway Rd Center Conway (03813) *(G-14051)*

Emme Controls LLC................................ 503 793-3792
  32 Valley St Fl C Bristol (06010) *(G-437)*

Emme E2ms LLC................................... 860 845-8810
  32 Valley St Fl C Bristol (06010) *(G-438)*

Emme E2ms LLC................................... 860 845-8810
  32 Valley St Bristol (06010) *(G-439)*

Emosyn America Inc............................... 203 794-1100
  7 Commerce Dr Danbury (06810) *(G-735)*

Emotionrx, Cambridge *Also Called: Emotionrx Inc (G-7561)*

Emotionrx Inc..................................... 617 500-5976
  245 Main St Fl 2 Cambridge (02142) *(G-7561)*

Emp Co Inc **(PA)**............................... **860 589-3233**
  147 Terryville Rd Bristol (06010) *(G-440)*

Empath Labs, Providence *Also Called: Sproutel Inc (G-16615)*

Empco Prcision Swiss Screw Mch, Bristol *Also Called: Emp Co Inc (G-440)*

Empiramed, Maynard *Also Called: Empiramed Inc (G-10262)*

Empiramed Inc.................................... 978 344-4300
  1 Mill And Main Pl Ste 100 Maynard (01754) *(G-10262)*

Empire Industries Inc............................. 860 647-1431
  180 Olcott St Manchester (06040) *(G-1596)*

Empire Manufacturing, South Windsor *Also Called: Agreda Industries LLC (G-3110)*

Empire Sheetmetal Inc............................ 603 622-4439
  155 Baker St Manchester (03103) *(G-14847)*

Ems Engnred Mtls Solutions LLC **(DH)**........... **508 342-2100**
  39 Perry Ave Attleboro (02703) *(G-6012)*

Emseal Joint Systems Ltd.......................... 508 836-0280
  25 Bridle Ln Westborough (01581) *(G-13100)*

Emtec Metal Products, Bridgeport *Also Called: Hispanic Enterprises Inc (G-329)*

Emtex Inc... 978 907-4500
  58 Pulaski St Peabody (01960) *(G-11309)*

Emuge Corp....................................... 508 595-3600
  1800 Century Dr West Boylston (01583) *(G-12962)*

Emx Controls Inc................................. 508 876-9700
  100 Davis St # 1 East Douglas (01516) *(G-8350)*

En-Pro Management Inc........................... 866 352-5433
  269 Mill Rd Chelmsford (01824) *(G-7926)*

Enamel Pure Inc.................................. 508 335-4824
  17 Briden St Worcester (01605) *(G-13720)*

ENANTA, Watertown *Also Called: Enanta Pharmaceuticals Inc (G-12872)*

Enanta Pharmaceuticals Inc **(PA)**............... **617 607-0800**
  500 Arsenal St Watertown (02472) *(G-12872)*

Enbw North America Inc.......................... 857 753-4623
  311 Summer St Ste 200 Boston (02210) *(G-6714)*

Enco, Plaistow *Also Called: Environmental Container Svcs (G-15342)*

Encon Evaporators, Hooksett *Also Called: PSI Water Systems LLC (G-14470)*

Encore Fire Protection............................ 617 903-3191
  67 4th Ave Needham (02494) *(G-10509)*

Encore Optics.................................... 860 282-0082
  140 Commerce Way South Windsor (06074) *(G-3143)*

Encyte Systems Inc............................... 781 848-6772
  55 Messina Dr Braintree (02184) *(G-7180)*

Endeavor Robotic Holdings Inc **(DH)**........... **978 769-9333**
  19 Alpha Rd Ste 101 Chelmsford (01824) *(G-7927)*

Endeavor Seafood, Newport *Also Called: Endeavor Seafood LLC (G-16209)*

Endeavor Seafood LLC............................ 401 841-8637
  110 William St Newport (02840) *(G-16209)*

Endiprev Usa LLC................................ 401 519-3600
  10 Dorrance St Ste 700 Providence (02903) *(G-16514)*

(G-0000) Company's Geographic Section entry number

Endodynamix Inc... 978 740-0400
   121 Loring Ave Ste 910 Salem (01970) *(G-11713)*

Endowmentsolutions, Auburn *Also Called: Endowmentsolutions LLC (G-6112)*

Endowmentsolutions LLC.. 617 308-7231
   8 Booth Rd Auburn (01501) *(G-6112)*

Endurance, Burlington *Also Called: Newfold Dgtal Hldngs Group Inc (G-7399)*

Endurance Intl Group-West Inc....................................... 781 852-3200
   10 Corporate Dr Ste 300 Burlington (01803) *(G-7369)*

Endure Dgtal Intrmdate Hldngs....................................... 781 852-3200
   10 Corp Dr Ste 300 Burlington (01803) *(G-7370)*

Ene Systems Inc **(PA)**... **781 828-6770**
   480 Neponset St Ste 11d Canton (02021) *(G-7789)*

Ene Systems of Nh Inc... 603 856-0330
   155 River Rd Unit 10 Bow (03304) *(G-13996)*

Enefco International Inc **(PA)**...................................... **207 514-7218**
   1130 Minot Ave Auburn (04210) *(G-4428)*

Eneon US LLC **(HQ)**.. **312 724-6886**
   2150 Post Rd Fairfield (06824) *(G-1184)*

Ener-Tek International Inc.. 401 471-6580
   2000 S County Trl East Greenwich (02818) *(G-15985)*

Enercon.. 207 657-7001
   234 First Flight Dr Auburn (04210) *(G-4429)*

Enercon **(HQ)**.. **207 657-7000**
   25 Northbrook Dr Gray (04039) *(G-4841)*

Enercon Technologies, Gray *Also Called: Enercon (G-4841)*

Energizer, Shelton *Also Called: Edgewell Per Care Brands LLC (G-3002)*

Energizer Auto Sales Inc.. 203 205-2900
   44 Old Ridgebury Rd Ste 300 Danbury (06810) *(G-736)*

Energizer Holdings.. 314 985-2000
   6 Research Dr Ste 400 Shelton (06484) *(G-3004)*

Energy Beam Sciences, Niantic *Also Called: Ebs Acquisition Inc (G-2356)*

Energy Beam Sciences Inc... 860 653-0411
   2 Oak St Niantic (06357) *(G-2357)*

Energy MGT & Ctrl Svcs Inc.. 401 946-1440
   116 Budlong Rd Cranston (02920) *(G-15856)*

Energy Release, Leominster *Also Called: Uspack Inc (G-9714)*

Energy Release LLC.. 978 466-9700
   14 Brent Dr Hudson (01749) *(G-9363)*

Energy Resources Group Inc **(PA)**............................ **603 335-2535**
   23 Commerce Pkwy Farmington (03835) *(G-14309)*

Energy Saving Pdts & Sls Corp...................................... 860 675-6443
   713 George Washington Tpke Burlington (06013) *(G-549)*

Energy Sciences Inc.. 978 694-9000
   42 Industrial Way Ste 1 Wilmington (01887) *(G-13405)*

Enertgetic Baltic MI... 603 252-0804
   80 Baltic St Enfield (03748) *(G-14274)*

Enertrac Inc... 603 821-0003
   100 Market St Unit 302 Portsmouth (03801) *(G-15382)*

Enfield Collision, Enfield *Also Called: Adamczyk Enterprises Inc (G-1120)*

Enfield Stationers, Enfield *Also Called: Olympia Sales Inc (G-1140)*

Enfield Technologies LLC... 203 375-3100
   35 Nutmeg Dr Ste 130 Trumbull (06611) *(G-3719)*

Enfield Transit Mix Inc.. 860 763-0864
   84 Broadbrook Rd Enfield (06082) *(G-1129)*

Enflo Corporation **(PA)**... **860 589-0014**
   315 Lake Ave Bristol (06010) *(G-441)*

Engage2excel, Attleboro *Also Called: Robbins Company (G-6058)*

Engagesmart, Braintree *Also Called: Engagesmart Inc (G-7181)*

Engagesmart Inc **(PA)**.. **781 848-3733**
   30 Braintree Hill Park Ste 101 Braintree (02184) *(G-7181)*

Engelhard Surface Tech.. 978 658-0032
   201 Ballardvale St Wilmington (01887) *(G-13406)*

Engement Company Inc.. 603 537-2088
   58 Main St Ste 2 Topsfield (01983) *(G-12432)*

Engene Usa Inc... 857 246-8765
   201 Jones Rd Waltham (02451) *(G-12662)*

Engine Alliance, Glastonbury *Also Called: Engine Alliance LLC (G-1277)*

Engine Alliance LLC... 860 565-2239
   124 Hebron Ave Ste 200 Glastonbury (06033) *(G-1277)*

Engineered Building Pdts Inc... 860 243-1110
   18 Southwood Dr Bloomfield (06002) *(G-161)*

Engineered Coatings Inc... 860 567-5556
   272 Norfolk Rd Litchfield (06759) *(G-1557)*

Engineered Electric Company... 203 366-5211
   141 North Ave Bridgeport (06606) *(G-320)*

Engineered Fibers Tech LLC... 203 922-1810
   88 Long Hill Cross Rd Ste 4 Shelton (06484) *(G-3005)*

Engineered Inserts Systems Inc **(PA)**....................... **203 301-3334**
   26 Quirk Rd Milford (06460) *(G-1824)*

Engineered Materials Solutions, Attleboro *Also Called: Ems Engnred Mtls Solutions LLC (G-6012)*

Engineered Polymers Inds Inc.. 203 272-2233
   726 S Main St Cheshire (06410) *(G-590)*

Engineered Syntactic Systems, Attleboro *Also Called: Cmt Materials Inc (G-6005)*

Engineering, Andover *Also Called: Schneider Automation Inc (G-5915)*

Engineering Services & Pdts Co **(PA)**........................ **860 528-1119**
   1395 John Fitch Blvd South Windsor (06074) *(G-3144)*

Engineering Specialties Inc.. 203 488-2266
   452 Twin Lakes Rd North Branford (06471) *(G-2367)*

Engineing Wldg & Fabg Co Inc....................................... 401 884-1484
   120 Old Baptist Rd North Kingstown (02852) *(G-16252)*

Enginered Pressure Systems Inc.................................... 978 469-8280
   165 Ferry Rd Haverhill (01835) *(G-9094)*

Enginred Syntactic Systems LLC.................................... 508 226-3907
   107 Frank Mossberg Dr Attleboro (02703) *(G-6013)*

Enginuity Plm LLC **(DH)**.. **203 218-7225**
   440 Wheelers Farms Rd Milford (06461) *(G-1825)*

Enjet Aero Bloomfield LLC.. 860 242-2211
   3 Old Windsor Rd Bloomfield (06002) *(G-162)*

Enjet Aero Malden LLC.. 781 321-0366
   60 Winter St Malden (02148) *(G-10013)*

Enjet Aero Manchester LLC... 913 717-7396
   41 Progress Dr Manchester (06042) *(G-1597)*

Enjet Aero New Britain LLC... 860 356-0330
   150 John Downey Dr New Britain (06051) *(G-2026)*

Enjet Aero Newington Inc.. 860 953-0686
   111 Holmes Rd Newington (06111) *(G-2291)*

Enon Copy Inc **(PA)**.. **978 927-8757**
   409 Cabot St Ste 4 Beverly (01915) *(G-6346)*

Enos Engineering LLC... 978 654-6522
   914 Main St Acton (01720) *(G-5745)*

Enow Inc.. 401 732-7080
   3970 Post Rd Warwick (02886) *(G-16814)*

Ensem Therapeutics Inc.. 662 422-2488
   880 Winter St Ste 1003 Waltham (02451) *(G-12663)*

Ensign Bickford Industries.. 203 843-2126
   100 Grist Mill Ln Simsbury (06070) *(G-3087)*

Ensign-Bckford Rnwble Enrgies...................................... 860 843-2000
   125 Powder Forest Dr Simsbury (06070) *(G-3088)*

Ensign-Bickford Arospc Def Co **(HQ)**........................ **860 843-2289**
   640 Hopmeadow St Simsbury (06070) *(G-3089)*

Ensign-Bickford Company **(HQ)**................................. **860 843-2001**
   125 Powder Forest Dr Simsbury (06070) *(G-3090)*

Ensinger Prcsion Cmponents Inc **(DH)**...................... **860 928-7911**
   11 Danco Rd Putnam (06260) *(G-2854)*

Entasis Thrputics Holdings Inc **(HQ)**.......................... **781 810-0120**
   35 Gatehouse Dr Waltham (02451) *(G-12664)*

Entec Polymers.. 508 865-2001
   166 Stone School Rd Sutton (01590) *(G-12280)*

Entegris, Danbury *Also Called: Entegris Inc (G-737)*

ENTEGRIS, Billerica *Also Called: Entegris Inc (G-6443)*

Entegris Inc... 800 766-2681
   7 Commerce Dr Danbury (06810) *(G-737)*

Entegris Inc.. 978 436-6500
   129 Concord Rd Bldg 2 Billerica (01821) *(G-6442)*

Entegris Inc **(PA)**... **978 436-6500**
   129 Concord Rd Billerica (01821) *(G-6443)*

Entegris Prof Solutions Inc **(HQ)**............................... **203 794-1100**
   7 Commerce Dr Danbury (06810) *(G-738)*

Entelligence Computer Svcs LLC.................................... 603 893-4800
   287 Lawrence Rd Unit 1 Salem (03079) *(G-15520)*

Enterasys Networks Inc **(HQ)**................................... **603 952-5000**
   9 Northeastern Blvd Ste 300 Salem (03079) *(G-15521)*

Enterprise Casting Corporation.................................. 207 782-5511
  40 South Ave Lewiston (04240) *(G-4961)*

Enterprise Gvrnnce Systems Cor **(PA)**.................. **888 655-4125**
  399 Boylston St Boston (02116) *(G-6715)*

Enterprise Gvrnnce Systems Cor.......................... 888 655-4125
  33 Arch St Ste 1600 Boston (02110) *(G-6716)*

Enterprise Newsmedia LLC.................................. 781 769-5535
  1091 Washington St Norwood (02062) *(G-11172)*

Enterprise Power Conversion, Middleboro *Also Called: EPC Corporation (G-10358)*

Enterprise Publications **(PA)**.............................. 508 548-4700
  50 Depot Ave Falmouth (02540) *(G-8630)*

ENTERTAINMENT EDUCATION INSTIT, South Burlington *Also Called: Population Media Center Inc (G-17595)*

Entrada Therapeutics Inc **(PA)**............................ **857 520-9158**
  6 Tide St Ste 1 Boston (02210) *(G-6717)*

Entwistle Company LLC **(PA)**.............................. **508 481-4000**
  6 Bigelow St Hudson (01749) *(G-9364)*

Entwistle Trust.. 508 481-4000
  6 Bigelow St Hudson (01749) *(G-9365)*

Envases Usa Inc **(HQ)**...................................... **603 889-8311**
  12 Howe Dr Amherst (03031) *(G-13868)*

Envelopes & More Inc.. 860 286-7570
  124 Francis Ave Newington (06111) *(G-2292)*

Envirnmntal Office Sltions Inc **(PA)**.................... **860 291-1900**
  130 Prestige Park Rd East Hartford (06108) *(G-993)*

Enviro-Fuels LLC.. 860 242-2325
  700 Hale St Suffield (06078) *(G-3590)*

Enviro-Tote Inc.. 603 647-7171
  15 Industrial Dr Londonderry (03053) *(G-14749)*

Envirologix Inc **(PA)**.. **207 797-0300**
  500 Riverside Industrial Pkwy Portland (04103) *(G-5215)*

Enviromart Green Inds Inc.................................. 603 382-8481
  4 Wilder Dr Ste 7 Plaistow (03865) *(G-15340)*

Enviromart Industries Inc.................................... 603 378-0154
  4 Wilder Dr Plaistow (03865) *(G-15341)*

Environics Inc.. 860 872-1111
  69 Industrial Park Rd E Tolland (06084) *(G-3660)*

Environmantal Systems Cor.................................. 860 953-5167
  18 Jansen Ct Hartford (06110) *(G-1479)*

Environmental Building News, Brattleboro *Also Called: Buildinggreen Inc (G-17076)*

Environmental Container Svcs.............................. 603 382-8481
  4 Wilder Dr Ste 7 Plaistow (03865) *(G-15342)*

Environmental Ctrl Systems Inc............................ 401 437-8612
  41 Commercial Way East Providence (02914) *(G-16016)*

Environmental Division, Beverly *Also Called: TK&k Services LLC (G-6389)*

Environmental Interiors Inc.................................. 603 889-9290
  400 Amherst St Ste 201 Nashua (03063) *(G-15095)*

Environmental Monitor Svc Inc............................ 203 935-0102
  87 Gypsy Ln Meriden (06450) *(G-1667)*

Environmental Systems Corp................................ 860 953-8800
  18 Jansen Ct West Hartford (06110) *(G-4060)*

Environmental Systems Products Inc...................... 860 653-0081
  7 Kripes Rd East Granby (06026) *(G-933)*

Environmental Test Pdts Inc **(PA)**...................... **603 924-5010**
  29 Shipley Dr Hollis (03049) *(G-14451)*

Envision, Cumberland *Also Called: Plastics Plus Inc (G-15960)*

Eo Vista LLC.. 978 635-8080
  42 Nagog Park Ste 200 Acton (01720) *(G-5746)*

Eon Designs, Norwich *Also Called: One & Co Inc (G-2614)*

Eos Imaging Inc.. 678 564-5400
  185 Alewife Brook Pkwy Ste 210 Cambridge (02138) *(G-7562)*

Eows Midland Inc.. 203 358-5705
  1 Landmark Sq Fl 11 Stamford (06901) *(G-3343)*

EPC Corporation.. 508 923-9503
  25 Wareham St Middleboro (02346) *(G-10358)*

EPC Space LLC.. 978 208-1334
  200 Bulfinch Dr Andover (01810) *(G-5881)*

Epec LLC **(PA)**.. **508 995-5171**
  176 Samuel Barnet Blvd New Bedford (02745) *(G-10589)*

Ephemeral Solutions Inc.................................... 203 312-7337
  4 Oxford Rd Ste B1 Milford (06460) *(G-1826)*

Ephemeral Tattoo, Milford *Also Called: Ephemeral Solutions Inc (G-1826)*

Epi II Inc.. 978 462-1514
  30 Green St Newburyport (01950) *(G-10682)*

Epic Enterprises Inc.. 978 772-2340
  11 Copeland Dr Ayer (01432) *(G-6182)*

Epicenter.. 413 568-1360
  1 Arch Rd Westfield (01085) *(G-13164)*

Epicerie Azur, Shelburne *Also Called: Vermont Tortilla Company LLC (G-17564)*

Epicurean Feast Medtron O.................................. 203 492-5000
  195 Mcdermott Rd North Haven (06473) *(G-2410)*

Epirus Biopharmaceuticals Inc............................ 617 600-3497
  124 Washington St Ste 101 Foxboro (02035) *(G-8696)*

Epivax Inc.. 401 272-2123
  188 Valley St Ste 424 Providence (02909) *(G-16515)*

Epizyme, Cambridge *Also Called: Epizyme Inc (G-7563)*

Epizyme Inc.. 617 229-5872
  400 Technology Sq Ste 4 Cambridge (02139) *(G-7563)*

Epo-Tek, Billerica *Also Called: Epoxy Technology Inc (G-6444)*

Epoch Industries, West Bridgewater *Also Called: Thomas M Leonard Inc (G-12984)*

Epoxies Inc.. 401 946-5564
  21 Starline Way Cranston (02921) *(G-15857)*

Epoxies, Etc, Cranston *Also Called: Epoxies Inc (G-15857)*

Epoxies, Etc, Cranston *Also Called: Fri Resins Holding Company (G-15863)*

Epoxy Technology Inc **(PA)**.............................. **978 667-3805**
  14 Fortune Dr Billerica (01821) *(G-6444)*

Epoxyset, Woonsocket *Also Called: Epoxytech Inc (G-16958)*

Epoxytech Inc.. 401 726-4500
  718 Park East Dr Woonsocket (02895) *(G-16958)*

Eppendorf Inc **(DH)**.. **860 253-3400**
  175 Freshwater Blvd Enfield (06082) *(G-1130)*

Eppendorf Holding Inc **(DH)**............................ **860 253-3417**
  175 Freshwater Blvd Enfield (06082) *(G-1131)*

Eppendorf Manufacturing Corp............................ 860 253-3400
  175 Freshwater Blvd Enfield (06082) *(G-1132)*

Epping Vfd, Columbia Falls *Also Called: Epping Volunteer Fire District (G-4699)*

Epping Volunteer Fire District.............................. 207 483-2036
  392 Us Rte-1 Columbia Falls (04623) *(G-4699)*

Eptam Plastics Ltd **(PA)**.................................. **603 286-8009**
  2 Riverside Business Park Northfield (03276) *(G-15264)*

Eptam Precision Solutions, Northfield *Also Called: Eptam Plastics Ltd (G-15264)*

Eqrx, Cambridge *Also Called: Eqrx Inc (G-7564)*

Eqrx Inc **(HQ)**.. **617 315-2255**
  50 Hampshire St Ste 700 Cambridge (02139) *(G-7564)*

Equinor Pipelines LLC.. 203 978-6900
  600 Washington Blvd 8th Fl Stamford (06901) *(G-3344)*

Equinor US Holdings Inc **(DH)**.......................... **203 978-6900**
  600 Washington Blvd 8th Fl Stamford (06901) *(G-3345)*

Equinox Resort Associates, Manchester *Also Called: Diageo North America Inc (G-17323)*

Equipe Communications Corp.............................. 978 635-1999
  100 Nagog Park # 2 Acton (01720) *(G-5747)*

Equipment Depot, Bangor *Also Called: Vld Inc (G-4519)*

Equipment Technologies Inc................................ 603 548-0875
  15 Cardiff Rd Windham (03087) *(G-15725)*

ER Lewin Inc.. 508 384-0363
  25 Cushing Dr Wrentham (02093) *(G-13841)*

ERA Replica Automobiles, New Britain *Also Called: International Auto Entps Inc (G-2034)*

ERA Wire Inc.. 203 933-0480
  19 Locust St West Haven (06516) *(G-4106)*

Eratech Inc.. 413 628-3219
  225 Smith Rd Ashfield (01330) *(G-5954)*

Erbi Biosystems Inc.. 617 297-7422
  85 Maple St Stoneham (02180) *(G-12177)*

ERC Acquisition Inc.. 781 593-4000
  19 Bennett St Lynn (01905) *(G-9971)*

ERC Wiping Products, Lynn *Also Called: ERC Acquisition Inc (G-9971)*

Ercon Inc.. 508 291-1400
  7 Kendrick Rd Ste 3 Wareham (02571) *(G-12835)*

Erd Metal Inc.. 508 232-3684
  323 Lockhouse Rd Ste 1 Westfield (01085) *(G-13165)*

Erecruit, Boston *Also Called: Erecruit Holdings LLC (G-6718)*

Erecruit Holdings LLC.. 617 535-3720
   100 Summer St Ste 1700 Boston (02110) *(G-6718)*

Erg, Farmington *Also Called: Energy Resources Group Inc (G-14309)*

Ergonomic Products Inc.. 508 636-2263
   198 Airport Rd Fall River (02720) *(G-8542)*

Eric Goetz Custom Sailboats.. 401 253-2670
   15 Broadcommon Rd Bristol (02809) *(G-15763)*

Eric T Vannah... 207 631-2475
   8 Oakwood Ter Brunswick (04011) *(G-4645)*

Erica Wilson Inc **(PA)**.. **212 348-6196**
   16 N Liberty St Nantucket (02554) *(G-10463)*

Erica Wilson Needle Works, Nantucket *Also Called: Erica Wilson Inc (G-10463)*

Erickson Metals Corporation **(PA)**.................................. **203 272-2918**
   25 Knotter Dr Cheshire (06410) *(G-591)*

Ericsson... 203 776-0631
   310 Orange St New Haven (06510) *(G-2150)*

Erika of Texas Inc... 956 783-4689
   920 Winter St Waltham (02451) *(G-12665)*

Erin Flett.. 207 887-9253
   2 Main St Gorham (04038) *(G-4819)*

Erin Murphy... 928 525-2056
   824 Roosevelt Trl Windham (04062) *(G-5660)*

Erm LLC... 401 934-2544
   16 Sunnyside Ave Johnston (02919) *(G-16084)*

Ernest Johnson... 508 259-6727
   146 Phelps St Marlborough (01752) *(G-10148)*

Ernest Johnson Co, Marlborough *Also Called: Ernest Johnson (G-10148)*

Ernest R Palmer Lumber Co Inc.. 207 876-2725
   30 N Dexter Rd Sangerville (04479) *(G-5419)*

Ersa Inc... 401 348-4000
   83 Tom Harvey Rd Westerly (02891) *(G-16930)*

Erving Industries Inc **(PA)**.. **413 422-2700**
   97 E Main St Erving (01344) *(G-8469)*

Erving Paper Mills, Erving *Also Called: Erving Industries Inc (G-8469)*

Erving Paper Mills Inc... 413 422-2700
   97 E Main St Erving (01344) *(G-8470)*

Erytech, Cambridge *Also Called: Erytech Pharma Inc (G-7565)*

Erytech Pharma Inc.. 360 320-3325
   1 Main St Ste 300 Cambridge (02142) *(G-7565)*

Es Countertops LLC.. 413 732-8128
   3 Century Way West Springfield (01089) *(G-13024)*

ES Metal Fabrications Inc... 860 585-6067
   11 Allread Dr Terryville (06786) *(G-3602)*

Es Sports Corporation... 413 534-5634
   47 Jackson St Holyoke (01040) *(G-9253)*

Escalon Digital Solutions Inc.. 610 688-6830
   91 Montvale Ave Ste 320 Stoneham (02180) *(G-12178)*

Eschenbach Optik, Danbury *Also Called: Eschenbach Optik America Inc (G-739)*

Eschenbach Optik America Inc **(PA)**.............................. **203 702-1600**
   22 Shelter Rock Ln Ste 1 Danbury (06810) *(G-739)*

Esco Technologies Inc... 508 429-4441
   75 October Hill Rd Holliston (01746) *(G-9209)*

Esco Tool, Holliston *Also Called: Esco Technologies Inc (G-9209)*

Esi, North Branford *Also Called: Engineering Specialties Inc (G-2367)*

Esi, Wilmington *Also Called: Energy Sciences Inc (G-13405)*

ESI Electronic Products Corp.. 203 758-4401
   109 Waterbury Rd Prospect (06712) *(G-2834)*

Esico Triton LLC... 860 526-9535
   10 Denlar Dr Chester (06412) *(G-629)*

Eskill Corporation.. 978 649-8010
   177 Huntington Ave Ste 1703 Boston (02115) *(G-6719)*

Esm Software LLC.. 781 541-4462
   55 Old Bedford Rd Ste 107 Lincoln (01773) *(G-9795)*

Esm Software Group Inc.. 781 541-4465
   55 Old Bedford Rd Ste 107 Lincoln (01773) *(G-9796)*

Esmond Manufacturing Co Inc.. 401 942-9103
   169 N View Ave Cranston (02920) *(G-15858)*

Esoterix Genetic Labs LLC **(HQ)**.................................. **508 389-6650**
   3400 Computer Dr Westborough (01581) *(G-13101)*

ESP Solutions Inc... 508 285-0017
   580 Myles Standish Blvd Ste 1 Taunton (02780) *(G-12335)*

ESP Solutions Services LLC.. 508 285-0017
   580 Myles Standish Blvd Ste 2 Taunton (02780) *(G-12336)*

Esposito Jewelry Inc... 401 943-1900
   225 Dupont Dr Providence (02907) *(G-16516)*

Essel Dental... 860 254-6955
   44 S Main St Ste 14 East Windsor (06088) *(G-1073)*

Essemtec Usa LLC.. 856 218-1131
   300 5th Ave Ste 10 Waltham (02451) *(G-12666)*

Essential Trading Systems Corp... 860 295-8100
   188 Norwich Ave Ste 5 Colchester (06415) *(G-657)*

Essentra Porous Technologies, Chicopee *Also Called: Porex Cleanroom Products Inc (G-8056)*

Essex Bay Engineering Inc.. 978 412-9600
   19 Mitchell Rd Ipswich (01938) *(G-9486)*

Essex Concrete Products Inc... 860 767-1768
   141 Westbrook Rd Essex (06426) *(G-1163)*

Essex County Brewing Co LLC... 978 587-2254
   154 Ipswich Rd Boxford (01921) *(G-7160)*

Essex County Coop Farming Assn....................................... 978 887-2300
   146 S Main St Topsfield (01983) *(G-12433)*

Essex Engineering Inc... 781 595-2114
   20 Day St Lynn (01905) *(G-9972)*

Essex Engineering & Mfg Co, Lynn *Also Called: Essex Engineering Inc (G-9972)*

Essex LLC... 602 374-1890
   120 N Main St Branford (06405) *(G-253)*

Essex Printing, Methuen *Also Called: Essex Ruling & Printing Co (G-10331)*

Essex Ruling & Printing Co... 978 682-2457
   154 Haverhill St Ste 2 Methuen (01844) *(G-10331)*

Essex Silverline Corporation **(PA)**................................ **978 957-2116**
   1118 Lakeview Ave Dracut (01826) *(G-8305)*

Essex Wood Products Inc.. 860 537-3451
   75 Mill St Colchester (06415) *(G-658)*

Essity North America Inc.. 413 289-1221
   1st St Palmer (01069) *(G-11274)*

Esteem Manufacturing Corp... 860 282-9964
   175 S Satellite Rd South Windsor (06074) *(G-3145)*

Eta Devices Inc.. 617 577-8300
   245 1st St Cambridge (02142) *(G-7566)*

Etc, Colchester *Also Called: Essential Trading Systems Corp (G-657)*

Etchomatic Inc... 978 656-0011
   179 Old Canal Dr Lowell (01851) *(G-9877)*

Etco, Warwick *Also Called: Etco Incorporated (G-16815)*

Etco Incorporated **(PA)**.. **401 467-2400**
   25 Bellows St Warwick (02888) *(G-16815)*

Etec Inc... 617 477-4308
   25 Worley St West Roxbury (02132) *(G-13010)*

Etex, Braintree *Also Called: Etex Corporation (G-7182)*

Etex Corporation... 617 577-7270
   55 Messina Dr Ste 1 Braintree (02184) *(G-7182)*

Ethan Allen, Danbury *Also Called: Ethan Allen Interiors Inc (G-740)*

Ethan Allen Home Interiors, Danbury *Also Called: Ethan Allen Retail Inc (G-741)*

Ethan Allen Interiors Inc **(PA)**..................................... **203 743-8000**
   25 Lake Avenue Ext Danbury (06811) *(G-740)*

Ethan Allen Retail Inc **(HQ)**... **203 743-8000**
   25 Lake Avenue Ext Danbury (06811) *(G-741)*

Etherington Brothers Inc.. 860 585-5624
   33 Stafford Ave Ste 2 Bristol (06010) *(G-442)*

Ethicon Endo - Surgery, Southington *Also Called: Ethicon Inc (G-3208)*

Ethicon Inc... 860 621-9111
   201 W Queen St Southington (06489) *(G-3208)*

Ethosenergy Tc Inc **(DH)**... **802 257-2721**
   1310 Sheridan St Chicopee (01022) *(G-8031)*

Eti, Windham *Also Called: Equipment Technologies Inc (G-15725)*

ETM Manufacturing, Littleton *Also Called: Sajawi Corporation (G-9837)*

Etter Engineering Company Incorporated............................. 860 584-8842
   210 Century Dr Bristol (06010) *(G-443)*

Eugene Corson.. 207 446-6489
   38 Cottage Rd Sumner (04292) *(G-5538)*

Eureka Blank Book Co, Holyoke *Also Called: Eureka Lab Book Inc (G-9254)*

Eureka Lab Book Inc... 413 534-5671
   110 Winter St Holyoke (01040) *(G-9254)*

ALPHABETIC

Euro -Coiffeur, Stamford *Also Called: Conair LLC (G-3321)*

Euro International Ltd.. 617 670-2265
  150 Staniford St Apt 632 Boston (02114) *(G-6720)*

Euro Tech Metal Creations Inc....................................... 914 325-1760
  2 Broad St Danbury (06810) *(G-742)*

Euro-Pro Holdco LLC.. 617 243-0235
  89 A St # 100 Needham Heights (02494) *(G-10543)*

European Cubicles LLC.. 617 681-6700
  38 3rd Ave Ste 100w Boston (02129) *(G-6721)*

European Woodcraft, Norwalk *Also Called: European Woodcraft LLC (G-2498)*

European Woodcraft LLC.. 203 847-6195
  9 Crockett St Ste 1 Norwalk (06851) *(G-2498)*

Eurovia Atlantic Coast LLC.. 703 230-0850
  1067 Odlin Rd Hermon (04401) *(G-4881)*

Euthymics Bioscience Inc... 617 758-0300
  43 Thorndike St Ste 21 Cambridge (02141) *(G-7567)*

Ev Launchpad, Kittery *Also Called: Launchpad Electric Solutions (G-4936)*

Evan Webster Ink LLC... 802 222-0344
  442 Lewis Creek Rd Charlotte (05445) *(G-17177)*

Evans Capacitor Company LLC.. 401 435-3555
  72 Boyd Ave East Providence (02914) *(G-16017)*

Evans Company, East Providence *Also Called: Evans Findings Company Inc (G-16018)*

Evans Findings Company Inc.. 401 434-5600
  33 Eastern Ave East Providence (02914) *(G-16018)*

Evans Industries LLC.. 978 887-8561
  249 Boston St Topsfield (01983) *(G-12434)*

Evans Machine, Brockton *Also Called: Evans Machine Co Inc (G-7277)*

Evans Machine Co Inc... 508 584-8085
  32 N Manchester St Brockton (02302) *(G-7277)*

Evans Printing Co.. 603 856-8238
  155 River Rd Unit 15 Bow (03304) *(G-13997)*

Ever Better Eating Inc.. 603 435-5119
  5 Main St Pittsfield (03263) *(G-15331)*

Evercel Inc... 781 741-8800
  1055 Washington Blvd Fl 8 Stamford (06901) *(G-3346)*

Everest Halthcare Holdings Inc (DH)............................... 781 699-9000
  920 Winter St Waltham (02451) *(G-12667)*

Everest Isles LLC... 203 561-5128
  616 N Elm St Wallingford (06492) *(G-3804)*

Everett Aluminum Inc... 617 389-3839
  10 Everett Ave Everett (02149) *(G-8488)*

Everett Charles Tech LLC... 603 882-2621
  41 Simon St Ste 1b Nashua (03060) *(G-15096)*

Everett J Prescott Inc... 401 333-8588
  38 Albion Rd Lincoln (02865) *(G-16135)*

Everett McCabe.. 207 890-9174
  21 Smith Ave Bridgton (04009) *(G-4628)*

Everett Print, Bridgeport *Also Called: Integrated Print Solutions Inc (G-332)*

Evergage Inc... 888 310-0589
  212 Elm St Ste 4 Somerville (02144) *(G-11870)*

Evergreen Custom Printing Inc....................................... 207 782-2327
  63 Broad St Auburn (04210) *(G-4430)*

Evergreen Embroidery... 603 726-4271
  239 Riverside Dr Campton (03223) *(G-14043)*

Evergreen Home & Hearth, Brewer *Also Called: M & S Enterprises Inc (G-4617)*

Evergreen Manufacturing Group LLC................................. 207 728-4900
  791 Main St Madawaska (04756) *(G-5037)*

Evergreen Printing.. 203 323-4717
  61 Seaview Ave Stamford (06902) *(G-3347)*

Everhot, Watertown *Also Called: Therma-Flow Inc (G-12913)*

Eversolve LLC... 603 870-9739
  8 Woodvue Rd Windham (03087) *(G-15726)*

Everson Distributing Co Inc.. 413 533-9261
  108 Grove St Ste 200 Worcester (01605) *(G-13721)*

Everwideningcirclescom LLC.. 802 524-3757
  1364 Castle Rd Fairfield (05455) *(G-17266)*

Evident Scientific Inc (PA)... 781 419-3900
  48 Woerd Ave Ste 105 Waltham (02453) *(G-12668)*

Evogence, Rocky Hill *Also Called: Frontier Vision Tech Inc (G-2922)*

Evolv Tech Holdings Inc (PA).. 781 374-8100
  500 Totten Pond Rd Fl 4 Waltham (02451) *(G-12669)*

Evolv Technologies, Waltham *Also Called: Evolv Tech Holdings Inc (G-12669)*

Evolv Technologies Inc (HQ)... 781 374-8100
  500 Totten Pond Rd 4th Fl Waltham (02451) *(G-12670)*

Evolv Technology, Waltham *Also Called: Evolv Technologies Inc (G-12670)*

Evolveimmune Therapeutics Inc...................................... 203 858-7389
  23 Business Park Dr Branford (06405) *(G-254)*

Evonic Cyro, Wallingford *Also Called: Allnex USA Inc (G-3769)*

Evopoint Biosciences Usa Inc.. 646 750-2661
  300 Baker Ave Ste 300 Concord (01742) *(G-8117)*

Evoqua Water Technologies, Warwick *Also Called: Benson Neptune Inc (G-16790)*

Evoqua Water Technologies LLC...................................... 860 528-6512
  88 Nutmeg Rd S South Windsor (06074) *(G-3146)*

Evoqua Water Technologies LLC...................................... 978 863-4600
  558 Clark Rd Tewksbury (01876) *(G-12397)*

Evoqua Water Technologies LLC...................................... 908 851-4250
  558 Clark Rd Tewksbury (01876) *(G-12398)*

Evoqua Water Technologies LLC...................................... 978 934-9349
  558 Clark Rd Tewksbury (01876) *(G-12399)*

Evotext Inc.. 781 272-1830
  357 Boston Rd Billerica (01821) *(G-6445)*

Evs New Hampshire Inc... 603 352-3000
  50 Optical Ave Keene (03431) *(G-14598)*

Ewald Instruments Corp.. 860 491-9042
  331 Wells Hill Rd Lakeville (06039) *(G-1545)*

Ewp, Colchester *Also Called: Essex Wood Products Inc (G-658)*

Exa Corporation (DH).. 781 564-0200
  55 Network Dr Burlington (01803) *(G-7371)*

Exacom Inc.. 603 228-0706
  99 Airport Rd Concord (03301) *(G-14129)*

Exact Dispensing Systems, Newcastle *Also Called: Sheepscot Machine Works LLC (G-5096)*

Exail Defense Systems Inc.. 401 475-4400
  27 Wellington Rd Lincoln (02865) *(G-16136)*

Exari Group Inc... 617 938-3777
  745 Boylston St Boston (02116) *(G-6722)*

Exari Systems Inc... 617 938-3777
  745 Boylston St Ste 201 Boston (02116) *(G-6723)*

Exatel Visual Systems Inc.. 781 221-7400
  111 S Bedford St Ste 201 Burlington (01803) *(G-7372)*

Excalibur Shelving Systems Inc....................................... 603 746-6200
  292 Burnham Intervale Rd Contoocook (03229) *(G-14169)*

Excel Dryer, East Longmeadow *Also Called: Excel Dryer Inc (G-8375)*

Excel Dryer Inc... 413 525-4531
  357 Chestnut St East Longmeadow (01028) *(G-8375)*

Excel Homes of Maine LLC.. 207 539-8883
  56 Mechanic Falls Rd Oxford (04270) *(G-5143)*

Excel Spring & Stamping LLC... 860 585-1495
  61 E Main St Ste 2 Bristol (06010) *(G-444)*

Excel Technology Inc (HQ)... 781 266-5700
  125 Middlesex Tpke Bedford (01730) *(G-6226)*

Excel Tool & Die Co Inc.. 617 472-0473
  69 Sumner St Quincy (02169) *(G-11516)*

Excelera, Stoughton *Also Called: Excelerarx Corp (G-12203)*

Excelerarx Corp... 612 293-0378
  100 Technology Center Dr Ste 600 Stoughton (02072) *(G-12203)*

Excelergy Corp (PA)... 781 274-0420
  10 Maguire Rd Ste 111 Lexington (02421) *(G-9742)*

Excelitas Tech Holdg Corp... 781 522-5914
  200 West St Ste E403 Waltham (02451) *(G-12671)*

Excelitas Tech Holdings LLC (PA).................................. 781 522-5900
  200 West St Ste E403 Waltham (02451) *(G-12672)*

Excelitas Technologies Corp.. 978 262-0049
  1 Fortune Dr Billerica (01821) *(G-6446)*

Excelitas Technologies Corp.. 800 775-6786
  35 Congress St Ste 2021 Salem (01970) *(G-11714)*

Excelitas Technologies Corp (DH).................................. 855 382-2677
  200 W St 4th Fl E Waltham (02451) *(G-12673)*

Excell Solutions Inc.. 978 663-6100
  41 Simon St Ste 1d Nashua (03060) *(G-15097)*

Excellent Coffee Co Inc (PA)....................................... 401 724-6393
  259 East Ave Pawtucket (02860) *(G-16367)*

Excello Tool Engrg & Mfg Co... 203 878-4073
  37 Warfield St Milford (06461) *(G-1827)*

Excelsior Inc.. 203 491-2028
  120 Braemar Dr Cheshire (06410) *(G-592)*

Excelsior Printing, North Adams *Also Called: Ghp Media Inc (G-10808)*

Excelsior Printing Company.................................. 413 663-3771
  60 Roberts Dr North Adams (01247) *(G-10807)*

Executive Greetings Inc **(HQ)**............................... **860 379-9911**
  120 Industrial Park Rd New Hartford (06057) *(G-2100)*

Executrain, Needham *Also Called: International Data Group Inc (G-10514)*

Exemplar Laboratories LLC.................................... 508 676-6726
  200 Riggenbach Rd Fall River (02720) *(G-8543)*

Exemplar Pharma LLC... 508 676-6726
  927 Currant Rd Fall River (02720) *(G-8544)*

Exemplar Pharmaceuticals, Fall River *Also Called: Exemplar Pharma LLC (G-8544)*

Exergen, Watertown *Also Called: Exergen Corporation (G-12873)*

Exergen Corporation.. 617 923-9900
  400 Pleasant St Watertown (02472) *(G-12873)*

Exeter Analytical Inc... 978 251-1411
  7 Doris Dr Ste 6a North Chelmsford (01863) *(G-10975)*

Exhibitcenter.com, Manchester *Also Called: Image 4 Concepts Inc (G-14862)*

Exinda Inc... 617 973-6477
  8 Faneuil Hall Market Pl 3rd Fl Boston (02109) *(G-6724)*

Exo Therapeutics Inc... 860 908-6508
  150 Cambridgepark Dr Cambridge (02140) *(G-7568)*

Exony Inc.. 617 854-7486
  60 State St Ste 700 Boston (02109) *(G-6725)*

Exothermics Inc.. 603 821-5660
  14 Columbia Dr Amherst (03031) *(G-13869)*

Expanded Rubber Products Inc **(PA)**....................... **207 324-8226**
  41 Industrial Ave Sanford (04073) *(G-5395)*

Expansion Opportunities Inc................................... 508 393-8200
  35 Lyman St Ste 1 Northborough (01532) *(G-11095)*

Expermental Prototype Pdts Inc.............................. 860 289-4948
  248 Chapel Rd South Windsor (06074) *(G-3147)*

Expert Embroidery LLC.. 203 269-9675
  121 N Plains Industrial Rd Ste G Wallingford (06492) *(G-3805)*

Expertek Systems Inc... 508 624-0006
  4 Mount Royal Ave Ste 140 Marlborough (01752) *(G-10149)*

Explain Everything Sales Inc.................................. 646 825-8552
  54 Danbury Rd Unit 425 Ridgefield (06877) *(G-2897)*

Express Assemblyproducts LLC................................ 603 424-5590
  1 Chestnut St Ste 215 Nashua (03060) *(G-15098)*

Express Lube & Tire LLC.. 860 690-3066
  35 Philip Henry Cir Windsor (06095) *(G-4274)*

Express Oil Co, East Greenwich *Also Called: East Greenwich Oil Co Inc (G-15982)*

Express Printing, Fall River *Also Called: Paiva Corp (G-8593)*

Expressive Design Group Inc.................................. 413 315-6296
  49 Garfield St Holyoke (01040) *(G-9255)*

Expresso To Go, Quechee *Also Called: Fat Hat Clothing Co (G-17462)*

Expressway Lube Centers....................................... 203 744-2511
  225 White St Danbury (06810) *(G-743)*

Extec Corp.. 860 741-3435
  99 Phoenix Ave Enfield (06082) *(G-1133)*

Extech Instruments Corporation.............................. 877 439-8324
  9 Townsend W Nashua (03063) *(G-15099)*

Extile.com, Stamford *Also Called: Pauls Marble Depot LLC (G-3427)*

Extra Extra Daily, Quincy *Also Called: Driggin Sandra DBA Extra Extra (G-11512)*

Extra Origin Foods, Belmont *Also Called: Longrun LLC (G-6307)*

Extreme Adhesives Inc... 603 895-4028
  63 Epping St Raymond (03077) *(G-15452)*

Extreme Dim Wildlife Calls LLC............................... 207 862-2825
  208 Kennebec Rd Hampden (04444) *(G-4863)*

Extreme Protocol Solutions Inc............................... 508 278-3600
  10 River Rd Ste 102e Uxbridge (01569) *(G-12478)*

Extrusion Alternatives Inc..................................... 603 430-9600
  19 Post Rd Portsmouth (03801) *(G-15383)*

Eye Exam 2000.. 603 836-5353
  39 S River Rd Ste 1 Bedford (03110) *(G-13927)*

Eye Health Services, Plymouth *Also Called: Eye Health Services Inc (G-11459)*

Eye Health Services Inc.. 508 747-6425
  146 Industrial Park Rd # 2 Plymouth (02360) *(G-11459)*

Eye Health Services Inc **(PA)**............................... **617 472-5242**
  1900 Crown Colony Dr Ste 301 Quincy (02169) *(G-11517)*

Eye Pint Phrmctcals Scrties Co................................ 617 926-5000
  400 Pleasant St Watertown (02472) *(G-12874)*

Eyelet Design Inc.. 203 754-4141
  2223 Thomaston Ave Waterbury (06704) *(G-3911)*

Eyelet Tech LLC.. 203 879-5306
  10 Venus Dr Wolcott (06716) *(G-4365)*

Eyelet Toolmakers Inc.. 860 274-5423
  40 Callender Rd Watertown (06795) *(G-4012)*

Eyepoint Pharmaceuticals Inc **(PA)**........................ **617 926-5000**
  480 Pleasant St Ste B300 Watertown (02472) *(G-12875)*

Eyesaver International Inc...................................... 781 829-0808
  348 Circuit St Ste 2 Hanover (02339) *(G-9031)*

Eylward Timber Co... 203 265-4276
  13 Quince St Wallingford (06492) *(G-3806)*

EZ Welding LLC... 860 707-3100
  244 Garry Dr New Britain (06052) *(G-2027)*

Eze C.S., Boston *Also Called: Eze Castle Software LLC (G-6727)*

Eze Castle Software Inc **(DH)**............................... **617 316-1100**
  50 Milk St Fl 7 Boston (02109) *(G-6726)*

Eze Castle Software LLC **(DH)**.............................. **617 316-1000**
  50 Milk St Fl 7 Boston (02109) *(G-6727)*

Ezflow Limited Partnership **(DH)**........................... **860 577-7064**
  4 Business Park Rd Old Saybrook (06475) *(G-2647)*

Eztousecom Directories... 207 974-3171
  592 Hammond St Bangor (04401) *(G-4500)*

F & D Plastics Inc **(PA)**..................................... **978 668-5140**
  23 Jytek Dr Leominster (01453) *(G-9662)*

F & M Tool & Plastics Inc...................................... 978 840-1897
  175 Pioneer Dr Leominster (01453) *(G-9663)*

F & W Rentals Inc... 203 795-0591
  164 Boston Post Rd Orange (06477) *(G-2668)*

F C Work and Sons, Jackson *Also Called: FC Work & Sons Incorporated (G-4912)*

F D Grave & Son Inc.. 203 239-9394
  85 State St Ste C North Haven (06473) *(G-2411)*

F D I, Farmington *Also Called: Farmington Displays Inc (G-1219)*

F F I, Smithfield *Also Called: Fiberglass Fabricators Inc (G-16700)*

F F J, Pawtucket *Also Called: Discovery Mint Inc (G-16364)*

F F Screw Products Inc... 860 621-4567
  888 W Queen St Southington (06489) *(G-3209)*

F H Peterson Machine Corp.................................... 781 341-4930
  143 South St Stoughton (02072) *(G-12204)*

F L Tripp & Sons Inc.. 508 636-4058
  Cherry & Webb Lane Westport Point (02791) *(G-13303)*

F M C Marine Colloid Division, Rockland *Also Called: FMC Corporation (G-5329)*

F M Callahan and Son Inc...................................... 781 324-5101
  22 Sharon St Malden (02148) *(G-10014)*

F M I, Hudson *Also Called: Fabco Mfg Inc (G-9366)*

F M S, Billerica *Also Called: Fluid Management Systems Inc (G-6448)*

F O Bailey Co Inc... 207 781-8001
  35 Depot Rd Falmouth (04105) *(G-4768)*

F P, Leominster *Also Called: First Plastics Corp (G-9664)*

F R C, Stamford *Also Called: Frc Founders Corporation (G-3348)*

F R Carroll Inc... 207 793-8615
  25 Doles Ridge Rd Limerick (04048) *(G-5001)*

F S Industries, West Greenwich *Also Called: LK Goodwin Co Inc (G-16888)*

F V Tigger.. 207 721-0875
  45a Ellen Way South Harpswell (04079) *(G-5487)*

F W Bryce Inc **(DH)**.. **978 283-7080**
  8 Pond Rd Gloucester (01930) *(G-8934)*

F W Lombard Company **(PA)**................................. **978 827-5333**
  246 Lakeview Dr Winchendon (01475) *(G-13479)*

F W Manufacturing & Engrg Co................................ 860 291-8580
  1505 John Fitch Blvd South Windsor (06074) *(G-3148)*

F W Webb Company... 203 865-6124
  650 Ella T Grasso Blvd New Haven (06519) *(G-2151)*

F W Webb Company... 207 892-5302
  3 Danielle Dr Windham (04062) *(G-5661)*

F W Webb Company... 207 873-7741
  37 Heywood Rd Winslow (04901) *(G-5682)*

F W Webb Company...781 247-0300
   100 Highland Ave Needham (02494) *(G-10510)*

F W Webb Company...781 341-1100
   152 Will Dr Stoughton (02072) *(G-12205)*

F-K Bearings Inc..860 621-4567
   865 W Queen St Southington (06489) *(G-3210)*

F2nyc, Pawtucket *Also Called: Fiesta Jewelry Corporation (G-16369)*

FA Finale Inc...617 226-7888
   24 Prime Park Way Ste 305 Boston (02116) *(G-6728)*

Fab-Tech Inc..802 655-8800
   480 Hercules Dr Ste 2 Colchester (05446) *(G-17190)*

Fabbrica LLC **(PA)**...**860 253-4136**
   1 Market Cir Windsor (06095) *(G-4275)*

Fabco Inc...207 377-6909
   30 Summer St Ste G Winthrop (04364) *(G-5692)*

Fabco Mfg Inc...978 568-8519
   14 Bonazzoli Ave Hudson (01749) *(G-9366)*

Fabco Wrap, New London *Also Called: First Aid Bandage Co Inc (G-2228)*

Faber Industries LLC **(HQ)**......................................**603 681-0484**
   6 Northwestern Dr Salem (03079) *(G-15522)*

Faber Polivol LLC **(DH)**...**603 681-0484**
   6 Northwestern Dr Salem (03079) *(G-15523)*

Fablevision Learning LLC...781 320-3225
   368 Washington St Ste 207 Dedham (02026) *(G-8243)*

Fabreeka International Inc **(DH)**................................**781 341-3655**
   1023 Turnpike St Stoughton (02072) *(G-12206)*

Fabreeka Intl Holdings Inc **(DH)**................................**781 341-3655**
   1023 Turnpike St Stoughton (02072) *(G-12207)*

Fabric Craftsman, Veazie *Also Called: Collabric (G-5570)*

Fabricgraphics, Pawcatuck *Also Called: Guidera Marketing Services (G-2721)*

Fabrique, Branford *Also Called: Fabrique Ltd (G-255)*

Fabrique Ltd **(PA)**..**203 481-2266**
   764 E Main St Ste 1 Branford (06405) *(G-255)*

Fabrizio Corporation...781 396-1400
   410 Riverside Ave Medford (02155) *(G-10284)*

Fabtron Incorporated...860 410-1801
   80 Farmington Valley Dr Plainville (06062) *(G-2759)*

Fabtron Corporation..781 891-4430
   80 Calvary St Waltham (02453) *(G-12674)*

Factorial Inc **(PA)**...**617 315-9733**
   19 Presidential Way Ste 103 Woburn (01801) *(G-13563)*

Factory Five Racing Inc..508 291-3443
   9 Tow Rd Wareham (02571) *(G-12836)*

Fad Tool Company LLC...860 582-7890
   95 Valley St Ste 7 Bristol (06010) *(G-445)*

Fadden Chipping & Logging Inc......................................603 939-2462
   1708 E Conway Rd Center Conway (03813) *(G-14052)*

Fadden Trucking, Center Conway *Also Called: Fadden Chipping & Logging Inc (G-14052)*

FAF Inc **(PA)**...**401 949-3000**
   26 Lark Industrial Pkwy Greenville (02828) *(G-16058)*

Fafard, Agawam *Also Called: Conrad Fafard Inc (G-5788)*

Fafard Inc..413 786-4343
   770 Silver St Agawam (01001) *(G-5790)*

Fair Haven Slate, Poultney *Also Called: Taran Bros Inc (G-17452)*

Fairchild, Colebrook *Also Called: Famp Inc (G-666)*

Fairchild Auto-Mated Parts, Winsted *Also Called: Fairchild Industries Inc (G-4345)*

Fairchild Energy LLC...207 775-8100
   82 Running Hill Rd South Portland (04106) *(G-5499)*

Fairchild Industries Inc...860 379-2725
   10 White St Winsted (06098) *(G-4345)*

Fairchild Semiconductor Corp.......................................801 562-7000
   333 Western Ave South Portland (04106) *(G-5500)*

Fairchild Semiconductor Corp.......................................207 775-8100
   333 Western Ave South Portland (04106) *(G-5501)*

Fairchild Semiconductor Corp **(DH)**.............................**207 775-8100**
   82 Running Hill Rd South Portland (04106) *(G-5502)*

Fairdeal Mfg Co, Chepachet *Also Called: Josef Creations Inc (G-15805)*

Fairfield County Look LLC..203 869-0077
   6 Wyckham Hill Ln Greenwich (06831) *(G-1329)*

Fairfield Marketing Group Inc **(PA)**............................**203 261-0884**
   830 Sport Hill Rd Easton (06612) *(G-1095)*

Fairfield Processing, Danbury *Also Called: Fairfield Processing Corp (G-744)*

Fairfield Processing Corp **(PA)**................................**203 744-2090**
   88 Rose Hill Ave Danbury (06810) *(G-744)*

Fairfield Wood Works, Stratford *Also Called: Fairfield Woodworks LLC (G-3535)*

Fairfield Woodworks LLC..203 380-9842
   365 Sniffens Ln Stratford (06615) *(G-3535)*

Fairfix, Fairfield *Also Called: Fairfix CT Inc (G-1185)*

Fairfix CT Inc..203 516-4137
   1134 Post Rd Fairfield (06824) *(G-1185)*

Fairhaven Marine Corporation.......................................401 433-3010
   254 Riverside Dr Riverside (02915) *(G-16654)*

Fairmarkit Inc **(PA)**...**774 364-4446**
   1 Beacon St Fl 15 Boston (02108) *(G-6729)*

Fairmount Foundry Inc..401 769-1585
   25 2nd Ave Woonsocket (02895) *(G-16959)*

Fairview Machine Company Inc.......................................978 887-2141
   427 Boston St Topsfield (01983) *(G-12435)*

Falcon Performance Ftwr LLC..207 784-9186
   27 Wrights Lndg Auburn (04210) *(G-4431)*

Falk Built New England, Boston *Also Called: Fbne LLC (G-6733)*

Fall Machine Company, LLC, Somersworth *Also Called: Aero Precision East LLC (G-15609)*

Fall Prevention Alarms Inc...508 765-5050
   186 Hamilton St Apt 1l Southbridge (01550) *(G-12016)*

Fall River Apparel Inc...508 677-1975
   192 Anawan St Ste 201 Fall River (02721) *(G-8545)*

Fall River Hat Company...508 672-7033
   394 Kilburn St Fall River (02724) *(G-8546)*

Fall River Mfg Co Inc..508 675-1125
   540 Currant Rd Fall River (02720) *(G-8547)*

Fall River Modern Prtg Co Inc......................................508 673-9421
   798 Plymouth Ave Fall River (02721) *(G-8548)*

Fall River Ready-Mix Con LLC.......................................508 675-7540
   245 Tripp St Fall River (02724) *(G-8549)*

Fall River Tool & Die Co Inc.......................................508 674-4621
   994 Jefferson St Ste 2 Fall River (02721) *(G-8550)*

Fallon Fine Cabinetry Inc..781 453-6988
   171 Reservoir St Needham Heights (02494) *(G-10544)*

Falmouth Enterprise, Falmouth *Also Called: Enterprise Publications (G-8630)*

Falmouth Mar Yachting Ctr Inc......................................508 548-4600
   278 Scranton Ave Falmouth (02540) *(G-8631)*

Falmouth Marine, Falmouth *Also Called: Falmouth Mar Yachting Ctr Inc (G-8631)*

Falmouth Ready Mix Inc...508 548-6100
   475 Thomas B Landers Rd East Falmouth (02536) *(G-8359)*

Falmouth Scientific Inc **(PA)**..................................**508 564-7640**
   33 Jonathan Bourne Dr Pocasset (02559) *(G-11486)*

Family Education Network Inc.......................................617 671-3435
   50 Congress St Ste 1025 Boston (02109) *(G-6730)*

Family Yarns Inc...207 269-3852
   15 Family Cir Etna (04434) *(G-4763)*

Famp Inc..860 379-2725
   1 Thompson Rd Pmb 310 Colebrook (06021) *(G-666)*

Fanaras Elc & Indus Contrls..603 772-3425
   89 Amesbury Rd Kensington (03833) *(G-14630)*

Far Industries Inc...508 644-3122
   11 Ridge Hill Rd Assonet (02702) *(G-5973)*

Far Reach Graphics Inc...781 444-4889
   15 Kearney Rd Needham Heights (02494) *(G-10545)*

Faraday, Burlington *Also Called: Faraday Inc (G-17134)*

Faraday Inc...802 658-2034
   431 Pine St Ste 113 Burlington (05401) *(G-17134)*

Farber Industrial Fabricating......................................401 725-2492
   55 Moss St Pawtucket (02860) *(G-16368)*

Farganyd Inc..781 575-1700
   112 Will Dr Canton (02021) *(G-7790)*

Fargo Ta LLC..617 345-0066
   745 Atlantic Ave Fl 8 Boston (02111) *(G-6731)*

Faria Beede Instruments Inc..860 848-9271
   75 Frontage Rd Ste 106 North Stonington (06359) *(G-2448)*

Faria Marine Instruments, North Stonington *Also Called: Faria Beede Instruments Inc (G-2448)*

Farmer Willies Inc...401 441-2997
   50 Terminal St Bldg 1 Charlestown (02129) *(G-7872)*

Farmhand Express, Skowhegan *Also Called: Central Maine Dairy Eqp Inc (G-5465)*

Farmington Chipping Ent, Farmington *Also Called: Farmington Chipping Entp Inc (G-4778)*

Farmington Chipping Entp Inc.................................... 207 778-4888
   Town Farm Rd Farmington (04938) *(G-4778)*

Farmington Coca Cola Btlg Dstr.................................. 207 778-4733
   282 Farmington Falls Rd Farmington (04938) *(G-4779)*

Farmington Displays Inc.. 860 677-2497
   21 Hyde Rd Ste 2 Farmington (06032) *(G-1219)*

Farmington Engineering Inc.. 800 428-7584
   73 Defco Park Rd North Haven (06473) *(G-2412)*

Farmington Mtal Fbrication LLC................................... 860 402-5148
   26 Lewis St Bristol (06010) *(G-446)*

Farmington Ready Mix, Farmington *Also Called: Dp Concrete LLC (G-1214)*

Farnum Hill Sider, Lebanon *Also Called: Lane Poverty Orchard (G-14692)*

Farrel Corporation **(DH)**.. **203 736-5500**
   1 Farrell Blvd Ansonia (06401) *(G-14)*

Farrel Pomini, Ansonia *Also Called: Farrel Corporation (G-14)*

Farrell Prcsion Mtalcraft Corp.................................... 860 355-2651
   192 Danbury Rd New Milford (06776) *(G-2243)*

Fars Inc.. 413 586-1332
   32 Pleasant St Northampton (01060) *(G-11061)*

Fascias Chocolates Inc... 203 753-0515
   44 Chase River Rd Waterbury (06704) *(G-3912)*

Fashion Accents LLC **(PA)**...................................... **401 331-6626**
   100 Nashua St Providence (02904) *(G-16517)*

Fashion Accessories First, Greenville *Also Called: FAF Inc (G-16058)*

Fasprint Inc **(PA)**... **508 588-9961**
   195 Liberty St Ste 1 Brockton (02301) *(G-7278)*

Fasstech, North Billerica *Also Called: Functional Assessment Tech Inc (G-10912)*

Fast, Stratford *Also Called: Food Atmtn - Svc Tchniques LLC (G-3537)*

Fast Forward Composites Inc..................................... 207 350-1773
   91 Broadcommon Rd Bristol (02809) *(G-15764)*

Fast Signs of Plaistow.. 603 894-7446
   160 Plaistow Rd Ste 15 Plaistow (03865) *(G-15343)*

Fastachi Ltd... 617 924-8787
   598 Mount Auburn St Watertown (02472) *(G-12876)*

Fastcap Systems Corporation **(PA)**......................... **857 403-6031**
   7 Audubon Rd Wakefield (01880) *(G-12509)*

Fastcast Consortium Inc.. 508 853-4500
   40 Rockdale St Worcester (01606) *(G-13722)*

Fastco, Lincoln *Also Called: Fastco Fabrication Inc (G-5007)*

Fastco Fabrication Inc.. 207 794-3030
   675 W Broadway Lincoln (04457) *(G-5007)*

Fastech Inc.. 781 964-3010
   18 Washington St Ste 33 Canton (02021) *(G-7791)*

Fastforms, Boston *Also Called: BFI Print Communications Inc (G-6591)*

Fastrax Signs Inc.. 603 775-7500
   67 Route 27 Brentwood (03833) *(G-14021)*

Fastsigns... 781 444-4889
   15 Kearney Rd Needham Heights (02494) *(G-10546)*

Fastsigns, Middletown *Also Called: Youngs Communications Inc (G-1791)*

Fastsigns, Waterford *Also Called: Whaling City Graphics LLC (G-3999)*

Fastsigns, Needham Heights *Also Called: Far Reach Graphics Inc (G-10545)*

Fastsigns, Needham Heights *Also Called: Fastsigns (G-10546)*

Fastsigns, Quincy *Also Called: Fnsj Inc (G-11519)*

Fastsigns, Rehoboth *Also Called: Fastsigns of Attleboro (G-11608)*

Fastsigns, Woburn *Also Called: Business Signs LLC (G-13537)*

Fastsigns, Woburn *Also Called: Signs To Go Inc (G-13667)*

Fastsigns, Plaistow *Also Called: Fast Signs of Plaistow (G-15343)*

Fastsigns, South Burlington *Also Called: Fastsigns - 490101 (G-17578)*

Fastsigns - 490101... 802 238-1247
   1335 Shelburne Rd South Burlington (05403) *(G-17578)*

Fastsigns of Attleboro.. 508 699-6699
   5 Greenwood Dr Rehoboth (02769) *(G-11608)*

Fat Hat Clothing Co... 802 296-6646
   1 Quechee Main St Quechee (05059) *(G-17462)*

Fat Hen LLC... 617 764-1412
   124 Broadway Somerville (02145) *(G-11871)*

Faulkner Corporation... 207 989-3792
   146 Parkway S Brewer (04412) *(G-4612)*

Faux Designs Inc.. 617 965-0142
   46 High St Needham Heights (02494) *(G-10547)*

Faverco Inc.. 617 247-1440
   16 Aberdeen St Boston (02215) *(G-6732)*

Favorite Fuels LLC.. 603 967-4889
   1 Crank Rd Hampton Falls (03844) *(G-14418)*

Favreau Forestry LLC... 978 706-1038
   109 Chace Hill Rd Sterling (01564) *(G-12162)*

Faxon Engineering Company Inc **(PA)**..................... **860 236-4266**
   17 Britton Dr Bloomfield (06002) *(G-163)*

Fbn Plastics Inc.. 603 894-4326
   338 N Main St Salem (03079) *(G-15524)*

Fbne LLC... 617 571-6443
   112 Beach St Unit A Boston (02111) *(G-6733)*

FC Hammond & Son Co Inc....................................... 603 523-4353
   11 Hammonds Way Canaan (03741) *(G-14046)*

FC Meyer Packaging LLC **(HQ)**.............................. **203 847-8500**
   108 Main St Ste 3 Norwalk (06851) *(G-2499)*

FC Phillips Inc.. 781 344-9400
   471 Washington St Stoughton (02072) *(G-12208)*

FC Work & Sons Incorporated.................................... 207 722-3206
   774 Moosehead Trl Jackson (04921) *(G-4912)*

Fci Electrical-Brundy Products.................................... 603 444-6781
   150 Burndy Rd Littleton (03561) *(G-14718)*

Fci Ophthalmics Inc... 781 826-9060
   30 Corporate Park Dr Ste 310 Pembroke (02359) *(G-11365)*

Fcmii Inc... 203 393-9751
   20 Sargent Dr Bethany (06524) *(G-93)*

Fct, Torrington *Also Called: Fct Electronics LP (G-3678)*

Fct Electronics LP... 860 482-2800
   187 Commercial Blvd Torrington (06790) *(G-3678)*

Fct Electronics Management Inc.................................. 860 482-2800
   187 Commercial Blvd Torrington (06790) *(G-3679)*

Fd Plastics, Leominster *Also Called: F & D Plastics Inc (G-9662)*

FDA Group, North Grafton *Also Called: FDA Group LLC (G-11023)*

FDA Group LLC... 413 330-7476
   3 Bridle Ridge Dr North Grafton (01536) *(G-11023)*

Fdc Grafixx, Holyoke *Also Called: Valley Etching Engrv Dsign Inc (G-9289)*

FE Knight Inc **(PA)**... **508 520-1666**
   56 Monadnock Rd Chestnut Hill (02467) *(G-7999)*

Feature Products Ltd.. 603 669-0800
   34 Rundlett Hill Rd Ste 1 Bedford (03110) *(G-13928)*

Fed, Dedham *Also Called: Dedham Recycled Gravel Co Inc (G-8241)*

Fedele and Carter Inc.. 508 394-1791
   411 Main St Dennis Port (02639) *(G-8261)*

Federal Business Products Inc.................................... 860 482-6231
   368 Ella Grasso Ave Torrington (06790) *(G-3680)*

Federal Electronics Inc... 401 944-6200
   75 Stamp Farm Rd Cranston (02921) *(G-15859)*

Federal Prison Industries.. 203 743-6471
   Route 37 Danbury (06811) *(G-745)*

Federal Program Integrators LLC
   12 Wabanaki Way Indian Island (04468) *(G-4907)*

Federal Spice Corp **(PA)**....................................... **603 356-6381**
   3378 White Mountain Hwy North Conway (03860) *(G-15248)*

Federici Brands LLC **(PA)**...................................... **203 762-7667**
   195 Danbury Rd 3rd Fl Wilton (06897) *(G-4239)*

Fedex Office & Print Svcs Inc.................................... 603 644-2679
   119 S River Rd Ste 1 Bedford (03110) *(G-13929)*

Feed Commodities Intl Inc **(HQ)**............................. **800 639-3191**
   47 Feed Mill Ln Middlebury (05753) *(G-17343)*

Feeleys Company Inc... 617 773-1711
   232 Water St 238 Quincy (02169) *(G-11518)*

Feeney's Welding and Fence Co., Hyde Park *Also Called: Feeneys Fence Inc (G-9460)*

Feeneys Fence Inc... 617 364-1407
   120 Business St Ste 5 Hyde Park (02136) *(G-9460)*

Fellows Corporation.. 802 674-6500
   7 Everett Ln Windsor (05089) *(G-17758)*

Felton Inc.. 603 425-0200
   7 Burton Dr Londonderry (03053) *(G-14750)*

Feman Steel LLC... 860 982-6393
   107 Old Windsor Rd Ste F Bloomfield (06002) *(G-164)*

**A
L
P
H
A
B
E
T
I
C**

Femtonics Usa Inc 361 210-3349
  100 Cummings Ctr Ste 265f Beverly (01915) *(G-6347)*

Fence Lines Inc 781 331-2121
  457 Columbian St South Weymouth (02190) *(G-11976)*

Fenn LLC 860 259-6600
  80 Clark Dr Unit 5d East Berlin (06023) *(G-910)*

Fenway Cmmunications Group Inc 617 226-1900
  870 Commonwealth Ave Ste F Boston (02215) *(G-6734)*

Fergene Inc 973 796-1600
  245 Main St 11th Fl Cambridge (02142) *(G-7569)*

Ferguson Enterprises LLC 413 593-1219
  1125 Sheridan St Chicopee (01022) *(G-8032)*

Ferguson Perforating Company **(DH)** **401 941-8876**
  130 Ernest St Providence (02905) *(G-16518)*

Fernald Lumber Inc 603 679-2997
  Rte 152 Nottingham (03290) *(G-15276)*

Ferraiolo Construction Inc 207 594-9840
  262 Pleasant St Rockland (04841) *(G-5327)*

Ferraro Custom Woodwork LLC 203 876-1280
  29 Eastern Steel Rd Milford (06460) *(G-1828)*

Ferreira Concrete Forms Inc 401 639-0931
  7 Tallman Ave East Providence (02914) *(G-16019)*

Ferrex Industries, Westminster Station *Also Called: Burtco Inc (G-17702)*

Ferrite Microwave Tech LLC 603 881-5234
  104 Perimeter Rd Ste 1 Nashua (03063) *(G-15100)*

Ferro Corporation 413 743-3927
  34 Holly Ln Williamstown (01267) *(G-13366)*

Ferro-Ceramic Grinding Inc 781 245-1833
  5 Cornell Pl Wilmington (01887) *(G-13407)*

Ferron Mold and Tool LLC 860 774-5555
  154 Louisa Viens Dr Dayville (06241) *(G-862)*

Ferrotec (usa) Corporation 603 472-6800
  33 Constitution Dr Bedford (03110) *(G-13930)*

Feteria Tool & Findings 508 222-7788
  1285 County St Attleboro (02703) *(G-6014)*

Fev Tutor, Woburn *Also Called: Fev Tutor Inc (G-13564)*

Fev Tutor Inc 781 376-6925
  500 W Cummings Park Ste 2700 Woburn (01801) *(G-13564)*

Ff Screw Products, Southington *Also Called: F F Screw Products Inc (G-3209)*

Fg Signs LLC 203 612-4447
  1895 Stratford Ave Stratford (06615) *(G-3536)*

Fgc Plasma Solutions Inc 617 999-9078
  11 River St Ste 3 Middleton (01949) *(G-10383)*

Fgx International, Smithfield *Also Called: Fgx International Inc (G-16699)*

Fgx International Holdings Ltd **(HQ)** **401 231-3800**
  500 Washington Hwy Smithfield (02917) *(G-16698)*

Fgx International Inc **(DH)** **401 231-3800**
  500 Washington Hwy Smithfield (02917) *(G-16699)*

Fhc Inc **(PA)** **207 666-8190**
  1201 Main St Bowdoin (04287) *(G-4605)*

Fiba Tech 978 486-0586
  53 Ayer Rd Littleton (01460) *(G-9814)*

Fiba Technologies Inc **(PA)** **508 887-7100**
  53 Ayer Rd Littleton (01460) *(G-9815)*

Fiber Materials Inc **(DH)** **207 282-5911**
  5 Morin St Biddeford (04005) *(G-4564)*

Fiber Optic Hardware 603 325-4993
  21 Technology Way Ste 485 Nashua (03060) *(G-15101)*

Fiberglass Building Pdts Inc 847 650-3045
  546a Plymouth St Halifax (02338) *(G-9021)*

Fiberglass Fabricators Inc 401 231-3552
  964 Douglas Pike Smithfield (02917) *(G-16700)*

Fiberkraft Inc 603 621-0090
  3 Industrial Way Salem (03079) *(G-15525)*

Fiberlock Technologies Inc 978 623-9987
  150 Dascomb Rd Andover (01810) *(G-5882)*

Fibernext LLC 603 226-2400
  41 Locke Rd Concord (03301) *(G-14130)*

Fiberoptics Technology Inc **(PA)** **860 928-0443**
  1 Quasset Rd Pomfret (06258) *(G-2807)*

Fiberoptics Technology Inc 860 928-0443
  1 Fiber Rd Pomfret (06258) *(G-2808)*

Fiberqa LLC 860 254-7275
  10 Vista Dr Unit 101 Old Lyme (06371) *(G-2641)*

Fiberspar Linepipe LLC 281 854-2636
  800 Purchase St Ste 502 New Bedford (02740) *(G-10590)*

Fiberspar Spoolable Pdts Inc **(PA)** **508 291-9000**
  28 Pattersons Brook Rd West Wareham (02576) *(G-13064)*

Fibertec Inc 508 697-5100
  35 Scotland Blvd Bridgewater (02324) *(G-7229)*

Fibredyne, Dover *Also Called: Pentair Rsdntial Filtration LLC (G-14244)*

Fiddlehead Brewing Company LLC 802 489-5090
  31 Sage Ct Shelburne (05482) *(G-17557)*

Fiddlehead Focus 207 316-2243
  90 E Main St # 1 Fort Kent (04743) *(G-4787)*

Fidelity Ind Advser Newsletter 413 458-4700
  25 Main St Williamstown (01267) *(G-13367)*

Fidelux, Middletown *Also Called: Fidelux Lighting LLC (G-1746)*

Fidelux Lighting LLC **(PA)** **203 774-5653**
  180 Johnson St Middletown (06457) *(G-1746)*

Field Trip, Westport *Also Called: Provisionaire & Co LLC (G-4193)*

Fielding Manufacturing Inc 401 461-0400
  780 Wellington Ave Cranston (02910) *(G-15860)*

Fielding Mfg - Zinc Dcsting In 401 461-0400
  780 Wellington Ave Cranston (02910) *(G-15861)*

Fiery, Londonderry *Also Called: Electronics For Imaging Inc (G-14748)*

Fiesta Jewelry, East Providence *Also Called: Ldc Inc (G-16029)*

Fiesta Jewelry Corporation 212 564-6847
  250 East Ave Pawtucket (02860) *(G-16369)*

Fife Packaging LLC 603 753-2669
  77 Merrimack St Penacook (03303) *(G-15310)*

Fig City News Inc 617 610-1093
  389 Central St Auburndale (02466) *(G-6133)*

Fil-Tech Inc 617 227-1133
  6 Pinckney St Boston (02114) *(G-6735)*

Filabot, Barre *Also Called: Triex LLC (G-17021)*

Filmco Rust Protection LLC 203 483-5017
  63-5 N Branford Rd Branford (06405) *(G-256)*

Filtec Precision Ceramics Corp 978 204-2288
  37 Village View Rd Westford (01886) *(G-13236)*

Filter-Kleen Manufacturing Co 978 692-5137
  3 Broadway St Westford (01886) *(G-13237)*

Filtered Air Systems Inc 781 491-0508
  100 Ashburton Ave Ste 3 Woburn (01801) *(G-13565)*

Filtersense, Beverly *Also Called: Auburn Filtersense LLC (G-6327)*

Filtersense, Beverly *Also Called: Impolit Envmtl Ctrl Corp (G-6356)*

Filtration & Separation Div, Haverhill *Also Called: Parker-Hannifin Corporation (G-9120)*

Filtrine, Keene *Also Called: Filtrine Manufacturing Co Inc (G-14599)*

Filtrine Manufacturing Co Inc 603 352-5500
  15 Kit St Keene (03431) *(G-14599)*

Filtrona Extrusion of Massachusetts LLC 978 249-5343
  764 S Athol Rd Athol (01331) *(G-5979)*

Fimor North America, Cheshire *Also Called: Fimor North America Inc (G-593)*

Fimor North America Inc **(HQ)** **203 272-3219**
  50 Grandview Ct Cheshire (06410) *(G-593)*

Finally Free LLC 603 626-4388
  55 South Commercial St Manchester (03101) *(G-14848)*

Finally Light Bulb Company, Charlestown *Also Called: Lucidity Lights Inc (G-7878)*

Finalsite, Glastonbury *Also Called: Active Internet Tech LLC (G-1269)*

Financial Accnting Foundation **(PA)** **203 847-0700**
  801 Main Ave Norwalk (06851) *(G-2500)*

Financial Accnting Stndards Bd, Norwalk *Also Called: Financial Accnting Foundation (G-2500)*

Finastra USA Corporation 781 203-9200
  55 Network Dr Burlington (01803) *(G-7373)*

Finch Therapeutics, Somerville *Also Called: Finch Therapeutics Group Inc (G-11873)*

Finch Therapeutics Inc 617 229-6499
  200 Innerbelt Rd Ste 400 Somerville (02143) *(G-11872)*

Finch Therapeutics Group Inc 617 229-6499
  200 Innerbelt Rd Ste 400 Somerville (02143) *(G-11873)*

Findings Incorporated 508 222-7449
  1231 County St Attleboro (02703) *(G-6015)*

Fine Edge Tool Company Inc 508 222-7511
  13 Maynard St Attleboro (02703) *(G-6016)*

Fine Line, Smithfield *Also Called: Fine Line Graphics Inc (G-16701)*

Fine Line Graphics Inc **(PA)**..401 349-3300
  90 Douglas Pike Unit 3 Smithfield (02917) *(G-16701)*

Fine Magazine..617 721-7372
  9 Fowle St Woburn (01801) *(G-13566)*

Fine Print New England Inc..860 953-0660
  711 N Mountain Rd Newington (06111) *(G-2293)*

Finelines, Peabody *Also Called: Ksg Enterprises Inc (G-11322)*

Finestkind Brewing LLC..603 436-4026
  105 Towle Farm Rd Hampton (03842) *(G-14402)*

Finetone, Windham *Also Called: Tena Group LLC (G-5671)*

Finicky Pet Food Inc...508 991-8448
  68 Blackmer St New Bedford (02744) *(G-10591)*

Finish Solutions LLC...802 540-0326
  75 Swanton Rd Saint Albans (05478) *(G-17522)*

Finishield Corp...603 641-2164
  5 George Ave Londonderry (03053) *(G-14751)*

Finishing Touch Woodcraft...860 916-2642
  3 Noja Trl Canton (06019) *(G-561)*

Finlay EXT Ingredients USA Inc **(DH)**.................................**800 288-6272**
  10 Blackstone Valley Pl Lincoln (02865) *(G-16137)*

Fire Defenses New England LLC...978 304-1506
  44 Garden St Ste 1 Danvers (01923) *(G-8186)*

Fire Dept, White River Junction *Also Called: Town of Hartford (G-17710)*

Fire Prevention Services..203 866-6357
  20 Indian Rd Trumbull (06611) *(G-3720)*

Fire-Lite, Northford *Also Called: Fire-Lite Alarms Inc (G-2452)*

Fire-Lite Alarms Inc...203 484-7161
  1 Fire Lite Pl Northford (06472) *(G-2452)*

Fireball Heat Treating Co Inc..508 222-2617
  34 John Williams St Attleboro (02703) *(G-6017)*

Firebrand Technologies, Newburyport *Also Called: Quality Solutions Inc (G-10710)*

Firecracker Sports LLC..401 595-0233
  8 Windsong Rd Cumberland (02864) *(G-15939)*

Fireslate 2 Inc...508 273-0047
  3065 Cranberry Hwy A24 East Wareham (02538) *(G-8422)*

Firestable Insulation Co..860 767-8773
  36 Plains Rd Essex (06426) *(G-1164)*

Firestone, Bristol *Also Called: Bridgestone Ret Operations LLC (G-417)*

Firestone, Hamden *Also Called: Bridgestone Ret Operations LLC (G-1414)*

Firestone, Milford *Also Called: Bridgestone Ret Operations LLC (G-1803)*

Firestone, New Britain *Also Called: Bridgestone Ret Operations LLC (G-2009)*

Firestone, New Haven *Also Called: Bridgestone Ret Operations LLC (G-2132)*

Firestone, Newington *Also Called: Bridgestone Ret Operations LLC (G-2277)*

Firestone, Southington *Also Called: Bridgestone Ret Operations LLC (G-3205)*

Firestone, Waterbury *Also Called: Bridgestone Ret Operations LLC (G-3893)*

Firestone, West Haven *Also Called: Bridgestone Ret Operations LLC (G-4095)*

Firestone, Auburn *Also Called: Bridgestone Ret Operations LLC (G-6110)*

Firestone, Boston *Also Called: Bridgestone Ret Operations LLC (G-6622)*

Firestone, Braintree *Also Called: Bridgestone Ret Operations LLC (G-7172)*

Firestone, Brockton *Also Called: Bridgestone Ret Operations LLC (G-7262)*

Firestone, Hingham *Also Called: Bridgestone Ret Operations LLC (G-9145)*

Firestone, Northampton *Also Called: Bridgestone Ret Operations LLC (G-11054)*

Firestone, Quincy *Also Called: Bridgestone Ret Operations LLC (G-11508)*

Firestone, Springfield *Also Called: Bridgestone Ret Operations LLC (G-12080)*

Firestone, Watertown *Also Called: Bridgestone Ret Operations LLC (G-12864)*

Firestone, Wilmington *Also Called: Bridgestone Ret Operations LLC (G-13394)*

Firestone, Manchester *Also Called: Bridgestone Ret Operations LLC (G-14821)*

Firestone, North Smithfield *Also Called: Bridgestone Ret Operations LLC (G-16319)*

Firestone, Providence *Also Called: Bridgestone Ret Operations LLC (G-16491)*

Firestone Building Pdts Co LLC...860 584-4516
  780 James P Casey Rd Ste 4 Bristol (06010) *(G-447)*

Fireye Inc **(DH)**..**603 432-4100**
  3 Manchester Rd Derry (03038) *(G-14193)*

First Aid Bandage Co Inc...860 443-8499
  3 State Pier Rd New London (06320) *(G-2228)*

First Card Co Inc...401 434-6140
  1 Carding Ln Johnston (02919) *(G-16085)*

First Card Packaging, Johnston *Also Called: First Card Co Inc (G-16085)*

First Ch of Chrst Scientist, Boston *Also Called: First Ch of Chrst Scntist In B (G-6736)*

First Ch of Chrst Scntist In B **(PA)**...................................**617 450-2000**
  210 Massachusetts Ave Boston (02115) *(G-6736)*

First Chance Inc...860 346-3663
  598 Washington St Middletown (06457) *(G-1747)*

First Choice Printing Inc..207 353-8006
  60 Capital Ave Lisbon Falls (04252) *(G-5020)*

First Electric Motor Svc Inc...781 491-1100
  73 Olympia Ave Woburn (01801) *(G-13567)*

First Electronics Corporation...617 704-4248
  400 Wood Rd Braintree (02184) *(G-7183)*

First Electronics Corporation...617 288-2430
  222 Williams St Chelsea (02150) *(G-7981)*

First Electronics Corporation **(DH)**....................................**617 288-2430**
  71 Von Hillern St Ste 1 Dorchester (02125) *(G-8299)*

First Equity Group Inc **(PA)**...**203 291-7700**
  15 Riverside Ave Ste 2 Westport (06880) *(G-4168)*

First Impression Printing Inc...781 344-8855
  178 Tosca Dr Stoughton (02072) *(G-12209)*

First Light Technologies Inc..802 287-4195
  212 Ideal Way Poultney (05764) *(G-17447)*

First Mate Prtg Converting Inc **(HQ)**..................................**978 630-1028**
  164 Fredette St Gardner (01440) *(G-8886)*

First Mile Brewing Co LLC...207 231-4579
  28 Market St Ste 103 Fort Kent (04743) *(G-4788)*

First Plastics Corp...978 537-0367
  22 Jytek Rd Leominster (01453) *(G-9664)*

First Point Power, Cranston *Also Called: Fpp Holdings LLC (G-15862)*

First Print Inc...781 729-7714
  109 Cambridge St Winchester (01890) *(G-13484)*

First Quality Metal Pdts Corp..781 585-5820
  171 Palmer Rd Ste D Plympton (02367) *(G-11484)*

First Sail Group Inc..425 409-2783
  69 Neptune Ln South Yarmouth (02664) *(G-11983)*

First Step Print Shop LLC..802 899-2708
  115 North St Burlington (05401) *(G-17135)*

First Trax Sports Shop, West Dover *Also Called: Gw Ski Inc (G-17690)*

Fis Systems International LLC..617 728-7722
  75-101 Federal Street Boston (02110) *(G-6737)*

Fis Systems International LLC..603 898-6185
  9 Northeastern Blvd Ste 400 Salem (03079) *(G-15526)*

Fischer Technology Inc **(DH)**..**860 683-0781**
  750 Marshall Phelps Rd Windsor (06095) *(G-4276)*

Fisher, Rockland *Also Called: Fisher Engineering (G-5328)*

Fisher Contracting, Worcester *Also Called: Fisher Contracting Corporation (G-13723)*

Fisher Contracting Corporation..508 421-6989
  11 Webster Pl Worcester (01603) *(G-13723)*

Fisher Controls Intl LLC..860 599-1140
  95 Pendleton Hill Rd North Stonington (06359) *(G-2449)*

Fisher Engineering..207 701-4200
  50 Gordon Dr Rockland (04841) *(G-5328)*

Fisher Engineering Division, Rockland *Also Called: Douglas Dynamics LLC (G-5325)*

Fisher Footwear LLC..203 302-2800
  777 W Putnam Ave Greenwich (06830) *(G-1330)*

Fisher Scientific Intl LLC...978 670-7460
  900 Middlesex Tpke Bldg 8-1 Billerica (01821) *(G-6447)*

Fisher Scientific Intl LLC **(HQ)**.......................................**781 622-1000**
  81 Wyman St Waltham (02451) *(G-12675)*

Fisher Sigerson Morrison LLC...203 302-2800
  777 W Putnam Ave Ste 10 Greenwich (06830) *(G-1331)*

Fishing Hot Spots Inc..715 365-5555
  9 Townsend W Nashua (03063) *(G-15102)*

Fishman Corporation..508 435-2115
  192 South St Hopkinton (01748) *(G-9325)*

Fishman Transducers Inc..978 988-9199
  3 Riverside Dr Ste 1 Andover (01810) *(G-5883)*

Fit & Fresh, Providence *Also Called: Wcm LLC (G-16644)*

Fitbit Inc..857 277-0594
  1 Marina Park Dr Ste 701 Boston (02210) *(G-6738)*

FITBIT, INC., Boston *Also Called: Fitbit Inc (G-6738)*

Fitchburg Publishing.. 978 343-6911
  808 Main St Fitchburg (01420) *(G-8654)*

Fitchburg Welding Co Inc....................................... 978 874-2911
  4 Depot Rd Westminster (01473) *(G-13270)*

Fitness Em, Uxbridge *Also Called: Fitness Em LLC (G-12479)*

Fitness Em LLC
  660 Douglas St Uxbridge (01569) *(G-12479)*

Fitnow Inc.. 617 699-5585
  101 Tremont St Fl 9 Boston (02108) *(G-6739)*

Fitz Machine Inc.. 781 245-5966
  4 Railroad Ave Ste 5 Wakefield (01880) *(G-12510)*

Fitzgerald and Wood Inc.. 203 488-2553
  85 Rogers St Ste 3 Branford (06405) *(G-257)*

Fitzgerald-Norwalk Awng Co Inc........................... 203 847-5858
  131 Main St Norwalk (06851) *(G-2501)*

Fitzpatrick Company, The, Westwood *Also Called: Idex Mpt Inc (G-13312)*

Five Star Companies, New Bedford *Also Called: Five Star Surgical Inc (G-10593)*

Five Star Manufacturing Inc................................... 508 998-1404
  163 Samuel Barnet Blvd New Bedford (02745) *(G-10592)*

Five Star Plating LLC... 978 655-4081
  7a Broadway Lawrence (01840) *(G-9561)*

Five Star Products Inc... 203 336-7900
  2 Enterprise Dr Ste 303 Shelton (06484) *(G-3006)*

Five Star Surgical Inc.. 508 998-1404
  163 Samuel Barnet Blvd New Bedford (02745) *(G-10593)*

Fizz LLC.. 207 887-9618
  28 Colonial Rd Portland (04102) *(G-5216)*

Fizz Time.. 603 870-0000
  11 Industrial Way Bldg C Salem (03079) *(G-15527)*

Fka Orion Electronics, Devens *Also Called: Ox3 Corporation (G-8284)*

Fka Ppm Inc.. 781 871-4606
  225 Asylum St Fl 20 Hartford (06103) *(G-1480)*

Flabeg Technical Glass US Corp............................ 203 729-5227
  451 Church St Naugatuck (06770) *(G-1958)*

Flag Fables Inc... 413 747-0525
  113 Vermont St Springfield (01108) *(G-12095)*

Flag Hill Distillery LLC... 603 659-2949
  297 N River Rd Lee (03861) *(G-14705)*

Flag Hill Winery, Lee *Also Called: Flag Hill Winery & Vinyrd LLC (G-14706)*

Flag Hill Winery & Vinyrd LLC................................ 603 659-2949
  297 N River Rd Lee (03861) *(G-14706)*

Flagg Palmer Precast Inc....................................... 508 987-3400
  1 Industrial Park Rd W Oxford (01540) *(G-11253)*

Flagman of America LLC.. 860 678-0275
  22 E Main St Avon (06001) *(G-24)*

Flagraphics Inc... 617 776-7549
  30 Alston St Somerville (02143) *(G-11874)*

Flagship Automation, East Douglas *Also Called: Emx Controls Inc (G-8350)*

Flagship Converters Inc... 203 792-0034
  205 Shelter Rock Rd Danbury (06810) *(G-746)*

Flagship Press Inc... 978 975-3100
  150 Flagship Dr North Andover (01845) *(G-10831)*

Flagstone Inc.. 207 227-5883
  235 Griffin Ridge Rd Mapleton (04757) *(G-5045)*

Flame Grilling Products Inc.................................... 800 724-5510
  2500 Winslows Mills Rd Waldoboro (04572) *(G-5576)*

Flame Laminating Corporation............................... 978 725-9527
  2350 Turnpike St Bldg B North Andover (01845) *(G-10832)*

Flametech Steels Inc.. 978 686-9518
  10 Methuen St Lawrence (01840) *(G-9562)*

Flash Print, Cambridge *Also Called: Flashprint Graphics Inc (G-7570)*

Flashprint Graphics Inc... 617 492-7767
  99 Mount Auburn St Ste 3 Cambridge (02138) *(G-7570)*

Flatworld... 781 974-9927
  175 Portland St Fl 2 Boston (02114) *(G-6740)*

Fleecepro, Fall River *Also Called: Tri Textiles Corporation (G-8617)*

Fleming & Son Corp... 617 623-3047
  3 Marigold Ln Chelmsford (01824) *(G-7928)*

Fleming Industries Inc... 413 593-3300
  102 1st Ave Chicopee (01020) *(G-8033)*

Fleming Printing, Chelmsford *Also Called: Fleming & Son Corp (G-7928)*

Flemish Master Weavers Inc.................................. 207 324-6600
  96 Gate House Rd Sanford (04073) *(G-5396)*

Flemming Tinker Incorporated............................... 860 316-2589
  27 Parson Ln Ste G Durham (06422) *(G-900)*

Fletcher Granite LLC **(DH)**................................ **978 692-1312**
  535 Groton Rd Westford (01886) *(G-13238)*

Fletcher-Terry Company LLC **(PA)**.................... **860 828-3400**
  91 Clark Dr East Berlin (06023) *(G-911)*

Flex Leasing Power & Svc LLC.............................. 603 430-7000
  112 Corporate Dr Portsmouth (03801) *(G-15384)*

Flex-A-Seal.. 802 878-8307
  291 Hurricane Ln Ste 101 Williston (05495) *(G-17729)*

Flex-O-Graphic Prtg Plate Inc............................... 508 752-8100
  33 Arctic St Ste 4 Worcester (01604) *(G-13724)*

Flex-Print-Labels, Hampton *Also Called: Labels Inc (G-14405)*

Flexaseal, Williston *Also Called: Flexaseal Engnred Sals Systems (G-17730)*

Flexaseal Engnred Sals Systems........................... 800 426-3594
  291 Hurricane Ln Williston (05495) *(G-17730)*

Flexcon, Spencer *Also Called: Flexcon Company Inc (G-12058)*

Flexcon Company Inc **(PA)**................................ **508 885-8200**
  1 Flexcon Industrial Park Spencer (01562) *(G-12058)*

Flexcon Industrial LLC **(HQ)**............................. **210 798-1900**
  1 S Spencer Rd Spencer (01562) *(G-12059)*

Flexcon Industries Inc... 781 986-2424
  300 Pond St Randolph (02368) *(G-11557)*

Flexenergy, Portsmouth *Also Called: Flexenergy Green Solutions Inc (G-15387)*

Flexenergy Inc.. 603 430-7000
  112 Corporate Dr Ste 3 Portsmouth (03801) *(G-15385)*

Flexenergy Energy Systems Inc............................. 877 477-6937
  112 Corporate Dr Ste 3 Portsmouth (03801) *(G-15386)*

Flexenergy Green Solutions Inc **(PA)**................ **603 430-7000**
  112 Corporate Dr Portsmouth (03801) *(G-15387)*

Flexenergy Holdings LLC....................................... 603 430-7000
  30 Nh Ave Portsmouth (03801) *(G-15388)*

Flexenergy Power Solutions LLC............................ 603 430-7000
  112 Corporate Dr Ste 3 Portsmouth (03801) *(G-15389)*

Flexhead Industries Inc... 508 893-9596
  56 Lowland St Holliston (01746) *(G-9210)*

Flexhead Industries Massachusetts Business Trust........... 508 893-9596
  56 Lowland St Holliston (01746) *(G-9211)*

Flexiinternational, Shelton *Also Called: Flexiinternational Sftwr Inc (G-3007)*

Flexiinternational Sftwr Inc **(PA)**...................... **203 925-3040**
  2 Trap Falls Rd Shelton (06484) *(G-3007)*

Flexion Thrptics Scrities Corp................................ 781 305-7777
  10 Mall Rd Ste 301 Burlington (01803) *(G-7374)*

Flexo Concepts, Plymouth *Also Called: Blade Tech Systems Inc (G-11451)*

Flexo Converters, Meriden *Also Called: Duro Hilex Poly LLC (G-1665)*

Flextronics Lighting Solution, Hollis *Also Called: Lw Holding Lc (G-14453)*

Flexware Control Tech LLC..................................... 207 262-9682
  40 Johnson St Bangor (04401) *(G-4501)*

Flight Support Inc.. 203 562-1415
  101 Sackett Point Rd North Haven (06473) *(G-2413)*

Flimp Media.. 508 435-5220
  2 Hayden Rowe St Ste 2 Hopkinton (01748) *(G-9326)*

Flintec Inc.. 978 562-4548
  18 Kane Industrial Dr Hudson (01749) *(G-9367)*

Flir Maritime Us Inc... 603 324-7900
  110 Lowell Rd Hudson (03051) *(G-14496)*

Flir Surveillance, North Billerica *Also Called: Teledyne Flir LLC (G-10961)*

Flir Systems-Boston Inc **(DH)**........................... **978 901-8000**
  25 Esquire Rd North Billerica (01862) *(G-10911)*

Flitsai Inc... 203 586-8201
  3 Oak Hill Farms Rd Ellington (06029) *(G-1106)*

Flo Chemical Corp.. 978 827-5101
  20 Puffer St Ashburnham (01430) *(G-5952)*

Flo-Matic, Brattleboro *Also Called: C E Bradley Laboratories Inc (G-17077)*

Flo-Tech LLC **(PA)**... **860 613-3333**
  545 Long Wharf Dr Ste 602 New Haven (06511) *(G-2152)*

Flodesign Sonics Inc... 413 596-5900
  380 Main St Wilbraham (01095) *(G-13358)*

Flojet, Beverly *Also Called: Flow Control LLC (G-6348)*

Flooring Pro Fastening, Auburn *Also Called: Flooring Pro Industries LLC (G-6113)*

Flooring Pro Industries LLC.................... 704 736-1004
27 Elm St Auburn (01501) *(G-6113)*

Florence Crushed Stone, Colchester *Also Called: Troy Minerals Inc (G-17205)*

Florence Crushed Stone, Florence *Also Called: Troy Minerals Inc (G-17273)*

Florian Tools, Southington *Also Called: American Standard Company (G-3203)*

Florida Mega Mix, Shaftsbury *Also Called: Dailey Precast LLC (G-17549)*

Florlink, Newport *Also Called: Florlink Inc (G-16210)*

Florlink Inc.................... 617 221-2200
174 Bellevue Ave Ste 316 Newport (02840) *(G-16210)*

Flotation Technologies LLC.................... 207 282-7749
20 Morin St Biddeford (04005) *(G-4565)*

Flow Chemicals, Ashburnham *Also Called: Flo Chemical Corp (G-5952)*

Flow Control LLC.................... 978 281-0440
100 Cummings Ctr Beverly (01915) *(G-6348)*

Flow Resources Inc **(HQ)**.................... **860 666-1200**
135 Day St Ste 1 Newington (06111) *(G-2294)*

Flowers Boat Works Inc.................... 207 563-7404
21 Ridge Rd Walpole (04573) *(G-5581)*

Flowserve US Inc.................... 978 682-5248
280 Merrimack St Lawrence (01843) *(G-9563)*

Flowtron Outdoor Products Div, Medford *Also Called: Armatron International Inc (G-10280)*

Floyd Manufacturing Co Inc.................... 860 829-1920
5 Pasco Hill Rd Cromwell (06416) *(G-692)*

Flue Gas Solutions Inc.................... 207 893-1510
3161 Hotel Rd Auburn (04210) *(G-4432)*

Flue Master, Sanford *Also Called: Maine Stove & Chimney LLC (G-5399)*

Fluent Technologies Inc.................... 781 939-0900
331 Montvale Ave Ste 300 Woburn (01801) *(G-13568)*

Fluid Dynamics LLC.................... 860 791-6325
192 Sheldon Rd Manchester (06042) *(G-1598)*

Fluid Management Systems Inc.................... 617 393-2396
900 Technology Park Dr Ste 101 Billerica (01821) *(G-6448)*

Fluidform Inc.................... 978 287-4698
283 Bear Hill Rd Waltham (02451) *(G-12676)*

Fluigent Inc.................... 978 934-5283
73 Princeton St Ste 310 North Chelmsford (01863) *(G-10976)*

Fluorolite Plastics LLC.................... 508 788-1200
555 Main St Hudson (01749) *(G-9368)*

Fluoropolymer Resources LLC **(PA)**.................... **860 423-7622**
99 Eriver Dr Riverview Sq Ii East Hartford (06108) *(G-994)*

Fluted Partition Inc.................... 203 334-3500
850 Union Ave Bridgeport (06607) *(G-321)*

Fluted Partition Inc **(PA)**.................... **203 368-2548**
850 Union Ave Bridgeport (06607) *(G-322)*

Flux Cyber Inc.................... 617 440-4655
275 Newbury St Ste 3 Boston (02116) *(G-6741)*

Flw Associates, Walpole *Also Called: Frank W Whitcomb Cnstr Corp (G-15661)*

Fly Rod & Reel, Rockport *Also Called: D E Enterprise Inc (G-5346)*

Flying Colors, Boston *Also Called: Faverco Inc (G-6732)*

Flying Kites.................... 401 575-0009
103 Central St Unit G Wellesley (02482) *(G-12941)*

FMC, Topsfield *Also Called: Fairview Machine Company Inc (G-12435)*

FMC Corporation.................... 207 594-3200
341 Park St Rockland (04841) *(G-5329)*

Fms New York Services LLC **(DH)**.................... **781 699-9000**
920 Winter St Waltham (02451) *(G-12677)*

Fnsj Inc.................... 617 302-2882
70 Quincy Ave Quincy (02169) *(G-11519)*

Foam Brewers LLC.................... 802 399-2511
112 Lake St Burlington (05401) *(G-17136)*

Foam Laminates of Vermont, Starksboro *Also Called: Acer Holdings Starksboro Inc (G-17625)*

Foam Systems LLC.................... 800 853-1577
30 Muller Ave Ste 19 Norwalk (06851) *(G-2502)*

Foamtech LLC.................... 978 343-4022
1 Nursery Ln Fitchburg (01420) *(G-8655)*

Focal Metals.................... 203 743-4443
11 Trowbridge Dr Bethel (06801) *(G-115)*

Focus Fabrication LLC.................... 860 604-8018
76 Pole Bridge Rd Woodstock (06281) *(G-4394)*

Focus Medical LLC.................... 203 730-8885
23 Francis J Clarke Cir Bethel (06801) *(G-116)*

Focus Technologies Inc.................... 860 829-8998
600 Four Rod Rd Ste 5 Berlin (06037) *(G-65)*

Focused Impressions Tech LLC.................... 857 453-6771
800 Boylston St Fl 16 Boston (02199) *(G-6742)*

Fog Pharmaceuticals Inc.................... 617 945-9510
30 Acorn Park Dr Cambridge (02140) *(G-7571)*

FOGHORN THERAPEUTICS, Cambridge *Also Called: Foghorn Therapeutics Inc (G-7572)*

Foghorn Therapeutics Inc **(PA)**.................... **617 586-3100**
500 Technology Sq Ste 700 Cambridge (02139) *(G-7572)*

Foilmark Inc.................... 860 243-0343
40 E Newberry Rd Bloomfield (06002) *(G-165)*

Foilmark Inc **(HQ)**.................... **978 225-8200**
5 Malcolm Hoyt Dr Newburyport (01950) *(G-10683)*

Folder-Glr Techl Svs Grp LLC.................... 603 635-7400
30 Pulpit Rock Rd Pelham (03076) *(G-15288)*

Foldrx Pharmaceuticals Inc **(HQ)**.................... **617 252-5500**
100 Acorn Park Dr # 5 Cambridge (02140) *(G-7573)*

Foley Fish, New Bedford *Also Called: M F Fley Incrprtd-New Bdford (G-10616)*

Foley Marine & Industrial Engs, Worcester *Also Called: Js Sale Corp (G-13746)*

Foleys Pump Service Inc.................... 203 792-2236
30 Miry Brook Rd Danbury (06810) *(G-747)*

Folia Materials Inc.................... 315 559-2135
3 Loomis St Bedford (01730) *(G-6227)*

Folia Water, Bedford *Also Called: Folia Materials Inc (G-6227)*

Folio Associates, Hyannis *Also Called: Gatco Inc (G-9437)*

Food Atmtn - Svc Tchniques LLC **(PA)**.................... **203 377-4414**
905 Honeyspot Rd Stratford (06615) *(G-3537)*

Food Bevs Spclty Import Export, West Roxbury *Also Called: Inkamazon LLC (G-13012)*

Foodberry, Boston *Also Called: Foodberry Inc (G-6743)*

Foodberry Inc.................... 617 491-6600
75 Sprague St Boston (02136) *(G-6743)*

Foodscience LLC **(HQ)**.................... **800 451-5190**
929 Harvest Ln Williston (05495) *(G-17731)*

Footprint Pwr Acquisitions LLC.................... 978 740-8411
24 Fort Ave Salem (01970) *(G-11715)*

Footwear Specialties Inc.................... 207 284-5003
16 Pomerleau St Biddeford (04005) *(G-4566)*

Force3 Pro Gear, Stratford *Also Called: Force3 Pro Gear LLC (G-3538)*

Force3 Pro Gear LLC.................... 315 367-2331
240 Hathaway Dr Stratford (06615) *(G-3538)*

Forced Exposure Inc.................... 781 321-0320
60 Lowell St Arlington (02476) *(G-5940)*

Forecast International Inc.................... 203 426-0800
75 Glen Rd Ste 302 Sandy Hook (06482) *(G-2951)*

Forecast Pro, Waltham *Also Called: Business Forecast Systems Inc (G-12614)*

Forecaster, South Portland *Also Called: Forecaster Publishing Inc (G-5503)*

Forecaster Publishing Inc.................... 207 781-3661
295 Gannett Dr South Portland (04106) *(G-5503)*

Foredom Electric Co, Bethel *Also Called: Blackstone Industries LLC (G-101)*

Forefield Inc.................... 508 630-1100
33 Boston Post Rd W Ste 190 Marlborough (01752) *(G-10150)*

Forest Chester Products Inc.................... 207 794-2303
Rte 116 Lincoln (04457) *(G-5008)*

Forest Manufacturing Corp.................... 603 647-6991
8 Grey Point Ave Auburn (03032) *(G-13907)*

Forest Northland Products Inc **(PA)**.................... **603 642-3665**
16 Church St Kingston (03848) *(G-14635)*

Forestville Machine Company.................... 860 747-6000
355 S Washington St Plainville (06062) *(G-2760)*

Forge Baking Company Inc.................... 617 764-5365
12 Elder Ter Arlington (02474) *(G-5941)*

Form Centerless Grinding Inc.................... 508 520-0900
1 Kenwood Cir Franklin (02038) *(G-8837)*

Form Roll Die Corp **(PA)**.................... **508 755-2010**
217 Stafford St Worcester (01603) *(G-13725)*

Form Roll Die Corp.................... 508 755-5302
88 Webster Pl Worcester (01603) *(G-13726)*

Form-All Plastics Corp.................... 203 634-1137
104 Gracey Ave Meriden (06451) *(G-1668)*

Forma Therapeutics, Watertown *Also Called: Forma Therapeutics Inc (G-12877)*

Forma Therapeutics Inc **(DH)**.................................... **617 679-1970**
   300 North Beacon St Ste 501 Watertown (02472) *(G-12877)*

Forma Thrapeutics Holdings Inc **(HQ)**........................ **617 679-1970**
   300 North Beacon St Ste 501 Watertown (02472) *(G-12878)*

Formation Inc.. 650 257-2277
   200 Pier 4 Blvd Ste 1000 Boston (02210) *(G-6744)*

Formation Systems, Boston *Also Called: Formation Inc (G-6744)*

Formatron Ltd.. 860 676-0227
   21 Hyde Rd Ste 3 Farmington (06032) *(G-1220)*

Formed Fiber Technologies Inc...................................... 207 784-1118
   125 Allied Rd Auburn (04210) *(G-4433)*

Formex Inc... 401 885-9800
   3305 S County Trl East Greenwich (02818) *(G-15986)*

Formlabs Inc **(PA)**.. **617 932-5227**
   35 Medford St Ste 201 Somerville (02143) *(G-11875)*

Forrati Manufacturing & TI LLC...................................... 860 426-1105
   411 Summer St Plantsville (06479) *(G-2791)*

Forrest Machine Inc.. 860 563-1796
   236 Christian Ln Berlin (06037) *(G-66)*

Forsake Inc.. 585 576-6358
   219 Wood Rd Stowe (05672) *(G-17631)*

Fort Hill Sign Products Inc.. 781 321-4320
   3b Landing Ln Hopedale (01747) *(G-9297)*

Fort Point Cabinet Makers LLC...................................... 617 338-9487
   21 Drydock Ave Ste 340e Boston (02210) *(G-6745)*

Forte Carbon Fiber Products, Ledyard *Also Called: Forte Rts Inc (G-1551)*

Forte Rts Inc.. 860 464-5221
   14 Lorenz Industrial Pkwy Ledyard (06339) *(G-1551)*

Forte Technology Inc... 508 297-2363
   58 Norfolk Ave Ste 4 South Easton (02375) *(G-11943)*

Forterra Pipe & Precast LLC... 860 564-9000
   174 All Hallows Rd Wauregan (06387) *(G-4040)*

Forterra Pipe & Precast LLC... 508 881-2000
   400 Main St Ashland (01721) *(G-5958)*

Forterra Pipe & Precast LLC... 401 782-2600
   170 Fiore Industrial Dr Peace Dale (02879) *(G-16433)*

Forthill Resources LLC... 617 849-0768
   100 Westminster St # 1500 Providence (02903) *(G-16519)*

Fortifiber LLC.. 508 222-3500
   55 Starkey Ave Attleboro (02703) *(G-6018)*

Fortis Solutions Group LLC.. 860 872-6311
   374 Somers Rd Ellington (06029) *(G-1107)*

Fortress Biotech Inc.. 781 652-4500
   95 Sawyer Rd Ste 110 Waltham (02453) *(G-12678)*

Fortune Marketing, Barre *Also Called: Jet Service Envelope Co Inc (G-17010)*

Fortune Plastics Inc.. 800 243-0306
   1 Williams Ln Old Saybrook (06475) *(G-2648)*

Fortune Rope & Metal Co Inc **(PA)**.............................. **800 416-6595**
   67 Ballou Blvd Bristol (02809) *(G-15765)*

Forum Plastics LLC... 203 754-0777
   105 Progress Ln Waterbury (06705) *(G-3913)*

Forward Photonics LLC... 978 224-5488
   10c Commerce Way Woburn (01801) *(G-13569)*

Foss Performance Materials LLC, Hampton *Also Called: Aj Nonwovens - Hampton LLC (G-14397)*

Fosta-Tek Optics Inc **(PA)**.. **978 534-6511**
   320 Hamilton St Ste 1 Leominster (01453) *(G-9665)*

Foster Corporation **(HQ)**... **860 928-4102**
   45 Ridge Rd Putnam (06260) *(G-2855)*

Foster Corporation.. 860 377-7117
   38 Ridge Rd Putnam (06260) *(G-2856)*

Foster Delivery Science, Putnam *Also Called: Foster Corporation (G-2855)*

Foster Delivery Science Inc **(HQ)**............................... **860 541-5280**
   36 Ridge Rd Putnam (06260) *(G-2857)*

Foster Delivery Science Inc.. 860 630-4515
   45 Ridge Rd Putnam (06260) *(G-2858)*

Foster Industries Inc... 802 472-6147
   75 Cal Foster Dr Wolcott (05680) *(G-17774)*

Fosters Daily Democrat.. 603 332-2200
   90 N Main St Rochester (03867) *(G-15476)*

Fosters Daily Dmcrat Fstrs Sun...................................... 603 431-4888
   111 Nh Ave Portsmouth (03801) *(G-15390)*

Fougera Pharmaceuticals Inc... 203 265-2086
   524 S Cherry St Wallingford (06492) *(G-3807)*

Found Energy Co... 201 315-9955
   50 Terminal St Ste 2 Charlestown (02129) *(G-7873)*

Foundation Armor LLC.. 866 306-0246
   3 Howe Dr Ste 2 Amherst (03031) *(G-13870)*

Foundation Brewing Company.. 207 370-8187
   1 Industrial Way Portland (04103) *(G-5217)*

Foundation Cigar, Ellington *Also Called: Foundation Cigar Company LLC (G-1108)*

Foundation Cigar Company LLC..................................... 203 738-9377
   78 Abbott Rd Ellington (06029) *(G-1108)*

Foundation Devices Inc.. 617 283-8306
   6 Liberty Sq Ste 6018 Boston (02109) *(G-6746)*

Foundry Specialty Coatings LLC..................................... 978 518-9990
   200 Pleasant St Tewksbury (01876) *(G-12400)*

Foundtion For Dmcracy In Ukrin..................................... 617 496-8816
   79 Jfk St Cambridge (02138) *(G-7574)*

Fountain Dispensers Co Inc... 401 461-8400
   35 Greenwich St Providence (02907) *(G-16520)*

Fountain Plating Company LLC....................................... 413 781-4651
   492 Prospect Ave West Springfield (01089) *(G-13025)*

Four In One LLC.. 978 250-0751
   12 Alpha Rd Chelmsford (01824) *(G-7929)*

Four Phantoms Brewing Co LLC..................................... 931 247-0315
   33 Forest Ave Greenfield (01301) *(G-8991)*

Four Seasons Fence, Portsmouth *Also Called: Chasco Inc (G-15371)*

Four Star Manufacturing Co.. 860 583-1614
   400 Riverside Ave Bristol (06010) *(G-448)*

Fourslide Spring Stamping Inc.. 860 583-1688
   87 Cross St Bristol (06010) *(G-449)*

Fourstar Connections Inc.. 978 568-9800
   One Robert Bonazzoli Ave Hudson (01749) *(G-9369)*

Fowler D J Log Land Clearing.. 860 742-5842
   150 Plains Rd Coventry (06238) *(G-679)*

Fowler Printing & Graphics Inc....................................... 781 986-8900
   132 York Ave Randolph (02368) *(G-11558)*

Fowler Printing and Graphics, Randolph *Also Called: Fowler Printing & Graphics Inc (G-11558)*

Fox Homes Inc.. 413 243-1950
   225 Housatonic St Lee (01238) *(G-9613)*

Fox Steel Products LLC... 203 799-2356
   312 Boston Post Rd Orange (06477) *(G-2669)*

Fox Valley Paint Inc.. 844 627-5255
   5a Production Dr Brookfield (06804) *(G-520)*

Foxborough Taproom, Foxborough *Also Called: Wormtown Brewery LLC (G-8738)*

Foxees Co Inc.. 508 548-8485
   419 Palmer Ave Ste 6 Falmouth (02540) *(G-8632)*

Foxon Park Beverages Inc.. 203 467-7874
   103 Foxon Blvd East Haven (06513) *(G-1042)*

Foxrock Granite LLC... 617 249-8015
   100 Newport Ave Quincy (02171) *(G-11520)*

Foxx Life Sciences LLC **(PA)**...................................... **603 890-3699**
   6 Delaware Dr Salem (03079) *(G-15528)*

Fpp Holdings LLC.. 401 684-1443
   2000 Chapel View Blvd Ste 450 Cranston (02920) *(G-15862)*

Fraen, Reading *Also Called: Fraen Corporation (G-11601)*

Fraen Corporation **(PA)**... **781 205-5300**
   80 New Crossing Rd Reading (01867) *(G-11601)*

Fraen Corporation... 781 937-8825
   324 New Boston St Woburn (01801) *(G-13570)*

Fraen Machining Corporation **(PA)**............................. **781 205-5400**
   324 New Boston St Woburn (01801) *(G-13571)*

Framingham Tab, Framingham *Also Called: Gatehouse Media Mass I Inc (G-8764)*

Framingham Welding & Engineering Corporation
   120 Leland St Framingham (01702) *(G-8763)*

Francer Industries Inc
   77 Green St Carver (02330) *(G-7854)*

Frank B Struzik Inc.. 401 766-6880
   129 Ballou St Woonsocket (02895) *(G-16960)*

Frank I Rounds Company **(PA)**.................................... **401 333-5014**
   65 York Ave Randolph (02368) *(G-11559)*

Frank J Newman & Son Inc ... 401 231-0550
200 Rocky Hill Rd North Scituate (02857) ***(G-16315)***

Frank L Reed Inc ... 413 596-3861
2443 Boston Rd Wilbraham (01095) ***(G-13359)***

Frank Lombardo and Sons Inc ... 401 461-4547
78 Narragansett Ave Providence (02907) ***(G-16521)***

Frank Roth Co Inc ... 203 377-2155
1795 Stratford Ave Stratford (06615) ***(G-3539)***

Frank Shatz & Co ... 401 739-1822
61 Dewey Ave Ste D Warwick (02886) ***(G-16816)***

Frank Smith ... 203 729-6434
60 Great Hill Rd Naugatuck (06770) ***(G-1959)***

Frank W Whitcomb Cnstr Corp **(PA)** ... **603 445-5555**
187 Whitcomb Rd Walpole (03608) ***(G-15661)***

Frank W Whitcomb Cnstr Corp ... 802 655-1270
115 Whitcomb St Colchester (05446) ***(G-17191)***

Frank's Bake Shop & Catering, Bangor *Also Called: Franks Bake Shop Inc* ***(G-4502)***

Franklin Exeter Inc ... 603 836-8590
222 International Dr Ste 135 Portsmouth (03801) ***(G-15391)***

Franklin Fixtures Inc **(PA)** ... **508 291-1475**
20 Pattersons Brook Rd Ste 4 West Wareham (02576) ***(G-13065)***

Franklin Foods Inc **(DH)** ... **802 933-4338**
68 East St Enosburg Falls (05450) ***(G-17223)***

Franklin Grid Solutions LLC **(HQ)** ... **207 571-1123**
34 Spring Hill Rd Saco (04072) ***(G-5366)***

Franklin Group ... 207 778-2075
187 Wilton Rd Farmington (04938) ***(G-4780)***

Franklin Impressions Inc ... 860 887-1661
327 Laurel Hill Ave Norwich (06360) ***(G-2605)***

Franklin Journal, The, Farmington *Also Called: Franklin Group* ***(G-4780)***

Franklin Paint Company Inc ... 800 486-0304
259 Cottage St Franklin (02038) ***(G-8838)***

Franklin Products Inc **(PA)** ... **860 482-0266**
153 Water St Torrington (06790) ***(G-3681)***

Franklin Sheet Metal Works Inc ... 508 528-3600
231 Cottage St Franklin (02038) ***(G-8839)***

Franklin's Printing, Farmington *Also Called: Nemi Publishing Inc* ***(G-4782)***

Franks Bake Shop Inc ... 207 947-4594
199 State St Bangor (04401) ***(G-4502)***

Frasal Tool Co Inc ... 860 666-3524
14 Foster St Newington (06111) ***(G-2295)***

Frazier Signal Tech LLC **(PA)** ... **207 991-0543**
1506 State St Veazie (04401) ***(G-5571)***

Frc Founders Corporation **(PA)** ... **203 661-6601**
290 Harbor Dr Stamford (06902) ***(G-3348)***

Fred F Waltz Co Inc ... 401 769-4900
58 Silo Dr Cumberland (02864) ***(G-15940)***

Fred Ricci Tool Co Inc ... 401 464-9911
165 Dyerville Ave Unit 2 Johnston (02919) ***(G-16086)***

Fredenberg-Nok Seals Division, Ashland *Also Called: Freudenberg-Nok General Partnr* ***(G-13900)***

Frederick Purdue Company Inc **(PA)** ... **203 588-8000**
201 Tresser Blvd Stamford (06901) ***(G-3349)***

Fredericks Pastries **(PA)** ... **603 882-7725**
109 State Route 101a Ste 4 Amherst (03031) ***(G-13871)***

Free Press ... 413 587-3770
26 Center St Apt 2 Northampton (01060) ***(G-11062)***

Free Press Inc ... 207 594-4408
8 N Main St Ste 101 Rockland (04841) ***(G-5330)***

Free Software Foundation Inc ... 617 542-5942
51 Franklin St Ste 500 Boston (02110) ***(G-6747)***

Free Times, West Warwick *Also Called: Kent County Daily Times* ***(G-16911)***

Freeaire Refrigeration, Buzzards Bay *Also Called: Mv3 LLC* ***(G-7455)***

Freedom Auto and Tire, Plaistow *Also Called: Freedom Tire Inc* ***(G-15344)***

Freedom Digital Printing LLC ... 508 881-6940
200 Butterfield Dr Ste A2 Ashland (01721) ***(G-5959)***

Freedom Foods LLC ... 802 728-0070
300 Beanville Rd Randolph (05060) ***(G-17468)***

Freedom Grafix LLC ... 815 900-6189
457 Castle Ave Fairfield (06825) ***(G-1186)***

Freedom Technologies LLC ... 860 633-0452
80 Timrod Trl Glastonbury (06033) ***(G-1278)***

Freedom Tire Inc **(PA)** ... **603 382-7223**
37 Westville Rd Plaistow (03865) ***(G-15344)***

Freeds Bakery LLC ... 603 627-7746
299 Pepsi Rd Manchester (03109) ***(G-14849)***

Freepoint Eco-Systems LLC ... 203 542-6000
58 Commerce Rd Stamford (06902) ***(G-3350)***

Freethink Technologies Inc ... 860 237-5800
35 Ne Industrial Rd Branford (06405) ***(G-258)***

Freeze Operations Holding Corp **(PA)** ... **413 543-2445**
1855 Boston Rd Wilbraham (01095) ***(G-13360)***

Freight Farms, Boston *Also Called: Freight Farms Inc* ***(G-6748)***

Freight Farms Inc ... 877 687-4326
20 Old Colony Ave Ste 201 Boston (02127) ***(G-6748)***

Frelonic, Saco *Also Called: Der-Tex Corporation* ***(G-5365)***

Fremco LLC ... 203 857-0522
25 Washington Ct Apt 7-6 Stamford (06902) ***(G-3351)***

FREMONT ENGINEERING, Fremont *Also Called: Fremont Machine & Tool Co Inc* ***(G-14327)***

Fremont Machine & Tool Co Inc ... 603 895-9445
810 Main St Fremont (03044) ***(G-14327)***

French Packaging Services, Canton *Also Called: Abbott-Action Inc* ***(G-7765)***

French Press LLC ... 781 400-2660
74 Chapel St Needham (02492) ***(G-10511)***

French Webb & Co Inc ... 207 338-6706
21 Front St Belfast (04915) ***(G-4533)***

Frendzi Inc ... 617 899-0234
275 Grove St Newton (02466) ***(G-10756)***

Fresenius Kabi Compounding LLC ... 224 358-1150
20 Dan Rd Canton (02021) ***(G-7792)***

Fresenius Kabi Usa LLC ... 978 775-8050
50 High St Ste 50 North Andover (01845) ***(G-10833)***

Fresenius Med Care Hldings Inc **(DH)** ... **781 699-9000**
920 Winter St Ste A Waltham (02451) ***(G-12679)***

Fresenius Med Care Rnal Thrpie ... 781 699-9000
920 Winter St Ste A Waltham (02451) ***(G-12680)***

Fresenius Med Care Vntures LLC **(DH)** ... **781 699-9000**
920 Winter St Ste A Waltham (02451) ***(G-12681)***

Fresenius Med Svcs Group LLC ... 781 699-9000
920 Winter St Ste A Waltham (02451) ***(G-12682)***

Fresenius Medical Care, Waltham *Also Called: Fresenius Usa Inc* ***(G-12683)***

Fresenius Medical Care N Amer, Waltham *Also Called: Fresenius Med Care Hldings Inc* ***(G-12679)***

Fresenius Rnal Pharmaceuticals, Waltham *Also Called: Fresenius USA Marketing Inc* ***(G-12684)***

Fresenius Usa Inc **(DH)** ... **781 699-4191**
920 Winter St Waltham (02451) ***(G-12683)***

Fresenius USA Marketing Inc **(DH)** ... **781 699-9000**
920 Winter St Waltham (02451) ***(G-12684)***

Fresh Ink LLC ... 860 656-7013
216 Park Rd Ste 3 West Hartford (06119) ***(G-4061)***

Freshco ... 401 351-1911
15 Clarkson St Providence (02908) ***(G-16522)***

Freshwater Stone & Brickwork ... 207 469-6331
4 Upper Falls Rd Orland (04472) ***(G-5132)***

Freudenberg Medical LLC ... 978 281-2023
40 Sam Fonzo Dr Beverly (01915) ***(G-6349)***

Freudenberg Nok, Beverly *Also Called: Freudenberg Medical LLC* ***(G-6349)***

Freudenberg-Nok General Partnr ... 603 968-7187
125 Main St Ashland (03217) ***(G-13900)***

Freudenberg-Nok General Partnr ... 603 744-0371
450 Pleasant St Bristol (03222) ***(G-14034)***

Freudenberg-Nok General Partnr ... 603 934-7800
450 Pleasant St Bristol (03222) ***(G-14035)***

Freudenberg-Nok General Partnr ... 603 286-1600
6 Axle Dr Northfield (03276) ***(G-15265)***

Freudenberg-Nok General Partnr ... 603 286-1600
19 Axle Dr Northfield (03276) ***(G-15266)***

Freudenberg-Nok General Partnr, Northfield *Also Called: Technical Tool & Design LLC* ***(G-15269)***

Freudenberg-Nok Gnrl Prtnrshp ... 603 628-7023
11 Ricker Ave Londonderry (03053) ***(G-14752)***

Frevvo Inc ... 203 208-3117
500 E Main St Ste 330 Branford (06405) ***(G-259)***

Frevvo LLC ... 203 208-3117
82 Anderson Rd Wallingford (06492) ***(G-3808)***

ALPHABETIC

Frg Publications.. 413 734-3411
  12 Tatham Hill Rd West Springfield (01089) *(G-13026)*

Fri Resins Holding Company... 401 946-5564
  21 Starline Way Cranston (02921) *(G-15863)*

Friend Box Company Inc.. 978 774-0240
  90 High St Danvers (01923) *(G-8187)*

Friends Foundry Inc.. 401 769-0160
  416 Pond St Woonsocket (02895) *(G-16961)*

Frito-Lay, Wilmington *Also Called: Frito-Lay North America Inc (G-13408)*

Frito-Lay North America Inc... 978 657-8344
  337 Ballardvale St Wilmington (01887) *(G-13408)*

Fronek Anchor Darling Entp.. 603 528-1931
  86 Doris Ray Ct Laconia (03246) *(G-14651)*

Front Line Apparel Group LLC... 860 859-3524
  33 Pendleton Dr Hebron (06248) *(G-1527)*

Front Line Group, The, Hebron *Also Called: Front Line Apparel Group LLC (G-1527)*

Frontgrade Technologies Inc... 603 775-5200
  11 Continental Dr Exeter (03833) *(G-14292)*

Frontier Design Group LLC.. 603 448-6283
  31 Old Etna Rd Ste N5 Lebanon (03766) *(G-14688)*

Frontier Forge Inc.. 207 265-2151
  37 Depot St Kingfield (04947) *(G-4933)*

Frontier Vision Tech Inc.. 860 953-0240
  2049 Silas Deane Hwy Ste 1c Rocky Hill (06067) *(G-2922)*

Frost Cedar Products Inc... 207 566-5912
  Fahi Pond Rd North Anson (04958) *(G-5105)*

Frostbite Cupcakes.. 508 801-6706
  230 Chestnut Oak Rd Chepachet (02814) *(G-15804)*

Frozen Batters Inc.. 508 683-1414
  351 Willow St North Andover (01845) *(G-10834)*

Frozen Desserts, Winchester *Also Called: Philip RS Sorbet Co Inc (G-13491)*

Frs Company Inc... 781 322-6252
  11 Salem St Ste 12 Medford (02155) *(G-10285)*

Frs Roofing and Gutter Svcs, Medford *Also Called: Frs Company Inc (G-10285)*

Frugal Printer Inc... 603 894-6333
  47a Northwestern Dr Salem (03079) *(G-15529)*

Fruit & Nut House, Warwick *Also Called: Lady Ann Candies Inc (G-16832)*

Fsb Inc.. 203 404-4700
  24 New Park Dr Berlin (06037) *(G-67)*

Fsb North America, Berlin *Also Called: Fsb Inc (G-67)*

Fsm Plasticoid Mfg Inc... 860 623-1361
  400 Governor St East Hartford (06108) *(G-995)*

Fswh Intl Holdings LLC **(HQ)**... **781 622-1000**
  168 3rd Ave Waltham (02451) *(G-12685)*

Ftc Inc **(PA)**.. **207 354-2545**
  570 Cushing Rd Friendship (04547) *(G-4806)*

FTC Enterprises Inc... 508 378-2799
  170 W Union St East Bridgewater (02333) *(G-8340)*

Ftg Circuits Haverhill Inc.. 978 373-9190
  140 Hilldale Ave Haverhill (01832) *(G-9095)*

Fuccillo Ready Mix Inc.. 508 540-2821
  548 Thomas B Landers Rd East Falmouth (02536) *(G-8360)*

Fudge Factory Inc.. 888 669-7425
  4367 Main St Manchester Center (05255) *(G-17328)*

Fuel America.. 617 782-0999
  152 Chestnut Hill Ave Brighton (02135) *(G-7240)*

Fuel Cell Manufacturing, Torrington *Also Called: Fuelcell Energy Inc (G-3682)*

Fuel First Elm Inc... 413 732-5732
  173 Elm St West Springfield (01089) *(G-13027)*

Fuel For Fire Inc.. 508 975-4573
  60 Kendrick St Ste 200 Needham Heights (02494) *(G-10548)*

Fuel Source Inc... 781 469-8449
  960 Providence Hwy Norwood (02062) *(G-11173)*

Fuel Wholesale, New Milford *Also Called: Anz Petroleum Inc (G-2238)*

Fuelcell Energy, Danbury *Also Called: Fuelcell Energy Inc (G-748)*

Fuelcell Energy Inc **(PA)**... **203 825-6000**
  3 Great Pasture Rd Danbury (06810) *(G-748)*

Fuelcell Energy Inc.. 860 496-1111
  539 Technology Park Dr Torrington (06790) *(G-3682)*

Fueling Services LLC.. 401 764-0711
  141 Shun Pike Johnston (02919) *(G-16087)*

Fujifilm Dimatix Inc.. 603 443-5300
  109 Etna Rd Lebanon (03766) *(G-14689)*

Fujifilm Elctrnic Mtls USA Inc... 203 363-3360
  419 West Ave Stamford (06902) *(G-3352)*

Fujifilm Hlthcare Amricas Corp **(DH)**................................. **203 324-2000**
  81 Hartwell Ave Ste 300 Lexington (02421) *(G-9743)*

Fujifilm Microdisks U.S.a, Bedford *Also Called: Fujifilm Rcrding Media USA Inc (G-6228)*

Fujifilm NDT Systems, Stamford *Also Called: Fujifilm Elctrnic Mtls USA Inc (G-3352)*

Fujifilm Rcrding Media USA Inc **(DH)**................................. **781 271-4400**
  45 Crosby Dr Bedford (01730) *(G-6228)*

Fulcrum Speedworks LLC.. 401 524-3953
  310 Bourne Ave Ste 29 Rumford (02916) *(G-16667)*

Fulcrum Therapeutics Inc **(PA)**.. **617 651-8851**
  26 Landsdowne St Ste 525 Cambridge (02139) *(G-7575)*

Fulcrum Thrptics Scrities Corp.. 617 651-8851
  26 Landsdowne St Ste 525 Cambridge (02139) *(G-7576)*

Fulflex, Brattleboro *Also Called: Garware Fulflex USA Inc (G-17085)*

Fulford Findings, Providence *Also Called: Salvadore Tool & Findings Inc (G-16609)*

Fulford Manufacturing Company **(PA)**................................. **401 431-2000**
  65 Tripps Ln Riverside (02915) *(G-16655)*

Fulghum Fibres Inc.. 207 427-6560
  224 Main St Baileyville (04694) *(G-4483)*

Full Circle Padding Inc... 508 285-2500
  253 Mansfield Ave Norton (02766) *(G-11127)*

Full Circle Technologies Inc.. 617 722-0100
  11 Beacon St Ste 340 Boston (02108) *(G-6749)*

Full Court Press... 207 464-0002
  855 Main St Ste 2 Westbrook (04092) *(G-5626)*

Fuller Box, North Attleboro *Also Called: Fuller Box Co Inc (G-10871)*

Fuller Box Co Inc **(PA)**.. **508 695-2525**
  150 Chestnut St North Attleboro (02760) *(G-10871)*

Fuller Box Co Inc... 401 725-4300
  1152 High St Central Falls (02863) *(G-15788)*

Fuller Machine Co Inc.. 603 835-6559
  5 Gilsum Mine Rd Alstead (03602) *(G-13857)*

Fuller Packaging, Central Falls *Also Called: Fuller Box Co Inc (G-15788)*

Fully Rooted Inc... 401 429-8768
  560 Mineral Spring Ave Unit 120 Pawtucket (02860) *(G-16370)*

Functional Assessment Tech Inc... 978 663-2800
  76 Treble Cove Rd Ste 3 North Billerica (01862) *(G-10912)*

Functional Coatings LLC.. 978 462-0796
  13 Malcolm Hoyt Dr Newburyport (01950) *(G-10684)*

Functional Inks Inc.. 413 363-0770
  150 Front St Ste 2 West Springfield (01089) *(G-13028)*

Furbush Roberts Prtg Co Inc.. 207 945-9409
  435 Odlin Rd Bangor (04401) *(G-4503)*

Furci Communications Inc.. 203 961-1800
  652 Glenbrook Rd Ste 4-101 Stamford (06906) *(G-3353)*

Furlongs Cttage Cndies Ice Cre.. 781 762-4124
  1355 Boston Providence Tpke Norwood (02062) *(G-11174)*

Furnace Source LLC... 860 582-4201
  99 Agney Ave Terryville (06786) *(G-3603)*

Furnished Quarters LLC... 212 367-9400
  303 3rd St Cambridge (02142) *(G-7577)*

Furniture Concepts.. 781 324-8668
  7 Cross St Malden (02148) *(G-10015)*

Furniture Design Services Inc... 978 531-3250
  119 Foster St Bldg 13 Peabody (01960) *(G-11310)*

Fuse Builds LLC **(PA)**... **617 602-4001**
  65 Allerton St Roxbury (02119) *(G-11691)*

Fused Fiberoptics, Southbridge *Also Called: Fused Fiberoptics LLC (G-12017)*

Fused Fiberoptics LLC... 508 765-1652
  79 Golf St Southbridge (01550) *(G-12017)*

Fusion Optix Inc.. 781 995-0805
  17 Wheeling Ave Woburn (01801) *(G-13572)*

Fusion Paperboard, Versailles *Also Called: Fusion Paperboard Connecticut LLC (G-3764)*

Fusion Paperboard Connecticut LLC...................................... 888 283-3617
  130 Inland Rd Versailles (06383) *(G-3764)*

Fusion Paperboard US Inc.. 859 586-1100
  130 Inland Rd Versailles (06383) *(G-3765)*

Fusion Pharmaceuticals US Inc... 617 420-5698
  451 D St Ste 930 Boston (02210) *(G-6750)*

(G-0000) Company's Geographic Section entry number

Futuramik Industries Inc.................................... 860 951-3121
245 Hamilton St Hartford (06106) *(G-1481)*

Future Classics USA LLC **(PA)**........................ **860 838-4688**
1030 Washington Woodbury Rd Roxbury (06783) *(G-2944)*

Future Foam Inc.. 508 339-0354
47 Maple St Mansfield (02048) *(G-10052)*

Future Manufacturing Inc................................... 860 584-0685
75 Center St Bristol (06010) *(G-450)*

Futureguard Building Pdts Inc **(PA)**................... **800 858-5818**
101 Merrow Rd Auburn (04210) *(G-4434)*

Fwm Inc.. 603 578-3366
11 Friars Dr Hudson (03051) *(G-14497)*

Fx Group... 508 987-1366
2 Hawksley Rd Ste B Oxford (01540) *(G-11254)*

Fyc Apparel Group LLC...................................... 203 466-6525
158 Commerce St East Haven (06512) *(G-1043)*

Fyc Apparel Group LLC **(PA)**............................ **203 481-2420**
30 Thompson Rd Branford (06405) *(G-260)*

G & A Machine Inc.. 603 894-6965
168 Lawrence Rd Salem (03079) *(G-15530)*

G & A Plating & Polishing Co, Cranston *Also Called: Jrb Associates Inc (G-15881)*

G & D Tool Co Inc.. 978 745-0020
12 Proctor St Salem (01970) *(G-11716)*

G & G Beverage Distributors................................ 203 949-6220
207 Church St Yalesville (06492) *(G-4397)*

G & G Dissolution Corp...................................... 860 633-7099
137 National Dr Glastonbury (06033) *(G-1279)*

G & G Machining, Kennebunk *Also Called: G & G Products LLC (G-4925)*

G & G Products LLC.. 207 985-9100
70 Twine Mill Rd Ste 1 Kennebunk (04043) *(G-4925)*

G & G Recycling Center, Yalesville *Also Called: G & G Beverage Distributors (G-4397)*

G & G Silk Screening.. 508 830-1075
187 Court St Plymouth (02360) *(G-11460)*

G & W Foundry Corp... 508 581-8719
50 Howe Ave Ste G Millbury (01527) *(G-10434)*

G + O Logic LLC.. 413 588-8079
137 High St Belfast (04915) *(G-4534)*

G Austin Young Inc... 508 222-4700
35 County St Attleboro (02703) *(G-6019)*

G E C, Gloucester *Also Called: Gloucester Engineering Co Inc (G-8935)*

G H Bent Company... 617 322-9287
7 Pleasant St Milton (02186) *(G-10452)*

G L C Inc... 860 945-6166
1094 Echo Lake Rd Watertown (06795) *(G-4013)*

G L Roller Division, Weymouth *Also Called: W Oliver Tripp Company (G-13338)*

G M Allen, Orland *Also Called: G M Allen & Son Inc (G-5133)*

G M Allen & Son Inc... 207 469-7060
267 Front Ridge Rd Orland (04472) *(G-5133)*

G M I, Holyoke *Also Called: Gregory Manufacturing Inc (G-9257)*

G M T Manufacturing Co Inc................................ 860 628-6757
220 West St Plantsville (06479) *(G-2792)*

G N Netcom Unex, Lowell *Also Called: Gn Audio USA Inc (G-9881)*

G P Tool Co Inc... 203 744-0310
59 James St Danbury (06810) *(G-749)*

G Pro Industrial Services.................................... 207 766-1671
5 Drapeau St Biddeford (04005) *(G-4567)*

G R Sands Monumental Works............................. 617 522-1001
3859 Washington St Roslindale (02131) *(G-11666)*

G S I, Pascoag *Also Called: S G Inc (G-16340)*

G S P Coatings Inc... 802 257-5858
101 John Seitz Dr Brattleboro (05301) *(G-17083)*

G S Precision Inc **(PA)**................................... **802 257-5200**
101 John Seitz Dr Brattleboro (05301) *(G-17084)*

G Schoepferinc... 203 250-7794
460 Cook Hill Rd Cheshire (06410) *(G-594)*

G T R Finishing Corporation................................. 508 588-3240
1 Jonathan Dr Brockton (02301) *(G-7279)*

G Tanury Plating Co Inc..................................... 401 232-2330
1 Oak Grove Blvd North Providence (02911) *(G-16302)*

G V Logging Inc.. 207 231-1003
399 Aroostook Rd Fort Kent (04743) *(G-4789)*

G-Form LLC.. 401 769-0994
1 Tupperware Dr Ste 7 North Smithfield (02896) *(G-16323)*

G-Form LLC **(HQ)**... **401 250-5555**
139 Point St Providence (02903) *(G-16523)*

G. T. Safety Products, Somerset *Also Called: Tamer Industries Inc (G-11856)*

G.S. BLODGETT CORPORATION, Bow *Also Called: GS Blodgett Corporation (G-14000)*

G&E Steel Fabricators Inc................................... 978 741-0391
4 Florence St Unit 5 Salem (01970) *(G-11717)*

G&F Medical Inc.. 978 560-2622
709 Main St Fiskdale (01518) *(G-8638)*

G&F Precision Molding Inc.................................. 978 560-2622
33 Cherry Hill Dr Danvers (01923) *(G-8188)*

G&F Precision Molding Inc **(PA)**........................ **508 347-9132**
709 Main St Fiskdale (01518) *(G-8639)*

G&G Technologies Inc....................................... 401 295-4000
6 Grandview St Coventry (02816) *(G-15813)*

G&H Keene, Keene *Also Called: Gooch & Housego (keene) LLC (G-14601)*

G5 Infrared LLC... 603 304-5722
12 Executive Dr Unit A Hudson (03051) *(G-14498)*

GA Gear, Portland *Also Called: Blue Sky Inc (G-5190)*

GA Rel Manufacturing Company............................ 401 331-5455
564 Manton Ave Providence (02909) *(G-16524)*

Gabriel Business Group Co Ltd............................. 877 401-5544
52 Laurel Crest Dr Brookline (03033) *(G-14039)*

Gac, Agawam *Also Called: Governors America Corporation (G-5791)*

Gac Chemical, Searsport *Also Called: General Alum New England Corp (G-5454)*

Gac Chemical Corporation **(PA)**........................ **207 548-2525**
34 Kidder Point Rd Searsport (04974) *(G-5453)*

Gaftek Inc.. 207 217-6515
160 Perry Rd Bangor (04401) *(G-4504)*

Gagne & Son Con Blocks Inc............................... 207 495-3313
270 Riverside Dr Auburn (04210) *(G-4435)*

Gagne & Son Concrete Blocks Inc **(PA)**............... **207 495-3313**
28 Old Rte 27 Rd Belgrade (04917) *(G-4539)*

Gain Life Inc... 888 412-6041
55 Court St Ste 200 Boston (02108) *(G-6751)*

Galasso Materials LLC....................................... 860 527-1825
60 S Main St East Granby (06026) *(G-934)*

Galaxie Labs Inc... 781 272-3750
18 A St Burlington (01803) *(G-7375)*

Galaxy Fuel LLC.. 203 878-8173
180 New Haven Ave Milford (06460) *(G-1829)*

Galaxy Software Inc.. 617 773-7790
200 Falls Blvd Unit B301 Quincy (02169) *(G-11521)*

Galaxy Stone Inc... 617 461-2790
23 Noel St Amesbury (01913) *(G-5835)*

Galazan's Gun Shop, New Britain *Also Called: Connecticut Shotgun Manufacturing Co (G-2012)*

Galileo Press, Inc., Quincy *Also Called: Rheinwerk Publishing Inc (G-11537)*

Gallery Leather Direct Inc.................................. 207 667-9474
8 Industrial Way Trenton (04605) *(G-5554)*

Gallery Leather Mfg Inc..................................... 207 667-9474
27 Industrial Way Trenton (04605) *(G-5555)*

Galvanic Applied Scnces USA In........................... 978 848-2701
101 Billerica Ave Bldg 5ste104 North Billerica (01862) *(G-10913)*

Galvion Ballistics Ltd.. 802 334-2774
7 Corporate Dr Essex Junction (05452) *(G-17233)*

Galvion Ltd **(HQ)**.. **514 739-4444**
160 Corporate Dr Portsmouth (03801) *(G-15392)*

Gametime Fabrics, Lowell *Also Called: Ames Textile Corporation (G-9853)*

Gamewright, Canton *Also Called: Ceaco Inc (G-7777)*

Gamut Publishing... 860 296-6128
30 Arbor St Unit 101 Hartford (06106) *(G-1482)*

Ganado Storage LLC... 617 605-4322
100 Brickstone Sq Ste 300 Andover (01810) *(G-5884)*

Gandin Brothers Inc... 802 584-3521
87 Stoneshed Rd South Ryegate (05069) *(G-17614)*

Gangi Printing Inc.. 617 776-6071
151 Montvale Ave Woburn (01801) *(G-13573)*

Gannett River States Pubg Corp........................... 802 893-4214
57 Yankee Park Rd Fairfax (05454) *(G-17258)*

Gannon & Scott Inc (PA)... 800 556-7296
  33 Kenney Dr Cranston (02920) (G-15864)

Gapolymer, Woodstock Also Called: Aardvark Polymers (G-4390)

Gar Kenyor Aerospace & Defense, Meriden Also Called: Saf Industries LLC (G-1696)

Garan Enterprises Inc... 413 594-4991
  129 Broadway St Chicopee (01020) (G-8034)

Garaventa U S A Inc.. 603 669-6553
  999 Candia Rd Bldg 2 Manchester (03109) (G-14850)

Garbage Gone Inc.. 508 737-4995
  75 Old Phinneys Ln Barnstable (02630) (G-6200)

Garden By Artech, Leominster Also Called: Allied Resin Technologies LLC (G-9635)

Garden Fresh Salad, Chelsea Also Called: Garden Fresh Salad Co Inc (G-7982)

Garden Fresh Salad Co Inc... 617 889-1580
  15 New England Produce Ctr # 20 Chelsea (02150) (G-7982)

Garden Iron LLC... 860 767-9917
  47 Westbrook Indust Park Rd Westbrook (06498) (G-4138)

Gardener's Supply, Burlington Also Called: Innovtive Grdning Slutions Inc (G-17139)

Gardener's Supply Co, Milton Also Called: Americas Grdening Resource Inc (G-17354)

Gardener's Supply Company, Burlington Also Called: Americas Grdening Resource Inc (G-17117)

Gardenmats.. 802 498-3314
  374 Calais Rd Worcester (05682) (G-17781)

Gardner Chpmlls Mllinocket LLC....................................... 207 794-2223
  820 S Chesterrd Chester (04457) (G-4693)

Gardner Mattress Corporation (PA).................................... 978 744-1810
  254 Canal St Salem (01970) (G-11718)

Gardner Screw Corporation... 978 632-0850
  220 Union St Gardner (01440) (G-8887)

Gardoc Inc (DH).. 603 673-6400
  86 Powers St Milford (03055) (G-15022)

Gare Incorporated... 978 373-9131
  165 Rosemont St Haverhill (01832) (G-9096)

Garelco Sales Company Inc... 413 525-3316
  42 Maple Ct East Longmeadow (01028) (G-8376)

Garelick Farms LLC (DH)... 508 528-9000
  1199 W Central St Ste 1 Franklin (02038) (G-8840)

Garf Trucking Inc... 860 558-8487
  462 Palisado Ave Windsor (06095) (G-4277)

Garlan Chain Co Inc.. 508 399-7288
  417 John L Dietsch Blvd Attleboro Falls (02763) (G-6085)

Garland Lumber Company Inc... 603 356-5636
  636 E Conway Rd Center Conway (03813) (G-14053)

Garland Manufacturing Co.. 207 283-3693
  55 Industrial Park Rd Saco (04072) (G-5367)

Garland Mill, Lancaster Also Called: Southworth Timberframes Inc (G-14679)

Garland Transportation Corp... 603 356-5636
  636 E Conway Rd Center Conway (03813) (G-14054)

Garland Writing Instruments, Newport Also Called: Becker Manufacturing Company (G-16204)

Garlic Press Inc.. 802 864-0670
  614 Macrae Rd Colchester (05446) (G-17192)

Garlock Printing & Converting, Gardner Also Called: First Mate Prtg Converting Inc (G-8886)

Garlock Printing & Converting, Gardner Also Called: GP&c Operations LLC (G-8889)

Garmac Screw Machines Inc.. 203 723-6911
  70 Great Hill Rd Naugatuck (06770) (G-1960)

Garmco, Danbury Also Called: Republic Foil Inc (G-805)

Garmin International Inc... 800 561-5105
  2 Delorme Dr Yarmouth (04096) (G-5704)

Garneau USA Outlet, Derby Also Called: Louis Garneau USA Inc (G-17211)

Garrettcom Inc.. 978 688-8807
  25 Commerce Way Ste 1 North Andover (01845) (G-10835)

Garuka Bars, Burlington Also Called: Gorilla Bars Inc (G-17138)

Garvin Industries Incorporated.. 603 647-5410
  81 Priscilla Ln Auburn (03032) (G-13908)

Garware Fulflex USA Inc.. 802 257-5256
  32 Justin Holden Dr Brattleboro (05301) (G-17085)

Gary M Pomeroy Logging Inc... 207 848-3171
  1909 Hammond St Hermon (04401) (G-4882)

Gary Raymond... 207 498-2549
  1121 Presque Isle Rd Caribou (04736) (G-4675)

Gary Tool Company... 203 377-3077
  26 Grant St Stratford (06615) (G-3540)

Gary's Sales and Service, Caribou Also Called: Gary Raymond (G-4675)

Gas Path Solutions LLC.. 978 229-5460
  81 Old Boston Tpke Hubbardston (01452) (G-9348)

Gas Turbine Fuel Systems Div, Devens Also Called: Parker-Hannifin Corporation (G-8285)

Gasbarre Products Inc.. 401 467-5200
  81 Western Industrial Dr Ste A Cranston (02921) (G-15865)

Gasket Express Inc... 508 754-4076
  7 Harris Ct Worcester (01610) (G-13727)

Gaskin Manufacturing Corp.. 508 695-8949
  17 Cross St Unit 8 Plainville (02762) (G-11433)

Gasworld Publishing LLC... 781 862-0624
  5 Militia Dr Ste 16 Lexington (02421) (G-9744)

Gatco Inc... 508 815-4910
  297 North St Ste 212 Hyannis (02601) (G-9437)

Gatehouse Media LLC... 860 886-0106
  10 Railroad Ave Norwich (06360) (G-2606)

Gatehouse Media LLC... 508 676-8211
  207 Pocasset St Fall River (02721) (G-8551)

Gatehouse Media LLC... 508 829-5981
  1105 Main St Ste A Holden (01520) (G-9189)

Gatehouse Media LLC... 508 829-5981
  100 Front St Ste 500 Worcester (01608) (G-13728)

Gatehouse Media Mass I Inc (HQ)..................................... 585 598-0030
  48 Dunham Rd Beverly (01915) (G-6350)

Gatehouse Media Mass I Inc... 978 667-2156
  150 Baker Ave Ste 101 Concord (01742) (G-8118)

Gatehouse Media Mass I Inc... 508 626-4412
  33 New York Ave Framingham (01701) (G-8764)

Gatehouse Media Mass I Inc... 508 626-3859
  40 Mechanic St Marlborough (01752) (G-10151)

Gatehouse Media Mass I Inc... 508 634-7522
  197 Main St Milford (01757) (G-10403)

Gatehouse Media Mass I Inc... 781 433-6917
  10 Cordage Park Cir Ste 240 Plymouth (02360) (G-11461)

Gatehouse Media Mass I Inc... 781 235-4000
  15 Pacella Park Dr Randolph (02368) (G-11560)

Gates Mectrol, Inc., Salem Also Called: Gates Tpu Inc (G-15531)

Gates Tpu Inc... 603 890-1515
  9 Northwestern Dr Salem (03079) (G-15531)

Gateway, Norwalk Also Called: Gateway Digital Inc (G-2503)

Gateway Digital Inc... 203 853-4929
  16 Testa Pl Norwalk (06854) (G-2503)

Gateway Press, Lincoln Also Called: Lincoln News (G-5010)

Gault, Westport Also Called: LH Gault & Son Incorporated (G-4180)

Gauss Corporation.. 207 883-4121
  1 Gibson Rd Scarborough (04074) (G-5432)

Gavitt Wire and Cable Co Inc.. 508 867-6476
  62 Central St West Brookfield (01585) (G-12994)

Gawet Marble & Granite Inc (PA)...................................... 802 773-8868
  805 Business Route 4 Center Rutland (05736) (G-17174)

Gaylord, Richard N, Westfield Also Called: Westfield Grinding Wheel Co (G-13220)

Gazette Printing Co Inc.. 413 527-7700
  58 Oneil St Easthampton (01027) (G-8446)

Gbg Industries, Hinsdale Also Called: Continental Cable LLC (G-14443)

Gbr Systems Corporation... 860 526-9561
  6 Winter Ave Deep River (06417) (G-877)

Gcb Medical LLC.. 617 699-6715
  289 Saint George St Duxbury (02332) (G-8331)

Gcb Medical Supply, Duxbury Also Called: Gcb Medical LLC (G-8331)

Gcp Applied Technologies Inc.. 617 876-1400
  62 Whittemore Ave Cambridge (02140) (G-7578)

Gd-Ots Williston, Williston Also Called: General Dynamics Ots Cal Inc (G-17733)

Gdmc USA LLC.. 413 584-0065
  296 Nonotuck St Ste 11 Northampton (01062) (G-11063)

Gds Manufacturing Company.. 802 862-7610
  32 Boyer Cir Williston (05495) (G-17732)

GE, Bridgeport Also Called: General Electric Company (G-323)

GE, New Haven Also Called: GE Engine Svcs UNC Holdg I Inc (G-2153)

GE, Norwalk Also Called: General Electric Company (G-2504)

GE, Plainville Also Called: ABB Enterprise Software Inc (G-2744)

(G-0000) Company's Geographic Section entry number

GE, Stamford *Also Called: General Electric Company (G-3354)*

GE, Auburn *Also Called: General Electric Company (G-4436)*

GE, Bangor *Also Called: General Electric Company (G-4505)*

GE, Boston *Also Called: GE Medcal Systems Info Tech In (G-6753)*

GE, Boston *Also Called: General Electric Company (G-6754)*

GE, Medford *Also Called: General Electric Company (G-10286)*

GE, Hooksett *Also Called: General Electric Company (G-14465)*

GE, Rutland *Also Called: General Electric Company (G-17497)*

GE Aviation, Lynn *Also Called: GE Aviation Systems LLC (G-9973)*

GE Aviation Systems LLC 513 552-3272
1000 Western Ave Lynn (01901) *(G-9973)*

GE Digital LLC **(HQ)**.................................. **925 242-6200**
58 Charles St Cambridge (02141) *(G-7579)*

GE Energy Parts Intl LLC.......................... 617 443-3000
41 Farnsworth St Boston (02210) *(G-6752)*

GE Engine Svcs UNC Holdg I Inc............. 518 380-0767
71 Shelton Ave New Haven (06511) *(G-2153)*

GE Grid Solutions LLC 425 250-2695
175 Addison Rd Windsor (06095) *(G-4278)*

GE Health Care 413 586-7720
22 Industrial Dr E Northampton (01060) *(G-11064)*

GE Healthcare Inc **(HQ)**.......................... **732 457-8667**
251 Locke Dr Marlborough (01752) *(G-10152)*

GE Healthcare Life Sciences, Marlborough *Also Called: GE Healthcare Inc (G-10152)*

GE Healthcare Life Sciences, Marlborough *Also Called: Global Lf Scnces Sltons USA LL (G-10153)*

GE Lighting, Hyannis *Also Called: Savant Systems Inc (G-9449)*

GE Measurement & Control, Billerica *Also Called: Druck LLC (G-6432)*

GE Medcal Systems Info Tech In 617 424-6800
116 Huntington Ave Ste 903 Boston (02116) *(G-6753)*

GE Steam Power Inc **(HQ)**...................... **866 257-8664**
200 Great Pond Dr Windsor (06095) *(G-4279)*

GE Vernova International LLC **(HQ)**........ **617 443-3000**
58 Charles St Cambridge (02141) *(G-7580)*

Gear/Tronics Inc 781 933-1400
100 Chelmsford Rd North Billerica (01862) *(G-10914)*

Gear/Tronics Industries Inc....................... 781 933-1400
100 Chelmsford Rd North Billerica (01862) *(G-10915)*

Gebelein Group Inc.................................... 617 361-6611
1715 Hyde Park Ave Hyde Park (02136) *(G-9461)*

GEC Durham Industries Inc **(PA)**............ **508 995-2636**
255 Samuel Barnet Blvd New Bedford (02745) *(G-10594)*

Gecko Marine Inc....................................... 401 237-6117
33 Broadcommon Rd Ste 1 Bristol (02809) *(G-15766)*

Geeco, Milford *Also Called: The Gas Equipment Engineering Corporation (G-1894)*

Geesaman Software, Inc., Portland *Also Called: Comnav Engineering Inc (G-5201)*

Gefran Inc **(DH)**...................................... **781 729-5249**
400 Willow St North Andover (01845) *(G-10836)*

Gefran Isi Inc... 781 729-0842
400 Willow St North Andover (01845) *(G-10837)*

Geib Refining Corporation.......................... 401 738-8560
399 Kilvert St Warwick (02886) *(G-16817)*

Geiger Bros **(PA)**.................................... **207 755-2000**
70 Mount Hope Ave Lewiston (04240) *(G-4962)*

Geisel Software Inc.................................... 508 853-5310
67 Millbrook St Ste 520 Worcester (01606) *(G-13729)*

Gelato Fiasco Inc....................................... 207 607-4002
22 Vesper St Apt 1 Portland (04101) *(G-5218)*

Gelato Giuliana LLC................................... 203 772-0607
240 Sargent Dr Ste 9 New Haven (06511) *(G-2154)*

Gelder Aerospace LLC............................... 203 283-9524
50 Waterview Dr Ste 120 Shelton (06484) *(G-3008)*

Gelpac Poly Usa Inc **(PA)**..................... **978 372-3300**
60 Fondi Rd Haverhill (01832) *(G-9097)*

Gelpac Poly Usa Inc 603 685-8338
7 Raymond Ave Ste D Salem (03079) *(G-15532)*

Gem, Waterbury *Also Called: Gem Manufacturing LLC (G-3914)*

Gem Asset Acquisition LLC....................... 508 419-7710
110 Blackstone River Rd Worcester (01607) *(G-13730)*

Gem Gravure Co Inc **(PA)**..................... **781 878-0456**
112 School St Hanover (02339) *(G-9032)*

Gem Group Inc **(PA)**............................... **978 691-2000**
9 International Way Lawrence (01843) *(G-9564)*

Gem Label & Tape Company...................... 401 724-1300
73 Whitewood Dr Cranston (02920) *(G-15866)*

Gem Manufacturing LLC............................ 203 574-1466
78 Brookside Rd Waterbury (06708) *(G-3914)*

Gem Welding... 978 362-3873
12 Republic Rd North Billerica (01862) *(G-10916)*

Gem-Craft Inc... 401 854-1200
1420 Elmwood Ave Cranston (02910) *(G-15867)*

Gemco Manufacturing Co Inc..................... 860 628-5529
555 W Queen St Southington (06489) *(G-3211)*

Gemini Fairfield Screenprint, Keene *Also Called: Gemini Firfield Screenprinting (G-14600)*

Gemini Firfield Screenprinting.................... 603 357-3847
294 West St Ste 4 Keene (03431) *(G-14600)*

Gemini Investors V LP **(PA)**.................. **781 237-7001**
20 William St Ste 250 Wellesley (02481) *(G-12942)*

Gemini Valve, Raymond *Also Called: Parker & Harper Companies Inc (G-15455)*

Gemline, Lawrence *Also Called: Gem Group Inc (G-9564)*

Gems Sensors & Controls, Plainville *Also Called: Gems Sensors Inc (G-2761)*

Gems Sensors Inc **(HQ)**......................... **860 747-3000**
1 Cowles Rd Plainville (06062) *(G-2761)*

Gemseal Pvements Pdts - Boston, Worcester *Also Called: Gem Asset Acquisition LLC (G-13730)*

Gen-El-Mec Associates LLC...................... 203 828-6566
2 Fox Hollow Rd Oxford (06478) *(G-2694)*

Genconnex, Hingham *Also Called: New England Gen-Connect LLC (G-9155)*

Genelec Inc... 508 652-0900
7 Tech Cir Natick (01760) *(G-10481)*

General Abrasives Inc................................ 802 763-7264
Back River Rd Sharon (05065) *(G-17555)*

General Alum New England Corp................ 207 548-2525
34 Kidder Point Rd Searsport (04974) *(G-5454)*

General Datacomm Inds Inc **(PA)**......... **203 729-0271**
6 Rubber Ave Naugatuck (06770) *(G-1961)*

General Digital Corporation........................ 860 282-2900
60 Prestige Park Rd East Hartford (06108) *(G-996)*

General Display Inc.................................... 508 533-6676
6 Industrial Park Rd Medway (02053) *(G-10305)*

General Dynamics Aviation Svcs................ 413 562-5860
33 Elise St Westfield (01085) *(G-13166)*

General Dynamics Corp.............................. 703 876-3631
266 Queen City Park Rd Burlington (05401) *(G-17137)*

General Dynamics Corporation................... 860 433-3000
75 Eastern Point Rd Groton (06340) *(G-1372)*

General Dynamics Electric Boat, Groton *Also Called: Electric Boat Corporation (G-1370)*

General Dynamics Electric Boat, New London *Also Called: Electric Boat Corporation (G-2227)*

General Dynamics Info Tech Inc................. 860 441-2400
100 Mechanic St Pawcatuck (06379) *(G-2720)*

General Dynamics Mission.......................... 781 410-9635
150 Rustcraft Rd Dedham (02026) *(G-8244)*

General Dynamics Mission.......................... 508 880-4000
400 John Quincy Adams Rd Taunton (02780) *(G-12337)*

General Dynamics Ordnance....................... 860 404-0162
65 Sandscreen Rd Avon (06001) *(G-25)*

GENERAL DYNAMICS OTS (CALIFORNIA), INC., Saco *Also Called: General Dynamics Ots Cal Inc (G-5368)*

General Dynamics Ots Cal Inc................... 207 283-3611
291 North St Saco (04072) *(G-5368)*

General Dynamics Ots Cal Inc................... 802 662-7000
326 Ibm Rd Bldg 862 Williston (05495) *(G-17733)*

General Dynmics Def Systems In............... 413 494-1110
100 Plastics Ave Pittsfield (01201) *(G-11397)*

General Dynmics Mssion Systems.............. 954 846-3000
77 A St Needham Heights (02494) *(G-10549)*

General Dynmics Mssion Systems.............. 413 494-1110
100 Plastics Ave Pittsfield (01201) *(G-11398)*

General Dynmics Mssion Systems.............. 617 715-7000
553 South St Quincy (02169) *(G-11522)*

General Dynmics Mssion Systems.............. 508 880-4000
20 Constitution Dr Taunton (02780) *(G-12338)*

ALPHABETIC

General Dynmics Mssion Systems.................. 603 864-6300
  24 Simon St Nashua (03060) *(G-15103)*

General Electric Company.......................... 203 396-1572
  1285 Boston Ave Bridgeport (06610) *(G-323)*

General Electric Company.......................... 203 797-0840
  901 Main Ave Ste 103 Norwalk (06851) *(G-2504)*

General Electric Company.......................... 866 419-4096
  1600 Summer St Ste 2 Stamford (06905) *(G-3354)*

General Electric Company.......................... 207 786-5100
  135 Rodman Rd Auburn (04210) *(G-4436)*

General Electric Company.......................... 207 941-2500
  534 Griffin Rd Bangor (04401) *(G-4505)*

General Electric Company **(PA)**.................. **617 443-3000**
  1 Financial Ctr Ste 3700 Boston (02111) *(G-6754)*

General Electric Company.......................... 781 594-0100
  1000 Western Ave Lynn (01910) *(G-9974)*

General Electric Company.......................... 781 594-2218
  1000 Western Ave Lynn (01905) *(G-9975)*

General Electric Company.......................... 781 396-9600
  3960 Mystic Valley Pkwy Medford (02155) *(G-10286)*

General Electric Company.......................... 603 666-8300
  31 Industrial Park Dr Hooksett (03106) *(G-14465)*

General Electric Company.......................... 802 775-9842
  210 Columbian Ave Rutland (05701) *(G-17497)*

General Electric Intl Inc, Cambridge *Also Called: GE Vernova International LLC (G-7580)*

General Electro Components........................ 860 659-3573
  122 Naubuc Ave Ste A7 Glastonbury (06033) *(G-1280)*

General Findings, Attleboro *Also Called: EF Leach & Company (G-6011)*

General Instrs Wrline Networks, Lowell *Also Called: Ruckus Wireless Inc (G-9922)*

General Machine Inc............................... 413 533-5744
  56 Jackson St Holyoke (01040) *(G-9256)*

General Machine & Foundry, Wilton *Also Called: Aluminum Castings Inc (G-15701)*

General Machine Company Inc....................... 860 426-9295
  1223 Mount Vernon Rd Southington (06489) *(G-3212)*

General Manufacturing Corp........................ 978 667-5514
  154 Rangeway Rd North Billerica (01862) *(G-10917)*

General Marine Inc................................ 207 284-7517
  56 Landry St Biddeford (04005) *(G-4568)*

General Metal Finishing LLC....................... 508 222-9683
  42 Frank Mossberg Dr Attleboro (02703) *(G-6020)*

General Packaging Products Inc.................... 203 846-1340
  3 Valley View Rd Apt 9 Norwalk (06851) *(G-2505)*

General Products & Gear Corp...................... 978 948-8146
  445 Newburyport Tpke Rowley (01969) *(G-11674)*

General Seating Solutions LLC..................... 860 242-3307
  45 S Satellite Rd Ste 5 South Windsor (06074) *(G-3149)*

General Sheet Metal Works Inc..................... 203 333-6111
  120 Silliman Ave Bridgeport (06605) *(G-324)*

General Steel Products Co Inc..................... 617 387-5400
  16 Russell Rd Lexington (02420) *(G-9745)*

General Wire Products Inc......................... 508 752-8260
  425 Shrewsbury St Worcester (01604) *(G-13731)*

General Wldg & Fabrication Inc.................... 860 274-9668
  977 Echo Lake Rd Watertown (06795) *(G-4014)*

General Woodworking Inc........................... 978 251-4070
  299 Western Ave Lowell (01851) *(G-9878)*

General Woodworking Inc **(PA)**.................. **978 458-6625**
  105 Pevey St Lowell (01851) *(G-9879)*

Generation Bio Co **(PA)**........................ **617 655-7500**
  301 Binrey St Ste 3 Cambridge (02142) *(G-7581)*

Generation Four Inc............................... 781 899-3180
  713 Main St Waltham (02451) *(G-12686)*

Generators On Demand LLC.......................... 860 662-4090
  61-1 Buttonball Rd Old Lyme (06371) *(G-2642)*

Genere Food, Providence *Also Called: Plastic Services Entps Inc (G-16584)*

Genest Precast, Sanford *Also Called: Richard Genest Inc (G-5411)*

Geneve Corporation **(HQ)**....................... **203 358-8000**
  96 Cummings Point Rd Stamford (06902) *(G-3355)*

Genevieves Gift Wrap Sales Div, West Springfield *Also Called: McLaughlin Paper Co Inc (G-13033)*

Genfoot America Inc................................ 603 575-5114
  673 Industrial Park Rd Littleton (03561) *(G-14719)*

Genfoot America Inc., Milton *Also Called: Genfoot America LLC (G-17358)*

Genfoot America LLC............................... 802 893-4280
  33 Catamount Dr Milton (05468) *(G-17358)*

Genie Lease Management LLC........................ 203 222-7170
  200 Nyala Farms Rd Westport (06880) *(G-4169)*

Gennaro Inc....................................... 401 632-4100
  81 Western Industrial Dr Cranston (02921) *(G-15868)*

Genoa Sausage Co Inc.............................. 781 933-3115
  14 Industrial Pkwy Woburn (01801) *(G-13574)*

Genocea, Cambridge *Also Called: Genocea Biosciences Inc (G-7582)*

Genocea Biosciences Inc **(PA)**.................. **617 876-8191**
  100 Acorn Park Dr Fl 5 Cambridge (02140) *(G-7582)*

Genomic Solutions Inc............................. 734 975-4800
  84 October Hill Rd Ste 7 Holliston (01746) *(G-9212)*

Genovese Manufacturing Co......................... 860 582-9944
  8 Bombard Ct Terryville (06786) *(G-3604)*

Genplex Inc....................................... 207 474-3500
  7 Industrial Park Rd Ste 1 Skowhegan (04976) *(G-5467)*

Genscope Inc...................................... 413 526-0802
  18 Deer Park Dr East Longmeadow (01028) *(G-8377)*

Gentex Corporation................................ 617 670-3547
  12 Channel St Ste 901 Boston (02210) *(G-6755)*

Gentex Corporation................................ 603 657-1200
  645 Harvey Rd Ste 1 Manchester (03103) *(G-14851)*

Gentuity LLC...................................... 978 202-4108
  142 North Rd Ste G Sudbury (01776) *(G-12267)*

Genuine Parts Company............................. 860 623-4479
  508 Spring St Ste 2 Windsor Locks (06096) *(G-4325)*

Genzyme, Woburn *Also Called: Pluromed Inc (G-13638)*

Genzyme Biosurgery, Cambridge *Also Called: Genzyme Corporation (G-7583)*

Genzyme Biosurgery, Cambridge *Also Called: Genzyme Corporation (G-7587)*

Genzyme Corporation............................... 617 252-7500
  114 Western Ave Allston (02134) *(G-5821)*

Genzyme Corporation............................... 508 271-2919
  55 Cambridge Pkwy Ste 19 Cambridge (02142) *(G-7583)*

Genzyme Corporation............................... 617 494-8484
  500 Kendall St Cambridge (02142) *(G-7584)*

Genzyme Corporation **(DH)**...................... **617 252-7500**
  450 Water St Cambridge (02141) *(G-7585)*

Genzyme Corporation............................... 617 252-7500
  1 Kendall Sq Ste 113 Cambridge (02139) *(G-7586)*

Genzyme Corporation............................... 617 252-7999
  64 Sidney St Ste 400 Cambridge (02139) *(G-7587)*

Genzyme Corporation............................... 617 252-7500
  350 Water St Cambridge (02141) *(G-7588)*

Genzyme Corporation............................... 508 872-8400
  1 Kendall Sq Cambridge (02139) *(G-7589)*

Genzyme Corporation............................... 508 872-8400
  51 New York Ave Framingham (01701) *(G-8765)*

Genzyme Corporation............................... 508 872-8400
  76 New York Ave Framingham (01701) *(G-8766)*

Genzyme Corporation............................... 508 872-8400
  74 New York Ave Framingham (01701) *(G-8767)*

Genzyme Corporation............................... 508 872-8400
  45 New York Ave Framingham (01701) *(G-8768)*

Genzyme Corporation............................... 508 872-8400
  68 New York Ave Framingham (01701) *(G-8769)*

Genzyme Corporation............................... 508 271-2642
  200 Crossing Blvd Framingham (01702) *(G-8770)*

Genzyme Corporation............................... 508 370-9690
  80 New York Ave Framingham (01701) *(G-8771)*

Genzyme Corporation............................... 617 252-7500
  78 New York Ave Framingham (01701) *(G-8772)*

Genzyme Corporation............................... 617 252-7500
  8 New York Ave Framingham (01701) *(G-8773)*

Genzyme Corporation............................... 617 252-7500
  10 California Ave Framingham (01701) *(G-8774)*

Genzyme Corporation............................... 508 351-2699
  11 Forbes Rd Northborough (01532) *(G-11096)*

Genzyme Corporation............................... 781 487-5728
  153 2nd Ave Waltham (02451) *(G-12687)*

Genzyme Corporation.................................... 508 351-2600
  1 Research Dr Ste 200 Westborough (01581) *(G-13102)*

Genzyme Corporation.................................... 508 898-9001
  3400 Computer Dr Westborough (01581) *(G-13103)*

Genzyme Genetics, Westborough *Also Called: Genzyme Corporation (G-13103)*

Genzyme Securities Corporation......................... 617 252-7500
  50 Binney St Cambridge (02142) *(G-7590)*

Genzyme Therapeutic Products, Framingham *Also Called: Genzyme Corporation (G-8774)*

Genzyme Therapeutics Division, Cambridge *Also Called: Genzyme Corporation (G-7585)*

Geo Knight & Co Inc.................................... 508 588-0186
  52 Perkins St Brockton (02302) *(G-7280)*

Geographics Australia, Norwalk *Also Called: Royal Consumer Products LLC (G-2567)*

Geokon Inc... 603 448-1562
  48 Spencer St Lebanon (03766) *(G-14690)*

Geometric Informatics Inc.............................. 617 440-1078
  387 Somerville Ave Apt 2 Somerville (02143) *(G-11876)*

Geonautics Manufacturing Inc.......................... 978 462-7161
  506 Merrimac St Newburyport (01950) *(G-10685)*

Georbital Inc.. 617 651-1102
  17 Rev Nazareno Properzi Way Somerville (02143) *(G-11877)*

Geophysical Survey Systems Inc (DH)................. **603 893-1109**
  40 Simon St Nashua (03060) *(G-15104)*

George Apkin & Sons Inc................................ 413 664-4936
  17 Depot St Ste 1 Adams (01220) *(G-5772)*

George D Judd & Sons LLC.............................. 413 268-7590
  145 Berkshire Trl W Goshen (01032) *(G-8967)*

George Gordon Associates Inc........................... 603 424-5204
  12 Continental Blvd Merrimack (03054) *(G-14981)*

George H Dean Co....................................... 781 544-3782
  140 Wood Rd Ste 105 Braintree (02184) *(G-7184)*

George H Olson Steel Company........................... 203 375-5656
  245 Access Rd Stratford (06615) *(G-3541)*

George Howell Coffee Co LLC............................ 978 635-9033
  312 School St Acton (01720) *(G-5748)*

George Patton Associates Inc........................... 800 572-2194
  81 Commerce Dr Fall River (02720) *(G-8552)*

George Schmithet and Company, Guilford *Also Called: Schmitt Realty Holdings Inc (G-1408)*

George Schmitt & Co Inc (PA)....................... **203 453-4334**
  251 Boston Post Rd Guilford (06437) *(G-1394)*

George Sherman Sand Grav Inc........................... 401 789-6304
  881 Curtis Corner Rd Wakefield (02879) *(G-16741)*

Georges Bank LLC...................................... 617 423-3474
  310 Northern Ave Boston (02210) *(G-6756)*

Georgetown Pottery..................................... 207 371-2801
  755 Five Islands Rd Georgetown (04548) *(G-4814)*

Georgia Stone Industries Inc (HQ).................. **401 232-2040**
  15 Branch Pike Smithfield (02917) *(G-16702)*

Georgia-Pacific, Baileyville *Also Called: Georgia-Pacific LLC (G-4484)*

Georgia-Pacific, Leominster *Also Called: Georgia-Pacific LLC (G-9666)*

Georgia-Pacific LLC.................................... 207 427-4077
  144 Main St Baileyville (04694) *(G-4484)*

Georgia-Pacific LLC.................................... 978 537-4701
  149 Hamilton St Leominster (01453) *(G-9666)*

Georgia-Pacific LLC.................................... 603 433-8000
  170 Shattuck Way Newington (03801) *(G-15207)*

Geosonics Inc.. 203 271-2504
  416 Highland Ave Ste D Cheshire (06410) *(G-595)*

Gepp LLC... 401 808-8004
  83 Vermont Ave Bldg 3-4 Warwick (02888) *(G-16818)*

Gerber Coburn Optical Inc (DH)..................... **800 843-1479**
  55 Gerber Rd E South Windsor (06074) *(G-3150)*

Gerber Scientific, Tolland *Also Called: Gerber Technology LLC (G-3662)*

Gerber Scientific LLC (PA)......................... **860 871-8082**
  24 Industrial Park Rd W Tolland (06084) *(G-3661)*

Gerber Technology LLC (HQ)........................ **800 321-2448**
  24 Industrial Park Rd W Tolland (06084) *(G-3662)*

Gerdau Ameristeel US Inc............................... 860 351-9029
  75 Neal Ct Plainville (06062) *(G-2762)*

Germani Inc.. 802 862-3653
  1930 Williston Rd South Burlington (05403) *(G-17579)*

Gerrity Company Incorporated........................... 207 933-2804
  152 Bog Rd Leeds (04263) *(G-4948)*

Gerritystone Inc...................................... 781 938-1820
  100a Eames St Wilmington (01887) *(G-13409)*

Geskus Studios & Yrbk Pubg Inc......................... 800 948-1120
  10 Whitaker Way U2 Seabrook (03874) *(G-15591)*

Gessner Company, Charlton *Also Called: Ghm Industries Inc (G-7888)*

Getchell & Son Inc.................................... 401 231-3850
  950 Douglas Pike Smithfield (02917) *(G-16703)*

Getchell Bros Inc (PA)............................. **800 949-4423**
  1 Union St Brewer (04412) *(G-4613)*

Getchell Bros Inc...................................... 207 490-0809
  1913 Main St Sanford (04073) *(G-5397)*

Getinge AB, Merrimack *Also Called: Getinge Group Logis Ameri LLC (G-14982)*

Getinge Group Logis Ameri LLC.......................... 603 880-1433
  40 Continental Blvd Merrimack (03054) *(G-14982)*

Getreskilled.. 617 901-9268
  800 Boylston St Ste 1600 Boston (02199) *(G-6757)*

Gets LLC... 401 314-5550
  7 Thornwood Dr Lincoln (02865) *(G-16138)*

Gg Inks, South Hadley *Also Called: Ggs Custom Metals Inc (G-11962)*

Ggs Custom Metals Inc................................. 413 315-4344
  785 New Ludlow Rd South Hadley (01075) *(G-11962)*

Ghm Industries Inc (PA)........................... **508 248-3941**
  100 Sturbridge Rd Unit A Charlton (01507) *(G-7888)*

Ghost Tequila, Boston *Also Called: Gt Spirits Inc (G-6777)*

Ghp, West Haven *Also Called: Ghp Media Inc (G-4107)*

Ghp Media Inc (PA)................................. **203 479-7500**
  475 Heffernan Dr West Haven (06516) *(G-4107)*

Ghp Media Inc.. 413 663-3771
  123 Mass Moca Way North Adams (01247) *(G-10808)*

Ghs Data Management, Augusta *Also Called: Change Hlthcare Phrm Sltons In (G-4468)*

GI Plastek LLC... 603 569-5100
  5 Wickers Dr Wolfeboro (03894) *(G-15731)*

GI Plastek Ltd Partnership............................. 603 569-5100
  5 Wickers Dr Wolfeboro (03894) *(G-15732)*

GI Plastek Wolfeboro, Wolfeboro *Also Called: PSI Molded Plastics NH Inc (G-15735)*

Giering Metal Finishing Incorporated................... 203 248-5583
  2655 State St Hamden (06517) *(G-1426)*

Gigantum Inc.. 301 960-8012
  124 Washington St Foxboro (02035) *(G-8697)*

Gilberte Interiors LLC (PA)....................... **603 643-3727**
  10 Allen St Hanover (03755) *(G-14423)*

Gilchrist Metal Fabg Co Inc............................ 603 889-2600
  12 Park Ave Hudson (03051) *(G-14499)*

Gilchrist Metal Fabg Co Inc (PA)................... **603 889-2600**
  18 Park Ave Hudson (03051) *(G-14500)*

Gilcris Enterprises Inc................................ 802 226-7764
  283 Peaceful Valley Rd Proctorsville (05153) *(G-17461)*

Gilead Sciences Inc................................... 203 315-1222
  36 E Industrial Rd Ste 3 Branford (06405) *(G-261)*

Gill Design Inc....................................... 603 890-1237
  3 Industrial Dr Unit 5 Windham (03087) *(G-15727)*

Gill Metal Fab Inc.................................... 508 580-4445
  170 Oak Hill Way Brockton (02301) *(G-7281)*

Gilles Champagne....................................... 603 237-5272
  Edwards St Colebrook (03576) *(G-14105)*

Gillespie Corporation.................................. 413 967-4980
  34 Pine St Ware (01082) *(G-12825)*

Gillette, Boston *Also Called: Gillette Company (G-6758)*

Gillette Company (HQ).............................. **617 463-3000**
  1 Gillette Park Boston (02127) *(G-6758)*

Gillette De Mexico Inc................................ 617 421-7000
  800 Boylston St Boston (02199) *(G-6759)*

Gillians Foods Inc................................... 781 586-0086
  45 Congress St Ste 4 Salem (01970) *(G-11719)*

Gilman Corporation..................................... 860 887-7080
  1 Polly Ln Gilman (06336) *(G-1266)*

Gilman Gear, Bozrah *Also Called: Marty Gilman Incorporated (G-229)*

Gilman Gear, Gilman *Also Called: Marty Gilman Incorporated (G-1267)*

Gima LLC.. 860 296-4441
  241 Ledyard St Ste B10 Hartford (06114) *(G-1483)*

Gimasport, Hartford *Also Called: Gima LLC (G-1483)*

Giner Elx Sub LLC.. 781 392-0300
   89 Rumford Ave Auburndale (02466) *(G-6134)*

Giner Life Sciences Inc... 781 529-0576
   89 Rumford Ave Auburndale (02466) *(G-6135)*

Ginerlabs, Auburndale *Also Called: Giner Life Sciences Inc (G-6135)*

Ginger Acquisition Inc... 617 551-4000
   22 Boston Wharf Rd Fl 7 Boston (02210) *(G-6760)*

Ginger Software Inc... 617 755-0160
   128 Chestnut St Newton (02465) *(G-10757)*

Gingras Lumber Inc... 413 229-2182
   77 Clayton Rd Ashley Falls (01222) *(G-5970)*

Ginkgo Bioworks Inc (HQ).. **877 422-5362**
   27 Drydock Ave Boston (02210) *(G-6761)*

Ginkgo Bioworks Inc.. 617 633-7972
   45 Moulton St Cambridge (02138) *(G-7591)*

Ginkgo Bioworks Holdings Inc (PA)......................... **877 422-5362**
   27 Drydock Ave Ste 8 Boston (02210) *(G-6762)*

Ginsco Inc.. 508 677-4767
   1572 President Ave Fall River (02720) *(G-8553)*

Ginsco Inc (PA)... **508 677-4767**
   1706 President Ave Fall River (02720) *(G-8554)*

Ginsco Inc.. 508 990-3350
   272 State Rd North Dartmouth (02747) *(G-10996)*

Ginseng Up Corporation.. 508 799-6178
   75 E Worcester St Worcester (01604) *(G-13732)*

Ginseng Up Corporation (PA)................................... **508 799-6178**
   16 Plum St Worcester (01604) *(G-13733)*

Giovanni, Middleboro *Also Called: Malden Intl Designs Inc (G-10365)*

Girardin Moulding Inc... 860 623-4486
   564 Halfway House Rd Windsor Locks (06096) *(G-4326)*

Girouard Tool Corp.. 978 534-4147
   561 Research Dr Leominster (01453) *(G-9667)*

Giroux Body Shop Inc.. 802 482-2162
   10370 Route 116 Hinesburg (05461) *(G-17291)*

Giv, Barre *Also Called: Granite Industries Vermont Inc (G-17003)*

Givens Marine Survival Svc Co................................. 617 441-5400
   550 Main Rd Tiverton (02878) *(G-16736)*

GK Automatics Incorporated..................................... 860 283-5878
   437 S Main St Thomaston (06787) *(G-3620)*

GK Mechanical Systems LLC.................................... 203 775-4970
   934 Federal Rd Ste 1 Brookfield (06804) *(G-521)*

GKN Aerospace New England Inc.............................. 603 542-5135
   1105 River Rd Charlestown (03603) *(G-14063)*

GKN Aerospace Newington LLC................................. 860 830-5810
   76 Stanwell Rd Newington (06111) *(G-2296)*

GKN Aerospace Newington LLC (DH)......................... **860 667-8502**
   183 Lou s St Newington (06111) *(G-2297)*

GKN Arspace Svcs Strctures LLC.............................. 860 613-0236
   1000 Corporate Row Cromwell (06416) *(G-693)*

GKN Arspace Svcs Strctures LLC.............................. 203 303-1408
   14 Research Pkwy Wallingford (06492) *(G-3809)*

GL&v USA Inc.. 603 882-2711
   1 Cellu Dr Ste 200 Nashua (03063) *(G-15105)*

Glaccet Corporation... 508 752-7356
   54 Rockdale St Ste 2 Worcester (01606) *(G-13734)*

Glacier Computer LLC.. 603 882-1560
   46 Bridge St New Milford (06776) *(G-2244)*

Gladding-Hearn Shipbuilding, Somerset *Also Called: The Duclos Corporation (G-11857)*

Glass America Window Mfg Inc.................................. 401 231-6000
   2 Esmond St Smithfield (02917) *(G-16704)*

Glass Graphics Inc.. 603 447-1900
   56 Pleasant St Conway (03818) *(G-14179)*

Glass Industries America LLC................................... 203 269-6700
   340 Quinnipiac St Unit 9 Wallingford (06492) *(G-3810)*

Glass Technologies Division, Central Falls *Also Called: Osram Sylvania Inc (G-15794)*

Glasseal Products Inc... 732 370-9100
   50 Welby Rd New Bedford (02745) *(G-10595)*

Glastonbury Citizen, Glastonbury *Also Called: Glastonbury Citizen Inc (G-1281)*

Glastonbury Citizen Inc.. 860 633-4691
   87 Nutmeg Ln Glastonbury (06033) *(G-1281)*

Glastonbury Southern Gage Div, Colchester *Also Called: Q Alpha Inc (G-664)*

Glencore Recycling LLC.. 401 438-9220
   80 Commercial Way East Providence (02914) *(G-16020)*

Glenn Inc.. 800 521-0065
   300 Jefferson Blvd Warwick (02888) *(G-16819)*

Glenns Gardening & Woodworking.............................. 617 548-7977
   491 Arborway Apt 20 Boston (02130) *(G-6763)*

Glenpharmer Distillery LLC.. 508 654-6577
   860 W Central St Franklin (02038) *(G-8841)*

Glh Systems... 603 774-6374
   181 Stark Hwy S Dunbarton (03046) *(G-14264)*

Glidden Signs Inc... 207 396-6111
   40a Manson Libby Rd Scarborough (04074) *(G-5433)*

Glidecam Industries Inc (PA).................................... **508 577-6261**
   125 Church St Ste 90-131 Pembroke (02359) *(G-11366)*

Glines & Rhodes Inc.. 508 226-2000
   189 East St Attleboro (02703) *(G-6021)*

Global Advanced Metals USA Inc (PA)....................... **781 996-7300**
   100 Worcester St Ste 200 Wellesley Hills (02481) *(G-12951)*

Global Connector Tech Ltd.. 978 208-1618
   354 Merrimack St Ste 260 Lawrence (01843) *(G-9565)*

Global Filtration Systems.. 603 651-8777
   615 Center St Wolfeboro (03894) *(G-15733)*

Global Foundries, Essex Junction *Also Called: Globalfoundries US 2 LLC (G-17234)*

Global I.P. Net, Boston *Also Called: Computer Software Associates (G-6664)*

Global Interconnect Inc (PA)..................................... **508 563-6306**
   11 Jonathan Bourne Dr Pocasset (02559) *(G-11487)*

Global Laminates Inc... 603 373-8323
   300 Constitution Ave Portsmouth (03801) *(G-15393)*

Global Lf Scnces Sltons USA LL................................ 800 526-3593
   170 Locke Dr Marlborough (01752) *(G-10153)*

Global Lf Scnces Sltons USA LL................................ 413 586-7720
   22 Industrial Dr E Northampton (01060) *(G-11065)*

Global Materials Inc... 978 322-1900
   1449 Middlesex St Lowell (01851) *(G-9880)*

Global Metal Fabrication LLC.................................... 207 753-0001
   302b Auburn Rd Turner (04282) *(G-5562)*

Global Pallet & Packaging LLC.................................. 603 969-6660
   148 Batchelder Rd Seabrook (03874) *(G-15592)*

Global Photonix LLC.. 401 474-8158
   2639 S County Trl East Greenwich (02818) *(G-15987)*

Global Scenic Services Inc....................................... 203 334-2130
   46 Brookfield Ave Bridgeport (06610) *(G-325)*

Global Silicon Tech Inc.. 508 999-2001
   11 David St New Bedford (02744) *(G-10596)*

Global Tower Holdings LLC.. 617 375-7500
   116 Huntington Ave Boston (02116) *(G-6764)*

Global Trbine Cmpnent Tech LLC.............................. 860 528-4722
   125 S Satellite Rd South Windsor (06074) *(G-3151)*

Globaldie, Auburn *Also Called: Enefco International Inc (G-4428)*

Globalfoundries US 2 LLC... 408 462-4452
   1000 River St Essex Junction (05452) *(G-17234)*

Globe Composite Solutions LLC................................ 781 871-3700
   200 Shuman Ave Ste 100 Stoughton (02072) *(G-12210)*

Globe Composite Solutions Ltd.................................. 781 871-3700
   200 Shuman Ave Stoughton (02072) *(G-12211)*

Globe Footwear LLC (HQ).. **207 784-9186**
   27 Wrights Lndg Auburn (04210) *(G-4437)*

Globe Manufacturing Co LLC (DH)............................ **603 435-8323**
   37 Loudon Rd Pittsfield (03263) *(G-15332)*

Globe Tool & Met Stampg Co Inc.............................. 860 621-6807
   95 Robert Porter Rd Southington (06489) *(G-3213)*

Globenix Inc... 203 740-7070
   9 Lois St Norwalk (06851) *(G-2506)*

Gloucester Associates Inc.. 802 479-1088
   10 Transport Dr # 1 Barre (05641) *(G-17001)*

Gloucester Builders Inc.. 617 241-5513
   92 Arlington Ave Charlestown (02129) *(G-7874)*

Gloucester Daily Times, Gloucester *Also Called: Eagle-Tribune Publishing Co (G-8933)*

Gloucester Engineering Co Inc (DH)........................... **978 281-1800**
   11 Dory Rd Gloucester (01930) *(G-8935)*

Gloucester Engineering Co Inc................ 978 515-7008
  18 Sargent St Gloucester (01930) *(G-8936)*

Gloucester Graphics Inc **(PA)**................ **978 281-4500**
  19 Pond Rd Gloucester (01930) *(G-8937)*

Gloucester Pharmaceuticals Inc................ 617 583-1300
  1 Broadway Fl 14 Cambridge (02142) *(G-7592)*

Gloucester Transit Mix Inc................ 978 283-9649
  45 Emerson Ave Gloucester (01930) *(G-8938)*

Glover Company Inc................ 207 236-8644
  17 Rockville St Rockport (04856) *(G-5349)*

Gluer-TEC, Pelham *Also Called: Folder-Glr Techl Svs Grp LLC (G-15288)*

Glycozym, Beverly *Also Called: Glycozym Usa Inc (G-6351)*

Glycozym Usa Inc................ 425 985-2556
  100 Cummings Ctr Ste 430j Beverly (01915) *(G-6351)*

Glyne Manufacturing Co Inc................ 203 375-4495
  380 E Main St Stratford (06614) *(G-3542)*

Gmf Engineering Inc................ 781 233-0315
  15 Main St Saugus (01906) *(G-11758)*

Gmn Usa LLC................ 800 686-1679
  181 Business Park Dr Bristol (06010) *(G-451)*

Gmo Threshold Logging LLC................ 617 330-7500
  40 Rowes Wharf Ste 600 Boston (02110) *(G-6765)*

Gmo Thrshold Tmber Hldings LLC................ 617 330-7500
  40 Rowes Wharf Ste 600 Boston (02110) *(G-6766)*

Gmt Composites, Bristol *Also Called: Element Industries Inc (G-15762)*

Gmt Mfg, Plantsville *Also Called: G M T Manufacturing Co Inc (G-2792)*

Gn Audio USA Inc **(DH)**................ **800 826-4656**
  900 Chelmsford St 8th Fl Lowell (01851) *(G-9881)*

Gnaw Inc................ 603 418-8900
  391 Oak St Manchester (03104) *(G-14852)*

Gnomon Color, Boston *Also Called: Julesan Inc (G-6835)*

Go East Promotions, Warwick *Also Called: Gepp LLC (G-16818)*

Goamericago Beverages LLC................ 802 897-7700
  2139 Quiet Valley Rd Shoreham (05770) *(G-17567)*

Goetz Composites, Bristol *Also Called: Composite Energy Tech Inc (G-15760)*

Gold Line, Redding *Also Called: Gold Line Connector Inc (G-2882)*

Gold Line Connector Inc **(PA)**................ **203 938-2588**
  40 Great Pasture Rd Redding (06896) *(G-2882)*

Gold Medal Bakery Inc **(PA)**................ **508 674-5766**
  21 Penn St Fall River (02724) *(G-8555)*

Gold Water Technology Inc................ 781 551-3590
  25 Walpole Park S Walpole (02081) *(G-12559)*

Goldacre Realty Inc................ 508 885-2748
  291 Main St Spencer (01562) *(G-12060)*

Golden Fleece Mfg Group LLC **(DH)**................ **978 686-3833**
  25 Computer Dr Haverhill (01832) *(G-9098)*

Golden Sun Inc................ 800 575-7960
  5 High Ridge Park Ste 200 Stamford (06905) *(G-3356)*

Golden Sun Holdings Inc **(HQ)**................ **203 595-5228**
  5 High Ridge Park Ste 100 Stamford (06905) *(G-3357)*

Goldenrod Corporation................ 203 723-4400
  25 Lancaster Dr Beacon Falls (06403) *(G-40)*

Goldline Controls Inc **(DH)**................ **401 583-1100**
  61 Whitecap Dr North Kingstown (02852) *(G-16253)*

Goldman-Kolber Inc................ 781 769-6362
  185 Dean St Ste 204 Norwood (02062) *(G-11175)*

Golf Course News, Yarmouth *Also Called: United Publications Inc (G-5709)*

Golf Galaxy LLC................ 203 855-0500
  595 Connecticut Ave Ste 4 Norwalk (06854) *(G-2507)*

Golf Shop The, Manchester *Also Called: Tom Waters Golf Shop (G-10034)*

Golfsmith, Norwalk *Also Called: Golf Galaxy LLC (G-2507)*

Gonco Inc **(PA)**................ **508 833-3900**
  338 Route 130 Sandwich (02563) *(G-11750)*

Gooby Industries Corp................ 978 689-0100
  45 Chase St Ste 45 Methuen (01844) *(G-10332)*

Gooch & Housego (keene) LLC................ 603 358-5577
  17a Bradco St Keene (03431) *(G-14601)*

Gooch & Housego Baltimore, Bedford *Also Called: Em4 Inc (G-6223)*

Good Clothing Company Inc................ 508 419-6152
  28 Anawan St # 2 Fall River (02721) *(G-8556)*

Good Crust LLC................ 207 522-4872
  70 Pinnacle Rd Canaan (04924) *(G-4669)*

Good Earth Millwork LLC................ 203 226-7958
  292 Post Rd E Westport (06880) *(G-4170)*

Good To-Go, Kittery *Also Called: Good To-Go LLC (G-4935)*

Good To-Go LLC................ 207 451-9060
  484 Us Route 1 Kittery (03904) *(G-4935)*

Good Wives, Wilmington *Also Called: Innovative Foods Inc (G-13414)*

Goodcopy Printing & Graphics, New Haven *Also Called: Goodcopy Printing Center Inc (G-2155)*

Goodcopy Printing Center Inc................ 203 624-0194
  110 Hamilton St New Haven (06511) *(G-2155)*

Goodkind Pen Company Inc................ 207 594-6207
  500 Main St Rockland (04841) *(G-5331)*

Goodrich, West Hartford *Also Called: Triumph Eng Ctrl Systems LLC (G-4087)*

Goodrich Corporation................ 505 345-9031
  100 Wooster Hts Danbury (06810) *(G-750)*

Goodrich Corporation................ 704 423-7000
  100 Reserve Rd Ste F2100 Danbury (06810) *(G-751)*

Goodrich Corporation................ 203 797-5000
  100 Wooster Hts Danbury (06810) *(G-752)*

Goodrich Corporation................ 978 532-2350
  5th St Peabody (01960) *(G-11311)*

Goodrich Corporation................ 978 303-6700
  7 Technology Park Dr Westford (01886) *(G-13239)*

Goodrich Corporation................ 978 303-6700
  9 Technology Park Dr Westford (01886) *(G-13240)*

Goodrich Sensors and Integrate, Cheshire *Also Called: Atlantic Inertial Systems Inc (G-572)*

Goodrich Snsors Intgrted Syste, Vergennes *Also Called: Simmonds Precision Products (G-17661)*

Goodway, Stamford *Also Called: Goodway Technologies Corporation (G-3358)*

Goodway Technologies Corporation **(PA)**................ **203 359-4708**
  420 West Ave Stamford (06902) *(G-3358)*

Goodwill Industries Nthrn Neng **(PA)**................ **207 774-6323**
  34 Hutcherson Dr Gorham (04038) *(G-4820)*

Goodwill Northern New England, Gorham *Also Called: Goodwill Industries Nthrn Neng (G-4820)*

Goodwin-Bradley Pattern Co Inc................ 401 461-5220
  216 Oxford St Providence (02905) *(G-16525)*

Goodyear, Augusta *Also Called: Maine Tire & Appliance Co (G-4477)*

Goodyear, Falmouth *Also Called: Maine Tire & Appliance Co (G-4769)*

Goodyear, Lynn *Also Called: Goodyear Tire & Rubber Company (G-9976)*

Goodyear Tire & Rubber Company................ 781 598-4500
  205 Market St Lynn (01901) *(G-9976)*

Googleplex Technologies LLC................ 978 897-0880
  43 Broad St Ste A300 Hudson (01749) *(G-9370)*

Goose Hummock Shop, Orleans *Also Called: Outdoor Outfitters Inc (G-11241)*

Gordini USA Inc **(PA)**................ **802 879-5211**
  67 Allen Martin Dr Essex Junction (05452) *(G-17235)*

Gordon Brothers Intl LLC **(HQ)**................ **888 424-1903**
  800 Boylston St Spc 27 Boston (02199) *(G-6767)*

Gordon Corporation................ 860 628-4775
  170 Spring St Unit 3 Southington (06489) *(G-3214)*

Gordon Couresy & Sons, Rumney *Also Called: Custom Log Homes (G-15497)*

Gordon Engineering Corporation................ 203 775-4501
  67 Del Mar Dr Brookfield (06804) *(G-522)*

Gordon Industries Inc **(PA)**................ **857 401-8398**
  358 North St Randolph (02368) *(G-11561)*

Gordon Martin................ 351 201-6065
  80 Hanover St Newbury (01951) *(G-10665)*

Gordon Products Incorporated................ 203 775-4501
  67 Del Mar Dr Brookfield (06804) *(G-523)*

Gordon Rubber and Pkg Co Inc................ 203 735-7441
  10 Cemetery Ave Derby (06418) *(G-889)*

Gordons Window Decor Inc **(PA)**................ **802 655-7777**
  8 Leroy Rd Williston (05495) *(G-17734)*

Gordons Window Decor Centl V T, Williston *Also Called: Gordons Window Decor Inc (G-17734)*

Gorham Acquisition LLC................ 603 342-2000
  72 Cascade Flt Gorham (03581) *(G-14357)*

Gorham Paper and Tissue LLC
  70 Cascade Flt Gorham (03581) *(G-14358)*

Gorham Sand & Gravel................ 603 466-2291
  42 Lancaster Rd Gorham (03581) *(G-14359)*

A
L
P
H
A
B
E
T
I
C

Gorham Times Inc.. 207 839-8390
  77 South St Gorham (04038) *(G-4821)*

Gorilla Bars Inc.. 802 309-4997
  336 N Winooski Ave Burlington (05401) *(G-17138)*

Gorilla Circuits.. 603 864-0283
  207 Main St Nashua (03060) *(G-15106)*

Gorilla Graphics Inc **(PA)**.......................... **617 623-2838**
  1236 Eastern Ave Ste 1 Malden (02148) *(G-10016)*

Gorilla Graphics Inc..................................... 860 704-8208
  52 N Main St Middletown (06457) *(G-1748)*

Gorilla Grip, Westport *Also Called: Hills Point Industries LLC (G-4173)*

Gorman Machine Corp.................................... 508 923-9462
  122 E Grove St Middleboro (02346) *(G-10359)*

Gortons, Gloucester *Also Called: Gortons Inc (G-8939)*

Gortons Inc **(DH)**.................................... **978 283-3000**
  128 Rogers St Gloucester (01930) *(G-8939)*

Gosolar NH LLC.. 603 948-1189
  232 Calef Hwy Unit 9 Barrington (03825) *(G-13914)*

Goss Lumber Co Inc..................................... 603 428-3363
  841 Flanders Rd Henniker (03242) *(G-14434)*

Gossamer Press.. 207 827-9881
  6 Albion Rd Benton (04901) *(G-4545)*

Got Interface.. 781 547-5700
  2 Centennial Dr Ste 310b Peabody (01960) *(G-11312)*

Gotham Chemical Company Inc.......................... 203 854-6644
  21 South St Norwalk (06854) *(G-2508)*

Gotham Greens, Providence *Also Called: Gotham Greens Providence LLC (G-16526)*

Gotham Greens Providence LLC......................... 401 816-0245
  555 Harris Ave Providence (02909) *(G-16526)*

Gotham Ink In Color, Marlborough *Also Called: Gotham Ink of New England Inc (G-10154)*

Gotham Ink of New England Inc......................... 508 485-7911
  255 E Main St Marlborough (01752) *(G-10154)*

Gotham Technologies Inc................................ 800 468-4261
  21 South St Norwalk (06854) *(G-2509)*

Goto, Boston *Also Called: GoTo Group Inc (G-6768)*

GoTo Group Inc **(PA)**   333 Summer St Boston (02210) *(G-6768)*

Gotuit Media Corp....................................... 801 592-5575
  400 Tradecenter Ste 3890 Woburn (01801) *(G-13575)*

Gotuit Video, Woburn *Also Called: Gotuit Media Corp (G-13575)*

Goulet Enterprises Inc.................................. 860 379-0793
  115 New Hartford Rd Pleasant Valley (06063) *(G-2801)*

Goulet Printery, Pleasant Valley *Also Called: Goulet Enterprises Inc (G-2801)*

Government Sales, Hartford *Also Called: Government Surplus Sales Inc (G-1484)*

Government Surplus Sales Inc.......................... 860 247-7787
  69 Francis Ave Hartford (06106) *(G-1484)*

Governor Supply Co..................................... 978 870-6888
  22 Hunter Ln Lancaster (01523) *(G-9526)*

Governors America Corporation......................... 413 233-1888
  720 Silver St Agawam (01001) *(G-5791)*

Gowanda Rcd LLC.. 716 532-2234
  520 East Industrial Park Dr Manchester (03109) *(G-14853)*

Gowdey Reed, Central Falls *Also Called: Reed Gowdey Company (G-15795)*

Gowen Inc.. 207 773-1761
  400 Commercial St Ste 101 Portland (04101) *(G-5219)*

Gowen Marine, Portland *Also Called: Gowen Inc (G-5219)*

GP Aggregate Corp...................................... 978 283-5318
  19 Pond Rd Gloucester (01930) *(G-8940)*

GP Gypsum Corp... 603 433-8000
  170 Shattuck Way Portsmouth (03801) *(G-15394)*

GP Industries.. 860 859-9938
  500 Norwich Ave Ste 7 Taftville (06380) *(G-3597)*

GP&c Operations LLC.................................... 978 630-1028
  77 Industrial Rowe Gardner (01440) *(G-8888)*

GP&c Operations LLC **(PA)**.......................... **978 630-1028**
  164 Fredette St Gardner (01440) *(G-8889)*

GP&g, Rowley *Also Called: General Products & Gear Corp (G-11674)*

Gp2 Technologies, Bow *Also Called: Gp2 Technologies Inc (G-13998)*

Gp2 Technologies Inc.................................... 603 226-0336
  157 River Rd Unit 18 Bow (03304) *(G-13998)*

GPA Global US Holding Inc.............................. 800 334-1113
  774 Norfolk St Mansfield (02048) *(G-10053)*

Gpd Optoelectronics Corp............................... 603 894-6865
  7 Manor Pkwy Salem (03079) *(G-15533)*

Gpi Nh-T Inc... 603 624-1800
  33 Auto Center Rd Manchester (03103) *(G-14854)*

Gpx International, Wakefield *Also Called: Yokohama Tws North America Inc (G-12544)*

Grace Lee Designs Shilling.............................. 617 661-7090
  309 Huron Ave Cambridge (02138) *(G-7593)*

Grace Machine Company LLC............................ 860 828-8789
  46 Woodlawn Rd Berlin (06037) *(G-68)*

Gracenote Media Services LLC.......................... 518 223-1993
  40 Danbury Rd Wilton (06897) *(G-4240)*

Gracies Kitchens Inc.................................... 203 773-0795
  211 Food Terminal Plz New Haven (06511) *(G-2156)*

Graco Awards Manufacturing Inc........................ 281 255-2161
  177 Georgia Ave Providence (02905) *(G-16527)*

Gradiant Osmotics Inc................................... 781 819-5034
  130 New Boston St Ste 200 Woburn (01801) *(G-13576)*

Graduation Solutions LLC............................... 914 934-5991
  200 Pemberwick Rd Greenwich (06831) *(G-1332)*

Graduation Source, Greenwich *Also Called: Graduation Solutions LLC (G-1332)*

Grafted Coatings Inc.................................... 203 377-9979
  400 Surf Ave Stratford (06615) *(G-3543)*

Grafton Fund, The, Grafton *Also Called: Windham Foundation Inc (G-17275)*

Grand Embroidery Inc.................................... 203 888-7484
  225 Christian St Oxford (06478) *(G-2695)*

Grand Image, Hudson *Also Called: Grand Image Inc (G-9371)*

Grand Image Inc... 888 973-2622
  560 Main St Ste 3 Hudson (01749) *(G-9371)*

Grand Imprints, Oxford *Also Called: Grand Embroidery Inc (G-2695)*

Grandstream Networks Inc **(PA)**..................... **617 566-9300**
  126 Brookline Ave Ste 3 Boston (02215) *(G-6769)*

Grandten Distilling, Boston *Also Called: Grandten Distilling LLC (G-6770)*

Grandten Distilling LLC................................. 484 888-1323
  7 Clinton St Newton (02458) *(G-10758)*

Grandten Distilling LLC................................. 617 269-0497
  383 Dorchester Ave Ste 130 Boston (02127) *(G-6770)*

Grandy Organics LLC **(PA)**.......................... **207 935-7415**
  34 Schoolhouse Rd Hiram (04041) *(G-4890)*

Grandyoats, Hiram *Also Called: Grandy Organics LLC (G-4890)*

Granger Lynch Corp..................................... 508 756-6244
  18 Mccracken Rd Millbury (01527) *(G-10435)*

Granite Commercial RE LLC............................. 603 669-2770
  30 Temple St Ste 300 Nashua (03060) *(G-15107)*

Granite Forge LLC....................................... 603 589-9480
  32 Executive Dr Hudson (03051) *(G-14501)*

Granite Group Wholesalers LLC......................... 860 537-7600
  464 S Main St Ste 1 Colchester (06415) *(G-659)*

Granite Group, The, Colchester *Also Called: Granite Group Wholesalers LLC (G-659)*

Granite Importers Inc **(PA)**........................ **802 476-5812**
  16 S Vine St Barre (05641) *(G-17002)*

Granite Importers Transport, Barre *Also Called: Granite Importers Inc (G-17002)*

Granite Industries of Vermont, Graniteville *Also Called: Rock of Ages Corporation (G-17277)*

Granite Industries Vermont Inc......................... 800 451-3236
  Vanneti Place Barre (05641) *(G-17003)*

Granite Power Technologies, Manchester *Also Called: Vicor Corporation (G-14953)*

Granite Shore Power LLC................................ 603 634-2299
  431 River Rd Bow (03304) *(G-13999)*

Granite State Cabinetry, Bedford *Also Called: Granite State Ktchns Dstrs In (G-13931)*

Granite State Candy Shoppe LLC **(PA)**.............. **603 225-2591**
  13 Warren St Concord (03301) *(G-14131)*

Granite State Concrete Co Inc.......................... 603 673-3327
  408 Elm St Milford (03055) *(G-15023)*

Granite State Cover and Canvas........................ 603 382-5462
  144 Main St Plaistow (03865) *(G-15345)*

Granite State Ktchns Dstrs In.......................... 603 472-4080
  384 Route 101 Bedford (03110) *(G-13931)*

Granite State Log Homes Inc **(PA)**................. **603 536-4949**
  17 King Rd Campton (03223) *(G-14044)*

Granite State Manufacturing............................ 800 464-7646
  124 Joliette St Manchester (03102) *(G-14855)*

Granite State Manufacturing, Manchester *Also Called: Allard Nazarian Group Inc* **(G-14810)**

Granite State Manufacturing, Nashua *Also Called: Allard Nazarian Group Inc* **(G-15057)**

Granite State Plasma Cutting.. 603 536-4415
  10 Pleasant St Ste 400 Portsmouth (03801) **(G-15395)**

Granite State Plasma Cutting, Portsmouth *Also Called: Granite State Plasma Cutting* **(G-15395)**

Granite State Plastics, Hudson *Also Called: Granite State Plastics Inc* **(G-14502)**

Granite State Plastics Inc... 603 669-6715
  37 Executive Dr Hudson (03051) **(G-14502)**

Granite State Stamps Inc.. 603 669-9322
  8025 S Willow St Ste 102 Manchester (03103) **(G-14856)**

Grant Foster Group L P.. 401 231-4077
  500 Washington Hwy Smithfield (02917) **(G-16705)**

Grant Manufacturing and Mch Co...................................... 203 366-4557
  90 Silliman Ave Bridgeport (06605) **(G-326)**

Granta USA Ltd... 440 207-6051
  62 E Starrs Plain Rd Danbury (06810) **(G-753)**

Grape Island Inc... 978 432-1280
  41 Railroad Ave Rowley (01969) **(G-11675)**

Graphic Arts Finishers, Jamaica Plain *Also Called: Graphic Arts Finishers Inc* **(G-9501)**

Graphic Arts Finishers Inc... 617 241-9292
  241 Perkins St Unit D201 Jamaica Plain (02130) **(G-9501)**

Graphic Arts Institute of Neng... 508 804-4100
  5 Crystal Pond Rd Southborough (01772) **(G-11995)**

Graphic Developments Inc... 781 878-2222
  70 Mayflower Dr Hanover (02339) **(G-9033)**

Graphic Edge LLC... 802 855-8840
  155 Seward Rd Rutland (05701) **(G-17498)**

Graphic Excellence LLC.. 413 733-6691
  1441 Main St Springfield (01103) **(G-12096)**

Graphic Fullfillment & Finishing Inc.................................. 781 727-8845
  145 Union St Ste 3 Holbrook (02343) **(G-9173)**

Graphic Image Inc... 203 877-8787
  561 Boston Post Rd Milford (06460) **(G-1830)**

Graphic Impact Signs Inc.. 413 499-0382
  575 Dalton Ave Pittsfield (01201) **(G-11399)**

Graphic Ink Incorporated.. 401 431-5081
  629 Warren Ave East Providence (02914) **(G-16021)**

Graphic Litho, Lawrence *Also Called: High-Speed Process Prtg Corp* **(G-9568)**

Graphic Packaging Intl LLC.. 978 459-9328
  164 Meadowcroft St Lowell (01852) **(G-9882)**

Graphic Packaging Intl LLC.. 603 230-5100
  80 Commercial St Concord (03301) **(G-14132)**

Graphic Packaging Intl LLC.. 603 230-5100
  80 Commercial St Concord (03301) **(G-14133)**

Graphic Packaging Intl LLC.. 603 224-2333
  80 Commercial St Concord (03301) **(G-14134)**

Graphic Utilities Incorporated... 207 370-9178
  191 Development Dr Limestone (04750) **(G-5004)**

Graphicast Inc.. 603 532-4481
  36 Knight St Jaffrey (03452) **(G-14568)**

Graphics Press LLC... 203 272-9187
  1161 Sperry Rd Cheshire (06410) **(G-596)**

Graphics Source Co... 413 543-0700
  18 Pequot Rd Southampton (01073) **(G-11985)**

Graphisoft North America Inc... 617 485-4219
  1601 Trapelo Rd Ste 162 Waltham (02451) **(G-12688)**

Graphite Insulg Systems Inc.. 978 630-8988
  36 Lachance St Gardner (01440) **(G-8890)**

Graphix Plus Inc... 508 677-2122
  52 Queen St Fall River (02724) **(G-8557)**

Graphtec Press... 727 267-0940
  40 Russo St Providence (02904) **(G-16528)**

Graphx Copy & Printing, Watertown *Also Called: John K Dietrich & Assoc Inc* **(G-12884)**

Grass Roots Creamery... 860 653-6303
  4 Park Pl Granby (06035) **(G-1306)**

Grassetti Sales Associates Inc....................................... 413 737-2283
  160 Progress Ave Springfield (01104) **(G-12097)**

Grate Ideas of America LLC... 844 292-6044
  63 Marina Loop Colchester (05446) **(G-17193)**

Grate Products LLC... 800 649-6140
  31 Sanford Rd Westport (02790) **(G-13296)**

Gravel Public House... 508 384-0888
  36 South St Wrentham (02093) **(G-13842)**

Graves Concrete, East Templeton *Also Called: Ragged Hill Incorporated* **(G-8414)**

Gray Enterprises, Charlestown *Also Called: Pompanette LLC* **(G-14067)**

Gray Rock Concrete... 802 379-5393
  54 W Milton Rd Milton (05468) **(G-17359)**

Graybark Enterprises LLC.. 203 255-4503
  20 Governors Ln Fairfield (06824) **(G-1187)**

Graycer Screw Products Co Inc....................................... 508 966-1810
  113 Depot St Bellingham (02019) **(G-6290)**

Graywolf Sensing Solutions LLC **(PA)**.............................. **203 402-0477**
  6 Research Dr Ste 110 Shelton (06484) **(G-3009)**

Great American Recrtl Eqp.. 401 463-5587
  24 Stafford Ct Cranston (02920) **(G-15869)**

Great Bay Manufacturing LLC... 603 948-1212
  73 Pickering Rd Ste 101 Rochester (03839) **(G-15477)**

Great Harvest Bread, Burlington *Also Called: Queen Dog LLC* **(G-17154)**

Great Lakes Chemical Corp **(DH)**.................................. **203 573-2000**
  2 Armstrong Rd Ste 101 Shelton (06484) **(G-3010)**

Great Neck Saw Mfrs Inc.. 508 865-4482
  100 Riverlin St Millbury (01527) **(G-10436)**

Great Northern Docks Inc **(PA)**................................... **207 693-3770**
  1114 Roosevelt Trl Naples (04055) **(G-5080)**

Great Northern Dunnage LLC.. 978 343-2300
  291 Westminster St Fitchburg (01420) **(G-8656)**

Great Northern Industries Inc **(PA)**.............................. **617 262-4314**
  266 Beacon St Ste 2 Boston (02116) **(G-6771)**

Great Rhythm Brewing Co LLC.. 603 430-9640
  105 Bartlett St Ste 4b Portsmouth (03801) **(G-15396)**

Great Wine, The, Acton *Also Called: Hirsch Retail Store Inc* **(G-5753)**

Greco Bros Inc... 401 421-9306
  1 Greco Ln Providence (02909) **(G-16529)**

Greco Industries Inc.. 203 798-7804
  14 Trowbridge Dr Bethel (06801) **(G-117)**

Greeley Company, Middleton *Also Called: Hcpro Inc* **(G-10385)**

Green Brothers Fabricating **(PA)**................................. **508 880-3608**
  15 4th St Taunton (02780) **(G-12339)**

Green Development LLC... 401 295-4998
  2000 Chapel View Blvd Ste 500 Cranston (02920) **(G-15870)**

Green Manor Corporation **(PA)**................................... **860 643-8111**
  306 Progress Dr Manchester (06042) **(G-1599)**

Green Meadow Lumber Inc... 413 568-0056
  994 Western Ave Westfield (01085) **(G-13167)**

Green Mountain Baking Co, Auburn *Also Called: Lepage Bakeries Park St LLC* **(G-4441)**

Green Mountain Beerworks, Morrisville *Also Called: Green Mountain Distillers LLC* **(G-17382)**

Green Mountain Beverage, Brandon *Also Called: Vermont Hard Cider Company LLC* **(G-17071)**

Green Mountain Beverages, Middlebury *Also Called: Vermont Hard Cider Company LLC* **(G-17350)**

Green Mountain Cbd Inc.. 802 595-3258
  273 Kate Brook Rd Hardwick (05843) **(G-17283)**

Green Mountain Choclat Co Inc **(PA)**............................. **508 473-9060**
  1 Rosenfeld Dr Hopedale (01747) **(G-9298)**

Green Mountain Coffee Roasters, Burlington *Also Called: Keurig Green Mountain Inc* **(G-7385)**

Green Mountain Creamery, Guilford *Also Called: Commonwealth Dairy LLC* **(G-17280)**

Green Mountain Custom Barrels, Conway *Also Called: Green Mtn Rifle Barrel Co Inc* **(G-14180)**

Green Mountain Distillers LLC... 802 498-4848
  2919 Laporte Rd Morrisville (05661) **(G-17382)**

Green Mountain Forest Products...................................... 802 868-2306
  962 Morey Rd Highgate Center (05459) **(G-17289)**

Green Mountain Gazebo.. 802 869-1212
  237 Kimball Hill Rd Westminster (05158) **(G-17701)**

Green Mountain Knitting, Medway *Also Called: Plastic Monofil Co Ltd* **(G-10311)**

Green Mountain Knitting Inc... 800 361-1190
  25 Jonergin Dr Swanton (05488) **(G-17637)**

Green Mountain Metals of VT.. 603 542-0005
  2 Wentworth Pl Claremont (03743) **(G-14090)**

Green Mountain Monogram Inc.. 802 757-2553
  14 Creamery St Wells River (05081) **(G-17687)**

Green Mountain Risk MGT LLC.. 802 683-8586
  660 Central Ave Ste 201 Dover (03820) **(G-14229)**

A
L
P
H
A
B
E
T
I
C

Green Mountain Spinnery Inc.................................. 802 387-4528
  7 Brickyard Ln East Dummerston (05346) *(G-17216)*

Green Mtn Cof Cafe Visitor Ctr, Waterbury *Also Called: Keurig Green Mountain Inc (G-17675)*

Green Mtn Maple Sug Ref Co Inc.............................. 802 644-2625
  204 Boarding House Hill Rd Belvidere Center (05442) *(G-17034)*

Green Mtn Rifle Barrel Co Inc.................................. 603 447-1095
  153 W Main St Conway (03818) *(G-14180)*

Green Publishing, West Springfield *Also Called: Frg Publications (G-13026)*

Green Valley Packaging Inc.................................... 860 779-7970
  90 Wauregan Rd Danielson (06239) *(G-839)*

Greenbrier Games LLP... 978 618-8442
  12 Bicknell St Marlborough (01752) *(G-10155)*

Greene Marine Inc.. 207 846-3184
  343 Gilman Road Yarmouth (04096) *(G-5705)*

Greene Rubber Company Inc **(PA)**............................ **781 937-9909**
  20 Cross St Woburn (01801) *(G-13577)*

Greener Formulas LLC... 888 825-4460
  121 Church St North Walpole (03609) *(G-15257)*

Greenerd Press & Mch Co LLC **(PA)**.......................... **603 889-4101**
  41 Crown St Nashua (03060) *(G-15108)*

Greenfield Global USA Inc **(HQ)**............................ **203 740-3471**
  58 Vale Rd Brookfield (06804) *(G-524)*

Greenfield Industries Inc..................................... 413 772-3200
  34 Sanderson St Greenfield (01301) *(G-8992)*

Greenhaven Cabinetry Mllwk LLC................................ 860 535-1106
  338 Elm St Stonington (06378) *(G-3509)*

Greenleaf Bfuels New Haven LLC................................ 203 672-9028
  100 Waterfront St New Haven (06512) *(G-2157)*

Greenlght Bscnces Holdings Pbc **(PA)**....................... **617 616-8188**
  200 Boston Ave Medford (02155) *(G-10287)*

Greenlight Biosciences, Medford *Also Called: Greenlght Bscnces Holdings Pbc (G-10287)*

Greenmaker Industries, West Hartford *Also Called: Greenmaker Industries Conn LLC (G-4062)*

Greenmaker Industries Conn LLC................................ 860 761-2830
  697 Oakwood Ave West Hartford (06110) *(G-4062)*

Greenplanet Scientific, Littleton *Also Called: Alpha Tech Pet Inc (G-9800)*

Greenrange Furniture Company.................................. 802 747-8564
  2778 Shelburne Falls Rd Hinesburg (05461) *(G-17292)*

Greensight Inc.. 617 633-4919
  529 Main St Charlestown (02129) *(G-7875)*

Greensource Fabrication LLC **(PA)**.......................... **603 283-9880**
  81 Ceda Rd Bldg 1 Charlestown (03603) *(G-14064)*

Greenstone Slate Company Inc.................................. 802 287-4333
  325 Upper Rd Poultney (05764) *(G-17448)*

Greentree Marketing Inc....................................... 508 877-2581
  10 Central St Framingham (01701) *(G-8775)*

Greenville Ready Mix.. 401 231-3900
  79 Cedar Swamp Rd Smithfield (02917) *(G-16706)*

Greenville Ready Mix Inc...................................... 401 539-2333
  Skunk Hill Rd Ashaway (02804) *(G-15740)*

Greenwald Industries, Chester *Also Called: Blackwold Inc (G-624)*

Greenwich Fine Woodwork LLC................................... 203 987-0001
  7 Lexington Ave Norwalk (06854) *(G-2510)*

Greenwich Magazine, Westport *Also Called: Moffly Publications Inc (G-4187)*

Greenwich Sentinel.. 203 883-1430
  28 Bruce Park Ave Greenwich (06830) *(G-1333)*

Greenwich Time.. 203 253-2922
  44 Columbus Pl Apt 9 Stamford (06907) *(G-3359)*

Greenwich Triangle LLC **(DH)**............................... **800 634-5312**
  25 Computer Dr Haverhill (01832) *(G-9099)*

Greenwich Workshop Inc **(PA)**............................... **203 881-3336**
  151 Main St Seymour (06483) *(G-2961)*

Greenwood Associates, Wareham *Also Called: Electro-Prep Inc (G-12834)*

Greenwood Emrgncy Vehicles LLC **(HQ)**....................... **508 695-7138**
  530 John L Dietsch Blvd Attleboro Falls (02763) *(G-6086)*

Greenwood Mill Inc.. 802 626-0800
  599 Goose Green Rd Bradford (05033) *(G-17062)*

Greenwood Publishing Group Inc................................ 603 431-7894
  145 Maplewood Ave Ste 300 Portsmouth (03801) *(G-15397)*

Greenwood Publishing Group LLC **(DH)**....................... **617 351-5000**
  125 High St Boston (02110) *(G-6772)*

Greg Robbins and Associates................................... 888 699-8876
  15 Park Pl Branford (06405) *(G-262)*

Gregor Technologies LLC....................................... 860 482-2569
  529 Technology Park Dr Torrington (06790) *(G-3683)*

Gregory Engineering Corp...................................... 508 481-0480
  105 Bartlett St Marlborough (01752) *(G-10156)*

Gregory Manufacturing Inc..................................... 413 536-5432
  102 Cabot St Ste 2 Holyoke (01040) *(G-9257)*

Gregory Woodworks LLC... 203 794-0726
  6 Sympaug Park Rd Bethel (06801) *(G-118)*

Gregs Outboard Service LLC.................................... 860 339-5139
  304 Boston Post Rd Old Saybrook (06475) *(G-2649)*

Gregstrom Corporation... 781 935-6600
  64 Holton St Woburn (01801) *(G-13578)*

Greif Inc... 740 549-6000
  491 North St Windsor Locks (06096) *(G-4327)*

Greif Global Industrial Packg, Windsor Locks *Also Called: Greif Inc (G-4327)*

Gremarco Industries Inc....................................... 508 867-5244
  131 E Main St West Brookfield (01585) *(G-12995)*

Grey Barn Farm Enterprises LLC................................ 508 645-4854
  22 South Rd Chilmark (02535) *(G-8071)*

Grey Wall Software LLC.. 203 782-5944
  195 Church St Fl 14 New Haven (06510) *(G-2158)*

Greystone, North Providence *Also Called: Induplate Inc (G-16303)*

Greystone Gift Shop, Randolph *Also Called: Porter Music Box Co Inc (G-17473)*

Greystone Incorporated.. 401 333-0444
  7 Wellington Rd Lincoln (02865) *(G-16139)*

Greystone of Lincoln Inc **(PA)**............................. **401 333-0444**
  7 Wellington Rd Lincoln (02865) *(G-16140)*

Gridedge Networks Inc... 978 569-2000
  40 Nagog Park Ste 105 Acton (01720) *(G-5749)*

Griffin Manufacturing Co Inc.................................. 508 677-0048
  502 Bedford St Fall River (02720) *(G-8558)*

Griffin Publishing Co Inc..................................... 781 829-4700
  21 Chestnut St Duxbury (02332) *(G-8332)*

Griffin Report Food Marketing, Duxbury *Also Called: Griffin Publishing Co Inc (G-8332)*

Grill Daddy Brush Company..................................... 888 840-7552
  29 Arcadia Rd Old Greenwich (06870) *(G-2633)*

Grillo Services LLC... 203 877-5070
  1183 Oronoque Rd Milford (06461) *(G-1831)*

Grinnell Cabinet Makers Inc................................... 401 781-1080
  169 Mill St Cranston (02905) *(G-15871)*

Grip Security Inc... 757 439-5650
  50 Milk St Fl 16 Boston (02109) *(G-6773)*

Gripwet Inc... 207 239-0486
  55 Devereaux Cir South Portland (04106) *(G-5504)*

Grist For Mill LLC.. 603 744-0405
  2 Central St Bristol (03222) *(G-14036)*

Griswold LLC.. 845 986-2271
  1 River St Moosup (06354) *(G-1930)*

Griswold Rubber Company, Moosup *Also Called: Griswold LLC (G-1930)*

Griswold Textile Print Inc.................................... 401 596-2784
  84 White Rock Rd Westerly (02891) *(G-16931)*

Grob Inc.. 617 817-3123
  19 Fairhope Rd Weston (02493) *(G-13285)*

Grolier Telemarketing Inc..................................... 203 797-3500
  90 Sherman Turnpike Danbury (06816) *(G-754)*

Grooming Ventures - FL LLC **(HQ)**........................... **305 593-0667**
  1 Gillette Park Boston (02127) *(G-6774)*

Groov-Pin Corporation **(PA)**................................ **770 251-5054**
  331 Farnum Pike Smithfield (02917) *(G-16707)*

Grossman Marketing Group, Woburn *Also Called: Massachusetts Envelope Co Inc (G-13606)*

Grote & Weigel Inc **(PA)**................................... **860 242-8528**
  76 Granby St Bloomfield (06002) *(G-166)*

Groton Timberworks Inc.. 802 584-4446
  2126 Scott Hwy Groton (05046) *(G-17278)*

Grotto Always Inc... 203 754-0295
  634 Watertown Ave Waterbury (06708) *(G-3915)*

Group Four Transducers Inc **(PA)**........................... **413 525-2705**
  22 Deer Park Dr East Longmeadow (01028) *(G-8378)*

Groupglobalnet Corp... 857 212-4012
  768 Morton St Boston (02126) *(G-6775)*

Grove Labs Inc.. 703 608-8178
  28 Dane St Somerville (02143) *(G-11878)*

(G-0000) Company's Geographic Section entry number

Grove Products Inc. — 978 534-5188
17 Marguerite Ave Ste 1 Leominster (01453) *(G-9668)*

Grove Street Enterprises Inc. — 413 698-3301
508 Canaan Rd Richmond (01254) *(G-11626)*

Grover Gndrilling Holdings LLC **(PA)** — **207 743-7051**
59 Industrial Dr Oxford (04270) *(G-5144)*

Grover Gundrilling LLC — 207 743-7051
59 Industrial Dr Oxford (04270) *(G-5145)*

Growspan LLC — 877 835-9996
1395 John Fitch Blvd South Windsor (06074) *(G-3152)*

Growspan Greenhouse Structures, South Windsor *Also Called: Growspan LLC* *(G-3152)*

Growth I M33 L P — 617 877-0046
888 Boylston St Ste 500 Boston (02199) *(G-6776)*

Grs Group Inc. — 207 775-6139
98 Elm St Portland (04101) *(G-5220)*

GS Blodgett LLC **(HQ)** — **802 860-3700**
42 Allen Martin Dr Essex Junction (05452) *(G-17236)*

GS Blodgett Corporation — 603 225-5688
509 Route 3a Bow (03304) *(G-14000)*

GS Blodgett Corporation — 802 860-3700
42 Allen Martin Dr Essex Junction (05452) *(G-17237)*

GS Inc. — 207 593-7730
12 Moran Dr Ste A1 Rockland (04841) *(G-5332)*

GS Precision LLC-Keene Div. — 603 355-1166
18 Bradco St Keene (03431) *(G-14602)*

Gs Rubber Industries LLC — 508 672-0742
1 S Main St Coventry (02816) *(G-15814)*

Gs Thermal Solutions Inc. — 475 289-4625
144 Old Brookfield Rd Ste C Danbury (06811) *(G-755)*

GSC, Lancaster *Also Called: Governor Supply Co (G-9526)*

Gsk. — 781 795-4165
200 Cambridgepark Dr Cambridge (02140) *(G-7594)*

Gss Infotech Ct Inc. — 860 709-0933
41b New London Tpke Ste 7 Glastonbury (06033) *(G-1282)*

Gssi, Nashua *Also Called: Geophysical Survey Systems Inc (G-15104)*

Gt Advanced Technologies Inc **(DH)** — **603 883-5200**
5 Wentworth Dr Ste 1 Hudson (03051) *(G-14503)*

Gt Advanced Technologies Ltd. — 603 883-5200
5 Wentworth Dr Hudson (03051) *(G-14504)*

Gt Equipment Holdings Inc. — 603 883-5200
243 Daniel Webster Hwy Merrimack (03054) *(G-14983)*

Gt Spirits Inc. — 617 276-5209
862 E 2nd St Boston (02127) *(G-6777)*

Gta-Nht Inc **(HQ)** — **781 331-5900**
30 Commerce Rd Rockland (02370) *(G-11647)*

Gtat, Hudson *Also Called: Gt Advanced Technologies Inc (G-14503)*

Gtat Corporation **(DH)** — **603 883-5200**
5 Wentworth Dr # 1 Hudson (03051) *(G-14505)*

Gtb Innovative Solutions Inc. — 413 733-0146
507 Southampton Rd Ste 1 Westfield (01085) *(G-13168)*

GTC Biotherapeutics Inc. — 508 370-5429
175 Crossing Blvd Ste 410 Framingham (01702) *(G-8776)*

GTC Falcon Inc. — 508 746-0200
130 Industrial Park Rd Plymouth (02360) *(G-11462)*

Gtech, Braintree *Also Called: Igt Global Solutions Corp (G-7188)*

Gti Spindle Technology Inc **(DH)** — **603 669-5993**
33 Zachary Rd Manchester (03109) *(G-14857)*

Gtr Manufacturing LLC — 508 588-3240
1 Jonathan Dr Brockton (02301) *(G-7282)*

Gtxcel Inc. — 508 804-3092
144 Turnpike Rd Ste 140 Southborough (01772) *(G-11996)*

Gty Technology, Boston *Also Called: Gty Technology Holdings Inc (G-6778)*

Gty Technology Holdings Inc **(PA)** — **702 945-2898**
800 Boylston St Fl 16 Boston (02199) *(G-6778)*

Guardair Corporation — 413 594-4400
47 Veterans Dr Chicopee (01022) *(G-8035)*

Guardian Envmtl Tech Inc. — 860 350-2200
208 Sawyer Hill Rd New Milford (06776) *(G-2245)*

Guardian Indus Pdts Inc Mass. — 508 384-0060
150 Dedham St Norfolk (02056) *(G-10798)*

Guardian Industrial, Norfolk *Also Called: Guardian Indus Pdts Inc Mass (G-10798)*

Guardicore Inc. — 781 789-8904
100 Summer St Ste 1600 Boston (02110) *(G-6779)*

Guertin Graphics & Awards, Worcester *Also Called: Guertins Graphics Inc (G-13735)*

Guertins Graphics Inc. — 508 754-0200
134 Southbridge St Ste 136 Worcester (01608) *(G-13735)*

Guess Inc. — 781 843-3147
250 Granite St Ste B Braintree (02184) *(G-7185)*

GUESS?, INC., Braintree *Also Called: Guess Inc (G-7185)*

Guhring Inc. — 860 216-5948
121 W Dudley Town Rd Ste C Bloomfield (06002) *(G-167)*

Guia Commercial Portugues Inc. — 401 438-1740
100 Warren Ave East Providence (02914) *(G-16022)*

Guida-Seibert Dairy Company **(HQ)** — **800 832-8929**
433 Park St New Britain (06051) *(G-2028)*

Guida's Dairy, New Britain *Also Called: Guida-Seibert Dairy Company (G-2028)*

Guidant Corporation — 508 683-4000
300 Boston Scientific Way Marlborough (01752) *(G-10157)*

Guidera Marketing Services. — 860 599-8880
21 Pawcatuck Ave Pawcatuck (06379) *(G-2721)*

Guidewire Technologies Inc. — 603 894-4399
26 Keewaydin Dr Ste D Salem (03079) *(G-15534)*

Guild Optical Associates, Amherst *Also Called: Guild Optical Associates Inc (G-13872)*

Guild Optical Associates Inc. — 603 889-6247
11 Columbia Dr Unit 13 Amherst (03031) *(G-13872)*

Guill Tool & Engrg Co Inc. — 401 822-8186
10 Pike St West Warwick (02893) *(G-16908)*

Guill Tool and Engrg Co Inc. — 401 828-7600
20 Pike St West Warwick (02893) *(G-16909)*

Guillow, Wakefield *Also Called: Paul K Guillow Inc (G-12526)*

Gulemo Inc. — 860 456-1151
2 Birch St Willimantic (06226) *(G-4218)*

Gulf Manufacturing Inc. — 860 529-8601
645 Cromwell Ave Rocky Hill (06067) *(G-2923)*

Gulfstream Aerospace Corp. — 912 965-3000
95 Old County Rd East Granby (06026) *(G-935)*

Gulfstream Aerospace Corp. — 413 562-5866
33 Elise St Westfield (01085) *(G-13169)*

Gunboat. — 401 619-1055
11 Bowler Ln Unit A Newport (02840) *(G-16211)*

Guptill's Logging Supply, East Machias *Also Called: Lyle Guptill (G-4740)*

Gurit (usa) Inc. — 401 396-5008
115 Broadcommon Rd Bristol (02809) *(G-15767)*

Gurit Uk, Bristol *Also Called: Gurit (usa) Inc (G-15767)*

Gurnet Holding Company. — 617 588-4900
55 Cambridge Pkwy Ste 401 Cambridge (02142) *(G-7595)*

Gurney Brothers Construction. — 802 886-2210
19 Gurney Rd North Springfield (05150) *(G-17421)*

Gurukrupa I LLC. — 508 947-1080
422 W Grove St Middleboro (02346) *(G-10360)*

Gutor Electronic Americas LLC. — 713 397-3798
70 Mechanic St Foxboro (02035) *(G-8698)*

Gutz LLC. — 978 805-5001
71 Willie St Lowell (01854) *(G-9883)*

Guyot Brothers Company Inc. — 508 222-2000
20 John Williams St Attleboro (02703) *(G-6022)*

Gvd Corporation **(PA)** — **617 661-0060**
45 Spinelli Pl Cambridge (02138) *(G-7596)*

Gvs North America, Sanford *Also Called: Maine Manufacturing LLC (G-5398)*

Gw Ski Inc. — 802 464-3464
5 Mountain Park Plz West Dover (05356) *(G-17690)*

Gwilliam Company Inc. — 860 354-2884
46 Old State Rd New Milford (06776) *(G-2246)*

Gws Marketing Associates, Seymour *Also Called: Greenwich Workshop Inc (G-2961)*

Gws Tool Holdings LLC. — 800 523-8570
616 Dwight St Springfield (01104) *(G-12098)*

Gxt Green Inc. — 978 735-4367
20 Bryant St Cambridge (02138) *(G-7597)*

Gybenorth Industries LLC. — 203 876-9876
80 Wampus Ln Ste 13 Milford (06460) *(G-1832)*

Gypsum Systems LLC. — 860 470-3916
11 Hinman Meadow Rd Burlington (06013) *(G-550)*

A L P H A B E T I C

Gyre9 LLC..203 702-4010
1200 Main St S Southbury (06488) *(G-3194)*

Gyrus Acmi LLC **(DH)**..................................**508 804-2600**
800 W Park Dr Westborough (01581) *(G-13104)*

Gzsl Corp...508 695-0727
90 George Leven Dr North Attleboro (02760) *(G-10872)*

H & B Tool & Eng Co Inc..860 528-9341
481 Sullivan Ave South Windsor (06074) *(G-3153)*

H & H Engineering Company Inc..............................978 682-0567
6 Pine St Methuen (01844) *(G-10333)*

H & H Marine Inc...207 546-7477
932 Us Route 1 Ste 1 Steuben (04680) *(G-5532)*

H & M Crumpets, Ogunquit *Also Called: Harbor Candy Shop Inc (G-5123)*

H & S Machine Company Inc...................................978 686-2321
18 Hickory Ridge Dr Plaistow (03865) *(G-15346)*

H & S Tool and Engineering Inc...............................508 672-6509
777 Airport Rd Fall River (02720) *(G-8559)*

H & T Specialty Co Inc..781 893-3866
56 Clematis Ave Waltham (02453) *(G-12689)*

H & W Shoe Supplies, Pawtucket *Also Called: Stretch Products Corp (G-16418)*

H & W Test Products Inc..508 336-3200
58 Industrial Ct Seekonk (02771) *(G-11776)*

H A Manosh Corp..802 888-5722
120 Northgate Plz Ste A Morrisville (05661) *(G-17383)*

H Arthur York Logging Inc **(PA)**........................**207 746-5883**
157 Main Rd Medway (04460) *(G-5056)*

H Arthur York Logging Inc......................................207 746-5912
163 Turnpike Rd Medway (04460) *(G-5057)*

H B Smith Company Inc..413 568-3148
61 Union St Ste 7 Westfield (01085) *(G-13170)*

H B Welding Inc..401 727-0323
60 Dyerville Ave Johnston (02919) *(G-16088)*

H Barber & Sons Inc...203 729-9000
15 Raytkwich Rd Naugatuck (06770) *(G-1962)*

H C Haynes, Winn *Also Called: Herbert C Haynes Inc (G-5678)*

H G Steinmetz Mch Works Inc.................................203 794-1880
184 Jonathan Dr Stamford (06903) *(G-3360)*

H H Arnold Co Inc...781 878-0346
529 Liberty St Rockland (02370) *(G-11648)*

H Hirschmann Ltd..802 438-4447
467 Sheldon Ave West Rutland (05777) *(G-17695)*

H I Five Renewables..978 384-8032
8 Church St Merrimac (01860) *(G-10324)*

H J Baker & Bro Inc..203 682-9200
228 Saugatuck Ave Ste A Westport (06880) *(G-4171)*

H J Baker & Brother Inc...501 664-4870
2 Corporate Dr Ste 545 Shelton (06484) *(G-3011)*

H Krevit and Company Inc......................................203 772-3350
73 Welton St New Haven (06511) *(G-2159)*

H Larosee and Sons Inc...978 562-9417
35 Reilly Ave Blackstone (01504) *(G-6494)*

H Loeb Corporation...508 996-3745
419 Sawyer St Unit 2 New Bedford (02746) *(G-10597)*

H O Wire Co Inc...508 243-7177
215 Shrewsbury St West Boylston (01583) *(G-12963)*

H O Zimman Inc..781 598-9230
152 Lynnway Lynn (01902) *(G-9977)*

H P Hood-Booth Brothers Dairy...............................802 476-6605
219 Allen St Barre (05641) *(G-17004)*

H S Gere & Sons Inc...413 247-5010
33 Main St Hatfield (01038) *(G-9071)*

H V Holland Inc...401 423-0614
79 North Rd Jamestown (02835) *(G-16069)*

H-O Products Corporation......................................860 379-9875
12 Munro St Winsted (06098) *(G-4346)*

H.C. Starck Solutions, Newton *Also Called: Newton Materion Inc (G-10772)*

H.K. Klitzner Company Division, Lincoln *Also Called: Klitzner Industries Inc (G-16143)*

H.krevit, New Haven *Also Called: New Haven Chlor-Alkali LLC (G-2178)*

H&H Custom Metal Fabg Inc...................................603 382-2818
6 Duston Ave Plaistow (03865) *(G-15347)*

H&H Propeller and Shaft Inc...................................800 325-0117
0 Essex St Salem (01970) *(G-11720)*

H&H Propeller Shop Inc **(PA)**............................**978 744-3806**
0 Essex St Salem (01970) *(G-11721)*

H&L Instruments LLC...603 964-1818
34 Post Rd North Hampton (03862) *(G-15251)*

H&T Waterbury Inc..203 574-2240
984 Waterville St Waterbury (06710) *(G-3916)*

H&V, East Walpole *Also Called: Hollingsworth & Vose Company (G-8418)*

H2o Care Inc..978 777-8330
18 Lonergan Rd Middleton (01949) *(G-10384)*

H2o Wear, Wilton *Also Called: Waterwear Inc (G-15712)*

H2ohh, Saco *Also Called: Shed Happens Inc (G-5379)*

H32 Design and Development LLC **(PA)**...............**603 865-1000**
134 Hall St Ste F Concord (03301) *(G-14135)*

H4 Holdings LLC..207 494-8085
24 Industrial Park Rd Unit 2 Saco (04072) *(G-5369)*

Haartz, Acton *Also Called: Haartz Corporation (G-5750)*

Haartz Auto Fabric, Acton *Also Called: Haartz Corporation (G-5751)*

Haartz Corporation...978 264-2607
20 Craig Rd Acton (01720) *(G-5750)*

Haartz Corporation **(PA)**..................................**978 264-2600**
87 Hayward Rd Acton (01720) *(G-5751)*

Habasit Abt Inc...860 632-2211
150 Industrial Park Rd Middletown (06457) *(G-1749)*

Habasit America Inc..860 632-2211
150 Industrial Park Rd Middletown (06457) *(G-1750)*

Habco, Glastonbury *Also Called: Habco Industries LLC (G-1283)*

Habco Industries LLC..860 682-6800
172 Oak St Glastonbury (06033) *(G-1283)*

Habitat Post & Beam Inc..413 665-4006
21 Elm St South Deerfield (01373) *(G-11923)*

Habitat Virtual Village, South Deerfield *Also Called: Habitat Post & Beam Inc (G-11923)*

Hadco Corporation **(HQ)**..................................**603 421-3400**
12a Manor Pkwy Salem (03079) *(G-15535)*

Hadley Printing Company Inc...................................413 536-8517
58 N Canal St Holyoke (01040) *(G-9258)*

Haemonetics, Boston *Also Called: Haemonetics Corporation (G-6780)*

Haemonetics Asia Incorporated **(HQ)**.................**781 848-7100**
400 Wood Rd Braintree (02184) *(G-7186)*

Haemonetics Corporation **(PA)**..........................**781 848-7100**
125 Summer St Ste 1800 Boston (02110) *(G-6780)*

Hagan Design and Machine Inc...............................603 292-1101
8 Forbes Rd Newmarket (03857) *(G-15220)*

Hager Geoscience Inc...781 935-8111
596 Main St Woburn (01801) *(G-13579)*

Hahnel Bros Co **(PA)**.......................................**207 784-6477**
46 Strawberry Ave Lewiston (04240) *(G-4963)*

Hai Labs, Lexington *Also Called: Hightech Amercn Indus Labs Inc (G-9748)*

Haigh-Farr Inc..603 644-6170
43 Harvey Rd Bedford (03110) *(G-13932)*

Hailux Lighting, Warwick *Also Called: Ritronics Inc (G-16852)*

Haines Manufacturing Co, Presque Isle *Also Called: Harold Haines Inc (G-5300)*

Hairenik Association Inc...617 926-3974
80 Bigelow Ave Watertown (02472) *(G-12879)*

Hajan LLC..860 223-2005
788 W Main St New Britain (06053) *(G-2029)*

Halco Inc...203 575-9450
114 Porter St Waterbury (06708) *(G-3917)*

Haleos Montgomery Co, Marlborough *Also Called: Rohm Haas Electronic Mtls LLC (G-10206)*

Haley Construction Inc...207 778-9990
116 Pierpole Rd Farmington (04938) *(G-4781)*

HALEY CONSTRUCTION, INC., Farmington *Also Called: Haley Construction Inc (G-4781)*

Hall Inc...401 253-4858
33 Broadcommon Rd Bristol (02809) *(G-15768)*

Hall Mailing & Fulfillment Inc..................................978 372-6546
46 Rogers Rd Ste 1 Haverhill (01835) *(G-9100)*

Hall Spars & Rigging, Bristol *Also Called: Hall Inc (G-15768)*

Hallmark Woodworkers Inc.....................................203 730-0535
350 Fairfield Ave Ste 602 Bridgeport (06604) *(G-327)*

Hallowell EMC, Pittsfield *Also Called: Hallowell Engrg & Mfg Corp (G-11400)*

Hallowell Engrg & Mfg Corp....................................413 445-4263
35 Downing Industrial Park Pittsfield (01201) *(G-11400)*

(G-0000) Company's Geographic Section entry number

Halmark Systems LLC.. 781 630-0123
  354 Page St Stoughton (02072) *(G-12212)*

Halo Technology Holdings Inc....................................... 203 422-2950
  1266 E Main St Ste 700r Stamford (06902) *(G-3361)*

Ham Radio Outlet, Salem *Also Called: Hro Inc (G-15537)*

Hamar Laser Instruments Inc....................................... 203 730-4600
  5 Ye Olde Rd Danbury (06810) *(G-756)*

Hamden Metal Service Co Inc...................................... 203 281-1522
  2 Broadway Hamden (06518) *(G-1427)*

Hamden Packaging Inc.. 203 288-0200
  100 Sanford St Hamden (06514) *(G-1428)*

Hamilton Branch, South Hamilton *Also Called: Danversbank (G-11969)*

Hamilton Elevator Interiors.. 781 233-9540
  6 Belair St Saugus (01906) *(G-11759)*

Hamilton Orchards... 978 544-6867
  25 West St New Salem (01355) *(G-10664)*

Hamilton Orchards Apple Barn, New Salem *Also Called: Hamilton Orchards (G-10664)*

Hamilton Sign & Design Inc... 508 459-9731
  545 Sw Cutoff Worcester (01607) *(G-13736)*

Hamilton Sndstrand Space Syste................................. 860 654-6000
  1 Hamilton Rd Windsor Locks (06096) *(G-4328)*

Hamilton Standard Space... 860 654-6000
  1 Hamilton Rd Windsor Locks (06096) *(G-4329)*

Hamilton Storage Tech Inc.. 508 544-7000
  3 Forge Pkwy Franklin (02038) *(G-8842)*

Hamilton Storage Tech Inc **(DH)**............................... **508 544-7000**
  3 Forge Pkwy Franklin (02038) *(G-8843)*

Hamilton Sundstrand Corp **(HQ)**.............................. **619 714-9442**
  1 Hamilton Rd Windsor Locks (06096) *(G-4330)*

Hamilton Thorne Inc **(PA)**.. **978 921-2050**
  100 Cummings Ctr Ste 465e Beverly (01915) *(G-6352)*

Hamilton Tool, Providence *Also Called: United States Associates LLC (G-16632)*

Hamlin Cabinet Corp.. 508 384-8371
  112 Pond St Norfolk (02056) *(G-10799)*

Hammar & Sons Inc... 603 635-2292
  71 Bridge St Pelham (03076) *(G-15289)*

Hammond Lumber, Canaan *Also Called: FC Hammond & Son Co Inc (G-14046)*

Hammond Lumber Company **(PA)**.............................. **207 495-3303**
  2 Hammond Dr Belgrade (04917) *(G-4540)*

Hampden Engineering Corp... 413 525-3981
  99 Shaker Rd East Longmeadow (01028) *(G-8379)*

Hampden Fence Supply Inc... 413 786-4390
  80 Industrial Ln Agawam (01001) *(G-5792)*

Hampden Hat & Cap Co Division, Springfield *Also Called: Athletic Emblem Lettering Inc (G-12078)*

Hampford Research Inc **(PA)**..................................... **203 375-1137**
  54 Veterans Blvd Stratford (06615) *(G-3544)*

Hampshire Chemical Corp **(DH)**................................ **603 888-2320**
  2 E Spit Brook Rd Nashua (03060) *(G-15109)*

Hampshire Controls Corp... 603 749-9424
  1 Grove St Dover (03820) *(G-14230)*

Hampshire Fire Protection LLC **(PA)**......................... **603 432-8221**
  8 N Wentworth Ave Londonderry (03053) *(G-14753)*

Hampshire Hives LLC.. 603 313-0186
  659 Route 10 Gilsum (03448) *(G-14342)*

Hampstead Copy Center, East Hampstead *Also Called: Ram Printing Incorporated (G-14271)*

Hampton Gazette Inc... 860 455-0160
  218 W Old Route 6 Hampton (06247) *(G-1465)*

Hamworthy Peabody Combustn Inc **(DH)**.................. **203 922-1199**
  6 Armstrong Rd Ste 2 Shelton (06484) *(G-3012)*

Handy Pad Supply Inc... 508 791-2722
  57 Richards Ave Paxton (01612) *(G-11289)*

Handyscape LLC... 860 318-1067
  43 Sandy Pine Dr Southington (06489) *(G-3215)*

Hanford Cabinet & Wdwkg Co Inc............................... 860 388-5055
  102 Ingham Hill Rd Old Saybrook (06475) *(G-2650)*

Hanford Cabinet & Woodworking, Old Saybrook *Also Called: Hanford Cabinet & Wdwkg Co Inc (G-2650)*

Hanington Bros Inc... 207 765-2681
  488 Us Hwy 2 Macwahoc Plt (04451) *(G-5036)*

Hanington Timberlands.. 207 456-7003
  95 Main St Wytopitlock (04497) *(G-5701)*

Hanley Construction Inc.. 207 677-2207
  1829 Bristol Rd Bristol (04539) *(G-4630)*

Hanna Instruments Inc... 401 335-3677
  35 Industrial Rd Cumberland (02864) *(G-15941)*

Hanna Instruments Inc **(PA)**.................................... **401 765-7500**
  584 Park East Dr Woonsocket (02895) *(G-16962)*

Hanna Instruments US Inc.. 401 765-7500
  270 Washington Hwy Smithfield (02917) *(G-16708)*

Hannaford & Dumas Corporation................................ 781 503-0100
  26 Conn St Woburn (01801) *(G-13580)*

Hannah Boden Corp.. 508 992-3334
  132 Herman Melville Blvd New Bedford (02740) *(G-10598)*

Hannah Engineering Inc.. 978 777-5892
  36 Longbow Rd Danvers (01923) *(G-8189)*

Hannoush Jewelers, Farmington *Also Called: Joseph Hannoush Family Inc (G-1225)*

Hanover Review Inc.. 603 643-4370
  8 Webster Ave Hanover (03755) *(G-14424)*

Hans Kissle Company LLC.. 978 556-4500
  9 Creek Brook Dr Haverhill (01832) *(G-9101)*

Hansa Consult North Amer LLC **(PA)**....................... **603 422-8833**
  200 International Dr Ste 120 Portsmouth (03801) *(G-15398)*

Hanscom Construction Inc.. 207 255-8067
  384 Ridge Rd Marshfield (04654) *(G-5046)*

Hanson Commerce Center, Hanson *Also Called: A A A Metals Company Inc (G-9049)*

Hanwha Aerospace USA LLC **(DH)**........................... **203 806-2090**
  5 Mckee Pl Cheshire (06410) *(G-597)*

Hanwha Aerospace USA LLC....................................... 860 789-2500
  68 Prospect Hill Dr East Windsor (06088) *(G-1074)*

Hanwha Aerospace USA LLC....................................... 860 789-2511
  68 Prospect Hill Rd East Windsor (06088) *(G-1075)*

Hanwha Aerospace USA LLC....................................... 860 677-2603
  1790 New Britain Ave Farmington (06032) *(G-1221)*

Hanwha Aerospace USA LLC....................................... 860 633-9474
  81 National Dr Glastonbury (06033) *(G-1284)*

Hanwha Aerospace USA LLC....................................... 860 667-2134
  275 Richard St Newington (06111) *(G-2298)*

Hanwha Aerospace USA LLC....................................... 860 667-2134
  275 Richard St Newington (06111) *(G-2299)*

Hapco Inc.. 781 826-8801
  353 Circuit St Hanover (02339) *(G-9034)*

Happy House Amusement Inc...................................... 603 497-4151
  70 Depot St Goffstown (03045) *(G-14348)*

Har-Conn Chrome Company **(PA)**.............................. **860 236-6801**
  603 New Park Ave West Hartford (06110) *(G-4063)*

Harbar, Canton *Also Called: Harbar LLC (G-7793)*

Harbar LLC.. 781 828-0848
  320 Turnpike St Canton (02021) *(G-7793)*

Harbor Candy Shop Inc... 207 646-8078
  248 Main St Ogunquit (03907) *(G-5123)*

Harborside Printing Co Inc.. 978 462-2026
  3 Graf Rd Ste 5 Newburyport (01950) *(G-10686)*

Harbour Biomed Us Inc... 617 682-3679
  1 Broadway Ste 14 Cambridge (02142) *(G-7598)*

Harby Power Solutions LLC... 203 265-0012
  105 S Elm St Wallingford (06492) *(G-3811)*

Harcosemco, Branford *Also Called: Semco Instruments Inc (G-276)*

Harcosemco, Branford *Also Called: Semco Instruments Inc (G-277)*

Harcosemco LLC.. 203 483-3700
  186 Cedar St Branford (06405) *(G-263)*

Harcros Chemicals Inc.. 207 856-6756
  50 Larrabee Rd Westbrook (04092) *(G-5627)*

Hard Core Spral Tube Wnders In................................. 603 775-0230
  50 Pine Rd Brentwood (03833) *(G-14022)*

Hardigg Cases, South Deerfield *Also Called: Hardigg Industries LLC (G-11924)*

Hardigg Industries LLC **(HQ)**................................... **413 665-2163**
  147 N Main St South Deerfield (01373) *(G-11924)*

Harding Company Inc **(HQ)**...................................... **603 778-7070**
  58 Highland Dr Putnam (06260) *(G-2859)*

Harding Company Inc.. 860 928-0475
  58 Highland Dr Putnam (06260) *(G-2860)*

Harding Metals Inc... 603 942-5573
  42 Harding Dr Northwood (03261) *(G-15273)*

**A
L
P
H
A
B
E
T
I
C**

Harding Sails Inc..508 748-0334
  732 Mill St Marion (02738) *(G-10097)*

Harding Sails Nb, Marion *Also Called: Harding Sails Inc (G-10097)*

Hardline Heat Treating Inc....................................508 764-6669
  134 Ashland Ave Southbridge (01550) *(G-12018)*

Hardric Laboratories Inc.......................................978 251-1702
  22 Flagstone Dr Hudson (03051) *(G-14506)*

Hardshore Distilling, Portland *Also Called: Milne Spirit Works LLC (G-5245)*

Hardware Products Company, Bristol *Also Called: Hardware Products Company LP (G-452)*

Hardware Products Company LP................................617 884-9410
  95 Valley St Bristol (06010) *(G-452)*

Hardwater Industries LLC......................................603 867-9240
  15 Bramble Ln Gilford (03249) *(G-14336)*

Hardwick Dry Kilns, Brattleboro *Also Called: Cersosimo Lumber Company Inc (G-17081)*

Hardwick Gazette Newspaper, Hardwick *Also Called: Hardwick Gazette Print Shop (G-17284)*

Hardwick Gazette Print Shop..................................802 472-6521
  42 S Main St Hardwick (05843) *(G-17284)*

Hardwick Knitted Fabric Inc....................................413 436-7704
  81 South St Warren (01083) *(G-12851)*

Hardwick Laminators Inc..413 477-6600
  268 Main St Gilbertville (01031) *(G-8913)*

Hardwood Closet Company, Exeter *Also Called: Hardwood Design Inc (G-16051)*

Hardwood Design Inc..401 294-2235
  24 Dorset Mill Rd Exeter (02822) *(G-16051)*

Hardwood Lumber Manufacturing...............................860 423-2447
  111 Ziegler Rd Scotland (06247) *(G-2953)*

Hardwood Products Company LLC...............................207 876-3312
  30 School St Guilford (04443) *(G-4854)*

Hardy Doric Inc..978 250-1113
  22 Progress Ave Chelmsford (01824) *(G-7930)*

Harman, Stamford *Also Called: Harman International Inds Inc (G-3365)*

Harman Bcker Auto Systems Mfg...............................203 328-3501
  400 Atlantic St Ste 15 Stamford (06901) *(G-3362)*

Harman Consumer Inc...203 328-3500
  400 Atlantic St Ste 1500 Stamford (06901) *(G-3363)*

Harman Consumer Group Division, Stamford *Also Called: Harman International Inds Inc (G-3364)*

Harman International Inds Inc..................................203 328-3500
  400 Atlantic St Ste 15 Stamford (06901) *(G-3364)*

Harman International Inds Inc **(HQ)**........................**203 328-3500**
  400 Atlantic St Ste 15 Stamford (06901) *(G-3365)*

Harman KG Holding LLC **(DH)**..............................**203 328-3500**
  400 Atlantic St Ste 1500 Stamford (06901) *(G-3366)*

Harmonic Drive LLC **(HQ)**.................................**978 532-1800**
  42 Dunham Rd Beverly (01915) *(G-6353)*

Harmony Metal Products North Inc.............................603 536-6012
  10 Pleasant St Ste 400 Portsmouth (03801) *(G-15399)*

Harnum Crane Service, Salisbury *Also Called: MEI Rigging & Crating LLC (G-11742)*

Harodite Industries Inc **(PA)**.............................**508 824-6961**
  66 South St Taunton (02780) *(G-12340)*

Harold Haines Inc...207 762-1411
  243 Main St Presque Isle (04769) *(G-5300)*

Harold Macquinn Incorporated **(PA)**.......................**207 667-4654**
  127 Macquinn Rd Hancock (04640) *(G-4869)*

Harpoon Acquisition Corp.......................................860 815-5736
  455 Winding Brook Dr Glastonbury (06033) *(G-1285)*

Harpoon Brewery, Boston *Also Called: Mass Bay Brewing Company Inc (G-6870)*

Harpoon Brewery, Windsor *Also Called: Mbbc Vermont LLC (G-17760)*

Harpoon Distributing Co Inc....................................617 574-9551
  306 Northern Ave Ste 2 Boston (02210) *(G-6781)*

Harps Unlimited Intl LLC..860 675-0227
  21 Highfield Dr Burlington (06013) *(G-551)*

Harpswell House Inc..207 353-2385
  52 Capital Ave Lisbon Falls (04252) *(G-5021)*

Harrel, Pawcatuck *Also Called: Davis-Standard LLC (G-2717)*

Harrells LLC..863 680-2003
  458 Danbury Rd Ste D3 New Milford (06776) *(G-2247)*

Harrington Air Systems LLC....................................781 341-1999
  80 Rosedale Rd Watertown (02472) *(G-12880)*

Harrington's of Vermont, Richmond *Also Called: Harringtons In Vermont Inc (G-17479)*

Harringtons In Vermont Inc **(PA)**.........................**802 434-7535**
  210 E Main St Richmond (05477) *(G-17479)*

Harris Enterprise Corp..860 649-4663
  80 Colonial Rd Manchester (06042) *(G-1600)*

Harris Envmtl Systems Inc......................................978 470-8600
  11 Connector Rd Andover (01810) *(G-5885)*

Harris OH Cabinetmaker..603 781-1315
  63 Nottingham Rd Deerfield (03037) *(G-14186)*

Harris Rebar..781 575-8999
  136 Will Dr Canton (02021) *(G-7794)*

Harris Steel, South Deerfield *Also Called: Nucor Hrris Rbar Northeast LLC (G-11925)*

Harris Woodworking, Manchester *Also Called: Harris Enterprise Corp (G-1600)*

Harrison Concrete Cnstr Inc....................................802 849-6688
  1803 Skunk Hill Rd Fairfax (05454) *(G-17259)*

Harrison Publishing House Inc..................................603 444-0820
  995 Industrial Park Rd Littleton (03561) *(G-14720)*

Harrison Redi-Mix Corp...802 849-6688
  1803 Skunk Hill Rd Fairfax (05454) *(G-17260)*

Harrisville Designs Inc **(PA)**.............................**603 827-3333**
  69 Main St Fl 2 Harrisville (03450) *(G-14432)*

Harry Miller Co LLC..617 427-2300
  850 Albany St Boston (02119) *(G-6782)*

Harry Miller Co LLC **(PA)**................................**617 427-2300**
  19 Hampden St Boston (02119) *(G-6783)*

Hart Tool & Engineering...203 264-9776
  339 Christian St Oxford (06478) *(G-2696)*

Harte Hanks, Chelmsford *Also Called: Harte Hanks Inc (G-7931)*

Harte Hanks Inc **(PA)**....................................**512 434-1100**
  2 Executive Dr Ste 103 Chelmsford (01824) *(G-7931)*

Hartford, Newport *Also Called: Eichenauer Inc (G-15228)*

Hartford Aircraft Products Inc..................................860 242-8228
  94 Old Poquonock Rd Bloomfield (06002) *(G-168)*

Hartford Business Supply Inc....................................860 233-2138
  1718 Park St Hartford (06106) *(G-1485)*

Hartford Compressors Inc
  179 South St West Hartford (06110) *(G-4064)*

Hartford Courant, Avon *Also Called: Hartford Courant Company LLC (G-26)*

Hartford Courant Company LLC.................................860 678-1330
  80 Darling Dr Avon (06001) *(G-26)*

Hartford Courant Company LLC **(DH)**......................**860 241-6200**
  285 Broad St Hartford (06115) *(G-1486)*

Hartford Fine Art & Framing Co, East Hartford *Also Called: Picture This Hartford Inc (G-1011)*

Hartford Fire Equipment..860 747-2757
  394 East St Plainville (06062) *(G-2763)*

Hartford Jet Center LLC..860 548-9334
  20 Lindbergh Dr Hartford (06114) *(G-1487)*

Hartford Technologies Inc.......................................860 571-3602
  1022 Elm St Rocky Hill (06067) *(G-2924)*

Hartford Wire Works, North Haven *Also Called: New England Cage & Fence Corp (G-2427)*

Hartmann, Mansfield *Also Called: HI Operating LLC (G-10056)*

Hartmann Incorporated...508 851-1400
  575 West St Ste 110 Mansfield (02048) *(G-10054)*

Hartwell 131 Holdings Corp.....................................781 328-3220
  131 Hartwell Ave Ste 3 Lexington (02421) *(G-9746)*

Hartwell Asscoiates...617 686-7571
  24 Thorndike St Cambridge (02141) *(G-7599)*

Harvard Apparatus Inc..508 893-8999
  84 October Hill Rd Holliston (01746) *(G-9213)*

Harvard Apprtus Rgnrtive Tech **(PA)**......................**774 233-7300**
  84 October Hill Rd Ste 11 Holliston (01746) *(G-9214)*

Harvard Bus Schl Pubg Corp **(HQ)**........................**617 783-7400**
  20 Guest St Ste 700 Brighton (02135) *(G-7241)*

Harvard Bus Schl Stdnt Assn In.................................617 495-6812
  70 N Harvard St Boston (02163) *(G-6784)*

Harvard Business School, Boston *Also Called: President Fllows Hrvard Cllege (G-6976)*

Harvard Chemical LLC **(HQ)**..............................**404 761-0657**
  201 Boston Trnpk Bolton (06043) *(G-220)*

Harvard Debate Incorporated...................................617 876-5003
  490 Adams Mail Ctr Cambridge (02138) *(G-7600)*

Harvard Independent Inc..617 495-3682
  371 Harvard St Apt 2d Cambridge (02138) *(G-7601)*

(G-0000) Company's Geographic Section entry number

Harvard Lampoon Inc.. 617 495-7801
   44 Bow St Cambridge (02138) **(G-7602)**

Harvard Machinery, Harvard *Also Called: Harvard Products Inc* **(G-9063)**

Harvard Magazine.. 617 495-5746
   7 Ware St Cambridge (02138) **(G-7603)**

Harvard Products Inc... 978 772-0309
   325 Ayer Rd Ste A105 Harvard (01451) **(G-9063)**

Harvard Scientific Corporation................................. 617 876-5033
   799 Concord Ave Cambridge (02138) **(G-7604)**

HARVARD UNIVERSITY, Brighton *Also Called: Harvard Bus Schl Pubg Corp* **(G-7241)**

Harvard University, Cambridge *Also Called: President and Fellows of Harvard College* **(G-7688)**

Harvest Co-Operative Sprmkt, Cambridge *Also Called: Boston Food Cooperative* **(G-7520)**

Harvest Consumer Products LLC **(PA)**........................ **980 444-2000**
   1432 Main St Ste 1 Waltham (02451) **(G-12690)**

Harvest Hill Holdings LLC **(PA)**.............................. **203 914-1620**
   1 High Ridge Park Fl 2 Stamford (06905) **(G-3367)**

Harvest of Barnstable, Yarmouth Port *Also Called: Wendi C Smith* **(G-13846)**

Harvey Bigelow Designs, Fall River *Also Called: Ecin Industries Inc* **(G-8540)**

Harvey Building Products, Augusta *Also Called: Harvey Industries Inc* **(G-4472)**

Harvey Building Products, Waltham *Also Called: Harvey Industries LLC* **(G-12691)**

Harvey Industries Inc.. 207 629-3737
   80 Anthony Ave Augusta (04330) **(G-4472)**

Harvey Industries Inc.. 508 998-9779
   7 Ledgewood Blvd North Dartmouth (02747) **(G-10997)**

Harvey Industries LLC... 413 731-7700
   175 Carando Dr Springfield (01104) **(G-12099)**

Harvey Industries LLC **(PA)**.................................... **800 598-5400**
   1400 Main St Fl 3 Waltham (02451) **(G-12691)**

Harvey Industries LLC... 781 935-7990
   33 Commonwealth Ave Woburn (01801) **(G-13581)**

Harvey Industries LLC... 603 216-8300
   30 Jacks Bridge Rd Londonderry (03053) **(G-14754)**

HARVEY INDUSTRIES, INC., North Dartmouth *Also Called: Harvey Industries Inc* **(G-10997)**

Harwest Holdings One Inc... 860 423-8334
   1102 Windham Rd South Windham (06266) **(G-3102)**

Harwich Oracle... 508 247-3200
   5 Namskaket Rd Orleans (02653) **(G-11238)**

Hasbro, Pawtucket *Also Called: Hasbro Inc* **(G-16371)**

Hasbro, Pawtucket *Also Called: Hasbro Inc* **(G-16372)**

Hasbro, Pawtucket *Also Called: Hasbro Inc* **(G-16373)**

Hasbro, Providence *Also Called: Hasbro Inc* **(G-16530)**

Hasbro Inc.. 401 726-2090
   1011 Newport Ave Pawtucket (02861) **(G-16371)**

Hasbro Inc.. 401 431-8412
   200 Narragansett Park Dr Pawtucket (02861) **(G-16372)**

Hasbro Inc **(PA)**... **401 431-8697**
   1027 Newport Ave Pawtucket (02861) **(G-16373)**

Hasbro Inc.. 401 280-2127
   1 Hasbro Pl Providence (02903) **(G-16530)**

Hasbro International Inc **(HQ)**................................. **401 431-8697**
   1027 Newport Ave Pawtucket (02861) **(G-16374)**

Hasler Inc.. 203 301-3400
   478 Wheelers Farms Rd Milford (06461) **(G-1833)**

Hassay Savage Broach Co Inc..................................... 413 863-9052
   10 Industrial Blvd Turners Falls (01376) **(G-12446)**

Hastone Homestone Inc.. 617 784-3284
   115 E Cottage St Dorchester (02125) **(G-8300)**

Hat Attack Inc **(PA)**.. **718 994-1000**
   52b Poplar St Stamford (06907) **(G-3368)**

Hat Attack I Bujibaja, Stamford *Also Called: Hat Attack Inc* **(G-3368)**

Haufe Group... 781 376-3737
   15 Hersam St Stoneham (02180) **(G-12179)**

Hauser Chocolatier, Westerly *Also Called: Hauser Foods Inc* **(G-16932)**

Hauser Eqp & Wldg Svcs Inc....................................... 203 377-7072
   45 Embree St Stratford (06615) **(G-3545)**

Hauser Equipment & Welding, Stratford *Also Called: Hauser Eqp & Wldg Svcs Inc* **(G-3545)**

Hauser Foods Inc... 401 596-8866
   59 Tom Harvey Rd Westerly (02891) **(G-16932)**

Hauthane, Lynn *Also Called: C L Hauthaway & Sons Corp* **(G-9965)**

Haverhill Gazette, Haverhill *Also Called: Eagle-Tribune Publishing Co* **(G-9093)**

Haverhill House Publishing LLC................................... 781 879-3102
   643 E Broadway Haverhill (01830) **(G-9102)**

Hawk Integrated Plastics LLC..................................... 860 337-0310
   1 Commerce Dr Columbia (06237) **(G-670)**

Hawk Motors Inc.. 207 363-4716
   1100 Us Route 1 York (03909) **(G-5712)**

Hawk Quality Products Inc... 603 432-3319
   125 Rockingham Rd Derry (03038) **(G-14194)**

Hawk Ridge Winery LLC... 860 274-7440
   28 Plungis Rd Watertown (06795) **(G-4015)**

Hawkes & Huberdeau Wdwkg Inc..................................... 978 388-7747
   23 Noel St Ste 5 Amesbury (01913) **(G-5836)**

Hawkes Motorsports LLC.. 603 660-9864
   129a S Mast St Goffstown (03045) **(G-14349)**

Hawkeye Technologies, Milford *Also Called: He Technologies Inc* **(G-1835)**

Hawkin Dynamics LLC... 207 405-9142
   90 Bridge St Ste 230 Westbrook (04092) **(G-5628)**

Hawkins Machine Company Inc...................................... 401 828-1424
   374 Hopkins Hill Rd Unit 3 Coventry (02816) **(G-15815)**

Hawtan Leathers LLC... 978 465-3791
   75 Parker St Newburyport (01950) **(G-10687)**

Hawthorn Creative Group LLC...................................... 603 610-0533
   33 Jewell Ct Portsmouth (03801) **(G-15400)**

Hawthorne Cove Marina Inc.. 978 740-9890
   10 White St Salem (01970) **(G-11722)**

Hay Island Holding Corporation **(PA)**......................... **203 656-8000**
   20 Thorndal Cir Darien (06820) **(G-847)**

Hayden Corporation... 413 734-4981
   333 River St West Springfield (01089) **(G-13029)**

Hayden Laser, West Springfield *Also Called: Hayden Corporation* **(G-13029)**

Haydenville Wdwkg & Design Inc **(PA)**......................... **413 665-7402**
   35 Conz St Northampton (01060) **(G-11066)**

Haydon Kerk Mtion Slutions Inc **(HQ)**......................... **203 756-7441**
   1500 Meriden Rd Waterbury (06705) **(G-3918)**

Haydon Kerk Mtion Slutions Inc................................... 603 213-6290
   56 Meadowbrook Dr Milford (03055) **(G-15024)**

Haydon Motion Europe, Waterbury *Also Called: Tritex Corporation* **(G-3977)**

Hayes Pump Inc **(PA)**.. **978 369-8800**
   66 Old Powder Mill Rd I Concord (01742) **(G-8119)**

Hayes Recycled Pallets Inc.. 802 247-4620
   16 Maple St Brandon (05733) **(G-17066)**

Hayes Services LLC... 860 739-2273
   15 Colton Rd East Lyme (06333) **(G-1059)**

Hayford Logging, Hartford *Also Called: Terrence L Hayford* **(G-4877)**

Haymart LLC... 207 528-2058
   19 Mill St Patten (04765) **(G-5153)**

Haynes Aggrgtes - Deep Rver LL................................... 203 888-8100
   220 Main St Ste 2f Oxford (06478) **(G-2697)**

Haystack ID.. 617 422-0075
   100 Franklin St Boston (02110) **(G-6785)**

Hayward Industries, North Kingstown *Also Called: Hayward Industries Inc* **(G-16254)**

Hayward Industries Inc.. 401 583-1150
   61 Whitecap Dr North Kingstown (02852) **(G-16254)**

Hayward Turnstiles Inc.. 203 647-9144
   333 Quarry Rd Milford (06460) **(G-1834)**

Hayward Tyler Inc **(DH)**... **802 655-4444**
   480 Roosevelt Hwy Colchester (05446) **(G-17194)**

Hazelett Strip-Casting Corp **(HQ)**............................ **802 863-6376**
   135 W Lakeshore Dr Colchester (05446) **(G-17195)**

Hazen, Holyoke *Also Called: Hazen Paper Company* **(G-9259)**

Hazen Paper Company **(PA)**...................................... **413 538-8204**
   240 S Water St Holyoke (01040) **(G-9259)**

HB Precision Products Inc... 401 767-4340
   21 Lark Industrial Pkwy Unit A Greenville (02828) **(G-16059)**

HB Printing, Northborough *Also Called: Tomandtim Enterprises LLC* **(G-11113)**

Hbc, Lewiston *Also Called: Hahnel Bros Co* **(G-4963)**

Hbh Prestain Inc **(PA)**.. **802 375-9723**
   1223 E Arlington Rd Arlington (05250) **(G-16987)**

Hbio, Holliston *Also Called: Harvard Apparatus Inc* **(G-9213)**

Hbl America Inc (HQ)...**860 257-9800**
 169 Progress Dr Manchester (06042) *(G-1601)*

Hbl Batteries, Manchester *Also Called: Hbl America Inc (G-1601)*

Hbn Shoe LLC...603 622-0272
 395 Main St Ste 6b Salem (03079) *(G-15536)*

HC Starck Tungsten LLC...617 630-4843
 275 Grove St Ste 2400 Auburndale (02466) *(G-6136)*

Hcb Holdings Inc (PA)...**207 767-2136**
 190 Rumery St South Portland (04106) *(G-5505)*

HCC Aegis Inc (DH)...**508 998-3141**
 50 Welby Rd New Bedford (02745) *(G-10599)*

Hci Cleaning Products LLC...508 864-5510
 7 Grassy Ln Westford (01886) *(G-13241)*

Hcp Packaging Usa Inc...603 256-3141
 370 Monument Rd Hinsdale (03451) *(G-14444)*

Hcpro Inc (HQ)...**781 639-1872**
 35 Village Rd Ste 200 Middleton (01949) *(G-10385)*

Hcrx Investments Holdco LP...203 487-8300
 300 Atlantic St Ste 600 Stamford (06901) *(G-3369)*

Hcrx Master Gp LLC...203 487-8300
 300 Atlantic St Ste 600 Stamford (06901) *(G-3370)*

Hdb Inc...860 379-9901
 135 S Main St Ste 1 Thomaston (06787) *(G-3621)*

Hdm Systems Corporation...617 562-4054
 84 Lincoln St Brighton (02135) *(G-7242)*

He Technologies Inc...203 878-6892
 181 Research Dr Ste 8 Milford (06460) *(G-1835)*

Head 2 Toe LLC...781 944-0286
 167 Pleasant St Reading (01867) *(G-11602)*

Headwall Photonics Inc...978 353-4100
 580 Main St Bolton (01740) *(G-6497)*

Headwaters Inc...781 715-6404
 134 Pleasant St Marblehead (01945) *(G-10087)*

Health Monitor, Newtown *Also Called: The Bee Publishing Company (G-2351)*

Health Pro, Portland *Also Called: Casco Bay Sbstnce Abuse Rsrces (G-5196)*

Healthcare Royalty, Stamford *Also Called: Healthcare Royalty Inc (G-3371)*

Healthcare Royalty Inc (PA)...**203 487-8300**
 300 Atlantic St Ste 600 Stamford (06901) *(G-3371)*

Healthco International LLC...603 255-3771
 1 Wilderness Rd Colebrook (03576) *(G-14106)*

Healthedge, Burlington *Also Called: Healthedge Software Inc (G-7376)*

Healthedge Software Inc (HQ)...**781 285-1300**
 30 Corporate Dr Ste 150 Burlington (01803) *(G-7376)*

HealthFleet Inc...203 810-5400
 163 Highland Ave Ste 1105 Needham Heights (02494) *(G-10550)*

Healthper Inc...203 506-0957
 24 Guenevere Ct Hamden (06518) *(G-1429)*

Healthquarters Inc...978 922-4490
 900 Cummings Ctr Beverly (01915) *(G-6354)*

Healthstar Inc...781 428-3696
 62 Johnson Ln Braintree (02184) *(G-7187)*

Healthy Life, Canton *Also Called: Healthy Life Snack Inc (G-7795)*

Healthy Life Snack Inc...781 575-6744
 905 Turnpike St Ste D2 Canton (02021) *(G-7795)*

Healthy Mom LLC...855 588-6242
 2319 Whitney Ave Ste 1d Hamden (06518) *(G-1430)*

Healthy Truth, Walpole *Also Called: Healthy Truth LLC (G-12560)*

Healthy Truth LLC...774 256-5800
 87 West St Walpole (02081) *(G-12560)*

Healy Plaques, Manville *Also Called: Michael Healy Designs Inc (G-16165)*

Heart Valve Society...212 561-9879
 500 Cummings Ctr Ste 4400 Beverly (01915) *(G-6355)*

Hearth Kitchen Co, Stamford *Also Called: Hearth Kitchen Products Inc (G-3372)*

Hearth Kitchen Products Inc...203 325-8800
 226 Selleck St # B Stamford (06902) *(G-3372)*

Heartland Water Technology Inc...603 490-9203
 43 Broad St Ste B403 Hudson (01749) *(G-9372)*

Heartware International Inc (DH)...**508 739-0950**
 500 Old Connecticut Path Framingham (01701) *(G-8777)*

Heartwood Brouillette Building, Barrington *Also Called: Brouillette Woodworking Co Inc (G-15746)*

Heartwood Cabinetry...860 295-0304
 345 N Main St Marlborough (06447) *(G-1643)*

Heat and Control Inc...603 225-5190
 339 Commerce Way Pembroke (03275) *(G-15303)*

Heat Fab Inc...413 863-2242
 130 Industrial Blvd Turners Falls (01376) *(G-12447)*

Heat Trace Products LLC...978 534-2810
 233 Florence St Leominster (01453) *(G-9669)*

Heat Transfer Products, Providence *Also Called: Ariston Usa LLC (G-16474)*

Heat Treating, East Granby *Also Called: Specialty Steel Treating Inc (G-953)*

Heat Treating, Newington *Also Called: Sousa Corp (G-2326)*

Heat-Flo Inc...508 278-2400
 15 Megan Ct Uxbridge (01569) *(G-12480)*

Heavy Inc...646 806-2113
 55 Post Rd W Fl 2 Westport (06880) *(G-4172)*

Heavy.com, Westport *Also Called: Heavy Inc (G-4172)*

Heb Manufacturing Company Inc...802 685-4821
 67 Vt Rte 110 Chelsea (05038) *(G-17178)*

Hebert Candies, Shrewsbury *Also Called: Hebert Retail LLC (G-11834)*

Hebert Confections LLC
 574 Hartford Tpke Shrewsbury (01545) *(G-11833)*

Hebert Foundry & Machine Inc...603 524-2065
 113 Fair St Laconia (03246) *(G-14652)*

Hebert Foundry & Machine Co, Laconia *Also Called: Hebert Foundry & Machine Inc (G-14652)*

Hebert Manufacturing Company (PA)...**603 524-2065**
 113 Fair St Laconia (03246) *(G-14653)*

Hebert Retail LLC...508 845-8051
 574 Hartford Tpke Shrewsbury (01545) *(G-11834)*

Hebert's Candy Mansion, Shrewsbury *Also Called: Hebert Confections LLC (G-11833)*

Heckmann Building Products Inc...708 865-2403
 110 Richards Ave Ste 1 Norwalk (06854) *(G-2511)*

Hedge Hog Industries Corp...413 363-2528
 86 Princeton St Springfield (01109) *(G-12100)*

Hedges & Hedges Ltd...860 257-3170
 1155 Silas Deane Hwy Ste 4 Wethersfield (06109) *(G-4205)*

Heffron Asphalt Corp (PA)...**781 935-1455**
 68 Winter St North Reading (01864) *(G-11040)*

Heffron Materials, North Reading *Also Called: Heffron Asphalt Corp (G-11040)*

Hefring Engineering, Gloucester *Also Called: Hefring Inc (G-8941)*

Hefring Inc...617 938-9544
 417 Main St Gloucester (01930) *(G-8941)*

Heico, Glastonbury *Also Called: Turbine Kinetics Inc (G-1300)*

Heidelberg Materials Us Inc...800 833-4157
 55 Fields Point Dr Providence (02905) *(G-16531)*

Height Land Publications Ltd...802 644-6606
 60 Main St Jeffersonville (05464) *(G-17306)*

Heilind Electronics Inc (PA)...**978 657-4870**
 58 Jonspin Rd Wilmington (01887) *(G-13410)*

Heise Industries Inc...860 828-6538
 196 Commerce St East Berlin (06023) *(G-912)*

Heiwa Soy Beanery, Rockport *Also Called: Heiwa Tofu Inc (G-5350)*

Heiwa Tofu Inc...207 236-8638
 201 West St Rockport (04856) *(G-5350)*

Helander Products Inc...860 669-7953
 26 Knollwood Dr Clinton (06413) *(G-644)*

Heleka Companies LLC (PA)...**603 798-3674**
 160 Dover Rd Unit 10 Chichester (03258) *(G-14073)*

Heleka Companies LLC...303 856-5457
 1361 Elm St Manchester (03101) *(G-14858)*

Helfrich Bros Boiler Works Inc...978 975-2464
 39 Merrimack St Lawrence (01843) *(G-9566)*

Helfrich Construction Svcs LLC...978 683-7244
 39 Merrimack St Lawrence (01843) *(G-9567)*

Helical Solutions LLC...207 854-5581
 428 Newburyport Tpke Rowley (01969) *(G-11676)*

Helicopter Support Inc (DH)...**203 416-4000**
 124 Quarry Rd Trumbull (06611) *(G-3721)*

Hellier, Danbury *Also Called: Acuren Inspection Inc (G-704)*

Hello Tomorrow LLC...401 727-0070
 1005 Main St Ste 7050 Pawtucket (02860) *(G-16375)*

Helmers Publishing Inc.	603 563-1631
1283 Main St Dublin (03444) **(G-14261)**	
Helvetia LLC.	508 829-7607
269 Wachusett St Holden (01520) **(G-9190)**	
Hemanext, Lexington *Also Called: Hemanext Inc* **(G-9747)**	
Hemanext Inc.	240 301-7474
99 Hayden Ave Ste 620 Lexington (02421) **(G-9747)**	
Hemedex Inc.	617 577-1759
564 Main St Ste 300 Waltham (02452) **(G-12692)**	
Hemingway Custom Cabinetry LLC.	203 382-0300
3400 Fairfield Ave Bridgeport (06605) **(G-328)**	
Hemmings Motor News Inc.	802 442-3101
222 Main St Bennington (05201) **(G-17040)**	
Hendrick Manufacturing Corp **(PA)**.	**781 631-4400**
32 Commercial St Salem (01970) **(G-11723)**	
Hendrickson Publishers LLC.	978 532-6546
3 Centennial Dr Ste 130 Peabody (01960) **(G-11313)**	
Hendrickson Publishers Inc.	800 358-3111
3 Centennial Dr Ste 130 Peabody (01960) **(G-11314)**	
Henke Sass Wolf America Inc.	508 671-9300
135 Schofield Ave Dudley (01571) **(G-8318)**	
Henkel, Stamford *Also Called: Henkel Consumer Goods Inc* **(G-3373)**	
Henkel Consumer Goods Inc **(DH)**.	**475 210-0230**
200 Elm St Stamford (06902) **(G-3373)**	
Henkel Corporation.	781 737-1400
869 Washington St Canton (02021) **(G-7796)**	
Henkel Loctite, Rocky Hill *Also Called: Henkel Loctite Corporation* **(G-2925)**	
Henkel Loctite Corporation **(DH)**.	**860 571-5100**
1 Henkel Way Rocky Hill (06067) **(G-2925)**	
Henkel of America Inc **(HQ)**.	**860 615-3395**
1 Henkel Way Rocky Hill (06067) **(G-2926)**	
Henkel US Operations Corp.	203 655-8911
100 Tokeneke Rd Darien (06820) **(G-848)**	
Henkel US Operations Corp **(DH)**.	**860 571-5100**
1 Henkel Way Rocky Hill (06067) **(G-2927)**	
Henlay Co.	908 795-1007
615 W Johnson Ave Ste 104 Cheshire (06410) **(G-598)**	
Henry A Evers Corp.	401 781-4767
1655 Elmwood Ave Ste 34 Cranston (02910) **(G-15872)**	
Henry Furtera.	762 200-7318
45 Orchard St Fl 1 New Haven (06519) **(G-2160)**	
Henry Gonsalves Co.	401 231-6700
35 Thurber Blvd Smithfield (02917) **(G-16709)**	
Henry Perkins Company.	508 697-6978
180 Broad St Bridgewater (02324) **(G-7230)**	
Herald News, The, Fall River *Also Called: Gatehouse Media LLC* **(G-8551)**	
Herald of Randolph.	802 728-3232
30 Pleasant St Randolph (05060) **(G-17469)**	
Heraldapi Inc.	781 799-1165
246 Highland Ave Apt 3 Somerville (02143) **(G-11879)**	
Herb Chambers Brookline Inc.	617 278-3920
308 Boylston St Brookline (02445) **(G-7318)**	
Herb Chambers Medford Inc.	617 739-6600
60 Mystic Ave Medford (02155) **(G-10288)**	
Herbalife Distributor.	860 584-9721
607 King St Bristol (06010) **(G-453)**	
Herbasway, Wallingford *Also Called: Herbasway Laboratories LLC* **(G-3812)**	
Herbasway Laboratories LLC.	203 269-6991
101 N Plains Industrial Rd Ste 3 Wallingford (06492) **(G-3812)**	
Herbert C Haynes Inc **(PA)**.	**207 736-3412**
40 Route 168 Winn (04495) **(G-5678)**	
Herbert L Hardy & Son Inc.	207 757-8550
1454 Dyerbrook Smyrna Mills (04780) **(G-5480)**	
Hercules Press.	617 323-1950
91 Spring St Boston (02132) **(G-6786)**	
Hercules Slr (us) Inc.	508 992-9519
82 Macarthur Dr New Bedford (02740) **(G-10600)**	
Hercules Slr (us) Inc **(PA)**.	**508 993-0010**
44 South St New Bedford (02740) **(G-10601)**	
Herfco Inc.	978 772-4758
9 Great Rd Shirley (01464) **(G-11816)**	

Herff Jones LLC.	203 266-7170
39 Terrell Farm Rd Bethlehem (06751) **(G-143)**	
Herff Jones LLC.	203 368-9344
71 Vought Pl Stratford (06614) **(G-3546)**	
Herff Jones LLC.	401 331-1240
150 Herff Jones Way Warwick (02888) **(G-16820)**	
Herff Jones - Dieges & Clust, Warwick *Also Called: Herff Jones LLC* **(G-16820)**	
Heritage Concrete Corp.	401 294-1524
535 South County Trl Exeter (02822) **(G-16052)**	
Heritage Wharf Company LLC.	508 990-1011
218 Elm St Dartmouth (02748) **(G-8230)**	
Herley New England, Woburn *Also Called: Caes Mission Systems LLC* **(G-13538)**	
Herman Schmidt Precision Workh.	860 289-3347
26 Sea Pave Rd South Windsor (06074) **(G-3154)**	
Hermann Schmidt, South Windsor *Also Called: Hermann Schmidt Company Inc* **(G-3155)**	
Hermann Schmidt Company Inc.	860 289-3347
26 Sea Pave Rd South Windsor (06074) **(G-3155)**	
Hermell Products Inc.	860 242-6550
9 Britton Dr Bloomfield (06002) **(G-169)**	
Hermetic Solutions Group Inc **(HQ)**.	**215 645-9420**
16 Plains Rd Essex (06426) **(G-1165)**	
Hermit Thrush Brewery, Brattleboro *Also Called: Hermit Thrush Brewery LLC* **(G-17086)**	
Hermit Thrush Brewery LLC **(PA)**.	**585 781-0617**
29 High St Apt 101c Brattleboro (05301) **(G-17086)**	
Hermon Plant Site, Bangor *Also Called: Lane Construction Corporation* **(G-4508)**	
Hermon Sand & Gravel LLC.	207 848-5977
23 Timberview Dr Hermon (04401) **(G-4883)**	
Hero Coatings Inc.	978 462-0746
13 Malcolm Hoyt Dr Newburyport (01950) **(G-10688)**	
Herrick & White Ltd.	401 658-0440
3 Flat St Cumberland (02864) **(G-15942)**	
Herrick Industries Inc.	603 428-3636
54 Main St Henniker (03242) **(G-14435)**	
Herrick Mill Work Inc.	603 746-5092
290 Burnham Intervale Rd Contoocook (03229) **(G-14170)**	
Herring Inc.	401 837-3111
223 Barnstable Rd Hyannis (02601) **(G-9438)**	
Hersam Acorn Cmnty Pubg LLC **(HQ)**.	**203 438-6544**
16 Bailey Ave Ridgefield (06877) **(G-2898)**	
Hersam Acorn Cmnty Pubg LLC.	203 261-2548
205 Spring Hill Rd Trumbull (06611) **(G-3722)**	
Hersam Acorn Newspapers LLC **(PA)**.	**203 438-6000**
16 Bailey Ave Ridgefield (06877) **(G-2899)**	
Hersam Acorn Newspapers LLC.	802 362-3535
Rte 7 Manchester Center (05255) **(G-17329)**	
Hersey Clutch Company LLC.	508 255-2533
8 Commerce Dr Ste A Orleans (02653) **(G-11239)**	
Hershey Creamery Company.	508 399-8560
107 Pond St Seekonk (02771) **(G-11777)**	
Hershey Ice Cream, Seekonk *Also Called: Hershey Creamery Company* **(G-11777)**	
Hess Oil.	508 587-8325
296 N Pearl St Brockton (02301) **(G-7283)**	
Heuresis, Burlington *Also Called: Viken Detection Corporation* **(G-7445)**	
Heutz Oil Co., Portsmouth *Also Called: Sail Energy LLC* **(G-15434)**	
Heveatex Corporation.	508 675-0181
106 Ferry St Ste 1 Fall River (02721) **(G-8560)**	
Hexagon Mfg Intelligence, North Kingstown *Also Called: Hexagon Mfg Intelligence Inc* **(G-16255)**	
Hexagon Mfg Intelligence Inc **(DH)**.	**401 886-2000**
250 Circuit Dr North Kingstown (02852) **(G-16255)**	
Hexagon Mfg Intllgnce- Mtrlogy.	401 886-2000
250 Circuit Dr North Kingstown (02852) **(G-16256)**	
HEXCEL, Stamford *Also Called: Hexcel Corporation* **(G-3374)**	
Hexcel Corporation.	925 520-3232
250 Nutmeg Rd S South Windsor (06074) **(G-3156)**	
Hexcel Corporation **(PA)**.	**203 969-0666**
281 Tresser Blvd # 16 Stamford (06901) **(G-3374)**	
Hexcel Pottsville Corporation.	203 969-0666
Two Stamford Plaza 16th Floor 281 Tresser Boulevard Stamford (06901) **(G-3375)**	
Hexcelpack LLC.	855 439-2351
95 Wooster Ct Bristol (06010) **(G-454)**	

A
L
P
H
A
B
E
T
I
C

Hexplora LLC.. 860 760-7601
   10 Waterchase Dr Rocky Hill (06067) *(G-2928)*

Heyes Forest Products Inc.............................. 978 544-8801
   34 Daniel Shays Highway, Orange Industrial Park Orange (01364) *(G-11223)*

Hf Group LLC... 617 242-1100
   27 Woodcliff Dr Billerica (01821) *(G-6449)*

Hfo Chicago LLC.. 860 285-0709
   910 Day Hill Rd Windsor (06095) *(G-4280)*

Hfw Inc.. 203 854-9584
   18 Ludlow Mnr Norwalk (06855) *(G-2512)*

HH Brown Shoe Company Inc (DH).............. **203 661-2424**
   124 W Putnam Ave Ste 1a Greenwich (06830) *(G-1334)*

HH Brown Shoe Company Inc........................ 978 933-4700
   100 Brickstone Sq Ste 100 Andover (01810) *(G-5886)*

Hhc LLC... 860 456-0677
   340 Progress Dr Manchester (06042) *(G-1602)*

Hhp Inc (PA)... **603 428-3298**
   14 Buxton Industrial Dr Henniker (03242) *(G-14436)*

HI Stone & Son Inc.. 203 264-8656
   313 Main St N Southbury (06488) *(G-3195)*

HI Tech Profiles Inc....................................... 401 377-2040
   185 S Broad St Ste 301 Pawcatuck (06379) *(G-2722)*

HI Tech Profiles Inc....................................... 401 377-2040
   401 Main St Ashaway (02804) *(G-15741)*

HI Tune Wax, Whately *Also Called: HI Tunes* *(G-13339)*

HI Tunes... 435 962-0405
   207 River Rd Whately (01093) *(G-13339)*

Hi-Rel Group LLC.. 860 767-9031
   16 Plains Rd Essex (06426) *(G-1166)*

Hi-Rel Products Inc....................................... 860 767-9031
   16 Plains Rd Essex (06426) *(G-1167)*

Hi-Tech Inc.. 401 454-4086
   50 Perry Ave Attleboro (02703) *(G-6023)*

Hi-Tech Fabricators Inc................................. 603 672-3766
   10 Scarborough Ln Milford (03055) *(G-15025)*

Hi-Tech Metals Inc.. 508 966-0332
   139 Farm St Bellingham (02019) *(G-6291)*

Hi-Tech Mold & Tool Inc............................... 413 443-9184
   1 Technology Dr W Pittsfield (01201) *(G-11401)*

HI-Tech Packaging Inc.................................. 203 378-2700
   1 Bruce Ave Stratford (06615) *(G-3547)*

Hi-Tech Plating, Everett *Also Called: Duncan Galvanizing Corporation* *(G-8487)*

Hi-Tech Polishing Inc.................................... 860 665-1399
   50 Progress Cir Ste 3 # 5 Newington (06111) *(G-2300)*

Hi-Way Concrete Pdts Co Inc....................... 508 295-0834
   2746 Cranberry Hwy Wareham (02571) *(G-12837)*

Hibernation Holding Co Inc (PA)................. **802 985-3001**
   6655 Shelburne Rd Shelburne (05482) *(G-17558)*

Hicks and Otis Prints Inc.............................. 203 846-2087
   9 Wilton Ave Norwalk (06851) *(G-2513)*

Hicks Enterprises Inc.................................... 603 756-3671
   65 Maplewood Cir Walpole (03608) *(G-15662)*

Hid Global Corporation.................................. 617 581-6200
   1320 Centre St Ste 201a Newton (02459) *(G-10759)*

Hidden Moon Brewing, Londonderry *Also Called: Moonlight Meadery LLC* *(G-14774)*

Hideaways International Inc........................... 603 430-4433
   767 Islington St Ste 21 Portsmouth (03801) *(G-15401)*

Higgingbotham Management Corp................ 603 431-0142
   222 International Dr Ste 140 Portsmouth (03801) *(G-15402)*

Higgins Location LLC.................................... 978 266-1200
   898 Main St Acton (01720) *(G-5752)*

High Liner Foods USA Inc............................. 603 818-5555
   183 International Dr Portsmouth (03801) *(G-15403)*

High Purity Natural Pdts LLC........................ 508 864-6072
   328 Main St Ste 3 Southbridge (01550) *(G-12019)*

High Purity New England, Smithfield *Also Called: High Purity New England Inc* *(G-16710)*

High Purity New England Inc (PA).............. **401 349-4477**
   2 Thurber Blvd Smithfield (02917) *(G-16710)*

High Purity New England Inc......................... 401 349-4477
   14 Thurber Blvd Smithfield (02917) *(G-16711)*

High Ridge Copy Inc...................................... 203 329-1889
   351 Woodbine Rd Stamford (06903) *(G-3376)*

High Ridge Printing & Copy Ctr, Stamford *Also Called: High Ridge Copy Inc* *(G-3376)*

High Speed Routing LLC................................ 603 527-8027
   42 Newark St Haverhill (01832) *(G-9103)*

High Speed Technologies................................ 603 483-0333
   1357 Route 3a Unit 9 Bow (03304) *(G-14001)*

High Tech Machinists Inc............................... 978 256-1600
   177 Riverneck Rd Chelmsford (01824) *(G-7932)*

High Technology Inc...................................... 508 660-2221
   20 Alice Agnew Dr North Attleboro (02763) *(G-10873)*

High Voltage Engineering Corp..................... 781 224-1001
   401 Edgewater Pl Ste 680 Wakefield (01880) *(G-12511)*

High-Speed Process Prtg Corp...................... 978 683-2766
   130 Shepard St Lawrence (01843) *(G-9568)*

High-Tech Conversions LLC........................... 860 265-2633
   1699 King St Ste 108 Enfield (06082) *(G-1134)*

Highbyte Inc.. 844 328-2677
   52 Alder St Portland (04101) *(G-5221)*

Highland Belts & Fine Lea Gds...................... 207 989-2597
   96 Parkway S Brewer (04412) *(G-4614)*

Highland Farms Logging LLC......................... 207 239-2977
   104 Towles Hill Rd Cornish (04020) *(G-4705)*

Highland Imports, Fairfield *Also Called: Highland Imports LLC* *(G-1188)*

Highland Imports LLC.................................... 203 538-6818
   74 Linwood Ave Fairfield (06824) *(G-1188)*

Highland Labs Inc.. 508 429-2918
   163 Woodland St Holliston (01746) *(G-9215)*

Highland Manufacturing Inc.......................... 860 646-5142
   5 Glen Rd Ste 4 Manchester (06040) *(G-1603)*

Highland Sugarworks, Websterville *Also Called: Highland Sugarworks Inc* *(G-17684)*

Highland Sugarworks Inc............................... 802 479-1747
   49 Parker Rd Websterville (05678) *(G-17684)*

Highland Tool Co Inc..................................... 603 882-6907
   20 Simon St Nashua (03060) *(G-15110)*

Highland Woodworking LLC.......................... 203 758-6625
   21 Gramar Ave Prospect (06712) *(G-2835)*

Highlands Fuel Delivery LLC (HQ)............... **603 559-8700**
   190 Commerce Way Portsmouth (03801) *(G-15404)*

Highlands Lunchette....................................... 508 674-6206
   757 Robeson St Fall River (02720) *(G-8561)*

Highlands Lunchonette, Fall River *Also Called: Highlands Lunchette* *(G-8561)*

Highlights For Children Inc............................ 413 397-2800
   9 1/2 Market St Northampton (01060) *(G-11067)*

Hightech Amercn Indus Labs Inc.................. 781 862-9884
   320 Massachusetts Ave Lexington (02420) *(G-9748)*

Hightech Extracts LLC................................... 207 590-3251
   5 Drapeau St Biddeford (04005) *(G-4569)*

Highway Safety LLC (HQ).......................... **860 633-9445**
   239 Commerce St Glastonbury (06033) *(G-1286)*

Hil Technology Inc (DH)............................. **207 756-6200**
   94 Hutchins Dr Portland (04102) *(G-5222)*

Hilco, West Warwick *Also Called: Hilco Athletic & Graphics Inc* *(G-16910)*

Hilco Athletic & Graphics Inc........................ 401 822-1775
   55 Greenhill St West Warwick (02893) *(G-16910)*

Hilco Vision, Mansfield *Also Called: Hilsinger Company Parent LLC* *(G-10055)*

Hill Acme Company, Gorham *Also Called: Hill-Loma Inc* *(G-4822)*

Hill-Loma Inc... 207 854-9791
   20 Hutcherson Dr Gorham (04038) *(G-4822)*

Hiller Companies Inc...................................... 978 532-5730
   141 Summit St Ste 2 Peabody (01960) *(G-11315)*

Hillevax, Boston *Also Called: Hillevax Inc* *(G-6787)*

Hillevax Inc.. 617 213-5054
   321 Harrison Ave Ste 500 Boston (02118) *(G-6787)*

Hilliard Precision Products LLC..................... 508 541-9100
   125 Depot St Bellingham (02019) *(G-6292)*

Hilliard's Chocolate System, West Bridgewater *Also Called: Jimsan Enterprises Inc* *(G-12973)*

Hills Point Industries LLC (PA)................... **800 807-8579**
   20 Ketchum St Westport (06880) *(G-4173)*

Hillsgrove Machine Inc.................................. 603 776-5090
   45 Dudley Rd Alton (03809) *(G-13859)*

Hillside Engineering Inc................................ 978 762-6640
   10r Rainbow Ter Ste A Danvers (01923) *(G-8190)*

(G-0000) Company's Geographic Section entry number

Hillside Lumber Company Inc..	207 839-2575
781 County Rd Westbrook (04092) *(G-5629)*	
Hillside Plastics Inc...	413 863-2222
262 Millers Falls Rd Turners Falls (01376) *(G-12448)*	
Hillside Solid Surfaces...	802 479-2508
37 Gable Pl Barre (05641) *(G-17005)*	
Hillside Stone Product, Barre *Also Called: Hillside Solid Surfaces (G-17005)*	
Hilltop Orchard, Richmond *Also Called: Grove Street Enterprises Inc (G-11626)*	
Hilsinger Company Parent LLC **(PA)**...................................	**508 699-4406**
575 West St Mansfield (02048) *(G-10055)*	
Hinckley Co, Portsmouth *Also Called: Talaria Company LLC (G-16459)*	
Hinckley Company, The, Trenton *Also Called: Talaria Company LLC (G-5558)*	
Hinckley Company, The, Portsmouth *Also Called: Talaria Company LLC (G-16458)*	
Hinckley Yacht Services, Southwest Harbor *Also Called: Talaria Company LLC (G-5519)*	
Hindley Manufacturing Co Inc...	401 722-2550
9 Havens St Cumberland (02864) *(G-15943)*	
Hinesburg Record Inc..	802 482-2350
327 Charlotte Rd Hinesburg (05461) *(G-17293)*	
Hinesburg Sand & Gravel Co Inc..	802 482-2335
14818 Route 116 Hinesburg (05461) *(G-17294)*	
Hinman Lumber, Burlington *Also Called: E R Hinman & Sons Inc (G-548)*	
Hiper Global Us LLC **(PA)**..	**978 486-0300**
1616 Osgood St Ste 1001 North Andover (01845) *(G-10838)*	
Hipotronics, Shelton *Also Called: Hipotronics Inc (G-3013)*	
Hipotronics Inc **(HQ)**..	**845 279-3644**
40 Waterview Dr Shelton (06484) *(G-3013)*	
Hippopress LLC **(PA)**..	**603 625-1855**
195 Mcgregor St Ste 325 Manchester (03102) *(G-14859)*	
Hirezon Corporation...	508 836-3800
4 Bellows Rd Westborough (01581) *(G-13105)*	
Hirsch Retail Store Inc..	978 621-4634
52 Eaton Dr Acton (01719) *(G-5753)*	
Hirschmann Windows and Doors, West Rutland *Also Called: H Hirschmann Ltd (G-17695)*	
Hisco, Bloomfield *Also Called: Hisco Pump Incorporated (G-170)*	
Hisco Pump Incorporated **(PA)**..	**860 243-2705**
4 Mosey Dr Bloomfield (06002) *(G-170)*	
Hispanic Communications LLC...	203 674-6793
400 Main St Stamford (06901) *(G-3377)*	
Hispanic Enterprises Inc..	203 588-9334
200 Cogswell St Bridgeport (06610) *(G-329)*	
Historical Publications, Tunbridge *Also Called: Cutter & Locke Inc (G-17652)*	
Hitachi Aloka Medical, Wallingford *Also Called: Hitachi Aloka Medical Amer Inc (G-3814)*	
Hitachi Aloka Medical Ltd..	203 269-5088
10 Fairfield Blvd Wallingford (06492) *(G-3813)*	
Hitachi Aloka Medical Amer Inc..	800 872-5652
10 Fairfield Blvd Wallingford (06492) *(G-3814)*	
Hitachi Kokusai Electric Comark LLC......................................	413 998-1100
104 Feeding Hills Rd Southwick (01077) *(G-12043)*	
Hitachi Protection Platform, Marlborough *Also Called: Sepaton Inc (G-10210)*	
Hitchcock Press Inc..	413 538-8811
8 Hanover St Holyoke (01040) *(G-9260)*	
Hitchcock Printers, New Britain *Also Called: E R Hitchcock Company (G-2024)*	
Hitchiner LLC...	603 672-9630
117 Old Wilton Rd Milford (03055) *(G-15026)*	
Hitchiner Manufacturing Co Inc **(PA)**...................................	**603 673-1100**
594 Elm St Milford (03055) *(G-15027)*	
Hitec Products Inc..	978 772-6963
4 Lomar Park Pepperell (01463) *(G-11384)*	
Hitech Div, Peterborough *Also Called: New Hmpshire Ball Bearings Inc (G-15320)*	
Hitech Metals, Bellingham *Also Called: Hi-Tech Metals Inc (G-6291)*	
Hitpoint Inc **(PA)**...	**413 992-6663**
30 Olive St Greenfield (01301) *(G-8993)*	
Hittite Microwave LLC **(HQ)**...	**978 250-3343**
2 Elizabeth Dr Chelmsford (01824) *(G-7933)*	
Hivec Holdings Inc..	781 224-1001
401 Edgewater Pl Ste 680 Wakefield (01880) *(G-12512)*	
HJ Baker & Bro LLC **(PA)**..	**203 682-9200**
2 Corporate Dr Ste 545 Shelton (06484) *(G-3014)*	
HJ Baker International Inc...	203 682-9200
2 Corporate Dr Ste 545 Shelton (06484) *(G-3015)*	

HJ Hoffman Company...	203 853-7740
25 Hanford Pl Norwalk (06854) *(G-2514)*	
Hkd Snowmakers, Natick *Also Called: Snow Economics Inc (G-10498)*	
Hkd Turbo...	508 878-3798
15 Mercer Rd Natick (01760) *(G-10482)*	
HI Operating LLC **(DH)**...	**508 851-1400**
575 West St Ste 110 Mansfield (02048) *(G-10056)*	
HM Machine LLC..	603 617-3450
5 Faraday Dr Dover (03820) *(G-14231)*	
HM Publishing Corp..	617 251-5000
222 Berkeley St Boston (02116) *(G-6788)*	
HMC Corporation **(PA)**...	**603 746-3399**
284 Maple St Hopkinton (03229) *(G-14477)*	
HMC Enterprises Inc...	860 379-8506
37 Greenwoods Rd New Hartford (06057) *(G-2101)*	
HMC Solutions LLC...	501 255-0498
23 Vine St Peterborough (03458) *(G-15316)*	
Hmg, Biddeford *Also Called: Hyperlite Mountain Gear Inc (G-4570)*	
Hmh, Boston *Also Called: Houghton Mifflin Harcourt Co (G-6796)*	
Hmh, Portsmouth *Also Called: Houghton Mifflin Harcourt Co (G-15406)*	
Hmh Publishers LLC **(DH)**..	**617 351-5000**
125 High St Boston (02110) *(G-6789)*	
HMh Religious Mfg Inc..	508 699-9464
11 Mirimichi St Plainville (02762) *(G-11434)*	
HMK Enterprises Inc **(PA)**..	**781 891-6660**
750 Marrett Rd Ste 401 Lexington (02421) *(G-9749)*	
HMS...	508 831-8317
94 Hamilton St Worcester (01604) *(G-13737)*	
Hmtx Industries LLC **(PA)**..	**203 299-3100**
29 Oakwood Ave Norwalk (06850) *(G-2515)*	
Hnu, Sandwich *Also Called: Pid Analyzers LLC (G-11752)*	
Ho Toy Noodles Inc **(PA)**..	**617 426-0247**
1490 Central St Stoughton (02072) *(G-12213)*	
Ho Yuen Bakery Inc..	617 426-8320
54 Beach St Ste 1 Boston (02111) *(G-6790)*	
Hob Industries Inc..	203 879-3028
25 Knotter Dr Cheshire (06410) *(G-599)*	
Hobbs Medical Inc..	860 684-5875
8 Spring St Stafford Springs (06076) *(G-3256)*	
Hobbs Tavern & Brewing Co LLC...	603 539-2000
2415 Route 16 West Ossipee (03890) *(G-15694)*	
Hobo, Bourne *Also Called: Onset Computer Corporation (G-7141)*	
Hobson and Motzer Incorporated **(PA)**................................	**860 349-1756**
30 Airline Rd Durham (06422) *(G-901)*	
Hockey12com..	781 910-2877
12 Beaumont Ave Billerica (01821) *(G-6450)*	
Hodgdon Shipbuilding LLC..	207 563-7033
6 Angell Ln Damariscotta (04543) *(G-4715)*	
Hodgdon Yachts Inc **(PA)**..	**207 737-2802**
14 School St East Boothbay (04544) *(G-4736)*	
Hodges Badge Company Inc **(PA)**..	**401 682-2000**
205 Clock Tower Sq Portsmouth (02871) *(G-16443)*	
Hoffman Engineering LLC **(DH)**...	**203 425-8900**
8 Riverbend Dr Stamford (06907) *(G-3378)*	
Hoffman Press, The, New Haven *Also Called: The Hoffman Press Incorporated (G-2209)*	
Hogan & Bolas..	401 349-2988
202 King Philip St Providence (02909) *(G-16532)*	
Hogy Lure Company LLC...	617 699-5157
15 Simpson Ln Falmouth (02540) *(G-8633)*	
Holbrook Sun Inc..	781 767-4000
15 Pacella Park Dr # 200 Randolph (02368) *(G-11562)*	
Holcim - Ner Inc **(DH)**..	**781 941-7200**
1715 Broadway Saugus (01906) *(G-11760)*	
Holden, Keene *Also Called: Evs New Hampshire Inc (G-14598)*	
Holden Trap Rock Co, Holden *Also Called: Massachusetts Broken Stone Co (G-9193)*	
Holden Trap Rock Company, Berlin *Also Called: Massachusetts Broken Stone Co (G-6319)*	
Holdette..	301 412-3660
165 Hobart St Danvers (01923) *(G-8191)*	
Hole In One...	508 255-5359
4295 Us-6 Eastham (02642) *(G-8434)*	

A L P H A B E T I C

Hole In One Donut Shop, Eastham *Also Called: Hole In One* **(G-8434)**

Holiday Hill Miniature Golf, Hyannis *Also Called: Drive-O-Rama Inc* **(G-9434)**

Holland Company Inc.. 413 743-1292
153 Howland Ave Adams (01220) **(G-5773)**

Holland, H. V. Sheet Metal, Jamestown *Also Called: H V Holland Inc* **(G-16069)**

Hollingsworth & Vose Company **(PA)**............................ **508 850-2000**
112 Washington St East Walpole (02032) **(G-8418)**

Hollingsworth & Vose Company...................................... 978 448-7000
219 Townsend Rd West Groton (01472) **(G-13002)**

Hollis Line Machine Co Inc... 603 673-1166
128 Old Wilton Rd Milford (03055) **(G-15028)**

Hollrock Engineering Inc.. 413 586-2256
294 Russell St Hadley (01035) **(G-9018)**

Holm Corrugated Container Inc...................................... 860 628-5559
Metals Dr Southington (06489) **(G-3216)**

Holmris, Bedford *Also Called: Design Brand Partners Inc* **(G-13925)**

Holo-Krome USA.. 800 879-6205
61 Barnes Industrial Park N Wallingford (06492) **(G-3815)**

HOLOGIC, Marlborough *Also Called: Hologic Inc* **(G-10159)**

Hologic Inc.. 203 790-1188
37 Apple Ridge Rd Danbury (06810) **(G-757)**

Hologic Inc.. 508 263-2900
445 Simarano Dr Marlborough (01752) **(G-10158)**

Hologic Inc **(PA)**... **508 263-2900**
250 Campus Dr Marlborough (01752) **(G-10159)**

Hologic Inc.. 508 263-2900
14 Aegean Dr Unit A Methuen (01844) **(G-10334)**

Hologic Inc.. 508 263-2900
2 E Perimeter Rd Londonderry (03053) **(G-14755)**

Hologic Foreign Sales Corp.. 781 999-7300
250 Campus Dr Marlborough (01752) **(G-10160)**

Hologic Sales and Service LLC...................................... 508 263-2900
250 Campus Dr Marlborough (01752) **(G-10161)**

Holographix LLC.. 978 562-4474
140 Locke Dr Ste A Marlborough (01752) **(G-10162)**

Holt & Bugbee, Tewksbury *Also Called: Holt and Bugbee Company* **(G-12401)**

Holt and Bugbee Company **(PA)**.................................. **978 851-7201**
1600 Shawsheen St Tewksbury (01876) **(G-12401)**

Holton Family Maple.. 802 888-5183
651 Morey Hill Rd Wolcott (05680) **(G-17775)**

Holy Donut Inc **(PA)**.. **207 761-7775**
194 Park Ave Portland (04102) **(G-5223)**

Holyoke Machine Company.. 413 534-5612
514 Main St Holyoke (01040) **(G-9261)**

Holyoke Tire & Auto Svc Inc... 413 733-2141
435 Dwight St Springfield (01103) **(G-12101)**

Homa Pump Technology, Ansonia *Also Called: Pump Technology Incorporated* **(G-18)**

Home Brands LLC.. 866 616-2685
300 Constitution Ave Unit 200 Portsmouth (03801) **(G-15405)**

Home Heating Services Corp.. 617 625-8255
2 Alpine St Somerville (02144) **(G-11880)**

Home Improvement, Peabody *Also Called: Pro Touch Home Improvement Inc* **(G-11336)**

Home Market Foods Inc.. 781 948-1500
140 Morgan Dr Norwood (02062) **(G-11176)**

Homefree LLC.. 603 898-0172
10 Industrial Dr Unit 11 Windham (03087) **(G-15728)**

Homegrown For Good LLC... 857 540-6361
275 Cider Hill Rd York (03909) **(G-5713)**

Homeland Fuels Company LLC....................................... 781 737-1892
40 Shawmut Rd Ste 200 Canton (02021) **(G-7797)**

Homeland Fundraising.. 860 386-6698
38 Borrup Rd East Windsor (06088) **(G-1076)**

Homeportfolio Inc.. 617 559-1197
288 Walnut St Ste 500 Newton (02460) **(G-10760)**

Homer D Bronson Company, The, Thomaston *Also Called: Hdb Inc* **(G-3621)**

Homestead Baking Co.. 401 434-0551
145 N Broadway Rumford (02916) **(G-16668)**

Homology Medicines Inc.. 781 301-7277
1 Patriots Park Bedford (01730) **(G-6229)**

Honematic Machine Corporation..................................... 508 869-2131
222 Shrewsbury St Boylston (01505) **(G-7162)**

Hones LLC... 603 643-4223
12 South St Ste 3 Hanover (03755) **(G-14425)**

Honey Dew Rehoboth.. 508 431-2784
317 Tremont St Rehoboth (02769) **(G-11609)**

Honeywell, Northford *Also Called: Honeywell International Inc* **(G-2453)**

Honeywell, Northford *Also Called: Honeywell International Inc* **(G-2454)**

Honeywell, Canton *Also Called: Honeywell International Inc* **(G-7798)**

Honeywell, Danvers *Also Called: Honeywell DMC Services LLC* **(G-8192)**

Honeywell, Southborough *Also Called: Honeywell International Inc* **(G-11997)**

Honeywell, Smithfield *Also Called: Honeywell International Inc* **(G-16712)**

Honeywell, Williston *Also Called: Honeywell International Inc* **(G-17735)**

Honeywell Authorized Dealer, New Britain *Also Called: Link Mechanical Services Inc* **(G-2038)**

Honeywell Authorized Dealer, West Hartford *Also Called: Environmental Systems Corp* **(G-4060)**

Honeywell Authorized Dealer, Danvers *Also Called: Burnell Controls Inc* **(G-8171)**

Honeywell Authorized Dealer, West Tisbury *Also Called: South Mountain Company Inc*
(G-13055)

Honeywell Authorized Dealer, Exeter *Also Called: Palmer and Sicard Inc* **(G-14300)**

Honeywell Data Instruments Inc...................................... 978 264-9550
100 Discovery Way Acton (01720) **(G-5754)**

Honeywell DMC Services LLC.. 978 774-3007
199 Rosewood Dr Danvers (01923) **(G-8192)**

Honeywell International Inc... 203 484-7161
1 Fire Lite Pl Northford (06472) **(G-2453)**

Honeywell International Inc... 203 484-7161
12 Clintonville Rd Northford (06472) **(G-2454)**

Honeywell International Inc... 781 298-2700
65 Shawmut Rd Unit 5 Canton (02021) **(G-7798)**

Honeywell International Inc... 508 490-7100
250 Turnpike Rd Southborough (01772) **(G-11997)**

Honeywell International Inc... 401 757-2560
10 Thurber Blvd Smithfield (02917) **(G-16712)**

Honeywell International Inc... 877 841-2840
203 Cornerstone Dr Williston (05495) **(G-17735)**

Honeywell Safety Pdts USA Inc...................................... 401 757-2249
900 Douglas Pike Smithfield (02917) **(G-16713)**

Honeywell Safety Pdts USA Inc...................................... 401 757-2106
10 Thurber Blvd Smithfield (02917) **(G-16714)**

Honeywell Safety Products, Smithfield *Also Called: Norcross Safety Products LLC* **(G-16724)**

Honeywell Safety Products, Smithfield *Also Called: Sperian Protection Usa Inc* **(G-16731)**

Honle Uv America Inc... 508 229-7774
261 Cedar Hill St Ste 5 Marlborough (01752) **(G-10163)**

Honorcraft, Stoughton *Also Called: Honorcraft LLC* **(G-12214)**

Honorcraft LLC.. 781 341-0410
292 Page St Ste A Stoughton (02072) **(G-12214)**

Hood E Benson Laboratories.. 781 826-7573
575 Washington St Pembroke (02359) **(G-11367)**

Hood Reorganization, Lynnfield *Also Called: HP Hood LLC* **(G-9995)**

Hood Sailmakers Inc **(PA)**... **401 849-9400**
23 Johnny Cake Hill Rd Middletown (02842) **(G-16174)**

Hook-Fast Specialties Inc.. 401 781-4466
63 Seymour St Providence (02905) **(G-16533)**

Hooke Laboratories Inc.. 617 475-5114
439 S Union St Ste E3 Lawrence (01843) **(G-9569)**

Hope Inc... 781 455-1145
333 Reservoir St Needham (02494) **(G-10512)**

Hope & Main.. 401 245-7400
691 Main St Warren (02885) **(G-16758)**

Hope Association **(PA)**... **207 364-4561**
85 Lincoln Ave Rumford (04276) **(G-5356)**

Hope Global, Cumberland *Also Called: Nfa Corp* **(G-15955)**

Hope Valley, Lincoln *Also Called: Hope Valley Industries LLC* **(G-16141)**

Hope Valley Industries Inc.. 401 667-7780
338 Compass Cir North Kingstown (02852) **(G-16257)**

Hope Valley Industries LLC.. 401 333-3133
13 Powder Hill Rd Lincoln (02865) **(G-16141)**

Hope Woodworks Inc... 401 497-7714
684 Jillson Ave Woonsocket (02895) **(G-16963)**

Hope-Bffnton Pckging Group LLC.................................. 401 725-3646
575 Lonsdale Ave Central Falls (02863) **(G-15789)**

Hopewell Therapeutics Inc.. 781 218-3318
  310 W Cummings Park Woburn (01801) *(G-13582)*

Hopkinton Independent.. 508 435-5188
  32 South St Westborough (01581) *(G-13106)*

Hopkinton For Land Claring Inc.. 603 428-8400
  88 State Shed Rd Henniker (03242) *(G-14437)*

Hopkinton Mews Sales Office.. 508 625-1267
  1 Freedom Way Hopkinton (01748) *(G-9327)*

Hopp Companies Inc **(PA)**... **800 889-8425**
  519 Heritage Rd Ste 2e Southbury (06488) *(G-3196)*

Hoppe Technologies Inc.. 413 592-9213
  107 1st Ave Chicopee (01020) *(G-8036)*

HOPTO, Concord *Also Called: Hopto Inc (G-14136)*

Hopto Inc **(PA)**... **408 688-2674**
  189 N Main St Ste 102 Concord (03301) *(G-14136)*

Horacios Inc.. 508 985-9940
  64 John Vertente Blvd New Bedford (02745) *(G-10602)*

Horizon Fence Company Inc... 774 289-9254
  66 Thompson Pond Rd Spencer (01562) *(G-12061)*

Horizon House Publications Inc **(PA)**.......................... **781 769-9750**
  685 Canton St Norwood (02062) *(G-11177)*

Horizon International Inc... 617 489-6666
  385 Concord Ave Ste 104 Belmont (02478) *(G-6306)*

Horizon Sheet Metal Inc.. 413 734-6966
  109 Cadwell Dr Springfield (01104) *(G-12102)*

Horizon Vert Pure LLC... 857 236-0904
  51 Teed Dr Randolph (02368) *(G-11563)*

Horizons Unlimited Inc... 860 423-1931
  90 S Park St Ste 1 Willimantic (06226) *(G-4219)*

Horlick Company Inc.. 781 963-0090
  91 Pacella Park Dr Randolph (02368) *(G-11564)*

Horn Book Inc... 617 278-0225
  300 Fenway Ste P311 Boston (02115) *(G-6791)*

Horn Book Magazine, Boston *Also Called: Horn Book Inc (G-6791)*

Horn Corporation **(PA)**.. **800 832-7020**
  580 Fort Pond Rd Lancaster (01523) *(G-9527)*

Horn International Packg Inc **(HQ)**.............................. **978 667-8797**
  580 Fort Pond Rd Lancaster (01523) *(G-9528)*

Hornblower Shipyard LLC.. 203 572-0378
  731 Seaview Ave Bridgeport (06607) *(G-330)*

Horner Millwork Corp.. 781 826-7770
  55 Corporate Park Dr Ste 1 Pembroke (02359) *(G-11368)*

Horsepower Technologies Inc... 844 514-6773
  600 Suffolk St Ste 250 Lowell (01854) *(G-9884)*

Horseshoe Pond Place Commnty...................................... 603 224-8390
  26 Commercial St Concord (03301) *(G-14137)*

Horseshoe Sunday LLC.. 978 476-9766
  506 Amesbury Rd Haverhill (01830) *(G-9104)*

Horst Engineering, East Hartford *Also Called: Horst Engineering & Manufacturing Co (G-997)*

Horst Engineering & Manufacturing Co **(PA)**................ **860 289-8209**
  141 Prestige Park Rd East Hartford (06108) *(G-997)*

Hosokawa Alpine American Div, Northborough *Also Called: Hosokawa Micron Intl Inc (G-11098)*

Hosokawa Alpine American Inc.. 508 655-1123
  455 Whitney St Northborough (01532) *(G-11097)*

Hosokawa Micron Intl Inc.. 860 828-0541
  63 Fuller Way Berlin (06037) *(G-69)*

Hosokawa Micron Intl Inc.. 508 655-1123
  455 Whitney St Northborough (01532) *(G-11098)*

Hosokawa Polymer Systems Div, Berlin *Also Called: Hosokawa Micron Intl Inc (G-69)*

Hostar, Wareham *Also Called: Hostar Mar Trnspt Systems Inc (G-12838)*

Hostar Mar Trnspt Systems Inc.. 508 295-2900
  1 Kendrick Rd Wareham (02571) *(G-12838)*

Hot Mamas Foods Inc... 413 737-6572
  134 Avocado St Springfield (01104) *(G-12103)*

Hot Tools Incorporated.. 781 639-1000
  24 Tioga Way Marblehead (01945) *(G-10088)*

Hot Tops LLC.. 203 926-2067
  240 Long Hill Cross Rd Ste 4 Shelton (06484) *(G-3016)*

Hottinger Bruel & Kjaer Inc **(DH)**............................... **508 485-7480**
  19 Bartlett St Marlborough (01752) *(G-10164)*

Houghton Mfflin Hrcurt Fndtion.. 617 351-5000
  125 High St Ste 900 Boston (02110) *(G-6792)*

Houghton Mfflin Hrcurt Pbls In **(DH)**........................... **617 351-5000**
  125 High St Ste 900 Boston (02110) *(G-6793)*

Houghton Mfflin Hrcurt Pbls In, Boston *Also Called: Hmh Publishers LLC (G-6789)*

Houghton Mifflin LLC.. 617 351-5000
  222 Berkeley St Lbby 1 Boston (02116) *(G-6794)*

Houghton Mifflin Co Intl Inc... 617 351-5000
  222 Berkeley St Boston (02116) *(G-6795)*

Houghton Mifflin Harcourt, Boston *Also Called: Houghton Mifflin Holding Company Inc (G-6798)*

Houghton Mifflin Harcourt Co **(HQ)**............................ **617 351-5000**
  125 High St Ste 900 Boston (02110) *(G-6796)*

Houghton Mifflin Harcourt Co.. 630 467-7000
  361 Hanover St Portsmouth (03801) *(G-15406)*

Houghton Mifflin Harcourt Pubg **(DH)**......................... **617 351-5000**
  125 High St Ste 900 Boston (02110) *(G-6797)*

Houghton Mifflin Holding Company Inc.............................. 617 351-5000
  222 Berkeley St Boston (02116) *(G-6798)*

Houghton Mifflin Publishing, Boston *Also Called: Houghton Mifflin Harcourt Pubg (G-6797)*

Houle Bros Granite Co Inc... 802 476-6825
  25 S Front St Barre (05641) *(G-17006)*

Houlton Farms Dairy, Houlton *Also Called: Houlton Farms Dairy Inc (G-4900)*

Houlton Farms Dairy Inc **(PA)**.................................... **207 532-3170**
  25 Commonwealth Ave Houlton (04730) *(G-4900)*

Houlton Pioneer Times, Houlton *Also Called: Northeast Publishing Company (G-4903)*

House of Fermentology, Burlington *Also Called: Foam Brewers LLC (G-17136)*

House of Kobrin, Everett *Also Called: Reliable Fabrics Inc (G-8497)*

House of Primavera, Providence *Also Called: J Cal Inc (G-16545)*

House of Stainless Inc... 800 556-3470
  1637 Elmwood Ave Cranston (02910) *(G-15873)*

House of Troy, Hyde Park *Also Called: Light Logic Inc (G-17300)*

House of Van Otis, Manchester *Also Called: Van Otis Chocolates LLC (G-14949)*

House of Villeroy & Boch, Kittery *Also Called: Villeroy & Boch Usa Inc (G-4940)*

Housing Devices Inc.. 781 395-5200
  407 R Mystic Ave 32b Medford (02155) *(G-10289)*

Houston Lonza Inc.. 201 316-9200
  4 Hartwell Pl Lexington (02421) *(G-9750)*

Houston-Weber Systems Inc.. 203 481-0115
  31 Business Park Dr Ste 3 Branford (06405) *(G-264)*

Howard Engineering LLC.. 203 729-5213
  687 Wooster St Naugatuck (06770) *(G-1963)*

Howard P Fairfield LLC **(DH)**...................................... **207 474-9836**
  9 Green St Skowhegan (04976) *(G-5468)*

Howard Precision Inc... 603 293-8012
  359 Hounsell Ave Gilford (03249) *(G-14337)*

Howard Printing Inc... 802 254-3550
  14 Noahs Ln Brattleboro (05301) *(G-17087)*

Howard Products Incorporated... 508 757-2440
  4 Birchwood Rd Worcester (01609) *(G-13738)*

Howard S I Glass Co, Worcester *Also Called: S I Howard Glass Company Inc (G-13785)*

Howard Tool Company.. 207 942-1203
  78 Freedom Pkwy Hermon (04401) *(G-4884)*

Howden Amricas Cmpsr - Windsor, Windsor *Also Called: Howden Roots LLC (G-4281)*

Howden Roots LLC... 860 688-8361
  600 Day Hill Rd Windsor (06095) *(G-4281)*

Howe & Howe Technologies Inc....................................... 207 247-2777
  661 Main St Waterboro (04087) *(G-5591)*

Howe Press Perkins Sch Fo.. 617 924-3434
  175 North Beacon St Watertown (02472) *(G-12881)*

Howell Laboratories Inc **(PA)**..................................... **207 647-3327**
  188 Harrison Rd Bridgton (04009) *(G-4629)*

Howestemco, Taunton *Also Called: Howestemco Inc (G-12341)*

Howestemco Inc
  130 Dever Dr Taunton (02780) *(G-12341)*

Howies Wldg & Fabrication Inc.. 207 645-2581
  1148 Main St Jay (04239) *(G-4913)*

Howmet Aerospace Inc.. 860 379-3314
  145 Price Rd Winsted (06098) *(G-4347)*

HOWMET AEROSPACE INC, Winsted *Also Called: Howmet Aerospace Inc (G-4347)*

Howmet Corporation.. 203 315-6150
  2 Commercial St Branford (06405) *(G-265)*

Howmet Corporation.. 203 481-3451
  4 Commercial St Branford (06405) *(G-266)*

A L P H A B E T I C

Hoya Corporation.. 860 289-5379
   580 Nutmeg Rd N South Windsor (06074) *(G-3157)*

Hoya Optcal Labs Amrc-Hartford, South Windsor *Also Called: Hoya Corporation (G-3157)*

Hoya Vision Care, Lewiston *Also Called: Qsa Optical Co Inc (G-4988)*

Hoylu Inc.. 877 554-6958
   50 Corporate Park Dr Ste 270 Pembroke (02359) *(G-11369)*

Hoylu Boston, Pembroke *Also Called: Hoylu Inc (G-11369)*

Hoyt Elec Instr Works Inc................................... 603 753-6321
   23 Meter St Concord (03303) *(G-14138)*

HP, Littleton *Also Called: Hp Inc (G-9816)*

HP, Littleton *Also Called: HP Inc (G-9817)*

Hp Inc... 800 222-5547
   153 Taylor St Littleton (01460) *(G-9816)*

HP Hood LLC.. 860 623-4435
   1250 East St S Suffield (06078) *(G-3591)*

HP Hood LLC (PA).. **617 887-3000**
   6 Kimball Ln Ste 400 Lynnfield (01940) *(G-9995)*

HP Hood LLC.. 978 535-3385
   18 Blackstone St Peabody (01960) *(G-11316)*

HP Inc... 650 857-1501
   550 King St Littleton (01460) *(G-9817)*

Hpi, Gilford *Also Called: Howard Precision Inc (G-14337)*

Hpi Manufacturing Inc.. 203 777-5395
   375 Morse St Hamden (06517) *(G-1431)*

HPM NH LLC... 603 474-1879
   19 Batchelder Rd Seabrook (03874) *(G-15593)*

HRB Winddown Inc (HQ).................................. **203 674-8080**
   333 Ludlow St Ste 2 Stamford (06902) *(G-3379)*

Hrd Press, Belchertown *Also Called: Human Resource Dev Press (G-6280)*

HRF Fastener Systems Inc................................... 860 589-0750
   70 Horizon Dr Bristol (06010) *(G-455)*

Hro Inc... 603 898-3750
   224 N Broadway Ste D12 Salem (03079) *(G-15537)*

Hsb Aircraft Components LLC................................ 860 505-7349
   80 Production Ct New Britain (06051) *(G-2030)*

HT Machine Co Inc.. 508 949-1105
   15 Town Forest Rd Webster (01570) *(G-12926)*

Hti Medical, North Attleboro *Also Called: High Technology Inc (G-10873)*

Htp, Ashaway *Also Called: Htp Meds LLC (G-15742)*

Htp Meds LLC.. 401 315-0654
   15 Gray Ln Ashaway (02804) *(G-15742)*

Hub & Federal Sign, Providence *Also Called: Hub-Federal Inc (G-16534)*

Hub Folding Box Company Inc.............................. 508 339-0005
   774 Norfolk St Mansfield (02048) *(G-10057)*

Hub Technologies Inc.. 508 947-3513
   29 Abbey Ln Middleboro (02346) *(G-10361)*

Hub-Federal Inc... 401 421-3400
   135 Dean St Providence (02903) *(G-16534)*

Hubbard-Hall, Waterbury *Also Called: Hubbard-Hall Inc (G-3919)*

Hubbard-Hall Inc (PA).................................... **203 756-5521**
   563 S Leonard St Waterbury (06708) *(G-3919)*

Hubbard-Hall Inc.. 978 988-0077
   100 Progress Way Wilmington (01887) *(G-13411)*

Hubbardton Forge, Castleton *Also Called: Hubbardton Forge LLC (G-17172)*

Hubbardton Forge LLC.. 802 468-3090
   154 Route 30 S Castleton (05735) *(G-17172)*

Hubbell, Shelton *Also Called: Hubbell Incorporated (G-3017)*

Hubbell Incorporated... 203 426-2555
   14 Prospect Dr Newtown (06470) *(G-2338)*

Hubbell Incorporated (PA).............................. **475 882-4000**
   40 Waterview Dr Shelton (06484) *(G-3017)*

Hubbell Incorporated... 800 346-4175
   7 Aviation Park Dr Londonderry (03053) *(G-14756)*

Hubbell Incorporated... 603 647-5000
   47 East Industrial Park Dr Manchester (03109) *(G-14860)*

Hubbell Incorporated Delaware (HQ)................. **475 882-4000**
   40 Waterview Dr Shelton (06484) *(G-3018)*

Hubbell Power Systems Inc................................. 860 635-2200
   46 Nooks Hill Rd Cromwell (06416) *(G-694)*

Hubbell Raco Division, Shelton *Also Called: Hubbell Incorporated Delaware (G-3018)*

Hubbell-Electric Heater Co, Stratford *Also Called: The Electric Heater Company (G-3580)*

Hubcast Inc... 877 207-6665
   500 Edgewater Dr Ste 568 Wakefield (01880) *(G-12513)*

Hubengage Inc.. 877 704-6662
   1035 Cambridge St Ste 1 Cambridge (02141) *(G-7605)*

Huber + Shner Platis Photonics............................ 781 275-5080
   213 Burlington Rd Ste 123 Bedford (01730) *(G-6230)*

Huber Engineered Woods LLC.............................. 207 488-6700
   333 Station Rd Easton (04740) *(G-4742)*

Huber+suhner Polatis Inc (DH)....................... **781 275-5080**
   213 Burlington Rd Ste 123 Bedford (01730) *(G-6231)*

Hubspot Inc (PA)... **888 482-7768**
   25 1st St Ste 200 Cambridge (02141) *(G-7606)*

Hudson, Cranston *Also Called: Hudson Liquid Asphalts Inc (G-15874)*

Hudson Company, Cranston *Also Called: Hudson Terminal Corp (G-15875)*

Hudson Liquid Asphalts, Providence *Also Called: Hudson Terminal Corp (G-16535)*

Hudson Liquid Asphalts Inc (PA)...................... **401 274-2200**
   2000 Chapel View Blvd Ste 380 Cranston (02920) *(G-15874)*

Hudson Lock LLC (PA)................................... **978 562-3481**
   81 Apsley St Hudson (01749) *(G-9373)*

Hudson Lock/ESP, Hudson *Also Called: Hudson Lock LLC (G-9373)*

Hudson Ouarry, Hudson *Also Called: Hudson Quarry Corp (G-14507)*

Hudson Paper Company (PA)........................... **203 378-8759**
   1341 W Broad St Stratford (06615) *(G-3548)*

Hudson Poly Bag Inc.. 978 562-7566
   578 Main St Hudson (01749) *(G-9374)*

Hudson Quarry Corp... 603 598-0142
   6 Candy Ln Hudson (03051) *(G-14507)*

Hudson Terminal Corp.. 401 941-0500
   2000 Chapel View Blvd Ste 380 Cranston (02920) *(G-15875)*

Hudson Terminal Corp (PA)............................ **401 274-2200**
   29 Terminal Rd Providence (02905) *(G-16535)*

Huestis Machine Corporation............................... 401 253-5500
   68 Buttonwood St Bristol (02809) *(G-15769)*

Huestis Medical, Bristol *Also Called: Huestis Machine Corporation (G-15769)*

Hugger Design, Greenwich *Also Called: Puppy Hugger (G-1345)*

Hughes Brothers Inc.. 207 659-3417
   719 Main Rd N Hampden (04444) *(G-4864)*

Huhtamaki Inc.. 207 795-6000
   11 Fireslate Pl Lewiston (04240) *(G-4964)*

Hull Forest Products Inc..................................... 860 974-0127
   101 Hampton Rd Pomfret Center (06259) *(G-2812)*

Human Care Systems Inc (HQ)........................ **617 720-7838**
   1 Faneuil Hall Sq Boston (02109) *(G-6799)*

Human Care Systems Inc..................................... 781 587-0414
   120 Salem St Lynnfield (01940) *(G-9996)*

Human Care Systems Inc..................................... 781 609-2194
   703 Boston Post Rd Weston (02493) *(G-13286)*

Human Resource Dev Press (PA)...................... **413 253-3488**
   468 Amherst Rd Belchertown (01007) *(G-6280)*

Human Rights Defense Center.............................. 802 257-1342
   1013 Lucerne Ave Brattleboro (05303) *(G-17088)*

Human Systems Integration Inc............................ 508 660-2500
   153 Washington St Ste 4 East Walpole (02032) *(G-8419)*

Humanscale Corporation..................................... 617 338-0077
   179 South St Fl 1 Boston (02111) *(G-6800)*

Humble Screen Printing Llc................................. 802 399-5400
   1610 Troy Ave Colchester (05446) *(G-17196)*

Hummel Bros Inc.. 203 787-4113
   180 Sargent Dr New Haven (06511) *(G-2161)*

Humphreys Industrial Pdts Inc............................. 603 692-5005
   22 Nadeau Dr Rochester (03867) *(G-15478)*

Humphreys Pharmacal Inc................................... 860 267-8710
   31 E High St East Hampton (06424) *(G-962)*

Hungry Ghost Press LLC..................................... 978 677-1000
   60 Valley St Apt 2 Providence (02909) *(G-16536)*

Hunt Yachts LLC... 401 324-4201
   1909 Alden Lndg Portsmouth (02871) *(G-16444)*

Hunter Associates Inc.. 781 233-9100
   92 Walnut St Ste 3 Saugus (01906) *(G-11761)*

Hunter Dathan Hair Artistry................................ 207 774-8887
   4 Milk St Portland (04101) *(G-5224)*

(G-0000) Company's Geographic Section entry number

Hunter Editions, Kennebunk *Also Called: Rich Associates Incorporated (G-4929)*

Hunter Industries Inc... 508 695-6800
266 John L Dietsch Blvd Attleboro Falls (02763) *(G-6087)*

Hunter Panels, Portland *Also Called: Carlisle Construction Mtls LLC (G-5195)*

Hunter Panels, Portland *Also Called: Hunter Panels LLC (G-5225)*

Hunter Panels LLC... 888 746-1114
15 Franklin St Portland (04101) *(G-5225)*

Hunting Dearborn Inc... 207 935-2171
6 Dearborn Dr Fryeburg (04037) *(G-4809)*

Huntsman International LLC.. 603 421-3500
52 Kendall Pond Rd Derry (03038) *(G-14195)*

Hupaco, Stratford *Also Called: Hudson Paper Company (G-3548)*

Hurley Manufacturing, New Hartford *Also Called: New Hartford Industrial Pk Inc (G-2106)*

Hurley Mtal Fbrication Mfg LLC... 860 688-8844
725 Marshall Phelps Rd Windsor (06095) *(G-4282)*

Hurricane Farm LLC... 603 352-0053
735 West Swanzey Rd West Swanzey (03469) *(G-15695)*

Hurricane's Cafe and Deli, Greene *Also Called: Kjpl Restaurants Inc (G-4846)*

Husky Fuel LLC.. 203 783-0783
62 Larkey Rd Oxford (06478) *(G-2698)*

Hussey Corporation **(PA)**.. **207 676-2271**
38 Dyer St Ext North Berwick (03906) *(G-5108)*

Hussey Seating Co, North Berwick *Also Called: Hussey Corporation (G-5108)*

Hussey Seating Company.. 207 676-2271
38 Dyer St Ext North Berwick (03906) *(G-5109)*

Hussmann Corporation.. 603 893-7770
10 Industrial Way Salem (03079) *(G-15538)*

Hutchins Roofing Company Inc.. 802 476-5591
17 W Second St Barre (05641) *(G-17007)*

Hutchinson Arospc & Indust Inc.. 508 417-7000
82 South St Hopkinton (01748) *(G-9328)*

Hutchinson Arospc & Indust Inc.. 508 417-7000
82 South St Hopkinton (01748) *(G-9329)*

Hutchinson Arospc & Indust Inc **(DH)**................................. **508 417-7000**
82 South St Hopkinton (01748) *(G-9330)*

Hutchinson Sealing Systems Inc....................................... 603 772-3771
171 Rte 85 Newfields (03856) *(G-15205)*

Hutchison Company Advg Display, North Kingstown *Also Called: Hutchison Company Inc (G-16258)*

Hutchison Company Inc... 401 294-3503
376 Dry Bridge Rd Ste J1 North Kingstown (02852) *(G-16258)*

Hutzler Manufacturing Co Inc... 860 824-5117
4 Grace Way Canaan (06018) *(G-555)*

HW Machine LLC... 860 828-7679
37 Willow Brook Dr Berlin (06037) *(G-70)*

Hxi LLC... 978 772-7774
12 Lancaster County Rd Ste 1 Harvard (01451) *(G-9064)*

Hxi Millimeter Wave Products, Harvard *Also Called: Hxi LLC (G-9064)*

Hy Temp Inc.. 508 222-6626
34 John Williams St Attleboro (02703) *(G-6024)*

Hy-Ten Die & Development Corp.. 603 673-1611
38 Powers St Milford (03055) *(G-15029)*

Hy-Ten Plastics, Milford *Also Called: Hy-Ten Die & Development Corp (G-15029)*

Hy9 Corporation.. 508 698-1040
124 Washington St Ste 101 Foxboro (02035) *(G-8699)*

Hyaxiom Inc **(HQ)**.. **860 727-2200**
101 E River Dr East Hartford (06108) *(G-998)*

Hycu Inc **(DH)**... **617 681-9100**
27 Wormwood St Ste 600 Boston (02210) *(G-6801)*

Hyde Athletic Industries, Waltham *Also Called: Saucony Inc (G-12776)*

Hyde Group Inc **(PA)**... **800 872-4933**
54 Eastford Rd Southbridge (01550) *(G-12020)*

Hyde Specialty Products LLC.. 603 883-7400
12 Webb Dr Merrimack (03054) *(G-14984)*

Hyde Tools... 508 764-4344
54 Eastford Rd Southbridge (01550) *(G-12021)*

Hyde Tools, Southbridge *Also Called: Hyde Group Inc (G-12020)*

Hydration Labs Inc **(PA)**.. **617 315-4715**
529 Main St Ste 304 Charlestown (02129) *(G-7876)*

Hydro Honing Laboratories Inc **(PA)**.................................... **860 289-4328**
8 Eastern Park Rd East Hartford (06108) *(G-999)*

Hydro International Stormwater, Portland *Also Called: Hil Technology Inc (G-5222)*

Hydro Service & Supplies Inc... 203 265-3995
975 Middle St Ste K Middletown (06457) *(G-1751)*

Hydro-Test Products Inc.. 978 897-4647
85 Hudson Rd Stow (01775) *(G-12246)*

Hydrocision Inc... 978 474-9300
267 Boston Rd Ste 28 North Billerica (01862) *(G-10918)*

Hydrofera, Manchester *Also Called: Hhc LLC (G-1602)*

Hydrofera LLC... 860 456-0677
340 Progress Dr Manchester (06042) *(G-1604)*

Hydrogen Energy California Inc... 978 287-9529
30 Monument Sq Ste 235 Concord (01742) *(G-8120)*

Hydrogen Highway LLC.. 203 871-1000
242 Branford Rd North Branford (06471) *(G-2368)*

Hydroid LLC.. 508 563-6565
1 Henry Dr Pocasset (02559) *(G-11488)*

Hydrolevel Company.. 203 776-0473
126 Bailey Rd North Haven (06473) *(G-2414)*

Hydrolevel Div, North Haven *Also Called: C Cowles & Company (G-2396)*

Hydronics Manufacturing Inc.. 978 528-4335
150 Rangeway Rd North Billerica (01862) *(G-10919)*

Hydrotech Services Inc... 508 699-5977
38b George Leven Dr North Attleboro (02760) *(G-10874)*

Hyer Industries Inc... 781 826-8101
91 Schoosett St Pembroke (02359) *(G-11370)*

Hygrade, Plainville *Also Called: Eclas Realty Corporation (G-2756)*

Hygrade Precision Tech LLC.. 860 747-5773
329 Cooke St Plainville (06062) *(G-2764)*

Hylie Products Incorporated.. 203 439-8786
30 Grandview Ct Cheshire (06410) *(G-600)*

Hyman Brickle & Son Inc **(PA)**... **401 769-0189**
235 Singleton St Woonsocket (02895) *(G-16964)*

Hyora Publications Inc.. 508 430-2700
60 Munson Meeting Way Ste C Chatham (02633) *(G-7897)*

Hypack Inc **(HQ)**... **860 635-1500**
56 Bradley St Middletown (06457) *(G-1752)*

Hyperfine Inc **(PA)**.. **203 458-7100**
351 New Whitfield St Guilford (06437) *(G-1395)*

Hyperfine Operations Inc.. 866 796-6767
351 New Whitfield St Guilford (06437) *(G-1396)*

Hyperion Catalysis Intl Inc **(PA)**.. **617 354-9678**
38 Smith Pl Cambridge (02138) *(G-7607)*

Hyperlite Mountain Gear Inc.. 800 464-9208
40 Main St Ste 13-120 Biddeford (04005) *(G-4570)*

Hypertac, Hudson *Also Called: Hypertronics Corporation (G-9375)*

Hypertherm Inc **(PA)**... **603 643-3441**
21 Great Hollow Rd Hanover (03755) *(G-14426)*

Hypertherm Associates, Hanover *Also Called: Hypertherm Inc (G-14426)*

Hypertherm Inc... 716 434-3755
1699 Wall St Hanover (03755) *(G-14427)*

Hypertronics Corporation.. 978 568-0451
16 Brent Dr Hudson (01749) *(G-9375)*

Hytex Decorative Textiles, Randolph *Also Called: Hytex Industries Inc (G-11565)*

Hytex Industries Inc.. 781 963-4400
67 Pacella Park Dr Randolph (02368) *(G-11565)*

Hyzer Industries.. 802 223-8277
108 Main St Montpelier (05602) *(G-17372)*

I & I Sling Inc.. 781 575-0600
1400 Boston Providence Tpke Ste 3000 Norwood (02062) *(G-11178)*

I & J Machine Tool Company... 203 877-5376
230 Woodmont Rd Ste V Milford (06460) *(G-1836)*

I B A Inc **(PA)**.. **508 865-6911**
103 Gilmore Dr Sutton (01590) *(G-12281)*

I B S, Waltham *Also Called: Industrial Bmdcal Sensors Corp (G-12698)*

I C I, South Easton *Also Called: International Coil Inc (G-11946)*

I C T, Oxford *Also Called: International Contact Tech Inc (G-2700)*

I E A, Brookfield *Also Called: Imperial Elctrnic Assembly Inc (G-525)*

I F Engineering Corp... 860 935-0280
3 Foshay Rd Dudley (01571) *(G-8319)*

I G Marston Company.. 781 767-2894
8 Mear Rd Holbrook (02343) *(G-9174)*

ALPHABETIC (side tab)

I H T, North Quincy *Also Called: Industrial Heat Treating Inc (G-11036)*

I L S, Holyoke *Also Called: International Laser Systems (G-9262)*

I M P, Chicopee *Also Called: International Metal Pdts Inc (G-8040)*

I M S, Marlborough *Also Called: Novanta Motion USA Inc (G-1646)*

I M S, Leominster *Also Called: Innovative Mold Solutions Inc (G-9671)*

I P T, Devens *Also Called: Lewa Process Technologies Inc (G-8275)*

I Q Technology LLC.. 860 749-7255
  9 Moody Rd Ste 18 Enfield (06082) *(G-1135)*

I R Energy Systems, Portsmouth *Also Called: Ingersoll-Rand Energy Systems Corporation (G-15408)*

I Robot Corp - Closed.. 781 345-0200
  63 South Ave Burlington (01803) *(G-7377)*

I Shalom, Bristol *Also Called: New York Accessory Group Inc (G-15776)*

I T C, Lenox *Also Called: Innovative Tooling Company Inc (G-9625)*

I-Optics, Burlington *Also Called: I-Optics Corp (G-7378)*

I-Optics Corp.. 508 366-1600
  1 Wall St Fl 6 Burlington (01803) *(G-7378)*

I-Web, Avon *Also Called: Integrted Web Fnshg Systems In (G-6151)*

I2o Therapeutics Inc.. 303 596-0402
  700 Main St Cambridge (02139) *(G-7608)*

I2s LLC.. 203 265-5684
  1070 N Farms Rd Ste 3 Wallingford (06492) *(G-3816)*

Iae, East Hartford *Also Called: International Aero Engines LLC (G-1002)*

Iae International Aero Engs AG.. 860 565-1773
  400 Main St East Hartford (06108) *(G-1000)*

Iamaw.. 860 228-0049
  249 East St Hebron (06248) *(G-1528)*

Ian Ingersoll Cabinetmaker.. 860 672-6334
  422 Sharon Goshen Tpke West Cornwall (06796) *(G-4044)*

Ian Marie Inc.. 978 463-6742
  11 Malcolm Hoyt Dr Newburyport (01950) *(G-10689)*

Ians, Boston *Also Called: Institute For Applied Ntwrk SE (G-6814)*

IBC Advanced Alloys Inc-Belac.. 978 284-8900
  55 Jonspin Rd Wilmington (01887) *(G-13412)*

IBC Corporation.. 508 238-7941
  27 Belmont St South Easton (02375) *(G-11944)*

Ibcontrols.. 207 893-0080
  3 Pope Rd Windham (04062) *(G-5662)*

Ibex Outdoor Clothing LLC.. 802 359-4239
  132 Ballardvale Dr White River Junction (05001) *(G-17708)*

Ibis LLC.. 603 471-0951
  10 Corporate Dr Ste 100 Bedford (03110) *(G-13933)*

Ibmnh Inc **(PA)**.. **603 644-2326**
  850 East Industrial Park Dr Ste 4 Manchester (03109) *(G-14861)*

Ibnr LLC.. 860 676-8600
  190 Farmington Ave Farmington (06032) *(G-1222)*

Ica Northeast Inc.. 603 773-2386
  41 Industrial Dr Ste 1 Exeter (03833) *(G-14293)*

Icad, Nashua *Also Called: Icad Inc (G-15111)*

Icad Inc **(PA)**.. **603 882-5200**
  98 Spit Brook Rd Ste 100 Nashua (03062) *(G-15111)*

Icarus Corporation.. 508 832-3481
  93 Bancroft St Auburn (01501) *(G-6114)*

Ice Cream Machine Co.. 401 333-5053
  4288 Diamond Hill Rd Cumberland (02864) *(G-15944)*

Icf, Johnston *Also Called: Industrial & Commercial Finshg (G-16089)*

Icl Eb Luce, Framingham *Also Called: Icl Imaging Corp (G-8778)*

Icl Imaging Corp.. 508 872-3280
  51 Mellen St Framingham (01702) *(G-8778)*

Icon Capital Management LLC.. 203 542-7792
  500 W Putnam Ave Ste 400 Greenwich (06830) *(G-1335)*

Icon International Inc.. 401 295-2533
  500 Callahan Rd North Kingstown (02852) *(G-16259)*

Iconics Inc **(HQ)**   100 Foxboro Blvd Ste 130 Foxboro (02035) *(G-8700)*

Iconotech, Bloomfield *Also Called: Mallace Industries Corp (G-191)*

Icopy, Providence *Also Called: Ocean State Book Binding Inc (G-16579)*

ICP Construction Inc **(HQ)**.. **978 623-9980**
  150 Dascomb Rd Andover (01810) *(G-5887)*

ICP Group, Andover *Also Called: Innovative Chem Pdts Group LLC (G-5889)*

ID Bimedical Corp Northborough.. 508 351-9333
  30 Bearfoot Rd Northborough (01532) *(G-11099)*

ID Graphics Group Inc.. 508 238-8500
  9 Bristol Dr South Easton (02375) *(G-11945)*

ID Label Inc.. 508 809-6199
  160 Midway Rd Cranston (02920) *(G-15876)*

ID Mail Systems Inc.. 860 344-3333
  515 John Downey Dr New Britain (06051) *(G-2031)*

ID Products.com, Shelton *Also Called: Identification Products Corp (G-3019)*

ID Sign Group, South Easton *Also Called: ID Graphics Group Inc (G-11945)*

Id123 Inc.. 617 936-0210
  397 Moody St Ste 202 Waltham (02453) *(G-12693)*

Ida International Inc.. 203 736-9249
  200 Roosevelt Dr Derby (06418) *(G-890)*

Ide Acquisition Corp.. 781 326-5700
  377 University Ave Westwood (02090) *(G-13311)*

Ideal Box Company.. 978 683-2802
  15 Union St Ste 455 Lawrence (01840) *(G-9570)*

Ideal Concrete Block Co.. 781 894-3200
  232 Lexington St Waltham (02452) *(G-12694)*

Ideal Concrete Block Co **(PA)**.. **978 692-3076**
  45 Powers Rd Westford (01886) *(G-13242)*

Ideal Electric Co Inc.. 781 284-2525
  0 Centennial Dr Peabody (01960) *(G-11317)*

Ideal Industries Inc.. 978 422-3600
  13 Pratts Junction Rd Sterling (01564) *(G-12163)*

Ideal Instrument Co Inc.. 781 828-0881
  863 Washington St Canton (02021) *(G-7799)*

Ideal Kitchens, Chicopee *Also Called: Ideal Kitchens of Palmer (G-8037)*

Ideal Kitchens of Palmer **(PA)**.. **413 532-2253**
  838 Grattan St Chicopee (01020) *(G-8037)*

Ideal Plating & Polsg Co Inc.. 401 455-1700
  175 Public St Providence (02903) *(G-16537)*

Ideal Powder Coating Inc.. 802 345-7532
  218 Jones Dr Brandon (05733) *(G-17067)*

Ideal Printing Co Incorporated.. 203 777-7626
  228 Food Terminal Plz New Haven (06511) *(G-2162)*

Ideal Sheet Metal Corp.. 508 799-2781
  5 Winter St Worcester (01604) *(G-13739)*

Ideal Tape Co Inc.. 978 458-6833
  1400 Middlesex St Lowell (01851) *(G-9885)*

Ideal Tape Co-A Div Amercn Bil, Lowell *Also Called: Ideal Tape Co Inc (G-9885)*

Ideapaint, Boston *Also Called: Innovative Chem Pdts Group LLC (G-6812)*

Ideas Inc.. 978 453-6864
  160 Tanner St Lowell (01852) *(G-9886)*

Idelle Management Company
  100 Reserve Rd Ste Cc250 Danbury (06810) *(G-758)*

Idemia Identity & SEC USA LLC.. 860 529-2559
  101 Hammer Mill Rd Rocky Hill (06067) *(G-2929)*

Idenix Pharmaceuticals Inc **(HQ)**.. **617 995-9800**
  320 Bent St Cambridge (02141) *(G-7609)*

Identification Concepts, Concord *Also Called: Computype Inc (G-14122)*

Identification Products Corp.. 203 334-5969
  1073 State St Bridgeport (06605) *(G-331)*

Identification Products Corp **(PA)**.. **203 334-5969**
  1 Parrott Dr Ste 500 Shelton (06484) *(G-3019)*

Identity Group Holdings Corp.. 207 510-6800
  43 Bibber Pkwy Brunswick (04011) *(G-4646)*

Idevices LLC.. 860 352-5252
  50 Tower Ln Avon (06001) *(G-27)*

Idex Health & Science LLC.. 860 314-2880
  110 Halcyon Dr Bristol (06010) *(G-456)*

Idex Health & Science LLC.. 203 774-4422
  50 Barnes Park Rd N Wallingford (06492) *(G-3817)*

Idex Health & Science LLC.. 774 213-0200
  16 Leona Dr Middleboro (02346) *(G-10362)*

Idex Mpt Inc **(HQ)**.. **630 530-3333**
  90 Glacier Dr Ste 1000 Westwood (02090) *(G-13312)*

Idexx, Westbrook *Also Called: Idexx Laboratories Inc (G-5631)*

Idexx Distribution Inc.. 207 556-0300
  1 Idexx Dr Westbrook (04092) *(G-5630)*

Idexx Laboratories Inc **(PA)**..**207 556-0300**
  1 Idexx Dr Westbrook (04092) *(G-5631)*

Idexx Operations Inc **(HQ)**..**207 556-4388**
  1 Idexx Dr Westbrook (04092) *(G-5632)*

Idexx Reference Laboratories, Westbrook *Also Called: Idexx Distribution Inc (G-5630)*

Idg..508 875-5000
  1 Exeter Plz 15th Fl Boston (02116) *(G-6802)*

Idg Brokerage Services, Framingham *Also Called: Idg Communications Inc (G-8779)*

Idg Communications Inc..508 766-5300
  492 Old Connecticut Path Framingham (01701) *(G-8779)*

Idg Communications Inc **(DH)**..**508 872-8200**
  140 Kendrick St Bldg B Needham (02494) *(G-10513)*

Idg Corporate Sales..508 875-5000
  3 Speen St 2nd Fl Framingham (01701) *(G-8780)*

Idg Corporate Services Group..508 875-5000
  5 Speen St Ste 5 Framingham (01701) *(G-8781)*

Idg News Service..617 423-9030
  699 Boylston St Ste 15 Boston (02116) *(G-6803)*

IDI, Milford *Also Called: Interface Devices Incorporated (G-1839)*

IDI, Fitchburg *Also Called: Image Diagnostics Inc (G-8657)*

Idp Holdings Inc **(PA)**   1 Beacon St Boston (02108) *(G-6804)*

Idry LLC...800 406-1887
  29 Pitman Rd Barre (05641) *(G-17008)*

IDS, Manchester *Also Called: Integrated Deicing Svcs LLC (G-14863)*

IDS Highway Safety Inc..401 425-2205
  1230 Mendon Rd Cumberland (02864) *(G-15945)*

Idss Holdings Inc...978 237-0236
  85 Swanson Rd Ste 110 Boxboro (01719) *(G-7144)*

Ie Chemical Systems Inc...603 888-4777
  402 S Main St Nashua (03060) *(G-15112)*

IEC Centrifuge, Milford *Also Called: Thermo Ice Inc (G-10421)*

Iet Labs Inc...617 969-0804
  1202 Vfw Pkwy West Roxbury (02132) *(G-13011)*

Iet Solutions LLC **(DH)**..**818 838-0606**
  25 Dan Rd Canton (02021) *(G-7800)*

If Not Now When Inc..860 445-5276
  223 Thames St Groton (06340) *(G-1373)*

Iffland Lumber Company Inc...860 489-9218
  747 S Main St Torrington (06790) *(G-3684)*

Ifm Therapeutics LLC..857 327-9903
  855 Boylston St Ste 1103 Boston (02116) *(G-6805)*

Ifs Enterprises LLC...781 369-9500
  9 Executive Park Dr Ste 200 North Billerica (01862) *(G-10920)*

Igc Polycold Systems, Chelmsford *Also Called: Edwards Vacuum LLC (G-7924)*

Iggy's Bread of The World, Cambridge *Also Called: Iggys Bread Ltd (G-7610)*

Iggys Bread Ltd **(PA)**...**617 491-7600**
  130 Fawcett St Cambridge (02138) *(G-7610)*

Igitt Inc...401 841-5544
  210 Airport Access Rd Middletown (02842) *(G-16175)*

Igm, Holbrook *Also Called: I G Marston Company (G-9174)*

Igs Store Fixtures Inc..978 532-0010
  28 Cedar Swamp Rd Unit 2 Smithfield (02917) *(G-16715)*

Igt, Providence *Also Called: Igt Global Solutions Corporation (G-16538)*

Igt Global Solutions Corp..781 849-5642
  60 Columbian St Braintree (02184) *(G-7188)*

Igt Global Solutions Corp..401 392-7025
  55 Technology Way West Greenwich (02817) *(G-16885)*

Igt Global Solutions Corporation **(HQ)**.............................**401 392-7077**
  10 Memorial Blvd Providence (02903) *(G-16538)*

Igus Bearings Inc **(HQ)**..**800 521-2747**
  257 Ferris Ave Rumford (02916) *(G-16669)*

Igus, Inc., Rumford *Also Called: Igus Bearings Inc (G-16669)*

Ihs Herold Inc **(DH)**..**203 857-0215**
  200 Connecticut Ave Ste 3a Norwalk (06854) *(G-2516)*

Ii-VI Photonics (us) Inc **(HQ)**...**781 938-1222**
  78a Olympia Ave Woburn (01801) *(G-13583)*

Ike Micro, Nashua *Also Called: K E I Incorporated (G-15120)*

IKENA ONCOLOGY, Boston *Also Called: Ikena Oncology Inc (G-6806)*

Ikena Oncology Inc **(PA)**..**857 273-8343**
  645 Summer St Ste 1 Boston (02210) *(G-6806)*

Ilab Solutions LLC...617 297-2805
  217 W Springfield St # 2 Boston (02118) *(G-6807)*

Illinois Tool Works Inc..860 435-2574
  14 Brook St Lakeville (06039) *(G-1546)*

Illinois Tool Works Inc..860 646-8153
  375 New State Rd Manchester (06042) *(G-1605)*

Illinois Tool Works Inc..203 720-1676
  29 Rado Dr Naugatuck (06770) *(G-1964)*

Illinois Tool Works Inc..203 574-2119
  1240 Wolcott St Waterbury (06705) *(G-3920)*

Illinois Tool Works Inc..207 998-5140
  31 Winterbrook Rd Mechanic Falls (04256) *(G-5051)*

Illinois Tool Works Inc..978 777-1100
  30 Endicott St Danvers (01923) *(G-8193)*

Illinois Tool Works Inc..508 520-0083
  35 Parkwood Dr Ste 10 Hopkinton (01748) *(G-9331)*

Illinois Tool Works Inc..781 828-2500
  825 University Ave Norwood (02062) *(G-11179)*

Illinois Tool Works Inc..978 874-0151
  180 State Rd E Westminster (01473) *(G-13271)*

Illumination Devices, Randolph *Also Called: 4382412 Canada Inc (G-17465)*

Ils Business Services Inc...413 789-4555
  570 Silver St Agawam (01001) *(G-5793)*

Imabiotech Corp...978 362-1825
  44 Manning Rd Billerica (01821) *(G-6451)*

Imactis Inc..617 576-2005
  185 Alewife Brook Pkwy Ste 210 Cambridge (02138) *(G-7611)*

Image 4 Concepts Inc..603 644-0077
  7 Perimeter Rd Ste 10 Manchester (03103) *(G-14862)*

Image Award Ribbons, Portsmouth *Also Called: Hodges Badge Company Inc (G-16443)*

Image Awnings Incorporated...603 569-6680
  509 S Main St Wolfeboro (03894) *(G-15734)*

Image Diagnostics Inc..978 829-0009
  310 Authority Dr Fitchburg (01420) *(G-8657)*

Image Factory...508 295-3876
  50 Portside Dr Pocasset (02559) *(G-11489)*

Image Insight Inc..888 667-9244
  222 Pitkin St Ste 2 # 128 East Hartford (06108) *(G-1001)*

Image Printing & Copying Inc...401 737-9311
  33 Plan Way Bldg 7 Warwick (02886) *(G-16821)*

Image Processing..203 488-3252
  251 Boston Post Rd Guilford (06437) *(G-1397)*

Image Signs..774 328-8059
  126 River Rd New Bedford (02745) *(G-10603)*

Image Software Services Inc..978 425-3600
  2 Shaker Rd Ste D103 Shirley (01464) *(G-11817)*

Image Source Inc
  70 Princeton St Ste 3 North Chelmsford (01863) *(G-10977)*

Image Star LLC..888 632-5515
  35 Phil Mack Dr Middletown (06457) *(G-1753)*

Image Stream Medical Inc...978 486-8494
  1 Monarch Dr Ste 102 Littleton (01460) *(G-9818)*

Image Tek Mfg Inc...802 885-6208
  280 Clinton St Springfield (05156) *(G-17618)*

Imagene Technology Inc...603 448-9940
  85 Mechanic St Lebanon (03766) *(G-14691)*

Imagetek Manufacturing, Springfield *Also Called: Image Tek Mfg Inc (G-17618)*

Imagewise, Hampton Falls *Also Called: Kensington Group Incorporated (G-14419)*

Imagine Publishing, Watertown *Also Called: Charlesbridge Publishing Inc (G-12869)*

Imagineering Inc...207 596-6483
  6 Gordon Dr Rockland (04841) *(G-5333)*

Imaging Division, Burlington *Also Called: Zoran Corporation (G-7452)*

Imaging W Varex Holdings Inc...781 663-6900
  940 Winter St Waltham (02451) *(G-12695)*

Imanova, Leominster *Also Called: Nova Packaging Systems Inc (G-9688)*

Imanova Packaging...978 537-8534
  7 New Lancaster Rd Leominster (01453) *(G-9670)*

Imbellus Inc..203 710-4667
  672 Chestnut St Waban (02468) *(G-12496)*

Imbria Pharmaceuticals Inc...617 941-3000
  265 Franklin St Ste 1702 Boston (02110) *(G-6808)*

Imbrium Therapeutics LP **(DH)**.. 888 827-0622
   201 Tresser Blvd Stamford (06901) *(G-3380)*

IMC Internet, North Haven *Also Called: Interactive Marketing Corp (G-2416)*

IMD Soft Inc **(DH)**.. **781 449-5567**
   980-990 Washington St Ste 115 Dedham (02026) *(G-8245)*

Imed Mfg... 603 489-5184
   20 Waters Edge Atkinson (03811) *(G-13903)*

Imeldas Fabrics & Designs.. 207 778-0665
   5 Starks Rd New Sharon (04955) *(G-5090)*

Imerchandise LLC... 860 581-8700
   47 Industrial Park Rd Centerbrook (06409) *(G-562)*

Imerys... 207 548-0900
   70 Trundy Rd Searsport (04974) *(G-5455)*

Imerys Usa Inc... 207 238-9267
   1329 Waterville Rd Skowhegan (04976) *(G-5469)*

IMI Precision Engineering, Farmington *Also Called: Norgren LLC (G-1232)*

Imi, Inc., Haverhill *Also Called: Ftg Circuits Haverhill Inc (G-9095)*

Immedia Semiconductor Inc... 978 296-4950
   100 Riverpark Dr Fl 1 North Reading (01864) *(G-11041)*

Immucell Corporation.. 207 878-2770
   33 Caddie Ln Portland (04103) *(G-5226)*

Immucell Corporation **(PA)**.. **207 878-2770**
   56 Evergreen Dr Portland (04103) *(G-5227)*

Immucor Trnsplant Dgnstics Inc **(DH)**..................................... **203 328-9500**
   550 West Ave Stamford (06902) *(G-3381)*

Immuneering, Cambridge *Also Called: Immuneering Corporation (G-7612)*

Immuneering Corporation... 617 500-8080
   245 Main St Fl 2 Cambridge (02142) *(G-7612)*

Immunex Rhode Island Corp... 401 392-1200
   40 Technology Way West Greenwich (02817) *(G-16886)*

Immunmlecular Therapeutics Inc.. 617 356-8170
   299 Washington St Ste A Woburn (01801) *(G-13584)*

Immunogen, Waltham *Also Called: Immunogen Inc (G-12696)*

Immunogen Inc **(PA)**... **781 895-0600**
   830 Winter St Waltham (02451) *(G-12696)*

Impact Nano LLC... 508 380-8423
   153 Quabbin Blvd Orange (01364) *(G-11224)*

Impact Plastics, Cromwell *Also Called: Apogee Corporation (G-686)*

Impact Science & Technology Inc... 603 459-2200
   85 Northwest Blvd Ste B Nashua (03063) *(G-15113)*

Imperia Corporation... 508 894-3000
   306 Rumstick Rd Barrington (02806) *(G-15748)*

Imperial Elctrnic Assembly Inc.. 203 740-8425
   1000 Federal Rd Brookfield (06804) *(G-525)*

Imperial Graphics, Milford *Also Called: Imperial Grphic Cmmnctions Inc (G-1837)*

Imperial Grphic Cmmnctions Inc.. 203 650-3478
   22 Way St Milford (06460) *(G-1837)*

Imperial Image Inc... 978 251-0420
   55 Middlesex St North Chelmsford (01863) *(G-10978)*

Imperial Metal Finishing Inc... 203 377-1229
   920 Honeyspot Rd Stratford (06615) *(G-3549)*

Imperial Pearl, East Providence *Also Called: Bazar Group Inc (G-16006)*

Imperial Pearl Syndicate, East Providence *Also Called: Imperial-Deltah Inc (G-16023)*

Imperial Pools Inc.. 508 339-3830
   90 John Hancock Rd Taunton (02780) *(G-12342)*

Imperial-Deltah Inc.. 401 434-2597
   795 Waterman Ave East Providence (02914) *(G-16023)*

Implant Sciences Corp.. 978 752-1700
   500 Research Dr Ste 3 Wilmington (01887) *(G-13413)*

Impolit Envmtl Ctrl Corp.. 978 927-4304
   800 Cummings Ctr Ste 355 Beverly (01915) *(G-6356)*

Impreglon Inc... 401 766-3353
   222 Goldstein Dr Woonsocket (02895) *(G-16965)*

Impression Point Inc... 203 353-8800
   500 West Ave Stamford (06902) *(G-3382)*

Imprint Graphics Inc... 508 879-0544
   59 Fountain St Fl 4 Framingham (01702) *(G-8782)*

Imprivata Inc **(HQ)**... **781 674-2700**
   480 Totten Pond Rd Fl 6 Waltham (02451) *(G-12697)*

Improved Consumer Products Inc... 508 695-6841
   100 Towne St North Attleboro (02760) *(G-10875)*

IMS, Milford *Also Called: Enginuity Plm LLC (G-1825)*

IMS, Newton *Also Called: International Marketing Specialists Inc (G-10764)*

IMS, Portsmouth *Also Called: International Mfg Svcs Inc (G-16445)*

Imx, Boston *Also Called: Secure Point Technologies Inc (G-7031)*

In Silico Biosciences Inc... 781 861-1592
   405 Waltham St Lexington (02421) *(G-9751)*

In Store Experience, Westport *Also Called: In Store Experience Inc (G-4174)*

In Store Experience Inc... 203 221-4777
   37 Franklin St Westport (06880) *(G-4174)*

Inanycase.com, Pittsfield *Also Called: Apex Resource Technologies Inc (G-11390)*

Inbalance Inc.. 339 223-6636
   12 Manning St Lexington (02421) *(G-9752)*

Inc, Sun Gro Horticulture, Agawam *Also Called: Sun Gro Horticulture Dist Inc (G-5812)*

Inc, Wtrbury Cntract Eylets St, Waterbury *Also Called: Wces Inc (G-3983)*

Incisiontech, Cranston *Also Called: Cadence Science Inc (G-15840)*

Incjet.. 860 823-1427
   31 Clinton Ave Ste 2 Norwich (06360) *(G-2607)*

Incom Inc.. 508 909-2200
   294 Southbridge Rd Charlton (01507) *(G-7889)*

Incon Inc... 603 595-0550
   21 Flagstone Dr Hudson (03051) *(G-14508)*

INCOPORATED VILLGE OF ORLEAN, Orleans *Also Called: Village of Orleans (G-17440)*

Incord Ltd.. 860 537-1414
   430 Chapel Hill Rd Oakdale (06370) *(G-2622)*

Indeco North America Inc... 203 713-1030
   135 Research Dr Milford (06460) *(G-1838)*

Independant Newspaper Group... 781 485-0588
   385 Broadway Ste 105 Revere (02151) *(G-11619)*

Independent Explosives Inc.. 860 243-0137
   103 Old Windsor Rd Bloomfield (06002) *(G-171)*

Independent Fabrication Inc.. 617 666-3609
   86 Joy St Rear Somerville (02143) *(G-11881)*

Independent Newspaper Group... 781 485-0588
   385 Broadway Revere (02151) *(G-11620)*

Independent Rowing News Inc... 603 448-5090
   53 S Main St Ste 201 Hanover (03755) *(G-14428)*

Indepenent Plating Co... 508 756-0301
   35 New St Worcester (01605) *(G-13740)*

Index Millwork, Milton *Also Called: Index Packaging Inc (G-15046)*

Index Packaging Inc... 603 350-0018
   1055 White Mountain Hwy Milton (03851) *(G-15046)*

Indie617, Cambridge *Also Called: Off The Dial Media LLC (G-7673)*

Indigo Coast Inc.. 860 592-0088
   17 Meadow St Kent (06757) *(G-1541)*

Induplate, Lincoln *Also Called: Greystone of Lincoln Inc (G-16140)*

Induplate Inc **(PA)**... **401 231-5770**
   1 Greystone Ave North Providence (02911) *(G-16303)*

Indusol Inc... 508 865-9516
   11 Depot St Sutton (01590) *(G-12282)*

Industrial & Commercial Finshg.. 401 942-4680
   1339 Plainfield St Johnston (02919) *(G-16089)*

Industrial Bmdcal Sensors Corp.. 781 891-4201
   1377 Main St Waltham (02451) *(G-12698)*

Industrial Cnc LLC... 603 320-3484
   17d Clinton Dr Hollis (03049) *(G-14452)*

Industrial Cnnctons Sltons LLC... 678 216-5817
   45 Griffin Rd S Bloomfield (06002) *(G-172)*

Industrial Construction & Dev, Middletown *Also Called: Clarke International Bus Inc (G-1743)*

Industrial Cutting Tools Inc.. 413 562-2996
   351 N Elm St Westfield (01085) *(G-13171)*

Industrial Defender Inc.. 617 675-4206
   225 Foxboro Blvd Ste 202 Foxboro (02035) *(G-8701)*

Industrial Drives Contrls Inc **(PA)**.. **203 753-5103**
   165 Homer St Waterbury (06704) *(G-3921)*

Industrial Etching Inc... 413 525-4110
   21 Fisher Ave East Longmeadow (01028) *(G-8380)*

Industrial Floor Covering Inc.. 978 362-8655
   148 Rangeway Rd Unit C North Billerica (01862) *(G-10921)*

Industrial Floor Finishes, Div, Bedford *Also Called: Perma Incorporated (G-6252)*

Industrial Flow Sltons Oper LL.. 860 399-5937
   104 John W Murphy Dr New Haven (06513) *(G-2163)*

Industrial Foundry Corporation....................	508 278-5523
Elmdale Rd Uxbridge (01569) *(G-12481)*	
Industrial Heat Treating Inc....................	617 328-1010
22 Densmore St 26 North Quincy (02171) *(G-11036)*	
Industrial Heater Corp....................	203 250-0500
30 Knotter Dr Cheshire (06410) *(G-601)*	
Industrial Lbling Systems Corp....................	978 649-7004
100 Business Park Dr Tyngsboro (01879) *(G-12460)*	
Industrial Magnetics Inc....................	508 853-3232
600 Day Hill Rd Windsor (06095) *(G-4283)*	
Industrial Marking Systems Corp....................	802 752-3170
107 Catamount Dr Unit C Milton (05468) *(G-17360)*	
Industrial Metal Pdts Co Inc....................	781 762-3330
15 Merchant St Sharon (02067) *(G-11793)*	
Industrial Packaging, Webster *Also Called: Industrial Packaging Supply Inc* *(G-12927)*	
Industrial Packaging Sup Inc....................	978 514-9960
150 Industrial Rd Worcester (01605) *(G-13741)*	
Industrial Packaging Supply Inc **(PA)**....................	**508 499-1600**
5 Cudworth Rd Webster (01570) *(G-12927)*	
Industrial Pallet LLC....................	860 974-0093
27 Chaplin Rd Eastford (06242) *(G-1091)*	
Industrial Physics PDT Intgrit....................	978 772-0970
137 Barnum Rd Devens (01434) *(G-8273)*	
Industrial Polymers & Chem Inc **(PA)**....................	**508 845-6112**
508 Boston Tpke Shrewsbury (01545) *(G-11835)*	
Industrial Precision Inc....................	413 562-5161
1014 Southampton Rd Westfield (01085) *(G-13172)*	
Industrial Press Inc....................	888 528-7852
1 Chestnut St Norwalk (06854) *(G-2517)*	
Industrial Realty Trust, Newburyport *Also Called: Epi II Inc* *(G-10682)*	
Industrial Sales Corp **(PA)**....................	**203 227-5988**
727 Post Rd E Westport (06880) *(G-4175)*	
Industrial Sales Supply, Westport *Also Called: Industrial Sales Corp* *(G-4175)*	
Industrial Stl Boiler Svcs Inc....................	413 532-7788
939 Chicopee St Ste 2 Chicopee (01013) *(G-8038)*	
Industrial Tecto....................	310 537-3750
1 Tribiology Ctr Oxford (06478) *(G-2699)*	
Industrial Transfer & Stor Inc....................	508 765-9178
529 Ashland Ave Ste 1 Southbridge (01550) *(G-12022)*	
Industrial Trucks & Equipment, Brockton *Also Called: Ite LLC* *(G-7286)*	
Industrial Video & Ctrl Co LLC....................	617 467-3059
189 Wells Ave Ste 202 Newton (02459) *(G-10761)*	
Industrial Woodworking Co Inc....................	781 340-7474
143 Moore Rd East Weymouth (02189) *(G-8429)*	
Industrious Spirit Company LLC....................	401 450-9229
1 Sims Ave Unit 103 Providence (02909) *(G-16539)*	
Industronics Service, South Windsor *Also Called: Jad LLC* *(G-3158)*	
Ineoquest, Westwood *Also Called: Ineoquest Technologies Inc* *(G-13313)*	
Ineoquest Technologies Inc **(HQ)**....................	**508 339-2497**
247 Station Dr Ste Ne2 Westwood (02090) *(G-13313)*	
Ineos, Springfield *Also Called: Ineos Melamines LLC* *(G-12104)*	
Ineos Melamines LLC....................	413 730-3811
730b Worcester St Springfield (01151) *(G-12104)*	
Inert Corporation....................	978 462-4415
1 Industrial Way Amesbury (01913) *(G-5837)*	
Inertia Dynamics LLC....................	860 379-1252
31 Industrial Park Rd New Hartford (06057) *(G-2102)*	
Inertia Dynamics Inc....................	860 379-1252
31 Industrial Park Rd New Hartford (06057) *(G-2103)*	
Infab Refractories Inc....................	207 783-2075
150 Summer St Lewiston (04240) *(G-4965)*	
Infiltrator Water Technologies LLC **(HQ)**....................	**860 577-7000**
4 Business Park Rd Old Saybrook (06475) *(G-2651)*	
Infineon Tech Americas Corp....................	978 851-1298
35 New England Business Center Dr Ste 110 Andover (01810) *(G-5888)*	
Infineon Tech Americas Corp....................	401 773-7501
200 Crossings Blvd Ste 100 Warwick (02886) *(G-16822)*	
Infineon Technologies, Andover *Also Called: Infineon Tech Americas Corp* *(G-5888)*	
Infinidat Inc....................	781 907-7585
500 Totten Pond Rd Ste 61 Waltham (02451) *(G-12699)*	
Infinite Creative Entps Inc **(PA)**....................	**603 347-6006**
72 Stard Rd Seabrook (03874) *(G-15594)*	
Infinite Electronics Intl Inc....................	800 341-5266
50 High St Fl 3 North Andover (01845) *(G-10839)*	
Infinite Forest Inc **(PA)**....................	**617 299-1382**
172 Charles St Ste B Cambridge (02141) *(G-7613)*	
Infinite Imaging, Portsmouth *Also Called: Powerplay Management LLC* *(G-15431)*	
Infinite Imaging Inc....................	603 436-3030
933 Islington St Portsmouth (03801) *(G-15407)*	
Infinite Iq Inc....................	781 710-8696
26 Willow St Wellesley (02481) *(G-12943)*	
Infinity Massage Chairs, Seabrook *Also Called: Infinite Creative Entps Inc* *(G-15594)*	
Infinity Pharmaceuticals, Cambridge *Also Called: Infinity Pharmaceuticals Inc* *(G-7614)*	
Infinity Pharmaceuticals Inc **(PA)** 1100 Mass Ave Ste 4 Cambridge (02138) *(G-7614)*	
Infinity Stone Inc....................	203 575-9484
1261 Meriden Rd Ste 1 Waterbury (06705) *(G-3922)*	
Infirst Healthcare, Westport *Also Called: Infirst Healthcare Inc* *(G-4176)*	
Infirst Healthcare Inc....................	203 222-1300
8 Church Ln Westport (06880) *(G-4176)*	
Inflammasome Therapeutics Inc....................	617 331-1071
57 Chapel St Ste 100 Newton (02458) *(G-10762)*	
Inflight Corporation....................	800 853-7505
1 Cottage St Unit 39 Easthampton (01027) *(G-8447)*	
Infobionic Inc....................	978 674-8304
321 Billerica Rd Ste 5 Chelmsford (01824) *(G-7934)*	
Infogix, Burlington *Also Called: Infogix Inc* *(G-7379)*	
Infogix Inc **(HQ)**....................	**630 505-1800**
1700 District Ave Ste 300 Burlington (01803) *(G-7379)*	
Infogix Inc....................	508 366-1400
200 Friberg Pkwy Ste 3008 Westborough (01581) *(G-13107)*	
Infor (us) LLC....................	678 319-8000
175 Ledge St Ste 2 Nashua (03060) *(G-15114)*	
Infor Inc....................	678 319-8000
30 Porter Rd Littleton (01460) *(G-9819)*	
Infor Restaurant Systems, Nashua *Also Called: Infor (us) LLC* *(G-15114)*	
Inforce, North Kingstown *Also Called: Emissive Energy Corp* *(G-16251)*	
Inform Inc....................	203 924-9929
25 Brook St Ste 200 Shelton (06484) *(G-3020)*	
Informa Business Media Inc....................	203 358-9900
11 Riverbend Dr S Stamford (06906) *(G-3383)*	
Informa Financial Information Inc....................	508 616-5550
1 Research Dr Ste 400a Westborough (01581) *(G-13108)*	
Informa Tech Holdings LLC....................	203 662-6501
330 Post Rd Fl 2 Darien (06820) *(G-849)*	
Infors USA Inc....................	781 335-3108
25 Mathewson Dr Weymouth (02189) *(G-13326)*	
Infra-Red Bldg & Pwr Svc Inc **(PA)**....................	**781 767-0888**
152 Ctr St Holbrook (02343) *(G-9175)*	
Inframetrics, North Billerica *Also Called: Flir Systems-Boston Inc* *(G-10911)*	
Infraredx Inc....................	781 221-0053
28 Crosby Dr Ste 100 Bedford (01730) *(G-6232)*	
Ingenico Inc....................	888 589-5885
101 Federal St Ste 700 Boston (02110) *(G-6809)*	
Ingenven Flrplymer Sltions LLC....................	603 601-0877
70 High St Hampton (03842) *(G-14403)*	
Ingersoll-Rand, Rocky Hill *Also Called: Trane Technologies Company LLC* *(G-2939)*	
Ingersoll-Rand, Torrington *Also Called: Trane Technologies Company LLC* *(G-3702)*	
Ingersoll-Rand, Northborough *Also Called: Trane Technologies Company LLC* *(G-11115)*	
Ingersoll-Rand, Shrewsbury *Also Called: Trane Technologies Company LLC* *(G-11844)*	
Ingersoll-Rand Energy Systems Corporation....................	603 430-7000
32 Exeter Street Portsmouth (03801) *(G-15408)*	
Ingerson Transportation....................	603 586-4335
36 Alderbrook Dr Jefferson (03583) *(G-14584)*	
Ingleside Corporation....................	781 769-6656
89 Access Rd Ste 17 Norwood (02062) *(G-11180)*	
Ingredion Incorporated....................	207 472-1250
145 Presque Isle St Fort Fairfield (04742) *(G-4784)*	
Ingu LLC....................	603 770-5969
210 West Rd Portsmouth (03801) *(G-15409)*	
Initial Ideas Inc....................	802 775-1685
378 Quality Ln Rutland (05701) *(G-17499)*	
Initial Ideas Inc **(PA)**....................	**802 773-6310**
142 West St Rutland (05701) *(G-17500)*	

Injectech Engineering LLC **(PA)**..860 379-9781
  19 Pioneer Rd New Hartford (06057) *(G-2104)*

Injected Solutions Inc...413 499-5800
  840 Cheshire Rd Lanesborough (01237) *(G-9532)*

Injection Molding Entps LLC..978 339-4535
  20 Harvard Rd Littleton (01460) *(G-9820)*

Injectronics, Clinton *Also Called: Injectronics Corporation (G-8078)*

Injectronics Corporation..978 365-1200
  1 Union St Clinton (01510) *(G-8078)*

Ink Outside Box Incorporated...603 635-2292
  71 Bridge St Pelham (03076) *(G-15290)*

Inkamazon LLC...617 763-4656
  841 Lagrange St Unit 7 West Roxbury (02132) *(G-13012)*

Inkify LLC..617 304-6642
  25 Walpole Park S Ste 8 Walpole (02081) *(G-12561)*

Inkjetmallcom Ltd...802 439-3127
  17 Powder Spring Rd Topsham (05076) *(G-17649)*

Inkspot Press...802 447-1768
  736 Main St Bennington (05201) *(G-17041)*

Inkspot, The, Quincy *Also Called: Winter & Company Inc (G-11545)*

Inkstone Inc...508 587-5200
  129 Liberty St Brockton (02301) *(G-7284)*

Inkstone Printing, Brockton *Also Called: Inkstone Inc (G-7284)*

Inland Fresh Sfood Corp Amer I..207 546-7591
  116 Dartmouth St Ste 2 South Portland (04106) *(G-5506)*

Inline Plastics Corp..800 826-5567
  470 Bridgeport Ave Shelton (06484) *(G-3021)*

Inline Plastics Corp **(PA)**..203 924-5933
  42 Canal St Shelton (06484) *(G-3022)*

Inmetal, Sharon *Also Called: Industrial Metal Pdts Co Inc (G-11793)*

Inner Armour Black LLC..860 656-7720
  83 White Oak Dr Berlin (06037) *(G-71)*

Inner Traditions International **(PA)**...802 767-3174
  1 Park St Rochester (05767) *(G-17485)*

Inner-Tite Corp...508 829-6361
  110 Industrial Dr Holden (01520) *(G-9191)*

Innoneo Health Tech Inc **(PA)**..617 336-3202
  1 Boston Pl Ste 2600 Boston (02108) *(G-6810)*

Innov-X Systems Inc...781 938-5005
  48 Woerd Ave Waltham (02453) *(G-12700)*

Innovairre Studios Inc...603 579-1600
  528 Route 13 S Ste 200 Milford (03055) *(G-15030)*

Innovasea Systems Inc **(PA)**..207 322-3219
  266 Summer St Fl 2 Boston (02210) *(G-6811)*

Innovate Healthcare, Providence *Also Called: Trimed Media Group Inc (G-16630)*

Innovations In Optics Inc...781 933-4477
  10k Gill St Woburn (01801) *(G-13585)*

Innovativ Hoisting LLC...860 969-4477
  16 Tolland Tpke Willington (06279) *(G-4225)*

Innovative Chem Pdts Group LLC **(PA)**..................................978 623-9980
  150 Dascomb Rd Andover (01810) *(G-5889)*

Innovative Chem Pdts Group LLC..800 393-5250
  1 Beacon St Boston (02108) *(G-6812)*

Innovative Coatings Inc...508 533-6101
  24 Jayar Rd Medway (02053) *(G-10306)*

Innovative Coatings,, Medway *Also Called: Innovative Coatings Inc (G-10306)*

Innovative Designs, Ivoryton *Also Called: Richard Riggio and Sons Inc (G-1532)*

Innovative Designs & Disp Inc..413 586-9854
  157 Main St Hatfield (01038) *(G-9072)*

Innovative Environmental, Colchester *Also Called: Innovative Environmental LLC (G-660)*

Innovative Environmental LLC...860 871-7582
  367 Lebanon Ave Colchester (06415) *(G-660)*

Innovative Foods Inc...781 596-0070
  330 Ballardvale St Wilmington (01887) *(G-13414)*

Innovative Fusion Inc..203 729-3873
  60 Great Hill Rd Naugatuck (06770) *(G-1965)*

Innovative Machine & Sup Inc...603 239-8082
  40 Snow Rd Winchester (03470) *(G-15714)*

Innovative Media Group Inc..781 335-8773
  36 Finnell Dr Ste 3 Weymouth (02188) *(G-13327)*

Innovative Mold Solutions Inc...978 840-1503
  42 Jungle Rd Leominster (01453) *(G-9671)*

Innovative Paper Tech LLC...603 286-4891
  1 Paper Trail Tilton (03276) *(G-15653)*

Innovative Publishing Company...267 266-8876
  91 Litchfield Rd Edgartown (02539) *(G-8466)*

Innovative Solutions, Naugatuck *Also Called: Frank Smith (G-1959)*

Innovative Specialties LLC..207 948-1500
  140 Business Ct Pittsfield (04967) *(G-5160)*

Innovative Systems, Meriden *Also Called: Southwick & Meister Inc (G-1701)*

Innovative Test Solutions LLC...603 288-0280
  41 Simon St Ste 2f Nashua (03060) *(G-15115)*

Innovative Tooling Company Inc...413 637-1031
  180 Pittsfield Rd Lenox (01240) *(G-9625)*

Innovatorslink Corporation..860 446-8058
  973 North Rd Groton (06340) *(G-1374)*

Innovent Technologies LLC...978 538-0808
  6 Centennial Dr Peabody (01960) *(G-11318)*

Innovheart US Inc...858 349-8652
  55 Chapel St Ste 10 Newton (02458) *(G-10763)*

Innovion, Wilmington *Also Called: Innovion Corporation (G-13415)*

Innovion Corporation...978 267-4064
  265 Ballardvale St Wilmington (01887) *(G-13415)*

Innoviva Spclty Thrpeutics Inc..800 651-3861
  35 Gatehouse Dr Waltham (02451) *(G-12701)*

Innovive LLC..617 500-1691
  129 Concord Rd Billerica (01821) *(G-6452)*

Innovtive Grdning Slutions Inc...888 560-1037
  128 Intervale Rd Burlington (05401) *(G-17139)*

Inofab LLC...603 435-5082
  26 Broadway St Pittsfield (03263) *(G-15333)*

Inotek Pharmaceuticals Corp...781 676-2100
  131 Hartwell Ave Ste 2 Lexington (02421) *(G-9753)*

Inov-8 Inc..508 251-4904
  290 Turnpike Rd Ste 6-303 Westborough (01581) *(G-13109)*

Inphotonics Inc..781 440-0202
  111 Downey St Norwood (02062) *(G-11181)*

Inriver Tank & Boat Inc..978 287-9534
  152 Commonwealth Ave Ste 21 Concord (01742) *(G-8121)*

INSA Inc..877 500-4672
  35 Center St Ste 1a Chicopee (01013) *(G-8039)*

Insco, Groton *Also Called: Insco Corporation (G-9010)*

Insco Corporation...978 448-6368
  412 Main St Groton (01450) *(G-9010)*

Inscribe Inc..781 933-3331
  12 Linscott Rd Ste C Woburn (01801) *(G-13586)*

Inside Premier Health, Brunswick *Also Called: Medical Resources Inc (G-4650)*

Inside Track Cabling Inc...603 886-8013
  18 West Rd Hudson (03051) *(G-14509)*

Insight Plus Technology LLC...860 930-4763
  747 Stafford Ave Bristol (06010) *(G-457)*

Insightfulvr...978 429-7874
  160 Western Ave Unit 114 Lowell (01851) *(G-9887)*

Insignia Incorporated..978 372-3721
  40 Orchard St Haverhill (01830) *(G-9105)*

Insignia Incorporated..781 278-0150
  1400 Boston Providence Tpke Ste 2500 Norwood (02062) *(G-11182)*

Insignia Athletics LLC..508 756-3633
  60 Fremont St Worcester (01603) *(G-13742)*

Inspectrology LLC...978 212-3100
  35 Upton Dr Wilmington (01887) *(G-13416)*

Inspiremd Inc **(PA)**...857 305-2410
  321 Columbus Ave Boston (02116) *(G-6813)*

Installed Building Pdts LLC...603 645-1604
  62 King St Auburn (03032) *(G-13909)*

Instant Offset Press Inc..508 790-1100
  115 Enterprise Rd Hyannis (02601) *(G-9439)*

Instant Sign Center, Norwood *Also Called: Insignia Incorporated (G-11182)*

Institute For Applied Ntwrk SE..617 399-8100
  2 Center Plz Ste 500a Boston (02108) *(G-6814)*

Institute For Fgn Plicy Analis **(PA)**.......................................617 492-2116
  675 Massachusetts Ave Ste 10 Cambridge (02139) *(G-7615)*

Institute For Scial Cltral Cmm...339 236-1991
  942 Norwest Dr Norwood (02062) *(G-11183)*

(G-0000) Company's Geographic Section entry number

Instron Japan Company Ltd............................. 781 828-2500
825 University Ave Norwood (02062) *(G-11184)*

Instrumart LLC **(HQ)**.................................... **802 863-0085**
35 Green Mountain Dr South Burlington (05403) *(G-17580)*

Instrument Technology, Westfield *Also Called: Transom Scopes Inc (G-13213)*

Instrument Technology Inc............................... 413 562-3512
33 Airport Rd Westfield (01085) *(G-13173)*

Instrumentation Laboratory Co **(DH)**................ **781 861-0710**
180 Hartwell Rd Bedford (01730) *(G-6233)*

Insty-Prints, Bedford *Also Called: Insty-Prints of Bedford Inc (G-13934)*

Insty-Prints of Bedford Inc............................. 603 622-3821
25 S River Rd Bedford (03110) *(G-13934)*

Insulated Wire Inc.. 203 791-1999
2c Park Lawn Dr Bethel (06801) *(G-119)*

Insulation Technology Inc............................... 508 697-6926
35 1st St Bridgewater (02324) *(G-7231)*

Insulectro.. 603 629-4403
8 Akira Way Londonderry (03053) *(G-14757)*

Insulet Corporation **(PA)**.............................. **978 600-7000**
100 Nagog Park Acton (01720) *(G-5755)*

Insulet MA Securities Corp............................. 978 600-7000
600 Technology Park Dr Ste 200 Billerica (01821) *(G-6453)*

Insulfab Plastics Inc..................................... 603 934-2770
155 N Main St Franklin (03235) *(G-14320)*

Insulpane Connecticut Inc.............................. 800 922-3248
30 Edmund St Hamden (06517) *(G-1432)*

Insulsafe Textiles Inc.................................... 207 782-7011
55 Holland St Lewiston (04240) *(G-4966)*

Insys Micro Inc... 917 566-5045
40 Richards Ave Ste 3 Norwalk (06854) *(G-2518)*

Intact Solutions LLC..................................... 860 350-1900
201 Housatonic Ave New Milford (06776) *(G-2248)*

Intec Automation Inc..................................... 603 833-9329
6 Industrial Way Rochester (03867) *(G-15479)*

Intech Inc... 978 263-2210
979 Main St Acton (01720) *(G-5756)*

Integ Systems, Danbury *Also Called: On Line Building Systems LLC (G-792)*

Integer Holdings Corporation........................... 781 830-5800
670 Paramount Dr Canton (02021) *(G-7801)*

Integra Biosciences Corp............................... 603 578-5800
22 Friars Dr Hudson (03051) *(G-14510)*

Integra Biosciences Corp............................... 603 578-5800
2 Wentworth Dr Hudson (03051) *(G-14511)*

Integra Biosciences Corp............................... 603 578-5800
57 Daniel Webster Hwy Merrimack (03054) *(G-14985)*

Integra Biosciences USA, Merrimack *Also Called: Integra Biosciences Corp (G-14985)*

Integra Lfscnces Holdings Corp........................ 800 466-6814
207d Cambridge St Burlington (01803) *(G-7380)*

Integra Lifesciences...................................... 617 268-1616
7 Elkins St Boston (02127) *(G-6815)*

Integra Lifesciences, Mansfield *Also Called: Integra Lifesciences Prod Corp (G-10058)*

Integra Lifesciences Prod Corp........................ 781 971-5682
11 Cabot Blvd Mansfield (02048) *(G-10058)*

Integra-Cast Inc.. 860 225-7600
265 Newington Ave New Britain (06051) *(G-2032)*

Integral Biosystems LLC................................. 781 275-8059
23 Crosby Dr Ste 100a Bedford (01730) *(G-6234)*

Integral Technologies Inc **(DH)**..................... **860 741-2281**
120 Post Rd Enfield (06082) *(G-1136)*

Integratech Solutions Corp............................. 978 567-1000
34b Tower St Hudson (01749) *(G-9376)*

Integrated Deicing Svcs LLC **(DH)**.................. **603 647-1717**
175 Ammon Dr Manchester (03103) *(G-14863)*

Integrated Device Technology............................ 401 719-1686
37 Thurber Blvd Unit 103 Smithfield (02917) *(G-16716)*

Integrated Dynamic Metals Corp....................... 508 624-7271
66 Brigham St Unit A Marlborough (01752) *(G-10165)*

Integrated Dynamics Engrg Inc **(HQ)**............... **781 300-6561**
120 Forbes Blvd Ste 180 Mansfield (02048) *(G-10059)*

Integrated Electronics, Ayer *Also Called: Superconductivity Inc (G-6197)*

Integrated Genetics, Westborough *Also Called: Esoterix Genetic Labs LLC (G-13101)*

Integrated Medical Systems Inc........................ 860 949-2929
5 Little John Ct Gales Ferry (06335) *(G-1260)*

Integrated Print Solutions Inc.......................... 203 330-0200
35 Benham Ave Ste 2 Bridgeport (06605) *(G-332)*

Integrated Vision Solutions, Londonderry *Also Called: L3 Technologies Inc (G-14760)*

Integris Inc.. 978 294-2633
296 Concord Rd Ste 180 Billerica (01821) *(G-6454)*

Integrity Composites LLC................................ 207 571-0743
8 Morin St Biddeford (04005) *(G-4571)*

Integrity Graphics Inc.................................... 800 343-1248
42 Carver Cir Simsbury (06070) *(G-3091)*

Integrity Mfg LLC... 860 678-1599
1451 New Britain Ave Ste 1 Farmington (06032) *(G-1223)*

Integrity Mold Inc.. 978 669-0093
246 Suffolk Ln Gardner (01440) *(G-8891)*

Integrted Web Fnshg Systems In....................... 508 580-5809
175 Bodwell St Avon (02322) *(G-6151)*

Intel, Hudson *Also Called: INTEL Network Systems Inc (G-9378)*

Intel Massachusetts Inc.................................. 978 553-4000
75 Reed Rd Hudson (01749) *(G-9377)*

INTEL Network Systems Inc **(HQ)**................... **978 553-4000**
77 Reed Rd Hudson (01749) *(G-9378)*

Intelcoat Tech Dgtal Imging Hl.......................... 413 536-7800
69 William Frank Dr West Springfield (01089) *(G-13030)*

Intelisent, Newington *Also Called: Compu-Data LLC (G-2282)*

Intelitek Inc... 800 221-2763
18 Tsienneto Rd Derry (03038) *(G-14196)*

Intellgent Clearing Netwrk Inc.......................... 203 972-0861
110 Washington Ave North Haven (06473) *(G-2415)*

Intellgent Cmpression Tech Inc......................... 617 773-3369
1250 Hancock St Ste 701n Quincy (02169) *(G-11523)*

Intellia Therapeutics Inc **(PA)**....................... **857 285-6200**
40 Erie St Ste 130 Cambridge (02139) *(G-7616)*

Intellicut Inc.. 617 417-5236
2 De Bush Ave Unit A8 Middleton (01949) *(G-10386)*

Intelligent Building Controls, Windham *Also Called: Ibcontrols (G-5662)*

Intelligent Bus Entrmt Inc............................... 617 519-4172
480 Pleasant St Ste C210 Watertown (02472) *(G-12882)*

Intelligent Controls, Inc., Saco *Also Called: Franklin Grid Solutions LLC (G-5366)*

Intelligent Mfg Solutns LLC............................. 603 296-1160
645 Harvey Rd Manchester (03103) *(G-14864)*

Intelligent Network Sales LLC.......................... 508 446-3646
689 Main St Walpole (02081) *(G-12562)*

Intellihome of Vermont L L C............................ 802 464-2499
18 Coldbrook Rd Wilmington (05363) *(G-17754)*

Intellinet Corporation.................................... 860 677-4427
10 Stanford Dr Ste 1 Farmington (06032) *(G-1224)*

Intellisense Software Corp............................... 781 933-8098
220 Broadway Ste 102 Lynnfield (01940) *(G-9997)*

Intelon Optics Inc.. 310 804-9392
331 Montvale Ave Woburn (01801) *(G-13587)*

Intelycare, Quincy *Also Called: Intelycare Inc (G-11524)*

Intelycare Inc... 617 971-8344
1250 Hancock St Ste 501n Quincy (02169) *(G-11524)*

Intempo Software Inc **(PA)**............................ **800 950-2221**
191 Chestnut St 5th Fl Springfield (01103) *(G-12105)*

Intensity Therapeutics Inc............................... 203 221-7381
1 Enterprise Dr Ste 430 Shelton (06484) *(G-3023)*

Intent Ai LLC... 415 871-0605
739 Main St Bridgewater (02324) *(G-7232)*

Intent Solutions Group **(PA)**.......................... **617 909-4714**
194 Riverside Dr Norwell (02061) *(G-11142)*

Inteplast Engineered Films Inc.......................... 508 366-8884
5 Otis St Westborough (01581) *(G-13110)*

Inter-All Corporation..................................... 413 467-7181
25 W State St Granby (01033) *(G-8971)*

Inter-Ego Systems Inc **(PA)**........................... **516 576-9052**
131 Main St Ste 1 Hatfield (01038) *(G-9073)*

Interacter Inc... 203 949-0199
10 Beaumont St A Wallingford (06492) *(G-3818)*

Interactive Display Systems, East Hartford *Also Called: General Digital Corporation (G-996)*

Interactive Marketing Corp.................................... 203 248-5324
  399 Sackett Point Rd North Haven (06473) *(G-2416)*

Intercept Medical LLC...................................... 800 622-1114
  3560 Lafayette Rd Portsmouth (03801) *(G-15410)*

Intercntnental Enrgy Group LLC............................. 781 749-9800
  350 Lincoln St Ste 111 Hingham (02043) *(G-9151)*

Interconnect, Bellows Falls *Also Called: Whitney Blake Company (G-17033)*

Interface Devices Incorporated.............................. 203 878-4648
  230 Depot Rd Milford (06460) *(G-1839)*

Interface Engineering Corp.................................. 781 986-2600
  51 N Main St Ste 1 Randolph (02368) *(G-11566)*

Interface Technology, Bridgeport *Also Called: A J R Inc (G-290)*

Interior Design Center, Quincy *Also Called: New England Worldwide Export (G-11529)*

Interlab Incorporated....................................... 203 794-0209
  3 Precision Rd Danbury (06810) *(G-759)*

Interlace Medical Inc....................................... 800 442-9892
  250 Campus Dr Marlborough (01752) *(G-10166)*

Interleukin Genetics Inc.................................... 781 398-0700
  135 Beaver St Waltham (02452) *(G-12702)*

Interlink Publishing Group.................................. 413 582-7054
  46 Crosby St Northampton (01060) *(G-11068)*

Intermat.. 207 283-1156
  389 Hill St Biddeford (04005) *(G-4572)*

International Aero Engines, East Hartford *Also Called: Iae International Aero Engs AG (G-1000)*

International Aero Engines LLC.............................. 860 565-5515
  400 Main St East Hartford (06108) *(G-1002)*

International Auto Entps Inc................................ 860 223-7979
  21 Dewey St New Britain (06051) *(G-2033)*

International Auto Entps Inc **(PA)**...................... **860 224-0253**
  608 E Main St Ste 612 New Britain (06051) *(G-2034)*

International Beam Welding, West Springfield *Also Called: International Beam Wldg Corp (G-13031)*

International Beam Wldg Corp................................ 413 781-4368
  63 Doty Cir West Springfield (01089) *(G-13031)*

International Chromium Pltg Co.............................. 401 421-0205
  2 Addison Pl Providence (02909) *(G-16540)*

International Coil Inc...................................... 508 580-8515
  8 Norfolk Ave Unit 2 South Easton (02375) *(G-11946)*

International Contact Tech Inc.............................. 203 264-5757
  6 Pheasant Run Dr Unit 4 Oxford (06478) *(G-2700)*

International Cordage East Ltd **(PA)**................... **860 537-1414**
  226 Upton Rd Colchester (06415) *(G-661)*

International Crmic Engrg Corp **(PA)**................... **508 853-4700**
  235 Brooks St Worcester (01606) *(G-13743)*

International Data Group, Boston *Also Called: Idg (G-6802)*

International Data Group Inc **(HQ)**..................... **508 875-5000**
  140 Kendrick St Ste C110b Needham (02494) *(G-10514)*

International Dioxcide Inc.................................. 401 295-8800
  40 Whitecap Dr North Kingstown (02852) *(G-16260)*

International Etching Inc................................... 401 781-6800
  7 Ninigret Ave Providence (02907) *(G-16541)*

International Food Pdts Inc................................. 617 594-5955
  454 High Plain St Walpole (02081) *(G-12563)*

International Framers LLC................................... 203 723-4564
  100 Water St 102 Naugatuck (06770) *(G-1966)*

International Insignia Corp................................. 401 784-0000
  1280 Eddy St Providence (02905) *(G-16542)*

International Laser Systems................................. 413 533-4372
  362 Race St Holyoke (01040) *(G-9262)*

International Light, Peabody *Also Called: International Light Tech Inc (G-11319)*

International Light Tech Inc................................ 978 818-6180
  10 Technology Dr Peabody (01960) *(G-11319)*

International Marketing Specialists Inc..................... 617 965-3400
  1105 Washington St Newton (02465) *(G-10764)*

International Metal Pdts Inc................................ 413 532-2411
  1165 Montgomery St Chicopee (01013) *(G-8040)*

International Mfg Svcs Inc.................................. 401 683-9700
  50 Schoolhouse Ln Portsmouth (02871) *(G-16445)*

International Mktg Strategies............................... 203 406-0106
  62 Southfield Ave Ste 214 Stamford (06902) *(G-3384)*

International Packaging Corporation **(PA)**.............. **401 724-1600**
  517 Mineral Spring Ave Pawtucket (02860) *(G-16376)*

International Paper, Auburn *Also Called: International Paper Company (G-4438)*

International Paper Company................................. 860 928-7901
  175 Park Rd Putnam (06260) *(G-2861)*

International Paper Company................................. 207 784-4051
  175 Allied Rd Auburn (04210) *(G-4438)*

International Parallel Mchs................................. 508 990-2977
  50 Conduit St New Bedford (02745) *(G-10604)*

International Pipe & Stl Corp............................... 203 481-7102
  4 Enterprise Dr North Branford (06471) *(G-2369)*

International Provisions Inc
  14 Hamden Park Dr Hamden (06517) *(G-1433)*

International Robotics Inc.................................. 914 630-1060
  761 Stillwater Rd Stamford (06902) *(G-3385)*

International Security Assista.............................. 617 590-7942
  400 Tradecenter Ste 5900 Woburn (01801) *(G-13588)*

International Stone Inc..................................... 781 937-3300
  10 Ryan Rd Woburn (01801) *(G-13589)*

International Stone Products **(PA)**..................... **802 476-6636**
  21 Metro Way Barre (05641) *(G-17009)*

International Technologies Inc.............................. 401 467-6907
  115 Maple St Warwick (02888) *(G-16823)*

International Textile Mfg Inc
  30 Meeting St Unit 4 Cumberland (02864) *(G-15946)*

Internet Systems Cnsortium Inc **(PA)**.................. **650 423-1300**
  60 Exeter Rd Ste 104 Newmarket (03857) *(G-15221)*

Interntnal Br-Tech Sltions Inc **(PA)**.................. **413 739-2271**
  225 Armory St Springfield (01104) *(G-12106)*

Interntnal Hder Tol/ Crbide Pd, Smithfield *Also Called: Jfl Enterprises Inc (G-16718)*

Interntnal Turbine Systems Inc............................. 860 761-0358
  131 W Dudley Town Rd Bloomfield (06002) *(G-173)*

Interntonal Micro Photonix Inc............................. 978 685-3800
  120 Willow St North Andover (01845) *(G-10840)*

Interpak, Pawtucket *Also Called: International Packaging Corporation (G-16376)*

Interplex Engineered Pdts Inc.............................. 401 434-6543
  231 Ferris Ave Rumford (02916) *(G-16670)*

Interplex Engineered Pdts Inc.............................. 508 399-6810
  231 Ferris Ave Rumford (02916) *(G-16671)*

Interplex Etch Logic LLC................................... 508 399-6810
  54 Venus Way Attleboro (02703) *(G-6025)*

Interplex Industries Inc **(DH)**........................ **401 434-6543**
  231 Ferris Ave Rumford (02916) *(G-16672)*

Interprint Inc... 413 443-4733
  101 Central Berkshire Blvd Pittsfield (01201) *(G-11402)*

Intersense Incorporated.................................... 781 541-6330
  700 Technology Park Dr Ste 102 Billerica (01821) *(G-6455)*

Interspace Industries LLC.................................. 520 745-5009
  72 Grays Bridge Rd Ste 1c Brookfield (06804) *(G-526)*

Interstate All Battery Center.............................. 508 394-9400
  484 Station Ave South Yarmouth (02664) *(G-11984)*

Interstate Design Company Inc.............................. 413 786-7730
  84 Gold St Agawam (01001) *(G-5794)*

Interstate Elec Svcs Corp.................................. 860 243-5644
  800 Marshall Phelps Rd # 2 Windsor (06095) *(G-4284)*

Interstate Elec Svcs Corp.................................. 401 369-7890
  20 N Blossom St East Providence (02914) *(G-16024)*

Interstate Elevator Corp................................... 603 560-3377
  21s Olympia Ave Woburn (01801) *(G-13590)*

Interstate Gasket Company Inc.............................. 508 234-5500
  55 Gilmore Dr Sutton (01590) *(G-12283)*

Interstate Mfg Co Inc...................................... 413 789-8674
  84 Gold St Agawam (01001) *(G-5795)*

Interstate Specialty Pdts Inc.............................. 800 984-1811
  55 Gilmore Dr Sutton (01590) *(G-12284)*

Intersurface Dynamics Inc.................................. 203 778-9995
  21 Francis J Clarke Cir Bethel (06801) *(G-120)*

Intertech Process Technology............................... 603 893-9566
  3 Commerce Dr Ste 301 Atkinson (03811) *(G-13904)*

Intervala LLC.. 603 595-1987
  33 Constitution Dr Hudson (03051) *(G-14512)*

Interview Exchange, Westborough *Also Called: Hirezon Corporation (G-13105)*

Inteset Systems, Hanover *Also Called: Inteset Technologies LLC (G-9035)*

(G-0000) Company's Geographic Section entry number

Inteset Technologies LLC...... 781 826-1560
51 Mill St Ste 21 Hanover (02339) *(G-9035)*

Intest Thermal Solutions, Mansfield *Also Called: Temptronic Corporation* *(G-10079)*

Intralign Holdings LLC...... 602 773-8506
124 Washington St Ste 101 Foxboro (02035) *(G-8702)*

Intrmatl Chromium Plating Co, Providence *Also Called: International Chromium Pltg Co* *(G-16540)*

Intuvision Inc...... 781 497-1015
10 Tower Office Park Ste 200 Woburn (01801) *(G-13591)*

Inventec Prfmce Chem USA LLC...... 860 526-8300
500 Main St Ste 18 Deep River (06417) *(G-878)*

Inverness Corporation **(DH)**...... **774 203-1130**
49 Pearl St Attleboro (02703) *(G-6026)*

Inverness Medical - Biostar Inc...... 781 647-3900
51 Sawyer Rd Ste 200 Waltham (02453) *(G-12703)*

Inversant Inc...... 617 423-0331
120 Munroe St Ste 1 Lynn (01901) *(G-9978)*

Invetech Inc...... 508 475-3400
159 Swanson Rd Boxborough (01719) *(G-7152)*

Invetx Inc...... 802 233-3103
22 Strathmore Rd Natick (01760) *(G-10483)*

Invincible Metal Corp...... 781 536-4589
1775 Ocean St Marshfield (02050) *(G-10239)*

Invironments, Hermon *Also Called: Naheks Inc* *(G-4886)*

Invisible Universe, White River Junction *Also Called: Chelsea Green Publishing Co* *(G-17705)*

Iodine Holdings Inc...... 203 630-0500
550 Research Pkwy Meriden (06450) *(G-1669)*

Ion, Cumberland *Also Called: Ion Audio LLC* *(G-15947)*

Ion Audio LLC **(HQ)**...... **401 658-3743**
200 Scenic View Dr Ste 201 Cumberland (02864) *(G-15947)*

Ion Physics Corp...... 603 895-5100
373 Main St Fremont (03044) *(G-14328)*

Ionbond LLC...... 603 610-4460
195 Nh Ave Ste 190 Portsmouth (03801) *(G-15411)*

Ione Press Inc...... 617 236-1935
138 Ipswich St Boston (02215) *(G-6816)*

Ionsense Inc...... 781 231-1739
40 Manning Rd Billerica (01821) *(G-6456)*

IPC Information Systems, Fairfield *Also Called: IPC Systems Inc* *(G-1189)*

IPC Information Systems, Old Saybrook *Also Called: IPC Systems Inc* *(G-2652)*

IPC Systems Inc...... 860 271-4100
777 Commerce Dr Ste 100 Fairfield (06825) *(G-1189)*

IPC Systems Inc...... 860 952-9575
8 Custom Dr Old Saybrook (06475) *(G-2652)*

Iperia Inc...... 781 839-3800
235 Bear Hill Rd Ste 401 Waltham (02451) *(G-12704)*

Ipg, Marlborough *Also Called: Ipg Photonics Corporation* *(G-10169)*

Ipg Photonics Corporation...... 508 373-1100
257 Cedar Hill St Marlborough (01752) *(G-10167)*

Ipg Photonics Corporation...... 508 506-2812
259 Cedar Hill St Marlborough (01752) *(G-10168)*

Ipg Photonics Corporation **(PA)**...... **508 373-1100**
377 Simarano Dr Marlborough (01752) *(G-10169)*

Ipg Photonics Corporation...... 508 506-2585
16b Old Webster Rd Oxford (01540) *(G-11255)*

Ipg Photonics Corporation...... 603 518-3200
200 Innovative Way Ste 201 Nashua (03062) *(G-15116)*

Ipotec LLC...... 704 991-6978
35 Woodworkers Way Seabrook (03874) *(G-15595)*

Ippolito's Stone Craft, Seekonk *Also Called: Ippolitos Stone Craft Inc* *(G-11778)*

Ippolitos Stone Craft Inc...... 508 336-9616
1960 Fall River Ave Seekonk (02771) *(G-11778)*

Ipsen Biopharmaceuticals Inc **(HQ)**...... **973 903-4442**
1 Main St Ste 700 Cambridge (02142) *(G-7617)*

Ipsen Bioscience Inc...... 617 679-8500
1 Kendall Sq Ste B7401 Cambridge (02139) *(G-7618)*

Ipsumm Inc **(PA)**...... **603 570-4050**
10 Industrial Way Ste 1 Amesbury (01913) *(G-5838)*

Ipswich Bay Glass Co Inc...... 978 948-6644
420 Newburyport Tpke Rowley (01969) *(G-11677)*

Ipura Consulting Group LLC...... 603 294-4002
8 Mohawk St Hampton (03842) *(G-14404)*

Iqbal Shaheen...... 857 415-7585
315 Freeport St Apt 3 Boston (02122) *(G-6817)*

Iqe Kc LLC...... 508 824-6696
200 John Hancock Rd Taunton (02780) *(G-12343)*

IR Industries Inc...... 203 790-8273
21 Francis J Clarke Cir Bethel (06801) *(G-121)*

Ira Green Inc **(PA)**...... **800 663-7487**
177 Georgia Ave Providence (02905) *(G-16543)*

Ira Toyota of Manchester, Manchester *Also Called: Gpi Nh-T Inc* *(G-14854)*

Iredale Cosmetics Inc **(PA)**...... **413 644-9900**
50 Church St Great Barrington (01230) *(G-8976)*

Irex Machining Inc...... 860 870-1885
4 Midland Dr Tolland (06084) *(G-3663)*

Iris Sample Processing, Westwood *Also Called: Statspin Inc* *(G-13319)*

Irobot, Bedford *Also Called: Irobot Corporation* *(G-6235)*

Irobot Corporation **(PA)**...... **781 430-3000**
8 Crosby Dr Bedford (01730) *(G-6235)*

Iron Duck Division, Chicopee *Also Called: Fleming Industries Inc* *(G-8033)*

Iron Horse Standing Seam Roofg, Tunbridge *Also Called: E I J Inc* *(G-17653)*

Ironhorse Industries LLC...... 203 598-8720
357 Terryville Rd Harwinton (06791) *(G-1521)*

Ironman Inc...... 989 386-8975
150 Rumford Ave Apt 230 Mansfield (02048) *(G-10060)*

Ironwood, Boston *Also Called: Ironwood Pharmaceuticals Inc* *(G-6818)*

Ironwood Pharmaceuticals Inc **(PA)**...... **617 621-7722**
100 Summer St Ste 2300 Boston (02110) *(G-6818)*

Iroquois Manufacturing Company...... 802 482-2155
695 Richmond Rd Hinesburg (05461) *(G-17295)*

Irving Energy Dist & Mktg, Portsmouth *Also Called: Highlands Fuel Delivery LLC* *(G-15404)*

Irving Woodlands LLC **(HQ)**...... **207 834-5767**
1798 St John Road St J St John Plt (04743) *(G-5525)*

Irvings Home Center Inc...... 508 583-4421
10 N Main St Brockton (02301) *(G-7285)*

Irwin Industrial Tool Company...... 860 438-3460
700 Stanley Dr 2nd Fl New Britain (06053) *(G-2035)*

ISA Group, Woburn *Also Called: International Security Assista* *(G-13588)*

Iselann - Moss Industries Inc...... 401 463-5950
41 Slater Rd Cranston (02920) *(G-15877)*

Isf Trading Inc...... 207 879-1575
390 Commercial St Portland (04101) *(G-5228)*

Ishigaki USA Ltd...... 603 433-3334
280 Heritage Ave Unit J Portsmouth (03801) *(G-15412)*

Isilon Systems LLC...... 206 315-7500
176 South St Hopkinton (01748) *(G-9332)*

Island Ad-Vantages, Stonington *Also Called: Penobscot Bay Press* *(G-5534)*

Island Approaches...... 207 348-2459
300 Sunset Rd Sunset (04683) *(G-5539)*

Island Institute...... 207 594-9209
386 Main St Rockland (04841) *(G-5334)*

Island Mooring Supplies LLC...... 401 447-5387
68 John Oldham Rd Prudence Island (02872) *(G-16650)*

Island News Enterprise...... 401 423-3200
45 Narragansett Ave Jamestown (02835) *(G-16070)*

Island Oasis, Walpole *Also Called: Island Oasis Frz Cocktail Inc* *(G-12564)*

Island Oasis Frz Cocktail Inc **(HQ)**...... **508 660-1177**
141 Norfolk St Walpole (02081) *(G-12564)*

Island Pond Industries Inc...... 413 732-6625
270 Main St Agawam (01001) *(G-5796)*

Island Publishing Company...... 401 351-4320
255 Hope St Providence (02906) *(G-16544)*

Island Sand & Gravel Pit, Shelton *Also Called: Dan Beard Inc* *(G-2996)*

Island Woods Performance Inc...... 401 349-4644
1186 Douglas Pike Smithfield (02917) *(G-16717)*

Isle Brewers Guild LLC...... 774 766-9186
461 Main St Pawtucket (02860) *(G-16377)*

Isovolta Inc...... 802 775-5528
477 Windcrest Rd North Clarendon (05759) *(G-17414)*

Isovolta/Us Samica, North Clarendon *Also Called: Isovolta Inc* *(G-17414)*

Isp, Sutton *Also Called: Interstate Specialty Pdts Inc* *(G-12284)*

Isp Freetown Fine Chem Inc...... 508 672-0634
238 S Main St Assonet (02702) *(G-5974)*

ISS, Shirley *Also Called: Image Software Services Inc (G-11817)*

Istar Publishing LLC.. 781 885-7724
  21 Grove Sq Randolph (02368) *(G-11567)*

Isto Biologics, Hopkinton *Also Called: Arteriocyte Med Systems Inc (G-9307)*

Isubscribed Inc.. 617 750-4975
  15 Network Dr 3rd Fl Burlington (01803) *(G-7381)*

Isupportws Inc... 203 569-7600
  1 Barry Pl Stamford (06902) *(G-3386)*

Iswiss Corporation... 860 327-4200
  161 Sanrico Dr Manchester (06042) *(G-1606)*

Isystems LLC **(HQ)**.. **802 655-8347**
  800 Hinesburg Rd South Burlington (05403) *(G-17581)*

It Synergy Group LLC.. 866 767-4874
  2980 W Shore Rd Warwick (02886) *(G-16824)*

It'll Be Pizza, Scarborough *Also Called: Itllbe LLC (G-5434)*

Itaconix Corporation.. 603 775-4400
  2 Marin Way Ste 1 Stratham (03885) *(G-15636)*

Ital-Tech Engineering Co Inc...................................... 978 373-6773
  3 Federal Way Groveland (01834) *(G-9014)*

Ital-Tech Machined Pdts LLC...................................... 978 373-6773
  3 Federal Way Groveland (01834) *(G-9015)*

Italian Bakery Products, Lewiston *Also Called: Italian Bakery Products Co (G-4967)*

Italian Bakery Products Co.. 207 782-8312
  225 Bartlett St Lewiston (04240) *(G-4967)*

Itc Group LLC... 203 260-5101
  378 Boston Post Rd Ste 101 Orange (06477) *(G-2670)*

Ite LLC... 508 313-5600
  140 Manley St Brockton (02301) *(G-7286)*

Iteos Therapeutics, Watertown *Also Called: Iteos Therapeutics Inc (G-12883)*

Iteos Therapeutics Inc **(PA)**................................... **339 217-0161**
  321 Arsenal St Ste 301 Watertown (02472) *(G-12883)*

Iterum Therapeutics Inc.. 860 391-8349
  20 Research Pkwy Old Saybrook (06475) *(G-2653)*

Ithaca Peripherals Div, Wallingford *Also Called: Magnetec Corporation (G-3829)*

Ithaco Space Systems Inc... 607 272-7640
  100 Wooster Hts Danbury (06810) *(G-760)*

ITI, Westfield *Also Called: Instrument Technology Inc (G-13173)*

Itk Chemicals Inc... 978 531-2279
  10 Electronics Ave Danvers (01923) *(G-8194)*

Itllbe LLC.. 207 730-7301
  5 Lincoln Ave Scarborough (04074) *(G-5434)*

Itnh Inc... 603 669-6900
  150 Dow St Ste 200a Manchester (03101) *(G-14865)*

Itrica Corp.. 617 340-7777
  125 High St 2nd Fl Boston (02110) *(G-6819)*

Its New England Inc... 203 265-8100
  8 Capital Dr Wallingford (06492) *(G-3819)*

Itsg, Warwick *Also Called: It Synergy Group LLC (G-16824)*

ITT, Stamford *Also Called: ITT Inc (G-3388)*

ITT Exelis, Nashua *Also Called: Impact Science & Technology Inc (G-15113)*

ITT Goulds Pumps Inc **(HQ)**................................... **315 568-2811**
  100 Washington Blvd Fl 6 Stamford (06902) *(G-3387)*

ITT Inc **(PA)**.. **914 641-2000**
  100 Washington Blvd Fl 6 Stamford (06902) *(G-3388)*

ITT Industries Holdings Inc **(DH)**............................. **914 641-2000**
  100 Washington Blvd Fl 6 Stamford (06902) *(G-3389)*

ITT Water & Wastewater USA Inc **(HQ)**.................... **262 548-8181**
  1 Greenwich Pl Ste 2 Shelton (06484) *(G-3024)*

ITW Ark-Les Corporation **(HQ)**................................ **781 297-6000**
  95 Mill St Stoughton (02072) *(G-12215)*

ITW Devcon Inc... 978 777-1100
  30 Endicott St Danvers (01923) *(G-8195)*

ITW EF&c US, Westminster *Also Called: Illinois Tool Works Inc (G-13271)*

ITW Foilmark, Bloomfield *Also Called: Foilmark Inc (G-165)*

ITW Graphics, Manchester *Also Called: Electrocal Inc (G-1595)*

ITW Highland, Waterbury *Also Called: ITW Highland Manufacturing Inc (G-3923)*

ITW Highland Manufacturing Inc.................................. 203 574-3200
  1240 Wolcott St Waterbury (06705) *(G-3923)*

ITW Hlographic Specialty Films.................................... 860 243-0343
  40 E Newberry Rd Bloomfield (06002) *(G-174)*

ITW Nutmeg, Naugatuck *Also Called: Illinois Tool Works Inc (G-1964)*

ITW Performance Polymers.. 978 777-1100
  30 Endicott St Danvers (01923) *(G-8196)*

ITW Powertrain Fastening... 203 720-1676
  29 Rado Dr Naugatuck (06770) *(G-1967)*

ITW Shinemark, Newburyport *Also Called: Foilmark Inc (G-10683)*

Ivanhoe Tool & Die Company Inc................................. 860 923-9541
  590 Thompson Rd Thompson (06277) *(G-3650)*

Ivek Corp **(PA)**... **802 886-2238**
  10 Fairbanks Rd North Springfield (05150) *(G-17422)*

Ivenix, North Andover *Also Called: Fresenius Kabi Usa LLC (G-10833)*

Ivey Industries... 413 736-6464
  15 Main St Holyoke (01040) *(G-9263)*

Ivix, Lexington *Also Called: Ivix Tech Inc (G-9754)*

Ivix Tech Inc **(PA)**.. **702 561-5304**
  405 Waltham St Ste 224 Lexington (02421) *(G-9754)*

Ivory Onyx.. 617 454-4980
  320 D St Unit 403 Boston (02127) *(G-6820)*

Ivy Biomedical Systems Inc... 203 481-4183
  11 Business Park Dr Ste 10 Branford (06405) *(G-267)*

Ivy Computer Inc.. 802 244-7880
  2933 Waterbury-Stowe Rd # 1 Waterbury Center (05677) *(G-17681)*

Iwaki America, Holliston *Also Called: Iwaki America Incorporated (G-9216)*

Iwaki America Incorporated **(HQ)**............................ **508 429-1440**
  5 Boynton Rd Hopping Brook Park Holliston (01746) *(G-9216)*

Iwaki Pumps Inc **(DH)**... **508 429-1440**
  5 Boynton Rd Holliston (01746) *(G-9217)*

Iwave Software LLC
  176 South St Hopkinton (01748) *(G-9333)*

Ix Cameras Inc.. 617 225-0080
  8 Cabot Rd Woburn (01801) *(G-13592)*

Ixys Intgrted Circuits Div LLC **(DH)**......................... **978 524-6700**
  78 Cherry Hill Dr Beverly (01915) *(G-6357)*

Iyrs, Newport *Also Called: Iyrs School Tech & Trades (G-16212)*

Iyrs School Tech & Trades.. 401 846-2587
  449 Thames St Unit 100 Newport (02840) *(G-16212)*

Izon Science US Limited.. 617 945-5936
  196 Boston Ave Ste 3900 Medford (02155) *(G-10290)*

Izon Science US LLC.. 617 945-5936
  196 Boston Ave Ste 3900 Medford (02155) *(G-10291)*

J & B Service Company LLC.. 203 743-9357
  12 Trowbridge Dr Bethel (06801) *(G-122)*

J & G Hadeka Slate Flrg Inc.. 802 265-3351
  773 Briar Hill Rd West Pawlet (05775) *(G-17691)*

J & J Heating & AC Inc... 978 454-8197
  17 Arlington St Dracut (01826) *(G-8306)*

J & J Heating and AC, Dracut *Also Called: J & J Heating & AC Inc (G-8306)*

J & J Technologies Inc.. 508 291-3803
  18 Kendrick Rd Wareham (02571) *(G-12839)*

J & K Cabinets Ltd... 978 658-1888
  66 Industrial Way # 68 Wilmington (01887) *(G-13417)*

J & K Sales Co Inc... 508 252-6235
  225 Pleasant St Rehoboth (02769) *(G-11610)*

J & L, Springfield *Also Called: J & L Metrology Inc (G-17619)*

J & L Machine Co Inc **(PA)**...................................... **860 649-3539**
  62 Batson Dr Manchester (06042) *(G-1607)*

J & L Metrology Inc.. 802 885-8291
  280 Clinton St Springfield (05156) *(G-17619)*

J & L Mfg Watertown Inc... 203 591-9124
  2714 E Main St Waterbury (06705) *(G-3924)*

J & L Tool Company Inc.. 203 265-6237
  368 N Cherry Street Ext Wallingford (06492) *(G-3820)*

J & L Welding & Machine Co.. 978 283-3388
  19 Arthur St # 25 Gloucester (01930) *(G-8942)*

J & M Cabinet Shop Inc.. 508 660-6660
  2050 Main St Walpole (02081) *(G-12565)*

J & M Logging Inc.. 207 622-6353
  35 Harold Dr Sidney (04330) *(G-5459)*

J & M Machining Inc... 207 474-7300
  313 North Ave Skowhegan (04976) *(G-5470)*

J & M Plumbing & Cnstr LLC....................................... 860 319-3082
  16 West St Norwich (06360) *(G-2608)*

J & P Manufacturing LLC.. 860 919-8287
   125 Robert Jackson Way Unit F Plainville (06062) *(G-2765)*

J T R Graphics Inc.. 781 871-7577
   155 Webster St Ste L Hanover (02339) *(G-9036)*

J & R Langley Co Inc.. 603 622-9653
   169 S Main St Manchester (03102) *(G-14866)*

J & R Pre-Cast Inc.. 508 822-3311
   16 County St Berkley (02779) *(G-6316)*

J & R Senior Sheet Metal Inc.................................. 401 322-1509
   15 Langworthy Rd Westerly (02891) *(G-16933)*

J & T Printing LLC.. 860 529-4628
   81 Wolcott Hill Rd Wethersfield (06109) *(G-4206)*

J and L Sand.. 207 499-2545
   221 S Waterboro Rd Lyman (04002) *(G-5029)*

J Arakelian Inc.. 401 943-7366
   66 Mill St Johnston (02919) *(G-16090)*

J B J Machine Company.. 207 676-3380
   12 Elm St North Berwick (03906) *(G-5110)*

J B Sash & Door Company Inc.................................. 617 884-8940
   280 2nd St Chelsea (02150) *(G-7983)*

J B Sawmill & Landclearing Inc................................ 508 435-6877
   51 Fisher St Westborough (01581) *(G-13111)*

J Burdon Division, Milford *Also Called: Ridge View Associates Inc (G-1878)*

J C B Leasing Inc.. 603 529-7974
   14 B And B Ln Weare (03281) *(G-15671)*

J C Image, Saint Albans *Also Called: Mprp Inc (G-17523)*

J Cal Inc.. 401 941-7700
   1 Baker St Providence (02905) *(G-16545)*

J Cal Inc (PA)... 401 941-7700
   1 Baker St Providence (02905) *(G-16546)*

J F Griffin Publishing LLC...................................... 413 884-0085
   33 Main St Ste 2 North Adams (01247) *(G-10809)*

J F Hutchinson Co.. 207 926-3676
   616b Lewiston Rd New Gloucester (04260) *(G-5085)*

J F M, Merrimac *Also Called: James F Mullen Co Inc (G-10325)*

J F White Contracting Co.. 781 436-8497
   56 Old Page St Stoughton (02072) *(G-12216)*

J Foster Ice Cream.. 860 651-1499
   894 Hopmeadow St Simsbury (06070) *(G-3092)*

J G Maclellan Con Co Inc.. 978 458-1223
   91 Haverhill Rd Amesbury (01913) *(G-5839)*

J G Maclellan Con Co Inc (PA).................................. 978 458-1223
   180 Phoenix Ave Lowell (01852) *(G-9888)*

J Goodison Company (PA).. 401 667-5938
   125 Zarbo Ave North Kingstown (02852) *(G-16261)*

J H Breakell & Company Inc.................................... 401 849-3522
   132 Spring St Newport (02840) *(G-16213)*

J H Dunning Corporation.. 603 445-5591
   1 Dunning Dr North Walpole (03609) *(G-15258)*

J J Ryan Corporation.. 860 628-0393
   355 Atwater St Plantsville (06479) *(G-2793)*

J K Adams Company Inc.. 802 362-2303
   1430 Route 30 Dorset (05251) *(G-17214)*

J L Anthony & Company.. 401 467-9700
   115 Baker St Providence (02905) *(G-16547)*

J L Enterprises Inc.. 781 821-6300
   875 Washington St Canton (02021) *(G-7802)*

J L McIntosh, Canton *Also Called: J L Enterprises Inc (G-7802)*

J O Brown & Son Inc.. 207 867-4621
   1 Main St North Haven (04853) *(G-5114)*

J P Mfg Inc.. 508 764-2538
   13 Lovely St Southbridge (01550) *(G-12023)*

J P Ruthier Sons Recycl Corp (PA).............................. 978 772-4251
   256 Ayer Rd Littleton (01460) *(G-9821)*

J Palmero Sales Company Inc.................................. 203 377-6424
   120 Goodwin Pl Stratford (06615) *(G-3550)*

J R Felix Co, Richmond *Also Called: Keith A Gilpatrick (G-5321)*

J R Merritt Controls Inc (PA)................................... 203 381-0100
   55 Sperry Ave Stratford (06615) *(G-3551)*

J R S, Canton *Also Called: Jewelry Solutions LLC (G-7803)*

J S McCarthy Printing, Augusta *Also Called: Letter Systems Inc (G-4475)*

J Steele Services LLC.. 860 415-9720
   800 Flanders Rd Unit 5-1 Mystic (06355) *(G-1938)*

J T C Printing, Needham Heights *Also Called: D & L Associates Inc (G-10540)*

J T Gardner Inc (PA)... 800 540-4993
   190 Turnpike Rd Westborough (01581) *(G-13112)*

J T Inman Co Inc.. 508 226-0080
   31 Larsen Way Attleboro Falls (02763) *(G-6088)*

J Tool Inc.. 603 524-5813
   23 Fruite St Belmont (03220) *(G-13962)*

J W Fishers Mfg Inc.. 508 822-7330
   1953 County St East Taunton (02718) *(G-8407)*

J W I N Promotional Corp.. 508 636-1993
   767 Main Rd Ste 3 Westport (02790) *(G-13297)*

J W Machining Inc.. 978 562-5611
   17 Bonazzoli Ave Hudson (01749) *(G-9379)*

J W Raye & Co Inc.. 207 853-4451
   83 Washington St Eastport (04631) *(G-4745)*

J-K Tool Co Inc.. 413 789-0613
   41 Russo Cir Agawam (01001) *(G-5797)*

J-Pac LLC (HQ).. 603 692-9955
   25 Ctr Rd Somersworth (03878) *(G-15617)*

J-Pac Medical, Somersworth *Also Called: J-Pac LLC (G-15617)*

J. Goodison Company, Inc., North Kingstown *Also Called: J Goodison Company (G-16261)*

J. Weston Walch, Publisher, South Portland *Also Called: Mathemtics Problem Solving LLC (G-5508)*

J.A. Tyler Forest Products, South China *Also Called: Comprehensive Land Tech Inc (G-5485)*

J.S. McCarthy Printers, Augusta *Also Called: JS McCarthy Co Inc (G-4473)*

J&E Home Products LLC.. 401 464-8677
   21 Carrington St Ste 3 Lincoln (02865) *(G-16142)*

J&E Precision TI Holdings LLC (PA).............................. 413 527-8778
   107 Valley Rd Southampton (01073) *(G-11986)*

J&E Precision Tool LLC.. 413 527-8778
   107 Valley Rd Southampton (01073) *(G-11987)*

J&G (2021) Inc.. 508 865-1101
   71 Blackstone St Sutton (01590) *(G-12285)*

J&G 2021, Sutton *Also Called: Tx5877 Inc (G-12292)*

J&J Machine Company Inc...................................... 508 481-8166
   66b Brigham St Marlborough (01752) *(G-10170)*

J&J Precision Inc.. 860 283-8243
   116 Waterbury Rd Thomaston (06787) *(G-3622)*

J&L, Gloucester *Also Called: J & L Welding & Machine Co (G-8942)*

J&L Plastic Molding LLC.. 203 265-6237
   368 N Cherry Street Ext Wallingford (06492) *(G-3821)*

J&S Business Products Inc.................................... 877 425-4049
   17 Main St Ste 5 Ayer (01432) *(G-6183)*

Jab Industries Inc.. 401 447-9668
   185 Washington St Attleboro (02703) *(G-6027)*

Jabil Healthcare, Clinton *Also Called: Jabil Inc (G-8079)*

Jabil Inc.. 978 365-9721
   101 Union St Clinton (01510) *(G-8079)*

Jack Tarmy Lumber Co Inc...................................... 802 257-0427
   1077 Putney Rd Brattleboro (05301) *(G-17089)*

Jack's Machine Company, Hanson *Also Called: South Shore Manufacturing Inc (G-9056)*

Jackman Cash Fuel, Jackman *Also Called: Jackman Lumber Inc (G-4911)*

Jackman Lumber Inc (PA).. 207 668-4407
   548 Main St Jackman (04945) *(G-4911)*

Jackowitz, Mark A MD, Springfield *Also Called: Springfield Eye Associates (G-12134)*

Jackson Caldwell.. 207 539-2325
   266 Hebron Rd Oxford (04270) *(G-5146)*

Jackson Corrugated Cont Corp.................................. 860 767-3373
   45 River Rd Essex (06426) *(G-1168)*

Jackson Signsmith.. 603 383-8900
   Rte 16 Jackson (03846) *(G-14562)*

Jaco Inc.. 508 553-1000
   140 Constitution Blvd Franklin (02038) *(G-8844)*

Jacobs Vehicle Systems Inc.................................... 860 243-5222
   22 E Dudley Town Rd Bloomfield (06002) *(G-175)*

Jacoby.. 203 227-2220
   11 Blueberry Hill Rd Weston (06883) *(G-4150)*

Jacquier Welding LLC.. 413 248-1204
   79 Clayton Rd Ashley Falls (01222) *(G-5971)*

ALPHABETIC

Jad LLC.. 860 289-1551
   489 Sullivan Ave South Windsor (06074) *(G-3158)*

Jade, Warren *Also Called: Jade Engineered Plastics Inc (G-16759)*

Jade Engineered Plastics Inc................................ 401 253-4440
   15 New Industrial Way Warren (02885) *(G-16759)*

Jade Manufacturing Company Inc............................. 401 737-2400
   132 Meadow St Warwick (02886) *(G-16825)*

Jade Manufacturing Company LLC........................... 401 737-2400
   132 Meadow St Warwick (02886) *(G-16826)*

Jaeger Usa Inc... 603 332-5816
   198 Pickering Rd Rochester (03839) *(G-15480)*

Jagger Brothers.. 207 324-5622
   5 Water St Springvale (04083) *(G-5520)*

Jagger Spun Division, Springvale *Also Called: Jagger Brothers (G-5520)*

Jain America Foods Inc.................................... 413 593-8883
   1000 Sheridan St Chicopee (01022) *(G-8041)*

Jake Brake, Bloomfield *Also Called: Jacobs Vehicle Systems Inc (G-175)*

Jalbert Printing LLC...................................... 603 623-4677
   10 Northern Blvd Ste 17 Amherst (03031) *(G-13873)*

Jam Consultant Services, Bristol *Also Called: Applied Plastics Tech Inc (G-15753)*

Jam Plastics Inc... 978 537-2570
   22 Tucker Dr Leominster (01453) *(G-9672)*

Jameco Industries Inc..................................... 978 688-1811
   815 Chestnut St North Andover (01845) *(G-10841)*

James A Bean Corporation................................. 860 489-1404
   89 Commercial Blvd Ste 3 Torrington (06790) *(G-3685)*

James A Kiley Company................................... 617 776-0344
   15 Linwood St Somerville (02143) *(G-11882)*

James A McBrady Inc.................................... 207 883-4176
   29 Parkway Dr Scarborough (04074) *(G-5435)*

James Austin Company.................................... 413 589-1600
   203 West Ave Ludlow (01056) *(G-9946)*

James C Cannell Coffees Inc.............................. 508 295-7009
   21 Pattersons Brook Rd Unit E West Wareham (02576) *(G-13066)*

James Cable LLC.. 781 356-8701
   15 Braintree Hill Park Braintree (02184) *(G-7189)*

James Communications, Braintree *Also Called: James Cable LLC (G-7189)*

James Eaton.. 207 522-3944
   20 Shannons Way Standish (04084) *(G-5527)*

James F Mullen Co, Merrimac *Also Called: Nsd Metal Fabrication Inc (G-10326)*

James F Mullen Co Inc................................... 978 346-0045
   51 E Main St Merrimac (01860) *(G-10325)*

James F Stearns, Pembroke *Also Called: James F Stearns Co LLP (G-11371)*

James F Stearns Co LLP.................................. 781 829-0095
   42 Winter St Ste 35 Pembroke (02359) *(G-11371)*

James H Rich Boatyard.................................... 207 244-3208
   Rte 102 Main St Bernard (04612) *(G-4548)*

James Ippolito & Co Conn Inc.............................. 203 366-3840
   1069 Connecticut Ave Ste 16 Bridgeport (06607) *(G-333)*

James L Gallagher Inc.................................... 508 758-3102
   408 W Main Rd Little Compton (02837) *(G-16161)*

James L Howard and Company Inc.......................... 860 242-3581
   10 Britton Dr Bloomfield (06002) *(G-176)*

James Manufacturing, North Haven *Also Called: Jeskey LLC (G-2418)*

James Monroe Wire & Cable Corp **(PA)**.................. **978 368-0131**
   767 Sterling Rd South Lancaster (01561) *(G-11971)*

James Newspapers Inc **(PA)**............................ **207 743-7011**
   1 Pikes Hl Norway (04268) *(G-5116)*

James Newspapers Inc..................................... 207 364-7893
   69 Congress St Rumford (04276) *(G-5357)*

James W McClellan & Associates Inc....................... 603 644-1247
   70 Tirrell Hill Rd Bedford (03110) *(G-13935)*

James W Sewall Company................................. 207 817-5410
   77 Exchange St Ste 401 Bangor (04401) *(G-4506)*

James W Sewall Company **(PA)**......................... **207 827-4456**
   136 Center St Old Town (04468) *(G-5125)*

James Wright Precision Pdts............................... 860 928-7756
   20 Mechanics St Putnam (06260) *(G-2862)*

Jamesbrook Enterprises Inc............................... 978 425-6166
   2 Shaker Rd Ste D100 Shirley (01464) *(G-11818)*

Jamestown Press, Jamestown *Also Called: Island News Enterprise (G-16070)*

Jan Manufacturing Co..................................... 203 879-0580
   14 Town Line Rd Ste 8 Wolcott (06716) *(G-4366)*

Janco Inc **(PA)**...................................... **603 742-0043**
   50 Goodwin Rd Rollinsford (03869) *(G-15495)*

Janco Electronics Inc.................................... 603 742-1581
   50 Goodwin Rd Rollinsford (03869) *(G-15496)*

Jane Iredale, Great Barrington *Also Called: Iredale Cosmetics Inc (G-8976)*

Janice Miller... 603 629-9995
   150 Dow St Ste 4 Manchester (03101) *(G-14867)*

Janisult, Woburn *Also Called: American Ult Cryogenics LLC (G-13508)*

Janlynn Corporation...................................... 413 206-0002
   2078 Memorial Dr South Hadley (01075) *(G-11963)*

Jannel Manufacturing Inc.................................. 781 767-0666
   5 Mear Rd Holbrook (02343) *(G-9176)*

Janos Technology Inc..................................... 603 757-0070
   55 Black Brook Rd Keene (03431) *(G-14603)*

Janos Technology LLC **(DH)**........................... **603 757-0070**
   55 Black Brook Rd Keene (03431) *(G-14604)*

Japanese Products Corporation............................ 203 334-7537
   1525 Kings Hwy Fairfield (06824) *(G-1190)*

Jarden LLC.. 203 845-5300
   301 Merritt 7 Ste 5 Norwalk (06851) *(G-2519)*

Jarden LLC.. 207 645-2574
   5 Mill Street East Wilton (04234) *(G-4741)*

Jarden Plastic Solution, Norwalk *Also Called: Jarden LLC (G-2519)*

Jared Manufacturing Co Inc............................... 203 846-1732
   25 Perry Ave Norwalk (06850) *(G-2520)*

Jarvis, Middletown *Also Called: Jarvis Products Corporation (G-1754)*

Jarvis Airfoil Inc... 860 342-5000
   528 Glastonbury Tpke Portland (06480) *(G-2820)*

Jarvis Auto Machine LLC................................. 603 504-6144
   13 Bowen St Claremont (03743) *(G-14091)*

Jarvis Company Inc **(PA)**............................ **603 332-9000**
   100 Jarvis Ave Rochester (03868) *(G-15481)*

Jarvis Cutting Tools Inc.................................. 603 332-9000
   100 Jarvis Ave Rochester (03868) *(G-15482)*

Jarvis Pools & Spas, Turners Falls *Also Called: Jarvis Welding & Mfg Co (G-12449)*

Jarvis Precision Polishing................................. 860 589-5822
   190 Century Dr Bristol (06010) *(G-458)*

Jarvis Products Corporation **(HQ)**..................... **860 347-7271**
   33 Anderson Rd Middletown (06457) *(G-1754)*

Jarvis Surgical Inc...................................... 413 562-6659
   53 Airport Rd Westfield (01085) *(G-13174)*

Jarvis Welding & Mfg Co.................................. 413 863-9541
   72 Unity St Turners Falls (01376) *(G-12449)*

Jason Trucks Inc... 781 396-8300
   407 Mystic Ave Medford (02155) *(G-10292)*

Jasper Wyman & Son..................................... 207 546-3381
   Rte 193 Cherryfield (04622) *(G-4689)*

Jasper Wyman & Son..................................... 207 546-3381
   178 Main St Cherryfield (04622) *(G-4690)*

Jasper Wyman & Son..................................... 207 638-2201
   601 Rte 193 Deblois (04622) *(G-4721)*

Jasper Wyman & Son..................................... 207 546-3381
   37 Wymans Rd Hancock (04640) *(G-4870)*

Jasper Wyman & Son..................................... 207 546-3381
   10 Bluebird Dr Jonesboro (04648) *(G-4919)*

Jawor Lumber Inc....................................... 203 269-4431
   1068 N Farms Rd Ste 1 Wallingford (06492) *(G-3822)*

Jay Mountain Maples LLC................................ 802 988-4086
   962 N Jay Rd North Troy (05859) *(G-17429)*

Jay Packaging Group Inc **(DH)**....................... **401 244-1300**
   100 Warwick Industrial Dr Warwick (02886) *(G-16827)*

Jay Printing Company, Warwick *Also Called: Jay Packaging Group Inc (G-16827)*

Jay Salem Inc... 978 774-4999
   230 S Main St Middleton (01949) *(G-10387)*

Jay Sons Screw Mch Pdts Inc............................. 860 621-0141
   197 Burritt St Milldale (06467) *(G-1901)*

Jay Strongwater, Cranston *Also Called: Weingeroff Enterprises Inc (G-15929)*

Jaybird & Mais Inc...................................... 978 686-8659
   360 Merrimack St Ste 20 Lawrence (01843) *(G-9571)*

2024 Harris New England
Manufacturers Directory

(G-0000) Company's Geographic Section entry number

Jaymill, Manchester *Also Called: Janice Miller (G-14867)*

Jaypro Sports, Waterford *Also Called: Unified Sports Incorporated (G-3998)*

Jaypro Sports LLC.. 860 447-3001
  976 Hartford Tpke Ste B Waterford (06385) *(G-3990)*

Jaz Brush USA Inc.. 774 992-7996
  59 Tarkiln Pl New Bedford (02745) *(G-10605)*

Jaz USA, New Bedford *Also Called: Jaz Brush USA Inc (G-10605)*

JB Rails and Fabrication, Pawtucket *Also Called: Jebella LLC (G-16378)*

JBJS, Needham *Also Called: Journal of Bone Jint Srgery In (G-10515)*

Jbl, Stamford *Also Called: Harman Consumer Inc (G-3363)*

Jbm Services Inc... 978 939-8004
  686 Patriots Rd Templeton (01468) *(G-12380)*

JBM Sherman Carmel Inc.. 802 442-5115
  14 Morse Rd Bennington (05201) *(G-17042)*

Jbs Aves Ltda.. 203 357-5920
  680 E Main St Ste A Pmb 650 Stamford (06901) *(G-3390)*

Jbsbt LLC... 860 349-0631
  30 Ozick Dr Unit C Durham (06422) *(G-902)*

Jbt Aerotech Corp... 857 574-3170
  121 Frankfort St Boston (02128) *(G-6821)*

JC Clocks Company Inc... 508 998-8442
  9 Ventura Dr North Dartmouth (02747) *(G-10998)*

Jcc Residual Ltd... 508 699-4401
  811 Park East Dr Woonsocket (02895) *(G-16966)*

JCM Design & Display Inc... 401 781-0470
  610 Manton Ave Providence (02909) *(G-16548)*

JDM Company Inc... 978 251-1121
  210 Tyngsboro Rd North Chelmsford (01863) *(G-10979)*

Jebella LLC.. 401 475-1720
  16 Sabin St Pawtucket (02860) *(G-16378)*

Jedwards International Inc... 617 340-9461
  65 Bay State Dr Braintree (02184) *(G-7190)*

Jedwards International Inc (PA).................................. **617 340-9461**
  141 Campanelli Dr Braintree (02184) *(G-7191)*

Jedwards International Inc... 617 340-9461
  1025 Elm St Ste 2 Bridgewater (02324) *(G-7233)*

Jeep, Fairfield *Also Called: Scap Motors Inc (G-1200)*

Jeff Mfg Inc... 860 482-1387
  679 Riverside Ave Torrington (06790) *(G-3686)*

Jeffco Fibres Inc (PA)... **508 943-0440**
  12 Park St Webster (01570) *(G-12928)*

Jefferson Rubber Products, Worcester *Also Called: Jefferson Rubber Works Inc (G-13744)*

Jefferson Rubber Works Inc...................................... 508 791-3600
  17 Coppage Dr Worcester (01603) *(G-13744)*

Jeffrey Gold... 203 281-5737
  2415 Shepard Ave Apt 41 Hamden (06518) *(G-1434)*

Jeio Tech Inc.. 781 376-0700
  19 Alexander Rd Ste 7 Billerica (01821) *(G-6457)*

Jeld-Wen Inc.. 541 882-3451
  9 Teddy Dr Avon (02322) *(G-6152)*

Jeld-Wen Inc.. 802 886-1728
  36 Precision Dr Ste 130 North Springfield (05150) *(G-17423)*

Jeld-Wen Doors, North Springfield *Also Called: Jeld-Wen Inc (G-17423)*

Jelliff, Southport *Also Called: C O Jelliff Corporation (G-3244)*

Jem Electronics Inc... 508 520-3105
  23 National Dr Franklin (02038) *(G-8845)*

Jen Mfg Inc.. 508 753-1076
  3 Latti Farm Rd Millbury (01527) *(G-10437)*

Jenesco Inc.. 603 673-4830
  138 Herrick Rd Lyndeborough (03082) *(G-14800)*

Jenne Machine LLC... 802 626-1106
  180 Commercial Ln Lyndonville (05851) *(G-17318)*

Jenne Machine Shop, Lyndonville *Also Called: Jenne Machine LLC (G-17318)*

Jenray Products Inc.. 914 375-5596
  4 Production Dr Brookfield (06804) *(G-527)*

Jensen Dental, North Haven *Also Called: Jensen Industries Inc (G-2417)*

Jensen Industries Inc (PA).. **203 285-1402**
  50 Stillman Rd North Haven (06473) *(G-2417)*

Jensen Machine Company.. 860 666-5438
  721 Russell Rd Newington (06111) *(G-2301)*

Jentek Sensors Inc... 781 642-9666
  121 Bartlett St Marlborough (01752) *(G-10171)*

Jenzabar Inc (PA)... **617 492-9099**
  101 Huntington Ave Ste 2200 Boston (02199) *(G-6822)*

Jeol Usa Inc (HQ)... **978 535-5900**
  11 Dearborn Rd Peabody (01960) *(G-11320)*

Jera Industries LLC... 203 428-6588
  27 Wind Mill Cir Stamford (06903) *(G-3391)*

Jerrys At Misquamicut Inc... 401 596-3155
  39 Canal St Westerly (02891) *(G-16934)*

Jesco Iron Crafts Inc.. 201 488-4545
  116 Willenbrock Rd Oxford (06478) *(G-2701)*

Jescraft, Oxford *Also Called: Jesco Iron Crafts Inc (G-2701)*

Jeskey LLC... 203 772-6675
  69 Dodge Ave North Haven (06473) *(G-2418)*

JET Corporation.. 203 334-3317
  146 Davis Ave Bridgeport (06605) *(G-334)*

Jet Electric Motor Co Inc.. 401 725-9050
  688 School St Pawtucket (02860) *(G-16379)*

Jet Graphics LLC.. 508 580-5809
  175 Bodwell St Ste 1 Avon (02322) *(G-6153)*

Jet Industries Inc... 413 786-2010
  307 Silver St Agawam (01001) *(G-5798)*

Jet Machined Products LLC....................................... 508 378-3200
  221 Highland St East Bridgewater (02333) *(G-8341)*

Jet Process Corporation.. 203 985-6000
  126 S Turnpike Rd Wallingford (06492) *(G-3823)*

Jet Service Envelope Co Inc (PA).............................. **802 229-9335**
  80 East Rd Barre (05641) *(G-17010)*

Jet-Tech Incorporated... 781 599-8685
  52 Alley St Lynn (01902) *(G-9979)*

Jetct Inc.. 860 621-5381
  125 W Queen St Southington (06489) *(G-3217)*

Jeto Engineering Inc... 978 768-6472
  191 Western Ave Essex (01929) *(G-8475)*

Jewel Case, Providence *Also Called: Jewel Case Corporation (G-16549)*

Jewel Case Corporation... 401 943-1400
  110 Dupont Dr Providence (02907) *(G-16549)*

Jeweled Cross, Woonsocket *Also Called: Jcc Residual Ltd (G-16966)*

Jewell Instruments LLC (PA)..................................... **603 669-5121**
  850 Perimeter Rd Manchester (03103) *(G-14868)*

Jewelry Designs Inc.. 203 797-0389
  86 Mill Plain Rd Danbury (06811) *(G-761)*

Jewelry Solutions LLC... 781 821-6100
  448 Turnpike St Ste 2 Canton (02021) *(G-7803)*

Jewels of Fashion, Providence *Also Called: CJ International Inc (G-16499)*

Jewish Advocate Pubg Corp...................................... 617 523-6232
  15 School St Boston (02108) *(G-6823)*

Jewish Advocate Religious... 617 227-8200
  15 School St Boston (02108) *(G-6824)*

Jewish Journal.. 978 745-4111
  121 Loring Ave Salem (01970) *(G-11724)*

Jewish Journal, The, Salem *Also Called: North Shore Jewish Press Ltd (G-11727)*

Jewish Ledger, Hartford *Also Called: NRG Connecticut LLC (G-1497)*

Jewish Times, Boston *Also Called: Jewish Advocate Pubg Corp (G-6823)*

Jf2 LLC.. 508 429-1022
  215 Hopping Brook Rd Holliston (01746) *(G-9218)*

JFd Tube & Coil Products Inc.................................... 203 288-6941
  7 Hamden Park Dr Hamden (06517) *(G-1435)*

Jfl Enterprises Inc.. 401 231-1020
  339 Farnum Pike Smithfield (02917) *(G-16718)*

JG Machine Co Inc... 978 447-5279
  21b Concord St Wilmington (01887) *(G-13418)*

JG Maclellan.. 781 245-7756
  1 New Salem St Wakefield (01880) *(G-12514)*

Jgp Enterprises Inc.. 978 691-2737
  421 Merrimack St # 1 Lawrence (01843) *(G-9572)*

Jgpg Inc.. 781 891-9640
  39 Calvary St 2nd Fl Waltham (02453) *(G-12705)*

Jgs Properties LLC... 203 378-7508
  132 Shelland St Milford (06461) *(G-1840)*

JH Lynch & Sons Inc... 508 756-6244
  18 Mccracken Rd Millbury (01527) *(G-10438)*

JH Lynch & Sons Inc **(PA)**.................................... **401 333-4300**
  50 Lynch Pl Cumberland (02864) *(G-15948)*

JH Lynch & Sons Inc... 401 434-7100
  835 Taunton Ave East Providence (02914) *(G-16025)*

JH Westerbeke Corp... 508 823-7677
  150 John Hancock Rd Taunton (02780) *(G-12344)*

Jhb Enterprises, Marstons Mills *Also Called: Cape Cod Braided Rug Co Inc (G-10247)*

Jhs Restoration Inc... 860 757-3870
  170 Strong Rd South Windsor (06074) *(G-3159)*

Jibo Inc.. 617 542-5426
  230 Congress St Ste 900 Boston (02110) *(G-6825)*

Jiffy Lube... 508 539-8888
  60 Falmouth Rd Mashpee (02649) *(G-10252)*

Jiffy Lube, Mashpee *Also Called: Jiffy Lube (G-10252)*

Jiffy Print Inc... 207 947-4490
  494 Broadway Bangor (04401) *(G-4507)*

Jiffy Print Copy Center, Fall River *Also Called: Lincoln Press Co Inc (G-8569)*

Jim's Metal Fabrication, New Gloucester *Also Called: J F Hutchinson Co (G-5085)*

Jim's Organic Coffee, West Wareham *Also Called: James C Cannell Coffees Inc (G-13066)*

Jimsan Enterprises Inc.. 508 587-3666
  275 E Center St West Bridgewater (02379) *(G-12973)*

JJ Box Co Inc... 203 367-1211
  25 Admiral St Bridgeport (06605) *(G-335)*

Jji International Inc.. 401 780-8668
  1 Weingeroff Blvd Cranston (02910) *(G-15878)*

Jjioc Inc.. 860 628-4655
  125 W Queen St Southington (06489) *(G-3218)*

Jk Custom Woodworking LLC................................. 207 644-1127
  51 Sloop Nellie Rd South Bristol (04568) *(G-5483)*

Jk Lumber LLC... 603 539-4145
  71 Marcella Dr Rte 41 Madison (03849) *(G-14802)*

JKL Specialty Foods Inc...................................... 203 541-3990
  456 Glenbrook Rd Ste 2 Stamford (06906) *(G-3392)*

JL Lucas Machinery Co Inc.................................... 203 597-1300
  429 Brookside Rd Waterbury (06708) *(G-3925)*

Jl Services, Stamford *Also Called: Isupportws Inc (G-3386)*

Jlc-Tech LLC.. 781 826-8162
  130 Corporate Park Dr Pembroke (02359) *(G-11372)*

Jlp Machine and Welding LLC................................ 781 585-1744
  10 Winter St Kingston (02364) *(G-9508)*

JM Huber Corporation... 207 723-9291
  Rte 157 Millinocket (04462) *(G-5065)*

Jmc Asset Holdings Inc....................................... 781 447-9264
  162 Industrial Blvd Ste 7 Hanson (02341) *(G-9052)*

Jmd Duct Fabrication LLC..................................... 603 235-9314
  25 Brown Ridge Rd Weare (03281) *(G-15672)*

Jmd Industries Inc.. 603 882-3198
  1 Park Ave Hudson (03051) *(G-14513)*

Jmf Group LLC... 860 627-7003
  13 Revay Rd East Windsor (06088) *(G-1077)*

Jmk Inc... 603 886-4100
  15 Caldwell Dr Amherst (03031) *(G-13874)*

JMS Manufacturing Co Inc................................... 508 675-1141
  22 5th St Ste 8 Taunton (02780) *(G-12345)*

Jnj Global Enterprises LLC.................................... 508 455-4945
  47 Semple Village Rd Attleboro (02703) *(G-6028)*

Jnj Industries Inc... 508 553-0529
  290 Beaver St Franklin (02038) *(G-8846)*

Joa Tools LLC... 850 529-3567
  7 Tyler Dr Goffstown (03045) *(G-14350)*

Joan Imports, Johnston *Also Called: Arden Jewelry Mfg Co (G-16076)*

Jobart Inc **(PA)**... **978 689-4414**
  37 1/2 Oakland Ave Methuen (01844) *(G-10335)*

Jobin Machine Inc... 860 953-1631
  836 Farmington Ave West Hartford (06119) *(G-4065)*

Joe Miller Inc... 508 753-8581
  333 Sw Cutoff Worcester (01604) *(G-13745)*

Joel Gorkowski Inc... 203 877-3896
  215 Pepes Farm Rd Milford (06460) *(G-1841)*

Joes Cstm Mfg Qlty Mmrals Inc.............................. 800 787-4004
  874 E Barre Rd Barre (05641) *(G-17011)*

Joglo Inc... 603 880-4519
  15 Factory St Nashua (03060) *(G-15117)*

Johansons Boatworks... 207 596-7060
  11 Farwell Dr Rockland (04841) *(G-5335)*

John Brown US LLC.. 617 449-4354
  1 South Sta Fl 3 Boston (02110) *(G-6826)*

John C Whyte... 603 530-1168
  43 Mutton Rd Salisbury (03268) *(G-15576)*

John Canning & Co Ltd.. 203 272-9868
  150 Commerce Ct Cheshire (06410) *(G-602)*

John Covey... 978 535-4681
  6 Cobb Ave Peabody (01960) *(G-11321)*

John Crane Sealol Inc **(DH)**............................... **401 732-0715**
  75 Commerce Dr # 101 Warwick (02886) *(G-16828)*

John Deere Authorized Dealer, Essex *Also Called: Bell Power Systems LLC (G-1162)*

John Deere Authorized Dealer, Sanford *Also Called: North Country Tractor Inc (G-5403)*

John Deere Authorized Dealer, Marlborough *Also Called: Knm Holdings LLC (G-10177)*

John Deere Authorized Dealer, Dover *Also Called: North Country Tractor Inc (G-14241)*

John Deere Authorized Dealer, Narragansett *Also Called: Rhode Island Engine Co Inc (G-16195)*

John E Boeing Company Inc.................................. 603 897-8000
  169 Daniel Webster Hwy Nashua (03060) *(G-15118)*

John G Shelley Co Inc... 781 237-0900
  20 Cross St Woburn (01801) *(G-13593)*

John Harvard's Brew House, Braintree *Also Called: John Harvards Brewhouse Llc (G-7192)*

John Harvards Brewhouse Llc.................................. 508 875-2337
  36 Grove Cir Braintree (02184) *(G-7192)*

John Hazen Whote Corporation............................... 401 942-8000
  1160 Cranston St Cranston (02920) *(G-15879)*

John J Cahill Displays Inc..................................... 617 737-3232
  293 Libbey Industrial Pkwy East Weymouth (02189) *(G-8430)*

John June Custom Cabinetry LLC............................. 203 334-1720
  541 Fairfield Ave Bridgeport (06604) *(G-336)*

John K Dietrich & Assoc Inc.................................. 617 868-4140
  33 Warwick Rd Watertown (02472) *(G-12884)*

John Karl Dietrich & Assoc.................................... 617 868-4140
  26 Central Sq Cambridge (02139) *(G-7619)*

John Khiel III Log Chpping Inc............................... 207 452-2157
  65 Bull Ring Rd Denmark (04022) *(G-4722)*

John M Williams Company...................................... 207 244-7854
  17 Shipwright Ln Mount Desert (04660) *(G-5077)*

John McGillicuddy Inc... 617 388-6324
  65 Governors Rd Milton (02186) *(G-10453)*

John McLeod Ltd **(PA)**..................................... **802 464-8175**
  111 W Main St Wilmington (05363) *(G-17755)*

John Oldham Studios Inc...................................... 860 529-3331
  888 Wells Rd Wethersfield (06109) *(G-4207)*

John P Pow Company Inc...................................... 617 269-6040
  49 D St Boston (02127) *(G-6827)*

John Penfield Ltd... 802 254-5411
  558 Putney Rd Brattleboro (05301) *(G-17090)*

John Seavey Acadia Fuel....................................... 207 664-6050
  711 Bar Harbor Rd Trenton (04605) *(G-5556)*

John Williams Boat, Mount Desert *Also Called: John M Williams Company (G-5077)*

John Zink -Todd Combustn Group, Shelton *Also Called: John Zink Company LLC (G-3025)*

John Zink Company, Shelton *Also Called: Hamworthy Peabody Combustn Inc (G-3012)*

John Zink Company LLC... 203 925-0380
  2 Armstrong Rd Bldg 3 Shelton (06484) *(G-3025)*

Johncarlo Woodworking Inc.................................. 413 562-4002
  30 Clifton St Westfield (01085) *(G-13175)*

Johnny H Castonguay.. 207 897-5945
  140 Shackley Hill Rd Livermore (04253) *(G-5024)*

Johns Building Supply Co Inc................................. 413 442-7846
  891 Crane Ave Ste 1 Pittsfield (01201) *(G-11403)*

Johns Manville Corporation.................................... 207 784-0123
  51 Lexington St Lewiston (04240) *(G-4968)*

Johns Manville Corporation.................................... 207 283-8000
  15 Lund Rd Saco (04072) *(G-5370)*

Johnson & Johnson... 781 264-4804
  600 Unicorn Park Dr # 102 Woburn (01801) *(G-13594)*

Johnson & Johnson..	401 762-6751
1300 Highland Corporate Dr Cumberland (02864) *(G-15949)*	
Johnson & Johnson, Raynham *Also Called: Medical Device Bus Svcs Inc (G-11591)*	
Johnson & Johnson, Cumberland *Also Called: Johnson & Johnson (G-15949)*	
Johnson & Wales University..	401 598-1824
333 Harborside Blvd Providence (02905) *(G-16550)*	
Johnson Abrasives Co Inc..	603 532-4434
49 Fitzgerald Dr Jaffrey (03452) *(G-14569)*	
Johnson Brothers Rhode Island, North Kingstown *Also Called: Johnson Brothers RI Inc* *(G-16262)*	
Johnson Brothers RI Inc..	401 583-0050
120 Moscrip Ave North Kingstown (02852) *(G-16262)*	
Johnson Contrls Authorized Dlr, New Haven *Also Called: F W Webb Company (G-2151)*	
Johnson Contrls Authorized Dlr, Windham *Also Called: F W Webb Company (G-5661)*	
Johnson Contrls Authorized Dlr, Winslow *Also Called: F W Webb Company (G-5682)*	
Johnson Contrls Authorized Dlr, Canton *Also Called: Ene Systems Inc (G-7789)*	
Johnson Contrls Authorized Dlr, Stoughton *Also Called: F W Webb Company (G-12205)*	
Johnson Controls, Ledyard *Also Called: Johnson Controls Inc (G-1552)*	
Johnson Controls, Meriden *Also Called: Johnson Controls Inc (G-1670)*	
Johnson Controls, Rocky Hill *Also Called: Johnson Controls Inc (G-2930)*	
Johnson Controls, Portland *Also Called: Clarios LLC (G-5199)*	
Johnson Controls, Boston *Also Called: Johnson Controls Inc (G-6828)*	
Johnson Controls, Boston *Also Called: Johnson Controls Inc (G-6829)*	
Johnson Controls, Lynnfield *Also Called: Johnson Controls Inc (G-9998)*	
Johnson Controls, North Easton *Also Called: Johnson Controls Inc (G-11010)*	
Johnson Controls, Wrentham *Also Called: Johnson Controls Inc (G-13843)*	
Johnson Controls, Manchester *Also Called: Clarios LLC (G-14830)*	
Johnson Controls, Cranston *Also Called: Johnson Controls Inc (G-15880)*	
Johnson Controls, Lincoln *Also Called: Clarios LLC (G-16127)*	
Johnson Controls Inc...	860 886-9021
39 Norwich Westerly Rd Ledyard (06339) *(G-1552)*	
Johnson Controls Inc...	678 297-4040
71 Deerfield Ln Meriden (06450) *(G-1670)*	
Johnson Controls Inc...	617 424-6601
1 Copley Pl Fl 4 Boston (02116) *(G-6828)*	
Johnson Controls Inc...	617 992-2073
33 Avenue Louis Pasteur Boston (02115) *(G-6829)*	
Johnson Controls Inc...	781 246-5500
39 Salem St Lynnfield (01940) *(G-9998)*	
Johnson Controls Inc...	508 238-0536
28 Main St Bldg 8-7 North Easton (02356) *(G-11010)*	
Johnson Controls Inc...	401 275-2097
2 Starline Way Unit 8 Cranston (02921) *(G-15880)*	
Johnson Controls Inc...	860 571-3300
27 Inwood Rd Rocky Hill (06067) *(G-2930)*	
Johnson Controls Inc...	508 384-0018
78 South St Wrentham (02093) *(G-13843)*	
Johnson Filaments, Williston *Also Called: Astenjohnson Inc (G-17722)*	
Johnson Gage Company..	860 242-5541
534 Cottage Grove Rd Bloomfield (06002) *(G-177)*	
Johnson Johnson Healthcar...	508 828-6194
50 Scotland Blvd Bridgewater (02324) *(G-7234)*	
Johnson Marine, East Haddam *Also Called: C Sherman Johnson Company Inc (G-955)*	
Johnson Matthey Phrm Svcs, North Andover *Also Called: Veranova LP (G-10857)*	
Johnson Otdoors Watercraft Inc **(HQ)**..........................	**207 827-5513**
125 Gilman Falls Ave Bldg B Old Town (04468) *(G-5126)*	
Johnson Outdoors Inc..	603 518-1634
125 Gilman Falls Ave Old Town (04468) *(G-5127)*	
Johnson Precision, Hudson *Also Called: Mrpc Northeast LLC (G-14530)*	
Johnsons Food Products Corp.......................................	617 265-3400
1 Mount Vernon St Boston (02108) *(G-6830)*	
Johnston Blckwood Slmakers Inc...................................	401 884-4227
1 Division St East Greenwich (02818) *(G-15988)*	
Johnston Dandy Company **(PA)**.................................	**207 794-6571**
148 Main St Lincoln (04457) *(G-5009)*	
Johnstone Company Inc..	203 239-5834
222 Sackett Point Rd North Haven (06473) *(G-2419)*	
Joinery Shop Inc..	617 242-4718
92 Arlington Ave Charlestown (02129) *(G-7877)*	

Joining Tech Automtn Inc..	860 784-1967
17 Connecticut South Dr Ste B East Granby (06026) *(G-936)*	
Joining Technologies LLC..	860 653-0111
17 Connecticut South Dr Ste B East Granby (06026) *(G-937)*	
Joint Venture Madison Intl, Norwalk *Also Called: Myllykoski North America (G-2541)*	
Jolen Cream Bleach Corp..	203 259-8779
25 Walls Dr Fairfield (06824) *(G-1191)*	
Jolie Jewels, Cranston *Also Called: Jji International Inc (G-15878)*	
Jolley Precast Inc..	860 774-9066
463 Putnam Rd Danielson (06239) *(G-840)*	
Joma Incorporated..	203 759-0848
185 Interstate Ln Waterbury (06705) *(G-3926)*	
Joma LLC..	978 374-0034
12 Rogers Rd Ste 1 Haverhill (01835) *(G-9106)*	
Joma Diamond Tool LLC..	413 525-0760
46 Baldwin St Ste A East Longmeadow (01028) *(G-8381)*	
Jonal Laboratories Inc..	203 634-4444
456 Center St Meriden (06450) *(G-1671)*	
Jones & Bartlett Learning LLC **(PA)**..........................	**978 443-5000**
25 Mall Rd Burlington (01803) *(G-7382)*	
Jones & Company, East Providence *Also Called: Jones Safety Equipment Company (G-16026)*	
Jones & Vining Incorporated **(PA)**............................	**508 232-7470**
1115 W Chestnut St Ste 2 Brockton (02301) *(G-7287)*	
Jones Safety Equipment Company.................................	401 434-4010
325 Massasoit Ave East Providence (02914) *(G-16026)*	
Joraco Inc...	401 232-1710
347 Furnam Pike Smithfield (02917) *(G-16719)*	
Jordan Associates...	603 246-8998
Rte 145 Pittsburg (03592) *(G-15328)*	
Jordan Bros Seafood Co Inc..	508 583-9797
314 Northern Ave Boston (02210) *(G-6831)*	
Jordan Brothers Seafood, Boston *Also Called: Jordan Bros Seafood Co Inc (G-6831)*	
Jordan Enterprises Inc..	508 481-2948
40 Hudson St Ste B Marlborough (01752) *(G-10172)*	
Jordan Saw Mill LLC...	860 774-0247
201 Saw Mill Hill Rd Sterling (06377) *(G-3501)*	
Jordan Sawmill, Sterling *Also Called: Jordan Saw Mill LLC (G-3501)*	
Jordans Furniture Inc **(HQ)**....................................	**508 828-4000**
450 Revolutionary Dr East Taunton (02718) *(G-8408)*	
Jordi Labs LLC...	508 719-8543
200 Gilbert St Mansfield (02048) *(G-10061)*	
Jornik Manufacturing Corp..	203 969-0500
652 Glenbrook Rd Ste 8-201 Stamford (06906) *(G-3393)*	
Josef Creations Inc **(PA)**......................................	**401 421-4198**
141 Jackson School House Rd Chepachet (02814) *(G-15805)*	
Joseph A Cura..	508 254-4624
4q Snow Cir Nashua (03062) *(G-15119)*	
Joseph A Thomas Ltd..	401 253-1330
24 Broadcommon Rd Bristol (02809) *(G-15770)*	
Joseph Abboud Mfg Corp...	508 999-1301
689 Belleville Ave New Bedford (02745) *(G-10606)*	
Joseph C La Fond Co Inc..	401 769-3744
340 Old River Rd Manville (02838) *(G-16164)*	
Joseph Cohn Son Tile Trazo LLC..................................	203 772-2420
352 Sackett Point Rd North Haven (06473) *(G-2420)*	
Joseph Freedman Co Inc..	413 781-4444
40 Albany St Springfield (01105) *(G-12107)*	
Joseph Freedman Co Inc **(PA)**.................................	**888 677-7818**
115 Stevens St Springfield (01104) *(G-12108)*	
Joseph G Pulitano Insur Agcy.......................................	617 783-2622
313 Washington St Ste 225 Newton (02458) *(G-10765)*	
Joseph Hannoush Family Inc..	860 561-4651
500 Westfarms Mall Farmington (06032) *(G-1225)*	
Joseph Merritt & Company Inc......................................	203 743-6734
4c Christopher Columbus Ave Danbury (06810) *(G-762)*	
Joseph Merritt & Company Inc **(PA)**..........................	**860 296-2500**
650 Franklin Ave Ste 3 Hartford (06114) *(G-1488)*	
Joseph Muto..	413 568-3245
61 Bowdoin St Westfield (01085) *(G-13176)*	
Joseph P Carrara & Sons Inc.......................................	802 388-6363
2464 Case St Middlebury (05753) *(G-17344)*	

A
L
P
H
A
B
E
T
I
C

Joseph P Carrara & Sons Inc **(PA)**............................ **802 775-2301**
   167 N Shrewsbury Rd North Clarendon (05759) **(G-17415)**

Joseph P Stachura Company Inc................................... 508 278-6525
   435 Quaker Hwy Uxbridge (01569) **(G-12482)**

Joseph Palmer Inc... 781 376-0130
   7 Walnut Hill Park Woburn (01801) **(G-13595)**

Josephs Gourmet Pasta Company................................ 978 521-1718
   262 Primrose St Haverhill (01830) **(G-9107)**

Josh Smpson Cntemporary GL Inc................................ 413 625-6145
   30 Frank Williams Rd Shelburne Falls (01370) **(G-11805)**

Joshua Friedman & Co LLC.. 860 439-1637
   49 Jay St New London (06320) **(G-2229)**

Joshua LLC **(PA)**.. **203 624-0080**
   1930 Durham Rd Guilford (06437) **(G-1398)**

Jotul North America Inc.. 207 797-5912
   55 Hutcherson Dr Gorham (04038) **(G-4823)**

Joule Unlimited Technologies Inc.................................. 781 533-9100
   124 Washington St Ste 101 Foxboro (02035) **(G-8703)**

Jounce Therapeutics, Cambridge *Also Called: Jounce Therapeutics Inc* **(G-7620)**

Jounce Therapeutics Inc **(PA)**................................ **857 259-3840**
   780 Memorial Dr Cambridge (02139) **(G-7620)**

Journal Emergency Management, Weston *Also Called: Prime National Publishing Corp*
(G-13289)

Journal Inquirer, Manchester *Also Called: Green Manor Corporation* **(G-1599)**

Journal Inquirer, Manchester *Also Called: Journal Publishing Company Inc* **(G-1608)**

Journal Jewish, Salem *Also Called: Jewish Journal* **(G-11724)**

Journal of Antq & Collectibles.................................... 508 347-1960
   46 Hall Rd Sturbridge (01566) **(G-12250)**

Journal of Bone Jint Srgery In..................................... 781 449-9780
   20 Pickering St Ste 3 Needham (02492) **(G-10515)**

Journal Opinion, Bradford *Also Called: Cohasa Publishing Inc* **(G-17061)**

Journal Opinion Inc.. 802 222-5281
   48 Main St Bradford (05033) **(G-17063)**

Journal Publishing Company... 800 873-1272
   121 Free St Ste A Portland (04101) **(G-5229)**

Journal Publishing Company Inc................................... 860 646-0500
   306 Progress Dr Manchester (06042) **(G-1608)**

Journal Register Company.. 508 678-3844
   207 Pocasset St Fall River (02721) **(G-8562)**

Journeyman Press, The, Newburyport *Also Called: Ian Marie Inc* **(G-10689)**

Jouve of North America Inc **(DH)**............................ **802 254-6073**
   70 Landmark Hill Dr Brattleboro (05301) **(G-17091)**

Joval Machine Co Inc.. 203 284-0082
   515 Main St Yalesville (06492) **(G-4398)**

Jove, Cambridge *Also Called: Myjove Corporation* **(G-7658)**

Jovek Tool and Die... 860 261-5020
   474 Birch St Bristol (06010) **(G-459)**

Jovil Universal LLC.. 203 792-6700
   10 Precision Rd Danbury (06810) **(G-763)**

Jowa Usa Inc.. 978 486-9800
   59 Porter Rd Littleton (01460) **(G-9822)**

Joy & Robert Cromwell.. 413 224-1440
   243 Prospect St East Longmeadow (01028) **(G-8382)**

Joy Food Company... 917 549-6240
   138 Goodwives River Rd Darien (06820) **(G-850)**

Joyn Bio LLC.. 978 549-3723
   27 Drydock Ave Ste 8 Boston (02210) **(G-6832)**

Jozef Custom Ironworks Inc....................................... 203 384-6363
   250 Smith St Bridgeport (06607) **(G-337)**

JP Carrara & Sons, Middlebury *Also Called: Joseph P Carrara & Sons Inc* **(G-17344)**

JP Lillis Enterprises Inc **(PA)**................................. **508 888-8394**
   7 Jan Sebastian Dr Sandwich (02563) **(G-11751)**

JP Plastics Inc... 508 697-4202
   45 1st St Bridgewater (02324) **(G-7235)**

JP Plastics Inc.. 508 203-2420
   67 Green St Ste 1 Foxboro (02035) **(G-8704)**

JP Progressive Comm Group LLC.................................. 800 477-4681
   186 Duchaine Blvd New Bedford (02745) **(G-10607)**

JP Saw Mfg Inc... 508 567-0469
   192 Anawan St Fall River (02721) **(G-8563)**

JP Sercel Associates Inc.. 603 595-7048
   220 Hackett Hill Rd Manchester (03102) **(G-14869)**

Jpc Products, Fairfield *Also Called: Japanese Products Corporation* **(G-1190)**

JPS Elastomerics Corp... 413 779-1200
   412 Main St Easthampton (01027) **(G-8448)**

Jpsa, Manchester *Also Called: JP Sercel Associates Inc* **(G-14869)**

Jr Chemical Coatings LLC.. 508 896-3383
   139 Queen Anne Rd Harwich (02645) **(G-9068)**

Jr Hinds Const Serv.. 603 496-2344
   60 Ridge Rd Tilton (03276) **(G-15654)**

JR Poirier Tool & Machine Co....................................... 603 882-9279
   4 Manhattan Dr Amherst (03031) **(G-13875)**

Jrb Associates Inc.. 401 351-8693
   2 2nd Ave Cranston (02910) **(G-15881)**

Jrni Inc... 857 305-6477
   320 Congress St Boston (02210) **(G-6833)**

JRS Corp... 802 310-5253
   134 Church St Burlington (05401) **(G-17140)**

JS International Inc **(PA)**....................................... **508 675-4722**
   485 Commerce Dr Fall River (02720) **(G-8564)**

Js Machine... 603 329-3790
   319 Kent Farm Rd Hampstead (03841) **(G-14383)**

JS McCarthy Co Inc **(PA)**....................................... **207 622-6241**
   15 Darin Dr Augusta (04330) **(G-4473)**

Js Pallet Co Inc... 401 723-0223
   60 Lockbridge St Pawtucket (02860) **(G-16380)**

Js Sale Corp... 508 753-2979
   200 Summer St Worcester (01604) **(G-13746)**

Jsg Holdings Inc.. 401 738-3800
   80 Meadow St Warwick (02886) **(G-16829)**

Jsi Quality Cabinetry, Fall River *Also Called: JS International Inc* **(G-8564)**

Jsi Store Fixtures Inc **(HQ)**...................................... **207 943-5203**
   140 Park St Milo (04463) **(G-5070)**

Jsl Asphalt Inc **(PA)**... **413 568-8986**
   730 E Mountain Rd Westfield (01085) **(G-13177)**

Jt Automation LLC.. 860 784-1967
   17 Connecticut South Dr East Granby (06026) **(G-938)**

JT Machine Inc.. 508 476-1508
   175 Davis St East Douglas (01516) **(G-8351)**

Jt Machine Shop, East Douglas *Also Called: JT Machine Inc* **(G-8351)**

JT Manufacturing Corporation...................................... 603 821-5720
   60b Pulpit Rock Rd Pelham (03076) **(G-15291)**

Jubali, Boston *Also Called: Life Force Beverages LLC* **(G-6858)**

Judd Paper Company.. 413 534-5661
   55 Pawtucket Ave Ste H Rumford (02916) **(G-16673)**

Judd Wire Inc **(DH)**.. **800 545-5833**
   124 Turnpike Rd Turners Falls (01376) **(G-12450)**

Jugos... 617 418-9879
   145 Dartmouth St Ste 3 Boston (02116) **(G-6834)**

Jules A Gourdeau Inc.. 978 922-0102
   94 Corning St Beverly (01915) **(G-6358)**

Julesan Inc.. 617 437-6860
   325 Huntington Ave Boston (02115) **(G-6835)**

Julian Materials LLC **(PA)**...................................... **203 416-5308**
   418 Meadow St Fairfield (06824) **(G-1192)**

Julie Cecchini.. 413 562-2042
   74 Tannery Rd Southwick (01077) **(G-12044)**

Julie Industries Inc **(PA)**... **978 276-0820**
   2 Dundee Park Dr Ste 302a Andover (01810) **(G-5890)**

Juliet Marine Systems Inc.. 603 319-8412
   14 Manchester Sq Ste 275 Portsmouth (03801) **(G-15413)**

Julius Koch USA Inc.. 508 995-9565
   15 Crooks Way Mattapoisett (02739) **(G-10258)**

Jumo, New Haven *Also Called: Jumo Health Usa Inc* **(G-2164)**

Jumo Health Usa Inc **(PA)**....................................... **646 895-9319**
   470 James St New Haven (06513) **(G-2164)**

Jumptap Inc... 617 301-4550
   155 Seaport Blvd 8th Fl Boston (02210) **(G-6836)**

Jungle Inc **(PA)**... **978 356-7722**
   6 Dodge St Essex (01929) **(G-8476)**

Juniper Networks Inc.. 978 589-5800
   10 Technology Park Dr Westford (01886) **(G-13243)**

Juniper Networks Inc.. 508 523-0427
   74 S Quinsigamond Ave Shrewsbury (01545) **(G-11836)**

Juniper Pharmaceuticals, Boston *Also Called: Juniper Pharmaceuticals Inc (G-6837)*

Juniper Pharmaceuticals Inc **(DH)**... **617 639-1500**
33 Arch St Ste 3110 Boston (02110) *(G-6837)*

Junora Ltd.. 207 284-4900
16 Pomerleau St Biddeford (04005) *(G-4573)*

Jupiter Communications LLC.. 475 238-7082
755 1st Ave West Haven (06516) *(G-4108)*

Juriba Limited... 617 356-8681
30 Newbury St Boston (02116) *(G-6838)*

Jurman Metrics Inc... 203 261-9388
555 Hammertown Rd Monroe (06468) *(G-1914)*

Just Counters.. 603 627-2027
28 Daniel Plummer Rd Ste 3 Goffstown (03045) *(G-14351)*

Just Hit Print LLC... 603 279-5939
23 Main St Ste 1c Center Harbor (03226) *(G-14056)*

Just Publications Inc... 617 739-5878
8 Alton Pl Ste 2 Brookline (02446) *(G-7319)*

Just Rentals, Brookline *Also Called: Just Publications Inc (G-7319)*

Just Ur Way Screen Print.. 508 235-0422
248 Briggs Rd Westport (02790) *(G-13298)*

Jutras Manufacturing Company....................................... 401 949-8101
25 Lark Industrial Pkwy Greenville (02828) *(G-16060)*

Jutras Signs Inc.. 603 622-2344
30 Harvey Rd Unit 8 Bedford (03110) *(G-13936)*

Jutras Signs & Flags, Bedford *Also Called: Jutras Signs Inc (G-13936)*

Jutras Woodworking Co... 401 949-8101
103 Dike St Providence (02909) *(G-16551)*

JV Precision Machine Co... 203 888-0748
71 Cogwheel Ln Seymour (06483) *(G-2962)*

Jwc Steel Co LLC.. 860 296-5517
540 Ledyard St Hartford (06114) *(G-1489)*

Jz Inc.. 207 655-7520
46 Red Mill Rd Casco (04015) *(G-4681)*

K & B Rock Crushing LLC.. 603 622-1188
20 Commercial Ct Auburn (03032) *(G-13910)*

K & C Industries Inc.. 508 520-4600
2 Esmond St Smithfield (02917) *(G-16720)*

K & D Distributing, Windham *Also Called: K & D Millworks Inc (G-5663)*

K & D Millworks Inc... 207 892-5188
7 Danielle Dr Windham (04062) *(G-5663)*

K & E Auto Machine L L C... 203 723-7189
628 Prospect St Naugatuck (06770) *(G-1968)*

K & E Plastics Inc... 802 375-0011
141 Morse Rd Bennington (05201) *(G-17043)*

K & G Corp.. 860 643-1133
219 Adams St Manchester (06042) *(G-1609)*

K & H Products, Bennington *Also Called: Porta-Brace Inc (G-17055)*

K & J Interiors Inc... 508 830-0670
4 Court St Plymouth (02360) *(G-11463)*

K & K Thermoforming Inc.. 508 764-7700
380 Elm St Southbridge (01550) *(G-12024)*

K & M Engineering Inc.. 978 235-7923
583 Berlin Rd Marlborough (01752) *(G-10173)*

K & R Holdings Inc.. 207 797-7950
400 Warren Ave Portland (04103) *(G-5230)*

K & W Tire Company Inc.. 978 772-5700
6 Willow Rd Ayer (01432) *(G-6184)*

K A D Machine & Tool, Chicopee *Also Called: Kad Machine Inc (G-8042)*

K A F Manufacturing Co Inc... 203 324-3012
14 Fahey St Stamford (06907) *(G-3394)*

K Alger Woodworking Inc.. 401 228-5254
54 Argonne St Johnston (02919) *(G-16091)*

K and C Plastics Inc.. 978 537-0605
18 Crawford St Leominster (01453) *(G-9673)*

K and R Precision Grinding.. 860 505-8030
39 John St New Britain (06051) *(G-2036)*

K B C Electronics Inc... 203 298-9654
273 Pepes Farm Rd Milford (06460) *(G-1842)*

K B Logging Inc.. 207 757-8818
3276 Us Route 2 Smyrna Mills (04780) *(G-5481)*

K E I Incorporated... 978 656-2575
486 Amherst St Nashua (03063) *(G-15120)*

K F Brick Plant, South Windsor *Also Called: Redland Brick Inc (G-3177)*

K H Corrugated Case Copr.. 802 442-5455
473 Bowen Rd Bennington (05201) *(G-17044)*

K Irwin Construction Inc... 617 481-2420
82 Grove St Quincy (02169) *(G-11525)*

K L X, Northborough *Also Called: Ltp Corporation (G-11101)*

K P I, Wilton *Also Called: Kimball Physics Inc (G-15705)*

K S I, Salem *Also Called: Kaiser Systems Inc (G-11725)*

K V Sbardella Slate Inc.. 802 265-9955
105 Colvin Rd Fair Haven (05743) *(G-17251)*

K W Aggregates.. 207 452-8888
65 Bull Ring Rd Denmark (04022) *(G-4723)*

K W Griffen Company... 203 846-1923
100 Pearl St Norwalk (06850) *(G-2521)*

K-F Liquidation Inc... 508 528-2000
842 Union St Ste 1 Franklin (02038) *(G-8847)*

K-Tech International Inc.. 860 489-9399
56 Ella Grasso Ave Torrington (06790) *(G-3687)*

K&H Group Inc... 802 442-5455
473 Bowen Rd Bennington (05201) *(G-17045)*

K&J Construction, Plymouth *Also Called: K & J Interiors Inc (G-11463)*

K&M/Nordic Co Inc.. 401 431-9299
5 Tripps Ln Riverside (02915) *(G-16656)*

K&W Webbing Company... 401 725-4441
403 Roosevelt Ave Central Falls (02863) *(G-15790)*

K2b Therapeutics, Cambridge *Also Called: Labcentral Inc (G-7626)*

K2w LLC... 617 818-2613
30 Grant St Waltham (02453) *(G-12706)*

K4 Machining LLC... 203 437-8764
217 Interstate Ln Waterbury (06705) *(G-3927)*

Kabinet Korner Inc.. 781 324-9600
212 Maplewood St Malden (02148) *(G-10017)*

Kad Machine Inc... 413 538-8684
28 Holgate Ave Chicopee (01020) *(G-8042)*

Kad Models & Prototypes Inc.. 510 229-8764
313 Vt Route 14 S East Randolph (05041) *(G-17218)*

Kadant Fibergen Inc **(HQ)**.. **781 275-3600**
8 Alfred Cir Bedford (01730) *(G-6236)*

Kadant Inc.. 508 791-8171
35 Sword St Auburn (01501) *(G-6115)*

Kadant Inc.. 508 791-8171
35 Sword St Auburn (01501) *(G-6116)*

Kadant Inc **(PA)**... **978 776-2000**
1 Technology Park Dr Ste 210 Westford (01886) *(G-13244)*

Kafa Group LLC.. 475 275-0090
800 Union Ave Bridgeport (06607) *(G-338)*

Kaffeology Inc.. 407 722-0922
359 Thames St Ste D Newport (02840) *(G-16214)*

Kahn Industries Inc... 860 529-8643
11 Hurd Park Rd East Hampton (06424) *(G-963)*

Kahn Instruments Incorporated.. 860 529-8643
885 Wells Rd Wethersfield (06109) *(G-4208)*

Kaiser Systems Inc... 978 224-4135
35 Congress St Ste 202 Salem (01970) *(G-11725)*

Kal-Lite Division, Bow *Also Called: Kalwall Corporation (G-14002)*

KALA, Arlington *Also Called: Kala Pharmaceuticals Inc (G-5942)*

Kala Pharmaceuticals Inc **(PA)**.................................... **781 996-5252**
1167 Massachusetts Ave Arlington (02476) *(G-5942)*

Kaleido, Lexington *Also Called: Kaleido Biosciences Inc (G-9755)*

Kaleido Biosciences Inc **(PA)**....................................... **617 674-9000**
65 Hayden Ave Lexington (02421) *(G-9755)*

Kalow Technologies LLC.. 802 775-4633
155 Seward Rd Rutland (05701) *(G-17501)*

Kalt Incorporated **(PA)**.. **978 805-5001**
71 Willie St Lowell (01854) *(G-9889)*

Kalvista, Cambridge *Also Called: Kalvista Pharmaceuticals Inc (G-7621)*

Kalvista Pharmaceuticals Inc **(PA)**................................ **857 999-0075**
55 Cambridge Pkwy Ste 900 Cambridge (02142) *(G-7621)*

Kalwall Corporation... 603 224-6881
40 River Rd Bow (03304) *(G-14002)*

Kalwall Corporation **(PA)**.. **603 627-3861**
  1111 Candia Rd Manchester (03109) *(G-14870)*

Kam Weld Technologies, Norwood *Also Called: Kamweld Technologies Inc (G-11186)*

Kaman, Bloomfield *Also Called: Kaman Corporation (G-183)*

Kaman Acquisition Usa Inc **(HQ)**.................................. **860 243-7100**
  1332 Blue Hills Ave Bloomfield (06002) *(G-178)*

Kaman Aerospace Corporation **(DH)**............................. **860 242-4461**
  1332 Blue Hills Ave Bloomfield (06002) *(G-179)*

Kaman Aerospace Corporation....................................... 860 242-4461
  30 Old Windsor Rd Bloomfield (06002) *(G-180)*

Kaman Aerospace Corporation....................................... 860 242-4461
  30 Old Windsor Rd Bloomfield (06002) *(G-181)*

Kaman Aerospace Corporation....................................... 860 632-1000
  217 Smith St Middletown (06457) *(G-1755)*

Kaman Aerospace Group Inc **(HQ)**................................. **860 243-7100**
  1332 Blue Hills Ave Bloomfield (06002) *(G-182)*

Kaman Composites - Vermont Inc.................................... 802 442-9964
  25 Performance Dr Bennington (05201) *(G-17046)*

Kaman Corporation **(PA)**... **860 243-7100**
  1332 Blue Hills Ave Bloomfield (06002) *(G-183)*

Kaman Corporation... 860 632-1000
  217 Smith St Middletown (06457) *(G-1756)*

Kaman Precision Products Inc... 860 632-1000
  217 Smith St Middletown (06457) *(G-1757)*

Kamatics, Bloomfield *Also Called: Kamatics Corporation (G-184)*

Kamatics Corporation **(DH)**.. **860 243-9704**
  1330 Blue Hills Ave Bloomfield (06002) *(G-184)*

Kamatics Corporation.. 860 243-7230
  1331 Blue Hills Ave Bloomfield (06002) *(G-185)*

Kamel Peripherals Inc **(PA)**... **508 435-7771**
  88a Elm St Ste 7 Hopkinton (01748) *(G-9334)*

Kammetal Inc **(PA)**... **718 722-9991**
  300 Great Hill Rd Naugatuck (06770) *(G-1969)*

Kamrowski Metal Refinishing... 508 877-0367
  80 K Street Pl Boston (02127) *(G-6839)*

Kamrowski Metal Refinishing, Framingham *Also Called: Kamrowski Refinishing Co Inc (G-8783)*

Kamrowski Refinishing Co Inc... 508 877-0367
  12 Bradford Rd Framingham (01701) *(G-8783)*

Kamweld Industries Inc... 617 558-7500
  100 Access Rd Norwood (02062) *(G-11185)*

Kamweld Technologies Inc.. 781 762-6922
  90 Access Rd Norwood (02062) *(G-11186)*

Kana Software Inc.. 650 614-8300
  10 Corporate Dr Ste 2206 Bedford (03110) *(G-13937)*

Kane Motor Car Co Inc... 401 294-4634
  1028 Boston Neck Rd North Kingstown (02852) *(G-16263)*

Kane-Perkins, Wayland *Also Called: E H Perkins Construction Inc (G-12925)*

Kanes Atlantic, North Kingstown *Also Called: Kane Motor Car Co Inc (G-16263)*

Kanes Donuts, Saugus *Also Called: PDKD Enterprises Inc (G-11764)*

Kangas Inc... 207 635-3745
  51 New Portland Rd North Anson (04958) *(G-5106)*

Kania Darius.. 860 667-4400
  75 Rockwell Rd Newington (06111) *(G-2302)*

Kanthal Corporation **(DH)**... **203 744-1440**
  119 Wooster St Bethel (06801) *(G-123)*

Kanthal Corporation... 203 744-1440
  119 Wooster St Bethel (06801) *(G-124)*

Kanzaki Specialty Papers Inc **(DH)**............................... **413 967-6204**
  20 Cummings St Ware (01082) *(G-12826)*

Kaplan Tarps & Cargo Controls, Manchester *Also Called: 3333 LLC (G-1579)*

Karas Engineering Company Inc...................................... 860 355-3153
  44 Old State Rd Ste 20 New Milford (06776) *(G-2249)*

Karavas Fashions Ltd... 203 866-4000
  17 Wall St Norwalk (06850) *(G-2522)*

Kardex Remstar LLC **(HQ)**.. **207 854-1861**
  41 Eisenhower Dr Westbrook (04092) *(G-5633)*

Karen Callan Designs Inc.. 203 762-9914
  30 Field Point Dr Greenwich (06830) *(G-1336)*

Karl Gschwind Machineworks LLC.................................... 603 434-4211
  6 Tinkham Ave Derry (03038) *(G-14197)*

Karl Storz Endovision Inc... 508 248-9011
  91 Carpenter Hill Rd Charlton (01507) *(G-7890)*

Karl Storz Endscpy-America Inc...................................... 508 248-9011
  28 Millbury St Auburn (01501) *(G-6117)*

Karls Boat Shop Inc... 508 432-4488
  50 Great Western Rd Harwich (02645) *(G-9069)*

Karos Pharmaceuticals Inc... 203 535-0540
  5 Science Park Ste 2 New Haven (06511) *(G-2165)*

Karuna Therapeutics Inc **(PA)**...................................... **857 449-2244**
  99 High St Fl 26 Boston (02110) *(G-6840)*

Karyopharm Therapeutics Inc **(PA)**.............................. **617 658-0600**
  85 Wells Ave Ste 300 Newton (02459) *(G-10766)*

Kasalis Inc... 781 273-6200
  11 North Ave Burlington (01803) *(G-7383)*

Kasanof Bread, North Grosvenordale *Also Called: Superior Bakery Inc (G-2387)*

Kasc Inc.. 508 985-9898
  270 Samuel Barnet Blvd New Bedford (02745) *(G-10608)*

Kase Printing Inc.. 603 883-9223
  13 Hampshire Dr Ste 12 Hudson (03051) *(G-14514)*

Kasi Infrared, Newport *Also Called: R Filion Manufacturing Inc (G-15236)*

Kasten Inc.. 702 860-2407
  304 Bishop Ave Bridgeport (06610) *(G-339)*

Katahdin Cedar Log Homes, Oakfield *Also Called: Katahdin Forest Products Co (G-5119)*

Katahdin Forest Products Co **(PA)**................................ **800 845-4533**
  205 Smyrna Rd Oakfield (04763) *(G-5119)*

Katahdin Industries Inc **(PA)**... **781 329-1420**
  51 Parmenter Rd Hudson (01749) *(G-9380)*

Katona Bakery LLC... 203 337-5349
  1189 Post Rd Ste 3b Fairfield (06824) *(G-1193)*

Katy Industries Inc... 314 656-4321
  765 Straits Tpke Bldg 2 Middlebury (06762) *(G-1715)*

Kautex Inc.. 603 743-2431
  74 Industrial Park Dover (03820) *(G-14232)*

KAY DEE DESIGNS INC **(PA)**....................................... **401 539-2400**
  177 Skunk Hill Rd Hope Valley (02832) *(G-16067)*

Kay Gee Sign and Graphics Co, Worcester *Also Called: New England Sign Group Inc (G-13764)*

Kayaku Advanced Materials Inc....................................... 617 965-5511
  20 Ossipee Rd Newton (02464) *(G-10767)*

Kayaku Advanced Materials Inc **(PA)**............................. **617 965-5511**
  200 Flanders Rd Westborough (01581) *(G-13113)*

Kayem Foods Inc **(PA)**... **781 933-3115**
  75 Arlington St Chelsea (02150) *(G-7984)*

Kaz Inc **(HQ)**... **508 490-7000**
  400 Donald Lynch Blvd Ste 300 Marlborough (01752) *(G-10174)*

Kaz Usa Inc... 508 490-7000
  400 Donald Lynch Blvd Marlborough (01752) *(G-10175)*

KB Logging, Smyrna Mills *Also Called: K B Logging Inc (G-5481)*

KB Surfaces LLC.. 401 727-6792
  20 Providence Pike North Smithfield (02896) *(G-16324)*

Kbace Technologies Inc **(HQ)**....................................... **603 821-7000**
  6 Trafalgar Sq Nashua (03063) *(G-15121)*

Kbc Electronics, Milford *Also Called: K B C Electronics Inc (G-1842)*

Kbs Builders Inc... 207 739-2400
  300 Park St South Paris (04281) *(G-5488)*

Kc Precision Machining LLC.. 978 356-8900
  23 Old Right Rd Unit 1 Ipswich (01938) *(G-9487)*

Kcb Solutions LLC.. 978 425-0400
  900 Mount Laurel Cir Shirley (01464) *(G-11819)*

Kci, Newington *Also Called: Kinetic Concepts Inc (G-2303)*

Kco Numet Inc.. 203 375-4995
  235 Edison Rd Orange (06477) *(G-2671)*

KCR Tire & Auto Inc... 203 438-4042
  861 Ethan Allen Hwy Ridgefield (06877) *(G-2900)*

Ke Printing & Graphics, Canton *Also Called: Keating Communication Group (G-7804)*

Ke Tube Inc.. 978 630-1436
  79 Wilkins Rd Gardner (01440) *(G-8892)*

Ke Usa Inc... 802 388-7309
  38b Pond Ln Middlebury (05753) *(G-17345)*

Ke Usa Inc... 802 864-3009
  19 Echo Pl Williston (05495) *(G-17736)*

Keane's Wood-Fired Catering, Cranston *Also Called: Lost Art Cultured Foods LLC (G-15886)*

Kearflex Engineering Company.. 401 781-4900
  66 Cypress St Warwick (02888) *(G-16830)*

Kearney-National Inc. 401 943-2686
66 Whitecap Dr North Kingstown (02852) *(G-16264)*

Keating Communication Group 781 828-9030
956 Turnpike St Canton (02021) *(G-7804)*

Keating-Wilbert Vault Inc. 413 543-1226
1840 Boston Rd Wilbraham (01095) *(G-13361)*

Kedron Sugar Makers, South Woodstock *Also Called: Kendle Enterprises (G-17615)*

Keebler, Franklin *Also Called: Keebler Company (G-8848)*

Keebler Company 508 520-7223
17 Forge Pkwy Franklin (02038) *(G-8848)*

Keebowil Inc **(PA)** **603 352-4232**
353 West St Keene (03431) *(G-14605)*

Keebowil Inc. 802 775-3572
126 Spruce St Rutland (05701) *(G-17502)*

Keegan Construction, Wallingford *Also Called: Thomas Keegan & Sons Inc (G-3862)*

Keene Publishing Corporation 603 352-1234
60 West St Keene (03431) *(G-14606)*

Keene Sentinel, Keene *Also Called: Keene Publishing Corporation (G-14606)*

Keeney Holdings LLC 860 666-3342
74 Batterson Park Rd Ste 102 Farmington (06032) *(G-1226)*

Kefi Development Inc. 401 272-6513
800 Waterman Ave East Providence (02914) *(G-16027)*

Keimos 1988 US Inc **(PA)** **508 921-4590**
249 Vanderbilt Ave Norwood (02062) *(G-11187)*

Keiser Homes, Oxford *Also Called: Excel Homes of Maine LLC (G-5143)*

Keith A Gilpatrick 207 737-4286
373 Lincoln St Richmond (04357) *(G-5321)*

Keith II Sporting Goods, Pittsford *Also Called: Keiths II Sports Ltd (G-17444)*

Keith's Sports Ltd II, Rutland *Also Called: Graphic Edge LLC (G-17498)*

Keiths II Sports Ltd. 802 483-6050
3892 Us Route 7 Pittsford (05763) *(G-17444)*

Keiver Willard-Lumber Corp. 978 462-7193
11 Graf Rd 13 Newburyport (01950) *(G-10690)*

Kel-Log Inc **(PA)** **603 752-2000**
743 E Side River Rd Milan (03588) *(G-15009)*

Kelco Concrete, Pawlet *Also Called: Matt Waite Excavation Inc (G-17441)*

Kelco Industries 207 546-7562
58 Main St Milbridge (04658) *(G-5061)*

Kell-Strom Tool Co Inc **(PA)** **860 529-6851**
214 Church St Wethersfield (06109) *(G-4209)*

Kell-Strom Tool Intl Inc. 860 529-6851
214 Church St Wethersfield (06109) *(G-4210)*

Kelleher Marketing, East Windsor *Also Called: Homeland Fundraising (G-1076)*

Keller Products Incorporated 603 224-5502
38 River Rd Bow (03304) *(G-14003)*

Keller Products Incorporated **(PA)** **603 627-7887**
41 Union St Manchester (03103) *(G-14871)*

Keller Products Inc. 978 264-1911
180 Middlesex St North Chelmsford (01863) *(G-10980)*

Kellerhaus Inc. 603 366-4466
259 Endicott St N Laconia (03246) *(G-14654)*

Kelley and Hall Book Publicity 617 680-1976
5 Briar Ln Marblehead (01945) *(G-10089)*

Kelley Bros, Hudson *Also Called: Kelley Bros New England LLC (G-14515)*

Kelley Bros New England LLC **(HQ)** **603 881-5559**
17 Hampshire Dr Ste 20 Hudson (03051) *(G-14515)*

Kelley Direct Solutions, Rye *Also Called: Kelley Solutions Inc (G-15499)*

Kelley Metals Corp. 401 434-8795
115 Valley St East Providence (02914) *(G-16028)*

Kelley Solutions Inc. 603 431-3881
14 Browns Ct Rye (03870) *(G-15499)*

Kelley Wood Products Inc. 978 345-7531
85 River St Fitchburg (01420) *(G-8658)*

Kellsport Industries Inc. 508 646-0855
22 Boomer St Fall River (02720) *(G-8565)*

Kelly Corned Beef Co Chicago 773 588-2882
140 Morgan Dr Norwood (02062) *(G-11188)*

Kelly Eisenberg, Norwood *Also Called: Kelly Corned Beef Co Chicago (G-11188)*

Kelly Lumber Sales Inc. 207 435-4950
101 Brunswick St Old Town (04468) *(G-5128)*

Kelmeg Woodworking 401 762-3090
1067 Victory Hwy North Smithfield (02896) *(G-16325)*

Kelton Woodwork Inc. 617 997-7261
11b Colicum Dr Charlton (01507) *(G-7891)*

Keltron Corporation **(HQ)** **781 894-8710**
101 1st Ave Ste 4 # A Waltham (02451) *(G-12707)*

Kelyniam Global Inc. 800 280-8192
97 River Rd Ste A Collinsville (06019) *(G-667)*

Kem Liquidating Company Inc. 860 430-5100
172 Oak St Glastonbury (06033) *(G-1287)*

Kemp Technologies Inc. 631 418-8407
7 Virginia Dr Rochdale (01542) *(G-11627)*

Kemper Manufacturing Corp. 203 934-1600
5 Clinton Pl West Haven (06516) *(G-4109)*

Kemtuff, Williston *Also Called: Gds Manufacturing Company (G-17732)*

Ken-Labs, Higganum *Also Called: Kenyon Laboratories LLC (G-1529)*

Ken-Mar LLC 603 898-1268
2 Northwestern Dr Salem (03079) *(G-15539)*

Kendall Press, Cambridge *Also Called: M & C Press Inc (G-7636)*

Kendle Enterprises 802 457-3015
109 Kendle Rd South Woodstock (05071) *(G-17615)*

Kenexa Brassring Inc. 781 530-5000
550 King St Littleton (01460) *(G-9823)*

Kenexa Compensation Inc **(DH)** **877 971-9171**
160 Gould St Needham (02494) *(G-10516)*

Kennametal Inc. 802 626-3331
34 Sanderson St Greenfield (01301) *(G-8994)*

Kennebec Cabinet Company, Bath *Also Called: Kennebec Company (G-4528)*

Kennebec Cabinetry Inc. 207 442-0813
37 Wing Farm Pkwy Bath (04530) *(G-4527)*

Kennebec Company 207 443-2131
1 Front St Ste 3 Bath (04530) *(G-4528)*

Kennebec Company, The, Bath *Also Called: Kennebec Cabinetry Inc (G-4527)*

Kennebec River Biosciences, Richmond *Also Called: Kennebec River Biosciences Inc (G-5322)*

Kennebec River Biosciences Inc. 207 737-2637
41 Main St Richmond (04357) *(G-5322)*

Kennebec Technologies 207 626-0188
150 Church Hill Rd Augusta (04330) *(G-4474)*

Kennebunkport Brewing Company, Kennebunk *Also Called: Ashleigh Inc (G-4921)*

Kennedy Die Castings Inc. 508 791-5594
15 Coppage Dr Airport Industrial Park Worcester (01603) *(G-13747)*

Kennedy Gustafson and Cole Inc. 860 828-2594
100 White Oak Dr Berlin (06037) *(G-72)*

Kennedy Incorporated 401 295-7800
21 Circuit Dr North Kingstown (02852) *(G-16265)*

Kennedy Sheet Metal Inc. 781 331-7764
1319 Pleasant St East Weymouth (02189) *(G-8431)*

Kenneth Crosby Co Inc. 508 497-0048
103 South St Hopkinton (01748) *(G-9335)*

Kenneth Lynch & Sons Inc. 203 762-8363
114 Willenbrock Rd Oxford (06478) *(G-2702)*

Kenney Manufacturing Company **(PA)** **401 739-2200**
1000 Jefferson Blvd Warwick (02886) *(G-16831)*

Kennison Machine Company, Rockland *Also Called: Kenniston Machine & Engrg (G-5336)*

Kenniston Machine & Engrg. 207 594-7810
30 Moran Dr Rockland (04841) *(G-5336)*

Keno Graphic Services Inc. 203 925-7722
1 Parrott Dr Ste 100 Shelton (06484) *(G-3026)*

Kens Foods Inc **(PA)** **508 229-1100**
1 Dangelo Dr Marlborough (01752) *(G-10176)*

Kensco Inc **(PA)** **203 734-8827**
41 Clifton Ave Ansonia (06401) *(G-15)*

Kensington GL & Frmng Co Inc. 860 828-9428
124 Woodlawn Rd Berlin (06037) *(G-73)*

Kensington Group Incorporated 603 926-6742
113 Lafayette Rd Hampton Falls (03844) *(G-14419)*

Kent County Daily Times 401 789-9744
1353 Main St West Warwick (02893) *(G-16911)*

Kent Fabrications 339 244-4533
171 Mattakeesett St Pembroke (02359) *(G-11373)*

Kent Falls Brewing Company 860 398-9645
33 Camps Rd Kent (06757) *(G-1542)*

A L P H A B E T I C

Kent Nutrition Group Inc.................................. 860 482-7116
   99 Thomaston Rd Litchfield (06759) *(G-1558)*

Kent Nutrition Group Inc.................................. 603 225-6661
   520 Hall St Bow (03304) *(G-14004)*

Kent Nutrition Group Inc.................................. 802 848-7718
   1 Webster St Richford (05476) *(G-17475)*

Kent Nutrition Group Rtlstr, Bow *Also Called: Kent Nutrition Group Inc (G-14004)*

Kent Scientific Corporation.............................. 860 626-1172
   1116 Litchfield St Torrington (06790) *(G-3688)*

Kentek Corporation **(PA)**.............................. **603 223-4900**
   5 Jarado Way Boscawen (03303) *(G-13990)*

Kentico Software LLC..................................... 866 328-8998
   15 Constitution Dr Ste 2c Bedford (03110) *(G-13938)*

Kentron Technologies Inc................................. 978 988-9100
   155 West St Ste 10 Wilmington (01887) *(G-13419)*

Kenway Composites, Augusta *Also Called: Cpk Manufacturing LLC (G-4470)*

Kenyon Industries Inc.................................... 401 364-7761
   36 Sherman Ave Kenyon (02836) *(G-16112)*

Kenyon International, Clinton *Also Called: Kenyon International Inc (G-645)*

Kenyon International Inc................................... 860 664-4906
   8 Heritage Park Rd Clinton (06413) *(G-645)*

Kenyon Laboratories LLC................................ 860 345-2097
   12 Scovil Rd Higganum (06441) *(G-1529)*

Kenyon Woodworking Inc................................. 617 524-6883
   179 Boylston St Jamaica Plain (02130) *(G-9502)*

Kerber Farms Lumber Company......................... 802 451-6920
   3489 Coolidge Hwy Guilford (05301) *(G-17281)*

Kerfoot Technologies Inc................................ 508 539-3002
   49 Ransom Rd Falmouth (02540) *(G-8634)*

Kerissa Creations... 401 949-5100
   15 Lark Industrial Pkwy Unit E Greenville (02828) *(G-16061)*

Kerk Products Division, Milford *Also Called: Haydon Kerk Mtion Slutions Inc (G-15024)*

Keros, Lexington *Also Called: Keros Therapeutics Inc (G-9756)*

Keros Therapeutics Inc **(PA)**....................... **617 314-6297**
   1050 Waltham St Ste 302 Lexington (02421) *(G-9756)*

Kerr Corporation... 203 748-0030
   21 Commerce Dr Danbury (06810) *(G-764)*

Kerry Inc.. 207 775-7060
   40 Quarry Rd Ste 200 Portland (04103) *(G-5231)*

Kerry R Wood.. 203 221-7780
   2 Hideaway Ln Westport (06880) *(G-4177)*

Kervick Entreprises, Worcester *Also Called: Fastcast Consortium Inc (G-13722)*

Kervick Family Foundation Inc........................... 508 853-4500
   40 Rockdale St Worcester (01606) *(G-13748)*

Keryx Biopharmaceuticals Inc **(HQ)**................ **617 871-2098**
   245 1st St Cambridge (02142) *(G-7622)*

Ketcham Supply Co Inc................................... 508 997-4787
   111 Myrtle St New Bedford (02740) *(G-10609)*

Ketcham Traps... 508 997-4787
   111 Myrtle St New Bedford (02740) *(G-10610)*

Kettle Cuisine LLC **(PA)**............................. **617 409-1100**
   330 Lynnway Lynn (01901) *(G-9980)*

Kettle Cuisine Holdings LLC.............................. 617 409-1100
   330 Lynnway Ste 405 Lynn (01901) *(G-9981)*

Keurig Dr Pepper, Burlington *Also Called: Keurig Dr Pepper Inc (G-7384)*

Keurig Dr Pepper Inc **(PA)**........................... **781 418-7000**
   53 South Ave Burlington (01803) *(G-7384)*

Keurig Dr Pepper Inc...................................... 802 288-6022
   5 New England Dr Essex Junction (05452) *(G-17238)*

Keurig Green Mountain Inc.............................. 781 246-3466
   53 South Ave Burlington (01803) *(G-7385)*

Keurig Green Mountain Inc **(DH)**.................... **877 879-2326**
   1 Rotarian Pl Waterbury (05676) *(G-17675)*

Kevin Emery.. 603 433-5784
   1 Wilson St Farmington (03835) *(G-14310)*

Kevin L Woolbert.. 603 445-5222
   118 Church St North Walpole (03609) *(G-15259)*

Kevin S Boghigian.. 603 883-0236
   141 Canal St Unit 4 Nashua (03064) *(G-15122)*

Kevin S Hawes.. 207 495-3412
   652 Manchester Rd Belgrade (04917) *(G-4541)*

Kevlaur Industries Inc..................................... 207 868-2761
   336 Champlain St Van Buren (04785) *(G-5569)*

Kevlin Corporation... 978 689-8331
   596 Lowell St Methuen (01844) *(G-10336)*

Key Container Corporation **(PA)**..................... **401 723-2000**
   21 Campbell St Pawtucket (02861) *(G-16381)*

Key Graphics Inc.. 401 826-2425
   7 Caitlin Ct Kingston (02881) *(G-16113)*

Key Industries.. 603 369-9634
   65 Turnpike Rd Unit B New Ipswich (03071) *(G-15198)*

Key Polymer LLC.. 978 683-9411
   17 Shepard St Lawrence (01843) *(G-9573)*

Key Polymer Holdings LLC **(PA)**.................... **978 683-9411**
   17 Shepard St Lawrence (01843) *(G-9574)*

Keysight Technologies Inc................................. 800 829-4444
   22 Cotton Rd Ste 150 Nashua (03063) *(G-15123)*

Keyspin Manufacturing LLC.............................. 603 420-8508
   21 Continental Blvd Merrimack (03054) *(G-14986)*

Keystone Dental Inc **(PA)**........................... **781 328-3300**
   154 Middlesex Tpke Ste 2 Burlington (01803) *(G-7386)*

Keystone Elev Svc Mdrnztion LL........................ 781 340-3860
   320 Libbey Industrial Pkwy Ste 800 Weymouth (02189) *(G-13328)*

Keystone Paper & Box Co LLC **(HQ)**................ **860 291-0027**
   31 Edwin Rd South Windsor (06074) *(G-3160)*

Keystone Paper & Box Co LLC........................... 781 938-3801
   10 Tower Office Park Woburn (01801) *(G-13596)*

Keystone Paper & Box Co Inc, South Windsor *Also Called: Keystone Paper & Box Co LLC (G-3160)*

Keystone Precision & Engrg Inc.......................... 978 433-8484
   16 Lomar Park Ste 3 Pepperell (01463) *(G-11385)*

Keystone Precision Inc.................................... 978 433-8484
   16 Lomar Park Ste 3 Pepperell (01463) *(G-11386)*

Keystone Press, Manchester *Also Called: Dr Biron Incorporated (G-14844)*

Keza Media, Manchester *Also Called: Snap Site Studios LLC (G-14931)*

KG Pallet LLC.. 413 536-3511
   70 Orange St Chicopee (01013) *(G-8043)*

Kgc, Berlin *Also Called: Kennedy Gustafson and Cole Inc (G-72)*

Kheops International Inc **(PA)**....................... **603 237-8188**
   232 Us Route 3 Stewartstown (03576) *(G-15631)*

Ki Inc.. 203 641-5492
   342 Cedarwood Dr Orange (06477) *(G-2672)*

Kickit Sports, Brewer *Also Called: T J Ryan LLC (G-4620)*

Kidde Fire System, Ashland *Also Called: Kidde-Fenwal Inc (G-5960)*

Kidde-Fenwal Inc **(HQ)**.............................. **508 881-2000**
   400 Main St Ashland (01721) *(G-5960)*

Kids Discover LLC.. 212 677-4457
   606 Post Rd E Ste 3 Westport (06880) *(G-4178)*

Kielb Welding Enterprises Inc............................ 413 734-4544
   150 Brookdale Dr Springfield (01104) *(G-12109)*

Kik Consumer Products, Ludlow *Also Called: James Austin Company (G-9946)*

Kilder Corporation... 978 663-8800
   7 Executive Park Dr North Billerica (01862) *(G-10922)*

Killeen Machine and TI Co Inc........................... 508 754-1714
   43 Sword St Auburn (01501) *(G-6118)*

Kimball Bakery Feeds, New Haven *Also Called: Phoenix Feeds and Ntrtn Inc (G-17394)*

Kimball Hardwoods LLC................................... 401 300-9070
   83 King St Johnston (02919) *(G-16092)*

Kimball Midwest, Newtown *Also Called: Midwest Motor Supply Co (G-2342)*

Kimball Physics Inc...................................... 603 878-1616
   311 Kimball Hill Rd Wilton (03086) *(G-15705)*

Kimberly-Clark, New Milford *Also Called: Kimberly-Clark Corporation (G-2250)*

Kimberly-Clark, Franklin *Also Called: Kimberly-Clark Corporation (G-8849)*

Kimberly-Clark Corporation............................... 860 210-1602
   58 Pickett District Rd New Milford (06776) *(G-2250)*

Kimberly-Clark Corporation............................... 508 520-1355
   38 Pawn Street Ste 108 Franklin (02038) *(G-8849)*

Kimble Applications Inc................................... 617 651-5600
   99 Chauncy St Ste 500 Boston (02111) *(G-6841)*

Kimchuk, Danbury *Also Called: Kimchuk Incorporated (G-766)*

Kimchuk Incorporated.................................... 203 798-0799
   4 Finance Dr Danbury (06810) *(G-765)*

Kimchuk Incorporated **(PA)**............................... **203 790-7800**
   1 Corporate Dr Ste 1 Danbury (06810) *(G-766)*

Kimtek Corporation.. 802 754-9000
   326 Industrial Park Ln Orleans (05860) *(G-17438)*

Kinamor Incorporated...................................... 203 269-0380
   63 N Plains Industrial Rd Wallingford (06492) *(G-3824)*

Kinamor Plastics, Wallingford *Also Called: Kinamor Incorporated (G-3824)*

Kinaset Therapeutics Inc **(PA)**....................... **508 858-5810**
   10 Knollwood Rd Medfield (02052) *(G-10271)*

Kind Grind Incorporated................................... 413 367-2478
   178 N Pleasant St Amherst (01002) *(G-5861)*

Kinder Industries Inc....................................... 401 253-7076
   75 Tupelo St Bristol (02809) *(G-15771)*

Kinderwagon Company...................................... 617 256-7599
   5 Gooseberry Rd Newport (02840) *(G-16215)*

Kinefac Corporation... 508 754-6901
   156 Goddard Memorial Dr Worcester (01603) *(G-13749)*

Kinepower Company Division, Worcester *Also Called: Kinefac Corporation (G-13749)*

Kinetic Concepts Inc....................................... 860 594-1043
   65 Louis St Ste C Newington (06111) *(G-2303)*

Kinetic Systems Inc... 617 522-8700
   20 Arboretum Rd Boston (02131) *(G-6842)*

Kinetic Tool Co Inc.. 860 627-5882
   5 Craftsman Rd Ste 7 East Windsor (06088) *(G-1078)*

Kinetics Group Inc... 207 541-4712
   3 Glasgow Rd Scarborough (04074) *(G-5436)*

King Fisher Co Inc... 978 596-0214
   81 Old Ferry Rd Lowell (01854) *(G-9890)*

King Forest Industries Inc................................. 603 764-5711
   968 Route 25 Wentworth (03282) *(G-15676)*

King Industries... 203 527-7380
   800 Chase Pkwy Waterbury (06708) *(G-3928)*

King Industries Inc **(PA)**.............................. **203 866-5551**
   1 Science Rd Norwalk (06850) *(G-2523)*

King Koil Northeast, East Windsor *Also Called: Blue Bell Mattress Company LLC (G-1068)*

King Manufacturing Co Inc................................. 603 532-6455
   295 Squantum Rd Jaffrey (03452) *(G-14570)*

King Network Services Inc................................. 860 479-8029
   336 S Washington St Ste R Plainville (06062) *(G-2766)*

King Pine Industries, Wentworth *Also Called: King Forest Industries Inc (G-15676)*

King Printing Company Inc................................. 978 458-2345
   181 Industrial Ave E Lowell (01852) *(G-9891)*

Kingfield Wood Products, Kingfield *Also Called: Frontier Forge Inc (G-4933)*

Kingfisher Marine Ltd....................................... 602 409-1460
   70 Riverside Dr Clinton (06413) *(G-646)*

Kingsland Company.. 860 542-6981
   7 Colebrook Rd Norfolk (06058) *(G-2360)*

Kingsley Printing Assoc LLC.............................. 203 345-6046
   4883 Main St Stratford (06614) *(G-3552)*

Kingston Aluminum Foundry Inc.......................... 781 585-6631
   7 Pembroke St Kingston (02364) *(G-9509)*

Kingston Krafts... 401 272-0292
   15 Industrial Rd Unit 2 Cranston (02920) *(G-15882)*

Kingston Manufacturing Co Inc........................... 781 585-4476
   3 Pleasant St Kingston (02364) *(G-9510)*

Kingston Materials, Methuen *Also Called: Torromeo Industries Inc (G-10346)*

Kingston Materials, Kingston *Also Called: Torromeo Industries Inc (G-14637)*

Kingswood Kitchens Co Inc................................ 203 792-8700
   70 Beaver St Danbury (06810) *(G-767)*

Kiniksa Pharmaceuticals Corp............................ 781 431-9100
   100 Hayden Ave Ste 1 Lexington (02421) *(G-9757)*

Kink Pieces of A Dream LLC.............................. 508 748-5417
   550 Cochituate Rd Ste 25 Framingham (01701) *(G-8784)*

Kinotek Inc.. 207 805-1919
   22 Monument Sq Ste 201 Portland (04101) *(G-5232)*

Kintent Inc.. 512 294-4201
   16 Spy Pond Pkwy Arlington (02474) *(G-5943)*

Kip Inc... 860 677-0272
   72 Spring Ln Farmington (06032) *(G-1227)*

Kiq Bio LLC.. 617 945-5576
   200 Cambridgepark Dr Ste 3100 Cambridge (02140) *(G-7623)*

Kirby Corporation.. 413 363-0005
   784 Page Blvd Springfield (01104) *(G-12110)*

Kirchoff Wohlberg.. 212 644-2020
   897 Boston Post Rd Madison (06443) *(G-1562)*

Kirk Eastern Company, Gardner *Also Called: Ke Tube Inc (G-8892)*

Kirkwood Direct, Wilmington *Also Called: Kirkwood Holdings Inc (G-13420)*

Kirkwood Holdings Inc **(PA)**......................... **978 658-4200**
   904 Main St Wilmington (01887) *(G-13420)*

Kirwan Surgical Products LLC............................ 781 834-9500
   180 Enterprise Dr Marshfield (02050) *(G-10240)*

Kitchen Associates Inc..................................... 978 422-3322
   76 Leominster Rd Sterling (01564) *(G-12164)*

Kitchen Cab Resurfacing LLC............................ 203 334-2857
   136 Merriam St Bridgeport (06604) *(G-340)*

Kitchen Living LLC.. 860 819-5847
   21 Main St East Hampton (06424) *(G-964)*

Kitchen Options Inc... 508 987-3384
   193 Sutton Ave Oxford (01540) *(G-11256)*

Kitchen Options of New England, Oxford *Also Called: Kitchen Options Inc (G-11256)*

Kitchen Store, The, Dorset *Also Called: J K Adams Company Inc (G-17214)*

Kitewheel LLC.. 617 447-2138
   24 School St Fl 6 Boston (02108) *(G-6843)*

Kj Can, Nashua *Also Called: Can-One (usa) Inc (G-15075)*

Kjpl Restaurants Inc.. 207 577-1728
   682 Route 202 Greene (04236) *(G-4846)*

Kksp Precision Machining LLC............................ 860 274-6773
   1012 Buckingham St Watertown (06795) *(G-4016)*

KLA Systems Inc.. 508 644-5555
   31 Mill St Assonet (02702) *(G-5975)*

Klarmann Rulings Inc....................................... 603 424-2401
   1 Perimeter Rd Ste 900 Manchester (03103) *(G-14872)*

Klear-Vu Corporation **(PA)**.......................... **508 674-5723**
   600 Airport Rd Fall River (02720) *(G-8566)*

Kleeberg Sheet Metal Inc................................. 413 589-1854
   65 Westover Rd Ludlow (01056) *(G-9947)*

Kleenline LLC.. 978 463-0827
   6 Opportunity Way Rear Newburyport (01950) *(G-10691)*

Klein Marine Systems Inc................................. 603 893-6131
   11 Klein Dr Salem (03079) *(G-15540)*

Kliks Inc... 617 230-0544
   867 Boylston St Boston (02116) *(G-6844)*

Klingers Bread Company................................... 802 860-6322
   10 Farrell St Ste 4 South Burlington (05403) *(G-17582)*

Klitzner Industries Inc...................................... 800 621-0161
   26 Kirkbrae Dr Lincoln (02865) *(G-16143)*

Klone Lab, Newburyport *Also Called: Klone Lab LLC (G-10692)*

Klone Lab LLC.. 978 378-3434
   115a Water St Ste A Newburyport (01950) *(G-10692)*

Kluber Lubric North Amercia LP.......................... 603 647-4104
   32 Industrial Dr Londonderry (03053) *(G-14758)*

Kluber Lubrication North Ameri........................... 603 434-7704
   54 Wentworth Ave Londonderry (03053) *(G-14759)*

Km Holding Inc... 603 566-2704
   120 Derry Rd Hudson (03051) *(G-14516)*

KMC Music, Bloomfield *Also Called: Rokr Distribution Us Inc (G-207)*

KMC Systems Inc... 866 742-0442
   220 Daniel Webster Hwy Merrimack (03054) *(G-14987)*

Kms Machine Works Inc.................................... 508 822-3151
   447 Winthrop St Taunton (02780) *(G-12346)*

Kneeland Bros Inc... 978 948-3919
   51 Wethersfield St Rowley (01969) *(G-11678)*

Knickerbocker Group Inc................................... 207 541-9333
   8 Builders Sq Boothbay (04537) *(G-4598)*

Knight Industries.. 802 773-8777
   20 Innovation Dr North Clarendon (05759) *(G-17416)*

Knight Kitchens, North Clarendon *Also Called: Knight Industries Inc (G-17416)*

Knight Machine & Tool Co Inc............................ 413 532-2507
   11 Industrial Dr South Hadley (01075) *(G-11964)*

Knight Optical (usa) LLC.................................. 401 521-7000
   1130 Ten Rod Rd Ste D102 North Kingstown (02852) *(G-16266)*

Knm Holdings LLC... 508 229-1400
   410 Forest St Ste 3 Marlborough (01752) *(G-10177)*

A L P H A B E T I C

Knoa Pharma LLC **(PA)**... **203 588-8000**
   201 Tresser Blvd Stamford (06901) *(G-3395)*

Knobby Krafters Inc.. 508 222-7272
   129 Bank St Ste 5 Attleboro (02703) *(G-6029)*

Knowledge Ai Inc **(PA)**................................... **415 321-9059**
   58 Winter St Boston (02108) *(G-6845)*

Knowlton Machine Company................................ 207 854-8471
   5 Sanford Dr Gorham (04038) *(G-4824)*

Knowlton Machine Engineering, Gorham *Also Called: Knowlton Machine Company* *(G-4824)*

Knox Machine Company..................................... 207 273-2296
   936 Eastern Rd Warren (04864) *(G-5582)*

Kobuta Choppers LLC.. 203 234-6047
   439 Washington Ave North Haven (06473) *(G-2421)*

Kobyluck Ready-Mix Inc..................................... 860 444-9604
   24 Industrial Dr Waterford (06385) *(G-3991)*

Kobyluck Sand and Gravel Inc............................ 860 444-9600
   24 Industrial Dr Waterford (06385) *(G-3992)*

Koch Membrane Solutions, Wilmington *Also Called: Kovalus Spration Solutions LLC* *(G-13421)*

Kochlowy, Avon *Also Called: Chapman Manufacturing Company Inc* *(G-6147)*

Kochman Reidt & Haigh Inc................................ 781 573-1500
   471 Page St Ste 8 Stoughton (02072) *(G-12217)*

Kodiak Machining Co Inc.................................... 978 356-9876
   20 Hayward St Ipswich (01938) *(G-9488)*

Kognito, Burlington *Also Called: Kognito Solutions LLC* *(G-7387)*

Kognito Solutions LLC.. 212 675-2651
   25 Mall Rd Ste 600 Burlington (01803) *(G-7387)*

Kohler Sgnture Str By Sup Neng.......................... 781 365-0168
   19 3rd Ave Burlington (01803) *(G-7388)*

Kokos Machine Co, Dudley *Also Called: Ryszard A Kokosinski* *(G-8321)*

Kol LLC... 203 393-2924
   12 Cassway Rd Woodbridge (06525) *(G-4379)*

Kollmorgen Corporation..................................... 802 258-3020
   343 John Seitz Dr Brattleboro (05301) *(G-17092)*

Kollsman Inc **(DH)**.. **603 889-2500**
   220 Daniel Webster Hwy Merrimack (03054) *(G-14988)*

Kolltan Pharmaceuticals Inc **(HQ)**................... **203 773-3000**
   300 George St Ste 530 New Haven (06511) *(G-2166)*

Kolmar Americas.. 203 840-5337
   383 Main Ave Norwalk (06851) *(G-2524)*

Kolmar Americas Inc **(HQ)**............................. **203 873-2051**
   10 Middle St Ph Bridgeport (06604) *(G-341)*

Komor Mfg Co, Rehoboth *Also Called: J & K Sales Co Inc* *(G-11610)*

Komtek Forge LLC... 508 853-4500
   40 Rockdale St Worcester (01606) *(G-13750)*

Koncert LLC... 800 955-5040
   7 Stiles Rd Ste 102 Salem (03079) *(G-15541)*

Konecranes Inc.. 978 256-5525
   25 Industrial Ave Ste 1 Chelmsford (01824) *(G-7935)*

Kongsberg Acttion Systems II L **(PA)**............... **860 668-1285**
   1 Firestone Dr Suffield (06078) *(G-3592)*

Kongsberg Automotive, Suffield *Also Called: Kongsberg Acttion Systems II L* *(G-3592)*

Kongsberg Dgtal Simulation Inc.......................... 860 405-2300
   115b Leonard Dr Groton (06340) *(G-1375)*

Kookla Inc... 508 765-0442
   386 E Main St Southbridge (01550) *(G-12025)*

Kookla Inc **(PA)**... **508 347-2623**
   120 Main St Sturbridge (01566) *(G-12251)*

Kool Ink LLC.. 860 242-0303
   21 Old Windsor Rd Ste B Bloomfield (06002) *(G-186)*

Koovera International... 978 867-0867
   186 Cabot St Beverly (01915) *(G-6359)*

Kopin Corporation.. 508 824-6696
   200 John Hancock Rd Taunton (02780) *(G-12347)*

Kopin Corporation **(PA)**................................. **508 870-5959**
   125 North Dr Westborough (01581) *(G-13114)*

Kopin Targeting Corporation.............................. 508 870-5959
   125 North Dr Westborough (01581) *(G-13115)*

Koplow Games Inc... 617 482-4011
   369 Congress St Fl 5 Boston (02210) *(G-6846)*

Korber Hats, Fall River *Also Called: Fall River Hat Company* *(G-8546)*

Korber Hats, Fall River *Also Called: Whole Earth Hat Co Inc* *(G-8626)*

Koren Publishers, New Milford *Also Called: Toby Press LLC* *(G-2261)*

Korner Bagel Partnership.................................... 508 336-5204
   23 Circle Dr Seekonk (02771) *(G-11779)*

Korolath, Hudson *Also Called: Korolath of New England Inc* *(G-9381)*

Korolath of New England Inc.............................. 978 562-7366
   498 River Rd Hudson (01749) *(G-9381)*

Korro Bio Inc **(PA)**.. **617 468-1999**
   1 Kendall Sq Bldg 600-700 Cambridge (02139) *(G-7624)*

Koso America Inc.. 774 517-5300
   4 Manley St West Bridgewater (02379) *(G-12974)*

Koster Keunen, Watertown *Also Called: Koster Keunen Mfg Inc* *(G-4019)*

Koster Keunen Inc.. 860 945-3333
   1021 Echo Lake Rd Watertown (06795) *(G-4017)*

Koster Keunen LLC **(PA)**................................ **860 945-3333**
   1021 Echo Lake Rd Watertown (06795) *(G-4018)*

Koster Keunen Mfg Inc...................................... 860 945-3333
   1021 Echo Lake Rd Watertown (06795) *(G-4019)*

Kovacs Machine and Tool Co.............................. 203 269-4949
   50 N Plains Industrial Rd Wallingford (06492) *(G-3825)*

Kovalus Spration Solutions LLC **(PA)**................ **978 694-7000**
   850 Main St Wilmington (01887) *(G-13421)*

Kp Building Products Inc.................................... 866 850-4447
   402 Boyer Cir Williston (05495) *(G-17737)*

Kraft Foods, Waterbury *Also Called: Kraft Heinz Foods Company* *(G-3929)*

Kraft Foods, Mansfield *Also Called: Kraft Heinz Foods Company* *(G-10062)*

Kraft Foods, Woburn *Also Called: Kraft Heinz Foods Company* *(G-13597)*

Kraft Group LLC **(PA)**.................................... **508 384-4230**
   1 Patriot Pl Foxboro (02035) *(G-8705)*

Kraft Heinz Foods Company............................... 203 597-9109
   67 Freight St Waterbury (06702) *(G-3929)*

Kraft Heinz Foods Company............................... 508 763-3311
   111 Forbes Blvd Mansfield (02048) *(G-10062)*

Kraft Heinz Foods Company............................... 781 933-2800
   1 Hill St Woburn (01801) *(G-13597)*

Kramer Printing Company Inc............................. 203 933-5416
   270 Front Ave West Haven (06516) *(G-4110)*

Kramer Scientific LLC.. 978 388-7159
   91 High St Ste 1 Amesbury (01913) *(G-5840)*

Kramers Cstm Kitchens & Wdwkg....................... 508 429-9007
   47 October Hill Rd Holliston (01746) *(G-9219)*

Krazy Korner Bagel & Deli, Seekonk *Also Called: Korner Bagel Partnership* *(G-11779)*

Krell Industries LLC... 203 298-4000
   45 Connair Rd Orange (06477) *(G-2673)*

Krest Products Corp.. 978 537-1244
   707 Lancaster St Leominster (01453) *(G-9674)*

Kretetek Industries Inc...................................... 855 573-8383
   66b River Rd Hudson (03051) *(G-14517)*

Kretetek Industries LLC..................................... 603 402-3073
   66 River Rd Hudson (03051) *(G-14518)*

Krl Electronics, Manchester *Also Called: Bantry Components Inc* *(G-14817)*

Krohn-Hite Corporation..................................... 508 580-1660
   15 Jonathan Dr Ste 4 Brockton (02301) *(G-7288)*

Krohne America, Beverly *Also Called: Krohne Inc* *(G-6360)*

Krohne Inc **(DH)**... **978 535-6060**
   55 Cherry Hill Dr Beverly (01915) *(G-6360)*

Kronos Incorporated, Lowell *Also Called: Ukg Kronos Systems LLC* *(G-9931)*

Kronos International MGT LLC **(DH)**.................. **978 250-9800**
   900 Chelmsford St Unit 312 Lowell (01851) *(G-9892)*

Kronos Securities Corporation............................ 978 250-9800
   900 Chelmsford St Unit 312 Lowell (01851) *(G-9893)*

Kronos Solutions Inc **(DH)**............................. **978 805-9971**
   900 Chelmsford St Unit 312 Lowell (01851) *(G-9894)*

Kronos Tech Systems Ltd Partnr.......................... 978 250-9800
   900 Chelmsford St Lowell (01851) *(G-9895)*

Krueger International Inc.................................... 617 542-4043
   109 Broad St Boston (02110) *(G-6847)*

Krushco, Auburn *Also Called: Maine Metal Recycling Inc* *(G-4442)*

Krystal Inc LLC.. 860 844-1267
   9a Bank St Granby (06035) *(G-1307)*

Krystal Restaurant, Granby *Also Called: Krystal Inc LLC* *(G-1307)*

KS Baxter Logistics Co Inc................................ 607 203-5921 6 Liberty Sq Boston (02109) **(G-6848)**	L & J Enterprises Inc................................ 781 233-1966 67 Maplewood St Malden (02148) **(G-10018)**
KS Manufacturing Inc................................ 508 427-5727 9 Sawyer Ter Allston (02134) **(G-5822)**	L & L Capital Partners LLC................................ 203 834-6222 57 Danbury Rd Ste 3 Wilton (06897) **(G-4241)**
Ksaria, Hudson Also Called: Ksaria Corporation **(G-14519)**	L & L Concrete Products Inc................................ 508 987-8175 28 Linwood St Oxford (01540) **(G-11257)**
Ksaria Corporation................................ 866 457-2742 6 Wentworth Dr Hudson (03051) **(G-14519)**	L & L Mechanical LLC................................ 860 491-4007 28 Pie Hill Rd Goshen (06756) **(G-1303)**
Ksaria Service Corporation................................ 978 933-0000 6 Wentworth Dr Hudson (03051) **(G-14520)**	L & M Machine Inc................................ 617 294-0378 115 Tremont St Everett (02149) **(G-8489)**
KSd ATL Trnspt Systems Inc................................ 207 591-4150 84g Warren Ave Westbrook (04092) **(G-5634)**	L & M Manufacturing Co Inc................................ 860 379-2751 37 Greenwoods Rd New Hartford (06057) **(G-2105)**
KSD Custom Wood Products Inc................................ 603 796-2951 102 High St Boscawen (03303) **(G-13991)**	L & M Service Contractors LLC................................ 603 359-1956 126 Nh Route 10 Orford (03777) **(G-15281)**
Kse Inc................................ 413 549-5506 665 Amherst Rd Ste 1 Sunderland (01375) **(G-12274)**	L & P Paper Inc................................ 508 248-3265 267 Southbridge Rd Charlton (01507) **(G-7892)**
Ksew................................ 774 230-4995 100 Central St Southbridge (01550) **(G-12026)**	L & R Manufacturing Co Inc................................ 508 853-0562 340 Tacoma St Worcester (01605) **(G-13751)**
Ksg Enterprises Inc................................ 978 977-7357 77 Walnut St Ste 8 Peabody (01960) **(G-11322)**	**L & S Industries Inc (PA)................................ 508 995-4654** 32 Lambeth St New Bedford (02745) **(G-10612)**
Ksplice Inc................................ 765 577-5423 1 Main St Ste 7f Cambridge (02142) **(G-7625)**	L A B, Bristol Also Called: Lab Security Systems Corp **(G-460)**
Ktcr Holding................................ 203 227-4115 4 Pheasant Ln Westport (06880) **(G-4179)**	L Brown and Sons Printing Inc................................ 802 476-3164 14 Jefferson St # 20 Barre (05641) **(G-17012)**
Kti Inc (HQ)................................ 860 623-2511 3 Thompson Rd East Windsor (06088) **(G-1079)**	L C M Tool Co................................ 203 757-1575 68 Diane Ter Waterbury (06705) **(G-3930)**
Ktron Incorporated................................ 508 229-0919 90 Bartlett St Marlborough (01752) **(G-10178)**	L E Taylor and Sons Inc................................ 207 625-4056 37 Cross Rd Porter (04068) **(G-5166)**
Kub Technologies Inc................................ 203 364-8544 111 Research Dr Stratford (06615) **(G-3553)**	L E Weed and Son, Newport Also Called: Newport Concrete Block Co **(G-15232)**
Kubota Authorized Dealer, Saint Albans Also Called: Champlain Valley Equipment Inc **(G-17518)**	**L H C Inc (PA)................................ 781 592-6444** 638 Summer St Lynn (01905) **(G-9982)**
Kubotek Usa Inc................................ 508 229-2020 2 Mount Royal Ave Ste 500 Marlborough (01752) **(G-10179)**	L H Thompson Inc................................ 207 989-3280 54 Wilson St Brewer (04412) **(G-4615)**
Kubtec, Stratford Also Called: Kub Technologies Inc **(G-3553)**	**L Hardy Company Inc (PA)................................ 508 757-3480** 17 Mill St Worcester (01603) **(G-13752)**
Kuehne New Haven LLC................................ 203 508-6703 71 Welton St New Haven (06511) **(G-2167)**	L J Gentile & Sons Inc................................ 508 384-5156 228 Dedham St Rear Norfolk (02056) **(G-10800)**
Kullson Engineered Tech Inc................................ 207 576-9808 10 Gould Rd Lewiston (04240) **(G-4969)**	L K M Industries Woburn................................ 781 935-9210 44 6th Rd Woburn (01801) **(G-13598)**
Kvh Industries Inc................................ 401 847-3327 75 Enterprise Ctr Middletown (02842) **(G-16176)**	L L Bean Inc................................ 207 725-0300 8 Industrial Pkwy Brunswick (04011) **(G-4647)**
Kvh Industries Inc (PA)................................ 401 847-3327 50 Enterprise Ctr Middletown (02842) **(G-16177)**	L L Rowe Company................................ 781 729-7860 15 Gray Ln Ste 108 Ashaway (02804) **(G-15743)**
Kw Products LLC................................ 207 357-3798 4 Golden Pond Rd Canton (04221) **(G-4671)**	L M C, Southington Also Called: Light Metals Coloring Co Inc **(G-3219)**
KW Thompson Tool Company Inc................................ 603 330-8670 41 Old Dover Rd Rochester (03867) **(G-15483)**	L M C Light Iron Inc................................ 207 793-9957 151 E Range Rd Limerick (04048) **(G-5002)**
Kwik-Print Inc................................ 413 528-2885 35 Bridge St Great Barrington (01230) **(G-8977)**	**L M Gill Welding and Mfr LLC (PA)................................ 860 647-9931** 1422 Tolland Tpke Manchester (06042) **(G-1610)**
Kws Inc................................ 207 832-5095 110 One Pie Rd Waldoboro (04572) **(G-5577)**	L M Gill Welding and Mfr LLC................................ 860 647-9931 1422 Tolland Tpke Manchester (06042) **(G-1611)**
Kx Technologies LLC (DH)................................ 203 799-9000 55 Railroad Ave West Haven (06516) **(G-4111)**	L M I, Acton Also Called: Liquid Metronics Incorporated **(G-5757)**
Kyle Equipment Co Inc................................ 978 422-8448 14 Legate Hill Rd Sterling (01564) **(G-12165)**	L M T Magazine, Newtown Also Called: Lmt Communications Inc **(G-2339)**
Kyler Seafood Inc................................ 508 984-5150 2 Washburn St New Bedford (02740) **(G-10611)**	L P Macadams Company Inc................................ 203 366-3647 50 Austin St Bridgeport (06604) **(G-342)**
Kyler's, New Bedford Also Called: Kyler Seafood Inc **(G-10611)**	L Ray Packing Company................................ 207 546-2355 314 Wyman Rd Milbridge (04658) **(G-5062)**
Kymera Therapeutics Inc (PA)................................ 857 285-5300 200 Arsenal Yards Blvd Ste 230 Watertown (02472) **(G-12885)**	L T Technologies................................ 508 456-0315 612 Plymouth St Ste 12 East Bridgewater (02333) **(G-8342)**
Kyocera AVX Cmpnnts Bddford Co................................ 207 282-5111 401 Hill St Biddeford (04005) **(G-4574)**	L T X International Inc................................ 781 461-1000 825 University Ave Norwood (02062) **(G-11189)**
Kyra Medical Inc................................ 888 611-5972 102 Otis St Ste 1 Northborough (01532) **(G-11100)**	L W Tank Repair, Uxbridge Also Called: L W Tank Repair Incorporated **(G-12483)**
Kyromina Oil Corporation................................ 508 651-8284 2 Austin Way Natick (01760) **(G-10484)**	L W Tank Repair Incorporated................................ 508 234-6000 410 N Main St Uxbridge (01569) **(G-12483)**
Kyruus Inc................................ 617 419-2060 100 Franklin St Ste 803 Boston (02110) **(G-6849)**	L-Com, North Andover Also Called: Infinite Electronics Intl Inc **(G-10839)**
L & A Molding Corporation................................ 978 537-3538 50 Francis St Leominster (01453) **(G-9675)**	**L-Com Inc (DH)................................ 978 682-6936** 50 High St North Andover (01845) **(G-10842)**
L & A Tent Awning, Lewiston Also Called: Lewiston-Auburn Tent & Awng Co **(G-4974)**	L-Com Global Connectivity, North Andover Also Called: L-Com Inc **(G-10842)**
L & F Construction, Leverett Also Called: Lml Construction Inc **(G-9718)**	L.a Burdick Chocolate Shop, Boston Also Called: LA Burdick Boston LLC **(G-6850)**
L & G Fabricators Inc................................ 802 447-0965 137 Harwood Hill Rd Bennington (05201) **(G-17047)**	**L3 Oceanserver Inc (DH)................................ 508 678-0550** 275 Martine St Ste 103 Fall River (02723) **(G-8567)**
	L3 Technologies Inc................................ 413 586-2330 50 Prince St Northampton (01060) **(G-11069)**

A L P H A B E T I C

L3 Technologies Inc......................................978 694-9991
  65 Jonspin Rd Wilmington (01887) *(G-13422)*

L3 Technologies Inc......................................401 377-2300
  15 Gray Ln Ste 202 Ashaway (02804) *(G-15744)*

L3 Technologies Inc......................................603 626-4800
  9 Akira Way Londonderry (03053) *(G-14760)*

LA Burdick Boston LLC...................................617 303-0113
  220 Clarendon St Boston (02116) *(G-6850)*

La Chance Brick, Auburn *Also Called: Rjf - Morin Brick LLC (G-4459)*

La Joies Auto Scrap & Recycl, Norwalk *Also Called: Lajoie Auto Wrecking Co Inc (G-2525)*

La Jolla Pharmaceutical Co **(HQ)**...................**617 715-3600**
  35 Gatehouse Dr Ste E0 Waltham (02451) *(G-12708)*

La Patisserie Bakery Cafe, Revere *Also Called: La Patisserie Inc (G-11621)*

La Patisserie Inc...781 729-9441
  260 Proctor Ave Revere (02151) *(G-11621)*

La Pietra Custom Marble & Gran, Brookfield *Also Called: La Pietra Thinstone Veneer (G-528)*

La Pietra Thinstone of CT LLC...........................203 948-3756
  15 Franklin St Seymour (06483) *(G-2963)*

La Pietra Thinstone Veneer..............................203 775-6162
  1106 Federal Rd Brookfield (06804) *(G-528)*

Laars, Rochester *Also Called: Laars Heating Systems Company (G-15484)*

Laars Heating Systems Company.........................603 335-6300
  20 Industrial Way Rochester (03867) *(G-15484)*

Lab Frnture Instlltons Sls Inc............................978 646-0600
  11 River St Ste 2 Middleton (01949) *(G-10388)*

Lab Medical Manufacturing Inc...........................978 663-2475
  28 Cook St Billerica (01821) *(G-6458)*

Lab Security Systems Corp...............................860 589-6037
  700 Emmett St Bristol (06010) *(G-460)*

Labcentral Inc **(PA)**..................................**617 863-3650**
  700 Main St N Cambridge (02139) *(G-7626)*

Label Haus Inc..978 777-1773
  3 Southside Rd Ste B Danvers (01923) *(G-8197)*

Label Tech LLC..603 692-2005
  16 Interstate Dr Somersworth (03878) *(G-15618)*

Labelprint America Inc...................................978 463-4004
  8 Opportunity Way Newburyport (01950) *(G-10693)*

Labels Inc..603 929-3088
  10 Merrill Industrial Dr Hampton (03842) *(G-14405)*

Lablite LLC...860 355-8817
  8 S Main St New Milford (06776) *(G-2251)*

Labminds Inc..844 956-8327
  285 Washington St Ste 3 Somerville (02143) *(G-11883)*

Labonville Inc **(PA)**..................................**603 752-4030**
  504 Main St Gorham (03581) *(G-14360)*

Laborie, Portsmouth *Also Called: Laborie Medical Technologies Corp (G-15414)*

Laborie Medical Technologies Corp **(HQ)**..............**802 857-1300**
  180 International Dr Portsmouth (03801) *(G-15414)*

Laborsoft, Newton *Also Called: Stone Tablet LLC (G-10788)*

Labpulse Medical, Niantic *Also Called: Energy Beam Sciences Inc (G-2357)*

Labsphere Inc...603 927-4266
  231 Shaker St North Sutton (03260) *(G-15254)*

Labthink, Medford *Also Called: Labthink International Inc (G-10293)*

Labthink International Inc................................617 830-2190
  200 Rivers Edge Dr Ste 1 Medford (02155) *(G-10293)*

Lac Landscaping LLC....................................203 807-1067
  60 Country Ln Milford (06461) *(G-1843)*

Lacascias Bakery Inc....................................781 395-8612
  418 Main St Medford (02155) *(G-10294)*

Lacerta Group Inc.......................................508 339-3312
  50 Suffolk Rd Mansfield (02048) *(G-10063)*

Lacerta Group LLC **(PA)**..............................**508 339-3312**
  360 Forbes Blvd Mansfield (02048) *(G-10064)*

Lacerta Group, Inc., Mansfield *Also Called: Lacerta Group Inc (G-10063)*

Lacey Manufacturing Co LLC.............................203 336-0121
  1146 Barnum Ave Bridgeport (06610) *(G-343)*

Laconia Magnetics Inc...................................603 528-2766
  Prescott Hill Rd Laconia (03246) *(G-14655)*

Lactalis US Yogurt Inc...................................603 437-4040
  10 Burton Dr Londonderry (03053) *(G-14761)*

LAD Welding & Fabrication...............................603 228-6617
  5 Lehoux Dr Hooksett (03106) *(G-14466)*

Ladd Research Industries, Essex Junction *Also Called: Raj Communications Ltd (G-17243)*

Laddawn Inc **(HQ)**....................................**800 446-3639**
  155 Jackson Rd Devens (01434) *(G-8274)*

Ladesco Inc..603 623-3772
  150 Dow St Manchester (03101) *(G-14873)*

Lady Ann Candies Inc...................................401 738-4321
  86 Warwick Industrial Dr Ste 1 Warwick (02886) *(G-16832)*

Lady Dye Yarns, Hyde Park *Also Called: Diane L Ivey (G-9459)*

Laflamme Farms, Monroe *Also Called: Pete and Gerrys Organics LLC (G-15047)*

Lag Inc **(PA)**..**207 729-1676**
  27 Monument Pl Topsham (04086) *(G-5548)*

Laird Connectivity LLC..................................603 627-7877
  205 Pinebrook Pl Manchester (03109) *(G-14874)*

Laird Technologies Inc..................................603 627-7877
  205 Pinebrook Pl Manchester (03109) *(G-14875)*

Lajoie Auto Wrecking Co Inc.............................203 870-0641
  40 Meadow St Norwalk (06854) *(G-2525)*

Lake Boone Ice Co LLC..................................508 755-3099
  710 Main St Hudson (01749) *(G-9382)*

Lake Champlain Chocolates, Burlington *Also Called: Champlain Chocolate Company (G-17124)*

Lake Champlain Chocolates, Williston *Also Called: Champlain Chocolate Company (G-17725)*

Lake Champlain Trnsp Co................................802 660-3495
  King Street Dock Burlington (05401) *(G-17141)*

Lake Hvac, Stoneham *Also Called: Lake Industries Inc (G-12180)*

Lake Industries Inc......................................781 438-8814
  41 Pleasant St Stoneham (02180) *(G-12180)*

Lake Machine Co Inc.....................................603 542-8884
  12 Balcom Pl Claremont (03743) *(G-14092)*

Lake Manufacturing Co Inc...............................978 465-1617
  6 Opportunity Way Newburyport (01950) *(G-10694)*

Lake Region Manufacturing Inc **(HQ)**..................**952 361-2515**
  100 Fordham Rd Ste 3 Wilmington (01887) *(G-13423)*

Lake Region Medical, Wilmington *Also Called: Lake Region Manufacturing Inc (G-13423)*

Lake Region Medical, Wilmington *Also Called: Lake Region Medical Inc (G-13424)*

Lake Region Medical Inc **(HQ)**........................**978 570-6900**
  100 Fordham Rd Ste 3 Wilmington (01887) *(G-13424)*

Lake Region Medical Inc.................................603 528-1211
  45 Lexington Dr Laconia (03246) *(G-14656)*

Lakes Region Tubular Pdts Inc...........................603 528-2838
  51 Growth Rd Laconia (03246) *(G-14657)*

Lakeside Management Corp..............................508 695-3252
  3 Belcher St Plainville (02762) *(G-11435)*

Lakeside Software LLC **(PA)**..........................**248 686-1700**
  2 Oliver St Ste 700 Boston (02109) *(G-6851)*

Lakeville Journal Company LLC **(PA)**..................**860 435-9873**
  33 Bissell St Lakeville (06039) *(G-1547)*

Lakewood Industries Inc.................................413 499-3550
  40 Downing Industrial Park Pittsfield (01201) *(G-11404)*

Lakewood Mold, Pittsfield *Also Called: Lakewood Industries Inc (G-11404)*

Lamar Advertising, Windsor *Also Called: Lamar Advertising Company (G-4285)*

Lamar Advertising Company..............................860 246-6546
  32 Midland St Windsor (06095) *(G-4285)*

Lamarre Industries LLC..................................603 889-0165
  379 Amherst St Nashua (03063) *(G-15124)*

Lamb, Chicopee *Also Called: Lamb Knitting Machine Corp (G-8044)*

Lamb & Ritchie Company Inc.............................781 941-2700
  90 Broadway Saugus (01906) *(G-11762)*

Lamb Knitting Machine Corp..............................413 592-2501
  66 New Lombard Rd Chicopee (01020) *(G-8044)*

Lambda Investors LLC...................................203 862-7000
  411 W Putnam Ave Greenwich (06830) *(G-1337)*

Lambient Technologies LLC..............................857 242-3963
  649 Massachusetts Ave Ste 4 Cambridge (02139) *(G-7627)*

Lamell Lumber Corporation..............................802 878-2475
  82a Jericho Rd Essex Junction (05452) *(G-17239)*

Laminam USA Inc.......................................905 669-6679
  156 State St Fl 5 Boston (02109) *(G-6852)*

Laminated Films & Packaging, Portsmouth *Also Called: Intercept Medical LLC (G-15410)*

Laminted Plas Dstrs Fbricators, North Billerica *Also Called: Kilder Corporation (G-10922)*

Lamitech.. 781 878-7708
  800 Hingham St Ste 200 Rockland (02370) *(G-11649)*

Lamontagne Wilbert Burial Vlt............................ 508 476-0040
  9 Main St Ste LI9 Sutton (01590) *(G-12286)*

Lampin Corporation **(PA)**.................................. **508 278-2422**
  38 River Rd Uxbridge (01569) *(G-12484)*

Lamplighter Brewing Co LLC............................... 617 945-2743
  110 N First St Cambridge (02141) *(G-7628)*

Lamplighter Brewing Co LLC **(PA)**...................... **207 650-3325**
  284 Broadway Cambridge (02139) *(G-7629)*

Lamplighter Brewing Co LLC............................... 617 945-0450
  3 Green St Woburn (01801) *(G-13599)*

Lamplighter Brewing Co., Cambridge *Also Called: Lamplighter Brewing Co LLC (G-7629)*

Lamplighter Brewing Co., Woburn *Also Called: Lamplighter Brewing Co LLC (G-13599)*

Lamson and Goodnow LLC................................. 413 625-0201
  45 Conway St Shelburne Falls (01370) *(G-11806)*

Lamson and Goodnow Mfg, Shelburne Falls *Also Called: Lamson and Goodnow LLC (G-11806)*

Lamson and Goodnow Mfg Co.............................. 413 625-6311
  45 Conway St Shelburne Falls (01370) *(G-11807)*

Lamsonsharp, Shelburne Falls *Also Called: Lamson and Goodnow Mfg Co (G-11807)*

Lanair Research & Dev Inc................................. 603 433-6134
  521 Shattuck Way Portsmouth (03801) *(G-15415)*

Lancaster Herrald, Pittsburg *Also Called: Jordan Associates (G-15328)*

Lancaster Imageworks...................................... 802 399-2418
  60 Lyman Dr Williston (05495) *(G-17738)*

Lance Industries... 401 654-5394
  1119 Douglas Ave North Providence (02904) *(G-16304)*

Lance Industries Inc **(PA)**............................... **401 365-6272**
  55 Industrial Cir Ste 3 Lincoln (02865) *(G-16144)*

Lance International, Westport *Also Called: Robert Warren LLC (G-4195)*

Lance Smith Inc.. 802 655-3354
  85 Gonyeau Rd Milton (05468) *(G-17361)*

Lanco Assembly Systems Inc **(PA)**..................... **207 773-2060**
  12 Thomas Dr Westbrook (04092) *(G-5635)*

Lanco Integrated, Westbrook *Also Called: Lanco Assembly Systems Inc (G-5635)*

Land and Sea Inc.. 603 226-3966
  25 Henniker St Concord (03301) *(G-14139)*

Land of Nod Winery LLC................................... 860 824-5225
  99 Lower Rd East Canaan (06024) *(G-922)*

Lander Group LLC.. 207 974-3104
  36a Chipmunk Ln W Greenville (04441) *(G-4850)*

Landes Enterprises LLC.................................... 508 761-7800
  859 Washington St Attleboro (02703) *(G-6030)*

Landes Family Automobile Sales, Attleboro *Also Called: Landes Enterprises LLC (G-6030)*

Landmark Bio Pbllc... 617 894-8629
  300 North Beacon St Watertown (02472) *(G-12886)*

Landmark Document Services, Stamford *Also Called: Landmark Print Inc (G-3396)*

Landmark Print Inc... 800 499-3808
  375 Fairfield Ave Bldg 3 Stamford (06902) *(G-3396)*

Landmark Window Fashions Inc............................ 781 767-3535
  5 Mear Rd Ste 4 Holbrook (02343) *(G-9177)*

Landmark, The, Worcester *Also Called: Gatehouse Media LLC (G-13728)*

Landolfi Food Corp... 609 392-1830
  77 Servistar Indus Way Westfield (01085) *(G-13178)*

Landolfi Food Products, Westfield *Also Called: Landolfi Food Corp (G-13178)*

Lane, Cheshire *Also Called: Lane Construction Corporation (G-603)*

Lane Construction Corporation **(DH)**.................. **203 235-3351**
  90 Fieldstone Ct Cheshire (06410) *(G-603)*

Lane Construction Corporation............................ 207 945-0850
  953 Odlin Rd Bangor (04401) *(G-4508)*

Lane Construction Corporation............................ 207 764-4137
  458 Reach Rd Presque Isle (04769) *(G-5301)*

Lane Construction Corporation............................ 413 637-2511
  1 Willow Hill Rd Lee (01238) *(G-9614)*

Lane Construction Corporation............................ 413 498-5586
  216 Mt Hermon Station Rd Northfield (01360) *(G-11120)*

Lane Conveyors & Drives Inc.............................. 207 989-4560
  15 Industrial Plaza Dr Brewer (04412) *(G-4616)*

Lane Industries Incorporated **(DH)**.................... **203 235-3351**
  90 Fieldstone Ct Cheshire (06410) *(G-604)*

Lane Poverty Orchard...................................... 603 448-1511
  98 Poverty Ln Lebanon (03766) *(G-14692)*

Lane Press, South Burlington *Also Called: Lane Press Inc (G-17583)*

Lane Press Inc... 877 300-5933
  87 Meadowland Dr South Burlington (05403) *(G-17583)*

Lane Printing Co Inc....................................... 781 767-4450
  210 S Franklin St Holbrook (02343) *(G-9178)*

Lane PRInting& Advertising, Holbrook *Also Called: Lane Printing Co Inc (G-9178)*

Lane Supply Company, Brewer *Also Called: Lane Conveyors & Drives Inc (G-4616)*

Lanford Manufacturing Corp............................... 978 557-0240
  43 Merrimack St Lawrence (01843) *(G-9575)*

Lank Machining Co LLC.................................... 207 286-9549
  113 Mountain Rd Arundel (04046) *(G-4410)*

Lanoco Specialty Wire Pdts Inc........................... 508 865-1500
  7 John Rd Sutton (01590) *(G-12287)*

Lansea Systtems Inc....................................... 617 877-9773
  25 Fairmount Way Quincy (02169) *(G-11526)*

Lansen Mold Co Inc.. 413 443-5328
  1 Main St Hancock (01237) *(G-9025)*

Lantheus Holdings, North Billerica *Also Called: Lantheus Holdings Inc (G-10923)*

Lantheus Holdings Inc **(PA)**............................ **978 671-8001**
  331 Treble Cove Rd North Billerica (01862) *(G-10923)*

Lantheus Medical Imaging Inc **(HQ)**................... **800 362-2668**
  331 Treble Cove Rd Bldg 200-2 North Billerica (01862) *(G-10924)*

Lantheus MI Intermediate Inc.............................. 978 671-8001
  331 Treble Cove Rd North Billerica (01862) *(G-10925)*

Lantos Tech, Foxboro *Also Called: Lantos Technologies Inc (G-8706)*

Lantos Technologies Inc................................... 781 443-7633
  124 Washington St Ste 101 Foxboro (02035) *(G-8706)*

Lantos Technologies Inc................................... 781 443-7633
  34 Route 111 Ste 8 Derry (03038) *(G-14198)*

Lanxess Corporation....................................... 203 714-8669
  400 Elm St Naugatuck (06770) *(G-1970)*

Lanxess Solutions US Inc.................................. 203 573-2000
  2 Armstrong Rd Ste 101 Shelton (06484) *(G-3027)*

Laplume & Sons Printing Inc............................... 978 683-1009
  1 Farley St Lawrence (01843) *(G-9576)*

Lapoint Industries Inc **(PA)**............................ **207 777-3100**
  65 First Flight Dr Auburn (04210) *(G-4439)*

Lapointe Hudson Broach Co Inc........................... 978 562-7943
  11 Brent Dr Hudson (01749) *(G-9383)*

Laporte Division, Concord *Also Called: Graphic Packaging Intl LLC (G-14132)*

Lar Plastics LLC... 617 860-2020
  3 Arbor Ln Winchester (01890) *(G-13485)*

Larcoline Inc **(PA)**..................................... **802 864-5440**
  113 Acorn Ln Ste 2 Colchester (05446) *(G-17197)*

Largo Clean Energy Corp **(HQ)**........................ **978 566-8220**
  500 Research Dr Ste 1 Wilmington (01887) *(G-13425)*

Lariat Biosciences Inc..................................... 603 244-9657
  39 John St Chelsea (02150) *(G-7985)*

Larosa Manufacturing LLC................................. 860 819-7066
  15 Hultenius St Plainville (06062) *(G-2767)*

Larose Rf Systems, Millis *Also Called: Radio Frequency Company Inc (G-10450)*

Larry Dingee... 603 542-9682
  195 Nh Route 120 Cornish (03745) *(G-14183)*

Larry G Carabeau.. 802 446-3123
  59a East Rd Tinmouth (05773) *(G-17648)*

Larson Tool & Stamping Company......................... 508 222-0897
  90 Olive St Attleboro (02703) *(G-6031)*

Lase Innovation Inc.. 617 599-0003
  16 Tower Office Park Woburn (01801) *(G-13600)*

Laser Advantage LLC....................................... 603 886-9464
  4 Townsend W Ste 2 Nashua (03063) *(G-15125)*

Laser Body Solutions, Hamden *Also Called: Jeffrey Gold (G-1434)*

Laser Fare Inc **(PA)**.................................... **401 231-4400**
  1 Industrial Dr S Smithfield (02917) *(G-16721)*

Laser Group Publishing Inc................................ 603 880-8909
  177 East Industrial Park Dr Manchester (03109) *(G-14876)*

Laser Light Engines Inc.................................... 603 952-4550
  8 Industrial Way Ste C6 Salem (03079) *(G-15542)*

Laser Process Mfg Inc..................................... 978 531-6003
  2 Centennial Dr Ste 6 Peabody (01960) *(G-11323)*

A L P H A B E T I C

Laser Projection Technologies Inc.............................603 421-0209
  8 Delta Dr Unit 9 Londonderry (03053) *(G-14762)*

Laser Tool Co Inc...860 283-8284
  98 N Main St Thomaston (06787) *(G-3623)*

Lasercraze...978 689-7700
  1580 Osgood St Ste 2210 North Andover (01845) *(G-10843)*

Laservall North America LLC..................................401 724-0076
  136 Newell Ave Pawtucket (02860) *(G-16382)*

Laserwords Maine..207 782-9595
  1775 Lisbon St Lewiston (04240) *(G-4970)*

Lashway Firewood Co, Williamsburg *Also Called: Lashway Logging Inc (G-13365)*

Lashway Logging Inc...413 268-3600
  67 Main St Williamsburg (01096) *(G-13365)*

Lassy Tools Inc..860 747-2748
  96 Bohemia St Plainville (06062) *(G-2768)*

Latex Foam Products, Shelton *Also Called: Talalay Global Inc (G-3067)*

Laticrete International Inc **(PA)**...........................**203 393-0010**
  1 Laticrete Park N Bethany (06524) *(G-94)*

Laticrete Supercap LLC...203 393-4558
  91 Amity Rd Bethany (06524) *(G-95)*

Latin American Holding Inc **(HQ)**.........................**860 674-3000**
  1 Carrier Pl Farmington (06032) *(G-1228)*

Latino Multiservice LLC...203 691-9715
  552 Ferry St New Haven (06513) *(G-2168)*

Latva Machine LLC..603 863-5155
  744 John Stark Hwy Newport (03773) *(G-15229)*

Laughing Whale, Searsport *Also Called: Bluejacket Inc (G-5451)*

Launchpad Electric Solutions..................................603 828-2919
  24 Hillcrest Ave Kittery (03904) *(G-4936)*

Launchworks LLC..978 338-3045
  123 Brimbal Ave Beverly (01915) *(G-6361)*

Launchworks Manufacturing Lab, Beverly *Also Called: Launchworks LLC (G-6361)*

Laurence Cndle Mfg Ch Sups Inc **(PA)**...............**508 865-6061**
  10 West St Millbury (01527) *(G-10439)*

Lauretano Sign Group Inc.......................................860 582-0233
  1 Tremco Dr Terryville (06786) *(G-3605)*

Laurin Publishing Co Inc **(PA)**............................**413 499-0514**
  100 West St Pittsfield (01201) *(G-11405)*

Lauzon Machine and Engrg Inc.................................802 442-3116
  757 Main St Bennington (05201) *(G-17048)*

Lauzon's Machine & Engineering, Bennington *Also Called: Lauzon Machine and Engrg Inc (G-17048)*

Lavallee Machinery Inc...508 764-2896
  831 Main St Southbridge (01550) *(G-12027)*

Lavelle Machine & Tool Co Inc.................................978 692-8825
  485 Groton Rd Westford (01886) *(G-13245)*

Lavigne Manufacturing Inc......................................401 490-4627
  15 Western Industrial Dr Cranston (02921) *(G-15883)*

Lavo USA LLC..781 600-4123
  98 Thornberry Rd Winchester (01890) *(G-13486)*

Lavoie Industries LLC..508 542-1062
  969 Charles St Fall River (02724) *(G-8568)*

Lawrence & Co, Lewiston *Also Called: White Rock Distilleries Inc (G-4997)*

Lawrence Holdings Inc...203 949-1600
  34b Barnes Industrial Rd S Wallingford (06492) *(G-3826)*

Lawrence Parson..207 935-3737
  510 Hampshire Rd Brownfield (04010) *(G-4636)*

Lawrence Pumps, Lawrence *Also Called: Flowserve US Inc (G-9563)*

Lawrence Pumps Inc..978 682-5248
  371 Market St Lawrence (01843) *(G-9577)*

Lawrence Ready-Mix, Sandwich *Also Called: Boston Sand & Gravel Company (G-11747)*

Lawrence Sigler...510 782-6737
  314 Ball Hill Rd Princeton (01541) *(G-11495)*

Lawson Hemphill Inc...508 679-5364
  1658 Gar Hwy Ste 5 Swansea (02777) *(G-12305)*

Lawton Truck Equipment Inc....................................978 887-0005
  240 Boston St Topsfield (01983) *(G-12436)*

Lawyers Weekly LLC **(PA)**..................................**617 451-7300**
  40 Court St Fl 5 Boston (02108) *(G-6853)*

Laydon Industries LLC **(PA)**...............................**203 562-7283**
  299 Terminal Ln New Haven (06519) *(G-2169)*

Lbh Jr, Barre *Also Called: Hutchins Roofing Company Inc (G-17007)*

Lcd Lighting Inc..203 799-7877
  37 Robinson Blvd Orange (06477) *(G-2674)*

LCI Paper Company...508 281-5088
  399 River Rd Ste 3 Hudson (01749) *(G-9384)*

Lcs Controls Inc...802 767-3128
  1678 Vt Route 100 S Rochester (05767) *(G-17486)*

LD Plastics Inc...508 584-7651
  1130 Pearl St Brockton (02301) *(G-7289)*

Lda Construction LLC..203 469-3180
  459 Main St East Haven (06512) *(G-1044)*

Ldc Inc...401 861-4667
  22 First St East Providence (02914) *(G-16029)*

Ldg Corporation...781 337-7155
  143 Moore Rd East Weymouth (02189) *(G-8432)*

LDI Solutions LLC...603 436-0077
  145 Airport Dr Rochester (03867) *(G-15485)*

LDM Manufacturing Inc..860 410-9804
  20 Hultenius St Ste S Plainville (06062) *(G-2769)*

LDR Care Inc..978 786-5110
  162 Park Ln Concord (01742) *(G-8122)*

Ldr Inc..978 825-0020
  35 Congress St Salem (01970) *(G-11726)*

Le Bel Inc..781 878-7279
  380 North Ave Abington (02351) *(G-5725)*

LE Weed & Son LLC **(PA)**...............................**603 863-1540**
  187 S Main St Newport (03773) *(G-15230)*

Leader Dist Systems Inc...802 254-6093
  1566 Putney Rd Brattleboro (05301) *(G-17093)*

Leading Edge Aero LLC...203 797-1200
  15 Berkshire Blvd Ste A Bethel (06801) *(G-125)*

Leading Edge Concepts Inc.....................................203 797-1200
  15 Berkshire Blvd Ste A Bethel (06801) *(G-126)*

Leading Market Tech Inc...617 494-4747
  58 Winter St Ste 5 Boston (02108) *(G-6854)*

Leaf Pharmaceuticals LLC.......................................781 305-4192
  216 W Cummings Park Woburn (01801) *(G-13601)*

Leaktite, Leominster *Also Called: Leaktite Corporation (G-9676)*

Leaktite Corporation **(DH)**.................................**978 537-8000**
  40 Francis St Leominster (01453) *(G-9676)*

Leanix Inc **(DH)**...**781 321-6500**
  1 Kingsbury Ave Watertown (02472) *(G-12887)*

Leap Pond LLC..203 361-9200
  3 Schooner Ln Ste 15 Milford (06460) *(G-1844)*

Leap Therapeutics, Cambridge *Also Called: Leap Therapeutics Inc (G-7630)*

Leap Therapeutics Inc **(PA)**..............................**617 714-0360**
  47 Thorndike St Ste B1-1 Cambridge (02141) *(G-7630)*

Leap Year Publishing LLC.......................................978 688-9900
  54 Pleasant St Newburyport (01950) *(G-10695)*

Learjet Inc..860 627-9491
  85-173 Bradley Intl Airport Windsor Locks (06096) *(G-4331)*

Learning Pool Inc **(PA)**....................................**857 284-1420**
  77 Sleeper St Boston (02210) *(G-6855)*

Learntoprogram Media, Bridgeport *Also Called: Learntoprogramtv Incorporated (G-344)*

Learntoprogramtv Incorporated.................................860 840-7090
  1000 Lafayette Blvd Bridgeport (06604) *(G-344)*

Leavers Lace Corporation.......................................401 397-5555
  144 Mishnock Rd West Greenwich (02817) *(G-16887)*

Leavitt & Parris Inc...207 797-0100
  256 Read St Portland (04103) *(G-5233)*

Lebanon Screw Products Inc....................................802 674-6347
  39 Park Rd Windsor (05089) *(G-17759)*

Leblanc Enterprises Inc..978 682-5112
  11 Glenn St Lawrence (01843) *(G-9578)*

Lebon Press, West Hartford *Also Called: Lebon Press Incorporated (G-4066)*

Lebon Press Incorporated.......................................860 278-6355
  30 Osage Rd West Hartford (06117) *(G-4066)*

Leddynamics Inc..802 728-4533
  296 Beanville Rd Randolph (05060) *(G-17470)*

Ledgeview Printing, Westford *Also Called: May Graphics & Printing Inc (G-13250)*

Ledor Jewelry, Plainville *Also Called: Titus Engrv & Stonesetting Inc (G-11443)*

Ledsupply, Randolph *Also Called: Leddynamics Inc (G-17470)*

Lee Company.. 860 399-6281
22 Pequot Park Rd Westbrook (06498) *(G-4139)*

Lee Company **(PA)**.. **860 399-6281**
2 Pettipaug Rd Westbrook (06498) *(G-4140)*

Lee Company HC.. 860 399-6281
2 Pettipaug Rd Westbrook (06498) *(G-4141)*

Lee Electric Inc... 978 777-0070
128 Maple St Danvers (01923) *(G-8198)*

Lee Manufacturing Inc.. 203 284-0466
46 Barnes Industrial Rd S Wallingford (06492) *(G-3827)*

Lee Plastics Inc... 978 422-7611
102 Pratts Junction Rd Sterling (01564) *(G-12166)*

Lee Spring Company LLC.. 860 584-0991
245 Lake Ave Bristol (06010) *(G-461)*

Lee Tan Enterprise LLC.. 413 243-4717
265 Greylock St Lee (01238) *(G-9615)*

Lee Tire, Topsham *Also Called: Lag Inc (G-5548)*

Lee Tool Co Inc... 413 583-8750
40 Ravenwood Dr Ludlow (01056) *(G-9948)*

Leeco Inc.. 860 404-8876
5 Alexandra Ln Avon (06001) *(G-28)*

Leed - Himmel Industries Inc...................................... 203 288-8484
75 Leeder Hill Dr Hamden (06517) *(G-1436)*

Leedon Webbing Co Inc.. 401 722-1043
86 Tremont St Central Falls (02863) *(G-15791)*

Leejay Industries LLC... 203 847-3660
151 Woodward Ave Norwalk (06854) *(G-2526)*

Leek Building Products Inc.. 203 853-3883
205 Wilson Ave Ste 3 Norwalk (06854) *(G-2527)*

Lees Concrete Inc.. 207 974-4936
974 Odlin Rd Bangor (04401) *(G-4509)*

Lees Manufacturing Co Inc.. 401 275-2383
160 Niantic Ave Providence (02907) *(G-16552)*

Lees Tire.. 207 729-1676
27 Monument Pl Topsham (04086) *(G-5549)*

Lefort Fine Furniture, Halifax *Also Called: David Lefort (G-9020)*

Left-Tees Designs Bayou, Derry *Also Called: Left-Tees Designs Bayou LLC (G-14199)*

Left-Tees Designs Bayou LLC...................................... 603 437-6630
15 W Broadway Ste 2 Derry (03038) *(G-14199)*

Legacy Broadcast Inc... 978 330-9300
101 Billerica Ave North Billerica (01862) *(G-10926)*

Legacy Global Sports LP.. 603 373-7262
290 Heritage Ave Portsmouth (03801) *(G-15416)*

Legacy Machine & Mfg LLC... 978 388-0956
43 Clinton St Amesbury (01913) *(G-5841)*

Legacy Publishing Group Inc....................................... 800 322-3866
75 Green St Ste 1 Clinton (01510) *(G-8080)*

Legacy Woodworking LLC... 203 592-8807
49 Birchwood Ter Middlebury (06762) *(G-1716)*

Legal Affairs Inc... 203 865-2520
115 Blake Rd Hamden (06517) *(G-1437)*

LEGAL AFFAIRS MAGAZINE, Hamden *Also Called: Legal Affairs Inc (G-1437)*

Legere Group Ltd... 860 674-0392
80 Darling Dr Avon (06001) *(G-29)*

Legere Woodworking, Avon *Also Called: Legere Group Ltd (G-29)*

Leggett & Platt Incorporated....................................... 860 635-8811
422 Timber Ridge Rd Middletown (06457) *(G-1758)*

Leggett & Platt Incorporated....................................... 508 987-8706
23 Dana Rd Oxford (01540) *(G-11258)*

Leggett Platt Arspc Mddltown L.................................... 860 635-8811
422 Timber Ridge Rd Middletown (06457) *(G-1759)*

Legnos Boat Industries, Groton *Also Called: B I L Inc (G-1365)*

Lego Brand Retail, Enfield *Also Called: Lego Systems Inc (G-1137)*

Lego Systems Inc **(DH)**... **860 698-9367**
100 Print Shop Rd Enfield (06082) *(G-1137)*

Legrand, West Hartford *Also Called: Ortronics Inc (G-4076)*

Legrand Holding Inc **(DH)**....................................... **860 233-6251**
60 Woodlawn St West Hartford (06110) *(G-4067)*

Lehi, Westborough *Also Called: Lehi Sheet Metal Corporation (G-13116)*

Lehi Sheet Metal Corporation...................................... 508 366-8550
245 Flanders Rd Westborough (01581) *(G-13116)*

Lehvoss North America LLC... 860 495-2046
185 S Broad St Ste 2b Pawcatuck (06379) *(G-2723)*

Leica Biosystems.. 978 471-0625
38 Cherry Hill Dr Danvers (01923) *(G-8199)*

Leica Geosystems Inc.. 203 744-8362
81 Kenosia Ave Ste 6 Danbury (06810) *(G-768)*

LEICA GEOSYSTEMS, INC., Danbury *Also Called: Leica Geosystems Inc (G-768)*

Leidos Inc.. 781 221-7627
1 Radcliff Rd Tewksbury (01876) *(G-12402)*

Leidos Inc.. 401 849-8900
28 Jacome Way Ste A Middletown (02842) *(G-16178)*

Leidos SEC Dtction Automtn Inc................................... 781 939-3800
179 Ferry Rd 181 Haverhill (01835) *(G-9108)*

Leidos SEC Dtction Automtn Inc................................... 571 526-6000
1 Radcliff Rd Ste 300 Tewksbury (01876) *(G-12403)*

Leidos SEC Dtction Automtn Inc................................... 781 939-3800
1 Radcliff Rd Tewksbury (01876) *(G-12404)*

Leipold Inc... 860 298-9791
545 Marshall Phelps Rd Windsor (06095) *(G-4286)*

Leisure Group, Stamford *Also Called: Leisure Learning Products Inc (G-3397)*

Leisure Learning Products Inc..................................... 203 325-2800
652 Glenbrook Rd Bldg 8 Stamford (06906) *(G-3397)*

Leisure Time Canvas Inc.. 413 785-5500
140 Norman St West Springfield (01089) *(G-13032)*

Leisure Zone, Putnam *Also Called: Leisure Zone Stores Inc (G-2863)*

Leisure Zone Stores Inc... 860 963-1181
164 Providence Pike Putnam (06260) *(G-2863)*

Leland Boggs II... 207 273-2610
715 Camden Rd Warren (04864) *(G-5583)*

Lelanite Corporation **(PA)**...................................... **508 987-2637**
1 Cudworth Rd Webster (01570) *(G-12929)*

LEMAITRE, Burlington *Also Called: Lemaitre Vascular Inc (G-7389)*

Lemaitre Vascular Inc **(PA)**..................................... **781 221-2266**
63 2nd Ave Burlington (01803) *(G-7389)*

Lemon Press Market LLC.. 508 228-3800
29 Center St Nantucket (02554) *(G-10464)*

Len Libby Candy Shops, Scarborough *Also Called: Len Libbys Inc (G-5437)*

Len Libbys Inc.. 207 883-4897
419 Us Route 1 Scarborough (04074) *(G-5437)*

Len-Tex Corp.. 603 445-2342
18 Len Tex Ln North Walpole (03609) *(G-15260)*

Len-Tex Wallcoverings, North Walpole *Also Called: Len-Tex Corp (G-15260)*

Lenco Armored Vehicles, Pittsfield *Also Called: Lenco Industries Inc (G-11406)*

Lenco Industries Inc.. 413 443-7359
10 Betnr Industrial Dr Pittsfield (01201) *(G-11406)*

Leni's Textiles, Canton *Also Called: Lenis Inc (G-7805)*

Lenis Inc.. 781 401-3273
480 Neponset St Ste 4a Canton (02021) *(G-7805)*

Lenmarine Inc.. 508 678-1234
1 Main St Somerset (02726) *(G-11852)*

Lenmarine Inc **(PA)**... **401 253-2200**
99 Poppasquash Rd Ste 1 Bristol (02809) *(G-15772)*

Lennartz Enterprises LLC... 978 663-6100
41 Simon St Ste 1d Nashua (03060) *(G-15126)*

Lenox, East Longmeadow *Also Called: American Saw & Mfg Company Inc (G-8369)*

Lenox, East Longmeadow *Also Called: Newell Brands Inc (G-8388)*

Lenox Dale Hot Mix Asp Aggrgat, Lee *Also Called: Lane Construction Corporation (G-9614)*

Lenox Special Needs.. 413 637-5571
129 West St Lenox (01240) *(G-9626)*

Lenric Corp.. 603 886-6772
44 Simon St Nashua (03060) *(G-15127)*

Lenscrafters... 203 878-8511
1201 Boston Post Rd # 20 Milford (06460) *(G-1845)*

Lensesonly LLC.. 860 769-2020
812 Park Ave Bloomfield (06002) *(G-187)*

Lentros Engineering Inc... 508 881-1160
280 Eliot St Ashland (01721) *(G-5961)*

Lenze Americas Corporation **(DH)**............................ **508 278-9100**
630 Douglas St Uxbridge (01569) *(G-12485)*

Leo Algers NH Elc Mtrs Inc.................................... 603 524-3729
459 Province Rd Laconia (03246) *(G-14658)*

Leo Concrete Service Inc...................................... 413 536-3370
652 Prospect St Chicopee (01020) *(G-8045)*

Leo D Bernstein & Sons Inc.................................... 802 442-8029
372 Vt Route 67 E Shaftsbury (05262) *(G-17550)*

Leo D Bernstein and Sons Inc.................................. 212 337-9578
372 Vt Route 67 E Shaftsbury (05262) *(G-17551)*

Leo F Maciver Co Inc... 508 583-2501
75 Ames St Brockton (02302) *(G-7290)*

Leo's Bakery, Boston *Also Called: Begum Brands Corporation* *(G-6588)*

Leominster Champion.. 978 534-6006
285 Central St Ste 202b Leominster (01453) *(G-9677)*

Leominster Ice & Oil Co, Leominster *Also Called: Leominster Ice Company Inc* *(G-9678)*

Leominster Ice Company Inc.................................... 978 537-5322
5 Chestnut St Leominster (01453) *(G-9678)*

Leon Eg Company Inc... 617 482-8383
1234 Washington St Boston (02118) *(G-6856)*

Leon Electric, Boston *Also Called: Leon Eg Company Inc* *(G-6856)*

Leonard Valve Company LLC................................... 800 222-1208
1360 Elmwood Ave Cranston (02910) *(G-15884)*

Leos Kitchen and Stair Corp.................................. 860 225-7363
48 John St New Britain (06051) *(G-2037)*

Leos Small Engines Inc.. 802 888-7247
541 Vt Route 15 E Morrisville (05661) *(G-17384)*

Lepage Bakeries Inc.. 207 783-9161
11 Adamian Dr Auburn (04210) *(G-4440)*

Lepage Bakeries Park St LLC.................................. 207 783-9161
11 Adamian Dr Auburn (04210) *(G-4441)*

Lepage Bakeries Park St LLC (HQ)........................... **207 783-9161**
415 Lisbon St # 4 Lewiston (04240) *(G-4971)*

Lepage Bakeries Park St LLC.................................. 207 783-9161
354 Lisbon St Lewiston (04240) *(G-4972)*

Lepage Bakeries Park St LLC.................................. 603 880-4446
2 Security Dr Hudson (03051) *(G-14521)*

Leppert/Nutmeg Inc.. 860 243-1737
113 W Dudley Town Rd Bloomfield (06002) *(G-188)*

Lesco.. 203 353-0061
52b Poplar St Stamford (06907) *(G-3398)*

Lesro Industries Inc.. 800 275-7545
1 Griffin Rd S Bloomfield (06002) *(G-189)*

Lesser Evil.. 203 529-3555
18 Finance Dr Danbury (06810) *(G-769)*

Lessonbee Inc.. 646 582-2040
700 Canal St Ste 42a Stamford (06902) *(G-3399)*

Lestat Production 81 Corp..................................... 866 557-4478
3 Executive Park Dr Ste 223 Bedford (03110) *(G-13939)*

Lets Go Inc... 617 495-9659
67 Mount Auburn St Cambridge (02138) *(G-7631)*

Letter Systems Inc (PA)....................................... **207 622-7126**
15 Darin Dr Augusta (04330) *(G-4475)*

Lettering Inc of New York (PA)............................... **203 329-7759**
255 Mill Rd Stamford (06903) *(G-3400)*

Leusin Microwave LLC.. 603 329-7270
6 Gigante Dr Hampstead (03841) *(G-14384)*

Leveillee Archtctral Mllwk Inc................................ 508 885-9731
23 S Spencer Rd Spencer (01562) *(G-12062)*

Lew A Cummings Co Inc.. 603 625-6901
4 Peters Brook Dr Hooksett (03106) *(G-14467)*

Lewa Process Technologies Inc................................ 978 487-1100
8 Charlestown St Devens (01434) *(G-8275)*

Lewa-Nikkiso America Inc (DH)............................... **508 429-7403**
132 Hopping Brook Rd Holliston (01746) *(G-9220)*

Lewicki & Sons Excavating Inc................................ 508 695-0122
15 Wilmarth Ln Plainville (02762) *(G-11436)*

Lewis Bible Bindery, Hartland *Also Called: Darwin A Lewis Inc* *(G-17286)*

Lewis Machine LLC.. 860 289-3468
22 John St East Hartford (06108) *(G-1003)*

Lewiston Daily Sun (PA).. **207 784-3555**
104 Park St Lewiston (04240) *(G-4973)*

Lewiston-Auburn Tent & Awng Co............................ 207 784-7353
240 River Rd Lewiston (04240) *(G-4974)*

Lewmar Inc (DH)... **203 458-6200**
2351 Boston Post Rd Ste 503 Guilford (06437) *(G-1399)*

Lewmar Marine, Guilford *Also Called: Lewmar Inc* *(G-1399)*

Lewtan Industries Corporation................................ 860 278-9800
57 Loomis Dr Apt A1 West Hartford (06107) *(G-4068)*

Lex, Trumbull *Also Called: Lex Products LLC* *(G-3723)*

Lex Products LLC (PA)... **203 363-3738**
35 Nutmeg Dr Ste 205 Trumbull (06611) *(G-3723)*

Lexia Learning Systems LLC................................... 800 435-3942
300 Baker Ave Ste 320 Concord (01742) *(G-8123)*

Lexington Data Incorporated................................. 603 899-5673
316 Main St Rindge (03461) *(G-15460)*

Lexington Graphics Inc.. 781 863-9510
76 Bedford St Ste 6 Lexington (02420) *(G-9758)*

Lexington Lighting Group LLC................................ 860 564-4512
181 Narragansett Park Dr Rumford (02916) *(G-16674)*

Lexisnexis, Newton *Also Called: Relx Inc* *(G-10780)*

Lfb Usa Inc (DH)... **508 370-5100**
175 Crossing Blvd Ste 420 Framingham (01702) *(G-8785)*

Lfb Usa Inc... 508 370-5100
300 Charlton Rd Spencer (01562) *(G-12063)*

Lfi Inc (PA).. **401 231-4400**
1 Ind Dr S Smithfield (02917) *(G-16722)*

Lfr Chassis Inc.. 508 425-3117
20 Sewall St Shrewsbury (01545) *(G-11837)*

Lg Energy Solution Vertech Inc (DH)........................ **508 497-7319**
155 Flanders Rd Westborough (01581) *(G-13117)*

Lgc Clinical Diagnostics Inc.................................. 207 892-1300
221 Us Route 1 Cumberland Foreside (04110) *(G-4712)*

Lgntcs of England... 603 532-4666
141 Old Sharon Rd Jaffrey (03452) *(G-14571)*

LH Gault & Son Incorporated................................. 203 227-5181
11 Ferry Ln W Westport (06880) *(G-4180)*

Lh Liquidation LLC.. 207 893-8233
765 Roosevelt Trl Windham (04062) *(G-5664)*

Lhi Metals, Wallingford *Also Called: Tico Titanium Inc* *(G-3864)*

Liberty Compassion Inc.. 978 213-8757
179 Brook St Clinton (01510) *(G-8081)*

Liberty Cycle LLC... 603 620-1851
113 E Deering Rd Deering (03244) *(G-14188)*

Liberty Engineering Inc.. 617 965-6644
26 Farwell St Newton (02460) *(G-10768)*

Liberty Enrgy Utlities NH Corp (DH)......................... **905 287-2061**
15 Buttrick Rd Londonderry (03053) *(G-14763)*

Liberty Garage Inc.. 203 778-0222
51 Sugar Hollow Rd Ste 1 Danbury (06810) *(G-770)*

Liberty Glass and Met Inds Inc............................... 860 923-3623
339 Riverside Dr North Grosvenordale (06255) *(G-2384)*

Liberty Graphics, Liberty *Also Called: Liberty Graphics Inc* *(G-4999)*

Liberty Graphics Inc... 207 589-4596
Main St Liberty (04949) *(G-4999)*

Liberty Industries Inc.. 860 828-6361
133 Commerce St East Berlin (06023) *(G-913)*

Liberty Machine Inc.. 207 376-6224
189 Yarmouth Rd Gray (04039) *(G-4842)*

Liberty Mtals Min Holdings LLC.............................. 617 654-4374
175 Berkeley St Boston (02116) *(G-6857)*

Liberty Plastics Company, Attleboro *Also Called: Applied Precision Technology* *(G-5994)*

Liberty Printing Co Inc... 508 586-6810
99 Lawrence St Brockton (02302) *(G-7291)*

Liberty Publishing Inc... 978 777-8200
100 Cummings Ctr Beverly (01915) *(G-6362)*

Liberty Research Co Inc (PA)................................. **603 332-2730**
7 Nadeau Dr Rochester (03867) *(G-15486)*

Liberty Screen Print Co, Beacon Falls *Also Called: Liberty Screen Print Co LLC* *(G-41)*

Liberty Screen Print Co LLC................................... 203 632-5449
141 S Main St Beacon Falls (06403) *(G-41)*

Liberty Utilities, Londonderry *Also Called: Liberty Enrgy Utilities NH Corp* *(G-14763)*

Libring Technologies Inc...................................... 617 553-1015
1 Broadway Fl 14 Cambridge (02142) *(G-7632)*

Lie-Nielsen Toolworks Inc..................................... 800 327-2520
264 Stirling Rd Warren (04864) *(G-5584)*

Life Chemicals Usa Inc.. 203 693-4563
26 Selden St Ste B Woodbridge (06525) *(G-4380)*

Life Force Beverages LLC.. 551 265-9482
196 Quincy St Boston (02121) *(G-6858)*

Life Image Inc... 617 244-8411
300 Washington St Ste 200 Newton (02458) *(G-10769)*

Life Is Good Design Center, Hudson *Also Called: Life Is Good Wholesale Inc* *(G-14523)*

Life Is Good Retail Inc **(PA)**... **603 594-6100**
15 Hudson Park Dr Hudson (03051) *(G-14522)*

Life Is Good Wholesale Inc... 603 594-6100
15 Hudson Park Dr Hudson (03051) *(G-14523)*

Life Publications.. 860 953-0444
106 South St Ste 5 West Hartford (06110) *(G-4069)*

Life Study Fllwship Foundation.. 203 655-1436
90 Heights Rd Darien (06820) *(G-851)*

Life Technologies Corporation.. 508 383-7700
500 Old Connecticut Path Ste 10 Framingham (01701) *(G-8786)*

Life+gear Inc... 858 755-2099
21 Cushing Rd Wellesley Hills (02481) *(G-12952)*

Lifecloud Inc... 978 621-9572
6 Lancewood Dr Amesbury (01913) *(G-5842)*

Lifeglobal Group, The, Guilford *Also Called: Coopersurgical Inc* *(G-1390)*

Lifeimage, Newton *Also Called: Life Image Inc* *(G-10769)*

Lifeline, Framingham *Also Called: Lifeline Systems Company* *(G-8787)*

Lifeline Systems Company **(HQ)**....................................... **855 600-6127**
111 Lawrence St Framingham (01702) *(G-8787)*

Lifetoken Software Inc... 203 515-9686
22 Daffodil Ln Cos Cob (06807) *(G-678)*

Lifoam Industries, Peabody *Also Called: Lifoam Industries LLC* *(G-11324)*

Lifoam Industries LLC.. 978 278-0008
2 5th St Peabody (01960) *(G-11324)*

Liftbag Usa Inc... 401 884-8801
6946 Post Rd North Kingstown (02852) *(G-16267)*

Liftline Capital LLC... 860 395-0150
7 Center Rd W Old Saybrook (06475) *(G-2654)*

Liftwing LLC... 203 913-2308
12 Commerce Dr Shelton (06484) *(G-3028)*

Light Logic Inc.. 802 888-7984
902 Silver Ridge Rd Hyde Park (05655) *(G-17300)*

Light Metal Platers LLC.. 781 899-8855
70 Clematis Ave Waltham (02453) *(G-12709)*

Light Metals Coloring Co Inc.. 860 621-0145
270 Spring St Southington (06489) *(G-3219)*

Light Rock Beverage, Danbury *Also Called: Light Rock Spring Water Co* *(G-771)*

Light Rock Spring Water Co... 203 743-2251
9 Balmforth Ave Danbury (06810) *(G-771)*

Lightblocks Inc... 603 889-1115
33 Elm St Bldg 6 Merrimack (03054) *(G-14989)*

Lighthouse Distributors Inc... 781 319-9828
864 Plain St Marshfield (02050) *(G-10241)*

Lighthouse International LLC... 860 528-4722
125 S Satellite Rd South Windsor (06074) *(G-3161)*

Lighthouse Manufacturing LLC.. 978 532-5999
35 Mirona Road Ext Portsmouth (03801) *(G-15417)*

Lighting By Hammerworks **(PA)**....................................... **508 755-3434**
6 Fremont St Worcester (01603) *(G-13753)*

Lighting Quotient, The, West Haven *Also Called: Sylvan R Shemitz Designs LLC* *(G-4127)*

Lightlab Imaging Inc.. 978 577-3400
4 Robbins Rd Westford (01886) *(G-13246)*

Lightlife Foods Inc.. 413 774-9000
153 Industrial Blvd Turners Falls (01376) *(G-12451)*

Lightlines, Farmington *Also Called: Kevin Emery* *(G-14310)*

Lightmatter Inc... 857 244-0460
100 Summer St Ste 1850 Boston (02110) *(G-6859)*

Lightolier, Burlington *Also Called: Signify North America Corp* *(G-7428)*

Lightship Group LLC **(PA)**.. **401 294-3341**
606 Ten Rod Rd Unit 6 North Kingstown (02852) *(G-16268)*

Lightspeed Mfg Co LLC.. 978 521-7676
63 Neck Rd Haverhill (01835) *(G-9109)*

Lightstat Inc... 860 738-4111
22 W West Hill Rd Pleasant Valley (06063) *(G-2802)*

Lignetics New England Inc.. 413 284-1050
21 Wilbraham St Unit B13 Palmer (01069) *(G-11275)*

Lignetics New England Inc.. 603 532-4666
415 Squantum Rd Jaffrey (03452) *(G-14572)*

Lignetics New England Inc.. 603 532-4666
141 Old Sharon Rd Jaffrey (03452) *(G-14573)*

Lignetics of Maine.. 207 684-3457
30 Norton Hill Rd Strong (04983) *(G-5536)*

Like Nu Electric Motor Service, Fairfax *Also Called: Apex Sealing Inc* *(G-17254)*

Lilac and Finch, Chichester *Also Called: Heleka Companies LLC* *(G-14073)*

Lilac and Finch, Manchester *Also Called: Heleka Companies LLC* *(G-14858)*

Lilly's Fresh Pasta, Everett *Also Called: Lillys Gstronomia Italiana Inc* *(G-8490)*

Lillys Gstronomia Italiana Inc.. 617 387-9666
208 Main St Everett (02149) *(G-8490)*

Lima Fredy.. 781 599-3055
128 Spring St Everett (02149) *(G-8491)*

LImage Inc.. 401 369-7141
4 Industrial Ln Johnston (02919) *(G-16093)*

Limat Graphics Inc... 203 798-9771
128 E Liberty St Danbury (06810) *(G-772)*

Limelight Productions Inc... 413 243-4950
471 Pleasant St Lee (01238) *(G-9616)*

Limerick Machine Co, Limerick *Also Called: Limerick Machine Company Inc* *(G-5003)*

Limerick Machine Company Inc.. 207 793-2288
81 Central Ave Limerick (04048) *(G-5003)*

Limington Lumber, East Baldwin *Also Called: Robbins Lumber E Baldwin LLC* *(G-4735)*

Limlaws Pulpwood Inc... 802 439-3503
261 Vt Route 25 West Topsham (05086) *(G-17698)*

Limo Chipping and Land Query, West Topsham *Also Called: Limlaws Pulpwood Inc* *(G-17698)*

Limoge & Sons Garage Doors, Williston *Also Called: Limoge & Sons Garage Doors Inc* *(G-17739)*

Limoge & Sons Garage Doors Inc..................................... 802 878-4338
136 James Brown Dr Williston (05495) *(G-17739)*

Limra International Inc **(PA)**.. **860 688-3358**
300 Day Hill Rd Windsor (06095) *(G-4287)*

Lincoln County News, Newcastle *Also Called: Lincoln County Publishing Co* *(G-5093)*

Lincoln County Publishing Co.. 207 563-3171
116 Mills Rd Newcastle (04553) *(G-5093)*

Lincoln Hoist, North Grafton *Also Called: Lincoln Precision Machining Co* *(G-11024)*

Lincoln News... 207 794-6532
78 W Broadway Lincoln (04457) *(G-5010)*

Lincoln Packing Co... 401 943-0878
7 Industrial Rd Cranston (02920) *(G-15885)*

Lincoln Paper and Tissue LLC... 207 794-0600
50 Katadin Ave Lincoln (04457) *(G-5011)*

Lincoln Precision Machining Co....................................... 508 839-2175
121 Creeper Hill Rd North Grafton (01536) *(G-11024)*

Lincoln Press Co Inc... 508 673-3241
407 Pleasant St Fall River (02721) *(G-8569)*

Lincoln Thompson... 860 516-0472
220 Business Park Dr Bristol (06010) *(G-462)*

Lincoln Tool & Machine Corp... 508 485-2940
43 Parmenter Rd Hudson (01749) *(G-9385)*

Lincoln, RI Plant, Lincoln *Also Called: Prysmian Cbles Systems USA LLC* *(G-16151)*

Linde Advanced Mtl Tech Inc... 203 837-2000
10 Riverview Dr Danbury (06810) *(G-773)*

Linde Advanced Mtl Tech Inc... 860 646-0700
1366 Tolland Tpke Manchester (06042) *(G-1612)*

Linde Advanced Mtl Tech Inc... 207 282-3787
24 Landry St Biddeford (04005) *(G-4575)*

Linde Advanced Mtl Tech Inc... 603 224-9585
146 Pembroke Rd Ste 1 Concord (03301) *(G-14140)*

Linde Gas & Equipment Inc.. 203 837-2162
55 Old Ridgebury Rd Danbury (06810) *(G-774)*

Linde Gas & Equipment Inc **(DH)**.................................... **844 445-4633**
10 Riverview Dr Danbury (06810) *(G-775)*

Linde Gas & Equipment Inc.. 413 283-9906
19 2nd St Palmer (01069) *(G-11276)*

Linde Gas & Equipment Inc.. 401 767-3450
21 Steel St Slatersville (02876) *(G-16682)*

A
L
P
H
A
B
E
T
I
C

Linde Inc **(HQ)**.. **203 837-2000**
  10 Riverview Dr Danbury (06810) *(G-776)*

Linde Inc.. 800 772-9247
  10 Riverview Dr Danbury (06810) *(G-777)*

Linde Inc.. 860 623-8211
  Eastern Point Rd Groton (06340) *(G-1376)*

Linden Vft LLC.. 203 357-4740
  800 Long Ridge Rd Stamford (06902) *(G-3401)*

Lindt & Sprungli (usa) Inc **(HQ)**.......................... **603 778-8100**
  1 Fine Chocolate Pl Stratham (03885) *(G-15637)*

Line Bore Industries Inc...................................... 508 987-6509
  3 Harlan Dr Oxford (01540) *(G-11259)*

Line Electric, Glastonbury *Also Called: General Electro Components (G-1280)*

Line Sets Inc... 203 732-6700
  10 Hershey Dr Ansonia (06401) *(G-16)*

Line-X, Hartford *Also Called: Line-X of Hartford (G-1490)*

Line-X, New Milford *Also Called: Line-X of New England LLC (G-2252)*

Line-X of Hartford.. 860 216-6180
  192 Ledyard St Hartford (06114) *(G-1490)*

Line-X of New England LLC................................... 860 355-6997
  8 Spice Ln New Milford (06776) *(G-2252)*

Linear & Metric Co.. 603 432-1700
  37 Harvey Rd Londonderry (03053) *(G-14764)*

Linear Singapore Holding LLC................................ 781 329-4700
  1 Technology Way Norwood (02062) *(G-11190)*

Linear Technology LLC... 978 656-4750
  15 Research Pl North Chelmsford (01863) *(G-10981)*

Linemaster Switch Corporation............................... 860 564-7713
  16 Center Pkwy Plainfield (06374) *(G-2736)*

Linemaster Switch Corporation............................... 860 630-4920
  29 Plaine Hill Rd Woodstock (06281) *(G-4395)*

Linesider Brewing Company LLC............................. 401 398-7700
  1485 S County Trl Ste 201 East Greenwich (02818) *(G-15989)*

Lingol Corporation.. 203 265-3608
  415 S Cherry St Wallingford (06492) *(G-3828)*

Link Mechanical Services Inc................................. 860 826-5880
  60 Production Ct New Britain (06051) *(G-2038)*

Linkletter & Sons Inc.. 207 654-2301
  115 Harmony Rd Athens (04912) *(G-4414)*

Links Point Inc.. 203 853-4600
  1 Selleck St Ste 330 Norwalk (06855) *(G-2528)*

Linmel Associates Inc.. 508 481-6699
  160 Main St Marlborough (01752) *(G-10180)*

Lins Propane Trucks Corp..................................... 508 669-6665
  2281 Cedar St Dighton (02715) *(G-8293)*

Linx Consulting LLC.. 508 461-6333
  661 S Main St Ste 7 Webster (01570) *(G-12930)*

Lion Labels Inc.. 508 230-8211
  15 Hampden Dr South Easton (02375) *(G-11947)*

Liquid Blue Inc... 401 333-6200
  6 Linlew Dr Derry (03038) *(G-14200)*

Liquid Measurement Systems Inc........................... 802 528-8100
  141 Morse Dr Fairfax (05454) *(G-17261)*

Liquid Metronics Incorporated............................... 978 263-9800
  8 Post Office Sq Ste 1 Acton (01720) *(G-5757)*

Liquid Solids Control Inc **(PA)**.......................... **508 529-3377**
  10 Farm St Upton (01568) *(G-12473)*

Liquidpiston Inc.. 860 838-2677
  1292a Blue Hills Ave Bloomfield (06002) *(G-190)*

Liquidsky Technologies Inc................................... 857 389-9893
  321 Heath St Chestnut Hill (02467) *(G-8000)*

Liquiglide Inc.. 617 901-0700
  75 Sidney St 5th Fl Cambridge (02139) *(G-7633)*

Liquiglide Inc.. 617 833-8638
  34 Sullivan Rd North Billerica (01862) *(G-10927)*

Lisbon Sausage Co Inc... 508 993-7645
  433 S 2nd St New Bedford (02740) *(G-10613)*

Lisha & Nirali Fuel LLC.. 908 433-6504
  223 Maple St Middleton (01949) *(G-10389)*

Lista International, Holliston *Also Called: Stanley Industrial & Auto LLC (G-9230)*

Lista International Corporation................................ 508 429-1350
  106 Lowland St Holliston (01746) *(G-9221)*

Listen Inc... 617 556-4104
  580 Harrison Ave Ste 3w Boston (02118) *(G-6860)*

Litchfield Distillery... 860 361-6503
  569 Bantam Rd Litchfield (06759) *(G-1559)*

Lite Control, Plympton *Also Called: Litecontrol Corporation (G-11485)*

Litecontrol Corporation.. 781 294-0100
  65 Spring St Plympton (02367) *(G-11485)*

Litho-Craft Inc.. 781 729-1789
  74 Maple St Stoneham (02180) *(G-12181)*

Lithographics Inc... 860 678-1660
  55 Spring Ln Farmington (06032) *(G-1229)*

Litigation Analytics Inc **(PA)**............................ **203 431-0300**
  127 Main St Ridgefield (06877) *(G-2901)*

Litron LLC
  207 Bowles Rd Agawam (01001) *(G-5799)*

LITTELFUSE, Plainville *Also Called: Carling Technologies Inc (G-2750)*

Little Enterprises LLC.. 207 549-7232
  208 Rockland Rd Whitefield (04353) *(G-5655)*

Little Enterprises LLC **(DH)**............................. **978 356-7422**
  31 Locust Rd Ipswich (01938) *(G-9489)*

Little Enterprises North, Whitefield *Also Called: Little Enterprises LLC (G-5655)*

Little Harbor Window Co Inc.................................. 207 698-1332
  11 Little Harbor Rd Berwick (03901) *(G-4550)*

Little Harbor Window Company, Berwick *Also Called: Little Harbor Window Co Inc (G-4550)*

Little John's Sign Factory, Enfield *Also Called: Sign Factory (G-1151)*

Little Kids Inc.. 800 545-5437
  1015 Newman Ave Seekonk (02771) *(G-11780)*

Little Pttys Lawn Cr/Demolition, Morrisville *Also Called: Manufacturing Solutions Inc (G-17386)*

Little Rhody Brand, Johnston *Also Called: Rhode Island Provision Co (G-16105)*

Little Rhody Machine Repr Inc............................... 401 828-1919
  7 Alice St Coventry (02816) *(G-15816)*

Little Rhody Railings, Coventry *Also Called: Little Rhody Machine Repr Inc (G-15816)*

Little River Hot Glass Studio, Stowe *Also Called: Little Rver Htglass Studio Inc (G-17632)*

Little Rver Htglass Studio Inc................................ 802 253-0889
  593 Moscow Rd Stowe (05672) *(G-17632)*

Little Tokyo Express Inc....................................... 203 878-8814
  1201 Boston Post Rd Ste 2 Milford (06460) *(G-1846)*

Littlejohn Partners IV LP..................................... 203 552-3500
  115 E Putnam Ave Ste 2 Greenwich (06830) *(G-1338)*

Littleton Millwork Inc.. 603 444-2677
  44 Lafayette Ave Littleton (03561) *(G-14721)*

Liuzzi Cheese, Hamden *Also Called: Ndr Liuzzi Inc (G-1445)*

Liv Outdoor, Salem *Also Called: Birch Outfitters LLC (G-11703)*

Live Free or Die Alliance...................................... 210 232-8779
  1 Liberty Ln E Ste 100 Hampton (03842) *(G-14406)*

Living Cocoon, Cumberland *Also Called: Amber Style Inc (G-15932)*

Ljm Packaging Co Inc.. 401 295-2660
  330 Romano Vineyard Way North Kingstown (02852) *(G-16269)*

LK Goodwin Co Inc **(PA)**.................................. **401 781-5526**
  20 Technology Way West Greenwich (02817) *(G-16888)*

LKM, Woburn *Also Called: LKM Industries Inc (G-13602)*

LKM Industries Inc... 781 935-9210
  44 6th Rd Ste 2 Woburn (01801) *(G-13602)*

Lkq Precious Metals Inc....................................... 800 447-1034
  290 Curran Rd Cumberland (02864) *(G-15950)*

LL Bean Mfg Bus, Brunswick *Also Called: L L Bean Inc (G-4647)*

LLC Dow Gage... 860 828-5327
  169 White Oak Dr 06037 Berlin (06037) *(G-74)*

LLC Dow Gage... 860 828-5327
  169 White Oak Dr Berlin (06037) *(G-75)*

LLC Park Hill.. 207 239-7741
  40 Fieldstone Dr Westbrook (04092) *(G-5636)*

Llc, Carl Zeiss NTS, Peabody *Also Called: Carl Zeiss Nts LLC (G-11301)*

Lloyd & Bouvier Inc.. 978 365-5700
  10 Parker St Clinton (01510) *(G-8082)*

Lloyds Woodworking Inc....................................... 978 562-9007
  86 River St Hudson (01749) *(G-9386)*

Lm, Newport *Also Called: Latva Machine LLC (G-15229)*

Lm Gill Welding & Mfg, Manchester *Also Called: L M Gill Welding and Mfr LLC (G-1611)*

LM Gill Welding & Mfg LLC.. 860 647-9931
    1422 Tolland Tpke Manchester (06042) *(G-1613)*

Lm/Tarbell Inc.. 413 525-4166
    140 Industrial Dr East Longmeadow (01028) *(G-8383)*

Lm76 Linear Motion Bearings, East Longmeadow *Also Called: Lm/Tarbell Inc (G-8383)*

Lmg Rhode Island Holdings Inc **(HQ)**................................ **585 598-0030**
    119 Harris Ave Providence (02902) *(G-16553)*

Lml Construction Inc.. 413 665-3788
    608 Long Plain Rd Leverett (01054) *(G-9718)*

LMS, Fairfax *Also Called: Liquid Measurement Systems Inc (G-17261)*

Lmt Communications Inc.. 203 426-4568
    84 S Main St Ste B Newtown (06470) *(G-2339)*

Lna Laser Technology, Pawtucket *Also Called: Laservall North America LLC (G-16382)*

Lnx Corporation... 603 898-6800
    267 Lowell Rd Hudson (03051) *(G-14524)*

Loadspring Solutions Inc **(PA)**.................................... **978 685-9715**
    1500 District Ave Pmb 1060 Burlington (01803) *(G-7390)*

Loanworks Servicing LLC... 203 402-7304
    3 Corporate Dr Ste 208 Shelton (06484) *(G-3029)*

Local Guides Publishing, Portland *Also Called: Sunrise Guide LLC (G-5277)*

Local Media Group Inc... 508 775-1200
    319 Main St Hyannis (02601) *(G-9440)*

Local Media Group Inc... 508 997-7411
    25 Elm St New Bedford (02740) *(G-10614)*

Local Media Group Inc... 603 436-1800
    111 Nh Ave Portsmouth (03801) *(G-15418)*

Local207, Scarborough *Also Called: Thomas Hall (G-5445)*

Locallive Networks, Stamford *Also Called: Locallive Networks Inc (G-3402)*

Locallive Networks Inc.. 877 355-6225
    175 Atlantic St Ste 15 Stamford (06901) *(G-3402)*

Lock Inspection Systems Inc... 978 343-3716
    98 Adams St Ste 107 Leominster (01453) *(G-9679)*

Lock It Down Inc.. 203 313-6454
    54 Research Dr Stamford (06906) *(G-3403)*

Lockheed Archtctral Sltons Inc...................................... 401 568-3061
    925 S Main St Pascoag (02859) *(G-16339)*

Lockheed Archtctural Solutions, Pascoag *Also Called: Lockheed Archtctral Sltons Inc (G-16339)*

Lockheed Martin... 603 966-6031
    9 Craig Brook Trl Wayne (04284) *(G-5597)*

Lockheed Martin, Bedford *Also Called: Lockheed Martin Corporation (G-6237)*

Lockheed Martin, Chelmsford *Also Called: Lockheed Martin Corporation (G-7936)*

Lockheed Martin, Nashua *Also Called: Lockheed Martin Corporation (G-15128)*

Lockheed Martin Corporation... 207 442-3125
    700 Washington St Bath (04530) *(G-4529)*

Lockheed Martin Corporation... 407 356-2374
    160 Dascomb Rd Ste 1 Andover (01810) *(G-5891)*

Lockheed Martin Corporation... 781 863-5235
    Bedford (01730) *(G-6237)*

Lockheed Martin Corporation... 978 256-4113
    16 Maple Rd Chelmsford (01824) *(G-7936)*

Lockheed Martin Corporation... 603 885-5295
    144 Daniel Webster Hwy Bldg 26 Merrimack (03054) *(G-14990)*

Lockheed Martin Corporation... 603 885-4321
    410 Amherst St Ste 200 Nashua (03063) *(G-15128)*

Lockheed Martin Corporation... 802 503-8699
    45 Nco Dr South Burlington (05403) *(G-17584)*

Lockheed Mrtin Advnced Enrgy S...................................... 972 603-7611
    117 Beaver St Waltham (02452) *(G-12710)*

Lockheed/Ms2-Baltimore, Bath *Also Called: Lockheed Martin Corporation (G-4529)*

Lockwood Mfg Inc.. 207 764-4196
    135 Parsons St Presque Isle (04769) *(G-5302)*

Loctec Corporation.. 203 364-1000
    15 Commerce Rd Ste 2 Newtown (06470) *(G-2340)*

Locus Robotics Corp **(PA)**.. **844 562-8700**
    301 Ballardvale St Ste 4 Wilmington (01887) *(G-13426)*

Loftware Holdings Inc **(PA)**...................................... **603 766-3630**
    249 Corporate Dr Portsmouth (03801) *(G-15419)*

Log House Designs Inc **(PA)**...................................... **603 694-3373**
    184 Butter Hill Rd Chatham (03813) *(G-14070)*

Logan Instruments Inc... 617 394-0601
    101a French Ave Braintree (02184) *(G-7193)*

Logan Sandblasting, Meriden *Also Called: Logan Steel Inc (G-1672)*

Logan Stamp Works Inc... 617 569-2121
    104 Meridian St 106 Boston (02128) *(G-6861)*

Logan Steel Inc **(PA)**.. **203 235-0811**
    119 Empire Ave Meriden (06450) *(G-1672)*

Logic Supply, South Burlington *Also Called: Onlogic Inc (G-17587)*

Logical Therapeutics Inc.. 781 290-0900
    300 Second Ave Waltham (02451) *(G-12711)*

Logicbio Therapeutics Inc... 617 245-0399
    65 Hayden Ave Fl 2 Lexington (02421) *(G-9759)*

Logicmanager Inc.. 617 530-1200
    5 Drydock Ave Ste 2080 Boston (02210) *(G-6862)*

Lohmann Animal Health Intl Inc...................................... 207 873-3989
    375 China Rd Winslow (04901) *(G-5683)*

Londonderry Industrial Pk Inc....................................... 802 297-3760
    170 Winhall Station Rd South Londonderry (05155) *(G-17611)*

Lone Star Holdings Inc **(HQ)**..................................... **781 935-2224**
    180 2nd St Chelsea (02150) *(G-7986)*

Long Falls Paperboard LLC... 802 257-0365
    161 Wellington Rd Brattleboro (05301) *(G-17094)*

Long Island Pipe New Hampshire, Salem *Also Called: Long Island Pipe Supply NH Inc (G-15543)*

Long Island Pipe Supply NH Inc...................................... 603 685-3200
    50b Northwestern Dr Ste 5 Salem (03079) *(G-15543)*

Longcap Lamson Products LLC... 413 642-8135
    79 Mainline Dr Westfield (01085) *(G-13179)*

Longfin LLC... 508 228-4266
    Nantucket (02554) *(G-10465)*

Longhill Partners Inc **(PA)**...................................... **802 457-4000**
    4 Sunset Farms Woodstock (05091) *(G-17776)*

Longhini LLC.. 203 624-7110
    41 Longhini Ln New Haven (06519) *(G-2170)*

Longhini Sausage, New Haven *Also Called: Longhini LLC (G-2170)*

Longhorn Steel Inc.. 978 265-3646
    15 Price Rd Peabody (01960) *(G-11325)*

Longrun LLC... 617 758-8674
    464 Common St U 207 Belmont (02478) *(G-6307)*

Longview Holding Corporation **(HQ)**............................... **203 869-6734**
    43 Arch St Greenwich (06830) *(G-1339)*

Longworth Venture Partners LP **(PA)**.............................. **781 663-3600**
    17 Chickadee Dr Norfolk (02056) *(G-10801)*

Lonza, Portsmouth *Also Called: Lonza Biologics Inc (G-15422)*

Lonza Bio Science Rockland Inc...................................... 207 594-3400
    191 Thomaston St Rockland (04841) *(G-5337)*

Lonza Biologics Inc... 608 630-3758
    50 Hampshire St Ste 401 Cambridge (02139) *(G-7634)*

Lonza Biologics Inc... 508 435-2331
    4 Hartwell Pl Lexington (02421) *(G-9760)*

Lonza Biologics Inc... 603 610-4696
    40 Goosebay Dr Portsmouth (03801) *(G-15420)*

Lonza Biologics Inc... 201 316-9200
    101 International Dr Portsmouth (03801) *(G-15421)*

Lonza Biologics Inc **(DH)**.. **603 610-4500**
    101 International Dr Portsmouth (03801) *(G-15422)*

Lonza Cell and Gene, Lexington *Also Called: Lonza Biologics Inc (G-9760)*

Lonza Rockland Inc.. 207 594-3400
    191 Thomaston St Rockland (04841) *(G-5338)*

Looks Gourmet Food Co Inc **(HQ)**................................. **207 259-3341**
    17 Stackpole Dr Machias (04654) *(G-5031)*

Loos & Co Inc **(PA)**.. **860 928-7981**
    16b Mashamoquet Rd Pomfret (06258) *(G-2809)*

Loos & Co Inc... 860 928-6681
    Rte 101 Pomfret (06258) *(G-2810)*

Lorac Company Inc... 401 781-3330
    97 Johnson St Providence (02905) *(G-16554)*

Lorac Union Tool, Providence *Also Called: Lorac Company Inc (G-16554)*

Lorad Corporation... 203 790-5544
    36 Apple Ridge Rd Danbury (06810) *(G-778)*

Lorad Medical Systems, Danbury *Also Called: Lorad Corporation (G-778)*

Lord & Hodge Inc.. 860 632-7006
    362 Industrial Park Rd Ste 4 Middletown (06457) *(G-1760)*

**A
L
P
H
A
B
E
T
I
C**

Lorenco Industries Inc................................ 203 743-6962
  25 Henry St Bethel (06801) *(G-127)*

Lorex Plastics Co Inc................................ 203 286-0020
  221 Wilson Ave Norwalk (06854) *(G-2529)*

Lori Donuts Inc................................ 413 526-9944
  55 Maple St East Longmeadow (01028) *(G-8384)*

Loric Tool Inc................................ 860 928-0171
  95 Gaumond Rd North Grosvenordale (06255) *(G-2385)*

Lorimer Studios LLC................................ 401 714-0014
  35 Brown St North Kingstown (02852) *(G-16270)*

Lorusso Corp **(PA)**................................ **508 668-6520**
  320 South St Plainville (02762) *(G-11437)*

Lorusso-Bristol Stone, East Weymouth *Also Called: S M Lorusso & Sons Inc (G-8433)*

Lose It, Boston *Also Called: Fitnow Inc (G-6739)*

Lost Art Cultured Foods LLC................................ 401 437-6933
  1850 Broad St Unit 1 Cranston (02905) *(G-15886)*

Lost Brothers Pallet Corp................................ 401 585-7194
  333 River St Woonsocket (02895) *(G-16967)*

Lost Nation Brewing, Morrisville *Also Called: Lost Nation Brewing LLC (G-17385)*

Lost Nation Brewing LLC................................ 802 851-8041
  87 Old Creamery Rd Morrisville (05661) *(G-17385)*

Lostocco Refuse Service LLC................................ 203 748-9296
  79 Beaver Brook Rd Danbury (06810) *(G-779)*

Lostocco Services, Danbury *Also Called: Lostocco Refuse Service LLC (G-779)*

Lotuff Leather................................ 888 763-2247
  1 Sims Ave Unit 101 Providence (02909) *(G-16555)*

Lou-Jan Tool & Die Inc................................ 203 272-3536
  474 Birch St Bristol (06010) *(G-463)*

Loud Audio LLC................................ 508 234-6158
  1 Main St Ste 1 Whitinsville (01588) *(G-13341)*

Louie and Teds Blacktop Inc................................ 508 678-4948
  105 Buffington St Swansea (02777) *(G-12306)*

Louis A Green Corp................................ 781 535-6199
  121 Union St Ste 15 North Adams (01247) *(G-10810)*

Louis C Morin Co Inc................................ 978 670-1222
  19 Sterling Rd Ste 4 North Billerica (01862) *(G-10928)*

Louis Dreyfus Holdg Co US LLC **(HQ)**................................ **203 761-2000**
  40 Danbury Rd Wilton (06897) *(G-4242)*

Louis Garneau USA Inc................................ 802 334-5885
  3916 Us Route 5 Derby (05829) *(G-17211)*

Louis M Gerson Co Inc................................ 508 947-4000
  15 Sumner Ave Middleboro (02346) *(G-10363)*

Louis M Gerson Co Inc **(PA)**................................ **508 947-4000**
  16 Commerce Blvd Ste D Middleboro (02346) *(G-10364)*

LOUIS M. GERSON CO., INC, Middleboro *Also Called: Louis M Gerson Co Inc (G-10363)*

Louis Press Inc................................ 401 351-9229
  39 Greenville Ave Apt 1 Johnston (02919) *(G-16094)*

Louis W Mian Incorporated **(PA)**................................ **617 241-7900**
  547 Rutherford Ave Boston (02129) *(G-6863)*

Lovejoy LLC................................ 413 737-0281
  185 West Ave Ste 101 Ludlow (01056) *(G-9949)*

Lovejoy Tool Company Inc................................ 802 885-2194
  133 Main St Springfield (05156) *(G-17620)*

Lovell Lumber Company................................ 207 925-6455
  3 Mill Rd Lovell (04051) *(G-5027)*

Lovepop, Boston *Also Called: Lovepop Inc (G-6864)*

Lovepop Inc **(PA)**................................ **888 687-9589**
  68 Harrison Ave Ste 501 Boston (02111) *(G-6864)*

Lovesac Company **(PA)**................................ **888 636-1223**
  2 Landmark Sq Ste 300 Stamford (06901) *(G-3404)*

Low Impact Logging LLC................................ 603 487-5298
  141 Riverdale Rd New Boston (03070) *(G-15192)*

Lowell Corporation................................ 508 835-2900
  65 Hartwell St West Boylston (01583) *(G-12964)*

Lowell Sun, Lowell *Also Called: Dispatch News (G-9876)*

Lowell Sun, Lowell *Also Called: Lowell Sun Publishing Company (G-9896)*

Lowell Sun Publishing Company................................ 978 433-6685
  69 Fitchburg Rd Ayer (01432) *(G-6185)*

Lowell Sun Publishing Company................................ 978 772-0777
  78 Barnum Rd Devens (01434) *(G-8276)*

Lowell Sun Publishing Company **(DH)**................................ **978 459-1300**
  491 Dutton St Lowell (01854) *(G-9896)*

Loxo Oncology Inc **(HQ)**................................ **203 653-3880**
  281 Tresser Blvd Fl 9 Stamford (06901) *(G-3405)*

Loxsmith Bagel Corporation................................ 603 362-9060
  1 Washington St Dover (03820) *(G-14233)*

Loyal Fence Company LLC................................ 203 530-7046
  1 Lorraine Ter Rockfall (06481) *(G-2914)*

Loyal Nine, Wakefield *Also Called: Diageo Loyal Spirits Corp (G-16740)*

Loyalty Builders Inc **(PA)**................................ **603 610-8800**
  155 Lafayette Rd North Hampton (03862) *(G-15252)*

Lp81 Shirts, Bedford *Also Called: Lestat Production 81 Corp (G-13939)*

Lpg Metal Crafts LLC................................ 860 982-3573
  54 Carol Dr Plainville (06062) *(G-2770)*

LPI Printing and Graphic Inc................................ 781 438-5400
  18 Spencer St Stoneham (02180) *(G-12182)*

Lps Enterprises Inc................................ 508 763-3830
  128 Braley Rd Bldg A3 East Freetown (02717) *(G-8364)*

Lq Mechatronics Inc................................ 203 433-4430
  2 Sycamore Way Branford (06405) *(G-268)*

Lqc Inc................................ 617 586-5139
  916 Pleasant St Ste 22 Norwood (02062) *(G-11191)*

Ls Industries Inc................................ 781 844-8115
  28 Durham Dr Lynnfield (01940) *(G-9999)*

LS Starrett Company................................ 978 249-3551
  121 Crescent St Athol (01331) *(G-5980)*

LS Starrett Company **(PA)**................................ **978 249-3551**
  121 Crescent St Athol (01331) *(G-5981)*

Lsc Communications Inc................................ 978 251-6000
  15 Wellman Ave North Chelmsford (01863) *(G-10982)*

LSI Industries Inc................................ 401 766-7446
  601 Park East Dr Woonsocket (02895) *(G-16968)*

Lsne, Bedford *Also Called: Lyophilization Svcs Neng Inc (G-13940)*

Lsne, Bedford *Also Called: Lyophilization Svcs Neng Inc (G-13943)*

Lsne, Manchester *Also Called: Lyophilization Svcs Neng Inc (G-14877)*

Lsr Sealcoating................................ 603 715-4934
  6 Bicentennial Sq Concord (03301) *(G-14141)*

LTI Group, Pittsfield *Also Called: LTI Smart Glass Inc (G-11407)*

LTI Portfolio Management Corp................................ 203 563-1100
  221 Danbury Rd Wilton (06897) *(G-4243)*

LTI Smart Glass Inc................................ 413 637-5001
  14 Federico Dr Pittsfield (01201) *(G-11407)*

Ltp Corporation **(DH)**................................ **508 393-7660**
  70 Bearfoot Rd Northborough (01532) *(G-11101)*

Ltpc Holdings Inc................................ 781 893-6672
  30 Clematis Ave Waltham (02453) *(G-12712)*

Lts Inc................................ 207 774-1104
  37 Danforth St Portland (04101) *(G-5234)*

LTS Group Holdings LLC, Boxborough *Also Called: Crown Cstle Fibr Holdings Corp (G-7150)*

LTX Credence, Norwood *Also Called: L T X International Inc (G-11189)*

Lu-Dz LLC................................ 207 563-2669
  16 Osprey Point Rd Newcastle (04553) *(G-5094)*

Lubrication Management, Danbury *Also Called: Expressway Lube Centers (G-743)*

Lubrizol Global Management Inc................................ 978 642-5051
  207 Lowell St Wilmington (01887) *(G-13427)*

Luca + Danni Inc................................ 401 275-5337
  838 Dyer Ave Cranston (02920) *(G-15887)*

Lucas Fabrication Inc................................ 413 586-0941
  30 N Maple St Ste 2 Florence (01062) *(G-8684)*

Lucci Corp................................ 603 567-4301
  375 Jaffrey Rd Ste 7 Peterborough (03458) *(G-15317)*

Lucent Specialty Fiber Tech................................ 320 258-3035
  55 Darling Dr Avon (06001) *(G-30)*

Lucerne Farms................................ 207 488-2520
  40 Easton Line Rd Fort Fairfield (04742) *(G-4785)*

Lucidity Lights Inc **(PA)**................................ **781 995-2405**
  56 Roland St Ste 300 Charlestown (02129) *(G-7878)*

Luckey LLC................................ 203 747-5270
  184 Chapel St New Haven (06513) *(G-2171)*

Luckwel Pharmaceuticals Inc................................ 617 430-5222
  125 Cambridgepark Dr Ste 301 Cambridge (02140) *(G-7635)*

Ludlow Tool................................ 413 786-6360
  370 Fuller St Ludlow (01056) *(G-9950)*

Ludlow Tool Inc.	413 786-6415	
46 Moylan Ln Agawam (01001) *(G-5800)*		
Lujean Printing Co Inc.	508 428-8700	
4507 Falmouth Rd Cotuit (02635) *(G-8146)*		
Luke Harding U G Nason & Sons, Middletown *Also Called: Nasons Ug Inc (G-16180)*		
Lumber Manufacturer, Searsmont *Also Called: Robbins Lumber Inc (G-5450)*		
Lumber Outlet, Campton *Also Called: Granite State Log Homes Inc (G-14044)*		
Lumendi LLC	203 528-0316	
253 Post Rd W Westport (06880) *(G-4181)*		
Lumenpulse Lighting Corp	617 307-5700	
14 Beacon St Ste 301 Boston (02108) *(G-6865)*		
Lumetta Inc	401 691-3994	
33 Minnesota Ave Warwick (02888) *(G-16833)*		
Lumeway Products Inc	508 829-2112	
800 Main St Ste 205 Holden (01520) *(G-9192)*		
Lumina Power Inc	978 241-8260	
26 Ward Hill Ave Haverhill (01835) *(G-9110)*		
Luminescent Systems, Lebanon *Also Called: Luminescent Systems Inc (G-14693)*		
Luminescent Systems Inc	603 643-7766	
4 Lucent Dr Lebanon (03766) *(G-14693)*		
Lumonics Corp Indus Pdts Div, Bedford *Also Called: Novanta Corporation (G-6245)*		
Luna Pharmaceuticals Inc	401 383-0299	
244 Weybosset St Ste 3 Providence (02903) *(G-16556)*		
Lunder Manufacturing Inc	207 284-5961	
44 Spring Hill Rd Saco (04072) *(G-5371)*		
Lunder Manufacturing Company, Saco *Also Called: Lunder Manufacturing Inc (G-5371)*		
Lundys Company Inc	781 595-8639	
34 Boston St Lynn (01904) *(G-9983)*		
Lunt Silversmiths, Greenfield *Also Called: Silver Greenfield Inc (G-8999)*		
Lupine Inc	603 356-7371	
16 Lupine Ln Center Conway (03813) *(G-14055)*		
Lupis Incorporated	203 562-9491	
169 Washington Ave New Haven (06519) *(G-2172)*		
Luster-On Products Inc	413 739-2541	
54 Waltham Ave Springfield (01109) *(G-12111)*		
Lutco, Worcester *Also Called: Lutco Bearings Inc (G-13754)*		
Lutco Bearings Inc	508 756-6296	
677 Cambridge St Ste 1 Worcester (01610) *(G-13754)*		
Luther's Welding, Bristol *Also Called: Luthers Repair Shop Inc (G-15773)*		
Luthers Repair Shop Inc	401 253-5550	
500 Wood St Bristol (02809) *(G-15773)*		
Lutronic USA	888 588-7644	
19 Fortune Dr Billerica (01821) *(G-6459)*		
Luv2bu Inc	401 612-9585	
17 Yard St Cranston (02920) *(G-15888)*		
Luvata Waterbury Inc	203 488-5956	
8 Baldwin Dr Branford (06405) *(G-269)*		
Luvata Waterbury Inc (HQ)	**203 753-5215**	
2121 Thomaston Ave Waterbury (06704) *(G-3931)*		
Lux Box Company Inc	301 832-0622	
517 Forest Ave Ste 1 Portland (04101) *(G-5235)*		
Luzy Technologies LLC	514 577-2295	
778 Boylston St Apt 6b Boston (02199) *(G-6866)*		
Lv Controls Incorporated	401 228-3937	
1 Starline Way Cranston (02921) *(G-15889)*		
Lvr Inc	508 987-2337	
2 Hawksley Rd Unit C Oxford (01540) *(G-11260)*		
Lw Holding Lc	913 851-3000	
12 Silver Lake Rd Hollis (03049) *(G-14453)*		
Lwi Metalworks, Morrisville *Also Called: S & A Trombley Corporation (G-17388)*		
Lydall Inc (HQ)	**860 646-1233**	
1 Colonial Rd Manchester (06042) *(G-1614)*		
Lydall Thermal/Acoustical Inc	860 646-1233	
180 Glastonbury Blvd Glastonbury (06033) *(G-1288)*		
Lykan Bioscience Holdings LLC	774 341-4200	
97 South St Hopkinton (01748) *(G-9336)*		
Lyle Guptill	207 255-4130	
343 Scotts Hill Rd East Machias (04630) *(G-4740)*		
Lyman Conrad (PA)	**413 538-8200**	
228 Lathrop St South Hadley (01075) *(G-11965)*		

Lyman Farm Incorporated (PA)	**860 349-1793**	
7 Lyman Rd Middlefield (06455) *(G-1725)*		
Lyman Morse Boatbuilding Inc	207 236-4378	
59 Sea St Camden (04843) *(G-4667)*		
Lyman Morse Boatbuilding Inc	207 354-6904	
19 Elltee Cir Thomaston (04861) *(G-5545)*		
Lyman Morse Boatbuilding Inc (PA)	**207 354-6904**	
84 Knox St Thomaston (04861) *(G-5546)*		
Lyman Orchards, Middlefield *Also Called: Lyman Farm Incorporated (G-1725)*		
Lyman Products Corporation (PA)	**860 632-2020**	
475 Smith St Middletown (06457) *(G-1761)*		
Lyman Sheet Metal Co Inc	413 527-0848	
281 College Hwy Southampton (01073) *(G-11988)*		
Lyme Timber Company LP (PA)	**603 643-3300**	
23 S Main St Ste 3 Hanover (03755) *(G-14429)*		
Lymol Medical Corp (PA)	**781 935-0004**	
4 Plympton St Woburn (01801) *(G-13603)*		
Lyn-Lad Group Ltd (PA)	**781 598-6010**	
20 Boston St Lynn (01904) *(G-9984)*		
Lynch Companies, Cumberland *Also Called: JH Lynch & Sons Inc (G-15948)*		
Lynch Corp	203 452-3007	
140 Greenwich Ave Ste 3 Greenwich (06830) *(G-1340)*		
Lyndon Furniture, Saint Johnsbury *Also Called: Lyndon Woodworking Inc (G-17542)*		
Lyndon Woodworking Inc (PA)	**802 748-0100**	
1135 Industrial Pkwy Saint Johnsbury (05819) *(G-17542)*		
Lyndra Therapeutics Inc	857 201-5314	
60 Westview St Lexington (02421) *(G-9761)*		
Lyndra Therapeutics Inc (PA)	**339 222-6519**	
65 Grove St Ste 301 Watertown (02472) *(G-12888)*		
Lyne Laboratories Inc	508 583-8700	
10 Burke Dr Brockton (02301) *(G-7292)*		
Lynn Ladder Scaffolding Co Inc (HQ)	**781 598-6010**	
20 Boston St 24 Lynn (01904) *(G-9985)*		
Lynn Products Co	781 593-2500	
400 Boston St Ste 1 Lynn (01905) *(G-9986)*		
Lynn Welding Co Inc	860 667-4400	
75 Rockwell Rd Ste 1 Newington (06111) *(G-2304)*		
Lynx System Developers Inc	978 556-9780	
179 Ward Hill Ave Haverhill (01835) *(G-9111)*		
Lyons Slitting Inc	203 755-4564	
46 Mattatuck Heights Rd Waterbury (06705) *(G-3932)*		
Lyons Tnney Timber Harvstg Inc	802 384-2620	
14 Switzer Rd Bennington (03442) *(G-13976)*		
Lyophilization Svcs Neng Inc	603 668-5763	
25 Commerce Dr Bedford (03110) *(G-13940)*		
Lyophilization Svcs Neng Inc	603 626-9559	
19 Harvey Rd Unit 7 Bedford (03110) *(G-13941)*		
Lyophilization Svcs Neng Inc	603 626-5763	
29 Harvey Rd Bedford (03110) *(G-13942)*		
Lyophilization Svcs Neng Inc	603 668-5763	
7 Commerce Dr Bedford (03110) *(G-13943)*		
Lyophilization Svcs Neng Inc (HQ)	**603 626-5763**	
1 Sundial Ave Ste 112 Manchester (03103) *(G-14877)*		
Lyra Therapeutics Inc	617 393-4600	
480 Arsenal Way Watertown (02472) *(G-12889)*		
Lytron Fs Inc	781 933-7300	
55 Dragon Ct Woburn (01801) *(G-13604)*		
M & A Advnced Design Cnstr Inc (PA)	**603 329-9515**	
1 Gigante Dr Hampstead (03841) *(G-14385)*		
M & B Enterprise LLC	888 983-2670	
155 New Haven Ave Derby (06418) *(G-891)*		
M & C Press Inc	617 354-2584	
1 Main St Ste 105 Cambridge (02142) *(G-7636)*		
M & D Coatings LLC	203 380-9466	
300 Long Beach Blvd Stratford (06615) *(G-3554)*		
M & H Construction, Rangeley *Also Called: M & H Logging LLC (G-5312)*		
M & H Engineering Co Inc	978 777-1222	
183 Newbury St Danvers (01923) *(G-8200)*		
M & H Logging LLC	207 864-5617	
3039 Main St Rangeley (04970) *(G-5312)*		
M & J Sheet Metal LLC	860 379-2907	
41 Meadow St Winsted (06098) *(G-4348)*		

ALPHABETIC

M & K Engineering, Woburn *Also Called: Arch Med & Arospc Woburn LLC* **(G-13514)**

M & K Industries Inc................................ 978 514-9850
  177 Florence St Leominster (01453) **(G-9680)**

M & M Garment Manufacturing.................... 617 389-7787
  167 Bow St Ste 2 Everett (02149) **(G-8492)**

M & M Glass Blowing Co Inc....................... 603 598-8195
  2 Townsend W Ste 11a Nashua (03063) **(G-15129)**

M & M Glassblowing, Nashua *Also Called: M & M Glass Blowing Co Inc* **(G-15129)**

M & M Label Co Inc................................. 781 321-2737
  5 Electronics Ave Danvers (01923) **(G-8201)**

M & M Machine Inc.................................. 207 764-4199
  1215 Airport Dr Presque Isle (04769) **(G-5303)**

M & M Precast Corp................................. 203 743-5559
  39 Padanaram Rd Danbury (06811) **(G-780)**

M & M Scale Company Inc.......................... 781 321-2737
  5 Electronics Ave Danvers (01923) **(G-8202)**

M & O Corporation.................................. 203 367-4292
  164 Alex St Bridgeport (06607) **(G-345)**

M & P, Stoughton *Also Called: M & P Machine Company Inc* **(G-12218)**

M & P Machine Company Inc....................... 781 344-5888
  1438 Washington St Stoughton (02072) **(G-12218)**

M & R Screen Printing Inc.......................... 508 996-0419
  95 Rodney French Blvd New Bedford (02744) **(G-10615)**

M & S Electrical Contrs LLC........................ 781 389-4465
  116 Intervale St Brockton (02302) **(G-7293)**

M & S Enterprises Inc............................... 207 989-0077
  603 Wilson St Brewer (04412) **(G-4617)**

M & T Manufacturing................................ 401 789-0472
  30 Hopkins Ln Wakefield (02879) **(G-16742)**

M & W Industries Inc............................... 508 406-2100
  11 Forbes Blvd # 101 Mansfield (02048) **(G-10065)**

M & W Sheet Metal LLC............................ 860 642-7748
  841 Route 32 Ste 7 North Franklin (06254) **(G-2382)**

M A Haskell & Sons LLC............................ 207 993-2265
  174 Mann Rd China (04358) **(G-4696)**

M B Eastman Logging Inc........................... 207 625-8020
  146 North Rd Parsonsfield (04047) **(G-5151)**

M Braun Inc... 603 773-9333
  14 Marin Way Stratham (03885) **(G-15638)**

M C I, Orange *Also Called: MCI Transformer Corporation* **(G-11226)**

M C T, Milford *Also Called: Metal Casting Technology Inc* **(G-15033)**

M C Test Service Inc................................ 781 218-7550
  101 Billerica Ave Bldg 7 North Billerica (01862) **(G-10929)**

M Cohen and Sons................................... 774 228-2193
  20 Joy St Mashpee (02649) **(G-10253)**

M Cubed, Newtown *Also Called: M Cubed Technologies Inc* **(G-2341)**

M Cubed Technologies Inc.......................... 203 452-2333
  921 Main St Monroe (06468) **(G-1915)**

M Cubed Technologies Inc **(HQ)**............... **203 304-2940**
  31 Pecks Ln Ste 8 Newtown (06470) **(G-2341)**

M D L, Needham Heights *Also Called: Microwave Development Labs Inc* **(G-10551)**

M Drug LLC.. 207 973-9444
  33 Whiting Hill Rd Ste 4 Brewer (04412) **(G-4618)**

M E M, Madison *Also Called: Madison Medical LLC* **(G-1563)**

M F Engineering Company Inc...................... 401 253-6163
  7 Peter Rd Bristol (02809) **(G-15774)**

M F Fley Incrprtd-New Bdford...................... 508 997-0773
  77 Wright St New Bedford (02740) **(G-10616)**

M G A Cast Stone Inc............................... 207 926-5993
  7 Oxford Homes Ln Oxford (04270) **(G-5147)**

M H Humphrey & Sons Inc.......................... 207 625-4965
  92 Mudgett Rd Parsonsfield (04047) **(G-5152)**

M J Harrington & Co Inc **(PA)**.................. **603 863-1662**
  33 Main St Newport (03773) **(G-15231)**

M K S, Andover *Also Called: Mks Instruments Inc* **(G-5899)**

M K S Astex Products, Wilmington *Also Called: Mks Instruments Inc* **(G-13433)**

M P Brewing Company............................... 508 944-8531
  52 Ferry St Fall River (02721) **(G-8570)**

M P E, Branford *Also Called: Madison Polymeric Engrg Inc* **(G-271)**

M P I, Seymour *Also Called: Microboard Processing Inc* **(G-2965)**

M P I, Winchester *Also Called: MJW Mass Inc* **(G-13488)**

M Piette & Sons Lumber Inc........................ 802 754-8876
  6 Seminole Ln Irasburg (05845) **(G-17302)**

M R F, Allenstown *Also Called: Materials Research Frncs Inc* **(G-13853)**

M S C, Enfield *Also Called: MSC Filtration Tech Inc* **(G-1139)**

M S Company.. 508 222-1700
  61 School St Attleboro (02703) **(G-6032)**

M S G, Manchester *Also Called: Manufacturing Services Group* **(G-14878)**

M T D Corporation.................................. 203 261-3721
  171 Spring Hill Rd Trumbull (06611) **(G-3724)**

M T G, Westfield *Also Called: Manufacturing Tech Group Inc* **(G-13181)**

M T I, Brentwood *Also Called: Multi Technologies Industrial LLC* **(G-14024)**

M T I, Providence *Also Called: MTI Film LLC* **(G-16570)**

M-R Resources Inc.................................. 978 345-9010
  160 Authority Dr Fitchburg (01420) **(G-8659)**

M.P.I., New Britain *Also Called: Metallurgical Processing Incorporated* **(G-2044)**

M/A-Com, Lowell *Also Called: Macom Metelics LLC* **(G-9897)**

M/A-Com, Lowell *Also Called: Macom Technology Solutions Inc* **(G-9900)**

M&H Liquidating Company LLC...................... 603 889-8320
  9a Columbia Dr Amherst (03031) **(G-13876)**

M&M Label Company, Danvers *Also Called: M & M Scale Company Inc* **(G-8202)**

M8trix Tech LLC.................................... 617 925-7030
  45 Dan Rd Canton (02021) **(G-7806)**

M8trix Technology, Canton *Also Called: M8trix Tech LLC* **(G-7806)**

MA Industrial Fall River LLC....................... 508 672-5217
  81 Commerce Dr Fall River (02720) **(G-8571)**

MA Mfg LLC... 978 400-9991
  325 Authority Dr Fitchburg (01420) **(G-8660)**

Mac Battery, Watertown *Also Called: Atlantic Battery Company Inc* **(G-12860)**

Mac Lean-Fogg Company............................ 781 328-3220
  131 Hartwell Ave Ste 3 Lexington (02421) **(G-9762)**

Macdermid Incorporated **(HQ)**.................. **203 575-5700**
  245 Freight St Waterbury (06702) **(G-3933)**

Macdermid Acumen Inc............................. 203 575-5700
  245 Freight St Waterbury (06702) **(G-3934)**

Macdermid AG Solutions Inc **(HQ)**............. **203 575-5727**
  245 Freight St Waterbury (06702) **(G-3935)**

Macdermid Anion Inc............................... 203 575-5700
  245 Freight St Waterbury (06702) **(G-3936)**

Macdermid Autotype Inc............................ 847 818-8262
  245 Freight St Waterbury (06702) **(G-3937)**

Macdermid Brazil Inc............................... 203 575-5700
  245 Freight St Waterbury (06702) **(G-3938)**

Macdermid Enthone Inc **(HQ)**.................. **203 934-8611**
  350 Frontage Rd West Haven (06516) **(G-4112)**

Macdermid Enthone Indus Sltons, West Haven *Also Called: Macdermid Enthone Inc* **(G-4112)**

Macdermid Holdings LLC............................ 203 575-5700
  245 Freight St Waterbury (06702) **(G-3939)**

Macdermid Overseas Asia Ltd **(HQ)**........... **203 575-5799**
  245 Freight St Waterbury (06702) **(G-3940)**

Macdermid Prfmce Solutions, Waterbury *Also Called: Macdermid Incorporated* **(G-3933)**

Macdermid Prtg Sltons Acmen In.................... 203 575-5700
  245 Freight St Waterbury (06702) **(G-3941)**

Macdiarmid LLC.................................... 978 465-3546
  7 Perry Way Newburyport (01950) **(G-10696)**

Macdiarmid Machine Corp.......................... 978 465-3546
  7 Perry Way Ste 13 Newburyport (01950) **(G-10697)**

Macey's Car Care Center, Warwick *Also Called: Sullivan Tire Co Inc* **(G-16866)**

Mach 7 Technologies Inc........................... 802 861-7745
  120 Kimball Ave Ste 210 South Burlington (05403) **(G-17585)**

Mach Machine Inc.................................. 978 274-5700
  569 Main St Hudson (01749) **(G-9387)**

Machine Builders Neng LLC......................... 203 922-9446
  83 Erna Ave Milford (06461) **(G-1847)**

Machine Craft Company Inc........................ 603 225-0958
  114 Hall St Concord (03301) **(G-14142)**

Machine Incorporated.............................. 781 297-3700
  879 Turnpike St Stoughton (02072) **(G-12219)**

Machine Shop, Londonderry *Also Called: Micro-Tech Prod Mch Co Inc* **(G-14773)**

Machine Shop, Pascoag *Also Called: Sandberg Enterprises Inc* *(G-16341)*

Machine Technology Inc.. 978 927-1900
148 Sohier Rd Beverly (01915) *(G-6363)*

Machine Trailers, Winslow *Also Called: Alcom LLC* *(G-5680)*

Machined Integrations LLC.. 603 420-8871
1507 Columbia Cir Merrimack (03054) *(G-14991)*

Machinemetrics Inc... 413 341-5747
116 Pleasant St Easthampton (01027) *(G-8449)*

Machinery Service Co Inc... 207 882-6788
166 W Alna Rd Wiscasset (04578) *(G-5698)*

Machinex Company Inc... 401 231-3230
350 Washington Hwy Smithfield (02917) *(G-16723)*

Machining For Electronics Inc...................................... 978 562-7554
4 Bigelow St Hudson (01749) *(G-9388)*

Machining Innovations Inc... 207 465-2500
279 Summer St Oakland (04963) *(G-5120)*

Mack Group Inc **(PA)**... **802 375-2511**
608 Warm Brook Rd Arlington (05250) *(G-16988)*

Mack Molding Company Inc.. 802 375-0500
79 E Arlington Rd Arlington (05250) *(G-16989)*

Mack Molding Company Inc **(HQ)**............................. **802 375-2511**
608 Warm Brook Rd Arlington (05250) *(G-16990)*

Mack Prototype Inc... 978 632-3700
424 Main St Gardner (01440) *(G-8893)*

Mack Technologies Inc **(HQ)**.................................... **978 392-5500**
27 Carlisle Rd Westford (01886) *(G-13247)*

Mackenzie Machine & Design Inc................................. 339 933-8157
171 Mattakeesett St Ste 2 Pembroke (02359) *(G-11374)*

Mackenzie Vault Inc.. 413 525-8827
165 Benton Dr East Longmeadow (01028) *(G-8385)*

Mackeyrms, Boston *Also Called: Verity LLC* *(G-7098)*

Maclean Precision Mch Co Inc...................................... 603 367-9011
1928 Village Rd Madison (03849) *(G-14803)*

Maclellan Concrete Co, Amesbury *Also Called: J G Maclellan Con Co Inc* *(G-5839)*

Macmillan Publishing Group LLC.................................. 646 307-5617
75 Arlington St 8th Fl Boston (02116) *(G-6867)*

Macneill Engineering Co Inc... 508 481-8830
1700 W Park Dr Ste 310 Westborough (01581) *(G-13118)*

MACOM, Lowell *Also Called: Macom Tech Sltons Holdings Inc* *(G-9898)*

Macom, Lowell *Also Called: Macom Technology Solutions Inc* *(G-9899)*

Macom Metelics LLC... 978 656-2500
100 Chelmsford St Lowell (01851) *(G-9897)*

Macom Tech Sltons Holdings Inc **(PA)**...................... **978 656-2500**
100 Chelmsford St Lowell (01851) *(G-9898)*

Macom Tech Sltons Holdings Inc.................................. 603 641-3800
54 Grenier Field Rd Londonderry (03053) *(G-14765)*

Macom Technology Solutions Inc.................................. 978 656-2500
121 Hale St Lowell (01851) *(G-9899)*

Macom Technology Solutions Inc **(HQ)**..................... **978 656-2500**
100 Chelmsford St Lowell (01851) *(G-9900)*

Macristy Industries Inc **(PA)**................................... **860 225-4637**
610 N Mountain Rd Newington (06111) *(G-2305)*

MACS SEAFOOD, Eastham *Also Called: Wellfleet Shellfish Co Inc* *(G-8436)*

Macton Oxford LLC... 203 267-1500
116 Willenbrock Rd Oxford (06478) *(G-2703)*

Macy Industries Inc.. 603 623-5568
5 Lehoux Dr Hooksett (03106) *(G-14468)*

Mad River Distillers.. 802 496-6973
156 Cold Springs Farm Rd Warren (05674) *(G-17672)*

Mad River Distillers, Warren *Also Called: Cold Springs Spirits LLC* *(G-17671)*

Madd Gear LLC... 410 800-4423
8 Hedge Brook Ln Stamford (06903) *(G-3406)*

Madeira Asset Holdings Inc... 401 728-5903
9 Powder Hill Rd Lincoln (02865) *(G-16145)*

Madgetech, Warner *Also Called: Madgetech Inc* *(G-15665)*

Madgetech Inc **(PA)**.. **603 456-2011**
6 Warner Rd Warner (03278) *(G-15665)*

Madigan Millwork, Unionville *Also Called: Madigan Millworks Inc* *(G-3749)*

Madigan Millworks Inc... 860 673-7601
150 New Britain Ave Unionville (06085) *(G-3749)*

Madison Cable Corporation.. 800 522-6752
125 Goddard Memorial Dr Worcester (01603) *(G-13755)*

Madison Company **(PA)**... **203 488-4477**
27 Business Park Dr Branford (06405) *(G-270)*

Madison Medical LLC... 203 245-0306
8 Bishop Ln Ste 4 Madison (06443) *(G-1563)*

Madison Paper Industries, Madison *Also Called: Madison Upm* *(G-5042)*

Madison Polymeric Engrg Inc....................................... 203 488-4554
965 W Main St Ste 2 Branford (06405) *(G-271)*

Madison Upm.. 207 696-3307
1 Main St Madison (04950) *(G-5042)*

Madtown Logging LLC.. 207 728-6260
185 Lavoie Ave Madawaska (04756) *(G-5038)*

Mafcote Inc **(PA)**... **203 847-8500**
108 Main St Ste 3 Norwalk (06851) *(G-2530)*

Mafcote Industries.. 601 776-9006
108 Main St Ste 3 Norwalk (06851) *(G-2531)*

Mafcote International Inc **(HQ)**............................... **203 644-1200**
108 Main St Ste 3 Norwalk (06851) *(G-2532)*

Mag Jewelry Co Inc.. 401 942-1840
838 Dyer Ave Cranston (02920) *(G-15890)*

Magco Inc.. 207 324-8060
85 Spencer Dr Unit A Wells (04090) *(G-5600)*

Magellan Aerospace Usa Inc **(DH)**.......................... **978 774-6000**
20 Computer Dr Haverhill (01832) *(G-9112)*

Magellan Arospc Haverhill Inc...................................... 978 774-6000
20 Computer Dr Haverhill (01832) *(G-9113)*

Magellan Biosciences Inc **(HQ)**............................... **978 856-2345**
101 Billerica Ave Ste 4-2 North Billerica (01862) *(G-10930)*

Magellan Diagnostics, North Billerica *Also Called: Magellan Diagnostics Inc* *(G-10931)*

Magellan Diagnostics Inc **(HQ)**............................... **978 250-7000**
22 Alpha Rd Chelmsford (01824) *(G-7937)*

Magellan Diagnostics Inc.. 978 856-2345
101 Billerica Ave Ste 4-2 North Billerica (01862) *(G-10931)*

Magellan Distribution Corp.. 617 399-7900
12 Channel St Ste 803 Boston (02210) *(G-6868)*

Magic Kitch'n, Bow *Also Called: Pitco Frialator Inc* *(G-14008)*

Magik Eye Inc... 917 676-7436
1055 Washington Blvd Fl 5 Stamford (06901) *(G-3407)*

Magiq Technologies Inc **(PA)**.................................. **617 661-8300**
11 Ward St Ste 300 Somerville (02143) *(G-11884)*

Magma.. 978 381-3494
11 Pleasant St Gloucester (01930) *(G-8943)*

Magmotor, Worcester *Also Called: Magmotor Technologies Inc* *(G-13756)*

Magmotor Technologies Inc... 508 835-4305
10 Coppage Dr Worcester (01603) *(G-13756)*

Magna Elec Roadscape Auto LLC **(HQ)**.................... **978 656-2500**
1011 Pawtucket Blvd Lowell (01854) *(G-9901)*

Magna Electronics LLC.. 978 674-6500
1001 Pawtucket Blvd Lowell (01854) *(G-9902)*

Magna Steel Sales Inc... 203 888-0300
2 Alliance Cir Beacon Falls (06403) *(G-42)*

Magnat-Fairview Inc.. 413 593-5742
1102 Sheridan St Chicopee (01022) *(G-8046)*

Magnatech LLC... 860 653-2573
6 Kripes Rd East Granby (06026) *(G-939)*

Magnatech Dsd Co, The, East Granby *Also Called: Magnatech LLC* *(G-939)*

Magnemotion Inc.. 978 757-9100
139 Barnum Rd Devens (01434) *(G-8277)*

Magnetec Corporation... 203 949-9933
7 Laser Ln Wallingford (06492) *(G-3829)*

Magnetic Seal LLC.. 401 247-2800
365 Market St Warren (02885) *(G-16760)*

Magnetic Technologies Ltd.. 508 987-3303
31 Highland Dr Putnam (06260) *(G-2864)*

Magnetika/East Ltd Partnership................................... 508 485-7555
34 Saint Martin Dr Ste 11 Marlborough (01752) *(G-10181)*

Magnetometric Devices, Salem *Also Called: Stellar Manufacturing Inc* *(G-15564)*

Magnitude Software Inc... 781 202-3200
2400 District Ave Ste 320 Burlington (01803) *(G-7391)*

Magnum Machine Inc.. 603 895-0545
1 Infinity Dr Raymond (03077) *(G-15453)*

Magnus Molding, Pittsfield *Also Called: Modern Mold and Tool Inc* **(G-11412)**

Magnus Molding Inc... 413 443-1192
  1995 East St Pittsfield (01201) **(G-11408)**

Magris Talc Usa Inc... 802 228-6400
  73 E Hill Rd Ludlow (05149) **(G-17315)**

Mahar Excavating & Logging.. 802 442-2954
  592 Coleville Rd Bennington (05201) **(G-17049)**

Mahi Gold Inc... 508 348-5487
  465 Main St Chatham (02633) **(G-7898)**

Mahi Gold Outfitters, Chatham *Also Called: Mahi Gold Inc* **(G-7898)**

Mailly Mfg Co Inc.. 203 879-1445
  54 Wakelee Rd Wolcott (06716) **(G-4367)**

Main Industrial Tires Ltd **(PA)**................................. **713 676-0251**
  107 Audubon Rd Ste 2 Wakefield (01880) **(G-12515)**

Main Street Blanchard LLC.. 781 944-4000
  505 Main St Reading (01867) **(G-11603)**

Main Street Branch Co , The, West Kingston *Also Called: Arnold Lumber Co* **(G-16893)**

Maine & Maritimes Corporation **(PA)**............................. **207 760-2499**
  209 State St Presque Isle (04769) **(G-5304)**

Maine Alpaca Experience LLC.. 207 356-4146
  141 Crosby Brook Rd Unity (04988) **(G-5566)**

Maine Antique Digest Inc... 207 832-7534
  911 Main St Waldoboro (04572) **(G-5578)**

Maine Artfl Limb & Orthotics, Portland *Also Called: Maine Artfl Limb Orthotics Co* **(G-5236)**

Maine Artfl Limb Orthotics Co...................................... 207 773-4963
  959 Brighton Ave Rear Portland (04102) **(G-5236)**

Maine Bag Co, Caribou *Also Called: Maine Potato Growers Inc* **(G-4676)**

Maine Balsam Fir Prodcts... 207 674-5090
  16 Morse Hill Rd West Paris (04289) **(G-5612)**

Maine Balsam Fir Products, West Paris *Also Called: Maine Balsam Fir Prodcts* **(G-5612)**

Maine Bay Canvas Inc... 207 878-8888
  53 Industrial Way Portland (04103) **(G-5237)**

Maine Bedding & Furniture Co., Biddeford *Also Called: Portland Mattress Makers* **(G-4582)**

Maine Beer Company LLC... 207 221-5711
  525 Us Route 1 Freeport (04032) **(G-4801)**

Maine Beverage Association... 207 773-5505
  316 Western Ave South Portland (04106) **(G-5507)**

Maine Bio-Fuel Inc... 207 878-3001
  51 Ingersol Dr Portland (04103) **(G-5238)**

Maine Biotechnology Svcs Inc....................................... 207 797-5454
  1037r Forest Ave Portland (04103) **(G-5239)**

Maine Bracelet Company, The, Boothbay Harbor *Also Called: A Silver Lining Inc* **(G-4599)**

Maine Bunk Beds LLC.. 207 929-4499
  355 Joy Valley Rd Buxton (04093) **(G-4663)**

Maine Camp Outfitters, Sunset *Also Called: Island Approaches* **(G-5539)**

Maine Cat.. 207 529-6500
  380 Hope Rd Lincolnville (04849) **(G-5015)**

Maine Cedar Specialty Products..................................... 207 532-4034
  1938 Ludlow Rd Ludlow (04730) **(G-5028)**

Maine Coast Nordic... 207 255-6714
  133 Smalls Point Rd Machiasport (04655) **(G-5035)**

Maine Coast Sea Vegetables Inc..................................... 207 412-0094
  430 Washington Jctn Rd Hancock (04640) **(G-4871)**

Maine Commercial Tire Inc **(PA)**................................. **207 848-5540**
  55 Freedom Pkwy Hermon (04401) **(G-4885)**

Maine Commercial Tire Inc.. 207 622-3200
  30 Industrial St Waterville (04901) **(G-5595)**

Maine Container LLC.. 603 888-1315
  115 Poland Spring Dr Poland (04274) **(G-5161)**

Maine Craft Distilling LLC... 207 798-2528
  123 Washington Ave Ste 1 Portland (04101) **(G-5240)**

Maine Custom Woodlands LLC... 207 353-9020
  1326 Hallowell Rd Durham (04222) **(G-4733)**

Maine Grains Inc... 207 474-8001
  42 Court St Skowhegan (04976) **(G-5471)**

Maine Heritage Timber LLC.. 207 723-9200
  102 Penobscot Ave Millinocket (04462) **(G-5066)**

Maine Heritage Weavers... 207 933-2605
  904 Main St Monmouth (04259) **(G-5071)**

Maine Homestead, Lyman *Also Called: Maine Homestead Inc* **(G-5030)**

Maine Homestead Inc.. 207 344-9274
  1773 Alfred Rd Lyman (04002) **(G-5030)**

Maine Industrial P & R Corp.. 207 563-5532
  21 Teague St Newcastle (04553) **(G-5095)**

Maine Industrial Repair Service Inc................................ 207 623-7500
  60 Darin Dr Augusta (04330) **(G-4476)**

Maine Industrial Tire, Wakefield *Also Called: Maine Industrial Tire LLC* **(G-12516)**

Maine Industrial Tire LLC.. 781 914-3410
  107 Audubon Rd Ste 2 Wakefield (01880) **(G-12516)**

Maine Innkeepers Association, Skowhegan *Also Called: Maine Stitching Spc LLC* **(G-5472)**

Maine Island Trail Assctn-Cncl, Rockland *Also Called: Island Institute* **(G-5334)**

Maine Machine Products Company **(PA)**............................ **207 743-6344**
  79 Prospect Ave South Paris (04281) **(G-5489)**

Maine Manufacturing LLC.. 207 324-1754
  63 Community Dr Sanford (04073) **(G-5398)**

Maine Market Refrigeration LLC **(PA)**............................ **207 685-3504**
  98 Morris Springer Rd Fayette (04349) **(G-4783)**

Maine Metal Recycling Inc.. 207 786-3531
  522 Washington St N Auburn (04210) **(G-4442)**

Maine Mold & Machine Inc... 207 388-2732
  208 Town Farm Rd Hartford (04220) **(G-4876)**

Maine Natural Gas Corporation...................................... 207 729-0420
  9 Industrial Pkwy Brunswick (04011) **(G-4648)**

Maine Orthotic Lab, Portland *Also Called: Maine Orthtic Prsthtic Rhab Sv* **(G-5241)**

Maine Orthtic Prsthtic Rhab Sv..................................... 207 773-8818
  300 Park Ave Portland (04102) **(G-5241)**

Maine Parts & Machine Inc.. 207 797-0024
  68 Waldron Way Portland (04103) **(G-5242)**

Maine Pet Supply... 207 360-0005
  179 Sanford Rd Wells (04090) **(G-5601)**

Maine Plastics, Portland *Also Called: Altium Packaging LLC* **(G-5177)**

Maine Poly Aquisition Corp... 207 946-7000
  933 Route 202 Greene (04236) **(G-4847)**

Maine Potato Growers Inc... 207 764-3131
  56 Sincock St Caribou (04736) **(G-4676)**

Maine Radio.. 207 883-2929
  68 Mussey Rd Scarborough (04074) **(G-5438)**

Maine Rubber International.. 877 648-1949
  107 Audubon Rd Ste 2 Wakefield (01880) **(G-12517)**

Maine Scale LLC.. 207 777-9500
  4 Washington St N Ste 1 Auburn (04210) **(G-4443)**

Maine Seafood Ventures LLC... 207 303-0165
  1016 Portland Rd Saco (04072) **(G-5372)**

Maine Shipping & Packaging Sup, Portland *Also Called: Ship-Pac Corp* **(G-5270)**

Maine Standard Biofuels, Portland *Also Called: Maine Bio-Fuel Inc* **(G-5238)**

Maine Standards Company, LLC, Cumberland Foreside *Also Called: Lgc Clinical Diagnostics Inc* **(G-4712)**

Maine Stitching Spc LLC.. 207 812-5207
  40 Dane Ave Skowhegan (04976) **(G-5472)**

Maine Stove & Chimney LLC.. 207 324-4440
  1438 Main St Sanford (04073) **(G-5399)**

Maine Sunday Telegram, Portland *Also Called: Mtm Oldco Inc* **(G-5247)**

Maine Tire, Wakefield *Also Called: Maine Rubber International* **(G-12517)**

Maine Tire & Appliance Co.. 207 623-1171
  300 State St Augusta (04330) **(G-4477)**

Maine Tire & Appliance Co **(PA)**................................. **207 781-3136**
  251 Us Route 1 Ste 9 Falmouth (04105) **(G-4769)**

Maine Tool & Machine LLC... 207 576-4319
  27 Canal St Lisbon Falls (04252) **(G-5022)**

Maine Turnpike Authority... 207 829-4531
  108 Blackstrap Rd Cumberland Center (04021) **(G-4709)**

Maine Valve Rebuilders... 207 856-6735
  5 Sanford Dr Gorham (04038) **(G-4825)**

Maine Visual... 207 553-0798
  13 Emerson St Apt 204 Portland (04101) **(G-5243)**

Maine Wild Blueberry Company....................................... 207 255-8364
  50 Elm St Machias (04654) **(G-5032)**

Maine Wild Blueberry Company **(DH)**.............................. **207 255-8364**
  78 Elm St Machias (04654) **(G-5033)**

Maine Wood Flooring, Portage *Also Called: Maine Woods Company LLC* **(G-5164)**

Maine Wood Treaters Inc...	207 345-8411
58 Walker Rd Mechanic Falls (04256) *(G-5052)*	
Maine Wood Turning Inc...	207 652-2320
Lake Street Rte 234 New Vineyard (04956) *(G-5091)*	
Maine Woods Company LLC...	207 435-4393
92 Fish Lake Rd Portage (04768) *(G-5164)*	
Maine Woods Pellet Company LLC..	207 654-2237
164 Harmony Rd Athens (04912) *(G-4415)*	
Maine Woolens LLC...	207 725-7900
15 Paul St Brunswick (04011) *(G-4649)*	
Maine-OK Enterprises Inc...	207 633-4620
97 Townsend Ave Boothbay Harbor (04538) *(G-4602)*	
MAINE'S FIRST SHIP, Bath *Also Called: Virginia Project Inc (G-4531)*	
Mainecal, Auburn *Also Called: Maine Scale LLC (G-4443)*	
Maineline Graphics, Antrim *Also Called: Maineline Graphics LLC (G-13897)*	
Maineline Graphics LLC..	603 588-3177
1 High St Antrim (03440) *(G-13897)*	
Mainely Gates & Handrails..	207 314-1083
263 Neck Rd Benton (04901) *(G-4546)*	
Mainely Handrails LLC...	207 314-1083
52 West St Fairfield (04937) *(G-4764)*	
Mainely Media..	207 282-4337
457 Alfred St Biddeford (04005) *(G-4576)*	
Mainely Newspapers Inc...	207 282-4337
180 Main St Biddeford (04005) *(G-4577)*	
Mainline Tool & Grind Inc..	413 626-9601
66 Mainline Dr Ste C Westfield (01085) *(G-13180)*	
Mainstream Global Inc..	978 682-6767
91 Glenn St Lawrence (01843) *(G-9579)*	
Mainstream Inc **(PA)**...	**802 442-8859**
1003 Monument Ave Bennington (05201) *(G-17050)*	
Mair-Mac Machine Company Inc...	508 895-9001
86 N Montello St Brockton (02301) *(G-7294)*	
Majestic Marble & Granite Inc..	781 830-1020
253 Revere St Canton (02021) *(G-7807)*	
Majestic Medical Inc..	508 824-1944
44 Commercial St Ste 2 Raynham (02767) *(G-11590)*	
Majilite Corporation..	978 441-6800
1530 Broadway Rd Dracut (01826) *(G-8307)*	
Majilite Manufacturing Inc..	978 441-6800
1530 Broadway Rd Dracut (01826) *(G-8308)*	
Major Findings Div, Warwick *Also Called: Robert Baxter Associates Inc (G-16853)*	
Make Archtectural Metalworking..	508 273-7603
2358 Cranberry Hwy West Wareham (02576) *(G-13067)*	
Makers Natural Green Wreaths, Newport Center *Also Called: Vermont Center Wreaths Inc (G-17408)*	
Makers Tool and Mfg Co LLC..	774 633-0658
175 Main St Oxford (01540) *(G-11261)*	
Maki Building Centers Inc **(HQ)**..	**978 343-7422**
513 Betty Spring Rd Gardner (01440) *(G-8894)*	
Maki Corp **(PA)**..	**978 343-7422**
513 Betty Spring Rd Gardner (01440) *(G-8895)*	
Making Your Mark Inc...	617 479-0999
121 Liberty St Quincy (02169) *(G-11527)*	
Malco Saw Co Inc..	401 942-7380
22 Field St Cranston (02920) *(G-15891)*	
Malden Intl Designs Inc..	508 946-2270
19 Cowan Dr Middleboro (02346) *(G-10365)*	
Male Clerk, Providence *Also Called: Johnson & Wales University (G-16550)*	
Maley Laser, Warwick *Also Called: Maley Laser Processing Inc (G-16834)*	
Maley Laser Processing Inc..	303 952-8941
25 Graystone St Warwick (02886) *(G-16834)*	
Malings Welding Svc Inc...	207 985-9769
115 York St Kennebunk (04043) *(G-4926)*	
Mallace Industries Corp..	800 521-0194
460 Woodland Ave Bloomfield (06002) *(G-191)*	
Mallace Industries Corp..	860 669-9001
1 Heritage Park Rd Clinton (06413) *(G-647)*	
Mallard Printing Inc..	508 675-5733
657 Quarry St Ste 9 Fall River (02723) *(G-8572)*	
Malvern Panalytical, Westborough *Also Called: Panalytical Inc (G-13128)*	

Malvern Panalytical Inc..	413 586-7720
22 Industrial Dr E Northampton (01060) *(G-11070)*	
Mam Software Inc..	978 392-0941
163 Plain Rd Westford (01886) *(G-13248)*	
Mamava Inc..	802 347-2111
180 Battery St Ste 210 Burlington (05401) *(G-17142)*	
Mamco, Westerly *Also Called: Maxson Automatic Machinery Co (G-16935)*	
Manage Inc...	413 593-9128
1380 Main St Ste 500 Springfield (01103) *(G-12112)*	
Manchester Corporation..	978 772-2900
280 Ayer Rd Harvard (01451) *(G-9065)*	
Manchester Life, Arlington *Also Called: Old Mill Road Media LLC (G-16991)*	
Manchester Lumber Inc...	802 635-2315
66 River Rd E Johnson (05656) *(G-17309)*	
Manchester Marine, Manchester *Also Called: Northern Light Mar Group Inc (G-10033)*	
Manchester Molding and Mfg Co...	860 643-2141
96 Sheldon Rd Manchester (06042) *(G-1615)*	
Manchester Packing, Vernon *Also Called: Bravo LLC (G-3752)*	
Manchester Packing Company Inc...	860 646-5000
349 Wetherell St Manchester (06040) *(G-1616)*	
Manchester TI & Design ADP LLC...	860 296-6541
44 Hermitage Ln North Haven (06473) *(G-2422)*	
Manchester, NH Plant, Manchester *Also Called: Prysmian Cbles Systems USA LLC (G-14918)*	
Manco LLC...	603 485-5327
43 Allenstown Rd Ste 1 Allenstown (03275) *(G-13852)*	
Mandes Inc...	781 344-6915
593 Washington St Stoughton (02072) *(G-12220)*	
Mandeville, Lincoln *Also Called: Mandeville Signs Inc (G-16146)*	
Mandeville Signs Inc..	401 334-9100
676 George Washington Hwy Lincoln (02865) *(G-16146)*	
Manfucturer, Charlton *Also Called: Incom Inc (G-7889)*	
Mange, Somerville *Also Called: Mange LLC (G-11885)*	
Mange LLC...	917 880-2104
30 Summer St Apt 1 Somerville (02143) *(G-11885)*	
Manisses Cmmncations Group Inc..	401 273-5221
17 University Ave Providence (02906) *(G-16557)*	
Manning Way Cpitl Partners LLC...	508 966-4800
5 Williams Way Bellingham (02019) *(G-6293)*	
Mannkind, Danbury *Also Called: Mannkind Corporation (G-781)*	
Mannkind Corporation **(PA)**...	**818 661-5000**
1 Casper St Ste 330 Danbury (06810) *(G-781)*	
Manomet Manufacturing Inc...	508 997-1795
194 Riverside Ave New Bedford (02746) *(G-10617)*	
Manroland Goss Web Systems AMR **(DH)**............................	**603 750-6600**
22 Industrial Dr Exeter (03833) *(G-14294)*	
Manroland Web Systems Inc...	630 920-5850
22 Industrial Dr Exeter (03833) *(G-14295)*	
Mansir Printing LLC..	413 536-4250
24 Shawmut Ave Holyoke (01040) *(G-9264)*	
Mantrose-Haeuser Co Inc **(HQ)**..	**203 454-1800**
100 Nyala Farms Rd Westport (06880) *(G-4182)*	
Mantrose-Haeuser Co Inc...	203 454-1800
113 Olive St Attleboro (02703) *(G-6033)*	
Manufacturer, Greenfield *Also Called: Northeastern Metals LLC (G-8997)*	
Manufacturer, North Billerica *Also Called: Nextek LLC (G-10939)*	
Manufacturer, Norwood *Also Called: Lqc Inc (G-11191)*	
Manufacturer, Warwick *Also Called: Aquamotion Inc (G-16783)*	
Manufacturer of Goods, Pocasset *Also Called: Falmouth Scientific Inc (G-11486)*	
Manufacturers Associates Inc...	203 931-4344
45 Railroad Ave West Haven (06516) *(G-4113)*	
Manufacturers Coml Fin LLC...	860 242-6287
1022 Boulevard West Hartford (06119) *(G-4070)*	
Manufacturers Service Co Inc...	203 389-9595
5 Lunar Dr Woodbridge (06525) *(G-4381)*	
Manufacturers Services Limited..	617 330-7682
300 Baker Ave Concord (01742) *(G-8124)*	
Manufactures Technologies, West Springfield *Also Called: MTI Systems Inc (G-13035)*	
Manufacturing, Stamford *Also Called: Amerpet LLC (G-3280)*	
Manufacturing, Wallingford *Also Called: New Designz Inc (G-3834)*	

**A
L
P
H
A
B
E
T
I
C**

Manufacturing, North Anson *Also Called: Cousineau Wood Products ME LLC (G-5104)*

Manufacturing, Burlington *Also Called: Computer Imprntble Lbel System (G-7355)*

Manufacturing, Nashua *Also Called: W H Bagshaw Co Inc (G-15184)*

Manufacturing PDT Systems Inc..877 689-1860
910 Day Hill Rd Windsor (06095) *(G-4288)*

Manufacturing Services Group...603 883-1022
91 Lilac Ct Manchester (03103) *(G-14878)*

Manufacturing Solutions Inc..802 888-3289
153 Stafford Ave Morrisville (05661) *(G-17386)*

Manufacturing Tech Group Inc...413 562-4337
85 Servistar Industrial Way Westfield (01085) *(G-13181)*

Manufacturing/Distribution, Wilbraham *Also Called: Safehands Distribution Ne LLC (G-13363)*

Manufctring Resource Group Inc..781 440-9700
930 Washington St Norwood (02062) *(G-11192)*

Manup LLC...203 588-9861
345 Wilson Ave Norwalk (06854) *(G-2533)*

Manus Bio Inc **(HQ)**...**617 299-8466**
43 Foundry Ave Waltham (02453) *(G-12713)*

Maple Brook Farm, North Bennington *Also Called: Mountain Mozzarella LLC (G-17409)*

Maple Craft Foods LLC..203 913-7066
6 Cider Mill Rd Sandy Hook (06482) *(G-2952)*

Maple Grove Farms Vermont Inc **(HQ)**..............................**802 748-5141**
1052 Portland St Saint Johnsbury (05819) *(G-17543)*

Maple Guild, Island Pond *Also Called: Sweet Tree Holdings 1 LLC (G-17305)*

Maple Landmark Inc..802 388-0627
1297 Exchange St Middlebury (05753) *(G-17346)*

Maple Landmark Woodcraft, Middlebury *Also Called: Maple Landmark Inc (G-17346)*

Maple Leaf Industries..508 728-9581
102 Highland Rd Lakeville (02347) *(G-9517)*

Maple Print Services Inc...860 381-5470
39 Wedgewood Dr Jewett City (06351) *(G-1536)*

Maple Wind Farm Inc..802 434-7257
1149 E Main St Richmond (05477) *(G-17480)*

Maplegate Media Group Inc..203 826-7557
1503 Sienna Dr Danbury (06810) *(G-782)*

Maplewood Machine Co Inc...508 673-6710
271 Anthony St Fall River (02721) *(G-8573)*

MAR, Foxboro *Also Called: Massachusetts Assn Realtors (G-8707)*

Mar Lee Companies Tech Ctrs, Fitchburg *Also Called: Mar-Lee Companies Inc (G-8661)*

Mar-Lee Companies Inc...978 343-9600
190 Authority Dr Fitchburg (01420) *(G-8661)*

Mar-Lee Companies Inc **(HQ)**..**978 343-9600**
180 Authority Dr Fitchburg (01420) *(G-8662)*

Mar-Lees Seafood LLC..508 991-6026
98 Front St New Bedford (02740) *(G-10618)*

Marathon, Attleboro *Also Called: Marathon Co (G-6034)*

Marathon Co...508 222-5544
90 Oneil Blvd Attleboro (02703) *(G-6034)*

Marblehead Engineering...978 432-1386
7 Essex Park Rd Essex (01929) *(G-8477)*

Marblehead Weather Gmts LLC..781 639-1060
100 Hoods Ln Ste U8 Marblehead (01945) *(G-10090)*

Marbuo Inc...508 994-7700
634 State Rd Unit E2 North Dartmouth (02747) *(G-10999)*

Marc Fisher Footwear, Greenwich *Also Called: Fisher Footwear LLC (G-1330)*

Marc Fisher Footwear, Greenwich *Also Called: Mf-TFC LLC (G-1342)*

Marc Woodworks LLC...203 281-4700
51 Overlook Dr Hamden (06514) *(G-1438)*

Marca Machine Engineering, Gorham *Also Called: Phocam Manufacturing LLC (G-4830)*

Marcell Oil Company Inc...802 775-5050
740 Us Route 7 Pittsford (05763) *(G-17445)*

Marco Group LLC **(PA)**...**603 468-3600**
35 Woodworkers Way Seabrook (03874) *(G-15596)*

Marco International Inc..203 894-8000
100 Danbury Rd Ste 101 Ridgefield (06877) *(G-2902)*

Marco Manufacturing, Ridgefield *Also Called: Marco International Inc (G-2902)*

Marco Rubber, Seabrook *Also Called: Marco Group LLC (G-15596)*

Marcus Company Inc...413 534-3303
750 Main St Holyoke (01040) *(G-9265)*

Marcus Printing Co, Holyoke *Also Called: Marcus Company Inc (G-9265)*

Marel Corporation...203 934-8187
5 Saw Mill Rd West Haven (06516) *(G-4114)*

Marena Industries Inc...860 528-9701
433 School St East Hartford (06108) *(G-1004)*

Marena Machinery Sales Div, East Hartford *Also Called: Marena Industries Inc (G-1004)*

Marenna Amusements LLC..203 623-4386
88 Marsh Hill Rd Orange (06477) *(G-2675)*

Maretron LLP..602 861-1707
60 Johnson Ave Plainville (06062) *(G-2771)*

Mariah Group LLC..802 747-4000
92 Park St Rutland (05701) *(G-17503)*

Marian Heath, Wareham *Also Called: Marian Heath Greeting Cards LLC (G-12840)*

Marian Heath Greeting Cards LLC.......................................508 291-0766
9 Kendrick Rd Wareham (02571) *(G-12840)*

Marie Deprofio...781 894-9793
11 Harrington Rd Waltham (02452) *(G-12714)*

Marimed Inc **(PA)**..**781 277-0007**
10 Oceana Way Ste 2 Norwood (02062) *(G-11193)*

Marine Hydraulics Inc...508 990-2866
256 Herman Melville Blvd New Bedford (02740) *(G-10619)*

Marine Money, Stamford *Also Called: International Mktg Strategies (G-3384)*

Marine Polymer Tech Inc **(PA)**...**781 270-3200**
159 Lorum St Tewksbury (01876) *(G-12405)*

Marine Usa Inc...508 791-7116
200 Sw Cutoff Ste 1 Worcester (01604) *(G-13757)*

Marinero Express 809 East..203 487-0636
809 E Main St Stamford (06902) *(G-3408)*

Marion Drapery Workroom, Lincoln *Also Called: Marion Mfg Co (G-16147)*

Marion Manufacturing Company..203 272-5376
1675 Reinhard Rd Cheshire (06410) *(G-605)*

Marion Mfg Co..401 331-4343
1 Court Dr Lincoln (02865) *(G-16147)*

Marios Oil Corp..617 202-8259
22 Forest Ave Everett (02149) *(G-8493)*

Maritime Activity Reports **(PA)**...**212 477-6700**
60 Herrmann Ln Easton (06612) *(G-1096)*

Marja Corporation..207 324-2994
14 Dale St Sanford (04073) *(G-5400)*

Marjan Inc..203 573-1742
44 Railroad Hill St Waterbury (06708) *(G-3942)*

Mark Allen Cabinetry LLC...603 491-7570
13 Columbia Dr Unit 3 Amherst (03031) *(G-13877)*

Mark Belden, Keene *Also Called: Belden Inc (G-14590)*

Mark Richey Wdwkg & Design Inc.......................................978 499-3800
40 Parker St Newburyport (01950) *(G-10698)*

Markal Finishing Co Inc..203 384-8219
400 Bostwick Ave Bridgeport (06605) *(G-346)*

Markard Industries, Providence *Also Called: Contempo Card Co Inc (G-16505)*

Markarian Electric LLC..617 393-9700
586 Pleasant St Ste 5 Watertown (02472) *(G-12890)*

Markem-Imaje Corporation **(HQ)**......................................**603 352-1130**
150 Congress St Keene (03431) *(G-14607)*

Market Basket Produce Inc...603 224-5479
108 Fort Eddy Rd Concord (03301) *(G-14143)*

Market Forge Industries Inc..617 387-4100
35 Garvey St Everett (02149) *(G-8494)*

Marketing Worldwide Corp **(PA)**.......................................**631 444-8090**
423 Main St Ste 3 Rockland (04841) *(G-5339)*

Marketplace Inc Corporate..401 336-3000
816 Middle Rd East Greenwich (02818) *(G-15990)*

Markforged Inc **(HQ)**...**866 496-1805**
60 Tower Rd Waltham (02451) *(G-12715)*

Markforged Holding Corporation **(PA)**..............................**866 496-1805**
480 Pleasant St Watertown (02472) *(G-12891)*

Marklin Candle Design, Contoocook *Also Called: Marklin Candle Design LLC (G-14171)*

Marklin Candle Design LLC...603 746-2211
28 Riverside Dr Contoocook (03229) *(G-14171)*

Markwell Manufacturing Co Inc..781 769-6610
692 Pleasant St Norwood (02062) *(G-11194)*

Marland Mold Inc...413 443-4481
12 Betnr Industrial Dr Pittsfield (01201) *(G-11409)*

Marlboro Plastics, Marlborough *Also Called: Altium Packaging LP* **(G-10107)**	
Marlborough Foundry Inc...........	508 485-2848
555 Maple St Marlborough (01752) **(G-10182)**	
Marlborough Plastics Inc..........	860 295-9124
350 N Main St Marlborough (06447) **(G-1644)**	
Marlin Company, The, Wallingford *Also Called: TMC Liquidating Corp* **(G-3869)**	
Marmon Aerospace & Defense LLC.........	603 622-3500
655 Valley St Manchester (03103) **(G-14879)**	
Marmon Aerospace & Defense LLC **(DH)**.........	**603 622-3500**
680 Hayward St Manchester (03103) **(G-14880)**	
Marmon Engineered Wire & Cable, Hartford *Also Called: Marmon Engnered Wire Cable LLC* **(G-1491)**	
Marmon Engnered Wire Cable LLC.........	860 653-8300
280 Trumbull St Fl 23 Hartford (06103) **(G-1491)**	
Marmon Indus Enrgy Infrstrctur.........	860 653-8300
20 Bradley Park Rd East Granby (06026) **(G-940)**	
Marmon Utility...........	603 249-1302
53 Old Wilton Rd Milford (03055) **(G-15031)**	
Marmon Utility LLC.........	603 673-2040
116 State Route 101a Amherst (03031) **(G-13878)**	
Marmon Utility LLC **(DH)**.........	**603 673-2040**
53 Old Wilton Rd Milford (03055) **(G-15032)**	
Marox Corporation.........	413 536-1300
373 Whitney Ave Holyoke (01040) **(G-9266)**	
Marques Guitars LLC.........	603 321-4833
230 Laval St Manchester (03102) **(G-14881)**	
Mars 2000 Inc.........	401 421-5275
45 Troy St Providence (02909) **(G-16558)**	
Mars Plastics, Providence *Also Called: Mars 2000 Inc* **(G-16558)**	
Marsam Metal Finishing Co.........	860 826-5489
206 Newington Ave New Britain (06051) **(G-2039)**	
Marsars Wtr Rescue Systems Inc.........	203 924-7315
206 Skokorat Rd Beacon Falls (06403) **(G-43)**	
Marshall & Williams Plastics, Woonsocket *Also Called: Parkinson Machinery & Manufacturing Corp* **(G-16971)**	
Marshall Marine Corporation.........	508 994-0414
55 Shipyard Ln South Dartmouth (02748) **(G-11917)**	
Marshall Paper Tube Co, Avon *Also Called: CA J&L Enterprises Inc* **(G-6146)**	
Martel Electronics Corp.........	603 434-6033
3 Corporate Park Dr Unit 1 Derry (03038) **(G-14201)**	
Martel Welding & Sons Inc.........	978 458-0661
500 Woburn St Tewksbury (01876) **(G-12406)**	
Martha's Vineyard Printing Co, Oak Bluffs *Also Called: Da Rosas* **(G-11221)**	
Marthas Seastreak Vineyard LLC.........	617 896-0293
49 State Pier New Bedford (02740) **(G-10620)**	
Marthas Vineyard Furn Co LLC.........	508 687-9555
49 Main St Vineyard Haven (02568) **(G-12491)**	
Marthas Vineyard Intr Design, Vineyard Haven *Also Called: Marthas Vineyard Furn Co LLC* **(G-12491)**	
Marthas Vineyard Times.........	508 693-6100
30 Beach Rd Vineyard Haven (02568) **(G-12492)**	
Martignetti Companies, Central Falls *Also Called: Martignetti Companies RI* **(G-15792)**	
Martignetti Companies RI.........	401 722-8008
500 High St Central Falls (02863) **(G-15792)**	
Martin Benjamin Corporation.........	781 326-8311
115 Commerce Way Dedham (02026) **(G-8246)**	
Martin Cabinet Inc.........	860 747-5769
500 Broad St Bristol (06010) **(G-464)**	
Martin Cabinet Inc **(PA)**.........	**860 747-5769**
336 S Washington St Ste 2 Plainville (06062) **(G-2772)**	
Martin Interiors Inc.........	781 447-1022
22 Industrial Blvd Ste G Hanson (02341) **(G-9053)**	
Martin Intl Enclosures LLC.........	603 474-2626
14 Woodworkers Way Seabrook (03874) **(G-15597)**	
Martin Printing Inc.........	203 239-7991
100 Powdered Metal Rd North Haven (06473) **(G-2423)**	
Martin Rosols Inc.........	860 223-2707
45 Grove St New Britain (06053) **(G-2040)**	
Martins News Shop.........	617 267-1334
143 Hemenway St Apt 4 Boston (02115) **(G-6869)**	
Martins Soldering.........	401 521-2280
10 Alcazar Ave Johnston (02919) **(G-16095)**	

Martran Corp.........	508 699-7506
65 John L Dietsch Blvd Ste A Attleboro Falls (02763) **(G-6089)**	
Marty Gilman Incorporated.........	860 889-7334
1 Commerce Park Rd Bozrah (06334) **(G-229)**	
Marty Gilman Incorporated **(PA)**.........	**860 889-7334**
30 Gilman Rd Gilman (06336) **(G-1267)**	
Maru Ltd DBA Greenleaf Metals.........	802 985-5200
1022 Mason Hl N Starksboro (05487) **(G-17626)**	
Maruho Htsujyo Innovations Inc **(PA)**.........	**617 653-1617**
55 Accord Park Dr Norwell (02061) **(G-11143)**	
Marvel Abrasive Products, Lincoln *Also Called: Bates Abrasive Products Inc* **(G-16121)**	
Marvel Abrasives Products LLC.........	800 621-0673
6 Carol Dr Lincoln (02865) **(G-16148)**	
Marvel Screw Machine Pdts Inc.........	203 756-7058
58 Lafayette St Waterbury (06708) **(G-3943)**	
Marvell Gvrnment Solutions LLC.........	845 245-8066
128 Lakeside Ave Ste 403 Burlington (05401) **(G-17143)**	
Marver Med Inc.........	781 341-9372
1063 Turnpike St Stoughton (02072) **(G-12221)**	
Marvic Inc.........	508 798-2600
160 Southbridge St Auburn (01501) **(G-6119)**	
Mary Breen & Company Inc.........	207 646-4227
616 Post Rd Wells (04090) **(G-5602)**	
Marzae LLC.........	630 915-0352
55 Knox Trl Ste 407 Acton (01720) **(G-5758)**	
Marzae LLC **(PA)**.........	**619 915-0352**
8 Gould Rd Bedford (01730) **(G-6238)**	
Marzilli Machine Co.........	508 567-4145
621 S Almond St Fall River (02724) **(G-8574)**	
Masart Inc.........	781 786-8774
586 Pleasant St Watertown (02472) **(G-12892)**	
Masas Usa Inc.........	305 603-8868
192 Commerce St East Haven (06512) **(G-1045)**	
Maschino & Sons Lumber Co Inc.........	207 926-4288
79 Morse Rd New Gloucester (04260) **(G-5086)**	
Mascon Inc.........	781 938-5800
5 Commonwealth Ave Unit 3 Woburn (01801) **(G-13605)**	
Mascon Medical, Woburn *Also Called: Mascon Inc* **(G-13605)**	
Masimo Semiconductor Inc.........	603 595-8900
25 Sagamore Park Rd Hudson (03051) **(G-14525)**	
Mason & Hamlin, Haverhill *Also Called: Burgett Brothers Incorporated* **(G-9082)**	
Mason Box Company.........	800 842-9526
517 Mineral Spring Ave Pawtucket (02860) **(G-16383)**	
Mason's Racing Engines, North Scituate *Also Called: Rounds Service Station Inc* **(G-16316)**	
Masonite International Corp.........	978 534-4065
248 Industrial Rd Leominster (01453) **(G-9681)**	
Mass Bay Brewing Company Inc **(PA)**.........	**617 574-9551**
306 Northern Ave Boston (02210) **(G-6870)**	
Mass Brewing LLC **(PA)**.........	**617 800-7070**
175 Sterling St Clinton (01510) **(G-8083)**	
Mass Brewing LLC.........	617 800-7070
65 Jackson Rd Devens (01434) **(G-8278)**	
Mass Cabinets Inc.........	978 738-0600
99 Cross St Methuen (01844) **(G-10337)**	
Mass Design Inc **(PA)**.........	**603 886-6460**
12 Murphy Dr Nashua (03062) **(G-15130)**	
Mass Dry Ice Corporation **(DH)**.........	**413 283-9906**
19 2nd St Palmer (01069) **(G-11277)**	
Mass Engineering & Tank Inc.........	508 947-8669
29 Abbey Ln Middleboro (02346) **(G-10366)**	
Mass Machine Inc.........	781 467-3550
24 Walpole Park S Ste 14 Walpole (02081) **(G-12566)**	
Mass Printing Inc.........	781 396-1970
352 Park St Ste 202w North Reading (01864) **(G-11042)**	
Mass Tank Inspection Svcs LLC.........	508 923-3445
29 Abbey Ln Middleboro (02346) **(G-10367)**	
Mass Tank Sales Corp.........	508 947-8826
29 Abbey Ln Middleboro (02346) **(G-10368)**	
Mass Transfer Systems, Walpole *Also Called: North Amrcn Fltration Mass Inc* **(G-12570)**	
Mass Vac Inc.........	978 667-2393
247 Rangeway Rd North Billerica (01862) **(G-10932)**	

ALPHABETIC

Mass-Flex Research Inc... 781 391-3640
  18 Canal St Ste 3 Medford (02155) *(G-10295)*

Massa Products Corporation... 781 749-3120
  280 Lincoln St Hingham (02043) *(G-9152)*

Massachsetts Brewers Guild Inc.................................. 508 405-9115
  237 Belknap Rd Framingham (01701) *(G-8788)*

Massachstts Cntning Lgal Edcat................................. 617 482-2205
  10 Winter Pl Boston (02108) *(G-6871)*

Massachstts Rebuild Svc Export, West Brookfield *Also Called: Mrse Inc (G-12996)*

Massachstts Sign Instlltion Co...................................... 508 793-0956
  184 Main St Worcester (01608) *(G-13758)*

Massachstts Soc For Prvntion C **(PA)**........................ **617 522-7282**
  350 S Huntington Ave Boston (02130) *(G-6872)*

Massachusetts Aspen Tech Inc, Bedford *Also Called: Aspen Technology Inc (G-6211)*

Massachusetts Assn Realtors **(PA)**............................ **781 890-3700**
  18 Washington St Foxboro (02035) *(G-8707)*

Massachusetts Bay Tech Inc.. 781 344-8809
  378 Page St Ste 7 Stoughton (02072) *(G-12222)*

Massachusetts Bev Aliance LLC.................................. 617 701-6238
  190 Mechanic St Bellingham (02019) *(G-6294)*

Massachusetts Beverage Bus, Boston *Also Called: New Beverage Publications Inc (G-6914)*

Massachusetts Broken Stone Co **(PA)**........................ **978 838-9999**
  332 Sawyerhill Rd Berlin (01503) *(G-6319)*

Massachusetts Broken Stone Co.................................. 508 829-5353
  2077 N Main St Holden (01520) *(G-9193)*

Massachusetts Clean Energy Ctr.................................. 617 315-9355
  63 Franklin St 3rd Fl Boston (02110) *(G-6873)*

Massachusetts Container Corp...................................... 508 481-1100
  300 Cedar Hill St Marlborough (01752) *(G-10183)*

Massachusetts Contr Sups Inc...................................... 978 413-2578
  71 Parmenter Rd Hudson (01749) *(G-9389)*

Massachusetts Envelope Co Inc.................................... 860 727-9100
  10 Midland St Hartford (06120) *(G-1492)*

Massachusetts Envelope Co Inc **(PA)**.......................... **617 623-8000**
  10 State St Ste 100 Woburn (01801) *(G-13606)*

Massachusetts Institute Tech.. 617 253-5646
  1 Rogers St Cambridge (02142) *(G-7637)*

Massachusetts Institute Tech.. 617 253-7183
  77 Max Ave Ste E60 Cambridge (02139) *(G-7638)*

Massachusetts Mch Works Inc...................................... 781 467-3550
  24 Walpole Park S Ste 14 Walpole (02081) *(G-12567)*

Massachusetts Medical Society.................................... 617 734-9800
  10 Shattuck St Boston (02115) *(G-6874)*

Massachusetts Medical Society..................................... 781 434-7950
  108 Clematis Ave Ste E Waltham (02453) *(G-12716)*

Massachusetts Natural Fert Inc..................................... 978 874-0744
  65 Bean Porridge Hill Rd Westminster (01473) *(G-13272)*

Massachusetts Port Authority.. 617 561-9300
  200 Terminal B Boston (02128) *(G-6875)*

Massachusetts Repro Ltd.. 617 227-2237
  1 Milk St Lbby Lbby Boston (02109) *(G-6876)*

Massachusetts Review Inc.. 413 545-2689
  211 Hicks Way Amherst (01003) *(G-5862)*

MASSACHUSETTS REVIEW, THE, Amherst *Also Called: Massachusetts Review Inc (G-5862)*

Massachusetts Thermal Tstg Lab, Franklin *Also Called: Cold Chain Technologies LLC (G-8825)*

Massbiologics... 617 474-3000
  460 Walk Hill St Boston (02126) *(G-6877)*

Massbiologics, Boston *Also Called: Massbiologics (G-6877)*

Masscec, Boston *Also Called: Massachusetts Clean Energy Ctr (G-6873)*

Massconn Distribute Cpl... 860 882-0717
  12 Commerce Way South Windsor (06074) *(G-3162)*

MASSHEFA, Boston *Also Called: Poweroptions Inc (G-6973)*

Massmicroelectronics LLC... 781 828-6110
  50 Energy Dr Ste 202 Canton (02021) *(G-7808)*

Master Containers Inc... 800 881-6847
  200 Brickstone Sq Ste G05 Andover (01810) *(G-5892)*

Master Kitchens Center Inc.. 401 324-7100
  547 Thames St Unit B Newport (02840) *(G-16216)*

Master Millwork LLC.. 508 273-0500
  55 Charlotte Furnace Rd West Wareham (02576) *(G-13068)*

Mastercast Ltd.. 401 726-3100
  56 Barnes St Pawtucket (02860) *(G-16384)*

Mastercraft Inc... 207 431-2056
  371 W Front St Skowhegan (04976) *(G-5473)*

Mastercraft Tool and Mch Co.. 860 628-5551
  100 Newell St Southington (06489) *(G-3220)*

Mastermatic Inc.. 603 225-5190
  339 Commerce Way Pembroke (03275) *(G-15304)*

Masters Machine Company... 207 529-5191
  500 Lower Round Pond Rd Bristol (04539) *(G-4631)*

Mastro Lighting Mfg Co Inc **(PA)**............................... **401 467-7700**
  555 Elmwood Ave Providence (02907) *(G-16559)*

Mastv / El Planeta LLC.. 617 379-0210
  399 Boylston St Fl 6 Boston (02116) *(G-6878)*

Matec Instrument Companies Inc **(PA)**........................ **508 393-0155**
  56 Hudson St Northborough (01532) *(G-11102)*

Material Concrete Corp.. 401 765-0204
  618 Greenville Rd North Smithfield (02896) *(G-16326)*

Material Impact Inc... 617 917-4123
  131 Dartmouth St Fl 3 Boston (02116) *(G-6879)*

Materialise Dental Inc... 443 557-0121
  590 Lincoln St Waltham (02451) *(G-12717)*

Materials Development Corp.. 781 391-0400
  10 Lowell Junction Rd Andover (01810) *(G-5893)*

Materials Research Frncs Inc....................................... 603 435-2394
  65 Pinewood Rd Unit 2 Allenstown (03275) *(G-13853)*

Materials Systems Inc... 978 486-0404
  543 Great Rd Littleton (01460) *(G-9824)*

Materion Lrge Area Catings LLC **(DH)**........................ **216 486-4200**
  300 Lamberton Rd Windsor (06095) *(G-4289)*

Materion Prcsion Optics Thin F **(DH)**.......................... **978 692-7513**
  2 Lyberty Way Westford (01886) *(G-13249)*

Materion Technical Mtls Inc.. 401 333-1700
  5 Wellington Rd Lincoln (02865) *(G-16149)*

MATHEMATICAL COUNCIL OF THE AM, Providence *Also Called: American Mathematical Society Inc (G-16470)*

Mathemtics Problem Solving LLC.................................. 207 772-2846
  35 Foden Rd South Portland (04106) *(G-5508)*

Mathertops, South Windsor *Also Called: C Mather Company Inc (G-3124)*

Mathews Bakery Inc.. 207 773-9647
  5 Karen Dr Westbrook (04092) *(G-5637)*

Mathews Brothers, Belfast *Also Called: Mathews Brothers Company (G-4535)*

Mathews Brothers Company **(PA)**.............................. **207 338-3360**
  22 Perkins Rd Belfast (04915) *(G-4535)*

Mathsoft Corporate Holdings **(HQ)**............................ **617 444-8000**
  101 Main St Charlestown (02129) *(G-7879)*

Mathworks Inc.. 508 647-7000
  3 Apple Hill Dr Natick (01760) *(G-10485)*

Mathworks Inc **(PA)**... **508 647-7000**
  1 Apple Hill Dr Natick (01760) *(G-10486)*

Matkim, Oxford *Also Called: Matkim Industries Inc (G-11262)*

Matkim Industries Inc.. 508 987-3599
  2 Hawksley Rd Ste D Oxford (01540) *(G-11262)*

Matlet Group LLC... 401 834-3007
  60 Delta Dr Pawtucket (02860) *(G-16385)*

Matlet Group LLC... 401 834-3007
  1 Park Row Ste 300 Providence (02903) *(G-16560)*

Matouk Factory Store Inc... 508 997-3444
  925 Airport Rd Fall River (02720) *(G-8575)*

Matouk Textile Works Inc... 508 997-3444
  925 Airport Rd Fall River (02720) *(G-8576)*

Matrivax Research & Dev Corp...................................... 617 385-7640
  650 Albany St Ste 117 Boston (02118) *(G-6880)*

Matrix Aerospace Corp.. 603 542-0191
  421 River Rd Claremont (03743) *(G-14093)*

Matrix Air, Newport *Also Called: Pollution Research & Dev Corp (G-15234)*

Matrix I LLC.. 401 434-3040
  1 Catamore Blvd East Providence (02914) *(G-16030)*

Matrix Metal Products Inc.. 508 226-2374
  53 County St Attleboro (02703) *(G-6035)*

Matrix Technologies.. 603 521-0547
  2 Radcliff Rd Tewksbury (01876) *(G-12407)*

Matrix Technologies LLC... 603 595-0505
  22 Friars Dr Hudson (03051) *(G-14526)*

Matt Waite Excavation Inc.................................... 802 325-3668
236 Milaura Rd Pawlet (05761) *(G-17441)*

Matter Surfaces Inc **(PA)**.................................. **800 628-7462**
179 Campanelli Pkwy Stoughton (02072) *(G-12223)*

Matthew Porio.. 203 227-3695
367 Main St Westport (06880) *(G-4183)*

Matthew W Robinson.. 401 480-3975
34 Lakeside St Riverside (02915) *(G-16657)*

Matthew Warren Inc... 203 888-2133
95 Silvermine Rd Ste 1 Seymour (06483) *(G-2964)*

Matthew Warren Inc... 860 621-7358
75 Aircraft Rd Ste 1 Southington (06489) *(G-3221)*

Matthews Printing Co... 203 265-0363
10 Marshall St Wallingford (06492) *(G-3830)*

Mattingly Products Company.................................. 207 635-2719
25 Folon Rd North Anson (04958) *(G-5107)*

Mauna Kea Technologies Inc.................................. 617 216-4263
24 Denby Rd Ste 140 Allston (02134) *(G-5823)*

Maurer & Shepherd Joyners................................... 860 633-2383
122 Naubuc Ave Ste B4 Glastonbury (06033) *(G-1289)*

Maurer Metalcraft Inc.. 203 799-8800
22 Prindle Hill Rd Orange (06477) *(G-2676)*

Mauser Packg Solutions Holdg................................ 978 728-5000
25 Tucker Dr Leominster (01453) *(G-9682)*

Maverick Electronics, Wilmington *Also Called: Heilind Electronics Inc (G-13410)*

Maverick Work Wear Inc.. 860 944-3776
92 Concord St North Reading (01864) *(G-11043)*

Mavrck, Boston *Also Called: Apifia Inc (G-6550)*

Mavrikis Uphlstring Furn Dsign............................... 603 883-6868
45 Lake St Nashua (03060) *(G-15131)*

Max Analytical Technologies, East Windsor *Also Called: MLS Acq Inc (G-1082)*

Max Cohen & Sons Inc **(HQ)**.............................. **603 224-3532**
25 Sandquist St Concord (03301) *(G-14144)*

Max Cuff LLC... 413 553-3511
34 Churchill St Pittsfield (01201) *(G-11410)*

Max Pro-Police & Armor, Salem *Also Called: Newdtc LLC (G-15549)*

Max-Tek LLC.. 860 372-4900
59 Cherry Cir Prospect (06712) *(G-2836)*

Max-Tek Ue Superabrasive Mch, Prospect *Also Called: Max-Tek LLC (G-2836)*

Maxam Initiation Systems LLC................................ 860 556-4064
74 Dixon Rd Sterling (06377) *(G-3502)*

Maxam Tire North America Inc **(HQ)**..................... **844 629-2662**
300 Rosewood Dr Ste 102 Danvers (01923) *(G-8203)*

Maxant Industries Inc.. 978 772-0576
58 Barnum Rd Devens (01434) *(G-8279)*

Maxilon Laboratories Inc....................................... 603 594-9300
105 State Route 101a Unit 8 Amherst (03031) *(G-13879)*

Maxim Integrated Products Inc............................... 978 934-7600
8 Technology Dr North Chelmsford (01863) *(G-10983)*

Maximum Inc.. 508 995-2200
30 Samuel Barnet Blvd New Bedford (02745) *(G-10621)*

Maximus.. 978 728-8000
11 Mill St Ste 2 Lowell (01852) *(G-9903)*

Maxon Precision Motors Inc **(HQ)**....................... **508 677-0520**
125 Dever Rd Taunton (02780) *(G-12348)*

Maxson Automatic Machinery Co **(PA)**.................. **401 596-0162**
70 Airport Rd Westerly (02891) *(G-16935)*

May Graphics & Printing Inc
359 Littleton Rd Westford (01886) *(G-13250)*

Mayan Corporation.. 203 854-4711
79 Day St Norwalk (06854) *(G-2534)*

Mayarc Industries Inc... 860 871-1872
54 Minor Hill Rd Ellington (06029) *(G-1109)*

Mayborn Group, Stamford *Also Called: Mayborn Usa Inc (G-3409)*

Mayborn Usa Inc... 781 269-7490
1010 Washington Blvd Fl 9 Stamford (06901) *(G-3409)*

Maybrook Inc... 603 898-0811
20 A St Derry (03038) *(G-14202)*

Maybury Associates Inc... 413 525-4216
90 Denslow Rd East Longmeadow (01028) *(G-8386)*

Maybury Material Handling, East Longmeadow *Also Called: Maybury Associates Inc (G-8386)*

Mayfield Plastics Inc.. 508 865-8150
75 Whiting Farms Rd Holyoke (01040) *(G-9267)*

Mayflower Communications Inc............................... 781 359-9500
11 Oak Park Dr Ste 200 Bedford (01730) *(G-6239)*

Mayflower Poultry, Boston *Also Called: Somerville Live Poultry Co Inc (G-7045)*

Mayflower Sand & Gravel Co, Hanover *Also Called: P A Landers Inc (G-9039)*

Mayhew Basque Plastics LLC.................................. 978 537-5219
100 Simplex Dr Ste 3 Westminster (01473) *(G-13273)*

Mayhew Steel Products Inc **(PA)**......................... **413 625-6351**
199 Industrial Blvd Turners Falls (01376) *(G-12452)*

Mayhew Tools, Turners Falls *Also Called: Mayhew Steel Products Inc (G-12452)*

Maynesboro Industries Inc..................................... 603 752-3366
55 Maynesboro St Ste 1 Berlin (03570) *(G-13982)*

Mazu Networks LLC... 617 354-9292
125 Cambridgepark Dr Ste 14 Cambridge (02140) *(G-7639)*

MB Aerospace... 860 653-0569
99 Rainbow Rd East Granby (06026) *(G-941)*

MB Aerospace East Granby Limited Partnership........... 860 653-5041
39 Bradley Park Rd East Granby (06026) *(G-942)*

MB Aerspace Acp Hldngs III Cor **(PA)**.................. **586 772-2500**
39 Bradley Park Rd East Granby (06026) *(G-943)*

MB Machining Inc.. 508 251-8663
245 Flanders Rd Westborough (01581) *(G-13119)*

MB Sport LLC **(PA)**... **203 966-1985**
31 Grove St New Canaan (06840) *(G-2082)*

MB Westfield Inc... 413 568-8676
109 Apremont Way Westfield (01085) *(G-13182)*

Mbbc Vermont LLC.. 802 674-5491
336 Ruth Carney Dr Windsor (05089) *(G-17760)*

Mbf Holdings LLC.. 203 302-2812
777 W Putnam Ave Greenwich (06830) *(G-1341)*

MBI Graphics & Printing Corp................................. 508 765-0658
97 Worcester St Southbridge (01550) *(G-12028)*

MBL International Corporation **(DH)**...................... **781 939-6964**
15a Constitution Way Woburn (01801) *(G-13607)*

Mbm Building Systems Ltd..................................... 617 478-3466
160 Federal St Boston (02110) *(G-6881)*

Mbraun.. 603 773-9333
14 Marin Way Stratham (03885) *(G-15639)*

Mbs Fabrication Inc **(PA)**.................................. **508 765-0900**
270 Ashland Ave Southbridge (01550) *(G-12029)*

Mbsw Inc... 860 243-0303
41 Plainfield Rd West Hartford (06117) *(G-4071)*

Mbt, Stoughton *Also Called: Massachusetts Bay Tech Inc (G-12222)*

Mbw Incorporated.. 978 544-6462
184 Gov Dukakis Dr Orange (01364) *(G-11225)*

Mbw Tractor Sales LLC... 207 384-2001
540 Route 4 Berwick (03901) *(G-4551)*

Mc Assembly, North Billerica *Also Called: M C Test Service Inc (G-10929)*

Mc Assembly International LLC................................ 978 215-9501
101 Billerica Ave Bldg 7 North Billerica (01862) *(G-10933)*

Mc Cann Bros Inc.. 203 335-8630
490 Pepper St Monroe (06468) *(G-1916)*

Mc Cann Brothers Baskets, Monroe *Also Called: Mc Cann Bros Inc (G-1916)*

Mc Embossing Inc.. 781 821-3088
200 John L Dietsch Blvd Attleboro Falls (02763) *(G-6090)*

MC Faulkner & Sons Inc.. 207 929-4545
5 Shaws Mill Rd Gorham (04038) *(G-4826)*

Mc Kenney Machine & Tool Co, Corinna *Also Called: McKenney Machine & Tool Co (G-4701)*

Mc Millen Yachts... 401 682-2610
1909 Alden Lndg Portsmouth (02871) *(G-16446)*

Mc10 Inc... 617 234-4448
5 Mark Rd Tewksbury (01876) *(G-12408)*

McAllister Machine Inc.. 207 282-8655
7 Pomerleau St # 102 Biddeford (04005) *(G-4578)*

McAllister Optical Inc... 781 938-0456
17d Everberg Rd Woburn (01801) *(G-13608)*

MCB Inc.. 401 739-7020
289 Kilvert St Warwick (02886) *(G-16835)*

McCabe Logging and Tree Svc, Bridgton *Also Called: Everett McCabe (G-4628)*

McCabe Sand & Gravel Co Inc................................ 508 823-0771
120 Berkley St Taunton (02780) *(G-12349)*

A
L
P
H
A
B
E
T
I
C

McCain Foods Usa Inc...207 488-2561
  319 Richardson Rd Easton (04740) *(G-4743)*

McCain Foods Usa Inc...207 488-2561
  Station Rd Easton (04740) *(G-4744)*

McCann Fabrication..207 926-4118
  1027 Lewiston Rd New Gloucester (04260) *(G-5087)*

McClellan Automation Systems, Bedford *Also Called: James W McClellan & Associates Inc*
(G-13935)

McClure Newspapers Inc..802 863-3441
  426 Industrial Ave Ste 160 Williston (05495) *(G-17740)*

McCrea Capital Advisors Inc **(PA)**.............................**617 276-3388**
  202 Neponset Valley Pkwy Hyde Park (02136) *(G-9462)*

McCrea's Candies, Hyde Park *Also Called: McCrea Capital Advisors Inc (G-9462)*

McCue Memorial Co Inc...802 468-5636
  680 E Hubbardton Rd Castleton (05735) *(G-17173)*

McCullough Crushing Inc **(PA)**.................................**802 223-5693**
  548 Mccullough Hill Rd Middlesex (05602) *(G-17352)*

McDonald Stain Glass Ltd...207 633-4815
  7 Wall Point Rd Boothbay Harbor (04538) *(G-4603)*

McElroy Electronics Corp...978 425-4055
  27 Fredonian St # 33 Shirley (01464) *(G-11820)*

McGarvin Engineering Inc..978 454-2741
  35 Maple St Ste 1 Lowell (01852) *(G-9904)*

McGill Airflow LLC..802 442-1900
  452 Harwood Hill Rd Bennington (05201) *(G-17051)*

McGill Hose, East Longmeadow *Also Called: McGill Hose & Coupling Inc (G-8387)*

McGill Hose & Coupling Inc **(PA)**.............................**413 525-3977**
  45 Industrial D East Longmeadow (01028) *(G-8387)*

McGirr Graphics Incorporated.....................................508 747-6400
  19 Richards Rd Plymouth (02360) *(G-11464)*

McGuire Manufacturing Co Inc....................................203 699-1801
  60 Grandview Ct Cheshire (06410) *(G-606)*

McHolbe-Noonan Corporation.....................................802 865-0500
  144 College St Burlington (05401) *(G-17144)*

MCI Transformer Corporation......................................978 544-8272
  25 Blodgett St Orange (01364) *(G-11226)*

McIntire Brass Works Inc...617 547-1819
  35 Brooks Rd Lincoln (01773) *(G-9797)*

McIntire Company **(HQ)**...**860 585-8559**
  745 Clark Ave Bristol (06010) *(G-465)*

McKenney Machine & Tool Co.....................................207 278-7091
  400 Exeter Rd Corinna (04928) *(G-4701)*

McKernon Group Inc...802 247-8500
  381 New Rd Brandon (05733) *(G-17068)*

McKinnon Design LLC..860 677-7371
  72 Northwest Dr Plainville (06062) *(G-2773)*

McKnight Management Co Inc **(PA)**...........................**508 540-5051**
  505 Palmer Ave Falmouth (02540) *(G-8635)*

McLane Research Labs Inc **(PA)**..............................**508 495-4000**
  121 Bernard E Saint Jean East Falmouth (02536) *(G-8361)*

McLaughlin Oil Corp **(PA)**......................................**603 882-5500**
  20 Progress Ave Nashua (03062) *(G-15132)*

McLaughlin Paper Co Inc **(PA)**................................**413 732-7485**
  61 Progress Ave West Springfield (01089) *(G-13033)*

McLaughlin Research Corp..401 849-4010
  132 Johnny Cake Hill Rd Middletown (02842) *(G-16179)*

McLaughlin Upholstering Co Inc...................................617 389-0761
  1813 Revere Beach Pkwy Everett (02149) *(G-8495)*

MCLE, Boston *Also Called: Massachstts Cntning Lgal Edcat (G-6871)*

McLean Communications LLC.......................................603 624-1442
  50 Dow St Manchester (03101) *(G-14882)*

McLeod Optical Company Inc.......................................207 623-3841
  179 Mount Vernon Ave Augusta (04330) *(G-4478)*

McLeod Optical Company Inc **(PA)**............................**401 467-3000**
  50 Jefferson Park Rd Warwick (02888) *(G-16836)*

McLures Honey & Maple Products, Littleton *Also Called: Dutch Gold Honey Inc (G-14716)*

McLures's Honey & Maple Prdcts, Littleton *Also Called: Dutch Gold Honey Inc (G-14717)*

McM Stamping Corporation...203 792-3080
  66 Beaver Brook Rd Danbury (06810) *(G-783)*

MCM Technologies Inc...401 785-9204
  175 Dupont Dr Providence (02907) *(G-16561)*

McMellon Bros Incorporated.......................................203 375-5685
  915 Honeyspot Rd Stratford (06615) *(G-3555)*

McMullin Manufacturing Corp......................................203 740-3360
  70 Pocono Rd Brookfield (06804) *(G-529)*

McNeil Healthcare Inc..203 934-8187
  5 Saw Mill Rd West Haven (06516) *(G-4115)*

McNeills Manufacturing...802 246-1171
  22 Browne Ct Brattleboro (05301) *(G-17095)*

McNeilly Ems Educators Inc...978 278-3008
  125 Liberty St Danvers (01923) *(G-8204)*

McPherson, Chelmsford *Also Called: Schoeffel International Corp (G-7955)*

McQuade Tidd Industries..207 532-2675
  154 Steelstone St Houlton (04730) *(G-4901)*

McQuade Tidd Industries..207 532-6571
  76 Smyrna St Houlton (04730) *(G-4902)*

MCR Labs LLC...508 872-6666
  85 Speen St Ste 100 Framingham (01701) *(G-8789)*

MCS, Hudson *Also Called: Massachusetts Contr Sups Inc (G-9389)*

MCS, North Billerica *Also Called: Microwave Cmpnnts Spclists Inc (G-10937)*

MCS, Westborough *Also Called: Microwave Cmpnents Systems Inc (G-13121)*

MCS Industries Inc..508 651-3755
  202 N Main St Natick (01760) *(G-10487)*

McStowe Engrg & Met Pdts Co, East Bridgewater *Also Called: McStowe Engrg & Met Pdts Inc*
(G-8343)

McStowe Engrg & Met Pdts Inc....................................508 378-7400
  548 Spring St East Bridgewater (02333) *(G-8343)*

McSwain Manufacturing Inc..513 619-1222
  83 Verti Dr Winslow (04901) *(G-5684)*

McVac Environmental Svcs Inc......................................203 497-1960
  481 Grand Ave New Haven (06513) *(G-2173)*

McVan Inc...508 431-2400
  35 Frank Mossberg Dr Attleboro (02703) *(G-6036)*

McWeeney Marketing Group Inc.....................................203 891-8100
  53 Robinson Blvd Orange (06477) *(G-2677)*

MD Chemicals LLC...508 314-9664
  6 Dudley Rd Mendon (01756) *(G-10320)*

MD Solarsciences Corporation.......................................203 857-0095
  88 Post Rd W Ste 3 Westport (06880) *(G-4184)*

MD Stetson Company Inc...781 986-6161
  11 Norfolk St Ste 3 Mansfield (02048) *(G-10066)*

Mdc Signs Printing...401 654-5354
  70 Gansett Ave Cranston (02910) *(G-15892)*

Mdf Systems Inc...860 584-4750
  780 James P Casey Rd Bristol (06010) *(G-466)*

Mdi East Inc..603 532-5656
  81 Turnpike Rd Jaffrey (03452) *(G-14574)*

Mdm Products LLC..203 877-7070
  105 Woodmont Rd Milford (06460) *(G-1848)*

Mds Nxstage Corporation **(DH)**................................**866 697-8243**
  920 Winter St Waltham (02451) *(G-12718)*

ME and Ollies...603 319-1561
  64 Water St Exeter (03833) *(G-14296)*

ME Industries..207 286-2030
  19 Pomerleau St Biddeford (04005) *(G-4579)*

ME Products LLC..860 832-8960
  30 Peter Ct New Britain (06051) *(G-2041)*

ME Title...207 942-1988
  543 Hammond St Bangor (04401) *(G-4510)*

Me-92 Operations Inc...401 831-9200
  10 Houghton St Providence (02904) *(G-16562)*

Mead Papers Group...207 369-2390
  35 Hartford St Rumford (04276) *(G-5358)*

Meadow Manufacturing Inc..860 357-3785
  106 Enterprise Dr Ste B Bristol (06010) *(G-467)*

Meadowbrook Orchards Inc...978 365-7617
  209 Chace Hill Rd Sterling (01564) *(G-12167)*

Meadowbrook Prcsion Shtmtl Fab, Charlestown *Also Called: David Streeter (G-14061)*

Means Pre-Cast Co Inc...781 843-1909
  151 Adams St Braintree (02184) *(G-7194)*

Mearthane Products LLC **(PA)**.................................**401 946-4400**
  16 Western Industrial Dr Cranston (02921) *(G-15893)*

Measurement Computing Corp (DH)........................508 946-5100
  10 Commerce Way Ste C1 Norton (02766) *(G-11128)*

Measurement Systems, Glastonbury *Also Called: Cameron International Corp (G-1273)*

Measurement Systems Inc........................203 949-3500
  50 Barnes Park Rd N Ste 101 Wallingford (06492) *(G-3831)*

Mecha Noodle Bar........................203 691-9671
  201 Crown St New Haven (06510) *(G-2174)*

Mechancal Engnered Systems LLC........................203 400-4658
  180 Jonathan Rd New Canaan (06840) *(G-2083)*

Mechancal Engrg Met Fbrication, Methuen *Also Called: H & H Engineering Company Inc (G-10333)*

Med Associates Inc (PA)........................802 527-2343
  166 Industrial Park Rd Fairfax (05454) *(G-17262)*

Med Print, Ellington *Also Called: Ellington Printery Inc (G-1105)*

Med Tech Machine Company Inc........................781 878-2250
  100 Weymouth St Ste G2 Rockland (02370) *(G-11650)*

Med-Tech, North Billerica *Also Called: Medical-Technical Gases Inc (G-10934)*

Medalist Corp........................615 620-8280
  10 N Main St Burnham (04922) *(G-4660)*

Medalist Corp, Burnham *Also Called: Medalist Corp (G-4660)*

Medcon Biolab Technologies Inc........................508 839-4203
  50 Brigham Hill Rd Grafton (01519) *(G-8968)*

Meddata Group LLC........................978 887-0039
  300 Rosewood Dr Ste 250 Danvers (01923) *(G-8205)*

Medex Southington, Southington *Also Called: Smiths Medical Asd Inc (G-3232)*

Medi - Print Inc (PA)........................781 324-4455
  200 Maplewood St Malden (02148) *(G-10019)*

Media Links Inc........................860 206-9163
  431 Hayden Station Rd Ste C Windsor (06095) *(G-4290)*

Media One LLC........................203 745-5825
  44 Hawley Rd Hamden (06517) *(G-1439)*

Medianews Group Inc........................203 333-0161
  301 Merritt 7 Ste 1 Norwalk (06851) *(G-2535)*

Medianews Group Inc........................978 772-0777
  78 Barnum Rd Devens (01434) *(G-8280)*

Medianews Group Inc........................978 343-6911
  808 Main St Fitchburg (01420) *(G-8663)*

Mediatek USA Inc........................781 503-8000
  120 Presidential Way Woburn (01801) *(G-13609)*

Mediatek Woburn, Woburn *Also Called: Mediatek USA Inc (G-13609)*

Mediavue Systems Inc........................781 926-0676
  35 Pond Park Rd Ste 14 Hingham (02043) *(G-9153)*

Mediavue Systems LLC........................781 926-0676
  35 Pond Park Rd Ste 14 Hingham (02043) *(G-9154)*

Medica, Bedford *Also Called: Medica Corporation (G-6240)*

Medica Corporation (PA)........................781 275-4892
  5 Oak Park Dr Ste 1 Bedford (01730) *(G-6240)*

Medical Cmpnent Spcialists Inc (PA)........................508 966-0992
  42 William Way Bellingham (02019) *(G-6295)*

Medical Device Bus Svcs Inc........................508 828-2726
  15 Commerce Way Norton (02766) *(G-11129)*

Medical Device Bus Svcs Inc........................508 880-8100
  325 Paramount Dr Raynham (02767) *(G-11591)*

Medical Information Tech Inc (PA)........................781 821-3000
  Meditech Cir Westwood (02090) *(G-13314)*

Medical Manager Pcn Inc........................508 850-3500
  100 Elm St Walpole (02081) *(G-12568)*

Medical Products Mfg LLC........................508 291-1830
  4 Little Brook Rd West Wareham (02576) *(G-13069)*

Medical Research Networx........................508 530-4289
  101 Constitution Blvd Franklin (02038) *(G-8850)*

Medical Resources Inc........................207 721-1110
  11 Medical Center Dr Ste 1 Brunswick (04011) *(G-4650)*

Medical-Technical Gases Inc........................781 395-1946
  8 Executive Park Dr North Billerica (01862) *(G-10934)*

Medicametrix LLC........................617 488-9233
  500 Unicorn Park Dr Woburn (01801) *(G-13610)*

Medina Plating Corp........................330 725-4155
  17 Kestree Dr Londonderry (03053) *(G-14766)*

Medispend, Portsmouth *Also Called: Mmis Inc (G-15424)*

Mediterranean Snack Fd Co LLC........................973 402-2644
  1111 Summer St Stamford (06905) *(G-3410)*

Meditron Devices, Rochester *Also Called: Nextphase Medical Devices LLC (G-15487)*

Medline Industries LP........................847 949-5500
  81 Campanelli Dr Uxbridge (01569) *(G-12486)*

Medrhythms Inc........................207 447-2177
  183 Middle St Ste 300 Portland (04101) *(G-5244)*

Medrobotics Corporation........................508 692-6460
  475 Paramount Dr Raynham (02767) *(G-11592)*

Medsource Tech Holdings LLC (DH)........................978 570-6900
  100 Fordham Rd Bldg C Wilmington (01887) *(G-13428)*

Medsource Technologies LLC (DH)........................978 570-6900
  100 Fordham Rd Ste 1 Wilmington (01887) *(G-13429)*

Medtherapy Biotechnology Inc........................617 938-7082
  1250 Hancock St Ste 803n Quincy (02169) *(G-11528)*

Medtrnic Intrvntnal Vsclar Inc........................978 777-0042
  37a Cherry Hill Dr Danvers (01923) *(G-8206)*

Medtronic, North Haven *Also Called: Medtronic Inc (G-2424)*

Medtronic, Danvers *Also Called: Medtrnic Intrvntnal Vsclar Inc (G-8206)*

Medtronic, Danvers *Also Called: Medtronic Inc (G-8207)*

Medtronic, Danvers *Also Called: Medtronic Inc (G-8208)*

Medtronic, Woburn *Also Called: Covidien LP (G-13550)*

Medtronic Inc........................203 492-5764
  60 Middletown Ave North Haven (06473) *(G-2424)*

Medtronic Inc........................978 777-0042
  37 Cherry Hill Dr Danvers (01923) *(G-8207)*

Medtronic Inc........................978 739-3080
  35 Cherry Hill Dr Danvers (01923) *(G-8208)*

Medway Block Co Inc........................508 533-6701
  120 Main St Medway (02053) *(G-10307)*

Mega Na Inc........................781 784-7684
  175 Paramount Dr Raynham (02767) *(G-11593)*

Mega Precision LLC........................203 887-5718
  56 Budney Rd Unit B Newington (06111) *(G-2306)*

Mega Resveratrol, Danbury *Also Called: Candlewood Stars Inc (G-720)*

Mega Sound and Light LLC........................203 743-4200
  36 Mill Plain Rd Ste 312 Danbury (06811) *(G-784)*

Megadoor USA Inc........................203 238-2700
  140 Pond View Dr Meriden (06450) *(G-1673)*

Meganutra Inc (PA)........................781 762-9600
  128 Carnegie Row Ste 107 Norwood (02062) *(G-11195)*

Megaprint, Holderness *Also Called: Megaprint Inc (G-14447)*

Megaprint Inc........................603 536-2900
  1177 New Hampshire Rte 175 Holderness (03245) *(G-14447)*

Megapulse Incorporated........................781 538-5299
  23 Crosby Dr Bedford (01730) *(G-6241)*

Megatech Corporation........................978 937-9600
  525 Woburn St Ste 3 Tewksbury (01876) *(G-12409)*

Megatrnics US Ultmate Hldco LL (PA)........................888 706-0230
  1 Stiles Rd Salem (03079) *(G-15544)*

Meggitt (new Hampshire) Inc........................603 669-0940
  144 Harvey Rd Londonderry (03053) *(G-14767)*

Meggitt (orange County) Inc........................603 657-2603
  136 Harvey Rd A9 Londonderry (03053) *(G-14768)*

Meggitt Sensing Systems, Londonderry *Also Called: Meggitt (orange County) Inc (G-14768)*

Megowen LLC........................860 528-9701
  433 School St East Hartford (06108) *(G-1005)*

Megquier & Jones Inc........................207 799-8555
  72 Ivanhoe Dr Topsham (04086) *(G-5550)*

MEI Rigging & Crating LLC........................978 685-7700
  18 Fanaras Dr Salisbury (01952) *(G-11742)*

Meister Abrasives, North Kingstown *Also Called: Meister Abrasives Usa Inc (G-16271)*

Meister Abrasives Usa Inc........................401 294-4503
  201 Circuit Dr North Kingstown (02852) *(G-16271)*

Meitu........................781 898-7655
  275 Grove St Ste 2400 Auburndale (02466) *(G-6137)*

Mel-Co-Ed Inc........................401 724-2160
  381 Roosevelt Ave Pawtucket (02860) *(G-16386)*

Melanie Casey LLC........................781 640-8910
  18 Red Spring Rd Ste 102 Andover (01810) *(G-5894)*

Melanson Company, The, Keene *Also Called: Tecta America Corp (G-14627)*

Meletharb Homemade Ice Cream, Wakefield *Also Called: Meletharb Inc (G-12518)*

A L P H A B E T I C

Meletharb Inc.. 781 245-4946
   393 Lowell St Wakefield (01880) *(G-12518)*

Melexis Inc... 603 223-2362
   43 Pinehurst Ave Nashua (03062) *(G-15133)*

Mellen Company Inc **(PA)**.. **603 228-2929**
   40 Chenell Dr Concord (03301) *(G-14145)*

Meller Opti, Providence *Also Called: Adolf Meller Company (G-16465)*

Melros-Wakefield Answering Svc, Beverly *Also Called: Business and Prof Exch Inc (G-6336)*

Melton Sales and Service Inc..................................... 207 623-8895
   323 Water St Hallowell (04347) *(G-4860)*

Melville Candy Corporation... 800 638-8063
   28 York Ave Randolph (02368) *(G-11568)*

Melville Old Time Candy & Pdts, Randolph *Also Called: Melville Candy Corporation (G-11568)*

Melvin L Yoder.. 207 278-3539
   16 Bolstridge Rd Corinna (04928) *(G-4702)*

Mem-Co Fittings Inc.. 603 329-9633
   45 Gigante Dr Hampstead (03841) *(G-14386)*

Memed US Inc... 617 335-0349
   200 Brickstone Sq Ste 106 Andover (01810) *(G-5895)*

Memento Inc.. 781 221-3030
   55 Network Dr Burlington (01803) *(G-7392)*

Memorial Sandblast Inc.. 802 476-7086
   15 Blackwell St Barre (05641) *(G-17013)*

Memry Corporation **(HQ)**... **203 739-1100**
   3 Berkshire Blvd Bethel (06801) *(G-128)*

Memtec Corporation.. 603 893-8080
   17 Old Nashua Rd Amherst (03031) *(G-13880)*

Mendix Inc.. 857 263-8200
   22 Boston Wharf Rd Fl 8 Boston (02210) *(G-6882)*

Meninno Brothers Gourmet Foods, Danvers *Also Called: R Walters Foods Ltd Lblty Co (G-8216)*

Mentis Sciences Inc... 603 624-9197
   40 Depot St Warner (03278) *(G-15666)*

Menton Machine Co Inc... 781 293-8394
   1299 Main St Hanson (02341) *(G-9054)*

Mercantile Development Inc....................................... 203 922-8880
   10 Waterview Dr Shelton (06484) *(G-3030)*

Merchants Metals LLC... 413 562-9981
   390 Burnett Rd Chicopee (01020) *(G-8047)*

Merchbro Inc... 866 428-0095
   1005 Main St Unit 8130 Pawtucket (02860) *(G-16387)*

Merck Group... 781 858-3284
   80 Ashby Rd Bedford (01730) *(G-6242)*

Merck Group... 978 762-5280
   17 Cherry Hill Dr Danvers (01923) *(G-8209)*

Merck Research Laboratories..................................... 617 992-2000
   33 Avenue Louis Pasteur Boston (02115) *(G-6883)*

Merck Sharp & Dohme Corp...................................... 617 992-2000
   33 Avenue Louis Pasteur Boston (02115) *(G-6884)*

Merco Inc... 860 871-1888
   26 Village St Ellington (06029) *(G-1110)*

Mercury Brewing & Dist Co Inc................................... 978 356-3329
   23 Hayward St Ipswich (01938) *(G-9490)*

Mercury Cabling Systems LLC................................... 203 378-9008
   300 Avon St Stratford (06615) *(G-3556)*

Mercury Commercial Electronics Inc........................... 978 967-1364
   201 Riverneck Rd Chelmsford (01824) *(G-7938)*

Mercury Group The, Stratford *Also Called: Mercury Cabling Systems LLC (G-3556)*

Mercury Systems Inc **(PA)**...................................... **978 256-1300**
   50 Minuteman Rd Andover (01810) *(G-5896)*

Mercury Systems Inc... 603 883-2900
   267 Lowell Rd Ste 101 Hudson (03051) *(G-14527)*

Mercury Wire Products Inc... 508 885-6363
   Mercury Dr 1 Spencer (01562) *(G-12064)*

Mercury-Excelum Inc.. 860 292-1800
   215 S Main St East Windsor (06088) *(G-1080)*

Mereco Technologies, Londonderry *Also Called: Metachem Resins Corporation (G-14770)*

Mereco Technologies Group Inc **(HQ)**...................... **401 822-9300**
   8 Ricker Ave Londonderry (03053) *(G-14769)*

Merida LLC... 508 675-6572
   1 Currant Rd Ste 1 Fall River (02720) *(G-8577)*

Merida Meridian Inc... 617 464-5400
   1 Design Center Pl Ste 714 Boston (02210) *(G-6885)*

Meriden Fire Marshals Office...................................... 203 630-4010
   142 E Main St Meriden (06450) *(G-1674)*

Meriden Manufacturing Inc... 203 237-7481
   230 State Street Ext Meriden (06450) *(G-1675)*

Meridian Custom Wdwkg Inc...................................... 508 587-4400
   443 Summer St # 1 Brockton (02302) *(G-7295)*

Meridian Industrial Group LLC.................................... 413 538-9880
   529 S East St Holyoke (01040) *(G-9268)*

Meridian Life Science Inc **(HQ)**............................... **207 283-6500**
   60 Industrial Park Rd Saco (04072) *(G-5373)*

Meridian Printing Inc.. 401 885-4882
   1538 S County Trl East Greenwich (02818) *(G-15991)*

Merit Machine Mfg Inc.. 978 342-7677
   25 Willow St Fitchburg (01420) *(G-8664)*

Merit Medical Systems Inc **(HQ)**.............................. **781 681-7900**
   1050 Hingham St Fl 1 Rockland (02370) *(G-11651)*

Merlinone, Braintree *Also Called: Merlinone Inc (G-7195)*

Merlinone Inc **(PA)**... **617 328-6645**
   50 Braintree Hill Park Ste 308 Braintree (02184) *(G-7195)*

Merriam-Webster Incorporated **(DH)**........................ **413 734-3134**
   47 Federal St Springfield (01105) *(G-12113)*

Merrick Services.. 508 802-3751
   81 Plum Rd North Grosvenordale (06255) *(G-2386)*

Merrill Anderson Company Inc.................................... 203 377-4996
   1166 Barnum Ave Stratford (06614) *(G-3557)*

Merrill Blueberry Farms, Hancock *Also Called: Coastal Blueberry Service Inc (G-4868)*

Merrill Blueberry Farms Inc....................................... 207 667-2541
   63 Thorsen Rd Hancock (04640) *(G-4872)*

Merrill Corp.. 978 725-3700
   35 New England Business Center Dr Ste 150 Andover (01810) *(G-5897)*

Merrill Industries LLC.. 860 871-1888
   26 Village St Ellington (06029) *(G-1111)*

Merrill/Daniels, Everett *Also Called: Datasite Global Corporation (G-8486)*

Merrimac Industrial Sales Inc **(PA)**.......................... **978 372-6006**
   111 Neck Rd Haverhill (01835) *(G-9114)*

Merrimac Industrial Sales Inc **(PA)**.......................... **978 372-6006**
   111 Neck Rd Haverhill (01835) *(G-9115)*

Merrimac Spool and Reel Co Inc................................ 978 372-7777
   203 Essex St Haverhill (01832) *(G-9116)*

Merrimac Tool Company Inc **(PA)**............................ **978 388-7159**
   91 High St Ste 1 Amesbury (01913) *(G-5843)*

Merrimac, Cambridge *Also Called: Merrimack Pharmaceuticals Inc (G-7640)*

Merrimack County Customs.. 603 938-5855
   14 Steele Rd Bradford (03221) *(G-14017)*

Merrimack Manufacturing LLC.................................... 603 206-0200
   540 North Commercial St Manchester (03101) *(G-14883)*

Merrimack Micro LLC.. 603 809-4183
   76 Jessica Dr Merrimack (03054) *(G-14992)*

Merrimack Pharmaceuticals Inc **(PA)**....................... **617 441-1000**
   1 Broadway Fl 14 Cambridge (02142) *(G-7640)*

Merritt Extruder Corp.. 203 230-8100
   15 Marne St Hamden (06514) *(G-1440)*

Merritt, Joseph & Company, Danbury *Also Called: Joseph Merritt & Company Inc (G-762)*

Merrow Manufacturing LLC **(PA)**............................. **508 689-4095**
   502 Bedford St Ste 3 Fall River (02720) *(G-8578)*

Merrow Superior LLC.. 212 691-3400
   502 Bedford St Fall River (02720) *(G-8579)*

Merry Christmas From Heaven, Weymouth *Also Called: Mooneytunco Inc (G-13330)*

Mersana Therapeutics, Cambridge *Also Called: Mersana Therapeutics Inc (G-7641)*

Mersana Therapeutics Inc **(PA)**............................... **617 498-0020**
   840 Memorial Dr Cambridge (02139) *(G-7641)*

Mersen, Newburyport *Also Called: Mersen USA Ep Corp (G-10699)*

Mersen USA Ep Corp **(HQ)**..................................... **978 462-6662**
   374 Merrimac St Newburyport (01950) *(G-10699)*

Mersen USA Ev LLC... 978 518-7648
   374 Merrimac St Newburyport (01950) *(G-10700)*

Mery Manufacturing, Rockfall *Also Called: Rogers Manufacturing Company (G-2915)*

Mesco Corporation.. 401 683-2677
   1676 E Main Rd Ste Bay Portsmouth (02871) *(G-16447)*

Messenger Marketing, Saint Albans *Also Called: ORourke Media Group LLC (G-17527)*

Messer LLC.. 908 464-8100
10 Riverview Dr Danbury (06810) *(G-785)*

Messer LLC.. 207 475-3102
9 Ranger Dr Kittery (03904) *(G-4937)*

Messer LLC.. 508 966-3148
92a Depot St Bellingham (02019) *(G-6296)*

Messer LLC.. 781 341-4575
97 Maple St Stoughton (02072) *(G-12224)*

Messer LLC.. 802 878-6339
Ibm Plant Essex Junction (05452) *(G-17240)*

Messer Petroleum Equipment, Westbrook *Also Called: Messer Truck Equipment (G-5638)*

Messer Truck Equipment **(PA)**...................... **207 854-9751**
170 Warren Ave Westbrook (04092) *(G-5638)*

Mestek Inc.. 413 568-9571
260 N Elm St Westfield (01085) *(G-13183)*

Mestek Inc.. 413 564-5530
260 N Elm St Westfield (01085) *(G-13184)*

Mestek Inc.. 413 568-9571
260 N Elm St Westfield (01085) *(G-13185)*

Mestek Inc **(PA)**...................................... **470 898-4533**
260 N Elm St Westfield (01085) *(G-13186)*

Met-Craft, Oxford *Also Called: Cast Global Manufacturing Corp (G-2688)*

Meta Software Corporation **(PA)**.................. **781 238-0293**
15 New England Executive Park Burlington (01803) *(G-7393)*

Metachem Resins Corporation
8 Ricker Ave Londonderry (03053) *(G-14770)*

Metal Bellows, Sharon *Also Called: Senior Operations LLC (G-11795)*

Metal Casting Technology Inc...................... 603 673-9720
127 Old Wilton Rd Milford (03055) *(G-15033)*

Metal Clay Findings, North Providence *Also Called: APAC Tool Inc (G-16295)*

Metal Fabrications, Biddeford *Also Called: DSM Metal Fabrication Inc (G-4561)*

Metal Finish Eqp & Sup Co Inc.................... 860 668-1050
19 Kenny Roberts Memorial Dr Suffield (06078) *(G-3593)*

Metal Improvement Company LLC................ 860 523-9901
12 Thompson Rd East Windsor (06088) *(G-1081)*

Metal Improvement Company LLC................ 860 635-9994
20 Tuttle Pl Ste 6 Middletown (06457) *(G-1762)*

Metal Improvement Company LLC................ 860 224-9148
1 John Downey Dr New Britain (06051) *(G-2042)*

Metal Improvement Company LLC................ 860 688-6201
145 Addison Rd Windsor (06095) *(G-4291)*

Metal Improvement Company LLC................ 781 246-3848
1 Nablus Rd Wakefield (01880) *(G-12519)*

Metal Improvement Company LLC................ 978 658-0032
201 Ballardvale St Wilmington (01887) *(G-13430)*

Metal Men.. 413 533-0513
280 Ludlow Rd Chicopee (01020) *(G-8048)*

Metal Perfection, Hamden *Also Called: Charles K White (G-1417)*

Metal Processing Co Inc............................ 978 649-1289
75 Westech Dr Tyngsboro (01879) *(G-12461)*

Metal Specialties Inc................................ 207 786-4268
300 Rodman Rd Auburn (04210) *(G-4444)*

Metal Tech Industries Inc.......................... 508 566-8132
4 Katie Marie Dr Bourne (02532) *(G-7140)*

Metal Tronics Inc.................................... 978 659-6960
23 National Ave Georgetown (01833) *(G-8909)*

Metal Works, Tiverton *Also Called: Metalworks Corporation (G-16737)*

Metal Works Inc...................................... 603 669-6180
24 Industrial Dr Londonderry (03053) *(G-14771)*

Metal-Flex Welded Bellows Inc................... 802 334-5550
149 Lakemont Rd Newport (05855) *(G-17400)*

Metalcraft Door Co Inc............................. 781 933-2861
87 Olympia Ave Woburn (01801) *(G-13611)*

Metalcrafters Inc..................................... 978 683-7097
104 Pleasant Valley St Methuen (01844) *(G-10338)*

Metalenz Inc.. 844 770-1300
375 Highland St Weston (02493) *(G-13287)*

Metalform Acquisition LLC **(PA)**.................. **860 224-2630**
555 John Downey Dr New Britain (06051) *(G-2043)*

Metalform Company, New Britain *Also Called: Metalform Acquisition LLC (G-2043)*

Metalgrommets.com, Dighton *Also Called: Armin Innovative Products Inc (G-8291)*

Metallics Inc.. 860 589-4186
229 Cross St Bristol (06010) *(G-468)*

Metallizing Svc Holdings LLC **(PA)**............... **860 953-1144**
11 Cody St West Hartford (06110) *(G-4072)*

Metallon Inc.. 860 283-8265
1415 Waterbury Rd Thomaston (06787) *(G-3624)*

Metallurgical Processing............................ 860 916-5015
11 Ritoli Rdg West Hartford (06117) *(G-4073)*

Metallurgical Processing Incorporated.......... 860 224-2648
68 Arthur St New Britain (06053) *(G-2044)*

Metallurgical Solutions Inc......................... 401 941-2100
85 Aldrich St Providence (02905) *(G-16563)*

Metalmark Innovations Pbc........................ 617 714-4026
767 Concord Ave Ste 2-1 Cambridge (02138) *(G-7642)*

Metalogic Industries LLC........................... 508 461-6787
15 Wells St Southbridge (01550) *(G-12030)*

Metalogix Software Corp............................ 202 609-9100
690 Winter St Ste 115 Waltham (02451) *(G-12719)*

Metalor, North Attleboro *Also Called: Metalor USA Refining Corp (G-10877)*

Metalor Technologies USA Corp **(DH)**.......... **508 699-8800**
255 John L Dietsch Blvd North Attleboro (02763) *(G-10876)*

Metalor USA Refining Corp **(DH)**................. **508 699-8800**
255 John L Dietsch Blvd North Attleboro (02763) *(G-10877)*

Metalpro Inc.. 860 388-1811
50 School House Rd Old Saybrook (06475) *(G-2655)*

Metalpro USA Inc.................................... 508 942-9746
21 Bettencourt Rd Plymouth (02360) *(G-11465)*

Metalworks Corporation............................ 401 624-4400
3940 Main Rd Tiverton (02878) *(G-16737)*

Metamorphic Materials Inc......................... 860 738-8638
122 Colebrook River Rd Winsted (06098) *(G-4349)*

Metavac LLC.. 631 207-2344
20 Post Rd Portsmouth (03801) *(G-15423)*

Metelics Corp... 408 737-8197
100 Chelmsford St Lowell (01851) *(G-9905)*

Meter Health Inc..................................... 833 638-3777
69 Cougar Dr Manchester (06040) *(G-1617)*

Metfab Engineering Inc............................. 508 695-1007
332 John L Dietsch Blvd Attleboro Falls (02763) *(G-6091)*

Metfin Shot Blast Systems, Suffield *Also Called: Metal Finish Eqp & Sup Co Inc (G-3593)*

Methods 3d Inc....................................... 978 443-5388
65 Union Ave Sudbury (01776) *(G-12268)*

Metrica Interior Inc.................................. 413 587-2750
209 Earle St Northampton (01060) *(G-11071)*

Metro Inc **(PA)**....................................... **401 461-2200**
1 Metro Park Dr Cranston (02910) *(G-15894)*

Metro Glass & Metal LLC........................... 781 281-0667
10 Wheeling Ave Woburn (01801) *(G-13612)*

Metro Group Inc...................................... 781 932-9911
155 West St Ste 3 Wilmington (01887) *(G-13431)*

Metro Home Video, Cranston *Also Called: Metro Inc (G-15894)*

Metro Sign & Awning, Tewksbury *Also Called: C & D Signs Inc (G-12388)*

Metroblity Optical Systems Inc.................... 781 255-5300
101 Billerica Ave Bldg 7 North Billerica (01862) *(G-10935)*

Metromatic Manufacturing Company Inc........ 781 396-5300
78 Elm St Byfield (01922) *(G-7458)*

Metropower, Rocky Hill *Also Called: Cummins Inc (G-2920)*

Metsa Board Americas Corp........................ 203 229-0037
301 Merritt 7 Ste 2 Norwalk (06851) *(G-2536)*

Metso Fabric, Winthrop *Also Called: Valmet Inc (G-5696)*

Mettler Packaging LLC.............................. 860 628-6193
100 Queen St Ste 5 Southington (06489) *(G-3222)*

Mettler-Toledo Thornton Inc **(DH)**............... **978 262-0210**
900 Middlesex Tpke Bldg 8-1 Billerica (01821) *(G-6460)*

Mettlr-Tledo Prcess Anlytics I...................... 781 301-8800
900 Middlesex Tpke Bldg 8-1 Billerica (01821) *(G-6461)*

Metzger/Mcguire Inc................................. 603 224-6122
807 Route 3a Bow (03304) *(G-14005)*

Metzys Taqueria LLC................................ 978 992-1451
17 55th St Newburyport (01950) *(G-10701)*

Mevatec Corp... 603 885-4321
65 Spit Brook Rd Nashua (03060) *(G-15134)*

A
L
P
H
A
B
E
T
I
C

Mevion Medical Systems, Littleton *Also Called: Mevion Medical Systems Inc (G-9825)*

Mevion Medical Systems Inc **(PA)**................................ **978 486-1006**
  300 Foster St Ste 3 Littleton (01460) *(G-9825)*

Mexichem Spcalty Compounds Inc **(HQ)**.................... **978 537-8071**
  170 Pioneer Dr Leominster (01453) *(G-9683)*

Meyer Gage Co Inc... 860 528-6526
  230 Burnham St South Windsor (06074) *(G-3163)*

Meyer Wire & Cable Company LLC............................ 203 281-0817
  1072 Sherman Ave Hamden (06514) *(G-1441)*

Mezzanine Safeti-Gates Inc.................................... 978 768-3000
  174 Western Ave Essex (01929) *(G-8478)*

Mf Blouin Mdsg Solution.. 800 394-1632
  27 Production Dr Dover (03820) *(G-14234)*

Mf-TFC LLC.. 203 302-2820
  777 W Putnam Ave Greenwich (06830) *(G-1342)*

Mfb Holdings LLC.. 603 742-0104
  27 Production Dr Dover (03820) *(G-14235)*

Mfg Electronics Inc.. 978 671-5490
  70 Treble Cove Rd Ste 1 North Billerica (01862) *(G-10936)*

Mfg Mach Corp... 774 294-4285
  847 Pleasant St Fall River (02723) *(G-8580)*

Mfi Corp.. 802 658-6600
  44 Lakeside Ave Burlington (05401) *(G-17145)*

Mfm Enterprises Inc.. 858 571-1358
  50 Alewife Ln Weymouth (02189) *(G-13329)*

Mgb Us Inc.. 774 415-0060
  157 Grove St Ste 30 Franklin (02038) *(G-8851)*

Mgi Energy, Northborough *Also Called: Sundrum Solar Inc (G-11110)*

MH Rhodes Cramer LLC.. 860 291-8402
  105 Nutmeg Rd S South Windsor (06074) *(G-3164)*

MH Stallman Company Inc **(PA)**................................ **401 331-5129**
  292 Charles St Providence (02904) *(G-16564)*

Mhgc, Wareham *Also Called: Viabella Holdings LLC (G-12848)*

Mhq Inc.. 888 242-1118
  750 Newfield St Middletown (06457) *(G-1763)*

Mhq Inc **(PA)**.. **508 573-2600**
  401 Elm St Marlborough (01752) *(G-10184)*

Mhq Municipal Vehicles, Marlborough *Also Called: Mhq Inc (G-10184)*

Mi-Box Southern Mass LLC..................................... 774 719-7367
  20 High St Plainville (02762) *(G-11438)*

Miami Bay Beverage Company LLC............................ 203 453-0090
  66 High St Guilford (06437) *(G-1400)*

Miami Wabash Paper, Norwalk *Also Called: Mafcote Inc (G-2530)*

Miami Wabash Paper LLC **(HQ)**................................ **203 847-8500**
  108 Main St Ste 3 Norwalk (06851) *(G-2537)*

Miano Printing Services Inc.................................... 617 935-2830
  89 October Hill Rd Holliston (01746) *(G-9222)*

Mica Corporation... 203 922-8888
  9 Mountain View Dr Shelton (06484) *(G-3031)*

Mica-Tron Products Corp....................................... 781 767-2163
  275 Centre St Ste 13 Holbrook (02343) *(G-9179)*

Michael Brisebois... 413 527-9590
  6 Industrial Pkwy Easthampton (01027) *(G-8450)*

Michael Healy Designs Inc..................................... 401 597-5900
  60 New River Rd Manville (02838) *(G-16165)*

Michael Perra Inc.. 603 644-2110
  640 Harvard St Ste 2 Manchester (03103) *(G-14884)*

Michael Rogovsky... 508 487-3287
  244 Bellevue St New Bedford (02744) *(G-10622)*

Michael Zoppa... 860 289-5881
  23 Sea Pave Rd South Windsor (06074) *(G-3165)*

Michaels Dairy Inc.. 860 443-7617
  11 Harbor Ln New London (06320) *(G-2230)*

Micheal John... 857 239-0277
  1842 Beacon St Brookline (02445) *(G-7320)*

Micheals Provision, Fall River *Also Called: Miranda Brothers Inc (G-8584)*

Michele Robyn, Providence *Also Called: Rgt Inc (G-16601)*

Michie Corporation.. 603 428-7426
  173 Buxton Industrial Dr Henniker (03242) *(G-14438)*

Micrex Corporation.. 508 660-1900
  17 Industrial Rd Walpole (02081) *(G-12569)*

Micro Abrasives Corporation.................................. 413 562-3641
  720 Southampton Rd Westfield (01085) *(G-13187)*

Micro Bends Corp... 603 924-0022
  365 Jaffrey Rd Peterborough (03458) *(G-15318)*

Micro Electronics Inc... 508 761-9161
  1005 Newman Ave Seekonk (02771) *(G-11781)*

Micro Farmington Sub LLC.................................... 860 677-2646
  206 Newington Ave New Britain (06051) *(G-2045)*

Micro Insert Incorporated...................................... 860 621-5789
  183 Clark St Milldale (06467) *(G-1902)*

Micro Magnetics Inc.. 508 672-4489
  617 Airport Rd Fall River (02720) *(G-8581)*

Micro Matic, Naugatuck *Also Called: Advantage Sheet Metal Mfg LLC (G-1946)*

Micro Precision LLC.. 860 423-4575
  1102 Windham Rd South Windham (06266) *(G-3103)*

Micro Source Discovery Systems............................. 860 350-8078
  11 George Washington Plz Gaylordsville (06755) *(G-1265)*

Micro Wire Products Inc.. 508 584-0200
  5 Mear Rd Ste 3 Holbrook (02343) *(G-9180)*

Micro Wire Transm Systems Inc.............................. 802 876-7901
  8 Ewing Pl Essex Junction (05452) *(G-17241)*

Micro-Leads Inc... 617 580-3030
  255 Elm St Ste 300 Somerville (02144) *(G-11886)*

Micro-Lite Inc.. 413 289-1313
  2039 Bridge St Three Rivers (01080) *(G-12429)*

Micro-Mech Inc.. 978 356-2966
  33 Turnpike Rd Ipswich (01938) *(G-9491)*

Micro-Metrics Inc... 603 641-3800
  54 Grenier Field Rd Londonderry (03053) *(G-14772)*

Micro-Precision Tech Inc **(PA)**................................ **978 688-1299**
  439 S Union St Unit 105 Lawrence (01843) *(G-9580)*

Micro-Precision Tech Inc....................................... 603 893-7600
  10 Manor Pkwy Ste C Salem (03079) *(G-15545)*

Micro-Tech Prod Mch Co Inc.................................. 603 434-1743
  1 Commercial Ln Londonderry (03053) *(G-14773)*

Microbest, Waterbury *Also Called: Microbest Inc (G-3944)*

Microbest Inc... 203 597-0355
  670 Captain Neville Dr Ste 1 Waterbury (06705) *(G-3944)*

Microbiotix Inc... 508 757-2800
  1 Innovation Dr Ste 120c Worcester (01605) *(G-13759)*

Microboard Processing Inc..................................... 203 881-4300
  36 Cogwheel Ln Seymour (06483) *(G-2965)*

Microcad Trning Consulting Inc **(PA)**........................ **617 923-0500**
  440 Arsenal St Ste 3 Watertown (02472) *(G-12893)*

Microcal LLC... 413 586-7720
  22 Industrial Dr E Northampton (01060) *(G-11072)*

Microcut Inc.. 781 582-8090
  182 Standish Ave # 2 Plymouth (02360) *(G-11466)*

Microelectrodes Inc... 603 668-0692
  40 Harvey Rd Bedford (03110) *(G-13944)*

Microfab Inc.. 603 621-9522
  180 Zachary Rd Ste 1 Manchester (03109) *(G-14885)*

Microfibres Inc... 401 725-4883
  124 Washington St Ste 101 Foxboro (02035) *(G-8708)*

Microfluidics Intl Corp.. 617 969-5452
  90 Glacier Dr Ste 1000 Westwood (02090) *(G-13315)*

Microgroup Inc... 508 533-4925
  7 Industrial Park Rd Medway (02053) *(G-10308)*

Microline Surgical Inc **(HQ)**................................... **978 922-9810**
  50 Dunham Rd Ste 1500 Beverly (01915) *(G-6364)*

Micromatics Machine Co Inc.................................. 603 889-2115
  9 Clinton Dr Hollis (03049) *(G-14454)*

Micron Corporation... 781 769-5771
  89 Access Rd Ste 5 Norwood (02062) *(G-11196)*

Micron Plastics Inc.. 978 772-6900
  30 Faulkner St Ayer (01432) *(G-6186)*

Micron Products Inc... 978 345-5000
  25 Sawyer Passway Fitchburg (01420) *(G-8665)*

Micron Solutions Inc **(PA)**..................................... **978 345-5000**
  25 Sawyer Passway Fitchburg (01420) *(G-8666)*

Micronetixx Technologies LLC................................. 207 786-2000
  70 Commercial St Ste 1 Lewiston (04240) *(G-4975)*

Micronics Engnred Fltrtion Gro........................ 40 Winada Dr Winthrop (04364) *(G-5693)*	207 377-2626
Micronics Engnred Fltrtion Gro........................ 12 Winada Dr Winthrop (04364) *(G-5694)*	207 377-2626
Microphase Corporation........................ 100 Trap Falls Road Ext Ste 400 Shelton (06484) *(G-3032)*	203 866-8000
Microport Navibot Intl LLC........................ 300 Foxboro Blvd Foxborough (02035) *(G-8735)*	774 215-5471
Microprint, Lowell *Also Called: Desk Top Solutions Inc (G-9874)*	
Micros Systems Inc........................ 1800 W Park Dr Ste 250 Westborough (01581) *(G-13120)*	508 655-7500
Microsembly LLC........................ 21 Manchester St Merrimack (03054) *(G-14993)*	603 718-8445
Microsemi, Simsbury *Also Called: Microsemi Corporation (G-3093)*	
Microsemi, Beverly *Also Called: Microsemi Frequency Time Corp (G-6366)*	
Microsemi Corp- Massachusetts........................ 6 Lake St Ste 1 Lawrence (01841) *(G-9581)*	978 620-2600
Microsemi Corp- Massachusetts........................ 75 Technology Dr Lowell (01851) *(G-9906)*	978 442-5600
Microsemi Corp-Colorado........................ 6 Lake St Ste 1 Lawrence (01841) *(G-9582)*	480 941-6300
Microsemi Corporation........................ 90 Wolcott Rd Simsbury (06070) *(G-3093)*	860 651-0211
Microsemi Corporation........................ 163 Cabot St Beverly (01915) *(G-6365)*	978 232-0040
Microsemi Corporation........................ 6 Lake St Ste 1 Lawrence (01841) *(G-9583)*	781 665-1071
Microsemi Corporation........................ 75 Technology Dr Lowell (01851) *(G-9907)*	978 442-5637
Microsemi Corporation........................ 890 East St Ste 2 Tewksbury (01876) *(G-12410)*	978 232-3793
Microsemi Corporation........................ 48 Abby Rd Manchester (03103) *(G-14886)*	978 232-3793
Microsemi Frequency Time Corp........................ 34 Tozer Rd Beverly (01915) *(G-6366)*	978 232-0040
Microsemi Nes Inc........................ 6 Lake St Lawrence (01841) *(G-9584)*	978 794-1666
Microsemi-Cdi, Lawrence *Also Called: Microsemi Corporation (G-9583)*	
Microsemi-Lawrence, Lawrence *Also Called: Microsemi Corp- Massachusetts (G-9581)*	
Microsemi-Lowell, Lowell *Also Called: Microsemi Corp- Massachusetts (G-9906)*	
Microsense, Lowell *Also Called: Microsense LLC (G-9908)*	
Microsense LLC **(HQ)**........................ 205 Industrial Ave E Lowell (01852) *(G-9908)*	**978 843-7670**
Microsoft, Cambridge *Also Called: Microsoft Corporation (G-7643)*	
Microsoft, Cambridge *Also Called: Microsoft Corporation (G-7644)*	
Microsoft Corporation........................ 255 Main St Ste 401 Cambridge (02142) *(G-7643)*	781 398-4600
Microsoft Corporation........................ 1 Memorial Dr Ste 1 Cambridge (02142) *(G-7644)*	857 453-6000
Microsol........................ 2 Oliver St Ste 10c Boston (02109) *(G-6886)*	857 263-7249
Microspec Corporation........................ 327 Jaffrey Rd Peterborough (03458) *(G-15319)*	603 924-4300
Microspecialities Inc........................ 430 Smith St Middletown (06457) *(G-1764)*	203 874-1832
Microspecialties Inc........................ 264 Quarry Rd Milford (06460) *(G-1849)*	203 874-1832
Micross Components, Manchester *Also Called: NORTH PENN TECHNOLOGY INC (G-14903)*	
Micross Components, Manchester *Also Called: Premier Semiconductor Svcs LLC (G-14914)*	
Micross Components LLC........................ 1050 Perimeter Rd Ste 301 Manchester (03103) *(G-14887)*	603 893-9900
Microtech Inc........................ 1425 Highland Ave Cheshire (06410) *(G-607)*	203 272-3234
Microtek Inc........................ 2070 Westover Rd Chicopee (01022) *(G-8049)*	413 593-1025
Microtools Inc........................ 714 Hopmeadow St Ste 14 Simsbury (06070) *(G-3094)*	860 651-6170
Microtronic Inc........................ 5 Peases Point Rd Edgartown (02539) *(G-8467)*	508 627-8951
Microvision Inc **(PA)**........................ 20 London Ln Seabrook (03874) *(G-15598)*	**603 474-5566**
Microwave Cmpnents Systems Inc........................ 131 Flanders Rd Westborough (01581) *(G-13121)*	508 466-8400
Microwave Cmpnnts Spclists Inc........................ 34 Sullivan Rd Ste 10 North Billerica (01862) *(G-10937)*	978 667-1215
Microwave Development Labs Inc........................ 135 Crescent Rd Needham Heights (02494) *(G-10551)*	781 292-6600
Microwave Engineering Corp........................ 1551 Osgood St North Andover (01845) *(G-10844)*	978 685-2776
Microwave Radio Communications, North Billerica *Also Called: Legacy Broadcast Inc (G-10926)*	
Microway Inc........................ 12 Richards Rd Plymouth (02360) *(G-11467)*	508 746-7341
Mid State Machine Products **(PA)**........................ 83 Verti Dr Winslow (04901) *(G-5685)*	**207 873-6136**
Mid West Colour, Leominster *Also Called: L & A Molding Corporation (G-9675)*	
Mid-Cape Restoration Inc........................ 335 Cape Rd Hollis Center (04042) *(G-4894)*	207 929-4759
Mid-State Welding Inc........................ 150 Commercial Dr Southbridge (01550) *(G-12031)*	508 987-9410
Midac Corporation........................ 6 Coleman Ave Westfield (01085) *(G-13188)*	413 642-5595
Midas Muffler, Rutland *Also Called: T M Services Inc (G-17511)*	
Midas Technology Inc........................ 400 W Cummings Park Ste 6400 Woburn (01801) *(G-13613)*	781 938-0069
Middlbury Bee-Intelligencer-Ct........................ 2030 Straits Tpke Ste 1 Middlebury (06762) *(G-1717)*	203 577-6800
Middlesex General Inds Inc........................ 2 New Pasture Rd Ste 7 Newburyport (01950) *(G-10702)*	781 935-8870
Middlesex News........................ 33 New York Ave Framingham (01701) *(G-8790)*	508 626-3800
Middlesex Research Mfg Co Inc........................ 27 Apsley St Hudson (01749) *(G-9390)*	978 562-3697
Middlesex Truck & Auto Body........................ 65 Gerard St Boston (02119) *(G-6887)*	617 442-3000
Middlesex Truck & Coach, Boston *Also Called: Middlesex Truck & Auto Body (G-6887)*	
Middleton Aerospace, Haverhill *Also Called: Magellan Aerospace Usa Inc (G-9112)*	
Middleton Aerospace, Haverhill *Also Called: Magellan Arospc Haverhill Inc (G-9113)*	
Middleton Building Supply **(PA)**........................ 5 Kings Hwy Middleton (03887) *(G-15008)*	**603 473-2210**
Middletown Engine Center, East Hartford *Also Called: Pratt & Whitney Company Inc (G-1014)*	
Middletown Printing Co Inc........................ 512 Main St Middletown (06457) *(G-1765)*	860 347-5700
Midget Louver Company Inc........................ 671 Naugatuck Ave Milford (06461) *(G-1850)*	203 783-1444
Midstate Arc Inc........................ 20 Powers Dr Meriden (06451) *(G-1676)*	203 238-9001
Midstate Berkshire, Westfield *Also Called: MB Westfield Inc (G-13182)*	
Midstate Electronics Co........................ 71 S Turnpike Rd Ste 2 Wallingford (06492) *(G-3832)*	203 265-9900
Midstatemolding LLC........................ 20 Liberty Way Ste D Franklin (02038) *(G-8852)*	508 520-0011
Midsun Specialty Products Inc........................ 378 Four Rod Rd Berlin (06037) *(G-76)*	860 378-0111
Midwest Motor Supply Co........................ 14 Prospect Dr Newtown (06470) *(G-2342)*	800 233-1294
Midwood Quarry and Cnstr Inc **(PA)**........................ 200 Tolland St East Hartford (06108) *(G-1006)*	**860 289-1414**
Miedge, Bedford *Also Called: Ibis LLC (G-13933)*	
Mielke Confections Inc........................ 46 W Center Rd West Stockbridge (01266) *(G-13054)*	413 528-2510
Mighty Well Inc........................ 45 Catherine St Newport (02840) *(G-16217)*	617 804-1233
Mikco Manufacturing Inc........................ 14 Village Ln Wallingford (06492) *(G-3833)*	203 269-2250
Mike Murphy & Sons Inc........................ 57 Newton Junction Rd Kingston (03848) *(G-14636)*	603 362-4879
Mike Sadlak........................ 712 Bread And Milk St Unit A6 Coventry (06238) *(G-680)*	860 742-0227
Mike Sheas Cffhuse Trdtnals In........................ 37 Winsegansett Ave Fairhaven (02719) *(G-8509)*	508 807-5754
Mike's Engine Stand, Naugatuck *Also Called: K & E Auto Machine L L C (G-1968)*	

A
L
P
H
A
B
E
T
I
C

Mikel Inc **(PA)**...... 401 846-0052
589 Commerce Dr Fall River (02720) *(G-8582)*

Mikel Surfboards LLC.... 603 767-7662
5 Wheaton Lane Ter Hampton (03842) *(G-14407)*

Mikes Precision Machine Inc.... 978 667-9793
14 Hadley St North Billerica (01862) *(G-10938)*

Mikro Industrial Finishing Co.... 860 875-6357
170 W Main St Vernon (06066) *(G-3754)*

Mikrolar Inc.... 603 617-2508
7 Scott Rd Ste 5 Hampton (03842) *(G-14408)*

Mikros Technologies LLC.... 603 690-2020
24 Colonel Ashley Ln Claremont (03743) *(G-14094)*

Miks Mix LLC.... 203 521-7824
60 Corona Dr Milford (06460) *(G-1851)*

Mil-Con Inc.... 630 595-2366
22 Great Hill Rd Naugatuck (06770) *(G-1971)*

Milacron Marketing Company LLC.... 978 238-7100
428 Newburyport Tpke Rowley (01969) *(G-11679)*

Milani Industries Incorporated.... 781 344-3377
61 Marys Way Stoughton (02072) *(G-12225)*

Milara Inc.... 508 533-5322
49 Maple St Milford (01757) *(G-10404)*

Milara Inc.... 508 359-2786
71 West St Medfield (02052) *(G-10272)*

Milbar Labs Inc.... 203 467-1577
20 Commerce St East Haven (06512) *(G-1046)*

Mildred Coppola **(PA)**.... 203 967-9300
64 Research Dr Stamford (06906) *(G-3411)*

Miles Kedex Co Inc.... 978 874-1403
1 Rowtier Rd Westminster (01473) *(G-13274)*

Miles Press Inc.... 508 752-6430
14 Sword St Ste 5 Auburn (01501) *(G-6120)*

Milfoam Corporation.... 203 248-8011
23 Marne St Hamden (06514) *(G-1442)*

Milford Daily News, Milford *Also Called: Gatehouse Media Mass I Inc* **(G-10403)**

Milford Fabricating Co Inc.... 203 878-2476
500 Bic Dr Bldg 2 Milford (06461) *(G-1852)*

Milford Fabricating Co., Milford *Also Called: Valley Tool and Mfg LLC* **(G-1897)**

Milford Fabricating Co., Milford *Also Called: Valley Tool and Mfg LLC* **(G-1898)**

Milford Manufacturing Svcs LLC.... 508 478-8544
4 Business Way Hopedale (01747) *(G-9299)*

Milford Woodworking Co Inc.... 508 473-2335
294 West St Milford (01757) *(G-10405)*

Military Art China, Contoocook *Also Called: Bryant Group Inc* **(G-14167)**

Milite Bakery.... 203 753-9451
26 Evers Dr Wolcott (06716) *(G-4368)*

Milk Street Press Inc.... 617 742-7900
8 Faneuil Hall Market Pl 3rd Fl Boston (02109) *(G-6888)*

Mill City Iron.... 603 622-0042
101 Allard Dr Manchester (03102) *(G-14888)*

Mill City Iron Fabricators.... 978 957-6833
479 Textile Ave Dracut (01826) *(G-8309)*

Mill Fudge Factory, The, Bristol *Also Called: Grist For Mill LLC* **(G-14036)**

Mill Manufacturing Inc.... 203 367-9572
105 Willow St Bridgeport (06610) *(G-347)*

Mill River Lumber Ltd.... 802 775-0032
2639 Middle Rd North Clarendon (05759) *(G-17417)*

Mill Valley Molding Inc.... 413 247-9313
15 West St West Hatfield (01088) *(G-13005)*

Mill Works.... 978 692-8222
22 Town Farm Rd Westford (01886) *(G-13251)*

Millard Jewelry Division, Warwick *Also Called: Millard Wire Company* **(G-16838)**

Millard Wire Company.... 401 737-9330
259 Warwick Industrial Dr Warwick (02886) *(G-16837)*

Millard Wire Company **(PA)**.... 401 737-9330
449 Warwick Industrial Dr Warwick (02886) *(G-16838)*

Millennium Die Group Inc.... 413 283-3500
2022 Bridge St Three Rivers (01080) *(G-12430)*

Millennium Pharmaceuticals Inc.... 617 679-7000
640 Memorial Dr Ste 3w Cambridge (02139) *(G-7645)*

Millennium Pharmaceuticals Inc **(HQ)**.... 617 679-7000
40 Landsdowne St Cambridge (02139) *(G-7646)*

Millennium Pharmaceuticals Inc.... 617 679-7000
35 Landsdowne St Cambridge (02139) *(G-7647)*

Millennium Pharmaceuticals Inc.... 617 679-7000
300 Massachusetts Ave Cambridge (02139) *(G-7648)*

Millennium Pharmaceuticals Inc.... 617 679-7000
45 Sidney St Cambridge (02139) *(G-7649)*

Millennium Pharmaceuticals Inc.... 617 679-7000
1 Kendall Sq Bldg 200 Cambridge (02139) *(G-7650)*

Millennium Pharmaceuticals Inc.... 617 679-7000
125 Binney St Cambridge (02142) *(G-7651)*

Millennium Pharmaceuticals Inc.... 617 679-7000
45 Hayden Ave # 55 Lexington (02421) *(G-9763)*

Millennium Pharmaceuticals Inc.... 781 729-7435
50 Harvard St Winchester (01890) *(G-13487)*

Millennium Plastics Inc.... 978 372-4822
180 Middlesex St Ste 1 North Chelmsford (01863) *(G-10984)*

Millennium Power Services Inc **(PA)**.... 413 562-5332
80 Mainline Dr Westfield (01085) *(G-13189)*

Millennium Press Inc.... 413 821-0028
570 Silver St Agawam (01001) *(G-5801)*

Miller Drug Whiting Hill Phrm, Brewer *Also Called: M Drug LLC* **(G-4618)**

Miller H C Wood Working Inc.... 508 429-4220
93 Bartzak Dr Holliston (01746) *(G-9223)*

Miller Industries Inc.... 207 353-4371
Canal St Rr 196 Lisbon Falls (04252) *(G-5023)*

Miller-Stephenson Chemical Company Inc **(PA)**.... 800 442-3424
55 Backus Ave Danbury (06810) *(G-786)*

Millers Petroleum Systems Inc.... 413 499-2134
875 Crane Ave Pittsfield (01201) *(G-11411)*

Millham LLC.... 978 422-8621
2 Northeast Blvd Sterling (01564) *(G-12168)*

Millibar Inc.... 508 488-9870
1 Bonazzoli Ave Ste 2 Hudson (01749) *(G-9391)*

Millies Pierogi, Chicopee *Also Called: Garan Enterprises Inc* **(G-8034)**

Millincket Fabrication Mch Inc **(PA)**.... 207 723-9733
432 Katahdin Ave Millinocket (04462) *(G-5067)*

Millitech Inc.... 413 582-9620
29 Industrial Dr E Northampton (01060) *(G-11073)*

Millrite Machine Inc.... 413 562-9212
587 Southampton Rd Westfield (01085) *(G-13190)*

Mills & Co Inc.... 207 893-1115
778 Roosevelt Trl Ste 1 Windham (04062) *(G-5665)*

Mills Coffee Roasting Co.... 401 781-7860
1058 Broad St Providence (02905) *(G-16565)*

Mills Industries Inc.... 603 528-4217
167 Water St Laconia (03246) *(G-14659)*

Millstone Med Outsourcing LLC **(PA)**.... 508 679-8384
580 Commerce Dr Fall River (02720) *(G-8583)*

Millwood Inc.... 203 248-7902
33 Stiles Ln Ste 3 North Haven (06473) *(G-2425)*

Millwork Masters Ltd **(PA)**.... 603 358-3038
69 Island St Ste B Keene (03431) *(G-14608)*

Millwork One Inc.... 401 738-6990
60 Kenney Dr Cranston (02920) *(G-15895)*

Milne Spirit Works LLC.... 207 536-0592
53 Washington Ave Portland (04101) *(G-5245)*

Milpower Source, Belmont *Also Called: Milpower Source Inc* **(G-13963)**

Milpower Source Inc.... 603 267-8865
7 Field Ln Belmont (03220) *(G-13963)*

Milton & Goose LLC.... 203 539-1073
65 High Ridge Rd Ste 369 Stamford (06905) *(G-3412)*

Milton Vermont Sheet Metal Inc.... 802 893-1581
103 Gonyeau Rd Milton (05468) *(G-17362)*

Miltronics Mfg Svcs Inc.... 603 352-3333
95 Krif Rd Keene (03431) *(G-14609)*

Mimoco Inc.... 617 783-1100
475 Hillside Ave Ste 1 Needham Heights (02494) *(G-10552)*

Minarik Automation & Control, Bloomfield *Also Called: Minarik Corporation* **(G-192)**

Minarik Corporation.... 860 687-5000
1 Vision Way Bloomfield (06002) *(G-192)*

Mindedge Inc.... 781 250-1805
271 Waverley Oaks Rd Ste 404 Waltham (02452) *(G-12720)*

Mindsciences Inc.. 516 658-2985
  45 Hickory Dr Worcester (01609) *(G-13760)*

Mindstream, South Burlington *Also Called: Step Ahead Innovations Inc (G-17600)*

Mineral Technology, Canaan *Also Called: Minteq International Inc (G-556)*

Minerva Nrscnces Scrities Corp..................................... 617 600-7373
  1601 Trapelo Rd Ste 284 Waltham (02451) *(G-12721)*

Mini, Naugatuck *Also Called: Mini LLC (G-1972)*

Mini LLC.. 203 464-5495
  66 Church St Naugatuck (06770) *(G-1972)*

Mini Cast Precision Casting, Cranston *Also Called: Miniature Casting Corporation (G-15896)*

Mini-Systems Inc.. 508 695-0203
  45 Frank Mossberg Dr Attleboro (02703) *(G-6037)*

Mini-Systems Inc **(PA)**.. **508 695-1420**
  20 David Rd North Attleboro (02760) *(G-10878)*

Mini-Systems Inc... 508 695-2000
  168 E Bacon St Plainville (02762) *(G-11439)*

Miniature Casting Corporation...................................... 401 463-5090
  21 Slater Rd Cranston (02920) *(G-15896)*

Minim, Manchester *Also Called: Minim Inc (G-14889)*

Minim Inc **(PA)**... **833 966-4646**
  848 Elm St Manchester (03101) *(G-14889)*

Minimally Invasive Surgeon... 860 241-0870
  1000 Asylum Ave Lbby Hartford (06105) *(G-1493)*

Minit Print Inc... 203 776-6000
  27 Whitney Ave New Haven (06510) *(G-2175)*

Mint Printworks LLC.. 603 718-1100
  1 Pine Street Ext Ste 135 Nashua (03060) *(G-15135)*

Minteq International Inc.. 860 824-5435
  30 Daisy Hill Rd Canaan (06018) *(G-556)*

Minute Man Broaches, Greenfield *Also Called: Dumont Company LLC (G-8990)*

Minute Man Press.. 203 891-6251
  5 Hamden Park Dr Hamden (06517) *(G-1443)*

Minute-Man Printing Corp... 978 369-2808
  20 Beharrell St Ste 1 Concord (01742) *(G-8125)*

Minuteman Laboratories Inc... 978 263-2632
  7a Stuart Rd Chelmsford (01824) *(G-7939)*

Minuteman Land Services Inc.. 203 854-4949
  377 Highland Ave Norwalk (06854) *(G-2538)*

Minuteman Metal LLC.. 207 217-8908
  469 Depot St Wilton (04294) *(G-5658)*

Minuteman Newspaper **(PA)**....................................... **203 226-8877**
  1175 Post Rd E Ste 3e Westport (06880) *(G-4185)*

Minuteman Pre-Hung Door Co, Acton *Also Called: Sb Development Corp (G-5764)*

Minuteman Press... 860 674-8700
  195 W Main St Ste E Avon (06001) *(G-31)*

Minuteman Press... 973 748-7160
  12 Mill Plain Rd Ste 1 Danbury (06811) *(G-787)*

Minuteman Press... 860 646-0601
  757 Main St Manchester (06040) *(G-1618)*

Minuteman Press... 203 261-8318
  14 Kitcher Ct Trumbull (06611) *(G-3725)*

Minuteman Press... 860 529-4628
  81 Wolcott Hill Rd Wethersfield (06109) *(G-4211)*

Minuteman Press... 207 517-5355
  33 E Main St Denmark (04022) *(G-4724)*

Minuteman Press... 781 273-1155
  169 Bedford St Ste 4 Burlington (01803) *(G-7394)*

Minuteman Press... 508 775-9890
  1694 Falmouth Rd Centerville (02632) *(G-7860)*

Minuteman Press... 508 778-0220
  223 Barnstable Rd Hyannis (02601) *(G-9441)*

Minuteman Press... 617 361-7400
  1279 Hyde Park Ave Hyde Park (02136) *(G-9463)*

Minuteman Press... 603 513-4993
  93 Storrs St Concord (03301) *(G-14146)*

Minuteman Press, Avon *Also Called: Minuteman Press (G-31)*

Minuteman Press, Bristol *Also Called: Minuteman Press of Bristol (G-469)*

Minuteman Press, Danbury *Also Called: Minuteman Press (G-787)*

Minuteman Press, Danbury *Also Called: Minuteman Press of Danbury (G-788)*

Minuteman Press, Hamden *Also Called: Minute Man Press (G-1443)*

Minuteman Press, Hartford *Also Called: Capitol Printing Co Inc (G-1473)*

Minuteman Press, Middletown *Also Called: Middletown Printing Co Inc (G-1765)*

Minuteman Press, Norwich *Also Called: Norwich Printing Company Inc (G-2611)*

Minuteman Press, Wethersfield *Also Called: Minuteman Press (G-4211)*

Minuteman Press, Saco *Also Called: Minuteman Press of Saco (G-5374)*

Minuteman Press, Andover *Also Called: Andover Printing Inc (G-5870)*

Minuteman Press, Andover *Also Called: Seventy Nine N Main St Prtg (G-5917)*

Minuteman Press, Beverly *Also Called: Enon Copy Inc (G-6346)*

Minuteman Press, Boston *Also Called: Fenway Cmmunications Group Inc (G-6734)*

Minuteman Press, Burlington *Also Called: Minuteman Press (G-7394)*

Minuteman Press, Centerville *Also Called: Minuteman Press (G-7860)*

Minuteman Press, Concord *Also Called: Minute-Man Printing Corp (G-8125)*

Minuteman Press, Hyde Park *Also Called: Minuteman Press (G-9463)*

Minuteman Press, Lowell *Also Called: Bassett & Cassidy Inc (G-9860)*

Minuteman Press, North Dartmouth *Also Called: Marbuo Inc (G-10999)*

Minuteman Press, Plymouth *Also Called: Minuteman Printing (G-11468)*

Minuteman Press, Waltham *Also Called: Generation Four Inc (G-12686)*

Minuteman Press, Londonderry *Also Called: Bob Bean Company Inc (G-14733)*

Minuteman Press, North Conway *Also Called: P2k Printing LLC (G-15249)*

Minuteman Press, Portsmouth *Also Called: Cygnus Inc (G-15379)*

Minuteman Press, Providence *Also Called: Peak Printing Inc (G-16582)*

Minuteman Press, Colchester *Also Called: Larcoline Inc (G-17197)*

Minuteman Press of Bristol... 860 589-1100
  98 Farmington Ave Bristol (06010) *(G-469)*

Minuteman Press of Danbury... 203 743-6755
  12 Mill Plain Rd Ste 10 Danbury (06811) *(G-788)*

Minuteman Press of Saco.. 207 282-6480
  110 Main St Ste 1207 Saco (04072) *(G-5374)*

Minuteman Printing... 508 830-3500
  53 S Meadow Rd Plymouth (02360) *(G-11468)*

Minuteman Tress, Waterbury *Also Called: Byrne Group Inc (G-3894)*

Mirabello Holdings LLC... 860 582-9517
  60 Wooster Ct Bristol (06010) *(G-470)*

Miracle Instruments Co... 860 642-7745
  1667 Exeter Rd Lebanon (06249) *(G-1549)*

Miraco Inc... 603 665-9449
  102 Maple St Manchester (03103) *(G-14890)*

Miranda Brothers Inc... 508 672-0982
  317 Lindsey St Fall River (02720) *(G-8584)*

Mirion Tech Canberra Inc **(DH)**.................................. **203 238-2351**
  800 Research Pkwy Meriden (06450) *(G-1677)*

Mirror Polishing & Pltg Co Inc..................................... 203 574-5400
  346 Huntingdon Ave Waterbury (06708) *(G-3945)*

Mirs, Augusta *Also Called: Maine Industrial Repair Service Inc (G-4476)*

Mist Hill Property Maint LLC....................................... 203 648-7434
  32 Mist Hill Dr Brookfield (06804) *(G-530)*

Mistras Group Inc.. 508 832-5500
  2 Millbury St Auburn (01501) *(G-6121)*

Mistras Services, Auburn *Also Called: Mistras Group Inc (G-6121)*

Mit Press, The, Cambridge *Also Called: Massachusetts Institute Tech (G-7637)*

Mitch Rosen Extraordinary Gunl..................................... 603 647-2971
  540 North Commercial St Manchester (03101) *(G-14891)*

Mitchell Machine Incorporated **(PA)**............................. **413 739-9693**
  224 Hancock St Springfield (01109) *(G-12114)*

Mitchell-Bate Company.. 203 233-0862
  365 Thomaston Ave Waterbury (06702) *(G-3946)*

Mitee-Bite Products LLC.. 603 539-4538
  340 Route 16b Center Ossipee (03814) *(G-14058)*

Miti Manufacturing Co Inc.. 802 424-1671
  2176 Portland St Saint Johnsbury (05819) *(G-17544)*

Mitsubishi Chemical Amer Inc....................................... 978 657-0075
  229 Andover St Wilmington (01887) *(G-13432)*

Mitsubishi Power Aero LLC **(HQ)**................................. **860 368-5900**
  628 Hebron Ave Ste 400 Glastonbury (06033) *(G-1290)*

Mitsubshi Tnabe Phrma Amer Inc..................................... 210 897-3473
  21 Erie St Cambridge (02139) *(G-7652)*

Mittys LLC... 516 297-9219
  76 Granby St Bloomfield (06002) *(G-193)*

A
L
P
H
A
B
E
T
I
C

MIW Corp..508 672-4029
  1205 Bay St Fall River (02724) *(G-8585)*

Mix Marketing Corp...401 954-6121
  68 Old Pine Rd Narragansett (02882) *(G-16191)*

Mixfit Inc..617 902-8082
  51 Melcher St Boston (02210) *(G-6889)*

Mixx Frozen Yogurt Inc **(PA)**...................................**617 782-6499**
  66 Brighton Ave Allston (02134) *(G-5824)*

Miyoshi America Inc **(HQ)**....................................**860 779-3990**
  110 Louisa Viens Dr Dayville (06241) *(G-863)*

Mizkan Americas Inc..207 786-3200
  176 First Flight Dr Auburn (04210) *(G-4445)*

MJ Metal Inc...203 334-3484
  225 Howard Ave Bridgeport (06605) *(G-348)*

MJ Murphy and Sons Inc.......................................603 767-4200
  4 Granite St Dover (03820) *(G-14236)*

Mj Research Inc **(HQ)**...**510 724-7000**
  245 Winter St Ste 100 Waltham (02451) *(G-12722)*

MJM Marga LLC..203 729-0600
  28 Raytkwich Rd Naugatuck (06770) *(G-1973)*

MJW Mass Inc..781 721-0332
  37 East St Winchester (01890) *(G-13488)*

MK Fuel Inc...413 245-7507
  341 Sturbridge Rd Brimfield (01010) *(G-7250)*

Mk Millwork LLC...860 567-0173
  234 Thomaston Rd Morris (06763) *(G-1933)*

Mk North America Inc...860 769-5500
  105 Highland Park Dr Bloomfield (06002) *(G-194)*

Mk Services Corp..978 777-2196
  194 S Main St Middleton (01949) *(G-10390)*

Mk Wood Cabinets, Plainfield *Also Called: Stm Imp and Exp Corp (G-2740)*

Mkind Inc...603 493-6882
  150 Dow St Ste 4 Manchester (03101) *(G-14892)*

Mks Astex Products, Methuen *Also Called: Mks Instruments Inc (G-10339)*

Mks Instruments Inc..978 645-5500
  6 Shattuck Rd Andover (01810) *(G-5898)*

Mks Instruments Inc **(PA)**.....................................**978 645-5500**
  2 Tech Dr Ste 201 Andover (01810) *(G-5899)*

Mks Instruments Inc..978 284-4015
  55 Foundation Ave Unit 4 Haverhill (01835) *(G-9117)*

Mks Instruments Inc..978 975-2350
  17 Ballard Way Lawrence (01843) *(G-9585)*

Mks Instruments Inc..978 682-3512
  651 Lowell St Methuen (01844) *(G-10339)*

Mks Instruments Inc..978 284-4000
  90 Industrial Way Wilmington (01887) *(G-13433)*

Mks Msc Inc..978 284-4000
  90 Industrial Way Wilmington (01887) *(G-13434)*

ML Custom Wood Work Inc....................................508 360-2137
  105 Ferndoc St Unit Gf Hyannis (02601) *(G-9442)*

Mlk Business Forms Inc..203 624-6304
  25 James St New Haven (06513) *(G-2176)*

MLS Acq Inc..860 386-6878
  32 North Rd East Windsor (06088) *(G-1082)*

MLS Sheet Metal LLC...781 275-2265
  39 Crosby Dr Bedford (01730) *(G-6243)*

Mlt Technology Review, Cambridge *Also Called: Technology Review Inc (G-7736)*

MM Newman Corporation.......................................781 631-7100
  24 Tioga Way Marblehead (01945) *(G-10091)*

MM Reif Ltd...617 442-9500
  850 Albany St Boston (02119) *(G-6890)*

Mm-Apvh Acquisition Co LLC **(HQ)**..........................**978 516-7050**
  100 Simplex Dr Westminster (01473) *(G-13275)*

Mm-Apvh Acquisition Co LLC...................................401 753-7778
  1 Campbell St Pawtucket (02860) *(G-16388)*

Mmis Inc..603 929-5078
  100 International Dr Ste 350 Portsmouth (03801) *(G-15424)*

Mmj Biopharma Cultivation Inc................................800 586-7863
  1 Crosswind Dr Westerly (02891) *(G-16936)*

MMS, Boston *Also Called: Mobile Messaging Solutions (G-6891)*

Moab Oil Inc..203 857-6622
  20 Marshall St Ste 200 Norwalk (06854) *(G-2539)*

Moark LLC **(HQ)**..**951 332-3300**
  28 Under The Mountain Rd North Franklin (06254) *(G-2383)*

Moat Mtn Smoke Hse Brewing Co, North Conway *Also Called: Federal Spice Corp (G-15248)*

Mobile Global Esports Inc......................................475 666-8401
  500 Post Rd E Fl 2 Westport (06880) *(G-4186)*

Mobile Messaging Solutions....................................857 202-3132
  745 Atlantic Ave Fl 2 Boston (02111) *(G-6891)*

Mobile Mini Inc...860 668-1888
  911 S St Mach 1 Industrial Park Suffield (06078) *(G-3594)*

Mobile Mini Inc...508 427-5395
  125 Manley St West Bridgewater (02379) *(G-12975)*

Mobile Sense Technologies Inc................................203 914-5375
  24 Cliff Ave Darien (06820) *(G-852)*

Mobile Software Inc...617 719-8660
  110 K St Boston (02127) *(G-6892)*

Mobilityworks, Londonderry *Also Called: Ride-Away Inc (G-14782)*

Mobius Imaging LLC...978 796-5068
  2 Shaker Rd Ste F100 Shirley (01464) *(G-11821)*

Moca, Boston *Also Called: Moca Systems Inc (G-6893)*

Moca Systems Inc **(PA)**..**617 581-6622**
  50 Congress St Ste 630 Boston (02109) *(G-6893)*

Mocana Corporation...508 251-5086
  225 Cedar Hill St Ste 332 Marlborough (01752) *(G-10185)*

Modalis Therapeutics Inc.......................................617 219-9808
  43 Foundry Ave Waltham (02453) *(G-12723)*

Model Engineering, Marion *Also Called: Nadco International Inc (G-10098)*

Modelvision Inc..860 355-3884
  566 Danbury Rd Ste 4 New Milford (06776) *(G-2253)*

Modern Architechtural Glazing, Rochdale *Also Called: Modern Mfg Inc Worcester (G-11628)*

Modern Industries Inc...401 331-8000
  242 W Exchange St Providence (02903) *(G-16566)*

Modern Jewelry, Johnston *Also Called: Modern Manufacturing Inc (G-16096)*

Modern Manufacturing Inc......................................401 944-9230
  47 Homeland St Johnston (02919) *(G-16096)*

Modern Metal Finishing LLC....................................203 267-1510
  110 Willenbrock Rd Oxford (06478) *(G-2704)*

Modern Metal Solutions LLC....................................603 402-3022
  12 Park Ave Hudson (03051) *(G-14528)*

Modern Mfg Inc Worcester......................................508 791-7151
  82 Huntoon Memorial Hwy Rochdale (01542) *(G-11628)*

Modern Mold and Tool Inc **(PA)**.............................**413 443-1192**
  45 Downing Industrial Park Pittsfield (01201) *(G-11412)*

Modern Pastry, Hartford *Also Called: Modern Pastry Shop Inc (G-1494)*

Modern Pastry Shop Inc...860 296-7628
  422 Franklin Ave Hartford (06114) *(G-1494)*

Modern Plastics..401 732-0415
  380 Jefferson Blvd Ste A Warwick (02886) *(G-16839)*

Modern Shoe Company LLC.....................................617 333-7470
  101 Sprague St Ste 1 Hyde Park (02136) *(G-9464)*

Modern Woodcrafts, Plainville *Also Called: McKinnon Design LLC (G-2773)*

Moderna, Cambridge *Also Called: Moderna Inc (G-7653)*

Moderna Inc **(PA)**..**617 714-6500**
  200 Technology Sq Cambridge (02139) *(G-7653)*

Modernist Pantry LLC...207 200-3817
  25 Harold L Dow Hwy Eliot (03903) *(G-4750)*

Modine LLC...860 452-4194
  129 Chittenden Rd Killingworth (06419) *(G-1543)*

Modine Manufacturing Company................................401 792-1231
  604 Liberty Ln West Kingston (02892) *(G-16894)*

Modu Form Inc **(PA)**...**978 345-7942**
  172 Industrial Rd Fitchburg (01420) *(G-8667)*

Moduform, Fitchburg *Also Called: Modu Form Inc (G-8667)*

Modula Inc **(DH)**...**207 440-5100**
  90 Alfred A Plourde Pkwy Lewiston (04240) *(G-4976)*

Modular Air Filtration Systems.................................508 823-4900
  450 Richmond St Raynham (02767) *(G-11594)*

Modular Fun I Inc..207 739-2400
  300 Park St South Paris (04281) *(G-5490)*

Moduline, Brockton *Also Called: Gill Metal Fab Inc (G-7281)*

Modus Media Inc...781 663-5000
  1601 Trapelo Rd Ste 170 Waltham (02451) *(G-12724)*

Modutec, Manchester *Also Called: Jewell Instruments LLC (G-14868)*	
Moeller Instrument Company Inc.	800 243-9310
126 Main St Ivoryton (06442) *(G-1530)*	
Moffly Publications Inc.	203 222-0600
205 Main St Ste 1 Westport (06880) *(G-4187)*	
Mohawk Chicago Distribution.	781 334-4976
9 Mohawk Dr Leominster (01453) *(G-9684)*	
Mohawk Fence Company Inc.	508 614-5507
185 Oak St Shrewsbury (01545) *(G-11838)*	
Mohawk Manufacturing Company.	860 632-2345
1270 Newfield St Middletown (06457) *(G-1766)*	
Mohawk Tool and Die Mfg Co Inc.	203 367-2181
25 Wells St Ste 4 Bridgeport (06604) *(G-349)*	
Mohegan Digital Services LLC.	888 226-7711
1 Mohegan Sun Blvd Uncasville (06382) *(G-3741)*	
Mohican Valley, Fairfield *Also Called: Mohican Valley Concrete Corp (G-1194)*	
Mohican Valley Concrete Corp.	203 254-7133
195 Ardmore St Fairfield (06824) *(G-1194)*	
Moku Artisan Furniture, Oak Bluffs *Also Called: Ms Orbis Corporation (G-11222)*	
Molded Plastics Engrg Inc.	978 948-7153
58 Kittery Ave Rowley (01969) *(G-11680)*	
Moldmaster Engineering Inc.	413 442-5793
187 Newell St Pittsfield (01201) *(G-11413)*	
Moldvision LLC.	860 315-1025
316 County Home Rd Thompson (06277) *(G-3651)*	
Molecular Health Inc.	832 482-3898
1 Beacon St Fl 15 Boston (02108) *(G-6894)*	
Molnycke, Palmer *Also Called: Essity North America Inc (G-11274)*	
Momenta Pharmaceuticals Inc **(HQ)**.	**617 491-9700**
301 Binney St Cambridge (02142) *(G-7654)*	
Momentum Mfg Group - N LLC **(PA)**.	**802 748-5007**
210 Pierce Rd Saint Johnsbury (05819) *(G-17545)*	
Momentum Mfg Group LLC **(HQ)**.	**978 659-6960**
23 National Ave Georgetown (01833) *(G-8910)*	
Moms Organic Munchies Inc.	207 869-4078
174 Lower Main St Ste 21 Freeport (04032) *(G-4802)*	
Monadnock Associates Inc **(PA)**.	**617 924-7032**
3 Brook St Watertown (02472) *(G-12894)*	
Monadnock Grinding LLC.	603 585-7275
98 Royalston Rd Fitzwilliam (03447) *(G-14314)*	
Monadnock Land Clearing.	603 878-2803
932 Fitchburg Rd Greenville (03048) *(G-14373)*	
Monadnock Land Clearing & Chip, Greenville *Also Called: Monadnock Land Clearing (G-14373)*	
Monadnock Ledger, Concord *Also Called: Newspapers New Hampshire Inc (G-14149)*	
Monadnock Ledger, Peterborough *Also Called: Newspapers New Hampshire Inc (G-15321)*	
Monadnock Mountain Spring Water Inc.	603 654-2728
8 Mansur Rd Wilton (03086) *(G-15706)*	
Monadnock Paper Mills Inc **(HQ)**.	**603 588-3311**
117 Antrim Rd Bennington (03442) *(G-13977)*	
Monadnock Paper Mills Inc.	603 588-8220
231 Forest Rd Greenfield (03047) *(G-14364)*	
Monadnock Paper Warehouse, Greenfield *Also Called: Monadnock Paper Mills Inc (G-14364)*	
Monadnock Shopper News, Keene *Also Called: Shakour Publishers Inc (G-14618)*	
Monaghan Printing Company.	508 991-8087
59 Alden Rd Fairhaven (02719) *(G-8510)*	
Monahan Products LLC **(PA)**.	**844 823-3132**
276 Weymouth St Rockland (02370) *(G-11652)*	
Monalex Manufacturing Inc.	508 476-1200
10 Riedell Rd East Douglas (01516) *(G-8352)*	
Monarch Industries Inc.	401 247-5200
80 Faunce Dr Providence (02906) *(G-16567)*	
Monarch Instrument, Amherst *Also Called: Monarch International Inc (G-13881)*	
Monarch International Inc.	603 883-3390
15 Columbia Dr Amherst (03031) *(G-13881)*	
Monarch Metal Finishing Co Inc.	401 785-3200
189 Georgia Ave Providence (02905) *(G-16568)*	
Monarch Stone Inc.	978 954-7021
133 Main St North Reading (01864) *(G-11044)*	
Moneysworth & Best USA Inc.	603 968-3301
1 Cedar Ln Ashland (03217) *(G-13901)*	

Monks Manufacturing Co Inc.	978 657-8282
1 Upton Dr Wilmington (01887) *(G-13435)*	
Mono Die Cutting Co Inc.	401 434-1274
7 Hemingway Dr Riverside (02915) *(G-16658)*	
Mono-Crete Step Co Ct LLC.	203 748-8419
12 Trowbridge Dr Bethel (06801) *(G-129)*	
Monopol Corporation.	860 583-3852
394 Riverside Ave Bristol (06010) *(G-471)*	
Monotonyai Inc.	202 607-8193
480 Pleasant St Ste A310 Watertown (02472) *(G-12895)*	
Monotype, Woburn *Also Called: Monotype Imaging Holdings Inc (G-13614)*	
Monotype Imaging Holdings Inc **(DH)**.	**781 970-6000**
600 Unicorn Park Dr Woburn (01801) *(G-13614)*	
Monotype Imaging Inc **(DH)**.	**781 970-6000**
600 Unicorn Park Dr Ste 3f Woburn (01801) *(G-13615)*	
Monro Inc.	603 352-7822
1042 W Swanzey Rd Swanzey (03446) *(G-15644)*	
Monro Muffler Brake, Swanzey *Also Called: Monro Inc (G-15644)*	
Monroe Recycl & Aggregates LLC.	203 644-7748
485 Pepper St Monroe (06468) *(G-1917)*	
Monster Tech.	978 897-0832
133 Boston Post Rd 15 Weston (02493) *(G-13288)*	
Montague Corporation.	617 491-7200
1035 Cambridge St Ste 29 Cambridge (02141) *(G-7655)*	
Montague Industries Inc.	413 863-4301
15 Rastallis St Turners Falls (01376) *(G-12453)*	
Montague Machine Company, Turners Falls *Also Called: Montague Industries Inc (G-12453)*	
Montague USA, Cambridge *Also Called: Montague Corporation (G-7655)*	
Montai Health Inc.	617 293-0578
26 Landsdowne St Cambridge (02139) *(G-7656)*	
Montalvo Corporation.	207 856-2501
50 Hutcherson Dr Gorham (04038) *(G-4827)*	
Monte Rosa Therapeutics Inc **(PA)**.	**617 949-2643**
321 Harrison Ave Ste 900 Boston (02118) *(G-6895)*	
Monteferro Press.	508 944-8587
49 Half Crown Cir Ashland (01721) *(G-5962)*	
Montello Heel Mfg Inc.	508 586-0603
13 Emerson Ave Ste 4 Brockton (02301) *(G-7296)*	
Montilio Baking Co Inc.	508 894-8855
134 Spark St Brockton (02302) *(G-7297)*	
Montilio's Baking Company, Brockton *Also Called: Montilio Baking Co Inc (G-7297)*	
Montpelier Granite Works Inc.	802 223-2581
65 Granite Shed Ln Montpelier (05602) *(G-17373)*	
Montreal Fishing Corp.	508 993-0275
13 Centre St Unit 1 New Bedford (02740) *(G-10623)*	
Montville Sewer Plant, Uncasville *Also Called: Town of Montville (G-3745)*	
Monument Farms Inc.	802 545-2119
2107 James Rd Weybridge (05753) *(G-17703)*	
Monument Industries Inc.	802 442-8187
159 Phyllis Ln Bennington (05201) *(G-17052)*	
Monzite Corporation **(HQ)**.	**617 429-7050**
165 Ledge St Nashua (03060) *(G-15136)*	
Moo Inc.	401 519-7216
25 Fairmount Ave East Providence (02914) *(G-16031)*	
Moo.com, East Providence *Also Called: Moo Inc (G-16031)*	
Moody Machine Products Inc.	401 941-5130
141 Carolina Ave Providence (02905) *(G-16569)*	
Moody Tools, Cranston *Also Called: Central Tools Inc (G-15841)*	
Moon Cutter Co Inc.	203 288-9249
2969 State St Hamden (06517) *(G-1444)*	
Mooneytunco Inc.	781 331-4445
65 Mathewson Dr Ste C Weymouth (02189) *(G-13330)*	
Moonlight Ltd.	508 584-0094
244 Liberty St Ste 11 Brockton (02301) *(G-7298)*	
Moonlight Meadery LLC.	603 216-2162
23 Londonderry Rd Unit 17 Londonderry (03053) *(G-14774)*	
Moor Metals Inc **(PA)**.	**508 429-9446**
2 Kuniholm Dr Ste 2 Holliston (01746) *(G-9224)*	
Moore Company.	401 596-0219
48 Canal St Westerly (02891) *(G-16937)*	
Moore Company **(PA)**.	**401 596-2816**
36 Beach St Westerly (02891) *(G-16938)*	

**A
L
P
H
A
B
E
T
I
C**

Moore Company.. 401 596-2816
   36 Beach St Westerly (02891) *(G-16939)*

Moore Design Builders, Waitsfield *Also Called: William H Moore Inc (G-17668)*

Moore Nntechnology Systems LLC **(DH)**.......... **603 352-3030**
   230 Old Homestead Hwy Swanzey (03446) *(G-15645)*

Moore Tool Company Inc **(HQ)**........................ **203 366-3224**
   599 Hollister Ave Bridgeport (06607) *(G-350)*

Moore-Clark USA Inc.. 207 591-7077
   15 Saunders Way Ste 500 Westbrook (04092) *(G-5639)*

Mooring Systems Incorporated................................ 508 776-0254
   1227 Rt 28a Cataumet (02534) *(G-7859)*

Moose Mountain Food Co., Wells River *Also Called: Bread & Chocolate Inc (G-17686)*

Moose River Lumber Company, Moose River *Also Called: Boundary Co (G-5076)*

Moose River Lumber Company Inc........................... 207 668-4426
   432 Milo Rd Dover Foxcroft (04426) *(G-4729)*

Moose's Tale Food & Ale, Boston *Also Called: Sunday River Brewing Co Inc (G-7064)*

Moosehead Cedar Log Homes, Greenville Junction *Also Called: Moosehead Wood Components Inc (G-4852)*

Moosehead Country Log Homes................................ 207 695-3730
   Greenville Industrial Park Greenville (04441) *(G-4851)*

Moosehead Wood Components Inc........................... 207 695-3730
   441 Pritham Ave Greenville Junction (04442) *(G-4852)*

Moosewood Millworks LLC....................................... 207 435-4950
   42 American Realty Rd. Ashland (04732) *(G-4411)*

Mor-Wire & Cable Inc... 978 453-1782
   50 Newhall St Ste 1 Lowell (01852) *(G-9909)*

Moresi & Associates Dev Co LLC............................. 413 663-8677
   60 Roberts Dr Ste 201 North Adams (01247) *(G-10811)*

Morgan A M T.. 860 349-4444
   18 Airline Rd Durham (06422) *(G-903)*

Morgan Advanced Ceramics Inc.............................. 508 995-1725
   225 Theodore Rice Blvd New Bedford (02745) *(G-10624)*

Morgan Advanced Ceramics Inc.............................. 603 598-9122
   4 Park Ave Hudson (03051) *(G-14529)*

Morgan Enterprises Inc.. 985 377-3216
   110 Blackstone River Rd Worcester (01607) *(G-13761)*

Morgan Mill Metals LLC.. 401 270-9944
   25 Morgan Mill Rd Johnston (02919) *(G-16097)*

Morgan Scientific Inc **(PA)**............................ **978 521-4440**
   151 Essex St Ste 8 Haverhill (01832) *(G-9118)*

Morin Brothers.. 207 834-5361
   41 Charette Hill Rd Fort Kent (04743) *(G-4790)*

Morin Corporation **(DH)**.............................. **860 584-0900**
   685 Middle St Bristol (06010) *(G-472)*

Morin East, Bristol *Also Called: Morin Corporation (G-472)*

Morning Sentinel, Waterville *Also Called: Central Maine Morning Sentinel (G-5593)*

Morningstar Marble & Gran Inc................................ 207 725-7309
   47 Park Dr Topsham (04086) *(G-5551)*

Morningstar Stone & Tile, Topsham *Also Called: Morningstar Marble & Gran Inc (G-5551)*

Mornsun America LLC.. 978 293-3923
   13 Country Club Ln Milford (01757) *(G-10406)*

Moroney Bodyworks Inc... 508 792-2878
   20 Eskow Rd Worcester (01604) *(G-13762)*

Moroso, Guilford *Also Called: Moroso Performance Pdts Inc (G-1401)*

Moroso Performance Pdts Inc **(PA)**............... **203 453-6571**
   80 Carter Dr Guilford (06437) *(G-1401)*

Morphi, Boston *Also Called: Morphisec Inc (G-6896)*

Morphic Holding Inc **(PA)**............................. **781 996-0955**
   35 Gatehouse Dr A2 Waltham (02451) *(G-12725)*

MORPHIC THERAPEUTIC, Waltham *Also Called: Morphic Holding Inc (G-12725)*

Morphisec Inc.. 617 826-1212
   11 Beacon St Ste 735 Boston (02108) *(G-6896)*

Morrell Metalsmiths Ltd... 413 624-1200
   207 Greenfield Rd Colrain (01340) *(G-8096)*

Morrill Woodworking LLC... 603 540-3151
   38 Westford Dr Auburn (03032) *(G-13911)*

Morris & Broms LLC.. 401 781-3134
   14 Wychwood Pl Johnston (02919) *(G-16098)*

Morris Transparent Box Co...................................... 401 438-6116
   945 Warren Ave East Providence (02914) *(G-16032)*

Morris Yachts LLC.. 207 667-2499
   1 Little Harbor Lndg Ste 1 Portsmouth (02871) *(G-16448)*

Morrison Berkshire Inc.. 413 663-6501
   865 Church St North Adams (01247) *(G-10812)*

Morrison's Forest Products, Harmony *Also Called: Tracy J Morrison (G-4874)*

Morristown Star Struck LLC...................................... 203 778-4925
   8 Francis J Clarke Cir Bethel (06801) *(G-130)*

Morse Hardware & Lumber LLC............................... 207 646-5700
   1259 Post Rd Wells (04090) *(G-5603)*

Morse Ready Mix LLC.. 508 809-4644
   24 Cross St Plainville (02762) *(G-11440)*

Morse Sand & Gravel Corp....................................... 508 809-4644
   125 Tiffany St Attleboro (02703) *(G-6038)*

Morse Watchmans Inc.. 203 264-4949
   2 Morse Rd Oxford (06478) *(G-2705)*

Mortise and Tenon LLC.. 802 643-2227
   22 Varney Hill Rd Starksboro (05487) *(G-17627)*

Morton Buildings Inc.. 413 562-7028
   563 Southampton Rd Westfield (01085) *(G-13191)*

Morvillo Precision Products, Providence *Also Called: Alloy Holdings LLC (G-16467)*

Mosaic Prtg Signage Mktg Svcs.............................. 203 483-4598
   250 W Main St Branford (06405) *(G-272)*

Moseley Corporation.. 508 520-4004
   31 Hayward St Ste A2 Franklin (02038) *(G-8853)*

Mosher Company Inc... 413 598-8341
   15 Exchange St Chicopee (01013) *(G-8050)*

Mother Myricks, Manchester Center *Also Called: Fudge Factory Inc (G-17328)*

Motif Magazine... 401 312-3305
   729 Main St Pawtucket (02860) *(G-16389)*

Motion Industries Inc... 860 687-5000
   1 Vision Way Bloomfield (06002) *(G-195)*

Motion Industries Inc... 978 774-7100
   6 Cherry Hill Dr Danvers (01923) *(G-8210)*

Motion Technology Inc.. 508 460-9800
   1 Bonazzoli Ave Hudson (01749) *(G-9392)*

Motive Power.. 857 350-3765
   34 Farnsworth St Boston (02210) *(G-6897)*

Moto Tassinari LLC.. 603 298-6646
   2 Technology Dr West Lebanon (03784) *(G-15684)*

Motor Power Inc... 207 782-0616
   1505 Lisbon St Lewiston (04240) *(G-4977)*

Motor Service Inc... 508 832-6291
   38 Wachusett Ave Shrewsbury (01545) *(G-11839)*

Motorola, Lowell *Also Called: Motorola Mobility LLC (G-9910)*

Motorola Mobility LLC.. 978 614-2900
   900 Chelmsford St Ofc 1 Lowell (01851) *(G-9910)*

Motorway Engineering Inc.. 603 668-6315
   85 Hancock St Manchester (03101) *(G-14893)*

Mott Corporation **(PA)**................................ **860 864-5017**
   75 Spring Ln Farmington (06032) *(G-1230)*

Mouldcam Inc.. 401 396-5522
   115 Broadcommon Rd Bristol (02809) *(G-15775)*

Mount Desert Island Ice Cream............................... 207 460-5515
   325 Main St Bar Harbor (04609) *(G-4523)*

Mount Desert Islander... 207 288-0556
   1 Printing House Sq Ellsworth (04605) *(G-4759)*

Mount Sunapee Ski Resort, Newbury *Also Called: Sunapee Difference LLC (G-15204)*

Mount Tom Box Co Inc... 413 781-5300
   21 Campbell St Pawtucket (02861) *(G-16390)*

Mount Tom Box Company Inc................................... 413 781-5300
   190 Interstate Dr West Springfield (01089) *(G-13034)*

Mount Washington Vly Mtn Ear.................................. 603 447-6336
   79 Main St Lancaster (03584) *(G-14677)*

Mountain Base Mfg LLC... 413 527-9590
   180 Pleasant St Ste 1 Easthampton (01027) *(G-8451)*

Mountain Corporation **(HQ)**......................... **603 355-2272**
   59 Optical Ave Keene (03431) *(G-14610)*

Mountain Creek Energy Inc...................................... 512 990-7886
   6 Castle Hl Manchester (06040) *(G-1619)*

Mountain Dairy, Storrs Mansfield *Also Called: Willard J Stearns & Sons Inc (G-3513)*

Mountain Ear, Lancaster *Also Called: Mount Washington Vly Mtn Ear (G-14677)*

Mountain Fluid Power, Auburn *Also Called: Mountain Machine Works* *(G-4446)*

Mountain Machine Works...................................... 207 783-6680
   2589 Hotel Rd Auburn (04210) *(G-4446)*

Mountain Mozzarella LLC... 802 440-9950
   441 Water St North Bennington (05257) *(G-17409)*

Mountain Ridge Pet Supply, Nashua *Also Called: Kevin S Boghigian (G-15122)*

Mountain Times, The, Killington *Also Called: Outer Limits Publishing LLC (G-17313)*

Mountain Tire Corp.. 603 752-8473
   15 Industrial Park Dr Berlin (03570) *(G-13983)*

Mountainbase Mold & Mfg, Easthampton *Also Called: Michael Brisebois (G-8450)*

Mountainoga LLC.. 857 972-6446
   134 Gould Rd West Lebanon (03784) *(G-15685)*

Mountaintop Woodworking LLC.................................. 603 616-1160
   22 Dusty Dr Whitefield (03598) *(G-15699)*

Mousam Valley Millwork... 207 324-2951
   282 River St Springvale (04083) *(G-5521)*

Moveras LLC.. 877 866-8372
   22 Northwestern Dr Salem (03079) *(G-15546)*

Mowi Ducktrap LLC.. 207 338-6280
   61 Little River Dr Belfast (04915) *(G-4536)*

Mowi Ducktrap LLC.. 207 338-6280
   57 Little River Dr Belfast (04915) *(G-4537)*

Mowmedia LLC.. 203 240-6416
   85 Camp Ave Apt 10l Stamford (06907) *(G-3413)*

Mozzicato Fmly Investments LLC................................ 860 296-0426
   631 Ridge Rd Wethersfield (06109) *(G-4212)*

Mozzicato Pastry & Bake Sp Inc................................ 860 296-0426
   329 Franklin Ave Hartford (06114) *(G-1495)*

Mozzict-De Psqale Bky Pstry Sp, Hartford *Also Called: Mozzicato Pastry & Bake Sp Inc (G-1495)*

MP Manufacturing Inc... 203 915-2235
   136 Mishnock Rd West Greenwich (02817) *(G-16889)*

Mp Systems Inc... 860 687-3460
   34 Bradley Park Rd East Granby (06026) *(G-944)*

Mpac, Greene *Also Called: Maine Poly Aquisition Corp (G-4847)*

Mpb, Lebanon *Also Called: Mpb Corporation (G-14695)*

Mpb Corporation **(HQ)**...................................... **603 352-0310**
   7 Optical Ave Keene (03431) *(G-14611)*

Mpb Corporation... 603 448-3000
   334 Mechanic St Lebanon (03766) *(G-14694)*

Mpb Corporation... 603 448-3000
   336 Mechanic St Lebanon (03766) *(G-14695)*

MPingo Multi Casting... 413 241-2500
   146 Chestnut St Springfield (01103) *(G-12115)*

Mprp Inc... 802 527-1557
   88 Walnut St Saint Albans (05478) *(G-17523)*

MPS, Holliston *Also Called: Miano Printing Services Inc (G-9222)*

MPS Plastics Incorporated..................................... 860 295-1161
   351 N Main St Marlborough (06447) *(G-1645)*

MPS Products Corp... 978 817-2144
   453 Newburyport Tpke Rowley (01969) *(G-11681)*

Mpx.. 207 774-6116
   2301 Congress St Portland (04102) *(G-5246)*

Mpx, Portland *Also Called: Mpx (G-5246)*

Mr Boston Brands LLC **(HQ)**................................ **207 783-1433**
   21 Saratoga St Lewiston (04240) *(G-4978)*

Mr Idea Inc... 508 222-0155
   100 Frank Mossberg Dr Attleboro (02703) *(G-6039)*

Mra Laboratories, Williamstown *Also Called: Ferro Corporation (G-13366)*

Mra Laboratories Inc... 413 743-3927
   15 Printworks Dr Adams (01220) *(G-5774)*

MRC, Middletown *Also Called: McLaughlin Research Corp (G-16179)*

Mrg, Norwood *Also Called: Manufctring Resource Group Inc (G-11192)*

MRM Seller Entity LLC.. 978 568-1330
   577 Main St Ste 270 Hudson (01749) *(G-9393)*

Mrn Diagnostics, Franklin *Also Called: Medical Research Networx (G-8850)*

Mrnd LLC... 860 749-0256
   75 Hazard Ave Ste 1 Enfield (06082) *(G-1138)*

Mrp Trading Innovations LLC.................................... 978 762-3900
   85 Sam Fonzo Dr Beverly (01915) *(G-6367)*

Mrpc Northeast LLC.. 603 880-3616
   12 Executive Dr Hudson (03051) *(G-14530)*

Mrs Nelsons Candy House, Chelmsford *Also Called: Arthur Mapes Inc (G-7910)*

Mrs. Kavanaghs English Muffins, Rumford *Also Called: Homestead Baking Co (G-16668)*

Mrse Inc... 508 867-5083
   192 W Main St West Brookfield (01585) *(G-12996)*

Mrsi Systems LLC.. 978 667-9449
   554 Clark Rd Tewksbury (01876) *(G-12411)*

Mrv Commmunications, Chelmsford *Also Called: Mrv Communications Americas Inc (G-7940)*

Mrv Communications, Chelmsford *Also Called: Adtran Networks North Amer Inc (G-7902)*

Mrv Communications Americas Inc.............................. 978 674-6800
   300 Apollo Dr Chelmsford (01824) *(G-7940)*

Ms Ambrogio North America LLC................................ 832 834-3641
   135 Rodman Rd Auburn (04210) *(G-4447)*

Ms Orbis Corporation **(PA)**................................ **774 330-5323**
   8 Uncas Ave Oak Bluffs (02557) *(G-11222)*

MSC Filtration Tech Inc... 860 745-7475
   198 Freshwater Blvd Enfield (06082) *(G-1139)*

MSI, Beverly *Also Called: Microline Surgical Inc (G-6364)*

MSI Transducers Corp.. 978 486-0404
   543 Great Rd Littleton (01460) *(G-9826)*

Msj Investments Inc.. 860 684-9956
   72 W Stafford Rd Ste 3 Stafford Springs (06076) *(G-3257)*

Msm Protein Technologies, East Kingston *Also Called: Msm Protein Technologies Inc (G-14272)*

Msm Protein Technologies Inc.................................. 617 504-9548
   97 Giles Rd East Kingston (03827) *(G-14272)*

Msm Protein Technologies Inc.................................. 781 373-2405
   1393 Main St Waltham (02451) *(G-12726)*

Msn Corporation... 603 623-3528
   431 Somerville St Manchester (03103) *(G-14894)*

MSP Digital Marketing Mass Inc **(HQ)**...................... **978 567-6000**
   399 River Rd Hudson (01749) *(G-9394)*

Msr Utility... 978 649-0002
   209 Pleasant St Dunstable (01827) *(G-8328)*

MST, Cumberland *Also Called: Lkq Precious Metals Inc (G-15950)*

Mt Johnson Inc... 802 234-6827
   1567 Mt Hunger Rd Barnard (05031) *(G-16994)*

Mtd Micro Molding Inc.. 508 248-0111
   15 Trolley Crossing Rd Charlton (01507) *(G-7893)*

MTI, Georgetown *Also Called: Metal Tronics Inc (G-8909)*

MTI Film LLC **(HQ)**... **401 831-1315**
   209 Angell St Providence (02906) *(G-16570)*

MTI Polyexe Corporation....................................... 603 778-1449
   50 Pine Rd Brentwood (03833) *(G-14023)*

MTI Systems Inc... 413 733-1972
   1111 Elm St Ste 6 West Springfield (01089) *(G-13035)*

Mti-Milliren, Newburyport *Also Called: Mti-Milliren Technologies Inc (G-10703)*

Mti-Milliren Technologies Inc................................... 978 465-6064
   2 New Pasture Rd Ste 10 Newburyport (01950) *(G-10703)*

Mtl Print Solution LLC.. 603 479-2998
   50 Bloody Brook Rd Hampstead (03841) *(G-14387)*

MTM Corporation.. 860 742-9600
   643 Route 6 Andover (06232) *(G-2)*

Mtm Oldco Inc **(PA)**.. **207 791-6650**
   1 City Ctr Fl 5 Portland (04101) *(G-5247)*

Mtoz Biolabs Inc... 617 401-8103
   210 Broadway 201 Cambridge (02139) *(G-7657)*

Mtp Software LLC.. 508 353-6221
   145 Rosemary St Needham (02494) *(G-10517)*

Mtr Guns & Ammo, North Smithfield *Also Called: Mtr Machining Inc (G-16327)*

Mtr Machining Inc.. 401 766-0200
   229 Quaker Hwy North Smithfield (02896) *(G-16327)*

MTS Associates Londonderry LLC.............................. 603 425-2562
   55 Hall Rd Londonderry (03053) *(G-14775)*

Mtu Aero Engine Design Inc., Newington *Also Called: Hanwha Aerospace USA LLC (G-2299)*

Mtu Aero Engines N Amer Inc.................................. 860 258-9700
   795 Brook St # 5 Rocky Hill (06067) *(G-2931)*

Mueller Corporation... 508 456-4500
   530 Spring St East Bridgewater (02333) *(G-8344)*

Muffins On Main LLC... 978 788-4365
   40 Main St Westford (01886) *(G-13252)*

Muir Envelope Div, Newington *Also Called: Muir Envelope Plus Inc (G-2307)*

**A
L
P
H
A
B
E
T
I
C**

Muir Envelope Plus Inc.. 860 953-6847
    124 Francis Ave Newington (06111) *(G-2307)*

Mulholland Wldg & Fabrication.................................... 802 875-5500
    81 Gold River Ext Chester (05143) *(G-17181)*

Mulholland Wldg & Fabrication, Chester *Also Called: Mulholland Wldg & Fabrication (G-17181)*

Multi Technologies Industrial LLC............................... 603 778-1449
    50 Pine Rd Brentwood (03833) *(G-14024)*

Multi-Cable Corp... 860 589-9035
    37 Horizon Dr Bristol (06010) *(G-473)*

Multi-Concept Inc... 508 366-7676
    15 Victoria Ln Mansfield (02048) *(G-10067)*

Multi-Flow Industries LLC... 617 442-7777
    51 Morgan Dr Ste 1 Norwood (02062) *(G-11197)*

Multi-Med Inc... 603 357-8733
    26 Victoria Ct Keene (03431) *(G-14612)*

Multi-Metal Manufacturing Inc.................................... 203 723-8887
    550 Spring St Naugatuck (06770) *(G-1974)*

Multi-Weld Services, Contoocook *Also Called: Multi-Weld Services Inc (G-14172)*

Multi-Weld Services Inc.. 603 746-4604
    153 Riverside Dr Contoocook (03229) *(G-14172)*

Multiprints Inc.. 203 235-4409
    812 Old Colony Rd Meriden (06451) *(G-1678)*

Mums Cheesecake.. 207 351-8543
    463 Us Route 1 York (03909) *(G-5714)*

Mumster Engineering, Manchester *Also Called: Whale Water Systems Inc (G-17325)*

Municipal Market Analytics Inc **(PA)**....................... **617 968-5906**
    75 Main St Concord (01742) *(G-8126)*

Munis, Yarmouth *Also Called: Tyler Technologies Inc (G-5708)*

Muniz Custom Woodwork Inc...................................... 617 970-3430
    165 Chelsea St Everett (02149) *(G-8496)*

Munk Pack Inc.. 203 769-5005
    76 Progress Dr Ste 263 Stamford (06902) *(G-3414)*

Munson's Chocolates, Bolton *Also Called: Munsons Candy Kitchen Inc (G-221)*

Munsons Candy Kitchen Inc **(PA)**........................... **860 649-4332**
    174 Hopriver Rd Bolton (06043) *(G-221)*

Munters Cargocaire, Amesbury *Also Called: Munters USA Inc (G-5847)*

Munters Corporation... 978 388-2666
    79 Monroe St Amesbury (01913) *(G-5844)*

Munters Corporation **(DH)**..................................... **978 241-1100**
    79 Monroe St Amesbury (01913) *(G-5845)*

Munters Corporation... 978 241-1100
    79 Monroe St Amesbury (01913) *(G-5846)*

Munters USA Inc.. 978 241-1100
    79 Monroe St Amesbury (01913) *(G-5847)*

Munters Zeol, Amesbury *Also Called: Munters Corporation (G-5844)*

Mural Oncology Inc... 617 694-2481
    852 Winter St Waltham (02451) *(G-12727)*

Murata Power Solutions Inc **(DH)**........................... **508 339-3000**
    129 Flanders Rd Westborough (01581) *(G-13122)*

Murder Hill LLC **(PA)**.. **774 757-4411**
    670 Linwood Ave Whitinsville (01588) *(G-13342)*

Murdock Webbing Company Inc **(PA)**..................... **401 724-3000**
    27 Foundry St Central Falls (02863) *(G-15793)*

Murray's Auto Recycling Center, Londonderry *Also Called: MTS Associates Londonderry LLC (G-14775)*

Murroney's Printing, Amherst *Also Called: Jalbert Printing LLC (G-13873)*

Musano Inc... 203 879-4651
    373 Woodtick Rd Wolcott (06716) *(G-4369)*

Musette Bridal Inc.. 617 424-1070
    123 Newbury St Boston (02116) *(G-6898)*

Museum Collection, Providence *Also Called: Fashion Accents LLC (G-16517)*

Mushield Company Inc.. 603 666-4433
    9 Ricker Ave Londonderry (03053) *(G-14776)*

Music Stand The, Smithfield *Also Called: Island Woods Performance Inc (G-16717)*

Mussel Bound LLC... 774 212-5488
    80 Joe Long Rd Brewster (02631) *(G-7215)*

Mustang Motorcycle Pdts LLC.................................... 413 283-6236
    4 Springfield St Ste 1 Three Rivers (01080) *(G-12431)*

Mutti USA Inc... 844 664-2630
    83 Wooster Hts Ste 120 Danbury (06810) *(G-789)*

Mutual Beef Co Inc... 617 442-3238
    126 Newmarket Sq Boston (02118) *(G-6899)*

Mutual Oil Leasing Co Inc... 508 583-5777
    863 Crescent St Brockton (02302) *(G-7299)*

Mv Products Division, North Billerica *Also Called: Mass Vac Inc (G-10932)*

Mv Times Corporation... 508 693-6100
    30 Beach Rd Vineyard Haven (02568) *(G-12493)*

Mv3 LLC.. 617 658-4420
    11 Mizzen Ln Buzzards Bay (02532) *(G-7455)*

Mvp Visuals, Ellington *Also Called: Soapstone Media Inc (G-1116)*

Mw Life Sciences - Mansfield, Mansfield *Also Called: M & W Industries Inc (G-10065)*

Mw Trucking and Logging Inc...................................... 207 890-3592
    74 Frost Hill Rd Norway (04268) *(G-5117)*

Mwave Industries LLC.. 207 892-0011
    33r Main St Ste 1 Windham (04062) *(G-5666)*

My, Portsmouth *Also Called: Morris Yachts LLC (G-16448)*

My Citizens News... 203 729-2228
    389 Meadow St Waterbury (06702) *(G-3947)*

My Ease Inc **(PA)**.. **207 667-6235**
    53 Granville Rd Bass Harbor (04653) *(G-4524)*

My Ease Inc... 207 667-8237
    27 Ramp Rd Trenton (04605) *(G-5557)*

My Kidz App, Brookline *Also Called: Micheal John (G-7320)*

My Pet Chicken, Cheshire *Also Called: Henlay Co (G-598)*

My Slide Lines LLC... 203 324-1642
    173 Main St Norwalk (06851) *(G-2540)*

Mygrant Glass Company Inc....................................... 781 767-3289
    196 High St Randolph (02368) *(G-11569)*

Myjove Corporation... 617 945-9051
    625 Massachusetts Ave Fl 2 Cambridge (02139) *(G-7658)*

Mykrolis, Billerica *Also Called: Entegris Inc (G-6442)*

Mylan Technologies Inc.. 802 527-7792
    700 Ind Park Rd Saint Albans (05478) *(G-17524)*

Mylan Technologies Inc **(HQ)**................................. **802 527-7792**
    110 Lake St Saint Albans (05478) *(G-17525)*

Mylec Inc **(PA)**.. **978 297-0089**
    37 Commercial Dr Winchendon (01475) *(G-13480)*

Myllykoski North America
    101 Merritt Ste 7 Norwalk (06851) *(G-2541)*

Myomo, Boston *Also Called: Myomo Inc (G-6900)*

Myomo Inc **(PA)**.. **617 996-9058**
    137 Portland St Fl 4 Boston (02114) *(G-6900)*

Myperfectgig Inc.. 978 461-6700
    1 Clock Tower Pl Ste 200 Maynard (01754) *(G-10263)*

Myri, Quincy *Also Called: Bioenergy International LLC (G-11506)*

Myriad Engineering Co Inc... 508 731-6416
    96 Southbridge Rd North Oxford (01537) *(G-11033)*

Myriad Fiber Imaging Tech Inc.................................... 508 949-3000
    56 Southbridge Rd Dudley (01571) *(G-8320)*

Myriant Lake Providence Inc....................................... 617 657-5200
    45 Cummings Park Woburn (01801) *(G-13616)*

Myson, Williston *Also Called: Purmo Group USA Inc (G-17746)*

Mystic Knotwork LLC.. 860 889-3793
    25 Cottrell St Mystic (06355) *(G-1939)*

Mystic Millwork, Norwood *Also Called: Mystic Scenic Studios Inc (G-11198)*

Mystic Mountain Maples LLC...................................... 802 524-6163
    1888 Fire Hill Rd Florence (05744) *(G-17270)*

Mystic Parker Printing Inc... 781 321-4948
    66 Willow St Malden (02148) *(G-10020)*

Mystic Scenic Studios Inc... 781 440-0914
    293 Lenox St Norwood (02062) *(G-11198)*

MYSTIC SEAPORT, Mystic *Also Called: Mystic Seaport Museum Inc (G-1940)*

Mystic Seaport Museum Inc.. 860 572-0711
    75 Greenmanville Ave Mystic (06355) *(G-1940)*

Mystic Valley Foundry Inc... 617 547-1819
    35 Brooks Rd Lincoln (01773) *(G-9798)*

Mystic Valley Wheel Works Inc **(PA)**...................... **617 489-3577**
    480 Trapelo Rd Belmont (02478) *(G-6308)*

Mystockoptions.com, Brookline *Also Called: Mystockplancom Inc (G-7321)*

Mystockplancom Inc.. 617 734-1979
    124 Harvard St Ste 9 Brookline (02446) *(G-7321)*

Mythic Paint, Bethel *Also Called: Southern Diversified Pdts LLC (G-134)*

N & D Sports, Hamden *Also Called: Nicks Enterprises Inc (G-1447)*

N B C Solid Surfaces Inc..802 885-8677
200 Clinton St Springfield (05156) *(G-17621)*

N C Hunt Inc..207 563-8503
237 Route One Damariscotta (04543) *(G-4716)*

N C Hunt Inc **(PA)**...**207 549-0922**
200 S Clary Rd Jefferson (04348) *(G-4918)*

N C T Inc...860 666-8424
124 Upton Rd Colchester (06415) *(G-662)*

N E E, Fall River *Also Called: New England Elctrpolishing Inc (G-8587)*

N E K, Fitchburg *Also Called: New England Keyboard Inc (G-8668)*

N E O, Pawtucket *Also Called: New England Overseas Corp (G-16393)*

N E P, Norton *Also Called: New England Phtoconductor Corp (G-11130)*

N E Publishing Group..508 675-8883
1610 Gar Hwy Swansea (02777) *(G-12307)*

N E Tech-Air Inc..207 347-7577
16 Manson Libby Rd Scarborough (04074) *(G-5439)*

N Ferrara Inc...508 679-2440
10 Riverside Ave Somerset (02725) *(G-11853)*

N H Central Concrete Corp..603 428-7900
4 Bradford Rd Henniker (03242) *(G-14439)*

N Kamenske & Co Inc...603 888-1007
19 Fairhaven Rd Nashua (03060) *(G-15137)*

N P Medical Inc...978 365-9721
101 Union St Clinton (01510) *(G-8084)*

N R G Barriers, Saco *Also Called: Johns Manville Corporation (G-5370)*

N R M, Canton *Also Called: National Resource MGT Inc (G-7809)*

N T P Republic, Holyoke *Also Called: Ntp/Republic Clear Thru Corp (G-9272)*

N W P Inc..802 442-4749
171 Church St Pownal (05261) *(G-17455)*

N Y C O A, Manchester *Also Called: Nylon Corporation America Inc (G-14906)*

N-Able Inc **(PA)**...**781 328-6490**
301 Edgewater Pl Ste 306 Wakefield (01880) *(G-12520)*

N-Able Technologies Inc...855 679-0817
30 Corporate Dr Ste 400 Burlington (01803) *(G-7395)*

N.E. Tech Air, Scarborough *Also Called: N E Tech-Air Inc (G-5439)*

N12 Technologies Inc..857 259-6622
124 Washington St Ste 101 Foxboro (02035) *(G-8709)*

N2 Biomedical LLC..781 275-6001
One Patriots Pk Bedford (01730) *(G-6244)*

N3k, Boston *Also Called: N3k Informatik Inc (G-6901)*

N3k Informatik Inc...617 289-9282
470 Atlantic Ave Fl 4 Boston (02210) *(G-6901)*

NA Manosh Inc..802 888-5722
120 Northgate Plz Ste B Morrisville (05661) *(G-17387)*

Nab Tool, Bristol *Also Called: Rgd Technologies Corp (G-492)*

Nabco Entrances Inc...262 679-0045
1556 Barnum Ave Bridgeport (06610) *(G-351)*

Nabs Inc..781 899-7719
180 Elm St Ste 5 Waltham (02453) *(G-12728)*

Nabs Bindery, Waltham *Also Called: Nabs Inc (G-12728)*

Nabson Inc...617 323-1101
45 Independence Dr Taunton (02780) *(G-12350)*

Nac Industries Inc...845 214-0659
112 Hurley Rd Oxford (06478) *(G-2706)*

Nadco International Inc..781 767-1797
91 Allens Point Rd Marion (02738) *(G-10098)*

Nadeau Logging Inc..207 834-6338
48 Summer Ave Fort Kent (04743) *(G-4791)*

Nagel Machine Co Inc...401 827-8962
27 Wightman St West Warwick (02893) *(G-16912)*

Naheks Inc...207 848-7770
15 Elaine Dr Hermon (04401) *(G-4886)*

Nai Cranes LLC...781 897-4100
110 Winn St Ste 205 Woburn (01801) *(G-13617)*

Naiad Dynamics, Shelton *Also Called: Naiad Maritime Group Inc (G-3034)*

Naiad Dynamics Us Inc **(HQ)**....................................**203 929-6355**
50 Parrott Dr Shelton (06484) *(G-3033)*

Naiad Inflatables Newport Inc
4 Thurston Ave Newport (02840) *(G-16218)*

Naiad Marine Systems, Shelton *Also Called: Naiad Dynamics Us Inc (G-3033)*

Naiad Maritime Group Inc **(PA)**..................................**203 944-1932**
50 Parrott Dr Shelton (06484) *(G-3034)*

Nalas Engineering Services..860 861-3691
1 Winnenden Rd Norwich (06360) *(G-2609)*

Naley Inc...508 579-8378
774 W Boylston St Worcester (01606) *(G-13763)*

Namco, Somerset *Also Called: North Atlantic Corp (G-11854)*

Nameplates For Industry, New Bedford *Also Called: Nfi LLC (G-10632)*

Namco, Chelsea *Also Called: Nancy Sales Co Inc (G-7987)*

Nancy B, East Providence *Also Called: Carla Corp (G-16008)*

Nancy Larson Publishers Inc..860 434-0800
27 Talcott Farm Rd Old Lyme (06371) *(G-2643)*

Nancy Sales Co Inc...617 884-1700
22 Willow St Chelsea (02150) *(G-7987)*

Nanmac, Milford *Also Called: Patriot Worldwide Inc (G-10413)*

Nanmac Corp...508 872-4811
425 Fortune Blvd Ste 206 Milford (01757) *(G-10407)*

Nanni Manufacturing Co Inc
200 Price Rd Winsted (06098) *(G-4350)*

Nano Dimension 3d, Waltham *Also Called: Nano Dimension USA Inc (G-12729)*

Nano Dimension USA Inc...650 209-2866
300 5th Ave Ste 10 Waltham (02451) *(G-12729)*

Nanoal LLC **(HQ)**...**774 777-3369**
260 Eliot St # 4a Ashland (01721) *(G-5963)*

Nanobiosym Inc..781 391-7979
245 1st St Ste 18 Cambridge (02142) *(G-7659)*

Nanodiagnostics, Southborough *Also Called: Nanodx Inc (G-11998)*

Nanodx Inc...508 599-2400
144 Turnpike Rd Ste 110 Southborough (01772) *(G-11998)*

Nanoentek Inc...781 472-2559
220 Bear Hill Rd Waltham (02451) *(G-12730)*

Nanoramic Laboratories...857 403-6031
7 Audubon Rd Wakefield (01880) *(G-12521)*

Nanoramic Laboratories, Wakefield *Also Called: Fastcap Systems Corporation (G-12509)*

Nanoscale Components Inc...207 671-7028
Portland (04112) *(G-5248)*

Nanosemi Inc...781 472-2832
200 5th Ave Ste 2020 Waltham (02451) *(G-12731)*

Nanostone Water Inc...781 209-6900
1432 Main St Ste 1 Waltham (02451) *(G-12732)*

Nanotechsys, Swanzey *Also Called: Moore Nntechnology Systems LLC (G-15645)*

Nantero Inc..781 932-5338
25b Olympia Ave Woburn (01801) *(G-13618)*

Nantucket Looms, Nantucket *Also Called: E W Winship Ltd Inc (G-10462)*

Nantucket Pavers Inc..508 336-5800
71 Fall River Ave Rehoboth (02769) *(G-11611)*

NAPA, Rowley *Also Called: Atlantic Auto & Trck Parts LLC (G-11667)*

NAPA Auto Parts, Windsor Locks *Also Called: Genuine Parts Company (G-4325)*

NAPA Motor Parts, Holyoke *Also Called: Tebaldi Enterprises Inc (G-9283)*

Napco Plastics LLC..860 261-4819
75 Napco Dr Terryville (06786) *(G-3606)*

Naps, Danvers *Also Called: North Atlantic PCF Seafood LLC (G-8213)*

Nar Industries LLC...401 941-3000
1 Weingeroff Blvd Cranston (02910) *(G-15897)*

Nara Logics Inc...617 945-2049
186 South St Ste 402 Boston (02111) *(G-6902)*

Narragansett Bus Forms Inc...401 331-2000
21 Massasoit Ave East Providence (02914) *(G-16033)*

Narragansett Coated Paper, Pawtucket *Also Called: Ecological Fibers Inc (G-16366)*

Narragansett Creamery, Providence *Also Called: Providence Specialty Pdts Inc (G-16593)*

Narragansett Imaging Usa LLC......................................401 762-3800
51 Industrial Dr North Smithfield (02896) *(G-16328)*

Narragansett Improvement Co **(PA)**..........................**401 331-0051**
223 Allens Ave Providence (02903) *(G-16571)*

Narragansett Screw Co..860 379-4059
119 Rowley St Winsted (06098) *(G-4351)*

Narragasett Jewelry Inc.................................... 401 944-2200
    100 Dupont Dr Ste 1 Providence (02907) *(G-16572)*

Narrative 1 Software LLC................................ 603 968-2233
    1 Bridge St Ste 301 Plymouth (03264) *(G-15355)*

Nash Manufacturing, Springfield *Also Called: Nash Mfg & Grinding Svcs Inc (G-12116)*

Nash Mfg & Grinding Svcs Inc........................ 413 301-5416
    572 Saint James Ave Springfield (01109) *(G-12116)*

Nashoba Security Inc.................................... 978 486-8615
    474 Great Rd Littleton (01460) *(G-9827)*

Nashoba Valley Spirits Limited....................... 978 779-5521
    100 Wattaquadock Hill Rd Bolton (01740) *(G-6498)*

Nashoba Valley Winery, Bolton *Also Called: Nashoba Valley Spirits Limited (G-6498)*

Nashua Corporation....................................... 603 880-1100
    59 Daniel Webster Hwy Ste A Merrimack (03054) *(G-14994)*

Nashua Fabrication Co Inc............................. 603 889-2181
    7 Security Dr Hudson (03051) *(G-14531)*

Nashua Foundries Inc................................... 603 882-4811
    5 Foundry St Nashua (03060) *(G-15138)*

Nashua Specialty Coated Pdts, Merrimack *Also Called: Nashua Corporation (G-14994)*

Nason's Stone House Farm, West Boxford *Also Called: Stone House Farm Inc (G-12954)*

Nasons Ug Inc (PA)....................................... **401 847-2497**
    305 Oliphant Ln Unit B Middletown (02842) *(G-16180)*

Nasoya Foods Usa LLC................................. 978 772-6880
    1 New England Way Ayer (01432) *(G-6187)*

Natale Co Safetycare LL................................. 781 933-7205
    11 Eames St Wilmington (01887) *(G-13436)*

Natalia, Waltham *Also Called: Natalia Marketing Corp (G-12733)*

Natalia Marketing Corp................................... 781 693-4900
    170 High St Waltham (02453) *(G-12733)*

Natco, West Warwick *Also Called: Natco Products Corporation (G-16916)*

Natco Home Fashions Inc.............................. 401 828-0300
    155 Brookside Ave West Warwick (02893) *(G-16913)*

Natco Home Fashions Inc.............................. 401 828-0300
    155 Brookside Ave West Warwick (02893) *(G-16914)*

Natco Home Fashions Inc (PA)....................... **401 828-0300**
    155 Brookside Ave West Warwick (02893) *(G-16915)*

Natco Products Corporation (PA)..................... **401 828-0300**
    155 Brookside Ave West Warwick (02893) *(G-16916)*

Natgun Corporation....................................... 781 224-5180
    11 Teal Rd Wakefield (01880) *(G-12522)*

Natick Auto Sales, Middletown *Also Called: Mhq Inc (G-1763)*

National Aperture Inc.................................... 603 893-7393
    5 Industrial Way Ste 3a Salem (03079) *(G-15547)*

National Braille Press Inc.............................. 617 425-2400
    88 Saint Stephen St Boston (02115) *(G-6903)*

National Chain Company (PA).......................... **401 732-3634**
    55 Access Rd Warwick (02886) *(G-16840)*

National Chimney, South Burlington *Also Called: National Chmney Spply-Vrmont I (G-17586)*

National Chmney Spply-Vrmont I..................... 802 861-2217
    3 Green Tree Dr South Burlington (05403) *(G-17586)*

National Chromium Co Inc Conn, Putnam *Also Called: National Chromium Company Inc (G-2865)*

National Chromium Company Inc...................... 860 928-7965
    10 Senexet Rd Putnam (06260) *(G-2865)*

National Coating Corporation.......................... 781 878-2781
    105 Industrial Way Rockland (02370) *(G-11653)*

National Con Tnks / Frguard JV........................ 978 505-5533
    82 Tarbell Spring Rd Concord (01742) *(G-8127)*

National Default Servicing LLC......................... 858 300-0700
    500 S Broad St Ste 1 Meriden (06450) *(G-1679)*

National Dentex LLC..................................... 561 537-8301
    1050 Perimeter Rd Ste 101 Manchester (03103) *(G-14895)*

National Die Company.................................... 203 879-1408
    64 Wolcott Rd Wolcott (06716) *(G-4370)*

National Embroidery Corp............................... 603 647-1995
    140 Bouchard St Ste 3 Manchester (03103) *(G-14896)*

National Energy & Light LLC........................... 603 821-9954
    14 Celina Ave Unit 9 Nashua (03063) *(G-15139)*

National Filter Media Corp............................... 207 327-2626
    12 Winada Dr Winthrop (04364) *(G-5695)*

National Fish and Seafood Inc......................... 978 282-7880
    11-15 Parker St Gloucester (01930) *(G-8944)*

National Grape Coop Assn Inc......................... 978 371-1000
    555 Virginia Rd Concord (01742) *(G-8128)*

National Graphics Inc.................................... 203 481-2351
    248 Branford Rd North Branford (06471) *(G-2370)*

National Grid USA Svc Co Inc (DH).................. **800 260-0054**
    170 Data Dr Waltham (02451) *(G-12734)*

National Grid USA Svc Co Inc.......................... 401 784-7224
    280 Melrose St Providence (02907) *(G-16573)*

National Hanger Company Inc.......................... 800 426-4377
    276 Water St North Bennington (05257) *(G-17410)*

National Lumber Company............................... 617 244-8020
    15 Needham St Newton (02461) *(G-10770)*

National Lumber Company LLC (HQ)................. **508 339-8020**
    71 Maple St Mansfield (02048) *(G-10068)*

National Marker Company................................ 401 762-9700
    100 Providence Pike North Smithfield (02896) *(G-16329)*

National Nonwovens Inc................................. 413 527-3445
    180 Pleasant St Easthampton (01027) *(G-8452)*

National Nonwovens Inc (PA).......................... **413 527-3445**
    110 Pleasant St Easthampton (01027) *(G-8453)*

National Nonwovens Inc................................. 413 527-3445
    27 Mechanic St Easthampton (01027) *(G-8454)*

National Packing Supply, Rumford *Also Called: The Real Reel Corporation (G-16678)*

National Publisher Svcs LLC............................ 917 902-9590
    2 Enterprise Dr Ste 420 Shelton (06484) *(G-3035)*

National Publishing Co Inc.............................. 203 221-2300
    64 Post Rd W Westport (06880) *(G-4188)*

National Relocation & RE Mag, Norwalk *Also Called: Relocation Information Svc Inc (G-2564)*

National Reprographics Inc............................. 857 383-3700
    21 Drydock Ave Ste 310e Boston (02210) *(G-6904)*

National Resource MGT Inc (PA)...................... **781 828-8877**
    480 Neponset St Ste 2a Canton (02021) *(G-7809)*

National Screw Manufacturing.......................... 203 469-7109
    259 Commerce St East Haven (06512) *(G-1047)*

National Shting Spt Fndtion In.......................... 203 426-1320
    6 Corporate Dr Ste 650 Shelton (06484) *(G-3036)*

National Sign Corp.. 508 809-4638
    21 Larsen Way Attleboro Falls (02763) *(G-6092)*

National Sign Corporation (PA)........................ **860 829-9060**
    780 Four Rod Rd Berlin (06037) *(G-77)*

National Spring & Stamping Inc........................ 860 283-0203
    135 S Main St Ste 8 Thomaston (06787) *(G-3625)*

National Store Fronts Co Inc............................ 508 584-8880
    10 Tracy Dr Avon (02322) *(G-6154)*

National Store Supply, North Bennington *Also Called: National Hanger Company Inc (G-17410)*

National Van Sales Inc................................... 508 222-2272
    80 Pine St Attleboro (02703) *(G-6040)*

National Velour-Nk, Warwick *Also Called: Wintech Intl Corp - Nk (G-16880)*

National Vinyl LLC....................................... 413 420-0548
    7 Coburn St Chicopee (01013) *(G-8051)*

National Welding LLC.................................... 860 818-1240
    48 Industrial Park Access Rd Middlefield (06455) *(G-1726)*

Nationwide Die Cutng Svcs LLC....................... 617 306-6836
    59 Tyler Dr Uxbridge (01569) *(G-12487)*

Nationwide Tax & Business Svcs....................... 774 473-8444
    5 Dover St Ste 103 New Bedford (02740) *(G-10625)*

Native Instruments Usa Inc (PA)..................... **617 577-7799**
    2 Avenue De Lafayette Boston (02111) *(G-6905)*

Native Maine Operations Inc........................... 207 856-1100
    10 Bradley Dr Westbrook (04092) *(G-5640)*

Nats USA Incorporated.................................. 860 398-0035
    515 Centerpoint Dr Ste 108 Middletown (06457) *(G-1767)*

Natural Country Farms Inc............................. 860 872-8346
    58 West Rd Ellington (06029) *(G-1112)*

Natural Form Medical, Manchester Center *Also Called: Wcw Inc (G-17332)*

Natural Nutmeg LLC...................................... 860 206-9500
    53 Mountain View Ave Avon (06001) *(G-32)*

Natural Playgrounds Shop LLC........................ 888 290-8405
    10 Pine St Concord (03301) *(G-14147)*

Natural Selection Inc.................................... 207 725-6287
    166 Admiral Fitch Ave Brunswick (04011) *(G-4651)*

(G-0000) Company's Geographic Section entry number

Naturalase, Bethel *Also Called: Focus Medical LLC* **(G-116)**

Naturally Uncommon LLC.................................... 603 458-2209
  14 Industrial Way Atkinson (03811) **(G-13905)**

Natures First Inc **(PA)**.................................... **203 795-8400**
  58 Robinson Blvd Ste C Orange (06477) **(G-2678)**

Natures Harvest LLC....................................... 203 758-3725
  845 Carrington Rd Bethany (06524) **(G-96)**

Natureseal Inc... 203 454-1800
  1175 Post Rd E Ste 3b Westport (06880) **(G-4189)**

Natworks Inc.. 802 485-6818
  454 S Main St Northfield (05663) **(G-17433)**

Naugatuck Glass LLC....................................... 203 729-5227
  451 Church St Naugatuck (06770) **(G-1975)**

Naugatuck Stair Company Inc............................... 203 729-7134
  51 Elm St Naugatuck (06770) **(G-1976)**

Nauset Marine Inc **(PA)**.................................... **508 255-0777**
  45 Rt 6a Orleans (02653) **(G-11240)**

Nautel, Bangor *Also Called: Nautel Maine Inc* **(G-4511)**

Nautel Maine Inc.. 207 947-8200
  201 Target Cir Bangor (04401) **(G-4511)**

Navigator Publishing LLC................................... 207 822-4350
  30 Danforth St Ste 307 Portland (04101) **(G-5249)**

Navilyst Medical Inc....................................... 508 658-7990
  26 Forest St Ste 200 Marlborough (01752) **(G-10186)**

Navionics Inc... 508 291-6000
  6 Thacher Ln Wareham (02571) **(G-12841)**

Navionics Inc, Wareham *Also Called: Navionics Inc* **(G-12841)**

Navitar Industries LLC..................................... 781 933-6125
  30 Nashua St Woburn (01801) **(G-13619)**

Navitor Pharmaceuticals Inc................................ 857 285-4300
  1030 Massachusetts Ave Cambridge (02138) **(G-7660)**

Navtec Rigging Solutions Inc
  11 Lakeside Dr Groton (01450) **(G-9011)**

Navtech Systems Inc....................................... 203 661-7800
  322 Sound Beach Ave Old Greenwich (06870) **(G-2634)**

Nazarian Diamonds, Salem *Also Called: Nazarian Jewelers NH Inc* **(G-15548)**

Nazarian Jewelers NH Inc **(PA)**............................ **603 893-1600**
  203 S Broadway Ste 2 Salem (03079) **(G-15548)**

NBC Sports Boston, Needham Heights *Also Called: Comcast Sportsnet Neng LLC* **(G-10537)**

NBD Nano Technologies, Lexington *Also Called: NBD Nanotechnologies Inc* **(G-9764)**

NBD Nanotechnologies Inc.................................. 781 541-4192
  99 Hayden Ave Bldg C Lexington (02421) **(G-9764)**

NBOC, New Bedford *Also Called: New Bedford Ocean Cluster Inc* **(G-10627)**

Nbr Diamond Tool Corp..................................... 603 394-2113
  22 Exeter Rd Unit 2 South Hampton (03827) **(G-15629)**

NC Brands LP... 203 295-2300
  40 Richards Ave Ste 2 Norwalk (06854) **(G-2542)**

NC Hunt Lumber Company, Jefferson *Also Called: N C Hunt Inc* **(G-4918)**

Ncab Group Usa Inc **(DH)**................................ **603 329-4551**
  10 Starwood Dr Hampstead (03841) **(G-14388)**

Nci Holdings Inc **(PA)**.................................... **203 295-2300**
  40 Richards Ave Ste 2 Norwalk (06854) **(G-2543)**

Nci Woodworking LLC LLC.................................. 203 391-1614
  230 Hollydale Rd Fairfield (06824) **(G-1195)**

Nciea.. 603 749-0733
  31 Mount Vernon St Dover (03820) **(G-14237)**

Nct, Kennebunk *Also Called: Northeast Coating Tech Inc* **(G-4927)**

ND Otm LLC... 207 401-2879
  24 Portland St Old Town (04468) **(G-5129)**

ND Paper Inc... 207 401-2920
  24 Portland St Old Town (04468) **(G-5130)**

ND Paper Inc... 207 364-4521
  35 Hartford St Rumford (04276) **(G-5359)**

ND Paper LLC.. 207 364-4521
  35 Hartford St Rumford (04276) **(G-5360)**

Ndr Liuzzi Inc.. 203 287-8477
  86 Rossotto Dr Hamden (06514) **(G-1445)**

Ndx H&O, Manchester *Also Called: National Dentex LLC* **(G-14895)**

Ndz Performance, Cheshire *Also Called: New Designz Realty LLC* **(G-608)**

Ne - Xt Technologies, Greenfield *Also Called: New England Expert Tech Corp* **(G-8995)**

Ne Finest LLC.. 800 215-6640
  1372 Main St Coventry (02816) **(G-15817)**

Ne Media Group Inc **(PA)**................................ **617 929-2000**
  1 Exchange Pl Ste 201 Boston (02109) **(G-6906)**

Ne Stainless Steel Fab..................................... 781 335-0121
  86 Finnell Dr Ste 23 Weymouth (02188) **(G-13331)**

Ne Steel Fabricators LLC................................... 401 785-1234
  1120 Wellington Ave Cranston (02910) **(G-15898)**

Neal Specialty Compounding LLC............................ 207 777-1122
  258 Goddard Rd Lewiston (04240) **(G-4979)**

Near East Bakery, Brockton *Also Called: Elie Baking Corporation* **(G-7276)**

Near Oak LLC.. 203 329-6500
  1011 High Ridge Rd Stamford (06905) **(G-3415)**

Nearpeer Inc... 207 615-0414
  63 Federal St Portland (04101) **(G-5250)**

Nebs, Townsend *Also Called: New England Business Svc Inc* **(G-12441)**

Nec, Westborough *Also Called: Lg Energy Solution Vertech Inc* **(G-13117)**

Necco, Revere *Also Called: New England Confectionery Company Inc* **(G-11622)**

Neci, Canton *Also Called: Neci LLC* **(G-7810)**

Neci LLC.. 781 828-4883
  530 Turnpike St Canton (02021) **(G-7810)**

Necsel Intllctual Property Inc............................... 802 877-6432
  101 Panton Rd Ste 1 Vergennes (05491) **(G-17658)**

Necsel Ip, Vergennes *Also Called: Necsel Intllctual Property Inc* **(G-17658)**

Necst... 860 628-2515
  525 W Queen St Southington (06489) **(G-3223)**

Nectar Cappuccino Group, South Burlington *Also Called: Sunny Sky Products LLC* **(G-17602)**

Nedap Inc... 844 876-3327
  25 Corporate Dr Ste 101 Burlington (01803) **(G-7396)**

Nedap Light Controls N Amer, Hampstead *Also Called: ARC Electronics Inc* **(G-14380)**

Nedap Retail North America, Burlington *Also Called: Nedap Inc* **(G-7396)**

Nedc Sealing Solutions, Methuen *Also Called: New England Die Cutting Inc* **(G-10340)**

Needham Electric Supply LLC **(DH)**........................ **781 828-9494**
  5 Shawmut Rd Canton (02021) **(G-7811)**

Needletech Products Inc.................................... 508 431-4000
  452 John L Dietsch Blvd North Attleboro (02763) **(G-10879)**

Neeltran Inc... 860 350-5964
  71 Pickett District Rd New Milford (06776) **(G-2254)**

Neenah Northeast LLC **(DH)**.............................. **413 533-0699**
  70 Front St West Springfield (01089) **(G-13036)**

Neenah Technical Materials Inc **(DH)**...................... **678 518-3343**
  Ashuelot Park Ii 448 Hubbard Ave Dalton (01226) **(G-8151)**

Neenas Lighting.. 617 864-5757
  57 Jfk St Cambridge (02138) **(G-7661)**

Nefab Packaging North East LLC............................ 800 258-4692
  23 Williams Way Bellingham (02019) **(G-6297)**

Nefab Packaging North East LLC **(PA)**...................... **603 343-5750**
  115 Broadway Dover (03820) **(G-14238)**

Nefc.. 800 360-6332
  85 Avenue A Ste 204 Turners Falls (01376) **(G-12454)**

Nefm, Leominster *Also Called: New England Fab Mtls Inc* **(G-9685)**

Nehp Inc.. 802 652-1444
  1193 S Brownell Rd Ste 35 Williston (05495) **(G-17741)**

Nei, Canton *Also Called: Unicom Engineering Inc* **(G-7836)**

Nei Advanced Composite Tech, Brentwood *Also Called: Northern Elastomeric Inc* **(G-14025)**

Nei Stamping, Lebanon *Also Called: New England Industries Inc* **(G-14696)**

Neil H Daniels Inc.. 802 674-6323
  4409 Route 5 Ascutney (05030) **(G-16993)**

Neiss Corp.. 860 872-8528
  29 Naek Rd Vernon (06066) **(G-3755)**

Nel Hydrogen US, Wallingford *Also Called: Proton Energy Systems Inc* **(G-3841)**

Nelipak Corporation **(PA)**................................ **401 946-2699**
  21 Amflex Dr Cranston (02921) **(G-15899)**

Nelipak Healthcare Packaging, Cranston *Also Called: Nelipak Corporation* **(G-15899)**

Nellcor Puritan Bennett LLC **(DH)**......................... **508 261-8000**
  15 Hampshire St Mansfield (02048) **(G-10069)**

Nelson Heat Treating Co Inc................................ 203 754-0670
  2046 N Main St Waterbury (06704) **(G-3948)**

Nelson Tool & Machine Co Inc.............................. 860 589-8004
  675 Emmett St Bristol (06010) **(G-474)**

**A
L
P
H
A
B
E
T
I
C**

Nemi Publishing Inc.................................. 207 778-4801
  553 Wilton Rd Farmington (04938) *(G-4782)*

Nemosyne Therapeutics, Cambridge *Also Called: Cadent Therapeutics Inc (G-7526)*

Nemucore Med Innovations Inc.................... 617 943-9983
  33 Kirkland Cir Wellesley (02481) *(G-12944)*

Nenpa.. 781 281-2053
  1 Arrow Dr Ste 6 Woburn (01801) *(G-13620)*

Neo Tech... 508 329-6270
  125 Fisher St Westborough (01581) *(G-13123)*

Neokraft Signs Inc.................................. 207 782-9654
  647 Pleasant St Lewiston (04240) *(G-4980)*

Neolane Inc.. 617 467-6760
  275 Washington St 3rd Fl Newton (02458) *(G-10771)*

Neon Labs LLC....................................... 847 867-4370
  210 South St Unit 113 Boston (02111) *(G-6907)*

Neoperl Inc.. 203 756-8891
  171 Mattatuck Heights Rd Waterbury (06705) *(G-3949)*

Neopost, Milford *Also Called: Quadient Inc (G-1874)*

Neopost USA, Milford *Also Called: Quadient Finance Usa Inc (G-1875)*

Neoprint Inc... 978 256-9939
  11 Alpha Rd Chelmsford (01824) *(G-7941)*

Neotech, Westborough *Also Called: Oncore Manufacturing LLC (G-13125)*

Neovii Biotech Na Inc.............................. 781 966-3830
  6 Liberty Sq Boston (02109) *(G-6908)*

Nepco, Presque Isle *Also Called: Northeast Packaging Co (G-5305)*

Neptco Incorporated **(DH)**..................... **401 722-5500**
  295 University Ave Westwood (02090) *(G-13316)*

Neptco Laminated Tapes Co Inc, Westwood *Also Called: Neptco Incorporated (G-13316)*

Neptune Garment Company....................... 617 482-3980
  242 E Berkeley St Ste 3 Boston (02118) *(G-6909)*

Nepv LLC... 860 739-2200
  36 Industrial Park Rd Ste B Niantic (06357) *(G-2358)*

Nery Corporation.................................... 508 990-9800
  700 Pleasant St Ste 330 New Bedford (02740) *(G-10626)*

Nes Embroidery Inc................................. 603 293-4664
  100 Autumn Dr Tilton (03276) *(G-15655)*

Nes Worldwide Inc.................................. 413 562-8000
  3 Progress Ave Westfield (01085) *(G-13192)*

Nesco, Canton *Also Called: Needham Electric Supply LLC (G-7811)*

Neshobe Wood Products Inc...................... 802 247-3805
  56 Pearl St Brandon (05733) *(G-17069)*

Neslo Manufacturing, Wolcott *Also Called: Musano Inc (G-4369)*

Nest, Litchfield *Also Called: New England Small Tube Corp (G-14713)*

Nestech Machine Systems Inc.................... 802 482-4575
  223 Commerce St Hinesburg (05461) *(G-17296)*

Nestle.. 508 828-3954
  455 John Hancock Rd Taunton (02780) *(G-12351)*

Nestle Usa Inc....................................... 860 928-0082
  151 Mashamoquet Rd Pomfret Center (06259) *(G-2813)*

Nestor Inc **(PA)**.................................. **401 274-5345**
  42 Oriental St Fl 3 Providence (02908) *(G-16574)*

Nestor Traffic Systems Inc **(PA)**.............. **401 714-7781**
  1080 Main St Pawtucket (02860) *(G-16391)*

Net.com, Westford *Also Called: Network Equipment Tech Inc (G-13254)*

Netbrain Technologies Inc **(PA)**............... **781 221-7199**
  15 Network Dr Ste 2 Burlington (01803) *(G-7397)*

Netc Liquidating Corporation.................... 603 569-3100
  147 Middle Rd Center Tuftonboro (03816) *(G-14059)*

Netco Extruded Plastics, Hudson *Also Called: Xponent Global Inc (G-9426)*

Netco Extruded Plastics Inc...................... 978 562-3485
  30 Tower St Hudson (01749) *(G-9395)*

Netcracker, Waltham *Also Called: Netcracker Technology Corp (G-12735)*

Netcracker Technology Corp **(HQ)**............ **781 419-3300**
  95 Sawyer Rd University Office Park Iii Waltham (02453) *(G-12735)*

Netgalley LLC **(PA)**.............................. **978 465-7755**
  44 Merrimac St Ste 21 Newburyport (01950) *(G-10704)*

Netscout, Westford *Also Called: Netscout Systems Inc (G-13253)*

Netscout Systems Inc **(PA)**..................... **978 614-4000**
  310 Littleton Rd Westford (01886) *(G-13253)*

Netsilicon Inc **(HQ)**.............................. **781 647-1234**
  411 Waverley Oaks Rd Waltham (02452) *(G-12736)*

Netsource Inc **(PA)**.............................. **860 649-6000**
  260 Progress Dr Manchester (06042) *(G-1620)*

Netsuite... 877 638-7848
  268 Summer St Ste 400 Boston (02210) *(G-6910)*

Nettwerk Music Group LLC........................ 617 497-8200
  15 Richdale Ave Cambridge (02140) *(G-7662)*

Network Equipment Tech Inc **(DH)**........... **510 713-7300**
  4 Technology Park Dr Westford (01886) *(G-13254)*

Network World Inc.................................. 800 622-1108
  140 Kendrick St # B Needham Heights (02494) *(G-10553)*

Netzsch, Burlington *Also Called: Netzsch Instruments N Amer LLC (G-7398)*

Netzsch Instruments N Amer LLC **(DH)**..... **781 272-5353**
  129 Middlesex Tpke Burlington (01803) *(G-7398)*

Neu Spclty Engineered Mtls LLC................ 203 239-9629
  15 Corporate Dr North Haven (06473) *(G-2426)*

Neu-Tool Design Inc............................... 978 658-5881
  220 Ballardvale St Ste A Wilmington (01887) *(G-13437)*

Neudorfer Inc.. 802 244-5338
  183 Crossett Hl Waterbury (05676) *(G-17676)*

Neudorfer Tables, Waterbury *Also Called: Neudorfer Inc (G-17676)*

Neumora Therapeutics Inc **(PA)**............... **857 760-0900**
  490 Arsenal Way Ste 200 Watertown (02472) *(G-12896)*

Neuro Phage Phrmaceuticals Inc............... 617 941-7004
  222 3rd St Cambridge (02142) *(G-7663)*

Neurobo, Cambridge *Also Called: Neurobo Pharmaceuticals Inc (G-7664)*

Neurobo Pharmaceuticals Inc **(PA)**........... **617 864-2880**
  545 Concord Ave Ste 210 Cambridge (02138) *(G-7664)*

Neurobo Therapeutics Inc........................ 617 313-7331
  177 Huntington Ave Ste 1700 Boston (02115) *(G-6911)*

Neurologica Corp.................................... 978 564-8500
  14 Electronics Ave Danvers (01923) *(G-8211)*

Neurometrix Inc **(PA)**............................ **781 890-9989**
  4b Gill St Woburn (01801) *(G-13621)*

Neuromotion Inc.................................... 415 676-9326
  186 Lincoln St Boston (02111) *(G-6912)*

Neuromotion Labs, Boston *Also Called: Neuromotion Inc (G-6912)*

Neurotech Pharmaceuticals Inc.................. 617 694-5520
  900 Highland Corporate Dr Bldg 1 Cumberland (02864) *(G-15951)*

Neurotherm Inc...................................... 888 655-3500
  600 Research Dr Ste 1 Wilmington (01887) *(G-13438)*

Neutral Zone LLC.................................... 802 989-3133
  738 Rutland Rd West Rutland (05777) *(G-17696)*

Neutron Therapeutics LLC........................ 978 777-0846
  1 Industrial Dr Ste 1 Danvers (01923) *(G-8212)*

Nevada Heat Treating LLC........................ 978 365-4999
  90 Parker St Clinton (01510) *(G-8085)*

Nevamar Company LLC **(HQ)**.................. **203 925-1556**
  2 Corporate Dr Ste 946 Shelton (06484) *(G-3037)*

Nevamar Distributors, Shelton *Also Called: Nevamar Company LLC (G-3037)*

Nevron Plastics Inc................................. 781 233-1310
  124 Ballard St Saugus (01906) *(G-11763)*

Nevron Plastics and Metals, Saugus *Also Called: Nevron Plastics Inc (G-11763)*

Nevtec, Newport *Also Called: Nevtec Ltd (G-17401)*

Nevtec Ltd... 802 334-7800
  33 Airport Rd Newport (05855) *(G-17401)*

New Age Ems, Attleboro *Also Called: New Age Technologies Inc (G-6041)*

New Age Technologies Inc........................ 508 226-6090
  527 Pleasant St Attleboro (02703) *(G-6041)*

New Amtrol Holdings Inc **(DH)**................ **614 438-3210**
  1400 Division Rd West Warwick (02893) *(G-16917)*

New Annex Plating Inc............................. 401 349-0911
  9 Warren Ave North Providence (02911) *(G-16305)*

New Balance Athletics Inc........................ 207 634-3033
  20 Depot St Norridgewock (04957) *(G-5103)*

New Balance Athletics Inc........................ 207 474-2042
  10 Walnut St Skowhegan (04976) *(G-5474)*

New Balance Athletics Inc **(HQ)**.............. **617 783-4000**
  100 Guest St Boston (02135) *(G-6913)*

New Balance Athletics Inc........................ 978 685-8400
  5 S Union St Lawrence (01843) *(G-9586)*

New Bedford Ocean Cluster Inc.................. 508 474-8902
  1213 Purchase St Unit 2 New Bedford (02740) *(G-10627)*

New Bedford Scale Co Inc................................ 508 997-6730
144 Francis St New Bedford (02740) *(G-10628)*

New Bedford Thread Co Inc............................. 508 996-8584
10 Howland Rd Fairhaven (02719) *(G-8511)*

New Bedford Thread Company........................ 860 333-6700
3 State Pier Rd New London (06320) *(G-2231)*

New Beverage Publications Inc....................... 617 598-1900
55 Clarendon St Ste 1 Boston (02116) *(G-6914)*

New Brick Dryvit Systems................................ 401 822-4100
200 Frenchtown Rd North Kingstown (02852) *(G-16272)*

New Britain Herald , The, New Britain *Also Called: Central Conn Cmmunications LLC (G-2010)*

New Can Company, Holbrook *Also Called: New Can Holdings Inc (G-9182)*

New Can Company Inc **(HQ)**......................... **330 928-1191**
1 Mear Rd Holbrook (02343) *(G-9181)*

New Can Holdings Inc **(PA)**........................... **781 767-1650**
1 Mear Rd Holbrook (02343) *(G-9182)*

New Canaan News... 203 842-2582
301 Merritt 7 Ste 1 Norwalk (06851) *(G-2544)*

New Canaan Sports LLC................................... 866 629-2453
96 Park St New Canaan (06840) *(G-2084)*

New Chapter Inc **(HQ)**................................... **800 543-7279**
90 Technology Dr Brattleboro (05301) *(G-17096)*

New Charter Distribution, Brattleboro *Also Called: New Chapter Inc (G-17096)*

New Christie Ventures, Naugatuck *Also Called: Pastanch LLC (G-1979)*

New Christie Ventures LLC............................... 203 720-9478
31 Sheridan Dr Ste 31 Naugatuck (06770) *(G-1977)*

New Colt Holding Corp..................................... 860 236-6311
545 New Park Ave West Hartford (06110) *(G-4074)*

New Designz Inc.. 203 439-7784
1068 N Farms Rd Ste 2 Wallingford (06492) *(G-3834)*

New Designz Realty LLC................................... 860 384-1809
278 Sandbank Rd Cheshire (06410) *(G-608)*

New England Airfoil Pdts Inc........................... 860 677-1376
36 Spring Ln Farmington (06032) *(G-1231)*

New England Alpaca Fibr Pool I...................... 508 659-6731
115 N 7th St Fall River (02720) *(G-8586)*

New England Apple Products Co, Leominster *Also Called: Bevovations LLC (G-9642)*

New England Art Publishers Inc....................... 781 878-5151
10 Railroad St Abington (02351) *(G-5726)*

New England Beverages LLC........................... 203 208-4517
137 N Branford Rd Branford (06405) *(G-273)*

New England Bias Binding, Boston *Also Called: Color-Tex International Inc (G-6663)*

New England Boat & Motor Inc....................... 603 527-9435
28 Center St Laconia (03246) *(G-14660)*

New England Boatworks Inc............................ 401 683-4000
1 Lagoon Rd Ste 4 Portsmouth (02871) *(G-16449)*

New England Box Beef Company.................... 781 320-3232
305 Myles Standish Blvd Taunton (02780) *(G-12352)*

New England Brace Co Inc **(PA)**................... **508 588-6060**
2 Greenwood Ave Concord (03301) *(G-14148)*

New England Braiding Co Inc.......................... 603 669-1987
610 Gold St Manchester (03103) *(G-14897)*

New England Bridge Pdts Inc.......................... 781 592-2444
93 Brookline St Lynn (01902) *(G-9987)*

New England Building Materials LLC............... 207 324-3350
563 New Dam Rd Sanford (04073) *(G-5401)*

New England Business Svc Inc **(HQ)**............. **978 448-6111**
12 South St Townsend (01469) *(G-12441)*

New England Cabinet Co.................................. 860 225-8645
580 E Main St New Britain (06051) *(G-2046)*

New England Cage & Fence Corp.................... 860 688-8148
230 Clintonville Ln North Haven (06473) *(G-2427)*

New England Carbide Inc................................. 978 887-0313
428 Boston St Ste A Topsfield (01983) *(G-12437)*

New England Castings LLC.............................. 207 642-3029
234 Northeast Rd Ste 2 Standish (04084) *(G-5528)*

New England Chimney Supply, Williston *Also Called: New England Supply Inc (G-17742)*

New England Clock, North Haven *Also Called: Bonito Manufacturing Inc (G-2394)*

New England Cmpunding Phrm Inc................. 800 994-6322
100 High St Ste 2400 Boston (02110) *(G-6915)*

New England Cnc Inc....................................... 203 288-8241
46 Manila Ave Hamden (06514) *(G-1446)*

New England Coffee Company, Norwood *Also Called: New England Partnership Inc (G-11199)*

New England Compounding Center, Boston *Also Called: New England Cmpunding Phrm Inc (G-6915)*

New England Confectionery Company Inc....... 781 485-4500
135 American Legion Hwy Revere (02151) *(G-11622)*

New England Country Pies LLC....................... 781 596-0176
18 Knowlton Dr Acton (01720) *(G-5759)*

New England Crane Inc.................................... 207 782-7353
500 Potash Hill Rd Unit 1 Tyngsboro (01879) *(G-12462)*

New England Cstm Cabinets LLC.................... 401 667-2572
840 Ten Rod Rd North Kingstown (02852) *(G-16273)*

New England Die Co Inc.................................. 203 574-5140
48 Ford Ave Waterbury (06708) *(G-3950)*

New England Die Cutting Inc........................... 978 374-0789
96 Milk St Methuen (01844) *(G-10340)*

New England Door Closer Inc.......................... 413 733-7889
694 Union St West Springfield (01089) *(G-13037)*

New England Duplicator Inc............................. 603 623-6847
8030 S Willow St Unit 108 Manchester (03103) *(G-14898)*

New England Elc Mtr Svc Corp........................ 617 884-9200
25 Griffin Way Chelsea (02150) *(G-7988)*

New England Elctrpolishing Inc....................... 508 672-6616
220 Shove St Fall River (02724) *(G-8587)*

New England Etching Co Inc............................ 413 532-9482
23 Spring St Holyoke (01040) *(G-9269)*

New England Expert Tech Corp........................ 413 773-8200
15 Greenfield St Greenfield (01301) *(G-8995)*

New England Fab Mtls Inc............................... 978 466-7823
101 Crawford St Leominster (01453) *(G-9685)*

New England Fast Ferry, New Bedford *Also Called: Marthas Seastreak Vineyard LLC (G-10620)*

New England Flag & Banner............................ 617 782-1892
165 Dexter Ave Watertown (02472) *(G-12897)*

New England Foam, Hartford *Also Called: New England Foam Products LLC (G-1496)*

New England Foam Products LLC **(PA)**......... **860 524-0121**
760 Windsor St Hartford (06120) *(G-1496)*

New England Foundation Co Inc **(PA)**........... **617 361-9750**
1 Westinghouse Plz Ste 27 Hyde Park (02136) *(G-9465)*

New England Gen-Connect LLC...................... 617 571-6884
35 Pond Park Rd Ste 11 Hingham (02043) *(G-9155)*

New England Gravel, Rehoboth *Also Called: New England Gravel Haulers (G-11612)*

New England Gravel Haulers............................ 508 922-4518
42 Winthrop St Rehoboth (02769) *(G-11612)*

New England Grund Slutions LLC.................... 978 203-6277
127 Eastern Ave Ste 2 Gloucester (01930) *(G-8945)*

New England Homes Inc.................................. 603 436-8830
277 Locust St Dover (03820) *(G-14239)*

New England Industrial Sup LLC...................... 860 436-5959
127 Costello Rd Newington (06111) *(G-2308)*

New England Industries Inc.............................. 603 448-5330
85 Etna Rd Lebanon (03766) *(G-14696)*

New England Innovations Corp........................ 603 742-6247
4 Progress Dr Dover (03820) *(G-14240)*

New England Journal Medicine, Boston *Also Called: Massachusetts Medical Society (G-6874)*

New England Journal Medicine, Waltham *Also Called: Massachusetts Medical Society (G-12716)*

New England Keyboard Inc............................... 978 345-8332
1 Princeton Rd Ste 1 Fitchburg (01420) *(G-8668)*

New England Label... 978 281-3663
10 Centennial Dr Peabody (01960) *(G-11326)*

New England Lift Systems LLC........................ 860 372-4040
714 N Mountain Rd Newington (06111) *(G-2309)*

New England Lumber & Packaging, East Longmeadow *Also Called: Garelco Sales Company Inc (G-8376)*

New England Machine Tools Inc...................... 860 583-4001
597 Middle St Ste B Bristol (06010) *(G-475)*

New England Mar Holdings Inc....................... 508 758-6600
128 Union St New Bedford (02740) *(G-10629)*

New England Meat Packing LLC..................... 860 684-3505
30 Furnace Hollow Rd Stafford Springs (06076) *(G-3258)*

New England Metalform Inc............................ 508 695-9340
380 South St Plainville (02762) *(G-11441)*

New England Mktg & Prtg Inc.......................... 917 582-1029
41 Deerfield Rd Unit 11 Attleboro (02703) *(G-6042)*

A
L
P
H
A
B
E
T
I
C

New England Natural Bakers Inc............................. 413 772-2239
  74 Fairview St E Greenfield (01301) *(G-8996)*

New England Newspapers Inc **(DH)**......................... **413 447-7311**
  75 S Church St Ste L1 Pittsfield (01201) *(G-11414)*

New England Newspapers Inc................................. 401 722-4000
  2 Dexter St Ste 2 Pawtucket (02860) *(G-16392)*

New England Newspapers Inc................................. 802 254-2311
  62 Black Mountain Rd Brattleboro (05301) *(G-17097)*

New England Newsppr Press Assn............................ 781 281-2053
  1 Arrow Dr Ste 1 Woburn (01801) *(G-13622)*

New England Nonwovens LLC................................. 203 891-0851
  283 Dogburn Rd West Haven (06516) *(G-4116)*

New England Orthdontic Lab Inc............................. 800 922-6365
  3 Riverside Dr Ste 1 Andover (01810) *(G-5900)*

New England Orthopedics **(PA)**............................ **401 739-9838**
  220 Toll Gate Rd Ste A Warwick (02886) *(G-16841)*

New England Outdoor Wood Pdts, Methuen *Also Called: Jobart Inc (G-10335)*

New England Overseas Corp................................. 401 722-3800
  358 Lowden St Pawtucket (02860) *(G-16393)*

New England Pallets Skids Inc.............................. 413 583-6628
  250 West St Ludlow (01056) *(G-9951)*

New England Paper Tube, Pawtucket *Also Called: Weeden Street Associates LLC (G-16430)*

New England Paper Tube Co Inc............................. 401 725-2610
  200 Conant St Pawtucket (02860) *(G-16394)*

New England Partnership Inc................................ 800 225-3537
  30 Walpole St Norwood (02062) *(G-11199)*

New England Phtoconductor Corp............................ 508 285-5561
  253 Mansfield Ave Norton (02766) *(G-11130)*

New England Pipe & Supply Co, Loudon *Also Called: Capitol Fire Protection Co Inc (G-14794)*

New England Plasma Dev Corp.............................. 860 928-6561
  14 Highland Dr Putnam (06260) *(G-2866)*

New England Plastics Corp................................. 508 998-3111
  126 Duchaine Blvd New Bedford (02745) *(G-10630)*

New England Plastics Corp **(PA)**.......................... **781 933-6004**
  310 Salem St Woburn (01801) *(G-13623)*

New England Powder Coating............................... 207 432-6679
  172 Creamery Hill Rd Lebanon (04027) *(G-4945)*

New England Precision Inc................................. 800 293-4112
  281 Beanville Rd Randolph (05060) *(G-17471)*

New England Promotions, Westport *Also Called: J W I N Promotional Corp (G-13297)*

New England Prtzel Popcorn Inc............................ 978 687-0342
  15 Bay State Rd Lawrence (01841) *(G-9587)*

New England Publishing Group, Swansea *Also Called: New England RE Bulltin (G-12308)*

New England Pump and Valve, Niantic *Also Called: Nepv LLC (G-2358)*

New England RE Bulltin.................................... 508 675-8884
  1610 Gar Hwy Swansea (02777) *(G-12308)*

New England Real Estate Jurnl, Norwell *Also Called: East Coast Publications Inc (G-11141)*

New England Rent To Own LLC............................. 207 399-6181
  65 River Rd Chelsea (04330) *(G-4687)*

New England Sales Team, Brattleboro *Also Called: Carlton Newton Corporation LLC (G-17078)*

New England Sand & Grav Co Inc........................... 508 877-2460
  Corner Of Danforth St & Birch Rd Framingham (01701) *(G-8791)*

New England Sheets LLC **(PA)**............................ **978 487-2500**
  36 Saratoga Blvd Devens (01434) *(G-8281)*

New England Showcase, Brattleboro *Also Called: Howard Printing Inc (G-17087)*

New England Shrlines Companies........................... 781 826-0140
  107 Broadway Hanover (02339) *(G-9037)*

New England Sign Group Inc............................... 508 779-0821
  14a E Worcester St Worcester (01604) *(G-13764)*

New England Small Tube Corp.............................. 603 429-1600
  480 Charles Bancroft Hwy Unit 3 Litchfield (03052) *(G-14713)*

New England Spring, Bristol *Also Called: Dcp Spring Acquisition Co Inc (G-435)*

New England Spt Ventures LLC............................. 617 267-9440
  4 Jersey St Boston (02215) *(G-6916)*

New England Stair Company Inc............................ 203 924-0606
  1 White St Shelton (06484) *(G-3038)*

New England Stinless Distr LLC............................ 978 255-4830
  18 Fanaras Dr Salisbury (01952) *(G-11743)*

New England Stl Fbricators Inc............................ 207 324-1846
  342 Jordan Springs Rd Alfred (04002) *(G-4403)*

New England Stone Inc.................................... 203 876-8606
  35 Higgins Dr Milford (06460) *(G-1853)*

New England Stone Industries, Smithfield *Also Called: Georgia Stone Industries Inc (G-16702)*

New England Sugars LLC.................................. 508 792-3801
  1120 Millbury St Worcester (01607) *(G-13765)*

New England Supply Inc **(PA)**............................ **802 858-4577**
  34 Commerce St Williston (05495) *(G-17742)*

New England Tape Co, Hudson *Also Called: Netco Extruded Plastics Inc (G-9395)*

New England Technology Group............................. 617 864-5551
  1 Davenport St Ste 1 Cambridge (02140) *(G-7665)*

New England Tool Co., Smithfield *Also Called: Blackhawk Machine Products Inc (G-16689)*

New England Tool Corporation **(PA)**...................... **860 783-5555**
  161 Sanrico Dr Manchester (06042) *(G-1621)*

New England Tooling Inc.................................. 800 866-5105
  145 Chestnut Hill Rd Killingworth (06419) *(G-1544)*

New England Tortilla Inc.................................. 617 889-6462
  74a Clarendon St, Boston (02116) *(G-6917)*

New England Trck Tire Ctrs Inc **(PA)**..................... **207 324-2262**
  38 Rainbow Ln Sanford (04073) *(G-5402)*

New England Ultimate Finishing............................ 413 532-7777
  709 Main St Holyoke (01040) *(G-9270)*

New England Union Co Inc................................ 401 821-0800
  107 Hay St West Warwick (02893) *(G-16918)*

New England Vlts Monuments LLC.......................... 603 449-2165
  9 Industrial Park Dr Berlin (03570) *(G-13984)*

New England Water Heater Co.............................. 781 647-7004
  1101 Worcester Rd Ste 2 Framingham (01701) *(G-8792)*

New England Welding Inc................................. 508 580-2024
  145 Bodwell St Avon (02322) *(G-6155)*

New England Wheels, Billerica *Also Called: New England Wheels Inc (G-6462)*

New England Wheels Inc **(PA)**........................... **978 663-9724**
  33 Manning Rd Billerica (01821) *(G-6462)*

New England Wire Products Inc............................ 207 265-2176
  49 Depot St Kingfield (04947) *(G-4934)*

New England Wire Products Inc **(PA)**..................... **800 254-9473**
  9 Mohawk Dr Leominster (01453) *(G-9686)*

New England Wire Tech Corp **(HQ)**....................... **603 838-6624**
  130 N Main St Lisbon (03585) *(G-14710)*

New England Wire Technologies, Lisbon *Also Called: New England Wire Tech Corp (G-14710)*

New England Wirecloth Co LLC............................ 978 343-4998
  123 Kelly Ave Fitchburg (01420) *(G-8669)*

New England Wood Pellet LLC............................. 603 532-4666
  415 Squantum Rd Jaffrey (03452) *(G-14575)*

New England Wood Products LLC........................... 401 789-7474
  535 Liberty Ln West Kingston (02892) *(G-16895)*

New England Woodcraft Inc............................... 802 247-8211
  481 North St Brandon (05733) *(G-17070)*

New England Woodcraft Inc............................... 413 522-0137
  70 Main St Westford (01886) *(G-13255)*

New England Wooden Ware Corp **(PA)**..................... **978 632-3600**
  205 School St Ste 201 Gardner (01440) *(G-8896)*

New England Woodworkers................................ 603 562-7200
  New Ipswich (03071) *(G-15199)*

New England Woodworking Co, Middletown *Also Called: Igitt Inc (G-16175)*

New England Woodworks.................................. 207 324-6343
  10 Coleco Ln Springvale (04083) *(G-5522)*

New England Worldwide Export............................. 617 472-0251
  247 Water St Quincy (02169) *(G-11529)*

New Erie Scientific LLC **(DH)**........................... **603 430-6859**
  20 Post Rd Portsmouth (03801) *(G-15425)*

New Fairfield Press Inc.................................. 203 746-2700
  3 Dunham Dr New Fairfield (06812) *(G-2096)*

New Generation Research Inc.............................. 617 573-9550
  88 Broad St Fl 2 Boston (02110) *(G-6918)*

New Hampshire Bindery Inc............................... 603 224-0441
  81 Dow Rd Bow (03304) *(G-14006)*

New Hampshire Electric Motors, Laconia *Also Called: Leo Algers NH Elc Mtrs Inc (G-14658)*

New Hampshire Forge Inc................................. 603 357-5692
  15 Forge St Keene (03431) *(G-14613)*

New Hampshire Gateway Mdsg.............................. 603 216-7373
  1048 Hayward St Manchester (03103) *(G-14899)*

(G-0000) Company's Geographic Section entry number

New Hampshire Industries, Claremont *Also Called: Cascaded Purchase Holdings Inc* **(G-14083)**

New Hampshire Machine Pdts Inc...603 772-4404
   10 Kingston Rd Exeter (03833) *(G-14297)*

New Hampshire Novelty LLC **(PA)**..**413 325-7648**
   20 Snow Rd Winchester (03470) *(G-15715)*

New Hampshire Optical Co Inc **(PA)**...**603 268-0741**
   32 Library St Allenstown (03275) *(G-13854)*

New Hampshire Print Mail Svcs, Concord *Also Called: Argyle Associates Inc* **(G-14114)**

New Hampshire Stamping Co Inc..603 641-1234
   9 Lance Ln Ste 2 Goffstown (03045) *(G-14352)*

New Hampshire Stl Erectors LLC...603 668-3464
   17 Lamy Dr Goffstown (03045) *(G-14353)*

New Hampshire Union Leader, Manchester *Also Called: Union Leader Corporation* **(G-14947)**

New Hampshirecom..603 314-0447
   1662 Elm St Ste 100 Manchester (03101) *(G-14900)*

New Hartford Industrial Pk Inc...860 379-8506
   37 Greenwoods Rd New Hartford (06057) *(G-2106)*

New Haven Chemicals LLC..475 241-1150
   67 Welton St New Haven (06511) *(G-2177)*

New Haven Chlor-Alkali LLC...203 772-3350
   73 Welton St New Haven (06511) *(G-2178)*

New Haven Companies Inc..203 469-6421
   41 Washington Ave East Haven (06512) *(G-1048)*

New Haven Register LLC...203 789-5200
   100 Gando Dr New Haven (06513) *(G-2179)*

New Hmpshire Ball Bearings Inc...603 524-0004
   155 Lexington Dr Laconia (03246) *(G-14661)*

New Hmpshire Ball Bearings Inc...818 407-9300
   175 Jaffrey Rd Peterborough (03458) *(G-15320)*

New Hmpshire Cntry Campers LLC...802 223-6417
   2060 Dover Rd Epsom (03234) *(G-14280)*

New Hmpshire Stl Fbrcators LLC...603 668-3464
   17 Lamy Dr Goffstown (03045) *(G-14354)*

New Horizon Machine Co Inc...203 316-9355
   36 Ludlow St Stamford (06902) *(G-3416)*

New Leaf Pharmaceuticals LLC...203 270-4167
   77 S Main St Newtown (06470) *(G-2343)*

New Method Plating Co Inc..508 754-2671
   43 Hammond St Worcester (01610) *(G-13766)*

New Milford Commission...860 354-3758
   123 West St New Milford (06776) *(G-2255)*

New Milford Farms Inc..860 210-0250
   60 Boardman Rd New Milford (06776) *(G-2256)*

New Mlford Wtr Plltion Ctrl Au, New Milford *Also Called: New Milford Commission* **(G-2255)**

New Model Inc..603 267-8225
   40 Higgins Dr Belmont (03220) *(G-13964)*

New Objective Inc..781 933-9560
   295 Foster St # 110 Littleton (01460) *(G-9828)*

New Page Books, Newburyport *Also Called: Career Press Inc* **(G-10674)**

New Portland Publishing Inc..207 536-5210
   251 Us Route 1 Ste 204 Falmouth (04105) *(G-4770)*

New Precision Technology LLC...800 243-4565
   98 Fort Path Rd Ste B Madison (06443) *(G-1564)*

New Tek Design Group Inc...508 835-4544
   18 Worcester St West Boylston (01583) *(G-12965)*

New Valence Robotics Corp..857 529-6397
   480 Neponset St Ste 10c Canton (02021) *(G-7812)*

New Vectrix LLC..858 674-6099
   197 Portland St Ste 4 Boston (02114) *(G-6919)*

New View Surgical Inc..774 284-2283
   555 Massachusetts Ave Unit 5 Boston (02118) *(G-6920)*

New York Accessory Group Inc...401 245-6096
   500 Wood St Ste 21 Bristol (02809) *(G-15776)*

New York Bagel Co, Fall River *Also Called: Ginsco Inc* **(G-8554)**

New York Bagel Co, North Dartmouth *Also Called: Ginsco Inc* **(G-10996)**

New York Graphic Society, Norwalk *Also Called: Portfolio Arts Group Ltd* **(G-2559)**

New-Com Metal Pdts Group LLC...781 767-7520
   40c Teed Dr Randolph (02368) *(G-11570)*

New-Indy Cntinerboard Hold LLC **(HQ)**.....................................**508 384-4230**
   1 Patriot Pl Foxborough (02035) *(G-8736)*

New-Indy Containerboard LLC..508 384-4230
   1 Patriot Pl Foxboro (02035) *(G-8710)*

Newark America, Fitchburg *Also Called: Caraustar Industries Inc* **(G-8648)**

Newbury Port Olive Oil, West Newbury *Also Called: Andaluna Enterprises Inc* **(G-13006)**

Newcarb, Topsfield *Also Called: New England Carbide Inc* **(G-12437)**

Newcastle Systems Inc..781 935-3450
   34 S Hunt Rd Amesbury (01913) *(G-5848)*

Newco Condenser Inc..475 882-4000
   40 Waterview Dr Shelton (06484) *(G-3039)*

Newcomb Spring Corp..860 621-0111
   235 Spring St Southington (06489) *(G-3224)*

Newcomb Springs, Southington *Also Called: Newcomb Springs Connecticut* **(G-3225)**

Newcomb Springs Connecticut..860 621-0111
   235 Spring St Southington (06489) *(G-3225)*

Newcorr Packaging Inc..508 393-9256
   66 Lyman St Northborough (01532) *(G-11103)*

Newdtc LLC...603 893-0992
   7 Industrial Way Ste 6b Salem (03079) *(G-15549)*

Newedge Signal Solutions LLC **(PA)**.......................................**978 425-5400**
   323 W Main St Ste 1 Ayer (01432) *(G-6188)*

Newell Brands Inc..413 526-5150
   301 Chestnut St East Longmeadow (01028) *(G-8388)*

Newera Services Corporation **(PA)**...**508 995-9711**
   146 Duchaine Blvd New Bedford (02745) *(G-10631)*

Newfab, Auburn *Also Called: North E Wldg & Fabrication Inc* **(G-4448)**

Newfold Dgtal Hldngs Group Inc **(HQ)**......................................**781 852-3200**
   10 Corporate Dr Ste 300 Burlington (01803) *(G-7399)*

Newhall Labs, Stamford *Also Called: Golden Sun Inc* **(G-3356)**

Newhart Products Inc...203 878-3546
   80 Collingsdale Dr Milford (06461) *(G-1854)*

Newhomesale LLC..508 541-8900
   363 E Central St Ste 2 Franklin (02038) *(G-8854)*

Newington Meat Center..860 666-3431
   847 Main St Newington (06111) *(G-2310)*

Newman Associates, Canton *Also Called: Westwood Systems Inc* **(G-7840)**

Newman Enterprises Inc...508 875-7446
   2 Southville Rd Unit C Southborough (01772) *(G-11999)*

Newman's Own Organics, Westport *Also Called: Newmans Own Inc* **(G-4190)**

Newmans Own Inc **(PA)**..**203 222-0136**
   1 Morningside Dr N Ste 1 Westport (06880) *(G-4190)*

Newmark Medical Components Inc...203 753-1158
   2670 S Main St Waterbury (06706) *(G-3951)*

Newmarket Sand & Gravel, Newmarket *Also Called: Chick Trucking Inc* **(G-15218)**

Newmont Slate Co Inc **(PA)**..**802 645-0203**
   720 Vt Route 149 West Pawlet (05775) *(G-17692)*

Newport Concrete Block Co..603 863-1540
   187 S Main St Newport (03773) *(G-15232)*

Newport Corporation..508 553-5035
   8 Forge Pkwy Ste 2 Franklin (02038) *(G-8855)*

Newport Creamery LLC...401 946-4000
   35 Sockanosset Cross Rd Cranston (02920) *(G-15900)*

Newport Electric Corporation...401 293-0527
   200 Highpoint Ave Ste B5 Portsmouth (02871) *(G-16450)*

Newport Electronics, Norwalk *Also Called: Omega Engineering Inc* **(G-2548)**

Newport Furniture Parts Corp...802 334-5428
   450 Main St Newport (05855) *(G-17402)*

Newport Harbor Shuttle, Newport *Also Called: Oldport Marine Services Inc* **(G-16220)**

Newport Jerky Company, Newport *Also Called: Newport Jerky Company LLC* **(G-16219)**

Newport Jerky Company LLC..774 644-2350
   125 Swinburne Row Newport (02840) *(G-16219)*

Newport Rocking Chair Center, Newport *Also Called: Newport Furniture Parts Corp* **(G-17402)**

Newport Sand & Gravel Co Inc...603 826-4444
   368 Springfield Rd Charlestown (03603) *(G-14065)*

Newport Sand & Gravel Co Inc **(PA)**..**603 298-0199**
   8 Reeds Mill Rd Newport (03773) *(G-15233)*

Newport Sand & Gravel Co Inc...603 298-8777
   301 Plainfield Rd West Lebanon (03784) *(G-15686)*

Newport Sand & Gravel Co Inc...802 334-2000
   2014 Alderbrook Rd Newport (05855) *(G-17403)*

Newport Sand & Gravel Co Inc...802 868-4119
   1st St Swanton (05488) *(G-17638)*

Newport Sand and Gravel, Newport *Also Called: Carroll Concrete Co Inc* **(G-15226)**

Newport Tool & Die Inc.. 401 847-6711
  1219 Aquidneck Ave Middletown (02842) *(G-16181)*

Newport Vineyards, Middletown *Also Called: Newport Vineyards & Winery LLC (G-16182)*

Newport Vineyards & Winery LLC............................... 401 848-5161
  909 E Main Rd Middletown (02842) *(G-16182)*

Newprint Offset Inc.. 781 891-6002
  405 Waltham St Lexington (02421) *(G-9765)*

Newpro Designs Inc.. 781 762-4477
  90 Kerry Pl Ste 5 Norwood (02062) *(G-11200)*

Newpro Mfg, Bellingham *Also Called: Newpro Operating LLC (G-6298)*

Newpro Operating LLC.. 781 933-4100
  26 Williams Way Bellingham (02019) *(G-6298)*

News & Sentinel Inc.. 603 237-5501
  6 Bridge St Colebrook (03576) *(G-14107)*

News 12 Connecticut LLC.. 203 849-1321
  28 Cross St Norwalk (06851) *(G-2545)*

News America, Wilton *Also Called: 21st Century Fox America Inc (G-4228)*

Newspaper Space Buyers LLC.................................... 203 967-6452
  1 Station Pl Ste 5 Stamford (06902) *(G-3417)*

Newspapers New Hampshire Inc **(HQ)**...................... **603 224-5301**
  1 Monitor Dr Concord (03301) *(G-14149)*

Newspapers New Hampshire Inc................................. 603 924-7172
  20 Grove St Peterborough (03458) *(G-15321)*

Newsshop of Portsmouth LLC..................................... 603 431-5665
  50 Fox Run Rd Ste 55 Newington (03801) *(G-15208)*

Newstress Inc... 603 736-9000
  1640 Dover Rd Epsom (03234) *(G-14281)*

Newton, Natick *Also Called: Newton Distributing Co Inc (G-10488)*

Newton Design Center, Newton *Also Called: National Lumber Company (G-10770)*

Newton Distributing Co Inc... 617 969-4002
  245 W Central St Natick (01760) *(G-10488)*

Newton Materion Inc **(HQ)**....................................... **617 630-5800**
  45 Industrial Pl Newton (02461) *(G-10772)*

Nexcelom Bioscience LLC **(HQ)**............................... **978 327-5340**
  360 Merrimack St Ste 47 Lawrence (01843) *(G-9588)*

Next Generation Vending LLC..................................... 781 828-2345
  800 Technology Center Dr Ste 1a Stoughton (02072) *(G-12226)*

Next Step Bnics Prsthetics Inc **(PA)**......................... **603 668-3831**
  155 Dow St Ste 200 Manchester (03101) *(G-14901)*

Nextek LLC... 978 486-0582
  101 Billerica Ave Bldg 5 North Billerica (01862) *(G-10939)*

Nextgen Adhesive, Burlington *Also Called: Ngac LLC (G-7400)*

Nexthink Inc... 617 861-8257
  501 Boylston St Ste 4102 Boston (02116) *(G-6921)*

Nextmove Technologies LLC....................................... 603 654-1280
  1 Kerk St Hollis (03049) *(G-14455)*

Nextphase Medical Devices LLC **(PA)**....................... **201 968-9400**
  88 Airport Dr Rochester (03867) *(G-15487)*

Nextphase Medical Devices LLC................................. 603 332-8900
  88 Airport Dr Rochester (03867) *(G-15488)*

Nextpoint Therapeutics Inc... 917 208-0865
  238 Main St Ste 5 Cambridge (02142) *(G-7666)*

Nexus Energyguide, Wellesley *Also Called: Aclara Software Inc (G-12933)*

Nexus Technology Inc.. 877 595-8116
  78 Northeastern Blvd Ste 2 Nashua (03062) *(G-15140)*

Nexvac Inc **(PA)**.. **603 887-0015**
  56 Giordani Ln Sandown (03873) *(G-15580)*

Nexvue Information Systems Inc.................................. 203 327-0800
  65 Broad St Stamford (06901) *(G-3418)*

Nexx, Billerica *Also Called: Asmpt Nexx Inc (G-6406)*

Nfa Corp.. 401 333-8990
  50 Martin St Cumberland (02864) *(G-15952)*

Nfa Corp.. 401 333-8990
  50 Martin St Cumberland (02864) *(G-15953)*

Nfa Corp.. 401 333-8947
  50 Martin St Cumberland (02864) *(G-15954)*

Nfa Corp.. 401 333-8990
  50 Martin St Cumberland (02864) *(G-15955)*

Nfall Corp.. 978 615-4030
  10 Andrews Pkwy Devens (01434) *(G-8282)*

Nfi LLC.. 508 998-9021
  22 Logan St Unit 1 New Bedford (02740) *(G-10632)*

Ngac LLC... 781 258-0008
  25 B St Burlington (01803) *(G-7400)*

Ngc Inc **(PA)**... **401 789-2200**
  45 State St Narragansett (02882) *(G-16192)*

NH Learning Solutions Corp....................................... 781 224-1113
  600 W Cummings Park Ste 2250 Woburn (01801) *(G-13624)*

NH Rapid Machining LLC... 603 821-5200
  22 Charron Ave Nashua (03063) *(G-15141)*

NH Steel Fabricators... 603 213-6357
  44 Christian Hill Rd Amherst (03031) *(G-13882)*

Nhi Mechanical Motion LLC.. 603 448-1090
  35 Connecticut River Bend Rd Claremont (03743) *(G-14095)*

Nhrc LLC... 603 485-2248
  415 4th Range Rd Pembroke (03275) *(G-15305)*

Nhs Print, Franklin *Also Called: Newhomesale LLC (G-8854)*

Nhv America Inc... 978 682-4900
  100 Griffin Brook Dr Methuen (01844) *(G-10341)*

Niagara Bottling LLC... 909 226-7353
  380 Woodland Ave Bloomfield (06002) *(G-196)*

Niantic Seal Inc.. 401 334-6870
  17 Powder Hill Rd Lincoln (02865) *(G-16150)*

Niantic Seal Nrtheast Rbr Pdts, Lincoln *Also Called: Niantic Seal Inc (G-16150)*

Nibr, Cambridge *Also Called: Novartis Insttttes For Bmdcal R (G-7668)*

Nibr Novartis, Cambridge *Also Called: Novartis Corporation (G-7667)*

Niche Inc... 508 990-4202
  84 Gifford St New Bedford (02744) *(G-10633)*

Nicholas Ieronimo... 508 947-5363
  459 Wareham St Middleboro (02346) *(G-10369)*

Nichols Candies Inc.. 978 283-9850
  1 Crafts Rd Gloucester (01930) *(G-8946)*

Nichols Portland LLC **(PA)**...................................... **207 774-6121**
  2400 Congress St Portland (04102) *(G-5251)*

Nichols Woodworking LLC.. 860 350-4223
  Washington Depot (06794) *(G-3877)*

Nickel Corporaxion... 401 351-6555
  836 Hope St Providence (02906) *(G-16575)*

Nicks Enterprises Inc **(PA)**..................................... **203 287-9990**
  2951 State St Hamden (06517) *(G-1447)*

Nickson Industries Inc... 860 747-1671
  336 Woodford Ave Plainville (06062) *(G-2774)*

Nicolock Paving Stones Ne, North Haven *Also Called: Nicolock Paving Stones Ne LLC (G-2428)*

Nicolock Paving Stones Ne LLC.................................. 203 234-2800
  99 Stoddard Ave North Haven (06473) *(G-2428)*

Nicols Brothers Inc... 207 364-7032
  29 Industrial Park Rd Rumford (04276) *(G-5361)*

Nicols Brothers Logging Inc.. 207 364-8685
  197 Poplar Hill Rd Mexico (04257) *(G-5058)*

Nidalo F & B LLC... 401 596-9559
  87 Oak St Westerly (02891) *(G-16940)*

Nidec America Corporation **(HQ)**.............................. **781 848-0970**
  50 Braintree Hill Park Ste 110 Braintree (02184) *(G-7196)*

Niem Holdings Inc.. 203 267-1510
  569 Lake Winnemaug Rd Watertown (06795) *(G-4020)*

Nif Inc.. 207 368-4344
  445 Elm St Newport (04953) *(G-5097)*

Nikel Precision Group LLC... 207 282-6080
  19 Mill Brook Rd Saco (04072) *(G-5375)*

Niko Us LLC.. 401 683-7525
  300 Highpoint Ave Ste 1b Portsmouth (02871) *(G-16451)*

Nim-Cor Inc... 603 889-2153
  575 Amherst St Nashua (03063) *(G-15142)*

Nimbus, Boston *Also Called: Nimbus Lakshmi Inc (G-6922)*

Nimbus Lakshmi Inc.. 857 999-2009
  22 Boston Wharf Rd Boston (02210) *(G-6922)*

Nine Dragons Paper - Rumford, Rumford *Also Called: ND Paper Inc (G-5359)*

Nippon American Limited.. 401 885-7353
  3 Cedar Rock Mdws East Greenwich (02818) *(G-15992)*

Nira Skin, Danvers *Also Called: Dermal Photonics Corporation (G-8180)*

Nissha Medical Technologies, Wolcott *Also Called: Sequel Special Products LLC (G-4377)*

Nissha Mtllizing Solutions Ltd..................................... 508 541-7700
  24 National Dr Forge Park Franklin (02038) *(G-8856)*

Nissin Ion Equipment Usa Inc.............................. 978 362-2590
   34 Sullivan Rd North Billerica (01862) *(G-10940)*

Nitch To Stitch LLC... 203 948-9921
   419 Federal Rd Brookfield (06804) *(G-531)*

Nitro Trailers, Pittsfield *Also Called: Innovative Specialties LLC (G-5160)*

Nitrofreeze Cryogenic Services, Worcester *Also Called: Cryogenic Institute Neng Inc (G-13712)*

Nitromed Inc... 781 274-1248
   125 Spring St Lexington (02421) *(G-9766)*

Nitrosecurity Inc **(DH)**................................. **603 766-8160**
   230 Commerce Way Ste 325 Portsmouth (03801) *(G-15426)*

Nitto Denko Avecia Inc **(DH)**........................ **508 532-2500**
   125 Fortune Blvd Milford (01757) *(G-10408)*

Nixie Sparkling Water Inc.................................. 617 784-8671
   149 Cross St Chatham (02633) *(G-7899)*

Nixon Company Incorporated............................. 413 543-3701
   161 Main St Indian Orchard (01151) *(G-9472)*

Njm Packaging, Lebanon *Also Called: Njm Packaging LLC (G-14697)*

Njm Packaging LLC **(DH)**............................. **603 448-0300**
   77 Bank St Lebanon (03766) *(G-14697)*

Nkt Photonics Inc **(DH)**............................... **503 444-8404**
   23 Drydock Ave Ste 23-410e Boston (02210) *(G-6923)*

Nle, Monroe *Also Called: Northeast Laser Engraving Inc (G-1918)*

Nmc Solar LLC.. 401 762-9700
   100 Providence Pike North Smithfield (02896) *(G-16330)*

Nmg, Plaistow *Also Called: Plaistow Cabinet Co Inc (G-15348)*

Nmi, Wellesley *Also Called: Nemucore Med Innovations Inc (G-12944)*

Nmw Holding Co Inc... 617 269-5650
   250 West St Weymouth (02188) *(G-13332)*

Nn Inc... 203 793-7132
   6 Northrop Industrial Park Rd W Wallingford (06492) *(G-3835)*

Nn Inc... 508 406-2100
   111 Forbes Blvd Ste 101 Mansfield (02048) *(G-10070)*

Nn Inc... 508 695-7700
   262 Broad St North Attleboro (02760) *(G-10880)*

Nni Liquidation Corp... 203 929-2221
   7 Progress Dr Shelton (06484) *(G-3040)*

Nntechnology Moore Systems LLC..................... 203 366-3224
   800 Union Ave Bridgeport (06607) *(G-352)*

No Limits Metal Works, Laconia *Also Called: Shawn Dudek (G-14669)*

Noble Metal Services, Cranston *Also Called: Noble Metals Services Inc (G-15901)*

Noble Metals Services Inc................................. 866 695-4806
   10 Ross Simons Dr Cranston (02920) *(G-15901)*

Noble Tree LLC.. 978 590-5101
   37 Glen Forest Dr Boxford (01921) *(G-7161)*

Nocion Therapeutics Inc.................................... 781 812-6176
   100 Beaver St Ste 301 Waltham (02453) *(G-12737)*

Noeveon Inc.. 978 642-5004
   207 Lowell St Wilmington (01887) *(G-13439)*

Nofet LLC.. 203 848-9064
   227 Church St Apt 5j New Haven (06510) *(G-2180)*

Nokia of America Corporation............................ 978 952-1616
   1 Robbins Rd Westford (01886) *(G-13256)*

Nokona USA Baseball.. 508 309-3527
   60 Pleasant St Ashland (01721) *(G-5964)*

Nolato Gw Inc **(HQ)**................................... **802 234-9941**
   239 Pleasant St Bethel (05032) *(G-17060)*

Nolato Gw Inc.. 802 763-2194
   272 Waterman Rd South Royalton (05068) *(G-17612)*

Nomad Communications Inc............................... 802 649-1995
   2456 Christian St Ste 101 White River Junction (05001) *(G-17709)*

Nonesuch River Brewing LLC............................. 207 219-8948
   201 Gorham Rd Scarborough (04074) *(G-5440)*

Nonwovens Inc... 978 251-8612
   100 Wotton St North Chelmsford (01863) *(G-10985)*

Noodle Revolution, Westerly *Also Called: Nidalo F & B LLC (G-16940)*

Nops Metal Works... 802 382-9300
   1479 Route 7 S Middlebury (05753) *(G-17347)*

Nora Systems Inc **(DH)**............................... **603 894-1021**
   9 Northeastern Blvd Salem (03079) *(G-15550)*

Norad, North Kingstown *Also Called: North Atlantic Dist Inc (G-16274)*

Norade Inc **(DH)**.. **413 533-7159**
   100 Appleton St Holyoke (01040) *(G-9271)*

Noramco Coventry LLC...................................... 401 623-1174
   498 Washington St Coventry (02816) *(G-15818)*

Norco, Framingham *Also Called: Greentree Marketing Inc (G-8775)*

Norcross Safety Products LLC............................ 800 430-5490
   900 Douglas Pike Smithfield (02917) *(G-16724)*

Nordex, Brookfield *Also Called: Nordex Incorporated (G-532)*

Nordex Incorporated.. 203 775-4877
   426 Federal Rd Brookfield (06804) *(G-532)*

Nordic American Smokeless Inc.......................... 203 207-9977
   100 Mill Plain Rd Ste 115 Danbury (06811) *(G-790)*

Nordson Efd LLC.. 860 889-3383
   10 Connecticut Ave Norwich (06360) *(G-2610)*

Nordson Efd LLC **(HQ)**................................ **401 431-7000**
   40 Catamore Blvd East Providence (02914) *(G-16034)*

Nordson Medical (nh) Inc **(HQ)**.................... **603 327-0600**
   29 Northwestern Dr Salem (03079) *(G-15551)*

Noremac Manufacturing, Westborough *Also Called: Noremac Manufacturing Corp (G-13124)*

Noremac Manufacturing Corp............................. 508 366-8822
   62 Hopkinton Rd Westborough (01581) *(G-13124)*

Norfield Data Products Inc................................. 203 849-0292
   181 Main St Ste 2 Norwalk (06851) *(G-2546)*

Norfolk Asphalt Paving Inc................................. 617 293-9775
   1010 Turnpike St Canton (02021) *(G-7813)*

Norfolk Corporation... 781 319-0400
   145 Enterprise Dr Marshfield (02050) *(G-10242)*

Norgaard Machine Inc....................................... 413 789-1291
   370 Garden St Feeding Hills (01030) *(G-8636)*

Norgren, Farmington *Also Called: Kip Inc (G-1227)*

Norgren LLC.. 860 677-0272
   72 Spring Ln Farmington (06032) *(G-1232)*

Norking Company Inc.. 508 222-3100
   53 County St Attleboro (02703) *(G-6043)*

Norm Brown Logging... 802 537-4474
   240 Hulett Hill Rd Benson (05743) *(G-17058)*

Norman White Inc... 207 636-1636
   28 Grant Rd Shapleigh (04076) *(G-5458)*

Norpaco Gourmet Foods, Middletown *Also Called: Norpaco Inc (G-1768)*

Norpaco Inc... 860 632-2299
   80 Bysiewicz Dr Middletown (06457) *(G-1768)*

Norpin Mfg Co Inc.. 413 599-1628
   2342 Boston Rd Wilbraham (01095) *(G-13362)*

Nortek Inc... 413 781-4777
   70 Doty Cir West Springfield (01089) *(G-13038)*

Nortekusa Inc.. 617 206-5755
   21 Drydock Ave Ste 740e Boston (02210) *(G-6924)*

North Amercn Spring Tl Co Div, Berlin *Also Called: All Five Tool Co Inc (G-48)*

North American Chemical Co.............................. 978 687-9500
   19 S Canal St Ste 2 Lawrence (01843) *(G-9589)*

North American Coating Sciences Inc.................. 978 691-5622
   12 Osgood St Lawrence (01843) *(G-9590)*

North American Elev Svcs Co **(DH)**.............. **860 676-6000**
   1 Farm Springs Rd Farmington (06032) *(G-1233)*

North American Kelp, Waldoboro *Also Called: Atlantic Laboratories Inc (G-5574)*

North American Plastics Ltd............................... 603 644-1660
   349 East Industrial Park Dr Manchester (03109) *(G-14902)*

North American Supaflu Systems........................ 207 883-1155
   15 Holly St Ste 201b Scarborough (04074) *(G-5441)*

North American Technical Svcs, Middletown *Also Called: Nats USA Incorporated (G-1767)*

North American Tool & Mch Corp........................ 508 248-9862
   278 Southbridge Rd Charlton (01507) *(G-7894)*

North Amrcn Fltration Mass Inc.......................... 508 660-9016
   23 Walpole Park S Ste 12 Walpole (02081) *(G-12570)*

North Atlantic Inc... 207 774-6025
   2 Portland Fish Pier Ste 308 Portland (04101) *(G-5252)*

North Atlantic Corp... 508 235-4830
   1255 Grand Army Hwy Somerset (02726) *(G-11854)*

North Atlantic Dist Inc....................................... 401 667-7000
   100 Tidal Dr North Kingstown (02852) *(G-16274)*

North Atlantic PCF Seafood LLC......................... 401 969-3886
   8 Treetops Ln Danvers (01923) *(G-8213)*

North Attleboro Jewelry Co Inc.............................508 222-4660
　112 Bank St Attleboro (02703) *(G-6044)*

North Barre Granite, Websterville *Also Called: Adams Granite Co Inc (G-17683)*

North Chelmsford Digital, North Chelmsford *Also Called: Lsc Communications Inc (G-10982)*

North Coast Sea-Foods Corp **(PA)**..................**617 345-4400**
　5 Drydock Ave Boston (02210) *(G-6925)*

North Country Engineering Inc................................802 766-5396
　106 John Taplin Rd Derby (05829) *(G-17212)*

North Country Smokehouse, Claremont *Also Called: Butcher Block Inc (G-14080)*

North Country Tractor Inc......................................207 324-5646
　8 Shaws Ridge Rd Sanford (04073) *(G-5403)*

North Country Tractor Inc......................................603 742-5488
　10 Littleworth Rd Dover (03820) *(G-14241)*

North Country Wind Bells Inc.................................207 677-2224
　544 State Route 32 Round Pond (04564) *(G-5353)*

North E Wldg & Fabrication Inc...............................207 786-2446
　928 Minot Ave Auburn (04210) *(G-4448)*

North East Cutting Die, Dover *Also Called: North East Cutting Die Corp (G-14242)*

North East Cutting Die Corp...................................603 436-8952
　29 Industrial Park Dover (03820) *(G-14242)*

North East Indus Coatings Inc................................978 356-1200
　9 Old Right Rd Unit C Ipswich (01938) *(G-9492)*

North East Knitting Inc..401 727-0500
　179 Conant St Pawtucket (02860) *(G-16395)*

North East Materials Group LLC..............................802 479-7004
　751 Graniteville Rd Graniteville (05654) *(G-17276)*

North East Precision Inc..802 748-1440
　3606 Memorial Dr Saint Johnsbury (05819) *(G-17546)*

North East Products, Dover *Also Called: New England Innovations Corp (G-14240)*

North East Silicon Tech Inc....................................508 999-2001
　11 David St New Bedford (02744) *(G-10634)*

North Eastern Publishing Co...................................802 447-7567
　425 Main St Bennington (05201) *(G-17053)*

North Easton Machine Co Inc..................................508 238-6219
　218 Elm St North Easton (02356) *(G-11011)*

North End Composites LLC.....................................207 594-8427
　23 Merrill Dr Rockland (04841) *(G-5340)*

North Hartland Tool Corp **(PA)**..........................**802 295-3196**
　14 Evarts Rd North Hartland (05052) *(G-17420)*

NORTH PENN TECHNOLOGY INC.............................603 893-9900
　1050 Perimeter Rd Manchester (03103) *(G-14903)*

North Ridge Contracting Inc...................................603 942-6104
　14 Jug City Rd Epsom (03234) *(G-14282)*

North River Graphics Inc..781 826-6866
　100 Corporate Park Dr Ste 1730 Pembroke (02359) *(G-11375)*

North Safety Products, Cranston *Also Called: North Safety Products LLC (G-15902)*

North Safety Products, Smithfield *Also Called: Honeywell Safety Pdts USA Inc (G-16713)*

North Safety Products LLC......................................401 943-4400
　2000 Plainfield Pike Cranston (02921) *(G-15902)*

North Sails Group LLC **(DH)**...............................**203 874-7548**
　837 Seaview Ave Ste A Bridgeport (06607) *(G-353)*

North Sales Rhode Island, Portsmouth *Also Called: Rhode Northsales Island Inc (G-16455)*

North Shore Jewish Press Ltd.................................978 745-4111
　121 Loring Ave Salem (01970) *(G-11727)*

North Shore Laboratories Corp...............................978 531-5954
　44 Endicott St Peabody (01960) *(G-11327)*

North Shore Marble & Granite, Danvers *Also Called: Steven Tedesco (G-8222)*

North Shore News Company Inc **(PA)**..................**781 592-1300**
　90 Forest St Peabody (01960) *(G-11328)*

North Shore Press Inc..781 662-6757
　6 Eastman Pl Ste 104 Melrose (02176) *(G-10317)*

North Shore Steel Co Inc **(PA)**............................**781 598-1645**
　16 Oakville St Lynn (01905) *(G-9988)*

North Star Distributors Inc **(PA)**..........................**508 693-2000**
　294 State Rd Vineyard Haven (02568) *(G-12494)*

North Taste, Plymouth *Also Called: Northice (G-11469)*

North Technology Group, Bridgeport *Also Called: North Sails Group LLC (G-353)*

North Tecom LLC..603 851-5165
　1120 Bodwell Rd Manchester (03109) *(G-14904)*

North-East Fasteners Corp.....................................860 589-3242
　8 Tremco Dr Terryville (06786) *(G-3607)*

Northampton Machine Co Inc.................................413 529-2530
　16 Industrial Pkwy Easthampton (01027) *(G-8455)*

Northast Cab Cntrtop Dstrs Inc..............................617 296-2100
　140 Campanelli Dr Ste 1 Braintree (02184) *(G-7197)*

Northast Dcment Cnsrvtion Ctr...............................978 470-1010
　100 Brickstone Sq Ste 401 Andover (01810) *(G-5901)*

Northastern Communications Inc............................203 381-9008
　255 Hathaway Dr Ste 3 Stratford (06615) *(G-3558)*

Northeast, Milford *Also Called: Northeast Electronics Corp (G-1855)*

NORTHEAST BIG BUCK CLUB, Paxton *Also Called: Northeast Outdoors Inc (G-11290)*

Northeast Buffinton Group Inc.................................401 434-1107
　25 Woodruff Rd Walpole (02081) *(G-12571)*

Northeast Chemicals Inc..508 634-6900
　11 Princess Pine Ln Milford (01757) *(G-10409)*

Northeast Circuit Tech LLC.....................................860 633-1967
　112 Sherwood Dr Glastonbury (06033) *(G-1291)*

Northeast Coating Tech Inc....................................207 985-3232
　105 York St Kennebunk (04043) *(G-4927)*

Northeast Coffee Company, Skowhegan *Also Called: Northeast Merchandising Corp (G-5476)*

Northeast Companies Inc **(PA)**............................**203 630-9675**
　250 Pomeroy Ave Meriden (06450) *(G-1680)*

Northeast Doran Inc..207 474-2000
　North Ave Industrial Park Skowhegan (04976) *(G-5475)*

Northeast Earth Mechanics LLC..............................603 435-7989
　159 Barnstead Rd Pittsfield (03263) *(G-15334)*

Northeast Electronics Corp.....................................203 878-3511
　455 Bic Dr Milford (06461) *(G-1855)*

Northeast Equipment Inc..508 324-0083
　44 Probber Ln Fall River (02720) *(G-8588)*

Northeast Foods Inc..860 779-1117
　328 Lake Rd Dayville (06241) *(G-864)*

Northeast Hot-Fill Co-Op Inc..................................978 772-9287
　25 Copeland Dr Ayer (01432) *(G-6189)*

Northeast Industrial Tech Inc..................................617 360-7220
　39 Merrimack St Lawrence (01843) *(G-9591)*

Northeast Innovations Inc......................................603 226-4000
　145 Sheep Davis Rd Pembroke (03275) *(G-15306)*

Northeast Knitting Mills Inc **(PA)**.........................**508 678-7553**
　69 Alden St Fall River (02723) *(G-8589)*

Northeast Laboratory Svcs Inc **(PA)**.....................**207 873-7711**
　227 China Rd Winslow (04901) *(G-5686)*

Northeast Laser Engraving Inc................................203 268-7238
　246 C Main St Rte 25 Monroe (06468) *(G-1918)*

Northeast Ldscpg Tree Svcs Inc..............................860 405-5274
　128 Oak St Westerly (02891) *(G-16941)*

Northeast Manufacturing Co Inc.............................781 438-3022
　35 Spencer St Stoneham (02180) *(G-12183)*

Northeast Merchandising Corp................................207 474-3321
　60 Southgate Pkwy Skowhegan (04976) *(G-5476)*

Northeast Metals Tech LLC....................................978 948-2633
　289 Newburyport Tpke Rowley (01969) *(G-11682)*

Northeast Mill Work Inc...207 655-1202
　22 Industrial Way Casco (04015) *(G-4682)*

Northeast Outdoors Inc...508 752-8762
　390 Marshall St Paxton (01612) *(G-11290)*

Northeast Overhaul and Repair, Berlin *Also Called: Budney Industries Inc (G-55)*

Northeast Packaging Co **(PA)**.............................**207 764-6271**
　875 Skyway St Presque Isle (04769) *(G-5305)*

Northeast Patients Group.......................................855 848-6740
　29 Western Ave South Portland (04106) *(G-5509)*

Northeast Pellets LLC..207 435-6230
　53 Realty Rd Ashland (04732) *(G-4412)*

Northeast Plastics Inc..781 245-5512
　5 Del Carmine St Wakefield (01880) *(G-12523)*

Northeast Products, Peterborough *Also Called: Lucci Corp (G-15317)*

Northeast Publishing Company................................207 496-3251
　159 Bennett Dr Caribou (04736) *(G-4677)*

Northeast Publishing Company................................207 564-8355
　12 E Main St Ste A Dover Foxcroft (04426) *(G-4730)*

Northeast Publishing Company................................207 532-2281
　23 Court St Houlton (04730) *(G-4903)*

Northeast Publishing Company.. 207 768-5431
40 North St Ste 2 Presque Isle (04769) (G-5306)

Northeast Publishing Company (HQ).................................. **207 764-4471**
260 Missile St Presque Isle (04769) (G-5307)

Northeast Publishing Company.. 207 764-4471
260 Missile St Presque Isle (04769) (G-5308)

Northeast Reprographics, Bangor Also Called: Central Street Corporation (G-4495)

Northeast Reprographics, Bangor Also Called: Print Bangor (G-4515)

Northeast Sand & Gravel.. 603 213-6133
1637 Osgood St North Andover (01845) (G-10845)

Northeast Sand and Gravel LLC.. 603 305-9429
1 Harwich Ct Merrimack (03054) (G-14995)

Northeast Screen Graphics, East Longmeadow Also Called: Industrial Etching Inc (G-8380)

Northeast Sealcoat, Millbury Also Called: Granger Lynch Corp (G-10435)

Northeast Seat Company Inc... 413 283-6236
21 Wilbraham St Palmer (01069) (G-11278)

Northeast Stainless Inc.. 781 589-9000
2350 Turnpike St Ste 3 North Andover (01845) (G-10846)

Northeast Stihl, Oxford Also Called: Stihl Incorporated (G-2712)

Northeast Structures Barns LLC.. 207 512-0503
202 Colcord Pond Rd Porter (04068) (G-5167)

Northeast Thermography, Wallingford Also Called: E & A Enterprises Inc (G-3802)

Northeast Tire Service Inc.. 603 524-7973
174 Daniel Webster Hwy Belmont (03220) (G-13965)

Northeast Treaters Inc (HQ)... **413 323-7811**
201 Springfield Rd Belchertown (01007) (G-6281)

Northeast Wood Products, Pownal Also Called: N W P Inc (G-17455)

Northeast Wood Products LLC.. 860 862-6350
13 Crow Hill Rd Uncasville (06382) (G-3742)

Northeast Woodworking Pdts Inc... 603 895-4271
24 Old Manchester Rd Raymond (03077) (G-15454)

Northeastern Heating & Vent, Williston Also Called: Northeastern Htg Vent AC Corp (G-17743)

Northeastern Htg Vent AC Corp.. 802 865-8008
32 Boyer Cir Williston (05495) (G-17743)

Northeastern Metals LLC.. 800 506-7090
322 Wells St Greenfield (01301) (G-8997)

Northeastern Metals Corp.. 203 348-8088
130 Lenox Ave Ste 23 Stamford (06906) (G-3419)

Northeastern Nonwovens Inc.. 603 332-5900
7 Amarosa Dr Unit 3 Rochester (03868) (G-15489)

Northeastern Shaped Wire Inc.. 860 621-8991
411 N Main St Southington (06489) (G-3226)

Northeastern Sheet Metal Inc... 603 497-4166
31 Depot St Goffstown (03045) (G-14355)

Northern Design Precast Inc.. 603 783-8989
51 International Dr Loudon (03307) (G-14796)

Northern Elastomeric Inc... 603 778-8899
61 Pine Rd Brentwood (03833) (G-14025)

Northern Fbrction Slutions LLC... 603 539-4333
235 Ossipee Lake Rd Tamworth (03886) (G-15647)

Northern Light, Biddeford Also Called: Beacon Press Inc (G-4557)

Northern Light Mar Group Inc... 978 526-7911
17 Ashland Ave Manchester (01944) (G-10033)

Northern Lights Inc.. 978 258-7412
15 Aegean Dr Ste 4 Methuen (01844) (G-10342)

Northern Products Inc... 978 840-3383
1427 Main St Leominster (01453) (G-9687)

Northern Products Inc
153 Hamlet Ave Woonsocket (02895) (G-16969)

Northern Tier Energy LLC (DH)... **203 244-6550**
38c Grove St Ste 5 Ridgefield (06877) (G-2903)

Northern Tool Mfg Co Inc.. 413 732-5549
170 Progress Ave Springfield (01104) (G-12117)

Northern Turf Prfessionals Inc.. 207 522-8598
251 Old Portland Rd Brunswick (04011) (G-4652)

Northern VT Cnsld Pure Mple Pr, Belvidere Center Also Called: Green Mtn Maple Sug Ref Co Inc (G-17034)

Northern Wind LLC (HQ).. **508 997-0727**
16 Hassey St New Bedford (02740) (G-10635)

Northice.. 781 985-5225
624 Long Pond Rd Plymouth (02360) (G-11469)

Northlight Studio Press, Montpelier Also Called: The Leahy Press Inc (G-17375)

Northpoint Printing Svcs Inc.. 781 895-1900
18 Bonazzoli Ave Hudson (01749) (G-9396)

Northrop Grmmn Spce & Mssn Sys....................................... 207 442-5097
Bath (04530) (G-4530)

Northrop Grumman Corporation.. 860 282-4461
121 Prestige Park Cir East Hartford (06108) (G-1007)

Northrop Grumman Systems Corp....................................... 508 589-6291
65 South St Ste 105 Hopkinton (01748) (G-9337)

Northrop Grumman Systems Corp....................................... 603 886-4270
6 Chagnon Ln Hudson (03051) (G-14532)

Northrop Grumman Systems Corp....................................... 401 849-6270
88 Silva Ln Ste 3 Middletown (02842) (G-16183)

Northside Minis LLC.. 860 388-6871
27 Bellaire Dr Old Saybrook (06475) (G-2656)

Northstar, Manchester Also Called: Northstar Direct LLC (G-14905)

Northstar Direct LLC
249 Gay St Manchester (03103) (G-14905)

Northstar Pulp & Paper Co Inc.. 413 263-6000
89 Guion St Springfield (01104) (G-12118)

Northwest Confections Mass LLC... 971 666-8282
207 Daniel Shays Hwy Orange (01364) (G-11227)

Northwest Conn Mfg Co Inc... 860 379-1553
95 Beech Hill Rd Winsted (06098) (G-4352)

Northwest Woolen Mills, Woonsocket Also Called: Hyman Brickle & Son Inc (G-16964)

Northwoods Brewing Co LLC.. 603 942-6400
1334 1st Nh Tpke Northwood (03261) (G-15274)

Northwoods Publications LLC... 207 732-4880
57 Old County Rd N West Enfield (04493) (G-5610)

Northwoods Sporting Journal, West Enfield Also Called: Northwoods Publications LLC (G-5610)

Norton Door Controls, New Haven Also Called: Assa Abloy ACC Door Cntrls Gro (G-2121)

Norwalk Awning Company, Norwalk Also Called: Fitzgerald-Norwalk Awng Co Inc (G-2501)

Norwalk Compreseer Company.. 203 386-1234
1650 Stratford Ave Stratford (06615) (G-3559)

Norwalk Indus Components LLC.. 860 645-5340
135 Sheldon Rd Manchester (06042) (G-1622)

Norwalk Powdered Metals Inc... 203 338-8000
30 Moffitt St Stratford (06615) (G-3560)

Norwalk Vault Company, Oakville Also Called: Norwalk Wilbert Vault Co LLC (G-2624)

Norwalk Wilbert Vault Co LLC.. 203 366-5678
760 Frost Bridge Rd Oakville (06779) (G-2624)

Norwell Mfg Co Inc... 508 822-2831
82 Stevens St East Taunton (02718) (G-8409)

Norwich Printing Company Inc... 860 887-7468
595 W Main St Ste 2 Norwich (06360) (G-2611)

Norwix.. 860 823-3090
31 Clinton Ave Ste 2 Norwich (06360) (G-2612)

Norwix Marking Systems, Norwich Also Called: Norwix Inc (G-2612)

Norwood, Norwood Also Called: Kamweld Industries Inc (G-11185)

Norwood Bulletin, Norwood Also Called: Enterprise Newsmedia LLC (G-11172)

Norwood Sheet Metal Corp... 781 762-0720
744 Boston Providence Tpke Ste 2 Norwood (02062) (G-11201)

Notabli Inc.. 802 448-0810
209 College St Ste 3w Burlington (05401) (G-17146)

Notch Mtn Solar Inc.. 413 498-0018
158 Birnam Rd Northfield (01360) (G-11121)

Noujaim Tool Co Inc... 203 753-4441
412 Chase River Rd Waterbury (06704) (G-3952)

Nourish Deli & Bakery, Saint Albans Also Called: Nourish Llc (G-17526)

Nourish Llc.. 802 782-0012
112 N Main St Ste 5 Saint Albans (05478) (G-17526)

Nova Analytics Corporation.. 781 897-1208
100 Cummings Ctr Ste 535n Beverly (01915) (G-6368)

Nova Biomedical Corporation... 781 894-0800
39 Manning Rd Billerica (01821) (G-6463)

Nova Biomedical Corporation... 781 647-3700
4 Enterprise Rd Billerica (01821) (G-6464)

Nova Biomedical Corporation (PA)...................................... **781 894-0800**
200 Prospect St Waltham (02453) (G-12738)

Nova Machining LLC.. 860 675-8131
16 E Shore Blvd Unionville (06085) (G-3750)

Nova Metrix LLC 781 897-1200	
600 Unicorn Park Dr Ste 4 Woburn (01801) *(G-13625)*	
Nova Packaging Systems Inc 978 537-8534	
7 New Lancaster Rd Leominster (01453) *(G-9688)*	
Nova Sports Usa Inc 508 473-6540	
6 Industrial Rd Ste 2 Milford (01757) *(G-10410)*	
Novabiotics, Boston *Also Called: Novabiotics Inc (G-6926)*	
Novabiotics Inc 866 259-4527	
1 Boston Pl Boston (02108) *(G-6926)*	
Novacel, Palmer *Also Called: Novacel Inc (G-11279)*	
Novacel Inc **(DH)** **413 283-3468**	
21 3rd St Palmer (01069) *(G-11279)*	
Novagenesis LLC 781 784-1149	
77 Norwood St Sharon (02067) *(G-11794)*	
Novamont North America Inc 203 744-8801	
1000 Bridgeport Ave Ste 304 Shelton (06484) *(G-3041)*	
Novanta, Bedford *Also Called: Novanta Inc (G-6246)*	
Novanta Corporation **(HQ)** **781 266-5700**	
125 Middlesex Tpke Bedford (01730) *(G-6245)*	
Novanta Inc **(PA)** **781 266-5700**	
125 Middlesex Tpke Bedford (01730) *(G-6246)*	
Novanta Inc 781 266-5200	
125 Middlesex Tpke Bedford (01730) *(G-6247)*	
Novanta Inc 781 266-5700	
125 Middlesex Tpke Bedford (01730) *(G-6248)*	
Novanta Motion USA Inc **(HQ)** **860 295-6102**	
370 N Main St Marlborough (06447) *(G-1646)*	
Novartis Corporation 617 225-0820	
181 Massachusetts Ave Cambridge (02139) *(G-7667)*	
Novartis Instttes For Bmdcal R **(HQ)** **617 777-8276**	
700 Main St Cambridge (02139) *(G-7668)*	
Novartis Mlclar Dagnostics LLC 617 871-8441	
45 Sidney St Cambridge (02139) *(G-7669)*	
Novartis Vccnes Dagnostics Inc 617 871-7000	
350 Massachusetts Ave Ste 200 Cambridge (02139) *(G-7670)*	
Novel Beverage Co 207 798-9610	
137 Pleasant Hill Rd Scarborough (04074) *(G-5442)*	
Novel Iron Works Inc 603 436-7950	
250 Ocean Rd Greenland (03840) *(G-14369)*	
Novell Inc 781 464-8000	
404 Wyman St Ste 500 Waltham (02451) *(G-12739)*	
Novelsat Inc 617 658-1419	
25 Tanglewood Rd Newton (02459) *(G-10773)*	
Novelty Plastics, Cumberland *Also Called: Nfa Corp (G-15953)*	
Novia Corporation 603 898-8600	
1 Northwestern Dr Salem (03079) *(G-15552)*	
Novirio Pharmaceuticals Inc 617 250-3100	
60 Hampshire Cambridge (02139) *(G-7671)*	
Novo Nordisk Inc 463 209-3849	
33 Hayden Ave Lexington (02421) *(G-9767)*	
Novo Nordisk Research Center, Lexington *Also Called: Novo Nordisk Inc (G-9767)*	
Novo Nordisk US Bio Prod Inc 603 298-3169	
9 Technology Dr West Lebanon (03784) *(G-15687)*	
Novo Precision LLC 860 583-0517	
150 Dolphin Rd Bristol (06010) *(G-476)*	
Novotech Inc 978 929-9458	
916 Main St Acton (01720) *(G-5760)*	
Novotechnik US Inc 508 485-2244	
155 Northboro Rd Ste 31 Southborough (01772) *(G-12000)*	
Nowak Products Inc 860 666-9685	
8 Dean Dr Newington (06111) *(G-2311)*	
Noyes Sheet Metal 508 482-9302	
66 Sumner St Milford (01757) *(G-10411)*	
Npc Inserts, Westport *Also Called: National Publishing Co Inc (G-4188)*	
Npc Processing Inc 802 660-0496	
97 Executive Dr Shelburne (05482) *(G-17559)*	
Npi Medical, Ansonia *Also Called: Ansonia Plastics LLC (G-7)*	
Npm, Stratford *Also Called: Norwalk Powdered Metals Inc (G-3560)*	
NPS Media Group, Shelton *Also Called: National Publisher Svcs LLC (G-3035)*	
Nq Industries Inc 860 258-3466	
850 Sherman Ave Hamden (06514) *(G-1448)*	

NRG Connecticut LLC 860 231-2424	
36 Woodland St Ste 1 Hartford (06105) *(G-1497)*	
NRG Systems Inc 802 482-2255	
110 Riggs Rd Hinesburg (05461) *(G-17297)*	
Nrt Inc 508 533-4588	
74 Main St Unit 16 Medway (02053) *(G-10309)*	
NSA Industries L.L.C., Groveton *Also Called: Nsa Industries LLC (G-14377)*	
Nsa Industries LLC 802 748-5007	
48 Mechanic St Groveton (03582) *(G-14377)*	
Nsd Metal Fabrication Inc 978 346-0045	
51 E Main St Merrimac (01860) *(G-10326)*	
Nsd Seafood Inc **(PA)** **978 282-7880**	
159 E Main St Gloucester (01930) *(G-8947)*	
Nsight Inc 781 273-6300	
300 Brickstone Sq Ste 201 Andover (01810) *(G-5902)*	
NSK Steering Systems Amer Inc 802 442-5448	
110 Shields Dr Bennington (05201) *(G-17054)*	
Nssa, Bennington Plant, Bennington *Also Called: NSK Steering Systems Amer Inc (G-17054)*	
Ntension Corp 207 848-7700	
18 White Pine Rd Hermon (04401) *(G-4887)*	
Ntp Software of Ca Inc **(PA)** **603 641-6937**	
427 Amherst St Nashua (03063) *(G-15143)*	
Ntp/Republic Clear Thru Corp 413 493-6800	
475 Canal St Holyoke (01040) *(G-9272)*	
Ntt Data Inc 877 532-6312	
1099 Hingman St Rockland (02370) *(G-11654)*	
NTT Data Inc., Rockland *Also Called: Ntt Data Inc (G-11654)*	
Ntt Data Intl Svcs Inc **(DH)** **800 745-3263**	
100 City Sq Boston (02129) *(G-6927)*	
Nu Chocolat LLC 802 735-7770	
180 Battery St Ste 110 Burlington (05401) *(G-17147)*	
Nu Chrome Corp 508 557-1418	
32 Industrial Ct Seekonk (02771) *(G-11782)*	
Nu-Cast Inc 603 432-1600	
29 Grenier Field Rd Londonderry (03053) *(G-14777)*	
Nu-Lustre, Providence *Also Called: Nu-Lustre Finishing Corp (G-16576)*	
Nu-Lustre Finishing Corp 401 521-7800	
1 Magnolia St Providence (02909) *(G-16576)*	
Nu-Stone Mfg & Distrg LLC 860 564-6555	
160 Sterling Rd Sterling (06377) *(G-3503)*	
Nu-Truss Inc 413 562-3861	
52 Steiger Dr Westfield (01085) *(G-13193)*	
Nuance, Burlington *Also Called: Nuance Communications Inc (G-7401)*	
Nuance Communications Inc **(HQ)** **781 565-5000**	
1 Wayside Rd Burlington (01803) *(G-7401)*	
Nuance Hlthcare Dgnstics Slton 404 575-4222	
1 Wayside Rd Burlington (01803) *(G-7402)*	
Nucap US Inc **(DH)** **203 879-1423**	
238 Wolcott Rd Wolcott (06716) *(G-4371)*	
Nucedar Mills, Chicopee *Also Called: Jain America Foods Inc (G-8041)*	
Nucor Bar Mill Group, Wallingford *Also Called: Nucor Steel Connecticut Inc (G-3836)*	
Nucor Grating 724 934-5320	
55 Sumner St Milford (01757) *(G-10412)*	
Nucor Hrris Rbar Northeast LLC 860 282-1860	
30 Talbot Ln South Windsor (06074) *(G-3166)*	
Nucor Hrris Rbar Northeast LLC 413 665-2381	
73 Old State Rd South Deerfield (01373) *(G-11925)*	
Nucor Hrris Rbar Northeast LLC 413 568-7803	
287 Lockhouse Rd Westfield (01085) *(G-13194)*	
Nucor Hrris Rbar Northeast LLC 603 632-5222	
450 Us Route 4 Canaan (03741) *(G-14047)*	
Nucor Hrris Rbar Northeast LLC 401 724-9200	
30 Lockbridge St Pawtucket (02860) *(G-16396)*	
Nucor Steel Connecticut Inc 203 265-0615	
35 Toelles Rd Wallingford (06492) *(G-3836)*	
Nudd Cabinetry 603 286-3160	
133 March Rd Sanbornton (03269) *(G-15577)*	
Nudd Carpentry, Sanbornton *Also Called: Nudd Cabinetry (G-15577)*	
Nufern 860 408-5000	
7 Airport Park Rd East Granby (06026) *(G-945)*	
Nufern, East Granby *Also Called: Nufern (G-945)*	

Nuforj LLC.. 413 530-0349
  1350 Main St Springfield (01103) *(G-12119)*

Nuimage Awnings, Auburn *Also Called: Futureguard Building Pdts Inc (G-4434)*

Numa Tool Company **(PA)**.. **860 923-9551**
  646 Thompson Rd Thompson (06277) *(G-3652)*

Numaco Packaging LLC.. 401 438-4952
  82 Boyd Ave East Providence (02914) *(G-16035)*

Numark International Inc.. 954 761-7550
  200 Scenic View Dr Cumberland (02864) *(G-15956)*

Numark Sound, Cumberland *Also Called: Numark International Inc (G-15956)*

Numberall Stamp & Tool Co.. 207 876-3541
  1 High St Sangerville (04479) *(G-5420)*

Numeric Inc... 413 732-6544
  321 Munger Hill Rd Westfield (01085) *(G-13195)*

Numeric Machining Company, Westfield *Also Called: Numeric Inc (G-13195)*

Numerical Control Technology, Colchester *Also Called: N C T Inc (G-662)*

Numet Machining Techniques LLC............................. 203 375-4995
  235 Edison Rd Orange (06477) *(G-2679)*

Nummy LLC... 608 801-9850
  1160 New Britain Ave West Hartford (06110) *(G-4075)*

Numotion... 401 681-2153
  300 Myles Standish Blvd Ste 2 Taunton (02780) *(G-12353)*

Numotion, Rocky Hill *Also Called: United Seating & Mobility LLC (G-2940)*

Nuovo Pasta Productions Ltd.................................... 203 380-4090
  1330 Honeyspot Road Ext Stratford (06615) *(G-3561)*

Nursery Supplies Inc... 207 625-9373
  18 High Rd Cornish (04020) *(G-4706)*

Nustar, Stamford *Also Called: CPI Operations LLC (G-3323)*

Nutek Aerospace Corp.. 860 355-3169
  180 Sunny Valley Rd Ste 2 New Milford (06776) *(G-2257)*

Nutex Industries Inc.. 508 993-2501
  127 Rodney French Blvd Unit 4 New Bedford (02744) *(G-10636)*

Nutfield Publishing LLC... 603 537-2760
  118 Hardy Rd Londonderry (03053) *(G-14778)*

Nutmeg Architectural Wdwrk Inc............................... 203 325-4434
  48 Union St Ste 14 Stamford (06906) *(G-3420)*

Nutmeg Container Corporation **(HQ)**........................ **860 963-6727**
  100 Canal St Putnam (06260) *(G-2867)*

Nutmeg Utility Products Inc **(PA)**............................ **203 250-8802**
  1755 Highland Ave Cheshire (06410) *(G-609)*

Nutmeg Wire.. 860 822-8616
  14 Main St Baltic (06330) *(G-38)*

Nutrasweet, Waltham *Also Called: Manus Bio Inc (G-12713)*

Nutrasweet Company... 706 303-5600
  500 Totten Pond Rd Ste 61 Waltham (02451) *(G-12740)*

Nutron Manufacturing Inc.. 860 887-4550
  5 Wisconsin Ave Norwich (06360) *(G-2613)*

Nuttin Ordinary LLC.. 603 567-7916
  49 Vose Farm Rd Ste 120 Peterborough (03458) *(G-15322)*

Nuvalent Inc **(PA)**... **857 357-7000**
  1 Broadway Ste 14 Cambridge (02142) *(G-7672)*

Nuvera, Billerica *Also Called: Nuvera Fuel Cells LLC (G-6465)*

Nuvera Fuel Cells LLC **(HQ)**.................................... **617 245-7500**
  129 Concord Rd Bldg 1 Billerica (01821) *(G-6465)*

Nuway Tobacco Company.. 860 289-6414
  200 Sullivan Ave Ste 2 South Windsor (06074) *(G-3167)*

NV Bots, Canton *Also Called: New Valence Robotics Corp (G-7812)*

Nvi Weld Technology LLC.. 203 707-0587
  15 Maplerow Ave Waterbury (06705) *(G-3953)*

Nvision Medical Corporation..................................... 408 655-3577
  100 Boston Scientific Way Marlborough (01752) *(G-10187)*

Nxstage, Lawrence *Also Called: Nxstage Medical Inc (G-9592)*

Nxstage Medical Inc **(DH)**....................................... **978 687-4700**
  350 Merrimack St Lawrence (01843) *(G-9592)*

Nyacol Nano Technologies Inc.................................. 508 881-2220
  211 Megunko Rd Ashland (01721) *(G-5965)*

Nye Lubricants Inc **(HQ)**.. **508 996-6721**
  12 Howland Rd Fairhaven (02719) *(G-8512)*

Nylco, Nashua *Also Called: Worthen Industries Inc (G-15190)*

Nylco Division, Nashua *Also Called: Worthen Industries Inc (G-15189)*

Nyle International Corp **(PA)**.................................... **207 989-4335**
  195 Thatcher St Ste 2 Bangor (04401) *(G-4512)*

Nyle Systems, Bangor *Also Called: Nyle Systems LLC (G-4513)*

Nyle Systems LLC... 207 989-4335
  690 Maine Ave Bangor (04401) *(G-4513)*

Nylon Corporation America Inc.................................. 603 627-5150
  333 Sundial Ave Manchester (03103) *(G-14906)*

Nyltech North America.. 603 627-5150
  333 Sundial Ave Manchester (03103) *(G-14907)*

Nyobolt, Bedford *Also Called: Nyobolt Inc (G-6249)*

Nyobolt Inc.. 978 884-2220
  4 Crosby Dr Bedford (01730) *(G-6249)*

Nypro Healthcare Baja Inc **(DH)**.............................. **619 498-9250**
  101 Union St Clinton (01510) *(G-8086)*

Nypro Inc **(HQ)**.. **978 365-9721**
  101 Union St Clinton (01510) *(G-8087)*

Nypro Inc... 978 368-6021
  25 School St Clinton (01510) *(G-8088)*

Nypro Inc... 978 784-2006
  112 Barnum Rd Devens (01434) *(G-8283)*

Nypro Precision Assemblies, Clinton *Also Called: Nypro Healthcare Baja Inc (G-8086)*

Nypromold Inc **(PA)**.. **978 365-4547**
  144 Pleasant St Clinton (01510) *(G-8089)*

O & G Industries Inc... 203 881-5192
  105 Breault Rd Beacon Falls (06403) *(G-44)*

O & G Industries Inc... 203 729-4529
  Railroad Ave Ext Beacon Falls (06403) *(G-45)*

O & G Industries Inc... 203 366-4586
  240 Bostwick Ave Bridgeport (06605) *(G-354)*

O & G Industries Inc... 203 748-5694
  9 Segar St Danbury (06810) *(G-791)*

O & G Industries Inc... 860 485-6600
  255 Lower Bogue Rd Harwinton (06791) *(G-1522)*

O & G Industries Inc... 860 354-4438
  271 Danbury Rd New Milford (06776) *(G-2258)*

O & G Industries Inc... 203 263-2195
  236 Roxbury Rd Southbury (06488) *(G-3197)*

O & G Industries Inc... 203 977-1618
  686 Canal St Stamford (06902) *(G-3421)*

O & G Industries Inc... 203 323-1111
  40 Meadow St Stamford (06902) *(G-3422)*

O & G Industries Inc **(PA)**....................................... **860 489-9261**
  112 Wall St Torrington (06790) *(G-3689)*

O & W Heat Treat Inc... 860 528-9239
  1 Bidwell Rd South Windsor (06074) *(G-3168)*

O Berk Company Neng LLC....................................... 203 932-8000
  300 Callegari Dr West Haven (06516) *(G-4117)*

O Brien D G Inc.. 603 474-5571
  1 Chase Park Rd Seabrook (03874) *(G-15599)*

O C White Company.. 413 289-1751
  4226 Church St Thorndike (01079) *(G-12427)*

O E M Controls Inc **(PA)**.. **203 929-8431**
  10 Controls Dr Shelton (06484) *(G-3042)*

O F Mossberg & Sons Inc **(HQ)**............................... **203 230-5300**
  7 Grasso Ave North Haven (06473) *(G-2429)*

O K Engineering Inc.. 978 562-1010
  14 Main St Ste 10 Hudson (01749) *(G-9397)*

O M Y A Inc.. 802 499-8131
  62 Main St Proctor (05765) *(G-17458)*

O R M Inc... 508 393-7054
  71 Lyman St Ste 1 Northborough (01532) *(G-11104)*

O S Walker Company Inc **(HQ)**................................ **508 853-3232**
  600 Day Hill Rd Windsor (06095) *(G-4292)*

O W Landergren Inc.. 413 442-5632
  1500 W Housatonic St Pittsfield (01201) *(G-11415)*

O-A, Agawam *Also Called: 325 Silver Street Inc (G-5776)*

O-D Tool & Cutter Inc... 508 339-7507
  150 Gilbert St Mansfield (02048) *(G-10071)*

O.E.M. Concepts, Inc., Saco *Also Called: Meridian Life Science Inc (G-5373)*

O'Casey Trucking, Hinesburg *Also Called: Hinesburg Sand & Gravel Co Inc (G-17294)*

O'Reilly Media, Boston *Also Called: OReilly Media Inc (G-6944)*

O/K Machinery Corporation................ 508 303-8286
73 Bartlett St Marlborough (01752) *(G-10188)*

O&G Studio LLC............ 520 247-1820
30 Cutler St Warren (02885) *(G-16761)*

O2 Concepts LLC................ 877 867-4008
199 Park Road Ext Ste B Middlebury (06762) *(G-1718)*

Oak Barrel Imports LLC.............. 617 286-2524
421r Essex St Beverly (01915) *(G-6369)*

Oakcraft Pizza, Nashua *Also Called: Oakcraft Pizza Inc (G-15144)*

Oakcraft Pizza Inc.............. 603 521-8452
2 Cellu Dr Ste 111 Nashua (03063) *(G-15144)*

Oakhurst Dairy **(HQ)**.............. **207 772-7468**
364 Forest Ave Portland (04101) *(G-5253)*

Oakville Quality Products LLC............. 203 757-5525
1495 Thomaston Ave Ste 2 Waterbury (06704) *(G-3954)*

Oasis Coffee Corp.............. 203 847-0554
327 Main Ave Norwalk (06851) *(G-2547)*

Oasis Truck Tire Service LLC **(PA)**.......... **860 296-8749**
104 Old Sea Ln Old Saybrook (06475) *(G-2657)*

Oasys Water Inc.............. 617 963-0450
124 Washington St Ste 101 Foxboro (02035) *(G-8711)*

Oatmeal Studios Inc.............. 802 967-8014
Town Rd 35 Rochester (05767) *(G-17487)*

Oatsystems Inc.............. 781 907-6100
309 Waverley Oaks Rd Ste 306 Waltham (02452) *(G-12741)*

Oberdorfer LLC
6 Central Row Fl 1 Hartford (06103) *(G-1498)*

Oberlin, Providence *Also Called: Oberlin LLC (G-16577)*

Oberlin LLC.............. 401 588-8755
186 Union St Providence (02903) *(G-16577)*

Oberon Company, North Dartmouth *Also Called: Paramount Corp (G-11000)*

Object First (us) Inc.............. 844 569-0653
100 Cummings Ctr Ste 207p Beverly (01915) *(G-6370)*

Objectif Lune Inc.............. 203 878-7206
5 Eastern Steel Rd Milford (06460) *(G-1856)*

Obp Surgical Corporation.............. 978 291-6853
360 Merrimack St Lawrence (01843) *(G-9593)*

OBrien Consolidated Inds.............. 207 783-8543
680 Lisbon St Ste 1 Lewiston (04240) *(G-4981)*

Oce-USA Holding Inc.............. 773 714-8500
100 Oakview Dr Trumbull (06611) *(G-3726)*

Ocean, Providence *Also Called: Ocean Biomedical Holdings Inc (G-16578)*

Ocean and Common Inc.............. 978 537-4102
32 Jungle Rd Leominster (01453) *(G-9689)*

Ocean Approved Inc.............. 207 701-1576
20 Pomerleau St Biddeford (04005) *(G-4580)*

Ocean Biomedical Holdings Inc.............. 401 444-7375
55 Claverick St Ste 325 Providence (02903) *(G-16578)*

Ocean Crest Seafood Inc.............. 978 281-0232
88 Commercial St Gloucester (01930) *(G-8948)*

Ocean Crest Seafoods Inc **(PA)**.......... **978 281-0232**
88 Commercial St Gloucester (01930) *(G-8949)*

Ocean Navigator, Portland *Also Called: Navigator Publishing LLC (G-5249)*

Ocean Orthopedic Services Inc **(PA)**.......... **401 725-5240**
45 Oakhurst Rd Hopkinton (01748) *(G-9338)*

Ocean Spray (europe) Ltd.............. 508 946-1000
1 Ocean Spray Dr Middleboro (02349) *(G-10370)*

Ocean Spray Cooperative, Middleboro *Also Called: Ocean Spray Cranberries Inc (G-10371)*

Ocean Spray Cranberries Inc **(PA)**.......... **508 946-1000**
1 Ocean Spray Dr Middleboro (02349) *(G-10371)*

Ocean Spray International Inc **(HQ)**.......... **508 946-1000**
1 Ocean Spray Dr Middleboro (02349) *(G-10372)*

Ocean Spray International Sls.............. 508 946-1000
1 Ocean Spray Dr Lakeville (02347) *(G-9518)*

Ocean Spray Intl Svcs Inc **(HQ)**.......... **508 946-1000**
1 Ocean Spray Dr Lakeville (02347) *(G-9519)*

Ocean State Air LLC.............. 401 722-2447
33 Dale St Pawtucket (02860) *(G-16397)*

Ocean State Book Binding Inc.............. 401 528-1172
225 Dupont Dr Providence (02907) *(G-16579)*

Ocean State Cpl Inc.............. 401 431-0153
40 Jordan St East Providence (02914) *(G-16036)*

Ocean State Creations, North Providence *Also Called: Anatone Jewelry Co Inc (G-16294)*

Ocean State Innovations, Portsmouth *Also Called: Brand & Oppenheimer Co Inc (G-16440)*

Ocean State Off Road, Warwick *Also Called: Barrette Fabrication LLC (G-16787)*

Ocean State Shellfish Coop LLC.............. 401 789-2065
20 Walts Way Narragansett (02882) *(G-16193)*

Ocean State Tire Co Inc.............. 401 946-0880
51 Worthington Rd Cranston (02920) *(G-15903)*

Oceans Balance.............. 207 370-4874
10 W Point Ln Bldg 10 Biddeford (04005) *(G-4581)*

Ocm Inc.............. 508 675-7711
42 8th St Fall River (02720) *(G-8590)*

Oct, Whitinsville *Also Called: Omni Control Technology Inc (G-13343)*

Octo Telematics North Amer LLC.............. 617 916-1080
134 Rumford Ave Ste 302 Auburndale (02466) *(G-6138)*

October Company Inc **(PA)**.......... **413 527-9380**
51 Ferry St Easthampton (01027) *(G-8456)*

October Company Inc.............. 413 529-0718
39 Oneil St Easthampton (01027) *(G-8457)*

Octoscope Inc.............. 978 486-3130
305 Foster St Ste 104 Littleton (01460) *(G-9829)*

Ocular Therapeutix, Bedford *Also Called: Ocular Therapeutix Inc (G-6250)*

Ocular Therapeutix Inc **(PA)**.......... **781 357-4000**
24 Crosby Dr Bedford (01730) *(G-6250)*

Ocv Fabrics Us Inc.............. 207 729-7792
43 Bibber Pkwy Brunswick (04011) *(G-4653)*

Odat Machine Inc.............. 207 854-2455
20 Sanford Dr Gorham (04038) *(G-4828)*

Oddo Print Shop & Copy Center, Torrington *Also Called: Oddo Print Shop Inc (G-3690)*

Oddo Print Shop Inc.............. 860 489-6585
142 E Main St Torrington (06790) *(G-3690)*

Odm, Belmont *Also Called: Ripley Odm LLC (G-13971)*

Odorox Iaq Inc.............. 203 541-5577
1266 E Main St Ste 700r Stamford (06902) *(G-3423)*

Odwalla Inc.............. 336 877-1634
102 Longwood Ave Brookline (02446) *(G-7322)*

Odyssey Press Inc **(PA)**.......... **603 749-4433**
36 Fords Landing Dr Dover (03820) *(G-14243)*

OEM Design Services LLC.............. 203 467-5993
34 Panagrosi St East Haven (06512) *(G-1049)*

OEM Sources LLC.............. 203 283-5415
214 Broadway Milford (06460) *(G-1857)*

Oerlikon AM Medical Inc.............. 203 712-1030
10 Constitution Blvd S Shelton (06484) *(G-3043)*

Oesco Inc.............. 413 369-4335
8 Ashfield Rd Conway (01341) *(G-8143)*

Off Center Harbor LLC.............. 401 487-2090
7 Bay Rd Brooklin (04616) *(G-4634)*

Off The Dial Media LLC.............. 617 929-3424
36 Bay State Rd Ste 2 Cambridge (02138) *(G-7673)*

Officers Equipment Company.............. 703 221-1912
177 Georgia Ave Providence (02905) *(G-16580)*

Officeworks Inc **(PA)**.......... **781 270-9000**
149 Middlesex Tpke Burlington (01803) *(G-7403)*

Offset House Inc.............. 802 878-4440
89 Sandhill Rd Essex Junction (05452) *(G-17242)*

Offshore Fuel.............. 207 963-7068
130 Route 1 Gouldsboro (04607) *(G-4840)*

Offshore Marine Outfitters.............. 207 363-8862
15 Hannaford Dr York (03909) *(G-5715)*

Ofs Brightwave LLC.............. 508 347-2261
50 Hall Rd Sturbridge (01566) *(G-12252)*

Ofs Fitel LLC.............. 860 678-0371
55 Darling Dr Avon (06001) *(G-33)*

Ofs Fitel LLC.............. 508 347-2261
50 Hall Rd Sturbridge (01566) *(G-12253)*

Ofs Specialty Photonics Div, Avon *Also Called: Ofs Fitel LLC (G-33)*

OGS TECHNOLOGIES LLC.............. 203 271-9055
1855 Peck Ln Cheshire (06410) *(G-610)*

Ohlheiser, H R Jr Pe, South Windsor *Also Called: O & W Heat Treat Inc (G-3168)*

Ohmd Inc.............. 802 578-6369
50 Lakeside Ave Burlington (05401) *(G-17148)*

Oi Infusion Services LLC...	603 319-6224
111 Nh Ave Portsmouth (03801) *(G-15427)*	
Oi Sellers Fund LLC..	781 587-3242
607 North Ave # 12 Wakefield (01880) *(G-12524)*	
Oil Purification Systems Inc.......................................	203 346-1800
2176 Thomaston Ave Waterbury (06704) *(G-3955)*	
Oizero9 Inc...	207 324-3582
31 Smada Dr Sanford (04073) *(G-5404)*	
OK Durable Packaging Inc..	508 303-8067
73 Bartlett St Marlborough (01752) *(G-10189)*	
Okonite Company Inc...	401 333-3500
5 Industrial Rd Cumberland (02864) *(G-15957)*	
Old Bh Inc...	603 430-2111
100 Domain Dr Exeter (03833) *(G-14298)*	
Old Cambridge Products Corp..................................	860 243-1761
244 Woodland Ave Bloomfield (06002) *(G-197)*	
Old Creamery Grocery Store.....................................	413 634-5560
445 Berkshire Trl Cummington (01026) *(G-8147)*	
Old Dmfg Inc...	860 677-8561
1820 New Britain Ave Farmington (06032) *(G-1234)*	
Old Dublin Road Inc..	603 924-3861
130 Grove St Peterborough (03458) *(G-15323)*	
Old Dutch Mustard Co Inc..	603 878-2100
68 Old Wilton Rd Greenville (03048) *(G-14374)*	
Old Gate Automotive LLC..	203 878-7688
254 Old Gate Ln Milford (06460) *(G-1858)*	
Old Ironsides Energy LLC..	617 366-2030
500 Totten Pond Rd Ste 1 Waltham (02451) *(G-12742)*	
Old Lyme Gourmet Company....................................	860 434-7347
16 Grove St Deep River (06417) *(G-879)*	
Old Materials New England, Leominster *Also Called: Crh Americas Inc (G-9655)*	
Old Mill Road Media LLC...	802 375-1366
316 Old Mill Rd Arlington (05250) *(G-16991)*	
Old Neighborhood Foods Div, Lynn *Also Called: Demakes Enterprises Inc (G-9967)*	
Old Route Two Spirits Inc..	802 424-4864
69 Pitman Rd Barre (05641) *(G-17014)*	
Old San Juan Bakery Inc..	413 534-5555
408 High St Holyoke (01040) *(G-9273)*	
Old Town Canoe, Old Town *Also Called: Johnson Otdoors Watercraft Inc (G-5126)*	
Oldani Brothers LLC **(PA)**......................................	**203 630-6565**
735 Hanover Rd Meriden (06451) *(G-1681)*	
Oldcastle Apg Northeast Inc.....................................	781 506-9473
46 Spring St Holbrook (02343) *(G-9183)*	
Oldcastle Infrastructure Inc......................................	860 673-3291
151 Old Farms Rd Avon (06001) *(G-34)*	
Oldcastle Infrastructure Inc......................................	508 336-7600
41 Almeida Rd Rehoboth (02769) *(G-11613)*	
Oldcastle North Atlantic, Holbrook *Also Called: Oldcastle Apg Northeast Inc (G-9183)*	
Olde Bostonian...	617 282-9300
66 Von Hillern St Boston (02125) *(G-6928)*	
Oldport Marine Services Inc.....................................	401 847-9109
Sayer's Wharf Newport (02840) *(G-16220)*	
Oldsignsnstuffcom Inc...	978 407-6718
104 E Broadway Gardner (01440) *(G-8897)*	
Olimpia Industries Inc...	508 966-3392
175 North St Bellingham (02019) *(G-6299)*	
Olin Chlor Alkali Products, Wilton *Also Called: Olin Corporation (G-4244)*	
Olin Corporation...	203 750-3100
88 Danbury Rd Ste 1a Wilton (06897) *(G-4244)*	
Olive Capizzano Oils & Vinegar................................	860 495-2187
5 Coggswell St Ste 1 Pawcatuck (06379) *(G-2724)*	
Olive Oil Factory, Waterbury *Also Called: Olive Oil Factory LLC (G-3956)*	
Olive Oil Factory LLC..	203 437-8286
197 Huntingdon Ave Waterbury (06708) *(G-3956)*	
Olivenation LLC **(PA)**..	**781 351-1499**
13 Robbie Rd Unit A4 Avon (02322) *(G-6156)*	
Oliver Welding & Fabg Inc..	978 356-4488
30 Avery St Ipswich (01938) *(G-9493)*	
Oliveri & Associates Inc..	781 320-9090
22 Skipping Stone Plymouth (02360) *(G-11470)*	
Olsen & Silk Abrasives..	978 744-4720
35 Congress St Salem (01970) *(G-11728)*	

Olson Brothers Company...	860 747-6844
272 Camp St Plainville (06062) *(G-2775)*	
Olson S Logging LLC...	207 474-8835
15 Strickland Rd Canaan (04924) *(G-4670)*	
Olson, G H Steel, Stratford *Also Called: George H Olson Steel Company (G-3541)*	
Olympia Sales Inc...	860 749-0751
215 Moody Rd Enfield (06082) *(G-1140)*	
Olympic Adhesives Inc **(PA)**..................................	**800 829-1871**
670 Canton St Norwood (02062) *(G-11202)*	
Olympic Engineering, Haverhill *Also Called: Olympic Engineering Service (G-9119)*	
Olympic Engineering Service....................................	978 373-2789
65 Avco Rd Unit C Haverhill (01835) *(G-9119)*	
Olympic STEel-Ps&w, Milford *Also Called: Tinsley GROup-Ps&w Inc (G-1896)*	
Olympic Systems Corporation..................................	781 721-2740
15 Lowell Ave Winchester (01890) *(G-13489)*	
Olympus Innov-X, Waltham *Also Called: Innov-X Systems Inc (G-12700)*	
Olympus Surgical Tech Amer, Westborough *Also Called: Gyrus Acmi LLC (G-13104)*	
Omada Technologies LLC..	603 610-8282
36 Maplewood Ave Portsmouth (03801) *(G-15428)*	
Omar Coffee Company...	860 667-8889
41 Commerce Ct Newington (06111) *(G-2312)*	
Omega Engineering Inc...	714 540-4914
800 Connecticut Ave Ste 5n1 Norwalk (06854) *(G-2548)*	
Omega Engineering Inc **(DH)**.................................	**203 359-1660**
800 Connecticut Ave Ste 5n01 Norwalk (06854) *(G-2549)*	
Omega Engineering Inc...	203 359-7922
1 Omega Dr Stamford (06907) *(G-3424)*	
Omega Optical Holdings LLC **(PA)**.........................	**802 251-7300**
21 Omega Dr Brattleboro (05301) *(G-17098)*	
Omega Six Security LLC..	888 866-9954
1 Hardy Rd Ste 406 Bedford (03110) *(G-13946)*	
Omegadyne, Norwalk *Also Called: Omega Engineering Inc (G-2549)*	
Omerin Usa Inc...	475 343-3450
95 Research Pkwy Meriden (06450) *(G-1682)*	
Omg, Agawam *Also Called: Omg Inc (G-5802)*	
Omg Inc..	413 786-0516
95 Bowles Rd Agawam (01001) *(G-5802)*	
Omg Inc **(DH)**..	**413 789-0252**
153 Bowles Rd Agawam (01001) *(G-5803)*	
Omg Manufacturing, Inc., Agawam *Also Called: Omg Inc (G-5803)*	
Omni Components Corp **(HQ)**................................	**603 882-4467**
46 River Rd Ste 1 Hudson (03051) *(G-14533)*	
Omni Control Technology Inc....................................	508 234-9121
1 Main St Ste 4 Whitinsville (01588) *(G-13343)*	
Omni Life Science Inc **(DH)**..................................	**508 824-2444**
480 Paramount Dr Raynham (02767) *(G-11595)*	
Omni Measurement Systems Inc...............................	802 497-2253
808 Hercules Dr Colchester (05446) *(G-17198)*	
Omni Medical Systems, Colchester *Also Called: Omni Measurement Systems Inc (G-17198)*	
Omni Metals Company Inc.......................................	603 692-6664
14 Interstate Dr Somersworth (03878) *(G-15619)*	
Omni Spectra, Manchester *Also Called: Xma Corporation (G-14961)*	
Omnify Software Inc..	508 527-1956
1 Tech Dr Andover (01810) *(G-5903)*	
Omniglow LLC...	413 241-6010
865 Memorial Ave Ste 4 West Springfield (01089) *(G-13039)*	
Omniprobe Inc	
300 Baker Ave Ste 150 Concord (01742) *(G-8129)*	
Omnium Brewing, Somersworth *Also Called: Patel Brew LLC (G-15620)*	
Omniview, Boston *Also Called: Omniview Sports Inc (G-6929)*	
Omniview Sports Inc..	781 583-3534
6 Liberty Sq Boston (02109) *(G-6929)*	
Omsc, New Haven *Also Called: Overseas Ministries Study Ctr (G-2182)*	
Omtec Corp..	508 481-3322
181 Liberty St Marlborough (01752) *(G-10190)*	
Omtec Ball Transfers, Marlborough *Also Called: Omtec Corp (G-10190)*	
OMV...	508 243-6236
679 Washington St Attleboro (02703) *(G-6045)*	
Omya..	802 770-7537
206 Omya W Florence (05744) *(G-17271)*	

ALPHABETIC

Omya Inc.. 802 459-3311
206 Omya W Whipple Hollow Rd Florence (05744) *(G-17272)*

Omya Inc.. 802 459-3311
39 Main St Proctor (05765) *(G-17459)*

On Deck Sports, Randolph *Also Called: Promounds Inc (G-11572)*

On Line Building Systems LLC........................... 203 798-1194
22 Shelter Rock Ln Unit 4 Danbury (06810) *(G-792)*

On Semiconductor, South Portland *Also Called: Fairchild Semiconductor Corp (G-5501)*

On Site Gas Systems Inc................................ 860 667-8888
35 Budney Rd Newington (06111) *(G-2313)*

On Technology Corp **(PA)**............................. **781 487-3300**
880 Winter St Bldg 4 Waltham (02451) *(G-12743)*

On The Beat Inc.. 617 491-8878
43 Thorndike St Ste 2-4 Cambridge (02141) *(G-7674)*

On The Edge Nutrition Llc.............................. 617 752-4056
283 Old Colony Ave Boston (02127) *(G-6930)*

On The Road, Warren *Also Called: Perseus Partners LLC (G-5586)*

On The Road Inc.. 207 273-3780
2243 Camden Rd Warren (04864) *(G-5585)*

On Time Software, Groton *Also Called: Ebsnet Inc (G-9009)*

On-Sight Insight....................................... 617 502-5985
38 Chauncy St Boston (02111) *(G-6931)*

On-Site Analysis Inc **(DH)**.......................... **561 775-5756**
1 Executive Dr Ste 101 Chelmsford (01824) *(G-7942)*

Onapsis, Boston *Also Called: Onapsis Inc (G-6932)*

Onapsis Inc **(PA)**................................... **617 603-9932**
101 Federal St Ste 1800 Boston (02110) *(G-6932)*

Oncopeptides Inc....................................... 866 596-6626
111 Huntington Ave Boston (02199) *(G-6933)*

Oncore Manufacturing LLC............................... 978 737-3640
125 Fisher St Westborough (01581) *(G-13125)*

ONCORUS, Andover *Also Called: Oncorus Inc (G-5904)*

Oncorus Inc **(PA)**................................... **857 334-9077**
4 Corporate Dr Andover (01810) *(G-5904)*

Ondas Holdings, Waltham *Also Called: Ondas Holdings Inc (G-12744)*

Ondas Holdings Inc..................................... 617 862-2101
53 Brigham St Unit 4 Marlborough (01752) *(G-10191)*

Ondas Holdings Inc **(PA)**............................ **888 350-9994**
411 Waverley Oaks Rd Ste 114 Waltham (02452) *(G-12744)*

Ondrick Materials & Recycl LLC......................... 413 592-2566
22 Industry Rd Chicopee (01020) *(G-8052)*

One & Co Inc... 860 892-5180
154 N Main St Norwich (06360) *(G-2614)*

One Hippo.. 857 233-4886
71 Summer St Boston (02110) *(G-6934)*

One Mighty Mill LLC.................................... 781 588-0970
200 Meadow Rd # 115 Hyde Park (02136) *(G-9466)*

One-Pull Sltons Wire Cable LLC......................... 833 663-7855
44 Hull St Ste 2 Randolph (05060) *(G-17472)*

Onepin Inc... 508 475-1000
2200 W Park Dr Ste 440 Westborough (01581) *(G-13126)*

Oneview Commerce Inc................................... 617 279-0549
350 Lincoln St Ste 2400 Hingham (02043) *(G-9156)*

Onguard, Waltham *Also Called: K2w LLC (G-12706)*

Onix Corporation....................................... 866 290-5362
71 Main St Caribou (04736) *(G-4678)*

Online Marketing Solutions Inc......................... 978 937-2363
128 Warren St Lowell (01852) *(G-9911)*

Online Ret Bkg Cking Ingrdents, Avon *Also Called: Olivenation LLC (G-6156)*

Online River LLC....................................... 203 801-5900
606 Post Rd E Ste 723 Westport (06880) *(G-4191)*

Onlogic Inc.. 802 861-2300
35 Thompson St South Burlington (05403) *(G-17587)*

Ono Pharma Usa Inc..................................... 617 904-4500
1 Main St Cambridge (02142) *(G-7675)*

Onofrios Ultimate Foods Inc............................ 203 469-4014
35 Wheeler St New Haven (06512) *(G-2181)*

Onset Computer Corporation............................. 508 759-9500
470 Macarthur Blvd Bourne (02532) *(G-7141)*

Onset Dermatologics LLC................................ 401 762-2000
900 Highland Corporate Dr Cumberland (02864) *(G-15958)*

Onshape Inc.. 844 667-4273
121 Seaport Blvd Boston (02210) *(G-6935)*

Onsite Drug Testing Neng............................... 603 226-3858
56 Old Suncook Rd Ste 1 Concord (03301) *(G-14150)*

Onsite Services Inc.................................... 860 669-3988
23 Meadow Rd Clinton (06413) *(G-648)*

Onto Innovation, Wilmington *Also Called: Onto Innovation Inc (G-13440)*

Onto Innovation Inc **(PA)**........................... **978 253-6200**
16 Jonspin Rd Wilmington (01887) *(G-13440)*

Ontraget Promotional, Stoneham *Also Called: LPI Printing and Graphic Inc (G-12182)*

Onvio, Salem *Also Called: Onvio Servo LLC (G-15554)*

Onvio LLC **(PA)**..................................... **603 685-0404**
20 Northwestern Dr Salem (03079) *(G-15553)*

Onvio Servo LLC.. 603 685-0404
20 Northwestern Dr Salem (03079) *(G-15554)*

Onyx Environmental Svcs LLC **(DH)**................... **617 849-6600**
53 State St Ste 14 Boston (02109) *(G-6936)*

Onyx Marble & Granite.................................. 508 620-0775
93 Beaver St Framingham (01702) *(G-8793)*

Onyx Specialty Papers Inc.............................. 413 243-1231
40 Willow St South Lee (01260) *(G-11972)*

Opalala Inc.. 508 646-0950
994 Jefferson St Ste 10 Fall River (02721) *(G-8591)*

Opco Laboratory Inc.................................... 978 345-2522
704 River St Fitchburg (01420) *(G-8670)*

Open Sesame Publishing................................. 781 856-8142
45 Yale St Winchester (01890) *(G-13490)*

Openair Inc.. 617 351-0232
211 Congress St 8th Fl Boston (02110) *(G-6937)*

Openbridge Inc... 857 234-1008
119 Braintree St Ste 413 Boston (02134) *(G-6938)*

Openclinica LLC.. 617 621-8585
163 Highland Ave Needham Heights (02494) *(G-10554)*

Opendatasoft LLC....................................... 781 952-0515
185 Alewife Brook Pkwy Ste 210 Cambridge (02138) *(G-7676)*

Ophir, Wilmington *Also Called: Ophir Optics LLC (G-13441)*

Ophir Optics LLC....................................... 978 657-6410
90 Industrial Way Wilmington (01887) *(G-13441)*

Opi, Littleton *Also Called: Peak Technologies LLC (G-9832)*

OPPORTUNITY WORKS, Newburyport *Also Called: Opportunity Works Inc (G-10705)*

Opportunity Works Inc **(PA)**......................... **978 462-6144**
10 Opportunity Way Newburyport (01950) *(G-10705)*

Opportunityspace Inc................................... 857 366-1666
295 Devonshire St Fl 4 Boston (02110) *(G-6939)*

Ops-Core, Boston *Also Called: Gentex Corporation (G-6755)*

Ops-Core Inc... 617 670-3547
12 Channel St Ste 901b Boston (02210) *(G-6940)*

Opscode, Burlington *Also Called: Chef Software Inc (G-7346)*

Opsec Security Inc..................................... 617 226-3000
330 Congress St Fl 3 Boston (02210) *(G-6941)*

Optamark LLC... 877 888-3878
865 E Washington St North Attleboro (02760) *(G-10881)*

Optical Filter Corporation............................. 603 357-7662
69 Island St Keene (03431) *(G-14614)*

Optical Laboratory Inc................................. 508 997-9779
14 S 6th St Side New Bedford (02740) *(G-10637)*

Optical Polymers Lab Corp.............................. 401 722-0710
200 Weeden St Pawtucket (02860) *(G-16398)*

Optical Solutions Inc.................................. 603 826-4411
26 Bull Run Charlestown (03603) *(G-14066)*

Opticare, Waterbury *Also Called: Opticare Health Systems Inc (G-3957)*

Opticare Health Systems Inc **(DH)**.................. **203 574-2020**
87 Grandview Ave Waterbury (06708) *(G-3957)*

Opticonx Inc... 888 748-6855
45 Danco Rd Putnam (06260) *(G-2868)*

Opticraft Inc.. 781 938-0456
17d Everberg Rd Woburn (01801) *(G-13626)*

Optics 1, Bedford *Also Called: Optics 1 Inc (G-13947)*

Optics 1 Inc **(DH)**.................................. **603 296-0469**
2 Cooper Ln Bedford (03110) *(G-13947)*

Optikos Corporation.. 617 354-7557
  107 Audubon Rd Ste 25 Wakefield (01880) *(G-12525)*

Optim LLC... 508 347-5100
  64 Technology Park Rd Sturbridge (01566) *(G-12254)*

Optimum Bindery Services Neng, Nashua *Also Called: Optimum Bindery Svcs Neng Inc* *(G-15145)*

Optimum Bindery Svcs Neng Inc................................ 603 886-3889
  120 Northeastern Blvd Unit 1 Nashua (03062) *(G-15145)*

Optimum Parts Company... 413 273-1865
  104 Ramah Cir S Agawam (01001) *(G-5804)*

Optimum Sportswear Inc... 978 689-2290
  34 Groton St Fl 1 Lawrence (01843) *(G-9594)*

Optimum Technologies Inc... 508 765-8100
  114 Pleasant St Southbridge (01550) *(G-12032)*

Optirtc Inc... 844 678-4782
  98 N Washington St Boston (02114) *(G-6942)*

Opto-Line International Inc.. 978 658-7255
  265 Ballardvale St Ste 3 Wilmington (01887) *(G-13442)*

Optoglo Inc... 978 235-0201
  493 Lancaster St Leominster (01453) *(G-9690)*

Optometrics Corporation (HQ)................................ **978 772-1700**
  521 Great Rd Ste 1 Littleton (01460) *(G-9830)*

Optomistic Products Inc.. 207 865-9181
  61 N Main St Leominster (01453) *(G-9691)*

Optos Inc.. 508 787-1400
  500 Nickerson Rd Ste 201 Marlborough (01752) *(G-10192)*

Optos North America, Marlborough *Also Called: Optos Inc (G-10192)*

Optowares Incorporated.. 781 427-7106
  15 Presidential Way Woburn (01801) *(G-13627)*

Optra Inc.. 978 887-6600
  4 Jacquith Rd Wilmington (01887) *(G-13443)*

Opus Telecom Inc.. 508 875-4444
  119 Herbert St Framingham (01702) *(G-8794)*

Ora Holdings, Andover *Also Called: Rock-Tred 2 LLC (G-5912)*

Oracle, Boston *Also Called: Oracle Systems Corporation (G-6943)*

Oracle, Burlington *Also Called: Oracle Corporation (G-7406)*

Oracle, Burlington *Also Called: Oracle Corporation (G-7407)*

Oracle, Cambridge *Also Called: Oracle Corporation (G-7677)*

Oracle, Waltham *Also Called: Oracle Corporation (G-12745)*

Oracle, Manchester *Also Called: Oracle Corporation (G-14908)*

Oracle, Nashua *Also Called: Oracle Systems Corporation (G-15146)*

Oracle America Inc... 781 328-4770
  100 Crosby Dr Bedford (01730) *(G-6251)*

Oracle America Inc... 650 506-7000
  4 Van De Graaff Dr Ste 1 Burlington (01803) *(G-7404)*

Oracle America Inc... 281 710-2881
  95 Network Dr Burlington (01803) *(G-7405)*

Oracle Corporation.. 678 815-6637
  10 Van De Graaff Dr Ste 1 Burlington (01803) *(G-7406)*

Oracle Corporation.. 650 506-7000
  6 Van De Graaff Dr Burlington (01803) *(G-7407)*

Oracle Corporation.. 617 497-7713
  101 Main St Ste 1 Cambridge (02142) *(G-7677)*

Oracle Corporation.. 781 314-8001
  230 3rd Ave Waltham (02451) *(G-12745)*

Oracle Corporation.. 603 668-4998
  150 Dow St Ste 301 Manchester (03101) *(G-14908)*

Oracle Otc Subsidiary LLC.. 617 386-1000
  1 Main St Ste 7 Cambridge (02142) *(G-7678)*

Oracle Systems Corporation...................................... 617 247-7900
  222 Berkeley St Ste 1200 Boston (02116) *(G-6943)*

Oracle Systems Corporation...................................... 603 897-3000
  1 Oracle Dr Nashua (03062) *(G-15146)*

Orafol, Wallingford *Also Called: Sjd Tech Inc (G-3849)*

Orafol Americas Inc... 860 676-7100
  120 Darling Dr Avon (06001) *(G-35)*

Orange Bike Brewing Co... 207 391-4343
  31 Diamond St Ste D Portland (04101) *(G-5254)*

Orange Research Inc.. 203 877-5657
  140 Cascade Blvd Milford (06460) *(G-1859)*

Orbit Design LLC.. 203 393-0171
  290 Pratt St Meriden (06450) *(G-1683)*

Orbit Motion Systems, Bristol *Also Called: Atlantic Automation Group LLC (G-15754)*

Orbit Plastics Corp.. 978 465-5300
  45 Prince St Danvers (01923) *(G-8214)*

Orbotech, Billerica *Also Called: Orbotech Inc (G-6466)*

Orbotech Inc (DH)... **978 667-6037**
  44 Manning Rd Billerica (01821) *(G-6466)*

Orc Foods, Norwell *Also Called: The Original Rangoon Company Incorporated (G-11148)*

Orca Inc... 860 223-4180
  199 Whiting St New Britain (06051) *(G-2047)*

Orchard Equipment & Supply Co, Conway *Also Called: Oesco Inc (G-8143)*

Orchard Food Div, Woburn *Also Called: Rohtstein Corp (G-13655)*

Orchard Tool & Die Inc.. 413 433-1233
  34 Front St Ste 29 Indian Orchard (01151) *(G-9473)*

Ore Offshore, West Wareham *Also Called: Edgeone LLC (G-13062)*

OReilly Media Inc.. 617 354-5800
  2 Avenue De Lafayette Fl 6 Boston (02111) *(G-6944)*

Organogenesis, Canton *Also Called: Organogenesis Holdings Inc (G-7814)*

Organogenesis Holdings Inc (PA)............................ **781 575-0775**
  85 Dan Rd Canton (02021) *(G-7814)*

Organogenesis Inc (HQ).. **781 575-0775**
  85 Dan Rd Canton (02021) *(G-7815)*

Organomation Associates Inc.................................... 978 838-7300
  266 River Rd W Berlin (01503) *(G-6320)*

Orgenesis Inc (PA)... **480 659-6404**
  27 Strathmore Rd Ofc 5 Natick (01760) *(G-10489)*

Oriental Chow Mein Co, Fall River *Also Called: Ocm Inc (G-8590)*

Original Brdford Soap Wrks Inc (DH)....................... **401 821-2141**
  200 Providence St West Warwick (02893) *(G-16919)*

Origio Midatlantic Devices Inc................................... 856 762-2000
  75 Corporate Dr Trumbull (06611) *(G-3727)*

Orion Cordage, Winslow *Also Called: Orion Ropeworks Inc (G-5687)*

Orion Enterprises Inc (HQ).................................... **913 342-1653**
  1600 Osgood St Ste 2005 North Andover (01845) *(G-10847)*

Orion Entrance Control Inc.. 603 527-4187
  76a Lexington Dr Laconia (03246) *(G-14662)*

Orion Fittings, North Andover *Also Called: Orion Enterprises Inc (G-10847)*

Orion Industries Incorporated.................................... 978 772-0020
  1 Orion Park Dr Ayer (01432) *(G-6190)*

Orion Magazine, Great Barrington *Also Called: The Orion Society Inc (G-8979)*

Orion Manufacturing LLC.. 860 572-2921
  800 Flanders Rd Unit 4-8 Mystic (06355) *(G-1941)*

Orion Red, Smithfield *Also Called: Orion Ret Svcs & Fixturing Inc (G-16725)*

Orion Ret Svcs & Fixturing Inc.................................. 401 334-5000
  270 Jenckes Hill Rd Smithfield (02917) *(G-16725)*

Orion Ropeworks Inc (HQ)..................................... **207 877-2224**
  953 Benton Ave Winslow (04901) *(G-5687)*

Orion Ropeworks LLC... 207 877-2224
  953 Benton Ave Winslow (04901) *(G-5688)*

Orleans Packing, Hyde Park *Also Called: Gebelein Group Inc (G-9461)*

Ornamental Ironworks, Fall River *Also Called: Ornamental Ironworks Inc (G-8592)*

Ornamental Ironworks Inc... 508 678-0687
  75 Ferry St Ste 1 Fall River (02721) *(G-8592)*

Orogen, Woburn *Also Called: Orogen Therapeutics Inc (G-13628)*

Orogen Therapeutics Inc... 617 981-2156
  12 Gill St Ste 4200 Woburn (01801) *(G-13628)*

Orono House of Pizza... 207 866-5505
  154 Park St Orono (04473) *(G-5135)*

ORourke Media Group LLC (PA)............................. **802 524-9771**
  281 N Main St Saint Albans (05478) *(G-17527)*

Orpro Vision LLC... 617 676-1101
  44 Manning Rd Ste 1 Billerica (01821) *(G-6467)*

Ortiz Tool LLC.. 413 733-1206
  395 Liberty St Springfield (01104) *(G-12120)*

Ortronics, New London *Also Called: Ortronics Inc (G-2232)*

Ortronics Inc (DH).. **860 445-3900**
  125 Eugene Oneill Dr Ste 140 New London (06320) *(G-2232)*

Ortronics Inc.. 877 295-3472
  60 Woodlawn St West Hartford (06110) *(G-4076)*

A L P H A B E T I C

Ortronics Legrand.. 860 767-3515
14 Windermere Way Ivoryton (06442) *(G-1531)*

Orvis Company Inc.. 802 362-3750
4180 Main St Manchester (05254) *(G-17324)*

Orvis Sporting Traditions, Sunderland *Also Called: The Orvis Company Inc* *(G-17635)*

Orwell Sand & Gravel... 802 345-6028
1200 Park Hill Rd Benson (05743) *(G-17059)*

Osaap America LLC... 877 652-7227
10 Kidder Rd Chelmsford (01824) *(G-7943)*

Osborne Concrete.. 603 231-3604
148 Old Turnpike Rd Northwood (03261) *(G-15275)*

Oscar Jobs.. 860 583-7834
165 Riverside Ave Bristol (06010) *(G-477)*

Osda, Milford *Also Called: Tallinn Fulfillment Limited* *(G-1893)*

Osda Inc... 203 878-2155
98 Quirk Rd Milford (06460) *(G-1860)*

Osf Flavors Inc **(PA)**... **860 298-8350**
40 Baker Hollow Rd Windsor (06095) *(G-4293)*

Osgood Welding, Claremont *Also Called: Ralph L Osgood Inc* *(G-14096)*

Oshkosh, East Granby *Also Called: Oshkosh Corporation* *(G-946)*

Oshkosh Corporation.. 860 653-5548
35 Nicholson Rd East Granby (06026) *(G-946)*

OSI, Charlestown *Also Called: Optical Solutions Inc* *(G-14066)*

Osmo Labs Pbc... 508 439-4692
750 Main St Cambridge (02139) *(G-7679)*

Osram Sylvania, Wilmington *Also Called: Osram Sylvania Inc* *(G-13444)*

Osram Sylvania Inc **(DH)**...................................... **978 570-3000**
200 Ballardvale St Ste 305 Wilmington (01887) *(G-13444)*

Osram Sylvania Inc... 603 772-4331
131 Portsmouth Ave Exeter (03833) *(G-14299)*

Osram Sylvania Inc... 978 750-3900
275 W Main St Hillsborough (03244) *(G-14441)*

Osram Sylvania Inc... 603 464-7235
275 W Main St Hillsborough (03244) *(G-14442)*

Osram Sylvania Inc... 401 723-1378
1193 Broad St Central Falls (02863) *(G-15794)*

Ossa, Waltham *Also Called: Evident Scientific Inc* *(G-12668)*

Ossipee Mountain Land Co LLC................................ 603 323-7677
844 Whittier Rd Tamworth (03886) *(G-15648)*

Ost Services LLC... 401 467-8661
55 Chapman St Providence (02905) *(G-16581)*

Other Paper.. 802 864-6670
1340 Williston Rd Ste 201 South Burlington (05403) *(G-17588)*

Otis, Farmington *Also Called: Otis Elevator Company* *(G-1235)*

Otis, Farmington *Also Called: Otis Worldwide Corporation* *(G-1237)*

Otis Elevator Company... 860 242-3632
212 W Newberry Rd Bloomfield (06002) *(G-198)*

Otis Elevator Company **(HQ)**................................. **860 674-3000**
1 Carrier Pl Farmington (06032) *(G-1235)*

Otis Elevator Company... 401 232-7282
34 Sword St Auburn (01501) *(G-6122)*

Otis Elevator Company, Bloomfield *Also Called: Otis Elevator Company* *(G-198)*

Otis Elevator Company, Canton *Also Called: Delta Elevator Service Corp* *(G-560)*

Otis Elevator Intl Inc.. 860 676-6000
10 Farm Springs Rd Farmington (06032) *(G-1236)*

Otis Worldwide Corporation **(PA)**........................... **860 674-3000**
1 Carrier Pl Farmington (06032) *(G-1237)*

Ottaway Newspapers.. 508 775-1200
319 Main St Hyannis (02601) *(G-9443)*

Otter Creek Awning, Williston *Also Called: Ke Usa Inc* *(G-17736)*

Ouellette Industries Inc... 508 695-0964
100 John L Dietsch Blvd Ste B Attleboro Falls (02763) *(G-6093)*

Ouidad Products LLC
41b Eagle Rd Danbury (06810) *(G-793)*

Our Glass, Hampden *Also Called: Stained Glass Resources Inc* *(G-9023)*

Our Town Publishing, Medway *Also Called: Nrt Inc* *(G-10309)*

Out of Business Dec 2019, Framingham *Also Called: Waverly Tool Rental & Sales Co* *(G-8811)*

Outcomes4me Inc... 617 812-1010
33 Arch St Fl 17 Boston (02110) *(G-6945)*

Outdoor Industries LLC... 203 350-2275
80 Devonshire Ln Madison (06443) *(G-1565)*

Outdoor Outfitters Inc... 508 255-0455
15 Rt 6a Orleans (02653) *(G-11241)*

Outer Limits Publishing LLC..................................... 802 422-2399
5465 Rte 4 Killington (05751) *(G-17313)*

Outfitters Inc Corporate... 802 527-0204
12 Champlain Cmns Saint Albans (05478) *(G-17528)*

Outland Engineering Inc... 800 797-3709
167 Cherry St Pmb 280 Milford (06460) *(G-1861)*

Outlaw Audio LLC.. 508 286-4110
10b Commerce Way Ste B Norton (02766) *(G-11131)*

Outside Unlimited, Concord *Also Called: Rwc Landscape Services MGT* *(G-14154)*

Outsystems Inc **(PA)**... **617 837-6840**
55 Thomson Pl Fl 2 Boston (02210) *(G-6946)*

Oven Poppers Inc... 603 644-3773
99 Faltin Dr Manchester (03103) *(G-14909)*

Overhaul Support Services LLC **(PA)**..................... **860 264-2101**
5 Connecticut South Dr East Granby (06026) *(G-947)*

Overhead Door Co Bangor Inc.................................. 207 848-7200
56 Liberty Dr Hermon (04401) *(G-4888)*

Overhead Doors, Hermon *Also Called: Overhead Door Co Bangor Inc* *(G-4888)*

Overland Phrmaceuticals US Inc............................... 508 827-8686
200 Clarendon St 25th Fl Boston (02116) *(G-6947)*

Overlook Industries Inc... 413 527-4344
193 Northampton St Ste 2 Easthampton (01027) *(G-8458)*

Overseas Ministries Study Ctr.................................. 203 624-6672
342 Yale Ave New Haven (06515) *(G-2182)*

Overtone Studio Inc... 774 290-2900
492 Old Connecticut Path # 102 Framingham (01701) *(G-8795)*

Ovik Health, Salisbury *Also Called: Andover Healthcare Inc* *(G-11739)*

Ovr Tech LLC... 802 391-4172
50 Lakeside Ave Unit 750 Burlington (05401) *(G-17149)*

Ovr Technology, Burlington *Also Called: Ovr Tech LLC* *(G-17149)*

Ovtene Inc... 617 852-4828
11 Sassamon Trl Ste 221 Marion (02738) *(G-10099)*

Owen J Folsom Inc... 207 827-7625
299 Gilman Falls Ave Old Town (04468) *(G-5131)*

Owen Tool and Mfg Co Inc....................................... 860 628-6540
149 Aircraft Rd Southington (06489) *(G-3227)*

Owens Corning.. 603 773-4246
61 Pine Rd Brentwood (03833) *(G-14026)*

Owens Corning, East Hartford *Also Called: Owens Corning Sales LLC* *(G-1008)*

Owens Corning, Canton *Also Called: Owens Corning Sales LLC* *(G-7816)*

Owens Corning Sales LLC.. 304 353-6945
East Hartford (06128) *(G-1008)*

Owens Corning Sales LLC.. 800 438-7465
Canton (02021) *(G-7816)*

Owl Separation Systems LLC.................................... 603 559-9297
25 Nimble Hill Rd Newington (03801) *(G-15209)*

Owl Stamp Company Inc.. 978 452-4541
31 1st St Lowell (01850) *(G-9912)*

Owlstamp Visual Solutions, Lowell *Also Called: Owl Stamp Company Inc* *(G-9912)*

Owncloud Inc... 617 515-3664
124 Washington St Ste 101 Foxboro (02035) *(G-8712)*

Ox Paper Tube and Core Inc.................................... 508 879-1141
89 October Hill Rd Holliston (01746) *(G-9225)*

Ox3 Corporation.. 978 772-1222
31 Macarthur Ave Devens (01434) *(G-8284)*

Oxeia Biopharmaceuticals Inc.................................. 619 213-7697
361 Newbury St Ste 500 Boston (02115) *(G-6948)*

Oxford General Industries Inc................................... 203 758-4467
3 Gramar Ave Prospect (06712) *(G-2837)*

Oxford Graphics LLC.. 978 281-3663
10 Centennial Dr Peabody (01960) *(G-11329)*

Oxford Immunotec USA Inc...................................... 833 682-6933
293 Boston Post Rd W Ste 210 Marlborough (01752) *(G-10193)*

Oxford Industries Conn Inc...................................... 860 225-3700
221 South St New Britain (06051) *(G-2048)*

Oxford Instrs Msrement Systems.............................. 978 369-9933
300 Baker Ave Ste 150 Concord (01742) *(G-8130)*

Oxford Instruments, Concord *Also Called: Oxford Instruments America Inc* *(G-8131)*

Oxford Instruments America, Concord *Also Called: Oxford Instrs Msrement Systems* *(G-8130)*

Oxford Instruments America Inc **(HQ)**.................................... 978 369-9933
   300 Baker Ave Ste 150 Concord (01742) *(G-8131)*

Oxford Performance Mtls Inc... 860 698-9300
   30 S Satellite Rd South Windsor (06074) *(G-3169)*

Oxford Polymers, New Britain *Also Called: Oxford Industries Conn Inc (G-2048)*

Oxford Science Inc.. 203 881-3115
   1 Old Moose Hill Rd Oxford (06478) *(G-2707)*

Oxford Spring 5301, Oxford *Also Called: Leggett & Platt Incorporated (G-11258)*

Oxford Timber Inc.. 207 539-9656
   60 E Oxford Rd Oxford (04270) *(G-5148)*

Oxford Trading Company, Taunton *Also Called: New England Box Beef Company (G-12352)*

Oxpekk Performance Mtls Inc.. 860 698-9300
   30 S Satellite Rd South Windsor (06074) *(G-3170)*

OXY-Gon Industries Inc.. 603 736-8422
   42 Old Route 28 N Epsom (03234) *(G-14283)*

Oyo Sportstoys Inc... 978 264-2000
   1309 Beacon St Ste 300 Brookline (02446) *(G-7323)*

Oz Holding Corp.. 603 546-0090
   11 Continental Blvd Ste 104 Merrimack (03054) *(G-14996)*

Ozcan Jewelers Inc... 617 338-6844
   387 Washington St Ste 516 Boston (02108) *(G-6949)*

Ozone Technologies Inc.. 617 955-4188
   75 Arlington St Lbby Boston (02116) *(G-6950)*

P & B Manufacturing, Providence *Also Called: Reed Allison Group Inc (G-16599)*

P & K Sand and Gravel Inc.. 207 693-6765
   234 Casco Rd Naples (04055) *(G-5081)*

P & L Machine Company, Littleton *Also Called: Stoneridge Design Inc (G-9841)*

P & L Riendeau Inc.. 802 626-9302
   1640 Sutton Rd Lyndonville (05851) *(G-17319)*

P & M Brick & Block Inc.. 617 924-6020
   213 Arlington St Watertown (02472) *(G-12898)*

P A Landers Inc **(PA)**.. 781 826-8818
   351 Winter St Hanover (02339) *(G-9038)*

P A Landers Inc... 508 747-1800
   351 Winter St Hanover (02339) *(G-9039)*

P A S, Lee *Also Called: Protective Armored Systems Inc (G-9618)*

P and L Trucking... 802 875-2819
   31 Toma Rd Chester (05143) *(G-17182)*

P B Y A Inc... 508 255-0994
   45 Arey's Ln South Orleans (02662) *(G-11973)*

P C I Group... 203 327-0410
   652 Glenbrook Rd Ste 3-301 Stamford (06906) *(G-3425)*

P C S, Taunton *Also Called: Professnal Cntract Strlztion I (G-12356)*

P Craft Jewelry, Attleboro *Also Called: Plastic Craft Novelty Co Inc (G-6049)*

P E P, Attleboro *Also Called: Precision Engineered Pdts LLC (G-6051)*

P G L Industries Inc.. 508 679-8845
   1432 Gar Hwy Swansea (02777) *(G-12309)*

P G T, Franklin *Also Called: Princton Gamma-Tech Instrs Inc (G-8858)*

P I C, Windsor *Also Called: Purchasing Inventory Cons Inc (G-17761)*

P I Liquidating Inc **(PA)**.. 203 758-6651
   32 Gramar Ave Prospect (06712) *(G-2838)*

P J Albert Inc.. 978 345-7828
   199 Upham St Fitchburg (01420) *(G-8671)*

P M C, Malden *Also Called: Palmer Manufacturing Co Llc (G-10021)*

P M I, East Windsor *Also Called: Shoham Manufacturing Inc (G-1085)*

P M I, Woonsocket *Also Called: Blackstone Molding Inc (G-16950)*

P M Recycling... 401 765-0330
   24 E Mill St Woonsocket (02895) *(G-16970)*

P M S Manufactured Pdts Inc.. 978 281-2600
   10 Sadler St Gloucester (01930) *(G-8950)*

P M Tile and Grout Care, Bridgewater *Also Called: Paul McNamara (G-7236)*

P P I, Williamstown *Also Called: Progressive Plastics Inc (G-17717)*

P S Holding Company Inc.. 207 799-9290
   110 Dartmouth St South Portland (04106) *(G-5510)*

P S M P, Biddeford *Also Called: Precision Screw Mch Pdts Inc (G-4583)*

P Straker Ltd... 508 996-4804
   8 Middle St South Dartmouth (02748) *(G-11918)*

P T I, Enfield *Also Called: Pti Industries Inc (G-1143)*

P Wiles Inc **(PA)**.. 508 385-4321
   20 Lots Hollow Rd Orleans (02653) *(G-11242)*

P-A-R Precision Inc... 860 491-4181
   15 Town Line Rd Wolcott (06716) *(G-4372)*

P-Cube Inc... 207 318-3349
   125 John Roberts Rd Ste 11 South Portland (04106) *(G-5511)*

P-Q Controls Inc **(PA)**.. 860 583-6994
   95 Dolphin Rd Bristol (06010) *(G-478)*

P.J. Noyes, Lancaster *Also Called: Trividia Mfg Solutions Inc (G-14680)*

P.M.c, Danbury *Also Called: PMC Engineering LLC (G-798)*

P/A Industries Inc **(PA)**.. 860 243-8306
   522 Cottage Grove Rd Bldg B Bloomfield (06002) *(G-200)*

P&E Informatics, Waltham *Also Called: Revvity Signals Software Inc (G-12769)*

P&G Metal Components Corp.. 860 243-2220
   98 Filley St Bloomfield (06002) *(G-199)*

P&L Machine, Littleton *Also Called: Dakin Road Investments Inc (G-9809)*

P2k Printing LLC... 603 356-2010
   1305 White Mountain Hwy North Conway (03860) *(G-15249)*

Pa-Ted Spring Company LLC.. 860 582-6368
   137 Vincent P Kelly Rd Bristol (06010) *(G-479)*

Pac Machinery Group... 214 724-8523
   5 Gigante Dr Stoneham (02180) *(G-12184)*

Pac Products, Yalesville *Also Called: Joval Machine Co Inc (G-4398)*

Pace Anlytical Lf Sciences LLC... 603 437-4990
   13 Industrial Way Salem (03079) *(G-15555)*

Pace Industries LLC... 978 667-8400
   67 Faulkner St North Billerica (01862) *(G-10941)*

Pacific Global Packaging South, Wilmington *Also Called: Pacific Packaging Products Inc*
(G-13445)

Pacific Packaging Products Inc **(PA)**................................. 978 657-9100
   24 Industrial Way Wilmington (01887) *(G-13445)*

Pacific Pathway, Wellesley Hills *Also Called: Life+gear Inc (G-12952)*

Pack Center , The, Stratford *Also Called: Park City Packaging Inc (G-3564)*

Package Industries Inc... 508 865-5871
   15 Harback Rd Sutton (01590) *(G-12288)*

Package Machinery Company Inc... 413 315-3801
   80 Commercial St Holyoke (01040) *(G-9274)*

Package Printing Company Inc.. 413 736-2748
   33 Myron St West Springfield (01089) *(G-13040)*

Package Steel Buildings, Sutton *Also Called: Package Industries Inc (G-12288)*

Package Steel Systems Inc.. 508 865-5871
   15 Harback Rd Sutton (01590) *(G-12289)*

Packaging and Crating Tech LLC.. 203 759-1799
   1100 Buckingham St Ste 4 Watertown (06795) *(G-4021)*

Packaging Concepts, East Hartford *Also Called: PCL Fixtures Inc (G-1009)*

Packaging Concepts Ltd... 401 334-0344
   275 Ferris Ave Rumford (02916) *(G-16675)*

Packaging Corporation America.. 413 584-6132
   525 Mount Tom Rd Northampton (01060) *(G-11074)*

Packaging Corporation America.. 978 256-4586
   525 Mount Tom Rd Northampton (01060) *(G-11075)*

Packaging Devices Inc **(PA)**.. 508 548-0224
   61 Homestead Ln Teaticket (02536) *(G-12379)*

Packaging Graphics LLC.. 401 725-7700
   60 Delta Dr Pawtucket (02860) *(G-16399)*

Packaging Products Corporation **(PA)**................................ 508 997-5150
   47 N 2nd St Fl 3 New Bedford (02740) *(G-10638)*

Packaging Specialties Inc... 978 462-1300
   3 Opportunity Way Newburyport (01950) *(G-10706)*

Packard Inc... 203 758-6219
   6 Industrial Rd Prospect (06712) *(G-2839)*

Packard Biochip, Billerica *Also Called: Revvity Inc (G-6477)*

Packard Specialties, Prospect *Also Called: Packard Inc (G-2839)*

Packedge Inc... 203 288-0200
   54 Maple Ave S Westport (06880) *(G-4192)*

Packgen, Auburn *Also Called: Packgen Inc (G-4449)*

Packgen Inc.. 207 784-4195
   160 Cascades Dr Auburn (04210) *(G-4449)*

Paco Assensio Woodworking LLC.. 203 536-2608
   15 Meadow St Norwalk (06854) *(G-2550)*

Pacon Corporation... 508 370-0780
   79 Main St Ste 202 Framingham (01702) *(G-8796)*

Pact Inc 203 759-1799
   1100 Buckingham St Ste 4 Watertown (06795) *(G-4022)*

Pactolus Cmmnctions Sftwr Corp 508 616-0900
   200 Nickerson Rd Marlborough (01752) *(G-10194)*

Padakshep 801 652-5589
   1530 Beacon St Apt 201 Brookline (02446) *(G-7324)*

Padco Inc 508 753-8486
   19 Wells St Worcester (01604) *(G-13767)*

Padebco Custom Boats 207 529-5106
   Anchor Inn Rd Round Pond (04564) *(G-5354)*

Padlock Therapeutics, Cambridge *Also Called: Padlock Therapeutics Inc (G-7680)*

Padlock Therapeutics Inc 978 381-9601
   200 Cambridgepark Dr Cambridge (02140) *(G-7680)*

Page Belting Company Inc 603 796-2463
   104 High St Boscawen (03303) *(G-13992)*

Page McLellan Inc 401 397-2795
   136 Mishnock Rd West Greenwich (02817) *(G-16890)*

Page Street Publishing Company 978 594-8758
   27 Congress St Ste 105 Salem (01970) *(G-11729)*

Pagell Corporation 508 429-2998
   74 Lowland St Holliston (01746) *(G-9226)*

Pageworks, Cambridge *Also Called: Creamer Associates Inc (G-7544)*

Pain Davignon, Hyannis *Also Called: Pain DAvignon II Inc (G-9444)*

Pain DAvignon II Inc 508 771-9771
   15 Hinckley Rd Unit C Hyannis (02601) *(G-9444)*

Paine Incense Co, Auburn *Also Called: Paine Products Inc (G-4450)*

Paine Products Inc 207 782-0931
   17 Sunset Ave Auburn (04210) *(G-4450)*

Paines Patio Inc 508 563-7557
   674 Macarthur Blvd Pocasset (02559) *(G-11490)*

Paint & Powder Works LLC 860 225-2019
   35 M And S Ct New Britain (06051) *(G-2049)*

Pairpoint Crystal, Reading *Also Called: Pgc Acquisition LLC (G-11604)*

Paiva Corp 508 679-7921
   192 Anawan St Ste 602 Fall River (02721) *(G-8593)*

Pajama Gram Company, Shelburne *Also Called: Vermont Teddy Bear Co Inc (G-17563)*

Pak 2000 Inc 603 569-3700
   16 Page Hill Rd Lancaster (03584) *(G-14678)*

Palace Manufacturing Co, Nashua *Also Called: Lennartz Enterprises LLC (G-15126)*

Paladin Commercial Printers, West Hartford *Also Called: Paladin Commercial Prtrs LLC (G-4077)*

Paladin Commercial Prtrs LLC 860 953-4900
   109 Talcott Rd West Hartford (06110) *(G-4077)*

Palco Connector Inc 203 729-9090
   22 Great Hill Rd Naugatuck (06770) *(G-1978)*

Paleo Products Inc 833 476-3733
   2 Commerce Dr Warwick (02886) *(G-16842)*

Paleonola, Warwick *Also Called: Paleo Products Inc (G-16842)*

Pall Corporation 508 259-5107
   41 Berkeley Rd Framingham (01701) *(G-8797)*

Pall Corporation 508 871-5380
   20 Walkup Dr Westborough (01581) *(G-13127)*

Pall Northborough **(DH)** **978 263-9888**
   50 Bearfoot Rd Northborough (01532) *(G-11105)*

Pall Westborough Pal05, Westborough *Also Called: Pall Corporation (G-13127)*

Palladin Precision Pdts Inc 203 574-0246
   57 Bristol St Waterbury (06708) *(G-3958)*

Palleon Pharma Inc 857 285-5904
   266 Second Ave Fl 2 Waltham (02451) *(G-12746)*

Pallflex Products Company 860 928-7761
   125 Kennedy Dr Putnam (06260) *(G-2869)*

Pallian & Company, Wells *Also Called: Cynthia Carroll Pallian (G-5599)*

Palmer and Sicard Inc 603 778-1841
   89 Holland Way Exeter (03833) *(G-14300)*

Palmer Foundry, Palmer *Also Called: Black Bay Ventures Vi LLC (G-11271)*

Palmer Foundry Inc 413 283-2976
   22 Mount Dumplin Rd Palmer (01069) *(G-11280)*

Palmer Industries, North Providence *Also Called: 379 Charles RI Inc (G-16293)*

Palmer Industries Inc 800 398-9676
   862r Charles St North Providence (02904) *(G-16306)*

Palmer Lane Maple LLC 802 899-8199
   19 Old Pump Rd Jericho (05465) *(G-17308)*

Palmer Machine Company Inc 603 447-2069
   48 North Rd Conway (03818) *(G-14181)*

Palmer Manufacturing Co LLC 860 828-0344
   134 Commerce St East Berlin (06023) *(G-914)*

Palmer Manufacturing Co Llc **(DH)** **781 321-0480**
   243 Medford St Malden (02148) *(G-10021)*

Palmer Manufacturing Co 781 321-0480
   1 2nd St Ste 1 Peabody (01960) *(G-11330)*

PALMER MANUFACTURING CO., LLC, East Berlin *Also Called: Palmer Manufacturing Co LLC (G-914)*

PALMER MANUFACTURING CO., LLC, Peabody *Also Called: Palmer Manufacturing Co LLC (G-11330)*

Palmer Paving Corporation **(PA)** **413 283-8354**
   25 Blanchard St Palmer (01069) *(G-11281)*

Palmer Spring Co, Woburn *Also Called: Joseph Palmer Inc (G-13595)*

Palmero Health Care, Stratford *Also Called: J Palmero Sales Company Inc (G-3550)*

Palmero Healthcare LLC 203 377-6424
   120 Goodwin Pl Stratford (06615) *(G-3562)*

Palmers Elc Mtrs & Pumps Inc 203 348-7378
   40 Osborne Ave Norwalk (06855) *(G-2551)*

Palomar Medical Products Inc 781 993-2300
   15 Network Dr Burlington (01803) *(G-7408)*

Palomar Medical Tech LLC **(DH)** **781 993-2330**
   15 Network Dr Burlington (01803) *(G-7409)*

Pamco Machine Company Inc 207 783-1763
   41 Chestnut St Ste 1a Lewiston (04240) *(G-4982)*

Pan De Oro Brand, Hartford *Also Called: Severance Foods Inc (G-1506)*

Panache, Bennington *Also Called: Mainstream Inc (G-17050)*

Panacol-Usa Inc 860 738-7449
   142 Industrial Ln Torrington (06790) *(G-3691)*

Panagrafix Inc **(PA)** **203 878-7412**
   75 Cascade Blvd Milford (06460) *(G-1862)*

Panagrafix Inc 203 691-5529
   50 Fresh Meadow Rd West Haven (06516) *(G-4118)*

Panalgo LLC 781 290-0808
   265 Franklin St Ste 1101 Boston (02110) *(G-6951)*

Panalytical Inc 508 647-1100
   117 Flanders Rd Westborough (01581) *(G-13128)*

Panametrics LLC **(DH)** **978 437-1000**
   1100 Technology Park Dr Ste 100 Billerica (01821) *(G-6468)*

Panasnic DVC Slutions Lab Mass, Sudbury *Also Called: Qualtre Inc (G-12270)*

Pancon Corporation **(PA)** **781 297-6000**
   350 Revolutionary Dr East Taunton (02718) *(G-8410)*

Panda Plates Inc **(PA)** **888 997-6623**
   124 Washington St Ste 101 Foxboro (02035) *(G-8713)*

Panda Plates Inc 917 848-8777
   124 Washington St Ste 101 Foxboro (02035) *(G-8714)*

Pandolf-Perkins, Sterling *Also Called: E H Perkins Construction Inc (G-12161)*

PANDORA'S PICKLE PRODUCTS, North Providence *Also Called: Training Thru Placement Inc (G-16312)*

Paneloc Corporation 860 677-6711
   142 Brickyard Rd Farmington (06032) *(G-1238)*

Paneltek Inc 920 906-9457
   10 Larsen Way Attleboro Falls (02763) *(G-6094)*

Paneltek LLC 920 906-9457
   10 Larsen Way Attleboro Falls (02763) *(G-6095)*

Panolam Industries Inc **(HQ)** **203 925-1556**
   2 Corporate Dr Ste 946 Shelton (06484) *(G-3044)*

Panolam Industries Intl Inc **(PA)** **203 925-1556**
   2 Corporate Dr Ste 946 Shelton (06484) *(G-3045)*

Panolam Surface System, Shelton *Also Called: Panolam Industries Inc (G-3044)*

Panolam Surface Systems 203 925-1556
   1 Pionite Rd Auburn (04210) *(G-4451)*

Panolam Surface Systems, Shelton *Also Called: Panolam Industries Intl Inc (G-3045)*

Panoramic Publishing Group LLC 603 569-5257
   83 Center St Wolfeboro Falls (03896) *(G-15736)*

Pantheon Guitars LLC 207 755-0003
   41 Canal St Lewiston (04240) *(G-4983)*

Paper Mill and Indus Rbr Pdts, Farmington *Also Called: Schaeferrolls Inc (G-14311)*

Paper Source, Bangor *Also Called: Tissue Plus LLC (G-4516)*

Papergraphics, Merrimack *Also Called: Papergraphics Print & Copy Inc (G-14997)*

Papergraphics Print & Copy Inc 603 880-1835
  4 John Tyler St Ste A Merrimack (03054) *(G-14997)*

Par Manufacturing Inc 860 677-1797
  1824 New Britain Ave Farmington (06032) *(G-1239)*

Par Pharmaceutical Companies, Inc., Stratford *Also Called: Par Phrmceutical Companies Inc (G-3563)*

Par Phrmceutical Companies Inc 203 290-6261
  555 Lordship Blvd Stratford (06615) *(G-3563)*

Par Thread Grinding, Farmington *Also Called: Par Manufacturing Inc (G-1239)*

Para Research Inc 978 282-1100
  85 Eastern Ave Gloucester (01930) *(G-8951)*

Paraclete Press Inc (HQ) **508 255-4685**
  36 Southern Eagle Cartway Brewster (02631) *(G-7216)*

Paradigm Biodevices Inc 781 982-9950
  800 Hingham St Ste 207s Rockland (02370) *(G-11655)*

Paradigm Manchester Inc (DH) **772 287-7770**
  200 Adams St Manchester (06042) *(G-1623)*

Paradigm Manchester Inc 860 646-4048
  151 Sheldon Rd Manchester (06042) *(G-1624)*

Paradigm Manchester Inc 860 649-2888
  255 Sheldon Rd Bldg 4 Manchester (06042) *(G-1625)*

Paradigm Operating Company LLC 877 994-6369
  56 Milliken St Portland (04103) *(G-5255)*

Paradigm Prcision Holdings LLC 860 829-3663
  134 Commerce St East Berlin (06023) *(G-915)*

Paradigm Prcision Holdings LLC 860 649-2888
  967 Parker St Manchester (06042) *(G-1626)*

Paradigm Prcision Holdings LLC 781 321-0480
  243 Medford St Malden (02148) *(G-10022)*

Paradigm Prcision Holdings LLC 978 278-7100
  1 2nd St Peabody (01960) *(G-11331)*

Paradigm Precision, Manchester *Also Called: Paradigm Manchester Inc (G-1623)*

Paradigm Solutions, Portland *Also Called: K & R Holdings Inc (G-5230)*

Paragon Electronic Systems 603 645-7630
  255 Coolidge Ave Manchester (03102) *(G-14910)*

Paragon ID USA, Essex Junction *Also Called: Ask-Inttag LLC (G-17226)*

Paragon Medical - Bridgeport, Bridgeport *Also Called: Lacey Manufacturing Co LLC (G-343)*

Paragon Mfg Inc 413 562-7202
  61 Union St Westfield (01085) *(G-13196)*

Paragon Tool Company Inc 860 647-9935
  121 Adams St Manchester (06042) *(G-1627)*

Parallel Systems Corp. 978 352-7100
  118 Tenney St Georgetown (01833) *(G-8911)*

Parama Corporation 203 790-8155
  7 Trowbridge Dr Bethel (06801) *(G-131)*

Parametric Holdings Inc (HQ) **781 370-5000**
  140 Kendrick St Needham Heights (02494) *(G-10555)*

Parametric Technology Corp. 781 370-5000
  121 Seaport Blvd Boston (02210) *(G-6952)*

Paramount Corp. 508 999-4442
  375 Faunce Corner Rd Ste E North Dartmouth (02747) *(G-11000)*

Paramount Industries Inc 508 533-8480
  42 Milford St Medway (02053) *(G-10310)*

Paramount Machine Company Inc 860 643-5549
  138 Sanrico Dr Manchester (06042) *(G-1628)*

Paramount South Boston 617 269-9999
  667 E Broadway Boston (02127) *(G-6953)*

Paramount Tool LLC 508 672-0844
  473 Pleasant St Fall River (02721) *(G-8594)*

Parason Machine Inc 860 526-3565
  1000 Industrial Park Rd Deep River (06417) *(G-880)*

Paratek Pharmaceuticals Inc (DH) **617 807-6600**
  75 Park Plz Ste 3 Boston (02116) *(G-6954)*

Paratronix Inc 508 222-8979
  200 Flanders Rd Westborough (01581) *(G-13129)*

Paraxel International, Billerica *Also Called: Parexel International Corp (G-6469)*

Parchment Press, Island Pond *Also Called: Community Apostolic Order Inc (G-17304)*

Parent Lumber Company Inc 207 998-2322
  355 Pigeon Hill Rd Mechanic Falls (04256) *(G-5053)*

Parexel International Corp. 978 313-3900
  1 Federal St Billerica (01821) *(G-6469)*

Parfums De Coeur Ltd (PA) **203 655-8807**
  750 E Main St Ste 1000 Stamford (06902) *(G-3426)*

Paricon Technologies Corp. 508 823-0876
  500 Myles Standish Blvd Ste 2 Taunton (02780) *(G-12354)*

Paridise Foods LLC 203 283-3903
  828 New Haven Ave Milford (06460) *(G-1863)*

Parisi Associates LLC. 978 667-8700
  6 Omni Way Chelmsford (01824) *(G-7944)*

Park Assist, Cheshire *Also Called: Tkh Security LLC (G-619)*

Park Avenue Securities 860 677-2600
  197 Scott Swamp Rd Farmington (06032) *(G-1240)*

Park City Packaging Inc (PA) **203 378-7384**
  480 Sniffens Ln Stratford (06615) *(G-3564)*

Park Distributories Inc 203 366-7200
  347 Railroad Ave Bridgeport (06604) *(G-355)*

Park Distributories Inc 203 366-7200
  347 Railroad Ave Bridgeport (06604) *(G-356)*

Park Distributories Inc (PA) **203 579-2140**
  347 Railroad Ave Bridgeport (06604) *(G-357)*

Park Press Printers, Saugus *Also Called: Gmf Engineering Inc (G-11758)*

Parker & Bailey Corp. 508 660-0011
  4 Walpole Park S Ste 2 Walpole (02081) *(G-12572)*

Parker & Harper Companies Inc (PA) **603 895-4761**
  2 Otter Ct Raymond (03077) *(G-15455)*

Parker Hannifin Chomerics, Woburn *Also Called: Parker-Hannifin Corporation (G-13631)*

Parker Medical Inc 860 350-4304
  43 Old Ridgebury Rd Danbury (06810) *(G-794)*

Parker Saw Mill, Somers *Also Called: Parker Septic LLC (G-3099)*

Parker Septic LLC. 860 749-8220
  77 South Rd Somers (06071) *(G-3099)*

Parker-Hannifin Corporation 860 827-2300
  95 Edgewood Ave New Britain (06051) *(G-2050)*

Parker-Hannifin Corporation 203 239-3341
  33 Defco Park Rd North Haven (06473) *(G-2430)*

Parker-Hannifin Corporation 207 439-9511
  9 Cutts Rd Kittery (03904) *(G-4938)*

Parker-Hannifin Corporation 978 784-1200
  14 Robbins Pond Rd Devens (01434) *(G-8285)*

Parker-Hannifin Corporation 978 858-0505
  242 Neck Rd Haverhill (01835) *(G-9120)*

Parker-Hannifin Corporation 781 935-4850
  77 Dragon Ct Woburn (01801) *(G-13629)*

Parker-Hannifin Corporation 781 935-4850
  8 Commonwealth Ave Woburn (01801) *(G-13630)*

Parker-Hannifin Corporation 781 939-4278
  70 Dragon Ct Woburn (01801) *(G-13631)*

Parker-Hannifin Corporation 603 595-1500
  26 Clinton Dr Ste 103 Hollis (03049) *(G-14456)*

Parker-Hannifin Corporation 603 880-4807
  16 Flagstone Dr Hudson (03051) *(G-14534)*

Parker's Maple Barn, Mason *Also Called: Parkers Maple Barn Corn Crib (G-14967)*

Parkers Maple Barn Corn Crib 603 878-2308
  1316 Brookline Rd Mason (03048) *(G-14967)*

Parkinson Machinery & Manufacturing Corp. 401 762-2100
  100 Goldstein Dr Woonsocket (02895) *(G-16971)*

Parkinson Technologies, Woonsocket *Also Called: Parkinson Technologies Inc (G-16972)*

Parkinson Technologies Inc 401 762-2100
  100 Goldstein Dr Woonsocket (02895) *(G-16972)*

Parkway Manufacturing Co Inc 508 559-6686
  1 Bert Dr West Bridgewater (02379) *(G-12976)*

Parlee Composites Inc 978 998-4880
  69 Federal St Beverly (01915) *(G-6371)*

Parlee Cycles Inc, Beverly *Also Called: Parlee Composites Inc (G-6371)*

Parlex. 978 946-2500
  145 Milk St Methuen (01844) *(G-10343)*

Parmatech 3d Inc 401 739-0740
  55 Service Ave Warwick (02886) *(G-16843)*

Parshley Steel Fabricators Inc. 207 957-4040
  12 Elm St North Berwick (03906) *(G-5111)*

ALPHABETIC

Parson's Kitchen, Brownfield *Also Called: Lawrence Parson (G-4636)*

Parsonskellogg LLC.. 866 602-8398
  2290 Pawtucket Ave East Providence (02914) *(G-16037)*

Particles Plus Inc... 781 341-6898
  31 Tosca Dr Ste 8 Stoughton (02072) *(G-12227)*

Partner In Publishing LLC.. 860 430-9440
  1715 Main St Glastonbury (06033) *(G-1292)*

Partners Capital Inv Group LLP................................... 617 292-2570
  600 Atlantic Ave Ste 3001 Boston (02210) *(G-6955)*

Parts Tool and Die Inc... 413 821-9718
  344 Shoemaker Ln Agawam (01001) *(G-5805)*

Partylite Inc **(HQ)**.. **203 661-1926**
  59 Armstrong Rd Plymouth (02360) *(G-11471)*

Partylite Worldwide LLC **(DH)**............................... **888 999-5706**
  600 Cordwainer Dr Ste 202 Norwell (02061) *(G-11144)*

Pas, Bethany *Also Called: Plastic Assembly Systems LLC (G-97)*

Pas Technologies Inc.. 860 649-2727
  321 Progress Dr Manchester (06042) *(G-1629)*

Pascale Industries Inc.. 508 673-3307
  939 Currant Rd Fall River (02720) *(G-8595)*

Pasta Bene Inc.. 508 583-1515
  1050 Pearl St Ste 1 Brockton (02301) *(G-7300)*

Pasta Vita Inc.. 860 395-1452
  225 Elm St Old Saybrook (06475) *(G-2658)*

Pastanch LLC.. 203 720-9478
  31 Sheridan Dr Naugatuck (06770) *(G-1979)*

Pat Gagne Logging LLC.. 603 449-2479
  236 Ferry Rd Dummer (03588) *(G-14263)*

Pat Trap Inc.. 603 428-3396
  632 Western Ave Henniker (03242) *(G-14440)*

Patchology, Norwood *Also Called: Rare Beauty Brands Inc (G-11205)*

Patel Brew LLC.. 603 602-7455
  460 High St Somersworth (03878) *(G-15620)*

Pathai Inc **(PA)**.. **617 543-5250**
  1325 Boylston St Ste 1000 Boston (02215) *(G-6956)*

Pathiakis Nickolas... 207 864-3474
  94 Stratton Rd Rangeley (04970) *(G-5313)*

Pathway Lighting Products Inc.................................... 860 388-6881
  35 Research Pkwy Old Saybrook (06475) *(G-2659)*

Patio Barn... 603 673-2716
  272 State Route 101 Amherst (03031) *(G-13883)*

Patricia Barrett... 978 537-0458
  56 Marshall St Leominster (01453) *(G-9692)*

Patricia Spratt For Home LLC..................................... 860 434-9291
  60 Lyme St Old Lyme (06371) *(G-2644)*

Patricia Spratt For The Home, Old Lyme *Also Called: Patricia Spratt For Home LLC (G-2644)*

Patriot Armor, Lenox Dale *Also Called: Patriot Armored Systems LLC (G-9628)*

Patriot Armored Systems LLC **(PA)**........................ **413 637-1060**
  140 Crystal St Lenox Dale (01242) *(G-9628)*

Patriot Armred Systems Hldg LL................................. 413 637-1060
  100 Valley St Lee (01238) *(G-9617)*

Patriot Beverages LLC.. 978 486-4900
  20 Harvard Rd Littleton (01460) *(G-9831)*

Patriot Coating Inc.. 978 567-9006
  17 Kane Industrial Dr Ste 2 Hudson (01749) *(G-9398)*

Patriot Custom Mfg Inc.. 508 764-7342
  134 Ashland Ave Southbridge (01550) *(G-12033)*

Patriot Foundry & Castings LLC.................................. 603 934-3919
  20 Herrick Cir Pelham (03076) *(G-15292)*

Patriot Newspaper, Webster *Also Called: Yankee Shopper (G-12931)*

Patriot Seal Coating.. 774 386-8531
  9 Greendale Ave Worcester (01606) *(G-13768)*

Patriot Worldwide Inc.. 800 786-4669
  425 Fortune Blvd Ste 206 Milford (01757) *(G-10413)*

Patrol, Attleboro Falls *Also Called: Advanced Electronic Design Inc (G-6078)*

Patsys Bus Sales and Service..................................... 603 226-2222
  31 Hall St Concord (03301) *(G-14151)*

Patten Machine Inc.. 978 562-9847
  299 Central St Hudson (01749) *(G-9399)*

Patten Tool and Engrg Inc.. 207 439-1555
  22 Route 236 Kittery (03904) *(G-4939)*

Patwil LLC... 860 589-9085
  190 Century Dr Ste 102 Bristol (06010) *(G-480)*

Paul Dewitt.. 203 792-5610
  128 E Liberty St Ste 4 Danbury (06810) *(G-795)*

Paul H Gesswein & Company Inc................................. 860 388-0652
  40 River St Old Saybrook (06475) *(G-2660)*

Paul H Murphy & Co Inc... 617 472-7707
  634 Willard St Quincy (02169) *(G-11530)*

Paul K Guillow Inc.. 781 245-5255
  40 New Salem St Wakefield (01880) *(G-12526)*

Paul King Foundry Inc.. 401 231-3120
  92 Allendale Ave Johnston (02919) *(G-16099)*

Paul McNamara... 508 245-5654
  110 Dundee Dr Bridgewater (02324) *(G-7236)*

Paul Welding Company Inc... 860 229-9945
  157 Kelsey St Newington (06111) *(G-2314)*

Paul's Pasta Shop, Groton *Also Called: If Not Now When Inc (G-1373)*

Pauls Marble Depot LLC... 203 978-0669
  40 Warshaw Pl Ste 1 Stamford (06902) *(G-3427)*

Pauway Corp... 203 265-3939
  63 N Cherry St Ste 2 Wallingford (06492) *(G-3837)*

Pavement Warehouse.. 401 233-3200
  11 Calista St Greenville (02828) *(G-16062)*

Pavers By Ideal, Westford *Also Called: Ideal Concrete Block Co (G-13242)*

Pavestone LLC... 508 947-6001
  18 Cowan Dr Middleboro (02346) *(G-10373)*

Paw Print Offset/Digital, South Burlington *Also Called: Paw Prints Press Inc (G-17589)*

Paw Print Pantry LLC **(PA)**.................................... **860 447-8442**
  33 Gurley Rd East Lyme (06333) *(G-1060)*

Paw Prints Press Inc.. 802 865-2872
  12 Gregory Dr Ste 8 South Burlington (05403) *(G-17589)*

Pawtucket Hot Mix Asphalt Inc................................... 401 722-4488
  25 Concord St Pawtucket (02860) *(G-16400)*

Pawtucket Times, The, Pawtucket *Also Called: New England Newspapers Inc (G-16392)*

Payne Engrg Fabrication Co Inc.................................. 781 828-9046
  28 Draper Ln Ste 3 Canton (02021) *(G-7817)*

Payne/Bouchier Inc **(PA)**...................................... **617 445-4323**
  173a Norfolk Ave Roxbury (02119) *(G-11692)*

Pbd Productions LLC.. 508 482-9300
  3b Landing Ln Hopedale (01747) *(G-9300)*

Pbi, South Easton *Also Called: Pressure Biosciences Inc (G-11950)*

PBL Incorporated... 802 893-0111
  158 Brentwood Dr Ste 2 Colchester (05446) *(G-17199)*

PBM Nutritionals LLC **(DH)**.................................. **802 527-0521**
  147 Industrial Park Rd Milton (05468) *(G-17363)*

Pbs Plastics Inc.. 603 868-1717
  219 Old Concord Tpke Barrington (03825) *(G-13915)*

PCA, Northampton *Also Called: Packaging Corporation America (G-11074)*

PCA LLC.. 978 494-0550
  5 Harper Cir Andover (01810) *(G-5905)*

PCA Systems, Adams *Also Called: Holland Company Inc (G-5773)*

Pca/Chelmsford 310, Northampton *Also Called: Packaging Corporation America (G-11075)*

PCC Specialty Products Inc.. 503 417-4800
  28 Sword St Auburn (01501) *(G-6123)*

PCC Strcturals Alum Operations, Northfield *Also Called: PCC Structurals Groton (G-15267)*

PCC Structurals, Groton *Also Called: PCC Structurals Groton (G-1377)*

PCC Structurals Groton **(DH)**................................ **860 405-3700**
  839 Poquonnock Rd Groton (06340) *(G-1377)*

PCC Structurals Groton.. 603 286-4301
  35 Industrial Park Dr Franklin (03235) *(G-14321)*

PCC Structurals Groton.. 603 286-4301
  24 Granite St Northfield (03276) *(G-15267)*

PCF, Wakefield *Also Called: Publishers Crcltion Flfllment (G-12530)*

Pcg Machine Shop, Hartland *Also Called: Precision Cutter Grinding Inc (G-17287)*

PCI Synthesis, Newburyport *Also Called: Polycarbon Industries Inc (G-10707)*

PCL Fixtures Inc.. 401 334-4646
  95 Leggett St Ste 2 East Hartford (06108) *(G-1009)*

Pcx, Newington *Also Called: Pcx Aerostructures LLC (G-2316)*

Pcx Aerostructures LLC **(PA)**................................ **860 666-2471**
  300 Fenn Rd Newington (06111) *(G-2315)*

Pcx Aerostructures LLC...................................... 860 666-2471
  300 Fenn Rd Newington (06111) *(G-2316)*

Pcx Aerostructures LLC...................................... 508 869-2131
  222 Shrewsbury St Boylston (01505) *(G-7163)*

Pcx Aerosystems, Boylston *Also Called: Pcx Aerostructures LLC (G-7163)*

Pcx Aerosystems LLC....................................... 860 666-2471
  300 Fenn Rd Newington (06111) *(G-2317)*

Pcx Aerosystems-Manchester LLC.......................... 860 649-0000
  586 Hilliard St Manchester (06042) *(G-1630)*

PDC Brands, Stamford *Also Called: Parfums De Coeur Ltd (G-3426)*

PDC International Corp...................................... 203 853-1516
  8 Sheehan Ave Norwalk (06854) *(G-2552)*

Pdi, Middletown *Also Called: Plastic Design Intl Inc (G-1771)*

Pdk Worldwide, Fall River *Also Called: PDk Worldwide Entps Inc (G-8596)*

PDk Worldwide Entps Inc **(PA)**.......................... **508 676-2155**
  10 N Main St Ste 3g # 3 Fall River (02720) *(G-8596)*

PDKD Enterprises Inc....................................... 781 233-8499
  120 Lincoln Ave Saugus (01906) *(G-11764)*

Pdq Inc **(PA)**... **860 529-9051**
  24 Evans Rd Rocky Hill (06067) *(G-2932)*

Pds, Bloomfield *Also Called: Pds Engineering & Construction (G-201)*

Pds Engineering & Construction............................ 860 242-8586
  107 Old Windsor Rd Bloomfield (06002) *(G-201)*

Peaceful Meadows Ice Cream Inc **(PA)**.................. **781 447-3700**
  5 Russell Holmes Way Carver (02330) *(G-7855)*

Peachwave of Watertown.................................... 203 942-4949
  1156 Main St Watertown (06795) *(G-4023)*

Peak Manufacturing, Fitchburg *Also Called: MA Mfg LLC (G-8660)*

Peak Manufacturing, Fitchburg *Also Called: Portance Corp (G-8672)*

Peak Printing Inc... 401 351-0500
  88 Orange St Providence (02903) *(G-16582)*

Peak Scientific Inc **(DH)**............................... **978 234-4679**
  19 Sterling Rd Ste 1 North Billerica (01862) *(G-10942)*

Peak Technologies LLC..................................... 978 393-5900
  9 Beaver Brook Rd Littleton (01460) *(G-9832)*

Peale Ctr For Christn Living, Danbury *Also Called: A Guideposts Church Corp (G-699)*

Pearce, Simon Restaurant, Quechee *Also Called: Simon Pearce (us) Inc (G-17463)*

Pearl Die-Cutting & Finshg LLC............................ 781 721-6900
  110 Commerce Way Ste E Woburn (01801) *(G-13632)*

Pearl Meat Packing Co Inc.................................. 781 228-5100
  27 York Ave Randolph (02368) *(G-11571)*

Pearl Street Beverage Inc.................................. 802 658-1574
  240 Pearl St Burlington (05401) *(G-17150)*

Pearl Street Pipe & Beverage, Burlington *Also Called: Pearl Street Beverage Inc (G-17150)*

Pearlco of Boston Inc...................................... 781 821-1010
  5 Whitman Rd Canton (02021) *(G-7818)*

Pearpoint Inc.. 760 343-7350
  28 Tower Rd Raymond (04071) *(G-5314)*

Pearson Custom Publishing................................. 781 248-2721
  501 Boylston St Boston (02116) *(G-6957)*

Pearson Education Inc...................................... 617 848-6000
  501 Boylston St Boston (02116) *(G-6958)*

Pearson Education Holdings Inc............................ 617 671-2000
  501 Boylston St Ste 900 Boston (02116) *(G-6959)*

Pearson Eductl Measurement, Boston *Also Called: Pearson Education Inc (G-6958)*

Pearson Learning Solutions................................ 617 671-3253
  31 Saint James Ave # 725 Boston (02116) *(G-6960)*

Pease & Curren Incorporated............................... 401 738-6449
  75 Pennsylvania Ave Warwick (02888) *(G-16844)*

Peavey Manufacturing Company............................. 207 843-7861
  526 Main Rd Eddington (04428) *(G-4746)*

Peckham Enterprises LLC................................... 413 862-3252
  20 Chamberlain Rd Montgomery (01050) *(G-10459)*

Peckham Industries Inc.................................... 802 442-4418
  295 Airport Rd Shaftsbury (05262) *(G-17552)*

Peco Pallet... 845 642-2780
  34 Lake St Apt 2 Brighton (02135) *(G-7243)*

Peeled Inc.. 212 706-2001
  30 Martin St Ste 3b1 Cumberland (02864) *(G-15959)*

Peeled Snacks, Cumberland *Also Called: Peeled Inc (G-15959)*

Peeled Snacks Inc... 773 372-3223
  121 Mount Archer Rd Lyme (06371) *(G-1560)*

Peening Technologies Conn, East Hartford *Also Called: Hydro Honing Laboratories Inc (G-999)*

Peening Technologies Eqp LLC.............................. 860 289-4328
  8 Eastern Park Rd East Hartford (06108) *(G-1010)*

Peergrade Inc **(PA)**..................................... **857 302-4023**
  361 Newbury St Ste 412 Boston (02115) *(G-6961)*

Peerless, Stamford *Also Called: Peerless Systems Corporation (G-3428)*

Peerless Precision Inc..................................... 413 562-2359
  22 Mainline Dr Westfield (01085) *(G-13197)*

Peerless Systems Corporation **(DH)**..................... **203 350-0040**
  1055 Washington Blvd Fl 8 Stamford (06901) *(G-3428)*

Peg Kearsarge Co Inc...................................... 603 374-2341
  14 Mill St Bartlett (03812) *(G-13918)*

PEGA, Cambridge *Also Called: Pegasystems Inc (G-7681)*

Pegasus Capital Advisors LP **(PA)**...................... **203 869-4400**
  750 E Main St Ste 600 Stamford (06902) *(G-3429)*

Pegasus Glassworks Inc.................................... 508 347-5656
  66 Technology Park Rd Sturbridge (01566) *(G-12255)*

Pegasus Inc... 508 429-2461
  39 Locust St Holliston (01746) *(G-9227)*

Pegasus Manufacturing, Middletown *Also Called: Leggett Platt Arspc Mddltown L (G-1759)*

Pegasus Manufacturing, Middletown *Also Called: Pegasus Manufacturing Inc (G-1769)*

Pegasus Manufacturing Inc................................. 860 635-8811
  422 Timber Ridge Rd Middletown (06457) *(G-1769)*

Pegasystems Inc **(PA)**.................................. **617 374-9600**
  1 Main St Cambridge (02142) *(G-7681)*

Pegco Process Labs, Bartlett *Also Called: Peg Kearsarge Co Inc (G-13918)*

Peggy Lawton Kitchens Inc................................. 508 668-1215
  255 Washington St East Walpole (02032) *(G-8420)*

Pelham Plastics Inc....................................... 603 886-7226
  42 Dick Tracy Dr Pelham (03076) *(G-15293)*

Pelican Products Inc...................................... 413 665-2163
  147 N Main St South Deerfield (01373) *(G-11926)*

Pelletier & Pelletier...................................... 207 834-2296
  14 E Main St Fort Kent (04743) *(G-4792)*

Pelletier Manufacturing Inc............................... 207 723-6500
  400 Golden Rd Millinocket (04462) *(G-5068)*

Pellion Technologies Inc
  1337 Massachusetts Ave Arlington (02476) *(G-5944)*

Pemac Construction.. 860 437-0007
  15 Lakewood Dr Unit 17 Oakdale (06370) *(G-2623)*

Pemberton's Gourmet, Gray *Also Called: Pembertons Food Inc (G-4843)*

Pembertons Food Inc....................................... 207 657-6446
  32 Lewiston Rd Bldg 1b Gray (04039) *(G-4843)*

Pen Ro Group, Pittsfield *Also Called: Pen Ro Mold and Tool Inc (G-11416)*

Pen Ro Mold and Tool Inc.................................. 413 499-0464
  343 Pecks Rd Ste 5 Pittsfield (01201) *(G-11416)*

Pendar Technologies LLC **(PA)**.......................... **617 588-2128**
  30 Spinelli Pl Cambridge (02138) *(G-7682)*

Penfield Search Partners Ltd.............................. 203 307-2600
  1275 Post Rd Ste 200d Fairfield (06824) *(G-1196)*

Penmar Industries Inc..................................... 203 853-4868
  35 Ontario St Stratford (06615) *(G-3565)*

Penmor Lithographers Inc.................................. 207 784-1341
  8 Lexington St Lewiston (04240) *(G-4984)*

Pennsylvania Globe Gaslight Co............................ 203 484-7749
  300 Shaw Rd North Branford (06471) *(G-2371)*

Penny Marketing, Loudon *Also Called: Penny Publications LLC (G-14797)*

Penny Marketing Ltd Partnr **(PA)**....................... **203 866-6688**
  6 Prowitt St Norwalk (06855) *(G-2553)*

Penny Pinchers Brewing Co LLC............................. 774 696-7885
  75 Elm St Millbury (01527) *(G-10440)*

Penny Press Inc... 203 866-6688
  185 Plains Rd Ste 100e Milford (06461) *(G-1864)*

Penny Press Inc **(PA)**.................................. **203 866-6688**
  6 Prowitt St Norwalk (06855) *(G-2554)*

Penny Publications LLC.................................... 203 866-6688
  185 Plains Rd Ste 201 Milford (06461) *(G-1865)*

Penny Publications LLC **(PA)**........................... **203 866-6688**
  6 Prowitt St Norwalk (06855) *(G-2555)*

A L P H A B E T I C

Penny Publications LLC..................................603 783-9998
  570 Route 106 N Loudon (03307) *(G-14797)*

Penny Straker Gardens, South Dartmouth *Also Called: P Straker Ltd (G-11918)*

Pennysaver, The, Warwick *Also Called: Beacon Communications Inc (G-16789)*

Penobscot Bay Press **(PA)**...........................**207 367-2200**
  138 Main St Stonington (04681) *(G-5534)*

Penobscot McCrum LLC....................................207 338-4360
  2326 Parsons Rd Washburn (04786) *(G-5587)*

Pentair Electronic Packaging, Warwick *Also Called: Schroff Inc (G-16859)*

Pentair Rsdntial Fltration LLC.........................603 749-1610
  47 Crosby Rd Dover (03820) *(G-14244)*

Penwell..508 347-8245
  15 Country Hill Rd Sturbridge (01566) *(G-12256)*

Pep Be-St, Bridgeport *Also Called: Boston Endo-Surgical Tech LLC (G-303)*

Pep Brainin, Attleboro *Also Called: Brainin-Advance Industries LLC (G-5998)*

Pep Connecticut Plastics, Wallingford *Also Called: Precision Engineered Pdts LLC (G-3840)*

Pep Direct LLC..603 654-6141
  19 Stoney Brook Dr Wilton (03086) *(G-15707)*

Pep General Metal Finishing, Attleboro *Also Called: General Metal Finishing LLC (G-6020)*

Pep Industries LLC...508 226-5600
  110 Frank Mossberg Dr Attleboro (02703) *(G-6046)*

Pep Micropep, East Providence *Also Called: Matrix I LLC (G-16030)*

Pepco, Bristol *Also Called: The Plainville Electrical Products Co (G-500)*

Pepgen Inc...781 797-0979
  321 Harrison Ave Ste 800 Boston (02118) *(G-6962)*

Pepin Granite Company Inc..............................802 476-6103
  58 Granite St Barre (05641) *(G-17015)*

Pepin Precast Inc...207 324-6125
  59 Shaw Rd Sanford (04073) *(G-5405)*

Peppercorn Food Service Inc...........................781 639-6035
  91 Pitman Rd Marblehead (01945) *(G-10092)*

Pepperell Braiding Company Inc **(PA)**...........**978 433-2133**
  22 Lowell St Pepperell (01463) *(G-11387)*

Pepperidge Farm, Norwalk *Also Called: Pepperidge Farm Incorporated (G-2556)*

Pepperidge Farm Incorporated **(HQ)**..............**203 846-7000**
  595 Westport Ave Norwalk (06851) *(G-2556)*

Pepsi Cola Bottling Aroostook..........................207 760-3000
  52 Industrial St Presque Isle (04769) *(G-5309)*

Pepsi Cola Bottling Co......................................802 254-6093
  1566 Putney Rd Brattleboro (05301) *(G-17099)*

Pepsi Cola Bottling Co Bristol...........................860 628-8200
  110 Corporate Dr Southington (06489) *(G-3228)*

Pepsi-Cola, Uncasville *Also Called: Pepsi-Cola Metro Btlg Co Inc (G-3743)*

Pepsi-Cola, Auburn *Also Called: Pepsi-Cola Metro Btlg Co Inc (G-4452)*

Pepsi-Cola, Sagamore Beach *Also Called: Pepsi-Cola Metro Btlg Co Inc (G-11697)*

Pepsi-Cola, Wilmington *Also Called: Pepsi-Cola Metro Btlg Co Inc (G-13446)*

Pepsi-Cola, Manchester *Also Called: Pepsi-Cola Metro Btlg Co Inc (G-14911)*

Pepsi-Cola, Cranston *Also Called: Pepsi-Cola Metro Btlg Co Inc (G-15904)*

Pepsi-Cola Btlg Worcester Inc..........................860 774-4007
  135 Louisa Viens Dr Dayville (06241) *(G-865)*

Pepsi-Cola Btlg Worcester Inc **(PA)**...............**508 829-6551**
  90 Industrial Dr Holden (01520) *(G-9194)*

Pepsi-Cola Metro Btlg Co Inc...........................203 375-2484
  355 Benton St Stratford (06615) *(G-3566)*

Pepsi-Cola Metro Btlg Co Inc...........................860 848-1231
  260 Gallivan Ln Uncasville (06382) *(G-3743)*

Pepsi-Cola Metro Btlg Co Inc...........................860 688-6281
  55 International Dr Windsor (06095) *(G-4294)*

Pepsi-Cola Metro Btlg Co Inc...........................207 784-5791
  191 Merrow Rd Auburn (04210) *(G-4452)*

Pepsi-Cola Metro Btlg Co Inc...........................207 973-2217
  19 Penobscot Meadow Dr Hampden (04444) *(G-4865)*

Pepsi-Cola Metro Btlg Co Inc...........................508 833-5600
  103 State Rd Sagamore Beach (02562) *(G-11697)*

Pepsi-Cola Metro Btlg Co Inc...........................978 661-6150
  111 Eames St Wilmington (01887) *(G-13446)*

Pepsi-Cola Metro Btlg Co Inc...........................603 625-5764
  127 Pepsi Rd Manchester (03109) *(G-14911)*

Pepsi-Cola Metro Btlg Co Inc...........................401 468-3300
  1400 Pontiac Ave Cranston (02920) *(G-15904)*

Pepsico..203 974-8912
  150 Munson St New Haven (06511) *(G-2183)*

Pepsico..857 233-2421
  108 Jersey St Boston (02215) *(G-6963)*

Pepsico, Dayville *Also Called: Pepsi-Cola Btlg Worcester Inc (G-865)*

Pepsico, New Haven *Also Called: Pepsico (G-2183)*

Pepsico, Southington *Also Called: Pepsi Cola Bottling Co Bristol (G-3228)*

Pepsico, Stratford *Also Called: Pepsi-Cola Metro Btlg Co Inc (G-3566)*

Pepsico, Windsor *Also Called: Pepsi-Cola Metro Btlg Co Inc (G-4294)*

Pepsico, Presque Isle *Also Called: Pepsi Cola Bottling Aroostook (G-5309)*

Pepsico, Boston *Also Called: Pepsico (G-6963)*

Pepsico, Holden *Also Called: Pepsi-Cola Btlg Worcester Inc (G-9194)*

Percision Electronics, Marshfield *Also Called: Precision Electronics Corp (G-10244)*

Percussion, Burlington *Also Called: Percussion Software Inc (G-7410)*

Percussion Software Inc....................................781 438-9900
  100 Summit Dr Ste 100 Burlington (01803) *(G-7410)*

Peregrine Turbine Tech LLC..............................207 687-8333
  29 S Point Dr Wiscasset (04578) *(G-5699)*

Perey Turnstiles Inc...203 333-9400
  308 Bishop Ave Bridgeport (06610) *(G-358)*

Perfect Empanada LLC **(PA)**...........................**508 241-5150**
  8 Blackstone Rd Attleboro (02703) *(G-6047)*

Perfect Empanada LLC.....................................508 241-5150
  691 Main St Warren (02885) *(G-16762)*

Perfect Fit..207 278-3333
  39 Stetson Rd Corinna (04928) *(G-4703)*

Perfection Fence Corp **(PA)**............................**781 837-3600**
  635 Plain St Marshfield (02050) *(G-10243)*

Perfectsoftware, Norwalk *Also Called: Criterion Inc (G-2488)*

Performance Chemicals, Franklin *Also Called: Performance Chemicals LLC (G-14322)*

Performance Chemicals LLC..............................603 228-1200
  40 Industrial Park Dr Franklin (03235) *(G-14322)*

Performance Connection Systems.....................203 868-5517
  599 W Main St Meriden (06451) *(G-1684)*

Performance Motion Devices Inc.......................978 266-1210
  80 Central St Ste 200 Boxborough (01719) *(G-7153)*

Performance Products Painting..........................207 783-4222
  63 Omni Cir Auburn (04210) *(G-4453)*

Performance Textiles Inc....................................781 934-7055
  42 Tremont St Ste 3 Duxbury (02332) *(G-8333)*

Performer Publications Inc.................................617 627-9200
  24 Dane St Somerville (02143) *(G-11887)*

Period Lighting Fixtures Inc...............................413 664-7141
  167 River Rd Clarksburg (01247) *(G-8072)*

Perioq Inc...978 534-1249
  37 Hamilton St Apt 4 Leominster (01453) *(G-9693)*

Perkatory Productions LLC................................860 894-6040
  725 Main St Unit 32 Middletown (06457) *(G-1770)*

Perkinelmer, Hopkinton *Also Called: Revvity Inc (G-9343)*

Perkinelmer, Waltham *Also Called: Revvity Inc (G-12767)*

Perkinelmer Hlth Sciences Inc, Waltham *Also Called: Revvity Health Sciences Inc (G-12768)*

Perkinelmer US LLC **(PA)**...............................**203 925-4600**
  710 Bridgeport Ave Shelton (06484) *(G-3046)*

Perkins Brothers Corp.......................................781 858-3031
  358 Main St Medfield (02052) *(G-10273)*

Perkins Division, Franklin *Also Called: Automatic Press Inc (G-8818)*

Perkins Pre-Coat, Medfield *Also Called: Perkins Brothers Corp (G-10273)*

Perkins School For Blind....................................617 924-3434
  175 North Beacon St Watertown (02472) *(G-12899)*

Perleys Logging Inc...207 227-0513
  150 Rafford Rd Ashland (04732) *(G-4413)*

Perma Flex Engineering, Chicopee *Also Called: Pfe Rolls Inc (G-8053)*

Perma Incorporated...978 667-5161
  605 Springs Rd Bedford (01730) *(G-6252)*

Permentry, West Haven *Also Called: The Bilco Company (G-4128)*

Perosphere Inc...203 885-1111
  108 Mill Plain Rd Ste 3 Danbury (06811) *(G-796)*

Perosphere Technologies Inc.............................475 218-4600
  108 Mill Plain Rd Ste 3 Danbury (06811) *(G-797)*

Perras Lumber Co Inc.. 603 636-1830
  45 Perras Rd Groveton (03582) *(G-14378)*

Perrco Inc.. 617 933-5300
  70 Conn St Woburn (01801) *(G-13633)*

Perrier Water, Stamford *Also Called: Bluetriton Brands Inc (G-3296)*

Perrigo Nutritionals, Milton *Also Called: PBM Nutritionals LLC (G-17363)*

Perry Blackburne Inc... 401 231-7200
  330 Woonasquatucket Ave North Providence (02911) *(G-16307)*

Perry Paving... 401 732-1730
  20 Keystone Dr Warwick (02889) *(G-16845)*

Perry Technology Corporation................................ 860 738-2525
  120 Industrial Park Rd New Hartford (06057) *(G-2107)*

Perseus Partners LLC.. 207 273-3780
  2243 Camden Rd Warren (04864) *(G-5586)*

Persimmon Tech, Wakefield *Also Called: Persimmon Technologies Corp (G-12527)*

Persimmon Technologies Corp............................... 781 587-0677
  200 Harvard Mill Sq Ste 110 Wakefield (01880) *(G-12527)*

Personal Care Appliances Div, Stamford *Also Called: Conair LLC (G-3320)*

Persons Concrete... 603 524-4434
  3 Eastgate Park Dr Belmont (03220) *(G-13966)*

Perspecta Svcs & Solutions Inc **(DH)**.................... **781 684-4000**
  350 2nd Ave Bldg 1 Waltham (02451) *(G-12747)*

Perx LLC... 413 358-9020
  25 Downing Three Park Pittsfield (01201) *(G-11417)*

Pet Food Experts Inc **(PA)**............................... **401 721-5593**
  175 Main St Unit 2 Pawtucket (02860) *(G-16401)*

Pet Gear, West Rutland *Also Called: Vermont Juvenile Furn Mfg Inc (G-17697)*

Pet Pocketbook Inc... 857 246-9884
  398 Columbus Ave Pmb 341 Boston (02116) *(G-6964)*

Pete and Gerrys Organics LLC **(PA)**..................... **603 638-2827**
  140 Buffum Rd Monroe (03771) *(G-15047)*

Pete's Tire Barns, Orange *Also Called: Petes Tire Barns Inc (G-11228)*

Peter Forg Manufacturing Co................................ 617 625-0337
  50 Park St Somerville (02143) *(G-11888)*

Peter Paul Electronics Co Inc................................ 860 229-4884
  480 John Downey Dr New Britain (06051) *(G-2051)*

Peterboro Basket Company................................... 603 924-3861
  130 Grove St Peterborough (03458) *(G-15324)*

Peterboro Tool Company Inc................................. 603 924-3034
  Upper Union St Peterborough (03458) *(G-15325)*

Peterborough Basket Company, Peterborough *Also Called: Old Dublin Road Inc (G-15323)*

Peterborough Transcript...................................... 603 924-3333
  1 Phoenix Mill Ln Unit 100 Peterborough (03458) *(G-15326)*

Petermans Boards and Bowls Inc........................... 413 863-2116
  61 French King Hwy Gill (01354) *(G-8915)*

Peterson and Nash Inc....................................... 781 826-9085
  846 Main St Norwell (02061) *(G-11145)*

Petes Tire Barns Inc... 401 521-2240
  80 Public St Providence (02903) *(G-16583)*

Petes Tire Barns Inc **(PA)**............................... **978 544-8811**
  275 E Main St Orange (01364) *(G-11228)*

Petnet Solutions Inc... 781 937-3600
  268 W Cummings Park Woburn (01801) *(G-13634)*

Petricca Industries Inc **(PA)**............................. **413 499-1441**
  550 Cheshire Rd Pittsfield (01201) *(G-11418)*

Petron Automation Inc....................................... 860 274-9091
  65 Mountain View Rd Watertown (06795) *(G-4024)*

Petrunti Design & Wdwkg LLC.............................. 860 953-5332
  23c Andover Dr West Hartford (06110) *(G-4078)*

Pexagon, Guilford *Also Called: Pexagon Technology Inc (G-1402)*

Pexagon Technology Inc..................................... 203 458-3364
  1 Shoreline Dr Ste 7 Guilford (06437) *(G-1402)*

Pexco LLC... 978 249-5343
  764 S Athol Rd Athol (01331) *(G-5982)*

Pez, Orange *Also Called: Pez Candy Inc (G-2680)*

Pez Candy Inc **(HQ)**....................................... **203 795-0531**
  35 Prindle Hill Rd Orange (06477) *(G-2680)*

Pez Manufacturing Corp..................................... 203 795-0531
  35 Prindle Hill Rd Orange (06477) *(G-2681)*

PF Laboratories Inc **(DH)**................................. **973 256-3100**
  201 Tresser Blvd Ste 324 Stamford (06901) *(G-3430)*

Pf Pro Fnshg Silkscreening Inc.............................. 603 329-8344
  13 Gigante Dr Hampstead (03841) *(G-14389)*

PFC Logging Inc.. 207 448-7998
  46 Snow Farm Rd Danforth (04424) *(G-4719)*

PFC Publications LLC... 508 366-2984
  8 Ashford Trl Apt 831 Peabody (01960) *(G-11332)*

Pfe Rolls Inc.. 978 544-7803
  1102 Sheridan St Chicopee (01022) *(G-8053)*

Pfeiffer Vacuum Inc **(DH)**................................ **317 328-8492**
  24 Trafalgar Sq Nashua (03063) *(G-15147)*

Pferd Inc.. 978 840-6420
  30 Jytek Dr Leominster (01453) *(G-9694)*

Pfizer.. 203 584-2793
  111 Ledgewood Rd Groton (06340) *(G-1378)*

Pfizer, Groton *Also Called: Pfizer (G-1378)*

Pfizer, New Haven *Also Called: Pfizer Inc (G-2184)*

Pfizer, Andover *Also Called: Pfizer Inc (G-5906)*

Pfizer, Cambridge *Also Called: Pfizer Inc (G-7683)*

Pfizer, Cambridge *Also Called: Pfizer Inc (G-7684)*

Pfizer Inc... 860 441-4100
  257 Eastern Point Rd Groton (06340) *(G-1379)*

Pfizer Inc... 203 401-0100
  1 Howe St New Haven (06511) *(G-2184)*

Pfizer Inc... 978 247-1000
  1 Burtt Rd Andover (01810) *(G-5906)*

Pfizer Inc... 617 551-3000
  610 Main St Cambridge (02139) *(G-7683)*

Pfizer Inc... 617 674-7436
  1 Portland St Cambridge (02139) *(G-7684)*

Pfm Holding Co.. 203 335-3300
  418 Meadow St Ste 201 Fairfield (06824) *(G-1197)*

Pg, Pawtucket *Also Called: Packaging Graphics LLC (G-16399)*

PG Adams Inc... 802 862-8664
  1215 Airport Pkwy South Burlington (05403) *(G-17590)*

Pg Imtech of Californ... 401 521-2490
  27 Dexter Rd East Providence (02914) *(G-16038)*

Pg Technologies Inc.. 413 562-1354
  91 Servistar Industrial Way Westfield (01085) *(G-13198)*

Pgc Acquisition LLC.. 508 888-2344
  74 Pleasant St Reading (01867) *(G-11604)*

Pgc Wire & Cable, Derry *Also Called: Pgc Wire & Cable LLC (G-14203)*

Pgc Wire & Cable LLC.. 603 821-7300
  16 Lesley Cir Derry (03038) *(G-14203)*

Pgi, Lowell *Also Called: Plenus Group Inc (G-9914)*

Pgxhealthholding Inc **(PA)**............................... **203 786-3400**
  5 Science Park New Haven (06511) *(G-2185)*

PH Production CT LLC.. 860 205-0942
  46 Schwier Rd South Windsor (06074) *(G-3171)*

Pha Industries Incorporated................................. 978 544-8770
  34 R W Moore Ave Orange (01364) *(G-11229)*

Pharm Eco Laboratories, Devens *Also Called: Veranova LP (G-8288)*

Pharmacal Research Labs Inc................................ 203 755-4908
  562 Captain Neville Dr Ste 1 Waterbury (06705) *(G-3959)*

Pharmaceutical RES Assoc Inc.............................. 203 588-8000
  201 Tresser Blvd Stamford (06901) *(G-3431)*

Pharmaceutical Resources, Brockton *Also Called: Lyne Laboratories Inc (G-7292)*

Pharmasol Corporation....................................... 508 238-0105
  1 Norfolk Ave Ste 1 South Easton (02375) *(G-11948)*

Pharmatron Inc... 603 645-6766
  2400 Computer Dr Westborough (01581) *(G-13130)*

Pharmavite Corp.. 860 651-1885
  10 Station St Simsbury (06070) *(G-3095)*

Pharmco-Aaper, Brookfield *Also Called: Greenfield Global USA Inc (G-524)*

Pharmctcal Strtgies Stffing LL.............................. 781 835-2300
  477 Main St Stoneham (02180) *(G-12185)*

Pharmion Corporation.. 857 706-1311
  200 Cambridgepark Dr Cambridge (02140) *(G-7685)*

Phase Forward... 781 626-1256
  880 Winter St Waltham (02451) *(G-12748)*

Phe Investments LLC... 401 289-2900
  1 Carding Ln Johnston (02919) *(G-16100)*

ALPHABETIC

Phesi Inc... 800 679-0068
  6 Applewood Cmn East Lyme (06333) *(G-1061)*

Philip Machine, Pawtucket *Also Called: Philip Machine Company Inc (G-16402)*

Philip Machine Company Inc............................. 401 353-7383
  190 York Ave Pawtucket (02860) *(G-16402)*

Philip Morris, Stamford *Also Called: Philip Morris Intl Inc (G-3432)*

Philip Morris Intl Inc **(PA)**........................... **203 905-2410**
  677 Washington Blvd Ste 1100 Stamford (06901) *(G-3432)*

Philip RS Sorbet Co Inc..................................... 781 721-6330
  750 Main St Winchester (01890) *(G-13491)*

Philipp Manufacturing Company........................ 413 527-4444
  19 Ward Ave Easthampton (01027) *(G-8459)*

Philips... 978 258-7110
  285 Sutton St North Andover (01845) *(G-10848)*

Philips Advanced Metrology Sys....................... 508 647-8400
  47 Manning Rd Billerica (01821) *(G-6470)*

Philips Colorkinetics.. 323 251-4758
  3 Burlington Woods Dr Burlington (01803) *(G-7411)*

Philips Consumer Lifestyle, Cambridge *Also Called: Philips Holding USA Inc (G-7686)*

Philips Hlthcare Infrmtics Inc.......................... 508 988-1000
  200 Donald Lynch Blvd Marlborough (01752) *(G-10195)*

Philips Holding USA Inc **(HQ)**..................... **978 687-1501**
  222 Jacobs St Cambridge (02141) *(G-7686)*

Philips Medical Systems, Andover *Also Called: Respironics Novametrix LLC (G-5911)*

Philips North America LLC................................. 508 647-1130
  12 Michigan Dr Natick (01760) *(G-10490)*

Philips Ultrasound Inc....................................... 203 753-5215
  1875 Thomaston Ave Ste 5 Waterbury (06704) *(G-3960)*

Phillips Candy House Inc................................... 617 282-2090
  818 William T Morrissey Blvd Boston (02122) *(G-6965)*

Phillips Chocolates, Boston *Also Called: Phillips Candy House Inc (G-6965)*

Phillips Enterprises Inc..................................... 413 586-5860
  149 Easthampton Rd Northampton (01060) *(G-11076)*

Phillips Fuel Systems Inc.................................. 203 908-3323
  25 Sherman St Stratford (06615) *(G-3567)*

Phillips Precision Inc... 508 869-3344
  240 Shrewsbury St Boylston (01505) *(G-7164)*

Phillips Precision Inc... 508 869-0373
  141 Shrewsbury St Boylston (01505) *(G-7165)*

Phinney Lumber Co.. 207 839-3336
  519 Fort Hill Rd Gorham (04038) *(G-4829)*

Phocam Manufacturing LLC.............................. 207 854-8471
  5 Sanford Dr Gorham (04038) *(G-4830)*

Phocuswright Inc **(HQ)**................................. **860 350-4084**
  1 Route 37 E Ste 200 Sherman (06784) *(G-3082)*

Phoenix Inc.. 508 399-7100
  257 Pine St Seekonk (02771) *(G-11783)*

Phoenix Assets Holdings Ltd............................ 800 323-9562
  68 Water St Norwalk (06854) *(G-2557)*

Phoenix Company of Chicago Inc **(PA)**....... **630 595-2300**
  22 Great Hill Rd Naugatuck (06770) *(G-1980)*

Phoenix Electric Corp.. 781 821-0200
  40 Hudson Rd Canton (02021) *(G-7819)*

Phoenix Feeds and Ntrtn Inc **(PA)**.............. **802 453-6684**
  5482 Ethan Allen Hwy New Haven (05472) *(G-17394)*

Phoenix Feeds Organix LLC.............................. 802 453-6684
  5482 Ethan Allen Hwy New Haven (05472) *(G-17395)*

Phoenix Manufacturing Inc............................... 860 745-2080
  250 South Rd Enfield (06082) *(G-1141)*

Phoenix Press Inc.. 203 865-5555
  15 James St New Haven (06513) *(G-2186)*

Phoenix Screen Printing.................................... 603 578-9599
  61 Bridge St Nashua (03060) *(G-15148)*

Phoenix Sheet Metal.. 508 994-4046
  53 Cove Rd South Dartmouth (02748) *(G-11919)*

Phoenix Vintners LLC... 877 340-9869
  28 Northgate Rd Ipswich (01938) *(G-9494)*

Phoenix Wire Inc.. 802 372-4561
  31 Tracy Rd South Hero (05486) *(G-17609)*

Phoenix Woodworks Inc..................................... 603 812-6214
  42 Nash Corner Rd Gilsum (03448) *(G-14343)*

Phoenix Workstation Division, Lowell *Also Called: General Woodworking Inc (G-9879)*

Phoenix Workstations, Lowell *Also Called: General Woodworking Inc (G-9878)*

Phoenix-Times Publishing Co............................ 401 253-6000
  1 Bradford St Bristol (02809) *(G-15777)*

Phosphorex LLC... 508 435-9100
  35 Parkwood Dr Ste 210 Hopkinton (01748) *(G-9339)*

Photo Diagnostic Systems Inc......................... 978 266-0420
  85 Swanson Rd Ste 110 Boxborough (01719) *(G-7154)*

Photo Etch Technology, Lowell *Also Called: Kalt Incorporated (G-9889)*

Photo Fab Engineering, Milford *Also Called: Elenel Industries Inc (G-10401)*

Photo Tool Engineering Inc............................... 978 805-5000
  71 Willie St Lowell (01854) *(G-9913)*

Photofabrication Engrg Inc **(HQ)**................. **508 478-2025**
  500 Fortune Blvd Milford (01757) *(G-10414)*

Photomachining Inc.. 603 882-9944
  4 Industrial Park Dr Unit 40 Pelham (03076) *(G-15294)*

Photonex Corporation... 978 723-2200
  200 Metrowest Tech Dr Maynard (01754) *(G-10264)*

Photonic Systems Inc.. 978 670-4990
  900 Middlesex Tpke Ste 5-2 Billerica (01821) *(G-6471)*

Photonics Media, Pittsfield *Also Called: Laurin Publishing Co Inc (G-11405)*

Photonis Scientific Inc **(DH)**....................... **508 347-4000**
  660 Main St Sturbridge (01518) *(G-12257)*

Photonis Usa, Inc., Sturbridge *Also Called: Photonis Scientific Inc (G-12257)*

Photonwares Corporation **(PA)**.................... **781 935-1200**
  15 Presidential Way Woburn (01801) *(G-13635)*

Photop Aegis Inc... 781 904-4000
  78a Olympia Ave Woburn (01801) *(G-13636)*

Photronics, Brookfield *Also Called: Photronics Inc (G-533)*

Photronics Inc **(PA)**..................................... **203 775-9000**
  15 Secor Rd Brookfield (06804) *(G-533)*

Photronics Texas Inc.. 203 546-3039
  15 Secor Rd Brookfield (06804) *(G-534)*

Photronics Texas I LLC..................................... 203 775-9000
  15 Secor Rd Brookfield (06804) *(G-535)*

Physical Measurement Tech Inc....................... 603 876-9990
  4 Ling St Marlborough (03455) *(G-14965)*

Physical Sciences Inc **(PA)**......................... **978 689-0003**
  20 New England Business Center Dr Andover (01810) *(G-5907)*

Phytek Industries Inc.. 603 226-4197
  578 River Rd Unit B Bow (03304) *(G-14007)*

Piantedosi, Malden *Also Called: Piantedosi Baking Co Inc (G-10023)*

Piantedosi Baking Co Inc **(PA)**.................... **781 321-3400**
  240 Commercial St Malden (02148) *(G-10023)*

Piatek Machine Company Inc............................ 401 728-9930
  25 Monticello Rd Pawtucket (02861) *(G-16403)*

Pic Pharmaceutical Inc..................................... 617 947-3883
  40 Nouvelle Way Unit N947 Natick (01760) *(G-10491)*

Pic20 Group LLC.. 203 957-3555
  155 Woodward Ave Ste 3 Norwalk (06854) *(G-2558)*

Pica, Derry *Also Called: Pica Mfg Solutions Inc (G-14204)*

Pica Mfg Solutions Inc **(PA)**....................... **603 845-3258**
  4 Ash Street Ext Unit 3 Derry (03038) *(G-14204)*

Picis Clinical Solutions Inc **(DH)**................ **336 397-5336**
  100 Quannapowitt Pkwy Ste 405 Wakefield (01880) *(G-12528)*

Picken Printing Inc.. 978 251-0730
  10 Middlesex St North Chelmsford (01863) *(G-10986)*

Pickering Interfaces Inc.................................... 781 897-1710
  221 Chelmsford St Ste 6 Chelmsford (01824) *(G-7945)*

Pickup Patrol, Mont Vernon *Also Called: Pickup Patrol LLC (G-15048)*

Pickup Patrol LLC.. 877 394-7774
  2 Wallace Ln Mont Vernon (03057) *(G-15048)*

Piconics Inc.. 978 649-7501
  26 Cummings Rd Tyngsboro (01879) *(G-12463)*

Picture This Hartford Inc.................................. 860 528-1409
  80 Pitkin St East Hartford (06108) *(G-1011)*

Pid Analyzers LLC.. 774 413-5281
  2 Washington Cir Ste 4 Sandwich (02563) *(G-11752)*

Pie Guy The, Salem *Also Called: Withrow Inc (G-15573)*

Pie Guy, The, Manchester *Also Called: Souhegan Management Corp (G-14933)*

Pieceworks Inc.. 207 589-3451
418 Acadia Hwy Montville (04941) *(G-5075)*

Piecing Puzzle.. 508 450-0323
1 Hardhill Rd Carver (02330) *(G-7856)*

Piecing Puzzle Inc... 508 465-0417
25 Wareham St Bldg 4 Middleboro (02346) *(G-10374)*

Piecing Puzzle Inc... 508 465-0417
11 Riverside Dr Lakeville (02347) *(G-9520)*

Piela Electric Inc... 860 889-8476
16 Halls Mill Rd Preston (06365) *(G-2828)*

Piematrix, Burlington *Also Called: Piematrix Inc (G-17151)*

Piematrix Inc... 802 318-4891
106 Main St Burlington (05401) *(G-17151)*

Pierce Machine Co Inc **(PA)**........................ **413 684-0056**
74 E Housatonic St Dalton (01226) *(G-8152)*

Piesco Sporting Goods Inc............................. 508 238-5599
130 Washington St North Easton (02356) *(G-11012)*

Pig Rock Sausages LLC................................. 617 851-9422
52 Dyer Ave Milton (02186) *(G-10454)*

Pigments Division, Coventry *Also Called: Clariant Corporation (G-15809)*

Pika Energy Inc... 207 887-9105
35 Bradley Dr Stop 1 Westbrook (04092) *(G-5641)*

Pike Industries Inc.. 207 676-9973
81 Boyd Rd Wells (04090) *(G-5604)*

Pike Industries Inc **(DH)**.............................. **603 527-5100**
3 Eastgate Park Dr Belmont (03220) *(G-13967)*

Pike Industries Inc.. 603 466-2772
42 Lancaster Rd Gorham (03581) *(G-14361)*

Pike Industries Inc.. 603 436-4432
650 Peverly Hill Rd Portsmouth (03801) *(G-15429)*

Pike Industries Inc.. 802 658-0453
346 Avenue A Williston (05495) *(G-17744)*

Pilgrim Candle Company Inc **(PA)**............... **413 562-2635**
36 Union Ave Westfield (01085) *(G-13199)*

Pilgrim Foods Co, Greenville *Also Called: Old Dutch Mustard Co Inc (G-14374)*

Pilgrim Innovative Plas LLC............................ 508 732-0297
127 Industrial Park Rd Plymouth (02360) *(G-11472)*

Pilgrim Nuts, Oxford *Also Called: Walz & Krenzer Inc (G-2714)*

Pilgrim Plastics, Taunton *Also Called: Star Printing Corp (G-12369)*

Pilgrim Tool & Die Co Inc............................... 508 753-0190
565 Southbridge St Worcester (01610) *(G-13769)*

Pillar Biosciences Inc...................................... 781 856-5568
9 Strathmore Rd Natick (01760) *(G-10492)*

Pilot Precision, South Deerfield *Also Called: Pilot Precision Products LLC (G-11927)*

Pilot Precision Products LLC........................... 413 350-5200
15 Merrigan Way South Deerfield (01373) *(G-11927)*

Pin-Line, Warwick *Also Called: Wehr Industries Inc (G-16878)*

Pine and Baker, Tewksbury *Also Called: Pine and Baker Mfg Inc (G-12412)*

Pine and Baker Mfg Inc.................................. 978 851-1215
166 Lorum St Tewksbury (01876) *(G-12412)*

Pine Hill Press, Lowell *Also Called: Thomas & Thomas Inc (G-9928)*

Pine Tree Concrete Pdts Inc........................... 508 883-7072
151 Lincoln St Millville (01529) *(G-10451)*

Pine Tree Lumber, Chesterville *Also Called: Wood-Mizer Holdings Inc (G-4695)*

Pine Tree Orthopedic Lab Inc......................... 207 897-5558
175 Park St Livermore Falls (04254) *(G-5025)*

Pineland Farms Dairy Company...................... 207 922-4036
1 Milk St Bangor (04401) *(G-4514)*

Pinga Bakery Inc... 401 821-8007
30 Newell St West Warwick (02893) *(G-16920)*

Pinnacle Loud Speakers, Hatfield *Also Called: Inter-Ego Systems Inc (G-9073)*

Pinpoint Laser Systems Inc............................. 978 532-8001
56 Pulaski St Unit 5 Peabody (01960) *(G-11333)*

Pinto Manufacturing LLC................................. 860 659-9543
122 Naubuc Ave Glastonbury (06033) *(G-1293)*

Pion Inc... 978 528-2020
10 Cook St Ste 6 Billerica (01821) *(G-6472)*

Pioneer Basements, Westport *Also Called: Grate Products LLC (G-13296)*

Pioneer Motors and Drives Inc....................... 802 651-0114
30 Berard Dr Unit 6 South Burlington (05403) *(G-17591)*

Pioneer Optics Company Inc........................... 860 286-0071
20 Connecticut South Dr East Granby (06026) *(G-948)*

Pioneer Packaging Inc **(PA)**....................... **413 378-6930**
220 Padgette St Chicopee (01022) *(G-8054)*

Pioneer Plastics, Auburn *Also Called: Pioneer Plastics Corporation (G-4454)*

Pioneer Plastics Corporation **(HQ)**............. **203 925-1556**
2 Corporate Dr Ste 946 Shelton (06484) *(G-3047)*

Pioneer Plastics Corporation.......................... 207 784-9111
1 Pionite Rd Auburn (04210) *(G-4454)*

Pioneer Precision Optics Inc........................... 413 341-3992
296c Nonotuck St Florence (01062) *(G-8685)*

Pioneer Shade & Awning, Easthampton *Also Called: Chilsons Shops Inc (G-8441)*

Pioneer Valley Machine LLC........................... 413 204-0358
121 Summit Lock Rd Westfield (01085) *(G-13200)*

Pionite Decorative Surfaces, Shelton *Also Called: Pioneer Plastics Corporation (G-3047)*

PIP Foundation Inc.. 508 757-0103
7 Bishop St Framingham (01702) *(G-8798)*

PIP Printing, Middletown *Also Called: Richard E Personette (G-1778)*

PIP Printing, Portsmouth *Also Called: Higginbotham Management Corp (G-15402)*

Pipe Shields Inc.. 603 528-1931
86 Doris Ray Ct Laconia (03246) *(G-14663)*

Pipe Supports Group, Woburn *Also Called: Bergen Pipe Supports Inc (G-13522)*

Piping Specialties Inc...................................... 207 878-3955
36 Rainmaker Dr Portland (04103) *(G-5256)*

Piping Systems Inc.. 508 644-2221
32 Mill St Assonet (02702) *(G-5976)*

Piscataquis Observer, Dover Foxcroft *Also Called: Northeast Publishing Company (G-4730)*

Pison Technology Inc....................................... 540 394-0998
179 Lincoln St Boston (02111) *(G-6966)*

Pitco, Pembroke *Also Called: Pitco Frialator Inc (G-15307)*

Pitco Frialator Inc **(HQ)**.............................. **603 225-6684**
553 Route 3a Bow (03304) *(G-14008)*

Pitco Frialator Inc... 603 225-6684
39 Sheep Davis Rd Pembroke (03275) *(G-15307)*

Pith Products LLC... 860 487-4859
39 Nott Hwy Unit 1 Ashford (06278) *(G-21)*

Pitney Bowes, Shelton *Also Called: Pitney Bowes Inc (G-3049)*

Pitney Bowes, Stamford *Also Called: Pitney Bowes Inc (G-3433)*

Pitney Bowes, Stamford *Also Called: Pitney Bowes RE Fing Corp (G-3434)*

Pitney Bowes Inc... 203 356-5000
27 Waterview Dr Shelton (06484) *(G-3048)*

Pitney Bowes Inc... 203 922-4000
27 Waterview Dr Shelton (06484) *(G-3049)*

Pitney Bowes Inc **(PA)**................................ **203 356-5000**
3001 Summer St Stamford (06905) *(G-3433)*

Pitney Bowes RE Fing Corp........................... 203 356-5000
300 Stamford Pl Ste 200 Stamford (06902) *(G-3434)*

Piton Therapeutics Inc.................................... 857 327-7666
313 Pleasant St Watertown (02472) *(G-12900)*

Pittsfield Plastics Engrg LLC.......................... 413 442-0067
1510 W Housatonic St Pittsfield (01201) *(G-11419)*

Pittsfield Rye Bakery Inc................................. 413 443-9141
1010 South St Pittsfield (01201) *(G-11420)*

Pixelle Androscoggin LLC **(HQ)**.................. **207 897-3431**
300 Riley Rd Jay (04239) *(G-4914)*

Pixelle Spcialty Solutions LLC........................ 207 897-3431
300 Riley Rd Jay (04239) *(G-4915)*

Pizza Gourmet, Central Falls *Also Called: Top Shell LLC (G-15799)*

Pj Diversified Machining Inc............................ 603 459-8655
12b Star Dr Ste 3 Merrimack (03054) *(G-14998)*

PJ Keating Company.. 978 454-7878
2140 Bridge St Route 38 Dracut (01826) *(G-8310)*

PJ Schwalbenberg & Assoc Inc...................... 207 354-0700
26 Spear Mill Rd Cushing (04563) *(G-4714)*

Pj Specialties... 860 429-7626
7 Luchon Rd Willington (06279) *(G-4226)*

Pjf Trucking & Logging LLC............................ 802 463-3343
35 Schoolbus Depot Rd Bellows Falls (05101) *(G-17030)*

Place Tailor.. 617 639-0633
103 Terrace St Fl 3 Roxbury Crossing (02120) *(G-11693)*

Places To Go LLC.. 774 202-7756
   1 Wamsutta St New Bedford (02740) *(G-10639)*

Placon Corporation... 413 785-1553
   1227 Union Street Ext West Springfield (01089) *(G-13041)*

Plaice Cove Spirits, Dover *Also Called: Sea Hagg Distillery LLC (G-14249)*

Plainville Machine & TI Co Inc................................. 860 589-5595
   65 Ronzo Rd Bristol (06010) *(G-481)*

Plainville Plating Company Inc............................... 860 747-1624
   21 Forestville Ave Plainville (06062) *(G-2776)*

Plainville Special Tool LLC................................... 860 747-2736
   63 N Washington St Plainville (06062) *(G-2777)*

Plaistow Cabinet Co Inc.. 603 382-1098
   56 Newton Rd Plaistow (03865) *(G-15348)*

Plan & Sponsor, Greenwich *Also Called: Asset International Inc (G-1314)*

Plan B, Springfield *Also Called: Plan B Burger LLC (G-12121)*

Plan B Burger LLC.. 413 285-8296
   1000 W Columbus Ave Springfield (01105) *(G-12121)*

Plan Tech Inc... 603 783-4767
   7031 Shaker Rd Unit J Loudon (03307) *(G-14798)*

Planes Road Associates LLC................................ 860 469-3200
   38 Plains Rd Essex (06426) *(G-1169)*

Planet Biopharmaceuticals Inc.............................. 800 255-3749
   96 Danbury Rd Ridgefield (06877) *(G-2904)*

Planet Dog-Cancelled, Westbrook *Also Called: Planet Ventures Inc (G-5642)*

Planet Eclipse LLC.. 401 247-9061
   130 Franklin St Bldg L4 Warren (02885) *(G-16763)*

Planet Technologies Inc....................................... 800 255-3749
   96 Danbury Rd Ridgefield (06877) *(G-2905)*

Planet Ventures Inc **(PA)**.................................. **207 761-1515**
   85 Bradley Dr Westbrook (04092) *(G-5642)*

Plannuh Inc... 617 965-7393
   150 Gibbs St Newton (02459) *(G-10774)*

Planon Corporation.. 781 356-0999
   45 Braintree Hill Park Ste 400 Braintree (02184) *(G-7198)*

Plant Snacks LLC.. 617 480-6265
   60 Kendrick St Ste 200 Needham (02494) *(G-10518)*

Plantbased Innovations LLC.................................. 571 243-4646
   320 Hamilton St Ste 27 Leominster (01453) *(G-9695)*

Plas-TEC Coatings Inc... 860 289-6029
   68 Mascolo Rd South Windsor (06074) *(G-3172)*

Plaskolite LLC.. 800 628-5084
   113 Silver St Sheffield (01257) *(G-11798)*

Plaskolite LLC.. 800 628-5084
   119 Salisbury Rd Sheffield (01257) *(G-11799)*

Plaskolite Massachusetts LLC.............................. 413 229-8711
   119 Salisbury Rd Sheffield (01257) *(G-11800)*

Plasma Biolife Services L P................................... 508 761-2902
   287 Washington St Ste 5 Attleboro (02703) *(G-6048)*

Plasma Coatings, Middlebury *Also Called: American Roller Company LLC (G-1713)*

Plasma Coatings Inc.. 203 598-3100
   84 Turnpike Dr Middlebury (06762) *(G-1719)*

Plasma Coatings Inc... 203 598-3100
   758 E Main St Waterbury (06702) *(G-3961)*

Plasma Pen USA LLC... 855 568-3776
   800 W Cummings Park Ste 5950 Woburn (01801) *(G-13637)*

Plasma Technology Incorporated........................... 860 282-0659
   70 Rye St South Windsor (06074) *(G-3173)*

Plastech Machining Fabrication.............................. 603 228-7601
   25 Dunklee Rd Bow (03304) *(G-14009)*

Plastech Manufacturing, East Hartford *Also Called: Trento Group LLC (G-1029)*

Plastech Molding Solutions, Hopedale *Also Called: REc Manufacturing Corp (G-9301)*

Plasti-Clip Corporation.. 603 672-1166
   38 Perry Rd Milford (03055) *(G-15034)*

Plastic Assembly Corporation................................ 978 772-4725
   1 Sculley Rd Unit A Ayer (01432) *(G-6191)*

Plastic Assembly Systems LLC............................. 203 393-0639
   19 Sargent Dr Bethany (06524) *(G-97)*

Plastic Concepts Inc... 978 663-7996
   2 Sterling Rd Unit 2 North Billerica (01862) *(G-10943)*

Plastic Craft Novelty Co Inc.................................. 508 222-1486
   12 Dunham St Apt A Attleboro (02703) *(G-6049)*

Plastic Design Inc.. 978 251-4830
   180 Middlesex St Ste 1 North Chelmsford (01863) *(G-10987)*

Plastic Design Intl Inc **(PA)**............................. **860 632-2001**
   111 Industrial Park Rd Middletown (06457) *(G-1771)*

Plastic Distrs Fabricators Inc................................ 978 374-0300
   144 Hilldale Ave Haverhill (01832) *(G-9121)*

Plastic Forming Company Inc **(PA)**.................... **203 397-1338**
   20 S Bradley Rd Woodbridge (06525) *(G-4382)*

Plastic Group, The, Woonsocket *Also Called: Ralco Industries Inc (G-16973)*

Plastic Industries, Nashua *Also Called: Carr Management (G-15077)*

Plastic Industries Inc **(HQ)**............................. **603 888-1315**
   1 Tara Blvd Nashua (03062) *(G-15149)*

Plastic Met Components Co Inc............................. 203 877-2723
   381 Bridgeport Ave Milford (06460) *(G-1866)*

Plastic Molding Mfg Inc **(PA)**.......................... **978 567-1000**
   34 Tower St Hudson (01749) *(G-9400)*

Plastic Molding Technology................................... 203 881-1811
   92 Cogwheel Ln Seymour (06483) *(G-2966)*

Plastic Monofil Co Ltd... 732 629-7701
   8 Tulip Way Medway (02053) *(G-10311)*

Plastic Moulding Manufacturing, Hudson *Also Called: Restech Plastic Molding LLC (G-9407)*

Plastic Packaging Corporation............................... 413 785-1553
   1227 Union Street Ext West Springfield (01089) *(G-13042)*

Plastic Services Entps Inc.................................... 401 490-3811
   100 Niantic Ave Ste 104 Providence (02907) *(G-16584)*

Plastic Techniques Inc... 603 622-5570
   27 Springfield Rd Goffstown (03045) *(G-14356)*

Plastic Technologies MD Inc................................. 802 658-6588
   8 Arbor Rd South Burlington (05403) *(G-17592)*

Plastic Technologies NY LLC................................ 802 658-6588
   8 Harbor View Rd South Burlington (05403) *(G-17593)*

Plastic Technologies of Vermont Inc...................... 802 658-6588
   8 Harbor View Rd South Burlington (05403) *(G-17594)*

Plastic Technology Division, Mansfield *Also Called: Hub Folding Box Company Inc (G-10057)*

Plastican Inc... 978 728-5000
   196 Industrial Rd Leominster (01453) *(G-9696)*

Plastics and Concepts Conn Inc............................ 860 657-9655
   101 Laurel Trl Glastonbury (06033) *(G-1294)*

Plastics Color Corp Inc.. 800 922-9936
   349 Lake Rd Dayville (06241) *(G-866)*

Plastics Group of Whelen, The, Charlestown *Also Called: Whelen Engineering Co (G-14069)*

Plastics Plus Inc.. 401 727-1447
   51 Abbott St Ste 1 Cumberland (02864) *(G-15960)*

Plastics Unlimited of MA Inc................................. 508 752-7842
   55 Millbrook St Ste 5 Worcester (01606) *(G-13770)*

Plastilam Inc... 978 745-5563
   14 Proctor St Salem (01970) *(G-11730)*

Plastock, Putnam *Also Called: Ensinger Prcsion Cmponents Inc (G-2854)*

Plastonics Inc.. 860 249-5455
   230 Locust St Hartford (06114) *(G-1499)*

Plastron Company, Westfield *Also Called: Sonicron Systems Corporation (G-13209)*

Plataine Inc... 336 905-0900
   465 Waverley Oaks Rd Ste 420 Waltham (02452) *(G-12749)*

Platformq Education Inc....................................... 617 938-6000
   100 Crescent Rd Ste 4 Needham (02494) *(G-10519)*

Plating For Electronics LLC.................................. 781 893-2368
   94 Calvary St Waltham (02453) *(G-12750)*

Plating Technology Inc... 508 996-4006
   41 Coffin Ave New Bedford (02746) *(G-10640)*

Platinum Fire Protection, Marlborough *Also Called: Platinum Fire Prtction Svcs LL (G-10196)*

Platinum Fire Prtction Svcs LL **(PA)**................... **508 481-8242**
   34 Saint Martin Dr Ste 12 Marlborough (01752) *(G-10196)*

Platinum Investments Ltd...................................... 617 731-2447
   1357 Beacon St Brookline (02446) *(G-7325)*

Platt & Labonia Company LLC............................... 800 505-9099
   182 E Aurora St Waterbury (06708) *(G-3962)*

Platt Brothers & Company **(PA)**......................... **203 753-4194**
   2670 S Main St Waterbury (06706) *(G-3963)*

Platt-Labonia of N Haven Inc................................ 203 239-5681
   70 Stoddard Ave North Haven (06473) *(G-2431)*

Play-It Productions Inc... 212 695-6530
   167b Lebanon Ave Colchester (06415) *(G-663)*

Playtex Products LLC **(HQ)**.. **203 944-5500**
   6 Research Dr Ste 400 Shelton (06484) *(G-3050)*

PLC Medical Systems, Inc., Milford *Also Called: Renalguard Solutions Inc (G-10416)*

Pleasant River Lumber Company **(PA)**.................................. **207 564-8520**
   432 Milo Rd Dover Foxcroft (04426) *(G-4731)*

Pleasant River Lumber Company.. 207 403-1507
   542 Hammett Rd Enfield (04493) *(G-4762)*

Pleasant River Pine, Hancock *Also Called: Prl Hancock LLC (G-4873)*

Pleasant Valley Fence Co Inc.. 860 379-0088
   Route 181 Pleasant Valley (06063) *(G-2803)*

Pleasant View Gardens Inc **(PA)**.. **603 435-8361**
   7316 Pleasant St Loudon (03307) *(G-14799)*

Plenus Group Inc... 978 970-3832
   101 Phoenix Ave Lowell (01852) *(G-9914)*

Plp Composite Technologies.. 603 585-9100
   57 Creamery Rd Fitzwilliam (03447) *(G-14315)*

Plumb Pak, Winchester *Also Called: 2023 Holdings LLC (G-15713)*

Plumb Pak Medical, Newington *Also Called: 2023 Holdings LLC (G-2263)*

Plumriver LLC.. 781 431-7477
   94 Edmunds Rd Wellesley (02481) *(G-12945)*

Plumrose Usa Inc... 802 868-7314
   14 Jonergin Dr Swanton (05488) *(G-17639)*

Pluromed Inc... 781 932-0574
   175 New Boston St Ste F Woburn (01801) *(G-13638)*

Plus One Corporation.. 978 532-3700
   11 Mason St Peabody (01960) *(G-11334)*

Plw Inc.. 603 889-4126
   8 Autumn Pond Park Greenland (03840) *(G-14370)*

Plymouth Grating Lab Inc.. 508 465-2274
   5 Commerce Way Carver (02330) *(G-7857)*

Plymouth Rubber Company LLC.. 781 828-0220
   104 Revere St Canton (02021) *(G-7820)*

Plymouth Spring Company Inc.. 860 584-0594
   281 Lake Ave Bristol (06010) *(G-482)*

Plymtron Industries Inc... 508 746-1126
   9 Aldrin Rd Plymouth (02360) *(G-11473)*

Plz Corp.. 650 543-7600
   300 Riggenbach Rd Fall River (02720) *(G-8597)*

PMC Engineering LLC... 203 792-8686
   11 Old Sugar Hollow Rd Danbury (06810) *(G-798)*

PMC Lighting, Warwick *Also Called: PMC Lighting Inc (G-16846)*

PMC Lighting Inc.. 401 738-7266
   100 Gilbane St Warwick (02886) *(G-16846)*

PMC Technologies LLC.. 203 222-0000
   31 Glenwood Rd Weston (06883) *(G-4151)*

PMI, Danbury *Also Called: Parker Medical Inc (G-794)*

PMI, Wolcott *Also Called: Precision Methods Incorporated (G-4373)*

Pmp Corporation.. 860 677-9656
   25 Security Dr Avon (06001) *(G-36)*

PMS Mfg, Gloucester *Also Called: P M S Manufactured Pdts Inc (G-8950)*

Pmsi, Stratford *Also Called: Professional Mktg Svcs Inc (G-3568)*

Pmt Group Inc **(PA)**... **203 367-8675**
   800 Union Ave Bridgeport (06607) *(G-359)*

Pmweb Inc.. 617 207-7080
   1 Pope St Wakefield (01880) *(G-12529)*

Pneucleus Technologies LLC.. 603 465-7346
   169 Depot Rd Hollis (03049) *(G-14457)*

Pneutek Inc... 603 883-1660
   17 Friars Dr Ste D Hudson (03051) *(G-14535)*

Pobco, Worcester *Also Called: Pobco Inc (G-13771)*

Pobco Inc.. 508 791-6376
   99 Hope Ave Worcester (01603) *(G-13771)*

Poc, Gardner *Also Called: Precision Optics Corp Inc (G-8898)*

Pocasset Machine Corporation... 508 563-5572
   7 Commerce Park Rd Pocasset (02559) *(G-11491)*

Pocathane Technologies, Woburn *Also Called: A Group Inc (G-13495)*

PODGURSKI WELDING AND HEAVY EQUIPMENT REPAIR, Canton *Also Called: Podgurski Wldg & Hvy Eqp Repr (G-7821)*

Podgurski Wldg & Hvy Eqp Repr... 781 830-9901
   8 Springdale Ave Ste 2 Canton (02021) *(G-7821)*

Pohto Etch Tech, Lowell *Also Called: Photo Tool Engineering Inc (G-9913)*

Point Lighting Corporation... 860 243-0600
   61 W Dudley Town Rd 65 Bloomfield (06002) *(G-202)*

Point Machine Company.. 860 828-6901
   588 Four Rod Rd Berlin (06037) *(G-78)*

Point3 Farma LLC.. 719 733-3900
   48 Round Hill Rd # 23 Northampton (01060) *(G-11077)*

Pointillist Inc.. 617 752-2214
   321 Summer St Fl 8 Boston (02210) *(G-6967)*

Polamer Precision Inc... 860 259-6200
   105 Alton Brooks Way New Britain (06053) *(G-2052)*

Poland Spring Bottling, Poland Spring *Also Called: Bluetriton Brands Inc (G-5163)*

Polar Bear & Company, Solon *Also Called: Solon Ctr For RES & Publishig (G-5482)*

Polar Beverages, Worcester *Also Called: Polar Corp (G-13772)*

Polar Cap Ice Co, Sandwich *Also Called: JP Lillis Enterprises Inc (G-11751)*

Polar Controls Inc.. 978 425-2233
   2 Shaker Rd D-205 Shirley (01464) *(G-11822)*

Polar Corp... 860 225-6000
   33 Columbus Blvd New Britain (06051) *(G-2053)*

Polar Corp **(PA)**.. **508 753-6383**
   1001 Southbridge St Worcester (01610) *(G-13772)*

Polar Corporation.. 862 225-6000
   1790 New Britain Ave Farmington (06032) *(G-1241)*

Polar Corporation.. 860 223-7891
   59 High St Ste 11 New Britain (06051) *(G-2054)*

Polaris Management Inc.. 203 261-6399
   30 Silver Hill Rd Easton (06612) *(G-1097)*

Polhemus, Colchester *Also Called: Alken Inc (G-17185)*

Polka Dog Bakery, Boston *Also Called: Polka Dog Designs LLC (G-6968)*

Polka Dog Bakery, Boston *Also Called: Polka Dog Designs LLC (G-6969)*

Polka Dog Designs LLC **(PA)**.. **617 338-5155**
   256 Shawmut Ave Ste 1 Boston (02118) *(G-6968)*

Polka Dog Designs LLC... 617 307-6733
   212 Northern Ave Boston (02210) *(G-6969)*

Pollution Research & Dev Corp **(PA)**.................................. **603 863-7553**
   475 Sunapee St Ste 4 Newport (03773) *(G-15234)*

Polster Industries LLC.. 203 521-8517
   115 Verna Hill Rd Fairfield (06824) *(G-1198)*

Poly-Cel Inc.. 508 229-8310
   6 Eastern Rd Acton (01720) *(G-5761)*

Poly-Ject Inc... 603 882-6570
   8 Manhattan Dr Amherst (03031) *(G-13884)*

Poly-Metal Finishing Inc... 413 781-4535
   1 Allen St Ste 218 Springfield (01108) *(G-12122)*

Poly-Plating Inc... 413 593-5477
   2096 Westover Rd Chicopee (01022) *(G-8055)*

Poly-Tech Diamond Co Inc.. 508 695-3561
   4 East St North Attleboro (02760) *(G-10882)*

Poly-Vac Inc.. 603 647-7822
   253 Abby Rd Manchester (03103) *(G-14912)*

Poly6, Burlington *Also Called: Poly6 Technologies Inc (G-7412)*

Poly6 Technologies Inc... 339 234-9300
   164 Middlesex Tpke Ste 1 Burlington (01803) *(G-7412)*

Polycarbon Industries Inc.. 978 462-5555
   9 Opportunity Way Newburyport (01950) *(G-10707)*

Polycast, Stamford *Also Called: Spartech LLC (G-3467)*

Polychromix... 978 284-6000
   30 Upton Dr Wilmington (01887) *(G-13447)*

Polyexe Corporation... 603 778-1143
   50 Pine Rd Brentwood (03833) *(G-14027)*

Polyfoam LLC.. 508 234-6323
   2355 Providence Rd Northbridge (01534) *(G-11117)*

Polymedex Discovery Group Inc **(PA)**................................ **860 928-4102**
   45 Ridge Rd Putnam (06260) *(G-2870)*

Polymer Corporation.. 413 267-5524
   1 3rd St Palmer (01069) *(G-11282)*

Polymer Corporation **(HQ)**... **781 871-4606**
   180 Pleasant St Rockland (02370) *(G-11656)*

Polymer Films Inc.. 203 932-3000
   301 Heffernan Dr West Haven (06516) *(G-4119)*

ALPHABETIC

Polymer Injection Molding, Palmer *Also Called: Polymer Corporation* **(G-11282)**

Polymer Liquid Resin Casting, Rockland *Also Called: Polymer Corporation* **(G-11656)**

Polymer Resources, Farmington *Also Called: Polymer Resources Ltd* **(G-1242)**

Polymer Resources Ltd **(PA)**.. **800 243-5176**
   656 New Britain Ave Farmington (06032) **(G-1242)**

Polymer Technology, Wilmington *Also Called: Wilmington Partners LP* **(G-13476)**

Polymeric Converting LLC.. 860 623-1335
   5 Old Depot Hill Rd Enfield (06082) **(G-1142)**

Polymetallurgical LLC.. 508 695-9312
   262 Broad St North Attleboro (02760) **(G-10883)**

Polyonics Corporation.. 978 462-3600
   24 Graf Rd Newburyport (01950) **(G-10708)**

Polyonics Inc.. 603 352-1415
   28 Industrial Park Dr Westmoreland (03467) **(G-15698)**

Polypolish Products Div, Bethel *Also Called: Intersurface Dynamics Inc* **(G-120)**

Polytec Inc.. 508 417-1040
   1 Cabot Rd Ste 102 Hudson (01749) **(G-9401)**

Polytech Fltration Systems Inc.. 978 562-7700
   100 Forest Ave Hudson (01749) **(G-9402)**

Polytite Manufacturing Corp.. 603 952-9327
   4 Tinkham Ave Derry (03038) **(G-14205)**

Polyvinyl Films Inc.. 508 865-3558
   38 Providence Rd Ste 2 Sutton (01590) **(G-12290)**

Pomeroy & Co Inc.. 617 241-0234
   18 Spice St Ste 1 Charlestown (02129) **(G-7880)**

Pompanette LLC **(PA)**.. **717 569-2300**
   73 Southwest St Charlestown (03603) **(G-14067)**

Pond Cove Millwork Inc.. 207 773-6819
   22 Mill Brook Rd Saco (04072) **(G-5376)**

Ponn Machine Cutting Co.. 781 937-3373
   20 Cross St Woburn (01801) **(G-13639)**

Pool Environments Inc.. 207 839-8225
   10 Elm St Gorham (04038) **(G-4831)**

Pop Color, Colchester *Also Called: Garlic Press Inc* **(G-17192)**

Pop Tops Company Inc.. 508 580-2580
   10 Plymouth Dr South Easton (02375) **(G-11949)**

Pop Tops Sportswear, South Easton *Also Called: Pop Tops Company Inc* **(G-11949)**

Popcorn Movie Poster Co, East Hartford *Also Called: Popcorn Movie Poster Co LLC* **(G-1012)**

Popcorn Movie Poster Co LLC.. 860 610-0000
   1 Cherry St East Hartford (06108) **(G-1012)**

Poplar Hill Machine Inc.. 413 369-4252
   2077 Roaring Brook Rd Conway (01341) **(G-8144)**

Population Media Center Inc.. 802 985-8156
   30 Kimball Ave Ste 206 South Burlington (05403) **(G-17595)**

Popzup LLC.. 603 314-8314
   22 Canal St Unit 358 Somersworth (03878) **(G-15621)**

Porcelanosa New York Inc.. 203 698-7618
   1063 E Putnam Ave Riverside (06878) **(G-2910)**

Porcelen Limited Connecticut LLC **(PA)**.. **203 248-6346**
   333 Welton St Hamden (06517) **(G-1449)**

Porcelen Ltd Connecticut LLC.. 203 248-6346
   129 Leeder Hill Dr Hamden (06517) **(G-1450)**

Porex Cleanroom Products Inc.. 800 628-8606
   2255 Westover Rd Chicopee (01022) **(G-8056)**

Porobond Products LLC.. 203 288-7477
   80 Sanford St Hamden (06514) **(G-1451)**

Port Canvas Company, Arundel *Also Called: C B P Corp* **(G-4409)**

Port City Foods LLC.. 603 436-3001
   170 West Rd Ste 10 Portsmouth (03801) **(G-15430)**

Port City Pretzels, Portsmouth *Also Called: Port City Foods LLC* **(G-15430)**

Port Oil Corp.. 617 926-3500
   60 Carlisle Rd Bedford (01730) **(G-6253)**

Port Plastics Inc.. 978 259-0002
   101 Brick Kiln Rd Ste 13 Chelmsford (01824) **(G-7946)**

Port-Lite LLC.. 678 575-9065
   957 Alna Rd Alna (04535) **(G-4405)**

Port-O-Lite Company Inc.. 603 352-3205
   1 Railroad St West Swanzey (03469) **(G-15696)**

Porta Door Co.. 203 888-6191
   65 Cogwheel Ln Seymour (06483) **(G-2967)**

Porta Phone Co Inc.. 401 789-8700
   145 Dean Knauss Dr Narragansett (02882) **(G-16194)**

Porta Phones, Narragansett *Also Called: Porta Phone Co Inc* **(G-16194)**

Porta-Brace Inc.. 802 442-8171
   160 Benmont Ave Ste 11 Bennington (05201) **(G-17055)**

Portal Inc.. 800 966-3030
   10 Tracy Dr Avon (02322) **(G-6157)**

Portance Corp.. 978 400-9991
   325 Authority Dr Fitchburg (01420) **(G-8672)**

Porter Machine Inc.. 401 397-8889
   765 Victory Hwy Unit 1 West Greenwich (02817) **(G-16891)**

Porter Music Box Co Inc.. 802 728-9694
   79 Sunset Hill Rd Randolph (05060) **(G-17473)**

Porter-Ferguson, West Boylston *Also Called: Lowell Corporation* **(G-12964)**

Portfolio Arts Group Ltd.. 203 847-2000
   129 Glover Ave Norwalk (06850) **(G-2559)**

Portfolio Software Inc.. 802 434-4000
   1 Millet St Richmond (05477) **(G-17481)**

Portion Meat Associates Inc.. 401 421-2438
   356 Valley St Providence (02908) **(G-16585)**

Portland Company.. 207 774-1067
   100 W Commercial St Portland (04102) **(G-5257)**

Portland Connecticut Mch Sp, Portland *Also Called: Connecticut Department Tmsp* **(G-2818)**

Portland Dry Goods Inc.. 207 699-5575
   237 Commercial St Portland (04101) **(G-5258)**

Portland Magazine, Portland *Also Called: Portland Monthly Inc* **(G-5259)**

Portland Mattress Makers **(PA)**.. **207 282-9583**
   25 Edwards Ave Biddeford (04005) **(G-4582)**

Portland Monthly Inc.. 207 775-4339
   722 Congress St Portland (04102) **(G-5259)**

Portland Phoenix, Falmouth *Also Called: New Portland Publishing Inc* **(G-4770)**

Portland Plastic Pipe.. 207 774-0364
   444 Lincoln Street Ext South Portland (04106) **(G-5512)**

Portland Printing Group.. 207 347-5700
   116 Riverside Industrial Pkwy Portland (04103) **(G-5260)**

Portland Stone Ware Co Inc **(PA)**.. **978 459-7272**
   50 Mcgrath Rd Dracut (01826) **(G-8311)**

Portland Stone Works Inc.. 207 878-6832
   50 Allen Ave Portland (04103) **(G-5261)**

Portland Stoneworks, Portland *Also Called: Portland Stone Works Inc* **(G-5261)**

Portland Valve LLC **(DH)**.. **704 289-6511**
   82 Bridge St Warren (01083) **(G-12852)**

Portsmouth Naval Shipyard, Portsmouth *Also Called: United States Dept of Navy* **(G-15446)**

Portugues Channel, The, New Bedford *Also Called: Portuguese Times Inc* **(G-10641)**

Portuguese Times Inc.. 508 997-3118
   1501 Acushnet Ave New Bedford (02746) **(G-10641)**

Portwest Corporation **(PA)**.. **508 809-5112**
   30 Larsen Way North Attleboro (02763) **(G-10884)**

Porvair Filtration Group Inc.. 207 493-3027
   15 Armco Ave Caribou (04736) **(G-4679)**

Posh House, Keene *Also Called: Rk Parisi Enterprises Inc* **(G-14616)**

Positive News For You LLC.. 802 384-3993
   50 Woodburn St Apt 25 Keene (03431) **(G-14615)**

Post Road Iron Works Inc.. 203 869-6322
   345 W Putnam Ave Greenwich (06830) **(G-1343)**

Post Woodworking Inc.. 603 382-4951
   163 Kingston Rd Danville (03819) **(G-14185)**

Postdoc Ventures LLC.. 617 492-3555
   1668 Massachusetts Ave Cambridge (02138) **(G-7687)**

Potomac Electric Corp.. 617 364-0400
   1 Westinghouse Plz Ste 17 Boston (02136) **(G-6970)**

Potters Printing Inc.. 617 547-3161
   207 Pocasset St Fall River (02721) **(G-8598)**

Potters Yard Brasserie, Bennington *Also Called: Bennington Potters Inc* **(G-17036)**

Poulin Grain Inc.. 802 681-1605
   1873 Vt Route 67 E North Bennington (05257) **(G-17411)**

Poulin Grain Inc.. 802 868-3323
   24 Depot St Swanton (05488) **(G-17640)**

Poulin Grain Inc **(PA)**.. **802 334-6731**
   24 Railroad Sq Newport (05855) **(G-17404)**

Powder Hollow Brewery, South Windsor *Also Called: PH Production CT LLC (G-3171)*

Powder Pro Powder Coating Inc............................. 508 991-5999
195 Riverside Ave New Bedford (02746) *(G-10642)*

Powdered Metal Technology Corp............................ 617 642-4135
76 Northwest Blvd Ste 29-A Nashua (03063) *(G-15150)*

Powell and Mahoney LLC.................................... 978 745-4332
39 Norman St Salem (01970) *(G-11731)*

Powell Stone & Gravel Co Inc **(PA)**...................... **978 537-8100**
133 Leominster Shirley Rd Lunenburg (01462) *(G-9959)*

Powell Stone Gravel....................................... 603 673-8100
89 Route 13 Brookline (03033) *(G-14040)*

Power Advocate Inc **(HQ)**................................ **857 453-5700**
179 Lincoln St Boston (02111) *(G-6971)*

Power Chair Recyclers Neng LLC............................ 401 294-4111
6802 Post Rd North Kingstown (02852) *(G-16275)*

Power Equipment Co Inc **(PA)**........................... **508 226-3410**
7 Franklin R Mckay Rd Attleboro (02703) *(G-6050)*

Power Object Inc.. 617 630-5701
123 Ridge Ave Newton (02459) *(G-10775)*

Power Systems Integrity Inc............................... 508 393-1655
100 Otis St Ste 6 Northborough (01532) *(G-11106)*

Power-Dyne LLC.. 860 346-9283
2055 S Main St Middletown (06457) *(G-1772)*

Power-Dyne LLC/Bidwll Indstrl, Middletown *Also Called: Power-Dyne LLC (G-1772)*

Poweradvocate, Boston *Also Called: Power Advocate Inc (G-6971)*

Powerhold Inc... 860 349-1044
63 Old Indian Trl Middlefield (06455) *(G-1727)*

Powerhydrant LLC **(PA)**................................. **617 686-9632**
11 Elkins St Ste 310 Boston (02127) *(G-6972)*

Poweroptions Inc.. 617 737-8480
129 South St Fl 5 Boston (02111) *(G-6973)*

Powerphone Inc.. 203 245-8911
1321 Boston Post Rd Madison (06443) *(G-1566)*

Powerplay Management LLC.................................. 603 436-3030
933 Islington St Portsmouth (03801) *(G-15431)*

Powers Industries & Laserpro, Meriden *Also Called: Midstate Arc Inc (G-1676)*

Powertronics, Candia *Also Called: Eastern Time Designs Inc (G-14048)*

Powr Pt Generator Pwr Systems............................ 207 864-2787
11 Mill Brook Rd Saco (04072) *(G-5377)*

Powr2, Bethel *Also Called: TT Trade Group LLC (G-137)*

Poyant Signs Inc **(PA)**................................. **800 544-0961**
125 Samuel Barnet Blvd New Bedford (02745) *(G-10643)*

Pp Manufacturing Corporation............................. 508 766-2700
175 Crossing Blvd Ste 200 Framingham (01702) *(G-8799)*

Pp Systems, Amesbury *Also Called: Pp Systems International Inc (G-5849)*

Pp Systems International Inc.............................. 978 834-0505
110 Haverhill Rd Ste 301 Amesbury (01913) *(G-5849)*

Ppi Gas Distribution Inc
33 Great Hill Rd Naugatuck (06770) *(G-1981)*

Ppj LLC **(PA)**.. **508 650-3500**
2 Carsha Dr Natick (01760) *(G-10493)*

Ppm, Framingham *Also Called: Pp Manufacturing Corporation (G-8799)*

Ppoes Inc... 401 421-5160
102 Waterman St Providence (02906) *(G-16586)*

Pr-Mx Holdings Company LLC **(HQ)**....................... **203 925-0012**
25 Forest Pkwy Shelton (06484) *(G-3051)*

PRA Holdings Inc.. 203 853-0123
1 Stamford Forum Stamford (06901) *(G-3435)*

Practical Automation Inc **(HQ)**......................... **203 882-5640**
28 Woodmont Rd Milford (06460) *(G-1867)*

Praecis Pharmaceuticals Inc............................... 781 795-4100
830 Winter St Ste 1 Waltham (02451) *(G-12751)*

Pralines Inc.. 203 284-8847
30 N Plains Industrial Rd Ste 12 Wallingford (06492) *(G-3838)*

Pralines Central, Wallingford *Also Called: Pralines Inc (G-3838)*

Pralines of Plainville.................................... 860 410-1151
107 New Britain Ave Plainville (06062) *(G-2778)*

Pratt & Whitney... 800 742-5877
52 Pettengill Rd Londonderry (03053) *(G-14779)*

Pratt & Whitney, Cheshire *Also Called: Pratt & Whitney Eng Svcs Inc (G-611)*

Pratt & Whitney, Middletown *Also Called: Pratt & Whitney Eng Svcs Inc (G-1773)*

Pratt & Whitney, South Burlington *Also Called: Pratt & Whitney Eng Svcs Inc (G-17596)*

Pratt & Whitney Aircraft Nelc, Londonderry *Also Called: Pratt & Whitney (G-14779)*

Pratt & Whitney Cenco Inc................................. 860 565-4321
400 Main St East Hartford (06108) *(G-1013)*

Pratt & Whitney Company Inc............................... 860 565-4321
400 Main St East Hartford (06108) *(G-1014)*

Pratt & Whitney Eng Svcs Inc.............................. 203 250-4000
500 Knotter Dr Cheshire (06410) *(G-611)*

Pratt & Whitney Eng Svcs Inc.............................. 860 565-4321
400 Main St East Hartford (06118) *(G-1015)*

Pratt & Whitney Eng Svcs Inc.............................. 860 610-7478
411 Silver Ln East Hartford (06118) *(G-1016)*

Pratt & Whitney Eng Svcs Inc.............................. 860 344-4000
1 Aircraft Rd Middletown (06457) *(G-1773)*

Pratt & Whitney Eng Svcs Inc.............................. 207 676-4100
113 Wells St North Berwick (03906) *(G-5112)*

Pratt & Whitney Eng Svcs Inc.............................. 802 658-2208
15 Eagle Dr South Burlington (05403) *(G-17596)*

Pratt & Whitney Engine Lsg LLC............................ 860 565-4321
400 Main St Hartford (06118) *(G-1500)*

Pratt & Whitney Services Inc.............................. 860 565-5489
400 Main St East Hartford (06108) *(G-1017)*

Pratt Whtney Cstmer Trning Ctr, East Hartford *Also Called: Pratt & Whitney Eng Svcs Inc (G-1015)*

Pratt Whtney Msrment Systems I............................ 860 286-8181
66 Douglas St Bloomfield (06002) *(G-203)*

Prattville Machine & TI Co Inc............................ 978 538-5229
240 Jubilee Dr Fl 2 Peabody (01960) *(G-11335)*

Praxair, Danbury *Also Called: Linde Advanced Mtl Tech Inc (G-773)*

Praxair, Danbury *Also Called: Linde Gas & Equipment Inc (G-774)*

Praxair, Danbury *Also Called: Linde Gas & Equipment Inc (G-775)*

Praxair, Danbury *Also Called: Linde Inc (G-776)*

Praxair, Danbury *Also Called: Linde Inc (G-777)*

Praxair, Manchester *Also Called: Linde Advanced Mtl Tech Inc (G-1612)*

Praxair, Biddeford *Also Called: Linde Advanced Mtl Tech Inc (G-4575)*

Praxair, Slatersville *Also Called: Linde Gas & Equipment Inc (G-16682)*

Praxair Surface, Concord *Also Called: Tafa Incorporated (G-14162)*

Praxis, Boston *Also Called: Praxis Precision Medicines Inc (G-6974)*

Praxis Precision Medicines Inc **(PA)**................... **617 300-8460**
99 High St Ste 30 Boston (02110) *(G-6974)*

PRC Acquisition Company Inc............................... 207 854-3702
639 Main St Gorham (04038) *(G-4832)*

PRC Synergy Corp.. 203 331-9100
1100 Boston Ave Bldg 1 Bridgeport (06610) *(G-360)*

Prcess Critical Systems Group............................. 802 448-5860
480 Hercules Dr Colchester (05446) *(G-17200)*

Pre-Hung Doors Inc.. 207 783-3881
353 Riverside Dr Auburn (04210) *(G-4455)*

Pre-Tech Plastic, Williston *Also Called: Pre-Tech Plastics Inc (G-17745)*

Pre-Tech Plastics Inc **(PA)**............................ **802 879-9441**
209 Blair Park Rd Williston (05495) *(G-17745)*

Preava Inc.. 202 935-1566
22 Essex Way Unit 8203 Essex (05451) *(G-17225)*

Precast Specialties Corp.................................. 781 878-7220
999 Adams St Abington (02351) *(G-5727)*

Preci-Manufacturing Inc................................... 802 655-2414
400 Weaver St Winooski (05404) *(G-17768)*

Precidiag, Watertown *Also Called: Piton Therapeutics Inc (G-12900)*

Precinmac Precision Machining, South Paris *Also Called: Maine Machine Products Company (G-5489)*

Precipio Inc **(PA)**..................................... **203 787-7888**
4 Science Park Ste 3 New Haven (06511) *(G-2187)*

Precise Circuit Company Inc............................... 203 924-2512
155 Myrtle St Shelton (06484) *(G-3052)*

Precise Industries Inc.................................... 978 453-8490
639 Lakeview Ave Lowell (01850) *(G-9915)*

Precision Aerospace Inc................................... 203 888-3022
220 Rock Ln Milford (06460) *(G-1868)*

Precision Coating, Woonsocket *Also Called: Duralectra-Chn LLC (G-16957)*

Precision Coating Co Inc.. 978 562-7561
  51 Parmenter Rd Hudson (01749) *(G-9403)*

Precision Coating Co Inc **(HQ)**.............................. **781 329-1420**
  51 Parmenter Rd Hudson (01749) *(G-9404)*

Precision Combustion Inc... 203 287-3700
  410 Sackett Point Rd Ste B North Haven (06473) *(G-2432)*

Precision Composites VT LLC...................................... 802 626-5900
  630 Gilman Rd Lyndonville (05851) *(G-17320)*

Precision Cutter Grinding Inc...................................... 802 436-2039
  7 Ferry Rd Hartland (05048) *(G-17287)*

Precision Depaneling Mchs LLC.................................. 540 248-1381
  326 Main St Unit 11 Fremont (03044) *(G-14329)*

Precision Design, Milford *Also Called: Plasti-Clip Corporation (G-15034)*

Precision Devices Inc **(PA)**..................................... **203 265-9308**
  55 N Plains Industrial Rd Wallingford (06492) *(G-3839)*

Precision Digital Corporation..................................... 508 655-7300
  233 South St Hopkinton (01748) *(G-9340)*

Precision Door & Window Inc **(PA)**....................... **781 344-6900**
  466 Sumner St Stoughton (02072) *(G-12228)*

Precision Electronic Assembly.................................. 203 452-1839
  133 Bart Rd Monroe (06468) *(G-1919)*

Precision Electronic Hardware, Naugatuck *Also Called: Multi-Metal Manufacturing Inc (G-1974)*

Precision Electronics Corp.. 781 834-6677
  427 Plain St Marshfield (02050) *(G-10244)*

Precision Engineered Pdts LLC................................. 203 336-6479
  1146 Barnum Ave Bridgeport (06610) *(G-361)*

Precision Engineered Pdts LLC................................. 203 265-3299
  6 Northrop Industrial Park Rd W Wallingford (06492) *(G-3840)*

Precision Engineered Pdts LLC **(DH)** 110 Frank Mossberg Dr Attleboro (02703) *(G-6051)*

Precision Engineering LLC... 508 278-5700
  29 Industrial Dr Uxbridge (01569) *(G-12488)*

Precision Express Mfg LLC.. 860 584-2627
  80 Dolphin Rd Bristol (06010) *(G-483)*

Precision Feeding Systems Inc.................................. 413 525-9200
  45 Deer Park Dr East Longmeadow (01028) *(G-8389)*

Precision Finishing Svcs Inc...................................... 860 882-1073
  60 Ezra Silva Ln Windsor (06095) *(G-4295)*

Precision Fire Fabrication LLC.................................... 203 706-0749
  8 West St Plantsville (06479) *(G-2794)*

Precision Graphics Inc.. 860 828-6561
  10 Clark Dr East Berlin (06023) *(G-916)*

Precision Grinding Company...................................... 860 229-9652
  33 Charles St New Britain (06051) *(G-2055)*

Precision Letter LLC.. 603 625-9625
  396 Pepsi Rd Manchester (03109) *(G-14913)*

Precision Lumber Inc.. 603 764-9450
  576 Buffalo Rd Wentworth (03282) *(G-15677)*

Precision Machining, Whitman *Also Called: Dimark Incorporated (G-13349)*

Precision Machinists Co Inc....................................... 508 528-2325
  9 Forge Pkwy Franklin (02038) *(G-8857)*

Precision Medical Engineering, Wilmington *Also Called: Neurotherm Inc (G-13438)*

Precision Metal Fabrication, Newburyport *Also Called: AW Airflo Industries Inc (G-10668)*

Precision Metal Goods, Hatfield *Also Called: Innovative Designs & Disp Inc (G-9072)*

Precision Metal Products Inc...................................... 203 877-4258
  307 Pepes Farm Rd Milford (06460) *(G-1869)*

Precision Metal Works Inc... 978 667-0180
  100 Rangeway Rd North Billerica (01862) *(G-10944)*

Precision Metals and Plas Mfg, Winsted *Also Called: Precision Metals and Plastics (G-4353)*

Precision Metals and Plastics.................................... 860 238-4320
  118 Colebrook River Rd Ste 7 Winsted (06098) *(G-4353)*

Precision Methods Incorporated................................ 203 879-1429
  40 North St Wolcott (06716) *(G-4373)*

Precision Mfg Solutions, Saco *Also Called: Nikel Precision Group LLC (G-5375)*

Precision Millwork Inc... 207 761-3997
  12 Sky View Dr Cumberland Foreside (04110) *(G-4713)*

Precision Optics Corp Inc **(PA)**............................. **978 630-1800**
  22 E Broadway Gardner (01440) *(G-8898)*

Precision Placement Mchs Inc **(PA)**...................... **603 895-5112**
  326 Main St Unit 11 Fremont (03044) *(G-14330)*

Precision Plastic Products Inc.................................... 860 342-2233
  151 Freestone Ave Portland (06480) *(G-2821)*

Precision Plsg Ornamentals Inc................................. 401 728-9994
  601 Mineral Spring Ave Ste 2 Pawtucket (02860) *(G-16404)*

Precision Polishing, Pawtucket *Also Called: Precision Plsg Ornamentals Inc (G-16404)*

Precision Products... 401 766-0200
  445 Saint Paul St North Smithfield (02896) *(G-16331)*

Precision Programming, Skowhegan *Also Called: J & M Machining Inc (G-5470)*

Precision Punch + Tooling Corp **(PA)**.................... **860 229-9902**
  304 Christian Ln Berlin (06037) *(G-79)*

Precision Punch + Tooling Corp................................ 860 225-4159
  304 Christian Ln Berlin (06037) *(G-80)*

Precision Resource Inc **(PA)**................................. **203 925-0012**
  25 Forest Pkwy Shelton (06484) *(G-3053)*

Precision Resource Mexico, Shelton *Also Called: Pr-Mx Holdings Company LLC (G-3051)*

Precision Screw Mch Pdts Inc................................... 207 283-0121
  30 Gooch St Biddeford (04005) *(G-4583)*

Precision Sensing Devices Inc................................... 508 359-2833
  93 West St Ste D Medfield (02052) *(G-10274)*

Precision Sensors Inc... 203 877-2795
  340 Woodmont Rd Milford (06460) *(G-1870)*

Precision Speed Mfg LLC.. 860 635-8811
  422 Timber Ridge Rd Middletown (06457) *(G-1774)*

Precision Spools, Pittsfield *Also Called: Pittsfield Plastics Engrg LLC (G-11419)*

Precision Sportswear Inc.. 508 674-3034
  54 Front St Unit 3 Fall River (02721) *(G-8599)*

Precision Systems Inc... 508 655-7010
  16 Tech Cir Ste 100 Natick (01760) *(G-10494)*

Precision Tape & Label Co Inc.................................. 508 278-7700
  322 West St Uxbridge (01569) *(G-12489)*

Precision Technologies Inc.. 978 649-8715
  42 Westech Dr Tyngsboro (01879) *(G-12464)*

Precision Temperature Control................................... 603 471-9023
  24 Saw Mill Dr Jaffrey (03452) *(G-14576)*

Precision Threaded Products, Bristol *Also Called: Lincoln Thompson (G-462)*

Precision Threaded Products, Bristol *Also Called: Thompson Aerospace LLC (G-502)*

Precision Tool & Molding LLC.................................... 603 437-6685
  22 Manchester Rd Unit 10 Derry (03038) *(G-14206)*

Precision Tool and Die, Derry *Also Called: Precision Tool & Molding LLC (G-14206)*

Precision Trned Cmponents Corp.............................. 401 232-3377
  331 Farnum Pike Smithfield (02917) *(G-16726)*

Precision Wire Shapes Inc.. 508 867-3859
  11 Long Hill Rd West Brookfield (01585) *(G-12997)*

Precision Woodworking Inc.. 617 479-7604
  50 Samoset Ave Quincy (02169) *(G-11531)*

Precision X-Ray Inc.. 203 484-2011
  14 New Rd Madison (06443) *(G-1567)*

Precision X-Ray Inc.. 203 484-2011
  15 Comm Dr Unit 1 North Branford (06471) *(G-2372)*

Precision X-Ray Irradiation, Madison *Also Called: Precision X-Ray Inc (G-1567)*

Precix, New Bedford *Also Called: Acushnet Rubber Company Inc (G-10564)*

Precommissioning Unit TAC 1, Bath *Also Called: Northrop Grmmn Spce & Mssn Sys (G-4530)*

Preferred Concrete Corporation................................. 508 763-5500
  66 Braley Rd East Freetown (02717) *(G-8365)*

Preferred Instruments, Danbury *Also Called: Preferred Utilities Mfg Corp (G-799)*

Preferred Precast Inc... 401 475-5560
  2 Titus St Cumberland (02864) *(G-15961)*

Preferred Precision, Shelton *Also Called: Preferred Tool & Die Inc (G-3054)*

Preferred Printing Co Inc
  140 Corporate Dr Trumbull (06611) *(G-3728)*

Preferred Tool & Die Inc **(PA)**.............................. **203 925-8525**
  30 Forest Pkwy Shelton (06484) *(G-3054)*

Preferred Tool & Die Inc.. 203 925-8525
  19 Forest Pkwy Shelton (06484) *(G-3055)*

Preferred Utilities Mfg Corp **(HQ)**......................... **203 743-6741**
  31-35 South St Danbury (06810) *(G-799)*

Premama, Providence *Also Called: Luna Pharmaceuticals Inc (G-16556)*

Prematech Advanced Ceramics, Worcester *Also Called: Prematech LLC (G-13773)*

Prematech LLC... 508 791-9549
  160 Goddard Memorial Dr Worcester (01603) *(G-13773)*

Prematechnoligies LLC.. 508 791-9549
  160 Goddard Memorial Dr Worcester (01603) *(G-13774)*

Premco Inc.. 781 749-0333
55 Research Rd S Shore Park Hingham (02043) *(G-9157)*

Premier Packaging LLC................................... 603 485-7465
47 Post Rd Hooksett (03106) *(G-14469)*

Premier Prtg Mailing Solutions, Stratford Also Called: Clarity Output Solutions LLC *(G-3527)*

Premier Recycling Eqp Inc................................ 855 223-5859
239 Walton Rd Seabrook (03874) *(G-15600)*

Premier Roll & Tool Inc.................................. 508 695-2551
10 Alice Agnew Dr North Attleboro (02763) *(G-10885)*

Premier Semiconductor Svcs LLC **(DH)**............. **267 954-0130**
1050 Perimeter Rd Ste 201 Manchester (03103) *(G-14914)*

Premiere Packg Partners LLC.......................... 203 694-0003
197 Huntingdon Ave Waterbury (06708) *(G-3964)*

Premium Poultry Co....................................... 401 467-3200
850 Eddy St Providence (02905) *(G-16587)*

Premiumshield, Holliston Also Called: Eastman Performance Films LLC *(G-9208)*

Prepco, Colebrook Also Called: Prepco Inc *(G-14108)*

Prepco Inc.. 603 237-4080
57 Colby St Colebrook (03576) *(G-14108)*

Preppy Puppy Inc... 508 291-7555
2380 Cranberry Hwy Ste 3 West Wareham (02576) *(G-13070)*

Presby Plastics Inc....................................... 603 837-3826
143 Airport Rd Whitefield (03598) *(G-15700)*

Prescott Metal **(PA)**.................................. **207 283-0115**
565 Elm St Biddeford (04005) *(G-4584)*

Preservica Inc... 617 294-6676
50 Milk St Fl 16 Boston (02109) *(G-6975)*

President and Fellows of Harvard College **(PA)**.... **617 496-4873**
1350 Massachusetts Ave Cambridge (02138) *(G-7688)*

President Fllows Hrvard Cllege.......................... 617 495-5581
1 Soldiers Field Rd Ste 20 Boston (02134) *(G-6976)*

President Press Inc....................................... 617 773-1235
100 Columbia St Quincy (02169) *(G-11532)*

President Titanium Co Inc................................ 781 294-0000
243 Franklin St Hanson (02341) *(G-9055)*

Presidium USA Inc.. 203 803-2980
42 Beach Dr Darien (06820) *(G-853)*

Presort Express, Hermon Also Called: Snowman Group *(G-4889)*

Press Forward Inc.. 802 989-4383
228 Maple St Ste 31b Middlebury (05753) *(G-17348)*

Press Ganey Associates Inc............................. 781 295-5000
53 State St Fl 2 Boston (02109) *(G-6977)*

Pressed For Time Printing Inc........................... 617 267-4113
133 South St Boston (02111) *(G-6978)*

Pressure Biosciences Inc **(PA)**..................... **508 230-1828**
14 Norfolk Ave South Easton (02375) *(G-11950)*

Pressure Blast Mfg Co Inc............................... 800 722-5278
205 Nutmeg Rd S Ste E South Windsor (06074) *(G-3174)*

Pressure Signal Inc....................................... 781 871-5629
11 Commerce Rd Ste C Rockland (02370) *(G-11657)*

Prestige Cstm Mirror & GL Inc.......................... 781 647-0878
182 High St Waltham (02453) *(G-12752)*

Prestige Industrial Finshg Co........................... 203 924-7720
511 River Rd Shelton (06484) *(G-3056)*

Prestige Remodeling, Stratford Also Called: Chris Cross LLC *(G-3526)*

Prestige Remodeling LLC................................. 203 386-8426
66 Holland Ave Bridgeport (06605) *(G-362)*

Presto Lifts, Falmouth Also Called: WB Engineering Inc *(G-4775)*

Presto Lifts, Foxboro Also Called: WB Engineering Inc *(G-8731)*

Preston Engravers, East Windsor Also Called: Roto-Die Company Inc *(G-1084)*

Preston Leather Products, Ipswich Also Called: Ebinger Brothers Lea Co Inc *(G-9484)*

Presumpscot Water Power Co............................ 207 856-4000
89 Cumberland St Westbrook (04092) *(G-5643)*

Pretty Instant LLC.. 888 551-6765
300 Summer St Apt 14b Boston (02210) *(G-6979)*

Preusser Research Group Inc **(PA)**................. **203 459-8700**
115 Technology Dr Unit B307 Trumbull (06611) *(G-3729)*

Preventative Maintenance Corp.......................... 860 683-1180
55 Tunxis St Poquonock (06064) *(G-2815)*

Prfrred Lancaster Partners LLC.......................... 717 299-0782
200 Berkeley St Boston (02116) *(G-6980)*

Pride Manufacturing Co LLC **(PA)**.................. **207 487-3322**
10 N Main St Burnham (04922) *(G-4661)*

Pride Manufacturing Co LLC............................. 207 876-2719
169 Water St Guilford (04443) *(G-4855)*

Pride Manufacturing Machine Sp, Guilford Also Called: Pride Manufacturing Co LLC *(G-4855)*

Pride Sports, Burnham Also Called: Pride Manufacturing Co LLC *(G-4661)*

Prima America Corporation............................... 603 631-5407
248 State St Groveton (03582) *(G-14379)*

Prima Electro North Amer LLC, Chicopee Also Called: Convergent - Photonics LLC *(G-8020)*

Primary Colors Inc.. 508 839-3202
9 Millennium Dr North Grafton (01536) *(G-11025)*

Primary Flow Signal Inc **(PA)**...................... **401 461-6366**
800 Wellington Ave Unit 2 Cranston (02910) *(G-15905)*

Primary Graphics, Taunton Also Called: Primary Graphics Corporation *(G-12355)*

Primary Graphics Corporation........................... 781 575-0411
175 W Water St Taunton (02780) *(G-12355)*

Primary Pdc Inc **(PA)**............................... **781 386-2000**
1265 Main St Waltham (02451) *(G-12753)*

Primary Pdts Ingrdnts Amrcas L......................... 207 532-9523
48 Morningstar Rd Houlton (04730) *(G-4904)*

Primatics Financial LLC **(HQ)**...................... **703 342-0040**
80 Lamberton Rd Fl 1 Windsor (06095) *(G-4296)*

Primatope Therapeutics Inc............................. 617 413-3020
508 Dudley Rd Newton (02459) *(G-10776)*

Prime Electric Motors..................................... 207 591-7800
72 Sanford Dr Gorham (04038) *(G-4833)*

Prime Engineered Components, Watertown Also Called: Prime Engneered Components Inc *(G-4025)*

Prime Engneered Components Inc........................ 860 274-6773
1012 Buckingham St Watertown (06795) *(G-4025)*

Prime Engnred Cmpnnts - Brstol......................... 860 584-5964
231 Century Dr Bristol (06010) *(G-484)*

Prime Line, Bridgeport Also Called: PRC Synergy Corp *(G-360)*

Prime National Publishing Corp.......................... 781 899-2702
470 Boston Post Rd Weston (02493) *(G-13289)*

Prime Power Inc.. 603 329-4675
1 Owens Ct Ste 1 Hampstead (03841) *(G-14390)*

Prime Tanning Compan, Hartland Also Called: Tasman Industries Inc *(G-4878)*

Prime Technology LLC.................................... 203 481-5721
344 Twin Lakes Rd North Branford (06471) *(G-2373)*

Primo Medical Group Inc **(PA)**..................... **781 297-5700**
75 Mill St Stoughton (02072) *(G-12229)*

Primo Water North America, Watertown Also Called: Ds Services of America Inc *(G-4009)*

Primrose Medical Inc..................................... 508 660-8688
286 Union St East Walpole (02032) *(G-8421)*

Princeton Printing LLC................................... 617 530-0990
260 Elm St Somerville (02144) *(G-11889)*

Princeton Technology Corp.............................. 603 595-1987
33 Constitution Dr Hudson (03051) *(G-14536)*

Princton Gamma-Tech Instrs Inc........................ 609 924-7310
27 Forge Pkwy Franklin (02038) *(G-8858)*

Print B2b LLC... 203 744-5435
3 Hillcrest Rd Bethel (06801) *(G-132)*

Print Bangor.. 207 947-8049
80 Central St Bangor (04401) *(G-4515)*

Print House, Malden Also Called: Medi - Print Inc *(G-10019)*

Print Management Systems Inc........................... 781 944-1041
26 Conn St Woburn (01801) *(G-13640)*

Print Pro... 978 914-7619
34 Rogers Rd Haverhill (01835) *(G-9122)*

Print Promowear LLC..................................... 203 504-2858
169 Canfield Dr Stamford (06902) *(G-3436)*

Print Synergy Solutions LLC............................. 508 587-5200
129 Liberty St Brockton (02301) *(G-7301)*

Print Tech, Williston Also Called: Digital Press Printers LLC *(G-17727)*

Print Works, Presque Isle Also Called: Northeast Publishing Company *(G-5308)*

Print Works Inc... 508 589-4626
25 South St Ste 2b Hopkinton (01748) *(G-9341)*

Print-Mail of Maine Inc.................................. 207 878-8000
75 Bishop St Portland (04103) *(G-5262)*

A L P H A B E T I C

Printech, Stamford *Also Called: Furci Communications Inc (G-3353)*

Printed Communications.. 860 436-9619
   400 Chapel Rd Ste L1 South Windsor (06074) *(G-3175)*

Printemscom.. 207 490-5118
   2066 Main St Sanford (04073) *(G-5406)*

Printer Techs LLC.. 203 322-1160
   44 Commerce Rd Stamford (06902) *(G-3437)*

Printers, Hartford *Also Called: Hartford Business Supply Inc (G-1485)*

Printers Square Inc... 603 703-0795
   105 Faltin Dr Manchester (03103) *(G-14915)*

Printguard Inc... 508 890-8822
   1521 Grafton Rd Millbury (01527) *(G-10441)*

Printing, North Attleboro *Also Called: Artcraft Co Inc (G-10865)*

Printing & Graphic Services, New Haven *Also Called: Yale University (G-2221)*

Printing Dept... 617 349-4206
   795 Massachusetts Ave Cambridge (02139) *(G-7689)*

PRINTING INDUSTRIES OF NEW ENG, Southborough *Also Called: Graphic Arts Institute of Neng (G-11995)*

Printing Solutions Inc.. 978 392-9903
   6 Carlisle Rd Ste 6 Westford (01886) *(G-13257)*

Printmaster, Norwood *Also Called: Ingleside Corporation (G-11180)*

Printpro Silkscreen Co LLC... 978 556-1695
   233 Neck Rd Haverhill (01835) *(G-9123)*

Printsynergy Solutions, Brockton *Also Called: Print Synergy Solutions LLC (G-7301)*

Prior Scientific Inc **(HQ)**... **781 878-8442**
   80 Reservoir Park Dr Rockland (02370) *(G-11658)*

Priority Machine LLC.. 603 677-2507
   10 Chenell Dr Concord (03301) *(G-14152)*

Priority One Inc... 203 244-7093
   35 Eagle Rd Danbury (06810) *(G-800)*

Priority Print... 617 547-6919
   337 Cambridge St Cambridge (02141) *(G-7690)*

Priscilla of Boston Inc... 857 366-4109
   801 Boylston St Fl 3 Boston (02116) *(G-6981)*

Prismatrix Lighting, Rumford *Also Called: Lexington Lighting Group LLC (G-16674)*

Prismic Pharmaceuticals Inc... 971 506-6415
   650 South Rd Holden (01520) *(G-9195)*

Privateer LLC.. 860 526-1838
   5 Center Rd W Old Saybrook (06475) *(G-2661)*

Privateer International LLC.. 978 356-0477
   28 Mitchell Rd Ipswich (01938) *(G-9495)*

Prl Hancock LLC... 207 564-8520
   71 Salems Rd/Washington Jctn Rd Hancock (04640) *(G-4873)*

Pro Counters New England LLC.. 203 347-8663
   1 Chestnut St Ansonia (06401) *(G-17)*

Pro Design & Manufacturing.. 603 819-4131
   13 Elm St Newton (03858) *(G-15243)*

Pro Dough Inc... 603 623-6844
   8030 S Willow St Unit 2-7 Manchester (03103) *(G-14916)*

Pro Pel Plastech Inc **(PA)**... **413 665-3379**
   378 Long Plain Rd South Deerfield (01373) *(G-11928)*

Pro Scientific Inc.. 203 267-4600
   99 Willenbrock Rd Oxford (06478) *(G-2708)*

Pro Tool and Design Inc.. 860 828-4667
   45 Maselli Rd Newington (06111) *(G-2318)*

Pro Touch Home Improvement Inc... 617 378-1929
   118 Shore Dr Peabody (01960) *(G-11336)*

Pro-Line, Haverhill *Also Called: R W Hatfield Company Inc (G-9124)*

Pro-Manufactured Products Inc... 860 564-2197
   29 Center Pkwy Plainfield (06374) *(G-2737)*

Proampac, Claremont *Also Called: Ampac Holdings LLC (G-14076)*

Probatter Sports LLC.. 203 874-2500
   49 Research Dr Ste 1 Milford (06460) *(G-1871)*

Process Automtn Solutions Inc **(HQ)**....................................... **203 207-9917**
   107 Mill Plain Rd Ste 301 Danbury (06811) *(G-801)*

Process Cooling Systems Inc.. 978 537-1996
   800 Research Dr Leominster (01453) *(G-9697)*

Process Solutions Inc.. 413 525-5870
   198 Benton Dr East Longmeadow (01028) *(G-8390)*

Procraft Corporation.. 603 487-2080
   416 River Rd New Boston (03070) *(G-15193)*

Procter & Gamble, Auburn *Also Called: Procter & Gamble Company (G-4456)*

Procter & Gamble, Andover *Also Called: Procter & Gamble Mfg Co (G-5908)*

Procter & Gamble Company.. 207 753-4000
   2879 Hotel Rd Auburn (04210) *(G-4456)*

Procter & Gamble Mfg Co.. 978 749-5547
   30 Burtt Rd Andover (01810) *(G-5908)*

Proctor Gas Inc.. 802 459-3340
   2 Market St Proctor (05765) *(G-17460)*

Proctor Piper Log Homes, Proctorsville *Also Called: Gilcris Enterprises Inc (G-17461)*

Proctor Woodworks LLC.. 860 767-9881
   53 Grandview Ter Essex (06426) *(G-1170)*

Prodrive Technologies Inc... 617 475-1617
   15 University Rd Ste A Canton (02021) *(G-7822)*

Product Resources LLC... 978 524-8500
   4 Mulliken Way Newburyport (01950) *(G-10709)*

Production Basics Inc.. 617 926-8100
   31 Dunham Rd Ste 3 Billerica (01821) *(G-6473)*

Production Dept, New Britain *Also Called: International Auto Entps Inc (G-2033)*

Production Equipment Company.. 800 758-5697
   401 Liberty St Meriden (06450) *(G-1685)*

Production Tool & Grinding... 978 544-8206
   273 Main St Athol (01331) *(G-5983)*

Producto Corporation **(HQ)**... **203 366-3224**
   800 Union Ave Bridgeport (06607) *(G-363)*

Producto Machine Company, The, Bridgeport *Also Called: Producto Corporation (G-363)*

Prodways.. 763 568-7966
   316 Daniel Webster Hwy Merrimack (03054) *(G-14999)*

Professional Boat Builder, Brooklin *Also Called: Woodenboat Publications Inc (G-4635)*

Professional Graphics Inc.. 203 846-4291
   25 Perry Ave Norwalk (06850) *(G-2560)*

Professional Mktg Svcs Inc... 203 610-6222
   300 Long Beach Blvd Ste 6 Stratford (06615) *(G-3568)*

Professional TI Grinding Inc **(PA)**.. **508 230-3535**
   18 Plymouth Dr South Easton (02375) *(G-11951)*

Professional Trades Netwrk LLC.. 860 567-0173
   1100 Buckingham St Watertown (06795) *(G-4026)*

Professnal Cntract Strlztion I... 508 822-5524
   40 Myles Standish Blvd Taunton (02780) *(G-12356)*

Professnal Sftwr For Nrses Inc.. 800 889-7627
   4 Limbo Ln Amherst (03031) *(G-13885)*

Proficient Software Corp.. 617 964-3457
   396 Dedham St Newton (02459) *(G-10777)*

Profile Metal Forming, Newmarket *Also Called: Profile Metal Forming Inc (G-15222)*

Profile Metal Forming **(HQ)**... **603 659-8323**
   10 Forbes Rd Newmarket (03857) *(G-15222)*

Profile Precision Machine.. 603 692-4116
   350 Route 108 Unit 108 Somersworth (03878) *(G-15622)*

Profiles Incorporated... 413 283-7790
   7 First St Palmer (01069) *(G-11283)*

Profit Ect, Dedham *Also Called: Profitect Inc (G-8247)*

Profitect Inc **(HQ)**... **781 290-0009**
   3 Allied Dr Ste 220 Dedham (02026) *(G-8247)*

Profitkey International Inc.. 603 898-9800
   50 Stiles Rd Salem (03079) *(G-15556)*

Proflow Inc... 203 230-4700
   303 State St North Haven (06473) *(G-2433)*

Proflow Process Equipment, North Haven *Also Called: Proflow Inc (G-2433)*

Progderm Inc.. 617 419-1800
   33 Arch St Boston (02110) *(G-6982)*

Programmed Test Sources Inc... 978 486-3008
   9 Beaver Brook Rd Littleton (01460) *(G-9833)*

Progress, Burlington *Also Called: Progress Software Corporation (G-7413)*

Progress Enterprises LLC.. 413 562-2736
   3 Progress Ave Westfield (01085) *(G-13201)*

Progress Pallet Inc... 508 923-1930
   98 W Grove St Middleboro (02346) *(G-10375)*

Progress Software Corporation **(PA)**...................................... **781 280-4000**
   15 Wayside Rd Ste 4 Burlington (01803) *(G-7413)*

Progressive Displays Inc... 401 245-2909
   605 Main St Warren (02885) *(G-16764)*

(G-0000) Company's Geographic Section entry number

Progressive Manufacturing Inc......................... 603 298-5778
20 Airpark Rd West Lebanon (03784) *(G-15688)*

Progressive Plastics Inc................................. 802 433-1563
85 Industry St Williamstown (05679) *(G-17717)*

Progressive Sheetmetal LLC............................ 860 436-9884
36 Mascolo Rd South Windsor (06074) *(G-3176)*

Project Graphics, Woodbury *Also Called: Project Graphics Inc (G-4388)*

Project Graphics Inc.................................... 802 488-8789
41 Stone Pit Rd Woodbury (06798) *(G-4388)*

Project Plasma Holdings Corp........................... 508 244-6400
37 Birch St Milford (01757) *(G-10415)*

Project Resources Inc................................... 508 295-7444
16 Kendrick Rd Ste 6 Wareham (02571) *(G-12842)*

Projects Inc... 860 633-4615
65 Sequin Dr Glastonbury (06033) *(G-1295)*

Proknee, Whitefield *Also Called: Proknee Corp (G-5656)*

Proknee Corp.. 207 549-5018
137 Devine Rd Whitefield (04353) *(G-5656)*

Prolamina Corporation **(DH)**.......................... **413 562-2315**
132 N Elm St Westfield (01085) *(G-13202)*

Prolens Inc... 802 988-1018
47 Main St North Troy (05859) *(G-17430)*

Proliance International Inc.............................. 203 401-6450
100 Gando Dr New Haven (06513) *(G-2188)*

Proliance International Inc.............................. 860 688-7644
436 Hayden Station Rd Windsor (06095) *(G-4297)*

Prom Software Inc...................................... 802 862-7500
150 Dorset St Ste 294 South Burlington (05403) *(G-17597)*

Promax Supply LLC..................................... 781 620-1602
142 Franklin St Melrose (02176) *(G-10318)*

Promein Steel LLC...................................... 860 828-1944
76 Depot Rd Berlin (06037) *(G-81)*

Promet Marine Service Corp............................ 401 467-3730
242 Allens Ave Providence (02905) *(G-16588)*

Prometheus Group, Dover *Also Called: Prometheus Group of NH Ltd (G-14245)*

Prometheus Group of NH Ltd........................... 800 442-2325
1 Washington St Ste 3171 Dover (03820) *(G-14245)*

Promise Propane Llc................................... 860 685-0676
110 Holmes Rd Newington (06111) *(G-2319)*

Promisim Inc... 203 554-2707
500 W Putnam Ave Ste 400 Greenwich (06830) *(G-1344)*

Promounds Inc **(PA)**................................. **508 580-6171**
15 Pacella Park Dr Ste 240 Randolph (02368) *(G-11572)*

Proofing House Press, Salem *Also Called: Frugal Printer Inc (G-15529)*

Prophet Corp.. 774 253-0909
191 West St Auburn (01501) *(G-6124)*

Proprint, Boston *Also Called: Pressed For Time Printing Inc (G-6978)*

Proprint Incorporated.................................. 401 944-3855
1145 Atwood Ave Johnston (02919) *(G-16101)*

Proquip USA, Marblehead *Also Called: Marblehead Weather Gmts LLC (G-10090)*

Prosensing Inc.. 413 549-4402
107 Sunderland Rd Amherst (01002) *(G-5863)*

Prospect Hill Company, Brockton *Also Called: A W McMullen Co Inc (G-7251)*

Prospect Machine Products Inc.......................... 203 758-4448
139 Union City Rd Prospect (06712) *(G-2840)*

Prospect Press LLC.................................... 802 862-6717
47 Prospect Pkwy Burlington (05401) *(G-17152)*

Prospect Printing LLC................................. 203 758-6007
16 Waterbury Rd Prospect (06712) *(G-2841)*

Prospect Products Incorporated......................... 860 666-0323
43 Kelsey St Newington (06111) *(G-2320)*

Protac, New Haven *Also Called: Arvinas Inc (G-2119)*

Protagene Us Inc....................................... 857 829-3200
4 Burlington Woods Dr Burlington (01803) *(G-7414)*

Protavic America Inc................................... 603 623-8624
8 Ricker Ave Londonderry (03053) *(G-14780)*

Protection Industries Corp **(PA)**.................... **203 375-9393**
2897 Main St Stratford (06614) *(G-3569)*

Protective Armored Systems Inc......................... 413 637-1060
100 Valley St Lee (01238) *(G-9618)*

Protectowire, Pembroke *Also Called: Protectowire Co Inc (G-11376)*

Protectowire Co Inc.................................... 781 826-3878
60 Washington St Pembroke (02359) *(G-11376)*

Protegrity Usa Inc **(PA)**........................... **203 326-7200**
333 Ludlow St Ste 8 Stamford (06902) *(G-3438)*

Protein Holdings Inc **(PA)**......................... **207 771-0965**
10 Moulton St Ste 5 Portland (04101) *(G-5263)*

Protek Ski Racing Inc.................................. 860 628-9643
85 Ladyslipper Ln Southington (06489) *(G-3229)*

Protek-Sure, Orleans *Also Called: Hersey Clutch Company LLC (G-11239)*

Proteq Solutions LLC.................................. 603 888-6630
76 Northeastern Blvd Ste 38a Nashua (03062) *(G-15151)*

Proterial Cable America Inc............................ 603 669-4347
900 Holt Ave Manchester (03109) *(G-14917)*

Proteus Industries Inc................................. 978 281-9545
33 Commercial St Gloucester (01930) *(G-8952)*

Proteus Manufacturing Company Inc..................... 781 939-0919
100 Cummings Ctr Ste 327g Beverly (01915) *(G-6372)*

Proto Industrial Tools, New Britain *Also Called: Stanley Industrial & Auto LLC (G-2070)*

Proto Labs Inc... 763 479-2679
15 Charron Ave Nashua (03063) *(G-15152)*

Proto Part Inc... 603 883-6531
71 Pine Rd Unit F Hudson (03051) *(G-14537)*

Proto XYZ Inc... 508 525-6363
49 Potomska St New Bedford (02740) *(G-10644)*

Proton Energy Systems Inc............................. 203 678-2000
10 Technology Dr Wallingford (06492) *(G-3841)*

Protopac Inc... 860 274-6796
120 Echo Lake Rd Watertown (06795) *(G-4027)*

Protopac Printing Services, Watertown *Also Called: Protopac Inc (G-4027)*

Prototek Dgtal Mfg Concord LLC **(PA)**............... **603 746-2001**
244 Burnham Intervale Rd Contoocook (03229) *(G-14173)*

Prototek Intrmdate Hldings Inc......................... 800 403-9777
244 Burnham Intervale Rd Contoocook (03229) *(G-14174)*

Prototek Manufacturing, Contoocook *Also Called: Prototek Dgtal Mfg Concord LLC (G-14173)*

Protronix, Wallingford *Also Called: Protronix Inc (G-3842)*

Protronix Inc.. 203 269-5858
28 Parker St Wallingford (06492) *(G-3842)*

Proven Process Med Dvcs Inc........................... 508 261-0800
110 Forbes Blvd Mansfield (02048) *(G-10072)*

Proveris Scientific Corp **(PA)**..................... **508 460-8822**
2 Cabot Rd Ste 5 Hudson (01749) *(G-9405)*

Providence Braid Company............................. 401 722-2120
358 Lowden St Pawtucket (02860) *(G-16405)*

Providence Business News.............................. 401 273-2201
400 Westminster St Ste 600 Providence (02903) *(G-16589)*

Providence Casting Inc................................ 401 231-0860
3 Warren Ave North Providence (02911) *(G-16308)*

Providence Journal Company............................ 401 277-7000
75 Fountain St Providence (02902) *(G-16590)*

Providence Label & Tag Co............................. 401 751-6677
315 Harris Ave Providence (02909) *(G-16591)*

Providence Metallizing Co Inc **(PA)**............... **401 722-5300**
51 Fairlawn Ave Pawtucket (02860) *(G-16406)*

Providence Mint Inc................................... 401 272-7760
1205 Westminster St Providence (02909) *(G-16592)*

Providence Specialty Pdts Inc.......................... 401 272-4979
33 Dearborn St Providence (02909) *(G-16593)*

Providence Visitor, Providence *Also Called: Visitor Printing Company (G-16641)*

Providence Wire Creations Inc.......................... 401 490-3227
498 Kinsley Ave Providence (02909) *(G-16594)*

Providence Yarn Company Inc........................... 401 722-5600
50 Division St Pawtucket (02860) *(G-16407)*

Province Automation, Sanford *Also Called: Oizero9 Inc (G-5404)*

Province Kiln Dried Firewood........................... 603 524-4447
428 South Rd Belmont (03220) *(G-13968)*

Provincetown Banner Inc............................... 508 487-7400
167 Commercial St Ste 2 Provincetown (02657) *(G-11496)*

Provisionaire & Co LLC................................ 646 681-8600
151 Post Rd E Westport (06880) *(G-4193)*

Proxy Manufacturing Inc............................... 978 687-3138
55 Chase St Ste 7 Methuen (01844) *(G-10344)*

A L P H A B E T I C

Proxysoft Worldwide Inc................................... 203 730-0084
17c Trowbridge Dr Bethel (06801) *(G-133)*

Prr Enterprise Inc.. 207 783-2991
40 South Ave Lewiston (04240) *(G-4985)*

Prysm Inc.. 978 405-3091
45 Bartlett St Ste 2 Marlborough (01752) *(G-10197)*

Prysmian Cbles Systems USA LLC......................... 860 456-8000
1600 Main St Willimantic (06226) *(G-4220)*

Prysmian Cbles Systems USA LLC......................... 603 668-1620
345 Mcgregor St Manchester (03102) *(G-14918)*

Prysmian Cbles Systems USA LLC......................... 401 333-4848
3 Carol Dr Lincoln (02865) *(G-16151)*

Prysmian Group Spclty Cbles LL......................... 508 822-0246
761 Warner Blvd Taunton (02780) *(G-12357)*

Prysmian Group Spclty Cbles LL **(DH)**................. **774 501-7600**
656 Warner Blvd Taunton (02780) *(G-12358)*

Prysmian Group Spclty Cbles LL......................... 508 822-5444
656 Warner Blvd Taunton (02780) *(G-12359)*

Psg Framing, Somerville *Also Called: Pucker Gallery Inc (G-11891)*

Psg Framing Inc.. 617 261-1817
130 Broadway Somerville (02145) *(G-11890)*

PSI, Northborough *Also Called: Power Systems Integrity Inc (G-11106)*

PSI Controls, Portland *Also Called: Piping Specialties Inc (G-5256)*

PSI Molded Plastics NH Inc............................. 603 569-5100
5 Wickers Dr Wolfeboro (03894) *(G-15735)*

PSI Water Systems LLC **(PA)**......................... **603 624-5110**
1368 Hooksett Rd Hooksett (03106) *(G-14470)*

Psjl Corporation....................................... 978 313-2500
780 Boston Rd Ste 4 Billerica (01821) *(G-6474)*

Psp, Colchester *Also Called: Fab-Tech Inc (G-17190)*

Pta Corporation **(PA)**............................... **203 888-0585**
148 Christian St Oxford (06478) *(G-2709)*

Pta Plastics, Oxford *Also Called: Pta Corporation (G-2709)*

Ptc Inc **(PA)**...................................... **781 370-5000**
121 Seaport Blvd Boston (02210) *(G-6983)*

Ptc Inc... 617 792-7622
230 3rd Ave Prospect Place Waltham (02451) *(G-12754)*

Ptc Therapeutics Gt Inc............................... 781 799-9179
245 First St Ste 1800 Cambridge (02142) *(G-7691)*

Pte Precision Machining, Kittery *Also Called: Patten Tool and Engrg Inc (G-4939)*

Pti Industries Inc **(HQ)**........................... **800 318-8438**
2 Peerless Way Enfield (06082) *(G-1143)*

Pto Today, Wrentham *Also Called: School Family Media LLC (G-13844)*

Ptr - Precision Technologies Inc **(DH)**.............. **860 741-2281**
120 Post Rd Enfield (06082) *(G-1144)*

Pts, Littleton *Also Called: Programmed Test Sources Inc (G-9833)*

Pttgc Innovation America Corp **(HQ)**................ **617 657-5234**
45 Cummings Park Woburn (01801) *(G-13641)*

Public Scales... 207 784-9466
32 Lexington St Lewiston (04240) *(G-4986)*

Publishers Crcltion Flfllment......................... 978 671-1820
607 North Ave Ste 18-5 # 2c Wakefield (01880) *(G-12530)*

Publishing, Swansea *Also Called: N E Publishing Group (G-12307)*

Publishing Collaborative LLC.......................... 413 538-4170
475 Hadley St South Hadley (01075) *(G-11966)*

Publishing Solutions Group............................ 781 552-5568
15 Wall St Burlington (01803) *(G-7415)*

Pucker Gallery Inc.................................... 617 261-1817
130 Broadway Rear Somerville (02145) *(G-11891)*

Pucks Putters & Fuel LLC.............................. 203 877-5457
10 Robert Dennis Dr Milford (06461) *(G-1872)*

Puffin Boat Company, Hampden *Also Called: Puffin Boats LLC (G-4866)*

Puffin Boats LLC...................................... 207 907-4385
100 Marina Rd Hampden (04444) *(G-4866)*

Pulmatrix Inc **(PA)**............................... **781 357-2333**
36 Crosby Dr Ste 100 Bedford (01730) *(G-6254)*

Pulpdent Corporation.................................. 617 926-6666
80 Oakland St Watertown (02472) *(G-12901)*

Pulse Network Inc.................................... 781 688-8000
10 Oceana Way Norwood (02062) *(G-11203)*

Pumc Holding Corporation **(PA)**..................... **203 743-6741**
31-35 South St Danbury (06810) *(G-802)*

Pump Technology Incorporated.......................... 203 736-8890
390 Birmingham Blvd Ansonia (06401) *(G-18)*

Punchpops LLC... 508 344-7932
61 Harvard St Fl 3 Worcester (01609) *(G-13775)*

Puppy Hugger... 203 661-4858
15 Widgeon Way Greenwich (06830) *(G-1345)*

Puraclenz LLC.. 561 213-1411
30 Butler Ln New Canaan (06840) *(G-2085)*

Puratos Corporation.................................. 781 688-8560
83 Morse St Norwood (02062) *(G-11204)*

Purbeck Isle Inc **(PA)**............................ **207 623-5119**
36 Anthony Ave Ste 104 Augusta (04330) *(G-4479)*

Purchasing Inventory Cons Inc........................ 802 674-2620
1706 Brook Rd Windsor (05089) *(G-17761)*

Purdue Pharma, Stamford *Also Called: Frederick Purdue Company Inc (G-3349)*

Purdue Pharma, Stamford *Also Called: Purdue Pharma Technologies Inc (G-3441)*

Purdue Pharma LP **(HQ)**............................ **203 588-8000**
201 Tresser Blvd Stamford (06901) *(G-3439)*

Purdue Pharma LP..................................... 203 588-8000
498 Washington St Coventry (02816) *(G-15819)*

Purdue Pharma Manufacturing LP....................... 252 265-1924
201 Tresser Blvd Stamford (06901) *(G-3440)*

Purdue Pharma Technologies Inc....................... 203 588-8000
1 Stamford Forum Stamford (06901) *(G-3441)*

PURDUE PRODUCTS LP................................... 888 827-0624
201 Tresser Blvd Fl 1 Stamford (06901) *(G-3442)*

Purdy Corporation.................................... 860 649-0000
586 Hilliard St Manchester (06042) *(G-1631)*

Pure Country Products, Peabody *Also Called: Dunajski Dairy Inc (G-11308)*

Pure Element.. 603 235-4373
8 Birch St Derry (03038) *(G-14207)*

Pure Encapsulations LLC.............................. 800 753-2277
490 Boston Post Rd Sudbury (01776) *(G-12269)*

Pure Energy Apothecary, Williston *Also Called: Lancaster Imageworks Inc (G-17738)*

Pure Imaging.. 781 537-6992
9 Fowle St Woburn (01801) *(G-13642)*

Pure Source LLC..................................... 626 442-6784
291 Durham Point Rd Durham (03824) *(G-14267)*

Pure-Stat Technologies Inc.......................... 207 795-6000
11 Fireslate Pl Lewiston (04240) *(G-4987)*

Purecoat International LLC........................... 561 844-0100
30 Brighton St Belmont (02478) *(G-6309)*

Purecoat North LLC.................................. 617 489-2750
39 Hittinger St Belmont (02478) *(G-6310)*

Purestat, Lewiston *Also Called: Pure-Stat Technologies Inc (G-4987)*

Purestat Engineered Tech, Lewiston *Also Called: Kullson Engineered Tech Inc (G-4969)*

Puretech Health LLC **(HQ)**........................ **617 482-2333**
6 Tide St Ste 400 Boston (02210) *(G-6984)*

Puretech Health PLC................................. 617 482-2333
6 Tide St Ste 400 Boston (02210) *(G-6985)*

Purevita Labs LLC.................................. 401 258-8968
153 James P Murphy Ind Hwy West Warwick (02893) *(G-16921)*

Purification Technologies LLC **(DH)**.............. **860 526-7801**
67 Winthrop Rd Chester (06412) *(G-630)*

Puritan Capital, Hollis *Also Called: Puritan Press Inc (G-14458)*

Puritan Electronics Inc............................ 800 343-8649
920 Candia Rd Manchester (03109) *(G-14919)*

Puritan Ice Cream Boston Inc....................... 617 524-3580
3895 Washington St Boston (02131) *(G-6986)*

Puritan Industries Inc............................. 860 693-0791
122 Powder Mill Rd Collinsville (06019) *(G-668)*

Puritan Medical Pdts Co I LP....................... 207 876-3311
31 School St Guilford (04443) *(G-4856)*

Puritan Medical Pdts Co LLC **(PA)**............... **207 876-3311**
31 School St Guilford (04443) *(G-4857)*

Puritan Medical Products, Guilford *Also Called: Puritan Medical Pdts Co I LP (G-4856)*

Puritan Press Inc **(PA)**......................... **603 889-4500**
95 Runnells Bridge Rd Hollis (03049) *(G-14458)*

Purmo Group USA Inc................................ 802 654-7500
45 Krupp Dr Williston (05495) *(G-17746)*

Pursuit Aerospace, Eastford *Also Called: Whitcraft LLC* **(G-1093)**

Pussums Cat Company, Turner *Also Called: Two Rivers Pet Products Inc* **(G-5565)**

Pusterla Us Inc...... 401 245-5900
293 Child St Warren (02885) **(G-16765)**

Putnam Plastics Corporation...... 860 774-1559
40 Louisa Viens Dr Dayville (06241) **(G-867)**

Putnam Science Academy, Putnam *Also Called: D & M Group LLC* **(G-2852)**

Puzzle House...... 603 532-4442
426 Nutting Rd Jaffrey (03452) **(G-14577)**

Puzzle Pieces LLC...... 617 481-2304
1266 Furnace Brook Pkwy Ste 308 Quincy (02169) **(G-11533)**

Pv Engineering & Mfg Inc...... 978 465-1221
88 Rabbit Rd Salisbury (01952) **(G-11744)**

Pvd, Wilmington *Also Called: Pvd Products Inc* **(G-13448)**

Pvd Products Inc...... 978 694-9455
35 Upton Dr Ste 200 Wilmington (01887) **(G-13448)**

Pvf Maple LLC...... 802 492-3364
1368 Lincoln Hill Rd Cuttingsville (05738) **(G-17209)**

Pvh Corp...... 508 945-4063
1238 Main St Chatham (02633) **(G-7900)**

Pvk Inc...... 781 595-7771
86 Sanderson Ave Ste 130 Lynn (01902) **(G-9989)**

Pwb...... 508 497-3930
225 Wood St Hopkinton (01748) **(G-9342)**

PYC Deborring LLC F/K/A C &...... 860 828-6806
500 Four Rod Rd Ste 114 Berlin (06037) **(G-82)**

Pyne-Davidson Company...... 860 522-9106
237 Weston St Hartford (06120) **(G-1501)**

Pyramid Case Co Inc...... 401 273-0643
122 Manton Ave Providence (02909) **(G-16595)**

Pyramid Checks & Printing...... 207 878-9832
208 Riverside Industrial Pkwy Portland (04103) **(G-5264)**

Pyramid Printing and Advg Inc...... 781 337-7609
54 Mathewson Dr # 60 Weymouth (02189) **(G-13333)**

Pyramid Printing and Digital, Weymouth *Also Called: Pyramid Printing and Advg Inc* **(G-13333)**

Pyramid Technical Cons Inc...... 781 402-1700
135 Beaver St Ste 102 Waltham (02452) **(G-12755)**

Pyramid Time Systems LLC...... 203 238-0550
45 Gracey Ave Meriden (06451) **(G-1686)**

Pys Enterprises Inc...... 413 732-7470
616 Dwight St Springfield (01104) **(G-12123)**

Pyxis Oncology, Boston *Also Called: Pyxis Oncology Inc* **(G-6987)**

Pyxis Oncology Inc **(PA)**...... **617 221-9059**
321 Harrison Ave Boston (02118) **(G-6987)**

Q LLC...... 603 294-0047
110 Venture Dr Dover (03820) **(G-14246)**

Q A Technology Company Inc...... 603 926-1193
110 Towle Farm Rd Hampton (03842) **(G-14409)**

Q Alpha Inc...... 860 357-7340
87 Upton Rd Colchester (06415) **(G-664)**

Q E A, Chelmsford *Also Called: Quality Engineering Assoc Inc* **(G-7949)**

Q Pin2s Billiards...... 413 285-7971
885 Riverdale St West Springfield (01089) **(G-13043)**

Q S T, Saint Albans *Also Called: QST Inc* **(G-17529)**

Q-S Technologies Inc...... 203 237-2297
602 Pomeroy Ave Meriden (06450) **(G-1687)**

Q-Seal LLC...... 802 773-1228
92 Park St Rutland (05701) **(G-17504)**

Qbit Semiconductor Ltd...... 351 205-0005
1 Monarch Dr Ste 203 Littleton (01460) **(G-9834)**

Qbl Winddown LLC...... 617 219-8300
3 Speen St Ste 300 Framingham (01701) **(G-8800)**

Qc Industries Inc **(PA)**...... **781 344-1000**
60 Maple St Mansfield (02048) **(G-10073)**

Qci Engineering, Seekonk *Also Called: QCI Inc* **(G-11784)**

QCI Inc...... 508 399-8983
257 Pine St Seekonk (02771) **(G-11784)**

Qd Vision Inc...... 781 652-7500
124 Washington St Ste 101 Foxboro (02035) **(G-8715)**

Qds LLC...... 203 338-9668
120 Long Hill Cross Rd Shelton (06484) **(G-3057)**

QED, Woburn *Also Called: Queues Enforth Development Inc* **(G-13646)**

QEP Co Inc...... 978 368-8991
179 Brook St Clinton (01510) **(G-8090)**

Qg LLC...... 508 828-4400
1133 County St Taunton (02780) **(G-12360)**

Qg Printing Corp...... 978 534-8351
27 Nashua St Leominster (01453) **(G-9698)**

Qg Printing IL LLC...... 860 741-0150
96 Phoenix Ave Enfield (06082) **(G-1145)**

QG PRINTING IL LLC, Enfield *Also Called: Qg Printing IL LLC* **(G-1145)**

Qiagen Beverly LLC...... 978 927-7027
100 Cummings Ctr Ste 407) Beverly (01915) **(G-6373)**

Qinetiq North America, Inc., Waltham *Also Called: Perspecta Svcs & Solutions Inc* **(G-12747)**

Qmagiq LLC...... 603 821-3092
22 Cotton Rd Ste 180 Nashua (03063) **(G-15153)**

Qmd Medical, Swanton *Also Called: Green Mountain Knitting Inc* **(G-17637)**

Qnp Technologies, East Glastonbury *Also Called: Quality Name Plate Inc* **(G-923)**

Qol Publications, Manchester *Also Called: Hippopress LLC* **(G-14859)**

Qorvo, Chelmsford *Also Called: Qorvo Us Inc* **(G-7948)**

Qorvo Inc...... 978 770-2158
2 Executive Dr Ste 400 Chelmsford (01824) **(G-7947)**

Qorvo Us Inc...... 978 467-4290
300 Apollo Dr Ste 1 Chelmsford (01824) **(G-7948)**

Qpl, Chelmsford *Also Called: Quick Print Ltd Inc* **(G-7950)**

Qrst's, Somerville *Also Called: RAw Rinnigade Art Works LLC* **(G-11893)**

Qrsts LLC...... 617 625-3335
561 Windsor St Ste B101 Somerville (02143) **(G-11892)**

Qs Tehcnoligies Divison, Meriden *Also Called: Omerin Usa Inc* **(G-1682)**

Qsa Global Inc **(HQ)**...... **781 272-2000**
40 North Ave Ste 2 Burlington (01803) **(G-7416)**

Qsa Optical Co Inc...... 207 783-8523
1567 Lisbon St Ste 5 Lewiston (04240) **(G-4988)**

Qsi, Poultney *Also Called: Greenstone Slate Company Inc* **(G-17448)**

Qsimulate, Boston *Also Called: Quantum Simulation Tech Inc* **(G-6990)**

Qsonica LLC...... 203 426-0101
53 Church Hill Rd Newtown (06470) **(G-2344)**

Qsr Steel Corporation LLC...... 860 548-0248
121 Elliott St E Hartford (06114) **(G-1502)**

QST Inc...... 802 524-7704
300 Industrial Park Rd Saint Albans (05478) **(G-17529)**

Qtran Inc **(PA)**...... **203 367-8777**
155 Hill St Ste 3 Milford (06460) **(G-1873)**

Quabbin Inc...... 978 544-3872
158 Gov Dukakis Dr Orange (01364) **(G-11230)**

Quabbin Wire & Cable Co Inc **(PA)**...... **413 967-6281**
10 Maple St Ware (01082) **(G-12827)**

Quad/Graphics Inc...... 413 525-8552
245 Benton Dr East Longmeadow (01028) **(G-8391)**

Quad/Graphics Inc...... 978 534-8351
27 Nashua St Leominster (01453) **(G-9699)**

Quad/Graphics Inc...... 781 231-7200
110 Commerce Way Ste F Woburn (01801) **(G-13643)**

QUAD/GRAPHICS INC., Woburn *Also Called: Quad/Graphics Inc* **(G-13643)**

Quadgraphics, Leominster *Also Called: Quad/Graphics Inc* **(G-9699)**

Quadient Inc **(DH)**...... **203 301-3400**
478 Wheelers Farms Rd Milford (06461) **(G-1874)**

Quadient Finance Usa Inc **(DH)**...... **203 301-3400**
478 Wheelers Farms Rd Milford (06461) **(G-1875)**

Quadra-Tek, Arlington *Also Called: Arlington Industries Inc* **(G-16985)**

Quadramed Quantim Corporation...... 781 565-5000
1 Wayside Rd Burlington (01803) **(G-7417)**

Quadriga Art...... 603 654-6141
528 Route 13 S Ste 200 Milford (03055) **(G-15035)**

Quadtech...... 978 461-2100
734 Forest St Ste 500 Marlborough (01752) **(G-10198)**

Qual-Craft, Mansfield *Also Called: Qc Industries Inc* **(G-10073)**

Qualcomm Technologies Inc...... 617 447-9846
77 Summer St Fl 8-9 Boston (02110) **(G-6988)**

Qualcomm Technologies Inc...... 781 791-6000
1 Wall St Burlington (01803) **(G-7418)**

A L P H A B E T I C

Qualedi Inc.. 203 538-5320
  1 Trap Falls Rd Ste 206 Shelton (06484) *(G-3058)*

QUALEDI INC, Shelton *Also Called: Qualedi Inc (G-3058)*

Quality Air Control, Winooski *Also Called: Vhv Company (G-17771)*

Quality Air Metals, Holbrook *Also Called: Quality Air Metals Inc (G-9184)*

Quality Air Metals Inc.. 781 986-9967
  283 Centre St Ste B Holbrook (02343) *(G-9184)*

Quality Automatics Inc **(PA)**............................ **860 945-4795**
  15 Mclennan Dr Oakville (06779) *(G-2625)*

Quality Bead Craft Inc.. 860 242-2167
  25 Northwood Dr Bloomfield (06002) *(G-204)*

Quality Beef Co Inc.. 401 421-5668
  25 Bath St Providence (02908) *(G-16596)*

Quality Care Drg/Cntrbrook LLC........................ 860 767-0206
  33 Main St Centerbrook (06409) *(G-563)*

Quality Chain & Cable LLC................................ 401 575-8323
  70 Commercial Way East Providence (02914) *(G-16039)*

Quality Coils Incorporated **(PA)**...................... **860 584-0927**
  748 Middle St Bristol (06010) *(G-485)*

Quality Containers of Neng................................ 207 846-5420
  247 Portland St Ste 2 Yarmouth (04096) *(G-5706)*

Quality Controls Inc.. 603 286-3321
  200 Tilton Rd Ste 1 Northfield (03276) *(G-15268)*

Quality Copy Inc.. 207 622-7447
  4 North St Hallowell (04347) *(G-4861)*

Quality Copy and Digital Print, Hallowell *Also Called: Quality Copy Inc (G-4861)*

Quality Engineering Assoc Inc.......................... 978 528-2034
  6 Omni Way Chelmsford (01824) *(G-7949)*

Quality Engineering Svcs Inc............................ 203 269-5054
  122 N Plains Industrial Rd Wallingford (06492) *(G-3843)*

Quality Envelope, Middleboro *Also Called: Quality Envelope & Printing Co (G-10376)*

Quality Envelope & Printing Co.......................... 508 947-8878
  22 Cambridge St Ste H Middleboro (02346) *(G-10376)*

Quality Fabricators LLC.................................... 603 905-9012
  246 Calef Hwy Barrington (03825) *(G-13916)*

Quality Food Company, Providence *Also Called: Quality Beef Co Inc (G-16596)*

Quality Machine Inc.. 860 354-6794
  87 Danbury Rd New Milford (06776) *(G-2259)*

Quality Machine Inc.. 603 382-2334
  31 Kingston Rd Plaistow (03865) *(G-15349)*

Quality Name Plate Inc...................................... 860 633-9495
  22 Fisher Hill Rd East Glastonbury (06025) *(G-923)*

Quality Printing Company Inc............................ 413 442-4166
  3 Federico Dr Pittsfield (01201) *(G-11421)*

Quality Rolling Deburring Inc............................ 860 283-0271
  135 S Main St Ste 3 Thomaston (06787) *(G-3626)*

Quality Screw Machine Pdts Inc........................ 401 231-8900
  9 Industrial Dr S Smithfield (02917) *(G-16727)*

Quality Sheet Metal Inc.................................... 203 729-2244
  17 Clark Rd Naugatuck (06770) *(G-1982)*

Quality Sign Crafters, Willimantic *Also Called: Horizons Unlimited Inc (G-4219)*

Quality Solutions Inc **(DH)**............................ **978 465-7755**
  44 Merrimac St Ste 22 Newburyport (01950) *(G-10710)*

Quality Spraying Tech Inc................................ 401 861-2413
  150 Park Ln Providence (02907) *(G-16597)*

Quality Stairs Inc.. 203 367-8390
  70 Logan St Bridgeport (06607) *(G-364)*

Quality Stamping.. 401 272-7760
  1205 Westminster St Providence (02909) *(G-16598)*

Quality Stone Marble Inc **(PA)**...................... **774 813-4801**
  91 Court St Whitinsville (01588) *(G-13344)*

Quality Welding LLC.. 860 585-1121
  61 E Main St Bldg C Bristol (06010) *(G-486)*

Quality Wire Edm Inc.. 860 583-9867
  329 Redstone Hill Rd Bristol (06010) *(G-487)*

Qualtre Inc **(HQ)**.. **508 658-8360**
  144 North Rd Ste 2250 Sudbury (01776) *(G-12270)*

Quantifacts Inc.. 401 421-8300
  100 Amaral St Ste 2 Riverside (02915) *(G-16659)*

Quanttus Inc.. 617 401-2648
  2 Newton Executive Park Ste 104 Newton (02462) *(G-10778)*

Quantum Biopower, Southington *Also Called: Quantum Bpower Southington LLC (G-3230)*

Quantum Bpower Southington LLC...................... 860 201-0621
  49 Depaolo Dr Southington (06489) *(G-3230)*

Quantum Circuits Inc.. 203 872-4723
  150 Munson St Ste 203 New Haven (06511) *(G-2189)*

Quantum Discoveries Inc.................................. 857 272-9998
  53 State St Ste 500 Boston (02109) *(G-6989)*

Quantum Newport.. 401 849-7700
  1170 E Main Rd Portsmouth (02871) *(G-16452)*

Quantum Sails Newport, Portsmouth *Also Called: Quantum Newport (G-16452)*

Quantum Simulation Tech Inc............................ 847 626-5535
  20 Guest St Ste 101 Boston (02135) *(G-6990)*

Quarry Slate Industries Inc.............................. 802 287-9701
  325 Upper Rd Poultney (05764) *(G-17449)*

Quarry Tap Room LLC.. 207 213-6173
  122 Water St Hallowell (04347) *(G-4862)*

Quarter Point Woodworking LLC **(PA)**............ **207 926-1032**
  483 Intervale Rd New Gloucester (04260) *(G-5088)*

Quarter Point Woodworking LLC........................ 207 892-7022
  7b Commons Ave Windham (04062) *(G-5667)*

Quarto Pubg Group USA Inc.............................. 978 282-9590
  100 Cummings Ctr Ste 265g Beverly (01915) *(G-6374)*

Quarto Pubg Group USA Inc.............................. 425 827-7120
  100 Cummings Ctr Ste 253c Beverly (01915) *(G-6375)*

Quartzite Processing Inc.................................. 781 322-3611
  6 Holyoke St Malden (02148) *(G-10024)*

Quayside Publishing Group................................ 978 282-9590
  100 Cummings Ctr Ste 406l Beverly (01915) *(G-6376)*

Quayside Publishing Group................................ 978 282-9590
  33 Commercial St Gloucester (01930) *(G-8953)*

Queen Associates Inc...................................... 781 389-8494
  2 Banks St Woburn (01801) *(G-13644)*

Queen City Printers Inc.................................... 802 864-4566
  701 Pine St Burlington (05401) *(G-17153)*

Queen Dog LLC.. 802 660-2733
  382 Pine St Burlington (05401) *(G-17154)*

Queen Graphics, West Haven *Also Called: Queen Graphics Printworks Inc (G-4120)*

Queen Graphics Printworks Inc........................ 203 464-7337
  738 Washington Ave West Haven (06516) *(G-4120)*

Queen Screw & Mfg Inc.................................... 781 894-8110
  60 Farwell St Waltham (02453) *(G-12756)*

Quemere, Middletown *Also Called: Quemere International LLC (G-1775)*

Quemere International LLC................................ 914 934-8366
  234 Middle St Middletown (06457) *(G-1775)*

Quest Diagnostic Incorporated.......................... 617 547-8900
  200 Forest St Marlborough (01752) *(G-10199)*

Quest Drape.. 781 859-0300
  46 Cummings Park Woburn (01801) *(G-13645)*

Quest Machining & Mfg LLC.............................. 860 290-1145
  333 E River Dr Ste 500 East Hartford (06108) *(G-1018)*

Questech Corporation **(PA)**.......................... **802 773-1228**
  92 Park St Rutland (05701) *(G-17505)*

Questech Metals, Rutland *Also Called: Questech Corporation (G-17505)*

Queues Enforth Development Inc........................ 781 870-1100
  400 Tradecenter Ste 5900 Woburn (01801) *(G-13646)*

Quick Clean Car Wash Systems I **(PA)**.......... **781 245-6809**
  590 Main St Wakefield (01880) *(G-12531)*

Quick Copy, Fall River *Also Called: Fall River Modern Prtg Co Inc (G-8548)*

Quick Fitting Inc.. 401 734-9500
  655 Waterman Ave East Providence (02914) *(G-16040)*

Quick Machining Services LLC.......................... 203 634-8822
  290 Pratt St Ste 4 Meriden (06450) *(G-1688)*

Quick Manufacturing Co.................................... 978 750-4202
  4 Electronics Ave Danvers (01923) *(G-8215)*

Quick Print Ltd Inc.. 978 256-1822
  27 Industrial Ave Unit 4a Chelmsford (01824) *(G-7950)*

Quick Turn Machine Company Inc...................... 860 623-2569
  1000 Old County Cir Ste 105 Windsor Locks (06096) *(G-4332)*

Quick-Sling, Taunton *Also Called: Diversitech Corporation (G-12333)*

Quickbase Inc **(PA)**...................................... **855 725-2293**
  290 Congress St Fl 4 Boston (02210) *(G-6991)*

(G-0000) Company's Geographic Section entry number

Quickprint of Rutland , The, Rutland *Also Called: Edward Group Inc (G-17496)*

Quidel Corporation.. 866 800-5458
500 Cummings Ctr Ste 55500 Beverly (01915) *(G-6377)*

Quik-Pull, Randolph *Also Called: One-Pull Sltons Wire Cable LLC (G-17472)*

Quikrete Companies Inc.. 860 564-3308
541 Green Hollow Rd Wauregan (06387) *(G-4041)*

Quikrete Companies LLC... 603 778-2123
44 Pine Rd Brentwood (03833) *(G-14028)*

Quikrete Connecticut ME, Wauregan *Also Called: Quikrete Companies Inc (G-4041)*

Quince & Co., Saco *Also Called: Quince & Company Inc (G-5378)*

Quince & Company Inc.. 207 210-6630
102 Main St Saco (04072) *(G-5378)*

Quincy Electronics Co Inc... 617 471-7700
182 Washington St Quincy (02169) *(G-11534)*

Quincy Sun, Quincy *Also Called: Quincy Sun Publishing Co Inc (G-11535)*

Quincy Sun Publishing Co Inc...................................... 617 471-3100
1372 Hancock St Ste 102 Quincy (02169) *(G-11535)*

Quinn Bros of Essex Inc.. 978 768-6929
239 Western Ave Ste 1 Essex (01929) *(G-8479)*

Quinn Brothers, Essex *Also Called: Quinn Bros of Essex Inc (G-8479)*

Quintal Burial Vault Inc.. 508 669-5717
3425 Sharps Lot Rd Dighton (02715) *(G-8294)*

Quirion Luc.. 802 673-8386
495 Memphremagog Vw Newport (05855) *(G-17405)*

Quirion Luc **(PA)**... **802 673-8386**
96 Western Ave Newport (05855) *(G-17406)*

Quirk Wire Co Inc... 508 867-3155
146 E Main St West Brookfield (01585) *(G-12998)*

Quiver Spirits, Barre *Also Called: Old Route Two Spirits Inc (G-17014)*

Quonset Point Facility, North Kingstown *Also Called: Electric Boat Corporation (G-16250)*

Qwiklabs Inc.. 978 760-0732
37 Davis Rd Carlisle (01741) *(G-7846)*

R & B Splicer Systems Inc... 508 580-3500
145 Bodwell St Avon (02322) *(G-6158)*

R & D Manufacturing Co Inc... 401 305-7662
60 Dunnell Ln Pawtucket (02860) *(G-16408)*

R & D Precision Inc.. 203 284-3396
235 Cheshire Rd Meriden (06451) *(G-1689)*

R & D Precision Inc.. 203 284-3396
63 N Cherry St Ste 1 Wallingford (06492) *(G-3844)*

R & D Technologies Inc... 401 885-6400
60 Romano Vineyard Way Ste 112 North Kingstown (02852) *(G-16276)*

R & H Communications Inc **(PA)**................................. **781 893-6221**
187 Lexington St Ste 4 Waltham (02452) *(G-12757)*

R & I Manufacturing Co... 860 589-6364
118 Napco Dr Terryville (06786) *(G-3608)*

R & J Tool Inc **(PA)**.. **603 366-4925**
945 Scenic Rd Laconia (03246) *(G-14664)*

R & K Machine... 603 528-0221
53 Blaisdell Ave Laconia (03246) *(G-14665)*

R & M Associates Inc... 860 633-0721
277 Hebron Ave Glastonbury (06033) *(G-1296)*

R & N Inc... 207 948-2613
557 Albion Rd Unity (04988) *(G-5567)*

R & O, Jaffrey *Also Called: Radenhausen & ONeill Inc (G-14578)*

R & R Corrugated Container Inc..................................... 860 584-1194
360 Minor St Bristol (06010) *(G-488)*

R & R Machine Industries Inc....................................... 401 766-2505
660 Greenville Rd North Smithfield (02896) *(G-16332)*

R & R Pallet Corp.. 203 272-2784
120 Schoolhouse Rd Cheshire (06410) *(G-612)*

R & S Redco Inc.. 781 792-1717
106 Finnell Dr Ste 24 Weymouth (02188) *(G-13334)*

R A Cummings Inc.. 207 777-7100
82 Goldthwaite Rd Auburn (04210) *(G-4457)*

R A Lalli, Milford *Also Called: Jgs Properties LLC (G-1840)*

R A Thomas Logging Inc.. 207 876-2722
58 Butter St Guilford (04443) *(G-4858)*

R B Machine Co Inc.. 508 830-0567
2701 Cranberry Hwy Wareham (02571) *(G-12843)*

R C Brayshaw & Co LLC **(PA)**.................................. **603 456-3101**
45 Waterloo St Warner (03278) *(G-15667)*

R C McLucas Trucking Inc... 207 625-8915
Route 25 Porter (04068) *(G-5168)*

R D Fence Co, North Billerica *Also Called: RD Contractors Inc (G-10948)*

R D S Machine Inc **(PA)**.. **603 863-4131**
3 Putnam Rd Newport (03773) *(G-15235)*

R Ducharme Inc... 413 534-4516
451 Mckinstry Ave Chicopee (01020) *(G-8057)*

R E Lowell Lumber Co Inc... 207 336-2901
132 N Hill Rd Buckfield (04220) *(G-4658)*

R E M, Southington *Also Called: REM Chemicals Inc (G-3231)*

R F H Company Inc... 203 853-2863
79 Rockland Rd Ste 3 Norwalk (06854) *(G-2561)*

R F Integration Inc **(PA)**... **978 654-6770**
85 Rangeway Rd Ste 1 North Billerica (01862) *(G-10945)*

R F Sheet Metal and Mech Inc...................................... 508 367-0533
58 Homeport Dr Hyannis (02601) *(G-9445)*

R Filion Manufacturing Inc... 603 865-1893
931 John Stark Hwy Newport (03773) *(G-15236)*

R G Eaton Woodworks Inc.. 207 883-3398
12 Rochester St Westbrook (04092) *(G-5644)*

R G Tombs Door Company Inc....................................... 603 624-5040
38 West River Rd Hooksett (03106) *(G-14471)*

R H Le Mieur Corp... 978 939-8741
638 Patriots Rd Templeton (01468) *(G-12381)*

R I Baker Co Inc **(PA)**.. **413 663-3791**
163 River Rd Clarksburg (01247) *(G-8073)*

R I Fruit Syrup Co.. 401 231-0040
333 Waterman Ave Smithfield (02917) *(G-16728)*

R J McDonald Inc... 978 355-6649
71 Worcester Rd Barre (01005) *(G-6203)*

R John Wright Dolls Inc... 802 447-7072
2402 West Rd Bennington (05201) *(G-17056)*

R L Balla Inc.. 603 835-6529
338 Beryl Mountain Rd South Acworth (03607) *(G-15628)*

R L Barry Inc... 508 226-3350
60 Walton St Attleboro (02703) *(G-6052)*

R L Fisher Inc.. 860 951-8110
30 Bartholomew Ave Hartford (06106) *(G-1503)*

R M Precision Machine Corp... 978 640-2900
120 Lumber Ln Unit 7 Tewksbury (01876) *(G-12413)*

R N Haskins Printing Inc... 207 465-2155
1795 Pond Rd Sidney (04330) *(G-5460)*

R P A, Hamden *Also Called: Record Products America Inc (G-1453)*

R P Williams & Sons Inc... 603 744-5446
400 Summer St Bristol (03222) *(G-14037)*

R Pepin & Sons Inc.. 207 324-6125
59 Shaw Rd Sanford (04073) *(G-5407)*

R R Donnelley & Sons Company..................................... 617 345-4300
20 Custom House St Ste 650 Boston (02110) *(G-6992)*

R R Donnelley & Sons Company..................................... 617 360-2000
65 Sprague St Hyde Park (02136) *(G-9467)*

R R I, Billerica *Also Called: Resonance Research Inc (G-6476)*

R R Leduc Corp... 413 536-4329
100 Bobala Rd Holyoke (01040) *(G-9275)*

R S Machine Inc.. 603 880-3177
315 Derry Rd Ste 11 Hudson (03051) *(G-14538)*

R T G, Manchester *Also Called: K & G Corp (G-1609)*

R W E Inc.. 860 974-1101
91 Highland Dr Putnam (06260) *(G-2871)*

R W Hatfield Company Inc **(PA)**................................ **978 521-2600**
10 Avco Rd Ste 1 Haverhill (01835) *(G-9124)*

R Walters Foods Ltd Lblty Co **(PA)**............................ **978 646-8950**
144 Pine St Danvers (01923) *(G-8216)*

R-D Mfg Inc... 860 739-3986
6 Colton Rd East Lyme (06333) *(G-1062)*

R.A.w, Somerville *Also Called: Qrsts LLC (G-11892)*

R.D. Faulkner, Brewer *Also Called: Faulkner Corporation (G-4612)*

R&D Dynamics Corporation.. 860 726-1204
49 W Dudley Town Rd Bloomfield (06002) *(G-205)*

ALPHABETIC

R&R Tool & Die, East Windsor *Also Called: R&R Tool & Die LLC (G-1083)*

R&R Tool & Die LLC.. 860 627-9197
  94 Newberry Rd East Windsor (06088) *(G-1083)*

R&V Industries Inc... 207 324-5200
  90 Community Dr Sanford (04073) *(G-5408)*

R4 Technologies Inc **(PA)**..................................... **203 461-7100**
  38c Grove St Ste 201 Ridgefield (06877) *(G-2906)*

R4v, Westport *Also Called: Recycle 4 Vets LLC (G-4194)*

Ra Pharmaceuticals, Cambridge *Also Called: Ra Pharmaceuticals Inc (G-7692)*

Ra Pharmaceuticals Inc **(DH)**................................ **617 401-4060**
  87 Cambridgepark Dr Cambridge (02140) *(G-7692)*

Raaga Go LLC... 505 983-5555
  213 Burlington Rd Bedford (01730) *(G-6255)*

Racecar Jewelry Co.. 401 475-5701
  19 Mendon Ave Pawtucket (02861) *(G-16409)*

Rachad Fuel Inc... 781 273-0292
  161 Bedford St Burlington (01803) *(G-7419)*

Racing Times.. 203 298-2899
  428 Main St Wallingford (06492) *(G-3845)*

Rack Attack USA LLP... 508 665-4361
  745 Worcester Rd Framingham (01701) *(G-8801)*

Radar Technology Inc
  2 New Pasture Rd Newburyport (01950) *(G-10711)*

Radar Wind Up Corporation **(HQ)**.......................... **917 488-6050**
  30 Kelley St Cambridge (02138) *(G-7693)*

Radcliff Wire Inc.. 312 876-1754
  97 Ronzo Rd Bristol (06010) *(G-489)*

Radeco Inc.. 860 823-1220
  17 West Pkwy Plainfield (06374) *(G-2738)*

Radenhausen & ONeill Inc...................................... 603 532-4879
  32 Fitzgerald Dr Ste 6 Jaffrey (03452) *(G-14578)*

Rader's Engraving, Boston *Also Called: Raders Engraving Inc (G-6993)*

Raders Engraving Inc... 617 227-2921
  333 Washington St Ste 539 Boston (02108) *(G-6993)*

Radiant Sage Ventures LLC..................................... 855 723-7243
  464 Common St Pmb 133 Belmont (02478) *(G-6311)*

Radiation Monitoring Dvcs Inc **(HQ)**..................... **617 668-6800**
  44 Hunt St Ste 2 Watertown (02472) *(G-12902)*

Radical Plastics Inc... 781 631-7924
  6 Saturn Rd Marblehead (01945) *(G-10093)*

Radio Act Corporation... 617 731-6542
  101 Winthrop Rd Brookline (02445) *(G-7326)*

Radio Frequency Company Inc................................. 508 376-9555
  150 Dover Rd Millis (02054) *(G-10450)*

Radio Frequency Systems Inc **(DH)**...................... **203 630-3311**
  200 Pondview Dr Meriden (06450) *(G-1690)*

Radio Waves Inc... 978 459-8800
  495r Billerica Ave North Billerica (01862) *(G-10946)*

Radiodetection, Raymond *Also Called: SPX Corporation (G-5317)*

Radius, Boston *Also Called: Radius Health Inc (G-6994)*

Radius Health Inc **(PA)**.. **617 551-4000**
  22 Boston Wharf Rd Fl 7 Boston (02210) *(G-6994)*

Radius Medical Tech Inc.. 978 263-4466
  46 Edson St Stow (01775) *(G-12247)*

Radley Corp of Grand Rapids, Lincoln *Also Called: Radley Corporation (G-16152)*

Radley Corporation.. 616 554-9060
  24 Albion Rd Lincoln (02865) *(G-16152)*

Radlo Foods LLC **(PA)**... **617 926-7070**
  313 Pleasant St Ste 5 Watertown (02472) *(G-12903)*

Radonaway, Haverhill *Also Called: Spruce Environmental Tech Inc (G-9134)*

Rae Js... 413 625-9228
  2231 Mohawk Trl Shelburne Falls (01370) *(G-11808)*

Raf Electronic Hardware, Seymour *Also Called: Matthew Warren Inc (G-2964)*

Rag & Bone Bindery Ltd... 401 728-0762
  1088 Main St Frnt 1 Pawtucket (02860) *(G-16410)*

Ragged Hill Incorporated... 978 939-5712
  147 Gardner Rd East Templeton (01438) *(G-8414)*

Ragged Mountain Equipment, Intervale *Also Called: Ragged Mountain Equipment Inc (G-14561)*

Ragged Mountain Equipment Inc............................. 603 356-3042
  279 Nh Route 16 And 302 Intervale (03845) *(G-14561)*

Ragnar Inc.. 603 382-0556
  22 Whittier St Newton (03858) *(G-15244)*

Ragnartech Inc... 603 244-7575
  44 Iron Horse Dr Fremont (03044) *(G-14331)*

Ragozzino, Meriden *Also Called: Ragozzino Foods Inc (G-1691)*

Ragozzino Foods Inc **(PA)**................................... **203 238-2553**
  10 Ames Ave Meriden (06451) *(G-1691)*

Raid Inc.. 978 683-6444
  439 S Union St Ste 2 Lawrence (01843) *(G-9595)*

Rain Commodities (usa) Inc..................................... 203 406-0535
  10 Signal Rd Stamford (06902) *(G-3443)*

Rainbow Graphics Inc.. 413 733-3376
  267 Allen St Springfield (01108) *(G-12124)*

Rainbow Intl Greater Portland, Scarborough *Also Called: Barringer Industries LLC (G-5424)*

Rainbow Visions Inc... 617 787-4084
  161 Harvard Ave Ste 13b Boston (02134) *(G-6995)*

Rainsford Type, Danbury *Also Called: Westchster Bk/Rnsford Type Inc (G-837)*

Rainville Printing Entps Inc...................................... 603 225-6649
  45 S State St Concord (03301) *(G-14153)*

Rainville Printing Entps Inc...................................... 603 485-3422
  272 Cross Rd Pembroke (03275) *(G-15308)*

Raj Communications Ltd.. 802 658-4961
  3 Ewing Pl Essex Junction (05452) *(G-17243)*

Ralco Electric Inc... 508 679-3363
  101 State Rd Westport (02790) *(G-13299)*

Ralco Electric & Generator, Westport *Also Called: Ralco Electric Inc (G-13299)*

Ralco Industries Inc **(PA)**.................................... **401 765-1000**
  1112 River St Woonsocket (02895) *(G-16973)*

Rallybio, New Haven *Also Called: Rallybio Corporation (G-2190)*

Rallybio Corporation **(PA)**................................... **203 859-3820**
  234 Church St Ste 1020 New Haven (06510) *(G-2190)*

Ralph Industries Inc... 860 666-5621
  33 Stafford Ave Ste 5 Bristol (06010) *(G-490)*

Ralph L Osgood Inc.. 603 543-1703
  144 Grissom Ln Claremont (03743) *(G-14096)*

Ralph's Blacksmith Shop, Northampton *Also Called: Smj Metal Company Inc (G-11081)*

Ram Printing Incorporated **(PA)**........................... **603 382-7045**
  Rte 111 East Hampstead (03826) *(G-14271)*

Ram Specialty Fabrication, Naugatuck *Also Called: Ram Welding Co Inc (G-1983)*

Ram Technologies LLC... 203 453-3916
  29 Soundview Rd Ste 12 Guilford (06437) *(G-1403)*

Ram Welding Co Inc... 203 720-0535
  93 Rado Dr Naugatuck (06770) *(G-1983)*

Ramar-Hall, Middlefield *Also Called: Ramar-Hall Inc (G-1728)*

Ramar-Hall Inc... 860 349-1081
  26 Old Indian Trl Middlefield (06455) *(G-1728)*

Ramblers Way Farm Inc **(PA)**.............................. **207 467-8118**
  2 Storer St Ste 207 Kennebunk (04043) *(G-4928)*

Ramco Machine LLC.. 978 948-3778
  27 Turcotte Memorial Dr Rowley (01969) *(G-11683)*

Ramdy Corporation.. 860 274-3716
  40 Mclennan Dr Oakville (06779) *(G-2626)*

Rampage LLC... 203 521-1645
  38 Palisade Ave Trumbull (06611) *(G-3730)*

Rampage Systems Inc... 781 891-1001
  411 Waverley Oaks Rd Ste 138 Waltham (02452) *(G-12758)*

Ramsays Welding & Machine Inc............................. 207 794-8839
  289 Enfield Rd Lincoln (04457) *(G-5012)*

Ramsbottom Printing Inc... 508 730-2220
  135 Waldron Rd Fall River (02720) *(G-8600)*

Ramtel Corporation.. 401 231-3340
  115 Railroad Ave Johnston (02919) *(G-16102)*

Ran/All Metal Technology Inc................................... 603 668-1907
  7a E Point Dr Hooksett (03106) *(G-14472)*

Rancourt & Co Shoecrafters Inc.............................. 855 999-3544
  9 Bridge St Lewiston (04240) *(G-4989)*

Rancourt & Co., Lewiston *Also Called: Rancourt & Co Shoecrafters Inc (G-4989)*

Rand Machine & Fabrication Co............................... 203 272-1352
  1486 Highland Ave Ste 2 Cheshire (06410) *(G-613)*

Rand Sheaves & Pulleys LLC................................... 203 272-1352
  1486 Highland Ave Cheshire (06410) *(G-614)*

(G-0000) Company's Geographic Section entry number

Rand Whitney-Greenwood St, Worcester *Also Called: Rand-Whitney Container LLC (G-13776)*

Rand-Whitney Container LLC.. 203 597-1707
118 Railroad Hill St Waterbury (06708) *(G-3965)*

Rand-Whitney Container LLC.. 774 420-2425
2 Rand Whitney Way Worcester (01607) *(G-13776)*

Rand-Whitney Container LLC **(DH)**.. **508 890-7000**
1 Rand Whitney Way Worcester (01607) *(G-13777)*

Rand-Whitney Container LLC.. 603 822-7300
15 Stonewall Dr Dover (03820) *(G-14247)*

Rand-Whitney Container LLC.. 401 729-7900
455 Narragansett Park Dr Pawtucket (02861) *(G-16411)*

Rand-Whitney Container Newtown, Newtown *Also Called: Rand-Whitney Group LLC (G-2345)*

Rand-Whitney Group LLC... 203 426-5871
1 Edmund Rd Newtown (06470) *(G-2345)*

Rand-Whitney Group LLC **(HQ)**.. **508 791-2301**
1 Rand Whitney Way Worcester (01607) *(G-13778)*

Rand-Whitney Industries LLC.. 508 791-2301
1 Rand Whitney Way Worcester (01607) *(G-13779)*

Rand-Whitney Packaging Corp... 508 929-3400
150 Grove St Worcester (01605) *(G-13780)*

Rand-Whitney Recycling LLC.. 860 848-1900
370 Route 163 Montville (06353) *(G-1927)*

Rand-Whitney Cntnrbard Ltd Prtn... 860 848-1900
370 Route 163 Montville (06353) *(G-1928)*

Randolph Engineering Inc... 781 961-6070
26 Thomas Patten Dr Randolph (02368) *(G-11573)*

Randolph Sunglasses, Randolph *Also Called: Randolph Engineering Inc (G-11573)*

Ranfac Corp.. 508 588-4400
30 Doherty Ave Ste A Avon (02322) *(G-6159)*

Ranger Automation Systems Inc... 508 842-6500
9 Railroad Ave Millbury (01527) *(G-10442)*

Ranger Ready Repellents, Norwalk *Also Called: Pic20 Group LLC (G-2558)*

Rangeway Supply LLC.. 978 667-8500
149 Rangeway Rd North Billerica (01862) *(G-10947)*

Rankin Textile Printing Inc.. 203 743-1317
37 Newtown Rd Danbury (06810) *(G-803)*

Ranor Inc... 978 874-0591
1 Bella Dr Westminster (01473) *(G-13276)*

Rapid Coatings Inc.. 339 227-6490
35 Avco Rd Haverhill (01835) *(G-9125)*

Rapid Finishing LLC.. 603 889-4234
43 Simon St Nashua (03060) *(G-15154)*

Rapid Finishing North.. 603 641-2164
5 George Ave Londonderry (03053) *(G-14781)*

Rapid Group.. 603 821-7300
15 Charron Ave Nashua (03063) *(G-15155)*

Rapid Manufacturing Group LLC.. 603 686-8980
15a Charron Ave Nashua (03063) *(G-15156)*

Rapid Micro Biosystems Inc **(PA)**... **978 349-3200**
1001 Pawtucket Blvd Ste 28 Lowell (01854) *(G-9916)*

Rapid Press, Stamford *Also Called: Tech-Repro Inc (G-3478)*

Rapid Sheet Metal, Nashua *Also Called: Rapid Manufacturing Group LLC (G-15156)*

Rapid Usa Inc.. 203 461-7121
2 High Ridge Park Fl 1 Stamford (06905) *(G-3444)*

Rapid7 Inc **(PA)**... **617 247-1717**
120 Causeway St Ste 400 Boston (02114) *(G-6996)*

Rapid7 LLC **(HQ)**.. **617 247-1717**
120 Causeway St Ste 400 Boston (02114) *(G-6997)*

Rapidprint, Middletown *Also Called: Bidwell Industrial Group Inc (G-1740)*

Rapiscan Systems Inc.. 978 933-4375
829 Middlesex Tpke Billerica (01821) *(G-6475)*

Rapport Therapeutics Inc.. 512 636-1706
1325 Boylston St Ste 401 Boston (02215) *(G-6998)*

Rare Beauty Brands Inc **(PA)**... **888 243-0646**
83 Morse Ste 8a Norwood (02062) *(G-11205)*

Rare Reminder Incorporated... 860 563-9386
222 Dividend Rd Rocky Hill (06067) *(G-2933)*

Rasa Incorporated.. 508 425-3261
268 Boston Tpke Shrewsbury (01545) *(G-11840)*

Ravago Americas LLC.. 203 855-6000
10 Westport Rd Wilton (06897) *(G-4245)*

Raven Technology LLC... 207 729-7904
14 Industrial Pkwy Brunswick (04011) *(G-4654)*

RAw Rinnigade Art Works LLC.. 617 625-3335
561 Windsor St Ste A301 Somerville (02143) *(G-11893)*

Rawson Development Inc... 860 928-4536
205 Munyan Rd Putnam (06260) *(G-2872)*

Rawz Natural Pet Food **(PA)**.. **207 363-0684**
40 Adams Rd Cape Neddick (03902) *(G-4672)*

Ray Murray Inc **(PA)**... **413 243-2164**
50 Limestone Lee (01238) *(G-9619)*

Ray-Tech Infrared Corporation.. 603 826-3030
198 Springfield Rd Ste 198 Charlestown (03603) *(G-14068)*

Ray's Extrusion Dies Tubing Co, Swanton *Also Called: Raymond Gadues Inc (G-17641)*

Raybern Utility Solutions LLC... 303 775-5041
125 Power St Portsmouth (02871) *(G-16453)*

Rayco Inc... 860 357-4693
48 Atlantic St New Britain (06053) *(G-2056)*

Rayco Metal Finishing Inc... 860 347-7434
134 Mill St Middletown (06457) *(G-1776)*

Raye's Mustard, Eastport *Also Called: J W Raye & Co Inc (G-4745)*

Raym-Co Inc... 860 678-8292
62 Spring Ln Farmington (06032) *(G-1243)*

Raymon Tool LLC... 203 248-2199
79 Rossotto Dr Hamden (06514) *(G-1452)*

Raymond Gadues Inc... 802 868-2033
Route78 East Swanton (05488) *(G-17641)*

Raymond L Martin, Webster *Also Called: Linx Consulting LLC (G-12930)*

Rays Electric & Gen Contg Inc.. 603 752-1370
33 Jericho Rd Berlin (03570) *(G-13985)*

Rays Tool & Die Co Inc.. 603 692-5978
360 Route 108 Somersworth (03878) *(G-15623)*

Raytech Industries Div, Middletown *Also Called: Lyman Products Corporation (G-1761)*

Raytheon, Andover *Also Called: Raytheon Company (G-5909)*

Raytheon, Andover *Also Called: Raytheon Italy Liaison Company (G-5910)*

Raytheon, Waltham *Also Called: Raytheon Company (G-12759)*

Raytheon, Waltham *Also Called: Raytheon Sutheast Asia Systems (G-12762)*

Raytheon, Woburn *Also Called: Raytheon Company (G-13647)*

Raytheon, Woburn *Also Called: Raytheon Company (G-13648)*

Raytheon, Merrimack *Also Called: Raytheon Company (G-15000)*

Raytheon, Pelham *Also Called: Raytheon Company (G-15295)*

Raytheon Company.. 978 470-5000
350 Lowell St Andover (01810) *(G-5909)*

Raytheon Company.. 978 440-1000
1001 Boston Post Rd E Marlborough (01752) *(G-10200)*

Raytheon Company.. 508 490-1000
1001 Boston Post Rd E Marlborough (01752) *(G-10201)*

Raytheon Company **(HQ)**... **781 522-3000**
870 Winter St Waltham (02451) *(G-12759)*

Raytheon Company.. 781 933-1863
235 Presidential Way Woburn (01801) *(G-13647)*

Raytheon Company.. 339 645-6000
225 Presidential Way Woburn (01801) *(G-13648)*

Raytheon Company.. 978 313-0201
59 Daniel Webster Hwy Merrimack (03054) *(G-15000)*

Raytheon Company.. 603 635-6800
50 Bush Hill Rd Pelham (03076) *(G-15295)*

Raytheon Company.. 401 847-8000
1847 W Main Rd Portsmouth (02871) *(G-16454)*

Raytheon International Inc **(PA)**... **781 522-3000**
870 Winter St Waltham (02451) *(G-12760)*

Raytheon Italy Liaison Company.. 978 684-5300
358 Lowell St Andover (01810) *(G-5910)*

Raytheon Korean Support Co **(DH)**... **339 645-6111**
870 Winter St Waltham (02451) *(G-12761)*

Raytheon Lgstics Spport Trning **(DH)**.. **310 647-9438**
180 Hartwell Rd Bedford (01730) *(G-6256)*

Raytheon Sutheast Asia Systems **(DH)**.. **978 470-5000**
870 Winter St Waltham (02451) *(G-12762)*

Raytheon Systems Support Co **(DH)**.. **978 851-2134**
50 Apple Hill Dr Tewksbury (01876) *(G-12414)*

Raytheon Technologies RES Ctr, East Hartford *Also Called: Rtx Corporation* **(G-1020)**

Razberi Technologies Inc.. 469 828-3380
　3 Corporate Dr Ste 1 Danbury (06810) **(G-804)**

RB Graphics Inc.. 603 624-4025
　45 Londonderry Tpke Hooksett (03106) **(G-14473)**

Rbc, Oxford *Also Called: Rbc Bearings Incorporated* **(G-2710)**

Rbc Aircraft Products Inc... 860 626-7800
　2788 Winsted Rd Torrington (06790) **(G-3692)**

Rbc Bearings Incorporated **(PA)**.................................. **203 267-7001**
　1 Tribiology Ctr Oxford (06478) **(G-2710)**

Rbc Epoxy, Cranston *Also Called: Nar Industries LLC* **(G-15897)**

Rbc Industries Inc... 401 941-3000
　1 Weingeroff Blvd Cranston (02910) **(G-15906)**

Rbw Inc.. 207 786-2446
　113 Nash Rd Windham (04062) **(G-5668)**

RC Connectors LLC... 860 413-2196
　146 Hopmeadow St Weatogue (06089) **(G-4042)**

RC Industries Inc.. 203 423-9419
　4 Erdmann Ln Wilton (06897) **(G-4246)**

Rcd Chambers Inc.. 203 775-4416
　878 Federal Rd Brookfield (06804) **(G-536)**

Rcd Components, Manchester *Also Called: Gowanda Rcd LLC* **(G-14853)**

Rcd LLC.. 203 712-1900
　230 Long Hill Cross Rd Shelton (06484) **(G-3059)**

RD Contractors Inc.. 978 667-6545
　220 Boston Rd Rte 3a North Billerica (01862) **(G-10948)**

Rd Ventures Inc... 860 747-2709
　1 Northwest Dr Plainville (06062) **(G-2779)**

RDF, Hudson *Also Called: RDF Corporation* **(G-14539)**

RDF Corporation... 603 882-5195
　23 Elm Ave Hudson (03051) **(G-14539)**

Rdp Manufacturing Inc.. 413 525-7700
　70 Maple St East Longmeadow (01028) **(G-8392)**

Rea Inc... 802 527-7437
　211 Lake St Ste 5 Saint Albans (05478) **(G-17530)**

REA Associates Inc.. 209 521-2727
　325 Boston Rd North Billerica (01862) **(G-10949)**

REA Magnet Wire Company Inc.. 203 738-6100
　129 Soundview Rd Guilford (06437) **(G-1404)**

REA-Craft Press Incorporated.. 508 543-8710
　10 Wall St Foxboro (02035) **(G-8716)**

Reac Ready LLC.. 860 550-5049
　51 Clovercrest Rd Wethersfield (06109) **(G-4213)**

Read Display.. 401 889-2139
　1600 Division Rd Unit 1 West Warwick (02893) **(G-16922)**

Readcube... 857 265-4945
　25 1st St Ste 104 Cambridge (02141) **(G-7694)**

Reade Advanced Materials, East Providence *Also Called: Reade International Corp* **(G-16041)**

Reade International Corp **(PA)**...................................... **401 433-7000**
　850 Waterman Ave Ste 4 East Providence (02914) **(G-16041)**

Readers Hardwood Supply LLC... 508 301-3206
　250 Cape Hwy Ste 9 East Taunton (02718) **(G-8411)**

Reading Diagnostic Center... 781 942-9876
　20 Pondmeadow Dr Ste 106 Reading (01867) **(G-11605)**

Reading Health Center, Reading *Also Called: Reading Diagnostic Center* **(G-11605)**

Ready 2 Run Graphics Signs Inc.. 508 459-9977
　240 Barber Ave Ste 5 Worcester (01606) **(G-13781)**

Ready Tool Company... 860 524-7811
　1 Carney Rd West Hartford (06110) **(G-4079)**

Real Estate Investment and MGT, Brookline *Also Called: Platinum Investments Ltd* **(G-7325)**

Real Good Toys Inc.. 802 479-2217
　22 Gallison Hill Rd Unit 1 Montpelier (05602) **(G-17374)**

Real Pickles, Greenfield *Also Called: Real Pickles Coperative Inc* **(G-8998)**

Real Pickles Coperative Inc.. 413 774-2600
　311 Wells St Greenfield (01301) **(G-8998)**

Real Relational Solutions LLC... 781 646-7326
　754 Massachusetts Ave Arlington (02476) **(G-5945)**

Real Vermont Roofing Slate.. 802 884-8091
　720 Vt Route 149 West Pawlet (05775) **(G-17693)**

Real-Time Analyzers Inc.. 860 635-9800
　362 Industrial Park Rd Ste 8 Middletown (06457) **(G-1777)**

Realejo Donuts Inc.. 860 342-5120
　860 Portland Cobalt Rd Portland (06480) **(G-2822)**

Realhub Inc... 650 461-9210
　30 Old Kings Hwy S Ste 155 Darien (06820) **(G-854)**

Reasons To Be Cheerful... 978 610-6248
　110 Commonwealth Ave Concord (01742) **(G-8132)**

Rebars & Mesh Inc.. 978 374-2244
　111 Avco Rd Haverhill (01835) **(G-9126)**

Rebion, Boston *Also Called: Rebiscan Inc* **(G-6999)**

Rebiscan Inc.. 857 600-0982
　100 Cambridge St # 14 Boston (02114) **(G-6999)**

Rec Components, Stafford Springs *Also Called: Ei-Rec LLC* **(G-3255)**

REc Manufacturing Corp... 508 634-7999
　50 Mellen St Hopedale (01747) **(G-9301)**

Recognition Products, Lebanon *Also Called: Ann S Davis* **(G-1548)**

Recolor Paints LLC.. 833 732-6567
　149 Winter St Ste B Hanover (02339) **(G-9040)**

Record Products America Inc... 203 248-6371
　700 Sherman Ave Hamden (06514) **(G-1453)**

Record-Journal Newspaper **(PA)**.................................... **203 235-1661**
　500 S Broad St Ste 2 Meriden (06450) **(G-1692)**

Recreational Equipment Inc.. 860 313-0128
　1417 New Britain Ave West Hartford (06110) **(G-4080)**

Rectorseal LLC... 508 673-7561
　1244 Davol St Fall River (02720) **(G-8601)**

Rectrac LLC.. 802 879-6993
　12 Market Pl Essex Junction (05452) **(G-17244)**

Recycle 4 Vets LLC... 203 222-7300
　518 Riverside Ave Ste 1 Westport (06880) **(G-4194)**

Recycled Paper Company Inc.. 617 737-9911
　37 Whitcomb St Waltham (02453) **(G-12763)**

Recycled Paper Printing, Waltham *Also Called: Recycled Paper Company Inc* **(G-12763)**

Recycling Mechanical Neng LLC... 603 268-8028
　44 Ferry St Allenstown (03275) **(G-13855)**

Red 7 Media LLC **(HQ)**.. **203 853-2474**
　10 Norden Pl Ste 202 Norwalk (06855) **(G-2562)**

Red Corp... 802 862-4500
　180 Queen City Park Rd Burlington (05401) **(G-17155)**

Red Derby Incorporated Embrdry....................................... 978 927-4838
　140 Elliott St Bldg E Beverly (01915) **(G-6378)**

Red Fish - Blue Fish Dye Wrks... 603 692-3900
　145 Green St Somersworth (03878) **(G-15624)**

Red Frames Inc... 617 477-8740
　285 Summer St Fl 2 Boston (02210) **(G-7000)**

Red Hat Inc.. 978 392-1000
　314 Little 10 Rd Westford (01886) **(G-13258)**

Red Lion Inn Resort, Hull *Also Called: Sarro Cohasset Incorporated* **(G-9427)**

Red Mill Graphics Incorporated.. 978 251-4081
　14 Alpha Rd Chelmsford (01824) **(G-7951)**

Red Oak Sourcing LLC... 401 742-0701
　2 Hampshire St Ste 200 Foxborough (02035) **(G-8737)**

Red Point Positioning Corp **(PA)**.................................. **339 222-0261**
　313 Washington St Newton (02458) **(G-10779)**

Red Slate Quarry, Poultney *Also Called: Taran Bros Inc* **(G-17453)**

Red Sun Press Inc.. 617 524-6822
　94 Green St Jamaica Plain (02130) **(G-9503)**

Red-E-Made, Brockton *Also Called: Concord Foods LLC* **(G-7269)**

Redblack Software LLC **(HQ)**.. **603 232-9404**
　1 Bedford Farms Dr Ste 104 Bedford (03110) **(G-13948)**

Redco Audio Inc.. 203 502-7600
　515 Fan Hill Rd Monroe (06468) **(G-1920)**

Redco Corporation **(HQ)**.. **203 363-7300**
　100 Stamford Pl Stamford (06902) **(G-3445)**

Redcoat Publishing... 978 761-0877
　21 8th Ave Lowell (01854) **(G-9917)**

Redden Publishing Co LLC.. 207 236-0767
　160 Mistic Ave Rockport (04856) **(G-5351)**

Redi-Mix LP.. 508 295-5111
　South Carver (02366) **(G-11915)**

Redi-Mix Services Incorporated.. 508 823-0771
　490 Winthrop St Taunton (02780) **(G-12361)**

Redi2 Technologies Inc **(HQ)**........................ **617 910-3282**
205 Portland St Ste 202 Boston (02114) *(G-7001)*

Redifoils LLC........................ 860 342-1500
193 Pickering St Portland (06480) *(G-2823)*

Redimix Companies Inc **(DH)**........................ **603 524-4434**
3 Eastgate Park Dr Belmont (03220) *(G-13969)*

Redimix Concrete........................ 603 581-1805
3 Eastgate Park Dr Belmont (03220) *(G-13970)*

Redland Brick Inc........................ 860 528-1311
1440 John Fitch Blvd South Windsor (06074) *(G-3177)*

Redline Welding Inc........................ 603 489-2266
25 Emmert Dr Hampstead (03841) *(G-14391)*

Redpoint, Newton *Also Called: Red Point Positioning Corp (G-10779)*

Redstone Aggregator LP........................ 781 515-5000
174 Middlesex Tpke Bedford (01730) *(G-6257)*

Redstone Buyer LLC........................ 781 515-5000
174 Middlesex Tpke Bedford (01730) *(G-6258)*

Redstone GP Holdco 1 LLC........................ 781 515-5000
174 Middlesex Tpke Bedford (01730) *(G-6259)*

Redstone GP Holdco 2 LLC........................ 781 515-5000
174 Middlesex Tpke Bedford (01730) *(G-6260)*

Redstone Holdco 1 LP........................ 781 515-5000
174 Middlesex Tpke Bedford (01730) *(G-6261)*

Redstone Holdco 2 LP........................ 781 515-5000
174 Middlesex Tpke Bedford (01730) *(G-6262)*

Redstone Intrmdate Archer Hldc........................ 781 515-5000
174 Middlesex Tpke Bedford (01730) *(G-6263)*

Redstone Intrmdate Fri Hldco L........................ 781 515-5000
174 Middlesex Tpke Bedford (01730) *(G-6264)*

Redstone Intrmdate Scrid Hldco........................ 781 515-5000
174 Middlesex Tpke Bedford (01730) *(G-6265)*

Redstone Parent LP........................ 781 515-5000
174 Middlesex Tpke Bedford (01730) *(G-6266)*

Redwave Technology, Danbury *Also Called: Cam2 Technologies LLC (G-719)*

Redwheel/Weiser LLC **(PA)**........................ **978 465-0504**
65 Parker St Ste 7 Newburyport (01950) *(G-10712)*

Ree Machine Works Inc........................ 978 663-9105
34 Sullivan Rd Ste 7 North Billerica (01862) *(G-10950)*

Reebok International Ltd LLC **(HQ)**........................ **781 401-5000**
25 Drydock Ave Ste 110e Boston (02210) *(G-7002)*

Reebok International Ltd., Boston *Also Called: Reebok International Ltd LLC (G-7002)*

Reed & Prince Mfg Corp........................ 978 466-6903
272 Nashua St Leominster (01453) *(G-9700)*

Reed Allison Group Inc........................ 617 846-1237
144 Wayland Ave Ste 1 Providence (02906) *(G-16599)*

Reed and Stefanow Mch Tl Co........................ 860 583-7834
165 Riverside Ave Bristol (06010) *(G-491)*

Reed Gowdey Company........................ 401 723-6114
325 Illinois St Central Falls (02863) *(G-15795)*

Reed Machinery Inc **(PA)**........................ **508 595-9090**
10a New Bond St Worcester (01606) *(G-13782)*

Reed Semiconductor Corp **(PA)**........................ **401 886-0857**
875 Centerville Rd Warwick (02886) *(G-16847)*

Reed Truck Services Inc........................ 603 542-5032
287 Washington St Claremont (03743) *(G-14097)*

Reed Wax, Reading *Also Called: Roger A Reed Inc (G-11607)*

Reeds Inc........................ 800 997-3337
201 Merritt 7 Norwalk (06851) *(G-2563)*

Reeds Ferry Small Buildings........................ 603 883-1362
3 Tracy Ln Hudson (03051) *(G-14540)*

Reeves Company Inc........................ 508 222-2877
51 Newcomb St Attleboro (02703) *(G-6053)*

Reflex Ltg Group of CT LLC........................ 860 666-1548
1290 Silas Deane Hwy Ste 1a Wethersfield (06109) *(G-4214)*

Reframe Systems Inc........................ 781 417-9061
444 Somerville Ave Somerville (02143) *(G-11894)*

Refresco Beverages US Inc........................ 508 763-3515
65 Chace Rd East Freetown (02717) *(G-8366)*

Refrigerated Structures Neng, Lakeville *Also Called: Watka Corporation (G-9523)*

Regal Components Inc........................ 727 299-0800
10 Almeida Ave Ste D East Providence (02914) *(G-16042)*

Regal Press Incorporated **(PA)**........................ **781 769-3900**
79 Astor Ave Norwood (02062) *(G-11206)*

Regan S Pingree........................ 207 639-5706
989 Park St Phillips (04966) *(G-5157)*

Regco Corporation........................ 978 521-4370
46 Rogers Rd Haverhill (01835) *(G-9127)*

Regdox Solutions Inc........................ 603 589-4830
1 Elm St Ste 201 Nashua (03060) *(G-15157)*

Regen Med, Greenwich *Also Called: Regenerative Medicine LLC (G-1346)*

Regenacy Pharmaceuticals LLC........................ 617 245-1306
303 Wyman St Ste 300 Waltham (02451) *(G-12764)*

Regenerative Medicine LLC **(PA)**........................ **203 969-4877**
125 Field Point Rd Apt B5 Greenwich (06830) *(G-1346)*

Regenie's All Natural Snacks, Haverhill *Also Called: Regco Corporation (G-9127)*

Regenocell Therapeutics Inc........................ 508 651-1598
16 David Dr Natick (01760) *(G-10495)*

Regent Controls Inc........................ 203 732-6200
29 Lark Industrial Pkwy Greenville (02828) *(G-16063)*

Reggies Oil Company Inc........................ 617 471-2095
92-R Franklin St Quincy (02169) *(G-11536)*

Reggies Sales & Service........................ 207 783-0558
1334 Minot Ave Auburn (04210) *(G-4458)*

Regine Printing Co Inc........................ 401 943-3404
208 Laurel Hill Ave Providence (02909) *(G-16600)*

Regional Industries Inc........................ 978 750-8787
301 Newbury St # 332 Danvers (01923) *(G-8217)*

Regional Industries LLC........................ 860 227-3627
41 Commerce St Clinton (06413) *(G-649)*

Register Citizen Publishing........................ 860 489-3121
59 Field St Torrington (06790) *(G-3693)*

Register, The, Orleans *Also Called: Harwich Oracle (G-11238)*

Regor Therapeutics Inc........................ 617 407-4737
50 Soldiers Field Pl Brighton (02135) *(G-7244)*

Rehrig Pacific Company........................ 603 490-8722
153 Mitchell Rd Nottingham (03290) *(G-15277)*

Reidville Hydraulics & Mfg Inc........................ 860 496-1133
175 Industrial Ln Torrington (06790) *(G-3694)*

Reifenhauser Incorporated........................ 847 669-9972
27 Garden St Ste B Danvers (01923) *(G-8218)*

Reify Health Inc **(PA)**........................ **617 861-8261**
33 Arch St Fl 17 Boston (02110) *(G-7003)*

Reilly Foam Corp........................ 860 243-8200
16 Britton Dr Bloomfield (06002) *(G-206)*

Reily Foods Company........................ 504 524-6131
100 Charles St Malden (02148) *(G-10025)*

Reinforced Structures For Elec........................ 508 754-5316
50 Suffolk St Worcester (01604) *(G-13783)*

Reiser Creations........................ 508 259-5794
222 Loudville Rd Easthampton (01027) *(G-8460)*

Reistone Biopharma Inc........................ 978 429-5824
1 Lincoln St Fl 24 Boston (02111) *(G-7004)*

Rek Inc........................ 978 388-1826
73 Merrimac St Amesbury (01913) *(G-5850)*

Rel-Tech Electronics Inc........................ 203 877-8770
215 Pepes Farm Rd Milford (06460) *(G-1876)*

RELAY THERAPEUTICS, Cambridge *Also Called: Relay Therapeutics Inc (G-7695)*

Relay Therapeutics Inc **(PA)**........................ **617 670-8837**
399 Binney St Fl 2 Cambridge (02142) *(G-7695)*

Relays Unlimited, East Granby *Also Called: Computer Components Inc (G-931)*

Relentless Inc........................ 401 295-2585
100 Davisville Pier Rd North Kingstown (02852) *(G-16277)*

Reliable........................ 978 230-2689
77 Mill St Winchendon (01475) *(G-13481)*

Reliable Auto Tire Company Inc........................ 860 247-7977
711 Maple Ave Hartford (06114) *(G-1504)*

Reliable Electric Motor Inc........................ 860 522-2257
285 Murphy Rd Hartford (06114) *(G-1505)*

Reliable Electro Plating Inc........................ 508 222-0620
304 W Main St Chartley (02712) *(G-7896)*

Reliable Fabrics Inc........................ 617 387-5321
29 Henderson St Everett (02149) *(G-8497)*

A L P H A B E T I C

Reliable Fnce C/Wstern Div Inc.................... 508 877-1200
  231 Pond St Ashland (01721) *(G-5966)*

Reliable Plating, Chartley *Also Called: Reliable Electro Plating Inc (G-7896)*

Reliable Plating & Polishing, Bridgeport *Also Called: Reliable Pltg & Polsg Co Inc (G-365)*

Reliable Pltg & Polsg Co Inc....................... 203 366-5261
  80 Bishop Ave Bridgeport (06607) *(G-365)*

Reliable Silver Corporation........................ 203 574-7732
  302 Platts Mill Rd Naugatuck (06770) *(G-1984)*

Reliable Spring Company, Bristol *Also Called: Oscar Jobs (G-477)*

Reliance Electric Svc Co Inc....................... 413 533-3557
  573 S Canal St Holyoke (01040) *(G-9276)*

Reliance Engineering, Leominster *Also Called: CE Baird Corporation (G-9650)*

Reliance Engineering Division, Leominster *Also Called: CE Baird Corporation (G-9649)*

Relocation Information Svc Inc...................... 203 855-1234
  69 East Ave Ste 4 Norwalk (06851) *(G-2564)*

Relx Inc.. 203 840-4800
  383 Main Ave Fl 3 Norwalk (06851) *(G-2565)*

Relx Inc.. 617 558-4925
  313 Washington St Ste 401 Newton (02458) *(G-10780)*

Relx Inc.. 603 431-7894
  361 Hanover St Portsmouth (03801) *(G-15432)*

Relyco Sales Inc **(PA)**........................... **603 742-0999**
  121 Broadway Dover (03820) *(G-14248)*

REM Chemicals Inc **(PA)**......................... **860 621-6755**
  325 W Queen St Southington (06489) *(G-3231)*

Rema Dri-Vac Corp.................................. 203 847-2464
  45 Ruby St Norwalk (06850) *(G-2566)*

Remarc LLC... 860 844-8939
  46 Twilight Dr Granby (06035) *(G-1308)*

Remcon/North Corporation........................... 603 279-7091
  7-9 Enterprise Ct Meredith (03253) *(G-14969)*

Remediation Lockwood Tech.......................... 404 666-5857
  691 Research Dr Leominster (01453) *(G-9701)*

Reminder Broadcaster............................... 860 875-3366
  37 Cardinal Dr Glastonbury (06033) *(G-1297)*

Reminder Media, Glastonbury *Also Called: Reminder Broadcaster (G-1297)*

Reminder Publications.............................. 413 525-3947
  280 N Main St Ste 1 East Longmeadow (01028) *(G-8393)*

Remix Organics Company, Providence *Also Called: Compost Plant L3c (G-16503)*

Remote Sensing Solutions Inc....................... 508 362-9400
  1 Technology Park Dr Ste A Buzzards Bay (02532) *(G-7456)*

Remsport Mfg LLC................................... 413 589-1911
  566 Holyoke St Ludlow (01056) *(G-9952)*

Remtec Incorporated **(PA)**....................... **781 762-9191**
  100 Morse St Ste 7 Norwood (02062) *(G-11207)*

Renaisance Cornice................................. 401 275-6500
  1010 Plainfield St Johnston (02919) *(G-16103)*

Renaissance Greeting Cards, Sanford *Also Called: Renaissance Greeting Cards Inc (G-5409)*

Renaissance Greeting Cards Inc..................... 207 324-4153
  10 Renaissance Way Sanford (04073) *(G-5409)*

Renaissance Sheet Metal L.......................... 401 294-3703
  8 Fishing Cove Rd North Kingstown (02852) *(G-16278)*

Renalguard Solutions Inc **(HQ)**.................. **508 541-8800**
  459 Fortune Blvd Milford (01757) *(G-10416)*

Renbrandt Inc...................................... 617 445-8910
  32 Blackburn Ctr Gloucester (01930) *(G-8954)*

Renchel Tool LLC................................... 860 315-9017
  51 Ridge Rd Putnam (06260) *(G-2873)*

Renesas Electronics Amer Inc....................... 978 577-6340
  515 Groton Rd Ste 102 Westford (01886) *(G-13259)*

Renewable Energy Systems LLC....................... 781 545-3320
  15 Wigwam Ln Scituate (02066) *(G-11769)*

Renewable NRG Systems, Hinesburg *Also Called: NRG Systems Inc (G-17297)*

Reno Machine Company Inc........................... 860 666-5641
  170 Pane Rd Ste 1 Newington (06111) *(G-2321)*

Renova Lighting Systems Inc........................ 800 635-6682
  36 Bellair Ave Unit 4 Warwick (02886) *(G-16848)*

Renovators Supply Inc.............................. 413 423-3300
  1 River St Erving (01344) *(G-8471)*

Rens Welding & Fabricating......................... 508 828-1702
  988 Crane Ave S Ste 1 Taunton (02780) *(G-12362)*

Rensup.com, Old Mill Marketing, Erving *Also Called: Renovators Supply Inc (G-8471)*

Rentschler Biopharma Inc........................... 508 282-5800
  27 Maple St Milford (01757) *(G-10417)*

Repair Dept, Athol *Also Called: LS Starrett Company (G-5980)*

Repiper US Inc..................................... 802 230-5703
  448 Woodstock Rd Woodstock (05091) *(G-17777)*

Repjtm LLC... 508 406-2100
  111 Forbes Blvd Ste 101 Mansfield (02048) *(G-10074)*

Replica Works Inc.................................. 978 544-7000
  61 R W Moore Ave Orange (01364) *(G-11231)*

Repligen, Waltham *Also Called: Repligen Corporation (G-12765)*

Repligen Corporation............................... 508 845-6400
  111 Locke Dr Ste 100 Marlborough (01752) *(G-10202)*

Repligen Corporation **(PA)**...................... **781 250-0111**
  41 Seyon St Ste 100 Waltham (02453) *(G-12765)*

Replimune Group Inc **(PA)**....................... **781 222-9600**
  500 Unicorn Park Dr Ste 300 Woburn (01801) *(G-13649)*

Republic Foil Inc.................................. 203 743-2731
  58 Longview Ave Danbury (06811) *(G-805)*

Republic Iron Works Inc............................ 413 594-8819
  40 Champion Dr Chicopee (01020) *(G-8058)*

Republic Midstream Mktg LLC........................ 617 531-6300
  200 Clarendon St Boston (02116) *(G-7005)*

Republican Company **(HQ)**........................ **413 788-1000**
  1860 Main St Springfield (01103) *(G-12125)*

Republican-American, Waterbury *Also Called: American-Republican Inc (G-3884)*

RES-Tech Corporation **(HQ)**...................... **978 567-1000**
  34 Tower St Hudson (01749) *(G-9406)*

Resavue Inc.. 203 878-0944
  48 Grannis Rd Orange (06477) *(G-2682)*

Resavue Exhibits, Orange *Also Called: Resavue Inc (G-2682)*

Rescor Inc **(PA)**................................ **617 723-3635**
  254 Faneuil Hall Mkt Pl Boston (02109) *(G-7006)*

Research Applctons Fncl Trckin..................... 800 939-7238
  3 Center Plz Ste 501 Boston (02108) *(G-7007)*

Research Cmpt Cnsulting Servic, Canton *Also Called: Research Cmpt Consulting Svcs (G-7823)*

Research Cmpt Consulting Svcs **(PA)**............. **781 821-1221**
  960 Turnpike St Foxford Business Center Canton (02021) *(G-7823)*

Research Engineering & Mfg Inc..................... 401 841-8880
  55 Hammarlund Way Middletown (02842) *(G-16184)*

Research In Motion Rf Inc **(HQ)**................. **603 598-8880**
  22 Technology Way Fl 5 Nashua (03060) *(G-15158)*

Resin Designs LLC **(DH)**......................... **781 935-3133**
  11 State St Woburn (01801) *(G-13650)*

Resin Distribution Inc............................. 978 772-1616
  1 Sculley Rd Unit A Ayer (01432) *(G-6192)*

Resin Systems Corporation.......................... 603 673-1234
  62 State Route 101a Ste 1 Amherst (03031) *(G-13886)*

Resin Technology Group, Seabrook *Also Called: Resin Technology Group LLC (G-15601)*

Resin Technology Group LLC......................... 508 230-8070
  167 Batchelder Rd Seabrook (03874) *(G-15601)*

Resin Technology LLC **(DH)**...................... **978 448-6926**
  824 Constitution Ave Littleton (01460) *(G-9835)*

Resinall Corp North Carolina **(DH)**.............. **203 329-7100**
  3065 High Ridge Rd Stamford (06903) *(G-3446)*

Resinall Corp., Stamford *Also Called: Resinall Corp North Carolina (G-3446)*

Resolute Racing LLC................................ 401 253-7384
  77 Broadcommon Rd Bristol (02809) *(G-15778)*

Resonance Research Inc............................. 978 671-0811
  31 Dunham Rd Ste 1 Billerica (01821) *(G-6476)*

Resource Colors LLC................................ 978 537-3700
  517 Lancaster St Leominster (01453) *(G-9702)*

Respiratory Motion Inc............................. 508 954-2706
  80 Coolidge Hill Rd Watertown (02472) *(G-12904)*

Respironics Novametrix LLC......................... 724 882-4120
  3000 Minuteman Rd Andover (01810) *(G-5911)*

Response Technologies LLC.......................... 401 585-5918
  537 Main St Coventry (02816) *(G-15820)*

REST LLC... 781 788-8113
  3 Bridle Way North Reading (01864) *(G-11045)*

Rest Ensured Medical Inc........................... 603 225-2860
  661 Pleasant St Ste 99 Norwood (02062) *(G-11208)*

Restech Plastic Molding, Hudson *Also Called: RES-Tech Corporation (G-9406)*

Restech Plastic Molding LLC **(DH)**.................... **978 567-1000**
   34 Tower St Hudson (01749) *(G-9407)*

Restmore Inc.. 508 559-9944
   135 Spark St Brockton (02302) *(G-7302)*

Resurrection Defense LLC................................. 603 313-1040
   71 Richmond Rd Winchester (03470) *(G-15716)*

Retcomm Inc... 203 453-2389
   29 Soundview Rd Guilford (06437) *(G-1405)*

Retcomp Inc... 603 487-5010
   2nd New Hampshire Tpke S New Boston (03070) *(G-15194)*

Rethink Robotics Inc...................................... 617 500-2487
   27-43 Wormwood St Boston (02210) *(G-7008)*

Retina Systems Inc.. 203 881-1311
   146 Day St Seymour (06483) *(G-2968)*

Retrieve LLC.. 603 413-0022
   50 Commercial St Ste 35s Manchester (03101) *(G-14920)*

Retrieve Technologies, Manchester *Also Called: Retrieve LLC (G-14920)*

Retro-Fit, Taunton *Also Called: Retro-Fit Technologies Inc (G-12363)*

Retro-Fit Technologies Inc................................ 508 478-2222
   350 Myles Standish Blvd Ste 202 Taunton (02780) *(G-12363)*

Rettig USA Inc.. 802 654-7500
   948 Hercules Dr Colchester (05446) *(G-17201)*

Revbio Inc.. 617 460-6675
   600 Suffolk St Ste 250 Lowell (01854) *(G-9918)*

Revela Inc.. 716 725-2657
   500 W Cummings Park Ste 2150 Woburn (01801) *(G-13651)*

Revere Independent....................................... 781 485-0588
   385 Broadway Ste 105 Revere (02151) *(G-11623)*

Revered Metal Roofing, Marshfield *Also Called: Invincible Metal Corp (G-10239)*

Revision Heat LLC.. 207 221-5677
   188 Emerson Mill Rd Hampden (04444) *(G-4867)*

Revision Military Ltd **(PA)**............................. **802 879-7002**
   7 Corporate Dr Essex Junction (05452) *(G-17245)*

Revo Biologics Inc **(DH)**............................... **508 620-9700**
   175 Crossing Blvd Framingham (01702) *(G-8802)*

Revo Biologics Inc.. 508 370-5451
   300 Charlton Rd Spencer (01562) *(G-12065)*

Revolution Cooking LLC................................... 301 710-0590
   100 Sylvan Rd Ste 100 Woburn (01801) *(G-13652)*

Revolution Furnishings LLC............................... 603 606-6123
   9050 S Willow St Manchester (03103) *(G-14921)*

Revolution Lighting, Stamford *Also Called: Seesmart Inc (G-3454)*

Revolution Lighting Tech Inc **(PA)**..................... **877 578-2536**
   177 Broad St Fl 12 Stamford (06901) *(G-3447)*

Revulytics, Waltham *Also Called: Revulytics Inc (G-12766)*

Revulytics Inc **(DH)**................................... **781 398-3400**
   130 Turner St Waltham (02453) *(G-12766)*

Revvity Inc... 203 925-4600
   710 Bridgeport Ave Shelton (06484) *(G-3060)*

Revvity Inc... 978 439-5511
   40 Linnell Cir Billerica (01821) *(G-6477)*

Revvity Inc... 617 596-9909
   549 Albany St Boston (02118) *(G-7009)*

Revvity Inc... 508 435-9500
   68 Elm St Bldg 2 Hopkinton (01748) *(G-9343)*

Revvity Inc **(PA)**...................................... **781 663-6900**
   940 Winter St Waltham (02451) *(G-12767)*

Revvity Health Sciences Inc.............................. 203 925-4600
   710 Bridgeport Ave Shelton (06484) *(G-3061)*

Revvity Health Sciences Inc **(DH)**...................... **781 663-6900**
   940 Winter St Waltham (02451) *(G-12768)*

Revvity Signals Software Inc **(DH)**..................... **781 663-6900**
   940 Winter St Waltham (02451) *(G-12769)*

Rewalk Robotics Inc **(HQ)**............................. **508 251-1154**
   200 Donald Lynch Blvd Marlborough (01752) *(G-10203)*

Rex Cut, Fall River *Also Called: Rex Cut Products Incorporated (G-8602)*

Rex Cut Products Incorporated............................ 508 678-1985
   960 Airport Rd Fall River (02720) *(G-8602)*

Rex Forge Div, Plantsville *Also Called: J J Ryan Corporation (G-2793)*

Rex Lumber Company **(PA)**............................. **800 343-0567**
   840 Main St Acton (01720) *(G-5762)*

Rexa, West Bridgewater *Also Called: Koso America Inc (G-12974)*

Rexa Inc... 508 584-1199
   4 Manley St West Bridgewater (02379) *(G-12977)*

Rexa Electraulic Actuation, West Bridgewater *Also Called: Rexa Inc (G-12977)*

Rexx Company Inc... 207 200-9000
   18 Frye Dr Cumberland Center (04021) *(G-4710)*

Rexx Home Systems, Inc., Cumberland Center *Also Called: Rexx Company Inc (G-4710)*

Reynolds Carbide Die Co Inc.............................. 860 283-8246
   27 Reynolds Bridge Rd Thomaston (06787) *(G-3627)*

Reynolds D-Rap Corp...................................... 800 477-4681
   186 Duchaine Blvd New Bedford (02745) *(G-10645)*

Reynolds Dewalt, New Bedford *Also Called: JP Progressive Comm Group LLC (G-10607)*

Rf Aero LLC.. 508 910-3500
   167 John Vertente Blvd New Bedford (02745) *(G-10646)*

Rf Logic LLC... 603 578-9876
   21 Park Ave Hudson (03051) *(G-14541)*

RF McManus Company Inc.................................. 617 241-8081
   7 Sherman St Charlestown (02129) *(G-7881)*

Rf Venue Inc... 800 795-0817
   24 Walpole Park S Ste 1 Walpole (02081) *(G-12573)*

Rfbf Dye Works, Somersworth *Also Called: Red Fish - Blue Fish Dye Wrks (G-15624)*

Rgb Industries Inc....................................... 413 536-3100
   11 Berkshire St Holyoke (01040) *(G-9277)*

Rgc Millwork Incorporated................................ 978 275-9529
   175a Old Canal Dr Lowell (01851) *(G-9919)*

Rgd Technologies Corp.................................... 860 589-0756
   50 Emmett St Bristol (06010) *(G-492)*

Rgl Inc.. 860 653-7254
   290 Pratt St Ste 51 Meriden (06450) *(G-1693)*

Rgm Metals Inc.. 978 562-9773
   5 Parmenter Rd Hudson (01749) *(G-9408)*

Rgt Inc.. 401 431-5016
   1 W Exchange St Unit 2304 Providence (02903) *(G-16601)*

RH Laboratories Inc...................................... 603 459-5900
   1 Tanguay Ave Nashua (03063) *(G-15159)*

RH Rosenfield Co... 207 324-1798
   2066 Main St Sanford (04073) *(G-5410)*

Rhealth Corporation...................................... 617 913-7630
   1 Oak Park Dr Ste 2 Bedford (01730) *(G-6267)*

Rhee Gold Company Inc................................... 508 285-6650
   155 Pine St Norton (02766) *(G-11132)*

Rheinwerk Publishing Inc................................. 781 228-5070
   2 Heritage Dr Ste 305 Quincy (02171) *(G-11537)*

Rhema 320 LLC **(PA)**.................................. **475 434-8581**
   263 Grand Ave # 101 New Haven (06513) *(G-2191)*

Rhino, Burlington *Also Called: Rhino Foods Inc (G-17156)*

Rhino Foods Inc **(PA)**................................. **802 862-0252**
   179 Queen City Park Rd Burlington (05401) *(G-17156)*

Rhino Shelters, Milford *Also Called: Mdm Products LLC (G-1848)*

Rhode Island Assn Realtors Inc **(PA)**.................. **401 785-3650**
   100 Bignall St Warwick (02888) *(G-16849)*

Rhode Island Centerless Inc.............................. 401 942-0403
   24 Morgan Mill Rd Johnston (02919) *(G-16104)*

Rhode Island Chemical Corp............................... 401 274-3905
   754 Branch Ave Providence (02904) *(G-16602)*

Rhode Island Engine Co Inc............................... 401 789-1021
   79 State St Narragansett (02882) *(G-16195)*

Rhode Island Frt Syrup Co Inc............................ 401 231-0040
   250 Putnam Pike Smithfield (02917) *(G-16729)*

Rhode Island Fruit & Syrup, Smithfield *Also Called: Rhode Island Frt Syrup Co Inc (G-16729)*

Rhode Island Mktg & Prtg Inc............................. 917 582-1029
   41 Deerfield Rd Unit 11 Attleboro (02703) *(G-6054)*

Rhode Island Monthly..................................... 401 649-4898
   22 Bowens Wharf Newport (02840) *(G-16221)*

Rhode Island Monthly..................................... 401 649-4800
   717 Allens Ave Ste 105 Providence (02905) *(G-16603)*

Rhode Island Newsppr Group Inc........................... 401 732-3100
   1944 Warwick Ave Warwick (02889) *(G-16850)*

Rhode Island Precision Co................................ 401 421-6661
   25 Dorr St Providence (02908) *(G-16604)*

Rhode Island Provision Co................................ 401 831-0815
   5 Day St Johnston (02919) *(G-16105)*

A L P H A B E T I C

Rhode Island Textile Company.................... 401 722-3700
   35 Martin St Cumberland (02864) *(G-15962)*

Rhode Island Textile Company **(PA)**.................... **401 722-3700**
   35 Martin St Cumberland (02864) *(G-15963)*

Rhode Island Wiring Svc Inc.................... 401 789-1955
   567 Liberty Ln West Kingston (02892) *(G-16896)*

Rhode Island's Own, Pawtucket *Also Called: Catanzaro Food Products Inc (G-16353)*

Rhode Northsales Island Inc.................... 401 683-7997
   1 Maritime Dr Ste 1 Portsmouth (02871) *(G-16455)*

Rhode Runner Homes LLC.................... 401 489-8501
   40 Rosner Ave North Providence (02904) *(G-16309)*

Rhodes Pharmaceuticals LP.................... 888 827-0616
   201 Tresser Blvd Stamford (06901) *(G-3448)*

RI Knitting Co Inc.................... 508 822-5333
   20 Cushman St Taunton (02780) *(G-12364)*

RI Knitting Group LLC.................... 508 822-5333
   1 Main St Ste 10 Whitinsville (01588) *(G-13345)*

RI Realtors, Warwick *Also Called: Rhode Island Assn Realtors Inc (G-16849)*

Ribco Supply Co, Clarksburg *Also Called: R I Baker Co Inc (G-8073)*

Ribcraft, Marblehead *Also Called: Ribcraft Usa LLC (G-10094)*

Ribcraft Usa LLC.................... 781 639-9065
   88 Hoods Ln Marblehead (01945) *(G-10094)*

Ribon Therapeutics Inc.................... 617 914-8700
   35 Cambridgepark Dr Ste 300 Cambridge (02140) *(G-7696)*

Ricciardi Marble & Granite Inc.................... 508 790-2734
   174 Airport Rd Hyannis (02601) *(G-9446)*

Ricco Vishnu Brew House, Bridgeport *Also Called: Swagnificent Ent LLC (G-378)*

Rice Packaging Inc.................... 860 870-7057
   356 Somers Rd Ellington (06029) *(G-1113)*

Rich Associates Incorporated.................... 207 985-5999
   759 Alewive Rd Kennebunk (04043) *(G-4929)*

Rich Plastic Products Inc.................... 203 235-4241
   339 Fleming Rd Meriden (06450) *(G-1694)*

Rich Products Corporation.................... 866 737-8884
   263 Myrtle St New Britain (06053) *(G-2057)*

Richard Cantwell Woodworking.................... 508 984-7921
   611 Belleville Ave New Bedford (02745) *(G-10647)*

Richard E Personette.................... 860 344-9001
   179 Main Street Ext Middletown (06457) *(G-1778)*

Richard Gaudreau Engraving.................... 508 240-2940
   County Rd Eastham (02642) *(G-8435)*

Richard Genest Inc.................... 207 324-7215
   238 Country Club Rd Sanford (04073) *(G-5411)*

Richard H Bird & Co Inc.................... 781 894-0160
   1 Spruce St Waltham (02453) *(G-12770)*

Richard Manufacturing Co Inc.................... 203 874-3617
   250 Rock Ln Milford (06460) *(G-1877)*

Richard Mrchssult DBA Bngtson.................... 802 266-9666
   240 Gale St Canaan (05903) *(G-17169)*

Richard Riggio and Sons Inc.................... 860 767-0812
   90 Pond Meadow Rd Ivoryton (06442) *(G-1532)*

Richards Machine Tool Co Inc.................... 860 436-2938
   187 Stamm Rd Newington (06111) *(G-2322)*

Richards Metal Products Inc.................... 203 879-2555
   14 Swiss Ln Wolcott (06716) *(G-4374)*

Richards Micro-Tool LLC.................... 508 746-6900
   250 Cherry St Plymouth (02360) *(G-11474)*

Richardson Mfg Co Inc.................... 603 367-9018
   4 High St Silver Lake (03875) *(G-15607)*

Richardson-Allen Inc.................... 207 284-8402
   38 Pearl St Biddeford (04005) *(G-4585)*

Richardson's Maptech, New Bedford *Also Called: Edgewater Marine Inds LLC (G-10588)*

Richardsons Ice Cream.................... 781 944-9121
   50 Walkers Brook Dr Reading (01867) *(G-11606)*

Richelieu Foods Inc **(DH)**.................... **781 786-6800**
   222 Forbes Rd Ste 401 Braintree (02184) *(G-7199)*

Richie Navigation, Pembroke *Also Called: E S Ritchie & Sons Inc (G-11364)*

Richline Group Inc.................... 774 203-1199
   49 Pearl St Attleboro (02703) *(G-6055)*

Richmond Contract Mfg.................... 207 737-4385
   85 White Rd Bowdoinham (04008) *(G-4606)*

Richmond Graphic Products Inc.................... 401 233-2700
   188 Progress Ave Providence (02909) *(G-16605)*

Richmond Sand & Stone LLC.................... 401 539-7770
   35 Stilson Rd Richmond (02898) *(G-16651)*

Richmond Sand and Gravel Inc.................... 508 224-2231
   70 Minuteman Ln Plymouth (02360) *(G-11475)*

Ricks Mtorsport Electrics Inc.................... 603 329-9901
   48 Gigante Dr Hampstead (03841) *(G-14392)*

Ricks Sheet Metal Inc.................... 774 488-9576
   82 Lea Ln Fall River (02721) *(G-8603)*

Ricor Usa Inc.................... 603 718-8903
   200 Main St Ste 1 Salem (03079) *(G-15557)*

Ridco Casting Co.................... 401 724-0400
   6 Beverage Hill Ave Pawtucket (02860) *(G-16412)*

Ride-Away Inc **(HQ)**.................... **603 437-4444**
   54 Wentworth Ave Londonderry (03053) *(G-14782)*

Ridge View Associates Inc.................... 203 878-8560
   122 Cascade Blvd Milford (06460) *(G-1878)*

Riding Enhancement Designs, Burlington *Also Called: Burton Corporation (G-17123)*

Ridlons Metal Shop.................... 207 655-7997
   627 Roosevelt Trl Casco (04015) *(G-4683)*

Rig Grip Incorporated.................... 800 770-2666
   665 Centre St Newton (02458) *(G-10781)*

Rigaku Analytical Devices Inc.................... 855 785-1064
   30 Upton Dr Ste 2 Wilmington (01887) *(G-13449)*

Right Height Manufacturing, Manchester *Also Called: Mkind Inc (G-14892)*

Right of Way Solutions LLC.................... 860 917-0608
   595 Norwich Rd Salem (06420) *(G-2945)*

Rihani Plastics Inc.................... 401 942-7393
   14 Suez St Cranston (02920) *(G-15907)*

Rika Denshi America Inc.................... 508 226-2080
   112 Frank Mossberg Dr Attleboro (02703) *(G-6056)*

Riley Mountain Products Inc.................... 603 588-7234
   10 Water St Antrim (03440) *(G-13898)*

Riley Power Inc.................... 508 852-7100
   26 Forest St Ste 300 Marlborough (01752) *(G-10204)*

Riley Pwr A Babcock Pwr Inc Co, Marlborough *Also Called: Riley Power Inc (G-10204)*

Rimol Greenhouse Systems Inc.................... 603 629-9004
   40 Londonderry Tpke Ste 2d Hooksett (03106) *(G-14474)*

Ring Therapeutics Inc **(PA)**.................... **617 218-1549**
   140 1st St Ste 401 Cambridge (02141) *(G-7697)*

Ringfeder, Bolton *Also Called: Ringfeder Pwr Transm USA Corp (G-222)*

Ringfeder Pwr Transm USA Corp **(HQ)**.................... **201 666-3320**
   291 Boston Tpke Bolton (06043) *(G-222)*

Ringmaster Software Corp.................... 802 383-1050
   70 S Winooski Ave Ste 1w Burlington (05401) *(G-17157)*

Rings Wire Inc **(PA)**.................... **203 874-6719**
   257 Depot Rd Milford (06460) *(G-1879)*

Rintec Corporation.................... 860 274-3697
   165 Haddad Rd Waterbury (06708) *(G-3966)*

Ripano Stoneworks Ltd.................... 603 886-6655
   90 E Hollis St Nashua (03060) *(G-15160)*

Ripley, Cromwell *Also Called: Crrc LLC (G-691)*

Ripley Odm LLC.................... 603 524-8350
   171 Daniel Webster Hwy Unit 1 Belmont (03220) *(G-13971)*

Rise Brewing Co, Stamford *Also Called: Riseandshine Corporation (G-3449)*

Riseandshine Corporation **(PA)**.................... **917 599-7541**
   425 Fairfield Ave 1a11 Stamford (06902) *(G-3449)*

Rising Tide Brewing Co LLC.................... 207 370-2337
   103 Fox St Portland (04101) *(G-5265)*

Rite-Solutions Inc **(PA)**.................... **401 847-3399**
   185 S Broad St Pawcatuck (06379) *(G-2725)*

Ritec Inc.................... 401 738-3660
   60 Alhambra Rd Ste 5 Warwick (02886) *(G-16851)*

Ritronics Inc.................... 401 732-8175
   60 Alhambra Rd Ste 1 Warwick (02886) *(G-16852)*

River Falls Manufacturing Co.................... 508 646-2900
   40 County St Fall River (02723) *(G-8604)*

River Point Station, Warwick *Also Called: International Technologies Inc (G-16823)*

River St Metal Finishing Inc.................... 781 843-9351
   35 Johnson Ln Braintree (02184) *(G-7200)*

Riverbed Technology Inc.................................... 603 402-5200
  15 N Southwood Dr Nashua (03063) *(G-15161)*

Riverbend Fiberglass Inc................................... 207 562-7103
  16 Carter Rd Dixfield (04224) *(G-4727)*

Riverdale Mills Corporation................................ 508 234-8715
  130 Riverdale St Northbridge (01534) *(G-11118)*

Rivermeadow Software Inc................................. 617 448-4990
  319 Littleton Rd Ste 305 Westford (01886) *(G-13260)*

Riverside Engineering Co Inc.............................. 978 531-1556
  12 County St Peabody (01960) *(G-11337)*

Riverside Shtmtl & Contg Inc.............................. 781 396-0070
  15 Reardon Rd 15 Medford (02155) *(G-10296)*

Riverside Specialty Foods Inc............................. 603 474-5805
  1 Depot Ln Seabrook (03874) *(G-15602)*

Riverton Memorial Inc...................................... 802 485-3371
  2074 Rte #12 Riverton (05663) *(G-17483)*

Riverton Memorial Company, Riverton *Also Called: Riverton Memorial Inc* *(G-17483)*

Rivinius & Sons Inc... 781 933-5620
  225 Salem St Woburn (01801) *(G-13653)*

Rivkind Associates Inc **(PA)**........................... **781 269-2415**
  30 Twin Brooks Dr South Easton (02375) *(G-11952)*

Rj 15 Inc.. 860 585-0111
  115 Cross St Bristol (06010) *(G-493)*

Rj Fountain Group Inc...................................... 508 429-9950
  1376 W Central St Ste 130 Franklin (02038) *(G-8859)*

RJ Mansour Inc... 401 521-7800
  1 Magnolia St Providence (02909) *(G-16606)*

Rjd Woodworking LLC....................................... 508 984-4315
  92 Long Rd Fairhaven (02719) *(G-8513)*

Rjf - Morin Brick LLC....................................... 207 784-9375
  130 Morin Brick Rd Auburn (04210) *(G-4459)*

Rjtb Initiatives Inc... 203 531-7216
  200 Pemberwick Rd Greenwich (06831) *(G-1347)*

RK Manufacturing Corp Conn.............................. 203 797-8700
  34 Executive Dr Ste 2 Danbury (06810) *(G-806)*

RK Miles Inc **(PA)**...................................... **802 362-1952**
  618 Depot St Manchester Center (05255) *(G-17330)*

Rk Parisi Enterprises Inc.................................. 844 438-7674
  104 Emerald St Keene (03431) *(G-14616)*

Rl Controls LLC... 781 932-3349
  2 Gill St Woburn (01801) *(G-13654)*

RLB Industries Inc... 508 226-3350
  115 Berwick Rd Attleboro (02703) *(G-6057)*

Rlcp Inc... 401 461-6560
  262 New Meadow Rd Barrington (02806) *(G-15749)*

Rlf Homes, Hartford *Also Called: R L Fisher Inc (G-1503)*

Rm Dissolution Co LLC..................................... 203 699-9125
  151 Moss Farms Rd Cheshire (06410) *(G-615)*

RMA Manufacturing LLC.................................... 603 352-0053
  735 W Swanzey Rd West Swanzey (03469) *(G-15697)*

Rmb Ltd... 401 245-3700
  36 Franklin St Warren (02885) *(G-16766)*

Rmd Instruments Corp...................................... 617 668-6900
  44 Hunt St Ste 2 Watertown (02472) *(G-12905)*

Rme Filters Inc... 603 595-4573
  98 State Route 101a Amherst (03031) *(G-13887)*

Rmg Stone Products, Castleton *Also Called: McCue Memorial Co Inc (G-17173)*

Rmi, Stafford Springs *Also Called: Msj Investments Inc (G-3257)*

Rmi Inc... 860 875-3366
  130 Old Town Rd Vernon Rockville (06066) *(G-3761)*

Rmk Brewers LLC... 603 601-8196
  836 Lafayette Rd Hampton (03842) *(G-14410)*

RMS Media Group Inc...................................... 978 623-8020
  21 Middle St Newburyport (01950) *(G-10713)*

Rna Medical Division, Devens *Also Called: Bionostics Inc (G-8270)*

Ro-59 Inc... 781 341-1222
  1 Cabot Pl Ste 3 Stoughton (02072) *(G-12230)*

Roadsafe Traffic Systems.................................. 781 436-5006
  331 Page St Stoughton (02072) *(G-12231)*

Roadsafe Traffic Systems Inc............................. 508 580-6700
  55 Bodwell St Avon (02322) *(G-6160)*

Roar Industries Inc... 508 429-5952
  2 Rosenfeld Dr Ste A Hopedale (01747) *(G-9302)*

Rob Roy Foods Inc... 508 755-8393
  500 Cambridge St Ste 3 Worcester (01610) *(G-13784)*

Robbins Beef Co Inc....................................... 617 269-1826
  35 Food Mart Rd 37 Boston (02118) *(G-7010)*

Robbins Company... 508 222-2900
  400 Oneil Blvd Attleboro (02703) *(G-6058)*

Robbins Lumber Inc **(PA)**.............................. **207 342-5221**
  53 Ghent Rd Searsmont (04973) *(G-5450)*

Robbins Lumber E Baldwin LLC............................ 207 625-3286
  411 Pequawket Trl East Baldwin (04024) *(G-4735)*

Robbins Manufacturing Co Inc............................. 508 675-2555
  1200 Airport Rd Fall River (02720) *(G-8605)*

Robert Baxter Associates Inc.............................. 401 739-8222
  200 Jefferson Blvd Warwick (02888) *(G-16853)*

Robert Bentley Inc... 617 547-4170
  1734 Massachusetts Ave Cambridge (02138) *(G-7698)*

Robert Dugrenier Associates, Townshend *Also Called: Crest Studios (G-17650)*

Robert E Glidden... 508 775-6812
  30 Perseverance Way Ste 3 Hyannis (02601) *(G-9447)*

Robert J Moran Inc... 978 486-4718
  410 Great Rd Littleton (01460) *(G-9836)*

Robert L Lovallo.. 203 324-6655
  127 Myrtle Ave Stamford (06902) *(G-3450)*

Robert McBrearity Jr Sons................................. 207 834-3257
  260 St John Rd Fort Kent (04743) *(G-4793)*

Robert McBrearity Jr Sons Inc............................. 207 834-3257
  1013 Main St Saint Francis (04774) *(G-5388)*

Robert Miller Associates LLC.............................. 718 392-1640
  127 Lords Hwy Weston (06883) *(G-4152)*

Robert Mitchell Co Inc **(DH)**.......................... **207 797-6771**
  423 Riverside Industrial Pkwy Portland (04103) *(G-5266)*

Robert W Libby... 207 625-8285
  483 Old Meetinghouse Rd Porter (04068) *(G-5169)*

Robert W Libby & Sons Inc................................ 207 284-3668
  483 Old Meetinghouse Rd Porter (04068) *(G-5170)*

Robert W Libby and Sons, Porter *Also Called: Robert W Libby (G-5169)*

Robert Warren LLC **(PA)**............................... **203 247-3347**
  1 Sprucewood Ln Westport (06880) *(G-4195)*

Robert-Kenneth Andrade LLC.............................. 203 937-8697
  975 Campbell Ave West Haven (06516) *(G-4121)*

Roberts & Sons Printing Inc............................... 413 283-9356
  1791 Boston Rd Springfield (01129) *(G-12126)*

Roberts Brothers Lumber Co Inc........................... 413 628-3333
  1450 Spruce Corner Rd Ashfield (01330) *(G-5955)*

Roberts Ldscp Design & Cnstr............................. 508 364-4878
  120 Cobblestone Rd Barnstable (02630) *(G-6201)*

Roberts Machine Shop Inc.................................. 978 927-6111
  117 Elliott St Ste 7 Beverly (01915) *(G-6379)*

Roberts Manufacturing Company, Springfield *Also Called: Grassetti Sales Associates Inc (G-12097)*

Roberts Welding Inc.. 508 867-7640
  32 W Main St Brookfield (01506) *(G-7315)*

Robertson-Chase Fibers LLC............................... 978 453-2837
  16 Esquire Rd Ste 2 North Billerica (01862) *(G-10951)*

Robes Dana Wood Craftsmen **(PA)**.................... **603 643-9355**
  3 Great Hollow Rd Hanover (03755) *(G-14430)*

Robin Industries Inc....................................... 401 253-8350
  125 Thames St Bristol (02809) *(G-15779)*

Robin Rug, Bristol *Also Called: Robin Industries Inc (G-15779)*

Robinson Precision Tool Corp.............................. 603 889-1625
  315 Derry Rd Ste 15 Hudson (03051) *(G-14542)*

Robinson Tape & Label Inc................................ 203 481-5581
  32 E Industrial Rd Ste 1 Branford (06405) *(G-274)*

Roblo Woodworks, Stamford *Also Called: Robert L Lovallo (G-3450)*

Robotics, Stamford *Also Called: International Robotics Inc (G-3385)*

Roche Bros Barrel Drum Co Inc........................... 978 454-9135
  161 Phoenix Ave Lowell (01852) *(G-9920)*

Roche Bros Supermarkets LLC............................. 508 285-3600
  175 Mansfield Ave Unit 1 Norton (02766) *(G-11133)*

A L P H A B E T I C

Roche Dgnostics Hematology Inc........................ 508 329-2450
80 Guest St # 6 Brighton (02135) *(G-7245)*

Roche Manufacturing Inc................................ 978 454-9135
161 Phoenix Ave Lowell (01852) *(G-9921)*

Rocheleau Blow Molding Systems, Fitchburg *Also Called: Rocheleau Tool and Die Co Inc* *(G-8673)*

Rocheleau Tool and Die Co Inc........................ 978 345-1723
117 Indl Rd Fitchburg (01420) *(G-8673)*

Rochester Electronics, Newburyport *Also Called: Rochester Electronics LLC (G-10715)*

Rochester Electronics LLC.............................. 978 462-1248
18 Malcolm Hoyt Dr Newburyport (01950) *(G-10714)*

Rochester Electronics LLC **(PA)**..................... **978 462-9332**
16 Malcolm Hoyt Dr Newburyport (01950) *(G-10715)*

Rochester Shoe Tree Co Inc **(PA)**................... **603 968-3301**
1 Cedar Ln Ashland (03217) *(G-13902)*

Rochester USA... 603 332-0717
73 Allen St Rochester (03867) *(G-15490)*

Rochette Fmly Cstm Wdwkg & REM.................... 603 895-2181
2 Prevere Rd Raymond (03077) *(G-15456)*

Rock of Ages Corporation **(DH)**..................... **802 476-3115**
560 Graniteville Rd Graniteville (05654) *(G-17277)*

Rock Valley Tool LLC................................... 413 527-2350
54 Oneil St Easthampton (01027) *(G-8461)*

Rock-Tenn Missisquoi Mill, Sheldon Springs *Also Called: Westrock Cp LLC (G-17566)*

Rock-Tred 2 LLC... 888 762-5873
150 Dascomb Rd Andover (01810) *(G-5912)*

Rockbestos, East Granby *Also Called: Rscc Wire & Cable LLC (G-950)*

Rocket Software Inc **(PA)**........................... **781 577-4323**
77 4th Ave Waltham (02451) *(G-12771)*

Rocket Software Systems Inc........................... 248 833-9000
77 4th Ave Waltham (02451) *(G-12772)*

Rockingham Sheet Metal Inc............................ 603 886-1799
1 Industrial Park Dr Unit 22 Pelham (03076) *(G-15296)*

Rockland Equipment Company LLC...................... 781 871-4400
171 Vfw Dr Rockland (02370) *(G-11659)*

Rockland Industries Inc................................ 781 849-7918
405 Washington St Ste 3 Braintree (02184) *(G-7201)*

Rockland Marine Corporation........................... 207 594-7860
79 Mechanic St Rockland (04841) *(G-5341)*

Rockport Publishing, Beverly *Also Called: Quayside Publishing Group (G-6376)*

Rockport Steel, Rockport *Also Called: Glover Company Inc (G-5349)*

Rockstar New England Inc.............................. 978 409-6272
3 Dundee Park Dr Ste 102 Andover (01810) *(G-5913)*

Rockstep Solutions Inc **(PA)**....................... **844 800-7625**
48 Free St Ste 200 Portland (04101) *(G-5267)*

Rockville Technology LLC.............................. 860 871-6883
129 Reservoir Rd Vernon (06066) *(G-3756)*

Rockwell Automation Inc............................... 978 441-9500
2 Executive Dr Chelmsford (01824) *(G-7952)*

Rockwell Automation Inc............................... 508 357-8400
100 Nickerson Rd Fl 1 Marlborough (01752) *(G-10205)*

Rockwell Collins Inc................................... 978 532-2350
1 5th St Peabody (01960) *(G-11338)*

Rockwood Manufacturing Co............................ 800 582-2424
100 Sargent Dr New Haven (06511) *(G-2192)*

Rockwood Service Corporation **(PA)**............... **203 869-6734**
43 Arch St Greenwich (06830) *(G-1348)*

Rodco Enterprises...................................... 207 786-2931
9 Westminster St Lewiston (04240) *(G-4990)*

Rodin Therapeutics Inc................................. 857 201-2770
852 Winter St Waltham (02451) *(G-12773)*

Rodney Hunt-Fontaine Inc **(HQ)**.................... **978 544-2511**
46 Mill St Orange (01364) *(G-11232)*

Roehm America LLC..................................... 203 269-4481
528 S Cherry St Wallingford (06492) *(G-3846)*

Roehm America LLC..................................... 207 324-6000
1796 Main St Sanford (04073) *(G-5412)*

Roehr Tool Corp.. 978 562-4488
7 Chocksett Rd Sterling (01564) *(G-12169)*

Rofin-Baasel Inc **(HQ)**.............................. **978 635-9100**
68 Barnum Rd Devens (01434) *(G-8286)*

Roger A Reed Inc....................................... 781 944-4640
167 Pleasant St Reading (01867) *(G-11607)*

Rogers Corporation..................................... 860 774-9605
1 Technology Dr Rogers (06263) *(G-2943)*

Rogers Corporation..................................... 860 928-3622
245 Woodstock Rd Woodstock (06281) *(G-4396)*

Rogers Foam Automotive Corp.......................... 617 623-3010
20 Vernon St Ste 1 Somerville (02145) *(G-11895)*

Rogers Foam Corporation **(PA)**..................... **617 623-3010**
20 Vernon St Somerville (02145) *(G-11896)*

Rogers General Machining Inc.......................... 413 532-4673
181 Ludlow Rd Chicopee (01020) *(G-8059)*

Rogers Manufacturing Company......................... 860 346-8648
72 Main St Rockfall (06481) *(G-2915)*

Rogerson Orthopedic Appls Inc......................... 617 268-1135
483 Southampton St Boston (02127) *(G-7011)*

Rogue Amoeba Software Inc............................ 609 213-4380
536 Commercial St Boston (02109) *(G-7012)*

Rogue Industries, Standish *Also Called: Tower Publishing (G-5529)*

Rogue Space Systems Corp............................. 603 460-5069
131 Lake St Laconia (03246) *(G-14666)*

Rogue Wear, Lewiston *Also Called: Rodco Enterprises (G-4990)*

Rohm Haas Electronic Mtls LLC **(HQ)**.............. **508 481-7950**
455 Forest St Marlborough (01752) *(G-10206)*

Rohm Haas Electronic Mtls LLC........................ 508 481-7950
455 Forest St Marlborough (01752) *(G-10207)*

Rohtstein Corp **(PA)**............................... **781 935-8300**
70 Olympia Ave Woburn (01801) *(G-13655)*

Rokap Inc.. 203 265-6895
127 Comstock Trl East Hampton (06424) *(G-965)*

Rokon, Rochester *Also Called: Rokon International Inc (G-15491)*

Rokon International Inc................................ 603 335-3200
50 Railroad Ave Rochester (03839) *(G-15491)*

Rokr Distribution Us Inc............................... 860 509-8888
310 W Newberry Rd Bloomfield (06002) *(G-207)*

Rol-Flo Engineering Inc................................ 401 596-0060
85a Tom Harvey Rd Westerly (02891) *(G-16942)*

Rol-Vac Limited Partnership............................ 860 928-9929
207 Tracy Rd Dayville (06241) *(G-868)*

Roland and Whytock Company Inc...................... 401 781-1234
75 Oxford St Ste 202 Providence (02905) *(G-16607)*

Roland Gatchell.. 978 352-6132
119 Thurlow St Georgetown (01833) *(G-8912)*

Roland H Tyler Logging Inc............................ 207 562-7282
Canton Point Rd Dixfield (04224) *(G-4728)*

Rolands Tire Service Inc **(PA)**..................... **508 997-4501**
11 Howland Rd Fairhaven (02719) *(G-8514)*

Rollease Acmeda Inc **(HQ)**......................... **203 964-1573**
750 E Main St Fl 7 Stamford (06902) *(G-3451)*

Roller Bearing Co Amer Inc............................ 203 758-8272
86 Benson Rd Middlebury (06762) *(G-1720)*

Rolling Thunder Express, Newport *Also Called: Rolling Thunder Press Inc (G-5098)*

Rolling Thunder Press Inc.............................. 207 368-2028
134 Main St A Newport (04953) *(G-5098)*

Rollins Transmission Service, Stratford *Also Called: Connecticut Machine & Welding (G-3530)*

Rolls-Royce Marine North Amer **(DH)**.............. **508 668-9610**
110 Norfolk St Walpole (02081) *(G-12574)*

Rolltech Precision Metals.............................. 412 246-8846
193 Pickering St Portland (06480) *(G-2824)*

Roly Safeti-Gate, Essex *Also Called: Mezzanine Safeti-Gates Inc (G-8478)*

Rolyn Inc **(PA)**.................................... **401 944-0844**
189 Macklin St Cranston (02920) *(G-15908)*

Rom Technologies Inc.................................. 888 374-0855
101 Silvermine Rd Brookfield (06804) *(G-537)*

Roma Marble Inc....................................... 413 583-5017
15 Westover Rd Ludlow (01056) *(G-9953)*

Romano Investments Inc................................ 401 691-3400
333 Strawberry Field Rd Ste 11 Warwick (02886) *(G-16854)*

Romanow Inc **(DH)**................................. **781 320-9200**
346 University Ave Westwood (02090) *(G-13317)*

Romanow Container, Westwood *Also Called: Romanow Inc (G-13317)*

Romco Contractors Inc... 860 243-8872
   12 E Newberry Rd Bloomfield (06002) *(G-208)*

Rome Fastener Corporation... 203 874-6719
   257 Depot Rd Milford (06460) *(G-1880)*

Ronald Pratt Company Inc.. 508 222-9601
   50 Perry Ave Attleboro (02703) *(G-6059)*

Rondo America Incorporated.. 203 723-5831
   209 Great Hill Rd Naugatuck (06770) *(G-1985)*

Rondo Packaging Systems, Naugatuck *Also Called: Rondo America Incorporated (G-1985)*

Ronnie Sellers Productions, South Portland *Also Called: Sellers Publishing Inc (G-5514)*

Ronstan, Portsmouth *Also Called: Ronstan International Inc (G-16456)*

Ronstan International Inc... 401 293-0539
   1170 E Main Rd Ste 3 Portsmouth (02871) *(G-16456)*

Rontex America Inc.. 603 883-5076
   1 Caldwell Dr Amherst (03031) *(G-13888)*

Rootpath Genomics... 857 209-1060
   65 Grove St Watertown (02472) *(G-12906)*

Ropeless Systems Inc... 207 468-8545
   6 Apostolic Way Biddeford (04005) *(G-4586)*

Ropes Wealth Advisors LLC... 617 951-7217
   800 Boylston St Boston (02199) *(G-7013)*

Rosalie Gendron LLC.. 603 836-3692
   289 Pine St Manchester (03103) *(G-14922)*

Rosario Cabinets Inc... 781 329-0639
   49 Lower East St Ste 2 Dedham (02026) *(G-8248)*

Roscid Technologies Inc.. 781 933-4007
   215 Salem St Ste L Woburn (01801) *(G-13656)*

Rosco, Stamford *Also Called: Rosco Laboratories Inc (G-3452)*

Rosco Laboratories Inc **(HQ)**..................................... **203 708-8900**
   52 Harbor View Ave Stamford (06902) *(G-3452)*

Rosco Manufacturing, Central Falls *Also Called: Rosco Manufacturing LLC (G-15796)*

Rosco Manufacturing LLC.. 401 228-0120
   500 High St Central Falls (02863) *(G-15796)*

Rose Disp A Div Visual Creat, Pawtucket *Also Called: Visual Creations Inc (G-16429)*

Rose Displays... 978 219-8120
   500 Narragansett Park Dr Pawtucket (02861) *(G-16413)*

Rose Office Carl.. 508 833-8758
   8 Pinecone Dr East Sandwich (02537) *(G-8405)*

Rose Selavy Vermont, Manchester Center *Also Called: Applejack Art Partners Inc (G-17326)*

Rose Sisters Brands Inc.. 475 999-8115
   480 Barnum Ave Ste 5 Bridgeport (06608) *(G-366)*

Rose Sisters Chips, Bridgeport *Also Called: Rose Sisters Brands Inc (G-366)*

Rose's Marine Service, Gloucester *Also Called: Roses Oil Service Inc (G-8955)*

Rosellis Machine & Mfg Co... 413 562-4317
   248 Root Rd Westfield (01085) *(G-13203)*

Rosemathree Inc...
   10 Dorrance St Boston (02129) *(G-7014)*

Rosemount Inc... 508 261-2928
   9 Oxford Rd Mansfield (02048) *(G-10075)*

Rosencrntz Gldnstern Banknotes.. 603 654-6160
   6 Burns Hill Rd Wilton (03086) *(G-15708)*

Rosenfeld Concrete Corp **(HQ)**..................................... **508 473-7200**
   75 Plain St Hopedale (01747) *(G-9303)*

Roses Oil Service Inc **(PA)**...................................... **877 283-3334**
   375 Main St Gloucester (01930) *(G-8955)*

Roslynct US, Hopkinton *Also Called: Lykan Bioscience Holdings LLC (G-9336)*

Ross Mfg & Design LLC... 203 878-0187
   124 Research Dr Ste A Milford (06460) *(G-1881)*

Rossi Group LLC **(PA)**.. **860 632-3505**
   162 West St Ste A Cromwell (06416) *(G-695)*

Rotad Inc... 203 708-8900
   52 Harbor View Ave Stamford (06902) *(G-3453)*

Rotair Aerospace Corporation.. 203 576-6545
   964 Crescent Ave Bridgeport (06607) *(G-367)*

Rotary Vacuum Products Inc.. 603 890-6001
   7a Raymond Ave Salem (03079) *(G-15558)*

Rotating Composite Tech LLC... 860 829-6809
   49 Cambridge Hts Kensington (06037) *(G-1540)*

Rotek Instrument Corp... 781 899-4611
   390 Main St Waltham (02452) *(G-12774)*

Rothstein Associates Inc.. 203 740-7400
   4 Arapaho Rd Brookfield (06804) *(G-538)*

Rothstein Ctlog On Dsster Rcve, Brookfield *Also Called: Rothstein Associates Inc (G-538)*

Roto Hardware Systems, Chester *Also Called: Roto-Frank of America Inc (G-631)*

Roto-Die Company Inc... 860 292-7030
   7d Pasco Dr East Windsor (06088) *(G-1084)*

Roto-Frank of America Inc.. 860 526-4996
   14 Inspiration Ln Chester (06412) *(G-631)*

Rotondo Precast, Avon *Also Called: Oldcastle Infrastructure Inc (G-34)*

Rotondo Precast, Rehoboth *Also Called: Oldcastle Infrastructure Inc (G-11613)*

Round Rock Concrete, Old Town *Also Called: Owen J Folsom Inc (G-5131)*

Round Top Ice Cream Inc... 207 563-5307
   526 Main St Damariscotta (04543) *(G-4717)*

Rounds Service Station Inc... 401 934-9877
   53 Hartford Ave North Scituate (02857) *(G-16316)*

Roundtown Inc.. 415 425-6891
   45 Prospect St Cambridge (02139) *(G-7699)*

Rousselot Peabody Inc... 978 573-3700
   227 Washington St Peabody (01960) *(G-11339)*

Rowe Contracting Co... 781 620-0052
   90 Woodcrest Dr Melrose (02176) *(G-10319)*

Rowe Machine, Hampton *Also Called: Rowe Machine Co (G-14411)*

Rowe Machine Co... 603 926-0029
   143 N Shore Rd Hampton (03842) *(G-14411)*

Rowe Timber Harvesting LLC... 603 344-0302
   1467 Route 114 North Sutton (03260) *(G-15255)*

Rowley Concrete, Rowley *Also Called: Rowley Ready Mix Inc (G-11684)*

Rowley Ready Mix Inc... 978 948-2544
   84 Central St Rowley (01969) *(G-11684)*

Rowley Spring & Stamping Corp... 860 582-8175
   210 Redstone Hill Rd Ste 2 Bristol (06010) *(G-494)*

Roy and Laurel Amey Inc.. 603 538-7767
   Tabor Rd Pittsburg (03592) *(G-15329)*

Roy Tech, Meriden *Also Called: S J Pappas Inc (G-1695)*

Royal Adhesives & Sealants LLC.. 860 788-3380
   63 Epping St Raymond (03077) *(G-15457)*

Royal Business Group Inc.. 617 542-4100
   8 Newbury St Frnt Boston (02116) *(G-7015)*

Royal Consumer Products LLC **(HQ)**................................. **203 847-8500**
   108 Main St Ste 3 Norwalk (06851) *(G-2567)*

Royal Diversified Products.. 401 245-6900
   287 Market St Warren (02885) *(G-16767)*

Royal Food Import Corporation... 617 482-3826
   100 Franklin St Ste 702 Boston (02110) *(G-7016)*

Royal Group Inc **(PA)**... **802 773-3313**
   150 Woodstock Ave Rutland (05701) *(G-17506)*

Royal Ice Cream Company Inc **(PA)**................................ **860 649-5358**
   27 Warren St Manchester (06040) *(G-1632)*

Royal Label Co Inc... 617 825-6050
   50 Park St Ste 3 Boston (02122) *(G-7017)*

Royal Machine and Tool Corp... 860 828-6555
   4 Willow Brook Dr Berlin (06037) *(G-83)*

Royal Screw Machine Pdts Co... 860 845-8920
   409 Lake Ave Bristol (06010) *(G-495)*

Royal Technologies, Rutland *Also Called: Royal Group Inc (G-17506)*

Royal Woodcraft Inc.. 203 847-3461
   1 Riverside Dr Ansonia (06401) *(G-19)*

Royale Limousines, Haverhill *Also Called: Cabot Coach Builders Inc (G-9083)*

Royalty Brdcstg Svcs & Trnsp.. 413 777-7868
   484 White St Springfield (01108) *(G-12127)*

Royalty Consulting, Rocky Hill *Also Called: Royalty Consulting LLC (G-2934)*

Royalty Consulting LLC.. 800 474-5157
   750 Old Main St Rocky Hill (06067) *(G-2934)*

Roymal Inc... 603 863-2410
   475 Sunapee St Newport (03773) *(G-15237)*

Royston Laboratories... 412 828-1500
   26 Summer St Bridgewater (02325) *(G-7237)*

Rozelle Inc.. 802 744-2270
   4260 Loop Rd Westfield (05874) *(G-17699)*

RP Abrasives & Machine Inc... 603 335-2132
   20 Spaulding Ave Unit 2 Rochester (03868) *(G-15492)*

Rph Enterprises Inc.. 508 238-3351
  50 Earls Way Franklin (02038) *(G-8860)*

RPI Printing, Fall River *Also Called: Ramsbottom Printing Inc (G-8600)*

RPM Wood Finishes Group Inc.......................... 413 562-9655
  221 Union St Westfield (01085) *(G-13204)*

Rpp, Lawrence *Also Called: Emerson Prcess MGT Pwr Wtr Slt (G-9560)*

Rpt Holdings LLC... 877 997-3674
  30 Log Bridge Rd Bldg 200 Middleton (01949) *(G-10391)*

Rrk Walker Inc.. 508 541-8100
  22 Park St Mendon (01756) *(G-10321)*

RSA Corp.. 203 790-8100
  36 Old Sherman Tpke Danbury (06810) *(G-807)*

Rsa Security LLC **(PA)**.................................. **800 995-5095**
  176 Middlesex Tpke Bedford (01730) *(G-6268)*

Rsa Security LLC... 781 515-6258
  6 Potter Pond Lexington (02421) *(G-9768)*

Rscc, East Granby *Also Called: Rscc Wire & Cable LLC (G-949)*

Rscc Aerospace & Defense, Manchester *Also Called: Marmon Aerospace & Defense LLC (G-14880)*

Rscc Wire & Cable LLC.................................... 860 653-8300
  27 Bradley Park Rd East Granby (06026) *(G-949)*

Rscc Wire & Cable LLC **(DH)**........................... **860 653-8300**
  20 Bradley Park Rd East Granby (06026) *(G-950)*

Rscc Wire & Cable LLC.................................... 603 622-3500
  680 Hayward St Manchester (03103) *(G-14923)*

RSD America Inc... 201 996-1000
  77 4th Ave Fl 1 Waltham (02451) *(G-12775)*

RSI Metal Fabrication LLC................................ 603 382-8367
  213 Haverhill Rd Bldg 9 East Kingston (03827) *(G-14273)*

Rsl Fiber Systems LLC.................................... 860 282-4930
  473 Silver Ln East Hartford (06118) *(G-1019)*

Rst, Springfield *Also Called: Royalty Brdcstg Svcs & Trnsp (G-12127)*

Rsvp, Chelsea *Also Called: Rsvp Press (G-7989)*

Rsvp Press... 917 334-3102
  300 Commandants Way Apt 314 Chelsea (02150) *(G-7989)*

Rt Engineering Corporation.............................. 800 343-1182
  1 Kenwood Cir Franklin (02038) *(G-8861)*

RT Vanderbilt Holding Co Inc **(PA)**................... **203 295-2141**
  30 Winfield St Norwalk (06855) *(G-2568)*

Rtas Systems, Bedford *Also Called: Sudbury Systems Inc (G-6272)*

RTC Holdings Inc... 401 728-6980
  211 Weeden St Pawtucket (02860) *(G-16414)*

RTD Technologies, Somersworth *Also Called: Rays Tool & Die Co Inc (G-15623)*

Rtg Coatings.. 860 643-1133
  219 Adams St Manchester (06042) *(G-1633)*

Rtx Corporation... 860 610-7000
  411 Silver Ln East Hartford (06118) *(G-1020)*

Rtx Corporation... 860 565-7622
  400 Main St East Hartford (06108) *(G-1021)*

Rtx Corporation... 954 485-6501
  9 Farm Springs Rd Ste 3 Farmington (06032) *(G-1244)*

Rtx Corporation... 860 678-4500
  4 Farm Springs Rd Farmington (06032) *(G-1245)*

Rtx Corporation... 860 704-7133
  Aircraft Rd Bldg 220 Middletown (06457) *(G-1779)*

Rtx Corporation... 860 654-7519
  1 Hamilton Rd Windsor Locks (06096) *(G-4333)*

Rubb Building Systems, Sanford *Also Called: Rubb Inc (G-5413)*

Rubb Inc... 207 324-2877
  1 Rubb Ln Sanford (04073) *(G-5413)*

Rubber Group, The, Rochester *Also Called: Humphreys Industrial Pdts Inc (G-15478)*

Rubber Right Rollers Inc................................. 617 466-1447
  120 Eastern Ave Ste 206 Chelsea (02150) *(G-7990)*

Rubber-Right Rollers Inc................................. 617 387-6060
  101 Tileston St Everett (02149) *(G-8498)*

Rubil Associates Inc...................................... 978 670-7192
  34 Dunham Rd Billerica (01821) *(G-6478)*

Rubius Therapeutics....................................... 401 349-0818
  124 Washington St Foxboro (02035) *(G-8717)*

Rubix Composites Inc..................................... 781 856-0342
  10 Hancock St Woburn (01801) *(G-13657)*

Ruby Electric, Worcester *Also Called: Dkd Solutions Inc (G-13717)*

Ruckus Wireless Inc....................................... 978 614-2900
  900 Chelmsford St Lowell (01851) *(G-9922)*

Ruckus Wireless Inc....................................... 508 870-1184
  8 Technology Dr Ste 200 Westborough (01581) *(G-13131)*

Rudolph Technologies, Wilmington *Also Called: Rudolph Technologies Inc (G-13450)*

Rudolph Technologies Inc **(HQ)**....................... **978 253-6200**
  16 Jonspin Rd Wilmington (01887) *(G-13450)*

Ruger, Southport *Also Called: Sturm Ruger & Company Inc (G-3247)*

Ruger Records Dept, Newport *Also Called: Sturm Ruger & Company Inc (G-15239)*

Ruggles-Klingemann Mfg Co............................... 603 474-8500
  34 Folly Mill Rd Ste 400 Seabrook (03874) *(G-15603)*

Ruland Manufacturing Co Inc............................. 508 485-1000
  6 Hayes Memorial Dr Marlborough (01752) *(G-10208)*

Rule Industries LLC....................................... 978 281-0440
  1 Kondelin Rd Cape Ann Industrial Pk Gloucester (01930) *(G-8956)*

Rumas Pallet World LLC................................... 617 389-8090
  124 2nd St Ste 2 Chelsea (02150) *(G-7991)*

Rumford Falls Times, Rumford *Also Called: James Newspapers Inc (G-5357)*

Rumford Stone Inc **(PA)**.............................. **603 224-9876**
  278 River Rd Bow (03304) *(G-14010)*

Runamok, Fairfax *Also Called: Runamok Maple LLC (G-17263)*

Runamok Maple LLC.. 802 849-7943
  293 Fletcher Rd Fairfax (05454) *(G-17263)*

Runco Capital Corporation............................... 978 462-0320
  25 Storey Ave Ste 3 Newburyport (01950) *(G-10716)*

Runtal North America Inc................................. 800 526-2621
  187 Neck Rd Haverhill (01835) *(G-9128)*

Rupe Slate Co Inc... 802 287-9692
  54 New Boston Rd Poultney (05764) *(G-17450)*

Rusco Steel Company...................................... 401 732-0548
  25 Bleachery Ct Warwick (02886) *(G-16855)*

Russelectric A Siemens Bus, Hingham *Also Called: Siemens Industry Inc (G-9159)*

Russelectric Inc... 781 749-6000
  99 Industrial Park Rd Hingham (02043) *(G-9158)*

Russell James Engineering Works Inc.................... 617 265-2240
  9 Dewar St Boston (02125) *(G-7018)*

Russell Organics LLC...................................... 203 285-6633
  329 Main St Ste 208 Wallingford (06492) *(G-3847)*

Russell Partition Co Inc.................................. 203 239-5749
  20 Dodge Ave North Haven (06473) *(G-2434)*

Russo Woodworking Inc.................................... 508 428-1772
  80 Pine Grove Avenue Hyannis (02601) *(G-9448)*

Russo Woodworking Inc **(PA)**.......................... **908 351-2200**
  162 Cinderella Ter Marstons Mills (02648) *(G-10248)*

Russos Inc... 781 233-1737
  329 Main St Saugus (01906) *(G-11765)*

Russound/Fmp Inc.. 603 659-5170
  200 International Dr Ste 155 Portsmouth (03801) *(G-15433)*

Rustic Crust, Pittsfield *Also Called: Ever Better Eating Inc (G-15331)*

Rustic Marlin Designs LLC................................ 508 376-1004
  389 Columbia Rd Ste 40 Hanover (02339) *(G-9041)*

Rustoleum Attleboro Plant................................ 508 222-3710
  113 Olive St Attleboro (02703) *(G-6060)*

Rutland Business Journal, Rutland *Also Called: Creative Marketing Services (G-17493)*

Rutland Fire Clay Co **(PA)**........................... **802 775-5519**
  8 Madison St Rutland (05701) *(G-17507)*

Rutland Plywood Corp..................................... 802 747-4000
  92 Park St Rutland (05701) *(G-17508)*

Rutland Plywood Corp..................................... 802 747-4000
  92 Park St Rutland (05701) *(G-17509)*

Rutland Products, Rutland *Also Called: Rutland Fire Clay Co (G-17507)*

Ruwac Inc.. 413 532-4030
  54 Winter St Holyoke (01040) *(G-9278)*

Rv Manufacturing Inc...................................... 508 488-6612
  20 Harding St Middleboro (02346) *(G-10377)*

Rwc Landscape Services MGT............................... 603 279-1411
  2 Whitney Rd Unit 21 Concord (03301) *(G-14154)*

RWK Tool Inc.. 860 635-0116
  200 Corporate Row Cromwell (06416) *(G-696)*

Rwt Corporation.. 203 245-2731
32 New Rd Madison (06443) *(G-1568)*

Rxvantage Inc... 866 464-2157
225 Dyer St Providence (02903) *(G-16608)*

Ryan Iron Works Inc.................................... 508 821-2058
1830 Bdwy Raynham (02767) *(G-11596)*

Ryca Inc.. 978 851-3265
1768 Main St Ste 2 Tewksbury (01876) *(G-12415)*

Rynel Inc... 207 882-0200
11 Twin Rivers Dr Wiscasset (04578) *(G-5700)*

Rypos, Franklin *Also Called: Rypos Inc (G-8862)*

Rypos Inc **(PA)**...................................... **508 429-4552**
40 Kenwood Cir Ste 8 Franklin (02038) *(G-8862)*

Ryszard A Kokosinski.................................. 508 943-2700
75 Oxford Ave Dudley (01571) *(G-8321)*

S & A Trombley Corporation.......................... 802 888-2394
76 Houle Ave Morrisville (05661) *(G-17388)*

S & D Rubber Co Div, Hanover *Also Called: Standard Rubber Products Inc (G-9043)*

S & E Fuels Inc.. 617 407-9977
113 Dean St Taunton (02780) *(G-12365)*

S & F Machine Co Inc.................................. 978 374-1552
1405 River St Haverhill (01832) *(G-9129)*

S & H Precision, Newmarket *Also Called: S&H Precision Mfg Co Inc (G-15223)*

S & K Unlimited LLC.................................... 207 965-6137
33 Front St Brownville (04414) *(G-4638)*

S & M Fuels Inc.. 508 746-1495
86 Sandwich St Plymouth (02360) *(G-11476)*

S & P Heat Treating Inc............................... 401 737-9272
16a Dewey Ave Warwick (02886) *(G-16856)*

S & P Metallurgy Service, Warwick *Also Called: S & P Heat Treating Inc (G-16856)*

S & Q Printers Inc...................................... 603 654-2888
88 Elaine Dr Belmont (03220) *(G-13972)*

S & S Concrete Forms Cnstr, Swansea *Also Called: S and S Concrete Forms Cnstr (G-12310)*

S & S Fabric Products, Portsmouth *Also Called: Black Dog Corporation (G-16439)*

S & S Machine LLC..................................... 603 204-5542
11 Caldwell Dr Ste 4 Amherst (03031) *(G-13889)*

S & S Machine and Welding Inc..................... 413 743-5714
128 Windsor Rd Savoy (01256) *(G-11768)*

S & S Worldwide Inc................................... 860 537-3451
75 Mill St Colchester (06415) *(G-665)*

S and S Concrete Forms Cnstr....................... 508 379-0191
2224 Gar Hwy Swansea (02777) *(G-12310)*

S D Ireland Con Cnstr Corp........................... 802 863-6222
193 Industrial Ave Williston (05495) *(G-17747)*

S G Inc... 401 568-1110
885 S Main St Pascoag (02859) *(G-16340)*

S H P, Wilton *Also Called: Special Hermetic Products Inc (G-15710)*

S I Howard Glass Company Inc....................... 508 753-8146
379 Sw Cutoff Worcester (01604) *(G-13785)*

S J Pappas Inc... 203 237-7701
718 Old Colony Rd Meriden (06451) *(G-1695)*

S L Chasse Welding & Fabg Inc...................... 603 886-3436
8 Christine Dr Hudson (03051) *(G-14543)*

S Lane John & Son Incorporated..................... 508 987-3959
Off Clara Barton Oxford (01540) *(G-11263)*

S Lane John & Son Incorporated **(PA)**.......... **413 568-8986**
311 E Mountain Rd Westfield (01085) *(G-13205)*

S M Engineering Co Inc................................ 508 699-4484
83 Chestnut St North Attleboro (02760) *(G-10886)*

S M Lorusso & Sons Inc............................... 617 323-6380
10 Grove St Boston (02132) *(G-7019)*

S M Lorusso & Sons Inc............................... 781 337-6770
611 Pleasant St East Weymouth (02189) *(G-8433)*

S M Lorusso & Sons Inc **(PA)**.................... **508 668-2600**
331 West St Walpole (02081) *(G-12575)*

S M Services Inc... 603 883-3381
14 Progress Ave Nashua (03062) *(G-15162)*

S P, Windsor *Also Called: Specialty Printing LLC (G-4300)*

S P E, Danbury *Also Called: Society Plastics Engineers Inc (G-819)*

S P Holt Corporation................................... 207 866-4867
20 Water St Orono (04473) *(G-5136)*

S P I, Haverhill *Also Called: Specialized Plating Inc (G-9131)*

S Ralph Cross and Sons Inc.......................... 508 865-8112
75 Whiting Farms Rd Holyoke (01040) *(G-9279)*

S W Collins... 207 794-6113
431 Main St Lincoln (04457) *(G-5013)*

S W Granite Inc.. 713 933-0501
331 Central St Northfield (05663) *(G-17434)*

S&E Specialty Polymers LLC......................... 978 537-8261
140 Leominster Shirley Rd Ste 100 Lunenburg (01462) *(G-9960)*

S&H Engineering Inc.................................... 978 256-7231
248 Mill Rd Ste 4 Chelmsford (01824) *(G-7953)*

S&H Precision Mfg Co Inc **(PA)**.................. **603 659-8323**
10 Forbes Rd Newmarket (03857) *(G-15223)*

S&S Industries Inc **(PA)**........................... **914 885-1500**
1551 Central St Stoughton (02072) *(G-12232)*

SA Candelora Enterprises Inc........................ 203 484-2863
250 Totoket Rd North Branford (06471) *(G-2374)*

SA Manchester LLC..................................... 860 533-7500
41 Progress Dr Manchester (06042) *(G-1634)*

Saar Corporation.. 860 674-9440
81 Spring Ln Farmington (06032) *(G-1246)*

Sabatino North America LLC **(PA)**.............. **718 328-4120**
135 Front Ave West Haven (06516) *(G-4122)*

Sabattus Machine Works Inc.......................... 207 375-6222
62 Greene St Sabattus (04280) *(G-5362)*

Sabbow and Co Inc...................................... 603 444-6724
390 Highland Ave Littleton (03561) *(G-14722)*

Sabic Innovative Plas US LLC......................... 413 448-7110
1240 Tyler St Extention Pittsfield (01201) *(G-11422)*

Sabic Innovative Plas US LLC......................... 978 772-5900
65 Middlesex Rd Tyngsboro (01879) *(G-12465)*

Sabic Polymershapes, Tyngsboro *Also Called: Sabic Innovative Plas US LLC (G-12465)*

Sabra Corporation...................................... 207 655-3831
12 Hawthorne Rd Raymond (04071) *(G-5315)*

Sabra Foods, Walpole *Also Called: International Food Pdts Inc (G-12563)*

Sabre Yachts, Raymond *Also Called: Sabra Corporation (G-5315)*

Sabre Yachts Inc.. 207 655-3831
Hawthorne Rd South Casco (04077) *(G-5484)*

Saccuzzo Company Inc................................. 860 665-1101
149 Louis St Newington (06111) *(G-2323)*

Saco Bay Millwork Co................................... 207 929-8400
20 Tory Hill Dr Buxton (04093) *(G-4664)*

Saco Bay Provisioners, Portland *Also Called: York-Cmbrland Assn For Hndcppe (G-5292)*

Saco River Brewing LLC................................ 207 256-3028
10 Jockey Cap Ln Fryeburg (04037) *(G-4810)*

Sacred Profane LLC..................................... 508 259-3052
50 Washington St Biddeford (04005) *(G-4587)*

Sadlak Industries LLC.................................. 860 742-0227
712 Bread And Milk St Unit A9 Coventry (06238) *(G-681)*

Sadlak Innovative Design, Coventry *Also Called: Mike Sadlak (G-680)*

Sadlak Manufacturing LLC............................. 860 742-0227
712 Bread And Milk St Apt 7 Coventry (06238) *(G-682)*

Saeilo Inc.. 508 799-9809
130 Goddard Memorial Dr Worcester (01603) *(G-13786)*

Saeilo USA Inc... 508 795-3919
130 Goddard Memorial Dr Worcester (01603) *(G-13787)*

Saes Memry, Bethel *Also Called: Memry Corporation (G-128)*

Saf Industries LLC **(HQ)**............................ **203 729-4900**
106 Evansville Ave Meriden (06451) *(G-1696)*

Safariland LLC... 413 684-3104
401 South St Dalton (01226) *(G-8153)*

Safc Biosciences Inc.................................... 978 715-1700
400 Summit Dr Burlington (01803) *(G-7420)*

Safc Hitech Inc.. 978 374-5200
1429 Hilldale Ave Haverhill (01832) *(G-9130)*

Safe-Approach Inc...................................... 207 345-9900
206 Mechanic Falls Rd Poland (04274) *(G-5162)*

Safe-T-Cut Inc... 413 267-9984
97 Main St Monson (01057) *(G-10456)*

Safecor Health LLC..................................... 781 933-8780
317 New Boston St # 100 Woburn (01801) *(G-13658)*

ALPHABETIC

Safecor Health LLC... 781 933-8780
  317 New Boston St Ste 100 Woburn (01801) *(G-13659)*

Safehands Distribution Ne LLC............................ 413 244-1452
  35 Post Office Park Ste 3505 Wilbraham (01095) *(G-13363)*

Saferecipes LLC **(PA)**..................................... **617 448-6085**
  37 Varnum St Arlington (02474) *(G-5946)*

Safety 1st, Foxboro *Also Called: Dorel Juvenile Group Inc (G-8694)*

Safety Flag Company, Central Falls *Also Called: Vogue Industries Ltd Partnr (G-15800)*

Safety Seals, Peabody *Also Called: North Shore Laboratories Corp (G-11327)*

Safety-Kleen, Norwell *Also Called: Safety-Kleen Systems Inc (G-11146)*

Safety-Kleen Systems Inc **(HQ)**........................ **800 669-5740**
  42 Longwater Dr Norwell (02061) *(G-11146)*

Safeworld International, Canton *Also Called: Spectrowax Corporation (G-7832)*

Saft America Inc... 203 234-8333
  3 Powdered Metal Rd North Haven (06473) *(G-2435)*

Safve, Scituate *Also Called: Safve Inc (G-11770)*

Safve Inc... 781 545-3546
  24 Ladds Way Scituate (02066) *(G-11770)*

Saga Packaging Machinery Div, Southbridge *Also Called: A & M Tool & Die Company Inc (G-12008)*

Sage Learning Inc.. 778 951-9312
  125 Western Ave Boston (02163) *(G-7020)*

Sage Publications Inc... 805 499-9774
  285 Old Westport Rd North Dartmouth (02747) *(G-11001)*

Sage Science Inc... 617 922-1832
  500 Cummings Ctr Ste 2400 Beverly (01915) *(G-6380)*

Sage Therapeutics Inc **(PA)**............................ **617 299-8380**
  215 1st St Cambridge (02142) *(G-7700)*

Sagemaker Inc... 203 368-4888
  883 Black Rock Tpke Ste 200 Fairfield (06825) *(G-1199)*

Sail Energy LLC... 844 301-7245
  210 Commerce Way Ste 210 Portsmouth (03801) *(G-15434)*

Saint Germain.. 401 738-2800
  675 W Shore Rd Warwick (02889) *(G-16857)*

Saint Vincent De Paul Place................................ 860 889-7374
  120 Cliff St Norwich (06360) *(G-2615)*

Saint-Gobain Abrasives Inc **(HQ)**.................... **508 795-5000**
  1 New Bond St Worcester (01606) *(G-13788)*

Saint-Gobain Adfors Amer Inc............................. 508 795-2500
  1 New Bond St Worcester (01606) *(G-13789)*

Saint-Gobain Ceramic Materials, Worcester *Also Called: Saint-Gobain Ceramics Plas Inc (G-13790)*

Saint-Gobain Ceramics Plas Inc.......................... 413 586-8167
  175 Industrial Dr Northampton (01060) *(G-11078)*

Saint-Gobain Ceramics Plas Inc.......................... 508 351-7754
  9 Goddard Rd Northborough (01532) *(G-11107)*

Saint-Gobain Ceramics Plas Inc.......................... 508 795-5000
  1 New Bond St Worcester (01606) *(G-13790)*

Saint-Gobain Ceramics Plas Inc.......................... 508 795-5000
  351 Stores St Worcester (01606) *(G-13791)*

Saint-Gobain Ceramics Plas Inc.......................... 603 673-5831
  33 Powers St Milford (03055) *(G-15036)*

Saint-Gobain Corporation.................................... 508 351-7112
  9 Goddard Rd Northborough (01532) *(G-11108)*

Saint-Gobain Crystals, Milford *Also Called: Saint-Gobain Ceramics Plas Inc (G-15036)*

Saint-Gobain Glass Corporation........................... 603 673-7560
  47 Powers St Milford (03055) *(G-15037)*

Saint-Gobain Igniter Products, Milford *Also Called: Saint-Gobain Glass Corporation (G-15037)*

Saint-Gobain Prfmce Plas Corp........................... 508 823-7701
  250 Revolutionary Dr East Taunton (02718) *(G-8412)*

Saint-Gobain Prfmce Plas Corp........................... 508 823-7701
  700 Warner Blvd Taunton (02780) *(G-12366)*

Saint-Gobain Prfmce Plas Corp........................... 508 852-3072
  717 Plantation St Worcester (01605) *(G-13792)*

Saint-Gobain Prfmce Plas Corp........................... 603 424-9000
  701 Daniel Webster Hwy Merrimack (03054) *(G-15001)*

Sajawi Corporation... 978 486-9050
  24 Porter Rd Littleton (01460) *(G-9837)*

Sakonnet Vineyards LP....................................... 401 635-8486
  162 W Main Rd Little Compton (02837) *(G-16162)*

Sal Steel, New Britain *Also Called: Sal Steel Inc (G-2058)*

Sal Steel Inc.. 860 826-2755
  221 South St Ste 5 New Britain (06051) *(G-2058)*

Salamander Designs, Bloomfield *Also Called: Salamander Designs Ltd (G-209)*

Salamander Designs Ltd..................................... 860 761-9500
  811 Blue Hills Ave Bloomfield (06002) *(G-209)*

Salem Beer Works, Boston *Also Called: Slesar Bros Brewing Co Inc (G-7040)*

Salem Metal Inc... 978 774-2100
  177 N Main St Middleton (01949) *(G-10392)*

Salem News Archives.. 978 922-8303
  112 Sohier Rd Beverly (01915) *(G-6381)*

Salem Preferred Partners LLC **(PA)**................. **540 389-3922**
  200 Berkeley St Ste 1 Boston (02116) *(G-7021)*

Salem Prime Cuts Incorporated........................... 860 859-0741
  12 New London Rd Ste 5 Salem (06420) *(G-2946)*

Salem Stone Design, Waterford *Also Called: Singer Company Inc (G-3995)*

Salem Village Craftsmen Inc **(PA)**................... **833 827-7267**
  14 S Pleasant St Ashburnham (01430) *(G-5953)*

Salem Vly Farms Ice Cream Inc........................... 860 859-2980
  20 Darling Rd Salem (06420) *(G-2947)*

Sales Solutions Inc.. 781 588-2703
  266 Old Oaken Bucket Rd Scituate (02066) *(G-11771)*

SALESFORCE.COM, INC., Boston *Also Called: Salesforcecom Inc (G-7022)*

Salesforcecom Inc.. 857 415-3510
  500 Boylston St Fl 19 Boston (02116) *(G-7022)*

Salform Inc.. 860 559-6359
  250 John Downey Dr New Britain (06051) *(G-2059)*

Saliga Machine Co Inc.. 978 562-7959
  10 Bonazzoli Ave Hudson (01749) *(G-9409)*

Salisbury Sales Inc.. 508 907-6610
  214 N Main St Ste 103 Natick (01760) *(G-10496)*

Salk Company Inc.. 617 782-4030
  119 Braintree St Ste 151 Allston (02134) *(G-5825)*

Salmon Press LLC **(PA)**................................. **603 279-4516**
  5 Water St Meredith (03253) *(G-14970)*

Saloom Furniture Co Inc..................................... 800 297-1901
  256 Murdock Ave Winchendon (01475) *(G-13482)*

Sals Clothing & Fabric Restor.............................. 617 387-6726
  15 Henderson St Everett (02149) *(G-8499)*

Salsa Fresca New Haven..................................... 301 675-6226
  51 Broadway New Haven (06511) *(G-2193)*

Salsco Inc... 203 271-1682
  105 Schoolhouse Rd Cheshire (06410) *(G-616)*

Salt & Pepper... 508 755-1113
  268 Lincoln St Ste B Worcester (01605) *(G-13793)*

Salt & Pepper and Sugar Too, Wilton *Also Called: Salt and Pepper Me LLC (G-5659)*

Salt and Pepper Me LLC..................................... 207 645-7035
  843 Us Route 2 E Wilton (04294) *(G-5659)*

Salty Cultivation LLC.. 207 752-7549
  72 Emery St Ste 14 Sanford (04073) *(G-5414)*

Salvadore Tool & Findings Inc **(PA)**................. **401 331-6000**
  24 Althea St Providence (02907) *(G-16609)*

Sam & Ty LLC **(PA)**....................................... **212 840-1871**
  12 S Main St Ste 403 Norwalk (06854) *(G-2569)*

Sam Maulucci & Sons, Wethersfield *Also Called: Mozzicato Fmly Investments LLC (G-4212)*

Sam's & Son, Stoughton *Also Called: Sams Drapery Workroom Inc (G-12234)*

Sam's Good News, Rutland *Also Called: Eastview Associates Inc (G-17495)*

Sam's Italian Sandwich Shop, Lewiston *Also Called: Sams Italian Foods Inc (G-4991)*

Samar Co Inc... 781 297-7264
  220 Cushing St Stoughton (02072) *(G-12233)*

SAMPANN NEWSPAPER, Boston *Also Called: Asian American Civic Assn Inc (G-6560)*

Sampco Inc **(PA)**... **413 442-4043**
  56 Downing Pkwy Pittsfield (01201) *(G-11423)*

Sams Drapery Workroom Inc............................... 617 364-9440
  15 Smyth St Stoughton (02072) *(G-12234)*

Sams Food Stores, Rocky Hill *Also Called: Cco Llc (G-2917)*

Sams Italian Foods Inc **(PA)**........................... **207 782-9145**
  268 Main St Lewiston (04240) *(G-4991)*

Samsara.. 413 570-4130
  26 Strong Ave Northampton (01060) *(G-11079)*

Samsara Fitness LLC.. 860 895-8533
  10 Denlar Dr Chester (06412) *(G-632)*

Samson Manufacturing Corp.................................. 603 355-3903
  32 Optical Ave Keene (03431) *(G-14617)*

Samsonite, Warren *Also Called: Samsonite Company Stores LLC (G-16768)*

Samsonite Company Stores LLC.......................... 401 247-3301
  95 Main St Warren (02885) *(G-16768)*

Samtan Engineering Corp.................................... 781 322-7880
  127 Wyllis Ave Malden (02148) *(G-10026)*

Samuel Holmes Incorporated.............................. 617 269-5740
  56 Garden St Everett (02149) *(G-8500)*

San Franciso Market.. 781 780-3731
  2 Lafayette Park Lynn (01902) *(G-9990)*

San-Tron Inc **(PA)**.. **978 356-1585**
  4 Turnpike Rd Ipswich (01938) *(G-9496)*

Sana Biotechnology Inc **(PA)**.......................... **202 790-0313**
  300 Technology Sq Cambridge (02139) *(G-7701)*

Sancliff Inc.. 508 795-0747
  97 Temple St Worcester (01604) *(G-13794)*

Sand 9 Inc... 617 358-0957
  1 Kendall Sq Ste B2305 Cambridge (02139) *(G-7702)*

Sand A Industries... 508 943-1178
  137 Schofield Ave Dudley (01571) *(G-8322)*

Sandberg Enterprises Inc **(PA)**........................ **401 568-1602**
  806 Broncos Hwy Mapleville (02839) *(G-16168)*

Sandberg Enterprises Inc.................................... 401 568-1602
  806 Broncos Hwy Pascoag (02859) *(G-16341)*

Sandberg Machine, Mapleville *Also Called: Sandberg Enterprises Inc (G-16168)*

Sandbox Medical LLC.. 781 826-6905
  50 Corporate Park Dr # 750 Pembroke (02359) *(G-11377)*

Sandcastle Publishing LLC.................................. 508 398-3100
  434 Route 134 Ste A2 South Dennis (02660) *(G-11935)*

Sandelin Foundation Inc...................................... 207 725-7004
  82 Old Augusta Rd Topsham (04086) *(G-5552)*

Sanders Archtectural Wdwkg LLC........................ 860 682-5607
  150 Episcopal Rd Berlin (06037) *(G-84)*

Sanders- A Lockheed Martin Co, Merrimack *Also Called: Lockheed Martin Corporation (G-14990)*

Sanderson-Macleod Incorporate.......................... 413 283-3481
  1199 S Main St Palmer (01069) *(G-11284)*

Sands Business Eqp & Sups LLC.......................... 207 351-3334
  11 Payneton Hill Rd York (03909) *(G-5716)*

Sandstrom Crbide Pdts Corp Inc.......................... 401 739-5220
  140 Imera Ave Warwick (02886) *(G-16858)*

Sandur Tool Co.. 203 753-0004
  853 Hamilton Ave Waterbury (06706) *(G-3967)*

Sandvik Wire and Heating Tech, Bethel *Also Called: Kanthal Corporation (G-124)*

Sandviks Inc **(PA)**.. **866 984-0188**
  4 Mountainview Ter Ste 200 Danbury (06810) *(G-808)*

Sandy Bay Machine Inc....................................... 978 546-1331
  11 Dory Rd # 2 Gloucester (01930) *(G-8957)*

Sanford Manufacturing Facility, Sanford *Also Called: Roehm America LLC (G-5412)*

Sangari Active Science, Greenwich *Also Called: Sasc LLC (G-1349)*

Sanger Equipment Corporation............................ 413 625-8304
  Wilder Hill Road Conway (01341) *(G-8145)*

Sanmina Corporation.. 603 621-1800
  140 Abby Rd Manchester (03103) *(G-14924)*

Sanner... 603 577-9087
  2 Troy St Nashua (03064) *(G-15163)*

Sanofi Genzyme, Cambridge *Also Called: Genzyme Corporation (G-7588)*

Sanofi Pasteur Biologics LLC **(HQ)**.................. **617 866-4400**
  38 Sidney St Ste 370 Cambridge (02139) *(G-7703)*

Sanofi Pasteur Biologics LLC.............................. 781 302-3000
  50 Shawmut Rd Canton (02021) *(G-7824)*

Sanofi US Services Inc....................................... 617 562-4555
  500 Kendall St Ste 500 Cambridge (02142) *(G-7704)*

Sanofi US Services Inc....................................... 800 981-2491
  450 Water St Cambridge (02141) *(G-7705)*

Sanofi US Services Inc....................................... 508 424-4485
  51 New York Ave Framingham (01701) *(G-8803)*

Sanoil LLC.. 401 942-5000
  101 Corliss St Providence (02904) *(G-16610)*

Sanova Bioscience Inc.. 978 429-8079
  42 Nagog Park Acton (01720) *(G-5763)*

Sant Bani Press Inc.. 603 286-3114
  60 Buckley Cir Ste 3 Manchester (03109) *(G-14925)*

Santa Cruz Gunlocks LLC................................... 603 746-7740
  450 Tyler Rd Webster (03303) *(G-15674)*

Santacroce Graphics Inc..................................... 802 447-0020
  47 E Baylies Rd Charlton (01507) *(G-7895)*

Santec Corporation.. 203 878-1379
  84 Old Gate Ln Milford (06460) *(G-1882)*

Santhera Pharmaceuticals usa.............................. 781 552-5145
  25 Corporate Dr Burlington (01803) *(G-7421)*

Santo C De Spirt Marble & Gran.......................... 413 786-7073
  2 S Bridge Dr Agawam (01001) *(G-5806)*

Sanwa Technologies Inc...................................... 508 616-9500
  287 Turnpike Rd Westborough (01581) *(G-13132)*

Sanwa Technologies MA, Westborough *Also Called: Sanwa Technologies Inc (G-13132)*

Sap Press.. 617 481-0448
  2 Heritage Dr Quincy (02171) *(G-11538)*

Sap Professional Journal **(PA)**........................ **781 407-0360**
  20 Carematrix Dr Dedham (02026) *(G-8249)*

Sapphire Engineering, Middleboro *Also Called: Idex Health & Science LLC (G-10362)*

Sapphiros Ai Bio LLC... 617 297-7993
  27 Drydock Ave Boston (02210) *(G-7023)*

Sappi, Skowhegan *Also Called: Sappi North America Inc (G-5477)*

Sappi Fine Paper North America, Skowhegan *Also Called: Sappi North America Inc (G-5478)*

Sappi Fine Paper North America, South Portland *Also Called: Sappi North America Inc (G-5513)*

Sappi Fine Paper Tech Ctr................................... 207 239-6071
  300 Warren Ave Westbrook (04092) *(G-5645)*

Sappi Fine Ppr Westbrook Mill, Westbrook *Also Called: Sappi North America Inc (G-5647)*

Sappi NA Finance LLC.. 617 423-5439
  255 State St Boston (02109) *(G-7024)*

Sappi North America, Westbrook *Also Called: Sappi North America Inc (G-5646)*

Sappi North America Inc..................................... 207 858-4201
  98 North Ave Skowhegan (04976) *(G-5477)*

Sappi North America Inc..................................... 207 238-3000
  1329 Waterville Rd Skowhegan (04976) *(G-5478)*

Sappi North America Inc..................................... 207 854-7000
  179 John Roberts Rd South Portland (04106) *(G-5513)*

Sappi North America Inc..................................... 207 856-4000
  89 Cumberland St Westbrook (04092) *(G-5646)*

Sappi North America Inc..................................... 207 856-4911
  89 Cumberland St Westbrook (04092) *(G-5647)*

Sara Campbell Ltd **(PA)**.................................. **617 423-3134**
  67 Kemble St Ste 4 Boston (02119) *(G-7025)*

Saratoga Salad Dressing, Canton *Also Called: Pearlco of Boston Inc (G-7818)*

Sarepta, Cambridge *Also Called: Sarepta Therapeutics Inc (G-7706)*

Sarepta Therapeutics.. 781 221-7805
  55 Network Dr Burlington (01803) *(G-7422)*

Sarepta Therapeutics Inc.................................... 978 662-4800
  100 Federal St Andover (01810) *(G-5914)*

Sarepta Therapeutics Inc **(PA)**........................ **617 274-4000**
  215 1st St Ste 415 Cambridge (02142) *(G-7706)*

Sargeant & Wilbur Inc.. 401 726-0013
  20 Monticello Pl Pawtucket (02861) *(G-16415)*

Sargent Controls and Aerospace.......................... 520 744-1000
  1 Tribiology Ctr Oxford (06478) *(G-2711)*

Sargent Manufacturing Company.......................... 203 562-2151
  100 Sargent Dr New Haven (06511) *(G-2194)*

Sarid Inc.. 781 315-1105
  66 Middle St Lexington (02421) *(G-9769)*

Sarnafil Services Inc.. 781 828-5400
  100 Dan Rd Canton (02021) *(G-7825)*

Sarro Cohasset Incorporated............................... 781 383-1704
  30 Stoney Beach Rd Hull (02045) *(G-9427)*

Sasc LLC.. 203 846-2274
  44 Amogerone Crossway Unit 7862 Greenwich (06836) *(G-1349)*

Satellite Aerospace Inc....................................... 860 643-2771
  240 Chapel Rd Manchester (06042) *(G-1635)*

Satellite Tool & Mch Co Inc................................. 860 290-8558
  571 Nutmeg Rd N South Windsor (06074) *(G-3178)*

Sathorn Corporation.. 802 860-2121
  581 Industrial Ave Williston (05495) *(G-17748)*

ALPHABETIC

Saucony Inc **(DH)** **617 824-6000**
500 Totten Pond Rd Ste 1 Waltham (02451) *(G-12776)*

Saunders At Locke Mills LLC 207 875-2853
256 Main St Greenwood (04255) *(G-4853)*

Saunders Electronics, South Portland *Also Called: David Saunders Inc (G-5497)*

Saunders Manufacturing & Mktg, Readfield *Also Called: Saunders Mfg Co Inc (G-5318)*

Saunders Mfg Co Inc **(PA)** **207 685-9860**
65 Nickerson Hill Rd Readfield (04355) *(G-5318)*

Savage & Savage Logging Inc 207 528-2974
20 Valley St Patten (04765) *(G-5154)*

Savage Arms, Westfield *Also Called: Caliber Company (G-13156)*

Savage Arms Inc **(DH)** **413 642-4135**
100 Springdale Rd Westfield (01085) *(G-13206)*

Savage Latina Magazine LLC 800 260-3525
12 11th St Derby (06418) *(G-892)*

Savage Range Systems Inc 413 568-7001
100 Springdale Rd Westfield (01085) *(G-13207)*

Savage Sports Corporation **(HQ)** **413 568-7001**
100 Springdale Rd Westfield (01085) *(G-13208)*

Savant Systems Inc **(PA)** **508 683-2500**
45 Perseverance Way Hyannis (02601) *(G-9449)*

Savetime Corporation 203 382-2991
2710 North Ave Ste 105b Bridgeport (06604) *(G-368)*

Savin Products Company Inc 781 961-2743
214 High St Randolph (02368) *(G-11574)*

Savin Rock Printing 203 500-1577
145 Boston Post Rd West Haven (06516) *(G-4123)*

Savory Creations International 650 638-1024
330 Lynnway Ste 401 Lynn (01901) *(G-9991)*

Savron Graphics Inc **(PA)** **603 532-7726**
4 Stratton Rd Jaffrey (03452) *(G-14579)*

Savvy Workshop 603 792-0080
55 South Commercial St Manchester (03101) *(G-14926)*

Sawmill, New Vineyard *Also Called: Maine Wood Turning Inc (G-5091)*

Sawmill Park 413 569-3393
1 Saw Mill Park Southwick (01077) *(G-12045)*

Sawtech, Lawrence *Also Called: Leblanc Enterprises Inc (G-9578)*

Sawyer Bentwood Inc 802 368-2357
247 Maple Dr Whitingham (05361) *(G-17713)*

Sawyers Jewelry Inc 603 527-1000
520 Main St Laconia (03246) *(G-14667)*

Say It In Stitches Inc 603 224-6470
128 Hall St Ste B Concord (03301) *(G-14155)*

Saybrook Press Incorporated 203 458-3637
39 Chaffinch Island Rd Guilford (06437) *(G-1406)*

Saylent Technologies Inc 508 570-2161
122 Grove St Ste 300 Franklin (02038) *(G-8863)*

Sb Development Corp 978 263-2744
17 Craig Rd Acton (01720) *(G-5764)*

Sbarzola Construction Corp 781 817-6485
1183 Main St South Weymouth (02190) *(G-11977)*

SBE Vision Inc 612 237-0128
1 Albion St Ste 1 Wakefield (01880) *(G-12532)*

SBE-CT, Stafford Springs *Also Called: Division 5 LLC (G-3254)*

SBwinsor Creamery LLC 401 231-5113
58 Pine Hill Ave Johnston (02919) *(G-16106)*

Scan Soft Inc 781 565-5000
1 Wayside Rd Burlington (01803) *(G-7423)*

Scan Tool & Mold Inc 203 459-4950
2 Trefoil Dr Trumbull (06611) *(G-3731)*

Scan-Optics LLC 860 645-7878
169 Progress Dr Manchester (06042) *(G-1636)*

Scandia Kitchens Inc 508 966-0300
38 Maple St Bellingham (02019) *(G-6300)*

Scandia Plastics Inc 603 382-6533
55 Westville Rd Plaistow (03865) *(G-15350)*

Scandinavian Panel Systems 774 530-6340
370 Main St Ste 950 Worcester (01608) *(G-13795)*

Scannell Boiler Works 978 454-5629
50 Tanner St Ste 1 Lowell (01852) *(G-9923)*

Scap Motors Inc 203 384-0005
562 Rock Ridge Rd Fairfield (06824) *(G-1200)*

Scapa Holdings Inc **(DH)** **860 688-8000**
111 Great Pond Dr Windsor (06095) *(G-4298)*

Scarborough Faire Inc 401 724-4200
1151 Main St Pawtucket (02860) *(G-16416)*

Scarlet Aspen LLC 603 509-3990
105 Bartlett St Portsmouth (03801) *(G-15435)*

Schaefer Marine Inc 508 995-9511
158 Duchaine Blvd., Industrial Park New Bedford (02745) *(G-10648)*

Schaeferrolls Inc 603 335-1786
23 Plank Industrial Dr Farmington (03835) *(G-14311)*

Schaeffler Aerospace USA Corp **(DH)** **203 744-2211**
200 Park Ave Danbury (06810) *(G-809)*

Schaeffler Aerospace USA Corp. 860 379-7558
159 Colebrook River Rd Winsted (06098) *(G-4354)*

Schaeffler Holding LLC **(DH)** **203 790-5474**
200 Park Ave Danbury (06810) *(G-810)*

Scharf and Breit Inc 516 282-0287
9 High Ridge Rd Redding (06896) *(G-2883)*

Scheduling Systems Inc 508 620-0390
85 Speen St Ste 300 Framingham (01701) *(G-8804)*

Schenck USA Corp. 978 562-6017
571 Main St Hudson (01749) *(G-9410)*

Schiavi Homes, Oxford *Also Called: Schiavi Homes LLC (G-5149)*

Schiavi Homes LLC. 207 539-9600
754 Main St Oxford (04270) *(G-5149)*

Schlage Lock Company LLC 781 828-6655
5 Shawmut Rd Canton (02021) *(G-7826)*

Schleifring, Chelmsford *Also Called: Schleifring North America LLC (G-7954)*

Schleifring North America LLC 978 677-2500
222 Mill Rd Chelmsford (01824) *(G-7954)*

Schlumberger Technology Corp 617 768-2000
1 Hampshire St Ste 1 Cambridge (02139) *(G-7707)*

Schlumberger-Doll Research, Cambridge *Also Called: Schlumberger Technology Corp (G-7707)*

Schmitt Realty Holdings Inc 203 488-3252
746 E Main St Branford (06405) *(G-275)*

Schmitt Realty Holdings Inc **(PA)** **203 453-4334**
251 Boston Post Rd Guilford (06437) *(G-1407)*

Schmitt Realty Holdings Inc 203 453-4334
251 Boston Post Rd Guilford (06437) *(G-1408)*

Schneder Elc Systems Argntina 508 543-8750
38 Neponset Ave Foxboro (02035) *(G-8718)*

Schneeberger Inc **(DH)** **781 271-0140**
44 6th Rd Ste 3 Woburn (01801) *(G-13660)*

Schneider Automation Inc 978 975-9600
800 Federal St Andover (01810) *(G-5915)*

Schneider Elc Systems USA Inc 508 543-8750
38 Neponset Ave Foxboro (02035) *(G-8719)*

Schneider Elc Systems USA Inc. 508 543-8750
70 Mechanic St Foxboro (02035) *(G-8720)*

Schneider Elc Systems USA Inc **(DH)** **508 543-8750**
70 Mechanic St Foxboro (02035) *(G-8721)*

Schneider Electric, Boston *Also Called: Schneider Electric Usa Inc (G-7026)*

Schneider Electric, Foxboro *Also Called: Schneider Elc Systems USA Inc (G-8721)*

Schneider Electric, Foxboro *Also Called: Schneider Electric Usa Inc (G-8724)*

Schneider Electric Foxboro 508 543-8750
38 Neponset Ave Foxboro (02035) *(G-8722)*

Schneider Electric It Corp **(DH)** **508 543-8750**
70 Mechanic St Foxboro (02035) *(G-8723)*

Schneider Electric Usa Inc **(DH)** **978 975-9600**
1 Boston Pl Ste 2700 Boston (02108) *(G-7026)*

Schneider Electric Usa Inc. 508 549-3385
15 Pond Ave Foxboro (02035) *(G-8724)*

Schoeffel International Corp. 978 256-4512
7a Stuart Rd Chelmsford (01824) *(G-7955)*

Scholar Rock Holding Corp **(PA)** **857 259-3860**
301 Binney St Ste 3 Cambridge (02142) *(G-7708)*

Scholastic Corporation 617 924-3846
1200 Soldiers Field Rd # 1 Allston (02134) *(G-5826)*

Scholastic Inc **(DH)** **212 343-6100**
90 Old Sherman Tpke Danbury (06810) *(G-811)*

Scholastic Library Pubg Inc **(HQ)** **203 797-3500**
90 Sherman Tpke Danbury (06816) *(G-812)*

Scholz Frank X Ray Corp
244 Liberty St Ste 3a Brockton (02301) *(G-7303)*

School Family Media LLC..................................508 384-0394
100 Stonewall Blvd Ste 3 Wrentham (02093) *(G-13844)*

Schott North America Inc..................................508 765-9744
122 Charlton St Southbridge (01550) *(G-12034)*

Schrader Electronics Inc..................................615 384-0089
529 Pleasant St Attleboro (02703) *(G-6061)*

Schrafel Pprbd Converting Corp..................................203 931-1700
82 W Clark St Ste 1 West Haven (06516) *(G-4124)*

Schrimpf Welding, Woburn *Also Called: Schrimpf Wldg Fabrication Inc (G-13661)*

Schrimpf Wldg Fabrication Inc..................................339 298-2311
3 Breed Ave Unit J Woburn (01801) *(G-13661)*

Schroff Inc **(HQ)**..................................**763 204-7700**
170 Commerce Dr Warwick (02886) *(G-16859)*

Schuco International, Newington *Also Called: Schuco USA Lllp (G-2324)*

Schuco USA Lllp **(HQ)**..................................**860 666-0505**
240 Pane Rd Newington (06111) *(G-2324)*

Schuerch Corporation..................................781 982-7000
452 Randolph St Abington (02351) *(G-5728)*

Schul International Co LLC..................................603 889-6872
34 Executive Dr Hudson (03051) *(G-14544)*

Schulz Electric Company..................................203 562-5811
30 Gando Dr New Haven (06513) *(G-2195)*

Schuremed, Abington *Also Called: Schuerch Corporation (G-5728)*

Schweizer Aircraft Corp..................................203 386-4356
6900 Main St Stratford (06614) *(G-3570)*

Schwerdtle, Bridgeport *Also Called: Schwerdtle Stamp Company (G-369)*

Schwerdtle Stamp Company..................................203 330-2750
41 Benham Ave Bridgeport (06605) *(G-369)*

Schwing Bioset Technologies..................................203 744-2100
98 Mill Plain Rd Ste A Danbury (06811) *(G-813)*

Sciaps Inc **(PA)**..................................**339 222-2585**
7 Constitution Way Ste 105 Woburn (01801) *(G-13662)*

Scidose LLC..................................866 956-4333
196 N Pleasant St Ste 16 Amherst (01002) *(G-5864)*

Science Fction Fntsy Wrters AM..................................860 698-0536
24 Nutmeg Ave Enfield (06082) *(G-1146)*

Scienceopen Inc..................................781 222-5200
155 Middlesex Tpke Ste 4 Burlington (01803) *(G-7424)*

Scientific Instrument Facility..................................617 353-5056
590 Commonwealth Ave Rm 255 Boston (02215) *(G-7027)*

Scientific Solutions Inc..................................978 251-4554
55 Middlesex St Unit 210 North Chelmsford (01863) *(G-10988)*

Scion Medical Techologies LLC..................................617 455-5186
90 Oak St # 1 Newton Upper Falls (02464) *(G-10795)*

Scituate Concrete Pipe Corp..................................781 545-0564
1 Buckeye Ln Scituate (02066) *(G-11772)*

Scituate Concrete Products..................................781 837-1747
120 Clay Pit Rd Marshfield (02050) *(G-10245)*

Scituate Concrete Products Cor..................................617 837-1747
120 Clay Pit Rd Marshfield (02050) *(G-10246)*

Scmt Inc, Cranston *Also Called: Signature Cable Mfg Tech Inc (G-15910)*

Scope Display & Box Co Inc **(PA)**..................................**401 942-7150**
1840 Cranston St Cranston (02920) *(G-15909)*

Scope Technology Incorporated..................................860 963-1141
8 Center Pkwy Plainfield (06374) *(G-2739)*

Scotia Technology, Laconia *Also Called: Lakes Region Tubular Pdts Inc (G-14657)*

Scotia Woodworking..................................978 212-5379
571 Main St Hudson (01749) *(G-9411)*

Scotland Hardwoods, Scotland *Also Called: Hardwood Lumber Manufacturing (G-2953)*

Scotland Hardwoods, Scotland *Also Called: Scotland Hardwoods LLC (G-2954)*

Scotland Hardwoods LLC..................................860 423-1233
117 Ziegler Rd Scotland (06247) *(G-2954)*

Scott Brass, Cranston *Also Called: House of Stainless Inc (G-15873)*

Scott Electronics Inc **(PA)**..................................**603 893-2845**
5 Industrial Way Ste 2d Salem (03079) *(G-15559)*

Scott Metal Finishing, Bristol *Also Called: Scott Metal Finishing LLC (G-496)*

Scott Metal Finishing LLC..................................860 589-3778
310 Birch St Bristol (06010) *(G-496)*

Scott Woodford..................................203 245-4266
817 Boston Post Rd Madison (06443) *(G-1569)*

Scotts Company LLC..................................860 642-7591
20 Industrial Rd Lebanon (06249) *(G-1550)*

Scp Management LLC..................................860 738-2600
29 Industrial Park Rd New Hartford (06057) *(G-2108)*

SCPHARMACEUTICALS, Burlington *Also Called: Scpharmaceuticals Inc (G-7425)*

Scpharmaceuticals Inc..................................617 517-0730
25 Mall Rd Ste 203 Burlington (01803) *(G-7425)*

Scrapbook Clubhouse..................................860 399-4443
20 Westbrook Pl Westbrook (06498) *(G-4142)*

Scratch Art Company Inc **(PA)**..................................**508 583-8085**
11 Robbie Rd Ste A Avon (02322) *(G-6161)*

Screen Gems Inc..................................603 474-5353
34 Folly Mill Rd Ste 2 Seabrook (03874) *(G-15604)*

Screen Tek, Hamden *Also Called: Screen Tek Printing Co Inc (G-1454)*

Screen Tek Printing Co Inc..................................203 248-6248
130 Welton St Hamden (06517) *(G-1454)*

Screencraft, Lincoln *Also Called: Screencraft Tileworks LLC (G-16153)*

Screencraft Graphics, Lincoln *Also Called: Abar Color Labs Neng Inc (G-16114)*

Screencraft Tileworks LLC..................................401 427-2816
9 Powder Hill Rd Lincoln (02865) *(G-16153)*

Screenprint/Dow Inc..................................978 657-7290
200 Research Dr Ste 6 Wilmington (01887) *(G-13451)*

Screw-Matic Corporation..................................603 468-1610
10 Primrose Dr S Laconia (03246) *(G-14668)*

Scribl.com, Orange *Also Called: Scribliotech Inc (G-15280)*

Scribliotech Inc..................................603 306-9000
527 Tuttle Hill Rd Orange (03741) *(G-15280)*

Scully Data Systems, Wilmington *Also Called: Scully Signal Company (G-13452)*

Scully Signal Company **(PA)**..................................**617 692-8600**
70 Industrial Way Wilmington (01887) *(G-13452)*

SCW Corporation..................................401 808-6849
126 Chestnut St Warwick (02888) *(G-16860)*

SD Goodspeed Inc..................................860 526-3200
12 Bridge St Deep River (06417) *(G-881)*

SD Ireland Companies, Williston *Also Called: S D Ireland Con Cnstr Corp (G-17747)*

SDA Laboratories Inc..................................203 861-0005
280 Railroad Ave Ste 207 Greenwich (06830) *(G-1350)*

Sdl Xyenterprise LLC **(PA)**..................................**781 756-4400**
201 Edgewater Dr Ste 225 Wakefield (01880) *(G-12533)*

Sdpd Holdings Inc..................................781 893-2368
94 Calvary St Waltham (02453) *(G-12777)*

SDR Logging Inc..................................207 564-8534
629 Sebec Village Rd Sebec (04481) *(G-5457)*

SDS Logging Inc..................................603 586-7098
180 Presidential Hwy Jefferson (03583) *(G-14585)*

Sdv Software Inc..................................603 329-8164
32 Anne Dr Hampstead (03841) *(G-14393)*

SDW Holdings Corporation..................................617 423-5400
255 State St Fl 7 Boston (02109) *(G-7028)*

SE Mass Devlopment LLC..................................401 434-3329
930 Waterman Ave East Providence (02914) *(G-16043)*

SE Shires Inc..................................508 634-6805
260 Hopping Brook Rd Holliston (01746) *(G-9228)*

Sea & Reef Aquaculture, Franklin *Also Called: Sea & Reef Aquaculture LLC (G-4796)*

Sea & Reef Aquaculture LLC..................................207 422-2422
33 Salmon Farm Rd Franklin (04634) *(G-4796)*

Sea Bags Inc..................................207 939-3679
6 Bow St Freeport (04032) *(G-4803)*

Sea Bags LLC **(PA)**..................................**207 780-0744**
25 Custom House Wharf Portland (04101) *(G-5268)*

SEA BAGS, INC., Freeport *Also Called: Sea Bags Inc (G-4803)*

Sea Hagg Distillery LLC..................................603 343-1717
119 Broadway Dover (03820) *(G-14249)*

Sea Star Seafood Corp
128 Bartlett St Marlborough (01752) *(G-10209)*

Sea Street Technologies Inc..................................617 600-5150
779 Washington St Ste 2c Canton (02021) *(G-7827)*

Sea-Band International Inc..................................401 841-5900
580 Thames St # 440 Newport (02840) *(G-16222)*

Sea-Land Envmtl Svcs Inc.............................. 508 359-1085
  18 N Meadows Rd Ste 1 Medfield (02052) *(G-10275)*

Seaboard Folding Box Co Inc........................ 978 342-8921
  100 Simplex Dr Westminster (01473) *(G-13277)*

Seaboard Folding Box Company, Westminster *Also Called: Mm-Apvh Acquisition Co LLC*
(G-13275)

Seaboard Metal Finishing Co.......................... 203 933-1603
  410 John Downey Dr New Britain (06051) *(G-2060)*

Seaboard Plating, New Britain *Also Called: Seaboard Metal Finishing Co* *(G-2060)*

Seaborn Networks, Beverly *Also Called: Seaborn Networks Holdings LLC* *(G-6382)*

Seaborn Networks Holdings LLC **(PA)**............. **978 471-3171**
  600 Cummings Ctr Fl 2 Beverly (01915) *(G-6382)*

Seabrook Medical LLC................................... 603 474-1919
  15 Woodworkers Way Seabrook (03874) *(G-15605)*

Seabury Splash Inc....................................... 508 830-3440
  10 Cordage Park Cir Ste 212 Plymouth (02360) *(G-11477)*

Seachange, Boston *Also Called: Seachange International Inc* *(G-7029)*

Seachange International Inc **(PA)**.................... **978 897-0100**
  177 Huntington Ave Ste 1703 Pmb 73480 Boston (02115) *(G-7029)*

Seacoast Machine Company LLC..................... 603 659-3404
  80a Exeter Rd Newmarket (03857) *(G-15224)*

Seacoast Newspapers, Portsmouth *Also Called: Local Media Group Inc* *(G-15418)*

Seacoast Redimix Concrete LLC **(PA)**............. **603 742-4441**
  349 Mast Rd Dover (03820) *(G-14250)*

Seacoast Technologies Inc.............................. 603 766-9800
  222 International Dr Ste 145 Portsmouth (03801) *(G-15436)*

Seacolors.. 207 845-2587
  45 Hopkins Rd Washington (04574) *(G-5588)*

Seagate Technology LLC................................ 508 770-3111
  333 South St Shrewsbury (01545) *(G-11841)*

Sealed Air Corporation.................................. 203 791-3597
  10 Old Sherman Tpke Danbury (06810) *(G-814)*

Sealed Air Corporation.................................. 508 521-5694
  100 Westford Rd Ayer (01432) *(G-6193)*

Sealed Air Corporation.................................. 413 534-0231
  2030 Homestead Ave Lowr Holyoke (01040) *(G-9280)*

Sealite Usa LLC... 603 737-1310
  61 Business Park Dr Tilton (03276) *(G-15656)*

Sealmaster... 508 926-8080
  110 Blackstone River Rd Worcester (01607) *(G-13796)*

Seals-It Inc... 860 979-0060
  164 Maple St Ellington (06029) *(G-1114)*

Seaman Paper Company, Gardner *Also Called: Seaman Paper Company Mass Inc* *(G-8899)*

Seaman Paper Company Mass Inc.................... 978 939-5356
  51 Main St Baldwinville (01436) *(G-6198)*

Seaman Paper Company Mass Inc **(PA)**.......... **978 632-1513**
  35 Wilkins Rd Gardner (01440) *(G-8899)*

Seaman Paper Company Mass Inc.................... 978 544-2455
  184 Gov Dukakis Dr Orange (01364) *(G-11233)*

Seamark International LLC.............................. 603 546-0100
  16 Celina Ave Unit 5 Nashua (03063) *(G-15164)*

Seamless North America................................ 401 714-2925
  259 Franklin St Bristol (02809) *(G-15780)*

Seaport Marine Inc....................................... 860 536-9651
  2 Washington St Mystic (06355) *(G-1942)*

Seaside Casual Furniture, Coventry *Also Called: Arnold Lumber Co* *(G-15806)*

Seasmoke Extracts Inc.................................. 207 819-4114
  230 Merrow Rd Auburn (04210) *(G-4460)*

Seatrade International Co LLC......................... 774 305-4948
  10 N Front St New Bedford (02740) *(G-10649)*

Seattle Times Company................................. 207 623-3811
  274 Western Ave Augusta (04330) *(G-4480)*

Seaview Plastic Recycling Inc......................... 203 367-0070
  938 Crescent Ave Bridgeport (06607) *(G-370)*

Seavus Group... 978 623-7221
  45 W Parish Dr Andover (01810) *(G-5916)*

Seavus Usa Inc... 888 573-2887
  179 High St Acton (01720) *(G-5765)*

Seaway Boats Inc.. 207 539-8116
  59 Industrial Dr Oxford (04270) *(G-5150)*

Sebabo South Inc.. 603 881-8720
  15 Progress Ave Nashua (03062) *(G-15165)*

Sebago Brewing Company **(PA)**..................... **207 856-2537**
  616 Main St Gorham (04038) *(G-4834)*

Sebasticook Lumber LLC................................ 207 660-1360
  446 Hartland Rd Saint Albans (04971) *(G-5386)*

SEC Electrical Inc.. 203 562-5811
  30 Gando Dr New Haven (06513) *(G-2196)*

Seceon Inc... 978 923-0040
  238 Littleton Rd Ste 206 Westford (01886) *(G-13261)*

Second Wind, Newton *Also Called: Second Wind Systems Inc* *(G-10782)*

Second Wind, Newton *Also Called: Second Wind Systems Inc* *(G-10783)*

Second Wind Media Limited............................ 203 781-3480
  315 Front St New Haven (06513) *(G-2197)*

Second Wind Systems Inc.............................. 617 581-6090
  15 Riverdale Ave Newton (02458) *(G-10782)*

Second Wind Systems Inc.............................. 617 467-1500
  15 Riverdale Ave Newton (02458) *(G-10783)*

Secondaries Inc.. 203 879-4633
  15 Venus Dr Wolcott (06716) *(G-4375)*

Seconn Automation Solutions......................... 860 442-4325
  147 Cross Rd Waterford (06385) *(G-3993)*

Seconn Fabrication LLC................................. 860 443-0000
  180 Cross Rd Waterford (06385) *(G-3994)*

Secure Care Products LLC.............................. 603 223-0745
  39 Chenell Dr Concord (03301) *(G-14156)*

Secure Code Warrior Inc................................ 617 901-3005
  265 Franklin St Ste 1702 Boston (02110) *(G-7030)*

Secure Pnt Inc.. 201 401-4207
  135 Pond Rd Shelburne (05482) *(G-17560)*

Secure Point Technologies Inc........................ 978 752-1700
  207 Union Wharf Boston (02109) *(G-7031)*

Securecash Advantage.................................. 207 797-4838
  200 Riverside Industrial Pkwy Portland (04103) *(G-5269)*

Securemark Decal Corp................................. 203 333-5503
  20 Nutmeg Dr Trumbull (06611) *(G-3732)*

Securities Software & Consulti......................... 860 298-4500
  80 Lamberton Rd Windsor (06095) *(G-4299)*

Security Engineered Machinery, Westborough *Also Called: Security Engineered McHy Inc*
(G-13133)

Security Engineered McHy Inc **(PA)**............... **508 366-1488**
  5 Walkup Dr Westborough (01581) *(G-13133)*

Securos, Sturbridge *Also Called: Wotton Enterprises Inc* *(G-12259)*

Seekonk Manufacturing Co Inc........................ 508 761-8284
  87 Perrin Ave Seekonk (02771) *(G-11785)*

Seekonk Precision Tools, Seekonk *Also Called: Seekonk Manufacturing Co Inc* *(G-11785)*

Seesmart Inc.. 203 504-1111
  263 Tresser Blvd Stamford (06901) *(G-3454)*

Sega Ready Mix, New Milford *Also Called: Sega Ready Mix Incorporated* *(G-2260)*

Sega Ready Mix, Waterbury *Also Called: Sega Ready Mix Incorporated* *(G-3968)*

Sega Ready Mix Incorporated **(PA)**................. **860 354-3969**
  519 Danbury Rd New Milford (06776) *(G-2260)*

Sega Ready Mix Incorporated.......................... 203 465-1052
  310 Chase River Rd Waterbury (06704) *(G-3968)*

Segue LLC... 970 274-9801
  163 Front St Marion (02738) *(G-10100)*

Segue Manufacturing Svcs LLC........................ 978 970-1200
  101 Billerica Ave Bldg 3 North Billerica (01862) *(G-10952)*

SEI II Inc.. 203 877-8488
  60 Commerce Park Ste 1 Milford (06460) *(G-1883)*

Seica.. 978 376-7254
  50a Northwestern Dr Salem (03079) *(G-15560)*

Seidel LLC... 203 757-7349
  2223 Thomaston Ave Waterbury (06704) *(G-3969)*

Seifert Systems Inc...................................... 401 294-6960
  75 Circuit Dr North Kingstown (02852) *(G-16279)*

Seismic Monitoring Svcs LLC.......................... 860 753-6363
  70 Black Rock Ave Danielson (06239) *(G-841)*

Seitz LLC... 860 489-0476
  212 Industrial Ln Torrington (06790) *(G-3695)*

Seize Sur Vingt, Lenox *Also Called: 16sur20 Management LLC* *(G-9624)*

Sekisui Diagnostics LLC **(DH)**....................... **781 652-7800**
  1 Wall St Ste 301 Burlington (01803) *(G-7426)*

Select Design Ltd...................................... 802 864-9075
208 Flynn Ave Ste 1a Burlington (05401) *(G-17158)*

Selectcom Manufacturing Co Inc....................... 203 879-9900
29 Nutmeg Valley Rd Wolcott (06716) *(G-4376)*

Selection Unlimited, South Burlington *Also Called: Sentar Inc (G-17598)*

Selectives LLC.. 860 585-1956
166 Litchfield St Thomaston (06787) *(G-3628)*

Sellers Publishing Inc................................. 207 772-6833
161 John Roberts Rd Ste 1 South Portland (04106) *(G-5514)*

Selvita Inc... 857 998-4075
100 Cambridge St Ste 14010 Boston (02114) *(G-7032)*

Sem-Tec Inc.. 508 798-8551
47 Lagrange St Worcester (01610) *(G-13797)*

Semco, Plainville *Also Called: Semco Machine Corp (G-11442)*

Semco Instruments Inc................................. 661 362-6117
186 Cedar St Branford (06405) *(G-276)*

Semco Instruments Inc (DH)....................... 203 483-3700
186 Cedar St Branford (06405) *(G-277)*

Semco Machine Corp.................................... 508 384-8303
14 High St Plainville (02762) *(G-11442)*

Semi-General Inc....................................... 603 641-3800
54 Grenier Field Rd Londonderry (03053) *(G-14783)*

Semiconsoft, Southborough *Also Called: Semiconsoft Inc (G-12001)*

Semiconsoft Inc.. 617 388-6832
83 Pine Hill Rd Southborough (01772) *(G-12001)*

Semigear Inc... 781 213-3066
107 Audubon Rd Ste 2 Wakefield (01880) *(G-12534)*

Semigen, Londonderry *Also Called: Semi-General Inc (G-14783)*

Semikron Inc (HQ)................................. 603 883-8102
11 Executive Dr Hudson (03051) *(G-14545)*

Semilab USA LLC....................................... 508 647-8400
47 Manning Rd Billerica (01821) *(G-6479)*

Semilab USA LLC....................................... 508 647-8400
101 Billerica Ave Bldg 5 North Billerica (01862) *(G-10953)*

Seminex Corporation................................... 978 326-7700
153 Andover St Ste 201 Danvers (01923) *(G-8219)*

Semma Therapeutics Inc (HQ)...................... 857 529-6430
100 Technology Sq Fl 3 Cambridge (02139) *(G-7709)*

Sempco Inc... 603 889-1830
51 Lake St Ste 7 Nashua (03060) *(G-15166)*

Semper FI Power Supply Inc............................ 603 656-9729
21 W Auburn St Ste 29 Manchester (03101) *(G-14927)*

Semrush Holdings Inc (PA)......................... 800 815-9959
800 Boylston St Ste 2475 Boston (02199) *(G-7033)*

Semtech Solutions Inc................................. 978 663-9822
3 Executive Park Dr Ste 1 North Billerica (01862) *(G-10954)*

Semya Corp (PA)................................... 802 875-6564
53 Duncan Rd Alstead (03602) *(G-13858)*

Semya Corp... 802 875-6564
4333 Vt Route 103 N Chester (05143) *(G-17183)*

Sencorp Inc.. 508 771-9400
400 Kidds Hill Rd Hyannis (02601) *(G-9450)*

Sencorpwhite, Hyannis *Also Called: Sencorpwhite Inc (G-9451)*

Sencorpwhite Inc (HQ)............................. 508 771-9400
400 Kidds Hill Rd Hyannis (02601) *(G-9451)*

Sencorpwhite Holdings LLC............................. 508 771-9400
400 Kidds Hill Rd Hyannis (02601) *(G-9452)*

Senesco Marine LLC.................................... 401 295-0373
10 Macnaught St North Kingstown (02852) *(G-16280)*

Senior Aerospace Connecticut, Enfield *Also Called: Senior Operations LLC (G-1147)*

Senior Flexonics Pthwy, Lewiston *Also Called: Wahlcometroflex Inc (G-4995)*

Senior Flxnics Pthway Mtroflex, Lewiston *Also Called: Senior Operations LLC (G-4992)*

Senior Network Inc..................................... 203 969-2700
777 Summer St Ste 103 Stamford (06901) *(G-3455)*

Senior Operations LLC................................. 860 741-2546
4 Peerless Way Enfield (06082) *(G-1147)*

Senior Operations LLC................................. 860 741-2546
4 Peerless Way Enfield (06082) *(G-1148)*

Senior Operations LLC................................. 207 784-2338
29 Lexington St Lewiston (04240) *(G-4992)*

Senior Operations LLC................................. 781 784-1400
1075 Providence Hwy Sharon (02067) *(G-11795)*

Senix, Hinesburg *Also Called: Senix Corporation (G-17298)*

Senix Corporation..................................... 802 489-7300
10516 Route 116 Ste 300 Hinesburg (05461) *(G-17298)*

Senko Advanced Components Inc (HQ)............... 508 481-9999
2 Cabot Rd Ste 103 Hudson (01749) *(G-9412)*

Senko America, Hudson *Also Called: Senko Advanced Components Inc (G-9412)*

Sensar Marine Us Inc.................................. 800 910-2150
15 Depot Sq Lexington (02420) *(G-9770)*

Sensata Technologies Inc (HQ).................... 508 236-3800
529 Pleasant St Attleboro (02703) *(G-6062)*

Sensata Technologies Ind Inc (DH)............... 508 236-3800
529 Pleasant St Attleboro (02703) *(G-6063)*

Sensata Technologies Mass Inc (DH).............. 508 236-3800
529 Pleasant St Attleboro (02703) *(G-6064)*

Sensera Inc.. 978 606-2600
15 Presidential Way Woburn (01801) *(G-13663)*

Sensing Systems Corporation........................... 508 992-0872
7 Commerce Way Dartmouth (02747) *(G-8231)*

Sensitech Inc (DH)............................... 978 927-7033
800 Cummings Ctr Ste 258x Beverly (01915) *(G-6383)*

Sensor Engineering, Westborough *Also Called: Sensortech Systems Inc (G-13134)*

Sensor Research and Dev Corp.......................... 207 866-0100
5 Godfrey Dr Orono (04473) *(G-5137)*

Sensor Switch Inc (DH).......................... 203 265-2842
265 Church St Fl 15 New Haven (06510) *(G-2198)*

Sensortech Systems Inc................................ 805 981-3735
8 Technology Dr Ste 100 Westborough (01581) *(G-13134)*

Sensorworx, Wallingford *Also Called: Blp Technologies Inc (G-3781)*

Sensory Acquisition Co, Billerica *Also Called: Durridge Company Inc (G-6433)*

Sentar Inc... 802 861-6004
102 Kimball Ave Ste 2 South Burlington (05403) *(G-17598)*

Sentinel and Enterprise, Fitchburg *Also Called: Medianews Group Inc (G-8663)*

Sentinel Process Systems Inc.......................... 508 624-5577
10 Southville Rd Southborough (01772) *(G-12002)*

Seongyun Corporation.................................. 203 668-6803
21 Elm St West Haven (06516) *(G-4125)*

Sepaton Inc.. 508 490-7900
400 Nickerson Rd Marlborough (01752) *(G-10210)*

Seqirus Inc.. 617 871-5734
225 Wyman St Waltham (02451) *(G-12778)*

Sequel Industrial Products Inc, Colchester *Also Called: Prcess Critical Systems Group (G-17200)*

Sequel Med Tech LLC (PA)......................... 212 883-1007
50 Commercial St Fl 3 Manchester (03101) *(G-14928)*

Sequel Special Products LLC........................... 203 759-1020
1 Hillside Dr Wolcott (06716) *(G-4377)*

Ser Exposition Services, Worcester *Also Called: Ser Logistics Inc (G-13798)*

Ser Logistics Inc..................................... 508 757-3397
35b New St Worcester (01605) *(G-13798)*

Seres Therapeutics Inc (PA)..................... 617 945-9626
200 Sidney St Fl 4 Cambridge (02139) *(G-7710)*

Serono Inc... 781 681-2137
1 Technology Pl Rockland (02370) *(G-11660)*

Serpentino Stned Leaded GL Inc........................ 781 449-2074
21 Highland Cir Ste 6 Needham Heights (02494) *(G-10556)*

Serrato Signs, Worcester *Also Called: Serrato Signs LLC (G-13799)*

Serrato Signs LLC..................................... 508 756-7004
15 Dewey St Worcester (01609) *(G-13799)*

Servers Storage Networking LLC........................ 203 433-0808
26 Pearl St Ste 101 Norwalk (06850) *(G-2570)*

Service Experts LLC................................... 603 332-6466
38 Milton Rd Rochester (03868) *(G-15493)*

Service Network Inc................................... 860 679-7432
21 Spring Ln Farmington (06032) *(G-1247)*

Service Press, Newington *Also Called: The Hartford Press Inc (G-2327)*

Service Tech Inc (PA)........................... 401 353-3664
1164 Douglas Ave North Providence (02904) *(G-16310)*

Servier US Inc (PA)............................. 610 506-8203
200 Pier 4 Blvd 7th Fl Boston (02210) *(G-7034)*

SES, Woburn *Also Called: Solidenergy Systems LLC (G-13670)*

SES America Inc....................................... 401 232-3370
21 Quinton St Warwick (02888) *(G-16861)*

(PA)=Parent Co (HQ)=Headquarters (DH)=Div Headquarters

Set Americas, Easthampton *Also Called: Set Americas Inc (G-8462)*

Set Americas Inc.. 413 203-6130
  180 Pleasant St Ste 207 Easthampton (01027) *(G-8462)*

Set Connectors Inc... 207 527-2876
  36 Holman Ln Norway (04268) *(G-5118)*

Setra Systems Inc... 978 263-1400
  159 Swanson Rd Ste 1 Boxboro (01719) *(G-7145)*

Settle Shop, The, West Townsend *Also Called: Albert E Cadrette (G-13056)*

Sevcon, Northborough *Also Called: Borgwarner Massachusetts Inc (G-11092)*

Seven Days Newspaper, Burlington *Also Called: Da Capo Publishing Inc (G-17130)*

Seven Sweets Inc.. 781 631-0303
  154 Atlantic Ave Marblehead (01945) *(G-10095)*

SEVENTH GENERATION, Burlington *Also Called: Seventh Generation Inc (G-17159)*

Seventh Generation Inc **(DH)**..................................... **802 658-3773**
  60 Lake St Ste 3n Burlington (05401) *(G-17159)*

Seventy Nine N Main St Prtg.. 978 475-4945
  79 N Main St Andover (01810) *(G-5917)*

Sever Pharma Solutions, Putnam *Also Called: Foster Delivery Science Inc (G-2857)*

Severance Foods Inc... 860 724-7063
  3478 Main St Hartford (06120) *(G-1506)*

Sewickley LLC... 203 661-2511
  340 North St Greenwich (06830) *(G-1351)*

Sewn In America Inc **(PA)**.. **203 438-9149**
  54 Danbury Rd Ste 240 Ridgefield (06877) *(G-2907)*

Seymour - Sheridan Incorporated....................................... 203 261-4009
  15 Commerce Dr Monroe (06468) *(G-1921)*

SF Madden Inc... 207 852-2525
  183 Greenfield Rd Greenbush (04418) *(G-4845)*

SF Tools LLC... 603 863-7719
  460 Sunapee St Newport (03773) *(G-15238)*

Sfc Koenig LLC... 203 245-1100
  73 Defco Park Rd North Haven (06473) *(G-2436)*

SFE Mfg, Limestone *Also Called: Stainless Fdsrvice Eqp Mfg Inc (G-5005)*

Sfwa.. 508 320-5293
  24 Nutmeg Ave Enfield (06082) *(G-1149)*

Sga Components Group LLC... 203 758-3702
  13 Gramar Ave Prospect (06712) *(G-2842)*

Sh Consulting Co... 508 695-6611
  55 Access Rd Ste 500 Warwick (02886) *(G-16862)*

Shaans Panini & Roast Beef LLC.. 617 230-3166
  99 Chelmsford Rd Unit 9rte North Billerica (01862) *(G-10955)*

Shackletonthomas, Bridgewater *Also Called: Charles Shcklton Mrnda Thmas L (G-17111)*

Shacksbury Holdings Inc... 802 458-0530
  75 Meigs Rd Vergennes (05491) *(G-17659)*

Shafiis Inc **(PA)**.. **413 224-2100**
  50 Industrial Dr East Longmeadow (01028) *(G-8394)*

Shaft Current Solutions Inc... 413 267-0590
  34 N Maple St Ste 7 Florence (01062) *(G-8686)*

Shaidzon Beer Company LLC... 401 314-8730
  141 Fairgrounds Rd West Kingston (02892) *(G-16897)*

Shain's of Maine Ice Cream, Sanford *Also Called: Shains (G-5415)*

Shains.. 207 324-1449
  1491 Main St Sanford (04073) *(G-5415)*

Shaker Workshops, Ashburnham *Also Called: Salem Village Craftsmen Inc (G-5953)*

Shakour Publishers Inc.. 603 352-5250
  445 West St Keene (03431) *(G-14618)*

Shambhala Publications.. 617 424-0030
  300 Massachusetts Ave Boston (02115) *(G-7035)*

Shanklin, Ayer *Also Called: Shanklin Research Corporation (G-6195)*

Shanklin Corporation **(HQ)**....................................... **978 487-2204**
  100 Westford Rd Ayer (01432) *(G-6194)*

Shanklin Research Corporation... 978 772-2090
  100 Westford Rd Ayer (01432) *(G-6195)*

Shannon Boat Company Inc.. 401 253-2441
  19 Broadcommon Rd Bristol (02809) *(G-15781)*

Shannon Drilling.. 207 255-6149
  684 Route 1 Machias (04654) *(G-5034)*

Shannon Yachts, Bristol *Also Called: Shannon Boat Company Inc (G-15781)*

Shape Global Technologies, Sanford *Also Called: R&V Industries Inc (G-5408)*

Share Coffee, Amherst *Also Called: Kind Grind Incorporated (G-5861)*

Sharkninja Inc... 617 243-0235
  89 A St Ste 100 Needham (02494) *(G-10520)*

Sharkninja Operating LLC **(PA)**............................... **617 243-0235**
  89 A St Ste 100 Needham (02494) *(G-10521)*

Sharoc Realty Inc... 508 238-0151
  55 Bristol Dr Ste 1 South Easton (02375) *(G-11953)*

Sharon Dinette Inc.. 413 593-6731
  118 Dulong Cir Chicopee (01022) *(G-8060)*

Sharon Vacuum Co Inc.. 508 588-2323
  69 Falmouth Ave Brockton (02301) *(G-7304)*

Sharp Manufacturing Inc... 508 583-4080
  415 N Elm St West Bridgewater (02379) *(G-12978)*

Sharp Services Inc.. 781 854-3334
  222 Central St Saugus (01906) *(G-11766)*

Sharpe Hill Vineyard Inc.. 860 974-3549
  108 Wade Rd Pomfret (06258) *(G-2811)*

Shaw & Tenney, Orono *Also Called: S P Holt Corporation (G-5136)*

Shaw Brothers Construction Inc **(PA)**...................... **207 839-2552**
  341 Mosher Rd Gorham (04038) *(G-4835)*

Shaw Welding Company Inc.. 978 667-0197
  7 Innis Dr Billerica (01821) *(G-6480)*

Shaw Woodworking Inc.. 508 563-1242
  150 Highland Ave Pocasset (02559) *(G-11492)*

Shawmut, Peabody *Also Called: Shawmut Advertising Inc (G-11340)*

Shawmut Advertising Inc **(PA)**................................. **978 762-7500**
  310 Jubilee Dr Peabody (01960) *(G-11340)*

Shawmut Engineering Company.. 508 850-9500
  38 Weber Farm Rd Wrentham (02093) *(G-13845)*

Shawmut LLC **(PA)**... **508 588-3300**
  208 Manley St West Bridgewater (02379) *(G-12979)*

Shawmut Metal, Swansea *Also Called: Shawmut Metal Products Inc (G-12311)*

Shawmut Metal Products Inc... 508 379-0803
  1914 Gar Hwy Swansea (02777) *(G-12311)*

Shawmut Printing... 978 762-7500
  310 Jubilee Dr Peabody (01960) *(G-11341)*

Shawn Dudek... 603 387-1859
  334 White Oaks Rd Laconia (03246) *(G-14669)*

Shawn Roberts Woodworking.. 413 477-0060
  830 Lower Rd Gilbertville (01031) *(G-8914)*

Shawnee Steps, Bangor *Also Called: American Concrete Inds Inc (G-4488)*

Shawsheen Rubber Co Inc... 978 470-1760
  220 Andover St Andover (01810) *(G-5918)*

Shea Concrete Products Inc **(PA)**............................ **978 658-2645**
  87 Haverhill Rd Amesbury (01913) *(G-5851)*

Shea Concrete Products Inc.. 978 388-1509
  87 Haverhill Rd Amesbury (01913) *(G-5852)*

Sheaffer Pen Corporation.. 319 372-7444
  1 Albion Rd Ste 100 Lincoln (02865) *(G-16154)*

Sheaffer Pen U.S., Lincoln *Also Called: Sheaffer Pen Corporation (G-16154)*

Shear Color Printing Inc... 781 376-9607
  30d 6th Rd Woburn (01801) *(G-13664)*

Shearwater Allergy LLC... 207 846-7676
  10 Forest Falls Dr Stop 9 Yarmouth (04096) *(G-5707)*

Sheaumann Laser Inc.. 508 970-0600
  5 Federal St Ste 1 Billerica (01821) *(G-6481)*

Shed Happens Inc **(PA)**... **207 494-7546**
  730 Portland Rd Saco (04072) *(G-5379)*

Sheds USA, Portsmouth *Also Called: Home Brands LLC (G-15405)*

Sheehan & Sons Lumber... 802 263-5545
  251 Stoughton Pond Rd Perkinsville (05151) *(G-17442)*

Sheepscot Machine Works LLC... 207 563-2299
  1130 Route 1 Newcastle (04553) *(G-5096)*

Sheepscot River Pottery **(PA)**.................................. **207 882-9410**
  34 Route One Edgecomb (04556) *(G-4748)*

Sheergard Cmpsite Slutions Inc.. 954 661-7372
  6 Industrial Way Salem (03079) *(G-15561)*

Sheet Metal Design.. 802 288-9700
  3 Corporate Dr Essex Junction (05452) *(G-17246)*

Sheffield Pharmaceuticals, New London *Also Called: Sheffield Pharmaceuticals LLC (G-2233)*

Sheffield Pharmaceuticals LLC **(PA)**....................... **860 442-4451**
  170 Broad St New London (06320) *(G-2233)*

Sheffield Pharmaceuticals LLC... 860 442-4451
  9 Wisconsin Ave Norwich (06360) *(G-2616)*

Sheffield Plastic Division, Sheffield *Also Called: Plaskolite LLC (G-11799)*

Sheffield Pottery Inc... 413 229-7700
  995 N Main St Us Sheffield (01257) *(G-11801)*

Shelborne Plastics, South Burlington *Also Called: Plastic Technologies NY LLC (G-17593)*

Shelbrack Woodworking.. 860 431-5028
  15 Nod Brook Dr Simsbury (06070) *(G-3096)*

Shelburne Corporation **(PA)**.. **802 985-3321**
  6221 Shelburne Rd Shelburne (05482) *(G-17561)*

Shelburne Farms.. 802 985-8498
  1611 Harbor Rd Shelburne (05482) *(G-17562)*

Shelburne Farms Market Garden, Shelburne *Also Called: Shelburne Farms (G-17562)*

Shelburne Limestone, Swanton *Also Called: Shelburne Limestone Corp (G-17642)*

Shelburne Limestone Corp.. 802 878-2656
  1975 Route 7 S Colchester (05446) *(G-17202)*

Shelburne Limestone Corp **(PA)**.. **802 878-2656**
  1949 Main St Colchester (05446) *(G-17203)*

Shelburne Limestone Corp.. 802 868-3357
  30 Jewett St Swanton (05488) *(G-17642)*

Shelburne News, Shelburne *Also Called: Wind Ridge Publishing (G-17565)*

Shelburne Plastics, Londonderry *Also Called: Altium Packaging LLC (G-14731)*

Shelburne Plastics, South Burlington *Also Called: Altium Packaging LLC (G-17569)*

Shelburne Plastics, South Burlington *Also Called: Plastic Technologies MD Inc (G-17592)*

Shelburne Plastics, South Burlington *Also Called: Plastic Technologies of Vermont Inc (G-17594)*

Shelco Filters Division, Middletown *Also Called: Tinny Corporation (G-1786)*

Sheldon Precision LLC.. 203 758-4441
  10 Industrial Rd Prospect (06712) *(G-2843)*

Sheldon Slate Products Co Inc... 207 997-3615
  38 Farm Quarry Rd Monson (04464) *(G-5074)*

Shelmar Inc... 781 245-1206
  187 Water St Wakefield (01880) *(G-12535)*

Shelpak Plastics Inc.. 781 844-2046
  339 N Main St Middleton (01949) *(G-10393)*

Shelterlogic Corp **(HQ)**... **860 945-6442**
  150 Callender Rd Watertown (06795) *(G-4028)*

Shemin Landscape Supply Co, Lexington *Also Called: Shemin Nurseries Inc (G-9771)*

Shemin Nurseries Inc... 781 861-1111
  1265 Massachusetts Ave Lexington (02420) *(G-9771)*

Shenitech, Marlborough *Also Called: Spire Metering Technology LLC (G-10215)*

Shepard Steel, Hartford *Also Called: Shepard Steel Co Inc (G-1507)*

Shepard Steel Co Inc **(PA)**... **860 525-4446**
  110 Meadow St Hartford (06114) *(G-1507)*

Shepard Steel Co Inc.. 860 525-4446
  55 Shepard Dr Newington (06111) *(G-2325)*

Sheppard Envelope Company Inc... 508 791-5588
  133 Southbridge St Auburn (01501) *(G-6125)*

Sheridan Corporation **(HQ)**.. **207 453-9311**
  33 Sheridan Rd Fairfield (04937) *(G-4765)*

Sheridan Journal Services, Waterbury *Also Called: Dartmouth Journal Services Inc (G-17674)*

Sheridan Me Inc.. 207 353-1500
  119 Lisbon St Lisbon (04250) *(G-5016)*

Sheridan New Hampshire, Hanover *Also Called: Dartmouth Printing Company (G-14422)*

Sherle Wagner Intl LLC... 212 758-3300
  1 Lewiston St Unit 2 Fall River (02721) *(G-8606)*

Sherman Printing Co Inc.. 781 828-8855
  9 Kelly Way Canton (02021) *(G-7828)*

Sherwin Dodge Printers Inc.. 603 444-6552
  365 Union St Littleton (03561) *(G-14723)*

Shibumicom Inc.. 855 744-2864
  50 Washington St Ste 302e Norwalk (06854) *(G-2571)*

Shield CA, Canton *Also Called: Shield Realty California Inc (G-7829)*

Shield Packaging Co Inc... 508 949-0900
  50 Oxford Rd Dudley (01571) *(G-8323)*

Shield Realty California Inc **(PA)**... **909 628-4707**
  99 University Rd Canton (02021) *(G-7829)*

Shields Mri At Umass Memorial, Worcester *Also Called: Umass Mem Mri Imaging Ctr LLC (G-13814)*

Shiller and Company Inc... 203 210-5208
  258 Thunder Lake Rd Wilton (06897) *(G-4247)*

Shillermath, Wilton *Also Called: Shiller and Company Inc (G-4247)*

Shiner Signs Inc.. 203 634-4331
  38 Elm St Ste 3 Meriden (06450) *(G-1697)*

Shintron Co Inc... 617 491-8701
  144 Rogers St Cambridge (02142) *(G-7711)*

Shintron Co Interligua Div, Cambridge *Also Called: Shintron Co Inc (G-7711)*

Ship Street Capital LLC.. 508 995-9711
  146 Duchaine Blvd New Bedford (02745) *(G-10650)*

Ship-Pac Corp.. 207 797-7444
  460 Riverside St Portland (04103) *(G-5270)*

Shippinginsight.. 203 260-0480
  21 Davis Hill Rd Weston (06883) *(G-4153)*

Shipyard In Boothbay Hbr LLC... 207 633-3171
  120 Commercial St Boothbay Harbor (04538) *(G-4604)*

Shire... 508 282-5731
  27 Maple St Milford (01757) *(G-10418)*

Shire City Herbals Inc.. 413 344-4740
  87 Old State Rd Berkshire (01224) *(G-6317)*

Shire Humn Gntic Therapies Inc **(DH)**... **617 349-0200**
  300 Shire Way Lexington (02421) *(G-9772)*

Shire Pharmaceuticals, Lexington *Also Called: Shire Humn Gntic Therapies Inc (G-9772)*

Shire Pharmaceuticals, Lexington *Also Called: Shire US Inc (G-9775)*

Shire Pharmaceuticals LLC... 617 588-8800
  650 E Kendall St Cambridge (02142) *(G-7712)*

Shire Pharmaceuticals LLC... 781 482-9245
  185 Alewife Brook Pkwy Cambridge (02138) *(G-7713)*

Shire Pharmaceuticals LLC **(HQ)**.. **617 349-0200**
  300 Shire Way Lexington (02421) *(G-9773)*

Shire Pharmaceuticals LLC... 617 349-0200
  235 Wyman St Lexington (02421) *(G-9774)*

Shire US Inc **(HQ)**.. **781 482-9222**
  300 Shire Way Lexington (02421) *(G-9775)*

Shirtmasters Screen Printing, Chichester *Also Called: Business Shirtmasters (G-14072)*

Shlomo Enterprises Inc **(PA)**... **860 265-7995**
  1699 King St Enfield (06082) *(G-1150)*

Shoham Manufacturing Inc... 860 623-1361
  32 North Rd Rear East Windsor (06088) *(G-1085)*

Shookus Special Tools Inc.. 603 895-1200
  11 Center St Raymond (03077) *(G-15458)*

Shop Smart Central Inc... 914 962-3871
  31 Pecks Ln Newtown (06470) *(G-2346)*

Shop Therapy Imports.. 508 487-8970
  20 Province Rd Provincetown (02657) *(G-11497)*

Shopper-Turnpike Corporation... 860 928-3040
  70 Main St Putnam (06260) *(G-2874)*

Shoppers Guide, Putnam *Also Called: Shopper-Turnpike Corporation (G-2874)*

Shoppers Guide, Great Barrington *Also Called: Southern Brkshire Shppers Gide (G-8978)*

Shore Publishing LLC... 203 245-1877
  724 Boston Post Rd Madison (06443) *(G-1570)*

Shoreline Metal Services LLC... 203 466-7372
  250 Dodge Ave East Haven (06512) *(G-1050)*

Shoreline Publications.. 207 646-8448
  952 Post Rd Unit 10 Wells (04090) *(G-5605)*

Shorelink Publications LLC... 413 320-3611
  31 West St Newport (02840) *(G-16223)*

Shorey Precast Division, Harwich *Also Called: Acme-Shorey Precast Co Inc (G-9066)*

Show Management Associates LLC.. 203 939-9901
  10 Wall St Apt 201 Norwalk (06850) *(G-2572)*

Show Motion Inc... 203 866-1866
  1034 Bridgeport Ave Milford (06460) *(G-1884)*

Showhegan New Balance, Skowhegan *Also Called: New Balance Athletics Inc (G-5474)*

Shrink Equipment, Ayer *Also Called: Shanklin Corporation (G-6194)*

Shufro Engineering Labs, Newton *Also Called: Shufro Security Company Inc (G-10784)*

Shufro Security Company Inc... 617 244-3355
  1231 Washington St Newton (02460) *(G-10784)*

Shuster Machines, Plainville *Also Called: Shuster-Mettler Corp (G-2780)*

Shuster-Mettler Corp... 203 562-3178
  10 Sparks St Plainville (06062) *(G-2780)*

Shuttercraft Inc.. 203 245-2608
  15 Orchard Park Rd Ste A5 Madison (06443) *(G-1571)*

Shyft Group Inc.. 207 692-7178
   977 W River Rd Unit 3 Waterville (04901) *(G-5596)*

Si Group Inc.. 203 702-6140
   4 Mountainview Ter Ste 200 Danbury (06810) *(G-815)*

Si Group USA Hldings Usha Corp **(DH)**.............. **203 702-6140**
   4 Mountainview Ter Ste 200 Danbury (06810) *(G-816)*

Si-Rel Inc.. 978 455-8737
   101 Brick Kiln Rd Ste 2 Chelmsford (01824) *(G-7956)*

Sia, Ridgefield *Also Called: Sewn In America Inc (G-2907)*

Sical.. 508 898-1800
   11 Walkup Dr Westborough (01581) *(G-13135)*

Sick, Stoughton *Also Called: Sick Auto Ident Inc (G-12236)*

Sick Inc... 781 302-2500
   800 Technology Center Dr Ste 5 Stoughton (02072) *(G-12235)*

Sick Auto Ident Inc **(DH)**................................. **781 302-2500**
   800 Technology Center Dr Ste 5 Stoughton (02072) *(G-12236)*

Sickday, Wellfleet *Also Called: Sickday Inc (G-12953)*

Sickday Inc... 508 214-4158
   3 W Main St Wellfleet (02667) *(G-12953)*

Sidechannel Inc... 508 925-0114
   146 Main St Rm 405 Worcester (01608) *(G-13800)*

Sie Computing Solutions Inc............................... 508 588-6110
   10 Mupac Dr Brockton (02301) *(G-7305)*

Siemens Energy Inc.. 978 577-6413
   20 Villanova Dr Westford (01886) *(G-13262)*

Siemens Hlthcare Dgnostics Inc.......................... 212 258-4000
   6 Tech Dr Andover (01810) *(G-5919)*

Siemens Industry Inc.. 207 878-3367
   9 Sunset Rd Falmouth (04105) *(G-4771)*

Siemens Industry Inc.. 781 749-6000
   99 Industrial Park Rd Hingham (02043) *(G-9159)*

Siemon Company **(PA)**.................................... **860 945-4200**
   101 Siemon Company Dr Watertown (06795) *(G-4029)*

Siemon Global Project Services, Watertown *Also Called: Siemon Company (G-4029)*

Sierra Nevada Corporation.................................. 775 331-0222
   43 Constitution Dr Ste 202 Bedford (03110) *(G-13949)*

Sierra Peaks Corporation................................... 207 236-3301
   5 Colcord Ave Camden (04843) *(G-4668)*

Siftex Equipment Company................................. 860 289-8779
   52 Connecticut Ave Ste D South Windsor (06074) *(G-3179)*

Sig Sauer Inc.. 603 610-3000
   12 Industrial Dr Exeter (03833) *(G-14301)*

Sig Sauer Inc.. 603 772-2302
   18 Industrial Dr Exeter (03833) *(G-14302)*

Sig Sauer Inc **(DH)**.. **603 610-3000**
   72 Pease Blvd Newington (03801) *(G-15210)*

Sig Sauer US Holding LP.................................... 603 610-3000
   72 Pease Blvd Newington (03801) *(G-15211)*

Sigco, Westbrook *Also Called: Sigco LLC (G-5649)*

Sigco LLC.. 207 775-2676
   600 County Rd Westbrook (04092) *(G-5648)*

Sigco LLC **(HQ)**... **207 775-2676**
   48 Spiller Dr Westbrook (04092) *(G-5649)*

Sigcom, Woburn *Also Called: Signal Communications Corp (G-13666)*

Sige Semiconductor Inc **(HQ)**........................... **978 327-6850**
   300 Federal St Andover (01810) *(G-5920)*

Sigg Switzerland (usa) Inc.................................. 203 321-1232
   1177 High Ridge Rd Stamford (06905) *(G-3456)*

Sigilon Therapeutics, Cambridge *Also Called: Sigilon Therapeutics Inc (G-7714)*

Sigilon Therapeutics Inc **(HQ)**.......................... **617 336-7540**
   100 Binney St Ste 600 Cambridge (02142) *(G-7714)*

Siglab Industries LLC.. 603 860-2931
   9 Greenwich Dr Merrimack (03054) *(G-15002)*

Sigler Machine Co.. 978 422-7868
   3 Northeast Blvd Sterling (01564) *(G-12170)*

Sigler Machine Co, Princeton *Also Called: Lawrence Sigler (G-11495)*

Sigma Research Biochemicals.............................. 781 237-3828
   1 Strathmore Rd Natick (01760) *(G-10497)*

Sigma Systems Corp... 781 688-2354
   41 Hampden Rd Mansfield (02048) *(G-10076)*

Sigma Tankers Inc
   20 Glover Ave Ste 5 Norwalk (06850) *(G-2573)*

Sigma-Aldrich Corporation.................................. 978 715-1804
   400 Summit Dr Burlington (01803) *(G-7427)*

Sigmavoip Llc... 203 541-5450
   980 Post Rd E Westport (06880) *(G-4196)*

Sigmet, Westford Operations, Woburn *Also Called: Vaisala Inc (G-13683)*

Sigmund Software LLC....................................... 800 448-6975
   83 Wooster Hts Ste 210 Danbury (06810) *(G-817)*

Sign Art Inc.. 781 322-3785
   60 Sharon St Malden (02148) *(G-10027)*

Sign By Tommorrow.. 508 222-1900
   400 Old Colony Rd Norton (02766) *(G-11134)*

Sign Company.. 508 760-5400
   343 Main St Dennis Port (02639) *(G-8262)*

Sign Concepts LLC... 207 699-2920
   342 Warren Ave Portland (04103) *(G-5271)*

Sign Design Inc... 508 580-0094
   170 Liberty St Brockton (02301) *(G-7306)*

Sign Design Inc... 207 856-2600
   306 Warren Ave Ste 3 Portland (04103) *(G-5272)*

Sign Factory.. 860 763-1085
   25 Dust House Rd Enfield (06082) *(G-1151)*

Sign Fast... 203 549-8500
   3841 Main St Bridgeport (06606) *(G-371)*

Sign Pro Inc... 860 229-1812
   60 Westfield Dr Plantsville (06479) *(G-2795)*

Sign Services Inc... 207 296-2400
   512 Wolfboro Rd Stetson (04488) *(G-5531)*

Sign Solutions, Portland *Also Called: Print-Mail of Maine Inc (G-5262)*

Sign Solutions Unlimited..................................... 781 537-6156
   30 6th Rd Woburn (01801) *(G-13665)*

Sign Stop, East Hampton *Also Called: Rokap Inc (G-965)*

Sign Tech, Chicopee *Also Called: Sign Techniques Inc (G-8061)*

Sign Techniques Inc.. 413 594-8240
   361 Chicopee St Chicopee (01013) *(G-8061)*

Sign-A-Rama, Danbury *Also Called: Priority One Inc (G-800)*

Sign-A-Rama, Braintree *Also Called: Speedy Sign-A-Rama USA (G-7203)*

Sign-A-Rama, Kingston *Also Called: Titus & Bean Graphics Inc (G-9513)*

Sign-A-Rama, Southborough *Also Called: Newman Enterprises Inc (G-11999)*

Sign-A-Rama, Worcester *Also Called: Signarama (G-13801)*

Signage US, Meriden *Also Called: Shiner Signs Inc (G-1697)*

Signal Communications Corp................................ 781 933-0998
   4 Wheeling Ave Woburn (01801) *(G-13666)*

Signal Integrity Journal, Norwood *Also Called: Horizon House Publications Inc (G-11177)*

Signalquest LLC... 603 448-6266
   10 Water St Lebanon (03766) *(G-14698)*

Signamerica, Berlin *Also Called: National Sign Corporation (G-77)*

Signarama... 508 459-9731
   545 Sw Cutoff Ste A Worcester (01607) *(G-13801)*

Signarama Saco, Saco *Also Called: H4 Holdings LLC (G-5369)*

Signature Cable Mfg Tech Inc.............................. 401 383-1008
   14 Suez St Cranston (02920) *(G-15910)*

Signature Engrv Systems Inc............................... 413 533-7500
   120 Whiting Farms Rd Holyoke (01040) *(G-9281)*

Signature Graphics & Signs, Weymouth *Also Called: Innovative Media Group Inc (G-13327)*

Signature Press & Blue Prtg, Hooksett *Also Called: RB Graphics Inc (G-14473)*

Signature Printing Inc....................................... 401 438-1200
   5 Almeida Ave East Providence (02914) *(G-16044)*

Signet Products Corporation............................... 650 592-3575
   521 Mount Hope St North Attleboro (02760) *(G-10887)*

Signify North America Corp................................. 617 423-9999
   10 Milk St Boston (02108) *(G-7036)*

Signify North America Corp................................. 508 679-8131
   300 Burlington Woods Dr Fl 4 Burlington (01803) *(G-7428)*

Signify North America Corp................................. 603 645-6061
   386 Commercial St Manchester (03101) *(G-14929)*

Signity Americas, Cranston *Also Called: Swarovski North America Ltd (G-15915)*

Signode Industrial Group LLC.............................. 401 438-5203
   50 Taylor Dr Rumford (02916) *(G-16676)*

Signs By J Inc... 617 825-9855
   100 Tenean St Boston (02122) *(G-7037)*

Signs Now New Hampshire, Pelham *Also Called: Ink Outside Box Incorporated* **(G-15290)**	
Signs On Demand Usa LLC..	860 346-1720
777 Laurel Grove Rd Middletown (06457) **(G-1780)**	
Signs Plus Inc **(PA)**...	**860 653-0547**
3 Turkey Hills Rd East Granby (06026) **(G-951)**	
Signs To Go Inc..	781 808-3153
400 W Cummings Park Ste 1975 Woburn (01801) **(G-13667)**	
Signworks Group, Watertown *Also Called: Signworks Group Inc* **(G-12907)**	
Signworks Group Inc...	617 924-0292
60 Arsenal St Ste 2 Watertown (02472) **(G-12907)**	
Sigtech, Providence *Also Called: Cambridge Signal Tech Inc* **(G-16493)**	
Sihl, Fiskeville *Also Called: Arkwright Advanced Coating Inc* **(G-16053)**	
Sikorsky, Stratford *Also Called: Sikorsky Aircraft Corporation* **(G-3571)**	
Sikorsky Aircraft Corporation..	203 384-7532
1201 South Ave Bridgeport (06604) **(G-372)**	
Sikorsky Aircraft Corporation..	203 386-7861
1 Far Mill Xing Shelton (06484) **(G-3062)**	
Sikorsky Aircraft Corporation..	203 386-4000
33 Platt Rd Shelton (06484) **(G-3063)**	
Sikorsky Aircraft Corporation **(HQ)**.......................................	**203 386-4000**
6900 Main St Stratford (06614) **(G-3571)**	
Sikorsky Aircraft Corporation..	203 386-4000
1825 Main St Stratford (06615) **(G-3572)**	
Sikorsky Aircraft Corporation..	203 380-3142
3191 Broadbridge Ave Stratford (06614) **(G-3573)**	
Sikorsky Aircraft Corporation..	203 386-7794
124 Quarry Rd Trumbull (06611) **(G-3733)**	
Sikorsky Commercial, Trumbull *Also Called: Helicopter Support Inc* **(G-3721)**	
Sikorsky Export Corporation..	203 386-4000
6900 Main St Stratford (06614) **(G-3574)**	
Silex Microsystems Inc...	617 834-7197
9 Hamilton Pl Ste 300 Boston (02108) **(G-7038)**	
Silgan, Deep River *Also Called: Silgan Plastics LLC* **(G-882)**	
Silgan, Stamford *Also Called: Silgan Containers Corporation* **(G-3458)**	
Silgan Closures Intl Holdg Co..	203 975-7110
4 Landmark Sq Stamford (06901) **(G-3457)**	
Silgan Containers Corporation...	203 975-7110
4 Landmark Sq Stamford (06901) **(G-3458)**	
Silgan Dispensing...	860 283-2025
669 Prospect St Torrington (06790) **(G-3696)**	
Silgan Dspnsing Systems Cvit A...	860 274-6791
60 Electric Ave Thomaston (06787) **(G-3629)**	
Silgan Dspnsing Systems Sltrsv **(DH)**...................................	**401 767-2400**
110 Graham Dr Slatersville (02876) **(G-16683)**	
Silgan Dspnsing Systems Thmsto...	860 283-2000
60 Electric Ave Thomaston (06787) **(G-3630)**	
Silgan Holdings Inc **(PA)**..	**203 975-7110**
4 Landmark Sq Ste 400 Stamford (06901) **(G-3459)**	
Silgan Plastics LLC..	860 526-6300
38 Bridge St Deep River (06417) **(G-882)**	
Silgan White Cap Corporation...	630 515-8383
4 Landmark Sq Ste 400 Stamford (06901) **(G-3460)**	
Silicon Integration Inc...	203 876-2844
241 Research Dr Ste 9 Milford (06460) **(G-1885)**	
Silicon Transistor Corporation...	978 256-3321
27 Katrina Rd Chelmsford (01824) **(G-7957)**	
Silk Technologies Inc...	877 982-2555
75 2nd Ave Ste 620 Needham Heights (02494) **(G-10557)**	
Sillycow Farms Llc..	802 429-2920
293 Industrial Park Wells River (05081) **(G-17688)**	
Silpro LLC **(PA)**..	**978 772-4444**
2 New England Way Ayer (01432) **(G-6196)**	
Silva Jewelers of Osterville...	508 428-2872
1112 Main St Ste 1 Osterville (02655) **(G-11246)**	
Silver Bear Distillery LLC..	413 242-4892
63 Flansburg Ave Dalton (01226) **(G-8154)**	
Silver City, Taunton *Also Called: Silver City Aluminum Corp* **(G-12367)**	
Silver City Aluminum Corp..	508 824-8631
704 W Water St Taunton (02780) **(G-12367)**	
Silver City Manufacturing, Meriden *Also Called: Silver City Manufacturing LLC* **(G-1698)**	

Silver City Manufacturing LLC...	203 238-0027
85 Tremont St Ste 5 Meriden (06450) **(G-1698)**	
Silver Greenfield Inc..	413 774-2774
298 Federal St Greenfield (01301) **(G-8999)**	
Silver Leaf Books LLC..	781 799-6609
13 Temi Rd Holliston (01746) **(G-9229)**	
Silver Screen Design Inc..	413 773-1692
324 Wells St Ste 3 Greenfield (01301) **(G-9000)**	
Silver Sweet Candies Co, Lawrence *Also Called: Silver Sweet Products Co* **(G-9596)**	
Silver Sweet Products Co..	978 688-0474
522 Essex St Lawrence (01840) **(G-9596)**	
Silverlining Holding Corp **(PA)**...	**617 986-4600**
368 Hillside Ave Bsmt Needham (02494) **(G-10522)**	
Silverside Detectors Inc...	617 684-5925
117 Beaver St Waltham (02452) **(G-12779)**	
Silverthread Inc..	800 674-9366
1 Broadway Ste 14 Cambridge (02142) **(G-7715)**	
Silvex Incorporated...	207 761-0392
45 Thomas Dr Westbrook (04092) **(G-5650)**	
Simbex LLC...	603 448-2367
10 Water St Ste 410 Lebanon (03766) **(G-14699)**	
Simfer Precision Machine Co..	978 667-1138
42 Manning Rd Billerica (01821) **(G-6482)**	
Similarweb Inc...	800 540-1086
800 District Ave Ste 120 Burlington (01803) **(G-7429)**	
Simkins Industries Inc..	203 787-7171
260 East St New Haven (06511) **(G-2199)**	
Simmonds Precision Pdts Inc...	203 797-5000
100 Wooster Hts Danbury (06810) **(G-818)**	
Simmonds Precision Pdts Inc...	802 877-2911
100 Panton Rd Vergennes (05491) **(G-17660)**	
Simmonds Precision Products **(DH)**.......................................	**802 877-4000**
100 Panton Rd Vergennes (05491) **(G-17661)**	
Simon & Schuster Inc..	617 492-1220
10 Fawcett St Ste 4 Cambridge (02138) **(G-7716)**	
SIMON & SCHUSTER, INC., Cambridge *Also Called: Simon & Schuster Inc* **(G-7716)**	
Simon Holding, Leominster *Also Called: Simonds Saw LLC* **(G-9704)**	
Simon Pearce (us) Inc...	802 295-2711
Main Street Quechee (05059) **(G-17463)**	
Simon Pearce (us) Inc **(PA)**..	**802 674-6280**
109 Park Rd Windsor (05089) **(G-17762)**	
Simon Pearce Glass and Pottery, Windsor *Also Called: Simon Pearce (us) Inc* **(G-17762)**	
Simon Pearce PA, Windsor *Also Called: Simon Pearce US Inc* **(G-17763)**	
SIMON PEARCE U.S., INC., Boston *Also Called: Simon Pearce US Inc* **(G-7039)**	
Simon Pearce US Inc...	617 450-8388
115 Newbury St Ste 1 Boston (02116) **(G-7039)**	
Simon Pearce US Inc...	802 674-6280
109 Park Rd Windsor (05089) **(G-17763)**	
Simon's Stamps, Turners Falls *Also Called: Simons Stamps Inc* **(G-12455)**	
Simonds Industries Intl...	978 424-0100
135 Intervale Rd Fitchburg (01420) **(G-8674)**	
Simonds International LLC **(HQ)**...	**978 424-0100**
135 Intervale Rd Fitchburg (01420) **(G-8675)**	
Simonds Saw - Louisville, Leominster *Also Called: Simonds Saw LLC* **(G-9703)**	
Simonds Saw LLC..	800 343-1616
435 Lancaster St Leominster (01453) **(G-9703)**	
Simonds Saw LLC **(PA)**...	**800 343-1616**
435 Lancaster St Ste 211 Leominster (01453) **(G-9704)**	
Simoniz USA Inc **(PA)**...	**860 646-0172**
201 Boston Tpke Bolton (06043) **(G-223)**	
Simons Stamps Inc...	413 863-6800
320 Avenue A Turners Falls (01376) **(G-12455)**	
Simpatico Software Systems Inc...	401 246-1358
15 Blanding Ave Barrington (02806) **(G-15750)**	
Simplex Time Recorder LLC **(DH)** 50 Technology Dr Westminster (01441) **(G-13278)**	
Simply Birkenstock, Concord *Also Called: Simply Footwear Utah LLC* **(G-14157)**	
Simply Footwear Utah LLC..	603 715-2259
31 N Main St Concord (03301) **(G-14157)**	
Simply Safer Products LLC..	401 474-4957
69 Tingley St Providence (02903) **(G-16611)**	

ALPHABETIC

Simpson Auto & Truck Supply, Lawrence *Also Called: Simpsons Inc of Lawrence* **(G-9597)**

Simpson Cabinetry, Essex Junction *Also Called: Catamount North Cabinetry LLC* **(G-17230)**

Simpson Spring Corp, South Easton *Also Called: Easton Springs Corporation* **(G-11942)**

Simpson Strong-Tie Company Inc.............................. 860 741-8923
  7 Pearson Way Enfield (06082) *(G-1152)*

Simpsons Inc of Lawrence.. 978 683-2417
  26 International Way Lawrence (01843) *(G-9597)*

Sims Portex Inc.. 603 352-3812
  10 Bowman Dr Keene (03431) *(G-14619)*

Simsbury Precision Pdts Inc..................................... 860 658-6909
  11 Herman Dr Ste C Simsbury (06070) *(G-3097)*

Simsoft Corp.. 508 366-5451
  1 Butterfield Dr Westborough (01581) *(G-13136)*

Simson Corporation.. 203 265-9882
  50 N Plains Industrial Rd Wallingford (06492) *(G-3848)*

Simulconsult Inc.. 617 566-5383
  27 Crafts Rd Ste 101 Chestnut Hill (02467) *(G-8001)*

Simunition Operations, Avon *Also Called: General Dynamics Ordnance* **(G-25)**

Sinauer Associates Inc.. 413 549-4300
  23 Plumtree Rd Sunderland (01375) *(G-12275)*

Sinclair Manufacturing Co LLC................................. 508 222-7440
  12 S Worcester St Norton (02766) *(G-11135)*

Singer Company Inc... 860 439-1234
  18a Industrial Dr Waterford (06385) *(G-3995)*

Singulrity Elctrnic Systems In.................................. 603 430-6000
  300 Heritage Ave Unit 2 Portsmouth (03801) *(G-15437)*

Sinicon Plastics Inc... 413 684-5290
  455 Housatonic St Dalton (01226) *(G-8155)*

Sionyx LLC **(PA)**.. **978 922-0684**
  100 Cummings Ctr Ste 303b Beverly (01915) *(G-6384)*

Sir Speedy.. 781 848-0990
  529 Washington St Braintree (02184) *(G-7202)*

Sir Speedy.. 401 351-7400
  50 Nashua St Providence (02904) *(G-16612)*

Sir Speedy, Bloomfield *Also Called: Kool Ink LLC* **(G-186)**

Sir Speedy, Boston *Also Called: Massachusetts Repro Ltd* **(G-6876)**

Sir Speedy, Lexington *Also Called: Lexington Graphics Inc* **(G-9758)**

Sir Speedy, Marlborough *Also Called: Linmel Associates Inc* **(G-10180)**

Sir Speedy, Orleans *Also Called: W S Walcott Inc* **(G-11244)**

Sir Speedy, Springfield *Also Called: Graphic Excellence LLC* **(G-12096)**

Sir Speedy, Waltham *Also Called: Descal Inc* **(G-12651)**

Sir Speedy, Portsmouth *Also Called: Southport Management Group LLC* **(G-15438)**

Sir Speedy, Cranston *Also Called: Sir Speedy Printing Inc* **(G-15911)**

Sir Speedy, Providence *Also Called: Sir Speedy* **(G-16612)**

Sir Speedy Printing Inc.. 401 781-5650
  969 Park Ave Cranston (02910) *(G-15911)*

Sira Naturals Inc... 508 422-0145
  13 Commercial Way Milford (01757) *(G-10419)*

Siren Marine Inc.. 401 619-4774
  221 3rd St Ste 200 Newport (02840) *(G-16224)*

Siri Manufacturing Co Inc.. 860 236-5901
  90 Wauregan Rd Danielson (06239) *(G-842)*

Siri Wire Co... 860 774-0607
  90 Wauregan Rd Danielson (06239) *(G-843)*

Sirois Tool Company Inc **(PA)**................................ **860 828-5327**
  169 White Oak Dr Berlin (06037) *(G-85)*

Sirtex, Woburn *Also Called: Sirtex Medical US Holdings Inc* **(G-13668)**

Sirtex Medical US Holdings Inc................................ 888 474-7839
  300 Unicorn Park Dr Woburn (01801) *(G-13668)*

SIS Ergo, Londonderry *Also Called: SIS-USA Inc* **(G-14784)**

SIS-USA Inc.. 603 432-4495
  55 Wentworth Ave Londonderry (03053) *(G-14784)*

Sisson Engineering Corp.. 413 498-2840
  450 W River St Orange (01364) *(G-11234)*

Sisters Salsa Inc.. 207 374-2170
  689 Hinckley Ridge Rd Blue Hill (04614) *(G-4596)*

Six One Cmmodities US Trdg LLC............................ 203 409-2079
  1 Dock St Ste 412 Stamford (06902) *(G-3461)*

Sixmil Holdings Inc **(PA)**....................................... **203 708-8900**
  52 Harbor View Ave Stamford (06902) *(G-3462)*

Sjd Tech Inc.. 203 269-9500
  320 Barnes Rd Wallingford (06492) *(G-3849)*

Sjm Properties... 860 979-0060
  164 Maple St Ellington (06029) *(G-1115)*

Sjogren Industries Inc.. 508 987-3206
  982 Southbridge St Worcester (01610) *(G-13802)*

Skaff Cryogenics Inc.. 603 775-0350
  48 Pine Rd Brentwood (03833) *(G-14029)*

Skelmir LLC... 617 625-1551
  81 Park Ave Arlington (02476) *(G-5947)*

Skew Products Incorporated..................................... 508 580-5800
  4 Bert Dr Ste 6 West Bridgewater (02379) *(G-12980)*

Skeyetrac LLC... 603 898-8000
  70 N Broadway Salem (03079) *(G-15562)*

SKF... 207 454-8078
  35 Sandy Beach Ln Charlotte (04666) *(G-4686)*

SKF Specialty Balls.. 860 379-8511
  149 Colebrook River Rd Winsted (06098) *(G-4355)*

SKF USA Inc.. 860 379-8511
  149 Colebrook River Rd Winsted (06098) *(G-4356)*

Skg Associates Inc.. 781 878-7250
  59 Mcdonald St Dedham (02026) *(G-8250)*

Skico Manufacturing, Hamden *Also Called: Skico Manufacturing Co LLC* **(G-1455)**

Skico Manufacturing Co LLC.................................... 203 230-1305
  3 Industrial Cir Hamden (06517) *(G-1455)*

Skidmore Co, Randolph *Also Called: Vent-Rite Valve Corp* **(G-11578)**

Skillcraft Machine Tool Co.. 860 953-1246
  255 Nutmeg Rd S South Windsor (06074) *(G-3180)*

Skillsoft (US) LLC **(DH)**.. **603 324-3000**
  300 Innovative Way Ste 201 Nashua (03062) *(G-15167)*

Skillsoft Corp.. 603 889-8834
  220 Daniel Webster Hwy Nashua (03060) *(G-15168)*

Skillsoft Ltd.. 603 324-3000
  300 Innovative Way Ste 201 Nashua (03062) *(G-15169)*

Skin & Co North America LLC................................... 888 444-9971
  135 Front Ave West Haven (06516) *(G-4126)*

Skin Catering Inc... 413 349-8199
  1500 Main St., Ste 220 Springfield (01115) *(G-12128)*

Skineez Skincarewear, Sudbury *Also Called: Cause For Change LLC* **(G-12262)**

Skowhegan Machine, Skowhegan *Also Called: Howard P Fairfield LLC* **(G-5468)**

Skowhegan Press, Skowhegan *Also Called: Bromar* **(G-5463)**

Skull Kingdom Entrmt LLC....................................... 262 804-8193
  4e Flintlock Rd Ledyard (06339) *(G-1553)*

Skurge of Sea LLC.. 860 887-7679
  11 Barnsider Ln Norwich (06360) *(G-2617)*

Sky & Telescope, Cambridge *Also Called: Sky Publishing Corporation* **(G-7717)**

Sky Computers Inc... 978 250-2420
  27 Industrial Ave Unit 1 Chelmsford (01824) *(G-7958)*

Sky Publishing Corporation...................................... 617 864-7360
  90 Sherman St Ste D Cambridge (02140) *(G-7717)*

Skyline Exhibits Graphics Inc................................... 860 635-2400
  362 Industrial Park Rd Ste 6 Middletown (06457) *(G-1781)*

Skyline Quarry LLC.. 860 875-3580
  110 Conklin Rd Stafford Springs (06076) *(G-3259)*

Skyray Instrument Inc.. 617 202-3879
  95 Mill St Stoughton (02072) *(G-12237)*

Skytrans Mfg LLC.. 802 230-7783
  106 Burnham Intervale Rd Contoocook (03229) *(G-14175)*

Skyworks Luxembourg S.A.R.L., Woburn *Also Called: Skyworks Solutions Inc* **(G-13669)**

Skyworks Solutions Inc.. 978 327-6850
  300 Federal St # 100 Andover (01810) *(G-5921)*

Skyworks Solutions Inc.. 781 935-5150
  20 Sylvan Rd Woburn (01801) *(G-13669)*

SL 301b LLC... 888 315-9598
  301 Binney St Cambridge (02142) *(G-7718)*

SL Chasse Steel, Hudson *Also Called: S L Chasse Welding & Fabg Inc* **(G-14543)**

Slab LLC... 207 245-3088
  25 Preble St Portland (04101) *(G-5273)*

Slab Sicilian Street Food, Portland *Also Called: Slab LLC* **(G-5273)**

Slate Corporation.. 603 234-5943
  236 Rockingham Rd Auburn (03032) *(G-13912)*

Slattery Bros Inc.. 617 269-3025
697 High St Unit 460 Westwood (02090) *(G-13318)*

Sleep Management Solutions LLC **(DH)**............ **888 497-5337**
20 Church St Ste 900 Hartford (06103) *(G-1508)*

Sleepnet Corp.. 603 758-6600
5 Merrill Industrial Dr Hampton (03842) *(G-14412)*

Slesar Bros Brewing Co Inc.............................. 978 745-2337
90 Canal St Boston (02114) *(G-7040)*

Slesar Bros Brewing Co Inc.............................. 781 749-2337
18 Shipyard Dr Hingham (02043) *(G-9160)*

Slickbar Products Corp..................................... 203 888-7700
18 Beach St Seymour (06483) *(G-2969)*

Slideways Inc.. 508 854-0799
705 Plantation St Ste 1 Worcester (01605) *(G-13803)*

Slinky Stainless Steel....................................... 603 673-1104
20 Mont Vernon St Milford (03055) *(G-15038)*

Sloan MGT Review, Cambridge *Also Called: Massachusetts Institute Tech* *(G-7638)*

Sloan Valve Company.. 617 796-9001
19 Connector Rd Ste 4 Andover (01810) *(G-5922)*

Slogic Holding Corp **(PA)**................................ **203 966-2800**
36 Grove St New Canaan (06840) *(G-2086)*

Slt Logic, Boston *Also Called: Coredge Networks Inc* *(G-6671)*

SM Heat Treating, North Attleboro *Also Called: S M Engineering Co Inc* *(G-10886)*

Small Batch Organics LLC.................................. 802 367-1054
53b Manchester Valley Rd Manchester Center (05255) *(G-17331)*

Small Plnet Communications Inc......................... 978 794-2201
15 Union St Ste 5 Lawrence (01840) *(G-9598)*

Small Water Systems Svcs LLC.......................... 978 486-1008
80 Taylor St Littleton (01460) *(G-9838)*

Smart Modular Technologies Inc......................... 978 221-3513
2 Highwood Dr Ste 101 Tewksbury (01876) *(G-12416)*

Smart Software Inc.. 617 489-2743
4 Hill Rd Ste 2 Belmont (02478) *(G-6312)*

Smart Source LLC.. 781 890-0110
280 Bear Hill Rd Waltham (02451) *(G-12780)*

Smartco Services LLC....................................... 508 880-0816
200 Myles Standish Blvd Ste A Taunton (02780) *(G-12368)*

Smarter Living, Boston *Also Called: Smarter Travel Media LLC* *(G-7041)*

Smarter Travel Media LLC.................................. 617 886-5555
226 Causeway St Ste 3 Boston (02114) *(G-7041)*

Smartfan, Littleton *Also Called: Control Resources Inc* *(G-9806)*

Smartlabs, Cambridge *Also Called: SL 301b LLC* *(G-7718)*

Smartlipo, Westford *Also Called: Cynosure LLC* *(G-13233)*

Smartpak, Plymouth *Also Called: Smartpak Equine LLC* *(G-11478)*

Smartpak Equine LLC **(DH)**............................ **774 773-1100**
40 Grissom Rd Ste 500 Plymouth (02360) *(G-11478)*

Smartpay Solutions LLC.................................... 860 986-7659
470 James St Ste 7 New Haven (06513) *(G-2200)*

Smartpro, Saint Johnsbury *Also Called: 4smartpro LLC* *(G-17537)*

Smartware Products, Leominster *Also Called: F & M Tool & Plastics Inc* *(G-9663)*

SMC Aerospace, Laconia *Also Called: Screw-Matic Corporation* *(G-14668)*

SMC Corporation of America.............................. 978 767-2328
99 Rosewood Dr Ste 180 Danvers (01923) *(G-8220)*

SMC Ltd... 978 422-6800
18 Independence Dr Devens (01434) *(G-8287)*

Smcc, Stratford *Also Called: Schweizer Aircraft Corp* *(G-3570)*

Sme Ltd... 617 842-4682
14 Atkins St Dedham (02026) *(G-8251)*

SMI Podwer Coating, Amesbury *Also Called: Specialty Manufacturing Inc* *(G-5853)*

Smiley's Dairy, Portland *Also Called: Oakhurst Dairy* *(G-5253)*

Smith & Nephew Inc... 978 749-1000
150 Minuteman Rd Andover (01810) *(G-5923)*

Smith & Nephew Endoscopy Inc......................... 978 749-1000
150 Minuteman Rd Andover (01810) *(G-5924)*

Smith & Town Printers LLC................................ 603 752-2150
42 Main St Berlin (03570) *(G-13986)*

Smith & Wesson Brands Inc **(PA)**.................... **800 331-0852**
2100 Roosevelt Ave Springfield (01104) *(G-12129)*

Smith Hill of Delaware Inc................................. 860 767-7502
34 Plains Rd Essex (06426) *(G-1171)*

Smith Microwave Company, North Billerica *Also Called: Radio Waves Inc* *(G-10946)*

Smithfamily1938 LLC.. 424 341-8876
14 Hazard Ave Ste 23 Enfield (06082) *(G-1153)*

Smithfield Direct LLC.. 413 781-5620
20 Carando Dr Springfield (01104) *(G-12130)*

Smithfield Foods Inc... 413 781-5620
20 Carando Dr Springfield (01104) *(G-12131)*

Smiths Interconnect Inc.................................... 413 582-9620
29 Industrial Dr E Northampton (01060) *(G-11080)*

Smiths Intrcnnect Americas Inc.......................... 978 568-0451
16 Brent Dr Hudson (01749) *(G-9413)*

Smiths Medical.. 860 413-3230
133 Hartford Ave Ste 3 East Granby (06026) *(G-952)*

Smiths Medical Asd Inc..................................... 860 621-9111
201 W Queen St Southington (06489) *(G-3232)*

Smiths Medical Asd Inc..................................... 603 352-3812
Production Ave Keene (03431) *(G-14620)*

Smiths Medical Asd Inc..................................... 603 352-3812
10 Bowman Dr Keene (03431) *(G-14621)*

Smiths Tblar Systms-Lconia Inc.......................... 603 524-2064
93 Lexington Dr Laconia (03246) *(G-14670)*

Smj Metal Company Inc..................................... 413 586-3535
36 Smith St Northampton (01060) *(G-11081)*

Sml Inc.. 207 784-2961
777 Main St Lewiston (04240) *(G-4993)*

Smm New England Corporation........................... 203 777-7445
808 Washington Ave New Haven (06519) *(G-2201)*

Smokeloudz LLC **(PA)**.................................. **203 909-3556**
1367 Hanover Ave Apt 801 Meriden (06451) *(G-1699)*

Smokey Mountain Chew Inc............................... 203 304-9200
365 Post Rd Darien (06820) *(G-855)*

Smoothie Bus LLC... 603 303-7353
85 Faltin Dr Ste 35 Manchester (03103) *(G-14930)*

Smoothie King... 860 574-9382
106 Boston Post Rd Ste A Waterford (06385) *(G-3996)*

Smoothie King, Waterford *Also Called: Smoothie King* *(G-3996)*

SMP DBA A BAND FOR BROTHERS, Attleboro *Also Called: Sweet Metal Finishing Inc* *(G-6068)*

SMR Metal Technology LLC................................ 860 291-8259
524 Sullivan Ave Ste 15 South Windsor (06074) *(G-3181)*

Smt International LLC.. 860 526-8300
500 Main St Ste 18 Deep River (06417) *(G-883)*

Smtc Manufacturing.. 508 207-6355
101 Billerica Ave Bldg 7 North Billerica (01862) *(G-10956)*

Smudge Ink Incorporated.................................. 617 242-8228
50 Terminal St Ste 2 Charlestown (02129) *(G-7882)*

Smugglers Notch Distillery LLC........................... 860 670-1838
5087 Route 15 Jeffersonville (05464) *(G-17307)*

Smurfit-Stone, Concord *Also Called: Graphic Packaging Intl LLC* *(G-14133)*

Smuttynose Brewing Company, Hampton *Also Called: Finestkind Brewing LLC* *(G-14402)*

Smuttynose Brewing Company Inc....................... 603 436-4026
105 Towle Farm Rd Hampton (03842) *(G-14413)*

Smyth Companies LLC....................................... 800 776-1201
271 Ballardvale St Wilmington (01887) *(G-13453)*

Snackergy, Fairfax *Also Called: Bariatrix Nutrition Corp* *(G-17255)*

Snap Site Studios LLC....................................... 603 782-3395
55 South Commercial St Ste 99 Manchester (03101) *(G-14931)*

Snapple Juices, Bridgeport *Also Called: B & E Juices Inc* *(G-299)*

Snf Finishing LLC.. 603 355-3903
32 Optical Ave Keene (03431) *(G-14622)*

Snow & Stars Corporation................................. 401 421-4134
18 Delaine St Providence (02909) *(G-16613)*

Snow Economics Inc... 508 655-3232
15 Mercer Rd Natick (01760) *(G-10498)*

Snow Farm Winery... 802 372-9463
190 W Shore Rd South Hero (05486) *(G-17610)*

Snow Goose 2019 Inc....................................... 203 237-3444
235 Cheshire Rd Meriden (06451) *(G-1700)*

Snow Mountain Jwly & Graphics, Wilmington *Also Called: John McLeod Ltd* *(G-17755)*

Snow Plowing / Landscaping, Westerly *Also Called: Northeast Ldscpg Tree Svcs Inc* *(G-16941)*

Snow-Nbstedt Pwr Transmissions, Manchester *Also Called: Allard Nazarian Group Inc* *(G-14809)*

Snowbound Software Corporation............................ 617 607-2000
   128 1st Ave Needham (02494) *(G-10523)*

Snowman Group.. 207 848-7300
   1 Printers Dr Hermon (04401) *(G-4889)*

Snowman's Printing & Stamps, Hermon *Also Called: Armstrong Family Inds Inc (G-4880)*

Snowshoe Pond Mple Sgrwrks LLC........................... 802 777-9676
   431 Barnes Rd Enosburg Falls (05450) *(G-17224)*

Snyder Machine Co Inc.. 978 356-4488
   30 Avery St Ipswich (01938) *(G-9497)*

Snyk Inc **(HQ)**.. **786 506-2615**
   100 Summer St Fl 7 Boston (02110) *(G-7042)*

So. Wallingford Limestone, Colchester *Also Called: Shelburne Limestone Corp (G-17203)*

Soapstone Media Inc... 860 749-0455
   92 West Rd Ellington (06029) *(G-1116)*

Soapstone Networks Inc... 617 719-3897
   15 New England Executive Park Burlington (01803) *(G-7430)*

Sobi Inc **(HQ)**... **781 786-7370**
   77 4th Ave Fl 3 Waltham (02451) *(G-12781)*

Society of St John The Evang.................................... 617 876-3037
   980 Memorial Dr Cambridge (02138) *(G-7719)*

Society Plastics Engineers Inc **(PA)**......................... **203 740-5422**
   83 Wooster Hts Ste 125 Danbury (06810) *(G-819)*

Sock Shack.. 207 805-1348
   564 Congress St Portland (04101) *(G-5274)*

Socomec Inc **(DH)**.. **617 245-0447**
   9 Galen St Ste 120 Watertown (02472) *(G-12908)*

Sodexo Abbott Bioresearch, Worcester *Also Called: Abbott Laboratories (G-13696)*

SOF Holdings Inc.. 802 244-7644
   40 Foundry St Ste 1a Waterbury (05676) *(G-17677)*

Sofnet Technology Inc... 857 272-2568
   5 North St Newton (02460) *(G-10785)*

Soft Robotics Inc.. 617 391-0612
   32 Crosby Dr Ste 101 Bedford (01730) *(G-6269)*

Soft Serve CT LLC.. 203 367-3000
   325 Cherry St Bridgeport (06605) *(G-373)*

Soft-As-A-grape Inc **(PA)**.. **508 295-9900**
   328 Marion Rd Wareham (02571) *(G-12844)*

Soft10 Inc.. 857 263-7375
   83 Chestnut St Boston (02108) *(G-7043)*

Softech Inc **(HQ)**... **513 942-7100**
   1 Tara Blvd Ste 104 Nashua (03062) *(G-15170)*

Softinway Inc... 781 328-4310
   20 Mall Rd Ste 450 Burlington (01803) *(G-7431)*

Software Experts Inc... 978 692-5343
   4 Grey Fox Ln Westford (01886) *(G-13263)*

Software Outside Inc... 603 820-1994
   369 Summer St Peterborough (03458) *(G-15327)*

Sogle Property LLC... 802 849-7943
   189 Glenn Dr Cambridge (05444) *(G-17168)*

Sohre Turbomachinery, Florence *Also Called: Shaft Current Solutions Inc (G-8686)*

Soil Exploration Corp **(PA)**....................................... **978 840-0391**
   148 Pioneer Dr Leominster (01453) *(G-9705)*

Soitec Usa Inc **(HQ)**.. **978 531-2222**
   2 Blackburn Ctr Gloucester (01930) *(G-8958)*

Solais Lighting Inc.. 203 683-6222
   650 West Ave Stamford (06902) *(G-3463)*

Solar Five LLC... 781 301-7233
   420 Bedford St Ste 335 Lexington (02420) *(G-9776)*

Solar Seal Company, South Easton *Also Called: Sharoc Realty Inc (G-11953)*

Solar Seal of Connecticut, Hamden *Also Called: Insulpane Connecticut Inc (G-1432)*

Solar Source, Keene *Also Called: Keebowil Inc (G-14605)*

Solchroma Technologies Inc....................................... 401 829-0024
   12 Dunham Rd Ste 1 Billerica (01821) *(G-6483)*

Soldream Inc.. 860 871-6883
   129 Reservoir Rd Vernon Rockville (06066) *(G-3762)*

Soldream Spcial Process - Wldg................................. 860 858-5247
   203 Hartford Tpke Tolland (06084) *(G-3664)*

Sole Proprietorship, New Bedford *Also Called: Blue Fleet Welding Service (G-10572)*

Solect, Hopkinton *Also Called: Solect Energy Development LLC (G-9344)*

Solect Energy Development LLC **(PA)**....................... **508 598-3511**
   89 Hayden Rowe St Ste E Hopkinton (01748) *(G-9344)*

Solectria Renewables LLC... 978 683-9700
   360 Merrimack St Ste 9 Lawrence (01843) *(G-9599)*

Soleo Health Inc... 781 298-3427
   5 Shawmut Rd Ste 103 Canton (02021) *(G-7830)*

Soleras Advanced Coatings Ltd **(PA)**........................ **207 282-5699**
   589 Elm St Biddeford (04005) *(G-4588)*

Solico, West Hartford *Also Called: Sorenson Lighted Controls Inc (G-4081)*

Solid Biosciences, Charlestown *Also Called: Solid Biosciences Inc (G-7883)*

Solid Biosciences Inc **(PA)**...................................... **617 337-4680**
   500 Rutherford Ave Fl 3 Charlestown (02129) *(G-7883)*

Solid Earth Technologies Inc...................................... 603 882-5319
   3 Howe Dr Ste 3 Amherst (03031) *(G-13890)*

Solid State Heating, Westbrook *Also Called: Sshc Inc (G-4143)*

Solidenergy Systems LLC.. 617 972-3412
   35 Cabot Rd Woburn (01801) *(G-13670)*

Solidification Pdts Intl Inc.. 203 484-9494
   215 Village St Northford (06472) *(G-2455)*

Solidification Pdts Intl Inc.. 203 484-9494
   524 Forest Rd Northford (06472) *(G-2456)*

Solidification Products Intl, Northford *Also Called: Solidification Pdts Intl Inc (G-2455)*

Solidscape Inc... 603 424-0590
   316 Daniel Webster Hwy Merrimack (03054) *(G-15003)*

Solion, Walpole *Also Called: Medical Manager Pcn Inc (G-12568)*

Solla Eyelet Products, Watertown *Also Called: Solla Eyelet Products Inc (G-4030)*

Solla Eyelet Products Inc.. 860 274-5729
   50 Seemar Rd Watertown (06795) *(G-4030)*

Solon Ctr For RES & Publishig.................................... 207 319-4727
   8 Brook St Solon (04979) *(G-5482)*

Solon Manufacturing... 203 230-5300
   7 Grasso Ave North Haven (06473) *(G-2437)*

Solos Endoscopy, Boston *Also Called: Cyduct Diagnostics Inc (G-6682)*

Solusoft Inc... 978 375-6021
   300 Willow St North Andover (01845) *(G-10849)*

Solutek Corporation.. 617 445-5335
   94 Shirley St Boston (02119) *(G-7044)*

Solutia Inc... 734 676-4400
   730 Worcester St Indian Orchard (01151) *(G-9474)*

Solutia Inc... 413 788-6911
   730 Worcester St Springfield (01151) *(G-12132)*

Solvay.. 203 321-2292
   1937 W Main St Stamford (06902) *(G-3464)*

Solve Advisors Inc **(PA)**.. **646 699-5041**
   600 Summer St Ste 503 Stamford (06901) *(G-3465)*

Somalabs Inc... 802 355-3000
   308 Industrial Park Rd Milton (05468) *(G-17364)*

Somatex Inc.. 207 487-6141
   70 North Rd Detroit (04929) *(G-4725)*

Somerset Industries Inc.. 978 667-3355
   137 Phoenix Ave Lowell (01852) *(G-9924)*

Somerset Plastics Company Inc.................................. 860 635-1601
   454 Timber Ridge Rd Middletown (06457) *(G-1782)*

Somerville Live Poultry Co Inc.................................... 617 547-9191
   139 Newmarket Sq Boston (02118) *(G-7045)*

Somerville Office.. 617 776-0738
   344 Somerville Ave Somerville (02143) *(G-11897)*

Somerville Orna Ir Works Inc...................................... 617 666-8872
   7 George St Somerville (02145) *(G-11898)*

Somic America Inc.. 207 989-1759
   6 Baker Blvd Brewer (04412) *(G-4619)*

Somma Tool Company.. 203 753-2114
   109 Scott Rd Waterbury (06705) *(G-3970)*

Sonalysts Inc **(PA)**.. **860 442-4355**
   215 Parkway N Waterford (06385) *(G-3997)*

Sonare Winds, Maynard *Also Called: Verne Q Powell Flutes Inc (G-10265)*

Sonco Worldwide Inc... 401 406-3761
   450 Pavilion Ave Warwick (02888) *(G-16863)*

Sonesys LLC... 603 423-9000
   21 Continental Blvd Merrimack (03054) *(G-15004)*

Sonic Blue Aerospace Inc.. 207 776-2471
   80 Exchange St Ste 36 Portland (04101) *(G-5275)*

Sonic Corp.. 203 375-0063
   1 Research Dr Stratford (06615) *(G-3575)*

Sonic Manufacturing Co Inc.................... 603 882-1020
  35 Sagamore Park Rd Hudson (03051) *(G-14546)*

Sonicators, Newtown *Also Called: Qsonica LLC (G-2344)*

Sonicron Systems Corporation.................... 413 562-5218
  382 Southampton Rd Ste 102 Westfield (01085) *(G-13209)*

Sonics & Materials Inc (PA).................... 203 270-4600
  53 Church Hill Rd Newtown (06470) *(G-2347)*

Sonitek, Milford *Also Called: Sonitek Corporation (G-1886)*

Sonitek Corporation.................... 203 878-9321
  84 Research Dr Milford (06460) *(G-1886)*

Sonivie Inc.................... 857 415-4814
  50 Milk St Fl 16 Boston (02109) *(G-7046)*

Sonnax, Bellows Falls *Also Called: Sonnax Transmission Company (G-17032)*

Sonnax Industries Inc.................... 802 463-0240
  1 Automatic Dr Bellows Falls (05101) *(G-17031)*

Sonnax Transmission Company (DH).................... 802 463-9722
  2 Imtec Ln Bellows Falls (05101) *(G-17032)*

Sonoco Products Company.................... 413 536-4546
  200 S Water St Holyoke (01040) *(G-9282)*

Sonoco Prtective Solutions Inc.................... 860 928-7795
  29 Park Rd Putnam (06260) *(G-2875)*

Sonolite Plastics Corporation.................... 978 281-0662
  10 Fernwood Lake Ave Gloucester (01930) *(G-8959)*

Sonomedescalon, Stoneham *Also Called: Escalon Digital Solutions Inc (G-12178)*

Sonosystems N Schunk Amer Corp (DH).................... 978 658-9400
  250 Andover St Wilmington (01887) *(G-13454)*

Sophia Institute.................... 603 641-9344
  525 Greeley St Manchester (03102) *(G-14932)*

Sophya, Boston *Also Called: Sage Learning Inc (G-7020)*

Sorbus Inc.................... 203 481-2810
  20 Baldwin Dr Branford (06405) *(G-278)*

Sorenson Lighted Controls Inc (PA).................... 860 527-3092
  100 Shield St West Hartford (06110) *(G-4081)*

Sorrento Fine Woodwork LLC.................... 203 741-9263
  340 Quinnipiac St Bldg 43l Wallingford (06492) *(G-3850)*

SOS Group Inc.................... 978 496-7947
  529 Main St Ste 102 Boston (02129) *(G-7047)*

Soto Holdings Inc.................... 203 781-8020
  300 East St New Haven (06511) *(G-2202)*

Soucy Industries Inc (PA).................... 603 883-4500
  5 Dick Tracy Dr Pelham (03076) *(G-15297)*

Souhegan Management Corp (PA).................... 603 898-8868
  99 Faltin Dr Manchester (03103) *(G-14933)*

Souhegan Wood Products Inc.................... 603 654-2311
  10 Souhegan St Wilton (03086) *(G-15709)*

Sound Construction & Engrg Co.................... 860 242-2109
  522 Cottage Grove Rd Bldg H Bloomfield (06002) *(G-210)*

Sound Manufacturing Inc.................... 860 388-4466
  1 Williams Ln Old Saybrook (06475) *(G-2662)*

Sound Oasis Company, Marblehead *Also Called: Headwaters Inc (G-10087)*

Sound View Plastics LLC.................... 860 322-4139
  500 Main St Ste 25a Deep River (06417) *(G-884)*

Soundown Corporation (PA).................... 978 745-7000
  16 Broadway Salem (01970) *(G-11732)*

Soundview Paper Mills LLC (DH).................... 201 796-4000
  1 Sound Shore Dr Ste 203 Greenwich (06830) *(G-1352)*

Soundview Vermont Holdings LLC.................... 802 387-5571
  67 Kathan Meadow Rd East Dummerston (05346) *(G-17217)*

Source Inc (PA).................... 203 488-6400
  101 Fowler Rd North Branford (06471) *(G-2375)*

Source Code LLC (PA).................... 781 688-2248
  232 Vanderbilt Ave Norwood (02062) *(G-11209)*

Source Code Midco LLC (PA).................... 781 255-2022
  232 Vanderbilt Ave Norwood (02062) *(G-11210)*

Source International Corp.................... 800 722-0474
  17 Gilmore Dr Sutton (01590) *(G-12291)*

Sousa & Demayo, Attleboro Falls *Also Called: Cape House Realty Inc (G-6081)*

Sousa Corp.................... 860 523-9090
  565 Cedar St Newington (06111) *(G-2326)*

Sousa Signs LLC.................... 603 622-5067
  225 East Industrial Park Dr Manchester (03109) *(G-14934)*

South Boston Today.................... 617 268-4032
  396 W 4th St Boston (02127) *(G-7048)*

South Carolina Elastic, Cumberland *Also Called: Rhode Island Textile Company (G-15963)*

South County Independent, The, Wakefield *Also Called: South County Newspaper Inc (G-16743)*

South County Newspaper Inc.................... 401 789-6000
  10 High St Unit H Wakefield (02879) *(G-16743)*

South Hallow Spirits, North Truro *Also Called: Truro Vineyards Cape Cod LLC (G-11051)*

South Main Manchester Housing.................... 603 626-3034
  198 Hanover St Manchester (03104) *(G-14935)*

South Mountain Company Inc.................... 508 693-4850
  15 Red Arrow Rd West Tisbury (02575) *(G-13055)*

South Pier Fish Company Inc.................... 401 783-6611
  20 Walts Way Narragansett (02882) *(G-16196)*

South Poultney Slate.................... 802 287-9278
  376 York St Poultney (05764) *(G-17451)*

South Shore Manufacturing Inc.................... 781 447-9264
  162 Industrial Blvd Ste 2b Hanson (02341) *(G-9056)*

South Shore Meat, Brockton *Also Called: South Shore Packing Inc (G-7307)*

South Shore Meats, East Bridgewater *Also Called: Crocetti Oakdale Pkg Co Inc (G-8338)*

South Shore Millwork Inc.................... 508 226-5500
  7 Maple St Norton (02766) *(G-11136)*

South Shore Packing Inc.................... 508 941-0458
  12 Taylor Ave Brockton (02302) *(G-7307)*

South Windsor Golf Course LLC.................... 860 648-4653
  516 Griffin Rd South Windsor (06074) *(G-3182)*

Southborough Villager, Marlborough *Also Called: Gatehouse Media Mass I Inc (G-10151)*

Southbridge News, Southbridge *Also Called: Stonebridge Press Inc (G-12035)*

Southbridge Shtmtl Works Inc.................... 508 347-7800
  441 Main St Sturbridge (01566) *(G-12258)*

Southbridge Tool & Mfg Inc.................... 508 764-6819
  181 Southbridge Rd Dudley (01571) *(G-8324)*

Southbury Printing Centre Inc.................... 203 264-0102
  385 Main St S Southbury (06488) *(G-3198)*

Southeast Railing Co Inc.................... 781 828-7088
  901 Turnpike St Unit A Canton (02021) *(G-7831)*

Southeast Shellfish Inc.................... 508 273-0323
  22 Kendrick Rd Wareham (02571) *(G-12845)*

Southeastern Concrete Inc.................... 617 227-9000
  399 Elm St Kingston (02364) *(G-9511)*

Southeastern Concrete Inc.................... 781 848-9390
  611 Pleasant St Weymouth (02189) *(G-13335)*

Southeastern Container Inc.................... 603 324-1204
  36 Executive Dr Hudson (03051) *(G-14547)*

Southeastern Millwork Co Inc.................... 508 888-6038
  150 State Rd Sagamore Beach (02562) *(G-11698)*

Southeastern Millwork Co Inc.................... 508 888-6038
  150 State Rd Bourne (02532) *(G-7142)*

Southeastern Sand and Grav Inc.................... 781 413-6884
  27 Pine Hill Rd Kingston (02364) *(G-9512)*

Southern Almnum Intrmdte Hldin.................... 870 234-8660
  130 Main St New Canaan (06840) *(G-2087)*

Southern Brkshire Shppers Gide.................... 413 528-0095
  271 Main St Ste 4 Great Barrington (01230) *(G-8978)*

Southern Conn Newspapers Inc.................... 203 964-2200
  1055 Washington Blvd L Stamford (06901) *(G-3466)*

Southern Conn Pallet Co Inc.................... 203 265-1313
  346 Quinnipiac St Wallingford (06492) *(G-3851)*

Southern Diversified Pdts LLC.................... 917 306-4138
  5 2nd Ln Bethel (06801) *(G-134)*

Southern Maine Atv Club.................... 207 676-1152
  43 Mckinnon Ln North Berwick (03906) *(G-5113)*

Southern Maine Industries Corp.................... 207 856-7391
  68 Outlet Cove Rd Windham (04062) *(G-5669)*

Southern Neng Telecom Corp (HQ).................... 203 771-5200
  2 Science Park New Haven (06511) *(G-2203)*

Southern New England Wldg LLC.................... 401 822-0596
  7 Acorn St Coventry (02816) *(G-15821)*

Southern New Hampshire Univ.................... 603 629-4631
  2500 N River Rd Manchester (03106) *(G-14963)*

Southern RI Newspapers (HQ).................... 401 789-9744
  187 Main St Wakefield (02879) *(G-16744)*

A L P H A B E T I C

Southfield Carton, Concord *Also Called: Graphic Packaging Intl LLC (G-14134)*

Southington Metal Fabg Co.................................... 860 621-0149
  95 Corporate Dr Southington (06489) *(G-3233)*

Southington Tool & Mfg Corp................................. 860 276-0021
  300 Atwater St Plantsville (06479) *(G-2796)*

Southpack LLC... 860 224-2242
  1 Hartford Sq Ste 14w New Britain (06052) *(G-2061)*

Southport Management Group LLC........................... 603 433-4664
  738 Islington St 800 Portsmouth (03801) *(G-15438)*

Southport Printing Company, Portsmouth *Also Called: Spirit Advisory LLC (G-15439)*

Southside Media, Hartford *Also Called: Gamut Publishing (G-1482)*

Southstern Mtal Fbricators Inc.............................. 781 878-1505
  Air Station Industrial Park Rockland (02370) *(G-11661)*

Southwick, Haverhill *Also Called: Golden Fleece Mfg Group LLC (G-9098)*

Southwick & Meister Inc...................................... 203 237-0000
  1455 N Colony Rd Meriden (06450) *(G-1701)*

Southwick Clothing LLC, Haverhill *Also Called: Greenwich Triangle LLC (G-9099)*

Southworth, Falmouth *Also Called: Southworth Products Corp (G-4773)*

Southworth Company.. 413 789-1200
  265 Main St Agawam (01001) *(G-5807)*

Southworth Intl Group Inc **(PA)**......................... **207 878-0700**
  11 Gray Rd Falmouth (04105) *(G-4772)*

Southworth Products Corp **(HQ)**........................ **207 878-0700**
  11 Gray Rd Falmouth (04105) *(G-4773)*

Southworth Timberframes Inc................................ 603 788-2619
  273 Garland Rd Lancaster (03584) *(G-14679)*

Soyaz.. 207 453-4911
  7 Truss Ln Fairfield (04937) *(G-4766)*

Sp Machine Inc.. 978 562-2019
  526 Main St Hudson (01749) *(G-9414)*

Space Age Accessories Inc................................... 508 543-3661
  131 Morse St Foxboro (02035) *(G-8725)*

Space Age Americana, Foxboro *Also Called: Space Age Accessories Inc (G-8725)*

Space Age Electronics Inc **(PA)**....................... **800 486-1723**
  58 Chocksett Rd Sterling (01564) *(G-12171)*

Space Age Electronics Inc.................................... 978 652-5421
  283 Baldwinville Rd Templeton (01468) *(G-12382)*

Space Building Corp... 508 947-7277
  8 Harding St Ste 107 Lakeville (02347) *(G-9521)*

Space Electronics LLC.. 860 829-0001
  81 Fuller Way Berlin (06037) *(G-86)*

Space Optics Research Labs LLC............................ 978 250-8640
  15 Caron St Merrimack (03054) *(G-15005)*

Spaceclaim Corporation...................................... 978 482-2100
  150 Baker Avenue Ext Concord (01742) *(G-8133)*

Spantech Software Inc... 603 589-4044
  20 Trafalgar Sq Ste 422 Nashua (03063) *(G-15171)*

Spargo Machine Products Inc................................ 860 583-3925
  6 Gear Dr Terryville (06786) *(G-3609)*

Sparkcharge Inc... 866 906-2330
  455 Grand Union Blvd Pmb 5 Somerville (02145) *(G-11899)*

Sparkman & Stephens LLC **(PA)**........................ **401 847-5449**
  26 Washington Sq Ste 3 Newport (02840) *(G-16225)*

Spartech, Ossipee *Also Called: Tufpak Inc (G-15285)*

Spartech LLC.. 203 327-6010
  69 Southfield Ave Stamford (06902) *(G-3467)*

Spartech Polycast Inc... 203 327-6010
  70 Carlisle Pl Stamford (06902) *(G-3468)*

Sparton Beckwood, Plaistow *Also Called: Spartronics Plaistow Inc (G-15352)*

Sparton Beckwood LLC.. 603 382-3840
  27 Hale Spring Rd Plaistow (03865) *(G-15351)*

Sparton Technology Corp..................................... 603 880-3692
  8 Hampshire Dr Hudson (03051) *(G-14548)*

Spartronics Plaistow Inc...................................... 603 382-3840
  27 Hale Spring Rd Plaistow (03865) *(G-15352)*

Spatter Inc... 617 510-0498
  21 Randolph St Newton (02461) *(G-10786)*

Spaulding Composites Inc **(PA)**........................ **603 332-0555**
  55 Nadeau Dr Rochester (03867) *(G-15494)*

Spc Marcom Studio, North Springfield *Also Called: Springfield Printing Corp (G-17425)*

Spear Farms Inc... 207 832-4488
  14 Eugley Hill Rd Nobleboro (04555) *(G-5101)*

Spear Systems, Milford *Also Called: Gardoc Inc (G-15022)*

Spec Label Systems, Stratford *Also Called: Penmar Industries Inc (G-3565)*

Spec Plating Inc.. 203 366-3638
  740 Seaview Ave Bridgeport (06607) *(G-374)*

Spec Tools, West Bridgewater *Also Called: Skew Products Incorporated (G-12980)*

Special Hermetic Products Inc............................... 603 654-2002
  Riverview Mill 39 Souhegan St Wilton (03086) *(G-15710)*

Special Metals Corporation................................... 270 365-9551
  80 Hermon St Worcester (01610) *(G-13804)*

Special Projects Group LLC.................................. 603 391-9700
  221 Intervale Rd B2 Gilford (03249) *(G-14338)*

Specialized Coating Svcs LLC............................... 978 362-0346
  16 Esquire Rd Unit A North Billerica (01862) *(G-10957)*

Specialized Plating Inc....................................... 978 373-8030
  15 Ward Hill Ave Haverhill (01835) *(G-9131)*

Specialized Ppr Converting Inc............................. 978 632-5524
  21 Industrial Rowe Gardner (01440) *(G-8900)*

Specialized Turning Inc....................................... 978 977-0444
  147 Summit St Ste 7 Peabody (01960) *(G-11342)*

Specialty Cable Corp.. 203 265-7126
  2 Tower Dr Wallingford (06492) *(G-3852)*

Specialty Coating Systems................................... 603 883-3339
  10 Columbia Dr Ste 2 Amherst (03031) *(G-13891)*

Specialty Coating Systems Inc.............................. 203 283-0087
  98 Quirk Rd Milford (06460) *(G-1887)*

Specialty Components Inc.................................... 203 284-9112
  14 Village Ln Ste 1 Wallingford (06492) *(G-3853)*

Specialty Manufacturing Inc................................. 978 388-1601
  40 Water St Amesbury (01913) *(G-5853)*

Specialty Materials, Lowell *Also Called: Global Materials Inc (G-9880)*

Specialty Minerals Inc.. 860 824-5435
  30 Daisy Hill Rd Canaan (06018) *(G-557)*

Specialty Minerals Inc.. 207 897-4492
  Riley Rd Gate 15 Jay (04239) *(G-4916)*

Specialty Minerals Inc.. 413 743-0591
  260 Columbia St Adams (01220) *(G-5775)*

Specialty Printing LLC.. 860 654-1850
  15 Thompson Rd East Windsor (06088) *(G-1086)*

Specialty Printing LLC **(PA)**............................ **860 623-8870**
  123 Day Hill Rd Windsor (06095) *(G-4300)*

Specialty Restoration Inc..................................... 978 365-1700
  32 Greeley St Clinton (01510) *(G-8091)*

Specialty Shop Inc... 860 647-1477
  18 Sanrico Dr Manchester (06042) *(G-1637)*

Specialty Steel Treating Inc.................................. 860 653-0061
  12 Kripes Rd East Granby (06026) *(G-953)*

Specialty Tool Company USA LLC........................... 203 874-2009
  61 Erna Ave Milford (06461) *(G-1888)*

Specialty Truss Inc.. 603 886-5523
  12 Mercier Ln Nashua (03062) *(G-15172)*

Specialty Wholesale Sup Corp.............................. 978 632-1472
  101 Linus Allain Ave Gardner (01440) *(G-8901)*

Specialty Wire & Cord Sets Inc............................ 203 498-2932
  1 Gallagher Rd Hamden (06517) *(G-1456)*

Specrail, Hamden *Also Called: Porcelen Limited Connecticut LLC (G-1449)*

Specter Aerospace, Middleton *Also Called: Fgc Plasma Solutions Inc (G-10383)*

Spector Metal Products Co Inc.............................. 781 767-5600
  608 South St Holbrook (02343) *(G-9185)*

Spector Textile Products Inc **(PA)**.................... **978 688-3501**
  10 Embankment St Ste 1 Lawrence (01841) *(G-9600)*

Spectra Analysis Inc **(PA)**.............................. **508 281-6232**
  257 Simarano Dr Ste 100 Marlborough (01752) *(G-10211)*

Spectra Medical Devices LLC............................... 978 657-0889
  299 Ballardvale St Ste 1 Wilmington (01887) *(G-13455)*

Spectragraphic New England Inc........................... 617 737-3575
  451 D St Ste 200 Boston (02210) *(G-7049)*

Spectral Evolution Inc.. 978 687-1833
  26 Parkridge Rd Ste 1a Haverhill (01835) *(G-9132)*

Spectral LLC... 860 928-7726
  111 Highland Dr Putnam (06260) *(G-2876)*

Spectral Products, Putnam *Also Called: Spectral LLC (G-2876)*

Spectris Inc **(HQ)**...**508 768-6400**
117 Flanders Rd Westborough (01581) *(G-13137)*

Spectro Analytical Instrs Inc...203 778-8837
15 Roger Ave Danbury (06810) *(G-820)*

Spectro Analytical Instruments Inc **(HQ)**....................**201 642-3000**
50 Fordham Rd Wilmington (01887) *(G-13456)*

SPECTRO ANALYTICAL INSTRUMENTS, INC., Danbury *Also Called: Spectro Analytical Instrs Inc (G-820)*

Spectro Coating Corp..978 534-6191
107 Scott Dr Leominster (01453) *(G-9706)*

Spectro Coating Corp **(PA)**...**978 534-1800**
68 Main St Leominster (01453) *(G-9707)*

Spectro Scientific Inc **(HQ)**.......................................**978 486-0123**
1 Executive Dr Ste 101 Chelmsford (01824) *(G-7959)*

Spectro-Film, Billerica *Also Called: Rubil Associates Inc (G-6478)*

Spectrowax Corporation **(PA)**....................................**617 543-0400**
330 Pine St Canton (02021) *(G-7832)*

Spectrsite Bradcast Towers Inc.....................................888 498-3667
116 Huntington Ave 11th Fl Boston (02116) *(G-7050)*

Spectrum, Boston *Also Called: Spectrum Pharmaceuticals Inc (G-7051)*

Spectrum Associates Inc...203 878-4618
440 New Haven Ave Ste 1 Milford (06460) *(G-1889)*

Spectrum Coatings Labs Inc...401 781-4847
217 Chapman St Providence (02905) *(G-16614)*

Spectrum Controls Inc...603 686-4442
112 N Shore Rd Hampton (03842) *(G-14414)*

Spectrum Graphix, East Haven *Also Called: Spectrum Press (G-1051)*

Spectrum Lighting Inc..508 678-2303
994 Jefferson St Ste 5 Fall River (02721) *(G-8607)*

Spectrum Machine & Design LLC...................................860 386-6490
800 Old County Cir Windsor Locks (06096) *(G-4334)*

Spectrum Management, Lexington *Also Called: HMK Enterprises Inc (G-9749)*

Spectrum Marketing Companies, Manchester *Also Called: Spectrum Monthly LLC (G-14936)*

Spectrum Microwave Inc..508 485-0336
400 Nickerson Rd Ste 1 Marlborough (01752) *(G-10212)*

Spectrum Microwave Inc..508 251-6400
400 Nickerson Rd Ste 1 Marlborough (01752) *(G-10213)*

Spectrum Microwave Inc..603 459-1600
400 Nickerson Rd Ste 1 Marlborough (01752) *(G-10214)*

Spectrum Monthly LLC..603 627-0042
95 Eddy Rd Ste 101 Manchester (03102) *(G-14936)*

Spectrum Pharmaceuticals Inc **(PA)**.........................**617 586-3900**
2 Atlantic Ave Fl 6 Boston (02110) *(G-7051)*

Spectrum Plastics Group...203 736-5230
149 Marshall St Paxton (01612) *(G-11291)*

Spectrum Press..203 878-9090
875 Foxon Rd East Haven (06513) *(G-1051)*

Spectrum Thermal Proc LLC...401 808-6249
818 Wellington Ave Cranston (02910) *(G-15912)*

Spectrum Virtual LLC..203 303-7540
55 Realty Dr Ste 315 Cheshire (06410) *(G-617)*

Speechworks International..781 565-5000
1 Wayside Rd Burlington (01803) *(G-7432)*

Speedboard Usa Inc..978 884-3900
39 Kittery Ave Rowley (01969) *(G-11685)*

Speeder & Earl's, Burlington *Also Called: Speeder & Earls Inc (G-17160)*

Speeder & Earls Inc...802 660-3996
412 Pine St Burlington (05401) *(G-17160)*

Speedline Technologies Inc...508 541-4867
16 Forge Pkwy Franklin (02038) *(G-8864)*

Speedy Food Group USA, West Haven *Also Called: Sabatino North America LLC (G-4122)*

Speedy Sign-A-Rama USA...781 849-1181
130 Wood Rd Braintree (02184) *(G-7203)*

Spence & Co Ltd..508 427-5577
76 Campanelli Industrial Dr Brockton (02301) *(G-7308)*

Spencer Industrial Painting...508 885-5406
60 Wire Village Rd Spencer (01562) *(G-12066)*

Spencer Metal Finishing Inc **(HQ)**.............................**508 885-6477**
55 Mill St Brookfield (01506) *(G-7316)*

Spencer Norb..860 231-8079
17 Oakwood Ave Ste 2 West Hartford (06119) *(G-4082)*

Spencer Turbine Company **(DH)**.................................**860 688-8361**
600 Day Hill Rd Windsor (06095) *(G-4301)*

Sperian Eye & Face Protection Inc.................................401 232-1200
10 Thurber Blvd Smithfield (02917) *(G-16730)*

Sperian Protection Usa Inc **(DH)**...............................**401 232-1200**
900 Douglas Pike Smithfield (02917) *(G-16731)*

Sperian Prtction Instrmntion..860 344-1079
651 S Main St Middletown (06457) *(G-1783)*

Sperry Automatics Co Inc...203 729-4589
1372 New Haven Rd Naugatuck (06770) *(G-1986)*

Sperry Product Innovation Inc...781 271-1400
12 Deangelo Dr Bedford (01730) *(G-6270)*

Sperry Sails, Marion *Also Called: Sperry Sails Inc (G-10101)*

Sperry Sails Inc...508 748-2581
11 Marconi Ln Marion (02738) *(G-10101)*

SPI LLC..603 745-3911
1366 Daniel Webster Hwy North Woodstock (03262) *(G-15262)*

Spike Aerospace Inc..617 338-1400
292 Newbury St Boston (02115) *(G-7052)*

Spilldam, Brockton *Also Called: Spilldam Environmental Inc (G-7309)*

Spilldam Environmental Inc...508 583-7850
89 N Montello St Brockton (02301) *(G-7309)*

Spinal Technology LLC **(PA)**......................................**508 775-0990**
191 Mid Tech Dr West Yarmouth (02673) *(G-13073)*

Spindle City Precious Metals...508 567-1597
161 Wilbur Ave Somerset (02725) *(G-11855)*

Spine Wave Inc..203 944-9494
3 Enterprise Dr Ste 210 Shelton (06484) *(G-3064)*

Spinefrontier Inc..978 232-3990
350 Main St 2nd Fl Malden (02148) *(G-10028)*

Spinelli Bky Ravioli Pastry Sp, Boston *Also Called: Spinelli Ravioli Mfg Co Inc (G-7053)*

Spinelli Ravioli Mfg Co Inc..617 567-1992
282 Bennington St Boston (02128) *(G-7053)*

Spinnaker Contract Mfg Inc..603 286-4366
95 Business Park Dr Tilton (03276) *(G-15657)*

Spinnakervideo Inc..617 591-2200
529 Main St Ste 109 Boston (02129) *(G-7054)*

Spiral Air Manufacturing LLC..603 624-6647
1 B St Derry (03038) *(G-14208)*

Spiral Software, Newton *Also Called: Stuart Karon (G-10789)*

Spire, Peabody *Also Called: Digipress Inc (G-11306)*

Spire Inc..617 474-8800
1 1st Ave Ste 1 Peabody (01960) *(G-11343)*

Spire Corporation **(PA)**..**978 584-3958**
25 Linnell Cir Billerica (01821) *(G-6484)*

Spire Express, Portland *Also Called: Desk Top Graphics Inc (G-5208)*

Spire Express, Peabody *Also Called: Desk Top Graphics Inc (G-11305)*

Spire Metering Technology LLC.......................................978 263-7100
34 Saint Martin Dr Marlborough (01752) *(G-10215)*

Spire Solar Inc **(HQ)**..**781 275-6000**
1 Patriots Park Bedford (01730) *(G-6271)*

Spire Solar LLC...617 332-4040
2020 Commonwealth Ave Ste 200 Newton (02466) *(G-10787)*

Spire Technology Solutions LLC......................................603 594-0005
3 Capitol St Nashua (03063) *(G-15173)*

Spirent Communications Inc..774 463-0281
305 Foster St Littleton (01460) *(G-9839)*

Spirit Advisory LLC...603 433-4664
738 Islington St Ste C Portsmouth (03801) *(G-15439)*

Spirit Foodservice LLC..978 964-1551
200 Brickstone Sq Ste G05 Andover (01810) *(G-5925)*

Spirit Recognition Inc **(PA)**..**401 722-6400**
639 Central Ave Pawtucket (02861) *(G-16417)*

Spirol, Danielson *Also Called: Spirol International Corp (G-844)*

Spirol International Corp **(HQ)**....................................**860 774-8571**
30 Rock Ave Danielson (06239) *(G-844)*

Spirol Intl Holdg Corp **(PA)**..**860 774-8571**
30 Rock Ave Danielson (06239) *(G-845)*

Spirometrics, Gray *Also Called: Vuetek Scientific LLC (G-4844)*

Spitjack, Shrewsbury *Also Called: Rasa Incorporated (G-11840)*

ALPHABETIC

Split Rock Distilling, Newcastle *Also Called: Lu-Dz LLC (G-5094)*

Spm Management Inc.. 203 847-1112
3 Enterprise Dr Shelton (06484) *(G-3065)*

Spoiler Alert, Boston *Also Called: Material Impact Inc (G-6879)*

Sponge-Jet, Newington *Also Called: Sponge-Jet Inc (G-15212)*

Sponge-Jet Inc (PA).. **603 610-7950**
14 Patterson Ln Newington (03801) *(G-15212)*

Spoontiques Inc.. 781 344-9530
111 Island St Stoughton (02072) *(G-12238)*

Sports Event and Products Co, Cumberland *Also Called: Firecracker Sports LLC (G-15939)*

Sports Fields Inc... 207 933-3547
242 Warren Rd Monmouth (04259) *(G-5072)*

Sports Systems Custom Bags................................. 401 767-3770
44 Hazel St Woonsocket (02895) *(G-16974)*

Sports Visio Inc... 603 774-1339
9 Tucker Hill Rd Dunbarton (03046) *(G-14265)*

Spotbus Inc.. 774 262-4052
114 Turnpike Rd Ste 106 Westborough (01581) *(G-13138)*

Spotlight LLC.. 978 762-8352
6 Southside Rd Danvers (01923) *(G-8221)*

Spray Foam Insulation, Norwalk *Also Called: Foam Systems LLC (G-2502)*

Spray Maine Inc... 207 384-2273
104 Parker St Newburyport (01950) *(G-10717)*

Spraying Systems Co... 603 471-0505
174 Route 101 Bedford (03110) *(G-13950)*

Spraying Systems Co... 603 517-1854
243 Daniel Webster Hwy Merrimack (03054) *(G-15006)*

Spread Cheese Co LLC... 203 982-1674
386 Main St Middletown (06457) *(G-1784)*

Spring Air Ohio LLC.. 617 884-0041
124 2nd St Chelsea (02150) *(G-7992)*

Spring Computerized Inds LLC................................ 860 605-9206
93 Oakwood Dr Harwinton (06791) *(G-1523)*

Spring Fill... 802 846-5900
1775 Williston Rd Ste 250 South Burlington (05403) *(G-17599)*

Spring Hill Machine Co Inc.................................... 978 374-4461
48 Laurier St Haverhill (01832) *(G-9133)*

Spring Manufacturing Corp.................................... 978 658-7396
2235 Main St Tewksbury (01876) *(G-12417)*

Spring Tollman Company Incorporated (PA)............... **860 583-1326**
91 Enterprise Dr Bristol (06010) *(G-497)*

Springboard Technology Corporation
1 Federal St Springfield (01105) *(G-12133)*

Springfield Eye Associates.................................... 413 739-7367
3640 Main St Ste 205 Springfield (01107) *(G-12134)*

Springfield Fence, North Springfield *Also Called: Springfield Fence Company Inc (G-17424)*

Springfield Fence Company Inc............................... 802 886-2221
50 Route 106 North Springfield (05150) *(G-17424)*

Springfield Label Tape Co Inc................................ 413 733-6634
430 Saint James Ave Springfield (01109) *(G-12135)*

Springfield Newspaper, Springfield *Also Called: Republican Company (G-12125)*

Springfield Pallet Inc.. 413 593-0044
1819 Page Blvd Indian Orchard (01151) *(G-9475)*

Springfield Printing Corp...................................... 802 886-2201
19 Precision Dr North Springfield (05150) *(G-17425)*

Springfield Spring Corporation................................ 860 584-6560
24 Dell Manor Dr Bristol (06010) *(G-498)*

Springfield Spring Corporation (PA)....................... **413 525-6837**
311 Shaker Rd East Longmeadow (01028) *(G-8395)*

Springfield Tire & Auto, Springfield *Also Called: Holyoke Tire & Auto Svc Inc (G-12101)*

Springfield Wire Inc.. 413 385-0115
100 Moody St Ste 2 Ludlow (01056) *(G-9954)*

Springleaf Therapeutics Inc
8 Saint Marys St Ste 601 Boston (02215) *(G-7055)*

Springs Manufacturer Supply Co, Southington *Also Called: Necst Inc (G-3223)*

Springworks Farm Maine Inc.................................. 207 407-4207
347 Lisbon St Lisbon (04250) *(G-5017)*

Sprout USA LLC... 617 650-1958
117 Huntington Ave Boston (02199) *(G-7056)*

Sproutel Inc... 914 806-6514
60 Valley St Apt 29 Providence (02909) *(G-16615)*

Spruce Environmental Tech Inc............................... 978 521-0901
3 Saber Way Haverhill (01835) *(G-9134)*

Spruce Mountian Granites Inc................................. 802 476-7474
84 Pitman Rd Barre (05641) *(G-17016)*

Spruce Mtn Grntes Cstm Sndblas............................ 802 476-7474
84 Pitman Rd Barre (05641) *(G-17017)*

SPS, Manchester *Also Called: Summit Packaging Systems LLC (G-14937)*

Spurwink Cordage Inc.. 207 284-5894
27 Landry St Biddeford (04005) *(G-4589)*

Spv Industries LLC... 860 953-5928
9 Tolles St West Hartford (06110) *(G-4083)*

SPX Corporation.. 207 655-8525
28 Tower Rd Raymond (04071) *(G-5316)*

SPX Corporation.. 207 655-8100
22 Tower Rd Raymond (04071) *(G-5317)*

Sq Innovation Inc... 617 500-0121
20 Mall Rd Ste 220 Burlington (01803) *(G-7433)*

Sqdm.. 888 993-9674
100 Tower Office Park Ste M Woburn (01801) *(G-13671)*

Squadlocker Inc... 888 885-6253
240 Bald Hill Rd Warwick (02886) *(G-16864)*

Square Robot Inc... 617 274-8389
50 Dangelo Dr Ste 5 Marlborough (01752) *(G-10216)*

Squareworks Consulting LLC.................................. 800 779-6285
101 Arch St Fl 8 Boston (02110) *(G-7057)*

Squirrel Works LLC... 401 247-3000
75 Taylor Rd Portsmouth (02871) *(G-16457)*

SQZ BIOTECH, Watertown *Also Called: Sqz Biotechnologies Company (G-12909)*

Sqz Biotechnologies Company (PA)........................ **617 758-8672**
200 Arsenal Yards Blvd Fl 2 Watertown (02472) *(G-12909)*

SRC Medical Inc.. 781 826-9100
263 Winter St Hanover (02339) *(G-9042)*

SRC Publishing Inc... 508 749-3212
23 Midstate Dr Ste 114 Auburn (01501) *(G-6126)*

Srd, Orono *Also Called: Sensor Research and Dev Corp (G-5137)*

Srd Holdings Inc.. 508 695-5656
211 John L Dietsch Sq North Attleboro (02763) *(G-10888)*

Srg Inc... 802 479-2508
37 Gable Pl Barre (05641) *(G-17018)*

SRS Medical Systems Inc (PA)............................. **978 663-2800**
76 Treble Cove Rd Ste 3 North Billerica (01862) *(G-10958)*

SS Fabrications Inc... 860 974-1910
82 County Rd Eastford (06242) *(G-1092)*

SS&C HOLDINGS, Windsor *Also Called: SS&c Technologies Holdings Inc (G-4303)*

SS&c Technologies Inc (HQ)................................ **800 234-0556**
80 Lamberton Rd Windsor (06095) *(G-4302)*

SS&c Technologies Inc... 781 654-6498
3 Burlington Woods Dr Burlington (01803) *(G-7434)*

SS&c Technologies Holdings Inc (PA)..................... **860 298-4500**
80 Lamberton Rd Windsor (06095) *(G-4303)*

Ssg Optronics.. 978 694-9991
65 Jonspin Rd Wilmington (01887) *(G-13457)*

Sshc Inc.. 860 399-5434
1244 Old Clinton Rd Westbrook (06498) *(G-4143)*

Ssi Liquidating Inc... 617 547-6706
625 Mount Auburn St Ste 4 Cambridge (02138) *(G-7720)*

Ssi Manufacturing Tech Corp.................................. 860 589-8004
106 Enterprise Dr Bristol (06010) *(G-499)*

Sst Components Inc (PA).................................... **978 670-7300**
9 Hampshire St Ste 1 Lawrence (01840) *(G-9601)*

St Albans Cooperative Creamery Inc......................... 802 524-9366
140 Federal St Saint Albans (05478) *(G-17531)*

St Albans Creamery LLC....................................... 802 524-9366
138 Federal St Saint Albans (05478) *(G-17532)*

St Albans Messenger, Saint Albans *Also Called: Vermont Publishing Comany (G-17536)*

St Associates Inc
1 Teal Rd Wakefield (01880) *(G-12536)*

St Cyr Inc.. 508 752-2222
235 Park Ave Worcester (01609) *(G-13805)*

St Cyr Salon Spa, Worcester *Also Called: St Cyr Inc (G-13805)*

St Equipment & Technology LLC.............................. 781 972-2319
101 Hampton Ave Needham (02494) *(G-10524)*

St Joseph's Abbey, Spencer *Also Called: Cistercian Abbey Spencer Inc (G-12056)*

St Jude Medical LLC... 978 577-3400
   4 Robbins Rd Westford (01886) *(G-13264)*

St Liquidation Corporation... 860 628-9090
   445 W Queen St Ste 100 Southington (06489) *(G-3234)*

St Pierre Chain & Wire Rope, Worcester *Also Called: St Pierre Manufacturing Corp (G-13806)*

St Pierre Manufacturing Corp.. 508 853-8010
   317 E Mountain St Worcester (01606) *(G-13806)*

St Regis Sportswear Ltd.. 518 725-6767
   3 Ironwood Rd North Andover (01845) *(G-10850)*

St. Albans Creamery, Saint Albans *Also Called: St Albans Creamery LLC (G-17532)*

St. Josephs, Boston *Also Called: Bedrock Brands LLC (G-6587)*

STA Cruz Gun Locks, Webster *Also Called: Santa Cruz Gunlocks LLC (G-15674)*

Staban Engineering Corp... 203 294-1997
   65 N Plains Industrial Rd Wallingford (06492) *(G-3854)*

Stabil, Biddeford *Also Called: 32 North Corporation (G-4553)*

Stache Co LLC.. 860 719-1727
   71 Edwin Rd Ste 2 South Windsor (06074) *(G-3183)*

Stackbin Corporation... 401 333-1600
   29 Powder Hill Rd Lincoln (02865) *(G-16155)*

Stacys Pita Chip Company Inc....................................... 781 961-2800
   1 Posturepedic Dr Randolph (02368) *(G-11575)*

Staffall Inc.. 401 461-5554
   1468 Elmwood Ave Cranston (02910) *(G-15913)*

Stafford Manufacturing Corp (PA)................................ **978 657-8000**
   256 Andover St Wilmington (01887) *(G-13458)*

Stafford Reminder, Vernon Rockville *Also Called: Rmi Inc (G-3761)*

Stafford Special Tool, Worcester *Also Called: Form Roll Die Corp (G-13726)*

Stage Stop Candy, Dennis Port *Also Called: Fedele and Carter Inc (G-8261)*

Stage Stop Candy Ltd Inc.. 508 394-1791
   411 Main St Dennis Port (02639) *(G-8263)*

Stahl (usa) Inc (DH)... **978 968-1382**
   13 Corwin St Peabody (01960) *(G-11344)*

Stained Glass Resources Inc (PA)............................... **413 566-5053**
   15 Commercial Dr Hampden (01036) *(G-9023)*

Stainless Fdsrvice Eqp Mfg Inc..................................... 207 227-7747
   14 Connecticut Rd Limestone (04750) *(G-5005)*

Stainless Steel Coatings Inc.. 978 365-9828
   835 Sterling Rd Lancaster (01523) *(G-9529)*

Stairs Unlimited Inc.. 802 848-7030
   484 Hardwood Hill Rd Richford (05476) *(G-17476)*

Stairway Manufacturers Assoc....................................... 508 646-1313
   657 Quarry St Ste 3 Fall River (02723) *(G-8608)*

Stallrgenes Greer Holdings Inc...................................... 617 588-4900
   55 Cambridge Pkwy Cambridge (02142) *(G-7721)*

Stamford Advocate, The, Stamford *Also Called: Southern Conn Newspapers Inc (G-3466)*

Stamford Capital Group Inc (PA)................................. **800 977-7837**
   1266 E Main St Stamford (06902) *(G-3469)*

Stamford Iron & Stl Works Inc....................................... 203 324-6751
   347 Courtland Ave Stamford (06906) *(G-3470)*

Stamford Mdia Ctr Prdctons LLC.................................... 203 905-4000
   307 Atlantic St Stamford (06901) *(G-3471)*

Stamford Risk Analytics LLC.. 203 559-0883
   263 Tresser Blvd 9th Fl Stamford (06901) *(G-3472)*

Stamping Technologies Inc.. 603 524-5958
   20 Growtth Rd Laconia (03246) *(G-14671)*

Stan Rubinstein Associates Inc...................................... 508 668-6044
   24 Walpole Park S Ste 10 Walpole (02081) *(G-12576)*

Stan-Allen Co., Three Rivers *Also Called: Millennium Die Group Inc (G-12430)*

Stanchem Incorporated.. 860 828-0571
   401 Berlin St East Berlin (06023) *(G-917)*

Stanchem Incorporated (HQ)....................................... **860 828-0571**
   401 Berlin St East Berlin (06023) *(G-918)*

Stanchem Polymers, East Berlin *Also Called: Stanchem Incorporated (G-917)*

Stancor LP.. 203 268-7513
   515 Fan Hill Rd Monroe (06468) *(G-1922)*

Stancor Pumps, Monroe *Also Called: Stancor LP (G-1922)*

Standard Bellows Co (PA).. **860 623-2307**
   375 Ella Grasso Tpke Windsor Locks (06096) *(G-4335)*

Standard Box Co Inc... 617 884-4200
   28 Gerrish Ave Chelsea (02150) *(G-7993)*

Standard Chair Gardner Inc... 978 632-1301
   1 S Main St Gardner (01440) *(G-8902)*

Standard Knapp Inc... 860 342-1100
   63 Pickering St Portland (06480) *(G-2825)*

Standard Lock Washer & Mfg Co.................................... 508 757-4508
   1451 Grafton St Worcester (01604) *(G-13807)*

Standard Merger Sub LLC.. 207 856-6151
   52 Anderson Rd Windham (04062) *(G-5670)*

Standard Mfg Co LLC... 860 225-3401
   100 Burritt St New Britain (06053) *(G-2062)*

Standard Mill Machinery Corp.. 401 822-7871
   1370 Main St Ste C West Warwick (02893) *(G-16923)*

Standard Modern Company.. 774 425-3537
   186 Duchaine Blvd New Bedford (02745) *(G-10651)*

Standard Modern Company Inc...................................... 508 586-4300
   186 Duchaine Blvd New Bedford (02745) *(G-10652)*

Standard Publishing Corp (PA)................................... **617 457-0600**
   10 High St Ste 1107 Boston (02110) *(G-7058)*

Standard Repair Co Division, Wareham *Also Called: R B Machine Co Inc (G-12843)*

Standard Rubber Products Inc.. 781 878-2626
   64 B St Hanover (02339) *(G-9043)*

Standard Times, Wakefield *Also Called: Southern RI Newspapers (G-16744)*

Standard Washer & Mat Inc.. 860 643-5125
   299 Progress Dr Manchester (06042) *(G-1638)*

Standard Welding Company Inc...................................... 860 528-9628
   212 Prospect St East Hartford (06108) *(G-1022)*

Standard-Knapp, Inc., Portland *Also Called: Standard Knapp Inc (G-2825)*

Standex, Salem *Also Called: Standex International Corp (G-15563)*

Standex Elctrnic Magnetics Inc...................................... 800 805-8991
   24 Chenell Dr Concord (03301) *(G-14158)*

Standex International Corp.. 978 667-2771
   500 Iron Horse Park North Billerica (01862) *(G-10959)*

Standex International Corp.. 978 538-0808
   107 Audubon Rd Ste 20 Wakefield (01880) *(G-12537)*

Standex International Corp (PA)................................... **603 893-9701**
   23 Keewaydin Dr Ste 205 Salem (03079) *(G-15563)*

Standex International Corp... 864 963-3471
   42 Allen Martin Dr Essex Junction (05452) *(G-17247)*

Standley Bros Machine Co Inc.. 978 927-0278
   96 Park St Beverly (01915) *(G-6385)*

Stanley Access Technologies, Farmington *Also Called: Stanley Black & Decker Inc (G-1248)*

Stanley Black & Decker.. 781 460-4511
   23 Drydock Ave Ste 720w Boston (02210) *(G-7059)*

Stanley Black & Decker, New Britain *Also Called: Stanley Black & Decker Inc (G-2065)*

Stanley Black & Decker Inc.. 860 677-2861
   65 Scott Swamp Rd (Corner Of Rte 6 & Hyde Rd) Farmington (06032) *(G-1248)*

Stanley Black & Decker Inc.. 860 225-5111
   480 Myrtle St New Britain (06053) *(G-2063)*

Stanley Black & Decker Inc.. 860 225-5111
   100 Curtis St New Britain (06052) *(G-2064)*

Stanley Black & Decker Inc (PA).................................. **860 225-5111**
   1000 Stanley Dr New Britain (06053) *(G-2065)*

Stanley Black & Decker Inc.. 860 827-5025
   600 Myrtle St New Britain (06053) *(G-2066)*

Stanley Black & Decker Inc.. 860 225-5111
   480 Myrtle St New Britain (06053) *(G-2067)*

Stanley Black & Decker Inc.. 860 460-9122
   400 Executive Blvd Southington (06489) *(G-3235)*

Stanley Black and Decker, New Britain *Also Called: Black & Decker (us) Inc (G-2008)*

Stanley Black Dcker Asia Hldng (HQ)......................... **860 225-5111**
   1000 Stanley Dr New Britain (06053) *(G-2068)*

Stanley Engineered Fastening, Danbury *Also Called: Stanley Engnered Fastening LLC (G-821)*

Stanley Engnered Fastening LLC (HQ)........................ **800 783-6427**
   4 Shelter Rock Ln Danbury (06810) *(G-821)*

Stanley Fastening Systems LP....................................... 860 225-5111
   480 Myrtle St New Britain (06053) *(G-2069)*

Stanley Fastening Systems LP (HQ)............................ **401 884-2500**
   2 Briggs Dr East Greenwich (02818) *(G-15993)*

Stanley Industrial & Auto LLC.. 800 800-8005
   480 Myrtle St New Britain (06053) *(G-2070)*

Stanley Industrial & Auto LLC.. 508 429-1350
   106 Lowland St Holliston (01746) *(G-9230)*

A L P H A B E T I C

Stanley-Bostitch, New Britain *Also Called: Stanley Fastening Systems LP (G-2069)*

Stanlok, Worcester *Also Called: Stanlok Corporation (G-13808)*

Stanlok Corporation..508 757-4508
1451 Grafton St Worcester (01604) *(G-13808)*

Star Base Technologies Inc..413 499-4005
343 Pecks Rd Pittsfield (01201) *(G-11424)*

Star Engineering Inc...508 316-1492
1 Vaillancourt Dr North Attleboro (02763) *(G-10889)*

Star Equity Holdings, Old Greenwich *Also Called: Star Equity Holdings Inc (G-2635)*

Star Equity Holdings Inc **(PA)**...............................**203 489-9500**
53 Forest Ave Ste 101 Old Greenwich (06870) *(G-2635)*

Star Group LP **(PA)**..**203 328-7310**
9 W Broad St Ste 310 Stamford (06902) *(G-3473)*

Star Kitchen Cabinets Inc.......................................508 510-3123
75 Stockwell Dr Ste H Avon (02322) *(G-6162)*

Star Litho Inc..781 340-9401
360 Libbey Industrial Pkwy Weymouth (02189) *(G-13336)*

Star Pickling Corp...508 672-8535
941 Wood St Swansea (02777) *(G-12312)*

Star Plating, New Bedford *Also Called: Plating Technology Inc (G-10640)*

Star Printing Corp...508 583-9046
10 Mozzone Blvd Taunton (02780) *(G-12369)*

Star Steel Structures Inc..860 763-5681
392 Four Bridges Rd Somers (06071) *(G-3100)*

Star Struck, Bethel *Also Called: Morristown Star Struck LLC (G-130)*

Star Tires Plus Wheels LLC......................................860 296-9799
888 Wethersfield Ave Hartford (06114) *(G-1509)*

Starburst Prtg & Graphics Inc....................................508 893-0900
300 Hopping Brook Rd Holliston (01746) *(G-9231)*

Starc Systems Inc...844 596-1784
112 Orion St Ste 100 Brunswick (04011) *(G-4655)*

Starensier Inc **(PA)**..**978 462-7311**
12 Kent Way Ste 201 Byfield (01922) *(G-7459)*

Starent Networks LLC **(HQ)**...................................**978 851-1100**
30 International Pl Tewksbury (01876) *(G-12418)*

Starfish Storage Corporation.....................................781 250-3000
271 Waverley Oaks Rd Ste 301 Waltham (02452) *(G-12782)*

Starherald Newspaper Pubg, Presque Isle *Also Called: Northeast Publishing Company (G-5306)*

Stark Mountain Woodworking Co, New Haven *Also Called: Stark Mountain Woodworks Co (G-17396)*

Stark Mountain Woodworks Co......................................802 453-5549
359 South St New Haven (05472) *(G-17396)*

Starkey Welding Crane Service....................................603 679-2553
444 Route 125 Brentwood (03833) *(G-14030)*

Starkweather Engineering Inc.....................................978 858-3700
1615 Shawsheen St Ste 14 Tewksbury (01876) *(G-12419)*

Starlink North America Inc.......................................877 823-1566
100 Sylvan Rd Ste G700 Woburn (01801) *(G-13672)*

Starmet Corporation **(PA)**....................................**978 369-5410**
2229 Main St Concord (01742) *(G-8134)*

Starrett, Athol *Also Called: LS Starrett Company (G-5981)*

Startech Environmental Corp **(PA)**............................**203 762-2499**
88 Danbury Rd Ste 2b Wilton (06897) *(G-4248)*

Stat Products Inc...508 881-8022
200 Butterfield Dr Ste D Ashland (01721) *(G-5967)*

State Military Reservation.......................................603 225-1230
1 Minuteman Way Concord (03301) *(G-14159)*

State Road Cement Block Co Inc...................................508 993-9473
656 State Rd North Dartmouth (02747) *(G-11002)*

State Sand & Gravel Co Inc.......................................207 338-4070
185 Belmont Ave Belfast (04915) *(G-4538)*

State Welding & Fabg Inc...203 294-4071
10 W Main St Clinton (06413) *(G-650)*

State-Line Graphics Inc...617 389-1200
6 Victoria St Ste 109 Everett (02149) *(G-8501)*

State-Wide Mltple Lsting Svc I...................................401 785-3650
100 Bignall St Warwick (02888) *(G-16865)*

Stately Stair Co Inc...203 575-1966
91 Great Hill Rd Naugatuck (06770) *(G-1987)*

Statham Woodwork..203 831-0629
38 Hemlock Pl Norwalk (06854) *(G-2574)*

Static Clean International Inc...................................781 229-7799
267 Boston Rd Ste 8 North Billerica (01862) *(G-10960)*

Static Safe Products Company.....................................203 937-6391
8 Cook Rd Cornwall Bridge (06754) *(G-672)*

Static Solutions Inc **(PA)**.................................**978 310-7251**
399 River Rd Ste C1 Hudson (01749) *(G-9415)*

Staticsmart Flooring, Andover *Also Called: Julie Industries Inc (G-5890)*

Statisy, Boston *Also Called: Statisys Inc (G-7060)*

Statisys Inc..617 804-1284
33 Arch St Boston (02110) *(G-7060)*

Statspin Inc..781 551-0100
60 Glacier Dr Ste 2000 Westwood (02090) *(G-13319)*

Stauffer Sheet Metal, Windsor *Also Called: Stauffer Sheet Metal LLC (G-4304)*

Stauffer Sheet Metal LLC..860 623-0518
56 Depot St Windsor (06006) *(G-4304)*

Stave Puzzles Incorporated.......................................802 295-5200
163 Olcott Dr Wilder (05088) *(G-17715)*

Std Manufacturing Inc...781 828-4400
1063 Turnpike St Stoughton (02072) *(G-12239)*

Std Med Inc..781 828-4400
375 West St West Bridgewater (02379) *(G-12981)*

Std Precision Gear & Instr Inc...................................508 580-0035
318 Manley St Ste 5 West Bridgewater (02379) *(G-12982)*

Stead-Fast Custom Linings LLC...................................203 466-8000
641 Main St East Haven (06512) *(G-1052)*

Stealth Biotherapeutics Inc **(HQ)**...........................**617 600-6888**
123 Highland Ave Ste 201 Needham Heights (02494) *(G-10558)*

Stealth Microwave, Hudson *Also Called: Vectronics Microwave Corp (G-14558)*

Stearns Perry & Smith Company....................................617 423-4775
33 Fayette St Ste 1 Quincy (02171) *(G-11539)*

Stearns Tool Company...401 351-4765
56 Sprague St Providence (02907) *(G-16616)*

Stedagio LLC...401 568-6228
1000 Danielle Dr Mapleville (02839) *(G-16169)*

Steel, Rowley *Also Called: MPS Products Corp (G-11681)*

Steel Art Company Inc..617 566-4079
189 Dean St Norwood (02062) *(G-11211)*

Steel Connections Inc...508 958-5129
101 Jefferson Rd Franklin (02038) *(G-8865)*

Steel Fabrication, Wareham *Also Called: Cape Cod Iron Corp (G-12831)*

Steel Modular Inc...310 227-3714
124 Westbrook Rd Ste 101 Essex (06426) *(G-1172)*

Steel Pro Services, Rockland *Also Called: Steel-Pro Inc (G-5342)*

Steel Root Inc..978 312-7668
16 Front St Ste 202 Salem (01970) *(G-11733)*

Steel-Fab Inc...978 345-1112
430 Crawford St Fitchburg (01420) *(G-8676)*

Steel-Fab Engineering & Sales....................................978 345-0035
552 Oak Hill Rd Fitchburg (01420) *(G-8677)*

Steel-It, Lancaster *Also Called: Stainless Steel Coatings Inc (G-9529)*

Steel-Pro Inc...207 596-0061
771 Main St Rockland (04841) *(G-5342)*

Steele Canvas Basket Corp..800 541-8929
201 Williams St Chelsea (02150) *(G-7994)*

Steelstone Industries, Houlton *Also Called: McQuade Tidd Industries (G-4901)*

Steeltech Building Pdts Inc......................................860 290-8930
636 Nutmeg Rd N South Windsor (06074) *(G-3184)*

Steinerfilm Inc...413 458-9525
987 Simonds Rd Williamstown (01267) *(G-13368)*

Steinerfilm USA, Williamstown *Also Called: Steinerfilm Inc (G-13368)*

Steinmetz Machine Works, Stamford *Also Called: H G Steinmetz Mch Works Inc (G-3360)*

Stella DOro Biscuit Co Inc.......................................718 549-3700
8 Sound Shore Dr Ste 265 Greenwich (06830) *(G-1353)*

Stellant PST Corp..978 887-5754
417 Boston St Topsfield (01983) *(G-12438)*

Stellar Industries Corp..508 865-1668
50 Howe Ave Millbury (01527) *(G-10443)*

Stellar Lasers LLC...802 299-5411
46 Worcester Village Rd Worcester (05682) *(G-17782)*

Stellar Manufacturing Inc.......................................978 241-9537
10 Manor Pkwy Ste A Salem (03079) *(G-15564)*

Stellar Menus Inc... 617 882-2800
14 Brewster St Provincetown (02657) *(G-11498)*

Stelray Plastic Products Inc... 203 735-2331
50 Westfield Ave Ansonia (06401) *(G-20)*

Stencil Ease, Old Saybrook *Also Called: Liftline Capital LLC* *(G-2654)*

Stenhouse Publishers... 207 253-1600
282 Corporate Dr Ste 1 Portsmouth (03801) *(G-15440)*

Stent Metal Corp... 203 287-9007
9 Hamden Park Dr Hamden (06517) *(G-1457)*

Stentech Inc **(PA)**... **603 505-4470**
22 Manchester Rd Unit 8b Derry (03038) *(G-14209)*

Step Ahead Innovations Inc... 802 233-0211
54 Royal Dr South Burlington (05403) *(G-17600)*

Stephane Inkel Inc... 603 331-3296
279 Rt 114 Canaan (05903) *(G-17170)*

Stephen C Dematrick... 401 789-4712
201p Gravelly Hill Rd Narragansett (02879) *(G-16197)*

Stephen F Madden... 207 827-5737
183 Greenfield Rd Cardville (04418) *(G-4673)*

Stephen Gould Corporation... 978 851-2500
30 Commerce Way Ste 1 Tewksbury (01876) *(G-12420)*

Stephen Plaud Inc... 401 625-5909
381 State Ave Tiverton (02878) *(G-16738)*

Stephen Terhune Woodworking In... 978 768-0106
106 Western Ave Essex (01929) *(G-8480)*

Stephens Pipe & Steel LLC... 877 777-8721
776 N Main St Manchester (06042) *(G-1639)*

Stephens Precision Inc... 802 222-9600
293 Industrial Dr Bradford (05033) *(G-17064)*

Stephens, Waring and White, Brooklin *Also Called: Brooklin Boat Yard Inc (G-4632)*

Stergis Aluminum Products Corp... 508 455-0661
79 Walton St Attleboro (02703) *(G-6065)*

Stergis/Alliance, Attleboro *Also Called: Stergis Aluminum Products Corp (G-6065)*

Sterilite Corporation **(PA)**... **978 597-1000**
30 Scales Ln Townsend (01469) *(G-12442)*

Steris Corporation... 508 393-9323
435 Whitney St Northborough (01532) *(G-11109)*

Sterling Architectural Mllwk, Springfield *Also Called: Triseptagon LLC (G-12144)*

Sterling Business Products Inc... 781 481-1234
214 Main St Stoneham (02180) *(G-12186)*

Sterling Concrete Corp... 978 422-8282
10 Sterling Way North Oxford (01537) *(G-11034)*

Sterling Custom Cabinetry LLC... 203 335-5151
323 North Ave Bridgeport (06606) *(G-375)*

Sterling Engineering Corp... 860 379-3366
236 New Hartford Rd Pleasant Valley (06063) *(G-2804)*

Sterling Gas Drlg Fund 1982 LP... 203 358-5700
1 Landmark Sq Stamford (06901) *(G-3474)*

Sterling Gun Drills Inc... 802 442-3525
940 Water St North Bennington (05257) *(G-17412)*

Sterling Hydraulics, Haverhill *Also Called: Runtal North America Inc (G-9128)*

Sterling Machine Division, Enfield *Also Called: Senior Operations LLC (G-1148)*

Sterling Manufacturing Co Inc... 978 368-8733
640 Sterling St Lancaster (01523) *(G-9530)*

Sterling Materials LLC... 203 315-6619
17 Tanglewood Dr Branford (06405) *(G-279)*

Sterling Prcsion Machining Inc... 860 564-4043
112 Industrial Park Rd Sterling (06377) *(G-3504)*

Sterling Precision Inc... 978 365-4999
99 Lawrence St Clinton (01510) *(G-8092)*

Sterling Precision Machining, Sterling *Also Called: Sterling Prcsion Machining Inc (G-3504)*

Sterling Printing, Stoneham *Also Called: Sterling Business Products Inc (G-12186)*

Sterling Rope Company Inc... 800 788-7673
26 Morin St Biddeford (04005) *(G-4590)*

Sterling Screw Machine Div, Milford *Also Called: Alinabal Inc (G-1796)*

Sterling Sintered Technologies Inc... 860 379-2753
249 Rockwell St Winsted (06098) *(G-4357)*

Sterling Street Brewery, Clinton *Also Called: Mass Brewing LLC (G-8083)*

Sterling Surfaces Div, Sterling *Also Called: Kitchen Associates Inc (G-12164)*

Sterling Technologies Inc... 802 888-4753
320 Wilkins St Morrisville (05661) *(G-17389)*

Sterling Technologies Inc... 802 363-6883
251 Harrel St Morrisville (05661) *(G-17390)*

Sterlingwear of Boston Inc **(PA)**... **617 567-2100**
175 William F Mcclellan Hwy Boston (02128) *(G-7061)*

Stern Seafood Inc... 207 303-8466
96 King St Scarborough (04074) *(G-5443)*

Sterngold Dental LLC... 508 226-5660
23 Frank Mossberg Dr Attleboro (02703) *(G-6066)*

Sterzingers Welding LLC... 203 685-1575
28 Alan Rd Danbury (06810) *(G-822)*

Steven Pelletier... 207 834-3191
82 W Main St Fort Kent (04743) *(G-4794)*

Steven Tedesco... 978 777-4070
100 Newbury St Ste A Danvers (01923) *(G-8222)*

Stevens Company Incorporated... 860 283-8201
1085 Waterbury Rd # 1 Thomaston (06787) *(G-3631)*

Stevens Electric Pump Service... 207 933-2143
18 Berry Rd Monmouth (04259) *(G-5073)*

Stevens Linen Associates Inc... 508 943-0813
137 Schofield Ave Ste 5 Dudley (01571) *(G-8325)*

Stevens Manufacturing Co Inc... 203 878-2328
220 Rock Ln Milford (06460) *(G-1890)*

Stevens Urethane, Easthampton *Also Called: JPS Elastomerics Corp (G-8448)*

Stevenson Group Corporation... 860 689-0011
120 Wilson Pond Rd Harwinton (06791) *(G-1524)*

Steward Pet Imaging LLC... 508 259-8919
795 Middle St Fall River (02721) *(G-8609)*

Stewart Efi LLC... 860 283-2523
332 Reynolds Bridge Rd Thomaston (06787) *(G-3632)*

Stewart Efi LLC **(PA)**... **860 283-8213**
45 Old Waterbury Rd Thomaston (06787) *(G-3633)*

Stewart Efi Connecticut LLC... 860 283-8213
45 Old Waterbury Rd Thomaston (06787) *(G-3634)*

Steyn Syndication... 603 359-1683
35 S Court St Woodsville (03785) *(G-15737)*

STI Incorporated... 860 577-7000
6 Business Park Rd Old Saybrook (06475) *(G-2663)*

Stickamayka Packaging Inc... 978 474-1930
7 Connector Rd Andover (01810) *(G-5926)*

Sticky Brnd Creative Group LLC... 609 731-0288
66 Bowdoin St South Burlington (05403) *(G-17601)*

Stihl Incorporated... 203 929-8488
2 Patriot Way Oxford (06478) *(G-2712)*

Stik-II Products, Easthampton *Also Called: Adhesive Applications Inc (G-8437)*

Stiles & Hart Brick Company... 508 697-6928
127 Cook St Bridgewater (02324) *(G-7238)*

Stilisti... 617 262-2234
116 Newbury St Fl 2 Boston (02116) *(G-7062)*

Stillwater Graphics Inc... 802 433-9898
71 Depot St Williamstown (05679) *(G-17718)*

Stirrings LLC... 508 324-9800
1 West St Unit 2 Fall River (02720) *(G-8610)*

Stirrings Better Cocktails, Fall River *Also Called: Stirrings LLC (G-8610)*

Stitchdx LLC... 617 818-8585
110 Canal St # 3 Lowell (01852) *(G-9925)*

Stm Imp and Exp Corp... 973 450-5110
55 Lathrop Road Ext Plainfield (06374) *(G-2740)*

Stmc, Plantsville *Also Called: Southington Tool & Mfg Corp (G-2796)*

Stmicroelectronics Inc... 781 861-2650
200 Summit Dr Burlington (01803) *(G-7435)*

Stockeryale Inc... 603 893-8778
13 Red Roof Ln Ste 200 Salem (03079) *(G-15565)*

Stockley Storage, Landaff *Also Called: Stockley Trucking Inc (G-14682)*

Stockley Trucking Inc... 603 838-2860
405 S Main St Landaff (03585) *(G-14682)*

Stokes Woodworking Co Inc **(PA)**... **508 481-0414**
12 Bonazzoli Ave Hudson (01749) *(G-9416)*

Stolberger Incorporated... 401 724-8800
1211 High St Central Falls (02863) *(G-15797)*

Stone Decor Galleria Inc... 781 937-9377
10 Ryan Rd Woburn (01801) *(G-13673)*

A
L
P
H
A
B
E
T
I
C

Stone Design Marble & Gran Co...................... 781 331-3000
   1235 Main St South Weymouth (02190) *(G-11978)*

Stone House Farm Inc...................... 978 352-2323
   276 Washington St West Boxford (01885) *(G-12954)*

Stone Image Custom Con LLC...................... 860 668-2434
   1186 Old Coach Xing Suffield (06078) *(G-3595)*

Stone Machine Co Inc...................... 603 887-4287
   45 E Derry Rd Chester (03036) *(G-14071)*

Stone Surfaces Inc...................... 781 270-4600
   275 Salem St Ste 2 Woburn (01801) *(G-13674)*

Stone Systems New England LLC...................... 401 766-3603
   9 Steel St North Smithfield (02896) *(G-16333)*

Stone Tablet LLC...................... 781 380-8800
   233 Needham St Ste 514 Newton (02464) *(G-10788)*

Stone Workshop LLC...................... 203 362-1144
   1108 Railroad Ave Bridgeport (06605) *(G-376)*

Stone Yard LLC...................... 978 742-9800
   265 Foster St Littleton (01460) *(G-9840)*

Stonebridge Press Inc **(PA)**...................... **508 764-4325**
   25 Elm St Southbridge (01550) *(G-12035)*

Stonecoast MARble& Granite, Westbrook *Also Called: R G Eaton Woodworks Inc (G-5644)*

Stonehouse Fine Cakes...................... 203 235-5091
   61 N 1st St Meriden (06451) *(G-1702)*

Stoneridge Design Inc...................... 978 486-9626
   162 Ayer Rd Littleton (01460) *(G-9841)*

Stonewall Cable Inc...................... 603 536-1601
   126 Hawkensen Dr Rumney (03266) *(G-15498)*

Stonewall Kitchen LLC...................... 207 251-4800
   90 Spencer Dr Wells (04090) *(G-5606)*

Stonewall Kitchen LLC **(PA)**...................... **207 351-2713**
   2 Stonewall Ln York (03909) *(G-5717)*

Stonington Services LLC...................... 860 464-1991
   39 Kings Hwy Gales Ferry (06335) *(G-1261)*

Stonington Vineyards, Groton *Also Called: Stonington Vineyards Inc (G-1380)*

Stonington Vineyards Inc...................... 860 535-1222
   328 Mitchell St Groton (06340) *(G-1380)*

Stony Creek Quarry Corporation...................... 203 483-3904
   7 Business Park Dr Ste A Branford (06405) *(G-280)*

Stonyfield Organic, Londonderry *Also Called: Lactalis US Yogurt Inc (G-14761)*

Stop N Go LLC...................... 860 206-3950
   432 New Britain Ave Hartford (06106) *(G-1510)*

Storage With Style, Danville *Also Called: Post Woodworking Inc (G-14185)*

Store 111, Norton *Also Called: Roche Bros Supermarkets LLC (G-11133)*

Store Brand Partner, Leominster *Also Called: Plantbased Innovations LLC (G-9695)*

Storey Publishing LLC **(DH)**...................... **413 346-2100**
   784 Middle Rd Clarksburg (01247) *(G-8074)*

Storm Duds Raingear, Attleboro *Also Called: Mr Idea Inc (G-6039)*

Stormalong Cider LLC **(PA)**...................... **213 280-4533**
   12 Sewall Brook Ln Sherborn (01770) *(G-11811)*

Stormtech LLC...................... 860 529-8188
   70 Inwood Rd Ste 3 Rocky Hill (06067) *(G-2935)*

Storymatic Studios, Brattleboro *Also Called: The Storymatic Corp (G-17101)*

Stoughton Steel Company Inc...................... 781 826-6496
   347 Circuit St Hanover (02339) *(G-9044)*

Stowaway Sweets, Marblehead *Also Called: Seven Sweets Inc (G-10095)*

Stowe Woodward Co-Div SW Ind, Concord *Also Called: Stowe Woodward LLC (G-14160)*

Stowe Woodward LLC...................... 603 224-6300
   60 Old Turnpike Rd Concord (03301) *(G-14160)*

Stowed LLC **(PA)**...................... **203 346-5687**
   12 Elm St Westport (06880) *(G-4197)*

Stowed Home, Westport *Also Called: Stowed LLC (G-4197)*

STP Bindery Services Inc...................... 860 528-1430
   265 Prestige Park Rd Ste 2 East Hartford (06108) *(G-1023)*

Str, Enfield *Also Called: Str Holdings Inc (G-1154)*

Str Grinnell GP Holding LLC...................... 978 731-2500
   50 Technology Dr Westminster (01441) *(G-13279)*

Str Holdings Inc **(PA)**...................... **860 272-4235**
   1559 King St Enfield (06082) *(G-1154)*

Strafello Precast Inc...................... 774 501-2628
   250 Cape Hwy East Taunton (02718) *(G-8413)*

Strafford Organic Creamery, Strafford *Also Called: Ebws LLC (G-17634)*

Strain Measurement Devices Inc...................... 203 294-5800
   55 Barnes Park Rd N Wallingford (06492) *(G-3855)*

Strainrite, Auburn *Also Called: United Fbrcnts Strainrite Corp (G-4463)*

Stran & Company Inc **(PA)**...................... **617 822-6950**
   2 Heritage Dr Ste 600 Quincy (02171) *(G-11540)*

Stran Promotional Solutions, Quincy *Also Called: Stran & Company Inc (G-11540)*

Stran Technologies LLC...................... 203 720-6500
   39 Great Hill Rd Naugatuck (06770) *(G-1988)*

Stratabond Co Inc...................... 802 747-4000
   92 Park St Rutland (05701) *(G-17510)*

Stratcomm Inc...................... 508 907-7000
   24 Superior Dr Ste 103 Natick (01760) *(G-10499)*

Strategic Bio Solutions, Windham *Also Called: Standard Merger Sub LLC (G-5670)*

Strategic Communications, Natick *Also Called: Stratcomm Inc (G-10499)*

Strategic Value Partners LLC **(PA)**...................... **203 618-3500**
   100 W Putnam Ave Ste 2 Greenwich (06830) *(G-1354)*

Stratford Publishing Services...................... 802 254-6073
   70 Landmark Hill Dr Brattleboro (05301) *(G-17100)*

Stratford Steel LLC...................... 203 612-7350
   185 Masarik Ave Stratford (06615) *(G-3576)*

Stratford Stl Fabrication LLC...................... 203 612-7350
   214 Benton St Stratford (06615) *(G-3577)*

Stratgic Corp Assssment System...................... 508 359-1966
   14 Hartford St Medfield (02052) *(G-10276)*

Stratis Visuals LLC **(PA)**...................... **860 482-1208**
   129 Industrial Ln Torrington (06790) *(G-3697)*

Straton Industries Inc...................... 203 375-4488
   180 Surf Ave Stratford (06615) *(G-3578)*

Stratton Lumber Inc **(HQ)**...................... **207 246-4500**
   66 Fontaine Rd Stratton (04982) *(G-5535)*

Straumann Usa LLC...................... 978 747-2500
   60 Minuteman Rd Andover (01810) *(G-5927)*

Streamline Plastics Co Inc...................... 718 401-4000
   35 Industrial Dr East Longmeadow (01028) *(G-8396)*

Streamware, Dedham *Also Called: Crane Mdsg Systems Inc (G-8240)*

Streetscan Inc...................... 617 399-8236
   605 Salem St Wakefield (01880) *(G-12538)*

Streetwise Media Inc...................... 857 265-3269
   1 Marina Park Dr Boston (02210) *(G-7063)*

Strem Chemicals Incorporated **(HQ)**...................... **978 499-1600**
   7 Mulliken Way Newburyport (01950) *(G-10718)*

Stretch Products Corp...................... 401 722-0400
   392 Pine St Pawtucket (02860) *(G-16418)*

Stretchable Solutions, Pawtucket *Also Called: North East Knitting Inc (G-16395)*

Stride Inc...................... 203 758-8307
   80 Turnpike Dr Ste 1 Middlebury (06762) *(G-1721)*

Stride Rite, Waltham *Also Called: Stride Rite Corporation (G-12783)*

Stride Rite Corporation **(HQ)**...................... **617 824-6000**
   500 Totten Pond Rd Ste 1 Waltham (02451) *(G-12783)*

Strocchia Iron Works...................... 203 296-4600
   116 Knowlton St Bridgeport (06608) *(G-377)*

Strolid Inc...................... 978 655-8550
   1 Stiles Rd Salem (03079) *(G-15566)*

Strong Group Inc **(PA)**...................... **978 281-3300**
   39 Grove St Gloucester (01930) *(G-8960)*

Strong Leather Co, Gloucester *Also Called: Strong Group Inc (G-8960)*

Stroud International Ltd...................... 781 631-8806
   123 Pleasant St Ste 300 Marblehead (01945) *(G-10096)*

Stroudwater Distillery...................... 207 272-7327
   Thompsons Pt Portland (04102) *(G-5276)*

Structural Stone LLC...................... 401 667-4969
   285 Smith St North Kingstown (02852) *(G-16281)*

Stryker Biotech, Hopkinton *Also Called: Stryker Corporation (G-9345)*

Stryker Corporation...................... 860 528-1111
   155 Founders Plz East Hartford (06108) *(G-1024)*

Stryker Corporation...................... 508 416-5200
   35 South St Ste C Hopkinton (01748) *(G-9345)*

Stuart Allyn Co Inc...................... 413 443-7306
   17 Taconic Park Dr Ste 2 Pittsfield (01201) *(G-11425)*

Stuart Karon.. 802 649-1911
  248 Park St Newton (02458) *(G-10789)*

Studley Press Inc.. 413 684-0441
  151 E Housatonic St Dalton (01226) *(G-8156)*

Stuffed Foods LLC.. 978 203-0370
  14 Jewel Dr Ste 3 Wilmington (01887) *(G-13459)*

Stultz Electric, Portland *Also Called: Timken Motor & Crane Svcs LLC (G-5284)*

Stupell Industries Ltd Inc.. 401 831-5640
  14 Industrial Ln Johnston (02919) *(G-16107)*

Sturm Ruger & Company Inc.. 203 256-3895
  1 Lazy Pl Southport (06890) *(G-3246)*

Sturm Ruger & Company Inc.. 603 865-2424
  529 Sunapee St Newport (03773) *(G-15239)*

Sturm Ruger & Company Inc **(PA)**............................ **203 259-7843**
  1 Lacey Pl Southport (06890) *(G-3247)*

Sturm Ruger & Company Inc.. 603 863-3300
  411 Sunapee St Newport (03773) *(G-15240)*

Sturtevant Inc **(PA)**.. **781 829-6501**
  348 Circuit St Ste 1 Hanover (02339) *(G-9045)*

Sturtevant Mill Company, Hanover *Also Called: Sturtevant Inc (G-9045)*

Stylair LLC.. 860 747-4588
  161 Woodford Ave Plainville (06062) *(G-2781)*

Stylecraft Inc... 401 463-9944
  1510 Pontiac Ave Cranston (02920) *(G-15914)*

Sua Prformance Fabrication LLC................................ 860 904-6068
  89 Charles St East Hartford (06108) *(G-1025)*

Subcom LLC.. 603 319-5041
  120 Shattuck Way Newington (03801) *(G-15213)*

Subcom Cable Systems LLC.. 603 436-6100
  100 Piscataqua Dr Newington (03801) *(G-15214)*

Subcon Technology, Leominster *Also Called: M & K Industries Inc (G-9680)*

Subinas USA LLC.. 860 298-0401
  4 Market Cir Windsor (06095) *(G-4305)*

Subsalve USA LLC.. 401 884-8801
  51 Circuit Dr North Kingstown (02852) *(G-16282)*

Subsurface Drlg Remediation Co................................ 401 275-2088
  5 Mill St Tiverton (02878) *(G-16739)*

Suburban Service, Westwood *Also Called: Suburban Service Corp Norwood (G-13320)*

Suburban Service Corp Norwood................................ 781 769-1515
  16 S West Park Westwood (02090) *(G-13320)*

Success Printing and Mailing, Shelton *Also Called: Spm Management Inc (G-3065)*

Sud-Chemie Protech Inc.. 781 444-5188
  32 Fremont St Ste 1 Needham Heights (02494) *(G-10559)*

Sudbury Systems Inc... 800 876-8888
  200 Great Rd Ste 211 Bedford (01730) *(G-6272)*

Suddekor LLC **(DH)**.. **413 821-9000**
  240 Bowles Rd Agawam (01001) *(G-5808)*

Suddekor LLC... 413 525-4070
  82 Deer Park Dr East Longmeadow (01028) *(G-8397)*

Sugar Plums, North Grafton *Also Called: Dance It Up Inc (G-11021)*

Sugarbush Farm, Woodstock *Also Called: Sugarbush Farm Inc (G-17778)*

Sugarbush Farm Inc... 802 457-1757
  591 Sugarbush Farm Rd Woodstock (05091) *(G-17778)*

Sugarhill Containers, Turners Falls *Also Called: Hillside Plastics Inc (G-12448)*

Sugarloaf Ambulance and Rescue.............................. 207 235-2222
  1003 Carriage Rd Carrabassett Valley (04947) *(G-4680)*

Suisman & Blumenthal, Hartford *Also Called: Aerospace Metals Inc (G-1468)*

Sukesha, Manchester *Also Called: Chuckles Inc (G-14828)*

Sullivan Associates, East Boothbay *Also Called: Williams Partners Ltd (G-4738)*

Sullivan Investment Co Inc **(PA)**............................. **781 982-1550**
  41 Accord Park Dr Norwell (02061) *(G-11147)*

Sullivan Paper Company Inc **(PA)**........................... **413 827-7030**
  42 Progress Ave West Springfield (01089) *(G-13044)*

Sullivan Tire Co, Norwell *Also Called: Sullivan Investment Co Inc (G-11147)*

Sullivan Tire Co Inc... 508 695-9920
  36 George Leven Dr North Attleboro (02760) *(G-10890)*

Sullivan Tire Co Inc... 401 737-5251
  1102 Jefferson Blvd Warwick (02886) *(G-16866)*

Sulzer Pump Solutions US Inc **(PA)**......................... **203 238-2700**
  108 Leigus Rd Wallingford (06492) *(G-3856)*

Sumake North America LLC... 603 402-2924
  10 Northern Blvd Ste 13 Amherst (03031) *(G-13892)*

Sumitomo Pharma America Inc **(HQ)**....................... **508 481-6700**
  84 Waterford Dr Marlborough (01752) *(G-10217)*

Summer Infant Inc **(HQ)**.. **401 671-6550**
  1275 Park East Dr Woonsocket (02895) *(G-16975)*

Summer Infant (usa) Inc... 401 671-6551
  1275 Park East Dr Woonsocket (02895) *(G-16976)*

Summit Corporation of America................................. 860 283-4391
  1430 Waterbury Rd Thomaston (06787) *(G-3635)*

Summit Finishing Division, Thomaston *Also Called: Summit Corporation of America (G-3635)*

Summit Packaging Systems LLC **(PA)**..................... **603 669-5410**
  400 Gay St Manchester (03103) *(G-14937)*

Summit Plastics LLC.. 860 740-4482
  91 Main St Portland (06480) *(G-2826)*

Summit Screw Machine Corp...................................... 203 693-2727
  49 Research Dr Ste 3 Milford (06460) *(G-1891)*

Summit Stair Inc.. 203 778-2251
  101 Wooster St Bethel (06801) *(G-135)*

Sumner Communications Inc...................................... 203 748-2050
  6 Research Dr Ste 420 Shelton (06484) *(G-3066)*

Sumner Printing Inc.. 603 692-7424
  433 Route 108 Somersworth (03878) *(G-15625)*

Sun Catalytix Corporation.. 617 374-3797
  61 Moulton St Cambridge (02138) *(G-7722)*

Sun Corp... 860 567-0817
  27 Anderson Road Ext Morris (06763) *(G-1934)*

Sun Country Foods Inc **(HQ)**.................................... **855 824-7645**
  1 Edgewater Dr Ste 200 Norwood (02062) *(G-11212)*

Sun Diagnostics LLC.. 207 926-1125
  60 Pineland Dr Ste 305 New Gloucester (04260) *(G-5089)*

Sun Gro Holdings Inc... 413 786-4343
  770 Silver St Agawam (01001) *(G-5809)*

Sun Gro Horticulture Dist Inc **(HQ)**......................... **413 786-4343**
  770 Silver St Agawam (01001) *(G-5810)*

Sun Gro Horticulture Dist Inc...................................... 800 732-8667
  770 Silver St Agawam (01001) *(G-5811)*

Sun Gro Horticulture Dist Inc...................................... 864 224-7989
  770 Silver St Agawam (01001) *(G-5812)*

Sun Gro Horticulture Proc, Agawam *Also Called: Sun Gro Horticulture Dist Inc (G-5811)*

Sun Hing Noodle Co, Boston *Also Called: United Foods Incorporated (G-7093)*

Sun Journal, Lewiston *Also Called: Lewiston Daily Sun (G-4973)*

Sunapee Difference LLC.. 603 763-3500
  1398 Route 103 Newbury (03255) *(G-15204)*

Sunbelt Microelectronics Div, North Attleboro *Also Called: Mini-Systems Inc (G-10878)*

Sunburst Elctrnic Mfg Sltons I **(PA)**........................ **508 580-1881**
  70 Pleasant St West Bridgewater (02379) *(G-12983)*

Sunburst Ems, West Bridgewater *Also Called: Sunburst Elctrnic Mfg Sltons I (G-12983)*

Suncor Stainless Inc.. 508 732-9191
  70 Armstrong Rd Plymouth (02360) *(G-11479)*

Sundance Newbridge Publishing................................ 508 303-1920
  33 Boston Post Rd W Ste 440 Marlborough (01752) *(G-10218)*

Sundance Wind Project LLC.. 978 409-9712
  100 Brickstone Sq Andover (01810) *(G-5928)*

Sunday River Brewing Co Inc..................................... 207 824-4253
  320 D St Unit 426 Boston (02127) *(G-7064)*

Sundensity Inc **(PA)**... **617 642-1767**
  100 William T Morrissey Blvd Ste 166 Boston (02125) *(G-7065)*

Sunderland Printing, Hyannis *Also Called: Instant Offset Press Inc (G-9439)*

Sundrum Solar Inc... 508 740-6256
  15 Hillside Rd Northborough (01532) *(G-11110)*

Sungard, Boston *Also Called: Fis Systems International LLC (G-6737)*

Sunny Side Land Holdings LLC.................................... 207 768-1020
  9 Parsons St Presque Isle (04769) *(G-5310)*

Sunny Sky Products LLC.. 802 861-6004
  102 Kimball Ave Ste 1 South Burlington (05403) *(G-17602)*

Sunnycor Incorporated... 860 582-9667
  60 Napco Dr Terryville (06786) *(G-3610)*

Sunovion Respiratory Dev, Marlborough *Also Called: Sumitomo Pharma America Inc (G-10217)*

Sunrise, Pembroke *Also Called: Apple Mill Holding Company Inc (G-11358)*

ALPHABETIC

Sunrise County Evergreens, Milbridge *Also Called: Kelco Industries (G-5061)*

Sunrise Foods Incorporated.. 603 772-4420
  25 Pine St Brentwood (03833) *(G-14031)*

Sunrise Group USA LLC.. 508 873-1519
  85 Commons Dr Unit 403 Shrewsbury (01545) *(G-11842)*

Sunrise Guide LLC.. 207 221-3450
  503 Woodford St Portland (04103) *(G-5277)*

Sunrise Technologies Inc... 508 821-1597
  370 Paramount Dr Ste 2 Raynham (02767) *(G-11597)*

Sunrise Technologies LLC... 508 884-9732
  54 Commercial St Ste 2 Raynham (02767) *(G-11598)*

Suns International LLC... 978 349-2329
  127 Riverneck Rd Chelmsford (01824) *(G-7960)*

Sunset Meadow Farm LLC... 860 201-4654
  599 Old Middle St Goshen (06756) *(G-1304)*

Sunset Tool Inc... 603 355-2246
  58 Optical Ave Keene (03431) *(G-14623)*

Sunsetter Products, Malden *Also Called: Sunsetter Products Ltd Partnr (G-10029)*

Sunsetter Products Ltd Partnr.. 781 321-9600
  184 Charles St Malden (02148) *(G-10029)*

Sunshine, Agawam *Also Called: Sun Gro Horticulture Dist Inc (G-5810)*

Sunshine Minting Inc.. 401 265-8383
  9 Warren Ave North Providence (02911) *(G-16311)*

Sunshine Sign Company Inc.. 508 839-5588
  121 Westboro Rd North Grafton (01536) *(G-11026)*

Sunstar Spa Covers Inc... 508 993-5830
  305 Nash Rd New Bedford (02746) *(G-10653)*

Sunu, Cambridge *Also Called: Sunu Inc (G-7723)*

Sunu Inc.. 617 980-9807
  245 Main St 2nd Fl Cambridge (02142) *(G-7723)*

Sunvent Industries, Pelham *Also Called: Sylro Sales Corporation (G-15298)*

Suominen Nonwoven, East Windsor *Also Called: Windsor Locks Nonwovens Inc (G-1090)*

Suominen Nonwovens, East Windsor *Also Called: Bethune Nonwovens Inc (G-1067)*

Suominen US Holding (HQ)... **860 386-8001**
  1 Hartfield Blvd Ste 101 East Windsor (06088) *(G-1087)*

Super Brush LLC.. 413 543-1442
  800 Worcester St Springfield (01151) *(G-12136)*

Super Dup'r Instant Printing, Marlborough *Also Called: Jordan Enterprises Inc (G-10172)*

Super Seal Company LLC... 203 378-5015
  45 Seymour St Stratford (06615) *(G-3579)*

Super Thin Saws, Waterbury *Also Called: T S S Inc (G-17678)*

Super-Tech Prosthetics, Essex Junction *Also Called: Biomedic Appliances Inc (G-17228)*

Super-Temp Wire & Cable Inc... 802 655-4211
  104 Bowdoin St South Burlington (05403) *(G-17603)*

Supercon Incorporated.. 508 842-0174
  830 Boston Tpke Shrewsbury (01545) *(G-11843)*

Superconductivity Inc (HQ).. **608 831-5773**
  114 E Main St Ayer (01432) *(G-6197)*

Superior, Cambridge *Also Called: Superior Nut Company Inc (G-7724)*

Superior Bakery Inc.. 860 923-9555
  72 Main St North Grosvenordale (06255) *(G-2387)*

Superior Baking Co Inc... 508 586-6601
  176 N Warren Ave Brockton (02301) *(G-7310)*

Superior Bindery Inc... 781 303-0022
  1 Federal Dr Braintree (02184) *(G-7204)*

Superior Cake Products Inc... 508 764-3276
  94 Ashland Ave Southbridge (01550) *(G-12036)*

Superior Die, Attleboro *Also Called: Superior Die & Stamping Inc (G-6067)*

Superior Die & Stamping Inc.. 774 203-3674
  96 County St Attleboro (02703) *(G-6067)*

Superior Docks, Ellsworth *Also Called: Superior Wldg Fabrication Inc (G-4760)*

Superior Ice Cream Eqp LLC.. 603 225-4207
  155 River Rd Unit 9 Bow (03304) *(G-14011)*

Superior Kitchen Designs Inc... 978 632-5072
  166 Mill St Gardner (01440) *(G-8903)*

Superior Nut Company Inc... 800 251-6060
  225 Monsignor Obrien Hwy Cambridge (02141) *(G-7724)*

Superior Packaging & Finishing, Braintree *Also Called: Superior Bindery Inc (G-7204)*

Superior Plas Extrusion Co Inc.. 860 234-1864
  154 West St Cromwell (06416) *(G-697)*

Superior Plas Extrusion Co Inc (PA)................................... **860 963-1976**
  5 Highland Dr Putnam (06260) *(G-2877)*

Superior Plating Company.. 203 255-1501
  2 Lacey Pl Southport (06890) *(G-3248)*

Superior Power Systems, Attleboro *Also Called: Power Equipment Co Inc (G-6050)*

Superior Printing Company Inc... 781 391-9090
  407 Rear Mystic Ave Unit 34a Medford (02155) *(G-10297)*

Superior Printing Ink Co Inc.. 203 281-1921
  800 Sherman Ave Hamden (06514) *(G-1458)*

Superior Printing Ink Co Inc.. 203 777-9055
  15 Bernhard Rd North Haven (06473) *(G-2438)*

Superior Printing Ink Co Inc.. 508 481-8250
  255 E Main St Marlborough (01752) *(G-10219)*

Superior Promotions, Medford *Also Called: Superior Printing Company Inc (G-10297)*

Superior Rail and Ir Works Inc... 508 378-4025
  350 West St East Bridgewater (02333) *(G-8345)*

Superior Sheet Metal LLC... 866 468-3828
  14 Flagstone Dr Hudson (03051) *(G-14549)*

Superior Steel Fabricators Inc... 603 673-7509
  46 Route 13 Brookline (03033) *(G-14041)*

Superior Tchncal Ceramics Corp (HQ)................................... **802 527-7726**
  600 Industrial Park Rd Saint Albans (05478) *(G-17533)*

Superior Technical Ceramics, Saint Albans *Also Called: Superior Tchncal Ceramics Corp (G-17533)*

Superior Technology Corp (PA)... **203 255-1501**
  Lacey Place Southport (06890) *(G-3249)*

Superior Wldg Fabrication Inc.. 207 664-2121
  420 Christian Ridge Rd Ellsworth (04605) *(G-4760)*

Superlative Printing Inc... 781 341-9000
  4 Cabot Pl Ste 3 Stoughton (02072) *(G-12240)*

Supermedia LLC.. 207 828-6100
  600 Southborough Dr Ste 101 South Portland (04106) *(G-5515)*

Supermedia LLC.. 781 849-7670
  186 Forbes Rd Braintree (02184) *(G-7205)*

Supermedia LLC.. 802 878-2336
  34 Blair Park Rd Williston (05495) *(G-17749)*

Supernova Diagnostics Inc.. 301 792-4345
  36 Richmond Hill Rd New Canaan (06840) *(G-2088)*

Superpedestrian Inc (PA)... **877 678-7518**
  84 Hamilton St Cambridge (02139) *(G-7725)*

Supfina Machine Co Inc.. 401 294-6600
  181 Circuit Dr North Kingstown (02852) *(G-16283)*

Supplyscape Corporation... 781 503-7426
  124 Washington St Ste 101 Foxboro (02035) *(G-8726)*

Supportive Therapeutics LLC.. 860 625-9226
  1 Broadway Fl 14 Cambridge (02142) *(G-7726)*

Supreme Dairy Farms... 401 739-8180
  171 Saint Augustin St Woonsocket (02895) *(G-16977)*

Supreme-Lake Mfg Inc... 860 621-8911
  455 Atwater St Plantsville (06479) *(G-2797)*

Suraci Corp... 203 624-1345
  90 River St Ste 2 New Haven (06513) *(G-2204)*

Suraci Paint & Powder Coating, New Haven *Also Called: Suraci Corp (G-2204)*

Surell Accessories Inc.. 603 242-7784
  198 N Main St Troy (03465) *(G-15658)*

Surelock Division, Shelton *Also Called: Inline Plastics Corp (G-3022)*

Surface Coatings Div, Providence *Also Called: Westwell Industries Inc (G-16646)*

Surface Mount Technology Ctr, North Billerica *Also Called: Smtc Manufacturing (G-10956)*

Surfari Inc... 978 283-7873
  88 Bass Ave Gloucester (01930) *(G-8961)*

Surfctcom Inc.. 203 720-9209
  1453 New Haven Rd Naugatuck (06770) *(G-1989)*

Surgical Devices, New Haven *Also Called: Covidien LP (G-2141)*

Surgical Devices, North Haven *Also Called: Covidien LP (G-2403)*

Surgical Specialties Corp (HQ).. **781 751-1000**
  247 Station Dr Ste Ne1 Westwood (02090) *(G-13321)*

Surgical Tables Incorporated.. 978 777-4031
  2 De Bush Ave Bldg A Middleton (01949) *(G-10394)*

Surgiquest Inc... 203 799-2400
  488 Wheelers Farms Rd Milford (06461) *(G-1892)*

Surmet Corp (PA).. **781 345-5721**
  31 B St Burlington (01803) *(G-7436)*

Suros Surgical Systems Inc.. 508 263-2900
  250 Campus Dr Marlborough (01752) *(G-10220)*

Surplus Solutions LLC... 401 526-0055
  2010 Diamond Hill Rd Woonsocket (02895) *(G-16978)*

Surry Licensing LLC... 603 354-7000
  7 Corporate Dr Keene (03431) *(G-14624)*

Survey Software Services... 781 849-8118
  220 Forbes Rd Ste 400 Braintree (02184) *(G-7206)*

Surys Inc.. 203 333-5503
  20 Nutmeg Dr Trumbull (06611) *(G-3734)*

Suse Linux, Cambridge *Also Called: Suse LLC (G-7727)*

Suse LLC.. 617 613-2000
  10 Canal Park Ste 200 Cambridge (02141) *(G-7727)*

Sustainable Minds LLC... 617 401-2269
  1 Bdwy Kendall Sq Cambridge (02142) *(G-7728)*

Sustainx, Exeter *Also Called: Sustainx Inc (G-14303)*

Sustainx Inc... 603 601-7800
  26 Exeter Highland Dr Exeter (03833) *(G-14303)*

Suzio York Hill Companies... 888 789-4626
  975 Westfield Rd Meriden (06450) *(G-1703)*

Svh Software Inc... 978 566-1812
  139 Billerica Rd Ste 1 Chelmsford (01824) *(G-7961)*

Svp Global, Greenwich *Also Called: Strategic Value Partners LLC (G-1354)*

SW Boatworks.. 207 667-7427
  358 Douglas Hwy Lamoine (04605) *(G-4944)*

Swagnificent Ent LLC... 203 449-0124
  79 Sage Ave Bridgeport (06610) *(G-378)*

Swampscott Fuel Inc.. 781 592-1065
  197 Essex St Swampscott (01907) *(G-12299)*

Swan Dyeing and Printing Corp... 508 674-4611
  372 Stevens St Fall River (02721) *(G-8611)*

Swan Fabrics, Fall River *Also Called: Swan Dyeing and Printing Corp (G-8611)*

Swan Finishing Company Inc **(PA)**....................................... **508 674-4611**
  372 Stevens St Fall River (02721) *(G-8612)*

Swan Valley Cheese Vermont LLC... 802 868-7181
  11 Jonergin Dr Swanton (05488) *(G-17643)*

Swanson Tool Manufacturing Inc... 860 953-1641
  71 Custer St West Hartford (06110) *(G-4084)*

Swarovski North America Ltd **(DH)**...................................... **401 463-6400**
  1 Kenney Dr Cranston (02920) *(G-15915)*

Swc, Hamden *Also Called: Specialty Wire & Cord Sets Inc (G-1456)*

Sweenors Chocolates Inc **(PA)**... **401 783-4433**
  21 Charles St Wakefield (02879) *(G-16745)*

Sweet Dreams, Clinton *Also Called: Cold Stone Creamery (G-639)*

Sweet Grass Farm, Greenland *Also Called: Sweet Grass Farm Inc (G-14371)*

Sweet Grass Farm Inc... 603 766-1651
  16 Autumn Pond Park Greenland (03840) *(G-14371)*

Sweet Leaf Tea Company **(DH)**... **203 863-0263**
  900 Long Ridge Rd Bldg 2 Stamford (06902) *(G-3475)*

Sweet Metal Finishing Inc... 508 226-4359
  28 John Williams St Attleboro (02703) *(G-6068)*

Sweet Tree Holdings 1 LLC.. 802 723-6753
  One Sweet Tree Ln Island Pond (05846) *(G-17305)*

Sweetgrass Farm Winery & Dist.. 207 761-8446
  324 Fore St Portland (04101) *(G-5278)*

Sweethearts Candy Co LLC.. 781 485-4500
  135 American Legion Hwy Revere (02151) *(G-11624)*

Sweets Logging & Land Clearin... 603 664-2349
  13 Scribner Rd Strafford (03884) *(G-15632)*

Swenson Granite Company LLC **(DH)**.................................... **603 225-4322**
  369 N State St Concord (03301) *(G-14161)*

Swenson Granite Company LLC... 802 476-7021
  54 Willey St Barre (05641) *(G-17019)*

Swift Textile Metalizing LLC **(HQ)**...................................... **860 243-1122**
  23 Britton Dr Bloomfield (06002) *(G-211)*

Swimex Inc.. 508 646-1600
  390 Airport Rd Fall River (02720) *(G-8613)*

Swing By Swing Golf Inc... 804 869-6983
  80 State House Sq Unit 158 Hartford (06123) *(G-1511)*

Swing Center Factory Outlet, Billerica *Also Called: April Twenty One Corporation (G-6405)*

Swingthing, Framingham *Also Called: Creative Playthings Ltd (G-8753)*

Swiss Concept Inc... 781 894-1281
  77 Felton St Waltham (02453) *(G-12784)*

Swiss Precision Products Inc **(DH)**...................................... **508 987-8003**
  627 Main St North Oxford (01537) *(G-11035)*

Swiss Technology New England, Plainville *Also Called: Gaskin Manufacturing Corp (G-11433)*

Swissbakers Inc.. 781 354-6989
  168 Western Ave Boston (02134) *(G-7066)*

Swissline Precision LLC... 216 362-3814
  23 Ashton Park Way Unit A Cumberland (02864) *(G-15964)*

Swissline Precision Mfg Inc... 401 333-8888
  23 Ashton Park Way Unit A Cumberland (02864) *(G-15965)*

Swissline Products LLC... 401 333-8888
  23 Ashton Park Way Unit A Cumberland (02864) *(G-15966)*

Swisstronics, Woburn *Also Called: Fraen Machining Corporation (G-13571)*

Swissturn/Usa Inc... 508 987-6211
  21 Dana Rd Oxford (01540) *(G-11264)*

Swm... 413 772-2564
  53 Silvio O Conte Dr Greenfield (01301) *(G-9001)*

Swnh Fire Mutual Aid Radio... 603 352-8635
  350 Marlboro St Keene (03431) *(G-14625)*

Swpc Plastics LLC **(DH)**... **860 526-9800**
  12 Bridge St Deep River (06417) *(G-885)*

Swyme, Lexington *Also Called: Swymed Incorporated (G-9777)*

Swymed Incorporated... 855 799-6366
  71 Hancock St Lexington (02420) *(G-9777)*

Sx Industries, Stoughton *Also Called: Timco Corporation (G-12243)*

Sx Industries Inc **(PA)**... **781 828-7111**
  1551 Central St Stoughton (02072) *(G-12241)*

Syam Software Incorporated... 603 598-9575
  12 Lantern Ln Londonderry (03053) *(G-14785)*

Sybase Inc.. 617 673-1200
  400 Talcott Ave Ste 200 Watertown (02472) *(G-12910)*

Syberworks Inc.. 781 891-1999
  1 Epping St Arlington (02474) *(G-5948)*

Sycamore Networks Inc... 978 250-2900
  220 Mill Rd Chelmsford (01824) *(G-7962)*

Sycast Inc... 860 308-2122
  148 Bartholomew Ave Hartford (06106) *(G-1512)*

Syferlock Technology Corp... 203 292-5441
  31 Stowe Rd Waterbury (06704) *(G-3971)*

Syl-Ver Logging Inc... 207 398-3158
  206 Allagash Rd Allagash (04774) *(G-4404)*

Syllametrics, Brunswick *Also Called: Syllaworks LLC (G-4656)*

Syllaworks LLC... 617 564-3727
  1 Laurel Rd Brunswick (04011) *(G-4656)*

Sylro Sales Corporation.. 603 595-4556
  1 Industrial Park Dr Unit 26 Pelham (03076) *(G-15298)*

Sylvan R Shemitz Designs LLC... 203 776-5577
  45 Spring St New Haven (06519) *(G-2205)*

Sylvan R Shemitz Designs LLC **(PA)**.................................... **203 931-4455**
  114 Boston Post Rd West Haven (06516) *(G-4127)*

Sylvester Products Division, Marlborough *Also Called: Gregory Engineering Corp (G-10156)*

Sylvester Sheet Metal LLC.. 603 624-4586
  451 Pepsi Rd Manchester (03109) *(G-14938)*

Sylvesters Sales, Marlborough *Also Called: Credit Card Supplies Corp (G-10139)*

Sylvestre Screw Machine Co., Smithfield *Also Called: Precision Trned Cmponents Corp (G-16726)*

Symbol Mattress Neng Inc... 860 779-3112
  312 Lake Rd Dayville (06241) *(G-869)*

Symbol Technologies LLC.. 203 359-5677
  6 Landmark Sq 4th Fl Stamford (06901) *(G-3476)*

Symbotic LLC **(HQ)**... **978 284-2800**
  200 Research Dr Wilmington (01887) *(G-13460)*

Symetrica Inc... 508 718-5610
  4 Lyberty Way Ste 1 Westford (01886) *(G-13265)*

Symmetry Med New Bedford Inc... 781 447-6661
  61 John Vertente Blvd New Bedford (02745) *(G-10654)*

Symmetry Medical Inc.. 508 998-1104
  61 John Vertente Blvd New Bedford (02745) *(G-10655)*

Symmetry Medical Manufacturing, Manchester *Also Called: Poly-Vac Inc (G-14912)*

Symmetry Products, Lincoln *Also Called: Lance Industries Inc (G-16144)*

A
L
P
H
A
B
E
T
I
C

Symmons Industries Inc....................................	508 857-2352
275 Bodwell St Avon (02322) *(G-6163)*	
Symmons Industries Inc **(PA)**...........................	**800 796-6667**
31 Brooks Dr Braintree (02184) *(G-7207)*	
Syn-Mar Products Inc......................................	860 872-8505
5 Nutmeg Dr Ellington (06029) *(G-1117)*	
Synageva Biopharma Corp..................................	781 357-9900
33 Hayden Ave Lexington (02421) *(G-9778)*	
Synap, Dover *Also Called: Synap Inc (G-14251)*	
Synap Inc..	888 572-1150
77 Fourth St Dover (03820) *(G-14251)*	
Syncote Chemical Company Inc..............................	203 426-5526
16 Greenbriar Ln Newtown (06470) *(G-2348)*	
Syndax, Waltham *Also Called: Syndax Pharmaceuticals Inc (G-12785)*	
Syndax Pharmaceuticals Inc **(PA)**........................	**781 419-1400**
35 Gatehouse Dr Bldg D Waltham (02451) *(G-12785)*	
Syndax Securities Corporation..............................	781 472-2985
35 Gatehouse Dr Waltham (02451) *(G-12786)*	
Syndexa Pharmaceuticals Corp..............................	617 607-7283
480 Arsenal St Watertown (02472) *(G-12911)*	
Syner-G Biopharma Group LLC **(PA)**.......................	**508 460-9700**
100 Pennsylvania Ave Ste 300 Framingham (01701) *(G-8805)*	
Synergy, Keene *Also Called: Synergy Sportswear Inc (G-14626)*	
Synergy Manufacturing LLC.................................	781 209-5538
1551 Central St Stoughton (02072) *(G-12242)*	
Synergy Printing..	207 703-2782
89 Goodwin Rd Kittery Point (03905) *(G-4942)*	
Synergy Signworks LLC....................................	603 440-3519
880 Candia Rd Unit 1 Manchester (03109) *(G-14939)*	
Synergy Sportswear Inc **(PA)**...........................	**603 352-8681**
5 Main St Keene (03431) *(G-14626)*	
Syneron Candela, Marlborough *Also Called: Candela Corporation (G-10127)*	
Synlogic, Cambridge *Also Called: Synlogic Inc (G-7729)*	
Synlogic Inc **(PA)**.....................................	**617 401-9975**
301 Binney St Ste 3 Cambridge (02142) *(G-7729)*	
Synopsys Inc...	508 870-6500
1800 W Park Dr Ste 410 Westborough (01581) *(G-13139)*	
Synostics Inc..	781 248-5699
3 Old Coach Rd Weston (02493) *(G-13290)*	
Synqor Inc **(PA)**.......................................	**978 849-0600**
155 Swanson Rd Boxborough (01719) *(G-7155)*	
Synqor Holdings LLC......................................	978 849-0600
155 Swanson Rd Boxborough (01719) *(G-7156)*	
Syntac Coated Products, New Hartford *Also Called: Scp Management LLC (G-2108)*	
Synthetic Labs Inc.......................................	978 957-2919
24 Victory Ln Dracut (01826) *(G-8312)*	
Synthomer Inc...	978 342-5831
83 Authority Dr Fitchburg (01420) *(G-8678)*	
Syntonic Microwave LLC...................................	408 866-5900
50 Minuteman Rd Andover (01810) *(G-5929)*	
Synventive Molding Solutions Inc **(HQ)**.................	**978 750-8065**
10 Centennial Dr Peabody (01960) *(G-11345)*	
Syqwest Inc...	401 432-7129
30 Kenney Dr Cranston (02920) *(G-15916)*	
Syratech Acquisition Corp **(HQ)**........................	**781 539-0100**
22 Blake St Medford (02155) *(G-10298)*	
Sysaid Technologies Inc..................................	800 686-7047
128 Chestnut St Newton (02465) *(G-10790)*	
Sysdyne Technologies LLC................................	203 327-3649
9 Riverbend Dr S Stamford (06907) *(G-3477)*	
Sysnova LLC...	508 309-9264
5 Boundry Rd Mansfield (02048) *(G-10077)*	
Systematic Automation Inc................................	310 218-3361
20 Executive Dr Farmington (06032) *(G-1249)*	
Systems & Software Inc...................................	802 655-4400
401 Watertower Cir Colchester (05446) *(G-17204)*	
Syzygy Global Technology LLC.............................	203 818-2166
17 Cutrone Rd Darien (06820) *(G-856)*	
Szr Fuel LLC...	978 649-2409
46 Anderson Dr Tyngsboro (01879) *(G-12466)*	
T & A Industries LLC.....................................	860 309-9211
3 Maple Ave Bloomfield (06002) *(G-212)*	

T & A Screw Products Inc.................................	203 756-2770
64 Avenue Of Industry Waterbury (06705) *(G-3972)*	
T & D Specialties Inc....................................	508 987-8344
35 Industrial Park Rd E Oxford (01540) *(G-11265)*	
T & J Manufacturing LLP..................................	860 632-8655
1385 Newfield St Middletown (06457) *(G-1785)*	
T & J Screw Machine Pdts LLC.............................	860 417-3801
27 Main St Oakville (06779) *(G-2627)*	
T & M Enterprises Inc....................................	802 447-0601
251 Church St Shaftsbury (05262) *(G-17553)*	
T & T Anodizing Inc......................................	978 454-9631
35 Maple St Lowell (01852) *(G-9926)*	
T & T Anodizing Incorporated.............................	978 454-9631
35 Maple St Ste 8 Lowell (01852) *(G-9927)*	
T & T Anonizing & Indus Spray, Lowell *Also Called: T & T Anodizing Inc (G-9926)*	
T & T Automation Inc....................................	860 683-8788
88 Pierson Ln Windsor (06095) *(G-4306)*	
T & T Machine Products Inc...............................	781 878-3861
254 Beech St Rockland (02370) *(G-11662)*	
T & T Woodworkers Inc...................................	401 766-2304
500 Pond St Woonsocket (02895) *(G-16979)*	
T and P Lumber Inc **(PA)**..............................	**207 825-3317**
60 Fowler Rd Orrington (04474) *(G-5139)*	
T C I, Oxford *Also Called: Turbine Components Inc (G-2713)*	
T D F Metal Finishing Co Inc.............................	978 223-4292
9 Electronics Ave Danvers (01923) *(G-8223)*	
T D L, Canton *Also Called: Tdl Inc (G-7833)*	
T E M, Buxton *Also Called: Tem Inc (G-4665)*	
T G G Inc..	978 777-5010
3 Birch Rd Middleton (01949) *(G-10395)*	
T H M, Attleboro *Also Called: Techncal Hrdfcing McHining Inc (G-6069)*	
T J Ryan LLC..	207 989-7183
90 Acme Rd Brewer (04412) *(G-4620)*	
T K Machining, Waterboro *Also Called: TK Machining Inc (G-5592)*	
T L Edwards Inc...	508 732-9148
300 Cherry St Plymouth (02360) *(G-11480)*	
T M C, Durham *Also Called: Technical Manufacturing Corp (G-904)*	
T M F, Wallingford *Also Called: Technical Metal Finishing Inc (G-3857)*	
T M I Liquidating Inc....................................	860 828-0344
134 Commerce St East Berlin (06023) *(G-919)*	
T M Services Inc..	802 775-2948
Route 4 East Woodstock Avenue Rutland (05701) *(G-17511)*	
T N Dickinson Company...................................	860 267-2279
31 E High St East Hampton (06424) *(G-966)*	
T P Engineering, Danbury *Also Called: TP Cycle & Engineering Inc (G-826)*	
T R D Specialities, Pine Meadow *Also Called: Trd Specialties Inc (G-2729)*	
T R Dillon Logging Inc **(PA)**..........................	**207 696-8137**
138 Main St Madison (04950) *(G-5043)*	
T R I, Milford *Also Called: Tech Resources Inc (G-15039)*	
T R Sign Design Inc.....................................	207 856-2600
306 Warren Ave Ste 3 Portland (04103) *(G-5279)*	
T Raymond Forest Products, Lee *Also Called: T Raymond Forest Products Inc (G-4946)*	
T Raymond Forest Products Inc............................	207 738-2313
260 Arab Rd Lee (04455) *(G-4946)*	
T S S Inc...	802 244-8101
80 Commercial Dr Ste 5 Waterbury (05676) *(G-17678)*	
T Sardelli and Sons Inc..................................	401 429-2144
195 Dupont Dr Providence (02907) *(G-16617)*	
T Stop, Wakefield *Also Called: All-City Screen Printing Inc (G-12498)*	
T Tech Machine Inc......................................	401 732-3590
11 Knight St Bldg A Warwick (02886) *(G-16867)*	
T Woodward Stair Building LLC............................	860 664-0515
10 Bailey Dr North Branford (06471) *(G-2376)*	
T-Shirts Authority Inc...................................	774 855-0000
20 Iyanough Rd West Yarmouth (02673) *(G-13074)*	
T-Shirts Etc Inc...	860 657-3551
74 Kreiger Ln Ste 1 Glastonbury (06033) *(G-1298)*	
T&J Manufacturing, Middletown *Also Called: T & J Manufacturing LLP (G-1785)*	
T2 Biosystems, Lexington *Also Called: T2 Biosystems Inc (G-9779)*	
T2 Biosystems Inc **(PA)**...............................	**781 761-4646**
101 Hartwell Ave Lexington (02421) *(G-9779)*	

T2 Biosystems Inc.. 978 447-1069
231 Andover St Wilmington (01887) *(G-13461)*

T2 Biosystems Manufacturing, Wilmington *Also Called: T2 Biosystems Inc (G-13461)*

Ta Property Maintenance LLC.. 207 289-7158
81 Sawyer Rd Scarborough (04074) *(G-5444)*

Ta Update Inc **(PA)**.. **802 479-4040**
47 N Main St Ste 200 Barre (05641) *(G-17020)*

Table Talk Pies, Worcester *Also Called: Table Talk Pies Inc (G-13810)*

Table Talk Pies Inc... 508 798-8811
25 Southgate St Worcester (01610) *(G-13809)*

Table Talk Pies Inc **(PA)**... **508 438-1556**
58 Gardner St Worcester (01610) *(G-13810)*

TAC Acquisition Corp.. 203 983-5276
8 Sound Shore Dr Greenwich (06830) *(G-1355)*

Tachwa Enterprises Inc... 203 691-5772
4 Industrial Cir Hamden (06517) *(G-1459)*

Taco Inc **(PA)**.. **401 942-8000**
1160 Cranston St Cranston (02920) *(G-15917)*

Taco Comfort Solutions, Cranston *Also Called: Taco Inc (G-15917)*

Taco Fasteners Inc... 860 747-5597
71 Northwest Dr Plainville (06062) *(G-2782)*

Taco International Ltd.. 401 942-8000
1160 Cranston St Cranston (02920) *(G-15918)*

Taconic Wire, North Branford *Also Called: SA Candelora Enterprises Inc (G-2374)*

Tactai Inc... 617 391-7915
225 Wyman St Waltham (02451) *(G-12787)*

Tafa Incorporated **(DH)**.. **603 224-9585**
146 Pembroke Rd Ste 1 Concord (03301) *(G-14162)*

Tag Global Systems LLC.. 800 630-4708
575 Washington St Ste 1 Pembroke (02359) *(G-11378)*

Taggart Ice Inc.. 603 888-4630
8 Taggart Dr Nashua (03060) *(G-15174)*

Tagup Inc... 513 262-0159
361 Newbury St Ste 300 Boston (02115) *(G-7067)*

Tahoe Jewelry Inc.. 401 435-4114
20 J Medeiros Way East Providence (02914) *(G-16045)*

Tailor Vintage, Norwalk *Also Called: Sam & Ty LLC (G-2569)*

Tak Systems, Wareham *Also Called: Cataki International Inc (G-12833)*

Takeda... 617 594-7199
33 Brighton St Belmont (02478) *(G-6313)*

Takeda... 781 266-5464
300 Shire Way Lexington (02421) *(G-9780)*

Takeda, Cambridge *Also Called: Takeda Pharmaceuticals USA Inc (G-7733)*

Takeda Building 35 5... 617 444-4352
35 Landsdowne St Cambridge (02139) *(G-7730)*

Takeda Dev Ctr Americas Inc... 617 349-0200
500 Kendall St Cambridge (02142) *(G-7731)*

Takeda Manufacturing USA Inc.. 877 825-3327
95 Hayden Ave Lexington (02421) *(G-9781)*

Takeda Oncology, Cambridge *Also Called: Millennium Pharmaceuticals Inc (G-7646)*

Takeda Pharmaceutical Co Ltd... 877 872-3700
200 Shire Way Lexington (02421) *(G-9782)*

Takeda Pharmaceuticals Inc.. 617 679-7348
35 Landsdowne St Cambridge (02139) *(G-7732)*

Takeda Pharmaceuticals USA Inc.. 781 733-5208
350 Massachusetts Ave Cambridge (02139) *(G-7733)*

Takeda Pharmaceuticals USA Inc.. 617 349-0200
300 Shire Way Lexington (02421) *(G-9783)*

Takeda Pharmaceuticals USA Inc **(HQ)**............................. **877 825-3327**
95 Hayden Ave Lexington (02421) *(G-9784)*

Takeda Pharmaceuticals USA Inc.. 781 482-1461
200 Riverpark Dr North Reading (01864) *(G-11046)*

Takeda Phrmaceuticals Amer Inc **(DH)**............................. **224 554-6500**
95 Hayden Ave Lexington (02421) *(G-9785)*

Takeda Vaccines Inc... 970 672-4918
40 Landsdowne St Cambridge (02139) *(G-7734)*

Talalay Global Inc **(DH)**... **203 924-0700**
510 River Rd Shelton (06484) *(G-3067)*

Talamas Broadcast Equipment, Waltham *Also Called: Talamas Company Inc (G-12788)*

Talamas Company Inc... 617 928-3437
280 Bear Hill Rd Waltham (02451) *(G-12788)*

Talaria Company LLC.. 207 244-5572
130 Shore Rd Southwest Harbor (04679) *(G-5519)*

Talaria Company LLC.. 207 667-1891
40 Industrial Way Trenton (04605) *(G-5558)*

Talaria Company LLC **(PA)**.. **401 683-7100**
1 Little Harbor Lndg Portsmouth (02871) *(G-16458)*

Talaria Company LLC.. 401 683-7280
1 Little Harbor Lndg Ste 1 Portsmouth (02871) *(G-16459)*

Talbot Hill Holdings Corp.. 603 357-2523
36 Denman Thompson Hwy Swanzey (03446) *(G-15646)*

Talco Enterprises LLC.. 603 765-8052
6 Freeman Hall Rd Nottingham (03290) *(G-15278)*

Talient Action Group, Manchester *Also Called: Printers Square Inc (G-14915)*

Tall Guy Woodworking Inc... 617 901-2166
1349 Commonwealth Ave Boston (02134) *(G-7068)*

Tallinn Fulfillment Limited... 203 878-2155
291 Pepes Farm Rd Milford (06460) *(G-1893)*

Tallon Lumber Inc... 860 824-0733
2 Tallon Dr Canaan (06018) *(G-558)*

Tally Transportation LLC... 781 510-2411
45 North St Randolph (02368) *(G-11576)*

Tamer Industries Inc... 508 677-0900
185 Riverside Ave Somerset (02725) *(G-11856)*

Tamworth Granite, Tamworth *Also Called: Windy Ridge Corporation (G-15650)*

Tandem Kross LLC.. 603 369-7060
490 S Stark Hwy Weare (03281) *(G-15673)*

Tandemkross, Weare *Also Called: Tandem Kross LLC (G-15673)*

Tangenx Technology, Marlborough *Also Called: Repligen Corporation (G-10202)*

Tango Modem LLC... 203 421-2245
303 Race Hill Rd Madison (06443) *(G-1572)*

TANGO THERAPEUTICS, Boston *Also Called: Tango Therapeutics Inc (G-7069)*

Tango Therapeutics Inc **(PA)**... **857 302-4900**
201 W Brookline St Ste 901 Boston (02215) *(G-7069)*

Tannin, Peabody *Also Called: Walnut 65 Holdings Inc (G-11352)*

Tantor Media Incorporated.. 860 395-1155
6 Business Park Rd Old Saybrook (06475) *(G-2664)*

Tanury Industries Inc.. 800 428-6213
6 New England Way Lincoln (02865) *(G-16156)*

Tanyx Measurements Inc.. 978 671-0183
505 Middlesex Tpke Unit 9 Billerica (01821) *(G-6485)*

Tapcoenpro Tracker LLC.. 781 270-1200
30 Corporate Dr Ste 200 Burlington (01803) *(G-7437)*

Tapecoat Company.. 781 332-0700
295 University Ave Westwood (02090) *(G-13322)*

Taproot... 802 472-1617
49 Fox St Portland (04101) *(G-5280)*

Taran Bros Inc... 802 287-9308
2522 Vt Route 30 N Poultney (05764) *(G-17452)*

Taran Bros Inc **(PA)**.. **802 287-5853**
Rte 30 Poultney (05764) *(G-17453)*

Target Custom Manufacturing Co.. 860 388-5848
27 Swain Johnson Trl Haddam (06438) *(G-1410)*

Target Flavors Inc.. 203 775-4727
7 Del Mar Dr Brookfield (06804) *(G-539)*

Target Therapeutics Inc **(HQ)**....................................... **508 683-4000**
300 Boston Scientific Way Marlborough (01752) *(G-10221)*

Tark Inc... 978 663-8074
35 Dunham Rd Ste 7 Billerica (01821) *(G-6486)*

Tarpon Biosystems Inc.. 978 979-4222
197m Boston Post Rd W Ste 273 Marlborough (01752) *(G-10222)*

Tarry Manufacturing, Danbury *Also Called: Tarry Medical Products Inc (G-823)*

Tarry Medical Products Inc... 203 791-9001
22 Shelter Rock Ln Unit 7 Danbury (06810) *(G-823)*

Tarveda Therapeutics Inc... 617 923-4100
134 Coolidge Ave Watertown (02472) *(G-12912)*

Tasco Engineering, North Dighton *Also Called: Taunton Stove Company Inc (G-11004)*

Tase-Rite Co Inc.. 401 783-7300
1211 Kingstown Rd Wakefield (02879) *(G-16746)*

Tasi Group, Marlborough *Also Called: Tasi Holdings Inc (G-10223)*

Tasi Holdings Inc **(PA)**... **513 202-5182**
40 Locke Dr Ste B Marlborough (01752) *(G-10223)*

A
L
P
H
A
B
E
T
I
C

Tasker Funeral Home, Dover *Also Called: Tfh Liquidation Company LLC* **(G-14252)**

Tasman Industries Inc.. 207 938-4491
  9 Main St Hartland (04943) **(G-4878)**

Tasman Leather Group LLC... 207 553-3700
  9 Main St Hartland (04943) **(G-4879)**

Tasteful Gift Baskets By Mrs G, Waterbury *Also Called: Grotto Always Inc* **(G-3915)**

Tastex Corporation... 401 727-2900
  467 469 Roosevelt Ave Central Falls (02863) **(G-15798)**

Tata Harper Labratory, Whiting *Also Called: Tatas Natural Alchemy LLC* **(G-17711)**

Tata Harper Skincare, Whiting *Also Called: Tatas Natural Alchemy LLC* **(G-17712)**

Tatas Natural Alchemy LLC... 802 462-3958
  1136 Wooster Rd Whiting (05778) **(G-17711)**

Tatas Natural Alchemy LLC **(PA)**.. **802 462-3814**
  1135 Wooster Rd Whiting (05778) **(G-17712)**

Tatte Bakery and Cafe, Boston *Also Called: Tatte Holdings LLC* **(G-7070)**

Tatte Holdings LLC.. 617 577-1111
  320 Congress St Fl 5 Boston (02210) **(G-7070)**

Tattersall Machining Inc.. 508 529-2300
  190 Milford St Upton (01568) **(G-12474)**

Taunton.. 774 501-2220
  30 Taunton Grn Ste 1 Taunton (02780) **(G-12370)**

Taunton Inc... 203 426-8171
  63 S Main St Newtown (06470) **(G-2349)**

Taunton Press, Newtown *Also Called: Taunton Inc* **(G-2349)**

Taunton Press Inc... 203 426-8171
  191 S Main St Newtown (06470) **(G-2350)**

Taunton Stove Company Inc.. 508 823-0786
  490 Somerset Ave Ste 490 North Dighton (02764) **(G-11004)**

Taurus Technologies Corp... 508 234-6372
  134 Ferry St South Grafton (01560) **(G-11957)**

Tausight Inc... 339 364-1246
  10-24 School St Boston (02108) **(G-7071)**

Tauten Inc... 978 961-3272
  100 Cummings Ctr Ste 215f Beverly (01915) **(G-6386)**

Taylor & Fenn Company.. 860 219-9393
  22 Deerfield Rd Windsor (06095) **(G-4307)**

Taylor Brooke Winery, Woodstock *Also Called: Brooke Taylor Farm LLC* **(G-4391)**

Taylor Coml Foodservice Inc.. 336 245-6400
  3 Farm Glen Blvd Ste 301 Farmington (06032) **(G-1250)**

Taylor Communications Inc... 860 875-0731
  311 Prestige Park Rd East Hartford (06108) **(G-1026)**

Taylor Communications Inc... 508 584-0102
  81 Uraco Way Avon (02322) **(G-6164)**

Taylor Communications Inc... 781 843-0250
  400 Washington St Braintree (02184) **(G-7208)**

Taylor Egg Products, Madbury *Also Called: Taylor Egg Products Inc* **(G-14801)**

Taylor Egg Products Inc.. 603 742-1050
  242 Littleworth Rd Madbury (03823) **(G-14801)**

Taylor Farms New England Inc... 877 323-7374
  320 Commerce Park Rd North Kingstown (02852) **(G-16284)**

Tb Woods Corporation.. 781 917-0600
  300 Granite St Ste 201 Braintree (02184) **(G-7209)**

Tcc, Concord *Also Called: Technical Communications Corp* **(G-8135)**

TCI, Seekonk *Also Called: Telco Communications Inc* **(G-11788)**

TCI America Inc... 508 336-6633
  21 Industrial Ct Seekonk (02771) **(G-11786)**

TCI Press Inc.. 508 336-6633
  21 Industrial Ct Seekonk (02771) **(G-11787)**

Tcr2 Therapeutics, Cambridge *Also Called: Tcr2 Therapeutics Inc* **(G-7735)**

Tcr2 Therapeutics Inc **(HQ)**... **617 949-5200**
  100 Binney St Ste 710 Cambridge (02142) **(G-7735)**

Tdc Americas, Cambridge *Also Called: Takeda Dev Ctr Americas Inc* **(G-7731)**

Tdf Metal Finishing Co Inc... 978 223-4292
  6 Electronics Ave Danvers (01923) **(G-8224)**

Tdi, Torrington *Also Called: Torrington Distributors Inc* **(G-3701)**

Tdl Inc.. 781 828-3366
  550 Turnpike St Canton (02021) **(G-7833)**

Te Connctvity Phenix Optix Inc.. 401 637-4600
  15 Gray Ln Ste 301 Ashaway (02804) **(G-15745)**

Te Connectivity Corporation.. 860 684-8000
  15 Tyco Dr Stafford Springs (06076) **(G-3260)**

Te Connectivity Corporation.. 717 592-4299
  20a Forbes Rd Northborough (01532) **(G-11111)**

Te Connectivity Corporation.. 781 278-5200
  63 Nahatan St Ste 100 Norwood (02062) **(G-11213)**

Te Connectivity Corporation.. 781 278-5273
  62 Nahatan St Norwood (02062) **(G-11214)**

Teachers Publishing Group, Portsmouth *Also Called: Stenhouse Publishers* **(G-15440)**

Team Augmented Reality Inc... 207 350-0460
  440 E Neck Rd Nobleboro (04555) **(G-5102)**

Team Bes, Plainville *Also Called: Building Envelope Systems LLC* **(G-11430)**

Team Eda Inc.. 603 656-5200
  1001 Elm St Bsmt 305 Manchester (03101) **(G-14940)**

TEAM INC.. 401 762-1500
  841 Park East Dr Woonsocket (02895) **(G-16980)**

Team Logic It.. 320 760-9084
  428 Hartford Tpke Ste 107 Vernon (06066) **(G-3757)**

Team Technologies, Haverhill *Also Called: Baril Corporation* **(G-9076)**

Team Technologies Inc... 860 945-9125
  162 Commercial St Watertown (06795) **(G-4031)**

Teamar, Nobleboro *Also Called: Team Augmented Reality Inc* **(G-5102)**

Tebaldi Enterprises Inc.. 413 532-3261
  2 Cabot St Holyoke (01040) **(G-9283)**

TEC, Oxford *Also Called: TEC Engineering Corp* **(G-11266)**

TEC Engineering Corp... 508 987-0231
  31 Town Forest Rd Oxford (01540) **(G-11266)**

TEC Mark Plating, Norwood *Also Called: Remtec Incorporated* **(G-11207)**

Teca-Print USA Corp... 781 369-1084
  2a Lowell Ave Winchester (01890) **(G-13492)**

Tecdocdigital Solutions, Hudson *Also Called: MSP Digital Marketing Mass Inc* **(G-9394)**

Tech Circuits, Wallingford *Also Called: Apct-Wallingford Inc* **(G-3773)**

Tech Fab Inc... 413 532-9022
  1 W Main St South Hadley (01075) **(G-11967)**

Tech II Business Services Inc... 518 587-1565
  400 Capital Blvd Rocky Hill (06067) **(G-2936)**

Tech Nh Inc **(PA)**... **603 424-4404**
  8 Continental Blvd Merrimack (03054) **(G-15007)**

Tech Resources Inc.. 603 673-9000
  1 Meadowbrook Dr Milford (03055) **(G-15039)**

Tech Ridge Inc.. 978 256-5741
  190 Hunt Rd Chelmsford (01824) **(G-7963)**

Tech-Air Incorporated.. 860 848-1287
  152 Route 163 Uncasville (06382) **(G-3744)**

Tech-Etch Inc.. 508 675-5757
  100 Riggenbach Rd Fall River (02720) **(G-8614)**

Tech-Etch Inc **(PA)**.. **508 747-0300**
  45 Aldrin Rd Plymouth (02360) **(G-11481)**

Tech-Repro Inc.. 203 348-8884
  555 Summer St Ste 1 Stamford (06901) **(G-3478)**

Tech180 Corp.. 413 203-6123
  180 Pleasant St Ste 211 Easthampton (01027) **(G-8463)**

Tech180 System, Easthampton *Also Called: Tech180 Corp* **(G-8463)**

Techfourfive LLC.. 603 438-5760
  45 Edgewood Ave Nashua (03064) **(G-15175)**

Techncal Hrdfcing McHining Inc.. 508 223-2900
  35 Extension St Attleboro (02703) **(G-6069)**

Techncal Metal Fabricators Inc.. 508 473-2223
  134 Uxbridge Rd Mendon (01756) **(G-10322)**

Techni-Products Inc.. 413 525-6321
  126 Industrial Dr East Longmeadow (01028) **(G-8398)**

Technic Inc **(PA)**.. **401 781-6100**
  47 Molter St Cranston (02910) **(G-15919)**

Technic Inc... 401 781-6100
  55 Maryland Ave Pawtucket (02860) **(G-16419)**

Technic Inc Equipment Division, Pawtucket *Also Called: Technic Inc* **(G-16419)**

Technical Communications Corp **(PA)**................................. **978 287-5100**
  100 Domino Dr Concord (01742) **(G-8135)**

Technical Industries Inc **(PA)**.. **860 489-2160**
  336 Pinewoods Rd Torrington (06790) **(G-3698)**

Technical Machine Components.. 603 880-0444
  4 Security Dr Hudson (03051) **(G-14550)**

Technical Manufacturing Corp................................ 860 349-1735
  645 New Haven Rd Durham (06422) *(G-904)*

Technical Manufacturing Corp **(HQ)**.................... **978 532-6330**
  15 Centennial Dr Peabody (01960) *(G-11346)*

Technical Metal Finishing Inc................................ 203 284-7825
  29 Capital Dr Wallingford (06492) *(G-3857)*

Technical Power Systems Inc................................ 630 719-1471
  19 Leona Dr Middleboro (02346) *(G-10378)*

Technical Publications Inc.................................... 781 899-0263
  45 Calvary St Waltham (02453) *(G-12789)*

Technical Reproductions Inc................................. 203 849-9100
  326 Main Ave Norwalk (06851) *(G-2575)*

Technical Research and Manufacturing Inc............... 603 627-6000
  280 S River Rd Bedford (03110) *(G-13951)*

Technical Sales & Svc of Neng.............................. 207 946-5506
  170 N Daggett Hill Rd Greene (04236) *(G-4848)*

Technical Services Inc....................................... 781 389-8342
  263 South St E Raynham (02767) *(G-11599)*

Technical Tool & Design LLC................................ 603 286-1600
  19 Axle Dr Northfield (03276) *(G-15269)*

Technicoil LLC.. 603 569-3100
  775 Route 16 Ossipee (03864) *(G-15283)*

Technique Printers Inc....................................... 860 669-2516
  36 Old Post Rd Clinton (06413) *(G-651)*

Technisonic Research Inc.................................... 203 368-3600
  328 Commerce Dr Fairfield (06825) *(G-1201)*

Technodic Inc... 401 467-6660
  245 Carolina Ave Providence (02905) *(G-16618)*

Technology Design Mfg Svcs LLC........................... 413 730-4444
  220 Brookdale Dr Springfield (01104) *(G-12137)*

Technology Plastics LLC..................................... 860 583-1590
  75 Napco Dr Terryville (06786) *(G-3611)*

Technology Review Inc....................................... 617 475-8000
  196 Broadway Ste 3 Cambridge (02139) *(G-7736)*

Technology Service Corporation............................ 508 275-5113
  656 Burke's Way Plymouth (02360) *(G-11482)*

Technology Service Corporation............................ 508 275-5113
  246 S Meadow Rd Plymouth (02360) *(G-11483)*

Technolutions Inc.. 203 404-4835
  157 Church St Fl 22a New Haven (06510) *(G-2206)*

Technomad Associates LLC................................. 413 665-6704
  37 Harvard St Ste 2 South Deerfield (01373) *(G-11929)*

Technometalpost Connecticut............................... 203 228-7094
  766 Marion Rd Cheshire (06410) *(G-618)*

Techprecision, Westminster *Also Called: Techprecision Corporation (G-13280)*

Techprecision Corporation **(PA)**........................ **978 874-0591**
  1 Bella Dr Westminster (01473) *(G-13280)*

Techprint Inc... 978 975-1245
  137 Marston St Lawrence (01841) *(G-9602)*

Techtrade Inc.. 781 724-7878
  935 Great Plain Ave Needham (02492) *(G-10525)*

Techtrak LLC... 401 397-3983
  2435 Nooseneck Hill Rd Ste A1b Coventry (02816) *(G-15822)*

Tecnau Inc **(DH)**... **978 608-0500**
  60 Willow St North Andover (01845) *(G-10851)*

Tecogen, Waltham *Also Called: Tecogen Inc (G-12790)*

Tecogen Inc **(PA)**....................................... **781 466-6402**
  45 1st Ave Waltham (02451) *(G-12790)*

Tecomet, Wilmington *Also Called: Tecomet Inc (G-13463)*

Tecomet Inc... 978 642-2400
  301 Ballardvale St Ste 3 Wilmington (01887) *(G-13462)*

Tecomet Inc **(HQ)**....................................... **978 642-2400**
  115 Eames St Wilmington (01887) *(G-13463)*

Tecomet Inc... 781 782-6400
  170 New Boston St Woburn (01801) *(G-13675)*

Tecostar Holdings Inc **(PA)**............................. **978 642-2400**
  18 Commerce Way Ste 500 Woburn (01801) *(G-13676)*

Tecta America Corp... 603 352-4232
  353 West St Keene (03431) *(G-14627)*

Ted Ondrick Company LLC **(PA)**........................ **413 592-2565**
  58 Industry Rd Chicopee (01020) *(G-8062)*

Teddys Tees Inc... 603 226-2762
  248 Sheep Davis Rd Ste 6 Concord (03301) *(G-14163)*

Tedor Pharma Inc... 401 658-5219
  400 Highland Corporate Dr Cumberland (02864) *(G-15967)*

Tee Enterprises... 603 447-5662
  Rte 16 Conway (03818) *(G-14182)*

Tees & More LLC.. 860 244-2224
  306 Murphy Rd Hartford (06114) *(G-1513)*

Teespring Inc... 855 833-7774
  3 Davol Sq Ste B300 Providence (02903) *(G-16619)*

Tego Inc.. 781 547-5680
  204 Second Ave Ste 1 Waltham (02451) *(G-12791)*

Tegra Medical LLC **(HQ)**................................ **508 541-4200**
  16 Forge Pkwy Franklin (02038) *(G-8866)*

Tegu... 877 834-8869
  319 Rowayton Ave Norwalk (06853) *(G-2576)*

Tei Biosciences Inc **(DH)**............................... **617 268-1616**
  7 Elkins St Boston (02127) *(G-7072)*

Tek Industries Inc.. 860 870-0001
  166 Tunnel Rd Vernon Rockville (06066) *(G-3763)*

Tek Wire and Cable Corp................................... 914 663-2100
  77 Havemeyer Ln Unit 422 Stamford (06902) *(G-3479)*

Tek-Air Systems Inc.. 203 791-1400
  600 Pepper St Monroe (06468) *(G-1923)*

Tek-Motive Inc.. 203 468-2224
  171 Turtle Bay Dr Branford (06405) *(G-281)*

Teka Interconnection Systems Inc.......................... 401 785-4110
  231 Ferris Ave Rumford (02916) *(G-16677)*

Tekcast Industries RI, Warwick *Also Called: Conley Casting Supply Corp (G-16797)*

Tekni-Plex Inc.. 508 881-2440
  150 Homer Ave Ashland (01721) *(G-5968)*

Teknikor Automtn & Contrls Inc............................ 508 679-9474
  595 Airport Rd Fall River (02720) *(G-8615)*

Teknor Apex.. 603 434-3056
  4 Meadowbrook Rd Derry (03038) *(G-14210)*

Teknor Apex Co... 802 524-7704
  300 Industrial Park Rd Saint Albans (05478) *(G-17534)*

Teknor Apex Co, Pawtucket *Also Called: Teknor Color Company (G-16421)*

Teknor Apex Company...................................... 978 534-1010
  31 Fuller St Leominster (01453) *(G-9708)*

Teknor Apex Company **(PA)**............................ **401 725-8000**
  505 Central Ave Pawtucket (02861) *(G-16420)*

Teknor Apex Elastomers Inc................................ 978 466-5344
  31 Fuller St Leominster (01453) *(G-9709)*

Teknor Color Company..................................... 401 725-8000
  505 Central Ave Pawtucket (02861) *(G-16421)*

Teknor Color Company LLC **(HQ)** 505 Central Ave Pawtucket (02861) *(G-16422)*

Teknor Prfmce Elastomers Inc.............................. 401 725-8000
  505 Central Ave Pawtucket (02861) *(G-16423)*

Tekon-Technical Cons Inc.................................. 603 335-3080
  110 Corporate Dr Ste 4 Portsmouth (03801) *(G-15441)*

Tekscan Inc... 617 464-4500
  333 Boston Providence Tpke Norwood (02062) *(G-11215)*

Tektron Inc... 978 887-0091
  424 Boston St Ste B Topsfield (01983) *(G-12439)*

Tektronix.. 203 730-2730
  100 Wooster Hts Danbury (06810) *(G-824)*

Tektronix, Danbury *Also Called: Tektronix (G-824)*

Tel Mnfacturing Engrg Amer Inc............................ 978 436-2300
  900 Middlesex Tpke Ste 6-1 Billerica (01821) *(G-6487)*

Telco Communications Inc.................................. 508 336-6633
  21 Industrial Ct Seekonk (02771) *(G-11788)*

Telcor.. 603 525-4769
  15 Forest Rd Hancock (03449) *(G-14420)*

Telecast Fibr Systems -An Unnc, Worcester *Also Called: Belden Inc (G-13703)*

Telecom Installation Svcs Inc.............................. 401 258-2095
  28 Jacome Way Middletown (02842) *(G-16185)*

Telect Mfg LLC... 877 858-3855
  358 Hall Ave Wallingford (06492) *(G-3858)*

Teledyne Benthos, North Falmouth *Also Called: Teledyne Instruments Inc (G-11014)*

Teledyne Benthos Inc....................................... 508 563-1000
  49 Edgerton Dr North Falmouth (02556) *(G-11013)*

Teledyne Bolt Inc.. 203 853-0700
  4 Duke Pl Norwalk (06854) *(G-2577)*

Teledyne D.G. O Brien, Hampton *Also Called: Teledyne Instruments Inc (G-14415)*

Teledyne D.G. O'Brien, Portsmouth *Also Called: Teledyne Instruments Inc (G-15442)*

Teledyne Flir LLC.. 978 901-8000
  25 Esquire Rd North Billerica (01862) *(G-10961)*

Teledyne Flir LLC.. 603 324-7783
  110 Lowell Rd Hudson (03051) *(G-14551)*

Teledyne Flir Coml Systems Inc............................ 603 324-7824
  110 Lowell Rd Hudson (03051) *(G-14552)*

Teledyne Flir Unmnned Grund Sy (DH)   **978 769-9333**
  19 Alpha Rd Ste 101 Chelmsford (01824) *(G-7964)*

Teledyne Instrs Leeman Labs.............................. 603 521-3299
  110 Lowell Rd Hudson (03051) *(G-14553)*

Teledyne Instruments Inc..................................... 508 563-1000
  49 Edgerton Dr North Falmouth (02556) *(G-11014)*

Teledyne Instruments Inc..................................... 508 563-1000
  49 Edgerton Dr North Falmouth (02556) *(G-11015)*

Teledyne Instruments Inc..................................... 508 548-2077
  49 Edgerton Dr North Falmouth (02556) *(G-11016)*

Teledyne Instruments Inc..................................... 508 563-1000
  49 Edgerton Dr North Falmouth (02556) *(G-11017)*

Teledyne Instruments Inc..................................... 603 474-5571
  1 Lafayette Rd Hampton (03842) *(G-14415)*

Teledyne Instruments Inc..................................... 603 886-8400
  110 Lowell Rd Hudson (03051) *(G-14554)*

Teledyne Instruments Inc..................................... 603 474-5571
  162 Corporate Dr Ste 100 Portsmouth (03801) *(G-15442)*

Teledyne Lecroy Inc.. 508 748-0103
  513 Mill St Marion (02738) *(G-10102)*

Teledyne Leeman Labs, Hudson *Also Called: Teledyne Tekmar Company Inc (G-14555)*

Teledyne Oceanscience, North Falmouth *Also Called: Teledyne Instruments Inc (G-11015)*

Teledyne Seabotix, North Falmouth *Also Called: Teledyne Instruments Inc (G-11017)*

Teledyne Tekmar Company Inc............................ 603 886-8400
  110 Lowell Rd Hudson (03051) *(G-14555)*

Teledyne Webb Research, North Falmouth *Also Called: Teledyne Instruments Inc (G-11016)*

Teleflex, Coventry *Also Called: Teleflex Incorporated (G-683)*

Teleflex, Chelmsford *Also Called: Arrow Interventional Inc (G-7909)*

Teleflex, Mansfield *Also Called: Teleflex Incorporated (G-10078)*

Teleflex Incorporated... 860 742-8821
  1295 Main St Coventry (06238) *(G-683)*

Teleflex Incorporated... 508 964-6021
  375 Forbes Blvd Mansfield (02048) *(G-10078)*

Teleflex Incorporated... 603 532-7706
  50 Plantation Dr Jaffrey (03452) *(G-14580)*

Teleflex Medical, Chelmsford *Also Called: Arrow International LLC (G-7908)*

Telefluent Communications Inc............................ 508 919-0902
  104 Otis St Ste 22 Northborough (01532) *(G-11112)*

Telefunken Elektro Acoustic, South Windsor *Also Called: Telefunken Usa LLC (G-3185)*

Telefunken Usa LLC.. 860 882-5919
  300 Pleasant Valley Rd Ste E South Windsor (06074) *(G-3185)*

Telenity Inc.. 203 445-2000
  755 Main St Ste 7 Monroe (06468) *(G-1924)*

Teletypesetting Company Inc............................... 617 542-6220
  10 Post Office Sq Ste 800s Boston (02109) *(G-7073)*

Televeh Inc... 857 400-1938
  132 Charles St Ste 201 Auburndale (02466) *(G-6139)*

Tell Tool Inc... 413 568-1671
  35 Turnpike Industrial Rd Westfield (01085) *(G-13210)*

Tell Tool Acquisition Inc (DH)............................. **413 568-1671**
  ⁻35 Turnpike Industrial Rd Westfield (01085) *(G-13211)*

Telling Industries LLC... 860 731-7975
  1050 Kennedy Rd Windsor (06095) *(G-4308)*

Telliris, Shelton *Also Called: Dac Systems Inc (G-2995)*

Telome Inc.. 617 383-7565
  1393 Main St Waltham (02451) *(G-12792)*

Teltron Engineering Inc....................................... 508 543-6600
  131 Morse St Ste 9 Foxboro (02035) *(G-8727)*

Tem Inc.. 207 929-8700
  8 Pierce Dr Buxton (04093) *(G-4665)*

Temco Tool Company Inc.................................... 603 622-6989
  800 Holt Ave Manchester (03109) *(G-14941)*

Temp-Flex LLC.. 508 839-3120
  26 Milford Rd South Grafton (01560) *(G-11958)*

Temp-Pro, Northampton *Also Called: Temp-Pro Incorporated (G-11082)*

Temp-Pro Incorporated.. 413 584-3165
  200 Industrial Dr Northampton (01060) *(G-11082)*

Tempshield, Trenton *Also Called: Tempshield LLC (G-5559)*

Tempshield LLC.. 207 667-9696
  23 Industrial Way Trenton (04605) *(G-5559)*

Temptronic Corporation (HQ).............................. **781 688-2300**
  41 Hampden Rd Mansfield (02048) *(G-10079)*

Ten Bamboo Studio, West Kennebunk *Also Called: William Arthur Inc (G-5611)*

Ten10 Products LLC (PA).................................... **603 770-0502**
  22 Wiggin Way Stratham (03885) *(G-15640)*

Tena Group LLC... 207 893-2920
  2 Plaza Dr Windham (04062) *(G-5671)*

Tenacity Medical Inc... 617 299-8001
  100 Trade Center Lexington (02421) *(G-9786)*

Tender Corporation (PA)...................................... **603 444-5464**
  944 Industrial Park Rd Littleton (03561) *(G-14724)*

Tenova Inc.. 203 265-5684
  1070 N Farms Rd Ste 3b Wallingford (06492) *(G-3859)*

Tensar, Greenwich *Also Called: TAC Acquisition Corp (G-1355)*

Tent Connection Inc... 508 234-8746
  1682 Providence Rd Northbridge (01534) *(G-11119)*

Tepha Inc (HQ).. **781 357-1700**
  99 Hayden Ave Ste 360 Lexington (02421) *(G-9787)*

Teradar Inc... 508 433-0269
  501 Massachusetts Ave Cambridge (02139) *(G-7737)*

Teradiode, Wilmington *Also Called: Teradiode Inc (G-13464)*

Teradiode Inc.. 978 988-1040
  30 Upton Dr Wilmington (01887) *(G-13464)*

Teradyne, North Reading *Also Called: Teradyne Inc (G-11048)*

Teradyne Inc... 978 370-2700
  Boston (02241) *(G-7074)*

Teradyne Inc... 978 370-2700
  600 Riverpark Dr North Reading (01864) *(G-11047)*

Teradyne Inc (PA)... **978 370-2700**
  600 Riverpark Dr North Reading (01864) *(G-11048)*

Teradyne Inc... 978 370-2700
  500 Riverpark Dr North Reading (01864) *(G-11049)*

Teradyne Inc... 978 370-2700
  36 Cabot Rd Woburn (01801) *(G-13677)*

Teranode Inc... 781 493-6900
  3 Allied Dr Ste 230 Dedham (02026) *(G-8252)*

Terason Ultrasound, Burlington *Also Called: Teratech Corporation (G-7438)*

Teratech Corporation... 781 270-4143
  77 Terrace Hall Ave Burlington (01803) *(G-7438)*

Tercat Tool and Die Co II Inc.............................. 401 421-3371
  31 Delaine St Providence (02909) *(G-16620)*

TEREX, Norwalk *Also Called: Terex Corporation (G-2578)*

Terex Advance Mixer Inc..................................... 203 222-7170
  500 Post Rd E Westport (06880) *(G-4198)*

Terex Awp North America, Norwalk *Also Called: Terex Usa LLC (G-2579)*

Terex Corporation (PA).. **203 222-7170**
  45 Glover Ave Fl 4 Norwalk (06850) *(G-2578)*

Terex Environmental Equipment, Newton *Also Called: Terex Usa LLC (G-15245)*

Terex Usa LLC (HQ)... **203 222-7170**
  45 Glover Ave Ste 4 Norwalk (06850) *(G-2579)*

Terex Usa LLC... 603 382-0556
  22 Whittier St Newton (03858) *(G-15245)*

Terika Smith Ministries Corp............................... 978 233-0576
  530 Broadway Fl 3 Lawrence (01841) *(G-9603)*

Tero Design Holdings LLC................................... 203 899-9950
  66 Fort Point St Ste 2 Norwalk (06855) *(G-2580)*

Teroforma, Norwalk *Also Called: Tero Design Holdings LLC (G-2580)*

Terra Americana, Southwick *Also Called: Julie Cecchini (G-12044)*

Terrafugia Inc... 781 491-0812
  23 Rainin Rd Ste 2 Woburn (01801) *(G-13678)*

Terrapin.. 508 487-8181
955 Massachusetts Ave Cambridge (02139) *(G-7738)*

Terrence L Hayford.. 207 357-0142
74 Moses Young Rd Hartford (04220) *(G-4877)*

Terroir Coffee, Acton *Also Called: George Howell Coffee Co LLC* *(G-5748)*

Tesaro, Waltham *Also Called: Tesaro Inc* *(G-12793)*

Tesaro Inc **(HQ)**... **339 970-0900**
1000 Winter St Ste 3300 Waltham (02451) *(G-12793)*

Tesaro Securities Corporation............................ 339 970-0900
1000 Winter St Waltham (02451) *(G-12794)*

Tesco Associates Incorporated **(PA)**.................. **978 649-5527**
500 Business Park Dr Unit 1 Tyngsboro (01879) *(G-12467)*

Teshima International Corp................................. 617 830-1886
1 Broadway Fl 14 Cambridge (02142) *(G-7739)*

Tessera Therapeutics Inc.................................. 860 910-6030
101 South St Ste 500 Somerville (02143) *(G-11900)*

Tessier Machine Company, Hudson *Also Called: Sp Machine Inc* *(G-9414)*

Tessis Pizza & Roast Beef................................. 978 851-8700
910 Andover St Ste 1 Tewksbury (01876) *(G-12421)*

Test Devices By Schenck, Hudson *Also Called: Schenck USA Corp* *(G-9410)*

Test Devices Inc.. 978 562-6017
571 Main St Ste 2 Hudson (01749) *(G-9417)*

Testing Machines Inc.. 302 613-5600
1658 Gar Hwy Ste 6 Swansea (02777) *(G-12313)*

TET Mfg Co Inc.. 860 349-1004
2 Old Indian Trl Middlefield (06455) *(G-1729)*

Tet Mfg Co/Machine Shop, Middlefield *Also Called: TET Mfg Co Inc* *(G-1729)*

Tetco Inc... 860 747-1280
4 Northwest Dr Plainville (06062) *(G-2783)*

Tethereducation Inc... 203 691-0131
102 Audubon St Fl 2 New Haven (06510) *(G-2207)*

Tetragenetics Inc.. 617 500-7471
91 Mystic St Ste 1 Arlington (02474) *(G-5949)*

Tetraphase Pharmaceuticals, Waltham *Also Called: Tetraphase Pharmaceuticals Inc* *(G-12795)*

Tetraphase Pharmaceuticals Inc.......................... 617 715-3600
35 Gatehouse Dr Waltham (02451) *(G-12795)*

Teufelberger, Fall River *Also Called: Teufelberger Fiber Rope Corp* *(G-8616)*

Teufelberger Fiber Rope Corp.............................. 508 678-8200
848 Airport Rd Fall River (02720) *(G-8616)*

Tevelle Pharmaceuticals LLC............................... 207 808-9771
200 John Roberts Rd South Portland (04106) *(G-5516)*

Tevtech LLC.. 978 667-4557
100 Billerica Ave North Billerica (01862) *(G-10962)*

Tex Elm Inc.. 860 873-9715
136 Town St East Haddam (06423) *(G-956)*

Tex Flock Inc.. 401 765-2340
200 Founders Dr Woonsocket (02895) *(G-16981)*

Tex-Tech Industries Inc..................................... 336 992-7495
105 N Main St North Monmouth (04265) *(G-5115)*

Texas Die Casting LLC....................................... 903 845-2224
8 Knobhill Rd Norwalk (06851) *(G-2581)*

Texas Instruments, Attleboro *Also Called: Texas Instruments Incorporated* *(G-6070)*

Texas Instruments, Manchester *Also Called: Texas Instruments Incorporated* *(G-14942)*

Texas Instruments Incorporated.......................... 508 236-3800
529 Pleasant St Attleboro (02703) *(G-6070)*

Texas Instruments Incorporated.......................... 603 222-8500
50 Phillippe Cote St Ste 100 Manchester (03101) *(G-14942)*

Texcel Inc.. 401 727-2113
18 Meeting St Cumberland (02864) *(G-15968)*

Texcel Industries Inc.. 401 727-2113
18 Meeting St Cumberland (02864) *(G-15969)*

Texon Usa Inc... 413 862-3652
1190 Huntington Rd Russell (01071) *(G-11695)*

Textile Buff & Wheel Co Inc............................... 617 241-8100
511 Medford St Boston (02129) *(G-7075)*

Textile Engineering & Mfg, Woonsocket *Also Called: TEAM INC* *(G-16980)*

Textile Waste Supply LLC................................... 617 241-8100
511 Medford St Boston (02129) *(G-7076)*

Textiles Coated Incorporated **(PA)**.................... **603 296-2221**
6 George Ave Londonderry (03053) *(G-14786)*

Textiles Coated Incorporated............................. 603 296-2221
200 Bouchard St Manchester (03103) *(G-14943)*

Textiles Coated International, Londonderry *Also Called: Textiles Coated Incorporated* *(G-14786)*

Textron, Providence *Also Called: Textron Inc* *(G-16623)*

Textron Aviation RI Inc...................................... 401 421-2800
40 Westminster St Providence (02903) *(G-16621)*

Textron Defense Systems, Wilmington *Also Called: Textron Systems Corporation* *(G-13466)*

Textron Fluid and Power Inc............................... 401 588-3400
40 Westminster St Providence (02903) *(G-16622)*

Textron Inc **(PA)**... **401 421-2800**
40 Westminster St Providence (02903) *(G-16623)*

Textron Inc... 401 457-2310
566 Airport Rd Warwick (02886) *(G-16868)*

Textron Lycoming Corp **(HQ)**............................ **401 421-2800**
40 Westminster St Providence (02903) *(G-16624)*

Textron Systems Corporation.............................. 978 657-5111
201 Lowell St Wilmington (01887) *(G-13465)*

Textron Systems Corporation **(DH)**.................... **978 657-5111**
201 Lowell St Wilmington (01887) *(G-13466)*

Textspeak Corporation...................................... 203 803-1069
55 Post Rd W Fl 2 Westport (06880) *(G-4199)*

Textspeak Design, Westport *Also Called: Textspeak Corporation* *(G-4199)*

Tfac LLC.. 203 776-6000
27 Whitney Ave New Haven (06510) *(G-2208)*

Tfh Liquidation Company LLC.............................. 603 742-4961
621 Central Ave Dover (03820) *(G-14252)*

Tfi Technologies, Greenfield *Also Called: Thin Film Imaging Technologies* *(G-9002)*

Tfx Medical Incorporated................................... 603 532-7706
50 Plantation Dr Jaffrey (03452) *(G-14581)*

TG Industries Inc... 203 235-3239
361 S Colony St Ste 1 Meriden (06451) *(G-1704)*

Thames Glass Inc... 401 846-0576
139 Old Beach Rd Newport (02840) *(G-16226)*

Thames Shipyard & Repair Co.............................. 860 442-5349
50 Farnsworth St New London (06320) *(G-2234)*

Thank-U Company Inc....................................... 401 739-3100
360 Callahan Rd North Kingstown (02852) *(G-16285)*

Thanksben10 LLC.. 603 206-5116
48 Powers St Milford (03055) *(G-15040)*

That Corporation **(PA)**................................... **508 478-9200**
45 Sumner St Milford (01757) *(G-10420)*

Thats Great News LLC....................................... 203 649-4900
900 Northrop Rd Ste F Wallingford (06492) *(G-3860)*

Thavenet Machine Company Inc........................... 860 599-4495
12 Chase St Ste 14 Pawcatuck (06379) *(G-2726)*

Thayer Scale, Pembroke *Also Called: Hyer Industries Inc* *(G-11370)*

Thayermahan Inc **(PA)**................................... **860 785-9994**
120b Leonard Dr Groton (06340) *(G-1381)*

The A H Emery Company **(PA)**.......................... **203 881-9333**
73 Cogwheel Ln Seymour (06483) *(G-2970)*

The Bee Publishing Company **(PA)**..................... **203 426-8036**
5 Church Hill Rd Newtown (06470) *(G-2351)*

The Bilco Company **(DH)**................................. **203 934-6363**
37 Water St West Haven (06516) *(G-4128)*

The Bridgeport Insulated Wire Company, Stratford *Also Called: Bridgeport Insulated Wire Co* *(G-3523)*

The Carby Corporation....................................... 860 274-6741
1121 Echo Lake Rd Watertown (06795) *(G-4032)*

The Childsplay, East Longmeadow *Also Called: Reminder Publications* *(G-8393)*

The Commercial Foundry Company........................ 860 224-1794
326 South St New Britain (06051) *(G-2071)*

The Cricket System Inc..................................... 617 905-1420
5 Perkins Way Ste 2 Newburyport (01950) *(G-10719)*

The Dingley Press Inc **(PA)**............................. **207 353-1500**
119 Lisbon St Lisbon (04250) *(G-5018)*

The Duclos Corporation..................................... 508 676-8596
168 Walker St Somerset (02725) *(G-11857)*

The E J Davis Company....................................... 203 239-5391
10 Dodge Ave North Haven (06473) *(G-2439)*

The Electric Heater Company.............................. 800 647-3165
45 Seymour St Stratford (06615) *(G-3580)*

ALPHABETIC

The Elliott Sales Group Inc... 401 944-0002
  111 Dupont Dr Providence (02907) *(G-16625)*

The Gas Equipment Engineering Corporation
  571 Plains Rd Milford (06461) *(G-1894)*

The Gilman Brothers Company... 860 889-8444
  9 Thomas Rd Gilman (06336) *(G-1268)*

The Great N Woods Assoc/ Blind...................................... 603 490-9877
  23 Gould St Colebrook (03576) *(G-14109)*

The Hartford Press Inc... 860 296-3588
  105 Day St Newington (06111) *(G-2327)*

The Hoffman Press Incorporated...................................... 203 865-0818
  30 Printers Ln New Haven (06519) *(G-2209)*

The L C Doane Company.. 860 767-8295
  110 Pond Meadow Rd Ivoryton (06442) *(G-1533)*

The L Suzio Asphalt Co Inc... 203 237-8421
  975 Westfield Rd Meriden (06450) *(G-1705)*

The L Suzio Concrete Co Inc **(PA)**................................. **203 237-8421**
  975 Westfield Rd Meriden (06450) *(G-1706)*

The Leahy Press Inc.. 802 223-2100
  79 River St Montpelier (05602) *(G-17375)*

The Lyons Tool & Die Company... 203 238-2689
  185 Research Pkwy Meriden (06450) *(G-1707)*

The Original Rangoon Company Incorporated............................ 781 596-0070
  200 Cordwainer Dr Norwell (02061) *(G-11148)*

The Orion Society Inc.. 413 528-4422
  187 Main St Great Barrington (01230) *(G-8979)*

The Orvis Company Inc **(PA)**....................................... **802 362-3622**
  178 Conservation Way Sunderland (05250) *(G-17635)*

The Petit Tool Co.. 860 283-9626
  1387 Waterbury Rd Thomaston (06787) *(G-3636)*

The Plainville Electrical Products Co................................ 860 583-1144
  435 Lake Ave Bristol (06010) *(G-500)*

The Pohly Company.. 617 451-1700
  42 Konohassett Cartway Brewster (02631) *(G-7217)*

The Real Reel Corporation.. 401 434-1070
  50 Taylor Dr Rumford (02916) *(G-16678)*

The Romatic Manufacturing Company.................................... 203 264-8203
  1200 Main St S Southbury (06488) *(G-3199)*

The Rumford Falls Times, Norway *Also Called: James Newspapers Inc* *(G-5116)*

The Savogran Company... 781 762-5400
  259 Lenox St Norwood (02062) *(G-11216)*

The Schundler Company.. 732 287-2244
  10 Central St Nahant (01908) *(G-10460)*

The Sentry Company... 508 543-5391
  65 Leonard St Foxboro (02035) *(G-8728)*

The Sharp Tool Co Inc.. 978 568-9292
  7 Bonazzoli Ave Hudson (01749) *(G-9418)*

The Stone Depot, Alstead *Also Called: Semya Corp* *(G-13858)*

The Storymatic Corp.. 917 842-9932
  74 Cotton Mill Hl Unit A300 Brattleboro (05301) *(G-17101)*

The Sun Products Corporation... 203 254-6700
  200 Elm St Ste 600 Stamford (06902) *(G-3480)*

The Taunton Press Inc **(PA)**....................................... **203 426-8171**
  63 S Main St Newtown (06470) *(G-2352)*

THE TAUNTON PRESS, INC., Newtown *Also Called: Taunton Press Inc* *(G-2350)*

The Tyler Co Inc... 978 568-3400
  10 Brent Dr Hudson (01749) *(G-9419)*

The Viking Tool Company.. 203 929-1457
  435 Access Rd Shelton (06484) *(G-3068)*

The Village Goldsmith, Warwick *Also Called: Village Goldsmith* *(G-16872)*

The Wakefield Corporation.. 781 587-1925
  29 Foundry St Wakefield (01880) *(G-12539)*

THE WIREMOLD COMPANY, Rocky Hill *Also Called: Wiremold Company* *(G-2942)*

The Wiremold Company, West Hartford *Also Called: Wiremold Company* *(G-4092)*

The Yofarm Company... 203 720-0000
  141a Sheridan Dr Ste A Naugatuck (06770) *(G-1990)*

Thea Pharma Inc.. 781 832-3667
  303 Wyman St Waltham (02451) *(G-12796)*

Theam, Brunswick *Also Called: Westcon Mfg Inc* *(G-4657)*

Thebeamer LLC.. 860 212-5071
  87 Church St East Hartford (06108) *(G-1027)*

Theis Precision Steel, Bristol *Also Called: Theis Precision Steel USA Inc* *(G-501)*

Theis Precision Steel USA Inc **(HQ)**.............................. **860 589-5511**
  300 Broad St Bristol (06010) *(G-501)*

Ther-A-Pedic Sleep Products, Brockton *Also Called: Restmore Inc* *(G-7302)*

Theracour Pharma Inc... 203 937-6137
  135 Wood St Ste 8 West Haven (06516) *(G-4129)*

Theracycle, Franklin *Also Called: Xthera Corporation* *(G-8877)*

Therap Techne LLC.. 203 596-7553
  333 Kennedy Dr Ste R101 Torrington (06790) *(G-3699)*

Therapedic of New England LLC.. 508 559-9944
  135 Spark St Brockton (02302) *(G-7311)*

Therma-Flow Inc.. 617 924-3877
  191 Arlington St Watertown (02472) *(G-12913)*

Thermacell Repellents Inc.. 781 541-6900
  32 Crosby Dr Ste 101 Bedford (01730) *(G-6273)*

Thermacut Inc.. 603 543-0585
  153 Charlestown Rd Claremont (03743) *(G-14098)*

Thermadyne, West Lebanon *Also Called: Thermal Dynamics Corporation* *(G-15690)*

Thermaglo, Uncasville *Also Called: Northeast Wood Products LLC* *(G-3742)*

Thermal Arc Inc.. 800 462-2782
  82 Benning St West Lebanon (03784) *(G-15689)*

Thermal Circuits Inc... 978 745-1162
  1 Technology Way Salem (01970) *(G-11734)*

Thermal Dynamics Corporation **(DH)**............................... **603 298-5711**
  82 Benning St West Lebanon (03784) *(G-15690)*

Thermal Seal Insulating GL Inc....................................... 508 278-4243
  47 Industrial Dr Uxbridge (01569) *(G-12490)*

Thermal Solutions, Hampton *Also Called: Tsi Group Inc* *(G-14416)*

Thermalogic Corporation.. 800 343-4492
  22 Kane Industrial Dr Hudson (01749) *(G-9420)*

Thermatool Corp **(HQ)**.. **203 468-4100**
  31 Commerce St East Haven (06512) *(G-1053)*

Thermatron, Methuen *Also Called: Thermatron Engineering Inc* *(G-10345)*

Thermatron Engineering Inc... 978 687-8844
  687 Lowell St Methuen (01844) *(G-10345)*

Thermaxx LLC **(HQ)**... **203 672-1021**
  14 Farwell St West Haven (06516) *(G-4130)*

Thermedetec Inc.. 508 520-0430
  21 Hickory Dr # 4 Waltham (02451) *(G-12797)*

Thermo Biostar Inc., Waltham *Also Called: Inverness Medical - Biostar Inc* *(G-12703)*

Thermo Detection, Waltham *Also Called: Thermedetec Inc* *(G-12797)*

Thermo Eberline LLC **(HQ)**.. **508 553-1582**
  27 Forge Pkwy Franklin (02038) *(G-8867)*

Thermo Egs Gauging LLC... 978 663-2300
  22 Alpha Rd Chelmsford (01824) *(G-7965)*

Thermo Electron, Franklin *Also Called: Thermo Process Instruments LP* *(G-8870)*

Thermo Electron F S C Inc.. 781 622-1000
  81 Wyman St Waltham (02451) *(G-12798)*

Thermo Envmtl Instrs LLC **(HQ)**................................... **508 520-0430**
  27 Forge Pkwy Franklin (02038) *(G-8868)*

Thermo Fisher.. 781 325-8726
  61 Medford St Somerville (02143) *(G-11901)*

Thermo Fisher, Waltham *Also Called: Thermo Fisher Scientific Inc* *(G-12800)*

Thermo Fisher Fincl Svcs Inc... 781 622-1000
  168 3rd Ave Waltham (02451) *(G-12799)*

Thermo Fisher Scientific, Franklin *Also Called: Thermo Eberline LLC* *(G-8867)*

Thermo Fisher Scientific, Hudson *Also Called: Matrix Technologies LLC* *(G-14526)*

Thermo Fisher Scientific, Newington *Also Called: Owl Separation Systems LLC* *(G-15209)*

Thermo Fisher Scientific Inc... 978 232-6000
  100 Cummings Ctr Ste 166 Beverly (01915) *(G-6387)*

Thermo Fisher Scientific Inc... 978 250-7000
  22 Alpha Rd Chelmsford (01824) *(G-7966)*

Thermo Fisher Scientific Inc... 713 272-0404
  27 Forge Pkwy Franklin (02038) *(G-8869)*

Thermo Fisher Scientific Inc... 781 622-1000
  2 Radcliff Rd Tewksbury (01876) *(G-12422)*

Thermo Fisher Scientific Inc **(PA)**............................... **781 622-1000**
  168 3rd Ave Waltham (02451) *(G-12800)*

Thermo Fisher Scientific Inc **(HQ)**............................... **603 431-8410**
  20 Post Rd Portsmouth (03801) *(G-15443)*

Thermo Fisher Scientific Inc... 401 294-1234
  1130 Ten Rod Rd North Kingstown (02852) *(G-16286)*

Thermo Ice Inc **(HQ)**   450 Fortune Blvd Milford (01757) *(G-10421)*

Thermo Instrument Systems Inc....................................... 781 622-1000
  81 Wyman St Waltham (02451) *(G-12801)*

Thermo Neslab LLC.. 603 436-9444
  25 Nimble Hill Rd Newington (03801) *(G-15215)*

Thermo Orion Inc **(HQ)**... **800 225-1480**
  22 Alpha Rd Chelmsford (01824) *(G-7967)*

Thermo Power Corporation... 781 622-1400
  45 1st Ave Waltham (02451) *(G-12802)*

Thermo Process Instruments LP....................................... 508 553-6913
  27 Forge Pkwy Franklin (02038) *(G-8870)*

Thermo Scientific, Tewksbury *Also Called: Thermo Scntfic Prtble Anlytcal (G-12423)*

Thermo Scntfic Prtble Anlytcal **(HQ)**............................ **978 657-5555**
  2 Radcliff Rd Tewksbury (01876) *(G-12423)*

Thermo Vision Corp **(HQ)**.. **508 520-0083**
  8 Forge Pkwy Ste 4 Franklin (02038) *(G-8871)*

Thermo Wave Technologies LLC....................................... 800 733-9615
  1 Centennial Dr Ste 1 Peabody (01960) *(G-11347)*

Thermo-Craft Engineering Corp....................................... 781 599-4023
  701 Western Ave Lynn (01905) *(G-9992)*

Thermoformed Plastics Neng LLC..................................... 207 286-1775
  362 Hill St Biddeford (04005) *(G-4591)*

Thermonics Inc... 408 542-5900
  41 Hampden Rd Mansfield (02048) *(G-10080)*

Thermoplastics Company Inc... 508 754-4668
  24 Woodward St Worcester (01610) *(G-13811)*

Thermoplastics Engineering Corp
  11 Spruce St Leominster (01453) *(G-9710)*

Thermopol Inc.. 603 692-6300
  13 Interstate Dr Somersworth (03878) *(G-15626)*

Thermospas Hot Tub Products... 203 303-0005
  47 N Plains Industrial Rd Wallingford (06492) *(G-3861)*

Thermoswitch International Ltd.. 401 467-7550
  25 Reservoir Ave Providence (02907) *(G-16626)*

Theseus, Cambridge *Also Called: Theseus Pharmaceuticals Inc (G-7740)*

Theseus Pharmaceuticals Inc **(PA)**............................... **857 400-9491**
  314 Main St Ste 04-200 Cambridge (02142) *(G-7740)*

Thibco Inc.. 603 623-3011
  41 Alpheus St Manchester (03103) *(G-14944)*

Thiel & Associates, Portsmouth *Also Called: Hideaways International Inc (G-15401)*

Thimble Island Brewing Company..................................... 203 208-2827
  16 Business Park Dr Branford (06405) *(G-282)*

Thin Film Division, Attleboro *Also Called: Mini-Systems Inc (G-6037)*

Thin Film Imaging Technologies....................................... 413 774-6692
  11 Blanker Ln Greenfield (01301) *(G-9002)*

Think Energy, Southport *Also Called: Think Energy LLC (G-3250)*

Think Energy LLC... 917 202-3574
  107 John St Southport (06890) *(G-3250)*

Thinkflood Inc... 617 299-2000
  295 Reservoir St Needham (02494) *(G-10526)*

Thinkmate, Norwood *Also Called: Source Code LLC (G-11209)*

Third Place Inc.. 802 861-2999
  115 Saint Paul St Burlington (05401) *(G-17161)*

Third Pole Inc **(PA)**.. **908 310-0596**
  309 Waverley Oaks Rd Ste 404 Waltham (02452) *(G-12803)*

Third Pole Therapeutics, Waltham *Also Called: Third Pole Inc (G-12803)*

Third Wave Technologies Inc **(HQ)**............................... **608 273-8933**
  250 Campus Dr Marlborough (01752) *(G-10224)*

This Old House Ventures LLC.. 475 209-8665
  2 Harbor Dr Stamford (06902) *(G-3481)*

Thl-Nortek Investors LLC **(PA)**..................................... **617 227-1050**
  100 Federal St Ste 3700 Boston (02110) *(G-7077)*

Thomann Steel LLC... 802 462-3066
  1006 Nortontown Rd Vergennes (05491) *(G-17662)*

Thomas & Thomas Inc.. 978 453-7444
  207 Industrial Ave E Lowell (01852) *(G-9928)*

Thomas & Thomas Rodmakers.. 413 475-3840
  627 Barton Rd Ste 1 Greenfield (01301) *(G-9003)*

Thomas Engineering.. 401 822-1235
  9 Morin Ave Coventry (02816) *(G-15823)*

Thomas H Lee Equity Fund V LP...................................... 617 227-1050
  100 Federal St Ste 3500 Boston (02110) *(G-7078)*

Thomas Hall.. 207 956-0020
  175 Black Point Rd Scarborough (04074) *(G-5445)*

Thomas Instruments.. 603 363-4500
  1453 Route 9 Spofford (03462) *(G-15630)*

Thomas J Cronin.. 508 510-2328
  107 Harding St Medfield (02052) *(G-10277)*

Thomas J Doane... 978 821-2361
  59 Ward Rd Orange (01364) *(G-11235)*

Thomas Keegan & Sons Inc.. 203 239-9248
  38 Evanwood Dr Wallingford (06492) *(G-3862)*

Thomas Logging & Forestry Inc....................................... 207 876-2722
  58 Butter St Guilford (04443) *(G-4859)*

Thomas M Leonard Inc
  319 Manley St Ste 301 West Bridgewater (02379) *(G-12984)*

Thomas Machine Works Inc.. 978 462-7182
  9 New Pasture Rd Newburyport (01950) *(G-10720)*

Thomas Products Ltd... 860 621-9101
  987 West St Southington (06489) *(G-3236)*

Thomas S Klise Co.. 860 536-4200
  42 Denison Ave Mystic (06355) *(G-1943)*

Thomas Scientific Inc.. 413 406-6588
  4226 Church St Thorndike (01079) *(G-12428)*

Thomas Smith Company Inc.. 508 792-5000
  288 Grove St Worcester (01605) *(G-13812)*

Thomas Spring Co Conn Inc.. 203 874-7030
  29 Seemans Ln Milford (06460) *(G-1895)*

Thomas Taylor Braid, Waldoboro *Also Called: David Bird LLC (G-5575)*

Thomas W Raftery Inc... 860 278-9870
  1055 Broad St Hartford (06106) *(G-1514)*

Thomastn-Mdtown Screw Mch Pdts.................................. 860 283-9796
  550 N Main St Thomaston (06787) *(G-3637)*

Thomaston Express, The Div, Torrington *Also Called: Bristol Press (G-3673)*

Thomaston Industries Inc... 860 283-4358
  41 Electric Ave Thomaston (06787) *(G-3638)*

Thomaston Swiss, Thomaston *Also Called: GK Automatics Incorporated (G-3620)*

Thompson Aerospace LLC.. 860 516-0472
  220 Business Park Dr Bristol (06010) *(G-502)*

Thompson Brands LLC... 203 235-2541
  80 S Vine St Meriden (06451) *(G-1708)*

Thompson Candy Company.. 203 235-2541
  80 S Vine St Meriden (06451) *(G-1709)*

Thompson Forest Services, Lincoln *Also Called: Thompson Trucking Inc (G-5014)*

Thompson Investment Casting, Rochester *Also Called: KW Thompson Tool Company Inc (G-15483)*

Thompson Printing, Brewer *Also Called: L H Thompson Inc (G-4615)*

Thompson Steel Company Inc.. 781 828-8800
  120 Royall St Canton (02021) *(G-7834)*

Thompson Trucking Inc... 207 794-6101
  725 Enfield Rd Lincoln (04457) *(G-5014)*

Thompson/Center Arms, Springfield *Also Called: Thompson/Center Arms Co Inc (G-12138)*

Thompson/Center Arms Co Inc **(HQ)**.............................. **800 331-0852**
  2100 Roosevelt Ave Springfield (01104) *(G-12138)*

Thomsen Enterprises LLC.. 401 431-2190
  141 Narragansett Park Dr Rumford (02916) *(G-16679)*

Thomsen Restaurant Paper Sup, Rumford *Also Called: Thomsen Enterprises LLC (G-16679)*

Thomson Group, The, Franklin *Also Called: Thomson Service Corp (G-8872)*

Thomson Linear, Bristol *Also Called: Abek LLC (G-390)*

Thomson Reuters Corporation... 203 466-5055
  250 Dodge Ave East Haven (06512) *(G-1054)*

Thomson Reuters Corporation... 781 250-4340
  950 Winter St Ste 1900 Waltham (02451) *(G-12804)*

Thomson Reuters Corporation... 781 331-6610
  805 Pleasant St Weymouth (02189) *(G-13337)*

Thomson Reuters Risk MGT Inc....................................... 203 539-8000
  1 Station Pl Stamford (06902) *(G-3482)*

Thomson Reuters US LLC **(DH)**..................................... **203 539-8000**
  1 Station Pl Ste 6 Stamford (06902) *(G-3483)*

Thomson Service Corp... 508 528-2000
  842 Union St Ste 1 Franklin (02038) *(G-8872)*

A L P H A B E T I C

Thomson Video Networks Americas LLC.................... 413 998-1200
  104 Feeding Hills Rd Southwick (01077) *(G-12046)*

Thor's Elegance, Brandon *Also Called: New England Woodcraft Inc (G-17070)*

Thoratec LLC.................... 781 272-0139
  168 Middlesex Tpke Burlington (01803) *(G-7439)*

Thoratec LLC.................... 781 272-0139
  23 4th Ave Ste 2 Burlington (01803) *(G-7440)*

Thorme Wall Inc.................... 203 583-2305
  1535 Central Ave Apt 107 Bridgeport (06610) *(G-379)*

Thorndike Corporation.................... 508 378-9797
  680 N Bedford St Ste 1 East Bridgewater (02333) *(G-8346)*

Thorndike Mills, Palmer *Also Called: TMI Industries Inc (G-11285)*

Thornton and Company Inc.................... 860 628-6771
  132 Main St Ste 2a # 3 Southington (06489) *(G-3237)*

Thors Skyr LLC.................... 315 955-9418
  68 Commercial St Portland (04101) *(G-5281)*

Thought Out Co LLC.................... 203 987-5452
  200 Main St Ste B Monroe (06468) *(G-1925)*

Threadhead Inc.................... 508 778-6516
  38 Plant Rd Hyannis (02601) *(G-9453)*

Three Dimensional Graphics Corp.................... 978 774-8595
  3 Austin Ln Byfield (01922) *(G-7460)*

Three Fins Cof Roasters & Merc.................... 508 246-5813
  581 Main St West Dennis (02670) *(G-12999)*

Three Twins Productions Inc.................... 617 926-0377
  18 Bridge St Watertown (02472) *(G-12914)*

Threshold Visitor MGT Systems, Unionville *Also Called: Data Management Incorporated (G-3748)*

Thrislington Cubicles, Boston *Also Called: European Cubicles LLC (G-6721)*

Thrive Bioscience Inc.................... 978 720-8048
  100 Cummings Ctr Beverly (01915) *(G-6388)*

Thule Inc **(DH)**.................... **203 881-9600**
  42 Silvermine Rd Seymour (06483) *(G-2971)*

Thule Holding Inc **(DH)**.................... **203 881-9600**
  42 Silvermine Rd Seymour (06483) *(G-2972)*

Thureon Inc.................... 774 249-8110
  37 Glen Rd Hopkinton (01748) *(G-9346)*

Thurston Manufacturing Company.................... 401 232-9100
  14 Thurber Blvd Smithfield (02917) *(G-16732)*

Thurston Sails Inc.................... 401 254-0970
  112 Tupelo St Bristol (02809) *(G-15782)*

Thyssenkrupp Materials NA Inc.................... 610 586-1800
  5 Sterling Dr Wallingford (06492) *(G-3863)*

Tibco Scribe, Manchester *Also Called: Cloud Software Group Inc (G-14831)*

Tiberio Manufacturing Corp.................... 508 429-4011
  79 Lowland St Holliston (01746) *(G-9232)*

Tiburio Therapeutics Inc.................... 617 231-6050
  700 Technology Sq Ste 2 Cambridge (02139) *(G-7741)*

Ticked Off Inc.................... 603 742-0925
  97 Spruce Ln Dover (03820) *(G-14253)*

Tico Titanium Inc **(PA)**.................... **248 446-0400**
  34b Barnes Industrial Rd S Wallingford (06492) *(G-3864)*

Tidal Communications LLC.................... 978 687-0900
  565 Turnpike St Ste 61 North Andover (01845) *(G-10852)*

Tienda Y Panaderia El Quiche.................... 401 521-5154
  1076 Chalkstone Ave Providence (02908) *(G-16627)*

Tier 7 Communications.................... 978 425-9543
  41 Holden Rd Shirley (01464) *(G-11823)*

Tiffany, Cumberland *Also Called: Tiffany & Co (G-15970)*

Tiffany & Co.................... 212 755-8000
  300 Maple Ridge Dr Cumberland (02864) *(G-15970)*

Tiger Enterprises Inc.................... 860 621-9155
  379 Summer St Plantsville (06479) *(G-2798)*

Tiger-Sul Products LLC.................... 203 635-0190
  4 Armstrong Rd Ste 220 Shelton (06484) *(G-3069)*

Tigerpress, East Longmeadow *Also Called: Shafiis Inc (G-8394)*

Tighitco Inc.................... 860 828-0298
  245 Old Brickyard Ln Berlin (06037) *(G-87)*

Tigpro Inc.................... 207 878-1190
  21 Tee Dr Portland (04103) *(G-5282)*

Tilcon Arthur Whitcomb Inc **(HQ)**.................... **603 352-0101**
  28 Old Homestead Hwy North Swanzey (03431) *(G-15256)*

Tilcon Connecticut, New Britain *Also Called: Tilcon Connecticut Inc (G-2072)*

Tilcon Connecticut Inc.................... 860 844-7000
  60 S Main St East Granby (06026) *(G-954)*

Tilcon Connecticut Inc **(DH)**.................... **860 224-6010**
  642 Black Rock Ave New Britain (06052) *(G-2072)*

Tilcon Connecticut Inc.................... 860 342-1096
  Black Rock Av Portland (06480) *(G-2827)*

Tilcon Connecticut Portland, Portland *Also Called: Tilcon Connecticut Inc (G-2827)*

Tilcon Inc **(DH)**.................... **860 223-3651**
  301 Hartford Ave Newington (06111) *(G-2328)*

Tillamook County Creamery Assn.................... 503 815-1300
  190 Riverside St Unit 6a Portland (04103) *(G-5283)*

Tillotson Corporation **(PA)**.................... **781 402-1731**
  159 Main St Nashua (03060) *(G-15176)*

Tillotson Rubber Co Inc.................... 781 402-1731
  1539 Fall River Ave Seekonk (02771) *(G-11789)*

Tilton - Nrthfeld Rcrtion Cnci.................... 603 286-8653
  61 Summer St Northfield (03276) *(G-15270)*

Timberchic, Millinocket *Also Called: Maine Heritage Timber LLC (G-5066)*

Timberland Company, The, Stratham *Also Called: Timberland LLC (G-15641)*

Timberland LLC **(HQ)**.................... **603 772-9500**
  200 Domain Dr Stratham (03885) *(G-15641)*

Timberpeg, Claremont *Also Called: Whs Homes Inc (G-14100)*

Timberpeg East Inc **(PA)**.................... **603 542-7762**
  61 Plains Rd Claremont (03743) *(G-14099)*

Timco Corporation.................... 781 821-1041
  1551 Central St Stoughton (02072) *(G-12243)*

Time-Out Sports Inc.................... 781 447-6670
  7 Marble St Whitman (02382) *(G-13350)*

Time4printing Inc.................... 207 838-1496
  588 Roosevelt Trl Windham (04062) *(G-5672)*

Timelinx Software Inc.................... 978 296-4090
  800 Turnpike St Ste 300 North Andover (01845) *(G-10853)*

Timelinx Software LLC.................... 978 662-1171
  800 Turnpike St Ste 300 North Andover (01845) *(G-10854)*

Timeout Sportswear Promotions, Whitman *Also Called: Time-Out Sports Inc (G-13350)*

Times Community News Group.................... 860 437-1150
  47 Eugene Oneill Dr New London (06320) *(G-2235)*

Times Fiber Communications Inc **(HQ)**.................... **800 677-2288**
  358 Hall Ave Wallingford (06492) *(G-3865)*

Times Microwave Systems, Wallingford *Also Called: Times Microwave Systems Inc (G-3866)*

Times Microwave Systems Inc **(HQ)**.................... **203 949-8400**
  358 Hall Ave Wallingford (06492) *(G-3866)*

Times Publishing LLC.................... 860 349-8532
  491 Main St Middlefield (06455) *(G-1730)*

Times Wire and Cable Company **(HQ)**.................... **203 949-8400**
  358 Hall Ave Wallingford (06492) *(G-3867)*

Timet, East Windsor *Also Called: Titanium Metals Corporation (G-1088)*

Timex Group Usa Inc **(HQ)**.................... **203 346-5000**
  555 Christian Rd Middlebury (06762) *(G-1722)*

Timken Motor & Crane Svcs LLC.................... 207 699-2501
  190 Riverside St Unit 4a Portland (04103) *(G-5284)*

Timken Super Precision, Keene *Also Called: Mpb Corporation (G-14611)*

Timna Manufacturing Inc.................... 203 265-4656
  208 N Plains Industrial Rd Wallingford (06492) *(G-3868)*

Tin Can Alley.................... 508 487-1648
  269 Commercial St Provincetown (02657) *(G-11499)*

Tinkergarten, Northampton *Also Called: Highlights For Children Inc (G-11067)*

Tinny Corporation.................... 860 854-6121
  100 Bradley St Middletown (06457) *(G-1786)*

Tinsley GROup-Ps&w Inc **(HQ)**.................... **919 742-5832**
  1 Eastern Steel Rd Milford (06460) *(G-1896)*

Tiny Homes of Maine LLC.................... 207 619-4108
  66 Industrial Dr # 4 Houlton (04730) *(G-4905)*

Tiny-Clutch, Clinton *Also Called: Helander Products Inc (G-644)*

Tire & Auto Service Centers.................... 508 559-6802
  98 Westgate Dr Ste 2 Brockton (02301) *(G-7312)*

Tire Chains Requiredcom.................... 207 465-7276
  1010 Kennedy Memorial Dr Oakland (04963) *(G-5121)*

Tire Country of Enfield Inc.................... 860 763-0846
  623 Hazard Ave Enfield (06082) *(G-1155)*

Tire King, Skowhegan *Also Called: Tki Inc (G-5479)*

Tis Brewer LLC..207 989-4560
15 Industrial Plaza Dr Brewer (04412) *(G-4621)*

Tisbury Printer Inc...508 693-4222
39 Lagoon Pond Rd Vineyard Haven (02568) *(G-12495)*

Tissue Plus LLC..978 524-0550
39 Hildreth St N Bangor (04401) *(G-4516)*

Titalist and Footjoy Worldwide, Brockton *Also Called: Acushnet Company (G-7252)*

Titan Advnced Enrgy Sltons Inc...........................561 654-5558
35 Congress St Ste 251 Salem (01970) *(G-11735)*

Titan Machine Products Inc...................................207 775-0011
600 County Rd Westbrook (04092) *(G-5651)*

Titanium Electric LLC..203 810-4050
15 Arbor Dr Norwalk (06854) *(G-2582)*

Titanium Metals Corporation................................860 627-7051
7 Craftsman Rd East Windsor (06088) *(G-1088)*

Titeflex, Springfield *Also Called: Titeflex Corporation (G-12140)*

Titeflex Aerospace, Laconia *Also Called: Smiths Tblar Systms-Lconia Inc (G-14670)*

Titeflex Commercial Inc.......................................413 739-5631
603 Hendee St Springfield (01104) *(G-12139)*

Titeflex Corporation **(HQ)**................................**413 739-5631**
603 Hendee St Springfield (01104) *(G-12140)*

Titi, Weston *Also Called: Tryxus Investment & Trdg Inc (G-13291)*

Titleist, New Bedford *Also Called: Acushnet Company (G-10561)*

Titleist & Footjoy Worldwide, New Bedford *Also Called: Acushnet Company (G-10563)*

Titus & Bean Graphics Inc...................................781 585-1355
62 Main St Ste 107 Kingston (02364) *(G-9513)*

Titus Engrv & Stonesetting Inc.............................508 695-6842
44 Washington St Unit 1 Plainville (02762) *(G-11443)*

Tivoli Audio, Boston *Also Called: Fargo Ta LLC (G-6731)*

Tivoly Inc..802 873-3106
434 Baxter Ave Derby Line (05830) *(G-17213)*

TJ Bark Mulch Inc..413 569-2400
25 Sam West Rd Southwick (01077) *(G-12047)*

Tk Cups-Sorg's, Fitchburg *Also Called: Visionstep Consulting Inc (G-8681)*

TK Machining Inc...207 247-3114
4 Dyer Ln Waterboro (04087) *(G-5592)*

Tk Sports and Associates Inc...............................603 442-6770
100 Whaleback Mountain Rd Enfield (03748) *(G-14275)*

TK&k Services LLC...770 844-8710
719 Hale St Ste 3 Beverly (01915) *(G-6389)*

Tkh Security LLC **(PA)**...................................**203 220-6544**
125 Commerce Ct Ste 11 Cheshire (06410) *(G-619)*

Tki Inc...207 474-5322
309 North Ave Skowhegan (04976) *(G-5479)*

Tl Partners LLC..203 956-6181
227 Wilson Ave Norwalk (06854) *(G-2583)*

TLC Vision (usa) Corporation...............................978 531-4114
201 Andover St Peabody (01960) *(G-11348)*

TLD America Corporation **(DH)**.......................**860 602-3400**
812 Bloomfield Ave Windsor (06095) *(G-4309)*

Tld Group, Windsor *Also Called: TLD America Corporation (G-4309)*

Tli Group Ltd...508 866-9825
35 Kennedy Dr Carver (02330) *(G-7858)*

Tls Printing LLC...508 234-2344
84 Tyler Rd Townsend (01469) *(G-12443)*

Tm & Tm, Livermore Falls *Also Called: Tm and Tm Inc (G-5026)*

Tm and Tm Inc...207 897-3442
49 Gilbert St Livermore Falls (04254) *(G-5026)*

Tm Electronics, Devens *Also Called: Industrial Physics PDT Intgrit (G-8273)*

Tm Ward Co Connecticut LLC...............................203 866-9203
5 Wilbur St Norwalk (06854) *(G-2584)*

TMC Liquidating Corp...800 344-5901
10 Research Pkwy Ste 100 Wallingford (06492) *(G-3869)*

TMC Rhode Island Company Inc...........................401 596-2816
36 Beach St Westerly (02891) *(G-16943)*

Tmcs, Peabody *Also Called: Technical Manufacturing Corp (G-11346)*

Tmd Technologies LLC..978 922-6000
150 Sohier Rd Beverly (01915) *(G-6390)*

Tme Co Inc..860 354-0686
315 Cole Ave Providence (02906) *(G-16628)*

Tmh Machining & Welding Corp............................508 580-6899
124 Turnpike St Ste 15 West Bridgewater (02379) *(G-12985)*

TMI Industries Inc..413 283-9021
25 Ware St Palmer (01069) *(G-11285)*

Tml Manufacturing Inc...508 264-0494
7 Perry Dr Foxboro (02035) *(G-8729)*

Tmlp Ernest Mello...508 823-4849
10 Benefit St Taunton (02780) *(G-12371)*

Tms International LLC...203 629-8383
165 W Putnam Ave Greenwich (06830) *(G-1356)*

Tne, Greene *Also Called: Technical Sales & Svc of Neng (G-4848)*

Tnemec, Wilmington *Also Called: Tnemec East Inc (G-13467)*

Tnemec East Inc...978 988-9500
11 Upton Dr Wilmington (01887) *(G-13467)*

TNT Precision, Hudson *Also Called: TNT Precision LLC (G-14556)*

TNT Precision LLC...603 595-6813
315 Derry Rd Ste 14 Hudson (03051) *(G-14556)*

To Wind Down LLC..203 426-3030
31 Pecks Ln Newtown (06470) *(G-2353)*

Toast, Boston *Also Called: Toast Inc (G-7079)*

Toast Inc **(PA)**...**617 297-1005**
401 Park Dr Ste 801 Boston (02215) *(G-7079)*

Toby Leary Fine Wdwkg Inc..................................508 957-2281
135 Barnstable Rd Ste A Hyannis (02601) *(G-9454)*

Toby Press LLC..203 830-8508
New Milford (06776) *(G-2261)*

TOC Finishing Corp..617 623-3310
22 Clifton St Somerville (02144) *(G-11902)*

Toce Brothers Incorporated **(PA)**....................**860 496-2080**
145 E Main St Torrington (06790) *(G-3700)*

Todd & Weld LLP..781 784-1026
4 Manns Hill Cres Sharon (02067) *(G-11796)*

Todd Clark and Associates Inc.............................978 774-7100
6 Cherry Hill Dr Danvers (01923) *(G-8225)*

Todrin Industries Inc...508 946-3600
305 Kenneth Welch Dr Lakeville (02347) *(G-9522)*

Toff Industry Inc..860 378-0532
323 Clark St Milldale (06467) *(G-1903)*

Tog Manufacturing Company Inc...........................949 888-7700
1454 S State St North Adams (01247) *(G-10813)*

Toggle-Aire, Smithfield *Also Called: Joraco Inc (G-16719)*

Toledo Woodworking Inc......................................508 280-3354
1246 Highland St Holliston (01746) *(G-9233)*

Tolerx Inc...617 354-8100
300 Technology Sq Ste 4 Cambridge (02139) *(G-7742)*

Tolles Communications Corp.................................603 627-9500
103 Bay St Manchester (03104) *(G-14945)*

Tom and Sallys Handmade Choco..........................800 289-8783
59 Tom Harvey Rd Westerly (02891) *(G-16944)*

Tom Berkowitz Trucking Inc **(PA)**....................**508 234-2920**
279 Douglas Rd Whitinsville (01588) *(G-13346)*

Tom Raredon Metal Work, Florence *Also Called: Lucas Fabrication Inc (G-8684)*

Tom Snyder Productions Inc **(HQ)**...................**617 600-2145**
100 Talcott Ave Ste 6 Watertown (02472) *(G-12915)*

Tom Waters Golf Shop...978 526-7311
153 School St Manchester (01944) *(G-10034)*

Tom's Natural Soap, Kennebunk *Also Called: Toms of Maine Inc (G-4930)*

Tomandtim Enterprises LLC..................................508 380-5550
75 W Main St Northborough (01532) *(G-11113)*

Tomatero Publications Inc.....................................207 474-6300
300 Beckwith Rd Cornville (04976) *(G-4707)*

Tomeli, Boston *Also Called: Opportunityspace Inc (G-6939)*

Tommila Brothers Inc..603 242-7774
487 Nh Fitzwilliam (03447) *(G-14316)*

Tommy Hilfiger Footwear Inc.................................617 824-6000
191 Spring St Fl 4 Lexington (02421) *(G-9788)*

Tommy Tape, Berlin *Also Called: Midsun Specialty Products Inc (G-76)*

Tomorrow Companies Inc......................................800 735-7075
9 Channel Ctr St Fl 7 Boston (02210) *(G-7080)*

Tomorrow.io, Boston *Also Called: Tomorrow Companies Inc (G-7080)*

A L P H A B E T I C

Toms of Maine Inc **(HQ)**.. **207 985-2944**
  2 Storer St Ste 302 Kennebunk (04043) *(G-4930)*

Tomtec, Hamden *Also Called: Tomtec Inc (G-1460)*

Tomtec Inc.. 203 281-6790
  1020 Sherman Ave Hamden (06514) *(G-1460)*

Tomtom, Lebanon *Also Called: Tomtom North America Inc (G-14700)*

Tomtom North America Inc... 978 405-1677
  21 Lafayette St Lebanon (03766) *(G-14700)*

Tomtom North America Inc... 603 643-0330
  11 Lafayette St Lebanon (03766) *(G-14701)*

Tomz Corporation... 860 829-0670
  47 Episcopal Rd Berlin (06037) *(G-88)*

Toner Plastics Inc... 413 789-1300
  35 Industrial Dr East Longmeadow (01028) *(G-8399)*

Tonix Phrmceuticals Holdg Corp...................................... 617 908-5040
  259 Samuel Barnet Blvd New Bradford Business Park New Bedford (02745) *(G-10656)*

Tonys Donut Shop.. 207 772-2727
  9 Bolton St Portland (04102) *(G-5285)*

Too Sweets LLC... 203 578-6493
  1348 N Main St Waterbury (06704) *(G-3973)*

Tool Logistics II... 203 855-9754
  46 Chestnut St Norwalk (06854) *(G-2585)*

Tool Technology Inc... 978 777-5006
  3 Ajootian Way Bldg A Middleton (01949) *(G-10396)*

Tooling Division, New Britain *Also Called: Cyient Defense Services Inc (G-2019)*

Tooling Research Inc.. 508 668-5583
  Walpole (02081) *(G-12577)*

Tooling Research Inc **(PA)**... **508 668-1950**
  81 Diamond St Walpole (02081) *(G-12578)*

Tooling Tech Center, Northfield *Also Called: Freudenberg-Nok General Partnr (G-15266)*

Toolmax Designing Tooling Inc.. 860 477-0373
  591 Ference Rd Ashford (06278) *(G-22)*

Toolmex, Northborough *Also Called: Toolmex Indus Solutions Inc (G-11114)*

Toolmex Indus Solutions Inc **(PA)**............................... **508 653-8897**
  34 Talbot Rd Northborough (01532) *(G-11114)*

Toolsgroup Inc... 617 263-0080
  75 Federal St Ste 920 Boston (02110) *(G-7081)*

Toomey's Rent-All Center, Worcester *Also Called: B R T Inc (G-13701)*

Tootsie Chambridge Plant.. 617 491-2500
  810 Main St Cambridge (02139) *(G-7743)*

Top Dead Center Apparel, Wells River *Also Called: Green Mountain Monogram Inc (G-17687)*

Top Flight Machine Tool LLC.. 860 747-4726
  90 Robert Jackson Way Plainville (06062) *(G-2784)*

Top Half Inc.. 978 454-5440
  15 Fairview Ave Tyngsboro (01879) *(G-12468)*

Top Shell LLC.. 401 726-7890
  55 Conduit St Unit 1 Central Falls (02863) *(G-15799)*

Top Shop Inc.. 802 658-1351
  87 Ethan Allen Dr South Burlington (05403) *(G-17604)*

Topaz Legal Inc... 802 540-2504
  29 Church St Ste 303 Burlington (05401) *(G-17162)*

Topcon Positioning Systems Inc...................................... 800 421-0125
  58 Chenell Dr Concord (03301) *(G-14164)*

Topek LLC.. 603 863-2400
  131 Yankee Barn Rd Grantham (03753) *(G-14363)*

Topex Inc... 203 748-5918
  10 Precision Rd Ste 2 Danbury (06810) *(G-825)*

Topper & Griggs Group LLC.. 860 747-5737
  36 Russo Cir Agawam (01001) *(G-5813)*

Topside Canvas & Uphl Inc... 860 399-4845
  768 Boston Post Rd Westbrook (06498) *(G-4144)*

Topstone Golf Course, South Windsor *Also Called: South Windsor Golf Course LLC (G-3182)*

Tor Project Inc.. 206 512-5312
  56 Waterhouse St Apt 1 Somerville (02144) *(G-11903)*

Toray Plastics (america) Inc **(DH)**................................ **401 294-4511**
  50 Belver Ave North Kingstown (02852) *(G-16287)*

Torino Systems, Madison *Also Called: Torino Systems LLC (G-1573)*

Torino Systems LLC... 203 871-1118
  44 Pent Rd Madison (06443) *(G-1573)*

Tornik Inc... 860 282-6081
  16 Old Forge Rd # B Rocky Hill (06067) *(G-2937)*

Tornik LLC... 860 282-6081
  16 Old Forge Rd Ste B Rocky Hill (06067) *(G-2938)*

Torqmaster Inc... 203 326-5945
  200 Harvard Ave Stamford (06902) *(G-3484)*

Torqmaster International, Stamford *Also Called: Torqmaster Inc (G-3484)*

Torque, Cambridge *Also Called: Torque Therapeutics Inc (G-7744)*

Torque Specialties, Windsor *Also Called: AKO Inc (G-4256)*

Torque Therapeutics Inc.. 617 945-1082
  1 Kendall Sq Bldg 1400 Cambridge (02139) *(G-7744)*

Torrey S Crane Company... 860 628-4778
  492 Summer St Plantsville (06479) *(G-2799)*

Torrington Distributors Inc **(PA)**.................................. **860 482-4464**
  43 Norfolk St Torrington (06790) *(G-3701)*

Torrington Register Citizen, Torrington *Also Called: Register Citizen Publishing (G-3693)*

Torromeo Industries Inc **(PA)**...................................... **978 686-5634**
  33 Old Ferry Rd Methuen (01844) *(G-10346)*

Torromeo Industries Inc.. 603 642-5564
  18 Dorre Rd Kingston (03848) *(G-14637)*

Tortilleria MI Nina, Boston *Also Called: New England Tortilla Inc (G-6917)*

Tortran Inc... 203 538-5062
  6 Waterview Dr Shelton (06484) *(G-3070)*

Total Air Supply LLC.. 603 889-0100
  171 E Hollis St Nashua (03060) *(G-15177)*

Total Basement Finishing, Seymour *Also Called: Connecticut Basement Systems Inc (G-2959)*

Total Communications Inc **(PA)**.................................... **860 282-9999**
  333 Burnham St East Hartford (06108) *(G-1028)*

Total Concept Tool Inc.. 203 483-1130
  2 Research Dr Ste 1 Branford (06405) *(G-283)*

Total Drilling Supply LLC... 860 923-1091
  144 New Rd Thompson (06277) *(G-3653)*

Total Fab, East Haven *Also Called: Total Fab LLC (G-1055)*

Total Fab LLC.. 475 238-8176
  140 Commerce St East Haven (06512) *(G-1055)*

Total Recoil Magnetics Inc.. 508 429-9600
  84 October Hill Rd Ste 6a Holliston (01746) *(G-9234)*

Total Register Inc... 860 210-0465
  180 Sunny Valley Rd Ste 1 New Milford (06776) *(G-2262)*

Total Specialty Chemicals Inc **(PA)**............................. **203 966-1525**
  47 Elm St New Canaan (06840) *(G-2089)*

Toth Inc **(PA)**... **617 577-6400**
  86 Baker Avenue Ext Ste 230 Concord (01742) *(G-8136)*

Toth Brand Imaging, Concord *Also Called: Toth Inc (G-8136)*

Toto LLC.. 203 776-6000
  27 Whitney Ave New Haven (06510) *(G-2210)*

Touch Inc... 781 894-8133
  27 Spring St Waltham (02451) *(G-12805)*

Touch Ahead Software LLC... 866 960-9301
  10 Post Office Sq Ste 800s Boston (02109) *(G-7082)*

Touch Bionics.. 774 719-2199
  35 Hampden Rd Mansfield (02048) *(G-10081)*

Touche Manufacturing Company..................................... 860 254-5080
  200 Glastonbury Blvd Glastonbury (06033) *(G-1299)*

Tova Industries Inc.. 413 569-5688
  10 Hudson Dr Southwick (01077) *(G-12048)*

Tower Brands, Centerbrook *Also Called: Tower Laboratories Ltd (G-564)*

Tower Laboratories Ltd.. 860 669-7078
  7 Heritage Park Rd Clinton (06413) *(G-652)*

Tower Laboratories Ltd **(PA)**.. **860 767-2127**
  8 Industrial Park Rd Centerbrook (06409) *(G-564)*

Tower Manufacturing Corp.. 401 467-7550
  25 Reservoir Ave Providence (02907) *(G-16629)*

Tower Optical Company Inc... 203 866-4535
  275 East Ave Fl 2 Norwalk (06855) *(G-2586)*

Tower Publishing **(PA)**.. **207 642-5400**
  650 Cape Rd Standish (04084) *(G-5529)*

Town Bookbindery.. 508 763-2713
  154 County Rd East Freetown (02717) *(G-8367)*

Town Common Inc... 978 948-8696
  77 Wethersfield St Rowley (01969) *(G-11686)*

Town Crier, Wilmington *Also Called: Daily Woburn Times Inc (G-13402)*

(G-0000) Company's Geographic Section entry number

Town Crier Publications Inc.................................. 508 529-7791
  48 Mechanic St Upton (01568) *(G-12475)*

Town Crier, The, Pittsfield *Also Called: New England Newspapers Inc (G-11414)*

Town Dock, The, Narragansett *Also Called: Ngc Inc (G-16192)*

Town of Billerica.. 978 671-0954
  365 Boston Rd Ste 207 Billerica (01821) *(G-6488)*

Town of Bristol.. 401 787-6763
  32 Ridge Rd Bristol (02809) *(G-15783)*

Town of Burrillville.. 401 568-6296
  141 Clear River Dr Oakland (02858) *(G-16335)*

Town of Gorham **(PA)**.. **207 222-1610**
  75 South St Ste 1 Gorham (04038) *(G-4836)*

Town of Hartford.. 802 295-9425
  812 Va Cutoff Rd White River Junction (05001) *(G-17710)*

Town of Ledyard... 860 464-9060
  889 Colonel Ledyard Hwy Gales Ferry (06339) *(G-1262)*

Town of Medyard, The, Gales Ferry *Also Called: Town of Ledyard (G-1262)*

Town of Montville... 860 848-3830
  83 Pink Row Uncasville (06382) *(G-3745)*

Town of North Reading.. 978 664-6027
  235 North St North Reading (01864) *(G-11050)*

Town of Putnam, Putnam *Also Called: Superior Plas Extrusion Co Inc (G-2877)*

Town of Vernon.. 860 870-3545
  100 Windsorville Rd Vernon (06066) *(G-3758)*

Town of Westborough.. 508 366-7615
  238 Turnpike Rd Westborough (01581) *(G-13140)*

Town of Westminster.. 978 874-2313
  7 South St Westminster (01473) *(G-13281)*

Town Times, Meriden *Also Called: Record-Journal Newspaper (G-1692)*

Townsend Welding Co Inc.. 978 657-5189
  815 Woburn St Wilmington (01887) *(G-13468)*

Toxikon Corporation.. 978 942-5554
  15 Wiggins Ave Bedford (01730) *(G-6274)*

Tozier Group Inc... 207 838-7939
  185 Mountain Rd Falmouth (04105) *(G-4774)*

Tozier Group, The, Falmouth *Also Called: Tozier Group Inc (G-4774)*

TP Cycle & Engineering Inc..................................... 203 744-4960
  4 Finance Dr Danbury (06810) *(G-826)*

Tph Inc.. 401 431-1791
  100 Kimberly Rd Taunton (02780) *(G-12372)*

Tpi Inc.. 401 247-4010
  373 Market St Unit B Warren (02885) *(G-16769)*

Tpi Composites, Warren *Also Called: Tpi Inc (G-16769)*

Tpi Composites Inc... 401 247-4010
  373 Market St Warren (02885) *(G-16770)*

Tpi Industries LLC **(HQ)**.................................... **845 692-2820**
  208 Manley St West Bridgewater (02379) *(G-12986)*

Tpi Solutions Ink, Waltham *Also Called: Technical Publications Inc (G-12789)*

Tpni, Norwood *Also Called: Pulse Network Inc (G-11203)*

Tr Enabling, Ludlow *Also Called: Remsport Mfg LLC (G-9952)*

Tr3 Solutions Inc.. 781 481-0642
  2 Main St Ste 200 Stoneham (02180) *(G-12187)*

Tracelink Inc **(PA)**.. **781 914-4900**
  200 Ballardvale St Ste 100 Wilmington (01887) *(G-13469)*

Tracer Technologies Inc.. 617 776-6410
  20 Assembly Square Dr Somerville (02145) *(G-11904)*

Tracey Gear Inc.. 401 725-3920
  740 York Ave Pawtucket (02861) *(G-16424)*

Tracey Gear & Precision Shaft, Pawtucket *Also Called: Tracey Gear Inc (G-16424)*

Trackcam LLC... 508 556-1955
  285 Winthrop St Unit 2b Rehoboth (02769) *(G-11614)*

Tracksmith Corporation **(PA)**............................... **781 235-0037**
  285 Newbury St Boston (02115) *(G-7083)*

Tracs Industrial Coolers....................................... 603 707-2241
  790 Route 16 Ossipee (03864) *(G-15284)*

Tracy Glover Objects & Ltg Inc................................. 401 724-1100
  59 Blackstone Ave Unit 11 Pawtucket (02860) *(G-16425)*

Tracy Glover Studio, Pawtucket *Also Called: Tracy Glover Objects & Ltg Inc (G-16425)*

Tracy J Morrison... 207 683-2371
  26 Wellington Rd Harmony (04942) *(G-4874)*

Tracy L Gordon... 207 684-4462
  68 Norton Hill Rd Strong (04983) *(G-5537)*

Tradebe Transportation, Meriden *Also Called: Tradebe Treatment and Recycling Northeast LLC (G-1710)*

Tradebe Treatment and Recycling Northeast LLC **(DH)**........ **203 238-8102**
  234 Hobart St Ste 1 Meriden (06450) *(G-1710)*

Tradeport USA LLC.. 603 692-2900
  3 Progress Dr Dover (03820) *(G-14254)*

Tradest1... 401 884-4949
  219 Main St East Greenwich (02818) *(G-15994)*

Tradewinds... 203 723-6966
  274 Bethany Rd Beacon Falls (06403) *(G-46)*

Trafa Pharmaceutical Inc....................................... 866 998-7232
  140 Padgette St Ste D Chicopee (01022) *(G-8063)*

Trail-Tex LLC.. 603 436-6326
  140 West Rd Ste 2 Portsmouth (03801) *(G-15444)*

Trailheads, Kent *Also Called: Indigo Coast Inc (G-1541)*

Traincroft Inc **(PA)**....................................... **781 393-6943**
  0 Governors Ave Ste 38 Medford (02155) *(G-10299)*

Training Thru Placement Inc.................................... 401 353-0220
  20 Marblehead Ave North Providence (02904) *(G-16312)*

Trane, Farmington *Also Called: Trane US Inc (G-1251)*

Trane, Westbrook *Also Called: Trane US Inc (G-5652)*

Trane, Springfield *Also Called: Trane Comercial Systems (G-12141)*

Trane, Wilmington *Also Called: Trane Inc (G-13470)*

Trane, Riverside *Also Called: Trane US Inc (G-16660)*

Trane Comercial Systems.. 413 271-3001
  90 Carando Dr Springfield (01104) *(G-12141)*

Trane Company... 802 864-3816
  177 Leroy Rd Williston (05495) *(G-17750)*

Trane Inc.. 860 437-6208
  178 Wallace St New Haven (06511) *(G-2211)*

Trane Inc.. 978 737-3900
  181 Ballardvale St Ste 201 Wilmington (01887) *(G-13470)*

Trane Supply, New Haven *Also Called: Trane Inc (G-2211)*

Trane Technologies Company LLC................................. 860 616-6600
  716 Brook St Ste 130 Rocky Hill (06067) *(G-2939)*

Trane Technologies Company LLC................................. 860 626-2085
  70 North St Torrington (06790) *(G-3702)*

Trane Technologies Company LLC................................. 781 961-2063
  70 Bearfoot Rd Northborough (01532) *(G-11115)*

Trane Technologies Company LLC................................. 508 842-5769
  908 Boston Tpke Shrewsbury (01545) *(G-11844)*

Trane US Inc... 860 470-3901
  135 South Rd Farmington (06032) *(G-1251)*

Trane US Inc... 844 807-2282
  860 Spring St # 1 Westbrook (04092) *(G-5652)*

Trane US Inc... 617 908-6710
  10 Hemingway Dr Riverside (02915) *(G-16660)*

Trans Form Plastics Corp....................................... 978 777-1440
  45 Prince St Danvers (01923) *(G-8226)*

Trans Mag Corp... 978 458-1487
  104 Canterbury Ct Carlisle (01741) *(G-7847)*

Trans Metrics Inc **(HQ)**.................................... **617 926-1000**
  180 Dexter Ave Watertown (02472) *(G-12916)*

Trans Utility Inc.. 207 454-1162
  197 Houlton Rd Baileyville (04694) *(G-4485)*

Trans-Tek Inc.. 860 872-8351
  10 Industrial Dr Ellington (06029) *(G-1118)*

Trans-Tex, Cranston *Also Called: Trans-Tex LLC (G-15920)*

Trans-Tex LLC.. 401 331-8483
  117 Pettaconsett Ave Cranston (02920) *(G-15920)*

Trans-Utility Services, Baileyville *Also Called: Trans Utility Inc (G-4485)*

Transatlantic Bubbles LLC...................................... 203 464-0051
  935 Greenway Rd Woodbridge (06525) *(G-4383)*

Transcat Inc... 888 975-5061
  149 River St Ste 3 Andover (01810) *(G-5930)*

Transcat Calibration Services, Andover *Also Called: Transcat Inc (G-5930)*

Transcend Aero, Carlisle *Also Called: Transcend Air Corporation (G-7848)*

Transcend Air Corporation...................................... 781 883-4818
  779 West St Carlisle (01741) *(G-7848)*

Transcendia Inc.. 207 786-4790
  21 Old Farm Rd Lewiston (04240) *(G-4994)*

Transcon Technologies Inc.. 413 562-7684
  53 Mainline Dr Westfield (01085) *(G-13212)*

Transene Company Inc **(PA)**.. **978 777-7860**
  10 Electronics Ave Danvers (01923) *(G-8227)*

Transformer Technology Inc... 860 349-1061
  60 Commerce Cir Durham (06422) *(G-905)*

Transformit **(PA)**... **207 856-9911**
  33 Sanford Dr Gorham (04038) *(G-4837)*

Transit Systems Inc... 860 747-3669
  161 Woodford Ave Ste 34 Plainville (06062) *(G-2785)*

Transitions Abroad Pubg Inc... 413 992-6486
  18 Hulst Rd Amherst (01002) *(G-5865)*

Translate, Lexington *Also Called: Translate Bio Inc (G-9789)*

Translate Bio Inc **(HQ)**... **617 945-7361**
  29 Hartwell Ave Lexington (02421) *(G-9789)*

Transmedics, Andover *Also Called: Transmedics Inc (G-5931)*

Transmedics **(PA)**.. **978 552-0443**
  200 Minuteman Rd Ste 302 Andover (01810) *(G-5931)*

Transmode USA, North Branford *Also Called: Transmonde USa Inc (G-2377)*

Transmonde USa Inc... 203 484-1528
  100 Shaw Rd North Branford (06471) *(G-2377)*

Transom Scopes Inc... 413 562-3606
  33 Airport Rd Westfield (01085) *(G-13213)*

Transom Symphony Opco LLC **(PA)**................................ **203 503-7938**
  120 Long Ridge Rd Stamford (06902) *(G-3485)*

Transparency-One Inc... 617 645-2176
  100 Cambridge St Ste 1310 Boston (02114) *(G-7084)*

Transparent Audio Inc.. 207 284-1100
  47 Industrial Park Rd Saco (04072) *(G-5380)*

Transtulit LLC... 413 737-2600
  138 Memorial Ave Ste 40 West Springfield (01089) *(G-13045)*

Transwitch Corporation.. 203 929-8810
  3 Enterprise Dr Shelton (06484) *(G-3071)*

Tranztape LLC.. 207 785-2467
  317 Town Hill Rd Appleton (04862) *(G-4406)*

Trash Flow, Waterbury Center *Also Called: Ivy Computer Inc (G-17681)*

Travel Wear, Norwalk *Also Called: Business Journals Inc (G-2478)*

Traveling Vineyard, Ipswich *Also Called: Phoenix Vintners LLC (G-9494)*

Traver Electric Motor Co Inc.. 203 753-5103
  151 Homer St Waterbury (06704) *(G-3974)*

Trawlworks Inc... 401 789-3964
  30 Walts Way Narragansett (02882) *(G-16198)*

Trd Specialties Inc... 860 738-4505
  8 Wickett St Pine Meadow (06061) *(G-2729)*

Treadwell Corporation.. 860 283-7600
  341 Railroad St Thomaston (06787) *(G-3639)*

Treasure Tees.. 855 438-8337
  165 Ledge St Ste 6 Nashua (03060) *(G-15178)*

Treasuretreats, Worcester *Also Called: Everson Distributing Co Inc (G-13721)*

Treasury & Risk Management, Shelton *Also Called: Wicks Business Information LLC (G-3078)*

Trebia Networks Inc.. 978 264-3700
  33 Nagog Park Acton (01720) *(G-5766)*

Tree Care Industry Assn Inc.. 603 314-5380
  670 North Commercial St Ste 201 Manchester (03101) *(G-14946)*

TREE CARE INDUSTRY ASSOCIATION, Manchester *Also Called: Tree Care Industry Assn Inc (G-14946)*

Treeline Timber.. 603 586-7725
  11 Nevers Ln Jefferson (03583) *(G-14586)*

Trees Ltd A Partnr Consisting...................................... 207 547-3168
  2506 Middle Rd Sidney (04330) *(G-5461)*

Treetop, South Easton *Also Called: Case Assembly Solutions Inc (G-11939)*

Trego Inc.. 508 291-3816
  5 Little Brook Rd Wareham (02571) *(G-12846)*

Treif USA Inc.. 203 929-9930
  50 Waterview Dr Ste 130 Shelton (06484) *(G-3072)*

Trellborg Engnered Ctd Fabrics, Monson *Also Called: Trelleborg Ctd Systems US Inc (G-10457)*

Trellborg Pipe Sals Mlford Inc..................................... 603 673-8680
  279 Riverway W Milford (03055) *(G-15041)*

Trelleborg Pipe Sals Mlford Inc **(DH)**........................... **800 626-2180**
  250 Elm St Milford (03055) *(G-15042)*

Trelleborg Applied Tech, Randolph *Also Called: Trelleborg Offshore Boston Inc (G-11577)*

Trelleborg Ctd Systems US Inc...................................... 203 468-0342
  30 Lenox St New Haven (06513) *(G-2212)*

Trelleborg Ctd Systems US Inc...................................... 413 267-4808
  152 Bethany Rd Monson (01057) *(G-10457)*

Trelleborg Offshore Boston Inc..................................... 774 719-1400
  290 Forbes Blvd Mansfield (02048) *(G-10082)*

Trelleborg Offshore Boston Inc **(HQ)**............................ **781 437-1171**
  24 Teed Dr Randolph (02368) *(G-11577)*

Trellis Structures Inc.. 888 285-4624
  25 N Main St East Templeton (01438) *(G-8415)*

Tremco Swiss Inc... 203 573-8584
  43 Mattatuck Heights Rd Waterbury (06705) *(G-3975)*

Tremeau Pharmaceuticals Inc.. 617 485-0250
  53 Main St Ste 202 Concord (01742) *(G-8137)*

Tremont Street Lq Group Inc **(PA)**.............................. **617 262-0379**
  607 Tremont St Boston (02118) *(G-7085)*

Trems Inc.. 207 596-6989
  19 Merrill Dr Rockland (04841) *(G-5343)*

Trento Group LLC... 860 623-1361
  400 Governor St East Hartford (06108) *(G-1029)*

Trevi, New Haven *Also Called: Trevi Therapeutics Inc (G-2213)*

Trevi Therapeutics Inc **(PA)**.................................... **203 304-2499**
  195 Church St Fl 14 New Haven (06510) *(G-2213)*

Trew Corp.. 413 773-9798
  901 River Rd Deerfield (01342) *(G-8256)*

Trexel Inc **(PA)**... **781 932-0202**
  100 Research Dr Ste 1 Wilmington (01887) *(G-13471)*

Tri Star Printing & Graphics....................................... 617 666-4480
  33 Park St Somerville (02143) *(G-11905)*

Tri Star Sheet Metal Company....................................... 207 225-2043
  1817 Auburn Rd Turner (04282) *(G-5563)*

Tri State Maintenance Svcs LLC..................................... 203 691-1343
  356 Old Maple Ave North Haven (06473) *(G-2440)*

Tri State Steel Inc.. 207 784-9371
  24 Chasse St Auburn (04210) *(G-4461)*

Tri TEC Electronics Inc.. 203 573-8491
  33 5th St Waterbury (06708) *(G-3976)*

Tri Textiles Corporation **(PA)**.................................. **631 420-0011**
  147 Plymouth Ave Fall River (02721) *(G-8617)*

Tri Town Cabinetry... 603 391-9276
  1261 Hooksett Rd Ste 3 Hooksett (03106) *(G-14475)*

Tri Town Precision Plastics, Deep River *Also Called: Swpc Plastics LLC (G-885)*

Tri-Angle Metal Fab, Milton *Also Called: Milton Vermont Sheet Metal Inc (G-17362)*

Tri-Bro Tool Co Inc.. 401 781-6323
  1370 Elmwood Ave Cranston (02910) *(G-15921)*

Tri-K, Derry *Also Called: Tri-K Industries Inc (G-14211)*

Tri-K Industries Inc... 973 298-8850
  20 A St Derry (03038) *(G-14211)*

Tri-K Industries Inc... 603 898-0811
  8 Willow St Ste 2 Salem (03079) *(G-15567)*

Tri-Mack Plastics Mfg Corp... 401 253-2140
  55 Broadcommon Rd Ste 1 Bristol (02809) *(G-15784)*

Tri-Mar Manufacturing Company...................................... 860 628-4791
  191 Captain Lewis Dr Southington (06489) *(G-3238)*

Tri-Mass Inc... 781 235-1075
  32 Monadnock Rd Wellesley (02481) *(G-12946)*

Tri-Star Industries Inc.. 860 828-7570
  95 Silvermine Rd # 1 Seymour (06483) *(G-2973)*

Tri-Star Plastics Corp **(PA)**.................................... **508 845-1111**
  906 Boston Tpke Shrewsbury (01545) *(G-11845)*

Tri-State Iron Works Inc... 603 228-0020
  24 Industrial Park Dr Concord (03301) *(G-14165)*

Tri-State Led Inc.. 203 813-3791
  255 Mill St Greenwich (06830) *(G-1357)*

Tri-State Logging LLC.. 603 499-1499
  46 Fullam Pond Rd Winchester (03470) *(G-15717)*

Tri-State Packing Supply... 207 883-5218
  158 Pleasant Hill Rd Scarborough (04074) *(G-5446)*

(G-0000) Company's Geographic Section entry number

Tri-State Seafoods Inc.. 603 692-7201
  23 Interstate Dr Somersworth (03878) *(G-15627)*

Triad Inc... 508 695-2247
  44 Washington St Plainville (02762) *(G-11444)*

Triad Concepts Inc... 860 399-4045
  51 Brookwood Dr Westbrook (06498) *(G-4145)*

Triangle Design Group LLC................................... 207 776-3177
  649 Elm St Biddeford (04005) *(G-4592)*

Triangle Engineering Inc.. 781 878-1500
  6 Industrial Way Hanover (02339) *(G-9046)*

Triatic Inc... 860 236-2298
  22 Grassmere Ave West Hartford (06110) *(G-4085)*

Tribe Mediterranean Foods Inc............................ 419 695-9925
  110 Prince Henry Dr Taunton (02780) *(G-12373)*

Tricab (usa) Inc... 508 421-4680
  15 Coppage Dr Worcester (01603) *(G-13813)*

Trickett Woodworks Company, Auburn *Also Called: Forest Manufacturing Corp (G-13907)*

Trico, Attleboro *Also Called: Schrader Electronics Inc (G-6061)*

Trico Millworks Inc.. 207 637-2711
  300 Hardscrabble Rd Limington (04049) *(G-5006)*

Trico Specialty Films LLC..................................... 401 294-7022
  310 Compass Cir North Kingstown (02852) *(G-16288)*

Trident Alloys Inc... 413 737-1477
  181 Abbe Ave Springfield (01107) *(G-12142)*

Tridyne Process Systems Inc............................... 802 863-6873
  80 Allen Rd South Burlington (05403) *(G-17605)*

Triem Industries LLC.. 203 888-1212
  105 Napco Dr Terryville (06786) *(G-3612)*

Triex LLC.. 802 505-6772
  81 Parker Rd Barre (05641) *(G-17021)*

Trigila Construction Inc.. 860 828-8444
  30 And A Half Ripple Ct Berlin (06037) *(G-89)*

Trilliam Solutions, Brownville *Also Called: S & K Unlimited LLC (G-4638)*

Trillium Brewing, Canton *Also Called: Trillium Brewing Company LLC (G-7835)*

Trillium Brewing Company LLC **(PA)**.............. **781 298-7126**
  100 Royall St Canton (02021) *(G-7835)*

Trillium Valves USA, Ipswich *Also Called: Valves and Controls Us Inc (G-9499)*

Trilog Group Inc.. 781 937-9963
  54 Cummings Park Ste 308 Woburn (01801) *(G-13679)*

Trimboard, Springfield *Also Called: Trimboard Inc (G-12143)*

Trimboard Inc... 413 886-0142
  983 Page Blvd Springfield (01104) *(G-12143)*

Trimech Advanced Manufacturing, Deep River *Also Called: Trimech Solutions LLC (G-886)*

Trimech Solutions LLC... 860 526-5869
  630 Industrial Park Rd Deep River (06417) *(G-886)*

Trimed Media Group Inc... 401 919-5165
  235 Promenade St Rm 298 Providence (02908) *(G-16630)*

Trimino, Guilford *Also Called: Miami Bay Beverage Company LLC (G-1400)*

Trine Access Technology Inc................................. 203 730-1756
  2 Park Lawn Dr Bethel (06801) *(G-136)*

Trine Pharmaceuticals Inc..................................... 617 558-8789
  1 Gateway Ctr Newton (02458) *(G-10791)*

Trinity Builders Inc **(PA)**.................................... **781 780-6168**
  217 Washington St Westwood (02090) *(G-13323)*

Trinken Brewing Co LLC... 207 389-6360
  144 State Rd West Bath (04530) *(G-5609)*

Trio Community Meals LLC.................................... 203 336-8407
  515 Lindley St Bridgeport (06606) *(G-380)*

Tripcraft LLC.. 781 588-9100
  15 Fiske Ave Waltham (02453) *(G-12806)*

Triple B Media LLC... 917 710-2222
  195 S Main St Cheshire (06410) *(G-620)*

Triple Crown Cbnets Mllwk Corp......................... 508 833-6500
  12b Jan Sebastian Dr Sandwich (02563) *(G-11753)*

Triple P Packg & Ppr Pdts Inc............................. 508 588-0444
  20 Burke Dr Brockton (02301) *(G-7313)*

Triple Play Sports... 860 417-2877
  16 Straits Tpke Watertown (06795) *(G-4033)*

Triple Seat Software LLC...................................... 978 635-0615
  6 Ashwood Rd Acton (01720) *(G-5767)*

Triple Stitch Sportswear, Prospect *Also Called: TSS & A Inc (G-2844)*

Tripleshot LLC... 646 812-7548
  21 School St Boston (02108) *(G-7086)*

Tripoli Bakery Inc.. 978 682-7754
  106 Common St Ste 6 Lawrence (01840) *(G-9604)*

Trireme Manufacturing Co Inc.............................. 978 887-2132
  245 Boston St Topsfield (01983) *(G-12440)*

Trirx Pharmaceutical Svcs LLC **(PA)**.............. **256 489-8867**
  101 Merritt 7 Norwalk (06851) *(G-2587)*

Triseptagon LLC.. 413 732-2131
  55 Avocado St Springfield (01104) *(G-12144)*

Tristar, Shrewsbury *Also Called: Tri-Star Plastics Corp (G-11845)*

Tritex Corporation... 203 756-7441
  1500 Meriden Rd Waterbury (06705) *(G-3977)*

Triumph Acttion Systems - Conn **(HQ)**........... **860 687-5412**
  175 Addison Rd Ste 4 Windsor (06095) *(G-4310)*

Triumph Actuation Systems; Windsor *Also Called: Triumph Acttion Systems - Conn (G-4310)*

Triumph Eng Ctrl Systems LLC............................ 860 597-7173
  110 Talcott Rd West Hartford (06110) *(G-4086)*

Triumph Eng Ctrl Systems LLC **(HQ)**.............. **860 236-0651**
  1 Charter Oak Blvd West Hartford (06110) *(G-4087)*

Triumph Group Inc.. 860 726-9378
  1395 Blue Hills Ave Bloomfield (06002) *(G-213)*

Triumph Interiors LLC.. 603 899-5184
  1090 Nh Rte 119 Rindge (03461) *(G-15461)*

Triumph Manufacturing Co Inc............................. 860 635-8811
  422 Timber Ridge Rd Middletown (06457) *(G-1787)*

Trivak Incorporated.. 978 453-7123
  280 Howard St Lowell (01852) *(G-9929)*

Trividia Mfg Solutions Inc **(DH)**....................... **603 788-2848**
  89 Bridge St Lancaster (03584) *(G-14680)*

TRM Microwave, Bedford *Also Called: Technical Research and Manufacturing Inc (G-13951)*

Tronox, Stamford *Also Called: Tronox LLC (G-3487)*

Tronox Incorporated **(DH)**................................. **203 705-3800**
  263 Tresser Blvd Ste 1100 Stamford (06901) *(G-3486)*

Tronox LLC **(PA)**.. **203 705-3800**
  263 Tresser Blvd Ste 1100 Stamford (06901) *(G-3487)*

Tropax Precision Manufacturing........................... 203 794-0733
  10 Precision Rd Danbury (06810) *(G-827)*

Tropical Paradise Inc.. 781 357-1210
  213 Burlington Rd Ste 109 Bedford (01730) *(G-6275)*

Tropical Products Inc.. 978 740-5665
  220 Highland Ave Salem (01970) *(G-11736)*

Tropical Smoothie of Bristol.................................. 508 636-1424
  14 Eliza Ln Dartmouth (02747) *(G-8232)*

Trow & Holden Co Inc.. 802 476-7221
  45 S Main St Ste 57 Barre (05641) *(G-17022)*

Troy Industrial Solutions, Brewer *Also Called: Tis Brewer LLC (G-4621)*

Troy Micro Five Inc.. 802 524-0076
  79 Walnut St Saint Albans (05478) *(G-17535)*

Troy Minerals Inc.. 802 878-5103
  312 Village Dr Colchester (05446) *(G-17205)*

Troy Minerals Inc.. 802 878-5103
  180 Fire Hill Rd Florence (05744) *(G-17273)*

Tru Chocolate Inc... 855 878-2462
  610 Kenoza St Haverhill (01830) *(G-9135)*

Tru Form Precision Mfg LLC................................. 603 974-2552
  2 Wilder Dr Plaistow (03865) *(G-15353)*

Tru Technologies Inc.. 978 532-0775
  245 Lynnfield St Peabody (01960) *(G-11349)*

Tru-Hitch Inc.. 860 379-7772
  16 W West Hill Rd Pleasant Valley (06063) *(G-2805)*

Tru-Precision Corporation...................................... 860 269-6230
  1451 New Britain Ave Ste 86 Farmington (06032) *(G-1252)*

Trucbrush Corporation.. 877 783-0237
  28 Renker Dr South Easton (02375) *(G-11954)*

Trucking , Distribution, Westbrook *Also Called: KSd ATL Trnspt Systems Inc (G-5634)*

True Machine Co Inc... 508 379-0329
  2222 Gar Hwy Swansea (02777) *(G-12314)*

True North Ale Company, Ipswich *Also Called: True North Ale Company LLC (G-9498)*

True North Ale Company LLC................................ 978 312-6473
  116 County Rd Ipswich (01938) *(G-9498)*

A L P H A B E T I C

True Position Mfg LLC... 860 291-2987
   40 Sandra Dr Ste 3 South Windsor (06074) *(G-3186)*

True Precision Inc.. 413 788-4226
   17 Allston Ave West Springfield (01089) *(G-13046)*

True Precision Industries Inc................................... 413 788-4226
   17 Allston Ave West Springfield (01089) *(G-13047)*

True Publishing Company.. 203 272-5316
   125 Grandview Ave Wallingford (06492) *(G-3870)*

True Value, Sanford *Also Called: New England Building Materials LLC* *(G-5401)*

True Words Tortillas Inc.. 508 255-3338
   136 Rt 6a Orleans (02653) *(G-11243)*

Trueform Runner, Chester *Also Called: Samsara Fitness LLC* *(G-632)*

Trueline Publishing LLC.. 207 510-4099
   561 Congress St Portland (04101) *(G-5286)*

Truelove & Maclean Inc... 860 274-9600
   57 Callender Rd Watertown (06795) *(G-4034)*

Truex Incorporated... 401 722-5023
   300 Armistice Blvd Pawtucket (02861) *(G-16426)*

Truex Machine Co Inc... 781 826-6875
   25 Pond St Hanover (02339) *(G-9047)*

Trumbull Printing, Trumbull *Also Called: Hersam Acorn Cmnty Pubg LLC* *(G-3722)*

Trumbull Printing Inc.. 203 261-2548
   205 Spring Hill Rd Trumbull (06611) *(G-3735)*

Trumpf Inc... 860 255-6000
   5 Johnson Ave Farmington (06032) *(G-1253)*

Trumpf Inc... 860 255-6000
   1 Johnson Ave Farmington (06032) *(G-1254)*

Trumpf Inc (DH)... 860 255-6000
   111 Hyde Rd Farmington (06032) *(G-1255)*

Trumpf Inc... 860 255-6000
   3 Johnson Ave Plainville (06062) *(G-2786)*

Trumpf Photonics Inc.. 860 255-6000
   111 Hyde Rd Farmington (06032) *(G-1256)*

Truro Vineyards Cape Cod LLC.................................. 508 487-6200
   11 Shore Road Rte 6a North Truro (02652) *(G-11051)*

TruRoots LLC (PA)... 800 288-3637
   117 Kendrick St Ste 300 Needham (02494) *(G-10527)*

Truss Engineering Corporation................................. 413 543-1298
   181 Goodwin St Indian Orchard (01151) *(G-9476)*

Truss Manufacturing Inc....................................... 860 665-0000
   97 Stanwell Rd Newington (06111) *(G-2329)*

Trustees of Boston College.................................... 617 552-2844
   22 Stone Ave Chestnut Hill (02467) *(G-8002)*

Trustees of Dartmouth College................................. 603 646-2256
   7 Lebanon St Ste 107 Hanover (03755) *(G-14431)*

Trustees of Dartmouth College................................. 603 448-1533
   1 Court St Ste 250 Lebanon (03766) *(G-14702)*

Trustees of Tufts College..................................... 617 628-5000
   520 Boston Ave Medford (02155) *(G-10300)*

Trustees of Tufts College (PA)............................... 617 628-5000
   169 Holland St Ste 318 Somerville (02144) *(G-11906)*

TRW Fastening Systems, Westminster *Also Called: ZF Active Safety & Elec US LLC* *(G-13283)*

Tryxus Investment & Trdg Inc.................................. 800 981-6616
   253 Highland St Weston (02493) *(G-13291)*

Tscan, Waltham *Also Called: Tscan Therapeutics Inc* *(G-12807)*

Tscan Therapeutics Inc.. 857 399-9500
   830 Winter St Waltham (02451) *(G-12807)*

Tsco Inc.. 401 295-0669
   25 Bonneau Rd North Kingstown (02852) *(G-16289)*

Tshb Inc.. 978 465-8950
   11 Malcolm Hoyt Dr Newburyport (01950) *(G-10721)*

Tsi Group Inc (DH)... 603 964-0296
   94 Tide Mill Rd Hampton (03842) *(G-14416)*

Tsi Liquidation Inc... 978 567-9033
   8 Kane Industrial Dr Hudson (01749) *(G-9421)*

Tsi/Protherm, Bridgewater *Also Called: Allen Morgan* *(G-7219)*

Tsmc Inc.. 860 283-8265
   100 Lawton St Torrington (06790) *(G-3703)*

TSS & A Inc... 203 758-6303
   100 Union City Rd Prospect (06712) *(G-2844)*

TSS-Maine LLC... 207 832-6344
   299 Atlantic Hwy Waldoboro (04572) *(G-5579)*

TT Trade Group LLC (PA)...................................... 800 354-4502
   185 Grassy Plain St Unit 1 Bethel (06801) *(G-137)*

Ttm Printed Circuit Group Inc................................. 860 684-8000
   15 Industrial Park Dr Stafford Springs (06076) *(G-3261)*

Ttm Technologies Inc.. 860 684-5881
   4 Old Monson Rd Stafford (06075) *(G-3251)*

Ttm Technologies Inc.. 860 684-8000
   20 Industrial Park Dr Stafford Springs (06076) *(G-3262)*

Tts Mexican Holding Company................................... 781 224-1001
   401 Edgewater Pl Ste 680 Wakefield (01880) *(G-12540)*

Tub's & Stuff Plumbing Supply, Ansonia *Also Called: Kensco Inc* *(G-15)*

Tube Hollows International.................................... 844 721-8823
   39 Enterprise Dr Ste 2 Windham (04062) *(G-5673)*

Tucel Industries Inc.. 802 247-6824
   2014 Forest Dale Rd Forest Dale (05745) *(G-17274)*

Tucker Engineering.. 978 532-5900
   4 5th St Peabody (01960) *(G-11350)*

Tucker Mountain Log Homes, Gouldsboro *Also Called: C A Construction Inc* *(G-4838)*

Tuckerman Steel Fabricators Inc............................... 617 569-8373
   256 Marginal St Ste 2 Boston (02128) *(G-7087)*

Tudor Converted Products Inc (PA)............................ 203 304-1875
   1305 Revere Rd Danbury (06811) *(G-828)*

Tudor House Furniture Co Inc.................................. 203 288-8451
   929 Sherman Ave Hamden (06514) *(G-1461)*

Tufin Software North Amer Inc................................. 877 270-7711
   10 Summer St Boston (02110) *(G-7088)*

Tufin Software Technologies, Boston *Also Called: Tufin Software North Amer Inc* *(G-7088)*

Tufpak Inc.. 603 539-4126
   698 Browns Ridge Rd Ossipee (03864) *(G-15285)*

Tuftane Eti, Fall River *Also Called: Tuftane Extrusion Tech Inc* *(G-8618)*

Tuftane Extrusion Tech Inc.................................... 978 921-8200
   96 Wordell St Fall River (02721) *(G-8618)*

Tufts Daily, Medford *Also Called: Trustees of Tufts College* *(G-10300)*

Tufts University, Somerville *Also Called: Trustees of Tufts College* *(G-11906)*

Tulip, Somerville *Also Called: Tulip Interfaces Inc* *(G-11907)*

Tulip Interfaces Inc (PA).................................... 833 468-8547
   77 Middlesex Ave Ste A Somerville (02145) *(G-11907)*

Tunstall Corporation (PA).................................... 413 594-8695
   118 Exchange St Chicopee (01013) *(G-8064)*

Tupelo Press Inc.. 413 664-9611
   60 Roberts Dr Ste 308 North Adams (01247) *(G-10814)*

Turbine Components Inc.. 858 678-8568
   102 Willenbrock Rd Oxford (06478) *(G-2713)*

Turbine Controls Inc (PA).................................... 860 242-0448
   5 Old Windsor Rd Bloomfield (06002) *(G-214)*

Turbine Kinetics Inc.. 860 633-8520
   60 Sequin Dr Ste 2 Glastonbury (06033) *(G-1300)*

Turbine Specialists LLC....................................... 207 947-9327
   55 Baker Blvd Brewer (04412) *(G-4622)*

Turbine Technologies Inc (PA)................................ 860 678-1642
   126 Hyde Rd Farmington (06032) *(G-1257)*

Turbocam Inc (PA).. 603 905-0200
   607 Calef Hwy Ste 100 Barrington (03825) *(G-13917)*

Turbocam Energy Solutions LLC................................. 603 905-0200
   5 Faraday Dr Dover (03820) *(G-14255)*

Turbocam International, Barrington *Also Called: Turbocam Inc* *(G-13917)*

Turley Publications Inc (PA)................................. 800 824-6548
   24 Water St Palmer (01069) *(G-11286)*

Turmoil Manufacturing, West Swanzey *Also Called: RMA Manufacturing LLC* *(G-15697)*

Turn Key Lumber, Fitzwilliam *Also Called: Turn Key Lumber Inc* *(G-14317)*

Turn Key Lumber Inc... 978 798-1370
   179 Nh Route 12 N 179 Fitzwilliam (03447) *(G-14317)*

Turnaround Letter, The, Boston *Also Called: New Generation Research Inc* *(G-6918)*

Turner Falls Paper, Agawam *Also Called: Southworth Company* *(G-5807)*

Turner Publishing Inc... 207 225-2076
   5 Fern St Turner (04282) *(G-5564)*

Turning Acquisitions LLC...................................... 207 336-2400
   46 John Ellingwood Rd Buckfield (04220) *(G-4659)*

Turning Leaf Ctrs Nrthmpton LL............................... 413 204-4749
   261 King St Northampton (01060) *(G-11083)*

(G-0000) Company's Geographic Section entry number

Turnstone Inc.. 203 625-0000
   500 W Putnam Ave Greenwich (06830) *(G-1358)*

Turtle Skin, New Ipswich *Also Called: Warwick Mills Inc (G-15201)*

Turtle Swamp Brewing LLC.. 617 314-2952
   3377 Washington St Boston (02130) *(G-7089)*

Tuscan Brands LLC **(PA)**.. **781 365-2800**
   63 Main St Salem (03079) *(G-15568)*

Tuttle Law Print Inc... 802 773-9171
   414 Quality Ln # 453 Rutland (05701) *(G-17512)*

Tuttle Printing & Engraving, Rutland *Also Called: Tuttle Law Print Inc (G-17512)*

Tuttle Publishing, North Clarendon *Also Called: Charles E Tuttle Co Inc (G-17413)*

Tvc Inc... 603 431-5251
   284 Constitution Ave Portsmouth (03801) *(G-15445)*

Tweave LLC... 508 285-6701
   1450 Brayton Ave Fall River (02721) *(G-8619)*

Twelve Percent Beer Project, North Haven *Also Called: Twelve Percent LLC (G-2441)*

Twelve Percent LLC... 203 745-3983
   341 State St North Haven (06473) *(G-2441)*

Twenty-Five Commerce Inc.. 203 866-0540
   25 Commerce St Norwalk (06850) *(G-2588)*

Twentyfrst Cntury Bchmcals Inc................................... 508 303-8222
   260 Cedar Hill St Marlborough (01752) *(G-10225)*

Twin City Machining Inc.. 978 874-1940
   4 Curtis Rd Westminster (01473) *(G-13282)*

Twin City Times.. 207 795-5017
   64 Jennifer Dr Auburn (04210) *(G-4462)*

Twin Cy Upholstering Mat Inc..................................... 781 843-1780
   476 Quincy Ave Braintree (02184) *(G-7210)*

Twin Mfg Co DBA Twin Mro... 860 289-6041
   273 Chapel Rd South Windsor (06074) *(G-3187)*

Twin Rivers Paper Company Corp................................... 207 523-2350
   82 Bridge Ave Madawaska (04756) *(G-5039)*

Twin Rivers Paper Company LLC **(PA)**........................... **207 728-3321**
   82 Bridge Ave Madawaska (04756) *(G-5040)*

Twin Rivers Tech Holdings Inc.................................... 617 472-9200
   780 Washington St Quincy (02169) *(G-11541)*

Twin Rivers Tech Ltd Partnr...................................... 617 472-9200
   780 Washington St Quincy (02169) *(G-11542)*

Twin Rivers Tech Mfg Corp.. 888 929-8780
   780 Washington St Quincy (02169) *(G-11543)*

Twin Rivers Technologies, Quincy *Also Called: Twin Rivers Tech Ltd Partnr (G-11542)*

Twin Rivers Technologies Mfg, Quincy *Also Called: Twin Rivers Technologies Us Inc (G-11544)*

Twin Rivers Technologies U.S., Quincy *Also Called: Twin Rivers Tech Holdings Inc (G-11541)*

Twin Rivers Technologies Us Inc.................................. 617 472-9200
   780 Washington St Quincy (02169) *(G-11544)*

Twin State Sand & Grav Co Inc.................................... 603 298-8705
   73 Elm St W West Lebanon (03784) *(G-15691)*

Twin State Signs, Essex Junction *Also Called: Twin State Signs Inc (G-17248)*

Twin State Signs Inc.. 802 872-8949
   14 Gauthier Dr Essex Junction (05452) *(G-17248)*

Twincraft Inc **(PA)**... **802 655-2200**
   2 Tigan St Winooski (05404) *(G-17769)*

Twincraft Soap, Winooski *Also Called: Twincraft Inc (G-17769)*

Twist & Shape/ Revere, Woburn *Also Called: Queen Associates Inc (G-13644)*

Two Brothers Maple LLC... 802 848-7042
   214 Max Rd Richford (05476) *(G-17477)*

Two Go Drycleaning Inc.. 802 658-9469
   1233 Shelburne Rd Ste 190 South Burlington (05403) *(G-17606)*

Two Hands Inc... 401 785-2727
   7 Ninigret Ave Providence (02907) *(G-16631)*

Two In One Manufacturing Inc.................................... 603 595-8212
   51 Lake St Ste 4 Nashua (03060) *(G-15179)*

Two Rivers Pet Products Inc...................................... 207 225-3965
   469 N Parish Rd Turner (04282) *(G-5565)*

Two Saints Inc... 401 490-5500
   81 Western Industrial Dr Ste B Cranston (02921) *(G-15922)*

Tx5877 Inc... 508 865-1101
   71 Blackstone St Sutton (01590) *(G-12292)*

Txv Aerospace Composites, Bristol *Also Called: Txv Aerospace Composites LLC (G-15785)*

Txv Aerospace Composites LLC.................................... 425 785-0883
   55 Broadcommon Rd Unit 2 Bristol (02809) *(G-15785)*

Ty-Wood Corporation.. 508 429-4011
   79 Lowland St Holliston (01746) *(G-9235)*

Tyca Corporation **(PA)**.. **978 612-0002**
   470 Main St Clinton (01510) *(G-8093)*

Tyco Adhesives.. 508 918-1600
   25 Forge Pkwy Franklin (02038) *(G-8873)*

Tyco Fire Products LP.. 508 583-8447
   27 Doherty Ave Avon (02322) *(G-6165)*

Tyco Fire Products LP.. 401 781-8220
   1467 Elmwood Ave Cranston (02910) *(G-15923)*

Tyco Fire Products LP **(DH)**................................... **215 362-0700**
   1467 Elmwood Ave Cranston (02910) *(G-15924)*

Tyco Fire Protection Products, Avon *Also Called: Tyco Fire Products LP (G-6165)*

Tyco Fire Protection Products, Cranston *Also Called: Tyco Fire Products LP (G-15923)*

Tyco Fire Sppression Bldg Pdts, Cranston *Also Called: Tyco Fire Products LP (G-15924)*

Tyger Tool Inc.. 203 375-4344
   45 Sperry Ave Stratford (06615) *(G-3581)*

Tylaska Marine Hardware, Mystic *Also Called: Vector Engineering Inc (G-1944)*

Tyler Technologies Inc.. 207 947-4494
   700 Mount Hope Ave Ste 101 Bangor (04401) *(G-4517)*

Tyler Technologies Inc.. 207 879-7243
   2275 Congress St Portland (04102) *(G-5287)*

Tyler Technologies Inc.. 207 781-2260
   1 Tyler Dr Yarmouth (04096) *(G-5708)*

Tylergraphics Inc... 603 524-6625
   14 Lexington Dr Ste 2 Laconia (03246) *(G-14672)*

Typesafe Inc.. 617 622-2200
   1 Brattle Sq Cambridge (02138) *(G-7745)*

U E I, Norwood *Also Called: Keimos 1988 US Inc (G-11187)*

U E T, Nashua *Also Called: Universal Envmtl Tech Inc (G-15180)*

U M S, Bow *Also Called: Unique Mechanical Services Inc (G-14013)*

U S Felt Company Inc.. 207 324-0063
   61 Industrial Ave Sanford (04073) *(G-5416)*

U S Glass Distributors Inc...................................... 860 741-3658
   7 Niblick Rd Enfield (06082) *(G-1156)*

U S Made Co Inc.. 978 777-8383
   76 Newbury St Danvers (01923) *(G-8228)*

U S Stucco LLC... 860 667-1935
   28 Costello Pl Newington (06111) *(G-2330)*

U S Tool Grinding Inc.. 203 797-5036
   100 Wooster Hts Danbury (06810) *(G-829)*

U-Haul, Somerville *Also Called: U-Haul Co Mass & Ohio Inc (G-11908)*

U-Haul Co Mass & Ohio Inc **(DH)**.............................. **617 625-2789**
   151 Linwood St Somerville (02143) *(G-11908)*

U-Sealusa LLC... 860 667-0911
   56 Fenn Rd Newington (06111) *(G-2331)*

U. S. Tank, West Warwick *Also Called: West Warwick Welding Inc (G-16926)*

U.S. Environmental Services, North Ferrisburgh *Also Called: Bowles Corporation (G-17419)*

Ua, Seymour *Also Called: United Avionics Inc (G-2974)*

Uav - America Inc... 603 389-6364
   240 Stage Rd Nottingham (03290) *(G-15279)*

Ubio Inc.. 401 541-9172
   1603 Plainfield Pike Apt B5 Johnston (02919) *(G-16108)*

Ucb Inc... 844 599-2273
   87 Cambridgepark Dr Cambridge (02140) *(G-7746)*

Ufp Londonderry LLC... 603 668-4113
   184 Rockingham Rd Londonderry (03053) *(G-14787)*

Ufp Shelf 1 LLC... 603 824-9690
   19 Stoney Brook Dr Wilton (03086) *(G-15711)*

Ufp Site Built, LLC, Wilton *Also Called: Ufp Shelf 1 LLC (G-15711)*

Ufp Technologies Inc.. 800 372-3172
   300 Burnett Rd Chicopee (01020) *(G-8065)*

Ufp Technologies Inc.. 978 352-2200
   175 Ward Hill Ave Haverhill (01835) *(G-9136)*

Ufp Technologies Inc **(PA)**................................... **978 352-2200**
   100 Hale St Newburyport (01950) *(G-10722)*

Ukg Inc **(HQ)**... **978 947-2855**
   900 Chelmsford St Lowell (01851) *(G-9930)*

Ukg Kronos Systems LLC **(DH)**................................ **978 250-9800**
   900 Chelmsford St Lowell (01851) *(G-9931)*

A
L
P
H
A
B
E
T
I
C

Ulbrich Stainless Steels.....................................203 269-2507
  1 Dudley Ave Wallingford (06492) **(G-3871)**

Ulbrich Steel, Wallingford *Also Called: Ulbrich Stainless Steels* **(G-3871)**

Ulbrich Stnless Stels Spcial M (PA)...................203 239-4481
  153 Washington Ave North Haven (06473) **(G-2442)**

Ullman Devices Corporation............................203 438-6577
  664 Danbury Rd Ridgefield (06877) **(G-2908)**

Ultimate Companies Inc (PA)...........................860 582-9111
  200 Central St Bristol (06010) **(G-503)**

Ultimate Kronos Group, Lowell *Also Called: Ukg Inc* **(G-9930)**

Ultimate Promotional Products, North Providence *Also Called: Perry Blackburne Inc* **(G-16307)**

Ultimate Windows Inc......................................978 687-9444
  130 Shepard St Lawrence (01843) **(G-9605)**

Ultimate Wireforms Inc....................................860 582-9111
  200 Central St Bristol (06010) **(G-504)**

Ultivue Inc (PA)...617 945-2662
  763d Concord Ave Cambridge (02138) **(G-7747)**

Ultra Clean Equipment Inc...............................860 669-1354
  64 Wall St Madison (06443) **(G-1574)**

Ultra Elec Measurement Systems, Wallingford *Also Called: Measurement Systems Inc* **(G-3831)**

Ultra Elec Ocean Systems Inc (DH)...................781 848-3400
  115 Bay State Dr Braintree (02184) **(G-7211)**

Ultra Fine Specialty Pdts LLC...........................401 488-4987
  500 Park East Dr Woonsocket (02895) **(G-16982)**

Ultra Flow Dispense LLC.................................866 827-2534
  820 Prospect Hill Rd Windsor (06095) **(G-4311)**

Ultra Food and Fuel..860 223-2005
  788 W Main St New Britain (06053) **(G-2073)**

Ultra Precision Machining, Smithfield *Also Called: D Simpson Inc* **(G-16693)**

Ultra Scientific Incorporated............................800 338-1754
  250 Smith St North Kingstown (02852) **(G-16290)**

Ultra Sonic Seal Co, Newtown *Also Called: Sonics & Materials Inc* **(G-2347)**

Ultraclad Corporation......................................978 358-7945
  10 Perry Way Newburyport (01950) **(G-10723)**

Ultrafryer Systems Inc....................................603 225-6684
  553 Route 3a Bow (03304) **(G-14012)**

Ultrasonic Systems Inc....................................978 521-0095
  135 Ward Hill Ave Haverhill (01835) **(G-9137)**

Ultrasource Inc..603 881-7799
  22 Clinton Dr Hollis (03049) **(G-14459)**

Ultrasystems Electronics Inc............................603 578-0444
  13 Columbia Dr Unit 10 Amherst (03031) **(G-13893)**

ULVAC NORTH AMERICA, Methuen *Also Called: Ulvac Technologies Inc* **(G-10347)**

Ulvac Technologies Inc (HQ)...........................978 686-7550
  401 Griffin Brook Dr Methuen (01844) **(G-10347)**

Um Food Sciences...413 545-2276
  228 Chenowith Amherst (01002) **(G-5866)**

Umami Noodle..207 947-9991
  1 Main St Bangor (04401) **(G-4518)**

Umass Mem Mri Imaging Ctr LLC......................508 756-7300
  214 Shrewsbury St Worcester (01604) **(G-13814)**

Unas Grinding Corporation...............................860 289-1538
  28 Cherry St East Hartford (06108) **(G-1030)**

Uncas International LLC (PA)...........................401 231-0266
  1600 Division Rd West Warwick (02893) **(G-16924)**

Uncle Bill's Tweezers, West Hartford *Also Called: El Mar Inc* **(G-4058)**

Uncle Sams Contractors LLC (PA)....................833 487-2776
  290 Roberts St Ste 302 East Hartford (06108) **(G-1031)**

Uncle Wileys Inc...203 256-9313
  1220 Post Rd Fairfield (06824) **(G-1202)**

Uncles Oil Company Corporation.......................401 383-0626
  1515 Elmwood Ave Ste 3 Cranston (02910) **(G-15925)**

Under Cover Inc..508 997-7600
  138 Hatch St New Bedford (02745) **(G-10657)**

Underground Systems Inc (PA).......................203 792-3444
  3a Trowbridge Dr Bethel (06801) **(G-138)**

Uneco Manufacturing Inc.................................413 594-2700
  330 Fuller Rd Chicopee (01020) **(G-8066)**

Unetixs Vascular Inc.......................................401 583-0089
  333 Strawberry Field Rd Ste 11 Warwick (02886) **(G-16869)**

Unger Enterprises LLC (PA)...........................203 366-4884
  425 Asylum St Bridgeport (06610) **(G-381)**

Unger Industrial, Bridgeport *Also Called: Unger Industrial LLC* **(G-382)**

Unger Industrial LLC.......................................203 336-3344
  425 Asylum St Bridgeport (06610) **(G-382)**

Unholtz-Dickie Corporation..............................203 265-3929
  6 Brookside Dr Wallingford (06492) **(G-3872)**

UNI Pac, Holyoke *Also Called: UNI-Pac Inc* **(G-9284)**

UNI-Cast LLC..603 625-5761
  11 Industrial Dr Londonderry (03053) **(G-14788)**

Uni-Graphic Inc..781 231-7200
  110j Commerce Way Woburn (01801) **(G-13680)**

UNI-Pac Inc...413 534-5284
  150 Middle Water St Holyoke (01040) **(G-9284)**

UNI-Sim, Windham *Also Called: Windham Millwork Inc* **(G-5675)**

Unica Corporation...781 839-8000
  1 Rogers St Cambridge (02142) **(G-7748)**

Unicast Development Co., Guilford *Also Called: Joshua LLC* **(G-1398)**

Unicom Engineering Inc (HQ).........................781 332-1000
  25 Dan Rd Canton (02021) **(G-7836)**

Unicor, Danbury *Also Called: Federal Prison Industries* **(G-745)**

Unicore LLC..413 284-9995
  6 Chamber Rd Palmer (01069) **(G-11287)**

Unicorr..508 481-1100
  300 Cedar Hill St Marlborough (01752) **(G-10226)**

Unicorr Group, North Haven *Also Called: Connecticut Container Corp* **(G-2399)**

Unicorr Packaging, Putnam *Also Called: Nutmeg Container Corporation* **(G-2867)**

Unicus Pharmaceuticals LLC (PA)...................508 659-7002
  30 Robert W Boyden Rd Ste 200a Taunton (02780) **(G-12374)**

Unified Sports Incorporated (PA)....................860 447-3001
  976 Hartford Tpke Ste B Waterford (06385) **(G-3998)**

Unified2 Globl Packg Group LLC........................508 865-1155
  580 Fort Pond Rd Lancaster (01523) **(G-9531)**

Unifirst, Wilmington *Also Called: Unifirst Corporation* **(G-13472)**

Unifirst Corporation (PA)...............................978 658-8888
  68 Jonspin Rd Wilmington (01887) **(G-13472)**

Unilever Ascc AG..203 381-2482
  3 Corporate Dr Shelton (06484) **(G-3073)**

Unilever Bestfoods North Amer.........................802 775-4986
  69 Park St Rutland (05701) **(G-17513)**

Unilever Home and Per Care NA........................203 502-0086
  75 Merritt Blvd Trumbull (06611) **(G-3736)**

Unilever Hpc NA, Trumbull *Also Called: Unilever Home and Per Care NA* **(G-3736)**

Unilever Hpc USA...203 381-3311
  45 Commerce Dr Trumbull (06611) **(G-3737)**

Unilever Hpc USA, Trumbull *Also Called: Unilever Trumbull RES Svcs Inc* **(G-3738)**

Unilever Trumbull RES Svcs Inc........................203 502-0086
  40 Merritt Blvd Trumbull (06611) **(G-3738)**

Unimacts Manufacturing Mx LLC.......................410 415-6070
  2 Sedge Rd Lexington (02420) **(G-9790)**

Unimark Plastics, East Wilton *Also Called: Jarden LLC* **(G-4741)**

Unimed-Midwest Inc.......................................800 347-9023
  100 Sylvan Rd Ste 100 Woburn (01801) **(G-13681)**

Unimetal Surface Finishing LLC.........................203 729-8244
  15 E Waterbury Rd Naugatuck (06770) **(G-1991)**

Unimetal Surface Finishing LLC.......................860 283-0271
  135 S Main St Thomaston (06787) **(G-3640)**

Unimin Specialty Minerals Inc, New Canaan *Also Called: Covia Specialty Minerals Inc* **(G-2080)**

Unimin Texas Co Ltd (HQ)..............................203 966-8880
  258 Elm St New Canaan (06840) **(G-2090)**

Unimin Wisconsin Eqp Corp.............................203 966-8880
  258 Elm St New Canaan (06840) **(G-2091)**

Union Biometrica Inc (PA)..............................508 893-3115
  84 October Hill Rd Ste 12 Holliston (01746) **(G-9236)**

Union Leader Corporation (PA)........................603 668-4321
  100 William Loeb Dr Unit 2 Manchester (03109) **(G-14947)**

Union Machine Company Lynn Inc (PA)............978 521-5100
  6 Federal Way Groveland (01834) **(G-9016)**

Union Miniere...617 960-5900
  12 Channel St Ste 702 Boston (02210) **(G-7090)**

Union Paper & Packaging Inc............................978 227-5868
  507 Lancaster St Leominster (01453) **(G-9711)**

Union Products, Fitchburg *Also Called: Cado Products Inc (G-8647)*

Union Specialties Inc... 978 465-1717
3 Malcolm Hoyt Dr Newburyport (01950) *(G-10724)*

Unipharm Inc.. 203 528-3230
75 Progress Ln Waterbury (06705) *(G-3978)*

Unipower LLC.. 203 740-8555
57 Commerce Dr Brookfield (06804) *(G-540)*

Uniprise International Inc... 860 589-7262
50 Napco Dr Terryville (06786) *(G-3613)*

Uniprise Sales, Terryville *Also Called: Uniprise International Inc (G-3613)*

Unique Extrusions Incorporated.................................... 860 632-1314
10 Countyline Dr Cromwell (06416) *(G-698)*

Unique Mechanical Services Inc.................................... 603 856-0057
162 W Main St Bow (03304) *(G-14013)*

Unique Plating Co.. 401 943-7366
66 Mill St Johnston (02919) *(G-16109)*

Unique Spiral Stairs Inc... 207 437-2415
117 Benton Rd Albion (04910) *(G-4401)*

Unique Woodworking, East Weymouth *Also Called: Ldg Corporation (G-8432)*

Unisil Corporation.. 203 966-8880
258 Elm St New Canaan (06840) *(G-2092)*

Unisite LLC.. 781 926-7135
116 Huntington Ave Ste 1750 Boston (02116) *(G-7091)*

Unisoft Medical Corporation.. 860 482-6848
65 New Litchfield St Torrington (06790) *(G-3704)*

Unistar Corporation.. 603 323-9327
Junction Of Rtes 25 & 113 East Tamworth (03886) *(G-15649)*

Unistress, Pittsfield *Also Called: Petricca Industries Inc (G-11418)*

Unistress Corp.. 413 499-1441
550 Cheshire Rd Pittsfield (01201) *(G-11426)*

Unit4 Business Software Inc **(PA)**................................. **877 704-5974**
3 Burlington Woods Dr Ste 201 Burlington (01803) *(G-7441)*

Unitarian Universalist Assn **(PA)**.................................. **617 742-2100**
24 Farnsworth St Boston (02210) *(G-7092)*

Unitec.. 203 778-0400
4 Larson Dr Danbury (06810) *(G-830)*

United Abrasives Inc **(PA)**... **860 456-7131**
185 Boston Post Rd North Windham (06256) *(G-2451)*

United Aero Group, Shelton *Also Called: Gelder Aerospace LLC (G-3008)*

United Avionics Inc.. 203 723-1404
181 Mountain Rd Seymour (06483) *(G-2974)*

United Box Co Division, Worcester *Also Called: United Paper Stock Co Inc (G-13816)*

United Comb & Novelty Corp **(PA)**................................ **978 537-2096**
33 Patriots Cir Leominster (01453) *(G-9712)*

United Communications Corp.. 508 222-7000
34 S Main St Attleboro (02703) *(G-6071)*

United Concrete Products Inc....................................... 203 269-3119
173 Church St Yalesville (06492) *(G-4399)*

United Curtain Co Inc **(PA)**....................................... **508 588-4100**
91 Wales Ave Ste 1 Avon (02322) *(G-6166)*

United Electric Controls Company **(PA)**.......................... **617 926-1000**
180 Dexter Ave Watertown (02472) *(G-12917)*

United Fbrcnts Strainrite Corp **(HQ)**............................. **207 376-1600**
65 First Flight Dr Auburn (04210) *(G-4463)*

United Foods Incorporated **(PA)**................................. **617 482-9879**
170 Lincoln St Boston (02111) *(G-7093)*

United Gear and Machine Co Inc.................................... 860 623-6618
1087 East St S Suffield (06078) *(G-3596)*

United GL To Met Sealing Inc....................................... 978 327-5880
15 Union St Ste G30 Lawrence (01840) *(G-9606)*

United Hvac Co Inc.. 781 871-1060
333 Weymouth St Rockland (02370) *(G-11663)*

United Industrial Tex Pdts Inc **(PA)**.............................. **413 737-0095**
321 Main St West Springfield (01089) *(G-13048)*

United Innovations Inc.. 413 533-7500
120 Whiting Farms Rd Ste 2 Holyoke (01040) *(G-9285)*

United Lens Company Inc... 508 765-5421
259 Worcester St Southbridge (01550) *(G-12037)*

United Machining Inc.. 508 865-3035
219 Whitins Rd Ste 5 Sutton (01590) *(G-12293)*

United Mch & Tl Design Co Inc...................................... 603 642-3601
18 River Rd Fremont (03044) *(G-14332)*

United Metal Fabracators Inc....................................... 508 754-1800
1021 Southbridge St Worcester (01610) *(G-13815)*

United Ophthalmics LLC... 203 500-3332
430 Smith St Middletown (06457) *(G-1788)*

United Paper Stock Co Inc.. 401 724-5700
2 Pullman St Worcester (01606) *(G-13816)*

United Plastic Fabricating Inc **(PA)**.............................. **978 975-4520**
165 Flagship Dr North Andover (01845) *(G-10855)*

United Plastics, Leominster *Also Called: United Comb & Novelty Corp (G-9712)*

United Plastics Group, Chicopee *Also Called: Viant Chicopee Inc (G-8068)*

United Plastics Tech Inc... 860 224-1110
6 Downing Way Madison (06443) *(G-1575)*

United Publications Inc.. 207 846-0600
106 Lafayette St Yarmouth (04096) *(G-5709)*

United Seating & Mobility LLC...................................... 806 761-0700
65 Inwood Rd Rocky Hill (06067) *(G-2940)*

United Sensor Corporation.. 603 672-0909
3 Northern Blvd Amherst (03031) *(G-13894)*

United Site Services Inc **(PA)**.................................... **508 594-2655**
118 Flanders Rd Westborough (01581) *(G-13141)*

United States Associates LLC....................................... 401 272-7760
1205 Westminster St Providence (02909) *(G-16632)*

United States Badge Company, Providence *Also Called: Hook-Fast Specialties Inc (G-16533)*

United States Biological Corp....................................... 978 744-0345
4 Technology Way Salem (01970) *(G-11737)*

United States Dept of Navy.. 207 438-2714
Portsmouth Naval Shipyard Code 1710 Portsmouth (03804) *(G-15446)*

United Steel, Wolcott *Also Called: Bellavance Welding LLC (G-17773)*

United Steel Erectors, East Hartford *Also Called: United Steel Inc (G-1032)*

United Steel Inc.. 860 289-2323
164 School St East Hartford (06108) *(G-1032)*

United Stretch Design Corp... 978 562-7781
11 Bonazzoli Ave Hudson (01749) *(G-9422)*

United Sttes Sign Fbrction Cor..................................... 203 601-1000
1 Trefoil Dr Ste 2 Trumbull (06611) *(G-3739)*

United Technologies, North Berwick *Also Called: Pratt & Whitney Eng Svcs Inc (G-5112)*

United Technologies Optical Systems Inc.......................... 860 654-6000
1 Hamilton Rd Windsor Locks (06096) *(G-4336)*

United Tool & Die Company **(PA)**................................. **860 246-6531**
1 Carney Rd West Hartford (06110) *(G-4088)*

United Tool & Machine Corp **(PA)**................................ **978 658-5500**
50 Shepard St Lawrence (01843) *(G-9607)*

United Tool & Machine Corp... 978 686-4181
50 Shepard St Lawrence (01843) *(G-9608)*

United-County Industries Corp..................................... 508 865-5885
32 Howe Ave Millbury (01527) *(G-10444)*

Unitex Textile Rental Service, Hartford *Also Called: A&P Coat Apron & Linen Sup LLC (G-1466)*

Unitrode Corporation **(HQ)**....................................... **603 222-8500**
50 Phillippe Cote St Ste 100 Manchester (03101) *(G-14948)*

Unity Scientific LLC.. 203 740-2999
8 Technology Dr Ste 100 Westborough (01581) *(G-13142)*

Univar Solutions USA Inc... 518 762-3500
175 Terminal Rd Providence (02905) *(G-16633)*

Univar USA, Providence *Also Called: Univar Solutions USA Inc (G-16633)*

Universal Bath Systems, Holyoke *Also Called: Universal Plastics Corporation (G-9286)*

Universal Body and Eqp Co LLC.................................... 860 274-7541
17 Di Nunzio Rd Oakville (06779) *(G-2628)*

Universal Color Corp Inc.. 978 658-2300
377 Ballardvale St Unit 1 Wilmington (01887) *(G-13473)*

Universal Envmtl Tech Inc.. 603 883-9312
87 Technology Way Nashua (03060) *(G-15180)*

Universal Foam Products LLC....................................... 860 216-3015
101 W Dudley Town Rd Unit C&D Bloomfield (06002) *(G-215)*

Universal Graphic, West Haven *Also Called: Universal Printing Svcs Inc (G-4131)*

Universal Hardwood Flooring.. 617 783-2307
85 Arlington St Boston (02135) *(G-7094)*

Universal Mch & Design Corp....................................... 978 343-4688
323 Princeton Rd Fitchburg (01420) *(G-8679)*

Universal Pharma Tech LLC... 978 975-7216
70 Flagship Dr Ste 3 North Andover (01845) *(G-10856)*

A L P H A B E T I C

Universal Plastics Corporation **(PA)** 413 592-4791
  75 Whiting Farms Rd Holyoke (01040) *(G-9286)*

Universal Plating Co Inc 401 861-3530
  25 River Ave Providence (02908) *(G-16634)*

Universal Printing Svcs Inc 203 934-4275
  375 Morgan Ln Ste 203 West Haven (06516) *(G-4131)*

Universal Prtg & Mailing Svcs, Fairfield *Also Called: Universal Prtg Miling Svcs Inc* *(G-1203)*

Universal Prtg Miling Svcs Inc 203 330-0611
  75 Ardmore St Fairfield (06824) *(G-1203)*

Universal Relay Company, Bridgeport *Also Called: Park Distributories Inc (G-357)*

Universal Relays, Bridgeport *Also Called: Park Distributories Inc (G-355)*

Universal Screening Studio Inc 617 387-1832
  175 Ferry St Everett (02149) *(G-8502)*

Universal Specialty Awards 401 272-7760
  1205 Westminster St Providence (02909) *(G-16635)*

Universal Tag Inc 508 949-2411
  36 Hall Rd Dudley (01571) *(G-8326)*

Universal Thread Grinding Co 203 336-1849
  30 Chambers St Fairfield (06825) *(G-1204)*

Universal Tool Co Inc 413 732-4807
  33 Rose Pl Springfield (01104) *(G-12145)*

Universal Voltronics, Brookfield *Also Called: Universal Voltronics Corp (G-541)*

Universal Voltronics Corp 203 740-8555
  57 Commerce Dr Brookfield (06804) *(G-541)*

Universal Wilde **(PA)** **781 251-2700**
  135 Will Dr Unit 2 Canton (02021) *(G-7837)*

Universal Wilde Inc 978 658-0800
  135 Will Dr Unit 2 Canton (02021) *(G-7838)*

Universal Wilde Inc 508 429-5515
  201 Summer St Holliston (01746) *(G-9237)*

Universal Wilde Inc 781 251-2700
  403 Vfw Dr Rockland (02370) *(G-11664)*

University NH Brewry, Durham *Also Called: University System NH (G-14268)*

University of Maine System 207 581-2843
  5755 Nutting Hall Orono (04469) *(G-5138)*

University Press New England, Lebanon *Also Called: Trustees of Dartmouth College (G-14702)*

University Products Inc **(PA)** **413 532-3372**
  517 Main St Holyoke (01040) *(G-9287)*

University Spirit, Pawtucket *Also Called: Spirit Recognition Inc (G-16417)*

University System NH 603 659-2825
  34 Sage Way Barton Hall 111 Durham (03824) *(G-14268)*

University Wafer Inc 800 713-9375
  11 Elkins St Ste 330 Boston (02127) *(G-7095)*

Univex Corporation 603 893-6191
  3 Old Rockingham Rd Salem (03079) *(G-15569)*

Uniworld Bus Publications Inc 201 384-4900
  35 Kensett Ln Darien (06820) *(G-857)*

Unlimited Plant Care Service, Waltham *Also Called: Marie Deprofio (G-12714)*

Uno Foods Inc 617 323-9200
  44 Industrial Way Norwood (02062) *(G-11217)*

Untold Brewing LLC **(PA)** **781 378-0559**
  6 Old Country Way Scituate (02066) *(G-11773)*

Unwrapped Inc 978 441-0242
  95 Rock St Fl 1 Lowell (01854) *(G-9932)*

Up Country Inc 401 431-2940
  76 Boyd Ave East Providence (02914) *(G-16046)*

Up North Corp 207 834-6178
  185 Pleasant St Fort Kent (04743) *(G-4795)*

Upaco Adhesives, Nashua *Also Called: Worthen Industries Inc (G-15188)*

Upc LLC 877 466-1137
  170 Research Pkwy Meriden (06450) *(G-1711)*

Upnovr Inc 603 625-8639
  31 Pulpit Rock Rd Unit A Pelham (03076) *(G-15299)*

Uppababy, Rockland *Also Called: Monahan Products LLC (G-11652)*

Upper Valley Press, North Haverhill *Also Called: Uvp Liquidation Inc (G-15253)*

Uprising LLC 860 960-3781
  207 Doman Dr Torrington (06790) *(G-3705)*

UPS, Fairfield *Also Called: UPS Authorized Retailer (G-1205)*

UPS Authorized Retailer 203 256-9991
  857 Post Rd Fairfield (06824) *(G-1205)*

Upstart Power Inc 614 877-8278
  153 Northboro Rd Ste 1 Southborough (01772) *(G-12003)*

Uptite Company Inc 978 377-0451
  1001 Hilldale Ave Haverhill (01832) *(G-9138)*

Uptodate Inc **(DH)** **781 392-2000**
  230 3rd Ave Ste 1000 Waltham (02451) *(G-12808)*

Upton & Mendon Town Crier, Upton *Also Called: Town Crier Publications Inc (G-12475)*

Urban Exposition LLC **(DH)** **203 242-8717**
  6 Research Dr Shelton (06484) *(G-3074)*

Uretek, New Haven *Also Called: Trelleborg Ctd Systems US Inc (G-2212)*

Urg Graphics Inc **(PA)** **860 928-0835**
  12 Fox Hill Dr Stafford Springs (06076) *(G-3263)*

Ursa Navigation Solutions Inc 781 538-5299
  85 Rangeway Rd Ste 3 North Billerica (01862) *(G-10963)*

Ursanav, North Billerica *Also Called: Ursa Navigation Solutions Inc (G-10963)*

Urthpact Innovations LLC 978 847-9747
  42 Jungle Rd Leominster (01453) *(G-9713)*

US Athletic Equipment, Waterford *Also Called: Jaypro Sports LLC (G-3990)*

US Avionics, South Windsor *Also Called: US Avionics Inc / Superabr (G-3188)*

US Avionics Inc / Superabr 860 528-1114
  1265 John Fitch Blvd Ste 3 South Windsor (06074) *(G-3188)*

US Bedding Inc 508 678-6988
  451 Quarry St Fall River (02723) *(G-8620)*

US Biochips Corp 617 504-5502
  14 Hillcrest Cir Waban (02468) *(G-12497)*

US Button Corporation 860 928-2707
  328 Kennedy Dr Putnam (06260) *(G-2878)*

US Chemicals Inc 203 655-8878
  280 Elm St New Canaan (06840) *(G-2093)*

US Emblem LLC 401 487-4327
  1503 S County Trl East Greenwich (02818) *(G-15995)*

US Extruders Inc 401 584-4710
  87 Tom Harvey Rd Westerly (02891) *(G-16945)*

US Games Systems Inc 800 544-2637
  179 Ludlow St Stamford (06902) *(G-3488)*

US Mailing Systems Inc 802 891-1020
  15 Catamount Dr Milton (05468) *(G-17365)*

US Nortek Inc 774 314-4006
  4 Farnum St Worcester (01602) *(G-13817)*

US Oceans LLC 207 596-3603
  230 Park St Rockland (04841) *(G-5344)*

US Packaging Specialties 508 674-3636
  117 Tripp St Fall River (02724) *(G-8621)*

US Polymers Inc 978 921-8000
  100 Cummings Ctr Ste 326g Beverly (01915) *(G-6391)*

US Reflector, East Hartford *Also Called: Ecu & US International (G-991)*

US Sheetmetal Inc 508 427-0500
  420 West St West Bridgewater (02379) *(G-12987)*

US Sign, Trumbull *Also Called: United Sttes Sign Fbrction Cor (G-3739)*

US Tsubaki Automotive LLC **(DH)** **413 593-1100**
  106 Lonczak St Chicopee (01022) *(G-8067)*

US Tsubaki Power Transm LLC 413 536-1576
  821 Main St Holyoke (01040) *(G-9288)*

USA Builders Inc 843 321-9618
  12 Belmont Ave Deep River (06417) *(G-887)*

USA Notepads, West Haven *Also Called: Panagrafix Inc (G-4118)*

Usei, Amherst *Also Called: Ultrasystems Electronics Inc (G-13893)*

USG Services Corporation 401 644-7098
  1005 Main St Unit 1201 Pawtucket (02860) *(G-16427)*

USI, Bethel *Also Called: Underground Systems Inc (G-138)*

USI Education & Government Sls, Madison *Also Called: New Precision Technology LLC* *(G-1564)*

Uspack Inc 978 466-9700
  300 Whitney St Leominster (01453) *(G-9714)*

Uspack Inc 978 562-8522
  14 Brent Dr Hudson (01749) *(G-9423)*

UST 203 661-1100
  100 W Putnam Ave Greenwich (06830) *(G-1359)*

UST LLC 203 817-3000
  6 High Ridge Park Bldg A Stamford (06905) *(G-3489)*

UTC Aerospace Systems, Danbury *Also Called: Simmonds Precision Pdts Inc* (*G-818*)

UTC Aerospace Systems, Peabody *Also Called: Goodrich Corporation* (*G-11311*)

UTC Aerospace Systems, Vergennes *Also Called: Collins Aerospace* (*G-17657*)

UTC Climate Controls & SEC, Farmington *Also Called: Rtx Corporation* (*G-1244*)

UTC Corporation.. 860 665-1770
  25 Holly Dr Newington (06111) (*G-2332*)

Utility Cloud, Boston *Also Called: Advanced Entp Systems Corp* (*G-6517*)

Utility Mfg Co, Wilbraham *Also Called: Frank L Reed Inc* (*G-13359*)

Utility Systems Inc.. 401 351-6681
  123 King Philip St Johnston (02919) (*G-16110*)

Utitec Inc (HQ).. **860 945-0605**
  169 Callender Rd Ste 3 Watertown (06795) (*G-4035*)

Utitec Holdings Inc.. 860 945-0601
  169 Callender Rd Ste 3 Watertown (06795) (*G-4036*)

Utz Quality Foods LLC.. 413 562-1102
  225 Root Rd Westfield (01085) (*G-13214*)

Utz Technologies Inc (PA).. **973 339-1100**
  71 Willie St Lowell (01854) (*G-9933*)

Uv III Systems Inc.. 508 883-4881
  59 Cedarvale Est Alburg (05440) (*G-16984*)

Uva Lidkoping, Milford *Also Called: Uva Lidkoping Inc* (*G-10422*)

Uva Lidkoping Inc.. 508 634-4301
  4 Industrial Rd Ste 4 Milford (01757) (*G-10422*)

Uvex Safety Manufacturing Ltd.. 401 232-1200
  10 Thurber Blvd Smithfield (02917) (*G-16733*)

Uvm Print Mail Center.. 802 656-8149
  85 S Prospect St Burlington (05401) (*G-17163*)

Uvp Liquidation Inc.. 603 787-7000
  446 Benton Rd North Haverhill (03774) (*G-15253*)

Uvtech Systems Inc.. 978 440-7282
  335 River Rd Carlisle (01741) (*G-7849*)

V & G Iron Works Inc.. 978 851-9191
  1500 Shawsheen St Tewksbury (01876) (*G-12424*)

V M F, Seymour *Also Called: Vernier Metal Fabricating Inc* (*G-2975*)

V P M S, Springfield *Also Called: Vermont Precision Machine Svcs* (*G-17623*)

V Power Equipment, Wareham *Also Called: V Power Equipment LLC* (*G-12847*)

V Power Equipment LLC.. 508 273-7596
  297 Charge Pond Rd Wareham (02571) (*G-12847*)

V-Tron Electronics Corp.. 508 761-9100
  10 Venus Way Attleboro (02703) (*G-6072*)

V&M Tool & Die Inc.. 978 534-8814
  138 Lincoln Ter Leominster (01453) (*G-9715*)

V&S Taunton Galvanizing LLC.. 508 828-9499
  585 John Hancock Rd Taunton (02780) (*G-12375*)

Vacca Architectural Wdwkg LLC.. 860 599-3677
  9 Coggswell St Pawcatuck (06379) (*G-2727*)

Vacuum Barrier Corporation.. 781 933-3570
  4 Barten Ln Woburn (01801) (*G-13682*)

Vacuum Engineering Inc.. 413 734-4400
  857 Elm St West Springfield (01089) (*G-13049*)

Vacuum Plus Manufacturing Inc.. 978 441-3100
  80 Turnpike Rd Chelmsford (01824) (*G-7968*)

Vacuum Process Technology LLC.. 508 732-7200
  1 Broadway Cambridge (02142) (*G-7749*)

Vacuum Technology Assoc Inc.. 781 740-8600
  110 Industrial Park Rd Hingham (02043) (*G-9161*)

Vacuum Technology Inc.. 510 333-6562
  15 Great Republic Dr Ste 4 Gloucester (01930) (*G-8962*)

Vae, North Kingstown *Also Called: Veterans Assembled Elec LLC* (*G-16291*)

Vagrants Inc.. 857 400-8870
  230 Somerville Ave Somerville (02143) (*G-11909*)

Vaillancourt Folk Art Inc.. 508 476-3601
  9 Main St Ste 1h Sutton (01590) (*G-12294*)

Vaisala Inc.. 617 467-1500
  15 Riverdale Ave Newton (02458) (*G-10792*)

Vaisala Inc.. 508 574-1163
  10d Gill St Woburn (01801) (*G-13683*)

Valcom Division, Walpole *Also Called: Tooling Research Inc* (*G-12577*)

Valcom Division, Walpole *Also Called: Tooling Research Inc* (*G-12578*)

Valde Systems Inc.. 603 577-1728
  4 Hobart Hill Rd Brookline (03033) (*G-14042*)

Valen Analytics, Hartford *Also Called: Valen Technologies Inc* (*G-1515*)

Valen Technologies Inc.. 720 570-3333
  170 Huyshope Ave Hartford (06106) (*G-1515*)

Valentine Plating Company Inc.. 413 732-0009
  155 Allston Ave West Springfield (01089) (*G-13050*)

Valentine Tool & Stamping Inc.. 508 285-6911
  171 W Main St Norton (02766) (*G-11137*)

Valeritas Inc.. 908 927-9920
  293 Boston Post Rd W Ste 330 Marlborough (01752) (*G-10227*)

Valiantys, Dedham *Also Called: Valiantys America Inc* (*G-8253*)

Valiantys America Inc.. 781 375-2494
  980 Washington St Dedham (02026) (*G-8253*)

Valid Mfg Inc.. 603 880-0948
  16 Vista Ridge Dr Unit 238 Londonderry (03053) (*G-14789*)

Validated Cloud Inc (PA).. **617 849-8650**
  330 Bear Hill Rd Ste 205 Waltham (02451) (*G-12809*)

Validus DC Systems LLC.. 203 448-3600
  50 Pocono Rd Brookfield (06804) (*G-542*)

Valkyrie Company Inc.. 508 756-3633
  60 Fremont St Worcester (01603) (*G-13818*)

Valkyrie Company Inc (PA).. **508 756-3633**
  60 Fremont St Worcester (01603) (*G-13819*)

Vallet Motors, Fort Kent *Also Called: Steven Pelletier* (*G-4794*)

Valley Advocate.. 413 584-0003
  115 Conz St Ste 2 Northampton (01060) (*G-11084*)

Valley Breeze, Lincoln *Also Called: Breeze Publications Inc* (*G-16122*)

Valley Container Inc.. 203 368-6546
  850 Union Ave Bridgeport (06607) (*G-383*)

Valley Enterprises Inc.. 413 737-0281
  4 Birnie Ave Springfield (01107) (*G-12146*)

Valley Etching Engrv Dsign Inc.. 413 536-2256
  120b Whiting Farms Rd Holyoke (01040) (*G-9289*)

Valley Fire Equipment, Bradford *Also Called: Valley Transportation Inc* (*G-14018*)

Valley Plating Inc.. 413 788-7375
  412 Albany St Springfield (01105) (*G-12147*)

Valley Publishing Company Inc.. 203 735-6696
  7 Francis St Derby (06418) (*G-893*)

Valley Reporter Incorporated.. 802 496-3607
  5222 Main St Ste 2 Waitsfield (05673) (*G-17667*)

Valley Sand & Gravel Corp.. 203 562-3192
  400 N Frontage Rd North Haven (06473) (*G-2443*)

Valley Times, Derby *Also Called: Valley Publishing Company Inc* (*G-893*)

Valley Tool & Manufacturing Inc.. 203 799-8800
  22 Prindle Hill Rd Orange (06477) (*G-2683*)

Valley Tool and Mfg LLC.. 203 878-2476
  500 Bic Dr Bldg 2 Milford (06461) (*G-1897*)

Valley Tool and Mfg LLC (HQ).. **203 799-8800**
  132 Shelland St Milford (06461) (*G-1898*)

Valley Transportation Inc (PA).. **603 938-2271**
  2345 State Route 114 Bradford (03221) (*G-14018*)

Valley Truck Parts and Service, Marshfield *Also Called: Hanscom Construction Inc* (*G-5046*)

Valley View Orchard Pies, Oxford *Also Called: C J Cranam Inc* (*G-5142*)

Valley Welding & Fabg Inc.. 603 465-3266
  261 Proctor Hill Rd Hollis (03049) (*G-14460*)

Valleylab.. 203 461-9075
  74 Putter Dr Stamford (06907) (*G-3490*)

Valmet Inc.. 207 282-1521
  516 Alfred St Biddeford (04005) (*G-4593*)

Valmet Inc.. 207 377-6909
  30 Summer St Ste G Winthrop (04364) (*G-5696*)

Valmet Inc.. 413 637-2424
  175 Crystal St Lenox (01240) (*G-9627*)

Valmet Inc.. 603 882-2711
  1 Cellu Dr Ste 200 Nashua (03063) (*G-15181*)

Valmet Flow Control Inc.. 508 852-0200
  42 Bowditch Dr Shrewsbury (01545) (*G-11846*)

Valmet Flow Control Inc (HQ).. **508 852-0200**
  44 Bowditch Dr Shrewsbury (01545) (*G-11847*)

Valmont Inc.. 413 583-8351
  656 Chapin St Ludlow (01056) (*G-9955*)

Valo Health Inc (PA).. **617 237-6080**
  399 Boylston St Ste 505 Boston (02116) (*G-7096*)

A
L
P
H
A
B
E
T
I
C

Valora Technologies Inc...................................... 781 229-2265
   81 Daniels Ln Carlisle (01741) *(G-7850)*

Valt Enterprizes Inc... 207 560-5188
   1030 Airport Dr Unit 1 Presque Isle (04769) *(G-5311)*

Value Print Incorporated...................................... 203 265-1371
   34 Mellor Dr Wallingford (06492) *(G-3873)*

Valve Components Division, Worcester *Also Called: Standard Lock Washer & Mfg Co* *(G-13807)*

Valves and Controls Us Inc................................... 978 744-5690
   29 Old Right Rd Ipswich (01938) *(G-9499)*

Van - Wal Machine Inc... 508 966-0733
   97 Depot St Bellingham (02019) *(G-6301)*

Van & Company Inc.. 401 722-9829
   547 Weeden St Pawtucket (02860) *(G-16428)*

Van Deusen & Levitt Assoc Inc............................. 203 445-6244
   14 Wood Hill Rd Weston (06883) *(G-4154)*

Van Heusen, Chatham *Also Called: Pvh Corp (G-7900)*

Van Otis Chocolates LLC **(PA)**........................... **603 627-1611**
   341 Elm St Manchester (03101) *(G-14949)*

Van Pelt Precision Inc... 413 527-1204
   66 S Broad St Ste 3 Westfield (01085) *(G-13215)*

Van Stry Design Inc.. 781 388-9998
   420 Pearl St Ste 2 Malden (02148) *(G-10030)*

Van-Go Graphics.. 508 865-7300
   94 Fitzpatrick Rd Grafton (01519) *(G-8969)*

Vance Cabinet & Carpentry.................................. 603 801-5221
   2 Shaker Rd Shirley (01464) *(G-11824)*

Vance Publishing, Hartford *Also Called: Vance Publishing Corporation (G-1516)*

Vance Publishing Corporation................................ 847 634-2600
   100 Pearl St Fl 13 Hartford (06103) *(G-1516)*

Vanderbilt Chemicals LLC..................................... 203 744-3900
   31 Taylor Ave Bethel (06801) *(G-139)*

Vanderbilt Chemicals LLC **(HQ)**.......................... **203 295-2141**
   30 Winfield St Norwalk (06855) *(G-2589)*

Vanderbilt Minerals LLC **(HQ)**............................ **203 295-2140**
   33 Winfield St Norwalk (06855) *(G-2590)*

Vanguard Manufacturing Inc.................................. 603 878-2083
   100 Temple Rd New Ipswich (03071) *(G-15200)*

Vanguard Plastics Corporation.............................. 860 628-4736
   100 Robert Porter Rd Southington (06489) *(G-3239)*

Vanguard Products Corporation............................. 203 744-7265
   87 Newtown Rd Danbury (06810) *(G-831)*

Vangy Tool Company Inc...................................... 508 754-2669
   621 Millbury St Worcester (01607) *(G-13820)*

Vanity World Inc... 508 668-1800
   348 Turnpike St Ste 1 Canton (02021) *(G-7839)*

Vannah Logging, Brunswick *Also Called: Eric T Vannah (G-4645)*

Vanson Leathers Inc... 508 678-2000
   951 Broadway Ste 1 Fall River (02724) *(G-8622)*

Vantage Reporting Inc... 212 750-2256
   3 Allied Dr Ste 303 Dedham (02026) *(G-8254)*

Vantage Software, Dedham *Also Called: Vantage Reporting Inc (G-8254)*

Vantec LLC... 508 726-2830
   428 Towne St North Attleboro (02760) *(G-10891)*

Vaporizer LLC... 860 564-7225
   245 Main St Moosup (06354) *(G-1931)*

Vapotherm Inc **(PA)**... **603 658-0011**
   100 Domain Dr Ste 102 Exeter (03833) *(G-14304)*

Varian Medical Systems Inc.................................. 650 493-4000
   200 Butterfield Dr Ste B Ashland (01721) *(G-5969)*

Varian Semicdtr Eqp Assoc Inc............................. 978 282-2807
   41 Juniper Rd Andover (01810) *(G-5932)*

Varian Semicdtr Eqp Assoc Inc **(HQ)**................... **978 282-2000**
   35 Dory Rd Gloucester (01930) *(G-8963)*

Varian Semicdtr Eqp Assoc Inc............................. 978 463-1500
   4 Stanley Tucker Dr Newburyport (01950) *(G-10725)*

Varitron Hudson, Hudson *Also Called: Varitron Technologies USA Inc (G-14557)*

Varitron Technologies USA Inc.............................. 603 577-8855
   12 Executive Dr Ste 2 Hudson (03051) *(G-14557)*

Varney Bros Concrete, Bellingham *Also Called: Varney Bros Sand & Gravel Inc (G-6302)*

Varney Bros Sand & Gravel................................... 508 966-1313
   79 Hartford Ave Bellingham (02019) *(G-6302)*

Varnum Enterprises LLC....................................... 203 743-4443
   11 Trowbridge Dr Bethel (06801) *(G-140)*

Varstreet Inc.. 781 262-0610
   67 S Bedford St Ste 400w Burlington (01803) *(G-7442)*

Vartanian Custom Cabinets................................... 413 283-3438
   10 Second St (Palmer Industrial Park) Palmer (01069) *(G-11288)*

Vas Integrated LLC... 860 748-4058
   600 Four Rod Rd Berlin (06037) *(G-90)*

Vasca Inc **(PA)**.. **978 640-0431**
   3 Highwood Dr Tewksbury (01876) *(G-12425)*

Vascular Technology Inc...................................... 603 594-9700
   12 Murphy Dr Unit C Nashua (03062) *(G-15182)*

Vaso Active Phrmaceuticals Inc............................. 978 750-1991
   100 Cummings Ctr Ste 243c Beverly (01915) *(G-6392)*

Vat Inc... 781 537-5402
   500 W Cummings Park Ste 5450 Woburn (01801) *(G-13684)*

Vater Percussion Inc... 781 767-1877
   270 Centre St Unit D Holbrook (02343) *(G-9186)*

Vaughn Thermal Corporation................................. 978 462-6683
   26 Old Elm St Salisbury (01952) *(G-11745)*

Vaunix Technology Corporation.............................. 978 662-7839
   7 New Pasture Rd Newburyport (01950) *(G-10726)*

Vaupell Industrial Plas Inc.................................... 413 233-3801
   101 Almgren Dr Agawam (01001) *(G-5814)*

Vbi, Cambridge *Also Called: Vbi Vaccines Inc (G-7750)*

Vbi Vaccines Inc **(PA)**...................................... **617 830-3031**
   222 3rd St Ste 2241 Cambridge (02142) *(G-7750)*

Vblearning LLC.. 617 527-9999
   109 Oak St Ste 203 Newton (02464) *(G-10793)*

Vce Company LLC... 831 247-1660
   350 Campus Dr Marlborough (01752) *(G-10228)*

Vck Best Machining LLC....................................... 603 880-8858
   4 Townsend W Ste 8 Nashua (03063) *(G-15183)*

Vdc Research Group Inc **(PA)**............................. **508 653-9000**
   144 Turnpike Rd Ste 230 Southborough (01772) *(G-12004)*

Vector Engineering Inc.. 860 572-0422
   800 Flanders Rd Unit 1-4 Mystic (06355) *(G-1944)*

Vector Itc Group, Cambridge *Also Called: Vector Software USA Corp (G-7751)*

Vector Software USA Corp..................................... 305 332-1703
   245 Frst St Rvrview Ii Fl Riverview Cambridge (02142) *(G-7751)*

Vectrix LLC.. 508 717-6510
   55 Samuel Barnet Blvd New Bedford (02745) *(G-10658)*

Vectronics Microwave Corp **(PA)**......................... **973 244-1040**
   267 Lowell Rd # 101 Hudson (03051) *(G-14558)*

Vectura Incorporated.. 508 573-5700
   371 Turnpike Rd Ste 120 Southborough (01772) *(G-12005)*

Veeam Software... 978 660-3276
   10 Reinsway Cir Westford (01886) *(G-13266)*

Veeam Software Corporation................................. 781 592-0752
   45 New Ocean St Swampscott (01907) *(G-12300)*

Veeder-Root, Weatogue *Also Called: Veeder-Root Company (G-4043)*

Veeder-Root Company **(HQ)**............................... **860 651-2700**
   125 Powder Forest Dr Fl 1 Weatogue (06089) *(G-4043)*

Velan Valve Corp **(DH)**..................................... **802 863-2561**
   94 Avenue C Williston (05495) *(G-17751)*

Velcro, Manchester *Also Called: Velcro Inc (G-14950)*

Velcro Inc **(HQ)**... **603 669-4880**
   95 Sundial Ave Manchester (03103) *(G-14950)*

Velcro USA Inc **(DH)**.. **800 225-0180**
   95 Sundial Ave Manchester (03103) *(G-14951)*

Vellumoid Inc.. 508 853-2500
   54 Rockdale St Worcester (01606) *(G-13821)*

Velocity LLC... 617 389-5452
   120 Tremont St Ste 2 Everett (02149) *(G-8503)*

Veloxint Corporation.. 774 777-3369
   125 Newbury St Ste 200 Framingham (01701) *(G-8806)*

Velux America LLC.. 207 216-4500
   85 Spencer Dr Unit A Wells (04090) *(G-5607)*

Vemas Corporation... 802 287-4100
   61 Beaman St Poultney (05764) *(G-17454)*

Vemployee.. 888 471-1982
   47 Taylor Rd Portsmouth (02871) *(G-16460)*

Vena's Fizz House, Portland *Also Called: Fizz LLC (G-5216)*

Venan Entertainment Inc.. 860 704-6330
  213 Court St Ste 102 Middletown (06457) *(G-1789)*

Venda Ravioli Inc.. 401 421-9105
  150 Royal Little Dr Providence (02904) *(G-16636)*

Venda Ravioli Inc **(PA)**.. **401 421-9105**
  265 Atwells Ave Providence (02903) *(G-16637)*

Vendome Guide.. 401 849-8025
  28 Pelham St Newport (02840) *(G-16227)*

Veneer Division, Presque Isle *Also Called: Columbia Forest Products Inc (G-5299)*

Venmill Industries Inc... 508 363-0410
  36 Town Forest Rd Oxford (01540) *(G-11267)*

Vensys Energy Inc.. 401 295-0006
  305 Lincoln Ave Warwick (02888) *(G-16870)*

Vent-Rite Valve Corp **(PA)**... **781 986-2000**
  300 Pond St Randolph (02368) *(G-11578)*

Ventech Industries Inc.. 207 439-0069
  384 Harold L Dow Hwy Unit 1 Eliot (03903) *(G-4751)*

Vention Medical, Salem *Also Called: Nordson Medical (nh) Inc (G-15551)*

Venture Tape, Rockland *Also Called: Gta-Nht Inc (G-11647)*

Venturi Inc... 401 781-2647
  101 Venturi Ave Warwick (02888) *(G-16871)*

Ventus Technologies LLC.. 203 642-2800
  333 Wilson Ave Norwalk (06854) *(G-2591)*

Venus, Hingham *Also Called: Venus Wafers Inc (G-9162)*

Venus Wafers Inc.. 781 740-1002
  100 Research Rd Hingham (02043) *(G-9162)*

Veoci Inc.. 203 782-5944
  195 Church St Ste 1401 New Haven (06510) *(G-2214)*

Veoci.com, New Haven *Also Called: Grey Wall Software LLC (G-2158)*

Veolia Es Tchncal Slutions LLC.. 203 748-9116
  53 Newtown Rd Danbury (06810) *(G-832)*

Veolia N Amer Rgnrtion Svcs LL **(DH)**.............................. **312 552-2800**
  53 State St Ste 14 Boston (02109) *(G-7097)*

Veoneer Roadscape Auto Inc.. 978 656-2500
  1011 Pawtucket Blvd Lowell (01854) *(G-9934)*

Veoneer Roadscape Auto Inc, Lowell *Also Called: Magna Elec Roadscape Auto LLC (G-9901)*

Veoneer Roadscape Lowell, Lowell *Also Called: Veoneer Roadscape Auto Inc (G-9934)*

Vera Roasting Company.. 603 969-7970
  99 Bow St Ste 100e Portsmouth (03801) *(G-15447)*

Veradigm Inc... 800 720-7351
  1 Burlington Woods Dr Ste 3 Burlington (01803) *(G-7443)*

Veralto Corporation.. 781 755-3655
  225 Wyman St Ste 250 Waltham (02451) *(G-12810)*

Veralto Enterprise LLC **(PA)**... **603 860-7300**
  225 Wyman St Ste 250 Waltham (02451) *(G-12811)*

Veranova LP **(HQ)**.. **484 581-0149**
  25 Patton Rd Devens (01434) *(G-8288)*

Veranova LP... 978 784-5000
  70 Flagship Dr North Andover (01845) *(G-10857)*

Verastem Inc **(PA)**.. **781 292-4200**
  117 Kendrick St Ste 500 Needham (02494) *(G-10528)*

Verax Biomedical Incorporated... 866 948-3729
  148 Bartlett St Marlborough (01752) *(G-10229)*

Verbio North America LLC **(PA)**.................................... **866 306-4777**
  9 W Broad St Ste 400 Stamford (06902) *(G-3491)*

Verbio North American Holdings... 866 306-4777
  9 W Broad St Ste 400 Stamford (06902) *(G-3492)*

Vericel Corporation **(PA)**.. **617 588-5555**
  64 Sidney St Cambridge (02139) *(G-7752)*

Verichem Laboratories Inc.. 401 461-0180
  90 Narragansett Ave Providence (02907) *(G-16638)*

Verico Technology LLC **(HQ)**... **860 871-1200**
  230 Shaker Rd Enfield (06082) *(G-1157)*

Veritas Medicine Inc.. 617 234-1500
  11 Cambridge Ctr Cambridge (02142) *(G-7753)*

Veritas Press Ltd... 603 379-2790
  271 Harbor Rd Rye (03870) *(G-15500)*

Verity LLC **(PA)**.. **617 482-2634**
  867 Boylston St Ste 500 Boston (02116) *(G-7098)*

Verizon... 802 879-4954
  12 York St Swanton (05488) *(G-17644)*

Verizon, Winchester *Also Called: Verizon New York Inc (G-13493)*

Verizon, Bedford *Also Called: Verizon Communications Inc (G-13952)*

Verizon, Swanton *Also Called: Verizon (G-17644)*

Verizon Communications Inc.. 603 472-2090
  35 Constitution Dr Bedford (03110) *(G-13952)*

Verizon New York Inc.. 781 721-5957
  954 Main St Winchester (01890) *(G-13493)*

Vermilion Software... 617 279-0799
  50 Congress St Ste 500 Boston (02109) *(G-7099)*

Vermod High Prfmce Mnfctred Hs...................................... 802 295-0042
  2677 Rt 5 Wilder (05088) *(G-17716)*

Vermod Homes, Wilder *Also Called: Vermod High Prfmce Mnfctred Hs (G-17716)*

Vermont Aerospace Inds LLC... 802 748-8705
  966 Industrial Pkwy Saint Johnsbury (05819) *(G-17547)*

Vermont Aerospace Manufacturing Inc................................. 802 748-8705
  966 Industrial Pkway Lyndonville (05851) *(G-17321)*

Vermont Beef Jerky Co.. 802 754-9412
  348 Industrial Park Ln New Orleans (05860) *(G-17439)*

Vermont Business Magazine, South Burlington *Also Called: Boutin/Mcquiston Inc (G-17574)*

Vermont Center Wreaths Inc... 802 334-6432
  44 Kimberly Ln Newport Center (05857) *(G-17408)*

Vermont Christmas Company.. 802 893-1670
  24 Clapper Rd Milton (05468) *(G-17366)*

Vermont Circuits Inc... 802 257-4571
  76 Technology Dr Brattleboro (05301) *(G-17102)*

Vermont Container Corp, Bennington *Also Called: K&H Group Inc (G-17045)*

Vermont Cottage Shop, South Londonderry *Also Called: Londonderry Industrial Pk Inc (G-17611)*

Vermont Country Soap Corp.. 802 388-4302
  183 Industrial Ave Ste 1 Middlebury (05753) *(G-17349)*

Vermont Creamery LLC... 802 479-9371
  40 Pitman Rd Websterville (05678) *(G-17685)*

Vermont Culinary Islands LLC... 802 387-8591
  22 Browne Ct Unit 115 Brattleboro (05301) *(G-17103)*

Vermont Culinary Islands LLC... 802 246-2277
  22 Browne Ct Unit 115 Brattleboro (05301) *(G-17104)*

Vermont Custom Cabinetry, North Walpole *Also Called: J H Dunning Corporation (G-15258)*

Vermont Custom Cabinetry, North Walpole *Also Called: Vermont Custom Wood Products (G-15261)*

Vermont Custom Wood Products.. 802 463-9930
  5 Dunning Dr North Walpole (03609) *(G-15261)*

Vermont Engine Service Inc.. 802 863-2326
  16 Krupp Dr Williston (05495) *(G-17752)*

Vermont Evaporator, Montpelier *Also Called: Vermont Evaporator Company LLC (G-17376)*

Vermont Evaporator Company LLC **(PA)**............................ **802 522-8499**
  157 Pioneer Ctr Ste 1 Montpelier (05602) *(G-17376)*

Vermont Flannel Co **(PA)**.. **802 476-5226**
  128 Mill St East Barre (05649) *(G-17215)*

Vermont Furn Hardwoods Inc... 802 875-2550
  386 Depot St Chester (05143) *(G-17184)*

Vermont Furniture Designs Inc.. 802 655-6568
  4 Tigan St Winooski (05404) *(G-17770)*

Vermont Gage, Swanton *Also Called: Vermont Precision Tools Inc (G-17645)*

Vermont Gage, Swanton *Also Called: Vermont Thread Gage LLC (G-17646)*

Vermont Glass Factory & Dg, Bennington *Also Called: Catamount Glassware Co Inc (G-17038)*

Vermont Hard Cider Company LLC...................................... 802 385-3656
  1 Tubbs Ave Brandon (05733) *(G-17071)*

Vermont Hard Cider Company LLC **(HQ)**............................ **802 388-0700**
  1321 Exchange St Middlebury (05753) *(G-17350)*

Vermont Hardwoods, Chester *Also Called: Vermont Furn Hardwoods Inc (G-17184)*

Vermont Hemp Processing Inc... 802 565-8025
  44 Hull St Ste 6 Randolph (05060) *(G-17474)*

Vermont Heritage Distrs Inc... 802 334-6503
  98 Johns River Dr Newport (05855) *(G-17407)*

Vermont Heritage Spring Water, Newport *Also Called: Vermont Heritage Distrs Inc (G-17407)*

Vermont Indexable Tooling Inc.. 802 752-2002
  331b Bryce Blvd Fairfax (05454) *(G-17264)*

Vermont Islands, Brattleboro *Also Called: Vermont Culinary Islands LLC (G-17104)*

Vermont Islands Kitchens Bars, Brattleboro *Also Called: Vermont Culinary Islands LLC (G-17103)*

Vermont Journalism Trust Ltd... 802 225-6224
  97 State St Ste 1 Montpelier (05602) *(G-17377)*

Vermont Juvenile Furn Mfg Inc................ 802 438-2231
  192 Sheldon Ave West Rutland (05777) *(G-17697)*

Vermont Machine Tool, Springfield *Also Called: Vermont Machine Tool Corp (G-17622)*

Vermont Machine Tool Corp.................... 802 885-5161
  65 Pearl St Springfield (05156) *(G-17622)*

Vermont Maple Sugar Co Inc.................... 802 888-3491
  29 Clay Hl Johnson (05656) *(G-17310)*

Vermont Maple Sugar Co Inc.................... 802 635-7483
  31 Main St Johnson (05656) *(G-17311)*

Vermont Maple Sugar Co Inc **(PA)**........... **802 888-3491**
  37 Industrial Park Dr Morrisville (05661) *(G-17391)*

Vermont Maturity, Williston *Also Called: Williston Pubg Promotions LLC (G-17753)*

Vermont Media Corp............................. 802 464-5757
  797 Vt Route 100 N Wilmington (05363) *(G-17756)*

Vermont Microtechnologies, Barnet *Also Called: Vermont Mold & Tool Corp (G-16995)*

Vermont Mold & Tool Corp...................... 802 633-2300
  4693 Garland Hl Barnet (05821) *(G-16995)*

Vermont News Guide, Manchester Center *Also Called: Hersam Acorn Newspapers LLC (G-17329)*

Vermont Nut Free Choclat Inc.................. 802 372-4654
  146 Brentwood Dr Colchester (05446) *(G-17206)*

Vermont Olde Tyme Kettle Corn, Newport *Also Called: Quirion Luc (G-17405)*

Vermont Olde Tyme Kettle Corn, Newport *Also Called: Quirion Luc (G-17406)*

Vermont Originals, Morrisville *Also Called: Washburn Company Inc (G-17393)*

Vermont Packinghouse LLC...................... 802 886-8688
  25 Fairbanks Rd North Springfield (05150) *(G-17426)*

Vermont Pallet and Skid Sp Inc................ 860 822-6949
  104 Baltic Rd Norwich (06360) *(G-2618)*

Vermont Plastic Specialties, Williston *Also Called: Dolliver Corporation (G-17728)*

Vermont Precision Machine Svcs................ 802 885-8291
  280 Clinton St Springfield (05156) *(G-17623)*

Vermont Precision Tools Inc **(PA)**.......... **802 868-4246**
  10 Precision Ln Swanton (05488) *(G-17645)*

Vermont Pub Brewry Burlington, Burlington *Also Called: McHolbe-Noonan Corporation (G-17144)*

Vermont Publishing Comany..................... 802 524-9771
  281 N Main St Saint Albans (05478) *(G-17536)*

Vermont Quarries Corp......................... 802 775-1065
  1591 Us Route 4 Rutland (05701) *(G-17514)*

Vermont Soap, Middlebury *Also Called: Vermont Country Soap Corp (G-17349)*

Vermont Soapstone, Perkinsville *Also Called: Williams & Co Mining Inc (G-17443)*

Vermont Soy, Hardwick *Also Called: Vermont Soy LLC (G-17285)*

Vermont Soy LLC............................... 802 472-8500
  180 Junction Rd Hardwick (05843) *(G-17285)*

Vermont Sportscar, Milton *Also Called: Lance Smith Inc (G-17361)*

Vermont Standard Inc.......................... 802 457-1313
  23 Elm St Woodstock (05091) *(G-17779)*

Vermont Stone Art LLC......................... 802 238-1498
  21 Metro Way Ste 1 Barre (05641) *(G-17023)*

Vermont Store Fixture Corporation **(PA)**.... **802 293-5126**
  1566 Us Route 7 Danby (05739) *(G-17210)*

Vermont Structural Slate Co **(PA)**.......... **802 265-4933**
  3 Prospect St Fair Haven (05743) *(G-17252)*

Vermont Systems, Essex Junction *Also Called: Rectrac LLC (G-17244)*

Vermont Teddy Bear Co Inc **(HQ)**............ **802 985-3001**
  6655 Shelburne Rd Shelburne (05482) *(G-17563)*

Vermont Teddy Bear Company, Shelburne *Also Called: Hibernation Holding Co Inc (G-17558)*

Vermont Thread Gage LLC....................... 802 868-4246
  10 Precision Ln Swanton (05488) *(G-17646)*

Vermont Timber Works Inc...................... 802 886-1917
  16 Fairbanks Rd North Springfield (05150) *(G-17427)*

Vermont Tortilla Company LLC.................. 802 399-2223
  22 Sage Ct Shelburne (05482) *(G-17564)*

Vermont Unfding Green Slate In **(PA)**....... **802 265-3200**
  963 S Main St Fair Haven (05743) *(G-17253)*

Vermont Verde Antique Intl.................... 802 767-4421
  2561 Sugar Hollow Rd Pittsford (05763) *(G-17446)*

Vermont Village, York *Also Called: Stonewall Kitchen LLC (G-5717)*

Vermont Village Applesauce, Barre *Also Called: Village Cannery Vermont Inc (G-17024)*

Vermont Ware Inc.............................. 802 482-4426
  157 Barber Rd # A St George (05495) *(G-17624)*

Vermont Wireform Inc.......................... 802 889-3200
  Rt. 110 Chelsea (05038) *(G-17179)*

Vermont Wood Pellet Co LLC.................... 802 747-1093
  1105 Vt Route 7b Central North Clarendon (05759) *(G-17418)*

Vermonts Orginal Ice Cream Inc................ 802 375-1133
  116 Sweet St E Arlington (05250) *(G-16992)*

Vermonts Original LLC......................... 802 626-3610
  91 Williams St Lyndonville (05851) *(G-17322)*

Verne Q Powell Flutes Inc..................... 978 461-6111
  3 Mill And Main Pl Ste 130 Maynard (01754) *(G-10265)*

Vernier Metal Fabricating Inc................. 203 881-3133
  26 Progress Ave Seymour (06483) *(G-2975)*

Verpol Plant, Florence *Also Called: Omya Inc (G-17272)*

Verrillon Inc................................. 508 890-7100
  15 Centennial Dr North Grafton (01536) *(G-11027)*

Versant Energy Services Inc **(DH)**.......... **781 792-5000**
  42 Longwater Dr Norwell (02061) *(G-11149)*

Versatile Subcontracting LLC.................. 603 286-8081
  200 Tilton Rd Unit A Northfield (03276) *(G-15271)*

Versimedia.................................... 203 604-8094
  63 Glover Ave Norwalk (06850) *(G-2592)*

Verso Corporation............................. 339 788-1343
  100 River Ridge Dr Ste 112 Norwood (02062) *(G-11218)*

Verso Paper Holding LLC....................... 207 897-3431
  300 Riley Rd Jay (04239) *(G-4917)*

Verso Paper Holding Llc, Jay *Also Called: Verso Paper Holding LLC (G-4917)*

Versum Materials Us LLC....................... 978 715-1614
  400 Summit Dr Burlington (01803) *(G-7444)*

Vertafore Inc................................. 860 602-6000
  5 Waterside Xing Fl 2 Windsor (06095) *(G-4312)*

Vertek, Randolph *Also Called: Applied Research Assoc Inc (G-17467)*

Vertex, Boston *Also Called: Vertex Pharmaceuticals Inc (G-7101)*

Vertex Cell Genetic Therapies, Cambridge *Also Called: Semma Therapeutics Inc (G-7709)*

Vertex Cell Genetic Therapies, Providence *Also Called: Vertex Pharmaceuticals Inc (G-16639)*

Vertex Fab & Design LLC....................... 508 947-3513
  29 Abbey Ln Middleboro (02346) *(G-10379)*

Vertex Pharmaceuticals Del LLC................ 617 341-6100
  50 Northern Ave Boston (02210) *(G-7100)*

Vertex Pharmaceuticals Inc **(PA)**........... **617 341-6100**
  50 Northern Ave Boston (02210) *(G-7101)*

Vertex Pharmaceuticals Inc.................... 857 529-6430
  225a Carolina Ave Providence (02905) *(G-16639)*

Vertex Pharmaceuticals PR LLC................. 617 341-6100
  50 Northern Ave Boston (02210) *(G-7102)*

Vertex Phrmaceuticals Dist Inc................ 617 341-6100
  50 Northern Ave Boston (02210) *(G-7103)*

Vertica Systems LLC........................... 617 386-4400
  150 Cambridgepark Dr Cambridge (02140) *(G-7754)*

Vertical & Mini Blind Factory................. 413 789-2343
  1443 Main St Agawam (01001) *(G-5815)*

Vertical Retail Solutions LLC................. 860 742-6464
  101 Hutchinson Rd Andover (06232) *(G-3)*

Vertical Ventures Intl LLC.................... 203 227-1364
  40 Hackberry Hill Rd Weston (06883) *(G-4155)*

Vertiv, Wallingford *Also Called: Vertiv Corporation (G-3874)*

Vertiv Corporation............................ 203 294-6020
  8 Fairfield Blvd Ste 4 Wallingford (06492) *(G-3874)*

Verve Therapeutics, Cambridge *Also Called: Verve Therapeutics Inc (G-7756)*

Verve Therapeutics Inc........................ 617 603-0070
  26 Landsdowne St Cambridge (02139) *(G-7755)*

Verve Therapeutics Inc **(PA)**............... **617 603-0070**
  500 Technology Sq Ste 1 Cambridge (02139) *(G-7756)*

Veryfine, Littleton *Also Called: Veryfine Products Inc (G-9842)*

Veryfine Products Inc **(DH)**................ **978 486-0812**
  20 Harvard Rd Littleton (01460) *(G-9842)*

Vespoli Usa Inc............................... 203 773-0311
  385 Clinton Ave New Haven (06513) *(G-2215)*

Vesuvius America Inc **(DH)** 1 Cookson Pl Providence (02903) *(G-16640)*

Veterans Assembled Elec LLC **(PA)**.......... **401 228-6165**
  106 Sea View Ave North Kingstown (02852) *(G-16291)*

Vette Thermal Solutions LLC (HQ)...... 603 635-2800
33 Bridge St Pelham (03076) (G-15300)

VH Blackinton & Co Inc...... 508 699-4436
221 John L Dietsch Blvd Attleboro Falls (02763) (G-6096)

Vhp, Randolph Also Called: Vermont Hemp Processing Inc (G-17474)

Vhv Company (PA)...... 802 655-8805
16 Tigan St Ste A Winooski (05404) (G-17771)

Via Science Inc (PA)...... 857 600-2171
49r Day St Somerville (02144) (G-11910)

Via Separations Inc...... 781 354-7945
165 Dexter Ave Watertown (02472) (G-12918)

Viabella Holdings LLC...... 978 855-8817
11 Twillingate Rd Sudbury (01776) (G-12271)

Viabella Holdings LLC (PA)...... 800 688-9998
9 Kendrick Rd Wareham (02571) (G-12848)

Viamed Corp...... 508 238-0220
15 Plymouth Dr Ste D South Easton (02375) (G-11955)

Viamet Phrmctcals Holdings LLC...... 919 467-8539
124 Washington St Ste 101 Foxboro (02035) (G-8730)

Vianor Inc (HQ)...... 802 864-7108
1945 Main St Colchester (05446) (G-17207)

Vianor Inc...... 802 223-1747
375 River St Montpelier (05602) (G-17378)

Vianor Inc...... 802 888-7961
13 Vt Route 15 E Morrisville (05661) (G-17392)

Viant AS&o Holdings LLC...... 866 899-1392
100 Fordham Rd Wilmington (01887) (G-13474)

Viant Chicopee Inc...... 413 612-2100
1040 Sheridan St Chicopee (01022) (G-8068)

Viant Medical LLC...... 603 528-1211
45 Lexington Dr Laconia (03246) (G-14673)

Viasat Inc...... 508 229-6500
300 Nickerson Rd Ste 100 Marlborough (01752) (G-10230)

Vibalogics US Inc...... 252 903-2213
1414 Massachusetts Ave Boxborough (01719) (G-7157)

Vibco Inc (PA)...... 401 539-2392
75 Stilson Rd Wyoming (02898) (G-16983)

Vibez Sunglasses LLC...... 603 818-2207
237 Londonderry Tpke Hooksett (03106) (G-14476)

Vibrac LLC (PA)...... 603 882-6777
1050 Perimeter Rd #6 Manchester (03103) (G-14952)

Vibracoustic Usa Inc...... 603 413-7262
11 Ricker Ave Londonderry (03053) (G-14790)

Vibram Corporation (HQ)...... 978 318-0000
9 Damonmill Sq Fl 2 Concord (01742) (G-8138)

Vibram Corporation (DH)...... 508 867-6494
18 School St North Brookfield (01535) (G-10964)

Vibram USA Inc., Concord Also Called: Vibram Corporation (G-8138)

Vibration & Shock Tech LLC...... 781 281-0721
13 Arbella Dr Beverly (01915) (G-6393)

Vic Firth Gourmet, Newport Also Called: Vic Firth Manufacturing Inc (G-5099)

Vic Firth Manufacturing Inc...... 207 368-4358
34 Progress Park S Newport (04953) (G-5099)

VICOR, Andover Also Called: Vicor Corporation (G-5933)

Vicor Corporation (PA)...... 978 470-2900
25 Frontage Rd Andover (01810) (G-5933)

Vicor Corporation...... 603 623-3222
540 North Commercial St Ste 110 Manchester (03101) (G-14953)

Victaulic Company...... 508 406-3220
145 Plymouth St Ste A Mansfield (02048) (G-10083)

Victor Microwave Inc...... 781 245-4472
38 W Water St Wakefield (01880) (G-12541)

Victoria Brand, Boston Also Called: Mutual Beef Co Inc (G-6899)

Victoria Gourmet Inc...... 781 935-2100
17a Gill St Woburn (01801) (G-13685)

Victory Fuel LLC...... 860 585-0532
248 Main St Terryville (06786) (G-3614)

Victory Productions Inc...... 508 755-0051
55 Linden St Ste 2 Worcester (01609) (G-13822)

Vidarr Inc...... 877 636-8432
280 Heritage Ave Unit G Portsmouth (03801) (G-15448)

Videndum Prod Solutions Inc (HQ)...... 203 929-1100
14 Progress Dr Shelton (06484) (G-3075)

Video Messenger Co, Stratford Also Called: Video Messengercom Corp (G-3582)

Video Messengercom Corp...... 203 358-8842
862 Judson Pl Stratford (06615) (G-3582)

Videoiq Inc...... 781 222-3069
450 Artisan Way Ste 200 Somerville (02145) (G-11911)

Vieste Rosa, Johnston Also Called: AG & G Inc (G-16073)

Vietaz Inc...... 617 322-1933
2288 Dorchester Ave Dorchester (02124) (G-8301)

View, The, Dedham Also Called: Sap Professional Journal (G-8249)

Viewpoint Sign & Awning, Northborough Also Called: Expansion Opportunities Inc (G-11095)

Views Record Label Inc...... 413 204-0930
102 E Alvord St Springfield (01108) (G-12148)

Vigil Neuroscience Inc (PA)...... 857 254-4445
100 Forge Rd Ste 7 Watertown (02472) (G-12919)

Vigilant Incoporated...... 603 285-0400
85 Industrial Park Dover (03820) (G-14256)

Vigue Holding Company Inc...... 860 747-6000
355 S Washington St Plainville (06062) (G-2787)

Viken Detection Corporation...... 617 467-5526
21 North Ave Burlington (01803) (G-7445)

Viking Industrial Products...... 508 481-4600
3 Brigham St Marlborough (01752) (G-10231)

Viking Kitchen Cabinets LLC (PA)...... 860 223-7101
33 John St 39 New Britain (06051) (G-2074)

Viking Seafoods Inc...... 781 322-2000
50 Crystal St Malden (02148) (G-10031)

Viking Systems Inc...... 508 366-3668
134 Flanders Rd Westborough (01581) (G-13143)

Viking Welding, Kensington Also Called: Viking Wldg & Fabrication LLC (G-14631)

Viking Wldg & Fabrication LLC...... 603 394-7887
243 Amesbury Rd Ste 1 Kensington (03833) (G-14631)

Vilex LLC...... 860 413-9875
18 Hartford Ave Granby (06035) (G-1309)

Villa Machine Associates Inc...... 781 326-5969
61 Mcdonald St Dedham (02026) (G-8255)

Village Cabinets, Bristol Also Called: Belmont Corporation (G-413)

Village Candle, Wells Also Called: Stonewall Kitchen LLC (G-5606)

Village Candle Inc...... 207 251-4800
90 Spencer Dr Wells (04090) (G-5608)

Village Cannery Vermont Inc...... 207 351-2713
698 S Barre Rd Barre (05641) (G-17024)

Village Forge Inc...... 617 361-2591
51 Industrial Dr Boston (02136) (G-7104)

Village Goldsmith...... 401 944-8404
55 Access Rd Ste 500 Warwick (02886) (G-16872)

Village Home Center, Saint Albans Also Called: City Feed and Lumber Co Inc (G-17519)

Village Industrial Power Inc...... 802 522-8584
330 Industrial Dr Bradford (05033) (G-17065)

Village of Orleans...... 802 754-8584
1 Memorial Sq Orleans (05860) (G-17440)

Village Woodturning...... 401 647-3091
39 Carue Dr North Scituate (02857) (G-16317)

Villanti & Sons Printers Inc...... 802 864-0723
15 Catamount Dr Milton (05468) (G-17367)

Villanti Printers, Milton Also Called: Villanti & Sons Printers Inc (G-17367)

Villarina Pasta & Fine Foods (PA)...... 203 917-4463
22 Shelter Rock Ln Unit 34 Danbury (06810) (G-833)

Ville Swiss Automatics Inc...... 203 756-2825
205 Cherry St Waterbury (06702) (G-3979)

Villeroy & Boch Usa Inc...... 207 439-6440
360 Us Route 1 Kittery (03904) (G-4940)

Vinegar Syndrome LLC...... 475 731-1778
100 Congress St Bridgeport (06604) (G-384)

Vineyard At Seven Birches LLC...... 603 745-7550
22 S Mountain Dr Lincoln (03251) (G-14707)

Vineyard Brands...... 617 901-3597
40 Adair Rd Brighton (02135) (G-7246)

Vineyard Brands LLC...... 508 653-5458
24 Elmwood Ave Natick (01760) (G-10500)

A
L
P
H
A
B
E
T
I
C

Vineyard Gazette LLC (PA)............................ **508 627-4311**
34 S Summer St Edgartown (02539) *(G-8468)*

Vintage Maine Kitchen LLC............................ 207 317-2536
83 Fickett Rd Pownal (04069) *(G-5294)*

Vintage Millwork Corporation............................ 978 957-1400
19 School St Dracut (01826) *(G-8313)*

Vintners Cellar Winery............................ 603 356-9463
1857 White Mountain Hwy North Conway (03860) *(G-15250)*

Vinyl Technologies Inc............................ 978 342-9800
195 Industrial Rd Fitchburg (01420) *(G-8680)*

Viola Associates Inc............................ 508 771-3457
110 Rosary Ln Ste A Hyannis (02601) *(G-9455)*

Virginia Project Inc............................ 207 443-4242
229 Washington St Bath (04530) *(G-4531)*

Virtual Publishing LLC............................ 603 627-9500
103 Bay St Manchester (03104) *(G-14954)*

Virtual Software Systems Inc............................ 781 424-4899
130 Black Bear Dr Unit 1315 Waltham (02451) *(G-12812)*

Vishay, Shelton *Also Called: Vishay Americas Inc (G-3076)*

Vishay Americas Inc (HQ)............................ **203 452-5648**
1 Greenwich Pl Shelton (06484) *(G-3076)*

Vishay Dale Electronics LLC............................ 603 881-7799
22 Clinton Dr Hollis (03049) *(G-14461)*

Vishay Efi Inc............................ 401 738-9150
111 Gilbane St Warwick (02886) *(G-16873)*

Vishay Electro-Film,, Warwick *Also Called: Vishay Efi Inc (G-16873)*

Vishay Hirel Systems LLC............................ 603 742-4375
140 Crosby Rd Dover (03820) *(G-14257)*

Vishay Intertechnology Inc............................ 802 440-8571
2813 West Rd Bennington (05201) *(G-17057)*

Vishay Tansitor, Bennington *Also Called: Vishay Intertechnology Inc (G-17057)*

Vishay Ultrasource, Hollis *Also Called: Vishay Dale Electronics LLC (G-14461)*

Visi-Flash Rentals Eastern............................ 508 583-9100
31 Pleasant St West Bridgewater (02379) *(G-12988)*

Visible Electrophysiology LLC............................ 802 847-4539
197 Moonlight Rdg Colchester (05446) *(G-17208)*

Visible Ep, Colchester *Also Called: Visible Electrophysiology LLC (G-17208)*

Visible Good, Newburyport *Also Called: The Cricket System Inc (G-10719)*

Visible Light Inc............................ 603 926-6049
6 Merrill Industrial Dr Unit 11 Hampton (03842) *(G-14417)*

Visible Measures Corp (PA)............................ **617 482-0222**
745 Atlantic Ave Fl 9 Boston (02111) *(G-7105)*

Visible Record Systems, Shelton *Also Called: Inform Inc (G-3020)*

Visible Systems Corporation (PA)............................ **617 902-0767**
24 School St Fl 2 Boston (02108) *(G-7106)*

Visimark Inc (PA)............................ **866 344-7721**
14a E Worcester St Worcester (01604) *(G-13823)*

Vision Designs, Brookfield *Also Called: Vision Designs LLC (G-543)*

Vision Designs LLC............................ 203 778-9898
1120 Federal Rd Ste 2 Brookfield (06804) *(G-543)*

Vision Dynamics LLC............................ 203 271-1944
799 W Boylston St Ste 1 Worcester (01606) *(G-13824)*

Vision Gvernment Solutions Inc............................ 800 628-1013
1 Cabot Rd Ste 100 Hudson (01749) *(G-9424)*

Vision Industries Corp............................ 401 764-0916
43 Hill Top Dr Johnston (02919) *(G-16111)*

Vision Technical Molding............................ 860 783-5050
20 Utopia Rd Manchester (06042) *(G-1640)*

Vision Technical Molding, Manchester *Also Called: Advance Mold & Mfg Inc (G-1583)*

Vision Technical Molding LLC............................ 860 647-7787
71 Utopia Rd Manchester (06042) *(G-1641)*

Vision Wine & Spirits LLC............................ 781 278-2000
540 N Coml St Ste 311 Manchester (03101) *(G-14955)*

Vision Wine & Spirits LLC............................ 781 278-2000
540 North Commercial St Ste 311 Manchester (03101) *(G-14956)*

Visionaid Inc............................ 508 295-3300
11 Kendrick Rd Wareham (02571) *(G-12849)*

Visionpoint LLC............................ 860 436-9673
152 Rockwell Rd Ste B6 Newington (06111) *(G-2333)*

Visionquest Holdings LLC............................ 978 776-9518
305 Foster St Ste 204 Littleton (01460) *(G-9843)*

Visionstep Consulting Inc............................ 978 422-1447
750 Crawford St Fitchburg (01420) *(G-8681)*

Visit WEI............................ 603 893-0900
43 Northwestern Dr Salem (03079) *(G-15570)*

Visitor Printing Company............................ 401 272-1010
1 Cathedral Sq Providence (02903) *(G-16641)*

Visonic Inc (HQ)............................ **860 243-0833**
6 Technology Park Dr # 101 Westford (01886) *(G-13267)*

Vistaprint............................ 866 614-8002
11 Bonney Ln Norwood (02062) *(G-11219)*

Vistaprint, Waltham *Also Called: Vistaprint Corp Solutions Inc (G-12813)*

Vistaprint Corp Solutions Inc............................ 844 347-4162
275 Wyman St Ste 100 Waltham (02451) *(G-12813)*

Visterra Inc............................ 617 498-1070
275 Second Ave Ste 300 Waltham (02451) *(G-12814)*

Visual Creations Inc............................ 401 588-5151
500 Narragansett Park Dr Pawtucket (02861) *(G-16429)*

Visual Magnetics Ltd............................ 508 381-2400
1 Emerson St Mendon (01756) *(G-10323)*

Visual Polymer Tech LLC............................ 603 488-5064
91 Brick Mill Rd Bedford (03110) *(G-13953)*

Vita Needle Company............................ 781 444-1780
919 Great Plain Ave Needham (02492) *(G-10529)*

Vital Biosciences Inc............................ 415 910-2994
268 Summer St Boston (02210) *(G-7107)*

Vital Wood Products Inc............................ 508 673-7976
218 Shove St Fall River (02724) *(G-8623)*

Vitamin 1 LLC............................ 617 523-9090
256 Ayer Rd Littleton (01460) *(G-9844)*

Vitaminsea LLC............................ 207 671-0955
369 Beech Plain Rd Buxton (04093) *(G-4666)*

Vitasoy USA Inc............................ 781 430-8988
57 Russell St Woburn (01801) *(G-13686)*

Vitec Production Solutions Inc, Shelton *Also Called: Videndum Prod Solutions Inc (G-3075)*

Vitek Research Corporation............................ 203 735-1813
33 Sheridan Dr Naugatuck (06770) *(G-1992)*

Vitreo Retinal Consultants, Quincy *Also Called: Eye Health Services Inc (G-11517)*

Vitta Corporation............................ 203 790-8155
7 Trowbridge Dr Ste 2 Bethel (06801) *(G-141)*

Viva Beverages Inc............................ 617 712-3488
1 Marina Park Dr Ste 1410 Boston (02210) *(G-7108)*

Vivantio Inc............................ 617 982-0390
200 Portland St Ste 500 Boston (02114) *(G-7109)*

Vivax Medical Corporation............................ 203 729-0514
54 Great Hill Rd Naugatuck (06770) *(G-1993)*

Vivido Natural LLC (PA)............................ **617 630-0131**
2 Central St Ste 161 Framingham (01701) *(G-8807)*

Vivox Inc............................ 508 650-3571
40 Speen St Ste 305 Framingham (01701) *(G-8808)*

VJ Electronix Inc............................ 631 589-8800
19 Alpha Rd Chelmsford (01824) *(G-7969)*

Vld Inc............................ 207 947-6148
163 Hildreth St N Bangor (04401) *(G-4519)*

VMS Software Inc............................ 425 766-1692
6 Liberty Sq Pmb 294 Boston (02109) *(G-7110)*

Vmt LLC............................ 802 592-3146
300 Field Rd Groton (05046) *(G-17279)*

Vmturbo Inc............................ 914 584-5263
1 Burlington Woods Dr Ste 101 Burlington (01803) *(G-7446)*

Vmware Carbon Black, Waltham *Also Called: Carbon Black LLC (G-12620)*

Voatz, Boston *Also Called: Voatz Inc (G-7111)*

Voatz Inc............................ 617 395-8091
50 Milk St Fl 16 Boston (02109) *(G-7111)*

Vocero Hispano Newspaper Inc............................ 866 846-6397
44 Hamilton St Southbridge (01550) *(G-12038)*

Voda Industries LLC............................ 908 531-8156
127 Tarn Rd Mont Vernon (03057) *(G-15049)*

Vogel Capital Inc (HQ)............................ **508 481-5944**
85 Hayes Memorial Dr Marlborough (01752) *(G-10232)*

Vogform Tool & Die Co Inc............................ 413 737-6947
56 Doty Cir West Springfield (01089) *(G-13051)*

Vogue Industries Ltd Partnr..	401 722-0900
82 Hadwin St Central Falls (02863) **(G-15800)**	
Voice Glance, Mystic *Also Called: Voice Glance LLC* **(G-1945)**	
Voice Glance LLC..	800 260-3025
12 Roosevelt Ave Mystic (06355) **(G-1945)**	
Voicescript Technologies..	401 524-2246
193 Crestwood Rd Warwick (02886) **(G-16874)**	
Voisine Bros Inc **(PA)**..	**207 231-0220**
768 Strip Rd New Canada (04743) **(G-5082)**	
Volicon Inc...	781 221-7400
99 S Bedford St Ste 209 Burlington (01803) **(G-7447)**	
Volk Packaging Corporation..	207 282-6151
11 Morin St Biddeford Industrial Park Biddeford (04005) **(G-4594)**	
Volo Aero Mro Inc...	413 525-7211
21 Fisher Ave East Longmeadow (01028) **(G-8400)**	
Volpe Cable Corporation..	203 623-1818
201 Linden Ave Branford (06405) **(G-284)**	
Voltarc, Orange *Also Called: Lcd Lighting Inc* **(G-2674)**	
Voltea Inc..	510 861-3719
1 Parkton Ave Worcester (01605) **(G-13825)**	
Voltserver Inc **(PA)**...	**401 885-8658**
42 Ladd St East Greenwich (02818) **(G-15996)**	
Vomax, Northampton *Also Called: Gdmc USA LLC* **(G-11063)**	
VOR BIOPHARMA, Cambridge *Also Called: Vor Biopharma Inc* **(G-7757)**	
Vor Biopharma Inc **(PA)**...	**617 655-6580**
100 Cambridgepark Dr Ste 101 Cambridge (02140) **(G-7757)**	
Vortex Inc..	978 535-8721
4 Dearborn Rd Peabody (01960) **(G-11351)**	
Voxel8 Inc...	916 396-3714
21 Rev Nazareno Properzi Way Ste N Somerville (02143) **(G-11912)**	
Voyager Pharmaceutical Corp...	781 592-1945
51 Berkshire St Swampscott (01907) **(G-12301)**	
Voyager Therapeutics Inc **(PA)**......................................	**570 329-6851**
75 Hayden Ave Lexington (02421) **(G-9791)**	
Vpt Components, Lawrence *Also Called: Sst Components Inc* **(G-9601)**	
Vpt RAD, Chelmsford *Also Called: Si-Rel Inc* **(G-7956)**	
Vr Industries Inc...	401 732-6800
333 Strawberry Field Rd Ste 6 Warwick (02886) **(G-16875)**	
Vr Industries LLC...	860 618-2772
27 Elton St Torrington (06790) **(G-3706)**	
Vsea Inc..	978 282-2000
35 Dory Rd Gloucester (01930) **(G-8964)**	
Vsg Snacks Inc..	401 536-1116
50 Hurdis St North Providence (02904) **(G-16313)**	
VT Industries Inc..	978 388-3792
12 Merrill Ave Amesbury (01913) **(G-5854)**	
VT LVSTK SLGTR & PROC CO..	802 877-3421
76 Depot Rd Ferrisburgh (05456) **(G-17269)**	
VTDIGGER.ORG, Montpelier *Also Called: Vermont Journalism Trust Ltd* **(G-17377)**	
Vuetek Scientific LLC...	207 657-6565
22 Shaker Rd Gray (04039) **(G-4844)**	
Vulcan, Porter *Also Called: Vulcan Electric Company* **(G-5171)**	
Vulcan Company Inc **(PA)**..	**781 337-5970**
51 Sharp St Hingham (02043) **(G-9163)**	
Vulcan Electric Company **(PA)**..	**207 625-3231**
28 Endfield St Porter (04068) **(G-5171)**	
Vulcan Flex Circuit Corp..	603 883-1500
28 Endfield St Porter (04068) **(G-5172)**	
Vulcan Industries Inc...	860 683-2005
651 Day Hill Rd Windsor (06095) **(G-4313)**	
Vulcan Industries Inc...	978 562-0003
4 Cabot Rd Hudson (01749) **(G-9425)**	
Vulcan Industries Inc...	413 525-8846
16 Deer Park Dr East Longmeadow (01028) **(G-8401)**	
Vulcan Tool Mfg, Hingham *Also Called: Vulcan Company Inc* **(G-9163)**	
Vulcanforms Inc...	781 472-0160
112 Barnum Rd Devens (01434) **(G-8289)**	
Vulncheck Inc...	781 879-6863
6 Longfellow Rd Lexington (02420) **(G-9792)**	
Vulplex Inc..	508 996-6787
305 Nash Rd New Bedford (02746) **(G-10659)**	

Vw Quality Coating...	617 963-6503
62 Cross St Norton (02766) **(G-11138)**	
Vx1 Corporation...	603 742-2888
271 Locust St Dover (03820) **(G-14258)**	
Vygon Corporation..	603 743-5988
87 Venture Dr Dover (03820) **(G-14259)**	
Vynorius Companies, The, Salisbury *Also Called: Vynorius Prestress Inc* **(G-11746)**	
Vynorius Prestress Inc..	978 462-7765
150 Elm St Salisbury (01952) **(G-11746)**	
Vystar, Worcester *Also Called: Vystar Corporation* **(G-13826)**	
Vystar Corporation...	508 791-9114
725 Southbridge St Worcester (01610) **(G-13826)**	
Vytek, Fitchburg *Also Called: Vinyl Technologies Inc* **(G-8680)**	
W & Mb Inc..	802 257-1935
74 Cotton Mill Hl Unit A108 Brattleboro (05301) **(G-17105)**	
W & W Machine Co Inc	
90 Woodmont Rd Milford (06460) **(G-1899)**	
W A M, South Windham *Also Called: Windham Automated Machines Inc* **(G-3105)**	
W and G Machine Company Inc...	203 288-3871
4 Hamden Park Dr Hamden (06517) **(G-1462)**	
W B Mason Co Inc..	888 926-2766
43 North Rd East Windsor (06088) **(G-1089)**	
W B Mason Co Inc..	888 926-2766
151 Woodward Ave Norwalk (06854) **(G-2593)**	
W B Mason Co Inc..	888 926-2766
2 Consumers Ave Norwich (06360) **(G-2619)**	
W B Mason Co Inc..	888 926-2766
188 Water St Augusta (04330) **(G-4481)**	
W B Mason Co Inc..	888 926-2766
78 Rice St Bangor (04401) **(G-4520)**	
W B Mason Co Inc..	888 926-2766
106 Pine Tree Industrial Pkwy Portland (04102) **(G-5288)**	
W B Mason Co Inc..	888 926-2766
1455 Concord St Ste 4a Framingham (01701) **(G-8809)**	
W B Mason Co Inc..	888 926-2766
121 Wells St Greenfield (01301) **(G-9004)**	
W B Mason Co Inc..	888 926-2766
8001 S Willow St Manchester (03103) **(G-14957)**	
W B Mason Co Inc..	888 926-2766
99 Bald Hill Rd Cranston (02920) **(G-15926)**	
W B Mason Co Inc..	888 926-2766
447 Canal St Brattleboro (05301) **(G-17106)**	
W B Mason Co Inc..	888 926-2766
68 Nesti Dr South Burlington (05403) **(G-17607)**	
W Craig Washburn..	603 237-8403
45 Diamond Pond Rd Colebrook (03576) **(G-14110)**	
W D C Holdings Inc...	508 699-4412
200 John J Dietsch Blvd Attleboro (02703) **(G-6073)**	
W E C, Warren *Also Called: Rmb Ltd* **(G-16766)**	
W E Richards Co Inc...	508 226-1036
40 John Williams St Attleboro (02703) **(G-6074)**	
W F Young Incorporated **(PA)**...	**800 628-9653**
302 Benton Dr East Longmeadow (01028) **(G-8402)**	
W G Fry Corp...	413 747-2551
28 Sylvan Ln Florence (01062) **(G-8687)**	
W Gillies Technologies LLC..	508 852-2502
250 Barber Ave Worcester (01606) **(G-13827)**	
W H Bagshaw Co Inc...	603 883-7758
1 Pine Street Ext Ste 135 Nashua (03060) **(G-15184)**	
W H Preuss Sons Incorporated...	860 643-9492
228 Boston Tpke Bolton (06043) **(G-224)**	
W J Roberts Co Inc...	781 233-8176
181 Central St Saugus (01906) **(G-11767)**	
W K Hillquist Inc..	603 595-7790
37 Executive Dr Hudson (03051) **(G-14559)**	
W L Fuller Inc..	401 467-2900
7 Cypress St Warwick (02888) **(G-16876)**	
W M Gulliksen Mfg Co Inc **(PA)**......................................	**617 323-5750**
30 Fairway Lndg South Weymouth (02190) **(G-11979)**	
W Oliver Tripp Company **(PA)**...	**781 848-1230**
86 Finnell Dr Ste 6 Weymouth (02188) **(G-13338)**	

ALPHABETIC

W R Cobb Company..401 438-7000
　800 Waterman Ave East Providence (02914) *(G-16047)*

W R Grace & Co..617 876-1400
　91 Hartwell Ave Ste 2 Lexington (02421) *(G-9793)*

W S Bessett Inc...207 324-9232
　1923 Main St Sanford (04073) *(G-5417)*

W S Emerson Company Inc **(PA)**...........................**207 989-3410**
　15 Acme Rd Brewer (04412) *(G-4623)*

W S Walcott Inc...508 240-0882
　180 Hilltop Plz Rte 6a Orleans (02653) *(G-11244)*

W. F. Young, East Longmeadow *Also Called: W F Young Incorporated (G-8402)*

W. K. Hillquist, Hudson *Also Called: W K Hillquist Inc (G-14559)*

WA Logging LLC...207 694-2921
　634 White Settlement Rd Hodgdon (04730) *(G-4892)*

Wabash Technologies Inc **(DH)**............................**260 355-4100**
　529 Pleasant St Attleboro (02703) *(G-6075)*

Wackerbarth Box Mfg Co Inc.................................413 357-8816
　383 Granby Rd Granville (01034) *(G-8972)*

Wackerbarth Box Shop, Granville *Also Called: Wackerbarth Box Mfg Co Inc (G-8972)*

Wad Inc..860 828-3331
　100 Clark Dr East Berlin (06023) *(G-920)*

Waddington North America Inc...............................978 256-6551
　6 Stuart Rd Chelmsford (01824) *(G-7970)*

Wadsworth Falls Mfg Co.......................................860 346-3644
　72 Main St Rockfall (06481) *(G-2916)*

Wafer LLC...978 304-3821
　32 Dunham Rd Beverly (01915) *(G-6394)*

Wagner Instruments, Riverside *Also Called: Weigh & Test Systems Inc (G-2911)*

Wagz Inc **(PA)**...**603 570-6015**
　100 Market St Unit 401 Portsmouth (03801) *(G-15449)*

Wahlcometroflex Inc...207 784-2338
　29 Lexington St Lewiston (04240) *(G-4995)*

Wahsburn Vault Company Inc.................................603 256-6891
　18 Washburn Way Hinsdale (03451) *(G-14445)*

Wai, Madison *Also Called: Wire Association Intl Inc (G-1577)*

Waja Associates Inc...508 543-6050
　38 Forge Pkwy Franklin (02038) *(G-8874)*

Wakefeld Thermal Solutions Inc **(HQ)**...................**603 635-2800**
　120 Northwest Blvd Nashua (03063) *(G-15185)*

Wakefield Daily Item, Wakefield *Also Called: Wakefield Item Company (G-12542)*

Wakefield Engineering...603 417-8310
　132 Sykes Rd Fall River (02720) *(G-8624)*

Wakefield Item Company.......................................781 245-0080
　26 Albion St Wakefield (01880) *(G-12542)*

Wakefield-Vette, Nashua *Also Called: Wakefeld Thermal Solutions Inc (G-15185)*

Wakefield-Vette, Pelham *Also Called: Vette Thermal Solutions LLC (G-15300)*

Walco Electric Company..401 467-6500
　303 Allens Ave Providence (02905) *(G-16642)*

Walcott Associates LLC..401 694-0153
　North Kingstown (02852) *(G-16292)*

Walden Biosciences Inc..617 794-2733
　1 Kendall Sq Ste 7102 Cambridge (02139) *(G-7758)*

Wales Copy Center, Boston *Also Called: Andrew T Johnson Company Inc (G-6548)*

Walgreen Co...781 244-9431
　475 E Washington St North Attleboro (02760) *(G-10892)*

Walgreens, North Attleboro *Also Called: Walgreen Co (G-10892)*

Walker Magnetics, Windsor *Also Called: Industrial Magnetics Inc (G-4283)*

Walker Magnetics Group Inc...................................508 853-3232
　600 Day Hill Rd Windsor (06095) *(G-4314)*

Walker Products Incorporated.................................860 659-3781
　80 Commerce Way Ste C Glastonbury (06033) *(G-1301)*

Walker-Clay Inc...781 294-1100
　211 Station St Hanson (02341) *(G-9057)*

Wall Goldfinger Furniture......................................802 278-5823
　168 N Main St Northfield (05663) *(G-17435)*

Wall Industries Inc...603 778-2300
　37 Industrial Dr Ste 3 Exeter (03833) *(G-14305)*

Wall Shotz..603 431-0900
　10 Autumn Pond Park Greenland (03840) *(G-14372)*

Wall Street Journal..800 369-5663
　84 2nd Ave Chicopee (01020) *(G-8069)*

Wallace Building Products Corp...............................603 768-5402
　40 Wallace Ln Danbury (03230) *(G-14184)*

Wallach Surgical, Trumbull *Also Called: Coopersurgical Inc (G-3715)*

Wallach Surgical Devices Inc **(PA)**.......................**203 799-2000**
　75 Corporate Dr Trumbull (06611) *(G-3740)*

Wallgoldfinger Inc...802 483-4200
　706 Garvey Hill Rd Northfield (05663) *(G-17436)*

Wallingford Industries Inc.....................................203 481-0359
　31 Business Park Dr Ste 3 Branford (06405) *(G-285)*

Wallingford Prtg Bus Forms Inc...............................203 481-1911
　758 E Main St Branford (06405) *(G-286)*

Walnut 65 Holdings Inc **(PA)**.............................**978 532-4010**
　65 Walnut St Peabody (01960) *(G-11352)*

Walpole Cabinetry...603 826-4100
　5 Lambro Ln Walpole (03608) *(G-15663)*

Walpole Creamery Ltd...603 445-5700
　532 Main St Walpole (03608) *(G-15664)*

Walpole Fence Company, Ridgefield *Also Called: Walpole Outdoors LLC (G-2909)*

Walpole Outdoors LLC...508 668-2800
　346 Ethan Allen Hwy Ridgefield (06877) *(G-2909)*

Walpole Outdoors LLC...207 794-2248
　235 N Chester Rd Chester (04457) *(G-4694)*

Walpole Outdoors LLC...508 540-0300
　958 E Falmouth Hwy East Falmouth (02536) *(G-8362)*

Walpole Outdoors LLC...978 658-3373
　168 Lowell St Wilmington (01887) *(G-13475)*

Walpole Times Inc...508 668-0243
　1 Speen St Ste 200 Framingham (01701) *(G-8810)*

Walrus Enteprises LLC...413 387-4387
　30 Aldrich St Northampton (01060) *(G-11085)*

Walsh Mechanical Conractors, Abington *Also Called: Le Bel Inc (G-5725)*

Walston Inc...203 453-5929
　131 Nut Plains Rd Guilford (06437) *(G-1409)*

Walter A Beach Inc..860 282-7440
　8 Eastern Park Rd East Hartford (06108) *(G-1033)*

Walter A Furman Co Inc..508 674-7751
　180 Liberty St Fall River (02724) *(G-8625)*

Walter De Gruyter Inc...857 284-7073
　121 High St Fl 3 Boston (02110) *(G-7112)*

Walter Drake Incorporated **(PA)**.........................**413 536-5463**
　85 Sargeant St Holyoke (01040) *(G-9290)*

Walts Tropper Factory LLC.....................................203 871-9254
　44 Circle Dr North Branford (06471) *(G-2378)*

Walz & Krenzer Inc..203 267-5712
　91 Willenbrock Rd Ste B4 Oxford (06478) *(G-2714)*

Wanderlust Group Inc..617 784-3696
　1035 Cambridge St Ste 30 Cambridge (02141) *(G-7759)*

Wanho Manufacturing LLC......................................203 759-3744
　154 Knotter Dr Cheshire (06410) *(G-621)*

Waniewski Farms Inc...413 786-1182
　409 S Westfield St Feeding Hills (01030) *(G-8637)*

Ward Cedar Log Homes, Houlton *Also Called: Wlhc Inc (G-4906)*

Ward Leonard CT LLC **(DH)**...............................**860 283-5801**
　401 Watertown Rd Thomaston (06787) *(G-3641)*

Ward Leonard CT LLC...860 283-2294
　401 Watertown Rd Thomaston (06787) *(G-3642)*

Ward Leonard Operating LLC **(DH)**........................**860 283-5801**
　401 Watertown Rd Thomaston (06787) *(G-3643)*

Ward Lonard Houma Holdings LLC.............................860 283-5801
　401 Watertown Rd Thomaston (06787) *(G-3644)*

Ward Process Inc..508 429-1165
　311 Hopping Brook Rd Holliston (01746) *(G-9238)*

Wards Manufacturing LLC......................................404 441-0453
　84 Cutler St Unit 7 Warren (02885) *(G-16771)*

Wardwell Braiding Co., Central Falls *Also Called: Stolberger Incorporated (G-15797)*

Wardwell Braiding Company, Central Falls *Also Called: Wardwell Braiding Machine Company (G-15801)*

Wardwell Braiding Machine Company **(PA)**................**401 724-8800**
　1211 High St Central Falls (02863) *(G-15801)*

Wardwell Piping Inc..207 892-0034
　194 Roosevelt Trl Windham (04062) *(G-5674)*

Ware Rite Distributors Inc.. 508 690-2145
40 Industrial Dr East Bridgewater (02333) *(G-8347)*

Warehouse, Newburyport *Also Called: Rochester Electronics LLC (G-10714)*

Warehouse, Westwood *Also Called: Cambridge Soundworks Inc (G-13307)*

Warick Management Company Inc... 603 538-7112
10 Farr Rd Pittsburg (03592) *(G-15330)*

Waring Products Division, Torrington *Also Called: Conair LLC (G-3676)*

Warmup Inc
52 Federal Rd Ste 1b Danbury (06810) *(G-834)*

Warner Electric... 781 917-0600
300 Granite St Ste 201 Braintree (02184) *(G-7212)*

Warner Instruments.. 203 776-0664
84 October Hill Rd Ste 10 Holliston (01746) *(G-9239)*

Warner Precision Machining & F... 203 281-3660
875 Shepard Ave Hamden (06514) *(G-1463)*

Warren Chair Works, Warren *Also Called: O&G Studio LLC (G-16761)*

Warren Pumps LLC.. 413 436-7711
82 Bridge St Warren (01083) *(G-12853)*

Warrior Sports, Boston *Also Called: Warrior Sports Inc (G-7113)*

Warrior Sports Inc **(DH)**.. **800 968-7845**
100 Guest St Boston (02135) *(G-7113)*

Warrior Trading Inc... 413 591-1100
47 Railroad St Great Barrington (01230) *(G-8980)*

Warwick Fasteners... 401 739-9200
255 Pleasant St West Bridgewater (02379) *(G-12989)*

Warwick Ice Cream Company... 401 821-8403
743 Bald Hill Rd Warwick (02886) *(G-16877)*

Warwick Mills Inc **(PA)**.. **603 291-1000**
301 Turnpike Rd New Ipswich (03071) *(G-15201)*

Warwick Poultry Co Inc... 401 421-8500
46 Bath St Providence (02908) *(G-16643)*

Wasco Products, Wells *Also Called: Velux America LLC (G-5607)*

Washburn & Doughty Assoc Inc.. 207 633-6517
7 Enterprise St East Boothbay (04544) *(G-4737)*

Washburn Company Inc... 802 888-3032
320 Wilkins St Morrisville (05661) *(G-17393)*

Washburn Vault Company Inc.. 802 254-9150
795 Meadowbrook Rd Brattleboro (05301) *(G-17107)*

Washing Equipment Technologies, Bolton *Also Called: Simoniz USA Inc (G-223)*

Washington ABC Imaging Inc.. 857 753-4241
274 Summer St Boston (02210) *(G-7114)*

Washington Concrete Pdts Inc... 860 747-5242
328 S Washington St Plainville (06062) *(G-2788)*

Washington Mills, North Grafton *Also Called: Washington Mills N Grafton Inc (G-11029)*

Washington Mills Group Inc **(PA)**...................................... **508 839-6511**
20 N Main St North Grafton (01536) *(G-11028)*

Washington Mills N Grafton Inc **(HQ)**................................. **508 839-6511**
20 N Main St North Grafton (01536) *(G-11029)*

Washington Terex Inc.. 203 222-7170
200 Nyala Farms Rd Ste 2 Westport (06880) *(G-4200)*

Wasik Associates Inc.. 978 454-9787
29 Diana Ln Dracut (01826) *(G-8314)*

Waste Management, Barnstable *Also Called: Garbage Gone Inc (G-6200)*

Waste Management Recycle Amer, Springfield *Also Called: Waste Mgmt Inc (G-12149)*

Waste Mgmt Inc.. 413 747-9294
84 Birnie Ave Springfield (01107) *(G-12149)*

Water Analytics Inc... 978 749-9949
100 School St Andover (01810) *(G-5934)*

Water Billing Dept, Billerica *Also Called: Town of Billerica (G-6488)*

Water Closet LLC.. 508 228-2828
9 Sparks Ave Nantucket (02554) *(G-10466)*

Water Street Printing LLC.. 603 595-1444
97 Main St Nashua (03060) *(G-15186)*

Water Treatment Plant, Vernon *Also Called: Town of Vernon (G-3758)*

Water Treatment Plant, Manchester *Also Called: City of Manchester (G-14829)*

Waterair Supply Co, Byfield *Also Called: Metromatic Manufacturing Company Inc (G-7458)*

Waterbury Button Company, Cheshire *Also Called: OGS TECHNOLOGIES LLC (G-610)*

Waterbury Companies Inc
64 Avenue of Industry Waterbury (06705) *(G-3980)*

Waterbury Leatherworks Co.. 203 755-7789
1 Rivington Way Unit 304 Danbury (06810) *(G-835)*

Waterbury Plating, Waterbury *Also Called: Halco Inc (G-3917)*

Waterbury Rolling Mills Inc.. 203 597-5000
215 Piedmont St Waterbury (06706) *(G-3981)*

Waterbury Screw Mch Pdts Co... 203 756-8084
311 Thomaston Ave Ste 319 Waterbury (06702) *(G-3982)*

Watercure Farm LLC... 860 208-4083
94 Hampton Rd Pomfret Center (06259) *(G-2814)*

Waterfront Graphics & Prtg LLC... 207 799-3519
104 Ocean St South Portland (04106) *(G-5517)*

Waterlac Coating Inc.. 573 885-2506
142 Starr Ave Lowell (01852) *(G-9935)*

Watermillpreferred Partners LP.. 781 790-5045
800 South St Ste 355 Waltham (02453) *(G-12815)*

Waterrower Inc.. 800 852-2210
560 Metacom Ave Warren (02885) *(G-16772)*

Waterrower International LLC... 800 852-2210
560 Metacom Ave Warren (02885) *(G-16773)*

Waters, Milford *Also Called: Waters Corporation (G-10424)*

Waters, Milford *Also Called: Waters Technologies Corp (G-10425)*

Waters Associates Inc... 508 634-4500
34 Maple St Milford (01757) *(G-10423)*

Waters Chromatography Div, Milford *Also Called: Waters Associates Inc (G-10423)*

Waters Corporation **(PA)**.. **508 478-2000**
34 Maple St Milford (01757) *(G-10424)*

Waters Technologies Corp.. 508 482-4807
210 Grove St Franklin (02038) *(G-8875)*

Waters Technologies Corp **(HQ)**.. **508 478-2000**
34 Maple St Milford (01757) *(G-10425)*

Waters Technologies Corp.. 508 482-5223
177 Robert Treat Paine Dr Taunton (02780) *(G-12376)*

Watertown Cremation Products, Whitman *Also Called: Watertown Engineering Corp (G-13351)*

Watertown Engineering Corp.. 781 857-2555
1200 Auburn St Whitman (02382) *(G-13351)*

Watertown Ironworks Inc... 781 491-0229
47 Henshaw St Woburn (01801) *(G-13687)*

Watertown Jig Bore Service Inc.. 860 274-5898
29 New Wood Rd Watertown (06795) *(G-4037)*

Watertown Plastics Inc.. 860 274-7535
830 Echo Lake Rd Watertown (06795) *(G-4038)*

Watertown Printers Inc.. 781 893-9400
21 Mcgrath Hwy Ste 3 Somerville (02143) *(G-11913)*

Waterville Window Co Inc.. 207 873-0159
22 Verti Dr Winslow (04901) *(G-5689)*

Waterwear Inc.. 603 654-5344
24 Howard St Wilton (03086) *(G-15712)*

Waterwheel Breakfast Gift Hse.. 603 586-4313
1955 Presidential Hwy Jefferson (03583) *(G-14587)*

Waterwood Corporation... 413 572-1010
77 Servistar Industrial Way Westfield (01085) *(G-13216)*

Waterworks... 207 941-8306
25 Dowd Rd Bangor (04401) *(G-4521)*

Watka Corporation.. 508 946-5555
155 Millenium Cir Ste 104 Lakeville (02347) *(G-9523)*

Watson, West Haven *Also Called: Watson LLC (G-4132)*

Watson Brothers Inc.. 978 774-7677
6 Birch Rd Middleton (01949) *(G-10397)*

Watson LLC **(DH)**.. **203 932-3000**
301 Heffernan Dr West Haven (06516) *(G-4132)*

Watson Materials.. 401 885-0600
1500 S County Trl East Greenwich (02818) *(G-15997)*

Watson Printing Co Inc.. 781 237-1336
118 Cedar St Ste 2 Wellesley (02481) *(G-12947)*

Watson Wheeler Cider LLC **(PA)**....................................... **435 602-9042**
4322 East Rd Shaftsbury (05262) *(G-17554)*

Watts Regulator Co... 978 688-1811
1600 Osgood St North Andover (01845) *(G-10858)*

Watts Regulator Co **(HQ)**... **978 689-6000**
815 Chestnut St North Andover (01845) *(G-10859)*

Watts Regulator Co... 603 934-5110
583 S Main St Franklin (03235) *(G-14323)*

Watts Sea Tech Inc... 978 688-1811
815 Chestnut St North Andover (01845) *(G-10860)*

A
L
P
H
A
B
E
T
I
C

Watts Water, North Andover *Also Called: Watts Water Technologies Inc (G-10861)*

Watts Water Technologies Inc **(PA)**...................... **978 688-1811**
815 Chestnut St North Andover (01845) *(G-10861)*

Watts Water Technologies Inc............................. 603 934-1369
583 S Main St Franklin (03235) *(G-14324)*

Waughs Mountainview Elec................................. 207 545-2421
246 Roxbury Rd Mexico (04257) *(G-5059)*

Wavefront Semiconductor, Cumberland *Also Called: Alesis LP (G-15931)*

Waveguide Corporation................................... 617 892-9700
135 Beaver St Ste 310 Waltham (02452) *(G-12816)*

Wavelink LLC.. 603 606-7489
724 East Industrial Park Dr Unit 6 Manchester (03109) *(G-14958)*

Waverly Tool Rental & Sales Co........................... 508 872-8866
28 Miller Ave Framingham (01702) *(G-8811)*

Way Out Wax Inc... 802 730-8069
68 Puffer Rd Montgomery Center (05471) *(G-17369)*

Waybest Foods Inc
1510 John Fitch Blvd South Windsor (06074) *(G-3189)*

Wayland Millwork Corporation............................ 508 485-4172
344 Boston Post Rd E Ste 1 Marlborough (01752) *(G-10233)*

Wayne Manufacturing Inds LLC........................... 978 416-0899
13 Prescott Rd Brentwood (03833) *(G-14032)*

Waynes Sheet Metal Inc.................................. 508 431-8057
157 Tremont St Rehoboth (02769) *(G-11615)*

Waypoint Distillery...................................... 860 519-5390
410 Woodland Ave Bloomfield (06002) *(G-216)*

Wayside Publishing...................................... 888 302-2519
2 Stonewood Dr Freeport (04032) *(G-4804)*

WB Engineering Inc **(HQ)**.............................. **207 878-0700**
11 Gray Rd Falmouth (04105) *(G-4775)*

WB Engineering Inc..................................... 508 952-4000
2 Hampshire St Foxboro (02035) *(G-8731)*

Wces Inc... 203 573-1325
225 S Leonard St Waterbury (06708) *(G-3983)*

Wcm LLC... 401 273-0444
23 Acorn St Providence (02903) *(G-16644)*

Wcw Inc **(PA)**.. **802 362-8053**
450 Natural Form Way Manchester Center (05255) *(G-17332)*

Wdss Corporation....................................... 203 854-5930
7 Old Well Ct Norwalk (06855) *(G-2594)*

Wdw Machine Inc....................................... 603 329-9604
17 Gigante Dr Ste 1 Hampstead (03841) *(G-14394)*

We Cork Inc.. 800 666-2675
16 Kingston Rd Unit 6 Exeter (03833) *(G-14306)*

We Make Paint, Stratford *Also Called: Grafted Coatings Inc (G-3543)*

We Palmer Co, Boston *Also Called: Harry Miller Co LLC (G-6782)*

We Print Today LLC..................................... 781 585-6021
66 Summer St Kingston (02364) *(G-9514)*

Wealth2kcom Inc....................................... 781 989-5200
75 Arlington St Ste 5000 Boston (02116) *(G-7115)*

Wear-Guard Corporation................................ 781 871-4100
141 Longwater Dr Norwell (02061) *(G-11150)*

Wear-Rite Corp.. 508 987-0361
Cudworth Rd Oxford (01540) *(G-11268)*

Wearspf LLC.. 203 466-4616
20 Commerce St East Haven (06512) *(G-1056)*

Weather Guard Industries LLC........................... 954 703-0563
36 Smith St Northampton (01060) *(G-11086)*

Weather Source LLC.................................... 844 813-2617
1 Stiles Rd Ste 305 Salem (03079) *(G-15571)*

Weatherend Estate Furniture, Rockland *Also Called: Imagineering Inc (G-5333)*

Weatherford International LLC........................... 203 294-0190
8 Enterprise Rd Wallingford (06492) *(G-3875)*

Weavr Health Corp...................................... 617 430-6920
44 Manning Rd Billerica (01821) *(G-6489)*

Web Closeout... 413 222-8302
360 El Paso St Springfield (01104) *(G-12150)*

Web Handling Equipment, West Bridgewater *Also Called: Double E Company LLC (G-12972)*

Web Industries Hartford Inc **(HQ)**................... **860 779-3197**
20 Louisa Viens Dr Dayville (06241) *(G-870)*

Web Industries Inc **(PA)**............................. **508 898-2988**
293 Boston Post Rd W Ste 510 Marlborough (01752) *(G-10234)*

WEB Printing Inc.. 401 334-3190
1300 Mendon Rd Cumberland (02864) *(G-15971)*

Webco Chestnut Corporation............................ 508 943-2337
420 W Main St Dudley (01571) *(G-8327)*

Webco Engineering Inc.................................. 508 303-0500
155 Northboro Rd Ste 20 Southborough (01772) *(G-12006)*

Weber Realty Trust...................................... 508 756-4290
4 Westec Dr Auburn (01501) *(G-6127)*

Webilent Technology Inc................................ 860 254-6169
225 Oakland Rd Ste 106 South Windsor (06074) *(G-3190)*

Webster Printing Company Inc **(PA)**.................. **781 447-5484**
1069 W Washington St Hanson (02341) *(G-9058)*

Wee Forest Folk Inc..................................... 978 369-0286
887 Bedford Rd Carlisle (01741) *(G-7851)*

Weeden Street Associates LLC........................... 401 725-2610
173 Weeden St Pawtucket (02860) *(G-16430)*

Weekly Reader Corp.................................... 203 705-3500
200 Stamford Pl Ste 200 Stamford (06902) *(G-3493)*

Weekly Sentinel, The, Wells *Also Called: Shoreline Publications (G-5605)*

Weetabix Co.. 508 683-3600
300 Nickerson Rd Marlborough (01752) *(G-10235)*

Weetabix Company Inc................................. 978 422-2905
12 Industrial Dr Sterling (01564) *(G-12172)*

Wegotsoccer, Taunton *Also Called: Arocam Inc (G-12319)*

Wehl Plant Drops, Medford *Also Called: Ballhaus Bev Co LLC (G-10281)*

Wehr Industries Inc.................................... 401 732-6565
14 Minnesota Ave Warwick (02888) *(G-16878)*

Wei Inc.. 401 781-3904
25 Webb St Cranston (02920) *(G-15927)*

Wei Inc **(PA)**.. **401 781-3904**
33 Webb St Cranston (02920) *(G-15928)*

Weidmann Electrical Technology Inc **(DH)**........... **802 748-8106**
1 Gordon Mills Way Saint Johnsbury (05819) *(G-17548)*

Weidner Services LLC.................................. 603 532-4833
5 Saw Mill Dr Jaffrey (03452) *(G-14582)*

Weigh & Test Systems Inc.............................. 203 698-9681
17 Wilmot Ln Ste 2 Riverside (06878) *(G-2911)*

Weight Wizards, Wilder *Also Called: Stave Puzzles Incorporated (G-17715)*

Weimann Brothers Mfg Co.............................. 203 735-3311
247 Roosevelt Dr Derby (06418) *(G-894)*

Weingeroff Enterprises Inc............................. 401 467-2200
1 Weingeroff Blvd Cranston (02910) *(G-15929)*

Weiss Sheet Metal Inc.................................. 508 583-8300
105 Bodwell St Avon (02322) *(G-6167)*

Weissenfels Usa Inc.................................... 401 683-2900
45 Highpoint Ave Ste 1 Portsmouth (02871) *(G-16461)*

Welch Fluorocarbon Inc................................ 603 742-0164
113 Crosby Rd Ste 10 Dover (03820) *(G-14260)*

Welch Foods Inc A Cooperative......................... 978 371-3762
300 Baker Ave Ste 101 Concord (01742) *(G-8139)*

Welch Foods Inc A Cooperative **(HQ)**................ **978 371-1000**
575 Virginia Rd Concord (01742) *(G-8140)*

Welch Stencil Company, Scarborough *Also Called: Davis-Joncas Enterprises Inc (G-5430)*

Welch Welding and Trck Eqp Inc........................ 978 251-8726
164 Middlesex St North Chelmsford (01863) *(G-10989)*

Welch Welding and Truck Eqp, North Chelmsford *Also Called: Welch Welding and Trck Eqp Inc (G-10989)*

Welch's, Concord *Also Called: Welch Foods Inc A Cooperative (G-8140)*

Weld Engineering Co Inc................................ 508 842-2224
34 Fruit St Shrewsbury (01545) *(G-11848)*

Weld Power Generator Inc.............................. 800 288-6016
1529 Grafton Rd Millbury (01527) *(G-10445)*

Weld Rite.. 617 524-9747
3371 Washington St Jamaica Plain (02130) *(G-9504)*

Weld-All Inc.. 860 621-3156
987 West St Southington (06489) *(G-3240)*

Welding Craftsmen Co Inc.............................. 508 230-7878
63 Norfolk Ave South Easton (02375) *(G-11956)*

Welding Works, Madison *Also Called: Rwt Corporation (G-1568)*

Welding Works Inc...................................... 203 245-2731
32 New Rd Madison (06443) *(G-1576)*

Wellcoin Inc... 617 512-8617
   11 Drumlin Rd Newton (02459) *(G-10794)*

Wellesley Information Svcs LLC........................ 781 407-9013
   50 Congress St Ste 300 Boston (02109) *(G-7116)*

Wellesley Townsman, Randolph *Also Called: Gatehouse Media Mass I Inc (G-11560)*

Wellfleet Shellfish Co Inc............................ 508 255-5300
   137 Holmes Rd Eastham (02642) *(G-8436)*

Wellington Manufacturing Inc......................... 401 461-2248
   100 Aldrich St Providence (02905) *(G-16645)*

Wellness Connection of Maine, South Portland *Also Called: Northeast Patients Group (G-5509)*

Wellness Pet LLC **(PA)**........................... **877 869-2971**
   77 S Bedford St Ste 201 Burlington (01803) *(G-7448)*

Wells Bindery, Gloucester *Also Called: Ckg Limited (G-8929)*

Wells Development L L C.............................. 781 727-5560
   32 Devereaux St Arlington (02476) *(G-5950)*

Wells Tool Company.................................. 413 773-3465
   106 Hope St Greenfield (01301) *(G-9005)*

Wells Wood Turning & Finishing, Buckfield *Also Called: Turning Acquisitions LLC (G-4659)*

Wellsky Humn Social Svcs Corp....................... 802 316-3000
   25 New England Dr Essex Junction (05452) *(G-17249)*

Wellspect Healthcare, Waltham *Also Called: Dentsply Ih Inc (G-12650)*

Welog Inc.. 603 237-8277
   11 Skyline Dr Colebrook (03576) *(G-14111)*

Welton Technology LLC............................... 978 425-0160
   517 Lancaster St Ste 102 Leominster (01453) *(G-9716)*

Wembly Nycoa Holdings LLC.......................... 603 627-5150
   333 Sundial Ave Manchester (03103) *(G-14959)*

Wen Industries, Merrimack *Also Called: Hyde Specialty Products LLC (G-14984)*

Wendell Enterprises Inc.............................. 860 846-0800
   4 Right Ln Farmington (06032) *(G-1258)*

Wendi C Smith...................................... 508 362-4595
   89 Willow St Yarmouth Port (02675) *(G-13846)*

Wendon Company Inc
   16 Wimbledon Ln Easton (06612) *(G-1098)*

Wentworth, South Windham *Also Called: Wentworth Manufacturing LLC (G-3104)*

Wentworth Laboratories Inc **(PA)**................. **203 775-0448**
   1087 Federal Rd Ste 4 Brookfield (06804) *(G-544)*

Wentworth Manufacturing LLC........................ 860 423-4575
   1102 Windham Rd South Windham (06266) *(G-3104)*

Wentworth Technology Inc............................ 207 571-9744
   331 North St Saco (04072) *(G-5381)*

Wepco, Westfield *Also Called: Westfield Electroplating Co (G-13219)*

Wepco Plastics Inc.................................. 860 349-3407
   27 Industrial Park Access Rd Middlefield (06455) *(G-1731)*

Werewolf Therapeutics, Watertown *Also Called: Werewolf Therapeutics Inc (G-12920)*

Werewolf Therapeutics Inc........................... 617 952-0555
   200 Talcott Ave Fl 2 Watertown (02472) *(G-12920)*

Werfen, Bedford *Also Called: Instrumentation Laboratory Co (G-6233)*

Werfen USA LLC..................................... 781 861-0710
   180 Hartwell Rd Bedford (01730) *(G-6276)*

Wes Press, Middletown *Also Called: Wesleyan University (G-1790)*

Wesco Building & Design Inc......................... 781 279-0490
   271 Main St Ste G01 Stoneham (02180) *(G-12188)*

Wescon Corp of Conn................................ 860 599-2500
   Elmata Ave Pawcatuck (06379) *(G-2728)*

Wesconn Stairs Inc.................................. 203 792-7367
   2 Mill Plain Rd Danbury (06811) *(G-836)*

Wescor Ltd **(PA)**................................ **781 279-0490**
   271 Main St Ste G01 Stoneham (02180) *(G-12189)*

Wesleyan University................................. 860 685-2980
   110 Mount Vernon St Middletown (06457) *(G-1790)*

Wesmac Custom Boats Inc............................ 207 667-4822
   Route 172 Surry (04684) *(G-5540)*

Wesmac Customs Bulds, Surry *Also Called: Wesmac Custom Boats Inc (G-5540)*

Wespire Inc... 617 531-8970
   50 Milk St Fl 16 Boston (02109) *(G-7117)*

West Bridgewater Fd Pantry Inc...................... 339 987-1684
   2 Spring St West Bridgewater (02379) *(G-12990)*

West End Firewood Inc............................... 508 234-4747
   496 Purgatory Rd Whitinsville (01588) *(G-13347)*

West Hartford Lock Co LLC........................... 860 236-0671
   11 Sherman St West Hartford (06110) *(G-4089)*

West Hrtford Stirs Cbinets Inc....................... 860 953-9151
   17 Main St Newington (06111) *(G-2334)*

West Roxbury Crushed Stone Div, Boston *Also Called: S M Lorusso & Sons Inc (G-7019)*

West Rxbury / Rslndale Bulltin, Hyde Park *Also Called: Bulletin Newspapers Inc (G-9458)*

West Shore LLC...................................... 860 267-1764
   70 N Main St East Hampton (06424) *(G-967)*

West Shore Metals LLC.............................. 860 749-8013
   28 W Shore Dr Enfield (06082) *(G-1158)*

West Side Metal Door Corp........................... 413 589-0945
   190 Moody St Ludlow (01056) *(G-9956)*

West Springfield Record Inc.......................... 413 736-1587
   516 Main St West Springfield (01089) *(G-13052)*

West St Intrmdate Hldings Corp **(PA)**............ **781 434-5051**
   195 West St Waltham (02451) *(G-12817)*

West Warwick Screw Pdts Co Inc..................... 401 821-4729
   21 Factory St West Warwick (02893) *(G-16925)*

West Warwick Welding Inc........................... 401 822-8200
   970 Main St West Warwick (02893) *(G-16926)*

West-Conn Tool and Die Inc.......................... 203 538-5081
   128 Long Hill Cross Rd Shelton (06484) *(G-3077)*

Westborough Books Inc **(PA)**..................... **508 366-4292**
   24 Lyman St Ste 200 Westborough (01581) *(G-13144)*

Westborough Bookseller, Westborough *Also Called: Westborough Books Inc (G-13144)*

Westbrook Con Block Co Inc.......................... 860 399-6201
   Cold Spring Brook Industrial Park Westbrook (06498) *(G-4146)*

Westbrook Manufacturing LLC........................ 860 767-2460
   1 Cheney St Ivoryton (06442) *(G-1534)*

Westchester Industries Inc........................... 203 661-0055
   485 W Putnam Ave Greenwich (06830) *(G-1360)*

Westchster Bk/Rnsford Type Inc...................... 203 791-0080
   4 Old Newtown Rd Danbury (06810) *(G-837)*

Westcon Mfg Inc..................................... 207 725-5537
   22 Bibber Pkwy Brunswick (04011) *(G-4657)*

Westcott Farm, West Warwick *Also Called: Pinga Bakery Inc (G-16920)*

Westek Architectural Wdwkg Inc...................... 413 562-6363
   97 Servistar Industrial Way Westfield (01085) *(G-13217)*

Westerbeke Corporation.............................. 508 823-7677
   41 Ledin Dr Avon Industrial Park Avon (02322) *(G-6168)*

Westerbeke Corporation **(PA)**.................... **508 977-4273**
   150 John Hancock Rd Taunton (02780) *(G-12377)*

Western Bronze Inc.................................. 413 737-1319
   54 Western Ave West Springfield (01089) *(G-13053)*

Western Maine Graphics, Lewiston *Also Called: Penmor Lithographers Inc (G-4984)*

Western Maine Timberlands Inc....................... 207 925-1138
   278 Mcneil Rd Fryeburg (04037) *(G-4811)*

Western Managment Co, Newport *Also Called: Vendome Guide (G-16227)*

Western Mass Compounding Ctr, West Springfield *Also Called: Transtulit LLC (G-13045)*

Western Mass Penny Saver........................... 413 655-9957
   55 Ashmere Rd Hinsdale (01235) *(G-9167)*

Western Mass Rendering Co Inc....................... 413 569-6265
   94 Foster Rd Southwick (01077) *(G-12049)*

Western Mass Truss, Westfield *Also Called: Nu-Truss Inc (G-13193)*

Western Progress, Bristol *Also Called: McIntire Company (G-465)*

Westfalia Inc....................................... 860 314-2920
   625 Middle St Bristol (06010) *(G-505)*

Westfall Manufacturing Co........................... 401 253-3799
   15 Broadcommon Rd Bristol (02809) *(G-15786)*

Westfield Concrete Inc.............................. 413 562-4814
   403 Paper Mill Rd Westfield (01085) *(G-13218)*

Westfield Electroplating Co **(PA)**............... **413 568-3716**
   68 N Elm St Westfield (01085) *(G-13219)*

Westfield Evening News, Westfield *Also Called: Westfield News Publishing Inc (G-13221)*

Westfield Gage Co Inc............................... 413 569-9444
   34 Hudson Dr Southwick (01077) *(G-12050)*

Westfield Grinding Wheel Co......................... 413 568-8634
   135 Apremont Way Westfield (01085) *(G-13220)*

Westfield News Publishing Inc **(DH)**............. **413 562-4181**
   64 School St Westfield (01085) *(G-13221)*

Westfield Ready-Mix Inc.. 413 594-4700
  652 Prospect St Chicopee (01020) *(G-8070)*

Westfield Tool & Die Co Inc... 413 562-2393
  55 Arnold St Westfield (01085) *(G-13222)*

Westfield Whip Mfg Co... 413 568-8244
  360 Elm St Westfield (01085) *(G-13223)*

Westgate Tire & Auto Center, Brockton *Also Called: Tire & Auto Service Centers (G-7312)*

Westinghouse Electric Co LLC... 802 254-9353
  49 Bennett Dr Brattleboro (05301) *(G-17108)*

Westminster Fire Department, Westminster *Also Called: Town of Westminster (G-13281)*

Westminster Tool Inc... 860 564-6966
  5 East Pkwy Plainfield (06374) *(G-2741)*

Westminster Tool Inc... 860 317-1039
  51 Industrial Park Rd Sterling (06377) *(G-3505)*

Westmor Industries LLC.. 207 989-0100
  42 Coffin Ave Brewer (04412) *(G-4624)*

Weston Communications, Hingham *Also Called: Weston Corporation (G-9164)*

Weston Corporation... 781 749-0936
  45 Industrial Park Rd Hingham (02043) *(G-9164)*

Weston Presidio Capital, Boston *Also Called: Weston Presidio MGT Co Inc (G-7118)*

Weston Presidio MGT Co Inc **(PA)**.............................. **617 988-2500**
  200 Clarendon St Ste 5000 Boston (02116) *(G-7118)*

Westport Precision, Stratford *Also Called: Westport Precision LLC (G-3583)*

Westport Precision LLC.. 203 378-2175
  280 Hathaway Dr Stratford (06615) *(G-3583)*

Westport Rivers Inc... 508 636-3423
  417 Hixbridge Rd Westport (02790) *(G-13300)*

Westport Rivers Vinyrd Winery, Westport *Also Called: Westport Rivers Inc (G-13300)*

Westport Summit 7 LLC.. 917 370-2244
  1365 Post Rd E Westport (06880) *(G-4201)*

Westrex International Inc... 617 254-1200
  25 Denby Rd Boston (02134) *(G-7119)*

Westrock.. 770 448-2193
  16 Washington Ave Scarborough (04074) *(G-5447)*

Westrock - Southern Cont LLC....................................... 978 772-5050
  84 State St Boston (02109) *(G-7120)*

Westrock Commercial LLC.. 203 595-3130
  1635 Coining Dr Stamford (06902) *(G-3494)*

Westrock Container LLC.. 413 733-2211
  320 Parker St Springfield (01129) *(G-12151)*

Westrock Cp LLC.. 802 933-7733
  369 Mill St Sheldon Springs (05485) *(G-17566)*

Westrock Mwv LLC... 413 736-7211
  2001 Roosevelt Ave Springfield (01104) *(G-12152)*

Westrock Rkt LLC... 413 543-7300
  320 Parker St Springfield (01129) *(G-12153)*

Westside Finishing, Holyoke *Also Called: Westside Finishing Co Inc (G-9291)*

Westside Finishing Co Inc... 413 533-4909
  15 Samosett St Holyoke (01040) *(G-9291)*

Westwell Incorporated **(DH)**....................................... **800 753-2277**
  12 Appian Dr Wellesley (02481) *(G-12948)*

Westwell Industries Inc... 401 467-2992
  26 Plymouth St Providence (02907) *(G-16646)*

Westwood Fences Inc... 802 754-8486
  5975 Vt Route 14 Irasburg (05845) *(G-17303)*

Westwood Mills Corp... 781 335-4466
  55 Sharp St Ste 6 Hingham (02043) *(G-9165)*

Westwood Products Inc... 860 379-9401
  167 Torrington Rd Winsted (06098) *(G-4358)*

Westwood Systems Inc.. 781 821-1117
  80 Hudson Rd Ste 200 Canton (02021) *(G-7840)*

Wethersfield Printing Co Inc.. 860 721-8236
  1795 Silas Deane Hwy Rocky Hill (06067) *(G-2941)*

Wexford Capital LP **(PA)**... **203 862-7000**
  777 W Putnam Ave Ste 10 Greenwich (06830) *(G-1361)*

Weyerhaeuser... 603 237-1639
  149 Main St Lancaster (03584) *(G-14681)*

Weymouth Gas LLC.. 781 826-4327
  33 Stockbridge Rd Hanover (02339) *(G-9048)*

Weymouths Garage Inc... 207 827-2069
  8 Weymouth Way Milford (04461) *(G-5063)*

Wgi Inc.. 413 569-9444
  34 Hudson Dr Southwick (01077) *(G-12051)*

Wgtech, Westbrook *Also Called: Workgroup Tech Partners Inc (G-5653)*

Wh Property Service LLC.. 802 257-8566
  287 Locust Hill Rd Guilford (05301) *(G-17282)*

WH Rose Inc... 860 228-8258
  9 Route 66 E Columbia (06237) *(G-671)*

Whale Water Systems Inc... 802 367-1091
  91 Manchester Valley Rd Bldg E Manchester (05254) *(G-17325)*

Whaling City Graphics LLC... 860 437-7446
  217 Boston Post Rd # 1 Waterford (06385) *(G-3999)*

Whalley Glass Company **(PA)**..................................... **203 735-9388**
  72 Chapel St Derby (06418) *(G-895)*

Whalley Precision Inc.. 413 569-1400
  28 Hudson Dr Southwick (01077) *(G-12052)*

Wharf Industries Printing Inc.. 603 421-2566
  3 Lexington Rd Unit 2 Windham (03087) *(G-15729)*

Wheelchair.. 207 782-8400
  192 Russell St Lewiston (04240) *(G-4996)*

Whelen Engineering Co... 860 526-9504
  99 Ceda Rd Charlestown (03603) *(G-14069)*

Whelen Engineering Company Inc.................................. 860 526-9504
  Rr 145 Chester (06412) *(G-633)*

Whelen Engineering Company Inc **(PA)**....................... **860 526-9504**
  51 Winthrop Rd Chester (06412) *(G-634)*

When Pigs Fly, York *Also Called: Wpf Liquidating Co Inc (G-5719)*

Where Inc... 617 502-3100
  1 International Pl Ste 315 Boston (02110) *(G-7121)*

Whetstone Beer, Brattleboro *Also Called: Whetstone Stn Rest Brewry LLC (G-17109)*

Whetstone Stn Rest Brewry LLC **(PA)**......................... **802 490-2354**
  36 Bridge St Brattleboro (05301) *(G-17109)*

Whetstone Workshop LLC.. 401 368-7410
  41 Dexter Rd East Providence (02914) *(G-16048)*

Whiff LLC.. 917 420-0397
  119 Jackman Ave Fairfield (06825) *(G-1206)*

Whiffle Tree Candle, Billerica *Also Called: Whiffletree Cntry Str Gift Sp (G-6490)*

Whiffletree Cntry Str Gift Sp... 978 663-6346
  101 Andover Rd Billerica (01821) *(G-6490)*

Whip City Tool & Die Corp.. 413 569-5528
  813 College Hwy Southwick (01077) *(G-12053)*

Whip-It Tire of Branford, Branford *Also Called: Derby Tire Company (G-249)*

Whipps, Athol *Also Called: Whipps Inc (G-5984)*

Whipps Inc.. 978 249-7924
  370 S Athol Rd Athol (01331) *(G-5984)*

Whisper Hills.. 802 296-7627
  5573 Woodstock Rd Quechee (05059) *(G-17464)*

Whistlekick LLC.. 802 225-6676
  2030 Jones Brook Rd Montpelier (05602) *(G-17379)*

Whistlepig LLC **(PA)**.. **802 897-7700**
  2139 Quiet Valley Rd Shoreham (05770) *(G-17568)*

Whitcraft Central Connecticut, Plainville *Also Called: Connecticut Tool & Mfg Co LLC (G-2751)*

Whitcraft LLC **(PA)**.. **860 974-0786**
  76 County Rd Eastford (06242) *(G-1093)*

Whitcraft Newburyport, Newburyport *Also Called: Berkshire Mnufactured Pdts Inc (G-10670)*

Whitcraft Scarborough, Newburyport *Also Called: Whitcraft Scrborough/Tempe LLC (G-10727)*

Whitcraft Scrborough/Tempe LLC **(HQ)**..................... **860 974-0786**
  76 County Rd Eastford (06242) *(G-1094)*

Whitcraft Scrborough/Tempe LLC................................. 763 780-0060
  116 Parker St Newburyport (01950) *(G-10727)*

Whitcraft South Windsor, South Windsor *Also Called: Whitcraft South Windsor LLC (G-3191)*

Whitcraft South Windsor LLC... 860 436-5551
  425 Sullivan Ave South Windsor (06074) *(G-3191)*

White Birch Paper Company, Greenwich *Also Called: Bear Island Paper Company LLC (G-1316)*

White Birch Paper Company, Greenwich *Also Called: Brant Industries Inc (G-1320)*

White Dog Press, Fall River *Also Called: A Bismark Company (G-8516)*

White Dog Woodworking LLC... 860 482-3776
  59 Field St Ste 140 Torrington (06790) *(G-3707)*

White Mountain Biodiesel LLC....................................... 603 444-0335
  83 Elm St Littleton (03561) *(G-14725)*

White Mountain Creamery, Chestnut Hill *Also Called: White Mountain Creamery Inc (G-8003)*

White Mountain Creamery Inc.......... 617 527-8790
19 Commonwealth Ave Chestnut Hill (02467) *(G-8003)*

White Mountain Distillery LLC.......... 603 391-1306
2072 Elm St Manchester (03104) *(G-14960)*

White Mountain Imaging.......... 603 228-2630
46 Chenell Dr Concord (03301) *(G-14166)*

White Mountain Imaging **(PA)**.......... **603 648-2124**
1617 Battle St Webster (03303) *(G-15675)*

White Mountain Intl LLC **(PA)**.......... **603 838-6694**
20 Whitcher St Lisbon (03585) *(G-14711)*

White Mountain Lumber Co Inc.......... 603 752-1000
30 E Milan Rd Berlin (03570) *(G-13987)*

White Mountain Paper Company, Gorham *Also Called: Gorham Acquisition LLC* **(G-14357)**

White Mountain Wood Grinding.......... 603 455-6931
576 Pine St Contoocook (03229) *(G-14176)*

White Publishing, West Hartford *Also Called: Life Publications* **(G-4069)**

White Rock Distilleries Inc.......... 207 783-1433
21 Saratoga St Lewiston (04240) *(G-4997)*

White Sign Division, Stillwater *Also Called: Central Equipment Company* **(G-5533)**

White Star Software LLC.......... 603 897-0396
131 Daniel Webster Hwy Pmb 440 Nashua (03060) *(G-15187)*

White Welding Company.......... 203 753-1197
44 N Elm St Waterbury (06702) *(G-3984)*

White's Logging & Chipping, Shapleigh *Also Called: Norman White Inc* **(G-5458)**

Whitegate Features Syndicate, Providence *Also Called: Whitegate International Corp* **(G-16647)**

Whitegate International Corp.......... 401 274-2149
71 Faunce Dr Providence (02906) *(G-16647)*

Whiteside Holdings Inc.......... 802 655-7654
11 Tigan St Winooski (05404) *(G-17772)*

Whiting & Davis LLC.......... 508 699-4412
33 York Ave Pawtucket (02860) *(G-16431)*

Whiting & Davis Safety, Attleboro *Also Called: W D C Holdings Inc* **(G-6073)**

Whitman Castings Inc **(PA)**.......... **781 447-4417**
40 Raynor Ave Whitman (02382) *(G-13352)*

Whitman Communications Inc.......... 603 448-2600
10 Water St Lebanon (03766) *(G-14703)*

Whitman Company Inc.......... 781 447-2422
356 South Ave Ste 1 Whitman (02382) *(G-13353)*

Whitman Controls LLC.......... 800 233-4401
201 Dolphin Rd Bristol (06010) *(G-506)*

Whitman Products Company Inc.......... 978 975-0502
93 Brookview Dr North Andover (01845) *(G-10862)*

Whitman Tool & Die Company Inc.......... 781 447-0421
72 Raynor Ave Whitman (02382) *(G-13354)*

Whitman Vault Inc.......... 781 857-3031
1200 Auburn St Whitman (02382) *(G-13355)*

Whitman's Feed Store, Newport *Also Called: Poulin Grain Inc* **(G-17404)**

Whitman's Feed Store, North Bennington *Also Called: Poulin Grain Inc* **(G-17411)**

Whitmor Company Inc **(PA)**.......... **781 284-8000**
15 Whitmore Rd Revere (02151) *(G-11625)*

Whitney & Son Inc.......... 978 343-6353
95 Kelly Ave Fitchburg (01420) *(G-8682)*

Whitney Blake Company **(PA)**.......... **800 323-0479**
20 Industrial Dr Bellows Falls (05101) *(G-17033)*

Whitney Bros Co LLC.......... 603 352-2610
93 Railroad St Keene (03431) *(G-14628)*

Whitney Learning Materials, Keene *Also Called: Whitney Bros Co LLC* **(G-14628)**

Whitney Originals.......... 207 255-5857
600 Us Route 1 Whitneyville (04654) *(G-5657)*

Whitney Pratt.......... 860 565-6431
64 Cemetery Rd Willington (06279) *(G-4227)*

Whittemore Company Inc.......... 978 681-8833
30 Glenn St Lawrence (01843) *(G-9609)*

Whittemore-Wright Company Inc.......... 617 242-1180
62 Alford St Charlestown (02129) *(G-7884)*

Whittet-Higgins Company.......... 401 728-0700
33 Higginson Ave Central Falls (02863) *(G-15802)*

Whittier Farms Inc.......... 508 865-1096
90 Douglas Rd Sutton (01590) *(G-12295)*

Whole Donut.......... 860 745-3041
920 Enfield St Ste A Enfield (06082) *(G-1159)*

Whole Earth Hat Co Inc.......... 508 672-7033
394 Kilburn St Fall River (02724) *(G-8626)*

Wholesale Bakery, Shirley *Also Called: Annies Gluten Free Bakery* **(G-11814)**

Wholesale Poster Frames, Derby *Also Called: M & B Enterprise LLC* **(G-891)**

Wholesale Printing Inc.......... 781 937-3357
2 Cedar St Ste 2 Woburn (01801) *(G-13688)*

Wholistic Pet, Bedford *Also Called: Wholistic Pet Organics LLC* **(G-13954)**

Wholistic Pet Organics LLC.......... 603 472-8300
341 Route 101 Bedford (03110) *(G-13954)*

Whoop Inc **(PA)**.......... **617 670-1074**
1 Kenmore Sq Ste 601 Boston (02215) *(G-7122)*

Whq Woodworks LLC.......... 203 756-3011
28 Main St Ste 3 Oakville (06779) *(G-2629)*

Whs Homes Inc **(PA)**.......... **603 542-5418**
61 Plains Rd Claremont (03743) *(G-14100)*

Whyco Finishing Tech LLC.......... 860 283-5826
670 Waterbury Rd Thomaston (06787) *(G-3645)*

Whyte Electric LLC.......... 781 348-6239
95 Shaw St Braintree (02184) *(G-7213)*

Wicked Local.......... 781 433-6905
15 Pacella Park Dr Randolph (02368) *(G-11579)*

Wicking Products, North Adams *Also Called: Louis A Green Corp* **(G-10810)**

Wicks Business Information LLC **(PA)**.......... **203 334-2002**
4 Research Dr Ste 402 Shelton (06484) *(G-3078)*

Wide Angle Marketing Inc.......... 978 928-5400
27d Old Colony Rd Hubbardston (01452) *(G-9349)*

Wiesner Chain, Warwick *Also Called: Wiesner Manufacturing Company* **(G-16879)**

Wiesner Manufacturing Company.......... 401 421-2406
55 Access Rd Ste 700 Warwick (02886) *(G-16879)*

Wiffle Ball Incorporated.......... 203 924-4643
275 Bridgeport Ave Shelton (06484) *(G-3079)*

Wiggin Means Precast Co Inc.......... 508 564-6776
79 Barlows Landing Rd Pocasset (02559) *(G-11493)*

Wiggin Precast Corp.......... 508 564-6776
79 Barlows Landing Rd Pocasset (02559) *(G-11494)*

Wiggly Bridge Distilleries LLC.......... 207 363-9322
441 Us Route 1 York (03909) *(G-5718)*

Wiiisdom Usa Inc.......... 617 319-3563
53 State St Ste 500 Boston (02109) *(G-7123)*

Wikoff Color Corporation.......... 603 864-6456
4 Hampshire Dr Hudson (03051) *(G-14560)*

Wilbert Swans Vault Co.......... 207 854-5324
13 Scott Dr Casco (04015) *(G-4684)*

Wilbur Technical Services LLC.......... 603 880-7100
97 S Main St Mont Vernon (03057) *(G-15050)*

Wilburs ME Choclat Confections.......... 207 865-4071
174 Lower Main St Freeport (04032) *(G-4805)*

Wilcom Inc.......... 603 524-2622
73 Daniel Webster Hwy Belmont (03220) *(G-13973)*

Wilcox Associates, North Kingstown *Also Called: Hexagon Mfg Intllgnce- Mtrlogy* **(G-16256)**

Wilcox Ice Cream, Arlington *Also Called: Vermonts Orginal Ice Cream Inc* **(G-16992)**

Wilcox Industries Corp **(PA)**.......... **603 431-1331**
25 Piscataqua Dr Newington (03801) *(G-15216)*

Wilcox Industries Corp.......... 603 431-1331
1 Wilcox Way Newington (03801) *(G-15217)*

Wild Apple, Woodstock *Also Called: Wild Apple Graphics Ltd* **(G-17780)**

Wild Apple Graphics Ltd.......... 802 457-3003
43 Lincoln Corners Way Ste 102 Woodstock (05091) *(G-17780)*

Wild Card Golf LLC.......... 860 296-1661
222 Murphy Rd Hartford (06114) *(G-1517)*

Wild Oats Bakery, Brunswick *Also Called: Natural Selection Inc* **(G-4651)**

Wild Ocean Aquaculture LLC.......... 207 458-6288
72 Commercial St # 15 Portland (04101) *(G-5289)*

Wilde Manufacturing LLC.......... 203 693-3939
5 Philip Pl North Haven (06473) *(G-2444)*

Wildlife Acoustics Inc.......... 978 369-5225
3 Mill And Main Pl Ste 210 Maynard (01754) *(G-10266)*

Wildtree Inc.......... 401 732-1856
15 Wellington Rd Lincoln (02865) *(G-16157)*

Wilevco Inc.......... 978 667-0400
10 Fortune Dr Billerica (01821) *(G-6491)*

A
L
P
H
A
B
E
T
I
C

Wilex Inc 617 492-3900
   100 Acorn Park Dr Fl 6 Cambridge (02140) *(G-7760)*

Wilkins Lumber Co Inc 603 673-2545
   495 Mont Vernon Rd Milford (03055) *(G-15043)*

Will-Mor Manufacturing LLC 603 474-8971
   153 Batchelder Rd Seabrook (03874) *(G-15606)*

Willard J Stearns & Sons Inc 860 423-9289
   50 Stearns Rd Storrs Mansfield (06268) *(G-3513)*

Willard S Hanington & Son Inc 207 456-7511
   1619 Military Rd Reed Plt (04497) *(G-5319)*

Willco Sales & Service Inc (PA) **203 366-3895**
   18 King St Stratford (06615) *(G-3584)*

Willconn Connections Inc 203 481-8080
   33 Fowler Rd North Branford (06471) *(G-2379)*

Willey Construction, Windsor *Also Called: Willey Earthmoving Corp (G-17764)*

Willey Earthmoving Corp 802 674-2500
   1335 Hunt Rd Windsor (05089) *(G-17764)*

William & Co Foods Inc 617 442-2112
   135 Newmarket Sq Boston (02118) *(G-7124)*

William A Day Jr & Sons Inc 207 625-8181
   28 Wild Turkey Ln Porter (04068) *(G-5173)*

William Arthur Inc 413 684-2600
   7 Alewive Park Rd West Kennebunk (04094) *(G-5611)*

William Blanchard Co Inc 781 245-8050
   486 Main St Wakefield (01880) *(G-12543)*

William Green Inc 413 475-2014
   18 Conway Rd Shelburne Falls (01370) *(G-11809)*

William H Moore Inc 802 496-3595
   6971 Main St Ste 1 Waitsfield (05673) *(G-17668)*

William J Hirten Co LLC 401 334-5370
   96 Frank Mossberg Dr Attleboro (02703) *(G-6076)*

William J. Hirten Co., Attleboro *Also Called: William J Hirten Co LLC (G-6076)*

William McCaskie Inc 508 636-8845
   197 Forge Rd Westport (02790) *(G-13301)*

William N Lamarre Con Pdts Inc 603 878-1340
   87 Adams Hill Rd Greenville (03048) *(G-14375)*

William-Sever Inc 617 651-2483
   61 Sever St Worcester (01609) *(G-13828)*

Williams & Co Mining Inc 802 263-5404
   248 Stoughton Pond Rd Perkinsville (05151) *(G-17443)*

Williams & Hussey Mch Co Inc 603 732-0219
   105 State Route 101a Unit 4 Amherst (03031) *(G-13895)*

Williams Lea Boston 617 371-2300
   260 Franklin St Ste 730 Boston (02110) *(G-7125)*

Williams Partners Ltd 207 633-3111
   29 Lincoln St East Boothbay (04544) *(G-4738)*

Williams Stone Co Inc 413 269-4544
   1158 Lee Westfield Rd East Otis (01029) *(G-8403)*

Williamson Corporation 978 369-9607
   70 Domino Dr Concord (01742) *(G-8141)*

Williamson Electrical Co Inc 617 884-9200
   334b Calef Hwy Epping (03042) *(G-14277)*

Williamson New England, Epping *Also Called: Williamson Electrical Co Inc (G-14277)*

Willie's Superbrew, Charlestown *Also Called: Farmer Willies Inc (G-7872)*

Willimantic Waste Paper Co Inc (HQ) **860 423-4527**
   121 Chronicle Rd Willimantic (06226) *(G-4221)*

Willimantic, CT Plant, Willimantic *Also Called: Prysmian Cbles Systems USA LLC (G-4220)*

Willimatic Instant Print, Willimantic *Also Called: Gulemo Inc (G-4218)*

Willington Companies, Stafford Springs *Also Called: Willington Nameplate Inc (G-3264)*

Willington Nameplate Inc 860 684-4281
   11 Middle River Dr Stafford Springs (06076) *(G-3264)*

Willis & Pham LLC 603 893-6029
   3 Scotts Ter Salem (03079) *(G-15572)*

Williston Pubg Promotions LLC 802 872-9000
   181 Wildflower Cir Williston (05495) *(G-17753)*

Willow Tree Poultry Farm Inc 508 222-2479
   997 S Main St Attleboro (02703) *(G-6077)*

Willseal, Hudson *Also Called: Schul International Co LLC (G-14544)*

Wilmington Compliance Week 617 570-8600
   129 Portland St Ste 600 Boston (02114) *(G-7126)*

Wilmington Compliance Week Inc 888 519-9200
   77 N Washington St Ste 201 Boston (02114) *(G-7127)*

Wilmington Partners LP 978 658-6111
   100 Research Dr Ste 2 Wilmington (01887) *(G-13476)*

Wilson Partitions Inc 203 316-8033
   120 Viaduct Rd Stamford (06907) *(G-3495)*

Wilton Pressed Metals 603 863-1488
   488 Oak St Newport (03773) *(G-15241)*

Win-Pressor LLC 207 948-4800
   336 Stagecoach Rd Unity (04988) *(G-5568)*

Winchester Industries Inc 860 379-5336
   106 John G Groppo Dr Winsted (06098) *(G-4359)*

Winchester Interconnect, Norwalk *Also Called: Winchester Interconnect Corp (G-2595)*

Winchester Interconnect, Norwalk *Also Called: Winchster Interconnect Rf Corp (G-2596)*

Winchester Interconnect, Peabody *Also Called: Winchester Interconnect Corp (G-11353)*

Winchester Interconnect CM Corporation 860 774-4812
   349 Lake Rd Dayville (06241) *(G-871)*

Winchester Interconnect Corp (DH) **203 741-5400**
   68 Water St Norwalk (06854) *(G-2595)*

Winchester Interconnect Corp 978 532-0775
   245 Lynnfield St Peabody (01960) *(G-11353)*

Winchester Interconnect Corp 978 532-0775
   245 Lynnfield St Peabody (01960) *(G-11354)*

Winchester Precision Tech Ltd 603 239-6326
   41 Hildreth St Winchester (03470) *(G-15718)*

Winchester Systems Inc (PA) **781 265-0200**
   305 Foster St Ste 100 Littleton (01460) *(G-9845)*

Winchster Interconnect Rf Corp (DH) **978 532-0775**
   68 Water St Norwalk (06854) *(G-2596)*

Wind Corporation 800 946-3267
   30 Pecks Ln Newtown (06470) *(G-2354)*

Wind Hardware, Newtown *Also Called: Wind Corporation (G-2354)*

Wind Ridge Publishing 802 985-3091
   233 Falls Rd Shelburne (05482) *(G-17565)*

Wind River Systems Inc 781 364-2200
   120 Royall St Canton (02021) *(G-7841)*

Windesco Inc 617 480-9379
   265 Franklin St Ste 1702 Boston (02110) *(G-7128)*

Windham Automated Machines Inc 860 208-5297
   1102 Windham Rd South Windham (06266) *(G-3105)*

Windham Container Corporation 860 928-7934
   30 Park Rd Putnam (06260) *(G-2879)*

Windham Foundation Inc (PA) **802 843-2211**
   225 Townshend Rd Grafton (05146) *(G-17275)*

Windham Materials LLC (PA) **860 456-4111**
   79 Boston Post Rd Willimantic (06226) *(G-4222)*

Windham Materials LLC 860 456-3277
   360 Plains Rd Willimantic (06226) *(G-4223)*

Windham Millwork Inc 207 892-3238
   4 Architectural Dr Windham (04062) *(G-5675)*

Windham Weaponry, Windham *Also Called: Windham Weaponry Inc (G-5676)*

Windham Weaponry Inc 207 893-2223
   999 Roosevelt Trl Ste 22 Windham (04062) *(G-5676)*

Windham Wood Interiors Inc 781 932-8572
   7 Marblehead Rd Windham (03087) *(G-15730)*

Windhover Information Inc (DH) **203 838-4401**
   383 Main Ave Norwalk (06851) *(G-2597)*

Windhver Rvw-Emerging Med Vent, Norwalk *Also Called: Windhover Information Inc (G-2597)*

Windle Industries Inc 508 865-5773
   94 Singletary Ave Sutton (01590) *(G-12296)*

Window Book Inc 617 395-4500
   300 Franklin St Cambridge (02139) *(G-7761)*

Windsong Farm, Tinmouth *Also Called: Larry G Carabeau (G-17648)*

Windsor Architectural Wdwkg, Malden *Also Called: Kabinet Korner Inc (G-10017)*

Windsor Locks Nonwovens Inc (DH) **860 292-5600**
   1 Hartfield Blvd Ste 101 East Windsor (06088) *(G-1090)*

Windward Power Systems Inc 774 992-0059
   379 Alden Rd Fairhaven (02719) *(G-8515)*

Windy Ridge Corporation 603 323-2323
   190 Ossipee Mountain Hwy Tamworth (03886) *(G-15650)*

Wine Emporium, The, Boston *Also Called: Tremont Street Lq Group Inc (G-7085)*

Winfield Brooks Company, Inc., Woburn *Also Called: Perrco Inc (G-13633)*

(G-0000) Company's Geographic Section entry number

Winfrey's Fudge & Candy, Rowley *Also Called: Winfreys Olde English Fdge Inc* **(G-11687)**

Winfreys Olde English Fdge Inc **(PA)**...... **978 948-7448**
40 Newburyport Tpke Ste 1 Rowley (01969) **(G-11687)**

Winged Pegasus Consulting Inc............ 978 667-0600
8 Bobby Jones Dr Andover (01810) **(G-5935)**

Wingsite Displays Inc............ 860 257-3300
1060 Silas Deane Hwy Wethersfield (06109) **(G-4215)**

Winkler Group Ltd **(PA)**............ **401 272-2885**
54 Taylor Dr Rumford (02916) **(G-16680)**

Winning Moves Inc............ 978 777-7464
75 Sylvan St Ste C104 Danvers (01923) **(G-8229)**

Winning Moves Games, Danvers *Also Called: Winning Moves Inc* **(G-8229)**

Winshuttle LLC **(HQ)**............ **425 368-2708**
1700 District Ave Ste 300 Burlington (01803) **(G-7449)**

Winslow Automatics Inc............ 860 225-6321
23 Saint Claire Ave New Britain (06051) **(G-2075)**

WINSTED JOURNAL, Lakeville *Also Called: Lakeville Journal Company LLC* **(G-1547)**

Winsted Precision Ball, Winsted *Also Called: Schaeffler Aerospace USA Corp* **(G-4354)**

Wintech Intl Corp - Nk............ 401 383-3307
36 Bellair Ave Warwick (02886) **(G-16880)**

Winter & Company Inc............ 617 773-7605
40 Oval Rd Quincy (02170) **(G-11545)**

Winter People, Cumberland Center *Also Called: Winter People Inc* **(G-4711)**

Winter People Inc............ 207 865-6636
389 Main St Cumberland Center (04021) **(G-4711)**

Winterstick Snowboards, Freeport *Also Called: Bigelow Mountain Partners LLC* **(G-4798)**

Winthrop Printing Company Inc............ 617 268-9660
124 Washington St Ste 101 Foxboro (02035) **(G-8732)**

Winthrop Tool LLC............ 860 526-9079
55 Plains Rd Essex (06426) **(G-1173)**

Wintriss Controls Group LLC............ 978 268-2700
100 Discovery Way Ste 110 Acton (01720) **(G-5768)**

Wipl-D (usa) LLC............ 860 570-0678
103 High Ridge Rd West Hartford (06117) **(G-4090)**

Wire Association Intl Inc **(PA)**............ **203 453-2777**
71 Bradley Rd Unit 9 Madison (06443) **(G-1577)**

Wire Belt Company of America **(PA)**............ **603 644-2500**
17 Colby Ct Bedford (03110) **(G-13955)**

Wire Belt Company of America, Bedford *Also Called: Wire Belt Company of America* **(G-13955)**

Wire Journal Inc............ 203 453-2777
71 Bradley Rd Unit 9 Madison (06443) **(G-1578)**

Wire Rope Div, Pomfret *Also Called: Loos & Co Inc* **(G-2809)**

Wire Techniques Ltd............ 978 372-1300
11 Chestnut St Amesbury (01913) **(G-5855)**

Wire Winders, Milford *Also Called: Wire Winders Inc* **(G-15044)**

Wire Winders Inc............ 603 673-1763
151 Mont Vernon Rd Milford (03055) **(G-15044)**

Wirecraft Products, West Brookfield *Also Called: Quirk Wire Co Inc* **(G-12998)**

Wirefab Inc............ 508 754-5359
75 Blackstone River Rd Bldg 75 Worcester (01607) **(G-13829)**

Wireless Construction Inc............ 207 642-5751
40 Blake Rd Standish (04084) **(G-5530)**

Wiremold Company............ 860 233-6251
777 Brook St Rocky Hill (06067) **(G-2942)**

Wiremold Company **(DH)**............ **860 233-6251**
60 Woodlawn St West Hartford (06110) **(G-4091)**

Wiremold Company............ 860 263-3115
21 Railroad Pl West Hartford (06110) **(G-4092)**

Wiretek Inc............ 860 242-9473
48 E Newberry Rd Bloomfield (06002) **(G-217)**

Wiscasset Newspaper, Boothbay Harbor *Also Called: Maine-OK Enterprises Inc* **(G-4602)**

Wise Business Forms Inc............ 207 774-6560
2301 Congress St Portland (04102) **(G-5290)**

Witec Instruments Corp............ 865 690-5550
300 Baker Ave Ste 150 Concord (01742) **(G-8142)**

With Weld............ 800 288-6016
11 Elkins St Ste 210 Boston (02127) **(G-7129)**

Withrow Inc............ 603 898-8868
9 Hemlock Ln Salem (03079) **(G-15573)**

Witkowsky John............ 203 483-0152
73 Branford Rd North Branford (06471) **(G-2380)**

Witricity, Watertown *Also Called: Witricity Corporation* **(G-12921)**

Witricity Corporation **(PA)**............ **617 926-2700**
57 Water St Watertown (02472) **(G-12921)**

Wittmann Usa Inc **(DH)**............ **860 496-9603**
1 Technology Park Dr Torrington (06790) **(G-3708)**

Wizards Nuts Holdings LLC **(PA)**............ **708 483-1315**
100 Northfield St Greenwich (06830) **(G-1362)**

WJ Graves Cnstr Co Inc **(PA)**............ **978 939-5568**
192 Depot Rd East Templeton (01438) **(G-8416)**

WJ Kettleworks LLC............ 203 377-5000
55 Sperry Ave Stratford (06615) **(G-3585)**

Wjb Associates Inc............ 207 293-2457
290 Belgrade Rd Mount Vernon (04352) **(G-5078)**

Wlhc Inc **(PA)**............ **207 532-6531**
37 Bangor St Houlton (04730) **(G-4906)**

Wna, Andover *Also Called: Spirit Foodservice LLC* **(G-5925)**

Wna, Chelmsford *Also Called: Waddington North America Inc* **(G-7970)**

Woburn Daily Times Inc **(PA)**............ **781 933-3700**
1 Arrow Dr Woburn (01801) **(G-13689)**

Wohrles Foods Inc **(PA)**............ **413 442-1518**
1619 East St Pittsfield (01201) **(G-11427)**

Wolf Colorprint, Newington *Also Called: Flow Resources Inc* **(G-2294)**

Wolf Organization LLC............ 508 393-2040
450 Whitney St Northborough (01532) **(G-11116)**

Wolf Worcester, Northborough *Also Called: Wolf Organization LLC* **(G-11116)**

Wollaston Alloys Inc............ 781 848-3333
205 Wood Rd Braintree (02184) **(G-7214)**

Woobo Inc............ 630 639-6326
198 River St Cambridge (02139) **(G-7762)**

Wood & Wood Inc............ 413 772-0889
19 Butternut St Greenfield (01301) **(G-9006)**

Wood & Wood Inc............ 802 496-3000
98 Carroll Rd Waitsfield (05673) **(G-17669)**

Wood & Wood Sign Systems, Waitsfield *Also Called: Wood & Wood Inc* **(G-17669)**

Wood Art Incorporated............ 508 892-8058
424 Main St Ste 1 Cherry Valley (01611) **(G-7995)**

Wood Art Exhibit Group, Cherry Valley *Also Called: Wood Art Incorporated* **(G-7995)**

Wood Geek Inc............ 508 858-5282
685 Orchard St New Bedford (02744) **(G-10660)**

Wood Grinding Unlimited............ 203 333-9047
10 Barnum Dyke Bridgeport (06604) **(G-385)**

Wood Group Pratt & Whitney............ 860 687-1686
147 Addison Rd Windsor Locks (06096) **(G-4337)**

Wood Science/Technology, Orono *Also Called: University of Maine System* **(G-5138)**

Wood Services LLC............ 203 983-5752
1 Sound Shore Dr Ste 203 Greenwich (06830) **(G-1363)**

Wood Works............ 603 436-3805
855 Islington St Ste 123 Portsmouth (03801) **(G-15450)**

Wood-Mizer Holdings Inc............ 207 645-2072
541 Borough Rd Chesterville (04938) **(G-4695)**

Woodbelly Pizza LLC **(PA)**............ **802 552-3476**
34 Lagune Rd Cabot (05647) **(G-17166)**

Woodbury Pewterers Inc............ 203 263-2668
860 Main St S Woodbury (06798) **(G-4389)**

Woodcraft Designers Bldrs LLC............ 508 584-4200
45 North St Canton (02021) **(G-7842)**

Woodcraft Millwork, Canton *Also Called: Woodcraft Designers Bldrs LLC* **(G-7842)**

Woodcrafters LLP............ 860 355-1022
118 Williams St Thomaston (06787) **(G-3646)**

Wooden Kiwi, Waltham *Also Called: Wooden Kiwi Productions LLC* **(G-12818)**

Wooden Kiwi Productions LLC............ 781 209-2623
99 Hammond St Rear Waltham (02451) **(G-12818)**

Woodenboat Publications Inc............ 207 359-4651
41 Wooden Boat Ln Brooklin (04616) **(G-4635)**

Woodex Bearing Company Inc............ 207 371-2210
216 Bay Point Rd Georgetown (04548) **(G-4815)**

Woodforms Inc............ 508 543-9417
131 Morse St Ste 10 Foxboro (02035) **(G-8733)**

Woodfree Crating Systems Inc............ 203 759-1799
150 Mattatuck Heights Rd Waterbury (06705) **(G-3985)**

Woodlab LLC.. 207 536-7542
　299 Presumpscot St Portland (04103) *(G-5291)*

Woodland Power Products Inc......................... 888 531-7253
　72 Acton St West Haven (06516) *(G-4133)*

Woodland Pulp LLC **(PA)**............................... **207 427-3311**
　144 Main St Baileyville (04694) *(G-4486)*

Woodland Studios Inc.................................... 207 667-3286
　406 State St Ellsworth (04605) *(G-4761)*

Woodman Precision Engrg Inc........................ 978 538-9544
　119 Foster St Peabody (01960) *(G-11355)*

Woodmeister Master Bldrs Inc **(PA)**............... **774 345-1000**
　1 Woodmeister Way Holden (01520) *(G-9196)*

Woods Hole Group, Bourne *Also Called: Woods Hole Group Inc (G-7143)*

Woods Hole Group Inc **(DH)**......................... **301 925-4411**
　107 Waterhouse Rd Bourne (02532) *(G-7143)*

Woodstock Soapstone Co Inc.......................... 800 866-4344
　66 Airpark Rd West Lebanon (03784) *(G-15692)*

Woodworkers Heaven Inc................................ 203 333-2778
　955 Connecticut Ave Ste 4106 Bridgeport (06607) *(G-386)*

Woodworking Thompson & Design..................... 401 369-7999
　100 Dupont Dr Ste 2 Providence (02907) *(G-16648)*

Woodworks.. 781 596-1563
　23 Mudge St Lynn (01902) *(G-9993)*

Woodworks Architectural Mllwk....................... 603 432-4050
　16 N Wentworth Ave Londonderry (03053) *(G-14791)*

Wool Advisor LLC.. 802 635-2271
　51 Lower Main St E Johnson (05656) *(G-17312)*

Wool Felt Division, Easthampton *Also Called: National Nonwovens Inc (G-8454)*

Woolworks International Ltd............................ 203 661-7076
　379 Old Long Ridge Rd Stamford (06903) *(G-3496)*

Worcester Chrome Furniture, Worcester *Also Called: Worcester Manufacturing Inc (G-13830)*

Worcester County Welding Inc......................... 508 892-4884
　112 Huntoon Memorial Hwy Rochdale (01542) *(G-11629)*

Worcester Envelope Company............................ 508 832-5394
　22 Millbury St Auburn (01501) *(G-6128)*

Worcester Manufacturing Inc........................... 508 756-0301
　35 New St Worcester (01605) *(G-13830)*

Worcester Sand and Grav Co Inc...................... 508 852-1683
　182 Holden St Shrewsbury (01545) *(G-11849)*

WORCESTER TELEGRAM & GAZETTE CORPORATION, Leominster *Also Called: Worcester Tlegram Gazette Corp (G-9717)*

Worcester Telegram Gazette Inc **(HQ)**............ **508 793-9100**
　100 Front St Fl 20 Worcester (01608) *(G-13831)*

Worcester Tlegram Gazette Corp...................... 978 840-0071
　27 Monument Sq Leominster (01453) *(G-9717)*

Worcester Tlegram Gazette Corp...................... 978 368-0176
　100 Front St Worcester (01608) *(G-13832)*

Worcester Tool & Stamping Co.......................... 508 892-8194
　11 Hankey St Rochdale (01542) *(G-11630)*

Worcester Tool & Stamping Co., Pawtucket *Also Called: Crystal Stamping LLC (G-16361)*

Wordstock Inc.. 781 646-7700
　1 Sherman Ln Bedford (01730) *(G-6277)*

Wordstream Inc... 617 963-0555
　101 Huntington Ave Fl 7 Boston (02199) *(G-7130)*

Work and Tactical Gear, Woburn *Also Called: Black Diamond Group Inc (G-13527)*

Workgroup Tech Partners Inc **(PA)**............... **207 856-5312**
　207 Larrabee Rd Westbrook (04092) *(G-5653)*

Workplace Modular Systems LLC...................... 603 622-3727
　562 Mammoth Rd Londonderry (03053) *(G-14792)*

Works Bakery Cafe, The, Amherst *Also Called: Bagel Works Inc (G-5860)*

Worksafe Traffic Ctrl Inds Inc **(PA)**............... **802 223-8948**
　115 Industrial Ln Barre (05641) *(G-17025)*

Workwise LLC... 802 881-8178
　121 S Pinnacle Ridge Rd Waterbury (05676) *(G-17679)*

World Asset Management LLC......................... 617 889-7300
　225 Franklin St Ste 2320 Boston (02110) *(G-7131)*

World Color (usa) Holding Company.................. 203 288-2468
　291 State St North Haven (06473) *(G-2445)*

World Cord Sets Inc...................................... 860 763-2100
　210 Moody Rd Enfield (06082) *(G-1160)*

World Enegry, Boston *Also Called: World Energy Rome LLC (G-7134)*

World Energy, Boston *Also Called: World Energy Biox Biofuels LLC (G-7133)*

World Energy LLC... 617 889-7300
　225 Franklin St Ste 2330 Boston (02110) *(G-7132)*

World Energy Biox Biofuels LLC **(PA)**............ **617 889-7300**
　225 Franklin St Ste 2330 Boston (02110) *(G-7133)*

World Energy Rome LLC................................ 706 291-4829
　225 Franklin St Ste 2320 Boston (02110) *(G-7134)*

World Harbors LLC.. 207 786-3200
　176 First Flight Dr Auburn (04210) *(G-4464)*

World Publications Inc................................... 802 479-2582
　403 Us Route 302 Barre (05641) *(G-17026)*

World Satellite Media, Ashfield *Also Called: Eratech Inc (G-5954)*

World Trophies, Providence *Also Called: World Trophies Company Inc (G-16649)*

World Trophies Company Inc........................... 401 272-5846
　275 Silver Spring St Providence (02904) *(G-16649)*

World Wide Distribution Corp.......................... 603 942-6032
　424 Route 125 Unit 7 Brentwood (03833) *(G-14033)*

World Wrestling Entrmt LLC **(DH)**................. **203 352-8600**
　1241 E Main St Stamford (06902) *(G-3497)*

World, The, Barre *Also Called: World Publications Inc (G-17026)*

Worldwide Fueling, Johnston *Also Called: Fueling Services LLC (G-16087)*

Worldwide Tooling LLC................................... 401 334-9806
　1 Christopher Dr Lincoln (02865) *(G-16158)*

Wormtown Atomic Propulsion.......................... 781 487-7777
　303 Bear Hill Rd Waltham (02451) *(G-12819)*

Wormtown Brewery LLC.................................. 774 215-5403
　250 Patriot Pl Foxborough (02035) *(G-8738)*

Wormtown Brewery LLC.................................. 774 239-1555
　72 Shrewsbury St Ste 4 Worcester (01604) *(G-13833)*

Worsted Spinning Neng LLC........................... 207 324-5622
　5 Water St Springvale (04083) *(G-5523)*

Worthen Industries Inc **(HQ)**........................ **603 888-5443**
　3 E Spit Brook Rd Nashua (03060) *(G-15188)*

Worthen Industries Inc................................... 603 886-0973
　34 Cellu Dr Nashua (03063) *(G-15189)*

Worthen Industries Inc................................... 978 365-6345
　3 E Spit Brook Rd Nashua (03060) *(G-15190)*

Worthington Assembly Inc.............................. 413 397-8265
　14 Industrial Dr E Unit 2 South Deerfield (01373) *(G-11330)*

Wotton Enterprises Inc.................................. 855 383-7678
　21 Main St Ste 1 Sturbridge (01566) *(G-12259)*

Wpcs International- Hartford Inc **(HQ)**　427 Hayden Station Rd Ste B Windsor (06095) *(G-4315)*

Wpf Liquidating Co Inc **(PA)**........................ **207 363-0612**
　40 Brickyard Ct York (03909) *(G-5719)*

Wpi-Sarasota Division, Chelsea *Also Called: Cooper Crouse-Hinds LLC (G-7979)*

Wrabacon Inc.. 207 465-2068
　150 Old Waterville Rd Oakland (04963) *(G-5122)*

Wrapsol LLC
　55 North St Ste 1 Canton (02021) *(G-7843)*

Wrentham Quarry Div, Walpole *Also Called: S M Lorusso & Sons Inc (G-12575)*

Wrentham Tool Group LLC.............................. 508 966-2332
　155 Farm St Bellingham (02019) *(G-6303)*

Wright Archtectural Mllwk Corp....................... 413 586-3528
　115 Industrial Dr Northampton (01060) *(G-11087)*

Wright Electric Motors, Bedford *Also Called: Chase Electric Motors LLC (G-13921)*

Wright Line LLC **(HQ)**.................................. **508 852-4300**
　160 Gold Star Blvd Worcester (01606) *(G-13834)*

Wright Scoop, The, North Smithfield *Also Called: Wrights Dairy Farm Inc (G-16334)*

Wright Trailers Inc.. 508 336-8530
　1825 Fall River Ave Seekonk (02771) *(G-11790)*

Wrights Dairy Farm Inc.................................. 401 767-3014
　200 Woonsocket Hill Rd North Smithfield (02896) *(G-16334)*

Wrobel Engineering Co Inc............................. 508 586-8338
　154 Bodwell St Avon (02322) *(G-6169)*

Wrought Iron Works LLC................................. 860 523-4457
　600 Oakwood Ave West Hartford (06110) *(G-4093)*

WS Anderson Associates Inc........................... 508 832-5550
　303 Washington St # 313 Auburn (01501) *(G-6129)*

WS Badger Company Inc................................. 603 357-2958
　768 Route 10 Gilsum (03448) *(G-14344)*

Ws Dennison Cabinets Inc.......................... 603 224-8434
779 Silver Hills Dr Pembroke (03275) *(G-15309)*

WSbadger Company Inc.............................. 603 357-2958
768 Route 10 Gilsum (03448) *(G-14345)*

Wsmd Inc.. 413 589-0945
190 Moody St Ludlow (01056) *(G-9957)*

Wte Recycling Inc.................................. 413 772-2200
75 Southern Ave Greenfield (01301) *(G-9007)*

Wti Systems, Pembroke *Also Called: Datanational Corporation (G-11361)*

Www.cwt-Usa.com, Rockland *Also Called: Clearwter Tech Cnslting Wtr Sv (G-11640)*

Www.naplasticsltd.com, Manchester *Also Called: North American Plastics Ltd (G-14902)*

Www.sand9.com, Cambridge *Also Called: Sand 9 Inc (G-7702)*

Wyebot Inc.. 508 481-2603
2 Mount Royal Ave Ste 310 Marlborough (01752) *(G-10236)*

Wyeth Biopharma Division, Andover *Also Called: Wyeth Pharmaceuticals LLC (G-5936)*

Wyeth Pharmaceuticals LLC.......................... 978 475-9214
1 Burtt Rd Andover (01810) *(G-5936)*

Wyman-Gordon Company............................... 800 343-6070
1537 Grafton Rd Millbury (01527) *(G-10446)*

Wyman-Gordon Company **(DH)**...................... **508 839-8252**
244 Worcester St North Grafton (01536) *(G-11030)*

Wyman-Gordon Company............................... 508 839-8253
80 Hermon St Worcester (01610) *(G-13835)*

Wyman-Gordon Company............................... 603 934-6630
35 Industrial Park Dr Franklin (03235) *(G-14325)*

Wyz Machine Co Inc................................. 413 786-6816
95 Industrial Ln Agawam (01001) *(G-5816)*

X Cafe, Portland *Also Called: Kerry Inc (G-5231)*

X Press In Stowe Inc............................... 802 253-9788
73 Pond St Stowe (05672) *(G-17633)*

X-4 Tool Div, North Billerica *Also Called: Gear/Tronics Industries Inc (G-10915)*

X4, Boston *Also Called: X4 Pharmaceuticals Inc (G-7135)*

X4 Pharmaceuticals Inc **(PA)**.................... **857 529-8300**
61 North Beacon St Fl 4 Boston (02134) *(G-7135)*

Xact Robotics Inc.................................. 781 252-9143
75 Sgt William B Terry Dr Ste 200 Hingham (02043) *(G-9166)*

Xactly, Lowell *Also Called: Centive Inc (G-9866)*

Xagd Inc.. 802 989-7359
88 Mainelli Rd Ste 1 Middlebury (05753) *(G-17351)*

Xam Online Inc **(PA)**............................ **781 662-9268**
25 1st St Cambridge (02141) *(G-7763)*

Xamax, Seymour *Also Called: Xamax Industries Inc (G-2976)*

Xamax Industries Inc............................... 203 888-7200
63 Silvermine Rd Seymour (06483) *(G-2976)*

Xander Performance, Albion *Also Called: Unique Spiral Stairs Inc (G-4401)*

Xcaliber, Brookfield *Also Called: Defeo Manufacturing Inc (G-517)*

Xcellerex Inc....................................... 508 480-9235
170 Locke Dr Marlborough (01752) *(G-10237)*

Xcerra, Norwood *Also Called: Xcerra Corporation (G-11220)*

Xcerra Corporation **(HQ)**........................ **781 461-1000**
825 University Ave Norwood (02062) *(G-11220)*

Xchange Imc LLC.................................... 978 298-2100
7 Mill And Main Pl Ste 250 Maynard (01754) *(G-10267)*

Xemplar Pharmaceuticals, Fall River *Also Called: Exemplar Laboratories LLC (G-8543)*

Xenith.. 978 328-5297
672 Suffolk St Lowell (01854) *(G-9936)*

Xenocs Inc.. 413 587-4000
4 Open Square Way Ste L101 Holyoke (01040) *(G-9292)*

Xenogen Corporation **(DH)**...................... **508 435-9500**
68 Elm St Hopkinton (01748) *(G-9347)*

Xenon, Wilmington *Also Called: Xenon Corporation (G-13477)*

Xenon Corporation **(PA)**........................ **978 661-9033**
37 Upton Dr Wilmington (01887) *(G-13477)*

Xenotherapeutics LLC............................... 617 750-1907
21 Drydock Ave Ste 610e Boston (02210) *(G-7136)*

Xerox, Norwalk *Also Called: Xerox Corporation (G-2598)*

Xerox, Norwalk *Also Called: Xerox Holdings Corporation (G-2600)*

Xerox Corporation **(HQ)**........................ **203 849-5216**
201 Merritt 7 Norwalk (06851) *(G-2598)*

Xerox Holdings Inc................................. 203 968-3000
201 Merritt 7 Norwalk (06851) *(G-2599)*

Xerox Holdings Corporation **(PA)**............... **203 849-5216**
201 Merritt 7 Norwalk (06851) *(G-2600)*

Xg Industries LLC.................................. 475 282-4643
53 Hancock St Stratford (06615) *(G-3586)*

Xilectric, Fall River *Also Called: Xilectric Inc (G-8627)*

Xilectric Inc....................................... 781 247-4567
151 Martine St Ste 125-1 Fall River (02723) *(G-8627)*

Xilinx Inc.. 603 891-1096
10 Tara Blvd Ste 410 Nashua (03062) *(G-15191)*

XILIO THERAPEUTICS, Waltham *Also Called: Xilio Therapeutics Inc (G-12820)*

Xilio Therapeutics Inc............................. 617 430-4680
828 Winter St Ste 300 Waltham (02451) *(G-12820)*

Xiphos Partners Inc................................ 508 991-1014
419 Elm St Dartmouth (02748) *(G-8233)*

Xl Fleet, Brighton *Also Called: Xl Hybrids Inc (G-7247)*

Xl Hybrids Inc **(HQ)**........................... **617 718-0329**
145 Newton St Brighton (02135) *(G-7247)*

Xl Technology Systems Inc.......................... 781 982-1220
401 Vfw Dr Rockland (02370) *(G-11665)*

Xma Corporation.................................... 603 222-2256
7 Perimeter Rd Ste 2 Manchester (03103) *(G-14961)*

Xor Media Inc....................................... 603 878-6400
32 Mill St Greenville (03048) *(G-14376)*

Xos Digital, Boston *Also Called: Catapult Sports Inc (G-6642)*

Xosoft Inc.. 800 225-5224
100 Staples Dr Framingham (01702) *(G-8812)*

Xp Comdel, Gloucester *Also Called: Xp Power LLC (G-8965)*

Xp Power LLC.. 978 282-0620
11 Kondelin Rd Gloucester (01930) *(G-8965)*

Xp Power LLC.. 603 894-4420
45 Northwestern Dr Salem (03079) *(G-15574)*

Xphotonics LLC...................................... 978 952-2568
32 Surrey Rd Littleton (01460) *(G-9846)*

Xponent Global Inc................................. 978 562-3485
30 Tower St Hudson (01749) *(G-9426)*

Xpression Prints Inc............................... 401 413-6930
31 Hayward St Ste B2 Franklin (02038) *(G-8876)*

Xray Aerospace Corp................................ 603 254-8051
75 Winter St Claremont (03743) *(G-14101)*

Xstrata Recycling Inc.............................. 401 438-9220
80 Commercial Way East Providence (02914) *(G-16049)*

Xtalic Corporation................................. 508 485-9730
260 Cedar Hill St Ste 4 Marlborough (01752) *(G-10238)*

Xtelligent Healthcare Media, Danvers *Also Called: Dixie Media LLC (G-8183)*

Xthera Corporation................................. 508 528-3100
31 Hayward St Ste B1 Franklin (02038) *(G-8877)*

Xtralis Inc... 800 229-4434
175 Bodwell St Northford (06472) *(G-2457)*

Xtreme Designs LLC................................. 203 773-9303
330 Main St East Haven (06512) *(G-1057)*

Xtreme Screen & Sportswear LLC..................... 207 857-9200
937 Main St Westbrook (04092) *(G-5654)*

Xtreme Tub Grinding Svcs Inc....................... 508 386-6015
2450 Chestnut St North Dighton (02764) *(G-11005)*

Xuron Corp.. 207 283-1401
62 Industrial Park Rd Saco (04072) *(G-5382)*

Xxpress Auto Repair Shop LLC....................... 800 591-2068
1318 River St Hyde Park (02136) *(G-9468)*

Xybol Interlynks Inc............................... 978 356-0750
89 Turnpike Rd Ste 204 Ipswich (01938) *(G-9500)*

Xyenterprise Henrico Co, Wakefield *Also Called: Sdl Xyenterprise LLC (G-12533)*

Xylem Water Solutions USA Inc...................... 203 450-3715
1000 Bridgeport Ave Ste 402 Shelton (06484) *(G-3080)*

Xylem Water Solutions USA Inc...................... 781 935-6515
78 Olympia Ave Woburn (01801) *(G-13690)*

XYZ Sheet Metal Inc................................ 781 878-1419
281 Washington St Abington (02351) *(G-5729)*

Y & Z Bristol Inc.................................. 508 991-7365
963 Kempton St New Bedford (02740) *(G-10661)*

**A
L
P
H
A
B
E
T
I
C**

Y'S Enterprises, East Ryegate *Also Called: YS Enterprises Inc (G-17219)*

Yale Alumni Publications Inc................................203 432-0645
149 York St Fl 2 New Haven (06511) *(G-2216)*

Yale Commercial Locks & Hdwr, Berlin *Also Called: Assa Abloy ACC Door Cntrls Gro (G-50)*

Yale Cordage Inc..207 282-3396
77 Industrial Park Rd Saco (04072) *(G-5383)*

Yale New Haven Hlth Svcs Corp.........................203 688-2100
150 Sargent Dr Ste 1 New Haven (06511) *(G-2217)*

Yale University...203 764-4333
135 College St Ste 200 New Haven (06510) *(G-2218)*

Yale University **(PA)**...............................**203 432-2550**
105 Wall St New Haven (06511) *(G-2219)*

Yale University...203 737-1244
333 Cedar St le90shm New Haven (06510) *(G-2220)*

Yale University...203 432-2880
149 York St New Haven (06511) *(G-2221)*

Yamaha Unfied Cmmnications Inc.......................978 610-4040
144 North Rd Ste 1100 Sudbury (01776) *(G-12272)*

Yankee Aluminum, Hamden *Also Called: Stent Metal Corp (G-1457)*

Yankee Barn Home, Grantham *Also Called: Topek LLC (G-14363)*

Yankee Barn Homes Inc.................................603 863-4545
61 Plains Rd Claremont (03743) *(G-14102)*

Yankee Builders..508 636-8660
1227 Russells Mills Rd Dartmouth (02748) *(G-8234)*

Yankee Builders & Woodworking, Dartmouth *Also Called: Yankee Builders (G-8234)*

Yankee Candle, South Deerfield *Also Called: Yankee Candle Company Inc (G-11931)*

Yankee Candle Company Inc **(DH)**...................**413 665-8306**
16 Yankee Candle Way South Deerfield (01373) *(G-11931)*

Yankee Candle Company Inc............................413 665-8306
102 Christian Ln Whately (01093) *(G-13340)*

Yankee Candle Investments LLC **(DH)**..............**413 665-8306**
16 Yankee Candle Way South Deerfield (01373) *(G-11932)*

Yankee Casting Co Inc..................................860 749-6171
243 Shaker Rd Enfield (06082) *(G-1161)*

Yankee Corporation.....................................802 527-0177
125 Yankee Park Rd Fairfax (05454) *(G-17265)*

Yankee Custom Inc **(PA)**............................**978 851-9024**
1271 Main St Tewksbury (01876) *(G-12426)*

Yankee Electrical Mfg Co...............................413 596-8256
600 Main St Wilbraham (01095) *(G-13364)*

Yankee Hill Machine Co Inc.............................413 584-1400
412 Main St Easthampton (01027) *(G-8464)*

Yankee Holding Corp **(DH)**..........................**413 665-8306**
16 Yankee Candle Way South Deerfield (01373) *(G-11933)*

Yankee Machine Inc....................................207 627-4277
1300 Poland Springs Rd Rte 11 Casco (04015) *(G-4685)*

Yankee Magazine, Dublin *Also Called: Yankee Publishing Incorporated (G-14262)*

Yankee Marina Inc.....................................207 846-9120
142 Lafayette St Yarmouth (04096) *(G-5710)*

Yankee Marina and Billliards, Yarmouth *Also Called: Yankee Marina Inc (G-5710)*

Yankee Medical Inc **(DH)**...........................**802 863-4591**
276 North Ave Burlington (05401) *(G-17164)*

Yankee Photo Service, Bridgeport *Also Called: Yankee Plak Co Inc (G-387)*

Yankee Plak Co Inc....................................203 333-3168
240 Alice St Bridgeport (06606) *(G-387)*

Yankee Pride Fisheries Inc.............................401 783-9647
81 Point Ave Wakefield (02879) *(G-16747)*

Yankee Printing Group Inc.............................413 532-9513
630 New Ludlow Rd South Hadley (01075) *(G-11968)*

Yankee Publishing Incorporated **(PA)**...............**603 563-8111**
1121 Main St Dublin (03444) *(G-14262)*

Yankee Shopper.......................................508 943-8784
168 Gore Rd Webster (01570) *(G-12931)*

Yankee Toy Box, Milford *Also Called: Thanksben10 LLC (G-15040)*

Yankee Trader Seafood Ltd.............................781 829-4350
1610 Corporate Park Pembroke (02359) *(G-11379)*

Yard Stick Decore.....................................203 330-0360
145 Hart St Bridgeport (06606) *(G-388)*

Yarde Metals Inc **(HQ)**............................**860 406-6061**
45 Newell St Southington (06489) *(G-3241)*

Yardney Technical Products Inc.........................401 471-6580
2000 S County Trl East Greenwich (02818) *(G-15998)*

Yarn Outlet , The, Pawtucket *Also Called: Providence Yarn Company Inc (G-16407)*

Yarra Design & Fabrication LLC.........................603 224-6880
1 Tallwood Dr Bow (03304) *(G-14014)*

Yaskawa - Solectria Solar, Lawrence *Also Called: Solectria Renewables LLC (G-9599)*

Yates Lumber Inc......................................207 738-2331
137 Winn Rd Lee (04455) *(G-4947)*

Ycc Holdings LLC.....................................413 665-8306
16 Yankee Candle Way South Deerfield (01373) *(G-11934)*

Yellow Sign Commercial Inc............................802 324-8500
18 Dover St South Burlington (05403) *(G-17608)*

Yellowfin Holdings Inc................................866 341-0979
160 West Rd Ellington (06029) *(G-1119)*

Yeuell Name Plate & Label, Woburn *Also Called: E V Yeuell Inc (G-13560)*

Yield10 Bioscience Inc **(PA)**.......................**617 583-1700**
19 Presidential Way Woburn (01801) *(G-13691)*

Yieldx Inc..646 328-9803
1 Marina Park Dr Boston (02210) *(G-7137)*

Ymc America Inc......................................978 487-1130
8 Charlestown St Devens (01434) *(G-8290)*

Ymc Process Technologies, Inc., Devens *Also Called: Ymc America Inc (G-8290)*

Yoc..207 363-9322
21 Railroad Ave York (03909) *(G-5720)*

Yocrunch, Naugatuck *Also Called: The Yofarm Company (G-1990)*

Yokogawa Fluid Imging Tech Inc.......................207 289-3200
200 Enterprise Dr Scarborough (04074) *(G-5448)*

Yokohama Tws North America Inc......................781 914-3410
107 Audubon Rd Ste 205 Wakefield (01880) *(G-12544)*

Yolanda Dubose Records and..........................203 823-6699
105 W Prospect St West Haven (06516) *(G-4134)*

York Athletics Mfg Inc................................617 777-3125
535 Albany St Ste 200 Boston (02118) *(G-7138)*

York County Coast Star Inc............................207 985-5901
39 Main St Kennebunk (04043) *(G-4931)*

York Harbor Brewing Company.........................207 703-8060
8 Blueberry Ln Kittery (03904) *(G-4941)*

York Hill Trap Rock Quarry Co..........................203 237-8421
975 Westfield Rd Meriden (06450) *(G-1712)*

York International Corporation..........................203 730-8100
86 Payne Rd Danbury (06810) *(G-838)*

York Manufacturing Inc................................207 324-1300
43 Community Dr Sanford (04073) *(G-5418)*

York Woods Tree and Products, Eliot *Also Called: York Woods Tree Service LLC (G-4752)*

York Woods Tree Service LLC..........................207 703-0150
300 Harold L Dow Hwy Eliot (03903) *(G-4752)*

York-Cmbrland Assn For Hndcppe **(PA)**..............**207 879-1140**
619 Brighton Ave Portland (04102) *(G-5292)*

Yosi Kosher Catering LLC..............................860 688-6677
598 Hayden Station Rd Windsor (06095) *(G-4316)*

Yost Manufacturing & Sup Inc..........................800 872-9678
1018 Hartford Tpke Waterford (06385) *(G-4000)*

Young Furniture Mfg Inc...............................603 224-8830
161 River Rd Bow (03304) *(G-14015)*

Young Writers Project Inc..............................802 324-9537
47 Maple St Ste 216 Burlington (05401) *(G-17165)*

Youngs Communications Inc...........................860 347-8569
182 Court St Middletown (06457) *(G-1791)*

Your Oil Tools LLC....................................701 645-8665
652 Hackett Hill Rd Manchester (03102) *(G-14962)*

Yoway LLC..617 505-5158
1376 Beacon St Brookline (02446) *(G-7327)*

YS Enterprises Inc....................................802 238-0902
201 Eastwood Ln East Ryegate (05042) *(G-17219)*

YSNC Fuel Inc...508 436-2716
64 N Montello St Brockton (02301) *(G-7314)*

Yumble, Foxboro *Also Called: Panda Plates Inc (G-8714)*

Yumble Kids, Foxboro *Also Called: Panda Plates Inc (G-8713)*

Yushin America Inc **(HQ)**...........................**401 463-1800**
35 Kenney Dr Cranston (02920) *(G-15930)*

Yxlon...234 284-7862
100 Trap Falls Road Ext Shelton (06484) *(G-3081)*

Yxlon International, Shelton *Also Called: Comet Technologies USA Inc* **(G-2993)**

Z M Weapons High Performance.................................. 802 777-8964
  1958 Wes White Hl Richmond (05477) **(G-17482)**

Z Magazine, Norwood *Also Called: Institute For Scial Cltral Cmm* **(G-11183)**

Z Thunderline Inc.. 603 329-4050
  11 Hazel Dr Hampstead (03841) **(G-14395)**

Z-Flex (us) Inc.. 603 669-5136
  20 Commerce Park North Bedford (03110) **(G-13956)**

Z-Flex Realty Inc **(DH)**...................................... 603 669-5136
  20 Commerce Park North Ste 107 Bedford (03110) **(G-13957)**

Z-Medica LLC.. 203 294-0000
  4 Fairfield Blvd Ste 1 Wallingford (06492) **(G-3876)**

Z-Tech LLC.. 603 228-1305
  56 Dow Rd Bow (03304) **(G-14016)**

Zackin Publications Inc.. 203 262-4670
  100 Willenbrock Rd Oxford (06478) **(G-2715)**

Zag Machine & Tool Co, New Britain *Also Called: Adam Z Golas* **(G-1996)**

Zajac LLC.. 207 286-9100
  92 Industrial Park Rd Saco (04072) **(G-5384)**

Zampell, Newburyport *Also Called: Zampell Refractories Inc* **(G-10728)**

Zampell Refractories Inc.. 207 786-2400
  192 First Flight Dr Auburn (04210) **(G-4465)**

Zampell Refractories Inc **(PA)**.............................. 978 465-0055
  9 Stanley Tucker Dr Newburyport (01950) **(G-10728)**

Zappix Inc... 781 214-8124
  25 Mall Rd Burlington (01803) **(G-7450)**

Zar Tech... 978 499-5122
  5 Stanley Tucker Dr Newburyport (01950) **(G-10729)**

Zatec LLC... 508 880-3388
  620 Spring St North Dighton (02764) **(G-11006)**

Zatorski Coating Co Inc.. 860 267-9889
  77 Wopowog Rd East Hampton (06424) **(G-968)**

Zavarella Woodworking Inc..................................... 860 666-6969
  48 Commerce Ct Newington (06111) **(G-2335)**

Zax Signage, Greenland *Also Called: Plw Inc* **(G-14370)**

Zd USA Holdings Inc... 508 998-4000
  744 Belleville Ave New Bedford (02745) **(G-10662)**

Zea Biosciences Corp.. 508 921-3280
  85 West St Ste 3 Walpole (02081) **(G-12579)**

Zeevee Inc **(PA)**.. 978 467-1395
  295 Foster St Ste 200 Littleton (01460) **(G-9847)**

Zen Art & Design Inc... 800 215-6010
  119 Rocky Hill Rd Hadley (01035) **(G-9019)**

Zenna Noodle Bar.. 781 883-8624
  1374 Beacon St Brookline (02446) **(G-7328)**

Zephyr Designs Ltd.. 802 254-2788
  129 Main St Brattleboro (05301) **(G-17110)**

Zephyr Lock LLC... 866 937-4971
  30 Pecks Ln Newtown (06470) **(G-2355)**

Zero Check, Thomaston *Also Called: Zero Check LLC* **(G-3647)**

Zero Check LLC.. 860 283-5629
  297 Reynolds Bridge Rd Thomaston (06787) **(G-3647)**

Zero Porosity Casting Inc...................................... 617 391-0008
  411 Waverley Oaks Rd Waltham (02452) **(G-12821)**

ZF Active Safety & Elec US LLC................................ 978 874-0151
  180 State Rd E Westminster (01473) **(G-13283)**

ZF Chassis Components LLC................................... 859 334-3834
  Boston (02212) **(G-7139)**

Zhongding Laconia Inc... 603 524-3367
  210 Fair St Laconia (03246) **(G-14674)**

Zibra Corporation.. 508 636-6606
  640 American Legion Hwy Westport (02790) **(G-13302)**

Zikani Therapeutics Inc.. 617 453-9091
  480 Arsenal Way Ste 130 Watertown (02472) **(G-12922)**

Zim Sailing, Bristol *Also Called: Gecko Marine Inc* **(G-15766)**

Zimmer & Rohde Ltd **(DH)**.................................. 203 327-1400
  30 Buxton Farm Rd Ste 110 Stamford (06905) **(G-3498)**

Zink Imaging Inc.. 781 761-5400
  37 Manning Rd Billerica (01821) **(G-6492)**

Ziprint Centers Inc... 781 963-2250
  217 N Main St Randolph (02368) **(G-11580)**

Zlink Inc... 978 309-3628
  141 Parker St Ste 311 Maynard (01754) **(G-10268)**

Zmetra Clarspan Structures LLC............................... 508 943-0940
  2 Old Worcester Rd Webster (01570) **(G-12932)**

Znlabs LLC **(HQ)**... 781 897-6966
  20 Cabot Rd Woburn (01801) **(G-13692)**

Zoll, Chelmsford *Also Called: Zoll Medical Corporation* **(G-7972)**

Zoll Medical Corporation....................................... 781 229-0020
  32 2nd Ave Burlington (01803) **(G-7451)**

Zoll Medical Corporation....................................... 978 421-9132
  11 Alpha Rd Chelmsford (01824) **(G-7971)**

Zoll Medical Corporation **(HQ)**............................. 978 421-9655
  269 Mill Rd Chelmsford (01824) **(G-7972)**

Zoll Medical Corporation....................................... 401 729-1400
  525 Narragansett Park Dr Pawtucket (02861) **(G-16432)**

Zoll Medical Corporation....................................... 401 729-1400
  201 Narragansett Park Dr Rumford (02916) **(G-16681)**

Zoom Information LLC **(DH)**................................. 781 693-7500
  275 Wyman St Ste 120 Waltham (02451) **(G-12822)**

Zootility Co.. 207 536-0639
  2301 Congress St Ste 3 Portland (04102) **(G-5293)**

Zoppa Studio, South Windsor *Also Called: Michael Zoppa* **(G-3165)**

Zoran Corporation.. 408 523-6500
  1 Wall St Ste 10 Burlington (01803) **(G-7452)**

Zorean Inc... 978 250-9144
  10 Elizabeth Dr Ste 3 Chelmsford (01824) **(G-7973)**

Zorvino Vineyards.. 603 887-8463
  226 Main St Sandown (03873) **(G-15581)**

Zoulamis Fine Woodworking.................................... 207 449-1680
  521 Water St Gardiner (04345) **(G-4813)**

Zrc Worldwide, Marshfield *Also Called: Norfolk Corporation* **(G-10242)**

Zschimmer Schwarz Intrplymer I **(DH)**...................... 781 828-7120
  200 Dan Rd Canton (02021) **(G-7844)**

Zurich Instruments Usa Inc..................................... 949 682-5172
  400 5th Ave Waltham (02451) **(G-12823)**

Zuse Inc... 203 458-3295
  54 E Industrial Rd Branford (06405) **(G-287)**

Zwitterco, Woburn *Also Called: Zwitterco Inc* **(G-13693)**

Zwitterco Inc.. 301 442-5662
  12 Cabot Rd Ste B Woburn (01801) **(G-13693)**

Zycal Bioceuticals Mfg LLC.................................... 888 779-9225
  3 Turning Leaf Cir Shrewsbury (01545) **(G-11850)**

Zygo, Middlefield *Also Called: Zygo Corporation* **(G-1732)**

Zygo Corporation **(HQ)**..................................... 860 347-8506
  21 Laurel Brook Rd Middlefield (06455) **(G-1732)**

Zylotech.. 845 802-3188
  101 Main St Fl 14 Cambridge (02142) **(G-7764)**

Zyno Medical LLC.. 508 650-2008
  177 Pine St Natick (01760) **(G-10501)**

A L P H A B E T I C

(PA)=Parent Co (HQ)=Headquarters (DH)=Div Headquarters
        2024 Harris New England
        Manufacturers Directory
                            1313

PRODUCT INDEX

• Product categories are listed in alphabetical order.

A

ABRASIVES
ABRASIVES: Coated
ACCELERATION INDICATORS & SYSTEM COMPONENTS: Aerospace
ACCELERATORS, RUBBER PROCESSING: Cyclic or Acyclic
ACCELEROMETERS
ACIDS: Inorganic
ACIDS: Sulfuric, Oleum
ACOUSTICAL BOARD & TILE
ACRYLIC RESINS
ACTUATORS: Indl, NEC
ADDITIVE BASED PLASTIC MATERIALS: Plasticizers
ADHESIVES
ADHESIVES & SEALANTS
ADHESIVES: Adhesives, plastic
ADHESIVES: Epoxy
ADVERTISING AGENCIES
ADVERTISING AGENCIES: Consultants
ADVERTISING CURTAINS
ADVERTISING DISPLAY PRDTS
ADVERTISING MATERIAL DISTRIBUTION
ADVERTISING REPRESENTATIVES: Electronic Media
ADVERTISING REPRESENTATIVES: Newspaper
ADVERTISING REPRESENTATIVES: Printed Media
ADVERTISING SPECIALTIES, WHOLESALE
ADVERTISING SVCS: Direct Mail
ADVERTISING SVCS: Display
ADVERTISING SVCS: Outdoor
ADVERTISING SVCS: Transit
AERIAL WORK PLATFORMS
AEROSOLS
AGENTS, BROKERS & BUREAUS: Personal Service
AGRICULTURAL EQPT: BARN, SILO, POULTRY, DAIRY/ LIVESTOCK MACH
AGRICULTURAL EQPT: Grade, Clean & Sort Machines, Fruit/ Veg
AGRICULTURAL EQPT: Harvesters, Fruit, Vegetable, Tobacco
AGRICULTURAL MACHINERY & EQPT: Wholesalers
AIR CLEANING SYSTEMS
AIR CONDITIONING & VENTILATION EQPT & SPLYS: Wholesales
AIR CONDITIONING EQPT
AIR CONDITIONING EQPT, WHOLE HOUSE: Wholesalers
AIR CONDITIONING REPAIR SVCS
AIR CONDITIONING UNITS: Complete, Domestic Or Indl
AIR COOLERS: Metal Plate
AIR MATTRESSES: Plastic
AIR POLLUTION MEASURING SVCS
AIR PURIFICATION EQPT
AIRCRAFT & AEROSPACE FLIGHT INSTRUMENTS & GUIDANCE SYSTEMS
AIRCRAFT & HEAVY EQPT REPAIR SVCS
AIRCRAFT ASSEMBLY PLANTS
AIRCRAFT CONTROL SYSTEMS:
AIRCRAFT DEALERS
AIRCRAFT ELECTRICAL EQPT REPAIR SVCS
AIRCRAFT ENGINES & ENGINE PARTS: Airfoils
AIRCRAFT ENGINES & ENGINE PARTS: Mount Parts
AIRCRAFT ENGINES & ENGINE PARTS: Pumps
AIRCRAFT ENGINES & ENGINE PARTS: Research & Development, Mfr
AIRCRAFT ENGINES & PARTS
AIRCRAFT LIGHTING
AIRCRAFT MAINTENANCE & REPAIR SVCS
AIRCRAFT PARTS & AUX EQPT: Panel Assy/Hydro Prop Test Stands
AIRCRAFT PARTS & AUXILIARY EQPT: Assys, Subassemblies/Parts
AIRCRAFT PARTS & AUXILIARY EQPT: Blades, Prop, Metal Or Wood
AIRCRAFT PARTS & AUXILIARY EQPT: Body & Wing Assys & Parts
AIRCRAFT PARTS & AUXILIARY EQPT: Body Assemblies & Parts
AIRCRAFT PARTS & AUXILIARY EQPT: Deicing Eqpt

AIRCRAFT PARTS & AUXILIARY EQPT: Gears, Power Transmission
AIRCRAFT PARTS & AUXILIARY EQPT: Lighting/Landing Gear Assy
AIRCRAFT PARTS & AUXILIARY EQPT: Military Eqpt & Armament
AIRCRAFT PARTS & EQPT, NEC
AIRCRAFT PARTS WHOLESALERS
AIRCRAFT PROPELLERS & PARTS
AIRCRAFT SEATS
AIRCRAFT SERVICING & REPAIRING
AIRCRAFT TURBINES
AIRCRAFT: Airplanes, Fixed Or Rotary Wing
AIRCRAFT: Motorized
AIRCRAFT: Research & Development, Manufacturer
AIRFRAME ASSEMBLIES: Guided Missiles
AIRLINE TRAINING
ALARMS: Burglar
ALARMS: Fire
ALCOHOL, GRAIN: For Beverage Purposes
ALCOHOL: Ethyl & Ethanol
ALKALIES & CHLORINE
ALLOYS: Additive, Exc Copper Or Made In Blast Furnaces
ALTERNATORS & GENERATORS: Battery Charging
ALTERNATORS: Automotive
ALUMINUM
ALUMINUM PRDTS
ALUMINUM: Pigs
ALUMINUM: Rolling & Drawing
AMBULANCE SVCS
AMMONIUM NITRATE OR AMMONIUM SULFATE
AMMUNITION: Cartridges Case, 30 mm & Below
AMMUNITION: Components
AMMUNITION: Small Arms
AMPLIFIERS
AMPLIFIERS: Parametric
AMPLIFIERS: RF & IF Power
AMUSEMENT & RECREATION SVCS: Amusement Mach Rental, Coin-Op
AMUSEMENT & RECREATION SVCS: Art Gallery, Commercial
AMUSEMENT & RECREATION SVCS: Golf Club, Membership
AMUSEMENT & RECREATION SVCS: Recreation Center
AMUSEMENT MACHINES: Coin Operated
AMUSEMENT PARK DEVICES & RIDES
ANALYZERS: Moisture
ANALYZERS: Network
ANALYZERS: Respiratory
ANESTHESIA EQPT
ANIMAL BASED MEDICINAL CHEMICAL PRDTS
ANIMAL FEED & SUPPLEMENTS: Livestock & Poultry
ANIMAL FEED: Wholesalers
ANIMAL FOOD & SUPPLEMENTS: Dog
ANIMAL FOOD & SUPPLEMENTS: Dog & Cat
ANIMAL FOOD & SUPPLEMENTS: Feed Supplements
ANIMAL FOOD & SUPPLEMENTS: Livestock
ANIMAL FOOD & SUPPLEMENTS: Pet, Exc Dog & Cat, Canned
ANIMAL FOOD & SUPPLEMENTS: Poultry
ANODIZING EQPT
ANODIZING SVC
ANTENNAS: Radar Or Communications
ANTENNAS: Receiving
ANTIBIOTICS
ANTIFREEZE
ANTISEPTICS, MEDICINAL
APPAREL ACCESS STORES
APPAREL DESIGNERS: Commercial
APPAREL FILLING MATERIALS: Cotton Waste, Kapok/ Related Matl
APPLIANCES, HOUSEHOLD: Kitchen, Major, Exc Refrigs & Stoves
APPLIANCES, HOUSEHOLD: Refrigs, Mechanical & Absorption
APPLIANCES, HOUSEHOLD: Sewing Machines & Attchmnts, Domestic

APPLIANCES: Household, Refrigerators & Freezers
APPLIANCES: Major, Cooking
APPLIANCES: Small, Electric
APPLICATIONS SOFTWARE PROGRAMMING
APPRAISAL SVCS, EXC REAL ESTATE
AQUARIUMS & ACCESS: Plastic
ARCHERY & SHOOTING RANGES
ARCHITECTURAL SVCS
ARMATURE REPAIRING & REWINDING SVC
ART DEALERS & GALLERIES
ART GOODS & SPLYS WHOLESALERS
ART GOODS, WHOLESALE
ART SPLY STORES
ARTIST'S MATERIALS & SPLYS
ARTISTS' MATERIALS, WHOLESALE
ARTISTS' MATERIALS: Frames, Artists' Canvases
ARTISTS' MATERIALS: Ink, Drawing, Black & Colored
ARTWORK: Framed
ASBESTOS PRDTS: Insulation, Molded
ASBESTOS REMOVAL EQPT
ASPHALT & ASPHALT PRDTS
ASPHALT COATINGS & SEALERS
ASPHALT MINING & BITUMINOUS STONE QUARRYING SVCS
ASPHALT MIXTURES WHOLESALERS
ASPHALT PLANTS INCLUDING GRAVEL MIX TYPE
ASSEMBLING & PACKAGING SVCS: Cosmetic Kits
ASSOCIATIONS: Business
ASSOCIATIONS: Engineering
ASSOCIATIONS: Real Estate Management
ASSOCIATIONS: Scientists'
ASSOCIATIONS: Trade
ATOMIZERS
ATTENUATORS
AUCTIONEERS: Fee Basis
AUDIO & VIDEO EQPT, EXC COMMERCIAL
AUDIO COMPONENTS
AUDIO ELECTRONIC SYSTEMS
AUDIO-VISUAL PROGRAM PRODUCTION SVCS
AUDIOLOGICAL EQPT: Electronic
AUTO & HOME SUPPLY STORES: Auto & Truck Eqpt & Parts
AUTO & HOME SUPPLY STORES: Automotive Access
AUTO & HOME SUPPLY STORES: Automotive parts
AUTO & HOME SUPPLY STORES: Batteries, Automotive & Truck
AUTO & HOME SUPPLY STORES: Speed Shops, Incl Race Car Splys
AUTO & HOME SUPPLY STORES: Truck Eqpt & Parts
AUTOMATIC REGULATING CONTROL: Building Svcs Monitoring, Auto
AUTOMATIC REGULATING CONTROLS: AC & Refrigeration
AUTOMATIC REGULATING CONTROLS: Hydronic Pressure Or Temp
AUTOMATIC REGULATING CONTROLS: Incinerator, Residential/Comm
AUTOMATIC REGULATING CONTROLS: Refrig/Air-Cond Defrost
AUTOMATIC REGULATING CONTROLS: Refrigeration, Pressure
AUTOMATIC REGULATING CTRLS: Damper, Pneumatic Or Electric
AUTOMATIC REGULATING CTRLS: Elec Heat Proportion, Modultg
AUTOMATIC TELLER MACHINES
AUTOMOBILES & OTHER MOTOR VEHICLES WHOLESALERS
AUTOMOTIVE & TRUCK GENERAL REPAIR SVC
AUTOMOTIVE BODY SHOP
AUTOMOTIVE BODY, PAINT & INTERIOR REPAIR & MAINTENANCE SVC
AUTOMOTIVE GLASS REPLACEMENT SHOPS
AUTOMOTIVE PAINT SHOP
AUTOMOTIVE PARTS, ACCESS & SPLYS
AUTOMOTIVE PARTS: Plastic
AUTOMOTIVE PRDTS: Rubber
AUTOMOTIVE REPAIR SHOPS: Electrical Svcs
AUTOMOTIVE REPAIR SHOPS: Engine Rebuilding

AUTOMOTIVE REPAIR SHOPS: Machine Shop
AUTOMOTIVE REPAIR SHOPS: Muffler Shop, Sale/Rpr/
Installation
AUTOMOTIVE REPAIR SHOPS: Rebuilding & Retreading
Tires
AUTOMOTIVE REPAIR SHOPS: Springs, Rebuilding & Repair
AUTOMOTIVE REPAIR SHOPS: Tire Recapping
AUTOMOTIVE REPAIR SHOPS: Tire Repair Shop
AUTOMOTIVE REPAIR SHOPS: Trailer Repair
AUTOMOTIVE REPAIR SHOPS: Truck Engine Repair, Exc
Indl
AUTOMOTIVE REPAIR SHOPS: Wheel Alignment
AUTOMOTIVE REPAIR SVC
AUTOMOTIVE SPLYS & PARTS, NEW, WHOL: Auto
Servicing Eqpt
AUTOMOTIVE SPLYS & PARTS, NEW, WHOLESALE: Splys
AUTOMOTIVE SPLYS & PARTS, WHOLESALE, NEC
AUTOMOTIVE SVCS, EXC REPAIR & CARWASHES:
Lubrication
AUTOMOTIVE SVCS, EXC REPAIR & CARWASHES: Road
Svc
AUTOMOTIVE SVCS, EXC REPAIR & CARWASHES: Trailer
Maintenance
AUTOMOTIVE SVCS, EXC RPR/CARWASHES: High Perf
Auto Rpr/Svc
AUTOMOTIVE TRANSMISSION REPAIR SVC
AUTOMOTIVE WELDING SVCS
AUTOMOTIVE: Bodies
AUTOMOTIVE: Seating
AVIATION PROPELLER & BLADE REPAIR SVCS
AWNINGS & CANOPIES
AWNINGS & CANOPIES: Awnings, Fabric, From Purchased
Matls
AWNINGS & CANOPIES: Canopies, Fabric, From Purchased
Matls
AWNINGS: Fiberglass
AWNINGS: Metal

B

BADGES: Identification & Insignia
BAGS & CONTAINERS: Textile, Exc Sleeping
BAGS & SACKS: Shipping & Shopping
BAGS: Canvas
BAGS: Cellophane
BAGS: Food Storage & Trash, Plastic
BAGS: Paper
BAGS: Paper, Made From Purchased Materials
BAGS: Plastic
BAGS: Plastic & Pliofilm
BAGS: Plastic, Made From Purchased Materials
BAGS: Rubber Or Rubberized Fabric
BAKERIES, COMMERCIAL: On Premises Baking Only
BAKERIES: On Premises Baking & Consumption
BAKERY MACHINERY
BAKERY PRDTS: Bagels, Fresh Or Frozen
BAKERY PRDTS: Bread, All Types, Fresh Or Frozen
BAKERY PRDTS: Cakes, Bakery, Exc Frozen
BAKERY PRDTS: Cakes, Bakery, Frozen
BAKERY PRDTS: Cookies
BAKERY PRDTS: Cookies & crackers
BAKERY PRDTS: Doughnuts, Exc Frozen
BAKERY PRDTS: Dry
BAKERY PRDTS: Frozen
BAKERY PRDTS: Pies, Bakery, Frozen
BAKERY PRDTS: Pretzels
BAKERY PRDTS: Rolls, Bread Type, Fresh Or Frozen
BAKERY PRDTS: Wholesalers
BAKERY: Wholesale Or Wholesale & Retail Combined
BALLOONS: Toy & Advertising, Rubber
BALLS: Steel
BANNERS: Fabric
BAR
BAR JOISTS & CONCRETE REINFORCING BARS:
Fabricated
BARBECUE EQPT
BARRICADES: Metal
BARS & BAR SHAPES: Steel, Hot-Rolled
BARS, PLATES & SHEETS: Zinc & Zinc Alloy Bars, Plates,
Etc
BARS: Concrete Reinforcing, Fabricated Steel
BASES, BEVERAGE
BATHROOM ACCESS & FITTINGS: Vitreous China &
Earthenware

BATHROOM FIXTURES: Plastic
BATHTUBS: Concrete
BATTERIES, EXC AUTOMOTIVE: Wholesalers
BATTERIES: Alkaline, Cell Storage
BATTERIES: Lead Acid, Storage
BATTERIES: Rechargeable
BATTERIES: Storage
BATTERIES: Wet
BATTERY CASES: Plastic Or Plastics Combination
BATTERY CHARGERS
BATTERY CHARGERS: Storage, Motor & Engine Generator
Type
BATTERY CHARGING GENERATORS
BEARINGS & PARTS Ball
BEARINGS: Ball & Roller
BEARINGS: Plastic
BEARINGS: Railroad Car Journal
BEARINGS: Roller & Parts
BEARINGS: Wooden
BEAUTY & BARBER SHOP EQPT
BEAUTY SALONS
BED SHEETING, COTTON
BEDDING & BEDSPRINGS STORES
BEDDING, BEDSPREAD, BLANKET/SHEET: Pillowcase,
Purchd Mtrl
BEDDING, BEDSPREADS, BLANKETS & SHEETS
BEDDING, FROM SILK OR MANMADE FIBER
BEDS & ACCESS STORES
BEER & ALE WHOLESALERS
BEER & ALE, WHOLESALE: Beer & Other Fermented Malt
Liquors
BEER, WINE & LIQUOR STORES
BEER, WINE & LIQUOR STORES: Beer, Packaged
BELLOWS
BELTING: Rubber
BELTS & BELT PRDTS
BELTS: Conveyor, Made From Purchased Wire
BENTONITE MINING
BEVERAGE BASES & SYRUPS
BEVERAGE PRDTS: Brewers' Grain
BEVERAGE PRDTS: Malt, Barley
BEVERAGE STORES
BEVERAGE, NONALCOHOLIC: Iced Tea/Fruit Drink, Bottled/
Canned
BEVERAGES, ALCOHOLIC: Ale
BEVERAGES, ALCOHOLIC: Applejack
BEVERAGES, ALCOHOLIC: Beer
BEVERAGES, ALCOHOLIC: Beer & Ale
BEVERAGES, ALCOHOLIC: Bourbon Whiskey
BEVERAGES, ALCOHOLIC: Distilled Liquors
BEVERAGES, ALCOHOLIC: Near Beer
BEVERAGES, ALCOHOLIC: Rum
BEVERAGES, ALCOHOLIC: Wines
BEVERAGES, MALT
BEVERAGES, NONALCOHOLIC: Bottled & canned soft drinks
BEVERAGES, NONALCOHOLIC: Carbonated
BEVERAGES, NONALCOHOLIC: Carbonated, Canned &
Bottled, Etc
BEVERAGES, NONALCOHOLIC: Cider
BEVERAGES, NONALCOHOLIC: Flavoring extracts &
syrups, nec
BEVERAGES, NONALCOHOLIC: Fruit Drnks, Under 100%
Juice, Can
BEVERAGES, NONALCOHOLIC: Soft Drinks, Canned &
Bottled, Etc
BEVERAGES, NONALCOHOLIC: Tea, Iced, Bottled &
Canned, Etc
BEVERAGES, WINE & DISTILLED ALCOHOLIC,
WHOLESALE: Liquor
BEVERAGES, WINE & DISTILLED ALCOHOLIC,
WHOLESALE: Wine
BICYCLES WHOLESALERS
BICYCLES, PARTS & ACCESS
BILLING & BOOKKEEPING SVCS
BINDING SVC: Books & Manuals
BINDINGS: Bias, Made From Purchased Materials
BINOCULARS
BIOLOGICAL PRDTS: Exc Diagnostic
BIOLOGICAL PRDTS: Serums
BIOLOGICAL PRDTS: Vaccines
BIOLOGICAL PRDTS: Vaccines & Immunizing
BIOLOGICAL PRDTS: Veterinary
BLADES: Knife

BLADES: Saw, Hand Or Power
BLANKBOOKS & LOOSELEAF BINDERS
BLANKBOOKS: Albums, Record
BLANKETS & BLANKETING, COTTON
BLASTING SVC: Sand, Metal Parts
BLINDS & SHADES: Mini
BLINDS & SHADES: Vertical
BLINDS : Window
BLOCKS & BRICKS: Concrete
BLOCKS: Landscape Or Retaining Wall, Concrete
BLOCKS: Paving
BLOCKS: Paving, Concrete
BLOCKS: Paving, Cut Stone
BLOCKS: Standard, Concrete Or Cinder
BLOWERS & FANS
BLOWERS & FANS
BLOWERS, TURBO: Indl
BLUEPRINTING SVCS
BOAT BUILDING & REPAIR
BOAT BUILDING & REPAIRING: Fiberglass
BOAT BUILDING & REPAIRING: Motorboats, Inboard Or
Outboard
BOAT BUILDING & REPAIRING: Motorized
BOAT BUILDING & REPAIRING: Non-Motorized
BOAT BUILDING & REPAIRING: Yachts
BOAT BUILDING & RPRG: Fishing, Small, Lobster, Crab,
Oyster
BOAT DEALERS
BOAT DEALERS: Marine Splys & Eqpt
BOAT DEALERS: Motor
BOAT REPAIR SVCS
BOATS & OTHER MARINE EQPT: Plastic
BODIES: Truck & Bus
BODY PARTS: Automobile, Stamped Metal
BOILER & HEATING REPAIR SVCS
BOILER REPAIR SHOP
BOILERS & BOILER SHOP WORK
BOILERS: Low-Pressure Heating, Steam Or Hot Water
BOLTS: Handle, Wooden, Hewn
BOLTS: Metal
BOOK STORES
BOOKS, WHOLESALE
BOOTS: Men's
BORING MILL
BOTTLED GAS DEALERS: Propane
BOTTLES: Plastic
BOWLING CENTERS
BOXES & CRATES: Rectangular, Wood
BOXES & SHOOK: Nailed Wood
BOXES: Corrugated
BOXES: Filing, Paperboard Made From Purchased Materials
BOXES: Outlet, Electric Wiring Device
BOXES: Packing & Shipping, Metal
BOXES: Paperboard, Folding
BOXES: Paperboard, Set-Up
BOXES: Plastic
BOXES: Stamped Metal
BOXES: Wooden
BRAKES & BRAKE PARTS
BRAKES: Electromagnetic
BRAKES: Metal Forming
BRASS & BRONZE PRDTS: Die-casted
BRASS FOUNDRY, NEC
BRAZING SVCS
BRAZING: Metal
BRICK, STONE & RELATED PRDTS WHOLESALERS
BRICKS & BLOCKS: Structural
BRICKS: Clay
BRIDGE COMPONENTS: Bridge sections, prefabricated,
highway
BROADCASTING & COMMS EQPT: Antennas, Transmitting/
Comms
BROADCASTING & COMMS EQPT: Trnsmttng TV Antennas/
Grndng Eqpt
BROADCASTING & COMMUNICATION EQPT: Transmit-
Receiver, Radio
BROADCASTING & COMMUNICATIONS EQPT: Cellular
Radio Telephone
BROADCASTING & COMMUNICATIONS EQPT: Light
Comms Eqpt
BROADCASTING & COMMUNICATIONS EQPT: Studio Eqpt,
Radio & TV

BROADCASTING & COMMUNICATIONS EQPT:
  Transmitting, Radio/TV
BROKERS & DEALERS: Securities
BROKERS' SVCS
BROKERS: Business
BROKERS: Food
BROKERS: Printing
BRONZE FOUNDRY, NEC
BRONZE ROLLING & DRAWING
BROOMS
BROOMS & BRUSHES
BROOMS & BRUSHES: Household Or Indl
BROOMS & BRUSHES: Street Sweeping, Hand Or Machine
BRUSHES
BUCKETS: Plastic
BUCKLES & PARTS
BUILDING & OFFICE CLEANING SVCS
BUILDING & STRUCTURAL WOOD MEMBERS
BUILDING CLEANING & MAINTENANCE SVCS
BUILDING COMPONENTS: Structural Steel
BUILDING ITEM REPAIR SVCS, MISCELLANEOUS
BUILDING PRDTS & MATERIALS DEALERS
BUILDING PRDTS: Concrete
BUILDING PRDTS: Stone
BUILDING SCALES MODELS
BUILDINGS & COMPONENTS: Prefabricated Metal
BUILDINGS: Portable
BUILDINGS: Prefabricated, Metal
BUILDINGS: Prefabricated, Wood
BULLETPROOF VESTS
BUOYS: Plastic
BURIAL VAULTS: Concrete Or Precast Terrazzo
BURNERS: Gas, Domestic
BURNERS: Gas, Indl
BURNERS: Oil, Domestic Or Indl
BURNT WOOD ARTICLES
BUS BARS: Electrical
BUSINESS ACTIVITIES: Non-Commercial Site
BUSINESS FORMS WHOLESALERS
BUSINESS FORMS: Printed, Continuous
BUSINESS FORMS: Printed, Manifold
BUSINESS MACHINE REPAIR, ELECTRIC
BUSINESS TRAINING SVCS
BUTTER WHOLESALERS

C

CABINETS & CASES: Show, Display & Storage, Exc Wood
CABINETS: Bathroom Vanities, Wood
CABINETS: Entertainment
CABINETS: Factory
CABINETS: Kitchen, Metal
CABINETS: Kitchen, Wood
CABINETS: Office, Wood
CABINETS: Show, Display, Etc, Wood, Exc Refrigerated
CABLE & OTHER PAY TELEVISION DISTRIBUTION
CABLE TELEVISION
CABLE TELEVISION PRDTS
CABLE: Coaxial
CABLE: Fiber
CABLE: Fiber Optic
CABLE: Noninsulated
CABLE: Ropes & Fiber
CABLE: Steel, Insulated Or Armored
CAFES
CAFETERIAS
CALCULATING & ACCOUNTING EQPT
CALIBRATING SVCS, NEC
CAMERA CARRYING BAGS
CAMPERS: Truck Mounted
CAMSHAFTS
CANDLE SHOPS
CANDLES
CANDLES: Wholesalers
CANDY & CONFECTIONS: Candy Bars, Including Chocolate
  Covered
CANDY & CONFECTIONS: Chocolate Candy, Exc Solid
  Chocolate
CANDY & CONFECTIONS: Popcorn Balls/Other Trtd
  Popcorn Prdts
CANDY, NUT & CONFECTIONERY STORES: Candy
CANDY: Soft
CANNED SPECIALTIES
CANOE BUILDING & REPAIR

CANS: Aluminum
CANS: Metal
CANS: Tin
CANVAS PRDTS
CAPACITORS & CONDENSERS
CAPACITORS: NEC
CAPS: Plastic
CARBIDES
CARBON & GRAPHITE PRDTS, NEC
CARBON BLACK
CARBON PAPER & INKED RIBBONS
CARDIOVASCULAR SYSTEM DRUGS, EXC DIAGNOSTIC
CARDS: Beveled
CARDS: Greeting
CARDS: Identification
CARPET & UPHOLSTERY CLEANING SVCS
CARPETS & RUGS: Tufted
CARPETS, RUGS & FLOOR COVERING
CARPETS: Textile Fiber
CARRIER EQPT: Telephone Or Telegraph
CARRIERS: Infant, Textile
CARTONS: Egg, Molded Pulp, Made From Purchased
  Materials
CARTS: Grocery
CASEMENTS: Aluminum
CASES: Attache'
CASES: Carrying
CASES: Carrying, Clothing & Apparel
CASES: Jewelry
CASES: Nonrefrigerated, Exc Wood
CASES: Plastic
CASH REGISTER REPAIR SVCS
CASINGS: Sheet Metal
CASINGS: Storage, Missile & Missile Components
CAST STONE: Concrete
CASTINGS GRINDING: For The Trade
CASTINGS: Aerospace Investment, Ferrous
CASTINGS: Aerospace, Aluminum
CASTINGS: Aerospace, Nonferrous, Exc Aluminum
CASTINGS: Aluminum
CASTINGS: Brass, NEC, Exc Die
CASTINGS: Bronze, NEC, Exc Die
CASTINGS: Commercial Investment, Ferrous
CASTINGS: Die, Aluminum
CASTINGS: Die, Nonferrous
CASTINGS: Ductile
CASTINGS: Gray Iron
CASTINGS: Machinery, Nonferrous, Exc Die or Aluminum
  Copper
CASTINGS: Precision
CASTINGS: Steel
CASTINGS: Titanium
CATALOG & MAIL-ORDER HOUSES
CATALOG SALES
CATALYSTS: Chemical
CATAPULTS
CATERERS
CEILING SYSTEMS: Luminous, Commercial
CEMENT: Hydraulic
CEMENT: Portland
CERAMIC FIBER
CHAIN: Tire, Made From Purchased Wire
CHAIN: Welded, Made From Purchased Wire
CHANGE MAKING MACHINES
CHARCOAL: Activated
CHASSIS: Motor Vehicle
CHEMICAL ELEMENTS
CHEMICAL PROCESSING MACHINERY & EQPT
CHEMICAL: Sodm Compnds/Salts, Inorg, Exc Rfnd Sodm
  Chloride
CHEMICALS & ALLIED PRDTS WHOLESALERS, NEC
CHEMICALS & ALLIED PRDTS, WHOLESALE: Acids
CHEMICALS & ALLIED PRDTS, WHOLESALE: Alkalines &
  Chlorine
CHEMICALS & ALLIED PRDTS, WHOLESALE: Chemicals,
  Indl
CHEMICALS & ALLIED PRDTS, WHOLESALE: Chemicals,
  Indl & Heavy
CHEMICALS & ALLIED PRDTS, WHOLESALE: Detergent/
  Soap
CHEMICALS & ALLIED PRDTS, WHOLESALE: Plastics Film
CHEMICALS & ALLIED PRDTS, WHOLESALE: Plastics
  Materials, NEC

CHEMICALS & ALLIED PRDTS, WHOLESALE: Plastics
  Prdts, NEC
CHEMICALS & ALLIED PRDTS, WHOLESALE: Plastics
  Sheets & Rods
CHEMICALS & ALLIED PRDTS, WHOLESALE: Resins
CHEMICALS & ALLIED PRDTS, WHOLESALE: Resins,
  Plastics
CHEMICALS & ALLIED PRDTS, WHOLESALE: Rubber,
  Synthetic
CHEMICALS & ALLIED PRDTS, WHOLESALE: Spec Clean/
  Sanitation
CHEMICALS & ALLIED PRDTS, WHOLESALE: Syn Resin,
  Rub/Plastic
CHEMICALS: Agricultural
CHEMICALS: Aluminum Sulfate
CHEMICALS: Caustic Potash & Potassium Hydroxide
CHEMICALS: Fire Retardant
CHEMICALS: High Purity, Refined From Technical Grade
CHEMICALS: Inorganic, NEC
CHEMICALS: Medicinal
CHEMICALS: Medicinal, Organic, Uncompounded, Bulk
CHEMICALS: NEC
CHEMICALS: Organic, NEC
CHEMICALS: Reagent Grade, Refined From Technical Grade
CHEMICALS: Silica Compounds
CHEMICALS: Silica, Amorphous
CHEMICALS: Water Treatment
CHICKEN SLAUGHTERING & PROCESSING
CHILDREN'S & INFANTS' CLOTHING STORES
CHILDREN'S WEAR STORES
CHOCOLATE, EXC CANDY FROM BEANS: Chips, Powder,
  Block, Syrup
CHOCOLATE, EXC CANDY FROM PURCH CHOC: Chips,
  Powder, Block
CHRISTMAS NOVELTIES, WHOLESALE
CHROMATOGRAPHY EQPT
CHUCKS
CHURCHES
CIGARETTE LIGHTERS
CIRCUIT BOARD REPAIR SVCS
CIRCUIT BOARDS, PRINTED: Television & Radio
CIRCUIT BOARDS: Wiring
CIRCUITS, INTEGRATED: Hybrid
CIRCUITS: Electronic
CIRCULAR KNIT FABRICS DYEING & FINISHING
CLAMPS: Metal
CLEANING EQPT: Commercial
CLEANING EQPT: High Pressure
CLEANING OR POLISHING PREPARATIONS, NEC
CLEANING PRDTS: Ammonia, Household
CLEANING PRDTS: Automobile Polish
CLEANING PRDTS: Disinfectants, Household Or Indl Plant
CLEANING PRDTS: Drain Pipe Solvents Or Cleaners
CLEANING PRDTS: Floor Waxes
CLEANING PRDTS: Sanitation Preps, Disinfectants/
  Deodorants
CLEANING PRDTS: Specialty
CLEANING PRDTS: Stain Removers
CLEANING SVCS: Industrial Or Commercial
CLIPS & FASTENERS, MADE FROM PURCHASED WIRE
CLOSURES: Closures, Stamped Metal
CLOSURES: Plastic
CLOTHING & ACCESS, WOMEN, CHILDREN & INFANT,
  WHOL: Handbags
CLOTHING & ACCESS, WOMEN, CHILDREN & INFANT,
  WHOL: Sweaters
CLOTHING & ACCESS, WOMEN, CHILDREN & INFANT,
  WHOL: Uniforms
CLOTHING & ACCESS: Handicapped
CLOTHING & ACCESS: Hospital Gowns
CLOTHING & ACCESS: Men's Miscellaneous Access
CLOTHING & ACCESS: Suspenders
CLOTHING & APPAREL STORES: Custom
CLOTHING & FURNISHINGS, MENS & BOYS, WHOL:
  Sportswear/Work
CLOTHING & FURNISHINGS, MENS & BOYS,
  WHOLESALE: Apprl Belts
CLOTHING STORES: Designer Apparel
CLOTHING STORES: T-Shirts, Printed, Custom
CLOTHING STORES: Uniforms & Work
CLOTHING STORES: Unisex
CLOTHING STORES: Work

CLOTHING: Aprons, Exc Rubber/Plastic, Women, Misses, Junior
CLOTHING: Athletic & Sportswear, Men's & Boys'
CLOTHING: Athletic & Sportswear, Women's & Girls'
CLOTHING: Belts
CLOTHING: Blouses, Women's & Girls'
CLOTHING: Brassieres
CLOTHING: Bridal Gowns
CLOTHING: Caps, Baseball
CLOTHING: Children & Infants'
CLOTHING: Children's, Girls'
CLOTHING: Coats & Jackets, Leather & Sheep-Lined
CLOTHING: Coats & Suits, Men's & Boys'
CLOTHING: Coats, Leatherette, Oiled Fabric, Etc, Mens & Boys
CLOTHING: Costumes
CLOTHING: Disposable
CLOTHING: Dresses
CLOTHING: Hats & Caps, NEC
CLOTHING: Hats & Caps, Uniform
CLOTHING: Hosiery, Pantyhose & Knee Length, Sheer
CLOTHING: Jackets, Overall & Work
CLOTHING: Jeans, Men's & Boys'
CLOTHING: Leather
CLOTHING: Men's & boy's underwear & nightwear
CLOTHING: Mens & Boys Jackets, Sport, Suede, Leatherette
CLOTHING: Neckwear
CLOTHING: Outerwear, Knit
CLOTHING: Outerwear, Lthr, Wool/Down-Filled, Men, Youth/Boy
CLOTHING: Outerwear, Women's & Misses' NEC
CLOTHING: Raincoats, Exc Vulcanized Rubber, Purchased Matls
CLOTHING: Robes & Dressing Gowns
CLOTHING: Shirts
CLOTHING: Shirts, Dress, Men's & Boys'
CLOTHING: Shirts, Sports & Polo, Men's & Boys'
CLOTHING: Socks
CLOTHING: Sportswear, Women's
CLOTHING: Suits & Skirts, Women's & Misses'
CLOTHING: Suits, Men's & Boys', From Purchased Materials
CLOTHING: Sweaters & Sweater Coats, Knit
CLOTHING: Sweatshirts & T-Shirts, Men's & Boys'
CLOTHING: Swimwear, Women's & Misses'
CLOTHING: T-Shirts & Tops, Knit
CLOTHING: T-Shirts & Tops, Women's & Girls'
CLOTHING: Trousers & Slacks, Men's & Boys'
CLOTHING: Underwear, Women's & Children's
CLOTHING: Uniforms, Ex Athletic, Women's, Misses' & Juniors'
CLOTHING: Uniforms, Firemen's, From Purchased Materials
CLOTHING: Uniforms, Men's & Boys'
CLOTHING: Uniforms, Military, Men/Youth, Purchased Materials
CLOTHING: Uniforms, Team Athletic
CLOTHING: Uniforms, Work
CLOTHING: Waterproof Outerwear
CLOTHING: Work Apparel, Exc Uniforms
CLOTHING: Work, Men's
CLUTCHES, EXC VEHICULAR
COAL MINING SERVICES
COAL MINING: Anthracite
COAL MINING: Bituminous & Lignite Surface
COAL MINING: Bituminous Coal & Lignite-Surface Mining
COAL, MINERALS & ORES, WHOLESALE: Coal
COAL, MINERALS & ORES, WHOLESALE: Sulfur
COATED OR PLATED PRDTS
COATING SVC: Metals, With Plastic Or Resins
COATINGS: Epoxy
COATINGS: Polyurethane
COFFEE SVCS
COIL WINDING SVC
COILS & TRANSFORMERS
COILS: Electric Motors Or Generators
COILS: Pipe
COKE: Produced In Chemical Recovery Coke Ovens
COLLEGE, EXC JUNIOR
COLORS: Pigments, Inorganic
COMMERCIAL & OFFICE BUILDINGS RENOVATION & REPAIR
COMMERCIAL ART & GRAPHIC DESIGN SVCS
COMMERCIAL ART & ILLUSTRATION SVCS
COMMERCIAL CONTAINERS WHOLESALERS

COMMERCIAL COOKING EQPT WHOLESALERS
COMMERCIAL EQPT WHOLESALERS, NEC
COMMERCIAL EQPT, WHOLESALE: Bakery Eqpt & Splys
COMMERCIAL EQPT, WHOLESALE: Display Eqpt, Exc Refrigerated
COMMERCIAL EQPT, WHOLESALE: Restaurant, NEC
COMMERCIAL EQPT, WHOLESALE: Scales, Exc Laboratory
COMMERCIAL LAUNDRY EQPT
COMMERCIAL PRINTING & NEWSPAPER PUBLISHING
COMMON SAND MINING
COMMUNICATIONS EQPT WHOLESALERS
COMMUNICATIONS EQPT: Microwave
COMMUNICATIONS EQPT: Radio, Marine
COMMUNICATIONS SVCS
COMMUNICATIONS SVCS: Data
COMMUNICATIONS SVCS: Electronic Mail
COMMUNICATIONS SVCS: Internet Connectivity Svcs
COMMUNICATIONS SVCS: Internet Host Svcs
COMMUNICATIONS SVCS: Online Svc Providers
COMMUNICATIONS SVCS: Proprietary Online Svcs Networks
COMMUNICATIONS SVCS: Signal Enhancement Network Svcs
COMMUNICATIONS SVCS: Telephone Or Video
COMMUNICATIONS SVCS: Telephone, Local
COMMUNICATIONS SVCS: Telephone, Local & Long Distance
COMMUNICATIONS SVCS: Telephone, Voice
COMMUNITY SVCS EMPLOYMENT TRAINING PROGRAM
COMMUTATORS: Electronic
COMPACT LASER DISCS: Prerecorded
COMPOST
COMPRESSORS: Air & Gas
COMPRESSORS: Air & Gas, Including Vacuum Pumps
COMPRESSORS: Refrigeration & Air Conditioning Eqpt
COMPUTER & COMPUTER SOFTWARE STORES
COMPUTER & COMPUTER SOFTWARE STORES: Peripheral Eqpt
COMPUTER & COMPUTER SOFTWARE STORES: Software & Access
COMPUTER & COMPUTER SOFTWARE STORES: Software, Bus/Non-Game
COMPUTER & COMPUTER SOFTWARE STORES: Software, Computer Game
COMPUTER & DATA PROCESSING EQPT REPAIR & MAINTENANCE
COMPUTER & OFFICE MACHINE MAINTENANCE & REPAIR
COMPUTER FACILITIES MANAGEMENT SVCS
COMPUTER FORMS
COMPUTER GRAPHICS SVCS
COMPUTER HARDWARE REQUIREMENTS ANALYSIS
COMPUTER PERIPHERAL EQPT REPAIR & MAINTENANCE
COMPUTER PERIPHERAL EQPT, NEC
COMPUTER PERIPHERAL EQPT, WHOLESALE
COMPUTER PERIPHERAL EQPT: Input Or Output
COMPUTER PROCESSING SVCS
COMPUTER PROGRAMMING SVCS: Custom
COMPUTER RELATED MAINTENANCE SVCS
COMPUTER SOFTWARE DEVELOPMENT
COMPUTER SOFTWARE DEVELOPMENT & APPLICATIONS
COMPUTER SOFTWARE SYSTEMS ANALYSIS & DESIGN: Custom
COMPUTER STORAGE DEVICES, NEC
COMPUTER STORAGE UNITS: Auxiliary
COMPUTER SYSTEMS ANALYSIS & DESIGN
COMPUTER TERMINALS
COMPUTER-AIDED SYSTEM SVCS
COMPUTERS, NEC
COMPUTERS, NEC, WHOLESALE
COMPUTERS, PERIPHERALS & SOFTWARE, WHOLESALE: Printers
COMPUTERS, PERIPHERALS & SOFTWARE, WHOLESALE: Software
COMPUTERS: Mainframe
COMPUTERS: Personal
CONCENTRATES, DRINK
CONCENTRATES, FLAVORING, EXC DRINK
CONCRETE BUILDING PRDTS WHOLESALERS
CONCRETE CURING & HARDENING COMPOUNDS
CONCRETE MIXERS
CONCRETE PLANTS

CONCRETE PRDTS
CONCRETE PRDTS, PRECAST, NEC
CONCRETE: Bituminous
CONCRETE: Ready-Mixed
CONDENSERS: Motors Or Generators
CONDENSERS: Refrigeration
CONDUITS & FITTINGS: Electric
CONFINEMENT SURVEILLANCE SYS MAINTENANCE & MONITORING SVCS
CONNECTORS: Cord, Electric
CONNECTORS: Electronic
CONSTRUCTION & MINING MACHINERY WHOLESALERS
CONSTRUCTION EQPT: Attachments, Snow Plow
CONSTRUCTION EQPT: Cranes
CONSTRUCTION EQPT: Grapples, Rock, Wood, Etc
CONSTRUCTION EQPT: Roofing Eqpt
CONSTRUCTION MATERIALS, WHOLESALE: Aggregate
CONSTRUCTION MATERIALS, WHOLESALE: Air Ducts, Sheet Metal
CONSTRUCTION MATERIALS, WHOLESALE: Awnings
CONSTRUCTION MATERIALS, WHOLESALE: Building Stone
CONSTRUCTION MATERIALS, WHOLESALE: Building Stone, Marble
CONSTRUCTION MATERIALS, WHOLESALE: Building, Exterior
CONSTRUCTION MATERIALS, WHOLESALE: Cement
CONSTRUCTION MATERIALS, WHOLESALE: Concrete Mixtures
CONSTRUCTION MATERIALS, WHOLESALE: Glass
CONSTRUCTION MATERIALS, WHOLESALE: Gravel
CONSTRUCTION MATERIALS, WHOLESALE: Limestone
CONSTRUCTION MATERIALS, WHOLESALE: Masons' Materials
CONSTRUCTION MATERIALS, WHOLESALE: Millwork
CONSTRUCTION MATERIALS, WHOLESALE: Molding, All Materials
CONSTRUCTION MATERIALS, WHOLESALE: Paving Materials
CONSTRUCTION MATERIALS, WHOLESALE: Prefabricated Structures
CONSTRUCTION MATERIALS, WHOLESALE: Roofing & Siding Material
CONSTRUCTION MATERIALS, WHOLESALE: Sand
CONSTRUCTION MATERIALS, WHOLESALE: Septic Tanks
CONSTRUCTION MATERIALS, WHOLESALE: Siding, Exc Wood
CONSTRUCTION MATERIALS, WHOLESALE: Stone, Crushed Or Broken
CONSTRUCTION MATERIALS, WHOLESALE: Windows
CONSTRUCTION SAND MINING
CONSTRUCTION: Agricultural Building
CONSTRUCTION: Airport Runway
CONSTRUCTION: Bridge
CONSTRUCTION: Commercial & Office Building, New
CONSTRUCTION: Commercial & Office Buildings, Prefabricated
CONSTRUCTION: Dam
CONSTRUCTION: Dams, Waterways, Docks & Other Marine
CONSTRUCTION: Drainage System
CONSTRUCTION: Elevated Highway
CONSTRUCTION: Food Prdts Manufacturing or Packing Plant
CONSTRUCTION: Foundation & Retaining Wall
CONSTRUCTION: Heavy Highway & Street
CONSTRUCTION: Indl Buildings, New, NEC
CONSTRUCTION: Indl Plant
CONSTRUCTION: Institutional Building
CONSTRUCTION: Marine
CONSTRUCTION: Pharmaceutical Manufacturing Plant
CONSTRUCTION: Pipeline, NEC
CONSTRUCTION: Power Plant
CONSTRUCTION: Residential, Nec
CONSTRUCTION: Sewer Line
CONSTRUCTION: Single-Family Housing
CONSTRUCTION: Single-family Housing, New
CONSTRUCTION: Street Sign Installation & Mntnce
CONSTRUCTION: Subway
CONSTRUCTION: Swimming Pools
CONSTRUCTION: Water & Sewer Line
CONSULTING SVC: Business, NEC
CONSULTING SVC: Educational
CONSULTING SVC: Financial Management
CONSULTING SVC: Management
CONSULTING SVCS, BUSINESS: Communications

CONSULTING SVCS, BUSINESS: Energy Conservation
CONSULTING SVCS, BUSINESS: Environmental
CONSULTING SVCS, BUSINESS: Sys Engnrg, Exc Computer/ Prof
CONSULTING SVCS, BUSINESS: Systems Analysis & Engineering
CONSULTING SVCS, BUSINESS: Systems Analysis Or Design
CONSULTING SVCS: Scientific
CONTACT LENSES
CONTACTS: Electrical
CONTAINERS, GLASS: Food
CONTAINERS: Food & Beverage
CONTAINERS: Glass
CONTAINERS: Laminated Phenolic & Vulcanized Fiber
CONTAINERS: Liquid Tight Fiber, From Purchased Materials
CONTAINERS: Plastic
CONTAINERS: Sanitary, Food
CONTAINERS: Wood
CONTAINMENT VESSELS: Reactor, Metal Plate
CONTRACTOR: Rigging & Scaffolding
CONTRACTORS: Acoustical & Ceiling Work
CONTRACTORS: Asbestos Removal & Encapsulation
CONTRACTORS: Boiler Maintenance Contractor
CONTRACTORS: Building Front Installation, Metal
CONTRACTORS: Building Site Preparation
CONTRACTORS: Carpentry Work
CONTRACTORS: Carpentry, Cabinet & Finish Work
CONTRACTORS: Coating, Caulking & Weather, Water & Fire
CONTRACTORS: Commercial & Office Building
CONTRACTORS: Communications Svcs
CONTRACTORS: Decontamination Svcs
CONTRACTORS: Dewatering
CONTRACTORS: Directional Oil & Gas Well Drilling Svc
CONTRACTORS: Drywall
CONTRACTORS: Electric Power Systems
CONTRACTORS: Electronic Controls Installation
CONTRACTORS: Excavating Slush Pits & Cellars Svcs
CONTRACTORS: Fence Construction
CONTRACTORS: Fiber Optic Cable Installation
CONTRACTORS: Fire Detection & Burglar Alarm Systems
CONTRACTORS: Floor Laying & Other Floor Work
CONTRACTORS: Foundation & Footing
CONTRACTORS: General Electric
CONTRACTORS: Grave Excavation
CONTRACTORS: Heating & Air Conditioning
CONTRACTORS: Heating Systems Repair & Maintenance Svc
CONTRACTORS: Highway & Street Construction, General
CONTRACTORS: Highway & Street Paving
CONTRACTORS: Kitchen Cabinet Installation
CONTRACTORS: Machine Rigging & Moving
CONTRACTORS: Machinery Installation
CONTRACTORS: Marble Installation, Interior
CONTRACTORS: Masonry & Stonework
CONTRACTORS: Oil & Gas Field Geological Exploration Svcs
CONTRACTORS: Oil & Gas Field Geophysical Exploration Svcs
CONTRACTORS: Oil & Gas Well Flow Rate Measurement Svcs
CONTRACTORS: Oil & Gas Wells Svcs
CONTRACTORS: Oil Field Pipe Testing Svcs
CONTRACTORS: Ornamental Metal Work
CONTRACTORS: Painting, Commercial
CONTRACTORS: Painting, Indl
CONTRACTORS: Plumbing
CONTRACTORS: Power Generating Eqpt Installation
CONTRACTORS: Prefabricated Window & Door Installation
CONTRACTORS: Process Piping
CONTRACTORS: Roustabout Svcs
CONTRACTORS: Seismograph Survey Svcs
CONTRACTORS: Septic System
CONTRACTORS: Sheet Metal Work, NEC
CONTRACTORS: Siding
CONTRACTORS: Store Front Construction
CONTRACTORS: Structural Iron Work, Structural
CONTRACTORS: Structural Steel Erection
CONTRACTORS: Tile Installation, Ceramic
CONTRACTORS: Ventilation & Duct Work
CONTRACTORS: Warm Air Heating & Air Conditioning
CONTRACTORS: Water Well Drilling
CONTRACTORS: Well Logging Svcs
CONTRACTORS: Windows & Doors

CONTRACTORS: Wood Floor Installation & Refinishing
CONTRACTORS: Wrecking & Demolition
CONTROL CIRCUIT DEVICES
CONTROL EQPT: Electric
CONTROL EQPT: Noise
CONTROLS & ACCESS: Indl, Electric
CONTROLS & ACCESS: Motor
CONTROLS: Automatic Temperature
CONTROLS: Crane & Hoist, Including Metal Mill
CONTROLS: Electric Motor
CONTROLS: Environmental
CONTROLS: Marine & Navy, Auxiliary
CONTROLS: Numerical
CONTROLS: Resistance Welder
CONTROLS: Thermostats
CONVERTERS: Frequency
CONVERTERS: Torque, Exc Auto
CONVEYOR SYSTEMS
CONVEYOR SYSTEMS: Belt, General Indl Use
CONVEYOR SYSTEMS: Robotic
CONVEYORS & CONVEYING EQPT
COOKING & FOODWARMING EQPT: Commercial
COOKWARE, STONEWARE: Coarse Earthenware & Pottery
COPPER ORES
COPPER PRDTS: Smelter, Primary
COPPER: Rolling & Drawing
COPYRIGHT BUYING & LICENSING
CORD & TWINE
CORES: Magnetic
CORK & CORK PRDTS
CORRECTION FLUID
COSMETIC PREPARATIONS
COSMETICS & TOILETRIES
COSMETICS WHOLESALERS
COUNTER & SINK TOPS
COUNTERS OR COUNTER DISPLAY CASES, EXC WOOD
COUNTERS OR COUNTER DISPLAY CASES, WOOD
COUNTERS: Mechanical
COUNTING DEVICES: Controls, Revolution & Timing
COUNTING DEVICES: Tachometer, Centrifugal
COUNTING DEVICES: Vehicle Instruments
COUPLINGS, EXC PRESSURE & SOIL PIPE
COUPLINGS: Shaft
COVERS: Hot Tub & Spa
CRANE & AERIAL LIFT SVCS
CRANES: Indl Truck
CRANES: Overhead
CROWNS & CLOSURES
CRUDE PETROLEUM PRODUCTION
CRYOGENIC COOLING DEVICES: Infrared Detectors, Masers
CRYSTALS: Piezoelectric
CULTURE MEDIA
CUPOLAS: Metal Plate
CUPS & PLATES: Foamed Plastics
CURBING: Granite Or Stone
CURTAIN WALLS: Building, Steel
CURTAINS: Window, From Purchased Materials
CUSHIONS & PILLOWS
CUSHIONS & PILLOWS: Bed, From Purchased Materials
CUSHIONS: Carpet & Rug, Foamed Plastics
CUSTOM COMPOUNDING OF RUBBER MATERIALS
CUT STONE & STONE PRODUCTS
CUTLERY
CYCLIC CRUDES & INTERMEDIATES
CYLINDER & ACTUATORS: Fluid Power
CYLINDERS: Pressure

D

DAIRY EQPT
DAIRY PRDTS STORE: Butter
DAIRY PRDTS STORE: Cheese
DAIRY PRDTS STORE: Ice Cream, Packaged
DAIRY PRDTS STORE: Milk
DAIRY PRDTS STORES
DAIRY PRDTS: Acidophilus Milk
DAIRY PRDTS: Butter
DAIRY PRDTS: Cheese
DAIRY PRDTS: Cream, Sweet
DAIRY PRDTS: Dairy Based Desserts, Frozen
DAIRY PRDTS: Dietary Supplements, Dairy & Non-Dairy Based
DAIRY PRDTS: Dried Milk

DAIRY PRDTS: Evaporated Milk
DAIRY PRDTS: Ice Cream & Ice Milk
DAIRY PRDTS: Ice Cream, Bulk
DAIRY PRDTS: Ice Cream, Packaged, Molded, On Sticks, Etc.
DAIRY PRDTS: Milk & Cream, Cultured & Flavored
DAIRY PRDTS: Milk, Condensed & Evaporated
DAIRY PRDTS: Milk, Fluid
DAIRY PRDTS: Natural Cheese
DAIRY PRDTS: Processed Cheese
DAIRY PRDTS: Spreads, Cheese
DAIRY PRDTS: Yogurt, Frozen
DATA PROCESSING & PREPARATION SVCS
DATA PROCESSING SVCS
DEALERS: Commodity Contracts
DECORATIVE WOOD & WOODWORK
DEFENSE SYSTEMS & EQPT
DEGREASING MACHINES
DENTAL EQPT
DENTAL EQPT & SPLYS
DENTAL EQPT & SPLYS WHOLESALERS
DENTAL EQPT & SPLYS: Dental Materials
DENTAL EQPT & SPLYS: Enamels
DENTAL EQPT & SPLYS: Orthodontic Appliances
DENTISTS' OFFICES & CLINICS
DEODORANTS: Personal
DEPARTMENT STORES
DERMATOLOGICALS
DESIGN SVCS, NEC
DESIGN SVCS: Commercial & Indl
DESIGN SVCS: Computer Integrated Systems
DETECTION APPARATUS: Electronic/Magnetic Field, Light/ Heat
DETECTIVE & ARMORED CAR SERVICES
DIAGNOSTIC SUBSTANCES
DIAGNOSTIC SUBSTANCES OR AGENTS: Blood Derivative
DIAGNOSTIC SUBSTANCES OR AGENTS: Enzyme & Isoenzyme
DIAGNOSTIC SUBSTANCES OR AGENTS: In Vitro
DIAGNOSTIC SUBSTANCES OR AGENTS: Microbiology & Virology
DIAGNOSTIC SUBSTANCES OR AGENTS: Radioactive
DIAGNOSTIC SUBSTANCES OR AGENTS: Veterinary
DIE CUTTING SVC: Paper
DIE SETS: Presses, Metal Stamping
DIES & TOOLS: Special
DIES: Cutting, Exc Metal
DIES: Extrusion
DIES: Plastic Forming
DIES: Steel Rule
DIODES & RECTIFIERS
DIODES: Light Emitting
DIODES: Solid State, Germanium, Silicon, Etc
DIRECT SELLING ESTABLISHMENTS, NEC
DIRECT SELLING ESTABLISHMENTS: Encyclopedias, House-To-House
DIRECT SELLING ESTABLISHMENTS: Food Svcs
DISCS & TAPE: Optical, Blank
DISPENSERS: Soap
DISPLAY FIXTURES: Wood
DISPLAY ITEMS: Corrugated, Made From Purchased Materials
DOCK EQPT & SPLYS, INDL
DOOR FRAMES: Wood
DOORS & WINDOWS: Screen & Storm
DOORS & WINDOWS: Storm, Metal
DOORS: Fiberglass
DOORS: Fire, Metal
DOORS: Folding, Plastic Or Plastic Coated Fabric
DOORS: Garage, Overhead, Metal
DOORS: Glass
DRAPERIES & CURTAINS
DRAPERIES: Plastic & Textile, From Purchased Materials
DRAPERY & UPHOLSTERY STORES: Draperies
DRILLS & DRILLING EQPT: Mining
DRINK MIXES, NONALCOHOLIC: Cocktail
DRINKING PLACES: Bars & Lounges
DRINKING PLACES: Beer Garden
DRINKING WATER COOLERS WHOLESALERS: Mechanical
DRIVE SHAFTS
DRUG STORES
DRUGS & DRUG PROPRIETARIES, WHOLESALE

DRUGS & DRUG PROPRIETARIES, WHOLESALE: Medicinals/ Botanicals
DRUGS & DRUG PROPRIETARIES, WHOLESALE: Pharmaceuticals
DRUGS & DRUG PROPRIETARIES, WHOLESALE: Vitamins & Minerals
DRUGS ACTING ON THE CENTRAL NERVOUS SYSTEM & SENSE ORGANS
DRUGS AFFECTING NEOPLASMS & ENDOCRINE SYSTEMS
DRUGS: Parasitic & Infective Disease Affecting
DRUMS: Shipping, Metal
DUCTING: Metal Plate
DUCTING: Plastic
DUCTS: Sheet Metal
DUMPSTERS: Garbage
DUST OR FUME COLLECTING EQPT: Indl
DYES & PIGMENTS: Organic

E

EATING PLACES
EDITING SVCS
EDITORIAL SVCS
EDUCATIONAL SVCS
ELECTRIC & OTHER SERVICES COMBINED
ELECTRIC MOTOR & GENERATOR AUXILIARY PARTS
ELECTRIC MOTOR REPAIR SVCS
ELECTRIC POWER DISTRIBUTION TO CONSUMERS
ELECTRIC POWER GENERATION: Fossil Fuel
ELECTRIC SERVICES
ELECTRIC SVCS, NEC: Power Generation
ELECTRICAL APPARATUS & EQPT WHOLESALERS
ELECTRICAL DISCHARGE MACHINING, EDM
ELECTRICAL EQPT REPAIR SVCS
ELECTRICAL EQPT REPAIR SVCS: High Voltage
ELECTRICAL EQPT: Automotive, NEC
ELECTRICAL GOODS, WHOLESALE: Air Conditioning Appliances
ELECTRICAL GOODS, WHOLESALE: Cable Conduit
ELECTRICAL GOODS, WHOLESALE: Electrical Entertainment Eqpt
ELECTRICAL GOODS, WHOLESALE: Electronic Parts
ELECTRICAL GOODS, WHOLESALE: Generators
ELECTRICAL GOODS, WHOLESALE: Lighting Fittings & Access
ELECTRICAL GOODS, WHOLESALE: Security Control Eqpt & Systems
ELECTRICAL GOODS, WHOLESALE: Semiconductor Devices
ELECTRICAL GOODS, WHOLESALE: Signaling, Eqpt
ELECTRICAL GOODS, WHOLESALE: Telephone & Telegraphic Eqpt
ELECTRICAL GOODS, WHOLESALE: Telephone Eqpt
ELECTRICAL GOODS, WHOLESALE: Wire & Cable
ELECTRICAL GOODS, WHOLESALE: Wire & Cable, Electronic
ELECTRICAL SPLYS
ELECTRICAL SUPPLIES: Porcelain
ELECTROMEDICAL EQPT
ELECTROMEDICAL EQPT WHOLESALERS
ELECTROMETALLURGICAL PRDTS
ELECTRON TUBES
ELECTRONIC DETECTION SYSTEMS: Aeronautical
ELECTRONIC DEVICES: Solid State, NEC
ELECTRONIC EQPT REPAIR SVCS
ELECTRONIC LOADS & POWER SPLYS
ELECTRONIC PARTS & EQPT WHOLESALERS
ELECTRONIC SHOPPING
ELECTRONIC TRAINING DEVICES
ELECTROPLATING & PLATING SVC
ELEVATORS & EQPT
ELEVATORS WHOLESALERS
ELEVATORS: Installation & Conversion
EMBLEMS: Embroidered
EMBROIDERY ADVERTISING SVCS
EMBROIDERY KITS
EMERGENCY ALARMS
ENCLOSURES: Electronic
ENCODERS: Digital
ENDOCRINE PRDTS
ENGINEERING SVCS
ENGINEERING SVCS: Acoustical
ENGINEERING SVCS: Civil

ENGINEERING SVCS: Construction & Civil
ENGINEERING SVCS: Electrical Or Electronic
ENGINEERING SVCS: Machine Tool Design
ENGINEERING SVCS: Mechanical
ENGINEERING SVCS: Structural
ENGINES: Diesel & Semi-Diesel Or Duel Fuel
ENGINES: Gasoline, NEC
ENGINES: Internal Combustion, NEC
ENGINES: Jet Propulsion
ENGINES: Marine
ENGRAVING SVC, NEC
ENGRAVING SVCS
ENVELOPES
ENVELOPES WHOLESALERS
EPOXY RESINS
EQUIPMENT: Pedestrian Traffic Control
EQUIPMENT: Rental & Leasing, NEC
ETCHING & ENGRAVING SVC
ETHYLENE-PROPYLENE RUBBERS: EPDM Polymers
EXHAUST SYSTEMS: Eqpt & Parts
EXPLOSIVES
EXTRACTS, FLAVORING
EYEGLASSES: Sunglasses

F

FABRIC STORES
FABRICS & CLOTHING: Rubber Coated
FABRICS: Apparel & Outerwear, Broadwoven
FABRICS: Apparel & Outerwear, Cotton
FABRICS: Automotive, From Manmade Fiber
FABRICS: Bonded-Fiber, Exc Felt
FABRICS: Broad Woven, Goods, Cotton
FABRICS: Broadwoven, Cotton
FABRICS: Broadwoven, Wool
FABRICS: Cloth, Warp Knit
FABRICS: Denims
FABRICS: Fiberglass, Broadwoven
FABRICS: Lace, Knit, NEC
FABRICS: Manmade Fiber, Narrow
FABRICS: Nonwoven
FABRICS: Pile, Circular Knit
FABRICS: Resin Or Plastic Coated
FABRICS: Rubberized
FABRICS: Scrub Cloths
FABRICS: Shoe Laces, Exc Leather
FABRICS: Specialty Including Twisted Weaves, Broadwoven
FABRICS: Trimmings, Textile
FABRICS: Upholstery, Cotton
FABRICS: Warp & Flat Knit Prdts
FABRICS: Weft Or Circular Knit
FABRICS: Wool, Broadwoven
FACILITIES SUPPORT SVCS
FAMILY CLOTHING STORES
FANS, BLOWING: Indl Or Commercial
FANS, EXHAUST: Indl Or Commercial
FARM & GARDEN MACHINERY WHOLESALERS
FARM PRDTS, RAW MATERIALS, WHOLESALE: Sugar
FARM SPLYS WHOLESALERS
FARM SPLYS, WHOLESALE: Feed
FARM SPLYS, WHOLESALE: Garden Splys
FARM SPLYS, WHOLESALE: Insecticides
FASTENERS WHOLESALERS
FASTENERS: Metal
FASTENERS: Metal
FASTENERS: Notions, Hooks & Eyes
FATTY ACID ESTERS & AMINOS
FAUCETS & SPIGOTS: Metal & Plastic
FEATHERS & FEATHER PRODUCTS
FELT, WHOLESALE
FELT: Acoustic
FENCES OR POSTS: Ornamental Iron Or Steel
FENCING MADE IN WIREDRAWING PLANTS
FENCING MATERIALS: Docks & Other Outdoor Prdts, Wood
FENCING MATERIALS: Wood
FENCING: Chain Link
FERTILIZER, AGRICULTURAL: Wholesalers
FIBER & FIBER PRDTS: Elastomeric
FIBER & FIBER PRDTS: Polyester
FIBER & FIBER PRDTS: Protein
FIBER OPTICS
FIBER: Vulcanized
FIBERS: Carbon & Graphite
FILTER ELEMENTS: Fluid & Hydraulic Line

FILTERS
FILTERS & SOFTENERS: Water, Household
FILTERS & STRAINERS: Pipeline
FILTERS: Air Intake, Internal Combustion Engine, Exc Auto
FILTERS: General Line, Indl
FILTERS: Oil, Internal Combustion Engine, Exc Auto
FILTRATION DEVICES: Electronic
FINISHING AGENTS
FINISHING AGENTS: Textile
FINISHING SVCS
FIRE ARMS, SMALL: Guns Or Gun Parts, 30 mm & Below
FIRE ARMS, SMALL: Pistols Or Pistol Parts, 30 mm & below
FIRE ARMS, SMALL: Rifles Or Rifle Parts, 30 mm & below
FIRE ARMS, SMALL: Shotguns Or Shotgun Parts, 30 mm & Below
FIRE DETECTION SYSTEMS
FIRE EXTINGUISHERS: Portable
FIRE OR BURGLARY RESISTIVE PRDTS
FIREARMS & AMMUNITION, EXC SPORTING, WHOLESALE
FIREFIGHTING APPARATUS
FIREPLACE EQPT & ACCESS
FIREWOOD, WHOLESALE
FIREWORKS
FISH & SEAFOOD PROCESSORS: Canned Or Cured
FISH & SEAFOOD PROCESSORS: Fresh Or Frozen
FISH & SEAFOOD WHOLESALERS
FISH FOOD
FISHING EQPT: Lures
FITTINGS & ASSEMBLIES: Hose & Tube, Hydraulic Or Pneumatic
FITTINGS: Pipe
FITTINGS: Pipe, Fabricated
FIXTURES & EQPT: Kitchen, Porcelain Enameled
FIXTURES: Bank, Metal, Ornamental
FLAGPOLES
FLAGS: Fabric
FLAGSTONES
FLAT GLASS: Construction
FLAT GLASS: Optical, Transparent, Exc Lenses
FLAT GLASS: Window, Clear & Colored
FLAVORS OR FLAVORING MATERIALS: Synthetic
FLOOR COVERING STORES
FLOOR COVERING STORES: Carpets
FLOOR COVERINGS: Textile Fiber
FLOORING: Hardwood
FLOORING: Rubber
FLOWERS, ARTIFICIAL, WHOLESALE
FLUES & PIPES: Stove Or Furnace
FLUID METERS & COUNTING DEVICES
FLUID POWER PUMPS & MOTORS
FLUID POWER VALVES & HOSE FITTINGS
FOAM RUBBER
FOAMS & RUBBER, WHOLESALE
FOIL & LEAF: Metal
FOIL: Aluminum
FOIL: Copper
FOIL: Laminated To Paper Or Other Materials
FOOD PRDTS, BREAKFAST: Cereal, Oatmeal
FOOD PRDTS, CANNED OR FRESH PACK: Fruit Juices
FOOD PRDTS, CANNED: Barbecue Sauce
FOOD PRDTS, CANNED: Fruit Juices, Fresh
FOOD PRDTS, CANNED: Fruits
FOOD PRDTS, CANNED: Fruits
FOOD PRDTS, CANNED: Fruits & Fruit Prdts
FOOD PRDTS, CANNED: Jams, Including Imitation
FOOD PRDTS, CANNED: Jams, Jellies & Preserves
FOOD PRDTS, CANNED: Soups, Exc Seafood
FOOD PRDTS, CANNED: Spaghetti & Other Pasta Sauce
FOOD PRDTS, CANNED: Tomato Sauce.
FOOD PRDTS, CANNED: Vegetables
FOOD PRDTS, CONFECTIONERY, WHOLESALE: Candy
FOOD PRDTS, CONFECTIONERY, WHOLESALE: Snack Foods
FOOD PRDTS, DAIRY, WHOLESALE: Frozen Dairy Desserts
FOOD PRDTS, FISH & SEAFOOD: Fish, Fresh, Prepared
FOOD PRDTS, FISH & SEAFOOD: Fish, Frozen, Prepared
FOOD PRDTS, FISH & SEAFOOD: Fish, Smoked
FOOD PRDTS, FROZEN: Ethnic Foods, NEC
FOOD PRDTS, FROZEN: Fruit Juice, Concentrates
FOOD PRDTS, FROZEN: Fruits
FOOD PRDTS, FROZEN: Fruits & Vegetables
FOOD PRDTS, FROZEN: Fruits, Juices & Vegetables
FOOD PRDTS, POULTRY, WHOLESALE: Poultry Prdts, NEC

FOOD PRDTS, WHOLESALE: Beverages, Exc Coffee & Tea
FOOD PRDTS, WHOLESALE: Chocolate
FOOD PRDTS, WHOLESALE: Cocoa
FOOD PRDTS, WHOLESALE: Coffee & Tea
FOOD PRDTS, WHOLESALE: Coffee, Green Or Roasted
FOOD PRDTS, WHOLESALE: Condiments
FOOD PRDTS, WHOLESALE: Flavorings & Fragrances
FOOD PRDTS, WHOLESALE: Grains
FOOD PRDTS, WHOLESALE: Juices
FOOD PRDTS, WHOLESALE: Natural & Organic
FOOD PRDTS, WHOLESALE: Organic & Diet
FOOD PRDTS, WHOLESALE: Pasta & Rice
FOOD PRDTS, WHOLESALE: Salad Dressing
FOOD PRDTS, WHOLESALE: Sauces
FOOD PRDTS, WHOLESALE: Specialty
FOOD PRDTS, WHOLESALE: Spices & Seasonings
FOOD PRDTS: Almond Pastes
FOOD PRDTS: Animal & marine fats & oils
FOOD PRDTS: Box Lunches, For Sale Off Premises
FOOD PRDTS: Bread Crumbs, Exc Made In Bakeries
FOOD PRDTS: Chicken, Processed, Fresh
FOOD PRDTS: Chocolate Bars, Solid
FOOD PRDTS: Cocoa, Instant
FOOD PRDTS: Coffee
FOOD PRDTS: Coffee Extracts
FOOD PRDTS: Coffee, Ground, Mixed With Grain Or Chicory
FOOD PRDTS: Corn Chips & Other Corn-Based Snacks
FOOD PRDTS: Dessert Mixes & Fillings
FOOD PRDTS: Dips, Exc Cheese & Sour Cream Based
FOOD PRDTS: Dough, Pizza, Prepared
FOOD PRDTS: Doughs, Frozen Or Refrig From Purchased Flour
FOOD PRDTS: Dressings, Salad, Raw & Cooked Exc Dry Mixes
FOOD PRDTS: Dried & Dehydrated Fruits, Vegetables & Soup Mix
FOOD PRDTS: Edible fats & oils
FOOD PRDTS: Flour
FOOD PRDTS: Flour & Other Grain Mill Products
FOOD PRDTS: Flour Mixes & Doughs
FOOD PRDTS: Fruit Juices
FOOD PRDTS: Fruits & Vegetables, Pickled
FOOD PRDTS: Ice, Cubes
FOOD PRDTS: Instant Coffee
FOOD PRDTS: Mixes, Pancake From Purchased Flour
FOOD PRDTS: Mustard, Prepared
FOOD PRDTS: Oil, Hydrogenated, Edible
FOOD PRDTS: Olive Oil
FOOD PRDTS: Pasta, Uncooked, Packaged With Other Ingredients
FOOD PRDTS: Peanut Butter
FOOD PRDTS: Pizza Doughs From Purchased Flour
FOOD PRDTS: Pizza, Refrigerated
FOOD PRDTS: Potato Chips & Other Potato-Based Snacks
FOOD PRDTS: Poultry, Processed, Frozen
FOOD PRDTS: Poultry, Slaughtered & Dressed
FOOD PRDTS: Seasonings & Spices
FOOD PRDTS: Soy Sauce
FOOD PRDTS: Sugar
FOOD PRDTS: Syrup, Maple
FOOD PRDTS: Syrups
FOOD PRDTS: Tea
FOOD PRDTS: Tofu, Exc Frozen Desserts
FOOD PRDTS: Vegetable Oil Mills, NEC
FOOD PRDTS: Vinegar
FOOD PRODUCTS MACHINERY
FOOD STORES: Convenience, Chain
FOOD STORES: Convenience, Independent
FOOD STORES: Cooperative
FOOD STORES: Delicatessen
FOOD STORES: Grocery, Chain
FOOD STORES: Grocery, Independent
FOOD STORES: Supermarkets, Chain
FOOTWEAR, WHOLESALE: Athletic
FOOTWEAR, WHOLESALE: Shoe Access
FOOTWEAR, WHOLESALE: Shoes
FOOTWEAR: Cut Stock
FORGINGS: Aircraft
FORGINGS: Aircraft, Ferrous
FORGINGS: Automotive & Internal Combustion Engine
FORGINGS: Construction Or Mining Eqpt, Ferrous
FORGINGS: Iron & Steel
FORGINGS: Machinery, Nonferrous

FORGINGS: Metal , Ornamental, Ferrous
FORGINGS: Nonferrous
FORMS: Concrete, Sheet Metal
FOUNDRIES: Aluminum
FOUNDRIES: Gray & Ductile Iron
FOUNDRIES: Iron
FOUNDRIES: Nonferrous
FOUNDRIES: Steel
FOUNDRIES: Steel Investment
FOUNDRY MACHINERY & EQPT
FRACTIONATION PRDTS OF CRUDE PETROLEUM, HYDROCARBONS, NEC
FRAMES: Chair, Metal
FRANCHISES, SELLING OR LICENSING
FREIGHT FORWARDING ARRANGEMENTS
FRICTION MATERIAL, MADE FROM POWDERED METAL
FRUIT & VEGETABLE MARKETS
FRUIT STANDS OR MARKETS
FRUITS & VEGETABLES WHOLESALERS: Fresh
FUEL ADDITIVES
FUEL CELLS: Solid State
FUEL OIL DEALERS
FUELS: Diesel
FUND RAISING ORGANIZATION, NON-FEE BASIS
FURNACE CASINGS: Sheet Metal
FURNACES & OVENS: Indl
FURNACES: Warm Air, Electric
FURNITURE PARTS: Metal
FURNITURE REPAIR & MAINTENANCE SVCS
FURNITURE STOCK & PARTS: Hardwood
FURNITURE STOCK & PARTS: Turnings, Wood
FURNITURE STORES
FURNITURE UPHOLSTERY REPAIR SVCS
FURNITURE WHOLESALERS
FURNITURE, HOUSEHOLD: Wholesalers
FURNITURE, MATTRESSES: Wholesalers
FURNITURE, OFFICE: Wholesalers
FURNITURE, OUTDOOR & LAWN: Wholesalers
FURNITURE, WHOLESALE: Beds & Bedding
FURNITURE, WHOLESALE: Racks
FURNITURE, WHOLESALE: Shelving
FURNITURE: Bean Bag Chairs
FURNITURE: Bedroom, Wood
FURNITURE: Box Springs, Assembled
FURNITURE: Cabinets & Vanities, Medicine, Metal
FURNITURE: Chairs, Household Wood
FURNITURE: Couches, Sofa/Davenport, Upholstered Wood Frames
FURNITURE: Desks, Household, Wood
FURNITURE: Desks, Wood
FURNITURE: Dining Room, Wood
FURNITURE: Fiberglass & Plastic
FURNITURE: Foundations & Platforms
FURNITURE: Hotel
FURNITURE: Household, Metal
FURNITURE: Juvenile, Metal
FURNITURE: Kitchen & Dining Room, Metal
FURNITURE: Laboratory
FURNITURE: Living Room, Upholstered On Wood Frames
FURNITURE: Mattresses & Foundations
FURNITURE: Mattresses, Box & Bedsprings
FURNITURE: Mattresses, Innerspring Or Box Spring
FURNITURE: Novelty, Wood
FURNITURE: Office, Exc Wood
FURNITURE: Office, Wood
FURNITURE: School
FURNITURE: Storage Chests, Household, Wood
FURNITURE: Table Tops, Marble
FURNITURE: Tables, Office, Wood
FURNITURE: Upholstered
FUSES: Electric

G

GAMES & TOYS: Baby Carriages & Restraint Seats
GAMES & TOYS: Craft & Hobby Kits & Sets
GAMES & TOYS: Electronic
GAMES & TOYS: Erector Sets
GARBAGE CONTAINERS: Plastic
GARBAGE DISPOSERS & COMPACTORS: Commercial
GAS & OIL FIELD EXPLORATION SVCS
GAS & OIL FIELD SVCS, NEC
GAS PROCESSING SVC
GASES & LIQUIFIED PETROLEUM GASES

GASES: Carbon Dioxide
GASES: Indl
GASES: Nitrogen
GASES: Oxygen
GASKET MATERIALS
GASKETS
GASKETS & SEALING DEVICES
GASOLINE FILLING STATIONS
GASOLINE WHOLESALERS
GASTROINTESTINAL OR GENITOURINARY SYSTEM DRUGS
GATES: Dam, Metal Plate
GAUGES: Pressure
GEARS
GEARS & GEAR UNITS: Reduction, Exc Auto
GEARS: Power Transmission, Exc Auto
GENERAL COUNSELING SVCS
GENERATING APPARATUS & PARTS: Electrical
GENERATION EQPT: Electronic
GENERATOR REPAIR SVCS
GENERATORS SETS: Steam
GENERATORS: Electrochemical, Fuel Cell
GENERATORS: Gas
GIFT SHOP
GIFT WRAP: Paper, Made From Purchased Materials
GIFT, NOVELTY & SOUVENIR STORES: Gifts & Novelties
GIFTS & NOVELTIES: Wholesalers
GLASS & GLASS CERAMIC PRDTS, PRESSED OR BLOWN: Tableware
GLASS PRDTS, FROM PURCHASED GLASS: Enameled
GLASS PRDTS, FROM PURCHASED GLASS: Glassware
GLASS PRDTS, FROM PURCHASED GLASS: Insulating
GLASS PRDTS, FROM PURCHASED GLASS: Mirrored
GLASS PRDTS, PRESSED OR BLOWN: Barware
GLASS PRDTS, PRESSED OR BLOWN: Furnishings & Access
GLASS PRDTS, PRESSED OR BLOWN: Glass Fibers, Textile
GLASS PRDTS, PRESSED OR BLOWN: Glassware, Art Or Decorative
GLASS PRDTS, PRESSED OR BLOWN: Optical
GLASS PRDTS, PRESSED OR BLOWN: Scientific Glassware
GLASS PRDTS, PRESSED OR BLOWN: Tubing
GLASS: Fiber
GLASS: Flat
GLASS: Laminated
GLASS: Pressed & Blown, NEC
GLASS: Safety
GLASSWARE WHOLESALERS
GLASSWARE: Laboratory
GLOVES: Safety
GOLD ORE MINING
GOLF COURSES: Public
GOLF EQPT
GOLF GOODS & EQPT
GOURMET FOOD STORES
GOVERNMENT, GENERAL: Administration
GRAIN & FIELD BEANS WHOLESALERS
GRANITE: Crushed & Broken
GRANITE: Cut & Shaped
GRAPHIC ARTS & RELATED DESIGN SVCS
GRATINGS: Open Steel Flooring
GRAVEL MINING
GREENHOUSES: Prefabricated Metal
GREETING CARDS WHOLESALERS
GRINDING SVC: Precision, Commercial Or Indl
GRINDING SVCS: Ophthalmic Lens, Exc Prescription
GROCERIES, GENERAL LINE WHOLESALERS
GUIDED MISSILES & SPACE VEHICLES
GUIDED MISSILES & SPACE VEHICLES: Research & Development
GUTTERS: Sheet Metal
GYPSUM PRDTS
GYROSCOPES

H

HAIR & HAIR BASED PRDTS
HAIR CARE PRDTS
HAIR CARE PRDTS: Hair Coloring Preparations
HAND TOOLS, NEC: Wholesalers
HANDBAGS
HANDBAGS: Women's
HARD RUBBER PRDTS, NEC
HARDWARE

HARDWARE & BUILDING PRDTS: Plastic
HARDWARE & EQPT: Stage, Exc Lighting
HARDWARE STORES
HARDWARE STORES: Builders'
HARDWARE STORES: Pumps & Pumping Eqpt
HARDWARE STORES: Tools
HARDWARE STORES: Tools, Hand
HARDWARE WHOLESALERS
HARDWARE, WHOLESALE: Builders', NEC
HARDWARE, WHOLESALE: Chains
HARDWARE, WHOLESALE: Furniture, NEC
HARDWARE, WHOLESALE: Power Tools & Access
HARDWARE, WHOLESALE: Screws
HARDWARE, WHOLESALE: Security Devices, Locks
HARDWARE: Aircraft
HARDWARE: Aircraft & Marine, Incl Pulleys & Similar Items
HARDWARE: Builders'
HARDWARE: Door Opening & Closing Devices, Exc Electrical
HARDWARE: Parachute
HARDWARE: Rubber
HARNESS ASSEMBLIES: Cable & Wire
HEALTH AIDS: Exercise Eqpt
HEARING AIDS
HEAT EMISSION OPERATING APPARATUS
HEAT EXCHANGERS: After Or Inter Coolers Or Condensers, Etc
HEAT TREATING: Metal
HEATERS: Swimming Pool, Electric
HEATERS: Swimming Pool, Oil Or Gas
HEATING & AIR CONDITIONING UNITS, COMBINATION
HEATING APPARATUS: Steam
HEATING EQPT: Complete
HEATING EQPT: Induction
HEATING PADS: Nonelectric
HEATING SYSTEMS: Radiant, Indl Process
HEATING UNITS & DEVICES: Indl, Electric
HELICOPTERS
HELMETS: Athletic
HELMETS: Steel
HOBBY, TOY & GAME STORES: Arts & Crafts & Splys
HOBBY, TOY & GAME STORES: Dolls & Access
HOISTS
HOISTS: Aircraft Loading
HOLDING COMPANIES: Investment, Exc Banks
HOLDING COMPANIES: Personal, Exc Banks
HOME HEALTH CARE SVCS
HOMEFURNISHING STORES: Fireplaces & Wood Burning Stoves
HOMEFURNISHING STORES: Lighting Fixtures
HOMEFURNISHING STORES: Pottery
HOMEFURNISHING STORES: Venetian Blinds
HOMEFURNISHINGS, WHOLESALE: Carpets
HOMEFURNISHINGS, WHOLESALE: Kitchenware
HOMEFURNISHINGS, WHOLESALE: Wood Flooring
HOMES: Log Cabins
HOODS: Range, Sheet Metal
HORSESHOES
HOSE: Flexible Metal
HOSE: Garden, Rubber
HOSE: Plastic
HOSE: Rubber
HOSPITALS: Medical & Surgical
HOT TUBS
HOT TUBS: Plastic & Fiberglass
HOTELS & MOTELS
HOUSEHOLD ARTICLES, EXC FURNITURE: Cut Stone
HOUSEHOLD ARTICLES, EXC KITCHEN: Pottery
HOUSEHOLD ARTICLES: Metal
HOUSEHOLD FURNISHINGS, NEC
HOUSEHOLD SEWING MACHINES WHOLESALERS: Electric
HOUSEWARES, ELECTRIC, EXC COOKING APPLIANCES & UTENSILS
HOUSEWARES, ELECTRIC: Air Purifiers, Portable
HOUSEWARES, ELECTRIC: Broilers
HOUSEWARES, ELECTRIC: Cooking Appliances
HOUSEWARES, ELECTRIC: Fans, Exhaust & Ventilating
HOUSEWARES, ELECTRIC: Heating Units, Electric Appliances
HOUSINGS: Business Machine, Sheet Metal
HUMIDIFIERS & DEHUMIDIFIERS
HYDRAULIC EQPT REPAIR SVC

I

ICE
ICE CREAM & ICES WHOLESALERS
IDENTIFICATION TAGS, EXC PAPER
IGNITION APPARATUS & DISTRIBUTORS
IGNITION SYSTEMS: High Frequency
INDL & PERSONAL SVC PAPER WHOLESALERS
INDL & PERSONAL SVC PAPER, WHOLESALE: Boxes & Containers
INDL & PERSONAL SVC PAPER, WHOLESALE: Shipping Splys
INDL EQPT SVCS
INDL GASES WHOLESALERS
INDL MACHINERY & EQPT WHOLESALERS
INDL PATTERNS: Foundry Cores
INDL PATTERNS: Foundry Patternmaking
INDL PROCESS INSTRUMENTS: Analyzers
INDL PROCESS INSTRUMENTS: Control
INDL PROCESS INSTRUMENTS: Elements, Primary
INDL PROCESS INSTRUMENTS: Moisture Meters
INDL PROCESS INSTRUMENTS: On-Stream Gas Or Liquid Analysis
INDL PROCESS INSTRUMENTS: Thermistors
INDL SALTS WHOLESALERS
INDL SPLYS WHOLESALERS
INDL SPLYS, WHOLESALE: Abrasives
INDL SPLYS, WHOLESALE: Bearings
INDL SPLYS, WHOLESALE: Fasteners & Fastening Eqpt
INDL SPLYS, WHOLESALE: Gaskets
INDL SPLYS, WHOLESALE: Gears
INDL SPLYS, WHOLESALE: Power Transmission, Eqpt & Apparatus
INDL SPLYS, WHOLESALE: Rubber Goods, Mechanical
INDL SPLYS, WHOLESALE: Seals
INDL SPLYS, WHOLESALE: Tools
INDL SPLYS, WHOLESALE: Tools, NEC
INDL SPLYS, WHOLESALE: Valves & Fittings
INERTIAL GUIDANCE SYSTEMS
INFORMATION RETRIEVAL SERVICES
INFORMATION SVCS: Consumer
INFRARED OBJECT DETECTION EQPT
INK OR WRITING FLUIDS
INK: Gravure
INK: Lithographic
INK: Printing
INSECT LAMPS: Electric
INSECTICIDES
INSECTICIDES & PESTICIDES
INSPECTION & TESTING SVCS
INSTRUMENTS & ACCESSORIES: Surveying
INSTRUMENTS & METERS: Measuring, Electric
INSTRUMENTS, LABORATORY: Analyzers, Automatic Chemical
INSTRUMENTS, LABORATORY: Blood Testing
INSTRUMENTS, LABORATORY: Liquid Chromatographic
INSTRUMENTS, LABORATORY: Mass Spectrometers
INSTRUMENTS, LABORATORY: Measuring, Specific Ion
INSTRUMENTS, LABORATORY: Spectrometers
INSTRUMENTS, MEASURING & CNTRL: Geophysical & Meteorological
INSTRUMENTS, MEASURING & CNTRL: Radiation & Testing, Nuclear
INSTRUMENTS, MEASURING & CNTRLG: Aircraft & Motor Vehicle
INSTRUMENTS, MEASURING & CONTROLLING: Gas Detectors
INSTRUMENTS, MEASURING & CONTROLLING: Ion Chambers
INSTRUMENTS, MEASURING & CONTROLLING: Spectrometers
INSTRUMENTS, MEASURING & CONTROLLING: Ultrasonic Testing
INSTRUMENTS, OPTICAL: Elements & Assemblies, Exc Ophthalmic
INSTRUMENTS, OPTICAL: Lenses, All Types Exc Ophthalmic
INSTRUMENTS, OPTICAL: Mirrors
INSTRUMENTS, OPTICAL: Sighting & Fire Control
INSTRUMENTS, OPTICAL: Test & Inspection
INSTRUMENTS, SURGICAL & MED: Fixation Appliances, Internal
INSTRUMENTS, SURGICAL & MED: Needles & Syringes, Hypodermic
INSTRUMENTS, SURGICAL & MEDICAL: Biopsy

INSTRUMENTS, SURGICAL & MEDICAL: Blood & Bone Work
INSTRUMENTS, SURGICAL & MEDICAL: Blood Pressure
INSTRUMENTS, SURGICAL & MEDICAL: Blood Transfusion
INSTRUMENTS, SURGICAL & MEDICAL: Catheters
INSTRUMENTS, SURGICAL & MEDICAL: Hemodialysis
INSTRUMENTS, SURGICAL & MEDICAL: Inhalation Therapy
INSTRUMENTS, SURGICAL & MEDICAL: IV Transfusion
INSTRUMENTS, SURGICAL & MEDICAL: Knives
INSTRUMENTS, SURGICAL & MEDICAL: Lasers, Surgical
INSTRUMENTS, SURGICAL & MEDICAL: Muscle Exercise, Ophthalmic
INSTRUMENTS, SURGICAL & MEDICAL: Needles, Suture
INSTRUMENTS, SURGICAL & MEDICAL: Ophthalmic
INSTRUMENTS, SURGICAL & MEDICAL: Stapling Devices, Surgical
INSTRUMENTS: Analytical
INSTRUMENTS: Digital Panel Meters, Electricity Measuring
INSTRUMENTS: Electrocardiographs
INSTRUMENTS: Electrolytic Conductivity, Laboratory
INSTRUMENTS: Endoscopic Eqpt, Electromedical
INSTRUMENTS: Flow, Indl Process
INSTRUMENTS: Indl Process Control
INSTRUMENTS: Infrared, Indl Process
INSTRUMENTS: Laser, Scientific & Engineering
INSTRUMENTS: Liquid Level, Indl Process
INSTRUMENTS: Measurement, Indl Process
INSTRUMENTS: Measuring & Controlling
INSTRUMENTS: Measuring, Electrical Energy
INSTRUMENTS: Measuring, Electrical Power
INSTRUMENTS: Medical & Surgical
INSTRUMENTS: Meteorological
INSTRUMENTS: Nautical
INSTRUMENTS: Optical, Analytical
INSTRUMENTS: Pressure Measurement, Indl
INSTRUMENTS: Radio Frequency Measuring
INSTRUMENTS: Temperature Measurement, Indl
INSTRUMENTS: Test, Electrical, Engine
INSTRUMENTS: Test, Electronic & Electric Measurement
INSTRUMENTS: Test, Electronic & Electrical Circuits
INSULATING BOARD, HARD PRESSED
INSULATING COMPOUNDS
INSULATION MATERIALS WHOLESALERS
INSULATION: Felt
INSULATION: Fiberglass
INSULATORS & INSULATION MATERIALS: Electrical
INSULATORS, PORCELAIN: Electrical
INSURANCE AGENTS, NEC
INSURANCE CARRIERS: Automobile
INSURANCE: Agents, Brokers & Service
INTEGRATED CIRCUITS, SEMICONDUCTOR NETWORKS, ETC
INTERIOR DECORATING SVCS
INTERIOR DESIGN SVCS, NEC
INTRAVENOUS SOLUTIONS
INVERTERS: Nonrotating Electrical
INVERTERS: Rotating Electrical
INVESTMENT ADVISORY SVCS
INVESTMENT RESEARCH SVCS
INVESTORS, NEC
IRON & STEEL PRDTS: Hot-Rolled

J

JACKS: Hydraulic
JARS: Plastic
JEWELERS' FINDINGS & MATERIALS
JEWELRY & PRECIOUS STONES WHOLESALERS
JEWELRY REPAIR SVCS
JEWELRY STORES
JEWELRY STORES: Precious Stones & Precious Metals
JEWELRY STORES: Silverware
JEWELRY, PRECIOUS METAL: Earrings
JEWELRY, PRECIOUS METAL: Necklaces
JEWELRY, PRECIOUS METAL: Pins
JEWELRY, PRECIOUS METAL: Rings, Finger
JEWELRY, PRECIOUS METAL: Settings & Mountings
JEWELRY, WHOLESALE
JEWELRY: Precious Metal
JIGS & FIXTURES
JOB PRINTING & NEWSPAPER PUBLISHING COMBINED
JOB TRAINING SVCS
JOINTS: Expansion, Pipe
JOINTS: Swivel & Universal, Exc Aircraft & Auto

JOISTS: Long-Span Series, Open Web Steel
JUNIOR COLLEGES

K

KAOLIN MINING
KEYBOARDS: Computer Or Office Machine
KIDNEY DIALYSIS CENTERS
KILNS & FURNACES: Ceramic
KITCHEN CABINETS WHOLESALERS
KITCHEN UTENSILS: Bakers' Eqpt, Wood
KITCHEN UTENSILS: Food Handling & Processing Prdts, Wood
KITCHENWARE STORES
KNIT OUTERWEAR DYEING & FINISHING, EXC HOSIERY & GLOVE
KNIVES: Agricultural Or Indl

L

LABELS: Paper, Made From Purchased Materials
LABELS: Woven
LABORATORIES, TESTING: Metallurgical
LABORATORIES, TESTING: Product Testing
LABORATORIES, TESTING: Product Testing, Safety/ Performance
LABORATORIES, TESTING: Radiation
LABORATORIES: Biological
LABORATORIES: Biological Research
LABORATORIES: Biotechnology
LABORATORIES: Commercial Nonphysical Research
LABORATORIES: Dental, Crown & Bridge Production
LABORATORIES: Electronic Research
LABORATORIES: Medical
LABORATORIES: Noncommercial Research
LABORATORIES: Physical Research, Commercial
LABORATORIES: Testing
LABORATORIES: Testing
LABORATORY APPARATUS & FURNITURE
LABORATORY APPARATUS & FURNITURE: Worktables
LABORATORY APPARATUS, EXC HEATING & MEASURING
LABORATORY APPARATUS: Freezers
LABORATORY APPARATUS: Heating
LABORATORY APPARATUS: Laser Beam Alignment Device
LABORATORY APPARATUS: Sample Preparation Apparatus
LABORATORY APPARATUS: Shakers & Stirrers
LABORATORY CHEMICALS: Organic
LABORATORY EQPT, EXC MEDICAL: Wholesalers
LABORATORY EQPT: Chemical
LABORATORY EQPT: Clinical Instruments Exc Medical
LABORATORY EQPT: Measuring
LABORATORY EQPT: Sterilizers
LABORATORY INSTRUMENT REPAIR SVCS
LADDERS: Metal
LAMINATED PLASTICS: Plate, Sheet, Rod & Tubes
LAMINATING MATERIALS
LAMINATING SVCS
LAMP & LIGHT BULBS & TUBES
LAMP BULBS & TUBES, ELECTRIC: Light, Complete
LAMP BULBS & TUBES/PARTS, ELECTRIC: Generalized Applications
LAMP SHADES: Glass
LAND SUBDIVIDERS & DEVELOPERS: Commercial
LAND SUBDIVIDERS & DEVELOPERS: Residential
LAND SUBDIVISION & DEVELOPMENT
LASER SYSTEMS & EQPT
LASERS: Welding, Drilling & Cutting Eqpt
LATEX: Foamed
LAUNDRY EQPT: Commercial
LAUNDRY SVC: Indl Clothing
LAUNDRY SVCS: Indl
LAWN & GARDEN EQPT
LAWN & GARDEN EQPT: Tractors & Eqpt
LEAD
LEAD PENCILS & ART GOODS
LEAF TOBACCO WHOLESALERS
LEASING & RENTAL SVCS: Cranes & Aerial Lift Eqpt
LEASING & RENTAL: Construction & Mining Eqpt
LEASING & RENTAL: Medical Machinery & Eqpt
LEASING & RENTAL: Trucks, Without Drivers
LEASING: Shipping Container
LEATHER & CUT STOCK WHOLESALERS
LEATHER GOODS, EXC FOOTWEAR, GLOVES, LUGGAGE/ BELTING, WHOL
LEATHER GOODS: Garments

LEATHER GOODS: Holsters
LEATHER GOODS: Personal
LEATHER GOODS: Wallets
LEATHER TANNING & FINISHING
LEATHER, LEATHER GOODS & FURS, WHOLESALE
LEATHER: Artificial
LEGAL OFFICES & SVCS
LIFE RAFTS: Rubber
LIFESAVING & SURVIVAL EQPT, EXC MEDICAL, WHOLESALE
LIGHTING EQPT: Flashlights
LIGHTING EQPT: Locomotive & Railroad Car Lights
LIGHTING EQPT: Motor Vehicle, Headlights
LIGHTING EQPT: Motor Vehicle, NEC
LIGHTING EQPT: Outdoor
LIGHTING EQPT: Strobe Lighting Systems
LIGHTING FIXTURES WHOLESALERS
LIGHTING FIXTURES, NEC
LIGHTING FIXTURES: Decorative Area
LIGHTING FIXTURES: Fluorescent, Commercial
LIGHTING FIXTURES: Indl & Commercial
LIGHTING FIXTURES: Residential
LIGHTING FIXTURES: Residential, Electric
LIGHTING FIXTURES: Street
LIME
LIMESTONE: Crushed & Broken
LIMESTONE: Dimension
LINEN SPLY SVC: Uniform
LINENS & TOWELS WHOLESALERS
LINENS: Table & Dresser Scarves, From Purchased Materials
LINERS & COVERS: Fabric
LINERS & LINING
LININGS: Fabric, Apparel & Other, Exc Millinery
LIQUEFIED PETROLEUM GAS WHOLESALERS
LIQUID CRYSTAL DISPLAYS
LOADS: Electronic
LOCKS
LOCKSMITHS
LOCOMOTIVES & PARTS
LOGGING
LOGGING CAMPS & CONTRACTORS
LOGGING: Timber, Cut At Logging Camp
LOGGING: Wooden Logs
LOGS: Gas, Fireplace
LOTIONS OR CREAMS: Face
LOTIONS: SHAVING
LOUDSPEAKERS
LUBRICANTS: Corrosion Preventive
LUBRICATING EQPT: Indl
LUBRICATION SYSTEMS & EQPT
LUGGAGE & BRIEFCASES
LUGGAGE: Wardrobe Bags
LUMBER & BLDG MATLS DEALER, RET: Garage Doors, Sell/ Install
LUMBER & BLDG MATLS DEALERS, RET: Energy Conservation Prdts
LUMBER & BLDG MATRLS DEALERS, RET: Bath Fixtures, Eqpt/Sply
LUMBER & BLDG MTRLS DEALERS, RET: Planing Mill Prdts/ Lumber
LUMBER & BUILDING MATERIAL DEALERS, RETAIL: Roofing Material
LUMBER & BUILDING MATERIALS DEALER, RET: Door & Window Prdts
LUMBER & BUILDING MATERIALS DEALER, RET: Masonry Matls/Splys
LUMBER & BUILDING MATERIALS DEALERS, RET: Sash, Wood/Metal
LUMBER & BUILDING MATERIALS DEALERS, RETAIL: Brick
LUMBER & BUILDING MATERIALS DEALERS, RETAIL: Cement
LUMBER & BUILDING MATERIALS DEALERS, RETAIL: Modular Homes
LUMBER & BUILDING MATERIALS DEALERS, RETAIL: Sand & Gravel
LUMBER & BUILDING MATERIALS DEALERS, RETAIL: Tile, Ceramic
LUMBER & BUILDING MATERIALS RET DEALERS: Millwork & Lumber
LUMBER & BUILDING MATLS DEALERS, RET: Concrete/ Cinder Block
LUMBER: Flooring, Dressed, Softwood
LUMBER: Hardboard

LUMBER: Hardwood Dimension
LUMBER: Hardwood Dimension & Flooring Mills
LUMBER: Kiln Dried
LUMBER: Plywood, Hardwood
LUMBER: Plywood, Hardwood or Hardwood Faced
LUMBER: Treated

M

MACHINE PARTS: Stamped Or Pressed Metal
MACHINE TOOL ACCESS: Broaches
MACHINE TOOL ACCESS: Cutting
MACHINE TOOL ACCESS: Drills
MACHINE TOOL ACCESS: Honing Heads
MACHINE TOOL ACCESS: Tools & Access
MACHINE TOOL ATTACHMENTS & ACCESS
MACHINE TOOLS & ACCESS
MACHINE TOOLS, METAL CUTTING: Drilling
MACHINE TOOLS, METAL CUTTING: Exotic, Including Explosive
MACHINE TOOLS, METAL CUTTING: Plasma Process
MACHINE TOOLS, METAL CUTTING: Saws, Power
MACHINE TOOLS, METAL CUTTING: Tool Replacement & Rpr Parts
MACHINE TOOLS, METAL CUTTING: Vertical Turning & Boring
MACHINE TOOLS, METAL FORMING: Bending
MACHINE TOOLS, METAL FORMING: Elastic Membrane
MACHINE TOOLS, METAL FORMING: Mechanical, Pneumatic Or Hyd
MACHINE TOOLS, METAL FORMING: Pressing
MACHINE TOOLS, METAL FORMING: Rebuilt
MACHINE TOOLS, METAL FORMING: Spring Winding & Forming
MACHINE TOOLS: Metal Cutting
MACHINE TOOLS: Metal Forming
MACHINERY & EQPT FINANCE LEASING
MACHINERY & EQPT, AGRICULTURAL, WHOLESALE: Agricultural, NEC
MACHINERY & EQPT, AGRICULTURAL, WHOLESALE: Landscaping Eqpt
MACHINERY & EQPT, INDL, WHOLESALE: Chemical Process
MACHINERY & EQPT, INDL, WHOLESALE: Conveyor Systems
MACHINERY & EQPT, INDL, WHOLESALE: Cranes
MACHINERY & EQPT, INDL, WHOLESALE: Engines & Parts, Diesel
MACHINERY & EQPT, INDL, WHOLESALE: Engines, Gasoline
MACHINERY & EQPT, INDL, WHOLESALE: Engs/ Transportation Eqpt
MACHINERY & EQPT, INDL, WHOLESALE: Fans
MACHINERY & EQPT, INDL, WHOLESALE: Heat Exchange
MACHINERY & EQPT, INDL, WHOLESALE: Hydraulic Systems
MACHINERY & EQPT, INDL, WHOLESALE: Indl Machine Parts
MACHINERY & EQPT, INDL, WHOLESALE: Instruments & Cntrl Eqpt
MACHINERY & EQPT, INDL, WHOLESALE: Lift Trucks & Parts
MACHINERY & EQPT, INDL, WHOLESALE: Machine Tools & Access
MACHINERY & EQPT, INDL, WHOLESALE: Machine Tools & Metalwork
MACHINERY & EQPT, INDL, WHOLESALE: Measure/Test, Electric
MACHINERY & EQPT, INDL, WHOLESALE: Packaging
MACHINERY & EQPT, INDL, WHOLESALE: Paper Manufacturing
MACHINERY & EQPT, INDL, WHOLESALE: Petroleum Industry
MACHINERY & EQPT, INDL, WHOLESALE: Processing & Packaging
MACHINERY & EQPT, INDL, WHOLESALE: Recycling
MACHINERY & EQPT, INDL, WHOLESALE: Safety Eqpt
MACHINERY & EQPT, INDL, WHOLESALE: Water Pumps
MACHINERY & EQPT, WHOLESALE: Construction, General
MACHINERY & EQPT, WHOLESALE: Road Construction & Maintenance
MACHINERY & EQPT: Electroplating
MACHINERY & EQPT: Farm
MACHINERY & EQPT: Liquid Automation

MACHINERY, EQPT & SUPPLIES: Parking Facility
MACHINERY, FOOD PRDTS: Confectionery
MACHINERY, FOOD PRDTS: Ovens, Bakery
MACHINERY, MAILING: Postage Meters
MACHINERY, METALWORKING: Coiling
MACHINERY, OFFICE: Paper Handling
MACHINERY, OFFICE: Pencil Sharpeners
MACHINERY, OFFICE: Stapling, Hand Or Power
MACHINERY, PACKAGING: Carton Packing
MACHINERY, PACKAGING: Packing & Wrapping
MACHINERY, PAPER INDUSTRY: Converting, Die Cutting & Stampng
MACHINERY, PAPER INDUSTRY: Paper Mill, Plating, Etc
MACHINERY, PAPER INDUSTRY: Pulp Mill
MACHINERY, PRINTING TRADES: Plates
MACHINERY, PRINTING TRADES: Presses, Gravure
MACHINERY, SEWING: Sewing & Hat & Zipper Making
MACHINERY, TEXTILE: Finishing
MACHINERY, TEXTILE: Printing
MACHINERY: Ammunition & Explosives Loading
MACHINERY: Automotive Related
MACHINERY: Bag & Envelope Making
MACHINERY: Bridge Or Gate, Hydraulic
MACHINERY: Concrete Prdts
MACHINERY: Construction
MACHINERY: Cryogenic, Industrial
MACHINERY: Custom
MACHINERY: Desalination Eqpt
MACHINERY: Electrical Discharge Erosion
MACHINERY: Electronic Component Making
MACHINERY: Gas Producers
MACHINERY: Gas Separators
MACHINERY: Gear Cutting & Finishing
MACHINERY: Ice Cream
MACHINERY: Metalworking
MACHINERY: Packaging
MACHINERY: Paint Making
MACHINERY: Plastic Working
MACHINERY: Printing Presses
MACHINERY: Recycling
MACHINERY: Road Construction & Maintenance
MACHINERY: Robots, Molding & Forming Plastics
MACHINERY: Rubber Working
MACHINERY: Screening Eqpt, Electric
MACHINERY: Semiconductor Manufacturing
MACHINERY: Separation Eqpt, Magnetic
MACHINERY: Textile
MACHINERY: Tobacco Prdts
MACHINERY: Woodworking
MACHINISTS' TOOLS & MACHINES: Measuring, Metalworking Type
MACHINISTS' TOOLS: Measuring, Precision
MACHINISTS' TOOLS: Precision
MACHINISTS' TOOLS: Scales, Measuring, Precision
MAGNETIC INK & OPTICAL SCANNING EQPT
MAGNETIC SHIELDS, METAL
MAGNETIC TAPE, AUDIO: Prerecorded
MAIL-ORDER HOUSE, NEC
MAIL-ORDER HOUSES: Computer Software
MAIL-ORDER HOUSES: Educational Splys & Eqpt
MAIL-ORDER HOUSES: Fitness & Sporting Goods
MAIL-ORDER HOUSES: Food
MAIL-ORDER HOUSES: Women's Apparel
MAILBOX RENTAL & RELATED SVCS
MAILING LIST: Compilers
MAILING MACHINES WHOLESALERS
MAILING SVCS, NEC
MANAGEMENT CONSULTING SVCS: Automation & Robotics
MANAGEMENT CONSULTING SVCS: Business
MANAGEMENT CONSULTING SVCS: Business Planning & Organizing
MANAGEMENT CONSULTING SVCS: Construction Project
MANAGEMENT CONSULTING SVCS: Food & Beverage
MANAGEMENT CONSULTING SVCS: General
MANAGEMENT CONSULTING SVCS: Hospital & Health
MANAGEMENT CONSULTING SVCS: Industrial
MANAGEMENT CONSULTING SVCS: Industrial & Labor
MANAGEMENT CONSULTING SVCS: Industry Specialist
MANAGEMENT CONSULTING SVCS: Information Systems
MANAGEMENT CONSULTING SVCS: Maintenance
MANAGEMENT CONSULTING SVCS: Manufacturing
MANAGEMENT CONSULTING SVCS: Public Utilities
MANAGEMENT CONSULTING SVCS: Real Estate

MANAGEMENT CONSULTING SVCS: Restaurant & Food
MANAGEMENT CONSULTING SVCS: Training & Development
MANAGEMENT SERVICES
MANAGEMENT SVCS: Business
MANAGEMENT SVCS: Construction
MANPOWER TRAINING
MANUFACTURING INDUSTRIES, NEC
MARBLE, BUILDING: Cut & Shaped
MARINAS
MARINE HARDWARE
MARINE RELATED EQPT
MARINE SPLYS WHOLESALERS
MARKING DEVICES
MARKING DEVICES: Embossing Seals & Hand Stamps
MARKING DEVICES: Embossing Seals, Corporate & Official
MATCHES & MATCH BOOKS
MATS, MATTING & PADS: Door, Paper, Grass, Reed, Coir, Etc
MEAT MARKETS
MEAT PRDTS: Frozen
MEAT PRDTS: Ham, Smoked, From Purchased Meat
MEAT PRDTS: Prepared Beef Prdts From Purchased Beef
MEAT PRDTS: Roast Beef, From Purchased Meat
MEAT PRDTS: Sausages & Related Prdts, From Purchased Meat
MEAT PRDTS: Sausages, From Purchased Meat
MEAT PRDTS: Smoked
MEAT PRDTS: Snack Sticks, Incl Jerky, From Purchased Meat
MEAT PROCESSING MACHINERY
MEDIA: Magnetic & Optical Recording
MEDICAL & HOSPITAL EQPT WHOLESALERS
MEDICAL & SURGICAL SPLYS: Bandages & Dressings
MEDICAL & SURGICAL SPLYS: Braces, Elastic
MEDICAL & SURGICAL SPLYS: Braces, Orthopedic
MEDICAL & SURGICAL SPLYS: Clothing, Fire Resistant & Protect
MEDICAL & SURGICAL SPLYS: Cosmetic Restorations
MEDICAL & SURGICAL SPLYS: Dressings, Surgical
MEDICAL & SURGICAL SPLYS: Ear Plugs
MEDICAL & SURGICAL SPLYS: Foot Appliances, Orthopedic
MEDICAL & SURGICAL SPLYS: Gynecological Splys & Appliances
MEDICAL & SURGICAL SPLYS: Ligatures
MEDICAL & SURGICAL SPLYS: Limbs, Artificial
MEDICAL & SURGICAL SPLYS: Models, Anatomical
MEDICAL & SURGICAL SPLYS: Orthopedic Appliances
MEDICAL & SURGICAL SPLYS: Personal Safety Eqpt
MEDICAL & SURGICAL SPLYS: Prosthetic Appliances
MEDICAL & SURGICAL SPLYS: Splints, Pneumatic & Wood
MEDICAL EQPT REPAIR SVCS, NON-ELECTRIC
MEDICAL EQPT: Cardiographs
MEDICAL EQPT: Diagnostic
MEDICAL EQPT: Electromedical Apparatus
MEDICAL EQPT: Electrotherapeutic Apparatus
MEDICAL EQPT: Heart & Lung
MEDICAL EQPT: Ultrasonic Scanning Devices
MEDICAL EQPT: Ultrasonic, Exc Cleaning
MEDICAL EQPT: X-Ray Apparatus & Tubes, Radiographic
MEDICAL EQPT: X-Ray Apparatus & Tubes, Therapeutic
MEDICAL SUNDRIES: Rubber
MEDICAL SVCS ORGANIZATION
MEDICAL, DENTAL & HOSP EQPT, WHOLESALE: X-ray Film & Splys
MEDICAL, DENTAL & HOSPITAL EQPT, WHOL: Surgical Eqpt & Splys
MEMBERSHIP ORGANIZATIONS, BUSINESS: Growers' Association
MEMBERSHIP ORGANIZATIONS, PROFESSIONAL: Accounting Assoc
MEMBERSHIP ORGANIZATIONS, PROFESSIONAL: Health Association
MEMBERSHIP ORGANIZATIONS, REL: Churches, Temples & Shrines
MEMBERSHIP ORGS, RELIGIOUS: Non-Denominational Church
MEMBERSHIP SPORTS & RECREATION CLUBS
MEN'S & BOYS' CLOTHING STORES
MEN'S & BOYS' CLOTHING WHOLESALERS, NEC
MEN'S & BOYS' HOSIERY WHOLESALERS
MEN'S & BOYS' SPORTSWEAR CLOTHING STORES
MERCHANDISING MACHINE OPERATORS: Vending

METAL COMPONENTS: Prefabricated
METAL FINISHING SVCS
METAL MINING SVCS
METAL OXIDE SILICONE OR MOS DEVICES
METAL SERVICE CENTERS & OFFICES
METAL STAMPING, FOR THE TRADE
METAL STAMPINGS: Perforated
METAL TREATING COMPOUNDS
METAL: Battery
METALS SVC CENTERS & WHOLESALERS: Bars, Metal
METALS SVC CENTERS & WHOLESALERS: Cable, Wire
METALS SVC CENTERS & WHOLESALERS: Ferrous Metals
METALS SVC CENTERS & WHOLESALERS: Forgings, Ferrous
METALS SVC CENTERS & WHOLESALERS: Foundry Prdts
METALS SVC CENTERS & WHOLESALERS: Pipe & Tubing, Steel
METALS SVC CENTERS & WHOLESALERS: Sheets, Metal
METALS SVC CENTERS & WHOLESALERS: Steel
METALS SVC CENTERS & WHOLESALERS: Tubing, Metal
METALS: Precious NEC
METALS: Precious, Secondary
METALS: Primary Nonferrous, NEC
METALWORK: Miscellaneous
METALWORK: Ornamental
METALWORKING MACHINERY WHOLESALERS
METERING DEVICES: Water Quality Monitoring & Control Systems
METERS: Turbine Flow, Indl Process
MICA PRDTS
MICROCIRCUITS, INTEGRATED: Semiconductor
MICROPHONES
MICROPROCESSORS
MICROSCOPES: Electron & Proton
MICROWAVE COMPONENTS
MILITARY INSIGNIA
MILITARY INSIGNIA, TEXTILE
MILK, FLUID: Wholesalers
MILL PRDTS: Structural & Rail
MILLING: Rice
MILLWORK
MINE DEVELOPMENT SVCS: Nonmetallic Minerals
MINERAL WOOL
MINERAL WOOL INSULATION PRDTS
MINERALS: Ground or Treated
MINING EXPLORATION & DEVELOPMENT SVCS
MISSILE GUIDANCE SYSTEMS & EQPT
MIXTURES & BLOCKS: Asphalt Paving
MOBILE COMMUNICATIONS EQPT
MOBILE HOMES
MOBILE HOMES: Personal Or Private Use
MODELS: General, Exc Toy
MODULES: Computer Logic
MODULES: Solid State
MOLDED RUBBER PRDTS
MOLDING COMPOUNDS
MOLDINGS & TRIM: Metal, Exc Automobile
MOLDINGS OR TRIM: Automobile, Stamped Metal
MOLDS: Indl
MONOFILAMENTS: Nontextile
MONUMENTS & GRAVE MARKERS, WHOLESALE
MOPS: Floor & Dust
MOTION PICTURE & VIDEO DISTRIBUTION
MOTION PICTURE & VIDEO PRODUCTION SVCS
MOTION PICTURE & VIDEO PRODUCTION SVCS: Educational
MOTION PICTURE EQPT
MOTOR & GENERATOR PARTS: Electric
MOTOR CONTROL CENTERS
MOTOR HOMES
MOTOR SCOOTERS & PARTS
MOTOR VEHICLE ASSEMBLY, COMPLETE: Ambulances
MOTOR VEHICLE ASSEMBLY, COMPLETE: Buses, All Types
MOTOR VEHICLE ASSEMBLY, COMPLETE: Fire Department Vehicles
MOTOR VEHICLE ASSEMBLY, COMPLETE: Military Motor Vehicle
MOTOR VEHICLE DEALERS: Automobiles, New & Used
MOTOR VEHICLE DEALERS: Vans, New & Used
MOTOR VEHICLE PARTS & ACCESS: Bearings
MOTOR VEHICLE PARTS & ACCESS: Body Components & Frames
MOTOR VEHICLE PARTS & ACCESS: Electrical Eqpt

MOTOR VEHICLE PARTS & ACCESS: Engines & Parts
MOTOR VEHICLE PARTS & ACCESS: Fifth Wheels
MOTOR VEHICLE PARTS & ACCESS: Gears
MOTOR VEHICLE PARTS & ACCESS: Lifting Mechanisms, Dump Truck
MOTOR VEHICLE PARTS & ACCESS: Pumps, Hydraulic Fluid Power
MOTOR VEHICLE PARTS & ACCESS: Tie Rods
MOTOR VEHICLE PARTS & ACCESS: Tops
MOTOR VEHICLE PARTS & ACCESS: Trailer Hitches
MOTOR VEHICLE PARTS & ACCESS: Transmission Housings Or Parts
MOTOR VEHICLE PARTS & ACCESS: Transmissions
MOTOR VEHICLE PARTS & ACCESS: Water Pumps
MOTOR VEHICLE PARTS & ACCESS: Wiring Harness Sets
MOTOR VEHICLE SPLYS & PARTS WHOLESALERS: New
MOTOR VEHICLE: Hardware
MOTOR VEHICLE: Shock Absorbers
MOTOR VEHICLE: Steering Mechanisms
MOTOR VEHICLES & CAR BODIES
MOTOR VEHICLES, WHOLESALE: Fire Trucks
MOTORCYCLE DEALERS
MOTORCYCLES & RELATED PARTS
MOTORS: Electric
MOTORS: Generators
MOTORS: Pneumatic
MULTIPLEXERS: Telephone & Telegraph
MUSIC DISTRIBUTION APPARATUS
MUSICAL INSTRUMENTS & ACCESS: NEC
MUSICAL INSTRUMENTS & ACCESS: Pianos
MUSICAL INSTRUMENTS & PARTS: Percussion
MUSICAL INSTRUMENTS WHOLESALERS
MUSICAL INSTRUMENTS: Guitars & Parts, Electric & Acoustic

N

NAILS: Steel, Wire Or Cut
NAME PLATES: Engraved Or Etched
NATURAL GAS LIQUIDS PRODUCTION
NATURAL GAS PRODUCTION
NATURAL GASOLINE PRODUCTION
NAVIGATIONAL SYSTEMS & INSTRUMENTS
NICKEL
NONCURRENT CARRYING WIRING DEVICES
NONFERROUS: Rolling & Drawing, NEC
NOTEBOOKS, MADE FROM PURCHASED MATERIALS
NOVELTIES
NOVELTIES & SPECIALTIES: Metal
NOVELTIES: Plastic
NOZZLES: Spray, Aerosol, Paint Or Insecticide
NUCLEAR FUELS SCRAP REPROCESSING
NURSERY STOCK, WHOLESALE
NUTS: Metal
NYLON FIBERS
NYLON RESINS

O

OFFICE EQPT WHOLESALERS
OFFICE EQPT, WHOLESALE: Photocopy Machines
OFFICE SPLY & STATIONERY STORES: Office Forms & Splys
OFFICE SPLYS, NEC, WHOLESALE
OIL & GAS FIELD MACHINERY
OIL FIELD MACHINERY & EQPT
OIL FIELD SVCS, NEC
OIL TREATING COMPOUNDS
OILS & ESSENTIAL OILS
OILS: Cutting
OILS: Lubricating
OINTMENTS
OLEFINS
OPERATOR TRAINING, COMPUTER
OPHTHALMIC GOODS
OPHTHALMIC GOODS WHOLESALERS
OPHTHALMIC GOODS: Frames & Parts, Eyeglass & Spectacle
OPHTHALMIC GOODS: Lenses, Ophthalmic
OPTICAL GOODS STORES
OPTICAL GOODS STORES: Contact Lenses, Prescription
OPTICAL INSTRUMENT REPAIR SVCS
OPTICAL INSTRUMENTS & APPARATUS
OPTICAL INSTRUMENTS & LENSES
ORAL PREPARATIONS

ORGANIZATIONS: Educational Research Agency
ORGANIZATIONS: Medical Research
ORGANIZATIONS: Physical Research, Noncommercial
ORGANIZATIONS: Professional
ORGANIZATIONS: Religious
ORGANIZATIONS: Research Institute
ORNAMENTS: Christmas Tree, Exc Electrical & Glass
OSCILLATORS
OUTBOARD MOTORS: Electric

P

PACKAGE DESIGN SVCS
PACKAGING & LABELING SVCS
PACKAGING MATERIALS, WHOLESALE
PACKAGING MATERIALS: Paper
PACKAGING MATERIALS: Paper, Coated Or Laminated
PACKAGING MATERIALS: Paper, Thermoplastic Coated
PACKAGING MATERIALS: Plastic Film, Coated Or Laminated
PACKAGING: Blister Or Bubble Formed, Plastic
PACKING & CRATING SVC
PACKING MATERIALS: Mechanical
PADDING: Foamed Plastics
PAINTS & ADDITIVES
PAINTS & ALLIED PRODUCTS
PAINTS, VARNISHES & SPLYS WHOLESALERS
PAINTS, VARNISHES & SPLYS, WHOLESALE: Paints
PAINTS: Oil Or Alkyd Vehicle Or Water Thinned
PAINTS: Waterproof
PALLETS & SKIDS: Wood
PANEL & DISTRIBUTION BOARDS & OTHER RELATED APPARATUS
PANELS: Building, Plastic, NEC
PAPER & BOARD: Die-cut
PAPER & PAPER PRDTS: Crepe, Made From Purchased Materials
PAPER PRDTS: Infant & Baby Prdts
PAPER PRDTS: Napkin Stock
PAPER PRDTS: Pressed & Molded Pulp & Fiber Prdts
PAPER PRDTS: Sanitary
PAPER PRDTS: Sanitary Tissue Paper
PAPER PRDTS: Tampons, Sanitary, Made From Purchased Material
PAPER, WHOLESALE: Printing
PAPER: Adhesive
PAPER: Bank Note
PAPER: Building, Insulating & Packaging
PAPER: Cardboard
PAPER: Chart & Graph, Ruled
PAPER: Cigarette
PAPER: Coated & Laminated, NEC
PAPER: Coated, Exc Photographic, Carbon Or Abrasive
PAPER: Corrugated
PAPER: Filter
PAPER: Gift Wrap
PAPER: Kraft
PAPER: Packaging
PAPER: Specialty
PAPER: Specialty Or Chemically Treated
PAPER: Tissue
PAPER: Uncoated
PAPER: Wallpaper
PAPERBOARD PRDTS: Container Board
PAPERBOARD PRDTS: Folding Boxboard
PAPERBOARD PRDTS: Packaging Board
PAPERBOARD: Boxboard
PARACHUTES
PARTICLEBOARD
PARTITIONS & FIXTURES: Except Wood
PARTITIONS: Solid Fiber, Made From Purchased Materials
PARTITIONS: Wood & Fixtures
PARTS: Metal
PATENT OWNERS & LESSORS
PATTERNS: Indl
PAVERS
PAVING MIXTURES
PENCILS & PENS WHOLESALERS
PENS & PARTS: Ball Point
PERFUME: Perfumes, Natural Or Synthetic
PERFUMES
PEST CONTROL IN STRUCTURES SVCS
PEST CONTROL SVCS
PESTICIDES
PET FOOD WHOLESALERS

PET SPLYS
PHARMACEUTICAL PREPARATIONS: Adrenal
PHARMACEUTICAL PREPARATIONS: Druggists' Preparations
PHARMACEUTICAL PREPARATIONS: Pills
PHARMACEUTICAL PREPARATIONS: Powders
PHARMACEUTICAL PREPARATIONS: Proprietary Drug
PHARMACEUTICAL PREPARATIONS: Solutions
PHARMACEUTICAL PREPARATIONS: Tablets
PHARMACEUTICALS
PHARMACEUTICALS: Mail-Order Svc
PHOTOCOPY MACHINES
PHOTOCOPYING & DUPLICATING SVCS
PHOTOGRAPHIC EQPT & SPLYS
PHOTOGRAPHIC EQPT & SPLYS WHOLESALERS
PHOTOGRAPHIC EQPT & SPLYS: Editing Eqpt, Motion Picture
PHOTOGRAPHIC EQPT & SPLYS: Graphic Arts Plates, Sensitized
PHOTOGRAPHIC SENSITIZED GOODS, NEC
PHOTOGRAPHY SVCS: Commercial
PHYSICIANS' OFFICES & CLINICS: Medical doctors
PICTURE FRAMES: Metal
PICTURE FRAMES: Wood
PICTURE FRAMING SVCS, CUSTOM
PIECE GOODS & NOTIONS WHOLESALERS
PIECE GOODS, NOTIONS & DRY GOODS, WHOL: Textiles, Woven
PIECE GOODS, NOTIONS & OTHER DRY GOODS, WHOLESALE: Fabrics
PIECE GOODS, NOTIONS/DRY GOODS, WHOL: Fabrics, Synthetic
PINS
PIPE & TUBES: Copper & Copper Alloy
PIPE & TUBES: Seamless
PIPE CLEANERS
PIPE FITTINGS: Plastic
PIPE SECTIONS, FABRICATED FROM PURCHASED PIPE
PIPE: Plastic
PIPE: Water, Cast Iron
PIPELINE TERMINAL FACILITIES: Independent
PIPES & TUBES
PIPES & TUBES: Steel
PIPES & TUBES: Welded
PISTONS & PISTON RINGS
PLACEMATS: Plastic Or Textile
PLAQUES: Picture, Laminated
PLASMAS
PLASTICIZERS, ORGANIC: Cyclic & Acyclic
PLASTICS FILM & SHEET
PLASTICS FILM & SHEET: Polyethylene
PLASTICS FILM & SHEET: Polypropylene
PLASTICS FILM & SHEET: Polyvinyl
PLASTICS FILM & SHEET: Vinyl
PLASTICS FINISHED PRDTS: Laminated
PLASTICS FOAM, WHOLESALE
PLASTICS MATERIAL & RESINS
PLASTICS MATERIALS, BASIC FORMS & SHAPES WHOLESALERS
PLASTICS PROCESSING
PLASTICS SHEET: Packing Materials
PLASTICS: Blow Molded
PLASTICS: Extruded
PLASTICS: Finished Injection Molded
PLASTICS: Molded
PLASTICS: Polystyrene Foam
PLASTICS: Thermoformed
PLATE WORK: Metalworking Trade
PLATFORMS: Cargo
PLATING & FINISHING SVC: Decorative, Formed Prdts
PLATING & POLISHING SVC
PLATING COMPOUNDS
PLATING SVC: Chromium, Metals Or Formed Prdts
PLAYGROUND EQPT
PLEATING & STITCHING SVC
PLUMBING FIXTURES
PLUMBING FIXTURES: Plastic
PLUMBING FIXTURES: Vitreous China
POINT OF SALE DEVICES
POLISHING SVC: Metals Or Formed Prdts
POLYESTERS
POLYETHYLENE RESINS
POLYPROPYLENE RESINS

POLYSTYRENE RESINS
POLYURETHANE RESINS
POLYVINYL CHLORIDE RESINS
POTTERY: Laboratory & Indl
POULTRY & POULTRY PRDTS WHOLESALERS
POULTRY & SMALL GAME SLAUGHTERING &
 PROCESSING
POWDER: Aluminum Atomized
POWDER: Iron
POWDER: Metal
POWER GENERATORS
POWER SPLY CONVERTERS: Static, Electronic Applications
POWER SUPPLIES: All Types, Static
POWER SWITCHING EQPT
PRECAST TERRAZZO OR CONCRETE PRDTS
PRECIOUS METALS
PRESTRESSED CONCRETE PRDTS
PRIMARY ROLLING MILL EQPT
PRINT CARTRIDGES: Laser & Other Computer Printers
PRINTED CIRCUIT BOARDS
PRINTERS & PLOTTERS
PRINTERS' SVCS: Folding, Collating, Etc
PRINTERS: Computer
PRINTERS: Magnetic Ink, Bar Code
PRINTING & BINDING: Books
PRINTING & EMBOSSING: Plastic Fabric Articles
PRINTING & ENGRAVING: Card, Exc Greeting
PRINTING & ENGRAVING: Financial Notes & Certificates
PRINTING & STAMPING: Fabric Articles
PRINTING & WRITING PAPER WHOLESALERS
PRINTING MACHINERY
PRINTING, COMMERCIAL: Bags, Plastic, NEC
PRINTING, COMMERCIAL: Business Forms, NEC
PRINTING, COMMERCIAL: Calendars, NEC
PRINTING, COMMERCIAL: Decals, NEC
PRINTING, COMMERCIAL: Envelopes, NEC
PRINTING, COMMERCIAL: Imprinting
PRINTING, COMMERCIAL: Labels & Seals, NEC
PRINTING, COMMERCIAL: Letterpress & Screen
PRINTING, COMMERCIAL: Literature, Advertising, NEC
PRINTING, COMMERCIAL: Magazines, NEC
PRINTING, COMMERCIAL: Periodicals, NEC
PRINTING, COMMERCIAL: Promotional
PRINTING, COMMERCIAL: Screen
PRINTING, COMMERCIAL: Stationery, NEC
PRINTING, COMMERCIAL: Tags, NEC
PRINTING, LITHOGRAPHIC: Calendars
PRINTING, LITHOGRAPHIC: Color
PRINTING, LITHOGRAPHIC: Forms, Business
PRINTING, LITHOGRAPHIC: Offset & photolithographic
 printing
PRINTING, LITHOGRAPHIC: Posters & Decals
PRINTING, LITHOGRAPHIC: Promotional
PRINTING: Books
PRINTING: Books
PRINTING: Broadwoven Fabrics. Cotton
PRINTING: Checkbooks
PRINTING: Commercial, NEC
PRINTING: Flexographic
PRINTING: Gravure, Cards, Exc Greeting
PRINTING: Gravure, Forms, Business
PRINTING: Gravure, Labels
PRINTING: Gravure, Rotogravure
PRINTING: Laser
PRINTING: Letterpress
PRINTING: Lithographic
PRINTING: Manmade Fiber & Silk, Broadwoven Fabric
PRINTING: Offset
PRINTING: Photo-Offset
PRINTING: Photolithographic
PRINTING: Rotogravure
PRINTING: Screen, Broadwoven Fabrics, Cotton
PRINTING: Screen, Fabric
PRINTING: Screen, Manmade Fiber & Silk, Broadwoven
 Fabric
PRINTING: Thermography
PROFESSIONAL EQPT & SPLYS, WHOLESALE: Analytical
 Instruments'
PROFESSIONAL EQPT & SPLYS, WHOLESALE: Engineers',
 NEC
PROFESSIONAL EQPT & SPLYS, WHOLESALE: Optical
 Goods
PROFESSIONAL INSTRUMENT REPAIR SVCS

PROFESSIONAL SCHOOLS
PROFILE SHAPES: Unsupported Plastics
PROMOTERS OF SHOWS & EXHIBITIONS
PROMOTION SVCS
PROPELLERS: Boat & Ship, Machined
PROTECTION EQPT: Lightning
PROTECTIVE FOOTWEAR: Rubber Or Plastic
PUBLISHERS: Art Copy & Poster
PUBLISHERS: Music Book & Sheet Music
PUBLISHERS: Music, Sheet
PUBLISHERS: Sheet Music
PUBLISHERS: Telephone & Other Directory
PUBLISHING & BROADCASTING: Internet Only
PUBLISHING & PRINTING: Books
PUBLISHING & PRINTING: Directories, NEC
PUBLISHING & PRINTING: Directories, Telephone
PUBLISHING & PRINTING: Magazines: publishing & printing
PUBLISHING & PRINTING: Newsletters, Business Svc
PUBLISHING & PRINTING: Newspapers
PUBLISHING & PRINTING: Pamphlets
PUBLISHING & PRINTING: Shopping News
PUBLISHING & PRINTING: Textbooks
PUBLISHING & PRINTING: Trade Journals
PULLEYS: Metal
PULLEYS: Power Transmission
PULP MILLS
PULP MILLS: Mechanical & Recycling Processing
PUMPS & PARTS: Indl
PUMPS & PUMPING EQPT REPAIR SVCS
PUMPS & PUMPING EQPT WHOLESALERS
PUMPS, HEAT: Electric
PUMPS: Domestic, Water Or Sump
PUMPS: Fluid Power
PUMPS: Hydraulic Power Transfer
PUMPS: Measuring & Dispensing
PUMPS: Vacuum, Exc Laboratory
PUNCHES: Forming & Stamping
PUPPETS & MARIONETTES
PURIFICATION & DUST COLLECTION EQPT

R

RACEWAYS
RACKS: Pallet, Exc Wood
RADAR SYSTEMS & EQPT
RADIATORS, EXC ELECTRIC
RADIO BROADCASTING & COMMUNICATIONS EQPT
RADIO BROADCASTING STATIONS
RADIO, TV & CONSUMER ELEC STORES: High Fidelity
 Stereo Eqpt
RAILINGS: Prefabricated, Metal
RAILROAD EQPT
RAILROAD EQPT: Brakes, Air & Vacuum
RAILS: Steel Or Iron
RAMPS: Prefabricated Metal
RAZORS, RAZOR BLADES
REAL ESTATE AGENCIES & BROKERS
REAL ESTATE AGENCIES: Rental
REAL ESTATE AGENTS & MANAGERS
REAL ESTATE INVESTMENT TRUSTS
RECEIVERS: Radio Communications
RECORDING HEADS: Speech & Musical Eqpt
RECORDING TAPE: Video, Blank
RECORDS & TAPES: Prerecorded
RECOVERY SVC: Iron Ore, From Open Hearth Slag
RECREATIONAL VEHICLE DEALERS
RECREATIONAL VEHICLE PARTS & ACCESS STORES
REELS: Cable, Metal
REFINERS & SMELTERS: Copper
REFINERS & SMELTERS: Platinum Group Metals, Secondary
REFINING: Petroleum
REFRACTORIES: Clay
REFRACTORIES: Graphite, Carbon Or Ceramic Bond
REFRACTORIES: Nonclay
REFRACTORIES: Tile & Brick, Exc Plastic
REFRIGERATION & HEATING EQUIPMENT
REFRIGERATION EQPT & SPLYS WHOLESALERS
REFRIGERATION EQPT & SPLYS, WHOLESALE: Ice
 Making Machines
REFRIGERATION EQPT: Complete
REFRIGERATION REPAIR SVCS
REFUSE SYSTEMS
REGULATORS: Line Voltage
RELAYS & SWITCHES: Indl, Electric

RELAYS: Electric Power
RELIGIOUS SPLYS WHOLESALERS
REMOVERS & CLEANERS
REMOVERS: Paint
RENTAL SVCS: Aircraft
RENTAL SVCS: Audio-Visual Eqpt & Sply
RENTAL SVCS: Business Machine & Electronic Eqpt
RENTAL SVCS: Sound & Lighting Eqpt
RENTAL SVCS: Tent & Tarpaulin
RENTAL SVCS: Work Zone Traffic Eqpt, Flags, Cones, Etc
RENTAL: Portable Toilet
RENTAL: Video Tape & Disc
REPRODUCTION SVCS: Video Tape Or Disk
RESEARCH & DEVELOPMENT SVCS, COMMERCIAL:
 Engineering Lab
RESEARCH, DEVELOPMENT & TESTING SVCS, COMM:
 Agricultural
RESEARCH, DEVELOPMENT & TESTING SVCS,
 COMMERCIAL: Business
RESEARCH, DEVELOPMENT & TESTING SVCS,
 COMMERCIAL: Energy
RESEARCH, DEVELOPMENT & TESTING SVCS,
 COMMERCIAL: Medical
RESEARCH, DEVELOPMENT & TESTING SVCS,
 COMMERCIAL: Physical
RESEARCH, DEVELOPMENT SVCS, COMMERCIAL: Indl
 Lab
RESINS: Custom Compound Purchased
RESISTORS & RESISTOR UNITS
RESTAURANT EQPT: Carts
RESTAURANT EQPT: Sheet Metal
RESTAURANTS: Fast Food
RESTAURANTS:Full Svc, American
RETAIL BAKERY: Bagels
RETAIL BAKERY: Bread
RETAIL BAKERY: Cakes
RETAIL BAKERY: Cookies
RETAIL BAKERY: Doughnuts
RETAIL BAKERY: Pastries
RETAIL STORES: Alcoholic Beverage Making Eqpt & Splys
RETAIL STORES: Artificial Limbs
RETAIL STORES: Audio-Visual Eqpt & Splys
RETAIL STORES: Business Machines & Eqpt
RETAIL STORES: Communication Eqpt
RETAIL STORES: Concrete Prdts, Precast
RETAIL STORES: Cosmetics
RETAIL STORES: Decals
RETAIL STORES: Electronic Parts & Eqpt
RETAIL STORES: Flags
RETAIL STORES: Foam & Foam Prdts
RETAIL STORES: Hair Care Prdts
RETAIL STORES: Ice
RETAIL STORES: Medical Apparatus & Splys
RETAIL STORES: Orthopedic & Prosthesis Applications
RETAIL STORES: Pet Splys
RETAIL STORES: Religious Goods
RETAIL STORES: Safety Splys & Eqpt
RETAIL STORES: Telephone & Communication Eqpt
RETAIL STORES: Water Purification Eqpt
RETAIL STORES: Welding Splys
REUPHOLSTERY & FURNITURE REPAIR
RIBBONS, NEC
RIVETS: Metal
ROBOTS: Assembly Line
RODS: Steel & Iron, Made In Steel Mills
ROLL FORMED SHAPES: Custom
ROLLED OR DRAWN SHAPES, NEC: Copper & Copper Alloy
ROLLING MILL MACHINERY
ROLLING MILL ROLLS: Cast Steel
ROLLS & BLANKETS, PRINTERS': Rubber Or Rubberized
 Fabric
ROOFING MATERIALS: Asphalt
ROOFING MEMBRANE: Rubber
RUBBER PRDTS: Appliance, Mechanical
RUBBER PRDTS: Automotive, Mechanical
RUBBER PRDTS: Medical & Surgical Tubing, Extrudd &
 Lathe-Cut
RUBBER PRDTS: Silicone
RUBBER PRDTS: Sponge
RUBBER STRUCTURES: Air-Supported
RUGS : Hand & Machine Made
RUST RESISTING

S

SAFE DEPOSIT BOXES
SAFES & VAULTS: Metal
SAFETY EQPT & SPLYS WHOLESALERS
SALES PROMOTION SVCS
SALT
SAND & GRAVEL
SAND MINING
SANITARY SVCS: Hazardous Waste, Collection & Disposal
SANITARY SVCS: Oil Spill Cleanup
SANITARY SVCS: Refuse Collection & Disposal Svcs
SANITARY SVCS: Rubbish Collection & Disposal
SANITARY SVCS: Waste Materials, Recycling
SASHES: Door Or Window, Metal
SATELLITES: Communications
SAWMILL MACHINES
SAWS & SAWING EQPT
SCAFFOLDS: Mobile Or Stationary, Metal
SCALE REPAIR SVCS
SCALES & BALANCES, EXC LABORATORY
SCALES: Indl
SCANNING DEVICES: Optical
SCHOOL FOR PHYSICALLY HANDICAPPED, NEC
SCHOOLS: Vocational, NEC
SCIENTIFIC EQPT REPAIR SVCS
SCIENTIFIC INSTRUMENTS WHOLESALERS
SCISSORS: Hand
SCRAP & WASTE MATERIALS, WHOLESALE: Ferrous Metal
SCRAP & WASTE MATERIALS, WHOLESALE: Junk & Scrap
SCRAP & WASTE MATERIALS, WHOLESALE: Metal
SCRAP & WASTE MATERIALS, WHOLESALE: Paper
SCREENS: Window, Metal
SCREW MACHINE PRDTS
SCREWS: Metal
SEALANTS
SEALING COMPOUNDS: Sealing, synthetic rubber or plastic
SEALS: Hermetic
SEALS: Oil, Asbestos
SEARCH & NAVIGATION SYSTEMS
SEATING: Stadium
SECURITY CONTROL EQPT & SYSTEMS
SECURITY DEVICES
SECURITY SYSTEMS SERVICES
SEMICONDUCTOR CIRCUIT NETWORKS
SEMICONDUCTOR DEVICES: Wafers
SEMICONDUCTORS & RELATED DEVICES
SENSORS: Infrared, Solid State
SENSORS: Radiation
SENSORS: Temperature, Exc Indl Process
SEPTIC TANK CLEANING SVCS
SEPTIC TANKS: Concrete
SEPTIC TANKS: Plastic
SEWAGE & WATER TREATMENT EQPT
SEWING, NEEDLEWORK & PIECE GOODS STORES: Knitting Splys
SHAFTS: Flexible
SHAPES & PILINGS, STRUCTURAL: Steel
SHAPES: Extruded, Aluminum, NEC
SHEET METAL SPECIALTIES, EXC STAMPED
SHEETS: Fabric, From Purchased Materials
SHIMS: Metal
SHIP BUILDING & REPAIRING: Cargo, Commercial
SHIP BUILDING & REPAIRING: Combat Vessels
SHIP BUILDING & REPAIRING: Ferryboats
SHIP BUILDING & REPAIRING: Military
SHIP BUILDING & REPAIRING: Rigging, Marine
SHIP BUILDING & REPAIRING: Submarine Tenders
SHOE & BOOT ACCESS
SHOE STORES
SHOE STORES: Athletic
SHOE STORES: Men's
SHOES: Athletic, Exc Rubber Or Plastic
SHOES: Men's
SHOES: Men's, Dress
SHOES: Men's, Work
SHOES: Plastic Or Rubber
SHOES: Women's
SHOES: Women's, Dress
SHOT PEENING SVC
SHOWCASES & DISPLAY FIXTURES: Office & Store
SHREDDERS: Indl & Commercial
SHUTTERS, DOOR & WINDOW: Metal
SIDING: Plastic

SIDING: Sheet Metal
SIGN PAINTING & LETTERING SHOP
SIGNALING APPARATUS: Electric
SIGNALS: Traffic Control, Electric
SIGNS & ADVERTISING SPECIALTIES
SIGNS & ADVERTISING SPECIALTIES: Artwork, Advertising
SIGNS & ADVERTISING SPECIALTIES: Letters For Signs, Metal
SIGNS & ADVERTISING SPECIALTIES: Novelties
SIGNS, EXC ELECTRIC, WHOLESALE
SIGNS: Electrical
SIGNS: Neon
SILICA MINING
SILICON WAFERS: Chemically Doped
SILICONE RESINS
SILK SCREEN DESIGN SVCS
SILO STAVES: Concrete Or Cast Stone
SILVERWARE, STERLING SILVER
SKIN CARE PRDTS: Suntan Lotions & Oils
SLINGS: Rope
SMOKERS' SPLYS, WHOLESALE
SNOWMOBILES
SOCIAL SERVICES INFORMATION EXCHANGE
SOCIAL SVCS CENTER
SODA ASH MINING: Natural
SODIUM CHLORIDE: Refined
SOFT DRINKS WHOLESALERS
SOFTWARE PUBLISHERS: Home Entertainment
SOFTWARE PUBLISHERS: Operating Systems
SOFTWARE PUBLISHERS: Word Processing
SOFTWARE TRAINING, COMPUTER
SOLAR CELLS
SOLAR HEATING EQPT
SOLES, BOOT OR SHOE: Rubber, Composition Or Fiber
SOLVENTS
SOLVENTS: Organic
SONAR SYSTEMS & EQPT
SOUND EQPT: Electric
SOUND EQPT: Underwater
SOUND REPRODUCING EQPT
SPACE PROPULSION UNITS & PARTS
SPACE VEHICLES
SPEAKER SYSTEMS
SPECIALTY FOOD STORES: Coffee
SPECIALTY FOOD STORES: Dried Fruit
SPECIALTY FOOD STORES: Eggs & Poultry
SPECIALTY FOOD STORES: Health & Dietetic Food
SPECIALTY FOOD STORES: Juices, Fruit Or Vegetable
SPECIALTY FOOD STORES: Soft Drinks
SPECIALTY SAWMILL PRDTS
SPORTING & ATHLETIC GOODS: Bags, Golf
SPORTING & ATHLETIC GOODS: Basketball Eqpt & Splys, NEC
SPORTING & ATHLETIC GOODS: Camping Eqpt & Splys
SPORTING & ATHLETIC GOODS: Cases, Gun & Rod
SPORTING & ATHLETIC GOODS: Fishing Eqpt
SPORTING & ATHLETIC GOODS: Fishing Tackle, General
SPORTING & ATHLETIC GOODS: Hockey Eqpt & Splys, NEC
SPORTING & ATHLETIC GOODS: Hunting Eqpt
SPORTING & ATHLETIC GOODS: Rods & Rod Parts, Fishing
SPORTING & ATHLETIC GOODS: Shafts, Golf Club
SPORTING & ATHLETIC GOODS: Shooting Eqpt & Splys, General
SPORTING & ATHLETIC GOODS: Snow Skis
SPORTING & ATHLETIC GOODS: Targets, Archery & Rifle Shooting
SPORTING & ATHLETIC GOODS: Track & Field Athletic Eqpt
SPORTING & ATHLETIC GOODS: Treadmills
SPORTING & ATHLETIC GOODS: Water Sports Eqpt
SPORTING & REC GOODS, WHOLESALE: Camping Eqpt & Splys
SPORTING & RECREATIONAL GOODS, WHOLESALE: Boat Access & Part
SPORTING GOODS STORES: Camping & Backpacking Eqpt
SPORTING GOODS STORES: Firearms
SPORTING GOODS STORES: Fishing Eqpt
SPORTING GOODS STORES: Playground Eqpt
SPORTING GOODS STORES: Specialty Sport Splys, NEC
SPORTING GOODS: Sleeping Bags
SPORTS APPAREL STORES
SPORTS CLUBS, MANAGERS & PROMOTERS
SPORTS PROMOTION SVCS
SPRINGS: Coiled Flat

SPRINGS: Instrument, Precision
SPRINGS: Mechanical, Precision
SPRINGS: Precision
SPRINGS: Steel
SPRINGS: Wire
SPRINKLER SYSTEMS: Field
SPROCKETS: Power Transmission
STAINLESS STEEL
STAINLESS STEEL WARE
STAIRCASES & STAIRS, WOOD
STAMPINGS: Automotive
STAMPINGS: Metal
STAPLES
STAPLES: Steel, Wire Or Cut
STATIONARY & OFFICE SPLYS, WHOLESALE: Office Filing Splys
STATIONERY & OFFICE SPLYS WHOLESALERS
STATIONERY: Made From Purchased Materials
STATORS REWINDING SVCS
STEEL & ALLOYS: Tool & Die
STEEL, COLD-ROLLED: Sheet Or Strip, From Own HotRolled
STEEL, COLD-ROLLED: Strip NEC, From Purchased HotRolled
STONE: Dimension, NEC
STONE: Quarrying & Processing, Own Stone Prdts
STONEWARE PRDTS: Pottery
STORE FIXTURES: Exc Wood
STORE FIXTURES: Wood
STORE FRONTS: Prefabricated, Metal
STORES: Auto & Home Supply
STOVES: Wood & Coal Burning
STRAPS: Braids, Textile
STRAPS: Webbing, Woven
STRUCTURAL SUPPORT & BUILDING MATERIAL: Concrete
SUNDRIES & RELATED PRDTS: Medical & Laboratory, Rubber
SUNGLASSES, WHOLESALE
SURFACE ACTIVE AGENTS
SURFACE ACTIVE AGENTS: Oils & Greases
SURGICAL APPLIANCES & SPLYS
SURGICAL APPLIANCES & SPLYS
SURGICAL IMPLANTS
SURGICAL INSTRUMENT REPAIR SVCS
SUSPENSION SYSTEMS: Acoustical, Metal
SVC ESTABLISHMENT EQPT, WHOLESALE: Firefighting Eqpt
SVC ESTABLISHMENT EQPT, WHOLESALE: Restaurant Splys
SWEEPING COMPOUNDS
SWIMMING POOL EQPT: Filters & Water Conditioning Systems
SWIMMING POOLS, EQPT & SPLYS: Wholesalers
SWITCHBOARDS & PARTS: Power
SWITCHES: Electric Power
SWITCHES: Electric Power, Exc Snap, Push Button, Etc
SWITCHES: Electronic
SWITCHES: Electronic Applications
SWITCHES: Flow Actuated, Electrical
SWITCHES: Stepping
SWITCHES: Time, Electrical Switchgear Apparatus
SWITCHGEAR & SWITCHBOARD APPARATUS
SWITCHGEAR & SWITCHGEAR ACCESS, NEC
SYRUPS, DRINK
SYRUPS, FLAVORING, EXC DRINK
SYSTEMS ENGINEERING: Computer Related
SYSTEMS INTEGRATION SVCS
SYSTEMS INTEGRATION SVCS: Local Area Network
SYSTEMS SOFTWARE DEVELOPMENT SVCS

T

TABLE OR COUNTERTOPS, PLASTIC LAMINATED
TABLECLOTHS & SETTINGS
TABLES: Lift, Hydraulic
TABLETS & PADS
TABLETS & PADS: Book & Writing, Made From Purchased Material
TAGS & LABELS: Paper
TAGS: Paper, Blank, Made From Purchased Paper
TALLOW: Animal
TANK TOWERS: Metal Plate
TANKS & OTHER TRACKED VEHICLE CMPNTS
TANKS: Concrete
TANKS: Cryogenic, Metal

TANKS: For Tank Trucks, Metal Plate
TANKS: Fuel, Including Oil & Gas, Metal Plate
TANKS: Lined, Metal
TANKS: Plastic & Fiberglass
TANKS: Standard Or Custom Fabricated, Metal Plate
TANKS: Water, Metal Plate
TANNERIES: Leather
TAPE DRIVES
TAPE MEASURES
TAPE STORAGE UNITS: Computer
TAPES: Fabric
TAPES: Pressure Sensitive, Rubber
TARPAULINS
TELECOMMUNICATION EQPT REPAIR SVCS, EXC
  TELEPHONES
TELEMETERING EQPT
TELEPHONE ANSWERING SVCS
TELEPHONE EQPT: Modems
TELEPHONE EQPT: NEC
TELEPHONE STATION EQPT & PARTS: Wire
TELEPHONE: Headsets
TELEVISION & VIDEO TAPE DISTRIBUTION
TELEVISION BROADCASTING & COMMUNICATIONS EQPT
TELEVISION BROADCASTING STATIONS
TELEVISION: Monitors
TEMPERING: Metal
TEMPORARY HELP SVCS
TERMINAL BOARDS
TEST BORING SVCS: Nonmetallic Minerals
TESTERS: Battery
TESTERS: Physical Property
TESTING SVCS
TEXTILE & APPAREL SVCS
TEXTILE FINISHING: Chemical Coating Or Treating, Narrow
TEXTILE FINISHING: Dyeing, Manmade Fiber & Silk,
  Broadwoven
TEXTILES: Crash, Linen
TEXTILES: Mill Waste & Remnant
THEATRICAL SCENERY
THERMISTORS, EXC TEMPERATURE SENSORS
THERMOCOUPLES
THERMOPLASTIC MATERIALS
THERMOSETTING MATERIALS
THIN FILM CIRCUITS
THREAD: Cotton
TILE: Brick & Structural, Clay
TILE: Fireproofing, Clay
TILE: Terrazzo Or Concrete, Precast
TILE: Wall & Floor, Ceramic
TIMING DEVICES: Electronic
TIRE CORD & FABRIC
TIRES & INNER TUBES
TIRES & TUBES WHOLESALERS
TIRES & TUBES, WHOLESALE: Automotive
TIRES: Agricultural, Pneumatic
TIRES: Cushion Or Solid Rubber
TOBACCO & PRDTS, WHOLESALE: Cigarettes
TOBACCO & TOBACCO PRDTS WHOLESALERS
TOBACCO: Chewing
TOBACCO: Chewing & Snuff
TOBACCO: Cigarettes
TOBACCO: Cigars
TOILET PREPARATIONS
TOILETRIES, WHOLESALE: Toilet Soap
TOILETRIES, WHOLESALE: Toiletries
TOILETS: Portable Chemical, Plastics
TOOL & DIE STEEL
TOOLS: Hand, Hammers
TOOLS: Hand, Mechanics
TOWING SVCS: Marine
TOYS & HOBBY GOODS & SPLYS, WHOLESALE: Balloons,
  Novelty
TOYS & HOBBY GOODS & SPLYS, WHOLESALE: Toys &
  Games
TOYS & HOBBY GOODS & SPLYS, WHOLESALE: Toys,
  NEC
TOYS: Dolls, Stuffed Animals & Parts
TOYS: Electronic
TRADE SHOW ARRANGEMENT SVCS
TRADERS: Commodity, Contracts
TRAILERS & PARTS: Boat
TRAILERS & TRAILER EQPT
TRAILERS: Camping, Tent-Type

TRAILERS: Demountable Cargo Containers
TRANSDUCERS: Electrical Properties
TRANSDUCERS: Pressure
TRANSFORMERS: Distribution
TRANSFORMERS: Distribution, Electric
TRANSFORMERS: Electronic
TRANSFORMERS: Specialty
TRANSISTORS
TRANSPORTATION BROKERS: Truck
TRANSPORTATION EPQT & SPLYS, WHOL: Aeronautical
  Eqpt & Splys
TRANSPORTATION EPQT & SPLYS, WHOLESALE:
  Helicopter Parts
TRANSPORTATION EQPT & SPLYS WHOLESALERS, NEC
TRAP ROCK: Crushed & Broken
TRAVEL AGENCIES
TRAVEL TRAILERS & CAMPERS
TRAYS: Cable, Metal Plate
TROPHIES, NEC
TROPHIES, WHOLESALE
TROPHIES: Metal, Exc Silver
TRUCK & BUS BODIES: Garbage Or Refuse Truck
TRUCK & BUS BODIES: Utility Truck
TRUCK & BUS BODIES: Van Bodies
TRUCK BODIES: Body Parts
TRUCK BODY SHOP
TRUCK GENERAL REPAIR SVC
TRUCK PARTS & ACCESSORIES: Wholesalers
TRUCKING & HAULING SVCS: Contract Basis
TRUCKING & HAULING SVCS: Hazardous Waste
TRUCKING & HAULING SVCS: Heavy, NEC
TRUCKING & HAULING SVCS: Lumber & Log, Local
TRUCKING: Except Local
TRUCKING: Local, With Storage
TRUCKING: Local, Without Storage
TRUCKS & TRACTORS: Industrial
TRUCKS: Indl
TRUST MANAGEMENT SVCS: Personal Investment
TUBES: Light Sensing & Emitting
TUBES: Steel & Iron
TUBES: Vacuum
TUBING: Flexible, Metallic
TUBING: Glass
TURBINES & TURBINE GENERATOR SET UNITS: Gas,
  Complete
TURBINES & TURBINE GENERATOR SETS
TURBINES & TURBINE GENERATOR SETS & PARTS
TURBINES: Steam
TURBO-GENERATORS
TURNKEY VENDORS: Computer Systems
TYPESETTING SVC
TYPESETTING SVC: Computer

U

UNIFORM STORES
UNISEX HAIR SALONS
UNIVERSITY
UNSUPPORTED PLASTICS: Floor Or Wall Covering
UPHOLSTERY FILLING MATERIALS
UPHOLSTERY MATERIALS, BROADWOVEN
UPHOLSTERY WORK SVCS
USED MERCHANDISE STORES
UTILITY TRAILER DEALERS

V

VACUUM CLEANERS: Indl Type
VACUUM SYSTEMS: Air Extraction, Indl
VALUE-ADDED RESELLERS: Computer Systems
VALVE REPAIR SVCS, INDL
VALVES
VALVES & PARTS: Gas, Indl
VALVES & PIPE FITTINGS
VALVES & REGULATORS: Pressure, Indl
VALVES Solenoid
VALVES: Aerosol, Metal
VALVES: Aircraft, Control, Hydraulic & Pneumatic
VALVES: Control, Automatic
VALVES: Fluid Power, Control, Hydraulic & pneumatic
VALVES: Indl
VALVES: Plumbing & Heating
VALVES: Regulating & Control, Automatic
VALVES: Water Works
VAN CONVERSIONS

VAULTS & SAFES WHOLESALERS
VEHICLES: Recreational
VENDING MACHINES & PARTS
VENTILATING EQPT: Metal
VENTILATING EQPT: Sheet Metal
VENTURE CAPITAL COMPANIES
VETERINARY PHARMACEUTICAL PREPARATIONS
VETERINARY PRDTS: Instruments & Apparatus
VIDEO & AUDIO EQPT, WHOLESALE
VIDEO TAPE PRODUCTION SVCS
VINYL RESINS, NEC
VISES: Machine
VISUAL COMMUNICATIONS SYSTEMS
VITAMINS: Natural Or Synthetic, Uncompounded, Bulk
VOCATIONAL REHABILITATION AGENCY

W

WALL COVERINGS WHOLESALERS
WALLBOARD: Gypsum
WALLPAPER & WALL COVERINGS
WALLPAPER STORE
WALLS: Curtain, Metal
WAREHOUSE CLUBS STORES
WAREHOUSING & STORAGE FACILITIES, NEC
WAREHOUSING & STORAGE, REFRIGERATED: Cold
  Storage Or Refrig
WAREHOUSING & STORAGE: General
WAREHOUSING & STORAGE: Miniwarehouse
WAREHOUSING & STORAGE: Refrigerated
WAREHOUSING & STORAGE: Self Storage
WARM AIR HEATING/AC EQPT/SPLY, WHOL Humidifier,
  Exc Portable
WARM AIR HEATING/AC EQPT/SPLYS, WHOL Warm Air
  Htg Eqpt/Splys
WARP KNIT FABRIC FINISHING
WASHERS: Metal
WASHERS: Plastic
WASTE CLEANING SVCS
WATCH STRAPS, EXC METAL
WATCHES
WATER HEATERS
WATER PURIFICATION EQPT: Household
WATER SUPPLY
WATER TREATMENT EQPT: Indl
WATER: Distilled
WATER: Mineral, Carbonated, Canned & Bottled, Etc
WATER: Pasteurized & Mineral, Bottled & Canned
WATER: Pasteurized, Canned & Bottled, Etc
WATERPROOFING COMPOUNDS
WAVEGUIDES & FITTINGS
WAXES: Petroleum, Not Produced In Petroleum Refineries
WEATHER STRIP: Sponge Rubber
WEIGHING MACHINERY & APPARATUS
WELDING & CUTTING APPARATUS & ACCESS, NEC
WELDING EQPT
WELDING EQPT & SPLYS WHOLESALERS
WELDING EQPT & SPLYS: Gas
WELDING EQPT REPAIR SVCS
WELDING EQPT: Electric
WELDING EQPT: Electrical
WELDING MACHINES & EQPT: Ultrasonic
WELDING REPAIR SVC
WELDING SPLYS, EXC GASES: Wholesalers
WELDING TIPS: Heat Resistant, Metal
WELDMENTS
WET CORN MILLING
WHEELCHAIR LIFTS
WHEELCHAIRS
WHEELS, GRINDING: Artificial
WHEELS: Abrasive
WINCHES
WINDINGS: Coil, Electronic
WINDMILLS: Electric Power Generation
WINDOW & DOOR FRAMES
WINDOW FRAMES & SASHES: Plastic
WINDOW FRAMES, MOLDING & TRIM: Vinyl
WINDOW SASHES, WOOD
WINDOWS: Frames, Wood
WINDOWS: Wood
WINE & DISTILLED ALCOHOLIC BEVERAGES
  WHOLESALERS
WIRE
WIRE & CABLE: Aluminum

PRODUCT SECTION

	CITY	ST	EMP	PHONE	ENTRY#
GADGETS: PLASTIC					
Nacomb Mfg Co	Decatur	IL	C	217 222-4000	29981
National Avon Inds (HQ)	Rome	GA	A	706 551-6060	30035
National Gadget Mfg (HQ)	Kansas City	KS	A	913 999-7777	39167
Nupone Plastics Inc	Dallas	TX	B	920 344-5522	30891

Employment codes
A = over 500 employees
B = 251-500, C = 101-250
D = 51-100, E = 20-50
F = 10-19, G = 1-9

Geographic Section entry number where full company information appears

Business phone

See footnotes for employment codes identifications.
- Refer to the Product Index preceding this section to locate product headings..

	CITY	ST	EMP	PHONE	ENTRY#
ABRASIVES					
Ahlstrom Nonwovens LLC (DH)	Windsor Locks	CT	B	860 654-8300	4318
Chessco Industries Inc (PA)	Westport	CT	E	203 255-2804	4160
Composition Materials Co Inc	Milford	CT	G	203 874-6500	1812
Pressure Blast Mfg Co Inc	South Windsor	CT	F	800 722-5278	3174
Syncote Chemical Company Inc	Newtown	CT	G	203 426-5526	2348
Aspen Systems LLC (PA)	Marlborough	MA	F	508 281-5322	10112
Chas G Allen Realty LLC	Barre	MA	D	978 355-2911	6202
Mosher Company Inc	Chicopee	MA	F	413 598-8341	8050
Olsen & Silk Abrasives	Salem	MA	F	978 744-4720	11728
Vogel Capital Inc (HQ)	Marlborough	MA	E	508 481-5944	10232
Best Machine Inc	Fremont	NH	E	603 895-4018	14326
Johnson Abrasives Co Inc	Jaffrey	NH	E	603 532-4434	14569
Peg Kearsarge Co Inc	Bartlett	NH	G	603 374-2341	13918
RP Abrasives & Machine Inc	Rochester	NH	F	603 335-2132	15492
Bates Abrasive Products Inc	Lincoln	RI	E	773 586-8700	16121
Bullard Abrasives Inc	Lincoln	RI	D	508 366-4300	16123
Marvel Abrasives Products LLC	Lincoln	RI	F	800 621-0673	16148
Meister Abrasives Usa Inc	North Kingstown	RI	F	401 294-4503	16271
Dessureau Machines Inc	Barre	VT	F	802 476-4561	17000
ABRASIVES: Coated					
General Abrasives Inc	Sharon	VT	F	802 763-7264	17555
ACCELERATION INDICATORS & SYSTEM COMPONENTS: Aerospace					
Kaman Corporation	Middletown	CT	E	860 632-1000	1756
Kaman Precision Products Inc	Middletown	CT	C	860 632-1000	1757
Saf Industries LLC (HQ)	Meriden	CT	E	203 729-4900	1696
Parts Tool and Die Inc	Agawam	MA	E	413 821-9718	5805
Hunting Dearborn Inc	Fryeburg	ME	F	207 935-2171	4809
ARC Technology Solutions LLC	Nashua	NH	D	603 883-3027	15064
ACCELERATORS, RUBBER PROCESSING: Cyclic or Acyclic					
Chasm Advanced Materials Inc (PA)	Canton	MA	G	781 821-0443	7778
ACCELEROMETERS					
Whoop Inc (PA)	Boston	MA	B	617 670-1074	7122
ACIDS: Inorganic					
Metamorphic Materials Inc	Winsted	CT	G	860 738-8638	4349
ACIDS: Sulfuric, Oleum					
Veolia N Amer Rgnrtion Svcs LL (DH)	Boston	MA	D	312 552-2800	7097
ACOUSTICAL BOARD & TILE					
Eckel Industries Inc (PA)	Ayer	MA	F	978 772-0840	6181
Soundown Corporation (PA)	Salem	MA	E	978 745-7000	11732
ACRYLIC RESINS					
Banzan Intl Group Corp	Acton	MA	F	978 263-3186	5739
Space Age Accessories Inc	Foxboro	MA	E	508 543-3661	8725
Optical Polymers Lab Corp	Pawtucket	RI	F	401 722-0710	16398
ACTUATORS: Indl, NEC					
Hamilton Sundstrand Corp (HQ)	Windsor Locks	CT	A	619 714-9442	4330
Asahi/America Inc (HQ)	Lawrence	MA	E	781 321-5409	9540
Koso America Inc	West Bridgewater	MA	D	774 517-5300	12974
Rexa Inc	West Bridgewater	MA	D	508 584-1199	12977
ADDITIVE BASED PLASTIC MATERIALS: Plasticizers					

	CITY	ST	EMP	PHONE	ENTRY#
Gxt Green Inc	Cambridge	MA	F	978 735-4367	7597
ADHESIVES					
Advanced Adhesive Systems Inc	Newington	CT	E	860 953-4100	2267
Apcm Manufacturing LLC	Plainfield	CT	G	860 564-7817	2731
Edison Coatings Inc	Plainville	CT	F	860 747-2220	2757
Henkel Loctite Corporation (DH)	Rocky Hill	CT	D	860 571-5100	2925
Henkel of America Inc (HQ)	Rocky Hill	CT	B	860 615-3395	2926
Henkel US Operations Corp (DH)	Rocky Hill	CT	B	860 571-5100	2927
Hexcel Corporation (PA)	Stamford	CT	E	203 969-0666	3374
Mica Corporation	Shelton	CT	E	203 922-8888	3031
Si Group Inc	Danbury	CT	C	203 702-6140	815
3M Company	Rockland	MA	E	781 871-1400	11632
Adhesive Applications Inc (PA)	Easthampton	MA	E	413 527-7120	8437
Allcoat Technology Inc	Wilmington	MA	E	978 988-0880	13376
American Adhesive Coatings LLC (PA)	Lawrence	MA	E	978 688-7400	9536
AP Plastics LLC	Peabody	MA	F	800 222-1117	11298
Bacon Industries Inc	Wrentham	MA	F	508 384-0780	13837
Bemis Associates Inc (PA)	Shirley	MA	C	978 425-6761	11815
Bostik Inc	Middleton	MA	C	978 777-0103	10382
Coatings Adhesives Inks	Georgetown	MA	F	978 352-7273	8907
Creative Materials Inc	Ayer	MA	F	978 391-4700	6180
Delo Industrial Adhesives LLC	Sudbury	MA	F	978 254-5275	12263
Diemat Inc	Byfield	MA	F	978 499-0900	7457
Eastman Performance Films LLC	Holliston	MA	E	508 474-6002	9208
Flexcon Company Inc (PA)	Spencer	MA	A	508 885-8200	12058
Functional Coatings LLC	Newburyport	MA	D	978 462-0796	10684
Innovative Chem Pdts Group LLC (PA)	Andover	MA	E	978 623-9980	5889
ITW Devcon Inc	Danvers	MA	E	978 777-1100	8195
Key Polymer LLC	Lawrence	MA	E	978 683-9411	9573
Key Polymer Holdings LLC (PA)	Lawrence	MA	F	978 683-9411	9574
L H C Inc (PA)	Lynn	MA	F	781 592-6444	9982
Olympic Adhesives Inc (PA)	Norwood	MA	E	800 829-1871	11202
Resin Designs LLC (DH)	Woburn	MA	E	781 935-3133	13650
Saint-Gobain Corporation	Northborough	MA	A	508 351-7112	11108
Tyco Adhesives	Franklin	MA	G	508 918-1600	8873
Sheepscot Machine Works LLC	Newcastle	ME	G	207 563-2299	5096
Adhesive Engineering & Supply	Seabrook	NH	F	603 895-4028	15582
Coating Systems Inc	Nashua	NH	G	603 883-0553	15082
Extreme Adhesives Inc	Raymond	NH	G	603 895-4028	15452
Protavic America Inc	Londonderry	NH	G	603 623-8624	14780
Resin Technology Group LLC	Seabrook	NH	D	508 230-8070	15601
Royal Adhesives & Sealants LLC	Raymond	NH	G	860 788-3380	15457
Worthen Industries Inc (HQ)	Nashua	NH	D	603 888-5443	15188
Worthen Industries Inc	Nashua	NH	E	603 886-0973	15189
Atom Adhesives LLC	Providence	RI	F	888 522-6742	16478
Fri Resins Holding Company	Cranston	RI	F	401 946-5564	15863
Mylan Technologies Inc (HQ)	Saint Albans	VT	C	802 527-7792	17525
ADHESIVES & SEALANTS					
Chessco Industries Inc (PA)	Westport	CT	E	203 255-2804	4160
Five Star Products Inc	Shelton	CT	E	203 336-7900	3006
Metamorphic Materials Inc	Winsted	CT	G	860 738-8638	4349
Panacol-Usa Inc	Torrington	CT	F	860 738-7449	3691
Stanchem Incorporated (HQ)	East Berlin	CT	E	860 828-0571	918
Vanderbilt Chemicals LLC	Bethel	CT	C	203 744-3900	139
Xg Industries LLC	Stratford	CT	F	475 282-4643	3586
Acton Research Corporation	Acton	MA	E	941 556-2601	5731
C L Hauthaway & Sons Corp	Lynn	MA	E	781 592-6444	9965
Coating House Inc	East Longmeadow	MA	F	413 525-3100	8372
Hapco Inc	Hanover	MA	E	781 826-8801	9034

PRODUCT

	CITY	ST	EMP	PHONE	ENTRY#
Henkel Corporation	Canton	MA	C	781 737-1400	7796
Illinois Tool Works Inc	Danvers	MA	C	978 777-1100	8193
ITW Performance Polymers	Danvers	MA	D	978 777-1100	8196
John G Shelley Co Inc	Woburn	MA	F	781 237-0900	13593
Mussel Bound LLC	Brewster	MA	G	774 212-5488	7215
Ngac LLC	Burlington	MA	E	781 258-0008	7400
Parker-Hannifin Corporation	Woburn	MA	B	781 935-4850	13629
Perrco Inc	Woburn	MA	F	617 933-5300	13633
Stahl (usa) Inc **(DH)**	Peabody	MA	E	978 968-1382	11344
Standard Rubber Products Inc	Hanover	MA	E	781 878-2626	9043
Surmet Corp **(PA)**	Burlington	MA	E	781 345-5721	7436
Transene Company Inc **(PA)**	Danvers	MA	E	978 777-7860	8227
Jnion Specialties Inc	Newburyport	MA	E	978 465-1717	10724
Appli-Tec Inc	Salem	NH	E	603 685-0500	15508
Hampshire Chemical Corp **(DH)**	Nashua	NH	E	603 888-2320	15109
Trellborg Pipe Sals Mlford Inc **(DH)**	Milford	NH	F	800 626-2180	15042
Epoxies Inc	Cranston	RI	F	401 946-5564	15857
Gurit (usa) Inc	Bristol	RI	D	401 396-5008	15767
Rutland Fire Clay Co **(PA)**	Rutland	VT	F	802 775-5519	17507

ADHESIVES: Adhesives, plastic

	CITY	ST	EMP	PHONE	ENTRY#
Indusol Inc	Sutton	MA	E	508 865-9516	12282
North American Coating Sciences Inc	Lawrence	MA	G	978 691-5622	9590
Northern Products Inc	Woonsocket	RI	F		16969

ADHESIVES: Epoxy

	CITY	ST	EMP	PHONE	ENTRY#
Laticrete International Inc **(PA)**	Bethany	CT	B	203 393-0010	94
Epoxy Technology Inc **(PA)**	Billerica	MA	E	978 667-3805	6444
Enterprise Casting Corporation	Lewiston	ME	E	207 782-5511	4961
Mereco Technologies Group Inc **(HQ)**	Londonderry	NH	E	401 822-9300	14769
Metachem Resins Corporation	Londonderry	NH	E		14770
Schul International Co LLC	Hudson	NH	E	603 889-6872	14544
Vesuvius America Inc **(DH)**	Providence	RI	E		16640

ADVERTISING AGENCIES

	CITY	ST	EMP	PHONE	ENTRY#
Carnegie Communications LLC	Westford	MA	E	978 692-5092	13227
Carnegie Dartlet LLC **(PA)**	Westford	MA	D	978 692-5092	13228
Monster Tech	Weston	MA	F	978 897-0832	13288
RMS Media Group Inc	Newburyport	MA	F	978 623-8020	10713
Vocero Hispano Newspaper Inc	Southbridge	MA	F	866 846-6397	12038
Northeast Publishing Company	Caribou	ME	G	207 496-3251	4677
Hideaways International Inc	Portsmouth	NH	F	603 430-4433	15401
Uvp Liquidation Inc	North Haverhill	NH	D	603 787-7000	15253
Scarborough Faire Inc	Pawtucket	RI	E	401 724-4200	16416

ADVERTISING AGENCIES: Consultants

	CITY	ST	EMP	PHONE	ENTRY#
Applied Advertising Inc	Danbury	CT	F	860 640-0800	708
Directory Assistants Inc	Avon	CT	F	860 633-0122	23
Adlife Advertising & Graphics	Walpole	MA	F	508 668-4109	12547
Allison Advertising Inc	Boston	MA	F	617 368-6800	6537
Toth Inc **(PA)**	Concord	MA	E	617 577-6400	8136

ADVERTISING CURTAINS

	CITY	ST	EMP	PHONE	ENTRY#
Screencraft Tileworks LLC	Lincoln	RI	G	401 427-2816	16153

ADVERTISING DISPLAY PRDTS

	CITY	ST	EMP	PHONE	ENTRY#
Solchroma Technologies Inc	Billerica	MA	G	401 829-0024	6483
Stran & Company Inc **(PA)**	Quincy	MA	E	617 822-6950	11540
Scope Display & Box Co Inc **(PA)**	Cranston	RI	E	401 942-7150	15909

ADVERTISING MATERIAL DISTRIBUTION

	CITY	ST	EMP	PHONE	ENTRY#
Liberty Publishing Inc	Beverly	MA	F	978 777-8200	6362
Verizon	Swanton	VT	G	802 879-4954	17644

ADVERTISING REPRESENTATIVES: Electronic Media

	CITY	ST	EMP	PHONE	ENTRY#
Comcast Sportsnet Neng LLC	Needham Heights	MA	D	617 630-5000	10537
Dixie Media LLC	Danvers	MA	E	508 739-1999	8183

ADVERTISING REPRESENTATIVES: Newspaper

	CITY	ST	EMP	PHONE	ENTRY#
Eagle-Tribune Publishing Co	Haverhill	MA	F	978 374-0321	9093
Local Media Group Inc	New Bedford	MA	C	508 997-7411	10614
Lowell Sun Publishing Company	Ayer	MA	C	978 433-6685	6185
Vocero Hispano Newspaper Inc	Southbridge	MA	F	866 846-6397	12038
Northeast Publishing Company	Dover Foxcroft	ME	G	207 564-8355	4730
North Eastern Publishing Co	Bennington	VT	D	802 447-7567	17053

ADVERTISING REPRESENTATIVES: Printed Media

	CITY	ST	EMP	PHONE	ENTRY#
Newhomesale LLC	Franklin	MA	F	508 541-8900	8854

ADVERTISING SPECIALTIES, WHOLESALE

	CITY	ST	EMP	PHONE	ENTRY#
McWeeney Marketing Group Inc	Orange	CT	G	203 891-8100	2677
Professional Mktg Svcs Inc	Stratford	CT	F	203 610-6222	3568

	CITY	ST	EMP	PHONE	ENTRY#
Ad-A-Day Company Inc	Taunton	MA	E	508 824-8676	12315
J W I N Promotional Corp	Westport	MA	G	508 636-1993	13297
Shawmut Advertising Inc **(PA)**	Peabody	MA	E	978 762-7500	11340
Superior Printing Company Inc	Medford	MA	F	781 391-9090	10297
Time-Out Sports Inc	Whitman	MA	F	781 447-6670	13350
Walker-Clay Inc	Hanson	MA	F	781 294-1100	9057
Geiger Bros **(PA)**	Lewiston	ME	B	207 755-2000	4962
Harpswell House Inc	Lisbon Falls	ME	G	207 353-2385	5021
E Print Inc	Hudson	NH	G	603 594-0009	14495
Powerplay Management LLC	Portsmouth	NH	E	603 436-3030	15431

ADVERTISING SVCS: Direct Mail

	CITY	ST	EMP	PHONE	ENTRY#
Better Lists Incorporated	Stamford	CT	E	203 324-4171	3294
Fairfield Marketing Group Inc **(PA)**	Easton	CT	F	203 261-0884	1095
Joseph Merritt & Company Inc **(PA)**	Hartford	CT	E	860 296-2500	1488
L P Macadams Company Inc	Bridgeport	CT	D	203 366-3647	342
Life Study Fllwship Foundation	Darien	CT	G	203 655-1436	851
Transmonde USa Inc	North Branford	CT	D	203 484-1528	2377
ABS Printing Inc	Swansea	MA	G	401 826-0870	12302
Carnegie Communications LLC	Westford	MA	E	978 692-5092	13227
Carnegie Dartlet LLC **(PA)**	Westford	MA	D	978 692-5092	13228
Communication Ink Inc	Peabody	MA	E	978 977-4595	11302
Harte Hanks Inc **(PA)**	Chelmsford	MA	E	512 434-1100	7931
Newhomesale LLC	Franklin	MA	F	508 541-8900	8854
Owl Stamp Company Inc	Lowell	MA	G	978 452-4541	9912
Quad/Graphics Inc	East Longmeadow	MA	D	413 525-8552	8391
Rivkind Associates Inc **(PA)**	South Easton	MA	F	781 269-2415	11952
Shawmut Advertising Inc **(PA)**	Peabody	MA	E	978 762-7500	11340
Tom Snyder Productions Inc **(HQ)**	Watertown	MA	D	617 600-2145	12915
Bangor Ltr Sp & Color Copy Ctr	Bangor	ME	G	207 945-9311	4490
Turner Publishing Inc	Turner	ME	F	207 225-2076	5564
Puritan Press Inc **(PA)**	Hollis	NH	E	603 889-4500	14458
Spectrum Monthly LLC	Manchester	NH	C	603 627-0042	14936
Villanti & Sons Printers Inc	Milton	VT	D	802 864-0723	17367

ADVERTISING SVCS: Display

	CITY	ST	EMP	PHONE	ENTRY#
Resavue Inc	Orange	CT	F	203 878-0944	2682
Valley Container Inc	Bridgeport	CT	E	203 368-6546	383
Carnegie Communications LLC	Westford	MA	E	978 692-5092	13227
Carnegie Dartlet LLC **(PA)**	Westford	MA	D	978 692-5092	13228
Parsonskellogg LLC	East Providence	RI	D	866 602-8398	16037

ADVERTISING SVCS: Outdoor

	CITY	ST	EMP	PHONE	ENTRY#
All American Signs Inc	Plymouth	MA	F	508 830-0505	11445
Lane Printing Co Inc	Holbrook	MA	F	781 767-4450	9178
Davis-Joncas Enterprises Inc	Scarborough	ME	F	207 883-6200	5430

ADVERTISING SVCS: Transit

	CITY	ST	EMP	PHONE	ENTRY#
Applied Advertising Inc	Danbury	CT	F	860 640-0800	708
Nomad Communications Inc	White River Junction	VT	F	802 649-1995	17709

AERIAL WORK PLATFORMS

	CITY	ST	EMP	PHONE	ENTRY#
Capewell Aerial Systems LLC **(PA)**	South Windsor	CT	D	860 610-0700	3126

AEROSOLS

	CITY	ST	EMP	PHONE	ENTRY#
Plz Corp	Fall River	MA	C	650 543-7600	8597
Shield Packaging Co Inc	Dudley	MA	E	508 949-0900	8323
Shield Realty California Inc **(PA)**	Canton	MA	E	909 628-4707	7829

AGENTS, BROKERS & BUREAUS: Personal Service

	CITY	ST	EMP	PHONE	ENTRY#
Federal Business Products Inc	Torrington	CT	E	860 482-6231	3680
Stone Tablet LLC	Newton	MA	F	781 380-8800	10788

AGRICULTURAL EQPT: BARN, SILO, POULTRY, DAIRY/LIVESTOCK MACH

	CITY	ST	EMP	PHONE	ENTRY#
Northeast Structures Barns LLC	Porter	ME	G	207 512-0503	5167

AGRICULTURAL EQPT: Grade, Clean & Sort Machines, Fruit/Veg

	CITY	ST	EMP	PHONE	ENTRY#
Harold Haines Inc	Presque Isle	ME	F	207 762-1411	5300

AGRICULTURAL EQPT: Harvesters, Fruit, Vegetable, Tobacco

	CITY	ST	EMP	PHONE	ENTRY#
Allagash Timberlands LP	St John Plt	ME	G	207 834-6348	5524

AGRICULTURAL MACHINERY & EQPT: Wholesalers

	CITY	ST	EMP	PHONE	ENTRY#
I B A Inc **(PA)**	Sutton	MA	E	508 865-6911	12281

AIR CLEANING SYSTEMS

	CITY	ST	EMP	PHONE	ENTRY#
Nq Industries Inc	Hamden	CT	F	860 258-3466	1448
Planet Technologies Inc	Ridgefield	CT	D	800 255-3749	2905
Weld Engineering Co Inc	Shrewsbury	MA	F	508 842-2224	11848
Ocean State Air LLC	Pawtucket	RI	G	401 722-2447	16397

	CITY	ST	EMP	PHONE	ENTRY#

AIR CONDITIONING & VENTILATION EQPT & SPLYS: Wholesales

	CITY	ST	EMP	PHONE	ENTRY#
Outland Engineering Inc	Milford	CT	F	800 797-3709	1861

AIR CONDITIONING EQPT

Alvest (usa) Inc (DH)	Windsor	CT	E	860 602-3400	4259
Thermo Power Corporation	Waltham	MA	A	781 622-1400	12802
Maine Market Refrigeration LLC (PA)	Fayette	ME	E	207 685-3504	4783

AIR CONDITIONING EQPT, WHOLE HOUSE: Wholesalers

Total Air Supply LLC	Nashua	NH	E	603 889-0100	15177

AIR CONDITIONING REPAIR SVCS

Jason Trucks Inc	Medford	MA	F	781 396-8300	10292
Tecogen Inc (PA)	Waltham	MA	E	781 466-6402	12790

AIR CONDITIONING UNITS: Complete, Domestic Or Indl

Tecogen Inc (PA)	Waltham	MA	E	781 466-6402	12790

AIR COOLERS: Metal Plate

Mastercraft Tool and Mch Co	Southington	CT	F	860 628-5551	3220

AIR MATTRESSES: Plastic

E F Inc	Gardner	MA	F	978 630-3800	8885
Riverbend Fiberglass Inc	Dixfield	ME	G	207 562-7103	4727

AIR POLLUTION MEASURING SVCS

Environmental Monitor Svc Inc	Meriden	CT	G	203 935-0102	1667
Acumentrics Rups LLC	Walpole	MA	E	617 932-7877	12546

AIR PURIFICATION EQPT

Clean Air Group Inc (PA)	Fairfield	CT	G	203 335-3700	1179
Environmental Monitor Svc Inc	Meriden	CT	G	203 935-0102	1667
Liberty Industries Inc	East Berlin	CT	E	860 828-6361	913
Treadwell Corporation	Thomaston	CT	E	860 283-7600	3639
Kovalus Spration Solutions LLC (PA)	Wilmington	MA	C	978 694-7000	13421
Metalmark Innovations Pbc	Cambridge	MA	G	617 714-4026	7642
Vacuum Technology Inc	Gloucester	MA	G	510 333-6562	8962
Pollution Research & Dev Corp (PA)	Newport	NH	G	603 863-7553	15234

AIRCRAFT & AEROSPACE FLIGHT INSTRUMENTS & GUIDANCE SYSTEMS

Alpha Q Inc (PA)	Colchester	CT	D	860 537-4681	654
Crane Company (PA)	Stamford	CT	D	203 363-7300	3326
Msj Investments Inc	Stafford Springs	CT	F	860 684-9956	3257
UTC Corporation	Newington	CT	F	860 665-1770	2332
3deo Inc	Norwood	MA	G	781 999-3447	11151
Adcole LLC (PA)	Marlborough	MA	C	508 485-9100	10103
Ametek Arospc Pwr Holdings Inc (HQ)	Wilmington	MA	D	978 988-4771	13378
Autonodyne LLC (PA)	Boston	MA	E	321 751-8402	6579
De-Ice Technologies Inc	Somerville	MA	F	857 829-7651	11868
Spike Aerospace Inc	Boston	MA	F	617 338-1400	7052
Aero Defense International LLC	Manchester	NH	E	603 644-0305	14807
Allard Nazarian Group Inc	Manchester	NH	F	603 314-0017	14809
Allard Nazarian Group Inc (PA)	Manchester	NH	E	603 668-1900	14810
American Ir Solutions LLC	Hudson	NH	F	662 626-2477	14483
CHI Aerospace	Portsmouth	NH	F	603 380-9951	15372
Kearflex Engineering Company	Warwick	RI	F	401 781-4900	16830
BF Goodrich Aerspce Aircrft In	Vergennes	VT	G	802 877-2911	17656
Liquid Measurement Systems Inc	Fairfax	VT	E	802 528-8100	17261

AIRCRAFT & HEAVY EQPT REPAIR SVCS

Doncasters Inc (PA)	Groton	CT	D	860 449-1603	1367
Skico Manufacturing Co LLC	Hamden	CT	G	203 230-1305	1455

AIRCRAFT ASSEMBLY PLANTS

Aircastle Advisor LLC	Stamford	CT	D	203 504-1020	3276
Amco Precision Tools Inc (PA)	Berlin	CT	E	860 828-5640	49
B & F Design Incorporated	New Britain	CT	E	860 357-4317	2005
Cs Group - Usa Inc	East Hartford	CT	E	860 944-0041	983
Cyient Defense Services Inc	New Britain	CT	E	860 357-4317	2019
Embraer Executive Jet Svcs LLC	Windsor Locks	CT	G	860 804-4600	4324
GKN Aerospace Newington LLC	Newington	CT	F	860 830-5810	2296
Gulfstream Aerospace Corp	East Granby	CT	F	912 965-3000	935
Hanwha Aerospace USA LLC	Glastonbury	CT	D	860 633-9474	1284
Hartford Jet Center LLC	Hartford	CT	F	860 548-9334	1487
Kaman Aerospace Corporation (DH)	Bloomfield	CT	A	860 242-4461	179
Kaman Aerospace Corporation	Bloomfield	CT	G	860 242-4461	181
Kaman Aerospace Group Inc (HQ)	Bloomfield	CT	F	860 243-7100	182
Learjet Inc	Windsor Locks	CT	C	860 627-9491	4331
MB Aerospace	East Granby	CT	E	860 653-0569	941
New England Airfoil Pdts Inc	Farmington	CT	E	860 677-1376	1231

	CITY	ST	EMP	PHONE	ENTRY#
Aerovironment Inc	Burlington	MA	E	805 520-8350	7333
Ascent Aerosystems Inc	Wilmington	MA	E	330 554-6334	13381
Bombardier Services Corp	Boston	MA	C	617 464-0323	6600
General Dynamics Aviation Svcs	Westfield	MA	D	413 562-5860	13166
Gulfstream Aerospace Corp	Westfield	MA	C	413 562-5866	13169
Liquiglide Inc	Cambridge	MA	E	617 901-0700	7633
Lockheed Martin Corporation	Andover	MA	E	407 356-2374	5891
Lockheed Mrtin Advnced Enrgy S	Waltham	MA	G	972 603-7611	12710
Northeast Seat Company Inc	Palmer	MA	G	413 283-6236	11278
Terrafugia Inc	Woburn	MA	F	781 491-0812	13678
Transcend Air Corporation	Carlisle	MA	G	781 883-4818	7848
Lockheed Martin	Wayne	ME	E	603 966-6031	5597
Sonic Blue Aerospace Inc	Portland	ME	G	207 776-2471	5275
Marmon Aerospace & Defense LLC	Manchester	NH	G	603 622-3500	14879
Uav - America Inc	Nottingham	NH	G	603 389-6364	15279
Bell Helicopter Miami Inc	Providence	RI	E	401 421-2800	16485
Bell Textron Rhode Island Inc	Providence	RI	E	401 421-2800	16486
Textron Aviation RI Inc	Providence	RI	F	401 421-2800	16621
Textron Fluid and Power Inc	Providence	RI	F	401 588-3400	16622
Textron Inc (PA)	Providence	RI	A	401 421-2800	16623
Textron Inc	Warwick	RI	E	401 457-2310	16868
Beta Technologies Inc	South Burlington	VT	E	802 281-3623	17572
Lockheed Martin Corporation	South Burlington	VT	F	802 503-8699	17584

AIRCRAFT CONTROL SYSTEMS:

Triumph Eng Ctrl Systems LLC (HQ)	West Hartford	CT	D	860 236-0651	4087

AIRCRAFT DEALERS

Sikorsky Aircraft Corporation (HQ)	Stratford	CT	A	203 386-4000	3571

AIRCRAFT ELECTRICAL EQPT REPAIR SVCS

Electro-Methods Inc (PA)	South Windsor	CT	C	860 289-8661	3141
TLD America Corporation (DH)	Windsor	CT	F	860 602-3400	4309

AIRCRAFT ENGINES & ENGINE PARTS: Airfoils

General Electric Company	Stamford	CT	F	866 419-4096	3354
General Electric Company (PA)	Boston	MA	A	617 443-3000	6754

AIRCRAFT ENGINES & ENGINE PARTS: Mount Parts

Agreda Industries LLC	South Windsor	CT	E	860 436-5551	3110
Pratt & Whitney Eng Svcs Inc	North Berwick	ME	B	207 676-4100	5112

AIRCRAFT ENGINES & ENGINE PARTS: Pumps

Columbia Manufacturing Inc	Columbia	CT	D	860 228-2259	669

AIRCRAFT ENGINES & ENGINE PARTS: Research & Development, Mfr

Pratt & Whitney Cenco Inc	East Hartford	CT	F	860 565-4321	1013
De-Ice Technologies Inc	Somerville	MA	F	857 829-7651	11868
Fountain Plating Company LLC	West Springfield	MA	D	413 781-4651	13025

AIRCRAFT ENGINES & PARTS

A-1 Machining Co LLC	New Britain	CT	D	860 223-6420	1994
Accupaulo Holding Corporation (PA)	Bristol	CT	E	860 666-5621	391
Acmt Inc	Manchester	CT	E	860 645-0592	1582
Aerospace Techniques Inc	Middletown	CT	D	860 347-1200	1733
AGC Acquisition LLC	Meriden	CT	C	203 639-7125	1653
Air Transport Intl Inc	Windsor Locks	CT	G	937 287-8455	4322
Alloy Specialties LLC	Manchester	CT	E	860 646-4587	1585
American Design & Mfg Inc	South Windsor	CT	E	860 282-2719	3112
ATI Ladish Machining Inc (DH)	East Hartford	CT	E	860 688-3688	973
ATI Ladish Machining Inc	East Hartford	CT	D	860 688-3688	974
ATI Ladish Machining Inc	South Windsor	CT	D	860 688-3688	3116
Barnes Group Inc	Bristol	CT	C	513 759-3503	405
Barnes Group Inc (PA)	Bristol	CT	C	860 583-7070	406
Beacon Group Inc (PA)	Newington	CT	E	860 594-5200	2275
Budney Industries Inc	Berlin	CT	C	860 828-1950	55
Cambridge Specialty Co Inc	Berlin	CT	D	860 828-3579	57
CBS Manufacturing Company	East Granby	CT	E	860 653-8100	927
Chromalloy Component Svcs Inc	Windsor	CT	E	860 688-7798	4266
Chromalloy Gas Turbine LLC	Windsor	CT	D	860 688-7798	4267
Deburring House Inc	East Berlin	CT	E	860 828-0889	909
Drt Aerospace LLC	Meriden	CT	D	203 781-8020	1664
Electro-Methods Inc	South Windsor	CT	E	860 289-8661	3140
Electro-Methods Inc (PA)	South Windsor	CT	C	860 289-8661	3141
Engine Alliance LLC	Glastonbury	CT	B	860 565-2239	1277
Enjet Aero Bloomfield LLC	Bloomfield	CT	E	860 242-2211	162
Enjet Aero Manchester LLC	Manchester	CT	F	913 717-7396	1597
First Equity Group Inc (PA)	Westport	CT	F	203 291-7700	4168
GKN Aerospace Newington LLC (DH)	Newington	CT	C	860 667-8502	2297
GKN Arspace Svcs Strctures LLC	Cromwell	CT	C	860 613-0236	693
GKN Arspace Svcs Strctures LLC	Wallingford	CT	B	203 303-1408	3809
Global Trbine Cmpnent Tech LLC	South Windsor	CT	E	860 528-4722	3151

Employee Codes: A=Over 500 employees, B=251-500
C=101-250, D=51-100, E=20-50, F=10-19, G=1-9

2024 Harris New England
Manufacturers Directory

PRODUCT

1333

	CITY	ST	EMP	PHONE	ENTRY#
Hanwha Aerospace USA LLC **(DH)**	Cheshire	CT	C	203 806-2090	597
Hanwha Aerospace USA LLC	East Windsor	CT	E	860 789-2500	1074
Hanwha Aerospace USA LLC	East Windsor	CT	D	860 789-2511	1075
Hanwha Aerospace USA LLC	Farmington	CT	D	860 677-2603	1221
Honeywell International Inc	Northford	CT	E	203 484-7161	2453
Honeywell International Inc	Northford	CT	B	203 484-7161	2454
Horst Engineering & Manufacturing Co **(PA)**	East Hartford	CT			D
860 289-8209	997				
Hsb Aircraft Components LLC	New Britain	CT	F	860 505-7349	2030
I & J Machine Tool Company	Milford	CT	F	203 877-5376	1836
Iae International Aero Engs AG	East Hartford	CT	C	860 565-1773	1000
International Aero Engines LLC	East Hartford	CT	F	860 565-5515	1002
Kaman Aerospace Corporation	Bloomfield	CT	G	860 242-4461	181
Kaman Aerospace Group Inc **(HQ)**	Bloomfield	CT	F	860 243-7100	182
Kamatics Corporation **(DH)**	Bloomfield	CT	E	860 243-9704	184
Leading Edge Aero LLC	Bethel	CT	F	203 797-1200	125
Lewis Machine LLC	East Hartford	CT	E	860 289-3468	1003
Lighthouse International LLC	South Windsor	CT	F	860 528-4722	3161
MB Aerspace Acp Hldngs III Cor **(PA)**	East Granby	CT	E	586 772-2500	943
Meadow Manufacturing Inc	Bristol	CT	F	860 357-3785	467
Micro Farmington Sub LLC	New Britain	CT	D	860 677-2646	2045
Msj Investments Inc	Stafford Springs	CT	F	860 684-9956	3257
New England Airfoil Pdts Inc	Farmington	CT	E	860 677-1376	1231
Numet Machining Techniques LLC	Orange	CT	E	203 375-4995	2679
Palmer Manufacturing Co LLC	East Berlin	CT	F	860 828-0344	914
Pcx Aerosystems-Manchester LLC	Manchester	CT	C	860 649-0000	1630
Pdq Inc **(PA)**	Rocky Hill	CT	E	860 529-9051	2932
Point Machine Company	Berlin	CT	G	860 828-6901	78
Polar Corp	New Britain	CT	G	860 225-6000	2053
Polar Corporation	New Britain	CT	E	860 223-7891	2054
Pratt & Whitney Company Inc	East Hartford	CT	A	860 565-4321	1014
Pratt & Whitney Eng Svcs Inc	Cheshire	CT	B	203 250-4000	611
Pratt & Whitney Eng Svcs Inc	East Hartford	CT	E	860 565-4321	1015
Pratt & Whitney Eng Svcs Inc	East Hartford	CT	E	860 610-7478	1016
Pratt & Whitney Eng Svcs Inc	Middletown	CT	B	860 344-4000	1773
Pratt & Whitney Engine Lsg LLC	Hartford	CT	D	860 565-4321	1500
Pratt & Whitney Services Inc	East Hartford	CT	D	860 565-5489	1017
Precision Speed Mfg LLC	Middletown	CT	E	860 635-8811	1774
Purdy Corporation	Manchester	CT	C	860 649-0000	1631
Rockville Technology LLC	Vernon	CT	E	860 871-6883	3756
Rtx Corporation	East Hartford	CT	A	860 610-7000	1020
Rtx Corporation	Farmington	CT	C	860 678-4500	1245
Rtx Corporation	Windsor Locks	CT	C	860 654-7519	4333
SA Manchester LLC	Manchester	CT	D	860 533-7500	1634
Saar Corporation	Farmington	CT	F	860 674-9440	1246
Scap Motors Inc	Fairfield	CT	E	203 384-0005	1200
Sikorsky Aircraft Corporation	Stratford	CT	E	203 386-4000	3572
Simmonds Precision Pdts Inc	Danbury	CT	F	203 797-5000	818
Soto Holdings Inc	New Haven	CT	E	203 781-8020	2202
Specialty Tool Company USA LLC	Milford	CT	E	203 874-2009	1888
Triumph Eng Ctrl Systems LLC **(HQ)**	West Hartford	CT	D	860 236-0651	4087
Tru-Precision Corporation	Farmington	CT	G	860 269-6230	1252
Turbine Kinetics Inc	Glastonbury	CT	F	860 633-8520	1300
Turbine Technologies Inc **(PA)**	Farmington	CT	D	860 678-1642	1257
United Gear and Machine Co Inc	Suffield	CT	F	860 623-6618	3596
United Tool & Die Company **(PA)**	West Hartford	CT	C	860 246-6531	4088
Whitney Pratt	Willington	CT	G	860 565-6431	4227
Winslow Automatics Inc	New Britain	CT	D	860 225-6321	2075
325 Silver Street Inc	Agawam	MA	E	413 789-1800	5776
Actronics Incorporated	Waltham	MA	F	781 890-7030	12583
Aerobond Composites LLC	Springfield	MA	E	413 734-2224	12071
Ametek Arospc Pwr Holdings Inc **(HQ)**	Wilmington	MA	D	978 988-4771	13378
General Electric Company	Lynn	MA	A	781 594-0100	9974
General Electric Company	Lynn	MA	A	781 594-2218	9975
Goodrich Corporation	Westford	MA	A	978 303-6700	13239
Honeywell International Inc	Canton	MA	G	781 298-2700	7798
Honeywell International Inc	Southborough	MA	C	508 490-7100	11997
Hutchinson Arospc & Indust Inc **(DH)**	Hopkinton	MA	D	508 417-7000	9330
Jet Industries Inc	Agawam	MA	E	413 786-2010	5798
LKM Industries Inc	Woburn	MA	D	781 935-9210	13602
Magellan Aerospace Usa Inc **(DH)**	Haverhill	MA	F	978 774-6000	9112
Magellan Arospc Haverhill Inc	Haverhill	MA	C	978 774-6000	9113
Materials Development Corp	Andover	MA	D	781 391-0400	5893
MB Westfield Inc	Westfield	MA	C	413 568-8676	13182
Palmer Manufacturing Co Llc **(DH)**	Malden	MA	C	781 321-0480	10021
Palmer Manufacturing Co LLC	Peabody	MA	F	781 321-0480	11330
Paradigm Prcision Holdings LLC	Peabody	MA	C	978 278-7100	11331
Parker-Hannifin Corporation	Devens	MA	C	978 784-1000	8285
Si-Rel Inc	Chelmsford	MA	G	978 455-8737	7956
Tell Tool Inc	Westfield	MA	D	413 568-1671	13210
Tell Tool Acquisition Inc **(DH)**	Westfield	MA	E	413 568-1671	13211
Traincroft Inc **(PA)**	Medford	MA	E	781 393-6943	10299

	CITY	ST	EMP	PHONE	ENTRY#
Union Machine Company Lynn Inc **(PA)**	Groveland	MA	E	978 521-5100	9016
Wgi Inc	Southwick	MA	C	413 569-9444	12051
Tem Inc	Buxton	ME	E	207 929-8700	4665
General Electric Company	Hooksett	NH	A	603 666-8300	14465
GKN Aerospace New England Inc	Charlestown	NH	D	603 542-5135	14063
Pratt & Whitney	Londonderry	NH	F	800 742-5877	14779
Avco Corporation **(DH)**	Providence	RI	C	401 421-2800	16480
Honeywell International Inc	Smithfield	RI	F	401 757-2560	16712
Textron Inc **(PA)**	Providence	RI	A	401 421-2800	16623
Textron Lycoming Corp **(HQ)**	Providence	RI	E	401 421-2800	16624
General Electric Company	Rutland	VT	A	802 775-9842	17497
Honeywell International Inc	Williston	VT	G	877 841-2840	17735
Pratt & Whitney Eng Svcs Inc	South Burlington	VT	E	802 658-2208	17596
Simmonds Precision Products **(DH)**	Vergennes	VT	A	802 877-4000	17661
Superior Tchncal Ceramics Corp **(HQ)**	Saint Albans	VT	C	802 527-7726	17533

AIRCRAFT LIGHTING

	CITY	ST	EMP	PHONE	ENTRY#
Hoffman Engineering LLC **(DH)**	Stamford	CT	D	203 425-8900	3378
B/E Aerospace Inc	Hampton	NH	F	603 926-5700	14399

AIRCRAFT MAINTENANCE & REPAIR SVCS

	CITY	ST	EMP	PHONE	ENTRY#
Aerospace Techniques Inc	Middletown	CT	D	860 347-1200	1733
Helicopter Support Inc **(DH)**	Trumbull	CT	B	203 416-4600	3721
Sikorsky Aircraft Corporation **(HQ)**	Stratford	CT	A	203 386-4000	3571
Turbine Controls Inc **(PA)**	Bloomfield	CT	D	860 242-0448	214

AIRCRAFT PARTS & AUX EQPT: Panel Assy/Hydro Prop Test Stands

	CITY	ST	EMP	PHONE	ENTRY#
Electro-Methods Inc **(PA)**	South Windsor	CT	C	860 289-8661	3141

AIRCRAFT PARTS & AUXILIARY EQPT: Assys, Subassemblies/Parts

	CITY	ST	EMP	PHONE	ENTRY#
A G C Incorporated	Meriden	CT	C	203 235-3361	1649
Athens Industries Inc	Plantsville	CT	G	860 621-8957	2789
B&N Aerospace Inc	Newington	CT	E	860 665-0134	2274
Budney Aerospace Inc	Berlin	CT	D	860 828-0585	54
Carey Manufacturing Co Inc	Cromwell	CT	F	860 829-1803	689
Connecticut Tool & Mfg Co LLC	Plainville	CT	D	860 846-0800	2751
Hanwha Aerospace USA LLC	Glastonbury	CT	D	860 633-9474	1284
Jarvis Airfoil Inc	Portland	CT	D	860 342-5000	2820
Metallon Inc	Thomaston	CT	E	860 283-8265	3624
Paradigm Manchester Inc **(DH)**	Manchester	CT	B	772 287-7770	1623
Pcx Aerostructures LLC **(PA)**	Newington	CT	C	860 666-2471	2315
Pratt & Whitney Eng Svcs Inc	Middletown	CT	B	860 344-4000	1773
Precision Metals and Plastics	Winsted	CT	G	860 238-4320	4353
Richard Manufacturing Co Inc	Milford	CT	E	203 874-3617	1877
Saf Industries LLC **(HQ)**	Meriden	CT	E	203 729-4900	1696
Tachwa Enterprises Inc	Hamden	CT	G	203 691-5772	1459
Pcx Aerostructures LLC	Boylston	MA	D	508 869-2131	7163
Whitcraft Scrborough/Tempe LLC	Newburyport	MA	C	763 780-0060	10727

AIRCRAFT PARTS & AUXILIARY EQPT: Blades, Prop, Metal Or Wood

	CITY	ST	EMP	PHONE	ENTRY#
Toolmax Designing Tooling Inc	Ashford	CT	F	860 477-0373	22

AIRCRAFT PARTS & AUXILIARY EQPT: Body & Wing Assys & Parts

	CITY	ST	EMP	PHONE	ENTRY#
Schweizer Aircraft Corp	Stratford	CT	B	203 386-4356	3570
Triumph Eng Ctrl Systems LLC **(HQ)**	West Hartford	CT	D	860 236-0651	4087
Anderson Airmotive Inc	Fall River	MA	F	508 646-0950	8521
Opalala Inc	Fall River	MA	F	508 646-0950	8591

AIRCRAFT PARTS & AUXILIARY EQPT: Body Assemblies & Parts

	CITY	ST	EMP	PHONE	ENTRY#
Airborne Industries Inc	Branford	CT	F	203 315-0200	232
I & J Machine Tool Company	Milford	CT	F	203 877-5376	1836
Pcx Aerosystems-Manchester LLC	Manchester	CT	C	860 649-0000	1630
Purdy Corporation	Manchester	CT	C	860 649-0000	1631

AIRCRAFT PARTS & AUXILIARY EQPT: Deicing Eqpt

	CITY	ST	EMP	PHONE	ENTRY#
De-Ice Technologies Inc	Somerville	MA	F	857 829-7651	11868
Integrated Deicing Svcs LLC **(DH)**	Manchester	NH	B	603 647-1717	14863

AIRCRAFT PARTS & AUXILIARY EQPT: Gears, Power Transmission

	CITY	ST	EMP	PHONE	ENTRY#
Aero Gear Incorporated	Windsor	CT	C	860 688-0888	4255
Hamilton Sundstrand Corp **(HQ)**	Windsor Locks	CT	A	619 714-9442	4330
Perry Technology Corporation	New Hartford	CT	D	860 738-2525	2107

AIRCRAFT PARTS & AUXILIARY EQPT: Lighting/Landing Gear Assy

	CITY	ST	EMP	PHONE	ENTRY#
Straton Industries Inc	Stratford	CT	D	203 375-4488	3578
Goodrich Corporation	Peabody	MA	E	978 532-2350	11311

AIRCRAFT PARTS & AUXILIARY EQPT: Military Eqpt & Armament

	CITY	ST	EMP	PHONE	ENTRY#
Blue Tactical LLC	Westfield	MA	F	413 315-6344	13153
Boniface Tool & Die Inc	Dudley	MA	E	508 764-3248	8317
General Dynamics Ots Cal Inc	Saco	ME	C	207 283-3611	5368
Exothermics Inc	Amherst	NH	F	603 821-5660	13869

	CITY	ST	EMP	PHONE	ENTRY#
General Dynamics Ots Cal Inc	Williston	VT	B	802 662-7000	17733

AIRCRAFT PARTS & EQPT, NEC

	CITY	ST	EMP	PHONE	ENTRY#
A-1 Machining Co LLC	New Britain	CT	D	860 223-6420	1994
AAR Government Services Inc	Windsor	CT	F	860 298-0144	4250
Acmt Inc	Manchester	CT	D	860 645-0592	1582
Admill Machine Co LLC	New Britain	CT	C	860 356-0330	1998
Aero Tube Technologies LLC	South Windsor	CT	E	860 289-2520	3107
Aerocision LLC	Chester	CT	D	860 526-9700	622
Aerospace Techniques Inc	Middletown	CT	D	860 347-1200	1733
Agreda Industries LLC	South Windsor	CT	E	860 436-5551	3110
Air-Lock Incorporated	Milford	CT	E	203 878-4691	1794
Alinabal Inc (HQ)	Milford	CT	C	203 877-3241	1796
Alken Industries Inc	Newington	CT	E	631 467-2000	2269
Arrow Diversified Tooling Inc	Ellington	CT	E	860 872-9072	1101
B/E Aerospace Inc	Farmington	CT	D	410 266-2048	1207
Barnes Group Inc	Windsor	CT	A	860 298-7740	4262
Beacon Industries Inc	Newington	CT	C	860 594-5200	2276
Brandstrom Instruments Inc	Ridgefield	CT	E	203 544-9341	2892
C V Tool Company Inc (PA)	Southington	CT	E	978 353-7901	3206
Cambridge Specialty Co Inc	Berlin	CT	D	860 828-3579	57
CBS Manufacturing Company	East Granby	CT	E	860 653-8100	927
Continental Machine TI Co Inc	New Britain	CT	D	860 223-2896	2014
Crane Aerospace Inc (DH)	Stamford	CT	C	860 363-7300	3325
Doncasters Inc (PA)	Groton	CT	D	860 449-1603	1367
Enjet Aero Bloomfield LLC	Bloomfield	CT	C	860 242-2211	162
Enjet Aero New Britain LLC	New Britain	CT	C	860 356-0330	2026
Flight Support Inc	North Haven	CT	E	203 562-1415	2413
Forrest Machine Inc	Berlin	CT	D	860 563-1796	66
Gelder Aerospace LLC	Shelton	CT	G	203 283-9524	3008
GKN Aerospace Newington LLC (DH)	Newington	CT	C	860 667-8502	2297
Global Trbine Cmpnent Tech LLC	South Windsor	CT	E	860 528-4722	3151
Glyne Manufacturing Co Inc	Stratford	CT	F	203 375-4495	3542
Goodrich Corporation	Danbury	CT	C	704 423-7000	751
Goodrich Corporation	Danbury	CT	B	203 797-5000	752
H & B Tool & Eng Co Inc	South Windsor	CT	E	860 528-9341	3153
Hanwha Aerospace USA LLC	Newington	CT	D	860 667-2134	2298
Hanwha Aerospace USA LLC	Newington	CT	C	860 667-2134	2299
Helicopter Support Inc (DH)	Trumbull	CT	B	203 416-4000	3721
Hexcel Corporation (PA)	Stamford	CT	E	203 969-0666	3374
Hexcel Pottsville Corporation	Stamford	CT	E	203 969-0666	3375
Horst Engineering & Manufacturing Co (PA) 860 289-8209	East Hartford	CT			D 997
Ithaco Space Systems Inc	Danbury	CT	E	607 272-7640	760
Jobin Machine Inc	West Hartford	CT	E	860 953-1631	4065
Kaman Acquisition Usa Inc (HQ)	Bloomfield	CT	F	860 243-7100	178
Kaman Aerospace Corporation (DH)	Bloomfield	CT	A	860 242-4461	179
Kaman Aerospace Corporation	Bloomfield	CT	E	860 242-4461	180
Kaman Aerospace Group Inc (HQ)	Bloomfield	CT	F	860 243-7100	182
Kaman Corporation (PA)	Bloomfield	CT	D	860 243-7100	183
Kamatics Corporation (DH)	Bloomfield	CT	E	860 243-9704	184
L M Gill Welding and Mfr LLC	Manchester	CT	D	860 647-9931	1611
Leading Edge Aero LLC	Bethel	CT	F	203 797-1200	125
Lee Company (PA)	Westbrook	CT	A	860 399-6281	4140
Liftwing LLC	Shelton	CT	F	203 913-2308	3028
LM Gill Welding & Mfg LLC	Manchester	CT	E	860 647-9931	1613
MB Aerospace East Granby Limited Partnership 860 653-5041	East Granby	CT			C 942
McMellon Bros Incorporated	Stratford	CT	E	203 375-5685	3555
MTM Corporation	Andover	CT	G	860 742-9600	2
Naiad Dynamics Us Inc (HQ)	Shelton	CT	E	203 929-6355	3033
Nanni Manufacturing Co Inc	Winsted	CT	E		4350
Nelson Tool & Machine Co Inc	Bristol	CT	G	860 589-8004	474
Overhaul Support Services LLC (PA)	East Granby	CT	D	860 264-2101	947
Paragon Tool Company Inc	Manchester	CT	G	860 647-9935	1627
Polamer Precision Inc	New Britain	CT	C	860 259-6200	2052
Polar Corporation	New Britain	CT	E	860 223-7891	2054
Precision Speed Mfg LLC	Middletown	CT	E	860 635-8811	1774
Ramar-Hall Inc	Middlefield	CT	E	860 349-1081	1728
Rbc Bearings Incorporated (PA)	Oxford	CT	C	203 267-7001	2710
Redco Corporation (HQ)	Stamford	CT	D	203 363-7300	3445
Rotair Aerospace Corporation	Bridgeport	CT	E	203 576-6545	367
Rotating Composite Tech LLC	Kensington	CT	G	860 829-6809	1540
Sargent Controls and Aerospace	Oxford	CT	E	520 744-1000	2711
Senior Operations LLC	Enfield	CT	D	860 741-2546	1147
Simmonds Precision Pdts Inc	Danbury	CT	F	203 797-5000	818
Thompson Aerospace LLC	Bristol	CT	F	860 516-0472	502
TLD America Corporation (DH)	Windsor	CT	F	860 602-3400	4309
Triumph Acttion Systems - Conn (HQ)	Windsor	CT	D	860 687-5412	4310
Triumph Eng Ctrl Systems LLC	West Hartford	CT	B	860 597-7173	4086
Triumph Group Inc	Bloomfield	CT	G	860 726-9378	213
United Avionics Inc	Seymour	CT	E	203 723-1404	2974

	CITY	ST	EMP	PHONE	ENTRY#
Valley Tool and Mfg LLC (HQ)	Milford	CT	E	203 799-8800	1898
W and G Machine Company Inc	Hamden	CT	F	203 288-3871	1462
Whitcraft LLC (PA)	Eastford	CT	C	860 974-0786	1093
Whitcraft Scrborough/Tempe LLC (HQ)	Eastford	CT	E	860 974-0786	1094
Whitcraft South Windsor LLC	South Windsor	CT	B	860 436-5551	3191
2is Inc	Walpole	MA	E	508 850-7520	12545
325 Silver Street Inc	Agawam	MA	E	413 789-1800	5776
Actronics Incorporated	Waltham	MA	F	781 890-7030	12583
Aerobond Composites LLC	Springfield	MA	E	413 734-2224	12071
B & E Tool Company Inc	Southwick	MA	D	413 569-5585	12042
Collins Aerospace	Westford	MA	E	978 303-6700	13231
Crane Nxt Co (PA)	Waltham	MA	C	610 430-2510	12644
Fgc Plasma Solutions Inc	Middleton	MA	E	617 999-9078	10383
GE Aviation Systems LLC	Lynn	MA	E	513 552-3272	9973
Goodrich Corporation	Westford	MA	A	978 303-6700	13239
Goodrich Corporation	Westford	MA	E	978 303-6700	13240
Jet Industries Inc	Agawam	MA	E	413 786-2010	5798
Ltp Corporation (DH)	Northborough	MA	D	508 393-7660	11101
Parker-Hannifin Corporation	Devens	MA	C	978 784-1200	8285
Parts Tool and Die Inc	Agawam	MA	E	413 821-9718	5805
Raytheon Company	Marlborough	MA	E	508 490-1000	10201
Rockwell Collins Inc	Peabody	MA	F	978 532-2350	11338
Rodney Hunt-Fontaine Inc (HQ)	Orange	MA	E	978 544-2511	11232
Union Machine Company Lynn Inc (PA)	Groveland	MA	E	978 521-5100	9016
Wyman-Gordon Company (DH)	North Grafton	MA	B	508 839-8252	11030
Clamar Floats Inc	Brunswick	ME	G	603 828-5373	4644
Elmet Technologies LLC (PA)	Lewiston	ME	C	207 333-6100	4960
B/E Aerospace Inc	Hampton	NH	F	603 926-5700	14399
Bae Systems Info Elctrnic Syst	Merrimack	NH	B	603 885-4321	14975
Brazonics Inc (DH)	Hampton	NH	C	603 758-6237	14400
Continental Cable LLC	Hinsdale	NH	E	800 229-5131	14443
General Electric Company	Hooksett	NH	A	603 666-8300	14465
Hardric Laboratories Inc	Hudson	NH	E	978 251-1702	14506
Lakes Region Tubular Pdts Inc	Laconia	NH	E	603 528-2838	14657
Lanair Research & Dev Inc	Portsmouth	NH	G	603 433-6134	15415
Matrix Aerospace Corp	Claremont	NH	D	603 542-0191	14093
Meggitt (new Hampshire) Inc	Londonderry	NH	C	603 669-0940	14767
Screw-Matic Corporation	Laconia	NH	E	603 468-1610	14668
Sierra Nevada Corporation	Bedford	NH	E	775 331-0222	13949
Avco Corporation (DH)	Providence	RI	C	401 421-2800	16480
Bell Helicopter Korea Inc	Providence	RI	E	401 421-2800	16484
Clear Carbon & Components Inc	Bristol	RI	E	401 254-5085	15758
Magnetic Seal LLC	Warren	RI	D	401 247-2800	16760
Textron Inc (PA)	Providence	RI	A	401 421-2800	16623
Textron Lycoming Corp (HQ)	Providence	RI	E	401 421-2800	16624
Collins Aerospace	Vergennes	VT	D	802 877-4000	17657
Liquid Measurement Systems Inc	Fairfax	VT	E	802 528-8100	17261
Preci-Manufacturing Inc	Winooski	VT	D	802 655-2414	17768
Sathorn Corporation	Williston	VT	E	802 860-2121	17748
Simmonds Precision Pdts Inc	Vergennes	VT	F	802 877-2911	17660
Simmonds Precision Products (DH)	Vergennes	VT	A	802 877-4000	17661
Vermont Aerospace Manufacturing Inc	Lyndonville	VT	C	802 748-8705	17321

AIRCRAFT PARTS WHOLESALERS

	CITY	ST	EMP	PHONE	ENTRY#
TLD America Corporation (DH)	Windsor	CT	F	860 602-3400	4309

AIRCRAFT PROPELLERS & PARTS

	CITY	ST	EMP	PHONE	ENTRY#
Aerocomposites Inc	Kensington	CT	F	860 829-6809	1537
Leading Edge Concepts Inc	Bethel	CT	G	203 797-1200	126

AIRCRAFT SEATS

	CITY	ST	EMP	PHONE	ENTRY#
Franklin Products Inc (PA)	Torrington	CT	E	860 482-0266	3681
Torrington Distributors Inc (PA)	Torrington	CT	E	860 482-4464	3701
B/E Aerospace Inc	Hampton	NH	F	603 926-5700	14399

AIRCRAFT SERVICING & REPAIRING

	CITY	ST	EMP	PHONE	ENTRY#
Integrated Deicing Svcs LLC (DH)	Manchester	NH	B	603 647-1717	14863

AIRCRAFT TURBINES

	CITY	ST	EMP	PHONE	ENTRY#
MB Aerospace East Granby Limited Partnership 860 653-5041	East Granby	CT			C 942
Turbine Components Inc	Oxford	CT	E	858 678-8568	2713
Aero Turbine Components Inc	Worcester	MA	G	508 755-2121	13698
Ingersoll-Rand Energy Systems Corporation 603 430-7000	Portsmouth	NH			D 15408

AIRCRAFT: Airplanes, Fixed Or Rotary Wing

	CITY	ST	EMP	PHONE	ENTRY#
Schweizer Aircraft Corp	Stratford	CT	B	203 386-4356	3570
Raytheon Sutheast Asia Systems (DH)	Waltham	MA	E	978 470-5000	12762
John E Boeing Company Inc	Nashua	NH	F	603 897-8000	15118

AIRCRAFT: Motorized

PRODUCT

	CITY	ST	EMP	PHONE	ENTRY#
American Robotics Inc	Marlborough	MA	E	617 862-2101	10108
Echelon Industries Corporation	Westfield	MA	E	413 562-6659	13163
Ondas Holdings Inc	Marlborough	MA	E	617 862-2101	10191

AIRCRAFT: Research & Development, Manufacturer

	CITY	ST	EMP	PHONE	ENTRY#
Straton Industries Inc	Stratford	CT	D	203 375-4488	3578
Greensight Inc	Charlestown	MA	E	617 633-4919	7875
Spike Aerospace Inc	Boston	MA	F	617 338-1400	7052
Thermo Fisher Scientific Inc	Franklin	MA	C	713 272-0404	8869

AIRFRAME ASSEMBLIES: Guided Missiles

	CITY	ST	EMP	PHONE	ENTRY#
Entwistle Company LLC (PA)	Hudson	MA	D	508 481-4000	9364
Raytheon International Inc (PA)	Waltham	MA	F	781 522-3000	12760
Wgi Inc	Southwick	MA	C	413 569-9444	12051

AIRLINE TRAINING

	CITY	ST	EMP	PHONE	ENTRY#
Syberworks Inc	Arlington	MA	E	781 891-1999	5948

ALARMS: Burglar

	CITY	ST	EMP	PHONE	ENTRY#
Carrier Fire SEC Americas Corp	Farmington	CT	E	941 739-4200	1211
Alarmsafe Inc	Chelmsford	MA	E	978 658-6717	7903
Keltron Corporation (HQ)	Waltham	MA	E	781 894-8710	12707
Shufro Security Company Inc	Newton	MA	G	617 244-3355	10784

ALARMS: Fire

	CITY	ST	EMP	PHONE	ENTRY#
Allstate Fire Systems LLC	Middletown	CT	E	860 246-7711	1734
King Fisher Co Inc	Lowell	MA	E	978 596-0214	9890
Space Age Electronics Inc (PA)	Sterling	MA	E	800 486-1723	12171
Space Age Electronics Inc	Templeton	MA	E	978 652-5421	12382

ALCOHOL, GRAIN: For Beverage Purposes

	CITY	ST	EMP	PHONE	ENTRY#
Mr Boston Brands LLC (HQ)	Lewiston	ME	F	207 783-1433	4978

ALCOHOL: Ethyl & Ethanol

	CITY	ST	EMP	PHONE	ENTRY#
Joule Unlimited Technologies Inc	Foxboro	MA	D	781 533-9100	8703

ALKALIES & CHLORINE

	CITY	ST	EMP	PHONE	ENTRY#
International Dioxide Inc	North Kingstown	RI	E	401 295-8800	16260

ALLOYS: Additive, Exc Copper Or Made In Blast Furnaces

	CITY	ST	EMP	PHONE	ENTRY#
Alent USA Holding Inc	Waterbury	CT	E	203 575-5727	3880
Desktop Metal Inc (PA)	Burlington	MA	C	978 224-1244	7361

ALTERNATORS & GENERATORS: Battery Charging

	CITY	ST	EMP	PHONE	ENTRY#
Liquidsky Technologies Inc	Chestnut Hill	MA	F	857 389-9893	8000

ALTERNATORS: Automotive

	CITY	ST	EMP	PHONE	ENTRY#
Gauss Corporation	Scarborough	ME	F	207 883-4121	5432

ALUMINUM

	CITY	ST	EMP	PHONE	ENTRY#
Angelos Aluminum	East Haven	CT	G	203 469-3117	1035
Howmet Aerospace Inc	Winsted	CT	E	860 379-3314	4347
Wilson Partitions Inc	Stamford	CT	F	203 316-8033	3495
Gear/Tronics Inc	North Billerica	MA	E	781 933-1400	10914
Wakefield Engineering	Fall River	MA	G	603 417-8310	8624
Bill Lztte Archtctral GL Alum	Riverside	RI	E	401 383-9535	16652

ALUMINUM PRDTS

	CITY	ST	EMP	PHONE	ENTRY#
Narragansett Screw Co	Winsted	CT	F	860 379-4059	4351
Porcelen Limited Connecticut LLC (PA)	Hamden	CT	D	203 248-6346	1449
Porcelen Ltd Connecticut LLC	Hamden	CT	E	203 248-6346	1450
Republic Foil Inc	Danbury	CT	D	203 743-2731	805
The Petit Tool Co	Thomaston	CT	E	860 283-9626	3636
Unique Extrusions Incorporated	Cromwell	CT	E	860 632-1314	698
Atrenne Cmpt Solutions LLC	Brockton	MA	E	508 588-6110	7258
Atrenne Cmpt Solutions LLC (DH)	Brockton	MA	B	508 588-6110	7259
Erd Metal Inc	Westfield	MA	F	508 232-3684	13165
Maki Building Centers Inc (HQ)	Gardner	MA	E	978 343-7422	8894
Silver City Aluminum Corp	Taunton	MA	E	508 824-8631	12367
Hall Inc	Bristol	RI	D	401 253-4858	15768

ALUMINUM: Pigs

	CITY	ST	EMP	PHONE	ENTRY#
All Steel LLC	Ellington	CT	G	860 871-6023	1099

ALUMINUM: Rolling & Drawing

	CITY	ST	EMP	PHONE	ENTRY#
Acme Monaco Corporation (PA)	New Britain	CT	C	860 224-1349	1995
Alpha-Core Inc	Shelton	CT	E	203 954-0050	2980
Erickson Metals Corporation (PA)	Cheshire	CT	G	203 272-2918	591
Republic Foil Inc	Danbury	CT	D	203 743-2731	805
IBC Corporation	South Easton	MA	E	508 238-7941	11944
Joseph Freedman Co Inc	Springfield	MA	E	413 781-4444	12107
Replica Works Inc	Orange	MA	E	978 544-7000	11231

AMBULANCE SVCS

	CITY	ST	EMP	PHONE	ENTRY#
Sugarloaf Ambulance and Rescue 4680	Carrabassett Valley	ME	F	207 235-2222	

AMMONIUM NITRATE OR AMMONIUM SULFATE

	CITY	ST	EMP	PHONE	ENTRY#
Gac Chemical Corporation (PA)	Searsport	ME	D	207 548-2525	5453

AMMUNITION: Cartridges Case, 30 mm & Below

	CITY	ST	EMP	PHONE	ENTRY#
Green Mtn Rifle Barrel Co Inc	Conway	NH	F	603 447-1095	14180

AMMUNITION: Components

	CITY	ST	EMP	PHONE	ENTRY#
Geneve Corporation (HQ)	Stamford	CT	E	203 358-8000	3355
Textron Systems Corporation (DH)	Wilmington	MA	E	978 657-5111	13466

AMMUNITION: Small Arms

	CITY	ST	EMP	PHONE	ENTRY#
General Dynamics Ordnance	Avon	CT	F	860 404-0162	25
Illinois Tool Works Inc	Waterbury	CT	C	203 574-2119	3920
Smith & Wesson Brands Inc (PA)	Springfield	MA	A	800 331-0852	12129
Starmet Corporation (PA)	Concord	MA	E	978 369-5410	8134
Bzgunz LLC	Gilmanton	NH	G	603 491-8019	14339
Green Mountain Risk MGT LLC	Dover	NH	G	802 683-8586	14229

AMPLIFIERS

	CITY	ST	EMP	PHONE	ENTRY#
Ki Inc	Orange	CT	D	203 641-5492	2672
Krell Industries LLC	Orange	CT	E	203 298-4000	2673
Bowers and Wilkins Group	North Reading	MA	E	978 357-0428	11038
Fishman Transducers Inc	Andover	MA	D	978 988-9199	5883

AMPLIFIERS: Parametric

	CITY	ST	EMP	PHONE	ENTRY#
Copley Controls Corporation (DH)	Canton	MA	B	781 828-8090	7779

AMPLIFIERS: RF & IF Power

	CITY	ST	EMP	PHONE	ENTRY#
Axiom Microdevices Inc	Woburn	MA	E	781 376-3000	13518

AMUSEMENT & RECREATION SVCS: Amusement Mach Rental, Coin-Op

	CITY	ST	EMP	PHONE	ENTRY#
Happy House Amusement Inc	Goffstown	NH	F	603 497-4151	14348

AMUSEMENT & RECREATION SVCS: Art Gallery, Commercial

	CITY	ST	EMP	PHONE	ENTRY#
Rich Associates Incorporated	Kennebunk	ME	G	207 985-5999	4929

AMUSEMENT & RECREATION SVCS: Golf Club, Membership

	CITY	ST	EMP	PHONE	ENTRY#
South Windsor Golf Course LLC	South Windsor	CT	D	860 648-4653	3182

AMUSEMENT & RECREATION SVCS: Recreation Center

	CITY	ST	EMP	PHONE	ENTRY#
Lyman Farm Incorporated (PA)	Middlefield	CT	C	860 349-1793	1725
Axe Play LLC	Hudson	NH	G	603 809-9081	14485

AMUSEMENT MACHINES: Coin Operated

	CITY	ST	EMP	PHONE	ENTRY#
Axard LLC	Grantham	NH	F	603 306-7679	14362
Happy House Amusement Inc	Goffstown	NH	F	603 497-4151	14348

AMUSEMENT PARK DEVICES & RIDES

	CITY	ST	EMP	PHONE	ENTRY#
EA Patten Co LLC	Manchester	CT	D	860 649-2851	1594
Microbest Inc	Waterbury	CT	C	203 597-0355	3944
Skytrans Mfg LLC	Contoocook	NH	F	802 230-7783	14175
Tilton - Nrthfeld Rcrtion Cnci	Northfield	NH	G	603 286-8653	15270

ANALYZERS: Moisture

	CITY	ST	EMP	PHONE	ENTRY#
Roscid Technologies Inc	Woburn	MA	G	781 933-4007	13656
Vacuum Technology Inc	Gloucester	MA	G	510 333-6562	8962

ANALYZERS: Network

	CITY	ST	EMP	PHONE	ENTRY#
Exinda Inc	Boston	MA	G	617 973-6477	6724

ANALYZERS: Respiratory

	CITY	ST	EMP	PHONE	ENTRY#
Acute Care Gases of Ct LLC	Wolcott	CT	F	855 399-1224	4360
Covidien LP (HQ)	Mansfield	MA	C	763 514-4000	10046
Third Pole Inc (PA)	Waltham	MA	F	908 310-0596	12803

ANESTHESIA EQPT

	CITY	ST	EMP	PHONE	ENTRY#
Draeger Medical Systems Inc	Andover	MA	B	800 437-2437	5880
Hallowell Engrg & Mfg Corp	Pittsfield	MA	G	413 445-4263	11400
Vascular Technology Inc	Nashua	NH	E	603 594-9700	15182

ANIMAL BASED MEDICINAL CHEMICAL PRDTS

	CITY	ST	EMP	PHONE	ENTRY#
Ticked Off Inc	Dover	NH	G	603 742-0925	14253

ANIMAL FEED & SUPPLEMENTS: Livestock & Poultry

	CITY	ST	EMP	PHONE	ENTRY#
H J Baker & Brother Inc	Shelton	CT	F	501 664-4870	3011
Channel Fish Co Inc	Boston	MA	D	617 569-3200	6648

	CITY	ST	EMP	PHONE	ENTRY#
Designing Health Inc	East Longmeadow MA		F	661 257-1705	8373
Atlantic Laboratories Inc	Waldoboro	ME	G	207 832-5376	5574
Trividia Mfg Solutions Inc **(DH)**	Lancaster	NH	C	603 788-2848	14680
Cargill Incorporated	Swanton	VT	G	802 868-3232	17636
Feed Commodities Intl Inc **(HQ)**	Middlebury	VT	E	800 639-3191	17343
Poulin Grain Inc	Swanton	VT	E	802 868-3323	17640
Poulin Grain Inc **(PA)**	Newport	VT	D	802 334-6731	17404

ANIMAL FEED: Wholesalers

Cargill Incorporated	Swanton	VT	G	802 868-3232	17636

ANIMAL FOOD & SUPPLEMENTS: Dog

Bravo LLC	Vernon	CT	F	860 896-1899	3752
Joy Food Company	Darien	CT	G	917 549-6240	850
2 Dogs Treats LLC	Dorchester	MA	G	617 286-4844	8295
Preppy Puppy Inc	West Wareham	MA	E	508 291-7555	13070

ANIMAL FOOD & SUPPLEMENTS: Dog & Cat

Blue Buffalo Company Ltd **(DH)**	Wilton	CT	D	203 762-9751	4233
Canidae LLC	Stamford	CT	D	475 208-1789	3301
Channel Fish Co Inc	Boston	MA	D	617 569-3200	6648
Polka Dog Designs LLC **(PA)**	Boston	MA	G	617 338-5155	6968
Polka Dog Designs LLC	Boston	MA	F	617 307-6733	6969
Wellness Pet LLC **(PA)**	Burlington	MA	D	877 869-2971	7448
Wholistic Pet Organics LLC	Bedford	NH	G	603 472-8300	13954
Pet Food Experts Inc **(PA)**	Pawtucket	RI	C	401 721-5593	16401

ANIMAL FOOD & SUPPLEMENTS: Feed Supplements

Bactana Corp	Farmington	CT	G	203 716-1230	1208
HJ Baker & Bro LLC **(PA)**	Shelton	CT	E	203 682-9200	3014
Source Inc **(PA)**	North Branford	CT	G	203 488-6400	2375
Smartpak Equine LLC **(DH)**	Plymouth	MA	D	774 773-1100	11478
Wholistic Pet Organics LLC	Bedford	NH	G	603 472-8300	13954

ANIMAL FOOD & SUPPLEMENTS: Livestock

Kent Nutrition Group Inc	Litchfield	CT	G	860 482-7116	1558
Kent Nutrition Group Inc	Bow	NH	G	603 225-6661	14004
Kent Nutrition Group Inc	Richford	VT	F	802 848-7718	17475
Phoenix Feeds Organix LLC	New Haven	VT	E	802 453-6684	17395
Poulin Grain Inc	North Bennington	VT	E	802 681-1605	17411

ANIMAL FOOD & SUPPLEMENTS: Pet, Exc Dog & Cat, Canned

Blue Buffalo Pet Products Inc **(HQ)**	Wilton	CT	E	203 762-9751	4234

ANIMAL FOOD & SUPPLEMENTS: Poultry

H J Baker & Bro Inc	Westport	CT	B	203 682-9200	4171
HJ Baker International Inc	Shelton	CT	F	203 682-9200	3015
Moark LLC **(HQ)**	North Franklin	CT	E	951 332-3300	2383

ANODIZING EQPT

Reliable	Winchendon	MA	G	978 230-2689	13481

ANODIZING SVC

Anomet Products Inc	Shrewsbury	MA	E	508 842-0174	11827
Central Metal Finishing Inc	North Andover	MA	D	978 291-0500	10823
CIL Inc	Lawrence	MA	D	978 685-8300	9550
Poly-Metal Finishing Inc	Springfield	MA	D	413 781-4535	12122
Qc Industries Inc **(PA)**	Mansfield	MA	D	781 344-1000	10073

ANTENNAS: Radar Or Communications

Cobham Defense Electronic Systems Corporation	Lowell	MA			A
978 779-7000	9869				
CPI Radant Tech Div Inc **(DH)**	Stow	MA	D	978 562-3866	12245
Hxi LLC	Harvard	MA	F	978 772-7774	9064

ANTENNAS: Receiving

Cbm Industries Inc	Taunton	MA	E	508 821-4555	12326

ANTIBIOTICS

Microbiotix Inc	Worcester	MA	E	508 757-2800	13759
Tetraphase Pharmaceuticals Inc	Waltham	MA	D	617 715-3600	12795
Biodesign International	Saco	ME	E	207 283-6500	5363

ANTIFREEZE

Camco Manufacturing Inc	Leominster	MA	D	978 537-6777	9646
Cristy Corporation	Fitchburg	MA	F	978 343-4330	8650

ANTISEPTICS, MEDICINAL

Aplicare Products LLC **(HQ)**	Meriden	CT	D	203 630-0500	1655

APPAREL ACCESS STORES

Bondi Band LLC	Simsbury	CT	F	207 576-4191	3084

APPAREL DESIGNERS: Commercial

	CITY	ST	EMP	PHONE	ENTRY#
Sara Campbell Ltd **(PA)**	Boston	MA	G	617 423-3134	7025
Blue Dolphin Screenprint Inc	Somersworth	NH	E	603 692-2500	15611

APPAREL FILLING MATERIALS: Cotton Waste, Kapok/Related Matl

Cornell Online LLC	Burlington	VT	E	802 448-3281	17128

APPLIANCES, HOUSEHOLD: Kitchen, Major, Exc Refrigs & Stoves

Clarke Distribution Corp	Norwalk	CT	G	203 838-9385	2482
Conair LLC **(HQ)**	Stamford	CT	B	203 351-9000	3320
Euro-Pro Holdco LLC	Needham Heights	MA	G	617 243-0235	10543
Sharkninja Inc	Needham	MA	A	617 243-0235	10520
Sharkninja Operating LLC **(PA)**	Needham	MA	E	617 243-0235	10521
Vaughn Thermal Corporation	Salisbury	MA	E	978 462-6683	11745
Vermont Culinary Islands LLC	Brattleboro	VT	F	802 387-8591	17103

APPLIANCES, HOUSEHOLD: Refrigs, Mechanical & Absorption

Raytheon Sutheast Asia Systems **(DH)**	Waltham	MA	E	978 470-5000	12762

APPLIANCES, HOUSEHOLD: Sewing Machines & Attchmnts, Domestic

W S Bessett Inc	Sanford	ME	E	207 324-9232	5417

APPLIANCES: Household, Refrigerators & Freezers

Coldsnap Corp	Billerica	MA	E	617 733-9935	6426
General Electric Company **(PA)**	Boston	MA	A	617 443-3000	6754

APPLIANCES: Major, Cooking

Conair LLC **(HQ)**	Stamford	CT	B	203 351-9000	3320
General Electric Company **(PA)**	Boston	MA	A	617 443-3000	6754
Ray Murray Inc **(PA)**	Lee	MA	D	413 243-2164	9619
Cooking Solutions Group Inc **(HQ)**	Salem	NH	F	603 893-9701	15516
Cooking Solutions Group Inc	Essex Junction	VT	C	864 963-3471	17231
GS Blodgett LLC **(HQ)**	Essex Junction	VT	C	802 860-3700	17236

APPLIANCES: Small, Electric

Conair LLC **(HQ)**	Stamford	CT	B	203 351-9000	3320
Conair LLC	Stamford	CT	F	203 348-6684	3321
Conair LLC	Torrington	CT	D	800 492-7464	3676
Jarden LLC	Norwalk	CT	E	203 845-5300	2519
McIntire Company **(HQ)**	Bristol	CT	F	860 585-8559	465
Convectronics Inc	Haverhill	MA	E	978 374-7714	9088
Gillette Company **(HQ)**	Boston	MA	A	617 463-3000	6758
Kaz Usa Inc	Marlborough	MA	D	508 490-7000	10175
Thl-Nortek Investors LLC **(PA)**	Boston	MA	D	617 227-1050	7077

APPLICATIONS SOFTWARE PROGRAMMING

Powerphone Inc	Madison	CT	E	203 245-8911	1566
Belle Artfl Intelligence Corp	Cambridge	MA	F	650 291-9410	7504
Bvsn LLC	Waltham	MA	F	781 290-0710	12616
Connected Auto Systems Neng In	South Easton	MA	E	508 238-5855	11940
Datarobot Inc **(PA)**	Boston	MA	D	617 765-4500	6684
Svh Software Inc	Chelmsford	MA	G	978 566-1812	7961
VMS Software Inc	Boston	MA	D	425 766-1692	7110
Xiphos Partners Inc	Dartmouth	MA	G	508 991-1014	8233
Mmis Inc	Portsmouth	NH	D	603 929-5078	15424

APPRAISAL SVCS, EXC REAL ESTATE

Silva Jewelers of Osterville	Osterville	MA	E	508 428-2872	11246
Bellman Jewelers Inc	Manchester	NH	G	603 625-4653	14819
Nazarian Jewelers NH Inc **(PA)**	Salem	NH	F	603 893-1600	15548

AQUARIUMS & ACCESS: Plastic

Governor Supply Co	Lancaster	MA	G	978 870-6888	9526

ARCHERY & SHOOTING RANGES

Sig Sauer Inc **(DH)**	Newington	NH	C	603 610-3000	15210

ARCHITECTURAL SVCS

Coreslab Structures Conn Inc	Thomaston	CT	D	860 283-8281	3617
Architctral Fireplaces of Neng	Auburn	MA	F	508 757-0622	6104
Boston Sign Company Inc	Boston	MA	G	617 338-2114	6618
Faverco Inc	Boston	MA	G	617 247-1440	6732
Moca Systems Inc **(PA)**	Boston	MA	E	617 581-6622	6893
South Mountain Company Inc	West Tisbury	MA	E	508 693-4850	13055
Zlink Inc	Maynard	MA	D	978 309-3628	10268
Barrett Made **(PA)**	Portland	ME	E	207 650-6500	5184
Northern Design Precast Inc	Loudon	NH	E	603 783-8989	14796
Universal Envmtl Tech Inc	Nashua	NH	G	603 883-9312	15180
Herrick & White Ltd	Cumberland	RI	D	401 658-0440	15942
William H Moore Inc	Waitsfield	VT	G	802 496-3595	17668

PRODUCT

	CITY	ST	EMP	PHONE	ENTRY#

ARMATURE REPAIRING & REWINDING SVC

	CITY	ST	EMP	PHONE	ENTRY#
Ward Leonard Operating LLC (DH)	Thomaston	CT	E	860 283-5801	3643
Ward Lonard Houma Holdings LLC	Thomaston	CT	D	860 283-5801	3644
Applied Dynamics Corporation (PA)	Greenfield	MA	E	413 774-7268	8981
Maxon Precision Motors Inc (HQ)	Taunton	MA	E	508 677-0520	12348

ART DEALERS & GALLERIES

Greenwich Workshop Inc (PA)	Seymour	CT	E	203 881-3336	2961
Arnold Art Inc (PA)	Newport	RI	F	401 847-2273	16203
Applejack Art Partners Inc	Manchester Center	VT	E	802 362-3662	17326

ART GOODS & SPLYS WHOLESALERS

National Reprographics Inc	Boston	MA	F	857 383-3700	6904
W Oliver Tripp Company (PA)	Weymouth	MA	E	781 848-1230	13338

ART GOODS, WHOLESALE

Greenwich Workshop Inc (PA)	Seymour	CT	E	203 881-3336	2961
S & S Worldwide Inc	Colchester	CT	B	860 537-3451	665

ART SPLY STORES

Chartpak (HQ)	Leeds	MA	D	413 584-5446	9621
Zephyr Designs Ltd	Brattleboro	VT	G	802 254-2788	17110

ARTIST'S MATERIALS & SPLYS

Color Craft Ltd	East Granby	CT	F	800 509-6563	929
Canson Inc	South Hadley	MA	F	413 538-9250	11959

ARTISTS' MATERIALS, WHOLESALE

Color Craft Ltd	East Granby	CT	F	800 509-6563	929

ARTISTS' MATERIALS: Frames, Artists' Canvases

Wood & Wood Inc	Waitsfield	VT	G	802 496-3000	17669

ARTISTS' MATERIALS: Ink, Drawing, Black & Colored

Chartpak Inc (HQ)	Leeds	MA	D	413 584-5446	9621

ARTWORK: Framed

Picture This Hartford Inc	East Hartford	CT	G	860 528-1409	1011

ASBESTOS PRDTS: Insulation, Molded

Bascom Environmental Co	Plymouth	MA	E	617 282-9500	11449

ASBESTOS REMOVAL EQPT

Tryxus Investment & Trdg Inc	Weston	MA	F	800 981-6616	13291

ASPHALT & ASPHALT PRDTS

Wescon Corp of Conn	Pawcatuck	CT	G	860 599-2500	2728
Westchester Industries Inc	Greenwich	CT	F	203 661-0055	1360
Alton E Gleason Company Inc (PA)	Springfield	MA	F	413 732-8207	12073
Bond Construction Corporation	Spencer	MA	F	508 885-2480	12055
Granger Lynch Corp	Millbury	MA	C	508 756-6244	10435
Heffron Asphalt Corp (PA)	North Reading	MA	F	781 935-1455	11040
JH Lynch & Sons Inc	Millbury	MA	E	508 756-6244	10438
Jsl Asphalt Inc (PA)	Westfield	MA	F	413 568-8986	13177
Lorusso Corp (PA)	Plainville	MA	E	508 668-6520	11437
Norfolk Asphalt Paving Inc	Canton	MA	F	617 293-9775	7813
Rose Office Carl	East Sandwich	MA	G	508 833-8758	8405
T L Edwards Inc	Plymouth	MA	F	508 732-9148	11480
Ted Ondrick Company LLC (PA)	Chicopee	MA	F	413 592-2565	8062
Eurovia Atlantic Coast LLC	Hermon	ME	E	703 230-0850	4881
Blaktop Inc (PA)	West Lebanon	NH	E	603 298-8885	15678
Pike Industries Inc (DH)	Belmont	NH	E	603 527-5100	13967
JH Lynch & Sons Inc (PA)	Cumberland	RI	E	401 333-4300	15948

ASPHALT COATINGS & SEALERS

Firestone Building Pdts Co LLC	Bristol	CT	F	860 584-4516	447
Owens Corning Sales LLC	East Hartford	CT	C	304 353-6945	1008
Omg Inc (DH)	Agawam	MA	B	413 789-0252	5803
Patriot Seal Coating	Worcester	MA	G	774 386-8531	13768
Thomas J Cronin	Medfield	MA	G	508 510-2328	10277
Ta Property Maintenance LLC	Scarborough	ME	F	207 289-7158	5444
Andrade Sealcoating LLC	Gilmanton Iron Works	NH	F	603 435-3704	14340
Cameron Sealcoating LLC	Jefferson	NH	F	603 586-7945	14583
Cherubino Sealcoating LMC LLC	Salem	NH	G	781 272-1020	15514
Lsr Sealcoating	Concord	NH	G	603 715-4934	14141
Newmont Slate Co Inc (PA)	West Pawlet	VT	E	802 645-0203	17692
Quarry Slate Industries Inc	Poultney	VT	E	802 287-9701	17449
Vermont Structural Slate Co (PA)	Fair Haven	VT	E	802 265-4933	17252

ASPHALT MINING & BITUMINOUS STONE QUARRYING SVCS

Galasso Materials LLC	East Granby	CT	C	860 527-1825	934
Brox Industries Inc (PA)	Dracut	MA	D	978 454-9105	8302

ASPHALT MIXTURES WHOLESALERS

Suzio York Hill Companies	Meriden	CT	F	888 789-4626	1703

ASPHALT PLANTS INCLUDING GRAVEL MIX TYPE

County Concrete & Cnstr Co	Columbia Falls	ME	E	207 483-4409	4698
Hudson Terminal Corp	Cranston	RI	G	401 941-0500	15875
Hudson Terminal Corp (PA)	Providence	RI	F	401 274-2200	16535

ASSEMBLING & PACKAGING SVCS: Cosmetic Kits

Skin & Co North America LLC	West Haven	CT	G	888 444-9971	4126
Evergreen Manufacturing Group LLC	Madawaska	ME	E	207 728-4900	5037

ASSOCIATIONS: Business

Chief Executive Group LLC (PA)	Stamford	CT	E	785 832-0303	3310

ASSOCIATIONS: Engineering

Society Plastics Engineers Inc (PA)	Danbury	CT	E	203 740-5422	819

ASSOCIATIONS: Real Estate Management

Louis Dreyfus Holdg Co US LLC (HQ)	Wilton	CT	B	203 761-2000	4242

ASSOCIATIONS: Scientists'

American Mteorological Soc Inc (PA)	Boston	MA	D	617 227-2425	6541
Archaeological Institute Amer	Boston	MA	F	617 353-9361	6555
American Mathematical Society Inc (PA)	Providence	RI	C	401 455-4000	16470

ASSOCIATIONS: Trade

Limra International Inc (PA)	Windsor	CT	E	860 688-3358	4287
National Shting Spt Fndtion In	Shelton	CT	D	203 426-1320	3036
Tree Care Industry Assn Inc	Manchester	NH	E	603 314-5380	14946
Rhode Island Assn Realtors Inc (PA)	Warwick	RI	G	401 785-3650	16849

ATOMIZERS

Boom LLC	New Canaan	CT	E	212 317-2005	2076
Marmon Engnered Wire Cable LLC	Hartford	CT	F	860 653-8300	1491
O & G Industries Inc	Beacon Falls	CT	E	203 881-5192	44
O & G Industries Inc	Harwinton	CT	E	860 485-6600	1522
Solidification Pdts Intl Inc	Northford	CT	G	203 484-9494	2456
Altium Packaging LP	Marlborough	MA	E	508 485-2109	10107
Lighthouse Distributors Inc	Marshfield	MA	G	781 319-9828	10241
Pieceworks Inc	Montville	ME	G	207 589-3451	5075
Valid Mfg Inc	Londonderry	NH	F	603 880-0948	14789
Cas America LLC	North Smithfield	RI	F	401 884-8556	16320

ATTENUATORS

Anaren Ceramics Inc	Salem	NH	D	603 898-2883	15505
IDS Highway Safety Inc	Cumberland	RI	D	401 425-2205	15945

AUCTIONEERS: Fee Basis

F O Bailey Co Inc	Falmouth	ME	G	207 781-8001	4768

AUDIO & VIDEO EQPT, EXC COMMERCIAL

Harman Bcker Auto Systems Mfg	Stamford	CT	G	203 328-3501	3362
Insight Plus Technology LLC	Bristol	CT	G	860 930-4763	457
Microphase Corporation	Shelton	CT	E	203 866-8000	3032
PMC Technologies LLC	Weston	CT	G	203 222-0000	4151
Whelen Engineering Company Inc (PA)	Chester	CT	B	860 526-9504	634
Artel Video Systems Corp	Westford	MA	E	978 263-5775	13224
Bose Corporation	Framingham	MA	E	508 879-7330	8747
Brown Innovations Inc (PA)	Boston	MA	G	773 477-7500	6625
Cco Holdings LLC	Harvard	MA	E	978 615-1032	9060
Cco Holdings LLC	Longmeadow	MA	E	413 754-0616	9849
Cco Holdings LLC	North Grafton	MA	C	774 293-4026	11020
Cco Holdings LLC	Upton	MA	C	774 462-6577	12470
Courtsmart Digital Systems Inc	North Chelmsford	MA	E	978 251-3300	10973
Metalpro USA Inc	Plymouth	MA	G	508 942-9746	11465
Mini-Systems Inc (PA)	North Attleboro	MA	D	508 695-1420	10878
Outlaw Audio LLC	Norton	MA	F	508 286-4110	11131
Philips	North Andover	MA	F	978 258-7110	10848
Runco Capital Corporation	Newburyport	MA	E	978 462-0320	10716
Thomson Video Networks Americas LLC	Southwick	MA	E	413 998-1200	12046
Venmill Industries Inc	Oxford	MA	E	508 363-0410	11267
Viking Industrial Products	Marlborough	MA	E	508 481-4600	10231
Volicon Inc	Burlington	MA	E	781 221-7400	7447
Cc1 Inc	Portsmouth	NH	E	603 319-2000	15368
Tradeport USA LLC	Dover	NH	F	603 692-2900	14254
Vx1 Corporation	Dover	NH	E	603 742-2888	14258
Constant Technologies Inc	North Kingstown	RI	E	800 518-7369	16240
Cco Holdings LLC	Montpelier	VT	C	802 778-0497	17371

	CITY	ST	EMP	PHONE	ENTRY#
Westinghouse Electric Co LLC	Brattleboro	VT	E	802 254-9353	17108

AUDIO COMPONENTS

	CITY	ST	EMP	PHONE	ENTRY#
Harman International Inds Inc	Stamford	CT	E	203 328-3500	3364
Harman International Inds Inc (HQ)	Stamford	CT	A	203 328-3500	3365
Harman KG Holding LLC (DH)	Stamford	CT	D	203 328-3500	3366
Redco Audio Inc	Monroe	CT	F	203 502-7600	1920
Bose Corporation (PA)	Framingham	MA	A	508 879-7330	8745
Bose Corporation	Framingham	MA	E	508 766-1265	8746
Bose Corporation	Stow	MA	E	508 766-7330	12244
Ion Audio LLC (HQ)	Cumberland	RI	F	401 658-3743	15947

AUDIO ELECTRONIC SYSTEMS

	CITY	ST	EMP	PHONE	ENTRY#
D&C Global Enterprise LLC	Bridgeport	CT	G	810 553-2360	313
Harman Consumer Inc	Stamford	CT	E	203 328-3500	3363
Visionpoint LLC	Newington	CT	E	860 436-9673	2333
Access Advance LLC	Boston	MA	E	617 367-4802	6510
Andover Audio LLC	North Andover	MA	F	978 775-3670	10818
Cambridge Soundworks Inc	Westwood	MA	E	781 329-2777	13307
Fargo Ta LLC	Boston	MA	E	617 345-0066	6731
Rf Venue Inc	Walpole	MA	G	800 795-0817	12573
Savant Systems Inc (PA)	Hyannis	MA	E	508 683-2500	9449
Yamaha Unified Cmmnications Inc	Sudbury	MA	E	978 610-4040	12272
Transparent Audio LLC	Saco	ME	E	207 284-1100	5380
Cambridge Signal Tech Inc	Providence	RI	F	401 490-5682	16493

AUDIO-VISUAL PROGRAM PRODUCTION SVCS

	CITY	ST	EMP	PHONE	ENTRY#
Play-It Productions Inc	Colchester	CT	F	212 695-6530	663

AUDIOLOGICAL EQPT: Electronic

	CITY	ST	EMP	PHONE	ENTRY#
Textspeak Corporation	Westport	CT	F	203 803-1069	4199
Imactis Inc	Cambridge	MA	G	617 576-2005	7611
Medrhythms Inc	Portland	ME	E	207 447-2177	5244

AUTO & HOME SUPPLY STORES: Auto & Truck Eqpt & Parts

	CITY	ST	EMP	PHONE	ENTRY#
Lynn Ladder Scaffolding Co Inc (HQ)	Lynn	MA	D	781 598-6010	9985
Coastal Metal Fab	Topsham	ME	E	207 729-5101	5547

AUTO & HOME SUPPLY STORES: Automotive Access

	CITY	ST	EMP	PHONE	ENTRY#
Yankee Custom Inc (PA)	Tewksbury	MA	F	978 851-9024	12426

AUTO & HOME SUPPLY STORES: Automotive parts

	CITY	ST	EMP	PHONE	ENTRY#
Genuine Parts Company	Windsor Locks	CT	G	860 623-4479	4325
Atlantic Auto & Trck Parts LLC	Rowley	MA	G	978 535-6777	11667
Consolidated Truck & Eqp Inc	Seekonk	MA	G	508 252-3330	11775
Lawton Truck Equipment Inc	Topsfield	MA	F	978 887-0005	12436
Tebaldi Enterprises Inc	Holyoke	MA	F	413 532-3261	9283
Reed Truck Services Inc	Claremont	NH	F	603 542-5032	14097
Scarborough Faire Inc	Pawtucket	RI	E	401 724-4200	16416

AUTO & HOME SUPPLY STORES: Batteries, Automotive & Truck

	CITY	ST	EMP	PHONE	ENTRY#
Interstate All Battery Center	South Yarmouth	MA	F	508 394-9400	11984

AUTO & HOME SUPPLY STORES: Speed Shops, Incl Race Car Splys

	CITY	ST	EMP	PHONE	ENTRY#
Lance Smith Inc	Milton	VT	D	802 655-3354	17361

AUTO & HOME SUPPLY STORES: Truck Eqpt & Parts

	CITY	ST	EMP	PHONE	ENTRY#
Line-X of Hartford	Hartford	CT	G	860 216-6180	1490
Line-X of New England LLC	New Milford	CT	G	860 355-6997	2252
Stead-Fast Custom Linings LLC	East Haven	CT	F	203 466-8000	1052
Middlesex Truck & Auto Body	Boston	MA	E	617 442-3000	6887
Hanscom Construction Inc	Marshfield	ME	F	207 255-8067	5046
Freedom Tire Inc (PA)	Plaistow	NH	F	603 382-7223	15344

AUTOMATIC REGULATING CONTROL: Building Svcs Monitoring, Auto

	CITY	ST	EMP	PHONE	ENTRY#
Johnson Controls Inc	Meriden	CT	F	678 297-4040	1670
Process Automtn Solutions Inc (HQ)	Danbury	CT	E	203 207-9917	801
Johnson Controls Inc	Wrentham	MA	E	508 384-0018	13843
On-Sight Insight	Boston	MA	G	617 502-5985	6931
Parker-Hannifin Corporation	Kittery	ME	D	207 439-9511	4938
Ene Systems of Nh Inc	Bow	NH	G	603 856-0330	13996
Avtech Software Inc (PA)	Warren	RI	F	401 628-1600	16752
Energy MGT & Ctrl Svcs Inc	Cranston	RI	F	401 946-1440	15856

AUTOMATIC REGULATING CONTROLS: AC & Refrigeration

	CITY	ST	EMP	PHONE	ENTRY#
Hurricane Farm LLC	West Swanzey	NH	E	603 352-0053	15695
RMA Manufacturing LLC	West Swanzey	NH	E	603 352-0053	15697

AUTOMATIC REGULATING CONTROLS: Hydronic Pressure Or Temp

	CITY	ST	EMP	PHONE	ENTRY#
J & B Service Company LLC	Bethel	CT	G	203 743-9357	122

AUTOMATIC REGULATING CONTROLS: Incinerator, Residential/Comm

	CITY	ST	EMP	PHONE	ENTRY#
Sud-Chemie Protech Inc	Needham Heights	MA	B	781 444-5188	10559

AUTOMATIC REGULATING CONTROLS: Refrig/Air-Cond Defrost

	CITY	ST	EMP	PHONE	ENTRY#
Belimo Aircontrols (usa) Inc (HQ)	Danbury	CT	C	800 543-9038	715
Belimo Automation AG	Danbury	CT	E	203 749-3319	716

AUTOMATIC REGULATING CONTROLS: Refrigeration, Pressure

	CITY	ST	EMP	PHONE	ENTRY#
Mv3 LLC	Buzzards Bay	MA	G	617 658-4420	7455
Amtrol Holdings Inc	West Warwick	RI	A	401 884-6300	16899

AUTOMATIC REGULATING CTRLS: Damper, Pneumatic Or Electric

	CITY	ST	EMP	PHONE	ENTRY#
Senior Operations LLC	Lewiston	ME	E	207 784-2338	4992
Wahlcometroflex Inc	Lewiston	ME	B	207 784-2338	4995

AUTOMATIC REGULATING CTRLS: Elec Heat Proportion, Modultg

	CITY	ST	EMP	PHONE	ENTRY#
Lee Electric Inc	Danvers	MA	C	978 777-0070	8198
Sigma Systems Corp	Mansfield	MA	E	781 688-2354	10076

AUTOMATIC TELLER MACHINES

	CITY	ST	EMP	PHONE	ENTRY#
Marinero Express 809 East	Stamford	CT	F	203 487-0636	3408
Danversbank	South Hamilton	MA	G	978 468-2243	11969
Diebold Nixdorf Incorporated	North Dartmouth	MA	D	508 984-5936	10994
Diebold Nixdorf Incorporated	Swansea	MA	D	508 646-4378	12304
Atlantic Precision Services	Gorham	ME	E	207 329-1043	4816
Diebold Nixdorf Incorporated	Hudson	NH	G	603 577-9519	14493
Diebold Nixdorf Incorporated	Warwick	RI	G	401 823-8665	16806
Diebold Nixdorf Incorporated	Woonsocket	RI	G	401 766-3606	16956

AUTOMOBILES & OTHER MOTOR VEHICLES WHOLESALERS

	CITY	ST	EMP	PHONE	ENTRY#
New Haven Companies Inc	East Haven	CT	F	203 469-6421	1048
Tel Mnfacturing Engrg Amer Inc	Billerica	MA	E	978 436-2300	6487

AUTOMOTIVE & TRUCK GENERAL REPAIR SVC

	CITY	ST	EMP	PHONE	ENTRY#
Bridgestone Ret Operations LLC	West Haven	CT	G	203 933-7750	4095
Danbury A LLC	Danbury	CT	E	203 744-5202	724
Tire Country of Enfield Inc	Enfield	CT	E	860 763-0846	1155
Holyoke Tire & Auto Svc Inc	Springfield	MA	G	413 733-2141	12101
Sullivan Tire Co Inc	North Attleboro	MA	E	508 695-9920	10890
Central Tire Co Inc (PA)	Sanford	ME	E	207 324-4250	5391
J O Brown & Son Inc	North Haven	ME	G	207 867-4621	5114
Lees Tire	Topsham	ME	E	207 729-1676	5549
Steven Pelletier	Fort Kent	ME	F	207 834-3191	4794
Weymouths Garage Inc	Milford	ME	F	207 827-2069	5063
Belknap Tire Co Holdings Inc	Laconia	NH	F	603 524-4517	14646
Northeast Tire Service Inc	Belmont	NH	G	603 524-7973	13965
Eagle Motors Inc	Harrisville	RI	F	401 568-2580	16065
Kane Motor Car Co Inc	North Kingstown	RI	F	401 294-4634	16263
Rounds Service Station Inc	North Scituate	RI	F	401 934-9877	16316
Sullivan Tire Co Inc	Warwick	RI	G	401 737-5251	16866

AUTOMOTIVE BODY SHOP

	CITY	ST	EMP	PHONE	ENTRY#
Bodyshop World By Wagner Inc	Worcester	MA	F	508 853-0300	13704
Kane Motor Car Co Inc	North Kingstown	RI	F	401 294-4634	16263
Giroux Body Shop Inc	Hinesburg	VT	F	802 482-2162	17291

AUTOMOTIVE BODY, PAINT & INTERIOR REPAIR & MAINTENANCE SVC

	CITY	ST	EMP	PHONE	ENTRY#
Special Projects Group LLC	Gilford	NH	G	603 391-9700	14338

AUTOMOTIVE GLASS REPLACEMENT SHOPS

	CITY	ST	EMP	PHONE	ENTRY#
Capitol Glass Company Inc	West Hartford	CT	F	860 236-1936	4050

AUTOMOTIVE PAINT SHOP

	CITY	ST	EMP	PHONE	ENTRY#
Marketing Worldwide Corp (PA)	Rockland	ME	G	631 444-8090	5339

AUTOMOTIVE PARTS, ACCESS & SPLYS

	CITY	ST	EMP	PHONE	ENTRY#
Aerospace Techniques Inc	Middletown	CT	D	860 347-1200	1733
Airpot Corporation	Norwalk	CT	E	800 848-7681	2459
Beacon Group Inc (PA)	Newington	CT	E	860 594-5200	2275
Cambridge Specialty Co Inc	Berlin	CT	D	860 828-3579	57
Cheshire Manufacturing Co Inc	Cheshire	CT	G	203 272-3586	580
Competition Engineering Inc	Guilford	CT	E	203 453-5200	1389
Continental Machine TI Co Inc	New Britain	CT	D	860 223-2896	2014
CT Driveshaft Service LLC	East Hartford	CT	G	860 289-6459	984
Danbury A LLC	Danbury	CT	E	203 744-5202	724
Energizer Auto Sales Inc	Danbury	CT	E	203 205-2900	736
Express Lube & Tire LLC	Windsor	CT	G	860 690-3066	4274
Expressway Lube Centers	Danbury	CT	F	203 744-2511	743

PRODUCT

	CITY	ST	EMP	PHONE	ENTRY#
Genuine Parts Company	Windsor Locks	CT	G	860 623-4479	4325
Inertia Dynamics Inc	New Hartford	CT	E	860 379-1252	2103
International Auto Entps Inc	New Britain	CT	F	860 223-7979	2033
International Auto Entps Inc **(PA)**	New Britain	CT	F	860 224-0253	2034
Jobin Machine Inc	West Hartford	CT	E	860 953-1631	4065
Kongsberg Acttion Systems II L **(PA)**	Suffield	CT	D	860 668-1285	3592
Lee Company **(PA)**	Westbrook	CT	A	860 399-6281	4140
Littlejohn Partners IV LP	Greenwich	CT	A	203 552-3500	1338
Lydall Inc **(HQ)**	Manchester	CT	E	860 646-1233	1614
Nickson Industries Inc	Plainville	CT	E	860 747-1671	2774
Nucap US Inc **(DH)**	Wolcott	CT	E	203 879-1423	4371
Park Avenue Securities	Farmington	CT	F	860 677-2600	1240
Platt-Labonia of N Haven Inc	North Haven	CT	D	203 239-5681	2431
Pratt & Whitney Eng Svcs Inc	Middletown	CT	B	860 344-4000	1773
Proliance International Inc	Windsor	CT	G	860 688-7644	4297
Turbine Technologies Inc **(PA)**	Farmington	CT	D	860 678-1642	1257
Unitec	Danbury	CT	C	203 778-0400	830
Vulcan Industries Inc	Windsor	CT	C	860 683-2005	4313
AAm Inc	Weston	MA	F	781 330-9857	13284
Blendco Systems LLC	Holyoke	MA	D	800 537-7797	9244
Boston Steel & Mfg Co	Haverhill	MA	E	781 324-3000	9080
Car Gold Inc	Holyoke	MA	E	800 537-7797	9246
Clearmotion Inc **(PA)**	Billerica	MA	G	617 313-0822	6423
Currex LLC	Newton	MA	F	206 883-0209	10751
Curtis Industries LLC **(PA)**	West Boylston	MA	F	508 853-2200	12958
Fabreeka International Inc **(DH)**	Stoughton	MA	G	781 341-3655	12206
Fabreeka Intl Holdings Inc **(DH)**	Stoughton	MA	E	781 341-3655	12207
Factory Five Racing Inc	Wareham	MA	E	508 291-3443	12836
General Electric Company	Lynn	MA	A	781 594-2218	9975
Geoorbital Inc	Somerville	MA	F	617 651-1102	11877
Gtb Innovative Solutions Inc	Westfield	MA	F	413 733-0146	13168
H&H Propeller Shop Inc **(PA)**	Salem	MA	E	978 744-3806	11721
Haufe Group	Stoneham	MA	G	781 376-3737	12179
Helvetia LLC	Holden	MA	G	508 829-7607	9190
Hi-Tech Inc	Attleboro	MA	F	401 454-4086	6023
High Voltage Engineering Corp	Wakefield	MA	E	781 224-1001	12511
Joseph Palmer Inc	Woburn	MA	F	781 376-0130	13595
Lfr Chassis Inc	Shrewsbury	MA	F	508 425-3117	11837
Newera Services Corporation **(PA)**	New Bedford	MA	F	508 995-9711	10631
North Shore Laboratories Corp	Peabody	MA	F	978 531-5954	11327
OMV	Attleboro	MA	G	508 243-6236	6045
XI Hybrids Inc **(HQ)**	Brighton	MA	F	617 718-0329	7247
ZF Active Safety & Elec US LLC	Westminster	MA	D	978 874-0151	13283
ZF Chassis Components LLC	Boston	MA	F	859 334-3834	7139
Coastal Metal Fab	Topsham	ME	E	207 729-5101	5547
Electrnic Mobility Contrls LLC	Augusta	ME	F	207 512-8009	4471
Marketing Worldwide Corp **(PA)**	Rockland	ME	G	631 444-8090	5339
Nichols Portland LLC **(PA)**	Portland	ME	B	207 774-6121	5251
Somic America Inc	Brewer	ME	D	207 989-1759	4619
Down To Fab LLC	Canaan	NH	G	603 728-8299	14045
Freudenberg-Nok General Partnr	Northfield	NH	C	603 286-1600	15265
Freudenberg-Nok General Partnr	Northfield	NH	D	603 286-1600	15266
General Electric Company	Hooksett	NH	A	603 666-8300	14465
Granite Shore Power LLC	Bow	NH	C	603 634-2299	13999
Kautex Inc	Dover	NH	B	603 743-2431	14232
Larry Dingee	Cornish	NH	G	603 542-9682	14183
Osram Sylvania Inc	Hillsborough	NH	B	603 464-7235	14442
Sanner	Nashua	NH	G	603 577-9087	15163
Vibracoustic Usa Inc	Londonderry	NH	F	603 413-7262	14790
Kennedy Incorporated	North Kingstown	RI	F	401 295-7800	16265
M & T Manufacturing	Wakefield	RI	G	401 789-0472	16742
Vensys Energy Inc	Warwick	RI	F	401 295-0006	16870
General Electric Company	Rutland	VT	A	802 775-9842	17497
JBM Sherman Carmel Inc	Bennington	VT	E	802 442-5115	17042
Sonnax Industries Inc	Bellows Falls	VT	G	802 463-0240	17031

AUTOMOTIVE PARTS: Plastic

	CITY	ST	EMP	PHONE	ENTRY#
Lawrence Holdings Inc	Wallingford	CT	F	203 949-1600	3826
Atlantic Auto & Trck Parts LLC	Rowley	MA	G	978 535-6777	11667
Clean Products LLC	Fall River	MA	F	508 676-9355	8529
Illinois Tool Works Inc	Westminster	MA	C	978 874-0151	13271
Poly6 Technologies Inc	Burlington	MA	F	339 234-9300	7412
Eagle Motors Inc	Harrisville	RI	F	401 568-2580	16065
Scarborough Faire Inc	Pawtucket	RI	E	401 724-4200	16416

AUTOMOTIVE PRDTS: Rubber

	CITY	ST	EMP	PHONE	ENTRY#
Hutchinson Sealing Systems Inc	Newfields	NH	C	603 772-3771	15205

AUTOMOTIVE REPAIR SHOPS: Electrical Svcs

	CITY	ST	EMP	PHONE	ENTRY#
Maine & Maritimes Corporation **(PA)**	Presque Isle	ME	F	207 760-2499	5304

AUTOMOTIVE REPAIR SHOPS: Engine Rebuilding

	CITY	ST	EMP	PHONE	ENTRY#
Motor Service Inc	Shrewsbury	MA	F	508 832-6291	11839

AUTOMOTIVE REPAIR SHOPS: Machine Shop

	CITY	ST	EMP	PHONE	ENTRY#
Centerline Machine Company Inc	Beverly	MA	F	978 524-8842	6338
Hagan Design and Machine Inc	Newmarket	NH	F	603 292-1101	15220
Vermont Engine Service Inc	Williston	VT	G	802 863-2326	17752

AUTOMOTIVE REPAIR SHOPS: Muffler Shop, Sale/Rpr/Installation

	CITY	ST	EMP	PHONE	ENTRY#
Monro Inc	Swanzey	NH	G	603 352-7822	15644
T M Services Inc	Rutland	VT	E	802 775-2948	17511

AUTOMOTIVE REPAIR SHOPS: Rebuilding & Retreading Tires

	CITY	ST	EMP	PHONE	ENTRY#
Bridgestone Ret Operations LLC	Bristol	CT	G	860 584-2727	417
Bridgestone Ret Operations LLC	Hamden	CT	G	203 288-1634	1414
Bridgestone Ret Operations LLC	Milford	CT	G	203 878-6859	1803
Bridgestone Ret Operations LLC	New Britain	CT	F	860 229-0348	2009
Bridgestone Ret Operations LLC	New Haven	CT	G	203 787-1208	2132
Bridgestone Ret Operations LLC	Southington	CT	G	860 628-9621	3205
Bridgestone Ret Operations LLC	Waterbury	CT	F	203 754-6193	3893
Bridgestone Ret Operations LLC	Auburn	MA	G	508 832-9671	6110
Bridgestone Ret Operations LLC	Boston	MA	G	617 327-1100	6622
Bridgestone Ret Operations LLC	Braintree	MA	G	781 843-2870	7172
Bridgestone Ret Operations LLC	Brockton	MA	G	508 588-8866	7262
Bridgestone Ret Operations LLC	Hingham	MA	G	781 749-6454	9145
Bridgestone Ret Operations LLC	Northampton	MA	G	413 586-1584	11054
Bridgestone Ret Operations LLC	Quincy	MA	G	617 479-3208	11508
Bridgestone Ret Operations LLC	Springfield	MA	G	413 543-1312	12080
Bridgestone Ret Operations LLC	Watertown	MA	F	617 924-3989	12864
Bridgestone Ret Operations LLC	Wilmington	MA	G	978 658-5660	13394
K & W Tire Company Inc	Ayer	MA	F	978 772-5700	6184
Petes Tire Barns Inc **(PA)**	Orange	MA	G	978 544-8811	11228
Sullivan Investment Co Inc **(PA)**	Norwell	MA	E	781 982-1550	11147
Central Tire Co Inc **(PA)**	Sanford	ME	E	207 324-4250	5391
Lag Inc **(PA)**	Topsham	ME	E	207 729-1676	5548
Bridgestone Ret Operations LLC	Manchester	NH	G	603 668-1123	14821
Freedom Tire Inc **(PA)**	Plaistow	NH	F	603 382-7223	15344
Bridgestone Ret Operations LLC	Providence	RI	F	401 521-6622	16491

AUTOMOTIVE REPAIR SHOPS: Springs, Rebuilding & Repair

	CITY	ST	EMP	PHONE	ENTRY#
Joseph Palmer Inc	Woburn	MA	F	781 376-0130	13595

AUTOMOTIVE REPAIR SHOPS: Tire Recapping

	CITY	ST	EMP	PHONE	ENTRY#
Bergson Tire Co Inc	Ellington	CT	F	860 872-7729	1102
City Tire Co Inc	Pittsfield	MA	G	413 445-5578	11396
City Tire Co Inc **(PA)**	Springfield	MA	F	413 737-1419	12084
Belknap Tire Co Holdings Inc	Laconia	NH	F	603 524-4517	14646
Mountain Tire Corp	Berlin	NH	F	603 752-8473	13983

AUTOMOTIVE REPAIR SHOPS: Tire Repair Shop

	CITY	ST	EMP	PHONE	ENTRY#
Oasis Truck Tire Service LLC **(PA)**	Old Saybrook	CT	G	860 296-8749	2657
Reliable Auto Tire Company Inc	Hartford	CT	G	860 247-7977	1504
Star Tires Plus Wheels LLC	Hartford	CT	F	860 296-9799	1509
Tire Country of Enfield Inc	Enfield	CT	G	860 763-0846	1155
American Tire Svc & Sls Inc	Springfield	MA	F	413 739-5369	12074
Autocraft Collision Inc	Reading	MA	G	781 670-9001	11600
BJs Wholesale Club Inc	Franklin	MA	D	508 553-9889	8821
Bodyshop World By Wagner Inc	Worcester	MA	F	508 853-0300	13704
Goodyear Tire & Rubber Company	Lynn	MA	F	781 598-4500	9976
Sullivan Tire Co Inc	North Attleboro	MA	G	508 695-9920	10890
Tire & Auto Service Centers	Brockton	MA	G	508 559-6802	7312
Lees Tire	Topsham	ME	E	207 729-1676	5549
Maine Tire & Appliance Co	Augusta	ME	G	207 623-1171	4477
Steven Pelletier	Fort Kent	ME	F	207 834-3191	4794
Tki Inc	Skowhegan	ME	E	207 474-5322	5479
Northeast Tire Service Inc	Belmont	NH	G	603 524-7973	13965
Ocean State Tire Co Inc	Cranston	RI	E	401 946-0880	15903
Sullivan Tire Co Inc	Warwick	RI	E	401 737-5251	16866
John Penfield Ltd	Brattleboro	VT	F	802 254-5411	17090
Vianor Inc **(HQ)**	Colchester	VT	E	802 864-7108	17207
Vianor Inc	Montpelier	VT	E	802 223-1747	17378
Vianor Inc	Morrisville	VT	E	802 888-7961	17392

AUTOMOTIVE REPAIR SHOPS: Trailer Repair

	CITY	ST	EMP	PHONE	ENTRY#
Boston Trailer Manufacturing	Walpole	MA	F	508 668-2242	12553
Daves Truck Repair Inc	Springfield	MA	F	413 734-8898	12089
U-Haul Co Mass & Ohio Inc **(DH)**	Somerville	MA	E	617 625-2789	11908
Wright Trailers Inc	Seekonk	MA	F	508 336-8530	11790

AUTOMOTIVE REPAIR SHOPS: Truck Engine Repair, Exc Indl

	CITY	ST	EMP	PHONE	ENTRY#
Ralph L Osgood Inc	Claremont	NH	F	603 543-1703	14096
Reed Truck Services Inc	Claremont	NH	F	603 542-5032	14097

	CITY	ST	EMP	PHONE	ENTRY#

AUTOMOTIVE REPAIR SHOPS: Wheel Alignment

	CITY	ST	EMP	PHONE	ENTRY#
Monro Inc	Swanzey	NH	G	603 352-7822	15644
T M Services Inc	Rutland	VT	E	802 775-2948	17511

AUTOMOTIVE REPAIR SVC

Seals-It Inc	Ellington	CT	G	860 979-0060	1114
Dattco Sales & Service	Saugus	MA	G	860 229-4878	11756
Tire & Auto Service Centers	Brockton	MA	G	508 559-6802	7312
Lance Smith Inc	Milton	VT	D	802 655-3354	17361

AUTOMOTIVE SPLYS & PARTS, NEW, WHOL: Auto Servicing Eqpt

Connected Auto Systems Neng In	South Easton	MA	E	508 238-5855	11940

AUTOMOTIVE SPLYS & PARTS, NEW, WHOLESALE: Splys

Blendco Systems LLC	Holyoke	MA	D	800 537-7797	9244
Car Gold Inc	Holyoke	MA	E	800 537-7797	9246
Beacon Rock Properties Inc	Providence	RI	D	401 421-3470	16482

AUTOMOTIVE SPLYS & PARTS, WHOLESALE, NEC

Genuine Parts Company	Windsor Locks	CT	G	860 623-4479	4325
Tek-Motive Inc	Branford	CT	F	203 468-2224	281
Consolidated Truck & Eqp Inc	Seekonk	MA	E	508 252-3330	11775
Factory Five Racing Inc	Wareham	MA	E	508 291-3443	12836
Ride-Away Inc (HQ)	Londonderry	NH	E	603 437-4444	14782
Scarborough Faire Inc	Pawtucket	RI	E	401 724-4200	16416

AUTOMOTIVE SVCS, EXC REPAIR & CARWASHES: Lubrication

Jiffy Lube	Mashpee	MA	G	508 539-8888	10252
East Greenwich Oil Co Inc	East Greenwich	RI	G	401 884-2454	15982

AUTOMOTIVE SVCS, EXC REPAIR & CARWASHES: Road Svc

Cross Country Motor Club Inc (HQ)	Medford	MA	A	781 393-9300	10283

AUTOMOTIVE SVCS, EXC REPAIR & CARWASHES: Trailer Maintenance

Standard Welding Company Inc	East Hartford	CT	G	860 528-9628	1022
Daves Truck Repair Inc	Springfield	MA	E	413 734-8898	12089

AUTOMOTIVE SVCS, EXC RPR/CARWASHES: High Perf Auto Rpr/Svc

Xxpress Auto Repair Shop LLC	Hyde Park	MA	F	800 591-2068	9468
Melton Sales and Service Inc	Hallowell	ME	G	207 623-8895	4860
North Atlantic Dist Inc	North Kingstown	RI	B	401 667-7000	16274

AUTOMOTIVE TRANSMISSION REPAIR SVC

Bridgestone Ret Operations LLC	West Haven	CT	G	203 933-7750	4095

AUTOMOTIVE WELDING SVCS

WH Rose Inc	Columbia	CT	E	860 228-8258	671
Martel Welding & Sons Inc	Tewksbury	MA	F	978 458-0661	12406
Weymouths Garage Inc	Milford	ME	G	207 827-2069	5063

AUTOMOTIVE: Bodies

North Atlantic Dist Inc	North Kingstown	RI	B	401 667-7000	16274

AUTOMOTIVE: Seating

Johnson Controls Inc	Ledyard	CT	F	860 886-9021	1552
Johnson Controls Inc	Meriden	CT	F	678 297-4040	1670
Johnson Controls Inc	Rocky Hill	CT	F	860 571-3300	2930
Johnson Controls Inc	Boston	MA	F	617 424-6601	6828
Johnson Controls Inc	Boston	MA	F	617 992-2073	6829
Johnson Controls Inc	North Easton	MA	F	508 238-0536	11010
Clarios LLC	Portland	ME	E	603 222-2400	5199
Clarios LLC	Manchester	NH	D	603 222-2400	14830
Clarios LLC	Lincoln	RI	E	401 235-6700	16127
Johnson Controls Inc	Cranston	RI	F	401 275-2097	15880

AVIATION PROPELLER & BLADE REPAIR SVCS

Amk Welding Inc	South Windsor	CT	E	860 289-5634	3113

AWNINGS & CANOPIES

Jay Salem Inc	Middleton	MA	G	978 774-4999	10387
Futureguard Building Pdts Inc (PA)	Auburn	ME	E	800 858-5818	4434
Ke Usa Inc	Middlebury	VT	E	802 388-7309	17345

AWNINGS & CANOPIES: Awnings, Fabric, From Purchased Matls

Eastern Awning Systems Inc	Watertown	CT	F	860 274-9218	4011
Fitzgerald-Norwalk Awng Co Inc	Norwalk	CT	G	203 847-5858	2501
Toff Industry Inc	Milldale	CT	G	860 378-0532	1903
W H Preuss Sons Incorporated	Bolton	CT	G	860 643-9492	224
Dartmouth Awning Co Inc	Westport	MA	G	508 636-6838	13295
Expansion Opportunities Inc	Northborough	MA	E	508 393-8200	11095

	CITY	ST	EMP	PHONE	ENTRY#
Harry Miller Co LLC	Boston	MA	F	617 427-2300	6782
Harry Miller Co LLC (PA)	Boston	MA	E	617 427-2300	6783
Jay Salem Inc	Middleton	MA	G	978 774-4999	10387
Lyman Conrad (PA)	South Hadley	MA	F	413 538-8200	11965
MM Reif Ltd	Boston	MA	D	617 442-9500	6890
Sunsetter Products Ltd Partnr	Malden	MA	D	781 321-9600	10029
William Blanchard Co Inc	Wakefield	MA	F	781 245-8050	12543
Canvasworks Inc	Kennebunk	ME	G	207 985-2419	4923
Collabric	Veazie	ME	F	207 945-5095	5570
Leavitt & Parris Inc	Portland	ME	F	207 797-0100	5233
Lewiston-Auburn Tent & Awng Co	Lewiston	ME	G	207 784-7353	4974
Image Awnings Incorporated	Wolfeboro	NH	G	603 569-6680	15734
Yarra Design & Fabrication LLC	Bow	NH	F	603 224-6880	14014
Kinder Industries Inc	Bristol	RI	F	401 253-7076	15771

AWNINGS & CANOPIES: Canopies, Fabric, From Purchased Matls

Soapstone Media Inc	Ellington	CT	F	860 749-0455	1116
Ke Usa Inc	Williston	VT	E	802 864-3009	17736

AWNINGS: Fiberglass

Lyman Conrad (PA)	South Hadley	MA	F	413 538-8200	11965
Robert E Glidden	Hyannis	MA	G	508 775-6812	9447

AWNINGS: Metal

Lyman Conrad (PA)	South Hadley	MA	F	413 538-8200	11965

BADGES: Identification & Insignia

Reeves Company Inc	Attleboro	MA	F	508 222-2877	6053
GA Rel Manufacturing Company	Providence	RI	F	401 331-5455	16524
Ira Green Inc (PA)	Providence	RI	C	800 663-7487	16543

BAGS & CONTAINERS: Textile, Exc Sleeping

Fleming Industries Inc	Chicopee	MA	E	413 593-3300	8033
Lapoint Industries Inc (PA)	Auburn	ME	D	207 777-3100	4439
Enviro-Tote Inc	Londonderry	NH	E	603 647-7171	14749

BAGS & SACKS: Shipping & Shopping

Accurate Services Inc	Fall River	MA	E	508 674-5773	8518

BAGS: Canvas

Jungle Inc (PA)	Essex	MA	F	978 356-7722	8476
Steele Canvas Basket Corp	Chelsea	MA	E	800 541-8929	7994

BAGS: Cellophane

Eastern Packaging Inc	Lawrence	MA	D	978 685-7723	9559

BAGS: Food Storage & Trash, Plastic

Inteplast Engineered Films Inc	Westborough	MA	D	508 366-8884	13110

BAGS: Paper

Hudson Paper Company (PA)	Stratford	CT	E	203 378-8759	3548
K&H Group Inc	Bennington	VT	C	802 442-5455	17045

BAGS: Paper, Made From Purchased Materials

Duro Hilex Poly LLC	Meriden	CT	D	203 639-7070	1665
Northeast Packaging Co (PA)	Presque Isle	ME	E	207 764-6271	5305

BAGS: Plastic

Amgraph Packaging Inc (PA)	Baltic	CT	D	860 822-2000	37
Armin Innovative Products Inc	Dighton	MA	E	508 822-4629	8291
Admiral Packaging Inc	Providence	RI	D	401 274-5588	16464
Liftbag Usa Inc	North Kingstown	RI	F	401 884-8801	16267
Subsalve USA LLC	North Kingstown	RI	F	401 884-8801	16282

BAGS: Plastic & Pliofilm

Pak 2000 Inc	Lancaster	NH	F	603 569-3700	14678

BAGS: Plastic, Made From Purchased Materials

Fortune Plastics Inc	Old Saybrook	CT	B	800 243-0306	2648
Ace-Lon Corporation	Malden	MA	E	781 322-7121	10000
Jannel Manufacturing Inc	Holbrook	MA	E	781 767-0666	9176
Laddawn Inc (HQ)	Devens	MA	D	800 446-3639	8274
Northeast Packaging Co (PA)	Presque Isle	ME	E	207 764-6271	5305
Tufpak Inc	Ossipee	NH	E	603 539-4126	15285
Monument Industries Inc	Bennington	VT	E	802 442-8187	17052

BAGS: Rubber Or Rubberized Fabric

Alimed Inc	Dedham	MA	C	781 329-2900	8235

BAKERIES, COMMERCIAL: On Premises Baking Only

Amoun Pita & Distribution LLC	South Windsor	CT	F	866 239-9990	3114
Apicellas Bakery Inc	New Haven	CT	E	203 865-6204	2116

PRODUCT

	CITY	ST	EMP	PHONE	ENTRY#
Katona Bakery LLC	Fairfield	CT	E	203 337-5349	1193
Modern Pastry Shop Inc	Hartford	CT	G	860 296-7628	1494
Mozzicato Pastry & Bake Sp Inc	Hartford	CT	E	860 296-0426	1495
Stella DOro Biscuit Co Inc	Greenwich	CT	C	718 549-3700	1353
Superior Bakery Inc	North Grosvenordale	CT	E	860 923-9555	
					2387
Watson LLC (DH)	West Haven	CT	E	203 932-3000	4132
Abp Corporation (PA)	Boston	MA	C	617 423-0629	6505
Artisan Chef Manufacturing LLC (HQ)	Lawrence	MA	F	978 691-6100	9538
Arts International Wholesale	Raynham	MA	G	508 822-7181	11581
Bake-N-Joy Foods Inc (PA)	North Andover	MA	D	978 683-1414	10821
Begum Brands Corporation	Boston	MA	E	617 269-8400	6588
Big Y Foods Inc	Longmeadow	MA	D	413 567-6231	9848
Boston Food Cooperative (PA)	Cambridge	MA	C	617 661-1580	7520
Chmuras Bakery Inc (PA)	Indian Orchard	MA	F	413 543-2521	9471
Cumberland Farms (DH)	Westborough	MA	B	800 225-9702	13097
Diannes Fine Desserts Inc (PA)	Newburyport	MA	C	800 435-2253	10678
Duva Distributors Inc	Shrewsbury	MA	E	508 841-8182	11831
Elie Baking Corporation	Brockton	MA	F	508 584-4890	7276
Forge Baking Company Inc	Arlington	MA	E	617 764-5365	5941
G H Bent Company	Milton	MA	D	617 322-9287	10452
Hamilton Orchards	New Salem	MA	F	978 544-6867	10664
La Patisserie Inc	Revere	MA	F	781 729-9441	11621
Lori Donuts Inc	East Longmeadow	MA	E	413 526-9944	8384
Meadowbrook Orchards Inc	Sterling	MA	F	978 365-7617	12167
Rob Roy Foods Inc	Worcester	MA	G	508 755-8393	13784
Roche Bros Supermarkets LLC	Norton	MA	C	508 285-3600	11133
Sarro Cohasset Incorporated	Hull	MA	D	781 383-1704	9427
Spinelli Ravioli Mfg Co Inc	Boston	MA	E	617 567-1992	7053
B&G Foods Inc	Portland	ME	C	207 772-8341	5180
Cape Whpie Mnes Grmet Whpie Pl	South Portland	ME	F	207 799-9207	5493
Donut Hole Inc	Buxton	ME	F	207 929-5060	4662
Lepage Bakeries Inc	Auburn	ME	A	207 783-9161	4440
Lepage Bakeries Park St LLC (HQ)	Lewiston	ME	E	207 783-9161	4971
Bagel Alley of NH Inc	Nashua	NH	F	603 882-9343	15069
Crosby Bakery Inc	Nashua	NH	F	603 882-1851	15086
Doughvinci Inc	Manchester	NH	G	603 494-8769	14843
Lepage Bakeries Park St LLC	Hudson	NH	F	603 880-4446	14521
Market Basket Produce Inc	Concord	NH	D	603 224-5479	14143
Tuscan Brands LLC (PA)	Salem	NH	F	781 365-2800	15568
Bristol Bagel Works Ltd	Bristol	RI	F	401 254-1390	15756
Calise & Sons Bakery Inc (PA)	Lincoln	RI	C	401 334-3444	16124
Cavanagh Company	Greenville	RI	E	401 949-4000	16057
Dunkin Donuts	Warwick	RI	F	401 822-2434	16810
Frostbite Cupcakes	Chepachet	RI	G	508 801-6706	15804
Wrights Dairy Farm Inc	North Smithfield	RI	F	401 767-3014	16334
Bakers Dozen Inc	Colchester	VT	F	802 879-4001	17186
Fudge Factory Inc	Manchester Center	VT	F	888 669-7425	17328
Harringtons In Vermont Inc (PA)	Richmond	VT	F	802 434-7535	17479
Klingers Bread Company	South Burlington	VT	E	802 860-6322	17582

BAKERIES: On Premises Baking & Consumption

	CITY	ST	EMP	PHONE	ENTRY#
Capricorn Investors II LP	Greenwich	CT	E	203 861-6600	1325
Lupis Incorporated	New Haven	CT	F	203 562-9491	2172
Milite Bakery	Wolcott	CT	G	203 753-9451	4368
Abp Corporation (PA)	Boston	MA	C	617 423-0629	6505
Chmuras Bakery Inc (PA)	Indian Orchard	MA	F	413 543-2521	9471
Concord Teacakes Etcetera Inc	Concord	MA	F	978 369-7644	8109
G H Bent Company	Milton	MA	D	617 322-9287	10452
Hamilton Orchards	New Salem	MA	F	978 544-6867	10664
Harbar LLC	Canton	MA	C	781 828-0848	7793
Lacascias Bakery Inc	Medford	MA	F	781 395-8612	10294
Meadowbrook Orchards Inc	Sterling	MA	F	978 365-7617	12167
Rob Roy Foods Inc	Worcester	MA	G	508 755-8393	13784
Spinelli Ravioli Mfg Co Inc	Boston	MA	E	617 567-1992	7053
Tripoli Bakery Inc	Lawrence	MA	F	978 682-7754	9604
Cape Whpie Mnes Grmet Whpie Pl	South Portland	ME	F	207 799-9207	5493
Lepage Bakeries Inc	Auburn	ME	A	207 783-9161	4440
Lepage Bakeries Park St LLC	Auburn	ME	E	207 783-9161	4441
Lepage Bakeries Park St LLC (HQ)	Lewiston	ME	E	207 783-9161	4971
Natural Selection Inc	Brunswick	ME	E	207 725-6287	4651
Eastern Food Industries Inc	East Greenwich	RI	G	401 884-8798	15983
Tienda Y Panaderia El Quiche	Providence	RI	F	401 521-5154	16627
Wrights Dairy Farm Inc	North Smithfield	RI	F	401 767-3014	16334
Fudge Factory Inc	Manchester Center	VT	F	888 669-7425	17328
Klingers Bread Company	South Burlington	VT	E	802 860-6322	17582

BAKERY MACHINERY

	CITY	ST	EMP	PHONE	ENTRY#
C H Babb Co Inc	Raynham	MA	E	508 977-0600	11582
Somerset Industries Inc	Lowell	MA	E	978 667-3355	9924

BAKERY PRDTS: Bagels, Fresh Or Frozen

	CITY	ST	EMP	PHONE	ENTRY#
Bagel Boy LLC	Lawrence	MA	D	978 682-8646	9541
Bagel Works Inc	Amherst	MA	F	413 835-0561	5860
Boston Bagel Inc	Hyde Park	MA	F	617 364-6900	9457
Foxees Co Inc	Falmouth	MA	F	508 548-8485	8632
Frozen Batters Inc	North Andover	MA	D	508 683-1414	10834
Ginsco Inc	Fall River	MA	F	508 677-4767	8553
Ginsco Inc (PA)	Fall River	MA	F	508 677-4767	8554
Korner Bagel Partnership	Seekonk	MA	G	508 336-5204	11779
Loxsmith Bagel Corporation	Dover	NH	F	603 362-9060	14233

BAKERY PRDTS: Bread, All Types, Fresh Or Frozen

	CITY	ST	EMP	PHONE	ENTRY#
Lupis Incorporated	New Haven	CT	F	203 562-9491	2172
Milite Bakery	Wolcott	CT	G	203 753-9451	4368
Gold Medal Bakery Inc (PA)	Fall River	MA	B	508 674-5766	8555
Lacascias Bakery Inc	Medford	MA	F	781 395-8612	10294
Piantedosi Baking Co Inc (PA)	Malden	MA	C	781 321-3400	10023
Pittsfield Rye Bakery Inc	Pittsfield	MA	G	413 443-9141	11420
Lepage Bakeries Park St LLC	Lewiston	ME	D	207 783-9161	4972
Mathews Bakery Inc	Westbrook	ME	F	207 773-9647	5637
Pinga Bakery Inc	West Warwick	RI	F	401 821-8007	16920

BAKERY PRDTS: Cakes, Bakery, Exc Frozen

	CITY	ST	EMP	PHONE	ENTRY#
North Star Distributors Inc (PA)	Vineyard Haven	MA	E	508 693-2000	12494
Superior Cake Products Inc	Southbridge	MA	D	508 764-3276	12036
Betty Reez Whoopiez	Freeport	ME	G	207 865-1735	4797
Natural Selection Inc	Brunswick	ME	E	207 725-6287	4651
ME and Ollies	Exeter	NH	G	603 319-1561	14296

BAKERY PRDTS: Cakes, Bakery, Frozen

	CITY	ST	EMP	PHONE	ENTRY#
Dutch Maid Bakery Inc	Dorchester	MA	C	617 265-5417	8298
Goldacre Realty Inc	Spencer	MA	E	508 885-2748	12060
Somerville Office	Somerville	MA	G	617 776-0738	11897
C J Cranam Inc	Oxford	ME	E	207 739-1016	5142

BAKERY PRDTS: Cookies

	CITY	ST	EMP	PHONE	ENTRY#
Bob The Baker LLC	Brookfield	CT	F	203 775-1032	510
Stella DOro Biscuit Co Inc	Greenwich	CT	C	718 549-3700	1353
Boston Chipyard The Inc	Boston	MA	E	617 742-9537	6607
Concord Teacakes Etcetera Inc	Concord	MA	F	978 369-7644	8109
Ho Toy Noodles Inc (PA)	Stoughton	MA	F	617 426-0247	12213
Julie Cecchini	Southwick	MA	F	413 562-2042	12044
Keebler Company	Franklin	MA	D	508 520-7223	8848
Peggy Lawton Kitchens Inc	East Walpole	MA	F	508 668-1215	8420
Tatte Holdings LLC	Boston	MA	C	617 577-1111	7070
Moms Organic Munchies Inc	Freeport	ME	G	207 869-4078	4802
Homefree LLC	Windham	NH	E	603 898-0172	15728

BAKERY PRDTS: Cookies & crackers

	CITY	ST	EMP	PHONE	ENTRY#
Beldotti Bakeries LLC	Stamford	CT	F	203 348-9029	3293
Modern Pastry Shop Inc	Hartford	CT	G	860 296-7628	1494
Mozzicato Pastry & Bake Sp Inc	Hartford	CT	E	860 296-0426	1495
Boston Food Cooperative (PA)	Cambridge	MA	C	617 661-1580	7520
La Patisserie Inc	Revere	MA	F	781 729-9441	11621
Rob Roy Foods Inc	Worcester	MA	G	508 755-8393	13784
A & M Donuts Inc	Plymouth	NH	E	603 536-7622	15354
Market Basket Produce Inc	Concord	NH	D	603 224-5479	14143
Catanzaro Food Products Inc	Pawtucket	RI	F	401 255-1700	16353
Harringtons In Vermont Inc (PA)	Richmond	VT	F	802 434-7535	17479

BAKERY PRDTS: Doughnuts, Exc Frozen

	CITY	ST	EMP	PHONE	ENTRY#
DAndrea Corporation (PA)	West Haven	CT	G	203 932-6000	4101
Daybrake Donuts Inc	Bridgeport	CT	G	203 368-4962	314
Massconn Distribute Cpl	South Windsor	CT	D	860 882-0717	3162
Realejo Donuts Inc	Portland	CT	G	860 342-5120	2822
Whole Donut	Enfield	CT	F	860 745-3041	1159
D D J	Oxford	MA	F	508 987-0417	11251
Depot Donuts Inc	North Easton	MA	E	508 230-2888	11009
Dunkin Donuts of Methuen	Methuen	MA	D	978 681-8123	10328
Ginsco Inc	North Dartmouth	MA	F	508 990-3350	10996
Highlands Lunchette	Fall River	MA	G	508 674-6206	8561
Honey Dew Rehobeth	Rehoboth	MA	F	508 431-2784	11609
Kookla Inc	Southbridge	MA	F	508 765-0442	12025
Kookla Inc (PA)	Sturbridge	MA	E	508 347-2623	12251
Dunkin Donuts (PA)	Auburn	ME	E	207 783-0408	4427
Holy Donut (PA)	Portland	ME	F	207 761-7775	5223
Tonys Donut Shop	Portland	ME	G	207 772-2727	5285
A & M Donuts Inc	Plymouth	NH	E	603 536-7622	15354
ANM Donuts Inc	Tilton	NH	E	603 286-2770	15651
Manco LLC	Allenstown	NH	F	603 485-5327	13852

BAKERY PRDTS: Dry

	CITY	ST	EMP	PHONE	ENTRY#
Bagelman III Inc	Danbury	CT	F	203 792-0030	711

	CITY	ST	EMP	PHONE	ENTRY#
Cherise Cpl LLC	Meriden	CT	G	203 238-3482	1660
PDKD Enterprises Inc	Saugus	MA	E	781 233-8499	11764
Swissbakers Inc	Boston	MA	F	781 354-6989	7066

BAKERY PRDTS: Frozen

	CITY	ST	EMP	PHONE	ENTRY#
Rich Products Corporation	New Britain	CT	F	866 737-8884	2057
Bake-N-Joy Foods Inc (PA)	North Andover	MA	D	978 683-1414	10821
Diannes Fine Desserts Inc	Newburyport	MA	C	978 463-3881	10679
Dimitria Delights Inc	North Grafton	MA	D	508 839-1638	11022
Ocean State Cpl Inc	East Providence	RI	C	401 431-0153	16036
Harringtons In Vermont Inc (PA)	Richmond	VT	F	802 434-7535	17479

BAKERY PRDTS: Pies, Bakery, Frozen

	CITY	ST	EMP	PHONE	ENTRY#
Aristocrat Products Inc	Upton	MA	G	626 287-4110	12469
New England Country Pies LLC	Acton	MA	F	781 596-0176	5759
Peppercorn Food Service Inc	Marblehead	MA	F	781 639-6035	10092
Stone House Farm Inc	West Boxford	MA	G	978 352-2323	12954

BAKERY PRDTS: Pretzels

	CITY	ST	EMP	PHONE	ENTRY#
New England Prtzel Popcorn Inc	Lawrence	MA	G	978 687-0342	9587
Port City Foods LLC	Portsmouth	NH	E	603 436-3001	15430

BAKERY PRDTS: Rolls, Bread Type, Fresh Or Frozen

	CITY	ST	EMP	PHONE	ENTRY#
Tm and Tm Inc	Livermore Falls	ME	F	207 897-3442	5026
Homestead Baking Co	Rumford	RI	D	401 434-0551	16668

BAKERY PRDTS: Wholesalers

	CITY	ST	EMP	PHONE	ENTRY#
Apicellas Bakery Inc	New Haven	CT	E	203 865-6204	2116
Mozzicato Pastry & Bake Sp Inc	Hartford	CT	E	860 296-0426	1495
Superior Bakery Inc	North Grosvenordale	CT	E	860 923-9555	2387
Chmuras Bakery Inc (PA)	Indian Orchard	MA	F	413 543-2521	9471
La Patisserie Inc	Revere	MA	F	781 729-9441	11621
Tatte Holdings LLC	Boston	MA	C	617 577-1111	7070
Ann Clark Ltd	Rutland	VT	F	802 773-7886	17489
BB&c Wholesale LLC (PA)	Bristol	VT	F	802 453-7708	17114
Fudge Factory Inc	Manchester Center	VT	F	888 669-7425	17328
Klingers Bread Company	South Burlington	VT	E	802 860-6322	17582

BAKERY: Wholesale Or Wholesale & Retail Combined

	CITY	ST	EMP	PHONE	ENTRY#
Beldotti Bakeries LLC	Stamford	CT	F	203 348-9029	3293
Cheshire Cml LLC	Cheshire	CT	F	203 238-3482	579
Northeast Foods Inc	Dayville	CT	D	860 779-1117	864
Perkatory Productions LLC	Middletown	CT	G	860 894-6040	1770
Stonehouse Fine Cakes	Meriden	CT	F	203 235-5091	1702
Annies Gluten Free Bakery	Shirley	MA	G	978 425-5385	11814
Atkins Fruit Bowl Inc	Amherst	MA	C	413 253-9528	5859
Bakery To Go Inc	Boston	MA	F	617 482-1015	6582
Bernardinos Bakery Inc (PA)	Chicopee	MA	D	413 592-1944	8010
C Q P Bakery	Lawrence	MA	F	978 557-5626	9544
Concord Teacakes Etcetera Inc (PA)	Concord	MA	F	978 369-2409	8108
Ho Yuen Bakery Inc	Boston	MA	F	617 426-8320	6790
Hole In One	Eastham	MA	F	508 255-5359	8434
Old San Juan Bakery Inc	Holyoke	MA	F	413 534-5555	9273
Olivenation LLC (PA)	Avon	MA	F	781 351-1499	6156
Pain DAvignon II Inc	Hyannis	MA	F	508 771-9771	9444
Italian Bakery Products Co	Lewiston	ME	F	207 782-8312	4967
Lepage Bakeries Park St LLC	Auburn	ME	F	207 783-9161	4441
Mary Breen & Company Inc	Wells	ME	G	207 646-4227	5602
Fredericks Pastries (PA)	Amherst	NH	F	603 882-7725	13871
Freeds Bakery LLC	Manchester	NH	E	603 627-7746	14849
Catanzaro Food Products Inc	Pawtucket	RI	G	401 255-1700	16353
Tienda Y Panaderia El Quiche	Providence	RI	F	401 521-5154	16627
Against Grn Gourmet Foods LLC	Brattleboro	VT	G	802 258-3838	17072
BB&c Wholesale LLC (PA)	Bristol	VT	F	802 453-7708	17114
Queen Dog LLC	Burlington	VT	F	802 660-2733	17154
Unilever Bestfoods North Amer	Rutland	VT	G	802 775-4986	17513

BALLOONS: Toy & Advertising, Rubber

	CITY	ST	EMP	PHONE	ENTRY#
Nordson Medical (nh) Inc (HQ)	Salem	NH	C	603 327-0600	15551

BALLS: Steel

	CITY	ST	EMP	PHONE	ENTRY#
Abbott Ball Company	West Hartford	CT	D	860 236-5901	4046
Hartford Technologies Inc	Rocky Hill	CT	E	860 571-3602	2924
Schaeffler Aerospace USA Corp (DH)	Danbury	CT	B	203 744-2211	809
Schaeffler Aerospace USA Corp	Winsted	CT	D	860 379-7558	4354
Trd Specialties Inc	Pine Meadow	CT	G	860 738-4505	2729
Sem-Tec Inc	Worcester	MA	E	508 798-8551	13797

BANNERS: Fabric

	CITY	ST	EMP	PHONE	ENTRY#
DS Sewing Inc	New Haven	CT	F	203 773-1344	2145
Faverco Inc	Boston	MA	G	617 247-1440	6732

	CITY	ST	EMP	PHONE	ENTRY#
Custom Banner & Graphics LLC	Rochester	NH	G	603 332-2067	15472

BAR

	CITY	ST	EMP	PHONE	ENTRY#
Nonesuch River Brewing LLC	Scarborough	ME	E	207 219-8948	5440
Lost Nation Brewing LLC	Morrisville	VT	F	802 851-8041	17385
McHolbe-Noonan Corporation	Burlington	VT	E	802 865-0500	17144

BAR JOISTS & CONCRETE REINFORCING BARS: Fabricated

	CITY	ST	EMP	PHONE	ENTRY#
Dominion Rebar Company	Pawtucket	RI	E	401 724-9200	16365
Rusco Steel Company	Warwick	RI	D	401 732-0548	16855

BARBECUE EQPT

	CITY	ST	EMP	PHONE	ENTRY#
Kenyon International Inc	Clinton	CT	E	860 664-4906	645
South Windsor Golf Course LLC	South Windsor	CT	D	860 648-4653	3182
M & S Enterprises Inc	Brewer	ME	G	207 989-0077	4617

BARRICADES: Metal

	CITY	ST	EMP	PHONE	ENTRY#
K-Tech International Inc	Torrington	CT	E	860 489-9399	3687
Visi-Flash Rentals Eastern	West Bridgewater	MA	E	508 583-9100	12988

BARS & BAR SHAPES: Steel, Hot-Rolled

	CITY	ST	EMP	PHONE	ENTRY#
Natale Co Safetycare LL	Wilmington	MA	G	781 933-7205	13436

BARS, PLATES & SHEETS: Zinc & Zinc Alloy Bars, Plates, Etc

	CITY	ST	EMP	PHONE	ENTRY#
Jarden LLC	East Wilton	ME	F	207 645-2574	4741

BARS: Concrete Reinforcing, Fabricated Steel

	CITY	ST	EMP	PHONE	ENTRY#
Eastern Metal Works Inc	Milford	CT	E	203 878-6995	1821
Nucor Hrris Rbar Northeast LLC	South Windsor	CT	D	860 282-1860	3166
Nucor Steel Connecticut Inc	Wallingford	CT	C	203 265-0615	3836
Building Envelope Systems LLC	Plainville	MA	D	508 381-0429	11430
Nucor Hrris Rbar Northeast LLC	Westfield	MA	F	413 568-7803	13194
Rebars & Mesh Inc	Haverhill	MA	E	978 374-2244	9126
Audette Group LLC	Providence	RI	F	401 667-5884	16479
Nucor Hrris Rbar Northeast LLC	Pawtucket	RI	D	401 724-9200	16396

BASES, BEVERAGE

	CITY	ST	EMP	PHONE	ENTRY#
Transatlantic Bubbles LLC	Woodbridge	CT	G	203 464-0051	4383

BATHROOM ACCESS & FITTINGS: Vitreous China & Earthenware

	CITY	ST	EMP	PHONE	ENTRY#
Kenney Manufacturing Company (PA)	Warwick	RI	B	401 739-2200	16831
Summer Infant Inc (HQ)	Woonsocket	RI	C	401 671-6550	16975

BATHROOM FIXTURES: Plastic

	CITY	ST	EMP	PHONE	ENTRY#
Roma Marble Inc	Ludlow	MA	F	413 583-5017	9953

BATHTUBS: Concrete

	CITY	ST	EMP	PHONE	ENTRY#
Future Classics USA LLC (PA)	Roxbury	CT	F	860 838-4688	2944

BATTERIES, EXC AUTOMOTIVE: Wholesalers

	CITY	ST	EMP	PHONE	ENTRY#
A123 Systems LLC	Waltham	MA	C	617 778-5700	12580
Interstate All Battery Center	South Yarmouth	MA	F	508 394-9400	11984

BATTERIES: Alkaline, Cell Storage

	CITY	ST	EMP	PHONE	ENTRY#
Duracell US Holding LLC (HQ)	Bethel	CT	E	203 796-4000	113
Evercel Inc	Stamford	CT	C	781 741-8800	3346

BATTERIES: Lead Acid, Storage

	CITY	ST	EMP	PHONE	ENTRY#
Johnson Controls Inc	Meriden	CT	F	678 297-4040	1670

BATTERIES: Rechargeable

	CITY	ST	EMP	PHONE	ENTRY#
Nofet LLC	New Haven	CT	F	203 848-9064	2180
Battery Resourcers LLC	Westborough	MA	F	206 948-6325	13081
Lg Energy Solution Vertech Inc (DH)	Westborough	MA	E	508 497-7319	13117
Technical Power Systems Inc	Middleboro	MA	E	630 719-1471	10378
Titan Advnced Enrgy Sltons Inc	Salem	MA	F	561 654-5558	11735

BATTERIES: Storage

	CITY	ST	EMP	PHONE	ENTRY#
Alcad Inc	North Haven	CT	E	203 985-2500	2389
B S T Systems Inc	Plainfield	CT	D	860 564-4078	2734
Duracell Company	Bethel	CT	E	203 796-4000	110
Duracell International Inc	Bethel	CT	A	203 796-4000	111
Duracell Manufacturing LLC	Bethel	CT	C	203 796-4000	112
Hbl America Inc (HQ)	Manchester	CT	G	860 257-9800	1601
Saft America Inc	North Haven	CT	E	203 234-8333	2435
24m Technologies Inc (PA)	Cambridge	MA	E	617 553-1012	7461
A123 Systems Inc	Watertown	MA	F	617 972-3400	12854
A123 Systems LLC	Hopkinton	MA	D	508 497-7200	9304
A123 Systems LLC	Waltham	MA	C	617 778-5700	12580
Atlantic Battery Company Inc	Watertown	MA	F	617 924-2868	12860
Avanti Battery Company	Watertown	MA	F	617 209-9434	12861
B456 Systems Inc	Waltham	MA	A	617 778-5700	12600

PRODUCT

	CITY	ST	EMP	PHONE	ENTRY#

BATTERIES: Storage

	CITY	ST	EMP	PHONE	ENTRY#
Factorial Inc (PA)	Woburn	MA	E	617 315-9733	13563
Fastcap Systems Corporation (PA)	Wakefield	MA	D	857 403-6031	12509
Integer Holdings Corporation	Canton	MA	C	781 830-5800	7801
Interstate All Battery Center	South Yarmouth	MA	F	508 394-9400	11984
Nyobolt Inc	Bedford	MA	F	978 884-2220	6249
Solidenergy Systems LLC	Woburn	MA	D	617 972-3412	13670
Tracer Technologies Inc	Somerville	MA	E	617 776-6410	11904
Xilectric Inc	Fall River	MA	G	781 247-4567	8627
Sustainx Inc	Exeter	NH	E	603 601-7800	14303
Eaglepicher Technologies LLC	East Greenwich	RI	F	401 471-6580	15981
Ener-Tek International Inc	East Greenwich	RI	E	401 471-6580	15985
Yardney Technical Products Inc	East Greenwich	RI	E	401 471-6580	15998
Edgewell Per Care Brands LLC	Bennington	VT	E	802 442-5551	17039

BATTERIES: Wet

	CITY	ST	EMP	PHONE	ENTRY#
B S T Systems Inc	Plainfield	CT	D	860 564-4078	2734
Videndum Prod Solutions Inc (HQ)	Shelton	CT	E	203 929-1100	3075
Electrochem Solutions Inc	Raynham	MA	C	781 575-0800	11589
Integer Holdings Corporation	Canton	MA	C	781 830-5800	7801
Largo Clean Energy Corp (HQ)	Wilmington	MA	E	978 566-8220	13425
Ener-Tek International Inc	East Greenwich	RI	E	401 471-6580	15985

BATTERY CASES: Plastic Or Plastics Combination

	CITY	ST	EMP	PHONE	ENTRY#
GP Industries	Taftville	CT	F	860 859-9938	3597

BATTERY CHARGERS

	CITY	ST	EMP	PHONE	ENTRY#
Control Module Inc (PA)	Enfield	CT	D	860 745-2433	1125
Digatron Power Electronics Inc	Shelton	CT	E	203 446-8000	3000
Interacter Inc	Wallingford	CT	F	203 949-0199	3818
Aak Power Supply Corporation	Plaistow	NH	F	603 382-2222	15335

BATTERY CHARGERS: Storage, Motor & Engine Generator Type

	CITY	ST	EMP	PHONE	ENTRY#
Sparkcharge Inc	Somerville	MA	E	866 906-2330	11899

BATTERY CHARGING GENERATORS

	CITY	ST	EMP	PHONE	ENTRY#
Pellion Technologies Inc	Arlington	MA	E		5944
Launchpad Electric Solutions	Kittery	ME	F	603 828-2919	4936

BEARINGS & PARTS Ball

	CITY	ST	EMP	PHONE	ENTRY#
Abek LLC	Bristol	CT	F	860 314-3905	390
Buswell Manufacturing Company	Bridgeport	CT	F	203 334-6069	307
Gwilliam Company Inc	New Milford	CT	F	860 354-2884	2246
Nn Inc	Wallingford	CT	F	203 793-7132	3835
Schaeffler Aerospace USA Corp (DH)	Danbury	CT	B	203 744-2211	809
Schaeffler Aerospace USA Corp	Winsted	CT	D	860 379-7558	4354
Schaeffler Holding LLC (DH)	Danbury	CT	B	203 790-5474	810
Nn Inc	North Attleboro	MA	E	508 695-7700	10880
Mpb Corporation (HQ)	Keene	NH	C	603 352-0310	14611
Mpb Corporation	Lebanon	NH	A	603 448-3000	14695
New Hmpshire Ball Bearings Inc	Laconia	NH	B	603 524-0004	14661
New Hmpshire Ball Bearings Inc	Peterborough	NH	E	818 407-9300	15320

BEARINGS: Ball & Roller

	CITY	ST	EMP	PHONE	ENTRY#
Ball & Roller Bearing Co LLC	New Milford	CT	F	860 355-4161	2239
C & S Engineering Inc	Meriden	CT	F	203 235-5727	1657
Hartford Technologies Inc	Rocky Hill	CT	E	860 571-3602	2924
K A F Manufacturing Co Inc	Stamford	CT	E	203 324-3012	3394
Kamatics Corporation (DH)	Bloomfield	CT	E	860 243-9704	184
Kamatics Corporation	Bloomfield	CT	C	860 243-7230	185
Nordex Incorporated	Brookfield	CT	E	203 775-4877	532
Rbc Aircraft Products Inc	Torrington	CT	D	860 626-7800	3692
Rbc Bearings Incorporated (PA)	Oxford	CT	C	203 267-7001	2710
SKF Specialty Balls	Winsted	CT	F	860 379-8511	4355
SKF USA Inc	Winsted	CT	E	860 379-8511	4356
Wind Corporation	Newtown	CT	E	800 946-3267	2354
Mpb Corporation	Lebanon	NH	A	603 448-3000	14694

BEARINGS: Plastic

	CITY	ST	EMP	PHONE	ENTRY#
Pobco Inc	Worcester	MA	E	508 791-6376	13771
Slideways Inc	Worcester	MA	E	508 854-0799	13803

BEARINGS: Railroad Car Journal

	CITY	ST	EMP	PHONE	ENTRY#
Cmhanb LLC	Hartford	CT	G	860 241-0112	1474

BEARINGS: Roller & Parts

	CITY	ST	EMP	PHONE	ENTRY#
Del-Tron Precision Inc	Bethel	CT	E	203 778-2727	107

BEARINGS: Wooden

	CITY	ST	EMP	PHONE	ENTRY#
Pobco Inc	Worcester	MA	E	508 791-6376	13771
Woodex Bearing Company Inc	Georgetown	ME	E	207 371-2210	4815

BEAUTY & BARBER SHOP EQPT

	CITY	ST	EMP	PHONE	ENTRY#
Components For Mfg LLC	Noank	CT	E	860 572-1671	2359
Conair LLC (HQ)	Stamford	CT	B	203 351-9000	3320
CV Industries Corporation	Oxford	CT	E	203 828-6566	2692
DRM Research Laboratories Inc	Branford	CT	F	203 488-5555	252
Outdoor Industries LLC	Madison	CT	E	203 350-2275	1565
Thomaston Industries Inc	Thomaston	CT	F	860 283-4358	3638
West-Conn Tool and Die Inc	Shelton	CT	E	203 538-5081	3077
10beauty Inc	Burlington	MA	E	215 356-8680	7329
Axial Industries	Wakefield	MA	G	781 224-0421	12499
Don-Jo Mfg Inc	Sterling	MA	E	978 422-3377	12160
Inverness Corporation (DH)	Attleboro	MA	G	774 203-1130	6026
Manomet Manufacturing Inc	New Bedford	MA	G	508 997-1795	10617
Skin Catering Inc	Springfield	MA	F	413 349-8199	12128
Technical Power Systems Inc	Middleboro	MA	E	630 719-1471	10378
Zycal Bioceuticals Mfg LLC	Shrewsbury	MA	E	888 779-9225	11850
Alexanders Welding & Mch Inc	Greenfield Twp	ME	F	207 827-3300	4849
Cellblock Fcs LLC	Standish	ME	E	800 440-4119	5526
Phocam Manufacturing LLC	Gorham	ME	F	207 854-8471	4830
Stonewall Kitchen LLC	Wells	ME	D	207 251-4800	5606
Village Candle Inc	Wells	ME	E	207 251-4800	5608
Enviromart Industries Inc	Plaistow	NH	F	603 378-0154	15341
GKN Aerospace New England Inc	Charlestown	NH	D	603 542-5135	14063
Key Industries	New Ipswich	NH	F	603 369-9634	15198
Champlain Industries Inc	Burlington	VT	F	802 651-0708	17125
Select Design Ltd	Burlington	VT	D	802 864-9075	17158

BEAUTY SALONS

	CITY	ST	EMP	PHONE	ENTRY#
Skin Catering Inc	Springfield	MA	F	413 349-8199	12128
Stilisti	Boston	MA	G	617 262-2234	7062

BED SHEETING, COTTON

	CITY	ST	EMP	PHONE	ENTRY#
Maine Heritage Weavers	Monmouth	ME	E	207 933-2605	5071

BEDDING & BEDSPRINGS STORES

	CITY	ST	EMP	PHONE	ENTRY#
US Bedding Inc	Fall River	MA	F	508 678-6988	8620

BEDDING, BEDSPREAD, BLANKET/SHEET: Pillowcase, Purchd Mtrl

	CITY	ST	EMP	PHONE	ENTRY#
Two Rivers Pet Products Inc	Turner	ME	E	207 225-3965	5565

BEDDING, BEDSPREADS, BLANKETS & SHEETS

	CITY	ST	EMP	PHONE	ENTRY#
Thomas W Raftery Inc	Hartford	CT	E	860 278-9870	1514
Matouk Factory Store Inc	Fall River	MA	E	508 997-3444	8575
PDk Worldwide Entps Inc (PA)	Fall River	MA	E	508 676-2155	8596
Therapedic of New England LLC	Brockton	MA	F	508 559-9944	7311

BEDDING, FROM SILK OR MANMADE FIBER

	CITY	ST	EMP	PHONE	ENTRY#
US Bedding Inc	Fall River	MA	F	508 678-6988	8620

BEDS & ACCESS STORES

	CITY	ST	EMP	PHONE	ENTRY#
Drive-O-Rama Inc	Dennis Port	MA	G	508 394-0028	8260
Maine Bunk Beds LLC	Buxton	ME	F	207 929-4499	4663
Wcw Inc (PA)	Manchester Center	VT	D	802 362-8053	17332

BEER & ALE WHOLESALERS

	CITY	ST	EMP	PHONE	ENTRY#
A & I Concentrate LLC	Shelton	CT	E	203 447-1938	2977
Murder Hill LLC (PA)	Whitinsville	MA	G	774 757-4411	13342
Fiddlehead Brewing Company LLC	Shelburne	VT	F	802 489-5090	17557

BEER & ALE, WHOLESALE: Beer & Other Fermented Malt Liquors

	CITY	ST	EMP	PHONE	ENTRY#
G & G Beverage Distributors	Yalesville	CT	E	203 949-6220	4397
Harpoon Distributing Co Inc	Boston	MA	F	617 574-9551	6781
Capitol Distributors Inc	Bow	NH	E	603 223-2086	13995
Finestkind Brewing LLC	Hampton	NH	D	603 436-4026	14402
Smuttynose Brewing Company Inc	Hampton	NH	D	603 436-4026	14413
Martignetti Companies RI	Central Falls	RI	C	401 722-8008	15792

BEER, WINE & LIQUOR STORES

	CITY	ST	EMP	PHONE	ENTRY#
Gt Spirits Inc	Boston	MA	E	617 276-5209	6777
Old Creamery Grocery Store	Cummington	MA	G	413 634-5560	8147
Sunday River Brewing Co Inc	Boston	MA	G	207 824-4253	7064

BEER, WINE & LIQUOR STORES: Beer, Packaged

	CITY	ST	EMP	PHONE	ENTRY#
Brockton Beer Company LLC	Brockton	MA	G	508 521-9711	7263
Mass Bay Brewing Company Inc (PA)	Boston	MA	C	617 574-9551	6870
True North Ale Company LLC	Ipswich	MA	F	978 312-6473	9498
Finestkind Brewing LLC	Hampton	NH	D	603 436-4026	14402
Smuttynose Brewing Company Inc	Hampton	NH	D	603 436-4026	14413
Mbbc Vermont LLC	Windsor	VT	E	802 674-5491	17760
Pearl Street Beverage Inc	Burlington	VT	F	802 658-1574	17150
Rea Inc	Saint Albans	VT	F	802 527-7437	17530

BELLOWS

	CITY	ST	EMP	PHONE	ENTRY#
Seymour - Sheridan Incorporated	Monroe	CT	D	203 261-4009	1921
Standard Bellows Co (PA)	Windsor Locks	CT	E	860 623-2307	4335
John Crane Sealol Inc (DH)	Warwick	RI	C	401 732-0715	16828
Metal-Flex Welded Bellows Inc	Newport	VT	E	802 334-5550	17400

BELTING: Rubber

Dresco Belting Co Inc	Hingham	MA	G	781 335-1350	9148

BELTS & BELT PRDTS

Kemper Manufacturing Corp	West Haven	CT	E	203 934-1600	4109

BELTS: Conveyor, Made From Purchased Wire

Habasit Abt Inc	Middletown	CT	C	860 632-2211	1749
Alvin Johnson	East Longmeadow	MA	G	413 525-6334	8368
Custom Convyrs Fabrication Inc	North Oxford	MA	F	508 922-0283	11032
O/K Machinery Corporation	Marlborough	MA	E	508 303-8286	10188
Wire Belt Company of America (PA)	Bedford	NH	E	603 644-2500	13955

BENTONITE MINING

Vanderbilt Minerals LLC (HQ)	Norwalk	CT	E	203 295-2140	2590

BEVERAGE BASES & SYRUPS

Jmf Group LLC	East Windsor	CT	D	860 627-7003	1077
Backbay Roasters	Wilmington	MA	G	844 532-6269	13387
Cape Cod Ginger LLC	Wareham	MA	F	508 295-2795	12830
Keurig Dr Pepper Inc (PA)	Burlington	MA	D	781 418-7000	7384
Multi-Flow Industries LLC	Norwood	MA	E	617 442-7777	11197
Powell and Mahoney LLC	Salem	MA	F	978 745-4332	11731
Bev-Tech Inc	Eliot	ME	F	207 439-8061	4749

BEVERAGE PRDTS: Brewers' Grain

Kent Falls Brewing Company	Kent	CT	G	860 398-9645	1542
Foundation Brewing Company	Portland	ME	F	207 370-8187	5217

BEVERAGE PRDTS: Malt, Barley

Blue Ox Malthouse LLC	Lisbon Falls	ME	F	207 649-0018	5019

BEVERAGE STORES

Miami Bay Beverage Company LLC	Guilford	CT	F	203 453-0090	1400

BEVERAGE, NONALCOHOLIC: Iced Tea/Fruit Drink, Bottled/Canned

Sweet Leaf Tea Company (DH)	Stamford	CT	F	203 863-0263	3475
Tropical Paradise Inc	Bedford	MA	F	781 357-1210	6275

BEVERAGES, ALCOHOLIC: Ale

Cambridge Brewing Co Inc	Cambridge	MA	E	617 494-1994	7528
Wormtown Brewery LLC	Worcester	MA	F	774 239-1555	13833
Ashleigh Inc (PA)	Kennebunk	ME	E	207 967-4311	4921
Craft Brew Alliance Inc	Portsmouth	NH	D	603 430-8600	15378

BEVERAGES, ALCOHOLIC: Applejack

Downeast Cider House LLC (PA)	Boston	MA	G	857 301-8881	6700
Downeast Cider House LLC	Mansfield	MA	D	650 279-2417	10049

BEVERAGES, ALCOHOLIC: Beer

Beerd Brewing Co LLC (PA)	Stonington	CT	E	860 857-1014	3507
Brewery Legitimus LLC	New Hartford	CT	F	860 810-8894	2099
East Rock Brewing Company LLC (PA)	New Haven	CT	E	203 530-3484	2147
Amherst Brewing Co Inc	Amherst	MA	E	413 253-4400	5856
Atlas Distributing Inc	Auburn	MA	C	508 791-6221	6106
Avson Brewing	West Springfield	MA	G	781 727-5789	13016
Bad Martha Farmers Brewery LLC	Edgartown	MA	F	978 335-9879	8465
Barrel House Z LLC	Hingham	MA	E	617 480-2880	9142
Berkshire Brewing Company Inc (PA)	South Deerfield	MA	F	413 665-6600	11921
Boston Beer Company Inc	Boston	MA	F	617 368-5080	6602
Boston Beer Company Inc (PA)	Boston	MA	A	617 368-5000	6603
Boston Beer Corporation (DH)	Boston	MA	C	617 368-5000	6604
Buzzards Bay Brewing Inc	Westport	MA	G	508 636-2288	13294
Castle Island Brewing Co LLC	Norwood	MA	E	781 951-2029	11168
Common Crossing Inc	Berkley	MA	G	508 822-8225	6314
Downeast Cider House LLC (PA)	Boston	MA	G	857 301-8881	6700
Essex County Brewing Co LLC	Boxford	MA	F	978 587-2254	7160
Four Phantoms Brewing Co LLC	Greenfield	MA	G	931 247-0315	8991
Harpoon Distributing Co Inc	Boston	MA	F	617 574-9551	6781
John Harvards Brewhouse Llc	Braintree	MA	B	508 875-2337	7192
Lamplighter Brewing Co LLC (PA)	Cambridge	MA	E	207 650-3325	7629
Lamplighter Brewing Co LLC	Woburn	MA	E	617 945-0450	13599
M P Brewing Company	Fall River	MA	F	508 944-8531	8570
Mass Bay Brewing Company Inc (PA)	Boston	MA	C	617 574-9551	6870
Mass Brewing LLC (PA)	Clinton	MA	G	617 800-7070	8083
Mass Brewing LLC	Devens	MA	G	617 800-7070	8278
Massachusetts Bev Alliance LLC	Bellingham	MA	F	617 701-6238	6294

	CITY	ST	EMP	PHONE	ENTRY#
Mercury Brewing & Dist Co Inc	Ipswich	MA	F	978 356-3329	9490
Plan B Burger LLC	Springfield	MA	F	413 285-8296	12121
Slesar Bros Brewing Co Inc	Boston	MA	F	978 745-2337	7040
Slesar Bros Brewing Co Inc	Hingham	MA	F	781 749-2337	9160
Trillium Brewing Company LLC (PA)	Canton	MA	G	781 298-7126	7835
True North Ale Company LLC	Ipswich	MA	F	978 312-6473	9498
Turtle Swamp Brewing LLC	Boston	MA	F	617 314-2952	7089
Untold Brewing LLC (PA)	Scituate	MA	F	781 378-0559	11773
Belleflower Brewing Co LLC	Portland	ME	F	617 365-9536	5186
Brays Brewing Company	Naples	ME	E	207 693-6806	5079
Definitive Brewing Company LLC	Portland	ME	F	207 446-4746	5207
Maine Beer Company LLC	Freeport	ME	E	207 221-5711	4801
Nonesuch River Brewing LLC	Scarborough	ME	E	207 219-8948	5440
Rising Tide Brewing Co LLC	Portland	ME	F	207 370-2337	5265
Saco River Brewing LLC	Fryeburg	ME	F	207 256-3028	4810
Sacred Profane LLC	Biddeford	ME	G	508 259-3052	4587
7th Settlement Brewery LLC	Dover	NH	E	603 534-5292	14212
Capitol Distributors Inc	Concord	NH	G	603 224-3348	14119
Craft Beer Guild LLC	Portsmouth	NH	E	603 319-8508	15377
Debra Rivest Ltd	Keene	NH	E	603 355-3335	14595
Finestkind Brewing LLC	Hampton	NH	D	603 436-4026	14402
Hobbs Tavern & Brewing Co LLC	West Ossipee	NH	E	603 539-2000	15694
Northwoods Brewing Co LLC	Northwood	NH	F	603 942-6400	15274
Smuttynose Brewing Company Inc	Hampton	NH	D	603 436-4026	14413
Apponaug Brewing Company	Warwick	RI	E	401 681-4321	16782
Linesider Brewing Company LLC	East Greenwich	RI	F	401 398-7700	15989
Shaidzon Beer Company LLC	West Kingston	RI	F	401 314-8730	16897
Alchemy Brewing Stowe LLC	Stowe	VT	F	802 882-8165	17629
Foam Brewers LLC	Burlington	VT	F	802 399-2511	17136
Lost Nation Brewing LLC	Morrisville	VT	F	802 851-8041	17385
Mbbc Vermont LLC	Windsor	VT	E	802 674-5491	17760
McHolbe-Noonan Corporation	Burlington	VT	G	802 865-0500	17144

BEVERAGES, ALCOHOLIC: Beer & Ale

Black Pond Brews	Dayville	CT	G	860 207-5295	858
Diageo Investment Corporation	Stamford	CT	E	203 229-2100	3337
Lock It Down Inc	Stamford	CT	G	203 313-6454	3403
Masas Usa Inc	East Haven	CT	E	305 603-8868	1045
PH Production CT LLC	South Windsor	CT	G	860 205-0942	3171
Swagnificent Ent LLC	Bridgeport	CT	G	203 449-0124	378
Bent Water Brewing Co	Lynn	MA	E	781 780-9948	9963
Brockton Beer Company LLC	Brockton	MA	F	508 521-9711	7263
Craft Beer Guild Distrg VT LLC (PA)	Kingston	MA	E	781 585-5165	9507
K Irwin Construction Inc	Quincy	MA	G	617 481-2420	11525
Lamplighter Brewing Co LLC	Cambridge	MA	E	617 945-2743	7628
Murder Hill LLC (PA)	Whitinsville	MA	G	774 757-4411	13342
Penny Pinchers Brewing Co LLC	Millbury	MA	F	774 696-7885	10440
Sunday River Brewing Co Inc	Boston	MA	E	207 824-4253	7064
Wormtown Brewery LLC	Foxborough	MA	F	774 215-5403	8738
First Mile Brewing Co LLC	Fort Kent	ME	G	207 231-4579	4788
Orange Bike Brewing Co	Portland	ME	G	207 391-4343	5254
Sebago Brewing Company (PA)	Gorham	ME	E	207 856-2537	4834
Trinken Brewing Co LLC	West Bath	ME	G	207 389-6360	5609
York Harbor Brewing Company	Kittery	ME	G	207 703-8060	4941
Capitol Distributors Inc	Bow	NH	E	603 223-2086	13995
Earth Eagle Brewings LLC	Portsmouth	NH	E	603 817-2773	15381
Federal Spice Corp (PA)	North Conway	NH	E	603 356-6381	15248
Gnaw Inc	Manchester	NH	G	603 418-8900	14852
Great Rhythm Brewing Co LLC	Portsmouth	NH	G	603 430-9640	15396
Patel Brew LLC	Somersworth	NH	F	603 602-7455	15620
Rmk Brewers LLC	Hampton	NH	G	603 601-8196	14410
University System NH	Durham	NH	E	603 659-2825	14268
Isle Brewers Guild LLC	Pawtucket	RI	F	774 766-9186	16377
Fiddlehead Brewing Company LLC	Shelburne	VT	F	802 489-5090	17557
Hermit Thrush Brewery LLC (PA)	Brattleboro	VT	G	585 781-0617	17086
Third Place Inc	Burlington	VT	E	802 861-2999	17161
Whetstone Stn Rest Brewry LLC (PA)	Brattleboro	VT	E	802 490-2354	17109

BEVERAGES, ALCOHOLIC: Bourbon Whiskey

Johnson Brothers RI Inc	North Kingstown	RI	E	401 583-0050	16262

BEVERAGES, ALCOHOLIC: Distilled Liquors

Litchfield Distillery	Litchfield	CT	G	860 361-6503	1559
Waypoint Distillery	Bloomfield	CT	G	860 519-5390	216
Black Infusions	Wellesley	MA	E	617 212-1046	12938
Cisco Brwers Dstlrs Vntners Sp	Boston	MA	E	508 325-5929	6656
Deacon Giles Inc	Salem	MA	G	781 883-8256	11710
Grandten Distilling LLC	Newton	MA	G	484 888-1323	10758
Gt Spirits Inc	Boston	MA	E	617 276-5209	6777
Silver Bear Distillery LLC	Dalton	MA	G	413 242-4892	8154
Viva Beverages Inc	Boston	MA	F	617 712-3488	7108
Lu-Dz LLC	Newcastle	ME	G	207 563-2669	5094

	CITY	ST	EMP	PHONE	ENTRY#		CITY	ST	EMP	PHONE	ENTRY#
Milne Spirit Works LLC	Portland	ME	G	207 536-0592	5245	Natural Country Farms Inc	Ellington	CT	C	860 872-8346	1112
Stroudwater Distillery	Portland	ME	F	207 272-7327	5276	Niagara Bottling LLC	Bloomfield	CT	G	909 226-7353	196
White Rock Distilleries Inc	Lewiston	ME	C	207 783-1433	4997	Sigg Switzerland (usa) Inc	Stamford	CT	F	203 321-1232	3456
Wiggly Bridge Distilleries LLC	York	ME	E	207 363-9322	5718	Coca-Cola Bevs Northeast Inc	Needham Heights	MA	E	978 459-9378	10535
Cathedral Ledge Distillery Inc	North Conway	NH	G	612 386-4829	15246	Coca-Cola Bevs Northeast Inc	Sandwich	MA	E	508 888-0001	11749
Doire Distilling LLC	Derry	NH	G	603 765-4353	14191	Coca-Cola Btlg Sthstern Neng I	Greenfield	MA	E	413 448-8296	8987
Sea Hagg Distillery LLC	Dover	NH	G	603 343-1717	14249	Coca-Cola Btlg Sthstern Neng I	Needham Heights	MA	F	781 449-4300	10536
White Mountain Distillery LLC	Manchester	NH	G	603 391-1306	14960	Coca-Cola Btlg Sthstern Neng I	Northampton	MA	E	413 586-8461	11055
Diageo Loyal Spirits Corp	Wakefield	RI	G	401 284-4006	16740	Coca-Cola Btlg Sthstern Neng I	Westborough	MA	D	508 836-5200	13088
Industrious Spirit Company LLC	Providence	RI	G	401 450-9229	16539	Coca-Cola Refreshments USA Inc	Greenfield	MA	F	413 772-2617	8988
Cold Springs Spirits LLC	Warren	VT	G	802 496-6973	17671	Coca-Cola Refreshments USA Inc	Northampton	MA	D	413 586-8461	11056
Diageo North America Inc	Manchester	VT	D	802 362-4700	17323	Cumberland Farms Inc **(DH)**	Westborough	MA	B	800 225-9702	13097
Green Mountain Distillers LLC	Morrisville	VT	G	802 498-4848	17382	Easton Springs Corporation	South Easton	MA	F	508 238-2741	11942
Mad River Distillers	Warren	VT	G	802 496-6973	17672	Keurig Dr Pepper Inc **(PA)**	Burlington	MA	D	781 418-7000	7384
Old Route Two Spirits Inc	Barre	VT	F	802 424-4864	17014	Nixie Sparkling Water Inc	Chatham	MA	G	617 784-8671	7899
Smugglers Notch Distillery LLC	Jeffersonville	VT	G	860 670-1838	17307	Patriot Beverages LLC	Littleton	MA	E	978 486-4900	9831
Vermont Hard Cider Company LLC	Brandon	VT	D	802 385-3656	17071	Pepsi-Cola Metro Btlg Co Inc	Sagamore Beach	MA	E	508 833-5600	11697
Vermont Hard Cider Company LLC **(HQ)**	Middlebury	VT	D	802 388-0700	17350	Pepsi-Cola Metro Btlg Co Inc	Wilmington	MA	D	978 661-6150	13446
Xagd Inc	Middlebury	VT	G	802 989-7359	17351	Coca-Cola Bevs Northeast Inc	Presque Isle	ME	E	207 764-4481	5298
						Coca-Cola Bevs Northeast Inc	South Portland	ME	E	207 773-5505	5495

BEVERAGES, ALCOHOLIC: Near Beer

	CITY	ST	EMP	PHONE	ENTRY#
Thimble Island Brewing Company	Branford	CT	E	203 208-2827	282
Dorchester Beer Holdings LLC	Boston	MA	F	617 869-7092	6698

	CITY	ST	EMP	PHONE	ENTRY#
Farmington Coca Cola Btlg Dstr	Farmington	ME	F	207 778-4733	4779
Maine Beverage Association	South Portland	ME	F	207 773-5505	5507
Coca-Cola Beverages Northeast Inc **(HQ)**	Bedford	NH	E	603 627-7871	13922
Coca-Cola Bevs Northeast Inc	Belmont	NH	E	603 267-8834	13961
Coca-Cola Bevs Northeast Inc	Londonderry	NH	E	603 437-3530	14735
Coca-Cola Bevs Northeast Inc	Manchester	NH	E	603 623-6033	14833
Coca-Cola Bevs Northeast Inc	Seabrook	NH	E	603 926-0404	15587
Craft Beer Guild LLC	Portsmouth	NH	E	603 319-8508	15377
Monadnock Mountain Spring Water Inc	Wilton	NH	D	603 654-2728	15706
Surry Licensing LLC	Keene	NH	E	603 354-7000	14624
Coca-Cola Refreshments USA Inc	Providence	RI	D	401 331-1981	16501
Martignetti Companies RI	Central Falls	RI	C	401 722-8008	15792
Coca-Cola Btlg Sthstern Neng I	Rutland	VT	F	802 773-2768	17492
Pearl Street Beverage Inc	Burlington	VT	F	802 658-1574	17150
Rea Inc	Saint Albans	VT	F	802 527-7437	17530
Watson Wheeler Cider LLC **(PA)**	Shaftsbury	VT	G	435 602-9042	17554

BEVERAGES, ALCOHOLIC: Rum

	CITY	ST	EMP	PHONE	ENTRY#
Privateer International LLC	Ipswich	MA	G	978 356-0477	9495

BEVERAGES, ALCOHOLIC: Wines

	CITY	ST	EMP	PHONE	ENTRY#
Brooke Taylor Farm LLC **(PA)**	Woodstock	CT	G	860 974-1263	4391
Donelan Fmly Wine Cellars LLC	Ridgefield	CT	G	707 591-0782	2896
Hawk Ridge Winery LLC	Watertown	CT	G	860 274-7440	4015
Land of Nod Winery LLC	East Canaan	CT	G	860 824-5225	922
Sharpe Hill Vineyard Inc	Pomfret	CT	F	860 974-3549	2811
Stonington Vineyards Inc	Groton	CT	G	860 535-1222	1380
Sunset Meadow Farm LLC	Goshen	CT	F	860 201-4654	1304
Twelve Percent LLC	North Haven	CT	F	203 745-3983	2441
59 Beecher Street LLC	Southbridge	MA	G	631 734-6200	12007
Archer Roose Inc	Boston	MA	F	646 283-4152	6556
Cape Cod Winery Inc	Teaticket	MA	F	508 457-5592	12378
Davies Family Selections Inc	East Falmouth	MA	G	508 317-6024	8358
Grape Island Inc	Rowley	MA	G	978 432-1280	11675
Grove Street Enterprises Inc	Richmond	MA	F	413 698-3301	11626
Marthas Seastreak Vineyard LLC	New Bedford	MA	F	617 896-0293	10620
Nashoba Valley Spirits Limited	Bolton	MA	E	978 779-5521	6498
Oak Barrel Imports LLC	Beverly	MA	G	617 286-2524	6369
Phoenix Vintners LLC	Ipswich	MA	F	877 340-9869	9494
Punchpops LLC	Worcester	MA	G	508 344-7932	13775
Truro Vineyards Cape Cod LLC	North Truro	MA	F	508 487-6200	11051
Vineyard Brands	Brighton	MA	G	617 901-3597	7246
Vineyard Brands LLC	Natick	MA	F	508 653-5458	10500
Westport Rivers Inc	Westport	MA	F	508 636-3423	13300
Blue Lobster Wine Company	Portland	ME	F	207 671-1154	5189
Cellars	Bar Harbor	ME	G	207 288-3907	4522
Maine Craft Distilling LLC	Portland	ME	G	207 798-2528	5240
Sweetgrass Farm Winery & Dist	Portland	ME	G	207 761-8446	5278
Appolo Vineyards LLC	Derry	NH	G	603 421-6052	14189
Averill House Vineyard LLC	Brookline	NH	F	603 371-2296	14038
Flag Hill Distillery LLC	Lee	NH	F	603 659-2949	14705
Flag Hill Winery & Vinyrd LLC	Lee	NH	F	603 659-2949	14706
Lane Poverty Orchard	Lebanon	NH	G	603 448-1511	14692
Moonlight Meadery LLC	Londonderry	NH	F	603 216-2162	14774
Vineyard At Seven Birches LLC	Lincoln	NH	F	603 745-7550	14707
Vintners Cellar Winery	North Conway	NH	F	603 356-9463	15250
Zorvino Vineyards	Sandown	NH	F	603 887-8463	15581
Douglas Wine & Spirits Inc	North Providence	RI	F	401 353-6400	16299
Newport Vineyards & Winery LLC	Middletown	RI	E	401 848-5161	16182
Caledonia Spirits Inc	Montpelier	VT	E	802 472-8000	17370
Shacksbury Holdings Inc	Vergennes	VT	F	802 458-0530	17659
Snow Farm Winery	South Hero	VT	F	802 372-9463	17610

BEVERAGES, MALT

	CITY	ST	EMP	PHONE	ENTRY#
Cold Harbor Brewing Co LLC	Westborough	MA	F	508 768-5232	13090
Life Force Beverages LLC	Boston	MA	G	551 265-9482	6858

BEVERAGES, NONALCOHOLIC: Bottled & canned soft drinks

	CITY	ST	EMP	PHONE	ENTRY#
B & E Juices Inc	Bridgeport	CT	E	203 333-1802	299
Cell Nique	Weston	CT	G	888 417-9343	4148
Coca-Cola Bevs Northeast Inc	East Hartford	CT	E	860 895-5100	981
Coca-Cola Bevs Northeast Inc	South Windsor	CT	E	800 241-2653	3131
Coca-Cola Btlg Sthstern Neng I	East Hartford	CT	F	860 569-0037	982
Crystal Rock Spring Water Co	Watertown	CT	B	860 945-0661	4007
G & G Beverage Distributors	Yalesville	CT	E	203 949-6220	4397

BEVERAGES, NONALCOHOLIC: Carbonated

	CITY	ST	EMP	PHONE	ENTRY#
Pepsi Cola Bottling Co Bristol	Southington	CT	E	860 628-8200	3228
Pepsi-Cola Btlg Worcester Inc	Dayville	CT	E	860 774-4007	865
Pepsi Cola Metro Btlg Co Inc	Stratford	CT	E	203 375-2484	3566
Pepsi Cola Metro Btlg Co Inc	Uncasville	CT	E	860 848-1231	3743
Pepsi Cola Metro Btlg Co Inc	Windsor	CT	D	860 688-6281	4294
Pepsico	New Haven	CT	E	203 974-8912	2183
Pepsi-Cola Btlg Worcester Inc **(PA)**	Holden	MA	G	508 829-6551	9194
Pepsico	Boston	MA	G	857 233-2421	6963
Pepsi Cola Bottling Aroostook	Presque Isle	ME	F	207 760-3000	5309
Pepsi Cola Metro Btlg Co Inc	Hampden	ME	F	207 973-2217	4865
Pepsi Cola Metro Btlg Co Inc	Manchester	NH	D	603 625-5764	14911
Leader Dist Systems Inc	Brattleboro	VT	D	802 254-6093	17093
Pepsi Cola Bottling Co	Brattleboro	VT	F	802 254-6093	17099

BEVERAGES, NONALCOHOLIC: Carbonated, Canned & Bottled, Etc

	CITY	ST	EMP	PHONE	ENTRY#
Als Beverage Company Inc	East Windsor	CT	E	860 627-7003	1065
Castle Beverages Inc	Ansonia	CT	G	203 732-0883	9
Miami Bay Beverage Company LLC	Guilford	CT	F	203 453-0090	1400
New England Beverages LLC	Branford	CT	E	203 208-4517	273
Epic Enterprises Inc	Ayer	MA	D	978 772-2340	6182
Keurig Green Mountain Inc	Burlington	MA	D	781 246-3466	7385
Mercury Brewing & Dist Co Inc	Ipswich	MA	F	978 356-3329	9490
Refresco Beverages US Inc	East Freetown	MA	F	508 763-3515	8366

BEVERAGES, NONALCOHOLIC: Cider

	CITY	ST	EMP	PHONE	ENTRY#
Lyman Farm Incorporated **(PA)**	Middlefield	CT	C	860 349-1793	1725
Lane Poverty Orchard	Lebanon	NH	G	603 448-1511	14692

BEVERAGES, NONALCOHOLIC: Flavoring extracts & syrups, nec

	CITY	ST	EMP	PHONE	ENTRY#
American Distilling Inc **(PA)**	East Hampton	CT	D	860 267-4444	959
Brookside Flvors Ingrdents LLC **(HQ)**	Stamford	CT	G	203 595-4520	3297
Carrubba Incorporated	Monroe	CT	D	203 878-0605	1908
Herbasway Laboratories LLC	Wallingford	CT	F	203 269-6991	3812
Osf Flavors Inc **(PA)**	Windsor	CT	F	860 298-8350	4293
Watson LLC **(DH)**	West Haven	CT	E	203 932-3000	4132
Ballhaus Bev Co LLC	Medford	MA	G	828 302-5837	10281
Brighams Inc **(HQ)**	Arlington	MA	F	800 242-2423	5939
Drink Maple Inc	Sudbury	MA	F	978 610-6408	12266
Northice	Plymouth	MA	F	781 985-5225	11469
Rohtstein Corp **(PA)**	Woburn	MA	F	781 935-8300	13655
B&G Foods Inc	Portland	ME	F	207 772-8341	5180
FMC Corporation	Rockland	ME	D	207 594-3200	5329
Dutch Gold Honey Inc	Littleton	NH	F	603 444-6246	14717
Sunrise Foods Incorporated	Brentwood	NH	F	603 772-4420	14031

	CITY	ST	EMP	PHONE	ENTRY#
Fountain Dispensers Co Inc	Providence	RI	G	401 461-8400	16520
R I Fruit Syrup Co	Smithfield	RI	G	401 231-0040	16728
Maple Grove Farms Vermont Inc (HQ)	Saint Johnsbury	VT	D	802 748-5141	17543
Runamok Maple LLC	Fairfax	VT	E	802 849-7943	17263

BEVERAGES, NONALCOHOLIC: Fruit Drnks, Under 100% Juice, Can

	CITY	ST	EMP	PHONE	ENTRY#
Harvest Hill Holdings LLC (PA)	Stamford	CT	F	203 914-1620	3367
Dunajski Dairy Inc	Peabody	MA	G	978 531-1457	11308
Veryfine Products Inc (DH)	Littleton	MA	D	978 486-0812	9842

BEVERAGES, NONALCOHOLIC: Soft Drinks, Canned & Bottled, Etc

	CITY	ST	EMP	PHONE	ENTRY#
Coca-Cola Bottling Company of Southeastern New England Inc (DH) 860 443-2816	Hartford	CT	F		3987
Foxon Park Beverages Inc	East Haven	CT	G	203 467-7874	1042
Light Rock Spring Water Co	Danbury	CT	F	203 743-2251	771
Reeds Inc	Norwalk	CT	E	800 997-3337	2563
Adirondack Beverages Corp	Worcester	MA	F	800 734-9800	13697
Coca Cola Btlg Co of Cape Cod	Sandwich	MA	D	508 888-0001	11748
Ginseng Up Corporation	Worcester	MA	G	508 799-6178	13732
Ginseng Up Corporation (PA)	Worcester	MA	G	508 799-6178	13733
Polar Corp (PA)	Worcester	MA	A	508 753-6383	13772
Dr Pepper Bottling Co Portland	Portland	ME	F	207 773-4258	5211
Pepsi-Cola Metro Btlg Co Inc	Auburn	ME	E	207 784-5791	4452
Pepsi-Cola Metro Btlg Co Inc	Cranston	RI	C	401 468-3300	15904
Aqua Vitea LLC	Middlebury	VT	F	802 453-8590	17336
Keurig Dr Pepper Inc	Essex Junction	VT	F	802 288-6022	17238

BEVERAGES, NONALCOHOLIC: Tea, Iced, Bottled & Canned, Etc

	CITY	ST	EMP	PHONE	ENTRY#
Northeast Hot-Fill Co-Op Inc	Ayer	MA	E	978 772-9287	6189

BEVERAGES, WINE & DISTILLED ALCOHOLIC, WHOLESALE: Liquor

	CITY	ST	EMP	PHONE	ENTRY#
Martignetti Companies RI	Central Falls	RI	C	401 722-8008	15792

BEVERAGES, WINE & DISTILLED ALCOHOLIC, WHOLESALE: Wine

	CITY	ST	EMP	PHONE	ENTRY#
Truro Vineyards Cape Cod LLC	North Truro	MA	F	508 487-6200	11051
Johnson Brothers RI Inc	North Kingstown	RI	E	401 583-0050	16262
Sakonnet Vineyards LP	Little Compton	RI	F	401 635-8486	16162

BICYCLES WHOLESALERS

	CITY	ST	EMP	PHONE	ENTRY#
CMI Restructuring Inc	Westfield	MA	D	413 562-3664	13160
Montague Corporation	Cambridge	MA	F	617 491-7200	7655

BICYCLES, PARTS & ACCESS

	CITY	ST	EMP	PHONE	ENTRY#
Cycling Sports Group Inc (HQ)	Wilton	CT	D	203 845-8300	4238
Mystic Valley Wheel Works Inc (PA)	Belmont	MA	E	617 489-3577	6308
Parlee Composites Inc	Beverly	MA	F	978 998-4880	6371

BILLING & BOOKKEEPING SVCS

	CITY	ST	EMP	PHONE	ENTRY#
Numeric Inc	Westfield	MA	F	413 732-6544	13195
Verizon New York Inc	Winchester	MA	F	781 721-5957	13493
Anodyne Health Partners Inc (HQ)	Falmouth	ME	E	207 347-7400	4767
Outer Limits Publishing LLC	Killington	VT	F	802 422-2399	17313

BINDING SVC: Books & Manuals

	CITY	ST	EMP	PHONE	ENTRY#
Adkins Printing Company	New Britain	CT	F	800 228-9745	1997
Allied Printing Services Inc (PA)	Manchester	CT	B	860 643-1101	1584
Chapin Packaging LLC	Darien	CT	G	203 202-2747	846
E R Hitchcock Company	New Britain	CT	E	860 229-2024	2024
Elm Press Incorporated	Terryville	CT	E	860 583-3600	3601
Imperial Grphic Cmmnctions Inc	Milford	CT	E	203 650-3478	1837
Joseph Merritt & Company Inc	Danbury	CT	G	203 743-6734	762
Kool Ink LLC	Bloomfield	CT	E	860 242-0303	186
Leejay Industries LLC	Norwalk	CT	E	203 847-3660	2526
Norwich Printing Company Inc	Norwich	CT	F	860 887-7468	2611
Paul Dewitt	Danbury	CT	G	203 792-5610	795
Phoenix Press Inc	New Haven	CT	E	203 865-5555	2186
Richard E Personette	Middletown	CT	F	860 344-9001	1778
Tech-Repro Inc	Stamford	CT	F	203 348-8884	3478
Universal Printing Svcs Inc	West Haven	CT	E	203 934-4275	4131
American Prtg & Envelope Inc	Auburn	MA	E	508 832-6100	6102
Andrew T Johnson Company Inc (PA)	Boston	MA	F	617 742-1610	6548
Belmont Printing Company	Belmont	MA	E	617 484-0833	6304
Copy Cop The Digital Printing Company LLC 617 267-8899	Boston	MA			6669
Copy Masters Inc	Taunton	MA	F	508 824-7187	12329
Courier Westford Inc	Westford	MA	B	978 251-6482	13232
D & L Associates Inc	Needham Heights	MA	G	781 400-5068	10540
D S Graphics Inc (PA)	Lowell	MA	C	978 970-1359	9873
Datasite Global Corporation	Everett	MA	B	617 389-7900	8486
Dmr Print Inc (PA)	Concord	MA	E	617 876-3688	8114
Elbonais Incorporated	Framingham	MA	G	508 626-2318	8761
Excelsior Printing Company	North Adams	MA	D	413 663-3771	10807

	CITY	ST	EMP	PHONE	ENTRY#
Flagship Press Inc	North Andover	MA	C	978 975-3100	10831
Generation Four Inc	Waltham	MA	G	781 899-3180	12686
Ghp Media Inc	North Adams	MA	D	413 663-3771	10808
Graphic Fullfillment & Finishing Inc	Holbrook	MA	G	781 727-8845	9173
Hf Group LLC	Billerica	MA	C	617 242-1100	6449
J T Gardner Inc (PA)	Westborough	MA	E	800 540-4993	13112
Keating Communication Group	Canton	MA	G	781 828-9030	7804
Kirkwood Holdings Inc (PA)	Wilmington	MA	B	978 658-4200	13420
Laplume & Sons Printing Inc	Lawrence	MA	F	978 683-1009	9576
Linmel Associates Inc	Marlborough	MA	F	508 481-6699	10180
LPI Printing and Graphic Inc	Stoneham	MA	F	781 438-5400	12182
Marcus Company Inc	Holyoke	MA	E	413 534-3303	9265
Massachusetts Repro Ltd	Boston	MA	F	617 227-2237	6876
Miles Press Inc	Auburn	MA	F	508 752-6430	6120
Minute-Man Printing Corp	Concord	MA	F	978 369-2808	8125
Modus Media Inc	Waltham	MA	B	781 663-5000	12724
Paiva Corp	Fall River	MA	G	508 679-7921	8593
Picken Printing Inc	North Chelmsford	MA	F	978 251-0730	10986
Pyramid Printing and Advg Inc	Weymouth	MA	E	781 337-7609	13333
R & H Communications Inc (PA)	Waltham	MA	F	781 893-6221	12757
Sherman Printing Co Inc	Canton	MA	E	781 828-8855	7828
Universal Wilde Inc	Canton	MA	C	978 658-0800	7838
Winthrop Printing Company Inc	Foxboro	MA	E	617 268-9660	8732
Yankee Printing Group Inc	South Hadley	MA	F	413 532-9513	11968
Davic Inc	Portland	ME	G	207 774-0093	5206
Geiger Bros (PA)	Lewiston	ME	B	207 755-2000	4962
Penmor Lithographers Inc	Lewiston	ME	F	207 784-1341	4984
The Dingley Press Inc (PA)	Lisbon	ME	C	207 353-1500	5018
Cdc Enterprises Llc	Windham	NH	G	603 437-3090	15722
Cygnus Inc	Portsmouth	NH	G	603 431-8989	15379
Fedex Office & Print Svcs Inc	Bedford	NH	F	603 644-2679	13929
Higgingbotham Management Corp	Portsmouth	NH	F	603 431-0142	15402
RB Graphics Inc	Hooksett	NH	G	603 624-4025	14473
A & H Composition and Prtg Inc	East Providence	RI	G	401 438-1200	15999
Branch Graphics Inc	Rumford	RI	F	401 861-1830	16663
Dome Enterprises Trust (PA)	Warwick	RI	G	401 738-7900	16807
Darwin A Lewis Inc	Hartland	VT	G	802 457-4521	17286
L Brown and Sons Printing Inc	Barre	VT	E	802 476-3164	17012
Queen City Printers Inc	Burlington	VT	E	802 864-4566	17153
Villanti & Sons Printers Inc	Milton	VT	D	802 864-0723	17367

BINDINGS: Bias, Made From Purchased Materials

	CITY	ST	EMP	PHONE	ENTRY#
A B E Enterprises LLC	Bedford	MA	D	781 271-0000	6204
Brand & Oppenheimer Co Inc	Bedford	MA	E	781 271-0000	6216
Color-Tex International Inc	Boston	MA	C	617 269-8020	6663
Tranztape LLC	Appleton	ME	G	207 785-2467	4406

BINOCULARS

	CITY	ST	EMP	PHONE	ENTRY#
Tower Optical Company Inc	Norwalk	CT	G	203 866-4535	2586
S I Howard Glass Company Inc	Worcester	MA	E	508 753-8146	13785

BIOLOGICAL PRDTS: Exc Diagnostic

	CITY	ST	EMP	PHONE	ENTRY#
Avian Vaccine Services LLC (PA)	Norwich	CT	D	860 889-1389	2602
Axiomx Inc	Branford	CT	E	203 208-1034	239
Biomx Inc	Branford	CT	C	203 408-3915	240
Coopersurgical Inc	Guilford	CT	E	203 453-1700	1390
Gilead Sciences Inc	Branford	CT	G	203 315-1222	261
Green Valley Packaging Inc	Danielson	CT	G	860 779-7970	839
Intensity Therapeutics Inc	Shelton	CT	F	203 221-7381	3023
3-D Matrix Inc (HQ)	Newton	MA	G	781 373-9020	10730
3dm Inc	Cambridge	MA	G	617 875-6204	7463
Acceleron Holding Ltd	Boston	MA	G	617 649-9200	6507
Acceleron Pharma Inc (HQ)	Boston	MA	D	617 649-9200	6508
ACS Division Biochemical Tech	Boston	MA	E	617 216-6144	6512
Agenus Inc (PA)	Lexington	MA	C	781 674-4400	9721
Allovir Inc (PA)	Waltham	MA	F	617 433-2605	12591
Ariad Pharmaceuticals Inc	Cambridge	MA	B		7490
Aura Biosciences Inc (PA)	Boston	MA		617 500-8864	6577
Axcella Health Inc (PA)	Cambridge	MA	G	857 320-2200	7496
Beam Therapeutics Inc (PA)	Cambridge	MA	D	857 327-8775	7500
Biogen Inc (PA)	Cambridge	MA	G	617 679-2000	7511
Biogen MA Inc	Cambridge	MA	D	781 464-2000	7513
Biogen MA Inc (HQ)	Cambridge	MA	G	617 679-2000	7514
Biohelix Corporation	Beverly	MA	F	978 927-5056	6333
Biontech US Inc (HQ)	Cambridge	MA	F	617 337-4701	7515
Biose Industrie	Woburn	MA	F	617 460-1842	13525
Black Diamond Therapeutics Inc (PA)	Cambridge	MA	F	617 252-0848	7517
Bluebird Bio Inc (PA)	Somerville	MA	A	339 499-9300	11864
C4 Therapeutics Inc (PA)	Watertown	MA	E	617 231-0700	12866
Captivate Bio LLC	Watertown	MA	G	617 607-4017	12867
Cellaria Biosciences LLC	Boxford	MA	G	617 981-4208	7158
Checkmate Pharmaceuticals Inc	Cambridge	MA	E	617 682-3625	7539

Employee Codes: A=Over 500 employees, B=251-500
C=101-250, D=51-100, E=20-50, F=10-19, G=1-9

2024 Harris New England
Manufacturers Directory

PRODUCT

1347

	CITY	ST	EMP	PHONE	ENTRY#
Codiak Biosciences Inc (PA)	Cambridge	MA	E	617 949-4100	7542
Compass Therapeutics Inc (PA)	Brighton	MA	G	617 500-8099	7239
Corium LLC	Boston	MA	C	855 253-2407	6672
Cullinan Oncology Inc (PA)	Cambridge	MA	F	617 410-4650	7546
Curia Global Inc	Burlington	MA	G	781 205-1691	7357
Diagnosys LLC (PA)	Lowell	MA	E	978 458-1600	9875
Dicerna Pharmaceuticals Inc (HQ)	Lexington	MA	C	617 621-8097	9739
Diversified Biotech Inc	Dedham	MA	F	781 326-6709	8242
Editas Medicine Inc (PA)	Cambridge	MA	C	617 401-9000	7555
Elevatebio LLC (PA)	Cambridge	MA	E	413 297-7151	7559
Finch Therapeutics Group Inc	Somerville	MA	C	617 229-6499	11873
Forma Thrapeutics Holdings Inc (HQ)	Watertown	MA	F	617 679-1970	12878
Fresenius Usa Inc (DH)	Waltham	MA	C	781 699-4191	12683
Genocea Biosciences Inc (PA)	Cambridge	MA	E	617 876-8191	7582
Genzyme Corporation (DH)	Cambridge	MA	A	617 252-7500	7585
Genzyme Corporation	Framingham	MA	E	617 252-7500	8773
Ginkgo Bioworks Inc (HQ)	Boston	MA	B	877 422-5362	6761
Ginkgo Bioworks Inc	Cambridge	MA	F	617 633-7972	7591
Ginkgo Bioworks Holdings Inc (PA)	Boston	MA	D	877 422-5362	6762
Greenlght Bscnces Holdings Pbc (PA)	Medford	MA	F	617 616-8188	10287
Hillevax Inc	Boston	MA	D	617 213-5054	6787
Ikena Oncology Inc (PA)	Boston	MA	E	857 273-8343	6806
Iteos Therapeutics Inc (PA)	Watertown	MA	F	339 217-0161	12883
Jounce Therapeutics Inc (PA)	Cambridge	MA	D	857 259-3840	7620
Joyn Bio LLC	Boston	MA	E	978 549-3723	6832
Kaleido Biosciences Inc (PA)	Lexington	MA	D	617 674-9000	9755
Kymera Therapeutics Inc (PA)	Watertown	MA	E	857 285-5300	12885
Lariat Biosciences Inc	Chelsea	MA	G	603 244-9657	7985
Logicbio Therapeutics Inc	Lexington	MA	D	617 245-0399	9759
Moderna Inc (PA)	Cambridge	MA	B	617 714-6500	7653
Monte Rosa Therapeutics Inc (PA)	Boston	MA	D	617 949-2643	6895
Neumora Therapeutics Inc (PA)	Watertown	MA	D	857 760-0900	12896
Organogenesis Inc (HQ)	Canton	MA	C	781 575-0775	7815
Pillar Biosciences Inc	Natick	MA	D	781 856-5568	10492
Project Plasma Holdings Corp	Milford	MA	E	508 244-6400	10415
Protagene Us Inc	Burlington	MA	E	857 829-3200	7414
Puretech Health LLC (HQ)	Boston	MA	D	617 482-2333	6984
Pyxis Oncology Inc (PA)	Boston	MA	E	617 221-9059	6987
Qiagen Beverly LLC	Beverly	MA	D	978 927-7027	6373
Relay Therapeutics Inc (PA)	Cambridge	MA	D	617 670-8837	7695
Repligen Corporation	Marlborough	MA	E	508 845-6400	10202
Repligen Corporation (PA)	Waltham	MA	C	781 250-0111	12765
Replimune Group Inc (PA)	Woburn	MA	F	781 222-9600	13649
Revbio Inc	Lowell	MA	F	617 460-6675	9918
Safc Biosciences Inc	Burlington	MA	F	978 715-1700	7420
Scholar Rock Holding Corp (PA)	Cambridge	MA	F	857 259-3860	7708
Seqirus Inc	Waltham	MA	B	617 871-5734	12778
Sigma Research Biochemicals	Natick	MA	G	781 237-3828	10497
Solid Biosciences Inc (PA)	Charlestown	MA	E	617 337-4680	7883
Sqz Biotechnologies Company (PA)	Watertown	MA	E	617 758-8672	12909
Synageva Biopharma Corp	Lexington	MA	B	781 357-9900	9778
Tcr2 Therapeutics Inc (HQ)	Cambridge	MA	D	617 949-5200	7735
Tscan Therapeutics Inc	Waltham	MA	D	857 399-9500	12807
Twentyfrst Cntury Bchmcals Inc	Marlborough	MA	E	508 303-8222	10225
Vericel Corporation (PA)	Cambridge	MA	B	617 588-5555	7752
Vor Biopharma Inc (PA)	Cambridge	MA	C	617 655-6580	7757
Voyager Therapeutics Inc (PA)	Lexington	MA	D	570 329-6851	9791
X4 Pharmaceuticals Inc (PA)	Boston	MA	D	857 529-8300	7135
Xcellerex Inc	Marlborough	MA	D	508 480-9235	10237
Zea Biosciences Corp	Walpole	MA	E	508 921-3280	12579
Kennebec River Biosciences Inc	Richmond	ME	F	207 737-2637	5322
Lohmann Animal Health Intl Inc	Winslow	ME	C	207 873-3989	5683
Avitide Inc	Lebanon	NH	E	603 965-2100	14683
Lyophilization Svcs Neng Inc	Bedford	NH	E	603 668-5763	13940
Lyophilization Svcs Neng Inc	Bedford	NH	E	603 626-9559	13941
Lyophilization Svcs Neng Inc	Bedford	NH	E	603 626-5763	13942
Lyophilization Svcs Neng Inc	Bedford	NH	E	603 668-5763	13943
Lyophilization Svcs Neng Inc (HQ)	Manchester	NH	E	603 626-5763	14877
Amgen Inc	West Greenwich	RI	D	401 392-1200	16882
Population Media Center Inc	South Burlington	VT	E	802 985-8156	17595

BIOLOGICAL PRDTS: Serums

	CITY	ST	EMP	PHONE	ENTRY#
Skin & Co North America LLC	West Haven	CT	G	888 444-9971	4126
Standard Merger Sub LLC	Windham	ME	D	207 856-6151	5670

BIOLOGICAL PRDTS: Vaccines

	CITY	ST	EMP	PHONE	ENTRY#
Affinivax Inc	Cambridge	MA	C	617 465-0865	7469
Biobohemia Inc	Cambridge	MA	E	617 958-7900	7508
ID Bimedical Corp Northborough	Northborough	MA	E	508 351-9333	11099
Massbiologics	Boston	MA	C	617 474-3000	6877
Tetragenetics Inc	Arlington	MA	F	617 500-7471	5949
Vbi Vaccines Inc (PA)	Cambridge	MA	G	617 830-3031	7750

	CITY	ST	EMP	PHONE	ENTRY#
Epivax Inc	Providence	RI	E	401 272-2123	16515

BIOLOGICAL PRDTS: Vaccines & Immunizing

	CITY	ST	EMP	PHONE	ENTRY#
Realhub Inc	Darien	CT	F	650 461-9210	854

BIOLOGICAL PRDTS: Veterinary

	CITY	ST	EMP	PHONE	ENTRY#
Bactana Corp	Farmington	CT	G	203 716-1230	1208
Launchworks LLC	Beverly	MA	E	978 338-3045	6361

BLADES: Knife

	CITY	ST	EMP	PHONE	ENTRY#
Zootility Co	Portland	ME	F	207 536-0639	5293
Colonial Cutlery Intl Inc	North Kingstown	RI	E	401 737-0024	16238

BLADES: Saw, Hand Or Power

	CITY	ST	EMP	PHONE	ENTRY#
Blackstone Industries LLC	Bethel	CT	D	203 792-8622	101
Disston Company	Chicopee	MA	E	800 272-4436	8025
LS Starrett Company (PA)	Athol	MA	A	978 249-3551	5981
Malco Saw Co Inc	Cranston	RI	G	401 942-7380	15891

BLANKBOOKS & LOOSELEAF BINDERS

	CITY	ST	EMP	PHONE	ENTRY#
Atlantic Bookbinders Inc	South Lancaster	MA	G	978 365-4524	11970
Nettwerk Music Group LLC	Cambridge	MA	E	617 497-8200	7662
W G Fry Corp	Florence	MA	E	413 747-2551	8687
Geiger Bros (PA)	Lewiston	ME	B	207 755-2000	4962

BLANKBOOKS: Albums, Record

	CITY	ST	EMP	PHONE	ENTRY#
Yolanda Dubose Records and	West Haven	CT	F	203 823-6699	4134

BLANKETS & BLANKETING, COTTON

	CITY	ST	EMP	PHONE	ENTRY#
Maine Woolens LLC	Brunswick	ME	E	207 725-7900	4649

BLASTING SVC: Sand, Metal Parts

	CITY	ST	EMP	PHONE	ENTRY#
Logan Steel Inc (PA)	Meriden	CT	E	203 235-0811	1672
Cryogenic Institute Neng Inc	Worcester	MA	F	508 459-7447	13712
Finish Solutions LLC	Saint Albans	VT	G	802 540-0326	17522

BLINDS & SHADES: Mini

	CITY	ST	EMP	PHONE	ENTRY#
Vertical & Mini Blind Factory	Agawam	MA	G	413 789-2343	5815
Kenney Manufacturing Company (PA)	Warwick	RI	B	401 739-2200	16831

BLINDS & SHADES: Vertical

	CITY	ST	EMP	PHONE	ENTRY#
Decorator Services Inc	Bridgeport	CT	G	203 384-8144	315
Vertical Retail Solutions LLC	Andover	CT	A	860 742-6464	3
Landmark Window Fashions Inc	Holbrook	MA	E	781 767-3535	9177
Gordons Window Decor Inc (PA)	Williston	VT	F	802 655-7777	17734

BLINDS : Window

	CITY	ST	EMP	PHONE	ENTRY#
Roto-Frank of America Inc	Chester	CT	C	860 526-4996	631
TLC Vision (usa) Corporation	Peabody	MA	E	978 531-4114	11348
Blind Pig Tavern	Gardiner	ME	G	207 592-0776	4812
Mums Cheesecake	York	ME	G	207 351-8543	5714
Blind Tiger LLP	Exeter	NH	G	603 498-7005	14286

BLOCKS & BRICKS: Concrete

	CITY	ST	EMP	PHONE	ENTRY#
Lda Construction LLC	East Haven	CT	F	203 469-3180	1044
Ideal Concrete Block Co	Waltham	MA	E	781 894-3200	12694
Stiles & Hart Brick Company	Bridgewater	MA	E	508 697-6928	7238
Cs-Ma Inc	Newport	NH	F	603 863-1000	15227

BLOCKS: Landscape Or Retaining Wall, Concrete

	CITY	ST	EMP	PHONE	ENTRY#
Roberts Ldscp Design & Cnstr	Barnstable	MA	F	508 364-4878	6201

BLOCKS: Paving

	CITY	ST	EMP	PHONE	ENTRY#
Shaw Brothers Construction Inc (PA)	Gorham	ME	C	207 839-2552	4835

BLOCKS: Paving, Concrete

	CITY	ST	EMP	PHONE	ENTRY#
Laydon Industries LLC (PA)	New Haven	CT	E	203 562-7283	2169
Crystal Brook Ldscp Cnstr Inc	Springfield	MA	F	413 596-0055	12087

BLOCKS: Paving, Cut Stone

	CITY	ST	EMP	PHONE	ENTRY#
Connecticut Stone Supplies Inc (PA)	Milford	CT	D	203 882-1000	1814

BLOCKS: Standard, Concrete Or Cinder

	CITY	ST	EMP	PHONE	ENTRY#
Connecticut Concrete Form Inc	Farmington	CT	F	860 674-1314	1213
Cromwell Concrete Products Incorporated 690	Cromwell	CT	E		
Kobyluck Ready-Mix Inc	Waterford	CT	F	860 444-9604	3991
Westbrook Con Block Co Inc	Westbrook	CT	E	860 399-6201	4146
Adolf Jandris & Sons Inc	Gardner	MA	E	978 632-0089	8878
Connecticut Valley Block Co Inc	West Springfield	MA	E		13018
Hi-Way Concrete Pdts Co Inc	Wareham	MA	F	508 295-0834	12837
Ideal Concrete Block Co (PA)	Westford	MA	F	978 692-3076	13242

	CITY	ST	EMP	PHONE	ENTRY#
Johns Building Supply Co Inc	Pittsfield	MA	F	413 442-7846	11403
Medway Block Co Inc	Medway	MA	E	508 533-6701	10307
Oldcastle Apg Northeast Inc	Holbrook	MA	D	781 506-9473	9183
P & M Brick & Block Inc	Watertown	MA	G	617 924-6020	12898
R Ducharme Inc	Chicopee	MA	F	413 534-4516	8057
State Road Cement Block Co Inc	North Dartmouth	MA	G	508 993-9473	11002
Gagne & Son Con Blocks Inc	Auburn	ME	G	207 495-3313	4435
Gagne & Son Concrete Blocks Inc (PA)	Belgrade	ME	G	207 495-3313	4539
Tilcon Arthur Whitcomb Inc (HQ)	North Swanzey	NH	F	603 352-0101	15256
Anchor Concrete	Cranston	RI	F	401 942-4800	15833

BLOWERS & FANS

	CITY	ST	EMP	PHONE	ENTRY#
Atlantic Vent & Eqp Co Inc	Cromwell	CT	E	860 635-1300	687
EBM-Papst Inc (DH)	Farmington	CT	B	860 674-1515	1217
Environmental Systems Products Inc	East Granby	CT	C	860 653-0081	933
Planet Biopharmaceuticals Inc	Ridgefield	CT	G	800 255-3749	2904
Stylair LLC	Plainville	CT	F	860 747-4588	2781
Bmac Inc	Ayer	MA	E	978 772-3310	6175
Heat Fab Inc	Turners Falls	MA	F	413 863-2242	12447
Impolit Envmtl Ctrl Corp	Beverly	MA	E	978 927-4304	6356
Manchester Corporation	Harvard	MA	E	978 772-2900	9065
Munters Corporation (DH)	Amesbury	MA	C	978 241-1100	5845
Pall Northborough (DH)	Northborough	MA	D	978 263-9888	11105
Parker-Hannifin Corporation	Haverhill	MA	F	978 858-0505	9120
Riley Power Inc	Marlborough	MA	B	508 852-7100	10204
Spruce Environmental Tech Inc	Haverhill	MA	F	978 521-0901	9134
N E Tech-Air Inc	Scarborough	ME	C	207 347-7577	5439
Parker-Hannifin Corporation	Kittery	ME	D	207 439-9511	4938
Brailsford & Company Inc	Antrim	NH	F	603 588-2880	13896
Electrocraft New Hampshire Inc (DH)	Dover	NH	E	603 742-3333	14228
McIntire Company (HQ)	Bristol	CT	F	860 585-8559	465
Jarvis Welding & Mfg Co	Turners Falls	MA	G	413 863-9541	12449

BLOWERS, TURBO: Indl

	CITY	ST	EMP	PHONE	ENTRY#
Howden Roots LLC	Windsor	CT	D	860 688-8361	4281
Mechancal Engnered Systems LLC	New Canaan	CT	G	203 400-4658	2083
Spencer Turbine Company (DH)	Windsor	CT	E	860 688-8361	4301

BLUEPRINTING SVCS

	CITY	ST	EMP	PHONE	ENTRY#
Bpi Reprographics	Norwalk	CT	F	203 866-5600	2475
Technical Reproductions Inc	Norwalk	CT	F	203 849-9100	2575
Andrew T Johnson Company Inc (PA)	Boston	MA	F	617 742-1610	6548
Weston Corporation	Hingham	MA	E	781 749-0936	9164
Central Street Corporation	Bangor	ME	F	207 947-8049	4495
Copy Center (PA)	Winthrop	ME	F	207 623-1452	5691
RB Graphics Inc	Hooksett	NH	G	603 624-4025	14473

BOAT BUILDING & REPAIR

	CITY	ST	EMP	PHONE	ENTRY#
Casavant Corporation	Burlington	CT	G	860 605-5937	546
Dodson Boatyard LLC	Stonington	CT	E	860 535-1507	3508
Allen Harbor Marine Svc Inc	Harwich Port	MA	E	508 432-0353	9070
Bctz Ltd	Lexington	MA	F	781 863-0405	9727
Concordia Co Inc	South Dartmouth	MA	E	508 999-1381	11916
Crosby Yacht Yard Inc	Osterville	MA	E	508 428-6900	11245
Falmouth Mar Yachting Ctr Inc	Falmouth	MA	F	508 548-4600	8631
Inriver Tank & Boat Inc	Concord	MA	F	978 287-9534	8121
Karls Boat Shop Inc	Harwich	MA	G	508 432-4488	9069
Marine Usa Inc	Worcester	MA	F	508 791-7116	13757
Montreal Fishing Corp	New Bedford	MA	F	508 993-0275	10623
Nauset Marine Inc (PA)	Orleans	MA	E	508 255-0777	11240
Northern Light Mar Group Inc	Manchester	MA	E	978 526-7911	10033
P B Y A Inc	South Orleans	MA	G	508 255-0994	11973
Ribcraft Usa LLC	Marblehead	MA	E	781 639-9065	10094
Sperry Sails Inc	Marion	MA	F	508 748-2581	10101
Alley Road LLC	Boothbay Harbor	ME	F	207 633-3171	4600
Belmont Boatworks LLC	Belmont	ME	F	207 342-2885	4542
Dana Robes Boat Builders	Round Pond	ME	F	207 529-2433	5352
Dark Harbor Boatyard Corp	Islesboro	ME	F	207 734-2246	4908
Ebw Windup	Edgecomb	ME	G	207 882-5038	4747
Ellis Boat Co Inc	Southwest Harbor	ME	F	207 244-9221	5518
Flowers Boat Works Inc	Walpole	ME	G	207 563-7404	5581
French Webb & Co Inc	Belfast	ME	F	207 338-6706	4533
Gowen Inc	Portland	ME	F	207 773-1761	5219
Greene Marine Inc	Yarmouth	ME	F	207 846-3184	5705
Hodgdon Shipbuilding LLC	Damariscotta	ME	D	207 563-7033	4715
J O Brown & Son Inc	North Haven	ME	F	207 867-4621	5114
James H Rich Boatyard	Bernard	ME	F	207 244-3208	4548
Johansons Boatworks	Rockland	ME	F	207 596-7060	5335
Lyman Morse Boatbuilding Inc	Thomaston	ME	F	207 354-6904	5545
Mastercraft Inc	Skowhegan	ME	F	207 431-2056	5473
My Ease Inc	Trenton	ME	F	207 667-8237	5557
Padebco Custom Boats	Round Pond	ME	G	207 529-5106	5354

	CITY	ST	EMP	PHONE	ENTRY#
Portland Company	Portland	ME	E	207 774-1067	5257
Seaway Boats Inc	Oxford	ME	F	207 539-8116	5150
Talaria Company LLC	Trenton	ME	D	207 667-1891	5558
Washburn & Doughty Assoc Inc	East Boothbay	ME	D	207 633-6517	4737
Wesmac Custom Boats Inc	Surry	ME	F	207 667-4822	5540
American Marine Products Inc	Charlestown	NH	E	954 782-1400	14060
Juliet Marine Systems Inc	Portsmouth	NH	G	603 319-8412	15413
Liberty Cycle LLC	Deering	NH	G	603 620-1851	14188
New England Boat & Motor Inc	Laconia	NH	G	603 527-9435	14660
Pompanette LLC (PA)	Charlestown	NH	D	717 569-2300	14067
Special Projects Group LLC	Gilford	NH	G	603 391-9700	14338
Viking Wldg & Fabrication LLC	Kensington	NH	G	603 394-7887	14631
Berthon Usa Inc	Newport	RI	F	401 846-8404	16206
C & C Fibrgls Components Inc	Bristol	RI	F	401 254-4342	15757
Clean Away Inc	East Greenwich	RI	F	860 985-6743	15979
Cove Haven Corp	Barrington	RI	F	401 246-1600	15747
Dur A Flex Motor Sports	Warwick	RI	G	401 739-0202	16811
Fairhaven Marine Corporation	Riverside	RI	F	401 433-3010	16654
Gunboat	Newport	RI	F	401 619-1055	16211
Hall Inc	Bristol	RI	F	401 253-4858	15768
Mc Millen Yachts	Portsmouth	RI	F	401 682-2610	16446
Morris Yachts LLC	Portsmouth	RI	G	207 667-2499	16448
New England Boatworks Inc	Portsmouth	RI	D	401 683-4000	16449
Resolute Racing LLC	Bristol	RI	F	401 253-7384	15778
Rhode Northsales Island Inc	Portsmouth	RI	F	401 683-7997	16455
Seamless North America	Bristol	RI	G	401 714-2925	15780
Squirrel Works LLC	Portsmouth	RI	E	401 247-3000	16457
Talaria Company LLC (PA)	Portsmouth	RI	F	401 683-7100	16458
Talaria Company LLC	Portsmouth	RI	D	401 683-7280	16459
Darlings Boatworks Inc	Charlotte	VT	G	802 425-2004	17176

BOAT BUILDING & REPAIRING: Fiberglass

	CITY	ST	EMP	PHONE	ENTRY#
B I L Inc	Groton	CT	F	860 446-8058	1365
Chester Boatworks	Deep River	CT	G	860 526-2227	874
Vespoli Usa Inc	New Haven	CT	F	203 773-0311	2215
Beetle Inc	Wareham	MA	G	508 295-8585	12829
Boston Boatworks LLC	Charlestown	MA	E	617 561-9111	7862
Marshall Marine Corporation	South Dartmouth	MA	F	508 994-0414	11917
Crossfox Inc	Brooklin	ME	F	207 664-2900	4633
John M Williams Company	Mount Desert	ME	F	207 244-7854	5077
North End Composites LLC	Rockland	ME	C	207 594-8427	5340
SW Boatworks	Lamoine	ME	F	207 667-7427	4944
Eastern Boats Inc	Milton	NH	E	603 652-9213	15045
Anchorage Inc	Warren	RI	F	401 245-3300	16750
Blount Boats Inc	Warren	RI	D	401 245-8300	16754
Element Industries Inc	Bristol	RI	F	401 253-8802	15762
Gecko Marine Inc	Bristol	RI	F	401 237-6117	15766
Naiad Inflatables Newport Inc	Newport	RI	F		16218
Oldport Marine Services Inc	Newport	RI	F	401 847-9109	16220

BOAT BUILDING & REPAIRING: Motorboats, Inboard Or Outboard

	CITY	ST	EMP	PHONE	ENTRY#
General Marine Inc	Biddeford	ME	G	207 284-7517	4568

BOAT BUILDING & REPAIRING: Motorized

	CITY	ST	EMP	PHONE	ENTRY#
Seaport Marine Inc	Mystic	CT	G	860 536-9651	1942
Chisletts Boating & Design LLC	Dover	NH	G	603 755-6815	14222

BOAT BUILDING & REPAIRING: Non-Motorized

	CITY	ST	EMP	PHONE	ENTRY#
Gregs Outboard Service LLC	Old Saybrook	CT	G	860 339-5139	2649
Hawthorne Cove Marina Inc	Salem	MA	G	978 740-9890	11722

BOAT BUILDING & REPAIRING: Yachts

	CITY	ST	EMP	PHONE	ENTRY#
CW Hood Yachts Inc	Marblehead	MA	G	781 631-0192	10086
Heritage Wharf Company LLC	Dartmouth	MA	G	508 990-1011	8230
The Duclos Corporation	Somerset	MA	D	508 676-8596	11857
Brooklin Boat Yard Inc (PA)	Brooklin	ME	E	207 359-2236	4632
Lyman Morse Boatbuilding Inc	Camden	ME	F	207 236-4378	4667
Lyman Morse Boatbuilding Inc (PA)	Thomaston	ME	C	207 354-6904	5546
Maine Cat	Lincolnville	ME	F	207 529-6500	5015
Talaria Company LLC	Southwest Harbor	ME	E	207 244-5572	5519
Alden Yachts Corporation	Bristol	RI	E	401 683-4200	15752
Eric Goetz Custom Sailboats	Bristol	RI	E	401 253-2670	15763
Hunt Yachts LLC	Portsmouth	RI	F	401 324-4201	16444
Iyrs School Tech & Trades	Newport	RI	E	401 846-2587	16212
Shannon Boat Company Inc	Bristol	RI	F	401 253-2441	15781
Sparkman & Stephens LLC (PA)	Newport	RI	F	401 847-5449	16225

BOAT BUILDING & RPRG: Fishing, Small, Lobster, Crab, Oyster

	CITY	ST	EMP	PHONE	ENTRY#
Hannah Boden Corp	New Bedford	MA	F	508 992-3334	10598
F V Tigger	South Harpswell	ME	G	207 721-0875	5487
H & H Marine Inc	Steuben	ME	F	207 546-7477	5532
Hodgdon Yachts Inc (PA)	East Boothbay	ME	D	207 737-2802	4736

Employee Codes: A=Over 500 employees, B=251-500   2024 Harris New England   1349
C=101-250, D=51-100, E=20-50, F=10-19, G=1-9   Manufacturers Directory

PRODUCT

	CITY	ST	EMP	PHONE	ENTRY#

BOAT DEALERS

	CITY	ST	EMP	PHONE	ENTRY#
F L Tripp & Sons Inc	Westport Point	MA	F	508 636-4058	13303
Karls Boat Shop Inc	Harwich	MA	G	508 432-4488	9069
P B Y A Inc	South Orleans	MA	E	508 255-0994	11973
Ribcraft Usa LLC	Marblehead	MA	E	781 639-9065	10094
Gowen Inc	Portland	ME	F	207 773-1761	5219
John M Williams Company	Mount Desert	ME	F	207 244-7854	5077
Navigator Publishing LLC	Portland	ME	E	207 822-4350	5249
Accutech Marine Propeller Inc	Dover	NH	G	603 617-3626	14213
Eastern Boats Inc	Milton	NH	E	603 652-9213	15045
Berthon Usa Inc	Newport	RI	E	401 846-8404	16206
Iyrs School Tech & Trades	Newport	RI	E	401 846-2587	16212

BOAT DEALERS: Marine Splys & Eqpt

	CITY	ST	EMP	PHONE	ENTRY#
Hercules Slr (us) Inc	New Bedford	MA	G	508 992-9519	10600
Hercules Slr (us) Inc (PA)	New Bedford	MA	F	508 993-0010	10601
Roses Oil Service Inc (PA)	Gloucester	MA	E	877 283-3334	8955
Windward Power Systems Inc	Fairhaven	MA	G	774 992-0059	8515
Howell Laboratories Inc (PA)	Bridgton	ME	E	207 647-3327	4629
Gecko Marine Inc	Bristol	RI	F	401 237-6117	15766

BOAT DEALERS: Motor

	CITY	ST	EMP	PHONE	ENTRY#
Allen Harbor Marine Svc Inc	Harwich Port	MA	E	508 432-0353	9070
Marine Usa Inc	Worcester	MA	E	508 791-7116	13757
Nauset Marine Inc (PA)	Orleans	MA	E	508 255-0777	11240

BOAT REPAIR SVCS

	CITY	ST	EMP	PHONE	ENTRY#
Rokap Inc	East Hampton	CT	G	203 265-6895	965
Concordia Co Inc	South Dartmouth	MA	E	508 999-1381	11916
Falmouth Mar Yachting Ctr Inc	Falmouth	MA	F	508 548-4600	8631
Marine Usa Inc	Worcester	MA	E	508 791-7116	13757
P B Y A Inc	South Orleans	MA	G	508 255-0994	11973

BOATS & OTHER MARINE EQPT: Plastic

	CITY	ST	EMP	PHONE	ENTRY#
Big Rock Oyster Company Inc	Harwich	MA	G	774 408-7951	9067

BODIES: Truck & Bus

	CITY	ST	EMP	PHONE	ENTRY#
Rj 15 Inc	Bristol	CT	F	860 585-0111	493
Bart Truck Equipment LLC	West Springfield	MA	G	413 737-2766	13017
Boston Trailer Manufacturing	Walpole	MA	F	508 668-2242	12553
Dattco Sales & Service	Saugus	MA	G	860 229-4878	11756
DC Bates Equipment Co Inc	Hopedale	MA	E	508 473-0041	9296
Hcb Holdings Inc (PA)	South Portland	ME	E	207 767-2136	5505
Donovan Equipment Company Inc	Londonderry	NH	D	603 669-2250	14743
Nashua Fabrication Co Inc	Hudson	NH	F	603 889-2181	14531
Vanguard Manufacturing Inc	New Ipswich	NH	D	603 878-2083	15200

BODY PARTS: Automobile, Stamped Metal

	CITY	ST	EMP	PHONE	ENTRY#
Energy Release LLC	Hudson	MA	G	978 466-9700	9363
Illinois Tool Works Inc	Westminster	MA	C	978 874-0151	13271

BOILER & HEATING REPAIR SVCS

	CITY	ST	EMP	PHONE	ENTRY#
Industrial Stl Boiler Svcs Inc	Chicopee	MA	E	413 532-7788	8038

BOILER REPAIR SHOP

	CITY	ST	EMP	PHONE	ENTRY#
Connectcut Boiler Repr Mfg Inc	West Hartford	CT	E	860 953-9117	4054
Bellingham Metal Works LLC	Franklin	MA	G	617 519-5958	8819
A D& D Wldg & Boiler Works Inc	Warwick	RI	F	401 732-5222	16774

BOILERS & BOILER SHOP WORK

	CITY	ST	EMP	PHONE	ENTRY#
Certuss America LP	Windsor	CT	G	440 454-6172	4265
Vent-Rite Valve Corp (PA)	Randolph	MA	E	781 986-2000	11578

BOILERS: Low-Pressure Heating, Steam Or Hot Water

	CITY	ST	EMP	PHONE	ENTRY#
Manufacturing PDT Systems Inc	Windsor	CT	F	877 689-1860	4288
H B Smith Company Inc	Westfield	MA	F	413 568-3148	13170

BOLTS: Handle, Wooden, Hewn

	CITY	ST	EMP	PHONE	ENTRY#
Pride Manufacturing Co LLC (PA)	Burnham	ME	C	207 487-3322	4661
Pride Manufacturing Co LLC	Guilford	ME	F	207 876-2719	4855

BOLTS: Metal

	CITY	ST	EMP	PHONE	ENTRY#
Ametek Inc	Wallingford	CT	C	203 265-6731	3770
Click Bond Inc	Watertown	CT	E	860 274-5435	4005
American Bolt & Nut Co Inc	Chelsea	MA	G	617 884-3331	7974
Robbins Manufacturing Co Inc	Fall River	MA	E	508 675-2555	8605

BOOK STORES

	CITY	ST	EMP	PHONE	ENTRY#
Westborough Books Inc (PA)	Westborough	MA	E	508 366-4292	13144
Sellers Publishing Inc	South Portland	ME	D	207 772-6833	5514

BOOKS, WHOLESALE

	CITY	ST	EMP	PHONE	ENTRY#
Scholastic Inc (DH)	Danbury	CT	D	212 343-6100	811
Scholastic Library Pubg Inc (HQ)	Danbury	CT	A	203 797-3500	812
Cheng & Tsui Co Inc	Boston	MA	F	617 988-2400	6649
Courier Companies Inc (PA)	North Chelmsford	MA	E	978 251-6000	10969
Horizon House Publications Inc (PA)	Norwood	MA	E	781 769-9750	11177
Redwheel/Weiser LLC (PA)	Newburyport	MA	G	978 465-0504	10712
Robert Bentley Inc	Cambridge	MA	E	617 547-4170	7698
Storey Publishing LLC (DH)	Clarksburg	MA	E	413 346-2100	8074
Sundance Newbridge Publishing	Marlborough	MA	F	508 303-1920	10218
Westborough Books Inc (PA)	Westborough	MA	E	508 366-4292	13144

BOOTS: Men's

	CITY	ST	EMP	PHONE	ENTRY#
C & J Clark America Inc (DH)	Waltham	MA	B	617 964-1222	12617
C & J Clark Latin America	Waltham	MA	E	617 243-4100	12618
Timberland LLC (HQ)	Stratham	NH	B	603 772-9500	15641

BORING MILL

	CITY	ST	EMP	PHONE	ENTRY#
National Screw Manufacturing	East Haven	CT	F	203 469-7109	1047

BOTTLED GAS DEALERS: Propane

	CITY	ST	EMP	PHONE	ENTRY#
Proctor Gas Inc	Proctor	VT	E	802 459-3340	17460

BOTTLES: Plastic

	CITY	ST	EMP	PHONE	ENTRY#
Altium Packaging	Windsor	CT	F	860 683-8560	4258
Mayborn Usa Inc	Stamford	CT	F	781 269-7490	3409
Silgan Holdings Inc (PA)	Stamford	CT	C	203 975-7110	3459
Camco Manufacturing Inc	Leominster	MA	D	978 537-6777	9646
Weston Presidio MGT Co Inc (PA)	Boston	MA	E	617 988-2500	7118
Quality Containers of Neng	Yarmouth	ME	G	207 846-5420	5706
Carr Management Inc (PA)	Nashua	NH	F	603 888-1315	15077
Envases Usa Inc (HQ)	Amherst	NH	F	603 889-8311	13868
Foxx Life Sciences LLC (PA)	Salem	NH	F	603 890-3699	15528
Southeastern Container Inc	Hudson	NH	E	603 324-1204	14547
Plastic Technologies MD Inc	South Burlington	VT	G	802 658-6588	17592
Plastic Technologies NY LLC	South Burlington	VT	F	802 658-6588	17593
Plastic Technologies of Vermont Inc	South Burlington	VT	D	802 658-6588	17594

BOWLING CENTERS

	CITY	ST	EMP	PHONE	ENTRY#
Bay Colony Associates (PA)	Boston	MA	G	617 287-9100	6584

BOXES & CRATES: Rectangular, Wood

	CITY	ST	EMP	PHONE	ENTRY#
Pith Products LLC	Ashford	CT	F	860 487-4859	21
Woodfree Crating Systems Inc	Waterbury	CT	F	203 759-1799	3985
Nefab Packaging North East LLC	Bellingham	MA	E	800 258-4692	6297

BOXES & SHOOK: Nailed Wood

	CITY	ST	EMP	PHONE	ENTRY#
Horn International Packg Inc (HQ)	Lancaster	MA	E	978 667-8797	9528
Nefab Packaging North East LLC	Bellingham	MA	E	800 258-4692	6297
Unified2 Globl Packg Group LLC	Lancaster	MA	B	508 865-1155	9531
Index Packaging Inc	Milton	NH	C	603 350-0018	15046

BOXES: Corrugated

	CITY	ST	EMP	PHONE	ENTRY#
AP Disposition LLC	Norwich	CT	F	860 889-1344	2601
Champlin-Packrite Inc	Manchester	CT	E	860 559-6373	1589
Colonial Corrugated Pdts Inc	Waterbury	CT	E	203 597-1707	3899
Connecticut Container Corp (PA)	North Haven	CT	C	203 248-2161	2399
Danbury Square Box Company	Danbury	CT	E	203 744-4611	727
General Packaging Products Inc	Norwalk	CT	G	203 846-1340	2505
HI-Tech Packaging Inc	Stratford	CT	E	203 378-2700	3547
Holm Corrugated Container Inc	Southington	CT	E	860 628-5559	3216
Jackson Corrugated Cont Corp	Essex	CT	F	860 767-3373	1168
Merco Inc	Ellington	CT	E	860 871-1888	1110
Merrill Industries LLC	Ellington	CT	E	860 871-1888	1111
Nutmeg Container Corporation (HQ)	Putnam	CT	D	860 963-6727	2867
R & R Corrugated Container Inc	Bristol	CT	D	860 584-1194	488
Rand-Whitney Container LLC	Waterbury	CT	E	203 597-1707	3965
Rand-Whitney Group LLC	Newtown	CT	E	203 426-5871	2345
Rand-Whitney Recycling LLC	Montville	CT	E	860 848-1900	1927
Windham Container Corporation	Putnam	CT	F	860 928-7934	2879
Abbott-Action Inc (PA)	Attleboro	MA	E	401 722-2100	5990
Commonwealth Packaging Corp	Chicopee	MA	D	413 593-1482	8019
Corrugated Packaging Inc	Fitchburg	MA	F	978 342-6076	8649
Corrugated Stitcher Service	Berkley	MA	G	508 823-2844	6315
Craft Corrugated Box Inc	New Bedford	MA	F	508 998-2115	10581
Creative Packaging Inc (PA)	Worcester	MA	E	508 756-7275	13711
Friend Box Company Inc	Danvers	MA	D	978 774-0240	8187
Horn Corporation (PA)	Lancaster	MA	E	800 832-7020	9527
Hub Folding Box Company Inc	Mansfield	MA	B	508 339-0005	10057
Ideal Box Company	Lawrence	MA	G	978 683-2802	9570
Kraft Group LLC (PA)	Foxboro	MA	C	508 384-4230	8705

	CITY	ST	EMP	PHONE	ENTRY#
Massachusetts Container Corp	Marlborough	MA	C	508 481-1100	10183
Mount Tom Box Company Inc	West Springfield	MA	F	413 781-5300	13034
New England Wooden Ware Corp (PA)	Gardner	MA	E	978 632-3600	8896
Newcorr Packaging Inc	Northborough	MA	D	508 393-9256	11103
Packaging Corporation America	Northampton	MA	C	413 584-6132	11074
Packaging Corporation America	Northampton	MA	D	978 256-4586	11075
Rand-Whitney Container LLC	Worcester	MA	F	774 420-2425	13776
Rand-Whitney Container LLC (DH)	Worcester	MA	C	508 890-7000	13777
Rand-Whitney Group LLC (HQ)	Worcester	MA	C	508 791-2301	13778
Rand-Whitney Industries LLC	Worcester	MA	E	508 791-2301	13779
Romanow Inc (DH)	Westwood	MA	D	781 320-9200	13317
Seaboard Folding Box Co Inc	Westminster	MA	D	978 342-8921	13277
Triple P Packg & Ppr Pdts Inc	Brockton	MA	D	508 588-0444	7313
Unicorr	Marlborough	MA	F	508 481-1100	10226
Westrock Container LLC	Springfield	MA	D	413 733-2211	12151
Ship-Pac Corp	Portland	ME	G	207 797-7444	5270
Volk Packaging Corporation	Biddeford	ME	D	207 282-6151	4594
Westrock	Scarborough	ME	F	770 448-2193	5447
Aegis Holdings LLC	Milford	NH	E	603 673-8900	15010
Mills Industries Inc	Laconia	NH	E	603 528-4217	14659
Rand-Whitney Container LLC	Dover	NH	E	603 822-7300	14247
Custom & Miller Box Company	East Providence	RI	D	401 431-9007	16012
Hope-Bffnton Pckging Group LLC	Central Falls	RI	F	401 725-3646	15789
Key Container Corporation (PA)	Pawtucket	RI	C	401 723-2000	16381
MCB Inc	Warwick	RI	F	401 739-7020	16835
Mount Tom Box Co Inc	Pawtucket	RI	F	413 781-5300	16390
Pusterla Us Inc	Warren	RI	E	401 245-5900	16765
K H Corrugated Case Copr	Bennington	VT	G	802 442-5455	17044
K&H Group Inc	Bennington	VT	C	802 442-5455	17045

BOXES: Filing, Paperboard Made From Purchased Materials

	CITY	ST	EMP	PHONE	ENTRY#
Westrock Rkt LLC	Springfield	MA	G	413 543-7300	12153

BOXES: Outlet, Electric Wiring Device

	CITY	ST	EMP	PHONE	ENTRY#
Hubbell Incorporated Delaware (HQ)	Shelton	CT	B	475 882-4000	3018

BOXES: Packing & Shipping, Metal

	CITY	ST	EMP	PHONE	ENTRY#
Case Future Corp	Johnston	RI	E	401 944-0402	16078
International Packaging Corporation (PA)	Pawtucket	RI	A	401 724-1600	16376
Jewel Case Corporation	Providence	RI	B	401 943-1400	16549

BOXES: Paperboard, Folding

	CITY	ST	EMP	PHONE	ENTRY#
Agi-Shorewood Group Us LLC	Stamford	CT	A	203 324-4839	3275
Curtis Corporation A Del Corp	Sandy Hook	CT	C	203 426-5861	2949
Curtis Packaging Corporation	Sandy Hook	CT	C	203 426-5861	2950
Fusion Paperboard US Inc	Versailles	CT	E	859 586-1100	3765
Hamden Packaging Inc	Hamden	CT	E	203 288-0200	1428
Keystone Paper & Box Co LLC (HQ)	South Windsor	CT	F	860 291-0027	3160
Mafcote Inc (PA)	Norwalk	CT	E	203 847-8500	2530
Rice Packaging Inc	Ellington	CT	D	860 870-7057	1113
Accutech Packaging Inc	Foxboro	MA	D	508 543-3800	8689
Bopkg Inc (HQ)	Fitchburg	MA	C	978 343-3067	8644
Fuller Box Co Inc (PA)	North Attleboro	MA	D	508 695-2525	10871
Gooby Industries Corp	Methuen	MA	C	978 689-0100	10332
Graphic Packaging Intl LLC	Lowell	MA	B	978 459-9328	9882
Northeast Buffinton Group Inc	Walpole	MA	F	401 434-1107	12571
Packaging Specialties Inc	Newburyport	MA	D	978 462-1300	10706
Pioneer Packaging Inc (PA)	Chicopee	MA	D	413 378-6930	8054
Rand-Whitney Group LLC (HQ)	Worcester	MA	C	508 791-2301	13778
Standard Box Inc	Chelsea	MA	F	617 884-4200	7993
UNI-Pac Inc	Holyoke	MA	D	413 534-5284	9284
Volk Packaging Corporation	Biddeford	ME	D	207 282-6151	4594
Graphic Packaging Intl LLC	Concord	NH	D	603 230-5100	14133
Graphic Packaging Intl LLC	Concord	NH	E	603 224-2333	14134
Campbell Enterprises Corp	Pawtucket	RI	E	401 753-7778	16352
Mm-Apvh Acquisition Co LLC	Pawtucket	RI	C	401 753-7778	16388
Numaco Packaging LLC	East Providence	RI	F	401 438-4952	16035

BOXES: Paperboard, Set-Up

	CITY	ST	EMP	PHONE	ENTRY#
Agi-Shorewood Group Us LLC	Stamford	CT	A	203 324-4839	3275
Fusion Paperboard Connecticut LLC	Versailles	CT	C	888 283-3617	3764
Rice Packaging Inc	Ellington	CT	D	860 870-7057	1113
Rondo America Incorporated	Naugatuck	CT	C	203 723-5831	1985
Friend Box Company Inc	Danvers	MA	D	978 774-0240	8187
Keystone Paper & Box Co LLC	Woburn	MA	E	781 938-3801	13596
Packaging Specialties Inc	Newburyport	MA	D	978 462-1300	10706
UNI-Pac Inc	Holyoke	MA	D	413 534-5284	9284
Volk Packaging Corporation	Biddeford	ME	D	207 282-6151	4594
Graphic Packaging Intl LLC	Concord	NH	D	603 230-5100	14132
Graphic Packaging Intl LLC	Concord	NH	D	603 230-5100	14133
Cjf Group Ltd	Providence	RI	D	401 421-2000	16500
Fuller Box Co Inc	Central Falls	RI	C	401 725-4300	15788

BOXES: Plastic

	CITY	ST	EMP	PHONE	ENTRY#
Packgen Inc	Auburn	ME	E	207 784-4195	4449
Mills Industries Inc	Laconia	NH	E	603 528-4217	14659
International Packaging Corporation (PA)	Pawtucket	RI	A	401 724-1600	16376
Morris Transparent Box Co	East Providence	RI	F	401 438-6116	16032

BOXES: Stamped Metal

	CITY	ST	EMP	PHONE	ENTRY#
Durham Manufacturing Company (PA)	Durham	CT	D	860 349-3427	899

BOXES: Wooden

	CITY	ST	EMP	PHONE	ENTRY#
Colonial Wood Products Inc	West Haven	CT	G	203 932-9003	4097
Merco Inc	Ellington	CT	E	860 871-1888	1110
Vermont Pallet and Skid Sp Inc	Norwich	CT	G	860 822-6949	2618
Westwood Products Inc	Winsted	CT	F	860 379-9401	4358
Atlas Box and Crating Co Inc (PA)	Sutton	MA	C	508 865-1155	12276
Kelley Wood Products Inc	Fitchburg	MA	F	978 345-7531	8658
KG Pallet LLC	Chicopee	MA	E	413 536-3511	8043
J H Dunning Corporation	North Walpole	NH	E	603 445-5591	15258

BRAKES & BRAKE PARTS

	CITY	ST	EMP	PHONE	ENTRY#
Tek-Motive Inc	Branford	CT	F	203 468-2224	281
Ryca Inc	Tewksbury	MA	F	978 851-3265	12415

BRAKES: Electromagnetic

	CITY	ST	EMP	PHONE	ENTRY#
Carlyle Johnson Machine Co LLC (DH)	Bolton	CT	F	860 643-1531	219
Dufrane Technologies LLC	Winsted	CT	F	860 379-2318	4341
Inertia Dynamics LLC	New Hartford	CT	C	860 379-1252	2102
Altra Industrial Motion Corp (HQ)	Braintree	MA	C	781 917-0600	7167
Warner Electric	Braintree	MA	D	781 917-0600	7212

BRAKES: Metal Forming

	CITY	ST	EMP	PHONE	ENTRY#
Eyelet Tech LLC	Wolcott	CT	E	203 879-5306	4365
Altra Industrial Motion Corp (HQ)	Braintree	MA	C	781 917-0600	7167
Warner Electric	Braintree	MA	D	781 917-0600	7212

BRASS & BRONZE PRDTS: Die-casted

	CITY	ST	EMP	PHONE	ENTRY#
Industrial Foundry Corporation	Uxbridge	MA	G	508 278-5523	12481
Kingston Aluminum Foundry Inc	Kingston	MA	G	781 585-6631	9509
Hebert Manufacturing Company (PA)	Laconia	NH	F	603 524-2065	14653

BRASS FOUNDRY, NEC

	CITY	ST	EMP	PHONE	ENTRY#
Truex Incorporated	Pawtucket	RI	D	401 722-5023	16426

BRAZING SVCS

	CITY	ST	EMP	PHONE	ENTRY#
DBF Industries Inc	New Britain	CT	F	860 827-8283	2021
Parama Corporation	Bethel	CT	G	203 790-8155	131
Aero Brazing Corporation	Woburn	MA	F	781 933-7511	13502
Aero Manufacturing Corp	Beverly	MA	D	978 720-1000	6323

BRAZING: Metal

	CITY	ST	EMP	PHONE	ENTRY#
Bodycote Thermal Proc Inc	South Windsor	CT	E	860 282-1371	3121
O & W Heat Treat Inc	South Windsor	CT	E	860 528-9239	3168
Bodycote Thermal Proc Inc	Ipswich	MA	E	978 356-3818	9478
United-County Industries Corp	Millbury	MA	E	508 865-5885	10444
Accurate Brazing Corporation (HQ)	Goffstown	NH	E	603 945-3750	14346
Tsi Group Inc (DH)	Hampton	NH	E	603 964-0296	14416
Trow & Holden Co Inc	Barre	VT	E	802 476-7221	17022

BRICK, STONE & RELATED PRDTS WHOLESALERS

	CITY	ST	EMP	PHONE	ENTRY#
Dan Beard Inc	Shelton	CT	E	203 924-4346	2996
Desiato Sand & Gravel Corp	Storrs Mansfield	CT	E	860 429-6479	3512
Midwood Quarry and Cnstr Inc (PA)	East Hartford	CT	F	860 289-1414	1006
Cape Cod Aggregates Corp (PA)	Hyannis	MA	E	508 775-3716	9429
International Stone Inc	Woburn	MA	D	781 937-3300	13589
Dailey Precast LLC (HQ)	Shaftsbury	VT	D	802 442-4418	17549

BRICKS & BLOCKS: Structural

	CITY	ST	EMP	PHONE	ENTRY#
Redi-Mix Services Incorporated	Taunton	MA	F	508 823-0771	12361
Ventech Industries Inc	Eliot	ME	G	207 439-0069	4751

BRICKS: Clay

	CITY	ST	EMP	PHONE	ENTRY#
Stiles & Hart Brick Company	Bridgewater	MA	E	508 697-6928	7238

BRIDGE COMPONENTS: Bridge sections, prefabricated, highway

	CITY	ST	EMP	PHONE	ENTRY#
Spector Metal Products Co Inc	Holbrook	MA	E	781 767-5600	9185

BROADCASTING & COMMS EQPT: Antennas, Transmitting/Comms

	CITY	ST	EMP	PHONE	ENTRY#
Radio Frequency Systems Inc (DH)	Meriden	CT	E	203 630-3311	1690
Aerial Wireless Services LLC	Bellingham	MA	D	508 657-1213	6282
Antenna Research Assoc Inc	Pembroke	MA	E	781 829-4740	11357
CPI Radant Tech Div Inc (DH)	Stow	MA	D	978 562-3866	12245

PRODUCT

	CITY	ST	EMP	PHONE	ENTRY#
Linx Consulting LLC	Webster	MA	F	508 461-6333	12930
Radio Waves Inc	North Billerica	MA	E	978 459-8800	10946
Howell Laboratories Inc (PA)	Bridgton	ME	E	207 647-3327	4629
SPX Corporation	Raymond	ME	C	207 655-8100	5317
Cobham Exeter Inc	Exeter	NH	E	714 841-4976	14288
Research In Motion Rf Inc (HQ)	Nashua	NH	E	603 598-8880	15158

BROADCASTING & COMMS EQPT: Trnsmttng TV Antennas/Grndng Eqpt

	CITY	ST	EMP	PHONE	ENTRY#
Atlantic Microwave Corporation	Lowell	MA	C		9856
Hitachi Kokusai Electric Comark LLC	Southwick	MA	D	413 998-1100	12043

BROADCASTING & COMMUNICATION EQPT: Transmit-Receiver, Radio

	CITY	ST	EMP	PHONE	ENTRY#
Ashcroft Inc (DH)	Stratford	CT	B	203 378-8281	3517

BROADCASTING & COMMUNICATIONS EQPT: Cellular Radio Telephone

	CITY	ST	EMP	PHONE	ENTRY#
Manufacturers Services Limited	Concord	MA	E	617 330-7682	8124
Laird Technologies Inc	Manchester	NH	E	603 627-7877	14875

BROADCASTING & COMMUNICATIONS EQPT: Light Comms Eqpt

	CITY	ST	EMP	PHONE	ENTRY#
Manage Inc	Springfield	MA	E	413 593-9128	12112

BROADCASTING & COMMUNICATIONS EQPT: Studio Eqpt, Radio & TV

	CITY	ST	EMP	PHONE	ENTRY#
Stamford Mdia Ctr Prdctons LLC	Stamford	CT	G	203 905-4000	3471
Cowbell Technologies Inc	Hudson	MA	F	508 733-1778	9360
Cowbell Technologies Inc (PA)	Westborough	MA	G	508 733-1778	13094
Royalty Brdcstg Svcs & Trnsp	Springfield	MA	F	413 777-7868	12127

BROADCASTING & COMMUNICATIONS EQPT: Transmitting, Radio/TV

	CITY	ST	EMP	PHONE	ENTRY#
Nautel Maine Inc	Bangor	ME	C	207 947-8200	4511

BROKERS & DEALERS: Securities

	CITY	ST	EMP	PHONE	ENTRY#
Debt Exchange Inc	Boston	MA	D	617 531-3400	6685
New Generation Research Inc	Boston	MA	F	617 573-9550	6918

BROKERS' SVCS

	CITY	ST	EMP	PHONE	ENTRY#
TMI Industries Inc	Palmer	MA	E	413 283-9021	11285

BROKERS: Business

	CITY	ST	EMP	PHONE	ENTRY#
First Equity Group Inc (PA)	Westport	CT	F	203 291-7700	4168
Nery Corporation	New Bedford	MA	G	508 990-9800	10626

BROKERS: Food

	CITY	ST	EMP	PHONE	ENTRY#
Albano Sales Inc	North Billerica	MA	F	978 667-9100	10895
Dahlicious Holdings LLC	Leominster	MA	F	978 401-2103	9656
B Del Toro & Sons Inc	Providence	RI	F	401 421-5820	16481

BROKERS: Printing

	CITY	ST	EMP	PHONE	ENTRY#
Bew Corp	Randolph	MA	F	781 963-0315	11550
A & R Sawyer Co Inc	Windham	NH	G	603 893-5752	15719

BRONZE FOUNDRY, NEC

	CITY	ST	EMP	PHONE	ENTRY#
Michael Healy Designs Inc	Manville	RI	G	401 597-5900	16165

BRONZE ROLLING & DRAWING

	CITY	ST	EMP	PHONE	ENTRY#
Waterbury Rolling Mills Inc	Waterbury	CT	D	203 597-5000	3981

BROOMS

	CITY	ST	EMP	PHONE	ENTRY#
Butler Home Products LLC (HQ)	Hudson	MA	F	508 597-8000	9359
Tucel Industries Inc	Forest Dale	VT	F	802 247-6824	17274

BROOMS & BRUSHES

	CITY	ST	EMP	PHONE	ENTRY#
Loos & Co Inc	Pomfret	CT	D	860 928-6681	2810
Angel Guard Products Inc	Worcester	MA	G	508 791-1073	13699
Cardinal Comb & Brush Mfg Corp	Leominster	MA	E	978 537-6330	9647
ACS Industries Inc (PA)	Lincoln	RI	E	401 769-4700	16116

BROOMS & BRUSHES: Household Or Indl

	CITY	ST	EMP	PHONE	ENTRY#
Jaz Brush USA Inc	New Bedford	MA	F	774 992-7996	10605
Felton Inc	Londonderry	NH	D	603 425-0200	14750

BROOMS & BRUSHES: Street Sweeping, Hand Or Machine

	CITY	ST	EMP	PHONE	ENTRY#
Atlantic Broom Service Inc	East Bridgewater	MA	E	774 226-1300	8335
Howard P Fairfield LLC (DH)	Skowhegan	ME	E	207 474-9836	5468
Northeast Ldscpg Tree Svcs Inc	Westerly	RI	F	860 405-5274	16941

BRUSHES

	CITY	ST	EMP	PHONE	ENTRY#
Sanderson-Macleod Incorporate	Palmer	MA	C	413 283-3481	11284

BUCKETS: Plastic

	CITY	ST	EMP	PHONE	ENTRY#
Mauser Packg Solutions Holdg	Leominster	MA	F	978 728-5000	9682
Plastican Inc	Leominster	MA	A	978 728-5000	9696

BUCKLES & PARTS

	CITY	ST	EMP	PHONE	ENTRY#
Buckleguycom LLC	Newburyport	MA	G	978 213-9989	10673

BUILDING & OFFICE CLEANING SVCS

	CITY	ST	EMP	PHONE	ENTRY#
4smartpro LLC	Saint Johnsbury	VT	F	802 745-8797	17537

BUILDING & STRUCTURAL WOOD MEMBERS

	CITY	ST	EMP	PHONE	ENTRY#
Country Carpenters Inc	Hebron	CT	G	860 228-2276	1526
Eastern Co (PA)	Shelton	CT	E	203 729-2255	3001
Architectural Timber Mllwk Inc	Hadley	MA	F	413 586-3045	9017
Caliper Woodworking Corp	Malden	MA	E	781 322-9760	10006
K & J Interiors Inc	Plymouth	MA	D	508 830-0670	11463
National Lumber Company	Newton	MA	E	617 244-8020	10770
Acer Holdings Starksboro Inc	Starksboro	VT	F	802 453-4438	17625

BUILDING CLEANING & MAINTENANCE SVCS

	CITY	ST	EMP	PHONE	ENTRY#
Cw Solutions LLC	New Britain	CT	D	860 229-7700	2018
Lps Enterprises Inc	East Freetown	MA	E	508 763-3830	8364
Maine Turnpike Authority	Cumberland Center	ME	D	207 829-4531	4709

BUILDING COMPONENTS: Structural Steel

	CITY	ST	EMP	PHONE	ENTRY#
All Phase Steel Works LLC	New Haven	CT	F	203 375-8881	2113
Boudreaus Welding Co Inc	Dayville	CT	F	860 774-2771	860
Feman Steel LLC	Bloomfield	CT	F	860 982-6393	164
Pds Engineering & Construction	Bloomfield	CT	F	860 242-8586	201
Qsr Steel Corporation LLC	Hartford	CT	E	860 548-0248	1502
Shepard Steel Co Inc (PA)	Hartford	CT	D	860 525-4446	1507
State Welding & Fabg Inc	Clinton	CT	G	203 294-4071	650
2I Inc	Hudson	MA	F	978 567-8867	9350
All Steel Fabricating Inc	North Grafton	MA	E	508 839-4471	11019
Auciello Iron Works Inc	Hudson	MA	E	978 568-8382	9355
Boston Steel Fabricators Inc	Holbrook	MA	G	781 767-1540	9170
Bradford Steel Co Inc	East Freetown	MA	F	508 763-5921	8363
Dublin Steel Corporation	Palmer	MA	E	413 289-1218	11273
Package Steel Systems Inc	Sutton	MA	E	508 865-5871	12289
Schrimpf Wldg Fabrication Inc	Woburn	MA	G	339 298-2311	13661
Nif Inc	Newport	ME	E	207 368-4344	5097
Canam Bridges US Inc	Claremont	NH	E	603 542-5202	14081
Novel Iron Works Inc	Greenland	NH	C	603 436-7950	14369
Nsa Industries LLC	Groveton	NH	D	802 748-5007	14377
Farber Industrial Fabricating	Pawtucket	RI	G	401 725-2492	16368
Regal Components Inc	East Providence	RI	F	727 299-0800	16042
K V Sbardella Slate Inc	Fair Haven	VT	G	802 265-9955	17251

BUILDING ITEM REPAIR SVCS, MISCELLANEOUS

	CITY	ST	EMP	PHONE	ENTRY#
Otis Elevator Company (HQ)	Farmington	CT	C	860 674-3000	1235

BUILDING PRDTS & MATERIALS DEALERS

	CITY	ST	EMP	PHONE	ENTRY#
Viking Kitchen Cabinets LLC (PA)	New Britain	CT	E	860 223-7101	2074
Baxter Sand & Gravel Inc	Chicopee	MA	F	413 536-3370	8009
Brightman Corporation	Assonet	MA	F	508 644-2620	5972
Creative Material Tech Ltd	Palmer	MA	G	413 284-0000	11272
Delano Saw Mill Inc	North Dartmouth	MA	G	508 994-8752	10992
Maki Building Centers Inc (HQ)	Gardner	MA	F	978 343-7422	8894
P A Landers Inc	Hanover	MA	F	508 747-1800	9039
Rebars & Mesh Inc	Haverhill	MA	E	978 374-2244	9126
Southeastern Millwork Co Inc	Bourne	MA	F	508 888-6038	7142
N C Hunt Inc	Damariscotta	ME	E	207 563-8503	4716
Goss Lumber Co Inc	Henniker	NH	G	603 428-3363	14434
Granite State Log Homes Inc (PA)	Campton	NH	F	603 536-4949	14044
Nucor Hrris Rbar Northeast LLC	Canaan	NH	D	603 632-5222	14047
Turn Key Lumber Inc	Fitzwilliam	NH	C	978 798-1370	14317
White Mountain Lumber Co Inc	Berlin	NH	E	603 752-1000	13987
Windy Ridge Corporation	Tamworth	NH	G	603 323-2323	15650
Mill River Lumber Ltd	North Clarendon	VT	D	802 775-0032	17417
RK Miles Inc (PA)	Manchester Center	VT	C	802 362-1952	17330

BUILDING PRDTS: Concrete

	CITY	ST	EMP	PHONE	ENTRY#
Lane Construction Corporation (DH)	Cheshire	CT	C	203 235-3351	603
Lane Industries Incorporated (DH)	Cheshire	CT	G	203 235-3351	604
Lane Construction Corporation	Lee	MA	E	413 637-2511	9614
Turn Key Lumber Inc	Fitzwilliam	NH	C	978 798-1370	14317
Ufp Londonderry LLC	Londonderry	NH	E	603 668-4113	14787

BUILDING PRDTS: Stone

	CITY	ST	EMP	PHONE	ENTRY#
Ippolitos Stone Craft Inc	Seekonk	MA	F	508 336-9616	11778

BUILDING SCALES MODELS

Safety-Kleen Systems Inc (HQ)	Norwell	MA	B	800 669-5740	11146

BUILDINGS & COMPONENTS: Prefabricated Metal

Eb Carports & Metal Structures	Newington	CT	F	860 263-3797	2287
Engineered Building Pdts Inc	Bloomfield	CT	E	860 243-1110	161
Illinois Tool Works Inc	Waterbury	CT	C	203 574-2119	3920
Morin Corporation (DH)	Bristol	CT	D	860 584-0900	472
Walpole Outdoors LLC	Ridgefield	CT	E	508 668-2800	2909
Longhorn Steel Inc	Peabody	MA	G	978 265-3646	11325
Morton Buildings Inc	Westfield	MA	F	413 562-7028	13191
New England Foundation Co Inc (PA)	Hyde Park	MA	B	617 361-9750	9465
The Cricket System Inc	Newburyport	MA	G	617 905-1420	10719
Walpole Outdoors LLC	East Falmouth	MA	E	508 540-0300	8362
Walpole Outdoors LLC	Wilmington	MA	E	978 658-3373	13475
Sheridan Corporation (HQ)	Fairfield	ME	E	207 453-9311	4765
Walpole Outdoors LLC	Chester	ME	E	207 794-2248	4694
Concrete Systems Inc	Hudson	NH	D	603 886-5472	14491
Concrete Systems Inc	Londonderry	NH	F	603 432-1840	14736
Inofab LLC	Pittsfield	NH	F	603 435-5082	15333
Ufp Shelf 1 LLC	Wilton	NH	F	603 824-9690	15711

BUILDINGS: Portable

Mobile Mini Inc	Suffield	CT	G	860 668-1888	3594
Freight Farms Inc	Boston	MA	F	877 687-4326	6748
Mobile Mini Inc	West Bridgewater	MA	F	508 427-5395	12975
Package Industries Inc	Sutton	MA	E	508 865-5871	12288
Space Building Corp	Lakeville	MA	E	508 947-7277	9521
Ekto Manufacturing Corp	Sanford	ME	E	207 324-4427	5394

BUILDINGS: Prefabricated, Metal

Cover-It Inc	West Haven	CT	C	203 931-4747	4100
Fabbrica LLC (PA)	Windsor	CT	C	860 253-4136	4275
Steel Modular Inc	Essex	CT	F	310 227-3714	1172
Rubb Inc	Sanford	ME	D	207 324-2877	5413

BUILDINGS: Prefabricated, Wood

Country Carpenters Inc	Hebron	CT	G	860 228-2276	1526
Trigila Construction Inc	Berlin	CT	F	860 828-8444	89
Walpole Outdoors LLC	Ridgefield	CT	E	508 668-2800	2909
Architectural Timber Mllwk Inc	Hadley	MA	E	413 586-3045	9017
Eggrock Inc	Littleton	MA	E	978 952-2800	9813
Emery Development Ltd	Springfield	MA	G	413 782-1990	12094
Jobart Inc (PA)	Methuen	MA	F	978 689-4414	10335
Walpole Outdoors LLC	East Falmouth	MA	E	508 540-0300	8362
Walpole Outdoors LLC	Wilmington	MA	E	978 658-3373	13475
Ecocor LLC	Searsmont	ME	E	207 342-2085	5449
Modular Fun I Inc	South Paris	ME	C	207 739-2400	5490
New England Rent To Own LLC	Chelsea	ME	G	207 399-6181	4687
Walpole Outdoors LLC	Chester	ME	E	207 794-2248	4694
Southworth Timberframes Inc	Lancaster	NH	D	603 788-2619	14679
Connor Homes LLC	Middlebury	VT	D	802 382-9082	17342
Mortise and Tenon LLC	Starksboro	VT	E	802 643-2227	17627

BULLETPROOF VESTS

Safariland LLC	Dalton	MA	E	413 684-3104	8153

BUOYS: Plastic

Island Mooring Supplies LLC	Prudence Island	RI	F	401 447-5387	16650

BURIAL VAULTS: Concrete Or Precast Terrazzo

Cv Custom Volt	Ridgefield	CT	G	203 431-7646	2895
Doric Vault Connecticut LLC	Branford	CT	G	203 494-0172	251
Elm-Cap Industries Inc	West Hartford	CT	E	860 953-1060	4059
Norwalk Wilbert Vault Co LLC	Oakville	CT	E	203 366-5678	2624
DAngelo Burial Vaults	Franklin	MA	E	508 528-0385	8830
Flagg Palmer Precast Inc	Oxford	MA	E	508 987-3400	11253
Hardy Doric Inc	Chelmsford	MA	G	978 250-1113	7930
Keating-Wilbert Vault Inc	Wilbraham	MA	F	413 543-1226	13361
Lamontagne Wilbert Burial Vlt	Sutton	MA	E	508 476-0000	12286
Quintal Burial Vault Inc	Dighton	MA	F	508 669-5717	8294
Watertown Engineering Corp	Whitman	MA	F	781 857-2555	13351
Whitman Vault Inc	Whitman	MA	F	781 857-3031	13355
Elm Street Vault Inc	Biddeford	ME	F	207 284-4855	4563
Wilbert Swans Vault Co	Casco	ME	E	207 854-5324	4684
Alex Vault Co	Epping	NH	G	603 944-0132	14276
New England Vlts Monuments LLC	Berlin	NH	G	603 449-2165	13984
Sabbow and Co Inc	Littleton	NH	F	603 444-6724	14722
Washburn Vault Company Inc	Brattleboro	VT	F	802 254-9150	17107

BURNERS: Gas, Domestic

Metromatic Manufacturing Company Inc	Byfield	MA	F	781 396-5300	7458

BURNERS: Gas, Indl

Cowles Operating Company	North Haven	CT	C	203 680-9401	2404
Hamworthy Peabody Combustn Inc (DH)	Shelton	CT	E	203 922-1199	3012
Preferred Utilities Mfg Corp	Danbury	CT	D	203 743-6741	799
Pumc Holding Corporation (PA)	Danbury	CT	F	203 743-6741	802

BURNERS: Oil, Domestic Or Indl

John Zink Company LLC	Shelton	CT	E	203 925-0380	3025

BURNT WOOD ARTICLES

Northeast Wood Products LLC	Uncasville	CT	F	860 862-6350	3742

BUS BARS: Electrical

Schneider Electric Usa Inc (DH)	Boston	MA	A	978 975-9600	7026
Schneider Electric Usa Inc	Foxboro	MA	E	508 549-3385	8724

BUSINESS ACTIVITIES: Non-Commercial Site

API Wizard LLC	Stamford	CT	E	800 691-8714	3283
Indigo Coast Inc	Kent	CT	G	860 592-0088	1541
Lifetoken Software Inc	Cos Cob	CT	G	203 515-9686	678
Nofet LLC	New Haven	CT	F	203 848-9064	2180
Regenerative Medicine LLC (PA)	Greenwich	CT	G	203 969-4877	1346
Uniworld Bus Publications Inc	Darien	CT	G	201 384-4900	857
Actifio Federal Inc	Needham	MA	F	781 795-9182	10503
Boston Sports Journal LLC	Medway	MA	G	617 306-0166	10303
CJS Workshop LLC	Groton	MA	E	323 445-5012	9008
Dinner Daily LLC	Westford	MA	F	978 392-5887	13234
Drizly LLC (HQ)	Boston	MA	E	774 234-1033	6703
East Basin Sports Inc (PA)	Newton	MA	E	781 492-2747	10754
Edge Embossing Inc	Charlestown	MA	G	617 850-2868	7870
Grey Barn Farm Enterprises LLC	Chilmark	MA	G	508 645-4854	8071
Infinite Iq Inc	Wellesley	MA	F	781 710-8696	12943
Intelon Optics Inc	Woburn	MA	F	310 804-9392	13587
Klone Lab LLC	Newburyport	MA	F	978 378-3434	10692
Lifecloud Inc	Amesbury	MA	G	978 621-9572	5842
North Shore Laboratories Corp	Peabody	MA	F	978 531-5954	11327
Nvision Medical Corporation	Marlborough	MA	G	408 655-3577	10187
Radar Wind Up Corporation (HQ)	Cambridge	MA	F	917 488-6050	7693
Red Point Positioning Corp (PA)	Newton	MA	F	339 222-0261	10779
Stellar Menus Inc	Provincetown	MA	G	617 882-2800	11498
Veloxint Corporation	Framingham	MA	F	774 777-3369	8806
Coursestorm Inc	Orono	ME	F	207 866-0328	5134
Valt Enterprizes Inc	Presque Isle	ME	F	207 560-5188	5311
A B Excavating Inc	Lancaster	NH	E	603 788-5110	14675
Hopkinton For Land Claring Inc	Henniker	NH	E	603 428-8400	14437
Lestat Production 81 Corp	Bedford	NH	E	866 557-4478	13939
Sports Visio Inc	Dunbarton	NH	F	603 774-1339	14265
Wagz Inc (PA)	Portsmouth	NH	F	603 570-6015	15449
Precision Cutter Grinding Inc	Hartland	VT	G	802 436-2039	17287
Sogle Property LLC	Cambridge	VT	E	802 849-7943	17168

BUSINESS FORMS WHOLESALERS

Compu-Data LLC	Newington	CT	D	800 666-0399	2282
Brady Business Forms Inc	Lowell	MA	G	978 458-2585	9865
Continuprint Inc	Woburn	MA	G	781 933-1800	13547
Massachusetts Envelope Co Inc (PA)	Woburn	MA	E	617 623-8000	13606
Medical Manager Pcn Inc	Walpole	MA	F	508 850-3500	12568
Sterling Business Products Inc	Stoneham	MA	F	781 481-1234	12186
Fiberkraft Inc	Salem	NH	E	603 621-0090	15525
Kelley Solutions Inc	Rye	NH	F	603 431-3881	15499

BUSINESS FORMS: Printed, Continuous

Full Circle Technologies Inc	Boston	MA	E	617 722-0100	6749

BUSINESS FORMS: Printed, Manifold

Beekley Corporation (PA)	Bristol	CT	D	860 583-4700	411
Federal Business Products Inc	Torrington	CT	E	860 482-6231	3680
Mlk Business Forms Inc	New Haven	CT	F	203 624-6304	2176
Taylor Communications Inc	East Hartford	CT	F	860 875-0731	1026
Wallingford Prtg Bus Forms Inc	Branford	CT	F	203 481-1911	286
Belmont Printing Company	Belmont	MA	G	617 484-0833	6304
BFI Print Communications Inc (PA)	Boston	MA	E	781 447-1199	6591
Continuprint Inc	Woburn	MA	G	781 933-1800	13547
George H Dean Co	Braintree	MA	D	781 544-3782	7184
Regal Press Incorporated (PA)	Norwood	MA	E	781 769-3900	11206
Taylor Communications Inc	Avon	MA	F	508 584-0102	6164
Taylor Communications Inc	Braintree	MA	F	781 843-0250	7208
Wise Business Forms Inc	Portland	ME	C	207 774-6560	5290

PRODUCT

	CITY	ST	EMP	PHONE	ENTRY#

BUSINESS MACHINE REPAIR, ELECTRIC

	CITY	ST	EMP	PHONE	ENTRY#
Agissar Corporation	Stratford	CT	E	203 375-8662	3516
Quadient Inc (DH)	Milford	CT	C	203 301-3400	1874
Xerox Corporation (HQ)	Norwalk	CT	B	203 849-5216	2598
Xerox Holdings Inc	Norwalk	CT	A	203 968-3000	2599
Xerox Holdings Corporation (PA)	Norwalk	CT	B	203 849-5216	2600

BUSINESS TRAINING SVCS

	CITY	ST	EMP	PHONE	ENTRY#
Cengage Learning Inc	Boston	MA	F	518 348-2300	6645
Kbace Technologies Inc (HQ)	Nashua	NH	D	603 821-7000	15121

BUTTER WHOLESALERS

	CITY	ST	EMP	PHONE	ENTRY#
Casco Bay Butter Company Inc	Westbrook	ME	G	207 712-9148	5620

CABINETS & CASES: Show, Display & Storage, Exc Wood

	CITY	ST	EMP	PHONE	ENTRY#
Bull Metal Products Inc	Middletown	CT	E	860 346-9691	1742
PCL Fixtures Inc	East Hartford	CT	E	401 334-4646	1009
Platt-Labonia of N Haven Inc	North Haven	CT	D	203 239-5681	2431
Packaging Concepts Ltd	Rumford	RI	C	401 334-0344	16675

CABINETS: Bathroom Vanities, Wood

	CITY	ST	EMP	PHONE	ENTRY#
Christopoulos Designs Inc	Bridgeport	CT	F	203 576-1110	311
Kingswood Kitchens Co Inc	Danbury	CT	D	203 792-8700	767
Martin Cabinet Inc	Bristol	CT	F	860 747-5769	464
Royal Woodcraft Inc	Ansonia	CT	F	203 847-3461	19
S J Pappas Inc	Meriden	CT	F	203 237-7701	1695
Hamlin Cabinet Corp	Norfolk	MA	G	508 384-8371	10799
Milford Woodworking Co Inc	Milford	MA	F	508 473-2335	10405
Vanity World Inc	Canton	MA	F	508 668-1800	7839
Crown Point Realty Corp Inc	Claremont	NH	E	603 543-1208	14087
Vermont Custom Wood Products	North Walpole	NH	F	802 463-9930	15261
Young Furniture Mfg Inc	Bow	NH	F	603 224-8830	14015
Catamount North Cabinetry LLC	Essex Junction	VT	F	802 264-9009	17230
Knight Industries Inc	North Clarendon	VT	E	802 773-8777	17416

CABINETS: Entertainment

	CITY	ST	EMP	PHONE	ENTRY#
Belmont Corporation	Bristol	CT	E	860 589-5700	413
European Woodcraft LLC	Norwalk	CT	G	203 847-6195	2498
Custom Ktchens By Chmpagne Inc	Franklin	MA	F	508 528-7919	8828
Metrica Interior Inc	Northampton	MA	F	413 587-2750	11071
Superior Kitchen Designs Inc	Gardner	MA	F	978 632-5072	8903
Crown Point Realty Corp Inc	Claremont	NH	E	603 543-1208	14087

CABINETS: Factory

	CITY	ST	EMP	PHONE	ENTRY#
Curtiss Woodworking Inc	Prospect	CT	D	203 527-9305	2832
Liberty Garage Inc	Danbury	CT	G	203 778-0222	770
Jamesbrook Enterprises Inc	Shirley	MA	F	978 425-6166	11818
JS International Inc (PA)	Fall River	MA	F	508 675-4722	8564
Lista International Corporation	Holliston	MA	C	508 429-1350	9221
Stanley Industrial & Auto LLC	Holliston	MA	B	508 429-1350	9230
Coast To Cast Ff E Instltns	Greenland	NH	F	603 433-0164	14368

CABINETS: Kitchen, Metal

	CITY	ST	EMP	PHONE	ENTRY#
CT Acquisitions LLC	Wallingford	CT	E	888 441-0537	3797
Coastal-N-Counters Inc	Mashpee	MA	F	508 539-3500	10251

CABINETS: Kitchen, Wood

	CITY	ST	EMP	PHONE	ENTRY#
B & L Finishing Shop Inc	Bristol	CT	G	860 583-1164	400
Belmont Corporation	Bristol	CT	E	860 589-5700	413
Bergan Architectural Wdwkg Inc	Middletown	CT	E	860 346-0869	1739
Bonito Manufacturing Inc	North Haven	CT	D	203 234-8786	2394
Brunarhans Inc	Woodstock	CT	G	860 928-0807	4392
Cabinet Harward Specialti	West Hartford	CT	G	860 231-1192	4049
Cabinets To Go LLC	Wallingford	CT	E	800 222-4638	3785
Captivating Kitchens	West Hartford	CT	G	860 236-6500	4051
Chris Cross LLC	Stratford	CT	F	203 386-8426	3526
Christopher Peacock Home LLC	Norwalk	CT	F	203 388-4022	2481
Connecticut Solid Surface LLC	Canton	CT	E	860 410-9800	559
Conway Hardwood Products LLC	Gaylordsville	CT	E	860 355-4030	1264
Custom Furniture & Design LLC	Litchfield	CT	F	860 567-3519	1555
Cyr Woodworking Inc	Newington	CT	G	860 232-1991	2284
Domestic Kitchens Inc	Fairfield	CT	E	203 368-1651	1181
European Woodcraft LLC	Norwalk	CT	G	203 847-6195	2498
Focal Metals	Bethel	CT	G	203 743-4443	115
Greenhaven Cabinetry Mllwk LLC	Stonington	CT	G	860 535-1106	3509
Hanford Cabinet & Wdwkg Co Inc	Old Saybrook	CT	G	860 388-5055	2650
Heartwood Cabinet	Marlborough	CT	G	860 295-0304	1643
Hemingway Custom Cabinetry LLC	Bridgeport	CT	F	203 382-0300	328
John June Custom Cabinetry LLC	Bridgeport	CT	F	203 334-1720	336
Kitchen Cab Resurfacing LLC	Bridgeport	CT	F	203 334-2857	340
Kitchen Living LLC	East Hampton	CT	G	860 819-5847	964

	CITY	ST	EMP	PHONE	ENTRY#
Legere Group Ltd	Avon	CT	D	860 674-0392	29
Leos Kitchen and Stair Corp	New Britain	CT	G	860 225-7363	2037
Martin Cabinet Inc (PA)	Plainville	CT	E	860 747-5769	2772
Milton & Goose LLC	Stamford	CT	G	203 539-1073	3412
Porta Door Co	Seymour	CT	E	203 888-6191	2967
Prestige Remodeling LLC	Bridgeport	CT	F	203 386-8426	362
Robert L Lovallo	Stamford	CT	G	203 324-6655	3450
Specialty Shop Inc	Manchester	CT	G	860 647-1477	1637
Statham Woodwork	Norwalk	CT	G	203 831-0629	2574
Sterling Custom Cabinetry LLC	Bridgeport	CT	F	203 335-5151	375
Stm Imp and Exp Corp	Plainfield	CT	G	973 450-5110	2740
Viking Kitchen Cabinets LLC (PA)	New Britain	CT	E	860 223-7101	2074
West Hrtford Stirs Cbinets Inc	Newington	CT	D	860 953-9151	2334
Anthony Manufacturing Co Inc	Medford	MA	F	781 396-1400	10279
Architectural Kitchens Inc	Wellesley	MA	F	781 239-9750	12936
Ashland Cabinet Corporation	Southborough	MA	F	508 303-8100	11989
B & G Cabinet	Newburyport	MA	F	978 465-6455	10669
Boston Stone and Cabinet	Norwood	MA	F	781 352-3623	11165
Cabinet Depot Outlet Inc	Southborough	MA	F	508 485-7777	11993
Camio Custom Cabinetry Inc	Canton	MA	F	781 562-1573	7775
Carousel Cabinets	Lancaster	MA	G	978 846-8763	9524
Classic Kitchen Design Inc	Hyannis	MA	F	508 775-3075	9431
Clever Green Cabinets LLC	Waltham	MA	G	508 963-6776	12632
Coastal-N-Counters Inc	Mashpee	MA	F	508 539-3500	10251
Counterra LLC	Canton	MA	F	781 821-2100	7780
Cronin Cabinets - Marine LLP	Charlton	MA	G	508 248-7026	7886
Custom Ktchens By Chmpagne Inc	Franklin	MA	F	508 528-7919	8828
Dedham Cabinet Shop Inc	Canton	MA	F	781 326-4090	7783
Dixon Bros Millwork Inc	Abington	MA	G	781 261-9962	5724
Eastern Woodworks Llc	Georgetown	MA	F	978 352-2005	8908
Fallon Fine Cabinetry Inc	Needham Heights	MA	F	781 453-6988	10544
Fort Point Cabinet Makers LLC	Boston	MA	G	617 338-9487	6745
Furniture Design Services Inc	Peabody	MA	F	978 531-3250	11310
Hastone Homestone Inc	Dorchester	MA	F	617 784-3284	8300
Ideal Kitchens of Palmer (PA)	Chicopee	MA	G	413 532-2253	8037
Industrial Woodworking Co Inc	East Weymouth	MA	F	781 340-7474	8429
Irvings Home Center Inc	Brockton	MA	G	508 583-4421	7285
J & K Cabinets Ltd	Wilmington	MA	G	978 658-1888	13417
J & M Cabinet Shop Inc	Walpole	MA	G	508 660-6660	12565
JC Clocks Company Inc	North Dartmouth	MA	E	508 998-8442	10998
JS International Inc (PA)	Fall River	MA	F	508 675-4722	8564
Kitchen Options Inc	Oxford	MA	G	508 987-3384	11256
Kochman Reidt & Haigh Inc	Stoughton	MA	E	781 573-1500	12217
Mass Cabinets Inc	Methuen	MA	E	978 738-0600	10337
Miller H C Wood Working Inc	Holliston	MA	G	508 429-4220	9223
Northast Cab Cntrtop Dstrs Inc	Braintree	MA	F	617 296-2100	7197
Payne/Bouchier Inc (PA)	Roxbury	MA	E	617 445-4323	11692
RF McManus Company Inc	Charlestown	MA	F	617 241-8081	7881
Rgc Millwork Incorporated	Lowell	MA	G	978 275-9529	9919
Rosario Cabinets Inc	Dedham	MA	G	781 329-0639	8248
Scandia Kitchens Inc	Bellingham	MA	E	508 966-0300	6300
Star Kitchen Cabinets Inc	Avon	MA	G	508 510-3123	6162
Stokes Woodworking Co Inc (PA)	Hudson	MA	G	508 481-0414	9416
Superior Kitchen Designs Inc	Gardner	MA	F	978 632-5072	8903
Toledo Woodworking Inc	Holliston	MA	G	508 280-3354	9233
Triple Crown Cbnets Mllwk Corp	Sandwich	MA	G	508 833-6500	11753
Vartanian Custom Cabinets	Palmer	MA	E	413 283-3438	11288
Water Closet LLC	Nantucket	MA	F	508 228-2828	10466
Watson Brothers Inc	Middleton	MA	F	978 774-7677	10397
Wells Development L L C	Arlington	MA	F	781 727-5560	5950
Wolf Organization LLC	Northborough	MA	D	508 393-2040	11116
Woodmeister Master Bldrs Inc (PA)	Holden	MA	C	774 345-1000	9196
Black Cove Cabinetry	Scarborough	ME	G	207 883-8965	5425
Directions To Maine Dovetail	Westbrook	ME	G	207 829-2759	5625
Kennebec Cabinetry Inc	Bath	ME	F	207 442-0813	4527
Kennebec Company	Bath	ME	F	207 443-2131	4528
Lawrence Parson	Brownfield	ME	G	207 935-3737	4636
Naheks Inc	Hermon	ME	F	207 848-7770	4886
R G Eaton Woodworks Inc	Westbrook	ME	G	207 883-3398	5644
Trico Millworks Inc	Limington	ME	G	207 637-2711	5006
Advanced Custom Cabinets Inc	Brentwood	NH	F	603 772-6211	14019
Cabinets For Less LLC	Manchester	NH	G	603 935-7551	14825
Counter Pro Inc	Manchester	NH	F	603 647-2444	14838
Crown Point Cabinetry Corp	Claremont	NH	D	603 542-1273	14086
Cw Keller & Associates LLC	Plaistow	NH	D	603 382-2028	15339
Granite State Ktchens Dstrs In	Bedford	NH	E	603 472-4080	13931
Mark Allen Cabinetry LLC	Amherst	NH	E	603 491-7570	13877
Northeast Woodworking Pdts Inc	Raymond	NH	F	603 895-4271	15454
Nudd Cabinetry	Sanbornton	NH	F	603 286-3160	15577
Plaistow Cabinet Co Inc	Plaistow	NH	F	603 382-1098	15348
Revolution Furnishings LLC	Manchester	NH	G	603 606-6123	14921
Tri Town Cabinetry	Hooksett	NH	G	603 391-9276	14475

	CITY	ST	EMP	PHONE	ENTRY#
Triumph Interiors LLC	Rindge	NH	F	603 899-5184	15461
Walpole Cabinetry	Walpole	NH	F	603 826-4100	15663
Ws Dennison Cabinets Inc	Pembroke	NH	F	603 224-8434	15309
Bella Cabinets Inc	Pawtucket	RI	G	401 722-0038	16348
Completely Custom LLC	North Kingstown	RI	G	401 667-0059	16239
Elmwood Countertop Inc	Cranston	RI	G	401 785-1677	15854
Hardwood Design Inc	Exeter	RI	E	401 294-2235	16051
Imperia Corporation	Barrington	RI	E	508 894-3000	15748
Master Kitchens Center Inc	Newport	RI	G	401 324-7100	16216
New England Cstm Cabinets LLC	North Kingstown	RI	G	401 667-2572	16273
Carlton Newton Corporation LLC	Brattleboro	VT	G	802 579-1413	17078
City Feed and Lumber Co Inc (PA)	Saint Albans	VT	E	802 524-2136	17519

CABINETS: Office, Wood

	CITY	ST	EMP	PHONE	ENTRY#
CFI Millwork Inc	Manchester	CT	F	860 643-7580	1588
Gregory Woodworks LLC	Bethel	CT	G	203 794-0726	118
Stm Imp and Exp Corp	Plainfield	CT	F	973 450-5110	2740
Gill Metal Fab Inc	Brockton	MA	E	508 580-4445	7281
Imperia Corporation	Barrington	RI	E	508 894-3000	15748

CABINETS: Show, Display, Etc, Wood, Exc Refrigerated

	CITY	ST	EMP	PHONE	ENTRY#
New England Cabinet Co	New Britain	CT	E	860 225-8645	2046
B&B Micro Manufacturing Inc	Adams	MA	E	413 281-9431	5771
Custom Kctchens By Chmpagne Inc	Franklin	MA	F	508 528-7919	8828
Eagle Woodworking Inc	Lawrence	MA	E	978 681-6194	9558
Jules A Gourdeau Inc	Beverly	MA	G	978 922-0102	6358
Kochman Reidt & Haigh Inc	Stoughton	MA	E	781 573-1500	12217
Pbd Productions LLC	Hopedale	MA	F	508 482-9300	9300
Yankee Builders	Dartmouth	MA	G	508 636-8660	8234
Tozier Group Inc	Falmouth	ME	F	207 838-7939	4774
Advanced Custom Cabinets Inc	Brentwood	NH	F	603 772-6211	14019
Cole Cabinet Co Inc	Cranston	RI	F	401 467-4343	15842

CABLE & OTHER PAY TELEVISION DISTRIBUTION

	CITY	ST	EMP	PHONE	ENTRY#
Hubbell Power Systems Inc	Cromwell	CT	D	860 635-2200	694

CABLE TELEVISION

	CITY	ST	EMP	PHONE	ENTRY#
Cco Holdings LLC	Harvard	MA	C	978 615-1032	9060
Cco Holdings LLC	Longmeadow	MA	C	413 754-0616	9849
Cco Holdings LLC	North Grafton	MA	C	774 293-4026	11020
Cco Holdings LLC	Upton	MA	C	774 462-6577	12470
Comcast Sportsnet Neng LLC	Needham Heights	MA	D	617 630-5000	10537
Cco Holdings LLC	Montpelier	VT	C	802 778-0497	17371

CABLE TELEVISION PRDTS

	CITY	ST	EMP	PHONE	ENTRY#
Fat Hen LLC	Somerville	MA	G	617 764-1412	11871

CABLE: Coaxial

	CITY	ST	EMP	PHONE	ENTRY#
A J R Inc	Bridgeport	CT	F	203 384-0400	290
Times Fiber Communications Inc (HQ)	Wallingford	CT	D	800 677-2288	3865
Volpe Cable Corporation	Branford	CT	C	203 623-1818	284
East Cast McRwave Sls Dist LLC	Woburn	MA	E	781 279-0900	13562
Electronic Assemblies Mfg Inc	Methuen	MA	E	978 374-6840	10329
James Monroe Wire & Cable Corp (PA)	South Lancaster	MA	D	978 368-0131	11971
Amphenol Corporation	Nashua	NH	B	603 879-3000	15061
Cable Assemblies Inc	Amherst	NH	F	603 889-4090	13863

CABLE: Fiber

	CITY	ST	EMP	PHONE	ENTRY#
Photonic Systems Inc	Billerica	MA	F	978 670-4990	6471

CABLE: Fiber Optic

	CITY	ST	EMP	PHONE	ENTRY#
Fiberqa LLC	Old Lyme	CT	E	860 254-7275	2641
Microspec Corporation	Peterborough	NH	E	603 924-4300	15319
Subcom Cable Systems LLC	Newington	NH	B	603 436-6100	15214

CABLE: Noninsulated

	CITY	ST	EMP	PHONE	ENTRY#
Armored Shield Technologies	Redding	CT	F	714 848-5796	2881
Redco Audio Inc	Monroe	CT	F	203 502-7600	1920
Saint-Gobain Prfmce Plas Corp	Worcester	MA	C	508 852-3072	13792
Amphenol Corporation	Nashua	NH	B	603 879-3000	15061
Continental Cable LLC	Hinsdale	NH	D	800 229-5131	14443
Ametek Scp Inc (HQ)	Westerly	RI	D	401 596-6658	16927
Signature Cable Mfg Tech Inc	Cranston	RI	E	401 383-1008	15910

CABLE: Ropes & Fiber

	CITY	ST	EMP	PHONE	ENTRY#
Ropes Wealth Advisors LLC	Boston	MA	E	617 951-7217	7013
Orion Ropeworks Inc (HQ)	Winslow	ME	F	207 877-2224	5687
Marmon Utility	Milford	NH	F	603 249-1302	15031
Two In One Manufacturing Inc	Nashua	NH	E	603 595-8212	15179

CABLE: Steel, Insulated Or Armored

	CITY	ST	EMP	PHONE	ENTRY#
Federal Prison Industries	Danbury	CT	E	203 743-6471	745

	CITY	ST	EMP	PHONE	ENTRY#
Lex Products LLC (PA)	Trumbull	CT	C	203 363-3738	3723
Rscc Wire & Cable LLC (DH)	East Granby	CT	B	860 653-8300	950
Specialty Cable Corp	Wallingford	CT	D	203 265-7126	3852
Heat Trace Products LLC	Leominster	MA	E	978 534-2810	9669
James Monroe Wire & Cable Corp (PA)	South Lancaster	MA	D	978 368-0131	11971
Temp-Flex LLC	South Grafton	MA	E	508 839-3120	11958
Micro Wire Transm Systems Inc	Essex Junction	VT	F	802 876-7901	17241

CAFES

	CITY	ST	EMP	PHONE	ENTRY#
Tatte Holdings LLC	Boston	MA	C	617 577-1111	7070
Westborough Books Inc (PA)	Westborough	MA	E	508 366-4292	13144
Coffee Exchange Ltd	Providence	RI	F	401 273-1198	16502
Klingers Bread Company	South Burlington	VT	E	802 860-6322	17582

CAFETERIAS

	CITY	ST	EMP	PHONE	ENTRY#
Battle Grounds Coffee Co LLC	Haverhill	MA	F	978 891-5860	9077

CALCULATING & ACCOUNTING EQPT

	CITY	ST	EMP	PHONE	ENTRY#
Blackwold Inc	Chester	CT	D	860 526-0800	624

CALIBRATING SVCS, NEC

	CITY	ST	EMP	PHONE	ENTRY#
Klarmann Rulings Inc	Manchester	NH	F	603 424-2401	14872

CAMERA CARRYING BAGS

	CITY	ST	EMP	PHONE	ENTRY#
Porta-Brace Inc	Bennington	VT	F	802 442-8171	17055

CAMPERS: Truck Mounted

	CITY	ST	EMP	PHONE	ENTRY#
Port-Lite LLC	Alna	ME	G	678 575-9065	4405

CAMSHAFTS

	CITY	ST	EMP	PHONE	ENTRY#
Westfalia Inc	Bristol	CT	E	860 314-2920	505

CANDLE SHOPS

	CITY	ST	EMP	PHONE	ENTRY#
Laurence Cndle Mfg Ch Sups Inc (PA)	Millbury	MA	E	508 865-6061	10439
Pilgrim Candle Company Inc (PA)	Westfield	MA	E	413 562-2635	13199
Yankee Candle Company Inc (DH)	South Deerfield	MA	C	413 665-8306	11931
Yankee Candle Investments LLC (DH)	South Deerfield	MA	E	413 665-8306	11932
Ycc Holdings LLC	South Deerfield	MA	A	413 665-8306	11934

CANDLES

	CITY	ST	EMP	PHONE	ENTRY#
CJ First Candle	New Canaan	CT	G	203 966-1300	2077
Crystal Journey Candles LLC	Branford	CT	F	203 433-4735	245
Nac Industries Inc	Oxford	CT	F	845 214-0659	2706
Couture Brands LLC	Marlborough	MA	G	512 626-7544	10138
HMh Religious Mfg Inc	Plainville	MA	G	508 699-9464	11434
Laurence Cndle Mfg Ch Sups Inc (PA)	Millbury	MA	E	508 865-6061	10439
Partylite Inc (HQ)	Plymouth	MA	D	203 661-1926	11471
Partylite Worldwide LLC (DH)	Norwell	MA	C	888 999-5706	11144
Pilgrim Candle Company Inc (PA)	Westfield	MA	E	413 562-2635	13199
Whiffletree Cntry Str Gift Sp	Billerica	MA	F	978 663-6346	6490
Yankee Candle Company Inc (DH)	South Deerfield	MA	C	413 665-8306	11931
Yankee Candle Company Inc	Whately	MA	G	413 665-8306	13340
Yankee Candle Investments LLC (DH)	South Deerfield	MA	E	413 665-8306	11932
Yankee Holding Corp (DH)	South Deerfield	MA	D	413 665-8306	11933
Ycc Holdings LLC	South Deerfield	MA	A	413 665-8306	11934
Danica Design	Rockport	ME	E	207 236-3060	5347
Alene Candles LLC (PA)	Milford	NH	C	603 673-5050	15014
Marklin Candle Design LLC	Contoocook	NH	F	603 746-2211	14171
Aunt Sadies Inc	Lunenburg	VT	F	802 892-5267	17316
Way Out Wax Inc	Montgomery Center	VT	F	802 730-8069	17369

CANDLES: Wholesalers

	CITY	ST	EMP	PHONE	ENTRY#
Partylite Inc (HQ)	Plymouth	MA	D	203 661-1926	11471

CANDY & CONFECTIONS: Candy Bars, Including Chocolate Covered

	CITY	ST	EMP	PHONE	ENTRY#
Hebert Confections LLC	Shrewsbury	MA	F		11833
Hebert Retail LLC	Shrewsbury	MA	D	508 845-8051	11834
Nu Chocolat LLC	Burlington	VT	F	802 735-7770	17147

CANDY & CONFECTIONS: Chocolate Candy, Exc Solid Chocolate

	CITY	ST	EMP	PHONE	ENTRY#
Wilburs ME Choclat Confections	Freeport	ME	F	207 865-4071	4805

CANDY & CONFECTIONS: Popcorn Balls/Other Trtd Popcorn Prdts

	CITY	ST	EMP	PHONE	ENTRY#
Quirion Luc (PA)	Newport	VT	G	802 673-8386	17406

CANDY, NUT & CONFECTIONERY STORES: Candy

	CITY	ST	EMP	PHONE	ENTRY#
Bridgewater Chocolate LLC	Brookfield	CT	G	203 775-2286	513
Munsons Candy Kitchen Inc (PA)	Bolton	CT	E	860 649-4332	221
Thompson Brands LLC	Meriden	CT	D	203 235-2541	1708
Thompson Candy Company	Meriden	CT	D	203 235-2541	1709
Arthur Mapes Inc	Chelmsford	MA	F	978 256-4061	7910

PRODUCT

	CITY	ST	EMP	PHONE	ENTRY#
Bb Walpole Liquidation NH Inc	Cambridge	MA	G	617 491-4340	7499
Ben & Bills Chocolate Emporium	Falmouth	MA	F	508 548-7878	8628
Ben & Blls Chclat Emporium Inc (PA)	Northampton	MA	F	413 584-5695	11053
C&J Dreams Inc (PA)	North Easton	MA	E	508 238-6231	11008
Dorothy Coxs Candies Inc	Fall River	MA	E	774 678-0654	8534
Fastachi Ltd	Watertown	MA	F	617 924-8787	12876
Fedele and Carter Inc	Dennis Port	MA	F	508 394-1791	8261
Furlongs Cttage Cndies Ice Cre	Norwood	MA	F	781 762-4124	11174
Russos Inc	Saugus	MA	F	781 233-1737	11765
Seven Sweets Inc	Marblehead	MA	F	781 631-0303	10095
Stage Stop Candy Ltd Inc	Dennis Port	MA	G	508 394-1791	8263
Wilburs ME Choclat Confections	Freeport	ME	F	207 865-4071	4805
Fredericks Pastries (PA)	Amherst	NH	C	603 882-7725	13871
Lindt & Sprungli (usa) Inc (HQ)	Stratham	NH	C	603 778-8100	15637
Van Otis Chocolates LLC (PA)	Manchester	NH	G	603 627-1611	14949
Anchor Toffee LLC	Newport	RI	E	401 619-1044	16201
Sweenors Chocolates Inc (PA)	Wakefield	RI	F	401 783-4433	16745
Tom and Sallys Handmade Choco	Westerly	RI	F	800 289-8783	16944
Tradest1	East Greenwich	RI	E	401 884-4949	15994
Champlain Chocolate Company (PA)	Burlington	VT	D	800 465-5909	17124
Champlain Chocolate Company	Williston	VT	D	802 864-1808	17725
Fudge Factory Inc	Manchester Center	VT	F	888 669-7425	17328

CANDY: Soft

Seven Sweets Inc	Marblehead	MA	F	781 631-0303	10095

CANNED SPECIALTIES

Royal Food Import Corporation	Boston	MA	F	617 482-3826	7016
Stonewall Kitchen LLC (PA)	York	ME	C	207 351-2713	5717

CANOE BUILDING & REPAIR

Johnson Otdoors Watercraft Inc (HQ)	Old Town	ME	E	207 827-5513	5126

CANS: Aluminum

CCL Label Inc	Shelton	CT	F	203 926-1253	2990
CCL Industries Corporation (HQ)	Framingham	MA	D	508 872-4511	8749
CCL Label Inc (HQ)	Framingham	MA	D	508 872-4511	8750
Can-One (usa) Inc	Nashua	NH	F	860 299-4608	15075

CANS: Metal

Silgan Closures Intl Holdg Co	Stamford	CT	F	203 975-7110	3457
Silgan Containers Corporation	Stamford	CT	A	203 975-7110	3458
Silgan White Cap Corporation	Stamford	CT	E	630 515-8383	3460
Leaktite Corporation (DH)	Leominster	MA	E	978 537-8000	9676

CANS: Tin

Tin Can Alley	Provincetown	MA	G	508 487-1648	11499

CANVAS PRDTS

American Sign Inc	New Haven	CT	F	203 624-2991	2115
Defender Industries Inc	Waterford	CT	C	860 701-3400	3989
Dimension-Polyant Inc	Putnam	CT	E	860 928-8314	2853
New Haven Companies Inc	East Haven	CT	F	203 469-6421	1048
Topside Canvas & Uphl Inc	Westbrook	CT	G	860 399-4845	4144
Columbia ASC Inc	Lawrence	MA	F	978 683-2205	9554
Leisure Time Canvas Inc	West Springfield	MA	G	413 785-5500	13032
Spector Textile Products Inc (PA)	Lawrence	MA	E	978 688-3501	9600
Steele Canvas Basket Corp	Chelsea	MA	F	800 541-8929	7994
United Industrial Tex Pdts Inc (PA)	West Springfield	MA	E	413 737-0095	13048
Byer Manufacturing Company	Bernard	ME	E	207 866-2171	4547
C B P Corp (PA)	Arundel	ME	F	207 985-9767	4409
Custom Canvas & Upholstery LLC	Bridgton	ME	F	207 241-8518	4627
Maine Bay Canvas Inc	Portland	ME	F	207 878-8888	5237
Enviro-Tote Inc	Londonderry	NH	E	603 647-7171	14749
Anchors and Thread LLC	Portsmouth	RI	E	401 248-8645	16435
Anchors Aweigh Together LLC	Warwick	RI	E	401 738-8055	16779
Stupell Industries Ltd Inc	Johnston	RI	F	401 831-5640	16107
Ke Usa Inc	Middlebury	VT	E	802 388-7309	17345

CAPACITORS & CONDENSERS

Aerovox Incorporated	New Bedford	MA	A	508 994-9661	10565
Kyocera AVX Cmpnnts Bddford Co	Biddeford	ME	C	207 282-5111	4574
Desco Industries Inc	Rochester	NH	F	603 332-0717	15473

CAPACITORS: NEC

Code Red Electronics LLC	North Branford	CT	G		2363
Hipotronics Inc (HQ)	Shelton	CT	C	845 279-3644	3013
Newco Condenser Inc	Shelton	CT	F	475 882-4000	3039
Aerovox Incorporated	New Bedford	MA	A	508 994-9661	10565
Cornell-Dubilier Elec Inc	New Bedford	MA	B	508 996-8561	10580
Magellan Distribution Corp	Boston	MA	F	617 399-7900	6868
Rf Aero LLC	New Bedford	MA	E	508 910-3500	10646

	CITY	ST	EMP	PHONE	ENTRY#
Steinerfilm Inc	Williamstown	MA	C	413 458-9525	13368
Tdl Inc	Canton	MA	E	781 828-3366	7833
Kyocera AVX Cmpnnts Bddford Co	Biddeford	ME	C	207 282-5111	4574
Standex International Corp (PA)	Salem	NH	E	603 893-9701	15563
Evans Capacitor Company LLC	East Providence	RI	E	401 435-3555	16017
Vishay Efi Inc	Warwick	RI	E	401 738-9150	16873

CAPS: Plastic

Bprex Halthcare Brookville Inc	Waterbury	CT	B	203 754-4141	3891
Summit Packaging Systems LLC (PA)	Manchester	NH	B	603 669-5410	14937
Silgan Dspnsing Systems Sltrsv (DH)	Slatersville	RI	E	401 767-2400	16683

CARBIDES

Carbide Solutions LLC	Windsor	CT	G	860 515-8665	4264
Cutting Edge Carbide Tech Inc	Athol	MA	G	888 210-9670	5977
Gws Tool Holdings LLC	Springfield	MA	E	800 523-8570	12098
The Sharp Tool Co Inc	Hudson	MA	E	978 568-9292	9418

CARBON & GRAPHITE PRDTS, NEC

Carbon Products Inc	Somersville	CT	G	860 749-0614	3101
Joshua LLC (PA)	Guilford	CT	F	203 624-0080	1398
Minteq International Inc	Canaan	CT	F	860 824-5435	556
Morgan A M T	Durham	CT	F	860 349-4444	903
Applied Nnstrctred Sltions LLC	Billerica	MA	E	978 670-6959	6403
Geonautics Manufacturing Inc	Newburyport	MA	E	978 462-7161	10685
Via Separations Inc	Watertown	MA	D	781 354-7945	12918
Clear Carbon & Components Inc	Bristol	RI	E	401 254-5085	15758
Hall Inc	Bristol	RI	D	401 253-4858	15768

CARBON BLACK

Cabot Corporation	Billerica	MA	E	978 671-4000	6421
Cabot Corporation (PA)	Boston	MA	C	617 345-0100	6631
Cabot Corporation	Haverhill	MA	C	978 556-8400	9084

CARBON PAPER & INKED RIBBONS

Avcarb LLC	Lowell	MA	D	978 452-8961	9857

CARDIOVASCULAR SYSTEM DRUGS, EXC DIAGNOSTIC

Boehrnger Inglheim Phrmctcals	Ridgefield	CT	C	203 798-9988	2890
Boehrnger Inglheim Phrmctcals (DH)	Ridgefield	CT	A	203 798-9988	2891
Bentley Pharmaceuticals Inc (HQ)	Exeter	NH	C	603 658-6100	14285

CARDS: Beveled

JS McCarthy Co Inc (PA)	Augusta	ME	D	207 622-6241	4473

CARDS: Greeting

Anothercreationbymichele	Stamford	CT	G	203 322-4277	3282
Caspari Inc (PA)	Seymour	CT	F	203 888-1100	2957
Olympia Sales Inc	Enfield	CT	B	860 749-0751	1140
Expressive Design Group Inc	Holyoke	MA	E	413 315-6296	9255
Lovepop Inc (PA)	Boston	MA	E	888 687-9589	6864
Marian Heath Greeting Cards LLC	Wareham	MA	E	508 291-0766	12840
New England Art Publishers Inc	Abington	MA	E	781 878-5151	5726
New England Business Svc Inc (HQ)	Townsend	MA	D	978 448-6111	12441
Viabella Holdings LLC	Sudbury	MA	D	978 855-8817	12271
Viabella Holdings LLC (PA)	Wareham	MA	E	800 688-9998	12848
Walgreen Co	North Attleboro	MA	E	781 244-9431	10892
Borealis Press Inc	Blue Hill	ME	G	800 669-6845	4595
Renaissance Greeting Cards Inc	Sanford	ME	E	207 324-4153	5409
William Arthur Inc	West Kennebunk	ME	D	413 684-2600	5611
Be Youneeq LLC	Raymond	NH	G	603 244-3933	15451
Pep Direct LLC	Wilton	NH	D	603 654-6141	15707
Quadriga Art	Milford	NH	E	603 654-6141	15035
E Frances Paper Inc	Middletown	RI	F	857 250-0036	16173
Mainstream Inc (PA)	Bennington	VT	F	802 442-8859	17050
Oatmeal Studios Inc	Rochester	VT	F	802 967-8014	17487
Vermont Christmas Company	Milton	VT	G	802 893-1670	17366

CARDS: Identification

Amplified Ink Co	Fairfield	CT	C	203 787-2184	1175
Idemia Identity & SEC USA LLC	Rocky Hill	CT	F	860 529-2559	2929
Andrew Rolden PC	Ayer	MA	G	978 391-4655	6172
Budgetcard Inc	Attleboro Falls	MA	F	508 695-8762	6080
Comprehensive Identification Products Inc 781 229-8780	Burlington	MA	C		7354
Reeves Company Inc	Attleboro	MA	F	508 222-2877	6053

CARPET & UPHOLSTERY CLEANING SVCS

Craftech Upton	Upton	MA	F	508 529-4505	12472

CARPETS & RUGS: Tufted

0 Mohawk LLC	Cos Cob	CT	G	203 622-7180	673

	CITY	ST	EMP	PHONE	ENTRY#
Mohawk Fence Company Inc	Shrewsbury	MA	G	508 614-5507	11838
East Providence Mohawks	East Providence	RI	G	401 829-1411	16015

CARPETS, RUGS & FLOOR COVERING

	CITY	ST	EMP	PHONE	ENTRY#
Alliance Carpet Cushion Co (HQ)	Torrington	CT	D	860 489-4273	3667
Apricot Home LLC	Greenwich	CT	G	203 552-1791	1312
Connecticut Clean Room Corp	Bristol	CT	E	860 589-0049	430
Ethan Allen Retail Inc (HQ)	Danbury	CT	B	203 743-8000	741
New Haven Companies Inc	East Haven	CT	F	203 469-6421	1048
Aladdin Manufacturing Corp	Walpole	MA	B	508 660-8913	12549
Delaware Valley Corp	Tewksbury	MA	E	978 459-6932	12393
Julie Industries Inc (PA)	Andover	MA	G	978 276-0820	5890
Merida LLC	Fall River	MA	E	508 675-6572	8577
Merida Meridian Inc	Boston	MA	E	617 464-5400	6885
Stevens Linen Associates Inc	Dudley	MA	E	508 943-0813	8325
International Textile Mfg Inc	Cumberland	RI	G		15946
A View of Vermont LLC	Saint Johnsbury	VT	G	802 748-0880	17538

CARPETS: Textile Fiber

	CITY	ST	EMP	PHONE	ENTRY#
Natco Products Corporation (PA)	West Warwick	RI	B	401 828-0300	16916

CARRIER EQPT: Telephone Or Telegraph

	CITY	ST	EMP	PHONE	ENTRY#
Telecom Installation Svcs Inc	Middletown	RI	E	401 258-2095	16185

CARRIERS: Infant, Textile

	CITY	ST	EMP	PHONE	ENTRY#
Summer Infant Inc (HQ)	Woonsocket	RI	C	401 671-6550	16975
Summer Infant (usa) Inc	Woonsocket	RI	C	401 671-6551	16976

CARTONS: Egg, Molded Pulp, Made From Purchased Materials

	CITY	ST	EMP	PHONE	ENTRY#
Henlay Co	Cheshire	CT	G	908 795-1007	598

CARTS: Grocery

	CITY	ST	EMP	PHONE	ENTRY#
Cco Llc	Rocky Hill	CT	F	860 757-3434	2917

CASEMENTS: Aluminum

	CITY	ST	EMP	PHONE	ENTRY#
Far Industries Inc	Assonet	MA	F	508 644-3122	5973

CASES: Attache'

	CITY	ST	EMP	PHONE	ENTRY#
Case Concepts Intl LLC	Stamford	CT	G	203 883-8602	3303

CASES: Carrying

	CITY	ST	EMP	PHONE	ENTRY#
Calzone Ltd (PA)	Bridgeport	CT	E	203 367-5766	309
Fabrique Ltd (PA)	Branford	CT	G	203 481-2266	255
Ats Cases Inc	Northborough	MA	G	508 393-9110	11089
Van & Company Inc	Pawtucket	RI	F	401 722-9829	16428

CASES: Carrying, Clothing & Apparel

	CITY	ST	EMP	PHONE	ENTRY#
Smithfamily1938 LLC	Enfield	CT	G	424 341-8876	1153
Dance It Up Inc	North Grafton	MA	F	508 839-1648	11021

CASES: Jewelry

	CITY	ST	EMP	PHONE	ENTRY#
Fuller Box Co Inc (PA)	North Attleboro	MA	D	508 695-2525	10871
Jewel Case Corporation	Providence	RI	B	401 943-1400	16549
Numaco Packaging LLC	East Providence	RI	F	401 438-4952	16035

CASES: Nonrefrigerated, Exc Wood

	CITY	ST	EMP	PHONE	ENTRY#
Pemac Construction	Oakdale	CT	F	860 437-0007	2623

CASES: Plastic

	CITY	ST	EMP	PHONE	ENTRY#
Hcp Packaging Usa Inc	Hinsdale	NH	C	603 256-3141	14444
Cabinet Gallery Ltd (PA)	Woonsocket	RI	G	401 762-4300	16952
Case Hard	Little Compton	RI	F	401 635-8201	16159

CASH REGISTER REPAIR SVCS

	CITY	ST	EMP	PHONE	ENTRY#
Dgf Indstrial Innvtons Group L	Gilford	NH	F	603 528-6591	14335

CASINGS: Sheet Metal

	CITY	ST	EMP	PHONE	ENTRY#
MB Aerospace East Granby Limited Partnership 860 653-5041	East Granby 942	CT			C
Brouillette Hvac & Shtmtl Inc	East Taunton	MA	G	508 822-4800	8406
Churchill Corporation	Melrose	MA	E	781 665-4700	10315

CASINGS: Storage, Missile & Missile Components

	CITY	ST	EMP	PHONE	ENTRY#
Geonautics Manufacturing Inc	Newburyport	MA	E	978 462-7161	10685

CAST STONE: Concrete

	CITY	ST	EMP	PHONE	ENTRY#
Dawn Enterprises LLC	Manchester	CT	G	860 646-8200	1591
Stone Image Custom Con LLC	Suffield	CT	G	860 668-2434	3595

CASTINGS GRINDING: For The Trade

	CITY	ST	EMP	PHONE	ENTRY#
A D Grinding	Plainville	CT	F	860 747-6630	2743
Unas Grinding Corporation	East Hartford	CT	E	860 289-1538	1030

	CITY	ST	EMP	PHONE	ENTRY#
Wood Grinding Unlimited	Bridgeport	CT	G	203 333-9047	385
Form Centerless Grinding Inc	Franklin	MA	F	508 520-0900	8837
Kind Grind Incorporated	Amherst	MA	F	413 367-2478	5861
Precision Machinists Co Inc	Franklin	MA	F	508 528-2325	8857
Xtreme Tub Grinding Svcs Inc	North Dighton	MA	G	508 386-6015	11005
Monadnock Grinding LLC	Fitzwilliam	NH	F	603 585-7275	14314
White Mountain Wood Grinding	Contoocook	NH	G	603 455-6931	14176

CASTINGS: Aerospace Investment, Ferrous

	CITY	ST	EMP	PHONE	ENTRY#
Alphacoin LLC	Bethel	CT	G	475 256-4050	99
Doncasters US Hldings 2018 Inc	Groton	CT	F	860 449-1603	1368
Hexcel Corporation	South Windsor	CT	D	925 520-3232	3156
Mascon Inc	Woburn	MA	E	781 938-5800	13605
Parts Tool and Die Inc	Agawam	MA	E	413 821-9718	5805
Tecomet Inc	Wilmington	MA	B	978 642-2400	13462
Wyman-Gordon Company (DH)	North Grafton	MA	B	508 839-8252	11030
PCC Structurals Groton	Franklin	NH	B	603 286-4301	14321
Xray Aerospace Corp	Claremont	NH	F	603 254-8051	14101

CASTINGS: Aerospace, Aluminum

	CITY	ST	EMP	PHONE	ENTRY#
Integra-Cast Inc	New Britain	CT	D	860 225-7600	2032
Pcx Aerosystems LLC	Newington	CT	C	860 666-2471	2317
Arcam Cad To Metal Inc	Woburn	MA	E	781 281-1718	13513
Industrial Bmdcal Sensors Corp	Waltham	MA	E	781 891-4201	12698
Parts Tool and Die Inc	Agawam	MA	E	413 821-9718	5805
Tecomet Inc	Wilmington	MA	B	978 642-2400	13462
Westfield Gage Co Inc	Southwick	MA	F	413 569-9444	12050
Jade Manufacturing Company LLC	Warwick	RI	E	401 737-2400	16826

CASTINGS: Aerospace, Nonferrous, Exc Aluminum

	CITY	ST	EMP	PHONE	ENTRY#
Consoldted Inds Acqsition Corp	Cheshire	CT	D	203 272-5371	582
Parts Tool and Die Inc	Agawam	MA	E	413 821-9718	5805
Tecomet Inc	Wilmington	MA	B	978 642-2400	13462
Component Technologies Corpora	Bristol	RI	G	401 965-2699	15759

CASTINGS: Aluminum

	CITY	ST	EMP	PHONE	ENTRY#
Marlborough Foundry Inc	Marlborough	MA	E	508 485-2848	10182
Nanoal LLC (HQ)	Ashland	MA	G	774 777-3369	5963
Diamond Casting and Mch Co LLC	Hollis	NH	E	603 465-2263	14450
Nu-Cast Inc	Londonderry	NH	E	603 432-1600	14777

CASTINGS: Brass, NEC, Exc Die

	CITY	ST	EMP	PHONE	ENTRY#
KW Thompson Tool Company Inc	Rochester	NH	D	603 330-8670	15483

CASTINGS: Bronze, NEC, Exc Die

	CITY	ST	EMP	PHONE	ENTRY#
Mystic Valley Foundry Inc	Lincoln	MA	G	617 547-1819	9798
Bronze Craft Corporation	Nashua	NH	D	603 883-7747	15074

CASTINGS: Commercial Investment, Ferrous

	CITY	ST	EMP	PHONE	ENTRY#
Howmet Corporation	Branford	CT	B	203 315-6150	265
Howmet Corporation	Branford	CT	A	203 481-3451	266
Sturm Ruger & Company Inc (PA)	Southport	CT	B	203 259-7843	3247
A Young Casting	Attleboro	MA	F	508 222-8188	5987
Kervick Family Foundation Inc	Worcester	MA	B	508 853-4500	13748
New England Castings LLC	Standish	ME	E	207 642-3029	5528

CASTINGS: Die, Aluminum

	CITY	ST	EMP	PHONE	ENTRY#
Arrow Diversified Tooling Inc	Ellington	CT	E	860 872-9072	1101
Custom Metal Crafters Inc	Newington	CT	E	860 953-4210	2283
Texas Die Casting LLC	Norwalk	CT	C	903 845-2224	2581
Diecast Connections Co Inc	Plymouth	MA	E	413 592-8444	11456
Kennedy Die Castings Inc	Worcester	MA	C	508 791-5594	13747
Kingston Aluminum Foundry Inc	Kingston	MA	G	781 585-6631	9509
Mystic Valley Foundry Inc	Lincoln	MA	G	617 547-1819	9798
Pace Industries LLC	North Billerica	MA	C	978 667-8400	10941
Connectcut Prcsion Cstings Inc	Claremont	NH	G	603 542-3373	14085
Diamond Casting and Mch Co LLC	Hollis	NH	E	603 465-2263	14450
Hebert Manufacturing Company (PA)	Laconia	NH	F	603 524-2065	14653
Wyman-Gordon Company	Franklin	NH	B	603 934-6630	14325
Miniature Casting Corporation	Cranston	RI	F	401 463-5090	15896

CASTINGS: Die, Nonferrous

	CITY	ST	EMP	PHONE	ENTRY#
Custom Metal Crafters Inc	Newington	CT	E	860 953-4210	2283
Integra-Cast Inc	New Britain	CT	D	860 225-7600	2032
Narragansett Screw Co	Winsted	CT	F	860 379-4059	4351
Advanced Metal Concepts Inc	North Attleboro	MA	E	508 695-6400	10864
Diamond Casting and Mch Co LLC	Hollis	NH	E	603 465-2263	14450
Watts Regulator Co	Franklin	NH	A	603 934-5110	14323
Fielding Manufacturing Inc	Cranston	RI	D	401 461-0400	15860
New England Precision Inc	Randolph	VT	D	800 293-4112	17471

CASTINGS: Ductile

Employee Codes: A=Over 500 employees, B=251-500
C=101-250, D=51-100, E=20-50, F=10-19, G=1-9

2024 Harris New England
Manufacturers Directory

1357

P R O D U C T

	CITY	ST	EMP	PHONE	ENTRY#
G & W Foundry Corp	Millbury	MA	E	508 581-8719	10434
Kadant Inc (PA)	Westford	MA	C	978 776-2000	13244

CASTINGS: Gray Iron

	CITY	ST	EMP	PHONE	ENTRY#
Taylor & Fenn Company	Windsor	CT	E	860 219-9393	4307
Henry Perkins Company	Bridgewater	MA	F	508 697-6978	7230
Whitman Castings Inc (PA)	Whitman	MA	E	781 447-4417	13352
Millincket Fabrication Mch Inc (PA)	Millinocket	ME	E	207 723-9733	5067
Nashua Foundries Inc	Nashua	NH	E	603 882-4811	15138
Cumberland Foundry Co Inc	Cumberland	RI	E	401 658-3300	15936
Fairmount Foundry Inc	Woonsocket	RI	E	401 769-1585	16959

CASTINGS: Machinery, Nonferrous, Exc Die or Aluminum Copper

	CITY	ST	EMP	PHONE	ENTRY#
The Commercial Foundry Company	New Britain	CT	E	860 224-1794	2071
Accent On Industrial Metal Inc	Springfield	MA	F	413 785-1654	12069

CASTINGS: Precision

	CITY	ST	EMP	PHONE	ENTRY#
Sycast Inc	Hartford	CT	F	860 308-2122	1512
Yankee Casting Co Inc	Enfield	CT	D	860 749-6171	1161
Kervick Family Foundation Inc	Worcester	MA	E	508 853-4500	13748
AI CU Met Inc	Londonderry	NH	E	603 432-6220	14729
Providence Casting Inc	North Providence	RI	G	401 231-0860	16308

CASTINGS: Steel

	CITY	ST	EMP	PHONE	ENTRY#
Frank Roth Co Inc	Stratford	CT	D	203 377-2155	3539
Trident Alloys Inc	Springfield	MA	E	413 737-1477	12142
Wollaston Alloys Inc	Braintree	MA	C	781 848-3333	7214
KW Thompson Tool Company Inc	Rochester	NH	D	603 330-8670	15483

CASTINGS: Titanium

	CITY	ST	EMP	PHONE	ENTRY#
Aerospace Metals Inc	Hartford	CT	A	860 522-3123	1468
Doncasters Inc (PA)	Groton	CT	D	860 449-1603	1367
Titanium Electric LLC	Norwalk	CT	G	203 810-4050	2582

CATALOG & MAIL-ORDER HOUSES

	CITY	ST	EMP	PHONE	ENTRY#
Flag Fables Inc	Springfield	MA	E	413 747-0525	12095
Partylite Worldwide LLC (DH)	Norwell	MA	C	888 999-5706	11144
Southworth Company	Agawam	MA	C	413 789-1200	5807
Storey Publishing LLC (DH)	Clarksburg	MA	E	413 346-2100	8074
J H Breakell & Company Inc	Newport	RI	F	401 849-3522	16213
Vermont Christmas Company	Milton	VT	G	802 893-1670	17366

CATALOG SALES

	CITY	ST	EMP	PHONE	ENTRY#
Renovators Supply Inc	Erving	MA	E	413 423-3300	8471
Orvis Company Inc	Manchester	VT	E	802 362-3750	17324
Speeder & Earls Inc	Burlington	VT	F	802 660-3996	17160
The Orvis Company Inc (PA)	Sunderland	VT	B	802 362-3622	17635

CATALYSTS: Chemical

	CITY	ST	EMP	PHONE	ENTRY#
Advanced Pwr Systems Intl Inc	New Hartford	CT	G	860 921-0009	2097
Joshua LLC (PA)	Guilford	CT	F	203 624-0080	1398
King Industries Inc (PA)	Norwalk	CT	C	203 866-5551	2523

CATAPULTS

	CITY	ST	EMP	PHONE	ENTRY#
Catapult Sports LLC	Boston	MA	E	312 762-5332	6643
Entwistle Company LLC (PA)	Hudson	MA	D	508 481-4000	9364
M & P Machine Company Inc	Stoughton	MA	E	781 344-5888	12218

CATERERS

	CITY	ST	EMP	PHONE	ENTRY#
Creole Jos LLC	Glastonbury	CT	F	203 893-2875	1276
Yosi Kosher Catering LLC	Windsor	CT	F	860 688-6677	4316
Bakery To Go Inc	Boston	MA	G	617 482-1015	6582
Diemand Egg Farm Inc	Millers Falls	MA	G	978 544-3806	10447
North Star Distributors Inc (PA)	Vineyard Haven	MA	E	508 693-2000	12494
Spinelli Ravioli Mfg Co Inc	Boston	MA	E	617 567-1992	7053
Franks Bake Shop Inc	Bangor	ME	G	207 947-4594	4502

CEILING SYSTEMS: Luminous, Commercial

	CITY	ST	EMP	PHONE	ENTRY#
C Cowles & Company (PA)	North Haven	CT	D	203 865-3117	2396
Asd Lighting Corp	Canton	MA	E	781 739-3977	7770

CEMENT: Hydraulic

	CITY	ST	EMP	PHONE	ENTRY#
Dragon Products Company LLC	Thomaston	ME	E	207 594-5555	5544

CEMENT: Portland

	CITY	ST	EMP	PHONE	ENTRY#
Andrews Holdings Inc	Ayer	MA	E	978 772-4444	6173
Dragon Products Company LLC (DH)	Biddeford	ME	E	207 594-5555	4560

CERAMIC FIBER

	CITY	ST	EMP	PHONE	ENTRY#
International Crmic Engrg Corp (PA)	Worcester	MA	E	508 853-4700	13743
Ceramco Inc	Center Conway	NH	E	603 447-2090	14050

CHAIN: Tire, Made From Purchased Wire

	CITY	ST	EMP	PHONE	ENTRY#
Tire Chains Requiredcom	Oakland	ME	G	207 465-7276	5121

CHAIN: Welded, Made From Purchased Wire

	CITY	ST	EMP	PHONE	ENTRY#
St Pierre Manufacturing Corp	Worcester	MA	E	508 853-8010	13806

CHANGE MAKING MACHINES

	CITY	ST	EMP	PHONE	ENTRY#
Crane Payment Solutions Inc (DH)	Bedford	NH	D	603 685-6999	13923

CHARCOAL: Activated

	CITY	ST	EMP	PHONE	ENTRY#
Carbtrol Corporation	Stratford	CT	E	203 337-4340	3525

CHASSIS: Motor Vehicle

	CITY	ST	EMP	PHONE	ENTRY#
Prfrred Lancaster Partners LLC	Boston	MA	F	717 299-0782	6980
Costello/April Design Inc	Dover	NH	E	603 749-6755	14224

CHEMICAL ELEMENTS

	CITY	ST	EMP	PHONE	ENTRY#
Element Care	Methuen	MA	G	978 655-6195	10330
Element All Stars	Lewiston	ME	G	207 576-6931	4958
Brunswick Square LLC	Burlington	VT	G	802 497-2575	17122

CHEMICAL PROCESSING MACHINERY & EQPT

	CITY	ST	EMP	PHONE	ENTRY#
Interlab Incorporated	Danbury	CT	E	203 794-0209	759
Artisan Industries Inc	Stoughton	MA	D	781 893-6800	12195
Celeros Inc	Newton	MA	E	248 478-2800	10742
Chemical Systems Services Inc	Attleboro	MA	F	508 431-9995	6003
Hosokawa Micron Intl Inc	Northborough	MA	E	508 655-1123	11098
Jgp Enterprises Inc	Lawrence	MA	E	978 691-2737	9572
Sturtevant Inc (PA)	Hanover	MA	E	781 829-6501	9045
White Mountain Imaging	Concord	NH	E	603 228-2630	14166
White Mountain Imaging (PA)	Webster	NH	F	603 648-2124	15675
Environmental Ctrl Systems Inc	East Providence	RI	F	401 437-8612	16016

CHEMICAL: Sodm Compnds/Salts, Inorg, Exc Rfnd Sodm Chloride

	CITY	ST	EMP	PHONE	ENTRY#
Tronox Incorporated (DH)	Stamford	CT	C	203 705-3800	3486
International Dioxcide Inc	North Kingstown	RI	E	401 295-8800	16260

CHEMICALS & ALLIED PRDTS WHOLESALERS, NEC

	CITY	ST	EMP	PHONE	ENTRY#
Airgas Usa LLC	Danbury	CT	C	203 792-1834	705
Kolmar Americas Inc (HQ)	Bridgeport	CT	F	203 873-2051	341
Lanxess Corporation	Naugatuck	CT	E	203 714-8669	1970
Miyoshi America Inc (HQ)	Dayville	CT	D	860 779-3990	863
Total Specialty Chemicals Inc (PA)	New Canaan	CT	E	203 966-1525	2089
Vanderbilt Chemicals LLC (HQ)	Norwalk	CT	E	203 295-2141	2589
Fisher Scientific Intl LLC (HQ)	Waltham	MA	C	781 622-1000	12675
Guardian Indus Pdts Inc Mass	Norfolk	MA	E	508 384-0060	10798
Lubrizol Global Management Inc	Wilmington	MA	C	978 642-5051	13427
Safc Hitech Inc	Haverhill	MA	E	978 374-5200	9130
Savin Products Company Inc	Randolph	MA	E	781 961-2743	11574
The Savogran Company	Norwood	MA	E	781 762-5400	11216
Gac Chemical Corporation (PA)	Searsport	ME	D	207 548-2525	5453
Appli-Tec Inc	Salem	NH	E	603 685-0500	15508
Gates Tpu Inc	Salem	NH	E	603 890-1515	15531
Electrolizing Inc	Providence	RI	E	401 861-5900	16513
Seventh Generation Inc (DH)	Burlington	VT	C	802 658-3773	17159

CHEMICALS & ALLIED PRDTS, WHOLESALE: Acids

	CITY	ST	EMP	PHONE	ENTRY#
New England Tooling Inc	Killingworth	CT	F	800 866-5105	1544
US Chemicals Inc	New Canaan	CT	G	203 655-8878	2093

CHEMICALS & ALLIED PRDTS, WHOLESALE: Alkalines & Chlorine

	CITY	ST	EMP	PHONE	ENTRY#
Arcadia Chem Preservative LLC	Shelton	CT	F	203 717-4750	2982

CHEMICALS & ALLIED PRDTS, WHOLESALE: Chemicals, Indl

	CITY	ST	EMP	PHONE	ENTRY#
Greenfield Global USA Inc (HQ)	Brookfield	CT	F	203 740-3471	524
Harcros Chemicals Inc	Westbrook	ME	G	207 856-6756	5627
Univar Solutions USA Inc	Providence	RI	E	518 762-3500	16633

CHEMICALS & ALLIED PRDTS, WHOLESALE: Chemicals, Indl & Heavy

	CITY	ST	EMP	PHONE	ENTRY#
Hubbard-Hall Inc (PA)	Waterbury	CT	D	203 756-5521	3919
Near Oak LLC	Stamford	CT	G	203 329-6500	3415
RT Vanderbilt Holding Co Inc (PA)	Norwalk	CT	F	203 295-2141	2568
Borden & Remington Corp	Fall River	MA	E	508 675-0096	8528
Hubbard-Hall Inc	Wilmington	MA	F	978 988-0077	13411

CHEMICALS & ALLIED PRDTS, WHOLESALE: Detergent/Soap

	CITY	ST	EMP	PHONE	ENTRY#
MD Stetson Company Inc	Mansfield	MA	E	781 986-6161	10066

CHEMICALS & ALLIED PRDTS, WHOLESALE: Plastics Film

	CITY	ST	EMP	PHONE	ENTRY#
Orafol Americas Inc	Avon	CT	C	860 676-7100	35

	CITY	ST	EMP	PHONE	ENTRY#
Web Industries Hartford Inc (HQ)	Dayville	CT	E	860 779-3197	870
Web Industries Inc (PA)	Marlborough	MA	G	508 898-2988	10234

CHEMICALS & ALLIED PRDTS, WHOLESALE: Plastics Materials, NEC

Edco Industries Inc	Bridgeport	CT	F	203 333-8982	319

CHEMICALS & ALLIED PRDTS, WHOLESALE: Plastics Prdts, NEC

Thornton and Company Inc	Southington	CT	E	860 628-6771	3237
Tri-Star Plastics Corp (PA)	Shrewsbury	MA	E	508 845-1111	11845
Seventh Generation Inc (DH)	Burlington	VT	C	802 658-3773	17159

CHEMICALS & ALLIED PRDTS, WHOLESALE: Plastics Sheets & Rods

Delmar Products Inc	Berlin	CT	F	860 828-6501	64
Plastics Unlimited of MA Inc	Worcester	MA	G	508 752-7842	13770
Morris Transparent Box Co	East Providence	RI	F	401 438-6116	16032

CHEMICALS & ALLIED PRDTS, WHOLESALE: Resins

Neu Spclty Engineered Mtls LLC	North Haven	CT	F	203 239-9629	2426
Covestro LLC	Wilmington	MA	C	800 458-0014	13399
DSM Neoresins Inc	Wilmington	MA	C	800 458-0014	13403
Eastman Performance Films LLC	Holliston	MA	E	508 474-6002	9208

CHEMICALS & ALLIED PRDTS, WHOLESALE: Resins, Plastics

Polymer Corporation (HQ)	Rockland	MA	D	781 871-4606	11656

CHEMICALS & ALLIED PRDTS, WHOLESALE: Rubber, Synthetic

Auburn Manufacturing Company	Middletown	CT	E	860 346-6677	1737

CHEMICALS & ALLIED PRDTS, WHOLESALE: Spec Clean/Sanitation

A W Chesterton Company (PA)	Groveland	MA	E	781 438-7000	9012

CHEMICALS & ALLIED PRDTS, WHOLESALE: Syn Resin, Rub/Plastic

Seaview Plastic Recycling Inc	Bridgeport	CT	F	203 367-0070	370
Avient Colorants USA LLC	Lewiston	ME	B	207 784-0733	4951
Allstate Polyethylene Corp (PA)	Alexandria	NH	G	800 288-7659	13851
QST Inc	Saint Albans	VT	E	802 524-7704	17529

CHEMICALS: Agricultural

Clinton Nursery Products Inc (PA)	Westbrook	CT	C	860 399-3000	4137
Rohm Haas Electronic Mtls LLC	Marlborough	MA	E	508 481-7950	10207
Shield Packaging Co Inc	Dudley	MA	E	508 949-0900	8323
Rosalie Gendron LLC	Manchester	NH	G	603 836-3692	14922
Augmentus Group LLC	Burlington	VT	F		17119

CHEMICALS: Aluminum Sulfate

Gac Chemical Corporation (PA)	Searsport	ME	D	207 548-2525	5453
General Alum New England Corp	Searsport	ME	D	207 548-2525	5454

CHEMICALS: Caustic Potash & Potassium Hydroxide

Driscolls Restaurant	Mansfield	MA	G	508 261-1574	10050

CHEMICALS: Fire Retardant

Command Chemical Corporation	Fairfield	CT	G	203 319-1857	1180
Great Lakes Chemical Corp (DH)	Shelton	CT	E	203 573-2000	3010
Lanxess Solutions US Inc	Shelton	CT	A	203 573-2000	3027

CHEMICALS: High Purity, Refined From Technical Grade

Americanbio Inc	Canton	MA	E	508 655-4336	7768
Northern Products Inc	Woonsocket	RI	F		16969

CHEMICALS: Inorganic, NEC

Auterra Inc	Guilford	CT	G	518 382-9600	1385
Chromatics Inc	Bethel	CT	D	203 743-6868	102
H Krevit and Company Inc	New Haven	CT	E	203 772-3350	2159
Miller-Stephenson Chemical Company Inc (PA)	Danbury	CT	E	800 442-3424	786
RT Vanderbilt Holding Co Inc (PA)	Norwalk	CT	F	203 295-2141	2568
Solidification Pdts Intl Inc	Northford	CT	G	203 484-9494	2456
Solvay	Stamford	CT	E	203 321-2292	3464
Specialty Minerals Inc	Canaan	CT	F	860 824-5435	557
Total Specialty Chemicals Inc (PA)	New Canaan	CT	E	203 966-1525	2089
Vanderbilt Chemicals LLC	Bethel	CT	C	203 744-3900	139
Vanderbilt Chemicals LLC (HQ)	Norwalk	CT	E	203 295-2141	2589
A W Chesterton Company	Groveland	MA	B	781 438-7000	9013
Avient Colorants USA LLC (HQ)	Holden	MA	E	508 829-6321	9187
Cabot Holdings LLC	Boston	MA	F	617 345-0100	6632
Cabot Ii-Tn1w09 LLC	Boston	MA	F	617 723-7400	6633
Cabot Specialty Chemicals Inc (HQ)	Boston	MA	F	617 345-0100	6634
CCL Industries Corporation (HQ)	Framingham	MA	D	508 872-4511	8749
CMC Materials Inc	Waltham	MA	F	781 530-3833	12633
Cmo Partners Inc	Billerica	MA	F	617 575-5449	6425
Dow Chemical Company	Marlborough	MA	C	508 229-7676	10147

	CITY	ST	EMP	PHONE	ENTRY#
Eidp Inc	Boston	MA	F	617 482-9595	6708
Fiberlock Technologies Inc	Andover	MA	F	978 623-9987	5882
Gcp Applied Technologies Inc	Cambridge	MA	E	617 876-1400	7578
Holland Company Inc	Adams	MA	E	413 743-1292	5773
MD Stetson Company Inc	Mansfield	MA	E	781 986-6161	10066
Metalor USA Refining Corp (DH)	North Attleboro	MA	E	508 699-8800	10877
Omniglow LLC	West Springfield	MA	B	413 241-6010	13039
Qsa Global Inc (HQ)	Burlington	MA	D	781 272-2000	7416
Rohm Haas Electronic Mtls LLC (HQ)	Marlborough	MA	A	508 481-7950	10206
Saint-Gobain Ceramics Plas Inc	Northborough	MA	E	508 351-7754	11107
Saint-Gobain Ceramics Plas Inc	Worcester	MA	D	508 795-5000	13790
Saint-Gobain Ceramics Plas Inc	Worcester	MA	C	508 795-5000	13791
Solutia Inc	Indian Orchard	MA	C	734 676-4400	9474
Strem Chemicals Incorporated (HQ)	Newburyport	MA	D	978 499-1600	10718
Sud-Chemie Protech Inc	Needham Heights	MA	B	781 444-5188	10559
Synthomer Inc	Fitchburg	MA	C	978 342-5831	8678
Transene Company Inc (PA)	Danvers	MA	E	978 777-7860	8227
Trelleborg Offshore Boston Inc	Mansfield	MA	E	774 719-1400	10082
Trelleborg Offshore Boston Inc (HQ)	Randolph	MA	E	781 437-1171	11577
Dalegip America Inc	Searsport	ME	E	207 323-1880	5452
Imerys Usa Inc	Skowhegan	ME	E	207 238-9267	5469
Hampshire Chemical Corp (DH)	Nashua	NH	E	603 888-2320	15109
Pure Chemical	Derry	NH	G	603 235-4373	14207
Saint-Gobain Ceramics Plas Inc	Milford	NH	C	603 673-5831	15036
Z-Tech LLC	Bow	NH	C	603 228-1305	14016
Agilent Technologies Inc	North Kingstown	RI	D	800 338-1754	16229
Cal Chemical Corporation	Coventry	RI	E	401 821-0320	15808
Clariant Corporation	Coventry	RI	E	401 823-2000	15809
Ne Finest LLC	Coventry	RI	F	800 215-6640	15817
Reade International Corp (PA)	East Providence	RI	F	401 433-7000	16041
Ultra Scientific Incorporated	North Kingstown	RI	E	800 338-1754	16290
Augmentus Group LLC	Burlington	VT	F		17119
O M Y A Inc	Proctor	VT	E	802 499-8131	17458
Omya	Florence	VT	E	802 770-7537	17271

CHEMICALS: Medicinal

Fulcrum Thrptics Scrities Corp	Cambridge	MA	E	617 651-8851	7576
Nova Biomedical Corporation	Billerica	MA	D	781 647-3700	6464
Valo Health Inc (PA)	Boston	MA	E	617 237-6080	7096
Veranova LP	North Andover	MA	E	978 784-5000	10857
Seasmoke Extracts Inc	Auburn	ME	F	207 819-4114	4460

CHEMICALS: Medicinal, Organic, Uncompounded, Bulk

Impact Nano LLC	Orange	MA	G	508 380-8423	11224

CHEMICALS: NEC

5n Plus Corp	Bridgeport	CT	F	608 846-1357	288
Advanced Pwr Systems Intl Inc	New Hartford	CT	G	860 921-0009	2097
Armored Autogroup Parent Inc	Danbury	CT	C	203 205-2900	710
Brand-Nu Laboratories LLC (PA)	Meriden	CT	E	203 235-7989	1656
Carrubba Incorporated	Milford	CT	D	203 878-0605	1809
Chemotex Prtctive Catings Corp (PA)	Durham	CT	F	860 349-0144	897
Chessco Industries Inc (PA)	Westport	CT	E	203 255-2804	4160
Crystal Rock Spring Water Co	Watertown	CT	B	860 945-0661	4007
Cytec Industries Inc	Stamford	CT	D	203 321-2200	3333
Dexsil Corporation	Hamden	CT	E	203 288-3509	1421
Filmco Rust Protection LLC	Branford	CT	E	203 483-5017	256
Five Star Products Inc	Shelton	CT	E	203 336-7900	3006
Harvard Chemical LLC (HQ)	Bolton	CT	F	404 761-0657	220
Henkel of America Inc (HQ)	Rocky Hill	CT	B	860 615-3395	2926
Henkel US Operations Corp (DH)	Rocky Hill	CT	B	860 571-5100	2927
Hubbard-Hall Inc (PA)	Waterbury	CT	D	203 756-5521	3919
Intersurface Dynamics Inc	Bethel	CT	F	203 778-9995	120
Lanxess Corporation	Naugatuck	CT	E	203 714-8669	1970
Laticrete International Inc (PA)	Bethany	CT	B	203 393-0010	94
Macdermid Acumen Inc	Waterbury	CT	E	203 575-5700	3934
Macdermid AG Solutions Inc (HQ)	Waterbury	CT	F	203 575-5727	3935
Macdermid Anion Inc	Waterbury	CT	C	203 575-5700	3936
Macdermid Autotype Inc	Waterbury	CT	C	847 818-8262	3937
Macdermid Enthone Inc (HQ)	West Haven	CT	C	203 934-8611	4112
Macdermid Holdings LLC	Waterbury	CT	E	203 575-5700	3939
Macdermid Overseas Asia Ltd (HQ)	Waterbury	CT	C	203 575-5799	3940
Macdermid Prtg Sltons Acmen In	Waterbury	CT	C	203 575-5700	3941
Near Oak LLC	Stamford	CT	G	203 329-6500	3415
Purification Technologies LLC (DH)	Chester	CT	F	860 526-7801	630
REM Chemicals Inc (PA)	Southington	CT	F	860 621-6755	3231
Stanchem Incorporated (HQ)	East Berlin	CT	E	860 828-0571	918
A W Chesterton Company	Groveland	MA	B	781 438-7000	9013
Adaptive Surface Tech Inc	Hopkinton	MA	G	617 360-7080	9306
Barclay Water Management Inc	Newton	MA	D	617 926-3400	10736
Bolger and OHearn Inc	Fall River	MA	E	508 676-1518	8527
Business and Prof Exch Inc	Beverly	MA	E	978 556-4100	6336

Employee Codes: A=Over 500 employees, B=251-500
C=101-250, D=51-100, E=20-50, F=10-19, G=1-9

2024 Harris New England
Manufacturers Directory

1359

PRODUCT

	CITY	ST	EMP	PHONE	ENTRY#
Cabot Corporation	Billerica	MA	E	978 671-4000	6421
Cold Chain Technologies LLC (HQ)	Franklin	MA	D	508 429-1395	8826
Creative Materials Inc	Ayer	MA	E	978 391-4700	6180
Emco Services Inc	Fall River	MA	G	508 674-5504	8541
Hiller Companies Inc	Peabody	MA	E	978 532-5730	11315
Holland Company Inc	Adams	MA	E	413 743-1292	5773
Hubbard-Hall Inc	Wilmington	MA	F	978 988-0077	13411
Katahdin Industries Inc (PA)	Hudson	MA	E	781 329-1420	9380
Kayaku Advanced Materials Inc	Newton	MA	E	617 965-5511	10767
Kayaku Advanced Materials Inc (PA)	Westborough	MA	E	617 965-5511	13113
Lubrizol Global Management Inc	Wilmington	MA	C	978 642-5051	13427
MD Chemicals LLC	Mendon	MA	E	508 314-9664	10320
MD Stetson Company Inc	Mansfield	MA	E	781 986-6161	10066
Mexichem Spcalty Compounds Inc (HQ)	Leominster	MA	C	978 537-8071	9683
Osmo Labs Pbc	Cambridge	MA	F	508 439-4692	7679
Rectorseal LLC	Fall River	MA	F	508 673-7561	8601
Rule Industries LLC	Gloucester	MA	E	978 281-0440	8956
Sigma-Aldrich Corporation	Burlington	MA	D	978 715-1804	7427
Thermo Fisher Scientific Inc	Beverly	MA	C	978 232-6000	6387
Transene Company Inc (PA)	Danvers	MA	G	978 777-7860	8227
United States Biological Corp	Salem	MA	E	978 744-0345	11737
FMC Corporation	Rockland	ME	D	207 594-3200	5329
Salt and Pepper Me LLC	Wilton	ME	F	207 645-7035	5659
Diversified Enterprises-ADT	Claremont	NH	G	603 543-0038	14088
Hampshire Chemical Corp (DH)	Nashua	NH	F	603 888-2320	15109
Performance Chemicals LLC	Franklin	NH	F	603 228-1200	14322
Aspen Aerogels RI LLC	East Providence	RI	E	401 432-2612	16005
Cranston Print Works Company (PA)	Cranston	RI	F	401 943-4800	15844
Dryvit Systems Inc (DH)	North Kingstown	RI	D	401 822-4100	16245
International Dioxcide Inc	North Kingstown	RI	E	401 295-8800	16260
New Brick Dryvit Systems	North Kingstown	RI	G	401 822-4100	16272
Technic Inc	Pawtucket	RI	E	401 781-6100	16419
Univar Solutions USA Inc	Providence	RI	E	518 762-3500	16633

CHEMICALS: Organic, NEC

	CITY	ST	EMP	PHONE	ENTRY#
Agilent Technologies Inc	North Kingstown	RI	D	800 338-1754	16229
Ultra Scientific Incorporated	North Kingstown	RI	E	800 338-1754	16290

CHEMICALS: Reagent Grade, Refined From Technical Grade

	CITY	ST	EMP	PHONE	ENTRY#
Captivate Bio LLC	Watertown	MA	G	617 607-4017	12867
Instrumentation Laboratory Co (DH)	Bedford	MA	A	781 861-0710	6233
Magellan Diagnostics Inc (HQ)	Chelmsford	MA	D	978 250-7000	7937
Twin Rivers Tech Holdings Inc	Quincy	MA	C	617 472-9200	11541
Twin Rivers Technologies Us Inc	Quincy	MA	C	617 472-9200	11544

CHEMICALS: Silica Compounds

	CITY	ST	EMP	PHONE	ENTRY#
Nyacol Nano Technologies Inc	Ashland	MA	E	508 881-2220	5965

CHEMICALS: Silica, Amorphous

	CITY	ST	EMP	PHONE	ENTRY#
Cabot Corporation (PA)	Boston	MA	C	617 345-0100	6631
Cabot Corporation	Haverhill	MA	C	978 556-8400	9084

CHEMICALS: Water Treatment

	CITY	ST	EMP	PHONE	ENTRY#
Gotham Chemical Company Inc	Norwalk	CT	D	203 854-6644	2508
Aqua Laboratories Inc	Amesbury	MA	E	978 388-3989	5829
Clearwter Tech Cnslting Wtr Sv	Rockland	MA	F	781 871-5157	11640
Duraflow LLC	Tewksbury	MA	F	978 851-7439	12394
Bardon Industries Inc	East Greenwich	RI	F	401 884-1814	15973
Town of Burrillville	Oakland	RI	G	401 568-6296	16335

CHICKEN SLAUGHTERING & PROCESSING

	CITY	ST	EMP	PHONE	ENTRY#
Advancepierre Foods Inc	Portland	ME	A	207 541-2800	5175
Baffonis Poultry Farm Inc	Johnston	RI	E	401 231-6315	16077
Maple Wind Farm Inc	Richmond	VT	G	802 434-7257	17480

CHILDREN'S & INFANTS' CLOTHING STORES

	CITY	ST	EMP	PHONE	ENTRY#
Chuck Roast Equipment Inc (PA)	Conway	NH	F	603 447-5492	14178

CHILDREN'S WEAR STORES

	CITY	ST	EMP	PHONE	ENTRY#
Classic Prep Childrenswear Inc	Norwalk	CT	G	203 286-6204	2483
Ragged Mountain Equipment Inc	Intervale	NH	E	603 356-3042	14561
Thanksben10 LLC	Milford	NH	F	603 206-5116	15040

CHOCOLATE, EXC CANDY FROM BEANS: Chips, Powder, Block, Syrup

	CITY	ST	EMP	PHONE	ENTRY#
Mantrose-Haeuser Co Inc (HQ)	Westport	CT	E	203 454-1800	4182
Munsons Candy Kitchen Inc (PA)	Bolton	CT	E	860 649-4332	221
Thompson Brands LLC	Meriden	CT	D	203 235-2541	1708
Arthur Mapes Inc	Chelmsford	MA	F	978 256-4061	7910
C&J Dreams Inc (PA)	North Easton	MA	E	508 238-6231	11008
Cambridge Brands Mfg Inc	Cambridge	MA	C	617 491-2500	7527
Dorothy Coxs Candies Inc	Fall River	MA	F	774 678-0654	8534

	CITY	ST	EMP	PHONE	ENTRY#
Mielke Confections Inc	West Stockbridge	MA	G	413 528-2510	13054
New England Confectionery Company Inc	Revere	MA			B
781 485-4500	11622				
Phillips Candy House Inc	Boston	MA	E	617 282-2090	6965
Russos Inc	Saugus	MA	E	781 233-1737	11765
Sweethearts Candy Co LLC	Revere	MA	B	781 485-4500	11624
Winfreys Olde English Fdge Inc (PA)	Rowley	MA	F	978 948-7448	11687
Bixby & Co LLC	Rockland	ME	F	207 691-1778	5323
Harbor Candy Shop Inc	Ogunquit	ME	F	207 646-8078	5123
Lady Ann Candies Inc	Warwick	RI	F	401 738-4321	16832
Birnn Chocolates Vermont Inc	South Burlington	VT	F	802 860-1047	17573
Sentar Inc	South Burlington	VT	D	802 861-6004	17598
Sunny Sky Products LLC	South Burlington	VT	F	802 861-6004	17602
Vermont Nut Free Choclat Inc	Colchester	VT	F	802 372-4654	17206

CHOCOLATE, EXC CANDY FROM PURCH CHOC: Chips, Powder, Block

	CITY	ST	EMP	PHONE	ENTRY#
Bb Walpole Liquidation NH Inc	Cambridge	MA	G	617 491-4340	7499
Green Mountain Choclat Co Inc (PA)	Hopedale	MA	G	508 473-9060	9298
LA Burdick Boston LLC	Boston	MA	G	617 303-0113	6850
Tru Chocolate Inc	Haverhill	MA	G	855 878-2462	9135
Lindt & Sprungli (usa) Inc (HQ)	Stratham	NH	C	603 778-8100	15637
World Wide Distribution Corp	Brentwood	NH	G	603 942-6032	14033
Barry Callebaut USA LLC	Saint Albans	VT	C	802 524-9711	17516

CHRISTMAS NOVELTIES, WHOLESALE

	CITY	ST	EMP	PHONE	ENTRY#
Ambrose G McCarthy Jr	Skowhegan	ME	G	207 474-8837	5462
Kelco Industries	Milbridge	ME	E	207 546-7562	5061

CHROMATOGRAPHY EQPT

	CITY	ST	EMP	PHONE	ENTRY#
Organomation Associates Inc	Berlin	MA	F	978 838-7300	6320
Waters Associates Inc	Milford	MA	A	508 634-4500	10423
Waters Corporation (PA)	Milford	MA	A	508 478-2000	10424
Waters Technologies Corp (HQ)	Milford	MA	A	508 478-2000	10425
Waters Technologies Corp	Taunton	MA	F	508 482-5223	12376
G&G Technologies Inc	Coventry	RI	F	401 295-4000	15813

CHUCKS

	CITY	ST	EMP	PHONE	ENTRY#
Miracle Instruments Co	Lebanon	CT	F	860 642-7745	1549
O S Walker Company Inc (HQ)	Windsor	CT	E	508 853-3232	4292
Royal Machine and Tool Corp	Berlin	CT	E	860 828-6555	83
Double E Company LLC (PA)	West Bridgewater	MA	C	508 588-8099	12972

CHURCHES

	CITY	ST	EMP	PHONE	ENTRY#
Unitarian Universalist Assn (PA)	Boston	MA	C	617 742-2100	7092

CIGARETTE LIGHTERS

	CITY	ST	EMP	PHONE	ENTRY#
Bic Corporation (HQ)	Shelton	CT	A	203 783-2000	2985
Bic USA Inc (DH)	Shelton	CT	C	203 783-2000	2986

CIRCUIT BOARD REPAIR SVCS

	CITY	ST	EMP	PHONE	ENTRY#
Microboard Processing Inc	Seymour	CT	C	203 881-4300	2965
AC Electric Corp (PA)	Auburn	ME	E	207 784-7341	4416
Singulrity Elctrnic Systems In	Portsmouth	NH	G	603 430-6000	15437

CIRCUIT BOARDS, PRINTED: Television & Radio

	CITY	ST	EMP	PHONE	ENTRY#
Portuguese Times Inc	New Bedford	MA	G	508 997-3118	10641

CIRCUIT BOARDS: Wiring

	CITY	ST	EMP	PHONE	ENTRY#
Murata Power Solutions Inc (DH)	Westborough	MA	C	508 339-3000	13122

CIRCUITS, INTEGRATED: Hybrid

	CITY	ST	EMP	PHONE	ENTRY#
Hi-Rel Group LLC	Essex	CT	G	860 767-9031	1166
Hi-Rel Products LLC	Essex	CT	E	860 767-9031	1167
Mini-Systems Inc	North Attleboro	MA	D	508 695-1420	10878
Spectrum Microwave Inc	Marlborough	MA	C	508 485-0336	10212
Stellar Industries Corp	Millbury	MA	E	508 865-1668	10443
Ibmnh Inc (PA)	Manchester	NH	G	603 644-2326	14861
Micro-Precision Tech Inc	Salem	NH	E	603 893-7600	15545
Vishay Efi Inc	Warwick	RI	E	401 738-9150	16873

CIRCUITS: Electronic

	CITY	ST	EMP	PHONE	ENTRY#
AB Electronics LLC	Brookfield	CT	E	203 740-2793	509
Arccos Golf LLC (PA)	Stamford	CT	E	844 692-7226	3286
Bead Industries Inc (PA)	Milford	CT	E	203 301-0270	1801
Doltronics LLC	Branford	CT	E	203 488-8766	250
Electro-Tech Inc	Cheshire	CT	E	203 271-1976	589
ESI Electronic Products Corp	Prospect	CT	E	203 758-4401	2834
General Electro Components	Glastonbury	CT	G	860 659-3573	1280
Goodrich Corporation	Danbury	CT	B	505 345-9031	750
Hermetic Solutions Group Inc (HQ)	Essex	CT	F	215 645-9420	1165
Imperial Elctrnic Assembly Inc	Brookfield	CT	D	203 740-8425	525

	CITY	ST	EMP	PHONE	ENTRY#
K B C Electronics Inc	Milford	CT	F	203 298-9654	1842
Mil-Con Inc	Naugatuck	CT	F	630 595-2366	1971
Osda Inc	Milford	CT	G	203 878-2155	1860
Park Distributories Inc	Bridgeport	CT	G	203 366-7200	356
Protronix Inc	Wallingford	CT	F	203 269-5858	3842
Qtran Inc (PA)	Milford	CT	E	203 367-8777	1873
Rogers Corporation	Rogers	CT	C	860 774-9605	2943
Adcotron Ems Inc	Boston	MA	C	617 598-3000	6514
American Sub Assmbly Prdcers I	Dudley	MA	E	508 949-2320	8315
Aved Electronics LLC	North Billerica	MA	D	978 453-6393	10898
Bae Systems Info Elctrnic Syst	Lexington	MA	C	603 885-4321	9726
Case Assembly Solutions Inc	South Easton	MA	C	508 238-5665	11939
Cirtec Medical Corp	Lowell	MA	C	978 703-6822	9867
Comprehensive Power Inc	Marlborough	MA	E	508 460-0010	10134
Cooper Crouse-Hinds LLC	Chelsea	MA	E	617 889-7700	7979
Creation Technologies Intl Inc (PA)	Boston	MA	E	877 734-7456	6676
Datacon Inc	Chelmsford	MA	E	781 273-5800	7922
Diamond Antenna Microwave Corp	Littleton	MA	D	978 486-0039	9811
DI Technology LLC	Haverhill	MA	E	978 374-6451	9092
East West Boston LLC	Boston	MA	D	617 598-3000	6706
Embr Labs Inc	Charlestown	MA	F	413 218-0629	7871
Excelitas Technologies Corp (DH)	Waltham	MA	E	855 382-2677	12673
Fraen Corporation (PA)	Reading	MA	C	781 205-5300	11601
Gutz LLC	Lowell	MA	G	978 805-5001	9883
Hdm Systems Corporation	Brighton	MA	F	617 562-4054	7242
Interface Engineering Corp	Randolph	MA	F	781 986-2600	11566
Keystone Precision Inc	Pepperell	MA	G	978 433-8484	11386
Kopin Targeting Corporation	Westborough	MA	D	508 870-5959	13115
Massmicroelectronics LLC	Canton	MA	D	781 828-6110	7808
Midas Technology Inc	Woburn	MA	F	781 938-0069	13613
Murata Power Solutions Inc (DH)	Westborough	MA	C	508 339-3000	13122
Nanosemi Inc	Waltham	MA	E	781 472-2832	12731
Nypro Healthcare Baja Inc (DH)	Clinton	MA	D	619 498-9250	8086
Orion Industries Incorporated	Ayer	MA	E	978 772-0020	6190
Paricon Technologies Corp	Taunton	MA	F	508 823-0876	12354
Parisi Associates LLC	Chelmsford	MA	F	978 667-8700	7944
Photonis Scientific Inc (DH)	Sturbridge	MA	F	508 347-4000	12257
Polyonics Corporation	Newburyport	MA	F	978 462-3600	10708
Sensata Technologies Inc (HQ)	Attleboro	MA	A	508 236-3800	6062
Sensata Technologies Mass Inc (DH)	Attleboro	MA	E	508 236-3800	6064
Sie Computing Solutions Inc	Brockton	MA	D	508 588-6110	7305
Skyworks Solutions Inc	Woburn	MA	D	781 935-5150	13669
Star Engineering Inc	North Attleboro	MA	E	508 316-1492	10889
Texas Instruments Incorporated	Attleboro	MA	E	508 236-3800	6070
That Corporation (PA)	Milford	MA	E	508 478-9200	10420
Ulvac Technologies Inc (HQ)	Methuen	MA	E	978 686-7550	10347
Utz Technologies Inc (PA)	Lowell	MA	E	973 339-1100	9933
Artel Inc	Westbrook	ME	E	207 854-0860	5614
603 Manufacturing LLC	Hudson	NH	D	603 578-9876	14478
Aavid Corporation	Laconia	NH	A	603 528-3400	14638
Amphenol Printed Circuits Inc (HQ)	Nashua	NH	D	603 324-4500	15062
Asia Direct LLC	Plaistow	NH	F	603 382-9485	15336
Bae Systems Info Elctrnic Syst	Hudson	NH	A	603 885-4321	14486
Bae Systems Info Elctrnic Syst	Merrimack	NH	B	603 885-4321	14975
Boyd Laconia LLC (DH)	Laconia	NH	D	603 528-3400	14649
Data Electronic Devices Inc	Salem	NH	C	603 893-2047	15517
Gill Design Inc	Windham	NH	G	603 890-1237	15727
Great Bay Manufacturing LLC	Rochester	NH	F	603 948-1212	15477
Impact Science & Technology Inc	Nashua	NH	C	603 459-2200	15113
Intervala LLC	Hudson	NH	D	603 595-1987	14512
Janco Electronics Inc	Rollinsford	NH	D	603 742-1581	15496
Jenesco Inc	Lyndeborough	NH	F	603 673-4830	14800
K E I Incorporated	Nashua	NH	C	978 656-2575	15120
Megatronics US Ultmate Hldco LL (PA)	Salem	NH	E	888 706-0230	15544
Miltronics Mfg Svcs Inc	Keene	NH	F	603 352-3333	14609
New Model Inc	Belmont	NH	E	603 267-8225	13964
Pgc Wire & Cable LLC	Derry	NH	F	603 821-7300	14203
Princeton Technology Corp	Hudson	NH	D	603 595-1987	14536
Remcon/North Corporation	Meredith	NH	D	603 279-7091	14969
Rotary Vacuum Products Inc	Salem	NH	G	603 890-6001	15558
Sonesys LLC	Merrimack	NH	F	603 423-9000	15004
Stellar Manufacturing Inc	Salem	NH	E	978 241-9537	15564
Vectronics Microwave Corp (PA)	Hudson	NH	E	973 244-1040	14558
Andon Electronics Corporation	Lincoln	RI	E	401 333-0388	16119
Cooliance Inc (PA)	Warwick	RI	F	401 921-6500	16798
Federal Electronics Inc	Cranston	RI	D	401 944-6200	15859
International Mfg Svcs Inc	Portsmouth	RI	E	401 683-9700	16445
Kearney-National Inc	North Kingstown	RI	C	401 943-2686	16264
L L Rowe Company	Ashaway	RI	E	781 729-7860	15743
Narragansett Imaging Usa LLC	North Smithfield	RI	E	401 762-3800	16328
Raytheon Company	Portsmouth	RI	D	401 847-8000	16454
Staffall Inc	Cranston	RI	E	401 461-5554	15913

	CITY	ST	EMP	PHONE	ENTRY#
Vesuvius America Inc (DH)	Providence	RI	E		16640
Veterans Assembled Elec LLC (PA)	North Kingstown	RI	G	401 228-6165	16291
Vishay Efi Inc	Warwick	RI	E	401 738-9150	16873
Aviatron Inc	South Burlington	VT	E	802 865-9318	17570
Necsel Intllctual Property Inc	Vergennes	VT	E	802 877-6432	17658
Prom Software Inc	South Burlington	VT	F	802 862-7500	17597

CIRCULAR KNIT FABRICS DYEING & FINISHING

	CITY	ST	EMP	PHONE	ENTRY#
Hardwick Knitted Fabric Inc	Warren	MA	G	413 436-7704	12851

CLAMPS: Metal

	CITY	ST	EMP	PHONE	ENTRY#
Lassy Tools Inc	Plainville	CT	G	860 747-2748	2768

CLEANING EQPT: Commercial

	CITY	ST	EMP	PHONE	ENTRY#
Rhema 320 LLC (PA)	New Haven	CT	G	475 434-8581	2191
Uncle Sams Contractors LLC (PA)	East Hartford	CT	F	833 487-2776	1031
Uvtech Systems Inc	Carlisle	MA	G	978 440-7282	7849

CLEANING EQPT: High Pressure

	CITY	ST	EMP	PHONE	ENTRY#
Goodway Technologies Corporation (PA)	Stamford	CT	D	203 359-4708	3358
Sponge-Jet Inc (PA)	Newington	NH	G	603 610-7950	15212

CLEANING OR POLISHING PREPARATIONS, NEC

	CITY	ST	EMP	PHONE	ENTRY#
Grill Daddy Brush Company	Old Greenwich	CT	E	888 840-7552	2633
Harvard Chemical LLC (HQ)	Bolton	CT	F	404 761-0657	220
Macdermid Incorporated (HQ)	Waterbury	CT	C	203 575-5700	3933
Simoniz USA Inc (PA)	Bolton	CT	D	860 646-0172	223
All-Way Service Corp	South Weymouth	MA	E	781 335-4533	11974
Brady Enterprises Inc (PA)	East Weymouth	MA	D	781 340-4571	8427
Parker & Bailey Corp	Walpole	MA	F	508 660-0011	12572
Perma Incorporated	Bedford	MA	F	978 667-5161	6252
Perrco Inc	Woburn	MA	F	617 933-5300	13633
Savin Products Company Inc	Randolph	MA	E	781 961-2743	11574
Webco Chemical Corporation	Dudley	MA	D	508 943-2337	8327

CLEANING PRDTS: Ammonia, Household

	CITY	ST	EMP	PHONE	ENTRY#
Versum Materials Us LLC	Burlington	MA	E	978 715-1614	7444

CLEANING PRDTS: Automobile Polish

	CITY	ST	EMP	PHONE	ENTRY#
Armored Autogroup Parent Inc	Danbury	CT	C	203 205-2900	710

CLEANING PRDTS: Disinfectants, Household Or Indl Plant

	CITY	ST	EMP	PHONE	ENTRY#
Detrapel Inc	Framingham	MA	F	617 514-7778	8757
Hci Cleaning Products LLC	Westford	MA	F	508 864-5510	13241

CLEANING PRDTS: Drain Pipe Solvents Or Cleaners

	CITY	ST	EMP	PHONE	ENTRY#
D J Bass Inc	New Bedford	MA	G	508 678-4499	10583
Allens Environmental Svcs Inc	Presque Isle	ME	G	207 764-9336	5295

CLEANING PRDTS: Floor Waxes

	CITY	ST	EMP	PHONE	ENTRY#
Koster Keunen LLC (PA)	Watertown	CT	E	860 945-3333	4018

CLEANING PRDTS: Sanitation Preps, Disinfectants/Deodorants

	CITY	ST	EMP	PHONE	ENTRY#
Great Lakes Chemical Corp (DH)	Shelton	CT	E	203 573-2000	3010
Lanxess Solutions US Inc	Shelton	CT	A	203 573-2000	3027
Safehands Distribution Ne LLC	Wilbraham	MA	F	413 244-1452	13363
Unimed-Midwest Inc	Woburn	MA	G	800 347-9023	13681
Eco Knight Group LLC (PA)	Lebanon	NH	G	802 318-8760	14687

CLEANING PRDTS: Specialty

	CITY	ST	EMP	PHONE	ENTRY#
Alpha Chemical Services Inc	Stoughton	MA	E	781 344-8688	12193
MD Stetson Company Inc	Mansfield	MA	E	781 986-6161	10066
Spectrowax Corporation (PA)	Canton	MA	D	617 543-0400	7832
Brown Country Services LLC	West Dover	VT	G	802 464-5200	17689

CLEANING PRDTS: Stain Removers

	CITY	ST	EMP	PHONE	ENTRY#
Amodex Products Incorporated	Bridgeport	CT	E	203 335-1255	296

CLEANING SVCS: Industrial Or Commercial

	CITY	ST	EMP	PHONE	ENTRY#
E & J Parts Cleaning Inc	Waterbury	CT	F	203 757-1716	3909
Hartford Fire Equipment	Plainville	CT	F	860 747-2757	2763
Innovative Environmental LLC	Colchester	CT	F	860 871-7582	660

CLIPS & FASTENERS, MADE FROM PURCHASED WIRE

	CITY	ST	EMP	PHONE	ENTRY#
Royal Diversified Products	Warren	RI	E	401 245-6900	16767

CLOSURES: Closures, Stamped Metal

	CITY	ST	EMP	PHONE	ENTRY#
Orca Inc	New Britain	CT	E	860 223-4180	2047
American Cord & Webbing Co Inc	Woonsocket	RI	E	401 762-5500	16948

CLOSURES: Plastic

	CITY	ST	EMP	PHONE	ENTRY#
Aptargroup Inc	Trumbull	CT	B	203 377-8100	3712

PRODUCT

	CITY	ST	EMP	PHONE	ENTRY#
American Cord & Webbing Co Inc	Woonsocket	RI	E	401 762-5500	16948

CLOTHING & ACCESS, WOMEN, CHILDREN & INFANT, WHOL: Handbags

	CITY	ST	EMP	PHONE	ENTRY#
Samsonite Company Stores LLC	Warren	RI	F	401 247-3301	16768

CLOTHING & ACCESS, WOMEN, CHILDREN & INFANT, WHOL: Sweaters

	CITY	ST	EMP	PHONE	ENTRY#
Nomad Communications Inc 17709	White River Junction	VT	F	802 649-1995	

CLOTHING & ACCESS, WOMEN, CHILDREN & INFANT, WHOL: Uniforms

	CITY	ST	EMP	PHONE	ENTRY#
Action Apparel Inc	Stoneham	MA	G	781 435-2342	12173
Officers Equipment Company	Providence	RI	F	703 221-1912	16580
Vermont Flannel Co (PA)	East Barre	VT	F	802 476-5226	17215

CLOTHING & ACCESS: Handicapped

	CITY	ST	EMP	PHONE	ENTRY#
Portland Dry Goods Inc	Portland	ME	G	207 699-5575	5258

CLOTHING & ACCESS: Hospital Gowns

	CITY	ST	EMP	PHONE	ENTRY#
Realhub Inc	Darien	CT	F	650 461-9210	854

CLOTHING & ACCESS: Men's Miscellaneous Access

	CITY	ST	EMP	PHONE	ENTRY#
Bondi Band LLC	Simsbury	CT	F	207 576-4191	3084
Robert Miller Associates LLC	Weston	CT	F	718 392-1640	4152
Highland Belts & Fine Lea Gds	Brewer	ME	F	207 989-2597	4614
Synergy Sportswear Inc (PA)	Keene	NH	G	603 352-8681	14626
Thanksben10 LLC	Milford	NH	F	603 206-5116	15040

CLOTHING & ACCESS: Suspenders

	CITY	ST	EMP	PHONE	ENTRY#
Chaucer Accessories Inc	Haverhill	MA	G	978 373-1566	9085

CLOTHING & APPAREL STORES: Custom

	CITY	ST	EMP	PHONE	ENTRY#
Chillybear Inc (PA)	Needham	MA	F	781 455-6321	10507
Vermont Teddy Bear Co Inc (HQ)	Shelburne	VT	C	802 985-3001	17563

CLOTHING & FURNISHINGS, MENS & BOYS, WHOL: Sportswear/Work

	CITY	ST	EMP	PHONE	ENTRY#
Sickday Inc	Wellfleet	MA	F	508 214-4158	12953
Squadlocker Inc	Warwick	RI	D	888 885-6253	16864

CLOTHING & FURNISHINGS, MENS & BOYS, WHOLESALE: Apprl Belts

	CITY	ST	EMP	PHONE	ENTRY#
Highland Belts & Fine Lea Gds	Brewer	ME	F	207 989-2597	4614

CLOTHING STORES: Designer Apparel

	CITY	ST	EMP	PHONE	ENTRY#
Birch Outfitters LLC	Salem	MA	F	978 498-4631	11703
Blue Dolphin Screenprint Inc	Somersworth	NH	E	603 692-2500	15611

CLOTHING STORES: T-Shirts, Printed, Custom

	CITY	ST	EMP	PHONE	ENTRY#
Guertins Graphics Inc	Worcester	MA	F	508 754-0200	13735
Rainbow Visions Inc	Boston	MA	G	617 787-4084	6995
Soft-As-A-grape Inc (PA)	Wareham	MA	E	508 295-9900	12844
Merchbro Inc	Pawtucket	RI	F	866 428-0095	16387
Teespring Inc	Providence	RI	E	855 833-7774	16619

CLOTHING STORES: Uniforms & Work

	CITY	ST	EMP	PHONE	ENTRY#
Maverick Work Wear Inc	North Reading	MA	E	860 944-3776	11043
Wear-Guard Corporation	Norwell	MA	A	781 871-4100	11150
Winter People Inc 4711	Cumberland Center	ME	E	207 865-6636	

CLOTHING STORES: Unisex

	CITY	ST	EMP	PHONE	ENTRY#
Chillybear Inc (PA)	Needham	MA	F	781 455-6321	10507
Synergy Sportswear Inc (PA)	Keene	NH	G	603 352-8681	14626
Thanksben10 LLC	Milford	NH	F	603 206-5116	15040

CLOTHING STORES: Work

	CITY	ST	EMP	PHONE	ENTRY#
Air Tool Sales & Svc Co Inc (PA)	Unionville	CT	G	860 673-2714	3746

CLOTHING: Aprons, Exc Rubber/Plastic, Women, Misses, Junior

	CITY	ST	EMP	PHONE	ENTRY#
Janlynn Corporation	South Hadley	MA	D	413 206-0002	11963

CLOTHING: Athletic & Sportswear, Men's & Boys'

	CITY	ST	EMP	PHONE	ENTRY#
Cycling Sports Group Inc (HQ)	Wilton	CT	D	203 845-8300	4238
Gima LLC	Hartford	CT	F	860 296-4441	1483
16sur20 Management LLC	Lenox	MA	F	413 637-5061	9624
Golden Fleece Mfg Group LLC (DH)	Haverhill	MA	B	978 686-3833	9098
M & M Garment Manufacturing	Everett	MA	G	617 389-7787	8492
Mahi Gold Inc	Chatham	MA	F	508 348-5487	7898

	CITY	ST	EMP	PHONE	ENTRY#
Pop Tops Company Inc	South Easton	MA	E	508 580-2580	11949
Saucony Inc (DH)	Waltham	MA	C	617 824-6000	12776
Sickday Inc	Wellfleet	MA	F	508 214-4158	12953
Tracksmith Corporation (PA)	Boston	MA	G	781 235-0037	7083
Chuck Roast Equipment Inc (PA)	Conway	NH	F	603 447-5492	14178
Legacy Global Sports LP	Portsmouth	NH	E	603 373-7262	15416
Bogner of America Inc (PA)	Burlington	VT	E	802 451-4417	17121
Forsake Inc	Stowe	VT	F	585 576-6358	17631
Louis Garneau USA Inc	Derby	VT	D	802 334-5885	17211

CLOTHING: Athletic & Sportswear, Women's & Girls'

	CITY	ST	EMP	PHONE	ENTRY#
Good Clothing Company Inc	Fall River	MA	E	508 419-6152	8556
Pop Tops Company Inc	South Easton	MA	E	508 580-2580	11949
Saucony Inc (DH)	Waltham	MA	C	617 824-6000	12776
Sickday Inc	Wellfleet	MA	F	508 214-4158	12953
Tracksmith Corporation (PA)	Boston	MA	G	781 235-0037	7083
Chuck Roast Equipment Inc (PA)	Conway	NH	F	603 447-5492	14178

CLOTHING: Belts

	CITY	ST	EMP	PHONE	ENTRY#
Dooney & Bourke Inc (HQ)	Norwalk	CT	E	203 853-7515	2492
Karen Callan Designs Inc	Greenwich	CT	G	203 762-9914	1336
Chaucer Accessories Inc	Haverhill	MA	G	978 373-1566	9085
Highland Belts & Fine Lea Gds	Brewer	ME	F	207 989-2597	4614

CLOTHING: Blouses, Women's & Girls'

	CITY	ST	EMP	PHONE	ENTRY#
Fyc Apparel Group LLC	East Haven	CT	E	203 466-6525	1043
Fyc Apparel Group LLC (PA)	Branford	CT	D	203 481-2420	260
American Power Source Inc (PA)	Fall River	MA	E	508 672-8847	8520
Shop Therapy Imports	Provincetown	MA	G	508 487-8970	11497
B Peachee Inc	Biddeford	ME	G	207 602-6262	4555
Imeldas Fabrics & Designs	New Sharon	ME	G	207 778-0665	5090

CLOTHING: Brassieres

	CITY	ST	EMP	PHONE	ENTRY#
Valmont Inc	Ludlow	MA	F	413 583-8351	9955

CLOTHING: Bridal Gowns

	CITY	ST	EMP	PHONE	ENTRY#
Musette Bridal Inc	Boston	MA	E	617 424-1070	6898

CLOTHING: Caps, Baseball

	CITY	ST	EMP	PHONE	ENTRY#
Athletic Emblem Lettering Inc	Springfield	MA	F	413 733-8151	12078

CLOTHING: Children & Infants'

	CITY	ST	EMP	PHONE	ENTRY#
Classic Prep Childrenswear Inc	Norwalk	CT	G	203 286-6204	2483

CLOTHING: Children's, Girls'

	CITY	ST	EMP	PHONE	ENTRY#
Accurate Services Inc	Fall River	MA	E	508 674-5773	8518
E-I-E-I-o Incorporated	Fall River	MA	G	508 324-9311	8537
Precision Sportswear Inc	Fall River	MA	G	508 674-3034	8599
Shop Therapy Imports	Provincetown	MA	G	508 487-8970	11497
Imeldas Fabrics & Designs	New Sharon	ME	G	207 778-0665	5090
Richardson Mfg Co Inc	Silver Lake	NH	G	603 367-9018	15607
Vermont Flannel Co (PA)	East Barre	VT	F	802 476-5226	17215

CLOTHING: Coats & Jackets, Leather & Sheep-Lined

	CITY	ST	EMP	PHONE	ENTRY#
Timberland LLC (HQ)	Stratham	NH	B	603 772-9500	15641

CLOTHING: Coats & Suits, Men's & Boys'

	CITY	ST	EMP	PHONE	ENTRY#
Burlington Coat Fctry Whse Cor	Danbury	CT	E	203 748-8583	718
Sterlingwear of Boston Inc (PA)	Boston	MA	C	617 567-2100	7061

CLOTHING: Coats, Leatherette, Oiled Fabric, Etc, Mens & Boys

	CITY	ST	EMP	PHONE	ENTRY#
Timberland LLC (HQ)	Stratham	NH	B	603 772-9500	15641

CLOTHING: Costumes

	CITY	ST	EMP	PHONE	ENTRY#
B R T Inc	Worcester	MA	E	508 791-2383	13701
CJS Workshop LLC	Groton	MA	E	323 445-5012	9008

CLOTHING: Disposable

	CITY	ST	EMP	PHONE	ENTRY#
Ntension Corp	Hermon	ME	E	207 848-7700	4887

CLOTHING: Dresses

	CITY	ST	EMP	PHONE	ENTRY#
Fyc Apparel Group LLC (PA)	Branford	CT	D	203 481-2420	260
Fall River Apparel Inc	Fall River	MA	E	508 677-1975	8545

CLOTHING: Hats & Caps, NEC

	CITY	ST	EMP	PHONE	ENTRY#
Fall River Hat Company	Fall River	MA	E	508 672-7033	8546
Whole Earth Hat Co Inc	Fall River	MA	F	508 672-7033	8626

CLOTHING: Hats & Caps, Uniform

	CITY	ST	EMP	PHONE	ENTRY#
Barker Advg Specialty Co Inc (PA)	Cheshire	CT	D	203 272-2222	575

CLOTHING: Hosiery, Pantyhose & Knee Length, Sheer

	CITY	ST	EMP	PHONE	ENTRY#
Cabot Hosiery Mills Inc (PA)	Northfield	VT	D	802 485-6066	17432

CLOTHING: Jackets, Overall & Work

Essex County Coop Farming Assn	Topsfield	MA	F	978 887-2300	12433
Tyca Corporation (PA)	Clinton	MA	E	978 612-0002	8093

CLOTHING: Jeans, Men's & Boys'

Guess Inc	Braintree	MA	E	781 843-3147	7185

CLOTHING: Leather

U S Made Co Inc	Danvers	MA	F	978 777-8383	8228

CLOTHING: Men's & boy's underwear & nightwear

L L Bean Inc	Brunswick	ME	F	207 725-0300	4647

CLOTHING: Mens & Boys Jackets, Sport, Suede, Leatherette

New Balance Athletics Inc (HQ)	Boston	MA	B	617 783-4000	6913
Tyca Corporation (PA)	Clinton	MA	E	978 612-0002	8093
Rodco Enterprises	Lewiston	ME	F	207 786-2931	4990

CLOTHING: Neckwear

Skurge of Sea LLC	Norwich	CT	G	860 887-7679	2617
New York Accessory Group Inc	Bristol	RI	D	401 245-6096	15776
Beau Ties of Vermont LLC	Middlebury	VT	E	802 388-0108	17337
Btl Holdings LLC	Middlebury	VT	E	917 596-3660	17339

CLOTHING: Outerwear, Knit

River Falls Manufacturing Co	Fall River	MA	D	508 646-2900	8604

CLOTHING: Outerwear, Lthr, Wool/Down-Filled, Men, Youth/Boy

Fat Hat Clothing Co	Quechee	VT	F	802 296-6646	17462

CLOTHING: Outerwear, Women's & Misses' NEC

Accurate Services Inc	Fall River	MA	E	508 674-5773	8518
Broder Bros Co	Middleboro	MA	C	508 923-4800	10352
Corporate Casuals LLC	Concord	MA	F	978 369-5935	8110
Northeast Knitting Mills Inc (PA)	Fall River	MA	E	508 678-7553	8589
Tyca Corporation (PA)	Clinton	MA	E	978 612-0002	8093
Vermont Flannel Co (PA)	East Barre	VT	F	802 476-5226	17215
Wool Advisor LLC	Johnson	VT	F	802 635-2271	17312

CLOTHING: Raincoats, Exc Vulcanized Rubber, Purchased Matls

Mr Idea Inc	Attleboro	MA	E	508 222-0155	6039
Neptune Garment Company	Boston	MA	D	617 482-3980	6909

CLOTHING: Robes & Dressing Gowns

Graduation Solutions LLC	Greenwich	CT	E	914 934-5991	1332
L L Bean Inc	Brunswick	ME	F	207 725-0300	4647

CLOTHING: Shirts

16sur20 Management LLC	Lenox	MA	F	413 637-5061	9624
Acme Merchandise and AP Inc	Gloucester	MA	E	978 282-4800	8917
Shop Therapy Imports	Provincetown	MA	G	508 487-8970	11497
Imeldas Fabrics & Designs	New Sharon	ME	G	207 778-0665	5090
Jenesco Inc	Lyndeborough	NH	F	603 673-4830	14800
Timberland LLC (HQ)	Stratham	NH	B	603 772-9500	15641

CLOTHING: Shirts, Dress, Men's & Boys'

Pvh Corp	Chatham	MA	G	508 945-4063	7900
Barry T Chouinard Inc (HQ)	Northfield	VT	E	802 485-8600	17431

CLOTHING: Shirts, Sports & Polo, Men's & Boys'

New Balance Athletics Inc (HQ)	Boston	MA	B	617 783-4000	6913

CLOTHING: Socks

Sock Shack	Portland	ME	G	207 805-1348	5274

CLOTHING: Sportswear, Women's

Arocam Inc	Taunton	MA	F	508 822-1220	12319
Chuck Roast Equipment Inc (PA)	Conway	NH	F	603 447-5492	14178
Spirit Recognition Inc (PA)	Pawtucket	RI	F	401 722-6400	16417

CLOTHING: Suits & Skirts, Women's & Misses'

Fyc Apparel Group LLC (PA)	Branford	CT	D	203 481-2420	260

CLOTHING: Suits, Men's & Boys', From Purchased Materials

Greenwich Triangle LLC (DH)	Haverhill	MA	C	800 634-5312	9099
Joseph Abboud Mfg Corp	New Bedford	MA	B	508 999-1301	10606

CLOTHING: Sweaters & Sweater Coats, Knit

Alps Sportswear Mfg Co Inc	Natick	MA	F	978 685-5159	10467
Northeast Knitting Mills Inc (PA)	Fall River	MA	E	508 678-7553	8589

	CITY	ST	EMP	PHONE	ENTRY#
Nomad Communications Inc 17709	White River Junction	VT	F	802 649-1995	

CLOTHING: Sweatshirts & T-Shirts, Men's & Boys'

MB Sport LLC (PA)	New Canaan	CT	E	203 966-1985	2082
Ibex Outdoor Clothing LLC 17708	White River Junction	VT	E	802 359-4239	

CLOTHING: Swimwear, Women's & Misses'

Waterwear Inc	Wilton	NH	E	603 654-5344	15712

CLOTHING: T-Shirts & Tops, Knit

Mountain Corporation (HQ)	Keene	NH	E	603 355-2272	14610
Teespring Inc	Providence	RI	E	855 833-7774	16619

CLOTHING: T-Shirts & Tops, Women's & Girls'

Acme Merchandise and AP Inc	Gloucester	MA	E	978 282-4800	8917
Barry T Chouinard Inc (HQ)	Northfield	VT	E	802 485-8600	17431

CLOTHING: Trousers & Slacks, Men's & Boys'

16sur20 Management LLC	Lenox	MA	F	413 637-5061	9624
American Power Source Inc (PA)	Fall River	MA	F	508 672-8847	8520
Timberland LLC (HQ)	Stratham	NH	B	603 772-9500	15641

CLOTHING: Underwear, Women's & Children's

L L Bean Inc	Brunswick	ME	F	207 725-0300	4647

CLOTHING: Uniforms, Ex Athletic, Women's, Misses' & Juniors'

Blauer Manufacturing Co Inc (PA)	Boston	MA	E	800 225-6715	6597

CLOTHING: Uniforms, Firemen's, From Purchased Materials

Sperian Protection Usa Inc (DH)	Smithfield	RI	E	401 232-1200	16731

CLOTHING: Uniforms, Men's & Boys'

Neptune Garment Company	Boston	MA	D	617 482-3980	6909
Squadlocker Inc	Warwick	RI	D	888 885-6253	16864

CLOTHING: Uniforms, Military, Men/Youth, Purchased Materials

Front Line Apparel Group LLC	Hebron	CT	F	860 859-3524	1527

CLOTHING: Uniforms, Team Athletic

Ames Textile Corporation	Lowell	MA	D	978 934-8850	9853
Precision Sportswear Inc	Fall River	MA	G	508 674-3034	8599
Hilco Athletic & Graphics Inc	West Warwick	RI	F	401 822-1775	16910

CLOTHING: Uniforms, Work

Maverick Work Wear Inc	North Reading	MA	E	860 944-3776	11043

CLOTHING: Waterproof Outerwear

Sterlingwear of Boston Inc (PA)	Boston	MA	C	617 567-2100	7061
Wear-Guard Corporation	Norwell	MA	A	781 871-4100	11150
Log House Designs Inc (PA)	Chatham	NH	F	603 694-3373	14070

CLOTHING: Work Apparel, Exc Uniforms

Tempshield LLC	Trenton	ME	F	207 667-9696	5559

CLOTHING: Work, Men's

Vermont Flannel Co (PA)	East Barre	VT	F	802 476-5226	17215

CLUTCHES, EXC VEHICULAR

Carlyle Johnson Machine Co LLC (DH)	Bolton	CT	F	860 643-1531	219
Helander Products Inc	Clinton	CT	F	860 669-7953	644
Inertia Dynamics LLC	New Hartford	CT	C	860 379-1252	2102
Magnetic Technologies Ltd	Putnam	CT	F	508 987-3303	2864
Rollease Acmeda (HQ)	Stamford	CT	D	203 964-1573	3451
Hersey Clutch Company LLC	Orleans	MA	F	508 255-2533	11239

COAL MINING SERVICES

Tronox LLC (PA)	Stamford	CT	F	203 705-3800	3487

COAL MINING: Anthracite

Hartford Fire Equipment	Plainville	CT	F	860 747-2757	2763

COAL MINING: Bituminous & Lignite Surface

Eagle Ship Management LLC (HQ)	Stamford	CT	C	203 276-8100	3340
Wexford Capital LP (PA)	Greenwich	CT	G	203 862-7000	1361

COAL MINING: Bituminous Coal & Lignite-Surface Mining

Cloud Peak Energy Inc (PA)	Westport	CT	D	307 687-6000	4161

COAL, MINERALS & ORES, WHOLESALE: Coal

American Metals Coal Intl Inc (HQ)	Greenwich	CT	F	203 625-9200	1311

Employee Codes: A=Over 500 employees, B=251-500
C=101-250, D=51-100, E=20-50, F=10-19, G=1-9

2024 Harris New England
Manufacturers Directory

PRODUCT

1363

	CITY	ST	EMP	PHONE	ENTRY#

COAL, MINERALS & ORES, WHOLESALE: Sulfur

	CITY	ST	EMP	PHONE	ENTRY#
H J Baker & Bro Inc	Westport	CT	B	203 682-9200	4171
HJ Baker & Bro LLC (PA)	Shelton	CT	E	203 682-9200	3014

COATED OR PLATED PRDTS

Scp Management LLC	New Hartford	CT	E	860 738-2600	2108

COATING SVC: Metals, With Plastic Or Resins

American Roller Company LLC	Middlebury	CT	E	203 598-3100	1713
Mitchell-Bate Company	Waterbury	CT	E	203 233-0862	3946
American Durafilm Co Inc	Holliston	MA	E	508 429-8000	9198
Applied Plastics Co Inc	Norwood	MA	E	781 762-1881	11161
Covestro LLC	Wilmington	MA	C	800 458-0014	13399
DSM Neoresins Inc	Wilmington	MA	C	800 458-0014	13403
Indepenent Plating Co	Worcester	MA	E	508 756-0301	13740
Innovative Coatings Inc	Medway	MA	F	508 533-6101	10306
Parker-Hannifin Corporation	Hudson	NH	C	603 880-4807	14534
Development Associates Inc	North Kingstown	RI	F	401 884-1350	16244
Gds Manufacturing Company	Williston	VT	G	802 862-7610	17732

COATINGS: Epoxy

Dur-A-Flex Inc (HQ)	East Hartford	CT	E	860 528-9838	989
A W Chesterton Company (PA)	Groveland	MA	E	781 438-7000	9012
Breakthrough Coatings Inc	Buzzards Bay	MA	F	866 608-7625	7453

COATINGS: Polyurethane

Foam Systems LLC	Norwalk	CT	G	800 853-1577	2502
C L Hauthaway & Sons Corp	Lynn	MA	E	781 592-6444	9965
Rock-Tred 2 LLC	Andover	MA	F	888 762-5873	5912

COFFEE SVCS

DC Enterprizes Inc	Hinesburg	VT	F	802 865-4480	17290

COIL WINDING SVC

Jan Manufacturing Co	Wolcott	CT	G	203 879-0580	4366

COILS & TRANSFORMERS

Bicron Electronics LLC (HQ)	Torrington	CT	D	860 482-2524	3672
Cable Technology Inc	Willington	CT	E	860 429-7889	4224
Coils Plus Inc	Wolcott	CT	E	203 879-0755	4362
Future Manufacturing Inc	Bristol	CT	F	860 584-0685	450
Hipotronics Inc (HQ)	Shelton	CT	C	845 279-3644	3013
Microphase Corporation	Shelton	CT	E	203 866-8000	3032
Microtech Inc	Cheshire	CT	D	203 272-3234	607
Qtran Inc (PA)	Milford	CT	E	203 367-8777	1873
Tortran Inc	Shelton	CT	F	203 538-5062	3070
Excelitas Technologies Corp	Salem	MA	C	800 775-6786	11714
Magellan Distribution Corp	Boston	MA	F	617 399-7900	6868
MCI Transformer Corporation	Orange	MA	F	978 544-8272	11226
Microwave Engineering Corp	North Andover	MA	D	978 685-2776	10844
Gowanda Rcd LLC	Manchester	NH	C	716 532-2234	14853
Technicoil LLC	Ossipee	NH	F	603 569-3100	15283
Gets LLC	Lincoln	RI	D	401 314-5550	16138
Kearney-National Inc	North Kingstown	RI	C	401 943-2686	16264
Dynapower Company LLC (DH)	South Burlington	VT	D	802 860-7200	17577
Vishay Intertechnology Inc	Bennington	VT	F	802 440-8571	17057

COILS: Electric Motors Or Generators

Coils Plus Inc	Wolcott	CT	E	203 879-0755	4362
Schulz Electric Company	New Haven	CT	C	203 562-5811	2195

COILS: Pipe

JFd Tube & Coil Products Inc	Hamden	CT	E	203 288-6941	1435

COKE: Produced In Chemical Recovery Coke Ovens

Rain Commodities (usa) Inc	Stamford	CT	F	203 406-0535	3443

COLLEGE, EXC JUNIOR

Trustees of Boston College	Chestnut Hill	MA	F	617 552-2844	8002
Trustees of Tufts College	Medford	MA	G	617 628-5000	10300
Trustees of Dartmouth College	Hanover	NH	G	603 646-2256	14431
Trustees of Dartmouth College	Lebanon	NH	E	603 448-1533	14702

COLORS: Pigments, Inorganic

Color Change Technology Inc	North Andover	MA	G	978 377-0050	10824
F & D Plastics Inc (PA)	Leominster	MA	E	978 668-5140	9662
Ecc Holdings Inc (HQ)	Providence	RI	E	401 331-9000	16511

COMMERCIAL & OFFICE BUILDINGS RENOVATION & REPAIR

Musano Inc	Wolcott	CT	E	203 879-4651	4369
Gloucester Builders Inc	Charlestown	MA	E	617 241-5513	7874

	CITY	ST	EMP	PHONE	ENTRY#
Limelight Productions Inc	Lee	MA	G	413 243-4950	9616
Lockheed Archtctral Sltons Inc	Pascoag	RI	C	401 568-3061	16339
William H Moore Inc	Waitsfield	VT	G	802 496-3595	17668

COMMERCIAL ART & GRAPHIC DESIGN SVCS

Gerber Scientific LLC (PA)	Tolland	CT	C	860 871-8082	3661
Lettering Inc of New York (PA)	Stamford	CT	E	203 329-7759	3400
Spm Management Inc	Shelton	CT	F	203 847-1112	3065
Argosy Publishing Inc (PA)	Newton	MA	D	617 527-9999	10733
Clayton LLC DBA Blbird Grphic	Woburn	MA	E	617 250-8500	13542
Creamer Associates Inc	Cambridge	MA	G	617 374-6000	7544
Desk Top Graphics Inc (HQ)	Peabody	MA	E	617 832-1927	11305
Digital Graphics Inc	North Billerica	MA	G	781 270-3670	10907
Elite Envelope & Graphics Inc	Randolph	MA	F	781 961-1800	11556
Icl Imaging Corp	Framingham	MA	E	508 872-3280	8778
Quarto Pubg Group USA Inc	Beverly	MA	F	425 827-7120	6375
St Associates Inc	Wakefield	MA	E		12536
Winter & Company Inc	Quincy	MA	F	617 773-7605	11545
S & K Unlimited LLC	Brownville	ME	F	207 965-6137	4638
Winter People Inc	Cumberland Center	ME	E	207 865-6636	4711
Franklin Exeter Inc	Portsmouth	NH	F	603 836-8590	15391
Savvy Workshop	Manchester	NH	G	603 792-0080	14926

COMMERCIAL ART & ILLUSTRATION SVCS

Weston Corporation	Hingham	MA	E	781 749-0936	9164

COMMERCIAL CONTAINERS WHOLESALERS

Quality Containers of Neng	Yarmouth	ME	G	207 846-5420	5706

COMMERCIAL COOKING EQPT WHOLESALERS

Heat and Control Inc	Pembroke	NH	E	603 225-5190	15303

COMMERCIAL EQPT WHOLESALERS, NEC

Capricorn Investors III LP (PA)	Greenwich	CT	F	203 861-6600	1326
Cummins - Allison Corp	Cheshire	CT	G	203 794-9200	585
Treif USA Inc	Shelton	CT	F	203 929-9930	3072
Fitness Em LLC	Uxbridge	MA	E		12479
Markwell Manufacturing Co Inc	Norwood	MA	F	781 769-6610	11194
Walco Electric Company	Providence	RI	D	401 467-6500	16642

COMMERCIAL EQPT, WHOLESALE: Bakery Eqpt & Splys

Ann Clark Ltd	Rutland	VT	E	802 773-7886	17489

COMMERCIAL EQPT, WHOLESALE: Display Eqpt, Exc Refrigerated

Ardent Inc (PA)	East Hartford	CT	F	860 528-6000	971

COMMERCIAL EQPT, WHOLESALE: Restaurant, NEC

American Marketing Intl LLC	Clinton	CT	E	860 669-4100	635

COMMERCIAL EQPT, WHOLESALE: Scales, Exc Laboratory

Public Scales	Lewiston	ME	F	207 784-9466	4986

COMMERCIAL LAUNDRY EQPT

Baystate Business Ventures LLC	Taunton	MA	F	508 828-9274	12324

COMMERCIAL PRINTING & NEWSPAPER PUBLISHING

Bristol Press	Torrington	CT	D	860 584-0501	3673
Chronicle Printing Company	Willimantic	CT	E	860 423-8466	4217
Day Publishing Company (HQ)	New London	CT	B	860 701-4200	2226
Green Manor Corporation (PA)	Manchester	CT	B	860 643-8111	1599
Hersam Acorn Newspapers LLC (PA)	Ridgefield	CT	F	203 438-6000	2899
New Haven Register LLC	New Haven	CT	A	203 789-5200	2179
Printed Communications	South Windsor	CT	G	860 436-9619	3175
Record-Journal Newspaper (PA)	Meriden	CT	C	203 235-1661	1692
Register Citizen Publishing	Torrington	CT	C	860 489-3121	3693
Shore Publishing LLC	Madison	CT	E	203 245-1877	1570
Bh Media Inc (HQ)	Lowell	MA	C	617 426-3000	9862
Boston Globe LLC	Boston	MA	A	617 929-2684	6608
Boston Neighborhood News Inc	Boston	MA	G	617 436-1222	6611
Gatehouse Media Mass I Inc (HQ)	Beverly	MA	A	585 598-0030	6350
Gatehouse Media Mass I Inc	Plymouth	MA	B	781 430-6917	11461
Jewish Advocate Pubg Corp	Boston	MA	F	617 523-6232	6823
Jewish Journal	Salem	MA	F	978 745-4111	11724
Journal Register Company	Fall River	MA	F	508 678-3844	8562
Leominster Champion	Leominster	MA	F	978 534-6006	9677
Middlesex News	Framingham	MA	G	508 626-3800	8790
Newhomesale LLC	Franklin	MA	F	508 541-8900	8854
Stonebridge Press LLC (PA)	Southbridge	MA	E	508 764-4325	12035
Turley Publications Inc (PA)	Palmer	MA	C	800 824-6548	11286
Valley Advocate	Northampton	MA	G	413 584-0003	11084
Vineyard Gazette LLC (PA)	Edgartown	MA	E	508 627-4311	8468

	CITY	ST	EMP	PHONE	ENTRY#
Bangor Publishing Company (PA)	Bangor	ME	C	207 990-8000	4493
Beacon Press Inc	Biddeford	ME	E	207 282-1535	4557
Forecaster Publishing Inc	South Portland	ME	E	207 781-3661	5503
Franklin Group	Farmington	ME	E	207 778-2075	4780
Lewiston Daily Sun (PA)	Lewiston	ME	C	207 784-3555	4973
Mtm Oldco Inc (PA)	Portland	ME	B	207 791-6650	5247
Northeast Publishing Company	Caribou	ME	G	207 496-3251	4677
RH Rosenfield Co	Sanford	ME	E	207 324-1798	5410
Caledonian Record Pubg Co Inc	Littleton	NH	G	603 444-7141	14715
Country News Club Inc	North Conway	NH	E	603 356-2999	15247
Eagle Publications Inc	Claremont	NH	E	603 543-3100	14089
Fosters Daily Democrat	Rochester	NH	F	603 332-2200	15476
Fosters Daily Dmcrat Fstrs Sun	Portsmouth	NH	F	603 431-4888	15390
Franklin Exeter Inc	Portsmouth	NH	F	603 836-8590	15391
Keene Publishing Corporation	Keene	NH	D	603 352-1234	14606
Local Media Group Inc	Portsmouth	NH	A	603 436-1800	15418
News & Sentinel Inc	Colebrook	NH	F	603 237-5501	14107
Union Leader Corporation (PA)	Manchester	NH	B	603 668-4321	14947
Kent County Daily Times	West Warwick	RI	F	401 789-9744	16911
Lmg Rhode Island Holdings Inc (HQ)	Providence	RI	F	585 598-0030	16553
Phoenix-Times Publishing Co	Bristol	RI	D	401 253-6000	15777
Providence Journal Company	Providence	RI	B	401 277-7000	16590
Herald of Randolph	Randolph	VT	F	802 728-3232	17469
Other Paper	South Burlington	VT	G	802 864-6670	17588
Ta Update Inc (PA)	Barre	VT	D	802 479-4040	17020

COMMON SAND MINING

	CITY	ST	EMP	PHONE	ENTRY#
Kobyluck Sand and Gravel Inc	Waterford	CT	F	860 444-9600	3992
Chick Trucking Inc	Newmarket	NH	G	603 659-3566	15218
Tilcon Arthur Whitcomb Inc (HQ)	North Swanzey	NH	F	603 352-0101	15256

COMMUNICATIONS EQPT WHOLESALERS

	CITY	ST	EMP	PHONE	ENTRY#
Connecticut Radio Inc	Rocky Hill	CT	G	860 563-4867	2919
Globenix Inc	Norwalk	CT	G	203 740-7070	2506
Altiostar Networks Inc (PA)	Lexington	MA	D	855 709-0701	9724
Socomec Inc (DH)	Watertown	MA	F	617 245-0447	12908

COMMUNICATIONS EQPT: Microwave

	CITY	ST	EMP	PHONE	ENTRY#
Microphase Corporation	Shelton	CT	E	203 866-8000	3032
Ainslie Corporation	Walpole	MA	G	781 848-0850	12548
Hxi LLC	Harvard	MA	F	978 772-7774	9064
Legacy Broadcast Inc	North Billerica	MA	B	978 330-9300	10926
Stellant PST Corp	Topsfield	MA	F	978 887-5754	12438
Syntonic Microwave LLC	Andover	MA	G	408 866-5900	5929
Victor Microwave Inc	Wakefield	MA	E	781 245-4472	12541
Applied Radar Inc	North Kingstown	RI	E	401 295-0062	16231

COMMUNICATIONS EQPT: Radio, Marine

	CITY	ST	EMP	PHONE	ENTRY#
Raytheon Sutheast Asia Systems (DH)	Waltham	MA	E	978 470-5000	12762

COMMUNICATIONS SVCS

	CITY	ST	EMP	PHONE	ENTRY#
Acacia Communications Inc (HQ)	Maynard	MA	C	978 938-4896	10259
Tr3 Solutions Inc	Stoneham	MA	F	781 481-0642	12187

COMMUNICATIONS SVCS: Data

	CITY	ST	EMP	PHONE	ENTRY#
Aquila Technology Corp	Burlington	MA	E	781 993-9004	7334
Cisco Systems Inc	Boxborough	MA	F	978 936-0000	7149

COMMUNICATIONS SVCS: Electronic Mail

	CITY	ST	EMP	PHONE	ENTRY#
Southern Neng Telecom Corp (HQ)	New Haven	CT	B	203 771-5200	2203

COMMUNICATIONS SVCS: Internet Connectivity Svcs

	CITY	ST	EMP	PHONE	ENTRY#
Cst Incorporated	Wallingford	CT	F	203 949-9900	3796
Atc Sequoia LLC	Boston	MA	F	617 375-7500	6569
Benu Networks Inc	Burlington	MA	D	978 223-4700	7340
Grandstream Networks Inc (PA)	Boston	MA	E	617 566-9300	6769

COMMUNICATIONS SVCS: Internet Host Svcs

	CITY	ST	EMP	PHONE	ENTRY#
20/20 Software Inc	Stamford	CT	G	203 316-5500	3266
Family Education Network Inc	Boston	MA	E	617 671-3435	6730

COMMUNICATIONS SVCS: Online Svc Providers

	CITY	ST	EMP	PHONE	ENTRY#
Brightcove Inc (PA)	Boston	MA	B	888 882-1880	6623

COMMUNICATIONS SVCS: Proprietary Online Svcs Networks

	CITY	ST	EMP	PHONE	ENTRY#
Blc Holdings LLC (PA)	Norwalk	CT	E	203 229-1007	2474
Evotext Inc	Billerica	MA	F	781 272-1830	6445
Gridedge Networks Inc	Acton	MA	F	978 569-2000	5749
Dataxoom Corp (PA)	Manchester	NH	F	510 474-0044	14840

COMMUNICATIONS SVCS: Signal Enhancement Network Svcs

	CITY	ST	EMP	PHONE	ENTRY#
Textspeak Corporation	Westport	CT	F	203 803-1069	4199

	CITY	ST	EMP	PHONE	ENTRY#
Millitech Inc	Northampton	MA	D	413 582-9620	11073
Smiths Interconnect Inc	Northampton	MA	D	413 582-9620	11080

COMMUNICATIONS SVCS: Telephone Or Video

	CITY	ST	EMP	PHONE	ENTRY#
Swymed Incorporated	Lexington	MA	F	855 799-6366	9777

COMMUNICATIONS SVCS: Telephone, Local

	CITY	ST	EMP	PHONE	ENTRY#
Verizon New York Inc	Winchester	MA	F	781 721-5957	13493

COMMUNICATIONS SVCS: Telephone, Local & Long Distance

	CITY	ST	EMP	PHONE	ENTRY#
Southern Neng Telecom Corp (HQ)	New Haven	CT	B	203 771-5200	2203

COMMUNICATIONS SVCS: Telephone, Voice

	CITY	ST	EMP	PHONE	ENTRY#
Mirion Tech Canberra Inc (DH)	Meriden	CT	D	203 238-2351	1677
Sigmavoip Llc	Westport	CT	G	203 541-5450	4196

COMMUNITY SVCS EMPLOYMENT TRAINING PROGRAM

	CITY	ST	EMP	PHONE	ENTRY#
Asian American Civic Assn Inc (PA)	Boston	MA	E	617 426-9492	6560

COMMUTATORS: Electronic

	CITY	ST	EMP	PHONE	ENTRY#
Sysdyne Technologies LLC	Stamford	CT	F	203 327-3649	3477
Aquila Technology Corp	Burlington	MA	E	781 993-9004	7334
Intellisense Software Corp	Lynnfield	MA	F	781 933-8098	9997

COMPACT LASER DISCS: Prerecorded

	CITY	ST	EMP	PHONE	ENTRY#
Image Software Services Inc	Shirley	MA	G	978 425-3600	11817

COMPOST

	CITY	ST	EMP	PHONE	ENTRY#
New Milford Farms Inc	New Milford	CT	F	860 210-0250	2256
Black Earth Compost LLC	Gloucester	MA	F	262 227-1067	8923
Bootstrap Compost Inc	Plainfield	MA	F	617 642-1979	11428
Diemand Egg Farm Inc	Millers Falls	MA	G	978 544-3806	10447
Divert Inc (PA)	Concord	MA	E	978 341-5430	8113
Massachusetts Natural Fert Inc	Westminster	MA	G	978 874-0744	13272

COMPRESSORS: Air & Gas

	CITY	ST	EMP	PHONE	ENTRY#
Afcon Products Inc	Bethany	CT	F	203 393-9301	91
Nordson Efd LLC	Norwich	CT	D	860 889-3383	2610
Norwalk Compreseer Company	Stratford	CT	E	203 386-1234	3559
Stylair LLC	Plainville	CT	F	860 747-4588	2781
Anver Corporation	Hudson	MA	D	978 568-0221	9354
Atlas Copco Compressors LLC	Ludlow	MA	G	413 589-7439	9938
Atlas Copco Compressors LLC	West Springfield	MA	G	413 493-7290	13015
Atlas Copco Compressors LLC	Westfield	MA	G	518 765-3344	13149
Brooks Automation Us LLC	Chelmsford	MA	C	978 262-4613	7916
Guardair Corporation	Chicopee	MA	E	413 594-4400	8035
V Power Equipment LLC	Wareham	MA	F	508 273-7596	12847
General Electric Company	Bangor	ME	A	207 941-2500	4505

COMPRESSORS: Air & Gas, Including Vacuum Pumps

	CITY	ST	EMP	PHONE	ENTRY#
P&G Metal Components Corp	Bloomfield	CT	F	860 243-2220	199

COMPRESSORS: Refrigeration & Air Conditioning Eqpt

	CITY	ST	EMP	PHONE	ENTRY#
Hartford Compressors Inc	West Hartford	CT	E		4064
Merrimac Industrial Sales Inc (PA)	Haverhill	MA	E	978 372-6006	9114

COMPUTER & COMPUTER SOFTWARE STORES

	CITY	ST	EMP	PHONE	ENTRY#
Glacier Computer LLC	New Milford	CT	F	603 882-1560	2244
E E S Companies Inc	Framingham	MA	F	508 653-6911	8758
Retro-Fit Technologies Inc	Taunton	MA	E	508 478-2222	12363
Valora Technologies Inc	Carlisle	MA	F	781 229-2565	7850
Electronics For Imaging Inc	West Lebanon	NH	B	603 279-6800	15683
Quantifacts Inc	Riverside	RI	G	401 421-8300	16659

COMPUTER & COMPUTER SOFTWARE STORES: Peripheral Eqpt

	CITY	ST	EMP	PHONE	ENTRY#
Mimoco Inc	Needham Heights	MA	F	617 783-1100	10552

COMPUTER & COMPUTER SOFTWARE STORES: Software & Access

	CITY	ST	EMP	PHONE	ENTRY#
Cimcon Software LLC (PA)	Westford	MA	D	978 464-9180	13229

COMPUTER & COMPUTER SOFTWARE STORES: Software, Bus/Non-Game

	CITY	ST	EMP	PHONE	ENTRY#
Covalent Networks Inc	Boston	MA	F	781 296-7952	6673
Free Software Foundation Inc	Boston	MA	F	617 542-5942	6747
Hawkin Dynamics LLC	Westbrook	ME	F	207 405-9142	5628
Infor (us) LLC	Nashua	NH	E	678 319-8000	15114
Tomtom North America Inc	Lebanon	NH	D	978 405-1677	14700

COMPUTER & COMPUTER SOFTWARE STORES: Software, Computer Game

	CITY	ST	EMP	PHONE	ENTRY#
Omniview Sports Inc	Boston	MA	G	781 583-3534	6929

Employee Codes: A=Over 500 employees, B=251-500
C=101-250, D=51-100, E=20-50, F=10-19, G=1-9

2024 Harris New England
Manufacturers Directory

1365

PRODUCT

	CITY	ST	EMP	PHONE	ENTRY#

COMPUTER & DATA PROCESSING EQPT REPAIR & MAINTENANCE

	CITY	ST	EMP	PHONE	ENTRY#
Complete Technology Resources	Marlborough	MA	F	508 909-5961	10133
Retro-Fit Technologies Inc	Taunton	MA	F	508 478-2222	12363
Tyler Technologies Inc	Bangor	ME	F	207 947-4494	4517
Igt Global Solutions Corporation (HQ)	Providence	RI	D	401 392-7077	16538

COMPUTER & OFFICE MACHINE MAINTENANCE & REPAIR

	CITY	ST	EMP	PHONE	ENTRY#
Frontier Vision Tech Inc	Rocky Hill	CT	E	860 953-0240	2922
Bull Data Systems Inc	Chelmsford	MA	A	978 294-6000	7919
Deerwalk Inc (HQ)	Lexington	MA	C	781 325-1775	9738
Sdl Xyenterprise LLC (PA)	Wakefield	MA	E	781 756-4400	12533
Valora Technologies Inc	Carlisle	MA	F	781 229-2265	7850
Techfourfive LLC	Nashua	NH	G	603 438-5760	15175

COMPUTER FACILITIES MANAGEMENT SVCS

	CITY	ST	EMP	PHONE	ENTRY#
Environmental Systems Corp	West Hartford	CT	C	860 953-8800	4060
Research Cmpt Consulting Svcs (PA)	Canton	MA	G	781 821-1221	7823
It Synergy Group LLC	Warwick	RI	F	866 767-4874	16824

COMPUTER FORMS

	CITY	ST	EMP	PHONE	ENTRY#
D B S Industries Inc	Haverhill	MA	D	978 373-4748	9090
Stat Products Inc	Ashland	MA	E	508 881-8022	5967

COMPUTER GRAPHICS SVCS

	CITY	ST	EMP	PHONE	ENTRY#
A To A Studio Solutions Ltd	Stamford	CT	F	203 388-9050	3267
Joseph Merritt & Company Inc (PA)	Hartford	CT	E	860 296-2500	1488
Desk Top Graphics Inc (HQ)	Peabody	MA	E	617 832-1927	11305
Homeportfolio Inc	Newton	MA	E	617 559-1197	10760
Edge Media Group	Bangor	ME	F	207 942-2901	4498
S & K Unlimited LLC	Brownville	ME	F	207 965-6137	4638
Snap Site Studios LLC	Manchester	NH	G	603 782-3395	14931

COMPUTER HARDWARE REQUIREMENTS ANALYSIS

	CITY	ST	EMP	PHONE	ENTRY#
Advanced Decisions Inc	Orange	CT	G	203 402-0603	2665
Automatech Inc (PA)	Plymouth	MA	G	508 830-0088	11447
Cybernorth LLC	South Portland	ME	G	207 331-3310	5496

COMPUTER PERIPHERAL EQPT REPAIR & MAINTENANCE

	CITY	ST	EMP	PHONE	ENTRY#
Xerox Corporation (HQ)	Norwalk	CT	B	203 849-5216	2598
Xerox Holdings Inc	Norwalk	CT	A	203 968-3000	2599
Xerox Holdings Corporation (PA)	Norwalk	CT	B	203 849-5216	2600
Xxpress Auto Repair Shop LLC	Hyde Park	MA	F	800 591-2068	9468

COMPUTER PERIPHERAL EQPT, NEC

	CITY	ST	EMP	PHONE	ENTRY#
Braxton Manufacturing Co Inc	Watertown	CT	C	860 274-6781	4003
Computer Express LLC	Berlin	CT	F	860 829-1310	62
Contek International Corp	New Canaan	CT	F	203 972-7330	2078
Data Technology Inc	Tolland	CT	A	860 871-8082	3656
Dictaphone Corporation (DH)	Stratford	CT	C	203 381-7000	3533
Dymo Corporation	Norwalk	CT	D		2494
Eloque LLC	Norwalk	CT	F	203 849-5567	2497
General Digital Corporation	East Hartford	CT	D	860 282-2900	996
LTI Portfolio Management Corp	Wilton	CT	F	203 563-1100	4243
Marco International Inc	Ridgefield	CT	D	203 894-8000	2902
Measurement Systems Inc	Wallingford	CT	E	203 949-3500	3831
Morse Watchmans Inc	Oxford	CT	E	203 264-4949	2705
O E M Controls Inc (PA)	Shelton	CT	C	203 929-8431	3042
Online River LLC	Westport	CT	F	203 801-5900	4191
Ortronics Inc (DH)	New London	CT	D	860 445-3900	2232
Ortronics Inc	West Hartford	CT	F	877 295-3472	4076
Ortronics Legrand	Ivoryton	CT	G	860 767-3515	1531
Syferlock Technology Corp	Waterbury	CT	G	203 292-5441	3971
Symbol Technologies LLC	Stamford	CT	E	203 359-5677	3476
Team Logic It	Vernon	CT	G	320 760-9084	3757
Ventus Technologies LLC	Norwalk	CT	F	203 642-2800	2591
Xerox Corporation (HQ)	Norwalk	CT	B	203 849-5216	2598
Xerox Holdings Inc	Norwalk	CT	A	203 968-3000	2599
Xerox Holdings Corporation (PA)	Norwalk	CT	B	203 849-5216	2600
3M Touch Systems Inc	Norwood	MA	E	781 386-2770	11152
3M Touch Systems Inc	Westborough	MA	D	508 871-1840	13075
Adaptive Optics Associates Inc (DH)	Devens	MA	D	978 757-9600	8269
Aereo Inc	Hopedale	MA	F	617 861-8287	9293
Bull Data Systems Inc	Chelmsford	MA	A	978 294-6000	7919
Corero Network Security Inc	Marlborough	MA	E	978 212-1500	10136
Cortron Inc	Lowell	MA	E	978 975-5445	9871
Csi Keyboards Inc	Peabody	MA	E	978 532-8181	11304
Csp Inc (PA)	Lowell	MA	E	978 954-5038	9872
Dowslake Microsystems Corp	North Andover	MA	G	978 691-5700	10826
EMC Corporation (HQ)	Hopkinton	MA	B	508 435-1000	9322
EMC International Holdings Inc	Hopkinton	MA	A	508 435-1000	9324
Equipe Communications Corp	Acton	MA	C	978 635-1999	5747
Evolv Tech Holdings Inc (PA)	Waltham	MA	G	781 374-8100	12669
Evolv Technologies Inc (HQ)	Waltham	MA	D	781 374-8100	12670
Garrettcom Inc	North Andover	MA	E	978 688-8807	10835
Humanscale Corporation	Boston	MA	D	617 338-0077	6800
Intel Massachusetts Inc	Hudson	MA	A	978 553-4000	9377
INTEL Network Systems Inc (HQ)	Hudson	MA	C	978 553-4000	9378
International Parallel Mchs	New Bedford	MA	G	508 990-2977	10604
Inteset Technologies LLC	Hanover	MA	G	781 826-1560	9035
Juniper Networks Inc	Shrewsbury	MA	F	508 523-0427	11836
Kamel Peripherals Inc (PA)	Hopkinton	MA	E	508 435-7771	9334
Kemp Technologies Inc	Rochdale	MA	G	631 418-8407	11627
Kentron Technologies Inc	Wilmington	MA	G	978 988-9100	13419
L-Com Inc (DH)	North Andover	MA	D	978 682-6936	10842
M8trix Tech LLC	Canton	MA	G	617 925-7030	7806
Mack Technologies Inc (HQ)	Westford	MA	C	978 392-5500	13247
Madison Cable Corporation	Worcester	MA	D	800 522-6752	13755
Manufacturers Services Limited	Concord	MA	E	617 330-7682	8124
Mazu Networks LLC	Cambridge	MA	E	617 354-9292	7639
Metroblity Optical Systems Inc	North Billerica	MA	F	781 255-5300	10935
Microway Inc	Plymouth	MA	F	508 746-7341	11467
Milford Manufacturing Svcs LLC	Hopedale	MA	E	508 478-8544	9299
Mimoco Inc	Needham Heights	MA	F	617 783-1100	10552
N3k Informatik Inc	Boston	MA	F	617 289-9282	6901
Netscout Systems Inc (PA)	Westford	MA	C	978 614-4000	13253
Network Equipment Tech Inc (DH)	Westford	MA	E	510 713-7300	13254
New England Keyboard Inc	Fitchburg	MA	E	978 345-8332	8668
New England Technology Group	Cambridge	MA	F	617 864-5551	7665
Parallel Systems Corp	Georgetown	MA	E	978 352-7100	8911
Power Systems Integrity Inc	Northborough	MA	G	508 393-1655	11106
Project Resources Inc	Wareham	MA	F	508 295-7444	12842
Psjl Corporation	Billerica	MA	C	978 313-2500	6474
Rampage Systems Inc	Waltham	MA	E	781 891-1001	12758
Rapiscan Systems Inc	Billerica	MA	F	978 933-4375	6475
Retro-Fit Technologies Inc	Taunton	MA	E	508 478-2222	12363
Rsa Security LLC (PA)	Bedford	MA	A	800 995-5095	6268
Samsara	Northampton	MA	G	413 570-4130	11079
Sky Computers Inc	Chelmsford	MA	F	978 250-2420	7958
Smart Modular Technologies Inc	Tewksbury	MA	D	978 221-3513	12416
Sycamore Networks Inc	Chelmsford	MA	C	978 250-2900	7962
Winchester Systems Inc (PA)	Littleton	MA	E	781 265-0200	9845
Wind River Systems Inc	Canton	MA	D	781 364-2200	7841
Wright Line LLC (HQ)	Worcester	MA	B	508 852-4300	13834
Allen Datagraph Systems Inc	Salem	NH	E	603 216-6344	15504
Allied Telesis Inc	Portsmouth	NH	D	603 334-6058	15358
Bantry Components Inc	Manchester	NH	E	603 668-3210	14817
Corportion For Lser Optics Res (PA)	Londonderry	NH	G	603 430-2023	14738
CTS Corporation	Londonderry	NH	D	603 421-2546	14740
Dutile Glines & Higgins Inc	Manchester	NH	F	603 622-0452	14846
Enterasys Networks Inc (HQ)	Salem	NH	D	603 952-5000	15521
H32 Design and Development LLC (PA)	Concord	NH	G	603 865-1000	14135
Memtec Corporation	Amherst	NH	D	603 893-8080	13880
Minim Inc (PA)	Manchester	NH	E	833 966-4646	14889
Riverbed Technology Inc	Nashua	NH	G	603 402-5200	15161
Seamark International LLC	Nashua	NH	F	603 546-0100	15164
Solidscape Inc	Merrimack	NH	E	603 424-0590	15003
Tech Resources Inc	Milford	NH	G	603 673-9000	15039
Xor Media Inc	Greenville	NH	F	603 878-6400	14376
Electro Standards Lab Inc	Cranston	RI	D	401 946-1164	15853
Florlink Inc	Newport	RI	F	617 221-2200	16210
Vishay Efi Inc	Warwick	RI	E	401 738-9150	16873
Alken Inc	Colchester	VT	E	802 655-3159	17185
Image Tek Mfg Inc	Springfield	VT	E	802 885-6208	17618
Mack Group (PA)	Arlington	VT	B	802 375-2511	16988
Mack Molding Company Inc (HQ)	Arlington	VT	C	802 375-2511	16990
Ovr Tech LLC	Burlington	VT	G	802 391-4172	17149
Preci-Manufacturing Inc	Winooski	VT	D	802 655-2414	17768

COMPUTER PERIPHERAL EQPT, WHOLESALE

	CITY	ST	EMP	PHONE	ENTRY#
Mimoco Inc	Needham Heights	MA	F	617 783-1100	10552
Morgan Scientific Inc (PA)	Haverhill	MA	F	978 521-4440	9118
Netsilicon Inc (HQ)	Waltham	MA	D	781 647-1234	12736
Source Code LLC (PA)	Norwood	MA	E	781 688-2248	11209
Source Code Midco LLC (PA)	Norwood	MA	E	781 255-2022	11210

COMPUTER PERIPHERAL EQPT: Input Or Output

	CITY	ST	EMP	PHONE	ENTRY#
OEM Design Services LLC	East Haven	CT	G	203 467-5993	1049
Pison Technology Inc	Boston	MA	G	540 394-0998	6966

COMPUTER PROCESSING SVCS

	CITY	ST	EMP	PHONE	ENTRY#
Tactai Inc	Waltham	MA	F	617 391-7915	12787

COMPUTER PROGRAMMING SVCS: Custom

	CITY	ST	EMP	PHONE	ENTRY#
Gerber Technology LLC (HQ)	Tolland	CT	B	800 321-2448	3662
SS&c Technologies Inc (HQ)	Windsor	CT	C	800 234-0556	4302
Visionpoint LLC	Newington	CT	E	860 436-9673	2333
American Business Systems Inc	Chelmsford	MA	F	978 250-0335	7905
Raytheon Company	Marlborough	MA	E	508 490-1000	10201
Kbace Technologies Inc (HQ)	Nashua	NH	D	603 821-7000	15121
McLaughlin Research Corp	Middletown	RI	C	401 849-4010	16179

COMPUTER RELATED MAINTENANCE SVCS

	CITY	ST	EMP	PHONE	ENTRY#
Environmental Systems Corp	West Hartford	CT	C	860 953-8800	4060
General Dynamics Info Tech Inc	Pawcatuck	CT	D	860 441-2400	2720
Norfield Data Products Inc	Norwalk	CT	F	203 846-0292	2546
21st Century Software Tech Inc	Boston	MA	D	610 341-9017	6499
Datarobot Inc (PA)	Boston	MA	D	617 765-4500	6684
Modus Media Inc	Waltham	MA	E	781 663-5000	12724
National Reprographics Inc	Boston	MA	F	857 383-3700	6904
Octo Telematics North Amer LLC	Auburndale	MA	G	617 916-1080	6138
Oneview Commerce Inc	Hingham	MA	D	617 279-0549	9156
Research Cmpt Consulting Svcs (PA)	Canton	MA	G	781 821-1221	7823
North Tecom LLC	Manchester	NH	F	603 851-5165	14904

COMPUTER SOFTWARE DEVELOPMENT

	CITY	ST	EMP	PHONE	ENTRY#
Active Internet Tech LLC (PA)	Glastonbury	CT	C	800 592-2469	1269
Cnc Engineering Inc	Enfield	CT	E	860 749-1780	1124
Compuweigh Corporation (PA)	Woodbury	CT	F	203 262-9400	4386
Microtools Inc	Simsbury	CT	G	860 651-6170	3094
Otis Elevator Company (HQ)	Farmington	CT	C	860 674-3000	1235
Scholastic Library Pubg Inc (HQ)	Danbury	CT	A	203 797-3500	812
Vertafore Inc	Windsor	CT	E	860 602-6000	4312
21st Century Software Tech Inc	Boston	MA	D	610 341-9017	6499
Aquila Technology Corp	Burlington	MA	E	781 993-9004	7334
Bellhawk Systems Corporation	Millbury	MA	G	508 865-8070	10428
Bridgeline Digital Inc (PA)	Woburn	MA	E	781 376-5555	13536
Cami Research Inc	Acton	MA	F	978 266-2655	5742
Cantata Technology Inc (DH)	Needham Heights	MA	C	781 449-4100	10533
Canvas Gfx Inc	Boston	MA	E	833 721-0829	6637
Cimcon Software LLC (PA)	Westford	MA	D	978 464-9180	13229
Circle Labs Bio Inc	Cambridge	MA	G	516 660-6045	7541
Claricode Inc	Dedham	MA	E	781 449-2450	8238
Creativestar Solution Inc	Waltham	MA	F	617 326-5308	12645
CST of America LLC	Framingham	MA	E	508 665-4400	8754
Forefield Inc	Marlborough	MA	E	508 630-1100	10150
Human Resource Dev Press (PA)	Belchertown	MA	F	413 253-3488	6280
Infinidat Inc	Waltham	MA	D	781 907-7585	12699
Inscribe Inc	Woburn	MA	E	781 933-3331	13586
Intuvision Inc	Woburn	MA	G	781 497-1015	13591
Kemp Technologies Inc	Rochdale	MA	G	631 418-8407	11627
King Fisher Co Inc	Lowell	MA	E	978 454-0214	9890
Mathworks Inc	Natick	MA	A	508 647-7000	10485
Mathworks Inc (PA)	Natick	MA	A	508 647-7000	10486
Meta Software Corporation (PA)	Burlington	MA	F	781 238-0293	7393
MTI Systems Inc	West Springfield	MA	F	413 733-1972	13035
Nara Logics Inc	Boston	MA	F	617 945-2049	6902
Pegasystems Inc (PA)	Cambridge	MA	A	617 374-9600	7681
Rampage Systems Inc	Waltham	MA	E	781 891-1001	12758
Research Applctns Fncl Trckin	Boston	MA	E	800 939-7238	7007
Rocket Software Systems Inc	Waltham	MA	E	248 833-9000	12772
Seachange International Inc (PA)	Boston	MA	D	978 897-0100	7029
Sepaton Inc	Marlborough	MA	D	508 490-7900	10210
Speechworks International	Burlington	MA	E	781 565-5000	7432
Superpedestrian Inc (PA)	Cambridge	MA	C	877 678-7518	7725
Ukg Kronos Systems LLC (DH)	Lowell	MA	B	978 250-9800	9931
Window Book Inc	Cambridge	MA	D	617 395-4500	7761
Covetrus North America LLC (PA)	Portland	ME	C	888 280-2221	5202
Tyler Technologies Inc	Bangor	ME	F	207 947-4494	4517
Loftware Holdings Inc (PA)	Portsmouth	NH	F	603 766-3630	15419
Softech Inc (HQ)	Nashua	NH	E	513 942-7100	15170
Tomtom North America Inc	Lebanon	NH	A	603 643-0330	14701
A2b Tracking Solutions Inc	Portsmouth	RI	E	401 683-5215	16434
Avtech Software Inc (PA)	Warren	RI	F	401 628-1600	16752
Hexagon Mfg Intllgnce- Mtrlogy	North Kingstown	RI	D	401 886-2000	16256
MTI Film LLC (HQ)	Providence	RI	E	401 831-1315	16570
Radley Corporation	Lincoln	RI	E	616 554-9060	16152
Datamann Inc	Wilder	VT	E	802 295-6600	17714
Ivy Computer Inc	Waterbury Center	VT	F	802 244-7880	17681
Wellsky Humn Social Svcs Corp	Essex Junction	VT	D	802 316-3000	17249

COMPUTER SOFTWARE DEVELOPMENT & APPLICATIONS

	CITY	ST	EMP	PHONE	ENTRY#
Isupportws Inc	Stamford	CT	F	203 569-7600	3386
Vinegar Syndrome LLC	Bridgeport	CT	G	475 731-1778	384
Biobright LLC (HQ)	Boston	MA	G	617 444-9007	6595
Catapult Sports Inc (HQ)	Boston	MA	E	978 447-5220	6642

	CITY	ST	EMP	PHONE	ENTRY#
Centerity Systems Inc	Newton	MA	F	339 225-7007	10743
Channelwave Software Inc (DH)	Cambridge	MA	E	617 621-1700	7538
Dinner Daily LLC	Westford	MA	F	978 392-5887	13234
Expertek Systems Inc	Marlborough	MA	E	508 624-0006	10149
Grove Labs Inc	Somerville	MA	F	703 608-8178	11878
Hirezon Corporation	Westborough	MA	F	508 836-3800	13105
Hottinger Bruel & Kjaer Inc (DH)	Marlborough	MA	D	508 485-7480	10164
Metalmark Innovations Pbc	Cambridge	MA	G	617 714-4026	7642
Neuromotion Inc	Boston	MA	F	415 676-9326	6912
Ptc Inc (PA)	Boston	MA	A	781 370-5000	6983
Sdl Xyenterprise LLC (PA)	Wakefield	MA	E	781 756-4400	12533
Squareworks Consulting LLC	Boston	MA	E	800 779-6285	7057
Tomorrow Companies Inc	Boston	MA	F	800 735-7075	7080
Voxel8 Inc	Somerville	MA	F	916 396-3714	11912
Hawkin Dynamics LLC	Westbrook	ME	F	207 405-9142	5628
Team Augmented Reality Inc	Nobleboro	ME	G	207 350-0460	5102
Dataxoom Corp (PA)	Manchester	NH	F	510 474-0044	14840
Loxsmith Bagel Corporation	Dover	NH	F	603 362-9060	14233
North Tecom LLC	Manchester	NH	F	603 851-5165	14904
Purevita Labs LLC	West Warwick	RI	F	401 258-8968	16921

COMPUTER SOFTWARE SYSTEMS ANALYSIS & DESIGN: Custom

	CITY	ST	EMP	PHONE	ENTRY#
Bynder LLC	Boston	MA	C	857 310-5434	6630
Demandware LLC (HQ)	Burlington	MA	D	888 553-9216	7360
Full Circle Technologies Inc	Boston	MA	E	617 722-0100	6749
Iet Solutions LLC (DH)	Canton	MA	E	818 838-0606	7800
Ivory Onyx	Boston	MA	F	617 454-4980	6820
Kognito Solutions LLC	Burlington	MA	E	212 675-2651	7387
Leanix Inc (DH)	Watertown	MA	F	781 321-6500	12887
Ntt Data Intl Svcs Inc (DH)	Boston	MA	B	800 745-3663	6927
Silverthread Inc	Cambridge	MA	A	800 674-9366	7715
Waters Corporation (PA)	Milford	MA	A	508 478-2000	10424
Cybernorth LLC	South Portland	ME	G	207 331-3310	5496
Garmin International Inc	Yarmouth	ME	B	800 561-5105	5704
Sproutel Inc	Providence	RI	G	914 806-6514	16615

COMPUTER STORAGE DEVICES, NEC

	CITY	ST	EMP	PHONE	ENTRY#
J R Merritt Controls Inc (PA)	Stratford	CT	E	203 381-0100	3551
Kaman Aerospace Corporation	Middletown	CT	C	860 632-1000	1755
Pexagon Technology Inc	Guilford	CT	E	203 458-3364	1402
Quantum Bpower Southington LLC	Southington	CT	F	860 201-0621	3230
Quantum Circuits Inc	New Haven	CT	E	203 872-4723	2189
ARA Dell EMC MA Rsa Bedfo	Bedford	MA	F	508 431-4084	6210
Cambex Corporation (PA)	Westborough	MA	F	508 983-1200	13085
EMC Corporation	Franklin	MA	E	800 275-8777	8834
EMC Corporation	Franklin	MA	D	508 435-1000	8835
EMC Corporation	Franklin	MA	D	866 438-3622	8836
EMC Corporation	Hopkinton	MA	F	508 435-0369	9317
EMC Corporation	Hopkinton	MA	F	800 445-2588	9318
EMC Corporation	Hopkinton	MA	E	508 346-2900	9319
EMC Corporation	Hopkinton	MA	D	508 435-2581	9320
EMC Corporation	Hopkinton	MA	D	508 249-5883	9321
EMC Corporation (HQ)	Hopkinton	MA	B	508 435-1000	9322
EMC Corporation	Milford	MA	E	508 634-2774	10402
EMC Corporation	Newton	MA	D	617 618-3400	10755
EMC Global Holdings Company	Hopkinton	MA	D	508 544-2852	9323
EMC International Holdings Inc	Hopkinton	MA	A	508 435-1000	9324
Emc1 Continental Ave LLC	Boston	MA	G	617 875-2687	6713
Infinidat Inc	Waltham	MA	D	781 907-7585	12699
Iwave Software LLC	Hopkinton	MA	E		9333
Manufacturers Services Limited	Concord	MA		617 330-7682	8124
Nanoramic Laboratories	Wakefield	MA	F	857 403-6031	12521
Raid Inc	Lawrence	MA	E	978 683-6444	9595
Seagate Technology LLC	Shrewsbury	MA	F	508 770-3111	11841
Sepaton Inc	Marlborough	MA	D	508 490-7900	10210
Silk Technologies Inc	Needham Heights	MA	D	877 982-2555	10557
Sudbury Systems Inc	Bedford	MA	E	800 876-8888	6272
Unicom Engineering Inc (HQ)	Canton	MA	E	781 332-1000	7836
Vagrants Inc	Somerville	MA	F	857 400-8870	11909
Vce Company LLC	Marlborough	MA	A	831 247-1660	10228
Winchester Systems Inc (PA)	Littleton	MA	E	781 265-0200	9845
Cybernorth LLC	South Portland	ME	G	207 331-3310	5496
Centilla Corporation	Windham	NH	F	603 658-3881	15723
Visit WEI	Salem	NH	G	603 893-0900	15570
It Synergy Group LLC	Warwick	RI	F	866 767-4874	16824

COMPUTER STORAGE UNITS: Auxiliary

	CITY	ST	EMP	PHONE	ENTRY#
Mini LLC	Naugatuck	CT	G	203 464-5495	1972
Sencorpwhite Inc (HQ)	Hyannis	MA	C	508 771-9400	9451

COMPUTER SYSTEMS ANALYSIS & DESIGN

	CITY	ST	EMP	PHONE	ENTRY#
Canvas Gfx Inc	Boston	MA	E	833 721-0829	6637

	CITY	ST	EMP	PHONE	ENTRY#
Diacritech Inc	Boston	MA	F	617 236-7500	6692

COMPUTER TERMINALS

	CITY	ST	EMP	PHONE	ENTRY#
General Digital Corporation	East Hartford	CT	D	860 282-2900	996
Omega Engineering Inc (DH)	Norwalk	CT	C	203 359-1660	2549
Actuality Systems Inc	Arlington	MA	F	617 325-9230	5938
EPC Space LLC	Andover	MA	F	978 208-1334	5881
Igt Global Solutions Corp	Braintree	MA	G	781 849-5642	7188
Rampage Systems Inc	Waltham	MA	E	781 891-1001	12758
Ferrite Microwave Tech LLC	Nashua	NH	F	603 881-5234	15100
Igt Global Solutions Corp	West Greenwich	RI	E	401 392-7025	16885
Igt Global Solutions Corporation (HQ)	Providence	RI	D	401 392-7077	16538

COMPUTER-AIDED SYSTEM SVCS

	CITY	ST	EMP	PHONE	ENTRY#
Bpi Reprographics	Norwalk	CT	F	203 866-5600	2475
Double-Take Software Inc (DH)	Burlington	MA	C	949 253-6500	7365
Ptc Inc (PA)	Boston	MA	A	781 370-5000	6983

COMPUTERS, NEC

	CITY	ST	EMP	PHONE	ENTRY#
Black Rock Tech Group LLC	Bridgeport	CT	F	203 916-7200	302
Cyberresearch Inc	Branford	CT	E	203 643-5000	247
Fairfix CT Inc	Fairfield	CT	F	203 516-4137	1185
General Digital Corporation	East Hartford	CT	D	860 282-2900	996
Hoffman Engineering LLC (DH)	Stamford	CT	D	203 425-8900	3378
Kimchuk Incorporated	Danbury	CT	C	203 798-0799	765
Abaco Systems Technology Corp	Wilmington	MA	D	256 382-8115	13369
Acbel (usa) Polytech Inc	Hopkinton	MA	G	508 625-1768	9305
Acumentrics Rups LLC	Walpole	MA	E	617 932-7877	12546
Biscom Inc	Westford	MA	D	978 250-1800	13226
Bull Data Systems Inc	Chelmsford	MA	A	978 294-6000	7919
Comark LLC (HQ)	Milford	MA	E	508 359-8161	10399
E E S Companies Inc	Framingham	MA	F	508 653-6911	8758
General Dynamics Mission	Dedham	MA	B	781 410-9635	8244
General Dynamics Mission	Taunton	MA	A	508 880-4000	12337
Hiper Global Us LLC (PA)	North Andover	MA	D	978 486-0300	10838
Industrial Bmdcal Sensors Corp	Waltham	MA	F	781 891-4201	12698
Keimos 1988 US Inc (PA)	Norwood	MA	F	508 921-4590	11187
Kinetic Systems Inc	Boston	MA	E	617 522-8700	6842
Mack Technologies Inc (HQ)	Westford	MA	C	978 392-5500	13247
Manufacturers Services Limited	Concord	MA	E	617 330-7682	8124
Mercury Commercial Electronics Inc	Chelmsford	MA	C	978 967-1364	7938
Power Systems Integrity Inc	Northborough	MA	G	508 393-1655	11106
Sie Computing Solutions Inc	Brockton	MA	D	508 588-6110	7305
Source Code LLC (PA)	Norwood	MA	E	781 688-2248	11209
Source Code Midco LLC (PA)	Norwood	MA	E	781 255-2022	11210
Sybase Inc	Watertown	MA	E	617 673-1200	12910
Tag Global Systems LLC	Pembroke	MA	G	800 630-4708	11378
Thinkflood Inc	Needham	MA	G	617 299-2000	10526
Advanced Programs Inc	Salem	NH	F	603 685-6748	15503
Celestica New England Inc	Newington	NH	B	603 334-3450	15206
Dutile Glines & Higgins Inc	Manchester	NH	F	603 622-0452	14846
Lexington Data Incorporated	Rindge	NH	G	603 899-5673	15460
Monarch International Inc	Amherst	NH	E	603 883-3390	13881
Wagz Inc (PA)	Portsmouth	NH	F	603 570-6015	15449
Onlogic Inc	South Burlington	VT	C	802 861-2300	17587

COMPUTERS, NEC, WHOLESALE

	CITY	ST	EMP	PHONE	ENTRY#
Cyberresearch Inc	Branford	CT	E	203 643-5000	247
Inteset Technologies LLC	Hanover	MA	G	781 826-1560	9035
Maynesboro Industries Inc	Berlin	NH	F	603 752-3366	13982
Rectrac LLC	Essex Junction	VT	D	802 879-6993	17244

COMPUTERS, PERIPHERALS & SOFTWARE, WHOLESALE: Printers

	CITY	ST	EMP	PHONE	ENTRY#
Envirnmntal Office Sltions Inc (PA)	East Hartford	CT	E	860 291-1900	993
Flo-Tech LLC (PA)	New Haven	CT	D	860 613-3333	2152
Westrex International Inc	Boston	MA	F	617 254-1200	7119

COMPUTERS, PERIPHERALS & SOFTWARE, WHOLESALE: Software

	CITY	ST	EMP	PHONE	ENTRY#
3M Company	Wallingford	CT	F	203 949-1630	3766
Online River LLC	Westport	CT	F	203 801-5900	4191
Syferlock Technology Corp	Waterbury	CT	G	203 292-5441	3971
American Well Corporation (PA)	Boston	MA	B	617 204-3500	6543
Bynder LLC	Boston	MA	F	857 310-5434	6630
Canvas Gfx Inc	Boston	MA	E	833 721-0829	6637
Cisco Systems Inc	Boxborough	MA	F	978 936-0000	7149
Compart North America Inc	Andover	MA	E	877 237-2725	5879
Datarobot Inc (PA)	Boston	MA	D	617 765-4500	6684
Double-Take Software Inc (DH)	Burlington	MA	C	949 253-6500	7365
Dynatrace LLC (HQ)	Waltham	MA	C	781 530-1000	12657
Evotext Inc	Billerica	MA	F	781 272-1830	6445
Fev Tutor Inc	Woburn	MA	D	781 376-6925	13564
Free Software Foundation Inc	Boston	MA	F	617 542-5942	6747

	CITY	ST	EMP	PHONE	ENTRY#
Full Circle Technologies Inc	Boston	MA	E	617 722-0100	6749
Ivory Onyx	Boston	MA	F	617 454-4980	6820
New England Business Svc Inc (HQ)	Townsend	MA	D	978 448-6111	12441
RSD America Inc	Waltham	MA	F	201 996-1000	12775
Visible Systems Corporation (PA)	Boston	MA	E	617 902-0767	7106
Wordstock Inc	Bedford	MA	F	781 646-7700	6277
A2b Tracking Solutions Inc	Portsmouth	RI	E	401 683-5215	16434

COMPUTERS: Mainframe

	CITY	ST	EMP	PHONE	ENTRY#
Glacier Computer LLC	New Milford	CT	F	603 882-1560	2244
Mediavue Systems LLC	Hingham	MA	E	781 926-0676	9154

COMPUTERS: Personal

	CITY	ST	EMP	PHONE	ENTRY#
Cyclone Microsystems Inc	Hamden	CT	E	203 786-5536	1420
Interactive Marketing Corp	North Haven	CT	G	203 248-5324	2416
Hp Inc	Littleton	MA	D	800 222-5547	9816
HP Inc	Littleton	MA	F	650 857-1501	9817

CONCENTRATES, DRINK

	CITY	ST	EMP	PHONE	ENTRY#
Coca-Cola Refreshments USA Inc	Northampton	MA	D	413 586-8450	11056
Mrp Trading Innovations LLC	Beverly	MA	F	978 762-3900	6367

CONCENTRATES, FLAVORING, EXC DRINK

	CITY	ST	EMP	PHONE	ENTRY#
Target Flavors Inc	Brookfield	CT	F	203 775-4727	539

CONCRETE BUILDING PRDTS WHOLESALERS

	CITY	ST	EMP	PHONE	ENTRY#
Connecticut Valley Block Co Inc	West Springfield	MA	E		13018
J G Maclellan Con Co Inc	Amesbury	MA	F	978 458-1223	5839
Washburn Vault Company Inc	Brattleboro	VT	G	802 254-9150	17107

CONCRETE CURING & HARDENING COMPOUNDS

	CITY	ST	EMP	PHONE	ENTRY#
Engineered Coatings Inc	Litchfield	CT	G	860 567-5556	1557
Ecpi Inc	Bolton	MA	F	774 823-6368	6496

CONCRETE MIXERS

	CITY	ST	EMP	PHONE	ENTRY#
Bonsal American Inc	Oxford	MA	G	508 987-8188	11249

CONCRETE PLANTS

	CITY	ST	EMP	PHONE	ENTRY#
Advanced Concrete Tech Inc	Greenland	NH	G	603 431-5661	14365

CONCRETE PRDTS

	CITY	ST	EMP	PHONE	ENTRY#
Bonsal American Inc	Canaan	CT	F	860 824-7733	553
Custom Vault Corporation	New Fairfield	CT	G	203 746-0506	2094
Nicolock Paving Stones Ne LLC	North Haven	CT	F	203 234-2800	2428
O & G Industries Inc	Stamford	CT	D	203 323-1111	3422
Oldcastle Infrastructure Inc	Avon	CT	E	860 673-3291	34
Quikrete Companies Inc	Wauregan	CT	F	860 564-3308	4041
Washington Concrete Pdts Inc	Plainville	CT	F	860 747-5242	2788
Bonsal American Inc	Oxford	MA	G	508 987-8188	11249
Diversitech Corporation	Taunton	MA	G	800 699-0453	12333
Dn Tanks LLC	Wakefield	MA	F	781 246-1133	12508
Fireslate 2 Inc	East Wareham	MA	F	508 273-0047	8422
Fletcher Granite LLC (DH)	Westford	MA	F	978 692-1312	13238
Forterra Pipe & Precast LLC	Ashland	MA	C	508 881-2000	5958
L J Gentile & Sons Inc	Norfolk	MA	G	508 384-5156	10800
Lorusso Corp (PA)	Plainville	MA	E	508 668-6520	11437
Massachusetts Contr Sups Inc	Hudson	MA	G	978 413-2578	9389
Nantucket Pavers Inc	Rehoboth	MA	F	508 336-5800	11611
Oldcastle Apg Northeast Inc	Holbrook	MA	D	781 506-9473	9183
Williams Stone Co Inc	East Otis	MA	E	413 269-4544	8403
Mattingly Products Company	North Anson	ME	F	207 635-2719	5107
Pepin Precast Inc	Sanford	ME	F	207 324-6125	5405
Bd Enterprises LLC	Claremont	NH	G	603 504-6231	14078
Concrete Systems Inc	Londonderry	NH	F	603 432-1840	14736
Conproco Corp (PA)	Somersworth	NH	F	603 743-5800	15613
E-Z Crete LLC	Keene	NH	F	603 313-6462	14596
E-Z Crete LLC	Swanzey	NH	F	603 313-6462	15643
Quikrete Companies LLC	Brentwood	NH	E	603 778-2123	14028
Wahsburn Vault Company Inc	Hinsdale	NH	G	603 256-6891	14445
Anchor Concrete	Cranston	RI	F	401 942-4800	15833
Preferred Precast Inc	Cumberland	RI	F	401 475-5560	15961
Joseph P Carrara & Sons Inc	Middlebury	VT	D	802 388-6363	17344

CONCRETE PRDTS, PRECAST, NEC

	CITY	ST	EMP	PHONE	ENTRY#
Atlas Concrete Products Inc	New Britain	CT	F	860 224-2244	2002
Cromwell Concrete Products Incorporated 690	Cromwell	CT			E
Eastern Precast Company Inc	Brookfield	CT	F	203 775-0230	519
Essex Concrete Products Inc	Essex	CT	F	860 767-1768	1163
Forterra Pipe & Precast LLC	Wauregan	CT	G	860 564-9000	4040
United Concrete Products Inc	Yalesville	CT	C	203 269-3119	4399
Acme-Shorey Precast Co Inc	Carver	MA	G	508 548-9607	7852

	CITY	ST	EMP	PHONE	ENTRY#
Acme-Shorey Precast Co Inc (PA)	Harwich	MA	F	508 432-0530	9066
Acme-Shorey Precast Co Inc	South Yarmouth	MA	G	508 430-0956	11980
County Concrete Corp (PA)	Dalton	MA	F	413 499-3359	8149
J & R Pre-Cast Inc	Berkley	MA	F	508 822-3311	6316
Means Pre-Cast Co Inc	Braintree	MA	G	781 843-1909	7194
Pavestone LLC	Middleboro	MA	D	508 947-6001	10373
Precast Specialties Corp	Abington	MA	E	781 878-7220	5727
Scituate Concrete Pipe Corp	Scituate	MA	E	781 545-0564	11772
Scituate Concrete Products	Marshfield	MA	D	781 837-1747	10245
Scituate Concrete Products Cor	Marshfield	MA	F	617 837-1747	10246
Wiggin Means Precast Co Inc	Pocasset	MA	G	508 564-6776	11493
Wiggin Precast Corp	Pocasset	MA	F	508 564-6776	11494
American Concrete Inds Inc (PA)	Auburn	ME	F	207 947-8334	4418
American Concrete Inds Inc	Bangor	ME	D	207 947-8334	4488
Aroostacast Inc	Presque Isle	ME	F	207 764-0077	5296
Gagne & Son Con Blocks Inc	Auburn	ME	G	207 495-3313	4435
East Coast Concrete Pdts LLC	Amherst	NH	F	603 883-3042	13867
Hudson Quarry Corp	Hudson	NH	F	603.598-0142	14507
Newstress Inc	Epsom	NH	F	603 736-9000	14281
Northern Design Precast Inc	Loudon	NH	F	603 783-8989	14796
Durastone Corporation	Lincoln	RI	F	401 723-7100	16134
Durastone Flexicore Inc	Smithfield	RI	E	401 231-4000	16696
Caledonia Inc (PA)	Saint Johnsbury	VT	F	802 748-2319	17539
Camp Precast Concrete Products Inc	Milton	VT	E	802 893-2401	17355
Dailey Precast LLC (HQ)	Shaftsbury	VT	D	802 442-4418	17549

CONCRETE: Bituminous

	CITY	ST	EMP	PHONE	ENTRY#
Holcim - Ner Inc (DH)	Saugus	MA	E	781 941-7200	11760
Massachusetts Broken Stone Co (PA)	Berlin	MA	G	978 838-9999	6319

CONCRETE: Ready-Mixed

	CITY	ST	EMP	PHONE	ENTRY#
A Aiudi & Sons LLC (PA)	Plainville	CT	G	860 747-5534	2742
Aiudi Concrete Inc	Westbrook	CT	G	860 399-9289	4136
B&R Sand and Gravel	Gales Ferry	CT	G	860 464-5099	1259
Barnes Concrete Co Inc	Putnam	CT	E	860 928-7242	2846
Builders Concrete East LLC	North Windham	CT	E	860 456-4111	2450
Century Acquisition	Canaan	CT	G	518 758-7229	554
Devine Brothers Incorporated	Norwalk	CT	E	203 866-4421	2490
Dp Concrete LLC	Farmington	CT	E	860 677-2626	1214
Enfield Transit Mix Inc	Enfield	CT	F	860 763-0864	1129
Essex Concrete Products Inc	Essex	CT	F	860 767-1768	1163
Federici Brands LLC (PA)	Wilton	CT	F	203 762-7667	4239
Five Star Products Inc	Shelton	CT	E	203 336-7900	3006
Iffland Lumber Company Inc	Torrington	CT	E	860 489-9218	3684
Miks Mix LLC	Milford	CT	G	203 521-7824	1851
Mohican Valley Concrete Corp	Fairfield	CT	E	203 254-7133	1194
O & G Industries Inc	Bridgeport	CT	B	203 366-4586	354
O & G Industries Inc	Danbury	CT	E	203 748-5694	791
O & G Industries Inc	Stamford	CT	D	203 977-1618	3421
O & G Industries Inc	Stamford	CT	E	203 323-1111	3422
Quikrete Companies Inc	Wauregan	CT	F	860 564-3308	4041
Sega Ready Mix Incorporated (PA)	New Milford	CT	F	860 354-3969	2260
Sega Ready Mix Incorporated	Waterbury	CT	G	203 465-1052	3968
Sterling Materials LLC	Branford	CT	E	203 315-6619	279
Suzio York Hill Companies	Meriden	CT	F	888 789-4626	1703
The L Suzio Asphalt Co Inc	Meriden	CT	E	203 237-8421	1705
The L Suzio Concrete Co Inc (PA)	Meriden	CT	E	203 237-8421	1706
Tilcon Connecticut Inc	East Granby	CT	E	860 844-7000	954
Tilcon Connecticut Inc (DH)	New Britain	CT	D	860 224-6010	2072
Tilcon Connecticut Inc	Portland	CT	G	860 342-1096	2827
Tilcon Inc (DH)	Newington	CT	B	860 223-3651	2328
Windham Materials LLC (PA)	Willimantic	CT	E	860 456-4111	4222
Windham Materials LLC	Willimantic	CT	D	860 456-3277	4223
York Hill Trap Rock Quarry Co	Meriden	CT	E	203 237-8421	1712
A Graziano Inc	Braintree	MA	E	781 843-7300	7166
Aggregate Industries	Swampscott	MA	F	781 596-4107	12297
Banas Sand and Gravel Co Inc	Ludlow	MA	E	413 583-8321	9941
Berkshire Concrete Corp (HQ)	Pittsfield	MA	E	413 443-4734	11392
Boro Sand & Stone Corp (PA)	North Attleboro	MA	E	508 699-2911	10869
Boston Sand & Gravel Company (PA)	Boston	MA	E	617 227-9000	6616
Boston Sand & Gravel Company	Charlestown	MA	C	617 242-5540	7863
Boston Sand & Gravel Company	Sandwich	MA	F	508 888-8002	11747
Boucher Con Foundation Sups	Middleboro	MA	E	508 947-4279	10351
Byrne Sand & Gravel Co Inc	Middleboro	MA	F	508 947-0724	10354
Cape Cod Ready Mix Inc	Orleans	MA	E	508 255-4600	11236
Chicopee Foundations Inc	Chicopee	MA	E	413 594-4700	8015
CP Dauphinais Inc	Sutton	MA	E	508 865-1755	12279
Crh Americas Inc	Leominster	MA	B	978 840-1176	9655
Cs-Ma LLC (PA)	Wilbraham	MA	E	413 733-6631	13356
Dauphinais & Son Inc	Wilbraham	MA	E	413 596-3964	13357
Dauphinais Concrete	Bellingham	MA	G	508 657-0941	6289
Dmjl Consulting LLC	Methuen	MA	F	978 989-0790	10327
E H Perkins Construction Inc	Sterling	MA	F	978 422-3388	12161
E H Perkins Construction Inc (PA)	Wayland	MA	E	978 562-3436	12925
Fall River Ready-Mix Con LLC	Fall River	MA	G	508 675-7540	8549
Falmouth Ready Mix Inc	East Falmouth	MA	F	508 548-6100	8359
Fuccillo Ready Mix Inc	East Falmouth	MA	F	508 540-2821	8360
Gloucester Transit Mix Inc	Gloucester	MA	G	978 283-9649	8938
GP Aggregate Corp	Gloucester	MA	F	978 283-5318	8940
Holcim - Ner Inc (DH)	Saugus	MA	E	781 941-7200	11760
J G Maclellan Con Co Inc	Amesbury	MA	F	978 458-1223	5839
J G Maclellan Con Co Inc (PA)	Lowell	MA	D	978 458-1223	9888
JG Maclellan	Wakefield	MA	G	781 245-7756	12514
L & S Industries Inc (PA)	New Bedford	MA	E	508 995-4654	10612
Lane Construction Corporation	Northfield	MA	D	413 498-5586	11120
Leo Concrete Service Inc	Chicopee	MA	F	413 536-3370	8045
McCabe Sand & Gravel Co Inc	Taunton	MA	E	508 823-0771	12349
Morse Ready Mix LLC	Plainville	MA	E	508 809-4644	11440
Morse Sand & Gravel Corp	Attleboro	MA	E	508 809-4644	6038
P A Landers Inc	Hanover	MA	E	508 747-1800	9039
Petricca Industries Inc (PA)	Pittsfield	MA	E	413 499-1441	11418
Preferred Concrete Corporation	East Freetown	MA	E	508 763-5500	8365
Ragged Hill Incorporated	East Templeton	MA	E	978 939-5712	8414
Redi-Mix LP	South Carver	MA	E	508 295-5111	11915
Redi-Mix Services Incorporated	Taunton	MA	F	508 823-0771	12361
Rosenfeld Concrete Corp (HQ)	Hopedale	MA	F	508 473-7200	9303
Rowley Ready Mix Inc	Rowley	MA	F	978 948-2544	11684
Southeastern Concrete Inc	Kingston	MA	E	617 227-9000	9511
Southeastern Concrete Inc	Weymouth	MA	F	781 848-9390	13335
Sterling Concrete Corp	North Oxford	MA	F	978 422-8282	11034
Torromeo Industries Inc (PA)	Methuen	MA	F	978 686-5634	10346
Varney Bros Sand & Gravel Inc	Bellingham	MA	F	508 966-1313	6302
Westfield Concrete Inc	Westfield	MA	G	413 562-4814	13218
Westfield Ready-Mix Inc	Chicopee	MA	F	413 594-4700	8070
Coleman Concrete	Bethel	ME	G	207 824-6300	4552
County Concrete & Cnstr Co	Columbia Falls	ME	E	207 483-4409	4698
Dayton Sand & Gravel Inc	Dayton	ME	D	207 499-2306	4720
Dragon Products Company LLC (DH)	Biddeford	ME	E	207 594-5555	4560
Dragon Products Company LLC	Portland	ME	E	207 879-2328	5212
Dragon Products Company LLC	Thomaston	ME	E	207 594-5555	5544
F R Carroll Inc	Limerick	ME	E	207 793-8615	5001
Ferraiolo Construction Inc	Rockland	ME	E	207 594-9840	5327
Haley Construction Inc	Farmington	ME	E	207 778-9990	4781
Lane Construction Corporation	Presque Isle	ME	E	207 764-4137	5301
Lees Concrete Inc	Bangor	ME	G	207 974-4936	4509
Mattingly Products Company	North Anson	ME	E	207 635-2719	5107
Owen J Folsom Inc	Old Town	ME	E	207 827-7625	5131
P & K Sand and Gravel Inc	Naples	ME	E	207 693-6765	5081
R A Cummings Inc	Auburn	ME	E	207 777-7100	4457
R Pepin & Sons Inc	Sanford	ME	E	207 324-6125	5407
State Sand & Gravel Co Inc	Belfast	ME	F	207 338-4070	4538
Alvin J Coleman & Son Inc (PA)	Albany	NH	F	603 447-5936	13847
Alvin J Coleman & Son Inc	Albany	NH	E	603 447-3056	13848
Boston Sand & Gravel Company	Rochester	NH	D	603 330-3999	15467
Carroll Concrete Co Inc	Newport	NH	F	603 863-1765	15226
Coleman Concrete Inc	Albany	NH	E	603 447-5936	13850
Crh Americas Inc	West Lebanon	NH	C	603 298-5959	15681
Crh Americas Materials Inc	Manchester	NH	E	603 669-2373	14839
Granite State Concrete Co Inc	Milford	NH	F	603 673-3327	15023
LE Weed & Son LLC (PA)	Newport	NH	G	603 863-1540	15230
Michie Corporation	Henniker	NH	D	603 428-7426	14438
N H Central Concrete Corp	Henniker	NH	F	603 428-7900	14439
Newport Concrete Block Co	Newport	NH	F	603 863-1540	15232
Newport Sand & Gravel Co Inc	Charlestown	NH	G	603 826-4444	14065
Newport Sand & Gravel Co Inc (PA)	Newport	NH	F	603 298-0199	15233
Newport Sand & Gravel Co Inc	West Lebanon	NH	F	603 298-8777	15686
Osborne Concrete	Northwood	NH	F	603 231-3604	15275
Persons Concrete	Belmont	NH	F	603 524-4434	13966
Redimix Companies Inc (DH)	Belmont	NH	E	603 524-4434	13968
Redimix Concrete	Belmont	NH	F	603 581-1805	13970
Seacoast Redimix Concrete LLC (PA)	Dover	NH	F	603 742-4441	14250
Tilcon Arthur Whitcomb Inc (HQ)	North Swanzey	NH	F	603 352-0101	15256
Torromeo Industries Inc	Kingston	NH	E	603 642-5564	14637
Consolidated Concrete Corp (PA)	East Providence	RI	G	401 438-4700	16009
Cumberland Quarry Corp	Cumberland	RI	F	401 658-4442	15937
Ferreira Concrete Forms Inc	East Providence	RI	F	401 639-0931	16019
Greenville Ready Mix	Smithfield	RI	G	401 231-3900	16706
Greenville Ready Mix Inc	Ashaway	RI	F	401 539-2333	15740
Heidelberg Materials Us Inc	Providence	RI	F	800 833-4157	16531
Heritage Concrete Corp	Exeter	RI	F	401 294-1524	16052
Material Concrete Corp	North Smithfield	RI	F	401 765-0204	16326
Mix Marketing Corp	Narragansett	RI	G	401 954-6121	16191
Pawtucket Hot Mix Asphalt Inc	Pawtucket	RI	E	401 722-4488	16400
Bourbeau Aggregate LLC	Saint Albans	VT	G	802 309-4699	17517

PRODUCT

	CITY	ST	EMP	PHONE	ENTRY#
Carroll Concrete Co	Barre	VT	G	802 229-0191	16999
Dailey Precast LLC (HQ)	Shaftsbury	VT	D	802 442-4418	17549
Gray Rock Concrete	Milton	VT	F	802 379-5393	17359
Harrison Concrete Cnstr Inc	Fairfax	VT	E	802 849-6688	17259
Harrison Redi-Mix Corp	Fairfax	VT	E	802 849-6688	17260
Joseph P Carrara & Sons Inc	Middlebury	VT	D	802 388-6363	17344
Joseph P Carrara & Sons Inc (PA)	North Clarendon	VT	E	802 775-2301	17415
Matt Waite Excavation Inc	Pawlet	VT	F	802 325-3668	17441
Newport Sand & Gravel Co Inc	Newport	VT	F	802 334-2000	17403
Newport Sand & Gravel Co Inc	Swanton	VT	G	802 868-4119	17638
S D Ireland Con Cnstr Corp	Williston	VT	C	802 863-6222	17747

CONDENSERS: Motors Or Generators

	CITY	ST	EMP	PHONE	ENTRY#
Proliance International Inc	New Haven	CT	E	203 401-6450	2188

CONDENSERS: Refrigeration

	CITY	ST	EMP	PHONE	ENTRY#
Filtrine Manufacturing Co Inc	Keene	NH	D	603 352-5500	14599

CONDUITS & FITTINGS: Electric

	CITY	ST	EMP	PHONE	ENTRY#
Bridgeport Fittings LLC	Stratford	CT	E	203 377-5944	3522

CONFINEMENT SURVEILLANCE SYS MAINTENANCE & MONITORING SVCS

	CITY	ST	EMP	PHONE	ENTRY#
Videoiq Inc	Somerville	MA	E	781 222-3069	11911

CONNECTORS: Cord, Electric

	CITY	ST	EMP	PHONE	ENTRY#
Gold Line Connector Inc (PA)	Redding	CT	E	203 938-2588	2882
Whitney Blake Company (PA)	Bellows Falls	VT	D	800 323-0479	17033

CONNECTORS: Electronic

	CITY	ST	EMP	PHONE	ENTRY#
Fct Electronics LP	Torrington	CT	D	860 482-2800	3678
Phoenix Company of Chicago Inc (PA)	Naugatuck	CT	D	630 595-2300	1980
Electronic Assemblies Mfg Inc	Methuen	MA	E	978 374-6840	10329
Nabson Inc	Taunton	MA	G	617 323-1101	12350

CONSTRUCTION & MINING MACHINERY WHOLESALERS

	CITY	ST	EMP	PHONE	ENTRY#
Bell Power Systems LLC	Essex	CT	D	860 767-7502	1162
Knm Holdings LLC	Marlborough	MA	G	508 229-1400	10177
North Country Tractor Inc	Sanford	ME	F	207 324-5646	5403
North Country Tractor Inc	Dover	NH	F	603 742-5488	14241
Rhode Island Engine Co Inc	Narragansett	RI	E	401 789-1021	16195

CONSTRUCTION EQPT: Attachments, Snow Plow

	CITY	ST	EMP	PHONE	ENTRY#
Atlantic Broom Service Inc	East Bridgewater	MA	E	774 226-1300	8335
Industrial Stl Boiler Svcs Inc	Chicopee	MA	E	413 532-7788	8038
Rwc Landscape Services MGT	Concord	NH	E	603 279-1411	14154

CONSTRUCTION EQPT: Cranes

	CITY	ST	EMP	PHONE	ENTRY#
Astro Welding & Fabg Inc	Boxborough	MA	F	978 429-8666	7148

CONSTRUCTION EQPT: Grapples, Rock, Wood, Etc

	CITY	ST	EMP	PHONE	ENTRY#
Champlain Construction Co Inc	Middlebury	VT	F	802 388-2652	17341

CONSTRUCTION EQPT: Roofing Eqpt

	CITY	ST	EMP	PHONE	ENTRY#
Amos Grt-Grt-Granddaughter Inc	Leominster	MA	E	413 773-5471	9636

CONSTRUCTION MATERIALS, WHOLESALE: Aggregate

	CITY	ST	EMP	PHONE	ENTRY#
Monroe Recycl & Aggregates LLC	Monroe	CT	G	203 644-7748	1917
Morningstar Marble & Gran Inc	Topsham	ME	F	207 725-7309	5551
Benevento Aggregates LLC	Loudon	NH	F	603 783-4723	14793

CONSTRUCTION MATERIALS, WHOLESALE: Air Ducts, Sheet Metal

	CITY	ST	EMP	PHONE	ENTRY#
Schrimpf Wldg Fabrication Inc	Woburn	MA	G	339 298-2311	13661

CONSTRUCTION MATERIALS, WHOLESALE: Awnings

	CITY	ST	EMP	PHONE	ENTRY#
Dartmouth Awning Co Inc	Westport	MA	G	508 636-6838	13295
Jay Salem Inc	Middleton	MA	G	978 774-4999	10387
Image Awnings Incorporated	Wolfeboro	NH	G	603 569-6680	15734
Ke Usa Inc	Williston	VT	E	802 864-3009	17736

CONSTRUCTION MATERIALS, WHOLESALE: Building Stone

	CITY	ST	EMP	PHONE	ENTRY#
Connecticut Stone Supplies Inc (PA)	Milford	CT	D	203 882-1000	1814
LH Gault & Son Incorporated	Westport	CT	D	203 227-5181	4180
Skyline Quarry LLC	Stafford Springs	CT	F	860 875-3580	3259
Portland Stone Ware Co Inc (PA)	Dracut	MA	E	978 459-7272	8311

CONSTRUCTION MATERIALS, WHOLESALE: Building Stone, Marble

	CITY	ST	EMP	PHONE	ENTRY#
Pauls Marble Depot LLC	Stamford	CT	F	203 978-0669	3427
Aldrich Marble & Granite Co	Norwood	MA	G	781 762-6111	11158
Cumar Inc	Everett	MA	E	617 389-7818	8484
Louis W Mian Incorporated (PA)	Boston	MA	E	617 241-7900	6863
Stone Design Marble & Gran Co	South Weymouth	MA	G	781 331-3000	11978

	CITY	ST	EMP	PHONE	ENTRY#
Stone Yard LLC	Littleton	MA	E	978 742-9800	9840
McCue Memorial Co Inc	Castleton	VT	E	802 468-5636	17173
Vermont Quarries Corp	Rutland	VT	E	802 775-1065	17514

CONSTRUCTION MATERIALS, WHOLESALE: Building, Exterior

	CITY	ST	EMP	PHONE	ENTRY#
Devine Brothers Incorporated	Norwalk	CT	E	203 866-4421	2490
Creative Material Tech Ltd	Palmer	MA	G	413 284-0000	11272
Maki Corp (PA)	Gardner	MA	E	978 343-7422	8895

CONSTRUCTION MATERIALS, WHOLESALE: Cement

	CITY	ST	EMP	PHONE	ENTRY#
Quikrete Companies Inc	Wauregan	CT	F	860 564-3308	4041

CONSTRUCTION MATERIALS, WHOLESALE: Concrete Mixtures

	CITY	ST	EMP	PHONE	ENTRY#
Devine Brothers Incorporated	Norwalk	CT	E	203 866-4421	2490
O & G Industries Inc (PA)	Torrington	CT	D	860 489-9261	3689
Ideal Concrete Block Co	Waltham	MA	E	781 894-3200	12694
JH Lynch & Sons Inc	Millbury	MA	E	508 756-6244	10438

CONSTRUCTION MATERIALS, WHOLESALE: Glass

	CITY	ST	EMP	PHONE	ENTRY#
Liberty Glass and Met Inds Inc	North Grosvenordale	CT	E	860 923-3623	2384
U S Glass Distributors Inc	Enfield	CT	E	860 741-3658	1156
Mygrant Glass Company Inc	Randolph	MA	F	781 767-3289	11569

CONSTRUCTION MATERIALS, WHOLESALE: Gravel

	CITY	ST	EMP	PHONE	ENTRY#
Dauphinais & Son Inc	Wilbraham	MA	E	413 596-3964	13357
George D Judd & Sons LLC	Goshen	MA	G	413 268-7590	8967
T L Edwards Inc	Plymouth	MA	E	508 732-9148	11480
R Pepin & Sons Inc	Sanford	ME	E	207 324-6125	5407

CONSTRUCTION MATERIALS, WHOLESALE: Limestone

	CITY	ST	EMP	PHONE	ENTRY#
New England Stone Inc	Milford	CT	F	203 876-8606	1853
Shelburne Limestone Corp	Swanton	VT	E	802 868-3357	17642

CONSTRUCTION MATERIALS, WHOLESALE: Masons' Materials

	CITY	ST	EMP	PHONE	ENTRY#
State Road Cement Block Co Inc	North Dartmouth	MA	G	508 993-9473	11002
Rjf - Morin Brick LLC	Auburn	ME	D	207 784-9375	4459
Tilcon Arthur Whitcomb Inc (HQ)	North Swanzey	NH	F	603 352-0101	15256

CONSTRUCTION MATERIALS, WHOLESALE: Millwork

	CITY	ST	EMP	PHONE	ENTRY#
Brockway-Smith Company	West Hatfield	MA	C	413 247-9674	13004
New England Shrlines Companies	Hanover	MA	F	781 826-0140	9037
R E Lowell Lumber Co Inc	Buckfield	ME	F	207 336-2901	4658
Fernald Lumber Inc	Nottingham	NH	F	603 679-2997	15276
Tommila Brothers Inc	Fitzwilliam	NH	F	603 242-7774	14316
Cas America LLC	North Smithfield	RI	F	401 884-8556	16320

CONSTRUCTION MATERIALS, WHOLESALE: Molding, All Materials

	CITY	ST	EMP	PHONE	ENTRY#
Stelray Plastic Products Inc	Ansonia	CT	E	203 735-2331	20

CONSTRUCTION MATERIALS, WHOLESALE: Paving Materials

	CITY	ST	EMP	PHONE	ENTRY#
Lane Construction Corporation (DH)	Cheshire	CT	C	203 235-3351	603
Lane Industries Incorporated (DH)	Cheshire	CT	G	203 235-3351	604
Lane Construction Corporation	Lee	MA	E	413 637-2511	9614

CONSTRUCTION MATERIALS, WHOLESALE: Prefabricated Structures

	CITY	ST	EMP	PHONE	ENTRY#
Bridgwell Rsources Holdings LLC (HQ)	Greenwich	CT	E	203 622-9138	1322
Laydon Industries LLC (PA)	New Haven	CT	E	203 562-7283	2169
Nucor Hrris Rbar Northeast LLC	Canaan	NH	D	603 632-5222	14047

CONSTRUCTION MATERIALS, WHOLESALE: Roofing & Siding Material

	CITY	ST	EMP	PHONE	ENTRY#
Dfs In-Home Services	Danbury	CT	G	845 405-6464	730
Britton Lumber Company Inc (PA)	Fairlee	VT	E	802 333-4388	17267

CONSTRUCTION MATERIALS, WHOLESALE: Sand

	CITY	ST	EMP	PHONE	ENTRY#
Adelman Sand & Gravel Inc	Bozrah	CT	F	860 889-3394	226
O & G Industries Inc	Southbury	CT	E	203 263-2195	3197
Rawson Development Inc	Putnam	CT	F	860 928-4536	2872
Tilcon Connecticut Inc (DH)	New Britain	CT	D	860 224-6010	2072
Tilcon Inc (DH)	Newington	CT	B	860 223-3651	2328
Windham Materials LLC (PA)	Willimantic	CT	E	860 456-4111	4222
A Graziano Inc	Braintree	MA	E	781 843-7300	7166
Boro Sand & Stone Corp (PA)	North Attleboro	MA	E	508 699-2911	10869
E H Perkins Construction Inc	Sterling	MA	F	978 422-3388	12161
E H Perkins Construction Inc (PA)	Wayland	MA	E	978 562-3436	12925
Heffron Asphalt Corp (PA)	North Reading	MA	G	781 935-1455	11040
Holcim - Ner Inc (DH)	Saugus	MA	E	781 941-7200	11760
McCabe Sand & Gravel Co Inc	Taunton	MA	E	508 823-0771	12349
Torromeo Industries Inc (PA)	Methuen	MA	F	978 686-5634	10346
WJ Graves Cnstr Co Inc (PA)	East Templeton	MA	E	978 939-5568	8416
Pike Industries Inc	Wells	ME	F	207 676-9973	5604

	CITY	ST	EMP	PHONE	ENTRY#
Alvin J Coleman & Son Inc (PA)	Albany	NH	F	603 447-5936	13847
Torromeo Industries Inc	Kingston	NH	E	603 642-5564	14637
Hinesburg Sand & Gravel Co Inc	Hinesburg	VT	E	802 482-2335	17294

CONSTRUCTION MATERIALS, WHOLESALE: Septic Tanks

Elm Street Vault Inc	Biddeford	ME	G	207 284-4855	4563
Gagne & Son Con Blocks Inc	Auburn	ME	G	207 495-3313	4435

CONSTRUCTION MATERIALS, WHOLESALE: Siding, Exc Wood

Mercury-Excelum Inc	East Windsor	CT	E	860 292-1800	1080
Beacon Sales Acquisition Inc	Portland	ME	F	207 797-7950	5185
K & R Holdings Inc	Portland	ME	C	207 797-7950	5230

CONSTRUCTION MATERIALS, WHOLESALE: Stone, Crushed Or Broken

Tilcon Connecticut Inc	East Granby	CT	E	860 844-7000	954
B R S Inc	Bridgewater	MA	E	508 697-5448	7221
Nicholas Ieronimo	Middleboro	MA	G	508 947-5363	10369
PJ Keating Company	Dracut	MA	D	978 454-7878	8310
S Lane John & Son Incorporated	Oxford	MA	F	508 987-3959	11263
Shelburne Limestone Corp (PA)	Colchester	VT	F	802 878-2656	17203

CONSTRUCTION MATERIALS, WHOLESALE: Windows

Harvey Industries LLC	Springfield	MA	E	413 731-7700	12099
Harvey Industries LLC (PA)	Waltham	MA	C	800 598-5400	12691
Bagala Window Works	Westbrook	ME	G	207 887-9231	5616
Harvey Industries LLC	Augusta	ME	F	207 629-3737	4472
Paradigm Operating Company LLC	Portland	ME	C	877 994-6369	5255
Harvey Industries LLC	Londonderry	NH	E	603 216-8300	14754

CONSTRUCTION SAND MINING

Baxter Sand & Gravel Inc	Chicopee	MA	F	413 536-3370	8009
Boston Sand & Gravel Company (PA)	Boston	MA	E	617 227-9000	6616
Brox Industries Inc (PA)	Dracut	MA	D	978 454-9105	8302
Cape Cod Aggregates Corp (PA)	Hyannis	MA	E	508 775-3716	9429
Classic Tractor Services LLC	Kingston	MA	G	781 585-2050	9506
Lorusso Corp (PA)	Plainville	MA	E	508 668-6520	11437
Rosenfeld Concrete Corp (HQ)	Hopedale	MA	E	508 473-7200	9303
S Lane John & Son Incorporated (PA)	Westfield	MA	F	413 568-8986	13205
S M Lorusso & Sons Inc (PA)	Walpole	MA	E	508 668-2600	12575

CONSTRUCTION: Agricultural Building

McKernon Group Inc	Brandon	VT	D	802 247-8500	17068

CONSTRUCTION: Airport Runway

Lane Construction Corporation (DH)	Cheshire	CT	C	203 235-3351	603
Lane Industries Incorporated (DH)	Cheshire	CT	G	203 235-3351	604
Lane Construction Corporation	Lee	MA	E	413 637-2511	9614

CONSTRUCTION: Bridge

E H Perkins Construction Inc	Sterling	MA	F	978 422-3388	12161
E H Perkins Construction Inc (PA)	Wayland	MA	E	978 562-3436	12925
Neil H Daniels Inc	Ascutney	VT	E	802 674-6323	16993

CONSTRUCTION: Commercial & Office Building, New

Brennan Realty LLC (PA)	Shelton	CT	C	203 929-6314	2987
Central Construction Inds LLC	Putnam	CT	E	860 963-8902	2848
Kafa Group LLC	Bridgeport	CT	G	475 275-0090	338
O & G Industries Inc	Beacon Falls	CT	F	203 729-4529	45
O & G Industries Inc	Bridgeport	CT	B	203 366-4586	354
O & G Industries Inc	Danbury	CT	E	203 748-5694	791
O & G Industries Inc	New Milford	CT	E	860 354-4438	2258
O & G Industries Inc	Southbury	CT	E	203 263-2195	3197
O & G Industries Inc	Stamford	CT	D	203 323-1111	3422
O & G Industries Inc (PA)	Torrington	CT	D	860 489-9261	3689
Pds Engineering & Construction	Bloomfield	CT	E	860 242-8586	201
Acton Woodworks Inc	Acton	MA	G	978 263-0222	5732
Silverlining Holding Corp (PA)	Needham	MA	F	617 986-4600	10522
Sheridan Corporation (HQ)	Fairfield	ME	E	207 453-9311	4765
Alvin J Coleman & Son Inc (PA)	Albany	NH	F	603 447-5936	13847
Dexter Sign Co	East Providence	RI	F	401 434-1100	16014

CONSTRUCTION: Commercial & Office Buildings, Prefabricated

Lander Group LLC	Greenville	ME	F	207 974-3104	4850

CONSTRUCTION: Dam

Absorbent Specialty Pdts LLC	Pawtucket	RI	F	401 722-1177	16342

CONSTRUCTION: Dams, Waterways, Docks & Other Marine

Chas G Allen Realty LLC	Barre	MA	D	978 355-2911	6202
Louie and Teds Blacktop Inc	Swansea	MA	F	508 678-4948	12306
Lander Group LLC	Greenville	ME	F	207 974-3104	4850

CONSTRUCTION: Drainage System

LH Gault & Son Incorporated	Westport	CT	D	203 227-5181	4180
A B Excavating Inc	Lancaster	NH	E	603 788-5110	14675

CONSTRUCTION: Elevated Highway

Lane Construction Corporation (DH)	Cheshire	CT	C	203 235-3351	603
Lane Industries Incorporated (DH)	Cheshire	CT	G	203 235-3351	604
Lane Construction Corporation	Lee	MA	E	413 637-2511	9614

CONSTRUCTION: Food Prdts Manufacturing or Packing Plant

Masas Usa Inc	East Haven	CT	E	305 603-8868	1045
Core Concepts Inc	Franklin	MA	E	508 528-0070	8827
Flo Chemical Corp	Ashburnham	MA	F	978 827-5101	5952
Thomsen Enterprises LLC	Rumford	RI	D	401 431-2190	16679

CONSTRUCTION: Foundation & Retaining Wall

Connecticut Basement Systems Inc	Seymour	CT	C	203 881-5090	2959

CONSTRUCTION: Heavy Highway & Street

M & H Logging LLC	Rangeley	ME	E	207 864-5617	5312
R A Thomas Logging Inc	Guilford	ME	G	207 876-2722	4858
A B Excavating Inc	Lancaster	NH	E	603 788-5110	14675
Narragansett Improvement Co (PA)	Providence	RI	D	401 331-0051	16571
Cersosimo Industries Inc (PA)	Brattleboro	VT	D	802 254-4500	17080

CONSTRUCTION: Indl Buildings, New, NEC

Kafa Group LLC	Bridgeport	CT	G	475 275-0090	338
O & G Industries Inc (PA)	Torrington	CT	D	860 489-9261	3689
Pds Engineering & Construction	Bloomfield	CT	E	860 242-8586	201
Sheridan Corporation (HQ)	Fairfield	ME	E	207 453-9311	4765
Neil H Daniels Inc	Ascutney	VT	E	802 674-6323	16993

CONSTRUCTION: Indl Plant

Raytheon Sutheast Asia Systems (DH)	Waltham	MA	E	978 470-5000	12762

CONSTRUCTION: Institutional Building

Windham Materials LLC (PA)	Willimantic	CT	E	860 456-4111	4222

CONSTRUCTION: Marine

Burnham Associates Inc	Salem	MA	F	978 745-1788	11706
Dock Doctors LLC	Ferrisburgh	VT	E	802 877-6756	17268

CONSTRUCTION: Pharmaceutical Manufacturing Plant

Transtulit LLC	West Springfield	MA	G	413 737-2600	13045

CONSTRUCTION: Pipeline, NEC

Northeast Earth Mechanics LLC	Pittsfield	NH	E	603 435-7989	15334

CONSTRUCTION: Power Plant

Apcompower Inc (PA)	Windsor	CT	E	860 688-1911	4260
Veolia Es Tchncal Slutions LLC	Danbury	CT	F	203 748-9116	832
Onyx Environmental Svcs LLC (DH)	Boston	MA	E	617 849-6600	6936
Tecomet Inc	Woburn	MA	A	781 782-6400	13675

CONSTRUCTION: Residential, Nec

Emery Development Ltd	Springfield	MA	G	413 782-1990	12094
Woodmeister Master Bldrs Inc (PA)	Holden	MA	C	774 345-1000	9196
Davis Zac Fine Woodworking	New Gloucester	ME	G	207 926-4710	5084
Ecocor LLC	Searsmont	ME	E	207 342-2085	5449

CONSTRUCTION: Sewer Line

O & G Industries Inc (PA)	Torrington	CT	D	860 489-9261	3689
A F Amorello & Sons Inc	Worcester	MA	E	508 791-8778	13694
Petricca Industries Inc (PA)	Pittsfield	MA	E	413 499-1441	11418
Harold Macquinn Incorporated (PA)	Hancock	ME	E	207 667-4654	4869

CONSTRUCTION: Single-Family Housing

Central Construction Inds LLC	Putnam	CT	E	860 963-8902	2848
Coastal Exteriors LLC	Wallingford	CT	F	203 626-5396	3790
Country Carpenters Inc	Hebron	CT	G	860 228-2276	1526
Country Log Homes Inc	Goshen	CT	F	413 229-8084	1302
Eastern Electric Cnstr Co	Harwinton	CT	G	860 485-1100	1519
Hanford Cabinet & Wdwkg Co Inc	Old Saybrook	CT	G	860 388-5055	2650
Chicopee Foundations Inc	Chicopee	MA	E	413 594-4700	8015
Emery Development Ltd	Springfield	MA	G	413 782-1990	12094
Pro Touch Home Improvement Inc	Peabody	MA	F	617 378-1929	11336
Harold Macquinn Incorporated (PA)	Hancock	ME	E	207 667-4654	4869
Schiavi Homes LLC	Oxford	ME	E	207 539-9600	5149
Slate Corporation	Auburn	NH	F	603 234-5943	13912
Timberpeg East Inc (PA)	Claremont	NH	E	603 542-7762	14099
Vermod High Prfmce Mnfctred Hs	Wilder	VT	G	802 295-0042	17716

Employee Codes: A=Over 500 employees, B=251-500
C=101-250, D=51-100, E=20-50, F=10-19, G=1-9

2024 Harris New England
Manufacturers Directory

1371

PRODUCT

	CITY	ST	EMP	PHONE	ENTRY#
Vermont Timber Works Inc	North Springfield	VT	F	802 886-1917	17427

CONSTRUCTION: Single-family Housing, New

	CITY	ST	EMP	PHONE	ENTRY#
American Building Systems Inc	Bristol	CT	G	860 589-0215	395
Richard Riggio and Sons Inc	Ivoryton	CT	F	860 767-0812	1532
Acton Woodworks Inc	Acton	MA	F	978 263-0222	5732
BP Logue & Co	Chelmsford	MA	F	978 251-4433	7915
EJ Jaxtimer Builder Inc	Hyannis	MA	E	508 778-4911	9436
South Mountain Company Inc	West Tisbury	MA	E	508 693-4850	13055
Trinity Builders Inc (PA)	Westwood	MA	G	781 780-6168	13323
Yankee Builders	Dartmouth	MA	G	508 636-8660	8234
C A Construction Inc	Gouldsboro	ME	G	207 422-3493	4838
Wlhc Inc (PA)	Houlton	ME	G	207 532-6531	4906
Custom Log Homes	Rumney	NH	F	603 786-9082	15497
McKernon Group Inc	Brandon	VT	D	802 247-8500	17068
William H Moore Inc	Waitsfield	VT	G	802 496-3595	17668

CONSTRUCTION: Street Sign Installation & Mntnce

	CITY	ST	EMP	PHONE	ENTRY#
Visi-Flash Rentals Eastern	West Bridgewater	MA	E	508 583-9100	12988

CONSTRUCTION: Subway

	CITY	ST	EMP	PHONE	ENTRY#
Lane Construction Corporation (DH)	Cheshire	CT	C	203 235-3351	603
Lane Industries Incorporated (DH)	Cheshire	CT	G	203 235-3351	604
Lane Construction Corporation	Lee	MA	E	413 637-2511	9614

CONSTRUCTION: Swimming Pools

	CITY	ST	EMP	PHONE	ENTRY#
Jarvis Welding & Mfg Co	Turners Falls	MA	G	413 863-9541	12449
Aquatic Solutions LLC	Hampton	NH	G	888 704-7665	14398

CONSTRUCTION: Water & Sewer Line

	CITY	ST	EMP	PHONE	ENTRY#
Small Water Systems Svcs LLC	Littleton	MA	F	978 486-1008	9838
A B Excavating Inc	Lancaster	NH	E	603 788-5110	14675

CONSULTING SVC: Business, NEC

	CITY	ST	EMP	PHONE	ENTRY#
Childrens Health Market Inc	Wilton	CT	G	203 762-2938	4236
Cobra Green LLC	Norwalk	CT	A	203 354-5000	2484
D&D Fltrtion Cons Sppliers Inc	Kensington	CT	F	860 829-3690	1539
Draught Technologies LLC	Farmington	CT	G	860 840-7555	1215
Dufrane Nuclear Shielding Inc	Winsted	CT	F	860 379-2318	4340
Penfield Search Partners Ltd	Fairfield	CT	G	203 307-2600	1196
R4 Technologies Inc (PA)	Ridgefield	CT	E	203 461-7100	2906
Royalty Consulting LLC	Rocky Hill	CT	F	800 474-5157	2934
Agrify Corporation (PA)	North Billerica	MA	F	617 896-5243	10894
Cisco Systems Inc	Boxborough	MA	F	978 936-0000	7149
D L Maher Co	North Reading	MA	F	781 933-3210	11039
Ercon Inc	Wareham	MA	E	508 291-1400	12835
Foundtion For Dmcracy In Ukrin	Cambridge	MA	G	617 496-8816	7574
Innovasea Systems Inc (PA)	Boston	MA	E	207 322-3219	6811
Moseley Corporation	Franklin	MA	E	508 520-4004	8853
Syberworks Inc	Arlington	MA	E	781 891-1999	5948
James W Sewall Company	Bangor	ME	G	207 817-5410	4506
James W Sewall Company (PA)	Old Town	ME	G	207 827-4456	5125
Actio Software Corporation	Portsmouth	NH	D	603 433-2300	15356
Lenric Corp	Nashua	NH	E	603 886-6772	15127
Universal Envmtl Tech Inc	Nashua	NH	G	603 883-9312	15180
Hope & Main	Warren	RI	G	401 245-7400	16758
Nestor Traffic Systems Inc (PA)	Pawtucket	RI	E	401 714-7781	16391

CONSULTING SVC: Educational

	CITY	ST	EMP	PHONE	ENTRY#
Evotext Inc	Billerica	MA	F	781 272-1830	6445
DCI Training Inc	West Lebanon	NH	G	603 643-6066	15682

CONSULTING SVC: Financial Management

	CITY	ST	EMP	PHONE	ENTRY#
Frc Founders Corporation (PA)	Stamford	CT	E	203 661-6601	3348

CONSULTING SVC: Management

	CITY	ST	EMP	PHONE	ENTRY#
Chief Executive Group LLC (PA)	Stamford	CT	E	785 832-0303	3310
Chief Executive Group LP (PA)	Stamford	CT	G	203 930-2700	3311
Computer Prgrm & Systems Inc (PA)	Stamford	CT	G	203 324-9203	3319
Enginuity Plm LLC (DH)	Milford	CT	F	203 218-7225	1825
Forecast International Inc	Sandy Hook	CT	E	203 426-0800	2951
Gss Infotech Ct Inc	Glastonbury	CT	C	860 709-0933	1282
O & W Heat Treat Inc	South Windsor	CT	G	860 528-9239	3168
Rothstein Associates Inc	Brookfield	CT	G	203 740-7400	538
Stonington Services LLC	Gales Ferry	CT	E	860 464-1991	1261
Acentech Incorporated (PA)	Cambridge	MA	E	617 499-8000	7466
Beacon Application Svcs Corp (PA)	Framingham	MA	E	508 663-4433	8742
Caliper Corporation	Newton	MA	E	617 527-4700	10740
Cape Cod Life LLC	Mashpee	MA	F	508 419-7381	10250
City Pblcations Greater Boston	Wayland	MA	G	617 549-7622	12924
Copley Global Services LLC	Waltham	MA	G	617 970-9617	12641
Graphic Arts Institute of Neng	Southborough	MA	F	508 804-4100	11995

	CITY	ST	EMP	PHONE	ENTRY#
Infogix Inc (HQ)	Burlington	MA	C	630 505-1800	7379
International Security Assista	Woburn	MA	C	617 590-7942	13588
Kognito Solutions LLC	Burlington	MA	E	212 675-2651	7387
Material Impact Inc	Boston	MA	E	617 917-4123	6879
Network World Inc	Needham Heights	MA	E	800 622-1108	10553
Stratcomm Inc	Natick	MA	C	508 907-7000	10499
Vdc Research Group Inc (PA)	Southborough	MA	E	508 653-9000	12004
Xiphos Partners Inc	Dartmouth	MA	G	508 991-1014	8233
Actio Software Corporation	Portsmouth	NH	D	603 433-2300	15356
Atlantic Turnkey Cons Corp	Amherst	NH	F	603 673-9447	13862
Universal Envmtl Tech Inc	Nashua	NH	G	603 883-9312	15180
Durastone Corporation	Lincoln	RI	F	401 723-7100	16134

CONSULTING SVCS, BUSINESS: Communications

	CITY	ST	EMP	PHONE	ENTRY#
Joseph Merritt & Company Inc (PA)	Hartford	CT	E	860 296-2500	1488
Mercury Cabling Systems LLC	Stratford	CT	E	203 378-9008	3556
Powerphone Inc	Madison	CT	E	203 245-8911	1566
Data Radio Management Co Inc	Merrimack	NH	G	603 598-1222	14979
Northrop Grumman Systems Corp	Hudson	NH	G	603 886-4270	14532

CONSULTING SVCS, BUSINESS: Energy Conservation

	CITY	ST	EMP	PHONE	ENTRY#
Dynamic Bldg Enrgy Sltions LLC (PA)	North Stonington	CT	F	860 599-1872	2447
Aqua Laboratories	Amesbury	MA	F	978 388-3989	5829
Complete Energy Services Corp	Raynham	MA	F	833 237-2677	11584
Honeywell DMC Services LLC	Danvers	MA	B	978 774-3007	8192
National Resource MGT Inc (PA)	Canton	MA	E	781 828-8877	7809

CONSULTING SVCS, BUSINESS: Environmental

	CITY	ST	EMP	PHONE	ENTRY#
Edgeone LLC (PA)	West Wareham	MA	F	508 291-0057	13063
Kerfoot Technologies Inc	Falmouth	MA	F	508 539-3002	8634

CONSULTING SVCS, BUSINESS: Sys Engnrg, Exc Computer/ Prof

	CITY	ST	EMP	PHONE	ENTRY#
Sonalysts Inc (PA)	Waterford	CT	B	860 442-4355	3997
Rt Engineering Corporation	Franklin	MA	E	800 343-1182	8861
Sofnet Technology Inc	Newton	MA	F	857 272-2568	10785
Cybernorth LLC	South Portland	ME	G	207 331-3310	5496
Entelligence Computer Svcs LLC	Salem	NH	D	603 893-4800	15520
Impact Science & Technology Inc	Nashua	NH	C	603 459-2200	15113
Ipura Consulting Group LLC	Hampton	NH	F	603 294-4002	14404

CONSULTING SVCS, BUSINESS: Systems Analysis & Engineering

	CITY	ST	EMP	PHONE	ENTRY#
Advanced Electronic Design Inc	Attleboro Falls	MA	E	508 699-0249	6078
Applied Science Group Inc	Billerica	MA	E	781 275-4000	6404
Elcom International Inc (PA)	Braintree	MA	F	781 501-4000	7179
Silverthread Inc	Cambridge	MA	G	800 674-9366	7715

CONSULTING SVCS, BUSINESS: Systems Analysis Or Design

	CITY	ST	EMP	PHONE	ENTRY#
Solectria Renewables LLC	Lawrence	MA	C	978 683-9700	9599
Visible Systems Corporation (PA)	Boston	MA	E	617 902-0767	7106

CONSULTING SVCS: Scientific

	CITY	ST	EMP	PHONE	ENTRY#
Chasm Advanced Materials Inc (PA)	Canton	MA	G	781 821-0443	7778
Hager Geoscience Inc	Woburn	MA	G	781 935-8111	13579

CONTACT LENSES

	CITY	ST	EMP	PHONE	ENTRY#
Wilmington Partners LP	Wilmington	MA	C	978 658-6111	13476

CONTACTS: Electrical

	CITY	ST	EMP	PHONE	ENTRY#
Deringer-Ney Inc (PA)	Bloomfield	CT	C	860 242-2281	158
Brainin-Advance Industries LLC (HQ)	Attleboro	MA	C	508 226-1200	5998
Pep Industries LLC	Attleboro	MA	F	508 226-5600	6046
Portwest Corporation (PA)	North Attleboro	MA	C	508 809-5112	10884
Precision Engineered Pdts LLC (DH)	Attleboro	MA	G		6051

CONTAINERS, GLASS: Food

	CITY	ST	EMP	PHONE	ENTRY#
Saint-Gobain Corporation	Northborough	MA	A	508 351-7112	11108

CONTAINERS: Food & Beverage

	CITY	ST	EMP	PHONE	ENTRY#
Silgan Holdings Inc (PA)	Stamford	CT	C	203 975-7110	3459

CONTAINERS: Glass

	CITY	ST	EMP	PHONE	ENTRY#
Emhart Glass Manufacturing Inc (DH)	Windsor	CT	E	860 298-7340	4273
New Erie Scientific LLC (DH)	Portsmouth	NH	E	603 430-6859	15425

CONTAINERS: Laminated Phenolic & Vulcanized Fiber

	CITY	ST	EMP	PHONE	ENTRY#
Barrday Corporation	Millbury	MA	B	508 581-2100	10427

CONTAINERS: Liquid Tight Fiber, From Purchased Materials

	CITY	ST	EMP	PHONE	ENTRY#
Replica Works Inc	Orange	MA	E	978 544-7000	11231
Lapoint Industries Inc (PA)	Auburn	ME	D	207 777-3100	4439

CONTAINERS: Plastic

	CITY	ST	EMP	PHONE	ENTRY#
Architectural Supplements LLC	Waterbury	CT	F	203 591-5505	3886
CKS Packaging Inc	Naugatuck	CT	E	203 729-0716	1952
Jarden LLC	Norwalk	CT	E	203 845-5300	2519
Silgan Dispensing	Torrington	CT	E	860 283-2025	3696
Silgan Holdings Inc (PA)	Stamford	CT	C	203 975-7110	3459
Silgan Plastics LLC	Deep River	CT	C	860 526-6300	882
Upc LLC	Meriden	CT	E	877 466-1137	1711
Air-Tite Holders Inc	North Adams	MA	E	413 664-2730	10802
Altium Packaging LLC	Franklin	MA	D	508 520-8800	8816
Altium Packaging LP	Marlborough	MA	E	508 485-2109	10107
Berry Global Inc	Easthampton	MA	E	812 424-2904	8439
Berry Global Inc	Franklin	MA	C	508 918-1714	8820
Berry Plastics Corp	Easthampton	MA	E	413 529-2183	8440
CDF Corporation (PA)	Plymouth	MA	D	508 747-5858	11454
Cheer Pack North America LLC	West Bridgewater	MA	F	508 927-7800	12968
Chesterfield Products Inc	Chesterfield	MA	E	413 296-0066	7997
Donahue Industries Inc	Shrewsbury	MA	E	508 845-6501	11830
Dupont Packaging Inc	Holyoke	MA	F	413 552-0048	9251
Fraen Corporation (PA)	Reading	MA	C	781 205-5300	11601
Hardigg Industries LLC (HQ)	South Deerfield	MA	C	413 665-2163	11924
Hillside Plastics Inc	Turners Falls	MA	E	413 863-2222	12448
Hytex Industries Inc	Randolph	MA	E	781 963-4400	11565
Leaktite Corporation (DH)	Leominster	MA	E	978 537-8000	9676
Millham LLC	Sterling	MA	E	978 422-8621	12168
New England Business Svc Inc (HQ)	Townsend	MA	D	978 448-6111	12441
Pep Industries LLC	Attleboro	MA	F	508 226-5600	6046
Precision Engineered Pdts LLC (DH)	Attleboro	MA	G		6051
Seabury Splash Inc	Plymouth	MA		508 830-3440	11477
Altium Packaging LLC	Portland	ME	E	207 772-7468	5177
Jarden LLC	East Wilton	ME	F	207 645-2574	4741
Maine Container LLC	Poland	ME	E	603 888-1315	5161
Altium Packaging LLC	Londonderry	NH	D	603 624-6055	14731
Aspects Inc	Warren	RI	E	401 247-1854	16751
Custom Design Incorporated	North Kingstown	RI	E	401 294-0200	16243
Altium Packaging LLC	South Burlington	VT	E	802 658-6588	17569
Questech Corporation (PA)	Rutland	VT	E	802 773-1228	17505

CONTAINERS: Sanitary, Food

	CITY	ST	EMP	PHONE	ENTRY#
Wcm LLC	Providence	RI	E	401 273-0444	16644

CONTAINERS: Wood

	CITY	ST	EMP	PHONE	ENTRY#
Vermont Pallet and Skid Sp Inc	Norwich	CT	G	860 822-6949	2618
Westwood Products Inc	Winsted	CT	F	860 379-9401	4358
Garelco Sales Company Inc	East Longmeadow	MA	G	413 525-3316	8376
E G W Bradbury Enterprises Inc	Bridgewater	ME	F	207 429-8141	4625
Index Packaging Inc	Milton	NH	C	603 350-0018	15046
Peterboro Basket Company	Peterborough	NH	F	603 924-3861	15324
Ljm Packaging Co Inc	North Kingstown	RI	D	401 295-2660	16269

CONTAINMENT VESSELS: Reactor, Metal Plate

	CITY	ST	EMP	PHONE	ENTRY#
Fiba Technologies Inc (PA)	Littleton	MA	B	508 887-7100	9815

CONTRACTOR: Rigging & Scaffolding

	CITY	ST	EMP	PHONE	ENTRY#
Industrial Transfer & Stor Inc	Southbridge	MA	E	508 765-9178	12022

CONTRACTORS: Acoustical & Ceiling Work

	CITY	ST	EMP	PHONE	ENTRY#
Environmental Interiors Inc	Nashua	NH	E	603 889-9290	15095

CONTRACTORS: Asbestos Removal & Encapsulation

	CITY	ST	EMP	PHONE	ENTRY#
Veolia Es Tchncal Slutions LLC	Danbury	CT	F	203 748-9116	832
Onyx Environmental Svcs LLC (DH)	Boston	MA	E	617 849-6600	6936
North Ridge Contracting Inc	Epsom	NH	E	603 942-6104	14282

CONTRACTORS: Boiler Maintenance Contractor

	CITY	ST	EMP	PHONE	ENTRY#
Riley Power Inc	Marlborough	MA	B	508 852-7100	10204

CONTRACTORS: Building Front Installation, Metal

	CITY	ST	EMP	PHONE	ENTRY#
All Phase Steel Works LLC	New Haven	CT	F	203 375-8881	2113
General Wldg & Fabrication Inc	Watertown	CT	E	860 274-9668	4014

CONTRACTORS: Building Site Preparation

	CITY	ST	EMP	PHONE	ENTRY#
On-Sight Insight	Boston	MA	G	617 502-5985	6931
P A Landers Inc	Hanover	MA	F	508 747-1800	9039
George Sherman Sand Grav Inc	Wakefield	RI	E	401 789-6304	16741

CONTRACTORS: Carpentry Work

	CITY	ST	EMP	PHONE	ENTRY#
Agw Clssic Hardwood Floors LLC	Westbrook	CT	G	203 640-3106	4135
Pemac Construction	Oakdale	CT	F	860 437-0007	2623
Bagala Window Works	Westbrook	ME	G	207 887-9231	5616
Brown Construction Inc	Houlton	ME	F	207 532-0910	4898
Advanced Custom Cabinets Inc	Brentwood	NH	F	603 772-6211	14019

CONTRACTORS: Carpentry, Cabinet & Finish Work

	CITY	ST	EMP	PHONE	ENTRY#
Kitchen Associates Inc	Sterling	MA	E	978 422-3322	12164
Master Millwork LLC	West Wareham	MA	E	508 273-0500	13068
Payne/Bouchier Inc (PA)	Roxbury	MA	E	617 445-4323	11692
Chamberlain Companies Inc	Salem	NH	E	603 893-2606	15512
Procraft Corporation	New Boston	NH	E	603 487-2080	15193
Thibco Inc	Manchester	NH	G	603 623-3011	14944

CONTRACTORS: Coating, Caulking & Weather, Water & Fire

	CITY	ST	EMP	PHONE	ENTRY#
Bells Powder Coating Inc	Attleboro Falls	MA	F	508 643-2222	6079
United GL To Met Sealing Inc	Lawrence	MA	E	978 327-5880	9606

CONTRACTORS: Commercial & Office Building

	CITY	ST	EMP	PHONE	ENTRY#
Sbarzola Construction Corp	South Weymouth	MA	G	781 817-6485	11977
Wesco Building & Design Inc	Stoneham	MA	G	781 279-0490	12188
Wescor Ltd (PA)	Stoneham	MA	G	781 279-0490	12189
Gabriel Business Group Co Ltd	Brookline	NH	F	877 401-5544	14039

CONTRACTORS: Communications Svcs

	CITY	ST	EMP	PHONE	ENTRY#
Exacom Inc	Concord	NH	E	603 228-0706	14129

CONTRACTORS: Decontamination Svcs

	CITY	ST	EMP	PHONE	ENTRY#
Connecticut Basement Systems Inc	Seymour	CT	C	203 881-5090	2959
Innovative Environmental LLC	Colchester	CT	F	860 871-7582	660
Alan S Bolster	Brewer	ME	F	207 989-5143	4608

CONTRACTORS: Dewatering

	CITY	ST	EMP	PHONE	ENTRY#
Remediation Lockwood Tech	Leominster	MA	E	404 666-5857	9701

CONTRACTORS: Directional Oil & Gas Well Drilling Svc

	CITY	ST	EMP	PHONE	ENTRY#
Directional Technologies Inc	Wallingford	CT	G	203 294-9200	3801

CONTRACTORS: Drywall

	CITY	ST	EMP	PHONE	ENTRY#
K & J Interiors Inc	Plymouth	MA	D	508 830-0670	11463

CONTRACTORS: Electric Power Systems

	CITY	ST	EMP	PHONE	ENTRY#
Ac/DC Industrial Electric LLC	Bozrah	CT	G	860 886-2232	225
Right of Way Solutions LLC	Salem	CT	G	860 917-0608	2945
Electrcal Installations LLC Ei	Moultonborough	NH	E	603 253-4525	15053

CONTRACTORS: Electronic Controls Installation

	CITY	ST	EMP	PHONE	ENTRY#
Interstate Elec Svcs Corp	Windsor	CT	E	860 243-5644	4284
Interstate Elec Svcs Corp	East Providence	RI	E	401 369-7890	16024

CONTRACTORS: Excavating Slush Pits & Cellars Svcs

	CITY	ST	EMP	PHONE	ENTRY#
Richmond Sand and Gravel Inc	Plymouth	MA	G	508 224-2231	11475
Copp Excavating Inc	Durham	ME	E	207 926-4988	4732
Dig Rite Company Inc	Johnston	RI	F	401 862-5895	16081

CONTRACTORS: Fence Construction

	CITY	ST	EMP	PHONE	ENTRY#
Cape Cod Fence Co (PA)	South Yarmouth	MA	F	508 398-6041	11982
Citiworks Corp	Attleboro	MA	F	508 761-7400	6004
Dogwatch Inc (PA)	Natick	MA	G	508 650-0600	10478
Feeneys Fence Inc	Hyde Park	MA	G	617 364-1407	9460
Joe Miller Inc	Worcester	MA	F	508 753-8581	13745
Perfection Fence Corp (PA)	Marshfield	MA	F	781 837-3600	10243
Anchor Corporation	Kennebunk	ME	F	207 985-6018	4920
Cosco LLC	Woonsocket	RI	D	401 765-0009	16955
Custom Iron Works Inc	Coventry	RI	E	401 826-3310	15812
Sogle Property LLC	Cambridge	VT	E	802 849-7943	17168
Springfield Fence Company Inc	North Springfield	VT	F	802 886-2221	17424
Westwood Fences Inc	Irasburg	VT	F	802 754-8486	17303

CONTRACTORS: Fiber Optic Cable Installation

	CITY	ST	EMP	PHONE	ENTRY#
Nashoba Security Inc	Littleton	MA	F	978 486-8615	9827
Fibernext LLC	Concord	NH	E	603 226-2400	14130

CONTRACTORS: Fire Detection & Burglar Alarm Systems

	CITY	ST	EMP	PHONE	ENTRY#
American Sub Assmbly Prdcers I	Dudley	MA	E	508 949-2320	8315
Hiller Companies Inc	Peabody	MA	E	978 532-5730	11315
Shufro Security Company Inc	Newton	MA	G	617 244-3355	10784

CONTRACTORS: Floor Laying & Other Floor Work

	CITY	ST	EMP	PHONE	ENTRY#
Proknee Corp	Whitefield	ME	E	207 549-5018	5656
Atlas Gran Countertop Flr Sup	Derry	NH	G	603 818-8899	14190

CONTRACTORS: Foundation & Footing

	CITY	ST	EMP	PHONE	ENTRY#
New England Foundation Co Inc (PA)	Hyde Park	MA	D	617 361-9750	9465
Sandelin Foundation Inc	Topsham	ME	F	207 725-7004	5552
Joseph P Carrara & Sons Inc (PA)	North Clarendon	VT	E	802 775-2301	17415

Employee Codes: A=Over 500 employees, B=251-500
C=101-250, D=51-100, E=20-50, F=10-19, G=1-9

2024 Harris New England
Manufacturers Directory

PRODUCT

1373

	CITY	ST	EMP	PHONE	ENTRY#

CONTRACTORS: General Electric

	CITY	ST	EMP	PHONE	ENTRY#
Tri State Maintenance Svcs LLC	North Haven	CT	F	203 691-1343	2440
BP Logue & Co	Chelmsford	MA	F	978 251-4433	7915
Dagle Electrical Cnstr Corp	Wilmington	MA	D	800 379-1459	13401
Dgi Communications LLC (PA)	North Billerica	MA	E	781 285-6972	10905
Giner Elx Sub LLC	Auburndale	MA	F	781 392-0300	6134
Ideal Electric Co Inc	Peabody	MA	F	781 284-2525	11317
Infra-Red Bldg & Pwr Svc Inc (PA)	Holbrook	MA	F	781 767-0888	9175
Leon Eg Company Inc	Boston	MA	E	617 482-8383	6856
Ralco Electric Inc	Westport	MA	D	508 679-3363	13299
Rays Electric & Gen Contg Inc	Berlin	NH	F	603 752-1370	13985
Dexter Sign Co	East Providence	RI	F	401 434-1100	16014

CONTRACTORS: Grave Excavation

	CITY	ST	EMP	PHONE	ENTRY#
Core Site Services LLC	New Haven	CT	G	475 227-9026	2140

CONTRACTORS: Heating & Air Conditioning

	CITY	ST	EMP	PHONE	ENTRY#
Dependable Energy Incorporated	Prospect	CT	G	203 758-5831	2833
McVac Environmental Svcs Inc	New Haven	CT	E	203 497-1960	2173
Brideau Shtmtl Fabrication Inc	Leominster	MA	E	978 537-3372	9643
Harrington Air Systems LLC	Watertown	MA	F	781 341-1999	12880
Century Sheet Metal Inc	Riverside	RI	F	401 433-1380	16653
H V Holland Inc	Jamestown	RI	F	401 423-0614	16069

CONTRACTORS: Heating Systems Repair & Maintenance Svc

	CITY	ST	EMP	PHONE	ENTRY#
Piping Systems Inc	Assonet	MA	E	508 644-2221	5976
Zampell Refractories Inc (PA)	Newburyport	MA	E	978 465-0055	10728

CONTRACTORS: Highway & Street Construction, General

	CITY	ST	EMP	PHONE	ENTRY#
O & G Industries Inc (PA)	Torrington	CT	D	860 489-9261	3689
Aerial Wireless Services LLC	Bellingham	MA	D	508 657-1213	6282
Bascom Environmental Co	Plymouth	MA	E	617 282-9500	11449
Lane Construction Corporation	Northfield	MA	D	413 498-5586	11120
P A Landers Inc (PA)	Hanover	MA	C	781 826-8818	9038
Petricca Industries Inc (PA)	Pittsfield	MA	E	413 499-1441	11418
Wells Development L L C	Arlington	MA	G	781 727-5560	5950
Shaw Brothers Construction Inc (PA)	Gorham	ME	C	207 839-2552	4835
Northeast Earth Mechanics LLC	Pittsfield	NH	E	603 435-7989	15334
Pike Industries Inc (DH)	Belmont	NH	E	603 527-5100	13967
Pike Industries Inc	Williston	VT	F	802 658-0453	17744
Worksafe Traffic Ctrl Inds Inc (PA)	Barre	VT	G	802 223-8948	17025

CONTRACTORS: Highway & Street Paving

	CITY	ST	EMP	PHONE	ENTRY#
Tilcon Connecticut Inc (DH)	New Britain	CT	D	860 224-6010	2072
Tilcon Inc (DH)	Newington	CT	B	860 223-3651	2328
Westchester Industries Inc	Greenwich	CT	F	203 661-0055	1360
A F Amorello & Sons Inc	Worcester	MA	F	508 791-8778	13694
Alton E Gleason Company Inc (PA)	Springfield	MA	F	413 732-8207	12073
Brox Industries Inc (PA)	Dracut	MA	D	978 454-9105	8302
E H Perkins Construction Inc	Sterling	MA	F	978 422-3388	12161
E H Perkins Construction Inc (PA)	Wayland	MA	E	978 562-3436	12925
Holcim - Ner Inc (DH)	Saugus	MA	E	781 941-7200	11760
JH Lynch & Sons Inc	Millbury	MA	E	508 756-6244	10438
Jsl Asphalt Inc (PA)	Westfield	MA	F	413 568-8986	13177
Lml Construction Inc	Leverett	MA	F	413 665-3788	9718
P J Albert Inc	Fitchburg	MA	D	978 345-7828	8671
Palmer Paving Corporation (PA)	Palmer	MA	E	413 283-8354	11281
T L Edwards Inc	Plymouth	MA	F	508 732-9148	11480
Ted Ondrick Company LLC (PA)	Chicopee	MA	F	413 592-2565	8062
Harold Macquinn Incorporated (PA)	Hancock	ME	E	207 667-4654	4869
Lane Construction Corporation	Bangor	ME	B	207 945-0850	4508
Lane Construction Corporation	Presque Isle	ME	E	207 764-4137	5301
Pike Industries Inc	Wells	ME	F	207 676-9973	5604
Blaktop Inc (PA)	West Lebanon	NH	E	603 298-8885	15678
Pike Industries Inc	Gorham	NH	F	603 466-2772	14361
Pike Industries Inc	Portsmouth	NH	G	603 436-4432	15429
JH Lynch & Sons Inc (PA)	Cumberland	RI	D	401 333-4300	15948

CONTRACTORS: Kitchen Cabinet Installation

	CITY	ST	EMP	PHONE	ENTRY#
Water Closet LLC	Nantucket	MA	F	508 228-2828	10466
Cabinet Gallery Ltd (PA)	Woonsocket	RI	G	401 762-4300	16952

CONTRACTORS: Machine Rigging & Moving

	CITY	ST	EMP	PHONE	ENTRY#
MEI Rigging & Crating LLC	Salisbury	MA	F	978 685-7700	11742

CONTRACTORS: Machinery Installation

	CITY	ST	EMP	PHONE	ENTRY#
Momentum Mfg Group - N LLC (PA)	Saint Johnsbury	VT	C	802 748-5007	17545

CONTRACTORS: Marble Installation, Interior

	CITY	ST	EMP	PHONE	ENTRY#
Louis W Mian Incorporated (PA)	Boston	MA	F	617 241-7900	6863
Morningstar Marble & Gran Inc	Topsham	ME	F	207 725-7309	5551

	CITY	ST	EMP	PHONE	ENTRY#
Rumford Stone Inc (PA)	Bow	NH	F	603 224-9876	14010

CONTRACTORS: Masonry & Stonework

	CITY	ST	EMP	PHONE	ENTRY#
John Canning & Co Ltd	Cheshire	CT	E	203 272-9868	602
Ted Ondrick Company LLC (PA)	Chicopee	MA	F	413 592-2565	8062
Freshwater Stone & Brickwork	Orland	ME	E	207 469-6331	5132

CONTRACTORS: Oil & Gas Field Geological Exploration Svcs

	CITY	ST	EMP	PHONE	ENTRY#
Hager Geoscience Inc	Woburn	MA	G	781 935-8111	13579

CONTRACTORS: Oil & Gas Field Geophysical Exploration Svcs

	CITY	ST	EMP	PHONE	ENTRY#
James W Sewall Company (PA)	Old Town	ME	E	207 827-4456	5125

CONTRACTORS: Oil & Gas Well Flow Rate Measurement Svcs

	CITY	ST	EMP	PHONE	ENTRY#
Sensing Systems Corporation	Dartmouth	MA	F	508 992-0872	8231

CONTRACTORS: Oil & Gas Wells Svcs

	CITY	ST	EMP	PHONE	ENTRY#
Schlumberger Technology Corp	Cambridge	MA	C	617 768-2000	7707
East Greenwich Oil Co Inc	East Greenwich	RI	G	401 884-2454	15982

CONTRACTORS: Oil Field Pipe Testing Svcs

	CITY	ST	EMP	PHONE	ENTRY#
Ost Services LLC	Providence	RI	C	401 467-8661	16581
Sanoil LLC	Providence	RI	G	401 942-5000	16610

CONTRACTORS: Ornamental Metal Work

	CITY	ST	EMP	PHONE	ENTRY#
Feman Steel LLC	Bloomfield	CT	F	860 982-6393	164
Garden Iron LLC	Westbrook	CT	G	860 767-9917	4138
Lundys Company Inc	Lynn	MA	F	781 595-8639	9983
Ornamental Ironworks Inc	Fall River	MA	F	508 678-0687	8592
Southeast Railing Co Inc	Canton	MA	F	781 828-7088	7831
Capco Steel LLC	Providence	RI	D	401 861-1220	16496

CONTRACTORS: Painting, Commercial

	CITY	ST	EMP	PHONE	ENTRY#
Bond Painting Company Inc	Old Greenwich	CT	E	212 944-0070	2630
John Canning & Co Ltd	Cheshire	CT	E	203 272-9868	602
Gabriel Business Group Co Ltd	Brookline	NH	F	877 401-5544	14039

CONTRACTORS: Painting, Indl

	CITY	ST	EMP	PHONE	ENTRY#
J Goodison Company (PA)	North Kingstown	RI	E	401 667-5938	16261

CONTRACTORS: Plumbing

	CITY	ST	EMP	PHONE	ENTRY#
J & M Plumbing & Cnstr LLC	Norwich	CT	G	860 319-3082	2608
Atlas Water Systems Inc	Waltham	MA	D	781 373-4700	12597
H2o Care Inc	Middleton	MA	F	978 777-8330	10384
R I Baker Co Inc (PA)	Clarksburg	MA	E	413 663-3791	8073
Palmer and Sicard Inc	Exeter	NH	D	603 778-1841	14300

CONTRACTORS: Power Generating Eqpt Installation

	CITY	ST	EMP	PHONE	ENTRY#
Waverly Tool Rental & Sales Co	Framingham	MA	F	508 872-8866	8811

CONTRACTORS: Prefabricated Window & Door Installation

	CITY	ST	EMP	PHONE	ENTRY#
All-Time Manufacturing Co Inc	Montville	CT	F	860 848-9258	1926
Aluminum Products Cape Cod Inc (PA)	Dennis Port	MA	F	508 398-8546	8259
Ultimate Windows Inc	Lawrence	MA	G	978 687-9444	9605

CONTRACTORS: Process Piping

	CITY	ST	EMP	PHONE	ENTRY#
New England Stinless Distr LLC	Salisbury	MA	F	978 255-4830	11743
Process Cooling Systems Inc	Leominster	MA	E	978 537-1996	9697
Tigpro Inc	Portland	ME	G	207 878-1190	5282
Wardwell Piping Inc	Windham	ME	F	207 892-0034	5674

CONTRACTORS: Roustabout Svcs

	CITY	ST	EMP	PHONE	ENTRY#
Loanworks Servicing LLC	Shelton	CT	F	203 402-7304	3029
National Default Servicing LLC	Meriden	CT	D	858 300-0700	1679

CONTRACTORS: Seismograph Survey Svcs

	CITY	ST	EMP	PHONE	ENTRY#
Geosonics Inc	Cheshire	CT	F	203 271-2504	595
Seismic Monitoring Svcs LLC	Danielson	CT	G	860 753-6363	841

CONTRACTORS: Septic System

	CITY	ST	EMP	PHONE	ENTRY#
Acme Precast Co Inc	West Falmouth	MA	F	508 548-9607	13000
Lml Construction Inc	Leverett	MA	F	413 665-3788	9718
Oldcastle Infrastructure Inc	Rehoboth	MA	E	508 336-7600	11613
Earl W Gerrish & Sons	Brownville	ME	F	207 965-2171	4637
Slate Corporation	Auburn	NH	F	603 234-5943	13912

CONTRACTORS: Sheet Metal Work, NEC

	CITY	ST	EMP	PHONE	ENTRY#
Fabtron Incorporated	Plainville	CT	G	860 410-1801	2759
Redco Audio Inc	Monroe	CT	F	203 502-7600	1920
Tech-Air Incorporated	Uncasville	CT	E	860 848-1287	3744
Arlowe Corporation	Littleton	MA	F	978 486-9050	9802
Cox Engineering Company (PA)	Canton	MA	C	781 302-3300	7781

	CITY	ST	EMP	PHONE	ENTRY#
Crocker Architectural Shtmtl	North Oxford	MA	E	508 987-9900	11031
K & J Interiors Inc	Plymouth	MA	D	508 830-0670	11463
Oliver Welding & Fabg Inc	Ipswich	MA	G	978 356-4488	9493
Phoenix Sheet Metal	South Dartmouth	MA	G	508 994-4046	11919
United Hvac Co Inc	Rockland	MA	E	781 871-1060	11663
Vulcan Industries Inc	Hudson	MA	E	978 562-0003	9425
N E Tech-Air Inc	Scarborough	ME	C	207 347-7577	5439
Eastern Metals Inc	Londonderry	NH	E	603 818-8639	14745
Empire Sheetmetal Inc	Manchester	NH	E	603 622-4439	14847
Ken-Mar LLC	Salem	NH	E	603 898-1268	15539
Northeastern Sheet Metal Inc	Goffstown	NH	D	603 497-4166	14355
Sylvester Sheet Metal LLC	Manchester	NH	E	603 624-4586	14938
Tekon-Technical Cons Inc	Portsmouth	NH	E	603 335-3080	15441
All-State Fabricators Limited Partnership	Cranston	RI	D	401 785-3900	15827
EMI Industries LLC	Cranston	RI	E	401 785-3900	15855
Vermont Aerospace Manufacturing Inc	Lyndonville	VT	C	802 748-8705	17321
Vhv Company (PA)	Winooski	VT	C	802 655-8805	17771

CONTRACTORS: Siding

	CITY	ST	EMP	PHONE	ENTRY#
Everett Aluminum Inc	Everett	MA	F	617 389-3839	8488

CONTRACTORS: Store Front Construction

	CITY	ST	EMP	PHONE	ENTRY#
Ultimate Windows Inc	Lawrence	MA	G	978 687-9444	9605

CONTRACTORS: Structural Iron Work, Structural

	CITY	ST	EMP	PHONE	ENTRY#
James F Stearns Co LLP	Pembroke	MA	E	781 829-0095	11371
Superior Rail and Ir Works Inc	East Bridgewater	MA	E	508 378-4025	8345

CONTRACTORS: Structural Steel Erection

	CITY	ST	EMP	PHONE	ENTRY#
Berlin Steel Construction Co (PA)	Kensington	CT	E	860 828-3531	1538
Engineered Building Pdts Inc	Bloomfield	CT	E	860 243-1110	161
George H Olson Steel Company	Stratford	CT	F	203 375-5656	3541
Jwc Steel Co LLC	Hartford	CT	E	860 296-5517	1489
Steeltech Building Pdts Inc	South Windsor	CT	D	860 290-8930	3184
United Steel Inc	East Hartford	CT	C	860 289-2323	1032
MPS Products Corp	Rowley	MA	F	978 817-2144	11681
Patricia Barrett	Leominster	MA	F	978 537-0458	9692
Quinn Bros of Essex Inc	Essex	MA	E	978 768-6929	8479
Schrimpf Wldg Fabrication Inc	Woburn	MA	G	339 298-2311	13661
Topper & Griggs Group LLC	Agawam	MA	E	860 747-5737	5813
James A McBrady Inc	Scarborough	ME	E	207 883-4176	5435
New Hampshire Stl Erectors LLC	Goffstown	NH	G	603 668-3464	14353
S L Chasse Welding & Fabg Inc	Hudson	NH	D	603 886-3436	14543
Capco Steel LLC	Providence	RI	D	401 861-1220	16496
Engineering Wldg & Fabg Co Inc	North Kingstown	RI	G	401 884-1484	16252
Ne Steel Fabricators LLC	Cranston	RI	E	401 785-1234	15898

CONTRACTORS: Tile Installation, Ceramic

	CITY	ST	EMP	PHONE	ENTRY#
Joseph Cohn Son Tile Trazo LLC	North Haven	CT	G	203 772-2420	2420
New England Stone Inc	Milford	CT	F	203 876-8606	1853
Atlantic MBL & Gran Group Inc	East Falmouth	MA	G	508 540-9770	8356
Bostonian Clg Restoration Inc	Braintree	MA	F	781 356-3303	7170

CONTRACTORS: Ventilation & Duct Work

	CITY	ST	EMP	PHONE	ENTRY#
Atlantic Vent & Eqp Co Inc	Cromwell	CT	E	860 635-1300	687
Innovative Environmental LLC	Colchester	CT	F	860 871-7582	660
L & L Mechanical LLC	Goshen	CT	F	860 491-4007	1303

CONTRACTORS: Warm Air Heating & Air Conditioning

	CITY	ST	EMP	PHONE	ENTRY#
Mestek Inc	Westfield	MA	F	413 568-9571	13183
Ray Murray Inc (PA)	Lee	MA	D	413 243-2164	9619

CONTRACTORS: Water Well Drilling

	CITY	ST	EMP	PHONE	ENTRY#
New England Foundation Co Inc (PA)	Hyde Park	MA	D	617 361-9750	9465
H A Manosh Corp	Morrisville	VT	D	802 888-5722	17383

CONTRACTORS: Well Logging Svcs

	CITY	ST	EMP	PHONE	ENTRY#
Hager Geoscience Inc	Woburn	MA	G	781 935-8111	13579

CONTRACTORS: Windows & Doors

	CITY	ST	EMP	PHONE	ENTRY#
A Plus Exterior LLC	Milford	CT	F	203 516-1729	1792
Stanley Black & Decker Inc	Farmington	CT	F	860 677-2861	1248
Nashoba Security Inc	Littleton	MA	F	978 486-8615	9827
Lockheed Archtctral Sltons Inc	Pascoag	RI	C	401 568-3061	16339

CONTRACTORS: Wood Floor Installation & Refinishing

	CITY	ST	EMP	PHONE	ENTRY#
Agw Clssic Hardwood Floors LLC	Westbrook	CT	G	203 640-3106	4135

CONTRACTORS: Wrecking & Demolition

	CITY	ST	EMP	PHONE	ENTRY#
Fisher Contracting Corporation	Worcester	MA	G	508 421-6989	13723
Earth Waste Systems Inc (PA)	Rutland	VT	E	802 775-7722	17494

CONTROL CIRCUIT DEVICES

	CITY	ST	EMP	PHONE	ENTRY#
Richmond Contract Mfg	Bowdoinham	ME	F	207 737-4385	4606

CONTROL EQPT: Electric

	CITY	ST	EMP	PHONE	ENTRY#
Altek Electronics Inc	Torrington	CT	C	860 482-7626	3669
Cet Inc	Milford	CT	G	203 882-8057	1810
Conveyco Technologies Inc (PA)	Bristol	CT	E	860 589-8215	432
Delta Elevator Service Corp (DH)	Canton	CT	E	860 676-6152	560
ITT Inc (PA)	Stamford	CT	C	914 641-2000	3388
Kimchuk Incorporated (PA)	Danbury	CT	F	203 790-7800	766
New England Machine Tools Inc	Bristol	CT	G	860 583-4001	475
New Haven Companies Inc	East Haven	CT	F	203 469-6421	1048
North American Elev Svcs Co (DH)	Farmington	CT	E	860 676-6000	1233
P-Q Controls Inc (PA)	Bristol	CT	E	860 583-6994	478
T & T Automation Inc	Windsor	CT	F	860 683-8788	4306
Airloc Corporation	Franklin	MA	G	508 528-0022	8814
Massa Products Corporation	Hingham	MA	D	781 749-3120	9152
Omni Control Technology Inc	Whitinsville	MA	E	508 234-9121	13343
Performance Motion Devices Inc	Boxborough	MA	E	978 266-1210	7153
Waja Associates Inc	Franklin	MA	E	508 543-6050	8874
Ie Chemical Systems Inc	Nashua	NH	F	603 888-4777	15112
Walco Electric Company	Providence	RI	D	401 467-6500	16642
Cooper Lighting Inc	Essex Junction	VT	E	800 767-3674	17232

CONTROL EQPT: Noise

	CITY	ST	EMP	PHONE	ENTRY#
Control Resources Inc	Littleton	MA	E	978 486-4160	9806

CONTROLS & ACCESS: Indl, Electric

	CITY	ST	EMP	PHONE	ENTRY#
Alinabal Inc (HQ)	Milford	CT	C	203 877-3241	1796
Clarktron Products Inc	Fairfield	CT	G	203 333-6517	1178
Devar Inc	Bridgeport	CT	E	203 368-6751	317
Gordon Products Incorporated	Brookfield	CT	E	203 775-4501	523
Measurement Systems Inc	Wallingford	CT	E	203 949-3500	3831
O E M Controls Inc (PA)	Shelton	CT	C	203 929-8431	3042
Complete Energy Services Corp	Raynham	MA	F	833 237-2677	11584
Control Technology Corporation (PA)	Hopkinton	MA	E	508 435-9596	9313
Emx Controls Inc	East Douglas	MA	E	508 876-9700	8350
Ideal Electric Co Inc	Peabody	MA	E	781 284-2525	11317
Manufctring Resource Group Inc	Norwood	MA	E	781 440-9700	11192
Rockwell Automation Inc	Chelmsford	MA	D	978 441-9500	7952
Antrim Controls & Systems	Bennington	NH	G	603 588-6297	13974
Hampshire Controls Corp	Dover	NH	F	603 749-9424	14230
Regent Controls Inc	Greenville	RI	F	203 732-6200	16063

CONTROLS & ACCESS: Motor

	CITY	ST	EMP	PHONE	ENTRY#
EPC Corporation	Middleboro	MA	G	508 923-9503	10358
Motion Industries Inc	Danvers	MA	E	978 774-7100	8210
Todd Clark and Associates Inc	Danvers	MA	E	978 774-7100	8225
Viking Industrial Products	Marlborough	MA	E	508 481-4600	10231
ME Title	Bangor	ME	G	207 942-1988	4510

CONTROLS: Automatic Temperature

	CITY	ST	EMP	PHONE	ENTRY#
Automated Logic Corporation	Wallingford	CT	E	203 284-0100	3779
Food Atmtn - Svc Tchniques LLC (PA)	Stratford	CT	E	203 377-4414	3537
Lightstat Inc	Pleasant Valley	CT	E	860 738-4111	2802
Omega Engineering Inc	Norwalk	CT	D	714 540-4914	2548
Automated Logic Corporation	Chicopee	MA	F	413 547-6595	8008
Burnell Controls Inc	Danvers	MA	E	978 646-9992	8171
Control Resources Inc	Littleton	MA	E	978 486-4160	9806
Division 15 Hvac Inc	Pembroke	MA	E	781 285-3115	11363
Nanmac Corp	Milford	MA	E	508 872-4811	10407
Hansa Consult North Amer LLC (PA)	Portsmouth	NH	F	603 422-8833	15398
Goldline Controls Inc (DH)	North Kingstown	RI	D	401 583-1100	16253

CONTROLS: Crane & Hoist, Including Metal Mill

	CITY	ST	EMP	PHONE	ENTRY#
New England Lift Systems LLC	Newington	CT	G	860 372-4040	2309
Applied Dynamics Corporation (PA)	Greenfield	MA	E	413 774-7268	8981

CONTROLS: Electric Motor

	CITY	ST	EMP	PHONE	ENTRY#
ABB Inc	Danbury	CT	E	203 798-6210	702
Digatron Power Electronics Inc	Shelton	CT	E	203 446-8000	3000
Ward Leonard CT LLC (DH)	Thomaston	CT	D	860 283-5801	3641

CONTROLS: Environmental

	CITY	ST	EMP	PHONE	ENTRY#
Emme E2ms LLC	Bristol	CT	F	860 845-8810	439
Environmental Systems Corp	West Hartford	CT	C	860 953-8800	4060
Hamilton Standard Space	Windsor Locks	CT	E	860 654-6000	4329
Hamilton Sundstrand Corp (HQ)	Windsor Locks	CT	A	619 714-9442	4330
Nats USA Incorporated	Middletown	CT	F	860 398-0035	1767
Tek-Air Systems Inc	Monroe	CT	E	203 791-1400	1923
Ene Systems Inc (PA)	Canton	MA	D	781 828-6770	7789

Employee Codes: A=Over 500 employees, B=251-500
C=101-250, D=51-100, E=20-50, F=10-19, G=1-9

2024 Harris New England
Manufacturers Directory

1375

PRODUCT

	CITY	ST	EMP	PHONE	ENTRY#
Kidde-Fenwal Inc (HQ)	Ashland	MA	A	508 881-2000	5960
Massachusetts Clean Energy Ctr	Boston	MA	E	617 315-9355	6873
Mestek Inc	Westfield	MA	E	413 568-9571	13185
Mettlr-Tledo Prcess Anlytics I	Billerica	MA	D	781 301-8800	6461
Product Resources LLC	Newburyport	MA	E	978 524-8500	10709
Sensitech Inc (DH)	Beverly	MA	D	978 927-7033	6383
Rexx Company Inc	Cumberland Center	ME	F	207 200-9000	4710
Hampshire Controls Corp	Dover	NH	F	603 749-9424	14230
Meggitt (new Hampshire) Inc	Londonderry	NH	C	603 669-0940	14767
Taco Inc (PA)	Cranston	RI	B	401 942-8000	15917

CONTROLS: Marine & Navy, Auxiliary

	CITY	ST	EMP	PHONE	ENTRY#
Naiad Dynamics Us Inc (HQ)	Shelton	CT	E	203 929-6355	3033

CONTROLS: Numerical

	CITY	ST	EMP	PHONE	ENTRY#
Ben Franklin Design Mfg Co Inc	Agawam	MA	F	413 786-4220	5781

CONTROLS: Resistance Welder

	CITY	ST	EMP	PHONE	ENTRY#
Ewald Instruments Corp	Lakeville	CT	F	860 491-9042	1545

CONTROLS: Thermostats

	CITY	ST	EMP	PHONE	ENTRY#
Energy MGT & Ctrl Svcs Inc	Cranston	RI	F	401 946-1440	15856

CONVERTERS: Frequency

	CITY	ST	EMP	PHONE	ENTRY#
Hamilton Sundstrand Corp (HQ)	Windsor Locks	CT	A	619 714-9442	4330
Data Electronic Devices Inc	Salem	NH	C	603 893-2047	15517
Megatrnics US Ultmate Hldco LL (PA)	Salem	NH	E	888 706-0230	15544
Wall Industries Inc	Exeter	NH	E	603 778-2300	14305

CONVERTERS: Torque, Exc Auto

	CITY	ST	EMP	PHONE	ENTRY#
Advanced Torque Products LLC	Newington	CT	G	860 828-1523	2268
Hersey Clutch Company LLC	Orleans	MA	F	508 255-2533	11239

CONVEYOR SYSTEMS

	CITY	ST	EMP	PHONE	ENTRY#
Alvest (usa) Inc (DH)	Windsor	CT	E	860 602-3400	4259
Magnemotion Inc	Devens	MA	D	978 757-9100	8277

CONVEYOR SYSTEMS: Belt, General Indl Use

	CITY	ST	EMP	PHONE	ENTRY#
Amazon Robotics LLC (HQ)	North Reading	MA	C	781 221-4640	11037

CONVEYOR SYSTEMS: Robotic

	CITY	ST	EMP	PHONE	ENTRY#
International Robotics Inc	Stamford	CT	F	914 630-1060	3385
Ascend Robotics LLC	Cambridge	MA	F	978 451-0170	7491
Barrett Technology Inc	Cambridge	MA	F	617 252-9000	7497

CONVEYORS & CONVEYING EQPT

	CITY	ST	EMP	PHONE	ENTRY#
Affordable Conveyor Svcs LLC	Southington	CT	F	860 582-1800	3202
ID Mail Systems Inc	New Britain	CT	F	860 344-3333	2031
Industrial Magnetics Inc	Windsor	CT	D	508 853-3232	4283
Mk North America Inc	Bloomfield	CT	F	860 769-5500	194
Roller Bearing Co Amer Inc	Middlebury	CT	F	203 758-8272	1720
Walker Magnetics Group Inc	Windsor	CT	D	508 853-3232	4314
AMA Engnring - Smrtmove Cnvyor	Westport	MA	F	508 636-7740	13292
Anaconda Usa Inc	Natick	MA	F	800 285-5721	10470
Belt Technologies Inc (PA)	Agawam	MA	E	413 786-9922	5780
Chelsea Industries Inc	Newton	MA	A	617 232-6060	10745
Dg Marshall Associates Inc	Charlton	MA	E	508 943-2394	7887
Fabreeka International Inc (DH)	Stoughton	MA	G	781 341-3655	12206
Fabreeka Intl Holdings Inc (DH)	Stoughton	MA	E	781 341-3655	12207
Kleenline LLC	Newburyport	MA	D	978 463-0827	10691
Omtec Corp	Marlborough	MA	F	508 481-3322	10190
TEC Engineering Corp	Oxford	MA	F	508 987-0231	11266
Modula Inc (DH)	Lewiston	ME	D	207 440-5100	4976
Plastic Techniques Inc	Goffstown	NH	E	603 622-5570	14356
Action Conveyor Tech Inc	Smithfield	RI	F	401 722-2300	16685
Hall Inc	Bristol	RI	D	401 253-4858	15768

COOKING & FOODWARMING EQPT: Commercial

	CITY	ST	EMP	PHONE	ENTRY#
Motion Technology Inc	Hudson	MA	E	508 460-9800	9392
Remediation Lockwood Tech	Leominster	MA	E	404 666-5857	9701
Ultrafryer Systems Inc	Bow	NH	C	603 225-6684	14012

COOKWARE, STONEWARE: Coarse Earthenware & Pottery

	CITY	ST	EMP	PHONE	ENTRY#
Singer Company Inc	Waterford	CT	F	860 439-1234	3995

COPPER ORES

	CITY	ST	EMP	PHONE	ENTRY#
Quantum Discoveries Inc	Boston	MA	G	857 272-9998	6989

COPPER PRDTS: Smelter, Primary

	CITY	ST	EMP	PHONE	ENTRY#
Materion Technical Mtls Inc	Lincoln	RI	C	401 333-1700	16149

COPPER: Rolling & Drawing

	CITY	ST	EMP	PHONE	ENTRY#
Data Guide Cable Corporation	Gardner	MA	D	978 632-0900	8883
Pep Industries LLC	Attleboro	MA	F	508 226-5600	6046
Precision Engineered Pdts LLC (DH)	Attleboro	MA	G		6051
Sanderson-Macleod Incorporate	Palmer	MA	C	413 283-3481	11284
Advanced Building Products Inc	Sanford	ME	F	207 490-2306	5389
York Manufacturing Inc	Sanford	ME	F	207 324-1300	5418
Aetna Insulated Wire LLC	Milford	NH	C	757 460-3381	15011
J L Anthony & Company	Providence	RI	G	401 467-9700	16547
Millard Wire Company (PA)	Warwick	RI	E	401 737-9330	16838

COPYRIGHT BUYING & LICENSING

	CITY	ST	EMP	PHONE	ENTRY#
Applejack Art Partners Inc	Manchester Center	VT	E	802 362-3662	17326

CORD & TWINE

	CITY	ST	EMP	PHONE	ENTRY#
Detotec North America Inc	Sterling	CT	G	860 564-1012	3500
Loos & Co Inc (PA)	Pomfret	CT	B	860 928-7981	2809
Comprehensive Identification Products Inc	Burlington	MA	C	781 229-8780	7354
Julius Koch USA Inc	Mattapoisett	MA	E	508 995-9565	10258
Pepperell Braiding Company Inc (PA)	Pepperell	MA	E	978 433-2133	11387
Teufelberger Fiber Rope Corp	Fall River	MA	C	508 678-8200	8616
Auburn Manufacturing Inc (PA)	Mechanic Falls	ME	E	207 345-8271	5049
David Bird LLC	Waldoboro	ME	F	207 832-0569	5575
American Cord & Webbing Co Inc	Woonsocket	RI	E	401 762-5500	16948
Rhode Island Textile Company (PA)	Cumberland	RI	C	401 722-3700	15963

CORES: Magnetic

	CITY	ST	EMP	PHONE	ENTRY#
Alpha-Core Inc	Shelton	CT	E	203 954-0050	2980
Bridgeport Magnetics Group Inc	Shelton	CT	E	203 954-0050	2988

CORK & CORK PRDTS

	CITY	ST	EMP	PHONE	ENTRY#
Cork Technologies LLC	Lawrence	MA	G	978 687-9500	9555

CORRECTION FLUID

	CITY	ST	EMP	PHONE	ENTRY#
Bic Consumer Pdts Mfg Co Inc	Milford	CT	C	203 783-2000	1802
Bic Corporation (HQ)	Shelton	CT	A	203 783-2000	2985
Bic USA Inc (DH)	Shelton	CT	C	203 783-2000	2986
Blank Industries LLC	Hudson	MA	E	855 887-3123	9356
Gillette Company (HQ)	Boston	MA	A	617 463-3000	6758

COSMETIC PREPARATIONS

	CITY	ST	EMP	PHONE	ENTRY#
Amodex Products Incorporated	Bridgeport	CT	E	203 335-1255	296
Bella Grace LLC	Fairfield	CT	E	929 533-2343	1177
Ecometics Inc	Norwalk	CT	E	203 853-7856	2495
Edgewell Per Care Brands LLC	Milford	CT	E	203 882-2300	1822
Ephemeral Solutions Inc	Milford	CT	E	203 312-7337	1826
Milbar Labs Inc	East Haven	CT	F	203 467-1577	1046
Miyoshi America Inc (HQ)	Dayville	CT	D	860 779-3990	863
Russell Organics LLC	Wallingford	CT	G	203 285-6633	3847
Silgan Dspnsing Systems Thmsto	Thomaston	CT	B	860 283-2000	3630
Wearspf LLC	East Haven	CT	G	203 466-4616	1056
Avava Inc (PA)	Waltham	MA	G	617 912-2680	12599
Candela Corporation	Wayland	MA	F	800 733-8550	12923
CCL Industries Corporation (HQ)	Framingham	MA	F	508 872-4511	8749
Iredale Cosmetics Inc (PA)	Great Barrington	MA	D	413 644-9900	8976
Pharmasol Corporation	South Easton	MA	C	508 238-0105	11948
Revela Inc	Woburn	MA	F	716 725-2657	13651
St Cyr Inc	Worcester	MA	F	508 752-2222	13805
Toms of Maine Inc (HQ)	Kennebunk	ME	D	207 985-2944	4930
Fizz Time	Salem	NH	F	603 870-0000	15527
Maybrook Inc	Derry	NH	F	603 898-0811	14202
Tri-K Industries Inc	Derry	NH	F	973 298-8850	14211
Rozelle Inc	Westfield	VT	E	802 744-2270	17699
Tatas Natural Alchemy LLC (PA)	Whiting	VT	E	802 462-3814	17712

COSMETICS & TOILETRIES

	CITY	ST	EMP	PHONE	ENTRY#
Carrubba Incorporated	Monroe	CT	D	203 878-0605	1908
Crabtree & Evelyn Ltd (DH)	Woodstock	CT	C	800 272-2873	4393
Durol Laboratories LLC	New Haven	CT	F	866 611-9694	2146
Edgewell Personal Care Company (PA)	Shelton	CT	E	203 944-5500	3003
Golden Sun Holdings Inc (HQ)	Stamford	CT	F	203 595-5228	3357
HRB Winddown Inc (HQ)	Stamford	CT	D	203 674-8080	3379
Rjtb Initiatives Inc	Greenwich	CT	F	203 531-7216	1347
T N Dickinson Company	East Hampton	CT	F	860 267-2279	966
Commonwlth Soap Toiletries Inc (PA)	Fall River	MA	E	508 676-9355	8531
Conopco Inc	Foxboro	MA	F	508 543-6767	8693
European Cubicles LLC	Boston	MA	F	617 681-6700	6721
Grooming Ventures - FL LLC (HQ)	Boston	MA	D	305 593-0667	6774
Novagenesis LLC	Sharon	MA	F	781 784-1149	11794
Rare Beauty Brands Inc (PA)	Norwood	MA	F	888 243-0646	11205

	CITY	ST	EMP	PHONE	ENTRY#
Brickell Brands LLC	South Portland	ME	D	877 598-0060	5492
Colgate - Palmolive Company	Sanford	ME	G	207 467-2224	5392
Evergreen Manufacturing Group LLC	Madawaska	ME	E	207 728-4900	5037
Greener Formulas LLC	North Walpole	NH	G	888 825-4460	15257
Heleka Companies LLC (PA)	Chichester	NH	G	603 798-3674	14073
Heleka Companies LLC	Manchester	NH	F	303 856-5457	14858
Naturally Uncommon LLC	Atkinson	NH	G	603 458-2209	13905
Trividia Mfg Solutions Inc (DH)	Lancaster	NH	C	603 788-2848	14680
WSbadger Company Inc	Gilsum	NH	D	603 357-2958	14345
Autumn Harp Inc	Bristol	VT	E	802 453-4807	17113
Autumn-Harp Inc	Essex Junction	VT	C	802 857-4600	17227
Lancaster Imageworks Inc	Williston	VT	F	802 399-2418	17738
Tatas Natural Alchemy LLC	Whiting	VT	D	802 462-3958	17711

COSMETICS WHOLESALERS

Iredale Cosmetics Inc (PA)	Great Barrington	MA	D	413 644-9900	8976

COUNTER & SINK TOPS

Custom Cft Ktchens By Rzio Bro	Monroe	CT	F	203 268-0271	1912
Pro Counters New England LLC	Ansonia	CT	G	203 347-8663	17
Specialty Shop Inc	Manchester	CT	G	860 647-1477	1637
Carriage Hse Developments LLC	Winchester	MA	F	339 221-4253	13483
Quality Stone Marble Inc (PA)	Whitinsville	MA	F	774 813-4801	13344
Ware Rite Distributors Inc	East Bridgewater	MA	D	508 690-2145	8347
K & D Millworks Inc	Windham	ME	E	207 892-5188	5663
Portland Stone Works Inc	Portland	ME	G	207 878-6832	5261
Just Counters	Goffstown	NH	G	603 627-2027	14351
Artisan Surfaces Inc	Springfield	VT	E	802 885-8677	17616
N B C Solid Surfaces Inc	Springfield	VT	G	802 885-8677	17621

COUNTERS OR COUNTER DISPLAY CASES, EXC WOOD

C Mather Company Inc	South Windsor	CT	G	860 528-5667	3124
Richard Riggio and Sons Inc	Ivoryton	CT	F	860 767-0812	1532
Top Shop Inc	South Burlington	VT	F	802 658-1351	17604

COUNTERS OR COUNTER DISPLAY CASES, WOOD

Top Shop Inc	South Burlington	VT	F	802 658-1351	17604

COUNTERS: Mechanical

Denominator Company Inc	Waterbury	CT	F	203 263-3210	3905

COUNTING DEVICES: Controls, Revolution & Timing

Kongsberg Dgtal Simulation Inc	Groton	CT	F	860 405-2300	1375
Druck LLC (HQ)	Billerica	MA	C	978 437-1000	6432

COUNTING DEVICES: Tachometer, Centrifugal

Faria Beede Instruments Inc	North Stonington	CT	C	860 848-9271	2448
Monarch International Inc	Amherst	NH	E	603 883-3390	13881

COUNTING DEVICES: Vehicle Instruments

Ametek Arizona Instrument LLC	Middleboro	MA	C	508 946-6200	10349

COUPLINGS, EXC PRESSURE & SOIL PIPE

Axenics Inc	Tyngsboro	MA	E	978 774-9393	12456
Scully Signal Company (PA)	Wilmington	MA	D	617 692-8600	13452

COUPLINGS: Shaft

Lovejoy LLC	Ludlow	MA	E	413 737-0281	9949
Renbrandt Inc	Gloucester	MA	F	617 445-8910	8954
Ruland Manufacturing Co Inc	Marlborough	MA	E	508 485-1000	10208
Stafford Manufacturing Corp (PA)	Wilmington	MA	E	978 657-8000	13458
Accutech Marine Propeller Inc	Dover	NH	G	603 617-3626	14213
Tracey Gear Inc	Pawtucket	RI	E	401 725-3920	16424

COVERS: Hot Tub & Spa

Sunstar Spa Covers Inc	New Bedford	MA	F	508 993-5830	10653

CRANE & AERIAL LIFT SVCS

Arnco Sign Company	Wallingford	CT	E	203 238-1224	3775
Serrato Signs LLC	Worcester	MA	G	508 756-7004	13799
Somatex Inc	Detroit	ME	E	207 487-6141	4725
Starkey Welding Crane Service	Brentwood	NH	G	603 679-2553	14030
Dexter Enterprises Corp	East Providence	RI	G	401 434-2300	16013
Dexter Sign Co	East Providence	RI	F	401 434-1100	16014

CRANES: Indl Truck

MEI Rigging & Crating LLC	Salisbury	MA	F	978 685-7700	11742

CRANES: Overhead

Production Equipment Company	Meriden	CT	E	800 758-5697	1685
American Crane and Hoist Corp	Boston	MA	C	617 482-8383	6540
Nai Cranes LLC	Woburn	MA	D	781 897-4100	13617

CROWNS & CLOSURES

	CITY	ST	EMP	PHONE	ENTRY#
Assa Abloy ACC Door Cntrls Gro	New Haven	CT	C	901 365-2160	2121
Eyelet Design Inc	Waterbury	CT	D	203 754-4141	3911

CRUDE PETROLEUM PRODUCTION

El Paso Prod Oil Gas Texas LP	Hartford	CT	E	860 293-1990	1478
Northern Tier Energy LLC (DH)	Ridgefield	CT	F	203 244-6550	2903
Kyromina Oil Corporation	Natick	MA	G	508 651-8284	10484
National Grid USA Svc Co Inc (DH)	Waltham	MA	G	800 260-0054	12734
National Grid USA Svc Co Inc	Providence	RI	A	401 784-7224	16573
Marcell Oil Company Inc	Pittsford	VT	G	802 775-5050	17445

CRYOGENIC COOLING DEVICES: Infrared Detectors, Masers

Vette Thermal Solutions LLC (HQ)	Pelham	NH	F	603 635-2800	15300

CRYSTALS: Piezoelectric

Ebl Products Inc	East Hartford	CT	F	860 290-3737	990

CULTURE MEDIA

Hockey12com	Billerica	MA	G	781 910-2877	6450
Northeast Laboratory Svcs Inc (PA)	Winslow	ME	D	207 873-7711	5686

CUPOLAS: Metal Plate

Cape Cod Cupola Co Inc	North Dartmouth	MA	F	508 994-2119	10990

CUPS & PLATES: Foamed Plastics

Georgia-Pacific LLC	Leominster	MA	D	978 537-4701	9666
Master Containers Inc	Andover	MA	D	800 881-6847	5892
Waddington North America Inc	Chelmsford	MA	C	978 256-6551	7970

CURBING: Granite Or Stone

Es Countertops LLC	West Springfield	MA	G	413 732-8128	13024
Williams Stone Co Inc	East Otis	MA	E	413 269-4544	8403
Memorial Sandblast Inc	Barre	VT	G	802 476-7086	17013

CURTAIN WALLS: Building, Steel

Feman Steel LLC	Bloomfield	CT	F	860 982-6393	164
Ne Steel Fabricators LLC	Cranston	RI	E	401 785-1234	15898

CURTAINS: Window, From Purchased Materials

R L Fisher Inc	Hartford	CT	E	860 951-8110	1503
A L Ellis Inc	Fall River	MA	D	508 672-4799	8517
Bloom & Company Inc	Framingham	MA	F	617 923-1526	8744
Natco Home Fashions Inc	West Warwick	RI	F	401 828-0300	16913
Natco Home Fashions Inc	West Warwick	RI	F	401 828-0300	16914
Natco Home Fashions Inc (PA)	West Warwick	RI	F	401 828-0300	16915

CUSHIONS & PILLOWS

Klear-Vu Corporation (PA)	Fall River	MA	D	508 674-5723	8566
Boston Billows Inc	Nashua	NH	G	603 598-1200	15073
Lucci Corp	Peterborough	NH	F	603 567-4301	15317

CUSHIONS & PILLOWS: Bed, From Purchased Materials

Ksg Enterprises Inc	Peabody	MA	F	978 977-7357	11322

CUSHIONS: Carpet & Rug, Foamed Plastics

HI-Tech Packaging Inc	Stratford	CT	E	203 378-2700	3547
Future Foam Inc	Mansfield	MA	E	508 339-0354	10052

CUSTOM COMPOUNDING OF RUBBER MATERIALS

Jonal Laboratories Inc	Meriden	CT	D	203 634-4444	1671
Avon Custom Mixing Svcs Inc	Holbrook	MA	E	781 767-0511	9169
Watermillpreferred Partners LP	Waltham	MA	F	781 790-5045	12815
Teknor Apex Company (PA)	Pawtucket	RI	A	401 725-8000	16420

CUT STONE & STONE PRODUCTS

Architectural Stone Group LLC	Bridgeport	CT	G	203 494-5451	298
Connecticut Solid Surface LLC	Canton	CT	E	860 410-9800	559
Dan Beard Inc	Shelton	CT	E	203 924-4346	2996
O & G Industries Inc	Stamford	CT	D	203 323-1111	3422
B R S Inc	Bridgewater	MA	E	508 697-5448	7221
Counterra LLC	Canton	MA	F	781 821-2100	7780
Crystal Gt Systems LLC	Salem	MA	F	978 745-0088	11708
Cumar Inc	Everett	MA	E	617 389-7818	8484
Discover Marble & Granite Inc (PA)	Millbury	MA	D	877 411-9900	10432
Fletcher Granite LLC (DH)	Westford	MA	G	978 692-1312	13238
G R Sands Monumental Works	Roslindale	MA	F	617 522-1001	11666
Galaxy Stone Inc	Amesbury	MA	G	617 461-2790	5835
Gerritstone Inc	Wilmington	MA	E	781 938-1820	13409
Hi-Way Concrete Pdts Co Inc	Wareham	MA	E	508 295-0834	12837
International Stone Inc	Woburn	MA	D	781 937-3300	13589

Employee Codes: A=Over 500 employees, B=251-500
C=101-250, D=51-100, E=20-50, F=10-19, G=1-9

2024 Harris New England
Manufacturers Directory

PRODUCT

1377

	CITY	ST	EMP	PHONE	ENTRY#
Monarch Stone Inc	North Reading	MA	G	978 954-7021	11044
Sherle Wagner Intl LLC	Fall River	MA	F	212 758-3300	8606
Stone Surfaces Inc	Woburn	MA	F	781 270-4600	13674
Stone Yard LLC	Littleton	MA	E	978 742-9800	9840
Dragon Products Company LLC (DH)	Biddeford	ME	E	207 594-5555	4560
Freshwater Stone & Brickwork	Orland	ME	E	207 469-6331	5132
Sheldon Slate Products Co Inc	Monson	ME	F	207 997-3615	5074
KB Surfaces LLC	North Smithfield	RI	F	401 727-6792	16324
Structural Stone LLC	North Kingstown	RI	E	401 667-4969	16281
Granite Importers Inc (PA)	Barre	VT	E	802 476-5812	17002
Greenstone Slate Company Inc	Poultney	VT	E	802 287-4333	17448
McCue Memorial Co Inc	Castleton	VT	E	802 468-5636	17173
Q-Seal LLC	Rutland	VT	G	802 773-1228	17504
S W Granite Inc	Northfield	VT	G	713 933-0501	17434
Vermont Stone Art LLC	Barre	VT	G	802 238-1498	17023

CUTLERY

	CITY	ST	EMP	PHONE	ENTRY#
Energizer Holdings	Shelton	CT	E	314 985-2000	3004
Donahue Industries Inc	Shrewsbury	MA	E	508 845-6501	11830
Georgia-Pacific LLC	Leominster	MA	D	978 537-4701	9666
Gillette De Mexico Inc	Boston	MA	E	617 421-7000	6759
Longcap Lamson Products LLC	Westfield	MA	F	413 642-8135	13179
York-Cmbrland Assn For Hndcppe (PA)	Portland	ME	E	207 879-1140	5292
Perry Blackburne Inc	North Providence	RI	F	401 231-7200	16307

CYCLIC CRUDES & INTERMEDIATES

	CITY	ST	EMP	PHONE	ENTRY#
Chemgenes Corporation	Billerica	MA	E	978 694-4500	6422

CYLINDER & ACTUATORS: Fluid Power

	CITY	ST	EMP	PHONE	ENTRY#
Airpot Corporation	Norwalk	CT	E	800 848-7681	2459
Parker & Harper Companies Inc (PA)	Raymond	NH	D	603 895-4761	15455
Quality Controls Inc	Northfield	NH	E	603 286-3321	15268
Watts Regulator Co	Franklin	NH	A	603 934-5110	14323

CYLINDERS: Pressure

	CITY	ST	EMP	PHONE	ENTRY#
Larson Tool & Stamping Company	Attleboro	MA	D	508 222-0897	6031

DAIRY EQPT

	CITY	ST	EMP	PHONE	ENTRY#
Engineering Services & Pdts Co (PA)	South Windsor	CT	D	860 528-1119	3144
I B A Inc (PA)	Sutton	MA	E	508 865-6911	12281
Central Maine Dairy Eqp Inc	Skowhegan	ME	G	207 453-6727	5465

DAIRY PRDTS STORE: Butter

	CITY	ST	EMP	PHONE	ENTRY#
Cabot Creamery Cooperative Inc	Waitsfield	VT	B	888 792-2268	17664

DAIRY PRDTS STORE: Cheese

	CITY	ST	EMP	PHONE	ENTRY#
Mozzicato Fmly Investments LLC	Wethersfield	CT	F	860 296-0426	4212
Ndr Liuzzi Inc	Hamden	CT	E	203 287-8477	1445
Colony Foods Inc	Lawrence	MA	E	978 794-1500	9553
Sunrise Foods Incorporated	Brentwood	NH	F	603 772-4420	14031
Cabot Creamery Cooperative Inc	Waitsfield	VT	B	888 792-2268	17664

DAIRY PRDTS STORE: Ice Cream, Packaged

	CITY	ST	EMP	PHONE	ENTRY#
Cold Stone Creamery	Clinton	CT	G	860 669-7025	639
C&J Dreams Inc (PA)	North Easton	MA	E	508 238-6231	11008
Meletharb Inc	Wakefield	MA	G	781 245-4946	12518
Russos Inc	Saugus	MA	G	781 233-1737	11765
White Mountain Creamery Inc	Chestnut Hill	MA	F	617 527-8790	8003
Franks Bake Shop Inc	Bangor	ME	G	207 947-4594	4502
Shains Inc	Sanford	ME	D	207 324-1449	5415
Walpole Creamery Ltd	Walpole	NH	G	603 445-5700	15664
Newport Creamery LLC	Cranston	RI	F	401 946-4000	15900

DAIRY PRDTS STORE: Milk

	CITY	ST	EMP	PHONE	ENTRY#
Peaceful Meadows Ice Cream Inc (PA)	Carver	MA	F	781 447-3700	7855
Wrights Dairy Farm Inc	North Smithfield	RI	E	401 767-3014	16334

DAIRY PRDTS STORES

	CITY	ST	EMP	PHONE	ENTRY#
295 Tremont Inc	Attleboro	MA	D	508 222-2884	5985
Whittier Farms Inc	Sutton	MA	G	508 865-1096	12295
Monument Farms Inc	Weybridge	VT	E	802 545-2119	17703

DAIRY PRDTS: Acidophilus Milk

	CITY	ST	EMP	PHONE	ENTRY#
Commonwealth Dairy LLC	Guilford	VT	D	802 251-2300	17280

DAIRY PRDTS: Butter

	CITY	ST	EMP	PHONE	ENTRY#
Grass Roots Creamery	Granby	CT	G	860 653-6303	1306
Casco Bay Butter Company Inc	Westbrook	ME	G	207 712-9148	5620
SBwinsor Creamery LLC	Johnston	RI	G	401 231-5113	16106
Co Op Creamery	Saint Albans	VT	F	802 524-6581	17520

DAIRY PRDTS: Cheese

	CITY	ST	EMP	PHONE	ENTRY#
Calabro Cheese Corporation	East Haven	CT	D	203 469-1311	1038
Mozzicato Fmly Investments LLC	Wethersfield	CT	F	860 296-0426	4212
Ndr Liuzzi Inc	Hamden	CT	E	203 287-8477	1445
Agri-Mark Inc (PA)	Andover	MA	D	978 552-5500	5869
Pineland Farms Dairy Company	Bangor	ME	F	207 922-4036	4514
Tillamook County Creamery Assn	Portland	ME	G	503 815-1300	5283
Supreme Dairy Farms	Woonsocket	RI	F	401 739-8180	16977
Shelburne Farms	Shelburne	VT	D	802 985-8498	17562
Windham Foundation Inc (PA)	Grafton	VT	F	802 843-2211	17275

DAIRY PRDTS: Cream, Sweet

	CITY	ST	EMP	PHONE	ENTRY#
HP Hood LLC (PA)	Lynnfield	MA	C	617 887-3000	9995
Houlton Farms Dairy Inc (PA)	Houlton	ME	F	207 532-3170	4900

DAIRY PRDTS: Dairy Based Desserts, Frozen

	CITY	ST	EMP	PHONE	ENTRY#
Gelato Giuliana LLC	New Haven	CT	F	203 772-0607	2154

DAIRY PRDTS: Dietary Supplements, Dairy & Non-Dairy Based

	CITY	ST	EMP	PHONE	ENTRY#
Bactana Corp	Farmington	CT	G	203 716-1230	1208
Inner Armour Black LLC	Berlin	CT	F	860 656-7720	71
Natures First Inc (PA)	Orange	CT	F	203 795-8400	2678
Unipharm Inc	Waterbury	CT	E	203 528-3230	3978
Ajinomoto Cambrooke Inc (DH)	Ayer	MA	E	508 782-2300	6170
Meganutra Inc (PA)	Norwood	MA	E	781 762-9600	11195
On The Edge Nutrition Llc	Boston	MA	G	617 752-4056	6930
Partylite Inc (HQ)	Plymouth	MA	D	203 661-1926	11471
Bariatrix Nutrition Corp	Fairfax	VT	E	802 527-2500	17255

DAIRY PRDTS: Dried Milk

	CITY	ST	EMP	PHONE	ENTRY#
St Albans Cooperative Creamery Inc	Saint Albans	VT	D	802 524-9366	17531
St Albans Creamery LLC	Saint Albans	VT	E	802 524-9366	17532

DAIRY PRDTS: Evaporated Milk

	CITY	ST	EMP	PHONE	ENTRY#
Nestle Usa Inc	Pomfret Center	CT	D	860 928-0082	2813

DAIRY PRDTS: Ice Cream & Ice Milk

	CITY	ST	EMP	PHONE	ENTRY#
Michaels Dairy Inc	New London	CT	E	860 443-7617	2230
Reeds Inc	Norwalk	CT	E	800 997-3337	2563
Royal Ice Cream Company Inc (PA)	Manchester	CT	F	860 649-5358	1632
Queen Associates Inc	Woburn	MA	D	781 389-8494	13644
Rhino Foods Inc (PA)	Burlington	VT	C	802 862-0252	17156

DAIRY PRDTS: Ice Cream, Bulk

	CITY	ST	EMP	PHONE	ENTRY#
Bucks Spumoni Company Inc	Milford	CT	F	203 874-2007	1804
Pralines Inc	Wallingford	CT	F	203 284-8847	3838
Pralines of Plainville	Plainville	CT	G	860 410-1151	2778
Salem Vly Farms Ice Cream Inc	Salem	CT	F	860 859-2980	2947
Meletharb Inc	Wakefield	MA	G	781 245-4946	12518
Philip RS Sorbet Co Inc	Winchester	MA	F	781 721-6330	13491
Reasons To Be Cheerful	Concord	MA	G	978 610-6248	8132
Richardsons Ice Cream	Reading	MA	F	781 944-9121	11606
Franks Bake Shop Inc	Bangor	ME	G	207 947-4594	4502
Ice Cream Machine Co	Cumberland	RI	F	401 333-5053	15944
Warwick Ice Cream Company	Warwick	RI	E	401 821-8403	16877

DAIRY PRDTS: Ice Cream, Packaged, Molded, On Sticks, Etc.

	CITY	ST	EMP	PHONE	ENTRY#
Berry Twist	Boston	MA	G	857 362-7455	6589
Rescor Inc (PA)	Boston	MA	F	617 723-3635	7006
Protein Holdings Inc (PA)	Portland	ME	F	207 771-0965	5263
Ben & Jerrys Homemade Inc (HQ)	South Burlington	VT	C	802 846-1500	17571

DAIRY PRDTS: Milk & Cream, Cultured & Flavored

	CITY	ST	EMP	PHONE	ENTRY#
A B Munroe Dairy Inc (PA)	East Providence	RI	D	401 438-4450	16000

DAIRY PRDTS: Milk, Condensed & Evaporated

	CITY	ST	EMP	PHONE	ENTRY#
Culture Fresh Foods Inc	Naugatuck	CT	F	203 632-8433	1955
Herbalife Distributor	Bristol	CT	G	860 584-9721	453
Native Maine Operations Inc	Westbrook	ME	E	207 856-1100	5640

DAIRY PRDTS: Milk, Fluid

	CITY	ST	EMP	PHONE	ENTRY#
Willard J Stearns & Sons Inc	Storrs Mansfield	CT	E	860 423-9289	3513
295 Tremont Inc	Attleboro	MA	D	508 222-2884	5985
Brighams Inc (HQ)	Arlington	MA	E	800 242-2423	5939
Cumberland Farms Inc (DH)	Westborough	MA	B	800 225-9702	13097
HP Hood LLC	Peabody	MA	F	978 535-3385	11316
Duhamel Family Farm LLC	Highgate Center	VT	G	802 868-4954	17288
Ebws LLC	Strafford	VT	E	802 765-4180	17634
H P Hood-Booth Brothers Dairy	Barre	VT	F	802 476-6605	17004
St Albans Cooperative Creamery Inc	Saint Albans	VT	D	802 524-9366	17531
St Albans Creamery LLC	Saint Albans	VT	E	802 524-9366	17532

DAIRY PRDTS: Natural Cheese

	CITY	ST	EMP	PHONE	ENTRY#
Elm City Cheese Company Inc	Hamden	CT	F	203 865-5768	1424
Grey Barn Farm Enterprises LLC	Chilmark	MA	G	508 645-4854	8071
Providence Specialty Pdts Inc	Providence	RI	D	401 272-4979	16593
Cabot Creamery Cooperative Inc	Waitsfield	VT	B	888 792-2268	17664
Franklin Foods Inc (DH)	Enosburg Falls	VT	E	802 933-4338	17223
Sugarbush Farm Inc	Woodstock	VT	G	802 457-1757	17778
Swan Valley Cheese Vermont LLC	Swanton	VT	G	802 868-7181	17643
Vermont Creamery LLC	Websterville	VT	E	802 479-9371	17685

DAIRY PRDTS: Processed Cheese

	CITY	ST	EMP	PHONE	ENTRY#
HP Hood LLC (PA)	Lynnfield	MA	C	617 887-3000	9995
Kraft Heinz Foods Company	Woburn	MA	D	781 933-2800	13597
Mountain Mozzarella LLC	North Bennington	VT	E	802 440-9950	17409

DAIRY PRDTS: Spreads, Cheese

	CITY	ST	EMP	PHONE	ENTRY#
Spread Cheese Co LLC	Middletown	CT	G	203 982-1674	1784

DAIRY PRDTS: Yogurt, Frozen

	CITY	ST	EMP	PHONE	ENTRY#
Smoothie Bus LLC	Manchester	NH	F	603 303-7353	14930

DATA PROCESSING & PREPARATION SVCS

	CITY	ST	EMP	PHONE	ENTRY#
Better Lists Incorporated	Stamford	CT	E	203 324-4171	3294
Shibumicom Inc	Norwalk	CT	F	855 744-2864	2571
Spectrum Virtual LLC	Cheshire	CT	G	203 303-7540	617
Xerox Corporation (HQ)	Norwalk	CT	B	203 849-5216	2598
Xerox Holdings Inc	Norwalk	CT	A	203 968-3000	2599
Xerox Holdings Corporation (PA)	Norwalk	CT	B	203 849-5216	2600
Akamai Technologies Inc (PA)	Cambridge	MA	B	617 444-3000	7473
Corporate Rmbursement Svcs Inc	Newton	MA	D	888 312-0788	10748
Creamer Associates Inc	Cambridge	MA	G	617 374-6000	7544
Diacritech Inc	Boston	MA	F	617 236-7500	6692
Gty Technology Holdings Inc (PA)	Boston	MA	F	702 945-2898	6778
Logicmanager Inc	Boston	MA	E	617 530-1200	6862
Research Cmpt Consulting Svcs (PA)	Canton	MA	D	781 821-1221	7823
Scully Signal Company (PA)	Wilmington	MA	D	617 692-8600	13452
Toast Inc (PA)	Boston	MA	A	617 297-1005	7079
Zlink Inc	Maynard	MA	D	978 309-3628	10268
Ipura Consulting Group LLC	Hampton	NH	F	603 294-4002	14404
Oracle Systems Corporation	Nashua	NH	E	603 897-3000	15146
Igt Global Solutions Corporation (HQ)	Providence	RI	D	401 392-7077	16538
Northrop Grumman Systems Corp	Middletown	RI	B	401 849-6270	16183

DATA PROCESSING SVCS

	CITY	ST	EMP	PHONE	ENTRY#
Aquiline Drones Corporation	Hartford	CT	E	973 980-6596	1471
Hexplora LLC	Rocky Hill	CT	D	860 760-7601	2928
Cgi Information Systems & Management Consultants Inc 978 946-3000	Andover 5878	MA			A
Material Impact Inc	Boston	MA	E	617 917-4123	6879
School Family Media LLC	Wrentham	MA	E	508 384-0394	13844
Weather Source LLC	Salem	NH	F	844 813-2617	15571
Datamann Inc	Wilder	VT	E	802 295-6600	17714

DEALERS: Commodity Contracts

	CITY	ST	EMP	PHONE	ENTRY#
Cofco Americas Resources Corp (HQ)	Stamford	CT	F	203 658-2820	3316

DECORATIVE WOOD & WOODWORK

	CITY	ST	EMP	PHONE	ENTRY#
Agw Clssic Hardwood Floors LLC	Westbrook	CT	G	203 640-3106	4135
Anne Queen Woodworking	Naugatuck	CT	F	203 720-1781	1948
Elm City Manufacturing LLC	North Haven	CT	F	203 248-1969	2409
European Woodcraft LLC	Norwalk	CT	G	203 847-6195	2498
Harris Enterprise Corp	Manchester	CT	E	860 649-4663	1600
Legere Group Ltd	Avon	CT	D	860 674-0392	29
Vacca Architectural Wdwkg LLC	Pawcatuck	CT	G	860 599-3677	2727
Wood Services LLC	Greenwich	CT	G	203 983-5752	1363
Butler Architectural Wdwkg Inc	New Bedford	MA	F	508 985-9980	10576
Eagle Woodworking Inc	Lawrence	MA	F	978 681-6194	9558
South Shore Millwork Inc	Norton	MA	D	508 226-5500	11136
Vance Cabinet & Carpentry	Shirley	MA	G	603 801-5221	11824
Watson Brothers Inc	Middleton	MA	F	978 774-7677	10397
Aroostook Woodsmiths	Saint Agatha	ME	G	207 728-7100	5385
Bagala Window Works	Westbrook	ME	G	207 887-9231	5616
Coastal Woodworking Inc	Nobleboro	ME	E	207 563-1072	5100
Davis Zac Fine Woodworking	New Gloucester	ME	G	207 926-4710	5084
Maine Heritage Timber LLC	Millinocket	ME	E	207 723-9200	5066
Barlow Architectural Mllwk LLC	Hampstead	NH	E	603 329-6026	14381
Vigilant Incoporated	Dover	NH	E	603 285-0400	14256
Stupell Industries Ltd Inc	Johnston	RI	F	401 831-5640	16107

DEFENSE SYSTEMS & EQPT

	CITY	ST	EMP	PHONE	ENTRY#
Defensecom Inc	Boston	MA	G	203 912-8679	6688
Idss Holdings Inc	Boxboro	MA	D	978 237-0236	7144
Mascon Inc	Woburn	MA	E	781 938-5800	13605

	CITY	ST	EMP	PHONE	ENTRY#
Perspecta Svcs & Solutions Inc (DH)	Waltham	MA	G	781 684-4000	12747
Raytheon Company (HQ)	Waltham	MA	B	781 522-3000	12759
Raytheon Korean Support Co (DH)	Waltham	MA	E	339 645-6111	12761
Raytheon Systems Support Co (DH)	Tewksbury	MA	E	978 851-2134	12414
Xiphos Partners Inc	Dartmouth	MA	G	508 991-1014	8233
American Rhnmetall Systems LLC	Biddeford	ME	F	207 571-5850	4554
Northrop Grmmn Spce & Mssn Sys	Bath	ME	C	207 442-5097	4530
Alex & Ryan Design LLC	Manchester	NH	F	603 518-8650	14808
Cubic Corporation	Concord	NH	F	603 369-5504	14127
Gentex Corporation	Manchester	NH	C	603 657-1200	14851
Raytheon Company	Merrimack	NH	G	978 313-0201	15000
Resurrection Defense LLC	Winchester	NH	G	603 313-1040	15716
Raytheon Company	Portsmouth	RI	D	401 847-8000	16454

DEGREASING MACHINES

	CITY	ST	EMP	PHONE	ENTRY#
A B Engineering & Co	Oxford	MA	G	508 987-0318	11247
Degreasing Devices Co	Southbridge	MA	G	508 765-0045	12013
Safety-Kleen Systems Inc (HQ)	Norwell	MA	B	800 669-5740	11146
Greco Bros Inc	Providence	RI	E	401 421-9306	16529

DENTAL EQPT

	CITY	ST	EMP	PHONE	ENTRY#
Centrix Inc	Shelton	CT	C	203 929-5582	2991
Benco Dental	Hopkinton	MA	E	508 435-3000	9309
Bicon LLC (PA)	Boston	MA	F	617 524-4443	6593
Enamel Pure Inc	Worcester	MA	F	508 335-4824	13720

DENTAL EQPT & SPLYS

	CITY	ST	EMP	PHONE	ENTRY#
Aero-Med LLC	South Windsor	CT	F	860 659-2270	3108
J Palmero Sales Company Inc	Stratford	CT	F	203 377-6424	3550
Palmero Healthcare LLC	Stratford	CT	F	203 377-6424	3562
Proxysoft Worldwide Inc	Bethel	CT	D	203 730-0084	133
Surfctcom Inc	Naugatuck	CT	E	203 720-9209	1989
Ultimate Companies Inc (PA)	Bristol	CT	G	860 582-9111	503
Ultimate Wireforms Inc	Bristol	CT	D	860 582-9111	504
Winslow Automatics Inc	New Britain	CT	C	860 225-6321	2075
3d Diagnostix Inc	Allston	MA	F	617 820-5279	5817
Apogent Technologies Inc	Waltham	MA	A	781 622-1300	12594
Cataki International Inc	Wareham	MA	F	508 295-9630	12833
Convergent Dental Inc (PA)	Waltham	MA	E	508 500-5656	12640
Dentovations Inc	Boston	MA	F	617 737-1199	6690
Dillon Laboratories Inc	Abington	MA	G	781 871-2333	5723
Ergonomic Products Inc	Fall River	MA	F	508 636-2263	8542
Pulpdent Corporation	Watertown	MA	D	617 926-6666	12901
Sterngold Dental LLC	Attleboro	MA	E	508 226-5660	6066
Straumann Usa LLC	Andover	MA	C	978 747-2500	5927
National Dentex LLC	Manchester	NH	C	561 537-8301	14895

DENTAL EQPT & SPLYS WHOLESALERS

	CITY	ST	EMP	PHONE	ENTRY#
Dentovations Inc	Boston	MA	G	617 737-1199	6691

DENTAL EQPT & SPLYS: Dental Materials

	CITY	ST	EMP	PHONE	ENTRY#
DRM Research Laboratories Inc	Branford	CT	F	203 488-5555	252

DENTAL EQPT & SPLYS: Enamels

	CITY	ST	EMP	PHONE	ENTRY#
Scott Woodford	Madison	CT	G	203 245-4266	1569
Keystone Dental Inc (PA)	Burlington	MA	D	781 328-3300	7386

DENTAL EQPT & SPLYS: Orthodontic Appliances

	CITY	ST	EMP	PHONE	ENTRY#
Acme Monaco Corporation (PA)	New Britain	CT	C	860 224-1349	1995
New England Orthdontic Lab Inc	Andover	MA	E	800 922-6365	5900

DENTISTS' OFFICES & CLINICS

	CITY	ST	EMP	PHONE	ENTRY#
Ultimate Wireforms Inc	Bristol	CT	D	860 582-9111	504

DEODORANTS: Personal

	CITY	ST	EMP	PHONE	ENTRY#
Unilever Hpc USA	Trumbull	CT	D	203 381-3311	3737
Procter & Gamble Company	Auburn	ME	C	207 753-4000	4456

DEPARTMENT STORES

	CITY	ST	EMP	PHONE	ENTRY#
Gordon Brothers Intl LLC (HQ)	Boston	MA	D	888 424-1903	6767

DERMATOLOGICALS

	CITY	ST	EMP	PHONE	ENTRY#
Sanova Bioscience Inc	Acton	MA	F	978 429-8079	5763
Tender Corporation (PA)	Littleton	NH	D	603 444-5464	14724
Onset Dermatologics LLC	Cumberland	RI	D	401 762-2000	15958
Mylan Technologies Inc	Saint Albans	VT	F	802 527-7792	17524
Mylan Technologies Inc (HQ)	Saint Albans	VT	C	802 527-7792	17525

DESIGN SVCS, NEC

	CITY	ST	EMP	PHONE	ENTRY#
20/20 Software Inc	Stamford	CT	G	203 316-5500	3266
Aerospace Alloys Inc	Bloomfield	CT	D	860 882-0019	144
Century Tool and Design Inc	Milldale	CT	F	860 621-6748	1900

PRODUCT

	CITY	ST	EMP	PHONE	ENTRY#
Dufrane Nuclear Shielding Inc	Winsted	CT	F	860 379-2318	4340
Gyre9 LLC	Southbury	CT	E	203 702-4010	3194
John Oldham Studios Inc	Wethersfield	CT	E	860 529-3331	4207
Karen Callan Designs Inc	Greenwich	CT	G	203 762-9914	1336
Bcg Connect LLC	Wilmington	MA	E	978 528-7999	13389
Carriage Hse Developments LLC	Winchester	MA	F	339 221-4253	13483
Chris Ploof Designs Inc	Leominster	MA	G	978 728-4905	9651
First Sail Group Inc	South Yarmouth	MA	G	425 409-2783	11983
George Patton Associates Inc	Fall River	MA	C	800 572-2194	8552
Jamesbrook Enterprises Inc	Shirley	MA	G	978 425-6166	11818
Tanyx Measurements Inc	Billerica	MA	G	978 671-0183	6485
Advanced Indus Solutions Inc (PA)	Augusta	ME	F	207 623-9599	4466
Erin Flett	Gorham	ME	E	207 887-9253	4819
Print Bangor	Bangor	ME	G	207 947-8049	4515
Alex & Ryan Design LLC	Manchester	NH	F	603 518-8650	14808
Prime Power Inc	Hampstead	NH	F	603 329-4675	14390
Cabinet Gallery Ltd (PA)	Woonsocket	RI	F	401 762-4300	16952
Constant Technologies Inc	North Kingstown	RI	E	800 518-7369	16240
Tsco Inc	North Kingstown	RI	F	401 295-0669	16289
Leo D Bernstein & Sons Inc	Shaftsbury	VT	D	802 442-8029	17550

DESIGN SVCS: Commercial & Indl

	CITY	ST	EMP	PHONE	ENTRY#
D&D Fltrtion Cons Sppliers Inc	Kensington	CT	F	860 829-3690	1539
Kimchuk Incorporated (PA)	Danbury	CT	F	203 790-7800	766
On Line Building Systems LLC	Danbury	CT	G	203 798-1194	792
Pta Corporation (PA)	Oxford	CT	D	203 888-0585	2709
Andritz Inc	Springfield	MA	C	413 733-6603	12075
Architects of Packaging Inc	Westfield	MA	E	413 568-3187	13148
Microwave Development Labs Inc	Needham Heights	MA	D	781 292-6600	10551
Monalex Manufacturing Inc	East Douglas	MA	G	508 476-1200	8352
Nypro Inc (HQ)	Clinton	MA	A	978 365-9721	8087
Sampco Inc (PA)	Pittsfield	MA	F	413 442-4043	11423
Transformit (PA)	Gorham	ME	E	207 856-9911	4837
Ingersoll-Rand Energy Systems Corporation	Portsmouth	NH			D
603 430-7000			15408		

DESIGN SVCS: Computer Integrated Systems

	CITY	ST	EMP	PHONE	ENTRY#
Cyberresearch Inc	Branford	CT	E	203 643-5000	247
General Dynamics Info Tech Inc	Pawcatuck	CT	D	860 441-2400	2720
Insys Micro Inc	Norwalk	CT	G	917 566-5045	2518
Kimchuk Incorporated (PA)	Danbury	CT	F	203 790-7800	766
Rite-Solutions Inc (PA)	Pawcatuck	CT	F	401 847-3399	2725
Vertafore Inc	Windsor	CT	C	860 602-6000	4312
Bellhawk Systems Corporation	Millbury	MA	G	508 865-8070	10428
Cgi Information Systems & Management Consultants Inc	Andover	MA			A
978 946-3000			5878		
Csp Inc (PA)	Lowell	MA	E	978 954-5038	9872
DCI Automation Inc	West Boylston	MA	D	508 752-3071	12960
Engement Company Inc	Topsfield	MA	G	603 537-2088	12432
Juniper Networks Inc	Westford	MA	B	978 589-5800	13243
L T X International Inc	Norwood	MA	D	781 461-1000	11189
Milford Manufacturing Svcs LLC	Hopedale	MA	E	508 478-8544	9299
On Technology Corp (PA)	Waltham	MA	D	781 487-3300	12743
Rsa Security LLC (PA)	Bedford	MA	A	800 995-5095	6268
Speechworks International	Burlington	MA	E	781 565-5000	7432
Superpedestrian Inc (PA)	Cambridge	MA	C	877 678-7518	7725
Syberworks Inc	Arlington	MA	E	781 891-1999	5948
Ukg Kronos Systems LLC (DH)	Lowell	MA	B	978 250-9800	9931
Verizon New York Inc	Winchester	MA	F	781 721-5957	13493
It Synergy Group LLC	Warwick	RI	F	866 767-4874	16824
Northrop Grumman Systems Corp	Middletown	RI	B	401 849-6270	16183

DETECTION APPARATUS: Electronic/Magnetic Field, Light/Heat

	CITY	ST	EMP	PHONE	ENTRY#
J W Fishers Mfg Inc	East Taunton	MA	F	508 822-7330	8407
Secure Point Technologies Inc	Boston	MA	D	978 752-1700	7031
Vacuum Barrier Corporation	Woburn	MA	E	781 933-3570	13682

DETECTIVE & ARMORED CAR SERVICES

	CITY	ST	EMP	PHONE	ENTRY#
International Security Assista	Woburn	MA	C	617 590-7942	13588

DIAGNOSTIC SUBSTANCES

	CITY	ST	EMP	PHONE	ENTRY#
Charles River Laboratories Inc	Storrs	CT	F	860 429-7261	3511
Abpro Corporation	Woburn	MA	F	617 225-0808	13497
Advandx Inc	Woburn	MA	E	866 376-0009	13500
Alere US Holdings LLC	Waltham	MA	F	781 647-3900	12588
Associates of Cape Cod Inc (PA)	East Falmouth	MA	D	508 540-3444	8355
Axis-Shield Poc As	Norton	MA	E	508 285-4870	11123
Biokit U S A Inc	Bedford	MA	G	781 861-4064	6215
Bionostics Inc	Devens	MA	C	978 772-7070	8270
Cellay LLC	Cambridge	MA	F	617 995-1307	7535
Daktari Diagnostics Inc	Cambridge	MA	F	617 336-3299	7549
Esoterix Genetic Labs LLC (HQ)	Westborough	MA	E	508 389-6650	13101

	CITY	ST	EMP	PHONE	ENTRY#
Glycozym Usa Inc	Beverly	MA	G	425 985-2556	6351
Instrumentation Laboratory Co (DH)	Bedford	MA	A	781 861-0710	6233
Intellia Therapeutics Inc (PA)	Cambridge	MA	C	857 285-6200	7616
Interleukin Genetics Inc	Waltham	MA	F	781 398-0700	12702
Inverness Medical - Biostar Inc	Waltham	MA	C	781 647-3900	12703
Lantheus Holdings Inc (PA)	North Billerica	MA	A	978 671-8001	10923
Memed US Inc	Andover	MA	E	617 335-0349	5895
Nanobiosym Inc	Cambridge	MA	E	781 391-7979	7659
Petnet Solutions Inc	Woburn	MA	E	781 937-3600	13634
Quest Diagnostic Incorporated	Marlborough	MA	A	617 547-8900	10199
Quidel Corporation	Beverly	MA	F	866 800-5458	6377
Regenocell Therapeutics Inc	Natick	MA	G	508 651-1598	10495
Third Wave Technologies Inc (HQ)	Marlborough	MA	E	608 273-8933	10224
Ultivue Inc (PA)	Cambridge	MA	E	617 945-2662	7747
Vital Biosciences Inc	Boston	MA	G	415 910-2994	7107
Alere Inc	Scarborough	ME	D	207 730-5714	5421
Bioprocessing Inc	Portland	ME	E	207 457-0025	5187
Idexx Distribution Inc	Westbrook	ME	D	207 556-0300	5630

DIAGNOSTIC SUBSTANCES OR AGENTS: Blood Derivative

	CITY	ST	EMP	PHONE	ENTRY#
Fresenius Usa Inc (DH)	Waltham	MA	C	781 699-4191	12683
Medical Research Networx	Franklin	MA	E	508 530-4289	8850

DIAGNOSTIC SUBSTANCES OR AGENTS: Enzyme & Isoenzyme

	CITY	ST	EMP	PHONE	ENTRY#
Genzyme Corporation (DH)	Cambridge	MA	A	617 252-7500	7585

DIAGNOSTIC SUBSTANCES OR AGENTS: In Vitro

	CITY	ST	EMP	PHONE	ENTRY#
Alere Inc (HQ)	Waltham	MA	A	781 647-3900	12587
Bostonmolecules Inc	Waltham	MA	F	617 651-1016	12610
Cellanyx Diagnostics LLC	Beverly	MA	G	571 212-9991	6337
Confer Health Inc	Charlestown	MA	G	617 433-8810	7866
Creatics LLC	Braintree	MA	F	781 843-2202	7175
High Technology Inc	North Attleboro	MA	E	508 660-2221	10873
T2 Biosystems Inc (PA)	Lexington	MA	D	781 761-4646	9779
Telome Inc	Waltham	MA	G	617 383-7565	12792
Werfen USA LLC	Bedford	MA	C	781 861-0710	6276
Lgc Clinical Diagnostics Inc	Cumberland Foreside	ME	D	207 892-1300	4712
Maine Biotechnology Svcs Inc	Portland	ME	F	207 797-5454	5239
Sun Diagnostics LLC	New Gloucester	ME	G	207 926-1125	5089

DIAGNOSTIC SUBSTANCES OR AGENTS: Microbiology & Virology

	CITY	ST	EMP	PHONE	ENTRY#
Asimov Inc	Boston	MA	E	339 532-9982	6561
Piton Therapeutics Inc	Watertown	MA	F	857 327-7666	12900
Rootpath Genomics	Watertown	MA	F	857 209-1060	12906
Meridian Life Science Inc (HQ)	Saco	ME	E	207 283-6500	5373

DIAGNOSTIC SUBSTANCES OR AGENTS: Radioactive

	CITY	ST	EMP	PHONE	ENTRY#
Cardinal Health 414 LLC	East Hartford	CT	G	860 291-9135	978
Qsa Global Inc (HQ)	Burlington	MA	D	781 272-2000	7416

DIAGNOSTIC SUBSTANCES OR AGENTS: Veterinary

	CITY	ST	EMP	PHONE	ENTRY#
Covetrus North America LLC (PA)	Portland	ME	C	888 280-2221	5202
Idexx Laboratories Inc (PA)	Westbrook	ME	A	207 556-0300	5631
Immucell Corporation	Portland	ME	E	207 878-2770	5226
Immucell Corporation (PA)	Portland	ME	E	207 878-2770	5227

DIE CUTTING SVC: Paper

	CITY	ST	EMP	PHONE	ENTRY#
C & T Print Finishing Inc	South Windsor	CT	F	860 282-0616	3123
New England Paper Tube Co Inc	Pawtucket	RI	E	401 725-2610	16394

DIE SETS: Presses, Metal Stamping

	CITY	ST	EMP	PHONE	ENTRY#
Globe Tool & Met Stampg Co Inc	Southington	CT	E	860 621-6807	3213
P&G Metal Components Corp	Bloomfield	CT	F	860 243-2220	199
Connell Limited Partnership (PA)	Boston	MA	F	617 737-2700	6665
GA Rel Manufacturing Company	Providence	RI	F	401 331-5455	16524

DIES & TOOLS: Special

	CITY	ST	EMP	PHONE	ENTRY#
A & H Tool Works LLC	Harwinton	CT	G	860 302-9284	1518
Accurate Tool & Die Inc	Stamford	CT	E	203 967-1200	3270
All Five Tool Co Inc	Berlin	CT	F	860 583-1693	48
Arrow Diversified Tooling Inc	Ellington	CT	E	860 872-9072	1101
B & D Machine Inc	Tolland	CT	F	860 871-9226	3655
B & P Plating Equipment LLC	Bristol	CT	F	860 589-5799	401
Bremser Technologies Inc	Stratford	CT	E	203 378-8486	3521
Bridgeport TI & Stamping Corp	Bridgeport	CT	E	203 336-2501	305
Bristol Tool & Die Company	Bristol	CT	F	860 582-2577	423
Candlewood Tool and Mch Sp Inc	Gaylordsville	CT	F	860 355-1892	1263
Century Tool Co Inc	Thompson	CT	F	860 923-9523	3648
D & B Tool Co LLC	Milford	CT	G	203 878-6026	1815
Delta Tool Co Inc	Thompson	CT	G	860 923-2012	3649
E & E Tool & Mfg Co Inc	Winsted	CT	F	860 738-8577	4342

	CITY	ST	EMP	PHONE	ENTRY#
Fad Tool Company LLC	Bristol	CT	E	860 582-7890	445
G L C Inc	Watertown	CT	F	860 945-6166	4013
G P Tool Co Inc	Danbury	CT	E	203 744-0310	749
Heise Industries Inc	East Berlin	CT	D	860 828-6538	912
Highland Manufacturing Inc	Manchester	CT	E	860 646-5142	1603
Hobson and Motzer Incorporated (PA)	Durham	CT	C	860 349-1756	901
Jovek Tool and Die	Bristol	CT	G	860 261-5020	459
Lassy Tools Inc	Plainville	CT	G	860 747-2748	2768
Lou-Jan Tool & Die Inc	Bristol	CT	F	203 272-3536	463
Manchester Molding and Mfg Co	Manchester	CT	E	860 643-2141	1615
Mastercraft Tool and Mch Co	Southington	CT	F	860 628-5551	3220
Paragon Tool Company Inc	Manchester	CT	G	860 647-9935	1627
Plainville Machine & TI Co Inc	Bristol	CT	E	860 589-5595	481
Precision Punch + Tooling Corp (PA)	Berlin	CT	D	860 229-9902	79
Preferred Tool & Die Inc (PA)	Shelton	CT	E	203 925-8525	3054
Quality Wire Edm Inc	Bristol	CT	G	860 583-9867	487
Ramar-Hall Inc	Middlefield	CT	E	860 349-1081	1728
Reynolds Carbide Die Co Inc	Thomaston	CT	E	860 283-8246	3627
Richards Machine Tool Co Inc	Newington	CT	F	860 436-2938	2322
Rintec Corporation	Waterbury	CT	F	860 274-3697	3966
SA Manchester LLC	Manchester	CT	D	860 533-7500	1634
Sandur Tool Co	Waterbury	CT	G	203 753-0004	3967
Skico Manufacturing Co LLC	Hamden	CT	G	203 230-1305	1455
Skillcraft Machine Tool Co	South Windsor	CT	F	860 953-1246	3180
Straton Industries Inc	Stratford	CT	D	203 375-4488	3578
Taco Fasteners Inc	Plainville	CT	F	860 747-5597	2782
The Lyons Tool & Die Company	Meriden	CT	E	203 238-2689	1707
Total Concept Tool Inc	Branford	CT	G	203 483-1130	283
Watertown Jig Bore Service Inc	Watertown	CT	E	860 274-5898	4037
Weimann Brothers Mfg Co	Derby	CT	F	203 735-3311	894
West-Conn Tool and Die Inc	Shelton	CT	E	203 538-5081	3077
A Luongo & Sons Incorporated	Bridgewater	MA	G	508 226-0788	7218
Abco Tool & Die Inc	Hyannis	MA	E	508 771-3225	9428
Adt/Diversity Inc	Attleboro	MA	G	508 222-9601	5991
Baril Corporation	Haverhill	MA	F	978 373-7910	9076
Brolan Tool Inc	Leominster	MA	E	978 537-0290	9644
CE Baird Corporation	Lancaster	MA	F	978 365-3867	9525
CE Baird Corporation	Leominster	MA	F	978 751-8432	9650
Columbia ASC Inc	Lawrence	MA	F	978 683-2205	9554
Diecutting Tooling Svcs Inc (PA)	Chicopee	MA	G	413 331-3500	8023
Fort Hill Sign Products Inc	Hopedale	MA	E	781 321-4320	9297
G&F Precision Molding Inc	Danvers	MA	F	978 560-2622	8188
G&F Precision Molding Inc (PA)	Fiskdale	MA	D	508 347-9132	8639
Hoppe Technologies Inc	Chicopee	MA	D	413 592-9213	8036
Interstate Design Company Inc	Agawam	MA	E	413 786-7730	5794
Interstate Mfg Co Inc	Agawam	MA	E	413 789-8674	5795
J-K Tool Co Inc	Agawam	MA	E	413 789-0613	5797
Millennium Die Group Inc	Three Rivers	MA	E	413 283-3500	12430
Mtd Micro Molding Inc	Charlton	MA	E	508 248-0111	7893
New England Die Cutting Inc	Methuen	MA	E	978 374-0789	10340
Orchard Tool & Die Inc	Indian Orchard	MA	E	413 433-1233	9473
Sancliff Inc	Worcester	MA	E	508 795-0747	13794
Skg Associates Inc	Dedham	MA	E	781 878-7250	8250
Southbridge Tool & Mfg Inc	Dudley	MA	E	508 764-6819	8324
Srd Holdings Inc	North Attleboro	MA	E	508 695-5656	10888
Superior Die & Stamping Inc	Attleboro	MA	G	774 203-3674	6067
Tech Ridge Inc	Chelmsford	MA	E	978 256-5741	7963
Ultraclad Corporation	Newburyport	MA	G	978 358-7945	10723
V&M Tool & Die Inc	Leominster	MA	E	978 534-8814	9715
Vogform Tool & Die Co Inc	West Springfield	MA	E	413 737-6947	13051
W M Gulliksen Mfg Co Inc (PA)	South Weymouth	MA	F	617 323-5750	11979
Westfield Tool & Die Co Inc	Westfield	MA	E	413 562-2393	13222
Whip City Tool & Die Corp	Southwick	MA	E	413 569-5528	12053
Whitman Tool & Die Company Inc	Whitman	MA	E	781 447-0421	13354
Kennebec Technologies	Augusta	ME	D	207 626-0188	4474
Atlantic Microtool	Salem	NH	G	603 898-3212	15509
Berube Tool & Die Inc	Plaistow	NH	G	603 382-2224	15337
Live Free or Die Alliance	Hampton	NH	E	210 232-8779	14406
New England Industries Inc	Lebanon	NH	E	603 448-5330	14696
North East Cutting Die Corp	Dover	NH	E	603 436-8952	14242
Rays Tool & Die Co Inc	Somersworth	NH	G	603 692-5978	15623
Sunset Tool Inc	Keene	NH	E	603 355-2246	14623
Temco Tool Company Inc	Manchester	NH	E	603 622-6989	14941
Guill Tool & Engrg Co Inc	West Warwick	RI	D	401 822-8186	16908
Henry A Evers Corp	Cranston	RI	F	401 781-4767	15872
Ldc Inc	East Providence	RI	F	401 861-4667	16029
Mono Die Cutting Co Inc	Riverside	RI	F	401 434-1274	16658
Newport Tool & Die Inc	Middletown	RI	F	401 847-6711	16181
Rol-Flo Engineering Inc	Westerly	RI	F	401 596-0060	16942
Stearns Tool Company	Providence	RI	G	401 351-4765	16616
North Hartland Tool Corp (PA)	North Hartland	VT	D	802 295-3196	17420
Richard Mrchssult DBA Bngtson	Canaan	VT	G	802 266-9666	17169

	CITY	ST	EMP	PHONE	ENTRY#
Vermont Mold & Tool Corp	Barnet	VT	G	802 633-2300	16995
Vmt LLC	Groton	VT	E	802 592-3146	17279

DIES: Cutting, Exc Metal

	CITY	ST	EMP	PHONE	ENTRY#
Bessette Holdings Inc	East Hartford	CT	E	860 289-6000	975
Advanced Indus Solutions Inc (PA)	Augusta	ME	F	207 623-9599	4466

DIES: Extrusion

	CITY	ST	EMP	PHONE	ENTRY#
American Kuhne Inc	North Stonington	CT	E	401 326-6200	2446
Raymond Gadues Inc	Swanton	VT	E	802 868-2033	17641

DIES: Plastic Forming

	CITY	ST	EMP	PHONE	ENTRY#
Aba-Pgt Inc (PA)	Manchester	CT	D	860 649-4591	1580
Acson Tool Company	Bridgeport	CT	F	203 334-8050	292
Bermer Tool & Die Inc	Southbridge	MA	F	508 764-2521	12011
Fall River Tool & Die Co Inc	Fall River	MA	F	508 674-4621	8550
Moldmaster Engineering Inc	Pittsfield	MA	E	413 442-5793	11413

DIES: Steel Rule

	CITY	ST	EMP	PHONE	ENTRY#
Bessette Holdings Inc	East Hartford	CT	E	860 289-6000	975
Hamden Packaging Inc	Hamden	CT	E	203 288-0200	1428
Barnard Die Inc	Wakefield	MA	F	781 246-3117	12500
Csw Inc (PA)	Ludlow	MA	D	413 589-1311	9943
Pearl Die-Cutting & Finshg LLC	Woburn	MA	F	781 721-6900	13632

DIODES & RECTIFIERS

	CITY	ST	EMP	PHONE	ENTRY#
Excelitas Technologies Corp (DH)	Waltham	MA	E	855 382-2677	12673
Ipg Photonics Corporation (PA)	Marlborough	MA	B	508 373-1100	10169
Sheaumann Laser Inc	Billerica	MA	E	508 970-0600	6481
Gpd Optoelectronics Corp	Salem	NH	E	603 894-6865	15533
Two In One Manufacturing Inc	Nashua	NH	E	603 595-8212	15179

DIODES: Light Emitting

	CITY	ST	EMP	PHONE	ENTRY#
Revolution Lighting Tech Inc (PA)	Stamford	CT	E	877 578-2536	3447
Specialty Coating Systems Inc	Milford	CT	C	203 283-0087	1887
Optomistic Products Inc	Leominster	MA	F	207 865-9181	9691
4382412 Canada Inc	Randolph	VT	F	802 225-5911	17465
Leddynamics Inc	Randolph	VT	D	802 728-4533	17470

DIODES: Solid State, Germanium, Silicon, Etc

	CITY	ST	EMP	PHONE	ENTRY#
Microsemi Corporation	Lawrence	MA	D	781 665-1071	9583
Microsemi Nes Inc	Lawrence	MA	E	978 794-1666	9584
Micro-Metrics Inc	Londonderry	NH	D	603 641-3800	14772

DIRECT SELLING ESTABLISHMENTS, NEC

	CITY	ST	EMP	PHONE	ENTRY#
Bluecatbio MA Inc	Concord	MA	G	978 405-2533	8106

DIRECT SELLING ESTABLISHMENTS: Encyclopedias, House-To-House

	CITY	ST	EMP	PHONE	ENTRY#
Scholastic Library Pubg Inc (HQ)	Danbury	CT	A	203 797-3500	812

DIRECT SELLING ESTABLISHMENTS: Food Svcs

	CITY	ST	EMP	PHONE	ENTRY#
Sogle Property LLC	Cambridge	VT	E	802 849-7943	17168

DISCS & TAPE: Optical, Blank

	CITY	ST	EMP	PHONE	ENTRY#
Adaptive Optics Associates Inc (DH)	Devens	MA	D	978 757-9600	8269

DISPENSERS: Soap

	CITY	ST	EMP	PHONE	ENTRY#
Highland Labs Inc	Holliston	MA	G	508 429-2918	9215

DISPLAY FIXTURES: Wood

	CITY	ST	EMP	PHONE	ENTRY#
Franklin Fixtures Inc (PA)	West Wareham	MA	E	508 291-1475	13065
Phillips Enterprises Inc	Northampton	MA	F	413 586-5860	11076
Jsi Store Fixtures Inc (HQ)	Milo	ME	C	207 943-5203	5070
Custom Design Incorporated	North Kingstown	RI	E	401 294-0200	16243
Kenney Manufacturing Company (PA)	Warwick	RI	B	401 739-2200	16831
The Elliott Sales Group Inc	Providence	RI	D	401 944-0002	16625

DISPLAY ITEMS: Corrugated, Made From Purchased Materials

	CITY	ST	EMP	PHONE	ENTRY#
E Ink Corporation	Billerica	MA	D	617 499-6000	6437
Amring Worldwide Inc	Johnston	RI	D	401 943-5040	16075
Contempo Card Co Inc (PA)	Providence	RI	D	401 272-4210	16505

DOCK EQPT & SPLYS, INDL

	CITY	ST	EMP	PHONE	ENTRY#
CCI Cyrus River Terminal LLC	Stamford	CT	G	203 761-8000	3305
Dock Doctors LLC	Ferrisburgh	VT	E	802 877-6756	17268

DOOR FRAMES: Wood

	CITY	ST	EMP	PHONE	ENTRY#
Harvey Industries LLC	Londonderry	NH	E	603 216-8300	14754
Kelley Bros New England LLC (HQ)	Hudson	NH	F	603 881-5559	14515

PRODUCT

DOORS & WINDOWS: Screen & Storm

	CITY	ST	EMP	PHONE	ENTRY#
Mercury-Excelum Inc	East Windsor	CT	E	860 292-1800	1080
Post Road Iron Works Inc	Greenwich	CT	E	203 869-6322	1343

DOORS & WINDOWS: Storm, Metal

	CITY	ST	EMP	PHONE	ENTRY#
All-Time Manufacturing Co Inc	Montville	CT	F	860 848-9258	1926
Aluminum Products Cape Cod Inc **(PA)**	Dennis Port	MA	F	508 398-8546	8259
Centco Architectural Mtls Inc	East Bridgewater	MA	F	508 456-1888	8336
Diamond Windows Doors Mfg Inc	Boston	MA	E	617 282-1688	6693
Harvey Industries LLC	Springfield	MA	E	413 731-7700	12099
Harvey Industries LLC **(PA)**	Waltham	MA	C	800 598-5400	12691
Harvey Industries LLC	Woburn	MA	F	781 935-7990	13581
Harvey Industries Inc	Augusta	ME	F	207 629-3737	4472
Jsg Holdings Inc	Warwick	RI	E	401 738-3800	16829

DOORS: Fiberglass

	CITY	ST	EMP	PHONE	ENTRY#
Hexcel Corporation **(PA)**	Stamford	CT	E	203 969-0666	3374
Countrywide National Services	Walpole	MA	G	508 346-3286	12558
Fiberglass Building Pdts Inc	Halifax	MA	F	847 650-3045	9021

DOORS: Fire, Metal

	CITY	ST	EMP	PHONE	ENTRY#
Stonington Services LLC	Gales Ferry	CT	E	860 464-1991	1261

DOORS: Folding, Plastic Or Plastic Coated Fabric

	CITY	ST	EMP	PHONE	ENTRY#
Beacon Sales Acquisition Inc	Portland	ME	F	207 797-7950	5185
K & R Holdings Inc	Portland	ME	C	207 797-7950	5230
Albany International Corp **(PA)**	Rochester	NH	D	603 330-5850	15464

DOORS: Garage, Overhead, Metal

	CITY	ST	EMP	PHONE	ENTRY#
Overhead Door Co Bangor Inc	Hermon	ME	F	207 848-7200	4888
R G Tombs Door Company Inc	Hooksett	NH	E	603 624-5040	14471
E I J Inc	Tunbridge	VT	F	802 889-3432	17653

DOORS: Glass

	CITY	ST	EMP	PHONE	ENTRY#
Capitol Glass Company Inc	West Hartford	CT	F	860 236-1936	4050
Prestige Cstm Mirror & GL Inc	Waltham	MA	F	781 647-0878	12752

DRAPERIES & CURTAINS

	CITY	ST	EMP	PHONE	ENTRY#
Draperies Intrors Grenwich LLC	Cos Cob	CT	G	203 489-3010	677
Yard Stick Decore	Bridgeport	CT	F	203 330-0360	388
Dra-Cor Industries Inc	Brockton	MA	E	508 580-3770	7273
Fall River Apparel Inc	Fall River	MA	G	508 677-1975	8545
Ksg Enterprises Inc	Peabody	MA	F	978 977-7357	11322
Limelight Productions Inc	Lee	MA	G	413 243-4950	9616
Quest Drape	Woburn	MA	G	781 859-0300	13645
Reliable Fabrics Inc	Everett	MA	F	617 387-5321	8497
United Curtain Co Inc **(PA)**	Avon	MA	E	508 588-4100	6166
Dirigo Stitching Inc	Skowhegan	ME	E	207 474-8421	5466
Gordons Window Decor Inc **(PA)**	Williston	VT	F	802 655-7777	17734

DRAPERIES: Plastic & Textile, From Purchased Materials

	CITY	ST	EMP	PHONE	ENTRY#
Decorator Services Inc	Bridgeport	CT	G	203 384-8144	315
Thomas W Raftery Inc	Hartford	CT	E	860 278-9870	1514
Sams Drapery Workroom Inc	Stoughton	MA	F	617 364-9440	12234
Gilberte Interiors LLC **(PA)**	Hanover	NH	F	603 643-3727	14423
J & R Langley Co Inc	Manchester	NH	E	603 622-9653	14866
Marion Mfg Co	Lincoln	RI	E	401 331-4343	16147

DRAPERY & UPHOLSTERY STORES: Draperies

	CITY	ST	EMP	PHONE	ENTRY#
Irvings Home Center Inc	Brockton	MA	G	508 583-4421	7285
Reliable Fabrics Inc	Everett	MA	F	617 387-5321	8497
Gilberte Interiors LLC **(PA)**	Hanover	NH	F	603 643-3727	14423
Drapery House Inc	North Providence	RI	E	401 724-3400	16300
Marion Mfg Co	Lincoln	RI	E	401 331-4343	16147

DRILLS & DRILLING EQPT: Mining

	CITY	ST	EMP	PHONE	ENTRY#
Numa Tool Company **(PA)**	Thompson	CT	D	860 923-9551	3652
Buckeye Blasting Corporation	Epsom	NH	G	603 736-4681	14279

DRINK MIXES, NONALCOHOLIC: Cocktail

	CITY	ST	EMP	PHONE	ENTRY#
Brady Enterprises Inc **(PA)**	East Weymouth	MA	D	781 340-4571	8427
Stirrings LLC	Fall River	MA	E	508 324-9800	8610
Fizz LLC	Portland	ME	E	207 887-9618	5216

DRINKING PLACES: Bars & Lounges

	CITY	ST	EMP	PHONE	ENTRY#
Beerd Brewing Co LLC **(PA)**	Stonington	CT	E	860 857-1014	3507
Swagnificent Ent LLC	Bridgeport	CT	G	203 449-0124	378
Thimble Island Brewing Company	Branford	CT	E	203 208-2827	282
Bad Martha Farmers Brewery LLC	Edgartown	MA	F	978 335-9879	8465
Berkshire Brewing Company Inc **(PA)**	South Deerfield	MA	F	413 665-6600	11921
Four Phantoms Brewing Co LLC	Greenfield	MA	G	931 247-0315	8991
Penny Pinchers Brewing Co LLC	Millbury	MA	F	774 696-7885	10440
Untold Brewing LLC **(PA)**	Scituate	MA	F	781 378-0559	11773
Wormtown Brewery LLC	Worcester	MA	F	774 239-1555	13833
Brays Brewing Company	Naples	ME	E	207 693-6806	5079
Rising Tide Brewing Co LLC	Portland	ME	F	207 370-2337	5265
Saco River Brewing LLC	Fryeburg	ME	F	207 256-3028	4810
Cisco Brewers Portsmouth LLC	Portsmouth	NH	E	603 380-7575	15373
Apponaug Brewing Company	Warwick	RI	E	401 681-4321	16782
Foam Brewers LLC	Burlington	VT	F	802 399-2511	17136

DRINKING PLACES: Beer Garden

	CITY	ST	EMP	PHONE	ENTRY#
Turtle Swamp Brewing LLC	Boston	MA	F	617 314-2952	7089

DRINKING WATER COOLERS WHOLESALERS: Mechanical

	CITY	ST	EMP	PHONE	ENTRY#
Bluedrop LLC	South Easton	MA	F	877 662-7873	11938
United Fbrcnts Strainrite Corp **(HQ)**	Auburn	ME	D	207 376-1600	4463

DRIVE SHAFTS

	CITY	ST	EMP	PHONE	ENTRY#
Shaft Current Solutions Inc	Florence	MA	G	413 267-0590	8686

DRUG STORES

	CITY	ST	EMP	PHONE	ENTRY#
Walgreen Co	North Attleboro	MA	F	781 244-9431	10892

DRUGS & DRUG PROPRIETARIES, WHOLESALE

	CITY	ST	EMP	PHONE	ENTRY#
Bedrock Brands LLC	Boston	MA	G	914 231-9550	6587
Genzyme Corporation **(DH)**	Cambridge	MA	A	617 252-7500	7585
Progderm Inc	Boston	MA	F	617 419-1800	6982
Sanofi Pasteur Biologics LLC	Canton	MA	D	781 302-3000	7824
Sea-Band International Inc	Newport	RI	G	401 841-5900	16222

DRUGS & DRUG PROPRIETARIES, WHOLESALE: Medicinals/ Botanicals

	CITY	ST	EMP	PHONE	ENTRY#
GE Healthcare Inc **(HQ)**	Marlborough	MA	B	732 457-8667	10152
Desert Harvest Inc	Ellsworth	ME	F	919 245-1853	4756

DRUGS & DRUG PROPRIETARIES, WHOLESALE: Pharmaceuticals

	CITY	ST	EMP	PHONE	ENTRY#
Frederick Purdue Company Inc **(PA)**	Stamford	CT	B	203 588-8000	3349
Knoa Pharma LLC **(PA)**	Stamford	CT	E	203 588-8000	3395
Pharmaceutical RES Assoc Inc	Stamford	CT	A	203 588-8000	3431
PRA Holdings Inc	Stamford	CT	A	203 853-0123	3435
Purdue Pharma LP **(HQ)**	Stamford	CT	C	203 588-8000	3439
Sheffield Pharmaceuticals LLC **(PA)**	New London	CT	C	860 442-4451	2233
Amylyx Pharmaceuticals Inc **(PA)**	Cambridge	MA	C	617 682-0917	7486
Batavia Biosciences Inc	Woburn	MA	G	781 305-3921	13521
Beigene Usa Inc **(HQ)**	Cambridge	MA	E	781 801-1887	7503
Central Admxture Phrm Svcs Inc	Woburn	MA	G	781 376-0032	13541
Corvidia Therapeutics Inc	Waltham	MA	G	781 205-4755	12642
Encyte Systems Inc	Braintree	MA	G	781 848-6772	7180
MBL International Corporation **(DH)**	Woburn	MA	F	781 939-6964	13607
Pure Encapsulations LLC	Sudbury	MA	E	800 753-2277	12269
Sobi Inc **(HQ)**	Waltham	MA	F	781 786-7370	12781
Westwell Incorporated **(DH)**	Wellesley	MA	D	800 753-2277	12948
G&G Technologies Inc	Coventry	RI	F	401 295-4000	15813
Surplus Solutions LLC	Woonsocket	RI	F	401 526-0055	16978

DRUGS & DRUG PROPRIETARIES, WHOLESALE: Vitamins & Minerals

	CITY	ST	EMP	PHONE	ENTRY#
Foodscience LLC **(HQ)**	Williston	VT	C	800 451-5190	17731

DRUGS ACTING ON THE CENTRAL NERVOUS SYSTEM & SENSE ORGANS

	CITY	ST	EMP	PHONE	ENTRY#
Biohaven Phrm Holdg Co Ltd **(HQ)**	New Haven	CT	D	203 404-0410	2129
Brands To Go Inc	Norwalk	CT	F		2476
Civitas Therapeutics Inc	Chelsea	MA	E	617 884-3004	7978
Elan Pharmaceuticals Inc	Cambridge	MA	A		7558
Euthymics Bioscience Inc	Cambridge	MA	F	617 758-0300	7567
Ptc Therapeutics Gt Inc	Cambridge	MA	E	781 799-9179	7691

DRUGS AFFECTING NEOPLASMS & ENDOCRINE SYSTEMS

	CITY	ST	EMP	PHONE	ENTRY#
Alcami Carolinas Corporation	Pepperell	MA	G	910 619-3952	11380
Alcami Carolinas Corporation	Pepperell	MA	G	910 619-3952	11381
Alcami Carolinas Corporation	Pepperell	MA	F	910 619-3952	11382
Alcami Carolinas Corporation	Shirley	MA	G	910 619-3952	11813
Alcami Carolinas Corporation	Amherst	NH	G	910 619-3952	13861

DRUGS: Parasitic & Infective Disease Affecting

	CITY	ST	EMP	PHONE	ENTRY#
Idenix Pharmaceuticals Inc **(HQ)**	Cambridge	MA	E	617 995-9800	7609
Trine Pharmaceuticals Inc	Newton	MA	F	617 558-8789	10791
Amgen Inc	West Greenwich	RI	D	401 392-1200	16882

DRUMS: Shipping, Metal

	CITY	ST	EMP	PHONE	ENTRY#
Mobile Mini Inc	Suffield	CT	G	860 668-1888	3594

	CITY	ST	EMP	PHONE	ENTRY#
DUCTING: Metal Plate					
L & L Mechanical LLC	Goshen	CT	F	860 491-4007	1303
DUCTING: Plastic					
Siftex Equipment Company	South Windsor	CT	E	860 289-8779	3179
DUCTS: Sheet Metal					
Buckley Associates Inc	Stratford	CT	G	203 380-2405	3524
General Sheet Metal Works Inc	Bridgeport	CT	F	203 333-6111	324
M & O Corporation	Bridgeport	CT	E	203 367-4292	345
Manufacturers Service Co Inc	Woodbridge	CT	G	203 389-9595	4381
Brideau Shtmtl Fabrication Inc	Leominster	MA	E	978 537-3372	9643
Buckley Associates Inc (PA)	Hanover	MA	D	781 878-5000	9027
Carl Fisher Co Inc	Springfield	MA	F	413 736-3661	12082
Dg Service Company Inc	Mattapoisett	MA	F	508 758-7906	10257
Duc-Pac Corporation	Springfield	MA	E	413 525-3302	12091
Gas Path Solutions LLC	Hubbardston	MA	F	978 229-5460	9348
Integrated Dynamic Metals Corp	Marlborough	MA	E	508 624-7271	10165
Spiral Air Manufacturing LLC	Derry	NH	G	603 624-6647	14208
McGill Airflow LLC	Bennington	VT	G	802 442-1900	17051
DUMPSTERS: Garbage					
Hayes Services LLC	East Lyme	CT	E	860 739-2273	1059
HI Stone & Son Inc	Southbury	CT	E	203 264-8656	3195
Fisher Contracting Corporation	Worcester	MA	F	508 421-6989	13723
Garbage Gone Inc	Barnstable	MA	G	508 737-4995	6200
Bear Pond Dumpster LLC	Turner	ME	G	207 224-0337	5560
Recycling Mechanical Neng LLC	Allenstown	NH	F	603 268-8028	13855
DUST OR FUME COLLECTING EQPT: Indl					
Hendrick Manufacturing Corp (PA)	Salem	MA	F	781 631-4400	11723
DYES & PIGMENTS: Organic					
Ferro Corporation	Williamstown	MA	F	413 743-3927	13366
Mra Laboratories Inc	Adams	MA	F	413 743-3927	5774
Walrus Enteprises LLC	Northampton	MA	G	413 587-1085	11085
Avient Colorants USA LLC	Lewiston	ME	B	207 784-0733	4951
Clariant Corporation	Coventry	RI	B	401 823-2000	15809
Teknor Color Company	Pawtucket	RI	E	401 725-8000	16421
EATING PLACES					
Capricorn Investors III LP (PA)	Greenwich	CT	F	203 861-6600	1326
If Not Now When Inc	Groton	CT	G	860 445-5276	1373
Olive Oil Factory LLC	Waterbury	CT	E	203 437-8286	3956
Sharpe Hill Vineyard Inc	Pomfret	CT	F	860 974-3549	2811
295 Tremont Inc	Attleboro	MA	D	508 222-2884	5985
Abp Corporation (PA)	Boston	MA	C	617 423-0629	6505
Amherst Brewing Co Inc	Amherst	MA	E	413 253-4400	5856
Barrel House Z LLC	Hingham	MA	E	617 480-2880	9142
Bay Colony Associates (PA)	Boston	MA	E	617 287-9100	6584
Cambridge Brewing Co Inc	Cambridge	MA	E	617 494-1994	7528
G H Bent Company	Milton	MA	D	617 322-9287	10452
Kookla Inc (PA)	Sturbridge	MA	E	508 347-2623	12251
Korner Bagel Partnership	Seekonk	MA	G	508 336-5204	11779
La Patisserie Inc	Revere	MA	E	781 729-9441	11621
Neovii Biotech Na Inc	Boston	MA	E	781 966-3830	6908
Paramount South Boston	Boston	MA	F	617 269-9999	6953
PDKD Enterprises Inc	Saugus	MA	E	781 233-8499	11764
Phillips Candy House Inc	Boston	MA	E	617 282-2090	6965
Piantedosi Baking Co Inc (PA)	Malden	MA	C	781 321-3400	10023
Rob Roy Foods Inc	Worcester	MA	G	508 755-8393	13784
Salt & Pepper	Worcester	MA	F	508 755-1113	13793
Sarro Cohasset Incorporated	Hull	MA	D	781 383-1704	9427
Slesar Bros Brewing Co Inc	Boston	MA	F	978 745-2337	7040
Sunday River Brewing Co Inc	Boston	MA	F	207 824-4253	7064
True North Ale Company LLC	Ipswich	MA	F	978 312-6473	9498
Ashleigh Inc (PA)	Kennebunk	ME	E	207 967-4311	4921
Wpf Liquidating Co Inc (PA)	York	ME	D	207 363-0612	5719
Federal Spice Corp (PA)	North Conway	NH	E	603 356-6381	15248
Nuttin Ordinary LLC	Peterborough	NH	F	603 567-7916	15322
Bennington Potters Inc (PA)	Bennington	VT	E	800 205-8033	17036
Community Apostolic Order Inc (PA)	Island Pond	VT	F	802 723-4452	17304
DC Enterprizes Inc	Hinesburg	VT	F	802 865-4480	17290
Lost Nation Brewing LLC	Morrisville	VT	F	802 851-8041	17385
McHolbe-Noonan Corporation	Burlington	VT	G	802 865-0500	17144
Nourish Llc	Saint Albans	VT	G	802 782-0012	17526
Simon Pearce (us) Inc	Quechee	VT	E	802 295-2711	17463
EDITING SVCS					
Nsight Inc	Andover	MA	E	781 273-6300	5902
EDITORIAL SVCS					
Scribliotech Inc	Orange	NH	G	603 306-9000	15280
EDUCATIONAL SVCS					
Harvard Debate Incorporated	Cambridge	MA	G	617 876-5003	7600
Massachstts Cntning Lgal Edcat	Boston	MA	E	617 482-2205	6871
Mathemtics Problem Solving LLC	South Portland	ME	D	207 772-2846	5508
DCI Training Inc	West Lebanon	NH	G	603 643-6066	15682
Nippon American Limited	East Greenwich	RI	F	401 885-7353	15992
Shelburne Farms	Shelburne	VT	D	802 985-8498	17562
ELECTRIC & OTHER SERVICES COMBINED					
Ace Residential Solar LLC	North Andover	MA	F	800 223-1462	10816
ELECTRIC MOTOR & GENERATOR AUXILIARY PARTS					
ACS Group Inc	Everett	MA	E	617 381-0822	8481
ELECTRIC MOTOR REPAIR SVCS					
B & J Electric Motor Repair Co Inc	Ansonia	CT	F	203 734-1695	8
Electric Enterprise Inc	Stratford	CT	F	203 378-7311	3534
Industrial Drives Contrls Inc (PA)	Waterbury	CT	F	203 753-5103	3921
Leppert/Nutmeg Inc	Bloomfield	CT	F	860 243-1737	188
Nepv LLC	Niantic	CT	F	860 739-2200	2358
Palmers Elc Mtrs & Pumps Inc	Norwalk	CT	G	203 348-7378	2551
Precision Devices Inc (PA)	Wallingford	CT	F	203 265-9308	3839
Reliable Electric Motor Inc	Hartford	CT	F	860 522-2257	1505
Schulz Electric Company	New Haven	CT	C	203 562-5811	2195
Traver Electric Motor Co Inc	Waterbury	CT	E	203 753-5103	3974
Anchor Electric LLC	Agawam	MA	E	413 786-6788	5778
First Electric Motor Svc Inc	Woburn	MA	E	781 491-1100	13567
General Electric Company	Medford	MA	G	781 396-9600	10286
New England Elc Mtr Svc Corp	Chelsea	MA	E	617 884-9200	7988
Potomac Electric Corp	Boston	MA	F	617 364-0400	6970
Ralco Electric Inc	Westport	MA	D	508 679-3363	13299
Reliance Electric Svc Co Inc	Holyoke	MA	G	413 533-3557	9276
Stearns Perry & Smith Company	Quincy	MA	E	617 423-4775	11539
AC Electric Corp	Bangor	ME	F	207 945-9487	4487
Maine Industrial Repair Service Inc	Augusta	ME	E	207 623-7500	4476
Motor Power Inc	Lewiston	ME	E	207 782-0616	4977
Prime Electric Motors	Gorham	ME	F	207 591-7800	4833
Timken Motor & Crane Svcs LLC	Portland	ME	F	207 699-2501	5284
Chase Electric Motors LLC	Bedford	NH	G	603 669-2565	13921
Leo Algers NH Elc Mtrs Inc	Laconia	NH	G	603 524-3729	14658
Rays Electric & Gen Contg Inc	Berlin	NH	F	603 752-1370	13985
Atlantic Automation Group LLC	Bristol	RI	E	401 424-1840	15754
Delta-Electro Power LLC	Cranston	RI	E	401 944-8350	15848
Pioneer Motors and Drives Inc	South Burlington	VT	F	802 651-0114	17591
ELECTRIC POWER DISTRIBUTION TO CONSUMERS					
Maine & Maritimes Corporation (PA)	Presque Isle	ME	F	207 760-2499	5304
Granite Shore Power LLC	Bow	NH	C	603 634-2299	13999
National Grid USA Svc Co Inc	Providence	RI	A	401 784-7224	16573
ELECTRIC POWER GENERATION: Fossil Fuel					
GE Steam Power Inc (HQ)	Windsor	CT	A	866 257-8664	4279
ELECTRIC SERVICES					
Direct Energy Inc (HQ)	Stamford	CT	E	800 260-0300	3338
Ace Residential Solar LLC	North Andover	MA	F	800 223-1462	10816
ELECTRIC SVCS, NEC: Power Generation					
Atlantic Pwr US GP Hldings Inc	Dedham	MA	G	617 977-2400	8236
Intercntnental Enrgy Group LLC	Hingham	MA	G	781 749-9800	9151
National Grid USA Svc Co Inc (DH)	Waltham	MA	G	800 260-0054	12734
Tecomet Inc	Woburn	MA	A	781 782-6400	13675
Simon Pearce (us) Inc (PA)	Windsor	VT	C	802 674-6280	17762
ELECTRICAL APPARATUS & EQPT WHOLESALERS					
Asea Brown Boveri Inc	Norwalk	CT	A	203 750-2200	2465
Hartford Fire Equipment	Plainville	CT	F	860 747-2757	2763
Joining Technologies LLC	East Granby	CT	D	860 653-0111	937
On Line Building Systems LLC	Danbury	CT	G	203 798-1194	792
Pathway Lighting Products Inc	Old Saybrook	CT	D	860 388-6881	2659
Precision Devices Inc (PA)	Wallingford	CT	F	203 265-9308	3839
Copley Global Services LLC	Waltham	MA	G	617 970-9617	12641
Lloyd & Bouvier Inc	Clinton	MA	E	978 365-5700	8082
Micro-Lite Inc	Three Rivers	MA	F	413 289-1313	12429
Multi-Concept Inc	Mansfield	MA	F	508 366-7676	10067
Period Lighting Fixtures Inc	Clarksburg	MA	F	413 664-7141	8072
Phoenix Electric Corp	Canton	MA	E	781 821-0200	7819
Polytec Inc	Hudson	MA	G	508 417-1040	9401

Employee Codes: A=Over 500 employees, B=251-500
C=101-250, D=51-100, E=20-50, F=10-19, G=1-9

2024 Harris New England
Manufacturers Directory

1383

PRODUCT

	CITY	ST	EMP	PHONE	ENTRY#
Schneider Electric Usa Inc **(DH)**	Boston	MA	A	978 975-9600	7026
Schneider Electric Usa Inc	Foxboro	MA	E	508 549-3385	8724
Soitec Usa Inc **(HQ)**	Gloucester	MA	G	978 531-2222	8958
Enercon	Auburn	ME	E	207 657-7001	4429
Enercon **(HQ)**	Gray	ME	D	207 657-7000	4841
Burndy Americas Inc **(HQ)**	Manchester	NH	B	603 647-5000	14822
Burndy Americas Intl Holdg LLC	Manchester	NH	A	603 647-5000	14823
Hubbell Incorporated	Londonderry	NH	E	800 346-4175	14756
Eaton Corporation	Rumford	RI	E	401 473-2214	16666
Walco Electric Company	Providence	RI	D	401 467-6500	16642

ELECTRICAL DISCHARGE MACHINING, EDM

	CITY	ST	EMP	PHONE	ENTRY#
Arcade Technology LLC	Bridgeport	CT	D	203 366-3871	297
G L C Inc	Watertown	CT	F	860 945-6166	4013
Quality Wire Edm Inc	Bristol	CT	G	860 583-9867	487
Tektron Inc	Topsfield	MA	F	978 887-0091	12439
Hagan Design and Machine Inc	Newmarket	NH	F	603 292-1101	15220
Newport Tool & Die Inc	Middletown	RI	F	401 847-6711	16181

ELECTRICAL EQPT REPAIR SVCS

	CITY	ST	EMP	PHONE	ENTRY#
Leppert/Nutmeg Inc	Bloomfield	CT	E	860 243-1737	188
On Line Building Systems LLC	Danbury	CT	G	203 798-1194	792
Dover Flexo Electronics Inc	Rochester	NH	E	603 332-6150	15475
Walco Electric Company	Providence	RI	D	401 467-6500	16642

ELECTRICAL EQPT REPAIR SVCS: High Voltage

	CITY	ST	EMP	PHONE	ENTRY#
Wasik Associates Inc	Dracut	MA	F	978 454-9787	8314

ELECTRICAL EQPT: Automotive, NEC

	CITY	ST	EMP	PHONE	ENTRY#
BBA Remanufacturing Inc	Taunton	MA	E	508 822-4490	12325
Magna Elec Roadscape Auto LLC **(HQ)**	Lowell	MA	G	978 656-2500	9901
Magna Electronics LLC	Lowell	MA	C	978 674-6500	9902
Veoneer Roadscape Auto Inc	Lowell	MA	G	978 656-2500	9934
Hubbell Incorporated	Manchester	NH	F	603 647-5000	14860
Antaya Inc	Warwick	RI	E	401 941-7050	16780
Antaya Technologies Corp	Warwick	RI	C	401 921-3197	16781

ELECTRICAL GOODS, WHOLESALE: Air Conditioning Appliances

	CITY	ST	EMP	PHONE	ENTRY#
Economy Plumbing & Htg Sup Co	Mattapan	MA	E	617 433-1200	10254

ELECTRICAL GOODS, WHOLESALE: Cable Conduit

	CITY	ST	EMP	PHONE	ENTRY#
Underground Systems Inc **(PA)**	Bethel	CT	E	203 792-3444	138

ELECTRICAL GOODS, WHOLESALE: Electrical Entertainment Eqpt

	CITY	ST	EMP	PHONE	ENTRY#
Philips Holding USA Inc **(HQ)**	Cambridge	MA	A	978 687-1501	7686

ELECTRICAL GOODS, WHOLESALE: Electronic Parts

	CITY	ST	EMP	PHONE	ENTRY#
Midstate Electronics Co	Wallingford	CT	F	203 265-9900	3832
Mil-Con Inc	Naugatuck	CT	F	630 595-2366	1971
Park Distributories Inc	Bridgeport	CT	D	203 366-7200	355
Park Distributories Inc **(PA)**	Bridgeport	CT	G	203 579-2140	357
Servers Storage Networking LLC	Norwalk	CT	G	203 433-0808	2570
Wanho Manufacturing LLC	Cheshire	CT	E	203 759-3744	621
Cbm Industries Inc	Taunton	MA	E	508 821-4555	12326
Heilind Electronics Inc **(PA)**	Wilmington	MA	D	978 657-4870	13410
Jem Electronics Inc	Franklin	MA	C	508 520-3105	8845
Mainstream Global Inc	Lawrence	MA	E	978 682-6767	9579
Psjl Corporation	Billerica	MA	E	978 313-2500	6474
Rochester Electronics LLC **(PA)**	Newburyport	MA	C	978 462-9332	10715
Intelligent Mfg Solutons LLC	Manchester	NH	E	603 296-1160	14864
Signature Cable Mfg Tech Inc	Cranston	RI	E	401 383-1008	15910

ELECTRICAL GOODS, WHOLESALE: Generators

	CITY	ST	EMP	PHONE	ENTRY#
Ac/DC Industrial Electric LLC	Bozrah	CT	G	860 886-2232	225
Cummins Northeast LLC **(HQ)**	Braintree	MA	E	781 801-1700	7176
Gowen Inc	Portland	ME	F	207 773-1761	5219
Chase Electric Motors LLC	Bedford	NH	G	603 669-2565	13921

ELECTRICAL GOODS, WHOLESALE: Lighting Fittings & Access

	CITY	ST	EMP	PHONE	ENTRY#
Fluorolite Plastics LLC	Hudson	MA	G	508 788-1200	9368

ELECTRICAL GOODS, WHOLESALE: Security Control Eqpt & Systems

	CITY	ST	EMP	PHONE	ENTRY#
Razberi Technologies Inc	Danbury	CT	E	469 828-3380	804
Critical Cmmnctons Cntrls Inst	Exeter	NH	F		14290
Klein Marine Systems Inc	Salem	NH	D	603 893-6131	15540

ELECTRICAL GOODS, WHOLESALE: Semiconductor Devices

	CITY	ST	EMP	PHONE	ENTRY#
Bruce Technologies Inc	North Billerica	MA	F	978 670-5501	10901
Semigear Inc	Wakefield	MA	E	781 213-3066	12534
Stmicroelectronics Inc	Burlington	MA	G	781 861-2650	7435
Varian Semicdtr Eqp Assoc Inc **(HQ)**	Gloucester	MA	C	978 282-2000	8963

	CITY	ST	EMP	PHONE	ENTRY#
Asml Us LLC	Westbrook	ME	G	207 541-5000	5615
Marvell Gvrnment Solutions LLC	Burlington	VT	E	845 245-8066	17143

ELECTRICAL GOODS, WHOLESALE: Signaling, Eqpt

	CITY	ST	EMP	PHONE	ENTRY#
SES America Inc	Warwick	RI	F	401 232-3370	16861

ELECTRICAL GOODS, WHOLESALE: Telephone & Telegraphic Eqpt

	CITY	ST	EMP	PHONE	ENTRY#
Tech II Business Services Inc	Rocky Hill	CT	E	518 587-1565	2936

ELECTRICAL GOODS, WHOLESALE: Telephone Eqpt

	CITY	ST	EMP	PHONE	ENTRY#
Southern Neng Telecom Corp **(HQ)**	New Haven	CT	B	203 771-5200	2203
Total Communications Inc **(PA)**	East Hartford	CT	D	860 282-9999	1028

ELECTRICAL GOODS, WHOLESALE: Wire & Cable

	CITY	ST	EMP	PHONE	ENTRY#
Autac Incorporated **(PA)**	Branford	CT	G	203 481-3444	238
Marmon Engnered Wire Cable LLC	Hartford	CT	F	860 653-8300	1491
Rel-Tech Electronics Inc	Milford	CT	D	203 877-8770	1876
Specialty Cable Corp	Wallingford	CT	D	203 265-7126	3852
Bay State Wire & Cable Co Inc	Lowell	MA	E	978 454-2444	9861
James Monroe Wire & Cable Corp **(PA)**	South Lancaster	MA	F	978 368-0131	11971
Burndy LLC **(DH)**	Manchester	NH	B	603 647-5000	14824
Igus Bearings Inc **(HQ)**	Rumford	RI	C	800 521-2747	16669

ELECTRICAL GOODS, WHOLESALE: Wire & Cable, Electronic

	CITY	ST	EMP	PHONE	ENTRY#
Phoenix Company of Chicago Inc **(PA)**	Naugatuck	CT	D	630 595-2300	1980
Times Wire and Cable Company **(HQ)**	Wallingford	CT	D	203 949-8400	3867
Miraco Inc	Manchester	NH	E	603 665-9449	14890

ELECTRICAL SPLYS

	CITY	ST	EMP	PHONE	ENTRY#
Circuit Breaker Sales Ne LLC	Seymour	CT	D	203 888-7500	2958
Mil-Con Inc	Naugatuck	CT	F	630 595-2366	1971
Traver Electric Motor Co Inc	Waterbury	CT	E	203 753-5103	3974
Concord Electric Supply Ltd	Hyannis	MA	A	774 552-2185	9432
Concord Electric Supply Ltd	Nantucket	MA	A	774 325-5142	10461
Infra-Red Bldg & Pwr Svc Inc **(PA)**	Holbrook	MA	E	781 767-0888	9175
Needham Electric Supply LLC **(DH)**	Canton	MA	D	781 828-9494	7811
Newton Distributing Co Inc	Natick	MA	F	617 969-4002	10488

ELECTRICAL SUPPLIES: Porcelain

	CITY	ST	EMP	PHONE	ENTRY#
Coorstek Inc	East Granby	CT	C	860 653-8071	932
Accumet Engineering Corp	Devens	MA	E	978 568-8311	8266
Coorstek Inc	Worcester	MA	B	774 317-2600	13710
Idex Health & Science LLC	Middleboro	MA	C	774 213-0200	10362
Ceramco Inc	Center Conway	NH	E	603 447-2090	14050
Coorstek Inc	Milford	NH	D	603 673-7560	15019
Superior Tchncal Ceramics Corp **(HQ)**	Saint Albans	VT	C	802 527-7726	17533

ELECTROMEDICAL EQPT

	CITY	ST	EMP	PHONE	ENTRY#
Atlantic Inertial Systems Inc	Cheshire	CT	C	203 250-3500	573
Bartron Medical Imaging LLC	New Haven	CT	G	203 498-2184	2124
Bio-Med Devices Inc	Guilford	CT	D	203 458-0202	1386
Coopersurgical Inc **(DH)**	Trumbull	CT	C	203 601-5200	3716
Digirad Health LLC	Old Greenwich	CT	B	800 947-6134	2632
General Electric Company	Norwalk	CT	A	203 797-0840	2504
General Electric Company	Stamford	CT	F	866 419-4096	3354
Hobbs Medical Inc	Stafford Springs	CT	E	860 684-5875	3256
Hyperfine Inc **(PA)**	Guilford	CT	C	203 458-7100	1395
Industrial Magnetics Inc	Windsor	CT	D	508 853-3232	4283
Integrated Medical Systems Inc	Gales Ferry	CT	F	860 949-2929	1260
Philips Ultrasound Inc	Waterbury	CT	C	203 753-5215	3960
Star Equity Holdings Inc **(PA)**	Old Greenwich	CT	D	203 489-9500	2635
Walker Magnetics Group Inc	Windsor	CT	D	508 853-3232	4314
Abiomed Cardiovascular Inc	Danvers	MA	D	978 777-5410	8158
Adeza Biomedical Corp	Marlborough	MA	F	508 263-8390	10104
AGFA Healthcare Corporation	Canton	MA	D	978 284-7900	7766
Arrhythmia Research Technology	Fitchburg	MA	F	978 602-1436	8642
Axya Medical Inc	Beverly	MA	F	978 232-9997	6331
Cambridge Heart Inc **(PA)**	Foxborough	MA	F	978 654-7600	8734
Candela Medical Inc	Marlborough	MA	A	508 358-7400	10128
Cardiofocus Inc	Marlborough	MA	E	508 658-7200	10129
Csa Medical Inc	Lexington	MA	D	443 921-8053	9734
Cytyc Corporation	Marlborough	MA	E	508 303-4746	10140
Cytyc Corporation **(HQ)**	Marlborough	MA	B	508 263-2900	10141
Cytyc Surgical Products LLC **(HQ)**	Marlborough	MA	E	508 263-2900	10142
Delsys Inc	Natick	MA	D	508 545-8200	10477
Diagnosys LLC **(PA)**	Lowell	MA	F	978 458-1600	9875
Docbox Inc	Waltham	MA	F	978 987-2569	12654
Eldersafe Technologies Inc	Harvard	MA	E	617 852-3018	9062
Electrosonics Medical Inc	Boston	MA	G	216 357-3310	6711
En-Pro Management Inc	Chelmsford	MA	F	866 352-5433	7926
General Electric Company **(PA)**	Boston	MA	A	617 443-3000	6754
Gentuity LLC	Sudbury	MA	E	978 202-4108	12267

(G-0000) Company's Geographic Section entry number

	CITY	ST	EMP	PHONE	ENTRY#
Haemonetics Asia Incorporated (HQ)	Braintree	MA	F	781 848-7100	7186
Haemonetics Corporation (PA)	Boston	MA	A	781 848-7100	6780
Hologic Foreign Sales Corp	Marlborough	MA	A	781 999-7300	10160
Hologic Sales and Service LLC	Marlborough	MA	A	508 263-2900	10161
Infraredx Inc	Bedford	MA	D	781 221-0053	6232
L3 Technologies Inc	Northampton	MA	A	413 586-2330	11069
Lake Region Manufacturing Inc (HQ)	Wilmington	MA	A	952 361-2515	13423
Lantos Technologies Inc	Foxboro	MA	G	781 443-7633	8706
M-R Resources Inc	Fitchburg	MA	E	978 345-9010	8659
Medical Products Mfg LLC	West Wareham	MA	F	508 291-1830	13069
Medtronic Inc	Danvers	MA	F	978 777-0042	8207
Medtronic Inc	Danvers	MA	E	978 739-3080	8208
Mettlr-Tledo Prcess Anlytics I	Billerica	MA	D	781 301-8800	6461
Micro-Leads Inc	Somerville	MA	F	617 580-3030	11886
Pendar Technologies LLC (PA)	Cambridge	MA	F	617 588-2128	7682
Precision Optics Corp Inc (PA)	Gardner	MA	D	978 630-1800	8898
Proven Process Med Dvcs Inc	Mansfield	MA	D	508 261-0800	10072
Pyramid Technical Cons Inc	Waltham	MA	F	781 402-1700	12755
Radiation Monitoring Dvcs Inc (HQ)	Watertown	MA	E	617 668-6800	12902
Respiratory Motion Inc	Watertown	MA	E	508 954-2706	12904
Respironics Novametrix LLC	Andover	MA	A	724 882-4120	5911
Revvity Inc (PA)	Waltham	MA	C	781 663-6900	12767
Smith & Nephew Endoscopy Inc	Andover	MA	C	978 749-1000	5924
Suros Surgical Systems Inc	Marlborough	MA	D	508 263-2900	10220
Tenacity Medical Inc	Lexington	MA	G	617 299-8001	9786
Thermo Envmtl Instrs LLC (HQ)	Franklin	MA	C	508 520-0430	8868
Thermo Fisher Scientific Inc (PA)	Waltham	MA	C	781 622-1000	12800
Thoratec LLC	Burlington	MA	C	781 272-0139	7439
Thoratec LLC	Burlington	MA	C	781 272-0139	7440
Transmedics Inc (PA)	Andover	MA	C	978 552-0443	5931
Tsi Liquidation Inc	Hudson	MA	E	978 567-9033	9421
Viking Systems Inc	Westborough	MA	E	508 366-3668	13143
Vita Needle Company	Needham	MA	E	781 444-1780	10529
Zoll Medical Corporation	Burlington	MA	C	781 229-0020	7451
Zoll Medical Corporation	Chelmsford	MA	E	978 421-9132	7971
Artel Inc	Westbrook	ME	E	207 854-0860	5614
David Saunders Inc	South Portland	ME	E	207 228-1888	5497
Electrnic Mobility Contrls LLC	Augusta	ME	F	207 512-8009	4471
Fhc Inc (PA)	Bowdoin	ME	D	207 666-8190	4605
Vuetek Scientific LLC	Gray	ME	G	207 657-6565	4844
Cytyc Corporation	Londonderry	NH	E	603 668-7688	14741
Memtec Corporation	Amherst	NH	F	603 893-8080	13880
Monarch International Inc	Amherst	NH	E	603 883-3390	13881
Sleepnet Corp	Hampton	NH	E	603 758-6600	14412
Criticare Technologies Inc	Warwick	RI	E	401 667-3837	16800
Hanna Instruments Inc (PA)	Woonsocket	RI	E	401 765-7500	16962
Zoll Medical Corporation	Pawtucket	RI	B	401 729-1400	16432
Raj Communications Ltd	Essex Junction	VT	E	802 658-4961	17243

ELECTROMEDICAL EQPT WHOLESALERS

	CITY	ST	EMP	PHONE	ENTRY#
Third Pole Inc (PA)	Waltham	MA	F	908 310-0596	12803

ELECTROMETALLURGICAL PRDTS

	CITY	ST	EMP	PHONE	ENTRY#
Newton Materion Inc (HQ)	Newton	MA	C	617 630-5800	10772
Purecoat International LLC	Belmont	MA	E	561 844-0100	6309

ELECTRON TUBES

	CITY	ST	EMP	PHONE	ENTRY#
Connecticut Coining Inc	Bethel	CT	D	203 743-3861	103
Whelen Engineering Company Inc (PA)	Chester	CT	B	860 526-9504	634
Adaptas Solutions LLC (PA)	Palmer	MA	E	413 284-9975	11269
Photonis Scientific Inc (DH)	Sturbridge	MA	F	508 347-4000	12257
Osram Sylvania Inc	Exeter	NH	B	603 772-4331	14299
Narragansett Imaging Usa LLC	North Smithfield	RI	E	401 762-3800	16328

ELECTRONIC DETECTION SYSTEMS: Aeronautical

	CITY	ST	EMP	PHONE	ENTRY#
Atk Space Systems LLC	Hopkinton	MA	D	508 497-9457	9308
Raytheon Company	Andover	MA	C	978 470-5000	5909

ELECTRONIC DEVICES: Solid State, NEC

	CITY	ST	EMP	PHONE	ENTRY#
Delcom Products Inc	Danbury	CT	G	914 934-5170	729
Servers Storage Networking LLC	Norwalk	CT	G	203 433-0808	2570
Aetruim Incorporated	Billerica	MA	E	651 773-4200	6397
Apple Mill Holding Company Inc	Pembroke	MA	F	781 826-9706	11358
Atlas Devices LLC	Chelmsford	MA	F	617 415-1657	7913
Borgwarner Massachusetts Inc (HQ)	Northborough	MA	E	508 281-5500	11092
Forward Photonics LLC	Woburn	MA	F	978 224-5488	13569
Orbotech Inc (DH)	Billerica	MA	D	978 667-6037	6466
Yankee Electrical Mfg Co	Wilbraham	MA	G	413 596-8256	13364

ELECTRONIC EQPT REPAIR SVCS

	CITY	ST	EMP	PHONE	ENTRY#
Hyaxiom Inc (HQ)	East Hartford	CT	E	860 727-2200	998
N C T Inc	Colchester	CT	F	860 666-8424	662

	CITY	ST	EMP	PHONE	ENTRY#
Applied Dynamics Corporation (PA)	Greenfield	MA	E	413 774-7268	8981
L T X International Inc	Norwood	MA	D	781 461-1000	11189

ELECTRONIC LOADS & POWER SPLYS

	CITY	ST	EMP	PHONE	ENTRY#
Topex Inc	Danbury	CT	F	203 748-5918	825
Csr Technology Inc	Burlington	MA	E	781 791-6000	7356
Tmd Technologies LLC	Beverly	MA	C	978 922-6000	6390
Vicor Corporation (PA)	Andover	MA	A	978 470-2900	5933
Xp Power LLC	Salem	NH	F	603 894-4420	15574
Fpp Holdings LLC	Cranston	RI	F	401 684-1443	15862
Ritronics Inc	Warwick	RI	F	401 732-8175	16852
Village of Orleans	Orleans	VT	G	802 754-8584	17440

ELECTRONIC PARTS & EQPT WHOLESALERS

	CITY	ST	EMP	PHONE	ENTRY#
Carrier Fire SEC Americas Corp	Farmington	CT	E	941 739-4200	1211
Fiberoptics Technology Inc (PA)	Pomfret	CT	C	860 928-0443	2807
Marco International Inc	Ridgefield	CT	D	203 894-8000	2902
Radio Frequency Systems Inc (DH)	Meriden	CT	E	203 630-3311	1690
Anderson Power Products Inc (HQ)	Sterling	MA	D	978 422-3600	12154
Assocted Electro-Mechanics Inc	Springfield	MA	C	413 781-4276	12076
Electrochem Solutions Inc	Raynham	MA	C	781 575-0800	11589
Elpakco Inc (PA)	Westford	MA	F	978 392-0400	13235
Etchomatic Inc	Lowell	MA	F	978 656-0011	9877
Ideal Industries Inc	Sterling	MA	G	978 422-3600	12163
Magellan Distribution Corp	Boston	MA	F	617 399-7900	6868
Orbotech Inc (DH)	Billerica	MA	D	978 667-6037	6466
Rf Aero LLC	New Bedford	MA	E	508 910-3500	10646
Static Clean International Inc	North Billerica	MA	F	781 229-7799	10960
Tdl Inc	Canton	MA	E	781 828-3366	7833
Comnav Engineering Inc	Portland	ME	E	207 221-8524	5201
CTS Corporation	Londonderry	NH	D	603 421-2546	14740
Ferrite Microwave Tech LLC	Nashua	NH	E	603 881-5234	15100
Gowanda Rcd LLC	Manchester	NH	C	716 532-2234	14853
Insulectro	Londonderry	NH	E	603 629-4403	14757
Prime Power Inc	Hampstead	NH	E	603 329-4675	14390
Rme Filters Inc	Amherst	NH	F	603 595-4573	13887
Xma Corporation	Manchester	NH	D	603 222-2256	14961
Advanced Interconnections Corp	West Warwick	RI	D	401 823-5200	16898
Andon Electronics Corporation	Lincoln	RI	E	401 333-0388	16119
Galvion Ballistics Ltd	Essex Junction	VT	D	802 334-2774	17233

ELECTRONIC SHOPPING

	CITY	ST	EMP	PHONE	ENTRY#
Kent Scientific Corporation	Torrington	CT	F	860 626-1172	3688
Mountain Corporation (HQ)	Keene	NH	E	603 355-2272	14610
Merchbro Inc	Pawtucket	RI	F	866 428-0095	16387

ELECTRONIC TRAINING DEVICES

	CITY	ST	EMP	PHONE	ENTRY#
Wrapsol LLC	Canton	MA	E		7843

ELECTROPLATING & PLATING SVC

	CITY	ST	EMP	PHONE	ENTRY#
Gybenorth Industries LLC	Milford	CT	F	203 876-9876	1832
Jarvis Precision Polishing	Bristol	CT	F	860 589-5822	458
Bay State Plating Inc	Holyoke	MA	E	413 533-6927	9243
Fountain Plating Company LLC	West Springfield	MA	D	413 781-4651	13025
Luster-On Products Inc	Springfield	MA	F	413 739-2541	12111
Pure Source LLC	Durham	NH	F	626 442-6784	14267

ELEVATORS & EQPT

	CITY	ST	EMP	PHONE	ENTRY#
Ascend Elevator Inc	Bloomfield	CT	D	215 703-0358	148
Bay State Elevator Company Inc	Bloomfield	CT	F	860 243-9030	150
K-Tech International Inc	Torrington	CT	E	860 489-9399	3687
Otis Elevator Company (HQ)	Farmington	CT	C	860 674-3000	1235
Bay State Elevator Company Inc (HQ)	Agawam	MA	E	413 786-7000	5779
Gillespie Corporation	Ware	MA	E	413 967-4980	12825
Hamilton Elevator Interiors	Saugus	MA	F	781 233-9540	11759
Keystone Elev Svc Mdrnztion LL	Weymouth	MA	G	781 340-3860	13328
Otis Elevator Company	Auburn	MA	F	401 232-7282	6122

ELEVATORS WHOLESALERS

	CITY	ST	EMP	PHONE	ENTRY#
Otis Elevator Company	Bloomfield	CT	B	860 242-3632	198
Otis Elevator Company	Auburn	MA	F	401 232-7282	6122

ELEVATORS: Installation & Conversion

	CITY	ST	EMP	PHONE	ENTRY#
Bay State Elevator Company Inc	Bloomfield	CT	F	860 243-9030	150
Otis Elevator Company	Bloomfield	CT	B	860 242-3632	198
Otis Elevator Company (HQ)	Farmington	CT	C	860 674-3000	1235
Stevenson Group Corporation	Harwinton	CT	F	860 689-0011	1524
Bay State Elevator Company Inc (HQ)	Agawam	MA	E	413 786-7000	5779
Draper Elevator Cab Co Inc	Holbrook	MA	F	781 961-3146	9171

EMBLEMS: Embroidered

	CITY	ST	EMP	PHONE	ENTRY#
Athletic Emblem Lettering Inc	Springfield	MA	F	413 733-8151	12078

PRODUCT

	CITY	ST	EMP	PHONE	ENTRY#
G & G Silk Screening	Plymouth	MA	G	508 830-1075	11460
Rodco Enterprises	Lewiston	ME	F	207 786-2931	4990
Woodland Studios Inc	Ellsworth	ME	F	207 667-3286	4761

EMBROIDERY ADVERTISING SVCS

	CITY	ST	EMP	PHONE	ENTRY#
Chillybear Inc (PA)	Needham	MA	F	781 455-6321	10507
Corporate Casuals LLC	Concord	MA	F	978 369-5935	8110
Three Twins Productions Inc	Watertown	MA	G	617 926-0377	12914
BBH Apparrel	Boothbay Harbor	ME	F	207 633-0601	4601
Classsick Custom LLC	Pawtucket	RI	F	401 475-7288	16355
Parsonskellogg LLC	East Providence	RI	D	866 602-8398	16037

EMBROIDERY KITS

	CITY	ST	EMP	PHONE	ENTRY#
Callenstitch LLC	Concord	MA	F	978 369-9080	8107

EMERGENCY ALARMS

	CITY	ST	EMP	PHONE	ENTRY#
Nutmeg Utility Products Inc (PA)	Cheshire	CT	E	203 250-8802	609
Fall Prevention Alarms Inc	Southbridge	MA	G	508 765-5050	12016
General Dynmics Mssion Systems	Needham Heights	MA	D	954 846-3000	10549
Lifeline Systems Company (HQ)	Framingham	MA	A	855 600-6127	8787
Philips Hlthcare Infrmtics Inc	Marlborough	MA	F	508 988-1000	10195
Signal Communications Corp	Woburn	MA	E	781 933-0998	13666
Simplex Time Recorder LLC (DH)	Westminster	MA	C		13278
Visonic Inc (HQ)	Westford	MA	E	860 243-0833	13267

ENCLOSURES: Electronic

	CITY	ST	EMP	PHONE	ENTRY#
Touche Manufacturing Company	Glastonbury	CT	F	860 254-5080	1299
Barber Elc Enclosures Mfg Inc	North Attleboro	MA	F	508 699-4872	10867
Schroff Inc (HQ)	Warwick	RI	B	763 204-7700	16859

ENCODERS: Digital

	CITY	ST	EMP	PHONE	ENTRY#
Catalog Technologies Inc	Boston	MA	F	617 768-7222	6641
Zeevee Inc (PA)	Littleton	MA	E	978 467-1395	9847

ENDOCRINE PRDTS

	CITY	ST	EMP	PHONE	ENTRY#
Ipsen Biopharmaceuticals Inc (HQ)	Cambridge	MA	C	973 903-4442	7617

ENGINEERING SVCS

	CITY	ST	EMP	PHONE	ENTRY#
Apcompower Inc (PA)	Windsor	CT	E	860 688-1911	4260
Asea Brown Boveri Inc	Norwalk	CT	A	203 750-2200	2465
Connecticut Analytical Corp	Bethany	CT	F	203 393-9666	92
Cs Group - Usa Inc	East Hartford	CT	E	860 944-0041	983
Electric Boat Corporation (HQ)	Groton	CT	B	860 433-3000	1370
Electric Boat Corporation	Groton	CT	A	860 433-3000	1371
Engineered Fibers Tech LLC	Shelton	CT	F	203 922-1810	3005
ESI Electronic Products Corp	Prospect	CT	E	203 758-4401	2834
GE Steam Power Inc (HQ)	Windsor	CT	A	866 257-8664	4279
General Digital Corporation	East Hartford	CT	D	860 282-2900	996
General Dynamics Info Tech Inc	Pawcatuck	CT	D	860 441-2400	2720
Goldenrod Corporation	Beacon Falls	CT	E	203 723-4400	40
Henkel Loctite Corporation (DH)	Rocky Hill	CT	D	860 571-5100	2925
John Zink Company LLC	Shelton	CT	E	203 925-0380	3025
Jonal Laboratories Inc	Meriden	CT	D	203 634-4444	1671
Mike Sadlak	Coventry	CT	G	860 742-0227	680
Pta Corporation (PA)	Oxford	CT	D	203 888-0585	2709
Rite-Solutions Inc (PA)	Pawcatuck	CT	F	401 847-3399	2725
Seals-It Inc	Ellington	CT	G	860 979-0060	1114
Stanley Engnered Fastening LLC (HQ)	Danbury	CT	C	800 783-6427	821
Vector Engineering Inc	Mystic	CT	F	860 572-0422	1944
Veolia Es Tchncal Slutions LLC	Danbury	CT	F	203 748-9116	832
Vertafore Inc	Windsor	CT	E	860 602-6000	4312
2is Inc	Walpole	MA	E	508 850-7520	12545
Ae Red Holdings LLC (PA)	Marlborough	MA	F	561 372-7820	10105
B & E Group LLC	Southwick	MA	E	413 569-5585	12041
Bluecatbio MA Inc	Concord	MA	F	978 405-2533	8106
Chemical Systems Services Inc	Attleboro	MA	F	508 431-9995	6003
Comdel Inc	Gloucester	MA	F	978 282-0620	8930
Concepts Nrec LLC	Chelmsford	MA	F	781 935-9050	7920
Dale Engineering & Son Inc	Bedford	MA	F	781 541-6055	6221
Division 15 Hvac Inc	Pembroke	MA	E	781 285-3115	11363
GE Vernova International LLC (HQ)	Cambridge	MA	C	617 443-3000	7580
Graphite Insulg Systems Inc	Gardner	MA	F	978 630-8988	8890
Improved Consumer Products Inc	North Attleboro	MA	F	508 695-6841	10875
Makers Tool and Mfg Co LLC	Oxford	MA	F	774 633-0658	11261
Marblehead Engineering	Essex	MA	F	978 432-1386	8477
Medsource Tech Holdings LLC (DH)	Wilmington	MA	F	978 570-6900	13428
Nn Inc	Mansfield	MA	E	508 406-2100	10070
Nypro Inc (HQ)	Clinton	MA	A	978 365-9721	8087
Onyx Environmental Svcs LLC (DH)	Boston	MA	F	617 849-6600	6936
Optikos Corporation	Wakefield	MA	D	617 354-7557	12525
Physical Sciences Inc (PA)	Andover	MA	D	978 689-0003	5907
Product Resources LLC	Newburyport	MA	E	978 524-8500	10709

	CITY	ST	EMP	PHONE	ENTRY#
Proto XYZ Inc	New Bedford	MA	G	508 525-6363	10644
Repjtm LLC	Mansfield	MA	E	508 406-2100	10074
Schneider Elc Systems USA Inc	Foxboro	MA	F	508 543-8750	8719
Surmet Corp (PA)	Burlington	MA	E	781 345-5721	7436
Triangle Engineering Inc	Hanover	MA	F	781 878-1500	9046
US Nortek Inc	Worcester	MA	F	774 314-4006	13817
Vacuum Process Technology LLC	Cambridge	MA	E	508 732-7200	7749
Xp Power LLC	Gloucester	MA	D	978 282-0620	8965
Cascades Auburn Fiber Inc	Auburn	ME	E	207 753-5300	4423
Comnav Engineering Inc	Portland	ME	E	207 221-8524	5201
Enercon (HQ)	Gray	ME	D	207 657-7000	4841
Intermat	Biddeford	ME	E	207 283-1156	4572
James W Sewall Company	Bangor	ME	G	207 817-5410	4506
James W Sewall Company (PA)	Old Town	ME	E	207 827-4456	5125
Knowlton Machine Company	Gorham	ME	E	207 854-8471	4824
Modula Inc (DH)	Lewiston	ME	D	207 440-5100	4976
Nichols Portland LLC (PA)	Portland	ME	B	207 774-6121	5251
S & K Unlimited LLC	Brownville	ME	F	207 965-6137	4638
Fronek Anchor Darling Entp	Laconia	NH	E	603 528-1931	14651
Gill Design Inc	Windham	NH	G	603 890-1237	15727
Newdtc LLC	Salem	NH	F	603 893-0992	15549
Premier Recycling Eqp Inc	Seabrook	NH	F	855 223-5859	15600
Simbex LLC	Lebanon	NH	E	603 448-2367	14699
Two In One Manufacturing Inc	Nashua	NH	E	603 595-8212	15179
Universal Envmtl Tech Inc	Nashua	NH	G	603 883-9312	15180
Eagle Industries Inc	Ashaway	RI	E	401 596-8111	15739
Electric Boat Corporation	North Kingstown	RI	A	401 268-2410	16250
Ersa Inc	Westerly	RI	E	401 348-4000	16930
Hall Inc	Bristol	RI	D	401 253-4858	15768
Leidos Inc	Middletown	RI	E	401 849-8900	16178
Palmer Industries Inc	North Providence	RI	E	800 398-9676	16306
Cersosimo Industries Inc (PA)	Brattleboro	VT	D	802 254-4500	17080

ENGINEERING SVCS: Acoustical

	CITY	ST	EMP	PHONE	ENTRY#
Brown Innovations Inc (PA)	Boston	MA	G	773 477-7500	6625
Cambridge Signal Tech Inc	Providence	RI	F	401 490-5682	16493

ENGINEERING SVCS: Civil

	CITY	ST	EMP	PHONE	ENTRY#
Applied Research Assoc Inc	Randolph	VT	E	802 728-4588	17467

ENGINEERING SVCS: Construction & Civil

	CITY	ST	EMP	PHONE	ENTRY#
Louie and Teds Blacktop Inc	Swansea	MA	F	508 678-4948	12306

ENGINEERING SVCS: Electrical Or Electronic

	CITY	ST	EMP	PHONE	ENTRY#
AB Electronics LLC	Brookfield	CT	E	203 740-2793	509
Dark Field Technologies Inc	Shelton	CT	F	203 298-0731	2997
Delcom Products Inc	Danbury	CT	G	914 934-5170	729
Silicon Integration Inc	Milford	CT	E	203 876-2844	1885
Tornik Inc	Rocky Hill	CT	C	860 282-6081	2937
Atomera Incorporated	Wellesley Hills	MA	E	617 219-0600	12950
Eclypses Inc	Boston	MA	E	719 323-6680	6707
Oncore Manufacturing LLC	Westborough	MA	D	978 737-3640	13125
Design Consultants Associates	Hampstead	NH	F	603 329-4541	14382
Applied Radar Inc	North Kingstown	RI	E	401 295-0062	16231
Sproutel Inc	Providence	RI	G	914 806-6514	16615
Veterans Assembled Elec LLC (PA)	North Kingstown	RI	G	401 228-6165	16291

ENGINEERING SVCS: Machine Tool Design

	CITY	ST	EMP	PHONE	ENTRY#
Johnson Gage Company	Bloomfield	CT	E	860 242-5541	177
Prospect Machine Products Inc	Prospect	CT	F	203 758-4448	2840
Ipsumm Inc (PA)	Amesbury	MA	E	603 570-4050	5838

ENGINEERING SVCS: Mechanical

	CITY	ST	EMP	PHONE	ENTRY#
Atp Industries LLC (PA)	Plainville	CT	F	860 479-5007	2748
Dufrane Nuclear Shielding Inc	Winsted	CT	F	860 379-2318	4340
Engineering Specialties Inc	North Branford	CT	E	203 488-2266	2367
Quality Engineering Svcs Inc	Wallingford	CT	E	203 269-5054	3843
Costello Dismantling Co Inc (PA)	West Wareham	MA	E	508 291-2324	13058
R & S Redco Inc	Weymouth	MA	G	781 792-1717	13334
Rt Engineering Corporation	Franklin	MA	E	800 343-1182	8861
Oizero9 Inc	Sanford	ME	E	207 324-3582	5404

ENGINEERING SVCS: Structural

	CITY	ST	EMP	PHONE	ENTRY#
Bay State Industrial Weldin	Hudson	NH	E	603 881-7663	14488
Celestial Monitoring Corp (HQ)	Narragansett	RI	E	401 782-1045	16187

ENGINES: Diesel & Semi-Diesel Or Duel Fuel

	CITY	ST	EMP	PHONE	ENTRY#
Bell Power Systems LLC	Essex	CT	D	860 767-7502	1162
JH Westerbeke Corp	Taunton	MA	F	508 823-7677	12344
Salem Preferred Partners LLC (PA)	Boston	MA	C	540 389-3922	7021

ENGINES: Gasoline, NEC

	CITY	ST	EMP	PHONE	ENTRY#
Westerbeke Corporation	Avon	MA	E	508 823-7677	6168

ENGINES: Internal Combustion, NEC

	CITY	ST	EMP	PHONE	ENTRY#
Cummins - Allison Corp	Cheshire	CT	G	203 794-9200	585
Cummins Enviro Tech Inc	Old Lyme	CT	G	860 388-6377	2638
Cummins Inc	Rocky Hill	CT	F	860 529-7474	2920
Liquidpiston Inc	Bloomfield	CT	E	860 838-2677	190
Smith Hill of Delaware Inc	Essex	CT	E	860 767-7502	1171
Cummins Inc	Springfield	MA	E	413 737-2659	12088
Cummins Northeast LLC (HQ)	Braintree	MA	E	781 801-1700	7176
Js Sale Corp	Worcester	MA	E	508 753-2979	13746
Thermo Power Corporation	Waltham	MA	A	781 622-1400	12802
Melton Sales and Service Inc	Hallowell	ME	G	207 623-8895	4860
Davis Village Solutions LLC	New Ipswich	NH	F	603 878-3662	15197

ENGINES: Jet Propulsion

	CITY	ST	EMP	PHONE	ENTRY#
CAM Group LLC	Manchester	CT	F	860 646-2378	1587
Kco Numet Inc	Orange	CT	E	203 375-4995	2671
Andy Collazzo	Danvers	MA	G	978 539-8962	8162

ENGINES: Marine

	CITY	ST	EMP	PHONE	ENTRY#
Westerbeke Corporation (PA)	Taunton	MA	E	508 977-4273	12377
Vitaminsea LLC	Buxton	ME	G	207 671-0955	4666

ENGRAVING SVC, NEC

	CITY	ST	EMP	PHONE	ENTRY#
Baron Technology Inc	Milford	CT	F	203 452-0515	1800
Tex Elm Inc	East Haddam	CT	G	860 873-9715	956
International Laser Systems	Holyoke	MA	G	413 533-4372	9262

ENGRAVING SVCS

	CITY	ST	EMP	PHONE	ENTRY#
A D Perkins Company	New Haven	CT	G	203 777-3456	2110
Ann S Davis	Lebanon	CT	F	860 642-7228	1548
Biomerics LLC	Monroe	CT	D	203 268-7238	1906
Northeast Laser Engraving Inc	Monroe	CT	E	203 268-7238	1918
Rokap Inc	East Hampton	CT	G	203 265-6895	965
Owl Stamp Company Inc	Lowell	MA	G	978 452-4541	9912
Raders Engraving Inc	Boston	MA	G	617 227-2921	6993
Glass Graphics Inc	Conway	NH	F	603 447-1900	14179

ENVELOPES

	CITY	ST	EMP	PHONE	ENTRY#
Cenveo Corporation	Stamford	CT	A	303 790-8023	3307
Cenveo Enterprises Inc (PA)	Stamford	CT	D	203 595-3000	3308
Cenveo Worldwide Limited (DH)	Stamford	CT	E	203 595-3000	3309
Cwl Enterprises Inc (HQ)	Stamford	CT	F	303 790-8023	3332
Accutech Packaging Inc	Foxboro	MA	D	508 543-3800	8689
American Prtg & Envelope Inc	Auburn	MA	E	508 832-6100	6102
B & W Press Inc	West Newbury	MA	E	978 352-6100	13007
Classic Envelope Inc	East Douglas	MA	D	508 731-6747	8349
Jannel Manufacturing Inc	Holbrook	MA	E	781 767-0666	9176
Opportunity Works Inc (PA)	Newburyport	MA	E	978 462-6144	10705
Sheppard Envelope Company Inc	Auburn	MA	E	508 791-5588	6125
Westrock Mwv LLC	Springfield	MA	D	413 736-7211	12152
Worcester Envelope Company	Auburn	MA	C	508 832-5394	6128
Fiberkraft Inc	Salem	NH	E	603 621-0090	15525
Tufpak Inc	Ossipee	NH	E	603 539-4126	15285
Fred F Waltz Co Inc	Cumberland	RI	G	401 769-4900	15940
The Leahy Press Inc	Montpelier	VT	E	802 223-2100	17375

ENVELOPES WHOLESALERS

	CITY	ST	EMP	PHONE	ENTRY#
Massachusetts Envelope Co Inc	Hartford	CT	F	860 727-9100	1492
Fred F Waltz Co Inc	Cumberland	RI	G	401 769-4900	15940

EPOXY RESINS

	CITY	ST	EMP	PHONE	ENTRY#
Hexcel Corporation (PA)	Stamford	CT	E	203 969-0666	3374
Barrday Corporation	Millbury	MA	B	508 581-2100	10427
Nar Industries LLC	Cranston	RI	E	401 941-3000	15897
Rbc Industries Inc	Cranston	RI	D	401 941-3000	15906

EQUIPMENT: Pedestrian Traffic Control

	CITY	ST	EMP	PHONE	ENTRY#
Onsite Services Inc	Clinton	CT	F	860 669-3988	648
Preusser Research Group Inc (PA)	Trumbull	CT	F	203 459-8700	3729
Nestor Inc (PA)	Providence	RI	E	401 274-5345	16574

EQUIPMENT: Rental & Leasing, NEC

	CITY	ST	EMP	PHONE	ENTRY#
Pastanch LLC	Naugatuck	CT	E	203 720-9478	1979
The Bilco Company (DH)	West Haven	CT	C	203 934-6363	4128
Thomas Keegan & Sons Inc	Wallingford	CT	F	203 239-9248	3862
Bluedrop LLC	South Easton	MA	F	877 662-7873	11938
Easton Springs Corporation	South Easton	MA	F	508 238-2741	11942
Lyn-Lad Group Ltd (PA)	Lynn	MA	E	781 598-6010	9984
Lynn Ladder Scaffolding Co Inc (HQ)	Lynn	MA	D	781 598-6010	9985
Maki Corp (PA)	Gardner	MA	E	978 343-7422	8895

	CITY	ST	EMP	PHONE	ENTRY#
MEI Rigging & Crating LLC	Salisbury	MA	F	978 685-7700	11742
Whitney & Son Inc	Fitchburg	MA	E	978 343-6353	8682
Wilevco Inc	Billerica	MA	E	978 667-0400	6491
Grs Group Inc	Portland	ME	F	207 775-6139	5220

ETCHING & ENGRAVING SVC

	CITY	ST	EMP	PHONE	ENTRY#
Metamorphic Materials Inc	Winsted	CT	G	860 738-8638	4349
Ariston Engraving & Mch Co Inc	Woburn	MA	G	781 935-2328	13515
Automated Finishing Co Inc	Attleboro	MA	E	508 222-6262	5996
Jr Chemical Coatings LLC	Harwich	MA	E	508 896-3383	9068
N2 Biomedical LLC	Bedford	MA	E	781 275-6001	6244
New England Etching Co Inc	Holyoke	MA	E	413 532-9482	9269
Tech-Etch Inc (PA)	Plymouth	MA	B	508 747-0300	11481
Futureguard Building Pdts Inc (PA)	Auburn	ME	E	800 858-5818	4434
American Trophy and Supply Inc	East Providence	RI	G	401 438-3060	16004
GA Rel Manufacturing Company	Providence	RI	F	401 331-5455	16524

ETHYLENE-PROPYLENE RUBBERS: EPDM Polymers

	CITY	ST	EMP	PHONE	ENTRY#
Aardvark Polymers	Woodstock	CT	G	609 483-1013	4390
Si Group Inc	Danbury	CT	C	203 702-6140	815
Stanchem Incorporated	East Berlin	CT	E	860 828-0571	917
Advanced Frp Systems Inc	East Weymouth	MA	G	508 927-6915	8423
Allcoat Technology Inc	Wilmington	MA	E	978 988-0880	13376
Labthink International Inc	Medford	MA	F	617 830-2190	10293
Sheergard Cmpsite Slutions Inc	Salem	NH	E	954 661-7372	15561
Cool Polymers Inc	North Kingstown	RI	E	401 667-7830	16241

EXHAUST SYSTEMS: Eqpt & Parts

	CITY	ST	EMP	PHONE	ENTRY#
Davico Inc	New Bedford	MA	F	508 998-1150	10584

EXPLOSIVES

	CITY	ST	EMP	PHONE	ENTRY#
Austin Powder Company	Sterling	CT	E	860 564-5466	3499
Independent Explosives Inc	Bloomfield	CT	G	860 243-0137	171
Maxam Initiation Systems LLC	Sterling	CT	E	860 556-4064	3502
Metal Finish Eqp & Sup Co Inc	Suffield	CT	E	860 668-1050	3593
Dj Semichem Inc	Nashua	NH	G	603 204-5101	15092

EXTRACTS, FLAVORING

	CITY	ST	EMP	PHONE	ENTRY#
America Extract Corporation	East Hampton	CT	F	860 267-4444	958

EYEGLASSES: Sunglasses

	CITY	ST	EMP	PHONE	ENTRY#
Costa Inc	Providence	RI	E	401 333-1200	16506

FABRIC STORES

	CITY	ST	EMP	PHONE	ENTRY#
R & M Associates Inc	Glastonbury	CT	F	860 633-0721	1296
E W Winship Ltd Inc	Nantucket	MA	G	508 228-1908	10462
Hardwick Knitted Fabric Inc	Warren	MA	G	413 436-7704	12851
North East Knitting Inc	Pawtucket	RI	C	401 727-0500	16395
Simon Pearce (us) Inc (PA)	Windsor	VT	C	802 674-6280	17762

FABRICS & CLOTHING: Rubber Coated

	CITY	ST	EMP	PHONE	ENTRY#
Tillotson Corporation (PA)	Nashua	NH	F	781 402-1731	15176
Worthen Industries Inc	Nashua	NH	E	978 365-6345	15190

FABRICS: Apparel & Outerwear, Broadwoven

	CITY	ST	EMP	PHONE	ENTRY#
Ramblers Way Farm Inc (PA)	Kennebunk	ME	G	207 467-8118	4928
Trail-Tex LLC	Portsmouth	NH	F	603 436-6326	15444
Wool Advisor LLC	Johnson	VT	F	802 635-2271	17312

FABRICS: Apparel & Outerwear, Cotton

	CITY	ST	EMP	PHONE	ENTRY#
Zimmer & Rohde Ltd (DH)	Stamford	CT	F	203 327-1400	3498
Birch Outfitters LLC	Salem	MA	F	978 498-4631	11703

FABRICS: Automotive, From Manmade Fiber

	CITY	ST	EMP	PHONE	ENTRY#
Ballard Material Products Inc	Lowell	MA	E	978 452-8961	9859

FABRICS: Bonded-Fiber, Exc Felt

	CITY	ST	EMP	PHONE	ENTRY#
Insulsafe Textiles Inc	Lewiston	ME	E	207 782-7011	4966

FABRICS: Broad Woven, Goods, Cotton

	CITY	ST	EMP	PHONE	ENTRY#
A Lyons & Company Inc	Manchester	MA	F	978 526-4244	10032

FABRICS: Broadwoven, Cotton

	CITY	ST	EMP	PHONE	ENTRY#
Cranston Print Works Company (PA)	Cranston	RI	E	401 943-4800	15844
Cranston Print Works Company	West Greenwich	RI	F	401 397-2442	16884

FABRICS: Broadwoven, Wool

	CITY	ST	EMP	PHONE	ENTRY#
E W Winship Ltd Inc	Nantucket	MA	G	508 228-1908	10462
Brand & Oppenheimer Co Inc (PA)	Portsmouth	RI	E	401 293-5500	16440

FABRICS: Cloth, Warp Knit

	CITY	ST	EMP	PHONE	ENTRY#
Sunrise Group USA LLC	Shrewsbury	MA	E	508 873-1519	11842

PRODUCT

	CITY	ST	EMP	PHONE	ENTRY#

FABRICS: Denims
Dune Denim LLC	Bethel	CT	G	203 241-5409	109

FABRICS: Fiberglass, Broadwoven
Claremont Sales Corporation	Durham	CT	E	860 349-4499	898
Duro-Fiber Co Inc	Hudson	NH	F	603 881-4200	14494
Pro Design & Manufacturing	Newton	NH	G	603 819-4131	15243

FABRICS: Lace, Knit, NEC
Leavers Lace Corporation	West Greenwich	RI	E	401 397-5555	16887

FABRICS: Manmade Fiber, Narrow
Avila Textiles Inc	North Dighton	MA	G	508 828-5882	11003
Moore Company (PA)	Westerly	RI	C	401 596-2816	16938
Moore Company	Westerly	RI	E	401 596-2816	16939
Garware Fulflex USA Inc	Brattleboro	VT	C	802 257-5256	17085

FABRICS: Nonwoven
Bethune Nonwovens Inc	East Windsor	CT	C	860 386-8001	1067
Lydall Thermal/Acoustical Inc	Glastonbury	CT	E	860 646-1233	1288
New England Nonwovens LLC	West Haven	CT	F	203 891-0851	4116
Suominen US Holding Inc (HQ)	East Windsor	CT	C	860 386-8001	1087
Swift Textile Metalizing LLC (HQ)	Bloomfield	CT	D	860 243-1122	211
Windsor Locks Nonwovens Inc (DH)	East Windsor	CT	F	860 292-5600	1090
Xamax Industries Inc	Seymour	CT	E	203 888-7200	2976
Boyd Biomedical Inc (PA)	Lee	MA	E	413 243-2000	9612
Clark-Cutler-Mcdermott Company	Franklin	MA	C	508 528-1200	8823
Delaware Valley Corp (PA)	Lawrence	MA	F	978 688-6995	9556
Delaware Valley Corp	Tewksbury	MA	E	978 459-6932	12393
Draper Knitting Company Inc	Canton	MA	E	781 828-0029	7786
Hollingsworth & Vose Company (PA)	East Walpole	MA	C	508 850-2000	8418
National Nonwovens Inc	Easthampton	MA	E	413 527-3445	8452
National Nonwovens Inc (PA)	Easthampton	MA	D	413 527-3445	8453
Nonwovens Inc	North Chelmsford	MA	F	978 251-8612	10985
Saint-Gobain Adfors Amer Inc	Worcester	MA	D	508 795-2500	13789
Vulplex Inc	New Bedford	MA	F	508 996-6787	10659
C Cramer & Co Inc	Dover	NH	E	603 742-3838	14219
Northeastern Nonwovens Inc	Rochester	NH	F	603 332-5900	15489
Rontex America Inc	Amherst	NH	E	603 883-5076	13888
TEAM INC	Woonsocket	RI	E	401 762-1500	16980

FABRICS: Pile, Circular Knit
Draper Knitting Company Inc	Canton	MA	E	781 828-0029	7786

FABRICS: Resin Or Plastic Coated
Defender Industries Inc	Waterford	CT	C	860 701-3400	3989
Trelleborg Ctd Systems US Inc	New Haven	CT	C	203 468-0342	2212
Foamtech LLC	Fitchburg	MA	F	978 343-4022	8655
Haartz Corporation	Acton	MA	E	978 264-2607	5750
Haartz Corporation (PA)	Acton	MA	B	978 264-2600	5751
Protavic America Inc	Londonderry	NH	G	603 623-8624	14780

FABRICS: Rubberized
Au Milford LLC	Milford	MA	D	508 473-1870	10398
Haartz Corporation (PA)	Acton	MA	B	978 264-2600	5751

FABRICS: Scrub Cloths
E-Cloth Inc	Dover	NH	E	603 765-9367	14227

FABRICS: Shoe Laces, Exc Leather
Rhode Island Textile Company	Cumberland	RI	C	401 722-3700	15962
Rhode Island Textile Company (PA)	Cumberland	RI	C	401 722-3700	15963

FABRICS: Specialty Including Twisted Weaves, Broadwoven
Green Mountain Knitting Inc	Swanton	VT	E	800 361-1190	17637

FABRICS: Trimmings, Textile
Emtex Inc	Peabody	MA	F	978 907-4500	11309

FABRICS: Upholstery, Cotton
New England Worldwide Export	Quincy	MA	G	617 472-0251	11529
Alfreds Uphlstring Cstm Fbrcti	Alfred	ME	F	207 536-5565	4402

FABRICS: Warp & Flat Knit Prdts
Charbert Inc	Chestnut Hill	MA	F	401 364-7751	7998

FABRICS: Weft Or Circular Knit
Swift Textile Metalizing LLC (HQ)	Bloomfield	CT	D	860 243-1122	211
Nfa Corp	Cumberland	RI	B	401 333-8990	15955

FABRICS: Wool, Broadwoven

Swan Finishing Company Inc (PA)	Fall River	MA	C	508 674-4611	8612

FACILITIES SUPPORT SVCS
Johnson Controls Inc	Meriden	CT	F	678 297-4040	1670
Pitney Bowes Inc (PA)	Stamford	CT	A	203 356-5000	3433
Milk Street Press Inc	Boston	MA	F	617 742-7900	6888
Universal Envmtl Tech Inc	Nashua	NH	G	603 883-9312	15180

FAMILY CLOTHING STORES
Fyc Apparel Group LLC (PA)	Branford	CT	D	203 481-2420	260
Good Clothing Company Inc	Fall River	MA	F	508 419-6152	8556
Image Factory	Pocasset	MA	G	508 295-3876	11489
Santacroce Graphics Inc	Charlton	MA	F	802 447-0020	7895
Wool Advisor LLC	Johnson	VT	F	802 635-2271	17312

FANS, BLOWING: Indl Or Commercial
APA LLC	Canton	MA	E	781 986-5900	7769

FANS, EXHAUST: Indl Or Commercial
Kennedy Gustafson and Cole Inc	Berlin	CT	E	860 828-2594	72

FARM & GARDEN MACHINERY WHOLESALERS
Stihl Incorporated	Oxford	CT	E	203 929-8488	2712
Oesco Inc	Conway	MA	E	413 369-4335	8143
Lyle Guptill	East Machias	ME	F	207 255-4130	4740
Champlain Valley Equipment Inc	Saint Albans	VT	G	802 524-6782	17518

FARM PRDTS, RAW MATERIALS, WHOLESALE: Sugar
CSC Sugar LLC (PA)	Westport	CT	E	203 846-5610	4163

FARM SPLYS WHOLESALERS
Conrad Fafard Inc	Agawam	MA	A	413 786-4343	5788
I B A Inc (PA)	Sutton	MA	E	508 865-6911	12281
Americas Grdening Resource Inc	Milton	VT	C	802 660-3500	17354

FARM SPLYS, WHOLESALE: Feed
Central Conn Cooperative Farme	South Windsor	CT	E	860 649-4523	3127
H J Baker & Bro Inc	Westport	CT	B	203 682-9200	4171
HJ Baker & Bro LLC (PA)	Shelton	CT	E	203 682-9200	3014

FARM SPLYS, WHOLESALE: Garden Splys
Sun Gro Holdings Inc	Agawam	MA	E	413 786-4343	5809
Americas Grdening Resource Inc (PA)	Burlington	VT	C	802 660-3500	17117
Mill River Lumber Ltd	North Clarendon	VT	D	802 775-0032	17417

FARM SPLYS, WHOLESALE: Insecticides
Pic20 Group LLC	Norwalk	CT	F	203 957-3555	2558

FASTENERS WHOLESALERS
ITW Powertrain Fastening	Naugatuck	CT	E	203 720-1676	1967
Manchester TI & Design ADP LLC	North Haven	CT	G	860 296-6541	2422
Midwest Motor Supply Co	Newtown	CT	E	800 233-1294	2342
Paneloc Corporation	Farmington	CT	E	860 677-6711	1238
Rome Fastener Corporation	Milford	CT	E	203 874-6719	1880
Icarus Corporation	Auburn	MA	F	508 832-3481	6114
Reed & Prince Mfg Corp	Leominster	MA	F	978 466-6903	9700
Warwick Fasteners	West Bridgewater	MA	G	401 739-9200	12989

FASTENERS: Metal
Lincoln Thompson	Bristol	CT	F	860 516-0472	462
Integratech Solutions Corp	Hudson	MA	D	978 567-1000	9376
J Arakelian Inc	Johnston	RI	F	401 943-7366	16090
Anderson Component Corporation	Malden	MA	F	781 324-0350	10001
Device Technologies Inc	Southborough	MA	E	508 229-2000	11994
McStowe Engrg & Met Pdts Inc	East Bridgewater	MA	F	508 378-7400	8343
Tph Inc	Taunton	MA	E	401 431-1791	12372

FASTENERS: Notions, Hooks & Eyes
Metalform Acquisition LLC (PA)	New Britain	CT	F	860 224-2630	2043

FATTY ACID ESTERS & AMINOS
Henkel of America Inc (HQ)	Rocky Hill	CT	B	860 615-3395	2926
Twin Rivers Tech Ltd Partnr	Quincy	MA	C	617 472-9200	11542

FAUCETS & SPIGOTS: Metal & Plastic
Symmons Industries Inc (PA)	Braintree	MA	C	800 796-6667	7207

FEATHERS & FEATHER PRODUCTS
Prysm Inc	Marlborough	MA	F	978 405-3091	10197

FELT, WHOLESALE
U S Felt Company Inc	Sanford	ME	E	207 324-0063	5416

	CITY	ST	EMP	PHONE	ENTRY#

FELT: Acoustic

	CITY	ST	EMP	PHONE	ENTRY#
Clark-Cutler-Mcdermott Company	Franklin	MA	C	508 528-1200	8823

FENCES OR POSTS: Ornamental Iron Or Steel

	CITY	ST	EMP	PHONE	ENTRY#
Edi Landscape LLC	Hartford	CT	F	860 216-6871	1477
Perfection Fence Corp (PA)	Marshfield	MA	F	781 837-3600	10243
Somerville Orna Ir Works Inc	Somerville	MA	E	617 666-8872	11898
Soucy Industries Inc (PA)	Pelham	NH	E	603 883-4500	15297

FENCING MADE IN WIREDRAWING PLANTS

	CITY	ST	EMP	PHONE	ENTRY#
Countrywide National Services	Walpole	MA	G	508 346-3286	12558

FENCING MATERIALS: Docks & Other Outdoor Prdts, Wood

	CITY	ST	EMP	PHONE	ENTRY#
April Twenty One Corporation	Billerica	MA	G	978 667-8472	6405
Federal Program Integrators LLC	Indian Island	ME	F		4907
Chasco Inc	Portsmouth	NH	F	603 436-2141	15371

FENCING MATERIALS: Wood

	CITY	ST	EMP	PHONE	ENTRY#
Pleasant Valley Fence Co Inc	Pleasant Valley	CT	G	860 379-0088	2803
Walpole Outdoors LLC	Ridgefield	CT	E	508 668-2800	2909
Perfection Fence Corp (PA)	Marshfield	MA	F	781 837-3600	10243
Pine and Baker Mfg Inc	Tewksbury	MA	F	978 851-1215	12412
RD Contractors Inc	North Billerica	MA	E	978 667-6545	10948
Reliable Fnce C/Wstern Div Inc	Ashland	MA	F	508 877-1200	5966
Walpole Outdoors LLC	East Falmouth	MA	E	508 540-0300	8362
Walpole Outdoors LLC	Wilmington	MA	E	978 658-3373	13475
Frost Cedar Products Inc	North Anson	ME	G	207 566-5912	5105
Katahdin Forest Products Co (PA)	Oakfield	ME	D	800 845-4533	5119
Walpole Outdoors LLC	Chester	ME	E	207 794-2248	4694

FENCING: Chain Link

	CITY	ST	EMP	PHONE	ENTRY#
Stephens Pipe & Steel LLC	Manchester	CT	D	877 777-8721	1639
Perfection Fence Corp (PA)	Marshfield	MA	F	781 837-3600	10243

FERTILIZER, AGRICULTURAL: Wholesalers

	CITY	ST	EMP	PHONE	ENTRY#
Clinton Nursery Products Inc (PA)	Westbrook	CT	C	860 399-3000	4137
Sports Fields Inc	Monmouth	ME	F	207 933-3547	5072

FIBER & FIBER PRDTS: Elastomeric

	CITY	ST	EMP	PHONE	ENTRY#
Texon Usa Inc	Russell	MA	E	413 862-3652	11695

FIBER & FIBER PRDTS: Polyester

	CITY	ST	EMP	PHONE	ENTRY#
Fairfield Processing Corp (PA)	Danbury	CT	C	203 744-2090	744
Conform Automotive LLC	Auburn	ME	B	207 784-1118	4424
Formed Fiber Technologies Inc	Auburn	ME	A	207 784-1118	4433

FIBER & FIBER PRDTS: Protein

	CITY	ST	EMP	PHONE	ENTRY#
Proteus Industries Inc	Gloucester	MA	G	978 281-9545	8952

FIBER OPTICS

	CITY	ST	EMP	PHONE	ENTRY#
Nufern	East Granby	CT	D	860 408-5000	945
O E M Controls Inc (PA)	Shelton	CT	C	203 929-8431	3042
Pioneer Optics Company Inc	East Granby	CT	F	860 286-0071	948
Stran Technologies LLC	Naugatuck	CT	F	203 720-6500	1988
Corning Incorporated	Tewksbury	MA	E	978 442-2200	12391
Diamond USA Inc (HQ)	North Billerica	MA	F	978 256-6544	10906
Ipg Photonics Corporation (PA)	Marlborough	MA	B	508 373-1100	10169
Myriad Fiber Imaging Tech Inc	Dudley	MA	F	508 949-3000	8320
Schott North America Inc	Southbridge	MA	B	508 765-9744	12034
T & T Machine Products Inc	Rockland	MA	F	781 878-3861	11662
Fiber Optic Hardware	Nashua	NH	F	603 325-4993	15101
Fibernext LLC	Concord	NH	E	603 226-2400	14130
Te Connctvity Phenix Optix Inc	Ashaway	RI	C	401 637-4600	15745

FIBER: Vulcanized

	CITY	ST	EMP	PHONE	ENTRY#
Conform Automotive LLC	Auburn	ME	B	207 784-1118	4424
Formed Fiber Technologies Inc	Auburn	ME	A	207 784-1118	4433

FIBERS: Carbon & Graphite

	CITY	ST	EMP	PHONE	ENTRY#
Hexcel Corporation (PA)	Stamford	CT	E	203 969-0666	3374
N12 Technologies Inc	Foxboro	MA	G	857 259-6622	8709
Composite Energy Tech Inc	Bristol	RI	E	401 253-2670	15760
TEAM INC	Woonsocket	RI	E	401 762-1500	16980

FILTER ELEMENTS: Fluid & Hydraulic Line

	CITY	ST	EMP	PHONE	ENTRY#
Avenger Inc	Gloucester	MA	F	978 356-7311	8920

FILTERS

	CITY	ST	EMP	PHONE	ENTRY#
3M Purification Inc (HQ)	Meriden	CT	B	203 237-5541	1648
D&D Fltrtion Cons Sppliers Inc	Kensington	CT	F	860 829-3690	1539
Mott Corporation (PA)	Farmington	CT	D	860 864-5017	1230

	CITY	ST	EMP	PHONE	ENTRY#
MSC Filtration Tech Inc	Enfield	CT	F	860 745-7475	1139
Armstrong Machine Co Inc	Beverly	MA	F	978 232-9466	6326
East Coast Filter Inc	Wrentham	MA	G	716 649-2326	13840
Isp Freetown Fine Chem Inc	Assonet	MA	D	508 672-0634	5974
Mestek Inc	Westfield	MA	D	413 564-5530	13184
Pall Corporation	Framingham	MA	G	508 259-5107	8797
Parker-Hannifin Corporation	Haverhill	MA	C	978 858-0505	9120
Rypos Inc (PA)	Franklin	MA	E	508 429-4552	8862
Comnav Engineering Inc	Portland	ME	E	207 221-8524	5201
Mikrolar Inc	Hampton	NH	F	603 617-2508	14408
Bioprocessh2o LLC	Portsmouth	RI	E	401 683-5400	16438

FILTERS & SOFTENERS: Water, Household

	CITY	ST	EMP	PHONE	ENTRY#
Guardian Envmtl Tech Inc	New Milford	CT	F	860 350-2200	2245
Atlas Water Systems Inc	Waltham	MA	D	781 373-4700	12597
Bluedrop LLC	South Easton	MA	F	877 662-7873	11938
Diamond Water Systems Inc	Chicopee	MA	F	413 536-8186	8022
Duraflow LLC	Tewksbury	MA	F	978 851-7439	12394
H2o Care Inc	Middleton	MA	F	978 777-8330	10384
Nanostone Water Inc	Waltham	MA	C	781 209-6900	12732
Safve Inc	Scituate	MA	G	781 545-3546	11770
Alan S Bolster	Brewer	ME	F	207 989-5143	4608
Pentair Rsdntial Fltration LLC	Dover	NH	B	603 749-1610	14244

FILTERS & STRAINERS: Pipeline

	CITY	ST	EMP	PHONE	ENTRY#
Triad Concepts Inc	Westbrook	CT	G	860 399-4045	4145

FILTERS: Air Intake, Internal Combustion Engine, Exc Auto

	CITY	ST	EMP	PHONE	ENTRY#
Accutrol LLC	Danbury	CT	E	203 445-9991	703
Melton Sales and Service Inc	Hallowell	ME	G	207 623-8895	4860

FILTERS: General Line, Indl

	CITY	ST	EMP	PHONE	ENTRY#
Applied Porous Tech Inc	Tariffville	CT	F	860 408-9793	3598
Pallflex Products Company	Putnam	CT	E	860 928-7761	2869
Tinny Corporation	Middletown	CT	E	860 854-6121	1786
Evoqua Water Technologies LLC	Tewksbury	MA	E	978 863-4600	12397
Filter-Kleen Manufacturing Co	Westford	MA	F	978 692-5137	13237
Munters Corporation (DH)	Amesbury	MA	C	978 241-1100	5845
Pall Corporation	Westborough	MA	B	508 871-5380	13127
Polytech Fltration Systems Inc	Hudson	MA	F	978 562-7700	9402
Lapoint Industries Inc (PA)	Auburn	ME	D	207 777-3100	4439
Micronics Engnred Fltrtion Gro	Winthrop	ME	F	207 377-2626	5693
Micronics Engnred Fltrtion Gro	Winthrop	ME	D	207 377-2626	5694
National Filter Media Corp	Winthrop	ME	C	207 327-2626	5695
United Fbrcnts Strainrite Corp (HQ)	Auburn	ME	D	207 376-1600	4463

FILTERS: Oil, Internal Combustion Engine, Exc Auto

	CITY	ST	EMP	PHONE	ENTRY#
Expressway Lube Centers	Danbury	CT	F	203 744-2511	743

FILTRATION DEVICES: Electronic

	CITY	ST	EMP	PHONE	ENTRY#
3M Purification Inc	Stafford Springs	CT	B	860 684-8628	3252
Able Coil and Electronics Co	Bolton	CT	E	860 646-5686	218
Ainslie Corporation	Walpole	MA	E	781 848-0850	12548
Atrex Energy Inc (PA)	Walpole	MA	E	781 461-8251	12551
Degreasing Devices Co	Southbridge	MA	G	508 765-0045	12013
Modular Air Filtration Systems	Raynham	MA	E	508 823-4900	11594
Schneider Electric It Corp (DH)	Foxboro	MA	A	508 543-8750	8723
Porvair Filtration Group Inc	Caribou	ME	F	207 493-3027	4679
Jmk Inc	Amherst	NH	E	603 886-4100	13874
Rme Filters Inc	Amherst	NH	F	603 595-4573	13887
Bioholdings Ltd	Portsmouth	RI	F	401 683-5400	16437

FINISHING AGENTS

	CITY	ST	EMP	PHONE	ENTRY#
Unimetal Surface Finishing LLC (PA)	Thomaston	CT	E	860 283-0271	3640
Peg Kearsarge Co Inc	Bartlett	NH	G	603 374-2341	13918

FINISHING AGENTS: Textile

	CITY	ST	EMP	PHONE	ENTRY#
Bethune Nonwovens Inc	East Windsor	CT	C	860 386-8001	1067

FINISHING SVCS

	CITY	ST	EMP	PHONE	ENTRY#
Bradford Finshg Powdr Coat Inc	Haverhill	MA	G	978 469-9965	9081
J & M Machining Inc	Skowhegan	ME	F	207 474-7300	5470

FIRE ARMS, SMALL: Guns Or Gun Parts, 30 mm & Below

	CITY	ST	EMP	PHONE	ENTRY#
Black Phoenix Customs LLC	Bristol	CT	G	860 681-3162	416
New Designz Realty LLC	Cheshire	CT	G	860 384-1809	608
Standard Mfg Co LLC	New Britain	CT	F	860 225-3401	2062
Sturm Ruger & Company Inc	Southport	CT	B	203 256-3895	3246
Mascon Inc	Woburn	MA	F	781 938-5800	13605
Remsport Mfg LLC	Ludlow	MA	F	413 589-1911	9952
Windham Weaponry Inc	Windham	ME	G	207 893-2223	5676
Alex & Ryan Design LLC	Manchester	NH	F	603 518-8650	14808

PRODUCT

	CITY	ST	EMP	PHONE	ENTRY#

FIRE ARMS, SMALL: Guns Or Gun Parts, 30 mm & Below

	CITY	ST	EMP	PHONE	ENTRY#
Sturm Ruger & Company Inc	Newport	NH	B	603 865-2424	15239
Z M Weapons High Performance	Richmond	VT	G	802 777-8964	17482

FIRE ARMS, SMALL: Pistols Or Pistol Parts, 30 mm & below

Thompson/Center Arms Co Inc (HQ)	Springfield	MA	D	800 331-0852	12138
Sturm Ruger & Company Inc	Newport	NH	C	603 863-3300	15240
Foster Industries Inc	Wolcott	VT	F	802 472-6147	17774

FIRE ARMS, SMALL: Rifles Or Rifle Parts, 30 mm & below

Mike Sadlak	Coventry	CT	G	860 742-0227	680
Caliber Company (PA)	Westfield	MA	F	413 642-4260	13156
Savage Arms Inc (DH)	Westfield	MA	C	413 642-4135	13206
Savage Sports Corporation (HQ)	Westfield	MA	F	413 568-7001	13208
Green Mtn Rifle Barrel Co Inc	Conway	NH	F	603 447-1095	14180

FIRE ARMS, SMALL: Shotguns Or Shotgun Parts, 30 mm & Below

Connecticut Shotgun Manufacturing Co	New Britain	CT	D	860 225-6581	2012

FIRE DETECTION SYSTEMS

Fire-Lite Alarms Inc	Northford	CT	B	203 484-7161	2452
Protection Industries Corp (PA)	Stratford	CT	E	203 375-9393	3569
Rtx Corporation	Farmington	CT	B	954 485-6501	1244
Kidde-Fenwal Inc (HQ)	Ashland	MA	A	508 881-2000	5960
Protectowire Co Inc	Pembroke	MA	F	781 826-3878	11376
Fireye Inc (DH)	Derry	NH	C	603 432-4100	14193

FIRE EXTINGUISHERS: Portable

Fire Prevention Services	Trumbull	CT	F	203 866-6357	3720
Fire Defenses New England LLC	Danvers	MA	F	978 304-1506	8186
Hydro-Test Products Inc	Stow	MA	F	978 897-4647	12246
Mooneytunco Inc	Weymouth	MA	F	781 331-4445	13330
Hampshire Fire Protection LLC (PA)	Londonderry	NH	D	603 432-8221	14753

FIRE OR BURGLARY RESISTIVE PRDTS

Feman Steel LLC	Bloomfield	CT	F	860 982-6393	164
General Wldg & Fabrication Inc	Watertown	CT	E	860 274-9668	4014
Industrial Transfer & Stor Inc	Southbridge	MA	E	508 765-9178	12022
Mooring Systems Incorporated	Cataumet	MA	E	508 776-0254	7859
Barrette Outdoor Living Inc	Biddeford	ME	E	800 866-8101	4556
Brooks Inc (PA)	Thomaston	ME	E	207 354-8763	5542

FIREARMS & AMMUNITION, EXC SPORTING, WHOLESALE

Barile Printers LLC	New Britain	CT	F	860 224-0127	2007
Lighthouse Distributors Inc	Marshfield	MA	G	781 319-9828	10241
Century International Arms Inc	Fairfax	VT	D	802 527-1252	17257

FIREFIGHTING APPARATUS

Hydro-Test Products Inc	Stow	MA	F	978 897-4647	12246
King Fisher Co Inc	Lowell	MA	F	978 596-0214	9890

FIREPLACE EQPT & ACCESS

Architctral Fireplaces of Neng	Auburn	MA	F	508 757-0622	6104
Grate Ideas of America LLC	Colchester	VT	G	844 292-6044	17193

FIREWOOD, WHOLESALE

Eylward Timber Co	Wallingford	CT	G	203 265-4276	3806
West End Firewood Inc	Whitinsville	MA	G	508 234-4747	13347
Ossipee Mountain Land Co LLC	Tamworth	NH	E	603 323-7677	15648

FIREWORKS

Atlas Pyrvsion Entrmt Group In (PA)	Jaffrey	NH	E	603 532-8324	14564

FISH & SEAFOOD PROCESSORS: Canned Or Cured

Kneeland Bros Inc	Rowley	MA	F	978 948-3919	11678
Cherry Point Products Inc	Milbridge	ME	F	207 546-0930	5060
Looks Gourmet Food Co Inc (HQ)	Machias	ME	F	207 259-3341	5031

FISH & SEAFOOD PROCESSORS: Fresh Or Frozen

Nsd Seafood Inc (PA)	Gloucester	MA	C	978 282-7880	8947

FISH & SEAFOOD WHOLESALERS

Hannah Boden Corp	New Bedford	MA	F	508 992-3334	10598
Jordan Bros Seafood Co Inc	Boston	MA	F	508 583-9797	6831
Looks Gourmet Food Co Inc (HQ)	Machias	ME	F	207 259-3341	5031
North Atlantic Inc	Portland	ME	G	207 774-6025	5252

FISH FOOD

Finicky Pet Food Inc	New Bedford	MA	E	508 991-8448	10591
Offshore Marine Outfitters	York	ME	G	207 363-8862	5715

FISHING EQPT: Lures

Hogy Lure Company LLC	Falmouth	MA	G	617 699-5157	8633

FITTINGS & ASSEMBLIES: Hose & Tube, Hydraulic Or Pneumatic

	CITY	ST	EMP	PHONE	ENTRY#
Faxon Engineering Company Inc (PA)	Bloomfield	CT	F	860 236-4266	163
Fluid Dynamics LLC	Manchester	CT	F	860 791-6325	1598
PRC Acquisition Company Inc	Gorham	ME	F	207 854-3702	4832

FITTINGS: Pipe

Redco Corporation (HQ)	Stamford	CT	D	203 363-7300	3445
Crane Nxt Co (PA)	Waltham	MA	C	610 430-2510	12644
Guill Tool & Engrg Co Inc	West Warwick	RI	D	401 822-8186	16908

FITTINGS: Pipe, Fabricated

Improved Consumer Products Inc	North Attleboro	MA	F	508 695-6841	10875
New England Union Co Inc	West Warwick	RI	E	401 821-0800	16918

FIXTURES & EQPT: Kitchen, Porcelain Enameled

Rk Parisi Enterprises Inc	Keene	NH	F	844 438-7674	14616

FIXTURES: Bank, Metal, Ornamental

Mf Blouin Mdsg Solution	Dover	NH	G	800 394-1632	14234
Mfb Holdings LLC	Dover	NH	E	603 742-0104	14235

FLAGPOLES

Flagraphics Inc	Somerville	MA	E	617 776-7549	11874
Sunsetter Products Ltd Partnr	Malden	MA	D	781 321-9600	10029

FLAGS: Fabric

Flagman of America LLC	Avon	CT	G	860 678-0275	24
Flag Fables Inc	Springfield	MA	E	413 747-0525	12095
Flagraphics Inc	Somerville	MA	E	617 776-7549	11874

FLAGSTONES

Flagstone Inc	Mapleton	ME	G	207 227-5883	5045

FLAT GLASS: Construction

Custom Glass and Alum Co Inc	Tewksbury	MA	G	978 640-5800	12392

FLAT GLASS: Optical, Transparent, Exc Lenses

Guild Optical Associates Inc	Amherst	NH	F	603 889-6247	13872

FLAT GLASS: Window, Clear & Colored

Metro Glass & Metal LLC	Woburn	MA	E	781 281-0667	13612
Glass America Window Mfg Inc	Smithfield	RI	F	401 231-6000	16704

FLAVORS OR FLAVORING MATERIALS: Synthetic

Bedoukian Research Inc (PA)	Danbury	CT	E	203 830-4000	713

FLOOR COVERING STORES

Agw Clssic Hardwood Floors LLC	Westbrook	CT	G	203 640-3106	4135
Irvings Home Center Inc	Brockton	MA	G	508 583-4421	7285
Proknee Corp	Whitefield	ME	E	207 549-5018	5656
Robin Industries Inc	Bristol	RI	E	401 253-8350	15779

FLOOR COVERING STORES: Carpets

Ethan Allen Retail Inc (HQ)	Danbury	CT	B	203 743-8000	741

FLOOR COVERINGS: Textile Fiber

Joseph Cohn Son Tile Trazo LLC	North Haven	CT	G	203 772-2420	2420

FLOORING: Hardwood

Conway Hardwood Products LLC	Gaylordsville	CT	E	860 355-4030	1264
Tallon Lumber Inc	Canaan	CT	E	860 824-0733	558
Hydronics Manufacturing Inc	North Billerica	MA	G	978 528-4335	10919
Universal Hardwood Flooring	Boston	MA	G	617 783-2307	7094
Kelly Lumber Sales Inc	Old Town	ME	G	207 435-4950	5128
Moosewood Millworks LLC	Ashland	ME	G	207 435-4950	4411
Dycem Corporation (DH)	Smithfield	RI	E	401 738-4420	16697
Appalchian Engineered Flrg Inc	North Troy	VT	F	802 988-1073	17428

FLOORING: Rubber

Nora Systems Inc (DH)	Salem	NH	D	603 894-1021	15550

FLOWERS, ARTIFICIAL, WHOLESALE

Mc Cann Bros Inc	Monroe	CT	F	203 335-8630	1916

FLUES & PIPES: Stove Or Furnace

Heat Fab Inc	Turners Falls	MA	F	413 863-2242	12447
New England Supply Inc (PA)	Williston	VT	D	802 858-4577	17742

FLUID METERS & COUNTING DEVICES

Gems Sensors Inc (HQ)	Plainville	CT	B	860 747-3000	2761
Habco Industries LLC	Glastonbury	CT	E	860 682-6800	1283

	CITY	ST	EMP	PHONE	ENTRY#
Kem Liquidating Company Inc	Glastonbury	CT	E	860 430-5100	1287
Acentech Incorporated **(PA)**	Cambridge	MA	E	617 499-8000	7466
Data Industrial Corporation	Mattapoisett	MA	E	508 758-6390	10256
High Voltage Engineering Corp	Wakefield	MA	E	781 224-1001	12511
Cei Flowmaster Products LLC	Hudson	NH	G	603 880-0094	14490

FLUID POWER PUMPS & MOTORS

Hamilton Sundstrand Corp **(HQ)**	Windsor Locks	CT	A	619 714-9442	4330
ITT Inc **(PA)**	Stamford	CT	C	914 641-2000	3388
Hostar Mar Trnspt Systems Inc	Wareham	MA	F	508 295-2900	12838
Marine Hydraulics Inc	New Bedford	MA	F	508 990-2866	10619
Navtec Rigging Solutions Inc	Groton	MA	E		9011
Apex Sealing Inc	Fairfax	VT	F	802 524-7100	17254

FLUID POWER VALVES & HOSE FITTINGS

Atp Industries LLC **(PA)**	Plainville	CT	F	860 479-5007	2748
Enfield Technologies LLC	Trumbull	CT	F	203 375-3100	3719
Parker-Hannifin Corporation	New Britain	CT	C	860 827-2300	2050
Conant Controls Inc	Woburn	MA	E	781 395-2240	13544
Guardair Corporation	Chicopee	MA	E	413 594-4400	8035
McGill Hose & Coupling Inc **(PA)**	East Longmeadow	MA	E	413 525-3977	8387
Microgroup Inc	Medway	MA	C	508 533-4925	10308
Portland Valve LLC **(DH)**	Warren	MA	E	704 289-6511	12852
Tapcoenpro Tracker LLC	Burlington	MA	G	781 270-1200	7437
Windward Power Systems Inc	Fairhaven	MA	F	774 992-0059	8515
Parker-Hannifin Corporation	Hollis	NH	F	603 595-1500	14456
Quality Controls Inc	Northfield	NH	E	603 286-3321	15268

FOAM RUBBER

New England Foam Products LLC **(PA)**	Hartford	CT	E	860 524-0121	1496
Reilly Foam Corp	Bloomfield	CT	F	860 243-8200	206
Talalay Global Inc **(DH)**	Shelton	CT	E	203 924-0700	3067
Bosal Foam and Fiber **(PA)**	Limerick	ME	E	207 793-2245	5000

FOAMS & RUBBER, WHOLESALE

Bosal Foam and Fiber **(PA)**	Limerick	ME	E	207 793-2245	5000

FOIL & LEAF: Metal

Cthru Metals Inc	North Branford	CT	F	203 884-1017	2364
Dexmet Corporation	Wallingford	CT	D	203 294-4440	3800
Foilmark Inc	Bloomfield	CT	G	860 243-0343	165
Republic Foil Inc	Danbury	CT	D	203 743-2731	805
Foilmark Inc **(HQ)**	Newburyport	MA	D	978 225-8200	10683

FOIL: Aluminum

Republic Foil Inc	Danbury	CT	D	203 743-2731	805
Boyd Biomedical Inc **(PA)**	Lee	MA	E	413 243-2000	9612

FOIL: Copper

Global Laminates Inc	Portsmouth	NH	F	603 373-8323	15393

FOIL: Laminated To Paper Or Other Materials

Hazen Paper Company **(PA)**	Holyoke	MA	C	413 538-8204	9259

FOOD PRDTS, BREAKFAST: Cereal, Oatmeal

Munk Pack Inc	Stamford	CT	F	203 769-5005	3414

FOOD PRDTS, CANNED OR FRESH PACK: Fruit Juices

Guida-Seibert Dairy Company **(HQ)**	New Britain	CT	C	800 832-8929	2028
National Grape Coop Assn Inc	Concord	MA	G	978 371-1000	8128
Odwalla Inc	Brookline	MA	E	336 877-1634	7322
Welch Foods Inc A Cooperative **(HQ)**	Concord	MA	B	978 371-1000	8140

FOOD PRDTS, CANNED: Barbecue Sauce

Kens Foods Inc **(PA)**	Marlborough	MA	B	508 229-1100	10176

FOOD PRDTS, CANNED: Fruit Juices, Fresh

Dunajski Dairy Inc	Peabody	MA	G	978 531-1457	11308
Jugos	Boston	MA	G	617 418-9879	6834
Smoothie Bus LLC	Manchester	NH	F	603 303-7353	14930

FOOD PRDTS, CANNED: Fruits

Ocean Spray (europe) Ltd	Middleboro	MA	F	508 946-1000	10370
Cherryfield Foods Inc **(DH)**	Cherryfield	ME	D	207 546-7573	4688
Jasper Wyman & Son	Deblois	ME	F	207 638-2201	4721
Maine Wild Blueberry Company **(DH)**	Machias	ME	D	207 255-8364	5033
Cosmos Food Products Inc	West Haven	CT	E	800 942-6766	4099
Kraft Heinz Foods Company	Waterbury	CT	G	203 597-9109	3929
Natural Country Farms Inc	Ellington	CT	C	860 872-8346	1112
Coca-Cola Btlg Sthstern Neng I	Northampton	MA	E	413 586-8450	11055
Ocean Spray International Sls	Lakeville	MA	F	508 946-1000	9518
Rohtstein Corp **(PA)**	Woburn	MA	D	781 935-8300	13655

	CITY	ST	EMP	PHONE	ENTRY#
Welch Foods Inc A Cooperative	Concord	MA	D	978 371-3762	8139
B&G Foods Inc	Portland	ME	C	207 772-8341	5180
Jasper Wyman & Son	Cherryfield	ME	F	207 546-3381	4689
Jasper Wyman & Son	Cherryfield	ME	E	207 546-3381	4690
Maine Wild Blueberry Company	Machias	ME	D	207 255-8364	5032
McCain Foods Usa Inc	Easton	ME	C	207 488-2561	4743
B Del Toro & Sons Inc	Providence	RI	F	401 421-5820	16481
Fully Rooted Inc	Pawtucket	RI	F	401 429-8768	16370
Village Cannery Vermont Inc	Barre	VT	E	207 351-2713	17024

FOOD PRDTS, CANNED: Fruits & Fruit Prdts

Gebelein Group Inc	Hyde Park	MA	F	617 361-6611	9461
Ocean Spray Cranberries Inc **(PA)**	Middleboro	MA	B	508 946-1000	10371
Ocean Spray International Inc **(HQ)**	Middleboro	MA	B	508 946-1000	10372
Ocean Spray Intl Svcs Inc **(HQ)**	Lakeville	MA	B	508 946-1000	9519
Maine Homestead Inc	Lyman	ME	F	207 344-9274	5030

FOOD PRDTS, CANNED: Jams, Including Imitation

Cistercian Abbey Spencer Inc	Spencer	MA	E	508 885-8700	12056

FOOD PRDTS, CANNED: Jams, Jellies & Preserves

Pembertons Food Inc	Gray	ME	G	207 657-6446	4843
Stonewall Kitchen LLC **(PA)**	York	ME	C	207 351-2713	5717

FOOD PRDTS, CANNED: Soups, Exc Seafood

Kettle Cuisine LLC **(PA)**	Lynn	MA	C	617 409-1100	9980
Kettle Cuisine Holdings LLC	Lynn	MA	C	617 409-1100	9981

FOOD PRDTS, CANNED: Spaghetti & Other Pasta Sauce

Onofrios Ultimate Foods Inc	New Haven	CT	F	203 469-4014	2181
Ragozzino Foods Inc **(PA)**	Meriden	CT	F	203 238-2553	1691
Catanzaro Food Products Inc	Pawtucket	RI	G	401 255-1700	16353
Eastern Food Industries Inc	East Greenwich	RI	G	401 884-8798	15983
Dellamore Enterprises Inc	Colchester	VT	G	802 655-6264	17188

FOOD PRDTS, CANNED: Tomato Sauce.

Sewickley LLC	Greenwich	CT	G	203 661-2511	1351
Spinelli Ravioli Mfg Co Inc	Boston	MA	E	617 567-1992	7053

FOOD PRDTS, CANNED: Vegetables

Spear Farms Inc	Nobleboro	ME	E	207 832-4488	5101
Taylor Farms New England Inc	North Kingstown	RI	E	877 323-7374	16284

FOOD PRDTS, CONFECTIONERY, WHOLESALE: Candy

Thompson Brands LLC	Meriden	CT	D	203 235-2541	1708
Everson Distributing Co Inc	Worcester	MA	E	413 533-9261	13721
Stage Stop Candy Ltd Inc	Dennis Port	MA	G	508 394-1791	8263
Fredericks Pastries **(PA)**	Amherst	NH	F	603 882-7725	13871
Tom and Sallys Handmade Choco	Westerly	RI	F	800 289-8783	16944
Tradest1	East Greenwich	RI	G	401 884-4949	15994

FOOD PRDTS, CONFECTIONERY, WHOLESALE: Snack Foods

Grandy Organics LLC **(PA)**	Hiram	ME	E	207 935-7415	4890

FOOD PRDTS, DAIRY, WHOLESALE: Frozen Dairy Desserts

Vermonts Orginal Ice Cream Inc	Arlington	VT	G	802 375-1133	16992

FOOD PRDTS, FISH & SEAFOOD: Fish, Fresh, Prepared

M F Fley Incrprtd-New Bdford	New Bedford	MA	E	508 997-0773	10616
Seatrade International Co LLC	New Bedford	MA	D	774 305-4948	10649
Sea & Reef Aquaculture LLC	Franklin	ME	F	207 422-2422	4796

FOOD PRDTS, FISH & SEAFOOD: Fish, Frozen, Prepared

High Liner Foods USA Inc	Portsmouth	NH	F	603 818-5555	15403

FOOD PRDTS, FISH & SEAFOOD: Fish, Smoked

Boston Smoked Fish Company LLC	Boston	MA	F	617 819-5476	6619
Spence & Co Ltd	Brockton	MA	E	508 427-5577	7308
Mowi Ducktrap LLC	Belfast	ME	D	207 338-6280	4536
Mowi Ducktrap LLC	Belfast	ME	C	207 338-6280	4537

FOOD PRDTS, FROZEN: Ethnic Foods, NEC

Chinamerica Fd Manufacture Inc	Boston	MA	F	617 426-1818	6652
Perfect Empanada LLC **(PA)**	Attleboro	MA	G	508 241-5150	6047
Perfect Empanada LLC	Warren	RI	F	508 241-5150	16762

FOOD PRDTS, FROZEN: Fruit Juice, Concentrates

Ocean Spray Cranberries Inc **(PA)**	Middleboro	MA	B	508 946-1000	10371
Ocean Spray International Inc **(HQ)**	Middleboro	MA	B	508 946-1000	10372
Ocean Spray Intl Svcs Inc **(HQ)**	Lakeville	MA	B	508 946-1000	9519

FOOD PRDTS, FROZEN: Fruits

PRODUCT

	CITY	ST	EMP	PHONE	ENTRY#
Allens Blueberry Freezer Inc (HQ)	Ellsworth	ME	E	207 667-5561	4753
G M Allen & Son Inc	Orland	ME	G	207 469-7060	5133
Jasper Wyman & Son	Hancock	ME	G	207 546-3381	4870
Jasper Wyman & Son	Jonesboro	ME	G	207 546-3381	4919
Maine Wild Blueberry Company (DH)	Machias	ME	D	207 255-8364	5033

FOOD PRDTS, FROZEN: Fruits & Vegetables

	CITY	ST	EMP	PHONE	ENTRY#
McCain Foods Usa Inc	Easton	ME	C	207 488-2561	4743
Purbeck Isle Inc (PA)	Augusta	ME	E	207 623-5119	4479

FOOD PRDTS, FROZEN: Fruits, Juices & Vegetables

	CITY	ST	EMP	PHONE	ENTRY#
Natureseal Inc	Westport	CT	F	203 454-1800	4189
Welch Foods Inc A Cooperative (HQ)	Concord	MA	B	978 371-1000	8140
Coastal Blueberry Service Inc (PA)	Hancock	ME	F	207 667-9750	4868
Maine Wild Blueberry Company	Machias	ME	D	207 255-8364	5032
Merrill Blueberry Farms Inc	Hancock	ME	F	207 667-2541	4872
B Del Toro & Sons Inc	Providence	RI	F	401 421-5820	16481

FOOD PRDTS, POULTRY, WHOLESALE: Poultry Prdts, NEC

	CITY	ST	EMP	PHONE	ENTRY#
Carls Boned Chicken Inc	New Haven	CT	E	203 777-9048	2135

FOOD PRDTS, WHOLESALE: Beverages, Exc Coffee & Tea

	CITY	ST	EMP	PHONE	ENTRY#
Cape Cod Ginger LLC	Wareham	MA	G	508 295-2795	12830
Lqc Inc	Norwood	MA	G	617 586-5139	11191
Vitasoy USA Inc	Woburn	MA	C	781 430-8988	13686
Craft Beer Guild LLC	Portsmouth	NH	E	603 319-8508	15377

FOOD PRDTS, WHOLESALE: Chocolate

	CITY	ST	EMP	PHONE	ENTRY#
Granite State Candy Shoppe LLC (PA)	Concord	NH	F	603 225-2591	14131
Lindt & Sprungli (usa) Inc (HQ)	Stratham	NH	C	603 778-8100	15637
Birnn Chocolates Vermont Inc	South Burlington	VT	F	802 860-1047	17573

FOOD PRDTS, WHOLESALE: Cocoa

	CITY	ST	EMP	PHONE	ENTRY#
Cofco Americas Resources Corp (HQ)	Stamford	CT	F	203 658-2820	3316

FOOD PRDTS, WHOLESALE: Coffee & Tea

	CITY	ST	EMP	PHONE	ENTRY#
New England Partnership Inc	Norwood	MA	C	800 225-3537	11199
Mills Coffee Roasting Co	Providence	RI	G	401 781-7860	16565

FOOD PRDTS, WHOLESALE: Coffee, Green Or Roasted

	CITY	ST	EMP	PHONE	ENTRY#
Battle Grounds Coffee Co LLC	Haverhill	MA	F	978 891-5860	9077
Comfort Foods Inc	North Andover	MA	F	978 557-0009	10825
George Howell Coffee Co LLC	Acton	MA	F	978 635-9033	5748
James C Cannell Coffees Inc	West Wareham	MA	F	508 295-7009	13066
Mike Sheas Cffhuse Trdtnals In	Fairhaven	MA	F	508 807-5754	8509
Northeast Merchandising Corp	Skowhegan	ME	F	207 474-3321	5476
Excellent Coffee Co Inc (PA)	Pawtucket	RI	C	401 724-6393	16367

FOOD PRDTS, WHOLESALE: Condiments

	CITY	ST	EMP	PHONE	ENTRY#
Omar Coffee Company	Newington	CT	E	860 667-8889	2312
Mange LLC	Somerville	MA	G	917 880-2104	11885

FOOD PRDTS, WHOLESALE: Flavorings & Fragrances

	CITY	ST	EMP	PHONE	ENTRY#
Saccuzzo Company Inc	Newington	CT	G	860 665-1101	2323

FOOD PRDTS, WHOLESALE: Grains

	CITY	ST	EMP	PHONE	ENTRY#
Central Conn Cooperative Farme	South Windsor	CT	E	860 649-4523	3127
Louis Dreyfus Holdg Co US LLC (HQ)	Wilton	CT	B	203 761-2000	4242
TruRoots LLC (PA)	Needham	MA	F	800 288-3637	10527
Feed Commodities Intl Inc (HQ)	Middlebury	VT	E	800 639-3191	17343

FOOD PRDTS, WHOLESALE: Juices

	CITY	ST	EMP	PHONE	ENTRY#
Guida-Seibert Dairy Company (HQ)	New Britain	CT	C	800 832-8929	2028
Cold Hollow Cider Mill Inc	Waterbury Center	VT	E	802 244-8771	17680

FOOD PRDTS, WHOLESALE: Natural & Organic

	CITY	ST	EMP	PHONE	ENTRY#
Maine Coast Sea Vegetables Inc	Hancock	ME	E	207 412-0094	4871

FOOD PRDTS, WHOLESALE: Organic & Diet

	CITY	ST	EMP	PHONE	ENTRY#
D & M Packing LLC	Waterbury	CT	E	203 591-8986	3903
Herbasway Laboratories LLC	Wallingford	CT	F	203 269-6991	3812

FOOD PRDTS, WHOLESALE: Pasta & Rice

	CITY	ST	EMP	PHONE	ENTRY#
Pasta Vita Inc	Old Saybrook	CT	G	860 395-1452	2658
Pasta Bene Inc	Brockton	MA	F	508 583-1515	7300

FOOD PRDTS, WHOLESALE: Salad Dressing

	CITY	ST	EMP	PHONE	ENTRY#
R & N Inc	Unity	ME	G	207 948-2613	5567

FOOD PRDTS, WHOLESALE: Sauces

	CITY	ST	EMP	PHONE	ENTRY#
Gracies Kitchens Inc	New Haven	CT	F	203 773-0795	2156

FOOD PRDTS, WHOLESALE: Specialty

	CITY	ST	EMP	PHONE	ENTRY#
Boyajian Inc	Canton	MA	F	781 828-9966	7774
Jedwards International Inc (PA)	Braintree	MA	E	617 340-9461	7191
Pvk Inc	Lynn	MA	F	781 595-7771	9989
Rohtstein Corp (PA)	Woburn	MA	D	781 935-8300	13655
Native Maine Operations Inc	Westbrook	ME	E	207 856-1100	5640
Runamok Maple LLC	Fairfax	VT	E	802 849-7943	17263

FOOD PRDTS, WHOLESALE: Spices & Seasonings

	CITY	ST	EMP	PHONE	ENTRY#
Olivenation LLC (PA)	Avon	MA	F	781 351-1499	6156
Stonewall Kitchen LLC (PA)	York	ME	C	207 351-2713	5717

FOOD PRDTS: Almond Pastes

	CITY	ST	EMP	PHONE	ENTRY#
City Fresh Foods Inc	Roxbury	MA	D	617 606-7123	11690
Healthy Truth LLC	Walpole	MA	E	774 256-5800	12560
Modernist Pantry LLC	Eliot	ME	G	207 200-3817	4750
Freedom Foods LLC	Randolph	VT	F	802 728-0070	17468

FOOD PRDTS: Animal & marine fats & oils

	CITY	ST	EMP	PHONE	ENTRY#
Baker Commodities Inc	Warwick	RI	G	401 821-3003	16786
Baker Commodities Inc	Williston	VT	G	802 658-0721	17723

FOOD PRDTS: Box Lunches, For Sale Off Premises

	CITY	ST	EMP	PHONE	ENTRY#
Yosi Kosher Catering LLC	Windsor	CT	F	860 688-6677	4316
City Fresh Foods Inc	Roxbury	MA	D	617 606-7123	11689

FOOD PRDTS: Bread Crumbs, Exc Made In Bakeries

	CITY	ST	EMP	PHONE	ENTRY#
Sun Country Foods Inc (HQ)	Norwood	MA	G	855 824-7645	11212

FOOD PRDTS: Chicken, Processed, Fresh

	CITY	ST	EMP	PHONE	ENTRY#
Npc Processing Inc	Shelburne	VT	E	802 660-0496	17559

FOOD PRDTS: Chocolate Bars, Solid

	CITY	ST	EMP	PHONE	ENTRY#
Champlain Chocolate Company (PA)	Burlington	VT	D	800 465-5909	17124
Champlain Chocolate Company	Williston	VT	D	802 864-1808	17725

FOOD PRDTS: Cocoa, Instant

	CITY	ST	EMP	PHONE	ENTRY#
Sillycow Farms Llc	Wells River	VT	E	802 429-2920	17688

FOOD PRDTS: Coffee

	CITY	ST	EMP	PHONE	ENTRY#
Als Beverage Company Inc	East Windsor	CT	E	860 627-7003	1065
Oasis Coffee Corp	Norwalk	CT	G	203 847-0554	2547
Backbay Roasters	Wilmington	MA	G	844 532-6269	13387
Battle Grounds Coffee Co LLC	Haverhill	MA	F	978 891-5860	9077
Farmer Willies Inc	Charlestown	MA	G	401 441-2997	7872
George Howell Coffee Co LLC	Acton	MA	F	978 635-9033	5748
James C Cannell Coffees Inc	West Wareham	MA	F	508 295-7009	13066
Mike Sheas Cffhuse Trdtnals In	Fairhaven	MA	F	508 807-5754	8509
Coffee By Design Inc (PA)	Portland	ME	G	207 879-2233	5200
Vera Roasting Company	Portsmouth	NH	G	603 969-7970	15447
Bolt Coffee Company LLC	Providence	RI	F	401 533-6506	16487
Coffee Exchange Ltd	Providence	RI	F	401 273-1198	16502
Daves Coffee LLC (PA)	Narragansett	RI	F	800 483-4436	16188
Excellent Coffee Co Inc (PA)	Pawtucket	RI	C	401 724-6393	16367
Speeder & Earls Inc	Burlington	VT	F	802 660-3996	17160

FOOD PRDTS: Coffee Extracts

	CITY	ST	EMP	PHONE	ENTRY#
Kerry Inc	Portland	ME	E	207 775-7060	5231
Finlay EXT Ingredients USA Inc (DH)	Lincoln	RI	D	800 288-6272	16137
Keurig Green Mountain Inc (DH)	Waterbury	VT	D	877 879-2326	17675

FOOD PRDTS: Coffee, Ground, Mixed With Grain Or Chicory

	CITY	ST	EMP	PHONE	ENTRY#
Reily Foods Company	Malden	MA	E	504 524-6131	10025

FOOD PRDTS: Corn Chips & Other Corn-Based Snacks

	CITY	ST	EMP	PHONE	ENTRY#
New England Tortilla Inc	Boston	MA	E	617 889-6462	6917

FOOD PRDTS: Dessert Mixes & Fillings

	CITY	ST	EMP	PHONE	ENTRY#
Cherrybrook Kitchen LLC	Burlington	MA	G	781 272-0400	7347
Concord Foods LLC (PA)	Brockton	MA	C	508 580-1700	7269

FOOD PRDTS: Dips, Exc Cheese & Sour Cream Based

	CITY	ST	EMP	PHONE	ENTRY#
Salsa Fresca New Haven	New Haven	CT	G	301 675-6226	2193
Drews LLC (HQ)	Chester	VT	G	802 875-1184	17180

FOOD PRDTS: Dough, Pizza, Prepared

	CITY	ST	EMP	PHONE	ENTRY#
Itllbe LLC	Scarborough	ME	G	207 730-7301	5434
Pro Dough Inc	Manchester	NH	G	603 623-6844	14916

FOOD PRDTS: Doughs, Frozen Or Refrig From Purchased Flour

	CITY	ST	EMP	PHONE	ENTRY#
Rhino Foods Inc (PA)	Burlington	VT	C	802 862-0252	17156

FOOD PRDTS: Dressings, Salad, Raw & Cooked Exc Dry Mixes

	CITY	ST	EMP	PHONE	ENTRY#
Kerry R Wood	Westport	CT	G	203 221-7780	4177
Newmans Own Inc (PA)	Westport	CT	F	203 222-0136	4190
Pearlco of Boston Inc	Canton	MA	E	781 821-1010	7818
World Harbors LLC	Auburn	ME	C	207 786-3200	4464
Drews LLC (HQ)	Chester	VT	G	802 875-1184	17180

FOOD PRDTS: Dried & Dehydrated Fruits, Vegetables & Soup Mix

	CITY	ST	EMP	PHONE	ENTRY#
Decas Cranberry Products Inc (PA)	Carver	MA	E	508 866-8506	7853
Maine Wild Blueberry Company	Machias	ME	D	207 255-8364	5032

FOOD PRDTS: Edible fats & oils

	CITY	ST	EMP	PHONE	ENTRY#
Baker Commodities Inc	North Billerica	MA	D	978 454-8811	10899

FOOD PRDTS: Flour

	CITY	ST	EMP	PHONE	ENTRY#
Bay State Milling Company (PA)	Quincy	MA	E	617 328-4400	11505

FOOD PRDTS: Flour & Other Grain Mill Products

	CITY	ST	EMP	PHONE	ENTRY#
ADM Group LLC	New Milford	CT	G	860 354-3208	2237
Central Conn Cooperative Farme	South Windsor	CT	E	860 649-4523	3127
One Mighty Mill LLC	Hyde Park	MA	G	781 588-0970	9466
Rohtstein Corp (PA)	Woburn	MA	D	781 935-8300	13655

FOOD PRDTS: Flour Mixes & Doughs

	CITY	ST	EMP	PHONE	ENTRY#
Nummy LLC	West Hartford	CT	G	608 801-9850	4075
Watson LLC (DH)	West Haven	CT	E	203 932-3000	4132
Bake-N-Joy Foods Inc (PA)	North Andover	MA	D	978 683-1414	10821
Concord Foods LLC (PA)	Brockton	MA	C	508 580-1700	7269
Raaga Go LLC	Bedford	MA	G	505 983-5555	6255
Ever Better Eating Inc	Pittsfield	NH	D	603 435-5119	15331

FOOD PRDTS: Fruit Juices

	CITY	ST	EMP	PHONE	ENTRY#
Bevovations LLC	Leominster	MA	F	978 227-5469	9642

FOOD PRDTS: Fruits & Vegetables, Pickled

	CITY	ST	EMP	PHONE	ENTRY#
Star Pickling Corp	Swansea	MA	F	508 672-8535	12312
Stonewall Kitchen LLC (PA)	York	ME	C	207 351-2713	5717

FOOD PRDTS: Ice, Cubes

	CITY	ST	EMP	PHONE	ENTRY#
Twenty-Five Commerce Inc	Norwalk	CT	G	203 866-0540	2588

FOOD PRDTS: Instant Coffee

	CITY	ST	EMP	PHONE	ENTRY#
Riseandshine Corporation (PA)	Stamford	CT	F	917 599-7541	3449

FOOD PRDTS: Mixes, Pancake From Purchased Flour

	CITY	ST	EMP	PHONE	ENTRY#
Maple Grove Farms Vermont Inc (HQ)	Saint Johnsbury	VT	D	802 748-5141	17543

FOOD PRDTS: Mustard, Prepared

	CITY	ST	EMP	PHONE	ENTRY#
J W Raye & Co Inc	Eastport	ME	F	207 853-4451	4745
Old Dutch Mustard Co Inc	Greenville	NH	D	603 878-2100	14374

FOOD PRDTS: Oil, Hydrogenated, Edible

	CITY	ST	EMP	PHONE	ENTRY#
Lqc Inc	Norwood	MA	G	617 586-5139	11191

FOOD PRDTS: Olive Oil

	CITY	ST	EMP	PHONE	ENTRY#
Olive Capizzano Oils & Vinegar	Pawcatuck	CT	G	860 495-2187	2724
Olive Oil Factory LLC	Waterbury	CT	E	203 437-8286	3956
Andaluna Enterprises Inc	West Newbury	MA	G	617 335-3204	13006

FOOD PRDTS: Pasta, Uncooked, Packaged With Other Ingredients

	CITY	ST	EMP	PHONE	ENTRY#
If Not Now When Inc	Groton	CT	G	860 445-5276	1373
Pasta Vita Inc	Old Saybrook	CT	G	860 395-1452	2658
Josephs Gourmet Pasta Company	Haverhill	MA	B	978 521-1718	9107
Pasta Bene Inc	Brockton	MA	F	508 583-1515	7300

FOOD PRDTS: Peanut Butter

	CITY	ST	EMP	PHONE	ENTRY#
East Baking Company Inc	Holyoke	MA	C	413 536-2300	9252
Superior Nut Company Inc	Cambridge	MA	E	800 251-6060	7724
Edesia Industries LLC	North Kingstown	RI	D	401 272-5521	16249

FOOD PRDTS: Pizza Doughs From Purchased Flour

	CITY	ST	EMP	PHONE	ENTRY#
Dough Connection Corp	Woburn	MA	G	877 693-6844	13558
Good Crust LLC	Canaan	ME	G	207 522-4872	4669

FOOD PRDTS: Pizza, Refrigerated

	CITY	ST	EMP	PHONE	ENTRY#
Uno Foods Inc	Norwood	MA	C	617 323-9200	11217
Top Shell LLC	Central Falls	RI	D	401 726-7890	15799

FOOD PRDTS: Potato Chips & Other Potato-Based Snacks

	CITY	ST	EMP	PHONE	ENTRY#
Old Lyme Gourmet Company	Deep River	CT	E	860 434-7347	879
Rose Sisters Brands Inc	Bridgeport	CT	F	475 999-8115	366
Plant Snacks LLC	Needham	MA	F	617 480-6265	10518

FOOD PRDTS: Poultry, Processed, Frozen

	CITY	ST	EMP	PHONE	ENTRY#
Barber Foods LLC (DH)	Portland	ME	E	207 482-5500	5183

FOOD PRDTS: Poultry, Slaughtered & Dressed

	CITY	ST	EMP	PHONE	ENTRY#
Somerville Live Poultry Co Inc	Boston	MA	G	617 547-9191	7045

FOOD PRDTS: Seasonings & Spices

	CITY	ST	EMP	PHONE	ENTRY#
Uncle Wileys Inc	Fairfield	CT	F	203 256-9313	1202
Beyond Shaker LLC	Woburn	MA	G	617 461-6608	13523
Brady Enterprises Inc (PA)	East Weymouth	MA	D	781 340-4571	8427
Custom Seasonings Inc	Gloucester	MA	E	978 762-6300	8931
Wildtree Inc	Lincoln	RI	D	401 732-1856	16157

FOOD PRDTS: Soy Sauce

	CITY	ST	EMP	PHONE	ENTRY#
Onofrios Ultimate Foods Inc	New Haven	CT	F	203 469-4014	2181

FOOD PRDTS: Sugar

	CITY	ST	EMP	PHONE	ENTRY#
Cofco Americas Resources Corp (HQ)	Stamford	CT	F	203 658-2820	3316

FOOD PRDTS: Syrup, Maple

	CITY	ST	EMP	PHONE	ENTRY#
Parkers Maple Barn Corn Crib	Mason	NH	A	603 878-2308	14967
C E Maple LLC	Westminster	VT	E	802 387-5944	17700
Green Mtn Maple Sug Ref Co Inc	Belvidere Center	VT	F	802 644-2625	17034
Highland Sugarworks Inc	Websterville	VT	F	802 479-1747	17684
Holton Family Maple	Wolcott	VT	G	802 888-5183	17775
Jay Mountain Maples LLC	North Troy	VT	G	802 988-4086	17429
Kendle Enterprises	South Woodstock	VT	F	802 457-3015	17615
Maple Grove Farms Vermont Inc (HQ)	Saint Johnsbury	VT	D	802 748-5141	17543
Mystic Mountain Maples LLC	Florence	VT	F	802 524-6163	17270
Palmer Lane Maple LLC	Jericho	VT	G	802 899-8199	17308
Pvf Maple LLC	Cuttingsville	VT	G	802 492-3364	17209
Runamok Maple LLC	Fairfax	VT	E	802 849-7943	17263
Sogle Property LLC	Cambridge	VT	E	802 849-7943	17168
Sugarbush Farm Inc	Woodstock	VT	G	802 457-1757	17778
Sweet Tree Holdings 1 LLC	Island Pond	VT	E	802 723-6753	17305
Two Brothers Maple LLC	Richford	VT	G	802 848-7042	17477
Vermont Maple Sugar Co Inc	Johnson	VT	G	802 888-3491	17310
Vermont Maple Sugar Co Inc	Johnson	VT	C	802 635-7483	17311
Vermont Maple Sugar Co Inc (PA)	Morrisville	VT	E	802 888-3491	17391
Wh Property Service LLC	Guilford	VT	F	802 257-8566	17282

FOOD PRDTS: Syrups

	CITY	ST	EMP	PHONE	ENTRY#
Unilever Ascc AG	Shelton	CT	B	203 381-2482	3073

FOOD PRDTS: Tea

	CITY	ST	EMP	PHONE	ENTRY#
Herbasway Laboratories LLC	Wallingford	CT	F	203 269-6991	3812
Fuel For Fire Inc	Needham Heights	MA	G	508 975-4573	10548
Reily Foods Company	Malden	MA	E	504 524-6131	10025
Coffee By Design Inc (PA)	Portland	ME	G	207 879-2233	5200

FOOD PRDTS: Tofu, Exc Frozen Desserts

	CITY	ST	EMP	PHONE	ENTRY#
Chang Shing Tofu Inc	Cambridge	MA	G	617 868-8878	7537
Nasoya Foods Usa LLC	Ayer	MA	C	978 772-6880	6187
Vitasoy USA Inc	Woburn	MA	C	781 430-8988	13686
Heiwa Tofu Inc	Rockport	ME	G	207 236-8638	5350

FOOD PRDTS: Vegetable Oil Mills, NEC

	CITY	ST	EMP	PHONE	ENTRY#
Baker Commodities Inc	North Billerica	MA	D	978 454-8811	10899

FOOD PRDTS: Vinegar

	CITY	ST	EMP	PHONE	ENTRY#
Vinegar Syndrome LLC	Bridgeport	CT	G	475 731-1778	384
Mange LLC	Somerville	MA	G	917 880-2104	11885
Old Dutch Mustard Co Inc	Greenville	NH	D	603 878-2100	14374

FOOD PRODUCTS MACHINERY

	CITY	ST	EMP	PHONE	ENTRY#
A & I Concentrate LLC	Shelton	CT	E	203 447-1938	2977
Capricorn Investors III LP (PA)	Greenwich	CT	F	203 861-6600	1326
Conair LLC	Torrington	CT	D	800 492-7464	3676
Treif USA Inc	Shelton	CT	F	203 929-9930	3072
Alfa Laval Inc	Newburyport	MA	D	978 465-5777	10666
Consolidated Machine Corporation	Billerica	MA	E	617 782-6072	6428
Electrolyzer Corp	West Newbury	MA	G	978 363-5349	13008
Jbt Aerotech Corp	Boston	MA	E	857 574-3170	6821
Maxant Industries Inc	Devens	MA	F	978 772-0576	8279
Reiser Creations	Easthampton	MA	G	508 259-5794	8460
Burlodge USA Inc	Litchfield	NH	E	336 776-1010	14712
Heat and Control Inc	Pembroke	NH	D	603 225-5190	15303
Mastermatic Inc	Pembroke	NH	G	603 225-5190	15304
Univex Corporation	Salem	NH	D	603 893-6191	15569
Mfi Corp	Burlington	VT	D	802 658-6600	17145

P R O D U C T

	CITY	ST	EMP	PHONE	ENTRY#

FOOD STORES: Convenience, Chain

	CITY	ST	EMP	PHONE	ENTRY#
Cumberland Farms Inc (DH)	Westborough	MA	B	800 225-9702	13097

FOOD STORES: Convenience, Independent

Cco Llc	Rocky Hill	CT	F	860 757-3434	2917
Old Creamery Grocery Store	Cummington	MA	G	413 634-5560	8147

FOOD STORES: Cooperative

Boston Food Cooperative (PA)	Cambridge	MA	C	617 661-1580	7520

FOOD STORES: Delicatessen

Atkins Fruit Bowl Inc	Amherst	MA	C	413 253-9528	5859
Lacascias Bakery Inc	Medford	MA	F	781 395-8612	10294
Natural Selection Inc	Brunswick	ME	G	207 725-6287	4651
Eastern Food Industries Inc	East Greenwich	RI	G	401 884-8798	15983

FOOD STORES: Grocery, Chain

Market Basket Produce Inc	Concord	NH	D	603 224-5479	14143

FOOD STORES: Grocery, Independent

North Star Distributors Inc (PA)	Vineyard Haven	MA	E	508 693-2000	12494
Pearl Street Beverage Inc	Burlington	VT	F	802 658-1574	17150

FOOD STORES: Supermarkets, Chain

Big Y Foods Inc	Longmeadow	MA	D	413 567-6231	9848
Roche Bros Supermarkets LLC	Norton	MA	C	508 285-3600	11133

FOOTWEAR, WHOLESALE: Athletic

Stride Rite Corporation (HQ)	Waltham	MA	B	617 824-6000	12783
Forsake Inc	Stowe	VT	G	585 576-6358	17631

FOOTWEAR, WHOLESALE: Shoe Access

Hbn Shoe LLC	Salem	NH	G	603 622-0272	15536

FOOTWEAR, WHOLESALE: Shoes

C & J Clark America Inc (DH)	Waltham	MA	B	617 964-1222	12617
C & J Clark Latin America	Waltham	MA	E	617 243-4100	12618
White Mountain Intl LLC (PA)	Lisbon	NH	E	603 838-6694	14711

FOOTWEAR: Cut Stock

Macneill Engineering Co Inc	Westborough	MA	E	508 481-8830	13118
Enefco International Inc (PA)	Auburn	ME	E	207 514-7218	4428

FORGINGS: Aircraft

Wyman-Gordon Company (DH)	North Grafton	MA	B	508 839-8252	11030
Granite Forge LLC	Hudson	NH	F	603 589-9480	14501

FORGINGS: Aircraft, Ferrous

Consoldted Inds Acqsition Corp	Cheshire	CT	D	203 272-5371	582

FORGINGS: Automotive & Internal Combustion Engine

Schrader Electronics Inc	Attleboro	MA	B	615 384-0089	6061

FORGINGS: Construction Or Mining Eqpt, Ferrous

J C B Leasing Inc	Weare	NH	F	603 529-7974	15671

FORGINGS: Iron & Steel

J J Ryan Corporation	Plantsville	CT	C	860 628-0393	2793

FORGINGS: Machinery, Nonferrous

Smiths Tblar Systms-Lconia Inc	Laconia	NH	C	603 524-2064	14670

FORGINGS: Metal , Ornamental, Ferrous

Schrimpf Wldg Fabrication Inc	Woburn	MA	G	339 298-2311	13661

FORGINGS: Nonferrous

Consolidated Industries Inc	Cheshire	CT	D	203 272-5371	583
Kervick Family Foundation Inc	Worcester	MA	E	508 853-4500	13748
Wyman-Gordon Company	Worcester	MA	D	508 839-8253	13835
Tem Inc	Buxton	ME	E	207 929-8700	4665

FORMS: Concrete, Sheet Metal

S and S Concrete Forms Cnstr	Swansea	MA	G	508 379-0191	12310
Gagne & Son Con Blocks Inc	Auburn	ME	G	207 495-3313	4435
Advance Concrete Form Inc	Manchester	NH	D	603 669-4496	14805
McKernon Group Inc	Brandon	VT	D	802 247-8500	17068

FOUNDRIES: Aluminum

JET Corporation	Bridgeport	CT	F	203 334-3317	334
Oberdorfer LLC	Hartford	CT	C		1498
Black Bay Ventures Vi LLC	Palmer	MA	F	413 283-2976	11271

	CITY	ST	EMP	PHONE	ENTRY#
Consoldted Precision Pdts Corp	Braintree	MA	E	781 848-3333	7174
Industrial Foundry Corporation	Uxbridge	MA	G	508 278-5523	12481
Kingston Aluminum Foundry Inc	Kingston	MA	G	781 585-6631	9509
Mystic Valley Foundry Inc	Lincoln	MA	E	617 547-1819	9798
Pace Industries LLC	North Billerica	MA	C	978 667-8400	10941
Bronze Craft Corporation	Nashua	NH	D	603 883-7747	15074
Patriot Foundry & Castings LLC	Pelham	NH	F	603 934-3919	15292
Michael Healy Designs Inc	Manville	RI	G	401 597-5900	16165

FOUNDRIES: Gray & Ductile Iron

Ulvac Technologies Inc (HQ)	Methuen	MA	E	978 686-7550	10347
Prr Enterprise Inc	Lewiston	ME	E	207 783-2991	4985

FOUNDRIES: Iron

G & W Foundry Corp	Millbury	MA	E	508 581-8719	10434
Rodney Hunt-Fontaine Inc (HQ)	Orange	MA	E	978 544-2511	11232

FOUNDRIES: Nonferrous

Custom Metal Crafters Inc	Newington	CT	E	860 953-4210	2283
Doncasters Inc	Groton	CT	D	860 446-4803	1366
PCC Structurals Groton (DH)	Groton	CT	C	860 405-3700	1377
Advanced Metal Concepts Inc	North Attleboro	MA	E	508 695-6400	10864
D W Clark Inc (PA)	East Bridgewater	MA	E	508 378-4014	8339
D W Clark Inc	Taunton	MA	G	508 378-4014	12330
Kennedy Die Castings Inc	Worcester	MA	C	508 791-5594	13747
Mack Prototype Inc	Gardner	MA	E	978 632-3700	8893
Pace Industries LLC	North Billerica	MA	C	978 667-8400	10941
Trident Alloys Inc	Springfield	MA	E	413 737-1477	12142
Whitman Castings Inc (PA)	Whitman	MA	E	781 447-4417	13352
Wollaston Alloys Inc	Braintree	MA	C	781 848-3333	7214
Hawk Motors Inc	York	ME	G	207 363-4716	5712
Diamond Casting and Mch Co LLC	Hollis	NH	E	603 465-2263	14450
PCC Structurals Groton	Northfield	NH	C	603 286-4301	15267
Fielding Manufacturing Inc	Cranston	RI	D	401 461-0400	15860
New England Union Co Inc	West Warwick	RI	E	401 821-0800	16918
Optical Polymers Lab Corp	Pawtucket	RI	F	401 722-0710	16398
Osram Sylvania Inc	Central Falls	RI	C	401 723-1378	15794
Ridco Casting Co	Pawtucket	RI	D	401 724-0400	16412

FOUNDRIES: Steel

D W Clark Inc (PA)	East Bridgewater	MA	E	508 378-4014	8339
D W Clark Inc	Taunton	MA	G	508 378-4014	12330
Doncasters Inc	Springfield	MA	D	413 785-1801	12090
HMK Enterprises Inc (PA)	Lexington	MA	F	781 891-6660	9749
Metal Casting Technology Inc	Milford	NH	E	603 673-9720	15033

FOUNDRIES: Steel Investment

Doncasters Inc	Groton	CT	D	860 446-4803	1366
Integra-Cast Inc	New Britain	CT	D	860 225-7600	2032
Consoldted Precision Pdts Corp	Braintree	MA	E	781 848-3333	7174
Hitchiner Manufacturing Co Inc (PA)	Milford	NH	A	603 673-1100	15027
KW Thompson Tool Company Inc	Rochester	NH	D	603 330-8670	15483
Sturm Ruger & Company Inc	Newport	NH	B	603 865-2424	15239
Sturm Ruger & Company Inc	Newport	NH	C	603 863-3300	15240

FOUNDRY MACHINERY & EQPT

Gerber Technology LLC (HQ)	Tolland	CT	B	800 321-2448	3662
Arcast Inc	Oxford	ME	G	207 539-9638	5140

FRACTIONATION PRDTS OF CRUDE PETROLEUM, HYDROCARBONS, NEC

Burtco Inc	Westminster Station	VT	F	802 722-3358	17702

FRAMES: Chair, Metal

Whetstone Workshop LLC	East Providence	RI	G	401 368-7410	16048

FRANCHISES, SELLING OR LICENSING

The Bilco Company (DH)	West Haven	CT	C	203 934-6363	4128
Brighams Inc (HQ)	Arlington	MA	F	800 242-2423	5939
Gordon Industries Inc (PA)	Randolph	MA	E	857 401-8398	11561
White Mountain Creamery Inc	Chestnut Hill	MA	F	617 527-8790	8003
Ben & Jerrys Homemade Inc (HQ)	South Burlington	VT	C	802 846-1500	17571

FREIGHT FORWARDING ARRANGEMENTS

Vermont Heritage Distrs Inc	Newport	VT	G	802 334-6503	17407

FRICTION MATERIAL, MADE FROM POWDERED METAL

Tek-Motive Inc	Branford	CT	F	203 468-2224	281
Torqmaster Inc	Stamford	CT	E	203 326-5945	3484
Capstan Atlantic	Wrentham	MA	C	508 384-3100	13838
Veloxint Corporation	Framingham	MA	F	774 777-3369	8806

	CITY	ST	EMP	PHONE	ENTRY#
Elmet Technologies LLC **(PA)**	Lewiston	ME	C	207 333-6100	4960

FRUIT & VEGETABLE MARKETS

	CITY	ST	EMP	PHONE	ENTRY#
Nashoba Valley Spirits Limited	Bolton	MA	E	978 779-5521	6498

FRUIT STANDS OR MARKETS

	CITY	ST	EMP	PHONE	ENTRY#
Lyman Farm Incorporated **(PA)**	Middlefield	CT	C	860 349-1793	1725
Atkins Fruit Bowl Inc	Amherst	MA	C	413 253-9528	5859
Training Thru Placement Inc	North Providence	RI	F	401 353-0220	16312

FRUITS & VEGETABLES WHOLESALERS: Fresh

	CITY	ST	EMP	PHONE	ENTRY#
Native Maine Operations Inc	Westbrook	ME	E	207 856-1100	5640
B Del Toro & Sons Inc	Providence	RI	F	401 421-5820	16481

FUEL ADDITIVES

	CITY	ST	EMP	PHONE	ENTRY#
Armored Autogroup Parent Inc	Danbury	CT	C	203 205-2900	710
Si Group Inc	Danbury	CT	C	203 702-6140	815

FUEL CELLS: Solid State

	CITY	ST	EMP	PHONE	ENTRY#
Clear Edge Power International Service LLC 860 727-2200	South Windsor 3128	CT			C
Fuelcell Energy Inc	Torrington	CT	E	860 496-1111	3682
Hyaxiom Inc **(HQ)**	East Hartford	CT	E	860 727-2200	998
Merrick Services 2386	North Grosvenordale	CT	F	508 802-3751	

FUEL OIL DEALERS

	CITY	ST	EMP	PHONE	ENTRY#
Devine Brothers Incorporated	Norwalk	CT	E	203 866-4421	2490
Falmouth Mar Yachting Ctr Inc	Falmouth	MA	F	508 548-4600	8631
R J McDonald Inc	Barre	MA	F	978 355-6649	6203
Reggies Oil Company Inc	Quincy	MA	F	617 471-2095	11536
Mike Murphy & Sons Inc	Kingston	NH	F	603 362-4879	14636
Sail Energy LLC	Portsmouth	NH	C	844 301-7245	15434

FUELS: Diesel

	CITY	ST	EMP	PHONE	ENTRY#
App Polonia LLC	Plainville	CT	G	860 747-3397	2747
Altair Paramount LLC	Boston	MA	G	617 889-7300	6538
Homeland Fuels Company LLC	Canton	MA	F	781 737-1892	7797
Gaftek Inc	Bangor	ME	E	207 217-6515	4504
Maine Bio-Fuel Inc	Portland	ME	F	207 878-3001	5238
White Mountain Biodiesel LLC	Littleton	NH	G	603 444-0335	14725

FUND RAISING ORGANIZATION, NON-FEE BASIS

	CITY	ST	EMP	PHONE	ENTRY#
Shelburne Farms	Shelburne	VT	D	802 985-8498	17562

FURNACE CASINGS: Sheet Metal

	CITY	ST	EMP	PHONE	ENTRY#
Advanced Air Systems Inc	Abington	MA	F	781 878-5733	5721

FURNACES & OVENS: Indl

	CITY	ST	EMP	PHONE	ENTRY#
Etter Engineering Company Incorporated	Bristol	CT	E	860 584-8842	443
Furnace Source LLC	Terryville	CT	F	860 582-4201	3603
Hamworthy Peabody Combustn Inc **(DH)**	Shelton	CT	E	203 922-1199	3012
Jad LLC	South Windsor	CT	E	860 289-1551	3158
Kanthal Corporation	Bethel	CT	E	203 744-1440	124
Preferred Utilities Mfg Corp **(HQ)**	Danbury	CT	D	203 743-6741	799
Bruce Technologies Inc	North Billerica	MA	F	978 670-5501	10901
Duc-Pac Corporation	Springfield	MA	E	413 525-3302	12091
H B Smith Company Inc	Westfield	MA	F	413 568-3148	13170
Mestek Inc	Westfield	MA	F	413 568-9571	13183
S M Engineering Co Inc	North Attleboro	MA	F	508 699-4484	10886
Arcast Inc	Oxford	ME	F	207 539-9638	5141
N E Tech-Air Inc	Scarborough	ME	C	207 347-7577	5439
Onix Corporation	Caribou	ME	F	866 290-5362	4678
Ebner Furnaces	Londonderry	NH	G	603 552-3806	14746
Hollis Line Machine Co Inc	Milford	NH	E	603 673-1166	15028
Mellen Company Inc **(PA)**	Concord	NH	E	603 228-2929	14145
Gasbarre Products Inc	Cranston	RI	F	401 467-5200	15865
Rmb Ltd	Warren	RI	E	401 245-3700	16766
Rettig USA Inc	Colchester	VT	G	802 654-7500	17201

FURNACES: Warm Air, Electric

	CITY	ST	EMP	PHONE	ENTRY#
Metromatic Manufacturing Company Inc	Byfield	MA	F	781 396-5300	7458

FURNITURE PARTS: Metal

	CITY	ST	EMP	PHONE	ENTRY#
October Company Inc **(PA)**	Easthampton	MA	D	413 527-9380	8456
October Company Inc	Easthampton	MA	E	413 529-0718	8457
Production Basics Inc	Billerica	MA	E	617 926-8100	6473

FURNITURE REPAIR & MAINTENANCE SVCS

	CITY	ST	EMP	PHONE	ENTRY#
Joshua Friedman & Co LLC	New London	CT	F	860 439-1637	2229
Copley Furniture Company Inc	Boston	MA	G	617 566-1000	6668

FURNITURE STOCK & PARTS: Hardwood

	CITY	ST	EMP	PHONE	ENTRY#
Elkins & Co Inc	Boothbay	ME	F	207 633-0109	4597

FURNITURE STOCK & PARTS: Turnings, Wood

	CITY	ST	EMP	PHONE	ENTRY#
Pride Manufacturing Co LLC	Guilford	ME	F	207 876-2719	4855
Turning Acquisitions LLC	Buckfield	ME	F	207 336-2400	4659
Vic Firth Manufacturing Inc	Newport	ME	E	207 368-4358	5099
We Cork Inc	Exeter	NH	G	800 666-2675	14306

FURNITURE STORES

	CITY	ST	EMP	PHONE	ENTRY#
Cerrito Furniture Inds Inc	Branford	CT	F	203 481-2580	244
Domino Media Group Inc	Westport	CT	F	877 223-7844	4165
Ethan Allen Interiors Inc **(PA)**	Danbury	CT	C	203 743-8000	740
Ethan Allen Retail Inc **(HQ)**	Danbury	CT	B	203 743-8000	741
Lovesac Company **(PA)**	Stamford	CT	D	888 636-1223	3404
Porta Door Co	Seymour	CT	E	203 888-6191	2967
Acton Woodworks Inc	Acton	MA	G	978 263-0222	5732
Albert E Cadrette	West Townsend	MA	F	978 597-2312	13056
Atlantic Furniture Inc	South Deerfield	MA	E	413 665-4700	11920
Ecin Industries Inc	Fall River	MA	E	508 675-6920	8540
Marthas Vineyard Furn Co LLC	Vineyard Haven	MA	G	508 687-9555	12491
Twin Cy Upholstering Mat Inc	Braintree	MA	F	781 843-1780	7210
Portland Mattress Makers **(PA)**	Biddeford	ME	F	207 282-9583	4582
Design Brand Partners Inc	Bedford	NH	G	603 232-3490	13925
Gilberte Interiors LLC **(PA)**	Hanover	NH	F	603 643-3727	14423
Arnold Lumber Co	Coventry	RI	E	401 792-0979	15806
Community Apostolic Order Inc **(PA)**	Island Pond	VT	F	802 723-4452	17304

FURNITURE UPHOLSTERY REPAIR SVCS

	CITY	ST	EMP	PHONE	ENTRY#
McLaughlin Upholstering Co Inc	Everett	MA	F	617 389-0761	8495

FURNITURE WHOLESALERS

	CITY	ST	EMP	PHONE	ENTRY#
Donghia Inc	Milford	CT	C	800 366-4442	1818
Focal Metals	Bethel	CT	G	203 743-4443	115
Jackson Caldwell	Oxford	ME	G	207 539-2325	5146
York-Cmbrland Assn For Hndcppe **(PA)**	Portland	ME	E	207 879-1140	5292
Cw Keller & Associates LLC	Plaistow	NH	D	603 382-2028	15339

FURNITURE, HOUSEHOLD: Wholesalers

	CITY	ST	EMP	PHONE	ENTRY#
Chapman Manufacturing Company Inc **(PA)** 508 588-3200	Avon 6147	MA			E
Marthas Vineyard Furn Co LLC	Vineyard Haven	MA	G	508 687-9555	12491
Classic Dsgns By Mtthew Brak I	Saint Johnsbury	VT	E	802 748-6062	17541

FURNITURE, MATTRESSES: Wholesalers

	CITY	ST	EMP	PHONE	ENTRY#
Drive-O-Rama Inc	Dennis Port	MA	G	508 394-0028	8260

FURNITURE, OFFICE: Wholesalers

	CITY	ST	EMP	PHONE	ENTRY#
CAM Office Services Inc **(PA)**	Marlborough	MA	F	781 932-9868	10125
Mkind Inc	Manchester	NH	G	603 493-6882	14892

FURNITURE, OUTDOOR & LAWN: Wholesalers

	CITY	ST	EMP	PHONE	ENTRY#
Baldwin Lawn Furniture LLC	Middletown	CT	F	860 347-1306	1738

FURNITURE, WHOLESALE: Beds & Bedding

	CITY	ST	EMP	PHONE	ENTRY#
Restmore Inc	Brockton	MA	D	508 559-9944	7302

FURNITURE, WHOLESALE: Racks

	CITY	ST	EMP	PHONE	ENTRY#
Di-Cor Industries Inc	Bristol	CT	E	860 585-5583	436
Thule Inc **(DH)**	Seymour	CT	C	203 881-9600	2971

FURNITURE, WHOLESALE: Shelving

	CITY	ST	EMP	PHONE	ENTRY#
Installed Building Pdts LLC	Auburn	NH	B	603 645-1604	13909

FURNITURE: Bean Bag Chairs

	CITY	ST	EMP	PHONE	ENTRY#
Lovesac Company **(PA)**	Stamford	CT	D	888 636-1223	3404

FURNITURE: Bedroom, Wood

	CITY	ST	EMP	PHONE	ENTRY#
Ethan Allen Interiors Inc **(PA)**	Danbury	CT	C	203 743-8000	740
Jordans Furniture Inc **(HQ)**	East Taunton	MA	A	508 828-4000	8408
Woodforms Inc	Foxboro	MA	G	508 543-9417	8733

FURNITURE: Box Springs, Assembled

	CITY	ST	EMP	PHONE	ENTRY#
Leggett & Platt Incorporated	Oxford	MA	D	508 987-8706	11258
Vital Wood Products Inc	Fall River	MA	E	508 673-7976	8623

FURNITURE: Cabinets & Vanities, Medicine, Metal

	CITY	ST	EMP	PHONE	ENTRY#
Edigene Inc	Cambridge	MA	F	617 682-5731	7554

FURNITURE: Chairs, Household Wood

	CITY	ST	EMP	PHONE	ENTRY#
Andre Furniture Industries LLC	South Windsor	CT	G	860 528-8826	3115

PRODUCT

	CITY	ST	EMP	PHONE	ENTRY#
Bonito Manufacturing Inc	North Haven	CT	D	203 234-8786	2394
Connecticut Solid Surface LLC	Canton	CT	E	860 410-9800	559
Custom Furniture & Design LLC	Litchfield	CT	F	860 567-3519	1555
European Woodcraft LLC	Norwalk	CT	G	203 847-6195	2498
Finishing Touch Woodcraft	Canton	CT	G	860 916-2642	561
Future Classics USA LLC (PA)	Roxbury	CT	F	860 838-4688	2944
L & L Capital Partners LLC	Wilton	CT	F	203 834-6222	4241
Madigan Millworks Inc	Unionville	CT	G	860 673-7601	3749
Salamander Designs Ltd	Bloomfield	CT	E	860 761-9500	209
Tudor House Furniture Co Inc	Hamden	CT	F	203 288-8451	1461
Walpole Outdoors LLC	Ridgefield	CT	E	508 668-2800	2909
Woodworkers Heaven Inc	Bridgeport	CT	F	203 333-2778	386
Abcrosby & Company Inc	Ashburnham	MA	G	978 827-6064	5951
Acton Woodworks Inc	Acton	MA	G	978 263-0222	5732
Atlantic Furniture Inc	South Deerfield	MA	E	413 665-4700	11920
Bellecraft Woodworking Co Inc	Winchendon	MA	F	978 297-2672	13478
Connors Design Ltd	Marlborough	MA	G	508 481-1930	10135
Countryside Woodcraft LLP	Russell	MA	F	413 862-3276	11694
Custom Ktchens By Chmpagne Inc	Franklin	MA	F	508 528-7919	8828
David Lefort	Halifax	MA	G	781 826-9033	9020
Drive-O-Rama Inc (PA)	Hyannis	MA	G	508 771-8100	9434
Drive-O-Rama Inc	Dennis Port	MA	G	508 394-0028	8260
Fabrizio Corporation	Medford	MA	E	781 396-1400	10284
Grace Lee Designs Shilling	Cambridge	MA	F	617 661-7090	7593
Marthas Vineyard Furn Co LLC	Vineyard Haven	MA	G	508 687-9555	12491
Metrica Interior Inc	Northampton	MA	F	413 587-2750	11071
Modu Form Inc (PA)	Fitchburg	MA	D	978 345-7942	8667
Paines Patio Inc	Pocasset	MA	G	508 563-7557	11490
Salem Village Craftsmen Inc (PA)	Ashburnham	MA	F	833 827-7267	5953
South Mountain Company Inc	West Tisbury	MA	E	508 693-4850	13055
Walpole Outdoors LLC	East Falmouth	MA	E	508 540-0300	8362
Walpole Outdoors LLC	Wilmington	MA	E	978 658-3373	13475
Ambassador Woodworks Inc	Walpole	ME	G	916 858-1092	5580
Anchor Corporation	Kennebunk	ME	F	207 985-6018	4920
Imagineering Inc	Rockland	ME	F	207 596-6483	5333
Jackson Caldwell	Oxford	ME	G	207 539-2325	5146
Maine Bunk Beds LLC	Buxton	ME	F	207 929-4499	4663
Shed Happens Inc (PA)	Saco	ME	F	207 494-7546	5379
Walpole Outdoors LLC	Chester	ME	F	207 794-2248	4694
Waterworks	Bangor	ME	F	207 941-8306	4521
York-Cmbrland Assn For Hndcppe (PA)	Portland	ME	F	207 879-1140	5292
Cw Keller & Associates LLC	Plaistow	NH	D	603 382-2028	15339
D R Dimes & Co Ltd	Northwood	NH	G	603 942-8050	15272
Design Contempo	Lisbon	NH	G	603 838-6544	14709
Janice Miller	Manchester	NH	G	603 629-9995	14867
Michael Perra Inc	Manchester	NH	F	603 644-2110	14884
Bess Home Fashions Inc	West Warwick	RI	C	401 828-0300	16906
Stephen Plaud Inc	Tiverton	RI	F	401 625-5909	16738
Two Saints Inc	Cranston	RI	F	401 490-5500	15922
Community Apostolic Order Inc (PA)	Island Pond	VT	F	802 723-4452	17304
Dock Doctors LLC	Ferrisburgh	VT	E	802 877-6756	17268
Greenrange Furniture Company	Hinesburg	VT	G	802 747-8564	17292
Lyndon Woodworking Inc (PA)	Saint Johnsbury	VT	F	802 748-0100	17542
Neudorfer Inc	Waterbury	VT	F	802 244-5338	17676
New England Woodcraft Inc	Brandon	VT	C	802 247-8211	17070
Vermont Furniture Designs Inc	Winooski	VT	F	802 655-6568	17770

FURNITURE: Couches, Sofa/Davenport, Upholstered Wood Frames

	CITY	ST	EMP	PHONE	ENTRY#
Barclay Furniture Associates	Holyoke	MA	G	413 536-8084	9242

FURNITURE: Desks, Household, Wood

	CITY	ST	EMP	PHONE	ENTRY#
Vermont Custom Wood Products	North Walpole	NH	F	802 463-9930	15261

FURNITURE: Desks, Wood

	CITY	ST	EMP	PHONE	ENTRY#
Haydenville Wdwkg & Design Inc (PA)	Northampton	MA	G	413 665-7402	11066

FURNITURE: Dining Room, Wood

	CITY	ST	EMP	PHONE	ENTRY#
Mainstream Inc (PA)	Bennington	VT	F	802 442-8859	17050

FURNITURE: Fiberglass & Plastic

	CITY	ST	EMP	PHONE	ENTRY#
Weston Presidio MGT Co Inc (PA)	Boston	MA	E	617 988-2500	7118

FURNITURE: Foundations & Platforms

	CITY	ST	EMP	PHONE	ENTRY#
Installed Building Pdts LLC	Auburn	NH	B	603 645-1604	13909

FURNITURE: Hotel

	CITY	ST	EMP	PHONE	ENTRY#
Cricket Radio LLC	Burlington	VT	G	802 825-8368	17129

FURNITURE: Household, Metal

	CITY	ST	EMP	PHONE	ENTRY#
Durham Manufacturing Company (PA)	Durham	CT	D	860 349-3427	899
Salamander Designs Ltd	Bloomfield	CT	E	860 761-9500	209
Southern Almnum Intrmdte Hldin	New Canaan	CT	C	870 234-8660	2087

	CITY	ST	EMP	PHONE	ENTRY#
Lucas Fabrication Inc	Florence	MA	F	413 586-0941	8684

FURNITURE: Juvenile, Metal

	CITY	ST	EMP	PHONE	ENTRY#
Summer Infant Inc (HQ)	Woonsocket	RI	C	401 671-6550	16975

FURNITURE: Kitchen & Dining Room, Metal

	CITY	ST	EMP	PHONE	ENTRY#
Bostoncounters LLC	Woburn	MA	G	781 281-1622	13533

FURNITURE: Laboratory

	CITY	ST	EMP	PHONE	ENTRY#
Lab Frnture Instlltons Sls Inc	Middleton	MA	F	978 646-0600	10388

FURNITURE: Living Room, Upholstered On Wood Frames

	CITY	ST	EMP	PHONE	ENTRY#
Tudor House Furniture Co Inc	Hamden	CT	F	203 288-8451	1461
Twin Cy Upholstering Mat Inc	Braintree	MA	F	781 843-1780	7210

FURNITURE: Mattresses & Foundations

	CITY	ST	EMP	PHONE	ENTRY#
Symbol Mattress Neng Inc	Dayville	CT	B	860 779-3112	869
Ecin Industries Inc	Fall River	MA	E	508 675-6920	8540
US Bedding Inc	Fall River	MA	F	508 678-6988	8620

FURNITURE: Mattresses, Box & Bedsprings

	CITY	ST	EMP	PHONE	ENTRY#
A&S Innersprings Usa LLC	Windsor	CT	F	860 298-0401	4249
Leggett & Platt Incorporated	Middletown	CT	F	860 635-8811	1758
Ppj LLC (PA)	Natick	MA	F	508 650-3500	10493
Therapedic of New England LLC	Brockton	MA	F	508 559-9944	7311
Wcw Inc (PA)	Manchester Center	VT	D	802 362-8053	17332

FURNITURE: Mattresses, Innerspring Or Box Spring

	CITY	ST	EMP	PHONE	ENTRY#
Blue Bell Mattress Company LLC (HQ)	East Windsor	CT	E	860 292-6372	1068
Subinas USA LLC	Windsor	CT	F	860 298-0401	4305
Gardner Mattress Corporation (PA)	Salem	MA	F	978 744-1810	11718
Restmore Inc	Brockton	MA	D	508 559-9944	7302
Spring Air Ohio LLC	Chelsea	MA	G	617 884-0041	7992
Twin Cy Upholstering Mat Inc	Braintree	MA	F	781 843-1780	7210
Bourdons Institutional Sls Inc	Claremont	NH	E	603 542-8709	14079

FURNITURE: Novelty, Wood

	CITY	ST	EMP	PHONE	ENTRY#
Ms Orbis Corporation (PA)	Oak Bluffs	MA	G	774 330-5323	11222

FURNITURE: Office, Exc Wood

	CITY	ST	EMP	PHONE	ENTRY#
Bonito Manufacturing Inc	North Haven	CT	D	203 234-8786	2394
Conco Wood Working Inc	West Haven	CT	G	203 934-9665	4098
Durham Manufacturing Company (PA)	Durham	CT	D	860 349-3427	899
One & Co Inc	Norwich	CT	G	860 892-5180	2614
Static Safe Products Company	Cornwall Bridge	CT	F	203 937-6391	672
Conklin Office Services Inc (PA)	Holyoke	MA	E	413 315-4924	9248
Krueger International Inc	Boston	MA	E	617 542-4043	6847
Modu Form Inc (PA)	Fitchburg	MA	D	978 345-7942	8667
Officeworks Inc (PA)	Burlington	MA	F	781 270-9000	7403
Production Basics Inc	Billerica	MA	E	617 926-8100	6473
R W Hatfield Company Inc (PA)	Haverhill	MA	E	978 521-2600	9124
Wright Line LLC (HQ)	Worcester	MA	B	508 852-4300	13834
Mkind Inc	Manchester	NH	G	603 493-6882	14892
SIS-USA Inc	Londonderry	NH	E	603 432-4495	14784
Workplace Modular Systems LLC	Londonderry	NH	E	603 622-3727	14792
Constant Technologies Inc	North Kingstown	RI	E	800 518-7369	16240
Walcott Associates LLC	North Kingstown	RI	F	401 694-0153	16292

FURNITURE: Office, Wood

	CITY	ST	EMP	PHONE	ENTRY#
Belmont Corporation	Bristol	CT	E	860 589-5700	413
Bergan Architectural Wdwkg Inc	Middletown	CT	E	860 346-0869	1739
Bloomfield Wood & Melamine Inc	Bloomfield	CT	F	860 243-3226	153
Bold Wood Interiors LLC	New Haven	CT	F	203 907-4077	2131
Conco Wood Working Inc	West Haven	CT	G	203 934-9665	4098
Cyr Woodworking Inc	Newington	CT	G	860 232-1991	2284
Lesro Industries Inc	Bloomfield	CT	D	800 275-7545	189
Professional Trades Netwrk LLC	Watertown	CT	G	860 567-0173	4026
S J Pappas Inc	Meriden	CT	G	203 237-7701	1695
Salamander Designs Ltd	Bloomfield	CT	E	860 761-9500	209
CAM Office Services Inc (PA)	Marlborough	MA	F	781 932-9868	10125
JC Clocks Company Inc	North Dartmouth	MA	E	508 998-8442	10998
Modu Form Inc (PA)	Fitchburg	MA	D	978 345-7942	8667
Officeworks Inc (PA)	Burlington	MA	F	781 270-9000	7403
Wright Line LLC (HQ)	Worcester	MA	B	508 852-4300	13834
Mavrikis Uphlstring Furn Dsign	Nashua	NH	G	603 883-6868	15131
Constant Technologies Inc	North Kingstown	RI	E	800 518-7369	16240
Modern Industries Inc	Providence	RI	E	401 331-8000	16566
Walcott Associates LLC	North Kingstown	RI	F	401 694-0153	16292
New England Woodcraft Inc	Brandon	VT	C	802 247-8211	17070

FURNITURE: School

	CITY	ST	EMP	PHONE	ENTRY#
Bouncyband LLC	Glastonbury	CT	G	860 916-9978	1271

	CITY	ST	EMP	PHONE	ENTRY#
CMI Restructuring Inc	Westfield	MA	D	413 562-3664	13160
Whitney Bros Co LLC	Keene	NH	E	603 352-2610	14628

FURNITURE: Storage Chests, Household, Wood

	CITY	ST	EMP	PHONE	ENTRY#
Wood Geek Inc	New Bedford	MA	G	508 858-5282	10660
Kenney Manufacturing Company (PA)	Warwick	RI	B	401 739-2200	16831

FURNITURE: Table Tops, Marble

	CITY	ST	EMP	PHONE	ENTRY#
East Coast Marble & Gran Corp	Lynn	MA	F	781 760-0207	9970
Onyx Marble & Granite LLC	Framingham	MA	F	508 620-0775	8793
Vanity World Inc	Canton	MA	F	508 668-1800	7839

FURNITURE: Tables, Office, Wood

	CITY	ST	EMP	PHONE	ENTRY#
Lorimer Studios LLC	North Kingstown	RI	F	401 714-0014	16270

FURNITURE: Upholstered

	CITY	ST	EMP	PHONE	ENTRY#
Cerrito Furniture Inds Inc	Branford	CT	F	203 481-2580	244
Ethan Allen Interiors Inc (PA)	Danbury	CT	C	203 743-8000	740
Copley Furniture Company Inc	Boston	MA	G	617 566-1000	6668
Crimson Upholstery Company Inc	Newton	MA	F	617 332-0758	10750
David Lefort	Halifax	MA	F	781 826-9033	9020
Grace Lee Designs Shilling	Cambridge	MA	F	617 661-7090	7593
Marthas Vineyard Furn Co LLC	Vineyard Haven	MA	G	508 687-9555	12491
McLaughlin Upholstering Co Inc	Everett	MA	F	617 389-0761	8495
New England Woodcraft Inc	Westford	MA	F	413 522-0137	13255
Alfreds Uphlstring Cstm Fbrcti	Alfred	ME	F	207 536-5565	4402
Custom Canvas & Upholstery LLC	Bridgton	ME	F	207 241-8518	4627
Jackson Caldwell	Oxford	ME	F	207 539-2325	5146
Harris OH Cabinetmaker	Deerfield	NH	G	603 781-1315	14186
Mavrikis Uphlstring Furn Dsign	Nashua	NH	G	603 883-6868	15131
New England Woodcraft Inc	Brandon	VT	C	802 247-8211	17070

FUSES: Electric

	CITY	ST	EMP	PHONE	ENTRY#
Mersen USA Ev LLC	Newburyport	MA	F	978 518-7648	10700

GAMES & TOYS: Baby Carriages & Restraint Seats

	CITY	ST	EMP	PHONE	ENTRY#
Monahan Products LLC (PA)	Rockland	MA	D	844 823-3132	11652

GAMES & TOYS: Craft & Hobby Kits & Sets

	CITY	ST	EMP	PHONE	ENTRY#
Essex Wood Products Inc	Colchester	CT	F	860 537-3451	658
Merida Meridian Inc	Boston	MA	E	617 464-5400	6885
Hasbro Inc	Providence	RI	E	401 280-2127	16530

GAMES & TOYS: Electronic

	CITY	ST	EMP	PHONE	ENTRY#
Greenbrier Games LLP	Marlborough	MA	G	978 618-8442	10155
Hitpoint Inc (PA)	Greenfield	MA	E	413 992-6663	8993
Neuromotion Inc	Boston	MA	F	415 676-9326	6912

GAMES & TOYS: Erector Sets

	CITY	ST	EMP	PHONE	ENTRY#
Lego Systems Inc (DH)	Enfield	CT	A	860 698-9367	1137

GARBAGE CONTAINERS: Plastic

	CITY	ST	EMP	PHONE	ENTRY#
Billy Hill Tubs LLC	Sterling	MA	G	978 422-8800	12156
Edward F Briggs Disposal Inc	East Greenwich	RI	G	401 294-6391	15984

GARBAGE DISPOSERS & COMPACTORS: Commercial

	CITY	ST	EMP	PHONE	ENTRY#
Devivo Industries Inc	Waterbury	CT	E	203 270-1552	3906
All-Way Service Corp	South Weymouth	MA	F	781 335-4533	11974

GAS & OIL FIELD EXPLORATION SVCS

	CITY	ST	EMP	PHONE	ENTRY#
Ace Energy LLC	Broad Brook	CT	F	860 623-3308	507
Economy Energy LLC	Westport	CT	G	203 227-5181	4167
El Paso Prod Oil Gas Texas LP	Hartford	CT	E	860 293-1990	1478
Equinor Pipelines LLC	Stamford	CT	C	203 978-6900	3344
Equinor US Holdings Inc (DH)	Stamford	CT	C	203 978-6900	3345
Moab Oil Inc	Norwalk	CT	F	203 857-6622	2539
Copenhgen Offshore Prtners Inc	New Bedford	MA	E	508 717-8964	10579
Hess Inc	Brockton	MA	E	508 587-8325	7283
Nuvera Fuel Cells LLC (HQ)	Billerica	MA	C	617 245-7500	6465
Quantum Discoveries Inc	Boston	MA	G	857 272-9998	6989
Republic Midstream Mktg LLC	Boston	MA	E	617 531-6300	7005
Schlumberger Technology Corp	Cambridge	MA	C	617 768-2000	7707
Stroud International Ltd	Marblehead	MA	F	781 631-8806	10096
Woods Hole Group Inc (DH)	Bourne	MA	E	301 925-4411	7143
Hunting Dearborn Inc	Fryeburg	ME	C	207 935-2171	4809
James W Sewall Company	Bangor	ME	G	207 817-5410	4506
D F Richard Inc	Dover	NH	D	603 742-2020	14225
Clean Water Ventures Inc	North Kingstown	RI	F	858 437-3294	16237

GAS & OIL FIELD SVCS, NEC

	CITY	ST	EMP	PHONE	ENTRY#
Buffalo Gulf Cast Trminals LLC	Greenwich	CT	E	203 930-3802	1323
Kolmar Americas	Norwalk	CT	G	203 840-5337	2524

	CITY	ST	EMP	PHONE	ENTRY#
Digital Stream Energy Inc	Boston	MA	G	310 488-2743	6697
Home Heating Services Corp	Somerville	MA	G	617 625-8255	11880
Jiffy Lube	Mashpee	MA	G	508 539-8888	10252
Msr Utility	Dunstable	MA	G	978 649-0002	8328

GAS PROCESSING SVC

	CITY	ST	EMP	PHONE	ENTRY#
Arclight Enrgy Prtners Fund VI (PA)	Boston	MA	E	617 531-6300	6557

GASES & LIQUIFIED PETROLEUM GASES

	CITY	ST	EMP	PHONE	ENTRY#
Weymouth Gas LLC	Hanover	MA	F	781 826-4327	9048

GASES: Carbon Dioxide

	CITY	ST	EMP	PHONE	ENTRY#
Linde Gas & Equipment Inc	Slatersville	RI	D	401 767-3450	16682

GASES: Indl

	CITY	ST	EMP	PHONE	ENTRY#
Airgas Usa LLC	Danbury	CT	C	203 792-1834	705
Aldlab Chemicals LLC	North Haven	CT	F	203 589-4934	2390
Linde Gas & Equipment Inc	Danbury	CT	G	203 837-2162	774
Linde Gas & Equipment Inc (DH)	Danbury	CT	F	844 445-4633	775
Linde Inc (HQ)	Danbury	CT	B	203 837-2000	776
Linde Inc	Groton	CT	F	860 623-8211	1376
Airgas Usa LLC	Billerica	MA	E	978 439-1344	6398
American Industrial & Med Pdts (PA)	Auburn	MA	F	508 832-5785	6101
Electric Hydrogen Co	Natick	MA	E	617 546-5710	10480
Linde Gas & Equipment Inc	Palmer	MA	G	413 283-9906	11276
Messer LLC	Bellingham	MA	F	508 966-3148	6296
Hanna Instruments Inc (PA)	Woonsocket	RI	E	401 765-7500	16962
Messer LLC	Essex Junction	VT	E	802 878-6339	17240

GASES: Nitrogen

	CITY	ST	EMP	PHONE	ENTRY#
Messer LLC	Kittery	ME	E	207 475-3102	4937

GASES: Oxygen

	CITY	ST	EMP	PHONE	ENTRY#
Messer LLC	Danbury	CT	E	908 464-8100	785
O2 Concepts LLC	Middlebury	CT	E	877 867-4008	1718
Hydro-Test Products Inc	Stow	MA	F	978 897-4647	12246
Messer LLC	Stoughton	MA	F	781 341-4575	12224

GASKET MATERIALS

	CITY	ST	EMP	PHONE	ENTRY#
Auburn Manufacturing Company	Middletown	CT	E	860 346-6677	1737
Hollingsworth & Vose Company (PA)	East Walpole	MA	C	508 850-2000	8418

GASKETS

	CITY	ST	EMP	PHONE	ENTRY#
Corru-Seals Inc	Wallingford	CT	F	203 265-9331	3795
Parker-Hannifin Corporation	North Haven	CT	D	203 239-3341	2430
Spirol International Corp (HQ)	Danielson	CT	C	860 774-8571	844
Standard Washer & Mat Inc	Manchester	CT	E	860 643-5125	1638
Vanguard Products Corporation	Danbury	CT	D	203 744-7265	831
A W Chesterton Company (PA)	Groveland	MA	E	781 438-7000	9012
Acushnet Rubber Company Inc	New Bedford	MA	B	508 998-4000	10564
Atlantic Rubber Company Inc	Littleton	MA	F	800 882-3666	9804
Boston Atlantic Corp	Worcester	MA	F	508 754-4076	13705
D V Die Cutting Inc	Danvers	MA	G	978 777-0300	8177
Gasket Express Inc	Worcester	MA	G	508 754-4076	13727
Greene Rubber Company Inc (PA)	Woburn	MA	D	781 937-9909	13577
I G Marston Company	Holbrook	MA	F	781 767-2894	9174
Interstate Gasket Company Inc	Sutton	MA	E	508 234-5500	12283
Interstate Specialty Pdts Inc	Sutton	MA	E	800 984-1811	12284
United Tool & Machine Corp	Lawrence	MA	E	978 686-4181	9608
Vellumoid Inc	Worcester	MA	E	508 853-2500	13821

GASKETS & SEALING DEVICES

	CITY	ST	EMP	PHONE	ENTRY#
American Seal and Engrg Co Inc	Orange	CT	E	203 789-8819	2667
Derby Cellular Products Inc	Shelton	CT	E	203 735-4661	2999
H-O Products Corporation	Winsted	CT	E	860 379-9875	4346
SKF USA Inc	Winsted	CT	E	860 379-8511	4356
Parker-Hannifin Corporation	Woburn	MA	B	781 939-4278	13631
Saint-Gobain Prfmce Plas Corp	Worcester	MA	C	508 852-3072	13792
Woodex Bearing Company Inc	Georgetown	ME	E	207 371-2210	4815
Ferrotec (usa) Corporation	Bedford	NH	E	603 472-6800	13930
Marco Group LLC (PA)	Seabrook	NH	E	603 468-3600	15596
Trellborg Pipe Sals Mlford Inc (DH)	Milford	NH	F	800 626-2180	15042
Flex-A-Seal Inc	Williston	VT	E	802 878-8307	17729

GASOLINE FILLING STATIONS

	CITY	ST	EMP	PHONE	ENTRY#
Cumberland Farms Inc (DH)	Westborough	MA	B	800 225-9702	13097
Old Creamery Grocery Store	Cummington	MA	G	413 634-5560	8147
Highlands Fuel Delivery LLC (HQ)	Portsmouth	NH	D	603 559-8700	15404
Rounds Service Station Inc	North Scituate	RI	F	401 934-9877	16316
Hemmings Motor News Inc	Bennington	VT	A	802 442-3101	17040

GASOLINE WHOLESALERS

Employee Codes: A=Over 500 employees, B=251-500
C=101-250, D=51-100, E=20-50, F=10-19, G=1-9

2024 Harris New England
Manufacturers Directory

1397

PRODUCT

	CITY	ST	EMP	PHONE	ENTRY#
Cumberland Farms Inc **(DH)**	Westborough	MA	B	800 225-9702	13097
Highlands Fuel Delivery LLC **(HQ)**	Portsmouth	NH	D	603 559-8700	15404

GASTROINTESTINAL OR GENITOURINARY SYSTEM DRUGS

	CITY	ST	EMP	PHONE	ENTRY#
Decichera Pharmaceuticals LLC	Waltham	MA	B	781 209-6400	12648
Sobi Inc **(HQ)**	Waltham	MA	F	781 786-7370	12781

GATES: Dam, Metal Plate

	CITY	ST	EMP	PHONE	ENTRY#
Rodney Hunt-Fontaine Inc **(HQ)**	Orange	MA	E	978 544-2511	11232
Steel-Fab Inc	Fitchburg	MA	E	978 345-1112	8676

GAUGES: Pressure

	CITY	ST	EMP	PHONE	ENTRY#
Ashcroft Inc **(DH)**	Stratford	CT	B	203 378-8281	3517
Pressure Signal Inc	Rockland	MA	E	781 871-5629	11657

GEARS

	CITY	ST	EMP	PHONE	ENTRY#
United Gear and Machine Co Inc	Suffield	CT	F	860 623-6618	3596
Boulevard Machine & Gear Inc	Westfield	MA	E	413 788-6466	13154

GEARS & GEAR UNITS: Reduction, Exc Auto

	CITY	ST	EMP	PHONE	ENTRY#
Onvio Servo LLC	Salem	NH	C	603 685-0404	15554

GEARS: Power Transmission, Exc Auto

	CITY	ST	EMP	PHONE	ENTRY#
JET Corporation	Bridgeport	CT	F	203 334-3317	334
Bendon Gear and Machine Inc	Rockland	MA	E	781 878-8100	11636
Commercial Gear Sprocket Inc	East Walpole	MA	E	508 668-1073	8417
Custom Machine & Tool Co Inc	Hanover	MA	E	781 924-1003	9029
Insco Corporation	Groton	MA	E	978 448-6368	9010
Std Precision Gear & Instr Inc	West Bridgewater	MA	E	508 580-0035	12982
Allard Nazarian Group Inc **(PA)**	Manchester	NH	C	603 668-1900	14810

GENERAL COUNSELING SVCS

	CITY	ST	EMP	PHONE	ENTRY#
Kevin Emery	Farmington	NH	G	603 433-5784	14310

GENERATING APPARATUS & PARTS: Electrical

	CITY	ST	EMP	PHONE	ENTRY#
Afcon Products Inc	Bethany	CT	F	203 393-9301	91
Polaris Management Inc	Easton	CT	G	203 261-6399	1097

GENERATION EQPT: Electronic

	CITY	ST	EMP	PHONE	ENTRY#
Advanced Sonics LLC	Oxford	CT	G	203 266-4440	2684
B S T Systems Inc	Plainfield	CT	D	860 564-4078	2734
Asco Power Technologies LP	Marlborough	MA	D	508 624-0466	10111
Phoenix Electric Corp	Canton	MA	E	781 821-0200	7819
Sun Catalytix Corporation	Cambridge	MA	E	617 374-3797	7722
Superconductivity Inc **(HQ)**	Ayer	MA	D	608 831-5773	6197
Tasi Holdings Inc **(PA)**	Marlborough	MA	F	513 202-5182	10223
Thermo Fisher Scientific Inc **(PA)**	Waltham	MA	C	781 622-1000	12800
Wafer LLC	Beverly	MA	F	978 304-3821	6394
Stentech Inc **(PA)**	Derry	NH	D	603 505-4470	14209
Vicor Corporation	Manchester	NH	E	603 623-3222	14953
International Technologies Inc	Warwick	RI	F	401 467-6907	16823
Veterans Assembled Elec LLC **(PA)**	North Kingstown	RI	G	401 228-6165	16291

GENERATOR REPAIR SVCS

	CITY	ST	EMP	PHONE	ENTRY#
Afcon Products Inc	Bethany	CT	F	203 393-9301	91
BP Logue & Co	Chelmsford	MA	F	978 251-4433	7915
Chase Electric Motors LLC	Bedford	NH	G	603 669-2565	13921

GENERATORS SETS: Steam

	CITY	ST	EMP	PHONE	ENTRY#
On Site Gas Systems Inc	Newington	CT	E	860 667-8888	2313
Babcock Power Inc **(PA)**	Danvers	MA	G	978 646-3300	8166
Riley Power Inc	Marlborough	MA	B	508 852-7100	10204
M & A Advnced Design Cnstr Inc **(PA)**	Hampstead	NH	F	603 329-9515	14385

GENERATORS: Electrochemical, Fuel Cell

	CITY	ST	EMP	PHONE	ENTRY#
Ballard Unmanned Systems Inc	Southborough	MA	F	508 687-4970	11990
El-Op US Inc	Merrimack	NH	C	603 889-2500	14980
KMC Systems Inc	Merrimack	NH	D	866 742-0442	14987
Kollsman Inc **(DH)**	Merrimack	NH	A	603 889-2500	14988

GENERATORS: Gas

	CITY	ST	EMP	PHONE	ENTRY#
Angstrom Advanced Inc	Stoughton	MA	D	781 519-4765	12194
New England Gen-Connect LLC	Hingham	MA	G	617 571-6884	9155

GIFT SHOP

	CITY	ST	EMP	PHONE	ENTRY#
Bovano Industries Incorporated	Cheshire	CT	F	203 272-3208	576
Mystic Seaport Museum Inc	Mystic	CT	B	860 572-0711	1940
Albert E Cadrette	West Townsend	MA	F	978 597-2312	13056
Celebrations	Falmouth	MA	F	508 457-0530	8629
Dance It Up Inc	North Grafton	MA	F	508 839-1648	11021
Drive-O-Rama Inc **(PA)**	Hyannis	MA	G	508 771-8100	9434
Laurence Cndle Mfg Ch Sups Inc **(PA)**	Millbury	MA	E	508 865-6061	10439

	CITY	ST	EMP	PHONE	ENTRY#
Vaillancourt Folk Art Inc	Sutton	MA	E	508 476-3601	12294
Whiffletree Cntry Str Gift Sp	Billerica	MA	G	978 663-6346	6490
Harbor Candy Shop Inc	Ogunquit	ME	F	207 646-8078	5123
Kellerhaus Inc	Laconia	NH	F	603 366-4466	14654
Parkers Maple Barn Corn Crib	Mason	NH	A	603 878-2308	14967
Sawyers Jewelry Inc	Laconia	NH	F	603 527-1000	14667
Lake Champlain Trnsp Co	Burlington	VT	D	802 660-3495	17141
Windham Foundation Inc **(PA)**	Grafton	VT	F	802 843-2211	17275

GIFT WRAP: Paper, Made From Purchased Materials

	CITY	ST	EMP	PHONE	ENTRY#
Marian Heath Greeting Cards LLC	Wareham	MA	C	508 291-0766	12840

GIFT, NOVELTY & SOUVENIR STORES: Gifts & Novelties

	CITY	ST	EMP	PHONE	ENTRY#
Nicks Enterprises Inc **(PA)**	Hamden	CT	F	203 287-9990	1447

GIFTS & NOVELTIES: Wholesalers

	CITY	ST	EMP	PHONE	ENTRY#
Concord Industries Inc	Norwalk	CT	E	203 750-6060	2485
Executive Greetings Inc **(HQ)**	New Hartford	CT	B	860 379-9911	2100
Nicks Enterprises Inc **(PA)**	Hamden	CT	F	203 287-9990	1447
Ketcham Traps	New Bedford	MA	G	508 997-4787	10610
Mooneytunco Inc	Weymouth	MA	G	781 331-4445	13330
Nancy Sales Co Inc	Chelsea	MA	D	617 884-1700	7987
Downeast Concepts Inc	Yarmouth	ME	E	207 846-3726	5703
Lux Box Company Inc	Portland	ME	G	301 832-0622	5235
Glass Graphics Inc	Conway	NH	F	603 447-1900	14179
Ann Clark Ltd	Rutland	VT	E	802 773-7886	17489

GLASS & GLASS CERAMIC PRDTS, PRESSED OR BLOWN: Tableware

	CITY	ST	EMP	PHONE	ENTRY#
Tero Design Holdings LLC	Norwalk	CT	G	203 899-9950	2580

GLASS PRDTS, FROM PURCHASED GLASS: Enameled

	CITY	ST	EMP	PHONE	ENTRY#
Bovano Industries Incorporated	Cheshire	CT	F	203 272-3208	576

GLASS PRDTS, FROM PURCHASED GLASS: Glassware

	CITY	ST	EMP	PHONE	ENTRY#
Tero Design Holdings LLC	Norwalk	CT	G	203 899-9950	2580
Pgc Acquisition LLC	Reading	MA	G	508 888-2344	11604
Simon Pearce (us) Inc **(PA)**	Windsor	VT	C	802 674-6280	17762

GLASS PRDTS, FROM PURCHASED GLASS: Insulating

	CITY	ST	EMP	PHONE	ENTRY#
Sigco LLC	Westbrook	ME	E	207 775-2676	5648
Sigco LLC **(HQ)**	Westbrook	ME	C	207 775-2676	5649

GLASS PRDTS, FROM PURCHASED GLASS: Mirrored

	CITY	ST	EMP	PHONE	ENTRY#
Naugatuck Glass LLC	Naugatuck	CT	E	203 729-5227	1975
Canner Incorporated	West Groton	MA	F	978 448-3063	13001

GLASS PRDTS, PRESSED OR BLOWN: Barware

	CITY	ST	EMP	PHONE	ENTRY#
Ao Glass LLC	Burlington	VT	E	802 735-5016	17118

GLASS PRDTS, PRESSED OR BLOWN: Furnishings & Access

	CITY	ST	EMP	PHONE	ENTRY#
Whalley Glass Company **(PA)**	Derby	CT	D	203 735-9388	895
Vaillancourt Folk Art Inc	Sutton	MA	E	508 476-3601	12294
Simon Pearce US Inc	Windsor	VT	E	802 674-6280	17763

GLASS PRDTS, PRESSED OR BLOWN: Glass Fibers, Textile

	CITY	ST	EMP	PHONE	ENTRY#
Fiberoptics Technology Inc	Pomfret	CT	F	860 928-0443	2808
Owens Corning Sales LLC	East Hartford	CT	C	304 353-6945	1008
Ward Process Inc	Holliston	MA	D	508 429-1165	9238

GLASS PRDTS, PRESSED OR BLOWN: Glassware, Art Or Decorative

	CITY	ST	EMP	PHONE	ENTRY#
Pgc Acquisition LLC	Reading	MA	G	508 888-2344	11604
Thames Glass Inc	Newport	RI	F	401 846-0576	16226
Crest Studios	Townshend	VT	G	802 365-4200	17650

GLASS PRDTS, PRESSED OR BLOWN: Optical

	CITY	ST	EMP	PHONE	ENTRY#
Flabeg Technical Glass US Corp	Naugatuck	CT	E	203 729-5227	1958

GLASS PRDTS, PRESSED OR BLOWN: Scientific Glassware

	CITY	ST	EMP	PHONE	ENTRY#
Apogent Technologies Inc	Waltham	MA	A	781 622-1300	12594

GLASS PRDTS, PRESSED OR BLOWN: Tubing

	CITY	ST	EMP	PHONE	ENTRY#
Sentinel Process Systems Inc	Southborough	MA	F	508 624-5577	12002

GLASS: Fiber

	CITY	ST	EMP	PHONE	ENTRY#
Advance Coatings Co **(PA)**	Westminster	MA	F	978 874-5921	13268
Catalyst Acustics Group Inc	Agawam	MA	C	413 789-1770	5785
Catalyst Acustics Holdings Inc **(HQ)**	Agawam	MA	D	413 789-1770	5786

GLASS: Flat

	CITY	ST	EMP	PHONE	ENTRY#
A B C Glass Co Inc	Springfield	MA	F	413 734-4524	12067
B & G Glass LLC	Pittsfield	MA	G	413 442-3113	11391
Mygrant Glass Company Inc	Randolph	MA	F	781 767-3289	11569

	CITY	ST	EMP	PHONE	ENTRY#
Glass Graphics Inc	Conway	NH	F	603 447-1900	14179
New Erie Scientific LLC (DH)	Portsmouth	NH	E	603 430-6859	15425

GLASS: Laminated

	CITY	ST	EMP	PHONE	ENTRY#
LTI Smart Glass Inc	Pittsfield	MA	D	413 637-5001	11407
Protective Armored Systems Inc	Lee	MA	F	413 637-1060	9618

GLASS: Pressed & Blown, NEC

	CITY	ST	EMP	PHONE	ENTRY#
Bovano Industries Incorporated	Cheshire	CT	F	203 272-3208	576
G Schoepferinc	Cheshire	CT	F	203 250-7794	594
Schaeffler Aerospace USA Corp	Winsted	CT	D	860 379-7558	4354
A B C Glass Co Inc	Springfield	MA	F	413 734-4524	12067
Eye Health Services Inc	Plymouth	MA	E	508 747-6425	11459
Eye Health Services Inc (PA)	Quincy	MA	E	617 472-5242	11517
Fused Fiberoptics LLC	Southbridge	MA	F	508 765-1652	12017
Josh Smpson Cntemporary GL Inc	Shelburne Falls	MA	F	413 625-6145	11805
Mini-Systems Inc	Plainville	MA	E	508 695-2000	11439
Optical Laboratory Inc	New Bedford	MA	E	508 997-9779	10637
Perx LLC	Pittsfield	MA	F	413 358-9020	11417
Simon Pearce US Inc	Boston	MA	E	617 450-8388	7039
Stiles & Hart Brick Company	Bridgewater	MA	G	508 697-6928	7238
Corning Incorporated	Kennebunk	ME	D	207 985-3111	4924
Corning Incorporated	Keene	NH	C	603 357-7662	14594
M & M Glass Blowing Co Inc	Nashua	NH	G	603 598-8195	15129
New Erie Scientific LLC (DH)	Portsmouth	NH	E	603 430-6859	15425
Little Rver Htglass Studio Inc	Stowe	VT	G	802 253-0889	17632
Simon Pearce (us) Inc	Quechee	VT	E	802 295-2711	17463

GLASS: Safety

	CITY	ST	EMP	PHONE	ENTRY#
American Marine Products Inc	Charlestown	NH	F	954 782-1400	14060

GLASSWARE WHOLESALERS

	CITY	ST	EMP	PHONE	ENTRY#
Whalley Glass Company (PA)	Derby	CT	D	203 735-9388	895
Pgc Acquisition LLC	Reading	MA	G	508 888-2344	11604
Swarovski North America Ltd (DH)	Cranston	RI	A	401 463-6400	15915

GLASSWARE: Laboratory

	CITY	ST	EMP	PHONE	ENTRY#
High-Tech Conversions LLC	Enfield	CT	E	860 265-2633	1134
Klarmann Rulings Inc	Manchester	NH	F	603 424-2401	14872

GLOVES: Safety

	CITY	ST	EMP	PHONE	ENTRY#
Playtex Products LLC (HQ)	Shelton	CT	D	203 944-5500	3050
Tillotson Rubber Co Inc	Seekonk	MA	B	781 402-1731	11789
W D C Holdings Inc	Attleboro	MA	E	508 699-4412	6073
Healthco International LLC	Colebrook	NH	G	603 255-3771	14106
Honeywell Safety Pdts USA Inc	Smithfield	RI	F	401 757-2249	16713
North Safety Products LLC	Cranston	RI	A	401 943-4400	15902

GOLD ORE MINING

	CITY	ST	EMP	PHONE	ENTRY#
Castle Gate Invstmnts Ltd Lblt	Walpole	MA	G	617 596-1126	12555

GOLF COURSES: Public

	CITY	ST	EMP	PHONE	ENTRY#
Lyman Farm Incorporated (PA)	Middlefield	CT	C	860 349-1793	1725

GOLF EQPT

	CITY	ST	EMP	PHONE	ENTRY#
Golf Galaxy LLC	Norwalk	CT	F	203 855-0500	2507
Acushnet Holdings Corp (HQ)	Fairhaven	MA	E	800 225-8500	8505
Hollrock Engineering Inc	Hadley	MA	E	413 586-2256	9018
Omniview Sports Inc	Boston	MA	G	781 583-3534	6929
Tom Waters Golf Shop	Manchester	MA	G	978 526-7311	10034

GOLF GOODS & EQPT

	CITY	ST	EMP	PHONE	ENTRY#
Golf Galaxy LLC	Norwalk	CT	F	203 855-0500	2507
Lyman Farm Incorporated (PA)	Middlefield	CT	C	860 349-1793	1725

GOURMET FOOD STORES

	CITY	ST	EMP	PHONE	ENTRY#
Boyajian Inc	Canton	MA	F	781 828-9966	7774
Bread & Chocolate Inc	Wells River	VT	G	802 429-2920	17686

GOVERNMENT, GENERAL: Administration

	CITY	ST	EMP	PHONE	ENTRY#
City of Boston	Boston	MA	C	617 635-3700	6657

GRAIN & FIELD BEANS WHOLESALERS

	CITY	ST	EMP	PHONE	ENTRY#
Bridgwell Rsources Holdings LLC (HQ)	Greenwich	CT	E	203 622-9138	1322
Cofco Americas Resources Corp (HQ)	Stamford	CT	F	203 658-2820	3316
Poulin Grain Inc	Swanton	VT	E	802 868-8323	17640
Poulin Grain Inc (PA)	Newport	VT	D	802 334-6731	17404

GRANITE: Crushed & Broken

	CITY	ST	EMP	PHONE	ENTRY#
Skyline Quarry LLC	Stafford Springs	CT	F	860 875-3580	3259
McCullough Crushing Inc (PA)	Middlesex	VT	E	802 223-5693	17352

GRANITE: Cut & Shaped

	CITY	ST	EMP	PHONE	ENTRY#
Singer Company Inc	Waterford	CT	F	860 439-1234	3995
Stone Workshop LLC	Bridgeport	CT	G	203 362-1144	376
Atlantic MBL & Gran Group Inc	East Falmouth	MA	G	508 540-9770	8356
Continental Stone MBL Gran Inc	Sterling	MA	E	978 422-8700	12159
Divine Stoneworks LLC	Ashland	MA	F	774 221-6006	5956
Foxrock Granite LLC	Quincy	MA	F	617 249-8015	11520
Majestic Marble & Granite Inc	Canton	MA	G	781 830-1020	7807
Nicholas Ieronimo	Middleboro	MA	G	508 947-5363	10369
Ricciardi Marble & Granite Inc	Hyannis	MA	G	508 790-2734	9446
Atlas Gran Countertop Flr Sup	Derry	NH	G	603 818-8899	14190
Barre Tile Inc	Lebanon	NH	F	802 476-0912	14684
Swenson Granite Company LLC (DH)	Concord	NH	E	603 225-4322	14161
Stone Systems New England LLC	North Smithfield	RI	E	401 766-3603	16333
Adams Granite Co Inc	Websterville	VT	D	802 476-5281	17683
Buttura & Sons Inc	Barre	VT	E	802 476-6646	16998
Gandin Brothers Inc	South Ryegate	VT	F	802 584-3521	17614
Gawet Marble & Granite Inc (PA)	Center Rutland	VT	G	802 773-8868	17174
Granite Industries Vermont Inc	Barre	VT	D	800 451-3236	17003
Hillside Solid Surfaces	Barre	VT	F	802 479-2508	17005
Rock of Ages Corporation (DH)	Graniteville	VT	C	802 476-3115	17277
Spruce Mountian Granites Inc	Barre	VT	F	802 476-7474	17016
Spruce Mtn Gmtes Cstm Sndblas	Barre	VT	F	802 476-7474	17017

GRAPHIC ARTS & RELATED DESIGN SVCS

	CITY	ST	EMP	PHONE	ENTRY#
A To A Studio Solutions Ltd	Stamford	CT	F	203 388-9050	3267
Arteffects Incorporated	Bloomfield	CT	E	860 242-0031	147
Franklin Impressions Inc	Norwich	CT	F	860 887-1661	2605
Image Processing	Guilford	CT	G	203 488-3252	1397
P C I Group	Stamford	CT	F	203 327-0410	3425
Play-It Productions Inc	Colchester	CT	F	212 695-6530	663
Project Graphics Inc	Woodbury	CT	E	802 488-8789	4388
Schwerdtle Stamp Company	Bridgeport	CT	E	203 330-2750	369
Xtreme Designs LLC	East Haven	CT	G	203 773-9303	1057
Allison Advertising Inc	Boston	MA	F	617 368-6800	6537
Creative Publishing Corp Amer (PA)	Peabody	MA	F	978 532-5880	11303
J L Enterprises Inc	Canton	MA	G	781 821-6300	7802
Pg Technologies Inc	Westfield	MA	G	413 562-1354	13198
Rainbow Graphics Inc	Springfield	MA	F	413 733-3376	12124
Silver Screen Design Inc	Greenfield	MA	F	413 773-1692	9000
Toth Inc (PA)	Concord	MA	E	617 577-6400	8136
Valley Etching Engrv Dsign Inc	Holyoke	MA	F	413 536-2256	9289
Insty-Prints of Bedford Inc	Bedford	NH	F	603 622-3821	13934
Lestat Production 81 Corp	Bedford	NH	E	866 557-4478	13939
P2k Printing LLC	North Conway	NH	G	603 356-2010	15249
Fine Line Graphics Inc (PA)	Smithfield	RI	E	401 349-3300	16701
S G Inc	Pascoag	RI	F	401 568-1110	16340
Garlic Press Inc	Colchester	VT	F	802 864-0670	17192
Oatmeal Studios Inc	Rochester	VT	F	802 967-8014	17487
Stillwater Graphics Inc	Williamstown	VT	F	802 433-9898	17718

GRATINGS: Open Steel Flooring

	CITY	ST	EMP	PHONE	ENTRY#
Nucor Grating	Milford	MA	F	724 934-5320	10412

GRAVEL MINING

	CITY	ST	EMP	PHONE	ENTRY#
Dedham Recycled Gravel Co Inc	Dedham	MA	F	781 329-1044	8241
S M Lorusso & Sons Inc	Boston	MA	F	617 323-6380	7019
Hanley Construction Inc	Bristol	ME	F	207 677-2207	4630
Frank W Whitcomb Cnstr Corp (PA)	Walpole	NH	F	603 445-5555	15661

GREENHOUSES: Prefabricated Metal

	CITY	ST	EMP	PHONE	ENTRY#
Star Steel Structures Inc	Somers	CT	G	860 763-5681	3100
Rimol Greenhouse Systems Inc	Hooksett	NH	F	603 629-9004	14474

GREETING CARDS WHOLESALERS

	CITY	ST	EMP	PHONE	ENTRY#
Executive Greetings Inc (HQ)	New Hartford	CT	B	860 379-9911	2100
Olympia Sales Inc	Enfield	CT	D	860 749-0751	1140
Expressive Design Group Inc	Holyoke	MA	E	413 315-6296	9255
Lovepop Inc (PA)	Boston	MA	G	888 687-9589	6864

GRINDING SVC: Precision, Commercial Or Indl

	CITY	ST	EMP	PHONE	ENTRY#
N C T Inc	Colchester	CT	F	860 666-8424	662
New England Tooling Inc	Killingworth	CT	F	800 866-5105	1544
Duval Precision Grinding Inc	Chicopee	MA	E	413 593-3060	8028
Idex Health & Science LLC	Middleboro	MA	C	774 213-0200	10362
Insco Corporation	Groton	MA	E	978 448-6368	9010
True Machine Co Inc	Swansea	MA	G	508 379-0329	12314
B & B Precise Products Inc	Benton	ME	E	207 453-8118	4544
Contour360 Corp	Cornish	ME	E	207 625-4000	4704
Nikel Precision Group LLC	Saco	ME	D	207 282-6080	5375

PRODUCT

	CITY	ST	EMP	PHONE	ENTRY#

GRINDING SVCS: Ophthalmic Lens, Exc Prescription

	CITY	ST	EMP	PHONE	ENTRY#
Bomas Machine Specialties Inc	Woburn	MA	F	617 628-3831	13528

GROCERIES, GENERAL LINE WHOLESALERS

	CITY	ST	EMP	PHONE	ENTRY#
Norpaco Inc	Middletown	CT	D	860 632-2299	1768
Cambridge Packing Co Inc	Boston	MA	D	617 464-6000	6635
Colony Foods Inc	Lawrence	MA	F	978 794-1500	9553
Pvk Inc	Lynn	MA	F	781 595-7771	9989
Wohrles Foods Inc (PA)	Pittsfield	MA	E	413 442-1518	11427
Portion Meat Associates Inc	Providence	RI	F	401 421-2438	16585
Supreme Dairy Farms	Woonsocket	RI	F	401 739-8180	16977
Back Roads Food Co LLC	Brattleboro	VT	F	802 579-1135	17074

GUIDED MISSILES & SPACE VEHICLES

	CITY	ST	EMP	PHONE	ENTRY#
Kaman Corporation (PA)	Bloomfield	CT	D	860 243-7100	183
Rogue Space Systems Corp	Laconia	NH	F	603 460-5069	14666

GUIDED MISSILES & SPACE VEHICLES: Research & Development

	CITY	ST	EMP	PHONE	ENTRY#
Raytheon Company (HQ)	Waltham	MA	B	781 522-3000	12759
Raytheon Korean Support Co (DH)	Waltham	MA	E	339 645-6111	12761
Raytheon Lgstics Spport Trning (DH)	Bedford	MA	F	310 647-9438	6256
Raytheon Company	Merrimack	NH	G	978 313-0201	15000

GUTTERS: Sheet Metal

	CITY	ST	EMP	PHONE	ENTRY#
A Plus Exterior LLC	Milford	CT	F	203 516-1729	1792
U-Sealusa LLC	Newington	CT	F	860 667-0911	2331
Yost Manufacturing & Sup Inc	Waterford	CT	F	800 872-9678	4000
Aluminum Products Cape Cod Inc (PA)	Dennis Port	MA	F	508 398-8546	8259
Frs Company Inc	Medford	MA	F	781 322-6252	10285

GYPSUM PRDTS

	CITY	ST	EMP	PHONE	ENTRY#
GP Gypsum Corp	Portsmouth	NH	G	603 433-8000	15394
USG Services Corporation	Pawtucket	RI	G	401 644-7098	16427

GYROSCOPES

	CITY	ST	EMP	PHONE	ENTRY#
Ais Global Holdings LLC	Cheshire	CT	E	203 250-3500	570
Atlantic Inertial Systems Inc (DH)	Cheshire	CT	B	203 250-3500	572
Atlantic Inertial Systems Inc	Cheshire	CT	C	203 250-3500	573

HAIR & HAIR BASED PRDTS

	CITY	ST	EMP	PHONE	ENTRY#
Idelle Management Company	Danbury	CT	E		758
Ouidad Products LLC	Danbury	CT	G		793

HAIR CARE PRDTS

	CITY	ST	EMP	PHONE	ENTRY#
Golden Sun Inc	Stamford	CT	E	800 575-7960	3356
Henkel US Operations Corp	Darien	CT	A	203 655-8911	848
Chuckles Inc	Manchester	NH	E	603 669-4228	14828

HAIR CARE PRDTS: Hair Coloring Preparations

	CITY	ST	EMP	PHONE	ENTRY#
Continental Fragrances Ltd	Stamford	CT	E	800 542-5903	3322
Hunter Dathan Hair Artistry	Portland	ME	G	207 774-8887	5224

HAND TOOLS, NEC: Wholesalers

	CITY	ST	EMP	PHONE	ENTRY#
Kell-Strom Tool Intl Inc	Wethersfield	CT	F	860 529-6851	4210

HANDBAGS

	CITY	ST	EMP	PHONE	ENTRY#
Blw Holdings Inc (PA)	Fairhaven	MA	C	508 994-4000	8507
Brahmin Leather Works LLC	Fairhaven	MA	C	509 994-4000	8508
W D C Holdings Inc	Attleboro	MA	E	508 699-4412	6073

HANDBAGS: Women's

	CITY	ST	EMP	PHONE	ENTRY#
Dooney & Bourke Inc (HQ)	Norwalk	CT	E	203 853-7515	2492

HARD RUBBER PRDTS, NEC

	CITY	ST	EMP	PHONE	ENTRY#
Standard Rubber Products Inc	Hanover	MA	E	781 878-2626	9043
Maine Industrial P & R Corp	Newcastle	ME	G	207 563-5532	5095

HARDWARE

	CITY	ST	EMP	PHONE	ENTRY#
Air-Lock Incorporated	Milford	CT	E	203 878-4691	1794
Brookfield Industries Inc	Thomaston	CT	E	860 283-6211	3615
Hdb Inc	Thomaston	CT	F	860 379-9901	3621
Hicks and Otis Prints Inc	Norwalk	CT	E	203 846-2087	2513
Incjet	Norwich	CT	F	860 823-1427	2607
Lewmar Inc (DH)	Guilford	CT	E	203 458-6200	1399
Outland Engineering Inc	Milford	CT	F	800 797-3709	1861
Paradigm Manchester Inc	Manchester	CT	C	860 649-2888	1625
Perry Technology Corporation	New Hartford	CT	D	860 738-2525	2107
Roller Bearing Co Amer Inc	Middlebury	CT	E	203 758-8272	1720
Stanley Black & Decker Inc	New Britain	CT	G	860 225-5111	2064
Stanley Industrial & Auto LLC	New Britain	CT	C	800 800-8005	2070
Tiger Enterprises Inc	Plantsville	CT	E	860 621-9155	2798

	CITY	ST	EMP	PHONE	ENTRY#
Unger Industrial LLC	Bridgeport	CT	G	203 336-3344	382
Vector Engineering Inc	Mystic	CT	F	860 572-0422	1944
Afc Cable Systems Inc	New Bedford	MA	B	508 998-1131	10566
Atlantic RES Mktg Systems Inc	West Bridgewater	MA	F	508 584-7816	12966
Atrenne Cmpt Solutions LLC (DH)	Brockton	MA	B	508 588-6110	7259
Craft Inc	Attleboro	MA	E	508 761-7917	6008
Delaware Valley Corp	Tewksbury	MA	E	978 459-6932	12393
Dorel Juvenile Group Inc	Foxboro	MA	C	800 544-1108	8694
Everett Aluminum Inc	Everett	MA	F	617 389-3839	8488
Gardner Screw Corporation	Gardner	MA	F	978 632-0850	8887
H&H Propeller and Shaft Inc	Salem	MA	F	800 325-0117	11720
Hostar Mar Trnspt Systems Inc	Wareham	MA	F	508 295-2900	12838
Jibo Inc	Boston	MA	D	617 542-5426	6825
Newera Services Corporation (PA)	New Bedford	MA	E	508 995-9711	10631
Rolls-Royce Marine North Amer (DH)	Walpole	MA	C	508 668-9610	12574
Roses Oil Service Inc (PA)	Gloucester	MA	E	877 283-3334	8955
Taunton Stove Company Inc	North Dighton	MA	E	508 823-0786	11004
W J Roberts Co Inc	Saugus	MA	E	781 233-8176	11767
Worcester Tool & Stamping Co	Rochdale	MA	E	508 892-8194	11630
Xcerra Corporation (HQ)	Norwood	MA	C	781 461-1000	11220
Morse Hardware & Lumber LLC	Wells	ME	F	207 646-5700	5603
Sands Business Eqp & Sups LLC	York	ME	F	207 351-3334	5716
Bronze Craft Corporation	Nashua	NH	D	603 883-7747	15074
American Cord & Webbing Co Inc	Woonsocket	RI	E	401 762-5500	16948
Beacon Rock Properties Inc	Providence	RI	D	401 421-3470	16482
Drapery House Inc	North Providence	RI	E	401 724-3400	16300
Fulford Manufacturing Company (PA)	Riverside	RI	F	401 431-2000	16655
Groov-Pin Corporation (PA)	Smithfield	RI	D	770 251-5054	16707
Hindley Manufacturing Co Inc	Cumberland	RI	D	401 722-2550	15943

HARDWARE & BUILDING PRDTS: Plastic

	CITY	ST	EMP	PHONE	ENTRY#
The Gilman Brothers Company	Gilman	CT	D	860 889-8444	1268
Westbrook Manufacturing LLC	Ivoryton	CT	F	860 767-2460	1534
Fibertec Inc	Bridgewater	MA	D	508 697-5100	7229
Flagraphics Inc	Somerville	MA	E	617 776-7549	11874
LD Plastics Inc	Brockton	MA	E	508 584-7651	7289
Millennium Plastics Inc	North Chelmsford	MA	F	978 372-4822	10984
Plastic Concepts Inc	North Billerica	MA	F	978 663-7996	10943
Carris Financial Corp (PA)	Proctor	VT	F	802 773-9111	17456
Carris Reels Inc (HQ)	Proctor	VT	E	802 773-9111	17457

HARDWARE & EQPT: Stage, Exc Lighting

	CITY	ST	EMP	PHONE	ENTRY#
Audiospectrum Inc	Randolph	MA	E	781 767-1331	11549

HARDWARE STORES

	CITY	ST	EMP	PHONE	ENTRY#
F W Webb Company	New Haven	CT	F	203 865-6124	2151
Plastic Met Components Co Inc	Milford	CT	F	203 877-2723	1866
Irvings Home Center Inc	Brockton	MA	G	508 583-4421	7285
Lyn-Lad Group Ltd (PA)	Lynn	MA	F	781 598-6010	9984
Maki Building Centers Inc (HQ)	Gardner	MA	E	978 343-7422	8894
Maki Corp (PA)	Gardner	MA	E	978 343-7422	8895
National Lumber Company	Newton	MA	E	617 244-8020	10770
National Lumber Company LLC (HQ)	Mansfield	MA	C	508 339-8020	10068
Renovators Supply Inc	Erving	MA	E	413 423-3300	8471
Hammond Lumber Company (PA)	Belgrade	ME	C	207 495-3303	4540
Lyle Guptill	East Machias	ME	F	207 255-4130	4740
N C Hunt Inc (PA)	Jefferson	ME	E	207 549-0922	4918
R E Lowell Lumber Co Inc	Buckfield	ME	E	207 336-2901	4658
S W Collins	Lincoln	ME	F	207 794-6113	5013
Gilberte Interiors LLC (PA)	Hanover	NH	F	603 643-3727	14423
White Mountain Lumber Co Inc	Berlin	NH	E	603 752-1000	13987
379 Charles RI Inc	North Providence	RI	F	401 521-1101	16293

HARDWARE STORES: Builders'

	CITY	ST	EMP	PHONE	ENTRY#
Essex County Coop Farming Assn	Topsfield	MA	F	978 887-2300	12433

HARDWARE STORES: Pumps & Pumping Eqpt

	CITY	ST	EMP	PHONE	ENTRY#
Proflow Inc	North Haven	CT	E	203 230-4700	2433
Sulzer Pump Solutions US Inc (PA)	Wallingford	CT	E	203 238-2700	3856
F W Webb Company	Needham	MA	F	781 247-0300	10510
F W Webb Company	Windham	ME	F	207 892-5302	5661

HARDWARE STORES: Tools

	CITY	ST	EMP	PHONE	ENTRY#
Chapman Manufacturing Company	Durham	CT	F	860 349-9228	896
Swanson Tool Manufacturing Inc	West Hartford	CT	F	860 953-1641	4084
Safe-T-Cut Inc	Monson	MA	F	413 267-9984	10456
Gary Raymond	Caribou	ME	G	207 498-2549	4675

HARDWARE STORES: Tools, Hand

	CITY	ST	EMP	PHONE	ENTRY#
Kelco Industries	Milbridge	ME	E	207 546-7562	5061

HARDWARE WHOLESALERS

	CITY	ST	EMP	PHONE	ENTRY#
Carey Manufacturing Co Inc	Cromwell	CT	F	860 829-1803	689
Plastic Met Components Co Inc	Milford	CT	F	203 877-2723	1866
Steeltech Building Pdts Inc	South Windsor	CT	D	860 290-8930	3184
Viking Kitchen Cabinets LLC (PA)	New Britain	CT	E	860 223-7101	2074
Wind Corporation	Newtown	CT	E	800 946-3267	2354
Apco Mossberg Co	Attleboro	MA	G	508 222-0340	5993
Coating House Inc	East Longmeadow	MA	F	413 525-3100	8372
F W Webb Company	Needham	MA	F	781 247-0300	10510
Hudson Lock LLC (PA)	Hudson	MA	D	978 562-3481	9373

HARDWARE, WHOLESALE: Builders', NEC

Columbus Door Company	Warwick	RI	D	401 781-7792	16796

HARDWARE, WHOLESALE: Chains

East Shore Wire Rope Rgging Su	North Haven	CT	F	203 469-5204	2407

HARDWARE, WHOLESALE: Furniture, NEC

Bloomfield Wood & Melamine Inc	Bloomfield	CT	F	860 243-3226	153

HARDWARE, WHOLESALE: Power Tools & Access

Air Tool Sales & Svc Co Inc (PA)	Unionville	CT	G	860 673-2714	3746
Disston Company	Chicopee	MA	E	800 272-4436	8025
Express Assemblyproducts LLC	Nashua	NH	F	603 424-5590	15098

HARDWARE, WHOLESALE: Screws

Allesco Industries Inc (PA)	Cranston	RI	F	401 943-0680	15828
Alloy Fasteners Inc (HQ)	Cranston	RI	E	401 943-0639	15830
Eastern Screw Company	Cranston	RI	C	401 943-0680	15852

HARDWARE, WHOLESALE: Security Devices, Locks

Loctec Corporation	Newtown	CT	G	203 364-1000	2340

HARDWARE: Aircraft

Hartford Aircraft Products Inc	Bloomfield	CT	E	860 242-8228	168
James Ippolito & Co Conn Inc	Bridgeport	CT	E	203 366-3840	333
Kell-Strom Tool Co Inc (PA)	Wethersfield	CT	F	860 529-6851	4209
Kell-Strom Tool Intl Inc	Wethersfield	CT	F	860 529-6851	4210
Meadow Manufacturing Inc	Bristol	CT	F	860 357-3785	467
Paneloc Corporation	Farmington	CT	F	860 677-6711	1238
De-Ice Technologies Inc	Somerville	MA	E	857 829-7651	11868

HARDWARE: Aircraft & Marine, Incl Pulleys & Similar Items

Autonomous Marine Systems Inc	Somerville	MA	G	703 348-4778	11862
Accutech Marine Propeller Inc	Dover	NH	G	603 617-3626	14213
Ronstan International Inc	Portsmouth	RI	F	401 293-0539	16456

HARDWARE: Builders'

Colonial Bronze Company	Torrington	CT	D	860 489-9233	3674
Heckmann Building Products Inc	Norwalk	CT	E	708 865-2403	2511
Stanley Black & Decker Inc	New Britain	CT	B	860 225-5111	2063
Stanley Black & Decker Inc (PA)	New Britain	CT	C	860 225-5111	2065
Stanley Black & Decker Inc	New Britain	CT	F	860 827-5025	2066
Stanley Black & Decker Inc	New Britain	CT	C	860 225-5111	2067
Stanley Black Dcker Asia Hldng (HQ)	New Britain	CT	C	860 225-5111	2068
Acorn Manufacturing Co Inc	Mansfield	MA	E	508 339-4500	10036
Qc Industries Inc (PA)	Mansfield	MA	D	781 344-1000	10073
Renovators Supply Inc	Erving	MA	F	413 423-3300	8471
Coyote Mountain Farm Inc	Ossipee	NH	G	603 662-2164	15282
J&E Home Products LLC	Lincoln	RI	E	401 464-8677	16142

HARDWARE: Door Opening & Closing Devices, Exc Electrical

New England Door Closer Inc	West Springfield	MA	E	413 733-7889	13037

HARDWARE: Parachute

Bourdon Forge Co Inc	Middletown	CT	C	860 632-2740	1741
Crrc LLC	Cromwell	CT	D	860 635-2200	691
Crrc LLC (PA)	South Windsor	CT	D	877 684-6464	3136

HARDWARE: Rubber

Ballard Away Corporation	Lawrence	MA	C	978 689-2800	9542

HARNESS ASSEMBLIES: Cable & Wire

Data Signal Corporation	Milford	CT	E	203 882-5393	1816
Lq Mechatronics Inc	Branford	CT	G	203 433-4430	268
Precision Electronic Assembly	Monroe	CT	F	203 452-1839	1919
Rel-Tech Electronics Inc	Milford	CT	D	203 877-8770	1876
Robert Warren LLC (PA)	Westport	CT	E	203 247-3347	4195
Siemon Company (PA)	Watertown	CT	A	860 945-4200	4029
Technical Manufacturing Corp	Durham	CT	E	860 349-1735	904
Tornik Inc	Rocky Hill	CT	C	860 282-6081	2937
Tornik LLC	Rocky Hill	CT	F	860 282-6081	2938
Desco Electronics Inc	Plainville	MA	E	508 643-1950	11431

	CITY	ST	EMP	PHONE	ENTRY#
Electronic Assemblies Mfg Inc	Methuen	MA	E	978 374-6840	10329
First Electronics Corporation	Braintree	MA	D	617 704-4248	7183
First Electronics Corporation	Chelsea	MA	D	617 288-2430	7981
First Electronics Corporation (DH)	Dorchester	MA	D	617 288-2430	8299
Fourstar Connections Inc	Hudson	MA	D	978 568-9800	9369
General Manufacturing Corp	North Billerica	MA	D	978 667-5514	10917
Global Interconnect Inc (PA)	Pocasset	MA	D	508 563-6306	11487
Heilind Electronics Inc (PA)	Wilmington	MA	D	978 657-4870	13410
Jem Electronics Inc	Franklin	MA	E	508 520-3105	8845
Manage Inc	Springfield	MA	E	413 593-9128	12112
Microtek Inc	Chicopee	MA	C	413 593-1025	8049
PCA LLC	Andover	MA	F	978 494-0550	5905
Sunburst Elctrnic Mfg Sltons I (PA)	West Bridgewater	MA	D	508 580-1881	12983
V-Tron Electronics Corp	Attleboro	MA	D	508 761-9100	6072
Advanced Design & Mfg Inc	Portsmouth	NH	E	603 430-7573	15357
Electronics Aid Inc	Marlborough	NH	G	603 876-4161	14964
Ica Northeast Inc	Exeter	NH	E	603 773-2386	14293
Ksaria Corporation	Hudson	NH	C	866 457-2742	14519
Miraco Inc	Manchester	NH	E	603 665-9449	14890
Scott Electronics Inc (PA)	Salem	NH	D	603 893-2845	15559
Versatile Subcontracting LLC	Northfield	NH	G	603 286-8081	15271
Igus Bearings Inc (HQ)	Rumford	RI	C	800 521-2747	16669
Image Tek Mfg Inc	Springfield	VT	E	802 885-6208	17618
Vemas Corporation	Poultney	VT	E	802 287-4100	17454

HEALTH AIDS: Exercise Eqpt

Aqua Massage International Inc	Mystic	CT	F	860 536-3735	1936
Cybex International Inc	Medway	MA	C	508 533-4167	10304
Advanced Fitnes Components LLC	Hudson	NH	G	603 595-1967	14480

HEARING AIDS

Tena Group LLC	Windham	ME	G	207 893-2920	5671

HEAT EMISSION OPERATING APPARATUS

Design Architectural Heating	Lewiston	ME	F	207 784-0309	4955

HEAT EXCHANGERS: After Or Inter Coolers Or Condensers, Etc

Mp Systems Inc	East Granby	CT	E	860 687-3460	944
Alfa Laval Inc	Newburyport	MA	D	978 465-5777	10666
Merrimac Industrial Sales Inc (PA)	Haverhill	MA	E	978 372-6006	9115
Taco Inc (PA)	Cranston	RI	B	401 942-8000	15917

HEAT TREATING: Metal

A G C Incorporated	Meriden	CT	C	203 235-3361	1649
A-1 Heat Treating Inc	Ansonia	CT	F	914 220-2179	4
Accurate Brazing Corporation	Manchester	CT	F	860 432-1840	1581
American Heat Treating Inc	Monroe	CT	E	203 268-1750	1904
Amk Welding Inc	South Windsor	CT	E	860 289-5634	3113
Bodycote Thermal Proc Inc	Berlin	CT	E	860 225-7691	52
Bodycote Thermal Proc Inc	Berlin	CT	D	508 754-1724	53
Eastern Metal Treating Inc	Enfield	CT	F	860 763-4311	1128
Johnstone Company Inc	North Haven	CT	E	203 239-5834	2419
Metallurgical Processing	West Hartford	CT	G	860 916-5015	4073
Metallurgical Processing Incorporated	New Britain	CT	D	860 224-2648	2044
Nelson Heat Treating Co Inc	Waterbury	CT	F	203 754-0670	3948
Paradigm Manchester Inc	Manchester	CT	C	860 649-2888	1625
Sousa Corp	Newington	CT	F	860 523-9090	2326
Specialty Steel Treating Inc	East Granby	CT	E	860 653-0061	953
Walter A Beach Inc	East Hartford	CT	G	860 282-7440	1033
Bodycote Imt Inc (DH)	Andover	MA	D	978 470-0876	5873
Engelhard Surface Tech	Wilmington	MA	D	978 658-0032	13406
Fireball Heat Treating Co Inc	Attleboro	MA	G	508 222-2617	6017
Hy Temp Inc	Attleboro	MA	F	508 222-6626	6024
Industrial Heat Treating Inc	North Quincy	MA	E	617 328-1010	11036
Materials Development Corp	Andover	MA	D	781 391-0400	5893
Metal Processing Co Inc	Tyngsboro	MA	G	978 649-1289	12461
Norking Company Inc	Attleboro	MA	E	508 222-3100	6043
Northeast Metals Tech LLC	Rowley	MA	G	978 948-2633	11682
S M Engineering Co Inc	North Attleboro	MA	F	508 699-4484	10886
Thermo Electron F S C Inc	Waltham	MA	C	781 622-1000	12798
Enterprise Casting Corporation	Lewiston	ME	F	207 782-5511	4961
Bodycote Thermal Proc Inc	Laconia	NH	E	603 524-7886	14647
Brazecom Industries LLC	Weare	NH	G	603 529-2080	15670
Mushield Company Inc	Londonderry	NH	E	603 666-4433	14776
Smiths Tblar Systms-Lconia Inc	Laconia	NH	C	603 524-2064	14470
Turbocam Energy Solutions LLC	Dover	NH	E	603 905-0200	14255
Windy Ridge Corporation	Tamworth	NH	G	603 323-2323	15650
Induplate Inc (PA)	North Providence	RI	D	401 231-5770	16303
Metallurgical Solutions Inc	Providence	RI	D	401 941-2100	16563
S & P Heat Treating Inc	Warwick	RI	F	401 737-9272	16856
Spectrum Thermal Proc LLC	Cranston	RI	F	401 808-6249	15912
Bodycote Surface Tech Inc	Rutland	VT	E	802 773-4278	17490

Employee Codes: A=Over 500 employees, B=251-500
C=101-250, D=51-100, E=20-50, F=10-19, G=1-9

2024 Harris New England
Manufacturers Directory

1401

PRODUCT

	CITY	ST	EMP	PHONE	ENTRY#

HEATERS: Swimming Pool, Electric

	CITY	ST	EMP	PHONE	ENTRY#
Siemens Hlthcare Dgnostics Inc	Andover	MA	F	212 258-4000	5919

HEATERS: Swimming Pool, Oil Or Gas

| Aquacomfort Solutions LLC | Wallingford | CT | G | 203 265-0100 | 3774 |
| Marios Oil Corp | Everett | MA | G | 617 202-8259 | 8493 |

HEATING & AIR CONDITIONING UNITS, COMBINATION

Pfm Holding Co	Fairfield	CT	B	203 335-3300	1197
7ac Technologies Inc	Beverly	MA	F	781 574-1348	6322
Harris Envmtl Systems Inc	Andover	MA	D	978 470-8600	5885
Heat-Flo Inc	Uxbridge	MA	G	508 278-2400	12480
Suburban Service Corp Norwood	Westwood	MA	F	781 769-1515	13320

HEATING APPARATUS: Steam

| Tunstall Corporation (PA) | Chicopee | MA | E | 413 594-8695 | 8064 |

HEATING EQPT: Complete

Alpha Instruments Inc	Acton	MA	G	978 264-2966	5735
Backer Hotwatt Inc	Danvers	MA	E	978 777-0070	8168
Mestek Inc (PA)	Westfield	MA	E	470 898-4533	13186
Renewable Energy Systems LLC	Scituate	MA	F	781 545-3320	11769
Rubix Composites Inc	Woburn	MA	G	781 856-0342	13657
Amtrol Holdings Inc	West Warwick	RI	A	401 884-6300	16899
Amtrol Inc (DH)	West Warwick	RI	B	401 884-6300	16900
Davidon Industries Inc	Warwick	RI	F	401 737-8380	16803
John Hazen Whote Corporation	Cranston	RI	F	401 942-8000	15879

HEATING EQPT: Induction

East Coast Induction Inc	Brockton	MA	F	508 587-2800	7274
Radio Frequency Company Inc	Millis	MA	E	508 376-9555	10450
Purmo Group USA Inc	Williston	VT	F	802 654-7500	17746

HEATING PADS: Nonelectric

| Graphite Insulg Systems Inc | Gardner | MA | F | 978 630-8988 | 8890 |

HEATING SYSTEMS: Radiant, Indl Process

Calorique LLC	West Wareham	MA	F	508 291-2000	13057
Dcaf of Massachusetts Inc	West Wareham	MA	F	508 291-2000	13060
Runtal North America Inc	Haverhill	MA	E	800 526-2621	9128

HEATING UNITS & DEVICES: Indl, Electric

Birk Manufacturing Inc	East Lyme	CT	D	800 531-2070	1058
Duralite Incorporated	Riverton	CT	F	860 379-3113	2912
Industrial Heater Corp	Cheshire	CT	D	203 250-0500	601
Manufacturers Coml Fin LLC	West Hartford	CT	E	860 242-6287	4070
Sshc Inc	Westbrook	CT	F	860 399-5434	4143
Warmup Inc	Danbury	CT	F		834
Allen Morgan	Bridgewater	MA	G	714 538-7492	7219
Dalton Electric Heating Co Inc	Ipswich	MA	E	978 356-9844	9483
The Sentry Company	Foxboro	MA	G	508 543-5391	8728
Vulcan Electric Company (PA)	Porter	ME	D	207 625-3231	5171
Sargeant & Wilbur Inc	Pawtucket	RI	F	401 726-0013	16415

HELICOPTERS

Kaman Aerospace Corporation	Bloomfield	CT	E	860 242-4461	180
Kaman Corporation (PA)	Bloomfield	CT	D	860 243-7100	183
Sikorsky Aircraft Corporation	Bridgeport	CT	D	203 384-7532	372
Sikorsky Aircraft Corporation	Shelton	CT	E	203 386-7861	3062
Sikorsky Aircraft Corporation	Shelton	CT	E	203 386-4000	3063
Sikorsky Aircraft Corporation (HQ)	Stratford	CT	A	203 386-4000	3571
Sikorsky Export Corporation	Stratford	CT	D	203 386-4000	3574

HELMETS: Athletic

| Old Bh Inc | Exeter | NH | B | 603 430-2111 | 14298 |

HELMETS: Steel

| Government Surplus Sales Inc | Hartford | CT | G | 860 247-7787 | 1484 |
| Norcross Safety Products LLC | Smithfield | RI | A | 800 430-5490 | 16724 |

HOBBY, TOY & GAME STORES: Arts & Crafts & Splys

| Sheepscot River Pottery (PA) | Edgecomb | ME | F | 207 882-9410 | 4748 |

HOBBY, TOY & GAME STORES: Dolls & Access

| American Girl Brands LLC | Natick | MA | D | 508 810-3461 | 10469 |

HOISTS

| St Pierre Manufacturing Corp | Worcester | MA | E | 508 853-8010 | 13806 |
| Somatex Inc | Detroit | ME | E | 207 487-6141 | 4725 |

HOISTS: Aircraft Loading

| Entwistle Company LLC (PA) | Hudson | MA | D | 508 481-4000 | 9364 |

HOLDING COMPANIES: Investment, Exc Banks

Avara US Holdings LLC (PA)	Norwalk	CT	E	203 655-1333	2468
Kco Numet Inc	Orange	CT	E	203 375-4995	2671
Legrand Holding Inc (DH)	West Hartford	CT	E	860 233-6251	4067
Polymedex Discovery Group Inc (PA)	Putnam	CT	C	860 928-4102	2870
Video Messengercom Corp	Stratford	CT	G	203 358-8842	3582
Wizards Nuts Holdings LLC (PA)	Greenwich	CT	D	708 483-1315	1362
Altium Acqisition Holdings Inc	Boston	MA	A	617 516-2000	6539
Connell Limited Partnership (PA)	Boston	MA	F	617 737-2700	6665
Dawson Forte Holdings LLC (PA)	Canton	MA	A	508 651-7910	7782
Euro-Pro Holdco LLC	Needham Heights	MA	D	617 243-0235	10543
Ginger Acquisition Inc	Boston	MA	B	617 551-4000	6760
Gurnet Holding Company	Cambridge	MA	C	617 588-4900	7595
Kettle Cuisine Holdings LLC	Lynn	MA	C	617 409-1100	9981
Source Code Midco LLC (PA)	Norwood	MA	E	781 255-2022	11210
Kullson Engineered Tech Inc	Lewiston	ME	E	207 576-9808	4969
Cooley Group Holdings Inc (PA)	Pawtucket	RI	C	401 724-0510	16358
Mack Group Inc (PA)	Arlington	VT	B	802 375-2511	16988

HOLDING COMPANIES: Personal, Exc Banks

Longview Holding Corporation (HQ)	Greenwich	CT	G	203 869-6734	1339
Naiad Maritime Group Inc (PA)	Shelton	CT	E	203 944-1932	3034
Ibmnh Inc (PA)	Manchester	NH	G	603 644-2326	14861

HOME HEALTH CARE SVCS

| Fev Tutor Inc | Woburn | MA | D | 781 376-6925 | 13564 |
| Kaz Inc (HQ) | Marlborough | MA | D | 508 490-7000 | 10174 |

HOMEFURNISHING STORES: Fireplaces & Wood Burning Stoves

| Architctral Fireplaces of Neng | Auburn | MA | F | 508 757-0622 | 6104 |

HOMEFURNISHING STORES: Lighting Fixtures

Acme Sign Co (PA)	Stamford	CT	F	203 324-2263	3272
Lighthouse Distributors Inc	Marshfield	MA	G	781 319-9828	10241
Lighting By Hammerworks (PA)	Worcester	MA	E	508 755-3434	13753

HOMEFURNISHING STORES: Pottery

| Georgetown Pottery | Georgetown | ME | G | 207 371-2801 | 4814 |
| Sheepscot River Pottery (PA) | Edgecomb | ME | F | 207 882-9410 | 4748 |

HOMEFURNISHING STORES: Venetian Blinds

| Arrow Win Shade Mfg of Mrden I | Wethersfield | CT | G | 860 563-4035 | 4202 |
| J & R Langley Co Inc | Manchester | NH | E | 603 622-9653 | 14866 |

HOMEFURNISHINGS, WHOLESALE: Carpets

| Matter Surfaces Inc (PA) | Stoughton | MA | F | 800 628-7462 | 12223 |
| Merida Meridian Inc | Boston | MA | E | 617 464-5400 | 6885 |

HOMEFURNISHINGS, WHOLESALE: Kitchenware

Glass Industries America LLC	Wallingford	CT	G	203 269-6700	3810
Tero Design Holdings LLC	Norwalk	CT	G	203 899-9950	2580
Architctral Fireplaces of Neng	Auburn	MA	F	508 757-0622	6104
Petermans Boards and Bowls Inc	Gill	MA	G	413 863-2116	8915
Sherle Wagner Intl LLC	Fall River	MA	F	212 758-3300	8606
KAY DEE DESIGNS INC (PA)	Hope Valley	RI	E	401 539-2400	16067

HOMEFURNISHINGS, WHOLESALE: Wood Flooring

| Cabinets For Less LLC | Manchester | NH | G | 603 935-7551 | 14825 |

HOMES: Log Cabins

Country Log Homes Inc	Goshen	CT	F	413 229-8084	1302
C A Construction Inc	Gouldsboro	ME	G	207 422-3493	4838
Katahdin Forest Products Co (PA)	Oakfield	ME	D	800 845-4533	5119
Moosehead Country Log Homes	Greenville	ME	G	207 695-3730	4851
Moosehead Wood Components Inc	Greenville Junction	ME	F	207 695-3730	4852
Wlhc Inc (PA)	Houlton	ME	G	207 532-6531	4906
Benson Woodworking Company Inc	Walpole	NH	D	603 756-3600	15659
Granite State Log Homes Inc (PA)	Campton	NH	F	603 536-4949	14044
Timberpeg East Inc (PA)	Claremont	NH	E	603 542-7762	14099
Whs Homes Inc (PA)	Claremont	NH	E	603 542-5418	14100
Gilcris Enterprises Inc	Proctorsville	VT	F	802 226-7764	17461
Groton Timberworks Inc	Groton	VT	G	802 584-4446	17278
Londonderry Industrial Pk Inc	South Londonderry	VT	E	802 297-3760	17611
William H Moore Inc	Waitsfield	VT	G	802 496-3595	17668

HOODS: Range, Sheet Metal

| Denlar Fire Protection LLC | Chester | CT | G | 860 526-9846 | 626 |
| Nevtec Ltd | Newport | VT | F | 802 334-7800 | 17401 |

HORSESHOES

	CITY	ST	EMP	PHONE	ENTRY#
Diamond Hrseshoe Dev Group LLC	Quincy	MA	G	617 755-6100	11510
Horseshoe Sunday LLC	Haverhill	MA	G	978 476-9766	9104
St Pierre Manufacturing Corp	Worcester	MA	E	508 853-8010	13806
Horseshoe Pond Place Commnty	Concord	NH	G	603 224-8390	14137
Blue Horseshoe LLC	Bristol	RI	G	401 253-0037	15755

HOSE: Flexible Metal

	CITY	ST	EMP	PHONE	ENTRY#
East Coast Metal Hose Inc	Naugatuck	CT	G	203 723-7459	1956
Senior Operations LLC	Enfield	CT	E	860 741-2546	1148
Afc Cable Systems Inc	New Bedford	MA	B	508 998-1131	10566
Senior Operations LLC	Sharon	MA	C	781 784-1400	11795
Titeflex Corporation (HQ)	Springfield	MA	B	413 739-5631	12140
Niantic Seal Inc	Lincoln	RI	E	401 334-6870	16150

HOSE: Garden, Rubber

	CITY	ST	EMP	PHONE	ENTRY#
Teknor Apex Company (PA)	Pawtucket	RI	A	401 725-8000	16420

HOSE: Plastic

	CITY	ST	EMP	PHONE	ENTRY#
Titeflex Corporation (HQ)	Springfield	MA	B	413 739-5631	12140
Contitech Thermopol LLC	Rochester	NH	E	603 692-6300	15471
Contitech Thermopol LLC	Somersworth	NH	E	603 692-6300	15614
Contitech Thermopol LLC (HQ)	Somersworth	NH	C	603 692-6300	15615

HOSE: Rubber

	CITY	ST	EMP	PHONE	ENTRY#
Greene Rubber Company Inc (PA)	Woburn	MA	D	781 937-9909	13577
Samar Co Inc	Stoughton	MA	E	781 297-7264	12233

HOSPITALS: Medical & Surgical

	CITY	ST	EMP	PHONE	ENTRY#
Bcpe Seminole Holdings LP (PA)	Boston	MA	F	617 516-2000	6585
Cistercian Abbey Spencer Inc	Spencer	MA	E	508 885-8700	12056

HOT TUBS

	CITY	ST	EMP	PHONE	ENTRY#
Thermospas Hot Tub Products	Wallingford	CT	E	203 303-0005	3861

HOT TUBS: Plastic & Fiberglass

	CITY	ST	EMP	PHONE	ENTRY#
Leisure Zone Stores Inc	Putnam	CT	F	860 963-1181	2863

HOTELS & MOTELS

	CITY	ST	EMP	PHONE	ENTRY#
Bay Colony Associates (PA)	Boston	MA	G	617 287-9100	6584
Jordan Associates	Pittsburg	NH	F	603 246-8998	15328

HOUSEHOLD ARTICLES, EXC FURNITURE: Cut Stone

	CITY	ST	EMP	PHONE	ENTRY#
Williams & Co Mining Inc	Perkinsville	VT	F	802 263-5404	17443

HOUSEHOLD ARTICLES, EXC KITCHEN: Pottery

	CITY	ST	EMP	PHONE	ENTRY#
Gare Incorporated	Haverhill	MA	E	978 373-9131	9096
Simon Pearce (us) Inc (PA)	Windsor	VT	C	802 674-6280	17762

HOUSEHOLD ARTICLES: Metal

	CITY	ST	EMP	PHONE	ENTRY#
Alvarez Industries LLC	Orange	CT	D	203 799-2356	2666
Hampden Fence Supply Inc	Agawam	MA	F	413 786-4390	5792
S & A Trombley Corporation	Morrisville	VT	E	802 888-2394	17388

HOUSEHOLD FURNISHINGS, NEC

	CITY	ST	EMP	PHONE	ENTRY#
Hills Point Industries LLC (PA)	Westport	CT	F	800 807-8579	4173
R L Fisher Inc	Hartford	CT	E	860 951-8110	1503
Talalay Global Inc (DH)	Shelton	CT	F	203 924-0700	3067
Beantown Bedding LLC	Hingham	MA	F	781 608-9915	9143
Berkshire Corporation (HQ)	Great Barrington	MA	F	413 528-2602	8973
Emotionrx Inc	Cambridge	MA	F	617 500-5976	7561
Fall River Apparel Inc	Fall River	MA	F	508 677-1975	8545
Dirigo Stitching Inc	Skowhegan	ME	E	207 474-8421	5466
Goodwill Industries Nthrn Neng (PA)	Gorham	ME	D	207 774-6323	4820
Maine Balsam Fir Prodcts	West Paris	ME	F	207 674-5090	5612
Anichini Inc	Tunbridge	VT	E	802 889-9430	17651

HOUSEHOLD SEWING MACHINES WHOLESALERS: Electric

	CITY	ST	EMP	PHONE	ENTRY#
Abisee Inc	Acton	MA	E	978 637-2900	5730

HOUSEWARES, ELECTRIC, EXC COOKING APPLIANCES & UTENSILS

	CITY	ST	EMP	PHONE	ENTRY#
Headwaters Inc	Marblehead	MA	G	781 715-6404	10087
QCI Inc	Seekonk	MA	F	508 399-8983	11784
Mills & Co Inc	Windham	ME	C	207 893-1115	5665

HOUSEWARES, ELECTRIC: Air Purifiers, Portable

	CITY	ST	EMP	PHONE	ENTRY#
Puraclenz LLC	New Canaan	CT	G	561 213-1411	2085
Aeris Health Inc	Bedford	MA	F	917 685-6504	6206

HOUSEWARES, ELECTRIC: Broilers

	CITY	ST	EMP	PHONE	ENTRY#
Bkmfg Corp	Winsted	CT	E	860 738-2200	4339

HOUSEWARES, ELECTRIC: Cooking Appliances

	CITY	ST	EMP	PHONE	ENTRY#
Black & Decker (us) Inc	New Britain	CT	G	860 225-5111	2008
Revolution Cooking LLC	Woburn	MA	F	301 710-0590	13652
Vaughn Thermal Corporation	Salisbury	MA	E	978 462-6683	11745

HOUSEWARES, ELECTRIC: Fans, Exhaust & Ventilating

	CITY	ST	EMP	PHONE	ENTRY#
Ecovent Corp	Charlestown	MA	F	620 983-6863	7869
Spruce Environmental Tech Inc	Haverhill	MA	D	978 521-0901	9134

HOUSEWARES, ELECTRIC: Heating Units, Electric Appliances

	CITY	ST	EMP	PHONE	ENTRY#
Springfield Wire Inc	Ludlow	MA	A	413 385-0115	9954
Eichenauer Inc	Newport	NH	E	603 863-1454	15228

HOUSINGS: Business Machine, Sheet Metal

	CITY	ST	EMP	PHONE	ENTRY#
South Main Manchester Housing	Manchester	NH	G	603 626-3034	14935

HUMIDIFIERS & DEHUMIDIFIERS

	CITY	ST	EMP	PHONE	ENTRY#
Controlled Envmt Systems LLC (PA)	Mansfield	MA	E	508 339-4237	10042
Munters Corporation (DH)	Amesbury	MA	C	978 241-1100	5845
Nyle International Corp (PA)	Bangor	ME	C	207 989-4335	4512
Pool Environments Inc	Gorham	ME	F	207 839-8225	4831

HYDRAULIC EQPT REPAIR SVC

	CITY	ST	EMP	PHONE	ENTRY#
Dependable Repair Inc	North Branford	CT	F	203 481-9706	2365
Faxon Engineering Company Inc (PA)	Bloomfield	CT	F	860 236-4266	163
Power-Dyne LLC	Middletown	CT	E	860 346-9283	1772

ICE

	CITY	ST	EMP	PHONE	ENTRY#
Grotto Always Inc	Waterbury	CT	F	203 754-0295	3915
Vaporizer LLC	Moosup	CT	E	860 564-7225	1931
Brito Ice LLC	Salem	MA	F	978 744-7727	11705
Cape Pond Ice Company (PA)	Gloucester	MA	E	978 283-0174	8927
Coldwell Banker	Tewksbury	MA	F	978 851-3731	12390
Crystal Ice Co Inc	New Bedford	MA	F	508 997-7522	10582
Eastern Ice Company Inc	Fall River	MA	E	508 672-1800	8538
JP Lillis Enterprises Inc (PA)	Sandwich	MA	F	508 888-8394	11751
Lake Boone Ice Co LLC	Hudson	MA	G	508 755-3099	9382
Leominster Ice Company Inc	Leominster	MA	G	978 537-5322	9678
Mass Dry Ice Corporation (DH)	Palmer	MA	F	413 283-9906	11277
Getchell Bros Inc	Sanford	ME	F	207 490-0809	5397
Taggart Ice Inc	Nashua	NH	F	603 888-4630	15174
Cape Cod Ice	Rumford	RI	E	401 438-4555	16664

ICE CREAM & ICES WHOLESALERS

	CITY	ST	EMP	PHONE	ENTRY#
295 Tremont Inc	Attleboro	MA	D	508 222-2884	5985
Brighams Inc (HQ)	Arlington	MA	F	800 242-2423	5939
Freeze Operations Holding Corp (PA)	Wilbraham	MA	A	413 543-2445	13360
Hershey Creamery Company	Seekonk	MA	F	508 399-8560	11777
Getchell Bros Inc (PA)	Brewer	ME	E	800 949-4423	4613
Shains	Sanford	ME	D	207 324-1449	5415
Annablles Ntral Ice Cream Ygur	Portsmouth	NH	G	603 436-3400	15359

IDENTIFICATION TAGS, EXC PAPER

	CITY	ST	EMP	PHONE	ENTRY#
Ann S Davis	Lebanon	CT	F	860 642-7228	1548
Currys Leather Shop Inc	Randolph	MA	G	781 963-0679	11554
Gzsl Corp	North Attleboro	MA	E	508 695-0727	10872
Ask-Inttag LLC	Essex Junction	VT	E	802 288-7210	17226

IGNITION APPARATUS & DISTRIBUTORS

	CITY	ST	EMP	PHONE	ENTRY#
Tanyx Measurements Inc	Billerica	MA	G	978 671-0183	6485

IGNITION SYSTEMS: High Frequency

	CITY	ST	EMP	PHONE	ENTRY#
Simmonds Precision Pdts Inc	Danbury	CT	F	203 797-5000	818
Simmonds Precision Products (DH)	Vergennes	VT	A	802 877-4000	17661

INDL & PERSONAL SVC PAPER WHOLESALERS

	CITY	ST	EMP	PHONE	ENTRY#
Boyd Biomedical Inc (PA)	Lee	MA	E	413 243-2000	9612
Diamond Water Systems Inc	Chicopee	MA	E	413 536-8186	8022
LCI Paper Company	Hudson	MA	F	508 281-5088	9384
McLaughlin Paper Co Inc (PA)	West Springfield	MA	F	413 732-7485	13033
Visionstep Consulting Inc	Fitchburg	MA	E	978 422-1447	8681
Judd Paper Company	Rumford	RI	F	413 534-5661	16673

INDL & PERSONAL SVC PAPER, WHOLESALE: Boxes & Containers

	CITY	ST	EMP	PHONE	ENTRY#
Fortis Solutions Group LLC	Ellington	CT	E	860 872-6311	1107

INDL & PERSONAL SVC PAPER, WHOLESALE: Shipping Splys

	CITY	ST	EMP	PHONE	ENTRY#
IR Industries Inc	Bethel	CT	F	203 790-8273	121
Penmar Industries Inc	Stratford	CT	F	203 853-4868	3565
Horn Corporation (PA)	Lancaster	MA	E	800 832-7020	9527
Pacific Packaging Products Inc (PA)	Wilmington	MA	C	978 657-9100	13445
Vidarr Inc	Portsmouth	NH	G	877 636-8432	15448

PRODUCT

	CITY	ST	EMP	PHONE	ENTRY#

INDL EQPT SVCS

	CITY	ST	EMP	PHONE	ENTRY#
Afcon Products Inc	Bethany	CT	F	203 393-9301	91
Environmental Monitor Svc Inc	Meriden	CT	G	203 935-0102	1667
Hydro Service & Supplies Inc	Middletown	CT	G	203 265-3995	1751
Machine Builders Neng LLC	Milford	CT	F	203 922-9446	1847
American Water Systems LLC	Canton	MA	F	781 830-9722	7767
Azenta Inc (PA)	Burlington	MA	A	978 262-2400	7339
B G Wickberg Company Inc	East Weymouth	MA	G	781 335-7800	8425
Liquid Solids Control Inc (PA)	Upton	MA	E	508 529-3377	12473
Thermo Egs Gauging LLC	Chelmsford	MA	C	978 663-2300	7965
Maine Industrial Repair Service Inc	Augusta	ME	E	207 623-7500	4476
Macy Industries Inc	Hooksett	NH	E	603 623-5568	14468

INDL GASES WHOLESALERS

	CITY	ST	EMP	PHONE	ENTRY#
Connecticut Analytical Corp	Bethany	CT	F	203 393-9666	92
Airgas Usa LLC	Billerica	MA	E	978 439-1344	6398
B&C Cryotech Services Inc	Sutton	MA	G	508 277-5440	12277

INDL MACHINERY & EQPT WHOLESALERS

	CITY	ST	EMP	PHONE	ENTRY#
Arthur G Russell Company Inc	Bristol	CT	D	860 583-4109	398
Bloomy Controls Inc (PA)	South Windsor	CT	E	860 298-9925	3120
Bremser Technologies Inc	Stratford	CT	F	203 378-8486	3521
Del-Tron Precision Inc	Bethel	CT	E	203 778-2727	107
Devar Inc	Bridgeport	CT	E	203 368-6751	317
Gems Sensors Inc (HQ)	Plainville	CT	B	860 747-3000	2761
Helander Products Inc	Clinton	CT	E	860 669-7953	644
Industrial Flow Sltons Oper LL	New Haven	CT	E	860 399-5937	2163
Interface Devices Incorporated	Milford	CT	G	203 878-4648	1839
ITT Goulds Pumps Inc (HQ)	Stamford	CT	E	315 568-2811	3387
Jovil Universal LLC	Danbury	CT	F	203 792-6700	763
L M Gill Welding and Mfr LLC (PA)	Manchester	CT	D	860 647-9931	1610
Novo Precision LLC	Bristol	CT	E	860 583-0517	476
Record Products America Inc	Hamden	CT	F	203 248-6371	1453
Ringfeder Pwr Transm USA Corp (HQ)	Bolton	CT	F	201 666-3320	222
Royal Machine and Tool Corp	Berlin	CT	E	860 828-6555	83
Tenova Inc	Wallingford	CT	E	203 265-5684	3859
The Viking Tool Company	Shelton	CT	E	203 929-1457	3068
Wittmann Usa Inc (DH)	Torrington	CT	D	860 496-9603	3708
Acme-Shorey Precast Co Inc (PA)	Harwich	MA	F	508 432-0530	9066
Anver Corporation	Hudson	MA	E	978 568-0221	9354
Assocted Electro-Mechanics Inc	Springfield	MA	D	413 781-4276	12076
Auburn Systems LLC	Beverly	MA	G	978 777-2460	6329
Baker Parts Inc	Westport	MA	G	508 878-5436	13293
Degreasing Devices Co	Southbridge	MA	G	508 765-0045	12013
Dienes Corporation	Spencer	MA	E	508 885-6301	12057
Dynisco Instruments LLC (HQ)	Franklin	MA	C	508 541-9400	8831
Emuge Corp	West Boylston	MA	E	508 595-3600	12962
Frank I Rounds Company (PA)	Randolph	MA	E	401 333-5014	11559
Gorman Machine Corp	Middleboro	MA	E	508 923-9462	10359
Jeio Tech Inc	Billerica	MA	G	781 376-0700	6457
JP Plastics Inc	Foxboro	MA	E	508 203-2420	8704
Kadant Inc	Auburn	MA	C	508 791-8171	6116
Liquid Solids Control Inc (PA)	Upton	MA	E	508 529-3377	12473
Luster-On Products Inc	Springfield	MA	F	413 739-2541	12111
Mettler-Toledo Thornton Inc (DH)	Billerica	MA	D	978 262-0210	6460
Omtec Corp	Marlborough	MA	F	508 481-3322	10190
Panametrics LLC (DH)	Billerica	MA	A	978 437-1000	6468
Polytech Fltration Systems Inc	Hudson	MA	F	978 562-7700	9402
Sanger Equipment Corporation	Conway	MA	F	413 625-8304	8145
Thomson Service Corp	Franklin	MA	F	508 528-2000	8872
Toolmex Indus Solutions Inc (PA)	Northborough	MA	D	508 653-8897	11114
Trans Metrics Inc (HQ)	Watertown	MA	F	617 926-1000	12916
Ulvac Technologies Inc (HQ)	Methuen	MA	E	978 686-7550	10347
Whitmor Company Inc (PA)	Revere	MA	F	781 284-8000	11625
Whitney & Son Inc	Fitchburg	MA	E	978 343-6353	8682
Centilla Corporation	Windham	NH	F	603 658-3881	15723
Controlair LLC	Amherst	NH	E	603 886-9400	13865
HMC Corporation (PA)	Hopkinton	NH	E	603 746-3399	14477
Hyde Specialty Products LLC	Merrimack	NH	F	603 883-7400	14984
Atlantic Automation Group LLC	Bristol	RI	E	401 424-1840	15754
Rbc Industries Inc	Cranston	RI	D	401 941-3000	15906
Walco Electric Company	Providence	RI	F	401 467-6500	16642
Fellows Corporation	Windsor	VT	F	802 674-6500	17758
Vermont Machine Tool Corp	Springfield	VT	F	802 885-5161	17622
Worksafe Traffic Ctrl Inds Inc (PA)	Barre	VT	G	802 223-8948	17025

INDL PATTERNS: Foundry Cores

	CITY	ST	EMP	PHONE	ENTRY#
Roehr Tool Corp	Sterling	MA	E	978 562-4488	12169

INDL PATTERNS: Foundry Patternmaking

	CITY	ST	EMP	PHONE	ENTRY#
Goodwin-Bradley Pattern Co Inc	Providence	RI	F	401 461-5220	16525

INDL PROCESS INSTRUMENTS: Analyzers

	CITY	ST	EMP	PHONE	ENTRY#
Pid Analyzers LLC	Sandwich	MA	F	774 413-5281	11752
Roscid Technologies Inc	Woburn	MA	G	781 933-4007	13656
Semilab USA LLC	Billerica	MA	E	508 647-8400	6479

INDL PROCESS INSTRUMENTS: Control

	CITY	ST	EMP	PHONE	ENTRY#
Dynamic Bldg Enrgy Sltions LLC (PA)	North Stonington	CT	F	860 599-1872	2447

INDL PROCESS INSTRUMENTS: Elements, Primary

	CITY	ST	EMP	PHONE	ENTRY#
Primary Flow Signal Inc (PA)	Cranston	RI	D	401 461-6366	15905

INDL PROCESS INSTRUMENTS: Moisture Meters

	CITY	ST	EMP	PHONE	ENTRY#
Kahn Instruments Incorporated	Wethersfield	CT	G	860 529-8643	4208
Laticrete Supercap LLC	Bethany	CT	G	203 393-4558	95
Panametrics LLC (DH)	Billerica	MA	A	978 437-1000	6468

INDL PROCESS INSTRUMENTS: On-Stream Gas Or Liquid Analysis

	CITY	ST	EMP	PHONE	ENTRY#
Lynn Products Co	Lynn	MA	F	781 593-2500	9986

INDL PROCESS INSTRUMENTS: Thermistors

	CITY	ST	EMP	PHONE	ENTRY#
Advanced Thermal Solutions Inc (PA)	Norwood	MA	E	781 769-2800	11157

INDL SALTS WHOLESALERS

	CITY	ST	EMP	PHONE	ENTRY#
Blank Industries LLC	Hudson	MA	E	855 887-3123	9356

INDL SPLYS WHOLESALERS

	CITY	ST	EMP	PHONE	ENTRY#
Automation Inc	West Hartford	CT	E	860 236-5991	4048
B I L Inc	Groton	CT	F	860 446-8058	1365
Kell-Strom Tool Intl Inc	Wethersfield	CT	F	860 529-6851	4210
Motion Industries Inc	Bloomfield	CT	A	860 687-5000	195
Nucor Hrris Rbar Northeast LLC	South Windsor	CT	D	860 282-1860	3166
Seals-It Inc	Ellington	CT	G	860 979-0060	1114
Spectrum Associates Inc	Milford	CT	F	203 878-4618	1889
Sperry Automatics Co Inc	Naugatuck	CT	E	203 729-4589	1986
Stanley Black & Decker Inc	New Britain	CT	C	860 225-5111	2067
Afc Cable Systems Inc	New Bedford	MA	B	508 998-1131	10566
Airgas Usa LLC	Billerica	MA	E	978 439-1344	6398
American Holt Corporation (PA)	Norwood	MA	F	781 440-9993	11160
Ar-Ro Engineering Company Inc	Uxbridge	MA	F	401 766-6669	12477
C F G Corporation	Saugus	MA	F	781 233-6110	11754
Esco Technologies Inc	Holliston	MA	E	508 429-4441	9209
Gardner Screw Corporation	Gardner	MA	F	978 632-0850	8887
Hope Inc	Needham	MA	E	781 455-1145	10512
Joma Diamond Tool LLC	East Longmeadow	MA	F	413 525-0760	8381
Kinefac Corporation	Worcester	MA	D	508 754-6901	13749
Safety-Kleen Systems Inc (HQ)	Norwell	MA	B	800 669-5740	11146
Ulvac Technologies Inc (HQ)	Methuen	MA	E	978 686-7550	10347
AC Electric Corp	Bangor	ME	F	207 945-9487	4487
Deepwater Buoyancy Inc	Biddeford	ME	F	207 468-2565	4559
Lane Conveyors & Drives Inc	Brewer	ME	F	207 989-4560	4616
Pieceworks Inc	Montville	ME	G	207 589-3451	5075
PRC Acquisition Company Inc	Gorham	ME	F	207 854-3702	4832
Tis Brewer LLC	Brewer	ME	E	207 989-4560	4621
New Hmpshire Ball Bearings Inc	Peterborough	NH	F	818 407-9300	15320
Bullard Abrasives Inc	Lincoln	RI	D	508 366-4300	16123
W L Fuller Inc	Warwick	RI	E	401 467-2900	16876

INDL SPLYS, WHOLESALE: Abrasives

	CITY	ST	EMP	PHONE	ENTRY#
Composition Materials Co Inc	Milford	CT	G	203 874-6500	1812
Essex Silverline Corporation (PA)	Dracut	MA	F	978 957-2116	8305
Abrasives & Tools NH Inc	Pembroke	NH	E	603 224-5376	15301
Meister Abrasives Usa Inc	North Kingstown	RI	F	401 294-4503	16271

INDL SPLYS, WHOLESALE: Bearings

	CITY	ST	EMP	PHONE	ENTRY#
F-K Bearings Inc	Southington	CT	F	860 621-4567	3210
Kaman Aerospace Corporation	Bloomfield	CT	E	860 242-4461	180
Kaman Corporation (PA)	Bloomfield	CT	D	860 243-7100	183
Rbc Aircraft Products Inc	Torrington	CT	D	860 626-7800	3692
Rbc Bearings Incorporated (PA)	Oxford	CT	C	203 267-7001	2710
Lm/Tarbell Inc	East Longmeadow	MA	F	413 525-4166	8383
Motion Industries Inc	Danvers	MA	E	978 774-7100	8210
Igus Bearings Inc (HQ)	Rumford	RI	C	800 521-2747	16669

INDL SPLYS, WHOLESALE: Fasteners & Fastening Eqpt

	CITY	ST	EMP	PHONE	ENTRY#
Cbm Industries Inc	Taunton	MA	E	508 821-4555	12326

INDL SPLYS, WHOLESALE: Gaskets

	CITY	ST	EMP	PHONE	ENTRY#
Boston Atlantic Corp	Worcester	MA	F	508 754-4076	13705
Greene Rubber Company Inc (PA)	Woburn	MA	D	781 937-9909	13577
Cogebi Inc	Dover	NH	F	603 749-6896	14223

	CITY	ST	EMP	PHONE	ENTRY#

INDL SPLYS, WHOLESALE: Gears

	CITY	ST	EMP	PHONE	ENTRY#
Protek Ski Racing Inc	Southington	CT	G	860 628-9643	3229

INDL SPLYS, WHOLESALE: Power Transmission, Eqpt & Apparatus

	CITY	ST	EMP	PHONE	ENTRY#
Altra Industrial Motion Corp	New Hartford	CT	E	860 379-1673	2098
Altra Industrial Motion Corp (HQ)	Braintree	MA	C	781 917-0600	7167
Altra Power Transmission Inc	Braintree	MA	B	781 917-0600	7168
Warner Electric	Braintree	MA	D	781 917-0600	7212

INDL SPLYS, WHOLESALE: Rubber Goods, Mechanical

	CITY	ST	EMP	PHONE	ENTRY#
Acmt Inc	Manchester	CT	D	860 645-0592	1582
Airex Rubber Products Corporation	Portland	CT	E	860 342-0850	2816
Applied Rubber & Plastics Inc	Windsor	CT	F	860 987-9018	4261
Vanguard Products Corporation	Danbury	CT	D	203 744-7265	831
Acushnet Rubber Company Inc	New Bedford	MA	B	508 998-4000	10564
Biltrite Corporation (PA)	Brockton	MA	F	781 647-1700	7261
Device Technologies Inc	Southborough	MA	E	508 229-2000	11994
Hutchinson Arospc & Indust Inc (DH)	Hopkinton	MA	B	508 417-7000	9330
Jefferson Rubber Works Inc	Worcester	MA	D	508 791-3600	13744
Pocasset Machine Corporation	Pocasset	MA	E	508 563-5572	11491
Freudenberg-Nok General Partnr	Northfield	NH	C	603 286-1600	15265
Z-Flex Realty Inc (DH)	Bedford	NH	E	603 669-5136	13957
Zhongding Laconia Inc	Laconia	NH	E	603 524-3367	14674

INDL SPLYS, WHOLESALE: Seals

	CITY	ST	EMP	PHONE	ENTRY#
Tri-State Packing Supply	Scarborough	ME	F	207 883-5218	5446
Marco Group LLC (PA)	Seabrook	NH	E	603 468-3600	15596
Niantic Seal Inc	Lincoln	RI	E	401 334-6870	16150
Apex Sealing Inc	Fairfax	VT	E	802 524-7100	17254
Flex-A-Seal Inc	Williston	VT	E	802 878-8307	17729

INDL SPLYS, WHOLESALE: Tools

	CITY	ST	EMP	PHONE	ENTRY#
Mrse Inc	West Brookfield	MA	F	508 867-5083	12996
C P Technologies Inc (PA)	Saco	ME	F	207 286-1167	5364

INDL SPLYS, WHOLESALE: Tools, NEC

	CITY	ST	EMP	PHONE	ENTRY#
Wadsworth Falls Mfg Co	Rockfall	CT	F	860 346-3644	2916
Safe-T-Cut Inc	Monson	MA	F	413 267-9984	10456

INDL SPLYS, WHOLESALE: Valves & Fittings

	CITY	ST	EMP	PHONE	ENTRY#
Carlyle Johnson Machine Co LLC (DH)	Bolton	CT	F	860 643-1531	219
Circor LLC	Burlington	MA	E	781 270-1200	7348
Crosby Valve & Gage Intl Inc	Mansfield	MA	E	508 384-3121	10048
Sentinel Process Systems Inc	Southborough	MA	F	508 624-5577	12002
Tyco Fire Products LP (DH)	Cranston	RI	C	215 362-0700	15924
Velan Valve Corp (DH)	Williston	VT	D	802 863-2561	17751

INERTIAL GUIDANCE SYSTEMS

	CITY	ST	EMP	PHONE	ENTRY#
Qualtre Inc (HQ)	Sudbury	MA	E	508 658-8360	12270

INFORMATION RETRIEVAL SERVICES

	CITY	ST	EMP	PHONE	ENTRY#
Aquila Technology Corp	Burlington	MA	E	781 993-9004	7334
Ebsco Publishing Inc (DH)	Ipswich	MA	A	978 356-6500	9485
Homeportfolio Inc	Newton	MA	E	617 559-1197	10760
Kyruus Inc	Boston	MA	C	617 419-2060	6849
Research Cmpt Consulting Svcs (PA)	Canton	MA	G	781 821-1221	7823
Bald Hill Reach Inc	Ellsworth	ME	D	207 667-2576	4754
Winter People Inc	Cumberland Center	ME	E	207 865-6636	4711
Actio Software Corporation	Portsmouth	NH	D	603 433-2300	15356
Caledonian Record Pubg Co Inc (PA)	Saint Johnsbury	VT	D	802 748-8121	17540

INFORMATION SVCS: Consumer

	CITY	ST	EMP	PHONE	ENTRY#
Cst Incorporated	Wallingford	CT	F	203 949-9900	3796
Surfctcom Inc	Naugatuck	CT	E	203 720-9209	1989

INFRARED OBJECT DETECTION EQPT

	CITY	ST	EMP	PHONE	ENTRY#
Brandstrom Instruments Inc	Ridgefield	CT	E	203 544-9341	2892
Sensor Switch Inc (DH)	New Haven	CT	E	203 265-2842	2198
Advanced Device Technology	Andover	MA	G	603 894-1402	5867
Flir Systems-Boston Inc (DH)	North Billerica	MA	B	978 901-8000	10911

INK OR WRITING FLUIDS

	CITY	ST	EMP	PHONE	ENTRY#
Coating Systems Inc	Nashua	NH	G	603 883-0553	15082

INK: Gravure

	CITY	ST	EMP	PHONE	ENTRY#
Gem Gravure Co Inc (PA)	Hanover	MA	D	781 878-0456	9032

INK: Lithographic

	CITY	ST	EMP	PHONE	ENTRY#
Gotham Ink of New England Inc	Marlborough	MA	G	508 485-7911	10154

INK: Printing

	CITY	ST	EMP	PHONE	ENTRY#
Superior Printing Ink Co Inc	Hamden	CT	E	203 281-1921	1458
Superior Printing Ink Co Inc	North Haven	CT	G	203 777-9055	2438
A I C Inc (PA)	Georgetown	MA	E	978 352-4510	8904
Coatings Adhesives Inks	Georgetown	MA	F	978 352-7273	8907
Functional Inks Inc	West Springfield	MA	G	413 363-0770	13028
RPM Wood Finishes Group Inc	Westfield	MA	D	413 562-9655	13204
Superior Printing Ink Co Inc	Marlborough	MA	E	508 481-8250	10219
Three Dimensional Graphics Corp	Byfield	MA	E	978 774-8595	7460
Universal Color Corp Inc	Wilmington	MA	F	978 658-2300	13473
Winged Pegasus Consulting Inc	Andover	MA	E	978 667-0600	5935
Graphic Utilities Incorporated	Limestone	ME	F	207 370-9178	5004
Markem-Imaje Corporation (HQ)	Keene	NH	B	603 352-1130	14607
Wikoff Color Corporation	Hudson	NH	F	603 864-6456	14560

INSECT LAMPS: Electric

	CITY	ST	EMP	PHONE	ENTRY#
Armatron International Inc (PA)	Medford	MA	D	781 321-2300	10280

INSECTICIDES

	CITY	ST	EMP	PHONE	ENTRY#
Chemtura USA Corporation	Middlebury	CT	A	203 573-2000	1714

INSECTICIDES & PESTICIDES

	CITY	ST	EMP	PHONE	ENTRY#
Bedoukian Research Inc (PA)	Danbury	CT	E	203 830-4000	713
Connecticut Tick Control LLC	Norwalk	CT	F	203 855-7849	2486
Mist Hill Property Maint LLC	Brookfield	CT	F	203 648-7434	530
Pic20 Group LLC	Norwalk	CT	F	203 957-3555	2558
Northern Turf Prfessionals Inc	Brunswick	ME	F	207 522-8598	4652
Bio-Concept Laboratories Inc	Salem	NH	E	603 437-4990	15510
Pace Anlytical Lf Sciences LLC	Salem	NH	E	603 437-4990	15555
Tender Corporation (PA)	Littleton	NH	D	603 444-5464	14724
Costa Enterprises Ltd Co	Waterville	VT	G	802 644-6782	17682

INSPECTION & TESTING SVCS

	CITY	ST	EMP	PHONE	ENTRY#
Accumet Engineering Corp	Devens	MA	E	978 568-8311	8266
Aetruim Incorporated	Billerica	MA	E	651 773-4200	6397
Americas Test Kitchen Limited Partnership 617 232-1000	Boston	MA	C		6544
Etec Inc	West Roxbury	MA	G	617 477-4308	13010
Sst Components Inc (PA)	Lawrence	MA	E	978 670-7300	9601
Fiber Materials Inc (DH)	Biddeford	ME	C	207 282-5911	4564

INSTRUMENTS & ACCESSORIES: Surveying

	CITY	ST	EMP	PHONE	ENTRY#
Data Technology Inc	Tolland	CT	A	860 871-8082	3656
Topcon Positioning Systems Inc	Concord	NH	G	800 421-0125	14164

INSTRUMENTS & METERS: Measuring, Electric

	CITY	ST	EMP	PHONE	ENTRY#
Altek Electronics Inc	Torrington	CT	C	860 482-7626	3669
Omega Engineering Inc	Norwalk	CT	D	714 540-4914	2548
Axiam Inc (PA)	Gloucester	MA	G	978 281-3550	8921
Central Tools Inc	Framingham	MA	G	781 893-0095	8752
Krohn-Hite Corporation	Brockton	MA	F	508 580-1660	7288

INSTRUMENTS, LABORATORY: Analyzers, Automatic Chemical

	CITY	ST	EMP	PHONE	ENTRY#
American Healthcare	Scarborough	ME	F	888 567-7733	5423

INSTRUMENTS, LABORATORY: Blood Testing

	CITY	ST	EMP	PHONE	ENTRY#
Medica Corporation (PA)	Bedford	MA	C	781 275-4892	6240
Nova Biomedical Corporation (PA)	Waltham	MA	A	781 894-0800	12738

INSTRUMENTS, LABORATORY: Liquid Chromatographic

	CITY	ST	EMP	PHONE	ENTRY#
Cohesive Technologies Inc (HQ)	Franklin	MA	E	508 528-7989	8824

INSTRUMENTS, LABORATORY: Mass Spectrometers

	CITY	ST	EMP	PHONE	ENTRY#
New Objective Inc	Littleton	MA	F	781 933-9560	9828

INSTRUMENTS, LABORATORY: Measuring, Specific Ion

	CITY	ST	EMP	PHONE	ENTRY#
Dewetron Inc	East Greenwich	RI	F	401 284-3750	15980

INSTRUMENTS, LABORATORY: Spectrometers

	CITY	ST	EMP	PHONE	ENTRY#
Bruker Corporation	Billerica	MA	C	978 663-3660	6415
Bruker Scientific LLC	Billerica	MA	A	978 667-9580	6418
Minuteman Laboratories Inc	Chelmsford	MA	F	978 263-2632	7939
Teledyne Instruments Inc	Hudson	NH	D	603 886-8400	14554
Teledyne Tekmar Company Inc	Hudson	NH	D	603 886-8400	14555

INSTRUMENTS, MEASURING & CNTRL: Geophysical & Meteorological

	CITY	ST	EMP	PHONE	ENTRY#
NRG Systems Inc	Hinesburg	VT	C	802 482-2255	17297

INSTRUMENTS, MEASURING & CNTRL: Radiation & Testing, Nuclear

	CITY	ST	EMP	PHONE	ENTRY#
Mirion Tech Canberra Inc (DH)	Meriden	CT	D	203 238-2351	1677

Employee Codes: A=Over 500 employees, B=251-500
C=101-250, D=51-100, E=20-50, F=10-19, G=1-9

2024 Harris New England
Manufacturers Directory

1405

PRODUCT

	CITY	ST	EMP	PHONE	ENTRY#
Frincton Gamma-Tech Instrs Inc	Franklin	MA	E	609 924-7310	8858
Radiation Monitoring Dvcs Inc (HQ)	Watertown	MA	E	617 668-6800	12902
Motorway Engineering Inc	Manchester	NH	F	603 668-6315	14893

INSTRUMENTS, MEASURING & CNTRLG: Aircraft & Motor Vehicle

	CITY	ST	EMP	PHONE	ENTRY#
Bauer Inc	Bristol	CT	D	860 583-9100	409
Harcosemco LLC	Branford	CT	C	203 483-3700	263
Simmonds Precision Pdts Inc	Danbury	CT	F	203 797-5000	818
Allard Nazarian Group Inc (PA)	Manchester	NH	E	603 668-1900	14810
ARC Technology Solutions LLC	Nashua	NH	D	603 883-3027	15064
Textron Inc (PA)	Providence	RI	A	401 421-2800	16623
Simmonds Precision Products (DH)	Vergennes	VT	A	802 877-4000	17661

INSTRUMENTS, MEASURING & CONTROLLING: Gas Detectors

	CITY	ST	EMP	PHONE	ENTRY#
Sperian Prtction Instrmnttion	Middletown	CT	D	860 344-1079	1783
Sensor Research and Dev Corp	Orono	ME	G	207 866-0100	5137

INSTRUMENTS, MEASURING & CONTROLLING: Ion Chambers

	CITY	ST	EMP	PHONE	ENTRY#
Axcelis Technologies Inc (PA)	Beverly	MA	A	978 787-4000	6330

INSTRUMENTS, MEASURING & CONTROLLING: Spectrometers

	CITY	ST	EMP	PHONE	ENTRY#
Waters Corporation (PA)	Milford	MA	A	508 478-2000	10424
Waters Technologies Corp (HQ)	Milford	MA	A	508 478-2000	10425

INSTRUMENTS, MEASURING & CONTROLLING: Ultrasonic Testing

	CITY	ST	EMP	PHONE	ENTRY#
Technisonic Research Inc	Fairfield	CT	G	203 368-3600	1201
CTS Valpey Corporation (HQ)	Hopkinton	MA	D	508 435-6831	9314
Spire Metering Technology LLC	Marlborough	MA	F	978 263-7100	10215
Proteq Solutions LLC	Nashua	NH	F	603 888-6630	15151

INSTRUMENTS, OPTICAL: Elements & Assemblies, Exc Ophthalmic

	CITY	ST	EMP	PHONE	ENTRY#
Adaptive Optics Associates Inc	East Hartford	CT	F	860 282-4401	969
McAllister Optical Inc	Woburn	MA	E	781 938-0456	13608
Transom Scopes Inc	Westfield	MA	E	413 562-3606	13213
Chroma Technology Corp	Bellows Falls	VT	E	802 428-2500	17029

INSTRUMENTS, OPTICAL: Lenses, All Types Exc Ophthalmic

	CITY	ST	EMP	PHONE	ENTRY#
Orafol Americas Inc	Avon	CT	C	860 676-7100	35
Retina Systems Inc	Seymour	CT	E	203 881-1311	2968
Adaptive Optics Associates Inc	Devens	MA	F	978 757-9600	8268
Adaptive Optics Associates Inc (DH)	Devens	MA	D	978 757-9600	8269
AMF Optical Solutions LLC	Woburn	MA	F	781 933-6125	13509
Bern Optics Inc	Westfield	MA	F	413 568-6800	13152
Eidolon Corporation	Natick	MA	G	781 400-0586	10479
J P Mfg Inc	Southbridge	MA	G	508 764-2538	12023
Opco Laboratory Inc	Fitchburg	MA	F	978 345-2522	8670
Optometrics Corporation (HQ)	Littleton	MA	E	978 772-1700	9830
Primary Pdc Inc (PA)	Waltham	MA	G	781 386-2000	12753
Bond Optics LLC	Lebanon	NH	E	603 448-2300	14685
General Dynmics Mssion Systems	Nashua	NH	F	603 864-6300	15103
Janos Technology LLC (DH)	Keene	NH	D	603 757-0070	14604

INSTRUMENTS, OPTICAL: Mirrors

	CITY	ST	EMP	PHONE	ENTRY#
Kensington GL & Frmng Co Inc	Berlin	CT	F	860 828-9428	73
Mirror Polishing & Pltg Co Inc	Waterbury	CT	E	203 574-5400	3945
A B C Glass Co Inc	Springfield	MA	F	413 734-4524	12067
Central FLS Plate & Win GL Co	Central Falls	RI	F	401 722-1267	15787

INSTRUMENTS, OPTICAL: Sighting & Fire Control

	CITY	ST	EMP	PHONE	ENTRY#
Diffraction Ltd	Waitsfield	VT	G	802 496-6640	17666

INSTRUMENTS, OPTICAL: Test & Inspection

	CITY	ST	EMP	PHONE	ENTRY#
4 D Technology Corporation	East Hampton	CT	E	860 365-0420	957
Enos Engineering LLC	Acton	MA	G	978 654-6522	5745

INSTRUMENTS, SURGICAL & MED: Fixation Appliances, Internal

	CITY	ST	EMP	PHONE	ENTRY#
Wotton Enterprises Inc	Sturbridge	MA	F	855 383-7678	12259

INSTRUMENTS, SURGICAL & MED: Needles & Syringes, Hypodermic

	CITY	ST	EMP	PHONE	ENTRY#
Becton Dickinson and Company	Canaan	CT	D	860 824-5487	552
Connecticut Hypodermics Inc	Wallingford	CT	D	203 265-4881	3792
Vita Needle Company	Needham	MA	E	781 444-1780	10529
Cadence Science Inc	Cranston	RI	F	401 942-1031	15840

INSTRUMENTS, SURGICAL & MEDICAL: Biopsy

	CITY	ST	EMP	PHONE	ENTRY#
Lorad Corporation	Danbury	CT	C	203 790-5544	778

INSTRUMENTS, SURGICAL & MEDICAL: Blood & Bone Work

	CITY	ST	EMP	PHONE	ENTRY#
Creo Medical Inc	Danbury	CT	F	860 670-6054	723
Furnace Source LLC	Terryville	CT	F	860 582-4201	3603
Newmark Medical Components Inc	Waterbury	CT	F	203 753-1158	3951
Vivax Medical Corporation	Naugatuck	CT	F	203 729-0514	1993

	CITY	ST	EMP	PHONE	ENTRY#
Arteriocyte Med Systems Inc	Hopkinton	MA	C	508 395-5998	9307
Cheetah Medical Inc (PA)	Newton	MA	D	617 964-0613	10744
Conformis Inc (HQ)	Billerica	MA	D	781 345-9001	6427
David Clark Company Inc (PA)	Worcester	MA	C	508 756-6216	13713
Etex Corporation	Braintree	MA	E	617 577-7270	7182
Haemonetics Asia Incorporated (HQ)	Braintree	MA	F	781 848-7100	7186
Haemonetics Corporation (PA)	Boston	MA	A	781 848-7100	6780
Hemedex Inc	Waltham	MA	F	617 577-1759	12692
Hightech Amercn Indus Labs Inc	Lexington	MA	F	781 862-9884	9748
Hologic Inc (PA)	Marlborough	MA	A	508 263-2900	10159
Hologic Inc	Methuen	MA	E	508 263-2900	10334
Medicametrix LLC	Woburn	MA	G	617 488-9233	13610
Microport Navibot Intl LLC	Foxborough	MA	E	774 215-5471	8735
Photo Diagnostic Systems Inc	Boxborough	MA	E	978 266-0420	7154
Stryker Corporation	Hopkinton	MA	F	508 416-5200	9345
Alcor Scientific LLC	Smithfield	RI	D	401 737-3774	16686
Biomedical Structures LLC	Warwick	RI	F	401 223-0990	16791

INSTRUMENTS, SURGICAL & MEDICAL: Blood Pressure

	CITY	ST	EMP	PHONE	ENTRY#
Cas Medical Systems Inc	Branford	CT	E	203 488-6056	242

INSTRUMENTS, SURGICAL & MEDICAL: Blood Transfusion

	CITY	ST	EMP	PHONE	ENTRY#
Erika of Texas Inc	Waltham	MA	F	956 783-4689	12665
Medtronic Inc	Danvers	MA	F	978 777-0042	8207
Medtronic Inc	Danvers	MA	E	978 739-3080	8208

INSTRUMENTS, SURGICAL & MEDICAL: Catheters

	CITY	ST	EMP	PHONE	ENTRY#
Cardiofocus Inc	Marlborough	MA	E	508 658-7200	10129
Clinical Instruments Intl	Burlington	MA	F	781 221-2266	7352
Lightlab Imaging Inc	Westford	MA	B	978 577-3400	13246
Medtrnic Intrvntnal Vsclar Inc	Danvers	MA	A	978 777-0042	8206
Viamed Corp	South Easton	MA	F	508 238-0220	11955

INSTRUMENTS, SURGICAL & MEDICAL: Hemodialysis

	CITY	ST	EMP	PHONE	ENTRY#
Fresenius Med Care Rnal Thrpie	Waltham	MA	G	781 699-9000	12680
Fresenius Usa Inc (DH)	Waltham	MA	C	781 699-4191	12683
Mds Nxstage Corporation (DH)	Waltham	MA	E	866 697-8243	12718

INSTRUMENTS, SURGICAL & MEDICAL: Inhalation Therapy

	CITY	ST	EMP	PHONE	ENTRY#
Kinaset Therapeutics Inc (PA)	Medfield	MA	G	508 858-5810	10271

INSTRUMENTS, SURGICAL & MEDICAL: IV Transfusion

	CITY	ST	EMP	PHONE	ENTRY#
Smiths Medical Asd Inc	Southington	CT	E	860 621-9111	3232

INSTRUMENTS, SURGICAL & MEDICAL: Knives

	CITY	ST	EMP	PHONE	ENTRY#
Nu-Lustre Finishing Corp	Providence	RI	E	401 521-7800	16576

INSTRUMENTS, SURGICAL & MEDICAL: Lasers, Surgical

	CITY	ST	EMP	PHONE	ENTRY#
Palomar Medical Tech LLC (DH)	Burlington	MA	F	781 993-2330	7409
Renalguard Solutions Inc (HQ)	Milford	MA	F	508 541-8800	10416

INSTRUMENTS, SURGICAL & MEDICAL: Muscle Exercise, Ophthalmic

	CITY	ST	EMP	PHONE	ENTRY#
Atrium Innovations	Sudbury	MA	E	978 579-2346	12260

INSTRUMENTS, SURGICAL & MEDICAL: Needles, Suture

	CITY	ST	EMP	PHONE	ENTRY#
Needletech Products Inc	North Attleboro	MA	C	508 431-4000	10879
Surgical Specialties Corp (HQ)	Westwood	MA	C	781 751-1000	13321

INSTRUMENTS, SURGICAL & MEDICAL: Ophthalmic

	CITY	ST	EMP	PHONE	ENTRY#
Avedro Inc (HQ)	Burlington	MA	C	781 768-3400	7337
Bvi Medical Inc (PA)	Waltham	MA	E	866 906-8080	12615
Intelon Optics Inc	Woburn	MA	F	310 804-9392	13587

INSTRUMENTS, SURGICAL & MEDICAL: Stapling Devices, Surgical

	CITY	ST	EMP	PHONE	ENTRY#
Southington Tool & Mfg Corp	Plantsville	CT	E	860 276-0021	2796
Design Standards Corp	Charlestown	NH	D	603 826-7744	14062

INSTRUMENTS: Analytical

	CITY	ST	EMP	PHONE	ENTRY#
Applied Biosystems LLC	Norwalk	CT	F	781 271-0045	2462
Buck Scientific Inc	Norwalk	CT	E	203 853-9444	2477
Carestream Hlth Mlclar Imging	New Haven	CT	E	888 777-2072	2134
Connecticut Analytical Corp	Bethany	CT	F	203 393-9666	92
Diasys Corp	Waterbury	CT	F	302 636-5400	3907
Energy Beam Sciences Inc	Niantic	CT	F	860 653-0411	2357
Idex Health & Science LLC	Bristol	CT	C	860 314-2880	456
Ihs Herold Inc (DH)	Norwalk	CT	D	203 857-0215	2516
K A F Manufacturing Co Inc	Stamford	CT	E	203 324-3012	3394
MLS Acq Inc	East Windsor	CT	F	860 386-6878	1082
Perkinelmer US LLC (PA)	Shelton	CT	E	203 925-4600	3046
Precipio Inc (PA)	New Haven	CT	F	203 787-7888	2187
Revvity Inc	Shelton	CT	G	203 925-4600	3060
Revvity Health Sciences Inc	Shelton	CT	C	203 925-4600	3061

	CITY	ST	EMP	PHONE	ENTRY#
Spectral LLC	Putnam	CT	F	860 928-7726	2876
Spectro Analytical Instrs Inc	Danbury	CT	F	203 778-8837	820
Tomtec Inc	Hamden	CT	D	203 281-6790	1460
AB Sciex Sales LP	Framingham	MA	D	508 383-7700	8739
Acton Research Corporation	Acton	MA	E	941 556-2601	5731
Advanced Instruments LLC (DH)	Norwood	MA	E	781 320-9000	11156
Advanced Thermal Solutions Inc (PA)	Norwood	MA	E	781 769-2800	11157
Agilone Inc (HQ)	Boston	MA	E	877 769-3047	6521
American Ult Cryogenics Inc (PA)	Woburn	MA	E	781 491-0888	13507
American Ult Cryogenics LLC	Woburn	MA	E	781 491-0999	13508
Analytik Jena US LLC (DH)	Tewksbury	MA	D	909 946-3197	12384
Andor Technology Inc	Concord	MA	E	978 405-1116	8098
Andor Technology Ltd (DH)	Concord	MA	E	860 290-9211	8099
Antec (usa) LLC	Boston	MA	G	888 572-0012	6549
Apogent Holding Company (HQ)	Waltham	MA	F	781 622-1300	12593
Applied Biosystems LLC	Bedford	MA	F	781 271-0045	6209
Applied Biosystems LLC	Framingham	MA	F	508 877-1307	8741
Autogen Inc	Holliston	MA	E	508 429-5965	9200
Brammer Bio Ma LLC (HQ)	Cambridge	MA	B	877 765-7676	7524
Bruker Biospin Corporation (HQ)	Billerica	MA	F	978 667-9580	6412
Bruker Biospin Mri Inc	Billerica	MA	F	978 667-9580	6413
Bruker Corporation (PA)	Billerica	MA	A	978 663-3660	6414
Bruker Detection Corporation	Billerica	MA	F	978 663-3660	6416
Bruker Enrgy Supercon Tech Inc (HQ)	Billerica	MA	D	978 901-7550	6417
Bruker Scientific LLC (HQ)	Billerica	MA	A	978 439-9899	6419
Business and Prof Exch Inc	Beverly	MA	E	978 556-4100	6336
Caliper Life Sciences Inc (DH)	Hopkinton	MA	C	203 954-9442	9310
Corning Incorporated	Tewksbury	MA	E	978 442-2200	12391
Covaris Inc	Woburn	MA	E	781 932-3959	13549
Day Zero Diagnostics Inc	Watertown	MA	E	857 770-1125	12870
Doble Engineering Company (HQ)	Marlborough	MA	E	617 926-4900	10145
DOE & Inglls Msschstts Oprting	Peabody	MA	E	781 391-0090	11307
Dpp Inc	Sudbury	MA	G	978 443-9995	12265
Duke River Engineering Co	Newton	MA	G	617 965-7255	10753
Edgeone LLC (PA)	West Wareham	MA	F	508 291-0057	13063
EMD Millipore Corporation	Bedford	MA	C	781 533-6000	6224
EMD Millipore Corporation	Bedford	MA	C	781 533-6000	6225
EMD Millipore Corporation	Danvers	MA	E	978 762-5100	8185
EMD Millipore Corporation	Quincy	MA	F	800 637-7872	11514
Endeavor Robotic Holdings Inc (DH)	Chelmsford	MA	F	978 769-9333	7927
Evident Scientific Inc (PA)	Waltham	MA	A	781 419-3900	12668
Exeter Analytical Inc	North Chelmsford	MA	F	978 251-1411	10975
Eyepoint Pharmaceuticals Inc (PA)	Watertown	MA	D	617 926-5000	12875
Fisher Scientific Intl LLC	Billerica	MA	F	978 670-7460	6447
Fluid Management Systems Inc	Billerica	MA	E	617 393-2396	6448
Fswh Intl Holdings LLC (HQ)	Waltham	MA	E	781 622-1000	12685
Genomic Solutions Inc	Holliston	MA	E	734 975-4800	9212
High Voltage Engineering Corp	Wakefield	MA	F	781 224-1001	12511
Illinois Tool Works Inc	Norwood	MA	B	781 828-2500	11179
Imaging W Varex Holdings Inc	Waltham	MA	E	781 663-9100	12695
International Light Tech Inc	Peabody	MA	E	978 818-6180	11319
Ionsense Inc	Billerica	MA	F	781 231-1739	6456
Izon Science US Limited	Medford	MA	G	617 945-5936	10290
Izon Science US LLC	Medford	MA	F	617 945-5936	10291
Jentek Sensors Inc	Marlborough	MA	F	781 642-9666	10171
Jeol Usa Inc (HQ)	Peabody	MA	C	978 535-5900	11320
Kramer Scientific LLC	Amesbury	MA	G	978 388-7159	5840
Krohn-Hite Corporation	Brockton	MA	F	508 580-1660	7288
Lase Innovation Inc	Woburn	MA	G	617 599-0003	13600
Leica Biosystems	Danvers	MA	D	978 471-0625	8199
Life Technologies Corporation	Framingham	MA	E	508 383-7700	8786
Listen Inc	Boston	MA	E	617 556-4104	6860
Magellan Biosciences Inc (HQ)	North Billerica	MA	F	978 856-2345	10930
Magellan Diagnostics Inc (HQ)	Chelmsford	MA	D	978 250-7000	7937
Magellan Diagnostics Inc	North Billerica	MA	F	978 856-2345	10931
Malvern Panalytical Inc	Northampton	MA	E	413 586-7720	11070
Matec Instrument Companies Inc (PA)	Northborough	MA	E	508 393-0155	11102
Memed US Inc	Andover	MA	E	617 335-0349	5895
Microcal LLC	Northampton	MA	F	413 586-7720	11072
Mj Research Inc (HQ)	Waltham	MA	C	510 724-7000	12722
Nova Metrix LLC	Woburn	MA	F	781 897-1200	13625
Omniprobe Inc	Concord	MA	E		8129
On-Site Analysis Inc (DH)	Chelmsford	MA	G	561 775-5756	7942
Optra Inc	Wilmington	MA	F	978 887-6600	13443
Particles Plus Inc	Stoughton	MA	E	781 341-6898	12227
Philips North America LLC	Natick	MA	D	508 647-1130	10490
Photonis Scientific Inc (DH)	Sturbridge	MA	F	508 347-4000	12257
Pion Inc	Billerica	MA	F	978 528-2020	6472
Pp Systems International Inc	Amesbury	MA	G	978 834-0505	5849
Precision Systems Inc	Natick	MA	E	508 655-7010	10494
Proveris Scientific Corp (PA)	Hudson	MA	E	508 460-8822	9405
Rapid Micro Biosystems Inc (PA)	Lowell	MA	C	978 349-3200	9916
Resonance Research Inc	Billerica	MA	E	978 671-0811	6476
Revvity Inc	Billerica	MA	E	978 439-5511	6477
Revvity Inc	Boston	MA	E	617 596-9909	7009
Revvity Inc	Hopkinton	MA	F	508 435-9500	9343
Revvity Health Sciences Inc (DH)	Waltham	MA	D	781 663-6900	12768
Sage Science Inc	Beverly	MA	F	617 922-1832	6380
Schoeffel International Corp	Chelmsford	MA	E	978 256-4512	7955
Sciaps Inc (PA)	Woburn	MA	E	339 222-2585	13662
Scientific Instrument Facility	Boston	MA	F	617 353-5056	7027
Semilab USA LLC	North Billerica	MA	F	508 647-8400	10953
Semtech Solutions Inc	North Billerica	MA	E	978 663-9822	10954
Sensortech Systems Inc	Westborough	MA	F	805 981-3735	13134
Sick Inc	Stoughton	MA	D	781 302-2500	12235
Skyray Instrument Inc	Stoughton	MA	F	617 202-3879	12237
Spectra Analysis Inc (PA)	Marlborough	MA	G	508 281-6232	10211
Spectral Evolution Inc	Haverhill	MA	F	978 687-1833	9132
Teledyne Flir LLC	North Billerica	MA	A	978 901-8000	10961
Thermedetec Inc	Waltham	MA	F	508 520-0430	12797
Thermo Eberline LLC (HQ)	Franklin	MA	E	508 553-1862	8867
Thermo Envmtl Instrs LLC (HQ)	Franklin	MA	C	508 520-0430	8868
Thermo Fisher	Somerville	MA	F	781 325-8726	11901
Thermo Fisher Fincl Svcs Inc	Waltham	MA	D	781 622-1000	12799
Thermo Fisher Scientific Inc	Chelmsford	MA	E	978 250-7000	7966
Thermo Fisher Scientific Inc	Franklin	MA	C	713 272-0404	8869
Thermo Fisher Scientific Inc	Tewksbury	MA	D	781 622-1000	12422
Thermo Fisher Scientific Inc (PA)	Waltham	MA	D	781 622-1000	12800
Thermo Ice Inc (HQ)	Milford	MA	D		10421
Thermo Orion Inc (HQ)	Chelmsford	MA	E	800 225-1480	7967
Thermo Scntfc Prtble Anlytcal (HQ)	Tewksbury	MA	C	978 657-5555	12423
Thoratec LLC	Burlington	MA	F	781 272-0139	7440
Thrive Bioscience Inc	Beverly	MA	G	978 720-8048	6388
Union Biometrica Inc (PA)	Holliston	MA	F	508 893-3115	9236
Unity Scientific LLC	Westborough	MA	E	203 740-2999	13142
Waters Technologies Corp	Franklin	MA	E	508 482-4807	8875
Waveguide Corporation	Waltham	MA	G	617 892-9700	12816
Williamson Corporation	Concord	MA	E	978 369-9607	8141
Xenogen Corporation (DH)	Hopkinton	MA	D	508 435-9500	9347
Artel Inc	Westbrook	ME	E	207 854-0860	5614
Fhc Inc (PA)	Bowdoin	ME	D	207 666-8190	4605
Idexx Distribution Inc	Westbrook	ME	D	207 556-0300	5630
Idexx Operations Inc (HQ)	Westbrook	ME	E	207 556-4388	5632
Yokogawa Fluid Imaging Tech Inc	Scarborough	ME	E	207 289-3200	5448
Allen Datagraph Systems Inc	Salem	NH	E	603 216-6344	15504
Diversified Enterprises-ADT	Claremont	NH	G	603 543-0038	14088
EMD Millipore Corporation	Jaffrey	NH	B	603 532-8711	14567
Integra Biosciences Corp	Hudson	NH	F	603 578-5800	14510
Integra Biosciences Corp	Hudson	NH	F	603 578-5800	14511
Integra Biosciences Corp	Merrimack	NH	G	603 578-5800	14985
Labsphere Inc	North Sutton	NH	C	603 927-4266	15254
M Braun Inc	Stratham	NH	D	603 773-9333	15638
Metavac LLC	Portsmouth	NH	F	631 207-2344	15423
Microelectrodes Inc	Bedford	NH	G	603 668-0692	13944
Owl Separation Systems LLC	Newington	NH	D	603 559-9297	15209
Poly-Vac Inc	Manchester	NH	C	603 647-7822	14912
Teledyne Flir LLC	Hudson	NH	E	603 324-7783	14551
Teledyne Flir Coml Systems Inc	Hudson	NH	C	603 324-7824	14552
Teledyne Instrs Leeman Labs	Hudson	NH	D	603 521-3299	14553
Thermo Fisher Scientific Inc (HQ)	Portsmouth	NH	E	603 431-8410	15443
Thermo Neslab LLC	Newington	NH	D	603 436-9444	15215
Agilent Technologies Inc	North Kingstown	RI	D	800 338-1754	16229
Hanna Instruments Inc (PA)	Woonsocket	RI	E	401 765-7500	16962
Thermo Fisher Scientific Inc	North Kingstown	RI	G	401 294-1234	16286
Ultra Scientific Incorporated	North Kingstown	RI	E	800 338-1754	16290
Biotek Instruments Inc (HQ)	Winooski	VT	C	802 655-4040	17767
Med Associates Inc (PA)	Fairfax	VT	D	802 527-2343	17262

INSTRUMENTS: Digital Panel Meters, Electricity Measuring

	CITY	ST	EMP	PHONE	ENTRY#
Think Energy LLC	Southport	CT	D	917 202-3574	3250
Analogic Corporation	Peabody	MA	F	978 977-3000	11297
Brewer Electric & Utilities In	South Yarmouth	MA	G	508 771-2040	11981

INSTRUMENTS: Electrocardiographs

	CITY	ST	EMP	PHONE	ENTRY#
Infobionic Inc	Chelmsford	MA	E	978 674-8304	7934

INSTRUMENTS: Electrolytic Conductivity, Laboratory

	CITY	ST	EMP	PHONE	ENTRY#
Prospect Products Incorporated	Newington	CT	E	860 666-0323	2320

INSTRUMENTS: Endoscopic Eqpt, Electromedical

	CITY	ST	EMP	PHONE	ENTRY#
American Dream Unlimited LLC	Andover	CT	G	860 742-5055	1
American Optics Limited	Wellesley Hills	MA	F	905 631-5377	12949
Cyduct Diagnostics Inc	Boston	MA	G	617 360-9700	6682
Myriad Fiber Imaging Tech Inc	Dudley	MA	F	508 949-3000	8320

PRODUCT

	CITY	ST	EMP	PHONE	ENTRY#
Lh Liquidation LLC	Windham	ME	E	207 893-8233	5664

INSTRUMENTS: Flow, Indl Process

	CITY	ST	EMP	PHONE	ENTRY#
Cidra Chemical Management Inc **(HQ)**	Wallingford	CT	D	203 265-0035	3786
Cidra Minerals Processing Inc	Wallingford	CT	E	203 265-0035	3789
Accusonic Technologies **(DH)**	New Bedford	MA	F	508 495-6600	10560
Data Industrial Corporation	Mattapoisett	MA	E	508 758-6390	10256
Krohne Inc **(DH)**	Beverly	MA	E	978 535-6060	6360
Schneider Elc Systems USA Inc **(DH)**	Foxboro	MA	E	508 543-8750	8721
Dover Flexo Electronics Inc	Rochester	NH	E	603 332-6150	15475
Teledyne Instruments Inc	Hampton	NH	G	603 474-5571	14415

INSTRUMENTS: Indl Process Control

	CITY	ST	EMP	PHONE	ENTRY#
Bristol Inc **(HQ)**	Watertown	CT	B	860 945-2200	4004
Gordon Engineering Corporation	Brookfield	CT	G	203 775-4501	522
Kem Liquidating Company Inc	Glastonbury	CT	E	860 430-5100	1287
Assembly Guidance Systems Inc	Chelmsford	MA	F	978 244-1166	7911
Controlled Envmt Systems LLC **(PA)**	Mansfield	MA	E	508 339-4237	10042
Dynisco Parent Inc	Billerica	MA	B	978 667-5301	6436
Honeywell Data Instruments Inc	Acton	MA	E	978 264-9550	5754
Rigaku Analytical Devices Inc	Wilmington	MA	E	855 785-1064	13449

INSTRUMENTS: Infrared, Indl Process

	CITY	ST	EMP	PHONE	ENTRY#
Flir Systems-Boston Inc **(DH)**	North Billerica	MA	B	978 901-8000	10911

INSTRUMENTS: Laser, Scientific & Engineering

	CITY	ST	EMP	PHONE	ENTRY#
Albrayco Technologies Inc	Cromwell	CT	G	860 635-3369	685
Crane Company **(PA)**	Stamford	CT	D	203 363-7300	3326
Corindus Inc **(HQ)**	Auburndale	MA	E	508 653-3335	6131
Innov-X Systems Inc	Waltham	MA	C	781 938-5005	12700
Pvd Products Inc	Wilmington	MA	E	978 694-9455	13448
Kentek Corporation **(PA)**	Boscawen	NH	E	603 223-4900	13990
Wilbur Technical Services LLC	Mont Vernon	NH	G	603 880-7100	15050

INSTRUMENTS: Liquid Level, Indl Process

	CITY	ST	EMP	PHONE	ENTRY#
Madison Company **(PA)**	Branford	CT	E	203 488-4477	270
Seymour - Sheridan Incorporated	Monroe	CT	D	203 261-4009	1921

INSTRUMENTS: Measurement, Indl Process

	CITY	ST	EMP	PHONE	ENTRY#
Norwalk Indus Components LLC	Manchester	CT	G	860 645-5340	1622
Applied Analytics Inc	Chelmsford	MA	E	978 294-8214	7907
Lewa Process Technologies Inc	Devens	MA	D	978 487-1100	8275
Ymc America Inc	Devens	MA	E	978 487-1130	8290
Extech Instruments Corporation	Nashua	NH	D	877 439-8324	15099

INSTRUMENTS: Measuring & Controlling

	CITY	ST	EMP	PHONE	ENTRY#
Jad LLC	South Windsor	CT	E	860 289-1551	3158

INSTRUMENTS: Measuring, Electrical Energy

	CITY	ST	EMP	PHONE	ENTRY#
Extech Instruments Corporation	Nashua	NH	D	877 439-8324	15099

INSTRUMENTS: Measuring, Electrical Power

	CITY	ST	EMP	PHONE	ENTRY#
Space Electronics LLC	Berlin	CT	E	860 829-0001	86
Doble Engineering Company **(HQ)**	Marlborough	MA	F	617 926-4900	10145
Everett Charles Tech LLC	Nashua	NH	E	603 882-2621	15096
Hanna Instruments Inc	Cumberland	RI	F	401 335-3677	15941
Hanna Instruments Inc **(PA)**	Woonsocket	RI	E	401 765-7500	16962

INSTRUMENTS: Medical & Surgical

	CITY	ST	EMP	PHONE	ENTRY#
Abbott Associates Inc	Milford	CT	C	203 878-2370	1793
Acme Monaco Corporation **(PA)**	New Britain	CT	C	860 224-1349	1995
Aegea Medical Inc	Trumbull	CT	E	650 701-1125	3709
Aerospace Techniques Inc	Middletown	CT	D	860 347-1200	1733
Apiject Systems Corp **(PA)**	Stamford	CT	D	203 461-7121	3284
Bartron Medical Imaging LLC	New Haven	CT	G	203 498-2184	2124
Beekley Medical	Bristol	CT	E	860 583-4700	412
Bio-Med Devices Inc	Guilford	CT	D	203 458-0202	1386
Biosig Technologies Inc **(PA)**	Westport	CT	E	203 409-5444	4158
Boston Endo-Surgical Tech LLC	Bridgeport	CT	B	203 336-6479	303
Carwild Corporation **(PA)**	New London	CT	E	860 442-4914	2224
CD Management LLC	Bristol	CT	F	203 269-0090	424
Cirtec Medical Corp	Enfield	CT	C	860 814-3973	1123
Clinical Dynamics Conn LLC	Bristol	CT	G	203 269-0090	428
Coopersurgical Inc **(DH)**	Trumbull	CT	C	203 601-5200	3716
Covidien Holding Inc	North Haven	CT	C	203 492-5000	2401
Covidien LP	New Haven	CT	C	781 839-1722	2141
Covidien LP	North Haven	CT	B	203 492-6332	2402
Covidien LP	North Haven	CT	A	203 492-5000	2403
Cygnus Medical LLC	Branford	CT	G	800 990-7489	248
Dcg-Pmi Inc	Bethel	CT	C	203 743-5525	106
Epicurean Feast Medtron O	North Haven	CT	C	203 492-5000	2410
Eppendorf Manufacturing Corp	Enfield	CT	C	860 253-3400	1132

	CITY	ST	EMP	PHONE	ENTRY#
Frank Roth Co Inc	Stratford	CT	D	203 377-2155	3539
Hitachi Aloka Medical Ltd	Wallingford	CT	F	203 269-5088	3813
Hitachi Aloka Medical Amer Inc	Wallingford	CT	D	800 872-5652	3814
Hobbs Medical Inc	Stafford Springs	CT	E	860 684-5875	3256
Hologic Inc	Danbury	CT	C	203 790-1188	757
Iodine Holdings Inc	Meriden	CT	F	203 630-0500	1669
K B C Electronics Inc	Milford	CT	F	203 298-9654	1842
Kinetic Concepts Inc	Newington	CT	F	860 594-1043	2303
Lambda Investors LLC	Greenwich	CT	F	203 862-7000	1337
Lee Company **(PA)**	Westbrook	CT	A	860 399-6281	4140
Lumendi LLC	Westport	CT	G	203 528-0316	4181
Madison Medical LLC	Madison	CT	E	203 245-0306	1563
Marel Corporation	West Haven	CT	D	203 934-8187	4114
Medtronic Inc	North Haven	CT	C	203 492-5764	2424
Memry Corporation **(HQ)**	Bethel	CT	B	203 739-1100	128
Microspecialties Inc	Milford	CT	D	203 874-1832	1849
Minimally Invasive Surgeon	Hartford	CT	G	860 241-0870	1493
Monopol Corporation	Bristol	CT	F	860 583-3852	471
Nordex Incorporated	Brookfield	CT	E	203 775-4877	532
Oxford Science Inc	Oxford	CT	F	203 881-3115	2707
Precision Engineered Pdts LLC	Bridgeport	CT	G	203 336-6479	361
Promisim Inc	Greenwich	CT	F	203 554-2707	1344
Putnam Plastics Corporation	Dayville	CT	C	860 774-1559	867
Rapid Usa Inc	Stamford	CT	F	203 461-7121	3444
Rom Technologies Inc	Brookfield	CT	A	888 374-0855	537
Saar Corporation	Farmington	CT	F	860 674-9440	1246
SEI II Inc	Milford	CT	F	203 877-8488	1883
Sequel Special Products LLC	Wolcott	CT	D	203 759-1020	4377
Smiths Medical	East Granby	CT	G	860 413-3230	952
Spine Wave Inc	Shelton	CT	D	203 944-9494	3064
Stryker Corporation	East Hartford	CT	F	860 528-1111	1024
Surgiquest Inc	Milford	CT	D	203 799-2400	1892
Tarry Medical Products Inc	Danbury	CT	F	203 791-9001	823
Team Technologies Inc	Watertown	CT	G	860 945-9125	4031
Teleflex Incorporated	Coventry	CT	E	860 742-8821	683
Ultimate Wireforms Inc	Bristol	CT	D	860 582-9111	504
Utitec Inc **(HQ)**	Watertown	CT	D	860 945-0605	4035
Utitec Holdings Inc	Watertown	CT	D	860 945-0601	4036
Valleylab	Stamford	CT	E	203 461-9075	3490
Vilex LLC	Granby	CT	E	860 413-9875	1309
Wallach Surgical Devices Inc **(PA)**	Trumbull	CT	E	203 799-2000	3740
Winslow Automatics Inc	New Britain	CT	D	860 225-6321	2075
3eo Health Inc	Beverly	MA	E	508 308-4805	6321
Accellent Acquisition Corp	Wilmington	MA	A	978 570-6900	13370
Accellent Holdings Corp	Wilmington	MA	A	978 570-6900	13371
Accellent LLC	Brimfield	MA	F	413 245-7144	7248
Activ Surgical Inc	Boston	MA	D	202 688-5648	6513
Advansource Biomaterials Corporation	Wilmington	MA	F	978 657-0075	13374
Akili Inc **(PA)**	Boston	MA	F	617 313-8853	6527
Allen Medical Systems Inc **(DH)**	Acton	MA	F	978 263-7727	5734
American Surgical Company LLC	Salem	MA	E	781 592-7200	11701
Amide Technologies Inc	Cambridge	MA	F	508 245-6839	7484
Amplitude Vascular Systems Inc	Boston	MA	F	754 755-1530	6546
Andover Healthcare Inc	Salisbury	MA	B	978 465-0044	11739
Anika Therapeutics Inc **(PA)**	Bedford	MA	C	781 457-9000	6207
Applied Tissue Tech LLC	Hingham	MA	B	781 366-3848	9141
Arrow Interventional Inc	Chelmsford	MA	D	919 433-4948	7909
Arthrosurface Incorporated	Franklin	MA	D	508 520-3003	8817
Atc Technologies Inc	Wilmington	MA	E	781 939-0725	13383
Axiomed LLC	Malden	MA	E	978 232-3990	10002
Axya Medical Inc	Beverly	MA	F	978 232-9997	6331
Beaver Group LLC	Waltham	MA	G	781 647-5775	12603
Belmont Instrument LLC **(PA)**	Billerica	MA	E	978 663-0212	6409
Bio Sphere Medical Inc	Rockland	MA	E	208 844-5008	11637
Biodevek Inc	Allston	MA	G	617 768-8246	5819
Boston Scientific Corporation	Marlborough	MA	B	508 382-0200	10118
Boston Scientific Corporation **(PA)**	Marlborough	MA	A	508 683-4000	10119
Boston Scientific Corporation	Quincy	MA	B	617 689-6000	11507
Boston Scientific Corporation	Watertown	MA	F	617 972-4000	12863
Boston Scientific Funding LLC	Marlborough	MA	G	508 683-4000	10120
Boston Scientific Intl Corp	Marlborough	MA	F	508 683-4000	10121
Brimfield Precision LLC	Brimfield	MA	C	413 245-7144	7249
Btl Industries Inc	Marlborough	MA	C	866 285-1656	10122
Cambridge Interventional LLC	Burlington	MA	F	978 793-2674	7342
Cerenovus	Raynham	MA	A	908 704-4024	11583
Chmc Otlrynglgic Fundation Inc **(PA)**	Boston	MA	F	617 355-8290	6654
Claret Medical Inc	Marlborough	MA	F	707 528-9300	10132
Codman & Shurtleff Inc	Bridgewater	MA	D	508 880-8100	7227
Concert Medical LLC	Attleboro Falls	MA	E	781 261-7400	6082
Confluent Surgical Inc	Waltham	MA	D	781 839-1700	12638
Conmed Corporation	Westborough	MA	F	508 366-3668	13093
Corindus Vascular Robotics Inc **(PA)**	Auburndale	MA	E	508 653-3335	6132

	CITY	ST	EMP	PHONE	ENTRY#
Covidien France Holdings Inc	Mansfield	MA	G	508 261-8000	10043
Covidien LLC	Mansfield	MA	F	508 261-8000	10044
Covidien LP	Mansfield	MA	B	508 261-8000	10045
Covidien LP (HQ)	Mansfield	MA	C	763 514-4000	10046
Covidien LP	Woburn	MA	D	800 962-9888	13550
Covidien Sales LLC	Mansfield	MA	E	508 261-8000	10047
Cytonome/St LLC	Bedford	MA	F	617 330-5030	6220
Dale Medical Products Inc (PA)	Franklin	MA	D	800 343-3980	8829
Dentsply Ih Inc (HQ)	Waltham	MA	C	781 890-6800	12650
Depuy Mitek LLC	Raynham	MA	B	508 880-8100	11586
Depuy Synthes Products Inc (DH)	Raynham	MA	F	508 880-8100	11588
Diagnosys LLC (PA)	Lowell	MA	E	978 458-1600	9875
Digilab Genomic Solutions Inc	Holliston	MA	F	508 893-3130	9207
Direx Systems Corp	Canton	MA	G	339 502-6013	7785
Domain Surgical Inc	Lexington	MA	E	801 924-4950	9740
Eagle Vision Inc	Dennis	MA	G	508 385-2283	8258
Earlysense Inc	Woburn	MA	F	781 373-3228	13561
Endodynamix Inc	Salem	MA	F	978 740-0400	11713
Eos Imaging Inc	Cambridge	MA	F	678 564-5400	7562
Escalon Digital Solutions Inc	Stoneham	MA	F	610 688-6830	12178
Everest Halthcare Holdings Inc (DH)	Waltham	MA	G	781 699-9000	12667
Eyepoint Pharmaceuticals Inc (PA)	Watertown	MA	D	617 926-5000	12875
Fci Ophthalmics Inc	Pembroke	MA	G	781 826-9060	11365
Five Star Manufacturing Inc	New Bedford	MA	D	508 998-1404	10592
Flodesign Sonics Inc	Wilbraham	MA	E	413 596-5900	13358
Fms New York Services LLC (DH)	Waltham	MA	F	781 699-9000	12677
Fresenius Med Care Hldings Inc (DH)	Waltham	MA	A	781 699-9000	12679
Fresenius Med Care Vntures LLC (DH)	Waltham	MA	F	781 699-9000	12681
Fresenius Med Svcs Group LLC	Waltham	MA	F	781 699-9000	12682
Fresenius USA Marketing Inc (DH)	Waltham	MA	E	781 699-9000	12684
Gcb Medical LLC	Duxbury	MA	E	617 699-6715	8331
Gregory Manufacturing Inc	Holyoke	MA	D	413 536-5432	9257
Guidant Corporation	Marlborough	MA	D	508 683-4000	10157
Gyrus Acmi LLC (DH)	Westborough	MA	C	508 804-2600	13104
Harvard Apparatus Inc	Holliston	MA	D	508 893-8999	9213
Hemanext Inc	Lexington	MA	F	240 301-7474	9747
Highland Labs Inc	Holliston	MA	G	508 429-2918	9215
Inspiremd Inc (PA)	Boston	MA	E	857 305-2410	6813
Insulet Corporation (PA)	Acton	MA	B	978 600-7000	5755
Insulet MA Securities Corp	Billerica	MA	E	978 600-7000	6453
Intech Inc	Acton	MA	E	978 263-2210	5756
Integra Lfscnces Holdings Corp	Burlington	MA	G	800 466-6814	7380
Integra Lifesciences	Boston	MA	F	617 268-1616	6815
Integra Lifesciences Prod Corp	Mansfield	MA	E	781 971-5682	10058
Intralign Holdings LLC	Foxboro	MA	G	602 773-8506	8702
Jarvis Surgical Inc	Westfield	MA	E	413 562-6659	13174
Johnson Johnson Healthcar	Bridgewater	MA	E	508 828-6194	7234
Karl Storz Endovision Inc	Charlton	MA	A	508 248-9011	7890
Karl Storz Endscpy-America Inc	Auburn	MA	C	508 429-9011	6117
Lake Region Medical Inc (HQ)	Wilmington	MA	E	978 570-6900	13424
LDR Care Inc	Concord	MA	G	978 786-5110	8122
Lemaitre Vascular Inc (PA)	Burlington	MA	E	781 221-2266	7389
Logan Instruments Inc	Braintree	MA	F	617 394-0601	7193
Lymol Medical Corp (PA)	Woburn	MA	G	781 935-0004	13603
M & W Industries Inc	Mansfield	MA	F	508 406-2100	10065
Majestic Medical Inc	Raynham	MA	F	508 824-1944	11590
Maruho Htsuyjo Innovations Inc (PA)	Norwell	MA	E	617 653-1617	11143
Medcon Biolab Technologies Inc	Grafton	MA	G	508 839-4203	8968
Medical Device Bus Svcs Inc	Raynham	MA	B	508 880-8100	11591
Medical-Technical Gases Inc	North Billerica	MA	F	781 395-1946	10934
Medrobotics Corporation	Raynham	MA	E	508 692-6460	11592
Medsource Tech Holdings LLC (DH)	Wilmington	MA	F	978 570-6900	13428
Medsource Technologies Inc (DH)	Wilmington	MA	F	978 570-6900	13429
Merit Medical Systems Inc (HQ)	Rockland	MA	E	781 681-7900	11651
Microline Surgical Inc (HQ)	Beverly	MA	C	978 922-9810	6364
Micron Products Inc	Fitchburg	MA	E	978 345-5000	8665
Mitsubishi Chemical Amer Inc	Wilmington	MA	F	978 657-0075	13432
Mobius Imaging LLC	Shirley	MA	D	978 796-5068	11821
N P Medical Inc	Clinton	MA	E	978 365-9721	8084
Navilyst Medical Inc	Marlborough	MA	D	508 658-7990	10186
Nellcor Puritan Bennett LLC (DH)	Mansfield	MA	B	508 261-8000	10069
Neurologica Corp	Danvers	MA	D	978 564-8500	8211
Neurometrix Inc (PA)	Woburn	MA	G	781 890-9989	13621
New View Surgical Inc	Boston	MA	F	774 284-2283	6920
Nn Inc	Mansfield	MA	E	508 406-2100	10070
Nvision Medical Corporation	Marlborough	MA	G	408 655-3577	10187
Nypro Healthcare Baja Inc (DH)	Clinton	MA	D	619 498-9250	8086
Nypro Inc (HQ)	Clinton	MA	A	978 365-9721	8087
Obp Surgical Corporation	Lawrence	MA	F	978 291-6853	9593
Optim LLC	Sturbridge	MA	E	508 347-5100	12254
Pep Industries LLC	Attleboro	MA	F	508 226-5600	6046
Precision Engineered Pdts LLC (DH)	Attleboro	MA	G		6051
Precision Systems Inc	Natick	MA	E	508 655-7010	10494
Pressure Biosciences Inc (PA)	South Easton	MA	G	508 230-1828	11950
Primo Medical Group Inc (PA)	Stoughton	MA	C	781 297-5700	12229
Primrose Medical Inc	East Walpole	MA	F	508 660-8688	8421
Professnal Cntract Strlztion I	Taunton	MA	F	508 822-5524	12356
QCI Inc	Seekonk	MA	F	508 399-8983	11784
Radius Medical Tech Inc	Stow	MA	F	978 263-4466	12247
Ranfac Corp	Avon	MA	D	508 588-4400	6159
Rebiscan Inc	Boston	MA	F	857 600-0982	6999
Respironics Novametrix LLC	Andover	MA	A	724 882-4120	5911
Rest Ensured Medical Inc	Norwood	MA	G	603 225-2860	11208
Rhealth Corporation	Bedford	MA	E	617 913-7630	6267
Schuerch Corporation	Abington	MA	E	781 982-7000	5728
Sonivie Inc	Boston	MA	E	857 415-4814	7046
Spectra Medical Devices LLC	Wilmington	MA	B	978 657-0889	13455
Spinefrontier Inc	Malden	MA	E	978 232-3990	10028
Starmet Corporation (PA)	Concord	MA	E	978 369-5410	8134
Statspin Inc	Westwood	MA	E	781 551-0100	13319
Steris Corporation	Northborough	MA	D	508 393-9323	11109
Surgical Tables Incorporated	Middleton	MA	E	978 777-4031	10394
T & T Machine Products Inc	Rockland	MA	F	781 878-3861	11662
T2 Biosystems Inc (PA)	Lexington	MA	D	781 761-4646	9779
T2 Biosystems Inc	Wilmington	MA	E	978 447-1069	13461
Tegra Medical LLC (HQ)	Franklin	MA	C	508 541-4200	8866
Teleflex Incorporated	Mansfield	MA	E	508 964-6021	10078
Tenacity Medical Inc	Lexington	MA	G	617 299-8001	9786
Tepha Inc (HQ)	Lexington	MA	D	781 357-1700	9793
Teratech Corporation	Burlington	MA	D	781 270-4143	7438
Thermo Fisher Scientific Inc	Beverly	MA	C	978 232-6000	6387
Toxikon Corporation	Bedford	MA	D	978 942-5554	6274
Tsi Liquidation Inc	Hudson	MA	G	978 567-9033	9421
Ufp Technologies Inc	Chicopee	MA	E	800 372-3172	8065
Valeritas Inc	Marlborough	MA	E	908 927-9920	10227
Varian Medical Systems Inc	Ashland	MA	D	650 493-4000	5969
Vasca Inc (PA)	Tewksbury	MA	E	978 640-0431	12425
Viant AS&o Holdings LLC	Wilmington	MA	E	866 899-1392	13474
Visionquest Holdings LLC	Littleton	MA	F	978 776-9518	9843
Warner Instruments	Holliston	MA	G	203 776-0664	9239
Xact Robotics Inc	Hingham	MA	G	781 252-9143	9166
Xenotherapeutics LLC	Boston	MA	G	617 750-1907	7136
Zyno Medical LLC	Natick	MA	E	508 650-2008	10501
Biotronik Inc	Brewer	ME	G	207 944-5515	4610
Idexx Distribution Inc	Westbrook	ME	D	207 556-0300	5630
Standard Merger Sub LLC	Windham	ME	D	207 856-6151	5670
Accellent Endoscopy Inc	Laconia	NH	E	603 528-1211	14641
Atrium Medical Corporation (HQ)	Merrimack	NH	B	973 709-7654	14973
Dutch Ophthalmic Usa Inc	Exeter	NH	F	603 778-6929	14291
Extrusion Alternatives Inc	Portsmouth	NH	E	603 430-9600	15383
Getinge Group Logis Ameri LLC	Merrimack	NH	A	603 880-1433	14982
KMC Systems Inc	Merrimack	NH	D	866 742-0442	14987
Laborie Medical Technologies Corp (HQ)	Portsmouth	NH	E	802 857-1300	15414
Lake Region Medical Inc	Laconia	NH	E	603 528-1211	14656
Maxilon Laboratories Inc	Amherst	NH	G	603 594-9300	13879
Merrimack Manufacturing LLC	Manchester	NH	E	603 206-0200	14883
Multi-Med Inc	Keene	NH	F	603 357-8733	14612
Nciea	Dover	NH	G	603 749-0733	14237
New England Small Tube Corp	Litchfield	NH	D	603 429-1600	14713
Nextphase Medical Devices LLC (PA)	Rochester	NH	E	201 968-9400	15487
Nextphase Medical Devices LLC	Rochester	NH	D	603 332-8900	15488
Prepco Inc	Colebrook	NH	G	603 237-4080	14108
Prometheus Group of NH Ltd	Dover	NH	F	800 442-2325	14245
Seacoast Technologies Inc	Portsmouth	NH	G	603 766-9800	15436
Sequel Med Tech LLC (PA)	Manchester	NH	E	212 883-1007	14928
Sims Portex Inc	Keene	NH	G	603 352-3812	14619
Smiths Medical Asd Inc	Keene	NH	F	603 352-3812	14620
Smiths Medical Asd Inc	Keene	NH	D	603 352-3812	14621
Teleflex Incorporated	Jaffrey	NH	D	603 532-7706	14580
Tfx Medical Incorporated	Jaffrey	NH	D	603 532-7706	14581
Ticked Off Inc	Dover	NH	G	603 742-0925	14253
Viant Medical LLC	Laconia	NH	D	603 528-1211	14673
Vygon Corporation	Dover	NH	G	603 743-5988	14255
Bnr Supplies	Cranston	RI	G	401 461-9132	15836
C R Bard Inc	Warwick	RI	E	401 825-8300	16794
Contech Medical Inc	Providence	RI	D	401 351-4890	16504
Davol Inc (DH)	Warwick	RI	E	401 825-8300	16804
Huestis Machine Corporation	Bristol	RI	E	401 253-5500	15769
RJ Mansour Inc	Providence	RI	F	401 521-7800	16606
Biotek Instruments Inc (HQ)	Winooski	VT	C	802 655-4040	17767
PBL Incorporated	Colchester	VT	E	802 893-0111	17199
Preci-Manufacturing Inc	Winooski	VT	D	802 655-2414	17768
Raj Communications Ltd	Essex Junction	VT	E	802 658-4961	17243
Stellar Lasers LLC	Worcester	VT	G	802 299-5411	17782

PRODUCT

	CITY	ST	EMP	PHONE	ENTRY#

INSTRUMENTS: Meteorological

	CITY	ST	EMP	PHONE	ENTRY#
Maximum Inc	New Bedford	MA	G	508 995-2200	10621

INSTRUMENTS: Nautical

Drs Naval Power Systems Inc	Danbury	CT	B	203 798-3000	734
E S Ritchie & Sons Inc	Pembroke	MA	E	781 826-5131	11364
Rule Industries LLC	Gloucester	MA	C	978 281-0440	8956

INSTRUMENTS: Optical, Analytical

Eye Pint Phrmctcals Scrties Co	Watertown	MA	E	617 926-5000	12874
Physical Sciences Inc (PA)	Andover	MA	D	978 689-0003	5907
Vacuum Process Technology LLC	Cambridge	MA	E	508 732-7200	7749

INSTRUMENTS: Pressure Measurement, Indl

Orange Research Inc	Milford	CT	D	203 877-5657	1859
PMC Engineering LLC	Danbury	CT	E	203 792-8686	798
Mks Instruments Inc	Andover	MA	E	978 645-5500	5898
Mks Instruments Inc (PA)	Andover	MA	B	978 645-5500	5899
Mks Instruments Inc	Haverhill	MA	F	978 284-4015	9117
Mks Instruments Inc	Methuen	MA	E	978 682-3512	10339
Mks Instruments Inc	Wilmington	MA	C	978 284-4000	13433
Mks Msc Inc	Wilmington	MA	G	978 284-4000	13434
Celestial Monitoring Corp (HQ)	Narragansett	RI	E	401 782-1045	16187

INSTRUMENTS: Radio Frequency Measuring

Hid Global Corporation	Newton	MA	E	617 581-6200	10759
Amphenol Corporation	Nashua	NH	B	603 879-3000	15061

INSTRUMENTS: Temperature Measurement, Indl

Moeller Instrument Company Inc	Ivoryton	CT	F	800 243-9310	1530
Omega Engineering Inc (DH)	Norwalk	CT	C	203 359-1660	2549
Dias Infrared Corp	West Boylston	MA	G	845 987-8152	12961
Thermonics Inc	Mansfield	MA	F	408 542-5900	10080

INSTRUMENTS: Test, Electrical, Engine

Ametek Arizona Instrument LLC	Middleboro	MA	C	508 946-6200	10349
Connected Auto Systems Neng In	South Easton	MA	E	508 238-5855	11940
Xilectric Inc	Fall River	MA	G	781 247-4567	8627

INSTRUMENTS: Test, Electronic & Electric Measurement

International Contact Tech Inc	Oxford	CT	G	203 264-5757	2700
Acentech Incorporated (PA)	Cambridge	MA	E	617 499-8000	7466
Advanced Mechanical Tech Inc (PA)	Watertown	MA	E	617 923-4414	12855
Analog Devices Intl Inc (HQ)	Wilmington	MA	A	800 262-5643	13380
Cami Research Inc	Acton	MA	F	978 266-2655	5742
Programmed Test Sources Inc	Littleton	MA	F	978 486-3008	9833
Quadtech Inc	Marlborough	MA	D	978 461-2100	10198
Rika Denshi America Inc	Attleboro	MA	E	508 226-2080	6056
Tech180 Corp	Easthampton	MA	F	413 203-6123	8463
ARC Technology Solutions LLC	Nashua	NH	D	603 883-3027	15064

INSTRUMENTS: Test, Electronic & Electrical Circuits

Bose Corporation	Framingham	MA	F	508 766-1265	8746
Pharmatron Inc	Westborough	MA	F	603 645-6766	13130
Vaunix Technology Corporation	Newburyport	MA	F	978 662-7839	10726
Zurich Instruments Usa Inc	Waltham	MA	F	949 682-5172	12823

INSULATING BOARD, HARD PRESSED

Bnz Materials Inc	North Billerica	MA	C	978 663-3401	10900

INSULATING COMPOUNDS

Lydall Inc (HQ)	Manchester	CT	E	860 646-1233	1614
Aspen Aerogels Inc (PA)	Northborough	MA	C	508 691-1111	11088
Albany International Corp (PA)	Rochester	NH	D	603 330-5850	15464

INSULATION MATERIALS WHOLESALERS

Aspen Aerogels Inc (PA)	Northborough	MA	C	508 691-1111	11088
Harvey Industries LLC	Woburn	MA	F	781 935-7990	13581

INSULATION: Felt

Fiber Materials Inc (DH)	Biddeford	ME	C	207 282-5911	4564

INSULATION: Fiberglass

Ecologic Energy Solutions LLC	Stamford	CT	D	203 889-0505	3342
Owens Corning Sales LLC	East Hartford	CT	C	304 353-6945	1008
The E J Davis Company	North Haven	CT	E	203 239-5391	2439
Owens Corning	Brentwood	NH	G	603 773-4246	14026

INSULATORS & INSULATION MATERIALS: Electrical

Wiremold Company	Rocky Hill	CT	D	860 233-6251	2942
Chase Corp Inc	Westwood	MA	F	781 332-0700	13308
Chase Corporation	Oxford	MA	G	508 731-2710	11250
Chase Corporation (HQ)	Westwood	MA	G	781 332-0700	13309
H Loeb Corporation	New Bedford	MA	E	508 996-3745	10597
Matkim Industries Inc	Oxford	MA	E	508 987-3599	11262
Isovolta Inc	North Clarendon	VT	E	802 775-5528	17414
Superior Tchncal Ceramics Corp (HQ)	Saint Albans	VT	C	802 527-7726	17533
Weidmann Electrical Technology Inc (DH)	Saint Johnsbury	VT	B	802 748-8106	17548

INSULATORS, PORCELAIN: Electrical

Newco Condenser Inc	Shelton	CT	F	475 882-4000	3039

INSURANCE AGENTS, NEC

Joseph G Pulitano Insur Agcy	Newton	MA	F	617 783-2622	10765

INSURANCE CARRIERS: Automobile

Cross Country Motor Club Inc (HQ)	Medford	MA	A	781 393-9300	10283

INSURANCE: Agents, Brokers & Service

Boston Software Corp	Needham Heights	MA	F	781 449-8585	10532
HMK Enterprises Inc (PA)	Lexington	MA	F	781 891-6660	9749

INTEGRATED CIRCUITS, SEMICONDUCTOR NETWORKS, ETC

Compugraphics USA Inc (HQ)	Waterbury	CT	D	510 249-2600	3900
Aceinna Inc	Tewksbury	MA	E	978 965-3200	12383
Analog Devices Inc (PA)	Wilmington	MA	A	781 935-5565	13379
Ase (us)inc	Woburn	MA	G	781 305-5900	13516
Broadcom Corporation	Andover	MA	C	978 719-1300	5874
Dover Microsystems Inc	Waltham	MA	G	781 577-0300	12655
Eastwind Communications Inc	Hyannis	MA	F	508 862-8600	9435
Gridedge Networks Inc	Acton	MA	F	978 569-2000	5749
Hittite Microwave LLC (HQ)	Chelmsford	MA	E	978 250-3343	7933
Microsemi Corporation	Lowell	MA	E	978 442-5637	9907
Piconics Inc	Tyngsboro	MA	E	978 649-7501	12463
Qualcomm Technologies Inc	Boston	MA	E	617 447-9846	6988
Qualcomm Technologies Inc	Burlington	MA	F	781 791-6000	7418
R F Integration Inc (PA)	North Billerica	MA	G	978 654-6770	10945
Renesas Electronics Amer Inc	Westford	MA	E	978 577-6340	13259
Rochester Electronics LLC	Newburyport	MA	F	978 462-1248	10714
Rochester Electronics LLC (PA)	Newburyport	MA	C	978 462-9332	10715
Sensera Inc	Woburn	MA	F	978 606-2600	13663
Tier 7 Communications	Shirley	MA	E	978 425-9543	11823
Paragon Electronic Systems	Manchester	NH	F	603 645-7630	14910
Qmagiq LLC	Nashua	NH	G	603 821-3092	15153
Veterans Assembled Elec LLC (PA)	North Kingstown	RI	G	401 228-6165	16291

INTERIOR DECORATING SVCS

Bloom & Company Inc	Framingham	MA	F	617 923-1526	8744
Gilberte Interiors LLC (PA)	Hanover	NH	F	603 643-3727	14423
Drapery House Inc	North Providence	RI	E	401 724-3400	16300
RK Miles Inc (PA)	Manchester Center	VT	C	802 362-1952	17330

INTERIOR DESIGN SVCS, NEC

Kink Pieces of A Dream LLC	Framingham	MA	F	508 748-5417	8784
Marthas Vineyard Furn Co LLC	Vineyard Haven	MA	G	508 687-9555	12491
Barrett Made (PA)	Portland	ME	E	207 650-6500	5184
Knickerbocker Group Inc	Boothbay	ME	D	207 541-9333	4598
McKernon Group Inc	Brandon	VT	D	802 247-8500	17068

INTRAVENOUS SOLUTIONS

Fresenius Usa Inc (DH)	Waltham	MA	C	781 699-4191	12683

INVERTERS: Nonrotating Electrical

Solectria Renewables LLC	Lawrence	MA	C	978 683-9700	9599

INVERTERS: Rotating Electrical

Dynapower Company LLC (DH)	South Burlington	VT	D	802 860-7200	17577

INVESTMENT ADVISORY SVCS

Compass Group Management LLC (PA)	Westport	CT	F	203 221-1703	4162
Eagle Investment Systems LLC	West Hartford	CT	F	860 561-4602	4057
Debt Exchange Inc	Boston	MA	D	617 531-3400	6685
Eagle Investment Systems LLC (HQ)	Wellesley	MA	E	781 943-2200	12940
Partners Capital Inv Group LLP	Boston	MA	F	617 292-2570	6955

INVESTMENT RESEARCH SVCS

Ihs Herold Inc (DH)	Norwalk	CT	D	203 857-0215	2516

INVESTORS, NEC

Gemini Investors V LP (PA)	Wellesley	MA	E	781 237-7001	12942
Platinum Investments Ltd	Brookline	MA	F	617 731-2447	7325

IRON & STEEL PRDTS: Hot-Rolled

	CITY	ST	EMP	PHONE	ENTRY#
Ccr Products LLC	West Hartford	CT	E	860 953-0499	4052
Gerdau Ameristeel US Inc	Plainville	CT	G	860 351-9029	2762
Empire Sheetmetal Inc	Manchester	NH	E	603 622-4439	14847

JACKS: Hydraulic

Hostar Mar Trnspt Systems Inc	Wareham	MA	F	508 295-2900	12838

JARS: Plastic

Colts Plastics Company Inc	Dayville	CT	C	860 774-2277	861

JEWELERS' FINDINGS & MATERIALS

EF Leach & Company	Attleboro	MA	C	508 643-3309	6011
M S Company	Attleboro	MA	D	508 222-1700	6032
APAC Tool Inc	North Providence	RI	F	401 724-6090	16295
Aro-Sac Inc	North Providence	RI	F	401 231-6655	16297
Crystal Hord Corporation	Pawtucket	RI	E	401 723-2989	16360
Discovery Mint Inc	Pawtucket	RI	E	401 722-6530	16364
Eagle Tool Inc	Warwick	RI	F	401 421-5105	16812
Fulford Manufacturing Company **(PA)**	Riverside	RI	F	401 431-2000	16655
Kefi Development Inc	East Providence	RI	E	401 272-6513	16027
Lorac Company Inc	Providence	RI	E	401 781-3330	16554
Robert Baxter Associates Inc	Warwick	RI	F	401 739-8222	16853
Salvadore Tool & Findings Inc **(PA)**	Providence	RI	F	401 331-6000	16609
Venturi Inc	Warwick	RI	G	401 781-2647	16871
W R Cobb Company	East Providence	RI	C	401 438-7000	16047

JEWELRY & PRECIOUS STONES WHOLESALERS

Findings Incorporated	Attleboro	MA	D	508 222-7449	6015
Ozcan Jewelers Inc	Boston	MA	F	617 338-6844	6949

JEWELRY REPAIR SVCS

Joseph Hannoush Family Inc	Farmington	CT	F	860 561-4651	1225
Ozcan Jewelers Inc	Boston	MA	F	617 338-6844	6949
Silva Jewelers of Osterville	Osterville	MA	G	508 428-2872	11246
Brown Goldsmiths & Co Inc	Freeport	ME	F	207 865-4126	4799
Sawyers Jewelry Inc	Laconia	NH	F	603 527-1000	14667
Village Goldsmith	Warwick	RI	F	401 944-8404	16872

JEWELRY STORES

Dt Holdings Incorporated	Stamford	CT	F	203 602-6969	3339
Charles Thomae & Son Inc	Attleboro	MA	F	508 222-0785	6001
Findings Incorporated	Attleboro	MA	D	508 222-7449	6015
Plastic Craft Novelty Co Inc	Attleboro	MA	F	508 222-1486	6049
Daunis	Portland	ME	F	207 773-6011	5205
APAC Tool Inc	North Providence	RI	F	401 724-6090	16295
Dina Inc	Cranston	RI	G	401 942-9633	15851
J Cal Inc **(PA)**	Providence	RI	D	401 941-7700	16546
Ldc Inc	East Providence	RI	F	401 861-4667	16029
Racecar Jewelry Co	Pawtucket	RI	G	401 475-5701	16409

JEWELRY STORES: Precious Stones & Precious Metals

Buisson Jewelers Inc	Greenwich	CT	G	203 869-8895	1324
Elm City Mfg Jewelers Inc	Hamden	CT	F	203 248-2195	1425
Jewelry Designs Inc	Danbury	CT	E	203 797-0389	761
Joseph Hannoush Family Inc	Farmington	CT	F	860 561-4651	1225
Artinian Garabet Corporation	Concord	MA	F	978 371-7110	8102
Barmakian Brothers Ltd Partnr	Boston	MA	E	617 227-3724	6583
G Austin Young Inc	Attleboro	MA	G	508 222-4700	6019
Mahi Gold Inc	Chatham	MA	F	508 348-5487	7898
Silva Jewelers of Osterville	Osterville	MA	G	508 428-2872	11246
A Silver Lining Inc	Boothbay Harbor	ME	F	207 633-4103	4599
Brown Goldsmiths & Co Inc	Freeport	ME	F	207 865-4126	4799
Bellman Jewelers Inc	Manchester	NH	G	603 625-4653	14819
M J Harrington & Co Inc **(PA)**	Newport	NH	F	603 863-1662	15231
Nazarian Jewelers NH Inc **(PA)**	Salem	NH	F	603 893-1600	15548
Sawyers Jewelry Inc	Laconia	NH	F	603 527-1000	14667
Robert Baxter Associates Inc	Warwick	RI	F	401 739-8222	16853

JEWELRY STORES: Silverware

Boardman Silversmiths Inc	Wallingford	CT	F	203 265-9978	3782
J T Inman Co Inc	Attleboro Falls	MA	E	508 226-0080	6088

JEWELRY, PRECIOUS METAL: Earrings

EF Leach & Company	Attleboro	MA	C	508 643-3309	6011
Reed Allison Group Inc	Providence	RI	D	617 846-1237	16599

JEWELRY, PRECIOUS METAL: Necklaces

Jcc Residual Ltd	Woonsocket	RI	F	508 699-4401	16966

JEWELRY, PRECIOUS METAL: Pins

Robbins Company	Attleboro	MA	C	508 222-2900	6058

JEWELRY, PRECIOUS METAL: Rings, Finger

	CITY	ST	EMP	PHONE	ENTRY#
Herff Jones LLC	Warwick	RI	F	401 331-1240	16820

JEWELRY, PRECIOUS METAL: Settings & Mountings

Ozcan Jewelers Inc	Boston	MA	F	617 338-6844	6949
Sawyers Jewelry Inc	Laconia	NH	F	603 527-1000	14667
First Card Co Inc	Johnston	RI	E	401 434-6140	16085

JEWELRY, WHOLESALE

Elm City Mfg Jewelers Inc	Hamden	CT	F	203 248-2195	1425
American Biltrite Inc **(PA)**	Wellesley	MA	G	781 237-6655	12935
Artinian Garabet Corporation	Concord	MA	F	978 371-7110	8102
A Silver Lining Inc	Boothbay Harbor	ME	F	207 633-4103	4599
Bazar Group Inc **(PA)**	East Providence	RI	F	401 434-2595	16006
Imperial-Deltah Inc	East Providence	RI	D	401 434-2597	16023
Ldc Inc	East Providence	RI	F	401 861-4667	16029
R & D Manufacturing Co Inc	Pawtucket	RI	E	401 305-7662	16408
Uncas International LLC **(PA)**	West Warwick	RI	D	401 231-0266	16924

JEWELRY: Precious Metal

Amy Kahn Russell LLC **(PA)**	Ridgefield	CT	F	203 438-2133	2885
Brannkey Inc	Old Saybrook	CT	E	860 510-0501	2646
Dt Holdings Incorporated	Stamford	CT	F	203 602-6969	3339
Elm City Mfg Jewelers Inc	Hamden	CT	F	203 248-2195	1425
Jewelry Designs Inc	Danbury	CT	E	203 797-0389	761
Joseph Hannoush Family Inc	Farmington	CT	F	860 561-4651	1225
Karavas Fashions Ltd	Norwalk	CT	F	203 866-4000	2522
AB Group Inc	Attleboro	MA	G	508 222-1404	5989
Adina Inc **(PA)**	Norwood	MA	F	781 762-4477	11154
Artinian Garabet Corporation	Concord	MA	F	978 371-7110	8102
Ashworth Assoc Mfg Whl Jwelers	North Attleboro	MA	F	508 695-1900	10866
B & L Manufacturing Inc	Bellingham	MA	G	508 966-3066	6286
Barmakian Brothers Ltd Partnr	Boston	MA	E	617 227-3724	6583
Charles Thomae & Son Inc	Attleboro	MA	F	508 222-0785	6001
Dilon Company Inc	Attleboro	MA	G	508 223-3400	6009
E A Dion Inc	Attleboro	MA	C	800 445-1007	6010
Findings Incorporated	Attleboro	MA	D	508 222-7449	6015
G Austin Young Inc	Attleboro	MA	G	508 222-4700	6019
J T Inman Co Inc	Attleboro Falls	MA	E	508 226-0080	6088
Jewelry Solutions LLC	Canton	MA	G	781 821-6100	7803
M S Company	Attleboro	MA	D	508 222-1700	6032
Marathon Co	Attleboro	MA	G	508 222-5544	6034
Melanie Casey LLC	Andover	MA	E	781 640-8910	5894
Natalia Marketing Corp	Waltham	MA	E	781 693-4900	12733
Newpro Designs Inc	Norwood	MA	E	781 762-4477	11200
North Attleboro Jewelry Co Inc	Attleboro	MA	G	508 222-4660	6044
Richline Group Inc	Attleboro	MA	F	774 203-1199	6055
Silva Jewelers of Osterville	Osterville	MA	G	508 428-2872	11246
Sweet Metal Finishing Inc	Attleboro	MA	F	508 226-4359	6068
Touch Inc	Waltham	MA	F	781 894-8133	12805
W E Richards Co Inc	Attleboro	MA	G	508 226-1036	6074
Zero Porosity Casting Inc	Waltham	MA	F	617 391-0008	12821
A Silver Lining Inc	Boothbay Harbor	ME	G	207 633-4103	4599
Brown Goldsmiths & Co Inc	Freeport	ME	F	207 865-4126	4799
Daunis	Portland	ME	F	207 773-6011	5205
Nazarian Jewelers NH Inc **(PA)**	Salem	NH	F	603 893-1600	15548
Accessories Assoc Inc	Smithfield	RI	G	401 231-3800	16684
Aetna Manufacturing Company	Providence	RI	G	401 751-3260	16466
Alviti Link - All Inc	Johnston	RI	G	401 861-6656	16074
Anatone Jewelry Co Inc	North Providence	RI	G	401 728-0490	16294
Arden Jewelry Mfg Co	Johnston	RI	E	401 274-9800	16076
Armbrust International Ltd	Providence	RI	C	401 781-3300	16475
Atamian Manufacturing Corp	Providence	RI	E	401 944-9614	16477
Bazar Group Inc **(PA)**	East Providence	RI	F	401 434-2595	16006
Bliss Manufacturing Co Inc	Pawtucket	RI	E	401 729-1690	16350
Carla Corp	East Providence	RI	C	401 438-7070	16008
Chronomatic Inc	East Greenwich	RI	E	401 884-6361	15978
CJ International Inc	Providence	RI	E	401 944-4700	16499
Discovery Mint Inc	Pawtucket	RI	E	401 722-6530	16364
Erm LLC	Johnston	RI	G	401 934-2544	16084
Esposito Jewelry Inc	Providence	RI	F	401 943-1900	16516
FAF Inc	Greenville	RI	D	401 949-3000	16058
Fashion Accents LLC **(PA)**	Providence	RI	E	401 331-6626	16517
Fiesta Jewelry Corporation	Pawtucket	RI	E	212 564-6847	16369
Gem-Craft Inc	Cranston	RI	G	401 854-1200	15867
Grant Foster Group L P	Smithfield	RI	F	401 231-4077	16705
Hogan & Bolas	Providence	RI	G	401 349-2988	16532
Imperial-Deltah Inc	East Providence	RI	D	401 434-2597	16023
J Arakelian Inc	Johnston	RI	F	401 943-7366	16090
J Cal Inc	Providence	RI	D	401 941-7700	16545
J Cal Inc **(PA)**	Providence	RI	D	401 941-7700	16546

	CITY	ST	EMP	PHONE	ENTRY#
J H Breakell & Company Inc	Newport	RI	F	401 849-3522	16213
Jji International Inc	Cranston	RI	E	401 780-8668	15878
Kennedy Incorporated	North Kingstown	RI	F	401 295-7800	16265
Kerissa Creations Inc	Greenville	RI	F	401 949-5100	16061
Klitzner Industries Inc	Lincoln	RI	E	800 621-0161	16143
Lees Manufacturing Co Inc	Providence	RI	E	401 275-2383	16552
LImage Inc	Johnston	RI	E	401 369-7141	16093
Luca + Danni Inc	Cranston	RI	E	401 275-5337	15887
Mag Jewelry Co Inc	Cranston	RI	E	401 942-1840	15890
Marketplace Inc Corporate	East Greenwich	RI	F	401 336-3000	15990
Martins Soldering	Johnston	RI	G	401 521-2280	16095
National Chain Company **(PA)**	Warwick	RI	D	401 732-3634	16840
Rolyn Inc **(PA)**	Cranston	RI	E	401 944-0844	15908
Stylecraft Inc	Cranston	RI	D	401 463-9944	15914
Sunshine Minting Inc	North Providence	RI	G	401 265-8383	16311
T Sardelli and Sons Inc	Providence	RI	E	401 429-2144	16617
Tahoe Jewelry Inc	East Providence	RI	F	401 435-4114	16045
Tme Co Inc	Providence	RI	F	860 354-0686	16628
Two Hands Inc	Providence	RI	F	401 785-2727	16631
Uncas International LLC **(PA)**	West Warwick	RI	D	401 231-0266	16924
US Emblem LLC	East Greenwich	RI	F	401 487-4327	15995
Village Goldsmith	Warwick	RI	F	401 944-8404	16872
Wehr Industries Inc	Warwick	RI	E	401 732-6565	16878
Wiesner Manufacturing Company	Warwick	RI	F	401 421-2406	16879
Bixler University	Burlington	VT	F	888 361-4558	17120
PBL Incorporated	Colchester	VT	F	802 893-0111	17199

JIGS & FIXTURES

	CITY	ST	EMP	PHONE	ENTRY#
Apex Machine Tool Company Inc	Cheshire	CT	D	860 677-2884	571
Gary Tool Company	Stratford	CT	G	203 377-3077	3540
Sirois Tool Company Inc **(PA)**	Berlin	CT	E	860 828-5327	85
A & M Tool & Die Company Inc	Southbridge	MA	E	508 764-3241	12008

JOB PRINTING & NEWSPAPER PUBLISHING COMBINED

	CITY	ST	EMP	PHONE	ENTRY#
Glastonbury Citizen Inc	Glastonbury	CT	F	860 633-4691	1281
Lakeville Journal Company LLC **(PA)**	Lakeville	CT	E	860 435-9873	1547
Middlbury Bee-Intelligencer-Ct	Middlebury	CT	G	203 577-6800	1717
Amherst College Public Affairs	Amherst	MA	F	413 542-2321	5857
Boston Globe Mdia Partners LLC	Boston	MA	B	617 929-2000	6609
Wakefield Item Company	Wakefield	MA	E	781 245-0080	12542
Lincoln News	Lincoln	ME	G	207 794-6532	5010
County Courier Inc	Enosburg Falls	VT	G	802 933-4375	17222
Journal Opinion Inc	Bradford	VT	F	802 222-5281	17063

JOB TRAINING SVCS

	CITY	ST	EMP	PHONE	ENTRY#
Powerphone Inc	Madison	CT	E	203 245-8911	1566
Training Thru Placement Inc	North Providence	RI	F	401 353-0220	16312

JOINTS: Expansion, Pipe

	CITY	ST	EMP	PHONE	ENTRY#
Flue Gas Solutions Inc	Auburn	ME	G	207 893-1510	4432
Fronek Anchor Darling Entp	Laconia	NH	F	603 528-1931	14651

JOINTS: Swivel & Universal, Exc Aircraft & Auto

	CITY	ST	EMP	PHONE	ENTRY#
Valley Enterprises Inc	Springfield	MA	E	413 737-0281	12146

JOISTS: Long-Span Series, Open Web Steel

	CITY	ST	EMP	PHONE	ENTRY#
Stairs Unlimited Inc	Richford	VT	G	802 848-7030	17476

JUNIOR COLLEGES

	CITY	ST	EMP	PHONE	ENTRY#
Mathworks Inc	Natick	MA	A	508 647-7000	10485
Mathworks Inc **(PA)**	Natick	MA	A	508 647-7000	10486

KAOLIN MINING

	CITY	ST	EMP	PHONE	ENTRY#
JM Huber Corporation	Millinocket	ME	E	207 723-9291	5065

KEYBOARDS: Computer Or Office Machine

	CITY	ST	EMP	PHONE	ENTRY#
Precision Electronic Assembly	Monroe	CT	F	203 452-1839	1919
Cortron Inc	Lowell	MA	E	978 975-5445	9871
Csi Keyboards Inc	Peabody	MA	E	978 532-8181	11304
Vesuvius America Inc **(DH)**	Providence	RI	E		16640

KIDNEY DIALYSIS CENTERS

	CITY	ST	EMP	PHONE	ENTRY#
Fresenius Med Care Hldings Inc **(DH)**	Waltham	MA	A	781 699-9000	12679
Fresenius Med Svcs Group LLC	Waltham	MA	F	781 699-9000	12682

KILNS & FURNACES: Ceramic

	CITY	ST	EMP	PHONE	ENTRY#
Hearth Kitchen Products Inc	Stamford	CT	G	203 325-8800	3372

KITCHEN CABINETS WHOLESALERS

	CITY	ST	EMP	PHONE	ENTRY#
Professional Trades Netwrk LLC	Watertown	CT	G	860 567-0173	4026
S J Pappas Inc	Meriden	CT	G	203 237-7701	1695
Viking Kitchen Cabinets LLC **(PA)**	New Britain	CT	E	860 223-7101	2074

	CITY	ST	EMP	PHONE	ENTRY#
Coastal-N-Counters Inc	Mashpee	MA	F	508 539-3500	10251
K & D Millworks Inc	Windham	ME	E	207 892-5188	5663
David D Douglas Inc	Londonderry	NH	G	603 437-1151	14742
Granite State Ktchens Dstrs In	Bedford	NH	E	603 472-4080	13931

KITCHEN UTENSILS: Bakers' Eqpt, Wood

	CITY	ST	EMP	PHONE	ENTRY#
Jsi Store Fixtures Inc **(HQ)**	Milo	ME	C	207 943-5203	5070

KITCHEN UTENSILS: Food Handling & Processing Prdts, Wood

	CITY	ST	EMP	PHONE	ENTRY#
Too Sweets LLC	Waterbury	CT	G	203 578-6493	3973
Andrew Pearce Bowls LLC	Taftsville	VT	E	802 356-4632	17647

KITCHENWARE STORES

	CITY	ST	EMP	PHONE	ENTRY#
Hearth Kitchen Products Inc	Stamford	CT	G	203 325-8800	3372
Petermans Boards and Bowls Inc	Gill	MA	E	413 863-2116	8915
Plastican Inc	Leominster	MA	A	978 728-5000	9696
J K Adams Company Inc	Dorset	VT	E	802 362-2303	17214

KNIT OUTERWEAR DYEING & FINISHING, EXC HOSIERY & GLOVE

	CITY	ST	EMP	PHONE	ENTRY#
Red Fish - Blue Fish Dye Wrks	Somersworth	NH	G	603 692-3900	15624

KNIVES: Agricultural Or indl

	CITY	ST	EMP	PHONE	ENTRY#
D & S Manufacturing Company Incorporated		Auburn		MA	F
508 799-7812	6111				
Dexter-Russell Inc	Southbridge	MA	C	508 765-0201	12014
Lamson and Goodnow Mfg Co	Shelburne Falls	MA	E	413 625-6311	11807
Peterson and Nash Inc	Norwell	MA	E	781 826-9085	11145
Silver Greenfield Inc	Greenfield	MA	C	413 774-2774	8999

LABELS: Paper, Made From Purchased Materials

	CITY	ST	EMP	PHONE	ENTRY#
Biomerics LLC	Monroe	CT	D	203 268-7238	1906
George Schmitt & Co Inc **(PA)**	Guilford	CT	E	203 453-4334	1394
Northeast Laser Engraving Inc	Monroe	CT	E	203 268-7238	1918
Specialty Printing LLC **(PA)**	Windsor	CT	D	860 623-8870	4300
Screenprint/Dow Inc	Wilmington	MA	D	978 657-7290	13451
Smyth Companies LLC	Wilmington	MA	E	800 776-1201	13453
Computype Inc	Concord	NH	G	603 225-5500	14122

LABELS: Woven

	CITY	ST	EMP	PHONE	ENTRY#
Bell Manufacturing Co	Lewiston	ME	G	207 784-2961	4953

LABORATORIES, TESTING: Metallurgical

	CITY	ST	EMP	PHONE	ENTRY#
Pti Industries Inc **(HQ)**	Enfield	CT	E	800 318-8438	1143

LABORATORIES, TESTING: Product Testing

	CITY	ST	EMP	PHONE	ENTRY#
AKO Inc	Windsor	CT	E	860 298-9765	4256
Sousa Corp	Newington	CT	E	860 523-9090	2326
Alcami Carolinas Corporation	Pepperell	MA	G	910 619-3952	11380
Alcami Carolinas Corporation	Pepperell	MA	G	910 619-3952	11381
Alcami Carolinas Corporation	Pepperell	MA	F	910 619-3952	11382
Alcami Carolinas Corporation	Shirley	MA	G	910 619-3952	11813
Aspen Systems LLC **(PA)**	Marlborough	MA	F	508 281-5322	10112
Barbour Stockwell Inc	Woburn	MA	E	781 933-5200	13520
Hardigg Industries LLC **(HQ)**	South Deerfield	MA	C	413 665-2163	11924
Kse Inc	Sunderland	MA	F	413 549-5506	12274
Alcami Carolinas Corporation	Amherst	NH	G	910 619-3952	13861
American Iron & Metal USA Inc **(HQ)**	Cranston	RI	F	401 463-5605	15831

LABORATORIES, TESTING: Product Testing, Safety/Performance

	CITY	ST	EMP	PHONE	ENTRY#
Parker-Hannifin Corporation	Woburn	MA	B	781 939-4278	13631

LABORATORIES, TESTING: Radiation

	CITY	ST	EMP	PHONE	ENTRY#
Nats USA Incorporated	Middletown	CT	F	860 398-0035	1767

LABORATORIES: Biological

	CITY	ST	EMP	PHONE	ENTRY#
Genzyme Corporation **(DH)**	Cambridge	MA	A	617 252-7500	7585
Genzyme Corporation	Framingham	MA	E	617 252-7500	8773
Genzyme Corporation	Framingham	MA	E	617 252-7500	8774
Kalvista Pharmaceuticals Inc **(PA)**	Cambridge	MA	E	857 999-0075	7621

LABORATORIES: Biological Research

	CITY	ST	EMP	PHONE	ENTRY#
Precipio Inc **(PA)**	New Haven	CT	F	203 787-7888	2187
Agenus Inc **(PA)**	Lexington	MA	C	781 674-4400	9721
Alcami Carolinas Corporation	Pepperell	MA	G	910 619-3952	11380
Alcami Carolinas Corporation	Pepperell	MA	G	910 619-3952	11381
Alcami Carolinas Corporation	Pepperell	MA	F	910 619-3952	11382
Alcami Carolinas Corporation	Shirley	MA	G	910 619-3952	11813
Biogen Inc **(PA)**	Cambridge	MA	B	617 679-2000	7511
C4 Therapeutics Inc **(PA)**	Watertown	MA	E	617 231-0700	12866
Corium LLC	Boston	MA	C	855 253-2407	6672
Dicerna Pharmaceuticals Inc **(HQ)**	Lexington	MA	C	617 621-8097	9739
Disc Medicine Inc **(PA)**	Watertown	MA	F	617 674-9274	12871

	CITY	ST	EMP	PHONE	ENTRY#
Folia Materials Inc	Bedford	MA	G	315 559-2135	6227
Gurnet Holding Company	Cambridge	MA	C	617 588-4900	7595
Homology Medicines Inc	Bedford	MA	C	781 301-7277	6229
Sanofi Pasteur Biologics LLC **(HQ)**	Cambridge	MA	C	617 866-4400	7703
Sarepta Therapeutics Inc	Andover	MA	C	978 662-4800	5914
Sensera Inc	Woburn	MA	F	978 606-2600	13663
Synlogic Inc **(PA)**	Cambridge	MA	E	617 401-9975	7729
Vigil Neuroscience Inc **(PA)**	Watertown	MA	E	857 254-4445	12919
Voltea Inc	Worcester	MA	E	510 861-3719	13825
Alcami Carolinas Corporation	Amherst	NH	G	910 619-3952	13861
Epivax Inc	Providence	RI	E	401 272-2123	16515

LABORATORIES: Biotechnology

	CITY	ST	EMP	PHONE	ENTRY#
Arvinas Inc **(PA)**	New Haven	CT	B	203 535-1456	2119
DRM Research Laboratories Inc	Branford	CT	F	203 488-5555	252
Adicet Bio Inc **(PA)**	Boston	MA	G	857 315-5528	6516
Agios Pharmaceuticals Inc **(PA)**	Cambridge	MA	B	617 649-8600	7470
Aileron Therapeutics Inc **(PA)**	Boston	MA	G	617 995-0900	6522
Alkermes Inc **(HQ)**	Waltham	MA	E	781 609-6000	12589
Alnylam Pharmaceuticals Inc **(PA)**	Cambridge	MA	B	617 551-8200	7478
Amylyx Pharmaceuticals Inc **(PA)**	Cambridge	MA	C	617 682-0917	7486
Ardelyx Inc	Waltham	MA	D	510 745-1700	12595
Arqule Inc **(HQ)**	Burlington	MA	E	781 994-0300	7335
Atea Pharmaceuticals Inc **(PA)**	Boston	MA	E	857 284-8891	6571
Aura Biosciences Inc **(PA)**	Boston	MA	F	617 500-8864	6577
Biontech US Inc **(HQ)**	Cambridge	MA	E	617 337-4701	7515
Bluebird Bio Inc **(PA)**	Somerville	MA	A	339 499-9300	11864
Bostonmolecules Inc	Waltham	MA	F	617 651-1016	12610
Brammer Bio Ma LLC **(HQ)**	Cambridge	MA	B	877 765-7676	7524
Cambridge Polymer Group Inc	Woburn	MA	E	617 629-4400	13539
Chemgenes Corporation	Billerica	MA	E	978 694-4500	6422
Cogent Biosciences Inc **(PA)**	Waltham	MA	F	617 945-5576	12634
Curia Global Inc	Burlington	MA	G	781 205-1691	7357
Elevatebio LLC **(PA)**	Cambridge	MA	E	413 297-7151	7559
Elevatebio Base Camp Inc	Waltham	MA	C	617 433-2600	12660
Enanta Pharmaceuticals Inc **(PA)**	Watertown	MA	D	617 607-0800	12872
Epizyme Inc	Cambridge	MA	C	617 229-5872	7563
Imbria Pharmaceuticals Inc	Boston	MA	G	617 941-3000	6808
Immuneering Corporation	Cambridge	MA	E	617 500-8080	7612
Integral Biosystems LLC	Bedford	MA	F	781 275-8059	6234
Intellia Therapeutics Inc **(PA)**	Cambridge	MA	C	857 285-6200	7616
Joule Unlimited Technologies Inc	Foxboro	MA	E	781 533-9100	8703
La Jolla Pharmaceutical Co **(HQ)**	Waltham	MA	E	617 715-3600	12708
Landmark Bio Pbllc	Watertown	MA	G	617 894-8629	12886
Manus Bio Inc **(HQ)**	Waltham	MA	E	617 299-8466	12713
Medtherapy Biotechnology Inc	Quincy	MA	E	617 938-7082	11528
Mersana Therapeutics Inc **(PA)**	Cambridge	MA	D	617 498-0020	7641
Microbiotix Inc	Worcester	MA	E	508 757-2800	13759
Mural Oncology Inc	Waltham	MA	E	617 694-2481	12727
Pepgen Inc	Boston	MA	E	781 797-0979	6962
Revela Inc	Woburn	MA	G	716 725-2657	13651
Solid Biosciences Inc **(PA)**	Charlestown	MA	E	617 337-4680	7883
T2 Biosystems Inc	Wilmington	MA	E	978 447-1069	13461
Tango Therapeutics Inc **(PA)**	Boston	MA	F	857 302-4900	7069
Torque Therapeutics Inc	Cambridge	MA	E	617 945-1082	7744
Vertex Pharmaceuticals Inc **(PA)**	Boston	MA	A	617 341-6100	7101
Voyager Therapeutics Inc **(PA)**	Lexington	MA	D	570 329-6851	9791
Werewolf Therapeutics Inc	Watertown	MA	E	617 952-0555	12920
Ipura Consulting Group LLC	Hampton	MA	F	603 294-4002	14404
Amgen Inc	West Greenwich	RI	A	401 392-1200	16882
Vertex Pharmaceuticals Inc	Providence	RI	F	857 529-6430	16639

LABORATORIES: Commercial Nonphysical Research

	CITY	ST	EMP	PHONE	ENTRY#
Angel Guard Products Inc	Worcester	MA	G	508 791-1073	13699
Idg Corporate Services Group	Framingham	MA	G	508 875-5000	8781
Power Advocate Inc **(HQ)**	Boston	MA	D	857 453-5700	6971
President Fllows Hrvard Cllege	Boston	MA	C	617 495-5581	6976
Population Media Center Inc	South Burlington	VT	E	802 985-8156	17595

LABORATORIES: Dental, Crown & Bridge Production

	CITY	ST	EMP	PHONE	ENTRY#
National Dentex LLC	Manchester	NH	C	561 537-8301	14895

LABORATORIES: Electronic Research

	CITY	ST	EMP	PHONE	ENTRY#
Connecticut Analytical Corp	Bethany	CT	F	203 393-9666	92
Doltronics LLC	Branford	CT	E	203 488-8766	250
Arichell Technologies Inc	Newton	MA	D	617 796-9001	10734
Eclypses Inc	Boston	MA	E	719 323-6680	6707
Empiramed Inc	Maynard	MA	G	978 344-4300	10262
Optra Inc	Wilmington	MA	E	978 887-6600	13443
Videoiq Inc	Somerville	MA	E	781 222-3069	11911
David Saunders Inc	South Portland	ME	E	207 228-1888	5497

LABORATORIES: Medical

	CITY	ST	EMP	PHONE	ENTRY#
Alere Inc **(HQ)**	Waltham	MA	A	781 647-3900	12587
Day Zero Diagnostics Inc	Watertown	MA	E	857 770-1125	12870
Massbiologics	Boston	MA	C	617 474-3000	6877
Reading Diagnostic Center	Reading	MA	F	781 942-9876	11605

LABORATORIES: Noncommercial Research

	CITY	ST	EMP	PHONE	ENTRY#
Valo Health Inc **(PA)**	Boston	MA	E	617 237-6080	7096
Sensor Research and Dev Corp	Orono	ME	G	207 866-0100	5137

LABORATORIES: Physical Research, Commercial

	CITY	ST	EMP	PHONE	ENTRY#
Accustandard Inc	New Haven	CT	D	203 786-5290	2111
Cara Therapeutics Inc	Stamford	CT	D	203 406-3700	3302
Charles River Laboratories Inc	Storrs	CT	F	860 429-7261	3511
Clear Edge Power International Service LLC 860 727-2200	South Windsor	CT			C
3128					
Cytec Industries Inc	Stamford	CT	F	203 321-2200	3333
Hampford Research Inc **(PA)**	Stratford	CT	E	203 375-1137	3544
Henkel Loctite Corporation **(DH)**	Rocky Hill	CT	D	860 571-5100	2925
Herbasway Laboratories LLC	Wallingford	CT	F	203 269-6991	3812
Imbrium Therapeutics LP **(DH)**	Stamford	CT	E	888 827-0622	3380
Jet Process Corporation	Wallingford	CT	G	203 985-6000	3823
Pratt & Whitney Eng Svcs Inc	East Hartford	CT	E	860 610-7478	1016
Thayermahan Inc **(PA)**	Groton	CT	E	860 785-9994	1381
2is Inc	Walpole	MA	E	508 850-7520	12545
Adaptive Optics Associates Inc **(DH)**	Devens	MA	D	978 757-9600	8269
Axcella Health Inc **(PA)**	Cambridge	MA	G	857 320-2200	7496
Barrett Technology LLC	Newton	MA	E	617 252-9000	10737
BASF Bioresearch Corp	Worcester	MA	E	508 849-2500	13702
Carpe Diem Technologies Inc	Franklin	MA	F	508 541-2055	8822
Concepts Nrec LLC	Chelmsford	MA	F	781 935-9050	7920
Dynasil Corporation America **(PA)**	Concord	MA	E	617 668-6855	8116
Esoterix Genetic Labs LLC **(HQ)**	Westborough	MA	E	508 389-6650	13101
Flintec Inc	Hudson	MA	E	978 562-4548	9367
ID Bimedical Corp Northborough	Northborough	MA	D	508 351-9333	11099
Immunmlecular Therapeutics Inc	Woburn	MA	G	617 356-8170	13584
Infinity Pharmaceuticals Inc **(PA)**	Cambridge	MA	F		7614
Instrumentation Laboratory Co **(DH)**	Bedford	MA	A	781 861-0710	6233
Interleukin Genetics Inc	Waltham	MA	F	781 398-0700	12702
Ironwood Pharmaceuticals Inc **(PA)**	Boston	MA	C	617 621-7722	6818
Jounce Therapeutics Inc **(PA)**	Cambridge	MA	D	857 259-3840	7620
Lyne Laboratories Inc	Brockton	MA	D	508 583-8700	7292
Micro Magnetics Inc	Fall River	MA	F	508 672-4489	8581
New Balance Athletics Inc	Lawrence	MA	B	978 685-8400	9586
Novirio Pharmaceuticals Inc	Cambridge	MA	D	617 250-3100	7671
Praxis Precision Medicines Inc **(PA)**	Boston	MA	E	617 300-8460	6974
Scientific Solutions Inc	North Chelmsford	MA	F	978 251-4554	10988
Sigma Research Biochemicals	Natick	MA	G	781 237-3828	10497
Soft Robotics Inc	Bedford	MA	E	617 391-0612	6269
Theseus Pharmaceuticals Inc **(PA)**	Cambridge	MA	F	857 400-9491	7740
Ultraclad Corporation	Newburyport	MA	G	978 358-7945	10723
Biodesign International	Saco	ME	E	207 283-6500	5363
Maine Orthtic Prsthtic Rhab Sv	Portland	ME	F	207 773-8818	5241
At Comm Corp	Manchester	NH	F	603 624-4424	14815
Bae Systems Info Elctrnc Syst	Hudson	NH	A	603 885-4321	14486
Corportion For Lser Optics Res **(PA)**	Londonderry	NH	G	603 430-2023	14738
Exothermics Inc	Amherst	NH	F	603 821-5660	13869
Ingersoll-Rand Energy Systems Corporation 603 430-7000	Portsmouth	NH			D
15408					
Mentis Sciences Inc	Warner	NH	E	603 624-9197	15666
Oracle Systems Corporation	Nashua	NH	E	603 897-3000	15146
Simbex LLC	Lebanon	NH	E	603 448-2367	14699
Bioprocessh2o LLC	Portsmouth	RI	E	401 683-5400	16438
McLaughlin Research Corp	Middletown	RI	C	401 849-4010	16179

LABORATORIES: Testing

	CITY	ST	EMP	PHONE	ENTRY#
Acuren Inspection Inc **(HQ)**	Danbury	CT	A	203 702-8740	704
Immucor Trnsplant Dgnstics Inc **(DH)**	Stamford	CT	D	203 328-9500	3381
Esoterix Genetic Labs LLC **(HQ)**	Westborough	MA	F	508 389-6650	13101
Labthink International Inc	Medford	MA	F	617 830-2190	10293
Magellan Diagnostics Inc **(HQ)**	Chelmsford	MA	D	978 250-7000	7937
Magellan Diagnostics Inc	North Billerica	MA	E	978 856-2345	10931
Quest Diagnostic Incorporated	Marlborough	MA	A	617 547-8900	10199
Kennebec River Biosciences Inc	Richmond	ME	F	207 737-2637	5322
Cogstate Sport Inc	New Haven	CT	F	203 773-5010	2137
Enginuity Plm LLC **(DH)**	Milford	CT	F	203 218-7225	1825
Hoffman Engineering LLC **(DH)**	Stamford	CT	D	203 425-8900	3378
Precipio Inc **(PA)**	New Haven	CT	F	203 787-7888	2187
Bmac Inc	Ayer	MA	E	978 772-3310	6175
Cambridge Polymer Group Inc	Woburn	MA	E	617 629-4400	13539
Cryogenic Institute Neng Inc	Worcester	MA	F	508 459-7447	13712

PRODUCT

	CITY	ST	EMP	PHONE	ENTRY#
Jordi Labs LLC	Mansfield	MA	E	508 719-8543	10061
Netzsch Instruments N Amer LLC (DH)	Burlington	MA	E	781 272-5353	7398
Schenck USA Corp	Hudson	MA	E	978 562-6017	9410
Test Devices Inc	Hudson	MA	E	978 562-6017	9417
Kennebec River Biosciences Inc	Richmond	ME	F	207 737-2637	5322
Northeast Laboratory Svcs Inc (PA)	Winslow	ME	D	207 873-7711	5686
Smiths Tblar Systms-Lconia Inc	Laconia	NH	C	603 524-2064	14670
Verichem Laboratories Inc	Providence	RI	G	401 461-0180	16638

LABORATORY APPARATUS & FURNITURE

	CITY	ST	EMP	PHONE	ENTRY#
Ebs Acquisition Inc	Niantic	CT	F	860 653-0411	2356
Idex Health & Science LLC	Bristol	CT	C	860 314-2880	456
Kent Scientific Corporation	Torrington	CT	E	860 626-1172	3688
Tomtec Inc	Hamden	CT	D	203 281-6790	1460
Aja International Inc	Hingham	MA	E	781 545-7365	9139
Bluecatbio MA Inc	Concord	MA	G	978 405-2533	8106
Bmac Inc	Ayer	MA	E	978 772-3310	6175
Corning Incorporated	Tewksbury	MA	E	978 442-2200	12391
Digilab Inc	Hopkinton	MA	D	508 305-2410	9315
Erbi Biosystems Inc	Stoneham	MA	E	617 297-7422	12177
Idex Health & Science LLC	Middleboro	MA	C	774 213-0200	10362
Inert Corporation	Amesbury	MA	E	978 462-4415	5837
Kinetic Systems Inc	Boston	MA	E	617 522-8700	6842
Matrix Technologies	Tewksbury	MA	G	603 521-0547	12407
Micro-Lite Inc	Three Rivers	MA	F	413 289-1313	12429
Microfluidics Intl Corp	Westwood	MA	E	617 969-5452	13315
Parallel Systems Corp	Georgetown	MA	E	978 352-7100	8911
Thermo Fisher Scientific Inc	Beverly	MA	C	978 232-6000	6387
Thomas Scientific LLC	Thorndike	MA	D	413 406-6588	12428
Wright Line LLC (HQ)	Worcester	MA	B	508 852-4300	13834
Baker Company Inc (PA)	Sanford	ME	C	207 324-8773	5390
Emerson Apparatus Company	Gorham	ME	F	207 856-0055	4818
Materials Research Frncs Inc	Allenstown	NH	F	603 485-2394	13853
New Erie Scientific LLC (DH)	Portsmouth	NH	E	603 430-6859	15425
Pre-Tech Plastics Inc (PA)	Williston	VT	E	802 879-9441	17745
Raj Communications Ltd	Essex Junction	VT	E	802 658-4961	17243

LABORATORY APPARATUS & FURNITURE: Worktables

	CITY	ST	EMP	PHONE	ENTRY#
Bnz Materials Inc	North Billerica	MA	C	978 663-3401	10900

LABORATORY APPARATUS, EXC HEATING & MEASURING

	CITY	ST	EMP	PHONE	ENTRY#
Labcentral Inc (PA)	Cambridge	MA	E	617 863-3650	7626

LABORATORY APPARATUS: Freezers

	CITY	ST	EMP	PHONE	ENTRY#
Hamilton Storage Tech Inc	Franklin	MA	G	508 544-7000	8842

LABORATORY APPARATUS: Heating

	CITY	ST	EMP	PHONE	ENTRY#
Apogent Technologies Inc	Waltham	MA	A	781 622-1300	12594

LABORATORY APPARATUS: Laser Beam Alignment Device

	CITY	ST	EMP	PHONE	ENTRY#
Pinpoint Laser Systems Inc	Peabody	MA	E	978 532-8001	11333

LABORATORY APPARATUS: Sample Preparation Apparatus

	CITY	ST	EMP	PHONE	ENTRY#
Extec Corp	Enfield	CT	F	860 741-3435	1133

LABORATORY APPARATUS: Shakers & Stirrers

	CITY	ST	EMP	PHONE	ENTRY#
Eppendorf Holding Inc (DH)	Enfield	CT	E	860 253-3417	1131

LABORATORY CHEMICALS: Organic

	CITY	ST	EMP	PHONE	ENTRY#
RT Vanderbilt Holding Co Inc (PA)	Norwalk	CT	F	203 295-2141	2568
Fisher Scientific Intl LLC (HQ)	Waltham	MA	C	781 622-1000	12675
Giner Life Sciences Inc	Auburndale	MA	E	781 529-0576	6135
Strem Chemicals Incorporated (HQ)	Newburyport	MA	D	978 499-1600	10718
Purevita Labs LLC	West Warwick	RI	F	401 258-8968	16921

LABORATORY EQPT, EXC MEDICAL: Wholesalers

	CITY	ST	EMP	PHONE	ENTRY#
Fisher Scientific Intl LLC (HQ)	Waltham	MA	C	781 622-1000	12675
High Technology Inc	North Attleboro	MA	E	508 660-2221	10873
Jeio Tech Inc	Billerica	MA	G	781 376-0700	6457
M-R Resources Inc	Fitchburg	MA	E	978 345-9010	8659
Organomation Associates Inc	Berlin	MA	F	978 838-7300	6320
Pion Inc	Billerica	MA	E	978 528-2020	6472
Raj Communications Ltd	Essex Junction	VT	E	802 658-4961	17243

LABORATORY EQPT: Chemical

	CITY	ST	EMP	PHONE	ENTRY#
Novamont North America Inc	Shelton	CT	F	203 744-8801	3041

LABORATORY EQPT: Clinical Instruments Exc Medical

	CITY	ST	EMP	PHONE	ENTRY#
Excelerarx Corp	Stoughton	MA	F	612 293-0378	12203
Openclinica LLC	Needham Heights	MA	E	617 621-8585	10554

LABORATORY EQPT: Measuring

	CITY	ST	EMP	PHONE	ENTRY#
Arecna Holdings Inc	Branford	CT	F	203 819-2322	236
Rochester USA	Rochester	NH	G	603 332-0717	15490

LABORATORY EQPT: Sterilizers

	CITY	ST	EMP	PHONE	ENTRY#
Mayborn Usa Inc	Stamford	CT	F	781 269-7490	3409
Consolidated Machine Corporation	Billerica	MA	E	617 782-6072	6428

LABORATORY INSTRUMENT REPAIR SVCS

	CITY	ST	EMP	PHONE	ENTRY#
High Technology Inc	North Attleboro	MA	E	508 660-2221	10873

LADDERS: Metal

	CITY	ST	EMP	PHONE	ENTRY#
Lynn Ladder Scaffolding Co Inc (HQ)	Lynn	MA	D	781 598-6010	9985
Nsd Metal Fabrication Inc	Merrimac	MA	G	978 346-0045	10326
St Pierre Manufacturing Corp	Worcester	MA	E	508 853-8010	13806

LAMINATED PLASTICS: Plate, Sheet, Rod & Tubes

	CITY	ST	EMP	PHONE	ENTRY#
Beckson Manufacturing Inc (PA)	Bridgeport	CT	E	203 366-3644	301
CT Composites & Marine Svc LLC	South Windsor	CT	G	860 282-0100	3137
Current Inc (PA)	East Haven	CT	D	203 469-1337	1039
Diba Industries Inc (HQ)	Danbury	CT	E	203 744-0773	731
Panolam Industries Inc (HQ)	Shelton	CT	E	203 925-1556	3044
Pioneer Plastics Corporation (HQ)	Shelton	CT	C	203 925-1556	3047
Polymedex Discovery Group Inc (PA)	Putnam	CT	E	860 928-4102	2870
Quality Name Plate Inc	East Glastonbury	CT	D	860 633-9495	923
The E J Davis Company	North Haven	CT	E	203 239-5391	2439
3M Company	Chelmsford	MA	E	978 256-3911	7901
Custom Extrusion Inc (HQ)	Sheffield	MA	E	413 229-8748	11797
Fort Hill Sign Products Inc	Hopedale	MA	G	781 321-4320	9297
Injectronics Corporation	Clinton	MA	D	978 365-1200	8078
MM Newman Corporation	Marblehead	MA	F	781 631-7100	10091
October Company Inc	Easthampton	MA	E	413 529-0718	8457
Samar Co Inc	Stoughton	MA	E	781 297-7264	12233
United Plastic Fabricating Inc (PA)	North Andover	MA	D	978 975-4520	10855
Pioneer Plastics Corporation	Auburn	ME	C	207 784-9111	4454
Nordson Medical (nh) Inc (HQ)	Salem	NH	C	603 327-0600	15551
Scandia Plastics Inc	Plaistow	NH	E	603 382-6533	15350
Tech Resources Inc	Milford	NH	E	603 673-9000	15039
Teleflex Incorporated	Jaffrey	NH	D	603 532-7706	14580
Tfx Medical Incorporated	Jaffrey	NH	D	603 532-7706	14581
Nelipak Corporation (PA)	Cranston	RI	E	401 946-2699	15899
Tpi Inc	Warren	RI	D	401 247-4010	16769
Tpi Composites Inc	Warren	RI	E	401 247-4010	16770
Kaman Composites - Vermont Inc	Bennington	VT	C	802 442-9964	17046

LAMINATING MATERIALS

	CITY	ST	EMP	PHONE	ENTRY#
Middlesex Research Mfg Co Inc	Hudson	MA	E	978 562-3697	9390

LAMINATING SVCS

	CITY	ST	EMP	PHONE	ENTRY#
Flagship Converters Inc	Danbury	CT	D	203 792-0034	746
Technical Reproductions Inc	Norwalk	CT	F	203 849-9100	2575
J L Enterprises Inc	Canton	MA	G	781 821-6300	7802
Plastilam Inc	Salem	MA	E	978 745-5563	11730
AP Dley Cstm Laminating Corp	Windham	NH	E	603 437-6666	15720

LAMP & LIGHT BULBS & TUBES

	CITY	ST	EMP	PHONE	ENTRY#
Electro-Lite Corporation	Bethel	CT	F	203 743-4059	114
Whelen Engineering Company Inc (PA)	Chester	CT	B	860 526-9504	634
Dolan-Jenner Industries Inc	Boxborough	MA	E	978 263-1400	7151
International Light Tech Inc	Peabody	MA	E	978 818-6180	11319
Neenas Lighting	Cambridge	MA	G	617 864-5757	7661
Osram Sylvania Inc (DH)	Wilmington	MA	A	978 570-3000	13444
Partylite Inc (HQ)	Plymouth	MA	D	203 661-1926	11471
Philips Holding USA Inc (HQ)	Cambridge	MA	A	978 687-1501	7686
Luminescent Systems Inc	Lebanon	NH	C	603 643-7766	14693
Osram Sylvania Inc	Exeter	NH	B	603 772-4331	14299
Osram Sylvania Inc	Hillsborough	NH	B	978 750-3900	14441
Osram Sylvania Inc	Hillsborough	NH	B	603 464-7235	14442
Brownlie Lamar Design Group	Warren	RI	E	401 714-9371	16756
Osram Sylvania Inc	Central Falls	RI	C	401 723-1378	15794

LAMP BULBS & TUBES, ELECTRIC: Light, Complete

	CITY	ST	EMP	PHONE	ENTRY#
Revolution Lighting Tech Inc (PA)	Stamford	CT	E	877 578-2536	3447

LAMP BULBS & TUBES/PARTS, ELECTRIC: Generalized Applications

	CITY	ST	EMP	PHONE	ENTRY#
Lcd Lighting Inc	Orange	CT	C	203 799-7877	2674

LAMP SHADES: Glass

	CITY	ST	EMP	PHONE	ENTRY#
Capitol Glass Company Inc	West Hartford	CT	F	860 236-1936	4050
A B C Glass Co Inc	Springfield	MA	F	413 734-4524	12067
Central FLS Plate & Win GL Co	Central Falls	RI	F	401 722-1267	15787

LAND SUBDIVIDERS & DEVELOPERS: Commercial

2024 Harris New England
Manufacturers Directory

(G-0000) Company's Geographic Section entry number

	CITY	ST	EMP	PHONE	ENTRY#
The Bilco Company (DH)	West Haven	CT	C	203 934-6363	4128
Emery Development Ltd	Springfield	MA	G	413 782-1990	12094
Wells Development L L C	Arlington	MA	G	781 727-5560	5950

LAND SUBDIVIDERS & DEVELOPERS: Residential

	CITY	ST	EMP	PHONE	ENTRY#
Fox Homes Inc	Lee	MA	F	413 243-1950	9613

LAND SUBDIVISION & DEVELOPMENT

	CITY	ST	EMP	PHONE	ENTRY#
Richard Riggio and Sons Inc	Ivoryton	CT	F	860 767-0812	1532
Wesco Building & Design Inc	Stoneham	MA	G	781 279-0490	12188
Wescor Ltd (PA)	Stoneham	MA	G	781 279-0490	12189
Narragansett Improvement Co (PA)	Providence	RI	D	401 331-0051	16571

LASER SYSTEMS & EQPT

	CITY	ST	EMP	PHONE	ENTRY#
Coherent-Deos LLC	Bloomfield	CT	D	860 243-9557	157
Hamar Laser Instruments Inc	Danbury	CT	E	203 730-4600	756
Total Register Inc	New Milford	CT	F	860 210-0465	2262
Convergent - Photonics LLC (DH)	Chicopee	MA	E	413 598-5200	8020
Excel Technology Inc (HQ)	Bedford	MA	D	781 266-5700	6226
Ipg Photonics Corporation	Marlborough	MA	F	508 373-1100	10167
Ipg Photonics Corporation	Marlborough	MA	E	508 506-2812	10168
Ipg Photonics Corporation (PA)	Marlborough	MA	B	508 373-1100	10169
Ipg Photonics Corporation	Oxford	MA	F	508 506-2585	11255
Novanta Corporation (HQ)	Bedford	MA	C	781 266-5700	6245
Novanta Inc (PA)	Bedford	MA	C	781 266-5700	6246
Polytec Inc	Hudson	MA	G	508 417-1040	9401
Rofin-Baasel Inc (HQ)	Devens	MA	E	978 635-9100	8286
Sancliff Inc	Worcester	MA	E	508 795-0747	13794
Teradiode Inc	Wilmington	MA	D	978 988-1040	13464
Ipg Photonics Corporation	Nashua	NH	F	603 518-3200	15116
JP Sercel Associates Inc	Manchester	NH	E	603 595-7048	14869
Laser Advantage LLC	Nashua	NH	F	603 886-9464	15125
Laser Light Engines Inc	Salem	NH	F	603 952-4550	15542
Laser Projection Technologies Inc	Londonderry	NH	E	603 421-0209	14762
Lenric Corp	Nashua	NH	F	603 886-6772	15127
Clariant Corporation	Coventry	RI	B	401 823-2000	15809
Laser Fare Inc (PA)	Smithfield	RI	E	401 231-4400	16721
Laservall North America LLC	Pawtucket	RI	G	401 724-0076	16382

LASERS: Welding, Drilling & Cutting Eqpt

	CITY	ST	EMP	PHONE	ENTRY#
Arcor Laser Services LLC	Suffield	CT	D	860 370-9780	3587
Cadence Ct Inc	Suffield	CT	D	860 370-9780	3589
Varnum Enterprises LLC	Bethel	CT	F	203 743-4443	140
Green Brothers Fabricating (PA)	Taunton	MA	E	508 880-3608	12339
Litron LLC	Agawam	MA	D		5799
Lfi Inc (PA)	Smithfield	RI	E	401 231-4400	16722
Maley Laser Processing Inc	Warwick	RI	F	303 952-8941	16834

LATEX: Foamed

	CITY	ST	EMP	PHONE	ENTRY#
Universal Foam Products LLC	Bloomfield	CT	F	860 216-3015	215
Vystar Corporation	Worcester	MA	D	508 791-9114	13826

LAUNDRY EQPT: Commercial

	CITY	ST	EMP	PHONE	ENTRY#
Gordon Brothers Intl LLC (HQ)	Boston	MA	D	888 424-1903	6767

LAUNDRY SVC: Indl Clothing

	CITY	ST	EMP	PHONE	ENTRY#
Unifirst Corporation (PA)	Wilmington	MA	B	978 658-8888	13472

LAUNDRY SVCS: Indl

	CITY	ST	EMP	PHONE	ENTRY#
A&P Coat Apron & Linen Sup LLC	Hartford	CT	D	914 840-3200	1466

LAWN & GARDEN EQPT

	CITY	ST	EMP	PHONE	ENTRY#
Woodland Power Products Inc	West Haven	CT	E	888 531-7253	4133
Armatron International Inc (PA)	Medford	MA	D	781 321-2300	10280
Essex County Coop Farming Assn	Topsfield	MA	F	978 887-2300	12433
Douglas Dynamics LLC	Rockland	ME	F	207 701-4200	5325
North Country Tractor Inc	Dover	NH	F	603 742-5488	14241
Country Home Products Inc	Charlotte	VT	E	802 771-7202	17175
Vermont Ware Inc	St George	VT	G	802 482-4426	17624

LAWN & GARDEN EQPT: Tractors & Eqpt

	CITY	ST	EMP	PHONE	ENTRY#
Salsco Inc	Cheshire	CT	D	203 271-1682	616
Aubin Equipment and Automotive	East Dennis	MA	G	508 385-3237	8348
R I Baker Co Inc (PA)	Clarksburg	MA	E	413 663-3791	8073
Machining Innovations Inc	Oakland	ME	G	207 465-2500	5120

LEAD

	CITY	ST	EMP	PHONE	ENTRY#
Alent USA Holding Inc	Waterbury	CT	E	203 575-5727	3880

LEAD PENCILS & ART GOODS

	CITY	ST	EMP	PHONE	ENTRY#
Bic Corporation (HQ)	Shelton	CT	A	203 783-2000	2985
Jen Mfg Inc	Millbury	MA	E	508 753-1076	10437
Pucker Gallery Inc	Somerville	MA	F	617 261-1817	11891
Scratch Art Company Inc (PA)	Avon	MA	F	508 583-8085	6161
Goodkind Pen Company Inc	Rockland	ME	E	207 594-6207	5331
Sheaffer Pen Corporation	Lincoln	RI	A	319 372-7444	16154

LEAF TOBACCO WHOLESALERS

	CITY	ST	EMP	PHONE	ENTRY#
Nuway Tobacco Company	South Windsor	CT	D	860 289-6414	3167

LEASING & RENTAL SVCS: Cranes & Aerial Lift Eqpt

	CITY	ST	EMP	PHONE	ENTRY#
Baxter Inc	West Yarmouth	MA	F	508 775-0375	13072
Acer Holdings Starksboro Inc	Starksboro	VT	F	802 453-4438	17625

LEASING & RENTAL: Construction & Mining Eqpt

	CITY	ST	EMP	PHONE	ENTRY#
Central Equipment Company	Stillwater	ME	F	207 827-6193	5533
Granite Shore Power LLC	Bow	NH	C	603 634-2299	13999
American Equipment & Fabg Corp	East Providence	RI	F	401 438-2626	16002

LEASING & RENTAL: Medical Machinery & Eqpt

	CITY	ST	EMP	PHONE	ENTRY#
Vivax Medical Corporation	Naugatuck	CT	F	203 729-0514	1993
Tenacity Medical Inc	Lexington	MA	G	617 299-8001	9786

LEASING & RENTAL: Trucks, Without Drivers

	CITY	ST	EMP	PHONE	ENTRY#
Standard Welding Company Inc	East Hartford	CT	G	860 528-9628	1022
U-Haul Co Mass & Ohio Inc (DH)	Somerville	MA	E	617 625-2789	11908
Baude Inc	Houlton	ME	F	207 532-6571	4896

LEASING: Shipping Container

	CITY	ST	EMP	PHONE	ENTRY#
Mobile Mini Inc	Suffield	CT	G	860 668-1888	3594

LEATHER & CUT STOCK WHOLESALERS

	CITY	ST	EMP	PHONE	ENTRY#
Tasman Industries Inc	Hartland	ME	G	207 938-4491	4878

LEATHER GOODS, EXC FOOTWEAR, GLOVES, LUGGAGE/ BELTING, WHOL

	CITY	ST	EMP	PHONE	ENTRY#
Strong Group Inc (PA)	Gloucester	MA	D	978 281-3300	8960

LEATHER GOODS: Garments

	CITY	ST	EMP	PHONE	ENTRY#
A X M S Inc	Woodbury	CT	G	203 263-5046	4384
Perfect Fit	Corinna	ME	F	207 278-3333	4703

LEATHER GOODS: Holsters

	CITY	ST	EMP	PHONE	ENTRY#
Currys Leather Shop Inc	Randolph	MA	G	781 963-0679	11554
Safariland LLC	Dalton	MA	E	413 684-3104	8153
Strong Group Inc (PA)	Gloucester	MA	D	978 281-3300	8960

LEATHER GOODS: Personal

	CITY	ST	EMP	PHONE	ENTRY#
Dooney & Bourke Inc (HQ)	Norwalk	CT	E	203 853-7515	2492
Mayan Corporation	Norwalk	CT	F	203 854-4711	2534
Alliance Leather Inc	Peabody	MA	F	978 531-6771	11295
Blw Holdings Inc (PA)	Fairhaven	MA	C	508 994-4000	8507
Brahmin Leather Works LLC	Fairhaven	MA	C	509 994-4000	8508
Charles Thomae & Son Inc	Attleboro	MA	F	508 222-0785	6001
HI Operating LLC (DH)	Mansfield	MA	E	508 851-1400	10056
Miles Kedex Co Inc	Westminster	MA	E	978 874-1403	13274
Montello Heel Mfg Inc	Brockton	MA	E	508 586-0603	7296
Strong Group Inc (PA)	Gloucester	MA	D	978 281-3300	8960
Valkyrie Company Inc	Worcester	MA	E	508 756-3633	13818
Perfect Fit	Corinna	ME	F	207 278-3333	4703
Appalachian Stitching Co LLC (PA)	Littleton	NH	E	603 444-4422	14714
Perry Blackburne Inc	North Providence	RI	F	401 231-7200	16307

LEATHER GOODS: Wallets

	CITY	ST	EMP	PHONE	ENTRY#
Valkyrie Company Inc (PA)	Worcester	MA	D	508 756-3633	13819

LEATHER TANNING & FINISHING

	CITY	ST	EMP	PHONE	ENTRY#
Alliance Leather Inc	Peabody	MA	F	978 531-6771	11295
Hawtan Leathers LLC	Newburyport	MA	C	978 465-3791	10687
Slattery Bros Inc	Westwood	MA	G	617 269-3025	13318
Tasman Leather Group LLC	Hartland	ME	C	207 553-3700	4879

LEATHER, LEATHER GOODS & FURS, WHOLESALE

	CITY	ST	EMP	PHONE	ENTRY#
Hawtan Leathers LLC	Newburyport	MA	C	978 465-3791	10687

LEATHER: Artificial

	CITY	ST	EMP	PHONE	ENTRY#
Coaters Inc	New Bedford	MA	G	508 996-5700	10578
Miles Kedex Co Inc	Westminster	MA	E	978 874-1403	13274
Vulplex Inc	New Bedford	MA	F	508 996-6787	10659

LEGAL OFFICES & SVCS

	CITY	ST	EMP	PHONE	ENTRY#
Massachstts Cntning Lgal Edcat	Boston	MA	E	617 482-2205	6871

	CITY	ST	EMP	PHONE	ENTRY#

LIFE RAFTS: Rubber

	CITY	ST	EMP	PHONE	ENTRY#
Dodson Boatyard LLC	Stonington	CT	E	860 535-1507	3508
Givens Marine Survival Svc Co	Tiverton	RI	F	617 441-5400	16736

LIFESAVING & SURVIVAL EQPT, EXC MEDICAL, WHOLESALE

Life+gear Inc	Wellesley Hills	MA	F	858 755-2099	12952

LIGHTING EQPT: Flashlights

Brite-Strike Technologies Inc	Duxbury	MA	G	781 585-3525	8329

LIGHTING EQPT: Locomotive & Railroad Car Lights

Ridge View Associates Inc	Milford	CT	D	203 878-8560	1878

LIGHTING EQPT: Motor Vehicle, Headlights

Osram Sylvania Inc (DH)	Wilmington	MA	A	978 570-3000	13444

LIGHTING EQPT: Motor Vehicle, NEC

Whelen Engineering Company Inc (PA)	Chester	CT	B	860 526-9504	634

LIGHTING EQPT: Outdoor

Pennsylvania Globe Gaslight Co	North Branford	CT	E	203 484-7749	2371
Point Lighting Corporation	Bloomfield	CT	E	860 243-0600	202
Excelitas Technologies Corp (DH)	Waltham	MA	E	855 382-2677	12673
Lighting By Hammerworks (PA)	Worcester	MA	E	508 755-3434	13753

LIGHTING EQPT: Strobe Lighting Systems

Tmlp Ernest Mello	Taunton	MA	G	508 823-4849	12371

LIGHTING FIXTURES WHOLESALERS

Pennsylvania Globe Gaslight Co	North Branford	CT	E	203 484-7749	2371
Current Lighting Solutions LLC	Boston	MA	F	713 521-6500	6678
Current Ltg Employeeco LLC	Boston	MA	A	216 266-2906	6679
Lighting By Hammerworks (PA)	Worcester	MA	E	508 755-3434	13753
Lucidity Lights Inc (PA)	Charlestown	MA	E	781 995-2405	7878
Merrimac Industrial Sales Inc (PA)	Haverhill	MA	E	978 372-6006	9114
Hubbardton Forge LLC	Castleton	VT	C	802 468-3090	17172

LIGHTING FIXTURES, NEC

Blp Technologies Inc	Wallingford	CT	E	203 678-4224	3781
Fidelux Lighting LLC (PA)	Middletown	CT	F	203 774-5653	1746
Pathway Lighting Products Inc	Old Saybrook	CT	D	860 388-6881	2659
Reflex Ltg Group of CT LLC	Wethersfield	CT	G	860 666-1548	4214
Rsl Fiber Systems LLC	East Hartford	CT	F	860 282-4930	1019
Sensor Switch Inc (DH)	New Haven	CT	E	203 265-2842	2198
Solais Lighting Inc	Stamford	CT	F	203 683-6222	3463
Sorenson Lighted Controls Inc (PA)	West Hartford	CT	D	860 527-3092	4081
Whelen Engineering Company Inc (PA)	Chester	CT	B	860 526-9504	634
Acton Research Corporation	Acton	MA	E	941 556-2601	5731
Ainslie Corporation	Walpole	MA	G	781 848-0850	12548
Color Kinetics	Burlington	MA	D	617 423-9999	7353
Current Lighting Solutions LLC	Boston	MA	F	713 521-6500	6678
Current Ltg Employeeco LLC	Boston	MA	A	216 266-2906	6679
Cyalume Technologies Inc (HQ)	West Springfield	MA	E	888 858-7881	13020
Dolan-Jenner Industries Inc	Boxborough	MA	E	978 263-1400	7151
Dorel Juvenile Group Inc	Foxboro	MA	A	800 544-1108	8694
Excelitas Tech Holdg Corp	Waltham	MA	A	781 522-5914	12671
Excelitas Tech Holdings LLC (PA)	Waltham	MA	F	781 522-5900	12672
Lansea Systtems Inc	Quincy	MA	G	617 877-9773	11526
Micro-Lite Inc	Three Rivers	MA	F	413 289-1313	12429
Nedap Inc	Burlington	MA	F	844 876-3327	7396
Pelican Products Inc	South Deerfield	MA	E	413 665-2163	11926
Period Lighting Fixtures Inc	Clarksburg	MA	F	413 664-7141	8072
Spotlight LLC	Danvers	MA	F	978 762-8352	8221
Xenon Corporation (PA)	Wilmington	MA	E	978 661-9033	13477
ARC Electronics Inc	Hampstead	NH	F	603 458-2089	14380
Luminescent Systems Inc	Lebanon	NH	C	603 643-7766	14693
Visible Light Inc	Hampton	NH	G	603 926-6049	14417
Emissive Energy Corp	North Kingstown	RI	D	401 294-2030	16251
Cooper Lighting Inc	Essex Junction	VT	E	800 767-3674	17232

LIGHTING FIXTURES: Decorative Area

Electrix LLC	New Haven	CT	D	203 776-5577	2149
Sylvan R Shemitz Designs LLC	New Haven	CT	D	203 776-5577	2205

LIGHTING FIXTURES: Fluorescent, Commercial

Litecontrol Corporation	Plympton	MA	C	781 294-0100	11485
Central Tools Inc (PA)	Cranston	RI	E	401 467-8211	15841
SCW Corporation	Warwick	RI	E	401 808-6849	16860

LIGHTING FIXTURES: Indl & Commercial

Lcd Lighting Inc	Orange	CT	C	203 799-7877	2674

	CITY	ST	EMP	PHONE	ENTRY#
Nutron Manufacturing Inc	Norwich	CT	E	860 887-4550	2613
Pathway Lighting Products Inc	Old Saybrook	CT	D	860 388-6881	2659
Pegasus Capital Advisors LP (PA)	Stamford	CT	F	203 869-4400	3429
Seesmart Inc	Stamford	CT	E	203 504-1111	3454
Sylvan R Shemitz Designs LLC (PA)	West Haven	CT	D	203 931-4455	4127
The L C Doane Company	Ivoryton	CT	D	860 767-8295	1533
Tri-State Led Inc	Greenwich	CT	F	203 813-3791	1357
Whelen Engineering Company Inc	Chester	CT	E	860 526-9504	633
Whelen Engineering Company Inc (PA)	Chester	CT	B	860 526-9504	634
Arch Lighting Group Inc	Taunton	MA	E		12317
Atlantic Lighting Inc	Fall River	MA	E	508 678-5411	8523
Dion Signs and Service Inc	New Bedford	MA	E	401 724-4459	10586
International Light Tech Inc	Peabody	MA	E	978 818-6180	11319
Jlc-Tech LLC	Pembroke	MA	E	781 826-8162	11372
Lumenpulse Lighting Corp	Boston	MA	E	617 307-5700	6865
Micro-Lite Inc	Three Rivers	MA	F	413 289-1313	12429
Norwell Mfg Co Inc	East Taunton	MA	E	508 822-2831	8409
O C White Company	Thorndike	MA	E	413 289-1751	12427
Osram Sylvania Inc (DH)	Wilmington	MA	A	978 570-3000	13444
Philips Colorkinetics	Burlington	MA	G	323 251-4758	7411
Renovators Supply Inc	Erving	MA	E	413 423-3300	8471
Rpt Holdings LLC	Middleton	MA	F	877 997-3674	10391
Signify North America Corp	Boston	MA	E	617 423-9997	7036
Signify North America Corp	Burlington	MA	B	508 679-8131	7428
Spectrum Lighting Inc	Fall River	MA	D	508 678-2303	8607
Affinity Led Light LLC	Dover	NH	F	978 378-5338	14214
Lw Holding Lc	Hollis	NH	E	913 851-3000	14453
National Energy & Light LLC	Nashua	NH	E	603 821-9954	15139
Plastic Techniques Inc	Goffstown	NH	E	603 622-5570	14356
Signify North America Corp	Manchester	NH	E	603 645-6061	14929
Icon International Inc	North Kingstown	RI	D	401 295-2533	16259
Lexington Lighting Group LLC	Rumford	RI	E	860 564-4512	16674
Lumetta Inc	Warwick	RI	E	401 691-3994	16833
Mastro Lighting Mfg Co Inc (PA)	Providence	RI	E	401 467-7700	16559
Orion Ret Svcs & Fixturing Inc	Smithfield	RI	D	401 334-5000	16725
PMC Lighting Inc	Warwick	RI	E	401 738-7266	16846
Renova Lighting Systems Inc	Warwick	RI	E	800 635-6682	16848
Authentic Designs Inc	West Rupert	VT	F	802 394-7715	17694
Cooper Lighting Inc	Essex Junction	VT	E	800 767-3674	17232

LIGHTING FIXTURES: Residential

Rk Parisi Enterprises Inc	Keene	NH	F	844 438-7674	14616

LIGHTING FIXTURES: Residential, Electric

Needham Electric Supply LLC (DH)	Canton	MA	D	781 828-9494	7811
Optoglo Inc	Leominster	MA	F	978 235-0201	9690

LIGHTING FIXTURES: Street

Pegasus Capital Advisors LP (PA)	Stamford	CT	F	203 869-4400	3429
Sunrise Technologies LLC	Raynham	MA	F	508 884-9732	11598

LIME

Specialty Minerals Inc	Adams	MA	C	413 743-0591	5775
Dragon Products Company LLC (DH)	Biddeford	ME	E	207 594-5555	4560

LIMESTONE: Crushed & Broken

Specialty Minerals Inc	Canaan	CT	F	860 824-5435	557
S Lane John & Son Incorporated	Oxford	MA	F	508 987-3959	11263
S M Lorusso & Sons Inc	East Weymouth	MA	E	781 337-6770	8433
Specialty Minerals Inc	Adams	MA	C	413 743-0591	5775
Dragon Products Company LLC (DH)	Biddeford	ME	E	207 594-5555	4560
Dragon Products Company LLC	Thomaston	ME	E	207 594-5555	5544
K & B Rock Crushing LLC	Auburn	NH	G	603 622-1188	13910
Shelburne Limestone Corp (PA)	Colchester	VT	F	802 878-2656	17203
Shelburne Limestone Corp	Swanton	VT	E	802 868-3357	17642

LIMESTONE: Dimension

Coccomo Brothers Drilling LLC	Berlin	CT	F	860 828-1632	60

LINEN SPLY SVC: Uniform

A&P Coat Apron & Linen Sup LLC	Hartford	CT	D	914 840-3200	1466

LINENS & TOWELS WHOLESALERS

Mr Idea Inc	Attleboro	MA	E	508 222-0155	6039
Anichini Inc	Tunbridge	VT	E	802 889-9430	17651

LINENS: Table & Dresser Scarves, From Purchased Materials

Bess Home Fashions Inc	West Warwick	RI	C	401 828-0300	16906

LINERS & COVERS: Fabric

Commercial Sewing Inc	Torrington	CT	C	860 482-5509	3675
Custom Covers LLC	Clinton	CT	G	860 669-4169	641

LINERS & LINING

	CITY	ST	EMP	PHONE	ENTRY#
Bath Systems Massachusetts Inc	West Bridgewater	MA	G	508 521-2700	12967

LININGS: Fabric, Apparel & Other, Exc Millinery

	CITY	ST	EMP	PHONE	ENTRY#
Fuller Box Co Inc	Central Falls	RI	C	401 725-4300	15788

LIQUEFIED PETROLEUM GAS WHOLESALERS

	CITY	ST	EMP	PHONE	ENTRY#
Arclight Enrgy Prtners Fund VI **(PA)**	Boston	MA	E	617 531-6300	6557
Ray Murray Inc **(PA)**	Lee	MA	D	413 243-2164	9619

LIQUID CRYSTAL DISPLAYS

	CITY	ST	EMP	PHONE	ENTRY#
Corning Incorporated	Tewksbury	MA	E	978 442-2200	12391
Leidos Inc	Tewksbury	MA	G	781 221-7627	12402

LOADS: Electronic

	CITY	ST	EMP	PHONE	ENTRY#
Advent Technologies Inc **(PA)**	Boston	MA	F	617 655-6000	6519

LOCKS

	CITY	ST	EMP	PHONE	ENTRY#
Assa Inc	New Haven	CT	F	800 235-7482	2120
Assa Abloy ACC Door Cntrls Gro	Berlin	CT	D	865 986-7511	50
Assa Abloy ACC Door Cntrls Gro	New Haven	CT	C	901 365-2160	2121
Eastern Co **(PA)**	Shelton	CT	E	203 729-2255	3001
Fsb Inc	Berlin	CT	F	203 404-4700	67
Loctec Corporation	Newtown	CT	G	203 364-1000	2340
Sargent Manufacturing Company	New Haven	CT	A	203 562-2151	2194
Zephyr Lock LLC	Newtown	CT	F	866 937-4971	2355
Hudson Lock LLC **(PA)**	Hudson	MA	D	978 562-3481	9373
Inner-Tite Corp	Holden	MA	D	508 829-6361	9191
Schlage Lock Company LLC	Canton	MA	G	781 828-6655	7826

LOCKSMITHS

	CITY	ST	EMP	PHONE	ENTRY#
Assa Abloy Inc **(HQ)**	New Haven	CT	B	203 562-2151	2122
Corbin Russwin	New Haven	CT	E	860 225-7411	2139
GK Mechanical Systems LLC	Brookfield	CT	G	203 775-4970	521
James L Howard and Company Inc	Bloomfield	CT	E	860 242-3581	176
Lab Security Systems Corp	Bristol	CT	E	860 589-6037	460

LOCOMOTIVES & PARTS

	CITY	ST	EMP	PHONE	ENTRY#
Motive Power	Boston	MA	F	857 350-3765	6897

LOGGING

	CITY	ST	EMP	PHONE	ENTRY#
Davis Tree & Logging LLC	Danbury	CT	F	203 938-2153	728
Witkowsky John	North Branford	CT	G	203 483-0152	2380
Favreau Forestry LLC	Sterling	MA	G	978 706-1038	12162
Lashway Logging Inc	Williamsburg	MA	F	413 268-3600	13365
Noble Tree LLC	Boxford	MA	G	978 590-5101	7161
Roberts Brothers Lumber Co Inc	Ashfield	MA	F	413 628-3333	5955
Thomas J Doane	Orange	MA	G	978 821-2361	11235
Ambrose G McCarthy Jr	Skowhegan	ME	G	207 474-8837	5462
Chopper One Inc	Eagle Lake	ME	G	207 444-5476	4734
Clinton G Bradbury Inc	Rumford	ME	G	207 562-8014	5355
D R Logging Inc	Fort Kent	ME	G	207 316-6434	4786
Davis Forestry Products Inc	Danforth	ME	F	207 448-2625	4718
Eric T Vannah	Brunswick	ME	G	207 631-2475	4645
Eugene Corson	Sumner	ME	G	207 446-6489	5538
Everett McCabe	Bridgton	ME	G	207 890-9174	4628
G V Logging Inc	Fort Kent	ME	G	207 231-1003	4789
Gary M Pomeroy Logging Inc	Hermon	ME	F	207 848-3171	4882
Herbert L Hardy & Son Inc	Smyrna Mills	ME	G	207 757-8550	5480
Highland Farms Logging LLC	Cornish	ME	F	207 239-2977	4705
Kevin S Hawes	Belgrade	ME	G	207 495-3412	4541
M & H Logging LLC	Rangeley	ME	E	207 864-5617	5312
M H Humphrey & Sons Inc	Parsonsfield	ME	F	207 625-4965	5152
Maine Custom Woodlands LLC	Durham	ME	F	207 353-9020	4733
Mw Trucking and Logging Inc	Norway	ME	G	207 890-3592	5117
Olson S Logging LLC	Canaan	ME	G	207 474-8835	4670
PFC Logging Inc	Danforth	ME	G	207 448-7998	4719
R C McLucas Trucking Inc	Porter	ME	E	207 625-8915	5168
Regan S Pingree	Phillips	ME	F	207 639-5706	5157
SF Madden Inc	Greenbush	ME	G	207 852-2525	4845
Terrence L Hayford	Hartford	ME	G	207 357-0142	4877
Tracy L Gordon	Strong	ME	G	207 684-4462	5537
Voisine Bros Inc **(PA)**	New Canada	ME	G	207 231-0220	5082
WA Logging LLC	Hodgdon	ME	G	207 694-2921	4892
William A Day Jr & Sons Inc	Porter	ME	F	207 625-8181	5173
3d Logging Co Inc	Berlin	NH	G	603 915-3020	13978
Benjamin D Knapp	Weare	NH	G	603 660-8172	15668
Chuck Rose Inc	Contoocook	NH	E	603 746-2311	14168
Cmd Logging	Center Barnstead	NH	G	603 986-5055	14049
Custom Log Homes	Rumney	NH	F	603 786-9082	15497
Dale E Crawford	Sanbornville	NH	G	603 473-2738	15578
David R Burl	Goffstown	NH	G	603 235-2661	14347
Dorman Logging LLC	Londonderry	NH	G	603 437-4403	14744
Hopkinton For Land Claring Inc	Henniker	NH	E	603 428-8400	14437
John C Whyte	Salisbury	NH	G	603 530-1168	15576
Kel-Log Inc **(PA)**	Milan	NH	E	603 752-2000	15009
Lyons Tnney Timber Harvstg Inc	Bennington	NH	G	802 384-2620	13976
Rowe Timber Harvesting LLC	North Sutton	NH	G	603 344-0302	15255
Roy and Laurel Amey Inc	Pittsburg	NH	G	603 538-7767	15329
Stockley Trucking Inc	Landaff	NH	G	603 838-2860	14682
Sweets Logging & Land Clearin	Strafford	NH	G	603 664-2349	15632
Treeline Timber	Jefferson	NH	G	603 586-7725	14586
Tri-State Logging LLC	Winchester	NH	G	603 499-1499	15717
W Craig Washburn	Colebrook	NH	G	603 237-8403	14110
Warick Management Company Inc	Pittsburg	NH	G	603 538-7112	15330
AS Hudak Lumber	Saint Albans	VT	G	802 527-9802	17515
Djs Tree Service & Log Inc	Colchester	VT	F	802 655-0264	17189
Mt Johnson Inc	Barnard	VT	G	802 234-6827	16994
P & L Riendeau Inc	Lyndonville	VT	G	802 626-9302	17319
Stephane Inkel Inc	Canaan	VT	G	603 331-3296	17170

LOGGING CAMPS & CONTRACTORS

	CITY	ST	EMP	PHONE	ENTRY#
C & C Logging	Windsor	CT	G	860 683-0071	4263
Fowler D J Log Land Clearing	Coventry	CT	G	860 742-5842	679
Gmo Threshold Logging LLC	Boston	MA	G	617 330-7500	6765
Gmo Thrshold Tmber Hldings LLC	Boston	MA	G	617 330-7500	6766
Andrew Irish Logging	Peru	ME	F	207 562-8839	5155
Ashley & Harmon Logging Inc	East Machias	ME	F	207 259-2043	4739
Ben Savage Logging Inc	Sebec	ME	G	207 735-6699	5456
BP Logging	Saint Francis	ME	G	207 398-4457	5387
Chipping & Logging	Porter	ME	G	207 625-4056	5165
Darrell C McGuire & Sons Inc	Houlton	ME	F	207 532-0511	4899
Delaite Trucking Inc	Chester	ME	F	207 794-6844	4692
E J Carrier Inc	Jackman	ME	E	207 668-4457	4909
Edmond Roy & Sons Inc	Jackman	ME	G	877 425-8491	4910
Ellen McLaughlin	Medway	ME	G	207 746-3398	5055
H Arthur York Logging Inc **(PA)**	Medway	ME	F	207 746-5883	5056
H Arthur York Logging Inc	Medway	ME	F	207 746-5912	5057
Hanington Bros Inc	Macwahoc Plt	ME	F	207 765-2681	5036
Hanington Timberlands	Wytopitlock	ME	F	207 456-7003	5701
Hanscom Construction Inc	Marshfield	ME	F	207 255-8067	5046
J & M Logging Inc	Sidney	ME	G	207 622-6353	5459
Jackman Lumber Inc **(PA)**	Jackman	ME	E	207 668-4407	4911
John Khiel III Log Chpping Inc	Denmark	ME	E	207 452-2157	4722
Johnny H Castonguay	Livermore	ME	G	207 897-5945	5024
K B Logging Inc	Smyrna Mills	ME	F	207 757-8818	5481
L E Taylor and Sons Inc	Porter	ME	G	207 625-4056	5166
Lyle Guptill	East Machias	ME	F	207 255-4130	4740
M B Eastman Logging Inc	Parsonsfield	ME	G	207 625-8020	5151
Madtown Logging LLC	Madawaska	ME	G	207 728-6260	5038
Nadeau Logging Inc	Fort Kent	ME	F	207 834-6338	4791
Nicols Brothers Inc	Rumford	ME	G	207 364-7032	5361
Nicols Brothers Logging Inc	Mexico	ME	F	207 364-8685	5058
Norman White Inc	Shapleigh	ME	G	207 636-1636	5458
Pelletier & Pelletier	Fort Kent	ME	F	207 834-2296	4792
Perleys Logging Inc	Ashland	ME	G	207 227-0513	4413
Robert McBreairty Jr Sons	Fort Kent	ME	G	207 834-3257	4793
Robert McBreairty Jr Sons Inc	Saint Francis	ME	F	207 834-3257	5388
Robert W Libby	Porter	ME	G	207 625-8285	5169
Robert W Libby & Sons Inc	Porter	ME	G	207 284-3668	5170
Roland H Tyler Logging Inc	Dixfield	ME	G	207 562-7282	4728
Savage & Savage Logging Inc	Patten	ME	G	207 528-2974	5154
SDR Logging Inc	Sebec	ME	E	207 564-8534	5457
Stephen F Madden	Cardville	ME	G	207 827-5737	4673
Syl-Ver Logging Inc	Allagash	ME	G	207 398-3158	4404
T R Dillon Logging Inc **(PA)**	Madison	ME	F	207 696-8137	5043
T Raymond Forest Products Inc	Lee	ME	F	207 738-2313	4946
Thomas Logging & Forestry Inc	Guilford	ME	G	207 876-2722	4859
Thompson Trucking Inc	Lincoln	ME	F	207 794-6101	5014
Tracy J Morrison	Harmony	ME	G	207 683-2371	4874
Trees Ltd A Partnr Consisting	Sidney	ME	G	207 547-3168	5461
Western Maine Timberlands Inc	Fryeburg	ME	F	207 925-1138	4811
Willard S Hanington & Son Inc	Reed Plt	ME	F	207 456-7511	5319
A B Excavating Inc	Lancaster	NH	E	603 788-5110	14675
DH Hardwick & Sons Inc	Bennington	NH	F	603 588-6618	13975
Fadden Chipping & Logging Inc	Center Conway	NH	F	603 939-2462	14052
Garland Lumber Company Inc	Center Conway	NH	E	603 356-5636	14053
Garland Transportation Corp	Center Conway	NH	G	603 356-5636	14054
Gilles Champagne	Colebrook	NH	G	603 237-5272	14105
Low Impact Logging LLC	New Boston	NH	G	603 487-5298	15192
Ossipee Mountain Land Co LLC	Tamworth	NH	E	603 323-7677	15648
Pat Gagne Logging LLC	Dummer	NH	G	603 449-2479	14263
SDS Logging Inc	Jefferson	NH	E	603 586-7098	14585

	CITY	ST	EMP	PHONE	ENTRY#
Welog Inc	Colebrook	NH	F	603 237-8277	14111
Canopy Timber Alternatives Inc	Middlebury	VT	F	802 388-1548	17340
Chief Logging & Cnstr Inc	South Ryegate	VT	F	802 584-3868	17613
Mahar Excavating & Logging	Bennington	VT	G	802 442-2954	17049
Norm Brown Logging	Benson	VT	G	802 537-4474	17058
P and L Trucking	Chester	VT	G	802 875-2819	17182
Pjf Trucking & Logging LLC	Bellows Falls	VT	G	802 463-3343	17030
Willey Earthmoving Corp	Windsor	VT	G	802 674-2500	17764

LOGGING: Timber, Cut At Logging Camp

	CITY	ST	EMP	PHONE	ENTRY#
Lyme Timber Company LP (PA)	Hanover	NH	F	603 643-3300	14429

LOGGING: Wooden Logs

	CITY	ST	EMP	PHONE	ENTRY#
Brightman Corporation	Assonet	MA	F	508 644-2620	5972
R A Thomas Logging Inc	Guilford	ME	G	207 876-2722	4858
Benjamin K Lepesqueur	Enosburg Falls	VT	G	802 933-5500	17220

LOGS: Gas, Fireplace

	CITY	ST	EMP	PHONE	ENTRY#
Rasa Incorporated	Shrewsbury	MA	F	508 425-3261	11840

LOTIONS OR CREAMS: Face

	CITY	ST	EMP	PHONE	ENTRY#
Beiersdorf Inc (DH)	Stamford	CT	G	203 563-5800	3291
Beiersdorf North America Inc (DH)	Stamford	CT	F	203 563-5800	3292
Conopco Inc	Clinton	CT	C	860 669-8601	640
Jolen Cream Bleach Corp	Fairfield	CT	E	203 259-8779	1191
Skin & Co North America LLC	West Haven	CT	G	888 444-9971	4126
Tropical Products Inc	Salem	MA	E	978 740-5665	11736
WS Badger Company Inc	Gilsum	NH	D	603 357-2958	14344

LOTIONS: SHAVING

	CITY	ST	EMP	PHONE	ENTRY#
Edgewell Per Care Brands LLC (HQ)	Shelton	CT	B	203 944-5500	3002

LOUDSPEAKERS

	CITY	ST	EMP	PHONE	ENTRY#
Genelec Inc	Natick	MA	F	508 652-0900	10481
Loud Audio LLC	Whitinsville	MA	C	508 234-6158	13341
Technomad Associates LLC	South Deerfield	MA	G	413 665-6704	11929

LUBRICANTS: Corrosion Preventive

	CITY	ST	EMP	PHONE	ENTRY#
New England Tooling Inc	Killingworth	CT	F	800 866-5105	1544
Ro-59 Inc	Stoughton	MA	G	781 341-1222	12230

LUBRICATING EQPT: Indl

	CITY	ST	EMP	PHONE	ENTRY#
Automation Inc	West Hartford	CT	E	860 236-5991	4048

LUBRICATION SYSTEMS & EQPT

	CITY	ST	EMP	PHONE	ENTRY#
Ltp Corporation (DH)	Northborough	MA	D	508 393-7660	11101

LUGGAGE & BRIEFCASES

	CITY	ST	EMP	PHONE	ENTRY#
Commercial Sewing Inc	Torrington	CT	C	860 482-5509	3675
Manup LLC	Norwalk	CT	G	203 588-9861	2533
Blw Holdings Inc (PA)	Fairhaven	MA	C	508 994-4000	8507
Brahmin Leather Works LLC	Fairhaven	MA	C	509 994-4000	8508
Byer Manufacturing Company	Bernard	ME	E	207 866-2171	4547
C B P Corp (PA)	Arundel	ME	E	207 985-9767	4409
L L Bean Inc	Brunswick	ME	F	207 725-0300	4647
Sea Bags Inc	Freeport	ME	F	207 939-3679	4803
Samsonite Company Stores LLC	Warren	RI	F	401 247-3301	16768

LUGGAGE: Wardrobe Bags

	CITY	ST	EMP	PHONE	ENTRY#
Hartmann Incorporated	Mansfield	MA	G	508 851-1400	10054
HI Operating LLC (DH)	Mansfield	MA	G	508 851-1400	10056

LUMBER & BLDG MATLS DEALER, RET: Garage Doors, Sell/Install

	CITY	ST	EMP	PHONE	ENTRY#
Boston Area Door Company	Bridgewater	MA	G	508 857-4722	7224
Champlain Door Company Inc	Milton	VT	F	802 524-7595	17356
Limoge & Sons Garage Doors Inc	Williston	VT	F	802 878-4338	17739

LUMBER & BLDG MATLS DEALERS, RET: Energy Conservation Prdts

	CITY	ST	EMP	PHONE	ENTRY#
Allearth Renewables Inc	Williston	VT	E	802 872-9600	17721

LUMBER & BLDG MATRLS DEALERS, RET: Bath Fixtures, Eqpt/Sply

	CITY	ST	EMP	PHONE	ENTRY#
Kensco Inc (PA)	Ansonia	CT	G	203 734-8827	15

LUMBER & BLDG MTRLS DEALERS, RET: Planing Mill Prdts/Lumber

	CITY	ST	EMP	PHONE	ENTRY#
Iffland Lumber Company Inc	Torrington	CT	E	860 489-9218	3684
Deweys Lumber LLC	Liberty	ME	F	207 589-4126	4998
Ernest R Palmer Lumber Co Inc	Sangerville	ME	F	207 876-2725	5419
Hillside Lumber Company Inc	Westbrook	ME	E	207 839-2575	5629
Parent Lumber Company Inc	Mechanic Falls	ME	G	207 998-2322	5053
Wilkins Lumber Co Inc	Milford	NH	G	603 673-2545	15043
M Piette & Sons Lumber Inc	Irasburg	VT	F	802 754-8876	17302

LUMBER & BUILDING MATERIAL DEALERS, RETAIL: Roofing Material

	CITY	ST	EMP	PHONE	ENTRY#
Cooley Group Holdings Inc (PA)	Pawtucket	RI	C	401 724-0510	16358

LUMBER & BUILDING MATERIALS DEALER, RET: Door & Window Prdts

	CITY	ST	EMP	PHONE	ENTRY#
Leek Building Products Inc	Norwalk	CT	E	203 853-3883	2527
Millwork Masters Ltd (PA)	Keene	NH	F	603 358-3038	14608
H Hirschmann Ltd	West Rutland	VT	F	802 438-4447	17695

LUMBER & BUILDING MATERIALS DEALER, RET: Masonry Matls/Splys

	CITY	ST	EMP	PHONE	ENTRY#
Midwood Quarry and Cnstr Inc (PA)	East Hartford	CT	F	860 289-1414	1006
Johns Building Supply Co Inc	Pittsfield	MA	F	413 442-7846	11403
Shea Concrete Products Inc	Amesbury	MA	E	978 388-1509	5852
American Concrete Inds Inc	Bangor	ME	D	207 947-8334	4488
Gagne & Son Con Blocks Inc	Auburn	ME	E	207 495-3313	4435
Rjf - Morin Brick LLC	Auburn	ME	D	207 784-9375	4459
Cs-Ma Inc	Newport	NH	F	603 863-1000	15227
Northern Design Precast Inc	Loudon	NH	F	603 783-8989	14796
Concrete Products Inc	Chepachet	RI	E	401 568-8874	15803
McCue Memorial Co Inc	Castleton	VT	E	802 468-5636	17173

LUMBER & BUILDING MATERIALS DEALERS, RET: Sash, Wood/Metal

	CITY	ST	EMP	PHONE	ENTRY#
J B Sash & Door Company Inc	Chelsea	MA	E	617 884-8940	7983

LUMBER & BUILDING MATERIALS DEALERS, RETAIL: Brick

	CITY	ST	EMP	PHONE	ENTRY#
O & G Industries Inc	Stamford	CT	D	203 323-1111	3422
P & M Brick & Block Inc	Watertown	MA	G	617 924-6020	12898

LUMBER & BUILDING MATERIALS DEALERS, RETAIL: Cement

	CITY	ST	EMP	PHONE	ENTRY#
Dauphinais Concrete	Bellingham	MA	G	508 657-0941	6289

LUMBER & BUILDING MATERIALS DEALERS, RETAIL: Modular Homes

	CITY	ST	EMP	PHONE	ENTRY#
Sunny Side Land Holdings LLC	Presque Isle	ME	F	207 768-1020	5310

LUMBER & BUILDING MATERIALS DEALERS, RETAIL: Sand & Gravel

	CITY	ST	EMP	PHONE	ENTRY#
Desiato Sand & Gravel Corp	Storrs Mansfield	CT	E	860 429-6479	3512
LH Gault & Son Incorporated	Westport	CT	D	203 227-5181	4180
Rawson Development Inc	Putnam	CT	E	860 928-4536	2872
Windham Materials LLC (PA)	Willimantic	CT	E	860 456-4111	4222
Berkshire Concrete Corp (HQ)	Pittsfield	MA	E	413 443-4734	11392
Dauphinais & Son Inc	Wilbraham	MA	F	413 596-3964	13357
Delta Sand and Gravel Inc	Sunderland	MA	F	413 665-4051	12273
Morse Sand & Gravel Corp	Attleboro	MA	F	508 809-4644	6038
State Sand & Gravel Co Inc	Belfast	ME	F	207 338-4070	4538
Alvin J Coleman & Son Inc (PA)	Albany	NH	F	603 447-5936	13847
DH Hardwick & Sons Inc	Bennington	NH	F	603 588-6618	13975
Dailey Precast LLC (HQ)	Shaftsbury	VT	D	802 442-4418	17549

LUMBER & BUILDING MATERIALS DEALERS, RETAIL: Tile, Ceramic

	CITY	ST	EMP	PHONE	ENTRY#
La Pietra Thinstone Veneer	Brookfield	CT	F	203 775-6162	528
Louis W Mian Incorporated (PA)	Boston	MA	F	617 241-7900	6863
Cabinets For Less LLC	Manchester	NH	G	603 935-7551	14825

LUMBER & BUILDING MATERIALS RET DEALERS: Millwork & Lumber

	CITY	ST	EMP	PHONE	ENTRY#
Bonito Manufacturing Inc	North Haven	CT	D	203 234-8786	2394
Chapman Lumber Inc	Thomaston	CT	E	860 283-6213	3616
Amherst Woodworking & Supply Inc	Northampton	MA	E	413 584-3003	11052
Maschino & Sons Lumber Co Inc	New Gloucester	ME	F	207 926-4288	5086
New England Building Materials LLC	Sanford	ME	B	207 324-3350	5401
R E Lowell Lumber Co Inc	Buckfield	ME	F	207 336-2901	4658
T and P Lumber Inc (PA)	Orrington	ME	E	207 825-3317	5139
Fernald Lumber Inc	Nottingham	NH	F	603 679-2997	15276
Tommila Brothers Inc	Fitzwilliam	NH	G	603 242-7774	14316
Triumph Interiors LLC	Rindge	NH	F	603 899-5184	15461

LUMBER & BUILDING MATLS DEALERS, RET: Concrete/Cinder Block

	CITY	ST	EMP	PHONE	ENTRY#
Devine Brothers Incorporated	Norwalk	CT	E	203 866-4421	2490
JH Lynch & Sons Inc	Millbury	MA	E	508 756-6244	10438
Medway Block Co Inc	Medway	MA	E	508 533-6701	10307
Gagne & Son Concrete Blocks Inc (PA)	Belgrade	ME	E	207 495-3313	4539
Wilbert Swans Vault Co	Casco	ME	E	207 854-5324	4684
Seacoast Redimix Concrete LLC (PA)	Dover	NH	F	603 742-4441	14250

LUMBER: Flooring, Dressed, Softwood

	CITY	ST	EMP	PHONE	ENTRY#
Hmtx Industries LLC (PA)	Norwalk	CT	G	203 299-3100	2515
Barrett Made (PA)	Portland	ME	E	207 650-6500	5184

	CITY	ST	EMP	PHONE	ENTRY#

LUMBER: Hardboard

	CITY	ST	EMP	PHONE	ENTRY#
Speedboard Usa Inc	Rowley	MA	G	978 884-3900	11685

LUMBER: Hardwood Dimension

	CITY	ST	EMP	PHONE	ENTRY#
Rossi Group LLC (PA)	Cromwell	CT	F	860 632-3505	695
Bear Paw Lumber Corp (PA)	Fryeburg	ME	F	207 935-3052	4807
Lovell Lumber Company	Lovell	ME	E	207 925-6455	5027

LUMBER: Hardwood Dimension & Flooring Mills

	CITY	ST	EMP	PHONE	ENTRY#
E R Hinman & Sons Inc	Burlington	CT	G	860 673-9170	548
Hull Forest Products Inc	Pomfret Center	CT	E	860 974-0127	2812
Architectural Timber Mllwk Inc	Hadley	MA	F	413 586-3045	9017
Bannish Lumber Inc	Chester	MA	F	413 354-2279	7996
Canner Incorporated	West Groton	MA	F	978 448-3063	13001
Roberts Brothers Lumber Co Inc	Ashfield	MA	F	413 628-3333	5955
Stiles & Hart Brick Company	Bridgewater	MA	E	508 697-6928	7238
Columbia Forest Products Inc	Presque Isle	ME	C	207 760-3800	5299
K B Logging Inc	Smyrna Mills	ME	F	207 757-8818	5481
S W Collins	Lincoln	ME	E	207 794-6113	5013
York-Cmbrland Assn For Hndcppe (PA)	Portland	ME	E	207 879-1140	5292
Forest Northland Products Inc (PA)	Kingston	NH	E	603 642-3665	14635
Precision Lumber Inc	Wentworth	NH	D	603 764-9450	15677
Tommila Brothers Inc	Fitzwilliam	NH	F	603 242-7774	14316
A Johnson Co	Bristol	VT	E	802 453-4884	17112
Classic Dsgns By Mtthew Brak I	Saint Johnsbury	VT	E	802 748-6062	17541
Columbia Forest Products Inc	Newport	VT	C	802 334-6711	17399
Jack Tarmy Lumber Co Inc	Brattleboro	VT	F	802 257-0427	17089
N W P Inc	Pownal	VT	G	802 442-4749	17455
Rutland Plywood Corp	Rutland	VT	C	802 747-4000	17509

LUMBER: Kiln Dried

	CITY	ST	EMP	PHONE	ENTRY#
Precision Lumber Inc	Wentworth	NH	D	603 764-9450	15677

LUMBER: Plywood, Hardwood

	CITY	ST	EMP	PHONE	ENTRY#
Bergan Architectural Wdwkg Inc	Middletown	CT	E	860 346-0869	1739
Bernhard Thmas Bldg Systems LL	Southport	CT	F	203 925-0414	3243
Bear Paw Lumber Corp (PA)	Fryeburg	ME	F	207 935-3052	4807
Columbia Forest Products Inc	Presque Isle	ME	C	207 760-3800	5299
Herrick Mill Work Inc	Contoocook	NH	F	603 746-5092	14170
Columbia Forest Products Inc	Newport	VT	C	802 334-6711	17399
Mariah Group LLC	Rutland	VT	F	802 747-4000	17503
Springfield Fence Company Inc	North Springfield	VT	F	802 886-2221	17424
Stratabond Co Inc	Rutland	VT	F	802 747-4000	17510

LUMBER: Plywood, Hardwood or Hardwood Faced

	CITY	ST	EMP	PHONE	ENTRY#
Readers Hardwood Supply LLC	East Taunton	MA	F	508 301-3206	8411
Keller Products Incorporated (PA)	Manchester	NH	E	603 627-7887	14871
Rutland Plywood Corp	Rutland	VT	G	802 747-4000	17508
Rutland Plywood Corp	Rutland	VT	C	802 747-4000	17509

LUMBER: Treated

	CITY	ST	EMP	PHONE	ENTRY#
Northeast Treaters Inc (HQ)	Belchertown	MA	E	413 323-7811	6281
Integrity Composites LLC	Biddeford	ME	F	207 571-0743	4571
University of Maine System	Orono	ME	F	207 581-2843	5138
Hbh Prestain Inc (PA)	Arlington	VT	E	802 375-9723	16987

MACHINE PARTS: Stamped Or Pressed Metal

	CITY	ST	EMP	PHONE	ENTRY#
Addamo Manufacturing Inc	Newington	CT	G	860 667-2601	2266
Consulting Engrg Dev Svcs Inc	Oxford	CT	D	203 828-6528	2691
Forrest Machine Inc	Berlin	CT	D	860 563-1796	66
Meriden Manufacturing Inc	Meriden	CT	D	203 237-7481	1675
Paradigm Prcision Holdings LLC	Manchester	CT	E	860 649-2888	1626
Pressure Blast Mfg Co Inc	South Windsor	CT	F	800 722-5278	3174
Record Products America Inc	Hamden	CT	F	203 248-6371	1453
Schaeffler Aerospace USA Corp (DH)	Danbury	CT	B	203 744-2211	809
Tru-Precision Corporation	Farmington	CT	F	860 269-6230	1252
Tyger Tool Inc	Stratford	CT	F	203 375-4344	3581
Cobra Precision Machining Corp	Petersham	MA	G	603 434-8424	11388
Cunningham Machine Co Inc	Chelmsford	MA	G	978 256-7541	7921
Dakin Road Investments Inc	Littleton	MA	F	978 443-4020	9809
Lee Tool Co Inc	Ludlow	MA	F	413 583-8750	9948
Pocasset Machine Corporation	Pocasset	MA	E	508 563-5572	11491
Sp Machine Inc	Hudson	MA	F	978 562-2019	9414
Techncal Hrdfcing McHining Inc	Attleboro	MA	F	508 223-2900	6069
The Wakefield Corporation	Wakefield	MA	E	781 587-1925	12539
Alan T Seeler Inc	New Hampton	NH	F	603 744-3736	15195
Ameriforge Group Inc	Newport	NH	E	603 863-1270	15225
Samson Manufacturing Corp	Keene	NH	E	603 355-3903	14617
Amt Acquisition Inc	Warren	RI	E	401 247-1680	16749
Everett J Prescott Inc	Lincoln	RI	G	401 333-8588	16135
Cold Hollow Precision Inc	Enosburg Falls	VT	G	802 933-5542	17221

MACHINE TOOL ACCESS: Broaches

	CITY	ST	EMP	PHONE	ENTRY#
Center Broach & Machine Co	Meriden	CT	G	203 235-6329	1659
Eastern Broach Inc	Plainville	CT	F	860 828-4800	2755
Lapointe Hudson Broach Co Inc	Hudson	MA	E	978 562-7943	9383
Pilot Precision Products LLC	South Deerfield	MA	E	413 350-5200	11927

MACHINE TOOL ACCESS: Cutting

	CITY	ST	EMP	PHONE	ENTRY#
Dahle North America Inc	Peterborough	NH	F	603 924-0003	15314

MACHINE TOOL ACCESS: Drills

	CITY	ST	EMP	PHONE	ENTRY#
W L Fuller Inc	Warwick	RI	E	401 467-2900	16876

MACHINE TOOL ACCESS: Honing Heads

	CITY	ST	EMP	PHONE	ENTRY#
Vogel Capital Inc (HQ)	Marlborough	MA	E	508 481-5944	10232

MACHINE TOOL ACCESS: Tools & Access

	CITY	ST	EMP	PHONE	ENTRY#
Southwick & Meister Inc	Meriden	CT	C	203 237-0000	1701
Ar-Ro Engineering Company Inc	Uxbridge	MA	F	401 766-6669	12477
Michael Brisebois	Easthampton	MA	F	413 527-9590	8450
Waverly Tool Rental & Sales Co	Framingham	MA	F	508 872-8866	8811
Fielding Mfg - Zinc Dcsting In	Cranston	RI	D	401 461-0400	15861

MACHINE TOOL ATTACHMENTS & ACCESS

	CITY	ST	EMP	PHONE	ENTRY#
Accu-Rite Tool & Mfg Co	Tolland	CT	F	860 688-4844	3654
Century Tool and Design Inc	Milldale	CT	F	860 621-6748	1900
Danjon Manufacturing Corp	Cheshire	CT	E	203 272-7258	587
Edrive Actuators Inc	Newington	CT	G	860 953-0588	2290
Industrial Magnetics Inc	Windsor	CT	D	508 853-3232	4283
Pmt Group Inc (PA)	Bridgeport	CT	C	203 367-8675	359
Ringfeder Pwr Transm USA Corp (HQ)	Bolton	CT	F	201 666-3320	222
Walker Magnetics Group Inc	Windsor	CT	D	508 853-3232	4314
Hassay Savage Broach Co Inc	Turners Falls	MA	F	413 863-9052	12446
Thomas Machine Works Inc	Newburyport	MA	G	978 462-7182	10720
Mid State Machine Products (PA)	Winslow	ME	C	207 873-6136	5685

MACHINE TOOLS & ACCESS

	CITY	ST	EMP	PHONE	ENTRY#
American Grippers Inc	Trumbull	CT	F	203 459-8345	3710
Edmunds Manufacturing Company (PA)	Farmington	CT	D	860 677-2813	1218
Fletcher-Terry Company LLC (PA)	East Berlin	CT	D	860 828-3400	911
Goldenrod Corporation	Beacon Falls	CT	E	203 723-4400	40
H & B Tool & Eng Co Inc	South Windsor	CT	E	860 528-9341	3153
Jetct Inc	Southington	CT	E	860 621-5381	3217
Jjioc Inc	Southington	CT	E	860 628-4655	3218
Leeco Inc	Avon	CT	G	860 404-8876	28
Meyer Gage Co Inc	South Windsor	CT	F	860 528-6526	3163
Moon Cutter Co Inc	Hamden	CT	E	203 288-9249	1444
Paradigm Prcision Holdings LLC	East Berlin	CT	D	860 829-3663	915
Perry Technology Corporation	New Hartford	CT	D	860 738-2525	2107
Preferred Utilities Mfg Corp (HQ)	Danbury	CT	D	203 743-6741	799
Producto Corporation	Bridgeport	CT	F	203 366-3223	363
Seals-It Inc	Ellington	CT	G	860 979-0060	1114
The Viking Tool Company	Shelton	CT	E	203 929-1457	3068
Thought Out Co LLC	Monroe	CT	G	203 987-5452	1925
Ade Technologies Inc (HQ)	Westwood	MA	D	781 467-3500	13305
American Saw & Mfg Company Inc	East Longmeadow	MA	C	413 525-3961	8369
Automec Inc	Waltham	MA	E	781 893-3403	12598
Cobra Precision Machining Corp	Petersham	MA	G	603 434-8424	11388
Columbia ASC Inc	Lawrence	MA	F	978 683-2205	9554
Coorstek Inc	Worcester	MA	B	774 317-2600	13710
Dmt Export Inc	Marlborough	MA	F	508 481-5944	10144
Dynisco Instruments LLC (HQ)	Franklin	MA	C	508 541-9400	8831
Emuge Corp	West Boylston	MA	E	508 595-3600	12962
Form Roll Die Corp (PA)	Worcester	MA	F	508 755-2010	13725
Hutchinson Arospc & Indust Inc	Hopkinton	MA	C	508 417-7000	9328
LS Starrett Company	Athol	MA	F	978 249-3551	5980
Standex International Corp	Wakefield	MA	D	978 538-0808	12537
Toolmex Indus Solutions Inc (PA)	Northborough	MA	D	508 653-8897	11114
Vulcan Company Inc (PA)	Hingham	MA	D	781 337-5970	9163
Contour360 Corp	Cornish	ME	E	207 625-4000	4704
Enercon (HQ)	Gray	ME	D	207 657-7000	4841
Peavey Manufacturing Company	Eddington	ME	E	207 843-7861	4746
Sands Business Eqp & Sups LLC	York	ME	F	207 351-3334	5716
Xuron Corp	Saco	ME	E	207 283-1401	5382
Abtech Inc	Fitzwilliam	NH	E	603 585-7106	14312
Chadwick & Trefethen Inc	Portsmouth	NH	F	603 436-2568	15370
Contour Fine Tooling Inc	Keene	NH	G	603 876-4908	14593
Cutting Tool Technologies Inc	Wilton	NH	G	603 654-2550	15704
Datron Dynamics Inc	Milford	NH	E	603 215-5850	15020
Jarvis Cutting Tools Inc	Rochester	NH	D	603 332-9000	15482
Durant Tool Company Inc	North Kingstown	RI	E	401 781-7800	16246
Mouldcam Inc	Bristol	RI	G	401 396-5522	15775

PRODUCT

	CITY	ST	EMP	PHONE	ENTRY#
Numaco Packaging LLC	East Providence	RI	F	401 438-4952	16035
Rol-Flo Engineering Inc	Westerly	RI	F	401 596-0060	16942
Wei Inc (PA)	Cranston	RI	E	401 781-3904	15928
Kollmorgen Corporation	Brattleboro	VT	E	802 258-3020	17092
Preci-Manufacturing Inc	Winooski	VT	D	802 655-2414	17768
Tivoly Inc	Derby Line	VT	C	802 873-3106	17213
Vermont Thread Gage LLC	Swanton	VT	F	802 868-4246	17646
Yankee Corporation	Fairfax	VT	D	802 527-0177	17265

MACHINE TOOLS, METAL CUTTING: Drilling

	CITY	ST	EMP	PHONE	ENTRY#
American Holt Corporation (PA)	Norwood	MA	F	781 440-9993	11160

MACHINE TOOLS, METAL CUTTING: Exotic, Including Explosive

	CITY	ST	EMP	PHONE	ENTRY#
Connecticut Tool & Cutter Co	Bristol	CT	F	860 314-1740	431
Gary Tool Company	Stratford	CT	G	203 377-3077	3540
Moore Tool Company Inc (HQ)	Bridgeport	CT	E	203 366-3224	350
Pmt Group Inc (PA)	Bridgeport	CT	C	203 367-8675	359
Datron Dynamics Inc	Milford	NH	E	603 215-5850	15020

MACHINE TOOLS, METAL CUTTING: Plasma Process

	CITY	ST	EMP	PHONE	ENTRY#
Centricut Manufacturing LLC	West Lebanon	NH	F	603 298-6191	15680
Thermacut Inc	Claremont	NH	E	603 543-0585	14098
Thermal Dynamics Corporation (DH)	West Lebanon	NH	B	603 298-5711	15690

MACHINE TOOLS, METAL CUTTING: Saws, Power

	CITY	ST	EMP	PHONE	ENTRY#
Hendrick Manufacturing Corp (PA)	Salem	MA	F	781 631-4400	11723

MACHINE TOOLS, METAL CUTTING: Tool Replacement & Rpr Parts

	CITY	ST	EMP	PHONE	ENTRY#
Sadlak Industries LLC	Coventry	CT	E	860 742-0227	681
Component Sources Intl Inc	Westborough	MA	F	508 986-2300	13092
JT Machine Inc	East Douglas	MA	E	508 476-1508	8351
Fabco Inc	Winthrop	ME	F	207 377-6909	5692
Valmet Inc	Winthrop	ME	D	207 377-6909	5696
Fremont Machine & Tool Co Inc	Fremont	NH	G	603 895-9445	14327
Piatek Machine Company Inc	Pawtucket	RI	F	401 728-9930	16403

MACHINE TOOLS, METAL CUTTING: Vertical Turning & Boring

	CITY	ST	EMP	PHONE	ENTRY#
Atp Industries LLC (PA)	Plainville	CT	F	860 479-5007	2748
Iamaw	Hebron	CT	G	860 228-0049	1528

MACHINE TOOLS, METAL FORMING: Bending

	CITY	ST	EMP	PHONE	ENTRY#
Sonolite Plastics Corporation	Gloucester	MA	F	978 281-0662	8959

MACHINE TOOLS, METAL FORMING: Elastic Membrane

	CITY	ST	EMP	PHONE	ENTRY#
Whitney Blake Company (PA)	Bellows Falls	VT	D	800 323-0479	17033

MACHINE TOOLS, METAL FORMING: Mechanical, Pneumatic Or Hyd

	CITY	ST	EMP	PHONE	ENTRY#
Laser Fare Inc (PA)	Smithfield	RI	E	401 231-4400	16721

MACHINE TOOLS, METAL FORMING: Pressing

	CITY	ST	EMP	PHONE	ENTRY#
Parkinson Machinery & Manufacturing Corp 401 762-2100	Woonsocket 16971	RI			C

MACHINE TOOLS, METAL FORMING: Rebuilt

	CITY	ST	EMP	PHONE	ENTRY#
Fenn LLC	East Berlin	CT	E	860 259-6600	910
Vermont Machine Tool Corp	Springfield	VT	F	802 885-5161	17622

MACHINE TOOLS, METAL FORMING: Spring Winding & Forming

	CITY	ST	EMP	PHONE	ENTRY#
L M Gill Welding and Mfr LLC (PA)	Manchester	CT	D	860 647-9931	1610

MACHINE TOOLS: Metal Cutting

	CITY	ST	EMP	PHONE	ENTRY#
Branson Ultrasonics Corp (DH)	Brookfield	CT	B	203 796-0400	512
C V Tool Company Inc (PA)	Southington	CT	E	978 353-7901	3206
Cnc Engineering Inc	Enfield	CT	E	860 749-1780	1124
Coastal Industrial Distrs Inc	Berlin	CT	F	207 286-3319	59
Fletcher-Terry Company LLC (PA)	East Berlin	CT	D	860 828-3400	911
Gmn Usa LLC	Bristol	CT	F	800 686-1679	451
Hanwha Aerospace USA LLC (DH)	Cheshire	CT	C	203 806-2090	597
Hanwha Aerospace USA LLC	East Windsor	CT	D	860 789-2511	1075
JL Lucas Machinery Co Inc	Waterbury	CT	F	203 597-1300	3925
Laser Tool Co Inc	Thomaston	CT	F	860 283-8284	3623
Microbest Inc	Waterbury	CT	C	203 597-0355	3944
Moon Cutter Co Inc	Hamden	CT	F	203 288-9249	1444
New England Cnc Inc	Hamden	CT	F	203 288-8241	1446
New England Machine Tools Inc	Bristol	CT	E	860 583-4001	475
New England Plasma Dev Corp	Putnam	CT	F	860 928-6561	2866
New England Tooling Inc	Killingworth	CT	F	800 866-5105	1544
Nowak Products Inc	Newington	CT	F	860 666-9685	2311
P-A-R Precision Inc	Wolcott	CT	F	860 491-4181	4372
Producto Corporation (HQ)	Bridgeport	CT	F	203 366-3224	363
Ramdy Corporation	Oakville	CT	F	860 274-3716	2626
Ready Tool Company	West Hartford	CT	E	860 524-7811	4079

	CITY	ST	EMP	PHONE	ENTRY#
Service Network Inc	Farmington	CT	D	860 679-7432	1247
Shuster-Mettler Corp	Plainville	CT	E	203 562-3178	2780
Sperry Automatics Co Inc	Naugatuck	CT	E	203 729-4589	1986
Stanley Engnered Fastening LLC (HQ)	Danbury	CT	F	800 783-6427	821
Syzygy Global Technology LLC	Darien	CT	G	203 818-2166	856
The Viking Tool Company	Shelton	CT	E	203 929-1457	3068
U S Tool Grinding Inc	Danbury	CT	G	203 797-5036	829
United Tool & Die Company (PA)	West Hartford	CT	C	860 246-6531	4088
Acp Waterjet Inc	Littleton	MA	F	800 951-5127	9799
Amherst Machine Co	Amherst	MA	F	413 549-4551	5858
Central MA Waterjet Inc	Millbury	MA	G	508 769-4308	10429
Compumachine Inc	Danvers	MA	F	978 777-8440	8173
Desktop Metal Operating Inc (HQ)	Burlington	MA	C	978 224-1244	7362
Donahue Industries Inc	Shrewsbury	MA	E	508 845-6501	11830
Dumont Company LLC	Greenfield	MA	F	413 773-3675	8990
Duval Precision Grinding Inc	Chicopee	MA	E	413 593-3060	8028
E T Duval & Sons Inc	Leominster	MA	G	978 537-7596	9660
Grob Inc	Weston	MA	G	617 817-3123	13285
Kinefac Corporation	Worcester	MA	D	508 754-6901	13749
Mainline Tool & Grind Inc	Westfield	MA	G	413 626-9601	13180
Merit Machine Mfg Inc	Fitchburg	MA	F	978 342-7677	8664
Mrse Inc	West Brookfield	MA	F	508 867-5083	12996
Peterson and Nash Inc	Norwell	MA	G	781 826-9085	11145
Phoenix Inc	Seekonk	MA	E	508 399-7100	11783
Production Tool & Grinding	Athol	MA	E	978 544-8206	5983
Professional TI Grinding Inc (PA)	South Easton	MA	E	508 230-3535	11951
Pys Enterprises Inc	Springfield	MA	F	413 732-7470	12123
Simonds Industries Intl	Fitchburg	MA	F	978 424-0100	8674
Toolmex Indus Solutions Inc (PA)	Northborough	MA	D	508 653-8897	11114
Uva Lidkoping Inc	Milford	MA	G	508 634-4301	10422
OBrien Consolidated Inds	Lewiston	ME	G	207 783-8543	4981
Sands Business Eqp & Sups LLC	York	ME	F	207 351-3334	5716
Airmar Technology Corp (PA)	Milford	NH	B	603 673-9570	15013
Ametek Precitech Inc (HQ)	Keene	NH	D	603 357-2510	14588
Centricut Inc	West Lebanon	NH	F	603 298-7849	15679
Express Assemblyproducts LLC	Nashua	NH	F	603 424-5590	15098
Hypertherm Inc (PA)	Hanover	NH	A	603 643-3441	14416
Hypertherm Inc	Hanover	NH	F	716 434-3755	14427
Jarvis Company Inc (PA)	Rochester	NH	D	603 332-9000	15481
Trellborg Pipe Sals Mlford Inc (DH)	Milford	NH	F	800 626-2180	15042
Williams & Hussey Mch Co Inc	Amherst	NH	F	603 732-0219	13895
Jfl Enterprises Inc	Smithfield	RI	E	401 231-1020	16718
Malco Saw Co Inc	Cranston	RI	G	401 942-7380	15891
Neil H Daniels Inc	Ascutney	VT	E	802 674-6323	16993
Yankee Corporation	Fairfax	VT	D	802 527-0177	17265

MACHINE TOOLS: Metal Forming

	CITY	ST	EMP	PHONE	ENTRY#
American Actuator Corporation	Redding	CT	G	203 324-6334	2880
Arna Machine Company	Bristol	CT	F	860 583-0628	396
Arrow Diversified Tooling Inc	Ellington	CT	E	860 872-9072	1101
Avna Inc (PA)	New Britain	CT	C	860 225-8707	2004
Deringer-Ney Inc (PA)	Bloomfield	CT	C	860 242-2281	158
Grant Manufacturing and Mch Co	Bridgeport	CT	F	203 366-4557	326
Joining Tech Automtn Inc	East Granby	CT	F	860 784-1967	936
Joshua LLC (PA)	Guilford	CT	D	203 624-0080	1398
Lou-Jan Tool & Die Inc	Bristol	CT	D	203 272-3536	463
Merritt Extruder Corp	Hamden	CT	E	203 230-8100	1440
Oxford General Industries Inc	Prospect	CT	F	203 758-4467	2837
Raymon Tool LLC	Hamden	CT	F	203 248-2199	1452
Sandviks Inc (PA)	Danbury	CT	G	866 984-0188	808
Sirois Tool Company Inc (PA)	Berlin	CT	E	860 828-5327	85
St Liquidation Corporation	Southington	CT	F	860 628-9090	3234
Ab-Wey Machine & Die Co Inc	Pembroke	MA	F	781 294-8031	11356
American Flwform Machining LLC (HQ)	Billerica	MA	E	978 667-0202	6399
Automatic Press Inc	Franklin	MA	G	508 528-2000	8818
Compumachine Inc	Danvers	MA	F	978 777-8440	8173
Form Roll Die Corp	Worcester	MA	F	508 755-5302	13726
Kinefac Corporation	Worcester	MA	D	508 754-6901	13749
Thomson Service Corp	Franklin	MA	F	508 528-2000	8872
Valentine Tool & Stamping Inc	Norton	MA	F	508 285-6911	11137
Westfield Tool & Die Co Inc	Westfield	MA	F	413 562-2393	13222
Whitman Castings Inc (PA)	Whitman	MA	E	781 447-4417	13352
Nbr Diamond Tool Corp	South Hampton	NH	G	603 394-2113	15629
Gasbarre Products Inc	Cranston	RI	F	401 467-5200	15865

MACHINERY & EQPT FINANCE LEASING

	CITY	ST	EMP	PHONE	ENTRY#
Southern Neng Telecom Corp (HQ)	New Haven	CT	B	203 771-5200	2203

MACHINERY & EQPT, AGRICULTURAL, WHOLESALE: Agricultural, NEC

	CITY	ST	EMP	PHONE	ENTRY#
Bascom Maple Farms Inc (PA)	Alstead	NH	D	603 835-2230	13856

	CITY	ST	EMP	PHONE	ENTRY#

MACHINERY & EQPT, AGRICULTURAL, WHOLESALE: Landscaping Eqpt

	CITY	ST	EMP	PHONE	ENTRY#
Mist Hill Property Maint LLC	Brookfield	CT	F	203 648-7434	530
Blacksmith Shop Farms Inc	East Falmouth	MA	G	508 548-7714	8357

MACHINERY & EQPT, INDL, WHOLESALE: Chemical Process

Gac Chemical Corporation **(PA)**	Searsport	ME	D	207 548-2525	5453

MACHINERY & EQPT, INDL, WHOLESALE: Conveyor Systems

TEC Engineering Corp	Oxford	MA	F	508 987-0231	11266

MACHINERY & EQPT, INDL, WHOLESALE: Cranes

CT Crane and Hoist Service LLC	Plymouth	CT	G	860 283-4320	2806
Somatex Inc	Detroit	ME	E	207 487-6141	4725

MACHINERY & EQPT, INDL, WHOLESALE: Engines & Parts, Diesel

Cummins Northeast LLC **(HQ)**	Braintree	MA	E	781 801-1700	7176
Js Sale Corp	Worcester	MA	E	508 753-2979	13746
Melton Sales and Service Inc	Hallowell	ME	E	207 623-8895	4860

MACHINERY & EQPT, INDL, WHOLESALE: Engines, Gasoline

Cummins Inc	Rocky Hill	CT	F	860 529-7474	2920
Gary Raymond	Caribou	ME	G	207 498-2549	4675
Leos Small Engines Inc	Morrisville	VT	F	802 888-7247	17384

MACHINERY & EQPT, INDL, WHOLESALE: Engs/Transportation Eqpt

Advanced Pwr Systems Intl Inc	New Hartford	CT	G	860 921-0009	2097

MACHINERY & EQPT, INDL, WHOLESALE: Fans

EBM-Papst Inc **(DH)**	Farmington	CT	B	860 674-1515	1217

MACHINERY & EQPT, INDL, WHOLESALE: Heat Exchange

Etter Engineering Company Incorporated	Bristol	CT	E	860 584-8842	443
Merrimac Industrial Sales Inc **(PA)**	Haverhill	MA	E	978 372-6006	9115
Ariston Usa LLC **(HQ)**	Providence	RI	E	508 763-8071	16474

MACHINERY & EQPT, INDL, WHOLESALE: Hydraulic Systems

Spectrum Associates Inc	Milford	CT	F	203 878-4618	1889
Controls For Automation Inc	Taunton	MA	E	508 802-6005	12328
Hope Inc	Needham	MA	E	781 455-1145	10512
Ltp Corporation **(DH)**	Northborough	MA	D	508 393-7660	11101
Marine Hydraulics Inc	New Bedford	MA	F	508 990-2866	10619
PRC Acquisition Company Inc	Gorham	ME	F	207 854-3702	4832

MACHINERY & EQPT, INDL, WHOLESALE: Indl Machine Parts

F & W Rentals Inc	Orange	CT	F	203 795-0591	2668
Goldenrod Corporation	Beacon Falls	CT	E	203 723-4400	40
Seitz LLC	Torrington	CT	C	860 489-0476	3695
Emx Controls Inc	East Douglas	MA	E	508 876-9700	8350

MACHINERY & EQPT, INDL, WHOLESALE: Instruments & Cntrl Eqpt

Kahn Instruments Incorporated	Wethersfield	CT	G	860 529-8643	4208
Kamweld Industries Inc	Norwood	MA	G	617 558-7500	11185
Merrimac Industrial Sales Inc **(PA)**	Haverhill	MA	E	978 372-6006	9114
The Tyler Co Inc	Hudson	MA	E	978 568-3400	9419
Primary Flow Signal Inc **(PA)**	Cranston	RI	D	401 461-6366	15905

MACHINERY & EQPT, INDL, WHOLESALE: Lift Trucks & Parts

Southworth Products Corp **(HQ)**	Falmouth	ME	E	207 878-0700	4773

MACHINERY & EQPT, INDL, WHOLESALE: Machine Tools & Access

JL Lucas Machinery Co Inc	Waterbury	CT	F	203 597-1300	3925
Shuster-Mettler Corp	Plainville	CT	E	203 562-3178	2780
Compumachine Inc	Danvers	MA	F	978 777-8440	8173
Harvard Products Inc	Harvard	MA	F	978 772-0309	9063
Jarvis Company Inc **(PA)**	Rochester	NH	D	603 332-9000	15481
Moore Nntechnology Systems LLC **(DH)**	Swanzey	NH	F	603 352-3030	15645

MACHINERY & EQPT, INDL, WHOLESALE: Machine Tools & Metalwork

Mikro Industrial Finishing Co	Vernon	CT	G	860 875-6357	3754
Nidec America Corporation **(HQ)**	Braintree	MA	E	781 848-0970	7196

MACHINERY & EQPT, INDL, WHOLESALE: Measure/Test, Electric

Baumer Ltd **(DH)**	Bristol	CT	F	860 621-2121	410
Hamar Laser Instruments Inc	Danbury	CT	E	203 730-4600	756
Testing Machines Inc	Swansea	MA	E	302 613-5600	12313
Martel Electronics Corp	Derry	NH	E	603 434-6033	14201

MACHINERY & EQPT, INDL, WHOLESALE: Packaging

Millwood Inc	North Haven	CT	D	203 248-7902	2425
Industrial Packaging Sup Inc	Worcester	MA	F	978 514-9960	13741

	CITY	ST	EMP	PHONE	ENTRY#
Industrial Packaging Supply Inc **(PA)**	Webster	MA	F	508 499-1600	12927
Pacific Packaging Products Inc **(PA)**	Wilmington	MA	C	978 657-9100	13445

MACHINERY & EQPT, INDL, WHOLESALE: Paper Manufacturing

Carpe Diem Technologies Inc	Franklin	MA	F	508 541-2055	8822

MACHINERY & EQPT, INDL, WHOLESALE: Petroleum Industry

Frc Founders Corporation **(PA)**	Stamford	CT	E	203 661-6601	3348

MACHINERY & EQPT, INDL, WHOLESALE: Processing & Packaging

Fortis Solutions Group LLC	Ellington	CT	E	860 872-6311	1107
BEE International Inc	South Easton	MA	E	508 238-5558	11937
Labthink International Inc	Medford	MA	F	617 830-2190	10293
Oizero9 Inc	Sanford	ME	E	207 324-3582	5404

MACHINERY & EQPT, INDL, WHOLESALE: Recycling

Premier Recycling Eqp Inc	Seabrook	NH	F	855 223-5859	15600
Glencore Recycling LLC	East Providence	RI	F	401 438-9220	16020
Triex LLC	Barre	VT	G	802 505-6772	17021

MACHINERY & EQPT, INDL, WHOLESALE: Safety Eqpt

Realhub Inc	Darien	CT	F	650 461-9210	854
American Industrial & Med Pdts **(PA)**	Auburn	MA	F	508 832-5785	6101
Mascon Inc	Woburn	MA	E	781 938-5800	13605
Mezzanine Safeti-Gates Inc	Essex	MA	G	978 768-3000	8478
Vogue Industries Ltd Partnr	Central Falls	RI	E	401 722-0900	15800
Galvion Ballistics Ltd	Essex Junction	VT	D	802 334-2774	17233

MACHINERY & EQPT, INDL, WHOLESALE: Water Pumps

Rema Dri-Vac Corp	Norwalk	CT	F	203 847-2464	2566
Apex Sealing Inc	Fairfax	VT	F	802 524-7100	17254

MACHINERY & EQPT, WHOLESALE: Construction, General

Numa Tool Company **(PA)**	Thompson	CT	D	860 923-9551	3652
Waverly Tool Rental & Sales Co	Framingham	MA	F	508 872-8866	8811
American Equipment & Fabg Corp	East Providence	RI	F	401 438-2626	16002

MACHINERY & EQPT, WHOLESALE: Road Construction & Maintenance

FC Work & Sons Incorporated	Jackson	ME	F	207 722-3206	4912

MACHINERY & EQPT: Electroplating

Modern Metal Finishing LLC	Oxford	CT	E	203 267-1510	2704
Tecomet Inc	Woburn	MA	A	781 782-6400	13675
Technic Inc **(PA)**	Cranston	RI	C	401 781-6100	15919

MACHINERY & EQPT: Farm

Salsco Inc	Cheshire	CT	D	203 271-1682	616
American Robotics Inc	Marlborough	MA	E	617 862-2101	10108
Innovasea Systems Inc **(PA)**	Boston	MA	E	207 322-3219	6811
Oesco Inc	Conway	MA	E	413 369-4335	8143
Ondas Holdings Inc	Marlborough	MA	E	617 862-2101	10191
Country Home Products Inc	Charlotte	VT	E	802 771-7202	17175

MACHINERY & EQPT: Liquid Automation

Alstom Power Co	Windsor	CT	E	860 688-1911	4257
Environmantal Systems Cor	Hartford	CT	E	860 953-5167	1479
Qsonica LLC	Newtown	CT	G	203 426-0101	2344
Sonics & Materials Inc **(PA)**	Newtown	CT	D	203 270-4600	2347
St Equipment & Technology LLC	Needham	MA	E	781 972-2319	10524

MACHINERY, EQPT & SUPPLIES: Parking Facility

Tkh Security LLC **(PA)**	Cheshire	CT	D	203 220-6544	619

MACHINERY, FOOD PRDTS: Confectionery

Jimsan Enterprises Inc	West Bridgewater	MA	G	508 587-3666	12973

MACHINERY, FOOD PRDTS: Ovens, Bakery

Baker Parts Inc	Westport	MA	G	508 878-5436	13293
Cooking Solutions Group Inc **(HQ)**	Salem	NH	F	603 893-9701	15516
Cooking Solutions Group Inc	Essex Junction	VT	C	864 963-3471	17231

MACHINERY, MAILING: Postage Meters

Pitney Bowes Inc	Shelton	CT	G	203 356-5000	3048
Pitney Bowes Inc	Shelton	CT	E	203 922-4000	3049
Pitney Bowes RE Fing Corp	Stamford	CT	C	203 356-5000	3434
Quadient Inc **(DH)**	Milford	CT	C	203 301-3400	1874

MACHINERY, METALWORKING: Coiling

P/A Industries Inc **(PA)**	Bloomfield	CT	E	860 243-8306	200
Broomfield Laboratories Inc **(PA)**	Bolton	MA	F	978 779-6600	6495

PRODUCT

	CITY	ST	EMP	PHONE	ENTRY#

MACHINERY, OFFICE: Paper Handling

	CITY	ST	EMP	PHONE	ENTRY#
Bell and Howell LLC	Deep River	CT	E	860 526-9561	873
Gbr Systems Corporation	Deep River	CT	E	860 526-9561	877
Xerox Corporation (HQ)	Norwalk	CT	B	203 849-5216	2598
Xerox Holdings Inc	Norwalk	CT	A	203 968-3000	2599
Xerox Holdings Corporation (PA)	Norwalk	CT	B	203 849-5216	2600

MACHINERY, OFFICE: Pencil Sharpeners

	CITY	ST	EMP	PHONE	ENTRY#
Acme United Corporation (PA)	Shelton	CT	D	203 254-6060	2978

MACHINERY, OFFICE: Stapling, Hand Or Power

	CITY	ST	EMP	PHONE	ENTRY#
Stanley Fastening Systems LP	New Britain	CT	E	860 225-5111	2069
Markwell Manufacturing Co Inc	Norwood	MA	G	781 769-6610	11194
Acme Staple Company Inc	Franklin	NH	F	603 934-2320	14318
Stanley Fastening Systems LP (HQ)	East Greenwich	RI	C	401 884-2500	15993

MACHINERY, PACKAGING: Carton Packing

	CITY	ST	EMP	PHONE	ENTRY#
Econocorp Inc	Randolph	MA	E	781 986-7500	11555

MACHINERY, PACKAGING: Packing & Wrapping

	CITY	ST	EMP	PHONE	ENTRY#
PDC International Corp	Norwalk	CT	D	203 853-1516	2552
Staban Engineering Corp	Wallingford	CT	F	203 294-1997	3854
Illinois Tool Works Inc	Hopkinton	MA	E	508 520-0083	9331
Nova Packaging Systems Inc	Leominster	MA	D	978 537-8534	9688
Package Machinery Company Inc	Holyoke	MA	G	413 315-3801	9274
Speedline Technologies Inc	Franklin	MA	B	508 541-4867	8864
Tooling Research Inc (PA)	Walpole	MA	F	508 668-1950	12578

MACHINERY, PAPER INDUSTRY: Converting, Die Cutting & Stampng

	CITY	ST	EMP	PHONE	ENTRY#
Bar-Plate Manufacturing Co	Hamden	CT	F	203 397-0033	1413
Dcg-Apvh Acquisition Co LLC	Newington	CT	E	636 488-3200	2286
Mm-Apvh Acquisition Co LLC (HQ)	Westminster	MA	F	978 516-7050	13275

MACHINERY, PAPER INDUSTRY: Paper Mill, Plating, Etc

	CITY	ST	EMP	PHONE	ENTRY#
Johnston Dandy Company (PA)	Lincoln	ME	E	207 794-6571	5009
Bfmc LLC	Berlin	NH	E	603 752-4550	13980

MACHINERY, PAPER INDUSTRY: Pulp Mill

	CITY	ST	EMP	PHONE	ENTRY#
Andritz Inc	Springfield	MA	C	413 733-6603	12075
Montague Industries Inc	Turners Falls	MA	E	413 863-4301	12453
Valmet Inc	Nashua	NH	C	603 882-2711	15181

MACHINERY, PRINTING TRADES: Plates

	CITY	ST	EMP	PHONE	ENTRY#
Verico Technology LLC (HQ)	Enfield	CT	E	860 871-1200	1157
Fine Line Graphics Inc (PA)	Smithfield	RI	E	401 349-3300	16701

MACHINERY, PRINTING TRADES: Presses, Gravure

	CITY	ST	EMP	PHONE	ENTRY#
Gem Gravure Co Inc (PA)	Hanover	MA	D	781 878-0456	9032

MACHINERY, SEWING: Sewing & Hat & Zipper Making

	CITY	ST	EMP	PHONE	ENTRY#
Bausch Advanced Tech Inc (PA)	Clinton	CT	C	860 669-7380	637

MACHINERY, TEXTILE: Finishing

	CITY	ST	EMP	PHONE	ENTRY#
Maine Stitching Spc LLC	Skowhegan	ME	F	207 812-5207	5472

MACHINERY, TEXTILE: Printing

	CITY	ST	EMP	PHONE	ENTRY#
Image Star LLC	Middletown	CT	G	888 632-5515	1753

MACHINERY: Ammunition & Explosives Loading

	CITY	ST	EMP	PHONE	ENTRY#
Lyman Products Corporation (PA)	Middletown	CT	D	860 632-2020	1761
Bisco Environmental Inc	Danvers	MA	F	508 738-5100	8169

MACHINERY: Automotive Related

	CITY	ST	EMP	PHONE	ENTRY#
Day Machine Systems Inc	New Britain	CT	F	860 229-3440	2020
Windham Automated Machines Inc	South Windham	CT	E	860 208-5297	3105
Uspack Inc	Leominster	MA	E	978 466-9700	9714
Uspack Inc	Hudson	MA	E	978 562-8522	9423

MACHINERY: Bag & Envelope Making

	CITY	ST	EMP	PHONE	ENTRY#
First Mate Prtg Converting Inc (HQ)	Gardner	MA	D	978 630-1028	8886

MACHINERY: Bridge Or Gate, Hydraulic

	CITY	ST	EMP	PHONE	ENTRY#
Terex Corporation (PA)	Norwalk	CT	F	203 222-7170	2578
Dresser Msnlah Ctrl Vlves Avon (DH)	Avon	MA	D	508 586-4600	6149

MACHINERY: Concrete Prdts

	CITY	ST	EMP	PHONE	ENTRY#
Saint-Gobain Abrasives Inc (HQ)	Worcester	MA	A	508 795-5000	13788

MACHINERY: Construction

	CITY	ST	EMP	PHONE	ENTRY#
Conair LLC	Torrington	CT	D	800 492-7464	3676
Ezflow Limited Partnership (DH)	Old Saybrook	CT	E	860 577-7064	2647

	CITY	ST	EMP	PHONE	ENTRY#
H Barber & Sons Inc	Naugatuck	CT	E	203 729-9000	1962
Megadoor USA Inc	Meriden	CT	C	203 238-2700	1673
Salsco Inc	Cheshire	CT	D	203 271-1682	616
Terex Advance Mixer Inc	Westport	CT	E	203 222-7170	4198
Terex Usa LLC (HQ)	Norwalk	CT	E	203 222-7170	2579
Tinsley GROup-Ps&w Inc (HQ)	Milford	CT	E	919 742-5832	1896
Washington Terex Inc	Westport	CT	F	203 222-7170	4200
Altec Inc	Shrewsbury	MA	D	508 752-0660	11826
Altec Inc	Natick	MA	E	508 545-8200	10468
American Crane and Hoist Corp	Boston	MA	C	617 482-8383	6540
Ghm Industries Inc (PA)	Charlton	MA	F	508 248-3941	7888
Omg Inc	Agawam	MA	G	413 786-0516	5802
Omg Inc (DH)	Agawam	MA	B	413 789-0252	5803
Roadsafe Traffic Systems	Stoughton	MA	G	781 436-5006	12231
Rockland Equipment Company LLC	Rockland	MA	F	781 871-4400	11659
Shemin Nurseries Inc	Lexington	MA	E	781 861-1111	9771
Douglas Dynamics LLC	Rockland	ME	F	207 701-4200	5325
North E Wldg & Fabrication Inc	Auburn	ME	E	207 786-2446	4448
Admix Inc	Londonderry	NH	E	603 627-2340	14727
Continental Biomass Industries	Newton	NH	E	603 382-0556	15242
Terex Usa LLC	Newton	NH	D	603 382-0556	15245
American Equipment & Fabg Corp	East Providence	RI	F	401 438-2626	16002

MACHINERY: Cryogenic, Industrial

	CITY	ST	EMP	PHONE	ENTRY#
Azenta Inc	Chelmsford	MA	B	978 262-2795	7914
Vacuum Barrier Corporation	Woburn	MA	E	781 933-3570	13682

MACHINERY: Custom

	CITY	ST	EMP	PHONE	ENTRY#
Arna Machine Company	Bristol	CT	F	860 583-0628	396
Darly Custom Technology Inc	Windsor	CT	F	860 298-7966	4269
Dufrane Nuclear Shielding Inc	Winsted	CT	F	860 379-2318	4340
Elks Manufacturing Corporation	Meriden	CT	F	203 235-2528	1666
Engineering Specialties Inc	North Branford	CT	E	203 488-2266	2367
Manchester TI & Design ADP LLC	North Haven	CT	G	860 296-6541	2422
Advanced Precision Engineering Incorporated 978 356-7303	Ipswich 9477	MA	E		
Anver Corporation	Hudson	MA	D	978 568-0221	9354
Enos Engineering LLC	Acton	MA	E	978 654-6522	5745
Eyesaver International Inc	Hanover	MA	D	781 829-0808	9031
Harvard Products Inc	Harvard	MA	F	978 772-0309	9063
Holyoke Machine Company	Holyoke	MA	E	413 534-5612	9261
Innovative Tooling Company Inc	Lenox	MA	F	413 637-1031	9625
K-F Liquidation Inc	Franklin	MA	G	508 528-2000	8847
Markforged Inc (HQ)	Waltham	MA	C	866 496-1805	12715
Midas Technology Inc	Woburn	MA	F	781 938-0069	13613
Psjl Corporation	Billerica	MA	C	978 313-2500	6474
Regional Industries Inc	Danvers	MA	G	978 750-8787	8217
Thomas M Leonard Inc	West Bridgewater	MA	G		12984
Kennebec Technologies	Augusta	ME	F	207 626-0188	4474
Nikel Precision Group LLC	Saco	ME	D	207 282-6080	5375
Soleras Advanced Coatings Ltd (PA)	Biddeford	ME	E	207 282-5699	4588
Allard Nazarian Group Inc (PA)	Manchester	NH	C	603 668-1900	14810
Dgf Indstrial Innvtons Group L	Gilford	NH	F	603 528-6591	14335
HMC Solutions LLC	Peterborough	NH	G	501 255-0498	15316
Intec Automation Inc	Rochester	NH	E	603 833-9329	15479
Abacus Automation Inc	Bennington	VT	E	802 442-3662	17035
Gloucester Associates Inc	Barre	VT	E	802 479-1088	17001

MACHINERY: Desalination Eqpt

	CITY	ST	EMP	PHONE	ENTRY#
Gradiant Osmotics Inc	Woburn	MA	G	781 819-5034	13576
Oasys Water Inc	Foxboro	MA	E	617 963-0450	8711

MACHINERY: Electrical Discharge Erosion

	CITY	ST	EMP	PHONE	ENTRY#
New England Die Co Inc	Waterbury	CT	F	203 574-5140	3950

MACHINERY: Electronic Component Making

	CITY	ST	EMP	PHONE	ENTRY#
Omega Engineering Inc	Norwalk	CT	D	714 540-4914	2548
Csi Mfg Inc	Westborough	MA	E	508 986-2300	13096
O K Engineering Inc	Hudson	MA	G	978 562-1010	9397
Rt Engineering Corporation	Franklin	MA	E	800 343-1182	8861
Witricity Corporation (PA)	Watertown	MA	F	617 926-2700	12921
CET Technology LLC	Windham	NH	E	603 894-6100	15724
Pica Mfg Solutions Inc (PA)	Derry	NH	E	603 845-3258	14204

MACHINERY: Gas Producers

	CITY	ST	EMP	PHONE	ENTRY#
Linde Inc (HQ)	Danbury	CT	B	203 837-2000	776

MACHINERY: Gas Separators

	CITY	ST	EMP	PHONE	ENTRY#
ACS Industries Inc (PA)	Lincoln	RI	E	401 769-4700	16116

MACHINERY: Gear Cutting & Finishing

	CITY	ST	EMP	PHONE	ENTRY#
Fellows Corporation	Windsor	VT	E	802 674-6500	17758

	CITY	ST	EMP	PHONE	ENTRY#

MACHINERY: Ice Cream

	CITY	ST	EMP	PHONE	ENTRY#
Taylor Coml Foodservice Inc	Farmington	CT	A	336 245-6400	1250
Acana Northeast Inc	Pembroke	NH	G	800 922-2629	15302
Superior Ice Cream Eqp LLC	Bow	NH	F	603 225-4207	14011

MACHINERY: Metalworking

	CITY	ST	EMP	PHONE	ENTRY#
Alpha-Core Inc	Shelton	CT	E	203 954-0050	2980
Fletcher-Terry Company LLC (PA)	East Berlin	CT	D	860 828-3400	911
Foilmark Inc	Bloomfield	CT	G	860 243-0343	165
L M Gill Welding and Mfr LLC (PA)	Manchester	CT	D	860 647-9931	1610
Merritt Extruder Corp	Hamden	CT	E	203 230-8100	1440
Nni Liquidation Corp	Shelton	CT	F	203 929-2221	3040
True Position Mfg LLC	South Windsor	CT	G	860 291-2987	3186
Tyger Tool Inc	Stratford	CT	F	203 375-4344	3581
Kamrowski Metal Refinishing	Boston	MA	G	508 877-0367	6839
Ktron Incorporated	Marlborough	MA	E	508 229-0919	10178
Lawrence Sigler	Princeton	MA	G	510 782-6737	11495
Mestek Inc	Westfield	MA	E	413 568-9571	13185
Mestek Inc (PA)	Westfield	MA	E	470 898-4533	13186
Micro Electronics Inc	Seekonk	MA	F	508 761-9161	11781
Shanklin Research Corporation	Ayer	MA	G	978 772-2090	6195
Hill-Loma Inc	Gorham	ME	E	207 854-9791	4822
Precision Depaneling Mchs LLC	Fremont	NH	F	540 248-1381	14329
Standex International Corp (PA)	Salem	NH	E	603 893-9701	15563
Custom Centric Machining LLC	Bristol	RI	E	401 952-1804	15761
Durant Tool Company Inc	North Kingstown	RI	E	401 781-7800	16246
Gasbarre Products Inc	Cranston	RI	F	401 467-5200	15865
Huestis Machine Corporation	Bristol	RI	E	401 253-5500	15769
Providence Wire Creations Inc	Providence	RI	F	401 490-3227	16594
Abacus Automation Inc	Bennington	VT	E	802 442-3662	17035

MACHINERY: Packaging

	CITY	ST	EMP	PHONE	ENTRY#
B & B Equipment LLC	Portland	CT	G	860 342-5773	2817
Bausch Advanced Tech Inc (PA)	Clinton	CT	C	860 669-7380	637
Hasler Inc	Milford	CT	B	203 301-3400	1833
Millwood Inc	North Haven	CT	D	203 248-7902	2425
OEM Sources LLC	Milford	CT	E	203 283-5415	1857
Packard Inc	Prospect	CT	E	203 758-6219	2839
Standard Knapp Inc	Portland	CT	D	860 342-1100	2825
Accutech Packaging Inc	Foxboro	MA	D	508 543-3800	8689
Butler Automatic Inc (PA)	Middleboro	MA	D	508 923-0544	10353
Chesterfield Products Inc	Chesterfield	MA	E	413 296-0066	7997
Dtm Massman LLC	Hingham	MA	E	781 749-1866	9149
Energy Sciences Inc	Wilmington	MA	E	978 694-9000	13405
Lock Inspection Systems Inc	Leominster	MA	E	978 343-3716	9679
Maruho Htsujyo Innovations Inc (PA)	Norwell	MA	E	617 653-1617	11143
Mrsi Systems LLC	Tewksbury	MA	E	978 667-9449	12411
O/K Machinery Corporation	Marlborough	MA	E	508 303-8286	10188
Pac Machinery Group	Stoneham	MA	G	214 724-8523	12184
Packaging Devices Inc (PA)	Teaticket	MA	F	508 548-0224	12379
Sencorp Inc	Hyannis	MA	E	508 771-9400	9450
Shanklin Corporation (HQ)	Ayer	MA	C	978 487-2204	6194
Sperry Product Innovation Inc	Bedford	MA	F	781 271-1400	6270
Eami Inc	Biddeford	ME	F	207 283-3001	4562
Oizero9 Inc	Sanford	ME	F	207 324-3582	5404
Wrabacon Inc	Oakland	ME	F	207 465-2068	5122
Zajac LLC	Saco	ME	E	207 286-9100	5384
Folder-Glr Techl Svs Grp LLC	Pelham	NH	G	603 635-7400	15288
George Gordon Associates Inc	Merrimack	NH	F	603 424-5204	14981
Labels Inc	Hampton	NH	E	603 929-3088	14405
Nestech Machine Systems Inc	Hinesburg	VT	G	802 482-4575	17296

MACHINERY: Paint Making

	CITY	ST	EMP	PHONE	ENTRY#
Highland Labs Inc	Holliston	MA	G	508 429-2918	9215

MACHINERY: Plastic Working

	CITY	ST	EMP	PHONE	ENTRY#
Davis-Standard Holdings Inc (PA)	Pawcatuck	CT	B	860 599-1010	2718
Gloucester Engineering Co Inc (DH)	Gloucester	MA	F	978 281-1800	8935
Gloucester Engineering Co Inc	Gloucester	MA	E	978 515-7008	8936
Hardigg Industries LLC (HQ)	South Deerfield	MA	C	413 665-2163	11924
Lacerta Group Inc	Mansfield	MA	G	508 339-3312	10063
Lacerta Group LLC (PA)	Mansfield	MA	C	508 339-3312	10064
Mitchell Machine Incorporated (PA)	Springfield	MA	F	413 739-9693	12114
Reifenhauser Incorporated	Danvers	MA	G	847 669-9972	8218
Rocheleau Tool and Die Co Inc	Fitchburg	MA	D	978 345-1723	8673
Sonicron Systems Corporation	Westfield	MA	F	413 562-5218	13209
Synventive Molding Solutions Inc (HQ)	Peabody	MA	C	978 750-8065	11345
TEC Engineering Corp	Oxford	MA	E	508 987-0231	11266
Thermoplastics Company Inc	Worcester	MA	E	508 754-4668	13811
US Extruders Inc	Westerly	RI	F	401 584-4710	16945

MACHINERY: Printing Presses

	CITY	ST	EMP	PHONE	ENTRY#
Image Star LLC	Middletown	CT	G	888 632-5515	1753
Aurora Imaging Technology Inc	Wellesley	MA	D	617 522-6900	12937
Nes Worldwide Inc	Westfield	MA	E	413 562-8000	13192
Manroland Goss Web Systems AMR (DH)	Exeter		NH		B
603 750-6600		14294			

MACHINERY: Recycling

	CITY	ST	EMP	PHONE	ENTRY#
Devivo Industries Inc	Waterbury	CT	E	203 270-1552	3906
Startech Environmental Corp (PA)	Wilton	CT	F	203 762-2499	4248
American Recycled Mtls Inc	Holliston	MA	G	508 429-1455	9199
Waste Mgmt Inc	Springfield	MA	F	413 747-9294	12149
Premier Recycling Eqp Inc	Seabrook	NH	F	855 223-5859	15600
Triex LLC	Barre	VT	G	802 505-6772	17021

MACHINERY: Road Construction & Maintenance

	CITY	ST	EMP	PHONE	ENTRY#
Town of Ledyard	Gales Ferry	CT	F	860 464-9060	1262
Ray-Tech Infrared Corporation	Charlestown	NH	F	603 826-3030	14068

MACHINERY: Robots, Molding & Forming Plastics

	CITY	ST	EMP	PHONE	ENTRY#
Wittmann Usa Inc (DH)	Torrington	CT	D	860 496-9603	3708
Nypro Inc (HQ)	Clinton	MA	A	978 365-9721	8087
Ranger Automation Systems Inc	Millbury	MA	E	508 842-6500	10442
Rethink Robotics Inc	Boston	MA	F	617 500-2487	7008
Lanco Assembly Systems Inc (PA)	Westbrook	ME	D	207 773-2060	5635
Yushin America Inc (HQ)	Cranston	RI	D	401 463-1800	15930

MACHINERY: Rubber Working

	CITY	ST	EMP	PHONE	ENTRY#
Farrel Corporation (DH)	Ansonia	CT	D	203 736-5500	14

MACHINERY: Screening Eqpt, Electric

	CITY	ST	EMP	PHONE	ENTRY#
Lambient Technologies LLC	Cambridge	MA	G	857 242-3963	7627

MACHINERY: Semiconductor Manufacturing

	CITY	ST	EMP	PHONE	ENTRY#
Asml Us LLC	Wilton	CT	A	203 761-4000	4231
Jet Process Corporation	Wallingford	CT	G	203 985-6000	3823
Prospect Products Incorporated	Newington	CT	E	860 666-0323	2320
Applied Materials Inc	Gloucester	MA	F	978 282-2000	8919
Axcelis Technologies Inc (PA)	Beverly	MA	A	978 787-4000	6330
Azenta Inc (PA)	Burlington	MA	A	978 262-2400	7339
Carpe Diem Technologies Inc	Franklin	MA	F	508 541-2055	8822
DCI Automation Inc	West Boylston	MA	D	508 752-3071	12960
Innovent Technologies LLC	Peabody	MA	E	978 538-0808	11318
Mediatek USA Inc	Woburn	MA	C	781 503-8000	13609
Optikos Corporation	Wakefield	MA	D	617 354-7557	12525
Varian Semicdtr Eqp Assoc Inc	Newburyport	MA	E	978 463-1500	10725
Welton Technology LLC	Leominster	MA	G	978 425-0160	9716
Puritan Electronics Inc	Manchester	NH	E	800 343-8649	14919
Advanced Illumination Inc	Rochester	VT	E	802 767-3830	17484

MACHINERY: Separation Eqpt, Magnetic

	CITY	ST	EMP	PHONE	ENTRY#
Industrial Magnetics Inc	Windsor	CT	D	508 853-3232	4283
Walker Magnetics Group Inc	Windsor	CT	D	508 853-3232	4314
Mushield Company Inc	Londonderry	NH	E	603 666-4433	14776

MACHINERY: Textile

	CITY	ST	EMP	PHONE	ENTRY#
Reynolds Carbide Die Co Inc	Thomaston	CT	E	860 283-8246	3627
Sonic Corp	Stratford	CT	F	203 375-0063	3575
Holyoke Machine Company	Holyoke	MA	E	413 534-5612	9261
Cove Metal Company Inc (PA)	Pawtucket	RI	F	401 724-3500	16359
Greystone Incorporated	Lincoln	RI	F	401 333-0444	16139
James L Gallagher Inc	Little Compton	RI	F	508 758-3102	16161
Texcel Inc	Cumberland	RI	F	401 727-2113	15968

MACHINERY: Tobacco Prdts

	CITY	ST	EMP	PHONE	ENTRY#
Smokeloudz LLC (PA)	Meriden	CT	G	203 909-3556	1699

MACHINERY: Woodworking

	CITY	ST	EMP	PHONE	ENTRY#
United Abrasives Inc (PA)	North Windham	CT	B	860 456-7131	2451
Lawrence Sigler	Princeton	MA	G	510 782-6737	11495
Simonds International LLC (HQ)	Fitchburg	MA	B	978 424-0100	8675
Williams & Hussey Mch Co Inc	Amherst	NH	F	603 732-0219	13895

MACHINISTS' TOOLS & MACHINES: Measuring, Metalworking Type

	CITY	ST	EMP	PHONE	ENTRY#
Tool Technology Inc	Middleton	MA	F	978 777-5006	10396

MACHINISTS' TOOLS: Measuring, Precision

	CITY	ST	EMP	PHONE	ENTRY#
Hermann Schmidt Company Inc	South Windsor	CT	F	860 289-3347	3155
B & E Group LLC	Southwick	MA	E	413 569-5585	12041
Boston Centerless Inc (PA)	Woburn	MA	D	781 994-5000	13530
Lee Tool Co Inc	Ludlow	MA	F	413 583-8750	9948

PRODUCT

	CITY	ST	EMP	PHONE	ENTRY#
LS Starrett Company **(PA)**	Athol	MA	A	978 249-3551	5981
Tektron Inc	Topsfield	MA	F	978 887-0091	12439
Onvio LLC **(PA)**	Salem	NH	F	603 685-0404	15553
Central Tools Inc **(PA)**	Cranston	RI	E	401 467-8211	15841
Hexagon Mfg Intelligence Inc **(DH)**	North Kingstown	RI	D	401 886-2000	16255

MACHINISTS' TOOLS: Precision

	CITY	ST	EMP	PHONE	ENTRY#
Apex Machine Tool Company Inc	Cheshire	CT	D	860 677-2884	571
Enjet Aero Newington Inc	Newington	CT	D	860 953-0686	2291
Floyd Manufacturing Co Inc	Cromwell	CT	E	860 829-1920	692
Johnson Gage Company	Bloomfield	CT	E	860 242-5541	177
Preferred Tool & Die Inc	Shelton	CT	E	203 925-8525	3055
Skico Manufacturing Co LLC	Hamden	CT	G	203 230-1305	1455
Ben Franklin Design Mfg Co Inc	Agawam	MA	F	413 786-4220	5781
D & R Products Co Inc	Hudson	MA	E	978 562-4137	9361
Dff Corp	Agawam	MA	E	413 786-8880	5789
G & D Tool Co Inc	Salem	MA	F	978 745-0020	11716
Hoppe Technologies Inc	Chicopee	MA	D	413 592-9213	8036
Martran Corp	Attleboro Falls	MA	F	508 699-7506	6089
Mk Services Corp	Middleton	MA	E	978 777-2196	10390
Nortek Inc	West Springfield	MA	E	413 781-4777	13038
Proto XYZ Inc	New Bedford	MA	G	508 525-6363	10644
Ametek Precitech Inc **(HQ)**	Keene	NH	D	603 357-2510	14588
Bocra Industries Inc	Seabrook	NH	E	603 474-3598	15585
Will-Mor Manufacturing LLC	Seabrook	NH	D	603 474-8971	15606
Vermont Precision Tools Inc **(PA)**	Swanton	VT	C	802 868-4246	17645

MACHINISTS' TOOLS: Scales, Measuring, Precision

	CITY	ST	EMP	PHONE	ENTRY#
Maine Scale LLC	Auburn	ME	F	207 777-9500	4443

MAGNETIC INK & OPTICAL SCANNING EQPT

	CITY	ST	EMP	PHONE	ENTRY#
Gerber Scientific LLC **(PA)**	Tolland	CT	C	860 871-8082	3661
Verico Technology LLC **(HQ)**	Enfield	CT	E	860 871-1200	1157
Data Translation Inc **(PA)**	Norton	MA	E	508 481-3700	11126

MAGNETIC SHIELDS, METAL

	CITY	ST	EMP	PHONE	ENTRY#
Kenney Manufacturing Company **(PA)**	Warwick	RI	B	401 739-2200	16831

MAGNETIC TAPE, AUDIO: Prerecorded

	CITY	ST	EMP	PHONE	ENTRY#
Porter Music Box Co Inc	Randolph	VT	G	802 728-9694	17473

MAIL-ORDER HOUSE, NEC

	CITY	ST	EMP	PHONE	ENTRY#
Defender Industries Inc	Waterford	CT	C	860 701-3400	3989
Olympia Sales Inc	Enfield	CT	D	860 749-0751	1140
Atlantic RES Mktg Systems Inc	West Bridgewater	MA	F	508 584-7816	12966
Erica Wilson Inc **(PA)**	Nantucket	MA	F	212 348-6196	10463
Leo F Maciver Co Inc	Brockton	MA	G	508 583-2501	7290
Kelco Industries	Milbridge	ME	E	207 546-7562	5061
Americas Grdening Resource Inc **(PA)**	Burlington	VT	C	802 660-3500	17117
Americas Grdening Resource Inc	Milton	VT	E	802 660-3500	17354
Beau Ties of Vermont LLC	Middlebury	VT	E	802 388-0108	17337
Cold Hollow Cider Mill Inc	Waterbury Center	VT	E	802 244-8771	17680
Country Home Products Inc	Charlotte	VT	E	802 771-7202	17175

MAIL-ORDER HOUSES: Computer Software

	CITY	ST	EMP	PHONE	ENTRY#
Cogz Systems LLC	Woodbury	CT	F	203 263-7882	4385

MAIL-ORDER HOUSES: Educational Splys & Eqpt

	CITY	ST	EMP	PHONE	ENTRY#
Geneve Corporation **(HQ)**	Stamford	CT	E	203 358-8000	3355

MAIL-ORDER HOUSES: Fitness & Sporting Goods

	CITY	ST	EMP	PHONE	ENTRY#
G-Form LLC **(HQ)**	Providence	RI	E	401 250-5555	16523

MAIL-ORDER HOUSES: Food

	CITY	ST	EMP	PHONE	ENTRY#
Bascom Maple Farms Inc **(PA)**	Alstead	NH	D	603 835-2230	13856
Butcher Block Inc	Claremont	NH	E	800 258-4304	14080
Granite State Candy Shoppe LLC **(PA)**	Concord	NH	F	603 225-2591	14131
Lady Ann Candies Inc	Warwick	RI	F	401 738-4321	16832

MAIL-ORDER HOUSES: Women's Apparel

	CITY	ST	EMP	PHONE	ENTRY#
Birch Outfitters LLC	Salem	MA	F	978 498-4631	11703

MAILBOX RENTAL & RELATED SVCS

	CITY	ST	EMP	PHONE	ENTRY#
UPS Authorized Retailer	Fairfield	CT	G	203 256-9991	1205

MAILING LIST: Compilers

	CITY	ST	EMP	PHONE	ENTRY#
Action Letter Inc **(PA)**	Stamford	CT	E	203 323-2466	3273

MAILING MACHINES WHOLESALERS

	CITY	ST	EMP	PHONE	ENTRY#
Agissar Corporation	Stratford	CT	E	203 375-8662	3516
Pitney Bowes Inc **(PA)**	Stamford	CT	A	203 356-5000	3433
Quadient Finance Usa Inc **(DH)**	Milford	CT	E	203 301-3400	1875

MAILING SVCS, NEC

	CITY	ST	EMP	PHONE	ENTRY#
Automated Mailing Services LLC	Cheshire	CT	G	203 439-2763	574
Brescias Printing Services Inc	East Hartford	CT	G	860 528-4254	976
Oddo Print Shop Inc	Torrington	CT	G	860 489-6585	3690
Technique Printers Inc	Clinton	CT	G	860 669-2516	651
Boston Business Printing Inc	Boston	MA	F	617 482-7955	6606
Clark Mailing Service Inc	Worcester	MA	E	508 752-1953	13708
Ils Business Services Inc	Agawam	MA	G	413 789-4555	5793
Massachusetts Envelope Co Inc **(PA)**	Woburn	MA	E	617 623-8000	13606
Red Mill Graphics Incorporated	Chelmsford	MA	F	978 251-4081	7951
Winter & Company Inc	Quincy	MA	F	617 773-7605	11545
Print-Mail of Maine Inc	Portland	ME	F	207 878-8000	5262
Echo Communications Inc	New London	NH	E	603 526-6006	15203
Johnson & Wales University	Providence	RI	E	401 598-1824	16550
L Brown and Sons Printing Inc	Barre	VT	E	802 476-3164	17012
Offset House Inc	Essex Junction	VT	C	802 878-4440	17242
Paw Prints Press Inc	South Burlington	VT	F	802 865-2872	17589

MANAGEMENT CONSULTING SVCS: Automation & Robotics

	CITY	ST	EMP	PHONE	ENTRY#
Berkshire Grey Inc **(PA)**	Bedford	MA	E	833 848-9900	6214
Square Robot Inc	Marlborough	MA	E	617 274-8389	10216
Ipura Consulting Group LLC	Hampton	NH	F	603 294-4002	14404
Eagle Industries Inc	Ashaway	RI	E	401 596-8111	15739
Triex LLC	Barre	VT	G	802 505-6772	17021

MANAGEMENT CONSULTING SVCS: Business

	CITY	ST	EMP	PHONE	ENTRY#
4tell Solutions LP	Foxboro	MA	E	207 828-7900	8688
Cerulli Associates Inc **(PA)**	Boston	MA	E	617 437-0084	6647
Kbace Technologies Inc **(HQ)**	Nashua	NH	D	603 821-7000	15121

MANAGEMENT CONSULTING SVCS: Business Planning & Organizing

	CITY	ST	EMP	PHONE	ENTRY#
Innovative Publishing Company	Edgartown	MA	F	267 266-8876	8466
Product Resources LLC	Newburyport	MA	E	978 524-8500	10709

MANAGEMENT CONSULTING SVCS: Construction Project

	CITY	ST	EMP	PHONE	ENTRY#
Sbarzola Construction Corp	South Weymouth	MA	G	781 817-6485	11977
Barrett Made **(PA)**	Portland	ME	E	207 650-6500	5184

MANAGEMENT CONSULTING SVCS: Food & Beverage

	CITY	ST	EMP	PHONE	ENTRY#
Endeavor Seafood LLC	Newport	RI	G	401 841-8637	16209

MANAGEMENT CONSULTING SVCS: General

	CITY	ST	EMP	PHONE	ENTRY#
Debt Exchange Inc	Boston	MA	D	617 531-3400	6685

MANAGEMENT CONSULTING SVCS: Hospital & Health

	CITY	ST	EMP	PHONE	ENTRY#
Alere Inc **(HQ)**	Waltham	MA	A	781 647-3900	12587
Hcpro Inc **(HQ)**	Middleton	MA	E	781 639-1872	10385
Innoneo Health Tech Inc **(PA)**	Boston	MA	D	617 336-3202	6810
Intralign Holdings LLC	Foxboro	MA	G	602 773-8506	8702
Change Hlthcare Phrm Sltons In	Augusta	ME	D	207 622-7153	4468
G&G Technologies Inc	Coventry	RI	F	401 295-4000	15813

MANAGEMENT CONSULTING SVCS: Industrial

	CITY	ST	EMP	PHONE	ENTRY#
YS Enterprises Inc	East Ryegate	VT	G	802 238-0902	17219

MANAGEMENT CONSULTING SVCS: Industrial & Labor

	CITY	ST	EMP	PHONE	ENTRY#
R & J Tool Inc **(PA)**	Laconia	NH	G	603 366-4925	14664

MANAGEMENT CONSULTING SVCS: Industry Specialist

	CITY	ST	EMP	PHONE	ENTRY#
Powerphone Inc	Madison	CT	E	203 245-8911	1566
PRA Holdings Inc	Stamford	CT	A	203 853-0123	3435
Relocation Information Svc Inc	Norwalk	CT	F	203 855-1234	2564
Sfc Koenig LLC	North Haven	CT	E	203 245-1100	2436
Clearwter Tech Cnslting Wtr Sv	Rockland	MA	F	781 871-5157	11640
Oliveri & Associates Inc	Plymouth	MA	F	781 320-9090	11470

MANAGEMENT CONSULTING SVCS: Information Systems

	CITY	ST	EMP	PHONE	ENTRY#
Apiphani Inc	Boston	MA	E	800 215-0811	6551

MANAGEMENT CONSULTING SVCS: Maintenance

	CITY	ST	EMP	PHONE	ENTRY#
Sunny Side Land Holdings LLC	Presque Isle	ME	F	207 768-1020	5310

MANAGEMENT CONSULTING SVCS: Manufacturing

	CITY	ST	EMP	PHONE	ENTRY#
D&D Fltrtion Cons Sppliers Inc	Kensington	CT	F	860 829-3690	1539
DC Enterprizes Inc	Hinesburg	VT	F	802 865-4480	17290

MANAGEMENT CONSULTING SVCS: Public Utilities

	CITY	ST	EMP	PHONE	ENTRY#
Physical Sciences Inc **(PA)**	Andover	MA	D	978 689-0003	5907
Raybern Utility Solutions LLC	Portsmouth	RI	G	303 775-5041	16453

MANAGEMENT CONSULTING SVCS: Real Estate

	CITY	ST	EMP	PHONE	ENTRY#
Granite Commercial RE LLC	Nashua	NH	F	603 669-2770	15107

MANAGEMENT CONSULTING SVCS: Restaurant & Food

	CITY	ST	EMP	PHONE	ENTRY#
Nsd Seafood Inc (PA)	Gloucester	MA	C	978 282-7880	8947

MANAGEMENT CONSULTING SVCS: Training & Development

	CITY	ST	EMP	PHONE	ENTRY#
Reac Ready LLC	Wethersfield	CT	G	860 550-5049	4213

MANAGEMENT SERVICES

	CITY	ST	EMP	PHONE	ENTRY#
Brennan Realty LLC (PA)	Shelton	CT	C	203 929-6314	2987
Cogstate Sport Inc	New Haven	CT	F	203 773-5010	2137
Conair LLC	Torrington	CT	D	800 492-7464	3676
Dt Holdings Incorporated	Stamford	CT	F	203 602-6969	3339
General Dynamics Ordnance	Avon	CT	F	860 404-0162	25
Hasler Inc	Milford	CT	B	203 301-3400	1833
Sleep Management Solutions LLC (DH)	Hartford	CT	F	888 497-5337	1508
SS&c Technologies Inc (HQ)	Windsor	CT	C	800 234-0556	4302
Urban Exposition LLC (DH)	Shelton	CT	E	203 242-8717	3074
Wexford Capital LP (PA)	Greenwich	CT	G	203 862-7000	1361
Automatic Press Inc	Franklin	MA	G	508 528-2000	8818
Biokit U S A Inc	Bedford	MA	F	781 861-4064	6215
Cross Country Motor Club Inc (HQ)	Medford	MA	A	781 393-9300	10283
Linx Consulting LLC	Webster	MA	F	508 461-6333	12930
Massachusetts Envelope Co Inc (PA)	Woburn	MA	E	617 623-8000	13606
Schneder Elc Systems Argntina	Foxboro	MA	C	508 543-8750	8718
Schneider Elc Systems USA Inc	Foxboro	MA	F	508 543-8750	8719
Schneider Elc Systems USA Inc (DH)	Foxboro	MA	E	508 543-8750	8721
Coca-Cola Bevs Northeast Inc	Belmont	NH	F	603 267-8834	13961
Ener-Tek International Inc	East Greenwich	RI	E	401 471-6580	15985

MANAGEMENT SVCS: Business

	CITY	ST	EMP	PHONE	ENTRY#
Logicmanager Inc	Boston	MA	E	617 530-1200	6862
Gabriel Business Group Co Ltd	Brookline	NH	F	877 401-5544	14039
Beacon Rock Properties Inc	Providence	RI	D	401 421-3470	16482
Douglas Wine & Spirits Inc	North Providence	RI	F	401 353-6400	16299

MANAGEMENT SVCS: Construction

	CITY	ST	EMP	PHONE	ENTRY#
John McGillicuddy Inc	Milton	MA	F	617 388-6324	10453

MANPOWER TRAINING

	CITY	ST	EMP	PHONE	ENTRY#
International Security Assista	Woburn	MA	C	617 590-7942	13588

MANUFACTURING INDUSTRIES, NEC

	CITY	ST	EMP	PHONE	ENTRY#
Advanced Specialist LLC	Watertown	CT	G	860 945-9125	4001
Aero-Precision Mfg LLC	Wallingford	CT	G	203 675-7625	3768
American Hydrogen Northeast	Bridgeport	CT	G	203 449-4614	294
Andher Mfg LLC	East Hartford	CT	G	860 874-8816	970
Arrow Lock Manufacturing Co	New Haven	CT	G	203 603-5959	2118
Bnl Manufacturing LLC	Vernon Rockville	CT	G	860 870-6222	3760
Carlin Mfg Kitchens To Go	Mystic	CT	G	413 519-2822	1937
Cici Bevin Gordon	Marlborough	CT	G	860 365-5731	1642
Concentric Tool and Mfg Co	Naugatuck	CT	G	203 756-9145	1954
Connecticut Metal Industries	Ansonia	CT	G	203 736-0790	11
Customized Foods Mfg LLC	Waterbury	CT	G	203 759-1645	3902
Ddk Industries LLC	Shelton	CT	G	203 641-4218	2998
Delcon Industries	Trumbull	CT	G	203 371-5711	3717
Delta-Source LLC	West Hartford	CT	F	860 461-1600	4056
Diversified Manufacturing LLC	Ansonia	CT	F	203 734-0379	13
East Coast Precision Mfg	Chester	CT	F	860 322-4624	627
Elite Group Manufacturing LLC	Portland	CT	G	860 788-6413	2819
Ellis Manufacturing LLC	Plainville	CT	G	865 518-0531	2758
Ensign Bickford Industries	Simsbury	CT	E	203 843-2126	3087
Firestable Insulation Co	Essex	CT	G	860 767-8773	1164
Hpi Manufacturing Inc	Hamden	CT	F	203 777-5395	1431
Incord Ltd	Oakdale	CT	F	860 537-1414	2622
Ironhorse Industries LLC	Harwinton	CT	G	203 598-8720	1521
Jera Industries LLC	Stamford	CT	G	203 428-6588	3391
Katy Industries Inc	Middlebury	CT	F	314 656-4321	1715
LDM Manufacturing Inc	Plainville	CT	G	860 410-9804	2769
Lesco	Stamford	CT	G	203 353-0061	3398
Line Sets Inc	Ansonia	CT	G	203 732-6700	16
Mafcote Industries	Norwalk	CT	F	601 776-9006	2531
Mk Millwork LLC	Morris	CT	F	860 567-0173	1933
Polster Industries LLC	Fairfield	CT	G	203 521-8517	1198
Precision Express Mfg LLC	Bristol	CT	F	860 584-2627	483
Precision Fire Fabrication LLC	Plantsville	CT	F	860 706-0749	2794
Qds LLC	Shelton	CT	G	203 338-9668	3057
RC Industries Inc	Wilton	CT	F	203 423-9419	4246
Regional Industries LLC	Clinton	CT	F	860 227-3627	649
Rockwood Manufacturing Co	New Haven	CT	G	800 582-2424	2192
Sadlak Manufacturing LLC	Coventry	CT	E	860 742-0227	682
Solon Manufacturing	North Haven	CT	F	203 230-5300	2437

	CITY	ST	EMP	PHONE	ENTRY#
Spv Industries LLC	West Hartford	CT	G	860 953-5928	4083
Vr Industries LLC	Torrington	CT	G	860 618-2772	3706
Whiff LLC	Fairfield	CT	F	917 420-0397	1206
99degrees Custom Inc	Lawrence	MA	E	978 655-3362	9533
Act Manufacturing Securities C	Foxboro	MA	F	508 481-5246	8690
Advanced CAM Manufacturing LLC	Hudson	MA	F	978 562-2825	9352
Anthony Industries Inc	Woburn	MA	G	781 305-3750	13511
Batch Inc	New Braintree	MA	G	203 948-9212	10663
Byblos Industries Corporation	Norwood	MA	F	781 727-4764	11167
Cassjack Industries Inc	Westfield	MA	G	413 786-1800	13157
Century-Tywood J3 Corp	Holliston	MA	F	508 429-4011	9204
CIM Industries Inc	Bridgewater	MA	E	800 543-3458	7226
Cory Manufacturing Inc	West Bridgewater	MA	F	508 680-2111	12970
Custom Group Ctr For Mfg Tech	Woburn	MA	G	781 935-4940	13553
Dalton Manufacturing Group Inc	Amesbury	MA	F	978 388-2227	5834
Diamondhead Usa Inc	West Springfield	MA	F	413 537-4806	13021
Greenfield Industries Inc	Greenfield	MA	G	413 772-3200	8992
Hedge Hog Industries Corp	Springfield	MA	F	413 363-2528	12100
Ivey Industries	Holyoke	MA	G	413 736-6464	9263
Jab Industries Inc	Attleboro	MA	F	401 447-9668	6027
Jameco Industries Inc	North Andover	MA	F	978 688-1811	10841
JP Saw Mfg Inc	Fall River	MA	G	508 567-0469	8563
Lavoie Industries LLC	Fall River	MA	G	508 542-1062	8568
Ls Industries Inc	Lynnfield	MA	F	781 844-8115	9999
Makers Tool and Mfg Co LLC	Oxford	MA	F	774 633-0658	11261
Maple Leaf Industries	Lakeville	MA	G	508 728-9581	9517
Market Forge Industries Inc	Everett	MA	F	617 387-4100	8494
MCS Industries Inc	Natick	MA	F	508 651-3755	10487
Milani Industries Incorporated	Stoughton	MA	G	781 344-3377	12225
Mountain Base Mfg LLC	Easthampton	MA	G	413 527-9990	8451
Navitar Industries LLC	Woburn	MA	G	781 933-6125	13619
Olimpia Industries Inc	Bellingham	MA	F	508 966-3392	6299
Patriot Custom Mfg Inc	Southbridge	MA	G	508 764-7342	12033
Pha Industries Incorporated	Orange	MA	F	978 544-8770	11229
Rgb Industries Inc	Holyoke	MA	G	413 536-3100	9277
Rockland Industries Inc	Braintree	MA	G	781 849-7918	7201
Rv Manufacturing Inc	Middleboro	MA	G	508 488-6612	10377
Sencorpwhite Holdings LLC	Hyannis	MA	F	508 771-9400	9452
Sjogren Industries Inc	Worcester	MA	F	508 987-3206	13802
Smtc Manufacturing	North Billerica	MA	F	508 207-6355	10956
Std Industries Inc	Stoughton	MA	G	781 828-4400	12239
Std Med Inc	West Bridgewater	MA	G	781 828-4400	12981
Tml Manufacturing Inc	Foxboro	MA	G	508 264-0494	8729
Weather Guard Industries LLC	Northampton	MA	G	954 703-0563	11086
York Athletics Mfg Inc	Boston	MA	F	617 777-3125	7138
Auburn Asphalt LLC	Auburn	ME	F	207 894-5040	4421
Barringer Industries LLC	Scarborough	ME	F	207 730-7125	5424
Gardner Chpmlls Mllinocket LLC	Chester	ME	F	207 794-2223	4693
LLC Park Hill	Westbrook	ME	G	207 239-7741	5636
Lockwood Mfg Inc	Presque Isle	ME	G	207 764-4196	5302
McSwain Manufacturing Inc	Winslow	ME	G	513 619-1222	5684
New Portland Publishing Inc	Falmouth	ME	G	207 536-5210	4770
Allard Nazarian Group Inc (PA)	Nashua	NH	E	603 320-8755	15057
and Fauna LLC	Holderness	NH	G	603 968-7490	14446
Cbms LLC	Hampton	NH	G	508 776-2647	14401
Hampshire Hives LLC	Gilsum	NH	G	603 313-0186	14342
Hardwater Industries LLC	Gilford	NH	G	603 867-9240	14336
Imed Mfg	Atkinson	NH	G	603 489-5184	13903
Ingu LLC	Portsmouth	NH	F	603 770-5969	15409
Keyspin Manufacturing LLC	Merrimack	NH	G	603 420-8508	14986
Lamarre Industries LLC	Nashua	NH	G	603 889-0165	15124
Marques Guitars LLC	Manchester	NH	G	603 321-4833	14881
Natural Playgrounds Shop LLC	Concord	NH	F	888 290-8405	14147
New Hampshire Novelty LLC (PA)	Winchester	NH	G	413 325-7648	15715
Polytite Manufacturing Corp	Derry	NH	G	603 952-9327	14205
Ricor Usa Inc	Salem	NH	G	603 718-8903	15557
Siglab Industries LLC	Merrimack	NH	G	603 860-2931	15002
Voda Industries LLC	Mont Vernon	NH	G	908 531-8156	15049
Aro Industrial Finishing LLC	North Providence	RI	G	401 349-4848	16296
Custom Built Window Mfg LLC	Warwick	RI	E	401 738-3800	16801
Hope Valley Industries Inc	North Kingstown	RI	G	401 667-7780	16257
Lance Industries	North Providence	RI	G	401 654-5394	16304
MP Manufacturing Inc	West Greenwich	RI	G	203 915-2235	16889
Vision Industries Corp	Johnston	RI	G	401 764-0916	16111
Hyzer Industries	Montpelier	VT	G	802 223-8277	17372
McNeills Manufacturing	Brattleboro	VT	G	802 246-1171	17095
Miti Manufacturing Co Inc	Saint Johnsbury	VT	F	802 424-1671	17544

MARBLE, BUILDING: Cut & Shaped

	CITY	ST	EMP	PHONE	ENTRY#
Eastern Marble and Granite LLC	Milford	CT	F	203 882-8221	1820
La Pietra Thinstone Veneer	Brookfield	CT	F	203 775-6162	528
Mildred Coppola (PA)	Stamford	CT	F	203 967-9300	3411

PRODUCT

	CITY	ST	EMP	PHONE	ENTRY#
New England Stone Inc	Milford	CT	F	203 876-8606	1853
Aldrich Marble & Granite Co	Norwood	MA	G	781 762-6111	11158
Louis W Mian Incorporated (PA)	Boston	MA	F	617 241-7900	6863
Santo C De Spirt Marble & Gran	Agawam	MA	G	413 786-7073	5806
Steven Tedesco	Danvers	MA	G	978 777-4070	8222
Stone Design Marble & Gran Co	South Weymouth	MA	F	781 331-3000	11978
Arens Stoneworks Inc	Greenland	NH	G	603 436-8000	14367

MARINAS

	CITY	ST	EMP	PHONE	ENTRY#
Dodson Boatyard LLC	Stonington	CT	E	860 535-1507	3508
Allen Harbor Marine Svc Inc	Harwich Port	MA	E	508 432-0353	9070
F L Tripp & Sons Inc	Westport Point	MA	F	508 636-4058	13303
Falmouth Mar Yachting Ctr Inc	Falmouth	MA	E	508 548-4600	8631
Northern Light Mar Group Inc	Manchester	MA	E	978 526-7911	10033
Roses Oil Service Inc (PA)	Gloucester	MA	E	877 283-3334	8955
Shipyard In Boothbay Hbr LLC	Boothbay Harbor	ME	E	207 633-3171	4604
Alden Yachts Corporation	Bristol	RI	E	401 683-4200	15752
Lenmarine Inc (PA)	Bristol	RI	E	401 253-2200	15772

MARINE HARDWARE

	CITY	ST	EMP	PHONE	ENTRY#
Beckson Manufacturing Inc (PA)	Bridgeport	CT	E	203 366-3644	301
C Sherman Johnson Company Inc	East Haddam	CT	F	860 873-8697	955
Cornell-Carr Co Inc	Monroe	CT	E	203 261-2529	1911
Dwyer Aluminum Mast Co Inc	North Branford	CT	F	203 484-0419	2366
Ketcham Traps	New Bedford	MA	G	508 997-4787	10610
Mooring Systems Incorporated	Cataumet	MA	G	508 776-0254	7859
Schaefer Marine Inc	New Bedford	MA	E	508 995-9511	10648
Watts Sea Tech Inc	North Andover	MA	E	978 688-1811	10860
New England Boatworks Inc	Portsmouth	RI	D	401 683-4000	16449
Siren Marine Inc	Newport	RI	F	401 619-4774	16224

MARINE RELATED EQPT

	CITY	ST	EMP	PHONE	ENTRY#
Maretron LLP	Plainville	CT	F	602 861-1707	2771
Naiad Dynamics Us Inc (HQ)	Shelton	CT	E	203 929-6355	3033
Naiad Maritime Group Inc (PA)	Shelton	CT	E	203 944-1932	3034
West Shore LLC	East Hampton	CT	G	860 267-1764	967
Hercules Slr (us) Inc	New Bedford	MA	G	508 992-9519	10600
Hercules Slr (us) Inc (PA)	New Bedford	MA	F	508 993-0010	10601
Ship Street Capital LLC	New Bedford	MA	E	508 995-9711	10650

MARINE SPLYS WHOLESALERS

	CITY	ST	EMP	PHONE	ENTRY#
B I L Inc	Groton	CT	F	860 446-8058	1365
Dawid Manufacturing Inc	Ansonia	CT	G	203 734-1800	12
Defender Industries Inc	Waterford	CT	C	860 701-3400	3989
Hercules Slr (us) Inc	New Bedford	MA	G	508 992-9519	10600
Hercules Slr (us) Inc (PA)	New Bedford	MA	F	508 993-0010	10601
Ronstan International Inc	Portsmouth	RI	F	401 293-0539	16456

MARKING DEVICES

	CITY	ST	EMP	PHONE	ENTRY#
American Sign Inc	New Haven	CT	F	203 624-2991	2115
Schwerdtle Stamp Company	Bridgeport	CT	E	203 330-2750	369
United Sttes Sign Fbrction Cor	Trumbull	CT	F	203 601-1000	3739
AA White Company	Uxbridge	MA	G	508 779-0821	12476
Kalt Incorporated (PA)	Lowell	MA	E	978 805-5001	9889
New England Expert Tech Corp	Greenfield	MA	F	413 773-8200	8995
Rofin-Baasel Inc (HQ)	Devens	MA	E	978 635-9100	8286
Titus & Bean Graphics Inc	Kingston	MA	F	781 585-1355	9513
Visimark Inc (PA)	Worcester	MA	E	866 344-7721	13823
Armstrong Family Inds Inc	Hermon	ME	E	207 848-7300	4880

MARKING DEVICES: Embossing Seals & Hand Stamps

	CITY	ST	EMP	PHONE	ENTRY#
A D Perkins Company	New Haven	CT	G	203 777-3456	2110
Logan Stamp Works Inc	Boston	MA	G	617 569-2121	6861
Making Your Mark Inc	Quincy	MA	F	617 479-0999	11527
Opsec Security Inc	Boston	MA	F	617 226-3000	6941
Granite State Stamps Inc	Manchester	NH	F	603 669-9322	14856

MARKING DEVICES: Embossing Seals, Corporate & Official

	CITY	ST	EMP	PHONE	ENTRY#
Owl Stamp Company Inc	Lowell	MA	G	978 452-4541	9912

MATCHES & MATCH BOOKS

	CITY	ST	EMP	PHONE	ENTRY#
D D Bean & Sons Co (PA)	Jaffrey	NH	C	603 532-8311	14565

MATS, MATTING & PADS: Door, Paper, Grass, Reed, Coir, Etc

	CITY	ST	EMP	PHONE	ENTRY#
Matter Surfaces Inc (PA)	Stoughton	MA	F	800 628-7462	12223

MEAT MARKETS

	CITY	ST	EMP	PHONE	ENTRY#
Manchester Packing Company Inc	Manchester	CT	D	860 646-5000	1616
Newington Meat Center	Newington	CT	G	860 666-3431	2310
Chair City Meats Inc	Gardner	MA	F	978 630-1050	8881
Tase-Rite Co Inc	Wakefield	RI	F	401 783-7300	16746

MEAT PRDTS: Frozen

	CITY	ST	EMP	PHONE	ENTRY#
Cambridge Packing Co Inc	Boston	MA	D	617 464-6000	6635

MEAT PRDTS: Ham, Smoked, From Purchased Meat

	CITY	ST	EMP	PHONE	ENTRY#
Harringtons In Vermont Inc (PA)	Richmond	VT	F	802 434-7535	17479

MEAT PRDTS: Prepared Beef Prdts From Purchased Beef

	CITY	ST	EMP	PHONE	ENTRY#
Newport Creamery LLC	Cranston	RI	F	401 946-4000	15900

MEAT PRDTS: Roast Beef, From Purchased Meat

	CITY	ST	EMP	PHONE	ENTRY#
Carando Gourmet Foods Corp (PA)	Agawam	MA	E	413 737-0183	5784
Shaans Panini & Roast Beef LLC	North Billerica	MA	F	617 230-3166	10955
Tessis Pizza & Roast Beef	Tewksbury	MA	F	978 851-8700	12421

MEAT PRDTS: Sausages & Related Prdts, From Purchased Meat

	CITY	ST	EMP	PHONE	ENTRY#
Baretta Provision Inc	East Berlin	CT	F	860 828-0802	908
Chair City Meats Inc	Gardner	MA	F	978 630-1050	8881
Diluigis Inc	Danvers	MA	D	978 750-9900	8182
Angostura International Ltd	Auburn	ME	F	207 786-3200	4419
Daniele International Inc	Pascoag	RI	C	401 568-6228	16337
Daniele International Inc	Pascoag	RI	C	401 568-6228	16338
Daniele International LLC (PA)	Mapleville	RI	C	401 371-2000	16167

MEAT PRDTS: Sausages, From Purchased Meat

	CITY	ST	EMP	PHONE	ENTRY#
Hummel Bros Inc	New Haven	CT	D	203 787-4113	2161
Lisbon Sausage Co Inc	New Bedford	MA	F	508 993-7645	10613
Smithfield Direct LLC	Springfield	MA	C	413 781-5620	12130
Waniewski Farms Inc	Feeding Hills	MA	F	413 786-1182	8637
Lincoln Packing Co	Cranston	RI	C	401 943-0878	15885
Rhode Island Provision Co	Johnston	RI	F	401 831-0815	16105

MEAT PRDTS: Smoked

	CITY	ST	EMP	PHONE	ENTRY#
Norpaco Inc	Middletown	CT	D	860 632-2299	1768
Kayem Foods Inc (PA)	Chelsea	MA	B	781 933-3115	7984

MEAT PRDTS: Snack Sticks, Incl Jerky, From Purchased Meat

	CITY	ST	EMP	PHONE	ENTRY#
Provisionaire & Co LLC	Westport	CT	E	646 681-8600	4193
Brothers Artisanal Inc	New Bedford	MA	G	508 938-9161	10575
Newport Jerky Company LLC	Newport	RI	F	774 644-2350	16219

MEAT PROCESSING MACHINERY

	CITY	ST	EMP	PHONE	ENTRY#
South Shore Packing Inc	Brockton	MA	E	508 941-0458	7307

MEDIA: Magnetic & Optical Recording

	CITY	ST	EMP	PHONE	ENTRY#
Dictaphone Corporation (DH)	Stratford	CT	C	203 381-7000	3533

MEDICAL & HOSPITAL EQPT WHOLESALERS

	CITY	ST	EMP	PHONE	ENTRY#
Lenscrafters	Milford	CT	G	203 878-8511	1845
Tarry Medical Products Inc	Danbury	CT	F	203 791-9001	823
Amatech Corporation	Acton	MA	D	978 263-5401	5737
Brownmed Inc (PA)	Boston	MA	E	857 317-3354	6626
Dlrc Incorporated	Cambridge	MA	G	617 999-3340	7552
Kaz Inc (HQ)	Marlborough	MA	D	508 490-7000	10174
Perx LLC	Pittsfield	MA	F	413 358-9020	11417
Philips Holding USA Inc (HQ)	Cambridge	MA	A	978 687-1501	7686
Maine Orthtic Prsthtic Rhab Sv	Portland	ME	F	207 773-8818	5241
Surplus Solutions LLC	Woonsocket	RI	F	401 526-0055	16978

MEDICAL & SURGICAL SPLYS: Bandages & Dressings

	CITY	ST	EMP	PHONE	ENTRY#
Beiersdorf North America Inc (DH)	Stamford	CT	F	203 563-5800	3292
Cellu Tissue Corporation	East Hartford	CT	A	860 289-7496	979
Hermell Products Inc	Bloomfield	CT	E	860 242-6550	169

MEDICAL & SURGICAL SPLYS: Braces, Elastic

	CITY	ST	EMP	PHONE	ENTRY#
Eddies Wheels Inc	Shelburne Falls	MA	F	413 625-0033	11804

MEDICAL & SURGICAL SPLYS: Braces, Orthopedic

	CITY	ST	EMP	PHONE	ENTRY#
At Surgical Company	Holyoke	MA	F	888 233-4069	9241
Cornell Orthotics Prosthetics (PA)	Beverly	MA	F	978 922-2866	6343
Spinal Technology LLC (PA)	West Yarmouth	MA	E	508 775-0990	13073

MEDICAL & SURGICAL SPLYS: Clothing, Fire Resistant & Protect

	CITY	ST	EMP	PHONE	ENTRY#
Blauer Manufacturing Co Inc (PA)	Boston	MA	E	800 225-6715	6597
David Clark Company Inc (PA)	Worcester	MA	C	508 756-6216	13713
Salk Company Inc	Allston	MA	F	617 782-4030	5825
Globe Manufacturing Co LLC (DH)	Pittsfield	NH	B	603 435-8323	15332
Labonville Inc (PA)	Gorham	NH	E	603 752-4030	14360
Cintas Corporation No 2	Pawtucket	RI	F	401 723-7300	16354

MEDICAL & SURGICAL SPLYS: Cosmetic Restorations

	CITY	ST	EMP	PHONE	ENTRY#
Progderm Inc	Boston	MA	F	617 419-1800	6982

	CITY	ST	EMP	PHONE	ENTRY#
Sals Clothing & Fabric Restor	Everett	MA	F	617 387-6726	8499

MEDICAL & SURGICAL SPLYS: Dressings, Surgical

	CITY	ST	EMP	PHONE	ENTRY#
Handy Pad Supply Inc	Paxton	MA	F	508 791-2722	11289

MEDICAL & SURGICAL SPLYS: Ear Plugs

	CITY	ST	EMP	PHONE	ENTRY#
Sperian Protection Usa Inc (DH)	Smithfield	RI	E	401 232-1200	16731

MEDICAL & SURGICAL SPLYS: Foot Appliances, Orthopedic

	CITY	ST	EMP	PHONE	ENTRY#
Allied Orthotic Inc	Londonderry	NH	G	603 434-7722	14730
AF Group Inc	Lincoln	RI	C	401 757-3910	16117
Atlantic Footcare Inc	North Smithfield	RI	D	401 568-4918	16318

MEDICAL & SURGICAL SPLYS: Gynecological Splys & Appliances

	CITY	ST	EMP	PHONE	ENTRY#
Coopersurgical Inc	Trumbull	CT	G	203 601-5200	3715
Coopersurgical Inc (DH)	Trumbull	CT	C	203 601-5200	3716

MEDICAL & SURGICAL SPLYS: Ligatures

	CITY	ST	EMP	PHONE	ENTRY#
Ethicon Inc	Southington	CT	B	860 621-9111	3208

MEDICAL & SURGICAL SPLYS: Limbs, Artificial

	CITY	ST	EMP	PHONE	ENTRY#
Stride Inc	Middlebury	CT	F	203 758-8307	1721
Maine Artfl Limb Orthotics Co	Portland	ME	F	207 773-4963	5236

MEDICAL & SURGICAL SPLYS: Models, Anatomical

	CITY	ST	EMP	PHONE	ENTRY#
Chamberlain Group LLC	Great Barrington	MA	F	413 528-7744	8975

MEDICAL & SURGICAL SPLYS: Orthopedic Appliances

	CITY	ST	EMP	PHONE	ENTRY#
Brownmed Inc (PA)	Boston	MA	E	857 317-3354	6626
Fleming Industries Inc	Chicopee	MA	E	413 593-3300	8033
Myomo Inc (PA)	Boston	MA	D	617 996-9058	6900
Ocean Orthopedic Services Inc (PA)	Hopkinton	MA	F	401 725-5240	9338
Omni Life Science Inc (DH)	Raynham	MA	E	508 824-2444	11595
Rogerson Orthopedic Appls Inc	Boston	MA	F	617 268-1135	7011
Rph Enterprises Inc	Franklin	MA	D	508 238-3351	8860
Pine Tree Orthopedic Lab Inc	Livermore Falls	ME	F	207 897-5558	5025
Cg Holdings LLC (PA)	Manchester	NH	E	603 623-3344	14827
New England Brace Co Inc (PA)	Concord	NH	F	508 588-6060	14148
Poly-Vac Inc	Manchester	NH	C	603 647-7822	14912
Yankee Medical Inc (DH)	Burlington	VT	F	802 863-4591	17164

MEDICAL & SURGICAL SPLYS: Personal Safety Eqpt

	CITY	ST	EMP	PHONE	ENTRY#
Angel Guard Products Inc	Worcester	MA	G	508 791-1073	13699
Honeywell Data Instruments Inc	Acton	MA	E	978 264-9550	5754
Lovepop Inc (PA)	Boston	MA	G	888 687-9589	6864
Galvion Ltd (HQ)	Portsmouth	NH	F	514 739-4444	15392
Simply Safer Products LLC	Providence	RI	F	401 474-4957	16611
Summer Infant Inc (HQ)	Woonsocket	RI	C	401 671-6550	16975

MEDICAL & SURGICAL SPLYS: Prosthetic Appliances

	CITY	ST	EMP	PHONE	ENTRY#
Cohen Slvstri Rogoff Hammer PC	Boston	MA	E	617 426-6011	6661
Freudenberg Medical LLC	Beverly	MA	C	978 281-2023	6349
Hood E Benson Laboratories	Pembroke	MA	F	781 826-7573	11367
Next Step Bnics Prsthetics Inc (PA)	Manchester	NH	F	603 668-3831	14901
New England Orthopedics Inc (PA)	Warwick	RI	G	401 739-9838	16841
Biomedic Appliances Inc	Essex Junction	VT	G	802 878-0930	17228

MEDICAL & SURGICAL SPLYS: Splints, Pneumatic & Wood

	CITY	ST	EMP	PHONE	ENTRY#
Gzsl Corp	North Attleboro	MA	E	508 695-0727	10872

MEDICAL EQPT REPAIR SVCS, NON-ELECTRIC

	CITY	ST	EMP	PHONE	ENTRY#
Inert Corporation	Amesbury	MA	E	978 462-4415	5837

MEDICAL EQPT: Cardiographs

	CITY	ST	EMP	PHONE	ENTRY#
Mobile Sense Technologies Inc	Darien	CT	F	203 914-5375	852

MEDICAL EQPT: Diagnostic

	CITY	ST	EMP	PHONE	ENTRY#
Star Equity Holdings Inc (PA)	Old Greenwich	CT	D	203 489-9500	2635
Allm USA Inc	Cambridge	MA	F	857 209-5065	7477
GTC Falcon Inc	Plymouth	MA	F	508 746-0200	11462
Microvision Inc (PA)	Seabrook	NH	E	603 474-5566	15598
Verichem Laboratories Inc	Providence	RI	G	401 461-0180	16638

MEDICAL EQPT: Electromedical Apparatus

	CITY	ST	EMP	PHONE	ENTRY#
Ram Technologies LLC	Guilford	CT	F	203 453-3916	1403
Tomtec Inc	Hamden	CT	D	203 281-6790	1460
Abiomed Inc (HQ)	Danvers	MA	B	978 646-1400	8157
Belmont Instrument LLC (PA)	Billerica	MA	E	978 663-0212	6409
Beta Bionics Inc	Concord	MA	E	855 745-3800	8105
Cardiovascular Instrument Corp	Wakefield	MA	F	781 245-7799	12504
Excelitas Tech Holdg Corp	Waltham	MA	A	781 522-5914	12671
Mevion Medical Systems Inc (PA)	Littleton	MA	C	978 486-1006	9825

MEDICAL EQPT: Electrotherapeutic Apparatus

	CITY	ST	EMP	PHONE	ENTRY#
Micron Solutions Inc (PA)	Fitchburg	MA	E	978 345-5000	8666
Quanttus Inc	Newton	MA	G	617 401-2648	10778
Cosman Medical LLC	Marlborough	MA	D	781 272-6561	10137

MEDICAL EQPT: Heart & Lung

	CITY	ST	EMP	PHONE	ENTRY#
Innovheart US Inc	Newton	MA	F	858 349-8652	10763

MEDICAL EQPT: Ultrasonic Scanning Devices

	CITY	ST	EMP	PHONE	ENTRY#
Arteriocyte Med Systems Inc	Hopkinton	MA	C	508 395-5998	9307
Axiomed Spine Corporation (PA)	Malden	MA	F	978 232-3900	10003
Bioview (usa) Inc	Billerica	MA	G	978 670-4741	6410
Clozex Medical Inc	West Bridgewater	MA	G	781 237-1673	12969
Henke Sass Wolf America Inc	Dudley	MA	D	508 671-9300	8318
Interlace Medical Inc	Marlborough	MA	E	800 442-9892	10166
Neutron Therapeutics LLC	Danvers	MA	E	978 777-0846	8212
US Biochips Corp	Waban	MA	G	617 504-5502	12497

MEDICAL EQPT: Ultrasonic, Exc Cleaning

	CITY	ST	EMP	PHONE	ENTRY#
Innovatorslink Corporation	Groton	CT	G	860 446-8058	1374
Biolucent LLC	Marlborough	MA	F	508 263-2900	10116
Hologic Inc (PA)	Marlborough	MA	A	508 263-2900	10159
Hologic Inc	Methuen	MA	E	508 263-2900	10334

MEDICAL EQPT: X-Ray Apparatus & Tubes, Radiographic

	CITY	ST	EMP	PHONE	ENTRY#
Lorad Corporation	Danbury	CT	F	203 790-5544	778
Qsa Global Inc (HQ)	Burlington	MA	D	781 272-2000	7416

MEDICAL EQPT: X-Ray Apparatus & Tubes, Therapeutic

	CITY	ST	EMP	PHONE	ENTRY#
Finch Therapeutics Inc	Somerville	MA	D	617 229-6499	11872

MEDICAL SUNDRIES: Rubber

	CITY	ST	EMP	PHONE	ENTRY#
Acutek Adhesive Specialties	Windsor	CT	F	310 419-0190	4254
Cataki International Inc	Wareham	MA	F	508 295-9630	12833
Cara Incorporated	East Greenwich	RI	G	401 732-6535	15976

MEDICAL SVCS ORGANIZATION

	CITY	ST	EMP	PHONE	ENTRY#
C S M S-I P A	North Haven	CT	G	203 562-7228	2397
Simulconsult Inc	Chestnut Hill	MA	G	617 566-5383	8001

MEDICAL, DENTAL & HOSP EQPT, WHOLESALE: X-ray Film & Splys

	CITY	ST	EMP	PHONE	ENTRY#
Fujifilm Hlthcare Amricas Corp (DH)	Lexington	MA	C	203 324-2000	9743

MEDICAL, DENTAL & HOSPITAL EQPT, WHOL: Surgical Eqpt & Splys

	CITY	ST	EMP	PHONE	ENTRY#
Boston Endo-Surgical Tech LLC	Bridgeport	CT	B	203 336-6479	303
Precision Engineered Pdts LLC	Bridgeport	CT	G	203 336-6479	361
Boston Medical Products Inc	Shrewsbury	MA	E	508 898-9300	11829
Image Stream Medical Inc	Littleton	MA	D	978 486-8494	9818

MEMBERSHIP ORGANIZATIONS, BUSINESS: Growers' Association

	CITY	ST	EMP	PHONE	ENTRY#
Decas Cranberry Products Inc (PA)	Carver	MA	E	508 866-8506	7853

MEMBERSHIP ORGANIZATIONS, PROFESSIONAL: Accounting Assoc

	CITY	ST	EMP	PHONE	ENTRY#
Financial Accnting Foundation (PA)	Norwalk	CT	C	203 847-0700	2500

MEMBERSHIP ORGANIZATIONS, PROFESSIONAL: Health Association

	CITY	ST	EMP	PHONE	ENTRY#
Massachusetts Medical Society	Boston	MA	E	617 734-9800	6874

MEMBERSHIP ORGANIZATIONS, REL: Churches, Temples & Shrines

	CITY	ST	EMP	PHONE	ENTRY#
A Guideposts Church Corp (PA)	Danbury	CT	C	203 749-0203	699

MEMBERSHIP ORGS, RELIGIOUS: Non-Denominational Church

	CITY	ST	EMP	PHONE	ENTRY#
Community of Jesus Inc (PA)	Orleans	MA	E	508 255-1094	11237

MEMBERSHIP SPORTS & RECREATION CLUBS

	CITY	ST	EMP	PHONE	ENTRY#
Southern Maine Atv Club	North Berwick	ME	G	207 676-1152	5113

MEN'S & BOYS' CLOTHING STORES

	CITY	ST	EMP	PHONE	ENTRY#
Sickday Inc	Wellfleet	MA	F	508 214-4158	12953
Top Half Inc	Tyngsboro	MA	F	978 454-5440	12468
Nomad Communications Inc	White River Junction	VT	F	802 649-1995	17709

MEN'S & BOYS' CLOTHING WHOLESALERS, NEC

	CITY	ST	EMP	PHONE	ENTRY#
Accurate Services Inc	Fall River	MA	E	508 674-5773	8518
Advanced Print Technology Inc	Fitchburg	MA	G	978 342-0093	8640
Top Half Inc	Tyngsboro	MA	F	978 454-5440	12468
New York Accessory Group Inc	Bristol	RI	D	401 245-6096	15776

P R O D U C T

	CITY	ST	EMP	PHONE	ENTRY#

MEN'S & BOYS' HOSIERY WHOLESALERS

Cabot Hosiery Mills Inc (PA)	Northfield	VT	D	802 485-6066	17432

MEN'S & BOYS' SPORTSWEAR CLOTHING STORES

Arocam Inc	Taunton	MA	F	508 822-1220	12319
Chuck Roast Equipment Inc (PA)	Conway	NH	F	603 447-5492	14178
Spirit Recognition Inc (PA)	Pawtucket	RI	F	401 722-6400	16417

MERCHANDISING MACHINE OPERATORS: Vending

Coca-Cola Bottling Company of Southeastern New England Inc (DH)	Waterford	CT	F	860 443-2816	3987
Thomson Service Corp	Franklin	MA	F	508 528-2000	8872

METAL COMPONENTS: Prefabricated

Rwt Corporation	Madison	CT	E	203 245-2731	1568
Welding Works Inc	Madison	CT	E	203 245-2731	1576
Green Brothers Fabricating (PA)	Taunton	MA	E	508 880-3608	12339
Marzilli Machine Co	Fall River	MA	E	508 567-4145	8574

METAL FINISHING SVCS

Mikro Industrial Finishing Co	Vernon	CT	G	860 875-6357	3754
PYC Deborring LLC F/K/A C &	Berlin	CT	E	860 828-6806	82
Bay State Plating Inc	Holyoke	MA	G	413 533-6927	9243
Purecoat International LLC	Belmont	MA	E	561 844-0100	6309
Mid-Cape Restoration Inc	Hollis Center	ME	F	207 929-4759	4894
Impreglon Inc	Woonsocket	RI	F	401 766-3353	16965

METAL MINING SVCS

Liberty Mtals Min Holdings LLC	Boston	MA	F	617 654-4374	6857
Polymetallurgical LLC	North Attleboro	MA	D	508 695-9312	10883
Buckeye Blasting Corporation	Epsom	NH	G	603 736-4681	14279
Forthill Resources LLC	Providence	RI	F	617 849-0768	16519

METAL OXIDE SILICONE OR MOS DEVICES

Fairchild Semiconductor Corp (DH)	South Portland	ME	B	207 775-8100	5502

METAL SERVICE CENTERS & OFFICES

Alloy Specialties LLC	Manchester	CT	E	860 646-4587	1585
M Cubed Technologies Inc (HQ)	Newtown	CT	E	203 304-2940	2341
Scott Metal Finishing LLC	Bristol	CT	F	860 589-3778	496
Smm New England Corporation	New Haven	CT	E	203 777-7445	2201
St Liquidation Corporation	Southington	CT	E	860 628-9090	3234
Titanium Metals Corporation	East Windsor	CT	C	860 627-7051	1088
Mersen USA Ep Corp (HQ)	Newburyport	MA	D	978 462-6662	10699
Portland Stone Ware Co Inc (PA)	Dracut	MA	E	978 459-7272	8311
Wakefield Engineering	Fall River	MA	G	603 417-8310	8624
New England Small Tube Corp	Litchfield	NH	D	603 429-1600	14713

METAL STAMPING, FOR THE TRADE

A & D Components Inc	Bristol	CT	G	860 582-9541	389
Acme Monaco Corporation (PA)	New Britain	CT	C	860 224-1349	1995
Arcade Technology LLC	Bridgeport	CT	D	203 366-3871	297
Arrow Manufacturing Company	Bristol	CT	E		397
Atlas Stamping & Mfg Corp	Newington	CT	E	860 757-3233	2273
Avna Inc (PA)	New Britain	CT	C	860 225-8707	2004
Barlow Metal Stamping Inc	Bristol	CT	E	860 583-1387	403
Barnes Group Inc (PA)	Bristol	CT	E	860 583-7070	406
Ben-Art Manufacturing Co Inc	Prospect	CT	G	203 758-4435	2829
Berkley Associates Inc	Waterbury	CT	E	203 757-9221	3890
Bessette Holdings Inc	East Hartford	CT	E	860 289-6000	975
Blase Manufacturing Company (PA)	Stratford	CT	E	203 375-5646	3520
Bml Tool & Mfg Corp	Monroe	CT	D	203 880-9485	1907
Bridgeport Tl & Stamping Corp	Bridgeport	CT	E	203 336-2501	305
Bristol Tool & Die Company	Bristol	CT	F	860 582-2577	423
Cly-Del Manufacturing Company	Waterbury	CT	C	203 574-2100	3898
Companion Industries Inc	Southington	CT	D	860 628-0504	3207
Component Engineers Inc	Wallingford	CT	D	203 269-0557	3791
Connectcut Spring Stmping Corp	Farmington	CT	B	860 677-1341	1212
Cowles Stamping Inc	North Haven	CT	E	203 865-3117	2406
Demsey Manufacturing Co Inc	Watertown	CT	E	860 274-6209	4008
Eyelet Design Inc	Waterbury	CT	D	203 754-4141	3911
Eyelet Toolmakers Inc	Watertown	CT	D	860 274-5423	4012
Four Star Manufacturing Co	Bristol	CT	E	860 583-1614	448
Gem Manufacturing LLC	Waterbury	CT	D	203 574-1466	3914
Gemco Manufacturing Co Inc	Southington	CT	E	860 628-5529	3211
Globe Tool & Met Stampg Co Inc	Southington	CT	E	860 621-6807	3213
H&T Waterbury Inc	Waterbury	CT	C	203 574-2240	3916
Hob Industries Inc	Cheshire	CT	E	203 879-3028	599
Hobson and Motzer Incorporated (PA)	Durham	CT	C	860 349-1756	901
Howard Engineering LLC	Naugatuck	CT	E	203 729-5213	1963
ITW Highland Manufacturing Inc	Waterbury	CT	D	203 574-3200	3923

	CITY	ST	EMP	PHONE	ENTRY#
J&J Precision Inc	Thomaston	CT	D	860 283-8243	3622
Joma Incorporated	Waterbury	CT	E	203 759-0848	3926
Lawrence Holdings Inc	Wallingford	CT	F	203 949-1600	3826
Marion Manufacturing Company	Cheshire	CT	E	203 272-5376	605
Mastercraft Tool and Mch Co	Southington	CT	F	860 628-5551	3220
Maurer Metalcraft Inc	Orange	CT	G	203 799-8800	2676
McM Stamping Corporation	Danbury	CT	E	203 792-3080	783
McMullin Manufacturing Corp	Brookfield	CT	E	203 740-3360	529
Metalform Acquisition LLC (PA)	New Britain	CT	F	860 224-2630	2043
Metallon Inc	Thomaston	CT	E	860 283-8265	3624
MJM Marga LLC	Naugatuck	CT	G	203 729-0600	1973
Mohawk Manufacturing Company	Middletown	CT	F	860 632-2345	1766
National Die Company	Wolcott	CT	G	203 879-1408	4370
National Spring & Stamping Inc	Thomaston	CT	F	860 283-0203	3625
Oscar Jobs	Bristol	CT	G	860 583-7834	477
Owen Tool and Mfg Co Inc	Southington	CT	G	860 628-6540	3227
P&G Metal Components Corp	Bloomfield	CT	F	860 243-2220	199
Pr-Mx Holdings Company LLC (HQ)	Shelton	CT	D	203 925-0012	3051
Precision Resource Inc (PA)	Shelton	CT	C	203 925-0012	3053
Preferred Tool & Die Inc (PA)	Shelton	CT	E	203 925-8525	3054
Prospect Machine Products Inc	Prospect	CT	F	203 758-4448	2840
Richards Metal Products Inc	Wolcott	CT	F	203 879-2555	4374
Satellite Aerospace Inc	Manchester	CT	E	860 643-2771	1635
Solla Eyelet Products Inc	Watertown	CT	E	860 274-5729	4030
Southington Tool & Mfg Corp	Plantsville	CT	E	860 276-0021	2796
Spirol International Corp (HQ)	Danielson	CT	C	860 774-8571	844
Spirol Intl Holdg Corp (PA)	Danielson	CT	C	860 774-8571	845
Stevens Company Incorporated	Thomaston	CT	D	860 283-8201	3631
Stewart Efi LLC	Thomaston	CT	F	860 283-2523	3632
Stewart Efi LLC (PA)	Thomaston	CT	C	860 283-8213	3633
Stewart Efi Connecticut LLC	Thomaston	CT	C	860 283-8213	3634
Taco Fasteners Inc	Plainville	CT	F	860 747-5597	2782
Target Custom Manufacturing Co	Haddam	CT	G	860 388-5848	1410
The Lyons Tool & Die Company	Meriden	CT	E	203 238-2689	1707
The Romatic Manufacturing Company	Southbury	CT	C	203 264-8203	3199
Tiger Enterprises Inc	Plantsville	CT	E	860 621-9155	2798
Truelove & Maclean Inc	Watertown	CT	C	860 274-9600	4034
Wces Inc	Waterbury	CT	F	203 573-1325	3983
Weimann Brothers Mfg Co	Derby	CT	F	203 735-3311	894
Aero Manufacturing Corp	Beverly	MA	D	978 720-1000	6323
Astron Inc (PA)	Pepperell	MA	E	978 433-9500	11383
Brainin-Advance Industries LLC (HQ)	Attleboro	MA	C	508 226-1200	5998
Carlstrom Pressed Metal Co Inc	Westborough	MA	E	508 366-4472	13086
Charles A Richardson Inc	Mansfield	MA	E	508 339-8600	10041
Crystal Engineering Co Inc (PA)	Newburyport	MA	F	978 465-7007	10677
Deltran Inc	Attleboro Falls	MA	F	508 699-7506	6083
Elite Metal Fabricators Inc	Ludlow	MA	G	413 547-2588	9944
Enjet Aero Malden LLC	Malden	MA	D	781 321-0366	10013
Excel Tool & Die Co Inc	Quincy	MA	E	617 472-0473	11516
Fraen Corporation (PA)	Reading	MA	C	781 205-5300	11601
Fraen Corporation	Woburn	MA	D	781 937-8825	13570
Hi-Tech Inc	Attleboro	MA	F	401 454-4086	6023
International Metal Pdts Inc	Chicopee	MA	E	413 532-2411	8040
Interplex Etch Logic LLC	Attleboro	MA	E	508 399-6810	6025
Killeen Machine and TI Co Inc	Auburn	MA	D	508 754-1714	6118
Larson Tool & Stamping Company	Attleboro	MA	D	508 222-0897	6031
Matrix Metal Products Inc	Attleboro	MA	F	508 226-2374	6035
New England Metalform Inc	Plainville	MA	E	508 695-9340	11441
Norking Company Inc	Attleboro	MA	E	508 222-3100	6043
Norpin Mfg Co Inc	Wilbraham	MA	F	413 599-1628	13362
P M S Manufactured Pdts Inc	Gloucester	MA	F	978 281-2600	8950
Paramount Tool LLC	Fall River	MA	E	508 672-0844	8594
Pep Industries LLC	Attleboro	MA	F	508 226-5600	6046
Peter Forg Manufacturing Co	Somerville	MA	F	617 625-0337	11888
Precision Engineered Pdts LLC (DH)	Attleboro	MA	G		6051
Replica Works Inc	Orange	MA	E	978 544-7000	11231
Shawmut Engineering Company	Wrentham	MA	F	508 850-9500	13845
Skg Associates Inc	Dedham	MA	G	781 878-7250	8250
Springfield Spring Corporation (PA)	East Longmeadow	MA	E	413 525-6837	8395
Thomas Smith Company Inc	Worcester	MA	E	508 792-5000	13812
Tiberio Manufacturing Corp	Holliston	MA	D	508 429-4011	9232
Timco Corporation	Stoughton	MA	F	781 821-1041	12243
United Tool & Machine Corp (PA)	Lawrence	MA	E	978 658-5500	9607
Universal Tool & Stamping Inc	Springfield	MA	A	413 732-4807	12145
Valentine Tool & Stamping Inc	Norton	MA	E	508 285-6911	11137
Whitman Tool & Die Company Inc	Whitman	MA	E	781 447-0421	13354
Worcester Manufacturing Inc	Worcester	MA	E	508 756-0301	13830
Numberall Stamp & Tool Co	Sangerville	ME	F	207 876-3541	5420
Laird Technologies Inc	Manchester	NH	E	603 627-7877	14875
New England Industries Inc	Lebanon	NH	E	603 448-5330	14696
New Hampshire Stamping Co Inc	Goffstown	NH	E	603 641-1234	14352
Stamping Technologies Inc	Laconia	NH	F	603 524-5958	14671

2024 Harris New England
Manufacturers Directory

(G-0000) Company's Geographic Section entry number

	CITY	ST	EMP	PHONE	ENTRY#
Sunset Tool Inc	Keene	NH	E	603 355-2246	14623
Wilton Pressed Metals	Newport	NH	G	603 863-1488	15241
Angelo Di Maria Inc	Providence	RI	E	401 274-0100	16472
Atamian Manufacturing Corp	Providence	RI	E	401 944-9614	16477
C Sjoberg & Son Inc	Cranston	RI	F	401 461-8220	15838
Crest Manufacturing Company	Lincoln	RI	F	401 333-1350	16129
Crystal Stamping LLC	Pawtucket	RI	F	401 724-5880	16361
Csc Inc	Pawtucket	RI	F	401 724-5880	16362
Demaich Industries Inc	Johnston	RI	F	401 944-3576	16080
Eastern Manufacturing Company	North Providence	RI	F	401 231-8330	16301
Etco Incorporated (PA)	Warwick	RI	D	401 467-2400	16815
Evans Findings Company Inc	East Providence	RI	E	401 434-5600	16018
Ferguson Perforating Company (DH)	Providence	RI	F	401 941-8876	16518
Interplex Industries Inc (DH)	Rumford	RI	F	401 434-6543	16672
Ira Green Inc (PA)	Providence	RI	C	800 663-7487	16543
Morris & Broms LLC	Johnston	RI	F	401 781-3134	16098
Quality Stamping	Providence	RI	G	401 272-7760	16598
Tercat Tool and Die Co II Inc	Providence	RI	E	401 421-3371	16620
Heb Manufacturing Company Inc	Chelsea	VT	E	802 685-4821	17178
New England Precision Inc	Randolph	VT	D	800 293-4112	17471

METAL STAMPINGS: Perforated

	CITY	ST	EMP	PHONE	ENTRY#
Excel Spring & Stamping LLC	Bristol	CT	G	860 585-1495	444
Hylie Products Incorporated	Cheshire	CT	E	203 439-8786	600
New Can Company Inc (HQ)	Holbrook	MA	E	330 928-1191	9181

METAL TREATING COMPOUNDS

	CITY	ST	EMP	PHONE	ENTRY#
Technic Inc (PA)	Cranston	RI	C	401 781-6100	15919

METAL: Battery

	CITY	ST	EMP	PHONE	ENTRY#
6k Energy LLC	North Andover	MA	F	978 258-1645	10815
Ascend Elements Inc (PA)	Westborough	MA	G	508 936-7701	13077

METALS SVC CENTERS & WHOLESALERS: Bars, Metal

	CITY	ST	EMP	PHONE	ENTRY#
Fox Steel Products LLC	Orange	CT	F	203 799-2356	2669

METALS SVC CENTERS & WHOLESALERS: Cable, Wire

	CITY	ST	EMP	PHONE	ENTRY#
Loos & Co Inc (PA)	Pomfret	CT	B	860 928-7981	2809
Tsmc Inc	Torrington	CT	A	860 283-8265	3703

METALS SVC CENTERS & WHOLESALERS: Ferrous Metals

	CITY	ST	EMP	PHONE	ENTRY#
I2s LLC	Wallingford	CT	C	203 265-5684	3816

METALS SVC CENTERS & WHOLESALERS: Forgings, Ferrous

	CITY	ST	EMP	PHONE	ENTRY#
A A A Metals Company Inc	Hanson	MA	F	781 447-1220	9049

METALS SVC CENTERS & WHOLESALERS: Foundry Prdts

	CITY	ST	EMP	PHONE	ENTRY#
KW Thompson Tool Company Inc	Rochester	NH	D	603 330-8670	15483

METALS SVC CENTERS & WHOLESALERS: Pipe & Tubing, Steel

	CITY	ST	EMP	PHONE	ENTRY#
International Pipe & Stl Corp	North Branford	CT	F	203 481-7102	2369
Stephens Pipe & Steel LLC	Manchester	CT	D	877 777-8721	1639
Microgroup Inc	Medway	MA	C	508 533-4925	10308
Capitol Fire Protection Co Inc	Loudon	NH	E	603 783-4713	14794

METALS SVC CENTERS & WHOLESALERS: Sheets, Metal

	CITY	ST	EMP	PHONE	ENTRY#
Aerospace Alloys Inc	Bloomfield	CT	D	860 882-0019	144
Innovative Designs & Disp Inc	Hatfield	MA	F	413 586-9854	9072

METALS SVC CENTERS & WHOLESALERS: Steel

	CITY	ST	EMP	PHONE	ENTRY#
American Metals Coal Intl Inc (HQ)	Greenwich	CT	F	203 625-9200	1311
ATI Flat Rlled Pdts Hldngs LLC	Waterbury	CT	F	203 756-7414	3888
Contractors Steel Supply Inc	North Haven	CT	F	203 782-1221	2400
Eastern Metal Works Inc	Milford	CT	E	203 878-6995	1821
Magna Steel Sales Inc	Beacon Falls	CT	F	203 888-0300	42
Baxter Inc	West Yarmouth	MA	F	508 775-0375	13072
Bradford Steel Co Inc	East Freetown	MA	F	508 763-5921	8363
Diversified Metals Inc	Monson	MA	D	413 267-5101	10455
Moor Metals Inc (PA)	Holliston	MA	G	508 429-9446	9224
Rebars & Mesh Inc	Haverhill	MA	E	978 374-2244	9126
Special Metals Corporation	Worcester	MA	D	270 365-9551	13804
Thompson Steel Company Inc	Canton	MA	C	781 828-8800	7834
Bangor Steel Service Inc	Bangor	ME	E	207 947-2773	4494
Nucor Hrris Rbar Northeast LLC	Canaan	NH	D	603 632-5222	14047

METALS SVC CENTERS & WHOLESALERS: Tubing, Metal

	CITY	ST	EMP	PHONE	ENTRY#
Vita Needle Company	Needham	MA	E	781 444-1780	10529
Micro Bends Corp	Peterborough	NH	G	603 924-0022	15318
Raymond Gadues Inc	Swanton	VT	E	802 868-2033	17641

METALS: Precious NEC

	CITY	ST	EMP	PHONE	ENTRY#
Bal International Inc	Stamford	CT	E	203 359-6775	3290
Northeastern Metals Corp	Stamford	CT	G	203 348-8088	3419
Glines & Rhodes Inc	Attleboro	MA	E	508 226-2000	6021
Metalor USA Refining Corp (DH)	North Attleboro	MA	C	508 699-9800	10877
Spindle City Precious Metals	Somerset	MA	G	508 567-1597	11855
Junora Ltd	Biddeford	ME	F	207 284-4900	4573
Apogee Coins Precious Mtls LLC	Manchester	NH	E	603 391-6417	14813
Colt Refining Inc (PA)	Merrimack	NH	E	603 429-9966	14978
Harding Metals Inc	Northwood	NH	E	603 942-5573	15273
Advanced Chemical Company	Warwick	RI	E	401 785-3434	16776
Geib Refining Corporation	Warwick	RI	E	401 738-8560	16817

METALS: Precious, Secondary

	CITY	ST	EMP	PHONE	ENTRY#
Pease & Curren Incorporated	Warwick	RI	E	401 738-6449	16844

METALS: Primary Nonferrous, NEC

	CITY	ST	EMP	PHONE	ENTRY#
Ulbrich Stainless Steels	Wallingford	CT	C	203 269-2507	3871
Aspen Systems LLC (PA)	Marlborough	MA	F	508 281-5322	10112
Cabot Corporation (PA)	Boston	MA	C	617 345-0100	6631
Cabot Corporation	Haverhill	MA	C	978 556-8400	9084
Global Advanced Metals USA Inc (PA)	Wellesley Hills	MA	F	781 996-7300	12951
HC Starck Tungsten LLC	Auburndale	MA	E	617 630-4843	6136
J T Inman Co Inc	Attleboro Falls	MA	E	508 226-0080	6088
Newton Materion Inc (HQ)	Newton	MA	C	617 630-5800	10772
Medalist Corp	Burnham	ME	E	615 620-8280	4660

METALWORK: Miscellaneous

	CITY	ST	EMP	PHONE	ENTRY#
Aerospace Alloys Inc	Bloomfield	CT	D	860 882-0019	144
Boudreaus Welding Co Inc	Dayville	CT	F	860 774-2771	860
C & S Engineering Inc	Meriden	CT	F	203 235-5727	1657
Conntech Products Corporation	Cheshire	CT	E	203 272-2261	581
Engineered Building Pdts Inc	Bloomfield	CT	E	860 243-1110	161
Quality Engineering Svcs Inc	Wallingford	CT	E	203 269-5054	3843
Simpson Strong-Tie Company Inc	Enfield	CT	D	860 741-8923	1152
The Carby Corporation	Watertown	CT	E	860 274-6741	4032
Artisan Industries Inc	Stoughton	MA	D	781 893-6800	12195
Cdp Manufacturing LLC	Brockton	MA	F	508 588-6400	7267
Marblehead Engineering	Essex	MA	F	978 432-1386	8477
Mill City Iron Fabricators	Dracut	MA	F	978 957-6833	8309
Schrimpf Wldg Fabrication Inc	Woburn	MA	G	339 298-2311	13661
Megguier & Jones Inc	Topsham	ME	E	207 799-8555	5550
Nucor Hrris Rbar Northeast LLC	Canaan	NH	D	603 632-5222	14047
Ne Steel Fabricators LLC	Cranston	RI	E	401 785-1234	15898

METALWORK: Ornamental

	CITY	ST	EMP	PHONE	ENTRY#
Connecticut Iron Works Inc	Greenwich	CT	G	203 869-0657	1327
Garden Iron LLC	Westbrook	CT	G	860 767-9917	4138
United Steel Inc	East Hartford	CT	C	860 289-2323	1032
Boston Steel Fabricators Inc	Holbrook	MA	G	781 767-1540	9170
Brayton Wilson Cole Corp	Hingham	MA	E	781 803-6624	9144
Quinn Bros of Essex Inc	Essex	MA	E	978 768-6929	8479

METALWORKING MACHINERY WHOLESALERS

	CITY	ST	EMP	PHONE	ENTRY#
N Ferrara Inc	Somerset	MA	F	508 679-2440	11853

METERING DEVICES: Water Quality Monitoring & Control Systems

	CITY	ST	EMP	PHONE	ENTRY#
Danaher Tool Group	Wallingford	CT	D	203 284-7000	3799
Ecochlor Inc	North Haven	CT	D	978 298-1463	2408
E Gs Gauging Incorporated	Wilmington	MA	G	978 262-3100	13404
Evoqua Water Technologies LLC	Tewksbury	MA	E	978 863-4600	12397
Water Analytics Inc	Andover	MA	F	978 749-9949	5934

METERS: Turbine Flow, Indl Process

	CITY	ST	EMP	PHONE	ENTRY#
Hamilton Sundstrand Corp (HQ)	Windsor Locks	CT	A	619 714-9442	4330

MICA PRDTS

	CITY	ST	EMP	PHONE	ENTRY#
Cogebi Inc	Dover	NH	F	603 749-6896	14223

MICROCIRCUITS, INTEGRATED: Semiconductor

	CITY	ST	EMP	PHONE	ENTRY#
Carten-Fujikin Incorporated	Cheshire	CT	F	203 699-2134	578
ABB Enterprise Software Inc	Boston	MA	E	617 574-1130	6502
Advanced Micro Devices Inc	Boxborough	MA	D	978 795-2500	7146
HCC Aegis Inc (DH)	New Bedford	MA	C	508 998-3141	10599
Maxim Integrated Products Inc	North Chelmsford	MA	F	978 934-7600	10983
Masimo Semiconductor Inc	Hudson	NH	E	603 595-8900	14525
Unitrode Corporation (HQ)	Manchester	NH	B	603 222-8500	14948
Xilinx Inc	Nashua	NH	F	603 891-1096	15191

MICROPHONES

	CITY	ST	EMP	PHONE	ENTRY#
Telefunken Usa LLC	South Windsor	CT	F	860 882-5919	3185

MICROPROCESSORS

	CITY	ST	EMP	PHONE	ENTRY#
Distron Corporation	Attleboro Falls	MA	C	508 695-8786	6084

P
R
O
D
U
C
T

	CITY	ST	EMP	PHONE	ENTRY#
Sparton Beckwood LLC	Plaistow	NH	D	603 382-3840	15351
Texas Instruments Incorporated	Manchester	NH	G	603 222-8500	14942

MICROSCOPES: Electron & Proton

	CITY	ST	EMP	PHONE	ENTRY#
Carl Zeiss Nts LLC (DH)	Peabody	MA	D	978 826-1500	11301
E Fjeld Co Inc	North Billerica	MA	G	978 667-1416	10909
Witec Instruments Corp	Concord	MA	F	865 690-5550	8142
Raj Communications Ltd	Essex Junction	VT	E	802 658-4961	17243

MICROWAVE COMPONENTS

	CITY	ST	EMP	PHONE	ENTRY#
Times Microwave Systems Inc (HQ)	Wallingford	CT	B	203 949-8400	3866
Accellent Acquisition Corp	Wilmington	MA	A	978 570-6900	13370
Accellent Holdings Corp	Wilmington	MA	A	978 570-6900	13371
Caes Mission Systems LLC	Woburn	MA	C	781 729-9450	13538
Delta Electronics Mfg Corp	Beverly	MA	C	978 927-1060	6345
Dss Circuits Inc	Worcester	MA	D	508 852-8061	13719
H & T Specialty Co Inc	Waltham	MA	E	781 893-3866	12689
Hxi LLC	Harvard	MA	F	978 772-7774	9064
Kevlin Corporation	Methuen	MA	C	978 689-8331	10336
Macom Technology Solutions Inc	Lowell	MA	B	978 656-2500	9899
Macom Technology Solutions Inc (HQ)	Lowell	MA	B	978 656-2500	9900
Microwave Cmpnents Systems Inc	Westborough	MA	F	508 466-8400	13121
Microwave Engineering Corp	North Andover	MA	D	978 685-2776	10844
Millitech Inc	Northampton	MA	D	413 582-9620	11073
O R M Inc	Northborough	MA	F	508 393-7054	11104
REA Associates Inc	North Billerica	MA	G	209 521-2727	10949
Smiths Interconnect Inc	Northampton	MA	D	413 582-9620	11080
Smiths Intrcnnect Americas Inc	Hudson	MA	C	978 568-0451	9413
Spectrum Microwave Inc	Marlborough	MA	D	508 485-0336	10212
Spectrum Microwave Inc	Marlborough	MA	C	508 251-6400	10213
Spectrum Microwave Inc	Marlborough	MA	A	603 459-1600	10214
Thorndike Corporation	East Bridgewater	MA	F	508 378-9797	8346
Tru Technologies Inc	Peabody	MA	F	978 532-0775	11349
Victor Microwave Inc	Wakefield	MA	E	781 245-4472	12541
Lnx Corporation	Hudson	NH	F	603 898-6800	14524
Monzite Corporation (HQ)	Nashua	NH	G	617 429-7050	15136
RH Laboratories Inc	Nashua	NH	E	603 459-5900	15159
Technical Research and Manufacturing Inc 603 627-6000	Bedford 13951	NH		NH	D
Precision Trned Cmponents Corp	Smithfield	RI	D	401 232-3377	16726

MILITARY INSIGNIA

	CITY	ST	EMP	PHONE	ENTRY#
Bryant Group Inc	Contoocook	NH	F	603 746-1166	14167
Graco Awards Manufacturing Inc	Providence	RI	F	281 255-2161	16527
International Insignia Corp	Providence	RI	D	401 784-0000	16542
Officers Equipment Company	Providence	RI	F	703 221-1912	16580

MILITARY INSIGNIA, TEXTILE

	CITY	ST	EMP	PHONE	ENTRY#
Airborne Industries Inc	Branford	CT	F	203 315-0200	232

MILK, FLUID: Wholesalers

	CITY	ST	EMP	PHONE	ENTRY#
Monument Farms Inc	Weybridge	VT	E	802 545-2119	17703

MILL PRDTS: Structural & Rail

	CITY	ST	EMP	PHONE	ENTRY#
Boudreaus Welding Co Inc	Dayville	CT	F	860 774-2771	860
Avilite LLC	Merrimack	NH	G	603 626-4388	14974

MILLING: Rice

	CITY	ST	EMP	PHONE	ENTRY#
Horizon Vert Pure LLC	Randolph	MA	F	857 236-0904	11563

MILLWORK

	CITY	ST	EMP	PHONE	ENTRY#
A-1 Stairs & Rails Llc	Danbury	CT	G	203 792-7367	700
American Wood Products	North Haven	CT	G	203 248-4433	2391
Anvil CT LLP	Oxford	CT	F	860 619-0589	2685
Atlantic Woodcraft Inc	Enfield	CT	F	860 749-4887	1121
Bergan Architectural Wdwkg Inc	Middletown	CT	E	860 346-0869	1739
Byrne Woodworking Inc	Bridgeport	CT	G	203 953-3205	308
Century Woodworking Inc	Pleasant Valley	CT	F	860 379-7538	2800
Chapman Lumber Inc	Thomaston	CT	F	860 283-6213	3616
CJS Millwork Inc	Stamford	CT	F	203 708-0080	3314
Cleary Woodwork Company Inc	Rocky Hill	CT	G	800 486-7600	2918
Colonial Wood Products Inc	West Haven	CT	G	203 932-9003	4097
Connecticut Carpentry LLC	Meriden	CT	F	203 639-8585	1661
Connecticut Millwork Inc	Vernon	CT	G	860 875-2860	3753
Curtiss Woodworking Inc	Prospect	CT	D	203 527-9305	2832
Custom Design Woodworks LLC	Old Lyme	CT	G	860 434-0515	2639
Daniel F Crapa	New Fairfield	CT	G	203 746-5706	2095
Deane Inc	Stamford	CT	E	203 327-7008	3335
Dlz Architectural Mill Work	Hartford	CT	G	860 883-7562	1476
Dooney Woodworks LLC (PA)	Cos Cob	CT	G	203 340-9770	676
Dooney Woodworks LLC	Greenwich	CT	F	203 869-5457	1328
Eco Millwork LLC	Newington	CT	F	860 266-5744	2288

	CITY	ST	EMP	PHONE	ENTRY#
Fairfield Woodworks LLC	Stratford	CT	F	203 380-9842	3535
Fcmii Inc	Bethany	CT	F	203 393-9751	93
Good Earth Millwork LLC	Westport	CT	G	203 226-7958	4170
Greenwich Fine Woodwork LLC	Norwalk	CT	F	203 987-0001	2510
Hallmark Woodworkers Inc	Bridgeport	CT	F	203 730-0535	327
Harris Enterprise Corp	Manchester	CT	E	860 649-4663	1600
Highland Woodworking LLC	Prospect	CT	F	203 758-6625	2835
Jawor Lumber Inc	Wallingford	CT	F	203 269-4431	3822
Joshua Friedman & Co LLC	New London	CT	F	860 439-1637	2229
Legacy Woodworking LLC	Middlebury	CT	G	203 592-8807	1716
Legere Group Ltd	Avon	CT	D	860 674-0392	29
Luckey LLC	New Haven	CT	F	203 747-5270	2171
Marc Woodworks LLC	Hamden	CT	G	203 281-4700	1438
McKinnon Design LLC	Plainville	CT	G	860 677-7371	2773
Nci Woodworking LLC LLC	Fairfield	CT	G	203 391-1614	1195
New England Cabinet Co	New Britain	CT	E	860 225-8645	2046
Nichols Woodworking LLC	Washington Depot	CT	E	860 350-4223	3877
Orion Manufacturing LLC	Mystic	CT	G	860 572-2921	1941
Paco Assensio Woodworking LLC	Norwalk	CT	G	203 536-2608	2550
Petrunti Design & Wdwkg LLC	West Hartford	CT	G	860 953-5332	4078
Porta Door Co	Seymour	CT	E	203 888-6191	2967
Proctor Woodworks LLC	Essex	CT	G	860 767-9881	1170
Sanders Archtctural Wdwkg LLC	Berlin	CT	G	860 682-5607	84
Shelbrack Woodworking	Simsbury	CT	F	860 431-5028	3096
Shuttercraft Inc	Madison	CT	G	203 245-2608	1571
Sorrento Fine Woodwork LLC	Wallingford	CT	F	203 741-9263	3850
White Dog Woodworking LLC	Torrington	CT	F	860 482-3776	3707
Whq Woodworks LLC	Oakville	CT	F	203 756-3011	2629
Zavarella Woodworking Inc	Newington	CT	G	860 666-6969	2335
Advanced Woodworking Tech LLC	Lowell	MA	F	978 937-1400	9851
Allen Woodworking LLC	Bellingham	MA	G	617 306-6479	6284
Amherst Woodworking & Supply Inc	Northampton	MA	E	413 584-3003	11052
Architectural Components Inc	Montague	MA	F	413 367-9441	10458
Architectural Timber Mllwk Inc	Hadley	MA	F	413 586-3045	9017
Brockway-Smith Company	West Hatfield	MA	C	413 247-9674	13004
Bwi of MA LLC	Leominster	MA	F	978 534-4065	9645
Caliper Woodworking Corp	Malden	MA	E	781 322-9760	10006
Charles River Door Works	Blackstone	MA	G	617 828-3946	6493
Continental Woodcraft Inc (PA)	Worcester	MA	E	508 581-9560	13709
Detail Millwork Inc	Waltham	MA	F	781 893-2250	12652
EJ Jaxtimer Builder Inc	Hyannis	MA	E	508 778-4911	9436
General Woodworking Inc (PA)	Lowell	MA	F	978 458-6625	9879
Glaccet Corporation	Worcester	MA	D	508 752-7356	13734
Glenns Gardening & Woodworking	Boston	MA	G	617 548-7977	6763
Gloucester Builders Inc	Charlestown	MA	E	617 241-5513	7874
Hawkes & Huberdeau Wdwkg Inc	Amesbury	MA	E	978 388-7747	5836
Holt and Bugbee Company (PA)	Tewksbury	MA	C	978 851-7201	12401
Horner Millwork Corp	Pembroke	MA	E	781 826-7770	11368
JC Clocks Company Inc	North Dartmouth	MA	E	508 998-8442	10998
Johncarlo Woodworking Inc	Westfield	MA	F	413 562-4002	13175
Joinery Shop Inc	Charlestown	MA	G	617 242-4718	7877
Joseph Muto	Westfield	MA	G	413 568-3245	13176
K & J Interiors Inc	Plymouth	MA	D	508 830-0670	11463
Kabinet Korner Inc	Malden	MA	E	781 324-9600	10017
Keiver Willard-Lumber Corp	Newburyport	MA	D	978 462-7193	10690
Kelton Woodwork Inc	Charlton	MA	F	617 997-7261	7891
Kenyon Woodworking Inc	Jamaica Plain	MA	F	617 524-6883	9502
Kramers Cstm Kitchens & Wdwkg	Holliston	MA	G	508 429-9007	9219
Leveillee Archtctral Mllwk Inc	Spencer	MA	F	508 885-9731	12062
Lloyds Woodworking Inc	Hudson	MA	G	978 562-9007	9386
Mark Richey Wdwkg & Design Inc	Newburyport	MA	D	978 499-3800	10698
Martin Interiors Inc	Hanson	MA	G	781 447-1022	9053
Meridian Custom Wdwkg Inc	Brockton	MA	E	508 587-4400	7295
Metrica Interior Inc	Northampton	MA	F	413 587-2750	11071
Mill Works	Westford	MA	G	978 692-8222	13251
ML Custom Wood Work Inc	Hyannis	MA	G	508 360-2137	9442
Muniz Custom Woodwork Inc	Everett	MA	F	617 970-3430	8496
National Lumber Company LLC (HQ)	Mansfield	MA	C	508 339-8020	10068
New England Shrlines Companies	Hanover	MA	F	781 826-0140	9037
Notch Mtn Solar Inc	Northfield	MA	G	413 498-0018	11121
Olde Bostonian	Boston	MA	G	617 282-9300	6928
Padco Inc	Worcester	MA	F	508 753-8486	13767
Payne/Bouchier Inc (PA)	Roxbury	MA	E	617 445-4323	11692
Precision Woodworking Inc	Quincy	MA	G	617 479-7604	11531
Rex Lumber Company (PA)	Acton	MA	D	800 343-0567	5762
Rgc Millwork Incorporated	Lowell	MA	G	978 275-9529	9919
Richard Cantwell Woodworking	New Bedford	MA	G	508 984-7921	10647
Rjd Woodworking LLC	Fairhaven	MA	G	508 984-4315	8513
Russo Woodworking Inc	Hyannis	MA	E	508 428-1772	9448
Russo Woodworking Inc (PA)	Marstons Mills	MA	G	908 351-2200	10248
Scotia Woodworking	Hudson	MA	G	978 212-5379	9411
Shaw Woodworking Inc	Pocasset	MA	G	508 563-1242	11492

Company	CITY	ST	EMP	PHONE	ENTRY#
Shawn Roberts Woodworking	Gilbertville	MA	G	413 477-0060	8914
South Mountain Company Inc	West Tisbury	MA	E	508 693-4850	13055
South Shore Millwork Inc	Norton	MA	D	508 226-5500	11136
Southeastern Millwork Co Inc	Sagamore Beach	MA	G	508 888-6038	11698
Southeastern Millwork Co Inc	Bourne	MA	F	508 888-6038	7142
Specialty Wholesale Sup Corp	Gardner	MA	E	978 632-1472	8901
Stephen Terhune Woodworking In	Essex	MA	G	978 768-0106	8480
Stokes Woodworking Co Inc (PA)	Hudson	MA	G	508 481-0414	9416
Tall Guy Woodworking Inc	Boston	MA	G	617 901-2166	7068
Thl-Nortek Investors LLC (PA)	Boston	MA	D	617 227-1050	7077
Toby Leary Fine Wdwkg Inc	Hyannis	MA	F	508 957-2281	9454
Trimboard Inc	Springfield	MA	E	413 886-0142	12143
Vintage Millwork Corporation	Dracut	MA	F	978 957-1400	8313
VT Industries Inc	Amesbury	MA	E	978 388-3792	5854
Walter A Furman Co Inc	Fall River	MA	D	508 674-7751	8625
Watson Brothers Inc	Middleton	MA	F	978 774-7677	10397
Wayland Millwork Corporation	Marlborough	MA	F	508 485-4172	10233
Wesco Building & Design Inc	Stoneham	MA	G	781 279-0490	12188
Wescor Ltd (PA)	Stoneham	MA	G	781 279-0490	12189
Westek Architectural Wdwkg Inc	Westfield	MA	F	413 562-6363	13217
Wide Angle Marketing Inc	Hubbardston	MA	F	978 928-5400	9349
William Green Inc	Shelburne Falls	MA	F	413 475-2014	11809
Woodcraft Designers Bldrs LLC	Canton	MA	E	508 584-4200	7842
Woodmeister Master Bldrs Inc (PA)	Holden	MA	D	774 345-1000	9196
Woodworks	Lynn	MA	G	781 596-1563	9993
Wsmd Inc	Ludlow	MA	G	413 589-0945	9957
Bangor Millwork & Supply Inc (PA)	Bangor	ME	F	207 947-6019	4491
Coastal Woodworking Inc	Nobleboro	ME	G	207 563-1072	5100
Georgia-Pacific LLC	Baileyville	ME	G	207 427-4077	4484
Jk Custom Woodworking LLC	South Bristol	ME	G	207 644-1127	5483
Mousam Valley Millwork	Springvale	ME	E	207 324-2951	5521
New England Woodworks	Springvale	ME	G	207 324-6343	5522
Northeast Mill Work Inc	Casco	ME	G	207 655-1202	4682
Pond Cove Millwork Inc	Saco	ME	E	207 773-6819	5376
Pre-Hung Doors Inc	Auburn	ME	F	207 783-3881	4455
Precision Millwork Inc	Cumberland Foreside	ME	G	207 761-3997	4713
Quarter Point Woodworking LLC (PA)	New Gloucester	ME	G	207 926-1032	5088
Quarter Point Woodworking LLC	Windham	ME	F	207 892-7022	5667
R G Eaton Woodworks Inc	Westbrook	ME	G	207 883-3398	5644
Saco Bay Millwork Co	Buxton	ME	G	207 929-8400	4664
Windham Millwork Inc	Windham	ME	D	207 892-3238	5675
Zoulamis Fine Woodworking	Gardiner	ME	G	207 449-1680	4813
Archangel Woodworks Inc	Kingston	NH	G	603 347-5345	14633
Audia Woodworking	Stratham	NH	F	603 817-1309	15633
Boulia-Gorrell Lumber Co LLC	Laconia	NH	F	603 524-1300	14648
Cw Keller & Associates LLC	Plaistow	NH	D	603 382-2028	15339
Ds Huntington Co LLC	Peterborough	NH	G	603 784-5136	15315
Forest Manufacturing Corp	Auburn	NH	F	603 647-6991	13907
Herrick Mill Work Inc	Contoocook	NH	F	603 746-5092	14170
Keller Products Incorporated	Bow	NH	F	603 224-5502	14003
Littleton Millwork Inc	Littleton	NH	E	603 444-2677	14721
Middleton Building Supply (PA)	Middleton	NH	C	603 473-2210	15008
Millwork Masters Ltd (PA)	Keene	NH	F	603 358-3038	14608
Morrill Woodworking LLC	Auburn	NH	E	603 540-3151	13911
Mountaintop Woodworking LLC	Whitefield	NH	G	603 616-1160	15699
New England Woodworkers	New Ipswich	NH	G	603 562-7200	15199
Phoenix Woodworks Inc	Gilsum	NH	G	603 812-6214	14343
Phytek Industries Inc	Bow	NH	F	603 226-4197	14007
Port-O-Lite Company Inc	West Swanzey	NH	F	603 352-3205	15696
Rochette Fmly Cstm Wdwkg & REM	Raymond	NH	G	603 895-2181	15456
Thibco Inc	Manchester	NH	G	603 623-3011	14944
Tommila Brothers Inc	Fitzwilliam	NH	F	603 242-7774	14316
Windham Wood Interiors Inc	Windham	NH	G	781 932-8572	15730
Wood Works	Portsmouth	NH	G	603 436-3805	15450
Woodworks Architectural Mllwk	Londonderry	NH	E	603 432-4050	14791
18th Century Woodworks	West Kingston	RI	G	401 829-8760	16892
BP Custom Woodworking	Cumberland	RI	G	401 787-8750	15934
Broden Millworks LLC	Middletown	RI	G	401 846-0271	16170
Brouillette Woodworking Co Inc	Barrington	RI	G	401 499-4867	15746
Cas America LLC	North Smithfield	RI	F	401 884-8556	16320
Chopmist Hill Woodworks Ltd	North Scituate	RI	G	401 374-3143	16314
Columbus Door Company	Warwick	RI	D	401 781-7792	16796
Constant Technologies Inc	North Kingstown	RI	E	800 518-7369	16240
Design Fabricators Inc	Cranston	RI	E	401 944-5294	15849
Grinnell Cabinet Makers Inc	Cranston	RI	E	401 781-1080	15871
Hope Woodworks Inc	Woonsocket	RI	G	401 497-7714	16963
Igitt Inc	Middletown	RI	F	401 841-5544	16175
Imperia Corporation	Barrington	RI	E	508 894-3000	15748
Jutras Woodworking Co	Providence	RI	G	401 949-8101	16551
K Alger Woodworking Inc	Johnston	RI	G	401 228-5254	16091
Kelmeg Woodworking	North Smithfield	RI	G	401 762-3090	16325
Millwork One Inc	Cranston	RI	D	401 738-6990	15895
Modern Industries Inc	Providence	RI	E	401 331-8000	16566
Monarch Industries Inc	Providence	RI	D	401 247-5200	16567
Orion Ret Svcs & Fixturing Inc	Smithfield	RI	D	401 334-5000	16725
Stephen C Dematrick	Narragansett	RI	G	401 789-4712	16197
T & T Woodworkers Inc	Woonsocket	RI	F	401 766-2304	16979
Village Woodturning	North Scituate	RI	G	401 647-3091	16317
Woodworking Thompson & Design	Providence	RI	G	401 369-7999	16648
Brattleboro Kiln Dry & Milling	Brattleboro	VT	F	802 254-4528	17075
Classic Dsgns By Mtthew Brak I	Saint Johnsbury	VT	E	802 748-6062	17541
Cypress Woodworks LLC	Waterbury	VT	G	802 338-0538	17673
Idry LLC	Barre	VT	G	800 406-1887	17008
Newport Furniture Parts Corp	Newport	VT	D	802 334-5428	17402
RK Miles Inc (PA)	Manchester Center	VT	C	802 362-1952	17330
Stark Mountain Woodworks Co	New Haven	VT	F	802 453-5549	17396
Vermont Furn Hardwoods Inc	Chester	VT	E	802 875-2550	17184
Wall Goldfinger Furniture	Northfield	VT	F	802 278-5823	17435
Wallgoldfinger Inc	Northfield	VT	E	802 483-4200	17436

MINE DEVELOPMENT SVCS: Nonmetallic Minerals

Company	CITY	ST	EMP	PHONE	ENTRY#
Rowe Contracting Co	Melrose	MA	G	781 620-0052	10319

MINERAL WOOL

Company	CITY	ST	EMP	PHONE	ENTRY#
Leek Building Products Inc	Norwalk	CT	E	203 853-3883	2527
Bnz Materials Inc	North Billerica	MA	C	978 663-3401	10900
Owens Corning Sales LLC	Canton	MA	G	800 438-7465	7816
Johns Manville Corporation	Lewiston	ME	E	207 784-0123	4968
Duxbury Composite Products Inc	Fitzwilliam	NH	E	603 585-9100	14313
Vemployee	Portsmouth	RI	F	888 471-1982	16460

MINERAL WOOL INSULATION PRDTS

Company	CITY	ST	EMP	PHONE	ENTRY#
Ward Process Inc	Holliston	MA	D	508 429-1165	9238

MINERALS: Ground or Treated

Company	CITY	ST	EMP	PHONE	ENTRY#
Micro-Mech Inc	Ipswich	MA	E	978 356-2966	9491
Dicaperl Minerals	Thomaston	ME	G	207 594-8225	5543
FMC Corporation	Rockland	ME	D	207 594-3200	5329
Imerys	Searsport	ME	G	207 548-0900	5455
Pike Industries Inc (DH)	Belmont	NH	E	603 527-5100	13967
Isovolta Inc	North Clarendon	VT	E	802 775-5528	17414

MINING EXPLORATION & DEVELOPMENT SVCS

Company	CITY	ST	EMP	PHONE	ENTRY#
Crown Point Excavation LLC	Springfield	VT	F	802 291-4817	17617

MISSILE GUIDANCE SYSTEMS & EQPT

Company	CITY	ST	EMP	PHONE	ENTRY#
Raytheon International Inc (PA)	Waltham	MA	F	781 522-3000	12760
Arundel Holdings Inc	Arundel	ME	D	207 985-8555	4408

MIXTURES & BLOCKS: Asphalt Paving

Company	CITY	ST	EMP	PHONE	ENTRY#
E B Asphalt & Landscaping LLC	Oakdale	CT	F	860 639-1921	2621
Firestone Building Pdts Co LLC	Bristol	CT	F	860 584-4516	447
O & G Industries Inc	Bridgeport	CT	B	203 366-4586	354
O & G Industries Inc	New Milford	CT	E	860 354-4438	2258
O & G Industries Inc	Southbury	CT	E	203 263-2195	3197
O & G Industries Inc (PA)	Torrington	CT	D	860 489-9261	3689
Tilcon Connecticut Inc (DH)	New Britain	CT	D	860 224-6010	2072
Tilcon Inc (DH)	Newington	CT	B	860 223-3651	2328
A F Amorello & Sons Inc	Worcester	MA	E	508 791-8778	13694
Brox Industries Inc (PA)	Dracut	MA	D	978 454-9105	8302
East Coast Pavers LLC	Tewksbury	MA	F	508 577-7832	12395
Fletcher Granite LLC (DH)	Westford	MA	G	978 692-1312	13238
Gem Asset Acquisition LLC	Worcester	MA	E	508 419-7710	13730
Lane Construction Corporation	Northfield	MA	D	413 498-5586	11120
Massachusetts Broken Stone Co	Holden	MA	E	508 829-5353	9193
New England Grund Slutions LLC	Gloucester	MA	G	978 203-6277	8945
Ondrick Materials & Recycl LLC	Chicopee	MA	E	413 592-2566	8052
P A Landers Inc	Hanover	MA	F	508 747-1800	9039
Palmer Paving Corporation (PA)	Palmer	MA	E	413 283-8354	11281
Peckham Enterprises LLC	Montgomery	MA	G	413 862-3252	10459
PJ Keating Company	Dracut	MA	D	978 454-7878	8310
Sbarzola Construction Corp	South Weymouth	MA	G	781 817-6485	11977
Sealmaster	Worcester	MA	G	508 926-8080	13796
Trew Corp	Deerfield	MA	F	413 773-9798	8256
Dayton Sand & Gravel Inc	Dayton	ME	D	207 499-2306	4720
F R Carroll Inc	Limerick	ME	E	207 793-8615	5001
Lane Construction Corporation	Bangor	ME	B	207 945-0850	4508
Lane Construction Corporation	Presque Isle	ME	E	207 764-4137	5301
Mattingly Products Company	North Anson	ME	E	207 635-2719	5107
Morin Brothers	Fort Kent	ME	E	207 834-5455	4790
Pike Industries Inc	Wells	ME	F	207 676-9973	5604
Pike Industries Inc	Gorham	NH	F	603 466-2772	14361
Pike Industries Inc	Portsmouth	NH	G	603 436-4432	15429

Employee Codes: A=Over 500 employees, B=251-500
C=101-250, D=51-100, E=20-50, F=10-19, G=1-9

2024 Harris New England
Manufacturers Directory

1431

PRODUCT

	CITY	ST	EMP	PHONE	ENTRY#
Hudson Liquid Asphalts Inc (PA)	Cranston	RI	D	401 274-2200	15874
JH Lynch & Sons Inc	East Providence	RI	F	401 434-7100	16025
Narragansett Improvement Co (PA)	Providence	RI	D	401 331-0051	16571
Pavement Warehouse	Greenville	RI	G	401 233-3200	16062
Perry Paving	Warwick	RI	G	401 732-1730	16845
Watson Materials	East Greenwich	RI	G	401 885-0600	15997
Peckham Industries Inc	Shaftsbury	VT	F	802 442-4418	17552
Pike Industries Inc	Williston	VT	G	802 658-0453	17744

MOBILE COMMUNICATIONS EQPT

	CITY	ST	EMP	PHONE	ENTRY#
Latino Multiservice LLC	New Haven	CT	G	203 691-9715	2168
Links Point Inc	Norwalk	CT	E	203 853-4600	2528
Benu Networks Inc	Burlington	MA	F	978 223-4700	7340
Comrex Corporation	Devens	MA	F	978 784-1776	8272
Edge Velocity Corporation	Salem	NH	G	603 912-5618	15519
Kvh Industries Inc	Middletown	RI	C	401 847-3327	16176
Kvh Industries Inc (PA)	Middletown	RI	C	401 847-3327	16177

MOBILE HOMES

	CITY	ST	EMP	PHONE	ENTRY#
Champion Enterprises Inc	Storrs	CT	G	860 429-3537	3510
Royal Business Group Inc	Boston	MA	C	617 542-4100	7015
Knickerbocker Group Inc	Boothbay	ME	D	207 541-9333	4598
Tiny Homes of Maine LLC	Houlton	ME	G	207 619-4108	4905

MOBILE HOMES: Personal Or Private Use

	CITY	ST	EMP	PHONE	ENTRY#
Topek LLC	Grantham	NH	F	603 863-2400	14363

MODELS: General, Exc Toy

	CITY	ST	EMP	PHONE	ENTRY#
Modelvision Inc	New Milford	CT	G	860 355-3884	2253
Atlantic Industrial Models LLC	Essex	MA	E	978 768-7686	8473
Village Goldsmith	Warwick	RI	F	401 944-8404	16872

MODULES: Computer Logic

	CITY	ST	EMP	PHONE	ENTRY#
Starlink North America Inc	Woburn	MA	G	877 823-1566	13672
Laird Connectivity LLC	Manchester	NH	C	603 627-7877	14874

MODULES: Solid State

	CITY	ST	EMP	PHONE	ENTRY#
Interface Engineering Corp	Randolph	MA	F	781 986-2600	11566
Springboard Technology Corporation	Springfield	MA	D		12133

MOLDED RUBBER PRDTS

	CITY	ST	EMP	PHONE	ENTRY#
Airex Rubber Products Corporation	Portland	CT	E	860 342-0850	2816
Gordon Rubber and Pkg Co Inc	Derby	CT	E	203 735-7441	889
Fabreeka International Inc (DH)	Stoughton	MA	G	781 341-3655	12206
Fabreeka Intl Holdings Inc (DH)	Stoughton	MA	E	781 341-3655	12207
Jefferson Rubber Works Inc	Worcester	MA	F	508 791-3600	13744
Diacom Corporation	Amherst	NH	D	603 880-1900	13866
Humphreys Industrial Pdts Inc	Rochester	NH	E	603 692-5005	15478

MOLDING COMPOUNDS

	CITY	ST	EMP	PHONE	ENTRY#
Bi-Qem Inc	Florence	MA	E	413 584-2472	8683
Cambridge Polymer Group Inc	Woburn	MA	E	617 629-4400	13539
Indusol Inc	Sutton	MA	E	508 865-9516	12282
Reinforced Structures For Elec	Worcester	MA	F	508 754-5316	13783
RES-Tech Corporation (HQ)	Hudson	MA	E	978 567-1000	9406
Unicore LLC	Palmer	MA	E	413 284-9995	11287
G & G Products LLC	Kennebunk	ME	E	207 985-9100	4925
Faber Industries LLC (HQ)	Salem	NH	F	603 681-0484	15522
QST Inc	Saint Albans	VT	E	802 524-7704	17529

MOLDINGS & TRIM: Metal, Exc Automobile

	CITY	ST	EMP	PHONE	ENTRY#
Watertown Engineering Corp	Whitman	MA	E	781 857-2555	13351

MOLDINGS OR TRIM: Automobile, Stamped Metal

	CITY	ST	EMP	PHONE	ENTRY#
C Cowles & Company (PA)	North Haven	CT	D	203 865-3117	2396

MOLDS: Indl

	CITY	ST	EMP	PHONE	ENTRY#
Advance Mold & Mfg Inc	Manchester	CT	C	860 432-5887	1583
American Molded Products Inc	Bridgeport	CT	F	203 333-0183	295
Ferron Mold and Tool LLC	Dayville	CT	G	860 774-5555	862
Ivanhoe Tool & Die Company Inc	Thompson	CT	E	860 923-9541	3650
J & L Tool Company Inc	Wallingford	CT	E	203 265-6237	3820
Moldvision LLC	Thompson	CT	G	860 315-1025	3651
R&R Tool & Die LLC	East Windsor	CT	G	860 627-9197	1083
Scan Tool & Mold Inc	Trumbull	CT	E	203 459-4950	3731
Watertown Plastics Inc	Watertown	CT	E	860 274-7535	4038
Westminster Tool Inc	Plainfield	CT	E	860 564-6966	2741
Accutech Packaging Inc	Foxboro	MA	D	508 543-3800	8689
Ar-Ro Engineering Company Inc	Uxbridge	MA	F	401 766-6669	12477
Atco Plastics Inc	Plainville	MA	F	508 695-3573	11429
Innovative Tooling Company Inc	Lenox	MA	F	413 637-1031	9625
Lansen Mold Co Inc	Hancock	MA	F	413 443-5328	9025

	CITY	ST	EMP	PHONE	ENTRY#
Mayhew Basque Plastics LLC	Westminster	MA	F	978 537-5219	13273
Pen Ro Mold and Tool Inc	Pittsfield	MA	E	413 499-0464	11416
Pittsfield Plastics Engrg LLC	Pittsfield	MA	D	413 442-0067	11419
S Ralph Cross and Sons Inc	Holyoke	MA	E	508 865-8112	9279
Star Base Technologies Inc	Pittsfield	MA	E	413 499-4005	11424
Stuart Allyn Co Inc	Pittsfield	MA	G	413 443-7306	11425
Aluminum Castings Inc	Wilton	NH	G	603 654-9695	15701
Freudenberg-Nok General Partnr	Ashland	NH	D	603 968-7187	13900
Hy-Ten Die & Development Corp	Milford	NH	E	603 673-1611	15029
Talbot Hill Holdings Corp	Swanzey	NH	E	603 357-2523	15646
Whelen Engineering Co	Charlestown	NH	A	860 526-9504	14069
Clear Carbon & Components Inc	Bristol	RI	E	401 254-5085	15758
Goodwin-Bradley Pattern Co Inc	Providence	RI	F	401 461-5220	16525
Nolato Gw Inc (HQ)	Bethel	VT	B	802 234-9941	17060

MONOFILAMENTS: Nontextile

	CITY	ST	EMP	PHONE	ENTRY#
Astenjohnson Inc	Williston	VT	D	802 658-2040	17722

MONUMENTS & GRAVE MARKERS, WHOLESALE

	CITY	ST	EMP	PHONE	ENTRY#
G R Sands Monumental Works	Roslindale	MA	G	617 522-1001	11666
McCue Memorial Co Inc	Castleton	VT	E	802 468-5636	17173

MOPS: Floor & Dust

	CITY	ST	EMP	PHONE	ENTRY#
Butler Home Products LLC (HQ)	Hudson	MA	F	508 597-8000	9359

MOTION PICTURE & VIDEO DISTRIBUTION

	CITY	ST	EMP	PHONE	ENTRY#
Wooden Kiwi Productions LLC	Waltham	MA	G	781 209-2623	12818

MOTION PICTURE & VIDEO PRODUCTION SVCS

	CITY	ST	EMP	PHONE	ENTRY#
Bff Holdings Inc (HQ)	Old Saybrook	CT	C	860 510-0100	2645
Blue Sky Studios Inc	Greenwich	CT	C	203 992-6000	1319

MOTION PICTURE & VIDEO PRODUCTION SVCS: Educational

	CITY	ST	EMP	PHONE	ENTRY#
GS Inc	Rockland	ME	G	207 593-7730	5332

MOTION PICTURE EQPT

	CITY	ST	EMP	PHONE	ENTRY#
Boston Light & Sound Inc (PA)	Malden	MA	F	617 787-3131	10005

MOTOR & GENERATOR PARTS: Electric

	CITY	ST	EMP	PHONE	ENTRY#
Dmi Technology Corp (PA)	Dover	NH	F	603 742-3330	14226
Electrocraft Inc (HQ)	Stratham	NH	E	855 697-7966	15634

MOTOR CONTROL CENTERS

	CITY	ST	EMP	PHONE	ENTRY#
Teknikor Automtn & Contrls Inc	Fall River	MA	F	508 679-9474	8615

MOTOR HOMES

	CITY	ST	EMP	PHONE	ENTRY#
National Van Sales Inc	Attleboro	MA	F	508 222-2272	6040

MOTOR SCOOTERS & PARTS

	CITY	ST	EMP	PHONE	ENTRY#
Madd Gear LLC	Stamford	CT	F	410 800-4423	3406
New Vectrix LLC	Boston	MA	E	858 674-6099	6919
Superpedestrian Inc (PA)	Cambridge	MA	C	877 678-7518	7725

MOTOR VEHICLE ASSEMBLY, COMPLETE: Ambulances

	CITY	ST	EMP	PHONE	ENTRY#
Sugarloaf Ambulance and Rescue	Carrabassett Valley	ME	F	207 235-2222	4680

MOTOR VEHICLE ASSEMBLY, COMPLETE: Buses, All Types

	CITY	ST	EMP	PHONE	ENTRY#
Patsys Bus Sales and Service	Concord	NH	F	603 226-2222	14151

MOTOR VEHICLE ASSEMBLY, COMPLETE: Fire Department Vehicles

	CITY	ST	EMP	PHONE	ENTRY#
Meriden Fire Marshals Office	Meriden	CT	F	203 630-4010	1674
Allegiance Fire & Rescue LLC	Walpole	MA	F	800 225-4808	12550
Epping Volunteer Fire District	Columbia Falls	ME	G	207 483-2036	4699
Larry Dingee	Cornish	NH	G	603 542-9682	14183
Swnh Fire Mutual Aid Radio	Keene	NH	G	603 352-8635	14625
Valley Transportation Irlc (PA)	Bradford	NH	G	603 938-2271	14018
Town of Hartford	White River Junction	VT	E	802 295-9425	17710

MOTOR VEHICLE ASSEMBLY, COMPLETE: Military Motor Vehicle

	CITY	ST	EMP	PHONE	ENTRY#
Wgi Inc	Southwick	MA	F	413 569-9444	12051

MOTOR VEHICLE DEALERS: Automobiles, New & Used

	CITY	ST	EMP	PHONE	ENTRY#
Danbury A LLC	Danbury	CT	E	203 744-5202	724
Scap Motors Inc	Fairfield	CT	E	203 384-0005	1200
Steven Pelletier	Fort Kent	ME	F	207 834-3191	4794
Gpi Nh-T Inc	Manchester	NH	D	603 624-1800	14854

MOTOR VEHICLE DEALERS: Vans, New & Used

	CITY	ST	EMP	PHONE	ENTRY#
Ride-Away Inc (HQ)	Londonderry	NH	E	603 437-4444	14782

	CITY	ST	EMP	PHONE	ENTRY#

MOTOR VEHICLE PARTS & ACCESS: Bearings

	CITY	ST	EMP	PHONE	ENTRY#
Alinabal Holdings Corporation (PA)	Milford	CT	B	203 877-3241	1797

MOTOR VEHICLE PARTS & ACCESS: Body Components & Frames

Johnson Controls Inc	Meriden	CT	F	678 297-4040	1670
Textron Systems Corporation	Wilmington	MA	E	978 657-5111	13465
Angstrom Fiber Auburn LLC	Auburn	ME	D	734 756-1164	4420

MOTOR VEHICLE PARTS & ACCESS: Electrical Eqpt

Armatron International Inc (PA)	Medford	MA	D	781 321-2300	10280
Borgwarner Massachusetts Inc (HQ)	Northborough	MA	E	508 281-5500	11092
Kirby Corporation	Springfield	MA	G	413 363-0005	12110
Crescent Industries Company	Auburn	ME	G	207 777-3500	4425

MOTOR VEHICLE PARTS & ACCESS: Engines & Parts

Callaway Cars Inc	Old Lyme	CT	F	860 434-9002	2636
Callaway Companies Inc (PA)	Old Lyme	CT	F	860 434-9002	2637
Moroso Performance Pdts Inc (PA)	Guilford	CT	C	203 453-6571	1401
Aptiv Services Us LLC	Boston	MA	D	781 864-9230	6553
Ms Ambrogio North America LLC	Auburn	ME	E	832 834-3641	4447
Moveras LLC	Salem	NH	F	877 866-8372	15546

MOTOR VEHICLE PARTS & ACCESS: Fifth Wheels

Tru-Hitch Inc	Pleasant Valley	CT	F	860 379-7772	2805

MOTOR VEHICLE PARTS & ACCESS: Gears

Insco Corporation	Groton	MA	E	978 448-6368	9010

MOTOR VEHICLE PARTS & ACCESS: Lifting Mechanisms, Dump Truck

Lac Landscaping LLC	Milford	CT	F	203 807-1067	1843

MOTOR VEHICLE PARTS & ACCESS: Pumps, Hydraulic Fluid Power

Dynex/Rivett Inc	Ashland	MA	G	508 881-5110	5957
T M Services Inc	Rutland	VT	E	802 775-2948	17511

MOTOR VEHICLE PARTS & ACCESS: Tie Rods

Alinabal Inc (HQ)	Milford	CT	C	203 877-3241	1796

MOTOR VEHICLE PARTS & ACCESS: Tops

Thule Inc (DH)	Seymour	CT	C	203 881-9600	2971
Thule Holding Inc (DH)	Seymour	CT	E	203 881-9600	2972

MOTOR VEHICLE PARTS & ACCESS: Trailer Hitches

Daves Truck Repair Inc	Springfield	MA	E	413 734-8898	12089

MOTOR VEHICLE PARTS & ACCESS: Transmission Housings Or Parts

Defeo Manufacturing Inc	Brookfield	CT	E	203 775-0254	517
Sonnax Transmission Company (DH)	Bellows Falls	VT	D	802 463-9722	17032

MOTOR VEHICLE PARTS & ACCESS: Transmissions

Borgwarner Inc	Northborough	MA	E	508 281-5500	11091
Magmotor Technologies Inc	Worcester	MA	F	508 835-4305	13756
Xxpress Auto Repair Shop LLC	Hyde Park	MA	F	800 591-2068	9468
Allard Nazarian Group Inc	Manchester	NH	F	603 314-0017	14809

MOTOR VEHICLE PARTS & ACCESS: Water Pumps

V Power Equipment LLC	Wareham	MA	F	508 273-7596	12847

MOTOR VEHICLE PARTS & ACCESS: Wiring Harness Sets

Jenesco Inc	Lyndeborough	NH	F	603 673-4830	14800
Rhode Island Wiring Svc Inc	West Kingston	RI	G	401 789-1955	16896

MOTOR VEHICLE SPLYS & PARTS WHOLESALERS: New

National Van Sales Inc	Attleboro	MA	F	508 222-2272	6040
Freudenberg-Nok General Partnr	Northfield	NH	D	603 286-1600	15266
Dejana Trck Utility Eqp Co LLC	Smithfield	RI	D	401 231-9797	16695

MOTOR VEHICLE: Hardware

Vectrix LLC	New Bedford	MA	G	508 717-6510	10658

MOTOR VEHICLE: Shock Absorbers

Hutchinson Arospc & Indust Inc (DH)	Hopkinton	MA	B	508 417-7000	9330

MOTOR VEHICLE: Steering Mechanisms

NSK Steering Systems Amer Inc	Bennington	VT	B	802 442-5448	17054

MOTOR VEHICLES & CAR BODIES

Oshkosh Corporation	East Granby	CT	F	860 653-5548	946
CPI Essco Inc	Ayer	MA	C	978 568-5100	6179
Greenwood Emrgncy Vehicles LLC (HQ)	Attleboro Falls	MA	D	508 695-7138	6086
Lawton Truck Equipment Inc	Topsfield	MA	F	978 887-0005	12436

MOTOR VEHICLES, WHOLESALE: Fire Trucks

Greenwood Emrgncy Vehicles LLC (HQ)	Attleboro Falls	MA	D	508 695-7138	6086

MOTORCYCLE DEALERS

Gary Raymond	Caribou	ME	G	207 498-2549	4675
Moto Tassinari LLC	West Lebanon	NH	F	603 298-6646	15684
Rowe Machine Co	Hampton	NH	F	603 926-0029	14411

MOTORCYCLES & RELATED PARTS

Kobuta Choppers LLC	North Haven	CT	G	203 234-6047	2421
Choppers of New England	Nashua	NH	G	603 809-4391	15079
Moto Tassinari LLC	West Lebanon	NH	F	603 298-6646	15684

MOTORS: Electric

Crrc LLC (PA)	South Windsor	CT	D	877 684-6464	3136
Tritex Corporation	Waterbury	CT	E	203 756-7441	3977
Ward Leonard CT LLC (DH)	Thomaston	CT	D	860 283-5801	3641
Ametek Arizona Instrument LLC	Middleboro	MA	C	508 946-6200	10349
Dkd Industries Inc	Worcester	MA	G	508 762-9114	13717
Ashland Electric Products Inc	Rochester	NH	E	603 335-1100	15466
Electrocraft New Hampshire Inc (DH)	Dover	NH	E	603 742-3330	14228
Electrocraft New Hampshire Inc	Stratham	NH	E	740 441-6208	15635

MOTORS: Generators

Cramer Company	South Windsor	CT	F	860 291-8402	3135
Elinco International Jpc Inc (PA)	Fairfield	CT	G	203 334-7537	1183
Fuelcell Energy Inc	Torrington	CT	E	860 496-1111	3682
GE Steam Power Inc (HQ)	Windsor	CT	A	866 257-8664	4279
Generators On Demand LLC	Old Lyme	CT	F	860 662-4090	2642
Japanese Products Corporation	Fairfield	CT	F	203 334-7537	1190
Kanthal Corporation	Bethel	CT	E	203 744-1440	124
Ktcr Holding	Westport	CT	G	203 227-4115	4179
Novanta Motion USA Inc (HQ)	Marlborough	CT	D	860 295-6102	1646
Rowley Spring & Stamping Corp	Bristol	CT	E	860 582-8175	494
Ward Leonard Operating LLC (DH)	Thomaston	CT	E	860 283-5801	3643
Ward Lonard Houma Holdings LLC	Thomaston	CT	D	860 283-5801	3644
American Superconductor Corp (PA)	Ayer	MA	D	978 842-3000	6171
Ametek Inc	Wilmington	MA	D	978 988-4101	13377
Comprehensive Power Inc	Marlborough	MA	E	508 460-0010	10134
Electro Switch Corp	Weymouth	MA	C	781 607-3306	13324
L3 Technologies Inc	Northampton	MA	A	413 586-2330	11069
Maxon Precision Motors Inc (HQ)	Taunton	MA	E	508 677-0520	12348
Nidec America Corporation (HQ)	Braintree	MA	E	781 848-0970	7196
Northern Lights Inc	Methuen	MA	G	978 258-7412	10342
Peak Scientific Inc (DH)	North Billerica	MA	E	978 234-4679	10942
Precision Electronics Corp	Marshfield	MA	F	781 834-6677	10244
Ion Physics Corp	Fremont	NH	G	603 895-5100	14328
Kearney-National Inc	North Kingstown	RI	C	401 943-2686	16264
Wei (PA)	Cranston	RI	E	401 781-3904	15928
Apex Sealing Inc	Fairfax	VT	F	802 524-7100	17254
Hayward Tyler Inc (DH)	Colchester	VT	E	802 655-4444	17194

MOTORS: Pneumatic

Sfc Koenig LLC	North Haven	CT	E	203 245-1100	2436

MULTIPLEXERS: Telephone & Telegraph

Freedom Technologies LLC	Glastonbury	CT	G	860 633-0452	1278
IPC Systems Inc	Fairfield	CT	E	860 271-4100	1189
IPC Systems Inc	Old Saybrook	CT	F	860 952-9575	2652
K-Tech International Inc	Torrington	CT	E	860 489-9399	3687
Microphase Corporation	Shelton	CT	E	203 866-8000	3032
Nutmeg Utility Products Inc (PA)	Cheshire	CT	E	203 250-8802	609
Radio Frequency Systems Inc (DH)	Meriden	CT	E	203 630-3311	1690
Total Communications Inc (PA)	East Hartford	CT	E	860 282-9999	1028
Adtran Networks North Amer Inc	Chelmsford	MA	C	978 674-6800	7902
Artel Video Systems Corp	Westford	MA	E	978 263-5775	13224
Avaya LLC	Billerica	MA	F	908 953-6000	6407
Biscom Inc	Westford	MA	D	978 250-1800	13226
Digital 128 First Avenue LLC	Needham	MA	E	781 726-7736	10508
Equipe Communications Corp	Acton	MA	C	978 635-1999	5747
General Dynmics Mssion Systems	Taunton	MA	F	508 880-4000	12338
Global Connector Tech Ltd	Lawrence	MA	F	978 208-1618	9565
Mayflower Communications Inc	Bedford	MA	E	781 359-9500	6239
MB Westfield Inc	Westfield	MA	C	413 568-8676	13182
Mrv Communications Americas Inc	Chelmsford	MA	F	978 674-6800	7940
Nokia of America Corporation	Westford	MA	D	978 952-1616	13256
Shintron Co Inc	Cambridge	MA	F	617 491-8701	7711
Signal Communications Corp	Woburn	MA	E	781 933-0998	13666

Employee Codes: A=Over 500 employees, B=251-500
C=101-250, D=51-100, E=20-50, F=10-19, G=1-9

2024 Harris New England
Manufacturers Directory

PRODUCT

1433

	CITY	ST	EMP	PHONE	ENTRY#
Spectrsite Bradcast Towers Inc	Boston	MA	F	888 498-3667	7050
SPX Corporation	Raymond	ME	E	207 655-8525	5316
At Comm Corp	Manchester	NH	F	603 624-4424	14815
Dialogic (us) Inc	Salem	NH	E	603 890-7240	15518
Exacom Inc	Concord	NH	F	603 228-0706	14129
Northeast Innovations Inc	Pembroke	NH	F	603 226-4000	15306
Subcom LLC	Newington	NH	D	603 319-5041	15213
Aldotech Corporation	Warwick	RI	E	401 467-6100	16777
Eartec Company Inc	Narragansett	RI	E	401 789-8700	16190
Electro Standards Lab Inc	Cranston	RI	D	401 946-1164	15853
Okonite Company Inc	Cumberland	RI	E	401 333-3500	15957

MUSIC DISTRIBUTION APPARATUS

	CITY	ST	EMP	PHONE	ENTRY#
Views Record Label LLC	Springfield	MA	F	413 204-0930	12148
Russound/Fmp Inc	Portsmouth	NH	C	603 659-5170	15433

MUSICAL INSTRUMENTS & ACCESS: NEC

	CITY	ST	EMP	PHONE	ENTRY#
Rokr Distribution Us Inc	Bloomfield	CT	B	860 509-8888	207
FA Finale Inc	Boston	MA	E	617 226-7888	6728
Fishman Transducers Inc	Andover	MA	E	978 988-9199	5883
Alesis LP	Cumberland	RI	C	401 658-4032	15931
Clear Carbon & Components Inc	Bristol	RI	E	401 254-5085	15758
Island Woods Performance Inc	Smithfield	RI	G	401 349-4644	16717

MUSICAL INSTRUMENTS & ACCESS: Pianos

	CITY	ST	EMP	PHONE	ENTRY#
Burgett Brothers Incorporated	Haverhill	MA	E	978 374-8888	9082

MUSICAL INSTRUMENTS & PARTS: Percussion

	CITY	ST	EMP	PHONE	ENTRY#
Avedis Zildjian Co (PA)	Norwell	MA	C	781 871-2200	11139

MUSICAL INSTRUMENTS WHOLESALERS

	CITY	ST	EMP	PHONE	ENTRY#
FA Finale Inc	Boston	MA	E	617 226-7888	6728
Verne Q Powell Flutes Inc	Maynard	MA	D	978 461-6111	10265
Pantheon Guitars LLC	Lewiston	ME	F	207 755-0003	4983

MUSICAL INSTRUMENTS: Guitars & Parts, Electric & Acoustic

	CITY	ST	EMP	PHONE	ENTRY#
Pantheon Guitars LLC	Lewiston	ME	F	207 755-0003	4983

NAILS: Steel, Wire Or Cut

	CITY	ST	EMP	PHONE	ENTRY#
Tsmc Inc	Torrington	CT	A	860 283-8265	3703

NAME PLATES: Engraved Or Etched

	CITY	ST	EMP	PHONE	ENTRY#
Ann S Davis	Lebanon	CT	F	860 642-7228	1548
Biomerics LLC	Monroe	CT	D	203 268-7238	1906
Identification Products Corp	Bridgeport	CT	F	203 334-5969	331
Identification Products Corp (PA)	Shelton	CT	E	203 334-5969	3019
Northeast Laser Engraving Inc	Monroe	CT	E	203 268-7238	1918
Willington Nameplate Inc	Stafford Springs	CT	D	860 684-4281	3264
Chemi-Graphic Inc	Ludlow	MA	E	413 589-0151	9942
E V Yeuell Inc	Woburn	MA	E	781 933-2984	13560
Eastern Etching and Mfg Co	Chicopee	MA	E	413 594-6601	8030
Pg Technologies Inc	Westfield	MA	G	413 562-1354	13198
Reeves Company Inc	Attleboro	MA	F	508 222-2877	6053
Stickamayka Packaging Inc	Andover	MA	F	978 474-1930	5926

NATURAL GAS LIQUIDS PRODUCTION

	CITY	ST	EMP	PHONE	ENTRY#
Six One Cmmodities US Trdg LLC	Stamford	CT	E	203 409-2079	3461

NATURAL GAS PRODUCTION

	CITY	ST	EMP	PHONE	ENTRY#
Direct Energy Inc (HQ)	Stamford	CT	E	800 260-0300	3338
Louis Dreyfus Holdg Co US LLC (HQ)	Wilton	CT	B	203 761-2000	4242
British Transco Capital Inc	Westborough	MA	E	781 907-3646	13083
Poweroptions Inc	Boston	MA	G	617 737-8480	6973
Maine Natural Gas Corporation	Brunswick	ME	F	207 729-0420	4648
Revision Heat LLC	Hampden	ME	G	207 221-5677	4867

NATURAL GASOLINE PRODUCTION

	CITY	ST	EMP	PHONE	ENTRY#
Eagle Ship Management LLC (HQ)	Stamford	CT	C	203 276-8100	3340
World Energy LLC	Boston	MA	B	617 889-7300	7132

NAVIGATIONAL SYSTEMS & INSTRUMENTS

	CITY	ST	EMP	PHONE	ENTRY#
Entwistle Company LLC (PA)	Hudson	MA	D	508 481-4000	9364
Megapulse Incorporated	Bedford	MA	E	781 538-5299	6241
Navionics Inc	Wareham	MA	E	508 291-6000	12841
Quincy Electronics Co Inc	Quincy	MA	G	617 471-7700	11534
Ursa Navigation Solutions Inc	North Billerica	MA	E	781 538-5299	10963
Xchange Imc LLC	Maynard	MA	F	978 298-2100	10267
Critical Cmmnctons Cntrls Inst	Exeter	NH	F		14290
Signalquest LLC	Lebanon	NH	E	603 448-6266	14698
Kvh Industries Inc (PA)	Middletown	RI	C	401 847-3327	16177

NICKEL

	CITY	ST	EMP	PHONE	ENTRY#
Nickel Corporaxion	Providence	RI	G	401 351-6555	16575

NONCURRENT CARRYING WIRING DEVICES

	CITY	ST	EMP	PHONE	ENTRY#
Wiremold Company	West Hartford	CT	E	860 263-3115	4092
Reinforced Structures For Elec	Worcester	MA	F	508 754-5316	13783
Signal Communications Corp	Woburn	MA	E	781 933-0998	13666
Transene Company Inc (PA)	Danvers	MA	G	978 777-7860	8227
Baker Company Inc (PA)	Sanford	ME	C	207 324-8773	5390
Continental Cable LLC	Hinsdale	NH	D	800 229-5131	14443

NONFERROUS: Rolling & Drawing, NEC

	CITY	ST	EMP	PHONE	ENTRY#
Doncasters Inc	Groton	CT	D	860 446-4803	1366
Tico Titanium Inc (PA)	Wallingford	CT	E	248 446-0400	3864
Titanium Metals Corporation	East Windsor	CT	C	860 627-7051	1088
Ulbrich Stainless Steels	Wallingford	CT	C	203 269-2507	3871
United Sttes Sign Fbrction Cor	Trumbull	CT	F	203 601-1000	3739
Newton Materion Inc (HQ)	Newton	MA	C	617 630-5800	10772
Replica Works Inc	Orange	MA	E	978 544-7000	11231
Special Metals Corporation	Worcester	MA	D	270 365-9551	13804
Sx Industries Inc (PA)	Stoughton	MA	F	781 828-7111	12241
Elmet Technologies LLC (PA)	Lewiston	ME	C	207 333-6100	4960
Dgf Indstrial Innvtons Group L	Gilford	NH	F	603 528-6591	14335
Microspec Corporation	Peterborough	NH	E	603 924-4300	15319
1st Casting Company	Johnston	RI	F	401 272-0750	16071
Callico Metals Inc	North Kingstown	RI	G	401 398-8238	16236
J L Anthony & Company	Providence	RI	G	401 467-9700	16547

NOTEBOOKS, MADE FROM PURCHASED MATERIALS

	CITY	ST	EMP	PHONE	ENTRY#
Connecticut Clean Room Corp	Bristol	CT	E	860 589-0049	430
Avery Products Corporation	Holliston	MA	C	508 893-1000	9201
Eureka Lab Book Inc	Holyoke	MA	F	413 534-5671	9254

NOVELTIES

	CITY	ST	EMP	PHONE	ENTRY#
Cartamundi East Longmeadow LLC	East Longmeadow	MA	B	413 526-2000	8371
David W Wallace	Shelburne Falls	MA	G	413 625-6523	11803
Sheffield Pottery Inc	Sheffield	MA	E	413 229-7700	11801
Lux Box Company Inc	Portland	ME	G	301 832-0622	5235
RJ Mansour Inc	Providence	RI	F	401 521-7800	16606

NOVELTIES & SPECIALTIES: Metal

	CITY	ST	EMP	PHONE	ENTRY#
Saunders Mfg Co Inc (PA)	Readfield	ME	E	207 685-9860	5318
Aspects Inc	Warren	RI	E	401 247-1854	16751
Cathedral Art Metal Co Inc	Providence	RI	E	401 273-7200	16498

NOVELTIES: Plastic

	CITY	ST	EMP	PHONE	ENTRY#
Plastic Monofil Co Ltd	Medway	MA	F	732 629-7701	10311
Rainbow Visions Inc	Boston	MA	G	617 787-4084	6995
Spirit Foodservice LLC	Andover	MA	C	978 964-1551	5925
Perry Blackburne Inc	North Providence	RI	F	401 231-7200	16307

NOZZLES: Spray, Aerosol, Paint Or Insecticide

	CITY	ST	EMP	PHONE	ENTRY#
Waterbury Companies Inc	Waterbury	CT	C		3980
Bete Fog Nozzle Inc (PA)	Greenfield	MA	E	413 772-0846	8985
Spraying Systems Co	Bedford	NH	F	603 471-0505	13950
Spraying Systems Co	Merrimack	NH	E	603 517-1854	15006

NUCLEAR FUELS SCRAP REPROCESSING

	CITY	ST	EMP	PHONE	ENTRY#
Starmet Corporation (PA)	Concord	MA	E	978 369-5410	8134

NURSERY STOCK, WHOLESALE

	CITY	ST	EMP	PHONE	ENTRY#
Clinton Nursery Products Inc (PA)	Westbrook	CT	C	860 399-3000	4137

NUTS: Metal

	CITY	ST	EMP	PHONE	ENTRY#
Metalform Acquisition LLC (PA)	New Britain	CT	F	860 224-2630	2043
A1 Screw Machine Products Inc	Chicopee	MA	F	413 594-8939	8004
Donahue Industries Inc	Shrewsbury	MA	E	508 845-6501	11830
Stanlok Corporation	Worcester	MA	F	508 757-4508	13808

NYLON FIBERS

	CITY	ST	EMP	PHONE	ENTRY#
Synergy Manufacturing LLC	Stoughton	MA	G	781 209-5538	12242

NYLON RESINS

	CITY	ST	EMP	PHONE	ENTRY#
Nylon Corporation America Inc	Manchester	NH	D	603 627-5150	14906

OFFICE EQPT WHOLESALERS

	CITY	ST	EMP	PHONE	ENTRY#
Agissar Corporation	Stratford	CT	E	203 375-8662	3516
C P Bourg Inc (PA)	New Bedford	MA	E	508 998-2171	10577
MBI Graphics & Printing Corp	Southbridge	MA	F	508 765-0658	12028
Dahle North America Inc	Peterborough	NH	F	603 924-0003	15314
Relyco Sales Inc (PA)	Dover	NH	E	603 742-0999	14248

OFFICE EQPT, WHOLESALE: Photocopy Machines

	CITY	ST	EMP	PHONE	ENTRY#
Sands Business Eqp & Sups LLC	York	ME	F	207 351-3334	5716

OFFICE SPLY & STATIONERY STORES: Office Forms & Splys

	CITY	ST	EMP	PHONE	ENTRY#
Adkins Printing Company	New Britain	CT	F	800 228-9745	1997
Hartford Business Supply Inc	Hartford	CT	E	860 233-2138	1485
W B Mason Co Inc	East Windsor	CT	D	888 926-2766	1089
W B Mason Co Inc	Norwalk	CT	E	888 926-2766	2593
W B Mason Co Inc	Norwich	CT	C	888 926-2766	2619
Da Rosas	Oak Bluffs	MA	E	508 693-0110	11221
W B Mason Co Inc	Framingham	MA	D	888 926-2766	8809
W B Mason Co Inc	Greenfield	MA	E	888 926-2766	9004
W B Mason Co Inc	Augusta	ME	E	888 926-2766	4481
W B Mason Co Inc	Bangor	ME	E	888 926-2766	4520
W B Mason Co Inc	Portland	ME	E	888 926-2766	5288
B & E Enterprises Inc	Peterborough	NH	G	603 924-7203	15312
W B Mason Co Inc	Manchester	NH	E	888 926-2766	14957
W B Mason Co Inc	Cranston	RI	D	888 926-2766	15926
Portfolio Software Inc	Richmond	VT	F	802 434-4000	17481
W B Mason Co Inc	Brattleboro	VT	E	888 926-2766	17106
W B Mason Co Inc	South Burlington	VT	E	888 926-2766	17607

OFFICE SPLYS, NEC, WHOLESALE

	CITY	ST	EMP	PHONE	ENTRY#
Adkins Printing Company	New Britain	CT	F	800 228-9745	1997
Envirnmntal Office Sltions Inc (PA)	East Hartford	CT	E	860 291-1900	993
Da Rosas	Oak Bluffs	MA	E	508 693-0110	11221
Ils Business Services Inc	Agawam	MA	G	413 789-4555	5793
State-Line Graphics Inc	Everett	MA	F	617 389-1200	8501

OIL & GAS FIELD MACHINERY

	CITY	ST	EMP	PHONE	ENTRY#
Cameron International Corp	Glastonbury	CT	F	860 633-0277	1273
General Electric Company	Norwalk	CT	A	203 797-0840	2504
General Electric Company	Stamford	CT	F	866 419-4096	3354
Numa Tool Company (PA)	Thompson	CT	D	860 923-9551	3652
Slickbar Products Corp	Seymour	CT	G	203 888-7700	2969
Solidification Pdts Intl Inc	Northford	CT	E	203 484-9494	2455
GE Vernova International LLC (HQ)	Cambridge	MA	C	617 443-3000	7580
General Electric Company (PA)	Boston	MA	A	617 443-3000	6754
Deepwater Buoyancy Inc	Biddeford	ME	F	207 468-2565	4559

OIL FIELD MACHINERY & EQPT

	CITY	ST	EMP	PHONE	ENTRY#
Oil Purification Systems Inc	Waterbury	CT	F	203 346-1800	3955

OIL FIELD SVCS, NEC

	CITY	ST	EMP	PHONE	ENTRY#
Frc Founders Corporation (PA)	Stamford	CT	E	203 661-6601	3348
Sigma Tankers Inc	Norwalk	CT	E		2573
Weatherford International LLC	Wallingford	CT	E	203 294-0190	3875
Baker Hughes Holdings LLC	Walpole	MA	C	508 668-0400	12552
Mutual Oil Leasing Co Inc	Brockton	MA	F	508 583-5777	7299
Old Ironsides Energy LLC	Waltham	MA	E	617 366-2030	12742
Port Oil Corp	Bedford	MA	G	617 926-3500	6253
Mike Murphy & Sons Inc	Kingston	NH	F	603 362-4879	14636
Uncles Oil Company Corporation	Cranston	RI	G	401 383-0626	15925

OIL TREATING COMPOUNDS

	CITY	ST	EMP	PHONE	ENTRY#
Walnut 65 Holdings Inc (PA)	Peabody	MA	E	978 532-4010	11352

OILS & ESSENTIAL OILS

	CITY	ST	EMP	PHONE	ENTRY#
Whittemore-Wright Company Inc	Charlestown	MA	F	617 242-1180	7884
Yankee Candle Company Inc (DH)	South Deerfield	MA	C	413 665-8306	11931
Yankee Holding Corp (DH)	South Deerfield	MA	D	413 665-8306	11933
Ycc Holdings LLC	South Deerfield	MA	A	413 665-8306	11934

OILS: Cutting

	CITY	ST	EMP	PHONE	ENTRY#
Chessco Industries Inc (PA)	Westport	CT	E	203 255-2804	4160
Homeland Fuels Company LLC	Canton	MA	F	781 737-1892	7797

OILS: Lubricating

	CITY	ST	EMP	PHONE	ENTRY#
Chessco Industries Inc (PA)	Westport	CT	E	203 255-2804	4160

OINTMENTS

	CITY	ST	EMP	PHONE	ENTRY#
Vermonts Original LLC	Lyndonville	VT	G	802 626-3610	17322

OLEFINS

	CITY	ST	EMP	PHONE	ENTRY#
Girouard Tool Corp	Leominster	MA	G	978 534-4147	9667

OPERATOR TRAINING, COMPUTER

	CITY	ST	EMP	PHONE	ENTRY#
Learntoprogramtv Incorporated	Bridgeport	CT	F	860 840-7090	344

OPHTHALMIC GOODS

	CITY	ST	EMP	PHONE	ENTRY#
Coburn Technologies Inc (DH)	South Windsor	CT	E	860 648-6600	3129
Gerber Coburn Optical Inc (DH)	South Windsor	CT	C	800 843-1479	3150
Hoya Corporation	South Windsor	CT	E	860 289-5379	3157

	CITY	ST	EMP	PHONE	ENTRY#
Aearo Technologies LLC	Auburn	MA	B	317 692-6645	6098
Bausch & Lomb Incorporated	Wilmington	MA	C	978 658-6111	13388
Bcpe Seminole Holdings LP (PA)	Boston	MA	F	617 516-2000	6585
Beaver-Visitec Intl Inc	Waltham	MA	F	781 906-8080	12604
Eye Health Services Inc	Plymouth	MA	E	508 747-6425	11459
Eye Health Services Inc (PA)	Quincy	MA	E	617 472-5242	11517
Fosta-Tek Optics Inc (PA)	Leominster	MA	D	978 534-6511	9665
Hilsinger Company Parent LLC (PA)	Mansfield	MA	E	508 699-4406	10055
Perx LLC	Pittsfield	MA	F	413 358-9020	11417
Thea Pharma Inc	Waltham	MA	D	781 832-3667	12796
Qsa Optical Co Inc	Lewiston	ME	E	207 783-8523	4988
New Hampshire Optical Co Inc (PA)	Allenstown	NH	E	603 268-0741	13854
Prolens Inc	North Troy	VT	G	802 988-1018	17430

OPHTHALMIC GOODS WHOLESALERS

	CITY	ST	EMP	PHONE	ENTRY#
Avedro Inc (HQ)	Burlington	MA	C	781 768-3400	7337
Perx LLC	Pittsfield	MA	F	413 358-9020	11417
New Hampshire Optical Co Inc (PA)	Allenstown	NH	E	603 268-0741	13854
McLeod Optical Company Inc (PA)	Warwick	RI	E	401 467-3000	16836

OPHTHALMIC GOODS: Frames & Parts, Eyeglass & Spectacle

	CITY	ST	EMP	PHONE	ENTRY#
Randolph Engineering Inc	Randolph	MA	E	781 961-6070	11573

OPHTHALMIC GOODS: Lenses, Ophthalmic

	CITY	ST	EMP	PHONE	ENTRY#
Gerber Scientific LLC (PA)	Tolland	CT	C	860 871-8082	3661
Optical Laboratory Inc	New Bedford	MA	E	508 997-9779	10637
Accu Rx Inc	Johnston	RI	E	401 454-2920	16072

OPTICAL GOODS STORES

	CITY	ST	EMP	PHONE	ENTRY#
Opticare Health Systems Inc (DH)	Waterbury	CT	C	203 574-2020	3957
BJs Wholesale Club Inc	Franklin	MA	D	508 553-9889	8821
Eye Health Services Inc	Plymouth	MA	E	508 747-6425	11459
Eye Health Services Inc (PA)	Quincy	MA	E	617 472-5242	11517
Perx LLC	Pittsfield	MA	F	413 358-9020	11417

OPTICAL GOODS STORES: Contact Lenses, Prescription

	CITY	ST	EMP	PHONE	ENTRY#
Eye Exam 2000	Bedford	NH	G	603 836-5353	13927

OPTICAL INSTRUMENT REPAIR SVCS

	CITY	ST	EMP	PHONE	ENTRY#
Coburn Technologies Intl Inc (DH)	South Windsor	CT	F	860 648-6600	3130
Cyduct Diagnostics Inc	Boston	MA	G	617 360-9700	6682
Henke Sass Wolf America Inc	Dudley	MA	E	508 671-9300	8318
Optical Laboratory Inc	New Bedford	MA	E	508 997-9779	10637
Contour Fine Tooling Inc	Keene	NH	G	603 876-4908	14593

OPTICAL INSTRUMENTS & APPARATUS

	CITY	ST	EMP	PHONE	ENTRY#
Conoptics Inc	Danbury	CT	F	203 743-3349	722
Fiberoptics Technology Inc (PA)	Pomfret	CT	C	860 928-0443	2807
United Technologies Optical Systems Inc	Windsor Locks	CT	C	860 654-6000	4336
Amplitude Laser Inc	Cambridge	MA	E	857 285-5952	7485
Angstrom Advanced Inc	Stoughton	MA	D	781 519-4765	12194
Atlantic Vision Inc	Shrewsbury	MA	G	508 845-8401	11828
Dynasil Corporation America (PA)	Concord	MA	E	617 668-6855	8116
Eo Vista LLC	Acton	MA	E	978 635-8080	5746
Excel Technology Inc (HQ)	Bedford	MA	D	781 266-5700	6226
Excelitas Technologies Corp (DH)	Waltham	MA	E	855 382-2677	12673
Innovations In Optics Inc	Woburn	MA	F	781 933-4477	13585
Ophir Optics LLC	Wilmington	MA	D	978 657-6410	13441
Optikos Corporation	Wakefield	MA	D	617 354-7557	12525
Optra Inc	Wilmington	MA	F	978 887-6600	13443
Polychromix	Wilmington	MA	F	978 284-6000	13447
Precision Optics Corp Inc (PA)	Gardner	MA	D	978 630-1800	8898
Prior Scientific Inc (HQ)	Rockland	MA	F	781 878-8442	11658
Sycamore Networks Inc	Chelmsford	MA	C	978 250-2900	7962
Lh Liquidation LLC	Windham	ME	E	207 893-8233	5664
Andover Corporation	Salem	NH	E	603 893-6888	15506
Guidewire Technologies Inc	Salem	NH	E	603 894-4399	15534
Km Holding Inc	Hudson	NH	F	603 566-2704	14516
National Aperture Inc	Salem	NH	F	603 893-7393	15547
Optics 1 Inc (DH)	Bedford	NH	F	603 296-0469	13947
Space Optics Research Labs LLC	Merrimack	NH	F	978 250-8640	15005
Wilcox Industries Corp (PA)	Newington	NH	D	603 431-1331	15216
Wilcox Industries Corp	Newington	NH	E	603 431-1331	15217
Nippon American Limited	East Greenwich	RI	F	401 885-7353	15992
Pyramid Case Co Inc	Providence	RI	D	401 273-0643	16595

OPTICAL INSTRUMENTS & LENSES

	CITY	ST	EMP	PHONE	ENTRY#
Aperture Optical Sciences Inc (PA)	Meriden	CT	E	860 316-2589	1654
Coating Design Group Inc	Stratford	CT	E	203 878-3663	3528
Coburn Technologies Inc (DH)	South Windsor	CT	E	860 648-6600	3129
Coburn Technologies Intl Inc (DH)	South Windsor	CT	F	860 648-6600	3130
Crystal Fairfield Tech LLC	New Milford	CT	G	860 354-2111	2241

PRODUCT

	CITY	ST	EMP	PHONE	ENTRY#
CT Fiberoptics Inc	Somers	CT	F	860 763-4341	3098
Data Technology Inc	Tolland	CT	A	860 871-8082	3656
Eschenbach Optik America Inc (PA)	Danbury	CT	F	203 702-1600	739
Flemming Tinker Incorporated	Durham	CT	F	860 316-2589	900
Gerber Coburn Optical Inc (DH)	South Windsor	CT	F	800 843-1479	3150
Lenscrafters	Milford	CT	G	203 878-8511	1845
Nntechnology Moore Systems LLC	Bridgeport	CT	D	203 366-3224	352
Zygo Corporation (HQ)	Middlefield	CT	G	860 347-8506	1732
Acton Research Corporation	Acton	MA		941 556-2601	5731
Adaptive Optics Associates Inc	Devens	MA	F	978 391-0000	8267
Applied Science Group Inc	Billerica	MA	E	781 275-4000	6404
Atlantic RES Mktg Systems Inc	West Bridgewater	MA	F	508 584-7816	12966
Axsun Technologies Inc	Billerica	MA	D	978 262-0049	6408
Bae Systems Info Elctrnic Syst	Lexington	MA	C	603 885-4321	9726
Boston Piezo-Optics Inc	Bellingham	MA	F	508 966-4988	6287
Cambrdge RES Instrmntation Inc	Hopkinton	MA	F	781 935-9099	9311
Carl Zeiss Vision Inc	Marlborough	MA	G	800 327-9735	10130
Excelitas Technologies Corp	Billerica	MA	D	978 262-0049	6446
Eye Health Services Inc	Plymouth	MA	E	508 747-6425	11459
Eye Health Services Inc (PA)	Quincy	MA	E	617 472-5242	11517
Genscope Inc	East Longmeadow	MA	F	413 526-0802	8377
Headwall Photonics Inc	Bolton	MA	D	978 353-4100	6497
Hilsinger Company Parent LLC (PA)	Mansfield	MA	E	508 699-4406	10055
Holographix LLC	Marlborough	MA	F	978 562-4474	10162
I-Optics Corp	Burlington	MA	G	508 366-1600	7378
Incom Inc	Charlton	MA	C	508 909-2200	7889
Kinetic Systems Inc	Boston	MA	E	617 522-8700	6842
L3 Technologies Inc	Northampton	MA	A	413 586-2330	11069
L3 Technologies Inc	Wilmington	MA	C	978 694-9991	13422
Materion Prcsion Optics Thin F (DH)	Westford	MA	F	978 692-7513	13249
Newport Corporation	Franklin	MA	D	508 553-5035	8855
Novotech Inc	Acton	MA	F	978 929-9458	5760
Opticraft Inc	Woburn	MA	F	781 938-0456	13626
Optimum Technologies Inc	Southbridge	MA	F	508 765-8100	12032
Opto-Line International Inc	Wilmington	MA	F	978 658-7255	13442
Optos Inc	Marlborough	MA	D	508 787-1400	10192
Orpro Vision LLC	Billerica	MA	G	617 676-1101	6467
Pioneer Precision Optics Inc	Florence	MA	F	413 341-3992	8685
Rubil Associates Inc	Billerica	MA	F	978 670-7192	6478
Scientific Solutions Inc	North Chelmsford	MA	F	978 251-4554	10988
Spectro Scientific Inc (HQ)	Chelmsford	MA	D	978 486-0123	7959
Tel Mnfacturing Engrg Amer Inc	Billerica	MA	E	978 436-2300	6487
Thermo Vision Corp (HQ)	Franklin	MA	E	508 520-0083	8871
Thin Film Imaging Technologies	Greenfield	MA	F	413 774-6692	9002
United Lens Company Inc	Southbridge	MA	C	508 765-5421	12037
Vacuum Process Technology LLC	Cambridge	MA	E	508 732-7200	7749
Ametek Precitech Inc (HQ)	Keene	NH	D	603 357-2510	14588
Bae Systems Oasys LLC	Hudson	NH	D	603 232-8221	14487
Clear Align LLC	Nashua	NH	F	603 889-2116	15081
Contour Fine Tooling Inc	Keene	NH	G	603 876-4908	14593
G5 Infrared LLC	Hudson	NH	E	603 304-5722	14498
Gooch & Housego (keene) LLC	Keene	NH	E	603 358-5577	14601
Janos Technology Inc	Keene	NH	F	603 757-0070	14603
L3 Technologies Inc	Londonderry	NH	A	603 626-4800	14760
Moore Nntechnology Systems LLC (DH)	Swanzey	NH	F	603 352-3030	15645
Optical Filter Corporation	Keene	NH	A	603 357-7662	14614
Optical Solutions Inc	Charlestown	NH	G	603 826-4411	14066
Adolf Meller Company (PA)	Providence	RI	E	800 821-0180	16465
Knight Optical (usa) LLC	North Kingstown	RI	G	401 521-7000	16266
89 North Inc	Williston	VT	F	802 881-0302	17719
J & L Metrology Inc	Springfield	VT	F	802 885-8291	17619
Omega Optical Holdings LLC (PA)	Brattleboro	VT	F	802 251-7300	17098

ORAL PREPARATIONS

	CITY	ST	EMP	PHONE	ENTRY#
Cabot Hill Naturals LLC	Lancaster	NH	F	800 747-4372	14676

ORGANIZATIONS: Educational Research Agency

	CITY	ST	EMP	PHONE	ENTRY#
Institute For Fgn Plicy Analis (PA)	Cambridge	MA	E	617 492-2116	7615

ORGANIZATIONS: Medical Research

	CITY	ST	EMP	PHONE	ENTRY#
Alexion Pharma LLC (DH)	New Haven	CT	D	203 272-2596	2112
Confluent Surgical Inc	Waltham	MA	D	781 839-1700	12638
In Silico Biosciences Inc	Lexington	MA	F	781 861-1592	9751
Inverness Medical - Biostar Inc	Waltham	MA	C	781 647-3900	12703
Lfb Usa Inc (DH)	Framingham	MA	E	508 370-5100	8785
Logan Instruments Inc	Braintree	MA	F	617 394-0601	7193
Medical Research Networx	Franklin	MA	E	508 530-4289	8850

ORGANIZATIONS: Physical Research, Noncommercial

	CITY	ST	EMP	PHONE	ENTRY#
Silverthread Inc	Cambridge	MA	G	800 674-9366	7715

ORGANIZATIONS: Professional

	CITY	ST	EMP	PHONE	ENTRY#
Wire Association Intl Inc (PA)	Madison	CT	F	203 453-2777	1577

ORGANIZATIONS: Religious

	CITY	ST	EMP	PHONE	ENTRY#
NRG Connecticut LLC	Hartford	CT	F	860 231-2424	1497
Cistercian Abbey Spencer Inc	Spencer	MA	E	508 885-8700	12056
Terika Smith Ministries Corp	Lawrence	MA	E	978 233-0576	9603
T J Ryan LLC	Brewer	ME	F	207 989-7183	4620
Community Apostolic Order Inc (PA)	Island Pond	VT	F	802 723-4452	17304

ORGANIZATIONS: Research Institute

	CITY	ST	EMP	PHONE	ENTRY#
Advanced Mechanical Tech Inc (PA)	Watertown	MA	E	617 923-4174	12855
Haigh-Farr Inc	Bedford	NH	D	603 644-6170	13932

ORNAMENTS: Christmas Tree, Exc Electrical & Glass

	CITY	ST	EMP	PHONE	ENTRY#
Syratech Acquisition Corp (HQ)	Medford	MA	C	781 539-0100	10298
Rgt Inc	Providence	RI	D	401 431-5016	16601

OSCILLATORS

	CITY	ST	EMP	PHONE	ENTRY#
Mti-Milliren Technologies Inc	Newburyport	MA	E	978 465-6064	10703

OUTBOARD MOTORS: Electric

	CITY	ST	EMP	PHONE	ENTRY#
Coherent Corp	Bloomfield	CT	C	860 243-9557	156
Enertgetic Baltic MI	Enfield	NH	G	603 252-0804	14274

PACKAGE DESIGN SVCS

	CITY	ST	EMP	PHONE	ENTRY#
Stephen Gould Corporation	Tewksbury	MA	E	978 851-2500	12420

PACKAGING & LABELING SVCS

	CITY	ST	EMP	PHONE	ENTRY#
Olive Oil Factory LLC	Waterbury	CT	E	203 437-8286	3956
Feteria Tool & Findings	Attleboro	MA	G	508 222-7788	6014
Horn Corporation (PA)	Lancaster	MA	E	800 832-7020	9527
Industrial Packaging Sup Inc	Worcester	MA	F	978 514-9960	13741
Industrial Packaging Supply Inc (PA)	Webster	MA	F	508 499-1600	12927
JP Progressive Comm Group LLC	New Bedford	MA	G	800 477-4681	10607
Rand-Whitney Packaging Corp	Worcester	MA	D	508 929-3400	13780
Safecor Health LLC	Woburn	MA	G	781 933-8780	13658
US Packaging Specialties	Fall River	MA	F	508 674-3636	8621
Packgen Inc	Auburn	ME	F	207 784-4195	4449
Cdc Enterprises Llc	Windham	NH	G	603 437-3090	15722
J-Pac LLC (HQ)	Somersworth	NH	D	603 692-9955	15617
New Model Inc	Belmont	NH	F	603 267-8225	13964
Resin Technology Group LLC	Seabrook	NH	D	508 230-8070	15601
Contech Medical Inc	Providence	RI	D	401 351-4890	16504
Matlet Group LLC	Pawtucket	RI	B	401 834-3007	16385
Select Design Ltd	Burlington	VT	D	802 864-9075	17158

PACKAGING MATERIALS, WHOLESALE

	CITY	ST	EMP	PHONE	ENTRY#
Hudson Paper Company (PA)	Stratford	CT	E	203 378-8759	3548
Park City Packaging Inc (PA)	Stratford	CT	E	203 378-7384	3564
Penmar Industries Inc	Stratford	CT	F	203 853-4868	3565
Danvers Industrial Packg Corp	Beverly	MA	E	978 777-0020	6344
Horn International Packg Inc (HQ)	Lancaster	MA	E	978 667-8797	9528
Pacific Packaging Products Inc (PA)	Wilmington	MA	C	978 657-9100	13445
Packaging Products Corporation	New Bedford	MA	F	508 997-5150	10638
Packaging Specialties Inc	Newburyport	MA	D	978 462-1300	10706
Prolamina Corporation (DH)	Westfield	MA	F	413 562-2315	13202
Sealed Air Corporation	Holyoke	MA	C	413 534-0231	9280
Maine Potato Growers Inc	Caribou	ME	F	207 764-3131	4676
Ship-Pac Corp	Portland	ME	G	207 797-7444	5270
Continental Plas & Packg Inc	Lincoln	RI	F	781 932-1115	16128

PACKAGING MATERIALS: Paper

	CITY	ST	EMP	PHONE	ENTRY#
Agi-Shorewood Group Us LLC	Stamford	CT	A	203 324-4839	3275
Amgraph	Lisbon	CT	G	860 822-2000	1554
Ansel Label and Packaging Corp	Trumbull	CT	E	203 452-0311	3711
Atlas Agi Holdings LLC	Greenwich	CT	A	203 622-9138	1315
Biomerics LLC	Monroe	CT	D	203 268-7238	1906
CCL Label Inc	Shelton	CT	F	203 926-1253	2990
Flagship Converters Inc	Danbury	CT	D	203 792-0034	746
Fluted Partition Inc (PA)	Bridgeport	CT	C	203 368-2548	322
Fortis Solutions Group LLC	Ellington	CT	E	860 872-6311	1107
Identification Products Corp	Bridgeport	CT	F	203 334-5969	331
Identification Products Corp (PA)	Shelton	CT	F	203 334-5969	3019
Northeast Laser Engraving Inc	Monroe	CT	E	203 268-7238	1918
Packaging and Crating Tech LLC	Watertown	CT	F	203 759-1799	4021
Penmar Industries Inc	Stratford	CT	F	203 853-4868	3565
Polymer Films Inc	West Haven	CT	E	203 932-3000	4119
Quality Name Plate Inc	East Glastonbury	CT	D	860 633-9495	923
Rol-Vac Limited Partnership	Dayville	CT	F	860 928-9929	868
Sealed Air Corporation	Danbury	CT	C	203 791-3597	814
Sonoco Prtective Solutions Inc	Putnam	CT	D	860 928-7795	2875
Windham Container Corporation	Putnam	CT	F	860 928-7934	2879

	CITY	ST	EMP	PHONE	ENTRY#
Bopkg Inc (HQ)	Fitchburg	MA	C	978 343-3067	8644
CCL Label Inc (HQ)	Framingham	MA	D	508 872-4511	8750
Cheer Pack North America LLC	West Bridgewater	MA	F	508 927-7800	12968
Comprehensive Identification Products Inc	Burlington	MA	C		
781 229-8780				7354	
Coveris Advnced Ctngs Mtthews (DH)	West Springfield	MA	E	413 539-5547	13019
E V Yeuell Inc	Woburn	MA	E	781 933-2984	13560
GP&c Operations LLC (PA)	Gardner	MA	E	978 630-1028	8889
GPA Global US Holding Inc	Mansfield	MA	F	800 334-1113	10053
Gta-Nht Inc (HQ)	Rockland	MA	C	781 331-5900	11647
Halmark Systems LLC	Stoughton	MA	E	781 630-0231	12212
Healthy Life Snack Inc	Canton	MA	F	781 575-6744	7795
Ideal Tape Co Inc	Lowell	MA	D	978 458-6833	9885
Industrial Lbling Systems Corp	Tyngsboro	MA	E	978 649-7004	12460
OK Durable Packaging Inc	Marlborough	MA	F	508 303-8067	10189
Opsec Security Inc	Boston	MA	G	617 226-3000	6941
Pacific Packaging Products Inc (PA)	Wilmington	MA	C	978 657-9100	13445
Pioneer Packaging Inc (PA)	Chicopee	MA	D	413 378-6930	8054
Sealed Air Corporation	Holyoke	MA	C	413 534-0231	9280
Stickamayka Packaging Inc	Andover	MA	E	978 474-1930	5926
Vangy Tool Company Inc	Worcester	MA	G	508 754-2669	13820
Walter Drake Incorporated (PA)	Holyoke	MA	G	413 536-5463	9290
Westrock Mwv LLC	Springfield	MA	D	413 736-7211	12152
Huhtamaki Inc	Lewiston	ME	E	207 795-6000	4964
Kullson Engineered Tech Inc	Lewiston	ME	E	207 576-9808	4969
Pure-Stat Technologies Inc	Lewiston	ME	E	207 795-6000	4987
Transcendia Inc	Lewiston	ME	D	207 786-4790	4994
Label Tech LLC	Somersworth	NH	C	603 692-2005	15618
Nefab Packaging North East LLC (PA)	Dover	NH	E	603 343-5750	14238
Pak 2000 Inc	Lancaster	NH	F	603 569-3700	14678
Roymal Inc	Newport	NH	E	603 863-2410	15237
Amring Worldwide Inc	Johnston	RI	D	401 943-5040	16075
Contempo Card Co Inc (PA)	Providence	RI	D	401 272-4210	16505
Jewel Case Corporation	Providence	RI	B	401 943-1400	16549
Mason Box Company	Pawtucket	RI	E	800 842-9526	16383
Morris Transparent Box Co	East Providence	RI	F	401 438-6116	16032
Nelipak Corporation (PA)	Cranston	RI	E	401 946-2699	15899
S G Inc	Pascoag	RI	E	401 568-1110	16340
Tex Flock Inc	Woonsocket	RI	E	401 765-2340	16981
Wintech Intl Corp - Nk	Warwick	RI	F	401 383-3307	16880

PACKAGING MATERIALS: Paper, Coated Or Laminated

	CITY	ST	EMP	PHONE	ENTRY#
Amgraph Packaging Inc (PA)	Baltic	CT	D	860 822-2000	37
Packedge Inc	Westport	CT	F	203 288-0200	4192
Fortifiber LLC	Attleboro	MA	E	508 222-3500	6018
Millstone Med Outsourcing LLC (PA)	Fall River	MA	C	508 679-8384	8583
Novacel Inc (DH)	Palmer	MA	E	413 283-3468	11279
Package Printing Company Inc	West Springfield	MA	E	413 736-2748	13040
Prolamina Corporation (DH)	Westfield	MA	F	413 562-2315	13202
Web Industries Inc (PA)	Marlborough	MA	G	508 898-2988	10234
Verso Paper Holding LLC	Jay	ME	A	207 897-3431	4917

PACKAGING MATERIALS: Paper, Thermoplastic Coated

	CITY	ST	EMP	PHONE	ENTRY#
Packaging Devices Inc (PA)	Teaticket	MA	F	508 548-0224	12379

PACKAGING MATERIALS: Plastic Film, Coated Or Laminated

	CITY	ST	EMP	PHONE	ENTRY#
Bollore Inc	Dayville	CT	D	860 774-2930	859
General Packaging Products Inc	Norwalk	CT	G	203 846-1340	2505
Polymeric Converting LLC	Enfield	CT	E	860 623-1335	1142
Industrial Packaging Sup Inc	Worcester	MA	F	978 514-9960	13741
Industrial Packaging Supply Inc (PA)	Webster	MA	F	508 499-1600	12927
K & K Thermoforming Inc	Southbridge	MA	E	508 764-7700	12024
Ovtene Inc	Marion	MA	E	617 852-4828	10099
Intercept Medical LLC	Portsmouth	NH	E	800 622-1114	15410
J-Pac LLC (HQ)	Somersworth	NH	D	603 692-9955	15617

PACKAGING: Blister Or Bubble Formed, Plastic

	CITY	ST	EMP	PHONE	ENTRY#
Packaging and Crating Tech LLC	Watertown	CT	F	203 759-1799	4021
Southpack LLC	New Britain	CT	E	860 224-2242	2061
Lacerta Group Inc	Mansfield	MA	G	508 339-3312	10063
Lacerta Group LLC (PA)	Mansfield	MA	C	508 303-3312	10064
Ntp/Republic Clear Thru Corp	Holyoke	MA	E	413 493-6800	9272
Walter Drake Incorporated (PA)	Holyoke	MA	G	413 536-5463	9290
Capco Plastics Inc (PA)	Providence	RI	E	401 272-3833	16494

PACKING & CRATING SVC

	CITY	ST	EMP	PHONE	ENTRY#
Abbott-Action Inc	Canton	MA	E	781 702-5710	7765
Big Foot Moving & Storage Inc	Acton	MA	E	781 488-3090	5740

PACKING MATERIALS: Mechanical

	CITY	ST	EMP	PHONE	ENTRY#
New England Braiding Co Inc	Manchester	NH	F	603 669-1987	14897

PADDING: Foamed Plastics

	CITY	ST	EMP	PHONE	ENTRY#
Der-Tex Corporation	Saco	ME	E	207 284-5931	5365
Wayne Manufacturing Inds LLC	Brentwood	NH	F	978 416-0899	14032
Eco Global Manufacturing LLC	Providence	RI	E	401 331-5129	16512
MH Stallman Company Inc (PA)	Providence	RI	E	401 331-5129	16564

PAINTS & ADDITIVES

	CITY	ST	EMP	PHONE	ENTRY#
Southern Diversified Pdts LLC	Bethel	CT	F	917 306-4138	134
Stanchem Incorporated (HQ)	East Berlin	CT	E	860 828-0571	918
Eastman Performance Films LLC	Holliston	MA	C	508 474-6002	9208
ICP Construction Inc (HQ)	Andover	MA	C	978 623-9980	5887
L & A Molding Corporation	Leominster	MA	D	978 537-3538	9675
NBD Nanotechnologies Inc	Lexington	MA	F	781 541-4192	9764
Recolor Paints LLC	Hanover	MA	F	833 732-6567	9040

PAINTS & ALLIED PRODUCTS

	CITY	ST	EMP	PHONE	ENTRY#
A G C Incorporated	Meriden	CT	C	203 235-3361	1649
Albert Kemperle Inc	Hartford	CT	F	860 727-0933	1469
Albi Protective Coatings LLC	East Berlin	CT	F	860 828-0571	906
Chromalloy Component Svcs Inc	Windsor	CT	E	860 688-7798	4266
Colonial Coatings Inc	Milford	CT	D	203 783-9933	1811
Five Star Products Inc	Shelton	CT	E	203 336-7900	3006
Fougera Pharmaceuticals Inc	Wallingford	CT	C	203 265-2086	3807
Fox Valley Paint Inc	Brookfield	CT	D	844 627-5255	520
Greenmaker Industries Conn LLC	West Hartford	CT	F	860 761-2830	4062
Jet Process Corporation	Wallingford	CT	G	203 985-6000	3823
Mantrose-Haeuser Co Inc (HQ)	Westport	CT	E	203 454-1800	4182
Minteq International Inc	Canaan	CT	F	860 824-5435	556
Acton Research Corporation	Acton	MA	E	941 556-2601	5731
California Paint	Andover	MA	F	978 965-2122	5876
Coveris Advnced Ctngs Mtthews (DH)	West Springfield	MA	E	413 539-5547	13019
Covestro LLC	Wilmington	MA	C	800 458-0014	13399
DSM Neoresins Inc	Wilmington	MA	C	800 458-0014	13403
F & D Plastics Inc (PA)	Leominster	MA	E	978 668-5140	9662
Franklin Paint Company Inc	Franklin	MA	E	800 486-0304	8838
Gare Incorporated	Haverhill	MA	E	978 373-9131	9096
Highland Labs Inc	Holliston	MA	G	508 429-2918	9215
Innovative Chem Pdts Group LLC	Boston	MA	F	800 393-5250	6812
Katahdin Industries Inc (PA)	Hudson	MA	E	781 329-1420	9380
Mantrose-Haeuser Co Inc	Attleboro	MA	E	203 454-1800	6033
Perrco Inc	Woburn	MA	F	617 933-5300	13633
Rustoleum Attleboro Plant	Attleboro	MA	E	508 222-3710	6060
Tnemec East Inc	Wilmington	MA	E	978 988-9500	13467
Union Specialties Inc	Newburyport	MA	E	978 465-1717	10724
Chilton Paint Co Inc ME	Freeport	ME	G	207 865-4443	4800
Hampshire Chemical Corp (DH)	Nashua	NH	E	603 888-2320	15109
Roymal Inc	Newport	NH	E	603 863-2410	15237
Development Associates Inc	North Kingstown	RI	F	401 884-1350	16244
Fri Resins Holding Company	Cranston	RI	F	401 946-5564	15863
Pg Imtech of Californ	East Providence	RI	E	401 521-2490	16038
Teknor Color Company	Pawtucket	RI	G	401 725-8000	16421

PAINTS, VARNISHES & SPLYS WHOLESALERS

	CITY	ST	EMP	PHONE	ENTRY#
Advanced Frp Systems Inc	East Weymouth	MA	G	508 927-6915	8423
Detrapel Inc	Framingham	MA	F	617 514-7778	8757
Chilton Paint Co Inc ME	Freeport	ME	G	207 865-4443	4800

PAINTS, VARNISHES & SPLYS, WHOLESALE: Paints

	CITY	ST	EMP	PHONE	ENTRY#
Color Craft Ltd	East Granby	CT	F	800 509-6563	929
Grafted Coatings Inc	Stratford	CT	G	203 377-9979	3543
Maki Corp (PA)	Gardner	MA	E	978 343-7422	8895

PAINTS: Oil Or Alkyd Vehicle Or Water Thinned

	CITY	ST	EMP	PHONE	ENTRY#
Durant Prfmce Coatings Inc	Revere	MA	F	781 289-1400	11618
Michael Rogovsky	New Bedford	MA	F	508 487-3287	10622

PAINTS: Waterproof

	CITY	ST	EMP	PHONE	ENTRY#
M & D Coatings LLC	Stratford	CT	G	203 380-9466	3554
Foundation Armor LLC	Amherst	NH	F	866 306-0246	13870

PALLETS & SKIDS: Wood

	CITY	ST	EMP	PHONE	ENTRY#
Atlas Box and Crating Co Inc (PA)	Sutton	MA	C	508 865-1155	12276
Great Northern Dunnage LLC	Fitchburg	MA	E	978 343-2300	8656
Horn International Packg Inc (HQ)	Lancaster	MA	E	978 667-8797	9528
Unified2 Globl Packg Group LLC	Lancaster	MA	B	508 865-1155	9531
Carris Reels Inc (HQ)	Proctor	VT	E	802 773-9111	17457

PANEL & DISTRIBUTION BOARDS & OTHER RELATED APPARATUS

	CITY	ST	EMP	PHONE	ENTRY#
Columbia Electrical Contrs Inc	Westborough	MA	C	508 366-8297	13091
Huber Engineered Woods LLC	Easton	ME	D	207 488-6700	4742
Bittware Inc (DH)	Concord	NH	E	603 226-0404	14115

Employee Codes: A=Over 500 employees, B=251-500
C=101-250, D=51-100, E=20-50, F=10-19, G=1-9

2024 Harris New England
Manufacturers Directory

1437

PRODUCT

PANELS: Building, Plastic, NEC

	CITY	ST	EMP	PHONE	ENTRY#
Nevamar Company LLC **(HQ)**	Shelton	CT	B	203 925-1556	3037
Panolam Industries Inc **(HQ)**	Shelton	CT	E	203 925-1556	3044
Panolam Industries Intl Inc **(PA)**	Shelton	CT	E	203 925-1556	3045
Kalwall Corporation	Bow	NH	C	603 224-6881	14002
Kalwall Corporation **(PA)**	Manchester	NH	B	603 627-3861	14870
Precision Letter LLC	Manchester	NH	F	603 625-9625	14913
Clear Carbon & Components Inc	Bristol	RI	E	401 254-5085	15758

PAPER & BOARD: Die-cut

Hamden Packaging Inc	Hamden	CT	E	203 288-0200	1428
Martin Printing Inc	North Haven	CT	E	203 239-7991	2423
Walker Products Incorporated	Glastonbury	CT	F	860 659-3781	1301
H Loeb Corporation	New Bedford	MA	E	508 996-3745	10597
J L Enterprises Inc	Canton	MA	G	781 821-6300	7802
Merrimac Spool and Reel Co Inc	Haverhill	MA	E	978 372-7777	9116
New England Ultimate Finishing	Holyoke	MA	E	413 532-7777	9270
United Paper Stock Co Inc	Worcester	MA	E	401 724-5700	13816
Winthrop Printing Company Inc	Foxboro	MA	E	617 268-9660	8732
Yankee Printing Group Inc	South Hadley	MA	E	413 532-9513	11968
Tissue Plus LLC	Bangor	ME	F	978 524-0550	4516
Cdc Enterprises Llc	Windham	NH	G	603 437-3090	15722
Fife Packaging LLC	Penacook	NH	G	603 753-2669	15310
Mono Die Cutting Co Inc	Riverside	RI	F	401 434-1274	16658
Mylan Technologies Inc **(HQ)**	Saint Albans	VT	C	802 527-7792	17525

PAPER & PAPER PRDTS: Crepe, Made From Purchased Materials

Dennecrepe Corporation	Gardner	MA	D	978 630-8669	8884

PAPER PRDTS: Infant & Baby Prdts

Kimberly-Clark Corporation	New Milford	CT	D	860 210-1602	2250
Kimberly-Clark Corporation	Franklin	MA	G	508 520-1355	8849
Seventh Generation Inc **(DH)**	Burlington	VT	C	802 658-3773	17159

PAPER PRDTS: Napkin Stock

Erving Industries Inc **(PA)**	Erving	MA	D	413 422-2700	8469
Soundview Vermont Holdings LLC	East Dummerston	VT	C	802 387-5571	17217

PAPER PRDTS: Pressed & Molded Pulp & Fiber Prdts

Kadant Inc **(PA)**	Westford	MA	C	978 776-2000	13244

PAPER PRDTS: Sanitary

Soundview Paper Mills LLC **(DH)**	Greenwich	CT	F	201 796-4000	1352
Erving Industries Inc **(PA)**	Erving	MA	D	413 422-2700	8469
Essity North America Inc	Palmer	MA	B	413 289-1221	11274
Sales Solutions Inc	Scituate	MA	G	781 588-2703	11771
Sumner Printing Inc	Somersworth	NH	E	603 692-7424	15625

PAPER PRDTS: Sanitary Tissue Paper

Kimberly-Clark Corporation	New Milford	CT	D	860 210-1602	2250
Georgia-Pacific LLC	Leominster	MA	D	978 537-4701	9666
Kimberly-Clark Corporation	Franklin	MA	G	508 520-1355	8849

PAPER PRDTS: Tampons, Sanitary, Made From Purchased Material

Edgewell Per Care Brands LLC **(HQ)**	Shelton	CT	B	203 944-5500	3002
Edgewell Personal Care Company **(PA)**	Shelton	CT	E	203 944-5500	3003
Playtex Products LLC **(HQ)**	Shelton	CT	D	203 944-5500	3050

PAPER, WHOLESALE: Printing

Judd Paper Company	Rumford	RI	F	413 534-5661	16673

PAPER: Adhesive

Design Label Manufacturing Inc	Old Lyme	CT	E	860 739-6266	2640
H-O Products Corporation	Winsted	CT	E	860 379-9875	4346
Illinois Tool Works Inc	Manchester	CT	C	860 646-8153	1605
Asp Fibermark Holdings LLC	West Springfield	MA	A	413 736-4554	13014
Industrial Lbling Systems Corp	Tyngsboro	MA	E	978 649-7004	12460
Pacon Corporation	Framingham	MA	E	508 370-0780	8796
Pg Technologies Inc	Westfield	MA	G	413 562-1354	13198
Electronic Imaging Mtls Inc	Keene	NH	E	603 357-1459	14597
Polyonics Inc	Westmoreland	NH	E	603 352-1415	15698
Trans-Tex LLC	Cranston	RI	E	401 331-8483	15920

PAPER: Bank Note

Crane & Co Inc **(HQ)**	Dalton	MA	B	617 648-3799	8150

PAPER: Building, Insulating & Packaging

Ampd Air Quality Servics LLC	Hamden	CT	G	203 387-1709	1411

PAPER: Cardboard

Lamitech	Rockland	MA	F	781 878-7708	11649
Jewel Case Corporation	Providence	RI	B	401 943-1400	16549

PAPER: Chart & Graph, Ruled

Chartpak Inc **(HQ)**	Leeds	MA	D	413 584-5446	9621

PAPER: Cigarette

UST LLC	Stamford	CT	A	203 817-3000	3489

PAPER: Coated & Laminated, NEC

Copy Cats Inc	New London	CT	F	860 442-8424	2225
Markal Finishing Co Inc	Bridgeport	CT	E	203 384-8219	346
Scapa Holdings Inc **(DH)**	Windsor	CT	D	860 688-8000	4298
Specialty Printing LLC **(PA)**	Windsor	CT	D	860 623-8870	4300
The E J Davis Company	North Haven	CT	E	203 239-5391	2439
Accucon Incorporated	Leominster	MA	G	978 840-0337	9631
American Biltrite Inc **(PA)**	Wellesley	MA	G	781 237-6655	12935
Arclin Surfaces - E Longmeadow	East Longmeadow	MA	F	678 781-5341	8370
Chesterfield Products Inc	Chesterfield	MA	E	413 296-0066	7997
Fortifiber LLC	Attleboro	MA	E	508 222-3500	6018
Neptco Incorporated **(DH)**	Westwood	MA	D	401 722-5500	13316
New England Ultimate Finishing	Holyoke	MA	E	413 532-7777	9270
Paiva Corp	Fall River	MA	G	508 679-7921	8593
Regal Press Incorporated **(PA)**	Norwood	MA	C	781 769-3900	11206
Shawsheen Rubber Co Inc	Andover	MA	D	978 470-1760	5918
Suddekor LLC **(DH)**	Agawam	MA	E	413 821-9000	5808
Suddekor LLC	East Longmeadow	MA	E	413 525-4070	8397
Tekni-Plex Inc	Ashland	MA	E	508 881-2440	5968
Verso Paper Holding LLC	Jay	ME	A	207 897-3431	4917
Avery Dennison Corporation	Belmont	NH	E	603 217-4144	13959
Label Tech LLC	Somersworth	NH	C	603 692-2005	15618
Ecological Fibers Inc	Pawtucket	RI	D	401 725-9700	16366

PAPER: Coated, Exc Photographic, Carbon Or Abrasive

The Gilman Brothers Company	Gilman	CT	D	860 889-8444	1268
Avery Dennison Corporation	Fitchburg	MA	C	978 353-2100	8643
Hazen Paper Company **(PA)**	Holyoke	MA	C	413 538-8204	9259
Visual Magnetics Ltd	Mendon	MA	E	508 381-2400	10323
Sappi North America Inc	Skowhegan	ME	A	207 238-3000	5478
Sappi North America Inc	South Portland	ME	D	207 854-7000	5513
Sappi North America Inc	Westbrook	ME	C	207 856-4911	5647

PAPER: Corrugated

Park City Packaging Inc **(PA)**	Stratford	CT	E	203 378-7384	3564
Valley Container Inc	Bridgeport	CT	E	203 368-6546	383
Westrock - Southern Cont LLC	Boston	MA	E	978 772-5050	7120

PAPER: Filter

Hollingsworth & Vose Company **(PA)**	East Walpole	MA	C	508 850-2000	8418

PAPER: Gift Wrap

Expressive Design Group Inc	Holyoke	MA	E	413 315-6296	9255

PAPER: Kraft

Ampac Holdings LLC	Claremont	NH	D	603 542-0411	14076
APC Paper Company Inc **(DH)**	Claremont	NH	D	603 542-0411	14077
Weeden Street Associates LLC	Pawtucket	RI	E	401 725-2610	16430

PAPER: Packaging

Hexcelpack LLC	Bristol	CT	G	855 439-2351	454
Packaging Specialties Inc	Newburyport	MA	D	978 462-1300	10706
Union Paper & Packaging Inc	Leominster	MA	G	978 227-5868	9711
Signode Industrial Group LLC	Rumford	RI	D	401 438-5203	16676
The Real Reel Corporation	Rumford	RI	A	401 434-1070	16678

PAPER: Specialty

A Group Inc	Woburn	MA	E	781 756-3163	13495
Asp Fibermark Holdings LLC	West Springfield	MA	A	413 736-4554	13014
Crocker Technical Papers Inc	Fitchburg	MA	E	978 345-7771	8651
Hollingsworth & Vose Company	West Groton	MA	C	978 448-7000	13002
Tissue Plus LLC	Bangor	ME	F	978 524-0550	4516
Monadnock Paper Mills Inc **(HQ)**	Bennington	NH	D	603 588-3311	13977
Nashua Corporation	Merrimack	NH	A	603 880-1100	14994

PAPER: Specialty Or Chemically Treated

Ahlstrom USA Inc **(DH)**	Windsor Locks	CT	F	860 654-8300	4319
Boston Paper Board Corp	Boston	MA	F	617 666-1154	6612
Pixelle Specialty Solutions LLC	Jay	ME	B	207 897-3431	4915

PAPER: Tissue

Cellu Tissue Corporation	East Hartford	CT	A	860 289-7496	979
Seaman Paper Company Mass Inc	Orange	MA	G	978 544-2455	11233
Lincoln Paper and Tissue LLC	Lincoln	ME	B	207 794-0600	5011

	CITY	ST	EMP	PHONE	ENTRY#
Gorham Acquisition LLC	Gorham	NH	E	603 342-2000	14357

PAPER: Uncoated

	CITY	ST	EMP	PHONE	ENTRY#
Gorham Paper and Tissue LLC	Gorham	NH	A		14358

PAPER: Wallpaper

	CITY	ST	EMP	PHONE	ENTRY#
Arlington Sample Book Co Inc (PA)	Sunapee	NH	F	603 763-9082	15642

PAPERBOARD PRDTS: Container Board

	CITY	ST	EMP	PHONE	ENTRY#
Rand-Whtney Cntnrbard Ltd Prtn	Montville	CT	D	860 848-1900	1928
Westrock Rkt LLC	Springfield	MA	G	413 543-7300	12153
Georgia-Pacific LLC	Baileyville	ME	G	207 427-4077	4484
Graphic Packaging Intl LLC	Concord	NH	E	603 224-2333	14134

PAPERBOARD PRDTS: Folding Boxboard

	CITY	ST	EMP	PHONE	ENTRY#
Graphic Packaging Intl LLC	Concord	NH	C	603 230-5100	14133
Rand-Whitney Container LLC	Pawtucket	RI	D	401 729-7900	16411

PAPERBOARD PRDTS: Packaging Board

	CITY	ST	EMP	PHONE	ENTRY#
Pact Inc	Watertown	CT	F	203 759-1799	4022
Georgia-Pacific LLC	Leominster	MA	D	978 537-4701	9666
Signode Industrial Group LLC	Rumford	RI	D	401 438-5203	16676
The Real Reel Corporation	Rumford	RI	A	401 434-1070	16678

PAPERBOARD: Boxboard

	CITY	ST	EMP	PHONE	ENTRY#
Fusion Paperboard Connecticut LLC	Versailles	CT	C	888 283-3617	3764
Hamden Packaging Inc	Hamden	CT	E	203 288-0200	1428

PARACHUTES

	CITY	ST	EMP	PHONE	ENTRY#
Niche Inc	New Bedford	MA	E	508 990-4202	10633

PARTICLEBOARD

	CITY	ST	EMP	PHONE	ENTRY#
Panolam Industries Intl Inc (PA)	Shelton	CT	E	203 925-1556	3045

PARTITIONS & FIXTURES: Except Wood

	CITY	ST	EMP	PHONE	ENTRY#
Displaycraft Inc	Plainville	CT	E	860 747-9110	2754
Durham Manufacturing Company (PA)	Durham	CT	D	860 349-3427	899
George Patton Associates Inc	Fall River	MA	C	800 572-2194	8552
M & P Machine Company Inc	Stoughton	MA	E	781 344-5888	12218
New England Wire Products Inc (PA)	Leominster	MA	D	800 254-9473	9686
Newton Distributing Co Inc	Natick	MA	F	617 969-4002	10488
Van Stry Design Inc	Malden	MA	E	781 388-9998	10030
E G W Bradbury Enterprises Inc	Bridgewater	ME	F	207 429-8141	4625
Jsi Store Fixtures Inc (HQ)	Milo	ME	C	207 943-5203	5070
Kardex Remstar LLC (HQ)	Westbrook	ME	E	207 854-1861	5633
Custom Design Incorporated	North Kingstown	RI	E	401 294-0200	16243
Frank Shatz & Co	Warwick	RI	E	401 739-1822	16816
Scope Display & Box Co Inc (PA)	Cranston	RI	E	401 942-7150	15909
Vermont Store Fixture Corporation (PA)	Danby	VT	D	802 293-5126	17210

PARTITIONS: Solid Fiber, Made From Purchased Materials

	CITY	ST	EMP	PHONE	ENTRY#
Westrock Rkt LLC	Springfield	MA	G	413 543-7300	12153

PARTITIONS: Wood & Fixtures

	CITY	ST	EMP	PHONE	ENTRY#
C Mather Company Inc	South Windsor	CT	G	860 528-5667	3124
Creative Dimensions Inc	Cheshire	CT	E	203 250-6500	584
McKinnon Design LLC	Plainville	CT	G	860 617-7371	2773
Mildred Coppola (PA)	Stamford	CT	F	203 967-9300	3411
One & Co Inc	Norwich	CT	G	860 892-5180	2614
Robert L Lovallo	Stamford	CT	G	203 324-6655	3450
Stevenson Group Corporation	Harwinton	CT	F	860 689-0011	1524
Viking Kitchen Cabinets LLC (PA)	New Britain	CT	E	860 223-7101	2074
Cape Cod Lumber Co Inc	Abington	MA	C	781 878-0715	5722
General Woodworking Inc (PA)	Lowell	MA	F	978 458-6625	9879
J H Dunning Corporation	North Walpole	NH	E	603 445-5591	15258
Completely Custom LLC	North Kingstown	RI	G	401 667-0059	16239
Herrick & White Ltd	Cumberland	RI	D	401 658-0440	15942
Igs Store Fixtures Inc	Smithfield	RI	C	978 532-0010	16715
Orion Ret Svcs & Fixturing Inc	Smithfield	RI	D	401 334-5000	16725
Scope Display & Box Co Inc (PA)	Cranston	RI	E	401 942-7150	15909

PARTS: Metal

	CITY	ST	EMP	PHONE	ENTRY#
SMR Metal Technology LLC	South Windsor	CT	G	860 291-8259	3181
Westbrook Manufacturing LLC	Ivoryton	CT	F	860 767-2460	1534
Alvin Johnson	East Longmeadow	MA	G	413 525-6334	8368
Atlantic Industrial Models LLC	Essex	MA	E	978 768-7686	8473
Mair-Mac Machine Company Inc	Brockton	MA	E	508 895-9001	7294
Mascon Inc	Woburn	MA	E	781 938-5800	13605
Burtco Inc	Westminster Station	VT	F	802 722-3358	17702

PATENT OWNERS & LESSORS

	CITY	ST	EMP	PHONE	ENTRY#
Capricorn Investors II LP	Greenwich	CT	E	203 861-6600	1325
Capricorn Investors III LP (PA)	Greenwich	CT	F	203 861-6600	1326

PATTERNS: Indl

	CITY	ST	EMP	PHONE	ENTRY#
Arrow Diversified Tooling Inc	Ellington	CT	E	860 872-9072	1101
S Ralph Cross and Sons Inc	Holyoke	MA	E	508 865-8112	9279
Clear Carbon & Components Inc	Bristol	RI	E	401 254-5085	15758

PAVERS

	CITY	ST	EMP	PHONE	ENTRY#
LH Gault & Son Incorporated	Westport	CT	D	203 227-5181	4180
Colebrook Intrlcking Pvers Wll	Little Compton	RI	F	401 835-6934	16160

PAVING MIXTURES

	CITY	ST	EMP	PHONE	ENTRY#
Bruce A Manzer Inc	Farmington	ME	E	207 696-5881	4777

PENCILS & PENS WHOLESALERS

	CITY	ST	EMP	PHONE	ENTRY#
Mega Sound and Light LLC	Danbury	CT	G	203 743-4200	784
AT Cross Company LLC (HQ)	Providence	RI	D	401 333-1200	16476
Sheaffer Pen Corporation	Lincoln	RI	A	319 372-7444	16154

PENS & PARTS: Ball Point

	CITY	ST	EMP	PHONE	ENTRY#
Bic Consumer Pdts Mfg Co Inc	Milford	CT	C	203 783-2000	1802
Bic Consumer Pdts Mfg Co Inc (DH)	Shelton	CT	D	203 783-2000	2984
Bic Corporation (HQ)	Shelton	CT	A	203 783-2000	2985
Bic USA Inc (DH)	Shelton	CT	C	203 783-2000	2986
EF Leach & Company	Attleboro	MA	C	508 643-3309	6011

PERFUME: Perfumes, Natural Or Synthetic

	CITY	ST	EMP	PHONE	ENTRY#
Parfums De Coeur Ltd (PA)	Stamford	CT	E	203 655-8807	3426

PERFUMES

	CITY	ST	EMP	PHONE	ENTRY#
American Distilling Inc (PA)	East Hampton	CT	D	860 267-4444	959

PEST CONTROL IN STRUCTURES SVCS

	CITY	ST	EMP	PHONE	ENTRY#
Connecticut Tick Control LLC	Norwalk	CT	F	203 855-7849	2486

PEST CONTROL SVCS

	CITY	ST	EMP	PHONE	ENTRY#
Pfm Holding Co	Fairfield	CT	B	203 335-3300	1197

PESTICIDES

	CITY	ST	EMP	PHONE	ENTRY#
Waterbury Companies Inc	Waterbury	CT	C		3980

PET FOOD WHOLESALERS

	CITY	ST	EMP	PHONE	ENTRY#
Blue Buffalo Company Ltd (DH)	Wilton	CT	D	203 762-9751	4233

PET SPLYS

	CITY	ST	EMP	PHONE	ENTRY#
Amerpet LLC	Stamford	CT	G	475 619-9512	3280
Pleasant Valley Fence Co Inc	Pleasant Valley	CT	G	860 379-0088	2803
Alpha Tech Pet Inc	Littleton	MA	G	978 486-3690	9800
P Wiles Inc (PA)	Orleans	MA	F	508 385-4321	11242
Maine Pet Supply	Wells	ME	G	207 360-0005	5601
Moore-Clark USA Inc	Westbrook	ME	G	207 591-7077	5639
Planet Ventures Inc (PA)	Westbrook	ME	F	207 761-1515	5642
Two Rivers Pet Products Inc	Turner	ME	E	207 225-3965	5565
Kevin S Boghigian	Nashua	NH	G	603 883-0236	15122
Lupine Inc	Center Conway	NH	D	603 356-7371	14055
Up Country Inc	East Providence	RI	E	401 431-2940	16046
Vermont Juvenile Furn Mfg Inc	West Rutland	VT	F	802 438-2231	17697

PHARMACEUTICAL PREPARATIONS: Adrenal

	CITY	ST	EMP	PHONE	ENTRY#
Polycarbon Industries Inc	Newburyport	MA	D	978 462-5555	10707
Tri-K Industries Inc	Derry	NH	E	973 298-8850	14211

PHARMACEUTICAL PREPARATIONS: Druggists' Preparations

	CITY	ST	EMP	PHONE	ENTRY#
Avara US Holdings LLC (PA)	Norwalk	CT	E	203 655-1333	2468
Brookfeld Mdcl/Srgical Sup Inc	Brookfield	CT	F	203 775-0862	514
Quality Care Drg/Cntrbrook LLC	Centerbrook	CT	F	860 767-0206	563
4th Dimension Bioprocess Inc	Gloucester	MA	G	978 979-4222	8916
Abbott Laboratories	Worcester	MA	F	508 849-2500	13696
Arranta Bio Holdings LLC (DH)	Watertown	MA	G	785 760-3128	12859
Colucid Pharmaceuticals Inc	Cambridge	MA	G	857 285-6495	7543
Deepcure Inc	Boston	MA	G	617 417-2345	6687
Erytech Pharma Inc	Cambridge	MA	F	360 320-3325	7565
In Silico Biosciences Inc	Lexington	MA	F	781 861-1592	9751
Merrimack Pharmaceuticals Inc (PA)	Cambridge	MA	E	617 441-1000	7640
Nimbus Lakshmi Inc	Boston	MA	D	857 999-2009	6922
Ocular Therapeutix Inc (PA)	Bedford	MA	E	781 357-4000	6250
Pulmatrix Inc (PA)	Bedford	MA	F	781 357-2333	6254
Soleo Health Inc	Canton	MA	E	781 298-3427	7830
Transtulit LLC	West Springfield	MA	E	413 737-2600	13045
Vietaz Inc	Dorchester	MA	G	617 322-1933	8301
Visterra Inc	Waltham	MA	E	617 498-1070	12814

PRODUCT

	CITY	ST	EMP	PHONE	ENTRY#

PHARMACEUTICAL PREPARATIONS: Pills

	CITY	ST	EMP	PHONE	ENTRY#
Nextpoint Therapeutics Inc	Cambridge	MA	G	917 208-0865	7666

PHARMACEUTICAL PREPARATIONS: Powders

	CITY	ST	EMP	PHONE	ENTRY#
Tolerx Inc	Cambridge	MA	E	617 354-8100	7742

PHARMACEUTICAL PREPARATIONS: Proprietary Drug

	CITY	ST	EMP	PHONE	ENTRY#
New Leaf Pharmaceuticals LLC	Newtown	CT	F	203 270-4167	2343
Bedrock Brands LLC	Boston	MA	G	914 231-9550	6587
Innoviva Spclty Thrpeutics Inc	Waltham	MA	E	800 651-3861	12701
Ipsen Bioscience Inc	Cambridge	MA	E	617 679-8500	7618
Supportive Therapeutics LLC	Cambridge	MA	G	860 625-9226	7726

PHARMACEUTICAL PREPARATIONS: Solutions

	CITY	ST	EMP	PHONE	ENTRY#
Citra Labs LLC	Braintree	MA	E	781 848-9386	7173
Cytosol Laboratories Inc	Braintree	MA	E	781 848-9386	7178
Wilmington Partners LP	Wilmington	MA	C	978 658-6111	13476

PHARMACEUTICAL PREPARATIONS: Tablets

	CITY	ST	EMP	PHONE	ENTRY#
Foster Delivery Science Inc	Putnam	CT	E	860 630-4515	2858

PHARMACEUTICALS

	CITY	ST	EMP	PHONE	ENTRY#
Abbott Diagnostics	Southington	CT	G	860 463-0767	3200
Aeromics Inc	Branford	CT	G	216 772-1004	231
Alexion Pharma LLC (DH)	New Haven	CT	D	203 272-2596	2112
Aptuit (scientific Operations) LLC	Greenwich	CT	A	203 422-6600	1313
Arvinas Inc (PA)	New Haven	CT	B	203 535-1456	2119
Asepsis Inc	Waterbury	CT	F	203 573-2000	3887
Avara Pharmaceutical Svcs Inc (HQ)	Norwalk	CT	F	405 217-7670	2467
Benefit Coatings Inc	Stratford	CT	F	203 572-0660	3519
Bioasis Biosciences Corp	Guilford	CT	G	203 533-7082	1387
Biohaven Pharmaceuticals Inc	New Haven	CT	D	203 404-0410	2127
Biohaven Phrm Holdg Co Ltd	New Haven	CT	F	203 691-6332	2128
Biomed Health Inc	Glastonbury	CT	G	860 657-2258	1270
Bioxcel Therapeutics Inc	New Haven	CT	C	475 238-6837	2130
Boehringer Ingelheim Data Dime	Ridgefield	CT	F	800 203-2916	2887
Boehrnger Ingelheim Roxane Inc	Ridgefield	CT	E	800 243-0127	2889
Cara Therapeutics Inc	Stamford	CT	D	203 406-3700	3302
Cardinal Health 414 LLC	East Hartford	CT	G	860 291-9135	978
Celldex Therapeutics Inc	New Haven	CT	F	203 483-3531	2136
Cogstate Sport Inc	New Haven	CT	F	203 773-5010	2137
Drug Farm Usa LLC	Guilford	CT	G	617 735-5205	1392
Evolveimmune Therapeutics Inc	Branford	CT	F	203 858-7389	254
Foster Delivery Science Inc (HQ)	Putnam	CT	F	860 541-5280	2857
Frederick Purdue Company Inc (PA)	Stamford	CT	B	203 588-8000	3349
Hcrx Investments Holdco LP	Stamford	CT	G	203 487-8300	3369
Hcrx Master Gp LLC	Stamford	CT	F	203 487-8300	3370
Healthcare Royalty Inc (PA)	Stamford	CT	G	203 487-8300	3371
Imbrium Therapeutics LP (DH)	Stamford	CT	E	888 827-0622	3380
Itc Group LLC	Orange	CT	G	203 260-5101	2670
Iterum Therapeutics Inc	Old Saybrook	CT	F	860 391-8349	2653
J&J Precision Inc	Thomaston	CT	D	860 283-8243	3622
Karos Pharmaceuticals Inc	New Haven	CT	F	203 535-0540	2165
Kasten Inc	Bridgeport	CT	G	702 860-2407	339
Knoa Pharma LLC (PA)	Stamford	CT	E	203 588-8000	3395
Kolltan Pharmaceuticals Inc (HQ)	New Haven	CT	E	203 773-3000	2166
Koster Keunen LLC (PA)	Watertown	CT	E	860 945-3333	4018
Life Chemicals Usa Inc	Woodbridge	CT	G	203 693-4563	4380
Loxo Oncology Inc (HQ)	Stamford	CT	E	203 653-3880	3405
Mannkind Corporation (PA)	Danbury	CT	D	818 661-5000	781
MD Solarsciences Corporation	Westport	CT	F	203 857-0095	4184
Meter Health Inc	Manchester	CT	G	833 638-3777	1617
Micro Source Discovery Systems	Gaylordsville	CT	G	860 350-8078	1265
Par Phrmceutical Companies Inc	Stratford	CT	D	203 290-6261	3563
Penfield Search Partners Ltd	Fairfield	CT	G	203 307-2600	1196
Perosphere Inc	Danbury	CT	F	203 885-1111	796
PF Laboratories Inc (DH)	Stamford	CT	C	973 256-3100	3430
Pfizer	Groton	CT	E	203 584-2793	1378
Pfizer Inc	Groton	CT	C	860 441-4100	1379
Pfizer Inc	New Haven	CT	F	203 401-0100	2184
Pgxhealthholding Inc (PA)	New Haven	CT	C	203 786-3400	2185
Pharmaceutical RES Assoc Inc	Stamford	CT	A	203 588-8000	3431
PRA Holdings LP	Stamford	CT	A	203 853-0123	3435
Purdue Pharma LP (HQ)	Stamford	CT	C	203 588-8000	3439
Purdue Pharma Technologies Inc	Stamford	CT	A	203 588-8000	3441
PURDUE PRODUCTS LP	Stamford	CT	A	888 827-0624	3442
Rallybio Corporation (PA)	New Haven	CT	E	203 859-3820	2190
Rhodes Pharmaceuticals LP	Stamford	CT	F	888 827-0616	3448
Sheffield Pharmaceuticals LLC	Norwich	CT	F	860 442-4451	2616
Theracour Pharma Inc	West Haven	CT	G	203 937-6137	4129
Tower Laboratories Ltd	Clinton	CT	E	860 669-7078	652
Trevi Therapeutics Inc (PA)	New Haven	CT	F	203 304-2499	2213
Trirx Pharmaceutical Svcs LLC (PA)	Norwalk	CT	E	256 489-8867	2587
Unipharm Inc	Waterbury	CT	E	203 528-3230	3978
2seventy Bio Inc (PA)	Cambridge	MA	D	339 499-9300	7462
AA Pharmaceuticals Inc	Woburn	MA	F	617 935-1241	13496
Abbott	Burlington	MA	G	978 387-5652	7330
Abfero Pharmaceuticals Inc (PA)	Boston	MA	G	781 266-7297	6504
Abpro Corporation	Woburn	MA	E	617 225-0808	13497
Acceleron Pharma Inc (HQ)	Boston	MA	D	617 649-9200	6508
Acceleron Pharma Inc	Cambridge	MA	C	617 576-2220	7465
Adicet Bio Inc (PA)	Boston	MA	G	857 315-5528	6516
Adnexus Therapeutics Inc	Waltham	MA	E	781 891-3745	12584
Adolor Corporation	Lexington	MA	B	781 860-8660	9720
Aerovate Therapeutics Inc (PA)	Boston	MA	G	858 443-2400	6520
Agios Pharmaceuticals Inc (PA)	Cambridge	MA	B	617 649-8600	7470
Aileron Therapeutics Inc (PA)	Boston	MA	G	617 995-0900	6522
Akebia Therapeutics Inc (PA)	Cambridge	MA	C	617 871-2098	7474
Akouos Inc (PA)	Boston	MA	E	857 410-1818	6528
Albireo Pharma Inc (DH)	Boston	MA	E	857 254-5555	6531
Aldeyra Therapeutics Inc (PA)	Lexington	MA	F	781 761-4904	9723
Alexion Pharmaceuticals Inc (HQ)	Boston	MA	A	475 230-2596	6532
Alkermes Inc	Cambridge	MA	C	617 441-3092	7475
Alkermes Inc (HQ)	Waltham	MA	F	781 609-6000	12589
Alkermes Cntrlled Therapeutics	Waltham	MA	B	877 706-0510	12590
Alnylam Pharmaceuticals Inc (PA)	Cambridge	MA	B	617 551-8200	7478
Alnylam Pharmaceuticals Inc	Cambridge	MA	F	617 551-8200	7479
Alnylam Pharmaceuticals Inc	Cambridge	MA	A	617 551-8200	7480
Alnylam US Inc (HQ)	Cambridge	MA	F	617 551-8200	7481
Alnylam US Inc	Norton	MA	D	617 551-8200	11122
Alopexx Pharmaceuticals LLC	Cambridge	MA	F	617 945-2510	7482
Alzheon Inc	Framingham	MA	E	508 861-7709	8740
Amgen Inc	Cambridge	MA	E	617 444-5000	7483
Amryt Pharmaceuticals Inc (DH)	Boston	MA	F	877 764-3131	6547
Amylyx Pharmaceuticals Inc (PA)	Cambridge	MA	C	617 682-0917	7486
Antolrx Inc	Cambridge	MA	G	617 902-0601	7487
Apellis Pharmaceuticals Inc (PA)	Waltham	MA	B	617 977-5700	12592
Aquinnah Pharmaceuticals Inc	Cambridge	MA	F	617 416-0530	7488
Aratana Therapeutics Inc	Boston	MA	G	617 425-9226	6554
Arbor Biotechnologies Inc	Cambridge	MA	E	857 301-6366	7489
Ardelyx Inc	Waltham	MA	D	510 745-1700	12595
Armstrong Pharmaceuticals Inc (HQ)	West Roxbury	MA	B	617 323-7404	13009
Army & Roche LLC	Boston	MA	G	617 936-0114	6558
Arqule Inc (HQ)	Burlington	MA	E	781 994-0300	7335
Astellas Inst For Rgnrtive Mdc (HQ)	Westborough	MA	F	800 727-7003	13078
Astrea Bioseparations US Inc	Canton	MA	F	919 899-9087	7771
Astria Therapeutics Inc (PA)	Boston	MA	E	617 349-1971	6562
Atea Pharmaceuticals Inc (PA)	Boston	MA	E	857 284-8891	6571
Avedro Inc (HQ)	Burlington	MA	C	781 768-3400	7337
Aveo Pharmaceuticals Inc (HQ)	Boston	MA	F	857 400-0101	6580
Avrobio Inc (PA)	Cambridge	MA	E	617 914-8420	7495
Azurity Pharmaceuticals Inc (HQ)	Wilmington	MA	F	800 461-7449	13385
Batavia Biosciences Inc	Woburn	MA	G	781 305-3921	13521
Baxalta US Inc	Cambridge	MA	B	312 656-8021	7498
Beigene US Mfg Co Inc	Cambridge	MA	D	781 801-1800	7502
Beigene Usa Inc (HQ)	Cambridge	MA	E	781 801-1887	7503
Berg LLC (HQ)	Framingham	MA	E	617 588-0083	8743
Berkshire Sterile Mfg LLC	Lee	MA	C	413 243-0330	9611
Bfs Pharma Inc	Randolph	MA	F	781 767-2020	11551
Bial - Biotech Investments Inc	Cambridge	MA	F	508 332-9103	7505
Bicara Therapeutics Inc	Cambridge	MA	G	860 882-7478	7506
Bind Biosciences Inc	Cambridge	MA	F	617 679-9600	7507
Biocon Biologics Inc	Cambridge	MA	D	857 706-2596	7509
Biocytogen Boston Corp	Waltham	MA	D	781 587-3558	12606
Biodelivery Sciences Intl Inc (HQ)	Stoughton	MA	E	919 582-9050	12198
Biofrontera Inc (HQ)	Woburn	MA	F	781 245-1325	13524
Biogen Inc (PA)	Cambridge	MA	B	617 679-2000	7511
Biogen Inc	Cambridge	MA	D	617 914-8888	7512
Biophysics Pharma Inc	Peabody	MA	F	781 608-7738	11299
Bioverativ Inc (HQ)	Waltham	MA	D	781 663-4400	12607
Bioverativ Therapeutics Inc (DH)	Waltham	MA	E	781 663-4400	12608
Black Diamond Therapeutics Inc (PA)	Cambridge	MA	F	617 252-0848	7517
Bluefin Biomedicine Inc	Beverly	MA	F	925 524-3417	6334
Blueprint Medicines Corp (PA)	Cambridge	MA	A	617 374-7580	7518
Bms Pizza Inc	Tewksbury	MA	F	978 851-0540	12386
Boston Oncology LLC	Cambridge	MA	F	857 209-5052	7521
Bpg Bio Inc (PA)	Framingham	MA	F	617 588-0083	8748
Bright Horizons At Biogen Idec	Cambridge	MA	F	617 621-3383	7525
Bristol-Myers Squibb Company	Devens	MA	B	978 588-6001	8271
Bryan Oncor Inc	Somerville	MA	G	617 957-9858	11865
Cadent Therapeutics Inc	Cambridge	MA	F	617 949-5529	7526
Cambrex	Agawam	MA	E	413 786-1680	5783
Cambrex Bio Science	Hopkinton	MA	G	508 497-0700	9312

	CITY	ST	EMP	PHONE	ENTRY#
Carisma Therapeutics Inc	Cambridge	MA	F	617 444-8550	7532
Cartesian Therapeutics Inc (PA)	Watertown	MA	F	617 923-1400	12868
Catalent Massachusetts LLC	Chelsea	MA	F	617 660-4110	7976
Cedilla Therapeutics Inc	Cambridge	MA	E	617 581-9333	7533
Celgene Corporation	Amesbury	MA	F	857 225-2309	5832
Celldex Therapeutics Inc	Needham Heights	MA	F	781 433-0771	10534
Celyad Inc	Boston	MA	G	857 990-6900	6644
Central Admxture Phrm Svcs Inc	Woburn	MA	G	781 376-0032	13541
Centrexion Therapeutics Corp	Boston	MA	F	617 837-6911	6646
Cerevel Thrputics Holdings Inc (PA)	Cambridge	MA	F	844 304-2048	7536
Checkpoint Therapeutics Inc	Waltham	MA	E	781 652-4500	12624
Chiasma Inc	Waltham	MA	E	617 928-5300	12625
Chiesi Ventures Inc	Boston	MA	F	919 998-3330	6651
CinCor Pharma Inc	Waltham	MA	F	513 800-2585	12628
Clade Therapeutics Inc	Boston	MA	E	617 546-7460	6659
Clementia Phrmcuticals USA Inc	Auburndale	MA	F	857 226-5588	6130
Cogent Biosciences Inc (PA)	Waltham	MA	F	617 945-5576	12634
Coley Pharmaceutical Group Inc	Wellesley	MA	D	781 431-9000	12939
Collegium Pharmaceutical Inc (PA)	Stoughton	MA	E	781 713-3699	12201
Concert Pharmaceuticals (HQ)	Lexington	MA	E	781 860-0045	9731
Constlltion Phrmaceuticals Inc (DH)	Boston	MA	E	844 667-1992	6666
Corbus Pharmaceuticals Inc	Norwood	MA	G	617 963-0100	11169
Corium LLC	Boston	MA	C	855 253-2407	6672
Corvidia Therapeutics Inc	Waltham	MA	F	781 205-4755	12642
Courage Therapeutics Inc	Newton	MA	G	617 216-9921	10749
Cpec LLC	Lexington	MA	D	781 861-8444	9733
Cubist Pharmaceuticals LLC	Lexington	MA	D	781 860-8660	9735
Cue Biopharma Inc (PA)	Cambridge	MA	E	617 949-2680	7545
Curagen Corporation (HQ)	Needham Heights	MA	F	908 200-7500	10538
Curia Massachusetts Inc (DH)	Burlington	MA	E	781 270-7900	7358
Curirx Inc	Wilmington	MA	E	978 658-2962	13400
Curis Inc (PA)	Lexington	MA	E	617 503-6500	9736
Cyclerion Therapeutics Inc (PA)	Cambridge	MA	E	857 327-8778	7547
Cyteir Therapeutics Inc (PA)	Lexington	MA	E	857 285-4140	9737
Decibel Therapeutics Inc (HQ)	Boston	MA	E	617 370-8701	6686
Deciphera Pharmaceuticals Inc (PA)	Waltham	MA	C	781 209-6400	12649
Dicerna Pharmaceuticals Inc (HQ)	Lexington	MA	C	617 621-8097	9739
Disc Medicine Inc (PA)	Watertown	MA	F	617 674-9274	12871
Dlrc Incorporated	Cambridge	MA	G	617 999-3340	7552
DSM Nutritional Products LLC	Lexington	MA	C	781 259-7600	9741
Dusa Pharmaceuticals Inc (DH)	Billerica	MA	D	978 657-7500	6434
Dyne Therapeutics Inc (PA)	Waltham	MA	E	781 786-8230	12658
Eisai Inc	Cambridge	MA	F	978 837-4616	7556
Elan Pharma	Cambridge	MA	F	415 885-6780	7557
Elevatebio LLC (PA)	Cambridge	MA	E	413 297-7151	7559
Elevatebio Base Camp Inc	Waltham	MA	C	617 433-2600	12660
EMD Accnting Sltons Svcs Amer	Rockland	MA	C	781 982-9000	11642
EMD Serono Inc	Billerica	MA	F	781 982-9000	6439
EMD Serono Inc	Burlington	MA	F	978 715-1804	7368
EMD Serono Inc (DH)	Rockland	MA	A	781 982-9000	11643
EMD Serono Biotech Center Inc	Billerica	MA	D	978 294-1100	6440
EMD Serono Biotech Center Inc	Quincy	MA	E	978 294-1100	11515
EMD Serono Biotech Center Inc (HQ)	Rockland	MA	D	800 283-8088	11644
EMD Serono Holding Inc	Rockland	MA	C	781 982-9000	11645
EMD Serono RES & Dev Inst Inc	Billerica	MA	D	978 294-1100	6441
EMD Serono RES & Dev Inst Inc (HQ)	Rockland	MA	E	781 982-9000	11646
Emergent Biosolutions Inc	Canton	MA	F	781 302-3000	7788
Empiramed Inc	Maynard	MA	G	978 344-4300	10262
Enanta Pharmaceuticals Inc (PA)	Watertown	MA	D	617 607-0800	12872
Encyte Systems Inc	Braintree	MA	G	781 848-6772	7180
Ensem Therapeutics Inc	Waltham	MA	F	662 422-2488	12663
Entasis Thrputics Holdings Inc (HQ)	Waltham	MA	F	781 810-0120	12664
Entrada Therapeutics Inc (PA)	Boston	MA	D	857 520-9158	6717
Epirus Biopharmaceuticals Inc	Foxboro	MA	E	617 600-3497	8696
Epizyme Inc	Cambridge	MA	C	617 229-5872	7563
Epoxy Technology Inc (PA)	Billerica	MA	E	978 667-3805	6444
Eqrx Inc (HQ)	Cambridge	MA	E	617 315-2255	7564
Evopoint Biosciences Usa Inc	Concord	MA	G	646 750-2661	8117
Excelerarx Corp	Stoughton	MA	F	612 293-0378	12203
Exemplar Laboratories LLC	Fall River	MA	G	508 676-6726	8543
Exemplar Pharma LLC	Fall River	MA	E	508 676-6726	8544
Exo Therapeutics Inc	Cambridge	MA	F	860 908-6508	7568
FDA Group LLC	North Grafton	MA	F	413 330-7476	11023
Fergene Inc	Cambridge	MA	F	973 796-1600	7569
Flexion Thrptics Scrities Corp	Burlington	MA	C	781 305-7777	7374
Flo Chemical Corp	Ashburnham	MA	F	978 827-5101	5952
Fog Pharmaceuticals Inc	Cambridge	MA	D	617 945-9510	7571
Foghorn Therapeutics Inc (PA)	Cambridge	MA	E	617 586-3100	7572
Foldrx Pharmaceuticals Inc (HQ)	Cambridge	MA	F	617 252-5500	7573
Forma Therapeutics Inc (DH)	Watertown	MA	E	617 679-1970	12877
Fortress Biotech Inc	Waltham	MA	F	781 652-4500	12678
Fresenius Kabi Compounding LLC	Canton	MA	E	224 358-1150	7792
Fresenius Kabi Usa LLC	North Andover	MA	D	978 775-8050	10833
Fulcrum Therapeutics Inc (PA)	Cambridge	MA	E	617 651-8851	7575
Fusion Pharmaceuticals US Inc	Boston	MA	F	617 420-5698	6750
Generation Bio Co (PA)	Cambridge	MA	D	617 655-7500	7581
Genocea Biosciences Inc (PA)	Cambridge	MA	E	617 876-8191	7582
Genzyme Corporation	Allston	MA	E	617 252-7500	5821
Genzyme Corporation	Cambridge	MA	C	508 271-2919	7583
Genzyme Corporation	Cambridge	MA	B	617 494-8484	7584
Genzyme Corporation (DH)	Cambridge	MA	A	617 252-7500	7585
Genzyme Corporation	Cambridge	MA	D	617 252-7500	7586
Genzyme Corporation	Cambridge	MA	D	617 252-7999	7587
Genzyme Corporation	Cambridge	MA	D	617 252-7500	7588
Genzyme Corporation	Cambridge	MA	C	508 872-8400	7589
Genzyme Corporation	Framingham	MA	E	508 872-8400	8765
Genzyme Corporation	Framingham	MA	E	508 872-8400	8766
Genzyme Corporation	Framingham	MA	E	508 872-8400	8767
Genzyme Corporation	Framingham	MA	D	508 872-8400	8768
Genzyme Corporation	Framingham	MA	D	508 872-8400	8769
Genzyme Corporation	Framingham	MA	D	508 271-2642	8770
Genzyme Corporation	Framingham	MA	D	508 370-9690	8771
Genzyme Corporation	Framingham	MA	D	617 252-7500	8772
Genzyme Corporation	Framingham	MA	E	617 252-7500	8773
Genzyme Corporation	Framingham	MA	E	617 252-7500	8774
Genzyme Corporation	Northborough	MA	C	508 351-2699	11096
Genzyme Corporation	Waltham	MA	C	781 487-5728	12687
Genzyme Corporation	Westborough	MA	D	508 351-2600	13102
Genzyme Corporation	Westborough	MA	C	508 898-9001	13103
Genzyme Securities Corporation	Cambridge	MA	F	617 252-7500	7590
Getreskilled	Boston	MA	G	617 901-9268	6757
Ginger Acquisition Inc	Boston	MA	B	617 551-4000	6760
Global Lf Scnces Sltons USA LL	Marlborough	MA	A	800 526-3593	10153
Global Lf Scnces Sltons USA LL	Northampton	MA	C	413 586-7720	11065
Gloucester Pharmaceuticals Inc	Cambridge	MA	F	617 583-1300	7592
Gsk	Cambridge	MA	F	781 795-4165	7594
GTC Biotherapeutics Inc	Framingham	MA	E	508 370-5429	8776
Gurnet Holding Company	Cambridge	MA	C	617 588-4900	7595
Harbour Biomed Us Inc	Cambridge	MA	F	617 682-3679	7598
Homology Medicines Inc	Bedford	MA	C	781 301-7277	6229
Hopewell Therapeutics Inc	Woburn	MA	E	781 218-3318	13582
Houston Lonza Inc	Lexington	MA	F	201 316-9200	9750
I2o Therapeutics Inc	Cambridge	MA	G	303 596-0402	7608
Ifm Therapeutics LLC	Boston	MA	E	857 327-9903	6805
Imabiotech Corp	Billerica	MA	F	978 362-1825	6451
Imbria Pharmaceuticals Inc	Boston	MA	G	617 941-3000	6808
Immuneering Corporation	Cambridge	MA	E	617 500-8080	7612
Immunmlecular Therapeutics Inc	Woburn	MA	G	617 356-8170	13584
Immunogen Inc (PA)	Waltham	MA	F	781 895-0600	12696
Infinity Pharmaceuticals Inc (PA)	Cambridge	MA	F		7614
Inflammasome Therapeutics Inc	Newton	MA	F	617 331-1071	10762
Inotek Pharmaceuticals Corp	Lexington	MA	F	781 676-2100	9753
Integral Biosystems LLC	Bedford	MA	F	781 275-8059	6234
Invetx Inc	Natick	MA	F	802 233-3103	10483
Ipsen Biopharmaceuticals Inc (HQ)	Cambridge	MA	C	973 903-4442	7617
Ironwood Pharmaceuticals Inc (PA)	Boston	MA	C	617 621-7722	6818
Iteos Therapeutics Inc (PA)	Watertown	MA	F	339 217-0161	12883
Jnj Global Enterprises LLC	Attleboro	MA	G	508 455-4945	6028
Johnson & Johnson	Woburn	MA	G	781 264-4804	13594
Juniper Pharmaceuticals Inc (DH)	Boston	MA	D	617 639-1500	6837
Kala Pharmaceuticals Inc (PA)	Arlington	MA	C	781 996-5252	5942
Kalvista Pharmaceuticals Inc (PA)	Cambridge	MA	G	857 999-0075	7621
Karuna Therapeutics Inc (PA)	Boston	MA	E	857 449-2244	6840
Karyopharm Therapeutics Inc (PA)	Newton	MA	C	617 658-0600	10766
Kaz Inc (HQ)	Marlborough	MA	D	508 490-7000	10174
Keros Therapeutics Inc (PA)	Lexington	MA	G	617 314-6297	9756
Keryx Biopharmaceuticals Inc (HQ)	Cambridge	MA	F	617 871-2098	7622
Kiniksa Pharmaceuticals Corp	Lexington	MA	C	781 431-9100	9757
Kiq Bio LLC	Cambridge	MA	D	617 945-5576	7623
Korro Bio Inc (PA)	Cambridge	MA	D	617 468-1999	7624
La Jolla Pharmaceutical Co (HQ)	Waltham	MA	E	617 715-3600	12708
Landmark Bio Pbllc	Watertown	MA	G	617 894-8629	12886
Lantheus Holdings Inc (PA)	North Billerica	MA	A	978 671-8001	10923
Lantheus Medical Imaging Inc (HQ)	North Billerica	MA	B	800 362-2668	10924
Lantheus MI Intermediate Inc	North Billerica	MA	A	978 671-8001	10925
Leaf Pharmaceuticals LLC	Woburn	MA	E	781 305-4192	13601
Leap Therapeutics Inc (PA)	Cambridge	MA	F	617 714-0360	7630
Lfb Usa Inc (DH)	Framingham	MA	E	508 370-5100	8785
Lfb Usa Inc	Spencer	MA	G	508 370-5100	12063
Logical Therapeutics Inc	Waltham	MA	F	781 290-0900	12711
Lonza Biologics Inc	Cambridge	MA	D	608 630-3758	7634
Lonza Biologics Inc	Lexington	MA	F	508 435-2331	9760
Luckwel Pharmaceuticals Inc	Cambridge	MA	G	617 430-5222	7635
Lutronic USA	Billerica	MA	F	888 588-7644	6459

Employee Codes: A=Over 500 employees, B=251-500
C=101-250, D=51-100, E=20-50, F=10-19, G=1-9

2024 Harris New England
Manufacturers Directory

PRODUCT

1441

	CITY	ST	EMP	PHONE	ENTRY#
Lykan Bioscience Holdings LLC	Hopkinton	MA	F	774 341-4200	9336
Lyndra Therapeutics Inc	Lexington	MA	D	857 201-5314	9761
Lyndra Therapeutics Inc **(PA)**	Watertown	MA	F	339 222-6519	12888
Lyne Laboratories Inc	Brockton	MA	D	508 583-8700	7292
Lyra Therapeutics Inc	Watertown	MA	E	617 393-4600	12889
Matrivax Research & Dev Corp	Boston	MA	G	617 385-7640	6880
MBL International Corporation **(DH)**	Woburn	MA	F	781 939-6964	13607
Medtherapy Biotechnology Inc	Quincy	MA	E	617 938-7082	11528
Merck Group	Bedford	MA	E	781 858-3284	6242
Merck Group	Danvers	MA	D	978 762-5280	8209
Merck Research Laboratories	Boston	MA	F	617 992-2000	6883
Merck Sharp & Dohme Corp	Boston	MA	E	617 992-2000	6884
Mersana Therapeutics Inc **(PA)**	Cambridge	MA	D	617 498-0020	7641
Millennium Pharmaceuticals Inc	Cambridge	MA	C	617 679-7000	7645
Millennium Pharmaceuticals Inc **(HQ)**	Cambridge	MA	C	617 679-7000	7646
Millennium Pharmaceuticals Inc	Cambridge	MA	C	617 679-7000	7647
Millennium Pharmaceuticals Inc	Cambridge	MA	D	617 679-7000	7648
Millennium Pharmaceuticals Inc	Cambridge	MA	D	617 679-7000	7649
Millennium Pharmaceuticals Inc	Cambridge	MA	D	617 679-7000	7650
Millennium Pharmaceuticals Inc	Cambridge	MA	D	617 679-7000	7651
Millennium Pharmaceuticals Inc	Lexington	MA	D	617 679-7000	9763
Millennium Pharmaceuticals Inc	Winchester	MA	D	781 729-7435	13487
Minerva Nrscnces Scrities Corp	Waltham	MA	G	617 600-7373	12721
Mitsubshi Tnabe Phrma Amer Inc	Cambridge	MA	F	210 897-3473	7652
Modalis Therapeutics Inc	Waltham	MA	E	617 219-9808	12723
Moderna Inc **(PA)**	Cambridge	MA	B	617 714-6500	7653
Momenta Pharmaceuticals Inc **(HQ)**	Cambridge	MA	D	617 491-9700	7654
Montai Health Inc	Cambridge	MA	E	617 293-0578	7656
Morphic Holding Inc **(PA)**	Waltham	MA	E	781 996-0955	12725
Msm Protein Technologies Inc	Waltham	MA	G	781 373-2405	12726
Mural Oncology Inc	Waltham	MA	E	617 694-2481	12727
Navitor Pharmaceuticals Inc	Cambridge	MA	F	857 285-4300	7660
Nemucore Med Innovations Inc	Wellesley	MA	G	617 943-9983	12944
Neovii Biotech Na Inc	Boston	MA	E	781 966-3830	6908
Neuro Phage Phrmaceuticals Inc	Cambridge	MA	F	617 941-7004	7663
Neurobo Pharmaceuticals Inc **(PA)**	Cambridge	MA	F	617 864-2880	7664
Neurobo Therapeutics Inc	Boston	MA	F	617 313-7331	6911
New England Cmpunding Phrm Inc	Boston	MA	E	800 994-6322	6915
Nitromed Inc	Lexington	MA	G	781 274-1248	9766
Nocion Therapeutics Inc	Waltham	MA	G	781 812-6176	12737
Novabiotics Inc	Boston	MA	D	866 259-4527	6926
Novartis Corporation	Cambridge	MA	E	617 225-0820	7667
Novartis Instttes For Bmdcal R **(HQ)**	Cambridge	MA	E	617 777-8276	7668
Novartis Mlclar Dagnostics LLC	Cambridge	MA	E	617 871-8441	7669
Novartis Vccnes Dagnostics Inc	Cambridge	MA	A	617 871-7000	7670
Novirio Pharmaceuticals Inc	Cambridge	MA	D	617 250-3100	7671
Novo Nordisk Inc	Lexington	MA	A	463 209-3849	9767
Nuvalent Inc **(PA)**	Cambridge	MA	E	857 357-7000	7672
Nypro Inc	Clinton	MA	C	978 368-6021	8088
Oncopeptides Inc	Boston	MA	C	866 596-6626	6933
Oncorus Inc **(PA)**	Andover	MA	E	857 334-9077	5904
Ono Pharma Usa Inc	Cambridge	MA	F	617 904-4500	7675
Organogenesis Holdings Inc **(PA)**	Canton	MA	F	781 575-0775	7814
Orgenesis Inc **(PA)**	Natick	MA	F	480 659-6404	10489
Orogen Therapeutics Inc	Woburn	MA	G	617 981-2156	13628
Overland Phrmaceuticals US Inc	Boston	MA	F	508 827-8686	6947
Oxeia Biopharmaceuticals Inc	Boston	MA	G	619 213-7697	6948
Padlock Therapeutics Inc	Cambridge	MA	F	978 381-9601	7680
Palleon Pharma Inc	Waltham	MA	E	857 285-5904	12746
Paratek Pharmaceuticals Inc **(DH)**	Boston	MA	G	617 807-6600	6954
Parexel International Corp	Billerica	MA	D	978 313-3900	6469
Pepgen Inc	Boston	MA	E	781 797-0979	6962
Pfizer Inc	Andover	MA	C	978 247-1000	5906
Pfizer Inc	Cambridge	MA	F	617 551-3000	7683
Pfizer Inc	Cambridge	MA	G	617 674-7436	7684
Pharmasol Corporation	South Easton	MA	C	508 238-0105	11948
Pharmctcal Strtgies Stffing LL	Stoneham	MA	F	781 835-2300	12185
Pharmion Corporation	Cambridge	MA	E	857 706-1311	7685
Phosphorex LLC	Hopkinton	MA	E	508 435-9100	9339
Pic Pharmaceutical Inc	Natick	MA	G	617 947-3883	10491
Plasma Biolife Services L P	Attleboro	MA	E	508 761-2902	6048
Pluromed Inc	Woburn	MA	E	781 932-0574	13638
Point3 Farma LLC	Northampton	MA	G	719 733-3900	11077
Praecis Pharmaceuticals Inc	Waltham	MA	A	781 795-4100	12751
Praxis Precision Medicines Inc **(PA)**	Boston	MA	E	617 300-8460	6974
Primatope Therapeutics Inc	Newton	MA	G	617 413-3020	10776
Prismic Pharmaceuticals Inc	Holden	MA	G	971 506-6415	9195
Puretech Health PLC	Boston	MA	D	617 482-2333	6985
Pyxis Oncology Inc **(PA)**	Boston	MA	E	617 221-9059	6987
Ra Pharmaceuticals Inc **(DH)**	Cambridge	MA	E	617 401-4060	7692
Radius Health Inc **(PA)**	Boston	MA	B	617 551-4000	6994
Rapid Micro Biosystems Inc **(PA)**	Lowell	MA	C	978 349-3200	9916
Rapport Therapeutics Inc	Boston	MA	E	512 636-1706	6998
Red Oak Sourcing LLC	Foxborough	MA	D	401 742-0701	8737
Regenacy Pharmaceuticals LLC	Waltham	MA	E	617 245-1306	12764
Regor Therapeutics Inc	Brighton	MA	F	617 407-4737	7244
Reistone Biopharma Inc	Boston	MA	F	978 429-5824	7004
Rentschler Biopharma Inc	Milford	MA	D	508 282-5800	10417
Revo Biologics Inc **(DH)**	Framingham	MA	F	508 620-9700	8802
Ribon Therapeutics Inc	Cambridge	MA	E	617 914-8700	7696
Ring Therapeutics Inc **(PA)**	Cambridge	MA	F	617 218-1549	7697
Roche Dgnostics Hematology Inc	Brighton	MA	D	508 329-2450	7245
Rodin Therapeutics Inc	Waltham	MA	G	857 201-2770	12773
Rubius Therapeutics	Foxboro	MA	F	401 349-0818	8717
Safecor Health LLC	Woburn	MA	G	781 933-8780	13658
Safecor Health LLC	Woburn	MA	E	781 933-8780	13659
Sage Therapeutics Inc **(PA)**	Cambridge	MA	A	617 299-8380	7700
Sana Biotechnology Inc **(PA)**	Cambridge	MA	G	202 790-0313	7701
Sanofi Pasteur Biologics LLC **(HQ)**	Cambridge	MA	C	617 866-4400	7703
Sanofi Pasteur Biologics LLC	Canton	MA	D	781 302-3000	7824
Sanofi US Services Inc	Cambridge	MA	C	617 562-4555	7704
Sanofi US Services Inc	Cambridge	MA	E	800 981-2491	7705
Sanofi US Services Inc	Framingham	MA	C	508 424-4485	8803
Santhera Pharmaceuticals usa	Burlington	MA	G	781 552-5145	7421
Sarepta Therapeutics	Burlington	MA	F	781 221-7805	7422
Sarepta Therapeutics Inc **(PA)**	Cambridge	MA	C	617 274-4000	7706
Scholar Rock Holding Corp **(PA)**	Cambridge	MA	F	857 259-3860	7708
Scidose LLC	Amherst	MA	F	866 956-4333	5864
Scpharmaceuticals Inc	Burlington	MA	E	617 517-0730	7425
Selvita Inc	Boston	MA	F	857 998-4075	7032
Semma Therapeutics Inc **(HQ)**	Cambridge	MA	E	857 529-6430	7709
Seres Therapeutics Inc **(PA)**	Cambridge	MA	D	617 945-9626	7710
Serono Inc	Rockland	MA	E	781 681-2137	11660
Servier US Inc **(PA)**	Boston	MA	F	610 506-8203	7034
Shire	Milford	MA	F	508 282-5731	10418
Shire Humn Gntic Therapies Inc **(DH)**	Lexington	MA	E	617 349-0200	9772
Shire Pharmaceuticals LLC	Cambridge	MA	A	617 588-8800	7712
Shire Pharmaceuticals LLC	Cambridge	MA	A	781 482-9245	7713
Shire Pharmaceuticals LLC **(HQ)**	Lexington	MA	C	617 349-0200	9773
Shire Pharmaceuticals LLC	Lexington	MA	A	617 349-0200	9774
Shire US Inc **(HQ)**	Lexington	MA	A	781 482-9222	9775
Sigilon Therapeutics Inc **(HQ)**	Cambridge	MA	D	617 336-7540	7714
Sirtex Medical US Holdings Inc	Woburn	MA	F	888 474-7839	13668
Spectrum Pharmaceuticals Inc **(PA)**	Boston	MA	E	617 586-3900	7051
Springleaf Therapeutics Inc	Boston	MA	F		7055
Sq Innovation Inc	Burlington	MA	G	617 500-0121	7433
Stallrgenes Greer Holdings Inc	Cambridge	MA	E	617 588-4900	7721
Stealth Biotherapeutics Inc **(HQ)**	Needham Heights	MA	F	617 600-6888	10558
Sumitomo Pharma America Inc **(HQ)**	Marlborough	MA	A	508 481-6700	10217
Syndax Pharmaceuticals Inc **(PA)**	Waltham	MA	E	781 419-1400	12785
Syndax Securities Corporation	Waltham	MA	F	781 472-2985	12786
Syndexa Pharmaceuticals Corp	Watertown	MA	F	617 607-7283	12911
Syner-G Biopharma Group LLC **(PA)**	Framingham	MA	E	508 460-9700	8805
Synlogic Inc **(PA)**	Cambridge	MA	E	617 401-9975	7729
Synostics Inc	Weston	MA	G	781 248-5699	13290
Takeda	Belmont	MA	G	617 594-7199	6313
Takeda	Lexington	MA	D	781 266-5464	9780
Takeda Building 35 5	Cambridge	MA	G	617 444-4352	7730
Takeda Dev Ctr Americas Inc	Cambridge	MA	A	617 349-0200	7731
Takeda Manufacturing USA Inc	Lexington	MA	E	877 825-3327	9781
Takeda Pharmaceutical Co Ltd	Lexington	MA	D	877 872-3700	9782
Takeda Pharmaceuticals Inc	Cambridge	MA	E	617 679-7348	7732
Takeda Pharmaceuticals USA Inc	Cambridge	MA	F	781 733-5208	7733
Takeda Pharmaceuticals USA Inc	Lexington	MA	E	617 349-0200	9783
Takeda Pharmaceuticals USA Inc **(HQ)**	Lexington	MA	A	877 825-3327	9784
Takeda Pharmaceuticals USA Inc	North Reading	MA	G	781 482-1461	11046
Takeda Phrmaceuticals Amer Inc **(DH)**	Lexington	MA	D	224 554-6500	9785
Takeda Vaccines Inc	Cambridge	MA	D	970 672-4918	7734
Tango Therapeutics Inc **(PA)**	Boston	MA	F	857 302-4900	7069
Tarpon Biosystems Inc	Marlborough	MA	F	978 979-4222	10222
Tarveda Therapeutics Inc	Watertown	MA	E	617 923-4100	12912
Tesaro Inc **(HQ)**	Waltham	MA	D	339 970-0900	12793
Tesaro Securities Corporation	Waltham	MA	A	339 970-0900	12794
Tessera Therapeutics Inc	Somerville	MA	D	860 910-6030	11900
Tetraphase Pharmaceuticals Inc	Waltham	MA	D	617 715-3600	12795
Theseus Pharmaceuticals Inc **(PA)**	Cambridge	MA	F	857 400-9491	7740
Tiburio Therapeutics Inc	Cambridge	MA	G	617 231-6050	7741
Tonix Phrmceuticals Holdg Corp	New Bedford	MA	G	617 908-5040	10656
Torque Therapeutics Inc	Cambridge	MA	E	617 945-1082	7744
Trafa Pharmaceutical Inc	Chicopee	MA	F	866 998-7232	8063
Translate Bio Inc **(HQ)**	Lexington	MA	E	617 945-7361	9789
Tremeau Pharmaceuticals Inc	Concord	MA	F	617 485-0250	8137
Ucb Inc	Cambridge	MA	E	844 599-2273	7746
Unicus Pharmaceuticals LLC **(PA)**	Taunton	MA	F	508 659-7002	12374

1442
2024 Harris New England Manufacturers Directory
(G-0000) Company's Geographic Section entry number

	CITY	ST	EMP	PHONE	ENTRY#
Valo Health Inc (PA)	Boston	MA	E	617 237-6080	7096
Vaso Active Phrmaceuticals Inc	Beverly	MA	G	978 750-1991	6392
Vbi Vaccines Inc (PA)	Cambridge	MA	G	617 830-3031	7750
Vectura Incorporated	Southborough	MA	G	508 573-5700	12005
Veranova LP (HQ)	Devens	MA	C	484 581-0149	8288
Veranova LP	North Andover	MA	E	978 784-5000	10857
Verastem Inc (PA)	Needham	MA	G	781 292-4200	10528
Vertex Pharmaceuticals Del LLC	Boston	MA	F	617 341-6100	7100
Vertex Pharmaceuticals Inc (PA)	Boston	MA	A	617 341-6100	7101
Vertex Pharmaceuticals PR LLC	Boston	MA	E	617 341-6100	7102
Vertex Phrmaceuticals Dist Inc	Boston	MA	E	617 341-6100	7103
Verve Therapeutics Inc	Cambridge	MA	F	617 603-0070	7755
Verve Therapeutics Inc (PA)	Cambridge	MA	E	617 603-0070	7756
Viamet Phrmctcals Holdings LLC	Foxboro	MA	E	919 467-8539	8730
Vibalogics US Inc	Boxborough	MA	F	252 903-2213	7157
Vigil Neuroscience Inc (PA)	Watertown	MA	E	857 254-4445	12919
Visionaid Inc	Wareham	MA	E	508 295-3300	12849
Voyager Pharmaceutical Corp	Swampscott	MA	F	781 592-1945	12301
Walden Biosciences Inc	Cambridge	MA	F	617 794-2733	7758
Werewolf Therapeutics Inc	Watertown	MA	E	617 952-0555	12920
West St Intrmdate Hldings Corp (PA)	Waltham	MA	D	781 434-5051	12817
Wilex Inc	Cambridge	MA	F	617 492-3900	7760
Wyeth Pharmaceuticals LLC	Andover	MA	E	978 475-9214	5936
Xilio Therapeutics Inc	Waltham	MA	D	617 430-4680	12820
Zikani Therapeutics Inc	Watertown	MA	E	617 453-9091	12922
Znlabs LLC (HQ)	Woburn	MA	E	781 897-6966	13692
Biodesign International	Saco	ME	E	207 283-6500	5363
Clearh2o Inc	Westbrook	ME	E	207 221-0039	5621
Dermalogix Partners Inc	Scarborough	ME	F	207 883-4103	5431
Lonza Bio Science Rockland Inc	Rockland	ME	E	207 594-3400	5337
Lonza Rockland Inc	Rockland	ME	D	207 594-3400	5338
M Drug LLC	Brewer	ME	G	207 973-9444	4618
Maine Biotechnology Svcs Inc	Portland	ME	F	207 797-5454	5239
Shearwater Allergy LLC	Yarmouth	ME	G	207 846-7676	5707
Tevelle Pharmaceuticals LLC	South Portland	ME	E	207 808-9771	5516
Critical Prcess Filtration Inc (PA)	Nashua	NH	E	603 595-0140	15085
Icad Inc (PA)	Nashua	NH	F	603 882-5200	15111
Ipura Consulting Group LLC	Hampton	NH	F	603 294-4002	14404
Lonza Biologics Inc	Portsmouth	NH	D	603 610-4696	15420
Lonza Biologics Inc	Portsmouth	NH	D	201 316-9200	15421
Lonza Biologics Inc (DH)	Portsmouth	NH	C	603 610-4500	15087
Lyophilization Svcs Neng Inc	Bedford	NH	E	603 626-5763	13942
Lyophilization Svcs Neng Inc	Bedford	NH	E	603 668-5763	13943
Lyophilization Svcs Neng Inc (HQ)	Manchester	NH	F	603 626-5763	14877
Msm Protein Technologies Inc	East Kingston	NH	F	617 504-9548	14272
Novo Nordisk US Bio Prod Inc	West Lebanon	NH	C	603 298-3169	15687
Tri-K Industries Inc	Salem	NH	E	603 898-0811	15567
Trividia Mfg Solutions Inc (DH)	Lancaster	NH	C	603 788-2848	14680
Aidance Scientific Inc	Woonsocket	RI	D	401 432-7750	16946
Denison Pharmaceuticals LLC	Lincoln	RI	C	401 723-5500	16131
Denison Pharmaceuticals LLC (PA)	Lincoln	RI	C	401 723-5500	16132
Immunex Rhode Island Corp	West Greenwich	RI	C	401 392-1200	16886
Luna Pharmaceuticals Inc	Providence	RI	G	401 383-0299	16556
Mmj Biopharma Cultivation Inc	Westerly	RI	F	800 586-7863	16936
Neurotech Pharmaceuticals Inc	Cumberland	RI	E	617 694-5520	15951
Noramco Coventry LLC	Coventry	RI	D	401 623-1174	15818
Ocean Biomedical Holdings Inc	Providence	RI	D	401 444-7375	16578
Phe Investments LLC	Johnston	RI	D	401 289-2900	16100
Purdue Pharma LP	Coventry	RI	F	203 588-8000	15819
Sea-Band International Inc	Newport	RI	G	401 841-5900	16222
Techtrak LLC	Coventry	RI	F	401 397-3983	15822
Tedor Pharma Inc	Cumberland	RI	E	401 658-5219	15967
Vertex Pharmaceuticals Inc	Providence	RI	F	857 529-6430	16639
PBM Nutritionals LLC (DH)	Milton	VT	C	802 527-0521	17363
Somalabs Inc	Milton	VT	F	802 355-3000	17364

PHARMACEUTICALS: Mail-Order Svc

	CITY	ST	EMP	PHONE	ENTRY#
Designing Health Inc	East Longmeadow	MA	F	661 257-1705	8373
Desert Harvest Inc	Ellsworth	ME	F	919 245-1853	4756

PHOTOCOPY MACHINES

	CITY	ST	EMP	PHONE	ENTRY#
Freedom Grafix LLC	Fairfield	CT	G	815 900-6189	1186
Xerox Corporation (HQ)	Norwalk	CT	B	203 849-5216	2598
Xerox Holdings Inc	Norwalk	CT	A	203 968-3000	2599
Xerox Holdings Corporation (PA)	Norwalk	CT	B	203 849-5216	2600

PHOTOCOPYING & DUPLICATING SVCS

	CITY	ST	EMP	PHONE	ENTRY#
Action Letter Inc (PA)	Stamford	CT	E	203 323-2466	3273
Alliance Graphics Inc	Newington	CT	F	860 666-7992	2270
Baker Graphics Corporation	Westport	CT	F	203 226-6928	4157
Brescias Printing Services Inc	East Hartford	CT	G	860 528-4254	976
Copy Cats Inc	New London	CT	F	860 442-8424	2225
Custom Printing & Copy Inc (PA)	Enfield	CT	F	860 290-6890	1127
Derosa Printing Company Inc	Manchester	CT	F	860 646-1698	1592
Hedges & Hedges Ltd	Wethersfield	CT	G	860 257-3170	4205
Oddo Print Shop Inc	Torrington	CT	G	860 489-6585	3690
Tech-Repro Inc	Stamford	CT	F	203 348-8884	3478
Apex Press Inc	Westborough	MA	F	508 366-1110	13076
Boston Business Printing Inc	Boston	MA	F	617 482-7955	6606
Copy Cop The Digital Printing Company LLC 617 267-8899	Boston	MA			E 6669
Fars Inc	Northampton	MA	E	413 586-1332	11061
Fasprint Inc (PA)	Brockton	MA	F	508 588-9961	7278
Flashprint Graphics Inc	Cambridge	MA	G	617 492-7767	7570
Gorilla Graphics Inc (PA)	Malden	MA	F	617 623-2838	10016
Hercules Press	Boston	MA	G	617 323-1950	6786
John K Dietrich & Assoc Inc	Watertown	MA	G	617 868-4140	12884
John Karl Dietrich & Assoc	Cambridge	MA	G	617 868-4140	7619
Marcus Company Inc	Holyoke	MA	E	413 534-3303	9265
Milk Street Press Inc	Boston	MA	F	617 742-7900	6888
Northast Dcment Cnsrvtion Ctr	Andover	MA	E	978 470-1010	5901
R & H Communications Inc (PA)	Waltham	MA	F	781 893-6221	12757
Shafiis Inc (PA)	East Longmeadow	MA	E	413 224-2100	8394
Smudge Ink Incorporated	Charlestown	MA	G	617 242-8228	7882
Thomas & Thomas Inc	Lowell	MA	F	978 453-7444	9928
Tri Star Printing & Graphics	Somerville	MA	G	617 666-4480	11905
We Print Today LLC	Kingston	MA	F	781 585-6021	9514
Coastal Business Center Inc	Wiscasset	ME	G	207 882-7197	5697
Curry Printing & Copy Center	Portland	ME	F	207 772-5897	5203
First Choice Printing Inc	Lisbon Falls	ME	F	207 353-8006	5020
Gossamer Press	Benton	ME	G	207 827-9881	4545
Northeast Publishing Company	Dover Foxcroft	ME	G	207 564-8355	4730
Print Bangor	Bangor	ME	F	207 947-8049	4515
Alpha Grphics Prntshop of Ftur	Nashua	NH	F	603 595-1444	15058
Baker Graphics Inc	Manchester	NH	G	603 625-5427	14816
Boles Enterprises Inc	Manchester	NH	G	603 622-4282	14820
Fedex Office & Print Svcs Inc	Bedford	NH	F	603 644-2679	13929
Jalbert Printing LLC	Amherst	NH	G	603 623-4677	13873
New England Duplicator Inc	Manchester	NH	G	603 623-6847	14898
P2k Printing LLC	North Conway	NH	G	603 356-2010	15249
Papergraphics Print & Copy Inc	Merrimack	NH	F	603 880-1835	14997
Ram Printing Incorporated (PA)	East Hampstead	NH	E	603 382-7045	14271
Southport Management Group LLC	Portsmouth	NH	G	603 433-4664	15438
Digital Press Printers LLC	Williston	VT	G	802 863-5579	17727
First Step Print Shop LLC	Burlington	VT	G	802 899-2708	17135

PHOTOGRAPHIC EQPT & SPLYS

	CITY	ST	EMP	PHONE	ENTRY#
Bidwell Industrial Group Inc	Middletown	CT	E	860 346-9283	1740
Bpi Reprographics	Norwalk	CT	F	203 866-5600	2475
Fujifilm Elctrnic Mtls USA Inc	Stamford	CT	E	203 363-3360	3352
Kenyon Laboratories LLC	Higganum	CT	G	860 345-2097	1529
Midstate Arc Inc	Meriden	CT	D	203 238-9001	1676
Fujifilm Hlthcare Amricas Corp (DH)	Lexington	MA	C	203 324-2000	9743
Intelligent Network Sales LLC	Walpole	MA	F	508 446-3646	12562
Kasalis Inc	Burlington	MA	E	781 273-6200	7383
Primary Pdc Inc (PA)	Waltham	MA	G	781 386-2000	12753

PHOTOGRAPHIC EQPT & SPLYS WHOLESALERS

	CITY	ST	EMP	PHONE	ENTRY#
Fujifilm Elctrnic Mtls USA Inc	Stamford	CT	E	203 363-3360	3352
Comprehensive Identification Products Inc 781 229-8780	Burlington	MA			C 7354

PHOTOGRAPHIC EQPT & SPLYS: Editing Eqpt, Motion Picture

	CITY	ST	EMP	PHONE	ENTRY#
Avid Technology Inc (PA)	Burlington	MA	A	978 640-3000	7338
R & B Splicer Systems Inc	Avon	MA	G	508 580-3500	6158
Spinnakervideo Inc	Boston	MA	F	617 591-2200	7054

PHOTOGRAPHIC EQPT & SPLYS: Graphic Arts Plates, Sensitized

	CITY	ST	EMP	PHONE	ENTRY#
Base-Line II Inc (PA)	Danbury	CT	E	203 826-7031	712
Verico Technology LLC (HQ)	Enfield	CT	F	860 871-1200	1157
Progress Enterprises LLC	Westfield	MA	E	413 562-2736	13201

PHOTOGRAPHIC SENSITIZED GOODS, NEC

	CITY	ST	EMP	PHONE	ENTRY#
Advance Reproductions Corp	North Andover	MA	D	978 685-2911	10817

PHOTOGRAPHY SVCS: Commercial

	CITY	ST	EMP	PHONE	ENTRY#
James W Sewall Company	Bangor	ME	G	207 817-5410	4506
James W Sewall Company (PA)	Old Town	ME	E	207 827-4456	5125

PHYSICIANS' OFFICES & CLINICS: Medical doctors

	CITY	ST	EMP	PHONE	ENTRY#
Innoneo Health Tech Inc (PA)	Boston	MA	D	617 336-3202	6810
Ranfac Corp	Avon	MA	D	508 588-4400	6159
Umass Mem Mri Imaging Ctr LLC	Worcester	MA	F	508 756-7300	13814
Uptodate Inc (DH)	Waltham	MA	D	781 392-2000	12808

PRODUCT

	CITY	ST	EMP	PHONE	ENTRY#
Cg Holdings LLC (PA)	Manchester	NH	E	603 623-3344	14827

PICTURE FRAMES: Metal

	CITY	ST	EMP	PHONE	ENTRY#
M & B Enterprise LLC	Derby	CT	F	888 983-2670	891
Malden Intl Designs Inc	Middleboro	MA	C	508 946-2270	10365
Martin Benjamin Corporation	Dedham	MA	E	781 326-8311	8246
Capco Steel Erection Company	Providence	RI	F	401 383-9388	16495
Fulford Manufacturing Company (PA)	Riverside	RI	F	401 431-2000	16655
Weingeroff Enterprises Inc	Cranston	RI	C	401 467-2200	15929

PICTURE FRAMES: Wood

	CITY	ST	EMP	PHONE	ENTRY#
Kensington GL & Frmng Co Inc	Berlin	CT	F	860 828-9428	73
Malden Intl Designs Inc	Middleboro	MA	C	508 946-2270	10365
Wood & Wood Inc	Greenfield	MA	E	413 772-0889	9006
Zephyr Designs Ltd	Brattleboro	VT	G	802 254-2788	17110

PICTURE FRAMING SVCS, CUSTOM

	CITY	ST	EMP	PHONE	ENTRY#
Church Hill Classics Ltd	Monroe	CT	D	800 477-9005	1909

PIECE GOODS & NOTIONS WHOLESALERS

	CITY	ST	EMP	PHONE	ENTRY#
Emtex Inc	Peabody	MA	F	978 907-4500	11309

PIECE GOODS, NOTIONS & DRY GOODS, WHOL: Textiles, Woven

	CITY	ST	EMP	PHONE	ENTRY#
Time-Out Sports Inc	Whitman	MA	F	781 447-6670	13350

PIECE GOODS, NOTIONS & OTHER DRY GOODS, WHOLESALE: Fabrics

	CITY	ST	EMP	PHONE	ENTRY#
Donghia Inc	Milford	CT	C	800 366-4442	1818

PIECE GOODS, NOTIONS/DRY GOODS, WHOL: Fabrics, Synthetic

	CITY	ST	EMP	PHONE	ENTRY#
Thomas W Raftery Inc	Hartford	CT	E	860 278-9870	1514
Custom Banner & Graphics LLC	Rochester	NH	G	603 332-2067	15472

PINS

	CITY	ST	EMP	PHONE	ENTRY#
Spirol International Corp (HQ)	Danielson	CT	C	860 774-8571	844
Spirol Intl Holdg Corp (PA)	Danielson	CT	C	860 774-8571	845
Q Pin2s Billiards	West Springfield	MA	G	413 285-7971	13043
Bobby Pins	Cranston	RI	G	401 461-3400	15837

PIPE & TUBES: Copper & Copper Alloy

	CITY	ST	EMP	PHONE	ENTRY#
Thermatron Engineering Inc	Methuen	MA	E	978 687-8844	10345

PIPE & TUBES: Seamless

	CITY	ST	EMP	PHONE	ENTRY#
Accellent Acquisition Corp	Wilmington	MA	A	978 570-6900	13370
Accellent Holdings Corp	Wilmington	MA	A	978 570-6900	13371

PIPE CLEANERS

	CITY	ST	EMP	PHONE	ENTRY#
UST LLC	Stamford	CT	A	203 817-3000	3489

PIPE FITTINGS: Plastic

	CITY	ST	EMP	PHONE	ENTRY#
F F Screw Products Inc	Southington	CT	E	860 621-4567	3209
Asahi/America Inc (HQ)	Lawrence	MA	E	781 321-5409	9540
Orion Enterprises Inc (HQ)	North Andover	MA	C	913 342-1653	10847

PIPE SECTIONS, FABRICATED FROM PURCHASED PIPE

	CITY	ST	EMP	PHONE	ENTRY#
Triangle Engineering Inc	Hanover	MA	F	781 878-1500	9046

PIPE: Plastic

	CITY	ST	EMP	PHONE	ENTRY#
Advanced Drainage Systems Inc	Ludlow	MA	B	413 589-0515	9937
Applied Nnstrctred Sltions LLC	Billerica	MA	E	978 670-6959	6403
Asahi/America Inc	Lawrence	MA	G	800 343-3618	9539
Asahi/America Inc (HQ)	Lawrence	MA	E	781 321-5409	9540
Cabot Corporation (PA)	Boston	MA	C	617 345-0100	6631
Cabot Corporation	Haverhill	MA	C	978 556-8400	9084
Fiberspar Spoolable Pdts Inc (PA)	West Wareham	MA	E	508 291-9000	13046
Orion Enterprises Inc (HQ)	North Andover	MA	C	913 342-1653	10847
Plastics Unlimited of MA Inc	Worcester	MA	G	508 752-7842	13770

PIPE: Water, Cast Iron

	CITY	ST	EMP	PHONE	ENTRY#
Tyco Fire Products LP (DH)	Cranston	RI	C	215 362-0700	15924

PIPELINE TERMINAL FACILITIES: Independent

	CITY	ST	EMP	PHONE	ENTRY#
Ethosenergy Tc Inc (DH)	Chicopee	MA	E	802 257-2721	8031

PIPES & TUBES

	CITY	ST	EMP	PHONE	ENTRY#
Joy & Robert Cromwell	East Longmeadow	MA	G	413 224-1440	8382
Ldc Inc	East Providence	RI	F	401 861-4667	16029

PIPES & TUBES: Steel

	CITY	ST	EMP	PHONE	ENTRY#
Gordon Corporation	Southington	CT	D	860 628-4775	3214
3M Company	Chelmsford	MA	E	978 256-3911	7901
Microgroup Inc	Medway	MA	C	508 533-4925	10308

	CITY	ST	EMP	PHONE	ENTRY#
New Can Holdings Inc (PA)	Holbrook	MA	E	781 767-1650	9182
Thermatron Engineering Inc	Methuen	MA	E	978 687-8844	10345
Grover Gndrilling Holdings LLC (PA)	Oxford	ME	E	207 743-7051	5144
Maxson Automatic Machinery Co (PA)	Westerly	RI	E	401 596-0162	16935
National Chmney Spply-Vrmont I	South Burlington	VT	D	802 861-2217	17586

PIPES & TUBES: Welded

	CITY	ST	EMP	PHONE	ENTRY#
Nvi Weld Technology LLC	Waterbury	CT	G	203 707-0587	3953
Unique Mechanical Services Inc	Bow	NH	G	603 856-0057	14013

PISTONS & PISTON RINGS

	CITY	ST	EMP	PHONE	ENTRY#
Schwing Bioset Technologies	Danbury	CT	C	203 744-2100	813

PLACEMATS: Plastic Or Textile

	CITY	ST	EMP	PHONE	ENTRY#
Stevens Linen Associates Inc	Dudley	MA	E	508 943-0813	8325

PLAQUES: Picture, Laminated

	CITY	ST	EMP	PHONE	ENTRY#
Nixon Company Incorporated	Indian Orchard	MA	F	413 543-3701	9472
Michael Healy Designs Inc	Manville	RI	G	401 597-5900	16165
Thank-U Company Inc	North Kingstown	RI	G	401 739-3100	16285

PLASMAS

	CITY	ST	EMP	PHONE	ENTRY#
Aqua Pulsar LLC	Norwalk	CT	G	772 320-9691	2463
Plasma Technology Incorporated	South Windsor	CT	E	860 282-0659	3173
Circle Labs Bio Inc	Cambridge	MA	G	516 660-6045	7541
Plasma Pen USA LLC	Woburn	MA	F	855 568-3776	13637

PLASTICIZERS, ORGANIC: Cyclic & Acyclic

	CITY	ST	EMP	PHONE	ENTRY#
RSA Corp	Danbury	CT	E	203 790-8100	807
Teknor Apex Company (PA)	Pawtucket	RI	A	401 725-8000	16420

PLASTICS FILM & SHEET

	CITY	ST	EMP	PHONE	ENTRY#
Atlas Metallizing Inc	New Britain	CT	F	860 827-9777	2003
Polymer Films Inc	West Haven	CT	E	203 932-3000	4119
Superior Plas Extrusion Co Inc	Cromwell	CT	E	860 234-1864	697
American Durafilm Co Inc	Holliston	MA	E	508 429-8000	9198
Applied Nnstrctred Sltions LLC	Billerica	MA	E	978 670-6959	6403
Argotec LLC	Greenfield	MA	B	413 772-2564	8982
Argotec LLC (HQ)	Greenfield	MA	C	413 772-2564	8983
Atlantic Poly Inc	Norwood	MA	E	781 769-4260	11163
Entegris Inc (PA)	Billerica	MA	A	978 436-6500	6443
Flexcon Company Inc (PA)	Spencer	MA	A	508 885-8200	12058
Hartwell Asscoiates	Cambridge	MA	G	617 686-7571	7599
New England Plastics Corp (PA)	Woburn	MA	E	781 933-6004	13623
Tel Mnfacturing Engrg Amer Inc	Billerica	MA	E	978 436-2300	6487
Tri-Star Plastics Corp (PA)	Shrewsbury	MA	E	508 845-1111	11845
Zatec LLC	North Dighton	MA	E	508 880-3388	11006
Multi Technologies Industrial LLC	Brentwood	NH	E	603 778-1449	14024
SF Tools LLC	Newport	NH	F	603 863-7719	15238
Textiles Coated Incorporated (PA)	Londonderry	NH	E	603 296-2221	14786
Teknor Apex Company (PA)	Pawtucket	RI	A	401 725-8000	16420

PLASTICS FILM & SHEET: Polyethylene

	CITY	ST	EMP	PHONE	ENTRY#
Engineering Services & Pdts Co (PA)	South Windsor	CT	D	860 528-1119	3144
Arlin Mfg Co Inc	Lowell	MA	F	978 454-9165	9854
Cabot Corporation (PA)	Boston	MA	C	617 345-0100	6631
Cabot Corporation	Haverhill	MA	C	978 556-8400	9084
Hudson Poly Bag Inc	Hudson	MA	F	978 562-7566	9374
Laddawn Inc (HQ)	Devens	MA	D	800 446-3639	8274

PLASTICS FILM & SHEET: Polypropylene

	CITY	ST	EMP	PHONE	ENTRY#
Toray Plastics (america) Inc (DH)	North Kingstown	RI	A	401 294-4511	16287

PLASTICS FILM & SHEET: Polyvinyl

	CITY	ST	EMP	PHONE	ENTRY#
Polyvinyl Films Inc	Sutton	MA	D	508 865-3558	12290
Ward Process Inc	Holliston	MA	D	508 429-1165	9238

PLASTICS FILM & SHEET: Vinyl

	CITY	ST	EMP	PHONE	ENTRY#
Orafol Americas Inc	Avon	CT	C	860 676-7100	35
Dielectrics Inc	Chicopee	MA	C	413 594-8111	8024
Waterville Window Co Inc	Winslow	ME	E	207 873-0159	5689

PLASTICS FINISHED PRDTS: Laminated

	CITY	ST	EMP	PHONE	ENTRY#
Alcat Incorporated	Milford	CT	E	203 878-0648	1795
Hicks and Otis Prints Inc	Norwalk	CT	E	203 846-2087	2513
General Woodworking Inc (PA)	Lowell	MA	E	978 458-6625	9879
Geonautics Manufacturing Inc	Newburyport	MA	E	978 462-7161	10685
High Speed Routing LLC	Haverhill	MA	F	603 527-8027	9103
Advanced Building Products Inc	Sanford	ME	F	207 490-2306	5389
York Manufacturing Inc	Sanford	ME	F	207 324-1300	5418
Plasti-Clip Corporation	Milford	NH	F	603 672-1166	15034
Riley Mountain Products Inc	Antrim	NH	F	603 588-7234	13898

2024 Harris New England
Manufacturers Directory

(G-0000) Company's Geographic Section entry number

	CITY	ST	EMP	PHONE	ENTRY#

PLASTICS FOAM, WHOLESALE

	CITY	ST	EMP	PHONE	ENTRY#
Jeffco Fibres Inc (PA)	Webster	MA	C	508 943-0440	12928
Eco Global Manufacturing LLC	Providence	RI	E	401 331-5129	16512

PLASTICS MATERIAL & RESINS

	CITY	ST	EMP	PHONE	ENTRY#
Allnex USA Inc	Wallingford	CT	D	203 269-4481	3769
Allread Products Co LLC	Terryville	CT	F	860 589-3566	3600
Arkadia Plastics Inc	New Britain	CT	E	860 612-0556	2001
Axel Plastics RES Labs Inc	Monroe	CT	E	718 672-8300	1905
Bakelite N Sumitomo Amer Inc (DH)	Manchester	CT	D	860 646-5500	1586
C Mather Company Inc	South Windsor	CT	G	860 528-5667	3124
Chessco Industries Inc (PA)	Westport	CT	E	203 255-2804	4160
Electric Cable Compounds Inc	Naugatuck	CT	D	203 723-2590	1957
Electrocal Inc	Manchester	CT	C	860 646-8153	1595
Engineered Polymers Inds Inc	Cheshire	CT	F	203 272-2233	590
Fimor North America Inc (HQ)	Cheshire	CT	E	203 272-3219	593
Henkel of America Inc (HQ)	Rocky Hill	CT	B	860 615-3395	2926
Henkel US Operations Corp (DH)	Rocky Hill	CT	A	860 571-5100	2927
Lanxess Solutions US Inc	Shelton	CT	A	203 573-2000	3027
Oxford Performance Mtls Inc	South Windsor	CT	E	860 698-9300	3169
Plastics Color Corp Inc	Dayville	CT	G	800 922-9936	866
Polymer Resources Ltd (PA)	Farmington	CT	D	800 243-5176	1242
Ravago Americas LLC	Wilton	CT	D	203 855-6000	4245
Roehm America LLC	Wallingford	CT	E	203 269-4481	3846
Rogers Corporation	Woodstock	CT	C	860 928-3622	4396
Seaview Plastic Recycling Inc	Bridgeport	CT	F	203 367-0070	370
Sjd Tech Inc	Wallingford	CT	D	203 269-9500	3849
Sonoco Prtective Solutions Inc	Putnam	CT	D	860 928-7795	2875
Spartech LLC	Stamford	CT	C	203 327-6010	3467
Stanchem Incorporated (HQ)	East Berlin	CT	E	860 828-0571	918
Summit Plastics LLC	Portland	CT	G	860 740-4482	2826
A Schulman Custom Compounding Ne Inc	Worcester	MA			C
508 756-0002	13695				
Accurate Composites LLC	East Falmouth	MA	D	508 457-9097	8353
Accurate Plastics Inc	East Falmouth	MA	E	508 457-9097	8354
Acushnet Rubber Company Inc	New Bedford	MA	B	508 998-4000	10564
Allied Resin Technologies LLC	Leominster	MA	F	978 401-2267	9635
Anchor-Seal Inc	Gloucester	MA	G	978 515-6004	8918
Argotec LLC	Greenfield	MA	B	413 772-2564	8982
Argotec LLC (HQ)	Greenfield	MA	C	413 772-2564	8983
Blueshift Materials Inc	Spencer	MA	E	888 350-7586	12054
CDF Corporation (PA)	Plymouth	MA	D	508 747-5858	11454
Chroma Color Corporation	Leominster	MA	E	978 537-3538	9652
Clinton BCI Inc	Clinton	MA	E	978 365-7335	8075
Cold Chain Technologies LLC (HQ)	Franklin	MA	D	508 429-1395	8826
Dj Microlaminates Inc	Sudbury	MA	F	978 261-3188	12264
Dow Chemical Company	Marlborough	MA	C	508 229-7676	10147
DSM Thermoplastics	Leominster	MA	E	978 537-6484	9659
Enginred Syntactic Systems LLC	Attleboro	MA	G	508 226-3907	6013
Entec Polymers	Sutton	MA	F	508 865-2001	12280
Ernest Johnson	Marlborough	MA	E	508 259-6727	10148
Gare Incorporated	Haverhill	MA	E	978 373-9131	9096
Gelpac Poly Usa Inc (PA)	Haverhill	MA	F	978 372-3300	9097
George Patton Associates Inc	Fall River	MA	C	800 572-2194	8552
Henkel Corporation	Canton	MA	C	781 737-1400	7796
Industrial Polymers & Chem Inc (PA)	Shrewsbury	MA	F	508 845-6112	11835
Ineos Melamines LLC	Springfield	MA	E	413 730-3811	12104
Isp Freetown Fine Chem Inc	Assonet	MA	D	508 672-0634	5974
Lifoam Industries Inc	Peabody	MA	E	978 278-0008	11324
Plaskolite LLC	Sheffield	MA	E	800 628-5084	11798
Plaskolite LLC	Sheffield	MA	C	800 628-5084	11799
Plaskolite Massachusetts LLC	Sheffield	MA	E	413 229-8711	11800
Plastic Design Inc	North Chelmsford	MA	E	978 251-4830	10987
Port Plastics Inc	Chelmsford	MA	G	978 259-0002	7946
Primary Colors Inc	North Grafton	MA	E	508 839-3202	11025
Resin Distribution Inc	Ayer	MA	F	978 772-1616	6192
Resin Technology LLC (DH)	Littleton	MA	E	978 448-6926	9835
Royston Laboratories	Bridgewater	MA	G	412 828-1500	7237
S&E Specialty Polymers LLC	Lunenburg	MA	D	978 537-8261	9960
Sabic Innovative Plas US LLC	Pittsfield	MA	B	413 448-7110	11422
Sabic Innovative Plas US LLC	Tyngsboro	MA	E	978 772-5900	12465
Saint-Gobain Prfmce Plas Corp	Taunton	MA	C	508 823-7701	12366
Solutia Inc	Indian Orchard	MA	C	734 676-4400	9474
Solutia Inc	Springfield	MA	A	413 788-6911	12132
Synthomer Inc	Fitchburg	MA	C	978 342-5831	8678
Tapecoat Company	Westwood	MA	G	781 332-0700	13322
Teknor Apex Elastomers Inc	Leominster	MA	D	978 466-5344	9709
Tuftane Extrusion Tech Inc	Fall River	MA	F	978 921-8200	8618
US Polymers Inc	Beverly	MA	G	978 921-8000	6391
Ware Rite Distributors Inc	East Bridgewater	MA	D	508 690-2145	8347
Bosal Foam and Fiber (PA)	Limerick	ME	E	207 793-2245	5000
Cyro Industry	Sanford	ME	F	207 324-6000	5393
Neal Specialty Compounding LLC	Lewiston	ME	D	207 777-1122	4979
Roehm America LLC	Sanford	ME	E	207 324-6000	5412
Core Elastomers LLC	Portsmouth	NH	G	603 319-6912	15376
Freudenberg-Nok General Partnr	Bristol	NH	B	603 744-0371	14034
Freudenberg-Nok General Partnr	Northfield	NH	E	603 286-1600	15265
Freudenberg-Nok General Partnr	Northfield	NH	D	603 286-1600	15266
Gates Tpu Inc	Salem	NH	E	603 890-1515	15531
Gelpac Poly Usa Inc	Salem	NH	E	603 685-8338	15532
Huntsman International LLC	Derry	NH	G	603 421-3500	14195
Metzger/Mcguire Inc	Bow	NH	E	603 224-6122	14005
Nyltech North America	Manchester	NH	G	603 627-5150	14907
Omni Metals Company Inc	Somersworth	NH	E	603 692-6664	15619
Plan Tech Inc	Loudon	NH	E	603 783-4767	14798
Resin Systems Corporation	Amherst	NH	D	603 673-1234	13886
Saint-Gobain Prfmce Plas Corp	Merrimack	NH	C	603 424-9000	15001
Scandia Plastics Inc	Plaistow	NH	B	603 382-6533	15350
Spaulding Composites Inc (PA)	Rochester	NH	D	603 332-0555	15494
Teknor Apex	Derry	NH	F	603 434-3056	14210
Textiles Coated Incorporated	Manchester	NH	C	603 296-2221	14943
Visual Polymer Tech LLC	Bedford	NH	G	603 488-5064	13953
Wembly Nycoa Holdings LLC	Manchester	NH	G	603 627-5150	14959
Amazing Mobile	Woonsocket	RI	G	401 597-0566	16947
Development Associates Inc	North Kingstown	RI	F	401 884-1350	16244
G-Form LLC	North Smithfield	RI	E	401 769-0994	16323
Ralco Industries Inc (PA)	Woonsocket	RI	E	401 765-1000	16973
Teknor Color Company LLC (HQ)	Pawtucket	RI	E		16422
Teknor Prfmce Elastomers Inc	Pawtucket	RI		401 725-8000	16423
Trico Specialty Films LLC	North Kingstown	RI	F	401 294-7022	16288

PLASTICS MATERIALS, BASIC FORMS & SHAPES WHOLESALERS

	CITY	ST	EMP	PHONE	ENTRY#
Extec Corp	Enfield	CT	F	860 741-3435	1133
Nevamar Company LLC (HQ)	Shelton	CT	B	203 925-1556	3037
Atlantic Poly Inc	Norwood	MA	E	781 769-4260	11163
Fluorolite Plastics LLC	Hudson	MA	G	508 788-1200	9368
Kilder Corporation	North Billerica	MA	E	978 663-8800	10922
Millennium Plastics Inc	North Chelmsford	MA	F	978 372-4822	10984
Pacific Packaging Products Inc (PA)	Wilmington	MA	C	978 657-9100	13445
Plastic Concepts Inc	North Billerica	MA	E	978 663-7996	10943
Plastic Design Inc	North Chelmsford	MA	E	978 251-4830	10987

PLASTICS PROCESSING

	CITY	ST	EMP	PHONE	ENTRY#
Connecticut Plastics Inc	Wallingford	CT	E	203 265-3299	3793
Entegris Inc	Danbury	CT	C	800 766-2681	737
Idex Health & Science LLC	Bristol	CT	C	860 314-2880	456
Spartech LLC	Stamford	CT	C	203 327-6010	3467
Custom Extrusion Inc (HQ)	Sheffield	MA	E	413 229-8748	11797
Entegris Inc (PA)	Billerica	MA	A	978 436-6500	6443
Gregory Manufacturing Inc	Holyoke	MA	D	413 536-5432	9257
Hapco Inc	Hanover	MA	E	781 826-8801	9034
Hartwell 131 Holdings Corp	Lexington	MA	E	781 328-3220	9746
JMS Manufacturing Co Inc	Taunton	MA	G	508 675-1141	12345
M & P Machine Company Inc	Stoughton	MA	G	781 344-5888	12218
Mac Lean-Fogg Company	Lexington	MA	D	781 328-3220	9762
Mair-Mac Machine Company Inc	Brockton	MA	F	508 895-9001	7294
MJW Mass Inc	Winchester	MA	D	781 721-0332	13488
Nevron Plastics Inc	Saugus	MA	E	781 233-1310	11763
Poly-Cel Inc	Acton	MA	F	508 229-8310	5761
Sencorp Inc	Hyannis	MA	C	508 771-9400	9450
Vantec LLC	North Attleboro	MA	E	508 726-2830	10891
Freudenberg-Nok Gnrl Prtnrshp	Londonderry	NH	F	603 628-7023	14752
Newdtc LLC	Salem	NH	F	603 893-0992	15549
Rehrig Pacific Company	Nottingham	NH	C	603 490-8722	15277
Worthen Industries Inc	Nashua	NH	E	978 365-6345	15190
Custom Molded Products Inc	North Providence	RI	G	401 464-9991	16298
Parkinson Machinery & Manufacturing Corp	Woonsocket		RI		C
401 762-2100	16971				
Parkinson Technologies Inc	Woonsocket	RI	D	401 762-2100	16972

PLASTICS SHEET: Packing Materials

	CITY	ST	EMP	PHONE	ENTRY#
Charter Next Generation Inc	Turners Falls	MA	C	413 863-3171	12444
Gregory Manufacturing Inc	Holyoke	MA	D	413 536-5432	9257
JP Plastics Inc	Bridgewater	MA	G	508 697-4202	7235
Packaging Products Corporation (PA)	New Bedford	MA	F	508 997-5150	10638
Tekni-Plex Inc	Ashland	MA	E	508 881-2440	5968
Walter Drake Incorporated (PA)	Holyoke	MA	G	413 536-5463	9290
Nelipak Corporation (PA)	Cranston	RI	E	401 946-2699	15899

PLASTICS: Blow Molded

	CITY	ST	EMP	PHONE	ENTRY#
Altium Packaging	Windsor	CT	F	860 683-8560	4258
Plastic Forming Company Inc (PA)	Woodbridge	CT	E	203 397-1338	4382
Plastic Assembly Corporation	Ayer	MA	F	978 772-4725	6191

Employee Codes: A=Over 500 employees, B=251-500
C=101-250, D=51-100, E=20-50, F=10-19, G=1-9

2024 Harris New England
Manufacturers Directory

1445

PRODUCT

	CITY	ST	EMP	PHONE	ENTRY#
North American Plastics Ltd	Manchester	NH	E	603 644-1660	14902

PLASTICS: Extruded

	CITY	ST	EMP	PHONE	ENTRY#
Cowles Products Company Inc	North Haven	CT	D	203 865-3110	2405
Davis-Standard LLC **(HQ)**	Pawcatuck	CT	B	860 300-3928	2717
Farrel Corporation **(DH)**	Ansonia	CT	D	203 736-5500	14
Merritt Extruder Corp	Hamden	CT	E	203 230-8100	1440
Bixby International Corp	Newburyport	MA	D	978 462-4100	10671
Filtrona Extrusion of Massachusetts LLC	Athol	MA	C	978 249-5343	5979
Pepperell Braiding Company Inc **(PA)**	Pepperell	MA	E	978 433-2133	11387
Xponent Global Inc	Hudson	MA	E	978 562-3485	9426
Genplex Inc	Skowhegan	ME	G	207 474-3500	5467
HI Tech Profiles Inc	Ashaway	RI	E	401 377-2040	15741

PLASTICS: Finished Injection Molded

	CITY	ST	EMP	PHONE	ENTRY#
Apex Machine Tool Company Inc	Cheshire	CT	D	860 677-2884	571
Marlborough Plastics Inc	Marlborough	CT	G	860 295-9124	1644
Mbsw Inc	West Hartford	CT	E	860 243-0303	4071
Rogers Manufacturing Company	Rockfall	CT	D	860 346-8648	2915
Schaeffler Aerospace USA Corp **(DH)**	Danbury	CT	B	203 744-2211	809
Seitz LLC	Torrington	CT	C	860 489-0476	3695
Art Plastics Mfg Corp	Leominster	MA	F	978 537-6640	9637
Cardinal Comb & Brush Mfg Corp	Leominster	MA	E	978 537-6330	9647
Castle Plastics Inc	Leominster	MA	G	978 534-6220	9648
First Plastics Corp	Leominster	MA	F	978 537-0367	9664
Globe Composite Solutions Ltd	Stoughton	MA	D	781 871-3700	12211
Lar Plastics LLC	Winchester	MA	B	617 860-2020	13485
Pilgrim Innovative Plas LLC	Plymouth	MA	E	508 732-0297	11472
Plastic Molding Mfg Inc **(PA)**	Hudson	MA	E	978 567-1000	9400
Plastic Packaging Corporation	West Springfield	MA	C	413 785-1553	13042
Super Brush LLC	Springfield	MA	D	413 543-1442	12136
United Comb & Novelty Corp **(PA)**	Leominster	MA	D	978 537-2096	9712
Web Industries Inc **(PA)**	Marlborough	MA	G	508 898-2988	10234
Maine Manufacturing LLC	Sanford	ME	D	207 324-1754	5398
GI Plastek LLC	Wolfeboro	NH	E	603 569-5100	15731
Hy-Ten Die & Development Corp	Milford	NH	E	603 673-1611	15029
Tech Nh Inc **(PA)**	Merrimack	NH	D	603 424-4404	15007
W K Hillquist Inc	Hudson	NH	E	603 595-7790	14559
Cadence Mfg Inc	Cranston	RI	E	508 746-6082	15839
Continental Plas & Packg Inc	Lincoln	RI	F	781 932-1115	16128

PLASTICS: Molded

	CITY	ST	EMP	PHONE	ENTRY#
Balfor Industries Inc	Oxford	CT	F	203 828-6473	2687
Canevari Plastics Inc	Milford	CT	G	203 878-4319	1807
J&L Plastic Molding LLC	Wallingford	CT	G	203 265-6237	3821
Milfoam Corporation	Hamden	CT	F	203 248-8011	1442
Spartech Polycast Inc	Stamford	CT	C	203 327-6010	3468
Super Seal Company LLC	Stratford	CT	F	203 378-5015	3579
Bacon Industries Inc	Wrentham	MA	F	508 384-0780	13837
F & D Plastics Inc **(PA)**	Leominster	MA	F	978 668-5140	9662
Integrity Mold Inc	Gardner	MA	F	978 669-0093	8891
Mar-Lee Companies Inc	Fitchburg	MA	G	978 343-9600	8661
Restech Plastic Molding LLC **(DH)**	Hudson	MA	E	978 567-1000	9407
Tyca Corporation **(PA)**	Clinton	MA	E	978 612-0002	8093
Urthpact Innovations LLC	Leominster	MA	F	978 847-9747	9713
W M Gulliksen Mfg Co Inc **(PA)**	South Weymouth	MA	F	617 333-5750	11979
Comstock Industries Inc	Meredith	NH	E	603 279-7045	14968
Keller Products Incorporated **(PA)**	Manchester	NH	E	603 627-7887	14871
Proto Labs Inc	Nashua	NH	C	763 479-2679	15152
Talbot Hill Holdings Corp	Swanzey	NH	E	603 357-2523	15646
Jade Engineered Plastics Inc	Warren	RI	D	401 253-4440	16759
Dolliver Corporation	Williston	VT	G	802 879-0072	17728

PLASTICS: Polystyrene Foam

	CITY	ST	EMP	PHONE	ENTRY#
Ansonia Plastics LLC	Ansonia	CT	D	203 736-5200	7
Gilman Corporation	Gilman	CT	E	860 887-7080	1266
Hhc LLC	Manchester	CT	E	860 456-0677	1602
Hopp Companies Inc **(PA)**	Southbury	CT	F	800 889-8425	3196
Hydrofera LLC	Manchester	CT	D	860 456-0677	1604
Madison Polymeric Engrg Inc	Branford	CT	E	203 488-4554	271
Merco Inc	Ellington	CT	E	860 871-1888	1110
New England Foam Products LLC **(PA)**	Hartford	CT	E	860 524-0121	1496
Plastic Forming Company Inc **(PA)**	Woodbridge	CT	E	203 397-1338	4382
Reilly Foam Corp	Bloomfield	CT	F	860 243-8200	206
The Gilman Brothers Company	Gilman	CT	D	860 889-8444	1268
Ashworth International Inc	Fall River	MA	E	508 674-4693	8522
Bbmc Inc	Hancock	MA	E	413 443-3333	9024
Concrete Block Insulg Systems	West Brookfield	MA	E	508 867-4241	12993
Flexcon Industrial LLC **(HQ)**	Spencer	MA	D	210 798-1900	12059
Fuller Box Co Inc **(PA)**	North Attleboro	MA	D	508 695-2525	10871
Geonautics Manufacturing Inc	Newburyport	MA	E	978 462-7161	10685
Jeffco Fibres Inc **(PA)**	Webster	MA	C	508 943-0440	12928

	CITY	ST	EMP	PHONE	ENTRY#
Rogers Foam Automotive Corp	Somerville	MA	F	617 623-3010	11895
Trexel Inc **(PA)**	Wilmington	MA	F	781 932-0202	13471
Ward Process Inc	Holliston	MA	D	508 429-1165	9238
Deepwater Buoyancy Inc	Biddeford	ME	F	207 468-2565	4559
Enefco International Inc **(PA)**	Auburn	ME	E	207 514-7218	4428
Index Packaging Inc	Milton	NH	C	603 350-0018	15046
Tex Flock Inc	Woonsocket	RI	E	401 765-2340	16981
Vesuvius America Inc **(DH)**	Providence	RI	E		16640

PLASTICS: Thermoformed

	CITY	ST	EMP	PHONE	ENTRY#
Lehvoss North America LLC	Pawcatuck	CT	F	860 495-2046	2723
Siemon Company **(PA)**	Watertown	CT	A	860 945-4200	4029
34 Tower Street Inc	Shirley	MA	E	978 425-2311	11812
Accutech Packaging Inc	Foxboro	MA	D	508 543-3800	8689
Black Diamond Mfg & Engrg Inc	Georgetown	MA	F	978 352-6716	8905
New England Plastics Corp **(PA)**	Woburn	MA	E	781 933-6004	13623
Pioneer Packaging Inc **(PA)**	Chicopee	MA	D	413 378-6930	8054
Saint-Gobain Prfmce Plas Corp	Worcester	MA	C	508 852-3072	13792
United Plastic Fabricating Inc **(PA)**	North Andover	MA	D	978 975-4520	10855
Universal Plastics Corporation **(PA)**	Holyoke	MA	E	413 592-4791	9286
Alex & Ryan Design LLC	Manchester	NH	F	603 518-8650	14808
Jay Packaging Group Inc **(DH)**	Warwick	RI	D	401 244-1300	16827
Packaging Concepts Ltd	Rumford	RI	C	401 334-0344	16675
Precision Composites VT LLC	Lyndonville	VT	E	802 626-5900	17320

PLATE WORK: Metalworking Trade

	CITY	ST	EMP	PHONE	ENTRY#
Momentum Mfg Group LLC **(HQ)**	Georgetown	MA	D	978 659-6960	8910

PLATFORMS: Cargo

	CITY	ST	EMP	PHONE	ENTRY#
Ada Fabricators Inc	Wilmington	MA	F	978 262-9900	13372

PLATING & FINISHING SVC: Decorative, Formed Prdts

	CITY	ST	EMP	PHONE	ENTRY#
Jarden LLC	East Wilton	ME	F	207 645-2574	4741

PLATING & POLISHING SVC

	CITY	ST	EMP	PHONE	ENTRY#
C & S Engineering Inc	Meriden	CT	F	203 235-5727	1657
Colonial Coatings Inc	Milford	CT	E	203 783-9933	1811
Deburring Laboratories Inc	New Britain	CT	F	860 829-6300	2022
Giering Metal Finishing Incorporated	Hamden	CT	E	203 248-5583	1426
P&G Metal Components Corp	Bloomfield	CT	F	860 243-2220	199
Plasma Technology Incorporated	South Windsor	CT	E	860 282-0659	3173
Sousa Corp	Newington	CT	E	860 523-9090	2326
The Romatic Manufacturing Company	Southbury	CT	C	203 264-8203	3199
Accumet Engineering Corp	Devens	MA	E	978 568-8311	8266
Berkshire Mnufactured Pdts Inc	Newburyport	MA	C	978 462-8161	10670
Katahdin Industries Inc **(PA)**	Hudson	MA	F	781 329-1420	9380
Lone Star Holdings Inc **(HQ)**	Chelsea	MA	E	781 935-2224	7986
Pep Industries LLC	Attleboro	MA	F	508 226-5600	6046
Precision Engineered Pdts LLC **(DH)**	Attleboro	MA	G		6051
R L Barry Inc	Attleboro	MA	F	508 226-3350	6052
Spencer Metal Finishing Inc **(HQ)**	Brookfield	MA	E	508 885-6477	7316
Sweet Metal Finishing Inc	Attleboro	MA	F	508 226-4359	6068
Transene Company Inc **(PA)**	Danvers	MA	G	978 777-7860	8227
Mbw Tractor Sales LLC	Berwick	ME	F	207 384-2001	4551
Peg Kearsarge Co Inc	Bartlett	NH	G	603 374-2341	13918
Chemart Company **(PA)**	Lincoln	RI	D	401 333-9200	16126
Interplex Engineered Pdts Inc	Rumford	RI	D	401 434-6543	16670
Precision Plsg Ornamentals Inc	Pawtucket	RI	F	401 728-9994	16404

PLATING COMPOUNDS

	CITY	ST	EMP	PHONE	ENTRY#
Macdermid Incorporated **(HQ)**	Waterbury	CT	C	203 575-5700	3933
Advanced Chemical Company	Warwick	RI	E	401 785-3434	16776

PLATING SVC: Chromium, Metals Or Formed Prdts

	CITY	ST	EMP	PHONE	ENTRY#
CRC Chrome Corporation	Meriden	CT	F	203 630-1008	1662
Mirror Polishing & Pltg Co Inc	Waterbury	CT	E	203 574-5400	3945
Induplate Inc **(PA)**	North Providence	RI	D	401 231-5770	16303

PLAYGROUND EQPT

	CITY	ST	EMP	PHONE	ENTRY#
Creative Playthings Ltd **(PA)**	Framingham	MA	F	508 620-0900	8753
Cedarworks of Maine Inc	Rockland	ME	E	207 596-0771	5324

PLEATING & STITCHING SVC

	CITY	ST	EMP	PHONE	ENTRY#
Hot Tops LLC	Shelton	CT	F	203 926-2067	3016
Zuse Inc	Branford	CT	D	203 458-3295	287
47 Brand LLC	Boston	MA	D	617 437-1384	6501
Callenstitch LLC	Concord	MA	F	978 369-9080	8107
Chillybear Inc **(PA)**	Needham	MA	F	781 455-6321	10507
Nixon Company Incorporated	Indian Orchard	MA	F	413 543-3701	9472
Pop Tops Company Inc	South Easton	MA	E	508 580-2580	11949
Silver Screen Design Inc	Greenfield	MA	F	413 773-1692	9000
Wear-Guard Corporation	Norwell	MA	A	781 871-4100	11150

(G-0000) Company's Geographic Section entry number

	CITY	ST	EMP	PHONE	ENTRY#
Winter People Inc	Cumberland Center	ME	E	207 865-6636	
4711					
Business Shirtmasters	Chichester	NH	F	603 798-3787	14072
National Embroidery Corp	Manchester	NH	F	603 647-1995	14896
GA Rel Manufacturing Company	Providence	RI	F	401 331-5455	16524
Ira Green Inc (PA)	Providence	RI	C	800 663-7487	16543
Kennedy Incorporated	North Kingstown	RI	F	401 295-7800	16265
Spirit Recognition Inc (PA)	Pawtucket	RI	F	401 722-6400	16417

PLUMBING FIXTURES

	CITY	ST	EMP	PHONE	ENTRY#
Bead Industries Inc (PA)	Milford	CT	E	203 301-0270	1801
Burt Process Equipment Inc (PA)	Hamden	CT	E	203 287-1985	1415
Colonial Bronze Company	Torrington	CT	D	860 489-9233	3674
F W Webb Company	New Haven	CT	F	203 865-6124	2151
Fitzgerald and Wood Inc	Branford	CT	G	203 488-2553	257
Granite Group Wholesalers LLC	Colchester	CT	G	860 537-7600	659
Macristy Industries Inc (PA)	Newington	CT	F	860 225-4637	2305
McGuire Manufacturing Co Inc	Cheshire	CT	E	203 699-1801	606
F W Webb Company	Needham	MA	F	781 247-0300	10510
Ferguson Enterprises LLC	Chicopee	MA	C	413 593-1219	8032
Idex Health & Science LLC	Middleboro	MA	C	774 213-0200	10362
Orion Enterprises Inc (HQ)	North Andover	MA	C	913 342-1653	10847
Renovators Supply Inc	Erving	MA	E	413 423-3300	8471
Sherle Wagner Intl LLC	Fall River	MA	F	212 758-3300	8606
Symmons Industries Inc	Avon	MA	D	508 857-2352	6163
F W Webb Company	Windham	ME	F	207 892-5302	5661
2023 Holdings LLC	Winchester	NH	D	603 239-6371	15713
Fulford Manufacturing Company (PA)	Riverside	RI	F	401 431-2000	16655
Quick Fitting Inc	East Providence	RI	D	401 734-9500	16040

PLUMBING FIXTURES: Plastic

	CITY	ST	EMP	PHONE	ENTRY#
Keeney Holdings LLC	Farmington	CT	B	860 666-3342	1226
Neoperl Inc	Waterbury	CT	D	203 756-8891	3949
Sherle Wagner Intl LLC	Fall River	MA	F	212 758-3300	8606

PLUMBING FIXTURES: Vitreous China

	CITY	ST	EMP	PHONE	ENTRY#
Clivus Multrum Inc	Lawrence	MA	G	978 725-5591	9551

POINT OF SALE DEVICES

	CITY	ST	EMP	PHONE	ENTRY#
Hopp Companies Inc (PA)	Southbury	CT	G	800 889-8425	3196
Displays By Garo Inc	Lincoln	RI	F	401 305-3511	16133
Plastics Plus Inc	Cumberland	RI	E	401 727-1447	15960

POLISHING SVC: Metals Or Formed Prdts

	CITY	ST	EMP	PHONE	ENTRY#
Nu-Lustre Finishing Corp	Providence	RI	E	401 521-7800	16576

POLYESTERS

	CITY	ST	EMP	PHONE	ENTRY#
Rig Grip Incorporated	Newton	MA	G	800 770-2666	10781

POLYETHYLENE RESINS

	CITY	ST	EMP	PHONE	ENTRY#
Thornton and Company Inc	Southington	CT	F	860 628-6771	3237
Covestro LLC	Wilmington	MA	C	800 458-0014	13399
DSM Neoresins Inc	Wilmington	MA	C	800 458-0014	13403
Eastern Packaging Inc	Lawrence	MA	D	978 685-7723	9559
Allstate Polyethylene Corp (PA)	Alexandria	NH	G	800 288-7659	13851
Polyexe Corporation	Brentwood	NH	E	603 778-1143	14027

POLYPROPYLENE RESINS

	CITY	ST	EMP	PHONE	ENTRY#
Bayer Corporation	Newton	MA	E	617 969-7690	10738

POLYSTYRENE RESINS

	CITY	ST	EMP	PHONE	ENTRY#
P I Liquidating Inc (PA)	Prospect	CT	E	203 758-6651	2838
Avilite LLC	Merrimack	NH	G	603 626-4388	14974
Branch River Plastics Inc	Smithfield	RI	E	401 232-0270	16690

POLYURETHANE RESINS

	CITY	ST	EMP	PHONE	ENTRY#
Presidium USA Inc	Darien	CT	F	203 803-2980	853
L H C Inc (PA)	Lynn	MA	F	781 592-6444	9982
Rynel Inc	Wiscasset	ME	D	207 882-0200	5700

POLYVINYL CHLORIDE RESINS

	CITY	ST	EMP	PHONE	ENTRY#
Altium Acqisition Holdings Inc	Boston	MA	A	617 516-2000	6539

POTTERY: Laboratory & Indl

	CITY	ST	EMP	PHONE	ENTRY#
Bodycote lmt Inc (DH)	Andover	MA	D	978 470-0876	5873
Saint-Gobain Corporation	Northborough	MA	A	508 351-7112	11108

POULTRY & POULTRY PRDTS WHOLESALERS

	CITY	ST	EMP	PHONE	ENTRY#
Samuel Holmes Incorporated	Everett	MA	F	617 269-5740	8500

POULTRY & SMALL GAME SLAUGHTERING & PROCESSING

	CITY	ST	EMP	PHONE	ENTRY#
Carls Boned Chicken Inc	New Haven	CT	E	203 777-9048	2135

	CITY	ST	EMP	PHONE	ENTRY#
Moark LLC (HQ)	North Franklin	CT	E	951 332-3300	2383
Nmw Holding Co Inc	Weymouth	MA	F	617 269-5650	13332
Radlo Foods LLC (PA)	Watertown	MA	G	617 926-7070	12903
Samuel Holmes Incorporated	Everett	MA	F	617 269-5740	8500
Willow Tree Poultry Farm Inc	Attleboro	MA	D	508 222-2479	6077
Premium Poultry Co	Providence	RI	F	401 467-3200	16587
Warwick Poultry Co Inc	Providence	RI	F	401 421-8500	16643

POWDER: Aluminum Atomized

	CITY	ST	EMP	PHONE	ENTRY#
US Packaging Specialties	Fall River	MA	F	508 674-3636	8621

POWDER: Iron

	CITY	ST	EMP	PHONE	ENTRY#
Ametek Inc	Wallingford	CT	C	203 265-6731	3770

POWDER: Metal

	CITY	ST	EMP	PHONE	ENTRY#
Allied Sinterings Incorporated	Danbury	CT	E	203 743-7502	706
Allread Products Co LLC	Terryville	CT	F	860 589-3566	3600
Conn Engineering Assoc Corp	Sandy Hook	CT	F	203 426-4733	2948
Norwalk Powdered Metals Inc	Stratford	CT	D	203 338-8000	3560
Sterling Sintered Technologies Inc	Winsted	CT	F	860 379-2753	4357
Capstan Industries Inc	Wrentham	MA	C	508 384-3100	13839
Starmet Corporation (PA)	Concord	MA	E	978 369-5410	8134
Powdered Metal Technology Corp	Nashua	NH	F	617 642-4135	15150

POWER GENERATORS

	CITY	ST	EMP	PHONE	ENTRY#
A-1 Machining Co LLC	New Britain	CT	D	860 223-6420	1994
Atlantic Pwr US GP Hldings Inc	Dedham	MA	G	617 977-2400	8236
Aurora Wind Project LLC	Andover	MA	F	978 409-9712	5871
Emergncy Pwr Gnrators Neng LLC	Chelmsford	MA	G	978 455-0461	7925
Hy9 Corporation	Foxboro	MA	G	508 698-1040	8699
New England Gen-Connect LLC	Hingham	MA	G	617 571-6884	9155
Power Equipment Co Inc (PA)	Attleboro	MA	E	508 226-3410	6050
Viking Industrial Products	Marlborough	MA	E	508 481-4600	10231
Weld Power Generator Inc	Millbury	MA	F	800 288-6016	10445
Bear Swamp Power Company LLC	Millinocket	ME	F	207 723-4341	5064
Powr Pt Generator Pwr Systems	Saco	ME	F	207 864-2787	5377

POWER SPLY CONVERTERS: Static, Electronic Applications

	CITY	ST	EMP	PHONE	ENTRY#
Neeltran Inc	New Milford	CT	C	860 350-5964	2254
Validus DC Systems LLC	Brookfield	CT	G	203 448-3600	542
Cape Light Compact	Barnstable	MA	F	508 375-6703	6199
Mornsun America LLC	Milford	MA	G	978 293-3923	10406
Dynapower Company LLC (DH)	South Burlington	VT	D	802 860-7200	17577

POWER SUPPLIES: All Types, Static

	CITY	ST	EMP	PHONE	ENTRY#
Dsaencore LLC	Brookfield	CT	D	203 740-4200	518
Hipotronics Inc (HQ)	Shelton	CT	C	845 279-3644	3013
Prime Technology LLC	North Branford	CT	E	203 481-5721	2373
Transformer Technology Inc	Durham	CT	F	860 349-1061	905
Excelitas Technologies Corp	Salem	MA	C	800 775-6786	11714
Kaiser Systems Inc	Salem	MA	D	978 224-4135	11725
Socomec Inc (DH)	Watertown	MA	F	617 245-0447	12908
Synqor Inc (PA)	Boxborough	MA	C	978 849-0600	7155
Synqor Holdings LLC	Boxborough	MA	F	978 849-0600	7156
Wasik Associates Inc	Dracut	MA	F	978 454-9787	8314

POWER SWITCHING EQPT

	CITY	ST	EMP	PHONE	ENTRY#
Russelectric Inc	Hingham	MA	B	781 749-6000	9158
Siemens Industry Inc	Hingham	MA	B	781 749-6000	9159

PRECAST TERRAZZO OR CONCRETE PRDTS

	CITY	ST	EMP	PHONE	ENTRY#
Coreslab Structures Conn Inc	Thomaston	CT	D	860 283-8281	3617
Mackenzie Vault Inc	East Longmeadow	MA	F	413 525-8827	8385
Oldcastle Infrastructure Inc	Rehoboth	MA	E	508 336-7600	11613
Strafello Precast Inc	East Taunton	MA	E	774 501-2628	8413
Michie Corporation	Henniker	NH	D	603 428-7426	14438
Concrete Products Inc	Chepachet	RI	E	401 568-8874	15803
Forterra Pipe & Precast LLC	Peace Dale	RI	G	401 782-2600	16433

PRECIOUS METALS

	CITY	ST	EMP	PHONE	ENTRY#
Cimini & Associates Inc	Westerly	RI	E	401 348-0388	16929

PRESTRESSED CONCRETE PRDTS

	CITY	ST	EMP	PHONE	ENTRY#
Blakeslee Prestress Inc (PA)	Branford	CT	C	203 315-7090	241
Petricca Industries Inc (PA)	Pittsfield	MA	E	413 499-1441	11418
Unistress Corp	Pittsfield	MA	B	413 499-1441	11426
Joseph P Carrara & Sons Inc (PA)	North Clarendon	VT	E	802 775-2301	17415

PRIMARY ROLLING MILL EQPT

	CITY	ST	EMP	PHONE	ENTRY#
Idex Mpt Inc (HQ)	Westwood	MA	D	630 530-3333	13312

PRINT CARTRIDGES: Laser & Other Computer Printers

P
R
O
D
U
C
T

	CITY	ST	EMP	PHONE	ENTRY#
Envirnmntal Office Sltions Inc (PA)	East Hartford	CT	E	860 291-1900	993
Electronics For Imaging Inc	Londonderry	NH	B	603 285-9800	14747
Electronics For Imaging Inc (HQ)	Londonderry	NH	E	650 357-3500	14748

PRINTED CIRCUIT BOARDS

	CITY	ST	EMP	PHONE	ENTRY#
AB Electronics LLC	Brookfield	CT	E	203 740-2793	509
Accutron Inc (PA)	Windsor	CT	D	860 683-8300	4253
Altek Electronics Inc	Torrington	CT	C	860 482-7626	3669
American Backplane Inc	Morris	CT	E	860 567-2360	1932
Argo Transdata Corp	Clinton	CT	E	860 669-2233	636
Carlton Industries Corp	Hamden	CT	E	203 288-5605	1416
Cyclone Microsystems Inc	Hamden	CT	E	203 786-5536	1420
Eastern Co	Clinton	CT	C	860 669-2233	642
Electronic Spc Conn Inc	Hamden	CT	E	203 288-1707	1423
Limat Graphics Inc	Danbury	CT	E	203 798-9771	772
Midstate Electronics Co	Wallingford	CT	F	203 265-9900	3832
Norfield Data Products Inc	Norwalk	CT	F	203 849-0292	2546
Northeast Circuit Tech LLC	Glastonbury	CT	G	860 633-1967	1291
Tallinn Fulfillment Limited	Milford	CT	E	203 878-2155	1893
Te Connectivity Corporation	Stafford Springs	CT		860 684-8000	3260
Technical Manufacturing Corp	Durham	CT	E	860 349-1735	904
Tek Industries Inc	Vernon Rockville	CT	E	860 870-0001	3763
Ttm Printed Circuit Group Inc	Stafford Springs	CT	C	860 684-8000	3261
Ttm Technologies Inc	Stafford	CT	B	860 684-5881	3251
Ttm Technologies Inc	Stafford Springs	CT	D	860 684-8000	3262
Accusemble Electronics Inc (PA)	North Billerica	MA	G	508 254-4538	10893
Adcotron Ems Inc	Boston	MA	E	617 598-3000	6514
Bitflow Inc	Woburn	MA	F	781 932-2900	13526
Boardtech Solutions Inc	North Attleboro	MA	G	508 643-3684	10868
Case Assembly Solutions Inc	South Easton	MA	E	508 238-5665	11939
Chase Corporation	Oxford	MA	G	508 731-2710	11250
Chase Corporation (HQ)	Westwood	MA	G	781 332-0700	13309
Circuit Technology Center Inc	Haverhill	MA	E	978 374-5000	9086
Coghlin Companies Inc (PA)	Westborough	MA	C	508 753-2354	13089
Creation Technologies Inc (PA)	Boston	MA	E	877 734-7456	6675
Creation Technologies Intl Inc (PA)	Boston	MA	E	877 734-7456	6676
Dilla St Corp	Milford	MA	G	508 478-3419	10400
Distron Corporation	Attleboro Falls	MA	E	508 695-8786	6084
East West Boston LLC	Boston	MA	D	617 598-3000	6706
Epec LLC (PA)	New Bedford	MA	D	508 995-5171	10589
Essemtec Usa LLC	Waltham	MA	F	856 218-1131	12666
Integratech Solutions Corp	Hudson	MA	E	978 567-1000	9376
J & J Technologies Inc	Wareham	MA	D	508 291-3803	12839
Jabil Inc	Clinton	MA	E	978 365-9721	8079
Jnj Industries Inc	Franklin	MA	E	508 553-0529	8846
Kalt Incorporated (PA)	Lowell	MA	E	978 805-5001	9889
Liberty Engineering Inc	Newton	MA	E	617 965-6644	10768
Ltpc Holdings Inc	Waltham	MA	E	781 893-6672	12712
M C Test Service Inc	North Billerica	MA	C	781 218-7550	10929
Mc Assembly International LLC	North Billerica	MA	B	978 215-9501	10933
Measurement Computing Corp (DH)	Norton	MA	E	508 946-5100	11128
Mercury Systems Inc (PA)	Andover	MA	B	978 256-1300	5896
Mfg Electronics Inc	North Billerica	MA	G	978 671-5490	10936
Micro-Precision Tech Inc (PA)	Lawrence	MA	F	978 688-1299	9580
Micron Corporation	Norwood	MA	E	781 769-5771	11196
Milford Manufacturing Svcs LLC	Hopedale	MA	E	508 478-8544	9299
Mini-Systems Inc (PA)	North Attleboro	MA	D	508 695-1420	10878
Nano Dimension USA Inc	Waltham	MA	E	650 209-2866	12729
Neo Tech	Westborough	MA	G	508 329-6270	13123
New Age Technologies Inc	Attleboro	MA	E	508 226-6090	6041
Oncore Manufacturing LLC	Westborough	MA	D	978 737-3640	13125
Parlex	Methuen	MA	F	978 946-2500	10343
Photo Tool Engineering Inc	Lowell	MA	F	978 805-5000	9913
Prodrive Technologies Inc	Canton	MA	E	617 475-1617	7822
Proxy Manufacturing Inc	Methuen	MA	E	978 687-3138	10344
Remtec Incorporated (PA)	Norwood	MA	E	781 762-9191	11207
RLB Industries Inc	Attleboro	MA	D	508 226-3350	6057
Specialized Coating Svcs LLC	North Billerica	MA	E	978 362-0346	10957
Sunburst Elctmic Mfg Sltons I (PA)	West Bridgewater	MA	D	508 580-1881	12983
Tech-Etch Inc (PA)	Plymouth	MA	B	508 747-0300	11481
Technical Services Inc	Raynham	MA	F	781 389-8342	11599
Techtrade Inc	Needham	MA	E	781 724-7878	10525
Whitman Products Company Inc	North Andover	MA	E	978 975-0502	10862
Worthington Assembly Inc	South Deerfield	MA	E	413 397-8265	11930
David Saunders Inc	South Portland	ME	E	207 228-1888	5497
Elscott Manufacturing LLC (PA)	Gouldsboro	ME	E	207 422-6747	4839
Enercon	Auburn	ME	E	207 657-7001	4429
Enercon (HQ)	Gray	ME	D	207 657-7000	4841
Marja Corporation	Sanford	ME	F	207 324-2994	5400
A Ttm Technologies Company	Salem	NH	G	603 870-4580	15501
Aci - Pcb Inc	Laconia	NH	G	603 528-7711	14642
Amphenol Corporation	Nashua	NH	B	603 879-3000	15060

	CITY	ST	EMP	PHONE	ENTRY#
Amphenol Printed Circuits Inc (HQ)	Nashua	NH	D	603 324-4500	15062
Anaren Ceramics Inc	Salem	NH	D	603 898-2883	15505
Azego Technology Svcs US Inc	Portsmouth	NH	E	603 610-0030	15363
Benchmark Electronics Inc	Nashua	NH	B	603 879-7000	15070
Circuit Technology LLC	Merrimack	NH	D	603 424-2200	14977
Cirtronics Corporation	Milford	NH	C	603 249-9190	15016
Colonial Electronic Mfrs Inc	Nashua	NH	E	603 881-8244	15083
Core Assemblies Inc	Gilford	NH	F	603 293-0270	14334
Data Electronic Devices Inc	Salem	NH	D	603 893-2047	15517
Electronics Aid Inc	Marlborough	NH	G	603 876-4161	14964
Equipment Technologies Inc	Windham	NH	F	603 548-0875	15725
Greensource Fabrication LLC (PA)	Charlestown	NH	D	603 283-9880	14064
Hadco Corporation (HQ)	Salem	NH	B	603 421-3400	15535
Insulectro	Londonderry	NH	E	603 629-4403	14757
Intelligent Mfg Solutons LLC	Manchester	NH	E	603 296-1160	14864
Intervala LLC	Hudson	NH	D	603 595-1987	14512
Manufacturing Services Group	Manchester	NH	F	603 883-1022	14878
Mass Design Inc (PA)	Nashua	NH	D	603 886-6460	15130
Megatrnics US Ultmate Hldco LL (PA)	Salem	NH	E	888 706-0230	15544
Mercury Systems Inc	Hudson	NH	A	603 883-2900	14527
Merrimack Micro LLC	Merrimack	NH	G	603 809-4183	14992
Miraco Inc	Manchester	NH	E	603 665-9449	14890
Pica Mfg Solutions Inc (PA)	Derry	NH	E	603 845-3258	14204
Precision Placement Mchs Inc (PA)	Fremont	NH	F	603 895-5112	14330
Princeton Technology Corp	Hudson	NH	D	603 595-1987	14536
Retcomp Inc	New Boston	NH	F	603 487-5010	15194
Sanmina Corporation	Manchester	NH	C	603 621-1800	14924
Seica	Salem	NH	F	978 376-7254	15560
Sonic Manufacturing Co Inc	Hudson	NH	E	603 882-1020	14546
Sparton Beckwood LLC	Plaistow	NH	D	603 382-3840	15351
Stellar Manufacturing Inc	Salem	NH	E	978 241-9537	15564
Two In One Manufacturing Inc	Nashua	NH	E	603 595-8212	15179
Varitron Technologies USA Inc	Hudson	NH	E	603 577-8855	14557
Aldotech Corporation	Warwick	RI	E	401 467-6100	16777
Vr Industries Inc	Warwick	RI	E	401 732-6800	16875
Image Tek Mfg Inc	Springfield	VT	E	802 885-6208	17618
Purchasing Inventory Cons Inc	Windsor	VT	F	802 674-2620	17761
Vemas Corporation	Poultney	VT	E	802 287-4100	17454
Vermont Circuits Inc	Brattleboro	VT	D	802 257-4571	17102

PRINTERS & PLOTTERS

	CITY	ST	EMP	PHONE	ENTRY#
Macdermid Incorporated (HQ)	Waterbury	CT	C	203 575-5700	3933
Voxel8 Inc	Somerville	MA	F	916 396-3714	11912
Williams Lea Boston	Boston	MA	E	617 371-2300	7125

PRINTERS' SVCS: Folding, Collating, Etc

	CITY	ST	EMP	PHONE	ENTRY#
Chapin Packaging LLC	Darien	CT	G	203 202-2747	846
Johnson & Wales University	Providence	RI	E	401 598-1824	16550

PRINTERS: Computer

	CITY	ST	EMP	PHONE	ENTRY#
Alinabal Holdings Corporation (PA)	Milford	CT	B	203 877-3241	1797
Flo-Tech LLC (PA)	New Haven	CT	D	860 613-3333	2152
Fremco LLC	Stamford	CT	F	203 857-0522	3351
Magnetec Corporation	Wallingford	CT	D	203 949-9933	3829
Omega Engineering Inc (DH)	Norwalk	CT	C	203 359-1660	2549
Bmf Precision Inc	Maynard	MA	E	978 637-2050	10261
Markforged Holding Corporation (PA)	Watertown	MA	E	866 496-1805	12891
Netsilicon Inc (HQ)	Waltham	MA	D	781 647-1234	12736
Extech Instruments Corporation	Nashua	NH	E	877 439-8324	15099
Fujifilm Dimatix Inc	Lebanon	NH	D	603 443-5300	14689
Astronova Inc (PA)	West Warwick	RI	C	401 828-4000	16902
Astronova Inc	West Warwick	RI	C	401 828-4000	16903

PRINTERS: Magnetic Ink, Bar Code

	CITY	ST	EMP	PHONE	ENTRY#
Yellowfin Holdings Inc	Ellington	CT	E	866 341-0979	1119

PRINTING & BINDING: Books

	CITY	ST	EMP	PHONE	ENTRY#
Courier Westford Inc	Westford	MA	B	978 251-6482	13232
Dunn & Co Inc	Clinton	MA	C	978 368-8505	8077
Quarto Pubg Group USA Inc	Beverly	MA	E	425 827-7120	6375

PRINTING & EMBOSSING: Plastic Fabric Articles

	CITY	ST	EMP	PHONE	ENTRY#
Advanced Visibility LLC	Fitchburg	MA	G	603 660-6033	8641

PRINTING & ENGRAVING: Card, Exc Greeting

	CITY	ST	EMP	PHONE	ENTRY#
Cannelli Printing Co Inc	West Haven	CT	G	203 932-1719	4096

PRINTING & ENGRAVING: Financial Notes & Certificates

	CITY	ST	EMP	PHONE	ENTRY#
R R Donnelley & Sons Company	Boston	MA	D	617 345-4300	6992
Connected Office Tech LLC	Portsmouth	NH	F	603 380-7333	15375

PRINTING & STAMPING: Fabric Articles

	CITY	ST	EMP	PHONE	ENTRY#
Bennettsville Holdings LLC	Hebron	CT	F	860 444-9400	1525
Industrial Lbling Systems Corp	Tyngsboro	MA	E	978 649-7004	12460
Swan Dyeing and Printing Corp	Fall River	MA	D	508 674-4611	8611

PRINTING & WRITING PAPER WHOLESALERS

	CITY	ST	EMP	PHONE	ENTRY#
Mega Sound and Light LLC	Danbury	CT	G	203 743-4200	784
Wallingford Prtg Bus Forms Inc	Branford	CT	F	203 481-1911	286
Medical Manager Pcn Inc	Walpole	MA	F	508 850-3500	12568

PRINTING MACHINERY

	CITY	ST	EMP	PHONE	ENTRY#
Dymo Corporation	Norwalk	CT	D		2494
I Q Technology LLC	Enfield	CT	E	860 749-7255	1135
Santec Corporation	Milford	CT	F	203 878-1379	1882
Systematic Automation Inc	Farmington	CT	E	310 218-3361	1249
Trimech Solutions LLC	Deep River	CT	F	508 526-5869	886
2I Inc	Hudson	MA	F	978 567-8867	9350
Armstrong Machine Co Inc	Beverly	MA	F	978 232-9466	6326
Art Swiss Corporation	New Bedford	MA	G	508 999-3281	10569
Autoroll Print Technologies LLC	Middleton	MA	E	978 777-2160	10380
Butler Automatic Inc (PA)	Middleboro	MA	E	508 923-0544	10353
Ecrm Incorporated (PA)	North Andover	MA	D	978 581-0207	10830
Flex-O-Graphic Prtg Plate Inc	Worcester	MA	E	508 752-8100	13724
Inscribe Inc	Woburn	MA	E	781 933-3331	13586
Integrted Web Fnshg Systems In	Avon	MA	E	508 580-5809	6151
Jet Graphics LLC	Avon	MA	G	508 580-5809	6153
Jnj Industries Inc	Franklin	MA	E	508 553-0529	8846
Milara Inc	Milford	MA	D	508 533-5322	10404
Signature Engrv Systems Inc	Holyoke	MA	E	413 533-7500	9281
Teca-Print USA Corp	Winchester	MA	F	781 369-1084	13492
Tecnau Inc (DH)	North Andover	MA	E	978 608-0500	10851
Thomas M Leonard Inc	West Bridgewater	MA	G		12984
Tooling Research Inc (PA)	Walpole	MA	F	508 668-1950	12578
W Gillies Technologies LLC	Worcester	MA	G	508 852-2502	13827
Westcon Mfg Inc	Brunswick	ME	E	207 725-5537	4657
Cc1 Inc	Portsmouth	NH	F	603 319-2000	15368
Electronics For Imaging Inc	West Lebanon	NH	B	603 279-6800	15683
Manroland Web Systems Inc	Exeter	NH	F	630 920-5850	14295
Prodways	Merrimack	NH	G	763 568-7966	14999
R & D Technologies Inc	North Kingstown	RI	F	401 885-6400	16276

PRINTING, COMMERCIAL: Bags, Plastic, NEC

	CITY	ST	EMP	PHONE	ENTRY#
Package Printing Company Inc	West Springfield	MA	E	413 736-2748	13040

PRINTING, COMMERCIAL: Business Forms, NEC

	CITY	ST	EMP	PHONE	ENTRY#
Beekley Corporation (PA)	Bristol	CT	D	860 583-4700	411
Mlk Business Forms Inc	New Haven	CT	F	203 624-6304	2176
New Fairfield Press Inc	New Fairfield	CT	F	203 746-2700	2096
A W McMullen Co Inc	Brockton	MA	F	508 583-2072	7251
Brady Business Forms Inc	Lowell	MA	G	978 458-2585	9865
Dgi Communications LLC (PA)	North Billerica	MA	E	781 285-6972	10905
Massachusetts Envelope Co Inc (PA)	Woburn	MA	E	617 623-8000	13606
New England Business Svc Inc (HQ)	Townsend	MA	D	978 448-6111	12441
Regal Press Incorporated (PA)	Norwood	MA	E	781 769-3900	11206
JS McCarthy Co Inc (PA)	Augusta	ME	D	207 622-6241	4473
Argyle Associates Inc	Concord	NH	E	603 226-4300	14114

PRINTING, COMMERCIAL: Calendars, NEC

	CITY	ST	EMP	PHONE	ENTRY#
Ad-A-Day Company Inc	Taunton	MA	E	508 824-8676	12315

PRINTING, COMMERCIAL: Decals, NEC

	CITY	ST	EMP	PHONE	ENTRY#
Eastern Etching and Mfg Co	Chicopee	MA	E	413 594-6601	8030

PRINTING, COMMERCIAL: Envelopes, NEC

	CITY	ST	EMP	PHONE	ENTRY#
Envelopes & More Inc	Newington	CT	F	860 286-7570	2292
Bay State Envelope Inc (PA)	Mansfield	MA	E	508 337-8900	10039
Classic Envelope Inc	East Douglas	MA	D	508 731-6747	8349
Quality Envelope & Printing Co	Middleboro	MA	G	508 947-8878	10376
Yankee Printing Group Inc	South Hadley	MA	E	413 532-9513	11968
Jet Service Envelope Co Inc (PA)	Barre	VT	G	802 229-9335	17010

PRINTING, COMMERCIAL: Imprinting

	CITY	ST	EMP	PHONE	ENTRY#
L P Macadams Company Inc	Bridgeport	CT	D	203 366-3647	342

PRINTING, COMMERCIAL: Labels & Seals, NEC

	CITY	ST	EMP	PHONE	ENTRY#
Ansel Label and Packaging Corp	Trumbull	CT	E	203 452-0311	3711
Cenveo Incorporated	Stamford	CT	A	303 790-8023	3307
Design Label Manufacturing Inc	Old Lyme	CT	E	860 739-6266	2640
Privateer LLC	Old Saybrook	CT	F	860 526-1838	2661
Robinson Tape & Label Inc	Branford	CT	E	203 481-5581	274
Schmitt Realty Holdings Inc	Guilford	CT	F	203 453-4334	1408
Specialty Printing LLC (PA)	Windsor	CT	D	860 623-8870	4300
Surys Inc	Trumbull	CT	C	203 333-5503	3734

	CITY	ST	EMP	PHONE	ENTRY#
Computer Imprntble Lbel System	Burlington	MA	F	877 512-8763	7355
Gloucester Graphics Inc (PA)	Gloucester	MA	G	978 281-4500	8937
Graphics Source Co	Southampton	MA	G	413 543-0700	11985
Label Haus Inc	Danvers	MA	F	978 777-1773	8197
M & M Label Co Inc	Danvers	MA	G	781 321-2737	8201
New England Label	Peabody	MA	G	978 281-3663	11326
Precision Tape & Label Co Inc	Uxbridge	MA	F	508 278-7700	12489
Stickamayka Packaging Inc	Andover	MA	E	978 474-1930	5926
Computype Inc	Concord	NH	F	603 225-5500	14122
Electronic Imaging Mtls Inc	Keene	NH	E	603 357-1459	14597
Labels Inc	Hampton	NH	E	603 929-3088	14405
Gem Label & Tape Company	Cranston	RI	F	401 724-1300	15866

PRINTING, COMMERCIAL: Letterpress & Screen

	CITY	ST	EMP	PHONE	ENTRY#
Morgan Enterprises Inc	Worcester	MA	G	985 377-3216	13761

PRINTING, COMMERCIAL: Literature, Advertising, NEC

	CITY	ST	EMP	PHONE	ENTRY#
Queen Graphics Printworks Inc	West Haven	CT	F	203 464-7337	4120
Washington ABC Imaging Inc	Boston	MA	F	857 753-4241	7114
Erin Murphy	Windham	ME	G	928 525-2056	5660

PRINTING, COMMERCIAL: Magazines, NEC

	CITY	ST	EMP	PHONE	ENTRY#
Trimed Media Group Inc	Providence	RI	F	401 919-5165	16630

PRINTING, COMMERCIAL: Periodicals, NEC

	CITY	ST	EMP	PHONE	ENTRY#
Bargain News Free Clssfied Adv	Stratford	CT	F	203 377-3000	3518
Bff Holdings Inc (HQ)	Old Saybrook	CT	C	860 510-0100	2645
Connecticut Forest Pk Assn Inc	Rockfall	CT	F	860 346-2372	2913
Gamut Publishing	Hartford	CT	G	860 296-6128	1482
Gracenote Media Services LLC	Wilton	CT	F	518 223-3993	4240
Informa Business Media Inc	Stamford	CT	C	203 358-9900	3383
Legal Affairs Inc	Hamden	CT	G	203 865-2520	1437
Limra International Inc (PA)	Windsor	CT	E	860 688-3358	4287
Relx Inc	Norwalk	CT	A	203 840-4800	2565
Woolworks International Ltd	Stamford	CT	G	203 661-7076	3496
73-75 Magazine Street LLC	Allston	MA	G	617 787-1913	5818
Biodata Inc	Cambridge	MA	F	512 593-5521	7510
Davis Corp Worcester Inc (PA)	Worcester	MA	E	508 754-7201	13714
Dow Jones & Company Inc	Chicopee	MA	D	413 598-4000	8027
East Coast Publications Inc (PA)	Norwell	MA	F	781 878-4540	11141
Ebsco Publishing Inc (DH)	Ipswich	MA	A	978 356-6500	9485
Enterprise Publications (PA)	Falmouth	MA	E	508 548-4700	8630
Free Software Foundation Inc	Boston	MA	F	617 542-5942	6747
Graphic Arts Institute of Neng	Southborough	MA	F	508 804-4100	11995
Idg	Boston	MA	E	508 875-5000	6802
Liberty Publishing Inc	Beverly	MA	F	978 777-8200	6362
Massachusetts Assn Realtors (PA)	Foxboro	MA	F	781 890-3700	8707
Massachusetts Institute Tech	Cambridge	MA	C	617 253-5646	7637
New Beverage Publications Inc	Boston	MA	G	617 598-1900	6914
New England RE Bulltin	Swansea	MA	F	508 675-8884	12308
President Fllows Hrvard Cllege	Boston	MA	C	617 495-5581	6976
Qbl Winndown LLC	Framingham	MA	F	617 219-8300	8800
Town of North Reading	North Reading	MA	E	978 664-6027	11050
Wilmington Compliance Week	Boston	MA	G	617 570-8600	7126
Echo Communications Inc	New London	NH	E	603 526-6006	15203
Hideaways International Inc	Portsmouth	NH	F	603 430-4433	15401
Relx Inc	Portsmouth	NH	F	603 431-7894	15432
Trustees of Dartmouth College	Hanover	NH	G	603 646-2256	14431
Vendome Guide	Newport	RI	F	401 849-8025	16227

PRINTING, COMMERCIAL: Promotional

	CITY	ST	EMP	PHONE	ENTRY#
Kramer Printing Company Inc	West Haven	CT	F	203 933-5416	4110
Martin Printing Inc	North Haven	CT	E	203 239-7991	2423
PRC Synergy Corp	Bridgeport	CT	B	203 331-9100	360
Data Associates Business Trust	Waltham	MA	D		12647
Walker-Clay Inc	Hanson	MA	F	781 294-1100	9057
D R Designs Inc	Manchester	ME	G	207 622-3303	5044
Trems Inc	Rockland	ME	G	207 596-6989	5343
Merchbro Inc	Pawtucket	RI	F	866 428-0095	16387

PRINTING, COMMERCIAL: Screen

	CITY	ST	EMP	PHONE	ENTRY#
Advanced Graphics Incorporated	Stratford	CT	E	203 378-0471	3515
Boltprintingcom	Brookfield	CT	G	203 885-0571	511
Colorgraphix LLC	Oxford	CT	G	203 264-5212	2690
Critical Scrn Printg & EMB	Waterford	CT	G	860 443-4327	3988
Custom Tees Plus	New Haven	CT	G	203 752-1071	2142
Custom TS n More LLC	Ridgefield	CT	G	203 438-1592	2894
E Cook Associates Inc	Watertown	CT	F	860 283-9849	4010
Electrocal Inc	Manchester	CT	C	860 646-8153	1595
Fresh Ink LLC	West Hartford	CT	G	860 656-7013	4061
George Schmitt & Co Inc (PA)	Guilford	CT	E	203 453-4334	1394
Integrated Print Solutions Inc	Bridgeport	CT	F	203 330-0200	332

PRODUCT

	CITY	ST	EMP	PHONE	ENTRY#
Liberty Screen Print Co LLC	Beacon Falls	CT	F	203 632-5449	41
Lorenco Industries Inc	Bethel	CT	F	203 743-6962	127
Multiprints Inc	Meriden	CT	G	203 235-4409	1678
O Berk Company Neng LLC	West Haven	CT	F	203 932-8000	4117
Print Promowear LLC	Stamford	CT	G	203 504-2858	3436
Quality Name Plate Inc	East Glastonbury	CT	D	860 633-9495	923
Rankin Textile Printing Inc	Danbury	CT	G	203 743-1317	803
Screen Tek Printing Co Inc	Hamden	CT	G	203 248-6248	1454
Stratis Visuals LLC (PA)	Torrington	CT	F	860 482-1208	3697
Vision Designs LLC	Brookfield	CT	F	203 778-9898	543
Xtreme Designs LLC	East Haven	CT	G	203 773-9303	1057
Albert Basse Associates Inc	Stoughton	MA	E	781 344-3555	12191
All-City Screen Printing Inc	Wakefield	MA	F	781 665-0000	12498
Applied Graphics Inc	Amesbury	MA	E	978 241-5300	5828
Astrella Ink	Millbury	MA	G	508 865-5028	10426
Austins Sportswear Inc	West Yarmouth	MA	F	508 775-0554	13071
Avon Cstm EMB & Screenprinting	Avon	MA	G	781 341-4663	6143
Bay State Apparel Inc	Leominster	MA	G	978 534-5810	9639
Bltees Inc	Chicopee	MA	F	413 594-7547	8011
Comdec Incorporated	Newburyport	MA	F	978 462-3399	10676
Customink LLC	Braintree	MA	F	781 205-4035	7177
First Sail Group Inc	South Yarmouth	MA	G	425 409-2783	11983
G & G Silk Screening	Plymouth	MA	G	508 830-1075	11460
Gem Group Inc (PA)	Lawrence	MA	B	978 691-2000	9564
Graphix Plus Inc	Fall River	MA	F	508 677-2122	8557
Guertins Graphics Inc	Worcester	MA	F	508 754-0200	13735
Hercules Press	Boston	MA	G	617 323-1950	6786
Image Factory	Pocasset	MA	F	508 295-3876	11489
Imprint Graphics Inc	Framingham	MA	F	508 879-0544	8782
Industrial Etching Inc	East Longmeadow	MA	F	413 525-4110	8380
Inkify LLC	Walpole	MA	F	617 304-6642	12561
Jungle Inc (PA)	Essex	MA	F	978 356-7722	8476
M & R Screen Printing Inc	New Bedford	MA	F	508 996-0419	10615
Milara Inc	Medfield	MA	G	508 359-2786	10272
Moonlight Ltd	Brockton	MA	G	508 584-0094	7298
New Tek Design Group Inc	West Boylston	MA	G	508 835-4544	12965
Optimum Sportswear Inc	Lawrence	MA	G	978 689-2290	9594
Plastilam Inc	Salem	MA	F	978 745-5563	11730
Printpro Silkscreen Co LLC	Haverhill	MA	D	978 556-1695	9123
Qrsts LLC	Somerville	MA	G	617 625-3335	11892
RAw Rinnigade Art Works LLC	Somerville	MA	G	617 625-3335	11893
Red Mill Graphics Incorporated	Chelmsford	MA	F	978 251-4081	7951
Salisbury Sales Inc	Natick	MA	G	508 907-6610	10496
Silver Screen Design Inc	Greenfield	MA	F	413 773-1692	9000
Smudge Ink Incorporated	Charlestown	MA	F	617 242-8228	7882
T-Shirts Authority Inc	West Yarmouth	MA	G	774 855-0000	13074
Techprint Inc	Lawrence	MA	D	978 975-1245	9602
Three Twins Productions Inc	Watertown	MA	G	617 926-0377	12914
Watertown Printers Inc	Somerville	MA	F	781 893-9400	11913
320 Ink LLC	Westbrook	ME	G	207 835-0038	5613
Action Screen Printing	Lewiston	ME	G	207 795-7786	4949
Allen Screen Printing	Scarborough	ME	E	207 510-6800	5422
Artforms (PA)	Brunswick	ME	G	800 828-8518	4640
Atlantic Sportswear Inc	Portland	ME	E	207 797-5028	5178
Blue Sky Inc	Portland	ME	G	207 772-0073	5190
Gossamer Press	Benton	ME	G	207 827-9881	4545
Identity Group Holdings Corp	Brunswick	ME	E	207 510-6800	4646
Island Approaches	Sunset	ME	F	207 348-2459	5539
Liberty Graphics Inc	Liberty	ME	F	207 589-4596	4999
Lts Inc	Portland	ME	F	207 774-1104	5234
T J Ryan LLC	Brewer	ME	F	207 989-7183	4620
W S Emerson Company Inc (PA)	Brewer	ME	E	207 989-3410	4623
Woodland Studios Inc	Ellsworth	ME	F	207 667-3286	4761
Xtreme Screen & Sportswear LLC	Westbrook	ME	F	207 857-9200	5654
Barn Door Screen Printers	Conway	NH	G	603 447-5369	14177
Beeze Tees LLC	Keene	NH	G	603 357-1400	14589
Bovie Screen Process Prtg Inc	Bow	NH	E	603 224-0651	13994
C K Productions Inc	Pelham	NH	G	603 893-5069	15287
Gemini Firfield Screenprinting	Keene	NH	G	603 357-3847	14600
Left-Tees Designs Bayou LLC	Derry	NH	F	603 437-6630	14199
Lestat Production 81 Corp	Bedford	NH	E	866 557-4478	13939
Life Is Good Retail Inc (PA)	Hudson	NH	D	603 594-6100	14522
Northstar Direct LLC	Manchester	NH	F		14905
Phoenix Screen Printing	Nashua	NH	F	603 578-9599	15148
Savvy Workshop	Manchester	NH	G	603 792-0080	14926
Say It In Stitches Inc	Concord	NH	G	603 224-6470	14155
Screen Gems Inc	Seabrook	NH	F	603 474-5353	15604
Teddys Tees Inc	Concord	NH	G	603 226-2762	14163
Treasure Tees	Nashua	NH	G	855 438-8337	15178
American Trophy and Supply Inc	East Providence	RI	G	401 438-3060	16004
Arkwear Inc	Newport	RI	F	401 846-9903	16202
Classsick Custom LLC	Pawtucket	RI	F	401 475-7288	16355

	CITY	ST	EMP	PHONE	ENTRY#
Cool Air Creations Inc	Smithfield	RI	E	401 830-5780	16692
Graphic Ink Incorporated	East Providence	RI	F	401 431-5081	16021
Griswold Textile Print Inc	Westerly	RI	F	401 596-2784	16931
Hilco Athletic & Graphics Inc	West Warwick	RI	F	401 822-1775	16910
K&M/Nordic Co Inc	Riverside	RI	E	401 431-9299	16656
RTC Holdings Inc	Pawtucket	RI	E	401 728-6980	16414
Squadlocker Inc	Warwick	RI	D	888 885-6253	16864
Bumwraps Inc (PA)	Montgomery Center	VT	G	802 326-4080	17368
Graphic Edge LLC	Rutland	VT	D	802 855-8840	17498
Humble Screen Printing Llc	Colchester	VT	G	802 399-5400	17196
Keiths II Sports Ltd	Pittsford	VT	F	802 483-6050	17444

PRINTING, COMMERCIAL: Stationery, NEC

	CITY	ST	EMP	PHONE	ENTRY#
Professional Mktg Svcs Inc	Stratford	CT	F	203 610-6222	3568
ESP Solutions Inc	Taunton	MA	F	508 285-0017	12335
LCI Paper Company	Hudson	MA	F	508 281-5088	9384
Downeast Concepts Inc	Yarmouth	ME	E	207 846-3726	5703
William Arthur Inc	West Kennebunk	ME	D	413 684-2600	5611

PRINTING, COMMERCIAL: Tags, NEC

	CITY	ST	EMP	PHONE	ENTRY#
Online River LLC	Westport	CT	F	203 801-5900	4191
Bell Manufacturing Co	Lewiston	ME	E	207 784-2961	4953

PRINTING, LITHOGRAPHIC: Calendars

	CITY	ST	EMP	PHONE	ENTRY#
Geiger Bros (PA)	Lewiston	ME	B	207 755-2000	4962

PRINTING, LITHOGRAPHIC: Color

	CITY	ST	EMP	PHONE	ENTRY#
Shear Color Printing Inc	Woburn	MA	E	781 376-9607	13664

PRINTING, LITHOGRAPHIC: Forms, Business

	CITY	ST	EMP	PHONE	ENTRY#
City of Boston	Boston	MA	C	617 635-3700	6657

PRINTING, LITHOGRAPHIC: Offset & photolithographic printing

	CITY	ST	EMP	PHONE	ENTRY#
Inform Inc	Shelton	CT	G	203 924-9929	3020
Macdermid Incorporated (HQ)	Waterbury	CT	C	203 575-5700	3933
Jam Plastics Inc	Leominster	MA	E	978 537-2570	9672

PRINTING, LITHOGRAPHIC: Posters & Decals

	CITY	ST	EMP	PHONE	ENTRY#
Gloucester Graphics Inc (PA)	Gloucester	MA	G	978 281-4500	8937

PRINTING, LITHOGRAPHIC: Promotional

	CITY	ST	EMP	PHONE	ENTRY#
Automated Mailing Services LLC	Cheshire	CT	G	203 439-2763	574
Vistaprint Corp Solutions Inc	Waltham	MA	E	844 347-4162	12813

PRINTING: Books

	CITY	ST	EMP	PHONE	ENTRY#
Landmark Print Inc	Stamford	CT	D	800 499-3808	3396
Baikar Association Inc (PA)	Watertown	MA	F	617 924-4420	12862
Book-Mart Press Inc	North Chelmsford	MA	F	978 251-6000	10966
Chand LLC	Roxbury	MA	G	310 483-5769	11688
Channing Bete Company Inc (PA)	South Deerfield	MA	C	413 665-7611	11922
Cistercian Abbey Spencer Inc	Spencer	MA	F	508 885-8700	12056
Courier Companies Inc (PA)	North Chelmsford	MA	C	978 251-6000	10969
Courier Corporation	North Chelmsford	MA	A	978 251-6000	10970
Courier Intl Holdings LLC	North Chelmsford	MA	C	978 251-6000	10971
Courier New Media Inc (PA)	North Chelmsford	MA	E	978 251-3945	10972
Lsc Communications Inc	North Chelmsford	MA	D	978 251-6000	10982
Mathemtics Problem Solving LLC	South Portland	ME	D	207 772-2846	5508
The Dingley Press Inc (PA)	Lisbon	ME	C	207 353-1500	5018
Copy Express LLC	Manchester	NH	E	603 625-4960	14836
Odyssey Press Inc (PA)	Dover	NH	E	603 749-4433	14243
Center Point Inc	Knox	ME	E	207 568-3717	4943
Kensington Group Incorporated	Hampton Falls	NH	F	603 926-6742	14419
Southern New Hampshire Univ	Manchester	NH	G	603 629-4631	14963
Johnson & Wales University	Providence	RI	E	401 598-1824	16550

PRINTING: Broadwoven Fabrics. Cotton

	CITY	ST	EMP	PHONE	ENTRY#
Duro Textiles LLC	Fall River	MA	C	508 679-0076	8536

PRINTING: Checkbooks

	CITY	ST	EMP	PHONE	ENTRY#
Rosencrntz Gldnstern Banknotes	Wilton	NH	G	603 654-6160	15708

PRINTING: Commercial, NEC

	CITY	ST	EMP	PHONE	ENTRY#
Allied Printing Services Inc (PA)	Manchester	CT	B	860 643-1101	1584
Amgraph Packaging Inc (PA)	Baltic	CT	D	860 822-2000	37
Better Lists Incorporated	Stamford	CT	E	203 324-4171	3294
Brook & Whittle Limited (PA)	Guilford	CT	B	203 483-5602	1388
Brook & Whittle Limited	North Branford	CT	F	203 483-5602	2361
Copy Cats Inc	New London	CT	F	860 442-8424	2225
Eastwood Printing Inc	Wethersfield	CT	E	860 529-6673	4204
Elm Press Incorporated	Terryville	CT	E	860 583-3600	3601
Executive Greetings Inc (HQ)	New Hartford	CT	B	860 379-9911	2100

	CITY	ST	EMP	PHONE	ENTRY#
Fairfield Marketing Group Inc (PA)	Easton	CT	F	203 261-0884	1095
Fusion Paperboard US Inc	Versailles	CT	C	859 586-1100	3765
Gateway Digital Inc	Norwalk	CT	F	203 853-4929	2503
Hamden Packaging Inc	Hamden	CT	E	203 288-0200	1428
Identification Products Corp (PA)	Shelton	CT	E	203 334-5969	3019
Imperial Grphic Cmmnctions Inc	Milford	CT	F	203 650-3478	1837
Kool Ink LLC	Bloomfield	CT	F	860 242-0303	186
Mallace Industries Corp	Bloomfield	CT	F	800 521-0194	191
McWeeney Marketing Group Inc	Orange	CT	G	203 891-8100	2677
Muir Envelope Plus Inc	Newington	CT	F	860 953-6847	2307
National Graphics Inc	North Branford	CT	B	203 481-2351	2370
Paul Dewitt	Danbury	CT	G	203 792-5610	795
Planes Road Associates LLC	Essex	CT	F	860 469-3200	1169
Richard E Personette	Middletown	CT	F	860 344-9001	1778
Roto-Die Company Inc	East Windsor	CT	E	860 292-7030	1084
Saint Vincent De Paul Place	Norwich	CT	G	860 889-7374	2615
Saybrook Press Incorporated	Guilford	CT	G	203 458-3637	1406
Schmitt Realty Holdings Inc (PA)	Guilford	CT	D	203 453-4334	1407
Universal Printing Svcs Inc	West Haven	CT	E	203 934-4275	4131
UPS Authorized Retailer	Fairfield	CT	G	203 256-9991	1205
Wallingford Prtg Bus Forms Inc	Branford	CT	F	203 481-1911	286
Yale University	New Haven	CT	E	203 737-1244	2220
Advanced Imaging Inc	Wilmington	MA	F	978 658-7776	13373
Apex Press Inc	Westborough	MA	F	508 366-1110	13076
Bcg Connect LLC	Wilmington	MA	E	978 528-7999	13389
Bold Maker LLC	Haverhill	MA	G	978 891-5920	9079
Bopkg Inc (HQ)	Fitchburg	MA	C	978 343-3067	8644
Bradford & Bigelow Realty LLC	Danvers	MA	E	978 777-1200	8170
Coatings Adhesives Inks	Georgetown	MA	F	978 352-7273	8907
Copy Masters Inc	Taunton	MA	F	508 824-7187	12329
Corporate Image Apparel Inc	Fall River	MA	E	508 676-3099	8532
Defiance Graphics Corp	Rowley	MA	F	978 948-2789	11673
Desk Top Graphics Inc (HQ)	Peabody	MA	E	617 832-1927	11305
Digital Graphics Inc	North Billerica	MA	G	781 270-3670	10907
Docuserve Inc	Marlborough	MA	E	508 786-5820	10146
Elbonais Incorporated	Framingham	MA	G	508 626-2318	8761
Elite Envelope & Graphics Inc	Randolph	MA	F	781 961-1800	11556
Excelsior Printing Company	North Adams	MA	D	413 663-3771	10807
Flashprint Graphics Inc	Cambridge	MA	F	617 492-7767	7570
Fluidform Inc	Waltham	MA	G	978 287-4698	12676
Formlabs Inc (PA)	Somerville	MA	B	617 932-5227	11875
Ghp Media Inc	North Adams	MA	D	413 663-3771	10808
Gorilla Graphics Inc (PA)	Malden	MA	F	617 623-2838	10016
Hannaford & Dumas Corporation	Woburn	MA	E	781 503-0100	13580
Hubcast Inc	Wakefield	MA	E	877 207-6665	12513
Icl Imaging Corp	Framingham	MA	E	508 872-3280	8778
Image Software Services Inc	Shirley	MA	G	978 425-3600	11817
Independant Newspaper Group	Revere	MA	F	781 485-0588	11619
Instant Offset Press Inc	Hyannis	MA	F	508 790-1100	9439
J L Enterprises Inc	Canton	MA	G	781 821-6300	7802
John Karl Dietrich & Assoc	Cambridge	MA	G	617 868-4140	7619
Kirkwood Holdings Inc (PA)	Wilmington	MA	B	978 658-4200	13420
Laplume & Sons Printing Inc	Lawrence	MA	E	978 683-1009	9576
Lujean Printing Co Inc	Cotuit	MA	F	508 428-8700	8146
McGirr Graphics Incorporated	Plymouth	MA	E	508 747-6400	11464
Medianews Group Inc	Devens	MA	F	978 772-0777	8280
Medical Manager Pcn Inc	Walpole	MA	F	508 850-3500	12568
Nfi LLC	New Bedford	MA	E	508 998-9021	10632
Paiva Corp	Fall River	MA	G	508 679-7921	8593
Paul H Murphy & Co Inc	Quincy	MA	F	617 472-7707	11530
Quad/Graphics Inc	East Longmeadow	MA	D	413 525-8552	8391
R R Donnelley & Sons Company	Hyde Park	MA	E	617 360-2000	9467
Ser Logistics Inc	Worcester	MA	F	508 757-3397	13798
Smart Source LLC	Waltham	MA	F	781 890-0110	12780
Specialty Manufacturing Inc	Amesbury	MA	F	978 388-1601	5853
Superior Printing Company Inc	Medford	MA	F	781 391-9090	10297
Taylor Communications Inc	Avon	MA	F	508 584-0102	6164
Tekni-Plex Inc	Ashland	MA	F	508 881-2440	5968
Tomandtim Enterprises LLC	Northborough	MA	G	508 380-5550	11113
Velocity LLC	Everett	MA	E	617 389-5452	8503
Vulcanforms Inc	Devens	MA	D	781 472-0160	8289
Walgreen Co	North Attleboro	MA	F	781 244-9431	10892
Winter & Company Inc	Quincy	MA	F	617 773-7605	11545
Allen Uniforms Inc	South Portland	ME	G	207 775-7364	5491
Bangor Ltr Sp & Color Copy Ctr	Bangor	ME	G	207 945-9311	4490
Creative Digital Imaging	Bangor	ME	G	207 973-0500	4496
Downeast Graphics & Prtg Inc	Ellsworth	ME	F	207 667-5582	4757
Mathemtics Problem Solving LLC	South Portland	ME	D	207 772-2846	5508
Northeast Publishing Company	Presque Isle	ME	G	207 764-4471	5308
Penobscot Bay Press (PA)	Stonington	ME	F	207 367-2200	5534
Print Bangor	Bangor	ME	G	207 947-8049	4515
Synergy Printing	Kittery Point	ME	G	207 703-2782	4942

	CITY	ST	EMP	PHONE	ENTRY#
Waterfront Graphics & Prtg LLC	South Portland	ME	G	207 799-3519	5517
B & E Enterprises Inc	Peterborough	NH	G	603 924-7203	15312
Brisco Graphics LLC	Bedford	NH	F		13919
Business Shirtmasters	Chichester	NH	F	603 798-3787	14072
Concord Photo Engraving Co Inc	Concord	NH	F	603 225-3681	14125
Electronics For Imaging Inc (HQ)	Londonderry	NH	E	650 357-3500	14748
Fedex Office & Print Svcs Inc	Bedford	NH	F	603 644-2679	13929
Fiberkraft Inc	Salem	NH	F	603 621-0090	15525
Jalbert Printing LLC	Amherst	NH	F	603 623-4677	13873
Joglo Inc	Nashua	NH	F	603 880-4519	15117
Powerplay Management LLC	Portsmouth	NH	E	603 436-3030	15431
RB Graphics Inc	Hooksett	NH	G	603 624-4025	14473
Red Fish - Blue Fish Dye Wrks	Somersworth	NH	G	603 692-3900	15624
Smith & Town Printers LLC	Berlin	NH	F	603 752-2150	13986
Sumner Printing Inc	Somersworth	NH	E	603 692-7424	15625
ID Label Inc	Cranston	RI	F	508 809-6199	15876
Matlet Group LLC	Pawtucket	RI	B	401 834-3007	16385
Moo Inc	East Providence	RI	D	401 519-7216	16031
Packaging Graphics LLC	Pawtucket	RI	C	401 725-7700	16399
Rlcp Inc	Barrington	RI	G	401 461-6560	15749
Paw Prints Press Inc	South Burlington	VT	F	802 865-2872	17589
The Leahy Press Inc	Montpelier	VT	E	802 223-2100	17375
Tuttle Law Print Inc	Rutland	VT	D	802 773-9171	17512

PRINTING: Flexographic

	CITY	ST	EMP	PHONE	ENTRY#
CCL Industries Corporation	Shelton	CT	A	203 926-1253	2989
CCL Label Inc	Shelton	CT	F	203 926-1253	2990
Identification Products Corp	Bridgeport	CT	F	203 334-5969	331
The Hoffman Press Incorporated	New Haven	CT	F	203 865-0818	2209
CCL Industries Corporation (HQ)	Framingham	MA	D	508 872-4511	8749
CCL Label Inc (HQ)	Framingham	MA	D	508 872-4511	8750
Design Mark Industries Inc	New Bedford	MA	D	800 451-3275	10585
First Mate Prtg Converting Inc (HQ)	Gardner	MA	D	978 630-1028	8886
GP&c Operations LLC	Gardner	MA	D	978 630-1028	8888
Maine Poly Aquisition Corp	Greene	ME	G	207 946-7000	4847
Amherst Label Inc	Milford	NH	D	603 673-7849	15015
S G Inc	Pascoag	RI	E	401 568-1110	16340

PRINTING: Gravure, Cards, Exc Greeting

	CITY	ST	EMP	PHONE	ENTRY#
Vermont Christmas Company	Milton	VT	G	802 893-1670	17366

PRINTING: Gravure, Forms, Business

	CITY	ST	EMP	PHONE	ENTRY#
D B S Industries Inc	Haverhill	MA	D	978 373-4748	9090

PRINTING: Gravure, Labels

	CITY	ST	EMP	PHONE	ENTRY#
Stat Products Inc	Ashland	MA	E	508 881-8022	5967
Label Tech LLC	Somersworth	NH	C	603 692-2005	15618

PRINTING: Gravure, Rotogravure

	CITY	ST	EMP	PHONE	ENTRY#
Brook & Whittle Limited (PA)	Guilford	CT	B	203 483-5602	1388
Brook & Whittle Limited	North Branford	CT	F	203 483-5602	2361
Massachusetts Envelope Co Inc	Hartford	CT	F	860 727-9100	1492
Interprint Inc	Pittsfield	MA	C	413 443-4733	11402

PRINTING: Laser

	CITY	ST	EMP	PHONE	ENTRY#
A To A Studio Solutions Ltd	Stamford	CT	F	203 388-9050	3267
Broadrdge Cstmer Cmmnctons E L (PA)	South Windsor	CT	E	860 290-7000	3122
Alltec Laser Technology	Southbridge	MA	F	508 765-6666	12009
Bigrep America Inc	Wilmington	MA	C	781 281-0569	13393
Julesan Inc	Boston	MA	E	617 437-6860	6835
Lasercraze	North Andover	MA	G	978 689-7700	10843
Relyco Sales Inc (PA)	Dover	NH	E	603 742-0999	14248

PRINTING: Letterpress

	CITY	ST	EMP	PHONE	ENTRY#
Ideal Printing Co Incorporated	New Haven	CT	G	203 777-7626	2162
Matthews Printing Co	Wallingford	CT	F	203 265-0363	3830
Barney Rabin Company Inc	Marblehead	MA	G	781 639-0593	10084
Belmont Printing Company	Belmont	MA	E	617 484-0833	6304
Bosworth Printing Co Inc	Stoughton	MA	F	781 341-2992	12199
Davol/Taunton Printing Inc	Taunton	MA	F	508 824-4305	12331
Fall River Modern Prtg Co Inc	Fall River	MA	F	508 673-3545	8548
Gazette Printing Co Inc	Easthampton	MA	F	413 527-7700	8446
Hadley Printing Company Inc	Holyoke	MA	E	413 536-8517	9258
Hitchcock Press Inc	Holyoke	MA	G	413 538-8811	9260
Liberty Printing Co Inc	Brockton	MA	G	508 586-6810	7291
Lincoln Press Co Inc	Fall River	MA	F	508 673-3241	8569
Mc Embossing Inc	Attleboro Falls	MA	G	781 821-3088	6090
Roberts & Sons Printing Inc	Springfield	MA	F	413 283-9356	12126
Winthrop Printing Company Inc	Foxboro	MA	E	617 268-9660	8732
Armstrong Family Inds Inc	Hermon	ME	E	207 848-7300	4880
Evans Printing Co	Bow	NH	G	603 856-8238	13997
Regine Printing Co Inc	Providence	RI	G	401 943-3404	16600

Employee Codes: A=Over 500 employees, B=251-500
C=101-250, D=51-100, E=20-50, F=10-19, G=1-9

2024 Harris New England
Manufacturers Directory

1451

PRODUCT

	CITY	ST	EMP	PHONE	ENTRY#
PRINTING: Lithographic					
Action Letter Inc **(PA)**	Stamford	CT	E	203 323-2466	3273
AlphaGraphics	Stamford	CT	G	203 847-8884	3278
American-Republican Inc **(PA)**	Waterbury	CT	C	203 574-3636	3884
Amgraph Packaging Inc **(PA)**	Baltic	CT	D	860 822-2000	37
Arch Parent Inc	Willimantic	CT	A	860 336-4856	4216
Better Lists Incorporated	Stamford	CT	E	203 324-4171	3294
Business Cards Tomorrow Inc	Naugatuck	CT	E	203 723-5858	1950
Byrne Group Inc	Waterbury	CT	F	203 573-0100	3894
Cadmus	Stamford	CT	F	203 595-3000	3300
Capitol Printing Co Inc	Hartford	CT	G	860 522-1547	1473
Cenveo Corporation	Stamford	CT	A	303 790-8023	3307
Cyberchrome Inc	Branford	CT	E	203 488-9594	246
Data-Graphics Inc	Newington	CT	D	860 667-0435	2285
Digitaldruker Inc	Oxford	CT	F	203 888-6001	2693
Fairfield Marketing Group Inc **(PA)**	Easton	CT	F	203 261-0884	1095
Fusion Paperboard US Inc	Versailles	CT	C	859 586-1100	3765
Gateway Digital Inc	Norwalk	CT	F	203 853-4929	2503
Herff Jones LLC	Bethlehem	CT	G	203 266-7170	143
Herff Jones LLC	Stratford	CT	F	203 368-9344	3546
J & T Printing LLC	Wethersfield	CT	F	860 529-4628	4206
Kingsley Printing Assoc LLC	Stratford	CT	F	203 345-6046	3552
Kool Ink LLC	Bloomfield	CT	F	860 242-0303	186
L P Macadams Company Inc	Bridgeport	CT	D	203 366-3647	342
Leejay Industries LLC	Norwalk	CT	E	203 847-3660	2526
Liberty Screen Print Co LLC	Beacon Falls	CT	F	203 632-5449	41
Massachusetts Envelope Co Inc	Hartford	CT	F	860 727-9100	1492
Mdf Systems Inc	Bristol	CT	D	860 584-4750	466
Middletown Printing Co Inc	Middletown	CT	F	860 347-5700	1765
Minute Man Press	Hamden	CT	G	203 891-6251	1443
Minuteman Press	Avon	CT	G	860 674-8700	31
Minuteman Press	Danbury	CT	G	973 748-7160	787
Minuteman Press	Manchester	CT	G	860 646-0601	1618
Minuteman Press	Trumbull	CT	G	203 261-8318	3725
Minuteman Press	Wethersfield	CT	F	860 529-4628	4211
Minuteman Press of Bristol	Bristol	CT	F	860 589-1100	469
Minuteman Press of Danbury	Danbury	CT	G	203 743-6755	788
Muir Envelope Plus Inc	Newington	CT	F	860 953-6847	2307
New Fairfield Press Inc	New Fairfield	CT	F	203 746-2700	2096
New Haven Register LLC	New Haven	CT	A	203 789-5200	2179
Norwich Printing Company Inc	Norwich	CT	F	860 887-7468	2611
Paw Print Pantry LLC **(PA)**	East Lyme	CT	G	860 447-8442	1060
Play-It Productions Inc	Colchester	CT	F	212 695-6530	663
Print B2b LLC	Bethel	CT	G	203 744-5435	132
Printer Techs LLC	Stamford	CT	G	203 322-1160	3437
Project Graphics Inc	Woodbury	CT	E	802 488-8789	4388
Savin Rock Printing	West Haven	CT	G	203 500-1577	4123
Stratis Visuals LLC **(PA)**	Torrington	CT	E	860 482-1208	3697
Tfac LLC	New Haven	CT	G	203 776-6000	2208
Toto LLC	New Haven	CT	F	203 776-6000	2210
Transmonde USa Inc	North Branford	CT	D	203 484-1528	2377
Turnstone Inc	Greenwich	CT	F	203 625-0000	1358
Universal Printing Svcs Inc	West Haven	CT	E	203 934-4275	4131
US Games Systems Inc	Stamford	CT	E	800 544-2637	3488
W B Mason Co Inc	East Windsor	CT	D	888 926-2766	1089
W B Mason Co Inc	Norwalk	CT	E	888 926-2766	2593
W B Mason Co Inc	Norwich	CT	C	888 926-2766	2619
World Color (usa) Holding Company	North Haven	CT	A	203 288-2468	2445
Yale New Haven Hlth Svcs Corp	New Haven	CT	A	203 688-2100	2217
A Bismark Company	Fall River	MA	G	508 675-2002	8516
Advanced Print Solutions Inc	Sharon	MA	F	508 655-8434	11791
AlphaGraphics	Concord	MA	G	508 380-8344	8097
AlphaGraphics	Watertown	MA	F	617 924-4091	12857
AM Lithography Corporation	Chicopee	MA	C	413 737-9412	8006
Andrew T Johnson Company Inc **(PA)**	Boston	MA	F	617 742-1610	6548
Arch Parent Inc	West Springfield	MA	A	413 504-1433	13013
B & W Press Inc	West Newbury	MA	E	978 352-6100	13007
Bassett & Cassidy Inc	Lowell	MA	G	978 452-9595	9860
BBC Printing and Products Inc	Waltham	MA	G	781 647-4646	12602
Ben Franklin Print Co Inc	Middleton	MA	G	978 624-7341	10381
Bew Corp	Randolph	MA	F	781 963-0315	11550
Bh Media Inc **(HQ)**	Lowell	MA	C	617 426-3000	9862
Boston Document Systems Inc **(PA)**	Marlborough	MA	E	800 616-8576	10117
Boston Print Specialists LLC	Boston	MA	G	617 742-9585	6613
Cimpress USA Incorporated	Waltham	MA	F	866 207-4955	12626
Cimpress USA Incorporated **(DH)**	Waltham	MA	E	781 652-6300	12627
Classic Envelope Inc	East Douglas	MA	G	508 731-6747	8349
Copy Masters Inc	Taunton	MA	F	508 824-7187	12329
Creative Print Products Inc	Leominster	MA	F	978 534-2030	9654
D B S Industries Inc	Haverhill	MA	D	978 373-4748	9090
Digipress Inc **(PA)**	Peabody	MA	C	617 832-1927	11306
Dion Label Printing Inc	Westfield	MA	D	413 568-3713	13162
Documents On Demand Inc	Worcester	MA	F	508 793-0956	13718
Docuserve Inc	Marlborough	MA	E	508 786-5820	10146
Elbonais Incorporated	Framingham	MA	G	508 626-2318	8761
Enon Copy Inc **(PA)**	Beverly	MA	G	978 927-8757	6346
Fenway Cmmunications Group Inc	Boston	MA	E	617 226-1900	6734
Footprint Pwr Acquisitions LLC	Salem	MA	F	978 740-8411	11715
Generation Four Inc	Waltham	MA	F	781 899-3180	12686
Ggs Custom Metals Inc	South Hadley	MA	F	413 315-4344	11962
Graphic Excellence LLC	Springfield	MA	G	413 733-6691	12096
Herring Inc	Hyannis	MA	G	401 837-3111	9438
John K Dietrich & Assoc Inc	Watertown	MA	G	617 868-4140	12884
Just Ur Way Screen Print	Westport	MA	F	508 235-0422	13298
Laplume & Sons Printing Inc	Lawrence	MA	E	978 683-1009	9576
Lincoln Press Co Inc	Fall River	MA	F	508 673-3241	8569
Linmel Associates Inc	Marlborough	MA	F	508 481-6699	10180
Lion Labels Inc	South Easton	MA	E	508 230-8211	11947
Marbuo Inc	North Dartmouth	MA	F	508 994-7700	10999
Massachusetts Repro Ltd	Boston	MA	F	617 227-2237	6876
Medianews Group Inc	Fitchburg	MA	E	978 343-6911	8663
Minuteman Press	Burlington	MA	G	781 273-1155	7394
Minuteman Press	Centerville	MA	G	508 775-9890	7860
Minuteman Press	Hyannis	MA	G	508 778-0220	9441
Minuteman Press	Hyde Park	MA	G	617 361-7400	9463
Minuteman Printing	Plymouth	MA	G	508 830-3500	11468
Modus Media Inc	Waltham	MA	E	781 663-5000	12724
MSP Digital Marketing Mass Inc **(HQ)**	Hudson	MA	E	978 567-6000	9394
Naley Inc	Worcester	MA	G	508 579-8378	13763
Neenah Technical Materials Inc **(DH)**	Dalton	MA	F	678 518-3343	8151
New England Mktg & Prtg Inc	Attleboro	MA	E	917 582-1029	6042
New Valence Robotics Corp	Canton	MA	G	857 529-6397	7812
Nfall Corp	Devens	MA	E	978 615-4030	8282
Oliveri & Associates Inc	Plymouth	MA	E	781 320-9090	11470
Oxford Graphics LLC	Peabody	MA	F	978 281-3663	11329
Paiva Corp	Fall River	MA	G	508 679-7921	8593
Pretty Instant LLC	Boston	MA	F	888 551-6765	6979
Princeton Printing LLC	Somerville	MA	G	617 530-0990	11889
Print Pro	Haverhill	MA	G	978 914-7619	9122
Quad/Graphics Inc	East Longmeadow	MA	D	413 525-8552	8391
Rhode Island Mktg & Prtg Inc	Attleboro	MA	G	917 582-1029	6054
Roberts & Sons Printing Inc	Springfield	MA	G	413 283-9356	12126
Seventy Nine N Main St Prtg	Andover	MA	G	978 475-4945	5917
Sir Speedy	Braintree	MA	G	781 848-0990	7202
Springfield Eye Associates	Springfield	MA	E	413 739-7367	12134
Stickamayka Packaging Inc	Andover	MA	F	978 474-1930	5926
Taylor Communications Inc	Avon	MA	F	508 584-0102	6164
Thomas & Thomas Inc	Lowell	MA	F	978 453-7444	9928
Titus & Bean Graphics Inc	Kingston	MA	F	781 585-1355	9513
Tls Printing LLC	Townsend	MA	G	508 234-2344	12443
Toth Inc **(PA)**	Concord	MA	E	617 577-6400	8136
Trustees of Tufts College **(PA)**	Somerville	MA	B	617 628-5000	11906
Uni-Graphic Inc	Woburn	MA	C	781 231-7200	13680
Van-Go Graphics	Grafton	MA	G	508 865-7300	8969
Vistaprint	Norwood	MA	F	866 614-8002	11219
W B Mason Co Inc	Framingham	MA	D	888 926-2766	8809
W B Mason Co Inc	Greenfield	MA	E	888 926-2766	9004
W S Walcott Inc	Orleans	MA	G	508 240-0882	11244
Wakefield Item Company	Wakefield	MA	E	781 245-0080	12542
Westfield News Publishing Inc **(DH)**	Westfield	MA	E	413 562-4181	13221
Winthrop Printing Company Inc	Foxboro	MA	E	617 268-9660	8732
Xpression Prints Inc	Franklin	MA	G	401 413-6930	8876
Arch Parent Inc	Connor Twp	ME	A	207 492-5414	4700
Lincoln County Publishing Co	Newcastle	ME	F	207 563-3171	5093
Minuteman Press	Denmark	ME	G	207 517-5355	4724
Minuteman Press of Saco	Saco	ME	G	207 282-6480	5374
Print-Mail of Maine Inc	Portland	ME	F	207 878-8000	5262
W B Mason Co Inc	Augusta	ME	E	888 926-2766	4481
W B Mason Co Inc	Bangor	ME	E	888 926-2766	4520
W B Mason Co Inc	Portland	ME	E	888 926-2766	5288
A & R Sawyer Co Inc	Windham	NH	E	603 893-5752	15179
Alpha Grphics Prntshop of Ftur	Nashua	NH	E	603 595-1444	15058
Bam Lab LLC	Somersworth	NH	G	603 973-9388	15610
Bob Bean Company Inc	Londonderry	NH	F	603 818-4390	14733
Capitol Screen Prtg & Embro	Concord	NH	G	603 234-7000	14120
Cygnus Inc	Portsmouth	NH	G	603 431-8989	15379
Eagle Publications Inc	Claremont	NH	E	603 543-3100	14089
Harrison Publishing House Inc	Littleton	NH	E	603 444-0820	14720
Insty-Prints of Bedford Inc	Bedford	NH	E	603 622-3821	13934
Minuteman Press	Concord	NH	E	603 513-4993	14146
Mtl Print Solution LLC	Hampstead	NH	G	603 479-2998	14387
New England Duplicator Inc	Manchester	NH	G	603 623-6847	14898
Odyssey Press Inc **(PA)**	Dover	NH	E	603 749-4433	14243

	CITY	ST	EMP	PHONE	ENTRY#
P2k Printing LLC	North Conway	NH	G	603 356-2010	15249
Rainville Printing Entps Inc	Concord	NH	F	603 225-6649	14153
W B Mason Co Inc	Manchester	NH	D	888 926-2766	14957
AlphaGraphics	Providence	RI	G	401 648-0078	16468
Arch Parent Inc	Westerly	RI	A	401 388-9802	16928
Branch Graphics Inc	Rumford	RI	E	401 861-1830	16663
Freshco	Providence	RI	G	401 351-1911	16522
Igt Global Solutions Corp	West Greenwich	RI	E	401 392-7025	16885
Igt Global Solutions Corporation (HQ)	Providence	RI	D	401 392-7077	16538
Matlet Group LLC	Providence	RI	G	401 834-3007	16560
Mdc Signs Printing	Cranston	RI	G	401 654-5354	15892
Mono Die Cutting Co Inc	Riverside	RI	F	401 434-1274	16658
Oberlin LLC	Providence	RI	G	401 588-8755	16577
Peak Printing Inc	Providence	RI	F	401 351-0500	16582
Sir Speedy	Providence	RI	G	401 351-7400	16612
Sir Speedy Printing Inc	Cranston	RI	E	401 781-5650	15911
W B Mason Co Inc	Cranston	RI	D	888 926-2766	15926
802 Print LLC	Vergennes	VT	G	802 598-0967	17655
Accura Printing	Barre	VT	G	802 476-4429	16996
Community Apostolic Order Inc (PA)	Island Pond	VT	F	802 723-4452	17304
Evan Webster Ink LLC	Charlotte	VT	F	802 222-0344	17177
Industrial Marking Systems Corp	Milton	VT	D	802 752-3170	17360
Inkjetmallcom Ltd	Topsham	VT	G	802 439-3127	17649
Larcoline Inc (PA)	Colchester	VT	F	802 864-5440	17197
McClure Newspapers Inc	Williston	VT	C	802 863-3441	17740
Uvm Print Mail Center	Burlington	VT	E	802 656-8149	17163
W B Mason Co Inc	Brattleboro	VT	E	888 926-2766	17106
W B Mason Co Inc	South Burlington	VT	E	888 926-2766	17607

PRINTING: Manmade Fiber & Silk, Broadwoven Fabric

	CITY	ST	EMP	PHONE	ENTRY#
Microfibres Inc	Foxboro	MA	A	401 725-4883	8708

PRINTING: Offset

	CITY	ST	EMP	PHONE	ENTRY#
ABC Printing Inc	East Haven	CT	F	203 468-1245	1034
Adkins Printing Company	New Britain	CT	F	800 228-9745	1997
Advanced Printing Services Inc	Bristol	CT	E	860 583-1906	393
Alliance Graphics Inc	Newington	CT	F	860 666-7992	2270
Allied Printing Services Inc (PA)	Manchester	CT	B	860 643-1101	1584
Appels Prtg & Mailing Bur Inc	Hartford	CT	F	860 522-8189	1470
Arga Prsnlzed Dcment Solutions	New Haven	CT	G	203 401-3650	2117
Baker Graphics Corporation	Westport	CT	F	203 226-6928	4157
Bardell Printing Corp	East Haven	CT	G	203 469-2441	1037
Barile Printers LLC	New Britain	CT	F	860 224-0127	2007
Brescias Printing Services Inc	East Hartford	CT	G	860 528-4254	976
Briarwood Printing Company Inc	Plainville	CT	F	860 747-6805	2749
Brody Printing Company Inc	Bridgeport	CT	F	203 384-9313	306
Cannelli Printing Co Inc	West Haven	CT	F	203 932-1719	4096
Chase Graphics Inc	Putnam	CT	F	860 315-9006	2849
Clarity Output Solutions LLC	Stratford	CT	G	800 414-1624	3527
Classic Label Inc	Woodbridge	CT	G	203 389-3535	4378
Craftsmen Printing Group Inc	Stamford	CT	G	203 327-2817	3324
Cricket Press Inc	West Hartford	CT	F	860 521-9279	4055
Custom Printing & Copy Inc (PA)	Enfield	CT	F	860 290-6890	1127
Data Management Incorporated	Unionville	CT	E	860 677-8586	3748
Derosa Printing Company Inc	Manchester	CT	F	860 646-1698	1592
Diversified Prtg Solutions Inc	Danbury	CT	G	203 826-7198	732
Docuprint & Imaging Inc	New Haven	CT	G	203 776-6000	2143
E & A Enterprises Inc	Wallingford	CT	G	203 250-8050	3802
E R Hitchcock Company	New Britain	CT	E	860 229-2024	2024
Ellington Printery Inc	Ellington	CT	G	860 875-3310	1105
Elm Press Incorporated	Terryville	CT	E	860 583-3600	3601
Evergreen Printing	Stamford	CT	E	203 323-4717	3347
Fine Print New England Inc	Newington	CT	G	860 953-0660	2293
Flow Resources Inc (HQ)	Newington	CT	F	860 666-1200	2294
Franklin Impressions Inc	Norwich	CT	F	860 887-1661	2605
Furci Communications Inc	Stamford	CT	E	203 961-1800	3353
Ghp Media Inc (PA)	West Haven	CT	D	203 479-7500	4107
Goodcopy Printing Center Inc	New Haven	CT	E	203 624-0194	2155
Goulet Enterprises Inc	Pleasant Valley	CT	F	860 379-0793	2801
Graphic Image Inc	Milford	CT	E	203 877-8787	1830
Gulemo Printing Inc	Willimantic	CT	G	860 456-1151	4218
Hartford Business Supply Inc	Hartford	CT	E	860 233-2138	1485
High Ridge Copy Inc	Stamford	CT	F	203 329-1889	3376
Ideal Printing Co Incorporated	New Haven	CT	G	203 777-7626	2162
Imperial Grphic Cmmnctions Inc	Milford	CT	E	203 650-3478	1837
Impression Point Inc	Stamford	CT	G	203 353-8800	3382
Integrity Graphics Inc	Simsbury	CT	C	800 343-1248	3091
Joseph Merritt & Company Inc	Danbury	CT	G	203 743-6734	762
Joseph Merritt & Company Inc (PA)	Hartford	CT	E	860 296-2500	1488
Jupiter Communications LLC	West Haven	CT	F	475 238-7082	4108
Keno Graphic Services Inc	Shelton	CT	E	203 925-7722	3026
Kramer Printing Company Inc	West Haven	CT	F	203 933-5416	4110

	CITY	ST	EMP	PHONE	ENTRY#
Landmark Print Inc	Stamford	CT	D	800 499-3808	3396
Lebon Press Incorporated	West Hartford	CT	E	860 278-6355	4066
Lithographics Inc	Farmington	CT	E	860 678-1660	1229
Maple Print Services Inc	Jewett City	CT	G	860 381-5470	1536
Martin Printing Inc	North Haven	CT	F	203 239-7991	2423
Matthews Printing Co	Wallingford	CT	F	203 265-0363	3830
Minit Print Inc	New Haven	CT	G	203 776-6000	2175
Minuteman Land Services Inc	Norwalk	CT	G	203 854-4949	2538
Mosaic Prtg Signage Mktg Svcs	Branford	CT	G	203 483-4598	272
Oddo Print Shop Inc	Torrington	CT	G	860 489-6585	3690
P C I Group	Stamford	CT	F	203 327-0410	3425
Paladin Commercial Prtrs LLC	West Hartford	CT	F	860 953-4900	4077
Panagrafix Inc (PA)	Milford	CT	F	203 878-7412	1862
Paul Dewitt	Danbury	CT	G	203 792-5610	795
Phoenix Press Inc	New Haven	CT	E	203 865-5555	2186
Preferred Printing Co Inc	Trumbull	CT	E		3728
Professional Graphics Inc	Norwalk	CT	F	203 846-4291	2560
Prospect Printing LLC	Prospect	CT	F	203 758-6007	2841
Protopac Inc	Watertown	CT	G	860 274-6796	4027
Pyne-Davidson Company	Hartford	CT	E	860 522-9106	1501
Qg Printing IL LLC	Enfield	CT	D	860 741-0150	1145
Rare Reminder Incorporated	Rocky Hill	CT	E	860 563-9386	2933
Record-Journal Newspaper (PA)	Meriden	CT	C	203 235-1661	1692
Richard E Personette	Middletown	CT	F	860 344-9001	1778
Rmi Inc	Vernon Rockville	CT	C	860 875-3366	3761
Southbury Printing Centre Inc	Southbury	CT	G	203 264-0102	3198
Specialty Printing LLC	East Windsor	CT	F	860 654-1850	1086
Spectrum Press	East Haven	CT	F	203 878-9090	1051
Spm Management Inc	Shelton	CT	F	203 847-1112	3065
Tech-Repro Inc	Stamford	CT	F	203 348-8884	3478
Technical Reproductions Inc	Norwalk	CT	F	203 849-9100	2575
Technique Printers Inc	Clinton	CT	G	860 669-2516	651
The Hartford Press Inc	Newington	CT	E	860 296-3588	2327
Trumbull Printing Inc	Trumbull	CT	C	203 261-2548	3735
Universal Prtg Miling Svcs Inc	Fairfield	CT	F	203 330-0611	1203
Value Print Incorporated	Wallingford	CT	G	203 265-1371	3873
Westrock Commercial LLC	Stamford	CT	G	203 595-3130	3494
Wethersfield Printing Co Inc	Rocky Hill	CT	F	860 721-8236	2941
Youngs Communications Inc	Middletown	CT	F	860 347-8569	1791
ABS Printing Inc	Swansea	MA	G	401 826-0870	12302
Accucon Incorporated	Leominster	MA	F	978 840-0337	9631
Adlife Advertising & Graphics	Walpole	MA	F	508 668-4109	12547
Alden-Hauk Inc	Woburn	MA	F	781 281-0154	13503
American Prtg & Envelope Inc	Auburn	MA	E	508 832-6100	6102
Andover Printing Inc	Andover	MA	F	978 475-4945	5870
Apex Press Inc	Westborough	MA	F	508 366-1110	13076
Applied Image Rprgrphics of Wt	Watertown	MA	G	617 924-6060	12858
Applied Image Rprographics Inc (PA)	Quincy	MA	F	617 471-3373	11503
Artcraft Co Inc	North Attleboro	MA	D	508 695-4042	10865
Atlantic Printing Co Inc	Medfield	MA	F	781 449-2700	10269
Bassette Printers LLC	Belchertown	MA	E	413 781-7140	6278
Belmont Printing Company	Belmont	MA	G	617 484-0833	6304
Bopkg Inc (HQ)	Fitchburg	MA	C	978 343-3067	8644
Boston Business Printing Inc	Boston	MA	F	617 482-7955	6606
Bosworth Printing Co Inc	Stoughton	MA	F	781 341-2992	12199
Bradford & Bigelow Inc	Newburyport	MA	C	978 904-3112	10672
Brady Business Forms Inc	Lowell	MA	G	978 458-2585	9865
Braintree Printing Inc	Braintree	MA	E	781 848-5300	7171
Bridgewater Prtg Copy Ctr LLC	Bridgewater	MA	G	508 697-5227	7125
Bruno Diduca	Waltham	MA	G	781 894-5300	12613
Business Resources Inc	Westborough	MA	F	508 433-4600	13084
Calendar Press Inc	Peabody	MA	E	508 531-1860	11300
Capeway Printing & Copy Center	Rockland	MA	F	781 878-1600	11638
Cenveo	Westfield	MA	G	203 595-3109	13158
Choice Graphics Inc	Rowley	MA	G	978 948-2789	11672
Citius Printing & Graphics LLC	Waltham	MA	F	781 547-5550	12629
Clark Mailing Service Inc	Worcester	MA	F	508 752-1953	13708
Connolly Printing LLC	Woburn	MA	F	781 932-8885	13545
Copy Cop The Digital Printing Company LLC	Boston	MA			E
		617 267-8899	6669		
Corporate Press	Norwood	MA	F	781 769-6656	11170
Country Press Inc	Lakeville	MA	F	508 947-4485	9516
Creamer Associates Inc	Cambridge	MA	G	617 374-6000	7544
Creative Imprints Inc	Norton	MA	E	508 285-7650	11125
D & L Associates Inc	Needham Heights	MA	G	781 400-5068	10540
D S Graphics Inc (PA)	Lowell	MA	C	978 970-1359	9873
Da Rosas	Oak Bluffs	MA	E	508 693-0110	11221
Data Print Inc	Woburn	MA	F	781 935-3350	13556
Datasite Global Corporation	Everett	MA	B	617 389-7900	8486
Davol/Taunton Printing Inc	Taunton	MA	F	508 824-4305	12331
Defiance Graphics Corp	Rowley	MA	F	978 948-2789	11673
Descal Inc	Waltham	MA	G	781 736-9400	12651

PRODUCT

	CITY	ST	EMP	PHONE	ENTRY#
Deschamps Printing Co Inc	Salem	MA	F	978 744-2152	11711
Desk Top Graphics Inc **(HQ)**	Peabody	MA	E	617 832-1927	11305
Devincentis Press Inc	Malden	MA	F	781 605-3796	10008
Digital Graphics Inc	North Billerica	MA	G	781 270-3670	10907
Digital On Demand LLC	Danvers	MA	G	978 224-7900	8181
Dmr Print Inc **(PA)**	Concord	MA	E	617 876-3688	8114
Duplication Management Inc	Woburn	MA	D	781 935-7224	13559
East Coast Printing Inc	Hingham	MA	G	781 331-5635	9150
Essex Ruling & Printing Co	Methuen	MA	G	978 682-2457	10331
Excelsior Printing Company	North Adams	MA	D	413 663-3771	10807
Fall River Modern Prtg Co Inc	Fall River	MA	F	508 673-9421	8548
Farganyd Inc	Canton	MA	C	781 575-1700	7790
Fars Inc	Northampton	MA	E	413 586-1332	11061
Fasprint Inc **(PA)**	Brockton	MA	F	508 588-9961	7278
First Impression Printing Inc	Stoughton	MA	G	781 344-8855	12209
Flagship Press Inc	North Andover	MA	C	978 975-3100	10831
Fleming & Son Corp	Chelmsford	MA	F	617 623-3047	7928
Fowler Printing & Graphics Inc	Randolph	MA	F	781 986-8900	11558
Freedom Digital Printing LLC	Ashland	MA	F	508 881-6940	5959
Gangi Printing Inc	Woburn	MA	E	617 776-6071	13573
Gazette Printing Co Inc	Easthampton	MA	F	413 527-7700	8446
George H Dean Co	Braintree	MA	D	781 544-3782	7184
Ghp Media Inc	North Adams	MA	D	413 663-3771	10808
Gmf Engineering Inc	Saugus	MA	F	781 233-0315	11758
Graphic Developments Inc	Hanover	MA	E	781 878-2222	9033
Greentree Marketing Inc	Framingham	MA	F	508 877-2581	8775
Hadley Printing Company Inc	Holyoke	MA	E	413 536-8517	9258
Hall Mailing & Fulfillment Inc	Haverhill	MA	F	978 372-6546	9100
Harborside Printing Co Inc	Newburyport	MA	F	978 462-2026	10686
High-Speed Process Prtg Corp	Lawrence	MA	F	978 683-2766	9568
Hitchcock Press Inc	Holyoke	MA	G	413 538-8811	9260
Ils Business Services Inc	Agawam	MA	G	413 789-4555	5793
Imperial Image Inc	North Chelmsford	MA	F	978 251-0420	10978
Ingleside Corporation	Norwood	MA	G	781 769-6656	11180
Inkstone Inc	Brockton	MA	F	508 587-5200	7284
Instant Offset Press Inc	Hyannis	MA	F	508 790-1100	9439
J & R Graphics Inc	Hanover	MA	F	781 871-7577	9036
J T Gardner Inc **(PA)**	Westborough	MA	E	800 540-4993	13112
J&S Business Products Inc	Ayer	MA	G	877 425-4049	6183
John P Pow Company Inc	Boston	MA	E	617 269-6040	6827
Jordan Enterprises Inc	Marlborough	MA	F	508 481-2948	10172
JP Progressive Comm Group LLC	New Bedford	MA	G	800 477-4681	10607
Keating Communication Group	Canton	MA	G	781 828-9030	7804
Kervick Family Foundation Inc	Worcester	MA	E	508 853-4500	13748
King Printing Company Inc	Lowell	MA	D	978 458-2345	9891
Kirkwood Holdings Inc **(PA)**	Wilmington	MA	B	978 658-4200	13420
Kwik-Print Inc	Great Barrington	MA	F	413 528-2885	8977
Labelprint America Inc	Newburyport	MA	F	978 463-4004	10693
Lane Printing Co Inc	Holbrook	MA	F	781 767-4450	9178
Lexington Graphics Inc	Lexington	MA	F	781 863-9510	9758
Liberty Printing Co Inc	Brockton	MA	G	508 586-6810	7291
Litho-Craft Inc	Stoneham	MA	F	781 729-1789	12181
Lujean Printing Co Inc	Cotuit	MA	F	508 428-8700	8146
M & C Press Inc	Cambridge	MA	F	617 354-2584	7636
Mallard Printing Inc	Fall River	MA	F	508 675-5733	8572
Mansir Printing LLC	Holyoke	MA	F	413 536-4250	9264
Marcus Company Inc	Holyoke	MA	E	413 534-3303	9265
Mass Printing Inc	North Reading	MA	G	781 396-1970	11042
May Graphics & Printing Inc	Westford	MA	G		13250
MBI Graphics & Printing Corp	Southbridge	MA	F	508 765-0658	12028
McGirr Graphics Incorporated	Plymouth	MA	E	508 747-6400	11464
Medi - Print Inc **(PA)**	Malden	MA	F	781 324-4455	10019
Miano Printing Services Inc	Holliston	MA	F	617 935-2830	9222
Miles Press Inc	Auburn	MA	F	508 752-6430	6120
Milk Street Press Inc	Boston	MA	F	617 742-7900	6888
Millennium Press Inc	Agawam	MA	E	413 821-0028	5801
Minute-Man Printing Corp	Concord	MA	F	978 369-2808	8125
Monaghan Printing Company	Fairhaven	MA	F	508 991-8087	8510
Mystic Parker Printing Inc	Malden	MA	F	781 321-4948	10020
Neoprint Inc	Chelmsford	MA	F	978 256-9939	7941
Newprint Offset Inc	Lexington	MA	F	781 891-6002	9765
North River Graphics Inc	Pembroke	MA	G	781 826-6866	11375
Northpoint Printing Svcs Inc	Hudson	MA	F	781 895-1900	9396
Owl Stamp Company Inc	Lowell	MA	F	978 452-4541	9912
Picken Printing Inc	North Chelmsford	MA	F	978 251-0730	10986
PIP Foundation Inc	Framingham	MA	D	508 757-0103	8798
Plastilam Inc	Salem	MA	E	978 745-5563	11730
Potters Printing Inc	Fall River	MA	F	617 547-3161	8598
President Press Inc	Quincy	MA	F	617 773-1235	11532
Pressed For Time Printing Inc	Boston	MA	F	617 267-4113	6978
Primary Graphics Corporation	Taunton	MA	F	781 575-0411	12355
Print Management Systems Inc	Woburn	MA	F	781 944-1041	13640
Print Synergy Solutions LLC	Brockton	MA	F	508 587-5200	7301
Print Works Inc	Hopkinton	MA	G	508 589-4626	9341
Printing Dept	Cambridge	MA	E	617 349-4206	7689
Printing Solutions Inc	Westford	MA	F	978 392-9903	13257
Priority Print	Cambridge	MA	G	617 547-6919	7690
Pyramid Printing and Advg Inc	Weymouth	MA	E	781 337-7609	13333
Qg LLC	Taunton	MA	B	508 828-4400	12360
Qg Printing Corp	Leominster	MA	E	978 534-8351	9698
Quad/Graphics Inc	Leominster	MA	G	978 534-8351	9699
Quad/Graphics Inc	Woburn	MA	C	781 231-7200	13643
Quality Envelope & Printing Co	Middleboro	MA	G	508 947-8878	10376
Quality Printing Company Inc	Pittsfield	MA	D	413 442-4166	11421
Quick Print Ltd Inc	Chelmsford	MA	G	978 256-1822	7950
R & H Communications Inc **(PA)**	Waltham	MA	F	781 893-6221	12757
Rainbow Graphics Inc	Springfield	MA	F	413 733-3376	12124
Ramsbottom Printing Inc	Fall River	MA	E	508 730-2220	8600
REA-Craft Press Incorporated	Foxboro	MA	F	508 543-8710	8716
Recycled Paper Company Inc	Waltham	MA	F	617 737-9911	12763
Red Sun Press Inc	Jamaica Plain	MA	F	617 524-6822	9503
Regal Press Incorporated **(PA)**	Norwood	MA	C	781 769-3900	11206
Reynolds D-Rap Corp	New Bedford	MA	E	800 477-4681	10645
Rivkind Associates Inc **(PA)**	South Easton	MA	F	781 269-2415	11952
Royal Label Co Inc	Boston	MA	F	617 825-6050	7017
Shafiis Inc **(PA)**	East Longmeadow	MA	E	413 224-2100	8394
Shawmut Advertising Inc **(PA)**	Peabody	MA	E	978 762-7500	11340
Shawmut Printing	Peabody	MA	E	978 762-7500	11341
Shear Color Printing Inc	Woburn	MA	E	781 376-9607	13664
Sherman Printing Co Inc	Canton	MA	E	781 828-8855	7828
Sical	Westborough	MA	F	508 898-1800	13135
Springfield Label Tape Co Inc	Springfield	MA	E	413 733-6634	12135
Standard Modern Company	New Bedford	MA	G	774 425-3537	10651
Star Litho Inc	Weymouth	MA	F	781 340-9401	13336
Star Printing Corp	Taunton	MA	F	508 583-9046	12369
Starburst Prtg & Graphics Inc	Holliston	MA	F	508 893-0900	9231
State-Line Graphics Inc	Everett	MA	F	617 389-1200	8501
Sterling Business Products Inc	Stoneham	MA	F	781 481-1234	12186
Studley Press Inc	Dalton	MA	F	413 684-0441	8156
Superlative Printing Inc	Stoughton	MA	G	781 341-9000	12240
TCI Press Inc	Seekonk	MA	E	508 336-6633	11787
Technical Publications Inc	Waltham	MA	F	781 899-0263	12789
Techprint Inc	Lawrence	MA	D	978 975-1245	9602
Tisbury Printer Inc	Vineyard Haven	MA	F	508 693-4222	12495
Tri Star Printing & Graphics	Somerville	MA	G	617 666-4480	11905
Tshb Inc	Newburyport	MA	E	978 465-8950	10721
Universal Tag Inc	Dudley	MA	E	508 949-2411	8326
Universal Wilde Inc **(PA)**	Canton	MA	C	781 251-2700	7837
Universal Wilde Inc	Canton	MA	C	978 658-0800	7838
Universal Wilde Inc	Holliston	MA	C	508 429-5515	9237
Universal Wilde Inc	Rockland	MA	C	781 251-2700	11664
Watson Printing Co Inc	Wellesley	MA	G	781 237-1336	12947
We Print Today LLC	Kingston	MA	F	781 585-6021	9514
Webster Printing Company Inc **(PA)**	Hanson	MA	F	781 447-5484	9058
Westrex International Inc	Boston	MA	F	617 254-1200	7119
Wholesale Printing Inc	Woburn	MA	F	781 937-3357	13688
Yankee Printing Group Inc	South Hadley	MA	E	413 532-9513	11968
Ziprint Centers Inc	Randolph	MA	F	781 963-2250	11580
Alliance Printers LLC	Brunswick	ME	G	207 504-8200	4639
Armstrong Family Inds Inc	Hermon	ME	E	207 848-7300	4880
Artco Offset Inc	Augusta	ME	E	781 830-7900	4467
Bromar	Skowhegan	ME	G	207 474-3784	5463
Checksforlesscom	Portland	ME	F	800 245-5775	5198
Coastal Business Center Inc	Wiscasset	ME	G	207 882-7197	5697
County Qwik Print Inc	Caribou	ME	F	207 492-0360	4674
Curry Printing & Copy Center	Portland	ME	F	207 772-5897	5203
Dale Rand Printing Inc	Portland	ME	G	207 773-8198	5204
Davic Inc	Portland	ME	F	207 774-0093	5206
Dingley Press Inc	Lewiston	ME	C	207 782-1529	4956
Dj Printing Inc	South Portland	ME	G	207 773-0439	5498
Downeast Graphics & Prtg Inc	Ellsworth	ME	F	207 667-5582	4757
E I Printing Co	Portland	ME	F	207 797-4838	5213
Evergreen Custom Printing Inc	Auburn	ME	E	207 782-2327	4430
First Choice Printing Inc	Lisbon Falls	ME	G	207 353-8006	5020
Full Court Press	Westbrook	ME	G	207 464-0002	5626
Furbush Roberts Prtg Co Inc	Bangor	ME	G	207 945-9409	4503
Jiffy Print Inc	Bangor	ME	G	207 947-4490	4507
JS McCarthy Co Inc **(PA)**	Augusta	ME	D	207 622-6241	4473
L H Thompson Inc	Brewer	ME	F	207 989-3280	4615
Letter Systems Inc **(PA)**	Augusta	ME	C	207 622-7126	4475
Mpx	Portland	ME	D	207 774-6116	5246
Nemi Publishing Inc	Farmington	ME	E	207 778-4801	4782
Northeast Publishing Company	Dover Foxcroft	ME	G	207 564-8355	4730
Portland Printing Group	Portland	ME	G	207 347-5700	5260

	CITY	ST	EMP	PHONE	ENTRY#
Printemscom	Sanford	ME	G	207 490-5118	5406
Pyramid Checks & Printing	Portland	ME	D	207 878-9832	5264
Quality Copy Inc	Hallowell	ME	G	207 622-7447	4861
R N Haskins Printing Inc	Sidney	ME	F	207 465-2155	5460
RH Rosenfield Co	Sanford	ME	E	207 324-1798	5410
Sheridan Me Inc	Lisbon	ME	G	207 353-1500	5016
Snowman Group	Hermon	ME	E	207 848-7300	4889
The Dingley Press Inc (PA)	Lisbon	ME	C	207 353-1500	5018
Time4printing Inc	Windham	ME	F	207 838-1496	5672
Waterfront Graphics & Prtg LLC	South Portland	ME	G	207 799-3519	5517
Baker Graphics Inc	Manchester	NH	G	603 625-5427	14816
Boles Enterprises Inc	Manchester	NH	G	603 622-4282	14820
Bridge & Byron Inc	Concord	NH	G	603 225-5221	14118
Capital Offset Co Inc	Hollis	NH	F	603 225-3308	14448
Concord Litho Group LLC (PA)	Concord	NH	C	603 224-1202	14123
Dartmouth Printing Company (DH)	Hanover	NH	E	603 643-2220	14422
Dr Biron Incorporated (PA)	Manchester	NH	F	603 622-5222	14844
E Print Inc	Hudson	NH	G	603 594-0009	14495
Echo Communications Inc	New London	NH	E	603 526-6006	15203
Evans Printing Co	Bow	NH	G	603 856-8238	13997
Frugal Printer Inc	Salem	NH	G	603 894-6333	15529
Higgingbotham Management Corp	Portsmouth	NH	F	603 431-0142	15402
Infinite Imaging Inc	Portsmouth	NH	F	603 436-3030	15407
Itnh Inc	Manchester	NH	E	603 669-6900	14865
Just Hit Print LLC	Center Harbor	NH	G	603 279-5939	14056
Kase Printing Inc	Hudson	NH	E	603 883-9223	14514
Kelley Solutions Inc	Rye	NH	G	603 431-3881	15499
Kensington Group Incorporated	Hampton Falls	NH	F	603 926-6742	14419
Lew A Cummings Co Inc	Hooksett	NH	C	603 625-6901	14467
Megaprint Inc	Holderness	NH	F	603 536-2900	14447
Papergraphics Print & Copy Inc	Merrimack	NH	F	603 880-1835	14997
Printers Square Inc	Manchester	NH	E	603 703-0795	14915
Puritan Press Inc	Hollis	NH	E	603 889-4500	14458
R C Brayshaw & Co LLC (PA)	Warner	NH	F	603 456-3101	15667
Rainville Printing Entps Inc	Pembroke	NH	G	603 485-3422	15308
Ram Printing Incorporated (PA)	East Hampstead	NH	E	603 382-7045	14271
RB Graphics Inc	Hooksett	NH	G	603 624-4025	14473
S & Q Printers Inc	Belmont	NH	G	603 654-2888	13972
Sant Bani Press Inc	Manchester	NH	E	603 286-3114	14925
Savron Graphics Inc (PA)	Jaffrey	NH	G	603 532-7726	14579
Sherwin Dodge Printers Inc	Littleton	NH	F	603 444-6552	14723
Smith & Town Printers LLC	Berlin	NH	F	603 752-2150	13986
Southport Management Group LLC	Portsmouth	NH	G	603 433-4664	15438
Spirit Advisory LLC	Portsmouth	NH	G	603 433-4664	15439
Sumner Printing Inc	Somersworth	NH	E	603 692-7424	15625
Tylergraphics Inc	Laconia	NH	G	603 524-6625	14672
Uvp Liquidation Inc	North Haverhill	NH	D	603 787-7000	15253
Wall Shotz	Greenland	NH	G	603 431-0900	14372
Water Street Printing LLC	Nashua	NH	F	603 595-1444	15186
Wharf Industries Printing Inc	Windham	NH	E	603 421-2566	15729
136 Express Printing Inc	Bristol	RI	G	401 253-0136	15751
A & H Composition and Prtg Inc	East Providence	RI	G	401 438-1200	15999
Advanced Print Tech LLC	East Providence	RI	G	401 434-8802	16001
Allied Group LLC (PA)	Cranston	RI	B	401 946-6100	15829
Barrington Enterprises LLC	Warwick	RI	F	401 943-8300	16788
Blazing Editions	East Greenwich	RI	E	401 885-4329	15974
Colonial Printing Inc (PA)	Warwick	RI	E	401 691-3400	16795
Copy World Inc	East Providence	RI	G	401 438-1200	16011
Crosstown Press Inc	Cranston	RI	G	401 941-4061	15845
Digital Printing Concepts Inc	Providence	RI	G	401 751-4953	16508
Image Printing & Copying Inc	Warwick	RI	F	401 737-9311	16821
Jay Packaging Group Inc (DH)	Warwick	RI	D	401 244-1300	16827
Key Graphics Inc	Kingston	RI	G	401 826-2425	16113
Louis Press Inc	Johnston	RI	G	401 351-9229	16094
Meridian Printing Inc	East Greenwich	RI	D	401 885-4882	15991
Narragansett Bus Forms Inc	East Providence	RI	F	401 331-2000	16033
Ppoes Inc	Providence	RI	G	401 421-5160	16586
Proprint Incorporated	Johnston	RI	F	401 944-3855	16101
Regine Printing Co Inc	Providence	RI	G	401 943-3404	16600
Romano Investments Inc	Warwick	RI	E	401 691-3400	16854
Signature Printing Inc	East Providence	RI	D	401 438-1200	16044
WEB Printing Inc	Cumberland	RI	G	401 334-3190	15971
Buyers Digest Press Inc	Fairfax	VT	F	802 893-4214	17256
Digital Press Printers LLC	Williston	VT	G	802 863-5579	17727
Edward Group Inc	Rutland	VT	F	802 775-1029	17496
Howard Printing Inc	Brattleboro	VT	G	802 254-3550	17087
Inkspot Press	Bennington	VT	E	802 447-1768	17041
L Brown and Sons Printing Inc	Barre	VT	E	802 476-3164	17012
Lane Press Inc	South Burlington	VT	B	877 300-5933	17583
Offset House Inc	Essex Junction	VT	C	802 878-4440	17242
Queen City Printers Inc	Burlington	VT	E	802 864-4566	17153
Springfield Printing Corp	North Springfield	VT	E	802 886-2201	17425

	CITY	ST	EMP	PHONE	ENTRY#
Stillwater Graphics Inc	Williamstown	VT	F	802 433-9898	17718
The Leahy Press Inc	Montpelier	VT	E	802 223-2100	17375
Tuttle Law Print Inc	Rutland	VT	D	802 773-9171	17512
US Mailing Systems Inc	Milton	VT	F	802 891-1020	17365
Vermont Publishing Comany	Saint Albans	VT	E	802 524-9771	17536
Villanti & Sons Printers Inc	Milton	VT	D	802 864-0723	17367
Whiteside Holdings Inc	Winooski	VT	E	802 655-7654	17772
X Press In Stowe Inc	Stowe	VT	G	802 253-9788	17633

PRINTING: Photo-Offset

	CITY	ST	EMP	PHONE	ENTRY#
Cag Imaging LLC	Norwich	CT	G	860 887-0836	2603
Cybercopy Inc	Westbrook	ME	G	207 775-2679	5623
Whitman Communications Inc	Lebanon	NH	G	603 448-2600	14703

PRINTING: Photolithographic

	CITY	ST	EMP	PHONE	ENTRY#
Central Street Corporation	Bangor	ME	F	207 947-8049	4495
First Step Print Shop LLC	Burlington	VT	G	802 899-2708	17135

PRINTING: Rotogravure

	CITY	ST	EMP	PHONE	ENTRY#
Schmitt Realty Holdings Inc	Branford	CT	F	203 488-3252	275

PRINTING: Screen, Broadwoven Fabrics, Cotton

	CITY	ST	EMP	PHONE	ENTRY#
Action Apparel Inc	Stoneham	MA	G	781 435-2342	12173
Chillybear Inc (PA)	Needham	MA	F	781 455-6321	10507
Gonco Inc (PA)	Sandwich	MA	F	508 833-3900	11750
Silver Screen Design Inc	Greenfield	MA	F	413 773-1692	9000
Collins Sports Center LLC	Rochester	NH	G	603 335-1470	15470
Life Is Good Wholesale Inc	Hudson	NH	D	603 594-6100	14523
Liquid Blue Inc	Derry	NH	D	401 333-6200	14200
KAY DEE DESIGNS INC (PA)	Hope Valley	RI	E	401 539-2400	16067

PRINTING: Screen, Fabric

	CITY	ST	EMP	PHONE	ENTRY#
Nicks Enterprises Inc (PA)	Hamden	CT	F	203 287-9990	1447
T-Shirts Etc Inc	Glastonbury	CT	G	860 657-3551	1298
Zuse Inc	Branford	CT	D	203 458-3295	287
Advanced Print Technology Inc	Fitchburg	MA	G	978 342-0093	8640
Es Sports Corporation	Holyoke	MA	D	413 534-5634	9253
ESP Solutions Services LLC	Taunton	MA	G	508 285-0017	12336
First Print Inc	Winchester	MA	F	781 729-7714	13484
Fleming Industries Inc	Chicopee	MA	E	413 593-3300	8033
Gloucester Graphics Inc (PA)	Gloucester	MA	G	978 281-4500	8937
J W I N Promotional Corp	Westport	MA	G	508 636-1993	13297
Janlynn Corporation	South Hadley	MA	D	413 206-0002	11963
Universal Screening Studio Inc	Everett	MA	G	617 387-1832	8502
Say It In Stitches Inc	Concord	NH	G	603 224-6470	14155
Squadlocker Inc	Warwick	RI	D	888 885-6253	16864
Keiths II Sports Ltd	Pittsford	VT	F	802 483-6050	17444

PRINTING: Screen, Manmade Fiber & Silk, Broadwoven Fabric

	CITY	ST	EMP	PHONE	ENTRY#
Tees & More LLC	Hartford	CT	G	860 244-2224	1513
Gloucester Graphics Inc (PA)	Gloucester	MA	G	978 281-4500	8937
Hammar & Sons Inc	Pelham	NH	F	603 635-2292	15289
Cooley Incorporated (HQ)	Pawtucket	RI	C	401 724-9000	16357

PRINTING: Thermography

	CITY	ST	EMP	PHONE	ENTRY#
Practical Automation Inc (HQ)	Milford	CT	D	203 882-5640	1867
Imperial Image Inc	North Chelmsford	MA	F	978 251-0420	10978
New England Art Publishers Inc	Abington	MA	C	781 878-5151	5726
Print Management Systems Inc	Woburn	MA	F	781 944-1041	13640
Van-Go Graphics	Grafton	MA	G	508 865-7300	8969

PROFESSIONAL EQPT & SPLYS, WHOLESALE: Analytical Instruments

	CITY	ST	EMP	PHONE	ENTRY#
Bruker Scientific LLC	Billerica	MA	A	978 667-9580	6418
Izon Science US LLC	Medford	MA	F	617 945-5936	10291
Witec Instruments Corp	Concord	MA	F	865 690-5550	8142

PROFESSIONAL EQPT & SPLYS, WHOLESALE: Engineers', NEC

	CITY	ST	EMP	PHONE	ENTRY#
Joseph Merritt & Company Inc	Danbury	CT	G	203 743-6734	762
Technical Reproductions Inc	Norwalk	CT	F	203 849-9100	2575

PROFESSIONAL EQPT & SPLYS, WHOLESALE: Optical Goods

	CITY	ST	EMP	PHONE	ENTRY#
Coburn Technologies Intl Inc (DH)	South Windsor	CT	F	860 648-6600	3130
Electro-Lite Corporation	Bethel	CT	F	203 743-4059	114
Globenix Inc	Norwalk	CT	G	203 740-7070	2506
Hoya Corporation	South Windsor	CT	E	860 289-5379	3157
AMF Optical Solutions LLC	Woburn	MA	F	781 933-6125	13509
Atlantic Vision Inc	Shrewsbury	MA	G	508 845-8401	11828
Boston Piezo-Optics Inc	Bellingham	MA	F	508 966-4988	6287
Cyduct Diagnostics Inc	Boston	MA	G	617 360-9700	6682
Qsa Optical Co Inc	Lewiston	ME	E	207 783-8523	4988
Contour Fine Tooling Inc	Keene	NH	G	603 876-4908	14593

PRODUCT

	CITY	ST	EMP	PHONE	ENTRY#
Optical Solutions Inc	Charlestown	NH	G	603 826-4411	14066

PROFESSIONAL INSTRUMENT REPAIR SVCS

	CITY	ST	EMP	PHONE	ENTRY#
Mainstream Global Inc	Lawrence	MA	E	978 682-6767	9579
Timken Motor & Crane Svcs LLC	Portland	ME	F	207 699-2501	5284

PROFESSIONAL SCHOOLS

	CITY	ST	EMP	PHONE	ENTRY#
Cengage Learning Inc	Boston	MA	F	518 348-2300	6645

PROFILE SHAPES: Unsupported Plastics

	CITY	ST	EMP	PHONE	ENTRY#
Web Industries Hartford Inc (HQ)	Dayville	CT	E	860 779-3197	870
Coorstek Inc	Worcester	MA	B	774 317-2600	13710
Fluorolite Plastics LLC	Hudson	MA	E	508 788-1200	9368
Kilder Corporation	North Billerica	MA	E	978 663-8800	10922
Teleflex Incorporated	Jaffrey	NH	D	603 532-7706	14580
Tfx Medical Incorporated	Jaffrey	NH	D	603 532-7706	14581

PROMOTERS OF SHOWS & EXHIBITIONS

	CITY	ST	EMP	PHONE	ENTRY#
Audiospectrum Inc	Randolph	MA	E	781 767-1331	11549
Telco Communications Inc	Seekonk	MA	F	508 336-6633	11788

PROMOTION SVCS

	CITY	ST	EMP	PHONE	ENTRY#
Innovairre Studios Inc	Milford	NH	E	603 579-1600	15030

PROPELLERS: Boat & Ship, Machined

	CITY	ST	EMP	PHONE	ENTRY#
Rolls-Royce Marine North Amer (DH)	Walpole	MA	C	508 668-9610	12574

PROTECTION EQPT: Lightning

	CITY	ST	EMP	PHONE	ENTRY#
East Coast Lightning Eqp Inc	Winsted	CT	E	860 379-9072	4343
Baystate Lghtning Prtction Inc	Bridgewater	MA	G	508 697-7727	7223
Paneltek Inc	Attleboro Falls	MA	F	920 906-9457	6094
Paneltek LLC	Attleboro Falls	MA	F	920 906-9457	6095

PROTECTIVE FOOTWEAR: Rubber Or Plastic

	CITY	ST	EMP	PHONE	ENTRY#
Klone Lab LLC	Newburyport	MA	F	978 378-3434	10692
32 North Corporation	Biddeford	ME	G	207 284-5010	4553
Simply Footwear Utah LLC	Concord	NH	F	603 715-2259	14157
Codet-Newport Corporation (HQ)	Newport	VT	F	802 334-5811	17398

PUBLISHERS: Art Copy & Poster

	CITY	ST	EMP	PHONE	ENTRY#
Rich Associates Incorporated	Kennebunk	ME	G	207 985-5999	4929
Fishing Hot Spots Inc	Nashua	NH	G	715 365-5555	15102
Applejack Art Partners Inc	Manchester Center	VT	E	802 362-3662	17326

PUBLISHERS: Music Book & Sheet Music

	CITY	ST	EMP	PHONE	ENTRY#
Skull Kingdom Entrmt LLC	Ledyard	CT	G	262 804-8193	1553

PUBLISHERS: Music, Sheet

	CITY	ST	EMP	PHONE	ENTRY#
Ione Press Inc	Boston	MA	G	617 236-1935	6816

PUBLISHERS: Sheet Music

	CITY	ST	EMP	PHONE	ENTRY#
Performer Publications Inc	Somerville	MA	G	617 627-9200	11887

PUBLISHERS: Telephone & Other Directory

	CITY	ST	EMP	PHONE	ENTRY#
Connectcut Hspnic Yellow Pages	Hartford	CT	F	860 560-8713	1475
Boxcar Media LLC	North Adams	MA	F	413 663-3384	10804
Eztosecom Directories	Bangor	ME	G	207 974-3171	4500
Connectcut Rver Vly Yllow Pges	Lebanon	NH	G	603 727-4700	14686
Supermedia LLC	Williston	VT	F	802 878-2336	17749
Verizon	Swanton	VT	G	802 879-4954	17644

PUBLISHING & BROADCASTING: Internet Only

	CITY	ST	EMP	PHONE	ENTRY#
Broadcastmed LLC (PA)	Farmington	CT	F	860 953-2900	1210
DCA Business Media LLC	Westport	CT	F	203 227-1699	4164
Heavy Inc	Westport	CT	F	646 806-2113	4172
Mowmedia LLC	Stamford	CT	G	203 240-6416	3413
Triple B Media LLC	Cheshire	CT	F	917 710-2222	620
943 Enteretainment Corp	Somerville	MA	F	617 608-6943	11858
Boston Sports Journal LLC	Medway	MA	G	617 306-0166	10303
Cambridge Brickhouse Inc	Lawrence	MA	G	978 725-8001	9545
Catapult Sports Inc (HQ)	Boston	MA	E	978 447-5220	6642
Clandestine Kitchen LLC	Hingham	MA	G	415 516-0378	9147
Ivix Tech Inc (PA)	Lexington	MA	G	702 561-5304	9754
Promax Supply LLC	Melrose	MA	F	781 620-1602	10318
Roundtown Inc	Cambridge	MA	G	415 425-6891	7699
Saferecipes LLC (PA)	Arlington	MA	G	617 448-6085	5946
Snyk Inc (HQ)	Boston	MA	D	786 506-2615	7042
TCI America Inc	Seekonk	MA	F	508 336-6633	11786
Zoom Information LLC (DH)	Waltham	MA	F	781 693-7500	12822
Alert Solutions Inc	Cranston	RI	F	401 427-2100	15826

PUBLISHING & PRINTING: Books

	CITY	ST	EMP	PHONE	ENTRY#
Air Age Inc	Wilton	CT	E	203 431-9000	4229
Comicana Inc	Stamford	CT	G	203 968-0748	3318
Charlesbridge Publishing Inc (PA)	Watertown	MA	E	617 926-0329	12869
Community of Jesus Inc (PA)	Orleans	MA	E	508 255-1094	11237
Harvard Bus Schl Stdnt Assn In	Boston	MA	D	617 495-6812	6784
Idg Communications Inc (DH)	Needham	MA	C	508 872-8200	10513
Mathemtics Problem Solving LLC	South Portland	ME	D	207 772-2846	5508

PUBLISHING & PRINTING: Directories, NEC

	CITY	ST	EMP	PHONE	ENTRY#
Direct Display Publishing Co	Bath	ME	G	207 443-4800	4526

PUBLISHING & PRINTING: Directories, Telephone

	CITY	ST	EMP	PHONE	ENTRY#
Southern Neng Telecom Corp (HQ)	New Haven	CT	B	203 771-5200	2203

PUBLISHING & PRINTING: Magazines: publishing & printing

	CITY	ST	EMP	PHONE	ENTRY#
Dulce Domum LLC	Norwalk	CT	E	203 227-1400	2493
Natural Nutmeg LLC	Avon	CT	G	860 206-9500	32
Racing Times	Wallingford	CT	G	203 298-2899	3845
Red 7 Media LLC (HQ)	Norwalk	CT	E	203 853-2474	2562
Savage Latina Magazine LLC	Derby	CT	G	800 260-3525	892
Show Management Associates LLC	Norwalk	CT	G	203 939-9901	2572
Urban Exposition LLC (DH)	Shelton	CT	E	203 242-8717	3074
Yale University	New Haven	CT	E	203 764-4333	2218
Yale University (PA)	New Haven	CT	E	203 432-2550	2219
Advanced Media Corporation	Quincy	MA	D	800 844-0599	11501
Atlantic Printing Co Inc	Medfield	MA	F	781 449-2700	10269
Community of Jesus Inc (PA)	Orleans	MA	E	508 255-1094	11237
Conquest Business Media Inc	Beverly	MA	E	978 299-1200	6341
Highlights For Children Inc	Northampton	MA	E	413 397-2800	11067
Massachusetts Review Inc	Amherst	MA	G	413 545-2689	5862
National Braille Press Inc	Boston	MA	D	617 425-2400	6903
Northeast Outdoors Inc	Paxton	MA	G	508 752-8762	11290
President and Fellows of Harvard College (PA) 617 496-4873	Cambridge	MA			A 7688
Rhee Gold Company Inc	Norton	MA	F	508 285-6650	11132
Technology Review Inc	Cambridge	MA	E	617 475-8000	7736
Spectrum Monthly LLC	Manchester	NH	C	603 627-0042	14936
Island Publishing Company	Providence	RI	F	401 351-4320	16544
Battenkill Communications LLP	Manchester Center	VT	G	802 362-3981	17327

PUBLISHING & PRINTING: Newsletters, Business Svc

	CITY	ST	EMP	PHONE	ENTRY#
Chief Executive Group LLC (PA)	Stamford	CT	E	785 832-0303	3310
Merrill Anderson Company Inc	Stratford	CT	E	203 377-4996	3557
Shop Smart Central Inc	Newtown	CT	G	914 962-3871	2346
Advisor Perspectives Inc	Woburn	MA	E	781 376-0050	13501
Assoction For Grvstone Studies	Greenfield	MA	G	413 772-0836	8984
Atlantic Printing Co Inc	Medfield	MA	F	781 449-2700	10269
Curriculum Associates LLC (PA)	North Billerica	MA	B	978 667-8000	10904
Liberty Publishing Inc	Beverly	MA	F	978 777-8200	6362
LPI Printing and Graphic Inc	Stoneham	MA	F	781 438-5400	12182
Quality Solutions Inc (DH)	Newburyport	MA	E	978 465-7755	10710
Quayside Publishing Group	Gloucester	MA	F	978 282-9590	8953
Constrction Smmary New Hmpshr/	Manchester	NH	G	603 627-8856	14835

PUBLISHING & PRINTING: Newspapers

	CITY	ST	EMP	PHONE	ENTRY#
Advisor	North Haven	CT	G	203 239-4121	2388
American-Republican Inc (PA)	Waterbury	CT	C	203 574-3636	3884
Bargain News Free Clssfied Adv	Stratford	CT	F	203 377-3000	3518
C S M S - I P A	North Haven	CT	G	203 562-7228	2397
Capital Cities Communications	New Haven	CT	G	203 784-8800	2133
Central Conn Cmmunications LLC	New Britain	CT	D	860 225-4601	2010
Comms At Mill River	Hamden	CT	G	203 287-0082	1418
Gatehouse Media LLC	Norwich	CT	D	860 886-0106	2606
Greenwich Sentinel	Greenwich	CT	G	203 883-1430	1333
Greenwich Time	Stamford	CT	G	203 253-2922	3359
Hampton Gazette Inc	Hampton	CT	G	860 455-0160	1465
Hartford Courant Company LLC (DH)	Hartford	CT	A	860 241-6200	1486
Hersam Acorn Cmnty Pubg LLC (HQ)	Ridgefield	CT	G	203 438-6544	2898
Hersam Acorn Cmnty Pubg LLC	Trumbull	CT	F	203 261-2548	3722
Hispanic Communications LLC	Stamford	CT	G	203 674-6793	3377
Journal Publishing Company Inc	Manchester	CT	A	860 646-0500	1608
Life Publications	West Hartford	CT	F	860 953-0444	4069
Medianews Group Inc	Norwalk	CT	F	203 333-0161	2535
Minuteman Newspaper (PA)	Westport	CT	E	203 226-8877	4185
New Canaan News	Norwalk	CT	G	203 842-2582	2544
New Canaan Sports LLC	New Canaan	CT	G	866 629-2453	2084
News 12 Connecticut LLC	Norwalk	CT	E	203 849-1321	2545
NRG Connecticut LLC	Hartford	CT	G	860 231-2424	1497
Reminder Broadcaster	Glastonbury	CT	F	860 875-3366	1297
Rmi Inc	Vernon Rockville	CT	C	860 875-3366	3761
Second Wind Media Limited	New Haven	CT	F	203 781-3480	2197
Southern Conn Newspapers Inc	Stamford	CT	B	203 964-2200	3466

2024 Harris New England
Manufacturers Directory

(G-0000) Company's Geographic Section entry number

	CITY	ST	EMP	PHONE	ENTRY#
Thats Great News LLC	Wallingford	CT	E	203 649-4900	3860
Thomson Reuters Risk MGT Inc	Stamford	CT	F	203 539-8000	3482
Thomson Reuters US LLC (DH)	Stamford	CT	D	203 539-8000	3483
Times Community News Group	New London	CT	F	860 437-1150	2235
Tradewinds	Beacon Falls	CT	F	203 723-6966	46
Valley Publishing Company Inc	Derby	CT	F	203 735-6696	893
Westport Summit 7 LLC	Westport	CT	G	917 370-2244	4201
Yale University	New Haven	CT	G	203 432-2880	2221
Bagdon Advertising Inc	Westborough	MA	E	508 366-5500	13080
Beverly Citizen	Beverly	MA	G	978 927-2777	6332
Boston Business Journal Inc	Boston	MA	B	617 330-1000	6605
Boston Irish Reporter	Dorchester	MA	F	617 436-1222	8297
Boston Korean	Allston	MA	F	617 254-4654	5820
Boston Legion LLC	Boston	MA	F	508 718-8912	6610
Bostoncom LLC	Boston	MA	G	617 929-8593	6620
Bulletin Newspapers Inc (PA)	Hyde Park	MA	F	617 361-8400	9458
Bulletin Newspapers Inc	Norwood	MA	F	617 361-8400	11166
Business West	Springfield	MA	G	413 781-8600	12081
Canton Citizen Inc	Canton	MA	G	781 821-4418	7776
Caribe Cmmnctons Pblctions Inc	Boston	MA	F	617 522-5060	6638
Cohasset Redemption Inc	Cohasset	MA	G	781 383-3100	8094
Colonial Times Publishing	Lexington	MA	F	781 274-9997	9730
Community Newspaper Inc	Marblehead	MA	F	781 639-4800	10085
Daily Hampshire Gazette	Easthampton	MA	G	413 527-4000	8442
Danvers Herald	Danvers	MA	G	978 774-0505	8178
Dig Publishing LLC	Boston	MA	F	617 426-8942	6694
Digboston	Boston	MA	F	617 426-8942	6695
Dinner Daily LLC	Westford	MA	F	978 392-5887	13234
Dispatch News	Lowell	MA	F	978 458-7100	9876
Dow Jones & Company Inc	Chicopee	MA	E	212 416-3858	8026
Driggin Sandra DBA Extra Extra	Quincy	MA	F	617 773-6996	11512
Eagle-Tribune Publishing Co	Gloucester	MA	F	978 282-0077	8933
Eagle-Tribune Publishing Co	Haverhill	MA	F	978 374-0321	9093
Eagle-Tribune Publishing Co	North Andover	MA	F	978 946-2000	10827
Eagle-Tribune Publishing Co (DH)	North Andover	MA	C	978 946-2000	10828
Gatehouse Media LLC	Fall River	MA	F	508 676-8211	8551
Gatehouse Media LLC	Holden	MA	F	508 829-5981	9189
Gatehouse Media Mass I Inc	Concord	MA	G	978 667-2156	8118
Gatehouse Media Mass I Inc	Framingham	MA	G	508 626-4412	8764
Gatehouse Media Mass I Inc	Marlborough	MA	G	508 626-3859	10151
Gatehouse Media Mass I Inc	Milford	MA	F	508 634-7522	10403
Gatehouse Media Mass I Inc	Randolph	MA	C	781 235-4000	11560
H S Gere & Sons Inc	Hatfield	MA	E	413 247-5010	9071
Harwich Oracle	Orleans	MA	F	508 247-3200	11238
Holbrook Sun Inc	Randolph	MA	G	781 767-4000	11562
Hyora Publications Inc	Chatham	MA	F	508 430-2700	7897
Independent Newspaper Group	Revere	MA	F	781 485-0588	11620
Jewish Advocate Religious	Boston	MA	G	617 227-8200	6824
Lawyers Weekly LLC (PA)	Boston	MA	F	617 451-7300	6853
Lee Tan Enterprise LLC	Lee	MA	G	413 243-4717	9615
Local Media Group Inc	Hyannis	MA	B	508 775-1200	9440
Lowell Sun Publishing Company	Ayer	MA	C	978 433-6685	6185
Lowell Sun Publishing Company	Devens	MA	C	978 772-0777	8276
Lowell Sun Publishing Company (DH)	Lowell	MA	C	978 459-1300	9896
Lujean Printing Co Inc	Cotuit	MA	E	508 428-8700	8146
Martins News Shop	Boston	MA	G	617 267-1334	6869
Massachusetts Institute Tech	Cambridge	MA	C	617 253-7183	7638
Massachusetts Port Authority	Boston	MA	C	617 561-9300	6875
Mastv / El Planeta LLC	Boston	MA	F	617 379-0210	6878
Ne Media Group Inc (PA)	Boston	MA	D	617 929-2000	6906
Nenpa	Woburn	MA	G	781 281-2053	13620
New England Newspapers Inc (DH)	Pittsfield	MA	C	413 447-7311	11414
New England Newspr Press Assn	Woburn	MA	F	781 281-2053	13622
North Shore News Company Inc (PA)	Peabody	MA	F	781 592-1300	11328
Nrt Inc	Medway	MA	F	508 533-4588	10309
Ottaway Newspapers	Hyannis	MA	E	508 775-1200	9443
Portuguese Times Inc	New Bedford	MA	G	508 997-3118	10641
Quincy Sun Publishing Co Inc	Quincy	MA	F	617 471-3100	11535
Republican Company (HQ)	Springfield	MA	A	413 788-1000	12125
Revere Independent	Revere	MA	F	781 485-0588	11623
Salem News Archives	Beverly	MA	G	978 922-8303	6381
South Boston Today	Boston	MA	G	617 268-4032	7048
Taunton	Taunton	MA	G	774 501-2220	12370
Terika Smith Ministries Corp	Lawrence	MA	E	978 233-0576	9603
Town Common Inc	Rowley	MA	F	978 948-8696	11686
Town Crier Publications Inc	Upton	MA	F	508 529-7791	12475
Trustees of Tufts College	Medford	MA	G	617 628-5000	10300
United Communications Corp	Attleboro	MA	C	508 222-7000	6071
Wall Street Journal	Chicopee	MA	E	800 369-5663	8069
Walpole Times Inc	Framingham	MA	F	508 668-0243	8810
West Springfield Record Inc	West Springfield	MA	G	413 736-1587	13052
Westfield News Publishing Inc (DH)	Westfield	MA	E	413 562-4181	13221

	CITY	ST	EMP	PHONE	ENTRY#
Woburn Daily Times Inc (PA)	Woburn	MA	D	781 933-3700	13689
Worcester Telegram Gazette Inc (HQ)	Worcester	MA	B	508 793-9100	13831
Worcester Tlegram Gazette Corp	Leominster	MA	F	978 840-0071	9717
Worcester Tlegram Gazette Corp	Worcester	MA	F	978 368-0176	13832
Yankee Shopper	Webster	MA	F	508 943-8784	12931
Bald Hill Reach Inc	Ellsworth	ME	D	207 667-2576	4754
Bangor Publishing Company	Ellsworth	ME	G	207 667-9393	4755
Blethen Maine Newspapers Inc	Portland	ME	F	207 791-6650	5188
Bottle King Redemption Center	Newcastle	ME	G	207 563-1520	5092
Bridgton News Corporation	Bridgton	ME	F	207 647-2851	4626
Brunswick Publishing LLC	Brunswick	ME	F	207 729-3311	4643
Central Maine Morning Sentinel	Waterville	ME	E	207 873-3341	5593
Citizen Printers Incorporated	Albany Twp	ME	G	207 824-2444	4400
Fiddlehead Focus	Fort Kent	ME	G	207 316-2243	4787
Free Press Inc	Rockland	ME	F	207 594-4408	5330
Gorham Times Inc	Gorham	ME	E	207 839-8390	4821
James Newspapers Inc (PA)	Norway	ME	E	207 743-7011	5116
Lincoln County Publishing Co	Newcastle	ME	E	207 563-3171	5093
Maine Visual	Portland	ME	G	207 553-0798	5243
Maine-OK Enterprises Inc	Boothbay Harbor	ME	F	207 633-4620	4602
Mainely Media	Biddeford	ME	E	207 282-4337	4576
Mainely Newspapers Inc	Biddeford	ME	E	207 282-4337	4577
Mount Desert Islander	Ellsworth	ME	G	207 288-0556	4759
Northeast Publishing Company	Houlton	ME	G	207 532-2281	4903
Northeast Publishing Company	Presque Isle	ME	G	207 768-5431	5306
Northeast Publishing Company (HQ)	Presque Isle	ME	D	207 764-4471	5307
Northwoods Publications LLC	West Enfield	ME	F	207 732-4880	5610
Rolling Thunder Press Inc	Newport	ME	G	207 368-2028	5098
Seattle Times Company	Augusta	ME	C	207 623-3811	4480
Shoreline Publications	Wells	ME	F	207 646-8448	5605
Sunrise Guide LLC	Portland	ME	F	207 221-3450	5277
York County Coast Star Inc	Kennebunk	ME	G	207 985-5901	4931
Concord Monitor	Concord	NH	G	603 224-5301	14124
Concordian LLC	Concord	NH	G	603 225-5660	14126
Eagle-Tribune Publishing Co	Derry	NH	F	603 437-7000	14192
Jordan Associates	Pittsburg	NH	F	603 246-8998	15328
McLean Communications LLC	Manchester	NH	D	603 624-1442	14882
New Hampshire Gateway Mdsg	Manchester	NH	G	603 216-7373	14899
Newspapers New Hampshire Inc (HQ)	Concord	NH	C	603 224-5301	14149
Newspapers New Hampshire Inc	Peterborough	NH	D	603 924-7172	15321
Panoramic Publishing Group LLC	Wolfeboro Falls	NH	F	603 569-5257	15736
Peterborough Transcript	Peterborough	NH	F	603 924-3333	15326
Shakour Publishers Inc	Keene	NH	F	603 352-5250	14618
Tolles Communications Corp	Manchester	NH	G	603 627-9500	14945
Beacon Communications Inc	Warwick	RI	E	401 732-3100	16789
Breeze Publications Inc	Lincoln	RI	E	401 334-9555	16122
Island News Enterprise	Jamestown	RI	G	401 423-3200	16070
New England Newspapers Inc	Pawtucket	RI	E	401 722-4000	16392
Providence Business News	Providence	RI	E	401 273-2201	16589
Rhode Island Newsppr Group Inc	Warwick	RI	F	401 732-5100	16850
South County Newspaper Inc	Wakefield	RI	F	401 789-6000	16743
Caledonian Record Pubg Co Inc (PA)	Saint Johnsbury	VT	D	802 748-8121	17540
Chronicle Inc	Barton	VT	F	802 525-3531	17027
Creative Marketing Services	Rutland	VT	F	802 775-9500	17493
Cutter & Locke Inc (PA)	Tunbridge	VT	G	802 889-3500	17652
Da Capo Publishing Inc	Burlington	VT	F	802 864-5684	17130
Daily Gardener	Calais	VT	G	802 223-7851	17167
Eastview Associates Inc	Rutland	VT	G	802 773-4040	17495
Gannett River States Pubg Corp	Fairfax	VT	E	802 893-4214	17258
Hardwick Gazette Print Shop	Hardwick	VT	E	802 472-6521	17284
McClure Newspapers Inc	Williston	VT	C	802 863-3441	17740
New England Newspapers Inc	Brattleboro	VT	E	802 254-2311	17097
ORourke Media Group LLC (PA)	Saint Albans	VT	F	802 524-9771	17527
Vermont Media Corp	Wilmington	VT	E	802 464-5757	17756
Vermont Publishing Comany	Saint Albans	VT	E	802 524-9771	17536
Williston Pubg Promotions LLC	Williston	VT	F	802 872-9000	17753
World Publications Inc	Barre	VT	G	802 479-2582	17026
Young Writers Project Inc	Burlington	VT	F	802 324-9537	17165

PUBLISHING & PRINTING: Pamphlets

	CITY	ST	EMP	PHONE	ENTRY#
Atlantic Printing Co Inc	Medfield	MA	F	781 449-2700	10269
Channing Bete Company Inc (PA)	South Deerfield	MA	C	413 665-7611	11922
Nsight Inc	Andover	MA	E	781 273-6300	5902
Kensington Group Incorporated	Hampton Falls	NH	F	603 926-6742	14419

PUBLISHING & PRINTING: Shopping News

	CITY	ST	EMP	PHONE	ENTRY#
Rare Reminder Incorporated	Rocky Hill	CT	E	860 563-9386	2933
Vermont Publishing Comany	Saint Albans	VT	E	802 524-9771	17536

PUBLISHING & PRINTING: Textbooks

	CITY	ST	EMP	PHONE	ENTRY#
Cengage Learning Inc	Boston	MA	F	518 348-2300	6645
Curriculum Associates LLC (PA)	North Billerica	MA	B	978 667-8000	10904

P
R
O
D
U
C
T

	CITY	ST	EMP	PHONE	ENTRY#
Flatworld	Boston	MA	E	781 974-9927	6740
Houghton Mfflin Hrcurt Pbls In **(DH)**	Boston	MA	A	617 351-5000	6793

PUBLISHING & PRINTING: Trade Journals

	CITY	ST	EMP	PHONE	ENTRY#
Vance Publishing Corporation	Hartford	CT	C	847 634-2600	1516
Archaeological Institute Amer	Boston	MA	F	617 353-9361	6555
Institute For Applied Ntwrk SE	Boston	MA	E	617 399-8100	6814
Massachusetts Medical Society	Waltham	MA	E	781 434-7950	12716
Trueline Publishing LLC	Portland	ME	E	207 510-4099	5286
Vermont Journalism Trust Ltd	Montpelier	VT	F	802 225-6224	17377

PULLEYS: Metal

	CITY	ST	EMP	PHONE	ENTRY#
Cascaded Purchase Holdings Inc **(PA)**	Claremont	NH	D	603 448-1090	14083
Tracey Gear Inc	Pawtucket	RI	E	401 725-3920	16424

PULLEYS: Power Transmission

	CITY	ST	EMP	PHONE	ENTRY#
Nhi Mechanical Motion LLC	Claremont	NH	F	603 448-1090	14095

PULP MILLS

	CITY	ST	EMP	PHONE	ENTRY#
ITT Industries Holdings Inc **(DH)**	Stamford	CT	G	914 641-2000	3389
Willimantic Waste Paper Co Inc **(HQ)**	Willimantic	CT	C	860 423-4527	4221
Capital Industries Corporation	East Weymouth	MA	F	781 337-9807	8428
Intercntnental Enrgy Group LLC	Hingham	MA	G	781 749-9800	9151
United Paper Stock Co Inc	Worcester	MA	E	401 724-5700	13816
Casella Recycling LLC **(HQ)**	Scarborough	ME	E	207 883-4600	5427
Georgia-Pacific LLC	Baileyville	ME	G	207 427-4077	4484
ND Otm LLC	Old Town	ME	C	207 401-2879	5129
Robbins Lumber Inc **(PA)**	Searsmont	ME	C	207 342-5221	5450
Woodland Pulp LLC **(PA)**	Baileyville	ME	B	207 427-3311	4486
Westrock Cp LLC	Sheldon Springs	VT	C	802 933-7733	17566

PULP MILLS: Mechanical & Recycling Processing

	CITY	ST	EMP	PHONE	ENTRY#
Freepoint Eco-Systems LLC	Stamford	CT	F	203 542-6000	3350
Sarid Inc	Lexington	MA	G	781 315-1105	9769
Lkq Precious Metals Inc	Cumberland	RI	C	800 447-1034	15950

PUMPS & PARTS: Indl

	CITY	ST	EMP	PHONE	ENTRY#
Idex Health & Science LLC	Wallingford	CT	E	203 774-4422	3817
Industrial Flow Sltons Oper LL	New Haven	CT	E	860 399-5937	2163
Megadoor USA Inc	Meriden	CT	C	203 238-2700	1673
Preferred Utilities Mfg Corp **(HQ)**	Danbury	CT	D	203 743-6741	799
Stancor LP	Monroe	CT	E	203 268-7513	1922
Sulzer Pump Solutions US Inc **(PA)**	Wallingford	CT	E	203 238-2700	3856
Iwaki America Incorporated **(HQ)**	Holliston	MA	E	508 429-1440	9216
Iwaki Pumps Inc **(DH)**	Holliston	MA	E	508 429-1440	9217
Lawrence Pumps Inc	Lawrence	MA	C	978 682-5248	9577
Monalex Manufacturing Inc	East Douglas	MA	G	508 476-1200	8352
Warren Pumps LLC	Warren	MA	E	413 436-7711	12853
Cascon Inc	Yarmouth	ME	E	207 846-6202	5702
Brailsford & Company Inc	Antrim	NH	F	603 588-2880	13896
Pfeiffer Vacuum Inc **(DH)**	Nashua	NH	E	317 328-8492	15147
Bsm Pump Corp	North Kingstown	RI	F	401 471-6350	16235
Mesco Corporation	Portsmouth	RI	C	401 683-2677	16447
Apex Sealing Inc	Fairfax	VT	F	802 524-7100	17254
Hayward Tyler Inc **(DH)**	Colchester	VT	E	802 655-4444	17194
Ivek Corp **(PA)**	North Springfield	VT	C	802 886-2238	17422
PBL Incorporated	Colchester	VT	F	802 893-0111	17199

PUMPS & PUMPING EQPT REPAIR SVCS

	CITY	ST	EMP	PHONE	ENTRY#
A V I International Inc	Torrington	CT	G	860 482-8345	3666
Hisco Pump Incorporated **(PA)**	Bloomfield	CT	F	860 243-2705	170
Chas G Allen Realty LLC	Barre	MA	D	978 355-2911	6202
Iwaki Pumps Inc **(DH)**	Holliston	MA	E	508 429-1440	9217
Mass Vac Inc	North Billerica	MA	E	978 667-2393	10932
Apex Sealing Inc	Fairfax	VT	F	802 524-7100	17254
Hayward Tyler Inc **(DH)**	Colchester	VT	E	802 655-4444	17194

PUMPS & PUMPING EQPT WHOLESALERS

	CITY	ST	EMP	PHONE	ENTRY#
2600 Albany Avenue LLC	Torrington	CT	G	336 632-0005	3665
A V I International Inc	Torrington	CT	G	860 482-8345	3666
Beckson Manufacturing Inc **(PA)**	Bridgeport	CT	E	203 366-3644	301
Draught Technologies LLC	Farmington	CT	G	860 840-7555	1215
Foleys Pump Service Inc	Danbury	CT	E	203 792-2236	747
Hamworthy Peabody Combustn Inc **(DH)**	Shelton	CT	E	203 922-1199	3012
Hisco Pump Incorporated **(PA)**	Bloomfield	CT	F	860 243-2705	170
ITT Goulds Pumps Inc **(HQ)**	Stamford	CT	E	315 568-2811	3387
ITT Water & Wastewater USA Inc **(HQ)**	Shelton	CT	D	262 548-8181	3024
McVac Environmental Svcs Inc	New Haven	CT	E	203 497-1960	2173
MSC Filtration Tech Inc	Enfield	CT	E	860 745-7475	1139
Omega Engineering Inc	Norwalk	CT	D	714 540-4914	2548
Proflow Inc	North Haven	CT	E	203 230-4700	2433
Sfc Koenig LLC	North Haven	CT	E	203 245-1100	2436

	CITY	ST	EMP	PHONE	ENTRY#
Sonic Corp	Stratford	CT	F	203 375-0063	3575
Trane Technologies Company LLC	Rocky Hill	CT	F	860 616-6600	2939
Trane Technologies Company LLC	Torrington	CT	G	860 626-2085	3702
Xylem Water Solutions USA Inc	Shelton	CT	E	203 450-3715	3080
A W Chesterton Company	Groveland	MA	B	781 438-7000	9013
Azenta Inc	Chelmsford	MA	B	978 262-2795	7914
BEE International Inc	South Easton	MA	E	508 238-5558	11937
Flow Control LLC	Beverly	MA	E	978 281-0440	6348
Flowserve US Inc	Lawrence	MA	C	978 682-5248	9563
Harvard Apparatus Inc	Holliston	MA	D	508 893-8999	9213
Hayes Pump Inc **(PA)**	Concord	MA	E	978 369-8800	8119
Lewa-Nikkiso America Inc **(DH)**	Holliston	MA	E	508 429-7403	9220
Mass Vac Inc	North Billerica	MA	E	978 667-2393	10932
Newera Services Corporation **(PA)**	New Bedford	MA	E	508 995-9711	10631
Northeast Equipment Inc	Fall River	MA	E	508 324-0083	8588
Rule Industries LLC	Gloucester	MA	C	978 281-0440	8956
Tark Inc	Billerica	MA	F	978 663-8074	6486
The Tyler Co Inc	Hudson	MA	E	978 568-3400	9419
Trane Technologies Company LLC	Northborough	MA	D	781 961-2063	11115
Trane Technologies Company LLC	Shrewsbury	MA	E	508 842-5769	11844
Xylem Water Solutions USA Inc	Woburn	MA	E	781 935-6515	13690
Bison Pumps	Houlton	ME	F	207 532-2600	4897
Stevens Electric Pump Service	Monmouth	ME	G	207 933-2143	5073
Universal Envmtl Tech Inc	Nashua	NH	G	603 883-9312	15180
Williamson Electrical Co Inc	Epping	NH	D	617 884-9200	14277
Aquamotion Inc	Warwick	RI	E	401 785-3000	16783
Boydco Inc **(PA)**	East Providence	RI	F	401 438-6900	16007
Taco Inc **(PA)**	Cranston	RI	B	401 942-8000	15917
Taco International Ltd	Cranston	RI	F	401 942-8000	15918
Whale Water Systems Inc	Manchester	VT	F	802 367-1091	17325

PUMPS, HEAT: Electric

	CITY	ST	EMP	PHONE	ENTRY#
Nyle Systems LLC	Bangor	ME	E	207 989-4335	4513

PUMPS: Domestic, Water Or Sump

	CITY	ST	EMP	PHONE	ENTRY#
Connecticut Basement Systems Inc	Seymour	CT	C	203 881-5090	2959
Marsars Wtr Rescue Systems Inc	Beacon Falls	CT	G	203 924-7315	43
Pump Technology Incorporated	Ansonia	CT	E	203 736-8890	18

PUMPS: Fluid Power

	CITY	ST	EMP	PHONE	ENTRY#
Kerfoot Technologies Inc	Falmouth	MA	F	508 539-3002	8634
Newera Services Corporation **(PA)**	New Bedford	MA	E	508 995-9711	10631

PUMPS: Hydraulic Power Transfer

	CITY	ST	EMP	PHONE	ENTRY#
Redco Corporation **(HQ)**	Stamford	CT	D	203 363-7300	3445
Crane Nxt Co **(PA)**	Waltham	MA	C	610 430-2510	12644

PUMPS: Measuring & Dispensing

	CITY	ST	EMP	PHONE	ENTRY#
Proflow Inc	North Haven	CT	E	203 230-4700	2433
Fishman Corporation	Hopkinton	MA	F	508 435-2115	9325
Lewa-Nikkiso America Inc **(DH)**	Holliston	MA	E	508 429-7403	9220
Liquid Metronics Incorporated	Acton	MA	E	978 263-9800	5757
Sensing Systems Corporation	Dartmouth	MA	F	508 992-0872	8231
Nordson Efd LLC **(HQ)**	East Providence	RI	C	401 431-7000	16034

PUMPS: Vacuum, Exc Laboratory

	CITY	ST	EMP	PHONE	ENTRY#
Artisan Industries Inc	Stoughton	MA	D	781 893-6800	12195
Azenta Inc **(PA)**	Burlington	MA	A	978 262-2400	7339
Azenta Inc	Chelmsford	MA	B	978 262-2795	7914
Mass Vac Inc	North Billerica	MA	E	978 667-2393	10932
Nexvac Inc **(PA)**	Sandown	NH	F	603 887-0015	15580

PUNCHES: Forming & Stamping

	CITY	ST	EMP	PHONE	ENTRY#
Royal Diversified Products	Warren	RI	E	401 245-6900	16767

PUPPETS & MARIONETTES

	CITY	ST	EMP	PHONE	ENTRY#
CJS Workshop LLC	Groton	MA	E	323 445-5012	9008

PURIFICATION & DUST COLLECTION EQPT

	CITY	ST	EMP	PHONE	ENTRY#
B G Wickberg Company Inc	East Weymouth	MA	G	781 335-7800	8425
Headwaters Inc	Marblehead	MA	G	781 715-6404	10087
Kse Inc	Sunderland	MA	F	413 549-5506	12274

RACEWAYS

	CITY	ST	EMP	PHONE	ENTRY#
Wiremold Company **(DH)**	West Hartford	CT	A	860 233-6251	4091
Speedboard Usa Inc	Rowley	MA	G	978 884-3900	11685

RACKS: Pallet, Exc Wood

	CITY	ST	EMP	PHONE	ENTRY#
Mamava Inc	Burlington	VT	E	802 347-2111	17142

RADAR SYSTEMS & EQPT

	CITY	ST	EMP	PHONE	ENTRY#
ITT Inc **(PA)**	Stamford	CT	C	914 641-2000	3388

	CITY	ST	EMP	PHONE	ENTRY#
Prosensing Inc	Amherst	MA	F	413 549-4402	5863
Radar Technology Inc	Newburyport	MA	E		10711
Raytheon Company	Woburn	MA	C	781 933-1863	13647
Raytheon Sutheast Asia Systems (DH)	Waltham	MA	E	978 470-5000	12762
Remote Sensing Solutions Inc	Buzzards Bay	MA	F	508 362-9400	7456
Where Inc	Boston	MA	F	617 502-3100	7121
Flir Maritime Us Inc	Hudson	NH	E	603 324-7900	14496

RADIATORS, EXC ELECTRIC

	CITY	ST	EMP	PHONE	ENTRY#
Mestek Inc	Westfield	MA	E	413 568-9571	13185

RADIO BROADCASTING & COMMUNICATIONS EQPT

	CITY	ST	EMP	PHONE	ENTRY#
Connecticut Radio Inc	Rocky Hill	CT	G	860 563-4867	2919
Northastern Communications Inc	Stratford	CT	F	203 381-9008	3558
Retcomm Inc	Guilford	CT	F	203 453-2389	1405
Wpcs International- Hartford Inc (HQ)	Windsor	CT	E		4315
Atc Ponderosa B-I LLC	Boston	MA	F	617 375-7500	6563
Atc Ponderosa B-II LLC	Boston	MA	F	617 375-7500	6564
Atc Ponderosa H-I LLC	Boston	MA	F	617 375-7500	6565
Atc Ponderosa H-II LLC	Boston	MA	F	617 375-7500	6566
Atc Ponderosa K LLC	Boston	MA	G	617 375-7500	6567
Atc Ponderosa K Ohio LLC	Boston	MA	F	617 375-7500	6568
Atc Sequoia LLC	Boston	MA	F	617 375-7500	6569
Burk Technology Inc	Littleton	MA	E	978 486-0086	9805
David Clark Company Inc (PA)	Worcester	MA	C	508 756-6216	13713
Global Tower Holdings LLC	Boston	MA	F	617 375-7500	6764
Ondas Holdings Inc (PA)	Waltham	MA	F	888 350-9994	12744
Starent Networks LLC (HQ)	Tewksbury	MA	E	978 851-1100	12418
Maine Radio	Scarborough	ME	F	207 883-2929	5438
Cellular Specialties Inc	Manchester	NH	D	603 626-6677	14826
Data Radio Management Co Inc	Merrimack	NH	F	603 598-1222	14979
Haigh-Farr Inc	Bedford	NH	D	603 644-6170	13932
Hro Inc	Salem	NH	G	603 898-3750	15537

RADIO BROADCASTING STATIONS

	CITY	ST	EMP	PHONE	ENTRY#
Christian Science Pubg Soc (PA)	Boston	MA	B	617 450-2000	6655
Off The Dial Media LLC	Cambridge	MA	F	617 929-3424	7673

RADIO, TV & CONSUMER ELEC STORES: High Fidelity Stereo Eqpt

	CITY	ST	EMP	PHONE	ENTRY#
Bose Corporation (PA)	Framingham	MA	A	508 879-7330	8745
Bose Corporation	Stow	MA	E	508 766-7330	12244

RAILINGS: Prefabricated, Metal

	CITY	ST	EMP	PHONE	ENTRY#
Mono-Crete Step Co Ct LLC	Bethel	CT	F	203 748-8419	129
Green Brothers Fabricating (PA)	Taunton	MA	E	508 880-3608	12339
379 Charles RI Inc	North Providence	RI	F	401 521-1101	16293

RAILROAD EQPT

	CITY	ST	EMP	PHONE	ENTRY#
James L Howard and Company Inc	Bloomfield	CT	E	860 242-3581	176
Winchester Industries Inc	Winsted	CT	G	860 379-5336	4359
RI Controls LLC	Woburn	MA	D	781 932-3349	13654
Okonite Company Inc	Cumberland	RI	E	401 333-3500	15957

RAILROAD EQPT: Brakes, Air & Vacuum

	CITY	ST	EMP	PHONE	ENTRY#
Winslow Automatics Inc	New Britain	CT	D	860 225-6321	2075

RAILS: Steel Or Iron

	CITY	ST	EMP	PHONE	ENTRY#
Arnio Welding LLC	Central Village	CT	F	860 564-7696	565
Concentric Fabrication LLC	Middleboro	MA	F	508 672-4098	10355
Jebella LLC	Pawtucket	RI	G	401 475-1720	16378

RAMPS: Prefabricated Metal

	CITY	ST	EMP	PHONE	ENTRY#
Gordon Industries Inc (PA)	Randolph	MA	E	857 401-8398	11561

RAZORS, RAZOR BLADES

	CITY	ST	EMP	PHONE	ENTRY#
Bic Corporation (HQ)	Shelton	CT	A	203 783-2000	2985
Bic USA Inc (DH)	Shelton	CT	C	203 783-2000	2986
Edgewell Per Care Brands LLC (HQ)	Shelton	CT	B	203 944-5500	3002
Edgewell Personal Care Company	Milford	CT	D	203 882-2308	1823
Edgewell Personal Care Company (PA)	Shelton	CT	E	203 944-5500	3003
Gillette Company (HQ)	Boston	MA	A	617 463-3000	6758
Grooming Ventures - FL LLC (HQ)	Boston	MA	D	305 593-0667	6774
Edgewell Per Care Brands LLC	Saint Albans	VT	E	802 524-2151	17521

REAL ESTATE AGENCIES & BROKERS

	CITY	ST	EMP	PHONE	ENTRY#
Chas G Allen Realty LLC	Barre	MA	D	978 355-2911	6202
Platinum Investments Ltd	Brookline	MA	F	617 731-2447	7325
Rowe Contracting Co	Melrose	MA	G	781 620-0052	10319
Weber Realty Trust	Auburn	MA	F	508 756-4290	6127

REAL ESTATE AGENCIES: Rental

	CITY	ST	EMP	PHONE	ENTRY#
Woodmeister Master Bldrs Inc (PA)	Holden	MA	C	774 345-1000	9196

REAL ESTATE AGENTS & MANAGERS

	CITY	ST	EMP	PHONE	ENTRY#
Icon Capital Management LLC	Greenwich	CT	G	203 542-7792	1335
Bruno Diduca	Waltham	MA	G	781 894-5300	12613
East Coast Publications Inc (PA)	Norwell	MA	F	781 878-4540	11141
Gordon Brothers Intl LLC (HQ)	Boston	MA	D	888 424-1903	6767
Just Publications Inc	Brookline	MA	F	617 739-5878	7319
Massachusetts Assn Realtors (PA)	Foxboro	MA	F	781 890-3700	8707
Southern Brkshire Shppers Gide	Great Barrington	MA	F	413 528-0095	8978
Ambrose G McCarthy Jr	Skowhegan	ME	G	207 474-8837	5462
Leland Boggs II	Warren	ME	G	207 273-2610	5583
Finally Free LLC	Manchester	NH	F	603 626-4388	14848
Granite Commercial RE LLC	Nashua	NH	F	603 669-2770	15107
Cersosimo Industries Inc (PA)	Brattleboro	VT	D	802 254-4500	17080

REAL ESTATE INVESTMENT TRUSTS

	CITY	ST	EMP	PHONE	ENTRY#
Smithfamily1938 LLC	Enfield	CT	G	424 341-8876	1153

RECEIVERS: Radio Communications

	CITY	ST	EMP	PHONE	ENTRY#
Nhrc LLC	Pembroke	NH	F	603 485-2248	15305

RECORDING HEADS: Speech & Musical Eqpt

	CITY	ST	EMP	PHONE	ENTRY#
Bowers and Wilkins Group	North Reading	MA	E	978 357-0428	11038

RECORDING TAPE: Video, Blank

	CITY	ST	EMP	PHONE	ENTRY#
Primary Pdc Inc (PA)	Waltham	MA	G	781 386-2000	12753

RECORDS & TAPES: Prerecorded

	CITY	ST	EMP	PHONE	ENTRY#
Bff Holdings Inc (HQ)	Old Saybrook	CT	C	860 510-0100	2645
Covalent Networks Inc	Boston	MA	F	781 296-7952	6673
Intent Solutions Group (PA)	Norwell	MA	G	617 909-4714	11142
Qwiklabs Inc	Carlisle	MA	F	978 760-0732	7846
Teranode Inc	Dedham	MA	F	781 493-6900	8252
Barefoot Technologies Corp	Henniker	NH	F	603 428-6255	14433

RECOVERY SVC: Iron Ore, From Open Hearth Slag

	CITY	ST	EMP	PHONE	ENTRY#
Eastern Metals Inc	Londonderry	NH	E	603 818-8639	14745

RECREATIONAL VEHICLE DEALERS

	CITY	ST	EMP	PHONE	ENTRY#
Lyle Guptill	East Machias	ME	F	207 255-4130	4740

RECREATIONAL VEHICLE PARTS & ACCESS STORES

	CITY	ST	EMP	PHONE	ENTRY#
Gary Raymond	Caribou	ME	G	207 498-2549	4675

REELS: Cable, Metal

	CITY	ST	EMP	PHONE	ENTRY#
William McCaskie Inc	Westport	MA	G	508 636-8845	13301
Carris Financial Corp (PA)	Proctor	VT	F	802 773-9111	17456
Carris Reels Inc (HQ)	Proctor	VT	E	802 773-9111	17457

REFINERS & SMELTERS: Copper

	CITY	ST	EMP	PHONE	ENTRY#
Ametek Inc	Wallingford	CT	C	203 265-6731	3770

REFINERS & SMELTERS: Platinum Group Metals, Secondary

	CITY	ST	EMP	PHONE	ENTRY#
Utitec Inc (HQ)	Watertown	CT	D	860 945-0605	4035

REFINING: Petroleum

	CITY	ST	EMP	PHONE	ENTRY#
CCI Corpus Christi LLC	Stamford	CT	F	203 564-8100	3304
CPI Operations LLC	Stamford	CT	C	210 249-9988	3323
Enviro-Fuels LLC	Suffield	CT	G	860 242-2325	3590
Mountain Creek Energy Inc	Manchester	CT	G	512 990-7886	1619
Star Group LP (PA)	Stamford	CT	D	203 328-7310	3473
Stop N Go LLC	Hartford	CT	G	860 206-3950	1510
Power Advocate Inc (HQ)	Boston	MA	D	857 453-5700	6971
Prima America Corporation	Groveton	NH	F	603 631-5407	14379
Proctor Gas Inc	Proctor	VT	E	802 459-3340	17460

REFRACTORIES: Clay

	CITY	ST	EMP	PHONE	ENTRY#
Bay State Crucible Co	Taunton	MA	E	508 824-5121	12323
Lynn Products Co	Lynn	MA	F	781 593-2500	9986
Zampell Refractories Inc (PA)	Newburyport	MA	E	978 465-0055	10728

REFRACTORIES: Graphite, Carbon Or Ceramic Bond

	CITY	ST	EMP	PHONE	ENTRY#
Saint-Gobain Abrasives Inc (HQ)	Worcester	MA	A	508 795-5000	13788

REFRACTORIES: Nonclay

	CITY	ST	EMP	PHONE	ENTRY#
Joshua LLC (PA)	Guilford	CT	F	203 624-0080	1398
Specialty Minerals Inc	Canaan	CT	F	860 824-5435	557
Lvr Inc	Oxford	MA	G	508 987-2337	11260
Saint-Gobain Ceramics Plas Inc	Northampton	MA	C	413 586-8167	11078
Zar Tech	Newburyport	MA	F	978 499-5122	10729
Infab Refractories Inc	Lewiston	ME	G	207 783-2075	4965
Newport Sand & Gravel Co Inc (PA)	Newport	NH	F	603 298-0199	15233

PRODUCT

	CITY	ST	EMP	PHONE	ENTRY#

REFRACTORIES: Tile & Brick, Exc Plastic

	CITY	ST	EMP	PHONE	ENTRY#
Zampell Refractories Inc	Auburn	ME	F	207 786-2400	4465

REFRIGERATION & HEATING EQUIPMENT

	CITY	ST	EMP	PHONE	ENTRY#
116 Lenox Eo LLC	Stamford	CT	G	973 854-1999	3265
Latin American Holding Inc (HQ)	Farmington	CT	F	860 674-3000	1228
Mechancal Engnered Systems LLC	New Canaan	CT	G	203 400-4658	2083
Rtx Corporation	East Hartford	CT	F	860 565-7622	1021
Rtx Corporation	Middletown	CT	C	860 704-7133	1779
Trane Inc	New Haven	CT	F	860 437-6208	2211
Trane US Inc	Farmington	CT	F	860 470-3901	1251
York International Corporation	Danbury	CT	F	203 730-8100	838
Airxchange Inc	Rockland	MA	D	781 871-4816	11633
Aspen Systems LLC (PA)	Marlborough	MA	E	508 281-5322	10112
Cambridgeport Air Systems Inc	Georgetown	MA	C	978 465-8481	8906
Cox Engineering Company (PA)	Canton	MA	C	781 302-3300	7781
Duc-Pac Corporation	Springfield	MA	E	413 525-3302	12091
Hkd Turbo	Natick	MA	F	508 878-3798	10482
J & J Heating & AC Inc	Dracut	MA	E	978 454-8197	8306
Lake Industries Inc	Stoneham	MA	D	781 438-8814	12180
Lenox Special Needs	Lenox	MA	G	413 637-5571	9626
Mestek Inc	Westfield	MA	D	413 564-5530	13184
Munters Corporation	Amesbury	MA	F	978 388-2666	5844
Tecomet Inc	Woburn	MA	A	781 782-6400	13675
Thermal Circuits Inc	Salem	MA	C	978 745-1162	11734
Thl-Nortek Investors LLC (PA)	Boston	MA	D	617 227-1050	7077
Thomas H Lee Equity Fund V LP	Boston	MA	E	617 227-1050	7078
Trane Comercial Systems	Springfield	MA	F	413 271-3001	12141
Trane Inc	Wilmington	MA	D	978 737-3900	13470
Flexware Control Tech LLC	Bangor	ME	G	207 262-9682	4501
N E Tech-Air Inc	Scarborough	ME	C	207 347-7577	5439
Trane US Inc	Westbrook	ME	F	844 807-2282	5652
Hussmann Corporation	Salem	NH	E	603 893-7770	15538
Precision Temperature Control	Jaffrey	NH	G	603 471-9023	14576
Tracs Industrial Coolers	Ossipee	NH	C	603 707-2241	15284
Amtrol Intl Investments Inc (DH)	West Warwick	RI	F	401 884-6300	16901
Nasons Ug Inc (PA)	Middletown	RI	F	401 847-2497	16180
Trane US Inc	Riverside	RI	E	617 908-6710	16660
Trane Company	Williston	VT	G	802 864-3816	17750

REFRIGERATION EQPT & SPLYS WHOLESALERS

	CITY	ST	EMP	PHONE	ENTRY#
Mv3 LLC	Buzzards Bay	MA	G	617 658-4420	7455

REFRIGERATION EQPT & SPLYS, WHOLESALE: Ice Making Machines

	CITY	ST	EMP	PHONE	ENTRY#
Bev-Tech Inc	Eliot	ME	F	207 439-8061	4749

REFRIGERATION EQPT: Complete

	CITY	ST	EMP	PHONE	ENTRY#
Demartino Fixture Co Inc	Windsor	CT	F	203 628-4899	4270
Aipco Inc	Taunton	MA	E	508 823-7003	12316
Munters USA Inc	Amesbury	MA	A	978 241-1100	5847
Watka Corporation	Lakeville	MA	F	508 946-5555	9523
Standex International Corp (PA)	Salem	NH	E	603 893-9701	15563
Standex International Corp	Essex Junction	VT	F	864 963-3471	17247

REFRIGERATION REPAIR SVCS

	CITY	ST	EMP	PHONE	ENTRY#
Watka Corporation	Lakeville	MA	F	508 946-5555	9523
Hussmann Corporation	Salem	NH	E	603 893-7770	15538

REFUSE SYSTEMS

	CITY	ST	EMP	PHONE	ENTRY#
MJ Metal Inc	Bridgeport	CT	E	203 334-3484	348
Copley Global Services LLC	Waltham	MA	G	617 970-9617	12641
Garbage Gone Inc	Barnstable	MA	C	508 737-4995	6200
Harding Metals Inc	Northwood	NH	E	603 942-5573	15273

REGULATORS: Line Voltage

	CITY	ST	EMP	PHONE	ENTRY#
Neeltran Inc	New Milford	CT	C	860 350-5964	2254

RELAYS & SWITCHES: Indl, Electric

	CITY	ST	EMP	PHONE	ENTRY#
Kenneth Crosby Co Inc	Hopkinton	MA	F	508 497-0048	9335

RELAYS: Electric Power

	CITY	ST	EMP	PHONE	ENTRY#
Coto Technology Inc	North Kingstown	RI	B	401 943-2686	16242

RELIGIOUS SPLYS WHOLESALERS

	CITY	ST	EMP	PHONE	ENTRY#
A W McMullen Co Inc	Brockton	MA	F	508 583-2072	7251
McVan Inc	Attleboro	MA	F	508 431-2400	6036
William J Hirten Co LLC	Attleboro	MA	F	401 334-5370	6076

REMOVERS & CLEANERS

	CITY	ST	EMP	PHONE	ENTRY#
Handyscape LLC	Southington	CT	G	860 318-1067	3215
Altri Junk Removal Services	Revere	MA	E	781 629-2500	11616

REMOVERS: Paint

	CITY	ST	EMP	PHONE	ENTRY#
The Savogran Company	Norwood	MA	E	781 762-5400	11216

RENTAL SVCS: Aircraft

	CITY	ST	EMP	PHONE	ENTRY#
Aircastle Advisor LLC	Stamford	CT	D	203 504-1020	3276

RENTAL SVCS: Audio-Visual Eqpt & Sply

	CITY	ST	EMP	PHONE	ENTRY#
Boston Light & Sound Inc (PA)	Malden	MA	F	617 787-3131	10005

RENTAL SVCS: Business Machine & Electronic Eqpt

	CITY	ST	EMP	PHONE	ENTRY#
Pitney Bowes Inc (PA)	Stamford	CT	A	203 356-5000	3433
Quadient Inc (DH)	Milford	CT	C	203 301-3400	1874
Doble Engineering Company (HQ)	Marlborough	MA	F	617 926-4900	10145

RENTAL SVCS: Sound & Lighting Eqpt

	CITY	ST	EMP	PHONE	ENTRY#
Audiospectrum Inc	Randolph	MA	E	781 767-1331	11549
Limelight Productions Inc	Lee	MA	E	413 243-4950	9616

RENTAL SVCS: Tent & Tarpaulin

	CITY	ST	EMP	PHONE	ENTRY#
3333 LLC	Manchester	CT	G	860 643-1384	1579
Tent Connection Inc	Northbridge	MA	G	508 234-8746	11119
Leavitt & Parris Inc	Portland	ME	F	207 797-0100	5233
Maine Bay Canvas Inc	Portland	ME	F	207 878-8888	5237

RENTAL SVCS: Work Zone Traffic Eqpt, Flags, Cones, Etc

	CITY	ST	EMP	PHONE	ENTRY#
Visi-Flash Rentals Eastern	West Bridgewater	MA	E	508 583-9100	12988
Sonco Worldwide Inc	Warwick	RI	F	401 406-3761	16863

RENTAL: Portable Toilet

	CITY	ST	EMP	PHONE	ENTRY#
United Site Services Inc (PA)	Westborough	MA	C	508 594-2655	13141

RENTAL: Video Tape & Disc

	CITY	ST	EMP	PHONE	ENTRY#
Cataki International Inc	Wareham	MA	F	508 295-9630	12833

REPRODUCTION SVCS: Video Tape Or Disk

	CITY	ST	EMP	PHONE	ENTRY#
Cine Magnetics Inc (HQ)	Stamford	CT	D	914 273-7600	3312
Play-It Productions Inc	Colchester	CT	F	212 695-6530	663

RESEARCH & DEVELOPMENT SVCS, COMMERCIAL: Engineering Lab

	CITY	ST	EMP	PHONE	ENTRY#
Perspecta Svcs & Solutions Inc (DH)	Waltham	MA	G	781 684-4000	12747
Electro Standards Lab Inc	Cranston	RI	D	401 946-1164	15853
Applied Research Assoc Inc	Randolph	VT	E	802 728-4588	17467

RESEARCH, DEVELOPMENT & TESTING SVCS, COMM: Agricultural

	CITY	ST	EMP	PHONE	ENTRY#
Wjb Associates Inc	Mount Vernon	ME	G	207 293-2457	5078

RESEARCH, DEVELOPMENT & TESTING SVCS, COMMERCIAL: Business

	CITY	ST	EMP	PHONE	ENTRY#
Sonalysts Inc (PA)	Waterford	CT	B	860 442-4355	3997
Vitek Research Corporation	Naugatuck	CT	F	203 735-1813	1992
Continuus Pharmaceuticals Inc	Woburn	MA	F	781 281-0115	13548
T & D Specialties Inc	Oxford	MA	E	508 987-8344	11265

RESEARCH, DEVELOPMENT & TESTING SVCS, COMMERCIAL: Energy

	CITY	ST	EMP	PHONE	ENTRY#
Frc Founders Corporation (PA)	Stamford	CT	E	203 661-6601	3348
Precision Combustion Inc	North Haven	CT	E	203 287-3700	2432
Advent Technologies Inc (PA)	Boston	MA	F	617 655-6000	6519
Spire Solar Inc (HQ)	Bedford	MA	G	781 275-6000	6271

RESEARCH, DEVELOPMENT & TESTING SVCS, COMMERCIAL: Medical

	CITY	ST	EMP	PHONE	ENTRY#
Lambda Investors LLC	Greenwich	CT	F	203 862-7000	1337
Pfizer Inc	Groton	CT	C	860 441-4100	1379
Ariad Pharmaceuticals Inc	Cambridge	MA	B		7490
Brammer Bio Holding Co LLC (HQ)	Cambridge	MA	E	386 418-8199	7523
Checkmate Pharmaceuticals Inc	Cambridge	MA	E	617 682-3625	7539
Ginger Acquisition Inc	Boston	MA	B	617 551-4000	6760
Kaleido Biosciences Inc (PA)	Lexington	MA	D	617 674-9000	9755
Radius Health Inc (PA)	Boston	MA	B	617 551-4000	6994
Tepha Inc (HQ)	Lexington	MA	D	781 357-1700	9787
Vaso Active Phrmaceuticals Inc	Beverly	MA	G	978 750-1991	6392
Lgc Clinical Diagnostics Inc	Cumberland Foreside	ME	D	207 892-1300	4712
Bio-Concept Laboratories Inc	Salem	NH	E	603 437-4990	15510
Pace Anlytical Lf Sciences LLC	Salem	NH	E	603 437-4990	15555

RESEARCH, DEVELOPMENT & TESTING SVCS, COMMERCIAL: Physical

	CITY	ST	EMP	PHONE	ENTRY#
Cambrdge RES Instrmntation Inc	Hopkinton	MA	E	781 935-9099	9311
CPI Radant Tech Div Inc (DH)	Stow	MA	D	978 562-3866	12245
Ferro Corporation	Williamstown	MA	F	413 743-3927	13366
Gentex Corporation	Boston	MA	F	617 670-3547	6755
Hood E Benson Laboratories	Pembroke	MA	F	781 826-7573	11367
Leidos Inc	Tewksbury	MA	G	781 221-7627	12402
Millennium Pharmaceuticals Inc	Cambridge	MA	C	617 679-7000	7647
Mra Laboratories Inc	Adams	MA	F	413 743-3927	5774
Physical Sciences Inc (PA)	Andover	MA	D	978 689-0003	5907
Thermo Power Corporation	Waltham	MA	A	781 622-1400	12802
Veranova LP (HQ)	Devens	MA	C	484 581-0149	8288
Veranova LP	North Andover	MA	E	978 784-5000	10857
Mikros Technologies LLC	Claremont	NH	E	603 690-2020	14094
Leidos Inc	Middletown	RI	E	401 849-8900	16178

RESEARCH, DEVELOPMENT SVCS, COMMERCIAL: Indl Lab

	CITY	ST	EMP	PHONE	ENTRY#
Integral Technologies Inc (DH)	Enfield	CT	G	860 741-2281	1136
Metal Casting Technology Inc	Milford	NH	E	603 673-9720	15033
Xstrata Recycling Inc	East Providence	RI	E	401 438-9220	16049

RESINS: Custom Compound Purchased

	CITY	ST	EMP	PHONE	ENTRY#
Byk USA Inc	North Haven	CT	E	475 234-5317	2395
Foster Corporation (HQ)	Putnam	CT	E	860 928-4102	2855
Foster Corporation	Putnam	CT	E	860 377-7117	2856
Neu Spclty Engineered Mtls LLC	North Haven	CT	F	203 239-9629	2426
Pioneer Plastics Corporation (HQ)	Shelton	CT	E	203 925-1556	3047
Ercon Inc	Wareham	MA	E	508 291-1400	12835
Mexichem Spcalty Compounds Inc (HQ)	Leominster	MA	C	978 537-8071	9683
Shield Packaging Co Inc	Dudley	MA	E	508 949-0900	8323
Teknor Apex Company	Leominster	MA	E	978 534-1010	9708
Pioneer Plastics Corporation	Auburn	ME	C	207 784-9111	4454
New Hampshire Stamping Co Inc	Goffstown	NH	E	603 641-1234	14352
Elite Custom Compounding Inc	Warwick	RI	G	401 921-2136	16813
Teknor Apex Company (PA)	Pawtucket	RI	A	401 725-8000	16420

RESISTORS & RESISTOR UNITS

	CITY	ST	EMP	PHONE	ENTRY#
RLB Industries Inc	Attleboro	MA	D	508 226-3350	6057
Elscott Manufacturing LLC (PA)	Gouldsboro	ME	E	207 422-6747	4839
Anaren Ceramics Inc	Salem	NH	D	603 898-2883	15505

RESTAURANT EQPT: Carts

	CITY	ST	EMP	PHONE	ENTRY#
Vermont Culinary Islands LLC	Brattleboro	VT	F	802 246-2277	17104

RESTAURANT EQPT: Sheet Metal

	CITY	ST	EMP	PHONE	ENTRY#
American Marketing Intl LLC	Clinton	CT	E	860 669-4100	635

RESTAURANTS: Fast Food

	CITY	ST	EMP	PHONE	ENTRY#
Orono House of Pizza	Orono	ME	F	207 866-5505	5135

RESTAURANTS:Full Svc, American

	CITY	ST	EMP	PHONE	ENTRY#
Krystal Inc LLC	Granby	CT	G	860 844-1267	1307
Highlands Lunchette	Fall River	MA	G	508 674-6206	8561
Debra Rivest Ltd	Keene	NH	E	603 355-3335	14595
Whetstone Stn Rest Brewry LLC (PA)	Brattleboro	VT	E	802 490-2354	17109

RETAIL BAKERY: Bagels

	CITY	ST	EMP	PHONE	ENTRY#
Bagel Works Inc	Amherst	MA	F	413 835-0561	5860
Driscolls Restaurant	Mansfield	MA	G	508 261-1574	10050
Ginsco Inc (PA)	Fall River	MA	F	508 677-4767	8554
Korner Bagel Partnership	Seekonk	MA	G	508 336-5204	11779
Loxsmith Bagel Corporation	Dover	NH	F	603 362-9060	14233
Bristol Bagel Works Ltd	Bristol	RI	F	401 254-1390	15756

RETAIL BAKERY: Bread

	CITY	ST	EMP	PHONE	ENTRY#
Amoun Pita & Distribution LLC	South Windsor	CT	F	866 239-9990	3114
Apicellas Bakery Inc	New Haven	CT	E	203 865-6204	2116
Oasis Coffee Corp	Norwalk	CT	G	203 847-0554	2547
Iggys Bread Ltd (PA)	Cambridge	MA	D	617 491-7600	7610
Superior Baking Co Inc	Brockton	MA	E	508 586-6601	7310
Franks Bake Shop Inc	Bangor	ME	G	207 947-4594	4502
Italian Bakery Products Co	Lewiston	ME	F	207 782-8312	4967
Crosby Bakery Inc	Nashua	NH	F	603 882-1851	15086
Queen Dog LLC	Burlington	VT	F	802 660-2733	17154

RETAIL BAKERY: Cakes

	CITY	ST	EMP	PHONE	ENTRY#
Modern Pastry Shop Inc	Hartford	CT	G	860 296-7628	1494
Mozzicato Pastry & Bake Sp Inc	Hartford	CT	E	860 296-0426	1495
La Patisserie Inc	Revere	MA	F	781 729-9441	11621

RETAIL BAKERY: Cookies

	CITY	ST	EMP	PHONE	ENTRY#
Boston Chipyard The Inc	Boston	MA	E	617 742-9537	6607

RETAIL BAKERY: Doughnuts

	CITY	ST	EMP	PHONE	ENTRY#
DAndrea Corporation (PA)	West Haven	CT	G	203 932-6000	4101
Realejo Donuts Inc	Portland	CT	F	860 342-5120	2822
Whole Donut	Enfield	CT	F	860 745-3041	1159
D D J	Oxford	MA	F	508 987-0417	11251
Depot Donuts Inc	North Easton	MA	F	508 230-2888	11009
Dunkin Donuts of Methuen	Methuen	MA	G	978 681-8123	10328
Hole In One	Eastham	MA	F	508 255-5359	8434
Kookla Inc	Southbridge	MA	F	508 765-0442	12025
Kookla Inc (PA)	Sturbridge	MA	E	508 347-2623	12251
Lori Donuts Inc	East Longmeadow	MA	E	413 526-9944	8384
Donut Hole Inc	Buxton	ME	F	207 929-5060	4662
Dunkin Donuts (PA)	Auburn	ME	E	207 783-0408	4427
Holy Donut Inc (PA)	Portland	ME	E	207 761-7775	5223
Tonys Donut Shop	Portland	ME	G	207 772-2727	5285
A & M Donuts Inc	Plymouth	NH	E	603 536-7622	15354
ANM Donuts Inc	Tilton	NH	E	603 286-2770	15651
Manco LLC	Allenstown	NH	G	603 485-5327	13852
Dunkin Donuts	Warwick	RI	F	401 822-2434	16810

RETAIL BAKERY: Pastries

	CITY	ST	EMP	PHONE	ENTRY#
Fredericks Pastries (PA)	Amherst	NH	F	603 882-7725	13871

RETAIL STORES: Alcoholic Beverage Making Eqpt & Splys

	CITY	ST	EMP	PHONE	ENTRY#
Universal Color Corp Inc	Wilmington	MA	F	978 658-2300	13473
Walgreen Co	North Attleboro	MA	F	781 244-9431	10892
D R Designs Inc	Manchester	ME	G	207 622-3303	5044

RETAIL STORES: Artificial Limbs

	CITY	ST	EMP	PHONE	ENTRY#
Maine Artfl Limb Orthotics Co	Portland	ME	F	207 773-4963	5236

RETAIL STORES: Audio-Visual Eqpt & Splys

	CITY	ST	EMP	PHONE	ENTRY#
Ion Audio LLC (HQ)	Cumberland	RI	F	401 658-3743	15947

RETAIL STORES: Business Machines & Eqpt

	CITY	ST	EMP	PHONE	ENTRY#
Automatic Press Inc	Franklin	MA	G	508 528-2000	8818

RETAIL STORES: Communication Eqpt

	CITY	ST	EMP	PHONE	ENTRY#
Motorola Mobility LLC	Lowell	MA	E	978 614-2900	9910

RETAIL STORES: Concrete Prdts, Precast

	CITY	ST	EMP	PHONE	ENTRY#
Washington Concrete Pdts Inc	Plainville	CT	F	860 747-5242	2788

RETAIL STORES: Cosmetics

	CITY	ST	EMP	PHONE	ENTRY#
Bella Grace LLC	Fairfield	CT	E	929 533-2343	1177

RETAIL STORES: Decals

	CITY	ST	EMP	PHONE	ENTRY#
Flag Fables Inc	Springfield	MA	E	413 747-0525	12095

RETAIL STORES: Electronic Parts & Eqpt

	CITY	ST	EMP	PHONE	ENTRY#
Carey Manufacturing Co Inc	Cromwell	CT	F	860 829-1803	689
East Cast McRwave Sls Dist LLC	Woburn	MA	E	781 279-0900	13562
Tech180 Corp	Easthampton	MA	F	413 203-6123	8463

RETAIL STORES: Flags

	CITY	ST	EMP	PHONE	ENTRY#
Flagman of America LLC	Avon	CT	G	860 678-0275	24
Accent Banner LLC	Medford	MA	F	781 391-7300	10278

RETAIL STORES: Foam & Foam Prdts

	CITY	ST	EMP	PHONE	ENTRY#
Foam Systems LLC	Norwalk	CT	G	800 853-1577	2502

RETAIL STORES: Hair Care Prdts

	CITY	ST	EMP	PHONE	ENTRY#
Grooming Ventures - FL LLC (HQ)	Boston	MA	D	305 593-0667	6774

RETAIL STORES: Ice

	CITY	ST	EMP	PHONE	ENTRY#
Eastern Ice Company Inc	Fall River	MA	E	508 672-1800	8538
Leominster Ice Company Inc	Leominster	MA	G	978 537-5322	9678
Getchell Bros Inc	Sanford	ME	F	207 490-0809	5397

RETAIL STORES: Medical Apparatus & Splys

	CITY	ST	EMP	PHONE	ENTRY#
Kent Scientific Corporation	Torrington	CT	F	860 626-1172	3688
Inert Corporation	Amesbury	MA	E	978 462-4415	5837

RETAIL STORES: Orthopedic & Prosthesis Applications

	CITY	ST	EMP	PHONE	ENTRY#
Biomedic Appliances Inc	Essex Junction	VT	G	802 878-0930	17228
Yankee Medical Inc (DH)	Burlington	VT	F	802 863-4591	17164

RETAIL STORES: Pet Splys

	CITY	ST	EMP	PHONE	ENTRY#
Clean Run Productions LLC	South Hadley	MA	F	413 532-1389	11960
Smartpak Equine LLC (DH)	Plymouth	MA	D	774 773-1100	11478
Rhode Island Textile Company (PA)	Cumberland	RI	C	401 722-3700	15963

P
R
O
D
U
C
T

	CITY	ST	EMP	PHONE	ENTRY#

RETAIL STORES: Religious Goods

	CITY	ST	EMP	PHONE	ENTRY#
Fred F Waltz Co Inc	Cumberland	RI	G	401 769-4900	15940

RETAIL STORES: Safety Splys & Eqpt

Ecu & US International	East Hartford	CT	F	860 906-3390	991
Sperian Protection Usa Inc (DH)	Smithfield	RI	E	401 232-1200	16731

RETAIL STORES: Telephone & Communication Eqpt

Northastern Communications Inc	Stratford	CT	F	203 381-9008	3558

RETAIL STORES: Water Purification Eqpt

American Water Systems LLC	Canton	MA	F	781 830-9722	7767
Atlas Water Systems Inc	Waltham	MA	D	781 373-4700	12597
Bluedrop LLC	South Easton	MA	F	877 662-7873	11938
H2o Care Inc	Middleton	MA	F	978 777-8330	10384

RETAIL STORES: Welding Splys

Linde Gas & Equipment Inc (DH)	Danbury	CT	F	844 445-4633	775
Linde Gas & Equipment Inc	Slatersville	RI	D	401 767-3450	16682

REUPHOLSTERY & FURNITURE REPAIR

Bonito Manufacturing Inc	North Haven	CT	D	203 234-8786	2394
Canner Incorporated	West Groton	MA	F	978 448-3063	13001
Columbia ASC Inc	Lawrence	MA	F	978 683-2205	9554
Conklin Office Services Inc (PA)	Holyoke	MA	E	413 315-4924	9248

RIBBONS, NEC

Graco Awards Manufacturing Inc	Providence	RI	F	281 255-2161	16527

RIVETS: Metal

Edson Manufacturing Inc	Wolcott	CT	F	203 879-1411	4364
Howard Engineering LLC	Naugatuck	CT	E	203 729-5213	1963
Nucap US Inc (DH)	Wolcott	CT	F	203 879-1423	4371
Alcoa Global Fasteners Inc	Stoughton	MA	C	412 553-4545	12192

ROBOTS: Assembly Line

Act Robots Inc	Bristol	CT	G	860 314-1557	392
Balyo Inc (HQ)	Woburn	MA	G	781 281-7957	13519
Barrett Technology LLC	Newton	MA	E	617 252-9000	10737
Barrett Technology Inc	Newtonville	MA	E	617 252-9000	10796
Berkshire Grey Inc (PA)	Bedford	MA	E	833 848-9900	6214
Corindus Inc (HQ)	Auburndale	MA	E	508 653-3335	6131
Irobot Corporation (PA)	Bedford	MA	B	781 430-3000	6235
Locus Robotics Corp (PA)	Wilmington	MA	F	844 562-8700	13426
Persimmon Technologies Corp	Wakefield	MA	F	781 587-0677	12527
Soft Robotics Inc	Bedford	MA	D	617 391-0612	6269
Teledyne Flir Unmnned Grund Sy (DH)	Chelmsford	MA	F	978 769-9333	7964
Wrabacon Inc	Oakland	ME	F	207 465-2068	5122
Devprotek Inc	Hollis	NH	G	603 577-5557	14449
JP Sercel Associates Inc	Manchester	NH	E	603 595-7048	14869

RODS: Steel & Iron, Made In Steel Mills

CMI Specialty Products Inc	Bristol	CT	F	860 585-0409	429
Nucor Steel Connecticut Inc	Wallingford	CT	C	203 265-0615	3836
Rivinius & Sons Inc	Woburn	MA	F	781 933-5620	13653

ROLL FORMED SHAPES: Custom

Ingenven Flrplymer Sltions LLC	Hampton	NH	F	603 601-0877	14403

ROLLED OR DRAWN SHAPES, NEC: Copper & Copper Alloy

Aimtek Inc (PA)	Auburn	MA	E	508 832-5035	6099

ROLLING MILL MACHINERY

Adam Z Golas (PA)	New Britain	CT	G	860 224-7178	1996
Compass Group Management LLC (PA)	Westport	CT	F	203 221-1703	4162
Ulbrich Stainless Steels	Wallingford	CT	C	203 269-2507	3871
Kinefac Corporation	Worcester	MA	D	508 754-6901	13749
N Ferrara Inc	Somerset	MA	F	508 679-2440	11853
Pfe Rolls Inc	Chicopee	MA	F	978 544-7803	8053
Winchester Precision Tech Ltd	Winchester	NH	F	603 239-6326	15718
Millard Wire Company	Warwick	RI	F	401 737-9330	16837
Millard Wire Company (PA)	Warwick	RI	E	401 737-9330	16838

ROLLING MILL ROLLS: Cast Steel

Tenova Inc	Wallingford	CT	E	203 265-5684	3859

ROLLS & BLANKETS, PRINTERS': Rubber Or Rubberized Fabric

Patten Machine Inc	Hudson	MA	F	978 562-9847	9399

ROOFING MATERIALS: Asphalt

Harvey Industries LLC	Springfield	MA	E	413 731-7700	12099

	CITY	ST	EMP	PHONE	ENTRY#
Harvey Industries LLC (PA)	Waltham	MA	C	800 598-5400	12691
Harvey Industries Inc	Augusta	ME	F	207 629-3737	4472

ROOFING MEMBRANE: Rubber

JPS Elastomerics Corp	Easthampton	MA	C	413 779-1200	8448
Cooley Incorporated (HQ)	Pawtucket	RI	C	401 724-9000	16357
Cooley Group Holdings Inc (PA)	Pawtucket	RI	C	401 724-0510	16358

RUBBER PRDTS: Appliance, Mechanical

Saint-Gobain Prfmce Plas Corp	Worcester	MA	C	508 852-3072	13792
Etco Incorporated (PA)	Warwick	RI	C	401 467-2400	16815
Moore Company	Westerly	RI	E	401 596-2816	16939
Garware Fulflex USA Inc	Brattleboro	VT	C	802 257-5256	17085

RUBBER PRDTS: Automotive, Mechanical

Greene Rubber Company Inc (PA)	Woburn	MA	D	781 937-9909	13577

RUBBER PRDTS: Medical & Surgical Tubing, Extrudd & Lathe-Cut

Htp Meds LLC	Ashaway	RI	C	401 315-0654	15742

RUBBER PRDTS: Silicone

Rbc Industries Inc	Cranston	RI	D	401 941-3000	15906

RUBBER PRDTS: Sponge

Griswold LLC	Moosup	CT	E	845 986-2271	1930
Expanded Rubber Products Inc (PA)	Sanford	ME	E	207 324-8226	5395

RUBBER STRUCTURES: Air-Supported

Gs Rubber Industries LLC	Coventry	RI	F	508 672-0742	15814
LK Goodwin Co Inc (PA)	West Greenwich	RI	F	401 781-5526	16888

RUGS : Hand & Machine Made

Flemish Master Weavers Inc	Sanford	ME	C	207 324-6600	5396
Colonial Mills Inc	Rumford	RI	D	401 724-6279	16665

RUST RESISTING

King Industries Inc (PA)	Norwalk	CT	C	203 866-5551	2523

SAFE DEPOSIT BOXES

Yarde Metals Inc (HQ)	Southington	CT	B	860 406-6061	3241

SAFES & VAULTS: Metal

Cvc II Inc (DH)	Bethel	CT	D	203 401-4205	105
Jaco Inc	Franklin	MA	C	508 553-1000	8844

SAFETY EQPT & SPLYS WHOLESALERS

Ecu & US International	East Hartford	CT	F	860 906-3390	991
New England Industrial Sup LLC	Newington	CT	F	860 436-5959	2308
Blauer Manufacturing Co Inc (PA)	Boston	MA	E	800 225-6715	6597
Spector Textile Products Inc (PA)	Lawrence	MA	E	978 688-3501	9600

SALES PROMOTION SVCS

Fairfield Marketing Group Inc (PA)	Easton	CT	F	203 261-0884	1095
Sales Solutions Inc	Scituate	MA	G	781 588-2703	11771
Zajac LLC	Saco	ME	E	207 286-9100	5384
Country Home Products Inc	Charlotte	VT	E	802 771-7202	17175

SALT

Salt & Pepper	Worcester	MA	F	508 755-1113	13793

SAND & GRAVEL

Adelman Sand & Gravel Inc	Bozrah	CT	F	860 889-3394	226
Dan Beard Inc	Shelton	CT	E	203 924-4346	2996
Desiato Sand & Gravel Corp	Storrs Mansfield	CT	E	860 429-6479	3512
Galasso Materials LLC	East Granby	CT	C	860 527-1825	934
Garf Trucking Inc	Windsor	CT	G	860 558-8487	4277
Midwood Quarry and Cnstr Inc (PA)	East Hartford	CT	F	860 289-1414	1006
Monroe Recycl & Aggregates LLC	Monroe	CT	G	203 644-7748	1917
O & G Industries Inc	Stamford	CT	D	203 323-1111	3422
Rawson Development Inc	Putnam	CT	F	860 928-4536	2872
Skyline Quarry LLC	Stafford Springs	CT	F	860 875-3580	3259
Thomas Keegan & Sons Inc	Wallingford	CT	F	203 239-9248	3862
Tradebe Treatment and Recycling Northeast LLC (DH) 203 238-8102	Meriden 1710	CT			D
Valley Sand & Gravel Corp	North Haven	CT	F	203 562-3192	2443
Attleboro Sand & Gravel Corp	Attleboro	MA	F	508 222-2870	5995
B R S Inc	Bridgewater	MA	E	508 697-5448	7221
Benevento Asphalt Corp	Wilmington	MA	F	978 658-5300	13391
Benevento Sand & Stone Corp	Wilmington	MA	F	978 658-4762	13392
Berkshire Concrete Corp (HQ)	Pittsfield	MA	E	413 443-4734	11392
Colrain Sand and Gravel Inc	Colrain	MA	F	413 624-5118	8095
Construction Source MGT LLC	Raynham	MA	F	508 484-5100	11585

	CITY	ST	EMP	PHONE	ENTRY#
Delta Sand and Gravel Inc	Sunderland	MA	F	413 665-4051	12273
Gravel Public House	Wrentham	MA	F	508 384-0888	13842
J G Maclellan Con Co Inc (PA)	Lowell	MA	D	978 458-1223	9888
Lakeside Management Corp	Plainville	MA	G	508 695-3252	11435
Lane Construction Corporation	Northfield	MA	D	413 498-5586	11120
Longfin LLC	Nantucket	MA	F	508 228-4266	10465
New England Gravel Haulers	Rehoboth	MA	G	508 922-4518	11612
New England Sand & Grav Co Inc	Framingham	MA	F	508 877-2460	8791
Northeast Sand & Gravel	North Andover	MA	G	603 213-6133	10845
P A Landers Inc (PA)	Hanover	MA	C	781 826-8818	9038
P A Landers Inc	Hanover	MA	F	508 747-1800	9039
Petricca Industries Inc (PA)	Pittsfield	MA	E	413 499-1441	11418
Powell Stone & Gravel Co Inc (PA)	Lunenburg	MA	F	978 537-8100	9959
Pro Touch Home Improvement Inc	Peabody	MA	F	617 378-1929	11336
Sanger Equipment Corporation	Conway	MA	F	413 625-8304	8145
Southeastern Sand and Grav Inc	Kingston	MA	G	781 413-6884	9512
WJ Graves Cnstr Co Inc (PA)	East Templeton	MA	E	978 939-5568	8416
Worcester Sand and Grav Co Inc	Shrewsbury	MA	E	508 852-1683	11849
Dayton Sand & Gravel Inc	Dayton	ME	D	207 499-2306	4720
Dragon Products Company LLC (DH)	Biddeford	ME	E	207 594-5555	4560
Dragon Products Company LLC	Thomaston	ME	E	207 594-5555	5544
Earl W Gerrish & Sons	Brownville	ME	F	207 965-2171	4637
F R Carroll Inc	Limerick	ME	F	207 793-8615	5001
Hermon Sand & Gravel LLC	Hermon	ME	F	207 848-5977	4883
Hughes Brothers Inc	Hampden	ME	E	207 659-3417	4864
J and L Sand	Lyman	ME	G	207 499-2545	5029
K W Aggregates	Denmark	ME	G	207 452-8888	4723
Lane Construction Corporation	Bangor	ME	B	207 945-0850	4508
McQuade Tidd Industries	Houlton	ME	F	207 532-2675	4901
P & K Sand and Gravel Inc	Naples	ME	F	207 693-6765	5081
State Sand & Gravel Co Inc	Belfast	ME	F	207 338-4070	4538
Sunny Side Land Holdings LLC	Presque Isle	ME	F	207 768-1020	5310
A B Excavating Inc	Lancaster	NH	E	603 788-5110	14675
Benevento Aggregates LLC	Loudon	NH	E	603 783-4723	14793
Big Foote Crushing LLC	Weare	NH	E	603 345-0695	15669
Columbia Sand & Gravel Inc	Colebrook	NH	G	603 237-5729	14103
Gorham Sand & Gravel	Gorham	NH	G	603 466-2291	14359
Granite State Concrete Co Inc	Milford	NH	F	603 673-3327	15023
Northeast Earth Mechanics LLC	Pittsfield	NH	E	603 435-7989	15334
Northeast Sand and Gravel LLC	Merrimack	NH	G	603 305-9429	14995
Pike Industries Inc	Portsmouth	NH	G	603 436-4432	15429
Powell Stone Gravel	Brookline	NH	G	603 673-8100	14040
Twin State Sand & Grav Co Inc	West Lebanon	NH	G	603 298-8705	15691
George Sherman Sand Grav Inc	Wakefield	RI	E	401 789-6304	16741
Richmond Sand & Stone LLC	Richmond	RI	F	401 539-7770	16651
Calkins Rock Products Inc	Lyndonville	VT	G	802 626-5755	17317
Calkins Sand & Gravel Inc	Newport	VT	F	802 334-8418	17397
Cersosimo Industries Inc (PA)	Brattleboro	VT	D	802 254-4500	17080
Dale E Percy Inc	Stowe	VT	F	802 253-8503	17630
Frank W Whitcomb Cnstr Corp	Colchester	VT	D	802 655-1270	17191
Gurney Brothers Construction	North Springfield	VT	E	802 886-2210	17421
H A Manosh Corp	Morrisville	VT	D	802 888-5722	17383
Hinesburg Sand & Gravel Co Inc	Hinesburg	VT	E	802 482-2335	17294
Orwell Sand & Gravel	Benson	VT	G	802 345-6028	17059

SAND MINING

Brennan Realty LLC (PA)	Shelton	CT	C	203 929-6314	2987
Tronox LLC (PA)	Stamford	CT	F	203 705-3800	3487
Varney Bros Sand & Gravel Inc	Bellingham	MA	F	508 966-1313	6302
Michie Corporation	Henniker	NH	D	603 428-7426	14438
Joseph P Carrara & Sons Inc (PA)	North Clarendon	VT	E	802 775-2301	17415

SANITARY SVCS: Hazardous Waste, Collection & Disposal

Veolia Es Tchncal Slutions LLC	Danbury	CT	F	203 748-9116	832
Onyx Environmental Svcs LLC (DH)	Boston	MA	E	617 849-6600	6936
Coating Systems Inc	Nashua	NH	G	603 883-0553	15082

SANITARY SVCS: Oil Spill Cleanup

Spilldam Environmental Inc	Brockton	MA	F	508 583-7850	7309

SANITARY SVCS: Refuse Collection & Disposal Svcs

City Carting Inc	Stamford	CT	D	888 413-3344	3313

SANITARY SVCS: Rubbish Collection & Disposal

Lostocco Refuse Service LLC	Danbury	CT	E	203 748-9296	779
Zwitterco Inc	Woburn	MA	E	301 442-5662	13693

SANITARY SVCS: Waste Materials, Recycling

G & G Beverage Distributors	Yalesville	CT	E	203 949-6220	4397
Seaview Plastic Recycling Inc	Bridgeport	CT	F	203 367-0070	370
Tradebe Treatment and Recycling Northeast LLC (DH)	Meriden	CT	D	203 238-8102	1710

	CITY	ST	EMP	PHONE	ENTRY#
American Recycled Mtls Inc	Holliston	MA	G	508 429-1455	9199
Blacksmith Shop Farms Inc	East Falmouth	MA	G	508 548-7714	8357
Divert Inc (PA)	Concord	MA	E	978 341-5430	8113
Northstar Pulp & Paper Co Inc	Springfield	MA	D	413 263-6000	12118
Ondrick Materials & Recycl LLC	Chicopee	MA	E	413 592-2566	8052
Safety-Kleen Systems Inc (HQ)	Norwell	MA	B	800 669-5740	11146
Ted Ondrick Company LLC (PA)	Chicopee	MA	F	413 592-2565	8062
Wte Recycling Inc	Greenfield	MA	F	413 772-2200	9007
Max Cohen & Sons Inc (HQ)	Concord	NH	E	603 224-3532	14144
Compost Plant L3c	Providence	RI	F	844 741-4653	16503
P M Recycling	Woonsocket	RI	E	401 765-0330	16970
Earth Waste Systems Inc (PA)	Rutland	VT	E	802 775-7722	17494

SASHES: Door Or Window, Metal

Liberty Glass and Met Inds Inc	North Grosvenordale	CT	E	860 923-3623	2384

SATELLITES: Communications

Accelerated Media Tech Inc	Auburn	MA	E	508 459-0300	6097
Comcast Sportsnet Neng LLC	Needham Heights	MA	D	617 630-5000	10537

SAWMILL MACHINES

Heyes Forest Products Inc	Orange	MA	G	978 544-8801	11223
Downeast Machine & Engrg Inc (PA)	Mechanic Falls	ME	F	207 345-8111	5050
Machinery Service Co Inc	Wiscasset	ME	G	207 882-6788	5698
HMC Corporation (PA)	Hopkinton	NH	E	603 746-3399	14477

SAWS & SAWING EQPT

Gary Raymond	Caribou	ME	G	207 498-2549	4675
Reggies Sales & Service	Auburn	ME	G	207 783-0558	4458
Champlain Valley Equipment Inc	Saint Albans	VT	G	802 524-6782	17518
Leos Small Engines Inc	Morrisville	VT	F	802 888-7247	17384

SCAFFOLDS: Mobile Or Stationary, Metal

DC Scaffold Inc	West Bridgewater	MA	G	508 580-5100	12971
Vanguard Manufacturing Inc	New Ipswich	NH	D	603 878-2083	15200

SCALE REPAIR SVCS

Commercial Scale Balance Inc	Agawam	MA	F	413 789-9990	5787
M & M Scale Company Inc	Danvers	MA	F	781 321-2737	8202

SCALES & BALANCES, EXC LABORATORY

Commercial Scale Balance Inc	Agawam	MA	F	413 789-9990	5787
Highland Labs Inc	Holliston	MA	G	508 429-2918	9215
M & M Scale Company Inc	Danvers	MA	F	781 321-2737	8202
Setra Systems Inc	Boxboro	MA	F	978 263-1400	7145
Public Scales	Lewiston	ME	F	207 784-9466	4986
Edlund Company LLC	Burlington	VT	D	802 862-9661	17133
Tridyne Process Systems Inc	South Burlington	VT	G	802 863-6873	17605

SCALES: Indl

Compuweigh Corporation (PA)	Woodbury	CT	F	203 262-9400	4386
Hasler Inc	Milford	CT	B	203 301-3400	1833
The A H Emery Company (PA)	Seymour	CT	E	203 881-9333	2970
New Bedford Scale Co Inc	New Bedford	MA	G	508 997-6730	10628

SCANNING DEVICES: Optical

Control Module Inc (PA)	Enfield	CT	D	860 745-2433	1125
Dark Field Technologies Inc	Shelton	CT	F	203 298-0731	2997
Scan-Optics LLC	Manchester	CT	D	860 645-7878	1636
Sick Inc	Stoughton	MA	D	781 302-2500	12235
Lantos Technologies Inc	Derry	NH	G	781 443-7633	14198

SCHOOL FOR PHYSICALLY HANDICAPPED, NEC

Perkins School For Blind	Watertown	MA	A	617 924-3434	12899

SCHOOLS: Vocational, NEC

Varian Semicdtr Eqp Assoc Inc	Newburyport	MA	E	978 463-1500	10725

SCIENTIFIC EQPT REPAIR SVCS

JDM Company Inc	North Chelmsford	MA	G	978 251-1121	10979

SCIENTIFIC INSTRUMENTS WHOLESALERS

Bruker Scientific LLC (HQ)	Billerica	MA	A	978 439-9899	6419
Edgeone LLC	West Wareham	MA	G	508 291-0960	13062
Harvard Apparatus Inc	Holliston	MA	D	508 893-8999	9213
Oxford Instruments America Inc (HQ)	Concord	MA	E	978 369-9933	8131
Princton Gamma-Tech Instrs Inc	Franklin	MA	E	609 924-7310	8858
Sage Science Inc	Beverly	MA	F	617 922-1832	6380

SCISSORS: Hand

Acme United Corporation (PA)	Shelton	CT	D	203 254-6060	2978

PRODUCT

	CITY	ST	EMP	PHONE	ENTRY#

SCRAP & WASTE MATERIALS, WHOLESALE: Ferrous Metal

	CITY	ST	EMP	PHONE	ENTRY#
MJ Metal Inc	Bridgeport	CT	E	203 334-3484	348
George Apkin & Sons Inc	Adams	MA	F	413 664-4936	5772

SCRAP & WASTE MATERIALS, WHOLESALE: Junk & Scrap

	CITY	ST	EMP	PHONE	ENTRY#
Maine Metal Recycling Inc	Auburn	ME	F	207 786-3531	4442

SCRAP & WASTE MATERIALS, WHOLESALE: Metal

	CITY	ST	EMP	PHONE	ENTRY#
Wte Recycling Inc	Greenfield	MA	E	413 772-2200	9007
Harding Metals Inc	Northwood	NH	E	603 942-5573	15273
Max Cohen & Sons Inc (HQ)	Concord	NH	E	603 224-3532	14144
Earth Waste Systems Inc (PA)	Rutland	VT	E	802 775-7722	17494

SCRAP & WASTE MATERIALS, WHOLESALE: Paper

	CITY	ST	EMP	PHONE	ENTRY#
Willimantic Waste Paper Co Inc (HQ)	Willimantic	CT	C	860 423-4527	4221
United Paper Stock Co Inc	Worcester	MA	E	401 724-5700	13816
Casella Recycling LLC (HQ)	Scarborough	ME	E	207 883-4600	5427

SCREENS: Window, Metal

	CITY	ST	EMP	PHONE	ENTRY#
Ultimate Windows Inc	Lawrence	MA	G	978 687-9444	9605
Lockheed Archtctral Sltons Inc	Pascoag	RI	C	401 568-3061	16339

SCREW MACHINE PRDTS

	CITY	ST	EMP	PHONE	ENTRY#
Atp Industries LLC (PA)	Plainville	CT	F	860 479-5007	2748
B&T Screw Machine Co Inc	Bristol	CT	F	860 314-4410	402
Bar Work Manufacturing Co Inc	Waterbury	CT	E	203 753-4103	3889
C & A Machine Co Inc	Newington	CT	E	860 667-0605	2278
Cadcom Inc	Milford	CT	F	203 877-0640	1806
Cole S Crew Machine Products	North Haven	CT	E	203 723-1418	2398
Creed 20 LLC	New Britain	CT	G	860 826-4004	2016
Creed Assets Inc	New Britain	CT	B	860 225-7884	2017
Curtis Products LLC	Bristol	CT	F	203 754-4155	433
Dacruz Manufacturing Inc	Bristol	CT	E	860 584-5315	434
Day Machine Systems Inc	New Britain	CT	F	860 229-3440	2020
Devon Precision Industries Inc	Wolcott	CT	D	203 879-1437	4363
Duda and Goodwin Incorporated	Woodbury	CT	F	203 263-4353	4387
Durco Manufacturing Co Inc	Waterbury	CT	G	203 575-0446	3908
Electro-Tech Inc	Cheshire	CT	E	203 271-1976	589
F F Screw Products Inc	Southington	CT	E	860 621-4567	3209
Forestville Machine Company	Plainville	CT	F	860 747-6000	2760
G M T Manufacturing Co Inc	Plantsville	CT	G	860 628-6757	2792
Garmac Screw Machines Inc	Naugatuck	CT	F	203 723-6911	1960
GK Automatics Incorporated	Thomaston	CT	F	860 283-5878	3620
Horst Engineering & Manufacturing Co (PA) 860 289-8209	East Hartford 997	CT			D
J J Ryan Corporation	Plantsville	CT	C	860 628-0393	2793
James Wright Precision Pdts	Putnam	CT	E	860 928-7756	2862
Jay Sons Screw Mch Pdts Inc	Milldale	CT	E	860 621-0141	1901
Kamatics Corporation (DH)	Bloomfield	CT	E	860 243-9704	184
Leipold Inc	Windsor	CT	E	860 298-9791	4286
Mailly Mfg Co Inc	Wolcott	CT	G	203 879-1445	4367
Manufacturers Associates Inc	West Haven	CT	E	203 931-4344	4113
Marvel Screw Machine Pdts Inc	Waterbury	CT	E	203 756-7058	3943
Matthew Warren Inc	Seymour	CT	G	203 888-2133	2964
Microbest Inc	Waterbury	CT	C	203 597-0355	3944
Multi-Metal Manufacturing Inc	Naugatuck	CT	C	203 723-8887	1974
OEM Sources LLC	Milford	CT	G	203 283-5415	1857
Olson Brothers Company	Plainville	CT	F	860 747-6844	2775
P-A-R Precision Inc	Wolcott	CT	F	860 491-4181	4372
Palladin Precision Pdts Inc	Waterbury	CT	E	203 574-0246	3958
Petron Automation Inc	Watertown	CT	E	860 274-9091	4024
Precision Methods Incorporated	Wolcott	CT	F	203 879-1429	4373
Prime Engneered Components Inc	Watertown	CT	D	860 274-6773	4025
Prime Engnred Cmpnnts - Brstol	Bristol	CT	E	860 584-5964	484
Pro-Manufactured Products Inc	Plainfield	CT	G	860 564-2197	2737
Quality Automatics Inc (PA)	Oakville	CT	F	860 945-4795	2625
Rgd Technologies Corp	Bristol	CT	D	860 589-0756	492
Royal Screw Machine Pdts Co	Bristol	CT	F	860 845-8920	495
Selectcom Manufacturing Co Inc	Wolcott	CT	G	203 879-9900	4376
Sga Components Group LLC	Prospect	CT	E	203 758-3702	2842
Sheldon Precision LLC	Prospect	CT	E	203 758-4441	2843
Sperry Automatics Co Inc	Naugatuck	CT	E	203 729-4589	1986
Sun Corp	Morris	CT	G	860 567-0817	1934
Supreme-Lake Mfg Inc	Plantsville	CT	D	860 621-8911	2797
T & A Screw Products Inc	Waterbury	CT	F	203 756-2770	3972
T & J Screw Machine Pdts LLC	Oakville	CT	F	860 417-3801	2627
Thomastn-Mdtown Screw Mch Pdts	Thomaston	CT	F	860 283-9796	3637
Thomaston Industries Inc	Thomaston	CT	F	860 283-4358	3638
Tomz Corporation	Berlin	CT	C	860 829-0670	88
Tremco Swiss Inc	Waterbury	CT	E	203 573-8584	3975
Tri-Star Industries Inc	Seymour	CT	E	860 828-7570	2973

	CITY	ST	EMP	PHONE	ENTRY#
Triem Industries LLC	Terryville	CT	E	203 888-1212	3612
Vigue Holding Company Inc	Plainville	CT	E	860 747-6000	2787
Ville Swiss Automatics Inc	Waterbury	CT	F	203 756-2825	3979
Waterbury Screw Mch Pdts Co	Waterbury	CT	E	203 756-8084	3982
Alpha Grainger Mfg Inc	Franklin	MA	C	508 520-4005	8815
Atc Screw Machine Inc	Haverhill	MA	F	781 939-0725	9075
Automatic Machine Pdts Sls Co	Taunton	MA	E	508 822-4226	12320
Berkmatics Inc	North Adams	MA	F	413 664-6152	10803
Boston Centerless Inc	Avon	MA	E	508 587-3500	6145
Burlington Machine Inc	Wilmington	MA	F	978 284-6525	13396
C F G Corporation	Saugus	MA	F	781 233-6110	11754
Condon Mfg Co Inc	Springfield	MA	E	413 543-1250	12085
Device Technologies Inc	Southborough	MA	E	508 229-2000	11994
E F Inc	Gardner	MA	F	978 630-3800	8885
FC Phillips Inc	Stoughton	MA	E	781 344-9400	12208
Fraen Corporation (PA)	Reading	MA	C	781 205-5300	11601
Geonautics Manufacturing Inc	Newburyport	MA	E	978 462-7161	10685
Louis C Morin Co Inc	North Billerica	MA	E	978 670-1222	10928
Lutco Bearings Inc	Worcester	MA	D	508 756-6296	13754
Marver Med Inc	Stoughton	MA	F	781 341-9372	12221
Mgb Us Inc	Franklin	MA	F	774 415-0060	8851
North Easton Machine Co Inc	North Easton	MA	E	508 238-6219	11011
Plymtron Industries Inc	Plymouth	MA	F	508 746-1126	11473
Rosellis Machine & Mfg Co	Westfield	MA	F	413 562-4317	13203
San-Tron Inc (PA)	Ipswich	MA	D	978 356-1585	9496
Specialized Turning Inc	Peabody	MA	E	978 977-0444	11342
Swissturn/Usa Inc	Oxford	MA	D	508 987-6211	11264
Weber Realty Trust	Auburn	MA	F	508 756-4290	6127
Yankee Hill Machine Co Inc	Easthampton	MA	D	413 584-1400	8464
Arundel Holdings Inc	Arundel	ME	E	207 985-8555	4408
Elmet Technologies Inc	Lewiston	ME	C	207 784-3591	4959
Barco Manufacturing Inc	Tilton	NH	E	603 286-3324	15652
D & E Screw Machine Pdts Inc	Colebrook	NH	E	508 658-7344	14104
Intelitek Inc	Derry	NH	E	800 221-2763	14196
JT Manufacturing Corporation	Pelham	NH	E	603 821-5720	15291
Liberty Research Co Inc (PA)	Rochester	NH	E	603 332-2730	15486
New Hampshire Machine Pdts Inc	Exeter	NH	E	603 772-4404	14297
Omni Components Corp (HQ)	Hudson	NH	C	603 882-4467	14533
Parker & Harper Companies Inc (PA)	Raymond	NH	D	603 895-4761	15455
W H Bagshaw Co Inc	Nashua	NH	E	603 883-7758	15184
Blackhawk Machine Products Inc	Smithfield	RI	E	401 232-7563	16689
Esmond Manufacturing Co Inc	Cranston	RI	G	401 942-9103	15858
Greystone Incorporated	Lincoln	RI	F	401 333-0444	16139
Greystone of Lincoln Inc (PA)	Lincoln	RI	C	401 333-0444	16140
Groov-Pin Corporation (PA)	Smithfield	RI	D	770 251-5054	16707
M F Engineering Company Inc	Bristol	RI	F	401 253-6163	15774
Machinex Company Inc	Smithfield	RI	G	401 231-3230	16723
Moody Machine Products Inc	Providence	RI	G	401 941-5130	16569
Precision Trned Cmponents Corp	Smithfield	RI	D	401 232-3377	16726
Quality Screw Machine Pdts Inc	Smithfield	RI	F	401 231-8900	16727
Rhode Island Precision Co	Providence	RI	F	401 421-6661	16604
Swissline Precision LLC	Cumberland	RI	F	216 362-3814	15964
Wellington Manufacturing Inc	Providence	RI	F	401 461-2248	16645
West Warwick Screw Pdts Co Inc	West Warwick	RI	G	401 821-4729	16925
Lebanon Screw Products Inc	Windsor	VT	F	802 674-6347	17759

SCREWS: Metal

	CITY	ST	EMP	PHONE	ENTRY#
Aerotech Fasteners Inc	Putnam	CT	F	860 928-6300	2845
Crescent Mnfacturing Operating	Burlington	CT	E	860 673-2591	547
L & M Manufacturing Co Inc	New Hartford	CT	F	860 379-2751	2105
Metallics Inc	Bristol	CT	E	860 589-4186	468
Narragansett Screw Co	Winsted	CT	F	860 379-4059	4351
North-East Fasteners Corp	Terryville	CT	E	860 589-3242	3607
Universal Thread Grinding Co	Fairfield	CT	F	203 336-1849	1204
Fall River Mfg Co Inc	Fall River	MA	D	508 675-1125	8547
Haydon Kerk Mtion Slutions Inc	Milford	NH	D	603 213-6290	15024
Allesco Industries Inc (PA)	Cranston	RI	F	401 943-0680	15828
Eastern Screw Company	Cranston	RI	C	401 943-0680	15852
Research Engineering & Mfg Inc	Middletown	RI	F	401 841-8880	16184

SEALANTS

	CITY	ST	EMP	PHONE	ENTRY#
Grafted Coatings Inc	Stratford	CT	G	203 377-9979	3543
Dorn Equipment Corp	Melrose	MA	F	781 662-9300	10316
Emseal Joint Systems Ltd	Westborough	MA	E	508 836-0280	13100
Granger Lynch Corp	Millbury	MA	C	508 756-6244	10435
Hero Coatings Inc	Newburyport	MA	G	978 462-0746	10688
Kretetek Industries Inc	Hudson	NH	F	855 573-8383	14517

SEALING COMPOUNDS: Sealing, synthetic rubber or plastic

	CITY	ST	EMP	PHONE	ENTRY#
Nova Sports Usa Inc	Milford	MA	F	508 473-6540	10410
Saint-Gobain Abrasives Inc (HQ)	Worcester	MA	A	508 795-5000	13788
Gripwet Inc	South Portland	ME	G	207 239-0486	5504

	CITY	ST	EMP	PHONE	ENTRY#
SEALS: Hermetic					
Northeast Electronics Corp	Milford	CT	D	203 878-3511	1855
Ceramic To Metal Seals Inc	Melrose	MA	F	781 665-5002	10314
Glasseal Products Inc	New Bedford	MA	E	732 370-9100	10595
Metal Processing Co Inc	Tyngsboro	MA	G	978 649-1289	12461
Sinclair Manufacturing Co LLC	Norton	MA	D	508 222-7440	11135
Special Hermetic Products Inc	Wilton	NH	E	603 654-2002	15710
SEALS: Oil, Asbestos					
Parker-Hannifin Corporation	Woburn	MA	B	781 935-4850	13629
SEARCH & NAVIGATION SYSTEMS					
Beacon Group Inc (PA)	Newington	CT	E	860 594-5200	2275
Chromalloy Component Svcs Inc	Windsor	CT	E	860 688-7798	4266
Connecticut Analytical Corp	Bethany	CT	F	203 393-9666	92
Drs Naval Power Systems Inc	Bethel	CT	B	203 366-5211	108
Electro-Methods Inc (PA)	South Windsor	CT	C	860 289-8661	3141
Ensign-Bickford Arospc Def Co (HQ)	Simsbury	CT	D	860 843-2289	3089
Ensign-Bickford Company (HQ)	Simsbury	CT	F	860 843-2001	3090
Gems Sensors Inc (HQ)	Plainville	CT	B	860 747-3000	2761
Hanwha Aerospace USA LLC	Glastonbury	CT	D	860 633-9474	1284
Hartford Aircraft Products Inc	Bloomfield	CT	E	860 242-8228	168
Lee Company (PA)	Westbrook	CT	A	860 399-6281	4140
Lewis Machine LLC	East Hartford	CT	E	860 289-3468	1003
Meriden Manufacturing Inc	Meriden	CT	D	203 237-7481	1675
Northrop Grumman Corporation	East Hartford	CT	D	860 282-4461	1007
Polar Corporation	New Britain	CT	E	860 223-7891	2054
Sikorsky Aircraft Corporation	Stratford	CT	B	203 380-3142	3573
Sikorsky Aircraft Corporation	Trumbull	CT	G	203 386-7794	3733
Sperian Prtction Instrmnttion	Middletown	CT	D	860 344-1079	1783
Thayermahan Inc (PA)	Groton	CT	E	860 785-9994	1381
Accusonic Technologies (DH)	New Bedford	MA	E	508 495-6600	10560
Ametek Inc	Wilmington	MA	D	978 988-4101	13377
Avwatch Inc	Plymouth	MA	F	508 274-7937	11448
Ba-Insight Inc	Boston	MA	D	339 368-7234	6581
Bascom-Turner Instruments Inc	Norwood	MA	F	781 769-9660	11164
Cobham Electronic Systems Inc	Lowell	MA	A	978 442-4700	9870
Drs Naval Power Systems Inc	Fitchburg	MA	C	978 343-9719	8653
Edgeone LLC	West Wareham	MA	G	508 291-0057	13061
Evolv Tech Holdings Inc (PA)	Waltham	MA	G	781 374-8100	12669
Evolv Technologies Inc (HQ)	Waltham	MA	D	781 374-8100	12670
Falmouth Scientific Inc (PA)	Pocasset	MA	F	508 564-7640	11486
General Dynmcs Mssion Systems	Pittsfield	MA	A	413 494-1110	11398
General Dynmcs Mssion Systems	Quincy	MA	D	617 715-7000	11522
Glasseal Products Inc	New Bedford	MA	E	732 370-9100	10595
Implant Sciences Corp	Wilmington	MA	A	978 752-1700	13413
L3 Technologies Inc	Northampton	MA	A	413 586-2330	11069
Leidos SEC Dtction Automtn Inc	Tewksbury	MA	F	571 526-6000	12403
Lockheed Martin Corporation	Bedford	MA	A	781 863-5235	6237
Lockheed Martin Corporation	Chelmsford	MA	F	978 256-4113	7936
Mettler-Toledo Thornton Inc (DH)	Billerica	MA	D	978 262-0210	6460
Mikel Inc (PA)	Fall River	MA	G	401 846-0052	8582
MSI Transducers Corp	Littleton	MA	F	978 486-0404	9826
Northrop Grumman Systems Corp	Hopkinton	MA	F	508 589-6291	9337
Photonis Scientific Inc (DH)	Sturbridge	MA	F	508 347-4000	12257
Princton Gamma-Tech Instrs Inc	Franklin	MA	E	609 924-7310	8858
Raytheon Italy Liaison Company	Andover	MA	D	978 684-5300	5910
Sensar Marine Us Inc	Lexington	MA	F	800 910-2150	9770
Spectrum Microwave Inc	Marlborough	MA	C	508 251-6400	10213
Ssg Optronics	Wilmington	MA	G	978 694-9991	13457
Symetrica Inc	Westford	MA	E	508 718-5610	13265
Teledyne Benthos Inc	North Falmouth	MA	F	508 563-1000	11013
Teledyne Instruments Inc	North Falmouth	MA	C	508 563-1000	11014
Tmd Technologies LLC	Beverly	MA	C	978 922-6000	6390
Tru Technologies Inc	Peabody	MA	F	978 532-0775	11349
Ultra Elec Ocean Systems Inc (DH)	Braintree	MA	D	781 848-3400	7211
General Dynamics Ots Cal Inc	Saco	ME	C	207 283-3611	5368
Lander Group LLC	Greenville	ME	F	207 974-3104	4850
Lockheed Martin Corporation	Bath	ME	G	207 442-3125	4529
Ropeless Systems Inc	Biddeford	ME	G	207 468-8545	4586
Bae Systems Elctronic Solution	Nashua	NH	D	603 885-3653	15066
Bae Systems Info Elctrnic Syst	Hudson	NH	A	603 885-4321	14486
Bae Systems Info Elctrnic Syst	Merrimack	NH	A	603 885-4321	14976
Bae Systems Info Elctrnic Syst	Nashua	NH	A	603 885-4321	15067
Bae Systems Info Elctrnic Syst (DH)	Nashua	NH	A	603 885-4321	15068
Cobham	Exeter	NH	D	603 418-9786	14287
Cobham Def Electronic Systems	Manchester	NH	G	603 518-2716	14832
Contintential Microwave	Exeter	NH	F	603 775-5200	14289
El-Op US Inc	Merrimack	NH	C	603 889-2500	14980
Fireye Inc (DH)	Derry	NH	C	603 432-4100	14193
Frontgrade Technologies Inc	Exeter	NH	B	603 775-5200	14292
KMC Systems Inc	Merrimack	NH	D	866 742-0442	14987
Kollsman Inc (DH)	Merrimack	NH	A	603 889-2500	14988
Lockheed Martin Corporation	Merrimack	NH	F	603 885-5295	14990
Lockheed Martin Corporation	Nashua	NH	D	603 885-4321	15128
Meggitt (new Hampshire) Inc	Londonderry	NH	C	603 669-0940	14767
Memtec Corporation	Amherst	NH	F	603 893-8080	13880
Mevatec Corp	Nashua	NH	G	603 885-4321	15134
Northrop Grumman Systems Corp	Hudson	NH	B	603 886-4270	14532
Research In Motion Rf Inc (HQ)	Nashua	NH	E	603 598-8880	15158
Sealite Usa LLC	Tilton	NH	F	603 737-1310	15656
Sierra Nevada Corporation	Bedford	NH	B	775 331-0222	13949
Tomtom North America Inc	Lebanon	NH	D	978 405-1677	14700
Tomtom North America Inc	Lebanon	NH	A	603 643-0330	14701
Northrop Grumman Systems Corp	Middletown	RI	B	401 849-6270	16183
Wei Inc (PA)	Cranston	RI	E	401 781-3904	15928
General Dynamics Ots Cal Inc	Williston	VT	B	802 662-7000	17733
SEATING: Stadium					
Hussey Corporation (PA)	North Berwick	ME	B	207 676-2271	5108
Hussey Seating Company	North Berwick	ME	B	207 676-2271	5109
SECURITY CONTROL EQPT & SYSTEMS					
Assa Abloy Inc (HQ)	New Haven	CT	B	203 562-2151	2122
Command Corporation	East Granby	CT	E	800 851-6012	930
Morse Watchmans Inc	Oxford	CT	E	203 264-4949	2705
AES Corporation	Peabody	MA	F	978 535-7310	11293
Byrna Technologies Inc (PA)	Andover	MA	C	978 868-5011	5875
Dogwatch Inc (PA)	Natick	MA	G	508 650-0600	10478
Oatsystems Inc	Waltham	MA	D	781 907-6100	12741
Chandler Security Systems Inc	Lewiston	ME	G	207 576-3418	4954
Namtek Corp	Bedford	NH	E	603 262-1630	13945
SECURITY DEVICES					
Insight Plus Technology LLC	Bristol	CT	G	860 930-4763	457
Isupportws Inc	Stamford	CT	F	203 569-7600	3386
Razberi Technologies Inc	Danbury	CT	E	469 828-3380	804
Rtx Corporation	Farmington	CT	B	954 485-6501	1244
Stanley Black & Decker Inc	New Britain	CT	C	860 225-5111	2063
Stanley Black & Decker Inc (PA)	New Britain	CT	C	860 225-5111	2065
AES International Corporation	Peabody	MA	F	978 535-7310	11294
All Security Co Inc	New Bedford	MA	E	508 993-4271	10567
Clearswift Corporation	Waltham	MA	B	781 839-7321	12630
Compu-Gard Inc	Swansea	MA	F	508 679-8845	12303
Dorel Juvenile Group Inc	Foxboro	MA	A	800 544-1108	8694
Inner-Tite Corp	Holden	MA	D	508 829-6361	9191
Interntnal Br-Tech Sltions Inc (PA)	Springfield	MA	G	413 739-2271	12106
Magiq Technologies Inc (PA)	Somerville	MA	F	617 661-8300	11884
Steel Root Inc	Salem	MA	F	978 312-7668	11733
Sysnova LLC	Mansfield	MA	G	508 309-9264	10077
Videoiq Inc	Somerville	MA	E	781 222-3069	11911
Omega Six Security LLC	Bedford	NH	F	888 866-9954	13946
Kenney Manufacturing Company (PA)	Warwick	RI	B	401 739-2200	16831
SECURITY SYSTEMS SERVICES					
Environmental Systems Corp	West Hartford	CT	C	860 953-8800	4060
Isupportws Inc	Stamford	CT	F	203 569-7600	3386
Manup LLC	Norwalk	CT	G	203 588-9861	2533
Mercury Cabling Systems LLC	Stratford	CT	E	203 378-9008	3556
AES International Corporation	Peabody	MA	F	978 535-7310	11294
Idss Holdings Inc	Boxboro	MA	D	978 237-0236	7144
Imprivata Inc (HQ)	Waltham	MA	B	781 674-2700	12697
Nashoba Security Inc	Littleton	MA	F	978 486-8615	9827
Simplex Time Recorder LLC (DH)	Westminster	MA	C		13278
Orion Entrance Control Inc	Laconia	NH	E	603 527-4187	14662
It Synergy Group LLC	Warwick	RI	F	866 767-4874	16824
SEMICONDUCTOR CIRCUIT NETWORKS					
Asmpt Nexx Inc	Billerica	MA	E	978 436-4600	6406
Axcel Photonics Inc	Marlborough	MA	E	508 481-9200	10115
MB Westfield Inc	Westfield	MA	C	413 568-8676	13182
Metelics Corp	Lowell	MA	E	408 737-8197	9905
Microsemi Corp-Colorado	Lawrence	MA	D	480 941-6300	9582
Trebia Networks Inc	Acton	MA	E	978 264-3700	5766
Interplex Industries Inc (DH)	Rumford	RI	F	401 434-6543	16672
SEMICONDUCTOR DEVICES: Wafers					
Iqe Kc LLC	Taunton	MA	D	508 824-6696	12343
Kopin Corporation (PA)	Westborough	MA	D	508 870-5959	13114
Macom Metelics LLC	Lowell	MA	C	978 656-2500	9897
Philips Advanced Metrology Sys	Billerica	MA	F	508 647-8400	6470
Macom Tech Sltons Holdings Inc	Londonderry	NH	D	603 641-3800	14765

P R O D U C T

	CITY	ST	EMP	PHONE	ENTRY#

SEMICONDUCTORS & RELATED DEVICES

Company	CITY	ST	EMP	PHONE	ENTRY#
AG Semiconductor Services LLC	Stamford	CT	E	203 322-5300	3274
Code Red Electronics LLC	North Branford	CT	G		2363
Coherent Inc	East Granby	CT	E	860 408-5066	928
Comet Technologies USA Inc (DH)	Shelton	CT	E	203 447-3200	2993
Edal Industries Inc	East Haven	CT	E	203 467-2591	1041
Emosyn America Inc	Danbury	CT	E	203 794-1100	735
Fuelcell Energy Inc (PA)	Danbury	CT	C	203 825-6000	748
Gordon Products Incorporated	Brookfield	CT	E	203 775-4501	523
Hipotronics Inc	Shelton	CT	E	845 279-3644	3013
Hoffman Engineering LLC (DH)	Stamford	CT	D	203 425-8900	3378
Luvata Waterbury Inc (HQ)	Waterbury	CT	D	203 753-5215	3931
Marco International Inc	Ridgefield	CT	D	203 894-8000	2902
Microphase Corporation	Shelton	CT	E	203 866-8000	3032
Newco Condenser Inc	Shelton	CT	F	475 882-4000	3039
Photronics Inc (PA)	Brookfield	CT	B	203 775-9000	533
Photronics Texas Inc	Brookfield	CT	E	203 546-3039	534
Photronics Texas I LLC	Brookfield	CT	G	203 775-9000	535
Strain Measurement Devices Inc	Wallingford	CT	E	203 294-5800	3855
Transwitch Corporation	Shelton	CT	C	203 929-8810	3071
Vishay Americas Inc (HQ)	Shelton	CT	E	203 452-5648	3076
Acacia Communications Inc (HQ)	Maynard	MA	C	978 938-4896	10259
Accuprobe Corporation	Salem	MA	F	978 745-7878	11699
Ace Residential Solar LLC	North Andover	MA	F	800 223-1462	10816
Advanced Microsensors Corp	Shrewsbury	MA	F	508 770-6600	11825
Allegro Microsystems LLC	Marlborough	MA	C	508 853-5000	10106
American Superconductor Corp (PA)	Ayer	MA	D	978 842-3000	6171
American Superconductor Corp	Westminster	MA	E	978 842-3000	13269
Ametek Inc	New Bedford	MA	D	508 998-4335	10568
Amkor Technology Inc	Stoneham	MA	G	781 438-7800	12174
Analog Devices Federal LLC (HQ)	Chelmsford	MA	B	978 250-3313	7906
Analog Devices Intl Inc (HQ)	Wilmington	MA	E	800 262-5643	13380
Anokiwave Inc	Billerica	MA	D	781 820-1049	6400
Applehill Systems Inc	Lynnfield	MA	G	781 334-7009	9994
Applied Materials Inc	Gloucester	MA	F	978 282-2000	8919
Ardeo Systems Inc	Haverhill	MA	G	978 373-4680	9074
Arm Inc	Waltham	MA	B	978 264-7300	12596
Arradiance LLC	Littleton	MA	F	508 202-0593	9803
Astex Plasmaquest Inc	Wilmington	MA	G	781 937-6272	13382
Athinia Technologies LLC	Cambridge	MA	F	781 491-4189	7494
Atomera Incorporated	Wellesley Hills	MA	G	617 219-0600	12950
Aware Inc (PA)	Bedford	MA	E	781 276-4000	6213
Bae Systems Info Elctrnic Syst	Lexington	MA	C	603 885-4321	9726
Black Earth Technologies Inc	Dighton	MA	G	508 397-1335	8292
Brooks Automation Us LLC (DH)	Chelmsford	MA	G	978 262-2400	7917
Bruce Technologies Inc	North Billerica	MA	F	978 670-5501	10901
Business and Prof Exch Inc	Beverly	MA	F	978 556-4100	6336
Ceramic Process Systems	Taunton	MA	G	508 222-0614	12327
Cicor Americas Inc	Cambridge	MA	F	617 576-2005	7540
CMC Materials Inc (HQ)	Billerica	MA	D	978 436-6500	6424
Comdel Inc	Gloucester	MA	F	978 282-0620	8930
Control Resources Inc	Littleton	MA	E	978 486-4160	9806
Crystal Gt Systems LLC	Salem	MA	F	978 745-0088	11708
Design Centers Com	Worcester	MA	F	800 570-1120	13716
Digital Lumens Incorporated	Boston	MA	C		6696
Drs Development LLC	Rochester	MA	G	774 271-0533	11631
Electronic Products Inds Inc	Newburyport	MA	E	978 462-8101	10681
Elpakco Inc (PA)	Westford	MA	F	978 392-0400	13235
Entegris Inc (PA)	Billerica	MA	A	978 436-6500	6443
Epi II Inc	Newburyport	MA	D	978 462-1514	10682
Gigantum Inc	Foxboro	MA	G	301 960-8012	8697
Global Silicon Tech Inc	New Bedford	MA	F	508 999-2001	10596
Googleplex Technologies LLC	Hudson	MA	G	978 897-0880	9370
Huber + Shner Platis Photonics	Bedford	MA	F	781 275-5080	6230
Ii-VI Photonics (us) Inc (HQ)	Woburn	MA	E	781 938-1222	13583
Immedia Semiconductor Inc	North Reading	MA	F	978 296-4950	11041
Infineon Tech Americas Corp	Andover	MA	G	978 851-1298	5888
Innovion Corporation	Wilmington	MA	F	978 267-4064	13415
Integris Inc	Billerica	MA	F	978 294-2633	6454
Isilon Systems LLC	Hopkinton	MA	C	206 315-7500	9332
Iwaki Pumps Inc (DH)	Holliston	MA	E	508 429-1440	9217
Ixys Intgrted Circuits Div LLC (DH)	Beverly	MA	D	978 524-6700	6357
Kcb Solutions LLC	Shirley	MA	F	978 425-0400	11819
Kopin Corporation	Taunton	MA	E	508 824-6696	12347
L T X International Inc	Norwood	MA	D	781 461-1000	11189
Lightmatter Inc	Boston	MA	D	857 244-0460	6859
Linear Singapore Holding LLC	Norwood	MA	F	781 329-4700	11190
Linear Technology LLC	North Chelmsford	MA	G	978 656-4750	10981
Macom Tech Sltons Holdings Inc (PA)	Lowell	MA	C	978 656-2500	9898
Macom Technology Solutions Inc (HQ)	Lowell	MA	B	978 656-2500	9900
Magellan Distribution Corp	Boston	MA	F	617 399-7900	6868
Massachusetts Bay Tech Inc	Stoughton	MA	F	781 344-8809	12222
Mediatek USA Inc	Woburn	MA	C	781 503-8000	13609
Metalenz Inc	Weston	MA	E	844 770-1300	13287
Micro Magnetics Inc	Fall River	MA	F	508 672-4489	8581
Micro-Precision Tech Inc (PA)	Lawrence	MA	F	978 688-1299	9580
Microsemi Corp- Massachusetts	Lawrence	MA	B	978 620-2600	9581
Microsemi Corp- Massachusetts	Lowell	MA	C	978 442-5600	9906
Microsemi Corporation	Beverly	MA	F	978 232-0040	6365
Microsemi Corporation	Tewksbury	MA	F	978 232-3793	12410
Microtronic Inc	Edgartown	MA	E	508 627-8951	8467
Mini-Systems Inc	Plainville	MA	E	508 695-2000	11439
Murata Power Solutions Inc (DH)	Westborough	MA	C	508 339-3000	13122
Nantero Inc	Woburn	MA	E	781 932-5338	13618
Nissin Ion Equipment Usa Inc	North Billerica	MA	F	978 362-2590	10940
North East Silicon Tech Inc	New Bedford	MA	D	508 999-2001	10634
Ox3 Corporation	Devens	MA	E	978 772-1222	8284
Panametrics LLC (DH)	Billerica	MA	A	978 437-1000	6468
Performance Motion Devices Inc	Boxborough	MA	E	978 266-1210	7153
Philips Holding USA Inc (HQ)	Cambridge	MA	A	978 687-1501	7686
Precision Sensing Devices Inc	Medfield	MA	G	508 359-2833	10274
Qbit Semiconductor Ltd	Littleton	MA	G	351 205-0005	9834
Qorvo Inc	Chelmsford	MA	E	978 770-2158	7947
Qorvo Us Inc	Chelmsford	MA	E	978 467-4290	7948
Reinforced Structures For Elec	Worcester	MA	F	508 754-5316	13783
Sand 9 Inc	Cambridge	MA	G	617 358-0957	7702
Semigear Inc	Wakefield	MA	E	781 213-3066	12534
Seminex Corporation	Danvers	MA	F	978 326-7700	8219
Sick Inc	Stoughton	MA	D	781 302-2500	12235
Sige Semiconductor Inc (HQ)	Andover	MA	E	978 327-6850	5920
Signet Products Corporation	North Attleboro	MA	E	650 592-3575	10887
Silex Microsystems Inc	Boston	MA	F	617 834-7197	7038
Sionyx LLC (PA)	Beverly	MA	F	978 922-0684	6384
Skyworks Solutions Inc	Andover	MA	F	978 327-6850	5921
Skyworks Solutions Inc	Woburn	MA	D	781 935-5150	13669
Spire Solar LLC	Newton	MA	E	617 332-4040	10787
Sst Components Inc (PA)	Lawrence	MA	E	978 670-7300	9601
Stmicroelectronics Inc	Burlington	MA	E	781 861-2650	7435
Tego Inc	Waltham	MA	G	781 547-5680	12791
Tel Mnfacturing Engrg Amer Inc	Billerica	MA	E	978 436-2300	6487
Teradyne Inc	Boston	MA	G	978 370-2700	7074
Teradyne Inc (PA)	North Reading	MA	A	978 370-2700	11048
Texas Instruments Incorporated	Attleboro	MA	E	508 236-3800	6070
That Corporation (PA)	Milford	MA	E	508 478-9200	10420
Transene Company Inc (PA)	Danvers	MA	G	978 777-7860	8227
Ulvac Technologies Inc (HQ)	Methuen	MA	E	978 686-7550	10347
Union Miniere	Boston	MA	E	617 960-5900	7090
University Wafer Inc	Boston	MA	E	800 713-9375	7095
Upstart Power Inc	Southborough	MA	E	614 877-8278	12003
Vacuum Plus Manufacturing Inc	Chelmsford	MA	F	978 441-3100	7968
Varian Semicdtr Eqp Assoc Inc	Andover	MA	G	978 282-2807	5932
Varian Semicdtr Eqp Assoc Inc (HQ)	Gloucester	MA	C	978 282-2000	8963
Vsea Inc	Gloucester	MA	E	978 282-2000	8964
Xosoft Inc	Framingham	MA	E	800 225-5224	8812
Xp Power LLC	Gloucester	MA	D	978 282-0620	8965
Asml Us LLC	Westbrook	ME	G	207 541-5000	5615
Delkin Inc	Cumberland Center	ME	G	207 370-0703	4708
Fairchild Energy LLC	South Portland	ME	E	207 775-8100	5499
Fairchild Semiconductor Corp	South Portland	ME	E	801 562-7000	5500
Fairchild Semiconductor Corp	South Portland	ME	C	207 775-8100	5501
Nanoscale Components Inc	Portland	ME	F	207 671-7028	5248
Allegro Microsystems Inc (HQ)	Manchester	NH	B	603 626-2300	14811
Allegro Microsystems LLC (HQ)	Manchester	NH	B	603 626-2300	14812
Analog Devices Inc	Nashua	NH	E	603 883-2430	15063
Bantry Components Inc	Manchester	NH	E	603 668-3210	14817
Bluglass Inc	Nashua	NH	E	617 869-5150	15072
Corfin Industries Inc	Manchester	NH	D	603 893-9900	14837
Cxe Equipment Services LLC	Seabrook	NH	G	603 437-2477	15589
Dutile Glines & Higgins Inc	Manchester	NH	F	603 622-0452	14846
Eigenlight Corporation	Newmarket	NH	E	603 692-9200	15219
Gt Advanced Technologies Ltd	Hudson	NH	G	603 883-5200	14504
Gt Equipment Holdings Inc	Merrimack	NH	D	603 883-5200	14983
Jenesco Inc	Lyndeborough	NH	F	603 673-4830	14800
Microfab Inc	Manchester	NH	F	603 621-9522	14885
Microsembly LLC	Merrimack	NH	A	603 718-8445	14993
Microsemi Corporation	Manchester	NH	F	978 232-3793	14886
Micross Components LLC	Manchester	NH	C	603 893-9900	14887
NORTH PENN TECHNOLOGY INC	Manchester	NH	E	603 893-9900	14903
Premier Semiconductor Svcs LLC (DH)	Manchester	NH	D	267 954-0130	14914
Saint-Gobain Glass Corporation	Milford	NH	E	603 673-7560	15037
Semi-General Inc	Londonderry	NH	D	603 641-3800	14783
Semikron Inc (HQ)	Hudson	NH	E	603 883-8102	14545

	CITY	ST	EMP	PHONE	ENTRY#
Stockeryale Inc	Salem	NH	G	603 893-8778	15565
Ampleon USA Inc	Smithfield	RI	E	401 830-5420	16687
ATW Companies Inc (PA)	Warwick	RI	D	401 244-1002	16785
Cherry Semiconductor Corp	East Greenwich	RI	F	401 885-3600	15977
Infineon Tech Americas Corp	Warwick	RI	G	401 773-7501	16822
Integrated Device Technology	Smithfield	RI	G	401 719-1686	16716
Narragansett Imaging Usa LLC	North Smithfield	RI	E	401 762-3800	16328
Numark International Inc	Cumberland	RI	F	954 761-7550	15956
Reed Semiconductor Corp (PA)	Warwick	RI	E	401 886-0857	16847
Wei Inc (PA)	Cranston	RI	E	401 781-3904	15928
Globalfoundries US 2 LLC	Essex Junction	VT	A	408 462-4452	17234
Marvell Gvrnment Solutions LLC	Burlington	VT	E	845 245-8066	17143
Nehp Inc	Williston	VT	D	802 652-1444	17741

SENSORS: Infrared, Solid State

	CITY	ST	EMP	PHONE	ENTRY#
Flir Systems-Boston Inc (DH)	North Billerica	MA	B	978 901-8000	10911
Spectris Inc (HQ)	Westborough	MA	E	508 768-6400	13137

SENSORS: Radiation

	CITY	ST	EMP	PHONE	ENTRY#
Radeco Inc	Plainfield	CT	G	860 823-1220	2738
Druck LLC (HQ)	Billerica	MA	C	978 437-1000	6432
Radio Act Corporation	Brookline	MA	G	617 731-6542	7326
Remote Sensing Solutions Inc	Buzzards Bay	MA	F	508 362-9400	7456

SENSORS: Temperature, Exc Indl Process

	CITY	ST	EMP	PHONE	ENTRY#
Omega Engineering Inc	Norwalk	CT	D	714 540-4914	2548
Thermalogic Corporation	Hudson	MA	E	800 343-4492	9420

SEPTIC TANK CLEANING SVCS

	CITY	ST	EMP	PHONE	ENTRY#
Coastline Environmental LLC	North Branford	CT	G	203 483-6898	2362
Parker Septic LLC	Somers	CT	G	860 749-8220	3099
Slate Corporation	Auburn	NH	F	603 234-5943	13912

SEPTIC TANKS: Concrete

	CITY	ST	EMP	PHONE	ENTRY#
Arrow Concrete Products Inc (PA)	Granby	CT	E	860 653-5063	1305
Connecticut Precast Corp	Monroe	CT	E	203 268-8688	1910
Jolley Precast Inc	Danielson	CT	E	860 774-9066	840
M & M Precast Corp	Danbury	CT	E	203 743-5559	780
Pine Tree Concrete Pdts Inc	Millville	MA	G	508 883-7072	10451
Richard Genest Inc	Sanford	ME	F	207 324-7215	5411
Sandelin Foundation Inc	Topsham	ME	F	207 725-7004	5552
Andrew J Foss Co LLC	Farmington	NH	F	603 755-2515	14307
Slate Corporation	Auburn	NH	F	603 234-5943	13912
William N Lamarre Con Pdts Inc	Greenville	NH	F	603 878-1340	14375

SEPTIC TANKS: Plastic

	CITY	ST	EMP	PHONE	ENTRY#
Infiltrator Water Technologies LLC (HQ)	Old Saybrook	CT	D	860 577-7000	2651
STI Incorporated	Old Saybrook	CT	E	860 577-7000	2663
Presby Plastics Inc	Whitefield	NH	E	603 837-3826	15700

SEWAGE & WATER TREATMENT EQPT

	CITY	ST	EMP	PHONE	ENTRY#
Gotham Technologies Inc	Norwalk	CT	F	800 468-4261	2509
New Milford Commission	New Milford	CT	G	860 354-3758	2255
Stormtech LLC	Rocky Hill	CT	E	860 529-8188	2935
Crosstek Membrane Tech LLC	Billerica	MA	F	978 761-9601	6430
Evoqua Water Technologies LLC	Tewksbury	MA	E	978 863-4600	12397
Sarid Inc	Lexington	MA	E	781 315-1105	9769
Town of Westborough	Westborough	MA	E	508 366-7615	13140
Veralto Corporation	Waltham	MA	G	781 755-3655	12810
City of Manchester	Manchester	NH	F	603 624-6482	14829

SEWING, NEEDLEWORK & PIECE GOODS STORES: Knitting Splys

	CITY	ST	EMP	PHONE	ENTRY#
P Straker Ltd	South Dartmouth	MA	G	508 996-4804	11918
Harrisville Designs Inc (PA)	Harrisville	NH	G	603 827-3333	14432
Providence Yarn Company Inc	Pawtucket	RI	G	401 722-5600	16407
Green Mountain Spinnery Inc	East Dummerston	VT	G	802 387-4528	17216

SHAFTS: Flexible

	CITY	ST	EMP	PHONE	ENTRY#
Double E Company LLC (PA)	West Bridgewater	MA	C	508 588-8099	12972
Mass-Flex Research Inc	Medford	MA	G	781 391-3640	10295
Nim-Cor Inc	Nashua	NH	E	603 889-2153	15142

SHAPES & PILINGS, STRUCTURAL: Steel

	CITY	ST	EMP	PHONE	ENTRY#
Ackles Steel and Iron Co Inc	Waltham	MA	F	781 893-6818	12581
Cmd Enterprises LLC	Dexter	ME	G	207 745-9985	4726
LK Goodwin Co Inc (PA)	West Greenwich	RI	F	401 781-5526	16888

SHAPES: Extruded, Aluminum, NEC

	CITY	ST	EMP	PHONE	ENTRY#
Mestek Inc (PA)	Westfield	MA	E	470 898-4533	13186
Wakefeld Thermal Solutions Inc (HQ)	Nashua	NH	C	603 635-2800	15185

SHEET METAL SPECIALTIES, EXC STAMPED

	CITY	ST	EMP	PHONE	ENTRY#
Anco Engineering Inc	Shelton	CT	D	203 925-9235	2981
Chapco Inc (PA)	Chester	CT	E	860 526-9535	625
Ductco LLC	Bloomfield	CT	E	860 243-0350	160
Farrell Prcsion Mtalcraft Corp	New Milford	CT	E	860 355-2651	2243
Hdb Inc	Thomaston	CT	E	860 379-9901	3621
Hispanic Enterprises Inc	Bridgeport	CT	E	203 588-9334	329
Jared Manufacturing Co Inc	Norwalk	CT	E	203 846-1732	2520
Jgs Properties LLC	Milford	CT	E	203 378-7508	1840
M & W Sheet Metal LLC	North Franklin	CT	G	860 642-7748	2382
Milford Fabricating Co Inc	Milford	CT	D	203 878-2476	1852
Paradigm Manchester Inc	Manchester	CT	G	860 646-4048	1624
Paradigm Manchester Inc	Manchester	CT	C	860 649-2888	1625
Quality Sheet Metal Inc	Naugatuck	CT	E	203 729-2244	1982
R & D Precision Inc	Wallingford	CT	F	203 284-3396	3844
R W E Inc	Putnam	CT	F	860 974-1101	2871
R-D Mfg Inc	East Lyme	CT	F	860 739-3986	1062
Seconn Fabrication LLC	Waterford	CT	D	860 443-0000	3994
A & D Metal Inc	Westfield	MA	F	413 485-7505	13145
Aero-Space Fabricators Inc	Waltham	MA	E	781 899-4535	12586
Allstate Hood & Duct Inc	Westfield	MA	F	413 568-4663	13147
Apahouser Inc	Marlborough	MA	E	508 786-0309	10110
Atlantic Air Products Mfg LLC	Quincy	MA	F	603 410-3900	11504
AW Airflo Industries Inc	Newburyport	MA	E	978 465-6260	10668
C S H Industries Inc	Plymouth	MA	E	508 747-1990	11452
Ceric Fabrication Co Inc	Ayer	MA	E	978 772-9034	6178
Computron Metal Products Inc	Whitman	MA	E	781 447-2265	13348
Crocker Architectural Shtmtl	North Oxford	MA	E	508 987-9900	11031
CTR Enterprises Inc	Haverhill	MA	G	978 794-2093	9089
D J Fabricators Inc	Ipswich	MA	F	978 356-0228	9482
Dosco Sheet Metal and Mfg Inc	Millbury	MA	G	508 865-9998	10433
Fabco Mfg Inc	Hudson	MA	E	978 568-8519	9366
Fabtron Corporation	Waltham	MA	E	781 891-4430	12674
Gtr Manufacturing LLC	Brockton	MA	D	508 588-3240	7282
Horizon Sheet Metal Inc	Springfield	MA	D	413 734-6966	12102
Howard Products Incorporated	Worcester	MA	E	508 757-2440	13738
Ideas Inc	Lowell	MA	G	978 453-6864	9886
Jgpg Inc	Waltham	MA	F	781 891-9640	12705
McGarvin Engineering Inc	Lowell	MA	F	978 454-2741	9904
Metal Tronics Inc	Georgetown	MA	E	978 659-6960	8909
Metalcrafters Inc	Methuen	MA	E	978 683-7097	10338
Momentum Mfg Group LLC (HQ)	Georgetown	MA	D	978 659-6960	8910
New England Fab Mtls Inc	Leominster	MA	F	978 466-7823	9685
P G L Industries Inc	Swansea	MA	E	508 679-8845	12309
Precise Industries Inc	Lowell	MA	E	978 453-8490	9915
Precision Engineering LLC	Uxbridge	MA	E	508 278-5700	12488
Southbridge Shtmtl Works Inc	Sturbridge	MA	E	508 347-7800	12258
Taunton Stove Company Inc	North Dighton	MA	E	508 823-0786	11004
Techncal Metal Fabricators Inc	Mendon	MA	E	508 473-2223	10322
Teltron Engineering Inc	Foxboro	MA	F	508 543-6600	8727
Collins Sheet Metal Inc	Berwick	ME	F	207 384-4428	4549
Down East Shtmtl & Certif Wldg	Brewer	ME	G	207 989-3443	4611
DSM Metal Fabrication Inc	Biddeford	ME	E	207 282-6740	4561
Dgf Indstrial Innvtons Group L	Gilford	NH	F	603 528-6591	14335
Garvin Industries Incorporated	Auburn	NH	G	603 647-5410	13908
H&H Custom Metal Fabg Inc	Plaistow	NH	G	603 382-2818	15347
M&H Liquidating Company LLC	Amherst	NH	D	603 889-8320	13876
Macy Industries Inc	Hooksett	NH	E	603 623-5568	14468
Nashua Fabrication Co Inc	Hudson	NH	E	603 889-2181	14531
Omni Metals Company Inc	Somersworth	NH	E	603 692-6664	15619
Ran/All Metal Technology Inc	Hooksett	NH	G	603 668-1907	14472
Sebabo South Inc	Nashua	NH	F	603 881-8720	15165
Renaisance Cornice	Johnston	RI	G	401 275-6500	16103
Momentum Mfg Group - N LLC (PA)	Saint Johnsbury	VT	C	802 748-5007	17545
Sheet Metal Group	Essex Junction	VT	G	802 288-9700	17246

SHEETS: Fabric, From Purchased Materials

	CITY	ST	EMP	PHONE	ENTRY#
Tiberio Manufacturing Corp	Holliston	MA	D	508 429-4011	9232

SHIMS: Metal

	CITY	ST	EMP	PHONE	ENTRY#
Beta Shim Co	Shelton	CT	E	203 926-1150	2983
Spirol International Corp (HQ)	Danielson	CT	C	860 774-8571	844
Spirol Intl Holdg Corp (PA)	Danielson	CT	C	860 774-8571	845

SHIP BUILDING & REPAIRING: Cargo, Commercial

	CITY	ST	EMP	PHONE	ENTRY#
LM Gill Welding & Mfg LLC	Manchester	CT	E	860 647-9931	1613

SHIP BUILDING & REPAIRING: Combat Vessels

	CITY	ST	EMP	PHONE	ENTRY#
Bath Iron Works Corporation (HQ)	Bath	ME	A	207 443-3311	4525

SHIP BUILDING & REPAIRING: Ferryboats

	CITY	ST	EMP	PHONE	ENTRY#
Lake Champlain Trnsp Co	Burlington	VT	D	802 660-3495	17141

PRODUCT

	CITY	ST	EMP	PHONE	ENTRY#

SHIP BUILDING & REPAIRING: Military

	CITY	ST	EMP	PHONE	ENTRY#
Naiad Dynamics Us Inc (HQ)	Shelton	CT	E	203 929-6355	3033

SHIP BUILDING & REPAIRING: Rigging, Marine

Navtec Rigging Solutions Inc	Groton	MA	E		9011
Aramid Rigging Inc	Portsmouth	RI	G	401 683-6966	16436

SHIP BUILDING & REPAIRING: Submarine Tenders

Hydroid LLC	Pocasset	MA	D	508 563-6565	11488

SHOE & BOOT ACCESS

Jones & Vining Incorporated (PA)	Brockton	MA	E	508 232-7470	7287

SHOE STORES

Reebok International Ltd LLC (HQ)	Boston	MA	B	781 401-5000	7002
Santacroce Graphics Inc	Charlton	MA	F	802 447-0020	7895
Stride Rite Corporation (HQ)	Waltham	MA	B	617 824-6000	12783
Vibram Corporation (HQ)	Concord	MA	E	978 318-0000	8138

SHOE STORES: Athletic

Arocam Inc	Taunton	MA	F	508 822-1220	12319
Pine Tree Orthopedic Lab Inc	Livermore Falls	ME	F	207 897-5558	5025

SHOE STORES: Men's

C & J Clark America Inc (DH)	Waltham	MA	B	617 964-1222	12617
C & J Clark Latin America	Waltham	MA	E	617 243-4100	12618
Wear-Guard Corporation	Norwell	MA	A	781 871-4100	11150

SHOES: Athletic, Exc Rubber Or Plastic

Acushnet Company (DH)	Fairhaven	MA	B	508 979-2000	8504
New Balance Athletics Inc	Lawrence	MA	B	978 685-8400	9586
Reebok International Ltd LLC (HQ)	Boston	MA	B	781 401-5000	7002
Saucony Inc (DH)	Waltham	MA	C	617 824-6000	12776
Warrior Sports Inc (DH)	Boston	MA	C	800 968-7845	7113
Callaway Golf Ball Oprtons Inc	Richmond	ME	C	207 737-4324	5320
New Balance Athletics Inc	Norridgewock	ME	E	207 634-3033	5103
New Balance Athletics Inc	Skowhegan	ME	F	207 474-2042	5474

SHOES: Men's

Bh Shoe Holdings Inc (HQ)	Greenwich	CT	E	203 661-2424	1318
Fisher Footwear LLC	Greenwich	CT	F	203 302-2800	1330
Mbf Holdings LLC	Greenwich	CT	F	203 302-2812	1341
Mf-TFC LLC	Greenwich	CT	F	203 302-2820	1342
Allbirds Inc	Boston	MA	F	617 430-4500	6535
Allbirds Inc	Boston	MA	F	857 990-1373	6536
Allbirds Inc	Cambridge	MA	F	617 315-4210	7476
Allbirds Inc	Hingham	MA	F	781 208-6094	9140
Allbirds Inc	Wrentham	MA	F	774 847-1330	13836
HH Brown Shoe Company Inc	Andover	MA	E	978 933-4700	5886
Saucony Inc (DH)	Waltham	MA	C	617 824-6000	12776
Falcon Performance Ftwr LLC	Auburn	ME	G	207 784-9186	4431
L L Bean Inc	Brunswick	ME	F	207 725-0300	4647
New Balance Athletics Inc	Norridgewock	ME	E	207 634-3033	5103

SHOES: Men's, Dress

Reebok International Ltd LLC (HQ)	Boston	MA	B	781 401-5000	7002
Rancourt & Co Shoecrafters Inc	Lewiston	ME	F	855 999-3544	4989

SHOES: Men's, Work

HH Brown Shoe Company Inc (DH)	Greenwich	CT	E	203 661-2424	1334
Footwear Specialties Inc	Biddeford	ME	G	207 284-5003	4566

SHOES: Plastic Or Rubber

Black Diamond Group Inc	Woburn	MA	F	781 939-7824	13527
Macneill Engineering Co Inc	Westborough	MA	E	508 481-8830	13118
New Balance Athletics Inc	Lawrence	MA	B	978 685-8400	9586
Homegrown For Good LLC	York	ME	F	857 540-6361	5713
New Balance Athletics Inc	Norridgewock	ME	E	207 634-3033	5103
New Balance Athletics Inc	Skowhegan	ME	F	207 474-2042	5474
Genfoot America Inc	Littleton	NH	D	603 575-5114	14719
Genfoot America LLC	Milton	VT	F	802 893-4280	17358

SHOES: Women's

Dooney & Bourke Inc (HQ)	Norwalk	CT	E	203 853-7515	2492
Fisher Footwear LLC	Greenwich	CT	F	203 302-2800	1330
Fisher Sigerson Morrison LLC	Greenwich	CT	E	203 302-2800	1331
HH Brown Shoe Company Inc (DH)	Greenwich	CT	E	203 661-2424	1334
Mf-TFC LLC	Greenwich	CT	F	203 302-2820	1342
Cardinal Shoe Corporation	Lawrence	MA	F	978 686-9706	9546
HH Brown Shoe Company Inc	Andover	MA	E	978 933-4700	5886
Modern Shoe Company LLC	Hyde Park	MA	F	617 333-7470	9464

	CITY	ST	EMP	PHONE	ENTRY#
Saucony Inc (DH)	Waltham	MA	C	617 824-6000	12776
Footwear Specialties Inc	Biddeford	ME	G	207 284-5003	4566
L L Bean Inc	Brunswick	ME	F	207 725-0300	4647
New Balance Athletics Inc	Norridgewock	ME	E	207 634-3033	5103
Colby Footwear Inc	Somersworth	NH	F	603 332-2283	15612
Timberland LLC (HQ)	Stratham	NH	B	603 772-9500	15641
White Mountain Intl LLC (PA)	Lisbon	NH	E	603 838-6694	14711

SHOES: Women's, Dress

Aj Casey LLC	Norwalk	CT	G	203 226-5961	2460
Reebok International Ltd LLC (HQ)	Boston	MA	B	781 401-5000	7002

SHOT PEENING SVC

Aqua Blasting Corp	Bloomfield	CT	F	860 242-8855	146
Hydro Honing Laboratories Inc (PA)	East Hartford	CT	E	860 289-4328	999
Metal Improvement Company LLC	East Windsor	CT	D	860 523-9901	1081
Metal Improvement Company LLC	Middletown	CT	E	860 635-9994	1762
Metal Improvement Company LLC	New Britain	CT	E	860 224-9148	2042
Metal Improvement Company LLC	Windsor	CT	E	860 688-6201	4291
P&G Metal Components Corp	Bloomfield	CT	F	860 243-2220	199
Peening Technologies Eqp LLC	East Hartford	CT	E	860 289-4328	1010
Metal Improvement Company LLC	Wakefield	MA	F	781 246-3848	12519
Metal Improvement Company LLC	Wilmington	MA	D	978 658-0032	13430

SHOWCASES & DISPLAY FIXTURES: Office & Store

Boston Retail Products Inc (PA)	Tewksbury	MA	D	781 395-7417	12387
Continental Woodcraft Inc (PA)	Worcester	MA	E	508 581-9560	13709
Stainless Fdsrvice Eqp Mfg Inc	Limestone	ME	F	207 227-7747	5005
Herrick & White Ltd	Cumberland	RI	D	401 658-0440	15942

SHREDDERS: Indl & Commercial

Security Engineered McHy Inc (PA)	Westborough	MA	E	508 366-1488	13133

SHUTTERS, DOOR & WINDOW: Metal

Jeld-Wen Inc	Avon	MA	F	541 882-3451	6152

SIDING: Plastic

Kp Building Products Inc	Williston	VT	D	866 850-4447	17737

SIDING: Sheet Metal

Rgm Metals Inc	Hudson	MA	G	978 562-9773	9408

SIGN PAINTING & LETTERING SHOP

American Sign Inc	New Haven	CT	F	203 624-2991	2115
Dion Signs and Service Inc	New Bedford	MA	F	401 724-4459	10586
Hammar & Sons Inc	Pelham	NH	F	603 635-2292	15289
Twin State Signs Inc	Essex Junction	VT	G	802 872-8949	17248

SIGNALING APPARATUS: Electric

Trans-Tek Inc	Ellington	CT	E	860 872-8351	1118
I F Engineering Corp	Dudley	MA	E	860 935-0280	8319
Suns International LLC	Chelmsford	MA	B	978 349-2329	7960

SIGNALS: Traffic Control, Electric

Coastal Traffic	York	ME	F	207 351-8673	5711
Frazier Signal Tech LLC (PA)	Veazie	ME	G	207 991-0543	5571
Nestor Traffic Systems Inc (PA)	Pawtucket	RI	E	401 714-7781	16391

SIGNS & ADVERTISING SPECIALTIES

Acme Sign Co (PA)	Stamford	CT	F	203 324-2263	3272
Adams Ahern Sign Solutions	West Hartford	CT	G	860 523-8835	4047
American Sign Inc	New Haven	CT	F	203 624-2991	2115
Asi Sign Systems Inc	East Berlin	CT	G	860 828-3331	907
Classic Graphics Corp	Stamford	CT	G	203 323-6635	3315
Concord Industries Inc	Norwalk	CT	E	203 750-6060	2485
Connecticut Container Corp (PA)	North Haven	CT	C	203 248-2161	2399
Connecticut Sign Service LLC	Deep River	CT	G	860 767-7446	875
CT Sign Service LLC	Deep River	CT	G	860 322-3954	876
Fg Signs LLC	Stratford	CT	G	203 612-4447	3536
Gerber Scientific LLC (PA)	Tolland	CT	C	860 871-8082	3661
Horizons Unlimited Inc	Willimantic	CT	F	860 423-1931	4219
Hot Tops LLC	Shelton	CT	F	203 926-2067	3016
Identification Products Corp (PA)	Shelton	CT	E	203 334-5969	3019
Jornik Manufacturing Corp	Stamford	CT	F	203 969-0500	3393
Lamar Advertising Company	Windsor	CT	G	860 246-6546	4285
Lewtan Industries Corporation	West Hartford	CT	E	860 278-9800	4068
McIntire Company (HQ)	Bristol	CT	F	860 585-8559	465
Michael Zoppa	South Windsor	CT	G	860 289-5881	3165
National Sign Corporation (PA)	Berlin	CT	F	860 829-9060	77
OGS TECHNOLOGIES LLC	Cheshire	CT	E	203 271-9055	610
PRC Synergy Corp	Bridgeport	CT	B	203 331-9100	360
Priority One Inc	Danbury	CT	G	203 244-7093	800

	CITY	ST	EMP	PHONE	ENTRY#
Project Graphics Inc	Woodbury	CT	E	802 488-8789	4388
Revolution Lighting Tech Inc (PA)	Stamford	CT	E	877 578-2536	3447
Sign Factory	Enfield	CT	F	860 763-1085	1151
Sign Fast	Bridgeport	CT	G	203 549-8500	371
Signs On Demand Usa LLC	Middletown	CT	E	860 346-1720	1780
Skyline Exhibits Graphics Inc	Middletown	CT	F	860 635-2400	1781
Spencer Norb	West Hartford	CT	F	860 231-8079	4082
The Gilman Brothers Company	Gilman	CT	D	860 889-8444	1268
United Sttes Sign Fbrction Cor	Trumbull	CT	F	203 601-1000	3739
Whaling City Graphics LLC	Waterford	CT	F	860 437-7446	3999
Wingsite Displays Inc	Wethersfield	CT	F	860 257-3300	4215
Yankee Plak Co Inc	Bridgeport	CT	F	203 333-3168	387
Accurate Graphics Inc	Lynn	MA	G	781 593-1630	9961
Ad-A-Day Company Inc	Taunton	MA	E	508 824-8676	12315
Advanced Signing LLC	Medway	MA	E	508 533-9000	10301
Aerial Skyvertising Inc	Brockton	MA	E	508 586-4076	7253
All American Signs Inc	Plymouth	MA	F	508 830-0505	11445
Apifia Inc	Boston	MA	E	585 506-2787	6550
Boston Sign Company Inc	Boston	MA	G	617 338-2114	6618
Business Signs LLC	Woburn	MA	E	781 808-3153	13537
C & D Signs Inc	Tewksbury	MA	E	978 851-2424	12388
Casey & Hayes Inc	Hingham	MA	C	617 269-5900	9146
Clayton LLC DBA Blbird Grphic	Woburn	MA	E	617 250-8500	13542
Dinn Bros Inc (PA)	West Springfield	MA	D	413 750-3466	13022
E A Dion Inc	Attleboro	MA	C	800 445-1007	6010
E V Yeuell Inc	Woburn	MA	E	781 933-2984	13560
Expansion Opportunities Inc	Northborough	MA	E	508 393-8200	11095
Far Reach Graphics Inc	Needham Heights	MA	G	781 444-4889	10545
Fastsigns	Needham Heights	MA	G	781 444-4889	10546
Fastsigns of Attleboro	Rehoboth	MA	F	508 699-6699	11608
Fnsj Inc	Quincy	MA	F	617 302-2882	11519
Grand Image Inc	Hudson	MA	E	888 973-2622	9371
Hamilton Sign & Design Inc	Worcester	MA	G	508 459-9731	13736
Higgins Location LLC	Acton	MA	E	978 266-1200	5752
John J Cahill Displays Inc	East Weymouth	MA	G	617 737-3232	8430
Keating Communication Group	Canton	MA	G	781 828-9030	7804
Lane Printing Co Inc	Holbrook	MA	F	781 767-4450	9178
Ldr Inc	Salem	MA	F	978 825-0020	11726
Massachstts Sign Instlltion Co	Worcester	MA	F	508 793-0956	13758
National Sign Corp	Attleboro Falls	MA	E	508 809-4638	6092
New England Flag & Banner	Watertown	MA	F	617 782-1892	12897
New England Sign Group Inc	Worcester	MA	G	508 779-0821	13764
New England Wire Products Inc (PA)	Leominster	MA	D	800 254-9473	9686
New England Wooden Ware Corp (PA)	Gardner	MA	E	978 632-3600	8896
Newman Enterprises Inc	Southborough	MA	G	508 875-7446	11999
Oldsignsnstuffcom Inc	Gardner	MA	F	978 407-6718	8897
Owl Stamp Company Inc	Lowell	MA	G	978 452-4541	9912
Pg Technologies Inc	Westfield	MA	G	413 562-1354	13198
Quick Print Ltd Inc	Chelmsford	MA	G	978 256-1822	7950
Raders Engraving Inc	Boston	MA	G	617 227-2921	6993
Ready 2 Run Graphics Signs Inc	Worcester	MA	F	508 459-9977	13781
Roadsafe Traffic Systems Inc	Avon	MA	D	508 580-6700	6160
Sign By Tommorrow	Norton	MA	G	508 222-1900	11134
Sign Company	Dennis Port	MA	F	508 760-5400	8262
Sign Solutions Unlimited	Woburn	MA	G	781 557-6156	13665
Signarama	Worcester	MA	G	508 459-9731	13801
Signs By J Inc	Boston	MA	G	617 825-9855	7037
Signs To Go Inc	Woburn	MA	G	781 808-3153	13667
Signworks Group Inc	Watertown	MA	F	617 924-0292	12907
Silver Screen Design Inc	Greenfield	MA	F	413 773-1692	9000
Space Age Accessories Inc	Foxboro	MA	F	508 543-3661	8725
Speedy Sign-A-Rama USA	Braintree	MA	G	781 849-1181	7203
Stickamayka Packaging Inc	Andover	MA	E	978 474-1930	5926
Sunshine Sign Company Inc	North Grafton	MA	C	508 839-5588	11026
Titus & Bean Graphics Inc	Kingston	MA	F	781 585-1355	9513
Wood Art Incorporated	Cherry Valley	MA	F	508 892-8058	7995
Affordable Exhibit Displays	Auburn	ME	F	207 782-6175	4417
American Nameplate	Brewer	ME	F	207 848-7187	4609
Davis-Joncas Enterprises Inc	Scarborough	ME	E	207 883-6200	5430
H4 Holdings LLC	Saco	ME	G	207 494-8085	5369
Print-Mail of Maine Inc	Portland	ME	F	207 878-8000	5262
Sign Concepts LLC	Portland	ME	F	207 699-2920	5271
T R Sign Design Inc	Portland	ME	G	207 856-2600	5279
Transformit (PA)	Gorham	ME	E	207 856-9911	4837
Winter People Inc	Cumberland Center	ME	E	207 865-6636	4711
American Flgging Trffic Ctrl I	Hudson	NH	D	603 890-1154	14482
Bigraphics Inc	Nashua	NH	G	603 594-8686	15071
Corportion For Lser Optics Res (PA)	Londonderry	NH	G	603 430-2023	14738
Db Signs LLC	Concord	NH	G	603 225-4081	14128
Fast Signs of Plaistow	Plaistow	NH	F	603 894-7446	15343
Fastrax Signs Inc	Brentwood	NH	G	603 775-7500	14021

	CITY	ST	EMP	PHONE	ENTRY#
Ink Outside Box Incorporated	Pelham	NH	G	603 635-2292	15290
J H Dunning Corporation	North Walpole	NH	E	603 445-5591	15258
Kevin L Woolbert	North Walpole	NH	G	603 445-5222	15259
Maineline Graphics LLC	Antrim	NH	G	603 588-3177	13897
Plw Inc	Greenland	NH	F	603 889-4126	14370
Powerplay Management LLC	Portsmouth	NH	E	603 436-3030	15431
Sousa Signs LLC	Manchester	NH	F	603 622-5067	14934
Spectrum Monthly LLC	Manchester	NH	C	603 627-0042	14936
Synergy Signworks LLC	Manchester	NH	F	603 440-3519	14939
Abar Color Labs Neng Inc	Lincoln	RI	F	401 351-8644	16114
Anchors Aweigh Together LLC	Warwick	RI	E	401 738-8055	16779
Dasko Identification Products	Warren	RI	F	401 435-6500	16757
Dexter Enterprises Corp	East Providence	RI	G	401 434-2300	16013
Josef Creations Inc (PA)	Chepachet	RI	E	401 421-4198	15805
Mastercast Ltd	Pawtucket	RI	F	401 726-3100	16384
Progressive Displays Inc	Warren	RI	F	401 245-2909	16764
Rose Displays	Pawtucket	RI	F	978 219-8120	16413
RTC Holdings Inc	Pawtucket	RI	E	401 728-6980	16414
Spirit Recognition Inc (PA)	Pawtucket	RI	F	401 722-6400	16417
The Elliott Sales Group Inc	Providence	RI	D	401 944-0002	16625
Fastsigns - 490101	South Burlington	VT	G	802 238-1247	17578
Wood & Wood Inc	Waitsfield	VT	G	802 496-3000	17669
Yellow Sign Commercial Inc	South Burlington	VT	G	802 324-8500	17608

SIGNS & ADVERTISING SPECIALTIES: Artwork, Advertising

	CITY	ST	EMP	PHONE	ENTRY#
Copy Cats Inc	New London	CT	F	860 442-8424	2225
Dg International Holdings Corp	Needham Heights	MA	G	781 577-2016	10541
Rustic Marlin Designs LLC	Hanover	MA	E	508 376-1004	9041

SIGNS & ADVERTISING SPECIALTIES: Letters For Signs, Metal

	CITY	ST	EMP	PHONE	ENTRY#
Gloucester Graphics Inc (PA)	Gloucester	MA	G	978 281-4500	8937
Steel Art Company Inc	Norwood	MA	D	617 566-4079	11211
Precision Letter LLC	Manchester	NH	F	603 625-9625	14913
Twin State Signs Inc	Essex Junction	VT	G	802 872-8949	17248

SIGNS & ADVERTISING SPECIALTIES: Novelties

	CITY	ST	EMP	PHONE	ENTRY#
A D Perkins Company	New Haven	CT	G	203 777-3456	2110
Strong Group Inc (PA)	Gloucester	MA	D	978 281-3300	8960
Geiger Bros (PA)	Lewiston	ME	B	207 755-2000	4962
Snap Site Studios LLC	Manchester	NH	G	603 782-3395	14931
Gepp LLC	Warwick	RI	F	401 808-8004	16818
Hutchison Company Inc	North Kingstown	RI	F	401 294-3503	16258

SIGNS, EXC ELECTRIC, WHOLESALE

	CITY	ST	EMP	PHONE	ENTRY#
Acme Sign Co (PA)	Stamford	CT	F	203 324-2263	3272
Vision Designs LLC	Brookfield	CT	F	203 778-9898	543
Visi-Flash Rentals Eastern	West Bridgewater	MA	E	508 583-9100	12988

SIGNS: Electrical

	CITY	ST	EMP	PHONE	ENTRY#
Adamsahern Sign Solutions Inc	Hartford	CT	F	860 523-8835	1467
Applied Advertising Inc	Danbury	CT	F	860 640-0800	708
Arnco Sign Company	Wallingford	CT	E	203 238-1224	3775
Camaro Signs Inc (PA)	Jewett City	CT	G	860 886-1553	1535
Creative Dimensions Inc	Cheshire	CT	E	203 250-6500	584
Lauretano Sign Group Inc	Terryville	CT	E	860 582-0233	3605
Shiner Signs Inc	Meriden	CT	E	203 634-4331	1697
Ace Signs Inc	Springfield	MA	F	413 739-3814	12070
Agnoli Sign Company Inc	Springfield	MA	E	413 732-5111	12072
Apple Mill Holding Company Inc	Pembroke	MA	F	781 826-9706	11358
Back Bay Sign LLC	Wilmington	MA	F	781 475-1001	13386
Baker Sign Works Inc	Fall River	MA	F	508 674-6600	8524
Batten Bros Inc	Wakefield	MA	F	781 245-4800	12501
Design Communications Ltd (PA)	Avon	MA	D	617 542-9620	6148
Graphic Impact Signs Inc	Pittsfield	MA	F	413 499-0382	11399
Image Signs	New Bedford	MA	G	774 328-8059	10603
Insignia Incorporated	Haverhill	MA	E	978 372-3721	9105
Insignia Incorporated	Norwood	MA	F	781 278-0150	11182
Mediavue Systems Inc	Hingham	MA	E	781 926-0676	9153
Poyant Signs Inc (PA)	New Bedford	MA	E	800 544-0961	10643
Sign Techniques Inc	Chicopee	MA	F	413 594-8240	8061
Bailey Sign Inc	Westbrook	ME	F	207 774-2843	5617
Bangor Neon	Bangor	ME	F	207 947-2766	4492
Burr Signs	Westbrook	ME	G	207 396-6111	5619
Glidden Signs Inc	Scarborough	ME	F	207 396-6111	5433
Sign Design Inc	Portland	ME	F	207 856-2600	5272
Sign Services Inc	Stetson	ME	F	207 296-2400	5531
Jutras Signs Inc	Bedford	NH	F	603 622-2344	13936
Dexter Sign Co	East Providence	RI	F	401 434-1100	16014
Hub-Federal Inc	Providence	RI	G	401 421-3400	16534
LSI Industries Inc	Woonsocket	RI	G	401 766-7446	16968
Mandeville Signs Inc	Lincoln	RI	E	401 334-9100	16146
SES America Inc	Warwick	RI	F	401 232-3370	16861

Employee Codes: A=Over 500 employees, B=251-500
C=101-250, D=51-100, E=20-50, F=10-19, G=1-9

2024 Harris New England
Manufacturers Directory

1469

PRODUCT

	CITY	ST	EMP	PHONE	ENTRY#

SIGNS: Neon

	CITY	ST	EMP	PHONE	ENTRY#
Neokraft Signs Inc	Lewiston	ME	E	207 782-9654	4980
National Marker Company	North Smithfield	RI	D	401 762-9700	16329

SILICA MINING

Covia Specialty Minerals Inc	New Canaan	CT	E	203 966-8880	2080

SILICON WAFERS: Chemically Doped

Soitec Usa Inc (HQ)	Gloucester	MA	G	978 531-2222	8958

SILICONE RESINS

MTI Polyexe Corporation	Brentwood	NH	F	603 778-1449	14023

SILK SCREEN DESIGN SVCS

Barker Advg Specialty Co Inc (PA)	Cheshire	CT	D	203 272-2222	575
HJ Hoffman Company	Norwalk	CT	G	203 853-7740	2514
Hot Tops LLC	Shelton	CT	F	203 926-2067	3016
Michael Zoppa	South Windsor	CT	F	860 289-5881	3165
Pj Specialties	Willington	CT	F	860 429-7626	4226
TSS & A Inc	Prospect	CT	F	203 758-6303	2844
Bay State Apparel Inc	Leominster	MA	G	978 534-5810	9639
Chesterfield Products Inc	Chesterfield	MA	F	413 296-0066	7997
ESP Solutions Inc	Taunton	MA	F	508 285-0017	12335
Light Metal Platers LLC	Waltham	MA	E	781 899-8855	12709
M & P Machine Company Inc	Stoughton	MA	F	781 344-5888	12218
Spray Maine Inc	Newburyport	MA	F	207 384-2273	10717
Top Half Inc	Tyngsboro	MA	F	978 454-5440	12468
Universal Screening Studio Inc	Everett	MA	G	617 387-1832	8502
BBH Apparel	Boothbay Harbor	ME	F	207 633-0601	4601
DVE Manufacturing Inc	Lewiston	ME	F	207 783-9895	4957
Pf Pro Fnshg Silkscreening Inc	Hampstead	NH	G	603 329-8344	14389
Rapid Finishing LLC	Nashua	NH	E	603 889-4234	15154
Tk Sports and Associates Inc	Enfield	NH	G	603 442-6770	14275

SILO STAVES: Concrete Or Cast Stone

M G A Cast Stone Inc	Oxford	ME	E	207 926-5993	5147

SILVERWARE, STERLING SILVER

Silver Greenfield Inc	Greenfield	MA	C	413 774-2774	8999
Syratech Acquisition Corp (HQ)	Medford	MA	C	781 539-0100	10298

SKIN CARE PRDTS: Suntan Lotions & Oils

Playtex Products LLC (HQ)	Shelton	CT	D	203 944-5500	3050

SLINGS: Rope

East Shore Wire Rope Rgging Su	North Haven	CT	F	203 469-5204	2407

SMOKERS' SPLYS, WHOLESALE

Smokeloudz LLC (PA)	Meriden	CT	G	203 909-3556	1699

SNOWMOBILES

Eagle Motors Inc	Harrisville	RI	F	401 568-2580	16065

SOCIAL SERVICES INFORMATION EXCHANGE

Stratcomm Inc	Natick	MA	C	508 907-7000	10499

SOCIAL SVCS CENTER

Saint Vincent De Paul Place	Norwich	CT	G	860 889-7374	2615

SODA ASH MINING: Natural

American Natural Soda Ash Corp (PA)	Westport	CT	E	203 226-9056	4156

SODIUM CHLORIDE: Refined

Kuehne New Haven LLC	New Haven	CT	E	203 508-6703	2167

SOFT DRINKS WHOLESALERS

G & G Beverage Distributors	Yalesville	CT	E	203 949-6220	4397
Polar Corp (PA)	Worcester	MA	A	508 753-6383	13772
Coca-Cola Bevs Northeast Inc	Londonderry	NH	E	603 437-3530	14735

SOFTWARE PUBLISHERS: Home Entertainment

Mobile Global Esports Inc	Westport	CT	F	475 666-8401	4186
Venan Entertainment Inc	Middletown	CT	G	860 704-6330	1789
Homeportfolio Inc	Newton	MA	F	617 559-1197	10760
Native Instruments Usa Inc (PA)	Boston	MA	D	617 577-7799	6905

SOFTWARE PUBLISHERS: Operating Systems

VMS Software Inc	Boston	MA	D	425 766-1692	7110
North Tecom LLC	Manchester	NH	F	603 851-5165	14904

SOFTWARE PUBLISHERS: Word Processing

	CITY	ST	EMP	PHONE	ENTRY#
Autovirt Inc	Nashua	NH	G	603 546-2900	15065

SOFTWARE TRAINING, COMPUTER

Compart North America Inc	Andover	MA	E	877 237-2725	5879
Datarobot Inc (PA)	Boston	MA	D	617 765-4500	6684
Microcad Trning Consulting Inc (PA)	Watertown	MA	F	617 923-0500	12893
Secure Code Warrior Inc	Boston	MA	E	617 901-3005	7030
Sunrise Group USA LLC	Shrewsbury	MA	E	508 873-1519	11842

SOLAR CELLS

Cubicpv Inc (PA)	Bedford	MA	F	781 861-1611	6218
Solar Five LLC	Lexington	MA	F	781 301-7233	9776
Spire Corporation (PA)	Billerica	MA	D	978 584-3958	6484
Gosolar NH LLC	Barrington	NH	G	603 948-1189	13914
Enow Inc	Warwick	RI	F	401 732-7080	16814
Allearth Renewables Inc	Williston	VT	E	802 872-9600	17721

SOLAR HEATING EQPT

Ganado Storage LLC	Andover	MA	D	617 605-4322	5884
Spire Solar Inc (HQ)	Bedford	MA	G	781 275-6000	6271
GS Inc	Rockland	ME	G	207 593-7730	5332
Bullrock Solar LLC	South Burlington	VT	F	802 985-1460	17575

SOLES, BOOT OR SHOE: Rubber, Composition Or Fiber

Vibram Corporation (HQ)	Concord	MA	E	978 318-0000	8138
Vibram Corporation (DH)	North Brookfield	MA	C	508 867-6494	10964

SOLVENTS

Purification Technologies LLC (DH)	Chester	CT	F	860 526-7801	630
US Chemicals Inc	New Canaan	CT	G	203 655-8878	2093
Isp Freetown Fine Chem Inc	Assonet	MA	E	508 672-0634	5974
Itk Chemicals Inc	Danvers	MA	F	978 531-2279	8194

SOLVENTS: Organic

Veolia Es Tchncal Slutions LLC	Danbury	CT	F	203 748-9116	832
Onyx Environmental Svcs LLC (DH)	Boston	MA	E	617 849-6600	6936

SONAR SYSTEMS & EQPT

Edgeone LLC	West Wareham	MA	G	508 291-0960	13062
Massa Products Corporation	Hingham	MA	D	781 749-3120	9152
Raytheon Company	Marlborough	MA	B	978 440-1000	10200
Raytheon Company	Marlborough	MA	E	508 490-1000	10201
Raytheon Company	Woburn	MA	C	339 645-6000	13648
Klein Marine Systems Inc	Salem	NH	D	603 893-6131	15540
Raytheon Company	Pelham	NH	F	603 635-6800	15295
Syqwest Inc	Cranston	RI	E	401 432-7129	15916

SOUND EQPT: Electric

Headwaters Inc	Marblehead	MA	G	781 715-6404	10087
Lightspeed Mfg Co LLC	Haverhill	MA	F	978 521-7676	9109
Thermal Circuits Inc	Salem	MA	C	978 745-1162	11734

SOUND EQPT: Underwater

McLane Research Labs Inc (PA)	East Falmouth	MA	G	508 495-4000	8361

SOUND REPRODUCING EQPT

Headwaters Inc	Marblehead	MA	G	781 715-6404	10087

SPACE PROPULSION UNITS & PARTS

United Gear and Machine Co Inc	Suffield	CT	F	860 623-6618	3596
Ae Red Holdings LLC (PA)	Marlborough	MA	F	561 372-7820	10105
Busek Co Inc	Natick	MA	E	508 655-5565	10471
Wormtown Atomic Propulsion	Waltham	MA	F	781 487-7777	12819

SPACE VEHICLES

Assurance Technology Corp (PA)	Carlisle	MA	D	978 369-8848	7845
Valt Enterprizes Inc	Presque Isle	ME	F	207 560-5188	5311

SPEAKER SYSTEMS

C Speaker Corp	Stamford	CT	C		3299
Aerial Acoustics Corporation	Lawrence	MA	F	978 988-1600	9535
Boston Acoustics Inc (DH)	Wakefield	MA	D	978 538-5000	12503
Inter-Ego Systems Inc (PA)	Hatfield	MA	F	516 576-9052	9073
Pine and Baker Mfg Inc	Tewksbury	MA	F	978 851-1215	12412

SPECIALTY FOOD STORES: Coffee

Masas Usa Inc	East Haven	CT	E	305 603-8868	1045
Bolt Coffee Company LLC	Providence	RI	E	401 533-6506	16487
Coffee Exchange Ltd	Providence	RI	F	401 273-1198	16502
Daves Coffee LLC (PA)	Narragansett	RI	F	800 483-4436	16188
Keurig Green Mountain Inc (DH)	Waterbury	VT	D	877 879-2326	17675
Speeder & Earls Inc	Burlington	VT	F	802 660-3996	17160

	CITY	ST	EMP	PHONE	ENTRY#

SPECIALTY FOOD STORES: Dried Fruit
	CITY	ST	EMP	PHONE	ENTRY#
Modernist Pantry LLC	Eliot	ME	G	207 200-3817	4750

SPECIALTY FOOD STORES: Eggs & Poultry
| Somerville Live Poultry Co Inc | Boston | MA | G | 617 547-9191 | 7045 |
| Willow Tree Poultry Farm Inc | Attleboro | MA | D | 508 222-2479 | 6077 |

SPECIALTY FOOD STORES: Health & Dietetic Food
| Designing Health Inc | East Longmeadow MA | F | | 661 257-1705 | 8373 |
| Perioq Inc | Leominster | MA | G | 978 534-1249 | 9693 |

SPECIALTY FOOD STORES: Juices, Fruit Or Vegetable
| Cold Hollow Cider Mill Inc | Waterbury Center | VT | E | 802 244-8771 | 17680 |

SPECIALTY FOOD STORES: Soft Drinks
Harvest Hill Holdings LLC (PA)	Stamford	CT	F	203 914-1620	3367
Ambrose G McCarthy Jr	Skowhegan	ME	G	207 474-8837	5462
Auburn Spring Water Company (PA)	Auburn	ME	G	207 782-1521	4422
Rea Inc	Saint Albans	VT	F	802 527-7437	17530

SPECIALTY SAWMILL PRDTS
| Carris Reels Inc (HQ) | Proctor | VT | E | 802 773-9111 | 17457 |

SPORTING & ATHLETIC GOODS: Bags, Golf
| Pride Manufacturing Co LLC (PA) | Burnham | ME | C | 207 487-3322 | 4661 |

SPORTING & ATHLETIC GOODS: Basketball Eqpt & Splys, NEC
| Unified Sports Incorporated (PA) | Waterford | CT | E | 860 447-3001 | 3998 |

SPORTING & ATHLETIC GOODS: Camping Eqpt & Splys
| Life+gear Inc | Wellesley Hills | MA | F | 858 755-2099 | 12952 |

SPORTING & ATHLETIC GOODS: Cases, Gun & Rod
| Santa Cruz Gunlocks LLC | Webster | NH | G | 603 746-7740 | 15674 |

SPORTING & ATHLETIC GOODS: Fishing Eqpt
Ei-Rec LLC	Stafford Springs	CT	F	860 851-9014	3255
Cns Outdoor Technologies LLC	Greenfield	MA	E	413 475-3840	8986
Johnson Outdoors Inc	Old Town	ME	F	603 518-1634	5127

SPORTING & ATHLETIC GOODS: Fishing Tackle, General
Outdoor Outfitters Inc	Orleans	MA	E	508 255-0455	11241
Kane Motor Car Co Inc	North Kingstown	RI	G	401 294-4634	16263
Orvis Company Inc	Manchester	VT	E	802 362-3750	17324
The Orvis Company Inc (PA)	Sunderland	VT	B	802 362-3622	17635

SPORTING & ATHLETIC GOODS: Hockey Eqpt & Splys, NEC
| Warrior Sports Inc (DH) | Boston | MA | C | 800 968-7845 | 7113 |

SPORTING & ATHLETIC GOODS: Hunting Eqpt
| Extreme Dim Wildlife Calls LLC | Hampden | ME | G | 207 862-2825 | 4863 |

SPORTING & ATHLETIC GOODS: Rods & Rod Parts, Fishing
| Thomas & Thomas Rodmakers | Greenfield | MA | F | 413 475-3840 | 9003 |

SPORTING & ATHLETIC GOODS: Shafts, Golf Club
Acushnet Company	Acushnet	MA	F	508 979-2000	5769
Acushnet Company	New Bedford	MA	F	508 979-2156	10561
Acushnet Company	New Bedford	MA	F	508 979-2000	10562
Acushnet Company	New Bedford	MA	E	508 979-2000	10563

SPORTING & ATHLETIC GOODS: Shooting Eqpt & Splys, General
| Savage Range Systems Inc | Westfield | MA | G | 413 568-7001 | 13207 |

SPORTING & ATHLETIC GOODS: Snow Skis
| Sunapee Difference LLC | Newbury | NH | D | 603 763-3500 | 15204 |

SPORTING & ATHLETIC GOODS: Targets, Archery & Rifle Shooting
| Sadlak Industries LLC | Coventry | CT | E | 860 742-0227 | 681 |

SPORTING & ATHLETIC GOODS: Track & Field Athletic Eqpt
| Sports Fields Inc | Monmouth | ME | F | 207 933-3547 | 5072 |

SPORTING & ATHLETIC GOODS: Treadmills
| Samsara Fitness LLC | Chester | CT | F | 860 895-8533 | 632 |

SPORTING & ATHLETIC GOODS: Water Sports Eqpt
| Imperial Pools Inc | Taunton | MA | F | 508 339-3830 | 12342 |
| Sickday Inc | Wellfleet | MA | F | 508 214-4158 | 12953 |

SPORTING & REC GOODS, WHOLESALE: Camping Eqpt & Splys
	CITY	ST	EMP	PHONE	ENTRY#
Shelterlogic Corp (HQ)	Watertown	CT	E	860 945-6442	4028
Slogic Holding Corp (PA)	New Canaan	CT	F	203 966-2800	2086

SPORTING & RECREATIONAL GOODS, WHOLESALE: Boat Access & Part
| Dock Doctors LLC | Ferrisburgh | VT | E | 802 877-6756 | 17268 |

SPORTING GOODS STORES: Camping & Backpacking Eqpt
| Ragged Mountain Equipment Inc | Intervale | NH | E | 603 356-3042 | 14561 |

SPORTING GOODS STORES: Firearms
Connecticut Shotgun Manufacturing Co	New Britain	CT	D	860 225-6581	2012
Liberty Industries Inc	East Berlin	CT	E	860 828-6361	913
Rosellis Machine & Mfg Co	Westfield	MA	F	413 562-4317	13203
Alex & Ryan Design LLC	Manchester	NH	F	603 518-8650	14808

SPORTING GOODS STORES: Fishing Eqpt
Thomas & Thomas Rodmakers	Greenfield	MA	F	413 475-3840	9003
Downeast Fishing Gear	Trenton	ME	E	207 667-3131	5553
Trawlworks Inc	Narragansett	RI	F	401 789-3964	16198

SPORTING GOODS STORES: Playground Eqpt
| Creative Playthings Ltd (PA) | Framingham | MA | F | 508 620-0900 | 8753 |

SPORTING GOODS STORES: Specialty Sport Splys, NEC
| Manup LLC | Norwalk | CT | G | 203 588-9861 | 2533 |
| Hyperlite Mountain Gear Inc | Biddeford | ME | D | 800 464-9208 | 4570 |

SPORTING GOODS: Sleeping Bags
| Black Dog Corporation | Portsmouth | RI | E | 401 683-5858 | 16439 |

SPORTS APPAREL STORES
Omniview Sports Inc	Boston	MA	G	781 583-3534	6929
Chuck Roast Equipment Inc (PA)	Conway	NH	F	603 447-5492	14178
Firecracker Sports LLC	Cumberland	RI	G	401 595-0233	15939

SPORTS CLUBS, MANAGERS & PROMOTERS
| Terika Smith Ministries Corp | Lawrence | MA | E | 978 233-0576 | 9603 |

SPORTS PROMOTION SVCS
| Video Messengercom Corp | Stratford | CT | G | 203 358-8842 | 3582 |

SPRINGS: Coiled Flat
| Excel Spring & Stamping LLC | Bristol | CT | G | 860 585-1495 | 444 |

SPRINGS: Instrument, Precision
Chestnut United Corporation	Bristol	CT	D	860 584-0594	426
Hardware Products Company LP	Bristol	CT	E	617 884-9410	452
Spring Manufacturing Corp	Tewksbury	MA	F	978 658-7396	12417

SPRINGS: Mechanical, Precision
Century Spring Mfg Co Inc	Bristol	CT	E	860 582-3344	425
Lee Spring Company LLC	Bristol	CT	F	860 584-0991	461
Rd Ventures Inc	Plainville	CT	F	860 747-2709	2779
Rowley Spring & Stamping Corp	Bristol	CT	C	860 582-8175	494
Thomas Spring Co Conn Inc	Milford	CT	G	203 874-7030	1895

SPRINGS: Precision
Barnes Group Inc (PA)	Bristol	CT	C	860 583-7070	406
Excel Spring & Stamping LLC	Bristol	CT	G	860 585-1495	444
Matthew Warren Inc	Southington	CT	D	860 621-7358	3221
Old Dmfg Inc	Farmington	CT	E	860 677-8561	1234

SPRINGS: Steel
Acme Monaco Corporation (PA)	New Britain	CT	C	860 224-1349	1995
Arrow Manufacturing Company	Bristol	CT	E		397
Century Spring Mfg Co Inc	Bristol	CT	E	860 582-3344	425
Connectcut Spring Stmping Corp	Farmington	CT	B	860 677-1341	1212
HMC Enterprises Inc	New Hartford	CT	E	860 379-8506	2101
Lee Spring Company LLC	Bristol	CT	F	860 584-0991	461
Matthew Warren Inc	Southington	CT	D	860 621-7358	3221
Newcomb Spring Corp	Southington	CT	D	860 621-0111	3224
Old Dmfg Inc	Farmington	CT	E	860 677-8561	1234
Oscar Jobs	Bristol	CT	G	860 583-7834	477
Pa-Ted Spring Company LLC	Bristol	CT	E	860 582-6368	479
Rowley Spring & Stamping Corp	Bristol	CT	C	860 582-8175	494
Spring Computerized Inds LLC	Harwinton	CT	G	860 605-9206	1523
Spring Tollman Company Incorporated (PA) 860 583-1326	Bristol 497	CT	D		
Leggett & Platt Incorporated	Oxford	MA	D	508 987-8706	11258
D & W Tool & Findings Inc	Pawtucket	RI	F	401 727-3030	16363

PRODUCT

	CITY	ST	EMP	PHONE	ENTRY#

SPRINGS: Wire

	CITY	ST	EMP	PHONE	ENTRY#
Atlantic Precision Spring Inc	Bristol	CT	E	860 583-1864	399
Barnes Group Inc	Bristol	CT	D	860 582-9581	404
Barnes Group Inc	Farmington	CT	G	860 298-7740	1209
Connectcut Spring Stmping Corp	Farmington	CT	B	860 677-1341	1212
Dcp Spring Acquisition Co Inc	Bristol	CT	E	860 589-3231	435
Engineering Specialties Inc	North Branford	CT	E	203 488-2266	2367
Fourslide Spring Stamping Inc	Bristol	CT	E	860 583-1688	449
Gemco Manufacturing Co Inc	Southington	CT	E	860 628-5529	3211
National Spring & Stamping Inc	Thomaston	CT	F	860 283-0203	3625
Newcomb Spring Corp	Southington	CT	D	860 621-0111	3224
Newcomb Springs Connecticut	Southington	CT	E	860 621-0111	3225
Oscar Jobs	Bristol	CT	G	860 583-7834	477
Plymouth Spring Company Inc	Bristol	CT	D	860 584-0594	482
Southington Tool & Mfg Corp	Plantsville	CT	E	860 276-0021	2796
Spring Computerized Inds LLC	Harwinton	CT	G	860 605-9206	1523
Spring Tollman Company Incorporated (PA)	Bristol	CT			D
860 583-1326	497				
Springfield Spring Corporation	Bristol	CT	F	860 584-6560	498
Device Technologies Inc	Southborough	MA	E	508 229-2000	11994
Leggett & Platt Incorporated	Oxford	MA	D	508 987-8706	11258
Springfield Spring Corporation (PA)	East Longmeadow	MA	E	413 525-6837	8395
D & W Tool & Findings Inc	Pawtucket	RI	F	401 727-3030	16363

SPRINKLER SYSTEMS: Field

	CITY	ST	EMP	PHONE	ENTRY#
C M S Landscaping Corporation	Holyoke	MA	F	413 533-3300	9245
F W Webb Company	Stoughton	MA	E	781 341-1100	12205

SPROCKETS: Power Transmission

	CITY	ST	EMP	PHONE	ENTRY#
Custom Machine & Tool Co Inc	Hanover	MA	E	781 924-1003	9029
Lampin Corporation (PA)	Uxbridge	MA	F	508 278-2422	12484

STAINLESS STEEL

	CITY	ST	EMP	PHONE	ENTRY#
ATI Flat Rlled Pdts Hldngs LLC	Waterbury	CT	F	203 756-7414	3888
Dufrane Nuclear Shielding Inc	Winsted	CT	F	860 379-2318	4340
A A A Metals Company Inc	Hanson	MA	F	781 447-1220	9049
Dakota Systems Inc	Dracut	MA	D	978 275-0600	8303
Ne Stainless Steel Fab	Weymouth	MA	G	781 335-0121	13331
New England Stinless Distr LLC	Salisbury	MA	F	978 255-4830	11743
Millincket Fabrication Mch Inc (PA)	Millinocket	ME	F	207 723-9733	5067
Slinky Stainless Steel	Milford	NH	G	603 673-1104	15038

STAINLESS STEEL WARE

	CITY	ST	EMP	PHONE	ENTRY#
Dipwell Company Inc	Northampton	MA	G	413 587-4673	11059
Hilliard Precision Products LLC	Bellingham	MA	E	508 541-9100	6292

STAIRCASES & STAIRS, WOOD

	CITY	ST	EMP	PHONE	ENTRY#
Colonial Woodworking Inc	Stamford	CT	E	203 866-5844	3317
Leos Kitchen and Stair Corp	New Britain	CT	G	860 225-7363	2037
Naugatuck Stair Company Inc	Naugatuck	CT	F	203 729-7134	1976
New England Stair Company Inc	Shelton	CT	E	203 924-0606	3038
Quality Stairs Inc	Bridgeport	CT	F	203 367-8390	364
Robert L Lovallo	Stamford	CT	G	203 324-6655	3450
Stately Stair Co Inc	Naugatuck	CT	E	203 575-1966	1987
Summit Stair Inc	Bethel	CT	F	203 778-2251	135
Walston Inc	Guilford	CT	G	203 453-5929	1409
Wesconn Stairs Inc	Danbury	CT	G	203 792-7367	836
West Hrtford Stirs Cbinets Inc	Newington	CT	D	860 953-9151	2334
AKa McHngelo Strbuilder LLC	North Easton	MA	G	508 238-9054	11007
Unique Spiral Stairs Inc	Albion	ME	G	207 437-2415	4401
Hardwood Design Inc	Exeter	RI	E	401 294-2235	16051

STAMPINGS: Automotive

	CITY	ST	EMP	PHONE	ENTRY#
3M Company	Meriden	CT	F	203 237-5541	1647

STAMPINGS: Metal

	CITY	ST	EMP	PHONE	ENTRY#
Newhart Products Inc	Milford	CT	E	203 878-3546	1854

STAPLES

	CITY	ST	EMP	PHONE	ENTRY#
Markwell Manufacturing Co Inc	Norwood	MA	G	781 769-6610	11194

STAPLES: Steel, Wire Or Cut

	CITY	ST	EMP	PHONE	ENTRY#
Flooring Pro Industries LLC	Auburn	MA	G	704 736-1004	6113
Acme Staple Company Inc	Franklin	NH	F	603 934-2320	14318
King Manufacturing Co Inc	Jaffrey	NH	F	603 532-6455	14570

STATIONARY & OFFICE SPLYS, WHOLESALE: Office Filing Splys

	CITY	ST	EMP	PHONE	ENTRY#
Ames Safety Envelope Company (DH)	Somerville	MA	F	617 684-1000	11860

STATIONERY & OFFICE SPLYS WHOLESALERS

	CITY	ST	EMP	PHONE	ENTRY#
Recycle 4 Vets LLC	Westport	CT	G	203 222-7300	4194

	CITY	ST	EMP	PHONE	ENTRY#
CAM Office Services Inc (PA)	Marlborough	MA	F	781 932-9868	10125
W G Fry Corp	Florence	MA	E	413 747-2551	8687
Wise Business Forms Inc	Portland	ME	C	207 774-6560	5290
Papergraphics Print & Copy Inc	Merrimack	NH	F	603 880-1835	14997
Relyco Sales Inc (PA)	Dover	NH	E	603 742-0999	14248
Savron Graphics Inc (PA)	Jaffrey	NH	G	603 532-7726	14579
Costa Inc	Providence	RI	E	401 333-1200	16506

STATIONERY: Made From Purchased Materials

	CITY	ST	EMP	PHONE	ENTRY#
Great Northern Industries Inc (PA)	Boston	MA	C	617 262-4314	6771
Marian Heath Greeting Cards LLC	Wareham	MA	C	508 291-0766	12840
Viabella Holdings LLC (PA)	Wareham	MA	E	800 688-9998	12848

STATORS REWINDING SVCS

	CITY	ST	EMP	PHONE	ENTRY#
Piela Electric Inc	Preston	CT	F	860 889-8476	2828
SEC Electrical Inc	New Haven	CT	F	203 562-5811	2196

STEEL & ALLOYS: Tool & Die

	CITY	ST	EMP	PHONE	ENTRY#
Plainville Special Tool LLC	Plainville	CT	F	860 747-2736	2777
Rcd LLC	Shelton	CT	E	203 712-1900	3059
New Hampshire Stamping Co Inc	Goffstown	NH	E	603 641-1234	14352
Stamping Technologies Inc	Laconia	NH	F	603 524-5958	14671

STEEL, COLD-ROLLED: Sheet Or Strip, From Own HotRolled

	CITY	ST	EMP	PHONE	ENTRY#
Kimchuk Incorporated (PA)	Danbury	CT	F	203 790-7800	766
Redifoils LLC	Portland	CT	F	860 342-1500	2823

STEEL, COLD-ROLLED: Strip NEC, From Purchased HotRolled

	CITY	ST	EMP	PHONE	ENTRY#
Ulbrich Stnless Stels Spcial M (PA)	North Haven	CT	D	203 239-4481	2442
ATI Allegheny Ludlum Inc	New Bedford	MA	D	508 992-4067	10570
Thompson Steel Company Inc	Canton	MA	C	781 828-8800	7834
New Amtrol Holdings Inc (DH)	West Warwick	RI	F	614 438-3210	16917

STONE: Dimension, NEC

	CITY	ST	EMP	PHONE	ENTRY#
Connecticut Stone Supplies Inc (PA)	Milford	CT	D	203 882-1000	1814
Midwood Quarry and Cnstr Inc (PA)	East Hartford	CT	F	860 289-1414	1006
Mildred Coppola (PA)	Stamford	CT	F	203 967-9300	3411
Cumar Inc	Everett	MA	E	617 389-7818	8484
George D Judd & Sons LLC	Goshen	MA	G	413 268-7590	8967
Adams Granite Co Inc	Websterville	VT	D	802 476-5281	17683
Houle Bros Granite Co Inc	Barre	VT	F	802 476-6825	17006
International Stone Products (PA)	Barre	VT	D	802 476-6636	17009
McCue Memorial Co Inc	Castleton	VT	E	802 468-5636	17173
Troy Minerals Inc	Florence	VT	F	802 878-5103	17273

STONE: Quarrying & Processing, Own Stone Prdts

	CITY	ST	EMP	PHONE	ENTRY#
Kenneth Lynch & Sons Inc	Oxford	CT	G	203 762-8363	2702
O & G Industries Inc	Beacon Falls	CT	F	203 729-4529	45
Paul H Gesswein & Company Inc	Old Saybrook	CT	E	860 388-0652	2660
Skyline Quarry LLC	Stafford Springs	CT	F	860 875-3580	3259
270 University Avenue LLC	Westwood	MA	G	781 407-0836	13304
All Granite & Marble Inc	Charlton	MA	E	508 434-0611	7885
Bates Bros Seam-Face Gran Co	East Weymouth	MA	E	781 337-1150	8426
E W Sykes General Contractors	Athol	MA	E	978 249-7655	5978
Newmont Slate Co Inc (PA)	West Pawlet	VT	E	802 645-0203	17692

STONEWARE PRDTS: Pottery

	CITY	ST	EMP	PHONE	ENTRY#
Sheffield Pottery Inc	Sheffield	MA	E	413 229-7700	11801
Bennington Potters Inc (PA)	Bennington	VT	E	800 205-8033	17036

STORE FIXTURES: Exc Wood

	CITY	ST	EMP	PHONE	ENTRY#
In Store Experience Inc	Westport	CT	E	203 221-4777	4174

STORE FIXTURES: Wood

	CITY	ST	EMP	PHONE	ENTRY#
Anthony Manufacturing Co Inc	Medford	MA	F	781 396-1400	10279
E G W Bradbury Enterprises Inc	Bridgewater	ME	F	207 429-8141	4625
Modern Industries Inc	Providence	RI	E	401 331-8000	16566
Monarch Industries Inc	Providence	RI	D	401 247-5200	16567
Vermont Store Fixture Corporation (PA)	Danby	VT	D	802 293-5126	17210

STORE FRONTS: Prefabricated, Metal

	CITY	ST	EMP	PHONE	ENTRY#
Capitol Glass Company Inc	West Hartford	CT	F	860 236-1936	4050
Stent Metal Corp	Hamden	CT	G	203 287-9007	1457
Central FLS Plate & Win GL Co	Central Falls	RI	F	401 722-1267	15787

STORES: Auto & Home Supply

	CITY	ST	EMP	PHONE	ENTRY#
International Auto Entps Inc (PA)	New Britain	CT	F	860 224-0253	2034
Holyoke Tire & Auto Svc Inc	Springfield	MA	G	413 733-2141	12101
Petes Tire Barns Inc	Providence	RI	F	401 521-2240	16583

STOVES: Wood & Coal Burning

	CITY	ST	EMP	PHONE	ENTRY#
Maine Stove & Chimney LLC	Sanford	ME	G	207 324-4440	5399

	CITY	ST	EMP	PHONE	ENTRY#
Woodstock Soapstone Co Inc	West Lebanon	NH	F	800 866-4344	15692
L & G Fabricators Inc	Bennington	VT	F	802 447-0965	17047

STRAPS: Braids, Textile

	CITY	ST	EMP	PHONE	ENTRY#
Conneaut Industries Inc	West Greenwich	RI	D	401 392-1110	16883

STRAPS: Webbing, Woven

	CITY	ST	EMP	PHONE	ENTRY#
Murdock Webbing Company Inc (PA)	Central Falls	RI	C	401 724-3000	15793
Nfa Corp	Cumberland	RI	E	401 333-8947	15954
Nfa Corp	Cumberland	RI	B	401 333-8990	15955
Texcel Industries Inc	Cumberland	RI	E	401 727-2113	15969

STRUCTURAL SUPPORT & BUILDING MATERIAL: Concrete

	CITY	ST	EMP	PHONE	ENTRY#
Growspan LLC	South Windsor	CT	F	877 835-9996	3152
WJ Kettleworks LLC	Stratford	CT	G	203 377-5000	3585

SUNDRIES & RELATED PRDTS: Medical & Laboratory, Rubber

	CITY	ST	EMP	PHONE	ENTRY#
Advent Medical Products Inc	Lincoln	MA	G	781 272-2813	9794
Hytex Industries Inc	Randolph	MA	E	781 963-4400	11565
Rubber-Right Rollers Inc	Everett	MA	G	617 387-6060	8498
Saint-Gobain Prfmce Plas Corp	Worcester	MA	C	508 852-3072	13792

SUNGLASSES, WHOLESALE

	CITY	ST	EMP	PHONE	ENTRY#
Fgx International Holdings Ltd (HQ)	Smithfield	RI	B	401 231-3800	16698
Fgx International Inc (DH)	Smithfield	RI	A	401 231-3800	16699

SURFACE ACTIVE AGENTS

	CITY	ST	EMP	PHONE	ENTRY#
Henkel of America Inc (HQ)	Rocky Hill	CT	B	860 615-3395	2926
Henkel US Operations Corp (DH)	Rocky Hill	CT	B	860 571-5100	2927
Lanxess Solutions US Inc	Shelton	CT	A	203 573-2000	3027
Isp Freetown Fine Chem Inc	Assonet	MA	D	508 672-0634	5974
CNc International Ltd Partnr	Woonsocket	RI	F	401 769-6100	16954
Ne Finest LLC	Coventry	RI	F	800 215-6640	15817

SURFACE ACTIVE AGENTS: Oils & Greases

	CITY	ST	EMP	PHONE	ENTRY#
Solidification Pdts Intl Inc	Northford	CT	G	203 484-9494	2456

SURGICAL APPLIANCES & SPLYS

	CITY	ST	EMP	PHONE	ENTRY#
Becton Dickinson and Company	Canaan	CT	D	860 824-5487	552
Cardiopulmonary Corp	Milford	CT	E	203 877-1999	1808
Carwild Corporation (PA)	New London	CT	E	860 442-4914	2224
Danbury Ortho	Danbury	CT	G	203 797-1500	725
Gordon Engineering Corporation	Brookfield	CT	G	203 775-4501	522
K B C Electronics Inc	Milford	CT	F	203 298-9654	1842
Kelyniam Global Inc	Collinsville	CT	G	800 280-8192	667
McIntire Company (HQ)	Bristol	CT	F	860 585-8559	465
McNeil Healthcare Inc	West Haven	CT	A	203 934-8187	4115
Seongyun Corporation	West Haven	CT	F	203 668-6803	4125
Unisoft Medical Corporation	Torrington	CT	F	860 482-6848	3704
Aearo Technologies LLC	Auburn	MA	B	317 692-6645	6098
Amatech Corporation (DH)	Acton	MA	E	978 263-5401	5736
Amatech Corporation	Acton	MA	D	978 263-5401	5737
Americal Sergical Company	Salem	MA	G	781 592-7200	11700
American Surgical Company LLC	Salem	MA	E	781 592-7200	11701
Axya Medical Inc	Beverly	MA	F	978 232-9997	6331
Bay State Elevator Company Inc (HQ)	Agawam	MA	E	413 786-7000	5779
Bionx Medical Technologies Inc	Cambridge	MA	D		7516
Bonesupport Inc	Needham Heights	MA	E	781 772-1756	10531
Boston Medical Products Inc	Shrewsbury	MA	E	508 898-9300	11829
Cardiotech International Inc	Wilmington	MA	F	978 657-0075	13397
Consolidated Machine Corporation	Billerica	MA	E	617 782-6072	6428
Consumer Hearing Cons Inc	Walpole	MA	G	866 658-8800	12557
Continental Metal Pdts Co Inc	Woburn	MA	E	781 935-4400	13546
Covidien LP (HQ)	Mansfield	MA	C	763 514-4000	10046
Emotionrx Inc	Cambridge	MA	F	617 500-5976	7561
Fosta-Tek Optics Inc (PA)	Leominster	MA	D	978 534-6511	9665
Genzyme Corporation (DH)	Cambridge	MA	A	617 252-7500	7585
Genzyme Corporation	Framingham	MA	E	617 252-7500	8773
Gta-Nht Inc (HQ)	Rockland	MA	C	781 331-5900	11647
Marine Polymer Tech Inc (PA)	Tewksbury	MA	E	781 270-3200	12405
Medical Device Bus Svcs Inc	Norton	MA	D	508 828-2726	11129
Medical Products Mfg LLC	West Wareham	MA	F	508 291-1830	13069
Medsource Technologies LLC (DH)	Wilmington	MA	F	978 570-6900	13429
Oi Sellers Fund LLC	Wakefield	MA	G	781 587-3242	12524
Palomar Medical Products LLC	Burlington	MA	E	781 993-2300	7408
Ranfac Corp	Avon	MA	D	508 588-4400	6159
Rewalk Robotics Inc (HQ)	Marlborough	MA	E	508 251-1154	10203
St Jude Medical LLC	Westford	MA	G	978 577-3400	13264
Visionaid Inc	Wareham	MA	E	508 295-3300	12849
Maine Orthtic Prsthtic Rhab Sv	Portland	ME	F	207 773-8818	5241
Puritan Medical Pdts Co I LP	Guilford	ME	B	207 876-3311	4856
Puritan Medical Pdts Co LLC (PA)	Guilford	ME	B	207 876-3311	4857

	CITY	ST	EMP	PHONE	ENTRY#
Qsa Optical Co Inc	Lewiston	ME	E	207 783-8523	4988
Fireye Inc (DH)	Derry	NH	C	603 432-4100	14193
Honeywell Safety Pdts USA Inc	Smithfield	RI	E	401 757-2106	16714
Johnson & Johnson	Cumberland	RI	C	401 762-6751	15949
Aadco Medical Inc	Randolph	VT	D	802 728-3400	17466
Bio Med Packaging Systems Inc	Norwalk	CT	F	203 846-1923	2472
K W Griffen Company	Norwalk	CT	E	203 846-1923	2521
Schaeffler Aerospace USA Corp (DH)	Danbury	CT	B	203 744-2211	809
Arrow Interventional Inc	Chelmsford	MA	C	919 433-4948	7909
Fresenius Usa Inc (DH)	Waltham	MA	C	781 699-4191	12683
Atrium Medical Corporation (HQ)	Merrimack	NH	B	973 709-7654	14973

SURGICAL IMPLANTS

	CITY	ST	EMP	PHONE	ENTRY#
Brimfield Precision LLC	Brimfield	MA	C	413 245-7144	7249
Depuy Spine LLC (HQ)	Raynham	MA	B	508 880-8100	11587
Medtronic Inc	Danvers	MA	F	978 777-0042	8207
Medtronic Inc	Danvers	MA	F	978 739-3080	8208
Tesco Associates Incorporated (PA)	Tyngsboro	MA	F	978 649-5527	12467
Seabrook Medical LLC	Seabrook	NH	C	603 474-1919	15605

SURGICAL INSTRUMENT REPAIR SVCS

	CITY	ST	EMP	PHONE	ENTRY#
Majestic Medical Inc	Raynham	MA	F	508 824-1944	11590

SUSPENSION SYSTEMS: Acoustical, Metal

	CITY	ST	EMP	PHONE	ENTRY#
Rolls-Royce Marine North Amer (DH)	Walpole	MA	C	508 668-9610	12574

SVC ESTABLISHMENT EQPT, WHOLESALE: Firefighting Eqpt

	CITY	ST	EMP	PHONE	ENTRY#
Greenwood Emrgncy Vehicles LLC (HQ)	Attleboro Falls	MA	D	508 695-7138	6086

SVC ESTABLISHMENT EQPT, WHOLESALE: Restaurant Splys

	CITY	ST	EMP	PHONE	ENTRY#
American Marketing Intl LLC	Clinton	CT	E	860 669-4100	635

SWEEPING COMPOUNDS

	CITY	ST	EMP	PHONE	ENTRY#
Absorbent Specialty Pdts LLC	Pawtucket	RI	F	401 722-1177	16342

SWIMMING POOL EQPT: Filters & Water Conditioning Systems

	CITY	ST	EMP	PHONE	ENTRY#
Aquatic Solutions LLC	Hampton	NH	G	888 704-7665	14398

SWIMMING POOLS, EQPT & SPLYS: Wholesalers

	CITY	ST	EMP	PHONE	ENTRY#
Jarvis Welding & Mfg Co	Turners Falls	MA	G	413 863-9541	12449

SWITCHBOARDS & PARTS: Power

	CITY	ST	EMP	PHONE	ENTRY#
Lex Products LLC (PA)	Trumbull	CT	C	203 363-3738	3723
Huber+suhner Polatis Inc (DH)	Bedford	MA	E	781 275-5080	6231
Whitmor Company Inc (PA)	Revere	MA	F	781 284-8000	11625

SWITCHES: Electric Power

	CITY	ST	EMP	PHONE	ENTRY#
Ashcroft Inc (DH)	Stratford	CT	B	203 378-8281	3517
Baumer Ltd (DH)	Bristol	CT	F	860 621-2121	410
Linemaster Switch Corporation	Woodstock	CT	C	860 630-4920	4395
High Voltage Engineering Corp	Wakefield	MA	E	781 224-1001	12511
Sick Inc	Stoughton	MA	D	781 302-2500	12235
Suns International LLC	Chelmsford	MA	B	978 349-2329	7960

SWITCHES: Electric Power, Exc Snap, Push Button, Etc

	CITY	ST	EMP	PHONE	ENTRY#
ABB Enterprise Software Inc	Plainville	CT	A	860 747-7111	2744
Control Concepts Inc (PA)	Brooklyn	CT	F	860 928-6551	545
Electro Switch Corp	Weymouth	MA	C	781 607-3306	13324
Pickering Interfaces Inc	Chelmsford	MA	G	781 897-1710	7945
Vicor Corporation (PA)	Andover	MA	A	978 470-2900	5933

SWITCHES: Electronic

	CITY	ST	EMP	PHONE	ENTRY#
Bloomy Controls Inc (PA)	South Windsor	CT	E	860 298-9925	3120
Linemaster Switch Corporation	Plainfield	CT	G	860 564-7713	2736
C & K Components LLC (HQ)	Waltham	MA	D	617 969-3700	12619
Coactive Technologies LLC	Newton	MA	C	617 969-3700	10747
Design Mark Industries Inc	New Bedford	MA	D	800 451-3275	10585
Metalogic Industries LLC	Southbridge	MA	F	508 461-6787	12030
Pickering Interfaces Inc	Chelmsford	MA	G	781 897-1710	7945
Meggitt (new Hampshire) Inc	Londonderry	NH	C	603 669-0940	14767

SWITCHES: Electronic Applications

	CITY	ST	EMP	PHONE	ENTRY#
Control Concepts Inc (PA)	Brooklyn	CT	F	860 928-6551	545

SWITCHES: Flow Actuated, Electrical

	CITY	ST	EMP	PHONE	ENTRY#
Thomas Products Ltd	Southington	CT	F	860 621-9101	3236
Sensata Technologies Ind Inc (DH)	Attleboro	MA	E	508 236-3800	6063
Wabash Technologies Inc (DH)	Attleboro	MA	D	260 355-4100	6075

SWITCHES: Stepping

	CITY	ST	EMP	PHONE	ENTRY#
Tritex Corporation	Waterbury	CT	C	203 756-7441	3977
High Voltage Engineering Corp	Wakefield	MA	E	781 224-1001	12511

PRODUCT

	CITY	ST	EMP	PHONE	ENTRY#

SWITCHES: Time, Electrical Switchgear Apparatus

	CITY	ST	EMP	PHONE	ENTRY#
MH Rhodes Cramer LLC	South Windsor	CT	G	860 291-8402	3164

SWITCHGEAR & SWITCHBOARD APPARATUS

	CITY	ST	EMP	PHONE	ENTRY#
ABB Finance (usa) Inc	Norwalk	CT	E	919 856-2360	2458
Allied Controls Inc	Stamford	CT	F	860 628-8443	3277
Asea Brown Boveri Inc	Norwalk	CT	A	203 750-2200	2465
Faria Beede Instruments Inc	North Stonington	CT	C	860 848-9271	2448
Gems Sensors Inc (HQ)	Plainville	CT	B	860 747-3000	2761
General Electro Components	Glastonbury	CT	G	860 659-3573	1280
Hubbell Incorporated Delaware (HQ)	Shelton	CT	B	475 882-4000	3018
Madison Company (PA)	Branford	CT	E	203 488-4477	270
Mil-Con Inc	Naugatuck	CT	F	630 595-2366	1971
Newco Condenser Inc	Shelton	CT	F	475 882-4000	3039
Omega Engineering Inc	Norwalk	CT	D	714 540-4914	2548
Quality Name Plate Inc	East Glastonbury	CT	D	860 633-9495	923
Siemon Company (PA)	Watertown	CT	A	860 945-4200	4029
C & K Components LLC (HQ)	Waltham	MA	E	617 969-3700	12619
Cgit Westboro Inc	Westborough	MA	E	508 836-4000	13087
Cole Hersee Company (HQ)	Boston	MA	D	617 268-2100	6662
Cordmaster Engineering Co Inc	North Adams	MA	E	413 664-9371	10805
Eaton Corporation	Franklin	MA	E	508 520-2444	8833
Echolab Inc	North Billerica	MA	E		10910
Electro Switch Corp	Weymouth	MA	F	781 335-1195	13325
Mettler-Toledo Thornton Inc (DH)	Billerica	MA	D	978 262-0210	6460
Pancon Corporation (PA)	East Taunton	MA	C	781 297-6000	8410
Power Systems Integrity Inc	Northborough	MA	G	508 393-1655	11106
Project Resources Inc	Wareham	MA	F	508 295-7444	12842
Stellant PST Corp	Topsfield	MA	F	978 887-5754	12438
Teknikor Automtn & Contrls Inc	Fall River	MA	F	508 679-9474	8615
Texas Instruments Incorporated	Attleboro	MA	E	508 236-3800	6070
Hoyt Elec Instr Works Inc	Concord	NH	E	603 753-6321	14138
Kearney-National Inc	North Kingstown	RI	C	401 943-2686	16264
SE Mass Devlopment LLC	East Providence	RI	F	401 434-3329	16043
Dynapower Company LLC (DH)	South Burlington	VT	D	802 860-7200	17577

SWITCHGEAR & SWITCHGEAR ACCESS, NEC

	CITY	ST	EMP	PHONE	ENTRY#
Capitol Electronics Inc	Wilton	CT	F	203 744-3300	4235
Suns International LLC	Chelmsford	MA	B	978 349-2329	7960
Siemens Industry Inc	Falmouth	ME	D	207 878-3367	4771

SYRUPS, DRINK

	CITY	ST	EMP	PHONE	ENTRY#
Coca-Cola Btlg Sthstern Neng I	Needham Heights	MA	F	781 449-4300	10536

SYRUPS, FLAVORING, EXC DRINK

	CITY	ST	EMP	PHONE	ENTRY#
Rhode Island Frt Syrup Co Inc	Smithfield	RI	E	401 231-0040	16729

SYSTEMS ENGINEERING: Computer Related

	CITY	ST	EMP	PHONE	ENTRY#
Crane Company (PA)	Stamford	CT	D	203 363-7300	3326
Sonalysts Inc (PA)	Waterford	CT	B	860 442-4355	3997
Belle Artfl Intelligence Corp	Cambridge	MA	F	650 291-9410	7504
EMC Corporation	Milford	MA	E	508 634-2774	10402
Mediavue Systems Inc	Hingham	MA	E	781 926-0676	9153

SYSTEMS INTEGRATION SVCS

	CITY	ST	EMP	PHONE	ENTRY#
Cst Incorporated	Wallingford	CT	F	203 949-9900	3796
Frontier Vision Tech Inc	Rocky Hill	CT	E	860 953-0240	2922
Harpoon Acquisition Corp	Glastonbury	CT	E	860 815-5736	1285
Process Automtn Solutions Inc (HQ)	Danbury	CT	E	203 207-9917	801
Visionpoint LLC	Newington	CT	E	860 436-9673	2333
Amazon Robotics LLC (HQ)	North Reading	MA	C	781 221-4640	11037
INTEL Network Systems Inc (HQ)	Hudson	MA	D	978 553-4000	9378
Sencorpwhite Inc (HQ)	Hyannis	MA	C	508 771-9400	9451
Caron Engineering Inc	Wells	ME	F	207 646-6071	5598
Namtek Corp	Bedford	NH	E	603 262-1630	13945
Softech Inc (HQ)	Nashua	NH	F	513 942-7100	15170

SYSTEMS INTEGRATION SVCS: Local Area Network

	CITY	ST	EMP	PHONE	ENTRY#
Interactive Marketing Corp	North Haven	CT	G	203 248-5324	2416
Ibcontrols	Windham	ME	E	207 893-0080	5662
Enterasys Networks Inc (HQ)	Salem	NH	D	603 952-5000	15521
Electro Standards Lab Inc	Cranston	RI	D	401 946-1164	15853

SYSTEMS SOFTWARE DEVELOPMENT SVCS

	CITY	ST	EMP	PHONE	ENTRY#
Enginuity Plm LLC (DH)	Milford	CT	F	203 218-7225	1825
Norfield Data Products Inc	Norwalk	CT	F	203 849-0292	2546
E E S Companies Inc	Framingham	MA	F	508 653-6911	8758
Eclypses Inc	Boston	MA	E	719 323-6680	6707
Infinite Iq Inc	Wellesley	MA	F	781 710-8696	12943
Netscout Systems Inc (PA)	Westford	MA	C	978 614-4000	13253
Paneltek LLC	Attleboro Falls	MA	F	920 906-9457	6095

	CITY	ST	EMP	PHONE	ENTRY#
Revvity Signals Software Inc (DH)	Waltham	MA	D	781 663-6900	12769
Soapstone Networks Inc	Burlington	MA	D	617 719-3897	7430
Tactai Inc	Waltham	MA	F	617 391-7915	12787
Timelinx Software LLC	North Andover	MA	G	978 662-1171	10854

TABLE OR COUNTERTOPS, PLASTIC LAMINATED

	CITY	ST	EMP	PHONE	ENTRY#
Leos Kitchen and Stair Corp	New Britain	CT	G	860 225-7363	2037
Boston Fabrications	Attleboro	MA	F	781 762-9185	5997
Bangor Millwork & Supply Inc	Portland	ME	G	207 878-8548	5181
David D Douglas Inc	Londonderry	NH	G	603 437-1151	14742

TABLECLOTHS & SETTINGS

	CITY	ST	EMP	PHONE	ENTRY#
Patricia Spratt For Home LLC	Old Lyme	CT	F	860 434-9291	2644

TABLES: Lift, Hydraulic

	CITY	ST	EMP	PHONE	ENTRY#
Southworth Intl Group Inc (PA)	Falmouth	ME	D	207 878-0700	4772

TABLETS & PADS

	CITY	ST	EMP	PHONE	ENTRY#
Bouncepad North America Inc	Charlestown	MA	G	617 804-0110	7864

TABLETS & PADS: Book & Writing, Made From Purchased Material

	CITY	ST	EMP	PHONE	ENTRY#
Panagrafix Inc	West Haven	CT	E	203 691-5529	4118

TAGS & LABELS: Paper

	CITY	ST	EMP	PHONE	ENTRY#
Cenveo Enterprises Inc (PA)	Stamford	CT	D	203 595-3000	3308
Cenveo Worldwide Limited (DH)	Stamford	CT	E	203 595-3000	3309
Cwl Enterprises Inc (HQ)	Stamford	CT	F	303 790-8023	3332
Royal Consumer Products LLC (HQ)	Norwalk	CT	E	203 847-8500	2567
Surys Inc	Trumbull	CT	C	203 333-5503	3734
D B S Industries Inc	Haverhill	MA	D	978 373-4748	9090
Dion Label Printing Inc	Westfield	MA	E	413 568-3713	13162
Nashua Corporation	Merrimack	NH	A	603 880-1100	14994
Dasko Identification Products	Warren	RI	F	401 435-6500	16757
Image Tek Mfg Inc	Springfield	VT	E	802 885-6208	17618

TAGS: Paper, Blank, Made From Purchased Paper

	CITY	ST	EMP	PHONE	ENTRY#
Universal Tag Inc	Dudley	MA	E	508 949-2411	8326
Cjf Group Ltd	Providence	RI	D	401 421-2000	16500

TALLOW: Animal

	CITY	ST	EMP	PHONE	ENTRY#
Baker Commodities Inc	North Billerica	MA	D	978 454-8811	10899

TANK TOWERS: Metal Plate

	CITY	ST	EMP	PHONE	ENTRY#
XI Technology Systems Inc	Rockland	MA	E	781 982-1220	11665
Hyde Specialty Products LLC	Merrimack	NH	F	603 883-7400	14984

TANKS & OTHER TRACKED VEHICLE CMPNTS

	CITY	ST	EMP	PHONE	ENTRY#
New England Airfoil Pdts Inc	Farmington	CT	E	860 677-1376	1231
General Dynmics Def Systems In	Pittsfield	MA	C	413 494-1110	11397
L W Tank Repair Incorporated	Uxbridge	MA	F	508 234-6000	12483
Natgun Corporation	Wakefield	MA	F	781 224-5180	12522
New England Stinless Distr LLC	Salisbury	MA	F	978 255-4830	11743
Howe & Howe Technologies Inc	Waterboro	ME	F	207 247-2777	5591

TANKS: Concrete

	CITY	ST	EMP	PHONE	ENTRY#
Dn Tanks Inc (PA)	Wakefield	MA	D	781 246-1133	12507
National Con Tnks / Frguard JV	Concord	MA	F	978 505-5533	8127

TANKS: Cryogenic, Metal

	CITY	ST	EMP	PHONE	ENTRY#
Russell James Engineering Works Inc	Boston	MA	E	617 265-2240	7018

TANKS: For Tank Trucks, Metal Plate

	CITY	ST	EMP	PHONE	ENTRY#
Boston Steel & Mfg Co	Haverhill	MA	E	781 324-3000	9080
Westmor Industries LLC	Brewer	ME	E	207 989-0100	4624

TANKS: Fuel, Including Oil & Gas, Metal Plate

	CITY	ST	EMP	PHONE	ENTRY#
Angel Fuel LLC	Waterbury	CT	G	203 597-8759	3885
Babcock Power Inc (PA)	Danvers	MA	G	978 646-3300	8166
Riley Power Inc	Marlborough	MA	B	508 852-7100	10204

TANKS: Lined, Metal

	CITY	ST	EMP	PHONE	ENTRY#
Boston Environmental LLC	Portsmouth	NH	E	603 334-1000	15366
Amtrol Holdings Inc	West Warwick	RI	A	401 884-6300	16899

TANKS: Plastic & Fiberglass

	CITY	ST	EMP	PHONE	ENTRY#
Rj Fountain Group Inc	Franklin	MA	F	508 429-9950	8859
Response Technologies LLC	Coventry	RI	E	401 585-5918	15820

TANKS: Standard Or Custom Fabricated, Metal Plate

	CITY	ST	EMP	PHONE	ENTRY#
Braden Manufacturing LLC	Auburn	MA	D	508 797-8000	6108
Flexcon Industries Inc	Randolph	MA	C	781 986-2424	11557
Mass Tank Inspection Svcs LLC	Middleboro	MA	E	508 923-3445	10367

	CITY	ST	EMP	PHONE	ENTRY#
Millincket Fabrication Mch Inc **(PA)**	Millinocket	ME	E	207 723-9733	5067
Fiberglass Fabricators Inc	Smithfield	RI	E	401 231-3552	16700
West Warwick Welding Inc	West Warwick	RI	F	401 822-8200	16926

TANKS: Water, Metal Plate

Walz & Krenzer Inc	Oxford	CT	G	203 267-5712	2714

TANNERIES: Leather

Tasman Industries Inc	Hartland	ME	G	207 938-4491	4878

TAPE DRIVES

Acbel (usa) Polytech Inc	Hopkinton	MA	G	508 625-1768	9305
Springboard Technology Corporation	Springfield	MA	D		12133

TAPE MEASURES

Acme United Corporation **(PA)**	Shelton	CT	D	203 254-6060	2978
LS Starrett Company **(PA)**	Athol	MA	A	978 249-3551	5981

TAPE STORAGE UNITS: Computer

Memtec Corporation	Amherst	NH	F	603 893-8080	13880

TAPES: Fabric

American Biltrite Inc **(PA)**	Wellesley	MA	G	781 237-6655	12935
Velcro Inc **(HQ)**	Manchester	NH	A	603 669-4880	14950
Velcro USA Inc **(DH)**	Manchester	NH	A	800 225-0180	14951
K&W Webbing Company	Central Falls	RI	F	401 725-4441	15790
Leedon Webbing Co Inc	Central Falls	RI	E	401 722-1043	15791

TAPES: Pressure Sensitive, Rubber

Beiersdorf North America Inc **(DH)**	Stamford	CT	F	203 563-5800	3292
Gta-Nht Inc **(HQ)**	Rockland	MA	C	781 331-5900	11647
Ideal Tape Co Inc	Lowell	MA	D	978 458-6833	9885
Jaybird & Mais Inc	Lawrence	MA	E	978 686-8659	9571
Dewal Industries LLC	Narragansett	RI	C	401 789-9736	16189

TARPAULINS

Cramaro Tarpaulin Systems Inc	Northborough	MA	G	508 393-3062	11094

TELECOMMUNICATION EQPT REPAIR SVCS, EXC TELEPHONES

Cowbell Technologies Inc	Hudson	MA	F	508 733-1778	9360
Cowbell Technologies Inc **(PA)**	Westborough	MA	G	508 733-1778	13094
Sandy Bay Machine Inc	Gloucester	MA	F	978 546-1331	8957
Schroff Inc **(HQ)**	Warwick	RI	B	763 204-7700	16859

TELEMETERING EQPT

Leidos SEC Dtction Automtn Inc	Haverhill	MA	F	781 939-3800	9108
Leidos SEC Dtction Automtn Inc	Tewksbury	MA	F	781 939-3800	12404
L3 Technologies Inc	Ashaway	RI	E	401 377-2300	15744
Lcs Controls Inc	Rochester	VT	G	802 767-3128	17486

TELEPHONE ANSWERING SVCS

Business and Prof Exch Inc	Beverly	MA	E	978 556-4100	6336

TELEPHONE EQPT: Modems

Canoga Perkins Corporation	Seymour	CT	G	203 888-7914	2956
Tango Modem LLC	Madison	CT	G	203 421-2245	1572
Minim Inc **(PA)**	Manchester	NH	E	833 966-4646	14889

TELEPHONE EQPT: NEC

Action-Dctgraph Tlecomuncation	Meriden	CT	G	203 238-2326	1651
Ahead Communications Systems	Naugatuck	CT	E	203 720-0227	1947
Dac Systems Inc	Shelton	CT	F	203 924-7000	2995
Sigmavoip Llc	Westport	CT	G	203 541-5450	4196
Opus Telecom Inc	Framingham	MA	F	508 875-4444	8794
Siemens Energy Inc	Westford	MA	E	978 577-6413	13262
Ramtel Corporation	Johnston	RI	F	401 231-3340	16102

TELEPHONE STATION EQPT & PARTS: Wire

Deborah Frost	Bedford	NH	F	603 882-3100	13924

TELEPHONE: Headsets

Gn Audio USA Inc **(DH)**	Lowell	MA	B	800 826-4656	9881
Grandstream Networks Inc **(PA)**	Boston	MA	E	617 566-9300	6769

TELEVISION & VIDEO TAPE DISTRIBUTION

Seachange International Inc **(PA)**	Boston	MA	D	978 897-0100	7029

TELEVISION BROADCASTING & COMMUNICATIONS EQPT

Media Links Inc	Windsor	CT	F	860 206-9163	4290
Seachange International Inc **(PA)**	Boston	MA	D	978 897-0100	7029

TELEVISION BROADCASTING STATIONS

	CITY	ST	EMP	PHONE	ENTRY#
Christian Science Pubg Soc **(PA)**	Boston	MA	B	617 450-2000	6655
Diversified Communications **(HQ)**	Portland	ME	E	207 842-5500	5209

TELEVISION: Monitors

Qd Vision Inc	Foxboro	MA	D	781 652-7500	8715

TEMPERING: Metal

Hardline Heat Treating Inc	Southbridge	MA	E	508 764-6669	12018

TEMPORARY HELP SVCS

Nsight Inc	Andover	MA	E	781 273-6300	5902
Traincroft Inc **(PA)**	Medford	MA	E	781 393-6943	10299

TERMINAL BOARDS

ITW Ark-Les Corporation **(HQ)**	Stoughton	MA	E	781 297-6000	12215

TEST BORING SVCS: Nonmetallic Minerals

Carr-Dee Corp	Medford	MA	F	781 391-4500	10282
Soil Exploration Corp **(PA)**	Leominster	MA	G	978 840-0391	9705

TESTERS: Battery

Digatron Power Electronics Inc	Shelton	CT	E	203 446-8000	3000
Ultrasystems Electronics Inc	Amherst	NH	F	603 578-0444	13893
Aurora Performance Pdts LLC	Jamestown	RI	G	401 398-2959	16068

TESTERS: Physical Property

Forte Technology Inc	South Easton	MA	F	508 297-2363	11943
Testing Machines Inc	Swansea	MA	D	302 613-5600	12313
Triangle Engineering Inc	Hanover	MA	F	781 878-1500	9046

TESTING SVCS

Assurance Technology Corp **(PA)**	Carlisle	MA	D	978 369-8848	7845
Labthink International Inc	Medford	MA	F	617 830-2190	10293
Kennebec River Biosciences Inc	Richmond	ME	F	207 737-2637	5322

TEXTILE & APPAREL SVCS

Merida Meridian Inc	Boston	MA	E	617 464-5400	6885
Tri Textiles Corporation **(PA)**	Fall River	MA	G	631 420-0011	8617
Enefco International Inc **(PA)**	Auburn	ME	E	207 514-7218	4428

TEXTILE FINISHING: Chemical Coating Or Treating, Narrow

Albany Engnered Composites Inc	Rochester	NH	G	603 330-5851	15462
Albany Engnered Composites Inc **(HQ)**	Rochester	NH	C	603 330-5800	15463

TEXTILE FINISHING: Dyeing, Manmade Fiber & Silk, Broadwoven

Swan Finishing Company Inc **(PA)**	Fall River	MA	C	508 674-4611	8612
Kenyon Industries Inc	Kenyon	RI	B	401 364-7761	16112

TEXTILES: Crash, Linen

Joel Gorkowski Inc	Milford	CT	F	203 877-3896	1841

TEXTILES: Mill Waste & Remnant

A&P Coat Apron & Linen Sup LLC	Hartford	CT	D	914 840-3200	1466

THEATRICAL SCENERY

Global Scenic Services Inc	Bridgeport	CT	E	203 334-2130	325
Show Motion Inc	Milford	CT	E	203 866-1866	1884
Mystic Scenic Studios Inc	Norwood	MA	D	781 440-0914	11198
Advanced Animations	Stockbridge	VT	E	802 746-8974	17628

THERMISTORS, EXC TEMPERATURE SENSORS

Sensata Technologies Ind Inc **(DH)**	Attleboro	MA	E	508 236-3800	6063
Wabash Technologies Inc **(DH)**	Attleboro	MA	D	260 355-4100	6075

THERMOCOUPLES

Projects Inc	Glastonbury	CT	C	860 633-4615	1295
Convectronics Inc	Haverhill	MA	E	978 374-7714	9088
Nanmac Corp	Milford	MA	E	508 872-4811	10407

THERMOPLASTIC MATERIALS

Forum Plastics LLC	Waterbury	CT	E	203 754-0777	3913
Neu Spclty Engineered Mtls LLC	North Haven	CT	F	203 239-9629	2426
Oxford Industries Conn Inc	New Britain	CT	E	860 225-3700	2048
Oxpekk Performance Mtls Inc	South Windsor	CT	E	860 698-9300	3170
Abcorp NA Inc	Boston	MA	B	617 325-9600	6503
Zschimmer Schwarz Intrplymer I **(DH)**	Canton	MA	E	781 828-7120	7844
Desmarais Plastics LLC	Manchester	NH	D	603 669-8523	14841
HI Tech Profiles Inc	Ashaway	RI	E	401 377-2040	15741
Teknor Apex Company **(PA)**	Pawtucket	RI	A	401 725-8000	16420
Txv Aerospace Composites LLC	Bristol	RI	F	425 785-0883	15785

THERMOSETTING MATERIALS

P
R
O
D
U
C
T

	CITY	ST	EMP	PHONE	ENTRY#
Current Inc (PA)	East Haven	CT	D	203 469-1337	1039
Resinall Corp North Carolina (DH)	Stamford	CT	F	203 329-7100	3446
Hapco Inc	Hanover	MA	E	781 826-8801	9034
Textiles Coated Incorporated (PA)	Londonderry	NH	E	603 296-2221	14786
Epoxytech Inc	Woonsocket	RI	E	401 726-4500	16958

THIN FILM CIRCUITS

	CITY	ST	EMP	PHONE	ENTRY#
Entegris Prof Solutions Inc (HQ)	Danbury	CT	C	203 794-1100	738
Vulcan Flex Circuit Corp	Porter	ME	D	603 883-1500	5172
Ultrasource Inc	Hollis	NH	D	603 881-7799	14459
Vishay Dale Electronics LLC	Hollis	NH	D	603 881-7799	14461

THREAD: Cotton

	CITY	ST	EMP	PHONE	ENTRY#
New Bedford Thread Co Inc	Fairhaven	MA	E	508 996-8584	8511

TILE: Brick & Structural, Clay

	CITY	ST	EMP	PHONE	ENTRY#
Redland Brick Inc	South Windsor	CT	E	860 528-1311	3177
Hi-Way Concrete Pdts Co Inc	Wareham	MA	E	508 295-0834	12837
Morgan Advanced Ceramics Inc	New Bedford	MA	D	508 995-1725	10624
Rjf - Morin Brick LLC	Auburn	ME	D	207 784-9375	4459
Morgan Advanced Ceramics Inc	Hudson	NH	E	603 598-9122	14529

TILE: Fireproofing, Clay

	CITY	ST	EMP	PHONE	ENTRY#
K & G Corp	Manchester	CT	F	860 643-1133	1609

TILE: Terrazzo Or Concrete, Precast

	CITY	ST	EMP	PHONE	ENTRY#
Pauls Marble Depot LLC	Stamford	CT	F	203 978-0669	3427

TILE: Wall & Floor, Ceramic

	CITY	ST	EMP	PHONE	ENTRY#
Aspecta North America LLC	Norwalk	CT	G	855 400-7732	2466
Cabinets For Less LLC	Manchester	NH	G	603 935-7551	14825

TIMING DEVICES: Electronic

	CITY	ST	EMP	PHONE	ENTRY#
Crrc LLC (PA)	South Windsor	CT	D	877 684-6464	3136
Idevices LLC	Avon	CT	D	860 352-5252	27
Lynx System Developers Inc	Haverhill	MA	E	978 556-9780	9111

TIRE CORD & FABRIC

	CITY	ST	EMP	PHONE	ENTRY#
United Abrasives Inc (PA)	North Windham	CT	B	860 456-7131	2451
Alvin Johnson	East Longmeadow	MA	G	413 525-6334	8368

TIRES & INNER TUBES

	CITY	ST	EMP	PHONE	ENTRY#
Toce Brothers Incorporated (PA)	Torrington	CT	E	860 496-2080	3700
BF Services Inc	Lexington	MA	F	781 862-9792	9728
Main Industrial Tires Ltd (PA)	Wakefield	MA	E	713 676-0251	12515

TIRES & TUBES WHOLESALERS

	CITY	ST	EMP	PHONE	ENTRY#
Derby Tire Company	Branford	CT	F	203 481-8473	249
Firestone Building Pdts Co LLC	Bristol	CT	F	860 584-4516	447
Reliable Auto Tire Company Inc	Hartford	CT	G	860 247-7977	1504
Toce Brothers Incorporated (PA)	Torrington	CT	E	860 496-2080	3700
Holyoke Tire & Auto Svc Inc	Springfield	MA	G	413 733-2141	12101
Maine Tire & Appliance Co (PA)	Falmouth	ME	F	207 781-3136	4769
Belknap Tire Co Holdings Inc	Laconia	NH	F	603 524-4517	14646
Northeast Tire Service Inc	Belmont	NH	G	603 524-7973	13965
Petes Tire Barns Inc	Providence	RI	G	401 521-2240	16583

TIRES & TUBES, WHOLESALE: Automotive

	CITY	ST	EMP	PHONE	ENTRY#
Bridgestone Ret Operations LLC	Bristol	CT	G	860 584-2727	417
Bridgestone Ret Operations LLC	Hamden	CT	G	203 288-1634	1414
Bridgestone Ret Operations LLC	Milford	CT	G	203 878-6859	1803
Bridgestone Ret Operations LLC	New Britain	CT	F	860 229-0348	2009
Bridgestone Ret Operations LLC	New Haven	CT	G	203 787-1208	2132
Bridgestone Ret Operations LLC	Newington	CT	G	860 594-0594	2277
Bridgestone Ret Operations LLC	Southington	CT	G	860 628-9621	3205
Bridgestone Ret Operations LLC	Waterbury	CT	F	203 754-6119	3893
Bridgestone Ret Operations LLC	West Haven	CT	G	203 933-7750	4095
Derby Tire Company	Branford	CT	F	203 481-8473	249
Firestone Building Pdts Co LLC	Bristol	CT	F	860 584-4516	447
Reliable Auto Tire Company Inc	Hartford	CT	G	860 247-7977	1504
Star Tires Plus Wheels LLC	Hartford	CT	F	860 296-9799	1509
Tire Country of Enfield Inc	Enfield	CT	G	860 763-0846	1155
Toce Brothers Incorporated (PA)	Torrington	CT	E	860 496-2080	3700
American Tire Svc & Sls Inc	Springfield	MA	G	413 739-5369	12074
Aronson Tire Company Inc	Auburn	MA	E	508 832-3244	6105
Bodyshop World By Wagner Inc	Worcester	MA	F	508 853-0300	13704
Bridgestone Ret Operations LLC	Auburn	MA	G	508 832-9671	6110
Bridgestone Ret Operations LLC	Boston	MA	G	617 327-1100	6622
Bridgestone Ret Operations LLC	Braintree	MA	G	781 843-2870	7172
Bridgestone Ret Operations LLC	Brockton	MA	G	508 588-8866	7262
Bridgestone Ret Operations LLC	Hingham	MA	G	781 749-6454	9145
Bridgestone Ret Operations LLC	Northampton	MA	G	413 586-1584	11054

	CITY	ST	EMP	PHONE	ENTRY#
Bridgestone Ret Operations LLC	Quincy	MA	G	617 479-3208	11508
Bridgestone Ret Operations LLC	Springfield	MA	F	413 543-1312	12080
Bridgestone Ret Operations LLC	Watertown	MA	F	617 924-3989	12864
Bridgestone Ret Operations LLC	Wilmington	MA	G	978 658-5660	13394
City Tire Co Inc	Chicopee	MA	E	413 534-2946	8018
City Tire Co Inc	Pittsfield	MA	G	413 445-5578	11396
City Tire Co Inc (PA)	Springfield	MA	E	413 737-1419	12084
Goodyear Tire & Rubber Company	Lynn	MA	F	781 598-4500	9976
K & W Tire Company Inc	Ayer	MA	F	978 772-5700	6184
Petes Tire Barns Inc (PA)	Orange	MA	D	978 544-8811	11228
Rolands Tire Service Inc (PA)	Fairhaven	MA	E	508 997-4501	8514
Sullivan Investment Inc (PA)	Norwell	MA	E	781 982-1550	11147
Sullivan Tire Co Inc	North Attleboro	MA	G	508 695-9920	10890
Baude Inc	Houlton	ME	F	207 532-6571	4896
Central Tire Co Inc (PA)	Sanford	ME	F	207 324-4250	5391
Lag Inc (PA)	Topsham	ME	G	207 729-1676	5548
Lees Tire	Topsham	ME	E	207 729-1676	5549
Maine Tire & Appliance Co	Augusta	ME	F	207 623-1171	4477
Maine Tire & Appliance Co (PA)	Falmouth	ME	F	207 781-3136	4769
McQuade Tidd Industries	Houlton	ME	F	207 532-6571	4902
Tki Inc	Skowhegan	ME	G	207 474-5322	5479
Belknap Tire Co Holdings Inc	Laconia	NH	F	603 524-4517	14646
Bridgestone Ret Operations LLC	Manchester	NH	G	603 668-1123	14821
DC Tire Service Inc	Milford	NH	G	603 673-9211	15021
Mountain Tire Corp	Berlin	NH	F	603 752-8473	13983
Northeast Tire Service Inc	Belmont	NH	G	603 524-7973	13965
Bec Corp	Pawtucket	RI	G	401 725-3535	16347
Bridgestone Ret Operations LLC	North Smithfield	RI	F	401 766-0233	16319
Bridgestone Ret Operations LLC	Providence	RI	F	401 521-6622	16491
Vianor Inc (HQ)	Colchester	VT	E	802 864-7108	17207

TIRES: Agricultural, Pneumatic

	CITY	ST	EMP	PHONE	ENTRY#
Maxam Tire North America Inc (HQ)	Danvers	MA	F	844 629-2662	8203

TIRES: Cushion Or Solid Rubber

	CITY	ST	EMP	PHONE	ENTRY#
Maine Rubber International	Wakefield	MA	B	877 648-1949	12517

TOBACCO & PRDTS, WHOLESALE: Cigarettes

	CITY	ST	EMP	PHONE	ENTRY#
Foundation Cigar Company LLC	Ellington	CT	G	203 738-9377	1108

TOBACCO & TOBACCO PRDTS WHOLESALERS

	CITY	ST	EMP	PHONE	ENTRY#
Consumer Product Distrs LLC	Stratford	CT	G	203 378-2193	3531
Hay Island Holding Corporation (PA)	Darien	CT	C	203 656-8000	847

TOBACCO: Chewing

	CITY	ST	EMP	PHONE	ENTRY#
Hay Island Holding Corporation (PA)	Darien	CT	C	203 656-8000	847

TOBACCO: Chewing & Snuff

	CITY	ST	EMP	PHONE	ENTRY#
Nordic American Smokeless Inc	Danbury	CT	F	203 207-9977	790
Nuway Tobacco Company	South Windsor	CT	D	860 289-6414	3167
UST LLC	Stamford	CT	A	203 817-3000	3489

TOBACCO: Cigarettes

	CITY	ST	EMP	PHONE	ENTRY#
Consumer Product Distrs LLC	Stratford	CT	G	203 378-2193	3531
Philip Morris Intl Inc (PA)	Stamford	CT	A	203 905-2410	3432
Smokey Mountain Chew Inc	Darien	CT	F	203 304-9200	855

TOBACCO: Cigars

	CITY	ST	EMP	PHONE	ENTRY#
F D Grave & Son Inc	North Haven	CT	G	203 239-9394	2411
Foundation Cigar Company LLC	Ellington	CT	G	203 738-9377	1108

TOILET PREPARATIONS

	CITY	ST	EMP	PHONE	ENTRY#
Transom Symphony Opco LLC (PA)	Stamford	CT	D	203 503-7938	3485
Unilever Trumbull RES Svcs Inc	Trumbull	CT	D	203 502-0086	3738
Gillette Company (HQ)	Boston	MA	A	617 463-3000	6758
Procter & Gamble Mfg Co	Andover	MA	D	978 749-5547	5908

TOILETRIES, WHOLESALE: Toilet Soap

	CITY	ST	EMP	PHONE	ENTRY#
Crabtree & Evelyn Ltd (DH)	Woodstock	CT	C	800 272-2873	4393
Downeast Concepts Inc	Yarmouth	ME	E	207 846-3726	5703

TOILETRIES, WHOLESALE: Toiletries

	CITY	ST	EMP	PHONE	ENTRY#
T N Dickinson Company	East Hampton	CT	F	860 267-2279	966

TOILETS: Portable Chemical, Plastics

	CITY	ST	EMP	PHONE	ENTRY#
Coastline Environmental LLC	North Branford	CT	G	203 483-6898	2362

TOOL & DIE STEEL

	CITY	ST	EMP	PHONE	ENTRY#
American Standard Company	Southington	CT	E	860 628-9643	3203
Ludlow Tool Inc	Agawam	MA	F	413 786-6415	5800
Vortex Inc	Peabody	MA	D	978 535-8721	11351
Shookus Special Tools Inc	Raymond	NH	F	603 895-1200	15458

	CITY	ST	EMP	PHONE	ENTRY#

TOOLS: Hand, Hammers

	CITY	ST	EMP	PHONE	ENTRY#
Mayhew Steel Products Inc (PA)	Turners Falls	MA	F	413 625-6351	12452
Garland Manufacturing Co	Saco	ME	E	207 283-3693	5367

TOOLS: Hand, Mechanics

	CITY	ST	EMP	PHONE	ENTRY#
Cambridge Specialty Co Inc	Berlin	CT	D	860 828-3579	57
J J Ryan Corporation	Plantsville	CT	C	860 628-0393	2793
Ullman Devices Corporation	Ridgefield	CT	D	203 438-6577	2908
Lowell Corporation	West Boylston	MA	E	508 835-2900	12964

TOWING SVCS: Marine

	CITY	ST	EMP	PHONE	ENTRY#
Cape Cod Shipbuilding Co	Wareham	MA	E	508 295-3550	12832

TOYS & HOBBY GOODS & SPLYS, WHOLESALE: Balloons, Novelty

	CITY	ST	EMP	PHONE	ENTRY#
Nicks Enterprises Inc (PA)	Hamden	CT	F	203 287-9990	1447

TOYS & HOBBY GOODS & SPLYS, WHOLESALE: Toys & Games

	CITY	ST	EMP	PHONE	ENTRY#
Leisure Learning Products Inc	Stamford	CT	F	203 325-2800	3397

TOYS & HOBBY GOODS & SPLYS, WHOLESALE: Toys, NEC

	CITY	ST	EMP	PHONE	ENTRY#
Beacon Wellness Brands Inc (PA)	Newton	MA	F	781 449-9500	10739
Catalystsmc Inc	Newton	MA	F	781 449-9500	10741
Nancy Sales Co Inc	Chelsea	MA	D	617 884-1700	7987

TOYS: Dolls, Stuffed Animals & Parts

	CITY	ST	EMP	PHONE	ENTRY#
Nancy Sales Co Inc	Chelsea	MA	D	617 884-1700	7987
Oyo Sportstoys Inc	Brookline	MA	D	978 264-2000	7323
Woobo Inc	Cambridge	MA	F	630 639-6326	7762
Hasbro Inc (PA)	Pawtucket	RI	A	401 431-8697	16373

TOYS: Electronic

	CITY	ST	EMP	PHONE	ENTRY#
Walts Tropper Factory LLC	North Branford	CT	G	203 871-9254	2378
Gold Water Technology Inc	Walpole	MA	G	781 551-3590	12559
Sproutel Inc	Providence	RI	G	914 806-6514	16615

TRADE SHOW ARRANGEMENT SVCS

	CITY	ST	EMP	PHONE	ENTRY#
Lmt Communications Inc	Newtown	CT	E	203 426-4568	2339
Show Management Associates LLC	Norwalk	CT	G	203 939-9901	2572
Institute For Applied Ntwrk SE	Boston	MA	E	617 399-8100	6814
International Data Group Inc (HQ)	Needham	MA	F	508 875-5000	10514
Mystic Scenic Studios Inc	Norwood	MA	D	781 440-0914	11198
Diversified Communications (HQ)	Portland	ME	E	207 842-5500	5209
Image 4 Concepts Inc	Manchester	NH	F	603 644-0077	14862

TRADERS: Commodity, Contracts

	CITY	ST	EMP	PHONE	ENTRY#
Boehringer Ingelheim Corp (DH)	Ridgefield	CT	A	203 798-9988	2886
Louis Dreyfus Holdg Co US LLC (HQ)	Wilton	CT	B	203 761-2000	4242

TRAILERS & PARTS: Boat

	CITY	ST	EMP	PHONE	ENTRY#
Hostar Mar Trnspt Systems Inc	Wareham	MA	F	508 295-2900	12838

TRAILERS & TRAILER EQPT

	CITY	ST	EMP	PHONE	ENTRY#
Wright Trailers Inc	Seekonk	MA	F	508 336-8530	11790
Eimskip USA Inc	Portland	ME	F	207 221-5268	5214
Davis Village Solutions LLC	New Ipswich	NH	F	603 878-3662	15197

TRAILERS: Camping, Tent-Type

	CITY	ST	EMP	PHONE	ENTRY#
American Keder Inc (PA)	Rindge	NH	G	603 899-3233	15459

TRAILERS: Demountable Cargo Containers

	CITY	ST	EMP	PHONE	ENTRY#
Jason Trucks Inc	Medford	MA	F	781 396-8300	10292

TRANSDUCERS: Electrical Properties

	CITY	ST	EMP	PHONE	ENTRY#
Ashcroft Inc (DH)	Stratford	CT	B	203 378-8281	3517
Flintec Inc	Hudson	MA	E	978 562-4548	9367
Hottinger Bruel & Kjaer Inc (DH)	Marlborough	MA	D	508 485-7480	10164
Massa Products Corporation	Hingham	MA	D	781 749-3120	9152

TRANSDUCERS: Pressure

	CITY	ST	EMP	PHONE	ENTRY#
Druck LLC (HQ)	Billerica	MA	C	978 437-1000	6432
Dynisco Parent Inc	Billerica	MA	B	978 667-5301	6436
Setra Systems Inc	Boxboro	MA	F	978 263-1400	7145
Trans Metrics Inc (HQ)	Watertown	MA	F	617 926-1000	12916

TRANSFORMERS: Distribution

	CITY	ST	EMP	PHONE	ENTRY#
Altus II LLC	Stamford	CT	G	203 698-0090	3279
Ethosenergy Tc Inc (DH)	Chicopee	MA	C	802 257-2721	8031
International Coil Inc	South Easton	MA	E	508 580-8515	11946
Magnetika/East Ltd Partnership	Marlborough	MA	F	508 485-7555	10181
Standex Elctrnic Magnetics Inc	Concord	NH	D	800 805-8991	14158
Voltserver Inc (PA)	East Greenwich	RI	E	401 885-8658	15996

TRANSFORMERS: Distribution, Electric

	CITY	ST	EMP	PHONE	ENTRY#
Linden Vft LLC	Stamford	CT	F	203 357-4740	3401
Micheal John	Brookline	MA	E	857 239-0277	7320

TRANSFORMERS: Electronic

	CITY	ST	EMP	PHONE	ENTRY#
MCI Transformer Corporation	Orange	MA	F	978 544-8272	11226

TRANSFORMERS: Specialty

	CITY	ST	EMP	PHONE	ENTRY#
Unipower LLC	Brookfield	CT	E	203 740-8555	540
Universal Voltronics Corp	Brookfield	CT	D	203 740-8555	541
Century Magnetics Holdings Inc	Northfield	NH	F	603 934-4931	15263
Dynapower Company LLC (DH)	South Burlington	VT	D	802 860-7200	17577

TRANSISTORS

	CITY	ST	EMP	PHONE	ENTRY#
Raytheon Sutheast Asia Systems (DH)	Waltham	MA	E	978 470-5000	12762
Silicon Transistor Corporation	Chelmsford	MA	F	978 256-3321	7957

TRANSPORTATION BROKERS: Truck

	CITY	ST	EMP	PHONE	ENTRY#
Evergreen Manufacturing Group LLC	Madawaska	ME	E	207 728-4900	5037

TRANSPORTATION EPQT & SPLYS, WHOL: Aeronautical Eqpt & Splys

	CITY	ST	EMP	PHONE	ENTRY#
New England Expert Tech Corp	Greenfield	MA	E	413 773-8200	8995
QCI Inc	Seekonk	MA	F	508 399-8983	11784

TRANSPORTATION EPQT & SPLYS, WHOLESALE: Helicopter Parts

	CITY	ST	EMP	PHONE	ENTRY#
Acmt Inc	Manchester	CT	D	860 645-0592	1582
Helicopter Support Inc (DH)	Trumbull	CT	B	203 416-4000	3721

TRANSPORTATION EQPT & SPLYS WHOLESALERS, NEC

	CITY	ST	EMP	PHONE	ENTRY#
Columbia Manufacturing Inc	Columbia	CT	D	860 228-2259	669
Textron Systems Corporation (DH)	Wilmington	MA	E	978 657-5111	13466

TRAP ROCK: Crushed & Broken

	CITY	ST	EMP	PHONE	ENTRY#
S Lane John & Son Incorporated (PA)	Westfield	MA	F	413 568-8986	13205

TRAVEL AGENCIES

	CITY	ST	EMP	PHONE	ENTRY#
Smarter Travel Media LLC	Boston	MA	C	617 886-5555	7041

TRAVEL TRAILERS & CAMPERS

	CITY	ST	EMP	PHONE	ENTRY#
Thule Holding Inc (DH)	Seymour	CT	E	203 881-9600	2972
Boston Trailer Manufacturing	Walpole	MA	F	508 668-2242	12553
Perseus Partners LLC	Warren	ME	F	207 273-3780	5586

TRAYS: Cable, Metal Plate

	CITY	ST	EMP	PHONE	ENTRY#
Wanho Manufacturing LLC	Cheshire	CT	E	203 759-3744	621

TROPHIES, NEC

	CITY	ST	EMP	PHONE	ENTRY#
Conference Medal & Trophy Co	Buzzards Bay	MA	F	508 563-3600	7454
Village Goldsmith	Warwick	RI	F	401 944-8404	16872

TROPHIES, WHOLESALE

	CITY	ST	EMP	PHONE	ENTRY#
Paramount Industries Inc	Medway	MA	F	508 533-8480	10310
Glass Graphics Inc	Conway	NH	F	603 447-1900	14179

TROPHIES: Metal, Exc Silver

	CITY	ST	EMP	PHONE	ENTRY#
Greco Industries Inc	Bethel	CT	G	203 798-7804	117
Conference Medal & Trophy Co	Buzzards Bay	MA	F	508 563-3600	7454
VH Blackinton & Co Inc	Attleboro Falls	MA	C	508 699-4436	6096
American Trophy and Supply Inc	East Providence	RI	G	401 438-3060	16004
World Trophies Company Inc	Providence	RI	F	401 272-5846	16649

TRUCK & BUS BODIES: Garbage Or Refuse Truck

	CITY	ST	EMP	PHONE	ENTRY#
Tom Berkowitz Trucking Inc (PA)	Whitinsville	MA	E	508 234-2920	13346

TRUCK & BUS BODIES: Utility Truck

	CITY	ST	EMP	PHONE	ENTRY#
Custom Truck One Source LP	Hooksett	NH	E	574 370-2740	14464
Utility Systems Inc	Johnston	RI	E	401 351-6681	16110

TRUCK & BUS BODIES: Van Bodies

	CITY	ST	EMP	PHONE	ENTRY#
New England Wheels Inc (PA)	Billerica	MA	E	978 663-9724	6462

TRUCK BODIES: Body Parts

	CITY	ST	EMP	PHONE	ENTRY#
Bostonian Body Inc	Everett	MA	F	617 944-0985	8483
Commonwlth Vntr Fnding Group I (PA)	Waltham	MA	G	781 684-0095	12636
Consolidated Truck & Eqp Inc	Seekonk	MA	G	508 252-3330	11775
Moroney Bodyworks Inc	Worcester	MA	F	508 792-2878	13762
Messer Truck Equipment (PA)	Westbrook	ME	F	207 854-9751	5638
Vld Inc	Bangor	ME	G	207 947-6148	4519
Gpi Nh-T Inc	Manchester	NH	D	603 624-1800	14854
Dejana Trck Utility Eqp Co LLC	Smithfield	RI	D	401 231-9797	16695

Employee Codes: A=Over 500 employees, B=251-500
C=101-250, D=51-100, E=20-50, F=10-19, G=1-9

2024 Harris New England
Manufacturers Directory

1477

PRODUCT

	CITY	ST	EMP	PHONE	ENTRY#

TRUCK BODY SHOP

	CITY	ST	EMP	PHONE	ENTRY#
Martel Welding & Sons Inc	Tewksbury	MA	F	978 458-0661	12406
Larry Dingee	Cornish	NH	G	603 542-9682	14183
Iroquois Manufacturing Company	Hinesburg	VT	E	802 482-2155	17295

TRUCK GENERAL REPAIR SVC

Boston Trailer Manufacturing	Walpole	MA	F	508 668-2242	12553
Daves Truck Repair Inc	Springfield	MA	E	413 734-8898	12089
U-Haul Co Mass & Ohio Inc (DH)	Somerville	MA	E	617 625-2789	11908
Hanscom Construction Inc	Marshfield	ME	E	207 255-8067	5046
Hcb Holdings Inc (PA)	South Portland	ME	E	207 767-2136	5505
Donovan Equipment Company Inc	Londonderry	NH	D	603 669-2250	14743

TRUCK PARTS & ACCESSORIES: Wholesalers

WH Rose Inc	Columbia	CT	E	860 228-8258	671
Moroney Bodyworks Inc	Worcester	MA	F	508 792-2878	13762
Simpsons Inc of Lawrence	Lawrence	MA	F	978 683-2417	9597
Vld Inc	Bangor	ME	G	207 947-6148	4519
Donovan Equipment Company Inc	Londonderry	NH	D	603 669-2250	14743

TRUCKING & HAULING SVCS: Contract Basis

Grillo Services LLC	Milford	CT	E	203 877-5070	1831

TRUCKING & HAULING SVCS: Hazardous Waste

Tradebe Treatment and Recycling Northeast LLC (DH)	Meriden	CT			D
203 238-8102	1710				
Safety-Kleen Systems Inc (HQ)	Norwell	MA	B	800 669-5740	11146
Coating Systems Inc	Nashua	NH	G	603 883-0553	15082

TRUCKING & HAULING SVCS: Heavy, NEC

On The Road Inc	Warren	ME	E	207 273-3780	5585
Padebco Custom Boats	Round Pond	ME	G	207 529-5106	5354
New England Boatworks Inc	Portsmouth	RI	E	401 683-4000	16449

TRUCKING & HAULING SVCS: Lumber & Log, Local

Roland H Tyler Logging Inc	Dixfield	ME	G	207 562-7282	4728
Thompson Trucking Inc	Lincoln	ME	F	207 794-6101	5014
Tracy J Morrison	Harmony	ME	G	207 683-2371	4874

TRUCKING: Except Local

Horn International Packg Inc (HQ)	Lancaster	MA	E	978 667-8797	9528
Roy and Laurel Amey Inc	Pittsburg	NH	G	603 538-7767	15329

TRUCKING: Local, With Storage

All-Way Service Corp	South Weymouth	MA	F	781 335-4533	11974
Casey & Hayes Inc	Hingham	MA	C	617 269-5900	9146

TRUCKING: Local, Without Storage

Thomas Keegan & Sons Inc	Wallingford	CT	F	203 239-9248	3862
Everson Distributing Co Inc	Worcester	MA	E	413 533-9261	13721
J P Ruthier Sons Recycl Corp (PA)	Littleton	MA	F	978 772-4251	9821
Hinesburg Sand & Gravel Co Inc	Hinesburg	VT	E	802 482-2335	17294
Sheehan & Sons Lumber	Perkinsville	VT	G	802 263-5545	17442

TRUCKS & TRACTORS: Industrial

Dri-Air Industries Inc	East Windsor	CT	E	860 627-5110	1071
Innovativ Hoisting LLC	Willington	CT	F	860 969-4477	4225
New Haven Companies Inc	East Haven	CT	F	203 469-6421	1048
Terex Corporation (PA)	Norwalk	CT	F	203 222-7170	2578
Greenwood Emrgncy Vehicles LLC (HQ)	Attleboro Falls	MA	D	508 695-7138	6086
Maybury Associates Inc	East Longmeadow	MA	D	413 525-4216	8386
WB Engineering Inc	Foxboro	MA	E	508 952-4000	8731
North Country Tractor Inc	Sanford	ME	F	207 324-5646	5403

TRUCKS: Indl

Masart Inc	Watertown	MA	F	781 786-8774	12892

TRUST MANAGEMENT SVCS: Personal Investment

Strategic Value Partners LLC (PA)	Greenwich	CT	D	203 618-3500	1354

TUBES: Light Sensing & Emitting

Motion Industries Inc	Danvers	MA	E	978 774-7100	8210
Todd Clark and Associates Inc	Danvers	MA	E	978 774-7100	8225

TUBES: Steel & Iron

Microgroup Inc	Medway	MA	C	508 533-4925	10308

TUBES: Vacuum

Fil-Tech Inc	Boston	MA	G	617 227-1133	6735

TUBING: Flexible, Metallic

	CITY	ST	EMP	PHONE	ENTRY#
Uniprise International Inc	Terryville	CT	E	860 589-7262	3613

TUBING: Glass

Omniglow LLC	West Springfield	MA	B	413 241-6010	13039

TURBINES & TURBINE GENERATOR SET UNITS: Gas, Complete

Peregrine Turbine Tech LLC	Wiscasset	ME	F	207 687-8333	5699
Flex Leasing Power & Svc LLC	Portsmouth	NH	F	603 430-7000	15384
Flexenergy Inc	Portsmouth	NH	D	603 430-7000	15385
Flexenergy Energy Systems Inc	Portsmouth	NH	G	877 477-6937	15386
Flexenergy Green Solutions Inc (PA)	Portsmouth	NH	E	603 430-7000	15387
Flexenergy Holdings LLC	Portsmouth	NH	D	603 430-7000	15388
Flexenergy Power Solutions LLC	Portsmouth	NH	D	603 430-7000	15389

TURBINES & TURBINE GENERATOR SETS

Advanced Turbine Services LLC	Wallingford	CT	G	203 269-7977	3767
Becon Incorporated (PA)	Bloomfield	CT	C	860 243-1428	151
GE Engine Svcs UNC Holdg I Inc	New Haven	CT	C	518 380-0767	2153
General Electric Company	Norwalk	CT	A	203 797-0840	2504
General Electric Company	Stamford	CT	F	866 419-4096	3354
Interntnal Turbine Systems Inc	Bloomfield	CT	F	860 761-0358	173
Mitsubishi Power Aero LLC (HQ)	Glastonbury	CT	C	860 368-5900	1290
Precision Combustion Inc	North Haven	CT	E	203 287-3700	2432
R&D Dynamics Corporation	Bloomfield	CT	D	860 726-1204	205
Wood Group Pratt & Whitney	Windsor Locks	CT	G	860 687-1686	4337
Camar Corp	Northborough	MA	F	508 845-9263	11093
Concepts Nrec LLC	Chelmsford	MA	F	781 935-9050	7920
Ethosenergy Tc Inc (DH)	Chicopee	MA	C	802 257-2721	8031
GE Vernova International LLC (HQ)	Cambridge	MA	C	617 443-3000	7580
General Electric Company (PA)	Boston	MA	A	617 443-3000	6754
LKM Industries Inc	Woburn	MA	D	781 935-9210	13602
New Bedford Ocean Cluster Inc	New Bedford	MA	F	508 474-8902	10627
Riley Power Inc	Marlborough	MA	B	508 852-7100	10204
General Electric Company	Bangor	ME	A	207 941-2500	4505
Pika Energy Inc	Westbrook	ME	F	207 887-9105	5641
Energy Resources Group Inc (PA)	Farmington	NH	E	603 335-2535	14309
Ingersoll-Rand Energy Systems Corporation	Portsmouth	NH			D
603 430-7000	15408				

TURBINES & TURBINE GENERATOR SETS & PARTS

Blastech Overhaul & Repr Corp	Bloomfield	CT	E	860 243-8811	152
Doncasters Inc (PA)	Groton	CT	D	860 449-1603	1367
Jet Industries Inc	Agawam	MA	E	413 786-2010	5798
Shaft Current Solutions Inc	Florence	MA	E	413 267-0950	8686
Trireme Manufacturing Co Inc	Topsfield	MA	E	978 887-2132	12440
Machining Innovations Inc	Oakland	ME	G	207 465-2500	5120
Concepts Nrec LLC (PA)	White River Junction	VT	D	802 296-2321	17707

TURBINES: Steam

GE Energy Parts Intl LLC	Boston	MA	E	617 443-3000	6752

TURBO-GENERATORS

Knm Holdings LLC	Marlborough	MA	G	508 229-1400	10177

TURNKEY VENDORS: Computer Systems

Environmental Systems Corp	West Hartford	CT	C	860 953-8800	4060
Tek Industries Inc	Vernon Rockville	CT	E	860 870-0001	3763
Jerrys At Misquamicut Inc	Westerly	RI	E	401 596-3155	16934
Nestor Inc (PA)	Providence	RI	F	401 274-5345	16574
Ivy Computer Inc	Waterbury Center	VT	F	802 244-7880	17681

TYPESETTING SVC

Action Letter Inc (PA)	Stamford	CT	E	203 323-2466	3273
Allied Printing Services Inc (PA)	Manchester	CT	B	860 643-1101	1584
Appels Prtg & Mailing Bur Inc	Hartford	CT	F	860 522-8189	1470
Brescias Printing Services Inc	East Hartford	CT	G	860 528-4254	976
E R Hitchcock Company	New Britain	CT	G	860 229-2024	2024
Elm Press Incorporated	Terryville	CT	E	860 583-3600	3601
Fairfield Marketing Group Inc (PA)	Easton	CT	F	203 261-0884	1095
Gateway Digital Inc	Norwalk	CT	F	203 853-4929	2503
Hedges & Hedges Ltd	Wethersfield	CT	G	860 257-3170	4205
Image Processing	Guilford	CT	G	203 488-3252	1397
Kool Ink LLC	Bloomfield	CT	F	860 242-0303	186
Lettering Inc of New York (PA)	Stamford	CT	E	203 329-7759	3400
Oddo Print Shop Inc	Torrington	CT	G	860 489-6585	3690
Paul Dewitt	Danbury	CT	G	203 792-5610	795
Phoenix Press Inc	New Haven	CT	E	203 865-5555	2186
Professional Graphics Inc	Norwalk	CT	F	203 846-4291	2560
Richard E Personette	Middletown	CT	F	860 344-9001	1778
Saybrook Press Incorporated	Guilford	CT	G	203 458-3637	1406
Tech-Repro Inc	Stamford	CT	F	203 348-8884	3478

	CITY	ST	EMP	PHONE	ENTRY#
Westchster Bk/Rnsford Type Inc	Danbury	CT	E	203 791-0080	837
Allison Advertising Inc	Boston	MA	F	617 368-6800	6537
American Prtg & Envelope Inc	Auburn	MA	E	508 832-6100	6102
Andrew T Johnson Company Inc **(PA)**	Boston	MA	F	617 742-1610	6548
Argosy Publishing Inc **(PA)**	Newton	MA	D	617 527-9999	10733
Belmont Printing Company	Belmont	MA	G	617 484-0833	6304
Copy Masters Inc	Taunton	MA	F	508 824-7187	12329
Creative Publishing Corp Amer **(PA)**	Peabody	MA	E	978 532-5880	11303
Cxo Media Inc **(DH)**	Needham Heights	MA	C	508 766-5696	10539
D & L Associates Inc	Needham Heights	MA	G	781 400-5068	10540
D S Graphics Inc	Lowell	MA	C	978 970-1359	9873
Desk Top Graphics Inc **(HQ)**	Peabody	MA	E	617 832-1927	11305
Dmr Print Inc **(PA)**	Concord	MA	E	617 876-3688	8114
Elbonais Incorporated	Framingham	MA	G	508 626-2318	8761
Excelsior Printing Company	North Adams	MA	D	413 663-3771	10807
Fasprint Inc **(PA)**	Brockton	MA	F	508 588-9961	7278
Flagship Press Inc	North Andover	MA	C	978 975-3100	10831
Generation Four Inc	Waltham	MA	G	781 899-3180	12686
Ghp Media Inc	North Adams	MA	D	413 663-3771	10808
Icl Imaging Corp	Framingham	MA	E	508 872-3280	8778
J T Gardner Inc **(PA)**	Westborough	MA	E	800 540-4993	13112
Keating Communication Group	Canton	MA	G	781 828-9030	7804
Kirkwood Holdings Inc **(PA)**	Wilmington	MA	B	978 658-4200	13420
Laplume & Sons Printing Inc	Lawrence	MA	E	978 683-1009	9576
Linmel Associates Inc	Marlborough	MA	F	508 481-6699	10180
LPI Printing and Graphic Inc	Stoneham	MA	F	781 438-5400	12182
Marcus Company Inc	Holyoke	MA	F	413 534-3303	9265
Massachusetts Repro Ltd	Boston	MA	F	617 227-2237	6876
Picken Printing Inc	North Chelmsford	MA	F	978 251-0730	10986
Pyramid Printing and Advg Inc	Weymouth	MA	E	781 337-7609	13333
R & H Communications Inc **(PA)**	Waltham	MA	E	781 893-6221	12757
Ramsbottom Printing Inc	Fall River	MA	E	508 730-2220	8600
Reminder Publications	East Longmeadow	MA	E	413 525-3947	8393
Sherman Printing Co Inc	Canton	MA	E	781 828-8855	7828
Southern Brkshire Shppers Gide	Great Barrington	MA	E	413 528-0095	8978
Teletypesetting Company Inc	Boston	MA	F	617 542-6220	7073
Trustees of Tufts College **(PA)**	Somerville	MA	B	617 628-5000	11906
Universal Wilde Inc	Canton	MA	C	978 658-0800	7838
Weston Corporation	Hingham	MA	E	781 749-0936	9164
Winthrop Printing Company Inc	Foxboro	MA	E	617 268-9660	8732
Yankee Printing Group Inc	South Hadley	MA	E	413 532-9513	11968
Davic Inc	Portland	ME	G	207 774-0093	5206
Cygnus Inc	Portsmouth	NH	G	603 431-8989	15379
Echo Communications Inc	New London	NH	E	603 526-6006	15203
Fedex Office & Print Svcs Inc	Bedford	NH	F	603 644-2679	13929
Higgingbotham Management Corp	Portsmouth	NH	F	603 431-0142	15402
Kensington Group Incorporated	Hampton Falls	NH	F	603 926-6742	14419
Puritan Press Inc	Hollis	NH	E	603 889-4500	14458
Ram Printing Incorporated **(PA)**	East Hampstead	NH	F	603 382-7045	14271
Smith & Town Printers LLC	Berlin	NH	F	603 752-2150	13986
Southport Management Group LLC	Portsmouth	NH	G	603 433-4664	15438
Whitman Communications Inc	Lebanon	NH	G	603 448-2600	14703
A & H Composition and Prtg Inc	East Providence	RI	E	401 438-1200	15999
Branch Graphics Inc	Rumford	RI	E	401 861-1830	16663
Southern RI Newspapers **(HQ)**	Wakefield	RI	E	401 789-9744	16744
Accura Printing	Barre	VT	F	802 476-4429	16996
L Brown and Sons Printing Inc	Barre	VT	E	802 476-3164	17012
McClure Newspapers Inc	Williston	VT	C	802 863-3441	17740
Offset House Inc	Essex Junction	VT	C	802 878-4440	17242
Queen City Printers Inc	Burlington	VT	E	802 864-4566	17153
Stillwater Graphics Inc	Williamstown	VT	F	802 433-9898	17718
Stratford Publishing Services	Brattleboro	VT	G	802 254-6073	17100
Tuttle Law Print Inc	Rutland	VT	D	802 773-9171	17512
Villanti & Sons Printers Inc	Milton	VT	D	802 864-0723	17367

TYPESETTING SVC: Computer

	CITY	ST	EMP	PHONE	ENTRY#
Jupiter Communications LLC	West Haven	CT	F	475 238-7082	4108
Universal Printing Svcs Inc	West Haven	CT	E	203 934-4275	4131
Crane Composition Inc	East Sandwich	MA	G	774 338-5183	8404
JS McCarthy Co Inc **(PA)**	Augusta	ME	D	207 622-6241	4473
Laserwords Maine	Lewiston	ME	F	207 782-9595	4970

UNIFORM STORES

	CITY	ST	EMP	PHONE	ENTRY#
Al-Lynn Sales LLC	Shelton	CT	G	203 922-7840	2979
Allen Uniforms Inc	South Portland	ME	G	207 775-7364	5491

UNISEX HAIR SALONS

	CITY	ST	EMP	PHONE	ENTRY#
Hunter Dathan Hair Artistry	Portland	ME	G	207 774-8887	5224

UNIVERSITY

	CITY	ST	EMP	PHONE	ENTRY#
Wesleyan University	Middletown	CT	G	860 685-2980	1790
Yale University	New Haven	CT	E	203 764-4333	2218

	CITY	ST	EMP	PHONE	ENTRY#
Yale University **(PA)**	New Haven	CT	E	203 432-2550	2219
Yale University	New Haven	CT	E	203 737-1244	2220
Yale University	New Haven	CT	G	203 432-2880	2221
Massachusetts Institute Tech	Cambridge	MA	C	617 253-5646	7637
Massachusetts Institute Tech	Cambridge	MA	G	617 253-7183	7638
President and Fellows of Harvard College **(PA)** 617 496-4873	Cambridge	MA			A 7688
President Fllows Hrvard Cllege	Boston	MA	C	617 495-5581	6976
Technology Review Inc	Cambridge	MA	E	617 475-8000	7736
Trustees of Tufts College **(PA)**	Somerville	MA	B	617 628-5000	11906
University of Maine System	Orono	ME	F	207 581-2843	5138
Southern New Hampshire Univ	Manchester	NH	G	603 629-4631	14963

UNSUPPORTED PLASTICS: Floor Or Wall Covering

	CITY	ST	EMP	PHONE	ENTRY#
Guardian Indus Pdts Inc Mass	Norfolk	MA	G	508 384-0060	10798
Hytex Industries Inc	Randolph	MA	E	781 963-4400	11565

UPHOLSTERY FILLING MATERIALS

	CITY	ST	EMP	PHONE	ENTRY#
Amber Style Inc	Cumberland	RI	E	401 405-0089	15932

UPHOLSTERY MATERIALS, BROADWOVEN

	CITY	ST	EMP	PHONE	ENTRY#
Microfibres Inc	Foxboro	MA	A	401 725-4883	8708
LDI Solutions LLC	Rochester	NH	E	603 436-0077	15485

UPHOLSTERY WORK SVCS

	CITY	ST	EMP	PHONE	ENTRY#
Furniture Concepts	Malden	MA	G	781 324-8668	10015

USED MERCHANDISE STORES

	CITY	ST	EMP	PHONE	ENTRY#
Maine Antique Digest Inc	Waldoboro	ME	F	207 832-7534	5578

UTILITY TRAILER DEALERS

	CITY	ST	EMP	PHONE	ENTRY#
Innovative Specialties LLC	Pittsfield	ME	F	207 948-1500	5160
On The Road Inc	Warren	ME	E	207 273-3780	5585

VACUUM CLEANERS: Indl Type

	CITY	ST	EMP	PHONE	ENTRY#
Howden Roots LLC	Windsor	CT	D	860 688-8361	4281
Spencer Turbine Company **(DH)**	Windsor	CT	E	860 688-8361	4301
Filtered Air Systems Inc	Woburn	MA	G	781 491-0508	13565

VACUUM SYSTEMS: Air Extraction, Indl

	CITY	ST	EMP	PHONE	ENTRY#
Craftech Upton	Upton	MA	F	508 529-4505	12472
Edwards Vacuum LLC	Chelmsford	MA	D	978 262-2400	7924
Millibar Inc	Hudson	MA	F	508 488-9870	9391
Ruwac Inc	Holyoke	MA	F	413 532-4030	9278
Vacuum Technology Assoc Inc	Hingham	MA	D	781 740-8600	9161
Aargo Environmental Inc	Exeter	RI	G	401 678-6444	16050

VALUE-ADDED RESELLERS: Computer Systems

	CITY	ST	EMP	PHONE	ENTRY#
Valiantys America Inc	Dedham	MA	F	781 375-2494	8253
Workgroup Tech Partners Inc **(PA)**	Westbrook	ME	E	207 856-5312	5653
Omada Technologies LLC	Portsmouth	NH	F	603 610-8282	15428
Profitkey International Inc	Salem	NH	E	603 898-9800	15556

VALVE REPAIR SVCS, INDL

	CITY	ST	EMP	PHONE	ENTRY#
Nepv LLC	Niantic	CT	F	860 739-2200	2358
Knowlton Machine Company	Gorham	ME	E	207 854-8471	4824

VALVES

	CITY	ST	EMP	PHONE	ENTRY#
Air Valves LLC	Bethlehem	CT	G	203 266-7175	142
Carten Controls Inc	Cheshire	CT	E	203 699-2100	577
Conant Controls Inc	Woburn	MA	E	781 395-2240	13544
Heart Valve Society	Beverly	MA	F	212 561-9879	6355
Tooling Research Inc	Walpole	MA	F	508 668-5583	12577
Valmet Flow Control Inc	Shrewsbury	MA	C	508 852-0200	11846
Valmet Flow Control Inc **(HQ)**	Shrewsbury	MA	C	508 852-0200	11847
Maine Valve Rebuilders	Gorham	ME	G	207 856-6735	4825
Butler Valve & Fittings	Portsmouth	RI	G	401 849-3833	16441

VALVES & PARTS: Gas, Indl

	CITY	ST	EMP	PHONE	ENTRY#
Broen-Lab Inc	Bedford	NH	F	603 310-5089	13920

VALVES & PIPE FITTINGS

	CITY	ST	EMP	PHONE	ENTRY#
Carten Controls Inc	Cheshire	CT	E	203 699-2100	577
Enfield Technologies LLC	Trumbull	CT	F	203 375-3100	3719
Fisher Controls Intl LLC	North Stonington	CT	F	860 599-1144	2449
Houston-Weber Systems Inc	Branford	CT	G	203 481-0115	264
Hydrolevel Company	North Haven	CT	F	203 776-0473	2414
Idex Health & Science LLC	Bristol	CT	C	860 314-2880	456
Ppi Gas Distribution Inc	Naugatuck	CT	G		1981
Automatic Machine Pdts Sls Co	Taunton	MA	E	508 822-4226	12320
Carpenter & Paterson Inc	Woburn	MA	E	781 935-7036	13540
Colfax Fluid Handling	Warren	MA	G	413 436-7711	12850

P
R
O
D
U
C
T

	CITY	ST	EMP	PHONE	ENTRY#
Conant Controls Inc	Woburn	MA	E	781 395-2240	13544
Ferguson Enterprises LLC	Chicopee	MA	G	413 593-1219	8032
Improved Consumer Products Inc	North Attleboro	MA	F	508 695-6841	10875
Ltp Corporation (DH)	Northborough	MA	D	508 393-7660	11101
Microgroup Inc	Medway	MA	E	508 533-4925	10308
Mks Instruments Inc	Andover	MA	E	978 645-5500	5898
Mks Instruments Inc (PA)	Andover	MA	B	978 645-5500	5899
Mks Msc Inc	Wilmington	MA	D	978 284-4000	13434
Portland Valve LLC (DH)	Warren	MA	E	704 289-6511	12852
Rodney Hunt-Fontaine Inc (HQ)	Orange	MA	E	978 544-2511	11232
Sem-Tec Inc	Worcester	MA	E	508 798-8551	13797
Sloan Valve Company	Andover	MA	C	617 796-9001	5922
Swiss Precision Products Inc (DH)	North Oxford	MA	E	508 987-8003	11035
Alan T Seeler Inc	New Hampton	NH	F	603 744-3736	15195
Controlair LLC	Amherst	NH	E	603 886-9400	13865
Mem-Co Fittings Inc	Hampstead	NH	G	603 329-9633	14386
Parker & Harper Companies Inc (PA)	Raymond	NH	D	603 895-4761	15455
Quality Controls Inc	Northfield	NH	E	603 286-3321	15268
Everett J Prescott Inc	Lincoln	RI	E	401 333-8588	16135
Tyco Fire Products LP (DH)	Cranston	RI	C	215 362-0700	15924

VALVES & REGULATORS: Pressure, Indl

	CITY	ST	EMP	PHONE	ENTRY#
Condon Mfg Co Inc	Springfield	MA	E	413 543-1250	12085
Crosby Valve & Gage Intl Inc	Mansfield	MA	E	508 384-3121	10048
Mks Msc Inc	Wilmington	MA	D	978 284-4000	13434
Watts Regulator Co	North Andover	MA	A	978 688-1811	10858
Watts Regulator Co (HQ)	North Andover	MA	C	978 689-6000	10859
Watts Water Technologies Inc (PA)	North Andover	MA	C	978 688-1811	10861
Controlair LLC	Amherst	NH	E	603 886-9400	13865

VALVES Solenoid

	CITY	ST	EMP	PHONE	ENTRY#
Kip Inc	Farmington	CT	C	860 677-0272	1227
Parker-Hannifin Corporation	New Britain	CT	C	860 827-2300	2050
Peter Paul Electronics Co Inc	New Britain	CT	C	860 229-4884	2051

VALVES: Aerosol, Metal

	CITY	ST	EMP	PHONE	ENTRY#
Aptargroup Inc	Trumbull	CT	B	203 377-8100	3712
Alloy Fabricators Neng Inc	Randolph	MA	F	781 986-6400	11547
Summit Packaging Systems LLC (PA)	Manchester	NH	B	603 669-5410	14937

VALVES: Aircraft, Control, Hydraulic & Pneumatic

	CITY	ST	EMP	PHONE	ENTRY#
Controls For Automation Inc	Taunton	MA	E	508 802-6005	12328
Hope Inc	Needham	MA	E	781 455-1145	10512
Eaton Corporation	Rumford	RI	E	401 473-2214	16666
John Crane Sealol Inc (DH)	Warwick	RI	C	401 732-0715	16828

VALVES: Control, Automatic

	CITY	ST	EMP	PHONE	ENTRY#
Fisher Controls Intl LLC	North Stonington	CT	F	860 599-1140	2449

VALVES: Fluid Power, Control, Hydraulic & pneumatic

	CITY	ST	EMP	PHONE	ENTRY#
Crane Aerospace Inc (DH)	Stamford	CT	C	203 363-7300	3325
Crane Controls Inc (DH)	Stamford	CT	C	203 363-7300	3327
Crane Intl Holdings Inc (HQ)	Stamford	CT	C	203 363-7300	3328
Crane Merger Co LLC	Stamford	CT	F	203 363-7300	3329
Crane Overseas LLC (HQ)	Stamford	CT	E	203 363-7300	3330
Norgren LLC	Farmington	CT	C	860 677-0272	1232
Redco Corporation (HQ)	Stamford	CT	D	203 363-7300	3445
Circor LLC	Burlington	MA	E	781 270-1200	7348
Crane Nxt Co (PA)	Waltham	MA	C	610 430-2510	12644
Navtec Rigging Solutions Inc	Groton	MA	E		9011

VALVES: Indl

	CITY	ST	EMP	PHONE	ENTRY#
Belimo Technology (usa) Inc	Danbury	CT	D	203 791-9915	717
BNL Industries Inc	Vernon	CT	E	860 870-6222	3751
Contemporary Products LLC	Middletown	CT	F	860 346-9283	1744
Conval Inc	Enfield	CT	C	860 749-0761	1126
Curtiss-Wright Corporation	East Windsor	CT	G	864 486-9311	1070
Motion Industries Inc	Bloomfield	CT	A	860 687-5000	195
Arichell Technologies Inc	Newton	MA	D	617 796-9001	10734
Asahi/America Inc (HQ)	Lawrence	MA	E	781 321-5409	9540
Circor Energy LLC	Burlington	MA	F	781 270-1200	7349
Circor German Holdings LLC (DH)	Burlington	MA	D	781 270-1200	7350
Circor International Inc (HQ)	Burlington	MA	E	781 270-1200	7351
Cobra Precision Machining Corp	Petersham	MA	G	603 434-8424	11388
Conant Controls Inc	Woburn	MA	E	781 395-2240	13544
Diebolt & Company	East Longmeadow	MA	G	860 434-2222	8374
Gordon Martin	Newbury	MA	G	351 201-6065	10665
Millennium Power Services Inc (PA)	Westfield	MA	E	413 562-5332	13189
Mks Instruments Inc	Andover	MA	E	978 645-5500	5898
Mks Instruments Inc (PA)	Andover	MA	B	978 645-5500	5899
Vent-Rite Valve Corp (PA)	Randolph	MA	E	781 986-2000	11578
Allagash International Inc	Portland	ME	G	207 781-8831	5176

	CITY	ST	EMP	PHONE	ENTRY#
Quality Controls Inc	Northfield	NH	E	603 286-3321	15268
Ruggles-Klingemann Mfg Co	Seabrook	NH	G	603 474-8500	15603
Watts Regulator Co	Franklin	NH	A	603 934-5110	14323
Watts Water Technologies Inc	Franklin	NH	E	603 934-1369	14324
Velan Valve Corp (DH)	Williston	VT	D	802 863-2561	17751

VALVES: Plumbing & Heating

	CITY	ST	EMP	PHONE	ENTRY#
Reggies Oil Company Inc	Quincy	MA	F	617 471-2095	11536
Symmons Industries Inc (PA)	Braintree	MA	C	800 796-6667	7207
Watts Regulator Co (HQ)	North Andover	MA	C	978 689-6000	10859
Watts Water Technologies Inc (PA)	North Andover	MA	C	978 688-1811	10861
Leonard Valve Company LLC	Cranston	RI	E	800 222-1208	15884

VALVES: Regulating & Control, Automatic

	CITY	ST	EMP	PHONE	ENTRY#
Emerson Atmtn Sltons Fnal Ctrl	Mansfield	MA	D	508 594-4411	10051

VALVES: Water Works

	CITY	ST	EMP	PHONE	ENTRY#
Rodney Hunt-Fontaine Inc (HQ)	Orange	MA	E	978 544-2511	11232
Valves and Controls Us Inc	Ipswich	MA	D	978 744-5690	9499

VAN CONVERSIONS

	CITY	ST	EMP	PHONE	ENTRY#
National Van Sales Inc	Attleboro	MA	F	508 222-2272	6040
Ride-Away Inc (HQ)	Londonderry	NH	E	603 437-4444	14782

VAULTS & SAFES WHOLESALERS

	CITY	ST	EMP	PHONE	ENTRY#
Cvc II Inc (DH)	Bethel	CT	D	203 401-4205	105

VEHICLES: Recreational

	CITY	ST	EMP	PHONE	ENTRY#
Rokon International Inc	Rochester	NH	F	603 335-3200	15491
Textron Inc (PA)	Providence	RI	A	401 421-2800	16623

VENDING MACHINES & PARTS

	CITY	ST	EMP	PHONE	ENTRY#
Century Food Service Inc	Acushnet	MA	F	508 995-3221	5770
Next Generation Vending LLC	Stoughton	MA	A	781 828-2345	12226
SOS Group Inc	Boston	MA	G	978 496-7947	7047

VENTILATING EQPT: Metal

	CITY	ST	EMP	PHONE	ENTRY#
Northeastern Metals LLC	Greenfield	MA	E	800 506-7090	8997
XYZ Sheet Metal Inc	Abington	MA	F	781 878-1419	5729
Sylro Sales Corporation	Pelham	NH	G	603 595-4556	15298

VENTILATING EQPT: Sheet Metal

	CITY	ST	EMP	PHONE	ENTRY#
Improved Consumer Products Inc	North Attleboro	MA	F	508 695-6841	10875
Nasons Ug Inc (PA)	Middletown	RI	F	401 847-2497	16180

VENTURE CAPITAL COMPANIES

	CITY	ST	EMP	PHONE	ENTRY#
Atlantic Street Capitl MGT LLC (PA)	Stamford	CT	E	203 428-3158	3289
Cobra Green LLC	Norwalk	CT	A	203 354-5000	2484
Abry Partners V L P	Boston	MA	A	617 859-2959	6506
Bcpe Seminole Holdings LP (PA)	Boston	MA	F	617 516-2000	6585
BV Investment Partners LP (PA)	Boston	MA	E	617 224-0057	6629
Weston Presidio MGT Co Inc (PA)	Boston	MA	E	617 988-2500	7118

VETERINARY PHARMACEUTICAL PREPARATIONS

	CITY	ST	EMP	PHONE	ENTRY#
Pp Manufacturing Corporation	Framingham	MA	F	508 766-2700	8799
Uptite Company Inc	Haverhill	MA	G	978 377-0451	9138
Covetrus North America LLC (PA)	Portland	ME	C	888 280-2221	5202
Idexx Laboratories Inc (PA)	Westbrook	ME	A	207 556-0300	5631

VETERINARY PRDTS: Instruments & Apparatus

	CITY	ST	EMP	PHONE	ENTRY#
Horsepower Technologies Inc	Lowell	MA	E	844 514-6773	9884
Swiss Precision Products Inc (DH)	North Oxford	MA	E	508 987-8003	11035

VIDEO & AUDIO EQPT, WHOLESALE

	CITY	ST	EMP	PHONE	ENTRY#
Audiospectrum Inc	Randolph	MA	E	781 767-1331	11549
Boston Light & Sound Inc (PA)	Malden	MA	F	617 787-3131	10005

VIDEO TAPE PRODUCTION SVCS

	CITY	ST	EMP	PHONE	ENTRY#
Taunton Inc	Newtown	CT	A	203 426-8171	2349
The Taunton Press Inc (PA)	Newtown	CT	C	203 426-8171	2352
Venan Entertainment Inc	Middletown	CT	G	860 704-6330	1789
Channing Bete Company Inc (PA)	South Deerfield	MA	C	413 665-7611	11922
Human Resource Dev Press (PA)	Belchertown	MA	E	413 253-3488	6280
Sinauer Associates Inc	Sunderland	MA	E	413 549-4300	12275

VINYL RESINS, NEC

	CITY	ST	EMP	PHONE	ENTRY#
Keller Products Incorporated	Bow	NH	F	603 224-5502	14003

VISES: Machine

	CITY	ST	EMP	PHONE	ENTRY#
Lord & Hodge Inc	Middletown	CT	F	860 632-7006	1760

VISUAL COMMUNICATIONS SYSTEMS

	CITY	ST	EMP	PHONE	ENTRY#
Essential Trading Systems Corp	Colchester	CT	F	860 295-8100	657
Magik Eye Inc	Stamford	CT	G	917 676-7436	3407
Visionpoint LLC	Newington	CT	E	860 436-9673	2333
Xtralis Inc	Northford	CT	E	800 229-4434	2457
Courtsmart Digital Systems Inc	North Chelmsford	MA	F	978 251-3300	10973
Image Stream Medical Inc	Littleton	MA	D	978 486-8494	9818
Talamas Company Inc	Waltham	MA	F	617 928-3437	12788
Vivox Inc	Framingham	MA	E	508 650-3571	8808

VITAMINS: Natural Or Synthetic, Uncompounded, Bulk

	CITY	ST	EMP	PHONE	ENTRY#
Biomed Health Inc	Glastonbury	CT	G	860 657-2258	1270
Watson LLC (DH)	West Haven	CT	E	203 932-3000	4132
Designing Health Inc	East Longmeadow	MA	F	661 257-1705	8373
Perioq Inc	Leominster	MA	G	978 534-1249	9693
Troy Micro Five Inc	Saint Albans	VT	G	802 524-0076	17535

VOCATIONAL REHABILITATION AGENCY

	CITY	ST	EMP	PHONE	ENTRY#
Goodwill Industries Nthrn Neng (PA)	Gorham	ME	D	207 774-6323	4820

WALL COVERINGS WHOLESALERS

	CITY	ST	EMP	PHONE	ENTRY#
Donghia Inc	Milford	CT	C	800 366-4442	1818
Merida Meridian Inc	Boston	MA	E	617 464-5400	6885

WALLBOARD: Gypsum

	CITY	ST	EMP	PHONE	ENTRY#
County Concrete & Cnstr Co	Columbia Falls	ME	E	207 483-4409	4698
Georgia-Pacific LLC	Newington	NH	C	603 433-8000	15207

WALLPAPER & WALL COVERINGS

	CITY	ST	EMP	PHONE	ENTRY#
Brewster Wallpaper LLC	Randolph	MA	D	800 366-1700	11552
Len-Tex Corp	North Walpole	NH	C	603 445-2342	15260

WALLPAPER STORE

	CITY	ST	EMP	PHONE	ENTRY#
Ethan Allen Retail Inc (HQ)	Danbury	CT	B	203 743-8000	741

WALLS: Curtain, Metal

	CITY	ST	EMP	PHONE	ENTRY#
Clarke International Bus Inc	Middletown	CT	E	860 632-1149	1743

WAREHOUSE CLUBS STORES

	CITY	ST	EMP	PHONE	ENTRY#
BJs Wholesale Club Inc	Franklin	MA	D	508 553-9889	8821

WAREHOUSING & STORAGE FACILITIES, NEC

	CITY	ST	EMP	PHONE	ENTRY#
Macristy Industries Inc (PA)	Newington	CT	F	860 225-4637	2305
Concordia Co Inc	South Dartmouth	MA	E	508 999-1381	11916
Holcim - Ner Inc (DH)	Saugus	MA	E	781 941-7200	11760
Pepsi-Cola Metro Btlg Co Inc	Sagamore Beach	MA	E	508 833-5600	11697
Sterilite Corporation (PA)	Townsend	MA	F	978 597-1000	12442

WAREHOUSING & STORAGE, REFRIGERATED: Cold Storage Or Refrig

	CITY	ST	EMP	PHONE	ENTRY#
Natural Country Farms Inc	Ellington	CT	C	860 872-8346	1112

WAREHOUSING & STORAGE: General

	CITY	ST	EMP	PHONE	ENTRY#
Dayleen Intimates Inc	Brookfield	CT	F	914 969-5900	516
L P Macadams Company Inc	Bridgeport	CT	D	203 366-3647	342
Big Foot Moving & Storage Inc	Acton	MA	E	781 488-3090	5740
Horn International Packg Inc (HQ)	Lancaster	MA	E	978 667-8797	9528
Pucker Gallery Inc	Somerville	MA	F	617 261-1817	11891

WAREHOUSING & STORAGE: Miniwarehouse

	CITY	ST	EMP	PHONE	ENTRY#
Coca-Cola Btlg Sthstern Neng I	Rutland	VT	F	802 773-2768	17492

WAREHOUSING & STORAGE: Refrigerated

	CITY	ST	EMP	PHONE	ENTRY#
Merrill Blueberry Farms Inc	Hancock	ME	F	207 667-2541	4872

WAREHOUSING & STORAGE: Self Storage

	CITY	ST	EMP	PHONE	ENTRY#
Cardinal Shoe Corporation	Lawrence	MA	F	978 686-9706	9546

WARM AIR HEATING/AC EQPT/SPLY, WHOL Humidifier, Exc Portable

	CITY	ST	EMP	PHONE	ENTRY#
Belimo Aircontrols (usa) Inc (HQ)	Danbury	CT	C	800 543-9038	715

WARM AIR HEATING/AC EQPT/SPLYS, WHOL Warm Air Htg Eqpt/Splys

	CITY	ST	EMP	PHONE	ENTRY#
Buckley Associates Inc	Stratford	CT	G	203 380-2405	3524
Buckley Associates Inc (PA)	Hanover	MA	D	781 878-5000	9027

WARP KNIT FABRIC FINISHING

	CITY	ST	EMP	PHONE	ENTRY#
Moore Company	Westerly	RI	E	401 596-0219	16937
Moore Company (PA)	Westerly	RI	C	401 596-2816	16938
Moore Company	Westerly	RI	E	401 596-2816	16939
Garware Fulflex USA Inc	Brattleboro	VT	C	802 257-5256	17085

WASHERS: Metal

	CITY	ST	EMP	PHONE	ENTRY#
Astron Inc (PA)	Pepperell	MA	E	978 433-9500	11383
Tiberio Manufacturing Corp	Holliston	MA	D	508 429-4011	9232

WASHERS: Plastic

	CITY	ST	EMP	PHONE	ENTRY#
Rcd Chambers Inc	Brookfield	CT	F	203 775-4416	536
Standard Washer & Mat Inc	Manchester	CT	E	860 643-5125	1638
I G Marston Company	Holbrook	MA	F	781 767-2894	9174

WASTE CLEANING SVCS

	CITY	ST	EMP	PHONE	ENTRY#
Acme Precast Co Inc	West Falmouth	MA	F	508 548-9607	13000

WATCH STRAPS, EXC METAL

	CITY	ST	EMP	PHONE	ENTRY#
Currys Leather Shop Inc	Randolph	MA	G	781 963-0679	11554

WATCHES

	CITY	ST	EMP	PHONE	ENTRY#
Morristown Star Struck LLC	Bethel	CT	E	203 778-4925	130
Timex Group Usa Inc (HQ)	Middlebury	CT	C	203 346-5000	1722

WATER HEATERS

	CITY	ST	EMP	PHONE	ENTRY#
Eemax Inc	Waterbury	CT	D	203 267-7890	3910
The Electric Heater Company	Stratford	CT	D	800 647-3165	3580
Therma-Flow Inc	Watertown	MA	E	617 924-3877	12913

WATER PURIFICATION EQPT: Household

	CITY	ST	EMP	PHONE	ENTRY#
3M Purification Inc (HQ)	Meriden	CT	B	203 237-5541	1648
Kx Technologies LLC (DH)	West Haven	CT	E	203 799-9000	4111
American Water Systems LLC	Canton	MA	F	781 830-9722	7767
Voltea Inc	Worcester	MA	F	510 861-3719	13825
Hil Technology Inc (DH)	Portland	ME	F	207 756-6200	5222
Filtrine Manufacturing Co Inc	Keene	NH	D	603 352-5500	14599

WATER SUPPLY

	CITY	ST	EMP	PHONE	ENTRY#
Evoqua Water Technologies LLC	Tewksbury	MA	E	978 863-4600	12397

WATER TREATMENT EQPT: Indl

	CITY	ST	EMP	PHONE	ENTRY#
Aqualogic Inc	North Haven	CT	E	203 248-8959	2393
Atlas Filtri North America LLC	Wallingford	CT	F	203 284-0080	3778
Evoqua Water Technologies LLC	South Windsor	CT	D	860 528-6512	3146
H Krevit and Company Inc	New Haven	CT	E	203 772-3350	2159
Hydro Service & Supplies Inc	Middletown	CT	G	203 265-3995	1751
Redco Corporation (HQ)	Stamford	CT	D	203 363-7300	3445
Town of Montville	Uncasville	CT	D	860 848-3830	3745
Town of Vernon	Vernon	CT	D	860 870-3545	3758
Barletta Fschbach Green Line D	Canton	MA	F	781 737-1705	7773
Crane Nxt Co (PA)	Waltham	MA	C	610 430-2510	12644
Evoqua Water Technologies LLC	Tewksbury	MA	A	908 851-4250	12398
Evoqua Water Technologies LLC	Tewksbury	MA	C	978 934-9349	12399
Heartland Water Technology Inc	Hudson	MA	F	603 490-9203	9372
Hydrotech Services Inc	North Attleboro	MA	F	508 699-5977	10874
JDM Company Inc	North Chelmsford	MA	G	978 251-1121	10979
Keller Products Inc	North Chelmsford	MA	F	978 264-1911	10980
Kerfoot Technologies Inc	Falmouth	MA	F	508 539-3002	8634
KLA Systems Inc	Assonet	MA	G	508 644-5555	5975
L T Technologies	East Bridgewater	MA	G	508 456-0315	8342
Metro Group Inc	Wilmington	MA	F	781 932-9911	13431
North Amrcn Fltration Mass Inc	Walpole	MA	F	508 660-9016	12570
Spilldam Environmental Inc	Brockton	MA	F	508 583-7850	7309
Williams Partners Ltd	East Boothbay	ME	G	207 633-3111	4738
Global Filtration Systems	Wolfeboro	NH	G	603 651-8777	15733
PSI Water Systems LLC (PA)	Hooksett	NH	F	603 624-5110	14470
Benson Neptune Inc (DH)	Warwick	RI	D	401 821-7140	16790
Service Tech Inc (PA)	North Providence	RI	G	401 353-3664	16310
Westfall Manufacturing Co	Bristol	RI	F	401 253-3799	15786

WATER: Distilled

	CITY	ST	EMP	PHONE	ENTRY#
Dunajski Dairy Inc	Peabody	MA	G	978 531-1457	11308
Monadnock Mountain Spring Water Inc	Wilton	NH	D	603 654-2728	15706

WATER: Mineral, Carbonated, Canned & Bottled, Etc

	CITY	ST	EMP	PHONE	ENTRY#
Crystal Rock Holdings Inc	Watertown	CT	B	860 945-0661	4006
Ds Services of America Inc	Watertown	CT	B	860 945-0661	4009
Bluetriton Brands Inc	Poland Spring	ME	C	207 998-4315	5163
Vermont Heritage Distrs Inc	Newport	VT	G	802 334-6503	17407

WATER: Pasteurized & Mineral, Bottled & Canned

	CITY	ST	EMP	PHONE	ENTRY#
Auburn Spring Water Company (PA)	Auburn	ME	G	207 782-1521	4422

WATER: Pasteurized, Canned & Bottled, Etc

	CITY	ST	EMP	PHONE	ENTRY#
Bluetriton Brands Inc	Stamford	CT	F	203 531-4100	3295
Bluetriton Brands Inc (HQ)	Stamford	CT	B	888 747-7437	3296

PRODUCT

	CITY	ST	EMP	PHONE	ENTRY#
Castle Seltzer Inc	Derby	CT	G	203 736-6887	888
Vitamin 1 LLC	Littleton	MA	G	617 523-9090	9844
Northeast Merchandising Corp	Skowhegan	ME	E	207 474-3321	5476
Cg Roxane LLC	Moultonborough	NH	F	603 476-8844	15051

WATERPROOFING COMPOUNDS

	CITY	ST	EMP	PHONE	ENTRY#
Caap Co Inc	Milford	CT	E	203 877-0375	1805
Grate Products LLC	Westport	MA	E	800 649-6140	13296
CIM Industries Inc	Peterborough	NH	D	603 924-9481	15313

WAVEGUIDES & FITTINGS

	CITY	ST	EMP	PHONE	ENTRY#
Microsemi Corporation	Simsbury	CT	D	860 651-0211	3093
Microtech Inc	Cheshire	CT	D	203 272-3234	607
Ainslie Corporation	Walpole	MA	G	781 848-0850	12548
Harvard Scientific Corporation	Cambridge	MA	F	617 876-5033	7604
Microwave Development Labs Inc	Needham Heights	MA	D	781 292-6600	10551

WAXES: Petroleum, Not Produced In Petroleum Refineries

	CITY	ST	EMP	PHONE	ENTRY#
Koster Keunen LLC (PA)	Watertown	CT	E	860 945-3333	4018
Cnc International Inc	Woonsocket	RI	G	401 769-6100	16953

WEATHER STRIP: Sponge Rubber

	CITY	ST	EMP	PHONE	ENTRY#
H-O Products Corporation	Winsted	CT	E	860 379-9875	4346

WEIGHING MACHINERY & APPARATUS

	CITY	ST	EMP	PHONE	ENTRY#
Hyer Industries Inc	Pembroke	MA	E	781 826-8101	11370

WELDING & CUTTING APPARATUS & ACCESS, NEC

	CITY	ST	EMP	PHONE	ENTRY#
Kamweld Technologies Inc	Norwood	MA	F	781 762-6922	11186
Stan Rubinstein Associates Inc	Walpole	MA	F	508 668-6044	12576
Triad Inc	Plainville	MA	G	508 695-2247	11444

WELDING EQPT

	CITY	ST	EMP	PHONE	ENTRY#
Branson Ultrasonics Corp (DH)	Brookfield	CT	B	203 796-0400	512
Jt Automation LLC	East Granby	CT	F	860 784-1967	938
Magnatech LLC	East Granby	CT	D	860 653-2573	939
Sonics & Materials Inc (PA)	Newtown	CT	D	203 270-4600	2347
Sonitek Corporation	Milford	CT	E	203 878-9321	1886
AGM Industries Inc	Brockton	MA	E	508 587-3900	7254
Mitchell Machine Incorporated (PA)	Springfield	MA	F	413 739-9693	12114
Precision Electronics Corp	Marshfield	MA	F	781 834-6677	10244
Bortech Corporation	Keene	NH	F	603 358-4030	14591
Centricut Manufacturing LLC	West Lebanon	NH	F	603 298-6191	15680
Contract Fusion Inc	East Providence	RI	F	401 438-1298	16010
Nordson Efd LLC (HQ)	East Providence	RI	C	401 431-7000	16034
YS Enterprises Inc	East Ryegate	VT	G	802 238-0902	17219

WELDING EQPT & SPLYS WHOLESALERS

	CITY	ST	EMP	PHONE	ENTRY#
Airgas Usa LLC	Danbury	CT	C	203 792-1834	705
Linde Gas & Equipment Inc (DH)	Danbury	CT	F	844 445-4633	775
Thavenet Machine Company Inc	Pawcatuck	CT	G	860 599-4495	2726
Ashmont Welding Company Inc	Bridgewater	MA	F	508 279-1977	7220
Stan Rubinstein Associates Inc	Walpole	MA	F	508 668-6044	12576
Weld Engineering Co Inc	Shrewsbury	MA	E	508 842-2224	11848
Thermal Dynamics Corporation (DH)	West Lebanon	NH	B	603 298-5711	15690
Contract Fusion Inc	East Providence	RI	F	401 438-1298	16010
Linde Gas & Equipment Inc	Slatersville	RI	D	401 767-3450	16682

WELDING EQPT & SPLYS: Gas

	CITY	ST	EMP	PHONE	ENTRY#
Hydro-Test Products Inc	Stow	MA	F	978 897-4647	12246

WELDING EQPT REPAIR SVCS

	CITY	ST	EMP	PHONE	ENTRY#
Ewald Instruments Corp	Lakeville	CT	F	860 491-9042	1545

WELDING EQPT: Electric

	CITY	ST	EMP	PHONE	ENTRY#
Linde Advanced Mtl Tech Inc	Manchester	CT	C	860 646-0700	1612
Kamweld Industries Inc	Norwood	MA	G	617 558-7500	11185
Weld Engineering Co Inc	Shrewsbury	MA	E	508 842-2224	11848

WELDING EQPT: Electrical

	CITY	ST	EMP	PHONE	ENTRY#
Luvata Waterbury Inc (HQ)	Waterbury	CT	D	203 753-5215	3931
Magnatech LLC	East Granby	CT	D	860 653-2573	939
Thermal Arc Inc	West Lebanon	NH	D	800 462-2782	15689

WELDING MACHINES & EQPT: Ultrasonic

	CITY	ST	EMP	PHONE	ENTRY#
Branson Ultrasonics Corp (DH)	Brookfield	CT	B	203 796-0400	512
Sonosystems N Schunk Amer Corp (DH)	Wilmington	MA	E	978 658-9400	13454

WELDING REPAIR SVC

	CITY	ST	EMP	PHONE	ENTRY#
24/7 LLC	Branford	CT	G	203 410-5151	230
Acceleron Inc	East Granby	CT	E	860 651-9333	924
Accurate Welding Services LLC	Windsor Locks	CT	F	860 623-9500	4317

	CITY	ST	EMP	PHONE	ENTRY#
Amk Welding Inc	South Windsor	CT	E	860 289-5634	3113
Ansonia Stl Fabrication Co Inc	Beacon Falls	CT	E	203 888-4509	39
Arp Welding LLC	Oxford	CT	F	203 344-7528	2686
B & F Machine Co Inc (PA)	New Britain	CT	C	860 225-6349	2006
C V Tool Company Inc (PA)	Southington	CT	F	978 353-7901	3206
Carlucci Wldg Fabrication Inc	Norwalk	CT	F	203 588-0746	2479
Cheshire Manufacturing Co Inc	Cheshire	CT	G	203 272-3586	580
Connecticut Machine & Welding	Stratford	CT	G	203 502-2605	3530
Dasco Welded Products Inc	Waterbury	CT	F	203 754-9353	3904
Dyco Industries Inc	South Windsor	CT	E	860 289-4957	3138
East Windsor Metal Fabg Inc	South Windsor	CT	F	860 528-7107	3139
Ebtec Corporation	East Windsor	CT	D	860 789-2462	1072
EZ Welding LLC	New Britain	CT	F	860 707-3100	2027
F & W Rentals Inc	Orange	CT	F	203 795-0591	2668
Fabtron Incorporated	Plainville	CT	G	860 410-1801	2759
Farrell Prcsion Mtalcraft Corp	New Milford	CT	E	860 355-2651	2243
H G Steinmetz Mch Works Inc	Stamford	CT	E	203 794-1880	3360
Hauser Eqp & Wldg Svcs Inc	Stratford	CT	F	203 377-7072	3545
Hurley Mtal Fbrication Mfg LLC	Windsor	CT	F	860 688-8844	4282
Innovative Fusion Inc	Naugatuck	CT	E	203 729-3873	1965
J & L Mfg Watertown Inc	Waterbury	CT	E	203 591-9124	3924
Jeff Mfg Inc	Torrington	CT	F	860 482-1387	3686
Joining Technologies LLC	East Granby	CT	D	860 653-0111	937
Kell-Strom Tool Intl Inc	Wethersfield	CT	F	860 529-6851	4210
Kti Inc (HQ)	East Windsor	CT	G	860 623-2511	1079
L M Gill Welding and Mfr LLC	Manchester	CT	D	860 647-9931	1611
Line-X of New England LLC	New Milford	CT	G	860 355-6997	2252
LM Gill Welding & Mfg LLC	Manchester	CT	E	860 647-9931	1613
Lostocco Refuse Service LLC	Danbury	CT	E	203 748-9296	779
Lynn Welding Co Inc	Newington	CT	F	860 667-4400	2304
N C T Inc	Colchester	CT	E	860 666-8424	662
National Welding LLC	Middlefield	CT	G	860 818-1240	1726
Paul Welding Company Inc	Newington	CT	G	860 229-9945	2314
Quality Welding LLC	Bristol	CT	G	860 585-1121	486
Ram Welding Co Inc	Naugatuck	CT	E	203 720-0535	1983
Reno Machine Company Inc	Newington	CT	D	860 666-5641	2321
Salsco Inc	Cheshire	CT	D	203 271-1682	616
SS Fabrications Inc	Eastford	CT	E	860 974-1910	1092
Standard Welding Company Inc	East Hartford	CT	D	860 528-9628	1022
State Welding & Fabg Inc	Clinton	CT	G	203 294-4071	650
Sterzingers Welding LLC	Danbury	CT	G	203 685-1575	822
Sua Prformance Fabrication LLC	East Hartford	CT	G	860 904-6068	1025
Tinsley GROup-Ps&w Inc (HQ)	Milford	CT	E	919 742-5832	1896
Total Fab LLC	East Haven	CT	F	475 238-8176	1055
United Steel Inc	East Hartford	CT	C	860 289-2323	1032
Weld-All Inc	Southington	CT	G	860 621-3156	3240
White Welding Company	Waterbury	CT	G	203 753-1197	3984
Advanced Welding & Design Inc	Woburn	MA	F	781 938-7644	13743
Alvin Johnson	East Longmeadow	MA	G	413 525-6334	8368
Ashmont Welding Company Inc	Bridgewater	MA	F	508 279-1977	7220
Assocted Electro-Mechanics Inc	Springfield	MA	D	413 781-4276	12076
Astro Welding & Fabg Inc	Boxborough	MA	F	978 429-8666	7148
B&C Cryotech Services Inc	Sutton	MA	G	508 277-5440	12277
Baxter Inc	West Yarmouth	MA	F	508 775-0375	13072
Blue Fleet Welding Service	New Bedford	MA	F	508 997-5513	10572
Boston Welding & Design Inc	Woburn	MA	F	781 932-0035	13532
Bostonia Welding Supply Inc	Boston	MA	G	617 268-1025	6621
Capeway Welding Inc	Plymouth	MA	F	508 747-6666	11453
City Welding & Fabrication Inc	Worcester	MA	G	508 853-6000	13707
Composite Company Inc	Sherborn	MA	G	508 651-1681	11810
David Gilbert	Framingham	MA	G	508 879-1507	8755
Dockside Repairs Inc	New Bedford	MA	G	508 993-6730	10587
East Cast Wldg Fabrication LLC	Newburyport	MA	E	978 465-2338	10680
Feeneys Fence Inc	Hyde Park	MA	G	617 364-1407	9460
Fitchburg Welding Co Inc	Westminster	MA	E	978 874-2911	13270
Framingham Welding & Engineering Corporation 8763	Framingham	MA			E
Gem Welding	North Billerica	MA	F	978 362-3873	10916
Gill Metal Fab Inc	Brockton	MA	E	508 580-4445	7281
Horacios Inc	New Bedford	MA	F	508 985-9940	10602
International Beam Wldg Corp	West Springfield	MA	F	413 781-4368	13031
J & L Welding & Machine Co	Gloucester	MA	E	978 283-3388	8942
Jacquier Welding LLC	Ashley Falls	MA	A	413 248-1204	5971
Kielb Welding Enterprises Inc	Springfield	MA	F	413 734-4544	12109
Lima Fredy	Everett	MA	F	781 599-3055	8491
Marblehead Engineering	Essex	MA	F	978 432-1386	8477
Morrell Metalsmiths Ltd	Colrain	MA	A	413 624-1200	8096
New England Welding Inc	Avon	MA	E	508 580-2024	6155
Noremac Manufacturing Corp	Westborough	MA	E	508 366-8822	13124
Northeast Stainless Inc	North Andover	MA	F	781 589-9000	10846
O W Landergren Inc	Pittsfield	MA	E	413 442-5632	11415
Oliver Welding & Fabg Inc	Ipswich	MA	G	978 356-4488	9493

	CITY	ST	EMP	PHONE	ENTRY#
Patricia Barrett	Leominster	MA	F	978 537-0458	9692
Podgurski Wldg & Hvy Eqp Repr	Canton	MA	E	781 830-9901	7821
Precision Metal Works Inc	North Billerica	MA	E	978 667-0180	10944
Rae Js	Shelburne Falls	MA	F	413 625-9228	11808
Rens Welding & Fabricating	Taunton	MA	F	508 828-1702	12362
Roar Industries Inc	Hopedale	MA	F	508 429-5952	9302
Schrimpf Wldg Fabrication Inc	Woburn	MA	G	339 298-2311	13661
Shaw Welding Company Inc	Billerica	MA	E	978 667-0197	6480
Standex International Corp	North Billerica	MA	D	978 667-2771	10959
Thermo-Craft Engineering Corp	Lynn	MA	E	781 599-4023	9992
Todd & Weld LLP	Sharon	MA	E	781 784-1026	11796
Townsend Welding Co Inc	Wilmington	MA	E	978 657-5189	13468
Triad Inc	Plainville	MA	G	508 695-2247	11444
Trivak Incorporated	Lowell	MA	E	978 453-7123	9929
Union Machine Company Lynn Inc (PA)	Groveland	MA	E	978 521-5100	9016
Villa Machine Associates Inc	Dedham	MA	F	781 326-5969	8255
Welch Welding and Trck Eqp Inc	North Chelmsford	MA	F	978 251-8726	10989
Weld Rite	Jamaica Plain	MA	G	617 524-9747	9504
Welding Craftsmen Co Inc	South Easton	MA	F	508 230-7878	11956
With Weld	Boston	MA	F	800 288-6016	7129
Worcester County Welding Inc	Rochdale	MA	G	508 892-4884	11629
Crosbys Welding LLC	Bangor	ME	G	207 974-7815	4497
Davis Brothers Inc	Chester	ME	F	207 794-1001	4691
Down East Shtmtl & Certif Wldg	Brewer	ME	G	207 989-3443	4611
Howies Wldg & Fabrication Inc	Jay	ME	G	207 645-2581	4913
Linde Advanced Mtl Tech Inc	Biddeford	ME	D	207 282-3787	4575
North E Wldg & Fabrication Inc	Auburn	ME	E	207 786-2446	4448
Ramsays Welding & Machine Inc	Lincoln	ME	F	207 794-8839	5012
Ace Welding Co Inc	Merrimack	NH	E	603 424-9936	14971
Anderson Welding LLC	Dover	NH	E	603 996-6225	14216
ARC Maintenance Machining	Londonderry	NH	G	603 626-8046	14732
Baron Machine Company Inc	Laconia	NH	D	603 524-6800	14645
Bay State Industrial Weldin	Hudson	NH	E	603 881-7663	14488
Bocra Industries Inc	Seabrook	NH	F	603 474-3598	15585
Bri-Weld Industries LLC	Auburn	NH	F	603 622-9480	13906
East Coast Metal Works Co Inc	Kingston	NH	G	603 642-9600	14634
Hollis Line Machine Co Inc	Milford	NH	E	603 673-1166	15028
Ken-Mar LLC	Salem	NH	E	603 898-1268	15539
Merrimack County Customs	Bradford	NH	G	603 938-5855	14017
Multi-Weld Services Inc	Contoocook	NH	F	603 746-4604	14172
Radenhausen & ONeill Inc	Jaffrey	NH	E	603 532-4879	14578
Ralph L Osgood Inc	Claremont	NH	F	603 543-1703	14096
Recycling Mechanical Neng LLC	Allenstown	NH	F	603 268-8028	13855
S L Chasse Welding & Fabg Inc	Hudson	NH	D	603 886-3436	14543
Shawn Dudek	Laconia	NH	F	603 387-1859	14669
Smiths Tblar Systms-Lconia Inc	Laconia	NH	C	603 524-2064	14670
Starkey Welding Crane Service	Brentwood	NH	G	603 679-2553	14030
Stone Machine Co Inc	Chester	NH	F	603 887-4287	14071
Valley Welding & Fabg Inc	Hollis	NH	E	603 465-3266	14460
Weidner Services LLC	Jaffrey	NH	G	603 532-4833	14582
Will-Mor Manufacturing LLC	Seabrook	NH	D	603 474-8971	15606
A D& D Wldg & Boiler Works Inc	Warwick	RI	F	401 732-5222	16774
Artic Tool & Engrg Co LLC	Greenville	RI	E	401 785-2210	16055
Formex Inc	East Greenwich	RI	E	401 885-9800	15986
Guill Tool & Engrg Co Inc	West Warwick	RI	D	401 822-8186	16908
H B Welding Inc	Johnston	RI	E	401 727-0323	16088
Laser Fare Inc (PA)	Smithfield	RI	E	401 231-4400	16721
Luthers Repair Shop Inc	Bristol	RI	F	401 253-5550	15773
Southern New England Wldg LLC	Coventry	RI	G	401 822-0596	15821
West Warwick Welding Inc	West Warwick	RI	F	401 822-8200	16926
Bellavance Welding LLC	Wolcott	VT	G	802 793-9327	17773
Browns Certified Welding Inc	Bristol	VT	F	802 453-3351	17115
Cave Manufacturing Inc	Brattleboro	VT	E	802 257-9253	17079
Giroux Body Shop Inc	Hinesburg	VT	F	802 482-2162	17291
Gloucester Associates Inc	Barre	VT	E	802 479-1088	17001
Milton Vermont Sheet Metal Inc	Milton	VT	D	802 893-1581	17362
Mulholland Wldg & Fabrication	Chester	VT	F	802 875-5500	17181
North Country Engineering Inc	Derby	VT	E	802 766-5396	17212
PG Adams Inc	South Burlington	VT	E	802 862-8664	17590
Pre-Tech Plastics Inc (PA)	Williston	VT	E	802 879-9441	17745

WELDING SPLYS, EXC GASES: Wholesalers

	CITY	ST	EMP	PHONE	ENTRY#
Airgas Usa LLC	Danbury	CT	C	203 792-1834	705

WELDING TIPS: Heat Resistant, Metal

Performance Connection Systems	Meriden	CT	G	203 868-5517	1684
Harmony Metal Products North Inc	Portsmouth	NH	E	603 536-6012	15399

WELDMENTS

Vitta Corporation	Bethel	CT	E	203 790-8155	141
Whitcraft LLC (PA)	Eastford	CT	C	860 974-0786	1093
Whitcraft Scrborough/Tempe LLC (HQ)	Eastford	CT	E	860 974-0786	1094

	CITY	ST	EMP	PHONE	ENTRY#
Alloy Fabricators Neng Inc	Randolph	MA	F	781 986-6400	11547
Green Brothers Fabricating (PA)	Taunton	MA	E	508 880-3608	12339
Steel-Fab Inc	Fitchburg	MA	E	978 345-1112	8676
United Metal Fabracators Inc	Worcester	MA	F	508 754-1800	13815

WET CORN MILLING

A E Staley Manufacturing Co	Houlton	ME	G	207 532-9523	4895
Primary Pdts Ingrdnts Amrcas L	Houlton	ME	E	207 532-9523	4904

WHEELCHAIR LIFTS

Garaventa U S A Inc	Manchester	NH	F	603 669-6553	14850
Ride-Away Inc (HQ)	Londonderry	NH	E	603 437-4444	14782
Yankee Medical Inc (DH)	Burlington	VT	F	802 863-4591	17164

WHEELCHAIRS

United Seating & Mobility LLC	Rocky Hill	CT	D	806 761-0700	2940
Numotion	Taunton	MA	G	401 681-2153	12353
Wheelchair	Lewiston	ME	F	207 782-8400	4996
Power Chair Recyclers Neng LLC	North Kingstown	RI	G	401 294-4111	16275

WHEELS, GRINDING: Artificial

Extec Corp	Enfield	CT	F	860 741-3435	1133
Westfield Grinding Wheel Co	Westfield	MA	F	413 568-8634	13220
Rhode Island Centerless Inc	Johnston	RI	F	401 942-0403	16104

WHEELS: Abrasive

Avery Abrasives Inc	Trumbull	CT	E	203 372-3513	3713
Rex Cut Products Incorporated	Fall River	MA	D	508 678-1985	8602
Saint-Gobain Abrasives Inc (HQ)	Worcester	MA	A	508 795-5000	13788
Joseph A Thomas Ltd	Bristol	RI	E	401 253-1330	15770

WINCHES

Show Motion Inc	Milford	CT	E	203 866-1866	1884
Rt Engineering Corporation	Franklin	MA	E	800 343-1182	8861

WINDINGS: Coil, Electronic

Classic Coil Company Inc	Bristol	CT	D	860 583-7600	427
Quality Coils Incorporated (PA)	Bristol	CT	C	860 584-0927	485
Transcon Technologies Inc	Westfield	MA	E	413 562-7684	13212
Ladesco Inc	Manchester	NH	C	603 623-3772	14873
Wire Winders Inc	Milford	NH	G	603 673-1763	15044
Crest Manufacturing Company	Lincoln	RI	E	401 333-1350	16129

WINDMILLS: Electric Power Generation

Cubico Palmetto Holdings LLC	Stamford	CT	E	646 513-4981	3331
Enbw North America Inc	Boston	MA	F	857 753-4623	6714
Green Development LLC	Cranston	RI	D	401 295-4998	15870

WINDOW & DOOR FRAMES

Advanced Window Systems LLC	Cromwell	CT	F	800 841-6544	684
Ckh Industries Inc	Wethersfield	CT	D	860 563-2999	4203
Cooper Group LLC	Pawcatuck	CT	F	860 599-2481	2716
Architctral Glzing Systems Inc	Avon	MA	E	508 588-4845	6142
Brunswick Enclosure Company	North Billerica	MA	G	978 670-1124	10902
ER Lewin Inc	Wrentham	MA	E	508 384-0363	13841
Modern Mfg Inc Worcester	Rochdale	MA	E	508 791-7151	11628
Win-Pressor LLC	Unity	ME	G	207 948-4800	5568

WINDOW FRAMES & SASHES: Plastic

All-Time Manufacturing Co Inc	Montville	CT	F	860 848-9258	1926
Paradigm Operating Company LLC	Portland	ME	C	877 994-6369	5255

WINDOW FRAMES, MOLDING & TRIM: Vinyl

Mercury-Excelum Inc	East Windsor	CT	E	860 292-1800	1080
Owens Corning Sales LLC	East Hartford	CT	C	304 353-6945	1008
Diamond Windows Doors Mfg Inc	Boston	MA	E	617 282-1688	6693
National Vinyl LLC	Chicopee	MA	E	413 420-0548	8051
Stergis Aluminum Products Corp	Attleboro	MA	E	508 455-0661	6065
Mathews Brothers Company (PA)	Belfast	ME	C	207 338-3360	4535
K & C Industries Inc	Smithfield	RI	F	508 520-4600	16720

WINDOW SASHES, WOOD

J B Sash & Door Company Inc	Chelsea	MA	E	617 884-8940	7983

WINDOWS: Frames, Wood

Mathews Brothers Company (PA)	Belfast	ME	C	207 338-3360	4535

WINDOWS: Wood

Schuco USA Lllp (HQ)	Newington	CT	E	860 666-0505	2324
Harvey Industries LLC	Springfield	MA	E	413 731-7700	12099
Harvey Industries LLC (PA)	Waltham	MA	C	800 598-5400	12691
Harvey Industries Inc	Augusta	ME	F	207 629-3737	4472

Employee Codes: A=Over 500 employees, B=251-500
C=101-250, D=51-100, E=20-50, F=10-19, G=1-9

2024 Harris New England
Manufacturers Directory

1483

PRODUCT

	CITY	ST	EMP	PHONE	ENTRY#

WINE & DISTILLED ALCOHOLIC BEVERAGES WHOLESALERS

	CITY	ST	EMP	PHONE	ENTRY#
Caledonia Spirits Inc	Montpelier	VT	E	802 472-8000	17370

WIRE

	CITY	ST	EMP	PHONE	ENTRY#
Accel Intl Holdings Inc	Meriden	CT	E	203 237-2700	1650
Lee Spring Company LLC	Bristol	CT	F	860 584-0991	461
Wiretek Inc	Bloomfield	CT	E	860 242-9473	217
Belden Inc	Leominster	MA	E	978 537-8911	9641
James Cable LLC	Braintree	MA	E	781 356-8701	7189
Mersen USA Ep Corp (HQ)	Newburyport	MA	D	978 462-6662	10699

WIRE & CABLE: Aluminum

	CITY	ST	EMP	PHONE	ENTRY#
Omerin Usa Inc	Meriden	CT	E	475 343-3450	1682
Joseph Freedman Co Inc (PA)	Springfield	MA	D	888 677-7818	12108

WIRE & CABLE: Nonferrous, Aircraft

	CITY	ST	EMP	PHONE	ENTRY#
Judd Wire Inc (DH)	Turners Falls	MA	B	800 545-5833	12450

WIRE & CABLE: Nonferrous, Automotive, Exc Ignition Sets

	CITY	ST	EMP	PHONE	ENTRY#
Autac Incorporated (PA)	Branford	CT	G	203 481-3444	238
Prysmian Cbles Systems USA LLC	Lincoln	RI	C	401 333-4848	16151

WIRE & CABLE: Nonferrous, Building

	CITY	ST	EMP	PHONE	ENTRY#
Hamden Metal Service Co Inc	Hamden	CT	F	203 281-1522	1427
Draka Cableteq Usa Inc	Boston	MA	B	888 520-1200	6702
General Wire Products Inc	Worcester	MA	E	508 752-8260	13731
Mor-Wire & Cable Inc	Lowell	MA	F	978 453-1782	9909
Prysmian Group Spclty Cbles LL (DH)	Taunton	MA	C	774 501-7600	12358
Prysmian Group Spclty Cbles LL	Taunton	MA	C	508 822-5444	12359
Taurus Technologies Corp	South Grafton	MA	E	508 234-6372	11957

WIRE & WIRE PRDTS

	CITY	ST	EMP	PHONE	ENTRY#
Acme Monaco Corporation (PA)	New Britain	CT	C	860 224-1349	1995
Acme Wire Products Co Inc	Mystic	CT	E	860 572-0511	1935
Arrow Manufacturing Company	Bristol	CT	E		397
Bes-Cut Inc	Bristol	CT	G	860 582-8660	414
Bridgeport Insulated Wire Co (PA)	Bridgeport	CT	F	203 333-3191	304
Bridgeport Insulated Wire Co	Stratford	CT	G	203 375-9579	3523
East Shore Wire Rope Rgging Su	North Haven	CT	F	203 469-5204	2407
ERA Wire Inc	West Haven	CT	F	203 933-0480	4106
Habasit America Inc	Middletown	CT	C	860 632-2211	1750
Harding Company Inc (HQ)	Putnam	CT	G	603 778-7070	2859
Harding Company Inc	Putnam	CT	F	860 928-0475	2860
International Pipe & Stl Corp	North Branford	CT	F	203 481-7102	2369
Luvata Waterbury Inc	Branford	CT	E	203 488-5956	269
Meyer Wire & Cable Company LLC	Hamden	CT	E	203 281-0817	1441
Netsource Inc (PA)	Manchester	CT	E	860 649-6000	1620
Northeastern Shaped Wire Inc	Southington	CT	E	860 621-8991	3226
Novo Precision LLC	Bristol	CT	E	860 583-0517	476
Pa-Ted Spring Company LLC	Bristol	CT	E	860 582-6368	479
Prysmian Cbles Systems USA LLC	Willimantic	CT	C	860 456-8000	4220
Radcliff Wire Inc	Bristol	CT	E	312 876-1754	489
Rowley Spring & Stamping Corp	Bristol	CT	C	860 582-8175	494
Siri Manufacturing Co Inc	Danielson	CT	E	860 236-5901	842
Siri Wire Co	Danielson	CT	G	860 774-0607	843
Specialty Wire & Cord Sets Inc	Hamden	CT	F	203 498-2932	1456
Spring Tollman Company Incorporated (PA) 860 583-1326	Bristol	CT	D		497
Tiger Enterprises Inc	Plantsville	CT	E	860 621-9155	2798
Ultimate Wireforms Inc	Bristol	CT	D	860 582-9111	504
Wiremold Company (DH)	West Hartford	CT	A	860 233-6251	4091
Atlee Delaware Incorporated	Melrose	MA	F	978 681-1003	10313
Automatic Specialties Inc	Marlborough	MA	E	508 481-2370	10114
Bay State Wire & Cable Co Inc	Lowell	MA	E	978 454-2444	9861
Cape Cod Fence Co (PA)	South Yarmouth	MA	F	508 398-6041	11982
Comprehensive Identification Products Inc 781 229-8780	Burlington	MA	C		7354
Dolan-Jenner Industries Inc	Boxborough	MA	E	978 263-1400	7151
Eastern Sling & Supply	Avon	MA	F	617 464-4422	6150
Ekiton Corporation	Boston	MA	G	617 464-4422	6709
Electro-Prep Inc	Wareham	MA	E	508 291-2880	12834
Frank L Reed Inc	Wilbraham	MA	E	413 596-3861	13359
General Wire Products Inc	Worcester	MA	E	508 752-8260	13731
Horizon Fence Company Inc	Spencer	MA	G	774 289-9254	12061
I & I Sling Inc	Norwood	MA	E	781 575-0600	11178
International Metal Pdts Inc	Chicopee	MA	E	413 532-2411	8040
Joe Miller Inc	Worcester	MA	E	508 753-8581	13745
Lanoco Specialty Wire Pdts Inc	Sutton	MA	E	508 865-1500	12287
Micro Wire Products Inc	Holbrook	MA	D	508 584-0200	9180
Profiles Incorporated	Palmer	MA	E	413 283-7790	11283
Quirk Wire Co Inc	West Brookfield	MA	E	508 867-3155	12998

	CITY	ST	EMP	PHONE	ENTRY#
S&S Industries Inc (PA)	Stoughton	MA	F	914 885-1500	12232
US Tsubaki Automotive LLC (DH)	Chicopee	MA	C	413 593-1100	8067
Viamed Corp	South Easton	MA	F	508 238-0220	11955
W D C Holdings Inc	Attleboro	MA	E	508 699-4412	6073
Whitney & Son Inc	Fitchburg	MA	E	978 343-6353	8682
Wirefab Inc	Worcester	MA	E	508 754-5359	13829
Worcester Manufacturing Inc	Worcester	MA	E	508 756-0301	13830
Anchor Corporation	Kennebunk	ME	F	207 985-6018	4920
Kardex Remstar LLC (HQ)	Westbrook	ME	F	207 854-1861	5633
Kelco Industries	Milbridge	ME	E	207 546-7562	5061
New England Wire Products Inc	Kingfield	ME	E	207 265-2176	4934
Elektrisola Incorporated (PA)	Boscawen	NH	C	603 796-2114	13989
Felton Inc	Londonderry	NH	D	603 425-0200	14750
Guidewire Technologies Inc	Salem	NH	E	603 894-4399	15534
New England Wire Tech Corp (HQ)	Lisbon	NH	B	603 838-6624	14710
Plasti-Clip Corporation	Milford	NH	F	603 672-1166	15034
Prysmian Cbles Systems USA LLC	Manchester	NH	D	603 668-1620	14918
Alloy Holdings LLC	Providence	RI	D	401 353-7500	16467
Ammega US Inc	Warwick	RI	G	401 732-8131	16778
Electro Standards Lab Inc	Cranston	RI	D	401 946-1164	15853
Fortune Rope & Metal Co Inc (PA)	Bristol	RI	F	800 416-6595	15765
Hindley Manufacturing Co Inc	Cumberland	RI	D	401 722-2550	15943
Perry Blackburne Inc	North Providence	RI	F	401 231-7200	16307
Quality Chain & Cable LLC	East Providence	RI	G	401 575-8323	16039
Weissenfels Usa Inc	Portsmouth	RI	F	401 683-2900	16461
Astenjohnson Inc	Williston	VT	D	802 658-0400	17722
One-Pull Sltons Wire Cable LLC	Randolph	VT	F	833 663-7855	17472
Vermont Wireform Inc	Chelsea	VT	F	802 889-3200	17179
Westwood Fences Inc	Irasburg	VT	F	802 754-8486	17303

WIRE CLOTH & WOVEN WIRE PRDTS, MADE FROM PURCHASED

	CITY	ST	EMP	PHONE	ENTRY#
New England Wire Products Inc (PA)	Leominster	MA	D	800 254-9473	9686

WIRE FABRIC: Welded Steel

	CITY	ST	EMP	PHONE	ENTRY#
Tool Logistics II	Norwalk	CT	F	203 855-9754	2585
Bergeron Machine LLC	Westford	MA	E	978 577-6235	13225

WIRE MATERIALS: Copper

	CITY	ST	EMP	PHONE	ENTRY#
Frank L Reed Inc	Wilbraham	MA	E	413 596-3861	13359

WIRE MATERIALS: Steel

	CITY	ST	EMP	PHONE	ENTRY#
Ametek Inc	Wallingford	CT	C	203 265-6731	3770
Bridgeport Insulated Wire Co (PA)	Bridgeport	CT	F	203 333-3191	304
International Pipe & Stl Corp	North Branford	CT	F	203 481-7102	2369
Kanthal Corporation	Bethel	CT	E	203 744-1440	124
Shuster-Mettler Corp	Plainville	CT	E	203 562-3178	2780
Wiremold Company (DH)	West Hartford	CT	A	860 233-6251	4091
Cape Cod Fence Co (PA)	South Yarmouth	MA	F	508 398-6041	11982
Fence Lines Inc	South Weymouth	MA	F	781 331-2121	11976
General Wire Products Inc	Worcester	MA	E	508 752-8260	13731
Joe Miller Inc	Worcester	MA	E	508 753-8581	13745
Quirk Wire Co Inc	West Brookfield	MA	E	508 867-3155	12998
S&S Industries Inc (PA)	Stoughton	MA	F	914 885-1500	12232
Sanderson-Macleod Incorporate	Palmer	MA	C	413 283-3481	11284
ACS Industries Inc (PA)	Lincoln	RI	D	401 769-4700	16116
Dayton Superior Corporation	Warwick	RI	G	401 885-1934	16805
Sonco Worldwide Inc	Warwick	RI	F	401 406-3761	16863

WIRE PRDTS: Ferrous Or Iron, Made In Wiredrawing Plants

	CITY	ST	EMP	PHONE	ENTRY#
Nutmeg Wire	Baltic	CT	F	860 822-8616	38
Accellent Acquisition Corp	Wilmington	MA	A	978 570-6900	13370
Accellent Holdings Corp	Wilmington	MA	A	978 570-6900	13371
Frank L Reed Inc	Wilbraham	MA	E	413 596-3861	13359
Moor Metals Inc (PA)	Holliston	MA	F	508 429-9446	9224
Precision Wire Shapes Inc	West Brookfield	MA	F	508 867-3859	12997
Kelco Industries	Milbridge	ME	E	207 546-7562	5061
Heb Manufacturing Company Inc	Chelsea	VT	E	802 685-4821	17178

WIRE PRDTS: Steel & Iron

	CITY	ST	EMP	PHONE	ENTRY#
Kanthal Corporation	Bethel	CT	E	203 744-1440	124
RSI Metal Fabrication LLC	East Kingston	NH	F	603 382-8367	14273
ACS Industries Inc (PA)	Lincoln	RI	D	401 769-4700	16116
Philip Machine Company Inc	Pawtucket	RI	E	401 353-7383	16402

WIRE WHOLESALERS

	CITY	ST	EMP	PHONE	ENTRY#
Ftc Inc (PA)	Friendship	ME	E	207 354-2545	4806
Whitney Blake Company (PA)	Bellows Falls	VT	D	800 323-0479	17033

WIRE WINDING OF PURCHASED WIRE

	CITY	ST	EMP	PHONE	ENTRY#
Protopac Inc	Watertown	CT	G	860 274-6796	4027

WIRE: Communication

	CITY	ST	EMP	PHONE	ENTRY#
King Network Services Inc	Plainville	CT	F	860 479-8029	2766
Ortronics Inc **(DH)**	New London	CT	D	860 445-3900	2232
Ortronics Inc	West Hartford	CT	F	877 295-3472	4076
Prysmian Cbles Systems USA LLC	Willimantic	CT	C	860 456-8000	4220
Winchester Interconnect CM Corporation	Dayville	CT	C	860 774-4812	871
American Insulated Wire Corporation **(HQ)**	Mansfield	MA			E
508 964-1200					10037
Belden Inc	Worcester	MA	G	508 754-4858	13703
Mercury Wire Products Inc	Spencer	MA	C	508 885-6363	12064
Quabbin Wire & Cable Co Inc **(PA)**	Ware	MA	D	413 967-6281	12827
Eldur Corporation	Bangor	ME	E	207 942-6592	4499
Enterasys Networks Inc **(HQ)**	Salem	NH	D	603 952-5000	15521
Marmon Utility LLC **(DH)**	Milford	NH	C	603 673-2040	15032
Stonewall Cable Inc	Rumney	NH	D	603 536-1601	15498

WIRE: Magnet

	CITY	ST	EMP	PHONE	ENTRY#
Bridgeport Magnetics Group Inc	Shelton	CT	E	203 954-0050	2988
Luvata Waterbury Inc **(HQ)**	Waterbury	CT	D	203 753-5215	3931
Tech-Etch Inc	Fall River	MA	E	508 675-5757	8614
Elektrisola Incorporated **(PA)**	Boscawen	NH	C	603 796-2114	13989

WIRE: Mesh

	CITY	ST	EMP	PHONE	ENTRY#
Nucor Steel Connecticut Inc	Wallingford	CT	C	203 265-0615	3836
Citiworks Corp	Attleboro	MA	F	508 761-7400	6004
Riverdale Mills Corporation	Northbridge	MA	C	508 234-8715	11118
ACS Industries Inc **(PA)**	Lincoln	RI	E	401 769-4700	16116

WIRE: Nonferrous

	CITY	ST	EMP	PHONE	ENTRY#
Algonquin Industries Inc **(HQ)**	Guilford	CT	D	203 453-4348	1384
Alpha-Core Inc	Shelton	CT	E	203 954-0050	2980
Altek Electronics Inc	Torrington	CT	C	860 482-7626	3669
Bellevue Private Equity Inc	Naugatuck	CT	G	781 893-6721	1949
Bridgeport Insulated Wire Co **(PA)**	Bridgeport	CT	F	203 333-3191	304
Bridgeport Insulated Wire Co	Stratford	CT	G	203 375-9579	3523
Cable Technology Inc	Willington	CT	E	860 429-7889	4224
Insulated Wire Inc	Bethel	CT	E	203 791-1999	119
Kanthal Corporation **(DH)**	Bethel	CT	D	203 744-1440	123
Kanthal Corporation	Bethel	CT	E	203 744-1440	124
Loos & Co Inc **(PA)**	Pomfret	CT	B	860 928-7981	2809
Lucent Specialty Fiber Tech	Avon	CT	G	320 258-3035	30
Multi-Cable Corp	Bristol	CT	F	860 589-9035	473
Norfield Data Products Inc	Norwalk	CT	E	203 849-0292	2546
Ofs Fitel LLC	Avon	CT	B	860 678-0371	33
Platt Brothers & Company **(PA)**	Waterbury	CT	D	203 753-4194	3963
Radcliff Wire Inc	Bristol	CT	E	312 876-1754	489
REA Magnet Wire Company Inc	Guilford	CT	D	203 738-6100	1404
Rscc Wire & Cable LLC	East Granby	CT	D	860 653-8300	949
Rscc Wire & Cable LLC **(DH)**	East Granby	CT	B	860 653-8300	950
Siemon Company **(PA)**	Watertown	CT	A	860 945-4200	4029
Specialty Cable Corp	Wallingford	CT	D	203 265-7126	3852
Tek Wire and Cable Corp	Stamford	CT	E	914 663-2100	3479
Wiretek Inc	Bloomfield	CT	F	860 242-9473	217
AFL Telecommunications LLC	North Grafton	MA	F	508 890-7100	11018
American Cable Assemblies Inc **(PA)**	Palmer	MA	F	413 283-2515	11270
Anomet Products Inc	Shrewsbury	MA	E	508 842-0174	11827
Belden Inc	Leominster	MA	E	978 537-8911	9641
Brookfield Wire Company Inc **(HQ)**	West Brookfield	MA	E	508 867-6474	12992
Caton Connector Corp	Kingston	MA	E	781 585-4315	9505
Champlain Cable Leeds Corporation	Leeds	MA	E	413 584-3853	9620
Cubit Wire & Cable Co Inc	Holyoke	MA	E	413 539-9892	9249
Data Guide Cable Corporation	Gardner	MA	D	978 632-0900	8883
Denardo Wire and Cable Co Inc	Fitchburg	MA	E	978 343-6412	8652
Dielectric Sciences Inc	Chelmsford	MA	E	978 250-1507	7923
Eis Wire & Cable Inc	South Hadley	MA	D	413 536-0152	11961
Gavitt Wire and Cable Co Inc	West Brookfield	MA	D	508 867-6476	12994
IBC Corporation	South Easton	MA	D	508 238-7941	11944
L-Com Inc **(DH)**	North Andover	MA	D	978 682-6936	10842
Madison Cable Corporation	Worcester	MA	D	800 522-6752	13755
Manage Inc	Springfield	MA	E	413 593-9128	12112
Milford Manufacturing Svcs LLC	Hopedale	MA	E	508 478-8544	9299
Mohawk Chicago Distribution	Leominster	MA	F	781 334-4976	9684
Motorola Mobility LLC	Lowell	MA	E	978 614-2900	9910
Ofs Brightwave LLC	Sturbridge	MA	F	508 347-2261	12252
Ofs Fitel LLC	Sturbridge	MA	B	508 347-2261	12253
Prysmian Group Spclty Cbles LL	Taunton	MA	C	508 822-0246	12357
Quirk Wire Co Inc	West Brookfield	MA	E	508 867-3155	12998
Saint-Gobain Prfmce Plas Corp	Worcester	MA	C	508 852-3072	13792
Segue Manufacturing Svcs LLC	North Billerica	MA	D	978 970-1200	10952
Senko Advanced Components Inc **(HQ)**	Hudson	MA	E	508 481-9999	9412
Supercon Incorporated	Shrewsbury	MA	E	508 842-0174	11843
Temp-Flex LLC	South Grafton	MA	C	508 839-3120	11958
Tricab (usa) Inc	Worcester	MA	E	508 421-4680	13813

	CITY	ST	EMP	PHONE	ENTRY#
V-Tron Electronics Corp	Attleboro	MA	D	508 761-9100	6072
Verrillon Inc	North Grafton	MA	D	508 890-7100	11027
Transparent Audio Inc	Saco	ME	E	207 284-1100	5380
Aetna Insulated Wire LLC	Milford	NH	C	757 460-3381	15011
AFL Telecommunications LLC	Belmont	NH	E	603 528-7780	13958
Amphenol Printed Circuits Inc **(HQ)**	Nashua	NH	D	603 324-4500	15062
Belden Inc	Keene	NH	G	603 359-7355	14590
Burton Wire & Cable LLC	Hooksett	NH	F	603 624-2427	14463
Marmon Aerospace & Defense LLC **(DH)**	Manchester	NH	F	603 622-3500	14880
Marmon Utility LLC	Amherst	NH	F	603 673-2040	13878
Proterial Cable America Inc	Manchester	NH	C	603 669-4347	14917
Prysmian Cbles Systems USA LLC	Manchester	NH	D	603 668-1620	14918
Retcomp Inc	New Boston	NH	F	603 487-5010	15194
Rscc Wire & Cable LLC	Manchester	NH	D	603 622-3500	14923
Teledyne Instruments Inc	Portsmouth	NH	C	603 474-5571	15442
Electro Standards Lab Inc	Cranston	RI	D	401 946-1164	15853
Okonite Company Inc	Cumberland	RI	E	401 333-3500	15957
Champlain Cable Corporation **(PA)**	Colchester	VT	C	802 654-4200	17187
Phoenix Wire Inc	South Hero	VT	G	802 372-4561	17609
Super-Temp Wire & Cable Inc	South Burlington	VT	E	802 655-4211	17603

WIRE: Nonferrous, Appliance Fixture

	CITY	ST	EMP	PHONE	ENTRY#
Times Microwave Systems Inc **(HQ)**	Wallingford	CT	B	203 949-8400	3866

WIRE: Steel, Insulated Or Armored

	CITY	ST	EMP	PHONE	ENTRY#
Q-S Technologies Inc	Meriden	CT	E	203 237-2297	1687
SA Candelora Enterprises Inc	North Branford	CT	F	203 484-2863	2374
Lanoco Specialty Wire Pdts Inc	Sutton	MA	E	508 865-1500	12287

WIRE: Wire, Ferrous Or Iron

	CITY	ST	EMP	PHONE	ENTRY#
Hamden Metal Service Co Inc	Hamden	CT	F	203 281-1522	1427
Loos & Co Inc **(PA)**	Pomfret	CT	B	860 928-7981	2809
Loos & Co Inc	Pomfret	CT	D	860 928-6681	2810
Radcliff Wire Inc	Bristol	CT	E	312 876-1754	489
Brookfield Wire Company Inc **(HQ)**	West Brookfield	MA	E	508 867-6474	12992
Profiles Incorporated	Palmer	MA	E	413 283-7790	11283

WIRING DEVICES WHOLESALERS

	CITY	ST	EMP	PHONE	ENTRY#
Hubbell Power Systems Inc	Cromwell	CT	D	860 635-2200	694

WOMEN'S & CHILDREN'S CLOTHING WHOLESALERS, NEC

	CITY	ST	EMP	PHONE	ENTRY#
Accurate Services Inc	Fall River	MA	E	508 674-5773	8518
Advanced Print Technology Inc	Fitchburg	MA	G	978 342-0093	8640
Austins Sportswear Inc	West Yarmouth	MA	F	508 775-0554	13071
Cause For Change LLC	Sudbury	MA	E	617 571-6990	12262
Mahi Gold Inc	Chatham	MA	F	508 348-5487	7898
Shop Therapy Imports	Provincetown	MA	G	508 487-8970	11497
Imeldas Fabrics & Designs	New Sharon	ME	D	207 778-0665	5090
New York Accessory Group Inc	Bristol	RI	D	401 245-6096	15776
Cornell Online LLC	Burlington	VT	E	802 448-3281	17128

WOMEN'S & GIRLS' SPORTSWEAR WHOLESALERS

	CITY	ST	EMP	PHONE	ENTRY#
Del Arbour LLC	Milford	CT	F	203 882-8501	1817
Broder Bros Co	Middleboro	MA	C	508 923-4800	10352
Piesco Sporting Goods Inc	North Easton	MA	F	508 238-5599	11012
Soft-As-A-grape Inc **(PA)**	Wareham	MA	E	508 295-9900	12844
Outfitters Inc Corporate	Saint Albans	VT	G	802 527-0204	17528

WOMEN'S CLOTHING STORES

	CITY	ST	EMP	PHONE	ENTRY#
Sickday Inc	Wellfleet	MA	F	508 214-4158	12953
Nomad Communications Inc	White River Junction	VT	F	802 649-1995	
17709					

WOMEN'S CLOTHING STORES: Ready-To-Wear

	CITY	ST	EMP	PHONE	ENTRY#
Dawson Forte Holdings LLC **(PA)**	Canton	MA	E	508 651-7910	7782
Lane Printing Co Inc	Holbrook	MA	F	781 767-4450	9178

WOOD & WOOD BY-PRDTS, WHOLESALE

	CITY	ST	EMP	PHONE	ENTRY#
Middleton Building Supply **(PA)**	Middleton	NH	C	603 473-2210	15008

WOOD CHIPS, PRODUCED AT THE MILL

	CITY	ST	EMP	PHONE	ENTRY#
Ensign-Bckford Rnwble Enrgies	Simsbury	CT	G	860 843-2000	3088
A W Chaffee	Clinton	ME	E	207 426-8588	4697
Linkletter & Sons Inc	Athens	ME	E	207 654-2301	4414
Yates Lumber Inc	Lee	ME	E	207 738-2331	4947
Hhp Inc **(PA)**	Henniker	NH	E	603 428-3298	14436
Green Mountain Forest Products	Highgate Center	VT	F	802 868-2306	17289

WOOD FENCING WHOLESALERS

	CITY	ST	EMP	PHONE	ENTRY#
Fiberglass Building Pdts Inc	Halifax	MA	F	847 650-3045	9021
Joe Miller Inc	Worcester	MA	F	508 753-8581	13745
Perfection Fence Corp **(PA)**	Marshfield	MA	F	781 837-3600	10243

**P
R
O
D
U
C
T**

	CITY	ST	EMP	PHONE	ENTRY#

WOOD PRDTS: Applicators

	CITY	ST	EMP	PHONE	ENTRY#
Avo Fence & Supply Inc **(PA)**	Stoughton	MA	F	781 341-2963	12196
Vermont Wood Pellet Co LLC	North Clarendon	VT	E	802 747-1093	17418

WOOD PRDTS: Battery Separators

	CITY	ST	EMP	PHONE	ENTRY#
Hollingsworth & Vose Company **(PA)**	East Walpole	MA	C	508 850-2000	8418
Moore Company	Westerly	RI	E	401 596-2816	16939
Garware Fulflex USA Inc	Brattleboro	VT	C	802 257-5256	17085

WOOD PRDTS: Box Shook

	CITY	ST	EMP	PHONE	ENTRY#
Herrick Mill Work Inc	Contoocook	NH	F	603 746-5092	14170

WOOD PRDTS: Flagpoles

	CITY	ST	EMP	PHONE	ENTRY#
Flagraphics Inc	Somerville	MA	E	617 776-7549	11874

WOOD PRDTS: Laundry

	CITY	ST	EMP	PHONE	ENTRY#
Cousineau Wood Products ME LLC	North Anson	ME	E	207 635-4445	5104
Maine Woods Pellet Company LLC	Athens	ME	E	207 654-2237	4415
Lignetics New England Inc	Jaffrey	NH	F	603 532-4666	14573

WOOD PRDTS: Moldings, Unfinished & Prefinished

	CITY	ST	EMP	PHONE	ENTRY#
Conway Hardwood Products LLC	Gaylordsville	CT	E	860 355-4030	1264
Boyce Highlands Furn Co Inc	Concord	NH	E	603 753-1042	14116

WOOD PRDTS: Mulch Or Sawdust

	CITY	ST	EMP	PHONE	ENTRY#
Nicholas Ieronimo	Middleboro	MA	G	508 947-5363	10369
Lucerne Farms	Fort Fairfield	ME	E	207 488-2520	4785
York Woods Tree Service LLC	Eliot	ME	F	207 703-0150	4752

WOOD PRDTS: Mulch, Wood & Bark

	CITY	ST	EMP	PHONE	ENTRY#
DR Charles Envmtl Cnstr LLC	Monroe	CT	G	203 445-0412	1913
Natures Harvest LLC	Bethany	CT	F	203 758-3725	96
Blacksmith Shop Farms Inc	East Falmouth	MA	E	508 548-7714	8357
Blank Industries LLC	Hudson	MA	E	855 887-3123	9356
Cook Forest Products Inc	Upton	MA	E	508 634-3300	12471
Harvest Consumer Products LLC **(PA)**	Waltham	MA	E	980 444-2000	12690
Lashway Logging Inc	Williamsburg	MA	F	413 268-3600	13365
Rangeway Supply LLC	North Billerica	MA	G	978 667-8500	10947
TJ Bark Mulch Inc	Southwick	MA	F	413 569-2400	12047
Kevlaur Industries Inc	Van Buren	ME	E	207 868-2761	5569
Ingerson Transportation	Jefferson	NH	G	603 586-4335	14584

WOOD PRDTS: Novelties, Fiber

	CITY	ST	EMP	PHONE	ENTRY#
Essex Wood Products Inc	Colchester	CT	F	860 537-3451	658
Maine Wood Turning Inc	New Vineyard	ME	G	207 652-2320	5091
Riley Mountain Products Inc	Antrim	NH	F	603 588-7234	13898

WOOD PRDTS: Outdoor, Structural

	CITY	ST	EMP	PHONE	ENTRY#
Downeast Concepts Inc	Yarmouth	ME	E	207 846-3726	5703
A & A Wheeler Mfg Inc	Lee	NH	G	603 659-4446	14704

WOOD PRDTS: Panel Work

	CITY	ST	EMP	PHONE	ENTRY#
Scandinavian Panel Systems	Worcester	MA	F	774 530-6340	13795

WOOD PRDTS: Rulers & Rules

	CITY	ST	EMP	PHONE	ENTRY#
Acme United Corporation **(PA)**	Shelton	CT	D	203 254-6060	2978

WOOD PRDTS: Signboards

	CITY	ST	EMP	PHONE	ENTRY#
Maine Turnpike Authority	Cumberland Center	ME	D	207 829-4531	4709
Wood & Wood Inc	Waitsfield	VT	G	802 496-3000	17669

WOOD PRDTS: Trophy Bases

	CITY	ST	EMP	PHONE	ENTRY#
Initial Ideas Inc	Rutland	VT	G	802 775-1685	17499

WOOD PRODUCTS: Reconstituted

	CITY	ST	EMP	PHONE	ENTRY#
Huber Engineered Woods LLC	Easton	ME	D	207 488-6700	4742
Saunders At Locke Mills LLC	Greenwood	ME	G	207 875-2853	4853
Souhegan Wood Products Inc	Wilton	NH	F	603 654-2311	15709
Neshobe Wood Products Inc	Brandon	VT	F	802 247-3805	17069

WOOD TREATING: Millwork

	CITY	ST	EMP	PHONE	ENTRY#
Amerifix LLC	West Haven	CT	G	203 931-7290	4094

WOOD TREATING: Structural Lumber & Timber

	CITY	ST	EMP	PHONE	ENTRY#
Oxford Timber Inc	Oxford	ME	F	207 539-9656	5148
BB&s Acquisition Corp	North Kingstown	RI	D	401 295-3200	16234
Vermont Timber Works Inc	North Springfield	VT	F	802 886-1917	17427

WOOD TREATING: Wood Prdts, Creosoted

	CITY	ST	EMP	PHONE	ENTRY#
Bridgwell Rsources Holdings LLC **(HQ)**	Greenwich	CT	E	203 622-9138	1322

	CITY	ST	EMP	PHONE	ENTRY#
Metalcraft Door Co Inc	Woburn	MA	E	781 933-2861	13611

WOODWORK & TRIM: Exterior & Ornamental

	CITY	ST	EMP	PHONE	ENTRY#
Trellis Structures Inc	East Templeton	MA	E	888 285-4624	8415

WOODWORK & TRIM: Interior & Ornamental

	CITY	ST	EMP	PHONE	ENTRY#
East Coast Interiors Inc	North Dartmouth	MA	F	508 995-4200	10995
Marie Deprofio	Waltham	MA	G	781 894-9793	12714
Alfreds Uphlstring Cstm Fbrcti	Alfred	ME	F	207 536-5565	4402
Chamberlain Companies Inc	Salem	NH	E	603 893-2606	15512
Eastern Design Inc	Manville	RI	G	401 765-0558	16163

WOODWORK: Interior & Ornamental, NEC

	CITY	ST	EMP	PHONE	ENTRY#
77 Mattatuck Heights LLC	Waterbury	CT	G	203 597-9338	3878
Ferraro Custom Woodwork LLC	Milford	CT	F	203 876-1280	1828
Madigan Millworks Inc	Unionville	CT	F	860 673-7601	3749
Maurer & Shepherd Joyners	Glastonbury	CT	F	860 633-2383	1289
Chilmark Archtctural Wdwkg LLC	Worcester	MA	F	508 856-9200	13706
Pomeroy & Co Inc	Charlestown	MA	E	617 241-0234	7880
Aubin Woodworking Inc	Bow	NH	F	603 224-5512	13993

WORD PROCESSING EQPT

	CITY	ST	EMP	PHONE	ENTRY#
Dmt Solutions Global Corp **(HQ)**	Danbury	CT	D	833 874-0552	733

WOVEN WIRE PRDTS, NEC

	CITY	ST	EMP	PHONE	ENTRY#
Amtec Corporation	Plainfield	CT	E	860 230-0006	2730
C O Jelliff Corporation **(PA)**	Southport	CT	E	203 259-1615	3244
Gemco Manufacturing Co Inc	Southington	CT	E	860 628-5529	3211
Garlan Chain Co Inc	Attleboro Falls	MA	G	508 399-7288	6085
Neptco Incorporated **(DH)**	Westwood	MA	D	401 722-5500	13316
New England Wirecloth Co LLC	Fitchburg	MA	F	978 343-4998	8669
Sh Consulting Co	Warwick	RI	F	508 695-6611	16862

WRENCHES

	CITY	ST	EMP	PHONE	ENTRY#
Easco Hand Tools Inc	Simsbury	CT	A	860 843-7351	3086
Power-Dyne LLC	Middletown	CT	E	860 346-9283	1772
Skillcraft Machine Tool Co	South Windsor	CT	F	860 953-1246	3180

X-RAY EQPT & TUBES

	CITY	ST	EMP	PHONE	ENTRY#
Associated X-Ray Corp **(PA)**	East Haven	CT	F	203 466-2446	1036
Bidwell Industrial Group Inc	Middletown	CT	E	860 346-9283	1740
Biowave Innovations LLC	Wilton	CT	C	203 982-8157	4232
Hologic Inc	Danbury	CT	C	203 790-1188	757
Kub Technologies Inc	Stratford	CT	E	203 364-8544	3553
Parker Medical Inc	Danbury	CT	D	860 350-4304	794
Precision X-Ray Inc	Madison	CT	E	203 484-2011	1567
Precision X-Ray Inc	North Branford	CT	F	203 484-2011	2372
Topex Inc	Danbury	CT	F	203 748-5918	825
Yxlon Inc	Shelton	CT	G	234 284-7862	3081
Biolucent LLC	Marlborough	MA	F	508 263-2900	10116
Bruker Corporation **(PA)**	Billerica	MA	A	978 663-3660	6414
Hologic Inc	Marlborough	MA	C	508 263-2900	10158
Hologic Inc **(PA)**	Marlborough	MA	A	508 263-2900	10159
Hologic Inc	Methuen	MA	E	508 263-2900	10334
Panalytical Inc	Westborough	MA	D	508 647-1100	13128
Princton Gamma-Tech Instrs Inc	Franklin	MA	E	609 924-7310	8858
Scholz Frank X Ray Corp	Brockton	MA	F		7303
VJ Electronix Inc	Chelmsford	MA	E	631 589-8800	7969
Xenocs Inc	Holyoke	MA	F	413 587-4000	9292
Hologic Inc	Londonderry	NH	E	508 263-2900	14755
Telcor Inc	Hancock	NH	G	603 525-4769	14420
Huestis Machine Corporation	Bristol	RI	E	401 253-5500	15769
Aadco Medical Inc	Randolph	VT	D	802 728-3400	17466

YARN & YARN SPINNING

	CITY	ST	EMP	PHONE	ENTRY#
St Regis Sportswear Ltd	North Andover	MA	G	518 725-6767	10850
Family Yarns Inc	Etna	ME	G	207 269-3852	4763
Jagger Brothers	Springvale	ME	E	207 324-5622	5520
Worsted Spinning Neng LLC	Springvale	ME	G	207 324-5622	5523
Harrisville Designs Inc **(PA)**	Harrisville	NH	G	603 827-3333	14432
Concordia Manufacturing LLC	Coventry	RI	D	401 828-1100	15811
Conneaut Industries Inc	West Greenwich	RI	F	401 392-1110	16883
Providence Yarn Company Inc	Pawtucket	RI	G	401 722-5600	16407

YARN WHOLESALERS

	CITY	ST	EMP	PHONE	ENTRY#
Quince & Company Inc	Saco	ME	E	207 210-6630	5378
Harrisville Designs Inc **(PA)**	Harrisville	NH	G	603 827-3333	14432

YARN: Knitting, Spun

	CITY	ST	EMP	PHONE	ENTRY#
Beal Manufacturing Inc	Swampscott	MA	E	704 824-9961	12298

YARN: Wool, Spun

	CITY	ST	EMP	PHONE	ENTRY#		CITY	ST	EMP	PHONE	ENTRY#
Quince & Company Inc	Saco	ME	E	207 210-6630	5378						
Green Mountain Spinnery Inc	East Dummerston	VT	G	802 387-4528	17216						

YARNS, INDL, WHOLESALE

	CITY	ST	EMP	PHONE	ENTRY#
Providence Yarn Company Inc	Pawtucket	RI	G	401 722-5600	16407

Employee Codes: A=Over 500 employees, B=251-500
C=101-250, D=51-100, E=20-50, F=10-19, G=1-9

2024 Harris New England
Manufacturers Directory

1487

PRODUCT